WHITAKER'S ALMANACK
2012

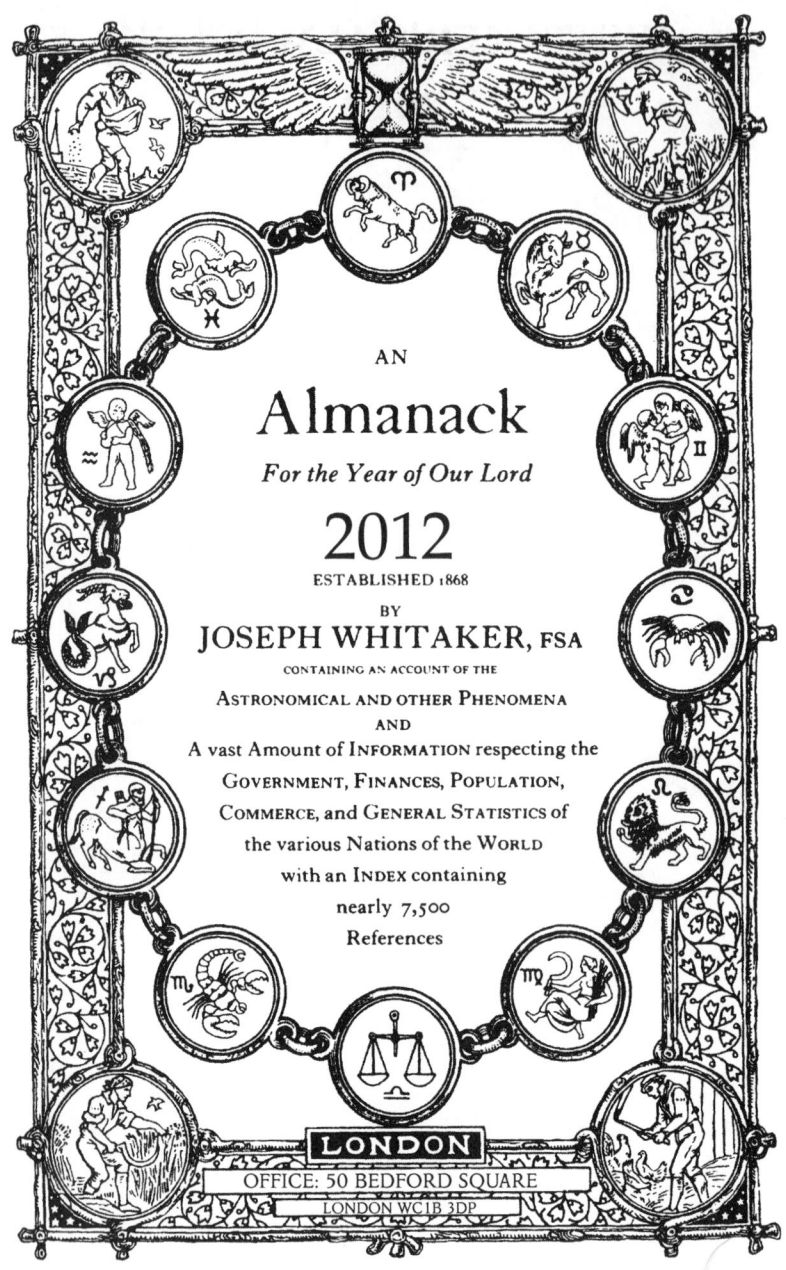

AN

Almanack

For the Year of Our Lord

2012

ESTABLISHED 1868

BY

JOSEPH WHITAKER, FSA

CONTAINING AN ACCOUNT OF THE

ASTRONOMICAL AND OTHER PHENOMENA

AND

A vast Amount of INFORMATION respecting the

GOVERNMENT, FINANCES, POPULATION,

COMMERCE, and GENERAL STATISTICS of

the various Nations of the WORLD

with an INDEX containing

nearly 7,500

References

LONDON

OFFICE: 50 BEDFORD SQUARE
LONDON WC1B 3DP

The traditional design of the title page for Whitaker's Almanack which has appeared in each edition since 1868

WHITAKER'S ALMANACK
2012

B L O O M S B U R Y

LONDON · BERLIN · NEW YORK · SYDNEY

Bloomsbury Publishing Plc.
50 Bedford Square, London WC1B 3DP

Whitaker's Almanack published annually since 1868
144th edition © 2011 Bloomsbury Publishing Plc.

www.bloomsbury.com

STANDARD EDITION
Cloth covers
978-1-4081-3012-4

CONCISE EDITION
Paperback
978-1-4081-4230-1

JACKET PHOTOGRAPHS
Main image: Riot police stand in line as fire rages
through a building in Tottenham, north London on
7 August 2011. © Lewis Whyld/PA Wire/Press
Association Images
Spine: Thousands of Egyptian demonstrators take part
in anti-government protests in February 2011. ©
KeystoneUSA-ZUMA/Rex Features
Top, from left to right:
1. A reader enjoys the final edition of the *News of the
World* newspaper, published on 10 July 2011. © Yui
Mok/PA Wire/Press Association Images
2. The Duke and Duchess of Cambridge arrive for a
reception with the British Consul General in Hancock
Park, Los Angeles, during the Royal Tour of the USA in
July 2011. © Stewart Cook/Rex Features
3. USA president Barack Obama gives a press
conference on the breakdown of the Debt Limit Talks in
Washington DC on 22 July 2011 © Rex Features
4. The waxwork figure of British singer Amy
Winehouse is unveiled at Madame Tussauds in central
London. © Joel Ryan/AP/Press Association Images

Typeset in the UK by RefineCatch Ltd, Bungay, Suffolk
NR35 1EF

Printed and bound in Italy by L.E.G.O. S.p.A.

FSC
www.fsc.org
MIX
Paper from
responsible sources
FSC® C023419

Whitaker's is a registered trade mark of J. Whitaker and
Sons Ltd, Registered Trade Mark Nos. (UK) 1322125/
09; 13422126/16 and 1322127/41; (EU)
19960401/09, 16, 41, licensed for use by A & C Black
(Publishers) Ltd, a subsidiary of Bloomsbury Publishing
Plc.

Whitaker's Almanack was compiled with the assistance
of: Amnesty International; Euromonitor International;
Keesing's Worldwide; Oxford Cartographers; Press
Association; Transparency International: the global
coalition against corruption; UK Hydrographic Office;
the UNESCO Institute for Statistics (UIS); WM/
Reuters; and the World Gazetteer/Stefan Helders
(W www.world-gazetteer.com).

Material was reproduced from (in addition to that
indicated): *CIA World Factbook 2011; The Diplomatic List
January 2011* © Crown Copyright; *Human Development
Indicators 2010* published by the UN Development
Programme; *International Financial Statistics Year Book
2010* and *World Economic Outlook Database* ©
International Monetary Fund; *The Military Balance 2011*
published by Routledge for the International Institute
for Strategic Studies (IISS); Ordnance Survey of
Northern Ireland, permit number 100036 © Crown
Copyright; 2011 *World Development Indicators* published
by The World Bank; the *World Health Organisation
Statistical Information System,* and *World Urbanisation
Prospects: The 2010 Revision* published by the UN
Population Division. Crown copyright material is
reproduced with the permission of the Controller of Her
Majesty's Stationery Office.

Government cabinet lists and embassy details are
sourced from *People in Power* ©, Cambridge
International Reference on Current Affairs Ltd
(W www.circaworld.com). *People in Power* provides a
constantly updated service at www.peopleinpower.com

EDITORIAL STAFF
Executive Editor: Ruth Northey
Project Editors: Nathan Joyce (UK); Matt Munday, Joel
Simons (International)
Editorial Assistant: Oli Lurie
Head of Yearbooks: Katy McAdam

Thanks to Omer Ali, Clare Bryant, Nicola Cutts, Rob
Hardy, Matt Rose

CONTENTS

6

PREFACE

Turbulent is the word that springs to mind when summing up the past year's events. In November 2010, against a backdrop of civil service job cuts and pay freezes, the UK government chose to announce proposals to raise the cap on university tuition fees to £9,000 a year. Student demonstrations and university sit-ins followed across the country, with the protests in London turning violent as an angry mob burst into the Conservative Party headquarters, vandalising the premises and hurling missiles from the roof of the building. Then in August 2011 came four days of unprecedented civil disorder – violent riots and looting across the capital and in other major cities around the country – forcing the prime minister to break off his holiday and recall parliament.

Meanwhile in North Africa and the Middle East, an individual act of self-immolation in Tunisia in December triggered the events of the 'Arab Spring', spreading through Egypt, Bahrain, Syria, Yemen and eventually Libya.

The media became part of the 'news' itself when allegations of widespread 'phone-hacking' at the *News of the World* led to arrests, resignations and the closure of the country's best-selling Sunday newspaper.

In the turmoil of such headline events it is easy to forget the detail. The 2012 edition of *Whitaker's Almanack* has all the facts, distilled into easily digestible chunks: a chapter on the UK education system; summaries of UK and World events throughout the year; the infrastructure of the UK in minute detail, including extensive coverage of the regional elections which took place in May; and a historical and political summary for every country of the world.

There are new colour plates further illustrating the regional elections and the flags of the world section has been fully updated to include the new National Transitional Council flag for Libya, even though at the time of going to press parts of Libya remain under Colonel Gaddafi's control and the whereabouts of Gaddafi himself are unknown.

It was also a busy year for the royal family – first the wedding of Prince William to Kate Middleton in April and then, in July, that of Zara Phillips, daughter of the Princess Royal, to England rugby player Mike Tindall. As always, the royal family chapter has been fully updated to include, not just the latest newcomers, but also information on the royal finances and the military ranks and titles currently held by members of the royal family, plus an up-to-date list of the order of succession.

Whatever your interests, you can be sure that *Whitaker's Almanack 2012* gives the complete picture.

It has also been a year of changes for *Whitaker's Almanack,* and we are now settled comfortably into our new offices in Bedford Square, with our parent company Bloomsbury Publishing. As usual I would like to thank the dedicated team of in-house editors and expert contributors for their efforts in compiling this year's edition. I hope you enjoy the new edition and please feel free to contact us with feedback and suggestions.

Ruth Northey
Executive Editor

THE YEAR 2012

CHRONOLOGICAL CYCLES AND ERAS

Dominical Letter	AG
Epact	6
Golden Number (Lunar Cycle)	XVIII
Julian Period	6725
Roman Indiction	5
Solar Cycle	5

	Beginning
Muslim year AH 1433*	26 Nov 2011
Japanese year Heisei 24	1 Jan
Roman year 2765 AUC	14 Jan
Regnal year 61	6 Feb
Chinese year of the Dragon	23 Jan
Sikh new year	14 Mar
Hindu new year (Chaitra)	23 Mar
Indian (Saka) year 1934	21 Mar
Jewish year AM 5773*	17 Sep

* Year begins at sunset on the previous day

RELIGIOUS CALENDARS

CHRISTIAN

Epiphany	6 Jan
Presentation of Christ in the Temple	2 Feb
Ash Wednesday	22 Feb
The Annunciation	25 Mar
Palm Sunday	1 Apr
Maundy Thursday	5 Apr
Good Friday	6 Apr
Easter Day (western churches)	8 Apr
Easter Day (Eastern Orthodox)	15 Apr
Rogation Sunday	13 May
Ascension Day	17 May
Pentecost (Whit Sunday)	27 May
Trinity Sunday	3 Jun
Corpus Christi	7 Jun
All Saints' Day	1 Nov
Advent Sunday	2 Dec
Christmas Day	25 Dec

HINDU

Makara Sankranti	14 Jan
Vasant Panchami (Sarasvati Puja)	28 Jan
Mahashivaratri	20 Feb
Holi	8 Mar
Chaitra (Spring new year)	23 Mar
Ramanavami	1 Apr
Raksha Bandhan	2 Aug
Janmashtami	10 Aug
Ganesh Chaturthi, first day	19 Sep
Navaratri festival (Durga Puja), first day	16 Oct
Dasara	24 Oct
Diwali (New Year festival of lights), first day	13 Nov

JEWISH

Purim	8 Mar
Pesach (Passover), first day	7 Apr
Shavuoth (Feast of Weeks), first day	27 May
Rosh Hashanah (Jewish new year)	17 Sep
Yom Kippur (Day of Atonement)	26 Sep
Succoth (Feast of Tabernacles), first day	1 Oct
Hanukkah, first day	9 Dec

MUSLIM

Al-Hijra (Muslim new year)	26 Nov 2011
Ashura	5 Dec 2011
Ramadan, first day	20 Jul
Eid-ul-Fitr	19 Aug
Hajj	24 Oct
Eid-ul-Adha	26 Oct

SIKH

Birthday of Guru Gobind Singh Ji	5 Jan
Hola Mohalla Mela	9 Mar†
1 Chet (Sikh new year)	14 Mar
Baisakhi Mela	13 Apr
Birthday of Guru Nanak Dev Ji	14 Apr†
Martyrdom of Guru Arjan Dev Ji	16 Jun
Martyrdom of Guru Tegh Bahadur Ji	24 Nov

† This festival is also currently celebrated according to the lunar calendar

CIVIL CALENDAR

Countess of Wessex's birthday	20 Jan
Accession of the Queen	6 Feb
Duke of York's birthday	19 Feb
St David's Day	1 Mar
Earl of Wessex's birthday	10 Mar
Commonwealth Day	12 Mar
St Patrick's Day	17 Mar
Birthday of the Queen	21 Apr
St George's Day	23 Apr
Europe Day	9 May
Coronation Day	2 Jun
Duke of Edinburgh's birthday	10 Jun
The Queen's Official Birthday	16 Jun
Duchess of Cornwall's birthday	17 Jul
Princess Royal's birthday	15 Aug
Lord Mayor's Day	10 Nov
Remembrance Sunday	11 Nov
Prince of Wales' birthday	14 Nov
Wedding Day of the Queen	20 Nov
St Andrew's Day	30 Nov

LEGAL CALENDAR

LAW TERMS

Hilary Term	11 Jan to 4 Apr
Easter Term	17 Apr to 1 Jun
Trinity Term	12 Jun to 31 Jul
Michaelmas Term	1 Oct to 21 Dec

QUARTER DAYS	TERM DAYS
England, Wales and Northern Ireland	Scotland
Lady – 25 Mar	Candlemas – 28 Feb
Midsummer – 24 Jun	Whitsunday – 28 May
Michaelmas – 29 Sep	Lammas – 28 Aug
Christmas – 25 Dec	Martinmas – 28 Nov

2012

JANUARY					
Sunday	1	8	15	22	29
Monday	2	9	16	23	30
Tuesday	3	10	17	24	31
Wednesday	4	11	18	25	
Thursday	5	12	19	26	
Friday	6	13	20	27	
Saturday	7	14	21	28	

FEBRUARY					
Sunday		5	12	19	26
Monday		6	13	20	27
Tuesday		7	14	21	28
Wednesday	1	8	15	22	29
Thursday	2	9	16	23	
Friday	3	10	17	24	
Saturday	4	11	18	25	

MARCH					
Sunday		4	11	18	25
Monday		5	12	19	26
Tuesday		6	13	20	27
Wednesday		7	14	21	28
Thursday	1	8	15	22	29
Friday	2	9	16	23	30
Saturday	3	10	17	24	31

APRIL					
Sunday	1	8	15	22	29
Monday	2	9	16	23	30
Tuesday	3	10	17	24	
Wednesday	4	11	18	25	
Thursday	5	12	19	26	
Friday	6	13	20	27	
Saturday	7	14	21	28	

MAY					
Sunday		6	13	20	27
Monday		7	14	21	28
Tuesday	1	8	15	22	29
Wednesday	2	9	16	23	30
Thursday	3	10	17	24	31
Friday	4	11	18	25	
Saturday	5	12	19	26	

JUNE					
Sunday		3	10	17	24
Monday		4	11	18	25
Tuesday		5	12	19	26
Wednesday		6	13	20	27
Thursday		7	14	21	28
Friday	1	8	15	22	29
Saturday	2	9	16	23	30

JULY					
Sunday	1	8	15	22	29
Monday	2	9	16	23	30
Tuesday	3	10	17	24	31
Wednesday	4	11	18	25	
Thursday	5	12	19	26	
Friday	6	13	20	27	
Saturday	7	14	21	28	

AUGUST					
Sunday		5	12	19	26
Monday		6	13	20	27
Tuesday		7	14	21	28
Wednesday	1	8	15	22	29
Thursday	2	9	16	23	30
Friday	3	10	17	24	31
Saturday	4	11	18	25	

SEPTEMBER					
Sunday		2	9	16	23	30
Monday		3	10	17	24	
Tuesday		4	11	18	25	
Wednesday		5	12	19	26	
Thursday		6	13	20	27	
Friday		7	14	21	28	
Saturday	1	8	15	22	29	

OCTOBER					
Sunday		7	14	21	28
Monday	1	8	15	22	29
Tuesday	2	9	16	23	30
Wednesday	3	10	17	24	31
Thursday	4	11	18	25	
Friday	5	12	19	26	
Saturday	6	13	20	27	

NOVEMBER					
Sunday		4	11	18	25
Monday		5	12	19	26
Tuesday		6	13	20	27
Wednesday		7	14	21	28
Thursday	1	8	15	22	29
Friday	2	9	16	23	30
Saturday	3	10	17	24	

DECEMBER					
Sunday		2	9	16	23	30
Monday		3	10	17	24	31
Tuesday		4	11	18	25	
Wednesday		5	12	19	26	
Thursday		6	13	20	27	
Friday		7	14	21	28	
Saturday	1	8	15	22	29	

PUBLIC HOLIDAYS	England and Wales	Scotland	Northern Ireland
New Year	2 January†	2, 3† January	2 January†
St Patrick's Day	—	—	17 March
*Good Friday	6 April	6 April	6 April
Easter Monday	9 April	—	9 April
Early May	7 May†	7 May	7 May†
Spring	4 June	28 May†	4 June
Queen's Diamond Jubilee	5 June	5 June	5 June
Battle of the Boyne	—	—	12 July‡
Summer	27 August	6 August	27 August
St Andrew's Day	—	30 Nov§	—
*Christmas	25, 26 December	25†, 26 December	25, 26 December

* In England, Wales and Northern Ireland, Christmas Day and Good Friday are common law holidays

† Subject to royal proclamation

‡ Subject to proclamation by the Secretary of State for Northern Ireland

§ The St Andrew's Day Holiday (Scotland) Bill was approved by parliament on 29 November 2006; it does not oblige employers to change their existing pattern of holidays but provides the legal framework in which the St Andrew's Day bank holiday could be substituted for an existing local holiday from another date in the year

Note: In the Channel Islands, Liberation Day is a bank and public holiday

2013

JANUARY				
Sunday	6	13	20	27
Monday	7	14	21	28
Tuesday	1	8	15	22	29
Wednesday	2	9	16	23	30
Thursday	3	10	17	24	31
Friday	4	11	18	25
Saturday	5	12	19	26

FEBRUARY				
Sunday	3	10	17	24
Monday	4	11	18	25
Tuesday	5	12	19	26
Wednesday	6	13	20	27
Thursday	7	14	21	28
Friday	1	8	15	22
Saturday	2	9	16	23

MARCH				
Sunday	3	10	17	24	31
Monday	4	11	18	25
Tuesday	5	12	19	26
Wednesday	6	13	20	27
Thursday	7	14	21	28
Friday	1	8	15	22	29
Saturday	2	9	16	23	30

APRIL				
Sunday	7	14	21	28
Monday	1	8	15	22	29
Tuesday	2	9	16	23	30
Wednesday	3	10	17	24
Thursday	4	11	18	25
Friday	5	12	19	26
Saturday	6	13	20	27

MAY				
Sunday	5	12	19	26
Monday	6	13	20	27
Tuesday	7	14	21	28
Wednesday	1	8	15	22	29
Thursday	2	9	16	23	30
Friday	3	10	17	24	31
Saturday	4	11	18	25

JUNE				
Sunday	2	9	16	23	30
Monday	3	10	17	24
Tuesday	4	11	18	25
Wednesday	5	12	19	26
Thursday	6	13	20	27
Friday	7	14	21	28
Saturday	1	8	15	22	29

JULY				
Sunday	7	14	21	28
Monday	1	8	15	22	29
Tuesday	2	9	16	23	30
Wednesday	3	10	17	24	31
Thursday	4	11	18	25
Friday	5	12	19	26
Saturday	6	13	20	27

AUGUST				
Sunday	4	11	18	25
Monday	5	12	19	26
Tuesday	6	13	20	27
Wednesday	7	14	21	28
Thursday	1	8	15	22	29
Friday	2	9	16	23	30
Saturday	3	10	17	24	31

SEPTEMBER				
Sunday	1	8	15	22	29
Monday	2	9	16	23	30
Tuesday	3	10	17	24
Wednesday	4	11	18	25
Thursday	5	12	19	26
Friday	6	13	20	27
Saturday	7	14	21	28

OCTOBER				
Sunday	6	13	20	27
Monday	7	14	21	28
Tuesday	1	8	15	22	29
Wednesday	2	9	16	23	30
Thursday	3	10	17	24	31
Friday	4	11	18	25
Saturday	5	12	19	26

NOVEMBER				
Sunday	3	10	17	24
Monday	4	11	18	25
Tuesday	5	12	19	26
Wednesday	6	13	20	27
Thursday	7	14	21	28
Friday	1	8	15	22	29
Saturday	2	9	16	23	30

DECEMBER				
Sunday	1	8	15	22	29
Monday	2	9	16	23	30
Tuesday	3	10	17	24	31
Wednesday	4	11	18	25
Thursday	5	12	19	26
Friday	6	13	20	27
Saturday	7	14	21	28

PUBLIC HOLIDAYS

	England and Wales	Scotland	Northern Ireland
New Year	1 January†	1, 2† January	1 January†
St Patrick's Day	—	—	17 March
*Good Friday	29 March	29 March	29 March
Easter Monday	1 April	—	1 April
Early May	6 May†	6 May	6 May†
Spring	27 May	27 May†	27 May
Battle of the Boyne	—	—	12 July‡
Summer	26 August	5 August	26 August
St Andrew's Day	—	30 Nov§	—
*Christmas	25, 26 December	25†, 26 December	25, 26 December

* In England, Wales and Northern Ireland, Christmas Day and Good Friday are common law holidays

† Subject to royal proclamation

‡ Subject to proclamation by the Secretary of State for Northern Ireland

§ The St Andrew's Day Holiday (Scotland) Bill was approved by parliament on 29 November 2006; it does not oblige employers to change their existing pattern of holidays but provides the legal framework in which the St Andrew's Day bank holiday could be substituted for an existing local holiday from another date in the year

Note: In the Channel Islands, Liberation Day is a bank and public holiday

FORTHCOMING EVENTS

* Provisional dates
† Venue not confirmed

JANUARY 2012
6–15	London Boat Show, Excel, London Docklands
11–29	London International Mime Festival
17–19	UK Open Dance Championships, Bournemouth International Centre
18–22	London Art Fair, Business Design Centre
19–5 Feb	Celtic Connections Music Festival, Glasgow
28–29	RSPB Big Garden Birdwatch

FEBRUARY
2–5	London Motorcycle Show, Excel, London Docklands
3–19	Leicester Comedy Festival
12	British Academy Film Awards, Royal Opera House, London
11–18	Jorvik Viking Festival, Jorvik Viking Centre, York
24–26	Ceramic Art London, Royal College of Art

MARCH
1	World Book Day
2–11	Bath Literature Festival
8	International Women's Day
8–11	Crufts Dog Show, NEC, Birmingham
9–18	National Science and Engineering Week
10–13	Affordable Art Fair, Battersea Park, London
16–1 Apr	Ideal Home Show, Earls Court, London
21–27	BADA Antiques and Fine Art Fair, Duke of York's Square, London

APRIL
2–10	Oxford Literary Festival
16–18	London Book Fair, Earls Court, London
22	Earth Day

MAY
20–26 Aug	Glyndebourne Festival
22–26	RHS Chelsea Flower Show, Royal Hospital, Chelsea
31 May–10 June	Hay Festival, Hay-on-Wye, Hereford

JUNE
4–12 Aug	Royal Academy of Arts Summer Exhibition, Burlington House, London
10–26	Aldeburgh Festival of Music and the Arts, Snape, Suffolk

16	Trooping the Colour, Horse Guards Parade, London
27–7 July	New Designers Exhibition, Business Design Centre, London

JULY
3–8	RHS Hampton Court Palace Flower Show, Surrey
4–15	Cheltenham Music Festival
6–14	York Early Music Festival
7	Pride Parade, London
7–25	Buxton Festival, Derbyshire
Mid-Jul–Mid-Sep	BBC Promenade Concerts, Royal Albert Hall, London
18–22	RHS Flower Show, Tatton Park, Cheshire
*21–30	The Welsh Proms, St David's Hall, Cardiff
26–29	Cambridge Folk Festival
27–29	WOMAD Festival, Charlton Park, Wiltshire
29–7 Aug	Edinburgh Jazz and Blues Festival

AUGUST
4–11	National Eisteddfod of Wales, Wrexham
5–27	Edinburgh Military Tattoo, Edinburgh Castle
*10–2 Sep	Edinburgh International Festival
21–28	Three Choirs Festival, Worcester
*28–29	Notting Hill Carnival, London
31–4 Nov	Blackpool Illuminations, Blackpool Promenade

SEPTEMBER
1	Braemar Royal Highland Gathering, Aberdeenshire
8	International Literacy Day
6–9	Heritage Open Days, England (nationwide)
6–9	RHS Wisley Flower Show, RHS Garden, Wisley
10–13	TUC Annual Congress, Brighton
*11	Mercury Music Prize
22–26	Liberal Democrat Party Conference, Brighton
30–4 Oct	Labour Party Conference, Manchester

OCTOBER
8–11	Conservative Party Conference, Birmingham
11–14	Frieze Art Fair, Regent's Park, London
Mid-Oct	Booker Prize
Mid-Oct	London Film Festival
Mid-Oct–Jan	Turner Prize Exhibition, Tate Britain, London

NOVEMBER
Mid-Nov   Classic Motor Show, NEC,
                 Birmingham
Mid-Nov   Lord Mayor's Procession and Show,
                 City of London
Mid-Nov   CBI Annual Conference

SPORTS EVENTS

JANUARY 2012
13–22   Winter Youth Olympics, Innsbruck,
                 Austria
15–22   Snooker: Masters, Alexandra Palace,
                 London
16–29   Tennis: Australian Open, Melbourne,
                 Australia
21–12 Feb   Football: African Cup of Nations,
                 Gabon and Equatorial Guinea

FEBRUARY
4–17 Mar   Rugby Union: Six Nations
                 Championship
7–12   Squash: British National
                 Championships, Manchester
12–13   Rugby League: Super League,
                 Millennium Stadium, Cardiff
26   Football: League Cup Final,
                 Wembley Stadium, London

MARCH
6–11   Badminton: English National
                 Championships, Birmingham

APRIL
7   Rowing: Oxford and Cambridge
                 Boat Race, Putney to Mortlake,
                 London
14   Horse racing: Grand National,
                 Aintree, Liverpool
21–7 May   Snooker: World Championship,
                 Crucible Theatre, Sheffield
22   Athletics: London Marathon

MAY
3–7   Equestrian: Badminton Horse Trials,
                 Badminton
Early May   Horse racing: Guineas Festival,
                 Newmarket
5   Football: FA Cup Final, Wembley
                 Stadium, London
9–13   Royal Windsor Horse Show, Home
                 Park, Windsor
19   Football: Scottish FA Cup Final,
                 Hampden Park, Glasgow
19–20   Rugby Union: Heineken Cup Final,
                 Twickenham, London
19   Football: UEFA Champions League
                 Final, Allianz Arena, Munich
†26   Football: FA Women's Cup Final

27–11 Jun   Tennis: French Open, Paris
*28–8 Jun   Motorcycling: TT Races, Isle of
                 Man

JUNE
2   Horse racing: The Derby, Epsom
                 Downs
8–1 July   Football: UEFA European
                 Championships, Poland and
                 Ukraine
18–23   Golf: British Amateur Golf
                 Championship, Royal Troon,
                 South Ayrshire
19–23   Horse racing: Royal Ascot
25–8 Jul   Tennis: Wimbledon Championship,
                 All England Lawn Tennis Club,
                 London
27–1 Jul   Rowing: Henley Royal Regatta,
                 Henley-on-Thames
30–22 Jul   Cycling: Tour de France

JULY
7–21   Shooting: NRA Imperial Meeting,
                 Bisley Camp, Surrey
15–22   Golf: Open Championship, Lytham,
                 Lancashire
Late Jul   Horse racing: King George VI and
                 Queen Elizabeth Diamond Stakes,
                 Ascot
27–12 Aug   Olympic Games, London

AUGUST
11–18   Sailing: Cowes Week, Isle of Wight
25   Rugby League: Challenge Cup Final,
                 Wembley Stadium, London
29–9 Sep   Paralympic Games, London
29–12 Sep   Tennis: US Open, New York

SEPTEMBER
Early Sep   Equestrian: Burghley Horse Trials,
                 Stamford, Lincolnshire
Early Sep   Horse racing: St Leger, Doncaster
13–16   Golf: Women's British Open, Royal
                 Liverpool, Hoylake
Mid-Sep   Cricket: Twenty20 World Cup,
                 Sri Lanka
Late Sep–   Horse racing: Cambridgeshire
Early Oct   Meeting, Newmarket
Late Sep–   Athletics: Great North Run,
Early Oct   Newcastle

OCTOBER
Early Oct   Equestrian: Horse of the Year Show,
                 NEC, Birmingham
Mid-Oct   Horse racing: Champions Meeting,
                 Newmarket
Early–Mid-Oct   Rugby League: Super League Final,
                 Old Trafford, Manchester

CENTENARIES

2012

1512
5 Mar   Gerardus Mercator, Flemish-German cartographer, born
10 Apr   King James V of Scotland, born

1612
17 Jan   Sir Thomas Fairfax, commander of the New Model Army, born

1712
28 Jun   Jean-Jacques Rousseau, French philosopher, born
12 Jul   Richard Cromwell, Lord Protector 1658–9, died
14 Oct   William Grenville, First Lord of the Treasury 1763–5, born

1812
7 Feb   Charles Dickens, novelist and essayist, born
1 Mar   Augustus Pugin, architect, born
6 Apr   Alexander Herzen, Russian political theorist and writer, born
7 May   Robert Browning, poet, born
11 May   Spencer Perceval, prime minister 1809–12, died
12 May   Edward Lear, poet and illustrator, born
19 Sep   Mayer Amschel Rothschild, German banker, died
16 Nov   John Walter, founder of *The Times,* died

1912
28 Jan   Jackson Pollock, painter, born
10 Feb   Sir Joseph Lister, surgeon, died
27 Feb   Lawrence Durrell, novelist and poet, born
14 Mar   Cliff Bastin, football player, born
27 Mar   James Callaghan, prime minister 1976–9, born
20 Apr   Bram Stoker, Irish novelist, died
28 May   Patrick White, Australian novelist, died
30 May   Wilbur Wright, American aviation pioneer, died
13 Jun   Sir Georg Solti, conductor, born
14 Jul   Woody Guthrie, American musician, born
17 Jul   Jules Henri Poincaré, French mathematican, died
13 Aug   Ben Hogan, American golfer, born
20 Aug   Gen. William Booth, founder of the Salvation Army, died
23 Aug   Gene Kelly, actor and choreographer, born

2013

1413
20 Mar   Henry IV, King of England 1399–1413, died

1513
9 Sep   James IV, King of Scotland 1488–1513, died

1813
26 Feb   Robert Livingston, American diplomat, died
19 Mar   David Livingstone, explorer, born
5 May   Soren Kierkegaard, Danish philospher, born
22 May   Richard Wagner, German composer, born

1913
4 Jan   Alfred von Schlieffen, German field marshal, died
6 Jan   Loretta Young, American actor, born
9 Jan   Richard Nixon, 37th president of USA, born
4 Feb   Rosa Parks, American civil rights activist, born
25 Feb   Gert Fröbe, German actor, born
13 Mar   William J. Casey, American director of the CIA, born
31 Mar   John Pierpont Morgan, American financier, died
25 May   Richard Dimbleby, journalist and broadcaster, born
8 Jun   Emily Davison, women's suffrage activist, died
11 Jun   Vince Lombardi, American football coach, born
14 Jul   Gerald Ford, 38th president of USA, born
23 Jul   Michael Foot, politician, born
16 Aug   Menachem Begin, Israeli prime minister, born
12 Sep   Jesse Owens, American athlete, born
29 Sep   Rudolf Diesel, inventor of the diesel engine, died
2 Nov   Burt Lancaster, American actor, born
5 Nov   Vivien Leigh, actor, born
7 Nov   Albert Camus, French novelist and essayist, born
22 Nov   Benjamin Britten, composer and conductor, born
18 Dec   Willy Brandt, German chancellor, born

THE UNITED KINGDOM

THE UK IN FIGURES

The United Kingdom comprises Great Britain (England, Wales and Scotland) and Northern Ireland. The Isle of Man and the Channel Islands are Crown dependencies with their own legislative systems and are not part of the UK.

ABBREVIATIONS
ONS   Office for National Statistics
NISRA   Northern Ireland Statistics and Research Agency
All data is for the UK unless otherwise stated.

AREA OF THE UNITED KINGDOM

	Sq. km	Sq. miles
United Kingdom	243,122	93,870
England	130,280	50,301
Wales	20,733	8,005
Scotland	77,958	30,100
Northern Ireland	14,150	5,463

Source: ONS (Crown copyright)

POPULATION

The first official census of population in England, Wales and Scotland was taken in 1801 and a census has been taken every ten years since, except in 1941 when there was no census because of Second World War. The last official census in the UK was taken on 29 April 2001 and the next is due in April 2011.

The first official census of population in Ireland was taken in 1841. However, all figures given below refer only to the area which is now Northern Ireland. Figures for Northern Ireland in 1921 and 1931 are estimates based on the censuses taken in 1926 and 1937 respectively.

Estimates of the population of England before 1801, calculated from the number of baptisms, burials and marriages, are:

1570	4,160,221	1670	5,773,646
1600	4,811,718	1700	6,045,008
1630	5,600,517	1750	6,517,035

Further details are available on the Office for National Statistics (ONS) website (W www.statistics.gov.uk).

CENSUS RESULTS *Thousands*

	United Kingdom			England and Wales			Scotland			Northern Ireland		
	Total	Male	Female	Total	Male	Female	Total	Male	Female	Total	Male	Female
1801	—	—	—	8,893	4,255	4,638	1,608	739	869	—	—	—
1811	13,368	6,368	7,000	10,165	4,874	5,291	1,806	826	980	—	—	—
1821	15,472	7,498	7,974	12,000	5,850	6,150	2,092	983	1,109	—	—	—
1831	17,835	8,647	9,188	13,897	6,771	7,126	2,364	1,114	1,250	—	—	—
1841	20,183	9,819	10,364	15,914	7,778	8,137	2,620	1,242	1,378	1,649	800	849
1851	22,259	10,855	11,404	17,928	8,781	9,146	2,889	1,376	1,513	1,443	698	745
1861	24,525	11,894	12,631	20,066	9,776	10,290	3,062	1,450	1,612	1,396	668	728
1871	27,431	13,309	14,122	22,712	11,059	11,653	3,360	1,603	1,757	1,359	647	712
1881	31,015	15,060	15,955	25,974	12,640	13,335	3,736	1,799	1,936	1,305	621	684
1891	34,264	16,593	17,671	29,003	14,060	14,942	4,026	1,943	2,083	1,236	590	646
1901	38,237	18,492	19,745	32,528	15,729	16,799	4,472	2,174	2,298	1,237	590	647
1911	42,082	20,357	21,725	36,070	17,446	18,625	4,761	2,309	2,452	1,251	603	648
1921	44,027	21,033	22,994	37,887	18,075	19,811	4,882	2,348	2,535	1,258	610	648
1931	46,038	22,060	23,978	39,952	19,133	20,819	4,843	2,326	2,517	1,243	601	642
1951	50,225	24,118	26,107	43,758	21,016	22,742	5,096	2,434	2,662	1,371	668	703
1961	52,709	25,481	27,228	46,105	22,304	23,801	5,179	2,483	2,697	1,425	694	731
1971	55,515	26,952	28,562	48,750	23,683	25,067	5,229	2,515	2,714	1,536	755	781
1981	55,848	27,104	28,742	49,155	23,873	25,281	5,131	2,466	2,664	1,533*	750	783
1991	56,467	27,344	29,123	49,890	24,182	25,707	4,999	2,392	2,607	1,578	769	809
2001	58,789	28,581	30,208	52,042	25,327	26,715	5,062	2,432	2,630	1,685	821	864

* Figure includes 44,500 non-enumerated persons

ISLANDS

	Isle of Man			Jersey			Guernsey†		
	Total	Male	Female	Total	Male	Female	Total	Male	Female
1901	54,752	25,496	29,256	52,576	23,940	28,636	40,446	19,652	20,794
1921	60,284	27,329	32,955	49,701	22,438	27,263	38,315	18,246	20,069
1951	55,123	25,749	29,464	57,296	27,282	30,014	43,652	21,221	22,431
1971	56,289	26,461	29,828	72,532	35,423	37,109	51,458	24,792	26,666
1991	69,788	33,693	36,095	84,082	40,862	43,220	58,867	28,297	30,570
2001	76,315	37,372	38,943	87,186	42,485	44,701	59,807	29,138	30,669
2006	80,058	39,523	40,535						

† Includes Herm, Jethou and Lithou
Source: ONS – Census Reports (Crown copyright)

RESIDENT POPULATION

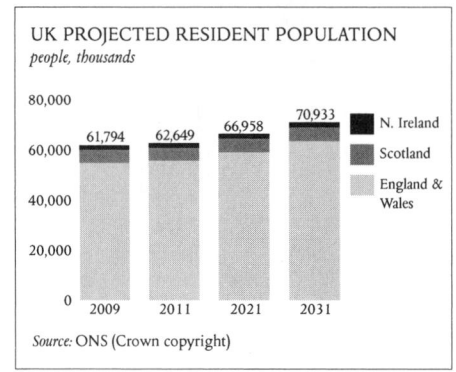

UK PROJECTED RESIDENT POPULATION
people, thousands

Source: ONS (Crown copyright)

UK PROJECTED RESIDENT POPULATION
by sex, thousands

Source: ONS (Crown copyright)

BY AGE AND SEX (UK)

	Male	Female
		Thousands
0–4	1,977	1,881
5–9	1,762	1,685
10–14	1,825	1,742
15–19	2,013	1,899
20–29	4,382	4,178
30–44	6,338	6,387
45–59	5,973	6,152
60–64	1,840	1,924
65–74	2,572	2,827
75–84	1,501	1,999
85+	460	951

Source: ONS (Crown copyright)

BY ETHNIC GROUP (ENGLAND AND WALES)

	Thousands
White	
British	45,682
Other	2,507
Mixed	
White and black Caribbean	311
White and black African	132
White and Asian	302
Other mixed	243
Asian	
Indian	1,434
Pakistani	1,007
Bangladeshi	392
Other Asian	386
Black	
Black Caribbean	615
Black African	799
Black other	126
Chinese	452
Other	423
ALL	54,809

Source: ONS (Crown copyright)

IMMIGRATION

ACCEPTANCES FOR SETTLEMENT IN THE UK

Geographical region	Number of persons	
	2007	*2009*
Europe*	8,660	10,580
Americas	10,435	15,120
Africa	34,050	47,730
Asia	67,955	116,740
Indian subcontinent	29,020	67,090
Middle East	10,655	9,390
Remainder of Asia	28,280	40,255
Oceania	3,615	4,365
Others	140	245
ALL NATIONALITIES	124,855	194,780

* Excluding European Economic Area and Swiss nationals
Source: Home Office

BIRTHS

	Live births	Birth rate*
United Kingdom	790,204	12.7
England and Wales	706,248	12.9
Scotland	59,046	11.4
Northern Ireland	24,910	13.9

* Live births per 1,000 population
Source: NISRA, ONS (Crown copyright), Scottish Government

FERTILITY RATES
Total fertility rate is the average number of children which
would be born to a woman if she experienced the
age-specific fertility rates of the period in question
throughout her child-bearing life span. The figures for the
years 1960–2 are estimates.

	1960–2	*1998*	*2009*
United Kingdom	2.80	1.71	1.94
England and Wales	2.77	1.72	1.95
Scotland	2.98	1.55	1.77
Northern Ireland	3.47	1.90	2.04

Source: ONS (Crown copyright)

MATERNITY RATES FOR ENGLAND AND WALES 2009

	All maternities*	Singleton	All multiplet	Twins	Triplets+
All ages	698,324	686,870	11,454	11,301	153
<20	43,216	42,920	296	294	2
20–24	135,404	134,068	1,336	1,323	13
25–29	192,422	189,832	2,590	2,562	28
30–34	188,767	185,074	3,693	3,639	54
35–39	112,134	109,382	2,752	2,712	40
40–44	24,906	24,275	631	619	12
45+	1,475	1,319	156	152	4

* Includes stillbirths
† Total inclues rates for twin, triplets, quads and above
Source: ONS (Crown copyright)

TOP TEN BABY NAMES

	1934 Girls	Boys	2009 Girls	Boys
1	Margaret	John	Olivia	Oliver
2	Jean	Peter	Ruby	Jack
3	Mary	William	Chloe	Harry
4	Joan	Brian	Emily	Alfie
5	Patricia	David	Sophie	Joshua
6	Sheila	James	Jessica	Thomas
7	Barbara	Michael	Grace	Charlie
8	Doreen	Ronald	Lily	William
9	June	Kenneth	Amelia	James
10	Shirley	George	Evie	Daniel

Source: ONS (Crown copyright)

LIVE BIRTHS BY AGE OF MOTHER AND REGISTRATION TYPE

Outside marriage

Year	under 20	20–29	30–39	40+	All ages
1971	21,600	33,500	9,500	1,100	65,700
1981	26,400	43,100	35,200	900	81,000
1991	43,400	130,200	35,500	2,100	211,300
2001	39,500	124,900	68,500	5,100	238,100
2009	40,900	185,700	89,900	9,600	326,200

Within marriage

1971	61,100	499,400	145,500	11,600	717,500
1981	30,100	367,200	150,200	6,000	553,500
1991	8,900	291,900	179,300	7,700	487,900
2001	4,600	143,800	196,900	11,100	356,500
2009	2,300	144,400	216,000	17,400	380,100

Source: ONS – Social Trends 2011 (Crown copyright)

LEGAL ABORTIONS

	1998	2010
England and Wales	177,871	189,574
Scotland	12,458	12,826

Source: Department of Health, NHS Scotland

DEATHS

Men	Deaths
United Kingdom	270,804
England and Wales	238,062
Scotland	25,828
Northern Ireland	6,914
Women	
United Kingdom	288,813
England and Wales	253,286
Scotland	28,028
Northern Ireland	7,499

Source: ONS (Crown copyright)

INFANT MORTALITY RATE*

United Kingdom	4.5
England and Wales	4.5
Scotland	4.0
Northern Ireland	5.1

* Deaths of infants under one year of age per 1,000 live births
Source: General Register Office for Scotland, NISRA, ONS (Crown copyright)

MARRIAGE AND DIVORCE

	Marriages	Divorces
United Kingdom	266,950*	126,496
England and Wales	231,490*	113,949
Scotland	27,524	10,371
Northern Ireland	7,931	2,176

* Provisional figures
Source: ONS (Crown copyright)

HOUSEHOLDS

BY TYPE (GREAT BRITAIN)

Percentages

	1971	1991	2010
One person	18	27	29
One family households			
Couple			
No children	27	28	28
1–2 dependent children	26	20	18
3 or more dependent children	9	5	3
Non-dependent children only	8	8	6
Lone parent			
Dependent children	3	6	7
Non-dependent children only	4	4	3
Two or more unrelated adults	4	3	3
Multi-family households	1	1	1
All households (=100%) (millions)	18.6	22.4	25.3

Source: ONS – Social Trends 2011 (Crown copyright)

BY SIZE (GREAT BRITAIN)

Percentages

	1971	1991	2010
One person	18	27	29
Two people	32	34	35
Three people	19	16	16
Four people	17	16	14
Five people	8	5	4
Six or more people	6	2	2
All households (=100%) (millions)	18.6	22.4	25.3
Average household size (people)	2.9	2.5	2.4

Source: ONS – Social Trends 2011 (Crown copyright)

20   The United Kingdom

DEPENDENT CHILDREN LIVING IN DIFFERENT FAMILY TYPES

Millions

	1997	2005	2009
Married couple	9.6	8.6	8.3
Cohabiting couple	1.0	1.5	1.7
Female lone parent	2.5	2.8	2.9
Male lone parent	0.2	0.3	0.3

Source: ONS – *Social Trends 2010* (Crown copyright)

MORTGAGES

	1999	2005	2009
Mortgages* *(thousands)*	10,987	11,608	11,401
Loans in arrears at end-period* *(thousands)*			
By 6–12 months	57	39	92
By 12+ months	30	15	68
Properties repossessed in period	30	15	48

*Estimates cover only members of the Council of Mortgage Lenders, which account for 98 per cent of all outstanding mortgages

Source: ONS – *Annual Abstract of Statistics 2010* (Crown copyright)

TENURE BY HOUSEHOLD COMPOSITION (GREAT BRTAIN), 2009

Percentages

	Owned outright	Owned with mortgage	Privately rented*	Rented from social sector
One person households				
Under state pension age†	18.9	36.6	18.7	25.8
Over state pension age	59.5	4.4	7.9	28.2
One family households				
Couple				
No children	48.5	33.6	9.9	8.0
Dependent children	8.3	65.9	12.5	13.2
Non-dependent children	36.2	49.8	4.6	9.5
Lone parent				
Dependent children	5.0	30.3	23.6	41.0
Non-dependent children	31.1	31.7	10.2	27.0
Other households‡	20.3	28.2	37.9	13.6
All households	31.9	37.1	12.9	18.1

* Includes tenants in rent-free accommodation and squatters

† Stage pension age in 2009 is 65 for men and 60 for women

‡ Comprising two or more unrelated adults or two or more families or a small number of same-sex couples

Source: ONS – *Social Trends 2011* (Crown copyright)

HEALTH

DEATHS BY CAUSE, 2009

	England and Wales	Scotland	N. Ireland
Total deaths	491,348	53,856	14,413
Deaths from natural causes	473,470	51,658	13,608
Certain infectious and parasitic diseases	5,750	838	164
Intestinal infectious diseases	1861	109	69*
Respiratory and other tuberculosis	305	29	6*
Meningococcal infection	60	5	2*
Viral hepatitis	258	25	2*
AIDS (HIV – disease)	256	17	–
Neoplasms	140,497	15,484	3,992
Malignant neoplasms	137,420	15,187	3,885
Malignant neoplasm of trachea, bronchus and lung	30,018	4,147	927*
Malignant neoplasm of skin	2,325	253	57*
Malignant neoplasm of breast	10,440	1,010	312*
Malignant neoplasm of cervix uteri	830	124	28*
Malignant neoplasm of prostate	9.402	790	226*
Leukaemia	3,990	388	102*
Diseases of the blood and blood-forming organs and certain disorders involving the immune mechanism	1,026	113	28
Endocrine, nutritional and metabolic diseases	7,123	873	319
Diabetes mellitus	5,278	632	229
Mental and behavioural disorders	18,021	3,327	525
Vascular and unspecified dementia	16,911	2,585	472
Alcohol abuse	645	312	46*
Drug dependence and non-dependent abuse of drugs	1,340	410	2*
Diseases of the nervous system and sense organs	17,408	1,652	618
Meningitis (excluding meningococcal)	154	22	3*
Alzheimer's disease	6,194	634	241
Diseases of the circulatory system	159,779	16,769	4,485
Ischaemic heart diseases	72,120	8,274	2,305
Cerebrovascular diseases	43,595	4,906	1,175
Diseases of the respiratory system	67,559	7,125	2,017
Influenza	227	62	2*
Pneumonia	26,741	2,345	900*
Bronchitis, emphysema and other chronic obstructive pulmonary diseases	23,318	2,801	680*
Asthma	991	75	31*
Diseases of the digestive system	25,230	3,006	686
Gastric and duodenal ulcer	2,714	220	52*
Chronic liver disease	7,326	1,110	204*
Diseases of the skin and subcutaneous tissue	1,849	157	24*
Diseases of the musculo-skeletal system and connective tissue	4,141	344	85*
Osteoporosis	1,565	73	15*
Diseases of the genito-urinary system	11,998	1,269	367
Complications of pregnancy, childbirth and the puerperium	63	7	5
Certain conditions originating in the perinatal period†	237	123	60
Congenital malformations, deformations and chromosomal abnormalities†	1,261	153	82
Symptoms, signs and abnormal findings not classified elsewhere	9,243	414	138
Senility without mention of psychosis (old age)	7,531	236	107*
Sudden infant death syndrome	156	23	3*
Deaths from external causes	17,878	2,198	805
Suicide and intentional self-harm	3,457	568	252*
Homicide and assault	318‡	72	40*

* 2008 figures

† Excludes neonatal deaths (those at age under 28 days): for England and Wales neonatal deaths are included in the total number of deaths but excluded from the cause figures

‡ This will not be a true figure as registration of homicide and assault deaths in England and Wales is often delayed by adjourned inquests

Source: General Register Office for Scotland, NISRA, ONS (Crown copyright)

22   The United Kingdom

ALCOHOL CONSUMPTION* BY AGE (GREAT BRITAIN)
Percentages

	16–24	25–44	45–64	65+	All 16+
Men					
No units	37	28	26	34	30
Up to 4 units	21	30	33	44	33
4–8 units	12	15	20	14	16
8+ units	30	27	21	7	21
Women					
No units	48	41	40	57	45
Up to 3 units	16	22	28	33	26
3–6 units	12	16	19	8	15
6+ units	24	20	13	2	14

* Maximum consumed on any one day in the previous week. Department of Health guidelines recommend that men should not regularly drink more than three to four units of alcohol per day and women should not regularly drink more than two to three units per day. A unit of alcohol is 8 grams by weight or 10ml by volume of pure alcohol, ie the amount contained in half a pint of ordinary strength beer or lager, a single pub measure of spirits or a small glass of ordinary strength wine
Source: ONS – *Social Trends 2010* (Crown copyright)

PREVALENCE OF SMOKING, DRINKING AND BINGE-DRINKING AMONG ADULTS
Percentages

	Men			Women		
	Regular smoker	Drank more than 4 units	Drank more than 8 units	Regular smoker	Drank more than 3 units	Drank more than 6 units
2000–1	29	39	21	25	23	10
2001–2	28	40	22	26	23	10
2002–3	27	38	21	25	23	10
2003–4	28	40	23	24	23	9
2004–5	26	39	22	23	22	9
2005	25	35	19	23	20	8
2006	23	40	23	21	33	15
2007	22	41	24	20	34	15
2008	22	37	21	21	29	14
2009	22	37	20	20	29	13

Source: ONS – *Social Trends 2011* (Crown copyright)

NOTIFICATIONS OF INFECTIOUS DISEASES

	2000	2008
Measles	2,865	5,331
Mumps	3,367	8,682
Rubella	2,064	1,230
Whooping cough	866	1,676
Scarlet fever	2,544	3,983
Dysentery	1,613	1,289
Food poisoning	98,076	77,854
Typhoid and paratyphoid fevers	205	418
Hepatitis	4,530	6,515
Tuberculosis	7,100	7,878
Malaria	1,166	403

Source: ONS – *Annual Abstract of Statistics 2010* (Crown copyright)

CIGARETTE SMOKING HABITS
Percentages

	2000	2008
Men		
Current cigarette smoker	29	22
Light to moderate (fewer than 20 cigarettes a day)	18	15
Heavy (20 or more a day)	10	7
Ex-regular smoker	27	30
Never or only occasionally smoked	44	49
Women		
Current cigarette smoker	25	21
Light to moderate (fewer than 20 cigarettes a day)	19	15
Heavy (20 or more a day)	6	5
Ex-regular smoker	20	22
Never or only occasionally smoked	54	58

Source: ONS – *Social Trends 2010* (Crown copyright)

BODY MASS INDEX (BMI)* BY WEIGHT CLASSIFICATION (ENGLAND)
Percentages

	2000	2008
Underweight (BMI less than 18.5)	1.5	1.8
Normal (18.5 to less than 25)	38.6	36.8
Overweight (25 to less than 30)	38.8	36.9
Obese† (30 and over)	21.2	24.5
Morbidly obese (40 and over)	1.5	2.0

* BMI is the most widely used measure of obesity among adults aged 16 and over. BMI standardises weight for height and is calculated as weight (kg)/height (m)^2
† Includes morbidly obese
Source: ONS – *Social Trends 2010* (Crown copyright)

THE NATIONAL FLAG

The national flag of the United Kingdom is the Union Flag, generally known as the Union Jack.

The Union Flag is a combination of the cross of St George, patron saint of England, the cross of St Andrew, patron saint of Scotland and the cross of St Patrick, patron saint of Ireland.

Cross of St George: cross Gules in a field Argent (red cross on a white ground)

Cross of St Andrew: saltire Argent in a field Azure (white diagonal cross on a blue ground)

Cross of St Patrick: saltire Gules in a field Argent (red diagonal cross on a white ground)

The Union Flag was first introduced in 1606 after the union of the kingdoms of England and Scotland under one sovereign. The cross of St Patrick was added in 1801 after the union of Great Britain and Ireland.

See also Flags of the World colour plates.

FLYING THE UNION FLAG

The correct orientation of the Union Flag when flying is with the broader diagonal band of white uppermost in the hoist (ie near the pole) and the narrower diagonal band of white uppermost in the fly (ie furthest from the pole).

The flying of the Union Flag on government buildings is decided by the Department for Culture, Media and Sport (DCMS) at the Queen's command. There is no formal definition of a government building but it is generally accepted to mean a building owned or used by the Crown and/or predominantly occupied or used by civil servants or the Armed Forces.

The Scottish or Welsh governments are responsible for drawing up their own flag-flying guidance for their buildings. In Northern Ireland, the flying of flags is constrained by The Flags Regulations (Northern Ireland) 2000 and the Police Emblems and Flag Regulations (Northern Ireland) 2002. Individuals, local authorities and other organisations may fly the Union Flag whenever they wish, subject to compliance with any local planning requirement.

FLAGS AT HALF-MAST

Flags are flown at half-mast (ie two-thirds up between the top and bottom of the flagstaff) on the following occasions:

• from the announcement of the death of the sovereign until the funeral
• the death or funeral of a member of the royal family*
• the funerals of foreign rulers*
• the funerals of prime ministers and ex-prime ministers of the UK*
• the funerals of first ministers and ex-first ministers of Scotland, Wales and Northern Ireland (unless otherwise commanded by the sovereign, this only applies to flags in their respective countries)*
• other occasions by special command from the Queen

* By special command from the Queen in each case

DAYS FOR FLYING FLAGS

On 25 March 2008 the DCMS announced that UK government departments in England, Scotland and Wales may fly the Union Flag on their buildings whenever they choose and not just on the designated days listed below. In addition, on the patron saints' days of Scotland and Wales, the appropriate national flag may be flown alongside the Union Flag on UK government buildings in the wider Whitehall area. When flying on designated days flags are hoisted from 8am to sunset.

Countess of Wessex's birthday	20 Jan
Accession of the Queen	6 Feb
Duke of York's birthday	19 Feb
St David's Day (in Wales only)*	1 Mar
Earl of Wessex's birthday	10 Mar
Commonwealth Day (2012)	12 Mar
St Patrick's Day (in Northern Ireland only)†	17 Mar
The Queen's birthday	21 Apr
St George's Day (in England only)*	23 Apr
Europe Day†	9 May
Coronation Day	2 Jun
Duke of Edinburgh's birthday	10 Jun
The Queen's official birthday (2012)	16 Jun
Duchess of Cornwall's birthday	17 Jul
Princess Royal's birthday	15 Aug
Remembrance Day (2012)	11 Nov
Prince of Wales' birthday	14 Nov
Wedding Day of the Queen	20 Nov
St Andrew's Day (in Scotland only)*	30 Nov
Opening of parliament by the Queen‡	
Prorogation of parliament by the Queen‡	

* The appropriate national flag, or the European flag, may be flown in addition to the Union Flag (where there are two or more flagpoles), but not in a superior position
† Only the Union Flag should be flown
‡ Only in the Greater London area, whether or not the Queen performs the ceremony in person

THE ROYAL STANDARD

The Royal Standard comprises four quarterings – two for England (three lions passant), one for Scotland* (a lion rampant) and one for Ireland (a harp).

The Royal Standard is flown when the Queen is in residence at a royal palace, on transport being used by the Queen for official journeys and from Victoria Tower when the Queen attends parliament. It may also be flown on any building (excluding ecclesiastical buildings) during a visit by the Queen. If the Queen is to be present in a building advice on flag flying can be obtained from the DCMS.

The Royal Standard is never flown at half-mast, even after the death of the sovereign, as the new monarch immediately succeeds to the throne.

* In Scotland a version with two Scottish quarterings is used

THE ROYAL FAMILY

THE SOVEREIGN

ELIZABETH II, by the Grace of God, of the United Kingdom of Great Britain and Northern Ireland and of her other Realms and Territories Queen, Head of the Commonwealth, Defender of the Faith
Her Majesty Elizabeth Alexandra Mary of Windsor, elder daughter of King George VI and of HM Queen Elizabeth the Queen Mother
Born 21 April 1926, at 17 Bruton Street, London W1
Ascended the throne 6 February 1952
Crowned 2 June 1953, at Westminster Abbey
Married 20 November 1947, in Westminster Abbey, HRH the Prince Philip, Duke of Edinburgh
Official residences Buckingham Palace, London SW1A 1AA; Windsor Castle, Berks; Palace of Holyroodhouse, Edinburgh
Private residences Sandringham, Norfolk; Balmoral Castle, Aberdeenshire

HUSBAND OF THE QUEEN

HRH THE PRINCE PHILIP, DUKE OF EDINBURGH, KG, KT, OM, GBE, Royal Victorian Chain, AC, QSO, PC, Ranger of Windsor Park
Born 10 June 1921, son of Prince and Princess Andrew of Greece and Denmark, naturalised a British subject 1947, created Duke of Edinburgh, Earl of Merioneth and Baron Greenwich 1947

CHILDREN OF THE QUEEN

HRH THE PRINCE OF WALES (Prince Charles Philip Arthur George), KG, KT, GCB, OM and Great Master of the Order of the Bath, AK, QSO, PC, ADC(P)
Born 14 November 1948, created Prince of Wales and Earl of Chester 1958, succeeded as Duke of Cornwall, Duke of Rothesay, Earl of Carrick and Baron Renfrew, Lord of the Isles and Great Steward of Scotland 1952
Married (1) 29 July 1981 Lady Diana Frances Spencer (Diana, Princess of Wales (1961–97), youngest daughter of the 8th Earl Spencer and the Hon. Mrs Shand Kydd), marriage dissolved 1996; (2) 9 April 2005 Mrs Camilla Rosemary Parker Bowles, now HRH the Duchess of Cornwall (*born* 17 July 1947, daughter of Major Bruce Shand and the Hon. Mrs Rosalind Shand)
Residences Clarence House, London SW1A 1BA; Highgrove, Doughton, Tetbury, Glos GL8 8TN; Birkhall, Ballater, Aberdeenshire
Issue
1. HRH the Duke of Cambridge (Prince William Arthur Philip Louis), KG, *born* 21 June 1982, *created* Duke of Cambridge, Earl of Strathearn, and Baron Carrickfergus 2011 *married* 29 April 2011 Catherine Elizabeth Middleton, now HRH the Duchess of Cambridge (*born* 9 January 1982, eldest daughter of Michael and Carole Middleton)
2. HRH Prince Henry of Wales (Prince Henry Charles Albert David), *born* 15 September 1984

HRH THE PRINCESS ROYAL (Princess Anne Elizabeth Alice Louise), KG, KT, GCVO
Born 15 August 1950, declared the Princess Royal 1987
Married (1) 14 November 1973 Captain Mark Anthony Peter Phillips, CVO (*born* 22 September 1948); marriage dissolved 1992; (2) 12 December 1992 Vice-Adm. Sir Timothy James Hamilton Laurence, KCVO, CB, ADC(P) (*born* 1 March 1955)
Residence Gatcombe Park, Minchinhampton, Glos GL6 9AT
Issue
1. Peter Mark Andrew Phillips, *born* 15 November 1977, *married* 17 May 2008 Autumn Patricia Kelly, and has issue, Savannah Phillips, *born* 29 December 2010
2. Zara Anne Elizabeth Phillips, MBE, *born* 15 May 1981, *married* 30 July 2011 Michael James Tindall, MBE

HRH THE DUKE OF YORK (Prince Andrew Albert Christian Edward), KG, GCVO, ADC(P)
Born 19 February 1960, created Duke of York, Earl of Inverness and Baron Killyleagh 1986
Married 23 July 1986 Sarah Margaret Ferguson, now Sarah, Duchess of York (*born* 15 October 1959, younger daughter of Major Ronald Ferguson and Mrs Hector Barrantes), marriage dissolved 1996
Residence Royal Lodge, Windsor Great Park, Berks
Issue
1. HRH Princess Beatrice of York (Princess Beatrice Elizabeth Mary), *born* 8 August 1988
2. HRH Princess Eugenie of York (Princess Eugenie Victoria Helena), *born* 23 March 1990

HRH THE EARL OF WESSEX (Prince Edward Antony Richard Louis), KG, GCVO, ADC(P)
Born 10 March 1964, created Earl of Wessex, Viscount Severn 1999
Married 19 June 1999 Sophie Helen Rhys-Jones, now HRH the Countess of Wessex, GCVO (*born* 20 January 1965, daughter of Mr and Mrs Christopher Rhys-Jones)
Residence Bagshot Park, Bagshot, Surrey GU19 5HS
Issue
1. Lady Louise Mountbatten-Windsor (Louise Alice Elizabeth Mary Mountbatten-Windsor), *born* 8 November 2003
2. Viscount Severn (James Alexander Philip Theo Mountbatten-Windsor), *born* 17 December 2007

NEPHEW AND NIECE OF THE QUEEN

Children of HRH the Princess Margaret, Countess of Snowdon and the Earl of Snowdon (*see* House of Windsor):

DAVID ALBERT CHARLES ARMSTRONG-JONES, VISCOUNT LINLEY, *born* 3 November 1961, *married* 8 October 1993 Hon. Serena Alleyne Stanhope, and has issue, Hon. Charles Patrick Inigo Armstrong-Jones, *born* 1 July 1999; Hon. Margarita Elizabeth Alleyne Armstrong-Jones, *born* 14 May 2002

LADY SARAH CHATTO (Sarah Frances Elizabeth), *born* 1 May 1964, *married* 14 July 1994 Daniel Chatto, and has issue, Samuel David Benedict Chatto, *born* 28 July 1996; Arthur Robert Nathaniel Chatto, *born* 5 February 1999

COUSINS OF THE QUEEN

Child of HRH the Duke of Gloucester and HRH Princess Alice, Duchess of Gloucester (*see* House of Windsor):

HRH THE DUKE OF GLOUCESTER (Prince Richard Alexander Walter George), KG, GCVO, Grand Prior of the Order of St John of Jerusalem
Born 26 August 1944
Married 8 July 1972 Birgitte Eva van Deurs, now HRH the Duchess of Gloucester, GCVO (*born* 20 June 1946, daughter of Asger Henriksen and Vivian van Deurs)
Residence Kensington Palace, London W8 4PU
Issue
1. Earl of Ulster (Alexander Patrick Gregers Richard), *born* 24 October 1974 *married* 22 June 2002 Dr Claire Alexandra Booth, and has issue, Lord Culloden (Xan Richard Anders), *born* 12 March 2007; Lady Cosima Windsor (Cosima Rose Alexandra), *born* 20 May 2010
2. Lady Davina Lewis (Davina Elizabeth Alice Benedikte), *born* 19 November 1977 *married* 31 July 2004 Gary Christie Lewis, and has issue, Senna Kowhai Lewis, *born* 22 June 2010
3. Lady Rose Gilman (Rose Victoria Birgitte Louise), *born* 1 March 1980 *married* 19 July 2008 George Edward Gilman, and has issue, Lyla Beatrix Christabel Gilman, *born* 30 May 2010

Children of HRH the Duke of Kent and Princess Marina, Duchess of Kent (*see* House of Windsor):

HRH THE DUKE OF KENT (Prince Edward George Nicholas Paul Patrick), KG, GCMG, GCVO, ADC(P)
Born 9 October 1935
Married 8 June 1961 Katharine Lucy Mary Worsley, now HRH the Duchess of Kent, GCVO (*born* 22 February 1933, daughter of Sir William Worsley, Bt.)
Residence Wren House, Palace Green, London W8 4PY
Issue
1. Earl of St Andrews (George Philip Nicholas), *born* 26 June 1962, *married* 9 January 1988 Sylvana Tomaselli, and has issue, Lord Downpatrick (Edward Edmund Maximilian George), *born* 2 December 1988; Lady Marina-Charlotte Windsor (Marina-Charlotte Alexandra Katharine Helen), *born* 30 September 1992; Lady Amelia Windsor (Amelia Sophia Theodora Mary Margaret), *born* 24 August 1995

2. Lady Helen Taylor (Helen Marina Lucy), *born* 28 April 1964, *married* 18 July 1992 Timothy Verner Taylor, and has issue, Columbus George Donald Taylor, *born* 6 August 1994; Cassius Edward Taylor, *born* 26 December 1996; Eloise Olivia Katharine Taylor, *born* 3 March 2003; Estella Olga Elizabeth Taylor, *born* 21 December 2004
3. Lord Nicholas Windsor (Nicholas Charles Edward Jonathan), *born* 25 July 1970, *married* 4 November 2006 Princess Paola Doimi de Lupis Frankopan Subic Zrinski, and has issue, Hon. Albert Louis Philip Edward Windsor, *born* 22 September 2007; Hon. Leopold Ernest Augustus Guelph Windsor, *born* 8 September 2009

HRH PRINCESS ALEXANDRA, THE HON. LADY OGILVY (Princess Alexandra Helen Elizabeth Olga Christabel), KG, GCVO
Born 25 December 1936
Married 24 April 1963 the Rt. Hon. Sir Angus Ogilvy, KCVO (1928–2004), second son of 12th Earl of Airlie
Residence Thatched House Lodge, Richmond Park, Surrey TW10 5HP
Issue
1. James Robert Bruce Ogilvy, *born* 29 February 1964, *married* 30 July 1988 Julia Rawlinson, and has issue, Flora Alexandra Ogilvy, *born* 15 December 1994; Alexander Charles Ogilvy, *born* 12 November 1996
2. Marina Victoria Alexandra Ogilvy, *born* 31 July 1966, *married* 2 February 1990 Paul Julian Mowatt (marriage dissolved 1997), and has issue, Zenouska May Mowatt, *born* 26 May 1990; Christian Alexander Mowatt, *born* 4 June 1993

HRH PRINCE MICHAEL OF KENT (Prince Michael George Charles Franklin), GCVO
Born 4 July 1942
Married 30 June 1978 Baroness Marie-Christine Agnes Hedwig Ida von Reibnitz, now HRH Princess Michael of Kent (*born* 15 January 1945, daughter of Baron Gunther von Reibnitz)
Residence Kensington Palace, London W8 4PU
Issue
1. Lord Frederick Windsor (Frederick Michael George David Louis), *born* 6 April 1979, *married* 12 September 2009 Sophie Winkleman
2. Lady Gabriella Windsor (Gabriella Marina Alexandra Ophelia), *born* 23 April 1981

ORDER OF SUCCESSION

1   HRH the Prince of Wales
2   HRH the Duke of Cambridge
3   HRH Prince Henry of Wales
4   HRH the Duke of York
5   HRH Princess Beatrice of York
6   HRH Princess Eugenie of York
7   HRH the Earl of Wessex
8   Viscount Severn
9   Lady Louise Mountbatten-Windsor
10   HRH the Princess Royal
11   Peter Phillips
12   Savannah Phillips
13   Zara Phillips
14   Viscount Linley
15   Hon. Charles Armstrong-Jones
16   Hon. Margarita Armstrong-Jones
17   Lady Sarah Chatto
18   Samuel Chatto
19   Arthur Chatto
20   HRH the Duke of Gloucester
21   Earl of Ulster
22   Lord Culloden
23   Lady Cosima Windsor
24   Lady Davina Lewis
25   Senna Lewis
26   Lady Rose Gilman
27   Lyla Gilman
28   HRH the Duke of Kent
29   Lady Amelia Windsor
30   Lady Helen Taylor
31   Columbus Taylor
32   Cassius Taylor
33   Eloise Taylor
34   Estella Taylor
35   Hon. Albert Windsor
36   Hon. Leopold Windsor
37   Lord Frederick Windsor
38   Lady Gabriella Windsor
39   HRH Princess Alexandra, the Hon. Lady Ogilvy

HRH Prince Michael of Kent, and the Earl of St Andrews both lost the right of succession to the throne through marriage to a Roman Catholic. Lord Nicholas Windsor, Lord Downpatrick and Lady Marina-Charlotte Windsor renounced their rights to the throne on converting to Roman Catholicism in 2001, 2003 and 2008 respectively. Their children remain in succession provided that they are in communion with the Church of England.

PRIVATE SECRETARIES

THE QUEEN
Office: Buckingham Palace, London SW1A 1AA
T 020-7930 4832 W www.royal.gov.uk
Private Secretary to the Queen, Rt. Hon. Sir Christopher Geidt, KCVO, OBE

PRINCE PHILIP, THE DUKE OF EDINBURGH
Office: Buckingham Palace, London SW1A 1AA
T 020-7930 4832
Private Secretary, Brig. Archie Miller-Bakewell

THE PRINCE OF WALES AND THE DUCHESS OF CORNWALL
Office: Clarence House, London SW1A 1BA
T 020-7930 4832
Principal Private Secretary, Sir Michael Peat, KCVO

THE DUKE AND DUCHESS OF CAMBRIDGE AND PRINCE HENRY OF WALES
Office: Clarence House, London SW1A 1BA
T 020-7930 4832
Private Secretary, James Lowther-Pinkerton, MVO, MBE

THE DUKE OF YORK
Office: Buckingham Palace, London SW1A 1AA
T 020-7930 4832
Private Secretary, Alastair Watson

THE EARL AND COUNTESS OF WESSEX
Office: Bagshot Park, Surrey GU19 5PL
T 01276-707040
Private Secretary, Brig. J. Smedley, LVO

THE PRINCESS ROYAL
Office: Buckingham Palace, London SW1A 1AA
T 020-7024 4199
Private Secretary, Capt. N. P. Wright, CVO, RN

THE DUKE AND DUCHESS OF GLOUCESTER
Office: Kensington Palace, London W8 4PU
T 020-7368 1000
Private Secretary, Alistair Wood, MBE

THE DUKE OF KENT
Office: St James's Palace, London SW1A 1BQ
T 020-7930 4872
Private Secretary, N. Marden

THE DUCHESS OF KENT
Office: Wren House, Palace Green, London W8 4PY
T 020-7937 2730
Personal Secretary, Chloe Hill

PRINCE AND PRINCESS MICHAEL OF KENT
Office: Kensington Palace, London W8 4PU
T 020-7938 3519
W www.princemichael.org.uk
Private Secretary, Nicholas Chance, LVO

PRINCESS ALEXANDRA, THE HON. LADY OGILVY
Office: Buckingham Palace, London SW1A 1AA
T 020-7024 4270
Private Secretary, Diane Duke

ROYAL HOUSEHOLD

The PRIVATE SECRETARY is responsible for:

- informing and advising the Queen on constitutional, governmental and political matters in the UK, her other Realms and the wider Commonwealth, including communications with the prime minister and government departments
- organising the Queen's domestic and overseas official programme
- the Queen's speeches, messages, patronage, photographs, portraits and official presents
- communications in connection with the role of the royal family
- dealing with correspondence to the Queen from members of the public
- royal travel policy
- coordinating and initiating research to support engagements by members of the royal family

The COMMUNICATIONS AND PRESS SECRETARY is in charge of Buckingham Palace's press office and reports to the private secretary. The press secretary is responsible for:

- developing communications strategies to enhance the public understanding of the role of the monarchy
- briefing the British and international media on the role and duties of the Queen and issues relating to the royal family
- responding to media enquiries
- arranging media facilities in the UK and overseas to support royal functions and engagements
- the management of the royal website

The private secretary is keeper of the royal archives and is responsible for the care of the records of the sovereign and the royal household from previous reigns, preserved in the royal archives at Windsor. As keeper, it is the private secretary's responsibility to ensure the proper management of the records of the present reign with a view to their transfer to the archives as and when appropriate. The private secretary is an *ex officio* trustee of the Royal Collection Trust.

The KEEPER OF THE PRIVY PURSE AND TREASURER to the Queen is responsible for:

- the Queen's Civil List, which is the money paid from the government's Consolidated Fund to meet official expenditure relating to the Queen's duties as head of state and head of the Commonwealth
- through the director of personnel, the planning and management of personnel policy across the royal household, the administration of all its pension schemes and private estates employees, and the allocation of employee and pensioner housing
- information technology systems
- internal audit services
- health and safety; insurance matters
- the privy purse, which is mainly financed by the net income of the Duchy of Lancaster, and meets both official and private expenditure incurred by the Queen
- liaison with other members of the royal family and their households on financial matters
- the Queen's private estates at Sandringham and Balmoral, the Queen's Racing Establishment and the Royal Studs and liaison with the Ascot Authority
- the Home Park at Windsor and liaison with the Crown

Estate Commissioners concerning the Home Park and the Great Park at Windsor
- the Royal Philatelic Collection
- administrative aspects of the Military Knights of Windsor
- administration of the Royal Victorian Order, of which the keeper of the privy purse is secretary, Long and Faithful Service Medals, and the Queen's cups, medals and prizes, and policy on commemorative medals

The keeper of the privy purse is one of three royal trustees (in respect of his responsibilities for the Civil List) and is receiver-general of the Duchy of Lancaster and a member of the Duchy's Council.

The keeper of the privy purse is responsible for property services at occupied royal palaces in England, comprising Buckingham Palace, St James's Palace, Clarence House, Marlborough House Mews, the residential and office areas of Kensington Palace, Windsor Castle and buildings in the Home and Great Parks of Windsor and Hampton Court Mews and Paddocks. The costs of property services for occupied royal palaces are met from a grant-in-aid from the Department for Culture, Media and Sport (DCMS).

The keeper of the privy purse also oversees royal communications and information expenditure, which is met from the property services grant-in-aid, and the financial aspects of royal travel, met from a grant-in-aid provided by the Department for Transport.

The keeper of the privy purse is an *ex officio* trustee of the Historic Royal Palaces Trust and the Royal Collection Trust.

The Queen's Civil List and the grants-in-aid for property services and royal travel are provided by the government in return for the net surplus from the Crown Estate and other hereditary revenues.

The DIRECTOR OF THE PROPERTY SECTION has day-to-day responsibility for the royal household's property section:

- fire and health and safety
- repairs and refurbishment of buildings and new building work
- utilities and telecommunications
- putting up stages, tents and other work in connection with ceremonial occasions, garden parties and other official functions

The property section is also responsible, on a sub-contract basis from the DCMS, for the maintenance of Marlborough House (which is occupied by the Commonwealth Secretariat).

The MASTER OF THE HOUSEHOLD is responsible for:

- delivering the majority of the official and private entertaining in the Queen's annual programme at residences in the UK, and on occasion overseas
- periodic support for entertaining by other members of the royal family
- furnishings and internal decorative refurbishment in conjunction with the director of the Royal Collection and Property Services
- housekeeping, catering and service provision for the royal household

The COMPTROLLER, LORD CHAMBERLAIN'S OFFICE is responsible for:

- the organisation of all ceremonial engagements, including state visits to the Queen in the UK, royal weddings and funerals, the state opening of parliament, Guards of Honour at Buckingham Palace, investitures, and the Garter and Thistle ceremonies
- garden parties at Buckingham Palace and the Palace of Holyroodhouse (except for catering and tents)
- the Crown Jewels, which are part of the Royal Collection, when they are in use on state occasions
- coordination of the arrangements for the Queen to be represented at funerals and memorial services and at the arrival and departure of visiting heads of state
- delivery of all official and approved travel operations
- advising on matters of precedence, style and titles, dress, flying of flags, gun salutes, mourning and other ceremonial issues
- supervising the applications from tradesmen for Royal Warrants of Appointment
- advising on the commercial use of royal emblems and contemporary royal photographs
- the ecclesiastical household, the medical household, the body guards and certain ceremonial appointments such as Gentlemen Ushers and Pages of Honour
- the lords in waiting, who represent the Queen on various occasions and escort visiting heads of state during incoming state visits
- the Queen's bargemaster and watermen and the Queen's swans
- the Royal Almonry

The comptroller is also responsible for the Royal Mews, assisted by the CROWN EQUERRY, who has day-to-day responsibility for:

- the provision of carriage processions for the state opening of parliament, state visits, Trooping of the Colour, Royal Ascot, the Garter Ceremony, the Thistle Service, the presentation of credentials to the Queen by incoming foreign ambassadors and high commissioners, and other state and ceremonial occasions
- the provision of chauffeur-driven cars
- coordinating travel arrangements by road, air, rail or sea in respect of the royal household
- supervision and administration of the Royal Mews at Buckingham Palace, Windsor Castle, Hampton Court and the Palace of Holyroodhouse

The comptroller also has overall responsibility for the MARSHAL OF THE DIPLOMATIC CORPS, who is responsible for the relationship between the royal household and the Diplomatic Heads of Mission in London; and the SECRETARY OF THE CENTRAL CHANCERY OF THE ORDERS OF KNIGHTHOOD, who administers the Orders of Chivalry, makes arrangements for investitures and the distribution of insignia, and ensures the proper public notification of awards through *The London Gazette*.

The DIRECTOR OF THE ROYAL COLLECTION is responsible for:

- the administration and custodial control of the Royal Collection in all royal residences
- the care, display, conservation and restoration of items in the collection
- initiating and assisting research into the collection and publishing catalogues and books on the collection
- making the collection accessible to the public and educating and informing the public about the collection

The Royal Collection, which contains a large number of works of art, is held by the Queen as sovereign in trust for her successors and the nation and is not owned by her as an individual. The administration, conservation and presentation of the Royal Collection are funded by the Royal Collection Trust solely from income from visitors to Windsor Castle, Buckingham Palace and the Palace of Holyroodhouse. The Royal Collection Trust is chaired by the Prince of Wales. The Lord Chamberlain, the private secretary and the keeper of the privy purse are *ex officio* trustees and there are three external trustees appointed by the Queen.

The director of the Royal Collection is also at present the SURVEYOR OF THE QUEEN'S WORKS OF ART. The ROYAL LIBRARIAN is responsible for all books, manuscripts, coins and medals, insignia and works of art on paper including the watercolours, prints and drawings in the Print Room at Windsor Castle, and the SURVEYOR OF THE QUEEN'S PICTURES is responsible for pictures and miniatures.

Royal Collection Enterprises Limited is the trading subsidiary of the Royal Collection Trust. The company, whose chair is the Keeper of the Privy Purse, is responsible for:

- managing access by the public to Windsor Castle (including Frogmore House), Buckingham Palace (including the Royal Mews and the Queen's Gallery) and the Palace of Holyroodhouse (including the Queen's Gallery)
- running shops at each location
- managing the images and intellectual property rights of the Royal Collection

The director of the Royal Collection is also an *ex officio* trustee of the Historic Royal Palaces Trust.

SENIOR MANAGEMENT OF THE ROYAL HOUSEHOLD

Lord Chamberlain, Earl Peel, GCVO, PC

HEADS OF DEPARTMENT
Private Secretary to The Queen, Rt. Hon. Sir Christopher Geidt, KCVO, OBE
Keeper of the Privy Purse, Sir Alan Reid, KCVO
Master of the Household, Air Vice-Marshal Sir David Walker, KCVO, OBE
Comptroller, Lord Chamberlain's Office, Lt.-Col. Andrew Ford
Director of the Royal Collection, Jonathan Marsden, LVO

NON-EXECUTIVE MEMBERS
Private Secretary to the Duke of Edinburgh, Brig. Archie Miller-Bakewell
Private Secretary to the Prince of Wales and the Duchess of Cornwall, Sir Michael Peat, KCVO

THE POET LAUREATE

The post of Poet Laureate was officially established when John Dryden was appointed by royal warrant as Poet Laureate and Historiographer Royal in 1668. The post is attached to the royal household and was originally conferred on the holder for life; in 1999 the length of appointment was changed to a ten-year term. It is customary for the Poet Laureate to write verse to mark events of national importance. The postholder currently receives an honorarium of £5,750 a year.
The Poet Laureate, Carol Ann Duffy, *apptd* 2009

ROYAL SALUTES

ENGLAND

The basic royal salute is 21 rounds with an extra 20 rounds fired at Hyde Park because it is a royal park. At the Tower of London 62 rounds are fired on royal anniversaries (21 plus a further 20 because the Tower is a royal palace and a further 21 'for the City of London') and 41 on other occasions. When the Queen's official birthday coincides with the Duke of Edinburgh's birthday, 124 rounds are fired from the Tower (62 rounds for each birthday). Gun salutes occur on the following royal anniversaries:

- Accession Day
- The Queen's birthday
- Coronation Day
- Duke of Edinburgh's birthday
- The Queen's Official Birthday
- The Prince of Wales' birthday
- State opening of parliament

Gun salutes also occur when parliament is prorogued by the sovereign, on royal births and when a visiting head of state meets the sovereign in London, Windsor or Edinburgh.

In London, salutes are fired at Hyde Park and the Tower of London although on some occasions (state visits, state opening of parliament and the Queen's birthday parade) Green Park is used instead of Hyde Park. Other military saluting stations in England are at Colchester, Dover, Plymouth, Woolwich and York.

Constable of the Royal Palace and Fortress of London, Gen. Lord Dannatt, GCB, CBE, MC
Lieutenant of the Tower of London, Lt. Gen. Peter Pearson, CB, CBE
Resident Governor and Keeper of the Jewel House, Col. Richard Harrold, OBE
Master Gunner of St James's Park, Gen. Sir Alex Harley, KBE, CB
Master Gunner within the Tower, HRH Prince Michael of Kent, GCVO

SCOTLAND

Royal salutes are authorised at Edinburgh Castle and Stirling Castle. A salute of 21 guns is fired on the following occasions:

- the anniversaries of the birth, accession and coronation of the sovereign
- the anniversary of the birth of the Duke of Edinburgh

A salute of 21 guns is fired in Edinburgh on the occasion of the opening of the general assembly of the Church of Scotland. A salute of 21 guns may also be fired in Edinburgh on the arrival of HM The Queen or a member of the royal family who is a Royal Highness on an official visit.

Military saluting stations are also situated at Cardiff Castle in Wales, Hillsborough Castle in Northern Ireland and in Gibraltar.

ROYAL FINANCES

FUNDING

CIVIL LIST

The Civil List dates back to the late 17th century. It was originally used by the sovereign to supplement hereditary revenues for paying the salaries of judges, ambassadors and other government officers as well as the expenses of the royal household. In 1760, on the accession of George III, it was decided that the Civil List would be provided by parliament to cover all relevant expenditure in return for the king surrendering the hereditary revenues of the Crown (principally the net surplus of the Crown Estate). At that time parliament undertook to pay the salaries of judges, ambassadors etc. In 1831 parliament agreed also to meet the costs of the royal palaces in return for a reduction in the Civil List. Each sovereign has agreed to continue this arrangement. The Civil List now meets the central staff costs and running expenses of the Queen's official household.

Until 1972, the amount of money allocated annually under the Civil List was set for the duration of a reign. The system was then altered to a fixed annual payment for ten years but from 1975 high inflation made an annual review necessary. The system of payments reverted to the practice of a fixed annual payment of £7.9m for a ten-year period to 31 December 2000; during this period annual Civil List expenditure reached £6.5m, and a reserve of £35m was established. In order to draw down the reserve, the annual Civil List payment has remained at £7.9m since 2001.

The legislative requirement is for Civil List accounts to be submitted to parliament, in the form of Royal Trustees Reports, at ten-yearly intervals, but from June 2002 accounts have been published annually. The ninth annual accounts for the year ending 31 December 2010 were published in June 2011:

	2009	2010
Civil List payment	£7,900,000	£7,900,000
Draw-down from the Civil List reserve	£6,500,000	£5,600,000
Net Receipts	£14,400,000	£13,500,000
Net Civil List Expenditure	(£14,200,000)	(£13,700,000)

PARLIAMENTARY ANNUITIES

The Civil List Acts provide for other members of the royal family to receive parliamentary annuities from government funds to meet the expenses of carrying out their official duties. Since 1993 the Queen has reimbursed all the annuities except those paid to the late Queen Elizabeth the Queen Mother and the Duke of Edinburgh.

The Prince of Wales does not receive a parliamentary annuity. He derives his income from the revenues of the Duchy of Cornwall and these monies meet the official and private expenses of the Prince of Wales and his family (*see* Prince of Wales' Funding).

In 2000 the annual amounts payable to members of the royal family, excluding the Earl of Wessex, were reset at their 1990 levels for the next ten years. The Earl of

Wessex had his annuity increased by £45,000 to £141,000 on the occasion of his marriage in 1999.

The annual payments remain as follows until December 2011:

The Duke of Edinburgh	£359,000
The Duke of York	£249,000
The Earl of Wessex	£141,000
The Princess Royal	£228,000
The Duke and Duchess of Gloucester	£175,000
The Duke and Duchess of Kent	£236,000
Princess Alexandra	£225,000
Subtotal	£1,613,000
Refunded to the Treasury by the Queen	(£1,254,000)
TOTAL	£359,000

GRANTS-IN-AID

Grants-in-aid are provided to the royal household annually by the Department for Culture, Media and Sport for property services and communications and information, and by the Department for Transport for royal travel. Property services meets the cost of property maintenance, utilities, telephones and related services at the occupied royal palaces in England (*see* Royal Household section for a list of occupied palaces). Communications and Information meets the cost of these services in connection with official royal functions and engagements in England and Scotland. Royal travel meets the cost of official royal travel by air and rail.

GRANTS-IN-AID 2010–11:

	Grant-in-aid voted by parliament	Total net expenditure
Property Services	£14,600,000	£11,900,000
Communications and Information	£500,000	£500,000
Royal Travel	£7,000,000	£6,000,000

THE PRIVY PURSE AND THE DUCHY OF LANCASTER

The funds received by the privy purse pay for official expenses incurred by the Queen as head of state and for some of the Queen's private expenditure. The revenues of the Duchy of Lancaster are the principal source of income for the privy purse. The revenues of the Duchy were retained by George III in 1760 when the hereditary revenues were surrendered in exchange for the Civil List. The Duchy's affairs are the responsibility of the Duchy Council which reports to the Chancellor of the Duchy of Lancaster, who in turn is accountable directly to the sovereign rather than to parliament. However the chancellor does answer parliamentary questions on matters relating to the Duchy of Lancaster's responsibilities.

THE DUCHY OF LANCASTER, 1 Lancaster Place, London WC2E 7ED

E info@duchyoflancaster.co.uk
W www.duchyoflancaster.com
Chancellor of the Duchy of Lancaster, Rt. Hon. Lord Strathclyde, *apptd* 2010
Chair of the Council, Lord Shuttleworth
Clerk and Chief Executive, Paul Clarke, CVO, FRICS
Receiver-General, Sir Alan Reid, KCVO
Attorney-General, Robert Hildyard, QC

PERSONAL INCOME

The Queen's personal income derives mostly from investments, and is used to meet private expenditure.

EXPENDITURE MET BY GOVERNMENT DEPARTMENTS AND THE CROWN ESTATE 2010–11:

Administration of honours	£500,000
Equerries, orderlies and other personnel	£1,000,000
Maintenance of Holyroodhouse	£1,100,000
State visits to and by the Queen and liaison with the Diplomatic Corps	£100,000
Ceremonial occasions	£400,000
Maintenance of Home Park, Windsor Castle	£600,000
Other	£100,000
Total	£3,800,000

PRINCE OF WALES' FUNDING

The Duchy Estate was created in 1337 by Edward III for his son and heir Prince Edward (the Black Prince) who became the Duke of Cornwall. The Duchy's primary function is to provide an income from its assets for the Prince of Wales. Under a 1337 charter, confirmed by subsequent legislation, the Prince of Wales is not entitled to the proceeds or profit on the sale of Duchy assets but only to the annual income which is generated from these assets. The Duchy is responsible for the sustainable and commercial management of its properties, investment portfolio and approximately 54,090 hectares of land, based mostly in the south-west of England. The Prince of Wales has chosen to use a proportion of his income to meet the cost of his public and charitable work in addition to providing a private source of income. The Duchy also funds the public, charitable and private activities of the Duchess of Cornwall and princes William and Harry. Proceeds from the Duchy are voluntarily subject to income tax.

THE DUCHY OF CORNWALL, 10 Buckingham Gate, London SW1E 6LA
T 020-7834 7346 E London@duchyofcornwall.org
W www.duchyofcornwall.org
Lord Warden of the Stannaries, Sir Nicholas Bacon, Bt.
Receiver-General, James Leigh-Pemberton
Attorney-General, Jonathan Crow, QC
Secretary and Keeper of the Records, Bertie Ross

TAXATION

The sovereign is not legally liable to pay income tax or capital gains tax. After income tax was reintroduced in 1842, some income tax was paid voluntarily by the sovereign but over a long period these payments were phased out. In 1992 the Queen offered to pay income and capital gains tax on a voluntary basis from 6 April 1993, and the Prince of Wales offered to pay tax on a voluntary basis on his income from the Duchy of Cornwall (he was already taxed in all other respects).

The main provisions for the Queen and the Prince of Wales to pay tax, set out in a Memorandum of Understanding on Royal Taxation presented to parliament on 11 February 1993, are that the Queen will pay income tax and capital gains tax in respect of her private income and assets, and on the proportion of the income and capital gains of the Privy Purse used for private purposes. Inheritance tax will be paid on the Queen's assets, except for those which pass to the next sovereign, whether automatically or by gift or bequest. The Prince of Wales will pay income tax on income from the Duchy of Cornwall used for private purposes.

The Prince of Wales has confirmed that he intends to pay tax on the same basis following his accession to the throne. Other members of the royal family are subject to tax as for any taxpayer.

MILITARY RANKS AND TITLES

THE QUEEN

ARMY
Colonel-in-Chief
The Life Guards; The Blues and Royals (Royal Horse Guards and 1st Dragoons); The Royal Scots Dragoon Guards (Carabiniers and Greys); The Queen's Royal Lancers; Royal Tank Regiment; Corps of Royal Engineers; Grenadier Guards; Coldstream Guards; Scots Guards; Irish Guards; Welsh Guards; The Royal Regiment of Scotland; The Duke of Lancaster's Regiment (King's, Lancashire and Border); The Royal Welsh; Adjutant General's Corps; The Royal Mercian and Lancastrian Yeomanry; The Governor General's Horse Guards (of Canada); The King's Own Calgary Regiment (Royal Canadian Armoured Corps); Canadian Military Engineers Branch; Royal 22e Regiment (of Canada); Governor General's Foot Guards (of Canada); The Canadian Grenadier Guards; Le Régiment de la Chaudière (of Canada); 2nd Battalion Royal New Brunswick Regiment (North Shore); 48th Highlanders of Canada; The Argyll and Sutherland Highlanders of Canada (Princess Louise's); The Calgary Highlanders; Royal Australian Engineers; Royal Australian Infantry Corps; Royal Australian Army Ordnance Corps; Royal Australian Army Nursing Corps; The Corps of Royal New Zealand Engineers; Royal New Zealand Infantry Regiment; The Malawi Rifles; The Royal Malta Artillery

Affiliated Colonel-in-Chief
The Queen's Gurkha Engineers

Captain-General
Royal Regiment of Artillery; The Honourable Artillery Company; Combined Cadet Force; Royal Regiment of Canadian Artillery; Royal Regiment of Australian Artillery; Royal Regiment of New Zealand Artillery; Royal New Zealand Armoured Corps

Royal Colonel
The Argyll and Sutherland Highlanders, 5th Battalion The Royal Regiment of Scotland

Patron
Royal Army Chaplains' Department

ROYAL AIR FORCE
Air Commodore-in-Chief
Royal Auxiliary Air Force; Royal Air Force Regiment; Air Reserve of Canada; Royal Australian Air Force Reserve; Territorial Air Force (of New Zealand)

Commandant-in-Chief
RAF College, Cranwell

Royal Honorary Air Commodore
RAF Marham; 603 (City of Edinburgh) Squadron Royal Auxiliary Air Force

PRINCE PHILIP, DUKE OF EDINBURGH
ROYAL NAVY
Lord High Admiral of the United Kingdom

Admiral of the Fleet
Admiral of the Fleet, Royal Australian Navy
Admiral of the Fleet, Royal New Zealand Navy
Admiral of the Royal Canadian Sea Cadets

ROYAL MARINES
Captain-General

ARMY
Field Marshal
Field Marshal, Australian Military Forces
Field Marshal, New Zealand Army
Colonel-in-Chief
The Queen's Royal Hussars (Queen's Own and Royal Irish); The Rifles; Corps of Royal Electrical and Mechanical Engineers; Intelligence Corps; Army Cadet Force Association; The Royal Canadian Regiment; The Royal Hamilton Light Infantry (Wentworth Regiment of Canada); The Cameron Highlanders of Ottawa; The Queen's Own Cameron Highlanders of Canada; The Seaforth Highlanders of Canada; The Royal Canadian Army Cadets; The Royal Australian Corps of Electrical and Mechanical Engineers; The Australian Army Cadet Corps

Colonel
Grenadier Guards

Royal Colonel
The Highlanders, 4th Battalion The Royal Regiment of Scotland

Honorary Colonel
City of Edinburgh University Officers' Training Corps; The Trinidad and Tobago Regiment

Member
Honourable Artillery Company

ROYAL AIR FORCE
Marshal of the Royal Air Force
Marshal of the Royal Australian Air Force
Marshal of the Royal New Zealand Air Force
Air Commodore-in-Chief
Air Training Corps; Royal Canadian Air Cadets

THE PRINCE OF WALES
ROYAL NAVY
Admiral
Commodore-in-Chief
    Royal Naval Command Plymouth

ARMY
General
Colonel-in-Chief
    The Royal Dragoon Guards; The Parachute Regiment;
    The Royal Gurkha Rifles; Army Air Corps; The Royal
    Canadian Dragoons; Lord Strathcona's Horse (Royal
    Canadians); The Royal Regiment of Canada; Royal
    Winnipeg Rifles; Royal Australian Armoured Corps;
    The Royal Pacific Islands Regiment; 1st The Queen's
    Dragoon Guards; The Black Watch (Royal Highland
    Regiment) of Canada; The Toronto Scottish Regiment
    (Queen Elizabeth The Queen Mother's Own); The
    Mercian Regiment

Royal Colonel
    The Black Watch, 3rd Battalion The Royal Regiment of
    Scotland; 51st Highland, 7th Battalion The Royal
    Regiment of Scotland (Territorial Army)

Colonel
    The Welsh Guards

Royal Honorary Colonel
    The Queen's Own Yeomanry

ROYAL AIR FORCE
Air Chief Marshal
Honorary Air Commodore
    RAF Valley

Air Commodore-in-Chief
    Royal New Zealand Air Force

Colonel-in-Chief
    Air Reserve Canada

THE DUCHESS OF CORNWALL
ROYAL NAVY
Commodore-in-Chief
    Naval Medical Services; Royal Naval Chaplaincy
    Services

ARMY
Royal Colonel
    4th Battalion The Rifles

ROYAL AIR FORCE
Honorary Air Commodore
    RAF Halton; RAF Leeming

THE DUKE OF CAMBRIDGE
ROYAL NAVY
Lieutenant
Commodore-in-Chief
    Scotland Command; Submarines Command

ARMY
Colonel
    Irish Guards

Captain
    The Blues and Royals (Royal Horse Guards and 1st
    Dragoons)

ROYAL AIR FORCE
Flight Lieutenant
Honorary Air Commandant
    RAF Coningsby

PRINCE HENRY OF WALES
ROYAL NAVY
Commodore-in-Chief
    Small Ships and Diving Command

ARMY
Lieutenant
    The Blues and Royals (Royal Horse Guards and 1st
    Dragoons)

ROYAL AIR FORCE
Honorary Air Commandant
    RAF Honington

THE DUKE OF YORK
ROYAL NAVY
Rear Admiral
Commodore-in-Chief
    Fleet Air Arm

Admiral of the Marine Society and Sea Cadets

ARMY
Colonel-in-Chief
    The Royal Irish Regiment (27th (Inniskilling), 83rd,
    87th and The Ulster Defence Regiment); 9th/12th
    Royal Lancers (The Prince of Wales's); The Royal
    Highland Fusiliers, 2nd Battalion The Royal Regiment
    of Scotland; The Yorkshire Regiment; Small Arms
    School Corps; The Queen's York Rangers (First
    Americans); Royal New Zealand Army Logistics
    Regiment; The Royal Highland Fusiliers of Canada;
    The Princess Louise Fusiliers (Canada)

ROYAL AIR FORCE
Honorary Air Commodore
    RAF Lossiemouth

THE EARL OF WESSEX
ROYAL NAVY
Commodore-in-Chief
    Royal Fleet Auxiliary

Patron
    Royal Fleet Auxiliary Association

ARMY
Colonel-in-Chief
    Hastings and Prince Edward Regiment; Saskatchewan
    Dragoons

Royal Colonel
    2nd Battalion, The Rifles

Royal Honorary Colonel
    Royal Wessex Yeomanry

ROYAL AIR FORCE
Honorary Air Commodore
    RAF Waddington

THE COUNTESS OF WESSEX
ARMY
Colonel-in-Chief
Queen Alexandra's Royal Army Nursing Corps; The Lincoln and Welland Regiment; South Alberta Light Horse Regiment

Royal Colonel
5th Battalion, The Rifles

ROYAL AIR FORCE
Honorary Air Commodore
RAF Wittering

THE PRINCESS ROYAL
ROYAL NAVY
Vice-Admiral
(Chief Commandant for Women in the Royal Navy)

Commodore-in-Chief
HM Naval Base Portsmouth

ARMY
Colonel-in-Chief
The King's Royal Hussars; Royal Corps of Signals; Royal Logistic Corps; The Royal Army Veterinary Corps; 8th Canadian Hussars (Princess Louise's); Royal Newfoundland Regiment; Canadian Forces Communications and Electronics Branch; The Grey and Simcoe Foresters (Royal Canadian Armoured Corps); The Royal Regina Rifle Regiment; Canadian Forces Medical Branch; Royal Australian Corps of Signals; Royal New Zealand Corps of Signals; Royal New Zealand Nursing Corps

Affiliated Colonel-in-Chief
The Queen's Gurkha Signals; The Queen's Own Gurkha Transport Regiment

Royal Colonel
1st Battalion The Royal Regiment of Scotland; 52nd Lowland, 6th Battalion The Royal Regiment of Scotland

Colonel
The Blues and Royals (Royal Horse Guards and 1st Dragoons)

Honorary Colonel
University of London Officers' Training Corps

Commandant-in-Chief
First Aid Nursing Yeomanry (Princess Royal's Volunteer Corps)

ROYAL AIR FORCE
Honorary Air Commodore
RAF Lyneham; University of London Air Squadron

THE DUKE OF GLOUCESTER
ARMY
Colonel-in-Chief
The Royal Anglian Regiment; Royal Army Medical Corps; Royal New Zealand Army Medical Corps

Deputy Colonel-in-Chief
The Royal Logistic Corps

Royal Colonel
6th Battalion, The Rifles

Honorary Royal Colonel
Royal Monmouthshire Royal Engineers (Militia)

ROYAL AIR FORCE
Honorary Air Marshal
Honorary Air Commodore
RAF Odiham; No. 501 (County of Gloucester) Squadron Royal Auxiliary Air Force

THE DUCHESS OF GLOUCESTER
ARMY
Colonel-in-Chief
Royal Army Dental Corps; Royal Australian Army Educational Corps; Royal New Zealand Army Educational Corps; Canadian Forces Dental Services

Deputy Colonel-in-Chief
Adjutant-General's Corps

Royal Colonel
7th Battalion, The Rifles

Vice-Patron
Adjutant General's Corps Regimental Association

Patron
Royal Army Educational Corps Association; Army Families Federation

THE DUKE OF KENT
ARMY
Field Marshal

Colonel-in-Chief
The Royal Regiment of Fusiliers; Lorne Scots (Peel, Dufferin and Hamilton Regiment)

Deputy Colonel-in-Chief
The Royal Scots Dragoon Guards (Carabiniers and Greys)

Royal Colonel
1st Battalion The Rifles

Colonel
Scots Guards

ROYAL AIR FORCE
Honorary Air Chief Marshal
Honorary Air Commodore
RAF Leuchars

THE DUCHESS OF KENT
ARMY
Deputy Colonel-in-Chief
The Royal Dragoon Guards; Adjutant-General's Corps; The Royal Logistic Corps

PRINCE MICHAEL OF KENT
ROYAL NAVY
Honorary Rear Admiral Royal Naval Reserve

ARMY
Colonel-in-Chief
Essex and Kent Scottish Regiment (Ontario)

Regimental Colonel
Honourable Artillery Company

Major (retired)
King's Royal Hussars

ROYAL AIR FORCE
Honorary Air Commodore
RAF Benson

PRINCESS ALEXANDRA, THE HON. LADY OGILVY
ROYAL NAVY
Patron
Queen Alexandra's Royal Naval Nursing Service

ARMY
Colonel-in-Chief
The Canadian Scottish Regiment (Princess Mary's)

Deputy Colonel-in-Chief
The Queen's Royal Lancers

Royal Colonel
3rd Battalion The Rifles

Royal Honorary Colonel
The Royal Yeomanry

ROYAL AIR FORCE
Patron and Air Chief Commandant
Princess Mary's RAF Nursing Service

Honorary Air Commodore
RAF Cottesmore

KINGS AND QUEENS

ENGLISH KINGS AND QUEENS 927 TO 1603

HOUSES OF CERDIC AND DENMARK

Reign

927–939 ÆTHELSTAN
Son of Edward the Elder, by Ecgwynn, and grandson of Alfred
Acceded to Wessex and Mercia c.924, established direct rule over Northumbria 927, effectively creating the Kingdom of England
Reigned 15 years

939–946 EDMUND I
Born 921, son of Edward the Elder, by Eadgifu
Married (1) Ælfgifu (2) Æthelflæd
Killed aged 25, *reigned* 6 years

946–955 EADRED
Son of Edward the Elder, by Eadgifu
Reigned 9 years

955–959 EADWIG
Born before 943, son of Edmund and Ælfgifu
Married Ælfgifu
Reigned 3 years

959–975 EDGAR I
Born 943, son of Edmund and Ælfgifu
Married (1) Æthelflæd (2) Wulfthryth (3) Ælfthryth
Died aged 32, *reigned* 15 years

975–978 EDWARD I (the Martyr)
Born c.962, son of Edgar and Æthelflæd
Assassinated aged c.16, *reigned* 2 years

978–1016 ÆTHELRED (the Unready)
Born 968/969, son of Edgar and Ælfthryth
Married (1) Ælfgifu (2) Emma, daughter of Richard I, Count of Normandy
1013–14 dispossessed of kingdom by Swegn Forkbeard (King of Denmark 987–1014)
Died aged c.47, *reigned* 38 years

1016 EDMUND II (Ironside)
(Apr–Nov) *Born* before 993, son of Æthelred and Ælfgifu
Married Ealdgyth
Died aged over 23, *reigned* 7 months

1016–1035 CNUT (Canute)
Born c.995, son of Swegn Forkbeard, King of Denmark, and Gunhild
Married (1) Ælfgifu (2) Emma, widow of Æthelred the Unready
Gained submission of West Saxons 1015, Northumbrians 1016, Mercia 1016, King of all England after Edmund's death, King of Denmark 1019–35, King of Norway 1028–35
Died aged c.40, *reigned* 19 years

1035–1040 HAROLD I (Harefoot)
Born 1016/17, son of Cnut and Ælfgifu
Married Ælfgifu
1035 recognised as regent for himself and his brother Harthacnut; 1037 recognised as king
Died aged c.23, *reigned* 4 years

1040–1042 HARTHACNUT (Harthacanute)
Born c.1018, son of Cnut and Emma
Titular king of Denmark from 1028
Acknowledged King of England 1035–7 with Harold I as regent; effective king after Harold's death
Died aged c.24, *reigned* 2 years

1042–1066 EDWARD II (the Confessor)
Born between 1002 and 1005, son of Æthelred the Unready and Emma
Married Eadgyth, daughter of Godwine, Earl of Wessex
Died aged over 60, *reigned* 23 years

1066 HAROLD II (Godwinesson)
(Jan–Oct) *Born* c.1020, son of Godwine, Earl of Wessex, and Gytha
Married (1) Eadgyth (2) Ealdgyth
Killed in battle aged c.46, *reigned* 10 months

THE HOUSE OF NORMANDY

1066–1087 WILLIAM I (the Conqueror)
Born 1027/8, son of Robert I, Duke of Normandy; obtained the Crown by conquest
Married Matilda, daughter of Baldwin, Count of Flanders
Died aged c.60, *reigned* 20 years

1087–1100 WILLIAM II (Rufus)
Born between 1056 and 1060, third son of William I; succeeded his father in England only
Killed aged c.40, *reigned* 12 years

1100–1135 HENRY I (Beauclerk)
Born 1068, fourth son of William I
Married (1) Edith or Matilda, daughter of Malcolm III of Scotland (2) Adela, daughter of Godfrey, Count of Louvain
Died aged 67, *reigned* 35 years

1135–1154 STEPHEN
Born not later than 1100, third son of Adela, daughter of William I, and Stephen, Count of Blois
Married Matilda, daughter of Eustace, Count of Boulogne
1141 (Feb–Nov) held captive by adherents of Matilda, daughter of Henry I, who contested the crown until 1153
Died aged over 53, *reigned* 18 years

THE HOUSE OF ANJOU (PLANTAGENETS)

1154–1189 HENRY II (Curtmantle)
Born 1133, son of Matilda, daughter of Henry I, and Geoffrey, Count of Anjou
Married Eleanor, daughter of William, Duke of Aquitaine, and divorced queen of Louis VII of France
Died aged 56, *reigned* 34 years

1189–1199 RICHARD I (Coeur de Lion)
Born 1157, third son of Henry II
Married Berengaria, daughter of Sancho VI, King of Navarre
Died aged 42, *reigned* 9 years

1199–1216	JOHN (Lackland) *Born* 1167, fifth son of Henry II *Married* (1) Isabella or Avisa, daughter of William, Earl of Gloucester (divorced) (2) Isabella, daughter of Aymer, Count of Angoulême *Died* aged 48, *reigned* 17 years
1216–1272	HENRY III *Born* 1207, son of John and Isabella of Angoulême *Married* Eleanor, daughter of Raymond, Count of Provence *Died* aged 65, *reigned* 56 years
1272–1307	EDWARD I (Longshanks) *Born* 1239, eldest son of Henry III *Married* (1) Eleanor, daughter of Ferdinand III, King of Castile (2) Margaret, daughter of Philip III of France *Died* aged 68, *reigned* 34 years
1307–1327	EDWARD II *Born* 1284, eldest surviving son of Edward I and Eleanor *Married* Isabella, daughter of Philip IV of France *Deposed* Jan 1327, *killed* Sep 1327 aged 43, *reigned* 19 years
1327–1377	EDWARD III *Born* 1312, eldest son of Edward II *Married* Philippa, daughter of William, Count of Hainault *Died* aged 64, *reigned* 50 years
1377–1399	RICHARD II *Born* 1367, son of Edward (the Black Prince), eldest son of Edward III *Married* (1) Anne, daughter of Emperor Charles IV (2) Isabelle, daughter of Charles VI of France *Deposed* Sep 1399, *killed* Feb 1400 aged 33, *reigned* 22 years

THE HOUSE OF LANCASTER

1399–1413	HENRY IV *Born* 1366, son of John of Gaunt, fourth son of Edward III, and Blanche, daughter of Henry, Duke of Lancaster *Married* (1) Mary, daughter of Humphrey, Earl of Hereford (2) Joan, daughter of Charles, King of Navarre, and widow of John, Duke of Brittany *Died* aged c.47, *reigned* 13 years
1413–1422	HENRY V *Born* 1387, eldest surviving son of Henry IV and Mary *Married* Catherine, daughter of Charles VI of France *Died* aged 34, *reigned* 9 years
1422–1471	HENRY VI *Born* 1421, son of Henry V *Married* Margaret, daughter of René, Duke of Anjou and Count of Provence *Deposed* Mar 1461, *restored* Oct 1470 *Deposed* Apr 1471, *killed* May 1471 aged 49, *reigned* 39 years

THE HOUSE OF YORK

1461–1483	EDWARD IV *Born* 1442, eldest son of Richard of York (grandson of Edmund, fifth son of Edward III; and son of Anne, great-granddaughter of Lionel, third son of Edward III)

	Married Elizabeth Woodville, daughter of Richard, Lord Rivers, and widow of Sir John Grey *Acceded* Mar 1461, *deposed* Oct 1470, *restored* Apr 1471 *Died* aged 40, *reigned* 21 years
1483 (Apr–Jun)	EDWARD V *Born* 1470, eldest son of Edward IV *Deposed* Jun 1483, *died* probably Jul–Sep 1483, aged 12, *reigned* 2 months
1483–1485	RICHARD III *Born* 1452, fourth son of Richard of York *Married* Anne Neville, daughter of Richard, Earl of Warwick, and widow of Edward, Prince of Wales, son of Henry VI *Killed* in battle aged 32, *reigned* 2 years

THE HOUSE OF TUDOR

1485–1509	HENRY VII *Born* 1457, son of Margaret Beaufort (great-granddaughter of John of Gaunt, fourth son of Edward III) and Edmund Tudor, Earl of Richmond *Married* Elizabeth, daughter of Edward IV *Died* aged 52, *reigned* 23 years
1509–1547	HENRY VIII *Born* 1491, second son of Henry VII *Married* (1) Catherine, daughter of Ferdinand II, King of Aragon, and widow of his elder brother Arthur (divorced) (2) Anne, daughter of Sir Thomas Boleyn (executed) (3) Jane, daughter of Sir John Seymour (died in childbirth) (4) Anne, daughter of John, Duke of Cleves (divorced) (5) Catherine Howard, niece of the Duke of Norfolk (executed) (6) Catherine, daughter of Sir Thomas Parr and widow of Lord Latimer *Died* aged 55, *reigned* 37 years
1547–1553	EDWARD VI *Born* 1537, son of Henry VIII and Jane Seymour *Died* aged 15, *reigned* 6 years
1553 *(6/10–19 Jul)	JANE *Born* 1537, daughter of Frances (daughter of Mary Tudor, the younger daughter of Henry VII) and Henry Grey, Duke of Suffolk *Married* Lord Guildford Dudley, son of the Duke of Northumberland *Deposed* Jul 1553, *executed* Feb 1554 aged 16, *reigned* 13/9 days
1553–1558	MARY I *Born* 1516, daughter of Henry VIII and Catherine of Aragon *Married* Philip II of Spain *Died* aged 42, *reigned* 5 years
1558–1603	ELIZABETH I *Born* 1533, daughter of Henry VIII and Anne Boleyn *Died* aged 69, *reigned* 44 years

* Depending on whether the date of her predecessor's death
(6 July) or that of her official proclamation as Queen (10 July) is
taken as the beginning of her reign.

BRITISH KINGS AND QUEENS SINCE 1603

THE HOUSE OF STUART

Reign

1603–1625   JAMES I (VI OF SCOTLAND)
Born 1566, son of Mary, Queen of Scots (granddaughter of Margaret Tudor, elder daughter of Henry VII), and Henry Stewart, Lord Darnley
Married Anne, daughter of Frederick II of Denmark
Died aged 58, *reigned* 22 years

1625–1649   CHARLES I
Born 1600, second son of James I
Married Henrietta Maria, daughter of Henry IV of France
Executed 1649 aged 48, *reigned* 23 years

INTERREGNUM 1649–1660
1649–1653   Government by a council of state
1653–1658   Oliver Cromwell, Lord Protector
1658–1659   Richard Cromwell, Lord Protector

Reign
1660–1685   CHARLES II
Born 1630, eldest son of Charles I
Married Catherine, daughter of John IV of Portugal
Died aged 54, *reigned* 24 years

1685–1688   JAMES II (VII OF SCOTLAND)
Born 1633, second son of Charles I
Married (1) Lady Anne Hyde, daughter of Edward, Earl of Clarendon (2) Mary, daughter of Alphonso, Duke of Modena
Reign ended with flight from kingdom Dec 1688
Died 1701 aged 67, *reigned* 3 years

INTERREGNUM
11 Dec 1688 to 12 Feb 1689

Reign
1689–1702   WILLIAM III
Born 1650, son of William II, Prince of Orange, and Mary Stuart, daughter of Charles I
Married Mary, elder daughter of James II
Died aged 51, *reigned* 13 years

and
1689–1694   MARY II
Born 1662, elder daughter of James II and Anne
Died aged 32, *reigned* 5 years

1702–1714   ANNE
Born 1665, younger daughter of James II and Anne
Married Prince George of Denmark, son of Frederick III of Denmark
Died aged 49, *reigned* 12 years

THE HOUSE OF HANOVER

1714–1727   GEORGE I (Elector of Hanover)
Born 1660, son of Sophia (daughter of Frederick, Elector Palatine, and Elizabeth Stuart, daughter of James I) and Ernest Augustus, Elector of Hanover
Married Sophia Dorothea, daughter of George William, Duke of Lüneburg-Celle
Died aged 67, *reigned* 12 years

1727–1760   GEORGE II
Born 1683, son of George I
Married Caroline, daughter of John Frederick, Margrave of Brandenburg-Anspach
Died aged 76, *reigned* 33 years

1760–1820   GEORGE III
Born 1738, son of Frederick, eldest son of George II
Married Charlotte, daughter of Charles Louis, Duke of Mecklenburg-Strelitz
Died aged 81, *reigned* 59 years

REGENCY 1811–1820
Prince of Wales regent owing to the insanity of George III

Reign
1820–1830   GEORGE IV
Born 1762, eldest son of George III
Married Caroline, daughter of Charles, Duke of Brunswick-Wolfenbüttel
Died aged 67, *reigned* 10 years

1830–1837   WILLIAM IV
Born 1765, third son of George III
Married Adelaide, daughter of George, Duke of Saxe-Meiningen
Died aged 71, *reigned* 7 years

1837–1901   VICTORIA
Born 1819, daughter of Edward, fourth son of George III
Married Prince Albert of Saxe-Coburg and Gotha
Died aged 81, *reigned* 63 years

THE HOUSE OF SAXE-COBURG AND GOTHA

1901–1910   EDWARD VII
Born 1841, eldest son of Victoria and Albert
Married Alexandra, daughter of Christian IX of Denmark
Died aged 68, *reigned* 9 years

THE HOUSE OF WINDSOR

1910–1936   GEORGE V
Born 1865, second son of Edward VII
Married Victoria Mary, daughter of Francis, Duke of Teck
Died aged 70, *reigned* 25 years

1936   EDWARD VIII
(20 Jan– 11 Dec)
Born 1894, eldest son of George V
Married (1937) Mrs Wallis Simpson
Abdicated 1936, *died* 1972 aged 77, *reigned* 10 months

1936–1952   GEORGE VI
Born 1895, second son of George V
Married Lady Elizabeth Bowes-Lyon, daughter of 14th Earl of Strathmore and Kinghorne
Died aged 56, *reigned* 15 years

1952–   ELIZABETH II
Born 1926, elder daughter of George VI
Married Philip, son of Prince Andrew of Greece

KINGS AND QUEENS OF SCOTS 1016 TO 1603

Reign

1016–1034   MALCOLM II
Born c.954, son of Kenneth II
Acceded to Alba 1005, secured Lothian
c.1016, obtained Strathclyde for his
grandson Duncan c.1016, thus reigning
over an area approximately the same as that
governed by later rulers of Scotland
Died aged c.80, *reigned* 18 years

THE HOUSE OF ATHOLL

1034–1040   DUNCAN I
Son of Bethoc, daughter of Malcolm II,
and Crinan, Mormaer of Atholl
Married a cousin of Siward, Earl of
Northumbria
Reigned 5 years

1040–1057   MACBETH
Born c.1005, son of a daughter of
Malcolm II and Finlaec, Mormaer of Moray
Married Gruoch, granddaughter of
Kenneth III
Killed aged c.52, *reigned* 17 years

1057–1058   LULACH
(Aug–Mar)   *Born* c.1032, son of Gillacomgan, Mormaer
of Moray, and Gruoch (and stepson of
Macbeth)
Died aged c.26, *reigned* 7 months

1058–1093   MALCOLM III (Canmore)
Born c.1031, elder son of Duncan I
Married (1) Ingibiorg (2) Margaret
(St Margaret), granddaughter of Edmund II
of England
Killed in battle aged c.62, *reigned* 35 years

1093–1097   DONALD III BÁN
Born c.1033, second son of Duncan I
Deposed May 1094, *restored* Nov
1094, *deposed* Oct 1097, *reigned* 3 years

1094   DUNCAN II
(May–Nov)   *Born* c.1060, elder son of Malcolm III and
Ingibiorg
Married Octreda of Dunbar
Killed aged c.34, *reigned* 6 months

1097–1107   EDGAR
Born c.1074, second son of Malcolm III and
Margaret
Died aged c.32, *reigned* 9 years

1107–1124   ALEXANDER I (the Fierce)
Born c.1077, fifth son of Malcolm III and
Margaret
Married Sybilla, illegitimate daughter of
Henry I of England
Died aged c.47, *reigned* 17 years

1124–1153   DAVID I (the Saint)
Born c.1085, sixth son of Malcolm III and
Margaret
Married Matilda, daughter of Waltheof, Earl
of Huntingdon
Died aged c.68, *reigned* 29 years

1153–1165   MALCOLM IV (the Maiden)
Born c.1141, son of Henry, Earl of
Huntingdon, second son of David I
Died aged c.24, *reigned* 12 years

1165–1214   WILLIAM I (the Lion)
Born c.1142, brother of Malcolm IV
Married Ermengarde, daughter of Richard,
Viscount of Beaumont
Died aged c.72, *reigned* 49 years

1214–1249   ALEXANDER II
Born 1198, son of William I
Married (1) Joan, daughter of John, King of
England (2) Marie, daughter of Ingelram de
Coucy
Died aged 50, *reigned* 34 years

1249–1286   ALEXANDER III
Born 1241, son of Alexander II and Marie
Married (1) Margaret, daughter of Henry III
of England (2) Yolande, daughter of the
Count of Dreux
Killed accidentally aged 44, *reigned* 36 years

1286–1290   MARGARET (the Maid of Norway)
Born 1283, daughter of Margaret (daughter
of Alexander III) and Eric II of Norway
Died aged 7, *reigned* 4 years

FIRST INTERREGNUM 1290–1292

Throne disputed by 13 competitors. Crown awarded to
John Balliol by adjudication of Edward I of England

THE HOUSE OF BALLIOL

Reign

1292–1296   JOHN (Balliol)
Born c.1250, son of Dervorguilla,
great-great-granddaughter of David I, and
John de Balliol
Married Isabella, daughter of John, Earl of
Surrey
Abdicated 1296, *died* 1313 aged c.63,
reigned 3 years

SECOND INTERREGNUM 1296–1306

Edward I of England declared John Balliol to have
forfeited the throne for contumacy in 1296 and took the
government of Scotland into his own hands

THE HOUSE OF BRUCE

Reign

1306–1329   ROBERT I (Bruce)
Born 1274, son of Robert Bruce and
Marjorie, countess of Carrick, and
great-grandson of the second daughter of
David, Earl of Huntingdon, brother of
William I
Married (1) Isabella, daughter of Donald,
Earl of Mar (2) Elizabeth, daughter of
Richard, Earl of Ulster
Died aged 54, *reigned* 23 years

1329–1371   DAVID II
Born 1324, son of Robert I and Elizabeth
Married (1) Joanna, daughter of Edward II
of England (2) Margaret Drummond,
widow of Sir John Logie (divorced)
Died aged 46, *reigned* 41 years

**1332 (Sep–   Edward Balliol, son of John
Dec)   Balliol**

1333–1336   Edward Balliol

THE HOUSE OF STEWART

1371–1390   ROBERT II (Stewart)
Born 1316, son of Marjorie (daughter of
Robert I) and Walter, High Steward of
Scotland
Married (1) Elizabeth, daughter of
Sir Robert Mure of Rowallan
(2) Euphemia, daughter of Hugh,
Earl of Ross
Died aged 74, *reigned* 19 years

1390–1406   ROBERT III
Born c.1337, son of Robert II and
Elizabeth

	Married Annabella, daughter of Sir John Drummond of Stobhall
	Died aged c.69, reigned 16 years
1406–1437	JAMES I
	Born 1394, son of Robert III
	Married Joan Beaufort, daughter of John, Earl of Somerset
	Assassinated aged 42, reigned 30 years
1437–1460	JAMES II
	Born 1430, son of James I
	Married Mary, daughter of Arnold, Duke of Gueldres
	Killed accidentally aged 29, reigned 23 years
1460–1488	JAMES III
	Born 1452, son of James II
	Married Margaret, daughter of Christian I of Denmark
	Assassinated aged 36, reigned 27 years
1488–1513	JAMES IV
	Born 1473, son of James III
	Married Margaret Tudor, daughter of Henry VII of England
	Killed in battle aged 40, reigned 25 years
1513–1542	JAMES V
	Born 1512, son of James IV
	Married (1) Madeleine, daughter of Francis I of France (2) Mary of Lorraine, daughter of the Duc de Guise
	Died aged 30, reigned 29 years
1542–1567	MARY
	Born 1542, daughter of James V and Mary
	Married (1) the Dauphin, afterwards Francis II of France (2) Henry Stewart, Lord Darnley (3) James Hepburn, Earl of Bothwell
	Abdicated 1567, prisoner in England from 1568, executed 1587, reigned 24 years
1567–1625	JAMES VI (and I of England)
	Born 1566, son of Mary, Queen of Scots, and Henry, Lord Darnley
	Acceded 1567 to the Scottish throne, reigned 58 years
	Succeeded 1603 to the English throne, so joining the English and Scottish crowns in one person. The two kingdoms remained distinct until 1707 when the parliaments of the kingdoms became conjoined

WELSH SOVEREIGNS AND PRINCES

Wales was ruled by sovereign princes from the earliest times until the death of Llywelyn in 1282. The first English Prince of Wales was the son of Edward I, who was born in Caernarvon town on 25 April 1284. According to a discredited legend, he was presented to the Welsh chieftains as their prince, in fulfilment of a promise that they should have a prince who 'could not speak a word of English' and should be native born. This son, who afterwards became Edward II, was created 'Prince of Wales and Earl of Chester' at the Lincoln Parliament on 7 February 1301.

The title Prince of Wales is borne after individual conferment and is not inherited at birth, though some Princes have been declared and styled Prince of Wales but never formally so created (s.). The title was conferred on Prince Charles by the Queen on 26 July 1958. He was invested at Caernarvon on 1 July 1969.

INDEPENDENT PRINCES AD 844 TO 1282

844–878	Rhodri the Great
878–916	Anarawd, son of Rhodri
916–950	Hywel Dda, the Good
950–979	Iago ab Idwal (or Ieuaf)
979–985	Hywel ab Ieuaf, the Bad
985–986	Cadwallon, his brother
986–999	Maredudd ab Owain ap Hywel Dda
999–1008	Cynan ap Hywel ab Ieuaf
1018–1023	Llywelyn ap Seisyll
1023–1039	Iago ab Idwal ap Meurig
1039–1063	Gruffydd ap Llywelyn ap Seisyll
1063–1075	Bleddyn ap Cynfyn
1075–1081	Trahaern ap Caradog
1081–1137	Gruffydd ap Cynan ab Iago
1137–1170	Owain Gwynedd
1170–1194	Dafydd ab Owain Gwynedd
1194–1240	Llywelyn Fawr, the Great
1240–1246	Dafydd ap Llywelyn
1246–1282	Llywelyn ap Gruffydd ap Llywelyn

ENGLISH PRINCES SINCE 1301

1301	Edward (Edward II)
1343	Edward the Black Prince, son of Edward III
1376	Richard (Richard II), son of the Black Prince
1399	Henry of Monmouth (Henry V)
1454	Edward of Westminster, son of Henry VI
1471	Edward of Westminster (Edward V)
1483	Edward, son of Richard III (d. 1484)
1489	Arthur Tudor, son of Henry VII
1504	Henry Tudor (Henry VIII)
1610	Henry Stuart, son of James I (d. 1612)
1616	Charles Stuart (Charles I)
c.1638 (s.)	Charles Stuart (Charles II)
1688 (s.)	James Francis Edward Stuart (The Old Pretender), son of James II (d. 1766)
1714	George Augustus (George II)
1729	Frederick Lewis, son of George II (d. 1751)
1751	George William Frederick (George III)
1762	George Augustus Frederick (George IV)
1841	Albert Edward (Edward VII)
1901	George (George V)
1910	Edward (Edward VIII)
1958	Charles, son of Elizabeth II

PRINCESSES ROYAL

The style Princess Royal is conferred at the sovereign's discretion on his or her eldest daughter. It is an honorary title, held for life, and cannot be inherited or passed on. It was first conferred on Princess Mary, daughter of Charles I, in approximately 1642.

c.1642	Princess Mary (1631–60), daughter of Charles I
1727	Princess Anne (1709–59), daughter of George II
1766	Princess Charlotte (1766–1828), daughter of George III
1840	Princess Victoria (1840–1901), daughter of Victoria
1905	Princess Louise (1867–1931), daughter of Edward VII
1932	Princess Mary (1897–1965), daughter of George V
1987	Princess Anne (b. 1950), daughter of Elizabeth II

DESCENDANTS OF QUEEN VICTORIA

I. HRH Princess Victoria Adelaide Mary Louisa, Princess Royal (1840–1901) *m* Friedrich III (1831–88), later German Emperor	II. HRH Prince Albert Edward (HM KING EDWARD VII) (1841– 1910) *succeeded* 22 Jan 1901 *m* HRH Princess Alexandra of Denmark (1844–1925)	III. HRH Princess Alice Maud Mary (1843–78) *m* Prince Ludwig (1837–92), later Grand Duke of Hesse	IV. HRH Prince Alfred Ernest Albert, Duke of Edinburgh (1844–1900) *succeeded* as Duke of Saxe-Coburg and Gotha 1893 *m* Grand Duchess Marie Alexandrovna of Russia (1853–1920)

1. HIM Wilhelm II (1859–1941), later German Emperor *m* (1) Princess Augusta Victoria of Schleswig-Holstein-Sonderburg-Augustenburg (1858–1921) (2) Princess Hermine of Reuss (1887–1947). *Issue* Wilhelm (1882–1951); Eitel-Friedrich (1883–1942); Adalbert (1884–1948); August Wilhelm (1887–1949); Oskar (1888–1958); Joachim (1890–1920); Viktoria Luise (1892–1980)

2. Charlotte (1860–1919) *m* Bernhard, Duke of Saxe-Meiningen (1851–1928). *Issue* Feodora (1879–1945)

1. Albert Victor, Duke of Clarence and Avondale (1864–92)

2. George (HM KING GEORGE V) (1865–1936) (*see* House of Windsor)

3. Louise (1867–1931), later Princess Royal *m* 1st Duke of Fife (1849–1912). *Issue* Alexandra (1891–1959); Maud (1893–1945)

4. Victoria (1868–1935)

5. Maud (1869–1938) *m* Prince Carl of Denmark (1872–1957), later King Haakon VII of Norway. *Issue* Olav V (1903–91)

6. Alexander (6–7 Apr 1871)

1. Victoria (1863–1950) *m* Prince Louis of Battenberg (1854–1921), later 1st Marquess of Milford Haven. *Issue* Alice (1885–1969); Louise (1889–1965); George (1892–1938); Louis (1900–79)

2. Elizabeth (1864–1918) *m* Grand Duke Sergius of Russia (1857–1905)

3. Irene (1866–1953) *m* Prince Heinrich of Prussia (*see* I.3)

4. Ernst Ludwig (1868–1937), Grand Duke of Hesse, *m* (1) Princess Victoria Melita of Saxe-Coburg (see IV.3) (2) Princess Eleonore of Solms-Hohensolms-Lich (1871–1937). *Issue* Elizabeth (1895–1903); George (1906–37); Ludwig (1908–68)

5. Frederick William (1870–3)

6. Alix (Tsaritsa of Russia) (1872–1918) *m* Nicholas II, Tsar of All the Russias (1868–1918). *Issue* Olga (1895–1918); Tatiana (1897–1918); Marie (1899–1918); Anastasia (1901–18); Alexis (1904–18)

7. Marie (1874–8)

3. Heinrich (1862–1929) *m* Princess Irene of Hesse (*see* III.3). *Issue* Waldemar (1889–1945); Sigismund (1896–1978); Heinrich (1900–4)

4. Sigismund (1864–6)

5. Victoria (1866–1929) *m* (1) Prince Adolf of Schaumburg-Lippe (1859–1916) (2) Alexander Zubkov (1900–36)

6. Waldemar (1868–79)

7. Sophie (1870–1932) *m* Constantine I (1868–1923), later King of the Hellenes. *Issue* George II (1890–1947); Alexander I (1893–1920); Helena (1896–1982); Paul I (1901–64); Irene (1904–74); Katherine (1913–2007)

8. Margarethe (1872–1954) *m* Prince Friedrich Karl of Hesse (1868–1940). *Issue* Friedrich Wilhelm (1893–1916); Maximilian (1894–1914); Philipp (1896–1980); Wolfgang (1896–1989); Richard (1901–69); Christoph (1901–43)

QUEEN VICTORIA (Alexandrina Victoria) (1819–1901) *succeeded* 20 Jun 1837 *m* (Francis) Albert Augustus Charles Emmanuel, Duke of Saxony, Prince of Saxe-Coburg and Gotha (HRH Albert, Prince Consort) (1819–61)

VI. HRH Princess Louise Caroline Alberta (1848–1939) *m* Marquess of Lorne (1845–1914), later 9th Duke of Argyll

VII. HRH Prince Arthur William Patrick Albert, Duke of Connaught (1850–1942) *m* Princess Louisa of Prussia (1860–1917)

VIII. HRH Prince Leopold George Duncan Albert, Duke of Albany (1853–84) *m* Princess Helena of Waldeck (1861–1922)

IX. HRH Princess Beatrice Mary Victoria Feodore (1857–1944) *m* Prince Henry of Battenberg (1858–96)

1. Alfred, Prince of Saxe-Coburg (1874–99)

2. Marie (1875–1938) *m* Ferdinand (1865–1927), later King of Roumania. *Issue* Carol II (1893–1953); Elisabeth (1894–1956); Marie (1900–61); Nicolas (1903–78); Ileana (1909–91); Mircea (1913–16)

3. Victoria Melita (1876–1936) *m* (1) Grand Duke Ernst Ludwig of Hesse (*see* III.4) (2) Grand Duke Kirill of Russia (1876–1938). *Issue* Marie (1907–51); Kira (1909–67); Vladimir (1917–92)

4. Alexandra (1878–1942) *m* Ernst, Prince of Hohenlohe Langenburg (1863–1950). *Issue* Gottfried (1897–1960); Maria (1899–1967); Alexandra (1901–63); Irma (1902–86)

5. Beatrice (1884–1966) *m* Alfonso of Orleans, Infante of Spain (1886–1975). *Issue* Alvaro (1910–97); Alonso (1912–36); Ataulfo (1913–74)

1. Margaret (1882–1920) *m* Crown Prince Gustaf Adolf (1882–1973), later King of Sweden. *Issue* Gustaf Adolf (1906–47); Sigvard (1907–2002); Ingrid (1910–2000); Bertil (1912–97); Count Carl Bernadotte (*b* 1916)

2. Arthur (1883–1938) *m* HH Duchess of Fife (1891–1959). *Issue* Alastair Arthur (1914–43)

3. (Victoria) Patricia (1886–1974) *m* Adm. Hon. Sir Alexander Ramsay (1881–1972). *Issue* Alexander (1919–2000)

1. Alice (1883–1981) *m* Prince Alexander of Teck (1874–1957), later 1st Earl of Athlone. *Issue* May (1906–94); Rupert (1907–28); Maurice (Mar–Sep 1910)

2. Charles Edward (1884–1954), Duke of Albany until title suspended 1917, Duke of Saxe-Coburg-Gotha, *m* Princess Victoria Adelheid of Schleswig-Holstein-Sonderburg-Glücksburg (1885–1970). *Issue* Johann Leopold (1906–72); Sibylla (1908–72); Dietmar Hubertus (1909–43); Caroline (1912–83); Friedrich Josias (1918–98)

1. Alexander, 1st Marquess of Carisbrooke (1886–1960) *m* Lady Irene Denison (1890–1956). *Issue* Iris (1920–82)

2. Victoria Eugénie (1887–1969) *m* Alfonso XIII, King of Spain (1886–1941). *Issue* Alfonso (1907–38); Jaime (1908–75); Beatriz (1909–2002); Maria (1911–96); Juan (1913–93); Gonzalo (1914–34)

3. Maj. Lord Leopold Mountbatten (1889–1922)

4. Maurice (1891–1914)

V. HRH Princess Helena Augusta Victoria (1846–1923) *m* Prince Christian of Schleswig-Holstein-Sonderburg-Augustenburg (1831–1917)

1. Christian Victor (1867–1900)

2. Albert (1869–1931), later Duke of Schleswig-Holstein

3. Helena (1870–1948)

4. Marie Louise (1872–1956), *m* Prince Aribert of Anhalt (1864–1933)

5. Harold (12–20 May 1876)

THE HOUSE OF WINDSOR

King George V assumed by royal proclamation (17 July 1917) for his House and family, as well as for all descendants in the male line of Queen Victoria who are subjects of these realms, the name of Windsor.

KING GEORGE V
(George Frederick Ernest Albert), second son of King Edward VII *born* 3 June 1865 *married* 6 July 1893 HSH Princess Victoria Mary Augusta Louise Olga Pauline Claudine Agnes of Teck (Queen Mary *born* 26 May 1867 *died* 24 March 1953) *succeeded* to the throne 6 May 1910 *died* 20 January 1936. *Issue*

1. HRH PRINCE EDWARD Albert Christian George Andrew Patrick David *born* 23 June 1894 *succeeded* to the throne as King Edward VIII, 20 January 1936 *abdicated* 11 December 1936 *created* Duke of Windsor 1937 *married* 3 June 1937 Mrs Wallis Simpson (Her Grace The Duchess of Windsor *born* 19 June 1896 *died* 24 April 1986) *died* 28 May 1972

2. HRH PRINCE ALBERT Frederick Arthur George *born* 14 December 1895 *created* Duke of York 1920 *married* 26 April 1923 Lady Elizabeth Bowes-Lyon, youngest daughter of the 14th Earl of Strathmore and Kinghorne (HM Queen Elizabeth the Queen Mother *born* 4 August 1900 *died* 30 March 2002) *succeeded* to the throne as King George VI, 11 December 1936 *died* 6 February 1952. *Issue*
   (1) HRH Princess Elizabeth Alexandra Mary *succeeded* to the throne as Queen Elizabeth II, 6 February 1952 (*see* Royal Family)
   (2) HRH Princess Margaret Rose (later HRH The Princess Margaret, Countess of Snowdon) *born* 21 August 1930 *married* 6 May 1960 Anthony Charles Robert Armstrong-Jones, GCVO *created* Earl of Snowdon 1961 (marriage dissolved 1978) *died* 9 February 2002, having had issue (*see* Royal Family)

3. HRH PRINCESS (Victoria Alexandra Alice) MARY *born* 25 April 1897 *created* Princess Royal 1932 *married* 28 February 1922 Viscount Lascelles, later the 6th Earl of Harewood (1882–1947) *died* 28 March 1965. *Issue*
   (1) George Henry Hubert Lascelles, 7th Earl of Harewood, KBE *born* 7 February 1923 *married* (1) 1949 Maria (Marion) Stein (marriage dissolved 1967) *issue (a)* David Henry George, Viscount Lascelles *born* 1950 *(b)* James Edward *born* 1953 *(c)* (Robert) Jeremy Hugh *born* 1955 (2) 1967 Patricia Tuckwell *issue (d)* Mark Hubert *born* 1964
   (2) Gerald David Lascelles (1924–98) *married* (1) 1952 Angela Dowding (marriage dissolved 1978) *issue (a)* Henry Ulick *born* 1953 (2) 1978 Elizabeth Collingwood (Elizabeth Colvin) *issue (b)* Martin David *born* 1962

4. HRH PRINCE HENRY William Frederick Albert *born* 31 March 1900 *created* Duke of Gloucester, Earl of Ulster and Baron Culloden 1928 *married* 6 November 1935 Lady Alice Christabel Montagu-Douglas-Scott, daughter of the 7th Duke of Buccleuch and Queensberry (HRH Princess Alice, Duchess of Gloucester *born* 25 December 1901 *died* 29 October 2004) *died* 10 June 1974. *Issue*
   (1) HRH Prince William Henry Andrew Frederick *born* 18 December 1941 accidentally *killed* 28 August 1972
   (2) HRH Prince Richard Alexander Walter George (HRH The Duke of Gloucester, *see* Royal Family)

5. HRH PRINCE GEORGE Edward Alexander Edmund *born* 20 December 1902 *created* Duke of Kent, Earl of St Andrews and Baron Downpatrick 1934 *married* 29 November 1934 HRH Princess Marina of Greece and Denmark (*born* 30 November 1906 *died* 27 August 1968) *killed* on active service 25 August 1942. *Issue*
   (1) HRH Prince Edward George Nicholas Paul Patrick (HRH The Duke of Kent, *see* Royal Family)
   (2) HRH Princess Alexandra Helen Elizabeth Olga Christabel (HRH Princess Alexandra, the Hon. Lady Ogilvy, *see* Royal Family)
   (3) HRH Prince Michael George Charles Franklin (HRH Prince Michael of Kent, *see* Royal Family)

6. HRH PRINCE JOHN Charles Francis *born* 12 July 1905 *died* 18 January 1919

PRECEDENCE

ENGLAND AND WALES

The Sovereign
The Prince Philip, Duke of
 Edinburgh
The Prince of Wales
The Sovereign's younger sons
The Sovereign's grandsons
The Sovereign's cousins
Archbishop of Canterbury
Lord High Chancellor
Archbishop of York
The Prime Minister
Lord President of the Council
Speaker of the House of Commons
Speaker of the House of Lords
President of the Supreme Court
Lord Chief Justice of England and
 Wales
Lord Privy Seal
Ambassadors and High
 Commissioners
Lord Great Chamberlain
Earl Marshal
Lord Steward of the Household
Lord Chamberlain of the Household
Master of the Horse
Dukes, according to their patent of
 creation:
 1. of England
 2. of Scotland
 3. of Great Britain
 4. of Ireland
 5. those created since the Union
Eldest sons of Dukes of the Blood
 Royal
Ministers, Envoys, and other
 important overseas visitors
Marquesses, according to their patent
 of creation:
 1. of England
 2. of Scotland
 3. of Great Britain
 4. of Ireland
 5. those created since the Union
Dukes' eldest sons
Earls, according to their patent of
 creation:
 1. of England
 2. of Scotland
 3. of Great Britain
 4. of Ireland
 5. those created since the Union
Younger sons of Dukes of Blood
 Royal
Marquesses' eldest sons

Dukes' younger sons
Viscounts, according to their patent
 of creation:
 1. of England
 2. of Scotland
 3. of Great Britain
 4. of Ireland
 5. those created since the Union
Earls' eldest sons
Marquesses' younger sons
Bishop of London
Bishop of Durham
Bishop of Winchester
Other English Diocesan Bishops,
 according to seniority of
 consecration
Retired Church of England Diocesan
 Bishops, according to seniority of
 consecration
Suffragan Bishops, according to
 seniority of consecration
Secretaries of State, if of the degree
 of a Baron
Barons, according to their patent of
 creation:
 1. of England
 2. of Scotland (Lords of
  Parliament)
 3. of Great Britain
 4. of Ireland
 5. those created since the Union,
  including Life Barons
Master of the Rolls
Deputy President of the Supreme
 Court
Justices of the Supreme Court,
 according to seniority of
 appointment
Treasurer of the Household
Comptroller of the Household
Vice-Chamberlain of the Household
Secretaries of State under the degree
 of Baron
Viscounts' eldest sons
Earls' younger sons
Barons' eldest sons
Knights of the Garter
Privy Counsellors
Chancellor of the Order of the
 Garter
Chancellor of the Exchequer
Chancellor of the Duchy of Lancaster
President of the Queen's Bench
 Division
President of the Family Division
Chancellor of the High Court

Lord Justices of Appeal, according to
 seniority of appointment
Judges of the High Court, according
 to seniority of appointment
Viscounts' younger sons
Barons' younger sons
Sons of Life Peers
Baronets, according to date of
 patent
Knights of the Thistle
Knights Grand Cross of the Bath
Knights Grand Cross of St Michael
 and St George
Knights Grand Cross of the Royal
 Victorian Order
Knights Grand Cross of the British
 Empire
Knights Commanders of the Bath
Knights Commanders of St Michael
 and St George
Knights Commanders of the Royal
 Victorian Order
Knights Commanders of the British
 Empire
Knights Bachelor
Circuit Judges, according to priority
 and order of their respective
 appointments
Master of the Court of Protection
Companions of the Bath
Companions of St Michael and St
 George
Commanders of the Royal Victorian
 Order
Commanders of the British
 Empire
Companions of the Distinguished
 Service Order
Lieutenants of the Royal Victorian
 Order
Officers of the British Empire
Companions of the Imperial Service
 Order
Eldest sons of younger sons of
 peers
Baronets' eldest sons
Eldest sons of knights, in the same
 order as their fathers
Members of the Royal Victorian
 Order
Members of the British Empire
Baronets' younger sons
Knights' younger sons, in the same
 order as their fathers
Esquires
Gentlemen

WOMEN

Women take the same rank as their husbands or as their brothers; but the daughter of a peer marrying a commoner retains her title as Lady or Honourable. Daughters of peers rank next immediately after the wives of their elder brothers, and before their younger brothers' wives. Daughters of peers marrying peers of a lower degree take the same order of precedence as that of their

husbands; thus the daughter of a Duke marrying a Baron becomes of the rank of Baroness only, while her sisters married to commoners retain their rank and take precedence over the Baroness. Merely official rank on the husband's part does not give any similar precedence to the wife.

Peeresses in their own right take the same precedence as peers of the same rank, ie from their date of creation.

SCOTLAND

The Sovereign
The Prince Philip, Duke of Edinburgh
The Lord High Commissioner to the General Assembly of the Church of Scotland (while that assembly is sitting)
The Duke of Rothesay (eldest son of the Sovereign)
The Sovereign's younger sons
The Sovereign's grandsons
The Sovereign's nephews
Lord-Lieutenants
Lord Provosts, during their term of office*
Sheriffs Principal, during their term of office and within the bounds of their respective sheriffdoms
Lord Chancellor of Great Britain
Moderator of the General Assembly of the Church of Scotland
Keeper of the Great Seal of Scotland (the First Minister)
Presiding Officer
The Secretary of State for Scotland
Hereditary High Constable of Scotland
Hereditary Master of the Household in Scotland
Dukes, as in England

Eldest sons of Dukes of the Blood Royal
Marquesses, as in England
Dukes' eldest sons
Earls, as in England
Younger sons of Dukes of Blood Royal
Marquesses' eldest sons
Dukes' younger sons
Lord Justice General
Lord Clerk Register
Lord Advocate
The Advocate General
Lord Justice Clerk
Viscounts, as in England
Earls' eldest sons
Marquesses' younger sons
Lords of Parliament or Barons, as in England
Eldest sons of Viscounts
Earls' younger sons
Eldest sons of Lords of Parliament or Barons
Knights and Ladies of the Garter
Knights and Ladies of the Thistle
Privy Counsellors
Senators of the College of Justice (Lords of Session)
Viscounts' younger sons
Younger sons of Lords of Parliament or Barons
Baronets
Knights and Dames Grand Cross and

Knights and Dames Grand Commanders of orders, as in England
Knights and Dames Commanders of orders, as in England
Solicitor-General for Scotland
Lord Lyon King of Arms
Sheriffs Principal, when not within own county
Knights Bachelor
Sheriffs
Companions of Orders, as in England
Commanders of the Royal Victorian Order
Commanders of the British Empire
Lieutenants of the Royal Victorian Order
Companions of the Distinguished Service Order
Officers of the British Empire
Companions of the Imperial Service Order
Eldest sons of younger sons of peers
Eldest sons of baronets
Eldest sons of knights, as in England
Members of the Royal Victorian Order
Members of the British Empire
Baronets' younger sons
Knights' younger sons
Queen's Counsel
Esquires
Gentlemen

* The Lord Provosts of Aberdeen, Dundee, Edinburgh and Glasgow are Lord-Lieutenants for these cities *ex officio* and take precedence as such

THE PEERAGE

The rules which govern the creation and succession of peerages are extremely complicated. There are, technically, five separate peerages, the Peerage of England, of Scotland, of Ireland, of Great Britain, and of the United Kingdom. The Peerage of Great Britain dates from 1707 when an Act of Union combined the two kingdoms of England and Scotland and separate peerages were discontinued. The Peerage of the United Kingdom dates from 1801 when Great Britain and Ireland were combined under an Act of Union. Some Scottish peers have received additional peerages of Great Britain or of the United Kingdom since 1707, and some Irish peers additional peerages of the United Kingdom since 1801.

The Peerage of Ireland was not entirely discontinued from 1801 but holders of Irish peerages, whether pre-dating or created subsequent to the Union of 1801, were not entitled to sit in the House of Lords if they had no additional English, Scottish, Great Britain or United Kingdom peerage. However, they are eligible for election to the House of Commons and to vote in parliamentary elections. An Irish peer holding a peerage of a lower grade which enabled him to sit in the House of Lords was introduced there by the title which enabled him to sit, though for all other purposes he was known by his higher title.

In the Peerage of Scotland there is no rank of Baron; the equivalent rank is Lord of Parliament, abbreviated to 'Lord' (the female equivalent is 'Lady').

All peers of England, Scotland, Great Britain or the United Kingdom who are 21 years or over, and of British, Irish or Commonwealth nationality were entitled to sit in the House of Lords until the House of Lords Act 1999, when hereditary peers lost the right to sit. However, section two of the act provided an exception for 90 hereditary peers plus the holders of the office of Earl Marshal and Lord Great Chamberlain to remain as members of the House of Lords for their lifetime or pending further reform. Of the 90 hereditary peers, 75 were elected by the hereditary peers in their political party, or Crossbench grouping, and the remaining 15 by the whole house. Until 7 November 2002 any vacancy arising due to the death of one of the 90 excepted hereditary peers was filled by the runner-up to the original election. From 7 November 2002 any vacancy due to a death has been filled by holding a by-election. By-elections are conducted in accordance with arrangements made by the Clerk of the Parliaments and have to take place within three months of a vacancy occurring. If the vacancy is among the 75, only the excepted hereditary peers in the relevant party or Crossbench grouping are entitled to vote. If the vacancy is among the other 15, the whole house is entitled to vote.

In the list below, peers currently holding one of the 92 hereditary places in the House of Lords are indicated by **.

HEREDITARY WOMEN PEERS

Most hereditary peerages pass on death to the nearest male heir, but there are exceptions, and several are held by women.

A woman peer in her own right retains her title after marriage, and if her husband's rank is the superior she is designated by the two titles jointly, the inferior one second. Her hereditary claim still holds good in spite of any marriage whether higher or lower. No rank held by a woman can confer any title or even precedence upon her husband but the rank of a hereditary woman peer in her own right is inherited by her eldest son (or in some cases daughter).

After the Peerage Act 1963, hereditary women peers in their own right were entitled to sit in the House of Lords, subject to the same qualifications as men, until the House of Lords Act 1999.

LIFE PEERS

From 1876 to 2009 non-hereditary or life peerages were conferred on certain eminent judges to enable the judicial functions of the House of Lords to be carried out. These lords were known as Lords of Appeal in Ordinary or law lords. The judicial role of the House of Lords as the highest appeal court in the UK ended on 30 July 2009 and since 1 October 2009, under the Constitutional Reform Act 2005, any peer who holds a senior judicial office is disqualified from sitting in the House of Lords until they retire from that office.

Justices of the Supreme Court currently disqualified from sitting or voting in the House of Lords until retirement are marked with a '§' in the list of life peerages which follows.

Since 1958 life peerages have been conferred upon distinguished men and women from all walks of life, giving them seats in the House of Lords in the degree of Baron or Baroness. They are addressed in the same way as hereditary lords and barons, and their children have similar courtesy titles.

PEERAGES EXTINCT SINCE THE LAST EDITION

EARLDOMS: Dunraven and Mount Earl (cr. 1822 I.); Halsbury (cr. 1898)

LIFE PEERAGES: Acton of Bridgnorth (cr. 2000); Bingham of Cornhill (cr. 1996); Boston of Faversham (cr. 1976); Carnegy of Lour (cr. 1982); Elliott of Morpeth (cr.1985); Fyfe of Fairfield (cr. 2000); Hennessy (cr. 1999); Livsey of Talgarth (cr. 2001); Marsh (cr.1981); Pilkington of Oxenford (cr.1996); Rodger of Earlsferry (cr. 1992)

DISCLAIMER OF PEERAGES

The Peerage Act 1963 enables peers to disclaim their peerages for life. Peers alive in 1963 could disclaim within twelve months after the passing of the act (31 July 1963); a person subsequently succeeding to a peerage may disclaim within 12 months (one month if an MP) after the date of succession, or of reaching 21, if later. The disclaimer is irrevocable but does not affect the descent of the peerage after the disclaimant's death, and children of a disclaimed peer may, if they wish, retain their precedence and any courtesy titles and styles borne as children of a peer. The disclaimer permitted the disclaimant to sit in the House of Commons if elected as an MP. As the House of Lords Act 1999 removed hereditary peers from the House of Lords, they are now entitled to sit in the House of Commons without having to disclaim their titles.

The following peerages are currently disclaimed:

EARLDOM: Selkirk (1994)
VISCOUNTCY: Stansgate (1963)
BARONIES: Merthyr (1977); Reith (1972); Sanderson of Ayot (1971); Silkin (2002)

PEERS WHO ARE MINORS (ie under 21 years of age)
VISCOUNT: Selby (b. 1993)
BARONS: Glenconner (b. 1994); Hawke (b. 1995)

FORMS OF ADDRESS

Forms of address are given under the style for each individual rank of the peerage. Both formal and social forms of address are given where usage differs; nowadays, the social form is generally preferred to the formal, which increasingly is used only for official documents and on very formal occasions.

ROLL OF THE PEERAGE

Crown Office, House of Lords, London SW1A 0PW

The Roll of the Peerage is kept at the Crown Office and maintained by the Registrar and Assistant Registrar of the Peerage in accordance with the terms of a 2004 royal warrant. The roll records the names of all living life peers and hereditary peers who have proved their succession to the satisfaction of the Lord Chancellor. The Roll of the Peerage is maintained in addition to the Clerk of the Parliaments' register of hereditary peers eligible to stand for election in House of Lords' by-elections.

A person whose name is not entered on the Roll of Peerage can not be addressed or mentioned by the title of a peer in any official document.

Registrar, Ian Denyer, MVO
Assistant Registrar, Grant Bavister

HEREDITARY PEERS

as at 31 August 2011

PEERS OF THE BLOOD ROYAL

Style, His Royal Highness the Duke of _/His Royal Highness the Earl of_/His Royal Highness the Lord_
Style of address (formal) May it please your Royal Highness; *(informal)* Sir

Created	Title, order of succession, name, etc	Heir
	Dukes	
1947	*Edinburgh (1st),* HRH the Prince Philip, Duke of Edinburgh	The Prince of Wales *
1337	*Cornwall,* HRH the Prince of Wales, *s.* 1952	‡
1398 S.	*Rothesay,* HRH the Prince of Wales, *s.* 1952	‡
2011	*Cambridge (1st),* HRH Prince William of Wales	None
1986	*York (1st),* Prince Andrew, HRH the Duke of York	None
1928	*Gloucester (2nd),* Prince Richard, HRH the Duke of Gloucester, *s.* 1974	Earl of Ulster
1934	*Kent (2nd),* Prince Edward, HRH the Duke of Kent, *s.* 1942	Earl of St Andrews
	Earl	
2011	*Strathearn (1st),* HRH Prince William of Wales	None
1999	*Wessex (1st),* Prince Edward, HRH the Earl of Wesex	Viscount Severn
	Baron	
2011	*Carrickfergus (1st),* HRH Prince William of Wales	None

* In June 1999 Buckingham Palace announced that the current Earl of Wessex will be granted the Dukedom of Edinburgh when the title reverts to the Crown. The title will only revert to the Crown on both the death of the current Duke of Edinburgh and the Prince of Wales' succession as king
‡ The title is held by the sovereign's eldest son from the moment of his birth or the sovereign's accession

DUKES

Coronet, Eight strawberry leaves

Style, His Grace the Duke of _
    Envelope (formal), His Grace the Duke of _; *(social),* The Duke of _. *Letter (formal),* My Lord Duke; *(social),* Dear Duke.
Spoken (formal), Your Grace; *(social),* Duke
Wife's style, Her Grace the Duchess of _
    Envelope (formal), Her Grace the Duchess of _; *(social),* The Duchess of _. *Letter (formal),* Dear Madam; *(social),* Dear Duchess. *Spoken,* Duchess
Eldest son's style, Takes his father's second title as a courtesy title *(see* Courtesy Titles*)*
Younger sons' style, 'Lord' before forename (F_) and surname (S_)
    Envelope, Lord F_ S_. *Letter (formal),* My Lord; *(social),* Dear Lord F_. *Spoken (formal),* My Lord; *(social),* Lord F_
Daughters' style, 'Lady' before forename (F_) and surname (S_)
    Envelope, Lady F_ S_. *Letter (formal),* Dear Madam; *(social),* Dear Lady F_. *Spoken,* Lady F_

Created	Title, order of succession, name, etc	Heir
1868 I.	*Abercorn (5th),* James Hamilton, KG, *b.* 1934, *s.* 1979, *m.*	Marquess of Hamilton, *b.* 1969
1701 S.	*Argyll (13th),* Torquhil Ian Campbell, *b.* 1968, *s.* 2001	Marquess of Lorne, *b.* 2004
1703 S.	*Atholl (11th),* John Murray, *b.* 1929, *s.* 1996, *m.*	Marquis of Tullibardine, *b.* 1960
1682	*Beaufort (11th),* David Robert Somerset, *b.* 1928, *s.* 1984, *m.*	Marquess of Worcester, *b.* 1952
1694	*Bedford (15th),* Andrew Ian Henry Russell, *b.* 1962, *s.* 2003, *m.*	Marquess of Tavistock, *b.* 2005
1663 S.	*Buccleuch (10th) and Queensberry (12th) (S. 1684),* Richard Walter John Montagu Douglas Scott, KBE, *b.* 1954, *s.* 2007, *m.*	Earl of Dalkeith, *b.* 1984
1694	*Devonshire (12th),* Peregrine Andrew Morny Cavendish, KCVO, CBE, *b.* 1944, *s.* 2004, *m.*	Earl of Burlington, *b.* 1969
1900	*Fife (3rd),* James George Alexander Bannerman Carnegie, *b.* 1929, *s.* 1959	Earl of Southesk, *b.* 1961
1675	*Grafton (12th),* Henry Oliver Charles FitzRoy, *b.* 1978, *s.* 2011, *m.*	Lord Charles P. H. F., *b.* 1957

1643 S.	*Hamilton (16th) and Brandon (13th) (1711)*, Alexander Douglas Douglas-Hamilton, *b.* 1978, *s.* 2010 *Premier Peer of Scotland*	Lord John W., *b.* 1979
1766 I.	*Leinster (9th)*, Maurice FitzGerald, *b.* 1948, *s.* 2004, *m. Premier Duke, Marquess and Earl of Ireland*	Lord John F., *b.* 1952
1719	*Manchester (13th)*, Alexander Charles David Drogo Montagu, *b.* 1962, *s.* 2002, *m.*	Lord Kimble W. D. M., *b.* 1964
1702	*Marlborough (11th)*, John George Vanderbilt Henry Spencer-Churchill, *b.* 1926, *s.* 1972, *m.*	Marquess of Blandford, *b.* 1955
1707 S.	** *Montrose (8th)*, James Graham, *b.* 1935, *s.* 1992, *m.*	Marquis of Graham, *b.* 1973
1483	** *Norfolk (18th)*, Edward Wiliam Fitzalan-Howard, *b.* 1956, *s.* 2002, *m. Premier Duke and Earl Marshal*	Earl of Arundel and Surrey, *b.* 1987
1766	*Northumberland (12th)*, Ralph George Algernon Percy, *b.* 1956, *s.* 1995, *m.*	Earl Percy, *b.* 1984
1675	*Richmond (10th) and Gordon (5th) (1876)*, Charles Henry Gordon Lennox, *b.* 1929, *s.* 1989, *m.*	Earl of March and Kinrara, *b.* 1955
1707 S.	*Roxburghe (10th)*, Guy David Innes-Ker, *b.* 1954, *s.* 1974, *m. Premier Baronet of Scotland*	Marquis of Bowmont and Cessford, *b.* 1981
1703	*Rutland (11th)*, David Charles Robert Manners, *b.* 1959, *s.* 1999, *m.*	Marquess of Granby, *b.*1999
1684	*St Albans (14th)*, Murray de Vere Beauclerk, *b.* 1939, *s.* 1988, *m.*	Earl of Burford, *b.* 1965
1547	*Somerset (19th)*, John Michael Edward Seymour, *b.* 1952, *s.* 1984, *m.*	Lord Seymour, *b.* 1982
1833	*Sutherland (7th)*, Francis Ronald Egerton, *b.* 1940, *s.* 2000, *m.*	Marquess of Stafford, *b.* 1975
1814	*Wellington (8th)*, Arthur Valerian Wellesley, KG, LVO, OBE, MC, *b.* 1915, *s.* 1972, *w.*	Marquess of Douro, *b.* 1945
1874	*Westminster (6th)*, Gerald Cavendish Grosvenor, KG, CB, OBE, *b.* 1951, *s.* 1979, *m.*	Earl Grosvenor, *b.* 1991

MARQUESSES

Coronet, Four strawberry leaves alternating with four silver balls

Style, The Most Hon. the Marquess (of) _ . In Scotland the spelling 'Marquis' is preferred for pre-Union creations
    Envelope (formal), The Most Hon. the Marquess of _; *(social),* The Marquess of _. *Letter (formal),* My Lord; *(social),* Dear Lord _. *Spoken (formal),* My Lord; *(social),* Lord _
Wife's style, The Most Hon. the Marchioness (of) _
    Envelope (formal), The Most Hon. the Marchioness of _; *(social),* The Marchioness of _. *Letter (formal),* Madam; *(social),* Dear Lady _. *Spoken,* Lady _
Eldest son's style, Takes his father's second title as a courtesy title (*see* Courtesy Titles)
Younger sons' style, 'Lord' before forename and surname, as for Duke's younger sons
Daughters' style, 'Lady' before forename and surname, as for Duke's daughter

Created	Title, order of succession, name, etc	Heir
1916	*Aberdeen and Temair (7th)*, Alexander George Gordon, *b.* 1955, *s.* 2002, *m.*	Earl of Haddo, *b.* 1983
1876	*Abergavenny (6th) and 10th Earl, Abergavenny, 1784*, Christopher George Charles Nevill, *b.* 1955, *s.* 2000, *m.*	To Earldom only, David M. R. N., *b.* 1941
1821	*Ailesbury (8th)*, Michael Sidney Cedric Brudenell-Bruce, *b.* 1926, *s.* 1974	Earl of Cardigan, *b.* 1952
1831	*Ailsa (8th)*, Archibald Angus Charles Kennedy, *b.* 1956, *s.* 1994	Lord David T. K., *b.* 1958
1815	*Anglesey (7th)*, George Charles Henry Victor Paget, *b.* 1922, *s.* 1947, *m.*	Earl of Uxbridge, *b.* 1950
1789	*Bath (7th)*, Alexander George Thynn, *b.* 1932, *s.* 1992, *m.*	Viscount Weymouth, *b.* 1974
1826	*Bristol (8th)*, Frederick William Augustus Hervey, *b.* 1979, *s.* 1999	Timothy H. H., *b.* 1960
1796	*Bute (7th)*, John Colum Crichton-Stuart, *b.* 1958, *s.* 1993, *m.*	Earl of Dumfries, *b.* 1989
1812	° *Camden (6th)*, David George Edward Henry Pratt, *b.* 1930, *s.* 1983	Earl of Brecknock, *b.* 1965
1815	** *Cholmondeley (7th)*, David George Philip Cholmondeley, KCVO, *b.* 1960, *s.* 1990, *m. Lord Great Chamberlain*	Earl of Rocksavage, *b.* 2010
1816 I.	° *Conyngham (8th)*, Henry Vivian Pierpoint Conyngham, *b.* 1951, *s.* 2009, *m.*	Earl of Mount Charles, *b.* 1975
1791 I.	*Donegall (8th)*, Arthur Patrick Chichester, *b.* 1952, *s.* 2007, *m.*	Earl of Belfast, *b.* 1990

1789 I.	*Downshire (9th),* (Arthur Francis) Nicholas Wills Hill, *b.* 1959, *s.* 2003, *m.*	Earl of Hillsborough, *b.* 1996
1801 I.	*Ely (9th),* Charles John Tottenham, *b.* 1943, *s.* 2006, *m.*	Lord Timothy C. T., *b.* 1948
1801	*Exeter (8th),* (William) Michael Anthony Cecil, *b.* 1935, *s.* 1988, *m.*	Lord Burghley, *b.* 1970
1800 I.	*Headfort (7th),* Thomas Michael Ronald Christopher Taylour, *b.* 1959, *s.* 2005, *m.*	Earl of Bective, *b.* 1989
1793	*Hertford (9th),* Henry Jocelyn Seymour, *b.* 1958, *s.* 1997, *m.*	Earl of Yarmouth, *b.* 1993
1599 S.	*Huntly (13th),* Granville Charles Gomer Gordon, *b.* 1944, *s.* 1987, *m. Premier Marquess of Scotland*	Earl of Aboyne, *b.* 1973
1784	*Lansdowne (9th),* Charles Maurice Mercer Nairne Petty-Fitzmaurice, LVO *b.* 1941, *s.* 1999, *m.*	Earl of Kerry, *b.* 1970
1902	*Linlithgow (4th),* Adrian John Charles Hope, *b.* 1946, *s.* 1987, *m.*	Earl of Hopetoun, *b.* 1969
1816 I.	*Londonderry (9th),* Alexander Charles Robert Vane-Tempest-Stewart, *b.* 1937, *s.* 1955, *m.*	Viscount Castlereagh, *b.* 1972
1701 S.	*Lothian (13th) and Baron Kerr of Monteviot (life peerage 2010),* Michael Andrew Foster Jude Kerr (Michael Ancram), PC, *b.* 1945, *s.* 2004, *m.*	Lord Ralph W. F. J. K., *b.* 1957
1917	*Milford Haven (4th),* George Ivar Louis Mountbatten, *b.* 1961, *s.* 1970, *m.*	Earl of Medina, *b.* 1991
1838	*Normanby (5th),* Constantine Edmund Walter Phipps, *b.* 1954, *s.* 1994, *m.*	Earl of Mulgrave, *b.* 1994
1812	*Northampton (7th),* Spencer Douglas David Compton, *b.* 1946, *s.* 1978, *m.*	Earl Compton, *b.* 1973
1682 S.	*Queensberry (12th),* David Harrington Angus Douglas, *b.* 1929, *s.* 1954	Viscount Drumlanrig, *b.* 1967
1926	*Reading (4th),* Simon Charles Henry Rufus Isaacs, *b.* 1942, *s.* 1980, *m.*	Viscount Erleigh, *b.* 1986
1789	*Salisbury (7th) and Baron Gascoyne-Cecil (life peerage, 1999),* Robert Michael James Gascoyne-Cecil, PC, *b.* 1946, *s.* 2003, *m.*	Viscount Cranborne, *b.* 1970
1800 I.	*Sligo (11th),* Jeremy Ulick Browne, *b.* 1939, *s.* 1991, *m.*	Sebastian U. B., *b.* 1964
1787	° *Townshend (8th),* Charles George Townshend, *b.* 1945, *s.* 2010, *m.*	Viscount Raynham, *b.* 1977
1694 S.	*Tweeddale (14th),* Charles David Montagu Hay, *b.* 1947, *s.* 2005	(Lord) Alistair J. M. H., *b.* 1955
1789 I.	*Waterford (8th),* John Hubert de la Poer Beresford, *b.* 1933, *s.* 1934, *m.*	Earl of Tyrone, *b.* 1958
1551	*Winchester (18th),* Nigel George Paulet, *b.* 1941, *s.* 1968, *m. Premier Marquess of England*	Earl of Wiltshire, *b.* 1969
1892	*Zetland (4th),* Lawrence Mark Dundas, *b.* 1937, *s.* 1989, *m.*	Earl of Ronaldshay, *b.* 1965

EARLS

Coronet, Eight silver balls on stalks alternating with eight gold strawberry leaves

Style, The Rt. Hon. the Earl (of) _
    Envelope (formal), The Rt. Hon. the Earl (of) _; *(social),* The Earl (of) _. *Letter (formal),* My Lord; *(social),* Dear Lord _. *Spoken (formal),* My Lord; *(social),* Lord _.
Wife's style, The Rt. Hon. the Countess (of) _
    Envelope (formal), The Rt. Hon. the Countess (of) _; *(social),* The Countess (of) _. *Letter (formal),* Madam; *(social),* Lady _. *Spoken (formal),* Madam; *(social),* Lady _.
Eldest son's style, Takes his father's second title as a courtesy title (*see* Courtesy Titles)
Younger sons' style, 'The Hon.' before forename and surname, as for Baron's children
Daughters' style, 'Lady' before forename and surname, as for Duke's daughter

Created	Title, order of succession, name, etc	Heir
1639 S.	*Airlie (13th),* David George Coke Patrick Ogilvy, KT, GCVO, PC, Royal Victorian Chain, *b.* 1926, *s.* 1968, *m.*	Lord Ogilvy, *b.* 1958
1696	*Albemarle (10th),* Rufus Arnold Alexis Keppel, *b.* 1965, *s.* 1979, *m.*	Viscount Bury, *b.* 2003
1952	° *Alexander of Tunis (2nd),* Shane William Desmond Alexander, *b.* 1935, *s.* 1969, *m.*	Hon. Brian J. A., *b.* 1939
1662 S.	*Annandale and Hartfell (11th),* Patrick Andrew Wentworth Hope Johnstone, *b.* 1941, *s.* 1983, *m.* claim established 1985	Lord Johnstone, *b.* 1971

1789 I.	° *Annesley (11th)*, Philip Harrison Annesley, *b.* 1927, *s.* 2001, *m.*	Hon. Michael R. A., *b.* 1933
1785 I.	*Antrim (9th)*, Alexander Randal Mark McDonnell, *b.* 1935, *s.* 1977, *m.*	Viscount Dunluce, *b.* 1967
1762 I.	** *Arran (9th)*, Arthur Desmond Colquhoun Gore, *b.* 1938, *s.* 1983, *m.*	Paul A. G., CMG, CVO, *b.* 1921
1955	° ** *Attlee (3rd)*, John Richard Attlee, *b.* 1956, *s.* 1991, *m.*	None
1714	*Aylesford (12th)*, Charles Heneage Finch-Knightley, *b.* 1947, *s.* 2008, *m.*	Lord Guernsey, *b.* 1985
1937	** *Baldwin of Bewdley (4th)*, Edward Alfred Alexander Baldwin, *b.* 1938, *s.* 1976, *w.*	Viscount Corvedale, *b.* 1973
1922	*Balfour (5th)*, Roderick Francis Arthur Balfour, *b.* 1948, *s.* 2003, *m.*	Charles G. Y. B., *b.* 1951
1772	° *Bathurst (8th)*, Henry Allen John Bathurst, *b.* 1927, *s.* 1943, *m.*	Lord Apsley, *b.* 1961
1919	° *Beatty (3rd)*, David Beatty, *b.* 1946, *s.* 1972, *m.*	Viscount Borodale, *b.* 1973
1797 I.	° *Belmore (8th)*, John Armar Lowry-Corry, *b.* 1951, *s.* 1960, *m.*	Viscount Corry, *b.* 1985
1739 I.	*Bessborough (12th)*, Myles Fitzhugh Longfield Ponsonby, *b.* 1941, *s.* 2002, *m.*	Viscount Duncannon, *b.* 1974
1815	*Bradford (7th)*, Richard Thomas Orlando Bridgeman, *b.* 1947, *s.* 1981, *m.*	Viscount Newport, *b.* 1980
1469 S.	*Buchan (17th)*, Malcolm Harry Erskine, *b.* 1930, *s.* 1984, *m.*	Lord Cardross, *b.* 1960
1746	*Buckinghamshire (10th)*, (George) Miles Hobart-Hampden, *b.* 1944, *s.* 1983, *m.*	Sir John Hobart, Bt., *b.* 1945
1800	° *Cadogan (8th)*, Charles Gerald John Cadogan, *b.* 1937, *s.* 1997, *m.*	Viscount Chelsea, *b.* 1966
1878	° *Cairns (6th)*, Simon Dallas Cairns, CVO, CBE, *b.* 1939, *s.* 1989, *m.*	Viscount Garmoyle, *b.* 1965
1455 S.	** *Caithness (20th)*, Malcolm Ian Sinclair, PC, *b.* 1948, *s.* 1965, *w.*	Lord Berriedale, *b.* 1981
1800 I.	*Caledon (7th)*, Nicholas James Alexander, *b.* 1955, *s.* 1980, *m.*	Viscount Alexander, *b.* 1990
1661	*Carlisle (13th)*, George William Beaumont Howard, *b.* 1949, *s.* 1994	Hon. Philip C. W. H., *b.* 1963
1793	*Carnarvon (8th)*, George Reginald Oliver Molyneux Herbert, *b.* 1956, *s.* 2001, *m.*	Lord Porchester, *b.* 1992
1748 I.	*Carrick (11th)*, Arion Thomas Piers Hamilton Butler, *b.* 1975, *s.* 2008	Hon. P. E. T. L. B., *b.* 1979
1800 I.	° *Castle Stewart (8th)*, Arthur Patrick Avondale Stuart, *b.* 1928, *s.* 1961, *m.*	Viscount Stuart, *b.* 1953
1814	°** *Cathcart (7th)*, Charles Alan Andrew Cathcart, *b.* 1952, *s.* 1999, *m.*	Lord Greenock, *b.* 1986
1647 I.	*Cavan*, The 12th Earl died in 1988.	†Roger C. Lambart, *b.* 1944
1827	° *Cawdor (7th)*, Colin Robert Vaughan Campbell, *b.* 1962, *s.* 1993, *m.*	Viscount Emlyn, *b.* 1998
1801	*Chichester (9th)*, John Nicholas Pelham, *b.* 1944, *s.* 1944, *m.*	Richard A. H. P., *b.* 1952
1803 I.	** *Clancarty (9th)*, Nicholas Power Richard Le Poer Trench, *b.* 1952, *s.* 1995, *m.*	None
1776 I.	*Clanwilliam (8th)*, Patrick James Meade, *b.* 1960, *s.* 2009, *m.*	Lord Gillford, *b.* 1998
1776	*Clarendon (8th)*, George Edward Laurence Villiers, *b.* 1976, *s.* 2009, *m.*	Lord Hyde, *b.* 2008
1620 I.	*Cork and Orrery (15th)*, John Richard Boyle, *b.* 1945, *s.* 2003, *m.*	Viscount Dungarvan, *b.* 1978
1850	*Cottenham (9th)*, Mark John Henry Pepys, *b.* 1983, *s.* 2000	Hon. Sam R. P., *b.* 1986
1762 I.	** *Courtown (9th)*, James Patrick Montagu Burgoyne Winthrop Stopford, *b.* 1954, *s.* 1975, *m.*	Viscount Stopford, *b.* 1988
1697	*Coventry (13th)*, George William Coventry, *b.* 1939, *s.* 2004, *m.*	David D. S. C., *b.* 1973
1857	° *Cowley (7th)*, Garret Graham Wellesley, *b.* 1934, *s.* 1975, *w.*	Viscount Dangan, *b.* 1965
1892	*Cranbrook (5th)*, Gathorne Gathorne-Hardy, *b.* 1933, *s.* 1978, *m.*	Lord Medway, *b.* 1968
1801 M.	*Craven (9th)*, Benjamin Robert Joseph Craven, *b.* 1989, *s.* 1990	Rupert J. E. C., *b.* 1926
1398 S.	*Crawford (29th) and Balcarres (12th) (S. 1651) and Baron Balniel (life peerage, 1974)*, Robert Alexander Lindsay, KT, GCVO, PC, *b.* 1927, *s.* 1975, *m. Premier Earl on Union Roll*	Lord Balniel, *b.* 1958
1861	*Cromartie (5th)*, John Ruaridh Blunt Grant Mackenzie, *b.* 1948, *s.* 1989, *m.*	Viscount Tarbat, *b.* 1987
1901	*Cromer (4th)*, Evelyn Rowland Esmond Baring, *b.* 1946, *s.* 1991, *m.*	Viscount Errington, *b.* 1994
1633 S.	*Dalhousie (17th)*, James Hubert Ramsay, *b.* 1948, *s.* 1999, *m., Lord Steward*	Lord Ramsay, *b.* 1981
1725 I.	*Darnley (11th)*, Adam Ivo Stuart Bligh, *b.* 1941, *s.* 1980, *m.*	Lord Clifton, *b.* 1968
1711	*Dartmouth (10th)*, William Legge, *b.* 1949, *s.* 1997, *m.*	Hon. Rupert L., *b.* 1951
1761	° *De La Warr (11th)*, William Herbrand Sackville, *b.* 1948, *s.* 1988, *m.*	Lord Buckhurst, *b.* 1979
1622	*Denbigh (12th) and Desmond (11th) (I. 1622)*, Alexander Stephen Rudolph Feilding, *b.* 1970, *s.* 1995, *m.*	Viscount Feilding, *b.* 2005
1485	*Derby (19th)*, Edward Richard William Stanley, *b.* 1962, *s.* 1994, *m.*	Lord Stanley, *b.* 1998
1553	*Devon (18th)*, Hugh Rupert Courtenay, *b.* 1942, *s.* 1998, *m.*	Lord Courtenay, *b.* 1975
1800 I.	*Donoughmore (8th)*, Richard Michael John Hely-Hutchinson, *b.* 1927, *s.* 1981, *w.*	Viscount Suirdale, *b.* 1952
1661 I.	*Drogheda (12th)*, Henry Dermot Ponsonby Moore, *b.* 1937, *s.* 1989, *m.*	Viscount Moore, *b.* 1983
1837	*Ducie (7th)*, David Leslie Moreton, *b.* 1951, *s.* 1991, *m.*	Lord Moreton, *b.* 1981
1860	*Dudley (4th)*, William Humble David Ward, *b.* 1920, *s.* 1969, *m.*	Viscount Ednam, *b.* 1947
1660 S.	** *Dundee (12th)*, Alexander Henry Scrymgeour, *b.* 1949, *s.* 1983, *m.*	Lord Scrymgeour, *b.* 1982

1669 S.	*Dundonald (15th)*, Iain Alexander Douglas Blair Cochrane, *b.* 1961, *s.* 1986, *m.*	Lord Cochrane, *b.* 1991
1686 S.	*Dunmore (12th)*, Malcolm Kenneth Murray, *b.* 1946, *s.* 1995, *m.*	Hon. Geoffrey C. M., *b.*1949
1833	*Durham (7th)*, Edward Richard Lambton, *b.* 1961, *s.* 2006, *m.*	Viscount Lambton, *b.* 1985
1837	*Effingham (7th)*, David Mowbray Algernon Howard, *b.* 1939, *s.* 1996, *m.*	Lord Howard of Effingham, *b.* 1971
1507 S.	*Eglinton (18th) and Winton (9th) (S. 1600)*, Archibald George Montgomerie, *b.* 1939, *s.* 1966, *m.*	Lord Montgomerie, *b.* 1966
1733 I.	*Egmont (12th)*, Thomas Frederick Gerald Perceval, *b.* 1934, *s.* 2001, *m.*	Hon. Donald W. P., *b.* 1954
1821	*Eldon (5th)*, John Joseph Nicholas Scott, *b.* 1937, *s.* 1976, *m.*	Viscount Encombe, *b.* 1962
1633 S.	*Elgin (11th) and Kincardine (15th) (S. 1647)*, Andrew Douglas Alexander Thomas Bruce, KT, *b.* 1924, *s.* 1968, *m.*	Lord Bruce, *b.* 1961
1789 I.	*Enniskillen (7th)*, Andrew John Galbraith Cole, *b.* 1942, *s.* 1989, *m.*	Arthur G. C., *b.* 1920
1789 I.	*Erne (6th)*, Henry George Victor John Crichton, *b.* 1937, *s.* 1940, *m.*	Viscount Crichton, *b.* 1971
1452 S.	** *Erroll (24th)*, Merlin Sereld Victor Gilbert Hay, *b.* 1948, *s.* 1978, *m.* *Hereditary Lord High Constable and Knight Marischal of Scotland*	Lord Hay, *b.* 1984
1661	*Essex (11th)*, Frederick Paul de Vere Capell, *b.* 1944, *s.* 2005	William J. C., *b.* 1952
1711	° ** *Ferrers (13th)*, Robert Washington Shirley, PC, *b.* 1929, *s.* 1954, *m.*	Viscount Tamworth, *b.* 1952
1789	° *Fortescue (8th)*, Charles Hugh Richard Fortescue, *b.* 1951, *s.* 1993, *m.*	John A. F. F., *b.* 1955
1841	*Gainsborough (6th)*, Anthony Baptist Noel, *b.* 1950, *s.* 2009, *m.*	Viscount Campden, *b.* 1977
1623 S.	*Galloway (13th)*, Randolph Keith Reginald Stewart, *b.* 1928, *s.* 1978, *w.*	Andrew C. S., *b.* 1949
1703 S.	** *Glasgow (10th)*, Patrick Robin Archibald Boyle, *b.* 1939, *s.* 1984, *m.*	Viscount of Kelburn, *b.* 1978
1806 I.	*Gosford (7th)*, Charles David Nicholas Alexander John Sparrow Acheson, *b.* 1942, *s.* 1966, *m.*	Nicholas H. C. A., *b.* 1947
1945	*Gowrie (2nd)*, Alexander Patrick Greysteil Hore-Ruthven, PC, *b.* 1939, *s.* 1955, *m.*	Viscount Ruthven of Canberra, *b.* 1964
1684 I.	*Granard (10th)*, Peter Arthur Edward Hastings Forbes, *b.* 1957, *s.* 1992, *m.*	Viscount Forbes, *b.* 1981
1833	° *Granville (6th)*, Granville George Fergus Leveson-Gower, *b.* 1959, *s.* 1996, *m.*	Lord Leveson, *b.* 1999
1806	° *Grey (6th)*, Richard Fleming George Charles Grey, *b.* 1939, *s.* 1963, *m.*	Philip K. G., *b.* 1940
1752	*Guilford (10th)*, Piers Edward Brownlow North, *b.* 1971, *s.* 1999, *m.*	Lord North, *b.* 2002
1619 S.	*Haddington (13th)*, John George Baillie-Hamilton, *b.* 1941, *s.* 1986, *m.*	Lord Binning, *b.* 1985
1919	° *Haig (3rd)*, Alexander Douglas Derrick Haig, *b.* 1961, *s.* 2009, *m.*	None
1944	*Halifax (3rd)*, Charles Edward Peter Neil Wood, *b.* 1944, *s.* 1980, *m.*	Lord Irwin, *b.* 1977
1754	*Hardwicke (10th)*, Joseph Philip Sebastian Yorke, *b.* 1971, *s.* 1974, *m.*	Viscount Royston, *b.* 2009
1812	*Harewood (8th)*, David Henry George Lascelles, *b.* 1950, *s.* 2011, *m.*	Viscount Lascelles, *b.* 1978
1742	*Harrington (12th)*, Charles Henry Leicester Stanhope, *b.* 1945, *s.* 2009, *m.*	Viscount Petersham, *b.* 1967
1809	*Harrowby (8th)*, Dudley Adrian Conroy Ryder, *b.* 1951, *s.* 2007, *m.*	Viscount Sandon, *b.* 1981
1605 S.	** *Home (15th)*, David Alexander Cospatrick Douglas-Home, CVO, CBE, *b.* 1943, *s.* 1995, *m.*	Lord Dunglass, *b.* 1987
1821	° ** *Howe (7th)*, Frederick Richard Penn Curzon, *b.* 1951, *s.* 1984, *m.*	Viscount Curzon, *b.* 1994
1529	*Huntingdon (16th)*, William Edward Robin Hood Hastings Bass, LVO, *b.* 1948, *s.* 1990, *m.*	Hon. Simon A. R. H. H. B., *b.* 1950
1885	*Iddesleigh (5th)*, John Stafford Northcote, *b.* 1957, *s.* 2004, *m.*	Viscount St Cyres, *b.* 1985
1756	*Ilchester (10th)*, Robin Maurice Fox-Strangways, *b.* 1942, *s.* 2006, *m.*	Lord Stavordale, *b.* 1972
1929	*Inchcape (4th)*, (Kenneth) Peter (Lyle) Mackay, *b.* 1943, *s.* 1994, *m.*	Viscount Glenapp, *b.* 1979
1919	*Iveagh (4th)*, Arthur Edward Rory Guinness, *b.* 1969, *s.* 1992	Viscount Elveden, *b.* 2003
1925	° *Jellicoe (3rd)*, Patrick John Bernard Jellicoe, *b.* 1950, *s.* 2007	Viscount Brocas, *b.* 1970
1697	*Jersey (10th)*, George Francis William Child Villiers, *b.* 1976, *s.* 1998 *m.*	Hon. Jamie C. C. V., *b.* 1994
1822 I.	*Kilmorey (6th)*, Sir Richard Francis Needham, PC, *b.* 1942, *s.* 1977, *m.*, (does not use title)	Viscount Newry and Mourne, *b.* 1966
1866	*Kimberley (5th)*, John Armine Wodehouse, *b.* 1951, *s.* 2002, *m.*	Lord Wodehouse, *b.*1978
1768 I.	*Kingston (12th)*, Robert Charles Henry King-Tenison, *b.* 1969, *s.* 2002, *m.*	Viscount Kingsborough, *b.* 2000
1633 S.	*Kinnoull (15th)*, Arthur William George Patrick Hay, *b.* 1935, *s.* 1938, *m.*	Viscount Dupplin, *b.* 1962
1677 S.	*Kintore (14th)*, James William Falconer Keith, *b.* 1976, *s.* 2004	Lady Iona D. M. G. K., *b.* 1978
1914	° *Kitchener of Khartoum (3rd)*, Henry Herbert Kitchener, TD, *b.* 1919, *s.* 1937	None
1624 S.	*Lauderdale (18th)*, Ian Maitland, *b.* 1937, *s.* 2008, *m.*	Viscount Maitland, *b.* 1965
1837	*Leicester (7th)*, Edward Douglas Coke, *b.* 1936, *s.* 1994, *m.*	Viscount Coke, *b.* 1965

1641 S.	*Leven (14th) and Melville (13th) (S. 1690)*, Alexander Robert Leslie Melville, *b.* 1924, *s.* 1947, *m.*	Lord Balgonie, *b.* 1984
1831	*Lichfield (6th)*, Thomas William Robert Hugh Anson, *b.* 1978, *s.* 2005, *m.*	Viscount Anson, *b.* 2011
1803 I.	*Limerick (7th)*, Edmund Christopher Pery, *b.* 1963, *s.* 2003, *m.*	Viscount Glentworth, *b.* 1991
1572	*Lincoln (19th)*, Robert Edward Fiennes-Clinton, *b.* 1972, *s.* 2001	Hon. William R. F.-C., *b.* 1980
1633 S.	** *Lindsay (16th)*, James Randolph Lindesay-Bethune, *b.* 1955, *s.* 1989, *m.*	Viscount Garnock, *b.* 1990
1626	*Lindsey (14th) and Abingdon (9th) (1682)*, Richard Henry Rupert Bertie, *b.* 1931, *s.* 1963, *m.*	Lord Norreys, *b.* 1958
1776 I.	*Lisburne (8th)*, John David Malet Vaughan, *b.* 1918, *s.* 1965, *m.*	Viscount Vaughan, *b.* 1945
1822 I.	** *Listowel (6th)*, Francis Michael Hare, *b.* 1964, *s.* 1997, *m.*	Hon. Timothy P. H., *b.* 1966
1905	** *Liverpool (5th)*, Edward Peter Bertram Savile Foljambe, *b.* 1944, *s.* 1969, *m.*	Viscount Hawkesbury, *b.* 1972
1945	° *Lloyd George of Dwyfor (4th)*, David Richard Owen Lloyd George, *b.* 1951, *s.* 2010, *m.*	Viscount Gwynedd, *b.* 1986
1785 I.	*Longford (8th)*, Thomas Frank Dermot Pakenham, *b.* 1933, *s.* 2001, *m.*, (does not use title)	Hon. Edward M. P., *b.* 1970
1807	*Lonsdale (8th)*, Hugh Clayton Lowther, *b.* 1949, *s.* 2006, *m.*	Hon. William J. L., *b.* 1957
1633 S.	*Loudoun (14th)*, Michael Edward Abney-Hastings, *b.* 1942, *s.* 2002, *m.*	Lord Mauchline, *b.* 1974
1838	*Lovelace (5th)*, Peter Axel William Locke King, *b.* 1951, *s.* 1964, *m.*	None
1795 I.	*Lucan (7th)*, Richard John Bingham, *b.* 1934, *s.* 1964, *m.* (missing since 8 November 1974)	Lord Bingham, *b.* 1967
1880	** *Lytton (5th)*, John Peter Michael Scawen Lytton, *b.* 1950, *s.* 1985, *m.*	Viscount Knebworth, *b.* 1989
1721	*Macclesfield (9th)*, Richard Timothy George Mansfield Parker, *b.* 1943, *s.* 1992, *m.*	Hon. J. David G. P., *b.* 1945
1800	*Malmesbury (7th)*, James Carleton Harris, *b.* 1946, *s.* 2000, *m.*	Viscount FitzHarris, *b.* 1970
1776	*Mansfield and Mansfield (8th) (1792)*, William David Mungo James Murray, *b.* 1930, *s.* 1971, *m.*	Viscount Stormont, *b.* 1956
1565 S.	*Mar (14th) and Kellie (16th) (S. 1616) and Baron Erskine of Alloa Tower (life peerage, 2000)*, James Thorne Erskine, *b.* 1949, *s.* 1994, *m.*	Hon. Alexander D. E., *b.* 1952
1785 I.	*Mayo (11th)*, Charles Diarmuidh John Bourke, *b.* 1953, *s.* 2006, *m.*	Lord Naas, *b.* 1985
1627 I.	*Meath (15th)*, John Anthony Brabazon, *b.* 1941, *s.* 1998, *m.*	Lord Ardee, *b.* 1977
1766 I.	*Mexborough (8th)*, John Christopher George Savile, *b.* 1931, *s.* 1980, *m.*	Viscount Pollington, *b.* 1959
1813	*Minto (7th)*, Gilbert Timothy George Lariston Elliot-Murray-Kynynmound, *b.* 1953, *s.* 2005, *m.*	Viscount Melgund, *b.* 1984
1562 S.	*Moray (20th)*, Douglas John Moray Stuart, *b.* 1928, *s.* 1974, *m.*	Lord Doune, *b.* 1966
1815	*Morley (6th)*, John St Aubyn Parker, KCVO, *b.* 1923, *s.* 1962, *m.*	Viscount Boringdon, *b.* 1956
1458 S.	*Morton (22nd)*, John Charles Sholto Douglas, *b.* 1927, *s.* 1976, *m.*	Lord Aberdour, *b.* 1952
1789	*Mount Edgcumbe (8th)*, Robert Charles Edgcumbe, *b.* 1939, *s.* 1982	Piers V. E., *b.* 1946
1805	° *Nelson (10th)*, Simon John Horatio Nelson, *b.* 1971, *s.* 2009, *m.*	Viscount Merton, *b.* 1994
1660 S.	*Newburgh (12th)*, Don Filippo Giambattista Camillo Francesco Aldo Maria Rospigliosi, *b.* 1942, *s.* 1986, *m.*	Princess Donna Benedetta F. M. R., *b.* 1974
1827 I.	*Norbury (7th)*, Richard James Graham-Toler, *b.* 1967, *s.* 2000	None
1806 I.	*Normanton (6th)*, Shaun James Christian Welbore Ellis Agar, *b.* 1945, *s.* 1967, *w.*	Viscount Somerton, *b.* 1982
1647 S.	*Northesk (15th)*, Patrick Charles Carnegy, *b.* 1940, *s.* 2010	Colin D. C., *b.* 1942
1801	*Onslow (8th)*, Rupert Charles William Bullard Onslow, *b.* 1967, *s.* 2011, *m.*	Anthony E. E. O., *b.* 1955
1696 S.	*Orkney (9th)*, (Oliver) Peter St John, *b.* 1938, *s.* 1998, *m.*	Viscount Kirkwall, *b.* 1969
1328 I.	*Ormonde and Ossory (I. 1527)*, The 25th/18th Earl (7th Marquess) died in 1988	†Viscount Mountgarret *b.* 1961 (*see* that title)
1925	*Oxford and Asquith (3rd)*, Raymond Benedict Bartholomew Michael Asquith, OBE, *b.* 1952, *s.* 2011, *m.*	Viscount Asquith, *b.* 1979
1929	° ** *Peel (3rd)*, William James Robert Peel, GCVO, PC, *b.* 1947, *s.* 1969, *m.* Lord Chamberlain	Viscount Clanfield, *b.* 1976
1551	*Pembroke (18th) and Montgomery (15th) (1605)*, William Alexander Sidney Herbert, *b.* 1978, *s.* 2003, *m.*	Earl of Carnarvon *b.* 1956 (*see* that title)
1605 S.	*Perth (18th)*, John Eric Drummond, *b.* 1935, *s.* 2002, *m.*	Viscount Strathallan, *b.* 1965
1905	*Plymouth (3rd)*, Other Robert Ivor Windsor-Clive, *b.* 1923, *s.* 1943, *m.*	Viscount Windsor, *b.* 1951
1785	*Portarlington (7th)*, George Lionel Yuill Seymour Dawson-Damer, *b.* 1938, *s.* 1959, *m.*	Viscount Carlow, *b.* 1965
1689	*Portland (12th)*, Count Timothy Charles Robert Noel Bentinck, *b.* 1953, *s.* 1997, *m.*	Viscount Woodstock, *b.* 1984
1743	*Portsmouth (10th)*, Quentin Gerard Carew Wallop, *b.* 1954, *s.* 1984, *m.*	Viscount Lymington, *b.* 1981
1804	*Powis (8th)*, John George Herbert, *b.* 1952, *s.* 1993, *m.*	Viscount Clive, *b.* 1979
1765	*Radnor (9th)*, William Pleydell-Bouverie, *b.* 1955, *s.* 2008, *m.*	Viscount Folkestone, *b.* 1999

1831 I.	*Ranfurly (7th)*, Gerald Françoys Needham Knox, *b.* 1929, *s.* 1988, *m.*	Viscount Northland, *b.* 1957
1771 I.	*Roden (10th)*, Robert John Jocelyn, *b.* 1938, *s.* 1993, *m.*	Viscount Jocelyn, *b.* 1989
1801	*Romney (8th)*, Julian Charles Marsham, *b.* 1948, *s.* 2004, *m.*	Viscount Marsham, *b.* 1977
1703 S.	*Rosebery (7th)*, Neil Archibald Primrose, *b.* 1929, *s.* 1974, *m.*	Lord Dalmeny, *b.* 1967
1806 I.	*Rosse (7th)*, William Brendan Parsons, *b.* 1936, *s.* 1979, *m.*	Lord Oxmantown, *b.* 1969.
1801	** *Rosslyn (7th)*, Peter St Clair-Erskine, *b.* 1958, *s.* 1977, *m.*	Lord Loughborough, *b.* 1986
1457 S.	*Rothes (22nd)*, James Malcolm David Leslie, *b.* 1958, *s.* 2005, *m.*	Hon. Alexander J. L., *b.* 1962
1861	° *Russell (6th)*, Nicholas Lyulph Russell, *b.* 1968, *s.* 2004	Hon. John F. R., *b.* 1971
1915	° *St Aldwyn (3rd)*, Michael Henry Hicks Beach, *b.* 1950, *s.* 1992, *m.*	Hon. David S. H. B., *b.* 1955
1815	*St Germans (10th)*, Peregrine Nicholas Eliot, *b.* 1941, *s.* 1988	Lord Eliot, *b.* 2004
1660	** *Sandwich (11th)*, John Edward Hollister Montagu, *b.* 1943, *s.* 1995, *m.*	Viscount Hinchingbrooke, *b.* 1969
1690	*Scarbrough (13th)*, Richard Osbert Lumley, *b.* 1973, *s.* 2004	Hon. Thomas H. L., *b.* 1980
1701 S.	*Seafield (13th)*, Ian Derek Francis Ogilvie-Grant, *b.* 1939, *s.* 1969, *m.*	Viscount Reidhaven, *b.* 1963
1882	** *Selborne (4th)*, John Roundell Palmer, GBE, *b.* 1940, *s.* 1971, *m.*	Viscount Wolmer, *b.* 1971
1646 S.	*Selkirk*, Disclaimed for life 1994. *(see* Lord Selkirk of Douglas, Life Peers)	Master of Selkirk, *b.* 1978
1672	*Shaftesbury (12th)*, Nicholas Edmund Anthony Ashley-Cooper, *b.* 1979, *s.* 2005, *m.*	Lord Ashley, *b.* 2011
1756 I.	*Shannon (9th)*, Richard Bentinck Boyle, *b.* 1924, *s.* 1963	Viscount Boyle, *b.* 1960
1442	** *Shrewsbury and Waterford (22nd) (I. 1446)*, Charles Henry John Benedict Crofton Chetwynd Chetwynd-Talbot, *b.* 1952, *s.* 1980, *m. Premier Earl of England and Ireland*	Viscount Ingestre, *b.* 1978
1961	*Snowdon (1st) and Baron Armstrong-Jones (life peerage, 1999)*, Antony Charles Robert Armstrong-Jones, GCVO, *b.* 1930, *m.*	Viscount Linley, *b.* 1961
1765	° *Spencer (9th)*, Charles Edward Maurice Spencer, *b.* 1964, *s.* 1992, *m.*	Viscount Althorp, *b.* 1994
1703 S.	** *Stair (14th)*, John David James Dalrymple, *b.* 1961, *s.* 1996, *m.*	Viscount Dalrymple, *b.* 2008
1984	*Stockton (2nd)*, Alexander Daniel Alan Macmillan, MEP, *b.* 1943, *s.* 1986, *m.*	Viscount Macmillan of Ovenden, *b.* 1974
1821	*Stradbroke (6th)*, Robert Keith Rous, *b.* 1937, *s.* 1983, *m.*	Viscount Dunwich, *b.* 1961
1847	*Strafford (8th)*, Thomas Edmund Byng, *b.* 1936, *s.* 1984, *m.*	Viscount Enfield, *b.* 1964
1606 S.	*Strathmore and Kinghorne (18th) (S. 1677)*, Michael Fergus Bowes Lyon, *b.* 1957, *s.* 1987, *m.*	Lord Glamis, *b.* 1986
1603	*Suffolk (21st) and Berkshire (14th) (1626)*, Michael John James George Robert Howard, *b.* 1935, *s.* 1941, *m.*	Viscount Andover, *b.* 1974
1955	*Swinton (3rd)*, Nicholas John Cunliffe-Lister, *b.* 1939, *s.* 2006, *m.*	Lord Masham *b.* 1970
1714	*Tankerville (10th)*, Peter Grey Bennet, *b.* 1956, *s.* 1980	Adrian G. B., *b.* 1958
1822	° *Temple of Stowe (8th)*, (Walter) Grenville Algernon Temple-Gore-Langton, *b.* 1924, *s.* 1988, *m.*	Lord Langton, *b.* 1955
1815	*Verulam (7th)*, John Duncan Grimston, *b.* 1951, *s.* 1973, *m.*	Viscount Grimston, *b.* 1978
1729	° *Waldegrave (13th)*, James Sherbrooke Waldegrave, *b.* 1940, *s.* 1995, *m.*	Viscount Chewton, *b.* 1986
1759	*Warwick (9th) and Brooke (9th) (1746)*, Guy David Greville, *b.* 1957, *s.* 1996, *m.*	Lord Brooke, *b.* 1982
1633 S.	*Wemyss (13th) and March (9th) (S. 1697)*, James Donald Charteris, *b.* 1948, *s.* 2008, *m.*	Lord Elcho, *b.* 1984
1621 I.	*Westmeath (13th)*, William Anthony Nugent, *b.* 1928, *s.* 1971, *m.*	Hon. Sean C. W. N., *b.* 1965
1624	*Westmorland (16th)*, Anthony David Francis Henry Fane, *b.* 1951, *s.* 1993, *m.*	Hon. Harry St C. F., *b.* 1953
1876	*Wharncliffe (5th)*, Richard Alan Montagu Stuart Wortley, *b.* 1953, *s.* 1987, *m.*	Viscount Carlton, *b.* 1980
1801	*Wilton (8th)*, Francis Egerton Grosvenor, *b.* 1934, *s.* 1999, *m.*	Viscount Grey de Wilton, *b.*1959
1628	*Winchilsea (17th) and Nottingham (12th) (1681)*, Daniel James Hatfield Finch Hatton, *b.* 1967, *s.* 1999, *m.*	Viscount Maidstone, *b.* 1998
1766	° *Winterton (8th)*, (Donald) David Turnour, *b.* 1943, *s.* 1991, *m.*	Robert C. T., *b.* 1950
1956	*Woolton (3rd)*, Simon Frederick Marquis, *b.* 1958, *s.* 1969, *m.*	None
1837	*Yarborough (8th)*, Charles John Pelham, *b.* 1963, *s.* 1991, *m.*	Lord Worsley, *b.* 1990

COUNTESSES IN THEIR OWN RIGHT

Style, The Rt. Hon. the Countess (of) _
   Envelope (formal), The Rt. Hon. the Countess (of) _; *(social),* The Countess (of) _. *Letter (formal),* Madam; *(social),*
   Lady _. *Spoken (formal),* Madam; *(social),* Lady _.
Husband, Untitled
Children's style, As for children of an Earl

Created	Title, order of succession, name, etc	Heir
1643 S.	*Dysart (12th in line),* Katherine Grant of Rothiemurchus, *b.* 1918, *s.* 2003 *w.*	Lord Huntingtower, *b.* 1946
c.1115 S.	** *Mar (31st in line),* Margaret of Mar, *b.* 1940, *s.* 1975, *m.* Premier Earldom of Scotland	Mistress of Mar, *b.* 1963
1947	° *Mountbatten of Burma (2nd in line),* Patricia Edwina Victoria Knatchbull, CBE, *b.* 1924, *s.* 1979, *w.*	Lord Romsey, *(also* Lord Brabourne (8th) *see* that title)
c.1235 S.	*Sutherland (24th in line),* Elizabeth Millicent Sutherland, *b.* 1921, *s.* 1963, *w.*	Lord Strathnaver, *b.* 1947

VISCOUNTS

Coronet, Sixteen silver balls

Style, The Rt. Hon. the Viscount _
   Envelope (formal), The Rt. Hon. the Viscount _; *(social),* The Viscount _. *Letter (formal),* My Lord; *(social),* Dear Lord
   _. *Spoken,* Lord _.
Wife's style, The Rt. Hon. the Viscountess _
   Envelope (formal), The Rt. Hon. the Viscountess _; *(social),* The Viscountess _. *Letter (formal),* Madam; *(social),* Dear
   Lady _. *Spoken,* Lady _.
Children's style, 'The Hon.' before forename and surname, as for Baron's children
In Scotland, the heir apparent to a Viscount may be styled 'The Master of _ (title of peer)'

Created	Title, order of succession, name, etc	Heir
1945	*Addison (4th),* William Matthew Wand Addison, *b.* 1945, *s.* 1992, *m.*	Hon. Paul W. A., *b.* 1973
1946	*Alanbrooke (3rd),* Alan Victor Harold Brooke, *b.* 1932, *s.* 1972	None
1919	** *Allenby (3rd),* Lt.-Col. Michael Jaffray Hynman Allenby, *b.* 1931, *s.* 1984, *m.*	Hon. Henry J. H. A., *b.* 1968
1911	*Allendale (4th),* Wentworth Peter Ismay Beaumont, *b.* 1948, *s.* 2002, *m.*	Hon. Wentworth A. I. B., *b.* 1979
1642 S.	*of Arbuthnott (16th),* John Campbell Arbuthnott, KT, CBE, DSC, *b.* 1924, *s.* 1966, *m.*	Master of Arbuthnott, *b.* 1950
1751 I.	*Ashbrook (11th),* Michael Llowarch Warburton Flower, *b.* 1935, *s.* 1995, *m.*	Hon. Rowland F. W. F., *b.* 1975
1917	** *Astor (4th),* William Waldorf Astor, *b.* 1951, *s.* 1966, *m.*	Hon. William W. A., *b.* 1979
1781 I.	*Bangor (8th),* William Maxwell David Ward, *b.* 1948, *s.* 1993, *m.*	Hon. E. Nicholas W., *b.* 1953
1925	*Bearsted (5th),* Nicholas Alan Samuel, *b.* 1950, *s.* 1996, *m.*	Hon. Harry R. S., *b.* 1988
1963	*Blakenham (2nd),* Michael John Hare, *b.* 1938, *s.* 1982, *m.*	Hon. Caspar J. H., *b.* 1972
1935	*Bledisloe (4th),* Rupert Edward Ludlow Bathurst, *b.* 1964, *s.* 2009, *m.*	Hon. Benjamin B., *b.* 2004
1712	*Bolingbroke (8th) and St John (9th) (1716),* Henry Fitzroy St John, *b.* 1957, *s.* 2010	Oliver J. B. St J., *b.* 1972
1960	*Boyd of Merton (2nd),* Simon Donald Rupert Neville Lennox-Boyd, *b.* 1939, *s.* 1983, *m.*	Hon. Benjamin A. L.-B., *b.* 1964
1717 I.	*Boyne (11th),* Gustavus Michael Stucley Hamilton-Russell, *b.* 1965, *s.* 1995, *m.*	Hon. Gustavus A. E. H.-R., *b.* 1999
1929	*Brentford (4th),* Crispin William Joynson-Hicks, *b.* 1933, *s.* 1983, *m.*	Hon. Paul W. J.-H., *b.* 1971
1929	** *Bridgeman (3rd),* Robin John Orlando Bridgeman, *b.* 1930, *s.* 1982, *m.*	Hon. Luke R. O. B., *b.* 1971

1868   *Bridport (4th) and 7th Duke, Bronte in Sicily, 1799*, Alexander Nelson Hood, *b.* 1948, *s.* 1969, *m.* — Hon. Peregrine A. N. H., *b.* 1974

1952   ** *Brookeborough (3rd)*, Alan Henry Brooke, *b.* 1952, *s.* 1987, *m.* — Hon. Christopher A. B., *b.* 1954

1933   *Buckmaster (4th)*, Adrian Charles Buckmaster, *b.* 1949, *s.* 2007, *m.* — Hon. Andrew N. B., *b.* 1980

1939   *Caldecote (3rd)*, Piers James Hampden Inskip, *b.* 1947, *s.* 1999, *m.* — Hon. Thomas J. H. I., *b.* 1985

1941   *Camrose (4th)*, Adrian Michael Berry, *b.* 1937, *s.* 2001, *m.* — Hon. Jonathan W. B., *b.* 1970

1954   *Chandos (3rd) and Baron Lyttelton of Aldershot (life peerage, 2000)*, Thomas Orlando Lyttelton, *b.* 1953, *s.* 1980, *m.* — Hon. Oliver A. L., *b.* 1986

1665 I. *Charlemont (15th)*, John Dodd Caulfeild, *b.* 1966, *s.* 2001, *m.* — Hon. Shane A. C., *b.* 1996

1921   *Chelmsford (4th)* Frederic Corin Piers Thesiger, *b.* 1962, *s.* 1999, *m.* — Hon. Frederic T. *b.* 2006

1717 I. *Chetwynd (10th)*, Adam Richard John Casson Chetwynd, *b.* 1935, *s.* 1965, *m.* — Hon. Adam D. C., *b.* 1969

1911   *Chilston (4th)*, Alastair George Akers-Douglas, *b.* 1946, *s.* 1982, *m.* — Hon. Oliver I. A.-D., *b.* 1973

1902   *Churchill (3rd) and 5th UK Baron Churchill (1815)*, Victor George Spencer, *b.* 1934, *s.* 1973 — To Barony only, Richard H. R. S., *b.* 1926

1718   *Cobham (12th)*, Christopher Charles Lyttelton, *b.* 1947, *s.* 2006, *m.* — Hon. Oliver C. L., *b.* 1976

1902   ** *Colville of Culross (5th)*, Charles Mark Townshend Colville, *b.* 1959, *s.* 2010 — Hon. Richmond J. I. C., *b.* 1961

1826   *Combermere (6th)*, Thomas Robert Wellington Stapleton-Cotton, *b.* 1969, *s.* 2000 — Hon. Laszlo M. W. S.-C., *b.* 2010

1917   *Cowdray (4th)*, Michael Orlando Weetman Pearson, *b.* 1944, *s.* 1995, *m.* — Hon. Peregrine J. D. P., *b.* 1994

1927   ** *Craigavon (3rd)*, Janric Fraser Craig, *b.* 1944, *s.* 1974 — None

1943   *Daventry (4th)*, James Edward FitzRoy Newdegate, *b.* 1960, *s.* 2000, *m.* — Hon. Humphrey J. F. N., *b.* 1995

1937   *Davidson (2nd)*, John Andrew Davidson, *b.* 1928, *s.* 1970, *m.* — Hon. Malcolm W. M. D., *b.* 1934

1956   *De L'Isle (2nd)*, Philip John Algernon Sidney, MBE, *b.* 1945, *s.* 1991, *m.* — Hon. Philip W. E. S., *b.* 1985

1776 I. *De Vesci (7th)*, Thomas Eustace Vesey, *b.* 1955, *s.* 1983, *m.* — Hon. Oliver I. V., *b.* 1991

1917   *Devonport (3rd)*, Terence Kearley, *b.* 1944, *s.* 1973 — Chester D. H. K., *b.* 1932

1964   *Dilhorne (2nd)*, John Mervyn Manningham-Buller, *b.* 1932, *s.* 1980, *m.* — Hon. James E. M.-B., *b.* 1956

1622 I. *Dillon (22nd)*, Henry Benedict Charles Dillon, *b.* 1973, *s.* 1982 — Hon. Richard A. L. D., *b.* 1948

1785 I. *Doneraile (10th)*, Richard Allen St Leger, *b.* 1946, *s.* 1983, *m.* — Hon. Nathaniel W. R. St J. St L., *b.* 1971

1680 I. *Downe (12th)*, Richard Henry Dawnay, *b.* 1967, *s.* 2002 — Thomas P. D., *b.* 1978

1959   *Dunrossil (3rd)*, Andrew William Reginald Morrison, *b.* 1953, *s.* 2000, *m.* — Hon. Callum A. B. M., *b.* 1994

1964   ** *Eccles (2nd)*, John Dawson Eccles, CBE, *b.* 1931, *s.* 1999, *m.* — Hon. William D. E., *b.* 1960

1897   *Esher (5th)*, Christopher Lionel Baliol Brett, *b.* 1936, *s.* 2004, *m.* — Hon. Matthew C. A. B., *b.* 1963

1816   *Exmouth (10th)*, Paul Edward Pellew, *b.* 1940, *s.* 1970, *m.* — Hon. Edward F. P., *b.* 1978

1620 S. ** *of Falkland (15th)*, Lucius Edward William Plantagenet Cary, *b.* 1935, *s.* 1984, *m. Premier Scottish Viscount on the Roll* — Master of Falkland, *b.* 1963

1720   *Falmouth (9th)*, George Hugh Boscawen, *b.* 1919, *s.* 1962, *w.* — Hon. Evelyn A. H. B., *b.* 1955

1720 I. *Gage (8th)*, (Henry) Nicolas Gage, *b.* 1934, *s.* 1993, *m.* — Hon. Henry W. G., *b.* 1975

1727 I. *Galway (12th)*, George Rupert Monckton-Arundell, *b.* 1922, *s.* 1980, *m.* — Hon. J. Philip M., *b.* 1952

1478 I. *Gormanston (17th)*, Jenico Nicholas Dudley Preston, *b.* 1939, *s.* 1940, *m. Premier Viscount of Ireland* — Hon. Jenico F. T. P., *b.* 1974

1816 I. *Gort (9th)*, Foley Robert Standish Prendergast Vereker, *b.* 1951, *s.* 1995, *m.* — Hon. Robert F. P. V., *b.* 1993

1900   ** *Goschen (4th)*, Giles John Harry Goschen, *b.* 1965, *s.* 1977, *m.* — Hon. Alexander J. E. G., *b.* 2001

1849   *Gough (5th)*, Shane Hugh Maryon Gough, *b.* 1941, *s.* 1951 — None

1929   *Hailsham (3rd)*, Douglas Martin Hogg, PC, QC, *b.* 1945, *s.* 2001, *m.* — Hon. Quintin J. N. M. H., *b.* 1973

1891   *Hambleden (4th)*, William Herbert Smith, *b.* 1930, *s.* 1948, *m.* — Hon. William H. B. S., *b.* 1955

1884   *Hampden (7th)*, Francis Anthony Brand, *b.* 1970, *s.* 2008, *m.* — Hon. Lucian A. B., *b.* 2005

1936   ** *Hanworth (3rd)*, David Stephen Geoffrey Pollock, *b.* 1946, *s.* 1996, *m.* — Harold W. C. P., *b.* 1988

1791 I. *Harberton (11th)*, Henry Robert Pomeroy, *b.* 1958, *s.* 2004, *m.* — Hon. Patrick C. P., *b.* 1995

1846   *Hardinge (7th)*, Andrew Hartland Hardinge, *b.* 1960, *s.* 2004, *m.* — Hon. Thomas H. de M. H., *b.* 1993

1791 I. *Hawarden (9th)*, (Robert) Connan Wyndham Leslie Maude, *b.* 1961, *s.* 1991, *m.* — Hon. Varian J. C. E. M., *b.* 1997

1960   *Head (2nd)*, Richard Antony Head, *b.* 1937, *s.* 1983, *m.* — Hon. Henry J. H., *b.* 1980

1550   *Hereford (19th)*, Charles Robin De Bohun Devereux, *b.* 1975, *s.* 2004, *Premier Viscount of England* — Hon. Edward M. de B. D., *b.* 1977

1842   *Hill (9th)*, Peter David Raymond Charles Clegg-Hill, *b.* 1945, *s.* 2003 — Hon. Michael C. D. C.-H., *b.* 1988

1796	*Hood (8th)*, Henry Lyttleton Alexander Hood, *b.* 1958, *s.* 1999, *m.*	Hon. Archibald L. S. H., *b.* 1993
1945	*Kemsley (3rd)*, Richard Gomer Berry, *b.* 1951, *s.* 1999, *m.*	Hon. Luke G. B., *b.* 1998
1911	*Knollys (3rd)*, David Francis Dudley Knollys, *b.* 1931, *s.* 1966, *m.*	Hon. Patrick N. M. K., *b.* 1962
1895	*Knutsford (6th)*, Michael Holland-Hibbert, *b.* 1926, *s.* 1986, *m.*	Hon. Henry T. H.-H., *b.* 1959
1954	*Leathers (3rd)*, Christopher Graeme Leathers, *b.* 1941, *s.* 1996, *m.*	Hon. James F. L., *b.* 1969
1781 I.	*Lifford (9th)*, (Edward) James Wingfield Hewitt, *b.* 1949, *s.* 1987, *m.*	Hon. James T. W. H., *b.* 1979
1921	*Long (4th)*, Richard Gerard Long, CBE, *b.* 1929, *s.* 1967, *m.*	Hon. James R. L., *b.* 1960
1957	*Mackintosh of Halifax (3rd)*, (John) Clive Mackintosh, *b.* 1958, *s.* 1980, *m.*	Hon. Thomas H. G. M., *b.* 1985
1955	*Malvern (3rd)*, Ashley Kevin Godfrey Huggins, *b.* 1949, *s.* 1978	Hon. M. James H., *b.* 1928
1945	*Marchwood (3rd)*, David George Staveley Penny, *b.* 1936, *s.* 1979, *w.*	Hon. Peter G. W. P., *b.* 1965
1942	*Margesson (2nd)*, Francis Vere Hampden Margesson, *b.* 1922, *s.* 1965, *m.*	Capt. Hon. Richard F. D. M., *b.* 1960
1660 I.	*Massereene (14th) and Ferrard (7th) (I. 1797)*, John David Clotworthy Whyte-Melville Foster Skeffington, *b.* 1940, *s.* 1992, *m.*	Hon. Charles J. C. W.-M. F. S., *b.* 1973
1802	*Melville (10th)*, Robert Henry Kirkpatrick Dundas, *b.* 1984, *s.* 2011	Hon. James D. B. D., *b.* 1986
1916	*Mersey (5th)*, Edward John Hallam Bigham, *b.* 1966, *s.* 2006, *m.*	Hon. David E. H. B., *b.* 1938
1717 I.	*Midleton (12th)*, Alan Henry Brodrick, *b.* 1949, *s.* 1988, *m.*	Hon. Ashley R. B., *b.* 1980
1962	*Mills (3rd)*, Christopher Philip Roger Mills, *b.* 1956, *s.* 1988, *m.*	None
1716 I.	*Molesworth (12th)*, Robert Bysse Kelham Molesworth, *b.* 1959, *s.* 1997	Hon. William J. C. M., *b.* 1960
1801 I.	*Monck (7th)*, Charles Stanley Monck, *b.* 1953, *s.* 1982 (Does not use title)	Hon. George S. M., *b.* 1957
1957	*Monckton of Brenchley (3rd)*, Christopher Walter Monckton, *b.* 1952, *s.* 2006, *m.*	Hon. Timothy D. R. M., *b.* 1955
1946	** *Montgomery of Alamein (2nd)*, David Bernard Montgomery, CMG, *b.* 1928, *s.* 1976, *m.*	Hon. Henry D. M., *b.* 1954
1550 I.	*Mountgarret (18th)*, Piers James Richard Butler, *b.* 1961, *s.* 2004	Hon. Edmund H. R. B., *b.* 1962
1952	*Norwich (2nd)*, John Julius Cooper, CVO, *b.* 1929, *s.* 1954, *m.*	Hon. Jason C. D. B. C., *b.* 1959
1651 S.	*of Oxfuird (14th)*, Ian Arthur Alexander Makgill, *b.* 1969, *s.* 2003	Hon. Robert E. G. M., *b.* 1969
1873	*Portman (10th)*, Christopher Edward Berkeley Portman, *b.* 1958, *s.* 1999, *m.*	Hon. Luke O. B. P., *b.* 1984
1743 I.	*Powerscourt (10th)*, Mervyn Niall Wingfield, *b.* 1935, *s.* 1973, *m.*	Hon. Mervyn A. W., *b.* 1963
1900	*Ridley (4th)*, Matthew White Ridley, KG, GCVO, TD, *b.* 1925, *s.* 1964, *w.*	Hon. Matthew W. R., *b.* 1958
1960	*Rochdale (2nd)*, St John Durival Kemp, *b.* 1938, *s.* 1993, *m.*	Hon. Jonathan H. D. K., *b.* 1961
1919	*Rothermere (4th)*, (Harold) Jonathan Esmond Vere Harmsworth, *b.* 1967, *s.* 1998, *m.*	Hon. Vere R. J. H. H., *b.* 1994
1937	*Runciman of Doxford (3rd)*, Walter Garrison Runciman (Garry), CBE, *b.* 1934, *s.* 1989, *m.*	Hon. David W. R., *b.* 1967
1918	*St Davids (4th)*, Rhodri Colwyn Philipps, *b.* 1966, *s.* 2009, *m.*	Hon. Roland A. J. E. P., *b.* 1970
1801	*St Vincent (8th)*, Edward Robert James Jervis, *b.* 1951, *s.* 2006, *m.*	Hon. James R. A. J., *b.* 1982
1937	*Samuel (3rd)*, David Herbert Samuel, OBE, PHD, *b.* 1922, *s.* 1978, *m.*	Hon. Dan J. S., *b.* 1925
1911	*Scarsdale (4th)*, Peter Ghislain Nathaniel Curzon, *b.* 1949, *s.* 2000, *m.*	Hon. David J. N. C., *b.* 1958
1905 M.	*Selby (6th)*, Christopher Rolf Thomas Gully, *b.* 1993, *s.* 2001	Hon. (James) Edward H. G. G., *b.* 1945
1805	*Sidmouth (8th)*, Jeremy Francis Addington, *b.* 1947, *s.* 2005, *w.*	Hon. Steffan A., *b.* 1966
1940	** *Simon (3rd)*, Jan David Simon, *b.* 1940, *s.* 1993, *m.*	None
1960	** *Slim (2nd)*, John Douglas Slim, OBE, *b.* 1927, *s.* 1970, *m.*	Hon. Mark W. R. S., *b.* 1960
1954	*Soulbury (4th)*, Oliver Peter Ramsbotham, *b.* 1943, *s.* 2010, *m.*	Hon. Edward H. R., *b.* 1966
1776 I.	*Southwell (7th)*, Pyers Anthony Joseph Southwell, *b.* 1930, *s.* 1960, *m.*	Hon. Richard A. P. S., *b.* 1956
1942	*Stansgate*, Anthony Neil Wedgwood Benn, *b.* 1925, *s.* 1960, *w.* Disclaimed for life 1963.	Stephen M. W. B., *b.* 1951
1959	*Stuart of Findhorn (3rd)*, James Dominic Stuart, *b.* 1948, *s.* 1999, *m.*	Hon. Andrew M. S., *b.* 1957
1957	** *Tenby (3rd)*, William Lloyd George, *b.* 1927, *s.* 1983, *m.*	Hon. Timothy H. G. L. G., *b.* 1962
1952	*Thurso (3rd)*, John Archibald Sinclair, MP, *b.* 1953, *s.* 1995, *m.*	Hon. James A. R. S., *b.* 1984
1721	*Torrington (11th)*, Timothy Howard St George Byng, *b.* 1943, *s.* 1961, *m.*	Colin H. C.-B., *b.* 1960
1936	** *Trenchard (3rd)*, Hugh Trenchard, *b.* 1951, *s.* 1987, *m.*	Hon. Alexander T. T., *b.* 1978
1921	** *Ullswater (2nd)*, Nicholas James Christopher Lowther, PC, LVO, *b.* 1942, *s.* 1949, *m.*	Hon. Benjamin J. L., *b.* 1975
1622 I.	*Valentia (16th)*, Frances William Dighton Annesley, *b.* 1959, *s.* 2005, *m.*	Hon. Peter J. A., *b.* 1967
1952	** *Waverley (3rd)*, John Desmond Forbes Anderson, *b.* 1949, *s.* 1990	Hon. Forbes A. R. A., *b.* 1996

1938	*Weir (3rd)*, William Kenneth James Weir, *b.* 1933, *s.* 1975, *m.*	Hon. James W. H. W., *b.* 1965
1918	*Wimborne (4th)*, Ivor Mervyn Vigors Guest, *b.* 1968, *s.* 1993	Hon. Julien J. G., *b.* 1945
1923	** *Younger of Leckie (5th)*, James Edward George Younger, *b.* 1955, *s.* 2003, *m.*	Hon. Alexander W. G. Y., *b.* 1993

BARONS/LORDS

Coronet, Six silver balls

Style, The Rt. Hon. the Lord _
  Envelope (formal), The Rt. Hon. Lord _; *(social)*, The Lord _. *Letter (formal)*, My Lord; *(social)*, Dear Lord _. *Spoken*, Lord _.
In the Peerage of Scotland there is no rank of Baron; the equivalent rank is Lord of Parliament and Scottish peers should always be styled 'Lord', never 'Baron'.
Wife's style, The Rt. Hon. the Lady _
  Envelope (formal), The Rt. Hon. Lady _; *(social)*, The Lady _. *Letter (formal)*, My Lady; *(social)*, Dear Lady _. *Spoken*, Lady _
Children's style, 'The Hon.' before forename (F_) and surname (S_)
  Envelope, The Hon. F_ S_. *Letter*, Dear Mr/Miss/Mrs S_. *Spoken*, Mr/Miss/Mrs S_
In Scotland, the heir apparent to a Lord may be styled 'The Master of _ (title of peer)'

Created	*Title, order of succession, name, etc*	*Heir*
1911	*Aberconway (4th)*, (Henry) Charles McLaren, *b.* 1948, *s.* 2003, *m.*	Hon. Charles S. M., *b.* 1984
1873	** *Aberdare (5th)*, Alastair John Lyndhurst Bruce, *b.* 1947, *s.* 2005, *m.*	Hon. Hector M. N. B., *b.* 1974
1835	*Abinger (9th)*, James Harry Scarlett, *b.* 1959, *s.* 2002, *m.*	Hon. Peter R. S., *b.* 1961
1869	*Acton (5th)*, John Charles Ferdinand Harold Lyon-Dalberg-Acton, *b.* 1966, *s.* 2010, *m.*	Hon. John C. L.-D.-A., *b.* 1943
1887	** *Addington (6th)*, Dominic Bryce Hubbard, *b.* 1963, *s.* 1982	Hon. Michael W. L. H., *b.* 1965
1896	*Aldenham (6th) and Hunsdon of Hunsdon (4th) (1923)*, Vicary Tyser Gibbs, *b.* 1948, *s.* 1986, *m.*	Hon. Humphrey W. F. G., *b.* 1989
1962	*Aldington (2nd)*, Charles Harold Stuart Low, *b.* 1948, *s.* 2000, *m.*	Hon. Philip T. A. L., *b.* 1990
1945	*Altrincham (3rd)*, Anthony Ulick David Dundas Grigg, *b.* 1934, *s.* 2001, *m.*	Hon. (Edward) Sebastian G., *b.* 1965
1929	*Alvingham (2nd)*, Maj.-Gen. Robert Guy Eardley Yerburgh, CBE, *b.* 1926, *s.* 1955, *m.*	Capt. Hon. Robert R. G. Y., *b.* 1956
1892	*Amherst of Hackney (5th)*, Hugh William Amherst Cecil, *b.* 1968, *s.* 2009, *m.*	Hon. Jack W. A. C., *b.* 2001
1881	*Ampthill (5th)*, David Whitney Erskine Russell, *b.* 1947, *s.* 2011	Hon. Anthony J. M. R., *b.* 1952
1947	*Amwell (3rd)*, Keith Norman Montague, *b.* 1943, *s.* 1990, *m.*	Hon. Ian K. M., *b.* 1973
1863	*Annaly (6th)*, Luke Richard White, *b.* 1954, *s.* 1990, *m.*	Hon. Luke H. W., *b.* 1990
1885	*Ashbourne (4th)*, Edward Barry Greynville Gibson, *b.* 1933, *s.* 1983, *m.*	Hon. Edward C. d'O. G., *b.* 1967
1835	*Ashburton (7th)*, John Francis Harcourt Baring, KG, KCVO, *b.* 1928, *s.* 1991, *m.*	Hon. Mark F. R. B., *b.* 1958
1892	*Ashcombe (4th)*, Henry Edward Cubitt, *b.* 1924, *s.* 1962, *m.*	Mark E. C., *b.* 1964
1911	** *Ashton of Hyde (4th)*, Thomas Henry Ashton, *b.* 1958, *s.* 2008, *m.*	Hon. John E. A., *b.* 1966
1800 I.	*Ashtown (8th)*, Roderick Nigel Godolphin Trench, *b.* 1944, *s.* 2010, *m.*	Hon. Timothy R. H. T., *b.* 1968
1956	** *Astor of Hever (3rd)*, John Jacob Astor, *b.* 1946, *s.* 1984, *m.*	Hon. Charles G. J. A., *b.* 1990
1789 I.	*Auckland (10th) and Auckland (10th) (1793)*, Robert Ian Burnard Eden, *b.* 1962, *s.* 1997, *m.*	Henry V. E., *b.* 1958
1313	*Audley*, Barony in abeyance between three co-heiresses since 1997	
1900	** *Avebury (4th)*, Eric Reginald Lubbock, *b.* 1928, *s.* 1971, *m.*	Hon. Lyulph A. J. L., *b.* 1954
1718 I.	*Aylmer (14th)*, (Anthony) Julian Aylmer, *b.* 1951, *s.* 2006, *m.*	Hon. Michael H. A., *b.* 1991
1929	*Baden-Powell (3rd)*, Robert Crause Baden-Powell, *b.* 1936, *s.* 1962, *w.*	Hon. David M. B.-P., *b.* 1940
1780	*Bagot (10th)*, (Charles Hugh) Shaun Bagot, *b.* 1944, *s.* 2001, *m.*	Richard C. V. B., *b.* 1941
1953	*Baillieu (3rd)*, James William Latham Baillieu, *b.* 1950, *s.* 1973, *m.*	Hon. Robert L. B., *b.* 1979
1607 S.	*Balfour of Burleigh (8th)*, Robert Bruce, *b.* 1927, *s.* 1967, *m.*	Hon. Victoria B., *b.* 1973
1945	*Balfour of Inchrye (2nd)*, Ian Balfour, *b.* 1924, *s.* 1988, *w.*	None
1924	*Banbury of Southam (3rd)*, Charles William Banbury, *b.* 1953, *s.* 1981, *m.*	None
1698	*Barnard (11th)*, Harry John Neville Vane, TD, *b.* 1923, *s.* 1964	Hon. Henry F. C. V., *b.* 1959

1887	*Basing (6th),* Stuart Anthony Whitfield Sclater-Booth, *b.* 1969, *s.* 2007, *m.*	Hon. Luke W. S.-B., *b.* 2000
1917	*Beaverbrook (3rd),* Maxwell William Humphrey Aitken, *b.* 1951, *s.* 1985, *m.*	Hon. Maxwell F. A., *b.* 1977
1647 S.	*Belhaven and Stenton (13th),* Robert Anthony Carmichael Hamilton, *b.* 1927, *s.* 1961, *m.*	Master of Belhaven, *b.* 1953
1848 I.	*Bellew (8th),* Bryan Edward Bellew, *b.* 1943, *s.* 2010, *m.*	Hon. Anthony R. B. B., *b.* 1972
1856	*Belper (5th),* Richard Henry Strutt, *b.* 1941, *s.* 1999, *m.*	Hon. Michael H. S., *b.* 1969
1421	*Berkeley (18th) and Gueterbock (life peerage, 2000),* Anthony Fitzhardinge Gueterbock, OBE, *b.* 1939, *s.* 1992, *m.*	Hon. Thomas F. G., *b.* 1969
1922	*Bethell (5th),* James Nicholas Bethell, *b.* 1967, *s.* 2007, *m.*	Hon. Jacob N. D. B., *b.* 200–
1938	*Bicester (3rd),* Angus Edward Vivian Smith, *b.* 1932, *s.* 1968	Hugh C. V. S., *b.* 1934
1903	*Biddulph (5th),* (Anthony) Nicholas Colin Maitland Biddulph, *b.* 1959, *s.* 1988, *m.*	Hon. Robert J. M. B., *b.* 1994
1938	*Birdwood (3rd),* Mark William Ogilvie Birdwood, *b.* 1938, *s.* 1962, *m.*	None
1958	*Birkett (2nd),* Michael Birkett, *b.* 1929, *s.* 1962, *w.*	Hon. Thomas B., *b.* 1982
1907	*Blyth (5th),* James Audley Ian Blyth, *b.* 1970, *s.* 2009, *m.*	Hon. Hugo A. J. B., *b.* 2006
1797	*Bolton (8th),* Harry Algar Nigel Orde-Powlett, *b.* 1954, *s.* 2001, *m.*	Hon. Thomas O.-P., *b.* 1979
1452 S.	*Borthwick (24th),* John Hugh Borthwick, *b.* 1940, *s.* 1996, *m.*	Hon. James H. A. B. of Glengelt, *b.* 1940
1922	*Borwick (5th),* (Geoffrey Robert) James Borwick, *b.* 1955, *s.* 2007, *m.*	Hon. Edwin D. W. B., *b.* 1984
1761	*Boston (11th),* George William Eustace Boteler Irby, *b.* 1971, *s.* 2007, *m.*	Hon. Thomas W. G. B. I., *b.* 1999
1942	** *Brabazon of Tara (3rd),* Ivon Anthony Moore-Brabazon, *b.* 1946, *s.* 1974, *m.*	Hon. Benjamin R. M.-B., *b.* 1983
1880	*Brabourne (8th),* Norton Louis Philip Knatchbull, *b.* 1947, *s.* 2005, *m.* (*also* Lord Romsey heir to Countess Mountbatten of Burma, *see* that title)	Hon. Nicholas L. C. N. K., *b.* 1981
1925	*Bradbury (3rd),* John Bradbury, *b.* 1940, *s.* 1994, *m.*	Hon. John B., *b.* 1973
1962	*Brain (2nd),* Christopher Langdon Brain, *b.* 1926, *s.* 1966, *m.*	Hon. Michael C. B., *b.* 1928
1938	*Brassey of Apethorpe (3rd),* David Henry Brassey, OBE, *b.* 1932, *s.* 1967, *m.*	Hon. Edward B., *b.* 1964
1788	*Braybrooke (10th),* Robin Henry Charles Neville, *b.* 1932, *s.* 1990, *m.*	Richard R. N., *b.* 1977
1957	** *Bridges (2nd),* Thomas Edward Bridges, GCMG, *b.* 1927, *s.* 1969, *m.*	Hon. Mark T. B., *b.* 1954
1945	*Broadbridge (4th),* Martin Hugh Broadbridge, *b.* 1929, *s.* 2000, *w.*	Hon. Richard J. M. B., *b.* 1959
1933	*Brocket (3rd),* Charles Ronald George Nall-Cain, *b.* 1952, *s.* 1967, *w.*	Hon. Alexander C. C. N.-C., *b.* 1984
1860	** *Brougham and Vaux (5th),* Michael John Brougham, CBE, *b.* 1938, *s.* 1967	Hon. Charles W. B., *b.* 1971
1776	*Brownlow (7th),* Edward John Peregrine Cust, *b.* 1936, *s.* 1978, *m.*	Hon. Peregrine E. Q. C., *b.* 1974
1942	*Bruntisfield (3rd),* Michael John Victor Warrender, *b.* 1949, *s.* 2007, *m.*	Hon. John M. P. C. W., *b.* 1996
1950	*Burden (4th),* Fraser William Elsworth Burden, *b.* 1964, *s.* 2000, *m.*	Hon. Ian S. B., *b.* 1967
1529	*Burgh (8th),* (Alexander) Gregory Disney Leith, *b.* 1958, *s.* 2001, *m.*	Hon. Alexander J. S. L., *b.* 1986
1903	*Burnham (7th),* Harry Frederick Alan Lawson, *b.* 1968, *s.* 2005	None
1897	*Burton (3rd),* Michael Evan Victor Baillie, *b.* 1924, *s.* 1962, *m.*	Hon. Evan M. R. B., *b.* 1949
1643	*Byron (13th),* Robert James Byron, *b.* 1950, *s.* 1989, *m.*	Hon. Charles R. G. B., *b.* 1990
1937	*Cadman (3rd),* John Anthony Cadman, *b.* 1938, *s.* 1966, *m.*	Hon. Nicholas A. J. C., *b.* 1977
1945	*Calverley (3rd),* Charles Rodney Muff, *b.* 1946, *s.* 1971, *m.*	Hon. Jonathan E. M., *b.* 1975
1383	*Camoys (7th),* (Ralph) Thomas Campion George Sherman Stonor, GCVO, PC, *b.* 1940, *s.* 1976, *m.*	Hon. R. William R. T. S., *b.* 1974
1715 I.	*Carbery (11th),* Peter Ralfe Harrington Evans-Freke, *b.* 1920, *s.* 1970, *w.*	Hon. Michael P. E.-F., *b.* 1942
1834 I.	*Carew (7th) and Carew (7th) (1838),* Patrick Thomas Conolly-Carew, *b.* 1938, *s.* 1994, *m.*	Hon. William P. C.-C., *b.* 1973
1916	*Carnock (5th),* Adam Nicolson, *b.* 1957, *s.* 2008, *m.*	Hon. Thomas N., *b.* 1984
1796 I.	*Carrington (6th) and Carrington (6th) (1797) and Carington of Upton (life peerage, 1999),* Peter Alexander Rupert Carington, KG, GCMG, CH, MC, PC, *b.* 1919, *s.* 1938, *w.*	Hon. Rupert F. J. C., *b.* 1948
1812 I.	*Castlemaine (8th),* Roland Thomas John Handcock, MBE, *b.* 1943, *s.* 1973, *m.*	Hon. Ronan M. E. H., *b.* 1989
1936	*Catto (3rd),* Innes Gordon Catto, *b.* 1950, *s.* 2001, *m.*	Hon. Alexander G. C., *b.* 1952
1918	*Cawley (4th),* John Francis Cawley, *b.* 1946, *s.* 2001, *m.*	Hon. William R. H. C., *b.* 1981
1858	*Chesham (7th),* Charles Gray Compton Cavendish, *b.* 1974, *s.* 2009, *m.*	Hon. Oliver N.B.C., *b.* 2007
1945	*Chetwode (2nd),* Philip Chetwode, *b.* 1937, *s.* 1950, *m.*	Hon. Roger C., *b.* 1968
1945	** *Chorley (2nd),* Roger Richard Edward Chorley, *b.* 1930, *s.* 1978, *m.*	Hon. Nicholas R. D. C., *b.* 1966
1858	*Churston (5th),* John Francis Yarde-Buller, *b.* 1934, *s.* 1991, *m.*	Hon. Benjamin F. A. Y.-B., *b.* 1974

1800 I.	*Clanmorris (8th)*, Simon John Ward Bingham, *b.* 1937, *s.* 1988, *m.*	Robert D. de B. B., *b.* 1942
1672	*Clifford of Chudleigh (14th)*, Thomas Hugh Clifford, *b.* 1948, *s.* 1988, *m.*	Hon. Alexander T. H. C., *b.* 1985
1299	*Clinton (22nd)*, Gerard Nevile Mark Fane Trefusis, *b.* 1934, *s.* 1965, *m.*	Hon. Charles P. R. F. T., *b.* 1962
1955	*Clitheroe (2nd)*, Ralph John Assheton, *b.* 1929, *s.* 1984, *m.*	Hon. Ralph C. A., *b.* 1962
1919	*Clwyd (4th)*, (John) Murray Roberts, *b.* 1971, *s.* 2006	Hon. Jeremy T. R., *b.* 1973
1948	*Clydesmuir (3rd)*, David Ronald Colville, *b.* 1949, *s.* 1996, *m.*	Hon. Richard C., *b.* 1980
1960	** *Cobbold (2nd)*, David Antony Fromanteel Lytton Cobbold, *b.* 1937, *s.* 1987, *m.*	Hon. Henry F. L. C., *b.* 1962
1919	*Cochrane of Cults (4th)*, (Ralph Henry) Vere Cochrane, *b.* 1926, *s.* 1990, *m.*	Hon. Thomas H. V. C., *b.* 1957
1954	*Coleraine (2nd)*, (James) Martin (Bonar) Law, *b.* 1931, *s.* 1980, *m.*	Hon. James P. B. L., *b.* 1975
1873	*Coleridge (5th)*, William Duke Coleridge, *b.* 1937, *s.* 1984, *m.*	Hon. James D. C., *b.* 1967
1946	*Colgrain (4th)*, Alastair Colin Leckie Campbell, *b.* 1951, *s.* 2008, *m.*	Hon. Thomas C. D. C., *b.* 1984
1917	** *Colwyn (3rd)*, (Ian) Anthony Hamilton-Smith, CBE, *b.* 1942, *s.* 1966, *m.*	Hon. Craig P. H.-S., *b.* 1968
1956	*Colyton (2nd)*, Alisdair John Munro Hopkinson, *b.* 1958, *s.* 1996, *m.*	Hon. James P. M. H., *b.* 1983
1841	*Congleton (8th)*, Christopher Patrick Parnell, *b.* 1930, *s.* 1967, *m.*	Hon. John P. C. P., *b.* 1959
1927	*Cornwallis (4th)*, Fiennes Wykeham Jeremy Cornwallis, *b.* 1946, *s.* 2010, *m.*	Hon. Fiennes A. W. M. C., *b.* 1987
1874	*Cottesloe (5th)*, John Tapling Fremantle, *b.* 1927, *s.* 1994, *m.*	Hon. Thomas F. H. F., *b.* 1966
1929	*Craigmyle (4th)*, Thomas Columba Shaw, *b.* 1960, *s.* 1998, *m.*	Hon. Alexander F. S., *b.* 1988
1899	*Cranworth (3rd)*, Philip Bertram Gurdon, *b.* 1940, *s.* 1964, *m.*	Hon. Sacha W. R. G., *b.* 1970
1959	** *Crathorne (2nd)*, Charles James Dugdale, *b.* 1939, *s.* 1977, *w.*	Hon. Thomas A. J. D., *b.* 1977
1892	*Crawshaw (5th)*, David Gerald Brooks, *b.* 1934, *s.* 1997, *m.*	Hon. John P. B., *b.* 1938
1940	*Croft (3rd)*, Bernard William Henry Page Croft, *b.* 1949, *s.* 1997, *m.*	None
1797 I.	*Crofton (8th)*, Edward Harry Piers Crofton, *b.* 1988, *s.* 2007	Hon. Charles M. G. C., *b.* 1988
1375	*Cromwell (7th)*, Godfrey John Bewicke-Copley, *b.* 1960, *s.* 1982, *m.*	Hon. David G. B.-C., *b.* 1997
1947	*Crook (3rd)*, Robert Douglas Edwin Crook, *b.* 1955, *s.* 2001, *m.*	Hon. Matthew R. C., *b.* 1990
1920	*Cullen of Ashbourne (3rd)*, Edmund Willoughby Marsham Cokayne, *b.* 1916, *s.* 2000, *w.*	(Hon.) John O'B. M. C., *b.*1920
1914	*Cunliffe (3rd)*, Roger Cunliffe, *b.* 1932, *s.* 1963, *m.*	Hon. Henry C., *b.* 1962
1332	*Darcy de Knayth (19th)*, Caspar David Ingrams, *b.* 1962, *s.* 2008, *m.*	Hon. Thomas R. I., *b.* 1999
1927	*Daresbury (4th)*, Peter Gilbert Greenall, *b.* 1953, *s.* 1996, *m.*	Hon. Thomas E. G., *b.* 1984
1924	*Darling (3rd)*, (Robert) Julian Henry Darling, *b.* 1944, *s.* 2003, *m.*	Hon. Robert J. C. D., *b.* 1972
1946	*Darwen (4th)*, Paul Davies, *b.* 1962, *s.* 2011	Hon. Benjamin D., *b.* 1966
1932	*Davies (3rd)*, David Davies, *b.* 1940, *s.* 1944, *m.*	Hon. David D. D., *b.* 1975
1812 I.	*Decies (7th)*, Marcus Hugh Tristram de la Poer Beresford, *b.* 1948, *s.* 1992, *m.*	Hon. Robert M. D. de la P. B., *b.* 1988
1299	*de Clifford (27th)*, John Edward Southwell Russell, *b.* 1928, *s.* 1982, *m.*	Hon. William S. R., *b.* 1930
1851	*De Freyne (8th)*, Fulke Charles Arthur John French, *b.* 1957, *s.* 2009	Hon. Alexander J. C. F., *b.* 1988
1821	*Delamere (5th)*, Hugh George Cholmondeley, *b.* 1934, *s.* 1979, *m.*	Hon. Thomas P. G. C., *b.* 1968
1838	** *de Mauley (7th)*, Rupert Charles Ponsonby, *b.* 1957, *s.* 2002, *m.*	Ashley G. P., *b.* 1959
1937	** *Denham (2nd)*, Bertram Stanley Mitford Bowyer, KBE, PC, *b.* 1927, *s.* 1948, *m.*	Hon. Richard G. G. B., *b.* 1959
1834	*Denman (5th)*, Charles Spencer Denman, CBE, MC, TD, *b.* 1916, *s.* 1971, *w.*	Hon. Richard T. S. D., *b.* 1946
1887	*De Ramsey (4th)*, John Ailwyn Fellowes, *b.* 1942, *s.* 1993, *m.*	Hon. Freddie J. F., *b.* 1978
1264	*de Ros (28th)*, Peter Trevor Maxwell, *b.* 1958, *s.* 1983, *m. Premier Baron of England*	Hon. Finbar J. M., *b.* 1988
1881	*Derwent (5th)*, Robin Evelyn Leo Vanden-Bempde-Johnstone, LVO, *b.* 1930, *s.* 1986, *m.*	Hon. Francis P. H. V.-B.-J., *b.* 1965
1831	*de Saumarez (7th)*, Eric Douglas Saumarez, *b.* 1956, *s.* 1991, *m.*	Hon. Victor T. S., *b.* 1956
1910	*de Villiers (4th)*, Alexander Charles de Villiers, *b.* 1940, *s.* 2001, *m.*	None
1930	*Dickinson (2nd)*, Richard Clavering Hyett Dickinson, *b.* 1926, *s.* 1943, *m.*	Hon. Martin H. D., *b.* 1961
1620 I.	*Digby (12th) and Digby (5th) (1765)*, Edward Henry Kenelm Digby, KCVO, *b.* 1924, *s.* 1964, *m.*	Hon. Henry N. K. D., *b.* 1954
1615	*Dormer (17th)*, Geoffrey Henry Dormer, *b.* 1920, *s.* 1995, *m.*	Hon. William R. D., *b.* 1960
1943	*Dowding (3rd)*, Piers Hugh Tremenheere Dowding, *b.* 1948, *s.* 1992	Hon. Mark D. J. D., *b.* 1949
1439	*Dudley (15th)*, Jim Anthony Hill Wallace, *b.* 1930, *s.* 2002, *m.*	Hon. Jeremy W. G. W., *b.* 1964
1800 I.	*Dufferin and Clandeboye (11th)*, John Francis Blackwood, *b.* 1944, *s.* 1991 (claim to the peerage not yet established), *m.*	Hon. Francis S. B., *b.* 1979
1929	*Dulverton (3rd)*, (Gilbert) Michael Hamilton Wills, *b.* 1944, *s.* 1992, *m.*	Hon. Robert A. H. W., *b.* 1983
1800 I.	*Dunalley (7th)*, Henry Francis Cornelius Prittie, *b.* 1948, *s.* 1992, *m.*	Hon. Joel H. P., *b.* 1981
1324 I.	*Dunboyne (29th)*, John Fitzwalter Butler, *b.* 1951, *s.* 2004, *m.*	Hon. Richard P. T. B., *b.* 1983
1892	*Dunleath (6th)*, Brian Henry Mulholland, *b.* 1950, *s.* 1997, *m.*	Hon. Andrew H. M., *b.* 1981
1439 I.	*Dunsany (21st)*, Randal Plunkett, *b.* 1983, *s.* 2011	Hon. Oliver P., *b.* 1985

1780	*Dynevor (10th)*, Hugo Griffith Uryan Rhys, *b.* 1966, *s.* 2008	Robert D. A. R., *b.* 1963
1963	*Egremont (2nd) and Leconfield (7th) (1859)*, John Max Henry Scawen Wyndham, *b.* 1948, *s.* 1972, *m.*	Hon. George R. V. W., *b.* 1983
1643	*Elibank (14th)*, Alan D'Ardis Erskine-Murray, *b.* 1923, *s.* 1973, *w.*	Master of Elibank, *b.* 1964
1802	*Ellenborough (8th)*, Richard Edward Cecil Law, *b.* 1926, *s.* 1945, *m.*	Maj. Hon. Rupert E. H. L., *b.* 1955
1509 S.	*Elphinstone (19th) and Elphinstone (5th) (1885)*, Alexander Mountstuart Elphinstone, *b.* 1980, *s.* 1994, *m.*	Master of Elphinstone, *b.* 2011
1934	** *Elton (2nd)*, Rodney Elton, TD, *b.* 1930, *s.* 1973, *m.*	Hon. Edward P. E., *b.* 1966
1627 S.	*Fairfax of Cameron (14th)*, Nicholas John Albert Fairfax, *b.* 1956, *s.* 1964, *m.*	Hon. Edward N. T. F., *b.* 1984
1961	*Fairhaven (3rd)*, Ailwyn Henry George Broughton, *b.* 1936, *s.* 1973, *m.*	Maj. Hon. James H. A. B., *b.* 1963
1916	*Faringdon (3rd)*, Charles Michael Henderson, KCVO, *b.* 1937, *s.* 1977, *m.*	Hon. James H. H., *b.* 1961
1756 I.	*Farnham (13th)*, Simon Kenlis Maxwell, *b.* 1933, *s.* 2001, *m.*	Hon. Robin S. M., *b.* 1965
1856 I.	*Fermoy (6th)*, Patrick Maurice Burke Roche, *b.* 1967, *s.* 1984, *m.*	Hon. E. Hugh B. R., *b.* 1972
1826	*Feversham (7th)*, Jasper Orlando Slingsby Duncombe, *b.* 1968, *s.* 2009	Hon. Jake B. D., *b.* 1972
1798 I.	*ffrench (8th)*, Robuck John Peter Charles Mario ffrench, *b.* 1956, *s.* 1986, *m.*	Hon. John C. M. J. F. ff., *b.* 1928
1909	*Fisher (3rd)*, John Vavasseur Fisher, DSC, *b.* 1921, *s.* 1955, *m.*	Hon. Patrick V. F., *b.* 1953
1295	*Fitzwalter (22nd)*, Julian Brook Plumptre, *b.* 1952, *s.* 2004, *m.*	Hon. Edward B. P., *b.* 1989
1776	*Foley (8th)*, Adrian Gerald Foley, *b.* 1923, *s.* 1927, *m.*	Hon. Thomas H. F., *b.* 1961
1445	*Forbes (22nd)*, Nigel Ivan Forbes, KBE, *b.* 1918, *s.* 1953, *m. Premier Lord of Scotland*	Master of Forbes, *b.* 1946
1821	*Forester (9th)*, Charles Richard George Weld-Forester, *b.* 1975, *s.* 2004,	Wolstan W. W.-F., *b.* 1941
1922	*Forres (4th)*, Alastair Stephen Grant Williamson, *b.* 1946, *s.* 1978, *m.*	Hon. George A. M. W., *b.* 1972
1917	*Forteviot (4th)*, John James Evelyn Dewar, *b.* 1938, *s.* 1993, *w.*	Hon. Alexander J. E. D., *b.* 1971
1951	** *Freyberg (3rd)*, Valerian Bernard Freyberg, *b.* 1970, *s.* 1993	Hon. Joseph J. F., *b.* 2007
1917	*Gainford (3rd)*, Joseph Edward Pease, *b.* 1921, *s.* 1971, *m.*	Hon. George P., *b.* 1926
1818 I.	*Garvagh (5th)*, (Alexander Leopold Ivor) George Canning, *b.* 1920, *s.* 1956, *m.*	Hon. Spencer G. S. de R. C., *b.* 1953
1942	** *Geddes (3rd)*, Euan Michael Ross Geddes, *b.* 1937, *s.* 1975, *m.*	Hon. James G. N. G., *b.* 1969
1876	*Gerard (5th)*, Anthony Robert Hugo Gerard, *b.* 1949, *s.* 1992, *m.*	Hon. Rupert B. C. G., *b.* 1981
1824	*Gifford (6th)*, Anthony Maurice Gifford, *b.* 1940, *s.* 1961, *m.*	Hon. Thomas A. G., *b.* 1967
1917	*Gisborough (3rd)*, Thomas Richard John Long Chaloner, *b.* 1927, *s.* 1951, *m.*	Hon. T. Peregrine L. C., *b.* 1961
1960	*Gladwyn (2nd)*, Miles Alvery Gladwyn Jebb, *b.* 1930, *s.* 1996	None
1899	*Glanusk (5th)*, Christopher Russell Bailey, *b.* 1942, *s.* 1997, *m.*	Hon. Charles H. B., *b.* 1976
1918	** *Glenarthur (4th)*, Simon Mark Arthur, *b.* 1944, *s.* 1976, *m.*	Hon. Edward A. A., *b.* 1973
1911	*Glenconner (4th)*, Cody Charles Edward Tennant, *b.* 1994, *s.* 2010	Hon. Christopher C. T., *b.* 1967
1964	*Glendevon (3rd)*, Jonathan Charles Hope, *b.* 1952, *s.* 2009	None
1922	*Glendyne (4th)*, John Nivison, *b.* 1960, *s.* 2008	None
1939	** *Glentoran (3rd)*, (Thomas) Robin (Valerian) Dixon, CBE, *b.* 1935, *s.* 1995, *m.*	Hon. Daniel G. D., *b.* 1959
1909	*Gorell (5th)*, John Picton Gorell Barnes, *b.* 1959, *s.* 2007, *m.*	Hon. Oliver G. B., *b.* 1993
1953	** *Grantchester (3rd)*, Christopher John Suenson-Taylor, *b.* 1951, *s.* 1995, *m.*	Hon. Jesse D. S.-T., *b.* 1977
1782	*Grantley (8th)*, Richard William Brinsley Norton, *b.* 1956, *s.* 1995	Hon. Francis J. H. N., *b.* 1960
1794 I.	*Graves (10th)*, Timothy Evelyn Graves, *b.* 1960, *s.* 2002	None
1445 S.	*Gray (23rd)*, Andrew Godfrey Diarmid Stuart Campbell-Gray, *b.* 1964, *s.* 2003, *m.*	Master of Gray, *b.* 1996
1950	*Greenhill (3rd)*, Malcolm Greenhill, *b.* 1924, *s.* 1989	None
1927	** *Greenway (4th)*, Ambrose Charles Drexel Greenway, *b.* 1941, *s.* 1975, *m.*	Hon. Nigel. P. G., *b.* 1944
1902	*Grenfell (3rd) and Grenfell of Kilvey (life peerage, 2000)*, Julian Pascoe Francis St Leger Grenfell, *b.* 1935, *s.* 1976, *m.*	Francis P. J. G., *b.* 1938
1944	*Gretton (4th)*, John Lysander Gretton, *b.* 1975, *s.* 1989	Hon. John F. B. G., *b.* 2008
1397	*Grey of Codnor (6th)*, Richard Henry Cornwall-Legh, *b.* 1936, *s.* 1996, *m.*	Hon. Richard S. C. C.-L., *b.* 1976
1955	*Gridley (3rd)*, Richard David Arnold Gridley, *b.* 1956, *s.* 1996, *m.*	Peter A. C. G., *b.* 1940
1964	*Grimston of Westbury (3rd)*, Robert John Sylvester Grimston, *b.* 1951, *s.* 2003, *m.*	Hon. Gerald C. W. G., *b.* 1953
1886	*Grimthorpe (5th)*, Edward John Beckett, *b.* 1954, *s.* 2003, *m.*	Hon. Harry M. B., *b.* 1993
1945	*Hacking (3rd)*, Douglas David Hacking, *b.* 1938, *s.* 1971, *m.*	Hon. Douglas F. H., *b.* 1968
1950	*Haden-Guest (5th)*, Christopher Haden-Guest, *b.* 1948, *s.* 1996, *m.*	Hon. Nicholas H.-G., *b.* 1951

1886   *Hamilton of Dalzell (5th)*, Gavin Goulburn Hamilton, *b.* 1968, *s.* 2006, *m.*   Hon. Francis A. J. G. H., *b.* 2009

1874   *Hampton (7th)*, John Humphrey Arnott Pakington, *b.* 1964, *s.* 2003, *m.*   Hon. Charles R. C. P., *b.* 2005

1939   *Hankey (3rd)*, Donald Robin Alers Hankey, *b.* 1938, *s.* 1996, *m.*   Hon. Alexander M. A. H., *b.* 1947

1958   *Harding of Petherton (2nd)*, John Charles Harding, *b.* 1928, *s.* 1989, *m.*   Hon. William A. J. H., *b.* 1969

1910   *Hardinge of Penshurst (4th)*, Julian Alexander Hardinge, *b.* 1945, *s.* 1997   Hon. Hugh F. H., *b.* 1948

1876   *Harlech (6th)*, Francis David Ormsby-Gore, *b.* 1954, *s.* 1985, *m.*   Hon. Jasset D. C. O.-G., *b.* 1986

1939   *Harmsworth (3rd)*, Thomas Harold Raymond Harmsworth, *b.* 1939, *s.* 1990, *m.*   Hon. Dominic M. E. H., *b.* 1973

1815   *Harris (8th)*, Anthony Harris, *b.* 1942, *s.* 1996, *m.*   Rear-Adm. Michael G. T. H., *b.* 1941

1954   *Harvey of Tasburgh (3rd)*, Charles John Giuseppe Harvey, *b.* 1951, *s.* 2010, *m.*   Hon. John H., *b.* 1993

1295   *Hastings (23rd)*, Delaval Thomas Harold Astley, *b.* 1960, *s.* 2007, *m.*   Hon. Jacob A. A., *b.* 1991

1835   *Hatherton (8th)*, Edward Charles Littleton, *b.* 1950, *s.* 1985, *m.*   Hon. Thomas E. L., *b.* 1977

1776   *Hawke (12th)*, William Martin Theodore Hawke, *b.* 1995, *s.* 2010   None

1927   *Hayter (4th)*, George William Michael Chubb, *b.* 1943, *s.* 2003, *m.*   Hon. Thomas F. F. C., *b.*1986

1945   *Hazlerigg (3rd)*, Arthur Grey Hazlerigg, *b.* 1951, *s.* 2002, *m.*   Hon. Arthur W. G. H. *b.* 1987

1943   *Hemingford (3rd)*, (Dennis) Nicholas Herbert, *b.* 1934, *s.* 1982, *m.*   Hon. Christopher D. C. H., *b.* 1973

1906   *Hemphill (5th)*, Peter Patrick Fitzroy Martyn Martyn-Hemphill, *b.* 1928, *s.* 1957, *m.*   Hon. Charles A. M. M.-H., *b.* 1954

1799 I.   ** *Henley (8th) and Northington (6th) (1885)*, Oliver Michael Robert Eden, *b.* 1953, *s.* 1977, *m.*   Hon. John W. O. E., *b.* 1988

1800 I.   *Henniker (9th) and Hartismere (6th) (1866)*, Mark Ian Philip Chandos Henniker-Major, *b.* 1947, *s.* 2004, *m.*   Hon. Edward G. M. H.-M., *b.* 1985

1461   *Herbert (19th)*, David John Seyfried Herbert, *b.* 1952, *s.* 2002, *m.*   Hon. Oliver R. S. H., *b.* 1976

1935   *Hesketh (3rd)*, Thomas Alexander Fermor-Hesketh, KBE, PC, *b.* 1950, *s.* 1955, *m.*   Hon. Frederick H. F.-H., *b.* 1988

1828   *Heytesbury (7th)*, James William Holmes à Court, *b.* 1967, *s.* 2004, *m.*   Peter M. H.. H. à. C., *b.* 1968

1886   *Hindlip (6th)*, Charles Henry Allsopp, *b.* 1940, *s.* 1993, *m.*   Hon. Henry W. A., *b.* 1973

1950   *Hives (3rd)*, Matthew Peter Hives, *b.* 1971, *s.* 1997   Hon. Michael B. H., *b.* 1926

1912   *Hollenden (4th)*, Ian Hampden Hope-Morley, *b.* 1946, *s.* 1999, *m.*   Hon. Edward H.-M., *b.* 1981

1897   *Holm Patrick (4th)*, Hans James David Hamilton, *b.* 1955, *s.* 1991, *m.*   Hon. Ion H. J. H., *b.* 1956

1797 I.   *Hotham (8th)*, Henry Durand Hotham, *b.* 1940, *s.* 1967, *m.*   Hon. William B. H., *b.* 1972

1881   *Hothfield (6th)*, Anthony Charles Sackville Tufton, *b.* 1939, *s.* 1991, *m.*   Hon. William S. T., *b.* 1977

1930   *Howard of Penrith (3rd)*, Philip Esme Howard, *b.* 1945, *s.* 1999, *m.*   Hon. Thomas Philip H., *b.* 1974

1960   *Howick of Glendale (2nd)*, Charles Evelyn Baring, *b.* 1937, *s.* 1973, *m.*   Hon. David E. C. B., *b.* 1975

1796 I.   *Huntingfield (7th)*, Joshua Charles Vanneck, *b.* 1954, *s.* 1994, *m.*   Hon. Gerard C. A. V., *b.* 1985

1866   ** *Hylton (5th)*, Raymond Hervey Jolliffe, *b.* 1932, *s.* 1967, *m.*   Hon. William H. M. J., *b.* 1967

1933   *Iliffe (3rd)*, Robert Peter Richard Iliffe, *b.* 1944, *s.* 1996, *m.*   Hon. Edward R. I., *b.* 1968

1543 I.   *Inchiquin (18th)*, Conor Myles John O'Brien, *b.* 1943, *s.* 1982, *m.*   Conor J. A. O'B., *b.* 1952

1962   *Inchyra (3rd)*, Christian James Charles Hoyer Millar, *b.* 1962, *s.* 2011, *m.*   Hon. Jake C. R. M., *b.* 1996

1964   ** *Inglewood (2nd)*, (William) Richard Fletcher-Vane, *b.* 1951, *s.* 1989, *m.*   Hon. Henry W. F. F.-V., *b.* 1990

1919   *Inverforth (4th)*, Andrew Peter Weir, *b.* 1966, *s.* 1982   Hon. Benjamin A. W., *b.* 1997

1941   *Ironside (2nd)*, Edmund Oslac Ironside, *b.* 1924, *s.* 1959, *m.*   Hon. Charles E. G. I., *b.* 1956

1952   *Jeffreys (3rd)*, Christopher Henry Mark Jeffreys, *b.* 1957, *s.* 1986, *m.*   Hon. Arthur M. H. J., *b.* 1989

1906   *Joicey (5th)*, James Michael Joicey, *b.* 1953, *s.* 1993, *m.*   Hon. William J. J., *b.* 1990

1937   *Kenilworth (4th)*, (John) Randle Siddeley, *b.* 1954, *s.* 1981, *m.*   Hon. William R. J. S., *b.* 1992

1935   *Kennet (3rd)*, William Aldus Thoby Young, *b.* 1957, *s.* 2009, *m.*   Hon. Archibald W. K. Y., *b.* 1992

1776 I.   *Kensington (8th) and Kensington (5th) (1886)*, Hugh Ivor Edwardes, *b.* 1933, *s.* 1981, *m.*   Hon. W. Owen A. E., *b.* 1964

1951   *Kenswood (2nd)*, John Michael Howard Whitfield, *b.* 1930, *s.* 1963, *m.*   Hon. Michael C. W., *b.* 1955

1788   *Kenyon (6th)*, Lloyd Tyrell-Kenyon, *b.* 1947, *s.* 1993, *m.*   Hon. Lloyd N. T.-K., *b.* 1972

1947   *Kershaw (4th)*, Edward John Kershaw, *b.* 1936, *s.* 1962, *m.*   Hon. John C. E. K., *b.* 1971

1943   *Keyes (3rd)*, Charles William Packe Keyes, *b.* 1951, *s.* 2005, *m.*   Hon. (Leopold R.) J. K., *b.* 1956

1909   *Kilbracken (4th)*, Christopher John Godley, *b.* 1945, *s.* 2006, *m.*   Hon. James J. G., *b.* 1972

1900   *Killanin (4th)*, (George) Redmond Fitzpatrick Morris, *b.* 1947, *s.* 1999, *m.*   Hon. Luke M. G. M., *b.* 1975

1943   *Killearn (3rd)*, Victor Miles George Aldous Lampson, *b.* 1941, *s.* 1996, *m.*   Hon. Miles H. M. L., *b.* 1977

1789 I.	*Kilmaine (7th)*, John David Henry Browne, *b.* 1948, *s.* 1978, *m.*	Hon. John F. S. B., *b.* 1983
1831	*Kilmarnock (8th)*, Dr Robin Jordan Boyd, *b.* 1941, *s.* 2009, *m.*	Hon. Simon J. B., *b.* 1978
1941	*Kindersley (3rd)*, Robert Hugh Molesworth Kindersley, *b.* 1929, *s.* 1976, *m.*	Hon. Rupert J. M. K., *b.* 1955
1223 I.	*Kingsale (36th)*, Nevinson Mark de Courcy, *b.* 1958, *s.* 2005, *m.*, *Premier Baron of Ireland*	Joseph K. C. de C., *b.* 1955
1902	*Kinross (5th)*, Christopher Patrick Balfour, *b.* 1949, *s.* 1985, *m.*	Hon. Alan I. B., *b.* 1978
1951	*Kirkwood (3rd)*, David Harvie Kirkwood, PHD, *b.* 1931, *s.* 1970, *m.*	Hon. James S. K., *b.* 1937
1800 I.	*Langford (9th)*, Col. Geoffrey Alexander Rowley-Conwy, OBE, *b.* 1912, *s.* 1953, *m.*	Hon. Owain G. R.-C., *b.* 1958
1942	*Latham (2nd)*, Dominic Charles Latham, *b.* 1954, *s.* 1970	Anthony M. L., *b.* 1954
1431	*Latymer (9th)*, Crispin James Alan Nevill Money-Coutts, *b.* 1955, *s.* 2003, *m.*	Hon. Drummond W. T. M.-C., *b.* 1986
1869	*Lawrence (5th)*, David John Downer Lawrence, *b.* 1937, *s.* 1968	None
1947	*Layton (3rd)*, Geoffrey Michael Layton, *b.* 1947, *s.* 1989, *m.*	Jonathan F., *b.* 1942
1839	*Leigh (6th)*, Christopher Dudley Piers Leigh, *b.* 1960, *s.* 2003, *m.*	Hon. Rupert D. L., *b.* 1994
1962	*Leighton of St Mellons (3rd)*, Robert William Henry Leighton Seager, *b.* 1955, *s.* 1998	Hon. Simon J. L. S., *b.* 1957
1797	*Lilford (8th)*, Mark Vernon Powys, *b.* 1975, *s.* 2005	Robert C. L. P., *b.* 1930
1945	*Lindsay of Birker (3rd)*, James Francis Lindsay, *b.* 1945, *s.* 1994, *m.*	Alexander S. L., *b.* 1940
1758 I.	*Lisle (9th)*, (John) Nicholas Geoffrey Lysaght, *b.* 1960, *s.* 2003	Hon. David J. L., *b.* 1963
1850	*Londesborough (9th)*, Richard John Denison, *b.* 1959, *s.* 1968, *m.*	Hon. James F. D., *b.* 1990
1541 I.	*Louth (16th)*, Otway Michael James Oliver Plunkett, *b.* 1929, *s.* 1950, *m.*	Hon. Jonathan O. P., *b.* 1952
1458 S.	*Lovat (16th) and Lovat (5th) (1837)*, Simon Fraser, *b.* 1977, *s.* 1995	Hon. Jack F., *b.* 1984
1946	*Lucas of Chilworth (3rd)*, Simon William Lucas, *b.* 1957, *s.* 2001, *m.*	Hon. John R. M. L., *b.* 1995
1663	** *Lucas (11th) and Dingwall (14th) (S. 1609)*, Ralph Matthew Palmer, *b.* 1951, *s.* 1991	Hon. Lewis E. P., *b.* 1987
1929	** *Luke (3rd)*, Arthur Charles St John Lawson-Johnston, *b.* 1933, *s.* 1996, *m.*	Hon. Ian J. St J. L.-J., *b.* 1963
1914	** *Lyell (3rd)*, Charles Lyell, *b.* 1939, *s.* 1943	None
1859	*Lyveden (7th)*, Jack Leslie Vernon, *b.* 1938, *s.* 1999, *m.*	Hon. Colin R. V., *b.* 1967
1959	*MacAndrew (3rd)*, Christopher Anthony Colin MacAndrew, *b.* 1945, *s.* 1989, *m.*	Hon. Oliver C. J. M., *b.* 1983
1776 I.	*Macdonald (8th)*, Godfrey James Macdonald of Macdonald, *b.* 1947, *s.* 1970, *m.*	Hon. Godfrey E. H. T. M., *b.* 1982
1937	*McGowan (4th)*, Harry John Charles McGowan, *b.* 1971, *s.* 2003, *m.*	Hon. Dominic J. W. McG., *b.* 1951
1922	*Maclay (3rd)*, Joseph Paton Maclay, *b.* 1942, *s.* 1969, *m.*	Hon. Joseph P. M., *b.* 1977
1955	*McNair (3rd)*, Duncan James McNair, *b.* 1947, *s.* 1989, *m.*	Hon. William S. A. M., *b.* 1958
1951	*Macpherson of Drumochter (3rd)*, James Anthony Macpherson, *b.* 1978, *s.* 2008	None
1937	** *Mancroft (3rd)*, Benjamin Lloyd Stormont Mancroft, *b.* 1957, *s.* 1987, *m.*	Hon. Arthur L. S. M., *b.* 1995
1807	*Manners (6th)*, John Hugh Robert Manners, *b.* 1956, *s.* 2008	Hon. Richard N. M., *b.* 1924
1922	*Manton (4th)*, Miles Ronald Marcus Watson, *b.* 1958, *s.* 2003, *m.*	Hon. Thomas N. C. D. W., *b.* 1985
1908	*Marchamley (4th)*, William Francis Whiteley, *b.* 1968, *s.* 1994	None
1964	*Margadale (3rd)*, Alastair John Morrison, *b.* 1958, *s.* 2003, *m.*	Hon. Declan J. M., *b.* 1993
1961	*Marks of Broughton (3rd)*, Simon Richard Marks, *b.* 1950, *s.* 1998, *m.*	Hon. Michael M., *b.* 1989
1964	*Martonmere (2nd)*, John Stephen Robinson, *b.* 1963, *s.* 1989	Hon. James I. R., *b.* 2003
1776 I.	*Massy (10th)*, David Hamon Somerset Massy, *b.* 1947, *s.* 1995	Hon. John H. M., *b.* 1950
1935	*May (4th)*, Jasper Bertram St John May, *b.* 1965, *s.* 2006	None
1928	*Melchett (4th)*, Peter Robert Henry Mond, *b.* 1948, *s.* 1973	None
1925	*Merrivale (4th)*, Derek John Philip Duke, *b.* 1948, *s.* 2007, *m.*	Hon. Thomas D., *b.* 1980
1911	*Merthyr*, Trevor Oswin Lewis, CBE, *b.* 1935, *s.* 1977, *m.* Disclaimed for life 1977	David T. L., *b.* 1977
1919	*Meston (3rd)*, James Meston, *b.* 1950, *s.* 1984, *m.*	Hon. Thomas J. D. M., *b.* 1977
1838	** *Methuen (7th)*, Robert Alexander Holt Methuen, *b.* 1931, *s.* 1994, *m.*	James P. A. M.-C., *b.* 1952
1711	*Middleton (12th)*, (Digby) Michael Godfrey John Willoughby, MC, *b.* 1921, *s.* 1970	Hon. Michael C. J. W., *b.* 1948
1939	*Milford (4th)*, Guy Wogan Philipps, *b.* 1961, *s.* 1999, *m.*	Hon. Archie S. P., *b.* 1997
1933	*Milne (3rd)*, George Alexander Milne, *b.* 1941, *s.* 2005	Hon. Iain C. L. M., *b.* 1949
1951	*Milner of Leeds (3rd)*, Richard James Milner, *b.* 1959, *s.* 2003, *m.*	None
1947	*Milverton (2nd)*, Revd Fraser Arthur Richard Richards, *b.* 1930, *s.* 1978, *m.*	Hon. Michael H. R., *b.* 1936
1873	*Moncreiff (6th)*, Rhoderick Harry Wellwood Moncreiff, *b.* 1954, *s.* 2002, *m.*	Hon. Harry J. W. M., *b.* 1986

1884	*Monk Bretton (3rd)*, John Charles Dodson, *b.* 1924, *s.* 1933, *m.*	Hon. Christopher M. D., *b.* 1958
1885	*Monkswell (5th)*, Gerard Collier, *b.* 1947, *s.* 1984, *m.*	Hon. James A. C., *b.* 1977
1728	*Monson (12th)*, Nicholas John Monson, *b.* 1955, *s.* 2011, *m.*	Hon. Alexander J. R. M., *b.* 1984
1885	** *Montagu of Beaulieu (3rd)*, Edward John Barrington Douglas-Scott-Montagu, *b.* 1926, *s.* 1929, *m.*	Hon. Ralph D.-S.-M., *b.* 1961
1839	*Monteagle of Brandon (6th)*, Gerald Spring Rice, *b.* 1926, *s.* 1946, *m.*	Hon. Charles J. S. R., *b.* 1953
1943	** *Moran (2nd)*, (Richard) John (McMoran) Wilson, KCMG, *b.* 1924, *s.* 1977, *m.*	Hon. James M. W., *b.* 1952
1918	*Morris (4th)*, Thomas Anthony Salmon Morris, *b.* 1982, *s.* 2011	Hon. John M. M., *b.* 1983
1950	*Morris of Kenwood (3rd)*, Jonathan David Morris, *b.* 1968, *s.* 2004, *m.*	Hon. Benjamin J. M., *b.* 1998
1831	*Mostyn (7th)*, Gregory Philip Roger Lloyd-Mostyn, *b.* 1984, *s.* 2011	Roger Hugh L.-M., *b.* 1941
1933	*Mottistone (4th)*, David Peter Seely, CBE, *b.* 1920, *s.* 1966, *w.*	Hon. Peter J. P. S., *b.* 1949
1945	*Mountevans (3rd)*, Edward Patrick Broke Evans, *b.* 1943, *s.* 1974, *m.*	Hon. Jeffrey de C. R. E., *b.* 1948
1283	*Mowbray (27th), Segrave (28th) (1295) and Stourton (24th) (1448)*, Edward William Stephen Stourton, *b.* 1953, *s.* 2006, *m.*	Hon. James C. P. S., *b.* 1991
1932	*Moyne (3rd)*, Jonathan Bryan Guinness, *b.* 1930, *s.* 1992, *m.*	Hon. Valentine G. B. G., *b.* 1959
1929	** *Moynihan (4th)*, Colin Berkeley Moynihan, *b.* 1955, *s.* 1997, *m.*	Hon. Nicholas E. B. M., *b.* 1994
1781 I.	*Muskerry (9th)*, Robert Fitzmaurice Deane, *b.* 1948, *s.* 1988, *m.*	Hon. Jonathan F. D., *b.* 1986
1627 S.	*Napier (14th) and Ettrick (5th) (1872)*, Francis Nigel Napier, KCVO, *b.* 1930, *s.* 1954, *m.*	Master of Napier, *b.* 1962
1868	*Napier of Magdala (6th)*, Robert Alan Napier, *b.* 1940, *s.* 1987, *m.*	Hon. James R. N., *b.* 1966
1940	*Nathan (3rd)*, Rupert Harry Bernard Nathan, *b.* 1957, *s.* 2007, *m.*	None
1960	*Nelson of Stafford (4th)*, Alistair William Henry Nelson, *b.* 1973, *s.* 2006	Hon. James J. N., *b.* 1947
1959	*Netherthorpe (3rd)*, James Frederick Turner, *b.* 1964, *s.* 1982, *m.*	Hon. Andrew J. E. T., *b.* 1993
1946	*Newall (2nd)*, Francis Storer Eaton Newall, *b.* 1930, *s.* 1963, *m.*	Hon. Richard H. E. N., *b.* 1961
1776 I.	*Newborough (8th)*, Robert Vaughan Wynn, *b.* 1949, *s.* 1998, *m.*	Antony C. V. W., *b.* 1949
1892	*Newton (5th)*, Richard Thomas Legh, *b.* 1950, *s.* 1992, *m.*	Hon. Piers R. L., *b.* 1979
1930	*Noel-Buxton (3rd)*, Martin Connal Noel-Buxton, *b.* 1940, *s.* 1980, *m.*	Hon. Charles C. N.-B., *b.* 1975
1957	*Norrie (2nd)*, (George) Willoughby Moke Norrie, *b.* 1936, *s.* 1977, *m.*	Hon. Mark W. J. N., *b.* 1972
1884	** *Northbourne (5th)*, Christopher George Walter James, *b.* 1926, *s.* 1982, *m.*	Hon. Charles W. H. J., *b.* 1960
1866	** *Northbrook (6th)*, Francis Thomas Baring, *b.* 1954, *s.* 1990, *m.*	To the Baronetcy, Peter B. *b.* 1939
1878	*Norton (8th)*, James Nigel Arden Adderley, *b.* 1947, *s.* 1993, *m.*	Hon. Edward J. A. A., *b.* 1982
1906	*Nunburnholme (6th)*, Stephen Charles Wilson, *b.* 1973, *s.* 2000	Hon. David M. W., *b.* 1954
1950	*Ogmore (3rd)*, Morgan Rees-Williams, *b.* 1937, *s.* 2004, *m.*	Hon. Tudor D. R.-W., *b.* 1991
1870	*O'Hagan (4th)*, Charles Towneley Strachey, *b.* 1945, *s.* 1961	Hon. Richard T. S., *b.* 1950
1868	*O'Neill (4th)*, Raymond Arthur Clanaboy O'Neill, KCVO, TD, *b.* 1933, *s.* 1944, *m.*	Hon. Shane S. C. O'N., *b.* 1965
1836 I.	*Oranmore and Browne (5th) and Mereworth (3rd) (1926)*, Dominick Geoffrey Thomas Browne, *b.* 1929, *s.* 2002	Hon. Martin M. D. B., *b.* 1931
1933	** *Palmer (4th)*, Adrian Bailie Nottage Palmer, *b.* 1951, *s.* 1990, *m.*	Hon. Hugo B. R. P., *b.* 1980
1914	*Parmoor (5th)*, Michael Leonard Seddon Cripps, *b.* 1942, *s.* 2008, *m.*	Hon. Henry W. A. C., *b.* 1976
1937	*Pender (3rd)*, John Willoughby Denison-Pender, *b.* 1933, *s.* 1965, *m.*	Hon. Henry J. R. D.-P., *b.* 1968
1866	*Penrhyn (7th)*, Simon Douglas-Pennant, *b.* 1938, *s.* 2003, *m.*	Hon. Edward S. D.-P., *b.* 1966
1603	*Petre (18th)*, John Patrick Lionel Petre, *b.* 1942, *s.* 1989, *m.*	Hon. Dominic W. P., *b.* 1966
1918	*Phillimore (5th)*, Francis Stephen Phillimore, *b.* 1944, *s.* 1994, *m.*	Hon. Tristan A. S. P., *b.* 1977
1945	*Piercy (3rd)*, James William Piercy, *b.* 1946, *s.* 1981	Hon. Mark E. P. P., *b.* 1953
1827	*Plunket (8th)*, Robin Rathmore Plunket, *b.* 1925, *s.* 1975, *m.*	Hon. Shaun A. F. S. P., *b.* 1931
1831	*Poltimore (7th)*, Mark Coplestone Bampfylde, *b.* 1957, *s.* 1978, *m.*	Hon. Henry A. W. B., *b.* 1985
1690 S.	*Polwarth (11th)*, Andrew Walter Hepburne-Scott, *b.* 1947, *s.* 2005, *m.*	Master of Polwarth, *b.* 1973
1930	*Ponsonby of Shulbrede (4th) and Ponsonby of Roehampton (life peerage, 2000)*, Frederick Matthew Thomas Ponsonby, *b.* 1958, *s.* 1990	None
1958	*Poole (2nd)*, David Charles Poole, *b.* 1945, *s.* 1993, *m.*	Hon. Oliver J. P., *b.* 1972
1852	*Raglan (6th)*, Geoffrey Somerset, *b.* 1932, *s.* 2010, *m.*	Hon. Arthur G. S., *b.* 1960
1932	*Rankeillour (5th)*, Michael Richard Hope, *b.* 1940, *s.* 2005, *m.*	James F. H., *b.* 1968
1953	*Rathcavan (3rd)*, Hugh Detmar Torrens O'Neill, *b.* 1939, *s.* 1994, *m.*	Hon. François H. N. O'N., *b.* 1968
1916	*Rathcreedan (3rd)*, Christopher John Norton, *b.* 1949, *s.* 1990, *m.*	Hon. Adam G. N., *b.* 1952
1868 I.	*Rathdonnell (5th)*, Thomas Benjamin McClintock-Bunbury, *b.* 1938, *s.* 1959, *m.*	Hon. William L. M.-B., *b.* 1966

1911	*Ravensdale (3rd)*, Nicholas Mosley, MC, *b.* 1923, *s.* 1966, *m.*	Daniel N. M., *b.* 1982
1821	*Ravensworth (9th)*, Thomas Arthur Hamish Liddell, *b.* 1954, *s.* 2004, *m.*	Hon. Henry A. T. L., *b.* 1987
1821	*Rayleigh (6th)*, John Gerald Strutt, *b.* 1960, *s.* 1988, *m.*	Hon. John F. S., *b.* 1993
1937	** *Rea (3rd)*, John Nicolas Rea, MD, *b.* 1928, *s.* 1981, *m.*	Hon. Matthew J. R., *b.* 1956
1628 S.	** *Reay (14th)*, Hugh William Mackay, *b.* 1937, *s.* 1963, *m.*	Master of Reay, *b.* 1965
1902	*Redesdale (6th) and Mitford (life peerage 2000)*, Rupert Bertram Mitford, *b.* 1967, *s.* 1991, *m.*	Hon. Bertram D. M., *b.* 2000
1940	*Reith*, Christopher John Reith, *b.* 1928, *s.* 1971, *m.* Disclaimed for life 1972.	Hon. James H. J. R., *b.* 1971
1928	*Remnant (3rd)*, James Wogan Remnant, CVO, *b.* 1930, *s.* 1967, *m.*	Hon. Philip J. R., CBE, *b.* 1954
1806 I.	*Rendlesham (9th)*, Charles William Brooke Thellusson, *b.* 1954, *s.* 1999, *m.*	Hon. Peter R. T., *b.* 1920
1933	*Rennell (4th)*, James Roderick David Tremayne Rodd, *b.* 1978, *s.* 2006	None
1964	*Renwick (2nd)*, Harry Andrew Renwick, *b.* 1935, *s.* 1973, *m.*	Hon. Robert J. R., *b.* 1966
1885	*Revelstoke (6th)*, James Cecil Baring, *b.* 1938, *s.* 2003, *m.*	Hon. Alexander R. B., *b.* 1970
1905	*Ritchie of Dundee (6th)*, Charles Rupert Rendall Ritchie, *b.* 1958, *s.* 2008, *m.*	Hon. Sebastian R., *b.* 2004
1935	*Riverdale (3rd)*, Anthony Robert Balfour, *b.* 1960, *s.* 1998	Arthur M. B., *b.* 1938
1961	*Robertson of Oakridge (3rd)*, William Brian Elworthy Robertson, *b.* 1975, *s.* 2009, *m.*	None
1938	*Roborough (3rd)*, Henry Massey Lopes, *b.* 1940, *s.* 1992, *m.*	Hon. Massey J. H. L., *b.* 1969
1931	*Rochester (2nd)*, Foster Charles Lowry Lamb, *b.* 1916, *s.* 1955, *w.*	Hon. David C. L., *b.* 1944
1934	*Rockley (3rd)*, James Hugh Cecil, *b.* 1934, *s.* 1976, *m.*	Hon. Anthony R. C., *b.* 1961
1782	*Rodney (11th)*, John George Brydges Rodney, *b.* 1999, *s.* 2011	Nicholas S. H. R., *b.* 1947
1651 S.	*Rollo (14th) and Dunning (5th) (1869)*, David Eric Howard Rollo, *b.* 1943, *s.* 1997, *m.*	Master of Rollo, *b.* 1972
1959	*Rootes (3rd)*, Nicholas Geoffrey Rootes, *b.* 1951, *s.* 1992, *m.*	William B. R., *b.* 1944
1796 I.	*Rossmore (7th) and Rossmore (6th) (1838)*, William Warner Westenra, *b.* 1931, *s.* 1958, *m.*	Hon. Benedict W. W., *b.* 1983
1939	** *Rotherwick (3rd)*, (Herbert) Robin Cayzer, *b.* 1954, *s.* 1996, *m.*	Hon. H. Robin C., *b.* 1989
1885	*Rothschild (4th)*, (Nathaniel Charles) Jacob Rothschild, OM, GBE, *b.* 1936, *s.* 1990, *m.*	Hon. Nathaniel P. V. J. R., *b.* 1971
1911	*Rowallan (4th)*, John Polson Cameron Corbett, *b.* 1947, *s.* 1993	Hon. Jason W. P. C. C., *b.* 1972
1947	*Rugby (3rd)*, Robert Charles Maffey, *b.* 1951, *s.* 1990, *m.*	Hon. Timothy J. H. M., *b.* 1975
1919	*Russell of Liverpool (3rd)*, Simon Gordon Jared Russell, *b.* 1952, *s.* 1981, *m.*	Hon. Edward C. S. R., *b.* 1985
1876	*Sackville (7th)*, Robert Bertrand Sackville-West, *b.* 1958, *s.* 2004, *m.*	Hon. Arthur S-W., *b.* 2000
1964	*St Helens (2nd)*, Richard Francis Hughes-Young, *b.* 1945, *s.* 1980, *m.*	Hon. Henry T. H.-Y., *b.* 1986
1559	** *St John of Bletso (21st)*, Anthony Tudor St John, *b.* 1957, *s.* 1978, *m.*	Hon. Oliver B. St J., *b.* 1995
1887	*St Levan (4th)*, John Francis Arthur St Aubyn, DSC, *b.* 1919, *s.* 1978, *w.*	James P. S. St. A., *b.* 1950
1885	*St Oswald (6th)*, Charles Rowland Andrew Winn, *b.* 1959, *s.* 1999, *m.*	Hon. Rowland C. S. H. W., *b.* 1986
1960	*Sanderson of Ayot (2nd)*, Alan Lindsay Sanderson, *b.* 1931, *s.* 1971, *m.* Disclaimed for life 1971.	Hon. Michael S., *b.* 1959
1945	*Sandford (3rd)*, James John Mowbray Edmondson, *b.* 1949, *s.* 2009, *m.*	Hon. Devon J. E., *b.* 1986
1871	*Sandhurst (6th)*, Guy Rees John Mansfield, *b.* 1949, *s.* 2002, *m.*	Hon. Edward J. M., *b.* 1982
1802	*Sandys (7th)*, Richard Michael Oliver Hill, *b.* 1931, *s.* 1961, *m.*	The Marquess of Downshire
1888	*Savile (4th)*, John Anthony Thornhill Lumley-Savile, *b.* 1947, *s.* 2008, *m.*	Hon. James G. A. L-S., *b.* 1975
1447	*Saye and Sele (21st)*, Nathaniel Thomas Allen Fiennes, *b.* 1920, *s.* 1968, *m.*	Hon. Martin G. F., *b.* 1961
1826	*Seaford (6th)*, Colin Humphrey Felton Ellis, *b.* 1946, *s.* 1999, *m.*	Hon. Benjamin F. T. E., *b.* 1976
1932	** *Selsdon (3rd)*, Malcolm McEacharn Mitchell-Thomson, *b.* 1937, *s.* 1963, *m.*	Hon. Callum M. M. M.-T., *b.* 1969
1489 S.	*Sempill (21st)*, James William Stuart Whitemore Sempill, *b.* 1949, *s.* 1995, *m.*	Master of Sempill, *b.* 1979
1916	*Shaughnessy (5th)*, Charles George Patrick Shaughnessy, *b.* 1955, *s.* 2007, *m.*	David J. S., *b.* 1957
1946	*Shepherd (3rd)*, Graham George Shepherd, *b.* 1949, *s.* 2001, *m.*	Hon. Patrick M. S., *b.* 19–
1964	*Sherfield (3rd)*, Dwight William Makins, *b.* 1951, *s.* 2006, *m.*	None
1902	*Shuttleworth (5th)*, Charles Geoffrey Nicholas Kay-Shuttleworth, KCVO, *b.* 1948, *s.* 1975, *m.*	Hon. Thomas E. K.-S., *b.* 1976
1950	*Silkin (3rd)*, Christopher Lewis Silkin, *b.* 1947, *s.* 2001. Disclaimed for life 2002.	Rory L. S., *b.* 1954
1963	*Silsoe (3rd)*, Simon Rupert Trustram Eve *b.* 1966, *s.* 2005	Hon. Peter N. T. E., *b.* 1930
1947	*Simon of Wythenshawe (3rd)*, Matthew Simon, *b.* 1955, *s.* 2002	Martin S., *b.* 1944

1449 S.	*Sinclair (18th)*, Matthew Murray Kennedy St Clair *b.* 1968, *s.* 2004, *m.*	Master of Sinclair, *b.* 2007
1957	*Sinclair of Cleeve (3rd)*, John Lawrence Robert Sinclair, *b.* 1953, *s.* 1985	None
1919	*Sinha (6th)*, Arup Kumar Sinha, *b.* 1966, *s.* 1999	Hon. Dilip K. S., *b.* 1967
1828	** *Skelmersdale (7th)*, Roger Bootle-Wilbraham, *b.* 1945, *s.* 1973, *m.*	Hon. Andrew B.-W., *b.* 1977
1916	*Somerleyton (3rd)*, Savile William Francis Crossley, GCVO, *b.* 1928, *s.* 1959, *m.*	Hon. Hugh F. S. C., *b.* 1971
1784	*Somers (9th)*, Philip Sebastian Somers Cocks, *b.* 1948, *s.* 1995	Alan B. C., *b.* 1930
1780	*Southampton (6th)*, Charles James FitzRoy, *b.* 1928, *s.* 1989, *m.*	Hon. Edward C. F., *b.* 1955
1959	*Spens (4th)*, Patrick Nathaniel George Spens, *b.* 1968, *s.* 2001, *m.*	Hon. Peter L. S., *b.* 2000
1640	*Stafford (15th)*, Francis Melfort William Fitzherbert, *b.* 1954, *s.* 1986, *m.*	Hon. Benjamin J. B. F., *b.* 1983
1938	*Stamp (4th)*, Trevor Charles Bosworth Stamp, MD, *b.* 1935, *s.* 1987, *m.*	Hon. Nicholas C. T. S., *b.* 1978
1839	*Stanley of Alderley (8th)*, *Sheffield (8th) (I. 1738)* and *Eddisbury (7th) (1848)*, Thomas Henry Oliver Stanley, *b.* 1927, *s.* 1971, *m.*	Hon. Richard O. S., *b.* 1956
1318	*Strabolgi (12th)*, Andrew David Whitley Kenworthy, *b.* 1967, *s.* 2010, *m.*	Hon. Joel B. K., *b.* 2004
1954	*Strang (2nd)*, Colin Strang, *b.* 1922, *s.* 1978, *m.*	None
1628	*Strange (17th)*, Adam Humphrey Drummond of Megginch, *b.* 1953, *s.* 2005 *m.*	Hon. John A. H. D. of M. *b.* 1992
1955	*Strathalmond (3rd)*, William Roberton Fraser, *b.* 1947, *s.* 1976, *m.*	Hon. William G. F., *b.* 1976
1936	*Strathcarron (3rd)*, Ian David Patrick Macpherson, *b.* 1949, *s.* 2006, *m.*	Hon. Rory D. A. M., *b.* 1982
1955	** *Strathclyde (2nd)*, Thomas Galloway Dunlop du Roy de Blicquy Galbraith, PC, *b.* 1960, *s.* 1985, *m.*	Hon. Charles W. du R. de B. G., *b.* 1962
1900	*Strathcona and Mount Royal (4th)*, Donald Euan Palmer Howard, *b.* 1923, *s.* 1959, *m.*	Hon. D. Alexander S. H., *b.* 1961
1836	*Stratheden (6th) and Campbell (6th) (1841)*, Donald Campbell, *b.* 1934, *s.* 1987, *m.*	Hon. David A. C., *b.* 1963
1884	*Strathspey (6th)*, James Patrick Trevor Grant of Grant, *b.* 1943, *s.* 1992, *m.*	Hon. Michael P. F. G., *b.* 1953
1838	*Sudeley (7th)*, Merlin Charles Sainthill Hanbury-Tracy, *b.* 1939, *s.* 1941	D. Andrew J. H.-T., *b.* 1928
1786	*Suffield (11th)*, Anthony Philip Harbord-Hamond, MC, *b.* 1922, *s.* 1951, *w.*	Hon. Charles A. A. H.-H., *b.* 1953
1893	*Swansea (5th)*, Richard Anthony Hussey Vivian, *b.* 1957, *s.* 2005, *m.*	Hon. James H. H. V., *b.* 1999
1907	*Swaythling (5th)*, Charles Edgar Samuel Montagu, *b.* 1954, *s.* 1998, *m.*	Hon. Anthony T. S. M., *b.* 1931
1919	** *Swinfen (3rd)*, Roger Mynors Swinfen Eady, *b.* 1938, *s.* 1977, *m.*	Hon. Charles R. P. S. E., *b.* 1971
1831 I.	*Talbot of Malahide (10th)*, Reginald John Richard Arundell, *b.* 1931, *s.* 1987, *m.*	Hon. Richard J. T. A., *b.* 1957
1946	*Tedder (3rd)*, Robin John Tedder, *b.* 1955, *s.* 1994, *m.*	Hon. Benjamin J. T., *b.* 1985
1884	*Tennyson (6th)*, David Harold Alexander Tennyson, *b.* 1960, *s.* 2006	Alan J. D. T., *b.* 1965
1918	*Terrington (6th)*, Christopher Richard James Woodhouse, MB, *b.* 1946, *s.* 2001, *m.*	Hon. Jack H. L. W., *b.* 1978
1940	*Teviot (2nd)*, Charles John Kerr, *b.* 1934, *s.* 1968, *m.*	Hon. Charles R. K., *b.* 1971
1616	*Teynham (20th)*, John Christopher Ingham Roper-Curzon, *b.* 1928, *s.* 1972, *m.*	Hon. David J. H. I. R.-C., *b.* 1965
1964	*Thomson of Fleet (3rd)*, David Kenneth Roy Thomson, *b.* 1957, *s.* 2006, *m.*	Hon. Benjamin T., *b.* 2006
1792	*Thurlow (8th)*, Francis Edward Hovell-Thurlow-Cumming-Bruce, KCMG, *b.* 1912, *s.* 1971, *w.*	Hon. Roualeyn R. H.-T.-C.-B., *b.* 1952
1876	*Tollemache (5th)*, Timothy John Edward Tollemache, *b.* 1939, *s.* 1975, *m.*	Hon. Edward J. H. T., *b.* 1976
1564 S.	*Torphichen (15th)*, James Andrew Douglas Sandilands, *b.* 1946, *s.* 1975, *m.*	Robert P. S., *b.* 1950
1947	** *Trefgarne (2nd)*, David Garro Trefgarne, PC, *b.* 1941, *s.* 1960, *m.*	Hon. George G. T., *b.* 1970
1921	*Trevethin (4th) and Oaksey (2nd) (1947)*, John Geoffrey Tristram Lawrence, OBE, *b.* 1929, *s.* 1971, *m.*	Hon. Patrick J. T. L., *b.* 1960
1880	*Trevor (5th)*, Marke Charles Hill-Trevor, *b.* 1970, *s.* 1997, *m.*	Hon. Iain R. H.-T., *b.* 1971
1461 I.	*Trimlestown (21st)*, Raymond Charles Barnewall, *b.* 1930, *s.* 1997	None
1940	*Tryon (3rd)*, Anthony George Merrik Tryon, *b.* 1940, *s.* 1976	Hon. Charles G. B. T., *b.* 1976
1935	*Tweedsmuir (4th)*, John William de l'Aigle (Toby) Buchan, *b.* 1950, *s.* 2008, *m.*	Hon. John A. G. B., *b.* 1986
1523	*Vaux of Harrowden (11th)*, Anthony William Gilbey, *b.* 1940, *s.* 2002, *m.*	Hon. Richard H. G. G., *b.* 1965
1800 I.	*Ventry (8th)*, Andrew Wesley Daubeny de Moleyns, *b.* 1943, *s.* 1987, *m.*	Hon. Francis W. D. de M., *b.* 1965
1762	*Vernon (11th)*, Anthony William Vernon-Harcourt, *b.* 1939, *s.* 2000, *m.*	Hon. Simon A. V.-H., *b.* 1969

1922	*Vestey (3rd)*, Samuel George Armstrong Vestey, KCVO, *b.* 1941, *s.* 1954, *m.*	Hon. William G. V., *b.* 1983
1841	*Vivian (7th)*, Charles Crespigny Hussey Vivian, *b.* 1966, *s.* 2004	Hon. Victor A. R. B. V., *b.* 1940
1934	*Wakehurst (3rd)*, (John) Christopher Loder, *b.* 1925, *s.* 1970, *m.*	Hon. Timothy W. L., *b.* 1958
1723	** *Walpole (10th) and Walpole of Wolterton (8th) (1756)*, Robert Horatio Walpole, *b.* 1938, *s.* 1989, *m.*	Hon. Jonathan R. H. W., *b.* 1967
1780	*Walsingham (9th)*, John de Grey, MC, *b.* 1925, *s.* 1965, *m.*	Hon. Robert de. G., *b.* 1969
1936	*Wardington (3rd)*, William Simon Pease, *b.* 1925, *s.* 2005, *m.*	None
1792 I.	*Waterpark (7th)*, Frederick Caryll Philip Cavendish, *b.* 1926, *s.* 1948, *m.*	Hon. Roderick A. C., *b.* 1959
1942	*Wedgwood (4th)*, Piers Anthony Weymouth Wedgwood, *b.* 1954, *s.* 1970, *m.*	Antony J. W., *b.* 1944
1861	*Westbury (6th)*, Richard Nicholas Bethell, MBE, *b.* 1950, *s.* 2001, *m.*	Hon. Alexander B., *b.* 1986
1944	*Westwood (3rd)*, (William) Gavin Westwood, *b.* 1944, *s.* 1991, *m.*	Hon. W. Fergus W., *b.* 1972
1544/5	*Wharton (12th)*, Myles Christopher David Robertson, *b.* 1964, *s.* 2000, *m.*	Hon. Christopher J. R., *b.* 1969
1935	*Wigram (2nd)*, (George) Neville (Clive) Wigram, MC, *b.* 1915, *s.* 1960, *w.*	Maj. Hon. Andrew F. C. W., *b.* 1949
1491	** *Willoughby de Broke (21st)*, Leopold David Verney, *b.* 1938, *s.* 1986, *m.*	Hon. Rupert G. V., *b.* 1966
1937	*Windlesham (4th)*, James Rupert Hennessy, *b.* 1968, *s.* 2010, *m.*	Hon. George R. J. H., *b.* 2006
1951	*Wise (2nd)*, John Clayton Wise, *b.* 1923, *s.* 1968, *m.*	Hon. Christopher J. C. W., *b.* 1949
1869	*Wolverton (8th)*, Miles John Glyn, *b.* 1966, *s.* 2011	Jonathan C. G., *b.* 1990
1928	*Wraxall (3rd)*, Eustace Hubert Beilby Gibbs, KCVO, CMG, *b.* 1929, *s.* 2001, *m.*	Hon. Anthony H. G., *b.* 1958
1915	*Wrenbury (3rd)*, Revd John Burton Buckley, *b.* 1927, *s.* 1940, *m.*	Hon. William E. B., *b.* 1966
1838	*Wrottesley (6th)*, Clifton Hugh Lancelot de Verdon Wrottesley, *b.* 1968, *s.* 1977, *m.*	Hon. Victor E. F. de V. W., *b.* 2004
1829	*Wynford (9th)*, John Philip Robert Best, *b.* 1950, *s.* 2002, *m.*	Hon. Harry R. F. B., *b.* 1987
1308	*Zouche (18th)*, James Assheton Frankland, *b.* 1943, *s.* 1965, *m.*	Hon. William T. A. F., *b.* 1984

BARONESSES/LADIES IN THEIR OWN RIGHT

Style, The Rt. Hon. the Lady _ , *or* The Rt. Hon. the Baroness _ , according to her preference. Either style may be used, except in the case of Scottish titles (indicated by S.), which are not baronies (*see* page 44) and whose holders are always addressed as Lady.
Envelope, may be addressed in same way as a Baron's wife or, if she prefers *(formal)*, The Rt. Hon. the Baroness _; *(social)*, The Baroness _. Otherwise as for a Baron's wife
Husband, Untitled
Children's style, As for children of a Baron

Created	*Title, order of succession, name, etc*	*Heir*
1664	*Arlington*, Jennifer Jane Forwood, *b.* 1939, *s.* 1999, *w.* Title called out of abeyance 1999	Hon. Patrick J. D. F., *b.* 1967
1455	*Berners (16th)*, Pamela Vivien Kirkham, *b.* 1929, *s.* 1995, *m.*	Hon. Rupert W. T. K., *b.* 1953
1529	*Braye (8th)*, Mary Penelope Aubrey-Fletcher, *b.* 1941, *s.* 1985, *m.*	Two co-heirs
1321	*Dacre (27th)*, Rachel Leila Douglas-Home, *b.* 1929, *s.* 1970, *w.*	Hon. James T. A. D.-H., *b.* 1952
1490 S.	*Herries of Terregles (14th)*, Anne Elizabeth Fitzalan-Howard, *b.* 1938, *s.* 1975, *w.*	Lady Mary Mumford, *b.* 1940
1597	*Howard de Walden (10th)*, Mary Hazel Caridwen Czernin, *b.* 1935, *s.* 2004, *m.* Title called out of abeyance 2004	Hon. Peter J. J. C. *b.* 1966
1602 S.	*Kinloss (12th)*, Beatrice Mary Grenville Freeman-Grenville, *b.* 1922, *s.* 1944, *w.*	Master of Kinloss, *b.* 1953
1445 S.	** *Saltoun (20th)*, Flora Marjory Fraser, *b.* 1930, *s.* 1979, *w.*	Hon. Katharine I. M. I. F., *b.* 1957
1313	*Willoughby de Eresby (27th)*, (Nancy) Jane Marie Heathcote-Drummond-Willoughby, *b.* 1934, *s.* 1983	Two co-heirs

LIFE PEERS

Style, The Rt. Hon. the Lord _ /The Rt. Hon. the Lady _ ,
or The Rt. Hon. the Baroness _ , according to her
preference
Envelope (formal), The Rt. Hon. Lord _/Lady_/
Baroness_; *(social),* The Lord _/Lady_/Baroness_
Letter (formal), My Lord/Lady; *(social),* Dear Lord/
Lady _. *Spoken,* Lord/Lady _
Wife's style, The Rt. Hon. the Lady _
Husband, Untitled
Children's style, 'The Hon.' before forename (F_) and
surname (S_)
Envelope, The Hon. F_ S_. *Letter,* Dear Mr/Miss/Mrs
S_. *Spoken,* Mr/Miss/Mrs S_

NEW LIFE PEERAGES

1 September 2010 to 31 August 2011:
Tariq Mahmood Ahmad; Dame Joan Dawson Bakewell,
DBE; Sir Robert George Alexander Balchin; Elizabeth
Rose Berridge; Sir Michael David Bishop, CBE; Sarah
Virginia Brinton; Raymond Edward Harry Collins;
Alistair Basil Cooke, OBE; Sir Patrick Thomas Cormack;
Gen. Sir (Francis) Richard Dannatt, GCB, CBE, MC;
Michael John Dobbs; Elizabeth Deirdre Doocey, OBE;
Robert Norman Edmiston; Sir Reginald Norman Morgan
Empey, OBE; Andrew Simon Feldman; Julian Alexander
Fellowes; Stanley Fink; Howard Emerson Flight; Rachel
Heyhoe Flint, OBE; Maurice Mark Glasman; Michael Ian
Grade; Stephen Keith Green; David Laurence Gold; Prof.
Peter John Hennessy; Prof. Sheila Clare Hollins; Qurban
Hussain; Anne Caroline Jenkin; Judith Anne Jolly;
Jonathan Andrew Kestenbaum; Oona Tamsyn King;
Susan Veronica Kramer; Margot Ruth Aline Lister, CBE;
Rajinder Paul Loomba; Sir Michael Nicholson Lord;
*Marquess of Lothian (Michael Ancram), PC, QC; David
John Maclean, PC; George Morgan Magan; Jonathan
Clive Marks, QC; Mair Eluned Morgan; Sir Gulam
Kaderbhoy Noon, MBE; Monroe Edward Palmer; Jennifer
Elizabeth Randerson; Sir Bernard Francisco Ribeiro, CBE;
Fiona Sarah Shackleton, LVO; John Kevin Sharkey;
Richard John Grenville Spring; Nicol Ross Stephen; Air
Chief Marshal Sir Graham Eric Stirrup, GCB, AFC;
Benjamin Russell Mackintosh Stoneham; Michael John
Storey; Tina Wendy Stowell, MBE; Paul Cline
Strasburger; Nicholas Edward True, CBE; Claire Tyler;
Gordon Joshua Wasserman; Patience Jane Wheatcroft;
Dafydd Wynne Wigley; Stewart Martin Wood; Bryony
Katherine Worthington

SYMBOLS
* Hereditary peer who has been granted a life peerage.
For further details, please refer to the Hereditary Peers
section. For example, life peer *Balniel* can be found
under his hereditary title *Earl of Crawford and
Balcarres*
§ Justices of the Supreme Court currently disqualified
from sitting or voting in the House of Lords until they
retire from the supreme court. For further information
see Law Courts and Offices
‡ Title not confirmed at time of going to press

CREATED UNDER THE APPELLATE JURISDICTION ACT 1876 (AS AMENDED)

BARONS
Created
2004 §*Brown of Eaton-under-Heywood,* Simon Denis
Brown, PC, *b.* 1937, *m.*
1991 *Browne-Wilkinson,* Nicolas Christopher Henry
Browne-Wilkinson, PC, *b.* 1930, *m.*
2004 *Carswell,* Robert Douglas Carswell, PC, *b.* 1934,
m.
2009 §*Collins of Mapesbury,* Lawrence Antony
Collins, PC, *b.* 1941
1986 *Goff of Chieveley,* Robert Lionel Archibald Goff,
PC, *b.* 1926, *m.*
1985 *Griffiths,* (William) Hugh Griffiths, MC, PC,
b. 1923, *m.*
1995 *Hoffmann,* Leonard Hubert Hoffmann, PC,
b. 1934, *m.*
1997 *Hutton,* (James) Brian (Edward) Hutton, PC,
b. 1931, *m.*
2009 §*Kerr of Tonaghmore,* Brian Francis Kerr, PC,
b. 1948, *m.*
1993 *Lloyd of Berwick,* Anthony John Leslie Lloyd,
PC, *b.* 1929, *m.*
2005 §*Mance,* Jonathan Hugh Mance, PC, *b.* 1943, *m.*
1998 *Millett,* Peter Julian Millett, PC, *b.* 1932, *m.*
1992 *Mustill,* Michael John Mustill, PC, *b.* 1931, *m.*
2007 *Neuberger of Abbotsbury,* David Edmond
Neuberger, PC, *b.* 1948, *m., Master of the
Rolls*
1994 *Nicholls of Birkenhead,* Donald James Nicholls,
PC, *b.* 1933, *m.*
1999 §*Phillips of Worth Matravers,* Nicholas Addison
Phillips, KG, *b.* 1938, *m.*
1997 §*Saville of Newdigate,* Mark Oliver Saville, PC,
b. 1936, *m.*
2000 *Scott of Foscote,* Richard Rashleigh Folliott Scott,
PC, *b.* 1934, *m.*
1995 *Steyn,* Johan van Zyl Steyn, PC, *b.* 1932, *m.*
1982 *Templeman,* Sydney William Templeman, MBE,
PC, *b.* 1920, *w.*
2003 §*Walker of Gestingthorpe,* Robert Walker, PC, *b.*
1938, *m.*
1992 *Woolf,* Harry Kenneth Woolf, PC, *b.* 1933, *m.*

BARONESSES
2004 §*Hale of Richmond,* Brenda Marjorie Hale, DBE,
PC, *b.* 1945, *m.*

CREATED UNDER THE LIFE PEERAGES ACT 1958

BARONS
Created
2001 *Adebowale,* Victor Olufemi Adebowale, CBE,
b. 1962
2005 *Adonis,* Andrew Adonis, PC, *b.* 1963, *m.*
2011 *Ahmad of Wimbledon,* Tariq Mahmood Ahmad,
b. 1968, *m.*

1998   Ahmed, Nazir Ahmed, b. 1957, m.
1996   Alderdice, John Thomas Alderdice, b. 1955, m.
2010   Allan of Hallam, Richard Beecroft Allan, b. 1966
1998   Alli, Waheed Alli, b. 1964
2004   Alliance, David Alliance, CBE, b. 1932
1997   Alton of Liverpool, David Patrick Paul Alton, b. 1951, m.
2005   Anderson of Swansea, Donald Anderson, PC, b. 1939, m.
1992   Archer of Sandwell, Peter Kingsley Archer, PC, QC, b. 1926, m.
1992   Archer of Weston-super-Mare, Jeffrey Howard Archer, b. 1940, m.
1988   Armstrong of Ilminster, Robert Temple Armstrong, GCB, CVO, b. 1927, m.
1999   *Armstrong-Jones, Earl of Snowdon, GCVO, b. 1930, m. (see Hereditary Peers)
2000   Ashcroft, Michael Anthony Ashcroft, KCMG,
2001   Ashdown of Norton-sub-Hamdon, Jeremy John Durham (Paddy) Ashdown, GCMG, KBE, PC, b. 1941, m.
1992   Ashley of Stoke, Jack Ashley, CH, PC, b. 1922, w.
1993   Attenborough, Richard Samuel Attenborough, CBE, b. 1923, m.
1998   Bach, William Stephen Goulden Bach, b. 1946, m.
1997   Bagri, Raj Kumar Bagri, CBE, b. 1930, m.
1997   Baker of Dorking, Kenneth Wilfred Baker, CH, PC, b. 1934, m.
2004   Ballyedmond, Dr Edward Haughey, OBE, b. 1944, m.
1974   *Balniel, The Earl of Crawford and Balcarres, b. 1927, m. (see Hereditary Peers)
2010   Bannside, Revd Ian Richard Kyle Paisley, PC, b. 1926, m.
1992   Barber of Tewkesbury, Derek Coates Barber, b. 1918, m.
1983   Barnett, Joel Barnett, PC, b. 1923, m.
1997   Bassam of Brighton, (John) Steven Bassam, PC, b. 1953
2008   Bates, Michael Walton Bates, b. 1961
2010   Beecham, Jeremy Hugh Beecham, b. 1944, m.
1998   Bell, Timothy John Leigh Bell, b. 1941, m.
2001   Best, Richard Stuart Best, OBE, b. 1945, m.
2007   Bew, Prof. Paul Anthony Elliott Bew, b. 1950, m.
2001   Bhatia, Amirali Alibhai Bhatia, OBE, b. 1932, m.
2004   Bhattacharyya, Prof. (Sushantha) Kumar Bhattacharyya, CBE b. 1932, m.
2010   Bichard, Michael George Bichard, KCB, b. 1947
2006   Bilimoria, Karan Faridoon Bilimoria, CBE, b. 1961, m.
2005   Bilston, Dennis Turner, b. 1942, m.
2000   Birt, John Francis Hodgess Birt, b. 1944, m.
2010   Black of Brentwood, Guy Vaughan Black, b. 1964, c. p.
2001   Black of Crossharbour, Conrad Moffat Black, OC, PC, b. 1944, m.
1997   Blackwell, Norman Roy Blackwell, b. 1952, m.
2010   Blair of Boughton, Ian Warwick Blair, QPM b. 1953, m.
2011   Blencathra, David John Maclean, PC, b. 1953
1995   Blyth of Rowington, James Blyth, b. 1940, m.
2010   Boateng, Paul Yaw Boateng, PC, b. 1951, m.
1996   Borrie, Gordon Johnson Borrie, QC, b. 1931, w.
2010   Boswell of Aynho, Timothy Eric Boswell, b. 1942, m.
1996   Bowness, Peter Spencer Bowness, CBE, b. 1943, m.

2003   Boyce, Michael Boyce, KG, GCB, OBE, b. 1943
2006   Boyd of Duncansby, Colin David Boyd, PC, b. 1953, m.
2006   Bradley, Keith John Charles Bradley, PC, b. 1950, m.
1999   Bradshaw, William Peter Bradshaw, b. 1936, m.
1998   Bragg, Melvyn Bragg, b. 1939, m.
1987   Bramall, Edwin Noel Westby Bramall, KG, GCB, OBE, MC, b. 1923, m.
2000   Brennan, Daniel Joseph Brennan, QC, b. 1942, m.
1999   Brett, William Henry Brett, b. 1942, m.
1976   Briggs, Asa Briggs, FBA, b. 1921, m.
2000   Brittan of Spennithorne, Leon Brittan, PC, QC, b. 1939, m.
2004   Broers, Prof. Alec (Nigel) Broers, b. 1938, m.
1997   Brooke of Alverthorpe, Clive Brooke, b. 1942, m.
2001   Brooke of Sutton Mandeville, Peter Leonard Brooke, CH, PC, b. 1934, m.
1998   Brookman, David Keith Brookman, b. 1937, m.
1979   Brooks of Tremorfa, John Edward Brooks, b. 1927, m.
2006   Browne of Belmont, Wallace Hamilton Browne, b. 1947
2010   Browne of Ladyton, Desmond Henry Browne, PC, b. 1952
2001   Browne of Madingley, Edmund John Phillip Browne, b. 1948
2006   Burnett, John Patrick Aubone Burnett, b. 1945, m.
1998   Burns, Terence Burns, GCB, b. 1944, m.
1998   Butler of Brockwell, (Frederick Edward) Robin Butler, KG, GCB, CVO, PC, b. 1938, m.
2004   Cameron of Dillington, Ewen (James Hanning) Cameron, b. 1949, m.
1984   Cameron of Lochbroom, Kenneth John Cameron, PC, b. 1931, m.
1981   Campbell of Alloway, Alan Robertson Campbell, QC, b. 1917, m.
2001   Campbell-Savours, Dale Norman Campbell-Savours, b. 1943, m.
2002   Carey of Clifton, Rt. Revd George Leonard Carey, PC, b. 1935, m.
1999   *Carington of Upton, Lord Carrington, GCMG, b. 1919, m. (see Hereditary Peers)
1999   Carlile of Berriew, Alexander Charles Carlile, QC, b. 1948, m.
1975   Carr of Hadley, (Leonard) Robert Carr, PC, b. 1916, m.
2008   Carter of Barnes, Stephen Andrew Carter, CBE, b. 1964, m.
2004   Carter of Coles, Patrick Robert Carter, b. 1946, m.
1990   Cavendish of Furness, (Richard) Hugh Cavendish, b. 1941, m.
1996   Chadlington, Peter Selwyn Gummer, b. 1942, m.
1964   Chalfont, (Alun) Arthur Gwynne Jones, OBE, MC, PC, b. 1919, w.
2005   Chidgey, David William George Chidgey, b. 1942, m.
1987   Chilver, (Amos) Henry Chilver, FRS, FRENG, b. 1926, m.
1977   Chitnis, Pratap Chidamber Chitnis, b. 1936, m.
1998   Christopher, Anthony Martin Grosvenor Christopher, CBE, b. 1925, m.
2001   Clark of Windermere, David George Clark, PC, PHD, b. 1939, m.
1998   Clarke of Hampstead, Anthony James Clarke, CBE, b. 1932, m.

2009 §*Clarke of Stone-Cum-Ebony,* Anthony Peter Clarke, PC, *b.* 1943, *m.*

1998 *Clement-Jones,* Timothy Francis Clement-Jones, CBE, *b.* 1949, *m.*

1990 *Clinton-Davis,* Stanley Clinton Clinton-Davis, PC, *b.* 1928, *m.*

2000 *Coe,* Sebastian Newbold Coe, KBE, *b.* 1956, *m.*

2011 *Collins of Highbury,* Raymond Edward Harry Collins, *b.* 1954

2001 *Condon,* Paul Leslie Condon, QPM, *b.* 1947, *m.*

1997 *Cope of Berkeley,* John Ambrose Cope, PC, *b.* 1937, *m.*

2001 *Corbett of Castle Vale,* Robin Corbett, *b.* 1933, *m.*

2010 *Cormack,* Patrick Thomas Cormack, *b.* 1939, *m.*

2006 *Cotter,* Brian Joseph Michael Cotter, *b.* 1939, *m.*

1991 *Craig of Radley,* David Brownrigg Craig, GCB, OBE, *b.* 1929, *m.*

1987 *Crickhowell,* (Roger) Nicholas Edwards, PC, *b.* 1934, *m.*

2006 *Crisp,* (Edmund) Nigel (Ramsay) Crisp, KCB, *b.* 1952, *m.*

1978 *Croham,* Douglas Albert Vivian Allen, GCB, *b.* 1917, *w.*

2003 *Cullen of Whitekirk,* William Douglas Cullen, KT, PC, *b.* 1935, *m.*

2005 *Cunningham of Felling,* John Anderson Cunningham, PC, *b.* 1939, *m.*

1996 *Currie of Marylebone,* David Anthony Currie, *b.* 1946, *m.*

2011 *Dannatt,* Gen. (Francis) Richard Dannatt, GCB, CBE, MC, *b.* 1950, *m.*

2007 *Darzi of Denham,* Ara Warkes Darzi, KBE, *b.* 1960, *m.*

2006 *Davidson of Glen Clova,* Neil Forbes Davidson, QC, *b.* 1950, *m.*

2009 *Davies of Abersoch,* Evan Mervyn Davies, CBE, *b.* 1952, *m.*

1997 *Davies of Coity,* (David) Garfield Davies, CBE, *b.* 1935, *m.*

1997 *Davies of Oldham,* Bryan Davies, PC, *b.* 1939, *m.*

2010 *Davies of Stamford,* John Quentin Davies, *b.* 1944, *m.*

2006 *Dear,* Geoffrey (James) Dear, QPM, *b.* 1937, *m.*

2010 *Deben,* John Selwyn Gummer, PC, *b.* 1939, *m.*

1991 *Desai,* Prof. Meghnad Jagdishchandra Desai, PHD, *b.* 1940, *m.*

1997 *Dholakia,* Navnit Dholakia, OBE, PC, *b.* 1937, *m.*

1997 *Dixon,* Donald Dixon, PC, *b.* 1929, *m.*

1993 *Dixon-Smith,* Robert William Dixon-Smith, *b.* 1934, *m.*

2010 *Dobbs,* Michael John Dobbs, *b.* 1948, *m.*

1985 *Donoughue,* Bernard Donoughue, DPHIL, *b.* 1934

2004 *Drayson,* Paul Rudd Drayson, PC, *b.* 1960, *m.*

1994 *Dubs,* Alfred Dubs, *b.* 1932, *m.*

2004 *Dykes,* Hugh John Maxwell Dykes, *b.* 1939, *m.*

1995 *Eames,* Robert Henry Alexander Eames, OM, PHD, *b.* 1937, *m.*

1992 *Eatwell,* John Leonard Eatwell, PHD, *b.* 1945

1983 *Eden of Winton,* John Benedict Eden, PC, *b.* 1925, *m.*

2011 *Edmiston,* Robert Norman Edmiston, *b.* 1946, *m.*

1999 *Elder,* Thomas Murray Elder, *b.* 1950

1992 *Elis-Thomas,* Dafydd Elis Elis-Thomas, PC, *b.* 1946, *m.*

1981 *Elystan-Morgan,* Dafydd Elystan Elystan-Morgan, *b.* 1932, *w.*

2011 *Empey,* Reginald Norman Morgan Empey, OBE, *b.* 1947, *m.*

2000 **Erskine of Alloa Tower,* Earl of Mar and Kellie, *b.* 1949, *m.* (*see* Hereditary Peers)

1997 *Evans of Parkside,* John Evans, *b.* 1930, *m.*

2000 *Evans of Temple Guiting,* Matthew Evans, CBE, *b.* 1941, *m.*

1998 *Evans of Watford,* David Charles Evans, *b.* 1942, *m.*

1983 *Ezra,* Derek Ezra, MBE, *b.* 1919, *m.*

1997 *Falconer of Thoroton,* Charles Leslie Falconer, QC, *b.* 1951, *m.*

1999 *Faulkner of Worcester,* Richard Oliver Faulkner, *b.* 1946, *m.*

2010 *Faulks,* Edward Peter Lawless Faulks, QC, *b.* 1950, *m.*

2001 *Fearn,* Ronald Cyril Fearn, OBE, *b.* 1931, *m.*

1996 *Feldman,* Basil Feldman, *b.* 1926, *m.*

2010 *Feldman of Elstree,* Andrew Simon Feldman, *b.* 1966, *m.*

1999 *Fellowes,* Robert Fellowes, GCB, GCVO, PC, *b.* 1941, *m.*

2011 *Fellowes of West Stafford,* Julian Alexander Fellowes, *b.* 1949, *m.*

1999 *Filkin,* David Geoffrey Nigel Filkin, CBE, *b.* 1944

2011 *Fink,* Stanley Fink, *b.* 1957, *m.*

2011 *Flight,* Howard Emerson Flight, *b.* 1948, *m.*

1999 *Forsyth of Drumlean,* Michael Bruce Forsyth, *b.* 1954, *m.*

2005 *Foster of Bishop Auckland,* Derek Foster, PC, *b.* 1937, *m.*

1999 *Foster of Thames Bank,* Norman Robert Foster, OM, *b.* 1935, *m.*

2005 *Foulkes of Cumnock,* George Foulkes, PC, *b.* 1942, *m.*

2001 *Fowler,* (Peter) Norman Fowler, PC, *b.* 1938, *m.*

2011 *Framlingham,* Michael Nicholson Lord, *b.* 1938, *m.*

1989 *Fraser of Carmyllie,* Peter Lovat Fraser, PC, QC, *b.* 1945, *m.*

1997 *Freeman,* Roger Norman Freeman, PC, *b.* 1942, *m.*

2009 *Freud,* David Anthony Freud, *b.* 1950 *m.*

2010 *Gardiner of Kimble,* John Gardiner, *b.* 1956, *m.*

1997 *Garel-Jones,* (William Armand) Thomas Tristan Garel-Jones, PC, *b.* 1941, *m.*

1999* *Gascoyne-Cecil,* The Marquess of Salisbury, PC , *b.* 1946, *m.* (*see* Hereditary Peers)

1999 *Gavron,* Robert Gavron, CBE, *b.* 1930, *m.*

2010 *German,* Michael James German, OBE, *b.* 1945, *m.*

2004 *Giddens,* Prof. Anthony Giddens, *b.* 1938, *m.*

1997 *Gilbert,* John William Gilbert, PC, PHD, *b.* 1927, *m.*

2011 *Glasman,* Maurice Mark Glasman, *b.* 1961, *m.*

1977 *Glenamara,* Edward Watson Short, CH, PC, *b.* 1912, *m.*

2011 *Glendonbrook,* Michael David Bishop, CBE, *b.* 1942

2011 *Gold,* David Laurence Gold, *b.* 1951, *m.*

1999 *Goldsmith,* Peter Henry Goldsmith, QC, *b.* 1950, *m.*

1997 *Goodhart,* William Howard Goodhart, QC, *b.* 1933, *m.*

2005   *Goodlad,* Alastair Robertson Goodlad, KCMG, b. 1943, *m.*

1997   *Gordon of Strathblane,* James Stuart Gordon, CBE, b. 1936, *m.*

2004   *Gould of Brookwood,* Philip Gould b. 1950 *m.*

1999   *Grabiner,* Anthony Stephen Grabiner, QC, b. 1945, *m.*

2011   *Grade of Yarmouth,* Michael Ian Grade, CBE, b. 1943, *m.*

1983   *Graham of Edmonton,* (Thomas) Edward Graham, b. 1925, *m.*

2000   *Greaves,* Anthony Robert Greaves, b. 1942, *m.*

2010   *Green of Hurstpierpoint,* Stephen Keith Green, b. 1948, *m.*

2000   **Grenfell of Kilvey,* Lord Grenfell, b. 1935, *m.* (*see* Hereditary Peers)

2004   *Griffiths of Burry Port,* Revd Dr Leslie John Griffiths, b. 1942, *m.*

1991   *Griffiths of Fforestfach,* Brian Griffiths, b. 1941, *m.*

2001   *Grocott,* Bruce Joseph Grocott, PC, b. 1940, *m.*

2000   **Gueterbock,* Lord Berkeley, OBE, b. 1939, *m.* (*see* Hereditary Peers)

2000   *Guthrie of Craigiebank,* Charles Ronald Llewelyn Guthrie, GCB, LVO, OBE b. 1938, *m.*

1995   *Habgood,* Rt. Revd John Stapylton Habgood, PC, PHD, b. 1927, *m.*

2010   *Hall of Birkenhead,* Anthony William Hall, CBE, b. 1951, *m.*

2007   *Hameed,* Dr Khalid Hameed, b. 1941, *m.*

2005   *Hamilton of Epsom,* Archibald Gavin Hamilton, PC, b. 1941, *m.*

2001   *Hannay of Chiswick,* David Hugh Alexander Hannay, GCMG, CH, b. 1935, *m.*

1998   *Hanningfield,* Paul Edward Winston White, b. 1940

1997   *Hardie,* Andrew Rutherford Hardie, QC, PC, b. 1946, *m.*

2006   *Harries of Pentregarth,* Rt. Revd Richard Douglas Harries, b. 1936, *m.*

1998   *Harris of Haringey,* (Jonathan) Toby Harris, b. 1953, *m.*

1996   *Harris of Peckham,* Philip Charles Harris, b. 1942, *m.*

1999   *Harrison,* Lyndon Henry Arthur Harrison, b. 1947, *m.*

2004   *Hart of Chilton,* Garry Richard Rushby Hart, b. 1940, *m.*

1993   *Haskel,* Simon Haskel, b. 1934, *m.*

1998   *Haskins,* Christopher Robin Haskins, b. 1937, *m.*

2005   *Hastings of Scarisbrick,* Michael John Hastings, CBE, b. 1958, *m.*

1997   *Hattersley,* Roy Sidney George Hattersley, PC, b. 1932, *m.*

2004   *Haworth,* Alan Robert Haworth, b. 1948, *m.*

1992   *Hayhoe,* Bernard John (Barney) Hayhoe, PC, b. 1925, *m.*

1992   *Healey,* Denis Winston Healey, CH, MBE, PC, b. 1917, *w.*

2010   *Hennessy of Nympsfield,* Prof. Peter John Hennessy, b. 1947, *m.*

2001   *Heseltine,* Michael Ray Dibdin Heseltine, CH, PC, b. 1933, *m.*

1997   *Higgins,* Terence Langley Higgins, KBE, PC, b. 1928, *m.*

2010   *Hill of Oareford,* Jonathan Hopkin Hill, CBE, b. 1960, *m.*

2000   *Hodgson of Astley Abbotts,* Robin Granville Hodgson, CBE, b. 1942, *m.*

1991   *Hollick,* Clive Richard Hollick, b. 1945, *m.*

1979   *Hooson,* (Hugh) Emlyn Hooson, QC, b. 1925, *m.*

2005   *Hope of Thornes,* Rt. Revd David Michael Hope, KCVO, PC, b. 1940

1995   *§Hope of Craighead,* (James Arthur) David Hope, KT, PC, b. 1938, *m.*

2010   *Howard of Lympne,* Michael Howard, CH, PC, QC, b. 1941, *m.*

2004   *Howard of Rising,* Greville Patrick Charles Howard, b. 1941, *m.*

2005   *Howarth of Newport,* Alan Thomas Howarth, CBE, PC, b. 1944

1992   *Howe of Aberavon,* (Richard Edward) Geoffrey Howe, CH, PC, QC, b. 1926, *m.*

1997   *Howell of Guildford,* David Arthur Russell Howell, PC, b. 1936, *m.*

1978   *Howie of Troon,* William Howie, b. 1924, *w.*

1997   *Hoyle,* (Eric) Douglas Harvey Hoyle, b. 1930, *w.*

1997   *Hughes of Woodside,* Robert Hughes, b. 1932, *m.*

2000   *Hunt of Chesterton,* Julian Charles Roland Hunt, CBE, b. 1941, *m.*

1997   *Hunt of Kings Heath,* Philip Alexander Hunt, OBE, PC, b. 1949, *m.*

1997   *Hunt of Wirral,* David James Fletcher Hunt, MBE, PC, b. 1942, *m.*

1997   *Hurd of Westwell,* Douglas Richard Hurd, CH, CBE, PC, b. 1930, *w.*

2011   *Hussain,* Qurban Hussain, *m.*

1978   *Hutchinson of Lullington,* Jeremy Nicolas Hutchinson, QC, b. 1915, *w.*

2010   *Hutton of Furness,* John Matthew Patrick Hutton, PC, b. 1955, *m.*

1999   *Imbert,* Peter Michael Imbert, CVO, QPM, b. 1933, *m.*

1997   *Inge,* Peter Anthony Inge, KG, GCB, PC, b. 1935, *m.*

1987   *Irvine of Lairg,* Alexander Andrew Mackay Irvine, PC, QC, b. 1940, *m.*

1997   *Jacobs,* (David) Anthony Jacobs, b. 1931, *m.*

2006   *James of Blackheath,* David Noel James, CBE, b. 1937, *m.*

1997   *Janner of Braunstone,* Greville Ewan Janner, QC, b. 1928, *w.*

2007   *Janvrin,* Robin Berry Janvrin, GCB, GCVO, PC, b. 1946, *m.*

2006   *Jay of Ewelme,* Michael (Hastings) Jay, GCMG, b. 1946, *m.*

1987   *Jenkin of Roding,* (Charles) Patrick (Fleeming) Jenkin, PC, b. 1926, *m.*

2000   *Joffe,* Joel Goodman Joffe, CBE, b. 1932, *m.*

2001   *Jones,* (Stephen) Barry Jones, b. 1937, *m.*

2007   *Jones of Birmingham,* Digby Marritt Jones, b. 1955, *m.*

2005,   *Jones of Cheltenham,* Nigel David Jones, b. 1948, *m.*

1997   *Jopling,* (Thomas) Michael Jopling, PC, b. 1930, *m.*

2000   *Jordan,* William Brian Jordan, CBE, b. 1936, *m.*

1991   *Judd,* Frank Ashcroft Judd, b. 1935, *m.*

2008   *Judge,* Igor Judge, PC, b. 1941, *m., Lord Chief Justice of England and Wales*

2010   *Kakkar,* Prof. Ajay Kumar Kakkar, b. 1964

2004   *Kalms,* Harold Stanley Kalms, b. 1931, *m.*

2010	*Kennedy of Southwark*, Roy Francis Kennedy, *b.* 1962
2004	*Kerr of Kinlochard*, John (Olav) Kerr, GCMG, *b.* 1942, *m.*
2010	**Kerr of Monteviot*, Marquess of Lothian (Michael Ancram), PC, QC, *b.* 1945, *m.* (*see* Hereditary Peers)
2011	*Kestenbaum*, Jonathan Andrew Kestenbaum, *b.* 1959, *m.*
2001	*Kilclooney*, John David Taylor, PC (NI), *b.* 1937, *m.*
1996	*Kilpatrick of Kincraig*, Robert Kilpatrick, CBE, *b.* 1926, *m.*
1985	*Kimball*, Marcus Richard Kimball, *b.* 1928, *m.*
2001	*King of Bridgwater*, Thomas Jeremy King, CH, PC, *b.* 1933, *m.*
1999	*King of West Bromwich*, Tarsem King, *b.* 1937
1993	*Kingsdown*, Robert (Robin) Leigh-Pemberton, KG, PC, *b.* 1927, *m.*
2005	*Kinnock*, Neil Gordon Kinnock, PC, *b.* 1942, *m.*
1999	*Kirkham*, Graham Kirkham, *b.* 1944, *m.*
1975	*Kirkhill*, John Farquharson Smith, *b.* 1930, *m.*
2005	*Kirkwood of Kirkhope*, Archibald Johnstone Kirkwood, *b.* 1946, *m.*
2007	*Krebs*, Prof. John (Richard) Krebs, FRS, *b.* 1945, *m.*
2010	*Knight of Weymouth*, James Philip Knight, PC, *b.* 1965, *m.*
1987	*Knights*, Philip Douglas Knights, CBE, QPM, *b.* 1920, *m.*
2004	*Laidlaw*, Irvine Alan Stewart Laidlaw, *b.* 1942, *m.*
1999	*Laird*, John Dunn Laird, *b.* 1944, *m.*
1998	*Laming*, (William) Herbert Laming, CBE, *b.* 1936, *m.*
1998	*Lamont of Lerwick*, Norman Stewart Hughson Lamont, PC, *b.* 1942, *m.*
1997	*Lang of Monkton*, Ian Bruce Lang, PC, *b.* 1940, *m.*
1992	*Lawson of Blaby*, Nigel Lawson, PC, *b.* 1932, *m.*
2000	*Layard*, Peter Richard Grenville Layard, *b.* 1934, *m.*
1999	*Lea of Crondall*, David Edward Lea, OBE, *b.* 1937
2006	*Leach of Fairford*, Charles Guy Rodney Leach, *b.* 1934, *m.*
2006	*Lee of Trafford*, John Robert Louis Lee, *b.* 1942, *m.*
2004	*Leitch*, Alexander Park Leitch, *b.* 1947, *m.*
1993	*Lester of Herne Hill*, Anthony Paul Lester, QC, *b.* 1936, *m.*
1997	*Levene of Portsoken*, Peter Keith Levene, KBE, *b.* 1941, *m.*
1997	*Levy*, Michael Abraham Levy, *b.* 1944, *m.*
1989	*Lewis of Newnham*, Jack Lewis, FRS, *b.* 1928, *m.*
2010	*Lexden*, Alistair Basil Cooke, OBE, *b.* 1945
2010	*Liddle*, Roger John Liddle, *b.* 1947, *m.*
2010	*Lingfield*, Robert George Alexander Balchin, *b.* 1942, *m.*
1999	*Lipsey*, David Lawrence Lipsey, *b.* 1948, *m.*
1997	*Lloyd-Webber*, Andrew Lloyd Webber, *b.* 1948, *m.*
1997	*Lofthouse of Pontefract*, Geoffrey Lofthouse, *b.* 1925, *w.*
2011	*Loomba*, Rajinder Paul Loomba, CBE, *b.* 1943, *m.*
2006	*Low of Dalston*, Prof. Colin Mackenzie Low, CBE, *b.* 1942, *m.*
2000	*Luce*, Richard Napier Luce, KG, GCVO, PC, *b.* 1936, *m.*
2000	**Lyttleton of Aldershot*, The Viscount Chandos, *b.* 1953, *m.* (*see* Hereditary Peers)
1984	*McAlpine of West Green*, (Robert) Alistair McAlpine, *b.* 1942, *m.*
2010	*McAvoy*, Thomas McLaughlin McAvoy, PC, *b.* 1943, *m.*
1988	*Macaulay of Bragar*, Donald Macaulay, QC, *b.* 1933, *m.*
1975	*McCarthy*, William Edward John McCarthy, DPHIL, *b.* 1925, *m.*
1976	*McCluskey*, John Herbert McCluskey, *b.* 1929, *m.*
1989	*McColl of Dulwich*, Ian McColl, CBE, FRCS, FRCSE, *b.* 1933, *m.*
2010	*McConnell of Glenscorrodale*, Dr Jack Wilson McConnell, PC, *b.* 1960, *m.*
2010	*MacDonald of River Glaven*, Kenneth Donald John MacDonald, QC, *b.* 1953, *m.*
1998	*Macdonald of Tradeston*, Angus John Macdonald, CBE, *b.* 1940, *m.*
2010	*McFall of Alcluith*, John Francis McFall, PC, *b.* 1944, *m.*
1991	*Macfarlane of Bearsden*, Norman Somerville Macfarlane, KT, FRSE, *b.* 1926, *m.*
2001	*MacGregor of Pulham Market*, John Roddick Russell MacGregor, CBE, PC, *b.* 1937, *m.*
1979	*Mackay of Clashfern*, James Peter Hymers Mackay, KT, PC, FRSE, *b.* 1927, *m.*
1995	*Mackay of Drumadoon*, Donald Sage Mackay, PC, *b.* 1946, *m.*
2004	*McKenzie of Luton*, William David McKenzie, *b.* 1946, *m.*
1999	*Mackenzie of Culkein*, Hector Uisdean MacKenzie, *b.* 1940
1998	*Mackenzie of Framwellgate*, Brian Mackenzie, OBE, *b.* 1943, *m.*
1974	*Mackie of Benshie*, George Yull Mackie, CBE, DSO, DFC, *b.* 1919, *m.*
1996	*MacLaurin of Knebworth*, Ian Charter MacLaurin, *b.* 1937, *m.*
2001	*Maclennon of Rogart*, Robert Adam Ross Maclennan, PC, *b.* 1936, *m.*
1995	*McNally*, Tom McNally, PC, *b.* 1943, *m.*
2011	*Magan of Castletown*, George Morgan Magan, *b.* 1945, *m.*
2001	*Maginnis of Drumglass*, Kenneth Wiggins Maginnis, *b.* 1938, *m.*
2007	*Malloch-Brown*, George Mark Malloch Brown, KCMG, PC, *b.* 1953, *m.*
2008	*Mandelson*, Peter Benjamin Mandelson, PC, *b.* 1953
2010	*Maples*, John Craddock Maples, *b.* 1943, *m.*
2011	*Marks of Henley-on-Thames*, Jonathan Clive Marks, QC, *b.* 1952, *m.*
2006	*Marland*, Jonathan Peter Marland, *b.* 1956, *m.*
1991	*Marlesford*, Mark Shuldham Schreiber, *b.* 1931, *m.*
1998	*Marshall of Knightsbridge*, Colin Marsh Marshall, *b.* 1933, *m.*
2009	*Martin of Springburn*, Michael Martin, PC, *b.* 1945, *m.*
1987	*Mason of Barnsley*, Roy Mason, PC, *b.* 1924, *m.*
2005	*Mawhinney*, Brian Stanley Mawhinney, PC, *b.* 1940, *m.*

2007   *Mawson,* Revd Andrew Mawson, OBE, b. 1954, *m.*

2004   *Maxton,* John Alston Maxton, b. 1936, *m.*

2001   *May of Oxford,* Robert McCredie May, OM, b. 1936, *m.*

1997   *Mayhew of Twysden,* Patrick Barnabas Burke Mayhew, QC, PC, b. 1929, *m.*

2000   *Mitchell,* Parry Andrew Mitchell, b. 1943, *m.*

2000   **Mitford,* Lord Redesdale, b. 1967, *m.* (*see* Hereditary Peers)

2008   *Mogg,* John (Frederick) Mogg, KCMG, b. 1943 *m.*

1997   *Molyneaux of Killead,* James Henry Molyneaux, KBE, PC, b. 1920

2010   *Monks,* John Stephen Monks, b. 1945, *m.*

2005   *Moonie,* Dr. Lewis George Moonie, b. 1947, *m.*

1992   *Moore of Lower Marsh,* John Edward Michael Moore, PC, b. 1937, *w.*

2000   *Morgan,* Kenneth Owen Morgan, b. 1934, *m.*

2001   *Morris of Aberavon,* John Morris, KG, QC, b. 1931, *m.*

2006   *Morris of Handsworth,* William Manuel Morris, b. 1938, *m.*

1997   *Morris of Manchester,* Alfred Morris, PC, b. 1928, *m.*

2006   *Morrow,* Maurice George Morrow, *m.*

2001   *Moser,* Claus Adolf Moser, KCB, CBE, b. 1922, *m.*

2008   *Myners,* Paul Myners, CBE, b. 1948, *m.*

1997   *Naseby,* Michael Wolfgang Laurence Morris, PC, b. 1936, *m.*

1997   *Neill of Bladen,* (Francis) Patrick Neill, QC, b. 1926, *m.*

1997   *Newby,* Richard Mark Newby, OBE, b. 1953, *m.*

1997   *Newton of Braintree,* Antony Harold Newton, OBE, PC, b. 1937, *m.*

1994   *Nickson,* David Wigley Nickson, KBE, FRSE, b. 1929, *m.*

2011   *Noon,* Gulam Kaderbhoy Noon, MBE, b. 1936, *m.*

1975   *Northfield,* (William) Donald Chapman, b. 1923

1998   *Norton of Louth,* Philip Norton, b. 1951

2000   *Oakeshott of Seagrove Bay,* Matthew Alan Oakeshott, b. 1947, *m.*

2005   *O'Neill of Clackmannan,* Martin John O'Neill, b. 1945, *m.*

2001   *Ouseley,* Herman George Ouseley, b. 1945, *m.*

1992   *Owen,* David Anthony Llewellyn Owen, CH, PC, b. 1938, *m.*

1999   *Oxburgh,* Ernest Ronald Oxburgh, KBE, FRS, PHD, b. 1934, *m.*

2011   *Palmer of Childs Hill,* Monroe Edward Palmer, OBE, b. 1938, *m.*

1991   *Palumbo,* Peter Garth Palumbo, b. 1935, *m.*

2008   *Pannick,* David Philip Pannick, QC, b. 1956, *m.*

2000   *Parekh,* Bhikhu Chhotalal Parekh, b. 1935, *m.*

1992   *Parkinson,* Cecil Edward Parkinson, PC, b. 1931, *m.*

1999   *Patel,* Narendra Babubhai Patel, b. 1938

2000   *Patel of Blackburn,* Adam Hafejee Patel, b. 1940

2006   *Patel of Bradford,* Prof. Kamlesh Kumar Patel, OBE, b. 1960 *m.*

2005   *Patten of Barnes,* Christopher Francis Patten, CH, PC, b. 1944, *m.*

1997   *Patten,* John Haggitt Charles Patten, PC, b. 1945, *m.*

1996   *Paul,* Swraj Paul, PC, b. 1931, *m.*

1990   *Pearson of Rannoch,* Malcolm Everard MacLaren Pearson, b. 1942, *m.*

2001   *Pendry,* Thomas Pendry, b. 1934, *m.*

1987   *Peston,* Maurice Harry Peston, b. 1931, *m.*

1998   *Phillips of Sudbury,* Andrew Wyndham Phillips, OBE, b. 1939, *m.*

1992   *Plant of Highfield,* Prof. Raymond Plant, PHD, b. 1945, *m.*

1987   *Plumb,* (Charles) Henry Plumb, b. 1925, *m.*

2000   **Ponsonby of Roehampton,* Lord Ponsonby of Shulbrede, b. 1958 (*see* Hereditary Peers)

2010   *Popat,* Dolar Amarshi Popat, b. 1953, *m.*

2000   *Powell of Bayswater,* Charles David Powell, KCMG, b. 1941

2010   *Prescott,* John Leslie Prescott, PC, b. 1938, *m.*

1987   *Prior,* James Michael Leathes Prior, PC, b. 1927, *m.*

1982   *Prys-Davies,* Gwilym Prys Prys-Davies, b. 1923, *m.*

1997   *Puttnam,* David Terence Puttnam, CBE, b. 1941, *m.*

1994   *Quirk,* Prof. (Charles) Randolph Quirk, CBE, FBA, b. 1920, *m.*

2001   *Radice,* Giles Heneage Radice, PC, b. 1936

2005   *Ramsbotham,* Gen. David John Ramsbotham, GCB, CBE, b. 1934, *m.*

2004   *Rana,* Dr Diljit Singh Rana, MBE, b. 1938, *m.*

1997   *Randall of St Budeaux,* Stuart Jeffrey Randall, b. 1938, *m.*

1997   *Razzall,* (Edward) Timothy Razzall, CBE, b. 1943, *m.*

2005   *Rees of Ludlow,* Prof. Martin John Rees, OM, b. 1942, *m.*

1988   *Rees-Mogg,* William Rees-Mogg, b. 1928, *m.*

2010   *Reid of Cardowan,* Dr John Reid, PC, b. 1947, *m.*

1991   *Renfrew of Kaimsthorn,* (Andrew) Colin Renfrew, FBA, b. 1937, *m.*

1999   *Rennard,* Christopher John Rennard, MBE, b. 1960

1997   *Renton of Mount Harry,* (Ronald) Timothy Renton, PC, b. 1932, *m.*

1997   *Renwick of Clifton,* Robin William Renwick, KCMG, b. 1937, *m.*

2010   *Ribeiro,* Bernard Francisco Ribeiro, CBE, b. 1944, *m.*

1990   *Richard,* Ivor Seward Richard, PC, QC, b. 1932, *m.*

2010   *Risby,* Richard John Grenville Spring, b. 1946, *m.*

1992   *Rix,* Brian Norman Roger Rix, CBE, b. 1924, *m.*

2004   *Roberts of Llandudno,* Revd John Roger Roberts, b. 1935, *m.*

1997   *Roberts of Conwy,* (Ieuan) Wyn (Pritchard) Roberts, PC, b. 1930, *m.*

1999   *Robertson of Port Ellen,* George Islay MacNeill Robertson, KT, GCMG, PC, b. 1946, *m.*

1992   *Rodgers of Quarry Bank,* William Thomas Rodgers, PC, b. 1928, *w.*

1999   *Rogan,* Dennis Robert David Rogan, b. 1942, *m.*

1996   *Rogers of Riverside,* Richard George Rogers, CH, RA, RIBA, b. 1933, *m.*

2001   *Rooker,* Jeffrey William Rooker, PC, b. 1941, *m.*

2000   *Roper,* John Francis Hodgess Roper, PC, b. 1935, *m.*

2004   *Rosser,* Richard Andrew Rosser, b. 1944, *m.*

2006   *Rowe-Beddoe,* David (Sydney) Rowe-Beddoe, b. 1937, *m.*

2004   *Rowlands,* Edward Rowlands, CBE, b. 1940, *m.*

1997   Ryder of Wensum, Richard Andrew Ryder, OBE, PC, b. 1949, m.

1996   Saatchi, Maurice Saatchi, b. 1946, w.

2009   ‡Sacks, Chief Rabbi Dr Jonathan Henry Sacks, b. 1948, m.

1989   Sainsbury of Preston Candover, John Davan Sainsbury, KG, b. 1927, m.

1997   Sainsbury of Turville, David John Sainsbury, b. 1940, m.

1987   St John of Fawsley, Norman Antony Francis St John-Stevas, PC, b. 1929

1997   Sandberg, Michael Graham Ruddock Sandberg, CBE, b. 1927, m.

1985   Sanderson of Bowden, Charles Russell Sanderson, b. 1933, m.

2010   Sassoon, James Meyer Sassoon, b. 1955, m.

1998   Sawyer, Lawrence (Tom) Sawyer, b. 1943

1997   Selkirk of Douglas, James Alexander Douglas-Hamilton, MSP, PC, QC, b. 1942, m.

1996   Sewel, John Buttifant Sewel, CBE, b. 1946

2010   Sharkey, John Kevin Sharkey, b. 1947, m.

1999   Sharman, Colin Morven Sharman, OBE, b. 1943, m.

1994   Shaw of Northstead, Michael Norman Shaw, b. 1920, m.

2006   Sheikh, Mohamed Iltaf Sheikh, b. 1941, m.

2001   Sheldon, Robert Edward Sheldon, PC, b. 1923, m.

1994   Sheppard of Didgemere, Allan John George Sheppard, KCVO, b. 1932, m.

2010   Shipley, John Warren Shipley, OBE, b. 1946

2000   Shutt of Greetland, David Trevor Shutt, OBE, PC, b. 1942

1997   Simon of Highbury, David Alec Gwyn Simon, CBE, b. 1939, m.

1997   Simpson of Dunkeld, George Simpson, b. 1942, m.

1991   Skidelsky, Robert Jacob Alexander Skidelsky, DPHIL, b. 1939, m.

1997   Smith of Clifton, Trevor Arthur Smith, b. 1937, m.

2005   Smith of Finsbury, Christopher Robert Smith, PC, b. 1951

2008   Smith of Kelvin, Robert (Haldane) Smith, b. 1944, m.

1999   Smith of Leigh, Peter Richard Charles Smith, b. 1945, m.

2004   Snape, Peter Charles Snape, b. 1942

2005   Soley, Clive Stafford Soley, b. 1939

1990   Soulsby of Swaffham Prior, Ernest Jackson Lawson Soulsby, PHD, b. 1926, m.

2010   Spicer, (William) Michael Hardy Spicer, b. 1943, m.

1997   Steel of Aikwood, David Martin Scott Steel, KT, KBE, PC, b. 1938, m.

2011   Stephen, Nicol Ross Stephen, b. 1960, m.

1991   Sterling of Plaistow, Jeffrey Maurice Sterling, GCVO, CBE, b. 1934, m.

2007   Stern of Brentford, Nicholas Herbert Stern, b. 1946, m.

2005   Stevens of Kirkwhelpington, John Arthur Stevens, b. 1942, m.

1987   Stevens of Ludgate, David Robert Stevens, b. 1936, m.

2010   Stevenson of Balmacara, Robert Wilfrid Stevenson, b. 1947, m.

1999   Stevenson of Coddenham, Henry Dennistoun Stevenson, CBE, b. 1945, m.

1992   Stewartby, (Bernard Harold) Ian (Halley) Stewart, RD, PC, FBA, FRSE, b. 1935, m.

2011   Stirrup, Air Chief Marshal Graham Eric Stirrup, GCB, AFC, b. 1949, m.

1983   Stoddart of Swindon, David Leonard Stoddart, b. 1926, m.

1997   Stone of Blackheath, Andrew Zelig Stone, b. 1942, m.

2011   Stoneham of Droxford, Benjamin Russell Mackintosh Stoneham 1940, m.

2011   Storey, Michael John Storey, CBE, b. 1949

2011   Strasburger, Paul Cline Strasburger, b. 1946

2009   Sugar, Alan Michael Sugar, b. 1947, m.

2001   Sutherland of Houndwood, Stewart Ross Sutherland, KT, b. 1941, m.

1971   Tanlaw, Simon Brooke Mackay, b. 1934, m.

1996   Taverne, Dick Taverne, QC, b. 1928, m.

2010   Taylor of Goss Moor, Matthew Owen John Taylor, b. 1963, m.

1978   Taylor of Blackburn, Thomas Taylor, CBE, b. 1929, m.

2006   Taylor of Holbeach, John Derek Taylor, CBE, b. 1943, m.

1996   Taylor of Warwick, John David Beckett Taylor, b. 1952, m.

1992   Tebbit, Norman Beresford Tebbit, CH, PC, b. 1931, m.

2001   Temple-Morris, Peter Temple-Morris, b. 1938, m.

2006   Teverson, Robin Teverson, b. 1952, m.

1996   Thomas of Gresford, Donald Martin Thomas, OBE, QC, b. 1937, m.

1997   Thomas of Macclesfield, Terence James Thomas, CBE, b. 1937, m.

1981   Thomas of Swynnerton, Hugh Swynnerton Thomas, b. 1931, m.

1990   Tombs, Francis Leonard Tombs, FENG, b. 1924, w.

1998   Tomlinson, John Edward Tomlinson, b. 1939

1994   Tope, Graham Norman Tope, CBE, b. 1943, m.

1981   Tordoff, Geoffrey Johnson Tordoff, b. 1928, m.

2010   Touhig, James Donnelly Touhig, PC, b. 1947, m.

2004   Triesman, David Maxim Triesman, b. 1943

2006   Trimble, William David Trimble, PC, b. 1944, m.

2010   True, Nicholas Edward True, CBE, b. 1951, m.

2004   Truscott, Dr Peter Derek Truscott, b. 1959, m.

1993   Tugendhat, Christopher Samuel Tugendhat, b. 1937, m.

2004   Tunnicliffe, Denis Tunnicliffe, CBE, b. 1943, m.

2000   Turnberg, Leslie Arnold Turnberg, MD, b. 1934, m.

2005   Turnbull, Andrew Turnbull, KCB, CVO, b. 1945, m.

2005   Turner of Ecchinswell, (Jonathan) Adair Turner, b. 1955, m.

2005   Tyler, Paul Archer Tyler, CBE, b. 1941, m.

2004   Vallance of Tummel, Iain (David Thomas) Vallance, b. 1943, m.

1996   Vincent of Coleshill, Richard Frederick Vincent, GBE, KCB, DSO, b. 1931, m.

1985   Vinson, Nigel Vinson, LVO, b. 1931, m.

1990   Waddington, David Charles Waddington, GCVO, PC, QC, b. 1929, m.

1990   Wade of Chorlton, (William) Oulton Wade, b. 1932, m.

1992   Wakeham, John Wakeham, PC, b. 1932, m.

1999   Waldegrave of North Hill, William Arthur Waldegrave, PC, b. 1946, m.

2007	*Walker of Aldringham,* Michael John Dawson Walker, GCB, CMG, CBE, *b.* 1944, *m.*
1995	*Wallace of Saltaire,* William John Lawrence Wallace, PHD, *b.* 1941, *m.*
2007	*Wallace of Tankerness,* James Robert Wallace, PC, QC, *b.* 1954, *m.*
1989	*Walton of Detchant,* John Nicholas Walton, TD, FRCP, *b.* 1922, *w.*
1998	*Warner,* Norman Reginald Warner, PC, *b.* 1940, *m.*
2011	*Wasserman,* Gordon Joshua Wasserman, *b.* 1938
1997	*Watson of Invergowrie,* Michael Goodall Watson, *b.* 1949, *m.*
1999	*Watson of Richmond,* Alan John Watson, CBE, *b.* 1941, *m.*
1977	*Wedderburn of Charlton,* (Kenneth) William Wedderburn, FBA, QC, *b.* 1927, *m.*
2010	*Wei,* Nathanael Ming-Yan Wei, *b.* 1977, *m.*
1976	*Weidenfeld,* (Arthur) George Weidenfeld, GBE, *b.* 1919, *m.*
2007	*West of Spithead,* Adm. Alan William John West, GCB, DSC, PC, *b.* 1948, *m.*
1996	*Whitty,* John Lawrence (Larry) Whitty, *b.* 1943, *m.*
2011	*Wigley,* Dafydd Wynne Wigley, *b.* 1943, *m.*
2010	*Williams of Baglan,* Michael Charles Williams, *b.* 1949
1985	*Williams of Elvel,* Charles Cuthbert Powell Williams, CBE, *b.* 1933, *m.*
1999	*Williamson of Horton,* David (Francis) Williamson, GCMG, CB, PC, *b.* 1934, *m.*
2010	*Willis of Knaresborough,* George Philip Willis, *b.* 1941, *m.*
2010	*Wills,* Michael David Wills, PC, *b.* 1952, *m.*
2002	*Wilson of Dinton,* Richard Thomas James Wilson, GCB, *b.* 1942, *m.*
1992	*Wilson of Tillyorn,* David Clive Wilson, KT, GCMG, PHD, *b.* 1935, *m.*
1995	*Winston,* Robert Maurice Lipson Winston, FRCOG, *b.* 1940, *m.*
2010	*Wolfson of Aspley Guise,* Simon David Wolfson, *b.* 1967
1991	*Wolfson of Sunningdale,* David Wolfson, *b.* 1935, *m.*
2011	*Wood of Anfield,* Stewart Martin Wood, *b.* 1968, *m.*
1999	*Woolmer of Leeds,* Kenneth John Woolmer, *b.* 1940, *m.*
1994	*Wright of Richmond,* Patrick Richard Henry Wright, GCMG, *b.* 1931, *m.*
2004	*Young of Norwood Green,* Anthony (Ian) Young, *b.* 1942, *m.*
1984	*Young of Graffham,* David Ivor Young, PC, *b.* 1932, *m.*

BARONESSES
Created

2005	*Adams of Craigielea,* Katherine Patricia Irene Adams, *b.* 1947, *w.*
1997	*Amos,* Valerie Ann Amos, *b.* 1954
2007	*Afshar,* Prof. Haleh Afshar, OBE, , *b.* 1944, *m.*
2000	*Andrews,* Elizabeth Kay Andrews, OBE, *b.* 1943, *m.*
1996	*Anelay of St Johns,* Joyce Anne Anelay, DBE, PC, *b.* 1947, *m.*
2010	*Armstrong of Hill Top,* Hilary Jane Armstrong, PC, *b.* 1945, *m.*
1999	*Ashton of Upholland,* Catherine Margaret Ashton, PC, *b.* 1956, *m.*
2011	*Bakewell,* Joan Dawson Bakewell, DBE, *b.* 1933
1999	*Barker,* Elizabeth Jean Barker, *b.* 1961
2010	*Benjamin,* Floella Karen Yunies Benjamin, OBE, *b.* 1949, *m.*
2011	*Berridge,* Elizabeth Rose Berridge, *b.* 1972
2000	*Billingham,* Angela Theodora Billingham, DPHIL, *b.* 1939, *w.*
1987	*Blackstone,* Tessa Ann Vosper Blackstone, PHD, *b.* 1942
1999	*Blood,* May Blood, MBE, *b.* 1938
2000	*Boothroyd,* Betty Boothroyd, OM, PC, *b.* 1929
2004	*Bonham-Carter of Yarnbury,* Jane Bonham Carter, *b.* 1957, *w.*
2005	*Bottomley of Nettlestone,* Virginia Hilda Brunette Maxwell Bottomley, PC, *b.* 1948, *m.*
2011	*Brinton,* Sarah Virginia Brinton, *b.* 1955, *m.*
2010	*Browning,* Angela Frances Browning, *b.* 1946, *m.*
1998	*Buscombe,* Peta Jane Buscombe, *b.* 1954, *m.*
2006	*Butler-Sloss,* (Ann) Elizabeth (Oldfield) Butler-Sloss, GBE, PC *b.* 1933, *m.*
1996	*Byford,* Hazel Byford, DBE, *b.* 1941, *m.*
2008	*Campbell of Loughborough,* Susan Catherine Campbell, CBE, *b.* 1948
2007	*Campbell of Surbiton,* Jane Susan Campbell, DBE, *b.* 1959, *m.*
1992	*Chalker of Wallasey,* Lynda Chalker, PC, *b.* 1942, *m.*
2005	*Clark of Calton,* Dr Lynda Margaret Clark, QC, *b.* 1949
2000	*Cohen of Pimlico,* Janet Cohen, *b.* 1940, *m.*
2005	*Corston,* Jean Ann Corston, PC, *b.* 1942, *w.*
2007	*Coussins,* Jean Coussins, *b.* 1950
1982	*Cox,* Caroline Anne Cox, *b.* 1937, *m.*
1998	*Crawley,* Christine Mary Crawley, *b.* 1950, *m.*
1990	*Cumberlege,* Julia Frances Cumberlege, CBE, *b.* 1943, *m.*
1993	*Dean of Thornton-le-Fylde,* Brenda Dean, PC, *b.* 1943, *m.*
2005	*Deech,* Ruth Lynn Deech, DBE, *b.* 1943, *m.*
2010	*Donaghy,* Rita Margaret Donaghy, CBE, *b.* 1944, *m.*
2010	*Doocey,* Elizabeth Deirdre Doocey, OBE, *m.*
2010	*Drake,* Jean Lesley Patricia Drake, CBE, *b.* 1948
2004	*D'Souza,* Dr Frances Gertrude Claire D'Souza, CMG, PC, *b.* 1944, *m.*
1990	*Dunn,* Lydia Selina Dunn, DBE, *b.* 1940, *m.*
2010	*Eaton,* Ellen Margaret Eaton, DBE
1990	*Eccles of Moulton,* Diana Catherine Eccles, *b.* 1933, *m.*
1997	*Emerton,* Audrey Caroline Emerton, DBE, *b.* 1935
1974	*Falkender,* Marcia Matilda Falkender, CBE, *b.* 1932
2004	*Falkner of Margravine,* Kishwer Falkner, *b.* 1955, *m.*
1994	*Farrington of Ribbleton,* Josephine Farrington, *b.* 1940, *m.*
2001	*Finlay of Llandaff,* Ilora Gillian Finlay, *b.* 1949, *m.*
1990	*Flather,* Shreela Flather, *m.*
1997	*Fookes,* Janet Evelyn Fookes, DBE, *b.* 1936
2006	*Ford,* Margaret Anne Ford, *b.* 1957, *m.*
2005	*Fritchie,* Irene Tordoff Fritchie, DBE, *b.* 1942, *m.*
1999	*Gale,* Anita Gale, *b.* 1940
2007	*Garden of Frognal,* Susan Elizabeth Garden, *b.* 1944, *m.*

1981   *Gardner of Parkes,* (Rachel) Trixie (Anne) Gardner, *b.* 1927, *w.*

2000   *Gibson of Market Rasen,* Anne Gibson, OBE, *b.* 1940, *m.*

2001   *Golding,* Llinos Golding, *b.* 1933, *m.*

1998   *Goudie,* Mary Teresa Goudie, *b.* 1946, *m.*

1993   *Gould of Potternewton,* Joyce Brenda Gould, *b.* 1932, *m.*

2001   *Greenfield,* Susan Adele Greenfield, CBE, *b.* 1950, *m.*

2000   *Greengross,* Sally Ralea Greengross, OBE, *b.* 1935, *m.*

2010   *Grey-Thompson,* Tanni Carys Davina Grey-Thompson, DBE, *b.* 1969, *m.*

1991   *Hamwee,* Sally Rachel Hamwee, *b.* 1947

1999   *Hanham,* Joan Brownlow Hanham, CBE, *b.* 1939, *m.*

1999   *Harris of Richmond,* Angela Felicity Harris, *b.* 1944

2011   *Heyhoe Flint,* Rachel Heyhoe Flint, OBE, *b.* 1939, *m.*

1996   *Hayman,* Helene Valerie Hayman, PC, *b.* 1949, *m.*

2010   *Hayter of Kentish Town,* Dr Dianne Hayter, *b.* 1949, *m.*

2010   *Healy of Primrose Hill,* Anna Healy, *b.* 1955, *m.*

2004   *Henig,* Ruth Beatrice Henig, CBE, *b.* 1943, *m.*

1991   *Hilton of Eggardon,* Jennifer Hilton, QPM, *b.* 1936

1995   *Hogg,* Sarah Elizabeth Mary Hogg, *b.* 1946, *m.*

2010   *Hollins,* Prof. Sheila Clare Hollins, *b.* 1946, *m.*

1990   *Hollis of Heigham,* Patricia Lesley Hollis, DPHIL, *b.* 1941, *m.*

1985   *Hooper,* Gloria Dorothy Hooper, CMG, *b.* 1939

2001   *Howarth of Breckland,* Valerie Georgina Howarth, OBE, *b.* 1940

2001   *Howe of Idlicote,* Elspeth Rosamond Morton Howe, CBE, *b.* 1932, *m.*

1999   *Howells of St Davids,* Rosalind Patricia-Anne Howells, *b.* 1931, *m.*

2010   *Hughes of Stretford,* Beverley Hughes, PC, *b.* 1950, *m.*

2010   *Hussein-Ece,* Meral Hussein Ece, OBE, *b.* 1953

1991   *James of Holland Park,* Phyllis Dorothy White (P. D. James), OBE, *b.* 1920, *w.*

1992   *Jay of Paddington,* Margaret Ann Jay, PC, *b.* 1939, *m.*

2011   *Jenkin of Kennington,* Anne Caroline Jenkin, *b.* 1955, *m.*

2010   *Jolly,* Judith Anne Jolly *m.*

2006   *Jones of Whitchurch,* Margaret Beryl Jones, *b.* 1955

1997   *Kennedy of the Shaws,* Helena Ann Kennedy, QC, *b.* 1950, *m.*

2011   *King of Bow,* Oona Tamsyn King, *b.* 1967, *m.*

2006   *Kingsmill,* Denise Patricia Byrne Kingsmill, CBE, *b.* 1947, *m.*

2009   *Kinnock of Holyhead,* Glenys Elizabeth Kinnock, *b.* 1944, *m.*

1997   *Knight of Collingtree,* (Joan Christabel) Jill Knight, DBE, *b.* 1927, *w.*

2010   *Kramer,* Susan Veronica Kramer, *b.* 1950, *w.*

2010   *Liddell of Coatdyke,* Helen Lawrie Liddell, PC, *b.* 1950, *m.*

1997   *Linklater of Butterstone,* Veronica Linklater, *b.* 1943, *m.*

2011   *Lister of Burtersett,* Margot Ruth Aline Lister, CBE, *b.* 1949, *m.*

1978   *Lockwood,* Betty Lockwood, *b.* 1924, *w.*

1997   *Ludford,* Sarah Ann Ludford, *b.* 1951

2004   *McDonagh,* Margaret Josephine McDonagh

1979   *McFarlane of Llandaff,* Jean Kennedy McFarlane, *b.* 1926

1999   *McIntosh of Hudnall,* Genista Mary McIntosh, *b.* 1946

1997   *Maddock,* Diana Margaret Maddock, *b.* 1945, *m.*

2008   *Manningham-Buller,* Elizabeth (Lydia) Manningham-Buller, DCB, *b.* 1948, *m.*

1991   *Mallalieu,* Ann Mallalieu, QC, *b.* 1945, *m.*

1970   *Masham of Ilton,* Susan Lilian Primrose Cunliffe-Lister, *b.* 1935, *w.*

1999   *Massey of Darwen,* Doreen Elizabeth Massey, *b.* 1938, *m.*

2006   *Meacher,* Molly Christine Meacher, *b.* 1940, *m.*

1998   *Miller of Chilthorne Domer,* Susan Elizabeth Miller, *b.* 1954

1993   *Miller of Hendon,* Doreen Miller, MBE, *b.* 1933, *m.*

2004   *Morgan of Drefelin,* Delyth Jane Morgan, *b.* 1961, *m.*

2011   *Morgan of Ely,* Mair Eluned Morgan, *b.* 1967, *m.*

2001   *Morgan of Huyton,* Sally Morgan, *b.* 1959, *m.*

2004   *Morris of Bolton,* Patricia Morris, OBE, *b.* 1953

2005   *Morris of Yardley,* Estelle Morris, PC, *b.* 1952

2004   *Murphy,* Elaine Murphy, *b.* 1947, *m.*

2004   *Neuberger,* Rabbi Julia (Babette Sarah) Neuberger, DBE, *b.* 1950, *m.*

2007   *Neville-Jones,* (Lilian) Pauline Neville-Jones, DCMG, PC, *b.* 1939

2010   *Newlove,* Helen Margaret Newlove, *w.*

1997   *Nicholson of Winterbourne,* Emma Harriet Nicholson, MEP, *b.* 1941, *m.*

1982   *Nicol,* Olive Mary Wendy Nicol, *b.* 1923, *m.*

2000   *Noakes,* Shiela Valerie Masters, DBE, *b.* 1949, *m.*

2000   *Northover,* Lindsay Patricia Granshaw, *b.* 1954

2010   *Nye,* Susan Nye, *b.* 1955, *m.*

1991   *O'Cathain,* Detta O'Cathain, OBE, *b.* 1938, *m.*

2009   *O'Loan,* Nuala Patricia, DBE, *b.* 1951, *m.*

1999   *O'Neill of Bengarve,* Onora Sylvia O'Neill, CBE, PHD, *b.* 1941

1989   *Oppenheim-Barnes,* Sally Oppenheim-Barnes, PC, *b.* 1930, *m.*

2006   *Paisley of St George's,* Eileen Emily Paisley, *m.*

2010   *Parminter,* Kathryn Jane Parminter, *b.* 1964, *m.*

1991   *Perry of Southwark,* Pauline Perry, *b.* 1931, *m.*

1997   *Pitkeathley,* Jill Elizabeth Pitkeathley, OBE, *b.* 1940

1981   *Platt of Writtle,* Beryl Catherine Platt, CBE, FENG, *b.* 1923, *m.*

1999   *Prashar,* Usha Kumari Prashar, CBE, PC, *b.* 1948, *m.*

2004   *Prosser,* Margaret Theresa Prosser, OBE, *b.* 1937

2006   *Quin,* Joyce Gwendoline Quin, PC *b.* 1944

1996   *Ramsay of Cartvale,* Margaret Mildred (Meta) Ramsay, *b.* 1936

2011   *Randerson,* Jennifer Elizabeth Randerson, *b.* 1948, *m.*

1994   *Rawlings,* Patricia Elizabeth Rawlings, *b.* 1939

1997   *Rendell of Babergh,* Ruth Barbara Rendell, CBE, *b.* 1930, *m.*

1998   *Richardson of Calow,* Kathleen Margaret Richardson, OBE, *b.* 1938, *m.*

2010   *Ritchie of Brompton,* Shireen Olive Ritchie,
        b. 1945

2004   *Royall of Blaisdon,* Janet Anne Royall, PC,
        b. 1955, *m.*

1997   *Scotland of Asthal,* Patricia Janet Scotland, QC,
        b. 1955, *m.*

2000   *Scott of Needham Market,* Rosalind Carol Scott,
        b. 1957

1991   *Seccombe,* Joan Anna Dalziel Seccombe, DBE,
        b. 1930, *m.*

2010   *Shackleton of Belgravia,* Fiona Sara Shackleton,
        LVO, *b.* 1956, *m.*

1998   *Sharp of Guildford,* Margaret Lucy Sharp,
        b. 1938, *m.*

1973   *Sharples,* Pamela Sharples, *b.* 1923, *m.*

2005   *Shephard of Northwold,* Gillian Patricia
        Shephard, PC, *b.* 1940, *m.*

2010   *Sherlock,* Maeve Christina Mary Sherlock, OBE,
        b. 1960

2010   *Smith of Basildon,* Angela Evans Smith, PC, *b.*
        1959, *m.*

1995   *Smith of Gilmorehill,* Elizabeth Margaret Smith,
        b. 1940, *w.*

2010   *Stedman-Scott,* Deborah Stedman-Scott, OBE,
        b. 1955

1999   *Stern,* Vivien Helen Stern, CBE, *b.* 1941

2011   *Stowell of Beeston,* Tina Wendy Stowell, MBE,
        b. 1967

1996   *Symons of Vernham Dean,* Elizabeth Conway
        Symons, *b.* 1951

2005   *Taylor of Bolton,* Winifred Ann Taylor, PC
        b. 1947, *m.*

1992   *Thatcher,* Margaret Hilda Thatcher, KG, OM,
        PC, FRS, *b.* 1925, *w.*

1994   *Thomas of Walliswood,* Susan Petronella
        Thomas, OBE, *b.* 1935, *m.*

2006   *Thomas of Winchester,* Celia Marjorie Thomas,
        MBE, *b.* 1945

1998   *Thornton,* (Dorothea) Glenys Thornton,
        b. 1952, *m.*

2005   *Tonge,* Dr. Jennifer Louise Tonge, *b.* 1941, *m.*

1980   *Trumpington,* Jean Alys Barker, DCVO, PC,
        b. 1922, *w.*

1985   *Turner of Camden,* Muriel Winifred Turner,
        b. 1927, *m.*

2011   *Tyler of Enfield,* Claire Tyler

1998   *Uddin,* Manzila Pola Uddin, *b.* 1959, *m.*

2007   *Vadera,* Shriti Vadera, PC

2005   *Valentine,* Josephine Clare Valentine

2006   *Verma,* Sandip Verma, *b.* 1959, *m.*

2004   *Wall of New Barnet,* Margaret Mary Wall,
        b. 1941, *m.*

2000   *Walmsley,* Joan Margaret Walmsley, *b.* 1943

1985   *Warnock,* Helen Mary Warnock, DBE,
        b. 1924, *w.*

2007   *Warsi,* Sayeeda Hussain Warsi, PC, *b.* 1971

1999   *Warwick of Undercliffe,* Diana Mary Warwick,
        b. 1945, *m.*

2010   *Wheatcroft,* Patience Jane Wheatcroft, *b.* 1951,
        m.

2010   *Wheeler,* Margaret Eileen Joyce Wheeler, MBE,
        b. 1949

1999   *Whitaker,* Janet Alison Whitaker, *b.* 1936

1996   *Wilcox,* Judith Ann Wilcox, *b.* 1940, *w.*

1999   *Wilkins,* Rosalie Catherine Wilkins, *b.* 1946

1993   *Williams of Crosby,* Shirley Vivien Teresa
        Brittain Williams, PC, *b.* 1930, *w.*

2011   *Worthington,* Bryony Katherine Worthington, *m.*

2004   *Young of Hornsey,* Prof. Margaret Omolola
        Young, OBE, *b.* 1951, *m.*

1997   *Young of Old Scone,* Barbara Scott Young,
        b. 1948

LORDS SPIRITUAL

The Lords Spiritual are the Archbishops of Canterbury and York and 24 diocesan bishops of the Church of England. The Bishops of London, Durham and Winchester always have seats in the House of Lords; the other 21 seats are filled by the remaining diocesan bishops in order of seniority. The Bishop of Sodor and Man and the Bishop of Gibraltar are not eligible to sit in the House of Lords.

ARCHBISHOPS

Style, The Most Revd and Rt. Hon. the Lord Archbishop of_
Addressed as Archbishop *or* Your Grace

INTRODUCED TO HOUSE OF LORDS

2003   *Canterbury* (104th), Rowan Douglas Williams, PC, DPHIL, *b.* 1950, *m., cons.* 1992, *elected* 2002
2005   *York* (97th), John Mugabi Tucker Sentamu, PC, PHD, *b.* 1949, *m., cons.* 1996, *elected* 2005, *trans.* 2005

BISHOPS

Style, The Rt. Revd the Lord Bishop of _
Addressed as My Lord
elected date of confirmation as diocesan bishop

INTRODUCED TO HOUSE OF LORDS
as at 31 August 2011

1996   *London* (132nd), Richard John Carew Chartres, KCVO, PC, *b.* 1947, *m., cons.* 1992, *elected* 1995
2011   *Durham* (72nd), Justin Welby, *b.* 1956, *m., cons.* 2011, *elected* 2011
1996   *Winchester* (96th), Michael Charles Scott-Joynt, *b.* 1943, *m., cons.* 1987, *elected* 1995
1997   *Manchester* (11th), Nigel Simeon McCulloch, *b.* 1942, *m., cons.* 1986, *elected* 1992, *trans.* 2002
2001   *Chester* (40th), Peter Robert Forster, PHD, *m., b.* 1950, *cons.* 1996, *elected* 1996
2003   *Newcastle* (11th), (John) Martin Wharton, *b.* 1944, *m., cons.* 1992, *elected* 1997
2003   *Liverpool* (7th), James Stuart Jones, *b.* 1948, *m., cons.* 1994, *elected* 1998
2003   *Leicester* (6th), Timothy John Stevens, *b.* 1946, *m., cons.* 1995, *elected* 1999
2004   *Norwich* (71st), Graham Richard James, *b.* 1951, *m., cons.* 1993, *elected* 1999
2005   *Exeter* (70th), Michael Lawrence Langrish, *b.* 1946, *m., cons.* 1993, *elected* 2000
2006   *Ripon and Leeds* (12th), John Richard Packer, *b.* 1946, *m., cons.* 1996, *elected* 2000
2008   *Chichester* (102nd), John William Hind, *b.* 1945, *m., cons.* 1991, *elected* 2001

2008   *Bath and Wells* (77th), Peter Bryan Price, *b.* 1944, *m., cons.* 1997, *elected* 2002
2009   *Wakefield* (12th), Stephen George Platten, *b.* 1947, *m., cons.* 2003, *elected* 2003
2009   *Bristol* (55th), Michael Arthur Hill, *b.* 1947, *m., cons.* 1998, *elected* 2003
2009   *Lichfield* (98th), Jonathan Michael Gledhill, *b.* 1949, *m., cons.* 1996, *elected* 2003
2009   *Blackburn* (8th), Nicholas Stewart Reade, *b.* 1946, *cons.* 2004, *elected* 2004
2009   *Hereford* (104th), Anthony Martin Priddis, *b.* 1948, *cons.* 1996, *elected* 2004
2009   *Gloucester* (40th), Michael Francis Perham, *b.* 1947, *m., cons.* 2004, *elected* 2004
2010   *Guildford* (9th), Christopher John Hill, *b.* 1945, *m., cons.* 1996, *elected* 2004
2010   *Derby* (7th), Alastair Llewellyn John Redfern, *b.* 1948, *m., cons.* 1997, *elected* 2005
2010   *Birmingham* (9th), David Andrew Urquhart, *b.* 1952, *cons.* 2000, *elected* 2006
2011   *Oxford* (42nd), John Lawrence Pritchard, *b.* 1948, *m., cons.* 2002, *elected* 2007
2011   *St Edmundsbury and Ipswich* (10th), (William) Nigel Stock, *b.* 1950, *m., cons.* 2000, *elected* 2007

BISHOPS AWAITING SEATS, in order of seniority
as at 31 August 2011

Worcester (113th), John Geoffrey Inge, PHD, *b.* 1955, *m., cons.* 2003, *elected* 2007
Coventry (9th), Christopher John Cocksworth, PHD, *b.* 1959, *m., cons.* 2008, *elected* 2008
Truro (15th), Timothy Martin Thornton, *b.* 1957, *m., cons.* 2001, *elected* 2008
Sheffield (7th), Stephen John Lindsey Croft, *b.* 1957, *m., cons.* 2009, *elected* 2009
St Albans (10th), Alan Gregory Clayton Smith, *b.* 1957, *cons.* 2001, *elected* 2009
Carlisle (66th), James Newcome, *b.* 1953, *m., cons.* 2002, *elected* 2009
Southwell and Nottingham (11th), Paul Butler, *b.* 1955, *cons.* 2004, *elected* 2009
Peterborough (38th), Donald Spargo Allister, *b.* 1952, *m., cons.* 2010, *elected* 2010
Portsmouth (9th), Christopher Richard James Foster, *b.* 1953, *m., cons.* 2001, *elected* 2010
Chelmsford (10th), Stephen Cottrell, *b.* 1958, *m., cons.* 2004, *elected* 2010
Rochester (107th), James Langstaff, *b.* 1956, *m., cons.* 2004, *elected* 2010
Ely (69th), Stephen Conway, *b.* 1957, *cons.* 2006, *elected* 2010
Southwark (10th), Christopher Chessun, *b.* 1956, *cons.* 2005, *elected* 2011
Bradford (10th), Nicholas Baines, *b.* 1957, *m., cons.* 2011, *elected* 2011
Salisbury (78th), Nicholas Holtam, *b.* 1954, *m., cons.* 2011, *elected* 2011
Lincoln (71st), Christopher Lowson, *b.* 1953, *m., cons.* 2011, *elected* 2011

COURTESY TITLES AND PEERS' SURNAMES

COURTESY TITLES

The heir apparent to a Duke, Marquess or Earl uses the highest of his father's other titles as a courtesy title. For example, the Marquess of Blandford is heir to the Dukedom of Marlborough, and Viscount Amberley to the Earldom of Russell. Titles of second heirs (when in use) are also given, and the courtesy title of the father of a second heir is indicated by * eg Earl of Mornington, eldest son of *Marquess of Douro.

The holder of a courtesy title is not styled 'the Most Hon.' or 'the Rt. Hon.', and in correspondence 'the' is omitted before the title. The heir apparent to a Scottish title may use the title 'Master'.

MARQUESSES
*Blandford –
  Marlborough, D.
Bowmont and Cessford –
  Roxburghe, D.
*Douro – *Wellington, D.*
Graham – *Montrose, D.*
*Hamilton – *Abercorn, D.*
Lorne – *Argyll, D.*
Stafford – *Sutherland, D.*
Tavistock – *Bedford, D.*
Tullibardine – *Atholl, D.*
*Worcester – *Beaufort, D.*

EARLS
Aboyne – *Huntly, M.*
Arundel and Surrey –
  Norfolk, D.
Bective – *Headfort, M.*
Belfast – *Donegall, M.*
Brecknock – *Camden, M.*
Burford – *St Albans, D.*
Burlington – *Devonshire, D.*
*Cardigan – *Ailesbury, M.*
Compton – *Northampton,
  M.*
*Dalkeith – *Buccleuch, D.*
Dumfries – *Bute, M.*
*Euston – *Grafton, D.*
Glamorgan – *Worcester,
  M.*
Grosvenor – *Westminster,
  D.*
Haddo – *Aberdeen and
  Temair, M.*
Hillsborough – *Downshire,
  M.*
Hopetoun – *Linlithgow, M.*
Kerry – *Lansdowne, M.*
March and Kinrara –
  Richmond, D.
Medina – *Milford Haven,
  M.*
*Mount Charles –
  Conyngham, M.*
Mornington – *Douro, M.*
Mulgrave – *Normanby, M.*
Percy – *Northumberland,
  D.*

Rocksavage –
  Cholmondeley, M.
Ronaldshay – *Zetland, M.*
*St Andrews – *Kent, D.*
*Southesk – *Fife, D.*
Sunderland – *Blandford,
  M.*
*Tyrone – *Waterford, M.*
Ulster – *Gloucester, D.*
*Uxbridge – *Anglesey, M.*
Wiltshire – *Winchester, M.*
Yarmouth – *Hertford, M.*

VISCOUNTS
Alexander – *Caledon, E.*
Althorp – *Spencer, E.*
Andover – *Suffolk and
  Berkshire, E.*
Anson – *Lichfield, E.*
Asquith – *Oxford and
  Asquith, E.*
Boringdon – *Morley, E.*
Borodale – *Beatty, E.*
Boyle – *Shannon, E.*
Brocas – *Jellicoe, E.*
Bury – *Albermarle, E.*
Campden – *Gainsborough,
  E.*
Carlow – *Portarlington, E.*
Carlton – *Wharncliffe, E.*
Castlereagh – *Londonderry,
  M.*
Chelsea – *Cadogan, E.*
Chewton – *Waldegrave, E.*
Clanfield – *Peel, E.*
Clive – *Powis, E.*
Coke – *Leicester, E.*
Corry – *Belmore, E.*
Corvedale – *Baldwin of
  Bewdley, E.*
Cranborne – *Salisbury,
  M.*
Cranley – *Onslow, E.*
Crichton – *Erne, E.*
Curzon – *Howe, E.*
Dalrymple – *Stair, E.*
Dangan – *Cowley, E.*
Drumlanrig – *Queensberry,
  M.*

Duncannon – *Bessborough,
  E.*
Dungarvan – *Cork and
  Orrery, E.*
Dunluce – *Antrim, E.*
Dunwich – *Stradbroke, E.*
Dupplin – *Kinnoull, E.*
Ednam – *Dudley, E.*
Elveden – *Iveagh, E.*
Emlyn – *Cawdor, E*
Encombe – *Eldon, E.*
Enfield – *Strafford, E.*
Erleigh – *Reading, M.*
Errington – *Cromer, E.*
Feilding – *Denbigh and
  Desmond, E.*
FitzHarris – *Malmesbury,
  E.*
Folkestone – *Radnor, E.*
Forbes – *Granard, E.*
Garmoyle – *Cairns, E.*
Garnock – *Lindsay, E.*
Glenapp – *Inchcape, E.*
Glentworth – *Limerick, E.*
Grey de Wilton – *Wilton,
  E.*
Grimstone – *Verulam, E.*
Gwynedd – *Lloyd George
  of Dwyfor, E.*
Hawkesbury – *Liverpool, E.*
Hinchingbrooke –
  Sandwich, E.
Ikerrin – *Carrick, E.*
Ingestre – *Shrewsbury, E.*
Jocelyn – *Roden, E.*
Kelburn – *Glasgow, E.*
Kingsborough – *Kingston,
  E.*
Kirkwall – *Orkney, E.*
Knebworth – *Lytton, E.*
Lambton – *Durham, E.*
Lascelles – *Harewood, E.*
Linley – *Snowdon, E.*
Lymington – *Portsmouth, E.*
Macmillan of Ovenden –
  Stockton, E.
Maidstone – *Winchilsea,
  E*
Maitland – *Lauderdale, E.*
Mandeville – *Manchester,
  D.*
Marsham – *Romney, E.*
Melgund – *Minto, E.*
Merton – *Nelson, E.*
Moore – *Drogheda, E.*
Newport – *Bradford, E.*
Northland – *Ranfurly, E*
Newry and Mourne –
  Kilmorey, E.
Petersham – *Harrington, E.*
Pollington – *Mexborough,
  E*

Raynham – *Townshend, M.*
Reidhaven – *Seafield, E.*
Royston – *Hardwicke, E.*
Ruthven of Canberra –
  Gowrie, E.
St Cyres – *Iddesleigh, E.*
Sandon – *Harrowby, E.*
Savernake – *Cardigan, E.*
Severn – *Wessex, E.*
Somerton – *Normanton, E.*
Stopford – *Courtown, E.*
Stormont – *Mansfield, E.*
Strabane – *Hamilton, M.*
Strathallan – *Perth, E.*
Stuart – *Castle Stewart, E.*
Suirdale – *Donoughmore, E.*
Tamworth – *Ferrers, E.*
Tarbat – *Cromartie, E.*
Vaughan – *Lisburne, E.*
Weymouth – *Bath, M.*
Windsor – *Plymouth, E.*
Wolmer – *Selborne, E.*
Woodstock – *Portland, E.*

BARONS (LORDS)
Aberdour – *Morton, E.*
Apsley – *Bathurst, E.*
Ardee – *Meath, E.*
Ashley – *Shaftesbury, E.*
Balgonie – *Leven and
  Melville, E.*
Balniel – *Crawford and
  Balcarres, E.*
Berriedale – *Caithness, E.*
Bingham – *Lucan, E.*
Binning – *Haddington, E.*
Brooke – *Warwick, E.*
Bruce – *Elgin, E.*
Burghley – *Exeter, M.*
Cardross – *Buchan, E.*
Carnegie – *Southesk, E.*
Clifton – *Darnley, E.*
Cochrane – *Dundonald, E.*
Courtenay – *Devon, E.*
Culloden – *Ulster, E.*
Dalmeny – *Rosebery, E.*
Doune – *Moray, E.*
Downpatrick – *St
  Andrews, E.*
Dunglass – *Home, E.*
Elcho – *Wemyss and
  March, E.*
Eliot – *St Germans, E.*
Formartine – *Haddo, E.*
Gillford – *Clanwilliam, E.*
Glamis – *Strathmore, E.*
Greenock – *Cathcart, E.*
Guernsey – *Aylesford, E.*
Hay – *Erroll, E.*
Howard of Effingham –
  Effingham, E.
Huntingtower – *Dysart, C.*

Irwin – *Halifax, E.*
Johnstone – *Annandale and Hartfell, E.*
Langton – *Temple of Stowe, E.*
La Poer – **Tyrone, E.*
Leveson – *Granville, E*
Loughborough – *Rosslyn, E.*

Masham – *Swinton, E.*
Mauchline – *Loudoun, C.*
Medway – *Cranbrook, E.*
Montgomerie – *Eglinton and Winton, E.*
Moreton – *Ducie, E.*
Naas – *Mayo, E.*
Norreys – *Lindsey and Abingdon, E.*

North – *Guilford, E.*
Ogilvy – *Airlie, E.*
Oxmantown – *Rosse, E.*
Paget de Beaudesert – **Uxbridge, E.*
Porchester – *Carnarvon, E.*
Ramsay – *Dalhousie, E.*
Romsey – *Mountbatten of Burma, C.*

Scrymgeour – *Dundee, E.*
Seymour – *Somerset, D.*
Stanley – *Derby, E.*
Stavordale – *Ilchester, E.*
Strathnaver – *Sutherland, C.*
Wodehouse – *Kimberley, E.*
Worsley – *Yarborough, E.*

PEERS' SURNAMES

The following symbols indicate the rank of the peer holding each title:

C.   Countess
D.   Duke
E.   Earl
M.   Marquess
V.   Viscount
*   Life Peer

Where no designation is given, the title is that of a hereditary Baron or Baroness.

Abney-Hastings – *Loudoun, C.*
Acheson – *Gosford, E.*
Adams – *A. of Craigielea**
Adderley – *Norton*
Addington – *Sidmouth, V.*
Adebowale – *A. of Thornes**
Agar – *Normanton, E.*
Ahmad – *A. of Wimbledon**
Aitken – *Beaverbrook*
Akers-Douglas – *Chilston, V.*
Alexander – *A. of Tunis, E.*
Alexander – *Caledon, E.*
Allan – *A. of Hallam**
Allen – *Croham**
Allsopp – *Hindlip*
Alton – *A. of Liverpool**
Ancram – *Kerr of Monteviot**
Anderson – *A. of Swansea**
Anderson – *Waverley, V.*
Anelay – *A. of St Johns**
Annesley – *Valentia, V.*
Anson – *Lichfield, E.*
Archer – *A. of Sandwell**
Archer – *A. of Weston-super-Mare**
Armstrong – *A. of Hill Top**
Armstrong – *A. of Ilminster**
Armstrong-Jones – *Snowdon, E.*
Arthur – *Glenarthur*
Arundell – *Talbot of Malahide*
Ashdown – *A. of Norton-sub-Hamdon**
Ashley – *A. of Stoke**

Ashley-Cooper – *Shaftesbury, E.*
Ashton – *A. of Hyde*
Ashton – *A. of Upholland**
Asquith – *Oxford and Asquith, E.*
Assheton – *Clitheroe*
Astley – *Hastings*
Astor – *A. of Hever*
Aubrey-Fletcher – *Braye*
Bailey – *Glanusk*
Baillie – *Burton*
Baillie Hamilton – *Haddington, E.*
Baker – *B. of Dorking**
Balchin – *Lingfield**
Baldwin – *B. of Bewdley, E.*
Balfour – *B. of Inchrye*
Balfour – *Kinross*
Balfour – *Riverdale*
Bampfylde – *Poltimore*
Banbury – *B. of Southam*
Barber – *B. of Tewkesbury**
Baring – *Ashburton*
Baring – *Cromer, E.*
Baring – *Howick of Glendale*
Baring – *Northbrook*
Baring – *Revelstoke*
Barker – *Trumpington**
Barnes – *Gorell*
Barnewall – *Trimlestown*
Bassam – *B. of Brighton**
Bathurst – *Bledisloe, V.*
Beauclerk – *St Albans, D.*
Beaumont – *Allendale, V.*
Beckett – *Grimthorpe*
Benn – *Stansgate, V.*
Bennet – *Tankerville, E.*
Bentinck – *Portland, E.*
Beresford – *Decies*
Beresford – *Waterford, M.*
Berry – *Camrose, V.*
Berry – *Kemsley, V.*
Bertie – *Lindsey, E.*
Best – *Wynford*
Bethell – *Westbury*
Bewicke-Copley – *Cromwell*
Bigham – *Mersey, V.*
Bingham – *Clanmorris*
Bingham – *Lucan, E.*
Bishop – *Glendonbrook**

Black – *B. of Brentwood**
Black – *B. of Crossharbour**
Blair – *B. of Boughton**
Bligh – *Darnley, E.*
Blyth – *B. of Rowington**
Bonham Carter – *B.-C. of Yarnbury**
Bootle-Wilbraham – *Skelmersdale*
Boscawen – *Falmouth, V.*
Boswell – *B. of Aynho**
Bottomley – *B. of Nettlestone**
Bourke – *Mayo, E.*
Bowes Lyon – *Strathmore, E.*
Bowyer – *Denham*
Boyd – *Kilmarnock*
Boyd – *B. of Duncansby**
Boyle – *Cork and Orrery, E.*
Boyle – *Glasgow, E.*
Boyle – *Shannon, E.*
Brabazon – *Meath, E.*
Brand – *Hampden, V.*
Brassey – *B. of Apethorpe*
Brett – *Esher, V.*
Bridgeman – *Bradford, E.*
Brittan – *B. of Spennithorne**
Brodrick – *Midleton, V.*
Brooke – *Alanbrooke, V.*
Brooke – *B. of Alverthorpe**
Brooke – *Brookeborough, V.*
Brooke – *B. of Sutton Mandeville**
Brooks – *B. of Tremorfa**
Brooks – *Crawshaw*
Brougham – *Brougham and Vaux*
Broughton – *Fairhaven*
Brown – *B. of Eaton-under-Heywood**
Browne – *B. of Belmont**
Browne – *B. of Ladyton**
Browne – *B. of Madingley**
Browne – *Kilmaine*
Browne – *Oranmore and Browne*
Browne – *Sligo, M.*
Bruce – *Aberdare*
Bruce – *Balfour of Burleigh*

Bruce – *Elgin and Kincardine, E.*
Brudenell-Bruce – *Ailesbury, M.*
Buchan – *Tweedsmuir*
Buckley – *Wrenbury*
Butler – *B. of Brockwell**
Butler – *Carrick, E.*
Butler – *Dunboyne*
Butler – *Mountgarret, V.*
Byng – *Strafford, E.*
Byng – *Torrington, V.*
Cambell-Savours – *C.-S. of Allerdale**
Cameron – *C. of Dillington**
Cameron – *C. of Lochbroom**
Campbell – *Argyll, D.*
Campbell – *C. of Alloway**
Campbell – *C. of Loughborough**
Campbell – *C. of Surbiton**
Campbell – *Cawdor, E.*
Campbell – *Colgrain*
Campbell – *Stratheden and Campbell*
Campbell-Gray – *Gray*
Canning – *Garvagh*
Capell – *Essex, E.*
Carey – *C. of Clifton**
Carington – *Carrington*
Carlisle – *C. of Berriew**
Carnegie – *Fife, D.*
Carnegy – *Northesk, E.*
Carr – *C. of Hadley**
Carter – *C. of Barnes**
Carter – *C. of Coles**
Cary – *Falkland, V.*
Caulfeild – *Charlemont, V.*
Cavendish – *C. of Furness**
Cavendish – *Chesham*
Cavendish – *Devonshire, D.*
Cavendish – *Waterpark*
Cayzer – *Rotherwick*
Cecil – *Amherst of Hackney*
Cecil – *Exeter, M.*
Cecil – *Rockley*
Chalker – *C. of Wallasey**
Chaloner – *Gisborough*
Chapman – *C. of Leeds**
Chapman – *Northfield**
Charteris – *Wemyss and March, E.*

Harbord-Hamond –
  Suffield
Harding – H. of Petherton
Hardinge – H. of Penshurst
Hare – Blakenham, V.
Hare – Listowel, E.
Harmsworth – Rothermere,
  V.
Harries – H. of
  Pentregarth*
Harris – H. of Haringey*
Harris – H. of Peckham*
Harris – H. of Richmond*
Harris – Malmesbury, E.
Hart – H. of Chilton*
Harvey – H. of Tasburgh
Hastings – H. of
  Scarisbrick*
Hastings Bass –
  Huntingdon, E.
Haughey – Ballyedmond*
Hay – Erroll, E.
Hay – Kinnoull, E.
Hay – Tweeddale, M.
Hayter – H. of Kentish
  Town*
Healy – H. of Primrose
  Hill*
Heathcote-Drummond-
  Willoughby –
  Willoughby de Eresby
Hely-Hutchinson –
  Donoughmore, E.
Henderson – Faringdon
Hennessy – H. of
  Nympsfield*
Hennessy – Windlesham
Henniker-Major –
  Henniker
Hepburne-Scott –
  Polwarth
Herbert – Carnarvon, E.
Herbert – Hemingford
Herbert – Pembroke, E.
Herbert – Powis, E.
Hervey – Bristol, M.
Heseltine – H. of
  Thenford*
Hewitt – Lifford, V.
Hicks Beach – St Aldwyn,
  E.
Hill – Downshire, M.
Hill – H. of Oareford*
Hill – Sandys
Hill-Trevor – Trevor
Hilton – H. of Eggardon*
Hobart-Hampden –
  Buckinghamshire, E.
Hodgson – H. of Astley
  Abbotts*
Hogg – Hailsham, V.
Holland-Hibbert –
  Knutsford, V.
Hollis – H. of Heigham*
Holmes à Court –
  Heytesbury
Hood – Bridport, V.
Hope – Glendevon

Hope – H. of Craighead*
Hope – H. of Thornes*
Hope – Linlithgow, M.
Hope – Rankeillour
Hope Johnstone –
  Annandale and Hartfell,
  E.
Hope-Morley – Hollenden
Hopkinson – Colyton
Hore Ruthven – Gowrie, E.
Hovell-Thurlow-
  Cumming-Bruce –
  Thurlow
Howard – Carlisle, E.
Howard – Effingham, E.
Howard – H. of Lympne*
Howard – H. of Penrith
Howard – H. of Rising*
Howard – Strathcona
Howard – Suffolk and
  Berkshire, E.
Howarth – H. of
  Breckland*
Howarth – H. of Newport*
Howe – H. of Aberavon*
Howe – H. of Idlicote*
Howell – H. of Guildford*
Howells – H. of St.
  Davids*
Howie – H. of Troon*
Hubbard – Addington
Huggins – Malvern, V.
Hughes – H. of Stretford*
Hughes – H. of Woodside*
Hughes-Young – St Helens
Hunt – H. of Chesterton*
Hunt – H. of Kings Heath*
Hunt – H. of Wirral*
Hurd – H. of Westwell*
Hutchinson – H. of
  Lullington*
Hutton – H. of Furness*
Ingrams – Darcy de Knayth
Innes-Ker – Roxburghe, D.
Inskip – Caldecote, V.
Irby – Boston
Irvine – I. of Lairg*
Isaacs – Reading, M.
James – J. of Blackheath*
James – J. of Holland Park*
James – Northbourne
Janner – J. of Braunstone*
Jay – J. of Ewelme*
Jay – J. of Paddington*
Jebb – Gladwyn
Jenkin – J. of Kennington*
Jenkin – J. of Roding*
Jervis – St Vincent, V.
Jocelyn – Roden, E.
Jolliffe – Hylton
Jones – J. of Birmingham*
Jones – J. of Cheltenham*
Jones – J. of Deeside*
Jones – J. of Whitchurch*
Joynson-Hicks – Brentford,
  V.
Kay-Shuttleworth –
  Shuttleworth

Kearley – Devonport, V.
Keith – Kintore, E.
Kemp – Rochdale, V.
Kennedy – Ailsa, M
Kennedy – K. of the
  Shaws*
Kennedy – K. of
  Southwark*
Kenworthy – Strabolgi
Keppel – Albemarle, E.
Kerr – K. of Kinlochard*
Kerr – K. of Tonaghmore*
Kerr – Lothian, M.
Kerr – Teviot
Kilpatrick – K. of
  Kincraig*
King – K. of Bow*
King – K. of West
  Bromwich*
King – Lovelace, E.
King-Tenison – Kingston,
  E.
Kinnock – K. of
  Holyhead*
Kirkham – Berners
Kirkwood – K. of
  Kirkhope*
Kitchener – K. of
  Khartoum, E.
Knatchbull – Brabourne
Knatchbull – Mountbatten
  of Burma, C.
Knight – K. of Collingtree*
Knight – K. of Weymouth*
Knox – Ranfurly, E.
Lamb – Rochester
Lambton – Durham, E.
Lamont – L. of Lerwick*
Lampson – Killearn
Lang – L. of Monkton*
Lascelles – Harewood, E.
Law – Coleraine
Law – Ellenborough
Lawrence – Trevethin and
  Oaksey
Lawson – Burnham
Lawson – L. of Blaby*
Lawson-Johnston – Luke
Lea – L. of Crondall*
Leach – L. of Fairford*
Lee – L. of Trafford*
Legge – Dartmouth, E.
Legh – Grey of Codnor
Legh – Newton
Leigh-Pemberton –
  Kingsdown*
Leith – Burgh
Lennox-Boyd – Boyd of
  Merton, V.
Le Poer Trench –
  Clancarty, E.
Leslie – Rothes, E.
Leslie Melville – Leven and
  Melville, E.
Lester – L. of Herne Hill*
Levene – L. of Portsoken*
Leveson-Gower –
  Granville, E.

Lewis – L. of Newnham*
Lewis – Merthyr
Liddell – L. of Coatdyke*
Liddell – Ravensworth
Lindesay-Bethune –
  Lindsay, E.
Lindsay – Crawford,
  E.
Lindsay – L. of Birker
Linklater – L. of
  Butterstone*
Lister – L. of Burtersett*
Littleton – Hatherton
Lloyd – L. of Berwick*
Lloyd George – Lloyd
  George of Dwyfor, E.
Lloyd George – Tenby, V.
Lloyd-Mostyn – Mostyn
Loder – Wakehurst
Lofthouse – L. of
  Pontefract*
Lopes – Roborough
Lord – Framlingham*
Lour – Carneggy of Lour*
Low – Aldington
Low – L. of Dalston*
Lowry-Corry – Belmore, E.
Lowther – Lonsdale, E.
Lowther – Ullswater, V.
Lubbock – Avebury
Lucas – L. of Chilworth
Lumley – Scarbrough, E.
Lumley-Savile – Savile
Lyon-Dalberg-Acton –
  Acton
Lysaght – Lisle
Lyttelton – Chandos, V.
Lyttelton – Cobham, V.
Lytton Cobbold – Cobbold
McAlpine – M. of West
  Green*
Macaulay – M. of Bragar*
Maclean – Blencathra*
McClintock-Bunbury –
  Rathdonnell
McColl – M. of Dulwich*
McConnell – M. of
  Glenscorrodale*
MacDonald – M. of River
  Glaven*
Macdonald – M. of
  Tradeston*
McDonnell – Antrim, E.
McFall – M. of Alcluith*
Macfarlane – M. of
  Bearsden*
McFarlane – M. of
  Llandaff*
MacGregor – M. of
  Pulham Market*
McIntosh – M. of
  Hudnall*
McKenzie – M. of Luton*
Mackay – Inchcape, E.
Mackay – M. of Clashfern*
Mackay – M. of
  Drumadoon*

St Leger – *Doneraile, V.*
Samuel – *Bearsted, V.*
Sanderson – *S. of Ayot*
Sanderson – *S. of Bowden**
Sandilands – *Torphichen*
Saumarez – *De Saumarez*
Savile – *Mexborough, E.*
Saville – *S. of Newdigate**
Scarlett – *Abinger*
Schreiber – *Marlesford**
Sclater-Booth – *Basing*
Scotland – *S. of Asthal**
Scott – *Eldon, E*
Scott – *S. of Foscotte**
Scott – *S. of Needham Market**.
Scrymgeour – *Dundee, E.*
Seager – *Leighton of St Mellons*
Seely – *Mottistone*
Seymour – *Hertford, M.*
Seymour – *Somerset, D.*
Shackleton – *S. of Belgravia**
Sharp – *S. of Guildford**
Shaw – *Craigmyle*
Shaw – *S. of Northstead**
Shephard – *S. of Northwood**
Sheppard – *S. of Didgemere**
Shirley – *Ferrers, E.*
Short – *Glenamara**
Shutt – *S. of Greetland**
Siddeley – *Kenilworth*
Sidney – *De L'Isle, V.*
Simon – *S. of Highbury**
Simon – *S. of Wythenshawe*
Simpson – *S. of Dunkeld**
Sinclair – *Caithness, E.*
Sinclair – *S. of Cleeve*
Sinclair – *S. of Thurso, V.*
Skeffington – *Massereene, V.*
Smith – *Bicester*
Smith – *Hambleden, V.*
Smith – *Kirkhill**
Smith – *S. of Basildon**
Smith – *S. of Clifton**
Smith – *Smith of Finsbury**
Smith – *S. of Gilmorehill**
Smith – *S. of Kelvin**
Smith – *S. of Leigh**
Somerset – *Beaufort, D.*
Somerset – *Raglan*
Soulsby – *S. of Swaffham Prior**
Spencer – *Churchill, V.*

Spencer-Churchill – *Marlborough, D.*
Spring – *Risby**
Spring Rice – *Monteagle of Brandon*
Stanhope – *Harrington, E.*
Stanley – *Derby, E.*
Stanley – *of Alderley and Sheffield*
Stapleton-Cotton – *Combermere, V.*
Steel – *S. of Aikwood**
Sterling – *S. of Plaistow**
Stern – *S. of Brentford**
Stevens – *S. of Kirkwhelpington**
Stevens – *S. of Ludgate**
Stevenson – *S. of Balmacara**
Stevenson – *S. of Coddenham**
Stewart – *Galloway, E.*
Stewart – *Stewartby**
Stoddart – *S. of Swindon**
Stone – *S. of Blackheath**
Stoneham – *S. of Droxford**
Stonor – *Camoys*
Stopford – *Courtown, E.*
Stourton – *Mowbray*
Stowell – *S. of Beeston**
Strachey – *O'Hagan*
Strutt – *Belper*
Strutt – *Rayleigh*
Stuart – *Castle Stewart, E.*
Stuart – *Moray, E.*
Stuart – *S. of Findhorn, V.*
Suenson-Taylor – *Grantchester*
Sutherland – *S. of Houndwood**
Symons – *S. of Vernham Dean**
Taylor – *Kilclooney**
Taylor – *T. of Blackburn**
Taylor – *T. of Bolton**
Taylor – *T. of Goss Moor**
Taylor – *T. of Holbeach**
Taylor – *T. of Warwick**
Taylour – *Headfort, M.*
Temple-Gore-Langton – *Temple of Stowe, E*
Temple-Morris – *Temple-Morris of Llandaff**
Tennant – *Glenconner*
Thellusson – *Rendlesham*
Thesiger – *Chelmsford, V.*

Thomas – *T. of Gresford**
Thomas – *T. of Macclesfield**
Thomas – *T. of Swynnerton**
Thomas – *T. of Walliswood**
Thomas – *T. of Winchester**
Thomson – *T. of Fleet*
Thynn – *Bath, M.*
Tottenham – *Ely, M.*
Trefusis – *Clinton*
Trench – *Ashtown*
Tufton – *Hothfield*
Turner – *Bilston**
Turner – *Netherthorpe*
Turner – *T. of Camden**
Turner – *T. of Ecchinswell**
Turnour – *Winterton, E.*
Tyler – *T. of Enfield**
Tyrell-Kenyon – *Kenyon*
Vanden-Bempde-Johnstone – *Derwent*
Vane – *Barnard*
Vane-Tempest-Stewart – *Londonderry, M.*
Vanneck – *Huntingfield*
Vaughan – *Lisburne, E.*
Vereker – *Gort, V.*
Verney – *Willoughby de Broke*
Vernon – *Lyveden*
Vesey – *De Vesci, V.*
Villiers – *Clarendon, E.*
Vincent – *V. of Coleshill**
Vivian – *Swansea*
Wade – *W. of Chorlton**
Waldegrave – *W. of North Hill**
Walker – *W. of Aldringham**
Walker – *W. of Gestingthorpe**
Wall – *W. of New Barnett**
Wallace – *Dudley*
Wallace – *W. of Saltaire**
Wallace – *W. of Tankerness**
Wallace – *W. of Tummel**
Wallop – *Portsmouth, E.*
Walton – *W. of Detchant**
Ward – *Bangor, V.*
Ward – *Dudley, E.*
Warrender – *Bruntisfield*
Warwick – *W. of Undercliffe**
Watson – *W. of Invergowrie**
Watson – *Manton*

Watson – *W. of Richmond**
Webber – *Lloyd-Webber**
Wedderburn – *W. of Charlton**
Weir – *Inverforth*
Weld-Forester – *Forester*
Wellesley – *Cowley, E.*
Wellesley – *Wellington, D.*
West – *W. of Spithead**
Westenra – *Rossmore*
White – *Annaly*
White – *Hanningfield**
Whiteley – *Marchamley*
Whitfield – *Kenswood*
Williams – *W. of Baglan**
Williams – *W. of Crosby**
Williams – *W. of Elve**
Williamson – *Forres*
Williamson – *W. of Horton**
Willis – *W. of Knaresborough**
Willoughby – *Middleton*
Wills – *Dulverton*
Wilson – *Moran*
Wilson – *Nunburnholme*
Wilson – *W. of Dinton**
Wilson – *W. of Tillyorn**
Windsor – *Gloucester, D.*
Windsor – *Kent, D.*
Windsor-Clive – *Plymouth, E.*
Wingfield – *Powerscourt, V.*
Winn – *St Oswald*
Wodehouse – *Kimberley, E.*
Wolfson – *W. of Aspley Guise**
Wolfson – *W. of Sunningdale**
Wood – *Halifax, E.*
Wood – *W. of Anfield**
Woodhouse – *Terrington*
Woolmer – *W. of Leeds**
Wright – *W. of Richmond**
Wyndham – *Egremont and Leconfield*
Wynn – *Newborough*
Yarde-Buller – *Churston*
Yerburgh – *Alvingham*
Yorke – *Hardwicke, E.*
Young – *Kennet*
Young – *Y. of Graffham**
Young – *Y. of Hornsey**
Young – *Y. of Norwood Green**
Young – *Y. of Old Scone**
Younger – *Y. of Leckie, V.*

ORDERS OF CHIVALRY

THE MOST NOBLE ORDER OF THE GARTER (1348)

KG
Ribbon, Blue
Motto, Honi soit qui mal y pense
(Shame on him who thinks evil of it)

The number of Knights and Lady Companions is limited to 24

SOVEREIGN OF THE ORDER
The Queen

LADIES OF THE ORDER
HRH The Princess Royal, 1994
HRH Princess Alexandra, The Hon. Lady Ogilvy, 2003

ROYAL KNIGHTS
HRH The Prince Philip, Duke of Edinburgh, 1947
HRH The Prince of Wales, 1958
HRH The Duke of Kent, 1985
HRH The Duke of Gloucester, 1997
HRH The Duke of York, 2006
HRH The Earl of Wessex, 2006
HRH The Duke of Cambridge, 2008

EXTRA KNIGHT COMPANIONS AND LADIES
Grand Duke Jean of Luxembourg, 1972
HM The Queen of Denmark, 1979
HM The King of Sweden, 1983
HM The King of Spain, 1988
HM The Queen of the Netherlands, 1989
HIM The Emperor of Japan, 1998
HM The King of Norway, 2001

KNIGHTS AND LADY COMPANIONS
Lord Carrington, 1985
Duke of Wellington, 1990
Lord Bramall, 1990
Viscount Ridley, 1992
Lord Sainsbury of Preston Candover, 1992
Lord Ashburton, 1994
Lord Kingsdown, 1994
Sir Ninian Stephen, 1994
Baroness Thatcher, 1995
Sir Timothy Colman, 1996
Duke of Abercorn, 1999
Sir William Gladstone, 1999
Lord Inge, 2001
Sir Anthony Acland, 2001
Duke of Westminster, 2003
Lord Butler of Brockwell, 2003
Lord Morris of Aberavon, 2003

Lady Soames, 2005
Sir John Major, 2005
Lord Luce, 2008
Sir Thomas Dunne, 2008
Lord Phillips of Worth Matravers, 2011
Lord Boyce, 2011

Prelate, Bishop of Winchester
Chancellor, Lord Carrington, KG, GCMG, CH, MC
Register, Dean of Windsor
Garter King of Arms, Thomas Woodcock, CVO
Gentleman Usher of the Black Rod, Lt.-Gen. David Leakey, CMG, CBE
Secretary, Patric Dickinson, LVO

THE MOST ANCIENT AND MOST NOBLE ORDER OF THE THISTLE (REVIVED 1687)

KT
Ribbon, Green
Motto, Nemo me impune lacessit
(No one provokes me with impunity)

The number of Knights and Ladies of the Thistle is limited to 16

SOVEREIGN OF THE ORDER
The Queen

ROYAL LADY OF THE ORDER
HRH The Princess Royal, 2000

ROYAL KNIGHTS
HRH The Prince Philip, Duke of Edinburgh, 1952
HRH The Prince of Wales, Duke of Rothesay, 1977

KNIGHTS AND LADIES
Earl of Elgin and Kincardine, 1981
Earl of Airlie, 1985
Viscount of Arbuthnott, 1996
Earl of Crawford and Balcarres, 1996
Lady Marion Fraser, 1996
Lord Macfarlane of Bearsden, 1996
Lord Mackay of Clashfern, 1997
Lord Wilson of Tillyorn, 2000
Lord Sutherland of Houndwood, 2002
Sir Eric Anderson, 2002
Lord Steel of Aikwood, 2004
Lord Robertson of Port Ellen, 2004

Lord Cullen of Whitekirk, 2007
Sir Garth Morrison, 2007
Lord Hope of Craighead, 2009
Lord Patel, 2009

Chancellor, Earl of Airlie, KT, GCVO, PC
Dean, Very Revd Gilleasbuig Macmillan, CVO
Secretary and Lord Lyon King of Arms, David Sellar
Gentleman Usher of the Green Rod, Rear-Adm. Christopher Layman, CB, DSO, LVO
Assistant Secretary, Mrs C. Roads, MVO

THE MOST HONOURABLE ORDER OF THE BATH (1725)

GCB *Military* GCB *Civil*

GCB Knight (or Dame) Grand Cross
KCB Knight Commander
DCB Dame Commander
CB Companion

Ribbon, Crimson
Motto, Tria juncta in uno
(Three joined in one)

Remodelled 1815, and enlarged many times since. The order is divided into civil and military divisions. Women became eligible for the order from 1 January 1971.

THE SOVEREIGN

GREAT MASTER AND FIRST OR PRINCIPAL KNIGHT GRAND CROSS
HRH The Prince of Wales, KG, KT, GCB, OM

Dean of the Order, Dean of Westminster
Bath King of Arms, Adm. Lord Boyce, KG, GCB, OBE
Registrar and Secretary, Rear-Adm. Iain Henderson, CB, CBE
Genealogist, Thomas Woodcock, CVO
Gentleman Usher of the Scarlet Rod, Maj.-Gen. Charles Vyvyan, CB, CBE
Deputy Secretary, Secretary of the Central Chancery of the Orders of Knighthood

Chancery, Central Chancery of the Orders of Knighthood, St James's Palace, London SW1A 1BH

THE ORDER OF MERIT (1902)

OM *Military*   OM *Civil*

OM
Ribbon, Blue and crimson

This order is designed as a special distinction for eminent men and women without conferring a knighthood upon them. The order is limited in numbers to 24, with the addition of foreign honorary members.

THE SOVEREIGN

HRH The Prince Philip, Duke of Edinburgh, 1968
Revd Prof. Owen Chadwick, KBE, 1983
Sir Andrew Huxley, 1983
Dr Frederick Sanger, 1986
Baroness Thatcher, 1990
Sir Michael Atiyah, 1992
Sir Aaron Klug, 1995
Lord Foster of Thames Bank, 1997
Sir Anthony Caro, 2000
Prof. Sir Roger Penrose, 2000
Sir Tom Stoppard, 2000
HRH The Prince of Wales, 2002
Lord May of Oxford, 2002
Lord Rothschild, 2002
Sir David Attenborough, 2005
Baroness Boothroyd, 2005
Sir Michael Howard, 2005
Sir Timothy Berners-Lee, KBE, 2007
Lord Eames, 2007
Lord Rees of Ludlow, 2007
Rt. Hon. Jean Chrétien, QC, 2009
Robert Neil MacGregor, 2010

Honorary Member, Nelson Mandela, 1995

Secretary and Registrar, Lord Fellowes, GCB, GCVO, PC, QSO
Chancery, Central Chancery of the Orders of Knighthood, St James's Palace, London SW1A 1BH

THE MOST DISTINGUISHED ORDER OF ST MICHAEL AND ST GEORGE (1818)

GCMG   KCMG

GCMG   Knight (or Dame) Grand Cross
KCMG   Knight Commander
DCMG   Dame Commander
CMG   Companion

Ribbon, Saxon blue, with scarlet centre
Motto, Auspicium melioris aevi
(Token of a better age)

THE SOVEREIGN

GRAND MASTER
HRH The Duke of Kent, KG, GCMG, GCVO, ADC

Prelate, Rt. Revd David Urquhart
Chancellor, Lord Robertson of Port Ellen, KT, GCMG
Secretary, Permanent Under-Secretary of State at the Foreign and Commonwealth Office and Head of the Diplomatic Service
Registrar, Sir David Manning, GCMG, CVO
King of Arms, Sir Jeremy Greenstock, GCMG
Gentleman Usher of the Blue Rod, Sir Anthony Figgis, KCVO, CMG
Dean, Dean of St Paul's
Deputy Secretary, Secretary of the Central Chancery of the Orders of Knighthood
Hon. Genealogist, Timothy Duke
Chancery, Central Chancery of the Orders of Knighthood, St James's Palace, London SW1A 1BH

THE IMPERIAL ORDER OF THE CROWN OF INDIA (1877) FOR LADIES

CI

Badge, the royal cipher of Queen Victoria in jewels within an oval, surmounted by an heraldic crown and attached to a bow of light blue watered ribbon, edged white

The honour does not confer any rank or title upon the recipient

No conferments have been made since 1947

HM The Queen, 1947

THE ROYAL VICTORIAN ORDER (1896)

GCVO   KCVO

GCVO   Knight or Dame Grand Cross
KCVO   Knight Commander
DCVO   Dame Commander
CVO   Commander
LVO   Lieutenant
MVO   Member

Ribbon, Blue, with red and white edges
Motto, Victoria

THE SOVEREIGN
GRAND MASTER
HRH The Princess Royal

Chancellor, Lord Chamberlain
Secretary, Keeper of the Privy Purse
Registrar, Secretary of the Central Chancery of the Orders of Knighthood
Chaplain, Chaplain of the Queen's Chapel of the Savoy
Hon. Genealogist, David White

THE MOST EXCELLENT ORDER OF THE BRITISH EMPIRE (1917)

GBE   KBE

The order was divided into military and civil divisions in December 1918

GBE	Knight or Dame Grand Cross
KBE	Knight Commander
DBE	Dame Commander
CBE	Commander
OBE	Officer
MBE	Member

Ribbon, Rose pink edged with pearl grey with vertical pearl stripe in centre (military division); without vertical pearl stripe (civil division)
Motto, For God and the Empire

THE SOVEREIGN

GRAND MASTER
HRH The Prince Philip, Duke of Edinburgh, KG, KT, OM, GBE, PC

Prelate, Bishop of London
King of Arms, Adm. Sir Peter Abbott, GBE, KCB
Registrar, Secretary of the Central Chancery of the Orders of Knighthood
Secretary, Secretary of the Cabinet and Head of the Home Civil Service
Dean, Dean of St Paul's
Gentleman Usher of the Purple Rod, Sir Alexander Michael Graham, GBE, DCL
Chancery, Central Chancery of the Orders of Knighthood, St James's Palace, London SW1A 1BH

ORDER OF THE COMPANIONS OF HONOUR (1917)

CH

Ribbon, Carmine, with gold edges

This order consists of one class only and carries with it no title. The number of awards is limited to 65 (excluding honorary members).

Anthony, Rt. Hon. John, 1981
Ashley of Stoke, Lord, 1975
Attenborough, Sir David, 1995
Baker, Dame Janet, 1993
Baker of Dorking, Lord, 1992
Birtwistle, Sir Harrison, 2000
Brenner, Sydney, 1986
Brook, Peter, 1998
Brooke of Sutton Mandeville, Lord, 1992
Carrington, Lord, 1983
Christie, Sir George, 2001
Davis, Sir Colin, 2001
De Chastelain, Gen. John, 1999
Dench, Dame Judi, 2005
Fraser, Rt. Hon. Malcolm, 1977
Glenamara, Lord, 1976
Hamilton, Richard, 1999
Hannay of Chiswick, Lord, 2003
Hawking, Prof. Stephen, 1989
Healey, Lord, 1979
Heseltine, Lord, 1997
Hobsbawm, Prof. Eric, 1998
Hockney, David, 1997
Hodgkin, Sir Howard, 2002
Howard, Sir Michael, 2002
Howard of Lympne, Lord, 2011
Howe of Aberavon, Lord, 1996
Hurd of Westwell, Lord, 1995
King of Bridgwater, Lord, 1992
Lessing, Doris, 1999
Lovelock, Prof. James, 2002
McKellen, Sir Ian Murray, 2008
McKenzie, Prof. Dan Peter, 2003
Major, Rt. Hon. Sir John, 1998
Owen, Lord, 1994
Patten of Barnes, Rt. Hon. Lord, 1997
Pawson, Prof. Anthony James, 2006
Riley, Bridget, 1998
Rogers of Riverside, Lord, 2008
Sanger, Dr. Frederick, 1981
Somare, Rt. Hon. Sir Michael, 1978
Talboys, Rt. Hon. Sir Brian, 1981
Tebbit, Lord, 1987

Honorary Members, Lee Kuan Yew, 1970; Prof. Amartya Sen, 2000; Bernard Haitink, 2002
Secretary and Registrar, Secretary of the Central Chancery of the Orders of Knighthood

THE DISTINGUISHED SERVICE ORDER (1886)

DSO

Ribbon, Red, with blue edges

Bestowed in recognition of especial services in action of commissioned officers in the Navy, Army and Royal Air Force and (since 1942) Mercantile Marine. The members are Companions only. A bar may be awarded for any additional act of service.

THE IMPERIAL SERVICE ORDER (1902)

ISO

Ribbon, Crimson, with blue centre

Appointment as companion of this order is open to members of the civil services whose eligibility is determined by the grade they hold. The order consists of the sovereign and companions to a number not exceeding 1,900, of whom 1,300 may belong to the home civil services and 600 to overseas civil services. The then prime minister announced in March 1993 that he would make no further recommendations for appointments to the order.

Secretary, Secretary of the Cabinet and Head of the Home Civil Service
Registrar, Secretary of the Central Chancery of the Orders of Knighthood

THE ROYAL VICTORIAN CHAIN (1902)

It confers no precedence on its holders

HM THE QUEEN

HM The King of Thailand, 1960
HM The Queen of Denmark, 1974
HM The King of Sweden, 1975
HM The Queen of the Netherlands, 1982
Gen. Antonio Eanes, 1985
HM The King of Spain, 1986
Dr Richard von Weizsäcker, 1992
HM The King of Norway, 1994
Earl of Airlie, 1997
Rt. Revd and Rt. Hon. Lord Carey of Clifton, 2002
HRH Prince Philip, Duke of Edinburgh, 2007
HM The King of Saudi Arabia, 2007
HM The Sultan of Oman, 2010

BARONETAGE AND KNIGHTAGE

BARONETS

Style, 'Sir' before forename and surname, followed by 'Bt'.
Envelope, Sir F_ S_, Bt. *Letter (formal)*, Dear Sir; *(social)*,
Dear Sir F_. *Spoken*, Sir F_
Wife's style, 'Lady' followed by surname
Envelope, Lady S_. *Letter (formal)*, Dear Madam; *(social)*,
Dear Lady S_. *Spoken*, Lady S_
Style of Baronetess, 'Dame' before forename and surname,
followed by 'Btss.' *(see also* Dames)

There are five different creations of baronetcies: Baronets
of England (creations dating from 1611); Baronets of
Ireland (creations dating from 1619); Baronets of
Scotland or Nova Scotia (creations dating from 1625);
Baronets of Great Britain (creations after the Act of Union
1707 which combined the kingdoms of England and
Scotland); and Baronets of the United Kingdom (creations
after the union of Great Britain and Ireland in 1801).

Badge of Baronets of the   *Badge of Baronets*
United Kingdom   *of Nova Scotia*

Badge of Ulster

The patent of creation limits the destination of a
baronetcy, usually to male descendants of the first
baronet, although special remainders allow the baronetcy
to pass, if the male issue of sons fail, to the male issue of
daughters of the first baronet. In the case of baronetcies of
Scotland or Nova Scotia, a special remainder of 'heirs
male and of tailzie' allows the baronetcy to descend to
heirs general, including women. There are four existing
Scottish baronets with such a remainder.

The Official Roll of the Baronetage is kept at the
Crown Office and maintained by the Registrar and
Assistant Registrar of the Baronetage. Anyone who
considers that he or she is entitled to be entered on the
roll may apply through the Crown Office to prove their
succession. Every person succeeding to a baronetcy must
exhibit proofs of succession to the Lord Chancellor. A
person whose name is not entered on the official roll will
not be addressed or mentioned by the title of baronet or
baronetess in any official document, nor will he or she be
accorded precedence as a baronet of baronetess.

BARONETCIES EXTINCT SINCE THE LAST EDITION
Beaumont (cr. 1661); Lawes (cr. 1882)

OFFICIAL ROLL OF THE BARONETAGE, Crown Office,
House of Lords, London SW1A 0PW T 020-7219 2632
Registrar, Ian Denyer, MVO
Assistant Registrar, Grant Bavister

KNIGHTS

Style, 'Sir' before forename and surname, followed by
appropriate post-nominal initials if a Knight Grand
Cross, Knight Grand Commander or Knight
Commander
Envelope, Sir F_ S_. *Letter (formal)*, Dear Sir; *(social)*, Dear
Sir F_. *Spoken*, Sir F_
Wife's style, 'Lady' followed by surname
Envelope, Lady S_. *Letter (formal)*, Dear Madam; *(social)*,
Dear Lady S_. *Spoken*, Lady S_

The prefix 'Sir' is not used by knights who are clerics of
the Church of England, who do not receive the accolade.
Their wives are entitled to precedence as the wife of a
knight but not to the style of 'Lady'.

ORDERS OF KNIGHTHOOD
Knight Grand Cross, Knight Grand Commander, and
Knight Commander are the higher classes of the Orders
of Chivalry (*see* Orders of Chivalry). Honorary
knighthoods of these orders may be conferred on men
who are citizens of countries of which the Queen is not
head of state. As a rule, the prefix 'Sir' is not used by
honorary knights.

KNIGHTS BACHELOR

The Knights Bachelor do not constitute a royal order, but
comprise the surviving representation of the ancient state
orders of knighthood. The Register of Knights Bachelor,
instituted by James I in the 17th century, lapsed, and in
1908 a voluntary association under the title of the Society
of Knights (now the Imperial Society of Knights
Bachelor) was formed with the primary objectives of
continuing the various registers dating from 1257 and
obtaining the uniform registration of every created
Knight Bachelor. In 1926 a design for a badge to be worn
by Knights Bachelor was approved and adopted; in 1974
a neck badge and miniature were added.

THE IMPERIAL SOCIETY OF KNIGHTS BACHELOR,
1 Throgmorton Avenue, London EC2N 2BY
Knight Principal, Lord Lingfield
Prelate, Rt. Revd and Rt. Hon. Bishop of London
Registrar, Sir Paul Judge
Hon. Treasurer, Sir Colin Berry
Clerk to the Council, Col. Simon Doughty

LIST OF BARONETS AND KNIGHTS *as at 31 August 2011*

†	Not registered on the Official Roll of the Baronetage at the time of going to press
()	The date of creation of the baronetcy is given in parentheses
I	Baronet of Ireland
NS	Baronet of Nova Scotia
S	Baronet of Scotland

A full entry in italic type indicates that the recipient of a knighthood died during the year in which the honour was conferred. The name is included for purposes of record. Peers are not included in this list.

Aaronson, Sir Michael John, Kt., CBE
Abbott, *Adm.* Sir Peter Charles, GBE, KCB
Abdy, Sir Valentine Robert Duff, Bt. (1850)
Abed, *Dr* Sir Fazle Hasan, KCMG
Ackroyd, Sir Timothy Robert Whyte, Bt. (1956)
Acland, Sir Antony Arthur, KG, GCMG, GCVO
Acland, *Lt.-Col.* Sir (Christopher) Guy (Dyke), Bt. (1890), MVO
†Acland, Sir Dominic Dyke, Bt. (1644)
Adam, Sir Kenneth Hugo, Kt., OBE
Adams, Sir Geoffrey Doyne, KCMG
Adams, Sir William James, KCMG
Adsetts, Sir William Norman, Kt., OBE
Adye, Sir John Anthony, KCMG
Aga Khan IV, HH Prince Karim, KBE
†Agnew, Sir Crispin Hamlyn, Bt. (S. 1629)
†Agnew, Sir George Anthony, Bt. (1895)
Agnew, Sir Rudolph Ion Joseph, Kt.
Agnew-Somerville, Sir James Lockett Charles, Bt. (1957)
Ah Koy, Sir James Michael, KBE
Aikens, *Rt. Hon.* Sir Richard John Pearson, Kt.
†Ainsworth, Sir Anthony Thomas Hugh, Bt. (1916)
Aird, Sir (George) John, Bt. (1901)
Airy, *Maj.-Gen.* Sir Christopher John, KCVO, CBE
Aitchison, Sir Charles Walter de Lancey, Bt. (1938)
Ajegbo, Sir Keith Onyema, Kt., OBE
Akenhead, *Hon.* Sir Robert, Kt.
Akers-Jones, Sir David, KBE, CMG
Alberti, *Prof.* Sir Kurt George Matthew Mayer, Kt.
Albu, Sir George, Bt. (1912)
Alcock, *Air Chief Marshal* Sir (Robert James) Michael, GCB, KBE
Aldous, *Rt. Hon.* Sir William, Kt.
†Alexander, Sir Richard, Bt. (1945)
Alexander, Sir Douglas, Bt. (1921)
Allen, *Prof.* Sir Geoffrey, Kt., PHD, FRS
Allen, Sir John Derek, Kt., CBE
Allen, Sir Mark John Spurgeon, Kt., CMG
Allen, *Hon.* Sir Peter Austin Philip Jermyn, Kt.
Allen, Sir Thomas Boaz, Kt., CBE
Allen, *Hon.* Sir William Clifford, KCMG

Allen, Sir William Guilford, Kt.
Alleyne, Sir George Allanmoore Ogarren, Kt.
Alleyne, *Revd* John Olpherts Campbell, Bt. (1769)
Allinson, Sir (Walter) Leonard, KCVO, CMG
Alliott, *Hon.* Sir John Downes, Kt.
Allison, *Air Chief Marshal* Sir John Shakespeare, KCB, CBE
Amet, *Hon.* Sir Arnold Karibone, Kt.
Amory, Sir Ian Heathcoat, Bt. (1874)
Anderson, *Dr* Sir James Iain Walker, Kt., CBE
Anderson, Sir John Anthony, KBE
Anderson, Sir Leith Reinsford Steven, Kt., CBE
Anderson, *Prof.* Sir Roy Malcolm, Kt.
Anderson, Sir (William) Eric Kinloch, KT.
Anderson, *Prof.* Sir (William) Ferguson, Kt., OBE
Anderton, Sir (Cyril) James, Kt., CBE, QPM
Andrew, Sir Robert John, KCB
Andrews, Sir Derek Henry, KCB, CBE
Andrews, Sir Ian Charles Franklin, Kt., CBE, TD
Annesley, Sir Hugh Norman, Kt., QPM
Anson, *Vice-Adm.* Sir Edward Rosebery, KCB
Anson, Sir John, KCB
Anson, *Rear-Adm.* Sir Peter, Bt. CB (1831)
Anstruther, Sir Sebastian Paten Campbell, Bt. (S. 1694)
Anstruther-Gough-Calthorpe, Sir Euan Hamilton, Bt. (1929)
Antrobus, Sir Edward Philip, Bt. (1815)
Appleyard, Sir Leonard Vincent, KCMG
Appleyard, Sir Raymond Kenelm, KBE
Arbib, Sir Martyn, Kt.
Arbuthnot, Sir Keith Robert Charles, Bt. (1823)
Arbuthnot, Sir William Reierson, Bt. (1964)
Arbuthnott, *Prof.* Sir John Peebles, Kt., PHD, FRSE
†Archdale, Sir Nicholas Edward, Bt. (1928)
Arculus, Sir Ronald, KCMG, KCVO
Arculus, Sir Thomas David Guy, Kt.

Armitage, *Air Chief Marshal* Sir Michael John, KCB, CBE
Armour, *Prof.* Sir James, Kt., CBE
Armstrong, Sir Christopher John Edmund Stuart, Bt. (1841), MBE
Armstrong, Sir Patrick John, Kt., CBE
Armstrong, Sir Richard, Kt., CBE
Armytage, Sir John Martin, Bt. (1738)
Arnold, *Hon.* Sir Richard David, Kt.
Arnold, Sir Thomas Richard, Kt.
Arnott, Sir Alexander John Maxwell, Bt. (1896)
†Arthur, Sir Benjamin Nathan Arthur, Bt. (1841)
Arthur, Sir Gavyn Farr, Kt.
Arthur, *Lt.-Gen.* Sir (John) Norman Stewart, KCB, CVO
Arthur, Sir Michael Anthony, KCMG
Arulkumaran, *Prof.* Sir Sabaratnam, Kt.
Asbridge, Sir Jonathan Elliott, Kt.
Ash, *Prof.* Sir Eric Albert, Kt., CBE, FRS, FRENG
Ashburnham, Sir James Fleetwood, Bt. (1661)
Ashmore, *Admiral of the Fleet* Sir Edward Beckwith, GCB, DSC
Ashworth, *Dr* Sir John Michael, Kt.
Aske, Sir Robert John Bingham, Bt. (1922)
Askew, Sir Bryan, Kt.
Asscher, Prof. Sir (Adolf) William, Kt., MD, FRCP
Astill, *Hon.* Sir Michael John, Kt.
Astley-Cooper, Sir Alexander Paston, Bt. (1821)
Astwood, *Hon.* Sir James Rufus, KBE
Atcherley, Sir Harold Winter, Kt.
Atiyah, Sir Michael Francis, Kt., OM, PHD, FRS
Atkins, *Rt. Hon.* Sir Robert James, Kt.
Atkinson, *Prof.* Sir Anthony Barnes, Kt.
Atkinson, *Air Marshal* Sir David William, KBE
Atkinson, Sir Frederick John, KCB
Atkinson, Sir John Alexander, KCB, DFC
Atkinson, Sir Robert, Kt., DSC, FRENG
Atkinson, Sir William Samuel, Kt.
Atopare, Sir Sailas, GCMG
Attenborough, Sir David Frederick, Kt., OM, CH, CVO, CBE, FRS
Aubrey-Fletcher, Sir Henry Egerton, Bt. (1782)

Audland, Sir Christopher John, KCMG
Augier, *Prof.* Sir Fitz-Roy Richard, Kt.
Auld, *Rt. Hon.* Sir Robin Ernest, Kt.
Austin, Sir Anthony Leonard, Bt. (1894)
Austin, *Air Marshal* Sir Roger Mark, KCB, AFC
Austen-Smith, *Air Marshal* Sir Roy David, KBE, CB, CVO, DFC
Avei, Sir Moi, KBE
Ayckbourn, Sir Alan, Kt., CBE
Aykroyd, Sir James Alexander Frederic, Bt. (1929)
†Aykroyd, Sir Henry Robert George, Bt. (1920)
Aylmer, Sir Richard John, Bt. (I. 1622)
Aylward, *Prof.* Sir Mansel, Kt., CB
Aynsley-Green, *Prof.* Sir Albert, Kt.

Bacha, Sir Bhinod, Kt., CMG
Backhouse, Sir Alfred James Stott, Bt. (1901)
Bacon, Sir Nicholas Hickman Ponsonby, Bt., OBE (1611 and 1627), *Premier Baronet of England*
Bacon, Sir Sidney Charles, Kt., CB, FRENG.
Baddeley, Sir John Wolsey Beresford, Bt. (1922)
Badge, Sir Peter Gilmour Noto, Kt.
Baer, Sir Jack Mervyn Frank, Kt.
Bagge, Sir (John) Jeremy Picton, Bt. (1867)
Bagnall, *Air Chief Marshal* Sir Anthony, GBE, KCB
Bailey, Sir Alan Marshall, KCB
Bailey, Sir Brian Harry, Kt., OBE
Bailey, Sir John Bilsland, KCB
†Bailey, Sir John Richard, Bt. (1919)
Bailhache, Sir Philip Martin, Kt.
Baillie, Sir Adrian Louis, Bt. (1823)
Bain, *Prof.* Sir George Sayers, Kt.
Baird, Sir Charles William Stuart, Bt. (1809)
†Baird, Sir James Andrew Gardiner, Bt. (S. 1695)
Baird, *Air Marshal* Sir John Alexander, KBE
Baird, *Vice-Adm.* Sir Thomas Henry Eustace, KCB
Bairsto, *Air Marshal* Sir Peter Edward, KBE, CB
Baker, Sir Bryan William, Kt.
Baker, *Prof.* Sir John Hamilton, Kt., QC
Baker, Sir John William, Kt., CBE
Baker, *Hon.* Sir Jonathan Leslie, Kt.
Baker, *Rt. Hon.* Sir (Thomas) Scott (Gillespie), Kt.
Balderstone, Sir James Schofield, Kt.
Baldwin, *Prof.* Sir Jack Edward, Kt., FRS
Ball, *Air Marshal* Sir Alfred Henry Wynne, KCB, DSO, DFC
Ball, Sir Christopher John Elinger, Kt.
Ball, *Prof.* Sir John Macleod, Kt.

Ball, Sir Richard Bentley, Bt. (1911)
Ball, *Prof.* Sir Robert James, Kt., PHD
Ballantyne, *Dr* Sir Frederick Nathaniel, GCMG
Bamford, Sir Anthony Paul, Kt.
Band, *Adm.* Sir Jonathon, GCB
Banham, Sir John Michael Middlecott, Kt.
Bannerman, Sir David Gordon, Bt., OBE (S. 1682)
Bannister, Sir Roger Gilbert, Kt., CBE, DM, FRCP
Barber, Sir Michael Bayldon, Kt.
Barber, Sir (Thomas) David, Bt. (1960)
Barbour, *Very Revd* Robert Alexander Stewart, KCVO, MC
Barclay, Sir David Rowat, Kt.
Barclay, Sir Frederick Hugh, Kt.
Barclay, Sir Peter Maurice, Kt., CBE
†Barclay, Sir Robert Colraine, Bt. (S. 1668)
Barder, Sir Brian Leon, KCMG
Baring, Sir John Francis, Bt. (1911)
Barker, Sir Colin, Kt.
Barker, *Hon.* Sir (Richard) Ian, Kt.
Barling, *Hon.* Sir Gerald Edward, Kt.
Barlow, Sir Christopher Hilaro, Bt. (1803)
Barlow, Sir Frank, Kt., CBE
Barlow, Sir (George) William, Kt., FRENG.
Barlow, Sir James Alan, Bt. (1902)
Barlow, Sir John Kemp, Bt. (1907)
Barnes, *The Most Revd* Brian James, KBE
Barnes, Sir (James) David (Francis), Kt., CBE
Barnett, *Hon.* Sir Michael Lancelot Patrick, Kt.
Barnewall, Sir Reginald Robert, Bt. (I. 1623)
Baron, Sir Thomas, Kt., CBE
†Barran, Sir John Ruthven, Bt. (1895)
Barratt, Sir Lawrence Arthur, Kt.
Barratt, Sir Richard Stanley, Kt., CBE, QPM
Barrett, Sir Stephen Jeremy, KCMG
Barrett-Lennard, Sir Peter John, Bt. (1801)
Barrington, Sir Benjamin, Bt. (1831)
Barrington, Sir Nicholas John, KCMG, CVO
Barrington-Ward, *Rt. Revd* Simon, KCMG
Barron, Sir Donald James, Kt.
Barrow, Sir Anthony John Grenfell, Bt. (1835)
Barry, Sir (Lawrence) Edward (Anthony Tress), Bt. (1899)
Barter, Sir Peter Leslie Charles, Kt., OBE
†Bartlett, Sir Andrew Alan, Bt. (1913)
Barttelot, *Col.* Sir Brian Walter de Stopham, Bt. (1875), OBE
Bates, Sir James Geoffrey, Bt. (1880)
Bates, Sir Richard Dawson Hoult, Bt. (1937)

Bateson, *Prof.* Sir Patrick, Kt.
Bather, Sir John Knollys, KCVO
Batho, Sir Peter Ghislain, Bt. (1928)
Bathurst, *Admiral of the Fleet* Sir (David) Benjamin, GCB
Batten, Sir John Charles, KCVO
Battersby, *Prof.* Sir Alan Rushton, Kt., FRS
Battishill, Sir Anthony Michael William, GCB
Baulcombe, *Prof.* Sir David Charles, Kt., FRS
Baxendell, Sir Peter Brian, Kt., CBE, FRENG.
Bayly, *Prof.* Sir Christopher Alan, Kt.
Bayne, Sir Nicholas Peter, KCMG
Baynes, Sir Christopher Rory, Bt. (1801)
Bazley, Sir Thomas John Sebastian, Bt. (1869)
Beach, *Gen.* Sir (William Gerald) Hugh, GBE, KCB, MC
Beache, *Hon.* Sir Vincent Ian, KCMG
Beale, *Lt.-Gen.* Sir Peter John, KBE, FRCP
Beamish, Sir Adrian John, KCMG
Bean, *Hon.* Sir David Michael, Kt
Beatson, *Hon.* Sir Jack, Kt.
Beavis, *Air Chief Marshal* Sir Michael Gordon, KCB, CBE, AFC
Beck, Sir Edgar Philip, Kt.
Beckett, Sir Richard Gervase, Bt. (1921), QC
Beckett, Sir Terence Norman, KBE, FRENG.
Beckwith, Sir John Lionel, Kt., CBE
Beddington, *Prof.* Sir John Rex, Kt., CMG
Beecham, Sir John Stratford Roland, Bt. (1914)
Beetham, *Marshal of the Royal Air Force* Sir Michael James, GCB, CBE, DFC, AFC
Beevor, Sir Thomas Agnew, Bt. (1784)
Beith, *Rt. Hon.* Sir Alan James, Kt.
Beldam, *Rt. Hon.* Sir (Alexander) Roy (Asplan), Kt.
Belich, Sir James, Kt.
Bell, Sir David Charles Maurice, Kt.
Bell, Sir David Robert, KCB
Bell, *Prof.* Sir John Irving, Kt.
Bell, Sir John Lowthian, Bt. (1885)
Bell, *Prof.* Sir Peter Robert Frank, Kt.
Bell, *Hon.* Sir Rodger, Kt.
Bell, Sir Stuart, Kt.
Bellamy, *Hon.* Sir Christopher William, Kt.
Bellingham, Sir Anthony Edward Norman, Bt. (1796)
Bender, Sir Brian Geoffrey, KCB
Benn, Sir (James) Jonathan, Bt. (1914)
Bennett, *Air Vice-Marshal* Sir Erik Peter, KBE, CB
Bennett, *Hon.* Sir Hugh Peter Derwyn, Kt.
Bennett, *Gen.* Sir Phillip Harvey, KBE, DSO

Bennett, Sir Richard Rodney, Kt., CBE
Bennett, Sir Ronald Wilfrid Murdoch, Bt. (1929)
Benson, Sir Christopher John, Kt.
Benyon, Sir William Richard, Kt.
Beresford, Sir (Alexander) Paul, Kt.
Beresford-Peirse, Sir Henry Grant de la Poer, Bt. (1814)
Berghuser, *Hon.* Sir Eric, Kt., MBE
Beringer, *Prof.* Sir John Evelyn, Kt., CBE
Berman, Sir Franklin Delow, KCMG
Berners-Lee, Sir Timothy John, OM, KBE, FRS
Bernard, Sir Dallas Edmund, Bt. (1954)
Bernstein, Sir Howard, Kt.
Berney, Sir Julian Reedham Stuart, Bt. (1620)
Berridge, *Prof.* Sir Michael John, Kt., FRS
Berriman, Sir David, Kt.
Berry, *Prof.* Sir Colin Leonard, Kt., FRCPATH
Berry, *Prof.* Sir Michael Victor, Kt., FRS
Berthoud, Sir Martin Seymour, KCVO, CMG
Best, Sir Richard Radford, KCVO, CBE
Best-Shaw, Sir John Michael Robert, Bt. (1665)
Bethel, Sir Baltron Benjamin, KCMG
Bethlehem, Sir Daniel, KCMG
Bett, Sir Michael, Kt., CBE
Bettison, Sir Norman George, Kt., QPM
Bevan, Sir Martyn Evan Evans, Bt. (1958)
Bevan, Sir Nicolas, Kt., CB
Bevan, Sir Timothy Hugh, Kt.
Beverley, *Lt.-Gen.* Sir Henry York La Roche, KCB, OBE, RM
Bibby, Sir Michael James, Bt. (1959)
Bickersteth, *Rt. Revd* John Monier, KCVO
Biddulph, Sir Ian D'Olier, Bt. (1664)
Bidwell, Sir Hugh Charles Philip, GBE
Biggam, Sir Robin Adair, Kt.
Bilas, Sir Angmai Simon, Kt., OBE
Bill, *Lt.-Gen.* Sir David Robert, KCB
Billière, *Gen.* Sir Peter Edgar de la Cour de la, KCB, KBE, DSO, MC
Bindman, Sir Geoffrey Lionel, Kt.
Bingham, *Hon.* Sir Eardley Max, Kt.
Birch, Sir John Allan, KCVO, CMG
Birch, Sir Roger, Kt., CBE, QPM
Bird, Sir Richard Geoffrey Chapman, Bt. (1922)
Birkin, Sir John Christian William, Bt. (1905)
Birkin, Sir (John) Derek, Kt., TD
Birkmyre, Sir James, Bt. (1921)
Birrell, Sir James Drake, Kt.
Birtwistle, Sir Harrison, Kt., CH
Bischoff, Sir Winfried Franz Wilhelm, Kt.

Black, *Adm.* Sir (John) Jeremy, GBE, KCB, DSO
Black, Sir Robert David, Bt. (1922)
Blackburn, *Vice-Adm.* Sir David Anthony James, KCVO, CB
Blackburne, *Hon.* Sir William Anthony, Kt.
Blackett, Sir Hugh Francis, Bt. (1673)
Blackham, *Vice-Adm.* Sir Jeremy Joe, KCB
Blackman, Sir Frank Milton, KCVO, OBE
†Blair, Sir Patrick David Hunter, Bt. (1786)
Blair, *Hon.* Sir William James Lynton, Kt.
Blake, Sir Alfred Lapthorn, KCVO, MC
Blake, Sir Francis Michael, Bt. (1907)
Blake, *Hon.* Sir Nicholas John Gorrod, Kt.
Blake, Sir Peter Thomas, Kt., CBE
Blake, Sir Anthony Teilo Bruce, Bt. (I. 1622)
Blaker, Sir John, Bt. (1919)
Blakiston, Sir Ferguson Arthur James, Bt. (1763)
Blanch, Sir Malcolm, KCVO
Bland, Sir (Francis) Christopher (Buchan), Kt.
Bland, *Lt.-Col.* Sir Simon Claud Michael, KCVO
Blank, Sir Maurice Victor, Kt.
Blatherwick, Sir David Elliott Spiby, KCMG, OBE
Blelloch, Sir John Nial Henderson, KCB
Blennerhassett, Sir (Marmaduke) Adrian Francis William, Bt. (1809)
Blewitt, *Maj.* Sir Shane Gabriel Basil, GCVO
Blofeld, *Hon.* Sir John Christopher Calthorpe, Kt.
Blois, Sir Charles Nicholas Gervase, Bt. (1686)
Blom-Cooper, Sir Louis Jacques, Kt., QC
Blomefield, Sir Thomas Charles Peregrine, Bt. (1807)
Bloomfield, Sir Kenneth Percy, KCB
Blundell, Sir Thomas Leon, Kt., FRS
Blunden, Sir George, Kt.
†Blunden, Sir Hubert Chisholm, Bt. (I. 1766)
Blunt, Sir David Richard Reginald Harvey, Bt. (1720)
Blyth, Sir Charles (Chay), Kt., CBE, BEM
Boardman, *Prof.* Sir John, Kt., FSA, FBA
Bodey, *Hon.* Sir David Roderick Lessiter, Kt.
Bodmer, Sir Walter Fred, Kt., PHD, FRS
Body, Sir Richard Bernard Frank Stewart, Kt.
Bogan, Sir Nagora, KBE
Boileau, Sir Guy (Francis), Bt. (1838)
Boles, Sir Jeremy John Fortescue, Bt. (1922)

Boles, Sir John Dennis, Kt., MBE
Bolt, *Air Marshal* Sir Richard Bruce, KBE, CB, DFC, AFC
Bona, Sir Kina, KBE
Bonallack, Sir Michael Francis, Kt., OBE
Bond, Sir John Reginald Hartnell, Kt.
Bond, *Prof.* Sir Michael Richard, Kt., FRCPSYCH, FRCPGLAS, FRCSE
Bone, *Prof.* Sir James Drummond, Kt., FRSE
Bone, Sir Roger Bridgland, KCMG
Bonfield, Sir Peter Leahy, Kt., CBE, FRENG
†Bonham, Sir George Martin Antony, Bt. (1852)
Bonington, Sir Christian John Storey, Kt., CVO, CBE
Bonsall, Sir Arthur Wilfred, KCMG, CBE
Bonsor, Sir Nicholas Cosmo, Bt. (1925)
Boord, Sir Nicolas John Charles, Bt. (1896)
Boorman, *Lt.-Gen.* Sir Derek, KCB
Booth, Sir Christopher Charles, Kt., MD, FRCP
Booth, Sir Clive, Kt.
Booth, Sir Douglas Allen, Bt. (1916)
Booth, Sir Gordon, KCMG, CVO
Boothby, Sir Brooke Charles, Bt. (1660)
Bore, Sir Albert, Kt.
Boreel, Sir Stephan Gerard, Bt. (1645)
Borthwick, Sir Anthony Thomas, Bt. (1908)
Borysiewicz, *Prof.* Sir Leszek Krzysztof, Kt.
Bossom, *Hon.* Sir Clive, Bt. (1953)
Boswell, *Lt.-Gen.* Sir Alexander Crawford Simpson, KCB, CBE
Bosworth, Sir Neville Bruce Alfred, Kt., CBE
Botham, Sir Ian Terence, Kt., OBE
Bottoms, *Prof.* Sir Anthony Edward, Kt.
Bottomley, Sir James Reginald Alfred, KCMG
Bottomley, Sir Peter James, Kt.
Boughey, Sir John George Fletcher, Bt. (1798)
Boulton, Sir Clifford John, GCB
†Boulton, Sir John Gibson, Bt. (1944)
Bouraga, Sir Phillip, KBE
Bourn, Sir John Bryant, KCB
Bowater, Sir Euan David Vansittart, Bt. (1939)
†Bowater, Sir Michael Patrick, Bt. (1914)
Bowden, Sir Andrew, Kt., MBE
Bowden, Sir Nicholas Richard, Bt. (1915)
Bowen, Sir Barry Manfield, KCMG
Bowen, Sir Geoffrey Fraser, Kt.
Bowen, Sir Mark Edward Mortimer, Bt. (1921)

Bowes Lyon, Sir Simon Alexander, KCVO

†Bowlby, Sir Richard Peregrine Longstaff, Bt. (1923)

Bowman, Sir Edwin Geoffrey, KCB

Bowman, Sir Jeffery Haverstock, Kt.

Bowman-Shaw, Sir (George) Neville, Kt.

Bowness, Sir Alan, Kt., CBE

Bowyer-Smyth, Sir Thomas Weyland, Bt. (1661)

Boyce, Sir Graham Hugh, KCMG

Boyce, Sir Robert Charles Leslie, Bt. (1952)

Boyd, Sir Alexander Walter, Bt. (1916)

Boyd, Sir John Dixon Iklé, KCMG

Boyd, *Prof.* Sir Robert David Hugh, Kt.

Boyd-Carpenter, Sir (Marsom) Henry, KCVO

Boyd-Carpenter, *Lt.-Gen. Hon.* Sir Thomas Patrick John, KBE

Boyle, *Prof.* Sir Roger Michael, Kt., CBE

Boyle, Sir Stephen Gurney, Bt. (1904)

Boyson, *Rt. Hon.* Sir Rhodes, Kt.

Brabham, Sir John Arthur, Kt., OBE

Bracewell-Smith, Sir Charles, Bt. (1947)

Bradbeer, Sir John Derek Richardson, Kt., OBE, TD

Bradfield, *Dr* Sir John Richard Grenfell, Kt., CBE

Bradford, Sir Edward Alexander Slade, Bt. (1902)

Brady, *Prof.* Sir John Michael, Kt., FRS

Braithwaite, Sir Rodric Quentin, GCMG

Bramley, *Prof.* Sir Paul Anthony, Kt.

Branson, Sir Richard Charles Nicholas, Kt.

Braithwaite, *Rt. Hon.* Sir Nicholas Alexander, Kt., OBE

Bratza, *Hon.* Sir Nicolas Dušan, Kt.

Breckenridge, *Prof.* Sir Alasdair Muir, Kt., CBE

Brennan, *Hon.* Sir (Francis) Gerard, KBE

Brenton, Sir Anthony Russell, KCMG

Brewer, Sir David William, Kt., CMG

Brierley, Sir Ronald Alfred, Kt.

Briggs, *Hon.* Sir Michael Townley Featherstone, Kt.

Brighouse, *Prof.* Sir Timothy Robert Peter, Kt.

Bright, Sir Graham Frank James, Kt.

Bright, Sir Keith, Kt.

Brigstocke, *Adm.* Sir John Richard, KCB

Brinckman, Sir Theodore George Roderick, Bt. (1831)

†Brisco, Sir Campbell Howard, Bt. (1782)

Briscoe, Sir Brian Anthony, Kt.

Briscoe, Sir John Geoffrey James, Bt. (1910)

Brittan, Sir Samuel, Kt.

Britton, Sir Paul John James, Kt., CB

†Broadbent, Sir Andrew George, Bt. (1893)

Broadbent, Sir Richard John, KCB

Brocklebank, Sir Aubrey Thomas, Bt. (1885)

Brodie, Sir Benjamin David Ross, Bt. (1834)

Brooke, Sir Rodney George, Kt., CBE

Brooking, Sir Trevor, Kt., CBE

Bromhead, Sir John Desmond Gonville, Bt. (1806)

Bromley, Sir Michael Roger, KBE

Bromley, Sir Rupert Charles, Bt. (1757)

Bromley-Davenport, Sir William Arthur, KCVO

Brook, *Prof.* Sir Richard John, Kt., OBE

†Brooke, Sir Alistair Weston, Bt. (1919)

Brooke, Sir Francis George Windham, Bt. (1903)

Brooke, *Rt. Hon.* Sir Henry, Kt.

Brooke, Sir (Richard) David Christopher, Bt. (1662)

Brooking, Sir Trevor David, Kt., CBE

Brooks, Sir Timothy Gerald Martin, KCVO

Brooksbank, Sir (Edward) Nicholas, Bt. (1919)

Broomfield, Sir Nigel Hugh Robert Allen, KCMG

†Broughton, Sir David Delves, Bt. (1661)

Broughton, Sir Martin Faulkner, Kt.

Broun, Sir Wayne Hercules, Bt. (S. 1686)

Brown, Sir (Austen) Patrick, KCB

Brown, *Adm.* Sir Brian Thomas, KCB, CBE

Brown, Sir David, Kt.

Brown, *Hon.* Sir Douglas Dunlop, Kt.

Brown, Sir George Francis Richmond, Bt. (1863)

Brown, Sir Mervyn, KCMG, OBE

Brown, Sir Peter Randolph, Kt.

Brown, *Rt. Hon.* Sir Stephen, GBE

Brown, Sir Stephen David Reid, KCVO

Browne, Sir Nicholas Walker, KBE, CMG

Brownrigg, Sir Nicholas (Gawen), Bt. (1816)

Browse, *Prof.* Sir Norman Leslie, Kt., MD, FRCS

Bruce, Sir (Francis) Michael Ian, Bt. (S. 1628)

†Bruce-Clifton, Sir Hervey Hamish Peter, Bt. (1804)

Bruce-Gardner, Sir Robert Henry, Bt. (1945)

Brunner, Sir Hugo Laurence Joseph, KCVO

Brunner, Sir John Henry Kilian, Bt. (1895)

Brunton, Sir Gordon Charles, Kt.

†Brunton, Sir James Lauder, Bt. (1908)

Bryant, *Air Chief Marshal* Sir Simon, KCB, CBE, ADC

Bubb, Sir Stephen John Limrick, Kt.

Buchan-Hepburn, Sir John Alastair Trant Kidd, Bt. (1815)

Buchanan, Sir Andrew George, Bt. (1878), KCVO

Buchanan, *Vice-Adm.* Sir Peter William, KBE

Buchanan, Sir Robert Wilson (Robin), Kt.

†Buchanan-Jardine, Sir John Christopher Rupert, Bt. (1885)

Buckland, Sir Ross, Kt.

Buckley, *Dr* Sir George William, Kt.

Buckley, Sir Michael Sidney, Kt.

Buckley, *Lt.-Cdr.* Sir (Peter) Richard, KCVO

Buckley, *Hon.* Sir Roger John, Kt.

Buckworth-Herne-Soame, Sir Charles John, Bt. (1697)

Budd, Sir Alan Peter, Kt.

Budd, Sir Colin Richard, KCMG

Bull, Sir George Jeffrey, Kt.

Bull, Sir Simeon George, Bt. (1922)

Bullock, Sir Stephen Michael, Kt.

Bultin, Sir Bato, Kt., MBE

Bunbury, Sir Michael William, Bt. (1681), KCVO

Bunyard, Sir Robert Sidney, Kt., CBE, QPM

Burbidge, Sir Peter Dudley, Bt. (1916)

Burden, Sir Anthony Thomas, Kt., QPM

Burdett, Sir Savile Aylmer, Bt. (1665)

Burgen, Sir Arnold Stanley Vincent, Kt., FRS

Burgess, *Gen.* Sir Edward Arthur, KCB, OBE

Burgess, Sir (Joseph) Stuart, Kt., CBE, PHD, FRSC

Burgess, *Prof.* Sir Robert George, Kt.

Burgh, Sir John Charles, KCMG, CB

Burke, Sir James Stanley Gilbert, Bt. (I. 1797)

Burke, Sir (Thomas) Kerry, Kt.

Burn, *Prof.* Sir John, Kt.

Burnell-Nugent, *Vice-Adm.* Sir James Michael, KCB, CBE, ADC

Burnet, Sir James William Alexander (Sir Alastair Burnet), Kt.

Burnett, *Air Chief Marshal* Sir Brian Kenyon, GCB, DFC, AFC

Burnett, Sir Charles David, Bt. (1913)

Burnett, *Hon.* Sir Ian Duncan, Kt.

Burnett, Sir Walter John, Kt.

Burney, Sir Nigel Dennistoun, Bt. (1921)

Burns, *Dr* Sir Henry, Kt.

Burns, Sir (Robert) Andrew, KCMG

Burnton, *Rt. Hon.* Sir Stanley Jeffrey, Kt.

Burrell, Sir Charles Raymond, Bt. (1774)

Burridge, *Air Chief Marshal* Sir Brian Kevin, KCB, CBE, ADC

Burston, Sir Samuel Gerald Wood, Kt., OBE

Burt, Sir Peter Alexander, Kt.

Burton, Sir Carlisle Archibald, Kt., OBE

Burton, Lt.-Gen. Sir Edmund Fortescue Gerard, KBE

Burton, Sir Graham Stuart, KCMG

Burton, Hon. Sir Michael John, Kt.

Burton, Sir Michael St Edmund, KCVO, CMG

Bush, Adm. Sir John Fitzroy Duyland, GCB, DSC

Butler, Hon. Sir Arlington Griffith, KCMG

Butler, Dr Sir David Edgeworth, Kt., CBE

Butler, Sir Michael Dacres, GCMG

Butler, Sir (Reginald) Michael (Thomas), Bt. (1922)

Butler, Sir Percy James, Kt., CBE

Butler, Hon. Sir Richard Clive, Kt.

Butler, Sir Richard Pierce, Bt. (1628)

Butterfield, Hon. Sir Alexander Neil Logie, Kt.

Butterfill, Sir John Valentine, Kt.

Buxton, Sir Jocelyn Charles Roden, Bt. (1840)

Buxton, Rt. Hon. Sir Richard Joseph, Kt.

Buzzard, Sir Anthony Farquhar, Bt. (1929)

Byatt, Sir Ian Charles Rayner, Kt.

Byford, Sir Lawrence, Kt., CBE, QPM

Byron, Rt. Hon. Sir Charles Michael Dennis, Kt.

†Cable-Alexander, Sir Patrick Desmond William, Bt. (1809)

Cadbury, Sir (George) Adrian (Hayhurst), Kt.

Cadbury, Sir (Nicholas) Dominic, Kt.

Cadogan, Prof. Sir John Ivan George, Kt., CBE, FRS, FRSE

Cahn, Sir Albert Jonas, Bt. (1934)

Cahn, Sir Andrew Thomas, KCMG

Caine, Sir Michael (Maurice Micklewhite), Kt., CBE

Caines, Sir John, KCB

Caldwell, Sir Edward George, KCB

Callaghan, Sir William Henry, Kt.

Callan, Sir Ivan Roy, KCVO, CMG

Calman, Prof. Sir Kenneth Charles, KCB, MD, FRCP, FRCS, FRSE

Calne, Prof. Sir Roy Yorke, Kt., FRS

Calvert-Smith, Sir David, Kt., QC

Cameron, Sir Hugh Roy Graham, Kt., QPM

Campbell, Prof. Sir Colin Murray, Kt.

Campbell, Sir Ian Tofts, Kt., CBE, VRD

Campbell, Sir Ilay Mark, Bt. (1808)

Campbell, Sir James Alexander Moffat Bain, Bt. (S. 1668)

Campbell, Sir Lachlan Philip Kemeys, Bt. (1815)

Campbell, Sir Roderick Duncan Hamilton, Bt. (1831)

Campbell, Sir Robin Auchinbreck, Bt. (S. 1628)

Campbell, Rt. Hon. Sir Walter Menzies, Kt., CBE, QC

Campbell, Rt. Hon. Sir William Anthony, Kt.

Campbell-Orde, Sir John Alexander, Bt. (1790)

Cannadine, Prof. Sir David Nicholas, Kt.

†Carden, Sir Christopher Robert, Bt. (1887)

†Carden, Sir John Craven, Bt. (I. 1787)

Carew, Sir Rivers Verain, Bt. (1661)

Carey, Sir de Vic Graham, Kt.

Carleton-Smith, Maj.-Gen. Sir Michael Edward, Kt., CBE

Carlisle, Sir James Beethoven, GCMG

Carlisle, Sir John Michael, Kt.

Carlisle, Sir Kenneth Melville, Kt.

Carnegie, Sir Roderick Howard, Kt.

Carnwath, Rt. Hon. Sir Robert John Anderson, Kt., CVO

Caro, Sir Anthony Alfred, Kt., OM, CBE

Carr, Sir (Albert) Raymond (Maillard), Kt.

Carr, Very Revd Dr Arthur Wesley, KCVO

Carr, Sir Peter Derek, Kt., CBE

Carr, Sir Roger Martyn, Kt.

Carr-Ellison, Col. Sir Ralph Harry, KCVO, TD

Carrick, Hon. Sir John Leslie, KCMG

Carrick, Sir Roger John, KCMG, LVO

Carruthers, Sir Ian James, Kt., OBE

Carsberg, Prof. Sir Bryan Victor, Kt.

Carter, Prof. Sir David Craig, Kt., FRCSE, FRCSGLAS, FRCPE

Carter, Sir John Alexander, Kt.

Carter, Sir John Gordon Thomas, Kt.

Carter, Sir Philip David, Kt., CBE

Cartledge, Sir Bryan George, KCMG

Cary, Sir Roger Hugh, Bt. (1955)

Casey, Rt. Hon. Sir Maurice Eugene, Kt.

Cash, Sir Andrew John, Kt., OBE

Cass, Sir Geoffrey Arthur, Kt.

Cassel, Sir Timothy Felix Harold, Bt. (1920)

Cassels, Sir John Seton, Kt., CB

Cassels, Adm. Sir Simon Alastair Cassillis, KCB, CBE

Cassidi, Adm. Sir (Arthur) Desmond, GCB

Castell, Sir William Martin, Kt.

Castledine, Prof. Sir George, Kt.

Catherwood, Sir (Henry) Frederick (Ross), Kt.

Catto, Prof. Sir Graeme Robertson Dawson, Kt.

Cave, Sir John Charles, Bt. (1896)

Cave-Browne-Cave, Sir Robert, Bt. (1641)

Cayley, Sir Digby William David, Bt. (1661)

Cayzer, Sir James Arthur, Bt. (1904)

Cazalet, Hon. Sir Edward Stephen, Kt.

Cazalet, Sir Peter Grenville, Kt.

Cecil, Sir Henry, Kt.

Cecil, Rear-Adm. Sir (Oswald) Nigel Amherst, KBE, CB

Chadwick, Rt. Hon. Sir John Murray, Kt.

Chadwick, Sir Joshua Kenneth Burton, Bt. (1935)

Chadwick, Revd Prof. (William) Owen, OM, KBE, FBA

Chadwyck-Healey, Sir Charles Edward, Bt. (1919)

Chakrabarti, Sir Sumantra, KCB

Chalmers, Sir Iain Geoffrey, Kt.

Chalmers, Sir Neil Robert, Kt.

Chalstrey, Sir (Leonard) John, Kt., MD, FRCS

Chan, Rt. Hon. Sir Julius, GCMG, KBE

Chan, Sir Thomas Kok, Kt., OBE

Chance, Sir (George) Jeremy ffolliott, Bt. (1900)

Chandler, Sir Colin Michael, Kt.

Chantler, Prof. Sir Cyril, Kt., MD, FRCP

Chaplin, Sir Malcolm Hilbery, Kt., CBE

Chapman, Sir David Robert Macgowan, Bt. (1958)

Chapman, Sir Frank, Kt.

Chapman, Sir George Alan, Kt.

Chapman, Sir Sidney Brookes, Kt., MP

Chapple, Field Marshal Sir John Lyon, GCB, CBE

Charles, Hon. Sir Arthur William Hessin, Kt.

Charlton, Sir Robert (Bobby), Kt., CBE

Charnley, Sir (William) John, Kt., CB, FRENG

Chartres, Rt. Revd and Rt. Hon. Richard John Carew, KCVO

Chataway, Rt. Hon. Sir Christopher, Kt.

†Chaytor, Sir Bruce Gordon, Bt. (1831)

Checketts, Sqn. Ldr. Sir David John, KCVO

Checkland, Sir Michael, Kt.

Cheshire, Air Chief Marshal Sir John Anthony, KBE, CB

Chessells, Sir Arthur David (Tim), Kt.

†Chetwynd, Sir Robin John Talbot, Bt. (1795)

Cheyne, Sir Patrick John Lister, Bt. (1908)

Chichester, Sir James Henry Edward, Bt. (1641)

Chichester-Clark, Sir Robin, Kt.

Chilcot, Rt. Hon. Sir John Anthony, GCB

Child, Sir (Coles John) Jeremy, Bt. (1919)

Chilwell, Hon. Sir Muir Fitzherbert, Kt.

Chinn, Sir Trevor Edwin, Kt., CVO

Chipperfield, Prof. Sir David Alan, Kt., CBE

Chipperfield, Sir Geoffrey Howes, KCB

Chisholm, Sir John Alexander Raymond, Kt., FRENG

Chitty, Sir Thomas Willes, Bt. (1924)

Cholmeley, Sir Hugh John Frederick Sebastian, Bt. (1806)
Chow, Sir Chung Kong, Kt.
Chow, Sir Henry Francis, Kt., OBE
Christie, Sir George William Langham, Kt., CH
Christopher, Sir Duncan Robin Carmichael, KBE, CMG
Chung, Sir Sze-yuen, GBE, FRENG
Clark, Sir Francis Drake, Bt. (1886)
Clark, Sir John Arnold, Kt.
Clark, Sir Jonathan George, Bt. (1917)
Clark, Sir Robert Anthony, Kt., DSC
Clark, Sir Terence Joseph, KBE, CMG, CVO
Clarke, Sir (Charles Mansfield) Tobias, Bt. (1831)
Clarke, Hon. Sir Christopher Simon Courtenay Stephenson, Kt.
Clarke, Hon. Sir David Clive, Kt.
Clarke, Sir Jonathan Dennis, Kt.
Clarke, Sir Robert Cyril, Kt.
†Clarke, Sir Rupert Grant Alexander, Bt. (1882)
Clay, Sir Edward, KCMG
Clay, Sir Richard Henry, Bt. (1841)
Clayton, Sir David Robert, Bt. (1732)
Cleaver, Sir Anthony Brian, Kt.
Clementi, Sir David Cecil, Kt.
Clerk, Sir Robert Maxwell, Bt. (1679), OBE
Clerke, Sir John Edward Longueville, Bt. (1660)
Clifford, Sir Roger Joseph, Bt. (1887)
Clifford, Sir Timothy Peter Plint, Kt.
Coates, Sir Anthony Robert Milnes, Bt. (1911)
Coates, Sir David Frederick Charlton, Bt. (1921)
Coats, Sir Alastair Francis Stuart, Bt. (1905)
Cochrane, Sir (Henry) Marc (Sursock), Bt. (1903)
Cockburn, Sir John Elliot, Bt. (S. 1671)
Cockburn-Campbell, Sir Alexander Thomas, Bt. (1821)
Cockell, Sir Merrick, Kt.
Cockshaw, Sir Alan, Kt., FRENG
†Codrington, Sir Christopher George Wayne, Bt. (1876)
†Codrington, Sir Giles Peter, Bt. (1721)
Coghill, Sir Patrick Kendal Farley, Bt. (1778)
Coghlin, Rt. Hon. Sir Patrick, Kt.
Cohen, Sir Edward, Kt.
Cohen, Sir Ivor Harold, Kt., CBE, TD
Cohen, Prof. Sir Philip, Kt., PHD, FRS
Cohen, Sir Ronald, Kt.
Cole, Sir (Robert) William, Kt.
Coleman, Sir Robert John, KCMG
Coleridge, Hon. Sir Paul James Duke, Kt.
Coles, Sir (Arthur) John, GCMG
Colfox, Sir (William) John, Bt. (1939)

Collett, Sir Christopher, GBE
Collett, Sir Ian Seymour, Bt. (1934)
Collins, Sir Alan Stanley, KCVO, CMG
Collins, Hon. Sir Andrew David, Kt.
Collins, Sir Bryan Thomas Alfred, Kt., OBE, QFSM
Collins, Sir John Alexander, Kt
Collins, Sir Kenneth Darlingston, Kt.
Collins, Prof. Sir Rory Edwards, Kt.
Collyear, Sir John Gowen, Kt.
Colman, Hon. Sir Anthony David, Kt.
Colman, Sir Michael Jeremiah, Bt. (1907)
Colman, Sir Timothy, KG
†Colquhoun of Luss, Sir Malcolm Rory, Bt. (1786)
Colt, Sir Edward William Dutton, Bt. (1694)
Colthurst, Sir Charles St John, Bt. (1744)
Conant, Sir John Ernest Michael, Bt. (1954)
Connell, Hon. Sir Michael Bryan, Kt.
Conner, Rt. Revd Sir David John, KCVO
Connery, Sir Sean, Kt.
Connor, Sir William Joseph, Kt.
Conran, Sir Terence Orby, Kt.
Cons, Hon. Sir Derek, Kt.
Conway, Prof. Sir Gordon Richard, KCMG, FRS
Cook, Sir Christopher Wymondham Rayner Herbert, Bt. (1886)
Cook, Prof. Sir Peter Frederic Chester, Kt.
Cooke, Col. Sir David William Perceval, Bt. (1661)
Cooke, Sir Howard Felix Hanlan, GCMG, GCVO
Cooke, Hon. Sir Jeremy Lionel, Kt.
Cooke, Prof. Sir Ronald Urwick, Kt.
Cooksey, Sir David James Scott, GBE
Cooper, Gen. Sir George Leslie Conroy, GCB, MC
Cooper, Sir Richard Adrian, Bt. (1905)
Cooper, Maj.-Gen. Sir Simon Christie, GCVO
Cooper, Sir William Daniel Charles, Bt. (1863)
Coote, Sir Christopher John, Bt. (I. 1621), Premier Baronet of Ireland
Copas, Most Revd Virgil, KBE
Copisarow, Sir Alcon Charles, Kt.
Corbett, Maj.-Gen. Sir Robert John Swan, KCVO, CB
Cordy-Simpson, Lt.-Gen. Sir Roderick Alexander, KBE, CB
Corfield, Sir Kenneth George, Kt., FRENG
Corness, Sir Colin Ross, Kt.
Cornforth, Sir John Warcup, Kt., CBE, DPHIL, FRS
Corry, Sir James Michael, Bt. (1885)
Cortazzi, Sir (Henry Arthur) Hugh, GCMG
Cory, Sir (Clinton Charles) Donald, Bt. (1919)

Cory-Wright, Sir Richard Michael, Bt. (1903)
Cossons, Sir Neil, Kt., OBE
Cotter, Sir Patrick Laurence Delaval, Bt. (I. 1763)
Cotterell, Sir John Henry Geers, Bt. (1805)
Cottrell, Sir Alan Howard, Kt., PHD, FRS, FRENG
†Cotts, Sir Richard Crichton Mitchell, Bt. (1921)
Coulson, Hon. Sir Peter David William, Kt.
Couper, Sir James George, Bt. (1841)
Courtenay, Sir Thomas Daniel, Kt.
Cousins, Air Chief Marshal Sir David, KCB, AFC
Coville, Air Marshal Sir Christopher Charles Cotton, KCB
Cowan, Gen. Sir Samuel, KCB, CBE
Coward, Vice-Adm. Sir John Francis, KCB, DSO
Cowen, Rt. Hon. Prof. Sir Zelman, GCMG, GCVO
Cowie, Sir Thomas (Tom), Kt., OBE
Cowper-Coles, Sir Sherard Louis, KCMG, LVO
Cox, Sir Alan George, Kt., CBE
Cox, Prof. Sir David Roxbee, Kt.
Cox, Sir George Edwin, Kt.
Craft, Prof. Sir Alan William, Kt.
Craig, Sir (Albert) James (Macqueen), GCMG
Craig-Cooper, Sir (Frederick Howard) Michael, Kt., CBE, TD
Crane, Hon. Sir Peter Francis, Kt.
Crane, Prof. Sir Peter Robert, Kt.
Cranston, Hon. Sir Ross Frederick, Kt.
Craufurd, Sir Robert James, Bt. (1781)
Craven, Sir John Anthony, Kt.
Craven, Sir Philip Lee, Kt., MBE
Crawford, Prof. Sir Frederick William, Kt., FRENG
Crawford, Sir Robert William Kenneth, Kt. CBE
Crawley-Boevey, Sir Thomas Michael Blake, Bt. (1784)
Crew, Sir (Michael) Edward, Kt., QPM
Crewe, Prof. Sir Ivor Martin, Kt.
Cresswell, Hon. Sir Peter John, Kt.
Crichton-Brown, Sir Robert, KCMG, CBE, TD
Crisp, Sir John Charles, Bt. (1913)
Critchett, Sir Charles George Montague, Bt. (1908)
Crockett, Sir Andrew Duncan, Kt.
Croft, Sir Owen Glendower, Bt. (1671)
Croft, Sir Thomas Stephen Hutton, Bt. (1818)
†Crofton, Sir Hugh Denis, Bt. (1801)
†Crofton, Sir Julian Malby, Bt. (1838)
Crombie, Sir Alexander, Kt.
Crompton, Sir Dan, Kt., CBE, QPM
Cropper, Sir James Anthony, KCVO
Crosby, Sir James Robert, Kt.

Crossley, Sir Sloan Nicholas, Bt. (1909)
Crowe, Sir Brian Lee, KCMG
Cruickshank, Sir Donald Gordon, Kt.
Cruthers, Sir James Winter, Kt.
Cubbon, Sir Brian Crossland, GCB
Cubie, *Dr* Sir Andrew, Kt., CBE
Cubitt, Sir Hugh Guy, Kt., CBE
Cubitt, *Maj.-Gen.* Sir William George, KCVO, CBE
Cullen, Sir (Edward) John, Kt., FRENG
Culme-Seymour, Sir Michael Patrick, Bt. (1809)
Culpin, Sir Robert Paul, Kt.
Cummins, Sir Michael John Austin, Kt.
Cunliffe, *Prof.* Sir Barrington, Kt., CBE
Cunliffe, Sir David Ellis, Bt. (1759)
Cunliffe, Sir Jonathan Stephen, Kt., CB
Cunliffe-Owen, Sir Hugo Dudley, Bt. (1920)
Cunningham, *Lt.-Gen.* Sir Hugh Patrick, KBE
Cunningham, Sir Roger Keith, Kt., CBE
Cunynghame, Sir Andrew David Francis, Bt. (S. 1702)
†Currie, Sir Donald Scott, Bt. (1847)
Curry, Sir Donald Thomas Younger, Kt., CBE
Curtain, Sir Michael, KBE
Curtis, Sir Barry John, Kt.
Curtis, *Hon.* Sir Richard Herbert, Kt.
Curtis, Sir William Peter, Bt. (1802)
Curtiss, *Air Marshal* Sir John Bagot, KCB, KBE
Curwen, Sir Christopher Keith, KCMG
Cuschieri, *Prof.* Sir Alfred, Kt.

Dain, Sir David John Michael, KCVO
Dales, Sir Richard Nigel, KCVO
Dalrymple-Hay, Sir Malcolm John Robert, Bt. (1798)
†Dalrymple-White, Sir Jan Hew, Bt. (1926)
Dalton, *Vice-Adm.* Sir Geoffrey Thomas James Oliver, KCB
Dalton, Sir Richard John, KCMG
Dalton, *Air Chief Marshal* Sir Stephen Gary George, KCB
Dalyell, Sir Tam (Thomas), Bt. (NS 1685)
Daniel, Sir John Sagar, Kt., DSC
Darell, Sir Jeffrey Lionel, Bt. (1795), MC
Darling, Sir Clifford, GCVO
Darrington, Sir Michael John, Kt.
Darroch, Sir Nigel Kim, KCMG
Dasgupta, *Prof.* Sir Partha Sarathi, Kt.
†Dashwood, Sir Edward John Francis, Bt. (1707), *Premier Baronet of Great Britain*
Dashwood, Sir Richard James, Bt. (1684)

Daunt, Sir Timothy Lewis Achilles, KCMG
Davenport-Handley, Sir David John, Kt., OBE
David, Sir Jean Marc, Kt., CBE, QC
David, *His Hon.* Sir Robin (Robert) Daniel George, Kt.
Davies, Sir Alan Seymour, Kt.
Davies, Sir (Charles) Noel, Kt.
Davies, *Prof.* Sir David Evan Naughton, Kt., CBE, FRS, FRENG
Davies, *Hon.* Sir (David Herbert) Mervyn, Kt., MC, TD
Davies, Sir David John, Kt.
Davies, Sir Frank John, Kt., CBE
Davies, *Prof.* Sir Graeme John, Kt., FRENG
Davies, Sir John Howard, Kt.
Davies, Sir John Michael, KCB
Davies, Sir Peter Maxwell, Kt., CBE
Davies, Sir Rhys Everson, Kt., QC
Davis, Sir Andrew Frank, Kt., CBE
Davis, Sir Colin Rex, Kt., CH, CBE
Davis, Sir Crispin Henry Lamert, Kt.
Davis, Sir John Gilbert, Bt. (1946)
Davis, *Hon.* Sir Nigel Anthony Lambert, Kt.
Davis, Sir Peter John, Kt.
Davis-Goff, Sir Robert (William), Bt. (1905)
Davison, *Rt. Hon.* Sir Ronald Keith, GBE, CMG
†Davson, Sir George Trenchard Simon, Bt. (1927)
Dawanincura, Sir John Norbert, Kt., OBE
Dawbarn, Sir Simon Yelverton, KCVO, CMG
Dawson, *Hon.* Sir Daryl Michael, KBE, CB
Dawson, Sir Nicholas Antony Trevor, Bt. (1920)
Dawtry, Sir Alan (Graham), Kt., CBE, TD
Day, Sir Derek Malcolm, KCMG
Day, *Air Chief Marshal* Sir John Romney, KCB, OBE, ADC
Day, Sir (Judson) Graham, Kt.
Day, Sir Michael John, Kt., OBE
Day, Sir Simon James, Kt.
Deane, *Hon.* Sir William Patrick, KBE
Dearlove, Sir Richard Billing, KCMG, OBE
de Bellaigue, Sir Geoffrey, GCVO
†Debenham, Sir Thomas Adam, Bt. (1931)
de Deney, Sir Geoffrey Ivor, KCVO
Deeny, *Hon.* Sir Donnell Justin Patrick, Kt.
De Halpert, *Rear-Adm.* Sir Jeremy Michael, KCVO, CB
de Hoghton, Sir (Richard) Bernard (Cuthbert), Bt. (1611)
De la Bère, Sir Cameron, Bt. (1953)
de la Rue, Sir Andrew George Ilay, Bt. (1898)
De Silva, Sir George Desmond Lorenz, Kt., QC

Dellow, Sir John Albert, Kt., CBE
Delves, *Lt.-Gen.* Sir Cedric Norman George, KBE
Denholm, Sir John Ferguson (Ian), Kt., CBE
Denison-Smith, *Lt.-Gen.* Sir Anthony Arthur, KBE
Denny, Sir Anthony Coningham de Waltham, Bt. (I. 1782)
Denny, Sir Charles Alistair Maurice, Bt. (1913)
Derbyshire, Sir Andrew George, Kt.
†de Trafford, Sir John Humphrey, Bt. (1841)
Deverell, *Gen.* Sir John Freegard, KCB, OBE
Devesi, Sir Baddeley, GCMG, GCVO
De Ville, Sir Harold Godfrey Oscar, Kt., CBE
Devitt, Sir James Hugh Thomas, Bt. (1916)
de Waal, Sir (Constant Henrik) Henry, KCB, QC
Dewey, Sir Anthony Hugh, Bt. (1917)
De Witt, Sir Ronald Wayne, Kt.
Dick-Lauder, Sir Piers Robert, Bt. (S. 1690)
Dilke, Sir Charles John Wentworth, Bt. (1862)
Dillon, Sir Andrew Patrick, Kt., CBE
Dillwyn-Venables-Llewelyn, Sir John Michael, Bt. (1890)
Dixon, Sir Jeremy, Kt.
Dixon, Sir Jonathan Mark, Bt. (1919)
Dixon, Sir Peter John Bellett, Kt.
Djanogly, Sir Harry Ari Simon, Kt., CBE
Dobson, *Vice-Adm.* Sir David Stuart, KBE
Dodds, Sir Ralph Jordan, Bt. (1964)
Dollery, Sir Colin Terence, Kt.
Don-Wauchope, Sir Roger (Hamilton), Bt. (S. 1667)
Donald, Sir Alan Ewen, KCMG
Donald, *Air Marshal* Sir John George, KBE
Donaldson, *Prof.* Sir Liam Joseph, Kt.
Donne, Sir John Christopher, Kt.
Donnelly, Sir Joseph Brian, KBE, CMG
Dorey, Sir Graham Martyn, Kt.
Dorman, Sir Philip Henry Keppel, Bt. (1923)
Doughty, Sir William Roland, Kt.
Douglas, *Prof.* Sir Neil James, Kt.
Douglas, *Hon.* Sir Roger Owen, Kt.
Dowell, Sir Anthony James, Kt., CBE
Dowling, Sir Robert, Kt.
Downey, Sir Gordon Stanley, KCB
Downs, Sir Diarmuid, Kt., CBE, FRENG
Downward, *Maj.-Gen.* Sir Peter Aldcroft, KCVO, CB, DSO, DFC
Dowson, Sir Philip Manning, Kt., CBE, PRA
Doyle, Sir Reginald Derek Henry, Kt., CBE

D'Oyly, Sir Hadley Gregory Bt. (1663)
Drake, *Hon.* Sir (Frederick) Maurice, Kt., DFC
Drewry, *Lt.-Gen.* Sir Christopher Francis, KCB, CBE
Drinkwater, Sir John Muir, Kt., QC
Drury, Sir (Victor William) Michael, Kt., OBE
Dryden, Sir John Stephen Gyles, Bt. (1733 and 1795)
du Cann, *Rt. Hon.* Sir Edward Dillon Lott, KBE
†Duckworth, Sir James Edward Dyce, Bt. (1909)
du Cros, Sir Claude Philip Arthur Mallet, Bt. (1916)
Dudley-Williams, Sir Alastair Edgcumbe James, Bt. (1964)
Duff, *Prof.* Sir Gordon William, Kt.
Duff-Gordon, Sir Andrew Cosmo Lewis, Bt. (1813)
Duffell, *Lt.-Gen.* Sir Peter Royson, KCB, CBE, MC
Duffy, Sir (Albert) (Edward) Patrick, Kt., PHD
Dugdale, Sir William Stratford, Bt. (1936), MC
Duggin, Sir Thomas Joseph, Kt.
Dummett, *Prof.* Sir Michael Anthony Eardley, Kt., FBA
Dunbar, Sir Archibald Ranulph, Bt. (S. 1700)
Dunbar, Sir Robert Drummond Cospatrick, Bt. (S. 1698)
Dunbar, Sir James Michael, Bt. (S. 1694)
Dunbar of Hempriggs, Sir Richard Francis, Bt. (S. 1706)
Dunbar-Nasmith, *Prof.* Sir James Duncan, Kt., CBE
Duncan, Sir James Blair, Kt.
Dunlop, Sir Thomas, Bt. (1916)
Dunn, *Rt. Hon.* Sir Robin Horace Walford, Kt., MC
Dunne, Sir Thomas Raymond, KG, KCVO
Dunning, Sir Simon William Patrick, Bt. (1930)
Dunnington-Jefferson, Sir Mervyn Stewart, Bt. (1958)
Dunstan, *Lt.-Gen.* Sir Donald Beaumont, KBE, CB
Dunt, *Vice-Adm.* Sir John Hugh, KCB
Duntze, Sir Daniel Evans Bt. (1774)
Dupre, Sir Tumun, Kt., MBE
Dupree, Sir (Thomas William James) David, Bt. (1921)
Durand, Sir Edward Alan Christopher David Percy, Bt. (1892)
Durant, Sir (Robert) Anthony (Bevis), Kt.
Durie, Sir David Robert Campbell, KCMG
Durrant, Sir William Alexander Estridge, Bt. (1784)
Duthie, *Prof.* Sir Herbert Livingston, Kt.

Duthie, Sir Robert Grieve (Robin), Kt., CBE
Dutton, *Lt-Gen.* Sir James Benjamin, KCB, CBE
Dwyer, Sir Joseph Anthony, Kt.
Dyke, Sir David William Hart, Bt. (1677)
Dymock, *Vice-Adm.* Sir Anthony Knox, KBE, CB
Dyson, Sir James, Kt., CBE
Dyson, *Rt. Hon.* Sir John Anthony, Kt.

Eady, *Hon.* Sir David, Kt.
Eardley-Wilmot, Sir Michael John Assheton, Bt. (1821)
Earle, Sir (Hardman) George (Algernon), Bt. (1869)
Eaton, *Adm.* Sir Kenneth John, GBE, KCB
Eberle, *Adm.* Sir James Henry Fuller, GCB
Ebrahim, Sir (Mahomed) Currimbhoy, Bt. (1910)
Eddington, Sir Roderick Ian, Kt.
Eder, *Hon.* Sir Henry Bernard, Kt.
Edge, *Capt.* Sir (Philip) Malcolm, KCVO
†Edge, Sir William, Bt. (1937)
Edmonstone, Sir Archibald Bruce Charles, Bt. (1774)
Edward, *Rt. Hon.* Sir David Alexander Ogilvy, KCMG
Edwardes, Sir Michael Owen, Kt.
Edwards, Sir Christopher John Churchill, Bt. (1866)
Edwards, *Prof.* Sir Christopher Richard Watkin, Kt.
Edwards, Sir Llewellyn Roy, Kt.
Edwards, *Prof.* Sir Robert Geoffrey, Kt., CBE
Edwards, Sir Robert Paul, Kt.
Edwards, *Prof.* Sir Samuel Frederick, Kt., FRS
†Edwards-Moss, Sir David John, Bt. (1868)
Edwards-Stuart, *Hon.* Sir Antony James Cobham, Kt.
Egan, Sir John Leopold, Kt.
Ehrman, Sir William Geoffrey, KCMG
Eichelbaum, *Rt. Hon.* Sir Thomas, GBE
Elder, Sir Mark Philip, Kt., CBE
Eldon, Sir Stewart Graham, KCMG, OBE
Elias, *Rt. Hon.* Sir Patrick, Kt.
Eliott of Stobs, Sir Charles Joseph Alexander, Bt. (S. 1666)
Elliot, Sir Gerald Henry, Kt.
Elliott, Sir Clive Christopher Hugh, Bt. (1917)
Elliott, Sir David Murray, KCMG, CB
Elliott, *Prof.* Sir John Huxtable, Kt., FBA
Elliott, *Prof.* Sir Roger James, Kt., FRS
Ellis, Sir Vernon James, Kt.
Ellwood, Sir Peter Brian, Kt., CBE
Elphinstone, Sir John, Bt. (S. 1701)
Elphinstone, Sir John Howard Main, Bt. (1816)

Elton, Sir Arnold, Kt., CBE
Elton, Sir Charles Abraham Grierson, Bt. (1717)
Elton, Sir Leslie, Kt.
Elvidge, Sir John, KCB
Elwes, *Dr* Sir Henry William, KCVO
Elwes, Sir Jeremy Vernon, Kt., CBE
Elwood, Sir Brian George Conway, Kt., CBE
Elworthy, *Air Cdre. Hon.* Sir Timothy Charles, KCVO, CBE
Enderby, *Prof.* Sir John Edwin, Kt. CBE, FRS
Engle, Sir George Lawrence Jose, KCB, QC
English, Sir Terence Alexander Hawthorne, KBE, FRCS
Ennals, Sir Paul Martin, Kt., CBE
Epstein, *Prof.* Sir (Michael) Anthony, Kt., CBE, FRS
Errington, *Col.* Sir Geoffrey Frederick, Bt. (1963), OBE
Errington, Sir Lancelot, KCB
Erskine, Sir (Thomas) Peter Neil, Bt. (1821)
Erskine-Hill, Sir Alexander Rodger, Bt. (1945)
Esmonde, Sir Thomas Francis Grattan, Bt. (I. 1629)
Esplen, Sir John Graham, Bt. (1921)
Esquivel, *Rt. Hon.* Sir Manuel, KCMG
Essenhigh, *Adm.* Sir Nigel Richard, GCB
Etherington, Sir Stuart James, Kt.
Etherton, *Rt. Hon.* Sir Terence Michael Elkan Barnet, Kt.
Evans, Sir Anthony Adney, Bt. (1920)
Evans, *Rt. Hon.* Sir Anthony Howell Meurig, Kt.
Evans, *Prof.* Sir Christopher Thomas, Kt., OBE
Evans, *Air Chief Marshal* Sir David George, GCB, CBE
Evans, *Hon.* Sir David Roderick, Kt.
Evans, Sir Harold Matthew, Kt.
Evans, *Hon.* Sir Haydn Tudor, Kt.
Evans, *Prof.* Sir John Grimley, Kt., FRCP
Evans, Sir John Stanley, Kt., QPM
Evans, *Prof.* Sir Martin John, Kt., FRS
Evans, Sir Richard Harry, Kt., CBE
Evans, Sir Richard Mark, KCMG, KCVO
Evans, Sir Robert, Kt., CBE, FRENG
Evans-Lombe, *Hon.* Sir Edward Christopher, Kt.
†Evans-Tipping, Sir David Gwynne, Bt. (1913)
Eveleigh, *Rt. Hon.* Sir Edward Walter, Kt., ERD
†Everard, Sir Henry Peter Charles, Bt. (1911)
Every, Sir Henry John Michael, Bt. (1641)
Ewans, Sir Martin Kenneth, KCMG
Ewart, Sir William Michael, Bt. (1887)

Eyre, Sir Reginald Edwin, Kt.
Eyre, Sir Richard Charles Hastings, Kt., CBE

Fagge, Sir John Christopher Frederick, Bt. (1660)
Fairbairn, Sir (James) Brooke, Bt. (1869)
Fairlie-Cuninghame, Sir Robert Henry, Bt. (S. 1630)
Fairweather, Sir Patrick Stanislaus, KCMG
Faldo, Sir Nicholas Alexander, Kt., MBE
†Falkiner, Sir Benjamin Simon Patrick, Bt. (I. 1778)
Fall, Sir Brian James Proetel, GCVO, KCMG
Falle, Sir Samuel, KCMG, KCVO, DSC
Fang, Prof. Sir Harry, Kt., CBE
Fareed, Sir Djamil Sheik, Kt.
Farmer, Sir Thomas, Kt., CVO, CBE
Farquhar, Sir Michael Fitzroy Henry, Bt. (1796)
Farquharson, Sir Angus Durie Miller, KCVO, OBE
Farrell, Sir Terence, Kt., CBE
Farrer, Sir (Charles) Matthew, GCVO
Farrington, Sir Henry William, Bt. (1818)
Fat, Sir (Maxime) Edouard (Lim Man) Lim, Kt.
Faulkner, Sir (James) Dennis (Compton), Kt., CBE, VRD
Fay, Sir (Humphrey) Michael Gerard, Kt.
Fayrer, Sir John Lang Macpherson, Bt. (1896)
Feachem, Prof. Sir Richard George Andrew, KBE
Fean, Sir Thomas Vincent, KCVO
†Feilden, Sir Henry Rudyard, Bt. (1846)
Feldmann, Prof. Sir Marc, Kt.
Fell, Sir David, KCB
Fender, Sir Brian Edward Frederick, Kt., CMG, PHD
Fenn, Sir Nicholas Maxted, GCMG
Fenwick, Sir Leonard Raymond, Kt., CBE
Fergus, Sir Howard Archibald, KBE
Ferguson, Sir Alexander Chapman, Kt., CBE
Ferguson-Davie, Sir Michael, Bt. (1847)
Fergusson of Kilkerran, Sir Charles, Bt. (S. 1703)
Fergusson, Sir Ewan Alastair John, GCMG, GCVO
Fersht, Prof. Sir Alan Roy, Kt., FRS
Ferris, Hon. Sir Francis Mursell, Kt., TD
ffolkes, Sir Robert Francis Alexander, Bt. (1774), OBE
Field, Sir Malcolm David, Kt.
Field, Hon. Sir Richard Alan, Kt.

Fielding, Sir Leslie, KCMG
Fields, Sir Allan Clifford, KCMG
Fieldsend, Hon. Sir John Charles Rowell, KBE
Fiennes, Sir Ranulph Twisleton-Wykeham, Bt. (1916), OBE
Figg, Sir Leonard Clifford William, KCMG
Figgis, Sir Anthony St John Howard, KCVO, CMG
Finch, Sir Robert Gerard, Kt.
Finlay, Sir David Ronald James Bell, Bt. (1964)
Finlayson, Sir Garet Orlando, KCMG, OBE
Finney, Sir Thomas, Kt., OBE
†Fison, Sir Charles William, Bt. (1905)
†Fitzgerald, Revd Daniel Patrick, Bt. (1903)
FitzGerald, Sir Adrian James Andrew, Bt. (1880)
FitzHerbert, Sir Richard Ranulph, Bt. (1784)
Fitzpatrick, Air Marshal Sir John Bernard, KBE, CB
Flanagan, Sir Ronald, GBE
Flanagan, Sir Maurice, KBE
Flaux, Hon. Sir Julian Martin, Kt.
Floud, Prof. Sir Roderick Castle, Kt.
Floyd, Hon. Sir Christopher David, Kt.
Floyd, Sir Giles Henry Charles, Bt. (1816)
Foley, Lt.-Gen. Sir John Paul, KCB, OBE, MC
Follett, Prof. Sir Brian Keith, Kt., FRS
Forbes, Sir James Thomas Stewart, Bt. (1823)
Forbes, Adm. Sir Ian Andrew, KCB, CBE
Forbes, Vice-Adm. Sir John Morrison, KCB
Forbes, Hon. Sir Thayne John, Kt.
†Forbes Adam, Revd Stephen Timothy Beilby, Bt. (1917)
Forbes-Leith, Sir George Ian David, Bt. (1923)
Forbes of Craigievar, Sir Andrew Iain Ochoncar, Bt. (S. 1630)
Ford, Sir Andrew Russell, Bt. (1929)
Ford, Sir David Robert, KBE, LVO
Ford, Sir John Archibald, KCMG, MC
Ford, Gen. Sir Robert Cyril, GCB, CBE
Foreman, Sir Philip Frank, Kt., CBE, FRENG
Forestier-Walker, Sir Michael Leolin, Bt. (1835)
Forman, Sir John Denis, Kt., OBE
Forrest, Prof. Sir (Andrew) Patrick (McEwen), Kt.
Forsyth-Johnson, Sir Bruce Joseph, Kt., CBE (Bruce Forsyth)
Forte, Hon. Sir Rocco John Vincent, Kt.
Forwood, Sir Peter Noel, Bt. (1895)
Foskett, Hon. Sir David Robert, Kt.
Foster, Sir Andrew William, Kt.

Foster, Prof. Sir Christopher David, Kt.
†Foster, Sir Saxby Gregory, Bt. (1930)
Foulkes, Sir Arthur Alexander, GCMG
Foulkes, Sir Nigel Gordon, Kt.
Fountain, Hon. Sir Cyril Stanley Smith, Kt.
Fowke, Sir David Frederick Gustavus, Bt. (1814)
Fowler, Sir (Edward) Michael Coulson, Kt.
Fox, Sir Christopher, Kt., QPM
Fox, Sir Paul Leonard, Kt., CBE
France, Sir Christopher Walter, GCB
Francis, Sir Horace William Alexander, Kt., CBE, FRENG
Frank, Sir Robert Andrew, Bt. (1920)
Franklin, Sir Michael David Milroy, KCB, CMG
Fraser, Sir Alasdair MacLeod, Kt.
Fraser, Sir Charles Annand, KCVO
Fraser, Gen. Sir David William, GCB, OBE
Fraser, Sir Iain Michael Duncan, Bt. (1943)
Fraser, Sir James Murdo, KBE
Fraser, Sir William Kerr, GCB
Frayling, Prof. Sir Christopher John, Kt.
Frederick, Sir Christopher St John, Bt. (1723)
Freedman, Rt. Hon. Prof. Sir Lawrence David, KCMG, CBE
Freeland, Sir John Redvers, KCMG
Freeman, Sir James Robin, Bt. (1945)
Freer, Air Chief Marshal Sir Robert William George, GBE, KCB
French, Air Marshal Sir Joseph Charles, KCB, CBE
Frere, Vice-Adm. Sir Richard Tobias, KCB
Fretwell, Sir (Major) John (Emsley), GCMG
Friend Prof. Sir Richard Henry, Kt.
Froggatt, Sir Peter, Kt.
Frossard, Sir Charles Keith, KBE
Frost, Sir David Paradine, Kt., OBE
Fry, Sir Graham Holbrook, KCMG
Fry, Sir Peter Derek, Kt.
Fry, Lt.-Gen. Sir Robert Allan, KCB, CBE
Fulford, Hon. Sir Adrian Bruce, Kt.
Fuller, Sir James Henry Fleetwood, Bt. (1910)
Fulton, Lt.-Gen. Sir Robert Henry Gervase, KBE
Furness, Sir Stephen Roberts, Bt. (1913)

Gage, Rt. Hon. Sir William Marcus, Kt., QC
Gains, Sir John Christopher, Kt.
Gainsford, Sir Ian Derek, Kt.
Galsworthy, Sir Anthony Charles, KCMG
Galway, Sir James, Kt., OBE

Gamble, Sir David Hugh Norman, Bt. (1897)

Gambon, Sir Michael John, Kt., CBE

Gammell, Sir William Benjamin Bowring, Kt.

Gardiner, Sir John Eliot, Kt., CBE

Gardner, *Prof.* Sir Richard Lavenham, Kt.

Gardner, Sir Roy Alan, Kt.

Garland, *Hon.* Sir Patrick Neville, Kt.

Garland, *Hon.* Sir Ransley Victor, KBE

Garland, *Dr* Sir Trevor, KBE

Garner, Sir Anthony Stuart, Kt.

Garnett, *Adm.* Sir Ian David Graham, KCB

Garnier, *Rear-Adm.* Sir John, KCVO, CBE

Garrard, Sir David Eardley, Kt.

Garrett, Sir Anthony Peter, Kt., CBE

Garrick, Sir Ronald, Kt., CBE, FRENG

Garthwaite, Sir (William) Mark (Charles), Bt. (1919)

Gaskell, Sir Richard Kennedy Harvey, Kt.

Gass, Sir Simon Lawrance, KCMG, CVO

Geidt, *Rt. Hon.* Sir Christopher, KCVO, OBE

Geno, Sir Makena Viora, KBE

Gent, Sir Christopher Charles, Kt.

George, Sir Arthur Thomas, Kt.

George, *Prof.* Sir Charles Frederick, MD, FRCP

George, Sir Richard William, Kt., CVO

Gerken, *Vice-Adm.* Sir Robert William Frank, KCB, CBE

Gershon, Sir Peter Oliver, Kt., CBE

Gethin, Sir Richard Joseph St Lawrence, Bt. (I. 1665)

Gibb, Sir Francis Ross (Frank), Kt., CBE, FRENG

Gibbings, Sir Peter Walter, Kt.

Gibbons, Sir (John) David, KBE

Gibbons, Sir William Edward Doran, Bt. (1752)

Gibbs, *Hon.* Sir Richard John Hedley, Kt.

Gibbs, Sir Roger Geoffrey, Kt.

†Gibson, *Revd* Christopher Herbert, Bt. (1931)

Gibson, Sir Ian, Kt., CBE

Gibson, *Rt. Hon.* Sir Peter Leslie, Kt.

Gibson-Craig-Carmichael, Sir David Peter William, Bt. (S. 1702 and 1831)

Gieve, Sir Edward John Watson, KCB

Giffard, Sir (Charles) Sydney (Rycroft), KCMG

Gilbart-Denham, *Lt.-Col.* Sir Seymour Vivian, KCVO

Gilbert, *Air Chief Marshal* Sir Joseph Alfred, KCB, CBE

Gilbert, *Rt. Hon.* Sir Martin John, Kt., CBE

†Gilbey, Sir Walter Gavin, Bt. (1893)

Gill, Sir Anthony Keith, Kt.

Gill, Sir Arthur Benjamin Norman, Kt., CBE

Gill, Sir Robin Denys, KCVO

Gillam, Sir Patrick John, Kt.

Gillen, *Hon.* Sir John de Winter, Kt.

Gillett, Sir Nicholas Danvers Penrose, Bt. (1959)

Gillinson, Sir Clive Daniel, Kt., CBE

Gilmore, *Prof.* Sir Ian Thomas, Kt.

Gilmour, Sir John, Bt. (1897)

Gina, Sir Lloyd Maepeza, KBE

Giordano, Sir Richard Vincent, KBE

Girolami, Sir Paul, Kt.

Girvan, *Rt. Hon.* Sir (Frederick) Paul, Kt.

Gladstone, Sir (Erskine) William, Bt. (1846), KG

Glean, Sir Carlyle Arnold, GCMG

Glenn, Sir (Joseph Robert) Archibald, Kt., OBE

Glidewell, *Rt. Hon.* Sir Iain Derek Laing, Kt.

Glover, Sir Victor Joseph Patrick, Kt.

Glyn, Sir Richard Lindsay, Bt. (1759 and 1800)

Gobbo, Sir James Augustine, Kt., AC

Goldberg, *Prof.* Sir David Paul Brandes, Kt.

Goldring, *Rt. Hon.* Sir John Bernard, Kt.

Gomersall, Sir Stephen John, KCMG

Gonsalves-Sabola, *Hon.* Sir Joaquim Claudino, Kt

Gooch, Sir Miles Peter, Bt. (1866)

Gooch, Sir Arthur Brian Sherlock Heywood, Bt. (1746)

Good, Sir John James Griffen, Kt., CBE

Goodall, Sir (Arthur) David Saunders, GCMG

Goodall, *Air Marshal* Sir Roderick Harvey, KBE, CB, AFC

Goode, *Prof.* Sir Royston Miles, Kt., CBE, QC

Goodenough, Sir Anthony Michael, KCMG

Goodenough, Sir William McLernon, Bt. (1943)

Goodhart, Sir Philip Carter, Kt.

Goodhart, Sir Robert Anthony Gordon, Bt. (1911)

Goodison, Sir Nicholas Proctor, Kt.

Goodman, Sir Patrick Ledger, Kt., CBE

Goodson, Sir Mark Weston Lassam, Bt. (1922)

Goodwin, Sir Frederick, KBE

Goodwin, Sir Frederick Anderson, Kt.

Goodwin, Sir Matthew Dean, Kt., CBE

Goody, *Prof.* Sir John Rankine, Kt.

†Goold, Sir George William, Bt. (1801)

Gordon, Sir Donald, Kt.

Gordon, Sir Gerald Henry, Kt., CBE, QC

Gordon, Sir Robert James, Bt. (S. 1706)

Gordon-Cumming, Sir Alexander Penrose, Bt. (1804)

Gore, Sir Hugh Frederick Corbet, Bt. (I. 1622)

Gore-Booth, Sir Josslyn Henry Robert, Bt. (I. 1760)

Goring, Sir William Burton Nigel, Bt. (1627)

Gorman, Sir John Reginald, Kt., CVO, CBE, MC

Goschen, Sir (Edward) Alexander, Bt. (1916)

Gosling, Sir (Frederick) Donald, KCVO

Goswell, Sir Brian Lawrence, Kt.

Gough, Sir Charles Brandon, Kt.

Goulden, Sir (Peter) John, GCMG

Goulding, Sir (William) Lingard Walter, Bt. (1904)

Gourlay, *Gen.* Sir (Basil) Ian (Spencer), KCB, OBE, MC, RM

Gourlay, Sir Simon Alexander, Kt.

Gow, *Gen.* Sir (James) Michael, GCB

Gowans, Sir James Learmonth, Kt., CBE, FRCP, FRS

Gozney, Sir Richard Hugh Turton, KCMG

†Graaff, Sir David de Villiers, Bt. (1911)

Grabham, Sir Anthony Henry, Kt.

Graham, Sir Alexander Michael, GBE

Graham, Sir James Bellingham, Bt. (1662)

Graham, Sir James Fergus Surtees, Bt. (1783)

Graham, Sir James Thompson, Kt., CMG

Graham, Sir John Alexander Noble, Bt. (1906), GCMG

Graham, Sir John Alistair, Kt.

Graham, Sir John Moodie, Bt. (1964)

Graham, Sir Peter, KCB, QC

Graham, *Lt.-Gen.* Sir Peter Walter, KCB, CBE

†Graham, Sir Ralph Stuart, Bt. (1629)

Graham-Moon, Sir Peter Wilfred Giles, Bt. (1855)

Graham-Smith, *Prof.* Sir Francis, Kt.

Grant, Sir Archibald, Bt. (S. 1705)

Grant, Sir Clifford, Kt.

Grant, Sir Ian David, Kt., CBE

Grant, Sir (John) Anthony, Kt.

Grant, Sir John Douglas Kelso, KCMG

Grant, Sir Patrick Alexander Benedict, Bt. (S. 1688)

Grant, Sir Paul Joseph Patrick, Kt.

Grant, *Lt.-Gen.* Sir Scott Carnegie, KCB

Grant-Suttie, Sir James Edward, Bt. (S. 1702)

Granville-Chapman, *Lt.-Gen.* Sir Timothy John, GBE, KCB, ADC

Gratton-Bellew, Sir Henry Charles, Bt. (1838)

Gray, *Hon.* Sir Charles Anthony St John, Kt.

Gray, Sir Charles Ireland, Kt., CBE
Gray, *Prof.* Sir Denis John Pereira, Kt., OBE, FRCGP
Gray, *Dr.* Sir John Armstrong Muir, Kt., CBE
Gray, Sir Robert McDowall (Robin), Kt.
Gray, Sir William Hume, Bt. (1917)
Graydon, *Air Chief Marshal* Sir Michael James, GCB, CBE
Grayson, Sir Jeremy Brian Vincent Harrington, Bt. (1922)
Green, Sir Allan David, KCB, QC
Green, Sir Andrew Fleming, KCMG
Green, Sir Edward Patrick Lycett, Bt. (1886)
Green, Sir Gregory David, KCMG
Green, *Hon.* Sir Guy Stephen Montague, KBE
Green, *Prof.* Sir Malcolm, Kt.
Green, Sir Owen Whitley, Kt.
Green, Sir Philip Green, Kt.
Green-Price, Sir Robert John, Bt. (1874)
Greenaway, Sir John Michael Burdick, Bt. (1933)
Greenbury, Sir Richard, Kt.
Greener, Sir Anthony Armitage, Kt.
Greengross, Sir Alan David, Kt.
Greenstock, Sir Jeremy Quentin, GCMG
Greenwell, Sir Edward Bernard, Bt. (1906)
Greenwood, *Prof.* Sir Christopher John, Kt., CMG
Gregory, *Prof.* Sir Michael John, Kt., CBE
Gregson, Sir Peter John, Kt.
Gregson, Sir Peter Lewis, GCB
Greig, Sir (Henry Louis) Carron, KCVO, CBE
Grey, Sir Anthony Dysart, Bt. (1814)
†Grey-Egerton, Sir William de Malpas, Bt. (1617), CB, OBE, MC
Grierson, Sir Ronald Hugh, Kt.
Griffiths, Sir Eldon Wylie, Kt.
Grigson, *Hon.* Sir Geoffrey Douglas, Kt.
Grimshaw, Sir Nicholas Thomas, Kt., CBE
Grimwade, Sir Andrew Sheppard, Kt., CBE
Grose, *Vice-Adm.* Sir Alan, KBE
Gross, *Rt. Hon.* Sir Peter Henry, Kt.
Grossart, Sir Angus McFarlane McLeod, Kt., CBE
Grotrian, Sir Philip Christian Brent, Bt. (1934)
Grove, Sir Charles Gerald, Bt. (1874)
Grundy, Sir Mark, Kt.
Guinness, Sir Howard Christian Sheldon, Kt., VRD
Guinness, Sir John Ralph Sidney, Kt., CB
†Guinness, Sir Kenelm Edward Lee, Bt. (1867)
†Guise, Sir Christopher James, Bt. (1783)
Gull, Sir Rupert William Cameron, Bt. (1872)

Gumbs, Sir Emile Rudolph, Kt.
Gunn, Sir Robert Norman, Kt.
†Gunning, Sir Charles Theodore, Bt. (1778)
Gunston, Sir John Wellesley, Bt. (1938)
Gurdon, *Prof.* Sir John Bertrand, Kt., DPHIL, FRS
Guthrie, Sir Malcolm Connop, Bt. (1936)

Haddacks, *Vice-Adm.* Sir Paul Kenneth, KCB
Hadfield, Sir Ronald, Kt., QPM
Hadlee, Sir Richard John, Kt., MBE
Hagart-Alexander, Sir Claud, Bt. (1886)
Hague, *Prof.* Sir Douglas Chalmers, Kt., CBE
Haines, *Prof.* Sir Andrew Paul, Kt.
Haji-Ioannou, Sir Stelios, Kt.
Halberg, Sir Murray Gordon, Kt., MBE
Hall, *Prof.* Sir David Michael Baldock, Kt.
Hall, Sir Ernest, Kt., OBE
Hall, Sir Graham Joseph, Kt.
Hall, Sir Iain Robert, Kt.
Hall, Sir (Frederick) John (Frank), Bt. (1923)
Hall, Sir John, Kt.
Hall, Sir John Bernard, Bt. (1919)
Hall, Sir John Douglas Hoste, Bt. (S. 1687)
Hall, HE *Prof.* Sir Kenneth Octavius, GCMG
Hall, Sir Peter Edward, KBE, CMG
Hall, *Prof.* Sir Peter Geoffrey, Kt., FBA
Hall, Sir Peter Reginald Frederick, Kt., CBE
Hall, Sir William Joseph, KCVO
Halpern, Sir Ralph Mark, Kt.
Halsey, *Revd* John Walter Brooke, Bt. (1920)
Halstead, Sir Ronald, Kt., CBE
Hamblen, *Hon.* Sir Nicholas Archibald, Kt.
†Hambling, Sir Herbert Peter Hugh, Bt. (1924)
Hamilton, Sir Andrew Caradoc, Bt. (S. 1646)
Hamilton, Sir James Arnot, KCB, MBE, FRENG
Hamilton, Sir Nigel, KCB
Hamilton-Dalrymple, *Maj.* Sir Hew Fleetwood, Bt. (S. 1697), GCVO
Hamilton-Spencer-Smith, Sir John, Bt. (1804)
Hammick, Sir Stephen George, Bt. (1834)
Hammond, Sir Anthony Hilgrove, KCB, QC
Hampel, Sir Ronald Claus, Kt.
Hampson, Sir Stuart, Kt.
Hampton, Sir (Leslie) Geoffrey, Kt.
Hampton, Sir Philip Roy, Kt.
Hanbury-Tenison, Sir Richard, KCVO

Hancock, Sir David John Stowell, KCB
†Hanham, Sir William John Edward, Bt. (1667)
Hankes-Drielsma, Sir Claude Dunbar, KCVO
Hanley, *Rt. Hon.* Sir Jeremy James, KCMG
Hanmer, Sir Wyndham Richard Guy, Bt. (1774)
Hannam, Sir John Gordon, Kt.
Hanson, Sir (Charles) Rupert (Patrick), Bt. (1918)
Hanson, Sir John Gilbert, KCMG, CBE
Harcourt-Smith, *Air Chief Marshal* Sir David, GBE, KCB, DFC
Hardie Boys, *Rt. Hon.* Sir Michael, GCMG
Harding, Sir George William, KCMG, CVO
Harding, *Marshal of the Royal Air Force* Sir Peter Robin, GCB
Harding, Sir Roy Pollard, Kt., CBE
Hardy, Sir David William, Kt.
Hardy, Sir James Gilbert, Kt., OBE
Hardy, Sir Richard Charles Chandos, Bt. (1876)
Hare, Sir David, Kt., FRSL
Hare, Sir Nicholas Patrick, Bt. (1818)
Haren, *Dr* Sir Patrick Hugh, Kt.
†Harford, Sir Mark John, Bt. (1934)
Harington, Sir Nicholas John, Bt. (1611)
Harkness, *Very Revd* James, KCVO, CB, OBE
Harland, *Air Marshal* Sir Reginald Edward Wynyard, KBE, CB
Harley, *Gen.* Sir Alexander George Hamilton, KBE, CB
Harman, *Hon.* Sir Jeremiah LeRoy, Kt.
Harman, Sir John Andrew, Kt.
Harmsworth, Sir Hildebrand Harold, Bt. (1922)
Harper, Sir Ewan William, Kt. CBE
Harper, *Prof.* Sir Peter Stanley, Kt., CBE
†Harris, Sir Christopher John Ashford, Bt. (1932)
Harris, *Prof.* Sir Henry, Kt., FRCP, FRCPATH, FRS
Harris, *Air Marshal* Sir John Hulme, KCB, CBE
Harris, *Prof.* Sir Martin Best, Kt., CBE
Harris, Sir Michael Frank, Kt.
Harris, Sir (Theodore) Wilson, Kt.
Harris, Sir Thomas George, KBE, CMG,
Harrison, *Prof.* Sir Brian Howard, Kt.
Harrison, Sir David, Kt., CBE, FRENG
Harrison, *Hon.* Sir Michael Guy Vicat, Kt.
Harrison, Sir Michael James Harwood, Bt. (1961)

Harrison, Sir (Robert) Colin, Bt. (1922)
Harrison, Sir Terence, Kt., FRENG
Harrop, Sir Peter John, KCB
Hart, *Hon.* Sir Anthony Ronald, Kt.
Hart, Sir David Michael, Kt., OBE
Hart, Sir Graham Allan, KCB
Hartwell, Sir (Francis) Anthony Charles Peter, Bt. (1805)
Harvey, Sir Charles Richard Musgrave, Bt. (1933)
Harvie, Sir John Smith, Kt., CBE
Harvie-Watt, Sir James, Bt. (1945)
Harwood, Sir Ronald, Kt., CBE
Haselhurst, *Rt. Hon.* Sir Alan Gordon Barraclough, Kt.
Haskard, Sir Cosmo Dugal Patrick Thomas, KCMG, MBE
Hastie, *Cdre* Sir Robert Cameron, KCVO, CBE, RD
Hastings, Sir Max Macdonald, Kt.
Hastings, *Dr* Sir William George, Kt., CBE
Hatter, Sir Maurice, Kt.
Havelock-Allan, Sir (Anthony) Mark David, Bt. (1858)
Hawkes, Sir John Garry, Kt., CBE
Hawkhead, Sir Anthony Gerard, Kt., CBE
Hawkins, Sir Richard Caesar, Bt. (1778)
†Hawley, Sir Henry Nicholas, Bt. (1795)
Hawley, Sir James Appleton, KCVO, TD
Haworth, Sir Philip, Bt. (1911)
Hawthorne, *Prof.* Sir William Rede, Kt., CBE, SCD, FRS, FRENG
Hay, Sir David Russell, Kt., CBE, FRCP, MD
Hay, Sir John Erroll Audley, Bt. (S. 1663)
†Hay, Sir Ronald Frederick Hamilton, Bt. (S. 1703)
Hayes, Sir Brian, Kt., CBE, QPM
Hayes, Sir Brian David, GCB
Hayman-Joyce, *Lt.-Gen.* Sir Robert John, KCB, CBE
Hayter, Sir Paul David Grenville, KCB, LVO
Hayward, Sir Jack Arnold, Kt., OBE
Head, Sir Richard Douglas Somerville, Bt. (1838)
Heap, Sir Peter William, KCMG
Heap, *Prof.* Sir Robert Brian, Kt., CBE, FRS
Hearne, Sir Graham James, Kt., CBE
Heathcote, *Brig.* Sir Gilbert Simon, Bt. (1733), CBE
†Heathcote, Sir Timothy Gilbert, Bt. (1733)
Heatley, Sir Peter, Kt., CBE
Hedley, *Hon.* Sir Mark, Kt.
Hegarty, Sir John Kevin, Kt.
Heiser, Sir Terence Michael, GCB
Henderson, Sir Denys Hartley, Kt.
Henderson, *Hon.* Sir Launcelot Dinadan James, Kt.
Henderson, *Maj.* Sir Richard Yates, KCVO

Hendry, *Prof.* Sir David Forbes, Kt.
Hennessy, Sir James Patrick Ivan, KBE, CMG
†Henniker, Sir Adrian Chandos, Bt. (1813)
Henniker-Heaton, Sir Yvo Robert, Bt. (1912)
Henriques, *Hon.* Sir Richard Henry Quixano, Kt.
Henry, *Hon.* Sir Geoffrey Arama, KBE
†Henry, Sir Patrick Denis, Bt. (1923)
Henshaw, Sir David George, Kt.
Hepple, *Prof.* Sir Bob Alexander, Kt.
Herbecq, Sir John Edward, KCB
Herbert, *Adm.* Sir Peter Geoffrey Marshall, KCB, OBE
Heron, Sir Conrad Frederick, KCB, OBE
Heron, Sir Michael Gilbert, Kt.
Heron-Maxwell, Sir Nigel Mellor, Bt. (S. 1683)
Hervey, Sir Roger Blaise Ramsay, KCVO, CMG
Hervey-Bathurst, Sir Frederick John Charles Gordon, Bt. (1818)
Heseltine, *Rt. Hon.* Sir William Frederick Payne, GCB, GCVO
Hewetson, Sir Christopher Raynor, Kt., TD
Hewett, Sir Richard Mark John, Bt. (1813)
Hewitt, Sir (Cyrus) Lenox (Simson), Kt., OBE
Hewitt, Sir Nicholas Charles Joseph, Bt. (1921)
Heygate, Sir Richard John Gage, Bt. (1831)
Heywood, Sir Peter, Bt. (1838)
Hickinbottom, *Hon.* Sir Gary Robert, Kt.
Hickman, Sir (Richard) Glenn, Bt. (1903)
Hicks, Sir Robert, Kt.
Hidden, *Hon.* Sir Anthony Brian, Kt.
Hielscher, Sir Leo Arthur, Kt.
Higgins, Sir Hartmann, Kt.
Higgins, *Rt. Hon.* Sir Malachy Joseph, Kt.
Higginson, Sir Gordon Robert, Kt., PHD, FRENG
Hill, Sir Arthur Alfred, Kt., CBE
Hill, Sir Brian John, Kt.
Hill, Sir James Frederick, Bt. (1917)
Hill, Sir John Alfred Rowley, Bt. (I. 1779)
Hill, *Vice-Adm.* Sir Robert Charles Finch, KBE, FRENG
Hill-Norton, *Vice-Adm. Hon.* Sir Nicholas John, KCB
Hill-Wood, Sir Samuel Thomas, Bt. (1921)
Hillhouse, Sir (Robert) Russell, KCB
Hills, Sir Graham John, Kt.
Hine, *Air Chief Marshal* Sir Patrick Bardon, GCB, GBE
Hirsch, *Prof.* Sir Peter Bernhard, Kt., PHD., FRS

Hirst, *Rt. Hon.* Sir David Cozens-Hardy, Kt.
Hirst, Sir Michael William, Kt.
Hoare, *Prof.* Sir Charles Anthony Richard, Kt., FRS
Hoare, Sir David John, Bt. (1786)
Hoare, Sir Charles James, Bt. (I. 1784)
Hobart, Sir John Vere, Bt. (1914)
Hobbs, *Maj.-Gen.* Sir Michael Frederick, KCVO, CBE
Hobday, Sir Gordon Ivan, Kt.
Hobhouse, Sir Charles John Spinney, Bt. (1812)
Hobson, Sir Ronald, KCVO
†Hodge, Sir Andrew Rowland, Bt. (1921)
Hodge, Sir James William, KCVO, CMG
Hodgkin, Sir (Gordon) Howard (Eliot), Kt., CH, CBE
Hodgkinson, Sir Michael Stewart, Kt.
Hodgson, Sir Maurice Arthur Eric, Kt., FRENG
Hodson, Sir Michael Robin Adderley, Bt. (I. 1789)
Hogg, Sir Christopher Anthony, Kt.
†Hogg, Sir Piers Michael James, Bt. (1846)
†Holcroft, Sir Charles Anthony Culcheth, Bt. (1921)
Holderness, Sir Martin William, Bt. (1920)
Holden, Sir Paul, Bt. (1893)
Holden, Sir John David, Bt. (1919)
Holden-Brown, Sir Derrick, Kt.
Holder, Sir John Henry, Bt. (1898)
Holdgate, Sir Martin Wyatt, Kt., CB, PHD
Holland, *Hon.* Sir Alan Douglas, Kt.
Holland, *Hon.* Sir Christopher John, Kt.
Holland, Sir Geoffrey, KCB
Holland, Sir John Anthony, Kt.
Holliday, *Prof.* Sir Frederick George Thomas, Kt., CBE, FRSE
Hollom, Sir Jasper Quintus, KBE
Holloway, *Hon.* Sir Barry Blyth, KBE
Holm, Sir Ian (Holm Cuthbert), Kt., CBE
Holman, *Hon.* Sir (Edward) James, Kt.
Holman, *Prof.* Sir John Stranger, Kt.
Holmes, *Prof.* Sir Frank Wakefield, Kt.
Holmes, Sir John Eaton, GCVO, KBE, CMG
Holroyd, *Air Marshal* Sir Frank Martyn, KBE, CB
Holroyd, Sir Michael De Courcy Fraser, Kt., CBE
Holroyde, *Hon.* Sir Timothy Victor, Kt.
Holt, *Prof.* Sir James Clarke, Kt.
Holt, Sir Michael, Kt., CBE
Home, Sir William Dundas, Bt. (S. 1671)
Honywood, Sir Filmer Courtenay William, Bt. (1660)

†Hood, Sir John Joseph Harold, Bt. (1922)

Hookway, Sir Harry Thurston, Kt.

Hooper, *Rt. Hon.* Sir Anthony, Kt.

Hope, Sir Colin Frederick Newton, Kt.

Hope, Sir Alexander Archibald Douglas, Bt. (S. 1628)

Hope-Dunbar, Sir David, Bt. (S. 1664)

Hopkin, *Prof.* Sir Deian Rhys, Kt.

Hopkin, Sir Royston Oliver, KCMG

Hopkins, Sir Anthony Philip, Kt., CBE

Hopkins, Sir Michael John, Kt., CBE, RA, RIBA

Hopwood, *Prof.* Sir David Alan, Kt., FRS

Hordern, *Rt. Hon.* Sir Peter Maudslay, Kt.

Horlick, *Vice-Adm.* Sir Edwin John, KBE, FRENG

Horlick, Sir James Cunliffe William, Bt. (1914)

Horlock, *Prof.* Sir John Harold, Kt., FRS, FRENG

Horn, *Prof.* Sir Gabriel, Kt., FRS

Horn-Smith, Sir Julian Michael, Kt.

Hornby, Sir Derek Peter, Kt.

Horne, Sir Alan Gray Antony, Bt. (1929)

Horne, *Dr* Sir Alistair Allan, Kt. CBE

Horsbrugh-Porter, Sir John Simon, Bt. (1902)

Horsfall, Sir Edward John Wright, Bt. (1909)

Hort, Sir Andrew Edwin Fenton, Bt. (1767)

Horton, Sir Robert Baynes, Kt.

Hosker, Sir Gerald Albery, KCB, QC

Hoskins, *Prof.* Sir Brian John, Kt. CBE, FRS

†Hoskyns, Sir Edwyn Wren, Bt. (1676)

Hoskyns, Sir John Austin Hungerford Leigh, Kt.

Hotung, Sir Joseph Edward, Kt.

Houghton, *Gen.* Sir John Nicholas Reynolds, GCB, CBE

Houghton, Sir John Theodore, Kt., CBE, FRS

Houldsworth, Sir Richard Thomas Reginald, Bt. (1887)

Hourston, Sir Gordon Minto, Kt.

Housden, Sir Peter James, KCB

House, *Lt.-Gen.* Sir David George, GCB, KCVO, CBE, MC

Houssemayne du Boulay, Sir Roger William, KCVO, CMG

Houstoun-Boswall, Sir (Thomas) Alford, Bt. (1836)

Howard, Sir David Howarth Seymour, Bt. (1955)

Howard, *Prof.* Sir Michael Eliot, Kt., OM, CH, CBE, MC

Howard-Lawson, Sir John Philip, Bt. (1841)

Howells, Sir Eric Waldo Benjamin, Kt., CBE

Howes, Sir Christopher Kingston, KCVO, CB

Howlett, *Gen.* Sir Geoffrey Hugh Whitby, KBE, MC

Hoy, Sir Christopher Andrew, Kt., MBE

Hugh-Jones, Sir Wynn Normington, Kt., LVO

Hugh-Smith, Sir Andrew Colin, Kt.

Hughes, *Rt. Hon.* Sir Anthony Philip Gilson, Kt.

Hughes, Sir Thomas Collingwood, Bt. (1773)

Hughes, Sir Trevor Poulton, KCB

†Hughes-Morgan, Sir (Ian) Parry David, Bt. (1925)

Hull, *Prof.* Sir David, Kt.

Hulse, Sir Edward Jeremy Westrow, Bt. (1739)

Hum, Sir Christopher Owen, KCMG

Humphreys, *Prof.* Sir Colin John, Kt., CBE

Hunt, Sir John Leonard, Kt.

Hunt, *Adm.* Sir Nicholas John Streynsham, GCB, LVO

Hunt, Sir Rex Masterman, Kt., CMG

Hunt, *Dr* Sir Richard Timothy, Kt.

Hunt-Davis, *Brig.* Sir Miles Garth, GCVO, CBE

Hunter, Sir Alistair John, KCMG

Hunter, *Prof.* Sir Laurence Colvin, Kt., CBE, FRSE

Hunter, *Dr* Sir Philip John, Kt., CBE

Hunter, Sir Thomas Blane, Kt.

Huntington-Whiteley, Sir Hugo Baldwin, Bt. (1918)

Hurn, Sir (Francis) Roger, Kt.

Hurst, Sir Geoffrey Charles, Kt., MBE

Husbands, Sir Clifford Straugh, GCMG

Hutchison, *Rt. Hon.* Sir Michael, Kt.

†Hutchison, Sir Peter Craft, CBE, Bt. (1956)

Hutchison, Sir Robert, Bt. (1939)

Hutt, Sir Dexter Walter, Kt.

Huxley, *Prof.* Sir Andrew Fielding, Kt., OM, FRS

Huxtable, *Gen.* Sir Charles Richard, KCB, CBE

Hytner, Sir Nicholas, Kt.

Ibbotson, *Vice-Adm.* Sir Richard Jeffrey, KBE, CB, DSC

Ibbs, Sir (John) Robin, KBE

Imbert-Terry, Sir Michael Edward Stanley, Bt. (1917)

Imray, Sir Colin Henry, KBE, CMG

Ingham, Sir Bernard, Kt.

Ingilby, Sir Thomas Colvin William, Bt. (1866)

Inglis, Sir Brian Scott, Kt.

Inglis of Glencorse, Sir Roderick John, Bt. (S. 1703)

Ingram, Sir James Herbert Charles, Bt. (1893)

Ingram, Sir John Henderson, Kt., CBE

Inkin, Sir Geoffrey David, Kt., OBE

†Innes, Sir Alastair Charles Deverell, Bt. (NS 1686)

Innes of Edingight, Sir Malcolm Rognvald, KCVO

Innes, Sir Peter Alexander Berowald, Bt. (S. 1628)

Insall, Sir Donald William, Kt., CBE

Irvine, Sir Donald Hamilton, Kt., CBE, MD, FRCGP

Irving, *Prof.* Sir Miles Horsfall, Kt., MD, FRCS, FRCSE

Irwin, *Lt.-Gen.* Sir Alistair Stuart Hastings, KCB, CBE

Irwin, *Hon.* Sir Stephen John, Kt.

Isaacs, Sir Jeremy Israel, Kt.

†Isham, Sir Norman Murray Crawford, Bt., OBE (1627)

Italeli, *HE* Sir Iakoba Taeia, GCMG

Ivory, Sir Brian Gammell, Kt., CBE

Jack, *Hon.* Sir Alieu Sulayman, Kt.

Jack, Sir David, Kt., CBE, FRS, FRSE

Jack, Sir Malcolm Roy, KCB

Jack, *Hon.* Sir Raymond Evan, Kt.

Jackling, Sir Roger Tustin, KCB, CBE

Jackson, Sir Barry Trevor, Kt.

Jackson, Sir Kenneth Joseph, Kt.

Jackson, *Gen.* Sir Michael David, GCB, CBE

Jackson, Sir Michael Roland, Bt. (1902)

†Jackson, Sir Neil Keith, Bt. (1815)

Jackson, Sir Nicholas Fane St George, Bt. (1913)

Jackson, *Hon.* Sir Peter Arthur Brian, Kt.

Jackson, *Rt. Hon.* Sir Rupert Matthew, Kt.

Jackson, Sir (William) Roland Cedric, Bt. (1869)

Jacob, *Rt. Hon.* Sir Robert Raphael Hayim (Robin), Kt.

Jacobi, Sir Derek George, Kt., CBE

Jacobs, Sir Cecil Albert, Kt., CBE

Jacobs, *Rt. Hon.* Sir Francis Geoffrey, KCMG, QC

Jacobs, *Hon.* Sir Kenneth Sydney, KBE

Jacomb, Sir Martin Wakefield, Kt.

Jaffray, Sir William Otho, Bt. (1892)

Jagger, Sir Michael Philip, Kt.

James, Sir Cynlais Morgan, KCMG

James, Sir Jeffrey Russell, KBE

James, Sir John Nigel Courtenay, KCVO, CBE

Jamieson, *Air Marshal* Sir David Ewan, KBE, CB

Jardine of Applegirth, Sir William Murray, Bt. (S. 1672)

Jardine, Sir Andrew Colin Douglas, Bt. (1916)

Jarman, *Prof.* Sir Brian, Kt., OBE

Jarratt, Sir Alexander Anthony, Kt., CB

Jawara, *Hon.* Sir Dawda Kairaba, Kt.

Jay, Sir Antony Rupert, Kt., CVO

Jeewoolall, Sir Ramesh, Kt.

Jefferson, Sir George Rowland, Kt., CBE, FRENG

Jeffrey, Sir William Alexander, KCB

Jeffreys, *Prof.* Sir Alec John, Kt., FRS

Jeffries, *Hon.* Sir John Francis, Kt.

Jehangir, Sir Cowasji, Bt. (1908)

†Jejeebhoy, Sir Jehangir, Bt. (1857)

Jenkins, Sir Brian Garton, GBE
Jenkins, Sir Elgar Spencer, Kt., OBE
Jenkins, Sir James Christopher, KCB, QC
Jenkins, Sir John, KCMG, LVO
Jenkins, Sir Michael Nicholas Howard, Kt., OBE
Jenkins, Sir Michael Romilly Heald, KCMG
Jenkins, Sir Simon, Kt.
Jenkinson, Sir John Banks, Bt. (1661)
Jenks, Sir (Richard) Peter, Bt. (1932)
Jenner, *Air Marshal* Sir Timothy Ivo, KCB
Jennings, Sir John Southwood, Kt., CBE, FRSE
Jennings, Sir Peter Neville Wake, Kt., CVO
Jephcott, Sir Neil Welbourn, Bt. (1962)
Jessel, Sir Charles John, Bt. (1883)
Jewkes, Sir Gordon Wesley, KCMG
Job, Sir Peter James Denton, Kt.
John, Sir David Glyndwr, KCMG
John, Sir Elton Hercules (Reginald Kenneth Dwight), Kt., CBE
Johns, *Vice-Adm.* Sir Adrian James, KCB, CBE, ADC
Johns, *Air Chief Marshal* Sir Richard Edward, GCB, KCVO, CBE
Johnson, Sir Colpoys Guy, Bt. (1755)
Johnson, *Gen.* Sir Garry Dene, KCB, OBE, MC
Johnson, Sir John Rodney, KCMG
†Johnson, Sir Patrick Eliot, Bt. (1818)
Johnson, *Hon.* Sir Robert Lionel, Kt.
Johnson-Ferguson, Sir Ian Edward, Bt. (1906)
Johnston, *Lt.-Gen.* Sir Maurice Robert, KCB, CVO, OBE
Johnston, Sir Thomas Alexander, Bt. (S. 1626)
Johnston, Sir William Ian Ridley, Kt., CBE, QPM
Johnstone, Sir Geoffrey Adams Dinwiddie, KCMG
Johnstone, Sir (George) Richard Douglas, Bt. (S. 1700)
Johnstone, Sir (John) Raymond, Kt., CBE
Jolliffe, Sir Anthony Stuart, GBE
Jolly, Sir Arthur Richard, KCMG
Jonas, Sir John Peter, Kt., CBE
Jones, Sir Alan Jeffrey, Kt.
Jones, Sir David Charles, Kt., CBE
Jones, Sir Harry George, Kt., CBE
Jones, Sir John Francis, Kt.
Jones, Sir Keith Stephen, Kt.
Jones, Sir Kenneth Lloyd, Kt., QPM
Jones, Sir Lyndon, Kt.
Jones, Sir Mark Ellis Powell, Kt.
Jones, Sir (Owen) Trevor, Kt.
Jones, Sir Richard Anthony Lloyd, KCB
Jones, Sir Robert Edward, Kt.
Jones, Sir Roger Spencer, Kt., OBE
Jones, Sir Simon Warley Frederick Benton, Bt. (1919)
†Joseph, *Hon.* Sir James Samuel, Bt. (1943)

Jowell, *Prof.* Sir Jeffrey Lionel, KCMG, QC
Jowell, *Prof.* Sir Roger Mark, Kt. CBE
Jowitt, *Hon.* Sir Edwin Frank, Kt.
Judge, Sir Paul Rupert, Kt.
Jugnauth, *Rt. Hon.* Sir Anerood, KCMG
Jungius, *Vice-Adm.* Sir James George, KBE

Kaberry, *Hon.* Sir Christopher Donald, Bt. (1960)
Kabui, Sir Frank Utu Ofagioro, GCMG, OBE
Kadoorie, *Hon.* Sir Michael David, Kt.
Kakaraya, Sir Pato, KBE
Kamit, Sir Leonard Wilson, Kt., CBE
Kan Yuet-Keung, Sir, GBE
Kao, *Prof.* Sir Charles Kuen, KBE
Kaputin, Sir John Rumet, KBE, CMG
Kaufman, *Rt. Hon.* Sir Gerald Bernard, Kt.
Kavali, Sir Thomas, Kt., OBE
Kay, *Rt. Hon.* Sir Maurice Ralph, Kt.
Kaye, Sir Paul Henry Gordon, Bt. (1923)
†Keane, Sir John Charles, Bt. (1801)
Kearney, *Hon.* Sir William John Francis, Kt., CBE
Keegan, Sir John Desmond Patrick, Kt., OBE
Keene, *Rt. Hon.* Sir David Wolfe, Kt.
Keith, *Hon.* Sir Brian Richard, Kt.
Keith, *Prof.* Sir James, KBE
†Kellett, Sir Stanley Charles, Bt. (1801)
Kelly, Sir Christopher William, KCB
Kelly, Sir David Robert Corbett, Kt., CBE
Kemakeza, Sir Allan, Kt.
Kemball, *Air Marshal* Sir (Richard) John, KCB, CBE
Kemp-Welch, Sir John, Kt.
Kenilorea, *Rt. Hon.* Sir Peter, KBE
Kennaway, Sir John Lawrence, Bt. (1791)
Kennedy, Sir Francis, KCMG, CBE
Kennedy, *Hon.* Sir Ian Alexander, Kt.
Kennedy, *Prof.* Sir Ian McColl, Kt.
†Kennedy, Sir Michael Edward, Bt. (1836)
Kennedy, *Rt. Hon.* Sir Paul Joseph Morrow, Kt.
Kennedy, *Air Chief Marshal* Sir Thomas Lawrie, GCB, AFC
Kenny, Sir Anthony John Patrick, Kt., DPHIL, DLITT, FBA
Kenny, *Gen.* Sir Brian Leslie Graham, GCB, CBE
Kentridge, Sir Sydney Woolf, KCMG, QC
Kenyon, Sir Nicholas Roger, Kt., CBE
Keogh, *Prof.* Sir Bruce Edward, KBE
Kerr, *Adm.* Sir John Beverley, GCB
Kerr, Sir Ronald James, Kt., CB

Kerry, Sir Michael James, KCB, QC
Kershaw, *Prof.* Sir Ian, Kt.
Kerslake, Sir Robert Walker, Kt.
Keswick, Sir Henry Neville Lindley, Kt.
Keswick, Sir John Chippendale Lindley, Kt.
Kevau, *Prof.* Sir Isi Henao, Kt., CBE
Kikau, *Ratu* Sir Jone Latianara, KBE
Kimber, Sir Timothy Roy Henry, Bt. (1904)
King, *Prof.* Sir David Anthony, Kt., FRS
King, Sir John Christopher, Bt. (1888)
King, *Prof.* Sir Mervyn Allister, GBE
King, *Vice-Adm.* Sir Norman Ross Dutton, KBE
King, *Hon.* Sir Timothy Roger Alan, Kt.
King, Sir Wayne Alexander, Bt. (1815)
Kingman, *Prof.* Sir John Frank Charles, Kt., FRS
Kingsland, Sir Richard, Kt., CBE, DFC
Kingsley, Sir Ben, Kt.
Kinloch, Sir David, Bt. (S. 1686)
Kinloch, Sir David Oliphant, Bt. (1873)
Kipalan, Sir Albert, Kt.
Kirkpatrick, Sir Ivone Elliott, Bt. (S. 1685)
Kirkwood, *Hon.* Sir Andrew Tristram Hammett, Kt.
Kiszely, *Lt.-Gen.* Sir John Panton, KCB, MC
Kitchin, *Hon.* Sir David James Tyson, Kt.
Kitson, *Gen.* Sir Frank Edward, GBE, KCB, MC
Kitson, Sir Timothy Peter Geoffrey, Kt.
Kleinwort, Sir Richard Drake, Bt. (1909)
Klug, Sir Aaron, Kt., OM
Knight, Sir Harold Murray, KBE, DSC
Knight, Sir Kenneth John, Kt., CBE, QFSM
Knight, *Air Chief Marshal* Sir Michael William Patrick, KCB, AFC
Knight, *Prof.* Sir Peter, Kt.
Knill, Sir Thomas John Pugin Bartholomew, Bt. (1893)
Knowles, Sir Charles Francis, Bt. (1765)
Knowles, Sir Durward Randolph, Kt., OBE
Knowles, Sir Nigel Graham, Kt.
Knox, Sir David Laidlaw, Kt.
Knox, *Hon.* Sir John Leonard, Kt.
Knox-Johnston, Sir William Robert Patrick (Sir Robin), Kt., CBE, RD
Kohn, *Dr* Sir Ralph, Kt., FRS
Koraea, Sir Thomas, Kt.
Kornberg, *Prof.* Sir Hans Leo, Kt., DSC, SCD, PHD, FRS
Korowi, Sir Wiwa, GCMG

Kroto, *Prof.* Sir Harold Walter, Kt., FRS

Kulukundis, Sir Elias George (Eddie), Kt., OBE

Kurongku, *Most Revd* Peter, KBE

Kwok-Po Li, *Dr* Sir David, Kt., OBE

Lachmann, *Prof.* Sir Peter Julius, Kt.

Lacon, Sir Edmund Vere, Bt. (1818)

Lacy, Sir Patrick Brian Finucane, Bt. (1921)

Laing, Sir (John) Martin (Kirby), Kt., CBE

Laird, Sir Gavin Harry, Kt., CBE

Lake, Sir (Atwell) Graham, Bt. (1711)

Lakin, Sir Michael, Bt. (1909)

Lamb, Sir Albert Thomas, KBE, CMG, DFC

Lamb, *Lt.-Gen.* Sir Graeme Cameron Maxwell, KBE, CMG, DSO

Lambert, Sir John Henry, KCVO, CMG

†Lambert, Sir Peter John Biddulph, Bt. (1711)

Lambert, Sir Richard Peter, Kt.

Lampl, Sir Peter, Kt., OBE

Lamport, Sir Stephen Mark Jeffrey, KCVO

Landale, Sir David William Neil, KCVO

Landau, Sir Dennis Marcus, Kt.

Lander, Sir Stephen James, KCB

Lane, Prof. Sir David Philip, Kt.

Langham, Sir John Stephen, Bt. (1660)

Langlands, Sir Robert Alan, Kt.

Langley, *Hon.* Sir Gordon Julian Hugh, Kt.

Langrishe, Sir James Hercules, Bt. (I. 1777)

Langstaff, *Hon.* Sir Brian Frederick James, Kt.

Lankester, Sir Timothy Patrick, KCB

Lapli, Sir John Ini, GCMG

Lapthorne, Sir Richard Douglas, Kt., CBE

Large, Sir Andrew McLeod Brooks, Kt.

Latasi, *Rt. Hon.* Sir Kamuta, KCMG, OBE

Latham, *Rt. Hon.* Sir David Nicholas Ramsey, Kt.

Latham, Sir Michael Anthony, Kt.

Latham, Sir Richard Thomas Paul, Bt. (1919)

Latimer, Sir Graham Stanley, KBE

Latour-Adrien, *Hon.* Sir Maurice, Kt.

Laughton, Sir Anthony Seymour, Kt.

Laurence, *Vice-Adm.* Sir Timothy James Hamilton, KCVO, CB, ADC

Laurie, Sir Robert Bayley Emilius, Bt. (1834)

Lauterpacht, Sir Elihu, Kt., CBE, QC

Lauti, *Rt. Hon.* Sir Toaripi, GCMG

Lawler, Sir Peter James, Kt., OBE

Lawrence, Sir Clive Wyndham, Bt. (1906)

Lawrence, Sir Edmund Wickham, KCMG, OBE

Lawrence, Sir Henry Peter, Bt. (1858)

Lawrence, Sir Ivan John, Kt., QC

Lawrence, Sir John Patrick Grosvenor, Kt., CBE

Lawrence, Sir William Fettiplace, Bt. (1867)

Lawrence-Jones, Sir Christopher, Bt. (1831)

Laws, *Rt. Hon.* Sir John Grant McKenzie, Kt.

Laws, Sir Stephen Charles, KCB

Lawson, Sir Charles John Patrick, Bt. (1900)

Lawson, *Gen.* Sir Richard George, KCB, DSO, OBE

†Lawson-Tancred, Sir Andrew Peter, Bt. (1662)

Lawton, *Prof.* Sir John Hartley, Kt., CBE, FRS

Layard, *Adm.* Sir Michael Henry Gordon, KCB, CBE

Lea, *Vice-Adm.* Sir John Stuart Crosbie, KBE

Lea, Sir Thomas William, Bt. (1892)

Leahy, Sir Daniel Joseph, Kt.

Leahy, Sir John Henry Gladstone, KCMG

Leahy, Sir Terence Patrick, Kt.

Learmont, *Gen.* Sir John Hartley, KCB, CBE

Leaver, Sir Christopher, GBE

Le Cheminant, *Air Chief Marshal* Sir Peter de Lacey, GBE, KCB, DFC

†Lechmere, Sir Nicholas Anthony Hungerford, Bt. (1818)

Ledger, Sir Philip Stevens, Kt., CBE, FRSE

Lee, Sir Christopher Frank Carandini, Kt., CBE

Lee, Sir Quo-wei, Kt., CBE

†Leeds, Sir John Charles Hildyard, Bt. (1812)

Lees, Sir David Bryan, Kt.

Lees, Sir Thomas Edward, Bt. (1897)

Lees, Sir Thomas Harcourt Ivor, Bt. (1804)

Lees, Sir (William) Antony Clare, Bt. (1937)

Leese, Sir Richard Charles, Kt., CBE

le Fleming, Sir David Kelland, Bt. (1705)

Legard, Sir Charles Thomas, Bt. (1660)

Legg, Sir Thomas Stuart, KCB, QC

Leggatt, *Rt. Hon.* Sir Andrew Peter, Kt.

Leggatt, Sir Hugh Frank John, Kt.

Leggett, *Prof.* Sir Anthony James, KBE

Leigh, Sir Geoffrey Norman, Kt.

Leigh, Sir Richard Henry, Bt. (1918)

Leighton, Sir Michael John Bryan, Bt. (1693)

Leith-Buchanan, Sir Gordon Kelly McNicol, Bt. (1775)

Le Marchant, Sir Francis Arthur, Bt. (1841)

Lennox-Boyd, The Hon. Sir Mark Alexander, Kt.

Leon, Sir John Ronald, Bt. (1911)

Lepping, Sir George Geria Dennis, GCMG, MBE

Le Quesne, Sir (John) Godfray, Kt., QC

Leslie, Sir John Norman Ide, Bt. (1876)

Lester, Sir James Theodore, Kt.

Lethbridge, Sir Thomas Periam Hector Noel, Bt. (1804)

Lever, Sir Jeremy Frederick, KCMG, QC

Lever, Sir Paul, KCMG

Lever, Sir (Tresham) Christopher Arthur Lindsay, Bt. (1911)

Leveson, *Rt. Hon.* Sir Brian Henry, Kt.

Levi, Sir Wasangula Noel, Kt., CBE

Levine, Sir Montague Bernard, Kt.

Levinge, Sir Richard George Robin, Bt. (I. 1704)

Lewinton, Sir Christopher, Kt.

Lewis, Sir David Thomas Rowell, Kt.

Lewis, Sir John Anthony, Kt., OBE

Lewis, Sir Lawrence Vernon Harcourt, KCMG, GCM

Lewis, Sir Leigh Warren, KCB

Lewis, Sir Terence Murray, Kt., OBE, GM, QPM

Lewison, *Hon.* Sir Kim Martin Jordan, Kt.

Ley, Sir Ian Francis, Bt. (1905)

Li, Sir Ka-Shing, KBE

Lickiss, Sir Michael Gillam, Kt.

Liddington, Sir Bruce, Kt.

Lightman, *Hon.* Sir Gavin Anthony, Kt.

Lighton, Sir Thomas Hamilton, Bt. (I. 1791)

Likierman, *Prof.* Sir John Andrew, Kt.

Lilleyman, *Prof.* Sir John Stuart, Kt.

Limon, Sir Donald William, KCB

Linacre, Sir (John) Gordon (Seymour), Kt., CBE, AFC, DFM

Lindblom, *Hon.* Sir Keith John, Kt.

Lindop, Sir Norman, Kt.

Lindsay, *Hon.* Sir John Edmund Frederic, Kt.

†Lindsay, Sir James Martin Evelyn, Bt. (1962)

†Lindsay-Hogg, Sir Michael Edward, Bt. (1905)

Lipton, Sir Stuart Anthony, Kt.

Lipworth, Sir (Maurice) Sydney, Kt.

Lister, Sir Edward Julian, Kt.

Lister-Kaye, Sir John Phillip Lister, Bt. (1812)

Lithgow, Sir William James, Bt. (1925)

Little, *Most Revd* Thomas Francis, KBE

Llewellyn, Sir Roderic Victor, Bt. (1922)

Llewellyn-Smith, *Prof.* Sir Christopher Hubert, Kt.

Lloyd, *Prof.* Sir Geoffrey Ernest Richard, Kt., FBA
Lloyd, Sir Nicholas Markley, Kt.
Lloyd, *Rt. Hon.* Sir Peter Robert Cable, Kt.
Lloyd, Sir Richard Ernest Butler, Bt. (1960)
Lloyd, *Hon.* Sir Timothy Andrew Wigram, Kt.
Lloyd-Edwards, *Capt.* Sir Norman, KCVO, RD
Lloyd Jones, Sir David, Kt.
Loader, Air Marshal Sir Clive Robert, KCB, OBE
Lobo, Sir Rogerio Hyndman, Kt., CBE
Lockhead, Sir Moir, Kt., OBE
†Loder, Sir Edmund Jeune, Bt. (1887)
Logan, Sir David Brian Carleton, KCMG
Lokoloko, Sir Tore, GCMG, GCVO, OBE
Longmore, *Rt. Hon.* Sir Andrew Centlivres, Kt.
Lorimer, Sir (Thomas) Desmond, Kt.
Los, *Hon.* Sir Kubulan, Kt., CBE
Loughran, Sir Gerald Finbar, KCB
Lovell, Sir (Alfred Charles) Bernard, Kt., OBE, FRS
Lovelock, Sir Douglas Arthur, KCB
Lovill, Sir John Roger, Kt., CBE
Lowa, *Rt. Revd* Sir Samson, KBE
Lowe, *Air Chief Marshal* Sir Douglas Charles, GCB, DFC, AFC
Lowe, Sir Frank Budge, Kt.
Lowe, Sir Thomas William Gordon, Bt. (1918)
Lowson, Sir Ian Patrick, Bt. (1951)
Lowther, *Col.* Sir Charles Douglas, Bt. (1824)
Loyd, Sir Julian St John, KCVO
Lu, Sir Tseng Chi, Kt.
Lucas, *Prof.* Sir Colin Renshaw, Kt.
Lucas, Sir Thomas Edward, Bt. (1887)
Lucas-Tooth, Sir (Hugh) John, Bt. (1920)
Lumsden, Sir David James, Kt.
Lushington, Sir John Richard Castleman, Bt. (1791)
Lyall Grant, Sir Mark Justin, KCMG
Lygo, *Adm.* Sir Raymond Derek, KCB
Lyle, Sir Gavin Archibald, Bt. (1929)
Lynch-Blosse, *Capt.* Sir Richard Hely, Bt. (1622)
Lynch-Robinson, Sir Dominick Christopher, Bt. (1920)
Lyne, *Rt. Hon.* Sir Roderic Michael John, KBE, CMG
Lyons, Sir John, Kt.
Lyons, Sir Michael Thomas, Kt.

McAllister, Sir Ian Gerald, Kt., CBE
McAlpine, Sir William Hepburn, Bt. (1918)
Macara, Sir Alexander Wiseman, Kt., FRCP, FRCGP
McCaffrey, Sir Thomas Daniel, Kt.

McCallum, Sir Donald Murdo, Kt., CBE, FRENG
McCamley, Sir Graham Edward, KBE
McCarthy, Sir Callum, Kt.
McCartney, *Rt. Hon.* Sir Ian, Kt.
McCartney, Sir (James) Paul, Kt., MBE
Macartney, Sir John Ralph, Bt. (I. 1799)
McClement, *Vice-Admiral* Sir Timothy Pentreath, KCB, OBE
McClintock, Sir Eric Paul, Kt.
McCloskey, *Hon.* Sir John Bernard, Kt.
McColl, Sir Colin Hugh Verel, KCMG
McColl, *Gen.* Sir John Chalmers, KCB, CBE, DSO
McCollum, *Rt. Hon.* Sir William, Kt.
McCombe, *Hon.* Sir Richard George Bramwell, Kt.
McConnell, Sir Robert Shean, Bt. (1900)
MacCormac, Sir Richard Cornelius, Kt., CBE
†McCowan, Sir David William, Bt. (1934)
McCullough, *Hon.* Sir (Iain) Charles (Robert), Kt.
MacDermott, *Rt. Hon.* Sir John Clarke, Kt.
Macdonald, Sir Alasdair Uist, Kt., CBE
Macdonald, Sir Kenneth Carmichael, KCB
McDonald, Sir Trevor, Kt., OBE
Macdonald of Sleat, Sir Ian Godfrey Bosville, Bt. (S. 1625)
McDowell, Sir Eric Wallace, Kt., CBE
MacDuff, *Hon.* Sir Alistair Geoffrey, Kt.
Mace, *Lt.-Gen.* Sir John Airth, KBE, CB
McEwen, Sir John Roderick Hugh, Bt. (1953)
McFarland, Sir John Talbot, Bt. (1914)
MacFarlane, *Prof.* Sir Alistair George James, Kt., CBE, FRS
McFarlane, Sir Andrew Ewart, Kt.
Macfarlane, Sir (David) Neil, Kt.
McGeechan, Sir Ian Robert, Kt., OBE
McGrath, Sir Brian Henry, GCVO
Macgregor, Sir Ian Grant, Bt. (1828)
McGregor, Sir James David, Kt., OBE
MacGregor of MacGregor, Sir Malcolm Gregor Charles, Bt. (1795)
McGrigor, Sir James Angus Rhoderick Neil, Bt. (1831)
McIntosh, Sir Neil William David, Kt., CBE
McIntosh, Sir Ronald Robert Duncan, KCB
McIntyre, Sir Donald Conroy, Kt.
McIntyre, Sir Meredith Alister, Kt.
Mackay, *Hon.* Sir Colin Crichton, Kt.
MacKay, *Prof.* Sir Donald Iain, Kt.

MacKay, Sir Francis Henry, Kt.
McKay, Sir Neil Stuart, Kt., CB
McKay, Sir William Robert, KCB
Mackay-Dick, *Maj.-Gen.* Sir Iain Charles, KCVO, MBE
Mackechnie, Sir Alistair John, Kt.
McKellen, Sir Ian Murray, Kt., CH, CBE
Mackenzie, Sir (James William) Guy, Bt. (1890)
Mackenzie, *Gen.* Sir Jeremy John George, GCB, OBE
†Mackenzie, Sir Peter Douglas, Bt. (S. 1673)
†Mackenzie, Sir Roderick McQuhae, Bt. (S. 1703)
Mackeson, Sir Rupert Henry, Bt. (1954)
McKillop, Sir Thomas Fulton Wilson, Kt.
McKinnon, *Rt. Hon.* Sir Donald Charles, GCVO
McKinnon, Sir James, Kt.
McKinnon, *Hon.* Sir Stuart Neil, Kt.
Mackintosh, Sir Cameron Anthony, Kt.
Mackworth, Sir Digby (John), Bt. (1776)
McLaughlin, Sir Richard, Kt.
Maclean of Dunconnell, Sir Charles Edward, Bt. (1957)
Maclean, Sir Lachlan Hector Charles, Bt. (NS 1631)
Maclean, Sir Murdo, Kt.
McLeod, Sir Charles Henry, Bt. (1925)
MacLeod, Sir (John) Maxwell Norman, Bt. (1924)
Macleod, Sir (Nathaniel William) Hamish, KBE
McLintock, Sir Michael William, Bt. (1934)
Maclure, Sir John Robert Spencer, Bt. (1898)
McMahon, Sir Brian Patrick, Bt. (1817)
McMahon, Sir Christopher William, Kt.
McMaster, Sir Brian John, Kt., CBE
McMichael, *Prof.* Sir Andrew James, Kt., FRS
MacMillan, *Lt.-Gen.* Sir John Richard Alexander, KCB, CBE
McMullin, *Rt. Hon.* Sir Duncan Wallace, Kt.
McMurtry, Sir David, Kt., CBE
Macnaghten, Sir Malcolm Francis, Bt. (1836)
McNair-Wilson, Sir Patrick Michael Ernest David, Kt.
McNamara, *Air Chief Marshal* Sir Neville Patrick, KBE
Macnaughton, *Prof.* Sir Malcolm Campbell, Kt.
McNee, Sir David Blackstock, Kt., QPM
McNulty, Sir (Robert William) Roy, Kt., CBE
MacPhail, Sir Bruce Dugald, Kt.
MacPherson, Sir Nicholas, KCB
Macpherson, Sir Ronald Thomas Steward (Tommy), CBE, MC, TD

Macpherson of Cluny, *Hon.* Sir William Alan, Kt., TD

McQuarrie, Sir Albert, Kt.

MacRae, Sir (Alastair) Christopher (Donald Summerhayes), KCMG

Macready, Sir Nevil John Wilfrid, Bt. (1923)

MacSween, *Prof.* Sir Roderick Norman McIver, Kt.

Mactaggart, Sir John Auld, Bt. (1938)

McWilliam, Sir Michael Douglas, KCMG

McWilliams, Sir Francis, GBE

Madden, Sir David Christopher Andrew, KCMG

†Madden, Sir Charles Jonathan, Bt. (1919)

Maddison, *Hon.* Sir David George, Kt.

Madejski, Sir John Robert, Kt., OBE

Madel, Sir (William) David, Kt.

Magee, Sir Ian Bernard Vaughan, Kt., CB

Magnus, Sir Laurence Henry Philip, Bt. (1917)

Mahon, Sir William Walter, Bt. (1819), LVO

Maiden, Sir Colin James, Kt., DPHIL

Maini, *Prof.* Sir Ravinder Nath, Kt.

Maino, Sir Charles, KBE

†Maitland, Sir Charles Alexander, Bt. (1818)

Major, *Rt. Hon.* Sir John, KG, CH

Malbon, *Vice-Adm.* Sir Fabian Michael, KBE

Malcolm, Sir James William Thomas Alexander, Bt. (S. 1665)

Malet, Sir Harry Douglas St Lo, Bt. (1791)

Mallaby, Sir Christopher Leslie George, GCMG, GCVO

Mallick, *Prof.* Sir Netar Prakash, Kt.

Mallinson, Sir William James, Bt. (1935)

Malpas, Sir Robert, Kt., CBE

Mancham, Sir James Richard Marie, KBE

†Mander, Sir (Charles) Nicholas, Bt. (1911)

Manduell, Sir John, Kt., CBE

Mann, *Hon.* Sir George Anthony, Kt.

Mann, *Rt. Revd* Michael Ashley, KCVO

Mann, Sir Rupert Edward, Bt. (1905)

Manning, Sir David Geoffrey, GCMG, CVO

Mano, Sir Koitaga, Kt., MBE

Mansel, Sir Philip, Bt. (1622)

Mansfield, *Prof.* Sir Peter, Kt.

Manuella, Sir Tulaga, GCMG, MBE

Manzie, Sir (Andrew) Gordon, KCB

Margetson, Sir John William Denys, KCMG

Margetts, Sir Robert John, Kt., CBE

Markesinis, *Prof.* Sir Basil Spyridonos, Kt. QC

Markham, *Prof.* Sir Alexander Fred, Kt.

Markham, Sir (Arthur) David, Bt. (1911)

Marling, Sir Charles William Somerset, Bt. (1882)

Marmot, Prof. Sir Michael Gideon, Kt.

Marr, Sir Leslie Lynn, Bt. (1919)

Marriner, Sir Neville, Kt., CBE

†Marsden, Sir Simon Neville Llewelyn, Bt. (1924)

Marsh, *Prof.* Sir John Stanley, Kt., CBE

Marshall, Sir Michael John, Kt., CBE

Marshall, *Prof.* Sir (Oshley) Roy, Kt., CBE

Marshall, Sir Peter Harold Reginald, KCMG

Marshall, *Prof. Emeritus* Sir Woodville Kemble, Kt.

Martin, Sir Clive Haydon, Kt., OBE

Martin, Sir George Henry, Kt., CBE

Martin, *Prof.* Sir Laurence Woodward, Kt.

Martin, Sir (Robert) Bruce, Kt., QC

Marychurch, Sir Peter Harvey, KCMG

Masefield, Sir Charles Beech Gordon, Kt.

Mason, *Hon.* Sir Anthony Frank, KBE

Mason, Sir (Basil) John, Kt., CB, DSC, FRS

Mason, *Prof.* Sir David Kean, Kt., CBE

Mason, Sir John Peter, Kt., CBE

Mason, Sir Peter James, KBE

Mason, *Prof.* Sir Ronald, KCB, FRS

Massey, *Vice-Adm.* Sir Alan, KCB, CBE, ADC

Massie, Sir Herbert William, Kt., CBE

Matane, HE Sir Paulias Nguna, GCMG, OBE

Matheson of Matheson, Sir Fergus John, Bt. (1882)

Mathewson, Sir George Ross, Kt., CBE, PHD, FRSE

Matthews, Sir Terence Hedley, Kt., OBE

Maud, *Hon.* Sir Humphrey John Hamilton, KCMG

Maughan, Sir Deryck, Kt.

Mawer, Sir Philip John Courtney, Kt.

Maxwell, Sir Michael Eustace George, Bt. (S. 1681)

†Maxwell Macdonald (formerly Stirling-Maxwell), Sir John Ronald, Bt. (NS 1682)

Maxwell-Scott, Sir Dominic James, Bt. (1642)

May, *Rt. Hon.* Sir Anthony Tristram Kenneth, Kt.

Mayhew-Sanders, Sir John Reynolds, Kt.

Meadow, *Prof.* Sir (Samuel) Roy, Kt., FRCP, FRCPE

Meale, Sir Joseph Alan, Kt.

Medlycott, Sir Mervyn Tregonwell, Bt. (1808)

Meeran, *His Hon.* Sir Goolam Hoosen Kader, Kt.

Meldrum, Sir Graham, Kt., CBE, QFSM

Melhuish, Sir Michael Ramsay, KBE, CMG

Mellars, *Prof.* Sir Paul Anthony, Kt., FBA

Mellon, Sir James, KCMG

Melmoth, Sir Graham John, Kt.

Melville, *Prof.* Sir David, Kt., CBE

Merifield, Sir Anthony James, KCVO, CB

†Meyer, Sir (Anthony) Ashley Frank, Bt. (1910)

Meyer, Sir Christopher John Rome, KCMG

Meyjes, Sir Richard Anthony, Kt.

†Meyrick, Sir Timothy Thomas Charlton, Bt. (1880)

Miakwe, *Hon.* Sir Akepa, KBE

Michael, Sir Duncan, Kt.

Michael, *Dr* Sir Jonathan, Kt.

Michael, Sir Peter Colin, Kt., CBE

Michels, Sir David Michael Charles, Kt.

Middleton, Sir John Maxwell, Kt.

Middleton, Sir Peter Edward, GCB

Miers, Sir (Henry) David Alastair Capel, KBE, CMG

Milbank, Sir Anthony Frederick, Bt. (1882)

Milborne-Swinnerton-Pilkington, Sir Thomas Henry, Bt. (S. 1635)

Milburn, Sir Anthony Rupert, Bt. (1905)

Miles, Sir Peter Tremayne, KCVO

†Miles, Sir Philip John, Bt. (1859)

Millais, Sir Geoffrey Richard Everett, Bt. (1885)

Millar, *Prof.* Sir Fergus Graham Burtholme, Kt.

Millard, Sir Guy Elwin, KCMG, CVO

Miller, Sir Albert Joel, KCMG, MVO, MBE, QPM, CPM

Miller, Sir Donald John, Kt., FRSE, FRENG

Miller, *Air Marshal* Sir Graham Anthony, KBE

†Miller, Sir Anthony Thomas, Bt. (1705)

Miller, Sir Hilary Duppa (Hal), Kt.

Miller, Sir Jonathan Wolfe, Kt., CBE

Miller, Sir Peter North, Kt.

Miller, Sir Robin Robert William, Kt.

Miller, Sir Ronald Andrew Baird, Kt., CBE

Miller of Glenlee, Sir Stephen William Macdonald, Bt. (1788)

Mills, Sir Ian, Kt.

Mills, Sir Keith, Kt.

Mills, Sir Peter Frederick Leighton, Bt. (1921)

Milman, Sir David Patrick, Bt. (1800)

Milne, Sir John Drummond, Kt.

Milne-Watson, Sir Andrew Michael, Bt. (1937)

Milner, Sir Timothy William Lycett, Bt. (1717)

Milton-Thompson, *Surgeon Vice-Adm.* Sir Godfrey James, KBE

Mirrlees, *Prof.* Sir James Alexander, Kt., FBA

Mitchell, Sir David Bower, Kt.

Mitchell, *Rt. Hon.* Sir James FitzAllen, KCMG

Mitchell, *Very Revd* Patrick Reynolds, KCVO

Mitchell, *Hon.* Sir Stephen George, Kt.

Mitting, *Hon.* Sir John Edward, Kt.

Moate, Sir Roger Denis, Kt.

Moberly, Sir Patrick Hamilton, KCMG

Moffat, Sir Brian Scott, Kt., OBE

Moffat, *Lt.-Gen.* Sir (William) Cameron, KBE

Moir, Sir Christopher Ernest, Bt. (1916)

†Molesworth-St Aubyn, Sir William, Bt. (1689)

†Molony, Sir Thomas Desmond, Bt. (1925)

Moncada, *Prof.* Sir Salvador, Kt.

Monck, Sir Nicholas Jeremy, KCB

Money-Coutts, Sir David Burdett, KCVO

Montagu, Sir Nicholas Lionel John, KCB

Montagu-Pollock, Sir Giles Hampden, Bt. (1872)

Montague, Sir Adrian Alastair, Kt., CBE

Montague-Browne, Sir Anthony Arthur Duncan, KCMG, CBE, DFC

Montgomery, Sir (Basil Henry) David, Bt. (1801), CVO

Montgomery, Sir (William) Fergus, Kt.

Montgomery-Cuninghame, Sir John Christopher Foggo, Bt. (NS 1672)

Moody-Stuart, Sir Mark, KCMG

Moollan, Sir Abdool Hamid Adam, Kt.

†Moon, Sir Roger, Bt. (1887)

Moorcroft, Sir William, Kt.

Moore, *Most Revd* Desmond Charles, KBE

Moore, Sir Francis Thomas, Kt.

Moore, Sir John Michael, KCVO, CB, DSC

Moore, *Vice Adm.* Sir Michael Antony Claës, KBE, LVO

Moore, *Prof.* Sir Norman Winfrid, Bt. (1919)

Moore, Sir Patrick Alfred Caldwell, Kt., CBE

Moore, Sir Patrick William Eisdell, Kt., OBE

Moore, Sir Roger George, KBE

Moore, Sir William Roger Clotworthy, Bt. (1932), TD

Moore-Bick, *Rt. Hon.* Sir Martin James, Kt.

Moores, Sir Peter, Kt., CBE

Morauta, Sir Mekere, KCMG

Mordaunt, Sir Richard Nigel Charles, Bt. (1611)

Moreton, Sir John Oscar, KCMG, KCVO, MC

Morgan, *Vice-Adm.* Sir Charles Christopher, KBE

Morgan, *Rt. Hon.* Sir (Charles) Declan, Kt.

Morgan, Sir Graham, Kt.

Morgan, Sir John Albert Leigh, KCMG

Morgan, *Hon.* Sir Paul Hyacinth, Kt.

Morgan-Giles, *Rear-Adm.* Sir Morgan Charles, Kt., DSO, OBE, GM

Morison, *Hon.* Sir Thomas Richard Atkin, Kt.

Morland, *Hon.* Sir Michael, Kt.

Morland, Sir Robert Kenelm, Kt.

Morpeth, Sir Douglas Spottiswoode, Kt., TD

†Morris, Sir Allan Lindsay, Bt. (1806)

Morris, *Air Marshal* Sir Arnold Alec, KBE, CB

Morris, Sir Derek James, Kt.

Morris, Sir Keith Elliot Hedley, KBE, CMG

Morris, *Prof.* Sir Peter John, Kt.

Morris, Sir Trefor Alfred, Kt., CBE, QPM

Morris, *Very Revd* William James, KCVO

Morrison, Sir (Alexander) Fraser, Kt., CBE

Morrison, Sir Kenneth Duncan, Kt., CBE

Morrison, Sir (William) Garth, KT, CBE

Morrison-Bell, Sir William Hollin Dayrell, Bt. (1905)

Morrison-Low, Sir James Richard, Bt. (1908)

Morritt, *Rt. Hon.* Sir (Robert) Andrew, Kt., CVO

Morse, Sir Christopher Jeremy, KCMG

Moseley, Sir George Walker, KCB

Moses, *Rt. Hon.* Sir Alan George, Kt.

Moses, *Very Revd* Dr John Henry, KCVO

Moss, Sir David Joseph, KCVO, CMG

Moss, Sir Stephen Alan, Kt.

Moss, Sir Stirling Craufurd, Kt., OBE

Mostyn, *Hon.* Sir Nicholas Anthony Joseph Ghislain, Kt.

Mostyn, Sir William Basil John, Bt. (1670)

Motion, Sir Andrew, Kt.

Mott, Sir John Harmer, Bt. (1930)

Mottram, Sir Richard Clive, GCB

†Mount, Sir (William Robert) Ferdinand, Bt. (1921)

†Mountain, Sir Edward Brian Stanford, Bt. (1922)

Mountfield, Sir Robin, KCB

Mowbray, Sir John Robert, Bt. (1880)

Moylan, *Hon.* Sir Andrew John Gregory, Kt.

†Muir, Sir Richard James Kay, Bt. (1892)

Muir-Mackenzie, Sir Alexander Alwyne Henry Charles Brinton, Bt. (1805)

Mulcahy, Sir Geoffrey John, Kt.

Mummery, *Rt. Hon.* Sir John Frank, Kt.

Munby, *Rt. Hon.* Sir James Lawrence, Kt.

Munro, Sir Alan Gordon, KCMG

†Munro, Sir Ian Kenneth, Bt. (S. 1634)

Munro, Sir Alasdair Thomas Ian, Bt. (1825)

Muria, *Hon.* Sir Gilbert John Baptist, Kt.

Murray, Sir David Edward, Kt.

Murray, *Rt. Hon.* Sir Donald Bruce, Kt.

Murray, *Prof.* Sir Kenneth, Kt.

Murray, Sir Nigel Andrew Digby, Bt. (S. 1628)

Murray, Sir Patrick Ian Keith, Bt. (S. 1673)

Murray, Sir Robert Sydney, Kt., CBE

Murray, Sir Robin MacGregor, Kt.

†Murray, Sir Rowland William, Bt. (S. 1630)

Musgrave, Sir Christopher John Shane, Bt. (1782)

Musgrave, Sir Christopher Patrick Charles, Bt. (1611)

Myers, Sir Philip Alan, Kt., OBE, QPM

Myers, *Prof.* Sir Rupert Horace, KBE

Mynors, Sir Richard Baskerville, Bt. (1964)

Naipaul, Sir Vidiadhar Surajprasad, Kt.

Nairn, Sir Michael, Bt. (1904)

Nairne, *Rt. Hon.* Sir Patrick Dalmahoy, GCB, MC

Naish, Sir (Charles) David, Kt.

Nalau, Sir Jerry Kasip, KBE

Nall, Sir Edward William Joseph Bt. (1954)

Namaliu, *Rt. Hon.* Sir Rabbie Langanai, KCMG

†Napier, Sir Charles Joseph, Bt. (1867)

Napier, Sir John Archibald Lennox, Bt. (S. 1627)

Naylor, Sir Robert, Kt.

Naylor-Leyland, Sir Philip Vyvyan, Bt. (1895)

Neal, Sir Eric James, Kt., CVO

Neale, Sir Gerrard Anthony, Kt.

Neave, Sir Paul Arundell, Bt. (1795)

Neill, *Rt. Hon.* Sir Brian Thomas, Kt.

Neill, Sir (James) Hugh, KCVO, CBE, TD

†Nelson, Sir Jamie Charles Vernon Hope, Bt. (1912)

Nelson, *Hon.* Sir Robert Franklyn, Kt.

Neubert, Sir Michael John, Kt.

New, *Maj.-Gen.* Sir Laurence Anthony Wallis, Kt., CB, CBE

Newall, Sir Paul Henry, Kt., TD

Newbigging, Sir David Kennedy, Kt., OBE

Newby, *Prof.* Sir Howard Joseph, Kt., CBE

Newey, *Hon.* Sir Guy Richard, Kt.

Newington, Sir Michael John, KCMG

Newman, Sir Francis Hugh Cecil, Bt. (1912)

Newman, Sir Geoffrey Robert, Bt. (1836)

Newman, *Hon.* Sir George Michael, Kt.

Newman, Sir Kenneth Leslie, GBE, QPM

Newman, *Vice-Adm.* Sir Roy Thomas, KCB

Newman Taylor, *Prof.* Sir Anthony John, Kt., CBE

Newsam, Sir Peter Anthony, Kt.

†Newson-Smith, Sir Peter Frank Graham, Bt. (1944)

Newton, Sir (Charles) Wilfred, Kt., CBE

†Newton, *Revd* George Peter Howgill, Bt. (1900)

Newton, Sir John Garnar, Bt. (1924)

Ngata, Sir Henare Kohere, KBE

Nice, Sir Geoffrey, Kt., QC

Nicol, *Hon.* Sir Andrew George Lindsay, Kt.

Nichol, Sir Duncan Kirkbride, Kt., CBE

Nicholas, Sir David, Kt., CBE

Nicholas, Sir John William, KCVO, CMG

Nicholls, Sir Nigel Hamilton, KCVO, CBE

Nichols, Sir Richard Everard, Kt.

Nicholson, Sir Bryan Hubert, GBE, Kt.

†Nicholson, Sir Charles Christian, Bt. (1912)

Nicholson, Sir David, KCB, CBE

Nicholson, *Rt. Hon.* Sir Michael, Kt.

Nicholson, Sir Paul Douglas, KCVO

Nicholson, Sir Robin Buchanan, Kt., PHD, FRS, FRENG

Nicoll, Sir William, KCMG

Nightingale, Sir Charles Manners Gamaliel, Bt. (1628)

Nixon, Sir Simon Michael Christopher, Bt. (1906)

Noble, Sir David Brunel, Bt. (1902)

†Noble, Sir Timothy Peter, Bt., OBE (1923)

Nombri, Sir Joseph Karl, Kt., ISO, BEM

Norman, Sir Arthur Gordon, KBE, DFC

Norman, Sir Mark Annesley, Bt. (1915)

Norman, Sir Ronald, Kt., OBE

Norman, Sir Torquil Patrick Alexander, Kt., CBE

Normington, Sir David John, GCB

Norrington, Sir Roger Arthur Carver, Kt., CBE

Norris, *Hon.* Sir Alastair Hubert, Kt.

Norriss, Air Marshal Sir Peter Coulson, KBE, CB, AFC

North, Sir Peter Machin, Kt., CBE, QC, DCL, FBA

North, Sir Thomas Lindsay, Kt.

North, Sir (William) Jonathan (Frederick), Bt. (1920)

Norton-Griffiths, Sir John, Bt. (1922)

Nossal, Sir Gustav Joseph Victor, Kt., CBE

Nott, *Rt. Hon.* Sir John William Frederic, KCB

Nourse, *Rt. Hon.* Sir Martin Charles, Kt.

†Nugent, Sir Christopher George Ridley, Bt. (1806)

†Nugent, Sir Nicholas Myles John, Bt. (I. 1795)

†Nugent, Sir (Walter) Richard Middleton, Bt. (1831)

Nunn, Sir Trevor Robert, Kt., CBE

Nunneley, Sir Charles Kenneth Roylance, Kt.

Nursaw, Sir James, KCB, QC

Nurse, Sir Paul Maxime, Kt.

†Nuttall, Sir Harry, Bt. (1922)

Nutting, Sir John Grenfell, Bt. (1903), QC

Oakeley, Sir John Digby Atholl, Bt. (1790)

Oakes, Sir Christopher, Bt. (1939)

†Oakshott, Hon. Sir Michael Arthur John, Bt. (1959)

Oates, Sir Thomas, Kt., CMG, OBE

O'Brien, Sir Frederick William Fitzgerald, Kt.

O'Brien, Sir Timothy John, Bt. (1849)

O'Brien, Sir William, Kt.

O'Brien, *Adm.* Sir William Donough, KCB, DSC

O'Connell, Sir Bernard, Kt.

O'Connell, Sir Maurice James Donagh MacCarthy, Bt. (1869)

O'Connor, Sir Denis Francis, Kt., CBE, QPM

Odell, Sir Stanley John, Kt.

Odgers, Sir Graeme David William, Kt.

O'Donnell, Sir Augustine Thomas, GCB

O'Donnell, Sir Christopher John, Kt.

O'Donoghue, *Lt.-Gen.* Sir Kevin, KCB, CBE

O'Dowd, Sir David Joseph, Kt., CBE, QPM

Ogden, *Dr* Sir Peter James, Kt.

Ogden, Sir Robert, Kt., CBE

Ogilvy, Sir Francis Gilbert Arthur, Bt. (S. 1626)

Ogilvy-Wedderburn, Sir Andrew John Alexander, Bt. (1803)

Ogio, *HE* Sir Michael, GCMG, CBE

Ognall, *Hon.* Sir Harry Henry, Kt.

Ohlson, Sir Brian Eric Christopher, Bt. (1920)

Oldham, *Dr* Sir John, Kt., OBE

Oliver, Sir James Michael Yorrick, Kt.

Oliver, Sir Stephen John Lindsay, Kt., QC

O'Loghlen, Sir Colman Michael, Bt. (1838)

Omand, Sir David Bruce, GCB

O'Nions, Prof. Sir Robert Keith, Kt., FRS, PHD

Ondaatje, Sir Christopher, Kt., CBE

†Onslow, Sir Richard Paul Atherton, Bt. (1797)

Oppenheimer, Sir Michael Bernard Grenville, Bt. (1921)

Oppenshaw, Sir Charles Peter Lawford, Kt., QC

Orde, Sir Hugh Stephen Roden, Kt., OBE, QPM

O'Regan, *Dr* Sir Stephen Gerard (Tipene), Kt.

O'Reilly, Sir Anthony John Francis, Kt.

O'Reilly, *Prof.* Sir John James, Kt.

Orr, Sir John, Kt., OBE

Orr-Ewing, Sir (Alistair) Simon, Bt. (1963)

Orr-Ewing, Sir Archibald Donald, Bt. (1886)

Osborn, Sir John Holbrook, Kt.

Osborn, Sir Richard Henry Danvers, Bt. (1662)

Osborne, Sir Peter George, Bt. (I. 1629)

O'Shea, *Prof.* Sir Timothy Michael Martin, Kt.

Osmotherly, Sir Edward Benjamin Crofton, Kt., CB

O'Sullevan, Sir Peter John, Kt., CBE

Oswald, Sir (William Richard) Michael, KCVO

Otton, Sir Geoffrey John, KCB

Otton, *Rt. Hon.* Sir Philip Howard, Kt.

Oulton, Sir Antony Derek Maxwell, GCB, QC

Ouseley, *Hon.* Sir Brian Walter, Kt.

Outram, Sir Alan James, Bt. (1858)

Owen, Sir Geoffrey, Kt.

Owen, *Hon.* Sir Robert Michael, Kt.

Owen-Jones, Sir Lindsay Harwood, KBE

Packer, Sir Richard John, KCB

Paget, Sir Julian Tolver, Bt. (1871), CVO

Paget, Sir Richard Herbert, Bt. (1886)

Paine, Sir Christopher Hammon, Kt., FRCP, FRCR

Pakenham, *Hon.* Sir Michael Aiden, KBE, CMG

Palin, *Air Chief Marshal* Sir Roger Hewlett, KCB, OBE

Palliser, *Rt. Hon.* Sir (Arthur) Michael, GCMG

Palmer, Sir Albert Rocky, Kt.

Palmer, Sir (Charles) Mark, Bt. (1886)

Palmer, Sir Geoffrey Christopher John, Bt. (1660)

Palmer, *Rt. Hon.* Sir Geoffrey Winston Russell, KCMG

Palmer, Sir John Edward Somerset, Bt. (1791)
Palmer, *Maj.-Gen.* Sir (Joseph) Michael, KCVO
Palmer, Sir Reginald Oswald, GCMG, MBE
Parbo, Sir Arvi Hillar, Kt.
Park, *Hon.* Sir Andrew Edward Wilson, Kt.
Parker, Sir Alan William, Kt., CBE
Parker, Sir Eric Wilson, Kt.
Parker, *Rt. Hon.* Sir Jonathan Frederic, Kt.
Parker, *Hon.* Sir Kenneth Blades, Kt.
Parker, *Maj.* Sir Michael John, KCVO, CBE
Parker, *Lt.-Gen.* Sir Nicholas Ralph, KCB, CBE
Parker, Sir Richard (William) Hyde, Bt. (1681)
Parker, Sir (Thomas) John, Kt.
Parker, Sir William Peter Brian, Bt. (1844)
Parkes, Sir Edward Walter, Kt., FRENG
Parkinson, Sir Michael, Kt., CBE
Parry, *Prof.* Sir Eldryd Hugh Owen, KCMG, OBE
Parry, Sir Emyr Jones, GCMG
Parry-Evans, *Air Chief Marshal* Sir David, GCB, CBE
Parsons, Sir John Christopher, KCVO
Parsons, Sir Richard Edmund (Clement Fownes), KCMG
Partridge, Sir Michael John Anthony, KCB
Partridge, Sir Nicholas Wyndham, Kt., OBE
Pascoe, *Gen.* Sir Robert Alan, KCB, MBE
Pasley, Sir Robert Killigrew Sabine, Bt. (1794)
†Paston-Bedingfeld, Sir Henry Edgar, Bt. (1661)
Paterson, Sir Dennis Craig, Kt.
Patey, Sir William Charters, KCMG
Patnick, Sir (Cyril) Irvine, Kt., OBE
Patten, *Rt. Hon.* Sir Nicholas John, Kt.
Pattie, *Rt. Hon.* Sir Geoffrey Edwin, Kt.
Pattison, *Prof.* Sir John Ridley, Kt., DM, FRCPATH
Pattullo, Sir (David) Bruce, Kt., CBE
Pauncefort-Duncombe, Sir Philip Digby, Bt. (1859)
Peace, Sir John Wilfrid, Kt.
Peach, Sir Leonard Harry, Kt.
Peach, *Air Marshal* Sir Stuart William, KCB, CBE
Peacock, *Prof.* Sir Alan Turner, Kt., DSC
Pearce, Sir (Daniel Norton) Idris, Kt., CBE, TD
Pearse, Sir Brian Gerald, Kt.
Pearson, Sir Francis Nicholas Fraser, Bt. (1964)
Pearson, Sir Keith, Kt.
Pearson, *Gen.* Sir Thomas Cecil Hook, KCB, CBE, DSO

Peart, *Prof.* Sir William Stanley, Kt., MD, FRS
Pease, Sir Joseph Gurney, Bt. (1882)
Pease, Sir Richard Thorn, Bt. (1920)
Peat, Sir Gerrard Charles, KCVO
Peat, Sir Michael Charles Gerrard, KCVO
Peckham, *Prof.* Sir Michael John, Kt.,
Peek, Sir Richard Grenville, Bt. (1874)
Peirse, *Air Vice-Marshal* Sir Richard Charles Fairfax, KCVO, CB
Pelgen, Sir Harry Friedrich, Kt., MBE
Pelham, *Dr* Sir Hugh Reginald Brentnall, Kt., FRS
Peliza, Sir Robert John, KBE, ED
Pelly, Sir Richard John, Bt. (1840)
Pemberton, Sir Francis Wingate William, Kt., CBE
Pendry, *Prof.* Sir John Brian, Kt., FRS
Penrose, *Prof.* Sir Roger, Kt., OM, FRS
Penry-Davey, *Hon.* Sir David Herbert, Kt.
Pepper, *Dr.* Sir David Edwin, KCMG
Pepper, *Prof.* Sir Michael, Kt.
Perowne, *Vice-Adm.* Sir James Francis, KBE
Perring, Sir John Raymond, Bt. (1963)
Perris, Sir David (Arthur), Kt., MBE
Perry, Sir David Howard, KCB
Perry, Sir Michael Sydney, GBE
Pervez, Sir Mohammed Anwar, Kt., OBE
Peters, *Prof.* Sir David Keith, Kt., FRCP
Peterson, Sir Christopher Matthew, Kt., CBE, TD
†Petit, Sir Jehangir, Bt. (1890)
†Peto, Sir Francis Michael Morton, Bt. (1855)
Peto, Sir Henry Christopher Morton Bampfylde, Bt. (1927)
Peto, *Prof.* Sir Richard, Kt., FRS
Petrie, Sir Peter Charles, Bt. (1918), CMG
Pettigrew, Sir Russell Hilton, Kt.
†Philipson-Stow, Sir (Robert) Matthew, Bt. (1907)
Phillips, Sir (Gerald) Hayden, GCB
Phillips, Sir John David, Kt., QPM
Phillips, Sir Jonathan, KCB
Phillips, Sir Peter John, Kt., OBE
Phillips, Sir Robin Francis, Bt. (1912)
Phillips, Sir Tom Richard Vaughan, KCMG
Pickard, Sir (John) Michael, Kt.
Pickthorn, Sir James Francis Mann, Bt. (1959)
Pidgeon, Sir John Allan Stewart, Kt.
†Piers, Sir James Desmond, Bt. (I. 1661)
Piggott-Brown, Sir William Brian, Bt. (1903)
Pigot, Sir George Hugh, Bt. (1764)
Pigott, *Lt.-Gen.* Sir Anthony David, KCB, CBE
Pigott, Sir Berkeley Henry Sebastian, Bt. (1808)
Pike, *Lt.-Gen.* Sir Hew William Royston, KCB, DSO, MBE

Pike, Sir Michael Edmund, KCVO, CMG
Pike, Sir Philip Ernest Housden, Kt., QC
Pilditch, Sir Richard Edward, Bt. (1929)
†Pile, Sir Anthony John Devereux, Bt. (1900), MC
Pill, *Rt. Hon.* Sir Malcolm Thomas, Kt.
Pilling, Sir Joseph Grant, KCB
Pinsent, Sir Christopher Roy, Bt. (1938)
Pinsent, Sir Matthew Clive, Kt., CBE
Pitakaka, Sir Moses Puibangara, GCMG
Pitcher, Sir Desmond Henry, Kt.
Pitchers, *Hon.* Sir Christopher (John), Kt.
Pitchford, *Rt. Hon.* Sir Christopher John, Kt.
Pitoi, Sir Sere, Kt., CBE
Pitt, Sir Michael Edward, Kt.
Plastow, Sir David Arnold Stuart, Kt.
Platt, Sir Martin Philip, Bt. (1959)
Pledger, *Air Chief Marshal* Sir Malcolm David, KCB, OBE, AFC
Plender, *Hon.* Sir Richard Owen, Kt.
Plumbly, Sir Derek John, KCMG
Pogo, *Most Revd* Ellison Leslie, KBE
Pohai, Sir Timothy, Kt., MBE
†Pole, Sir John Chandos, Bt. (1791)
Pole, Sir (John) Richard (Walter Reginald) Carew, Bt. (1628)
Polkinghorne, *Revd Canon* John Charlton, KBE, FRS
Pollard, Sir Charles, Kt.
†Pollen, Sir Richard John Hungerford, Bt. (1795)
Pollock, Sir George Frederick, Bt. (1866)
Ponder, *Prof.* Sir Bruce Anthony John, Kt.
†Ponsonby, Sir Charles Ashley, Bt. (1956)
Poore, Sir Roger Ricardo, Bt. (1795)
Pope, Sir Joseph Albert, Kt., DSC, PHD
Popplewell, *Hon.* Sir Oliver Bury, Kt.
†Porritt, Sir Jonathon Espie, Bt. (1963)
Portal, Sir Jonathan Francis, Bt. (1901)
Porter, *Prof.* Sir Keith Macdonald Porter, Kt.
Porter, *Rt. Hon.* Sir Robert Wilson, Kt., PC (NI)
Potter, *Rt. Hon.* Sir Mark Howard, Kt.
Potts, *Hon.* Sir Francis Humphrey, Kt.
Pound, Sir John David, Bt. (1905)
Povey, Sir Keith, Kt., QPM
Powell, Sir John Christopher, Kt.
Powell, Sir Nicholas Folliott Douglas, Bt. (1897)
Power, Sir Alastair John Cecil, Bt. (1924)
Pownall, Sir Michael Graham, KCB

Prance, *Prof.* Sir Ghillean Tolmie, Kt., FRS

Pratchett, Sir Terence David John, Kt., OBE

Prendergast, Sir (Walter) Kieran, KCVO, CMG

Prescott, Sir Mark, Bt. (1938)

†Preston, Sir Philip Charles Henry Hulton, Bt. (1815)

Prevost, Sir Christopher Gerald, Bt. (1805)

Price, Sir David Ernest Campbell, Kt.

Price, Sir Francis Caradoc Rose, Bt. (1815)

Price, Sir Frank Leslie, Kt.

Prideaux, Sir Humphrey Povah Treverbian, Kt., OBE

Priestly, Sir Julian Gordon, KCMG

†Primrose, Sir John Ure, Bt. (1903)

Pringle, *Air Marshal* Sir Charles Norman Seton, KBE, FRENG

Pringle, *Hon.* Sir John Kenneth, Kt.

Pringle, *Lt.-Gen.* Sir Steuart (Robert), Bt. (S. 1683), KCB

†Prichard-Jones, Sir David John Walter, Bt. (1910)

Proby, Sir William Henry, Bt. (1952)

Proctor-Beauchamp, Sir Christopher Radstock, Bt. (1745)

Prosser, Sir David John, Kt.

Prosser, Sir Ian Maurice Gray, Kt.

Pryke, Sir Christopher Dudley, Bt. (1926)

Puapua, *Rt. Hon.* Sir Tomasi, GCMG, KBE

Purves, Sir William, Kt., CBE, DSO

Purvis, *Vice-Adm.* Sir Neville, KCB

Quan, Sir Henry (Francis), KBE

Quigley, Sir (William) George (Henry), Kt., CB, PHD

Quilter, Sir Anthony Raymond Leopold Cuthbert, Bt. (1897)

Quinton, Sir James Grand, Kt.

Radcliffe, Sir Sebastian Everard, Bt. (1813)

Radda, *Prof.* Sir George Karoly, Kt., CBE, FRS

Rae, Sir William, Kt., QPM

Raeburn, Sir Michael Edward Norman, Bt. (1923)

Raikes, *Vice-Adm.* Sir Iwan Geoffrey, KCB, CBE, DSC

Raison, *Rt. Hon.* Sir Timothy Hugh Francis, Kt.

Rake, Sir Michael Derek Vaughan, Kt.

†Ralli, Sir David Charles, Bt. (1912)

Ramdanee, Sir Mookteswar Baboolall Kailash, Kt.

Ramphal, Sir Shridath Surendranath, GCMG

Ramphul, Sir Baalkhristna, Kt.

Ramphul, Sir Indurduth, Kt.

Ramsay, Sir Alexander William Burnett, Bt. (1806)

Ramsay, Sir Allan John (Hepple), KBE, CMG

Ramsay-Fairfax-Lucy, Sir Edmund John William Hugh, Bt. (1836)

Ramsden, Sir John Charles Josslyn, Bt. (1689)

Ramsey, *Dr* Sir Frank Cuthbert, KCMG

Ramsey, *Hon.* Sir Vivian Arthur, Kt.

Rankin, Sir Ian Niall, Bt. (1898)

Rasch, Sir Simon Anthony Carne, Bt. (1903)

Rashleigh, Sir Richard Harry, Bt. (1831)

Ratford, Sir David John Edward, KCMG, CVO

Rattee, *Hon.* Sir Donald Keith, Kt.

Rattle, Sir Simon Dennis, Kt., CBE

Rawlins, *Prof.* Sir Michael David, Kt., FRCP, FRCPED

Rawlinson, Sir Anthony Henry John, Bt. (1891)

Rea, *Prof.* Sir Desmond, Kt., OBE

Read, *Air Marshal* Sir Charles Frederick, KBE, CB, DFC, AFC

Read, *Prof.* Sir David John, Kt.

Read, Sir John Emms, Kt.

†Reade, Sir Kenneth Ray, Bt. (1661)

Reardon-Smith, Sir (William) Antony (John), Bt. (1920)

Reay, *Lt.-Gen.* Sir (Hubert) Alan John, KBE

Redgrave, Sir Steven Geoffrey, Kt., CBE

Redmayne, Sir Giles Martin, Bt. (1964)

Redmond, Sir Anthony Gerard, Kt.

Redwood, Sir Peter Boverton, Bt. (1911)

Reed, *Prof.* Sir Alec Edward, Kt., CBE

Reedie, Sir Craig Collins, Kt., CBE

Rees, Sir David Allan, Kt., PHD, DSC, FRS

Rees, Sir Richard Ellis Meuric, Kt., CBE

Reeve, Sir Anthony, KCMG, KCVO

Reffell, *Adm.* Sir Derek Roy, KCB

Reich, Sir Erich Arieh, Kt.

Reid, Sir Alexander James, Bt. (1897)

Reid, Sir Hugh, Bt. (1922)

Reid, Sir (Philip) Alan, KCVO

Reid, Sir Robert Paul, Kt.

Reid, Sir William Kennedy, KCB

Reiher, Sir Frederick Bernard Carl, KCMG, KBE

Reilly, *Lt.-Gen.* Sir Jeremy Calcott, KCB, DSO

Renals, Sir Stanley, Bt. (1895)

Renouf, Sir Clement William Bailey, Kt.

Renshaw, Sir John David Bine, Bt. (1903)

Renwick, Sir Richard Eustace, Bt. (1921)

Reporter, Sir Shapoor Ardeshirji, KBE

Reynolds, Sir David James, Bt. (1923)

Reynolds, Sir Peter William John, Kt., CBE

Rhodes, Sir John Christopher Douglas, Bt. (1919)

Rice, *Prof.* Sir Charles Duncan, Kt.

Rice, *Maj.-Gen.* Sir Desmond Hind Garrett, KCVO, CBE

Rice, Sir Timothy Miles Bindon, Kt.

Richard, Sir Cliff, Kt., OBE

Richards, Sir Brian Mansel, Kt., CBE, PHD

Richards, *Hon.* Sir David Anthony Stewart, Kt.

Richards, Sir David Gerald, Kt.

Richards, *Gen.* Sir David, Julian, GCB, CBE, DSO

Richards, Sir Francis Neville, KCMG, CVO

Richards, *Prof.* Sir Michael Adrian, Kt., CBE

Richards, Sir Rex Edward, Kt., DSC, FRS

Richards, *Rt. Hon.* Sir Stephen Price, Kt.

Richardson, Sir Anthony Lewis, Bt. (1924)

Richardson, *Rt. Hon.* Sir Ivor Lloyd Morgan, Kt.

Richardson, *Lt.-Gen.* Sir Robert Francis, KCB, CVO, CBE

Richardson, Sir Thomas Legh, KCMG

Richardson-Bunbury, Sir (Richard David) Michael, Bt. (I. 1787)

Richmond, Sir David Frank, KBE, CMG

Richmond, *Prof.* Sir Mark Henry, Kt., FRS

Ricketts, Sir Peter Forbes, GCMG

Ricketts, Sir Stephen Tristram, Bt. (1828)

Ricks, *Prof.* Sir Christopher Bruce, Kt.

†Riddell, Sir Walter John, Bt. (S. 1628)

Ridgway, *Lt.-Gen.* Sir Andrew Peter, KBE, CB

Ridley, Sir Adam (Nicholas), Kt.

Ridley, Sir Michael Kershaw, KCVO

Rifkind, *Rt. Hon.* Sir Malcolm Leslie, KCMG

Rigby, Sir Anthony John, Bt. (1929)

Rigby, Sir Peter, Kt.

Rimer, *Hon.* Sir Colin Percy Farquharson, Kt.

Ripley, Sir William Hugh, Bt. (1880)

Risk, Sir Thomas Neilson, Kt.

Ritako, Sir Thomas Baha, Kt., MBE

Ritblat, Sir John Henry, Kt.

Ritchie, *Prof.* Sir Lewis Duthie, Kt., OBE

†Rivett-Carnac, Sir Jonathan James, Bt. (1836)

Rix, *Rt. Hon.* Sir Bernard Anthony, Kt.

Robb, Sir John Weddell, Kt.

Roberts, *Hon.* Sir Denys Tudor Emil, KBE,

Roberts, Sir Derek Harry, Kt., CBE, FRS, FRENG

Roberts, *Prof.* Sir Edward Adam, KCMG

Roberts, Sir Gilbert Howland Rookehurst, Bt. (1809)

Roberts, Sir Hugh Ashley, GCVO
Roberts, Sir Ivor Anthony, KCMG
Roberts, *Dr* Sir Richard John, Kt.
Roberts, *Maj.-Gen.* Sir Sebastian John
  Lechmere, KCVO, OBE
Roberts, Sir Samuel, Bt. (1919)
Roberts, Sir William James Denby,
  Bt. (1909)
Robertson, Sir Simon Manwaring,
  Kt.
Robins, Sir Ralph Harry, Kt., FRENG
Robinson, Sir Bruce, KCB
†Robinson, Sir Christopher Philipse,
  Bt. (1854)
Robinson, Sir Gerrard Jude, Kt.
Robinson, Sir Ian, Kt.
Robinson, Sir John James Michael
  Laud, Bt. (1660)
Robinson, *Dr* Sir Kenneth, Kt.
Robinson, Sir Wilfred Henry
  Frederick, Bt. (1908)
Robson, Sir John Adam, KCMG
Robson, Sir Stephen Arthur, Kt.,
  CB
Roch, *Rt. Hon.* Sir John Ormond,
  Kt.
Roche, Sir David O'Grady, Bt.
  (1838)
Roche, Sir Henry John, Kt.
Rodgers, Sir (Andrew) Piers (Wingate
  Aikin-Sneath), Bt. (1964)
Rodley, *Prof.* Sir Nigel, KBE
Rogers, *Air Chief Marshal* Sir John
  Robson, KCB, CBE
Rogers, Sir Peter, Kt.
Rollo, *Lt.-Gen.* Sir William Raoul,
  KCB, CBE
Ropner, Sir John Bruce Woollacott,
  Bt. (1952)
Ropner, Sir Robert Clinton, Bt.
  (1904)
Rose, Sir Arthur James, Kt., CBE
Rose, *Rt. Hon.* Sir Christopher
  Dudley Roger, Kt.
Rose, Sir Clive Martin, GCMG
Rose, Sir David Lancaster, Bt. (1874)
Rose, *Gen.* Sir (Hugh) Michael, KCB,
  CBE, DSO, QGM
Rose, Sir John Edward Victor, Kt.
Rose, Sir Julian Day, Bt. (1872 and
  1909)
Rose, Sir Stuart Alan Ransom, Kt.
Rosenthal, Sir Norman Leon, Kt.
Ross, *Maj.* Sir Andrew Charles
  Paterson, Bt. (1960)
Ross, *Lt.-Gen.* Sir Robert Jeremy,
  KCB, OBE
Ross, *Lt.-Col.* Sir Walter Hugh
  Malcolm, GCVO, OBE
Rossi, Sir Hugh Alexis Louis, Kt.
Roth, *Hon.* Sir Peter Marcel, Kt.
Rothschild, Sir Evelyn Robert Adrian
  de, Kt.
Rove, *Revd* Ikan, KBE
Rowe, *Rear-Adm.* Sir Patrick Barton,
  KCVO, CBE
Rowe-Ham, Sir David Kenneth, GBE
Rowland, Sir (John) David, Kt.
Rowland, Sir Geoffrey Robert, Kt.
Rowlands, Sir David, KCB
Rowley, Sir Richard Charles, Bt.
  (1836)

Rowling, Sir John Reginald, Kt.
Rowlinson, *Prof.* Sir John Shipley,
  Kt., FRS
Royce, *Hon.* Sir Roger John, Kt.
Royden, Sir Christopher John, Bt.
  (1905)
Rubin *Prof.* Sir Peter Charles, Kt.
Rudd, Sir (Anthony) Nigel (Russell),
  Kt.
Rudge, Sir Alan Walter, Kt., CBE,
  FRS
Rugge-Price, Sir James Keith Peter,
  Bt. (1804)
Ruggles-Brise, Sir Timothy Edward,
  Bt. (1935)
Rumbold, Sir Henry John Sebastian,
  Bt. (1779)
Runchorelal, Sir (Udayan) Chinubhai
  Madhowlal, Bt. (1913)
Rusby, *Vice-Adm.* Sir Cameron, KCB,
  LVO
Rushdie, Sir (Ahmed) Salman, Kt.
†Russell, Sir (Arthur) Mervyn, Bt.
  (1812)
Russell, Sir Charles Dominic, Bt.
  (1916)
Russell, Sir George, Kt., CBE
Russell, Sir Muir, KCB
Rutter, *Prof.* Sir Michael Llewellyn,
  Kt., CBE, MD, FRS
Ryan, Sir Derek Gerald, Bt. (1919)
Rycroft, Sir Richard John, Bt. (1784)
Ryder, *Hon.* Sir Ernest Nigel Ryder,
  Kt., TD
Ryrie, Sir William Sinclair, KCB

Sacranie, Sir Iqbal Abdul Karim
  Mussa, Kt., OBE
Sainsbury, *Rt. Hon.* Sir Timothy Alan
  Davan, Kt.
†St Clair-Ford, Sir Colin Anson, Bt.
  (1793)
St George, Sir John Avenel Bligh, Bt.
  (I. 1766)
St John-Mildmay, Sir Walter John
  Hugh, Bt. (1772)
St Omer, *Hon. Dr* Sir Dunstan
  Gerbert Raphael, KCMG
Sainty, Sir John Christopher, KCB
Sales, *Hon.* Sir Philip James, Kt.
Salisbury, Sir Robert William, Kt.
Salt, Sir Patrick MacDonnell, Bt.
  (1869)
Salt, Sir (Thomas) Michael John, Bt.
  (1899)
†Salusbury-Trelawny, Sir John
  William Richard, Bt. (1628)
Sampson, Sir Colin, Kt., CBE,
  QPM
Samuel, Sir John Michael Glen, Bt.
  (1898)
Samuelson, Sir James Francis, Bt.
  (1884)
Samuelson, Sir Sydney Wylie, Kt.,
  CBE
Samworth, Sir David Chetwode, Kt.,
  CBE
Sanders, Sir Robert Tait, KBE, CMG
Sanders, Sir Ronald Michael, KCMG
Sanderson, Sir Frank Linton, Bt.
  (1920)
Sands, Sir Roger Blakemore, KCB

Sarei, Sir Alexis Holyweek, Kt.,
  CBE
Sargent, Sir William Desmond, Kt.,
  CBE
Satchwell, Sir Kevin Joseph, Kt.
Saunders, *Hon.* Sir John Henry
  Boulton, Kt.
Savile, Sir James Wilson Vincent, Kt.,
  OBE
Savill, *Prof.* Sir John Stewart, Kt.
Savory, Sir Michael Berry, Kt.
Sawers, Sir Robert John, KCMG
Saxby, *Prof.* Sir Robin Keith, Kt.
Scarlett, Sir John McLeod, KCMG,
  OBE
Scheele, Sir Nicholas Vernon, KCMG
Schiemann, *Rt. Hon.* Sir Konrad
  Hermann Theodor, Kt.
Scholar, Sir Michael Charles, KCB
Scholey, Sir David Gerald, Kt., CBE
Scholey, Sir Robert, Kt., CBE,
  FRENG
Schreier, Sir Bernard, Kt.
Schubert, Sir Sydney, Kt.
Scipio, Sir Hudson Rupert, Kt.
Scoon, Sir Paul, GCMG, GCVO,
  OBE
Scott, Sir Anthony Percy, Bt. (1913)
Scott, *Prof.* Sir George Peter, Kt.
Scott, Sir James Jervoise, Bt. (1962)
Scott, Sir John Hamilton, KCVO
Scott, Sir Kenneth Bertram Adam,
  KCVO, CMG
Scott, Sir Oliver Christopher
  Anderson, Bt. (1909)
Scott, *Prof.* Sir Philip John, KBE
Scott, Sir Ridley, Kt.
Scott, Sir Robert David Hillyer, Kt.
Scott, Sir Walter John, Bt. (1907)
Scott-Lee, Sir Paul Joseph, Kt., QPM
Seale, Sir Clarence David, Kt.
Seale, Sir John Henry, Bt. (1838)
Seaman, Sir Keith Douglas, KCVO,
  OBE
Sebastian, Sir Cuthbert Montraville,
  GCMG, OBE
†Sebright, Sir Rufus Hugo Giles, Bt.
  (1626)
Seccombe, Sir (William) Vernon
  Stephen, Kt.
Seconde, Sir Reginald Louis, KCMG,
  CVO
Sedley, *Rt. Hon.* Sir Stephen John,
  Kt.
Seely, Sir Nigel Edward, Bt. (1896)
Seeto, Sir Ling James, Kt., MBE
Seeyave, Sir Rene Sow Choung, Kt.,
  CBE
Seligman, Sir Peter Wendel, Kt., CBE
Semple, Sir John Laughlin, KCB
Sergeant, Sir Patrick, Kt.
Serota, Sir Nicholas Andrew, Kt.
†Seton, Sir Charles Wallace, Bt. (S.
  1683)
Seton, Sir Iain Bruce, Bt. (S. 1663)
Severne, *Air Vice-Marshal* Sir John de
  Milt, KCVO, OBE, AFC
Shaffer, Sir Peter Levin, Kt., CBE
Shakerley, Sir Geoffrey Adam, Bt.
  (1838)
Shakespeare, Sir Thomas William, Bt.
  (1942)

Sharp, Sir Adrian, Bt. (1922)
Sharp, Sir Leslie, Kt., QPM
Sharp, Sir Sheridan Christopher
 Robin, Bt. (1920)
Sharples, Sir James, Kt., QPM
Shaw, Sir Charles De Vere, Bt. (1821)
Shaw, Prof. Sir John Calman, Kt., CBE
Shaw, Sir Neil McGowan, Kt.
Shaw, Sir Roy, Kt.
Shaw, Sir Run Run, Kt., CBE
Shaw-Stewart, Sir Ludovic Houston,
 Bt. (S. 1667)
Shebbeare, Sir Thomas Andrew,
 KCVO
Sheehy, Sir Patrick, Kt.
Sheffield, Sir Reginald Adrian
 Berkeley, Bt. (1755)
Shehadie, Sir Nicholas Michael, Kt.,
 OBE
Sheil, Rt. Hon. Sir John, Kt.
Sheinwald, Sir Nigel Elton, GCMG
Shelley, Sir John Richard, Bt. (1611)
Shepherd, Sir Colin Ryley, Kt.
Shepherd, Sir John Alan, KCVO,
 CMG
Sher, Sir Antony, KBE
Sherbourne, Sir Stephen Ashley, Kt.,
 CBE
Sherston-Baker, Sir Robert George
 Humphrey, Bt. (1796)
Shiffner, Sir Henry David, Bt.
 (1818)
Silber, Hon. Sir Stephen Robert, Kt.
Shinwell, Sir (Maurice) Adrian, Kt.
Shirreff, Lt.-Gen. Sir Alexander
 Richard David, KCB, CBE
Shock, Sir Maurice, Kt.
Shortridge, Sir Jon Deacon, KCB
Shuckburgh, Sir Rupert Charles
 Gerald, Bt. (1660)
Sieff, Hon. Sir David, Kt.
Silber, Rt. Hon. Sir Stephen Robert,
 Kt.
Simeon, Sir Richard Edmund
 Barrington, Bt. (1815)
Simmonds, Rt. Hon. Dr Sir Kennedy
 Alphonse, KCMG
Simmons, Air Marshal Sir Michael
 George, KCB, AFC
Simmons, Sir Stanley Clifford, Kt.
Simms, Sir Neville Ian, Kt., FRENG
Simon, Hon. Sir Peregrine Charles
 Hugh, Kt.
Simonet, Sir Louis Marcel Pierre, Kt.,
 CBE
Simpson, Sir Peter Austin, Kt.,
 OBE
Simpson, Dr Sir Peter Jeffery, Kt.
Sims, Sir Roger Edward, Kt.
Sinclair, Sir Clive Marles, Kt.
Sinclair, Sir Ian McTaggart, KCMG,
 QC
Sinclair, Sir Robert John, Kt.
†Sinclair, Sir William Robert Francis,
 Bt. (S. 1704)
Sinclair-Lockhart, Sir Simon John
 Edward Francis, Bt. (S. 1636)
Sinden, Sir Donald Alfred, Kt.,
 CBE
Singer, Hon. Sir Jan Peter, Kt.
Singh, His Hon. Sir Mota, Kt., QC
Singh, Sir Pritpal, Kt.

Singleton, Sir Roger, Kt., CBE
Sione, Sir Tomu Malaefone, GCMG,
 OBE
†Sitwell, Sir George Reresby
 Sacheverell, Bt. (1808)
Skeggs, Sir Clifford George, Kt.
Skehel, Sir John James, Kt., FRS
Skingsley, Air Chief Marshal Sir
 Anthony Gerald, GBE, KCB
Skinner, Sir (Thomas) Keith (Hewitt),
 Bt. (1912)
Skipwith, Sir Patrick Alexander
 d'Estoteville, Bt. (1622)
Slack, Sir William Willatt, KCVO,
 FRCS
Slade, Sir Benjamin Julian Alfred, Bt.
 (1831)
Slade, Rt. Hon. Sir Christopher John,
 Kt.
Slaney, Prof. Sir Geoffrey, KBE
Slater, Adm. Sir John (Jock)
 Cunningham Kirkwood, GCB,
 LVO
Sleight, Sir Richard, Bt. (1920)
Sloman, Sir Albert Edward, Kt.,
 CBE
Smiley, Lt.-Col. Sir John Philip, Bt.
 (1903)
Smith, Prof. Sir Adrian Frederick
 Melhuish, Kt., FRS
Smith, Sir Alan, Kt., CBE, DFC
Smith, Hon. Sir Andrew Charles,
 Kt.
Smith, Sir Andrew Thomas, Bt.
 (1897)
Smith, Prof. Sir Colin Stansfield, Kt.,
 CBE
Smith, Prof. Sir David Cecil, Kt.,
 FRS
Smith, Sir David Iser, KCVO
Smith, Sir Dudley (Gordon), Kt.
Smith, Prof. Sir Eric Brian, Kt., PHD
Smith, Sir John Alfred, Kt., QPM
Smith, Sir Joseph William Grenville,
 Kt.
Smith, Sir Kevin, Kt., CBE
Smith, Sir Michael John Llewellyn,
 KCVO, CMG
Smith, Sir (Norman) Brian, Kt., CBE,
 PHD
Smith, Sir Paul Brierley, Kt., CBE
Smith, Hon. Sir Peter (Winston), Kt.
†Smith, Sir Robert Christopher
 Sydney Winwood, Bt. (1809)
Smith, Sir Robert Courtney, Kt., CBE
Smith, Sir Robert Hill, Bt. (1945)
Smith, Gen. Sir Rupert Anthony,
 KCB, DSO, OBE, QGM
Smith, Sir Steven Murray, Kt.
Smith-Dodsworth, Sir John
 Christopher, Bt. (1784)
Smith-Gordon, Sir (Lionel) Eldred
 (Peter), Bt. (1838)
Smith-Marriott, Sir Hugh Cavendish,
 Bt. (1774)
Smurfit, Dr. Sir Michael William
 Joseph, KBE
Smyth, Sir Timothy John, Bt.
 (1955)
Snyder, Sir Michael John, Kt.
Soar, Vice-Adm. Sir Trevor Alan,
 KCB, OBE

Sobers, Sir Garfield St Auburn, Kt.
Solomon, Sir Harry, Kt.
Somare, Rt. Hon. Sir Michael
 Thomas, GCMG, CH
Somerville, Brig. Sir John Nicholas,
 Kt., CBE
Songo, Sir Bernard Paul, Kt., CMG,
 OBE
Sorrell, Sir John William, Kt., CBE
Sorrell, Sir Martin Stuart, Kt.
Soulsby, Sir Peter Alfred, Kt.
Soutar, Air Marshal Sir Charles John
 Williamson, KBE
Souter, Sir Brian, Kt.
Southby, Sir John Richard Bilbe, Bt.
 (1937)
Southern, Prof. Sir Edwin Mellor, Kt.
Southgate, Sir Colin Grieve, Kt.
Southgate, Sir William David, Kt.
Southward, Dr Sir Nigel Ralph,
 KCVO
Sowrey, Air Marshal Sir Frederick
 Beresford, KCB, CBE, AFC
Sparrow, Sir John, Kt.
Spearman, Sir Alexander Young
 Richard Mainwaring, Bt. (1840)
Spedding, Prof. Sir Colin Raymond
 William, Kt., CBE
Speed, Sir (Herbert) Keith, Kt., RD
Speelman, Sir Cornelis Jacob, Bt.
 (1686)
Spencer, Sir Derek Harold, Kt., QC
Spencer, Vice-Adm. Sir Peter, KCB
Spencer, Hon. Sir Robin Godfrey,
 Kt.
Spencer-Nairn, Sir Robert Arnold,
 Bt. (1933)
Spicer, Sir James Wilton, Kt.
Spicer, Sir Nicholas Adrian Albert,
 Bt. (1906)
Spiers, Sir Donald Maurice, Kt., CB,
 TD
Spooner, Sir James Douglas, Kt.
Spratt, Col. Sir Greville Douglas,
 GBE, TD
Spring, Sir Dryden Thomas, Kt.
Squire, Air Chief Marshal Sir Peter
 Ted, GCB, DFC, AFC, ADC
Stadlen, Hon. Sir Nicholas Felix,
 Kt.
Stagg, Sir Charles Richard Vernon,
 KCMG
Stainton, Sir (John) Ross, Kt., CBE
Staite, Sir Richard John, Kt., OBE
Stamer, Sir (Lovelace) Anthony, Bt.
 (1809)
Stanhope, Adm. Sir Mark, GCB,
 OBE, ADC
Stanier, Sir Beville Douglas, Bt.
 (1917)
Stanley, Rt. Hon. Sir John Paul, Kt.,
 MP
Staples, Sir Richard Molesworth, Bt.
 (I. 1628)
Starkey, Sir John Philip, Bt. (1935)
Staughton, Rt. Hon. Sir Christopher
 Stephen Thomas Jonathan Thayer,
 Kt.
Stear, Air Chief Marshal Sir Michael
 James Douglas, KCB, CBE
Steel, Hon. Sir David William, Kt.
Steer, Sir Alan William, Kt.

Stephen, *Rt. Hon.* Sir Ninian Martin, KG, GCMG, GCVO, KBE
Stephens, Sir (Edwin) Barrie, Kt.
Stephens, Sir William Benjamin Synge, Kt.
Stephenson, Sir Henry Upton, Bt. (1936)
Stephenson, Sir Paul Robert, Kt., QPM
Sternberg, Sir Sigmund, Kt.
Stevens, Sir Jocelyn Edward Greville, Kt., CVO
Stevenson, Sir Hugh Alexander, Kt.
Stevenson, Sir Simpson, Kt.
Stewart, Sir Alan d'Arcy, Bt. (I. 1623)
Stewart, Sir Brian John, Kt., CBE
Stewart, Sir David James Henderson, Bt. (1957)
Stewart, Sir David John Christopher, Bt. (1803)
Stewart, Sir James Moray, KCB
Stewart, Sir (John) Simon (Watson), Bt. (1920)
Stewart, Sir John Young, Kt., OBE
Stewart, Sir Patrick, Kt., OBE
Stewart, *Lt.-Col.* Sir Robert Christie, KCVO, CBE, TD
Stewart, Sir Robin Alastair, Bt. (1960)
Stewart, *Prof.* Sir William Duncan Paterson, Kt., FRS, FRSE
Stewart-Clark, Sir John, Bt. (1918)
Stewart-Richardson, Sir Simon Alaisdair, Bt. (S. 1630)
Stibbon, *Gen.* Sir John James, KCB, OBE
Stirling, Sir Alexander John Dickson, KBE, CMG
Stirling, Sir Angus Duncan Aeneas, Kt.
Stirling-Hamilton, Sir Malcolm William Bruce, Bt. (S. 1673)
Stirling of Garden, *Col.* Sir James, KCVO, CBE, TD
Stockdale, Sir Thomas Minshull, Bt. (1960)
Stoddart, *Prof.* Sir James Fraser, Kt.
Stoker, *Prof.* Sir Michael George Parke, Kt., CBE, FRCP, FRS, FRSE
Stonhouse, *Revd* Michael Philip, Bt. (1628 and 1670)
Stonor, *Air Marshal* Sir Thomas Henry, KCB
Stoppard, Sir Thomas, Kt., OM, CBE
Storey, *Hon.* Sir Richard, Bt., CBE (1960)
Stothard, Sir Peter Michael, Kt.
Stott, Sir Adrian George Ellingham, Bt. (1920)
Stoute, Sir Michael Ronald, Kt.
Stowe, Sir Kenneth Ronald, GCB, CVO
Stracey, Sir John Simon, Bt. (1818)
Strachan, Sir Curtis Victor, Kt., CVO
Strachey, Sir Charles, Bt. (1801)
Straker, Sir Louis Hilton, KCMG
Strang Steel, Sir (Fiennes) Michael, Bt. (1938)
Street, *Hon.* Sir Laurence Whistler, KCMG

Streeton, Sir Terence George, KBE, CMG
Strickland-Constable, Sir Frederic, Bt. (1641)
Stringer, Sir Donald Edgar, Kt., CBE
Stringer, Sir Howard, Kt.
Strong, Sir Roy Colin, Kt., PHD, FSA
Stronge, Sir James Anselan Maxwell, Bt. (1803)
Stuart, Sir James Keith, Kt.
Stuart, Sir Kenneth Lamonte, Kt.
†Stuart, Sir Phillip Luttrell, Bt. (1660)
†Stuart-Forbes, Sir William Daniel, Bt. (S. 1626)
Stuart-Menteth, Sir Charles Greaves, Bt. (1838)
Stuart-Paul, *Air Marshal* Sir Ronald Ian, KBE
Stuart-Smith, *Rt. Hon.* Sir Murray, Kt.
Stubbs, Sir William Hamilton, Kt., PHD
Stucley, *Lt.* Sir Hugh George Coplestone Bampfylde, Bt. (1859)
Studd, Sir Edward Fairfax, Bt. (1929)
Studholme, Sir Henry William, Bt. (1956)
Sturridge, Sir Nicholas Anthony, KCVO
Stuttard, Sir John Boothman, Kt.
†Style, Sir William Frederick, Bt. (1627)
Sullivan, *Rt. Hon.* Sir Jeremy Mirth, Kt.
Sullivan, Sir Richard Arthur, Bt. (1804)
Sulston, Sir John Edward, Kt.
Sumner, *Hon.* Sir Christopher John, Kt.
Sunderland, Sir John Michael, Kt.
Supperstone, *Hon.* Sir Michael Alan, Kt.
Sutherland, Sir John Brewer, Bt. (1921)
Sutherland, Sir William George MacKenzie, Kt.
Sutton, *Air Marshal* Sir John Matthias Dobson, KCB
Sutton, Sir Richard Lexington, Bt. (1772)
Swaffield, Sir James Chesebrough, Kt., CBE, RD
Swaine, Sir John Joseph, Kt., CBE
Swan, Sir Conrad Marshall John Fisher, KCVO, PHD
Swan, Sir John William David, KBE
Swann, Sir Michael Christopher, Bt. (1906), TD
Sweeney, Sir George, Kt.
Sweeney, *Hon.* Sir Nigel Hamilton, Kt.
Sweeting, *Prof.* Sir Martin Nicholas, Kt., OBE, FRS
Sweetnam, Sir (David) Rodney, KCVO, CBE, FRCS
Swinburn, *Lt.-Gen.* Sir Richard Hull, KCB
Swinnerton-Dyer, *Prof.* Sir (Henry) Peter (Francis), Bt. (1678), KBE, FRS
Swinton, *Maj.-Gen.* Sir John, KCVO, OBE

Swire, Sir Adrian Christopher, Kt.
Swire, Sir John Anthony, Kt., CBE
Sykes, Sir David Michael, Bt. (1921)
Sykes, Sir Francis John Badcock, Bt. (1781)
Sykes, Sir Hugh Ridley, Kt.
Sykes, *Prof.* Sir (Malcolm) Keith, Kt.
Sykes, Sir Richard, Kt.
Sykes, Sir Tatton Christopher Mark, Bt. (1783)
Symons, *Vice-Adm.* Sir Patrick Jeremy, KBE
Synge, Sir Robert Carson, Bt. (1801)
Synnott, Sir Hilary Nicholas Hugh, KCMG

Talboys, *Rt. Hon.* Sir Brian Edward, CH, KCB
Tang, Sir David Wing-cheung, KBE
Tapps-Gervis-Meyrick, Sir George Christopher Cadafael, Bt. (1791)
Tapsell, Sir Peter Hannay Bailey, Kt., PC
Tate, Sir (Henry) Saxon, Bt. (1898)
Taureka, *Dr* Sir Reubeh, KBE
Tauvasa, Sir Joseph James, KBE
Tavare, Sir John, Kt., CBE
Tavener, *Prof.* Sir John Kenneth, Kt.
Taylor, Sir (Arthur) Godfrey, Kt.
Taylor, Sir Cyril Julian Hebden, GBE
Taylor, Sir Edward Macmillan (Teddy), Kt.
Taylor, Sir Hugh Henderson, KCB
Taylor, *Rt. Revd* John Bernard, KCVO
Taylor, *Dr* Sir John Michael, Kt., OBE
Taylor, *Prof.* Sir Martin John, Kt., FRS
Taylor, Sir Nicholas Richard Stuart, Bt. (1917)
Taylor, *Prof.* Sir William, Kt., CBE
Taylor, Sir William George, Kt.
Teagle, *Vice-Adm.* Sir Somerford Francis, KBE
Teare, *Hon.* Sir Nigel John Martin, Kt.
Teasdale, *Prof.* Sir Graham Michael, Kt.
Tebbit, Sir Kevin Reginald, KCB, CMG
Telito, *HE Revd* Filoimea, GCMG, MBE
Temple, *Prof.* Sir John Graham, Kt.
Temple, Sir Richard, Bt. (1876), Chartier
Temu, *Hon. Dr* Sir Puka, KBE, CMG
Tennyson-D'Eyncourt, Sir Mark Gervais, Bt. (1930)
Terry, *Air Marshal* Sir Colin George, KBE, CB
Terry, *Air Chief Marshal* Sir Peter David George, GCB, AFC
Thatcher, Sir Mark, Bt. (1990)
Thomas, Sir David John Godfrey, Bt. (1694)
Thomas, Sir Derek Morison David, KCMG
Thomas, Sir Gilbert Stanley, Kt., OBE

Thomas, Sir Jeremy Cashel, KCMG
Thomas, Sir (John) Alan, Kt.
Thomas, *Prof.* Sir John Meurig, Kt., FRS
Thomas, Sir Keith Vivian, Kt.
Thomas, *Dr* Sir Leton Felix, KCMG, CBE
Thomas, Sir Philip Lloyd, KCVO, CMG
Thomas, Sir Quentin Jeremy, Kt., CB
Thomas, *Rt. Hon.* Sir Roger John Laugharne, Kt.
Thomas, *Hon.* Sir Swinton Barclay, Kt.
Thomas, Sir William Michael, Bt. (1919)
Thomas, Sir (William) Michael (Marsh), Bt. (1918)
Thompson, Sir Christopher Peile, Bt. (1890)
Thompson, Sir Clive Malcolm, Kt.
Thompson, Sir David Albert, KCMG
Thompson, Sir Gilbert Williamson, Kt., OBE
Thompson, *Prof.* Sir Michael Warwick, Kt., DSC
Thompson, Sir Nicholas Annesley, Bt. (1963)
Thompson, Sir Nigel Cooper, KCMG, CBE
Thompson, Sir Paul Anthony, Bt. (1963)
Thompson, Sir Peter Anthony, Kt.
Thompson, *Dr* Sir Richard Paul Hepworth, KCVO
Thompson, Sir Thomas d'Eyncourt John, Bt. (1806)
Thomson, Sir (Frederick Douglas) David, Bt. (1929)
Thomson, Sir John Adam, GCMG
Thomson, Sir Mark Wilfrid Home, Bt. (1925)
Thomson, Sir Thomas James, Kt., CBE, FRCP
Thorne, Sir Neil Gordon, Kt., OBE, TD
Thornton, *Air Marshal* Sir Barry Michael, KCB
Thornton, Sir (George) Malcolm, Kt.
Thornton, Sir Peter Eustace, KCB
Thornton, Sir Richard Eustace, KCVO, OBE
†Thorold, Sir (Anthony) Oliver, Bt. (1642)
Thorpe, *Rt. Hon.* Sir Mathew Alexander, Kt.
Thurecht, Sir Ramon Richard, Kt., OBE
Thwaites, Sir Bryan, Kt., PHD
Tickell, Sir Crispin Charles Cervantes, GCMG, KCVO
Tidmarsh, Sir James Napier, KCVO, MBE
Tikaram, Sir Moti, KBE
Tilt, Sir Robin Richard, Kt.
Tiltman, Sir John Hessell, KCVO
Timmins, *Col.* Sir John Bradford, KCVO, OBE, TD
Tims, Sir Michael David, KCVO
Tindle, Sir Ray Stanley, Kt., CBE

Tirvengadum, Sir Harry Krishnan, Kt.
Tjoeng, Sir James Neng, KBE
Tod, *Vice-Adm.* Sir Jonathan James Richard, KCB, CBE
Todd, *Prof.* Sir David, Kt., CBE
Todd, Sir Ian Pelham, KBE, FRCS
Toka, Sir Mahuru Dadi, Kt., MBE
Tollemache, Sir Lyonel Humphry John, Bt. (1793)
Tomkys, Sir (William) Roger, KCMG
Tomlinson, *Prof.* Sir Bernard Evans, Kt., CBE
Tomlinson, Sir John Rowland, Kt., CBE
Tomlinson, Sir Michael John, Kt., CBE
Tomlinson, *Rt. Hon.* Sir Stephen Miles, Kt.
Tooke, *Prof.* Sir John Edward, Kt.
Tooley, Sir John, Kt.
ToRobert, Sir Henry Thomas, KBE
Torpy, *Air Marshal* Sir Glenn Lester, GCB, CBE, DSO
Torry, Sir Peter James, GCVO, KCMG
Tory, Sir Geofroy William, KCMG
Touche, Sir Anthony George, Bt. (1920)
Touche, Sir Rodney Gordon, Bt. (1962)
Toulson, *Rt. Hon.* Sir Roger Grenfell, Kt.
Tovadek, Sir Martin, Kt. CMG
Tovey, Sir Brian John Maynard, KCMG
ToVue, Sir Ronald, Kt., OBE
Towneley, Sir Simon Peter Edmund Cosmo William, KCVO
Townsend, Sir Cyril David, Kt.
Traill, Sir Alan Towers, GBE
Trainor, *Prof.* Sir Richard Hughes, KBE
Treacher, *Adm.* Sir John Devereux, KCB
Treacy, *Hon.* Sir Colman Maurice, Kt.
Treacy, *Hon.* Sir (James Mary) Seamus, Kt.
Treitel, *Prof.* Sir Guenter Heinz, Kt., FBA, QC
Trescowthick, Sir Donald Henry, KBE
†Trevelyan, Sir Andrew John, Bt. (1662 and 1874)
Trezise, Sir Kenneth Bruce, Kt., OBE
Trippier, Sir David Austin, Kt., RD
Tritton, Sir Anthony John Ernest, Bt. (1905)
Trollope, Sir Anthony Simon, Bt. (1642)
Trotman-Dickenson, Sir Aubrey Fiennes, Kt.
Trotter, Sir Neville Guthrie, Kt.
Troubridge, Sir Thomas Richard, Bt. (1799)
Trousdell, *Lt.-Gen.* Sir Philip Charles Cornwallis, KBE, CB
Truscott, Sir Ralph Eric Nicholson, Bt. (1909)
Tsang, Sir Donald Yam-keun, KBE
Tuamure-Maoate, *Dr* Sir Terepai, KBE

Tuck, Sir Bruce Adolph Reginald, Bt. (1910)
Tucker, *Hon.* Sir Richard Howard, Kt.
Tuckey, *Rt. Hon.* Sir Simon Lane, Kt.
Tugendhat, *Hon.* Sir Michael George, Kt.
Tuite, Sir Christopher Hugh, Bt. (1622), PHD
Tuivaga, Sir Timoci Uluiburotu, Kt.
Tully, Sir William Mark, KBE
†Tupper, Sir Charles Hibbert, Bt. (1888)
Turbott, Sir Ian Graham, Kt., CMG, CVO
Turing, Sir John Dermot, Bt. (S. 1638)
Turner, Sir Colin William Carstairs, Kt., CBE, DFC
Turner, *Hon.* Sir Michael John, Kt.
Turnquest, Sir Orville Alton, GCMG, QC
Tusa, Sir John, Kt.
Tweedie, *Prof.* Sir David Philip, Kt.
Tyree, Sir (Alfred) William, Kt., OBE
Tyrwhitt, Sir Reginald Thomas Newman, Bt. (1919)

Underhill, *Hon.* Sir Nicholas Edward, Kt.
Underwood, *Prof.* Sir James Cressee Elphinstone, Kt.
Unwin, Sir (James) Brian, KCB
Ure, Sir John Burns, KCMG, LVO
Urquhart, Sir Brian Edward, KCMG, MBE
Urwick, Sir Alan Bedford, KCVO, CMG
Usher, Sir Andrew John, Bt. (1899)
Utting, Sir William Benjamin, Kt., CB

Vardy, Sir Peter, Kt.
Varney, Sir David Robert, Kt.
Vasquez, Sir Alfred Joseph, Kt., CBE, QC
Vassar-Smith, Sir John Rathbone, Bt. (1917)
Vavasour, Sir Eric Michael Joseph Marmaduke, Bt. (1828)
Veness, Sir David, Kt., CBE, QPM
Venner, Sir Kenneth Dwight Vincent, KBE
Vereker, Sir John Michael Medlicott, KCB
†Verney, Sir John Sebastian, Bt. (1946)
Verney, *Hon.* Sir Lawrence John, Kt., TD
†Verney, Sir Edmund Ralph, Bt. (1818)
Vernon, Sir James William, Bt. (1914)
Vernon, Sir (William) Michael, Kt.
Vestey, Sir Paul Edmund, Bt. (1921)
Vickers, *Prof.* Sir Brian William, Kt.
Vickers, Sir John Stuart, Kt.
Vickers, *Lt.-Gen.* Sir Richard Maurice Hilton, KCB, CVO, OBE
Vickers, Sir Roger Henry, KCVO
Viggers, *Lt-Gen.* Sir Frederick Richard, KCB, CMG, MBE

Viggers, Sir Peter John, Kt.
Vincent, Sir William Percy Maxwell, Bt. (1936)
Vineall, Sir Anthony John Patrick, Kt.
Vos, *Hon.* Sir Geoffrey Michael, Kt.
†Vyvyan, Sir Ralph Ferrers Alexander, Bt. (1645)

Wade-Gery, Sir Robert Lucian, KCMG, KCVO
Waena, Sir Nathaniel Rahumaea, GCMG
Waine, *Rt. Revd* John, KCVO
Waite, *Rt. Hon.* Sir John Douglas, Kt.
Waka, Sir Lucas Joseph, Kt., OBE
Wake, Sir Hereward, Bt. (1621), MC
Wakefield, Sir (Edward) Humphry (Tyrell), Bt. (1962)
Wakefield, Sir Norman Edward, Kt.
Wakeford, Sir Geoffrey Michael Montgomery, Kt., OBE
Wakeham, *Prof.* Sir William Arnot, Kt.
Wakeley, Sir John Cecil Nicholson, Bt. (1952), FRCS
Wald, *Prof.* Sir Nicholas John, Kt.
Wales, Sir Robert Andrew, Kt.
Waley-Cohen, Sir Stephen Harry, Bt. (1961)
Walford, Sir Christopher Rupert, Kt.
Walker, *Gen.* Sir Antony Kenneth Frederick, KCB
†Walker, Sir Christopher Robert Baldwin, Bt. (1856)
Walker, Sir David Alan, Kt.
Walker, Air Vice-Marshal Sir David Allan, KCVO, OBE
Walker, Sir Harold Berners, KCMG
Walker, Sir John Ernest, Kt., DPHIL, FRS
Walker, *Air Marshal* Sir John Robert, KCB, CBE, AFC
Walker, Sir Miles Rawstron, Kt., CBE
Walker, Sir Patrick Jeremy, KCB
Walker, *Hon.* Sir Paul James, Kt.
Walker, Sir Rodney Myerscough, Kt.
Walker, Sir Roy Edward, Bt. (1906)
Walker, *Hon.* Sir Timothy Edward, Kt.
Walker, Sir Victor Stewart Heron, Bt. (1868)
Walker-Okeover, Sir Andrew Peter Monro, Bt. (1886)
Walker-Smith, Sir John Jonah, Bt. (1960)
Wall, Sir (John) Stephen, GCMG, LVO
Wall, *Rt. Hon.* Sir Nicholas Peter Rathbone, Kt.
Wall, *Gen.* Sir Peter Anthony, KCB, CBE
Wallace, *Lt.-Gen.* Sir Christopher Brooke Quentin, KBE
Wallace, *Prof.* David James, Kt., CBE, FRS
Waller, *Rt. Hon.* Sir (George) Mark, Kt.
Waller, Sir John Michael, Bt. (I. 1780)
Wallis, Sir Peter Gordon, KCVO

Wallis, Sir Timothy William, Kt.
Walmsley, *Vice-Adm.* Sir Robert, KCB
Walport, *Dr* Sir Mark Jeremy, Kt.
†Walsham, Sir Gerald Percy Robert, Bt. (1831)
Walters, Sir Dennis Murray, Kt., MBE
Walters, Sir Frederick Donald, Kt.
Walters, Sir Peter Ingram, Kt.
Wamiri, Sir Akapite, KBE
Wanless, Sir Derek, Kt.
Ward, *Rt. Hon.* Sir Alan Hylton, Kt.
Ward, Sir Austin, Kt., QC
Ward, *Prof.* Sir John MacQueen, Kt., CBE
Ward, Sir Joseph James Laffey, Bt. (1911)
Ward, Sir Timothy James, Kt.
Wardale, Sir Geoffrey Charles, KCB
Wardlaw, Sir Henry Justin, Bt. (NS. 1631)
Waring, Sir (Alfred) Holburt, Bt. (1935)
Warmington, Sir Rupert Marshall, Bt. (1908)
Warner, Sir Gerald Chierici, KCMG
†Warner, Sir Philip Courtenay Thomas, Bt. (1910)
Warren, Sir (Frederick) Miles, KBE
Warren, Sir Kenneth Robin, Kt.
Warren, Sir Nicholas Roger, Kt.
Wass, Sir Douglas William Gretton, GCB
Waterlow, Sir Christopher Rupert, Bt. (1873)
Waterlow, Sir (James) Gerard, Bt. (1930)
Waters, *Gen.* Sir (Charles) John, GCB, ·CBE
Waters, Sir (Thomas) Neil (Morris), Kt.
Waterworth, Sir Alan William, KCVO
Wates, Sir Christopher Stephen, Kt.
Watson, *Prof.* Sir David John, Kt., PHD
Watson, Sir Graham Robert, Kt.
Watson, Sir (James) Andrew, Bt. (1866)
Watson, Sir Ronald Matthew, Kt., CBE
Watson, Sir Simon Conran Hamilton, Bt. (1895)
Watt, *Gen.* Sir Charles Redmond, KCB, KCVO, CBE, ADC
Watts, Sir John Augustus Fitzroy, KCMG, CBE
Watts, Sir Philip Beverley, KCMG
Weatherall, *Prof.* Sir David John, Kt., FRS
Weatherall, *Vice-Adm.* Sir James Lamb, KCVO, KBE
Weatherup, *Hon.* Sir Ronald Eccles, Kt.
Webb, *Prof.* Sir Adrian Leonard, Kt.
Webb-Carter, *Gen.* Sir Evelyn John, KCVO, OBE

Webster, *Vice-Adm.* Sir John Morrison, KCB
†Wedgwood, Sir Ralph Nicholas, Bt. (1942)
Weekes, Sir Everton DeCourcey, KCMG, OBE
Weinberg, Sir Mark Aubrey, Kt.
Weir, *Hon.* Sir Reginald George, Kt.
Weir, Sir Roderick Bignell, Kt.
Welby, Sir (Richard) Bruno Gregory, Bt. (1801)
Welch, Sir John Reader, Bt. (1957)
Weldon, Sir Anthony William, Bt. (I. 1723)
Wellend, *Prof.* Sir Mark Edward, Kt.
Weller, Sir Arthur Burton, Kt., CBE
†Wells, Sir Christopher Charles, Bt. (1944)
Wells, Sir John Julius, Kt.
Wells, Sir William Henry Weston, Kt., FRICS
Wesker, Sir Arnold, Kt.
Westbrook, Sir Neil Gowanloch, Kt., CBE
Westmacott, Sir Peter John, KCMG
Weston, Sir Michael Charles Swift, KCMG, CVO
Weston, Sir (Philip) John, KCMG
Whalen, Sir Geoffrey Henry, Kt., CBE
Wheeler, Sir Harry Anthony, Kt., OBE
Wheeler, *Rt. Hon.* Sir John Daniel, Kt.
Wheeler, Sir John Frederick, Bt. (1920)
Wheeler, *Gen.* Sir Roger Neil, GCB, CBE
Wheeler-Booth, Sir Michael Addison John, KCB
Wheler, Sir Trevor Woodford, Bt. (1660)
Whitaker, Sir John James Ingham (Jack), Bt. (1936)
Whitbread, Sir Samuel Charles, KCVO
Whitchurch, Sir Graeme Ian, Kt., OBE
White, *Prof.* Sir Christopher John, Kt., CVO
White, Sir Christopher Robert Meadows, Bt. (1937)
White, Sir David (David Jason), Kt., OBE
White, Sir David Harry, Kt.
White, *Hon.* Sir Frank John, Kt.
White, Sir George Stanley James, Bt. (1904)
White, *Adm.* Sir Hugo Moresby, GCB, CBE
White, Sir John Woolmer, Bt. (1922)
White, Sir Nicholas Peter Archibald, Bt. (1802)
White, Sir Willard Wentworth, Kt., CBE
White-Spunner, *Lt.-Gen.* Sir Barnabas William Benjamin, KCB, CBE
Whitehead, Sir John Stainton, GCMG, CVO
Whitehead, Sir Philip Henry Rathbone, Bt. (1889)

Whiteley, *Gen.* Sir Peter John Frederick, GCB, OBE, RM

Whitfield, Sir William, Kt., CBE

Whitmore, Sir Clive Anthony, GCB, CVO

Whitmore, Sir John Henry Douglas, Bt. (1954)

Whitney, Sir Raymond William, Kt., OBE

Whitson, Sir Keith Roderick, Kt.

Wickerson, Sir John Michael, Kt.

Wicks, Sir Nigel Leonard, GCB, CVO, CBE

†Wigan, Sir Michael Iain, Bt. (1898)

Wiggin, Sir Alfred William (Jerry), Kt., TD

†Wiggin, Sir Charles Rupert John, Bt. (1892)

†Wigram, Sir John Woolmore, Bt. (1805)

Wilbraham, Sir Richard Baker, Bt. (1776)

Wild, Sir John Ralston, Kt., CBE

Wiles, *Prof.* Sir Andrew John, KBE

Wilkes, *Gen.* Sir Michael John, KCB, CBE

Wilkie, *Hon.* Sir Alan Fraser, Kt.

Wilkinson, Sir (David) Graham (Brook) Bt. (1941)

Wilkinson, *Prof.* Sir Denys Haigh, Kt., FRS

Willcocks, Sir David Valentine, Kt., CBE, MC

Willcocks, *Lt.-Gen.* Sir Michael Alan, KCB, CVO

Williams, Sir (Arthur) Gareth Ludovic Emrys Rhys, Bt. (1918)

Williams, Sir Charles Othniel, Kt.

Williams, Sir Daniel Charles, GCMG, QC

Williams, *Adm.* Sir David, GCB

Williams, Sir David Innes, Kt.

Williams, Sir David Reeve, Kt., CBE

Williams, *Hon.* Sir Denys Ambrose, KCMG

Williams, Sir Donald Mark, Bt. (1866)

Williams, *Prof.* Sir (Edward) Dillwyn, Kt., FRCP

Williams, Sir Francis Owen Garbett, Kt., CBE

Williams, *Hon.* Sir (John) Griffith, Kt.

Williams, Sir (Lawrence) Hugh, Bt. (1798)

Williams, Sir Osmond, Bt. (1909), MC

Williams, Sir Paul Michael, Kt., OBE

Williams, Sir Peter Michael, Kt.

Williams, Sir (Robert) Philip Nathaniel, Bt. (1915)

Williams, Sir Robin Philip, Bt. (1953)

Williams, *Prof.* Sir Roger, Kt.

Williams, Sir (William) Maxwell (Harries), Kt.

Williams, *Hon.* Sir Wyn Lewis

Williams-Bulkeley, Sir Richard Thomas, Bt. (1661)

Williams-Wynn, Sir David Watkin, Bt. (1688)

Williamson, Sir George Malcolm, Kt.

Williamson, *Marshal of the Royal Air Force* Sir Keith Alec, GCB, AFC

Williamson, Sir Robert Brian, Kt., CBE

Willink, Sir Edward Daniel, Bt. (1957)

Wills, Sir David James Vernon, Bt. (1923)

Wills, Sir David Seton, Bt. (1904)

Wilmot, Sir David, Kt., QPM

Wilmot, Sir Henry Robert, Bt. (1759)

Wilmut, *Prof.* Sir Ian, Kt., OBE

Wilsey, *Gen.* Sir John Finlay Willasey, GCB, CBE

Wilshaw, Sir Michael, Kt.

Wilson, *Prof.* Sir Alan Geoffrey, Kt.

Wilson, Sir Anthony, Kt.

Wilson, *Vice-Adm.* Sir Barry Nigel, KCB

Wilson, Sir David, Bt. (1920)

Wilson, Sir David Mackenzie, Kt.

Wilson, Sir James William Douglas, Bt. (1906)

Wilson, *Brig.* Sir Mathew John Anthony, Bt. (1874), OBE, MC

Wilson, *Rt. Hon.* Sir Nicholas Allan Roy, Kt.

Wilson, *Prof.* Sir Robert James Timothy, Kt.

Wilson, Sir Robert Peter, KCMG

Wilson, *Air Chief Marshal* Sir (Ronald) Andrew (Fellowes), KCB, AFC

Wingate, *Capt.* Sir Miles Buckley, KCVO

Winkley, Sir David Ross, Kt.

Winnington, Sir Anthony Edward, Bt. (1755)

Winship, Sir Peter James Joseph, Kt., CBE

Winter, *Dr* Sir Gregory Winter, Kt., CBE

Winterton, Sir Nicholas Raymond, Kt.

Wiseman, Sir John William, Bt. (1628)

Wolfendale, *Prof.* Sir Arnold Whittaker, Kt., FRS

Wolseley, Sir Charles Garnet Richard Mark, Bt. (1628)

†Wolseley, Sir James Douglas, Bt. (I. 1745)

†Wombell, Sir George Philip Frederick, Bt. (1778)

Womersley, Sir Peter John Walter, Bt. (1945)

Woo, Sir Leo Joseph, Kt.

Woo, Sir Po-Shing, Kt.

Wood, Sir Andrew Marley, GCMG

Wood, Sir Anthony John Page, Bt. (1837)

Wood, Sir Ian Clark, Kt., CBE

Wood, *Hon.* Sir John Kember, Kt., MC

Wood, Sir Martin Francis, Kt., OBE

Wood, Sir Michael Charles, KCMG

Wood, *Hon.* Sir Roderic Lionel James, Kt.

Woodard, *Rear Adm.* Sir Robert Nathaniel, KCVO

Woodcock, Sir John, Kt., CBE, QPM

Woodhead, *Vice-Adm.* Sir (Anthony) Peter, KCB

Woodhead, Sir Christopher Anthony, Kt.

Woodhouse, *Rt. Hon.* Sir (Arthur) Owen, KBE, DSC

Woodroffe, *Most Revd* George Cuthbert Manning, KBE

Woods, *Prof.* Sir Kent Linton, Kt.

Woods, Sir Robert Kynnersley, Kt., CBE

Woodward, Sir Clive Ronald, Kt., OBE

Woodward, *Adm.* Sir John Forster, GBE, KCB

Woodward, Sir Thomas Jones (Tom Jones), Kt., OBE

Worsley, *Gen.* Sir Richard Edward, GCB, OBE

Worsley, Sir (William) Marcus (John), Bt. (1838)

Worsthorne, Sir Peregrine Gerard, Kt.

Wratten, *Air Chief Marshal* Sir William John, GBE, CB, AFC

Wraxall, Sir Charles Frederick Lascelles, Bt. (1813)

Wrey, Sir George Richard Bourchier, Bt. (1628)

Wrigglesworth, Sir Ian William, Kt.

Wright, Sir Allan Frederick, KBE

Wright, Sir David John, GCMG, LVO

Wright, *Hon.* Sir (John) Michael, Kt.

Wright, *Prof.* Sir Nicholas Alcwyn, Kt.

Wright, Sir Peter Robert, Kt., CBE

Wright, *Air Marshal* Sir Robert Alfred, KBE, AFC

Wright, Sir Stephen John Leadbetter, KCMG

Wrightson, Sir Charles Mark Garmondsway, Bt. (1900)

Wrigley, *Prof.* Sir Edward Anthony (Sir Tony), Kt., PHD, PBA

Wrixon-Becher, Sir John William Michael, Bt. (1831)

Wroughton, Sir Philip Lavallin, KCVO

Wu, Sir Gordon Ying Sheung, KCMG

Wynne, Sir Graham Robert, Kt., CBE

Yacoub, *Prof.* Sir Magdi Habib, Kt., FRCS

Yaki, Sir Roy, KBE

Yang, *Hon.* Sir Ti Liang, Kt.

Yapp, Sir Stanley Graham, Kt.

Yardley, Sir David Charles Miller, Kt., LLD

Yarrow, Sir Eric Grant, Bt. (1916), MBE

Yocklunn, Sir John (Soong Chung), KCVO

Yoo Foo, Sir (François) Henri, Kt.

Young, Sir Brian Walter Mark, Kt.

Young, Sir Colville Norbert, GCMG, MBE

Young, Sir Dennis Charles, KCMG

Young, *Rt. Hon.* Sir George Samuel Knatchbull, Bt. (1813)

Young, Sir Jimmy Leslie Ronald, Kt., CBE

Young, Sir John Kenyon Roe, Bt. (1821)
Young, Sir John Robertson, GCMG
Young, Sir Leslie Clarence, Kt., CBE
Young, Sir Nicholas Charles, Kt.
Young, Sir Robin Urquhart, KCB

Young, Sir Roger William, Kt.
Young, Sir Stephen Stewart Templeton, Bt. (1945)
Young, Sir William Neil, Bt. (1769)
Younger, Sir Julian William Richard, Bt. (1911)
Yuwi, Sir Matiabe, KBE

Zeeman, *Prof.* Sir (Erik) Christopher, Kt., FRS
Zissman, Sir Bernard Philip, Kt.
Zochonis, Sir John Basil, Kt.
Zunz, Sir Gerhard Jacob (Jack), Kt., FRENG
Zurenuoc, Sir Zibang, KBE

THE ORDER OF ST JOHN

THE MOST VENERABLE ORDER OF THE HOSPITAL OF
ST JOHN OF JERUSALEM (1888)
GCStJ   Bailiff/Dame Grand Cross
KStJ   Knight of Justice/Grace
DStJ   Dame of Justice/Grace
CStJ   Commander
OstJ   Officer
SBStJ   Serving Brother
SSStJ   Serving Sister

Motto, Pro Fide, Pro Utilitate Hominum

The Order of St John, founded in the early 12th century
in Jerusalem, was a religious order with a particular duty
to care for the sick. In Britain the order was dissolved by
Henry VIII in 1540 but the British branch was revived in
the early 19th century. The branch was not accepted by
the Grand Magistracy of the Order in Rome but its search
for a role in the tradition of the hospitallers led to the
founding of the St John Ambulance Association in 1877
and later the St John Ambulance Brigade; in 1882 the St
John Ophthalmic Hospital was founded in Jerusalem. A
royal charter was granted in 1888 establishing the Order
of St John as a British Order of Chivalry with the
sovereign as its head.

Since October 1999 the whole order worldwide has
been governed by a Grand Council which includes a
representative from each of the eight priories (England,
Scotland, Wales, South Africa, New Zealand, Canada,
Australia and the USA). In addition there are also two
commanderies in Northern Ireland and Western Australia.
There are also branches in about 30 other
Commonwealth countries. Apart from the St John
Ambulance Foundation, the Order is also responsible for
the Jerusalem Eye Hospital. Admission to the order is
usually conferred in recognition of service to either one of
these institutions. Membership does not confer any rank,
style, title or precedence on a recipient.

SOVEREIGN HEAD OF THE ORDER
HM The Queen

GRAND PRIOR
HRH The Duke of Gloucester, KG, GCVO

Lord Prior, Prof. Anthony Mellows, OBE, TD
Prelate, Rt. Revd John Nicholls
Deputy Lord Prior, vacant
Sub Prior, Prof. Villis Marshall, AC
Secretary General, Rear-Adm. Andrew Gough, CB
Headquarters, 3 Charterhouse Mews, London EC1M 6BB
  T 020-7251 3292

DAMES

DAMES GRAND CROSS AND DAMES COMMANDERS

Style, 'Dame' before forename and surname, followed by appropriate post-nominal initials. Where such an award is made to a lady already in possession of a higher title, the appropriate initials follow her name *Envelope,* Dame F_ S_, followed by appropriate post-nominal letters. *Letter (formal),* Dear Madam; *(social),* Dear Dame F_. *Spoken,* Dame F_ *Husband,* Untitled

Dame Grand Cross and Dame Commander are the higher classes for women of the Order of the Bath, the Order of St Michael and St George, the Royal Victorian Order, and the Order of the British Empire. Dames Grand Cross rank after the wives of Baronets and before the wives of Knights Grand Cross. Dames Commanders rank after the wives of Knights Grand Cross and before the wives of Knights Commanders.

Honorary Dames Commanders may be conferred on women who are citizens of countries of which the Queen is not head of state.

LIST OF DAMES
As at 31 August 2011

Women peers in their own right and life peers are not included in this list. Female members of the royal family are not included in this list; details of the orders they hold can be found within the Royal Family section.

If a dame has a double barrelled or hyphenated surname, she is listed under the first element of the name. *A full entry in italic type* indicates that the recipient of an honour died during the year in which the honour was conferred. The name is included for the purposes of record.

Abaijah, Dame Josephine, DBE
Abramsky, Dame Jennifer Gita, DBE
Airlie, The Countess of, DCVO
Albemarle, The Countess of, DBE
Alexander, Dame Helen Anne, DBE
Allen, *Prof.* Dame Ingrid Victoria, DBE
Andrews, Dame Julie, DBE
Angiolini, *Rt. Hon.* Dame Elish, DBE, QC
Anglesey, The Marchioness of, DBE
Anson, Lady (Elizabeth Audrey), DBE
Anstee, Dame Margaret Joan, DCMG
Arden, *Rt. Hon.* Dame Mary Howarth (Mrs Mance), DBE
Atkins, Dame Eileen, DBE
Bacon, Dame Patricia Anne, DBE
Baker, Dame Janet Abbott (Mrs Shelley), CH, DBE
Barbour, Dame Margaret (Mrs Ash), DBE
Baron, *Hon.* Dame Florence Jacqueline, DBE
Barrow, Dame Jocelyn Anita (Mrs Downer), DBE
Barstow, Dame Josephine Clare (Mrs Anderson), DBE
Bassey, Dame Shirley, DBE
Beasley, *Prof.* Dame Christine Joan, DBE
Beaurepaire, Dame Beryl Edith, DBE
Beer, *Prof.* Dame Gillian Patricia Kempster, DBE, FBA
Begg, Dame Anne, DBE

Beral, *Prof.* Dame Valerie, DBE
Bertschinger, *Dr* Dame Claire, DBE
Bevan, Dame Yasmin, DBE
Bewley, Dame Beulah Rosemary, DBE
Bibby, Dame Enid, DBE
Black, *Prof.* Dame Carol Mary, DBE
Black, *Rt. Hon.* Dame Jill Margaret, DBE
Blackadder, Dame Elizabeth Violet, DBE
Blaize, Dame Venetia Ursula, DBE
Blaxland, Dame Helen Frances, DBE
Blume, Dame Hilary Sharon Braverman, DBE
Booth, *Hon.* Dame Margaret Myfanwy Wood, DBE
Bowtell, Dame Ann Elizabeth, DCB
Boyd, Dame Vivienne Myra, DBE
Brain, Dame Margaret Anne (Mrs Wheeler), DBE
Brennan, Dame Maureen, DBE
Brewer, *Dr* Dame Nicola Mary, DCMG
Bridges, Dame Mary Patricia, DBE
Brindley, Dame Lynne Janie, DBE
Brittan, Dame Diana (Lady Brittan of Spennithorne), DBE
Browne, Lady Moyra Blanche Madeleine, DBE
Buckland, Dame Yvonne Helen Elaine, DBE
Burnell, *Prof.* Dame Susan Jocelyn Bell, DBE
Burslem, Dame Alexandra Vivien, DBE
Byatt, Dame Antonia Susan, DBE, FRSL
Bynoe, Dame Hilda Louisa, DBE
Caldicott, Dame Fiona, DBE, FRCP, FRCPSYCH
Cameron, *Prof.* Dame Averil Millicent, DBE
Campbell-Preston, Dame Frances Olivia, DCVO
Carnall, Dame Ruth, DBE
Cartwright, Dame Silvia Rose, DBE
Clark, *Prof.* Dame Jill MacLeod, DBE
Clark, *Prof.* Dame (Margaret) June, DBE, PHD
Cleverdon, Dame Julia Charity, DCVO, CBE
Collarbone, Dame Patricia, DBE
Contreras, *Prof.* Dame Marcela, DBE
Corsar, *Hon.* Dame Mary Drummond, DBE
Coward, Dame Pamela Sarah, DBE
Cox, *Hon.* Dame Laura Mary, DBE
Cramp, *Prof.* Dame Rosemary Jean, DBE
Dacon, Dame Monica Jessie, DBE, CMG
Davies, *Prof.* Dame Kay Elizabeth, DBE
Davies, *Hon.* Dame Nicola Velfor, DBE
Davies, *Prof.* Dame Sally Claire, DBE
Davies, Dame Wendy Patricia, DBE
Davis, Dame Karlene Cecile, DBE
Dawson, *Prof.* Dame Sandra Jane Noble, DBE
Dell, Dame Miriam Patricia, DBE
Dench, Dame Judith Olivia (Mrs Williams), CH, DBE
Descartes, Dame Marie Selipha Sesenne, DBE, BEM
Devonshire, The Duchess of, DCVO
Digby, Lady, DBE
Dobbs, *Hon.* Dame Linda Penelope, DBE
Docherty, Dame Jacqueline, DBE
Donald, *Prof.* Dame Athene Margaret, DBE, FRS
Dowling, *Prof.* Dame Ann Patricia, DBE
Duffield, Dame Vivien Louise, DBE
Dumont, Dame Ivy Leona, DCMG
Dunnell, Dame Karen, DCB

Nelson, *Prof.* Dame Janet Laughland, DBE
Neville, Dame Elizabeth, DBE, QPM
Ogilvie, Dame Bridget Margaret, DBE, PHD, DSC
Oliver, Dame Gillian Frances, DBE
Ollerenshaw, Dame Kathleen Mary, DBE, DPHIL
Owers, Dame Anne Elizabeth (Mrs Cook), DBE
Oxenbury, Dame Shirley Anne, DBE
Palmer, Dame Felicity Joan, DBE
Paraskeva, *Rt. Hon.* Dame Janet, DBE
Park, Dame Merle Florence (Mrs Bloch), DBE
Parker, *Hon.* Dame Judith Mary Frances, DBE
Partridge, *Prof.* Dame Linda, DBE
Patel, Dame Indira, DBE
Pauffley, *Hon.* Dame Anna Evelyn Hamilton, DBE
Penhaligon, Dame Annette (Mrs Egerton), DBE
Perkins, Dame Mary Lesley, DBE
Peters, Dame Mary Elizabeth, DBE
Pindling, Lady (Marguerite M.), DCMG
Platt, Dame Denise, DBE
Plowright, Dame Joan Ann, DBE
Polak, *Prof.* Dame Julia Margaret, DBE
Poole, Dame Avril Anne Barker, DBE
Porter, Dame Shirley (Lady Porter), DBE
Powell, Dame Sally Ann Vickers, DBE
Prendergast, Dame Simone Ruth, DBE
Pringle, Dame Anne Fyfe, DCMG
Proudman, *Hon.* Dame Sonia Rosemary Susan, DBE
Pugh, *Dr* Dame Gillian Mary, DBE
Quinn, Dame Sheila Margaret Imelda, DBE
Rafferty, *Hon.* Dame Anne Judith, DBE
Rawson, *Prof.* Dame Jessica Mary, DBE
Rebuck, Dame Gail Ruth, DBE
Rees, *Prof.* Dame Lesley Howard, DBE
Reeves, Dame Helen May, DBE
Rego, Dame Paula Figueiroa, DBE
Reynolds, Dame Fiona Claire, DBE
Richardson, Dame Mary, DBE
Rigg, Dame Diana, DBE
Rimington, Dame Stella, DCB
Ritterman, Dame Janet, DBE
Roberts, Dame Jane Elisabeth, DBE
Robins, Dame Ruth Laura, DBE
Robottom, Dame Marlene, DBE
Roe, Dame Marion Audrey, DBE
Roe, Dame Raigh Edith, DBE
Ronson, Dame Gail, DBE
Rothwell, *Prof.* Dame Nancy Jane, DBE
Runciman of Doxford, The Viscountess, DBE
Russell, *Dr* Dame Philippa Margaret, DBE
Salas, Dame Margaret Laurence, DBE
Salmond, *Prof.* Dame Mary Anne, DBE
Savill, Dame Rosalind Joy, DBE
Sawyer, *Rt. Hon.* Dame Joan Augusta, DBE
Scardino, Dame Marjorie, DBE
Scott, Dame Catherine Margaret (Mrs Denton), DBE
Seward, Dame Margaret Helen Elizabeth, DBE
Sharp, *Hon.* Dame Victoria Madeleine, DBE
Shedrick, *Dr* Dame Daphne Marjorie, DBE
Shirley, Dame Stephanie, DBE
Shovelton, Dame Helena, DBE
Sibley, Dame Antoinette (Mrs Corbett), DBE

Silver, *Dr* Dame Ruth Muldoon, DBE
Slade, *Hon.* Dame Elizabeth Ann, DBE
Smith, Dame Dela, DBE
Smith, *Rt. Hon.* Dame Janet Hilary (Mrs Mathieson), DBE
Smith, *Hon.* Dame Jennifer Meredith, DBE
Smith, Dame Margaret Natalie (Maggie) (Mrs Cross), DBE
Soames, Lady Mary, KG, DBE
Southgate, *Prof.* Dame Lesley Jill, DBE
Spencer, Dame Rosemary Jane, DCMG
Steel, *Hon.* Dame (Anne) Heather (Mrs Beattie), DBE
Stocking, Dame Barbara Mary, DBE
Strachan, Dame Valerie Patricia Marie, DCB
Strathern, *Prof.* Dame Anne Marilyn, DBE
Strathie, Dame Lesley Ann, DCB
Street, Dame Susan Ruth, DCB
Stringer, *Prof.* Dame Joan Kathleen, DBE
Sutherland, Dame Veronica Evelyn, DBE, CMG
Suzman, Dame Janet, DBE
Swift, *Hon.* Dame Caroline Jane (Mrs Openshaw), DBE, QC
Symmonds, Dame Olga Patricia, DBE
Tanner, *Dr* Dame Mary Elizabeth, DBE
Taylor, Dame Meg, DBE
Te Kanawa, Dame Kiri Janette, DBE
Theis, *Hon.* Dame Lucy Morgan, DBE
Thirlwall, *Hon.* Dame Kathryn Mary, DBE
Thomas, *Prof.* Dame Jean Olwen, DBE
Thomas, Dame Maureen Elizabeth (Lady Thomas), DBE
Tickell, Dame Clare Oriana, DBE
Tinson, Dame Sue, DBE
Tizard, Dame Catherine Anne, GCMG, GCVO, DBE
Tokiel, Dame Rosa, DBE
Trotter, Dame Janet Olive, DBE
Turner-Warwick, Dame Margaret Elizabeth Harvey, DBE, FRCP, FRCPED
Twelftree, Dame Marcia, DBE
Uchida, Dame Mitsuko, DBE
Uprichard, Dame Mary Elizabeth, DBE
Varley, Dame Joan Fleetwood, DBE
Wagner, Dame Gillian Mary Millicent (Lady Wagner), DBE
Wall, Dame (Alice) Anne, (Mrs Michael Wall), DCVO
Wallace, *Prof.* Dame Helen Sarah, DBE, CMG
Wallis, Dame Sheila Ann, DBE
Walter, Dame Harriet Mary, DBE
Warburton, Dame Anne Marion, DCVO, CMG
Waterhouse, *Dr* Dame Rachel Elizabeth, DBE
Waterman, *Dr* Dame Fanny, DBE
Webb, *Prof.* Dame Patricia, DBE
Weir, Dame Gillian Constance (Mrs Phelps), DBE
Weller, Dame Rita, DBE
Weston, Dame Margaret Kate, DBE
Westwood, Dame Vivienne Isabel, DBE
Wheldon, Dame Juliet Louise, DCB, QC
Williams, Dame Josephine, DBE
Wilson, Dame Jacqueline, DBE
Wilson-Barnett, *Prof.* Dame Jenifer, DBE
Winstone, Dame Dorothy Gertrude, DBE, CMG
Wong Yick-ming, Dame Rosanna, DBE
Zaffar, Dame Naila, DBE

DECORATIONS AND MEDALS

PRINCIPAL DECORATIONS AND MEDALS
IN ORDER OF WEAR

VICTORIA CROSS (VC), 1856 (see below)
GEORGE CROSS (GC), 1940 (see below)

BRITISH ORDERS OF KNIGHTHOOD (see also Orders of
Chivalry)
Order of the Garter
Order of the Thistle
Order of St Patrick
Order of the Bath
Order of Merit
Order of the Star of India
Order of St Michael and George
Order of the Indian Empire
Order of the Crown of India
Royal Victorian Order (Classes I, II and III)
Order of the British Empire (Classes I, II and III)
Order of the Companions of Honour
Distinguished Service Order
Royal Victorian Order (Class IV)
Order of the British Empire (Class IV)
Imperial Service Order
Royal Victorian Order (Class V)
Order of the British Empire (Class V)

BARONET'S BADGE

KNIGHT BACHELOR'S BADGE

INDIAN ORDER OF MERIT (MILITARY)

DECORATIONS
Conspicuous Gallantry Cross (CGC), 1995
Royal Red Cross Class I (RRC), 1883
Distinguished Service Cross (DSC), 1914
Military Cross (MC), December 1914
Distinguished Flying Cross (DFC), 1918
Air Force Cross (AFC), 1918
Royal Red Cross Class II (ARRC)
Order of British India
Kaisar-i-Hind Medal
Order of St John

MEDALS FOR GALLANTRY AND DISTINGUISHED
CONDUCT
Union of South Africa Queen's Medal for Bravery, in Gold
Distinguished Conduct Medal (DCM), 1854
Conspicuous Gallantry Medal (CGM), 1874
Conspicuous Gallantry Medal (Flying)
George Medal (GM), 1940
Queen's Police Medal for Gallantry
Queen's Fire Service Medal for Gallantry
Royal West African Frontier Force Distinguished Conduct
  Medal
King's African Rifles Distinguished Conduct Medal
Indian Distinguished Service Medal
Union of South Africa Queen's Medal for Bravery, in Silver
Distinguished Service Medal (DSM), 1914
Military Medal (MM), 1916

Distinguished Flying Medal (DFM), 1918
Air Force Medal (AFM)
Constabulary Medal (Ireland)
Medal for Saving Life at Sea (Sea Gallantry Medal)
Indian Order of Merit (Civil)
Indian Police Medal for Gallantry
Ceylon Police Medal for Gallantry
Sierra Leone Police Medal for Gallantry
Sierra Leone Fire Brigades Medal for Gallantry
Colonial Police Medal for Gallantry (CPM)
Queen's Gallantry Medal (QGM), 1974
Royal Victorian Medal (RVM), Gold, Silver and Bronze
British Empire Medal (BEM)
Canada Medal
Queen's Police Medal for Distinguished Service (QPM)
Queen's Fire Service Medal for Distinguished Service
  (QFSM)
Queen's Volunteer Reserves Medal
Queen's Medal for Chiefs

CAMPAIGN MEDALS AND STARS
  Including authorised United Nations, European
  Community/Union and North Atlantic Treaty
  Organisation medals (in order of date of campaign for
  which awarded)

POLAR MEDALS (in order of date)

IMPERIAL SERVICE MEDAL

POLICE MEDALS FOR VALUABLE SERVICE
Indian Police Medal for Meritorious Service
Ceylon Police Medal for Merit
Sierra Leone Police Medal for Meritorious Service
Sierra Leone Fire Brigades Medal for Meritorious Service
Colonial Police Medal for Meritorious Service

BADGE OF HONOUR

JUBILEE, CORONATION AND DURBAR MEDALS
Queen Victoria, King Edward VII, King George V, King
  George VI, Queen Elizabeth II, Visit Commemoration and
  Long and Faithful Service Medals

EFFICIENCY AND LONG SERVICE DECORATIONS AND
MEDALS
Medal for Meritorious Service
Accumulated Campaign Service Medal
Medal for Long Service and Good Conduct (Military)
Naval Long Service and Good Conduct Medal
Medal for Meritorious Service (Royal Navy 1918–28)
Indian Long Service and Good Conduct Medal
Indian Meritorious Service Medal
Royal Marines Meritorious Service Medal (1849–1947)
Royal Air Force Meritorious Service Medal (1918–1928)
Royal Air Force Long Service and Good Conduct Medal
Medal for Long Service and Good Conduct (Ulster Defence
  Regiment)
Indian Long Service and Good Conduct Medal
Royal West African Frontier Force Long Service and Good
  Conduct Medal

Royal Sierra Leone Military Forces Long Service and Good
    Conduct Medal
King's African Rifles Long Service and Good Conduct
    Medal
Indian Meritorious Service Medal
Police Long Service and Good Conduct Medal
Fire Brigade Long Service and Good Conduct Medal
African Police Medal for Meritorious Service
Royal Canadian Mounted Police Long Service Medal
Ceylon Police Long Service Medal
Ceylon Fire Services Long Service Medal
Sierra Leone Police Long Service Medal
Colonial Police Long Service Medal
Sierra Leone Fire Brigades Long Service Medal
Mauritius Police Long Service and Good Conduct Medal
Mauritius Fire Services Long Service and Good Conduct
    Medal
Mauritius Prisons Service Long Service and Good Conduct
    Medal
Colonial Fire Brigades Long Service Medal
Colonial Prison Service Medal
Hong Kong Disciplined Services Medal
Army Emergency Reserve Decoration (ERD)
Volunteer Officers' Decoration (VD)
Volunteer Long Service Medal
Volunteer Officers' Decoration (for India and the Colonies)
Volunteer Long Service Medal (for India and the Colonies)
Colonial Auxiliary Forces Officers' Decoration
Colonial Auxiliary Forces Long Service Medal
Medal for Good Shooting (Naval)
Militia Long Service Medal
Imperial Yeomanry Long Service Medal
Territorial Decoration (TD), 1908
Ceylon Armed Services Long Service Medal
Efficiency Decoration (ED)
Territorial Efficiency Medal
Efficiency Medal
Special Reserve Long Service and Good Conduct Medal
Decoration for Officers of the Royal Navy Reserve (RD),
    1910
Decoration for Officers of the Royal Naval Volunteer Reserve
    (VRD)
Royal Naval Reserve Long Service and Good Conduct
    Medal
Royal Naval Volunteer Reserve Long Service and Good
    Conduct Medal
Royal Naval Auxiliary Sick Berth Reserve Long Service and
    Good Conduct Medal
Royal Fleet Reserve Long Service and Good Conduct Medal
Royal Naval Wireless Auxiliary Reserve Long Service and
    Good Conduct Medal
Royal Naval Auxiliary Service Medal
Air Efficiency Award (AE), 1942
Volunteer Reserves Service Medal
Ulster Defence Regiment Medal
Northern Ireland Home Service Medal
Queen's Medal (for Champion Shots of the RN and RM)
Queen's Medal (for Champion Shots of the New Zealand
    Naval Forces)
Queen's Medal (for Champion Shots in the Military
    Forces)
Queen's Medal (for Champion Shots of the Air Forces)
Cadet Forces Medal, 1950
Coastguard Auxiliary Service Long Service Medal
Special Constabulary Long Service Medal
Canadian Forces Decoration
Royal Observer Corps Medal
Civil Defence Long Service Medal

Ambulance Service (Emergency Duties) Long Service and
    Good Conduct Medal
Royal Fleet Auxiliary Service Medal
Prison Services (Operational Duties) Long Service and Good
    Conduct Medal
Rhodesia Medal
Royal Ulster Constabulary Service Medal
Northern Ireland Prison Service Medal
Union of South Africa Commemoration Medal
Indian Independence Medal
Pakistan Medal
Ceylon Armed Services Inauguration Medal
Ceylon Police Independence Medal (1948)
Sierra Leone Independence Medal
Jamaica Independence Medal
Uganda Independence Medal
Malawi Independence Medal
Fiji Independence Medal
Papua New Guinea Independence Medal
Solomon Islands Independence Medal
Service Medal of the Order of St John
Badge of the Order of the League of Mercy
Voluntary Medical Service Medal (1932)
Women's Royal Voluntary Service Medal
South African Medal for War Services
Colonial Special Constabulary Medal

HONORARY MEMBERSHIP OF COMMONWEALTH
ORDERS

OTHER COMMONWEALTH MEMBERS' ORDERS,
DECORATIONS AND MEDALS

FOREIGN ORDERS

FOREIGN DECORATIONS

FOREIGN MEDALS

THE VICTORIA CROSS (1856)
FOR CONSPICUOUS BRAVERY

VC

Ribbon, Crimson, for all Services (until 1918 it was blue
for the Royal Navy)

Instituted on 29 January 1856, the Victoria Cross was
awarded retrospectively to 1854, the first being held by
Lt. C. D. Lucas, RN, for bravery in the Baltic Sea on
21 June 1854 (gazetted 24 February 1857). The first 62
crosses were presented by Queen Victoria in Hyde Park,
London, on 26 June 1857.
    The Victoria Cross is worn before all other decorations,
on the left breast, and consists of a cross-pattée of bronze,
3.8cm in diameter, with the royal crown surmounted by a
lion in the centre, and beneath there is the inscription *For
Valour*. Holders of the VC currently receive a tax-free
annuity of £1,500, irrespective of need or other
conditions. In 1911, the right to receive the cross was
extended to Indian soldiers, and in 1920 to matrons,
sisters and nurses, the staff of the nursing services and
other services pertaining to hospitals and nursing, and to
civilians of either sex regularly or temporarily under the

orders, direction or supervision of the naval, military, or air forces of the crown.

SURVIVING RECIPIENTS OF THE VICTORIA CROSS
as at 31 August 2011

Apiata, Cpl. B. H. (New Zealand Special Air Service)
2004 *Afghanistan*
Beharry, Pte. J. G. (Princess of Wales's Royal Regiment)
2005 *Iraq*
Cruickshank, Flt. Lt. J. A. (RAFVR)
1944 *World War*
Donaldson, *Trooper* M. G. S. (Australian Special Air Service)
2008 *Afghanistan*
Payne, *WO* K., DSC (USA) (Australian Army Training Team)
1969 *Vietnam*
Rambahadur Limbu, *Capt.,* MVO (10th Princess Mary's Gurkha Rifles)
1965 *Sarawak*
Roberts-Smith, Cpl. B (Australian Special Air Service)
2010 *Afghanistan*
Speakman-Pitts, *Sgt.* W. (Black Watch, attached KOSB)
1951 *Korea*

THE GEORGE CROSS (1940)
FOR GALLANTRY

GC

Ribbon, Dark blue, threaded through a bar adorned with laurel leaves
Instituted 24 September 1940 (with amendments, 3 November 1942)

The George Cross is worn before all other decorations (except the VC) on the left breast (when worn by a woman it may be worn on the left shoulder from a ribbon of the same width and colour fashioned into a bow). It consists of a plain silver cross with four equal limbs, the cross having in the centre a circular medallion bearing a design showing St George and the Dragon. The inscription *For Gallantry* appears round the medallion and in the angle of each limb of the cross is the royal cypher 'G VI' forming a circle concentric with the medallion. The reverse is plain and bears the name of the recipient and the date of the award. The cross is suspended by a ring from a bar adorned with laurel leaves on dark blue ribbon 3.8cm wide.

The cross is intended primarily for civilians; awards to the fighting services are confined to actions for which purely military honours are not normally granted. It is awarded only for acts of the greatest heroism or of the most conspicuous courage in circumstances of extreme danger. From 1 April 1965, holders of the cross have received a tax-free annuity, which is currently £1,500. The cross has twice been awarded collectively rather than to an individual: to Malta (1942) and the Royal Ulster Constabulary (1999).

In October 1971 all surviving holders of the Albert Medal and the Edward Medal exchanged those decorations for the George Cross.

SURVIVING RECIPIENTS OF THE GEORGE CROSS
as at 31 August 2011

If the recipient originally received the Albert Medal (AM) or the Edward Medal (EM), this is indicated by the initials in parentheses.

Archer, *Col.* B. S. T., GC, OBE, ERD, 1941
Bamford, J., GC, 1952
Beaton, J., GC, CVO, 1974
Butson, *Lt.-Col.* A. R. C., GC, CD, MD (AM), 1948
Croucher, *Lance Cpl.* M., GC, 2008
Finney, C., GC, 2003
Flintoff, H. H., GC (EM), 1944
Gledhill, A. J., GC, 1967
Gregson, J. S., GC (AM), 1943
Hughes, *WO2* K. S., GC, 2010
Johnson, *WO1 (SSM)* B., GC, 1990
Kinne, D. G., GC, 1954
Lowe, A. R., GC (AM), 1949
Norton, *Maj.* P. A., GC, 2006
Pratt, M. K., GC, 1978
Purves, Mrs M., GC (AM), 1949
Raweng, Awang anak, GC, 1951
Stevens, H. W., GC, 1958
Walker, C., GC, 1972
Wooding, E. A., GC (AM), 1945

THE ELIZABETH CROSS (2009)

EC

Instituted 1 July 2009

The Elizabeth Cross consists of a silver cross with a laurel wreath passing between the arms, which bear the floral symbols of England (rose), Scotland (thistle), Ireland (shamrock) and Wales (daffodil). The centre of the cross bears the royal cypher and the reverse is inscribed with the name of the person for whom it is in honour. The cross is accompanied by a memorial scroll and a miniature.

The cross was created to commemorate UK armed forces personnel who have died on operations or as a result of an act of terrorism. It may be granted to and worn by the next of kin of any eligible personnel who died from 1 January 1948 to date. It offers the wearer no precedence. Those that are eligible include the next of kin of personnel who died while serving on a medal earning operation, as a result of an act of terrorism, or on a non-medal earning operation where death was caused by the inherent high risk of the task.

The Elizabeth Cross is not intended as a posthumous medal for the fallen but as an emblem of national recognition of the loss and sacrifice made by the personnel and their families.

CHIEFS OF CLANS IN SCOTLAND

Only chiefs of whole Names or Clans are included, except certain special instances (marked *) who, though not chiefs of a whole Name, were or are for some reason (eg the Macdonald forfeiture) independent. Under decision (*Campbell-Gray*, 1950) that a bearer of a 'double or triple-barrelled' surname cannot be held chief of a part of such, several others cannot be included in the list at present.

THE ROYAL HOUSE: HM The Queen

AGNEW: Sir Crispin Agnew of Lochnaw, Bt., QC
ANSTRUTHER: Tobias Anstruther of Anstruther and Balcaskie
ARBUTHNOTT: Viscount of Arbuthnott, KT, CBE, DSC
BANNERMAN: Sir David Bannerman of Elsick, Bt.
BARCLAY: Peter C. Barclay of Towie Barclay and of that Ilk
BORTHWICK: Lord Borthwick
BOYLE: Earl of Glasgow
BRODIE: Alexander Brodie of Brodie
BROUN OF COLSTOUN: Sir Wayne Broun of Colstoun, Bt.
BRUCE: Earl of Elgin and Kincardine, KT
BUCHAN: David Buchan of Auchmacoy
BURNETT: J. C. A. Burnett of Leys
CAMERON: Donald Cameron of Lochiel
CAMPBELL: Duke of Argyll
CARMICHAEL: Richard Carmichael of Carmichael
CARNEGIE: Duke of Fife
CATHCART: Earl Cathcart
CHARTERIS: Earl of Wemyss and March
CLAN CHATTAN: K. Mackintosh of Clan Chattan
CHISHOLM: Hamish Chisholm of Chisholm (*The Chisholm*)
COCHRANE: Earl of Dundonald
COLQUHOUN: Sir Malcolm Rory Colquhoun of Luss, Bt.
CRANSTOUN: David Cranstoun of that Ilk
CUMMING: Sir Alastair Cumming of Altyre, Bt.
DARROCH: Capt. Duncan Darroch of Gourock
DEWAR: Michael Dewar of that Ilk and Vogrie
DRUMMOND: Earl of Perth
DUNBAR: Sir James Dunbar of Mochrum, Bt.
DUNDAS: David Dundas of Dundas
DURIE: Andrew Durie of Durie, CBE
ELIOTT: Mrs Margaret Eliott of Redheugh
ERSKINE: Earl of Mar and Kellie
FARQUHARSON: Capt. A. Farquharson of Invercauld, MC
FERGUSSON: Sir Charles Fergusson of Kilkerran, Bt.
FORBES: Lord Forbes, KBE
FORSYTH: Alistair Forsyth of that Ilk
FRASER: Lady Saltoun
*FRASER (OF LOVAT): Lord Lovat
GAYRE: R. Gayre of Gayre and Nigg
GORDON: Marquess of Huntly
GRAHAM: Duke of Montrose
GRANT: Lord Strathspey
GUTHRIE: Alexander Guthrie of Guthrie
HAIG: Earl Haig

HALDANE: Martin Haldane of Gleneagles
HANNAY: David Hannay of Kirkdale and of that Ilk
HAY: Earl of Erroll
HENDERSON: Alistair Henderson of Fordell
HUNTER: Pauline Hunter of Hunterston
IRVINE OF DRUM: David Irvine of Drum
JARDINE: Sir William Jardine of Applegirth, Bt.
JOHNSTONE: Earl of Annandale and Hartfell
KEITH: Earl of Kintore
KENNEDY: Marquess of Ailsa
KERR: Marquess of Lothian, PC
KINCAID: Madam Arabella Kincaid of Kincaid
LAMONT: Revd Peter Lamont of that Ilk
LEASK: Jonathan Leask of that Ilk
LENNOX: Edward Lennox of that Ilk
LESLIE: Earl of Rothes
LINDSAY: Earl of Crawford and Balcarres, KT, GCVO, PC
LIVINGSTONE (or MACLEA): Niall Livingstone of the Bachuil
LOCKHART: Angus Lockhart of the Lee
LUMSDEN: Gillem Lumsden of that Ilk and Blanerne
MACALESTER: William St J. McAlester of Loup and Kennox
MACARTHUR; John MacArthur of that Ilk
MCBAIN: J. H. McBain of McBain
MACDONALD: Lord Macdonald (*The Macdonald of Macdonald*)
*MACDONALD OF CLANRANALD: Ranald Macdonald of Clanranald
*MACDONALD OF KEPPOCH: Ranald MacDonald of Keppoch
*MACDONALD OF SLEAT (CLAN HUSTEAIN): Sir Ian Macdonald of Sleat, Bt.
*MACDONELL OF GLENGARRY: Ranald MacDonell of Glengarry
MACDOUGALL: Morag MacDougall of MacDougall
MACDOWALL: Fergus Macdowall of Garthland
MACGREGOR: Sir Malcolm MacGregor of MacGregor, Bt.
MACINTYRE: Donald MacIntyre of Glenoe
MACKAY: Lord Reay
MACKENZIE: Earl of Cromartie
MACKINNON: Anne Mackinnon of Mackinnon
MACKINTOSH: John Mackintosh of Mackintosh (*The Mackintosh of Mackintosh*)
MACLACHLAN: Euan MacLachlan of MacLachlan
MACLAREN: Donald MacLaren of MacLaren and Achleskine
MACLEAN: Hon. Sir Lachlan Maclean of Duart, Bt., CVO
MACLENNAN: Ruaraidh MacLennan of MacLennan
MACLEOD: Hugh MacLeod of MacLeod
MACMILLAN: George MacMillan of MacMillan
MACNAB: J. C. Macnab of Macnab (*The Macnab*)
MACNAGHTEN: Sir Malcolm Macnaghten of Macnaghten and Dundarave, Bt.
MACNEACAIL: John Macneacail of Macneacail and Scorrybreac
MACNEIL OF BARRA: Rory Macneil of Barra (*The Macneil of Barra*)

MACPHERSON: Hon. Sir William Macpherson of
  Cluny, TD
MACTAVISH: Steven MacTavish of Dunardry
MACTHOMAS: Andrew MacThomas of Finegand
MAITLAND: Earl of Lauderdale
MAKGILL: Viscount of Oxfuird
MALCOLM (MACCALLUM): Robin N. L. Malcolm of
  Poltalloch
MAR: Countess of Mar
MARJORIBANKS: Andrew Marjoribanks of that Ilk
MATHESON: Maj. Sir Fergus Matheson of Matheson, Bt.
MENZIES: David Menzies of Menzies
MOFFAT: Madam Moffat of that Ilk
MONCREIFFE: Hon. Peregrine Moncreiffe of that Ilk
MONTGOMERIE: Earl of Eglinton and Winton
MORRISON: Dr Iain Morrison of Ruchdi
MUNRO: Hector Munro of Foulis
MURRAY: Duke of Atholl
NESBITT (or NISBET): Mark Nesbitt of that Ilk
OGILVY: Earl of Airlie, KT, GCVO, PC
OLIPHANT: Richard Oliphant of that Ilk
RAMSAY: Earl of Dalhousie

RIDDELL: Sir Walter Riddell of Riddell, Bt.
ROBERTSON: Alexander Robertson of Struan
  (Struan-Robertson)
ROLLO: Lord Rollo
ROSE: Miss Elizabeth Rose of Kilravock
ROSS: David Ross of that Ilk and Balnagowan
RUTHVEN: Earl of Gowrie, PC
SCOTT: Duke of Buccleuch and Queensberry, KBE
SCRYMGEOUR: Earl of Dundee
SEMPILL: Lord Sempill
SHAW: John Shaw of Tordarroch
SINCLAIR: Earl of Caithness
SKENE: Danus Skene of Skene
STIRLING: Fraser Stirling of Cader
STRANGE: Maj. Timothy Strange of Balcaskie
SUTHERLAND: Countess of Sutherland
SWINTON: John Swinton of that Ilk
TROTTER: Alexander Trotter of Mortonhall
URQUHART: Kenneth Urquhart of Urquhart
WALLACE: Ian Wallace of that Ilk
WEDDERBURN: Master of Dundee
WEMYSS: Michael Wemyss of that Ilk

THE PRIVY COUNCIL

The sovereign in council, or Privy Council, was the chief source of executive power until the system of cabinet government developed in the 18th century. Now the Privy Council's main functions are to advise the sovereign and to exercise its own statutory responsibilities independent of the sovereign in council.

Membership of the Privy Council is automatic upon appointment to certain government and judicial positions in the UK, eg cabinet ministers must be Privy Counsellors and are sworn in on first assuming office. Membership is also accorded by the Queen to eminent people in the UK and independent countries of the Commonwealth of which she is Queen, on the recommendation of the prime minister. Membership of the council is retained for life, except for very occasional removals.

The administrative functions of the Privy Council are carried out by the Privy Council Office under the direction of the president of the council, who is always a member of the cabinet. (*See also* Parliament)

President of the Council, Rt. Hon. Nick Clegg
Clerk of the Council, Judith Simpson

Style The Right (or Rt.) Hon._
    Envelope, The Right (or Rt.) Hon. F_ S_
    Letter, Dear Mr/Miss/Mrs S_
    *Spoken, Mr/Miss/Mrs S_*
It is incorrect to use the letters PC after the name in conjunction with the prefix The Rt. Hon., unless the Privy Counsellor is a peer below the rank of Marquess and so is styled The Rt. Hon. because of his/her rank.

MEMBERS *as at August 2011*

HRH The Duke of Edinburgh, 1951
HRH The Prince of Wales, 1977

Abernethy, *Hon.* Lord (Alastair Cameron), 2005
Adonis, Lord, 2009
Aikens, Sir Richard, 2008
Ainsworth, Robert, 2005
Airlie, Earl of, 1984
Aldous, Sir William, 1995
Alebua, Ezekiel, 1988
Alexander, Douglas, 2005
Alexander, Danny, 2010
Amos, Baroness, 2003
Anderson of Swansea, Lord, 2000
Anelay of St Johns, Baroness, 2009
Angiolini, Dame Elish, 2006
Anthony, Douglas, 1971
Arbuthnot, James, 1998
Archer of Sandwell, Lord, 1977
Arden, Dame Mary, 2000
Armstrong of Hill Top, Baroness, 1999
Arthur, *Hon.* Owen, 1995
Ashdown of Norton-sub-Hamdon, Lord, 1989
Ashley of Stoke, Lord, 1979
Ashton of Upholland, Baroness, 2006
Atkins, Sir Robert, 1995
Auld, Sir Robin, 1995
Baker, Sir Thomas, 2002
Baker of Dorking, Lord, 1984
Balls, Ed, 2007
Bannside, Lord, 2005
Barnett, Lord, 1975
Barron, Kevin, 2001
Bassam of Brighton, Lord, 2009
Battle, John, 2002
Beckett, Margaret, 1993
Beith, Sir Alan, 1992
Beldam, Sir Roy, 1989
Benn, Anthony, 1964
Benn, Hilary, 2003
Bercow, John, 2009

Birch, William, 1992
Black, Dame Jill, 2011
Blackstone, Baroness, 2001
Blair, Anthony, 1994
Blanchard, Peter, 1998
Blears, Hazel, 2005
Blencathra, Lord, 1995
Blunkett, David, 1997
Boateng, Lord, 1999
Bolger, James, 1991
Bonomy, *Hon.* Lord (Iain Bonomy), 2010
Boothroyd, Baroness, 1992
Boscawen, *Hon.* Robert, 1992
Bottomley of Nettlestone, Baroness, 1992
Boyd of Duncansby, Lord, 2000
Boyson, Sir Rhodes, 1987
Bradley, Lord, 2001
Bradshaw, Ben, 2009
Brake, Thomas, 2011
Brathwaite, Sir Nicholas, 1991
Brittan of Spennithorne, Lord, 1981
Brooke, Sir Henry, 1996
Brooke of Sutton Mandeville, Lord, 1988
Brown, Gordon, 1996
Brown, Nicholas, 1997
Brown, Sir Stephen, 1983
Brown of Eaton-under-Heywood, Lord, 1992
Browne of Ladyton, Lord, 2005
Browne-Wilkinson, Lord, 1983
Bruce, Malcolm, 2006
Burnham, Andy, 2007
Burns, Simon, 2011
Burnton, Sir Stanley, 2008
Butler of Brockwell, Lord, 2004
Butler-Sloss, Baroness, 1988
Buxton, Sir Richard, 1997
Byers, Stephen, 1998
Byrne, Liam, 2008
Byron, Sir Dennis, 2004
Cable, Vincent, 2010
Caborn, Richard, 1999

Caithness, Earl of, 1990
Cameron, David, 2005
Cameron of Lochbroom, Lord, 1984
Camoys, Lord, 1997
Campbell, Sir Walter Menzies, 1999
Campbell, Sir William, 1999
Canterbury, Archbishop of, 2002
Carey of Clifton, Lord, 1991
Carloway, *Hon.* Lord (Colin Sutherland), 2008
Carmichael, Alistair, 2010
Carnwath, Sir Robert, 2002
Carr of Hadley, Lord, 1963
Carrington, Lord, 1959
Carswell, Lord, 1993
Casey, Sir Maurice, 1986
Chadwick, Sir John, 1997
Chalfont, Lord, 1964
Chalker of Wallasey, Baroness, 1987
Chan, Sir Julius, 1981
Chataway, Sir Christopher, 1970
Chilcot, Sir John, 2004
Christie, Perry, 2004
Clark, Greg, 2010
Clark, Helen, 1990
Clark of Windermere, Lord, 1997
Clarke, Charles, 2001
Clarke, Kenneth, 1984
Clarke, *Hon.* Lord (Matthew Clarke), 2008
Clarke, Thomas, 1997
Clarke of Stone-Cum-Ebony, Lord, 1998
Clegg, Nicholas, 2008
Clinton-Davis, Lord, 1998
Clwyd, Ann, 2004
Coghlin, Sir Patrick, 2009
Collins of Mapesbury, Lord, 2007
Cooper, Yvette, 2007
Cope of Berkeley, Lord, 1988
Corston, Baroness, 2003
Cosgrove, *Hon.* Lady (Hazel Cosgrove), 2003

Laws, David, 2010
Laws, Sir John, 1999
Lawson of Blaby, Lord, 1981
Leggatt, Sir Andrew, 1990
Letwin, Oliver, 2002
Leveson, Sir Brian, 2006
Liddell of Coatdyke, Baroness, 1998
Lidington, David, 2010
Lilley, Peter, 1990
Lloyd of Berwick, Lord, 1984
Lloyd, Sir Peter, 1994
Lloyd, Sir Timothy, 2005
Llwyd, Elfyn, 2011
London, Bishop of, 1995
Longmore, Sir Andrew, 2001
Luce, Lord, 1986
Lyne, Sir Roderic, 2009
McAvoy, Lord, 2003
McCartney, Sir Ian, 1999
McCollum, Sir Liam, 1997
McConnell of Glenscorrodale, Lord, 2001
MacDermott, Sir John, 1987
Macdonald of Tradeston, Lord, 1999
McFadden, Patrick, 2008
McFall of Alcluith, Lord, 2004
MacGregor of Pulham Market, Lord, 1985
McGuire, Anne, 2008
Mackay, Andrew, 1998
McKay, Sir Ian, 1992
Mackay of Clashfern, Lord, 1979
Mackay of Drumadoon, Lord, 1996
McKinnon, Sir Donald, 1992
Maclean, Hon. Lord (Ranald MacLean), 2001
McLeish, Henry, 2000
Maclennan of Rogart, Lord, 1997
McLoughlin, Patrick, 2005
McMullin, Sir Duncan, 1980
McNally, Lord, 2005
McNulty, Anthony, 2007
MacShane, Denis, 2005
Major, Sir John, 1987
Malloch-Brown, Lord, 2007
Mance, Lord, 1999
Mandelson, Lord, 1998
Marnoch, Hon. Lord (Michael Marnoch), 2001
Martin of Springburn, Lord, 2000
Mason of Barnsley, Lord, 1968
Mates, Michael, 2004
Maude, Hon. Francis, 1992
Mawhinney, Lord, 1994
May, Sir Anthony, 1998
May, Theresa, 2003
Mayhew of Twysden, Lord, 1986
Meacher, Michael, 1997
Mellor, David, 1990
Michael, Alun, 1998
Milburn, Alan, 1998
Miliband, David, 2005
Miliband, Ed, 2007
Millan, Bruce, 1975
Millett, Lord, 1994
Mitchell, Andrew, 2010
Mitchell, Sir James, 1985
Mitchell, Dr Keith, 2004

Molyneaux of Killead, Lord, 1983
Moore, Michael, 1990
Moore, Michael, 2010
Moore of Lower Marsh, Lord, 1986
Moore-Bick, Sir Martin, 2005
Morgan, Sir Declan, 2009
Morgan, Rhodri, 2000
Morris, Charles, 1978
Morris of Aberavon, Lord, 1970
Morris of Manchester, Lord, 1979
Morris of Yardley, Baroness, 1999
Morritt, Sir Robert, 1994
Moses, Sir Alan, 2005
Moyle, Roland, 1978
Mulholland, Frank, 2011
Mummery, Sir John, 1996
Munby, Sir James, 2009
Mundell, David, 2010
Murphy, James, 2008
Murphy, Paul, 1999
Murray, Hon. Lord (Ronald Murray), 1974
Murray, Sir Donald, 1989
Musa, Wilbert, 2005
Mustill, Lord, 1985
Nairne, Sir Patrick, 1982
Namaliu, Sir Rabbie, 1989
Naseby, Lord, 1994
Needham, Sir Richard, 1994
Neill, Sir Brian, 1985
Neuberger of Abbotsbury, Lord, 2004
Neville-Jones, Baroness, 2010
Newton of Braintree, Lord, 1988
Nicholls of Birkenhead, Lord, 1995
Nicholson, Sir Michael, 1995
Nimmo Smith, Hon. Lord (William Nimmo Smith), 2005
Nott, Sir John, 1979
Nourse, Sir Martin, 1985
O'Brien, Mike, 2009
O'Donnell, Turlough, 1979
Oppenheim-Barnes, Baroness, 1979
Osborne, George, 2010
Osborne, Hon. Lord (Kenneth Osborne), 2001
Otton, Sir Philip, 1995
Owen, Lord, 1976
Paeniu, Bikenibeu, 1991
Paice, James, 2010
Palliser, Sir Michael, 1983
Palmer, Sir Geoffrey, 1986
Paraskeva, Dame Janet, 2010
Parker, Sir Jonathan, 2000
Parkinson, Lord, 1981
Paterson, Owen, 2010
Paton, Hon. Lady (Ann Paton), 2007
Patten, Lord, 1990
Patten, Sir Nicholas, 2009
Patten of Barnes, Lord, 1989
Patterson, Percival, 1993
Pattie, Sir Geoffrey, 1987
Paul, Lord, 2009
Peel, Earl, 2006
Pendry, Lord, 2000
Penrose, Hon. Lord (George Penrose), 2000

Peters, Winston, 1998
Philip, Hon. Lord (Alexander Philip), 2005
Phillips of Worth Matravers, Lord, 1995
Pickles, Eric, 2010
Pill, Sir Malcolm, 1995
Pitchford, Sir Christopher, 2010
Portillo, Michael, 1992
Potter, Sir Mark, 1996
Prashar, Baroness, 2009
Prescott, Lord, 1994
Price, George, 1982
Primarolo, Dawn, 2002
Prior, Lord, 1970
Prosser, Hon. Lord (William Prosser), 2000
Puapua, Sir Tomasi, 1982
Purnell, James, 2007
Quin, Baroness, 1998
Radice, Lord, 1999
Raison, Sir Timothy, 1982
Ramsden, James, 1963
Randall, John, 2010
Raynsford, Nick, 2001
Redwood, John, 1993
Reed, Lord, 2008
Reid, George, 2004
Reid of Cardowan, Lord, 1998
Renton of Mount Harry, Lord, 1989
Richard, Lord, 1993
Richards, Sir Stephen, 2005
Richardson, Sir Ivor, 1978
Riddell, Peter, 2010
Rifkind, Sir Malcolm, 1986
Rimer, Sir Colin, 2007
Rix, Sir Bernard, 2000
Robathan, Andrew, 2010
Roberts of Conwy, Lord, 1991
Robertson of Port Ellen, Lord, 1997
Robinson, Peter, 2007
Roch, Sir John, 1993
Rodgers of Quarry Bank, Lord, 1975
Rooker, Lord, 1999
Roper, Lord, 2005
Rose, Sir Christopher, 1992
Ross, Hon. Lord (Donald MacArthur), 1985
Royall of Blaisdon, Baroness, 2008
Ruddock, Joan, 2010
Ryan, Joan, 2007
Ryder of Wensum, Lord, 1990
Sainsbury, Sir Timothy, 1992
St John of Fawsley, Lord, 1979
Salisbury, Marquess of, 1994
Salmond, Alex, 2007
Sandiford, Erskine, 1989
Saville of Newdigate, Lord, 1994
Sawyer, Dame Joan, 2004
Schiemann, Sir Konrad, 1995
Scotland of Asthal, Baroness, 2001
Scott of Foscote, Lord, 1991
Seaga, Edward, 1981
Sedley, Sir Stephen, 1999
Selkirk of Douglas, Lord, 1996
Shapps, Grant, 2010
Sheldon, Lord, 1977

Shephard of Northwold, Baroness, 1992
Sheil, Sir John, 2005
Shipley, Jennifer, 1998
Short, Clare, 1997
Shutt of Greetland, Lord, 2009
Simmonds, Kennedy Sir, 1984
Sinclair, Ian, 1977
Slade, Sir Christopher, 1982
Smith, Andrew, 1997
Smith, Dame Janet, 2002
Smith, Jacqueline, 2003
Smith of Basildon, Baroness, 2009
Smith of Finsbury, Lord, 1997
Soames, *Hon.* (Arthur) Nicholas, 2011
Somare, Sir Michael, 1977
Spellar, John, 2001
Spelman, Caroline, 2010
Stanley, Sir John, 1984
Staughton, Sir Christopher, 1988
Steel of Aikwood, Lord, 1977
Stephen, Sir Ninian, 1979
Stewartby, Lord, 1989
Steyn, Lord, 1992
Strang, Gavin, 1997
Strathclyde, Lord, 1995
Straw, Jack, 1997
Stuart-Smith, Sir Murray, 1988
Sullivan, Sir Jeremy, 2009
Sutherland, *Hon.* Lord (Ranald Sutherland), 2000
Swayne, Desmond, 2011
Swire, Hugo, 2010

Symons of Vernham Dean, Baroness, 2001
Talboys, Sir Brian, 1977
Tapsell, Sir Peter, 2011
Taylor of Bolton, Baroness, 1997
Tebbit, Lord, 1981
Templeman, Lord, 1978
Thatcher, Baroness, 1970
Thomas, Edmund, 1996
Thomas, Sir Roger, 2003
Thomas, Sir Swinton, 1994
Thorpe, Jeremy, 1967
Thorpe, Sir Matthew, 1995
Timms, Stephen, 2006
Tipping, Andrew, 1998
Tizard, Robert, 1986
Tomlinson, Sir Stephen, 2011
Touhig, Lord, 2006
Toulson, Sir Roger, 2007
Trefgarne, Lord, 1989
Trimble, Lord, 1997
Trumpington, Baroness, 1992
Tuckey, Sir Simon, 1998
Ullswater, Viscount, 1994
Upton, Simon, 1999
Vadera, Baroness, 2009
Vaz, Keith, 2006
Villiers, Theresa, 2010
Waddington, Lord, 1987
Waite, Sir John, 1993
Wakeham, Lord, 1983
Waldegrave of North Hill, Lord, 1990

Walker of Gestingthorpe, Lord, 1997
Wall, Sir Nicholas, 2004
Wallace of Tankerness, Lord, 2000
Waller, Sir Mark, 1996
Ward, Sir Alan, 1995
Warner, Lord, 2006
Warsi, Baroness, 2010
West of Spithead, Lord, 2010
Wheatley, *Hon.* Lord (John Wheatley), 2007
Wheeler, Sir John, 1993
Whitty, Lord, 2005
Wicks, Malcolm, 2008
Widdecombe, Ann, 1997
Wigley, Dafydd, 1997
Willetts, David, 2010
Williams, Alan, 1977
Williams of Crosby, Baroness, 1974
Williamson of Horton, Lord, 2007
Wills, Lord, 2008
Wilson, Brian, 2003
Wilson, Sir Nicholas, 2005
Winterton, Rosie, 2006
Wingti, Paias, 1987
Withers, Reginald, 1977
Woodhouse, Sir Owen, 1974
Woodward, Shaun, 2007
Woolf, Lord, 1986
York, Archbishop of, 2005
Young, Sir George, 1993
Young of Graffham, Lord, 1984
Zacca, Edward, 1992

PRIVY COUNCIL OF NORTHERN IRELAND

The Privy Council of Northern Ireland had responsibilities in Northern Ireland similar to those of the Privy Council in Great Britain until the Northern Ireland Act 1974. Membership of the Privy Council of Northern Ireland is retained for life. Since the Northern Ireland Constitution Act 1973 no further appointments have been made. The postnominal initials PC (NI) are used to differentiate its members from those of the Privy Council.

MEMBERS *as at August 2011*
Bailie, Robin, 1971
Bleakley, David, 1971
Dobson, John, 1969
Kilclooney, Lord, 1970
Porter, Sir Robert, 1969

PARLIAMENT

The United Kingdom constitution is not contained in any single document but has evolved over time, formed partly by statute, partly by common law and partly by convention. A constitutional monarchy, the UK is governed by ministers of the crown in the name of the sovereign, who is head both of the state and of the government.

The organs of government are the legislature (parliament), the executive and the judiciary. The executive comprises HM government (the cabinet and other ministers), government departments and local authorities (*see* Government Departments, Public Bodies and Local Government sections). The judiciary (*see* Law Courts and Offices section) pronounces on the law, both written and unwritten, interprets statutes and is responsible for the enforcement of the law; the judiciary is independent of both the legislature and the executive.

THE MONARCHY

The sovereign personifies the state and is, in law, an integral part of the legislature, head of the executive, head of the judiciary, commander-in-chief of all armed forces of the crown and supreme governor of the Church of England. In the Channel Islands and the Isle of Man, which are crown dependencies, the sovereign is represented by a lieutenant-governor. In the member states of the Commonwealth of which the sovereign is head of state, her representative is a governor-general; in UK overseas territories the sovereign is usually represented by a governor, who is responsible to the British government.

Although in practice the powers of the monarchy are now very limited, and restricted mainly to the advisory and ceremonial, there are important acts of government which require the participation of the sovereign. These include summoning, proroguing and dissolving parliament, giving royal assent to bills passed by parliament, appointing important office-holders, eg government ministers, judges, bishops and governors, conferring peerages, knighthoods and other honours, and granting pardon to a person wrongly convicted of a crime. The sovereign appoints the prime minister; by convention this office is held by the leader of the political party which enjoys, or can secure, a majority of votes in the House of Commons. In international affairs the sovereign as head of state has the power to declare war and make peace, to recognise foreign states and governments, to conclude treaties and to annex or cede territory. However, as the sovereign entrusts executive power to ministers of the crown and acts on the advice of her ministers, which she cannot ignore, royal prerogative powers are in practice exercised by ministers, who are responsible to parliament.

Ministerial responsibility does not diminish the sovereign's importance to the smooth working of government. She holds meetings of the Privy Council (*see* below), gives audiences to her ministers and other officials at home and overseas, receives accounts of cabinet decisions, reads dispatches and signs state papers; she must be informed and consulted on every aspect of national life; and she must show complete impartiality.

COUNSELLORS OF STATE

If the sovereign travels abroad for more than a few days or suffers from a temporary illness, it is necessary to appoint members of the royal family, known as counsellors of state, under letters patent to carry out the chief functions of the monarch, including the holding of Privy Councils and giving royal assent to acts passed by parliament. The normal procedure is to appoint three or four members of the royal family among those members remaining in the UK, provided they are over 21. There are currently five counsellors of state.

In the event of the sovereign on accession being under the age of 18 years, or by infirmity of mind or body, rendered incapable of performing the royal functions, provision is made for a regency.

THE PRIVY COUNCIL

The sovereign in council, or Privy Council, was the chief source of executive power until the system of cabinet government developed. Its main function today is to advise the sovereign on the approval of various statutory functions and acts of the royal prerogative. These powers are exercised through orders in council and royal proclamations, approved by the Queen at meetings of the Privy Council. The council is also able to exercise a number of statutory duties without approval from the sovereign, including powers of supervision over registering bodies for the medical and allied professions. These duties are exercised through orders of council.

Although appointment as a privy counsellor is for life, only those who are currently government ministers are involved in the day-to-day business of the council. A full council is summoned only on the death of the sovereign or when the sovereign announces his or her intention to marry. (For a full list of privy counsellors, *see* the Privy Council section.)

There are a number of advisory Privy Council committees whose meetings the sovereign does not attend. Some are prerogative committees, such as those dealing with legislative matters submitted by the legislatures of the Channel Islands and the Isle of Man or with applications for charters of incorporation; and some are provided for by statute, eg those for the universities of Oxford and Cambridge and some Scottish universities.

Administrative work is carried out by the Privy Council Office under the direction of the Lord President of the Council, a cabinet minister.

JUDICIAL COMMITTEE OF THE PRIVY COUNCIL
Supreme Court Building, Parliament Square, London SW1P 3BD
T 020-7960 1500 W www.jcpc.gov.uk

The Judicial Committee of the Privy Council is the court of final appeal from courts of the UK dependencies, courts of independent Commonwealth countries which have retained the right of appeal and courts of the Channel Islands and the Isle of Man. It also hears very occasional appeals from a number of ancient and ecclesiastical courts.

The committee is composed of privy counsellors who hold, or have held, high judicial office. Only three or five judges hear each case, and these are usually justices of the Supreme Court.

PARLIAMENT

Parliament is the supreme law-making authority and can legislate for the UK as a whole or for any parts of it separately (the Channel Islands and the Isle of Man are crown dependencies and are not part of the UK). The main functions of parliament are to pass laws, to enable the government to raise taxes and to scrutinise government policy and administration, particularly proposals for expenditure. International treaties and agreements are customarily presented to parliament before ratification.

Parliament can trace its roots to two characteristics of Anglo-Saxon rule: the *witan* (a meeting of the king, nobles and advisors) and the *moot* (county meetings where local matters were discussed). However, it was the parliament that Simon de Montfort called in 1265 that is accepted as the forerunner to modern parliament, as it included non-noble representatives from counties, cities and towns alongside the nobility. The nucleus of early parliaments at the beginning of the 14th century were the officers of the king's household and the king's judges, joined by such ecclesiastical and lay magnates as the king might summon to form a prototype 'House of Lords', and occasionally by the knights of the shires, burgesses and proctors of the lower clergy. By the end of Edward III's reign a 'House of Commons' was beginning to appear; the first known Speaker was elected in 1377.

Parliamentary procedure is based on custom and precedent, partly formulated in the standing orders of both houses of parliament. Each house has the right to control its own internal proceedings and to commit for contempt. The system of debate in the two houses is similar; when a motion has been moved, the Speaker proposes the question as the subject of a debate. Members speak from wherever they have been sitting. Questions are decided by a vote on a simple majority. Draft legislation is introduced, in either house, as a bill. Bills can be introduced by a government minister or a private member, but in practice the majority of bills which become law are introduced by the government. To become law, a bill must be passed by each house (for parliamentary stages, *see* Parliamentary Information) and then sent to the sovereign for the royal assent, after which it becomes an act of parliament.

Proceedings of both houses are public, except on extremely rare occasions. The minutes (called *Votes and Proceedings in the Commons*, and *Minutes of Proceedings in the Lords)* and the speeches *(The Official Report of Parliamentary Debates,* Hansard) are published daily. Proceedings are also recorded for transmission on radio and television and stored in the Parliamentary Recording Unit before transfer to the National Sound Archive. Television cameras have been allowed into the House of Lords since 1985 and into the House of Commons since 1989; committee meetings may also be televised.

By the Parliament Act of 1911, the maximum duration of a parliament is five years (if not previously dissolved), the term being reckoned from the date given on the writs for the new parliament. The maximum life has been prolonged by legislation in such rare circumstances as the two world wars (31 January 1911 to 25 November 1918; 26 November 1935 to 15 June 1945). Dissolution and writs for a general election are ordered by the sovereign on the advice of the prime minister. The life of a parliament is divided into sessions, usually of one year in length, beginning and ending most often in October or November.

DEVOLUTION

The Scottish parliament and the National Assembly for Wales have legislative power over all devolved matters, ie matters not reserved to Westminster or otherwise outside its powers. The Northern Ireland Assembly has legislative authority in the fields previously administered by the Northern Ireland departments. The assembly was suspended in October 2002 and dissolved in April 2003, before being reinstated on 8 May 2007. For further information, *see* the Regional Government section.

THE HOUSE OF LORDS
London SW1A 0PW
T 020-7219 3000 Information Office 020-7219 3107
E hlinfo@parliament.uk W www.parliament.uk

The House of Lords is the second chamber, or 'Upper House', of the UK's bicameral parliament. Until the beginning of the 20th century, the House of Lords had considerable power, being able to veto any bill submitted to it by the House of Commons. Today the main functions of the House of Lords are to contribute to the legislative process, to act as a check on the government, and to provide a forum of independent expertise. Its judicial role as final court of appeal ended in 2009 as a result of the establishment of a new UK supreme court (*see* Law Courts and Offices section).

The House of Lords has a number of select committees. Some relate to the internal affairs of the house – such as its management and administration – while others carry out important investigative work on matters of public interest. The main areas of work are: Europe, science, the economy, the constitution and communications. House of Lords' investigative committees look at broader issues and do not mirror government departments as the select committees in the House of Commons do.

On 12 June 2003 the government announced reforms of the judicial function and the role of the Lord Chancellor as a judge and Speaker of the House of Lords. In 2006 the position of Lord Chancellor was significantly altered by the Constitutional Reform Act 2005. The office holder is no longer Speaker of the House of Lords nor head of the judiciary in England and Wales, but remains a cabinet minister (the Lord Chancellor and Secretary of State for Justice), currently in the House of Commons. The function of the Speaker of the House of Lords was devolved to the newly created post of Lord Speaker. The Rt. Hon. Baroness Hayman was elected as the first Lord Speaker by the house on 4 July 2006.

Members of the House of Lords comprise life peers created under the Life Peerages Act 1958, 92 hereditary peers under the House of Lords Act 1999 and Lords of Appeal in Ordinary, ie law lords, under the Appellate Jurisdiction Act 1876*. The Archbishops of Canterbury and York, the Bishops of London, Durham and Winchester, and the 21 senior diocesan bishops of the Church of England are also members.

The House of Lords Act provides for 90 elected hereditary peers to remain in the House of Lords until longer-term reform of the House has been carried out; 42 Conservative, 28 crossbench, three Liberal Democrat and two Labour. Elections for each of the party groups and the crossbenches were held in October and November 1999. Fifteen office holders were elected by the whole house. Two hereditary peers with royal duties, the Earl Marshal and the Lord Great Chamberlain, are also members.

Peers are disqualified from sitting in the house if they are:

• aliens, ie any peer who is not a British citizen, a Commonwealth citizen (under the British Nationality Act 1981) or a citizen of the Republic of Ireland
• under the age of 21
• undischarged bankrupts or, in Scotland, those whose estate is sequestered
• a non-domiciled resident in the UK for tax purposes
• convicted of treason

Bishops retire at the age of 70 and cease to be members of the house at that time.

Members who do not wish to attend sittings of the House of Lords may apply for leave of absence for the duration of a parliament.

Members of the House of Lords, who are not paid a salary, may claim a flat-rate daily attendance allowance of £300 (for peers that attend for a full sitting day) or £150 (for those peers that attend for less than a full sitting day), or may choose to make no claim for each sitting day they attend the house.

* Although the office of Lord of Appeal in Ordinary no longer exists, retired law lords remain in the House of Lords as life peers. Law lords who became justices of the UK supreme court are not permitted to sit or vote in the House of Lords until they retire.

COMPOSITION *as at 1 July 2011*

Archbishops and bishops	24
Life peers under the Appellate Jurisdiction Act 1876	23
Life peers under the Life Peerages Act 1958	690
Peers under the House of Lords Act 1999	90
Total	827

STATE OF THE PARTIES *as at 1 July 2011†*

Conservative	217
Labour	242
Liberal Democrat	92
Crossbench	184
Archbishops and bishops	24
Other	30
Total	789

† Excluding 22 peers on leave of absence, one currently suspended, 14 disqualified as senior members of the judiciary and one disqualified as an MEP

HOUSE OF LORDS PAY BANDS
Staff are placed in the following pay bands according to their level of responsibility and taking account of other factors such as experience and marketability.

Judicial group 4	£172,753
Senior band 3	£101,500–£145,629
Senior band 2	£82,900–£135,970
Senior band 1A	£67,600–£113,202
Senior band 1	£58,200–£100,374
Band A1	£56,723–£72,788
Band A2	£47,164–£60,221

OFFICERS AND OFFICIALS
The house is presided over by the Lord Speaker, whose powers differ from those of the Speaker of the House of Commons. The Lord Speaker has no power to maintain order because the House of Lords is self-regulating.

A panel of deputy speakers is appointed by Royal Commission. The first deputy speaker is the Chair of Committees, a salaried officer of the house appointed at the beginning of each session. He or she takes the chair when the whole house is in committee, as well as in some select committees. He or she is assisted by a panel of deputy chairs, headed by the salaried Principal Deputy Chair of Committees, who is also chair of the European Union Committee of the house.

The Clerk of the Parliaments is the accounting officer and the chief permanent official responsible for the administration of the house. The Gentleman Usher of the Black Rod is responsible for security and other services and also has royal duties as secretary to the Lord Great Chamberlain.

Lord Speaker (£101,038), Rt. Hon. Baroness Hayman
Chair of Committees (£84,524), Lord Brabazon of Tara
Principal Deputy Chair of Committees (£79,076), Lord Roper
Clerk of the Parliaments (Judicial Group 4), D. R. Beamish, LLM
Clerk Assistant (Senior Band 3), E. C. Ollard
Reading Clerk and Clerk of the Overseas Office (Senior Band 2), Dr R. H. Walters, DPHIL
Clerk of the Committees (Senior Band 2), Dr F. P Tudor
Director of Facilities (Senior Band 2), C. V. Woodall
Finance Director (Senior Band 1A), A. Makower
Head of Human Resources (Senior Band 1A), S. P. Burton
Clerk of the Judicial Office and Registrar of Members' Interests (Senior Band 1A), B. P. Keith
Director of Information Services and Librarian (Senior Band 2), Dr E. Hallam Smith
Clerk of Public and Private Bill Office and Examiner of Petitions for Private Bills in the House of Lords (Senior Band 1A), T. V. Mohan
Editor of the Official Report (Senior Band 1), A. S. Nicholls
Clerk of the Records (Senior Band 1), Dr C. Shenton
Deputy Finance Director and Head of Finance (Senior Band 1), J. P. Smith
Director of Public Information (Band A1), B. Hiscock
Counsel to the Chairman of Committees (Senior Band 2), M. Thomas
Second Counsel to the Chairman of Committees (Senior Band 2), A. Roberts
Legal Adviser to the Human Rights Committee (Senior Band 2), M. Hunt
Change Manager (Senior Band 1), Mrs M. E. Ollard
Clerk of the Journals (Senior Band 1), C. Johnson
Clerk of the European Union Committee (Senior Band 1A), J. Vaughan
Clerks of Select Committees (Senior Band 1), Ms C. Salmon Percival; Ms C. K. Mawson
Gentleman Usher of the Black Rod and Serjeant-at-Arms (Senior Band 2), Lt.-Gen. David Leakey, CMG, CBE
Yeoman Usher of the Black Rod and Deputy Serjeant-at-Arms (Band A2), T. Lloyd-Jukes

LORD GREAT CHAMBERLAIN'S OFFICE
Lord Great Chamberlain, Marquess of Cholmondeley
Secretary to the Lord Great Chamberlain, Lt.-Gen. David Leakey, CMG, CBE

SELECT COMMITTEES
The main House of Lords select committees, as at July 2011, are as follows:
Administration and Works Committee – Chair, vacant; *Clerk,* Tom Wilson
Communications Committee – Chair, Lord Inglewood; *Clerk,* Audrey Nelson

Constitution Committee – *Chair,* Baroness Jay of Paddington; *Clerk,* Emily Baldock

Delegated Powers and Regulatory Reform – *Chair,* Baroness Thomas of Winchester; *Clerk,* Kate Lawrence

Economic Affairs – *Chair,* Lord MacGregor of Pulham Market; *Clerk,* Bill Sinton

European Union – *Chair,* Lord Roper; *Clerks,* Jake Vaughan, Kate Meanwell

European Union – *Sub-committees:*

  A *(Economic and Financial Affairs and International Trade)* – *Chair,* Lord Harrison; *Clerk,* Antony Willott

  B *(Internal Market, Energy and Transport)* – *Chair,* Baroness O'Cathain; *Clerk,* John Turner

  C *(Foreign Affairs, Defence and Development Policy)* – *Chair,* Lord Teverson; *Clerk,* Kathryn Colvin

  D *(Agriculture, Fisheries and Environment)* – *Chair,* Lord Carter of Coles; *Clerk,* Paul Bristow

  E *(Justice and Institutions)* – *Chair,* Lord Bowness; *Clerk,* John Turner

  F *(Home Affairs)* – *Chair,* Lord Hannay of Chiswick; *Clerk,* Michael Collon

  G *(Social Policies and Consumer Protection)* – *Chair,* Baroness Young of Hornsey; *Clerk,* Talitha Rowland

House Committee – *Chair,* Baroness Hayman; *Clerk,* Chris Clarke

Liaison Committee – *Chair,* Lord Brabazon of Tara; *Clerk,* Edward Ollard

Privileges and Conduct – *Chair,* Lord Brabazon of Tara; *Clerk,* vacant

Lords' Conduct Sub-committee – *Chair,* Baroness Manningham-Buller; *Clerk,* vacant

Merits of Statutory Instruments – *Chair,* Rt. Hon. Lord Goodlad; *Clerk,* Kate Lawrence

National Security Strategy Joint Commitee – *Chair,* Rt. Hon. Margaret Beckett, MP; *Clerks,* Michael Collon *(Lords)*; Philippa Helme *(Commons)*

Refreshment Committee – *Chair,* Lord Brabazon of Tara; *Clerk,* vacant

Science and Technology – *Chair,* Lord Krebs; *Clerk,* Christine Salmon Percival

Science and Technology Sub-Committee I – *Chair,* Baroness Neuberger; *Clerk,* Daisy Ricketts

Selection Committee – *Chair,* Lord Brabazon of Tara; *Clerk,* vacant

Human Rights Joint Committee – *Chair,* Hywel Francis, MP; *Clerk,* Robert Whiteway *(Lords)*

Security Joint Committee – *Chair,* John Randall, MP; *Clerks,* Mr Wilson *(Commons)*; Mr Clarke *(Lords)*

Statutory Instruments Joint Committee – *Chair,* George Mudie, MP; *Clerk,* John Whatley

THE HOUSE OF COMMONS

London SW1A 0AA

T 020-7219 3000 W www.parliament.uk

HOUSE OF COMMONS INFORMATION OFFICE

Norman Shaw Building (North), London SW1A 2TT

T 020-7219 4272 E hcinfo@parliament.uk

The members of the House of Commons are elected by universal adult suffrage. For electoral purposes, the UK is divided into constituencies, each of which returns one member to the House of Commons, the member being the candidate who obtains the largest number of votes cast in the constituency. To ensure equitable representation, the four Boundary Commissions keep constituency boundaries under review and recommend any redistribution of seats which may seem necessary because of population movements etc. At the 2010 general election the number of seats increased from 646 to 650. Of the present 650 seats, there are 533 for England, 40 for Wales, 59 for Scotland and 18 for Northern Ireland.

NUMBER OF SEATS IN THE HOUSE OF COMMONS BY COUNTRY

	2005	2010
England	529	533
Wales	40	40
Scotland	59	59
Northern Ireland	18	18
Total	646	650

ELECTIONS

Elections are by secret ballot, each elector casting one vote; voting is not compulsory. (For entitlement to vote in parliamentary elections, *see* Legal Notes.) When a seat becomes vacant between general elections, a by-election is held.

British subjects and citizens of the Irish Republic can stand for election as MPs provided they are 18 or over and not subject to disqualification. Those disqualified from sitting in the house include:

• undischarged bankrupts

• people sentenced to more than one year's imprisonment

• members of the House of Lords (but hereditary peers not sitting in the Lords are eligible)

• holders of certain offices listed in the House of Commons Disqualification Act 1975, eg members of the judiciary, civil service, regular armed forces, police forces, some local government officers and some members of public corporations and government commissions

A candidate does not require any party backing but his or her nomination for election must be supported by the signatures of ten people registered in the constituency. A candidate must also deposit £500 with the returning officer, which is forfeit if the candidate does not receive more than 5 per cent of the votes cast. All election expenses at a general election, except the candidate's personal expenses, are subject to a statutory limit of £7,150, plus five pence for each elector in a borough constituency or seven pence for each elector in a county constituency.

See pages 140–185 for an alphabetical list of MPs and results of the general election in 2010.

STATE OF THE PARTIES *as at July 2011**

Party	Seats
Conservative	305
Labour	256
Liberal Democrats	57
Democratic Unionist Party	8
Scottish National Party	6
Sinn Fein (have not taken their seats)	5
Plaid Cymru	3
Social Democratic & Labour Party	3
Alliance	1
Green	1
Independent	1
The Speaker and three Deputy Speakers	4
Total	650

* Working majority of 84; 305 Conservative and 57 Liberal Democrat MPs less 279 of all other parties (excluding the speaker, deputy speakers and Sinn Fein)

BUSINESS

The week's business of the house is outlined each Thursday by the leader of the house, after consultation between the chief government whip and the chief opposition whip. A quarter to a third of the time will be taken up by the government's legislative programme and the rest by other business. As a rule, bills likely to raise political controversy are introduced in the Commons before going on to the Lords, and the Commons claims exclusive control in respect of national taxation and expenditure. Bills such as the finance bill, which imposes taxation, and the consolidated fund bills, which authorise expenditure, must begin in the Commons. A bill of which the financial provisions are subsidiary may begin in the Lords, and the Commons may waive its rights in regard to Lords' amendments affecting finance.

The Commons has a public register of MPs' financial and certain other interests; this is published annually as a House of Commons paper. Members must also disclose any relevant financial interest or benefit in a matter before the house when taking part in a debate, in certain other proceedings of the house, or in consultations with other MPs, with ministers or with civil servants.

MEMBERS' PAY AND ALLOWANCES

Since 1911 members of the House of Commons have received salary payments; facilities for free travel were introduced in 1924. Salary rates for the last 30 years are as follows:

1981 Jun	£13,950	1996 Jul	£43,000
1982 Jun	14,510	1997 Apr	43,860
1983 Jun	15,308	1998 Apr	45,066
1984 Jan	16,106	1999 Apr	47,008
1985 Jan	16,904	2000 Apr	48,371
1986 Jan	17,702	2001 Apr	49,822
1987 Jan	18,500	2002 Apr	55,118
1988 Jan	22,548	2003 Apr	56,358
1989 Jan	24,107	2004 Apr	57,485
1990 Jan	26,701	2005 Apr	59,095
1991 Jan	28,970	2006 Apr	59,686
1992 Jan	30,854	2007 Apr	61,181
1993 Jan	30,854	2008 Apr	63,291
1994 Jan	31,687	2009 Apr	64,766
1995 Jan	33,189	2010 Apr	65,738
1996 Jan	34,085	2011 Apr	65,738

The Independent Parliamentary Standards Authority (IPSA) was established under the Parliamentary Standards Act 2009 and is responsible for the independent regulation and administration of MPs' expenses, as well as for paying the salaries of MPs and their staff members. Since May 2011 IPSA has also been responsible for determining MPs' pay and setting the level of any increase to their salary.

For 2011–12, the office costs expenditure budget is £24,000 for London area MPs and £21,500 for non-London area MPs. The maximum annual staffing expenditure for each MP is set at £115,000.

Since 1972 MPs have been able to claim reimbursement for the additional cost of staying overnight away from their main residence while on parliamentary business. This is not payable to London area MPs and those MPs who reside in 'grace and favour' accommodation. Accommodation expenses for MPs claiming rental payments in the London area is capped at £19,900 per year; for MPs who own their own homes, mortgage interest and associated expenses up to £17,500 are payable.

For ministerial salaries *see* Government Departments.

MEMBERS' PENSIONS

Pension arrangements for MPs were first introduced in 1964. Under the Parliamentary Contributory Pension Fund (PCPF), MPs receive a pension on retirement based upon their salary in their final year, and upon their number of years' service as an MP. Members may pay a contribution rate of 5.9, 7.9 or 11.9 per cent and build up a pension of 1.6, 2 or 2.5 per cent of salary for each year of service. Pensions are normally payable upon retirement at age 65; the pension payable is subject to a maximum of 66.6 per cent of salary, inclusive of pensions from employment or self-employment prior to becoming an MP. There are provisions in place for: early retirement for those MPs who cease to serve between the ages of 55 and 65; MPs of any age who retire due to ill health; and pensions for widows/widowers of MPs. All pensions are index-linked. There is also an Exchequer contribution; currently 28.7 per cent of an MP's salary.

The House of Commons Members' Fund provides for annual or lump sum grants to ex-MPs, their widows or widowers, and children of those who either ceased to serve as an MP prior to the PCPF being established or who are experiencing hardship. Members contribute £24 a year and the Exchequer £215,000 a year to the fund.

HOUSE OF COMMONS PAY BANDS

Staff are placed in the following Senior Civil Service pay bands. These pay bands apply to the most senior staff in departments and agencies.

Pay Band 1	£58,200–£93,380
Pay Band 1A	£67,600–£105,560
Pay Band 2	£82,900–£124,845
Pay Band 3	£101,500–£139,829

OFFICERS AND OFFICIALS

The House of Commons is presided over by the Speaker, who has considerable powers to maintain order. A deputy speaker, called the Chairman of Ways and Means, and two deputy chairs may preside over sittings of the House of Commons; they are elected by the house, and, like the Speaker, neither speak nor vote other than in their official capacity.

The staff of the house are employed by a commission chaired by the Speaker. The heads of the six House of Commons departments are permanent officers of the house, not MPs. The Clerk of the House is the principal adviser to the Speaker on the privileges and procedures of the house, the conduct of the business of the house, and committees. The Serjeant-at-Arms is responsible for security and ceremonial functions of the house.

Speaker (£145,492)*, Rt. Hon. John Bercow, MP (Buckingham)

Chairman of Ways and Means (£107,108), Lindsay Hoyle, MP

First Deputy Chairman of Ways and Means (£102,098), Nigel Evans, MP

Second Deputy Chairman of Ways and Means (£102,098), Rt. Hon. Dawn Primarolo, MP

Parliamentary Commissioner for Standards in Public Life, John Lyon, CB

* Salaries in brackets are the maximum available. Ministers have opted not to take a pay rise for 2011–12

OFFICES OF THE SPEAKER AND CHAIRMAN OF WAYS
AND MEANS
Acting Speaker's Secretary, P. Barratt
Chaplain to the Speaker, Revd Rose Hudson-Wilkin
Secretary to the Chairman of Ways and Means, E. Wilson
Clerk of the House of Commons and Chief Executive,
    Robert Rogers

OFFICE OF THE CHIEF EXECUTIVE
Head of Office, M. Hamlyn
Director of Internal Audit, P. Dillon-Robinson

DEPARTMENT OF CHAMBER AND COMMITTEE
SERVICES
Director-General and Clerk Assistant, R. J. Rogers
Principal Clerks
    Table Office, A. R. Kennon
    Journals, L. Laurence Smyth
    Overseas Office, M. Hutton
Director of Departmental Services, N. Walker

VOTE OFFICE
Deliverer of the Vote, C. Fogarty
Deputy Deliverers of the Vote, O. B. T. Sweeney
    (Parliamentary); T. P. McVeagh *(Production)*

COMMITTEE DIRECTORATE
Clerk of Committees, Ms J. Sharpe
Principal Clerk and Deputy Head of Committee Office,
    Ms P. Helme
Clerk of Domestic Committees/Secretary to the Commission,
    D. J. Gerhold
Select Committees, P. A. Evans; C. J. Poyser
Head of Scrutiny Unit, C. A. Shaw
Director of Broadcasting, T. Jeffes

LEGISLATION DIRECTORATE
Clerk of Legislation, D. Natzler
Principal Clerks
    Delegated Legislation, J. Benger
    Bills, S. J. Patrick
    National Parliament Office (Brussels), E. J. Beale
    Ways and Means Office, E. Wilson

OFFICIAL REPORT DIRECTORATE
Editor, Miss L. Sutherland
Deputy Editors, Ms V. Widgery; A. Newton

SERJEANT-AT-ARMS DIRECTORATE
Serjeant-at-Arms, Mrs J. Pay
Deputy Serjeant-at-Arms, M. Naworynsky
Assistant Serjeant-at-Arms, Mrs T. Cullen

LEGAL SERVICES OFFICE
Speaker's Counsel and Head of Legal Services Office, M.
    Carpenter
Counsel for European Legislation, P. Hardy
Counsel for Legislation, P. Davis
Deputy Counsel, P. Brooksbank; P. Davies; D. Greenberg
Senior Assistant Counsel, Ms V. Daly
Assistant Counsel, Ms H. Emes

DEPARTMENT OF FACILITIES
Director-General, J. Borley
Director of Business Management, J. Greenaway
Parliamentary Director of Estates, M. Barlex
Director of Accommodation Services, J. Robertson
Director of Facilities Finance, P. Collins

Executive Officer, M. Trott
Director of Catering Services, Mrs S. Harrison
Operations Manager, R. Gibbs
Executive Chef, M. Hill

DEPARTMENT OF FINANCE
Director of Finance, Mrs. M. Barrett
Director of Financial Management, C. Ridley
Director of Commercial Services, vacant
Director of Savings, Ms. E. Honer
Head of Pensions, J. Walker

DEPARTMENT OF HUMAN RESOURCES AND
CHANGE
Director-General of HR and Change, A. J. Walker
Director of Business and Capability, Ms J. Rissen
Director of Human Resource Services, Mrs H. Bryson
Director of Change, vacant
Director of Commercial Services, Ms B. Mohan
Head of Occupational Safety, Health and Wellbeing Service,
    Dr M. McDougall

DEPARTMENT OF INFORMATION SERVICES
Director-General and Librarian, J. Pullinger
Directors, vacant *(Service Delivery)*; Prof. D. Cope
    (Parliamentary Office of Science and Technology);
    B. Morgan *(Research)*; R. Twigger *(Information
    Services)*; Ms A. Walker *(Public Information)*; S. Wise
    (Information Management); Ms H. Wood *(SPIRE
    Programme)*
Media and Communications Adviser, Ms E. Parratt
Parliamentary Outreach Officer, Ms C. Cowan
Visitor and Information Manager, C. Weeds

PARLIAMENTARY INFORMATION AND
COMMUNICATION TECHNOLOGY (ICT)
Director of Parliamentary ICT, Ms J. Miller
Director of Technology Directorate, S. O'Connor
Director of Operations and Members Services, M. Taylor
Director of Resources, F. Reid
Director of Programmes and Project Development, R. Ware
Director of Network Programme, I. Montgomery

SELECT COMMITTEES
The more significant committees, as at August 2011, are:

DEPARTMENTAL COMMITTEES
Business, Innovation and Skills – *Chair*, Adrian Bailey, MP;
    Clerk, James Davies
Communities and Local Government – *Chair*, Clive Betts,
    MP; *Clerk*, Huw Yardley
Culture, Media and Sport – *Chair*, John Whittingdale,
    MP; *Clerk*, Emily Commander
Defence – *Chair*, Rt. Hon. James Arbuthnot, MP; *Clerk*,
    Alda Barry
Education – *Chair*, Graham Stuart, MP; *Clerk*, Kenneth
    Fox
Energy and Climate Change – *Chair*, Tim Yeo, MP; *Clerk*,
    Nerys Welfoot
Environment, Food and Rural Affairs – *Chair*, Anne
    McIntosh, MP; *Clerk*, Richard Cooke
Foreign Affairs – *Chair*, Richard Ottaway, MP; *Clerk*,
    Dr Robin James
Health – *Chair*, Rt. Hon. Stephen Dorell, MP; *Clerk*,
    David Lloyd
Home Affairs – *Chair*, Rt. Hon. Keith Vaz, MP;
    Clerk, Elizabeth Flood
International Development – *Chair*, Rt. Hon. Malcolm
    Bruce, MP; *Clerk*, Dr David Harrison

Justice – *Chair,* Rt. Hon. Sir Alan Beith, MP; *Clerk,* Tom Goldsmith

Northern Ireland Affairs – *Chair,* Laurence Robertson, MP; *Clerk,* Mike Clark

Scottish Affairs – *Chair,* Ian Davidson, MP; *Clerk,* Dr Rebecca Davies

Transport – *Chair,* Louise Ellman, MP; *Clerk,* Dr Mark Egan

Treasury – *Chair,* Andrew Tyrie, MP; *Clerk,* Chris Stanton

Welsh Affairs – *Chair,* David T. C. Davies, MP; *Clerk,* Adrian Jenner

Work and Pensions – *Chair,* Dame Anne Begg, MP; *Clerk,* Carol Oxborough

NON-DEPARTMENTAL COMMITTEES

Environmental Audit – *Chair,* Joan Walley, MP; *Clerk,* Simon Fiander

Political and Constitutional Reform – *Chair,* Graham Allen, MP; *Clerk,* Steven Mark

Procedure – *Chair,* Rt. Hon. Greg Knight, MP; *Clerk,* Dr Lynn Gardner

Public Accounts – *Chair,* Rt. Hon. Margaret Hodge, MP; *Clerk,* Philip Aylett

Public Administration – *Chair,* Bernard Jenkin, MP; *Clerk,* Clive Porro

Science and Technology – *Chair,* Andrew Miller; *Clerk,* Glenn McKee

NATIONAL AUDIT OFFICE

157–197 Buckingham Palace Road, London SW1W 9SP
T 020-7798 7000
E enquiries@nao.gsi.gov.uk W www.nao.org.uk

The National Audit Office came into existence under the National Audit Act 1983 to replace and continue the work of the former Exchequer and Audit Department. The act reinforced the office's total financial and operational independence from the government and brought its head, the Comptroller and Auditor-General, into a closer relationship with parliament as an officer of the House of Commons.

The National Audit Office provides independent information, advice and assurance to parliament and the public about all aspects of the financial operations of government departments and many other bodies receiving public funds. It does this by examining and certifying the accounts of these organisations. It also regularly publishes reports to parliament on the results of its value for money investigations of the economy (the efficiency and effectiveness with which public resources have been used). The National Audit Office is also the auditor by agreement of the accounts of certain international and other organisations. In addition, the office authorises the issue of public funds to government departments.

Comptroller and Auditor-General, Amyas Morse
Private Secretary, Laura Brackwell
Chief Operating Officer, Michael Whitehouse
Leadership Team, Gabrielle Cohen; Ed Humpherson; Wendy Kenway-Smith; Martin Sinclair

PARLIAMENTARY INFORMATION

The following is a short glossary of aspects of the work of parliament. Unless otherwise stated, references are to House of Commons procedures.

BILL – Proposed legislation is termed a bill. The stages of a public bill (for private bills, *see* below) in the House of Commons are as follows:

First reading: This stage introduces the legislation to the house and, for government Bills, merely constitutes an order to have the bill printed.

Second reading: The debate on the principles of the bill.

Committee stage: The detailed examination of a bill, clause by clause. In most cases this takes place in a public bill committee, or the whole house may act as a committee. Public bill committees may take evidence before embarking on detailed scrutiny of the bill. Very rarely, a bill may be examined by a select committee.

Report stage: Detailed review of a bill as amended in committee, on the floor of the house, and an opportunity to make further changes.

Third reading: Final debate on the full bill in the Commons.

Public bills go through the same stages in the House of Lords, but with important differences: the committee stage is taken in committee of the whole house or in a grand committee, in which any peer may participate. There are no time limits, all amendments are debated, and further amendments can be made at third reading.

A bill may start in either house, and has to pass through both houses to become law. Both houses have to agree the final text of a bill, so that amendments made by the second house are then considered in the originating house, and if not agreed, sent back or themselves amended, until agreement is reached.

CHILTERN HUNDREDS – A nominal office of profit under the crown, the acceptance of which requires an MP to vacate his/her seat. The Manor of Northstead is similar. These are the only means by which an MP may resign.

CONSOLIDATED FUND BILL – A bill to authorise the issue of money to maintain government services. The bill is dealt with without debate.

EARLY DAY MOTION – A motion put on the notice paper by an MP without, in general, the real prospect of its being debated. Such motions are expressions of back-bench opinion.

FATHER OF THE HOUSE – The MP whose continuous service in the House of Commons is the longest. The present Father of the House is Sir Peter Tapsell, MP.

GRAND COMMITTEES – There are three grand committees in the House of Commons, one each for Northern Ireland, Scotland and Wales; they consider matters relating specifically to that country. In the House of Lords, bills may be sent to a grand committee instead of a committee of the whole house (*see also* Bill).

HOURS OF MEETING – The House of Commons normally meets on Mondays and Tuesdays at 2.30pm, Wednesdays at 11.30am, Thursdays at 10.30am and some Fridays at 9.30am. (*See also* Westminster Hall Sittings, below.) The House of Lords normally meets at 2.30pm Mondays and Tuesdays, 3pm on Wednesdays and at 11am on Thursdays. The House of Lords occasionally sits on Fridays at 10am.

LEADER OF THE OPPOSITION – In 1937 the office of leader of the opposition was recognised and a salary was assigned to the post. In 2011–12 this was £139,355 (including a parliamentary salary of £65,738). The present leader of the opposition is the Rt. Hon. Ed Miliband, MP.

THE LORD CHANCELLOR – The office of Lord High Chancellor of Great Britain was significantly altered by the Constitutional Reform Act 2005. Previously, the Lord Chancellor was (*ex officio*) the Speaker of the House of Lords, and took part in debates and voted in divisions in the House of Lords. The Department for Constitutional Affairs was created in 2003, which became the Ministry of Justice in 2007, incorporating most of the responsibilities of the Lord Chancellor's department. The role of Speaker has been transferred to the post of Lord Speaker. The Constitutional Reform Act 2005 also brought to an end the Lord Chancellor's role as head of the judiciary. A Judicial Appointments Commission was created in April 2006, and a supreme court (separate from the House of Lords) was established in 2009.

THE LORD SPEAKER – The first Lord Speaker of the House of Lords, the Rt. Hon. Baroness Hayman, took up office on 4 July 2006. Unlike in the case of the Lord Chancellor, the Lord Speaker is independent of the government and elected by members of the House of Lords rather than appointed by the prime minister. Although the Lord Speaker's primary role is to preside over proceedings in the House of Lords, she does not have the same powers as the Speaker of the House of Commons. For example, the Lord Speaker is not responsible for maintaining order during debates, as this is the responsibility of the house as a whole. The Lord Speaker sits in the Lords on one of the woolsacks, which are couches covered in red cloth and stuffed with wool.

THE LORD GREAT CHAMBERLAIN – The Lord Great Chamberlain is a Great Officer of State, the office being hereditary since the grant of Henry I to the family of De Vere, Earls of Oxford. It is now a joint hereditary office rotating on the death of the sovereign between the Cholmondeley, Carington and Ancaster families.

The Lord Great Chamberlain, currently the Marquess of Cholmondeley, is responsible for the royal apartments in the Palace of Westminster, the Royal Gallery, the administration of the Chapel of St Mary Undercroft and, in conjunction with the Lord Speaker and the Speaker of the House of Commons, Westminster Hall. The Lord Great Chamberlain has the right to perform specific services at a coronation, he carries out ceremonial duties in the Palace of Westminster when the sovereign visits the palace and has particular responsibility for the internal administrative arrangements within the House of Lords for state openings of parliament.

OPPOSITION DAY – A day on which the topic for debate is chosen by the opposition. There are 20 such days in a normal session. On 17 days, subjects are chosen by the leader of the opposition; on the remaining three days by the leader of the next largest opposition party.

PARLIAMENT ACTS 1911 AND 1949 – Under these acts, bills may become law without the consent of the Lords, though the House of Lords has the power to delay a public bill for a parliamentary session.

PRIME MINISTER'S QUESTIONS – The prime minister answers questions from 12 to 12.30pm on Wednesdays.

PRIVATE BILL – A bill promoted by a body or an individual to give powers additional to, or in conflict with, the general law, and to which a special procedure applies to enable people affected to object.

PRIVATE MEMBER'S BILL – A public bill promoted by an MP or peer who is not a member of the government.

PRIVATE NOTICE QUESTION – A question adjudged of urgent importance on submission to the Speaker (in the Lords, the Lord Speaker), answered at the end of oral questions.

PRIVILEGE – The House of Commons has rights and immunities to protect it from obstruction in carrying out its duties. These are known as parliamentary privilege and enable Members of Parliament to debate freely. The most important privilege is that of freedom of speech. MPs cannot be prosecuted for sedition or sued for libel or slander over anything said during proceedings in the house. This enables them to raise in the house questions affecting the public good which might be difficult to raise outside owing to the possibility of legal action against them. The House of Lords has similar privileges.

QUESTION TIME – Oral questions are answered by ministers in the Commons from 2.30 to 3.30pm on Mondays and Tuesdays, 11.30am to 12.30pm on Wednesdays, and 10.30 to 11.30am on Thursdays. Questions are also taken at the start of the Lords sittings, with a daily limit of four oral questions.

ROYAL ASSENT – The royal assent is signified by letters patent to such bills and measures as have passed both Houses of Parliament (or bills which have been passed under the Parliament Acts 1911 and 1949). The sovereign has not given royal assent in person since 1854. On occasion, for instance in the prorogation of parliament, royal assent may be pronounced to the two houses by Lords Commissioners. More usually royal assent is notified to each house sitting separately in accordance with the Royal Assent Act 1967. The old French formulae for royal assent are then endorsed on the acts by the Clerk of the Parliaments.

The power to withhold assent resides with the sovereign but has not been exercised in the UK since 1707.

SELECT COMMITTEES – Consisting usually of 10 to 15 members of all parties, select committees are a means used by both houses in order to investigate certain matters.

Most select committees in the House of Commons are tied to departments: each committee investigates subjects within a government department's remit. There are other select committees dealing with matters such as public accounts (ie the spending by the government of money voted by parliament) and European legislation, and also committees advising on procedures and domestic administration of the house. Major select committees usually take evidence in public; their evidence and reports are published on the parliament website and in hard copy by TSO (The Stationery Office). House of Commons select committees are reconstituted after a general election.

In the House of Lords, select committees do not mirror government departments but cover broader issues. There is a select committee on the European Union (EU), which has seven sub-committees dealing with specific areas of EU policy, a select committee on science and technology, a select committee on economic affairs and also one on the constitution. There is also a select committee on delegated powers and regulatory reform and one on privileges and conduct. In addition, *ad hoc* select committees have been set up from time to time to investigate specific subjects. There are also joint committees of the two houses, eg the committees on statutory instruments and on human rights.

THE SPEAKER – The Speaker of the House of Commons is the spokesperson and chair of the Chamber. He or she is elected by the house at the beginning of each parliament or when the previous Speaker retires or dies. The Speaker neither speaks in debates nor votes in divisions except when the voting is equal.

VACANT SEATS – When a vacancy occurs in the House of Commons during a session of parliament, the writ for the by-election is moved by a whip of the party to which the member whose seat has been vacated belonged. If the house is in recess, the Speaker can issue a warrant for a writ, should two members certify to him that a seat is vacant.

WESTMINSTER HALL SITTINGS – Following a report by the Modernisation of the House of Commons Select Committee, the Commons decided in May 1999 to set up a second debating forum. It is known as 'Westminster Hall' and sittings are in the Grand Committee Room on Tuesdays from 9.30 to 11.30am, Wednesdays from 9.30 to 11.30am and from 2 to 5pm, and Thursdays from 2.30 to 5.30pm. Sittings are open to the public at the times indicated.

WHIPS – In order to secure the attendance of members of a particular party in parliament, particularly on the occasion of an important vote, whips (originally known as 'whippers-in') are appointed. The written appeal or circular letter issued by them is also known as a 'whip', its urgency being denoted by the number of times it is underlined. Failure to respond to a three-line whip is tantamount in the Commons to secession (at any rate temporarily) from the party. Whips are provided with office accommodation in both houses, and government and some opposition whips receive salaries from public funds.

PARLIAMENTARY ARCHIVES
Houses of Parliament, London SW1A 0PW
T 020-7219 3074
E archives@parliament.uk W www.parliament.uk/archives

Since 1497, the records of parliament have been kept within the Palace of Westminster. They are in the custody of the Clerk of Parliaments. In 1946 the House of Lords Record Office, which became the Parliamentary Archives in 2006, was established to supervise their preservation and their availability to the public. Some three million documents are preserved, including acts of parliament from 1497, journals of the House of Lords from 1510, minutes and committee proceedings from 1610, and papers laid before parliament from 1531. Among the records are the Petition of Right, the death warrant of Charles I, the Declaration of Breda, and the Bill of Rights. Records are made available through a public search room.
Clerk of the Records, Dr Caroline Shenton

GOVERNMENT OFFICE

The government is the body of ministers responsible for the administration of national affairs, determining policy and introducing into parliament any legislation necessary to give effect to government policy. The majority of ministers are members of the House of Commons but members of the House of Lords, or of neither house, may also hold ministerial responsibility. The prime minister is, by current convention, always a member of the House of Commons.

THE PRIME MINISTER
The office of prime minister, which had been in existence for nearly 200 years, was officially recognised in 1905 and its holder was granted a place in the table of precedence. The prime minister, by tradition also First Lord of the Treasury and Minister for the Civil Service, is appointed by the sovereign and is usually the leader of the party which enjoys, or can secure, a majority in the House of Commons. Other ministers are appointed by the sovereign on the recommendation of the prime minister, who also allocates functions among ministers and has the power to dismiss ministers from their posts.

The prime minister informs the sovereign on state and political matters, advises on the dissolution of parliament, and makes recommendations for important crown appointments, ie the award of honours, etc.

As the chair of cabinet meetings and leader of a political party, the prime minister is responsible for translating party policy into government activity. As leader of the government, the prime minister is responsible to parliament and to the electorate for the policies and their implementation.

The prime minister also represents the nation in international affairs, eg summit conferences.

THE CABINET
The cabinet developed during the 18th century as an inner committee of the Privy Council, which was the chief source of executive power until that time. The cabinet is composed of about 20 ministers chosen by the prime minister, usually the heads of government departments (generally known as secretaries of state unless they have a special title, eg Chancellor of the Exchequer), the leaders of the two houses of parliament, and the holders of various traditional offices.

The cabinet's functions are the final determination of policy, control of government and coordination of government departments. The exercise of its functions is dependent upon the incumbent party's (or parties') majority support in the House of Commons. Cabinet meetings are held in private, taking place once or twice a week during parliamentary sittings and less often during a recess. Proceedings are confidential, the members being bound by their oath as privy counsellors not to disclose information about the proceedings.

The convention of collective responsibility means that the cabinet acts unanimously even when cabinet ministers do not all agree on a subject. The policies of departmental ministers must be consistent with the policies of the government as a whole, and once the government's policy has been decided, each minister is expected to support it or resign.

The convention of ministerial responsibility holds a minister, as the political head of his or her department, accountable to parliament for the department's work. Departmental ministers usually decide all matters within their responsibility, although on matters of political importance they normally consult their colleagues collectively. A decision by a departmental minister is binding on the government as a whole.

POLITICAL PARTIES

Before the reign of William and Mary the principal officers of state were chosen by and were responsible to the sovereign alone, and not to parliament or the nation at large. Such officers acted sometimes in concert with one another but more often independently, and the fall of one did not, of necessity, involve that of others, although all were liable to be dismissed at any moment.

In 1693 the Earl of Sunderland recommended to William III the advisability of selecting a ministry from the political party which enjoyed a majority in the House of Commons, and the first united ministry was drawn in 1696 from the Whigs, to which party the king owed his throne. This group became known as the 'junto' and was regarded with suspicion as a novelty in the political life of the nation, being a small section meeting in secret apart from the main body of ministers. It may be regarded as the forerunner of the cabinet and in the course of time it led to the establishment of the principle of joint responsibility of ministers, so that internal disagreement caused a change of personnel or resignation of the whole body of ministers.

The accession of George I, who was unfamiliar with the English language, led to a disinclination on the part of the sovereign to preside at meetings of his ministers and caused the emergence of a prime minister, a position first acquired by Robert Walpole in 1721 and retained by him without interruption for 20 years and 326 days. The office of prime minister was formally recognised in 1905 when it was established by royal warrant.

DEVELOPMENT OF PARTIES

In 1828 the Whigs became known as Liberals, a name originally given by opponents to imply laxity of principles, but gradually accepted by the party to indicate its claim to be pioneers and champions of political reform and progressive legislation. In 1861 a Liberal Registration Association was founded and Liberal Associations became widespread. In 1877 a National Liberal Federation was formed, with its headquarters in London. The Liberal Party was in power for long periods during the second half of the 19th century and for several years during the first quarter of the 20th century, but after a split in the party in 1931, the numbers elected remained small. In 1988 a majority of the Liberals agreed on a merger with the Social Democratic Party under the title Social and Liberal Democrats; since 1989 they have been known as the Liberal Democrats. A minority continue separately as the Liberal Party.

Soon after the change from Whig to Liberal, the Tory Party became known as Conservative, a name believed to have been invented by John Wilson Croker in 1830 and to have been generally adopted around the time of the passing of the Reform Act of 1832 – to indicate that the preservation of national institutions was the leading principle of the party. After the Home Rule crisis of 1886 the dissentient Liberals entered into a compact with the Conservatives, under which the latter undertook not to contest their seats, but a separate Liberal Unionist organisation was maintained until 1912, when it was united with the Conservatives.

Labour candidates for parliament made their first appearance at the general election of 1892, when there were 27 standing as Labour or Liberal-Labour. In 1900 the Labour Representation Committee (LRC) was set up in order to establish a distinct Labour group in parliament, with its own whips, its own policy, and a readiness to cooperate with any party which might be engaged in promoting legislation in the direct interests of labour. In 1906 the LRC became known as the Labour Party.

The Green Party was founded in 1973 and campaigns for social and environmental justice. The party began as 'People', was renamed the Ecology Party, and became the Green Party in 1985.

Plaid Cymru was founded in 1926 to provide an independent political voice for Wales and to campaign for self-government in Wales.

The Scottish National Party (SNP) was founded in 1934 to campaign for independence for Scotland.

The Social Democratic and Labour Party (SDLP) was founded in 1970, emerging from the civil rights movement of the 1960s, with the aim of promoting reform, reconciliation and partnership across the sectarian divide in Northern Ireland, and of opposing violence from any quarter.

The Democratic Unionist Party (DUP) was founded in 1971 to resist moves by the Ulster Unionist Party which were considered a threat to the Union. Its aim is to maintain Northern Ireland as an integral part of the UK.

The Alliance Party of Northern Ireland was formed in 1970 as a non-sectarian unionist party.

Sinn Fein first emerged in the 1900s as a federation of nationalist clubs. It is a left-wing republican and labour party that seeks to end British governance in Ireland and achieve a 32-county republic.

GOVERNMENT AND OPPOSITION

The government is formed by the party which wins the largest number of seats in the House of Commons at a general election, or which has the support of a majority of members in the House of Commons. By tradition, the leader of the majority party is asked by the sovereign to form a government, while the largest minority party becomes the official opposition with its own leader and a shadow cabinet. Leaders of the government and opposition sit on the front benches of the Commons with their supporters (the back-benchers) sitting behind them.

FINANCIAL SUPPORT

Financial support for opposition parties in the House of Commons was introduced in 1975 and is commonly known as Short Money, after Edward Short, the leader of the house at that time, who introduced the scheme. Short Money is only payable to those parties that have more than one sitting MP or 150,000 votes in total, and is only intended to provide assistance for parliamentary duties. Short Money allocations for 2011–12 are:

DUP	£149,823
Green	£59,501
Labour	£6,024,340
Plaid Cymru	£71,970
SDLP	£63,561
SNP	£168,795

A specific allocation for the leader of the opposition's office was introduced in April 1999 and has been set at £700,699 for the year 2011–12.

Financial support for opposition parties in the House of Lords was introduced in 1996 and is commonly known as Cranborne Money, after former leader of the house Viscount Cranbourne.

The following list of parties are those with MPs elected to the present parliament.

ALLIANCE PARTY OF NORTHERN IRELAND

88 University Street, Belfast BT7 1HE
T 028-9032 4274 E alliance@allianceparty.org
W www.allianceparty.org
Party Leader, David Ford
Deputy Party Leader, Naomi Long, MP
President, Colm Cavanagh
Chair, Stewart Dickson
Hon. Treasurer, Dan McGuinness

CONSERVATIVE PARTY

Conservative Campaign Headquarters, 30 Millbank, London SW1P 4DP
T 020-7222 9000
W www.conservatives.com

Parliamentary Party Leader, Rt. Hon. David Cameron, MP
Leader in the Lords and Chancellor of the Duchy of
Lancaster, Rt. Hon. Lord Strathclyde
Leader in the Commons and Lord Privy Seal, Rt. Hon. Sir
George Young, Bt., MP
Chairs, Lord Feldman of Elstree; Baroness Warsi
Party Treasurer, Lord Fink

GREEN PARTY
Development House, 56–64 Leonard Street, London, EC2A 4LT
T 020-7549 0310
E office@greenparty.org.uk W www.greenparty.org.uk
Party Leader, Dr Caroline Lucas, MP
Deputy Leader, Adrian Ramsay
Chair of Party Executive, Jayne Forbes
Finance Coordinator, Dean Walton

LABOUR PARTY
39 Victoria Street, London SW1H 0HA
T 0870-590 0200 W www.labour.org.uk
General Secretary, Ray Collins
General Secretary, Welsh Labour, Dave Hagendyk
General Secretary, Scottish Labour Party, Colin Smyth

SHADOW CABINET AS AT AUGUST 2011
Leader of the Opposition, Rt. Hon. Ed Miliband, MP
Deputy Leader and Secretary of State for International
Development, Rt. Hon. Harriet Harman, QC, MP
Chancellor of the Exchequer, Rt. Hon. Ed Balls, MP
Secretary of State for Foreign and Commonwealth Affairs,
Rt. Hon. Douglas Alexander, MP
Secretary of State for the Home Department and Minister for
Women and Equalities, Rt. Hon Yvette Cooper, MP
*Minister of State for the Cabinet Office, Jon Trickett,
MP
Minister for the Cabinet Office and Olympics, Rt. Hon.
Tessa Jowell, MP
Secretary of State for Communities and Local Government,
Rt. Hon. Caroline Flint, MP
Secretary of State for Culture, Media and Sport, Ivan Lewis,
MP
Secretary of State for Defence, Rt. Hon. Jim Murphy, MP
Secretary of State for Education and Election Co-ordinator,
Rt. Hon. Andy Burnham, MP
Secretary of State for Energy and Climate Change, Meg
Hiller, MP
Secretary of State for Environment, Food and Rural Affairs,
Mary Creagh, MP
Secretary of State for Health, Rt. Hon. John Healey, MP
Lord Chancellor, Secretary of State for Justice (with
responsibility for political/constitutional reform), Rt.
Hon. Sadiq Khan, MP
Secretary of State for Northern Ireland, Rt. Hon. Shaun
Woodward, MP
Secretary of State for Scotland, Ann McKechin, MP
Secretary of State for Transport, Maria Eagle, MP
Chief Secretary to the Treasury, Angela Eagle, MP
Secretary of State for Wales, Rt. Hon. Peter Hain, MP
Secretary of State for Work and Pensions, Rt. Hon. Liam
Byrne, MP
Leader of the House of Commons, Rt. Hon. Hilary Benn, MP
Leader of the House of Lords, Baroness Royall of Blaisdon
Attorney-General, Baroness Scotland of Asthal, QC
Parliamentary Party Chair, Tony Lloyd, MP

LABOUR WHIPS
House of Commons, Rt. Hon. Rosie Winterton, MP
House of Lords, Lord Bassam of Brighton
* Attends Cabinet meetings but is not a Cabinet member

LIBERAL DEMOCRATS
4 Cowley Street, London SW1P 3NB
T 020-7222 7999
E info@libdems.org.uk W www.libdems.org.uk
Parliamentary Party Leader, Rt. Hon. Nick Clegg, MP
Deputy Party Leader, Simon Hughes, MP
Leader in the Lords, Rt. Hon. Lord McNally
Deputy Leader in the Commons, David Heath, MP
President, Baroness Ros Scott
Chief Executive (interim), Chris Fox
Hon. Treasurer, Lord Razzall

NORTHERN IRELAND DEMOCRATIC UNIONIST PARTY
91 Dundela Avenue, Belfast BT4 3BU
T 028-9047 1155
E info@dup.org.uk W www.dup.org.uk
Parliamentary Party Leader, Rt. Hon. Peter Robinson,
MLA
Deputy Leader, Rt. Hon Nigel Dodds, OBE, MP, MLA
Chair, Lord Morrow, MLA
Treasurer, Gregory Campbell, MP, MLA
Party Secretary, Michelle McIlveen, MLA

PLAID CYMRU – THE PARTY OF WALES
Ty Gwynfor, Marine Chambers, Anson Court, Atlantic Wharf,
Caerdydd CF10 4AL
T 029-2047 2272
E post@plaidcymru.org W www.plaidcymru.org
Party Leader, Ieuan Wyn Jones
Party President, Jill Evans, MEP
Parliamentary Group Leader, Elfyn Llwyd, MP
Chief Executive, vacant

SCOTTISH NATIONAL PARTY
Gordon Lamb House, 3 Jackson's Entry, Edinburgh EH8 8PJ
T 0800-633 5432
E info@snp.org W www.snp.org
Westminster Parliamentary Party Leader, Angus Robertson,
MP
Westminster Parliamentary Party Chief Whip, Stewart
Hosie, MP
Scottish Parliamentary Party Leader, Alex Salmond, MSP
Scottish Parliamentary Party Chief Whip, Brian Adam, MSP
National Treasurer, Cllr Colin Beattie
National Secretary, William Henderson
Chief Executive, Peter Murrell

SINN FEIN
53 Falls Road, Belfast BT12 4PD
T 028-9034 7350
E sfadmin@eircom.net W www.sinnfein.ie
Party President, Gerry Adams
Vice-President, Mary Lou McDonald
Chair, Declan Kearney
Treasurers, Rita O'Hare; Maurice Quinlivan
General Secretary, Dawn Doyle

SOCIAL DEMOCRATIC AND LABOUR PARTY
121 Ormeau Road, Belfast BT7 1SH
T 028-9024 7700 E info@sdlp.ie W www.sdlp.ie
Parliamentary Party Leader, Margaret Ritchie, MP, MLA
Deputy Leader, Patsy McGlone, MLA
Party Whip, Pat Ramsey, MLA
Chair, Joe Byrne, MLA
Treasurer, Peter McEvoy
General Secretary, Gerry Cosgrove

MEMBERS OF PARLIAMENT as at 10 August 2011

* New MP
† Previously MP in another seat
‡ Previously MP for another party

Abbott, Diane (*b.* 1953) *Lab., Hackney North & Stoke Newington*, Maj. 14,461
***Abrahams**, Deborah (*b.* 1960) *Lab., Oldham East & Saddleworth*, Maj. 3,558
***Adams**, Nigel (*b.* 1966) *C., Selby & Ainsty*, Maj. 12,265
Afriyie, Adam (*b.* 1965) *C., Windsor*, Maj. 19,054
Ainsworth, Rt. Hon. Robert (*b.* 1952) *Lab., Coventry North East*, Maj. 11,775
***Aldous**, Peter (*b.* 1961) *C., Waveney*, Maj. 769
Alexander, Rt. Hon. Danny (*b.* 1972) *LD, Inverness, Nairn, Badenoch & Strathspey*, Maj. 8,765
Alexander, Rt. Hon. Douglas (*b.* 1967) *Lab., Paisley & Renfrewshire South*, Maj. 16,614
***Alexander**, Heidi (*b.* 1975) *Lab., Lewisham East*, Maj. 6,216
***Ali**, Rushanara, (*b.* 1975) *Lab., Bethnal Green & Bow*, Maj. 11,574
Allen, Graham (*b.* 1953) *Lab., Nottingham North*, Maj. 8,138
Amess, David (*b.* 1952) *C., Southend West*, Maj. 7,270
Anderson, David (*b.* 1953) *Lab., Blaydon*, Maj. 9,117
***Andrew**, Stuart (*b.* 1971) *C., Pudsey*, Maj. 1,659
Arbuthnot, Rt. Hon. James (*b.* 1952) *C., Hampshire North East*, Maj. 18,597
***Ashworth**, Jon (*b.* 1978) *Lab., Leicester South*, Maj. 12,078
Austin, Ian (*b.* 1965) *Lab., Dudley North*, Maj. 649
Bacon, Richard (*b.* 1962) *C., Norfolk South*, Maj. 10,940
***Bagshawe**, Louise (*b.* 1971) *C., Corby*, Maj. 1,951
Bailey, Adrian (*b.* 1945) *Lab. (Co-op), West Bromwich West*, Maj. 5,651
Bain, William (*b.* 1972) *Lab., Glasgow North East*, Maj. 15,942
Baker, Norman (*b.* 1957) *LD, Lewes*, Maj. 7,647
***Baker**, Steven (*b.* 1971) *C., Wycombe*, Maj. 9,560
Baldry, Tony (*b.* 1950) *C., Banbury*, Maj. 18,227
***Baldwin**, Harriett (*b.* 1960) *C., West Worcestershire*, Maj. 6,804
Balls, Rt. Hon. Ed (*b.* 1967) *Lab. (Co-op), Morley & Outwood*, Maj. 1,101
Banks, Gordon (*b.* 1955) *Lab., Ochil & Perthshire South*, Maj. 5,187
***Barclay**, Stephen (*b.* 1972) *C., Cambridgeshire North East*, Maj. 16,425
Barker, Gregory (*b.* 1966) *C., Bexhill & Battle*, Maj. 12,880
Baron, John (*b.* 1959) *C., Basildon & Billericay*, Maj. 12,398
Barron, Rt. Hon. Kevin (*b.* 1946) *Lab., Rother Valley*, Maj. 5,866
***Barwell**, Gavin (*b.* 1972) *C., Croydon Central*, Maj. 2,969
Bayley, Hugh (*b.* 1952) *Lab., York Central*, Maj. 6,451
***Bebb**, Guto (*b.* 1968) *C., Aberconwy*, Maj. 3,398
Beckett, Rt. Hon. Margaret (*b.* 1943) *Lab., Derby South*, Maj. 6,122
Begg, Anne (*b.* 1955) *Lab., Aberdeen South*, Maj. 3,506
Beith, Rt. Hon. Sir Alan (*b.* 1943) *LD, Berwick-upon-Tweed*, Maj. 2,690
Bell, Sir Stuart (*b.* 1938) *Lab., Middlesbrough*, Maj. 8,689

Bellingham, Henry (*b.* 1955) *C., Norfolk North West*, Maj. 14,810
Benn, Rt. Hon. Hilary (*b.* 1953) *Lab., Leeds Central*, Maj. 10,645
Benton, Joe (*b.* 1933) *Lab., Bootle*, Maj. 21,181
Benyon, Richard (*b.* 1960) *C., Newbury*, Maj. 12,248
Bercow, John (*b.* 1963) *The Speaker, Buckingham*, Maj. 12,529
Beresford, Sir Paul (*b.* 1946) *C., Mole Valley*, Maj. 15,653
***Berger**, Luciana (*b.* 1981) *Lab. (Co-op), Liverpool, Wavertree*, Maj. 7,167
***Berry**, Jake (*b.* 1978) *C., Rossendale & Darwen*, Maj. 4,493
Betts, Clive (*b.* 1950) *Lab., Sheffield South East*, Maj. 10,505
***Bingham**, Andrew (*b.* 1962) *C., High Peak*, Maj. 4,677
Binley, Brian (*b.* 1942) *C., Northampton South*, Maj. 6,004
***Birtwistle**, Gordon (*b.* 1943) *LD, Burnley*, Maj. 1,818
***Blackman**, Bob (*b.* 1956) *C., Harrow East*, Maj. 3,403
Blackman-Woods, Dr Roberta (*b.* 1957) *Lab., Durham, City of*, Maj. 3,067
***Blackwood**, Nicola (*b.* 1979) *C., Oxford West & Abingdon*, Maj. 176
Blears, Rt. Hon. Hazel (*b.* 1956) *Lab., Salford & Eccles*, Maj. 5,725
***Blenkinsop**, Tom (*b.* 1980) *Lab., Middlesbrough South & East Cleveland*, Maj. 1,677
***Blomfield**, Paul (*b.* 1953) *Lab., Sheffield Central*, Maj. 165
Blunkett, Rt. Hon. David (*b.* 1947) *Lab., Sheffield, Brightside & Hillsborough*, Maj. 13,632
Blunt, Crispin (*b.* 1960) *C., Reigate*, Maj. 13,591
***Boles**, Nick (*b.* 1965) *C., Grantham & Stamford*, Maj. 14,826
Bone, Peter (*b.* 1952) *C., Wellingborough*, Maj. 11,787
Bottomley, Peter (*b.* 1944) *C., Worthing West*, Maj. 11,729
***Bradley**, Karen (*b.* 1970) *C., Staffordshire Moorlands*, Maj. 6,689
Bradshaw, Ben (*b.* 1960) *Lab., Exeter*, Maj. 2,721
Brady, Graham (*b.* 1967) *C., Altrincham & Sale West*, Maj. 11,595
Brake, Tom (*b.* 1962) *LD, Carshalton & Wallington*, Maj. 5,260
***Bray**, Angie (*b.* 1953) *C., Ealing Central &Acton*, Maj. 3,716
Brazier, Julian (*b.* 1953) *C., Canterbury*, Maj. 6,048
Brennan, Kevin (*b.* 1959) *Lab., Cardiff West*, Maj. 4,750
***Bridgen**, Andrew (*b.* 1964) *C., Leicestershire North West*, Maj. 7,511
***Brine**, Steve (*b.* 1974) *C., Winchester*, Maj. 3,048
†**Brokenshire**, James (*b.* 1968) *C., Old Bexley & Sidcup*, Maj. 15,857
Brooke, Annette (*b.* 1947) *LD, Dorset Mid & Poole North*, Maj. 269
Brown, Rt. Hon. Gordon (*b.* 1951) *Lab., Kirkcaldy & Cowdenbeath*, Maj. 23,009
Brown, Lyn (*b.* 1960) *Lab., West Ham*, Maj. 22,534
Brown, Rt. Hon. Nicholas (*b.* 1950) *Lab., Newcastle upon Tyne East*, Maj. 4,453
Brown, Russell (*b.* 1951) *Lab., Dumfries & Galloway*, Maj. 7,449
Browne, Jeremy (*b.* 1970) *LD, Taunton Deane*, Maj. 3,993

Donohoe, Brian (b. 1948) Lab., Ayrshire Central, Maj. 12,007

Doran, Frank (b. 1949) Lab., Aberdeen North, Maj. 8,361

Dorrell, Rt. Hon. Stephen (b. 1952) C., Charnwood, Maj. 15,029

Dorries, Nadine (b. 1958) C., Bedfordshire Mid, Maj. 15,152

Dowd, Jim (b. 1951) Lab., Lewisham West & Penge, Maj. 5,828

*****Doyle**, Gemma (b. 1981) Lab. (Co-op), Dunbartonshire West, Maj. 17,408

*****Doyle-Price**, Jackie (b. 1969) C., Thurrock, Maj. 92

*****Drax**, Richard (b. 1958) C., Dorset South, Maj. 7,443

*****Dromey**, Jack (b. 1948) Lab., Birmingham Erdington, Maj. 3,277

Duddridge, James (b. 1971) C., Rochford & Southend East, Maj. 11,050

*****Dugher**, Michael (b. 1975) Lab., Barnsley East, Maj. 11,090

Duncan, Alan (b. 1957) C., Rutland & Melton, Maj. 14,000

Duncan Smith, Rt. Hon. Iain (b. 1954) C., Chingford & Woodford Green, Maj. 12,963

Dunne, Philip (b. 1958) C., Ludlow, Maj. 9,749

Durkan, Mark (b. 1960) SDLP, Foyle, Maj. 4,824

Eagle, Angela (b. 1961) Lab., Wallasey, Maj. 8,507

Eagle, Maria (b. 1961) Lab., Garston & Halewood, Maj. 16,877

*****Edwards**, Jonathan (b. 1976) PC, Carmarthen East & Dinefwr, Maj. 3,481

Efford, Clive (b. 1958) Lab., Eltham, Maj. 1,663

*****Elliott**, Julie (b. 1963) Lab., Sunderland Central, Maj. 6,725

*****Ellis**, Michael (b. 1967) C., Northampton North, Maj. 1,936

*****Ellison**, Jane (b.1964) C., Battersea, Maj. 5,977

Ellman, Louise (b. 1945) Lab. (Co-op), Liverpool Riverside, Maj. 14,173

Ellwood, Tobias (b. 1966) C., Bournemouth East, Maj. 7,728

*****Elphicke**, Charlie (b. 1971) C., Dover, Maj. 5,274

Engel, Natascha (b. 1967) Lab., Derbyshire North East, Maj. 2,445

*****Esterson**, Bill (b. 1966) Lab., Sefton Central, Maj. 3,862

*****Eustice**, George (b. 1971) C., Camborne & Redruth, Maj. 66

*****Evans**, Chris (b. 1976) Lab. (Co-op), Islwyn, Maj. 12,215

*****Evans**, Graham (b. 1963) C., Weaver Vale, Maj. 991

*****Evans**, Jonathan (b. 1950) C., Cardiff North, Maj. 194

Evans, Nigel (b. 1957) C., Deputy Speaker, Ribble Valley, Maj. 14,769

Evennett, David (b. 1949) C., Bexleyheath & Crayford, Maj. 10,344

Fabricant, Michael (b. 1950) C., Lichfield, Maj. 17,683

Fallon, Michael (b. 1952) C., Sevenoaks, Maj. 17,515

Farrelly, Paul (b. 1962) Lab., Newcastle-under-Lyme, Maj. 1,552

Farron, Tim (b. 1970) LD, Westmorland & Lonsdale, Maj. 12,264

Featherstone, Lynne (b. 1951) LD, Hornsey & Wood Green, Maj. 6,875

Field, Rt. Hon. Frank (b. 1942) Lab., Birkenhead, Maj. 15,195

Field, Mark (b. 1934) C., Cities of London & Westminster, Maj. 11,076

Fitzpatrick, Jim (b. 1952) Lab., Poplar & Limehouse, Maj. 6,030

Flello, Robert (b. 1966) Lab., Stoke-on-Trent South, Maj. 4,130

Flint, Rt. Hon. Caroline (b. 1961) Lab., Don Valley, Maj. 3,595

Flynn, Paul (b. 1935) Lab., Newport West, Maj. 3,544

Foster, Don (b. 1947) LD, Bath, Maj. 11,883

*****Fovargue**, Yvonne (b. 1956) Lab., Makerfield, Maj. 12,490

Fox, Rt. Hon. Dr Liam (b. 1961) C., North Somerset, Maj. 7,862

Francis, Dr Hywel (b. 1946) Lab., Aberavon, Maj. 11,039

Francois, Mark (b. 1965) C., Rayleigh & Wickford, Maj. 22,338

*****Freeman**, George (b. 1967) C., Norfolk Mid, Maj. 13,856

*****Freer**, Mike (b. 1960) C., Finchley & Golders Green, Maj. 5,809

*****Fullbrook**, Lorraine (b. 1959) C., Ribble South, Maj. 5,554

*****Fuller**, Richard (b. 1962) C., Bedford, Maj. 1,353

Gale, Roger (b. 1943) C., Thanet North, Maj. 13,528

Gapes, Mike (b. 1952) Lab. (Co-op), Ilford South, Maj. 11,297

Gardiner, Barry (b. 1957) Lab., Brent North, Maj. 8,028

Garnier, Edward (b. 1952) C., Harborough, Maj. 9,877

*****Garnier**, Mark (b. 1963) C. Wyre Forest, Maj. 2,643

Gauke, David (b. 1971) C., Hertfordshire South West, Maj. 14,920

George, Andrew (b. 1958) LD, St Ives, Maj. 1,719

Gibb, Nick (b. 1960) C., Bognor Regis & Littlehampton, Maj. 13,063

*****Gilbert**, Stephen (b. 1976) LD, St Austell & Newquay, Maj. 1,312

Gildernew, Michelle (b. 1970) SF, Fermanagh & South Tyrone, Maj. 4

Gillan, Rt. Hon. Cheryl (b. 1952) C., Chesham & Amersham, Maj. 16,710

*****Gilmore**, Sheila (b. 1950) Lab., Edinburgh East, Maj. 9,181

*****Glass**, Pat (b. 1956) Lab., Durham North West, Maj. 7,612

*****Glen**, John (b. 1974) C., Salisbury, Maj. 5,966

*****Glindon**, Mary (b. 1957) Lab., Tyneside North, Maj. 12,884

Godsiff, Roger (b. 1946) Lab., Birmingham Hall Green, Maj. 3,799

Goggins, Paul (b. 1953) Lab., Wythenshawe & Sale East, Maj. 7,575

*****Goldsmith**, Zac (b. 1975) C., Richmond Park, Maj. 4,091

Goodman, Helen (b. 1958) Lab., Bishop Auckland, Maj. 5,218

Goodwill, Robert (b. 1956) C., Scarborough & Whitby, Maj. 8,130

Gove, Rt. Hon. Michael (b. 1967) C., Surrey Heath, Maj. 17,289

*****Graham**, Richard (b. 1958) C., Gloucester, Maj. 2,420

*****Grant**, Helen (b. 1961) C., Maidstone & The Weald, Maj. 5,889

Gray, James (b. 1954) C., Wiltshire North, Maj. 7,483

Grayling, Chris (b. 1962) C., Epsom & Ewell, Maj. 16,134

*****Greatrex**, Tom (b. 1974) Lab. (Co-op), Rutherglen & Hamilton West, Maj. 21,002

Green, Damian (b. 1956) C., Ashford, Maj. 17,297

*****Green**, Kate (b. 1960) Lab., Stretford & Urmston, Maj. 8,935

Greening, Justine (b. 1969) C., Putney, Maj. 10,053

Kawczynski, Daniel (b. 1972) C., Shrewsbury & Atcham, Maj. 7,944

Keeley, Barbara (b. 1952) Lab., Worsley & Eccles South, Maj. 4,337

Keen, Alan (b. 1937) Lab. (Co-op), Feltham & Heston, Maj. 4,658

*Kelly, Chris (b. 1978) C., Dudley South, Maj. 3,856

*Kendall, Liz (b. 1971) Lab., Leicester West, Maj. 4,017

Kennedy, Rt. Hon. Charles (b. 1959) LD, Ross, Skye & Lochaber, Maj. 13,070

Khan, Rt. Hon. Sadiq (b. 1970) Lab., Tooting, Maj. 2,524

*Kirby, Simon (b. 1964) C., Brighton Kemptown, Maj. 1,328

Knight, Rt. Hon. Greg (b. 1949) C., Yorkshire East, Maj. 13,486

*Kwarteng, Kwasi (b. 1975) C., Spelthorne, Maj. 10,019

Laing, Eleanor (b. 1958) C., Epping Forest, Maj. 15,131

Lamb, Norman (b. 1957) LD, Norfolk North, Maj. 11,626

Lammy, Rt. Hon. David (b. 1972) Lab., Tottenham, Maj. 16,931

Lancaster, Mark (b. 1970) C., Milton Keynes North, Maj. 8,961

Lansley, Rt. Hon. Andrew (b. 1956) C., Cambridgeshire South, Maj. 7,838

*Latham, Pauline (b. 1948) C., Derbyshire Mid, Maj. 11,292

*Lavery, Ian (b. 1962) Lab., Wansbeck, Maj. 7,031

Laws, David (b. 1965) LD, Yeovil, Maj. 13,036

Lazarowicz, Mark (b. 1953) Lab. (Co-op), Edinburgh North & Leith, Maj. 1,724

*Leadsom, Andrea (b. 1963) C., Northamptonshire South, Maj. 20,478

*Lee, Jessica (b. 1976) C., Erewash, Maj. 2,501

*Lee, Phillip (b. 1970) C., Bracknell, Maj. 15,074

Leech, John (b. 1971) LD, Manchester Withington, Maj. 1,850

*Lefroy, Jeremy (b. 1959) C., Stafford, Maj. 5,460

Leigh, Edward (b. 1950) C., Gainsborough, Maj. 10,559

*Leslie, Charlotte (b. 1978) C., Bristol North West, Maj. 3,274

*Leslie, Chris (b. 1972) Lab. (Co-op), Nottingham East, Maj. 6,969

Letwin, Rt. Hon. Oliver (b. 1956) C., Dorset West, Maj. 3,923

*Lewis, Brandon (b. 1971) C., Great Yarmouth, Maj. 4,276

Lewis, Ivan (b. 1967) Lab., Bury South, Maj. 3,292

Lewis, Dr Julian (b. 1951) C., New Forest East, Maj. 11,307

Liddell-Grainger, Ian (b. 1959) C., Bridgwater & Somerset West, Maj. 9,249

Lidington, David (b. 1956) C., Aylesbury, Maj. 12,618

Lilley, Rt. Hon. Peter (b. 1943) C., Hitchin & Harpenden, Maj. 15,271

*Lloyd, Stephen (b. 1957) LD, Eastbourne, Maj. 3,435

Lloyd, Tony (b. 1950) Lab., Manchester Central, Maj. 10,439

Llwyd, Elfyn (b. 1951) PC, Dwyfor Meirionnydd, Maj. 6,367

*Long, Naomi (b. 1971) All. Belfast East, Maj. 1,533

*Lopresti, Jack (b. 1969) C., Filton & Bradley Stoke, Maj. 6,914

*Lord, Jonathan (b. 1962) C., Woking, Maj. 6,807

Loughton, Tim (b. 1962) C., Worthing East & Shoreham, Maj. 11,105

Love, Andy (b. 1949) Lab. (Co-op), Edmonton, Maj. 9,613

*Lucas, Caroline (b. 1960) Green, Brighton Pavilion, Maj. 1,252

Lucas, Ian (b. 1960) Lab., Wrexham, Maj. 3,658

Luff, Peter (b. 1955) C., Worcestershire Mid, Maj. 15,864

*Lumley, Karen (b. 1964) C., Redditch, Maj. 5,821

Maskey, Paul (b. 1967) SF, Belfast West, Maj. 13,123

McCabe, Steve (b. 1955) Lab., Birmingham Selly Oak, Maj. 3,482

*McCann, Michael (b. 1964) Lab., East Kilbride, Strathaven & Lesmahagow, Maj. 14,503

McCarthy, Kerry (b. 1965) Lab., Bristol East, Maj. 3,722

*McCartney, Jason (b. 1968) C., Colne Valley, Maj. 4,837

*McCartney, Karl (b. 1968) C., Lincoln, Maj. 1,058

*McClymont, Gregg (b. 1976) Lab., Cumbernauld, Kilsyth & Kirkintilloch East, Maj. 13,755

McCrea, Revd Dr William (b. 1948) DUP, Antrim South, Maj. 1,183

McDonagh, Siobhain (b. 1960) Lab., Mitcham & Morden, Maj. 13,666

McDonnell, Dr Alasdair (b. 1949) SDLP, Belfast South, Maj. 5,926

McDonnell, John (b. 1951) Lab., Hayes & Harlington, Maj. 10,824

McFadden, Rt. Hon. Pat (b. 1965) Lab., Wolverhampton South East, Maj. 6,593

*McGovern, Alison (b. 1980) Lab., Wirral South, Maj. 531

McGovern, James (b. 1956) Lab., Dundee West, Maj. 7,278

McGuinness, Martin (b. 1950) SF, Ulster Mid, Maj. 15,363

McGuire, Rt. Hon. Anne (b. 1949) Lab., Stirling, Maj. 8,354

McKechin, Ann (b. 1961) Lab., Glasgow North, Maj. 3,898

McKenzie, Iain (b. 1959) Lab., Inverclyde, Maj. 5,838

*McKinnell, Catherine (b. 1976) Lab., Newcastle upon Tyne North, Maj. 3,414

*MacLeod, Mary (b. 1969) C., Brentford & Isleworth, Maj. 1,958

McLoughlin, Rt. Hon. Patrick (b. 1957) C., Derbyshire Dales, Maj. 13,866

MacNeil, Angus (b. 1970) SNP, Na h-Eileanan an Iar, Maj. 1,885

*McPartland, Stephen (b. 1976) C., Stevenage, Maj. 3,578

MacShane, Rt. Hon. Denis (b. 1948) Lab., Rotherham, Maj. 10,462

Mactaggart, Fiona (b. 1953) Lab., Slough, Maj. 5,523

*McVey, Esther (b. 1967) C., Wirral West, Maj. 2,436

Mahmood, Khalid (b. 1961) Lab., Birmingham Perry Barr, Maj. 11,908

*Mahmood, Shabana (b. 1980) Lab., Birmingham Ladywood, Maj. 10,105

Main, Anne (b. 1957) C., St Albans, Maj. 2,305

Mann, John (b. 1960) Lab., Bassetlaw, Maj. 8,215

Marsden, Gordon (b. 1953) Lab., Blackpool South, Maj. 1,852

Maude, Rt. Hon. Francis (b. 1953) C., Horsham, Maj. 11,460

May, Rt. Hon. Theresa (b. 1956) C., Maidenhead, Maj. 16,769

*Maynard, Paul (b. 1975) C., Blackpool North & Cleveleys, Maj. 2,150

Meacher, Rt. Hon. Michael (b. 1939) Lab., Oldham West & Royton, Maj. 9,352

Meale, Alan (b. 1949) Lab., Mansfield, Maj. 6,012

*Mearns, Ian (b. 1957) Lab., Gateshead, Maj. 12,549

*Menzies, Mark (b. 1971) C., Fylde, Maj. 13,185

Mercer, Patrick (b. 1956) C., Newark, Maj. 16,152

*Reeves, Rachel (b. 1979) Lab., Leeds West, Maj. 7,016

Reid, Alan (b. 1954) LD, Argyll & Bute, Maj. 3,431

*Reynolds, Emma (b. 1977) Lab., Wolverhampton North East, Maj. 2,484

*Reynolds, Jonathan (b. 1980) Lab. (Co-op), Stalybridge & Hyde, Maj. 2,744

Rifkind, Rt. Hon. Sir Malcolm (b. 1946) C., Kensington, Maj. 8,616

Riordan, Linda (b. 1953) Lab. (Co-op), Halifax, Maj. 1,472

*Ritchie, Margaret (b. 1958) SDLP, South Down, Maj. 8,412

Robathan, Andrew (b. 1951) C., Leicestershire South, Maj. 15,524

Robertson, Angus (b. 1969) SNP, Moray, Maj. 5,590

Robertson, Hugh (b. 1962) C., Faversham & Kent Mid, Maj. 17,088

Robertson, John (b. 1952) Lab., Glasgow North West, Maj. 13,611

Robertson, Laurence (b. 1958) C., Tewkesbury, Maj. 6,310

Robinson, Geoffrey (b. 1938) Lab., Coventry North West, Maj. 6,288

Rogerson, Dan (b. 1975) LD, Cornwall North, Maj. 2,981

Rosindell, Andrew (b. 1966) C., Romford, Maj. 16,954

*Rotheram, Steve (b. 1961) Lab., Liverpool Walton, Maj. 19,818

Roy, Frank (b. 1958) Lab., Motherwell & Wishaw, Maj. 16,806

Roy, Lindsay (b. 1949) Lab., Glenrothes, Maj. 16,455

Ruane, Chris (b. 1958) Lab., Vale of Clwyd, Maj. 2,509

*Rudd, Amber (b. 1963) C., Hastings & Rye, Maj. 1,993

Ruddock, Joan (b. 1943) Lab., Lewisham Deptford, Maj. 12,499

Ruffley, David (b. 1962) C., Bury St Edmunds, Maj. 12,380

Russell, Bob (b. 1946) LD, Colchester, Maj. 6,982

*Rutley, David (b. 1961) C., Macclesfield, Maj. 11,959

Sanders, Adrian (b. 1959) LD, Torbay, Maj. 4,078

*Sandys, Laura (b. 1964) C., Thanet South, Maj. 7,617

*Sarwar, Anas (b. 1983) Lab., Glasgow Central, Maj. 10,551

Scott, Lee (b. 1956) C., Ilford North, Maj. 5,404

Seabeck, Alison (b. 1954) Lab., Plymouth Moor View, Maj. 1,588

Selous, Andrew (b. 1962) C., Bedfordshire South West, Maj. 16,649

*Shannon, Jim (b. 1955) DUP, Strangford, Maj. 5,876

Shapps, Grant (b. 1968) C., Welwyn Hatfield, Maj. 7,423

*Sharma, Alok (b. 1967) C., Reading West, Maj. 6,004

Sharma, Virendra (b. 1947) Lab., Ealing Southall, Maj. 9,291

Sheerman, Barry (b. 1940) Lab. (Co-op), Huddersfield, Maj. 4,472

*Shelbrooke, Alec (b. 1976) C., Elmet & Rothwell, Maj. 4,521

Shepherd, Richard (b. 1942) C., Aldridge-Brownhills, Maj. 15,256

Sheridan, Jim (b. 1952) Lab., Paisley & Renfrewshire North, Maj. 15,280

*Shuker, Gavin (b. 1981) Lab. (Co-op), Luton South, Maj. 2,339

Simmonds, Mark (b. 1964) C., Boston & Skegness, Maj. 12,426

Simpson, David (b. 1959) DUP, Upper Bann, Maj. 3,361

†Simpson, Keith (b. 1949) C., Broadland, Maj. 7,292

Singh, Marsha (b. 1954) Lab., Bradford West, Maj. 5,763

*Skidmore, Chris (b. 1981) C., Kingswood, Maj. 2,445

Skinner, Dennis (b. 1932) Lab., Bolsover, Maj. 11,182

†Slaughter, Andrew (b. 1960) Lab., Hammersmith, Maj. 3,549

Smith, Rt. Hon. Andrew (b. 1951) Lab., Oxford East, Maj. 4,581

Smith, Angela C. (b. 1961) Lab., Penistone & Stocksbridge, Maj. 3,049

Smith, Chloe (b. 1982) C., Norwich North, Maj. 3,901

*Smith, Henry (b. 1969) C., Crawley, Maj. 5,928

*Smith, Julian (b. 1971) C., Skipton & Ripon, Maj. 9,950

*Smith, Nick, (b. 1960) Lab., Blaenau Gwent, Maj. 10,516

*Smith, Owen (b. 1970) Lab., Pontypridd, Maj. 2,785

Smith, Sir Robert (b. 1958) LD, Aberdeenshire West & Kincardine, Maj. 6,684

Soames, Hon. Nicholas (b. 1948) C., Sussex Mid, Maj. 7,402

*Soubry, Anna (b. 1956) C., Broxtowe, Maj. 389

Spellar, Rt. Hon. John (b. 1947) Lab., Warley, Maj. 10,756

Spelman, Rt. Hon. Caroline (b. 1958) C., Meriden, Maj. 16,253

*Spencer, Mark (b. 1970) C., Sherwood, Maj. 214

Stanley, Rt. Hon. Sir John (b. 1942) C., Tonbridge & Malling, Maj. 18,178

*Stephenson, Andrew (b. 1981) C., Pendle, Maj. 3,585

*Stevenson, John (b. 1963) C., Carlisle, Maj. 853

*Stewart, Bob (b. 1949) C., Beckenham, Maj. 17,784

*Stewart, Iain (b. 1972) C., Milton Keynes South, Maj. 5,201

*Stewart, Rory (b. 1973) C., Penrith & The Border, Maj. 11,241

Straw, Rt. Hon. Jack (b. 1946) Lab., Blackburn, Maj. 9,856

Streeter, Gary (b. 1955) C., Devon South West, Maj. 15,874

*Stride, Mel (b. 1961) C., Devon Central, Maj. 9,230

Stringer, Graham (b. 1950) Lab., Blackley & Broughton, Maj. 12,303

Stuart, Gisela (b. 1955) Lab., Birmingham, Edgbaston, Maj. 1,274

Stuart, Graham (b. 1962) C., Beverley & Holderness, Maj. 12,987

Stunell, Andrew (b. 1942) LD, Hazel Grove, Maj. 6,371

*Sturdy, Julian (b. 1971) C., York Outer, Maj. 3,688

Sutcliffe, Gerry (b. 1953) Lab., Bradford South, Maj. 4,622

*Swales, Ian (b. 1953) LD, Redcar, Maj. 5,214

Swayne, Desmond (b. 1956) C., New Forest West, Maj. 16,896

Swinson, Jo (b. 1980) LD, Dunbartonshire East, Maj. 2,184

Swire, Hugo (b. 1959) C., Devon East, Maj. 9,114

Syms, Robert (b. 1956) C., Poole, Maj. 7,541

Tami, Mark (b. 1963) Lab., Alyn & Deeside, Maj. 2,919

Tapsell, Sir Peter (b. 1930) C., Louth & Horncastle, Maj. 13,871

Teather, Sarah (b. 1974) LD, Brent Central, Maj. 1,345

Thomas, Gareth (b. 1967) Lab. (Co-op), Harrow West, Maj. 3,143

Thornberry, Emily (b. 1960) Lab., Islington South & Finsbury, Maj. 3,569

Thurso, John (b. 1953) LD, Caithness, Sutherland & Easter Ross, Maj. 4,826

Timms, Rt. Hon. Stephen (b. 1955) Lab., East Ham, Maj. 27,826

GENERAL ELECTION RESULTS

The results of voting in each parliamentary division at the general election of 6 May 2010 are given below.

BOUNDARY CHANGES
The constituency boundaries were redrawn for the 2010 election in England, Wales and Northern Ireland. As a result of the review the number of constituencies increased from 646 to 650, with four new seats in England. Only 138 constituencies had no boundary changes, 59 of them in Scotland.

For the majority of constituencies where a boundary change has taken place, it is not appropriate to make a direct comparison between the results of 2005 and 2010. The seat of Hammersmith, for example, comprises 60 per cent of the old Hammersmith and Fulham constituency and 40 per cent of the old Ealing and Shepherds Bush constituency; it cannot therefore be described as a simple hold for the Labour party. The term 'notional' used here refers to a theoretical set of results, published by Professors Rallings and Thrasher of Plymouth University, which estimates the way each new constituency might have voted in the 2005 general election.

KEY
* New MP
† Previously MP in another seat
‡ Previously MP for another party
§ Notional result; see explanation of boundary changes
E. Electorate
T. Turnout

Abbreviations

AD	Apolitical Democrats	DUP	Democratic Unionist Party	LLPBPP	Local Liberals People Before Politics Party
Alliance	Alliance	Eng. Dem.	English Democrats	Loony	Monster Raving Loony Party
Animals	Animals Count	Eng. Ind.	English Independence Party	LTT	Lawfulness Trustworthiness and Transparency
Anti-War	Fight for an Anti-War Government	F and R	For Freedom and Responsibility		
APP	Animal Protection Party	FDP	Fancy Dress Party	Macc. Ind.	The Macclesfield Independent
Battersea	Putting the People of Battersea First	Good	The Common Good		
		Green	Green	Magna Carta	The Magna Carta Party
BB	A Better Britain for All	Green Belt	Independent Save Our Green Belt	Mansfield	Mansfield Independent Forum
BCP	Basingstoke Common Man			Ind.	
		Green Soc.	Alliance for Green Socialism	Meb. Ker.	Mebyon Kernow
Bean	New Millennium Bean			Med. Ind.	Medway Independent
Beer	Reduce Tax on Beer Party	Humanity	Humanity	Mid.	Middle England Party
Best	The Best of a Bad Bunch	Impact	Impact Party	England	
BIB	Bushra Irfan of Blackburn	Ind.	Independent	MP Expense	A Vote Against MP Expense Abuse
BIC	Bromsgrove Independent Conservative	Ind. CCF	New Independent Conservative Chelsea and Fulham	MRP	Money Reform Party
Blaenau Voice	Blaenau Gwent People's Voice	Ind. CHC	Independent Community and Health Concern	Nat. Dem.	National Democrat
				ND	No Description
Blue	Blue Environment Party	Ind. EACPS	Independent Ealing Action Communities Public Services	New Party	The New Party
BNP	British National Party			NF	National Front
BP Elvis	Bus-Pass Elvis Party			NFP	Nationwide Reform Party
C.	Conservative	Ind. Fed.	Independents Federation UK	No Vote	No Candidate Deserves My Vote
Ch. M.	Christian Movement for Great Britain	Ind. People	Independent People Together	Nobody	Nobody Party
Ch. P.	Christian Party			NSPS	Northampton – Save Our Public Services
Christian	Christian	Ind. Rantzen	Independent Rantzen		
CIP	Campaign for Independent Politicians	Ind. Voice	Independent Voice for Halifax	Parenting	Equal Parenting Alliance
City Ind.	City Independent	Integrity	Integrity UK	PBP	People Before Profit
Clause 28	Clause 28, Children's Protection Christian Democrats	IZB	Islam Zinda Baad Platform	PC	Plaid Cymru
		J & AC	Justice & Anti-Corruption Party	Pirate	Pirate Party UK
CNBPG	Community Need Before Private Greed	Jacobite	Scottish Jacobite Party	PNDP	People's National Democratic Party
Comm.	Communist Party	Joy	The Joy of Talk	Poetry	The True English (Poetry) Party
Comm. Brit.	Communist Party of Britain	JP	Justice Party		
		King George	Save King George Hospital	PP Essex	Peoples Party Essex
Comm. Lge	Communist League			PPN-V	Peace Party Non-Violence Justice Environment
Cornish D.	Cornish Democrats	Lab.	Labour		
CPA	Christian People's Alliance	Lab. (Co-op)	Labour and Co-operative	R and E	Citizens for Undead Rights and Equality
CSP	Common Sense Party	Land	Land is Power		
Currency	Virtue Currency Cognitive Appraisal Party	LD	Liberal Democrat	RA	Solihull and Meridien Residents' Association
		Leave EU	Independent Leave the EU Alliance	Reform	Reform 2000
D. Nat.	Democratic Nationalist			Respect	Respect the Unity Coalition
DDP	Direct Democracy Party	Lib.	Liberal		
Deficit	Cut the Deficit Party	Libertarian	Libertarian Party	RP	The Restoration Party
Dem. Lab.	Democratic Labour Party	Lincs. Ind.	Lincolnshire Independents	RRG	Radical Reform Group

SACL	Scotland Against Crooked Lawyers
Save QM	Independents to Save Queen Mary's Hospital
Science	The Science Party
SDLP	Social Democratic and Labour Party
SEP	Socialist Equality Party
SF	Sinn Fein
SMA	Scrap Members Allowances
Snouts	Get Snouts Out The Trough
SNP	Scottish National Party
Soc.	Socialist Party
Soc. Alt.	Socialist Alternative Party
Soc. Dem.	Social Democratic Party
Soc. Lab.	Socialist Labour Party
South Speaker	All the South Party The Speaker
SSP	Scottish Socialist Party
Staffs Ind.	Staffordshire Independent Group
Tendring	Tendring First
TOC	Tamsin Omond to the Commons
Trust	Trust
TUSC	Trade Unionist and Socialist Coalition
TUV	Traditional Unionist Voice
UCUNF	Ulster Conservatives and Unionists – New Force
UK Integrity	Independents Federation UK – Honest Integrity Democracy
UKIP	UK Independence Party
UPS	Unity for Peace and Socialism
Voice	United Voice
Wessex Reg.	Wessex Regionalist
Workers Lib.	Alliance for Workers Liberty
WP	Workers' Party
WRP	Workers' Revolutionary Party
You	You Party
Youth	Youth Party
YP	Go Mad and Vote For Yourself Party
YRDPL	Your Right to Democracy Party Limited

PARLIAMENTARY CONSTITUENCIES AS AT 6 MAY 2010 GENERAL ELECTION

UK Turnout
E. 45,533,536 T. 29,643,522 (65.1%)

ENGLAND

§ALDERSHOT
E. 71,469 T. 45,384 (63.50%) C. hold
Gerald Howarth, C.   21,203
Adrian Collett, LD   15,617
Jonathan Slater, Lab.   5,489
Robert Snare, UKIP   2,041
Gary Crowd, Eng. Ind.   803
Juliana Brimicombe, Ch. P.   231
C. majority 5,586 (12.31%)
Notional 1.41% swing C. to LD
(2005: C. majority 6,345 (15.12%))

§ALDRIDGE-BROWNHILLS
E. 59,355 T. 38,634 (65.09%) C. hold
Richard Shepherd, C.   22,913
Ashiq Hussain, Lab.   7,647
Ian Jenkins, LD   6,833
Karl Macnaughton, Green   847
Sue Gray, Ch. P.   394
C. majority 15,266 (39.51%)
Notional 12.01% swing Lab. to C.
(2005: C. majority 5,732 (15.49%))

§ALTRINCHAM & SALE WEST
E. 71,254 T. 49,393 (69.32%) C. hold
Graham Brady, C.   24,176
Jane Brophy, LD   12,581
Tom Ross, Lab.   11,073
Kenneth Bullman, UKIP   1,563
C. majority 11,595 (23.47%)
Notional 0.83% swing C. to LD
(2005: C. majority 7,618 (17.57%))

§AMBER VALLEY
E. 70,171 T. 45,958 (65.49%) C. gain
*Nigel Mills, C.   17,746
Judy Mallaber, Lab.   17,210
Tom Snowdon, LD   6,636
Michael Clarke, BNP   3,195
Sue Ransome, UKIP   906
Sam Thing, Loony   265
C. majority 536 (1.17%)
Notional 6.85% swing Lab. to C.
(2005: Lab. majority 5,512 (12.53%))

§ARUNDEL & SOUTH DOWNS
E. 77,564 T. 55,982 (72.18%) C. hold
Nick Herbert, C.   32,333
Derek Deedman, LD   15,642
Tim Lunnon, Lab.   4,835
Stuart Bower, UKIP   3,172
C. majority 16,691 (29.81%)
Notional 3.00% swing LD to C.
(2005: C. majority 12,291 (23.81%))

§ASHFIELD
E. 77,379 T. 48,196 (62.29%) Lab. hold
*Gloria De Piero, Lab.   16,239
Jason Zadrozny, LD   16,047
Garry Hickton, C.   10,698
Edward Holmes, BNP   2,781
Tony Ellis, Eng. Dem.   1,102
Terry Coleman, UKIP   933
Eddie Smith, Ind.   396
Lab. majority 192 (0.40%)
Notional 17.23% swing Lab. to LD
(2005: Lab. majority 10,370 (24.28%))

§ASHFORD
E. 81,269 T. 55,185 (67.90%) C. hold
Damian Green, C.   29,878
Chris Took, LD   12,581
Chris Clark, Lab.   9,204
Jeffrey Elenor, UKIP   2,508
Steve Campkin, Green   1,014
C. majority 17,297 (31.34%)
Notional 2.25% swing C. to LD
(2005: C. majority 12,268 (25.02%))

§ASHTON UNDER LYNE
E. 67,564 T. 38,432 (56.88%) Lab. hold
David Heyes, Lab.   18,604
Seema Kennedy, C.   9,510
Paul Larkin, LD   5,703
David Lomas, BNP   2,929
Angela McManus, UKIP   1,686
Lab. majority 9,094 (23.66%)
Notional 7.34% swing Lab. to C.
(2005: Lab. majority 13,199 (38.33%))

§AYLESBURY
E. 77,934 T. 53,162 (68.21%) C. hold
David Lidington, C.   27,736
Steven Lambert, LD   15,118
Kathryn White, Lab.   6,695
Chris Adams, UKIP   3,613
C. majority 12,618 (23.73%)
Notional 2.12% swing LD to C.
(2005: C. majority 9,314 (19.49%))

§BANBURY
E. 86,986 T. 56,241 (64.66%) C. hold
Tony Baldry, C.   29,703
David Rundle, LD   11,476
Les Sibley, Lab.   10,773
Dr David Fairweather, UKIP   2,806
Alastair White, Green   959
Roseanne Edwards, Ind.   524
C. majority 18,227 (32.41%)
Notional 1.51% swing LD to C.
(2005: C. majority 10,090 (18.79%))

§BARKING
E. 73,864 T. 45,343 (61.39%) Lab. hold
Margaret Hodge, Lab.   24,628
Simon Marcus, C.   8,073
Nick Griffin, BNP   6,620
Dominic Carman, LD   3,719
Frank Maloney, UKIP   1,300
George Hargreaves, Ch. P.   482
Jayne Forbes, Green   317
Crucial Chris Dowling, Loony   82
Thomas Darwood, Ind.   77
Dapo Sijuwola, RP   45
Lab. majority 16,555 (36.51%)
Notional 1.73% swing C. to Lab.
(2005: Lab. majority 12,183 (33.04%))

§BARNSLEY CENTRAL
E. 65,543 T. 37,001 (56.45%) Lab. hold
Eric Illsley, Lab.   17,487
Christopher Wiggin, LD   6,394
Piers Tempest, C.   6,388
Ian Sutton, BNP   3,307
David Silver, UKIP   1,727
Donald Wood, Ind.   732
Tony Devoy, Ind.   610
Terry Robinson, Soc. Lab.   356
Lab. majority 11,093 (29.98%)
Notional 4.17% swing Lab. to LD
(2005: Lab. majority 11,839 (38.32%))

§BARNSLEY EAST
E. 68,435 T. 38,386 (56.09%) Lab. hold
*Michael Dugher, Lab.   18,059
John Brown, LD   6,969
James Hockney, C.   6,329
Colin Porter, BNP   3,301
Tony Watson, UKIP   1,731
Kevin Hogan, Ind.   712
Eddie Devoy, Ind.   684
Ken Capstick, Soc. Lab.   601
Lab. majority 11,090 (28.89%)
Notional 14.02% swing Lab. to LD
(2005: Lab. majority 18,298 (56.94%))

§BARROW & FURNESS
E. 68,758 T. 44,124 (64.17%)
                      Lab. Co-op hold
*John Woodcock, Lab. Co-op   21,226
John Gough, C.   16,018
Barry Rabone, LD   4,424
John Smith, UKIP   841
Mike Ashburner, BNP   840
Christopher Loynes, Green   530
Brian Greaves, Ind.   245
Lab. Co-op majority 5,208 (11.80%)
Notional 0.37% swing Lab. to C.
(2005: Lab. majority 4,843 (12.54%))

§BASILDON & BILLERICAY
E. 65,482 T. 41,569 (63.48%) C. hold
John Baron, C.   21,922
Allan Davies, Lab.   9,584
Mike Hibbs, LD   6,538
Irene Bateman, BNP   1,934
Alan Broad, UKIP   1,591
C. majority 12,338 (29.68%)
Notional 9.23% swing Lab. to C.
(2005: C. majority 4,559 (11.22%))

§BASILDON SOUTH & THURROCK
EAST
E. 71,815 T. 44,735 (62.29%) C. gain
*Stephen Metcalfe, C.   19,624
Angela Smith, Lab. Co-op   13,852
Geoff Williams, LD   5,977
Kerry Smith, UKIP   2,639
Chris Roberts, BNP   2,518
None Of The Above X, ND   125
C. majority 5,772 (12.90%)
Notional 7.52% swing Lab. to C.
(2005: Lab. majority 905 (2.14%))

§BASINGSTOKE
E. 75,470 T. 50,654 (67.12%) C. hold
Maria Miller, C.   25,590
John Shaw, LD   12,414
Funda Pepperell, Lab.   10,327
Stella Howell, UKIP   2,076
Steve Saul, BCP   247
C. majority 13,176 (26.01%)
Notional 4.55% swing LD to C.
(2005: C. majority 2,651 (6.27%))

§BASSETLAW
E. 76,542 T. 49,577 (64.77%) Lab. hold
John Mann, Lab.   25,018
Keith Girling, C.   16,803
David Dobbie, LD   5,570
Andrea Hamilton, UKIP   1,779
Grahame Whithurst, Ind.   407
Lab. majority 8,215 (16.57%)
Notional 0.67% swing Lab. to C.
(2005: Lab. majority 8,256 (17.92%))

§BATH
E. 65,603 T. 47,086 (71.77%) LD hold
Don Foster, LD   26,651
Fabian Richter, C.   14,768
Hattie Ajderian, Lab.   3,251
Eric Lucas, Green   1,120
Ernie Warrender, UKIP   890
Steve Hewett, Ch. P.   250
ANON, ND   69
Sean Geddis, Ind.   56
Robert Craig, South   31
LD majority 11,883 (25.24%)
Notional 5.84% swing C. to LD
(2005: LD majority 5,624 (13.56%))

§BATLEY & SPEN
E. 76,732 T. 51,109 (66.61%) Lab. hold
Mike Wood, Lab.   21,565
Janice Small, C.   17,159
Neil Bentley, LD   8,095
David Exley, BNP   3,685
Matt Blakeley, Green   605
Lab. majority 4,406 (8.62%)
Notional 2.46% swing Lab. to C.
(2005: Lab. majority 6,060 (13.54%))

§BATTERSEA
E. 74,300 T. 48,792 (65.67%) C. gain
*Jane Ellison, C.   23,103
Martin Linton, Lab.   17,126
Layla Moran, LD   7,176
Guy Evans, Green   559
Christopher MacDonald, UKIP   505
Hugh Salmon, Battersea   168
Tom Fox, Ind.   155
C. majority 5,977 (12.25%)
Notional 6.53% swing Lab. to C.
(2005: Lab. majority 332 (0.81%))

§BEACONSFIELD
E. 74,982 T. 52,490 (70.00%) C. hold
Dominic Grieve, C.   32,053
John Edwards, LD   10,271
Jeremy Miles, Lab.   6,135
Delphine Gray-Fisk, UKIP   2,597
Jem Bailey, Green   768
Andrew Cowen, MP Expense   475
Quentin Baron, Ind.   191
C. majority 21,782 (41.50%)
Notional 4.70% swing LD to C.
(2005: C. majority 14,794 (32.09%))

§BECKENHAM
E. 66,219 T. 47,686 (72.01%) C. hold
*Bob Stewart, C.   27,597
Steve Jenkins, LD   9,813
Damien Egan, Lab.   6,893
Owen Brolly, UKIP   1,551
Roger Tonks, BNP   1,001
Ann Garrett, Green   608
Dan Eastgate, Eng. Dem.   223
C. majority 17,784 (37.29%)
Notional 3.15% swing C. to LD
(2005: C. majority 16,913 (40.40%))

§BEDFORD
E. 68,491 T. 45,102 (65.85%) C. gain
*Richard Fuller, C.   17,546
Patrick Hall, Lab.   16,193
Henry Vann, LD   8,957
Mark Adkin, UKIP   1,136
William Dewick, BNP   757
Ben Foley, Green   393
Samrat Bhandari, Ind.   120
C. majority 1,353 (3.00%)
Notional 5.52% swing Lab. to C.
(2005: Lab. majority 3,413 (8.04%))

§BEDFORDSHIRE MID
E. 76,023 T. 54,897 (72.21%) C. hold
Nadine Dorries, C.   28,815
Linda Jack, LD   13,663
David Reeves, Lab.   8,108
Bill Hall, UKIP   2,826
Malcolm Bailey, Green   773
John Cooper, Eng. Dem.   712
C. majority 15,152 (27.60%)
Notional 2.26% swing LD to C.
(2005: C. majority 11,593 (23.08%))

§BEDFORDSHIRE NORTH EAST
E. 78,060 T. 55,552 (71.17%) C. hold
Alistair Burt, C.   30,989
Mike Pitt, LD   12,047
Edward Brown,Lab.   8,957
Brian Capell, UKIP   2,294
Ian Seeby, BNP   1,265
C. majority 18,942 (34.10%)
Notional 2.55% swing LD to C.
(2005: C. majority 12,128 (24.59%))

BEDFORDSHIRE SOUTH WEST
E. 76,559 T. 50,774 (66.32%) C. hold
Andrew Selous, C.   26,815
Rod Cantrill, LD   10,166
Jennifer Bone, Lab.   9,948
Martin Newman, UKIP   2,142
Mark Tolman, BNP   1,703
C. majority 16,649 (32.79%)
0.69% swing LD to C.
(2005: C. majority 8,277 (18.07%))

§BERMONDSEY & OLD SOUTHWARK
E. 77,623 T. 44,651 (57.52%) LD hold
Simon Hughes, LD   21,590
Val Shawcross, Lab.   13,060
Loanna Morrison, C.   7,638
Stephen Tyler, BNP   1,370
Tom Chance, Green   718
Alan Kirkby, Ind.   155
Steve Freeman, ND   120
LD majority 8,530 (19.10%)
Notional 1.55% swing Lab. to LD
(2005: LD majority 5,769 (16.00%))

§BERWICK-UPON-TWEED
E. 57,403 T. 38,439 (66.96%) LD hold
Sir Alan Beith, LD   16,806
Anne-Marie Trevelyan, C.   14,116
Alan Strickland, Lab.   5,061
Michael Weatherley, UKIP   1,243
Peter Mailer, BNP   1,213
LD majority 2,690 (7.00%)
Notional 8.29% swing LD to C.
(2005: LD majority 8,585 (23.58%))

§BETHNAL GREEN & BOW
E. 81,243 T. 50,728 (62.44%) Lab. gain
*Rushanara Ali, Lab.   21,784
Ajmal Masroor, LD   10,210
Abjol Miah, Respect   8,532
Zakir Khan, C.   7,071
Jeffrey Marshall, BNP   1,405
Farid Bakht, Green   856
Patrick Brooks, Ind.   277
Alexander Van Terheyden, Pirate   213
Hasib Hikmat, Voice   209
Haji Choudhury, Ind.   100
Ahmed Malik, Ind.   71
Lab. majority 11,574 (22.82%)
Notional 14.11% swing Respect to Lab.
(2005: Respect majority 804 (2.10%))

§BEVERLEY & HOLDERNESS
E. 79,611 T. 53,199 (66.82%) C. hold
Graham Stuart, C. 25,063
Craig Dobson, LD 12,076
Ian Saunders, Lab. 11,224
Neil Whitelam, BNP 2,080
Andrew Horsfield, UKIP 1,845
Bill Rigby, Green 686
Ron Hughes, Ind. 225
C. majority 12,987 (24.41%)
Notional 1.58% swing LD to C.
(2005: C. majority 3,097 (6.23%))

§BEXHILL & BATTLE
E. 79,208 T. 54,587 (68.92%) C. hold
Greg Barker, C. 28,147
Mary Varrall, LD 15,267
James Royston, Lab. 6,524
Stuart Wheeler, Trust 2,699
Neil Jackson, BNP 1,950
C. majority 12,880 (23.60%)
Notional 3.96% swing C. to LD
(2005: C. majority 15,893 (31.52%))

§BEXLEYHEATH & CRAYFORD
E. 64,985 T. 43,182 (66.45%) C. hold
David Evennett, C. 21,794
Howard Dawber, Lab. 11,450
Karelia Scott, LD 5,502
Stephen James, BNP 2,042
John Dunford, UKIP 1,557
John Griffiths, Eng. Dem. 466
Adrian Ross, Green 371
C. majority 10,344 (23.95%)
Notional 5.81% swing Lab. to C.
(2005: C. majority 5,167 (12.33%))

§BIRKENHEAD
E. 62,773 T. 35,323 (56.27%) Lab. hold
Frank Field, Lab. 22,082
Andrew Gilbert, C. 6,687
Stuart Kelly, LD 6,554
Lab. majority 15,395 (43.58%)
Notional 2.34% swing Lab. to C.
(2005: Lab. majority 14,638 (46.21%))

§BIRMINGHAM EDGBASTON
E. 68,573 T. 41,571 (60.62%) Lab. hold
Gisela Stuart, Lab. 16,894
Deirdre Alden, C. 15,620
Roger Harmer, LD 6,387
Trevor Lloyd, BNP 1,196
Greville Warwick, UKIP 732
Phil Simpson, Green 469
Harry Takhar, Impact 146
Charith Fernando, Ch. P. 127
Lab. majority 1,274 (3.06%)
Notional 0.47% swing Lab. to C.
(2005: Lab. majority 1,555 (4.01%))

§BIRMINGHAM ERDINGTON
E. 66,405 T. 35,546 (53.53%) Lab. hold
*Jack Dromey, Lab. 14,869
Robert Alden, C. 11,592
Ann Holtom, LD 5,742
Kevin McHugh, BNP 1,815
Maria Foy, UKIP 842
Tony Tomkins, Ind. 240
Terry Williams, NF 229
Timothy Gray, Ch. P. 217
Lab. majority 3,277 (9.22%)
Notional 10.43% swing Lab. to C.
(2005: Lab. majority 9,677 (30.07%))

§BIRMINGHAM HALL GREEN
E. 76,580 T. 48,727 (63.63%) Lab. hold
Roger Godsiff, Lab. 16,039
Salma Yaqoob, Respect 12,240
Jerry Evans, LD 11,988
Jo Barker, C. 7,320
Alan Blumenthal, UKIP 950
Andrew Gardner, Ind. 190
Lab. majority 3,799 (7.80%)
Notional 11.07% swing Lab. to Respect
(2005: Lab. majority 6,649 (15.90%))

§BIRMINGHAM HODGE HILL
E. 75,040 T. 42,472 (56.60%) Lab. hold
Liam Byrne, Lab. 22,077
Tariq Khan, LD 11,775
Shailesh Parekh, C. 4,936
Richard Lumby, BNP 2,333
Waheed Rafiq, UKIP 714
Peter Johnson, Soc. Dem. 637
Lab. majority 10,302 (24.26%)
Notional 3.61% swing LD to Lab.
(2005: Lab. majority 7,063 (17.05%))

§BIRMINGHAM LADYWOOD
E. 73,646 T. 35,833 (48.66%) Lab. hold
*Shabana Mahmood, Lab. 19,950
Ayoub Khan, LD 9,845
Nusrat Ghani, C. 4,277
Christopher Booth, UKIP 902
Peter Beck, Green 859
Lab. majority 10,105 (28.20%)
Notional 2.49% swing LD to Lab.
(2005: Lab. majority 6,804 (23.23%))

§BIRMINGHAM NORTHFIELD
E. 71,338 T. 41,814 (58.61%) Lab. hold
Richard Burden, Lab. 16,841
Keely Huxtable, C. 14,059
Mike Dixon, LD 6,550
Les Orton, BNP 2,290
John Borthwick, UKIP 1,363
Susan Pearce, Green 406
Dick Rodgers, Good 305
Lab. majority 2,782 (6.65%)
Notional 6.64% swing Lab. to C.
(2005: Lab. majority 7,879 (19.93%))

§BIRMINGHAM PERRY BARR
E. 71,304 T. 42,045 (58.97%) Lab. hold
Khalid Mahmood, Lab. 21,142
Karen Hamilton, LD 9,234
William Norton, C. 8,960
Melvin Ward, UKIP 1,675
John Tyrrell, Soc. Lab. 527
Deborah Hey-Smith, Ch. P. 507
Lab. majority 11,908 (28.32%)
Notional 4.05% swing LD to Lab.
(2005: Lab. majority 7,825 (20.22%))

§BIRMINGHAM SELLY OAK
E. 74,805 T. 46,563 (62.25%) Lab. hold
Steve McCabe, Lab. 17,950
Nigel Dawkins, C. 14,468
David Radcliffe, LD 10,371
Lynette Orton, BNP 1,820
Jeffery Burgess, UKIP 1,131
James Burn, Green 664
Samuel Leeds, Ch. P. 159
Lab. majority 3,482 (7.48%)
Notional 4.83% swing Lab. to C.
(2005: Lab. majority 7,564 (17.14%))

§BIRMINGHAM YARDLEY
E. 72,321 T. 40,850 (56.48%) LD hold
John Hemming, LD 16,162
Lynnette Kelly, Lab. 13,160
Meirion Jenkins, C. 7,836
Tanya Lumby, BNP 2,153
Graham Duffen, UKIP 1,190
Paul Morris, NF 349
LD majority 3,002 (7.35%)
Notional 0.02% swing Lab. to LD
(2005: LD majority 2,864 (7.30%))

§BISHOP AUCKLAND
E. 68,370 T. 41,136 (60.17%) Lab. hold
Helen Goodman, Lab. 16,023
Barbara Harrison, C. 10,805
Mark Wilkes, LD 9,189
Adam Walker, BNP 2,036
Sam Zair, LLPBPP 1,964
Dave Brothers, UKIP 1,119
Lab. majority 5,218 (12.68%)
Notional 7.20% swing Lab. to C.
(2005: Lab. majority 10,047 (26.35%))

§BLACKBURN
E. 72,331 T. 45,499 (62.90%) Lab. hold
Jack Straw, Lab. 21,751
Michael Law-Riding, C. 11,895
Paul English, LD 6,918
Robin Evans, BNP 2,158
Bushra Irfanullah, BIB 1,424
Bobby Anwar, UKIP 942
Grace Astley, Ind. 238
Janis Sharp, Ind. 173
Lab. majority 9,856 (21.66%)
Notional 1.11% swing C. to Lab.
(2005: Lab. majority 8,048 (19.45%))

§BLACKLEY & BROUGHTON
E. 69,489 T. 34,204 (49.22%) Lab. hold
Graham Stringer, Lab. 18,563
James Edsberg, C. 6,260
William Hobhouse, LD 4,861
Derek Adams, BNP 2,469
Kay Phillips, Respect 996
Bob Willescroft, UKIP 894
Shafiq-Uz Zaman, Ch. P. 161
Lab. majority 12,303 (35.97%)
Notional 6.74% swing Lab. to C.
(2005: Lab. majority 13,060 (43.35%))

§BLACKPOOL NORTH & CLEVELEYS
E. 65,888 T. 40,591 (61.61%) C. gain
*Paul Maynard, C. 16,964
Penny Martin, Lab. 14,814
Bill Greene, LD 5,400
Roy Hopwood, UKIP 1,659
James Clayton, BNP 1,556
Tony Davies, Loony 198
C. majority 2,150 (5.30%)
Notional 6.89% swing Lab. to C.
(2005: Lab. majority 3,241 (8.48%))

§BLACKPOOL SOUTH
E. 63,025 T. 35,191 (55.84%) Lab. hold
Gordon Marsden, Lab. 14,448
Ron Bell, C. 12,597
Doreen Holt, LD 5,082
Roy Goodwin, BNP 1,482
Hamish Howitt, UKIP 1,352
Si Thu Tun, Integrity 230
Lab. majority 1,851 (5.26%)
Notional 6.21% swing Lab. to C.
(2005: Lab. majority 5,911 (17.67%))

§BLAYDON
E. 67,808 T. 44,913 (66.24%) Lab. hold
Dave Anderson, Lab.   22,297
Neil Bradbury, LD   13,180
Glenn Hall, C.   7,159
Keith McFarlane, BNP   2,277
Lab. majority 9,117 (20.30%)
Notional 3.28% swing LD to Lab.
(2005: Lab. majority 5,748 (13.75%))

BLYTH VALLEY
E. 64,263 T. 38,566 (60.01%) Lab. hold
Ronnie Campbell, Lab.   17,156
Jeffrey Reid, LD   10,488
Barry Flux, C.   6,412
Steve Fairbairn, BNP   1,699
James Condon, UKIP   1,665
Barry Elliott, Ind.   819
Allan White, Eng. Dem.   327
Lab. majority 6,668 (17.29%)
3.27% swing Lab. to LD
(2005: Lab. majority 8,527 (23.84%))

§BOGNOR REGIS &
LITTLEHAMPTON
E. 70,812 T. 46,852 (66.16%) C. hold
Nick Gibb, C.   24,087
Simon McDougall, LD   11,024
Michael Jones, Lab.   6,580
Douglas Denny, UKIP   3,036
Andrew Moffat, BNP   1,890
Melissa Briggs, Ind.   235
C. majority 13,063 (27.88%)
Notional 2.31% swing LD to C.
(2005: C. majority 8,617 (20.15%))

§BOLSOVER
E. 72,766 T. 43,988 (60.45%) Lab. hold
Dennis Skinner, Lab.   21,994
Lee Rowley, C.   10,812
Denise Hawksworth, LD   6,821
Martin Radford, BNP   2,640
Ray Calladine, UKIP   1,721
Lab. majority 11,182 (25.42%)
Notional 11.23% swing Lab. to C.
(2005: Lab. majority 19,260 (47.68%))

§BOLTON NORTH EAST
E. 67,281 T. 43,277 (64.32%) Lab. hold
David Crausby, Lab.   19,870
Deborah Dunleavy, C.   15,786
Paul Ankers, LD   5,624
Neil Johnson, UKIP   1,815
Norma Armston, You   182
Lab. majority 4,084 (9.44%)
Notional 1.27% swing Lab. to C.
(2005: Lab. majority 4,527 (11.99%))

§BOLTON SOUTH EAST
E. 69,928 T. 39,604 (56.64%) Lab. hold
*Yasmin Qureshi, Lab.   18,782
Andy Morgan, C.   10,148
Donal O'Hanlon, LD   6,289
Sheila Spink, BNP   2,012
Ian Sidaway, UKIP   1,564
Alan Johnson, Green   614
Navaid Syed, CPA   195
Lab. majority 8,634 (21.80%)
Notional 5.61% swing Lab. to C.
(2005: Lab. majority 11,483 (33.03%))

§BOLTON WEST
E. 71,250 T. 47,576 (66.77%) Lab. hold
*Julie Hilling, Lab.   18,327
Susan Williams, C.   18,235
Jackie Pearcey, LD   8,177
Harry Lamb, UKIP   1,901
Rachel Mann, Green   545
Jimmy Jones, Ind.   254
Doug Bagnall, You   137
Lab. majority 92 (0.19%)
Notional 5.88% swing Lab. to C.
(2005: Lab. majority 5,041 (11.95%))

§BOOTLE
E. 71,426 T. 41,277 (57.79%) Lab. hold
Joe Benton, Lab.   27,426
James Murray, LD   6,245
Sohail Qureshi, C.   3,678
Paul Nuttall, UKIP   2,514
Charles Stewart, BNP   942
Pete Glover, TUSC   472
Lab. majority 21,181 (51.31%)
Notional 1.59% swing Lab. to LD
(2005: Lab. majority 20,125 (54.48%))

§BOSTON & SKEGNESS
E. 70,529 T. 43,125 (61.15%) C. hold
Mark Simmonds, C.   21,325
Paul Kenny, Lab.   8,899
Philip Smith, LD   6,371
Christopher Pain, UKIP   4,081
David Owens, BNP   2,278
Peter Wilson, Ind.   171
C. majority 12,426 (28.81%)
Notional 7.00% swing Lab. to C.
(2005: C. majority 6,391 (14.81%))

§BOSWORTH
E. 77,296 T. 54,274 (70.22%) C. hold
David Tredinnick, C.   23,132
Michael Mullaney, LD   18,100
Rory Palmer, Lab.   8,674
John Ryde, BNP   2,458
Dutch Veldhuizen, UKIP   1,098
James Lampitt, Eng. Dem.   615
Michael Brooks, Science   197
C. majority 5,032 (9.27%)
Notional 5.87% swing C. to LD
(2005: C. majority 5,335 (10.72%))

§BOURNEMOUTH EAST
E. 71,125 T. 44,024 (61.90%) C. hold
Tobias Ellwood, C.   21,320
Lisa Northover, LD   13,592
David Stokes, Lab.   5,836
David Hughes, UKIP   3,027
Steven Humphrey, Ind.   249
C. majority 7,728 (17.55%)
Notional 1.76% swing LD to C.
(2005: C. majority 5,874 (14.04%))

§BOURNEMOUTH WEST
E. 71,753 T. 41,659 (58.06%) C. hold
*Conor Burns, C.   18,808
Alasdair Murray, LD   13,225
Sharon Carr-Brown, Lab.   6,171
Philip Glover, UKIP   2,999
Harvey Taylor, Ind.   456
C. majority 5,583 (13.40%)
Notional 2.92% swing LD to C.
(2005: C. majority 2,766 (7.55%))

§BRACKNELL
E. 76,885 T. 52,140 (67.82%) C. hold
*Phillip Lee, C.   27,327
Ray Earwicker, LD   11,623
John Piasecki, Lab.   8,755
Murray Barter, UKIP   2,297
Mark Burke, BNP   1,253
David Young, Green   825
Dan Haycocks, SMA   60
C. majority 15,704 (30.12%)
Notional 0.97% swing C. to LD
(2005: C. majority 10,037 (21.96%))

§BRADFORD EAST
E. 65,116 T. 40,457 (62.13%) LD gain
*David Ward, LD   13,637
Terry Rooney, Lab.   13,272
Mohammed Riaz, C.   10,860
Neville Poynton, BNP   1,854
Raja Hussain, Ind.   375
Peter Shields, Ind.   237
Gerry Robinson, NF   222
LD majority 365 (0.90%)
Notional 7.57% swing Lab. to LD
(2005: Lab. majority 5,227 (14.24%))

§BRADFORD SOUTH
E. 63,580 T. 37,995 (59.76%) Lab. hold
Gerry Sutcliffe, Lab.   15,682
Matt Palmer, C.   11,060
Alun Griffiths, LD   6,948
Sharon Sutton, BNP   2,651
Jamie Illingworth, UKIP   1,339
James Lewthwaite, D Nat   315
Lab. majority 4,622 (12.16%)
Notional 5.91% swing Lab. to C.
(2005: Lab. majority 8,444 (23.99%))

§BRADFORD WEST
E. 62,519 T. 40,576 (64.90%) Lab. hold
Marsha Singh, Lab.   18,401
Zahid Iqbal, C.   12,638
David Hall-Matthews, LD   4,732
Jenny Sampson, BNP   1,370
Arshad Ali, Respect   1,245
David Ford, Green   940
Jason Smith, UKIP   812
Neil Craig, D. Nat.   438
Lab. majority 5,763 (14.20%)
Notional 2.93% swing C. to Lab.
(2005: Lab. majority 3,050 (8.34%))

§BRAINTREE
E. 71,162 T. 49,203 (69.14%) C. hold
Brooks Newmark, C.   25,901
Bill Edwards, Lab.   9,780
Steve Jarvis, LD   9,247
Michael Ford, UKIP   2,477
Paul Hooks, BNP   1,080
Daisy Blench, Green   718
C. majority 16,121 (32.76%)
Notional 6.74% swing Lab. to C.
(2005: C. majority 8,658 (19.28%))

§BRENT CENTRAL
E. 74,076 T. 45,324 (61.19%) LD gain
Sarah Teather, LD   20,026
Dawn Butler, Lab.   18,681
Sachin Rajput, C.   5,068
Shahar Ali, Green   668
Errol Williams, Ch. P.   488
Abdi Duale, Respect   230
Dean McCastree, Ind.   163
LD majority 1,345 (2.97%)
Notional 10.99% swing Lab. to LD
(2005: Lab. majority 7,469 (19.02%))

§BRENT NORTH
E. 83,896 T. 52,298 (62.34%) Lab. hold
Barry Gardiner, Lab.   24,514
Harshadbhai Patel, C.   16,486
James Allie, LD   8,879
Atiq Malik, Ind.   734
Martin Francis, Green   725
Sunita Webb, UKIP   380
Jannen Vamadeva, Ind.   333
Arvind Tailor, Eng. Dem.   247
Lab. majority 8,028 (15.35%)
Notional 2.35% swing Lab. to C.
(2005: Lab. majority 8,830 (20.04%))

§BRENTFORD & ISLEWORTH
E. 83,546 T. 53,765 (64.35%) C. gain
*Mary Macleod, C.   20,022
Ann Keen, Lab.   18,064
Andrew Dakers, LD   12,718
Jason Hargreaves, UKIP   863
John Hunt, Green   787
Paul Winnet, BNP   704
David Cunningham, Eng. Dem.   230
Aamir Bhatti, Ch. P.   210
Evangeline Pillai, CPA   99
Teresa Vanneck-Surplice, Ind.   68
C. majority 1,958 (3.64%)
Notional 5.96% swing Lab. to C.
(2005: Lab. majority 3,633 (8.29%))

§BRENTWOOD & ONGAR
E. 73,224 T. 50,592 (69.09%) C. hold
Eric Pickles, C.   28,793
David Kendall, LD   11,872
Heidi Benzing, Lab.   4,992
Michael McGough, UKIP   2,037
Paul Morris, BNP   1,447
Jess Barnecutt, Green   584
Robin Tilbrook, Eng. Dem.   491
James Sapwell, Ind.   263
Danny Attfield, ND   113
C. majority 16,921 (33.45%)
Notional 3.12% swing LD to C.
(2005: C. majority 12,522 (27.21%))

§BRIDGWATER & SOMERSET WEST
E. 76,560 T. 54,493 (71.18%) C. hold
Ian Liddell-Grainger, C.   24,675
Theo Butt Philip, LD   15,426
Kathryn Pearce, Lab.   9,332
Peter Hollings, UKIP   2,604
Donna Treanor, BNP   1,282
Charles Graham, Green   859
Bob Cudlipp, Ind.   315
C. majority 9,249 (16.97%)
Notional 2.88% swing C. to LD
(2005: C. majority 10,081 (19.77%))

§BRIGG & GOOLE
E. 67,345 T. 43,874 (65.15%) C. gain
*Andrew Percy, C.   19,680
Ian Cawsey, Lab.   14,533
Richard Nixon, LD   6,414
Nigel Wright, UKIP   1,749
Stephen Ward, BNP   1,498
C. majority 5,147 (11.73%)
Notional 9.79% swing Lab. to C.
(2005: Lab. majority 3,217 (7.84%))

§BRIGHTON KEMPTOWN
E. 66,017 T. 42,705 (64.69%) C. gain
*Simon Kirby, C.   16,217
Simon Burgess, Lab. Co-op   14,889
Juliet Williams, LD   7,691
Ben Duncan, Green   2,330
James Chamberlain-Webber, UKIP   1,384
Dave Hill, TUSC   194
C. majority 1,328 (3.11%)
Notional 3.97% swing Lab. to C.
(2005: Lab. majority 1,853 (4.83%))

§BRIGHTON PAVILION
E. 74,004 T. 51,814 (70.04%) Green gain
*Dr Caroline Lucas, Green   16,238
Nancy Platts, Lab.   14,986
Charlotte Vere, C.   12,275
Bernadette Millam, LD   7,159
Nigel Carter, UKIP   948
Ian Fyvie, Soc. Lab.   148
Soraya Kara, R and E   61
Leo Atreides, ND   19
Green majority 1,252 (2.42%)
Notional 8.45% swing Lab. to Green
(2005: Lab. majority 5,867 (13.11%))

§BRISTOL EAST
E. 69,448 T. 45,017 (64.82%) Lab. hold
Kerry McCarthy, Lab.   16,471
Adeela Shafi, C.   12,749
Mike Popham, LD   10,993
Brian Jenkins, BNP   1,960
Philip Collins, UKIP   1,510
Glenn Vowles, Green   803
Stephen Wright, Eng. Dem.   347
Rae Lynch, TUSC   184
Lab. majority 3,722 (8.27%)
Notional 4.54% swing Lab. to C.
(2005: Lab. majority 7,335 (17.35%))

§BRISTOL NORTH WEST
E. 73,469 T. 50,336 (68.51%) C. gain
*Charlotte Leslie, C.   19,115
Paul Harrod, LD   15,841
Sam Townend, Lab.   13,059
Robert Upton, UKIP   1,175
Ray Carr, Eng. Dem.   635
Alex Dunn, Green   511
C. majority 3,274 (6.50%)
Notional 8.86% swing Lab. to C.
(2005: Lab. majority 2,781 (5.69%))

§BRISTOL SOUTH
E. 78,579 T. 48,377 (61.56%) Lab. hold
Dawn Primarolo, Lab.   18,600
Mark Wright, LD   13,866
Mark Lloyd Davies, C.   11,086
Colin Chidsey, BNP   1,739
Colin McNamee, UKIP   1,264
Charlie Bolton, Green   1,216
Craig Clarke, Eng. Dem.   400
Tom Baldwin, TUSC   206
Lab. majority 4,734 (9.79%)
Notional 7.53% swing Lab. to LD
(2005: Lab. majority 10,928 (24.86%))

§BRISTOL WEST
E. 82,728 T. 55,347 (66.90%) LD hold
Stephen Williams, LD   26,593
Paul Smith, Lab.   15,227
Nick Yarker, C.   10,169
Ricky Knight, Green   2,090
Chris Lees, UKIP   655
Danny Kushlick, Ind.   343
Jon Baker, Eng. Dem.   270
LD majority 11,366 (20.54%)
Notional 9.00% swing Lab. to LD
(2005: LD majority 1,147 (2.55%))

§BROADLAND
E. 73,168 T. 52,676 (71.99%) C. hold
Keith Simpson, C.   24,338
Daniel Roper, LD   17,046
Allyson Barron, Lab.   7,287
Stuart Agnew, UKIP   2,382
Edith Crowther, BNP   871
Susan Curran, Green   752
C. majority 7,292 (13.84%)
Notional 0.06% swing C. to LD
(2005: C. majority 6,573 (13.97%))

§BROMLEY & CHISLEHURST
E. 65,427 T. 44,037 (67.31%) C. hold
Bob Neill, C.   23,569
Sam Webber, LD   9,669
Chris Kirby, Lab.   7,295
Emmett Jenner, UKIP   1,451
Rowena Savage, BNP   1,070
Roisin Robertson, Green   607
Jon Cheeseman, Eng. Dem.   376
C. majority 13,900 (31.56%)
Notional 5.13% swing LD to C.
(2005: C. majority 8,236 (20.57%))

§BROMSGROVE
E. 73,086 T. 51,630 (70.64%) C. hold
*Sajid Javid, C.   22,558
Sam Burden, Lab.   11,250
Philip Ling, LD   10,124
Steven Morson, UKIP   2,950
Adrian Kriss, BIC   2,182
Elizabeth Wainwright, BNP   1,923
Mark France, Ind.   336
Ken Wheatley, Ind.   307
C. majority 11,308 (21.90%)
0.41% swing Lab. to C.
(2005: C. majority 10,080 (21.08%))

§BROXBOURNE
E. 71,391 T. 45,658 (63.95%) C. hold
Charles Walker, C.   26,844
Michael Watson, Lab.   8,040
Allan Witherick, LD   6,107
Steve McCole, BNP   2,159
Martin Harvey, UKIP   1,890
Debbie LeMay, Eng. Dem.   618
C. majority 18,804 (41.18%)
6.43% swing Lab. to C.
(2005: C. majority 11,509 (28.33%))

§BROXTOWE
E. 72,042 T. 52,727 (73.19%) C. gain
*Anna Soubry, C.   20,585
Nick Palmer, Lab.   20,196
David Watts, LD   8,907
Mike Shore, BNP   1,422
Chris Cobb, UKIP   1,194
David Mitchell, Green   423
C. majority 389 (0.74%)
Notional 2.59% swing Lab. to C.
(2005: Lab. majority 2,139 (4.44%))

§BUCKINGHAM
E. 74,996 T. 48,335 (64.45%)
                              Speaker hold
‡John Bercow, Speaker   22,860
John Stevens, Ind.   10,331
Nigel Farage, UKIP   8,401
Patrick Phillips, Ind.   2,394
Debbie Martin, Ind.   1,270
Lynne Mozar, BNP   980
Colin Dale, Loony   856
Geoff Howard, Ind.   435
David Hews, Ch. P.   369
Anthony Watts, Ind.   332
Simon Strutt, Deficit   107
Speaker majority 12,529 (25.92%)
(2005: C. majority 18,716 (37.83%))

BURNLEY
E. 66,616 T. 41,845 (62.82%) LD gain
*Gordon Birtwistle, LD   14,932
Julie Cooper, Lab.   13,114
Richard Ali, C.   6,950
Sharon Wilkinson, BNP   3,747
Andrew Brown, Ind.   1,876
John Wignall, UKIP   929
Andrew Hennessey, Ind.   297
LD majority 1,818 (4.34%)
9.58% swing Lab. to LD
(2005: Lab. majority 5,778 (14.82%))

§BURTON
E. 74,874 T. 49,823 (66.54%) C. gain
*Andrew Griffiths, C.   22,188
Ruth Smeeth, Lab.   15,884
Michael Rodgers, LD   7,891
Alan Hewitt, BNP   2,409
Philip Lancaster, UKIP   1,451
C. majority 6,304 (12.65%)
Notional 8.73% swing Lab. to C.
(2005: Lab. majority 2,132 (4.81%))

§BURY NORTH
E. 66,759 T. 44,961 (67.35%) C. gain
*David Nuttall, C.   18,070
Maryam Khan, Lab.   15,827
Richard Baum, LD   7,645
John Maude, BNP   1,825
Stephen Evans, UKIP   1,282
Bill Brison, Ind.   181
Graeme Lambert, Pirate   131
C. majority 2,243 (4.99%)
Notional 5.02% swing Lab. to C.
(2005: Lab. majority 2,059 (5.05%))

§BURY SOUTH
E. 73,544 T. 48,267 (65.63%) Lab. hold
Ivan Lewis, Lab.   19,508
Michelle Wiseman, C.   16,216
Vic D'Albert, LD   8,796
Jean Purdy, BNP   1,743
Paul Chadwick, UKIP   1,017
Valerie Morris, Eng. Dem.   494
George Heron, Green   493
Lab. majority 3,292 (6.82%)
Notional 8.01% swing Lab. to C.
(2005: Lab. majority 9,779 (22.84%))

§BURY ST EDMUNDS
E. 84,727 T. 58,718 (69.30%) C. hold
David Ruffley, C.   27,899
David Chappell, LD   15,519
Kevin Hind, Lab.   9,776
John Howlett, UKIP   3,003
Mark Ereira-Guyer, Green   2,521
C. majority 12,380 (21.08%)
Notional 2.76% swing C. to LD
(2005: C. majority 10,080 (19.03%))

§CALDER VALLEY
E. 76,903 T. 51,780 (67.33%) C. gain
*Craig Whittaker, C.   20,397
Steph Booth, Lab.   13,966
Hilary Myers, LD   13,037
John Gregory, BNP   1,823
Greg Burrows, UKIP   1,173
Kate Sweeny, Green   858
Tim Cole, Ind.   194
Barry Greenwood, Ind.   175
Paul Rogan, Eng. Dem.   157
C. majority 6,431 (12.42%)
Notional 7.58% swing Lab. to C.
(2005: Lab. majority 1,303 (2.73%))

§CAMBERWELL & PECKHAM
E. 78,618 T. 46,659 (59.35%) Lab. hold
Harriet Harman, Lab.   27,619
Columba Blango, LD   10,432
Andy Stranack, C.   6,080
Jenny Jones, Green   1,361
Yohara Robby Munilla, Eng. Dem.   435
Joshua Ogunleye, WRP   211
Margaret Sharkey, Soc. Lab.   184
Decima Francis, Ind.   93
Steven Robbins, Ind.   87
Patricia Knox, ND   82
Jill Mountford, Workers Lib   75
Lab. majority 17,187 (36.84%)
Notional 3.00% swing Lab. to LD
(2005: Lab. majority 16,608 (42.83%))

§CAMBORNE & REDRUTH
E. 63,968 T. 42,493 (66.43%) C. gain
*George Eustice, C.   15,969
Julia Goldsworthy, LD   15,903
Jude Robinson, Lab.   6,945
Derek Elliott, UKIP   2,152
Loveday Jenkin, Meb. Ker.   775
Euan McPhee, Green   581
Robert Hawkins, Soc. Lab.   168
C. majority 66 (0.16%)
Notional 5.21% swing LD to C.
(2005: LD majority 2,733 (7.08%))

§CAMBRIDGE
E. 77,081 T. 50,130 (65.04%) LD hold
*Julian Huppert, LD   19,621
Nick Hillman, C.   12,829
Daniel Zeichner, Lab.   12,174
Tony Juniper, Green   3,804
Peter Burkinshaw, UKIP   1,195
Martin Booth, TUSC   362
Holborn Old, Ind.   145
LD majority 6,792 (13.55%)
Notional 6.98% swing Lab. to LD
(2005: LD majority 5,834 (12.27%))

§CAMBRIDGESHIRE NORTH EAST
E. 73,224 T. 52,264 (71.38%) C. hold
*Stephen Barclay, C.   26,862
Lorna Spenceley, LD   10,437
Peter Roberts, Lab.   9,274
Robin Talbot, UKIP   2,991
Susan Clapp, BNP   1,747
Debra Jordan, Ind.   566
Graham Murphy, Eng. Dem.   387
C. majority 16,425 (31.43%)
Notional 0.79% swing LD to C.
(2005: C. majority 7,726 (16.30%))

§CAMBRIDGESHIRE NORTH WEST
E. 88,857 T. 58,283 (65.59%) C. hold
Shailesh Vara, C.   29,425
Kevin Wilkins, LD   12,748
Chris York, Lab.   9,877
Robert Brown, UKIP   4,826
Stephen Goldspink, Eng. Dem.   1,407
C. majority 16,677 (28.61%)
Notional 2.64% swing LD to C.
(2005: C. majority 10,925 (20.62%))

§CAMBRIDGESHIRE SOUTH
E. 78,995 T. 59,056 (74.76%) C. hold
Andrew Lansley, C.   27,995
Sebastian Kindersley, LD   20,157
Tariq Sadiq, Lab.   6,024
Robin Page, Ind.   1,968
Helene Davies-Green, UKIP   1,873
Simon Saggers, Green   1,039
C. majority 7,838 (13.27%)
Notional 2.46% swing C. to LD
(2005: C. majority 9,634 (18.20%))

§CAMBRIDGESHIRE SOUTH EAST
E. 83,068 T. 57,602 (69.34%) C. hold
Jim Paice, C.   27,629
Jonathan Chatfield, LD   21,683
John Cowan, Lab.   4,380
Andy Monk, UKIP   2,138
Simon Sedgwick-Jell, Green   766
Geoffrey Woollard, Ind.   517
Daniel Bell, CPA   489
C. majority 5,946 (10.32%)
Notional 2.67% swing C. to LD
(2005: C. majority 8,110 (15.66%))

§CANNOCK CHASE
E. 74,509 T. 45,559 (61.15%) C. gain
*Aidan Burley, C.   18,271
Susan Woodward, Lab.   15,076
Jon Hunt, LD   7,732
Terence Majorowicz, BNP   2,168
Malcolm McKenzie, UKIP   1,580
Ron Turville, Ind.   380
Royston Jenkins, Snouts   259
Mike Walters, Ind.   93
C. majority 3,195 (7.01%)
Notional 14.01% swing Lab. to C.
(2005: Lab. majority 8,726 (21.00%))

§CANTERBURY
E. 76,808 T. 49,209 (64.07%) C. hold
Julian Brazier, C.   22,050
Guy Voizey, LD   16,002
Jean Samuel, Lab.   7,940
Howard Farmer, UKIP   1,907
Geoff Meaden, Green   1,137
Anne Belsey, MRP   173
C. majority 6,048 (12.29%)
Notional 5.36% swing C. to LD
(2005: C. majority 7,579 (16.37%))

§CARLISLE
E. 65,263 T. 42,200 (64.66%) C. gain
*John Stevenson, C.   16,589
Michael Boaden, Lab.   15,736
Neil Hughes, LD   6,567
Paul Stafford, BNP   1,086
Michael Owen, UKIP   969
John Reardon, Green   614
John Metcalfe, TUSC   376
Peter Howe, ND   263
C. majority 853 (2.02%)
Notional 7.74% swing Lab. to C.
(2005: Lab. majority 5,085 (13.46%))

§CARSHALTON & WALLINGTON
E. 66,520 T. 45,918 (69.03%) LD hold
Tom Brake, LD   22,180
Dr Ken Andrew, C.   16,920
Shafi Khan, Lab.   4,015
Frank Day, UKIP   1,348
Charlotte Lewis, BNP   1,100
George Dow, Green   355
LD majority 5,260 (11.46%)
Notional 4.26% swing C. to LD
(2005: LD majority 1,225 (2.93%))

CASTLE POINT
E. 67,284 T. 45,026 (66.92%) C. gain
*Rebecca Harris, C.   19,806
Bob Spink, Green Belt   12,174
Julian Ware-Lane, Lab.   6,609
Brendan D'Cruz, LD   4,232
Philip Howell, BNP   2,205
C. majority 7,632 (16.95%)
(2005: C. majority 8,201 (17.91%))

§CHARNWOOD
E. 74,473 T. 53,542 (71.89%) C. hold
Stephen Dorrell, C.   26,560
Robin Webber-Jones, LD   11,531
Eric Goodyer, Lab.   10,536
Cathy Duffy, BNP   3,116
Miles Storier, UKIP   1,799
C. majority 15,029 (28.07%)
Notional 0.10% swing C. to LD
(2005: C. majority 8,613 (18.05%))

§CHATHAM & AYLESFORD
E. 71,122 T. 43,807 (61.59%) C. gain
*Tracey Crouch, C.   20,230
Jonathan Shaw, Lab.   14,161
John McClintock, LD   5,832
Colin McCarthy-Stewart, BNP   1,365
Steve Newton, UKIP   1,314
Sean Varnham, Eng. Dem.   400
Dave Arthur, Green   396
Maureen Smith, Ch. P.   109
C. majority 6,069 (13.85%)
Notional 11.05% swing Lab. to C.
(2005: Lab. majority 3,289 (8.25%))

§CHEADLE
E. 72,458 T. 52,512 (72.47%) LD hold
Mark Hunter, LD   24,717
Ben Jeffreys, C.   21,445
Martin Miller, Lab.   4,920
Tony Moore, UKIP   1,430
LD majority 3,272 (6.23%)
Notional 0.59% swing LD to C.
(2005: LD majority 3,672 (7.41%))

§CHELMSFORD
E. 77,529 T. 54,593 (70.42%) C. hold
Simon Burns, C.   25,207
Stephen Robinson, LD   20,097
Peter Dixon, Lab.   5,980
Ken Wedon, UKIP   1,527
Mike Bateman, BNP   899
Angela Thomson, Green   476
Claire Breed, Eng. Dem.   254
Ben Sherman, Beer   153
C. majority 5,110 (9.36%)
Notional 0.08% swing LD to C.
(2005: C. majority 4,358 (9.20%))

§CHELSEA & FULHAM
E. 66,295 T. 39,856 (60.12%) C. hold
Greg Hands, C.   24,093
Alexander Hilton, Lab.   7,371
Dirk Hazell, LD   6,473
Julia Stephenson, Green   671
Timothy Gittos, UKIP   478
Brian McDonald, BNP   388
Roland Courtenay, Ind. CCF   196
George Roseman, Eng. Dem.   169
Godfrey Spickernell, Blue   17
C. majority 16,722 (41.96%)
Notional 6.08% swing Lab. to C.
(2005: C. majority 10,253 (29.79%))

§CHELTENHAM
E. 78,998 T. 52,786 (66.82%) LD hold
Martin Horwood, LD   26,659
Mark Coote, C.   21,739
James Green, Lab.   2,703
Peter Bowman, UKIP   1,192
Dancing Ken Hanks, Loony   493
LD majority 4,920 (9.32%)
Notional 4.33% swing C. to LD
(2005: LD majority 316 (0.66%))

§CHESHAM & AMERSHAM
E. 70,333 T. 52,444 (74.57%) C. hold
Cheryl Gillan, C.   31,658
Tim Starkey, LD   14,948
Anthony Gajadharsingh, Lab.   2,942
Alan Stevens, UKIP   2,129
Nick Wilkins, Green   767
C. majority 16,710 (31.86%)
Notional 2.28% swing LD to C.
(2005: C. majority 12,974 (27.31%))

§CHESTER, CITY OF
E. 68,874 T. 46,790 (67.94%) C. gain
*Stephen Mosley, C.   18,995
Christine Russell, Lab.   16,412
Elizabeth Jewkes, LD   8,930
Allan Weddell, UKIP   1,225
Ed Abrams, Eng. Dem.   594
Tom Barker, Green   535
John Whittingham, Ind.   99
C. majority 2,583 (5.52%)
Notional 3.86% swing Lab. to C.
(2005: Lab. majority 973 (2.20%))

§CHESTERFIELD
E. 71,878 T. 45,839 (63.77%) Lab. gain
*Toby Perkins, Lab.   17,891
Paul Holmes, LD   17,342
Carolyn Abbott, C.   7,214
David Phillips, UKIP   1,432
Ian Jerram, Eng. Dem.   1,213
Duncan Kerr, Green   600
John Noneoftheabove Daramy, Ind.   147
Lab. majority 549 (1.20%)
Notional 3.78% swing LD to Lab.
(2005: LD majority 2,733 (6.36%))

§CHICHESTER
E. 81,462 T. 56,787 (69.71%) C. hold
Andrew Tyrie, C.   31,427
Martin Lury, LD   15,550
Simon Holland, Lab.   5,937
Andrew Moncrieff, UKIP   3,873
C. majority 15,877 (27.96%)
Notional 3.82% swing LD to C.
(2005: C. majority 10,457 (20.32%))

CHINGFORD & WOODFORD GREEN
E. 64,831 T. 43,106 (66.49%) C. hold
Iain Duncan Smith, C.   22,743
Cath Arakelian, Lab.   9,780
Geoffrey Seeff, LD   7,242
Julian Leppert, BNP   1,288
Nick Jones, UKIP   1,133
Lucy Craig, Green   650
None of The Above, Ind.   202
Barry White, Ind.   68
C. majority 12,963 (30.07%)
1.27% swing Lab. to C.
(2005: C. majority 10,641 (27.53%))

§CHIPPENHAM
E. 72,105 T. 52,385 (72.65%) LD hold
*Duncan Hames, LD   23,970
Wilfred Emmanuel-Jones, C.   21,500
Greg Lovell, Lab.   3,620
Julia Reid, UKIP   1,783
Michael Simpkins, BNP   641
Samantha Fletcher, Green   446
John Maguire, Eng. Dem.   307
Richard Sexton, Ch. P.   118
LD majority 2,470 (4.72%)
Notional 0.01% swing C. to LD
(2005: LD majority 2,183 (4.70%))

§CHIPPING BARNET
E. 77,798 T. 50,608 (65.05%) C. hold
Theresa Villiers, C.   24,700
Damien Welfare, Lab.   12,773
Stephen Barber, LD   10,202
James Fluss, UKIP   1,442
Kate Tansley, Green   1,021
Philip Clayton, Ind.   470
C. majority 11,927 (23.57%)
Notional 5.77% swing Lab. to C.
(2005: C. majority 5,457 (12.02%))

§CHORLEY
E. 70,950 T. 49,774 (70.15%) Lab. hold
Lindsay Hoyle, Lab.   21,515
Alan Cullens, C.   18,922
Stephen Fenn, LD   6,957
Nick Hogan, UKIP   2,021
Chris Curtis, Ind.   359
Lab. majority 2,593 (5.21%)
Notional 5.60% swing Lab. to C.
(2005: Lab. majority 7,285 (16.41%))

§CHRISTCHURCH
E. 68,861 T. 49,416 (71.76%) C. hold
Christopher Chope, C.   27,888
Martyn Hurll, LD   12,478
Robert Deeks, Lab.   4,849
David Williams, UKIP   4,201
C. majority 15,410 (31.18%)
Notional 0.05% swing C. to LD
(2005: C. majority 14,640 (31.28%))

§CITIES OF LONDON &
WESTMINSTER
E. 66,489 T. 36,931 (55.54%) C. hold
Mark Field, C.   19,264
David Rowntree, Lab.   8,188
Naomi Smith, LD   7,574
Dr Derek Chase, Green   778
Paul Weston, UKIP   664
Frank Roseman, Eng. Dem.   191
Dennis Delderfield, Ind.   98
Jack Nunn, Pirate   90
Mad Cap'n Tom, Ind.   84
C. majority 11,076 (29.99%)
Notional 3.51% swing Lab. to C.
(2005: C. majority 7,352 (22.96%))

§CLACTON
E. 67,194 T. 43,123 (64.18%) C. hold
Douglas Carswell, C.   22,867
Ivan Henderson, Lab.   10,799
Michael Green, LD   5,577
Jim Taylor, BNP   1,975
Terry Allen, Tendring   1,078
Chris Southall, Green   535
Christopher Humphrey, Ind.   292
C. majority 12,068 (27.99%)
Notional 9.74% swing Lab. to C.
(2005: C. majority 3,629 (8.50%))

CLEETHORPES
E. 70,214 T. 44,966 (64.04%) C. gain
*Martin Vickers, C.   18,939
Shona McIsaac, Lab.   14,641
Malcolm Morland, LD   8,192
Stephen Harness, UKIP   3,194
C. majority 4,298 (9.56%)
7.81% swing Lab. to C.
(2005: Lab. majority 2,642 (6.06%))

§COLCHESTER
E. 74,062 T. 46,139 (62.30%) LD hold
Bob Russell, LD   22,151
Will Quince, C.   15,169
Jordan Newell, Lab.   5,680
John Pitts, UKIP   1,350
Sidney Chaney, BNP   705
Peter Lynn, Green   694
Eddie Bone, Eng. Dem.   335
Garryck Noble, PP Essex   35
Paul Shaw, ND   20
LD majority 6,982 (15.13%)
Notional 0.24% swing LD to C.
(2005: LD majority 6,388 (15.60%))

§COLNE VALLEY
E. 80,062 T. 55,296 (69.07%) C. gain
*Jason McCartney, C.   20,440
Nicola Turner, LD   15,603
Debbie Abrahams, Lab.   14,589
Barry Fowler, BNP   1,893
Melanie Roberts, UKIP   1,163
Chas Ball, Green   867
Dr Jackie Grunsell, TUSC   741
C. majority 4,837 (8.75%)
Notional 6.55% swing Lab. to C.
(2005: Lab. majority 1,267 (2.51%))

CONGLETON
E. 73,692 T. 50,780 (68.91%) C. hold
*Fiona Bruce, C.   23,250
Peter Hirst, LD   16,187
David Bryant, Lab.   8,747
Lee Slaughter, UKIP   2,147
Paul Edwards, Ind.   276
Paul Rothwell, ND   94
Adam Parton, Ind.   79
C. majority 7,063 (13.91%)
2.30% swing C. to LD
(2005: C. majority 8,246 (17.66%))

§COPELAND
E. 63,291 T. 42,787 (67.60%) Lab. hold
Jamie Reed, Lab.   19,699
Christopher Whiteside, C.   15,866
Frank Hollowell, LD   4,365
Clive Jefferson, BNP   1,474
Ted Caley-Knowles, UKIP   994
Jill Perry, Green   389
Lab. majority 3,833 (8.96%)
Notional 2.14% swing Lab. to C.
(2005: Lab. majority 5,157 (13.24%))

CORBY
E. 78,305 T. 54,236 (69.26%) C. gain
*Louise Bagshawe, C.   22,886
Phil Hope, Lab.   20,991
Portia Wilson, LD   7,834
Roy Davies, BNP   2,525
C. majority 1,895 (3.49%)
3.31% swing Lab. to C.
(2005: Lab. (Co-op) majority 1,517
(3.13%))

§CORNWALL NORTH
E. 68,662 T. 46,844 (68.22%) LD hold
Dan Rogerson, LD   22,512
Sian Flynn, C.   19,531
Miriel O'Connor, UKIP   2,300
Janet Hulme, Lab.   1,971
Joanie Willett, Meb. Ker.   530
LD majority 2,981 (6.36%)
Notional 0.25% swing LD to C.
(2005: LD majority 2,892 (6.87%))

§CORNWALL SOUTH EAST
E. 72,237 T. 49,617 (68.69%) C. gain
*Sheryll Murray, C.   22,390
Karen Gillard, LD   19,170
Michael Sparling, Lab.   3,507
Stephanie McWilliam, UKIP   3,083
Roger Creagh-Osborne, Green   826
Roger Holmes, Meb. Ker.   641
C. majority 3,220 (6.49%)
Notional 9.13% swing LD to C.
(2005: LD majority 5,485 (11.77%))

§COTSWOLDS, THE
E. 76,728 T. 54,832 (71.46%) C. hold
Geoffrey Clifton-Brown, C.   29,075
Mike Collins, LD   16,211
Mark Dempsey, Lab.   5,886
Adrian Blake, UKIP   2,292
Kevin Lister, Green   940
Alex Steel, Ind.   428
C. majority 12,864 (23.46%)
Notional 1.08% swing LD to C.
(2005: C. majority 10,742 (21.29%))

§COVENTRY NORTH EAST
E. 73,035 T. 43,383 (59.40%) Lab. hold
Bob Ainsworth, Lab.   21,384
Hazel Noonan, C.   9,609
Russell Field, LD   7,210
Tom Gower, BNP   1,863
Dave Nellist, Soc. Alt.   1,592
Chris Forbes, UKIP   1,291
Ron Lebar, Ch. M.   434
Lab. majority 11,775 (27.14%)
Notional 5.47% swing Lab. to C.
(2005: Lab. majority 14,621 (38.08%))

§COVENTRY NORTH WEST
E. 72,871 T. 46,560 (63.89%) Lab. hold
Geoffrey Robinson, Lab.   19,936
Gary Ridley, C.   13,648
Vincent McKee, LD   8,344
Edward Sheppard, BNP   1,666
Mark Nattrass, UKIP   1,295
John Clarke, Ind.   640
Justin Wood, Green   497
Nikki Downes, Soc. Alt.   370
William Sidhu, Ch. M.   164
Lab. majority 6,288 (13.51%)
Notional 3.92% swing Lab. to C.
(2005: Lab. majority 8,934 (21.35%))

§COVENTRY SOUTH
E. 73,652 T. 45,924 (62.35%) Lab. hold
Jim Cunningham, Lab.   19,197
Kevin Foster, C.   15,352
Brian Patton, LD   8,278
Mark Taylor, UKIP   1,767
Judy Griffiths, Soc. Alt.   691
Stephen Gray, Green   639
Lab. majority 3,845 (8.37%)
Notional 3.41% swing Lab. to C.
(2005: Lab. majority 6,237 (15.18%))

CRAWLEY
E. 72,781 T. 47,504 (65.27%) C. gain
*Henry Smith, C.   21,264
Chris Oxlade, Lab.   15,336
John Vincent, LD   6,844
Richard Trower, BNP   1,672
Chris French, UKIP   1,382
Phil Smith, Green   598
Arshad Khan, JP   265
Andrew Hubner, Ind.   143
C. majority 5,928 (12.48%)
6.28% swing Lab. to C.
(2005: Lab. majority 37 (0.09%))

§CREWE & NANTWICH
E. 77,460 T. 51,084 (65.95%) C. hold
Edward Timpson, C.   23,420
David Williams, Lab.   17,374
Roy Wood, LD   7,656
James Clutton, UKIP   1,414
Phil Williams, BNP   1,043
Mike Parsons, Ind.   177
C. majority 6,046 (11.84%)
Notional 13.67% swing Lab. to C.
(2005: Lab. majority 6,999 (15.50%))

§CROYDON CENTRAL
E. 78,880 T. 49,757 (63.08%) C. gain
*Gavin Barwell, C.   19,657
Gerry Ryan, Lab. (Co-op)   16,688
Peter Lambell, LD   6,553
Andrew Pelling, Ind.   3,239
Cliff Le May, BNP   1,448
Ralph Atkinson, UKIP   997
Bernice Golberg, Green   581
James Gitau, Ch. P.   264
John Cartwright, Loony   192
Michael Castle, Ind.   138
C. majority 2,969 (5.97%)
Notional 3.34% swing Lab. to C.
(2005: Lab. majority 328 (0.72%))

§CROYDON NORTH
E. 85,212 T. 51,678 (60.65%) Lab. hold
Malcolm Wicks, Lab.   28,949
Jason Hadden, C.   12,466
Gerry Jerome, LD   7,226
Shasha Khan, Green   1,017
Jonathan Serter, UKIP   891
Novlette Williams, Ch. P.   586
Mohommad Shaikh, Respect   272
Ben Stevenson, Comm.   160
Mohamed Seyed, Ind.   111
Lab. majority 16,483 (31.90%)
Notional 0.27% swing C. to Lab.
(2005: Lab. majority 14,185 (31.37%))

§CROYDON SOUTH
E. 81,301 T. 56,322 (69.28%) C. hold
Richard Ottaway, C.   28,684
Simon Rix, LD   12,866
Jane Avis, Lab.   11,287
Jeffrey Bolter, UKIP   2,504
Gordon Ross, Green   981
C. majority 15,818 (28.08%)
Notional 1.75% swing C. to LD
(2005: C. majority 14,228 (27.95%))

§DAGENHAM & RAINHAM
E. 69,764 T. 44,232 (63.40%) Lab. hold
Jon Cruddas, Lab.   17,813
Simon Jones, C.   15,183
Michael Barnbrook, BNP   4,952
Joseph Bourke, LD   3,806
Craig Litwin, UKIP   1,569
Gordon Kennedy, Ind.   308
Paula Watson, Ch. P.   305
Debbie Rosaman, Green   296
Lab. majority 2,630 (5.95%)
Notional 4.87% swing Lab. to C.
(2005: Lab. majority 6,372 (15.69%))

§DARLINGTON
E. 69,352 T. 42,896 (61.85%) Lab. hold
*Jenny Chapman, Lab.   16,891
Edward Legard, C.   13,503
Mike Barker, LD   10,046
Amanda Foster, BNP   1,262
Charlotte Bull, UKIP   1,194
Lab. majority 3,388 (7.90%)
Notional 9.14% swing Lab. to C.
(2005: Lab. majority 10,417 (26.18%))

§DARTFORD
E. 76,271 T. 50,080 (65.66%) C. gain
*Gareth Johnson, C.   24,428
John Adams, Lab.   13,800
James Willis, LD   7,361
Gary Rogers, Eng. Dem.   2,178
Richard Palmer, UKIP   1,842
Stephane Tindame, Ind.   264
John Crockford, FDP   207
C. majority 10,628 (21.22%)
Notional 11.56% swing Lab. to C.
(2005: Lab. majority 860 (1.90%))

§DAVENTRY
E. 71,451 T. 51,774 (72.46%) C. hold
*Chris Heaton-Harris, C.   29,252
Christopher McGlynn, LD   10,064
Paul Corazzo, Lab.   8,168
Jim Broomfield, UKIP   2,333
Alan Bennett-Spencer, Eng. Dem.   1,187
Steve Whiffen, Green   770
C. majority 19,188 (37.06%)
Notional 0.71% swing C. to LD
(2005: C. majority 11,776 (25.15%))

§DENTON & REDDISH
E. 64,765 T. 37,635 (58.11%) Lab. hold
Andrew Gwynne, Lab.   19,191
Julie Searle, C.   9,360
Stephen Broadhurst, LD   6,727
William Robinson, UKIP   2,060
Jeff Dennis, Ind.   297
Lab. majority 9,831 (26.12%)
Notional 6.25% swing Lab. to C.
(2005: Lab. majority 13,128 (38.62%))

§DERBY NORTH
E. 71,484 T. 45,080 (63.06%) Lab. hold
*Chris Williamson, Lab.   14,896
Stephen Mold, C.   14,283
Lucy Care, LD   12,638
Peter Cheeseman, BNP   2,000
Elizabeth Ransome, UKIP   829
David Gale, Ind.   264
David Geraghty, Pirate   170
Lab. majority 613 (1.36%)
Notional 7.39% swing Lab. to C.
(2005: Lab. majority 5,691 (14.58%))

§DERBY SOUTH
E. 71,012 T. 41,188 (58.00%) Lab. hold
Margaret Beckett, Lab.   17,851
Jack Perschke, C.   11,729
David Batey, LD   8,430
Stephen Fowke, UKIP   1,821
Alan Graves, Ind.   1,357
Lab. majority 6,122 (14.86%)
Notional 9.26% swing Lab. to C.
(2005: Lab. majority 11,655 (28.99%))

§DERBYSHIRE DALES
E. 63,367 T. 46,780 (73.82%) C. hold
Patrick McLoughlin, C.   24,378
Joe Naitta, LD   10,512
Colin Swindell, Lab.   9,061
Ian Guiver, UKIP   1,779
Josh Stockell, Green   772
Nick The Flying Brick Delves,
   Loony   228
Amila Y'mech, Humanity   50
C. majority 13,866 (29.64%)
Notional 3.74% swing LD to C.
(2005: C. majority 8,810 (20.82%))

§DERBYSHIRE MID
E. 66,297 T. 47,342 (71.41%) C. hold
*Pauline Latham, C.   22,877
Hardyal Dhindsa, Lab.   11,585
Sally McIntosh, LD   9,711
Lewis Allsebrook, BNP   1,698
Anthony Kay, UKIP   1,252
RU Seerius, Loony   219
C. majority 11,292 (23.85%)
Notional 5.66% swing Lab. to C.
(2005: C. majority 5,329 (12.54%))

§DERBYSHIRE NORTH EAST
E. 71,422 T. 47,034 (65.85%) Lab. hold
Natascha Engel, Lab.   17,948
Huw Merriman, C.   15,503
Richard Bull, LD   10,947
James Bush, UKIP   2,636
Lab. majority 2,445 (5.20%)
Notional 8.56% swing Lab. to C.
(2005: Lab. majority 9,564 (22.31%))

§DERBYSHIRE SOUTH
E. 70,610 T. 50,419 (71.40%) C. gain
*Heather Wheeler, C.   22,935
Michael Edwards, Lab.   15,807
Alexis Diouf, LD   8,012
Peter Jarvis, BNP   2,193
Charles Swabey, UKIP   1,206
Paul Liversuch, Soc. Lab.   266
C. majority 7,128 (14.14%)
Notional 9.80% swing Lab. to C.
(2005: Lab. majority 2,436 (5.45%))

§DEVIZES
E. 67,374 T. 46,340 (68.78%) C. hold
*Claire Perry, C.   25,519
Fiona Hornby, LD   12,514
Jurab Ali, Lab.   4,711
Patricia Bryant, UKIP   2,076
Mark Fletcher, Green   813
Martin Houlden, Ind.   566
Nic Coombe, Libertarian   141
C. majority 13,005 (28.06%)
Notional 0.33% swing C. to LD
(2005: C. majority 12,259 (28.63%))

§DEVON CENTRAL
E. 71,204 T. 53,873 (75.66%) C. hold
*Mel Stride, C.   27,737
Philip Hutty, LD   18,507
Moira Macdonald, Lab.   3,715
Bob Edwards, UKIP   2,870
Colin Mathews, Green   1,044
C. majority 9,230 (17.13%)
Notional 6.07% swing LD to C.
(2005: C. majority 2,338 (4.99%))

§DEVON EAST
E. 73,109 T. 53,092 (72.62%) C. hold
Hugo Swire, C.   25,662
Paull Robathan, LD   16,548
Gareth Manson, Lab.   5,721
Mike Amor, UKIP   4,346
Sharon Pavey, Green   815
C. majority 9,114 (17.17%)
Notional 1.03% swing C. to LD
(2005: C. majority 9,168 (19.23%))

§DEVON NORTH
E. 74,508 T. 51,321 (68.88%) LD hold
Nick Harvey, LD   24,305
Philip Milton, C.   18,484
Stephen Crowther, UKIP   3,720
Mark Cann, Lab.   2,671
L'Anne Knight, Green   697
Gary Marshall, BNP   614
Rodney Cann, Ind.   588
Nigel Vidler, Eng. Dem.   146
Gerrard Sables, Comm. Brit.   96
LD majority 5,821 (11.34%)
Notional 0.32% swing C. to LD
(2005: LD majority 5,276 (10.71%))

§DEVON SOUTH WEST
E. 70,059 T. 49,860 (71.17%) C. hold
Gary Streeter, C.   27,908
Anna Pascoe, LD   12,034
Luke Pollard, Lab.   6,193
Hugh Williams, UKIP   3,084
Vaughan Brean, Green   641
C. majority 15,874 (31.84%)
Notional 5.64% swing LD to C.
(2005: C. majority 9,442 (20.12%))

§DEVON WEST & TORRIDGE
E. 76,574 T. 55,257 (72.16%) C. hold
Geoffrey Cox, C.   25,230
Adam Symons, LD   22,273
Robin Julian, UKIP   3,021
Darren Jones, Lab.   2,917
Cathrine Simmons, Green   1,050
Nick Baker, BNP   766
C. majority 2,957 (5.35%)
Notional 0.01% swing C. to LD
(2005: C. majority 2,732 (5.37%))

§DEWSBURY
E. 78,901 T. 54,008 (68.45%) C. gain
*Simon Reevell, C.   18,898
Shahid Malik, Lab.   17,372
Andrew Hutchinson, LD   9,150
Khizar Iqbal, Ind.   3,813
Roger Roberts, BNP   3,265
Adrian Cruden, Green   849
Michael Felse, Eng. Dem.   661
C. majority 1,526 (2.83%)
Notional 5.85% swing Lab. to C.
(2005: Lab. majority 3,999 (8.88%))

§DON VALLEY
E. 73,214 T. 43,430 (59.32%) Lab. hold
Caroline Flint, Lab.   16,472
Matthew Stephens, C.   12,877
Edward Simpson, LD   7,422
Erwin Toseland, BNP   2,112
William Shaw, UKIP   1,904
Bernie Aston, Eng. Dem.   1,756
Martin Williams, Ind.   887
Lab. majority 3,595 (8.28%)
Notional 10.64% swing Lab. to C.
(2005: Lab. majority 11,333 (29.56%))

§DONCASTER CENTRAL
E. 75,207 T. 41,745 (55.51%) Lab. hold
Rosie Winterton, Lab.   16,569
Gareth Davies, C.   10,340
Patrick Wilson, LD   8,795
Lawrence Parramore, Eng. Dem.   1,816
John Bettney, BNP   1,762
Michael Andrews, UKIP   1,421
Scott Pickles, Ind.   970
Derek Williams, R and E   72
Lab. majority 6,229 (14.92%)
Notional 8.72% swing Lab. to C.
(2005: Lab. majority 10,325 (27.33%))

§DONCASTER NORTH
E. 72,381 T. 41,483 (57.31%) Lab. hold
Ed Miliband, Lab.   19,637
Sophie Brodie, C.   8,728
Edward Sanderson, LD   6,174
Pamela Chambers, BNP   2,818
Wayne Crawshaw, Eng. Dem.   2,148
Liz Andrews, UKIP   1,797
Bill Rawcliffe, TUSC
Lab. majority 10,909 (26.30%)
Notional 2.77% swing Lab. to C.
(2005: Lab. majority 12,027 (31.85%))

§DORSET MID & POOLE NORTH
E. 72,647 T. 46,788 (64.40%) LD hold
Annette Brooke, LD   21,100
Nick King, C.   20,831
Darren Brown, Lab.   2,748
Dave Evans, UKIP   2,109
LD majority 269 (0.57%)
Notional 6.27% swing LD to C.
(2005: LD majority 5,931 (13.12%))

§DORSET NORTH
E. 73,698 T. 54,141 (73.46%) C. hold
Bob Walter, C.   27,640
Emily Gasson, LD   20,015
Mike Bunney, Lab.   2,910
Jeremy Nieboer, UKIP   2,812
Anna Hayball, Green   546
Roger Monksummers, Loony   218
C. majority 7,625 (14.08%)
Notional 2.75% swing LD to C.
(2005: C. majority 4,200 (8.58%))

DORSET SOUTH
E. 73,838 T. 50,310 (68.14%) C. gain
*Richard Drax, C.   22,667
Jim Knight, Lab.   15,224
Ros Kayes, LD   9,557
Mike Hobson, UKIP   2,034
Brian Heatley, Green   595
Andy Kirkwood, YP   233
C. majority 7,443 (14.79%)
9.26% swing Lab. to C.
(2005: Lab. majority 1,812 (3.73%))

DORSET WEST
E. 76,869 T. 57,337 (74.59%) C. hold
Oliver Letwin, C.   27,287
Sue Farrant, LD   23,364
Dr Steve Bick, Lab.   3,815
Oliver Chisholm, UKIP   2,196
Susan Greene, Green   675
C. majority 3,923 (6.84%)
1.11% swing LD to C.
(2005: C. majority 2,461 (4.62%))

§DOVER
E. 71,832 T. 50,385 (70.14%) C. gain
*Charlie Elphicke, C.   22,174
Gwyn Prosser, Lab.   16,900
John Brigden, LD   7,962
Victor Matcham, UKIP   1,747
Dennis Whiting, BNP   1,104
Michael Walters, Eng. Dem.   216
David Clark, CPA   200
George Lee-Delisle, Ind.   82
C. majority 5,274 (10.47%)
Notional 10.43% swing Lab. to C.
(2005: Lab. majority 5,005 (10.40%))

§DUDLEY NORTH
E. 60,838 T. 38,602 (63.45%) Lab. hold
Ian Austin, Lab.   14,923
Graeme Brown, C.   14,274
Mike Beckett, LD   4,066
Malcolm Davis, UKIP   3,267
Ken Griffiths, BNP   1,899
Kevin Inman, NF   173
Lab. majority 649 (1.68%)
Notional 4.73% swing Lab. to C.
(2005: Lab. majority 4,106 (11.14%))

§DUDLEY SOUTH
E. 60,572 T. 38,165 (63.01%) C. gain
*Chris Kelly, C.   16,450
Rachel Harris, Lab.   12,594
Jonathan Bramall, LD   5,989
Philip Rowe, UKIP   3,132
C. majority 3,856 (10.10%)
Notional 9.51% swing Lab. to C.
(2005: Lab. majority 3,222 (8.91%))

§DULWICH & WEST NORWOOD
E. 72,817 T. 48,214 (66.21%) Lab. hold
Tessa Jowell, Lab.   22,461
Jonathan Mitchell, LD   13,096
Kemi Adegoke, C.   10,684
Shane Collins, Green   1,266
Elizabeth Jones, UKIP   707
Lab. majority 9,365 (19.42%)
Notional 0.84% swing Lab. to LD
(2005: Lab. majority 7,853 (19.75%))

DURHAM, CITY OF
E. 68,832 T. 46,252 (67.20%) Lab. hold
Roberta Blackman-Woods, Lab.   20,496
Carol Woods, LD   17,429
Nick Varley, C.   6,146
Ralph Musgrave, BNP   1,153
Nigel Coghill-Marshall, UKIP   856
Jonathan Collings, Ind.   172
Lab. majority 3,067 (6.63%)
0.37% swing Lab. to LD
(2005: Lab. majority 3,274 (7.38%))

§DURHAM NORTH
E. 67,548 T. 40,967 (60.65%) Lab. hold
Kevan Jones, Lab.   20,698
David Skelton, C.   8,622
Ian Lindley, LD   8,617
Pete Molloy, BNP   1,686
Bruce Reid, UKIP   1,344
Lab. majority 12,076 (29.48%)
Notional 8.93% swing Lab. to C.
(2005: Lab. majority 16,781 (44.94%))

§DURHAM NORTH WEST
E. 70,618 T. 43,815 (62.05%) Lab. hold
*Pat Glass, Lab.   18,539
Owen Temple, LD   10,927
Michelle Tempest, C.   8,766
Watts Stelling, Ind.   2,472
Michael Stewart, BNP   1,852
Andrew McDonald, UKIP   1,259
Lab. majority 7,612 (17.37%)
Notional 8.33% swing Lab. to LD
(2005: Lab. majority 13,443 (34.03%))

§EALING CENTRAL & ACTON
E. 63,489 T. 47,200 (74.34%) C. gain
*Angie Bray, C.   17,944
Bassam Mahfouz, Lab.   14,228
Jon Ball, LD   13,041
Julie Carter, UKIP   765
Sarah Edwards, Green   737
Suzanne Fernandes, Ch. P.   295
Sam Akaki, Ind. EACPS   190
C. majority 3,716 (7.87%)
Notional 5.02% swing Lab. to C.
(2005: Lab. majority 839 (2.16%))

§EALING NORTH
E. 67,902 T. 47,678 (70.22%) Lab. hold
Stephen Pound, Lab.   24,023
Ian Gibb, C.   14,722
Chris Lucas, LD   6,283
Dave Furness, BNP   1,045
Ian De Wulverton, UKIP   685
Christopher Warleigh-Lack, Green   505
Petar Ljubisic, Ch. P.   415
Lab. majority 9,301 (19.51%)
Notional 0.45% swing C. to Lab.
(2005: Lab. majority 8,126 (18.61%))

§EALING SOUTHALL
E. 60,379 T. 42,756 (70.81%) Lab. hold
Virendra Sharma, Lab.   22,024
Gurcharan Singh, C.   12,733
Nigel Bakhai, LD   6,383
Suneil Basu, Green   705
Mehboob Anil, Ch. P.   503
Sati Chaggar, Eng. Dem.   408
Lab. majority 9,291 (21.73%)
Notional 8.30% swing Lab. to C.
(2005: Lab. majority 13,140 (38.33%))

§EASINGTON
E. 63,873 T. 34,914 (54.66%) Lab. hold
*Grahame Morris, Lab.   20,579
Tara Saville, LD   5,597
Richard Harrison, C.   4,790
Cheryl Dunn, BNP   2,317
Martyn Aiken, UKIP   1,631
Lab. majority 14,982 (42.91%)
Notional 7.74% swing Lab. to LD
(2005: Lab. majority 18,874 (58.39%))

§EAST HAM
E. 90,675 T. 50,373 (55.55%) Lab. hold
Stephen Timms, Lab.   35,471
Paul Shea, C.   7,645
Chris Brice, LD   5,849
Barry O'Connor, Eng. Dem.   822
Judy Maciejowska, Green   586
Lab. majority 27,826 (55.24%)
Notional 7.71% swing C. to Lab.
(2005: Lab. majority 13,649 (33.08%))

§EASTBOURNE
E. 77,840 T. 52,124 (66.96%) LD gain
*Stephen Lloyd, LD   24,658
Nigel Waterson, C.   21,223
Dave Brinson, Lab.   2,497
Stephen Shing, Ind.   1,327
Roger Needham, UKIP   1,305
Colin Poulter, BNP   939
Michael Baldry, Ind.   101
Keith Gell, Ind.   74
LD majority 3,435 (6.59%)
Notional 4.00% swing C. to LD
(2005: C. majority 672 (1.41%))

§EASTLEIGH
E. 77,435 T. 53,650 (69.28%) LD hold
Chris Huhne, LD	24,966
Maria Hutchings, C.	21,102
Leo Barraclough, Lab.	5,153
Ray Finch, UKIP	1,933
Tony Stephen Pewsey, Eng. Dem.	249
Dave Stone, Ind.	154
Keith Low, Nat. Dem.	93

LD majority 3,864 (7.20%)
Notional 3.04% swing C. to LD
(2005: LD majority 534 (1.12%))

§EDDISBURY
E. 65,306 T. 45,414 (69.54%) C. hold
Stephen O'Brien, C.	23,472
Robert Thompson, LD	10,217
Pat Merrick, Lab.	9,794
Charles Dodman, UKIP	1,931

C. majority 13,255 (29.19%)
Notional 0.13% swing LD to C.
(2005: C. majority 6,408 (14.83%))

§EDMONTON
E. 63,902 T. 40,377 (63.19%)
Lab. (Co-op) hold
Andy Love, Lab. (Co-op)	21,665
Andrew Charalambous, C.	12,052
Iarla Kilbane-Dawe, LD	4,252
Roy Freshwater, UKIP	1,036
Jack Johnson, Green	516
Erol Basarik, Green	379
Clive Morrison, Ch. P.	350
David Mclean, Ind.	127

Lab. (Co-op) majority 9,613 (23.81%)
Notional 2.26% swing Lab. (Co-op) to C.
(2005: Lab. (Co-op) majority 10,312 (28.33%))

§ELLESMERE PORT & NESTON
E. 63,097 T. 44,233 (70.10%) Lab. hold
Andrew Miller, Lab.	19,750
Stuart Penketh, C.	15,419
Denise Aspinall, LD	6,663
Henry Crocker, UKIP	1,619
Jonathan Starkey, Ind.	782

Lab. majority 4,331 (9.79%)
Notional 3.10% swing Lab. to C.
(2005: Lab. majority 6,713 (15.99%))

§ELMET & ROTHWELL
E. 77,724 T. 55,789 (71.78%) C. gain
*Alec Shelbrooke, C.	23,778
James Lewis, Lab.	19,257
Stewart Golton, LD	9,109
Sam Clayton, BNP	1,802
Darren Oddy, UKIP	1,593
Christopher Nolan, Ind.	250

C. majority 4,521 (8.10%)
Notional 9.77% swing Lab. to C.
(2005: Lab. majority 6,078 (11.43%))

§ELTHAM
E. 62,590 T. 41,964 (67.05%) Lab. hold
Clive Efford, Lab.	17,416
David Gold, C.	15,753
Steven Toole, LD	5,299
Roberta Woods, BNP	1,745
Ray Adams, UKIP	1,011
Arthur Hayles, Green	419
Mike Tibby, Eng. Dem.	217
Andrew Graham, Ind.	104

Lab. majority 1,663 (3.96%)
Notional 1.82% swing Lab. to C.
(2005: Lab. majority 2,904 (7.60%))

§ENFIELD NORTH
E. 66,258 T. 44,453 (67.09%) C. hold
*Nick de Bois, C.	18,804
Joan Ryan, Lab.	17,112
Paul Smith, LD	5,403
Tony Avery, BNP	1,228
Madge Jones, UKIP	938
Bill Linton, Green	489
Anthony Williams, Ch. P.	161
Raquel Weald, Eng. Dem.	131
Anna Athow, WRP	96
Gonul Daniels, Ind.	91

C. majority 1,692 (3.81%)
Notional 0.73% swing Lab. to C.
(2005: C. majority 937 (2.35%))

§ENFIELD SOUTHGATE
E. 64,138 T. 44,352 (69.15%) C. hold
David Burrowes, C.	21,928
Bambos Charalambous, Lab.	14,302
Johar Khan, LD	6,124
Peter Krakowiak, Green	632
Bob Brock, UKIP	505
Dr Asit Mukhopadhyay, Ind.	391
Samad Billoo, Respect	174
Ben Weald, Eng. Dem.	173
Mal Malakounides, ND	88
Jeremy Sturgess, BB	35

C. majority 7,626 (17.19%)
Notional 7.24% swing Lab. to C.
(2005: C. majority 1,127 (2.72%))

§EPPING FOREST
E. 72,198 T. 46,584 (64.52%) C. hold
Eleanor Laing, C.	25,148
Ann Haigh, LD	10,017
Katie Curtis, Lab.	6,641
Pat Richardson, BNP	1,982
Andrew Smith, UKIP	1,852
Simon Pepper, Green	659
Kim Sawyer, Eng. Dem.	285

C. majority 15,131 (32.48%)
Notional 1.08% swing C. to LD
(2005: C. majority 13,473 (31.33%))

§EPSOM & EWELL
E. 78,104 T. 54,955 (70.36%) C. hold
Chris Grayling, C.	30,868
Jonathan Lees, LD	14,734
Craig Montgomery, Lab.	6,538
Elizabeth Wallace, UKIP	2,549
Peter Ticher, RRG	266

C. majority 16,134 (29.36%)
Notional 2.05% swing C. to LD
(2005: C. majority 16,342 (33.47%))

§EREWASH
E. 69,654 T. 47,642 (68.40%) C. gain
*Jessica Lee, C.	18,805
Cheryl Pidgeon, Lab.	16,304
Martin Garnett, LD	8,343
Mark Bailey, BNP	2,337
Jodie Sutton, UKIP	855
Lee Fletcher, Green	534
Luke Wilkins, Ind.	464

C. majority 2,501 (5.25%)
Notional 10.45% swing Lab. to C.
(2005: Lab. majority 6,782 (15.66%))

§ERITH & THAMESMEAD
E. 69,918 T. 42,476 (60.75%) Lab. hold
*Teresa Pearce, Lab.	19,068
Colin Bloom, C.	13,365
Alexander Cunliffe, LD	5,116
Kevin Saunders, BNP	2,184
Pamela Perrin, UKIP	1,139
Laurence Williams, Eng. Dem.	465
Abbey Akinoshun, ND	438
Sid Cordle, CPA	379
Marek Powley, Green	322

Lab. majority 5,703 (13.43%)
Notional 6.34% swing Lab. to C.
(2005: Lab. majority 9,870 (26.11%))

ESHER & WALTON
E. 75,338 T. 54,543 (72.40%) C. hold
*Dominic Raab, C.	32,134
Lionel Blackman, LD	13,541
Francis Eldergill, Lab.	5,829
Bernard Collignon, UKIP	1,783
Tony Popham, Ind.	378
Chinners Chinnery, Loony	341
Mike Kearsley, Eng. Dem.	307
Andy Lear, Best	230

C. majority 18,593 (34.09%)
8.97% swing LD to C.
(2005: C. majority 7,727 (16.14%))

§EXETER
E. 77,157 T. 52,247 (67.72%) Lab. hold
Ben Bradshaw, Lab.	19,942
Hannah Foster, C.	17,221
Graham Oakes, LD	10,581
Keith Crawford, UKIP	1,930
Chris Gale, Lib.	1,108
Paula Black, Green	792
Robert Farmer, BNP	673

Lab. majority 2,721 (5.21%)
Notional 6.03% swing Lab. to C.
(2005: Lab. majority 8,559 (17.27%))

FAREHAM
E. 75,878 T. 54,345 (71.62%) C. hold
Mark Hoban, C.	30,037
Alex Bentley, LD	12,945
James Carr, Lab.	7,719
Steve Richards, UKIP	2,235
Peter Doggett, Green	791
Joe Jenkins, Eng. Dem.	618

C. majority 17,092 (31.45%)
1.73% swing LD to C.
(2005: C. majority 11,702 (24.09%))

§FAVERSHAM & KENT MID
E. 68,858 T. 46,712 (67.84%) C. hold
Hugh Robertson, C.	26,250
David Naghi, LD	9,162
Ash Rehal, Lab.	7,748
Sarah Larkins, UKIP	1,722
Tim Valentine, Green	890
Graham Kemp, NF	542
Hairy Knorm Davidson, Loony	398

C. majority 17,088 (36.58%)
Notional 1.62% swing LD to C.
(2005: C. majority 8,927 (21.00%))

§FELTHAM & HESTON
E. 81,058 T. 48,526 (59.87%)
Lab. (Co-op) hold

Alan Keen, Lab. (Co-op)	21,174
Mark Bowen, C.	16,516
Munira Wilson, LD	6,669
John Donnelly, BNP	1,714
Jerry Shadbolt, UKIP	992
Elizabeth Anstis, Green	530
Dharmendra Tripathi, Ind.	505
Asa Khaira, Ind.	180
Roger Williams, Ind.	168
Matthew Linley, WRP	78

Lab. (Co-op) majority 4,658 (9.60%)
Notional 4.83% swing Lab. (Co-op) to C.
(2005: Lab. (Co-op) majority 7,598
(19.25%))

§FILTON & BRADLEY STOKE
E. 69,003 T. 48,301 (70.00%) C. hold

*Jack Lopresti, C.	19,686
Ian Boulton, Lab.	12,772
Peter Tyzack, LD	12,197
John Knight, UKIP	1,506
David Scott, BNP	1,328
Jon Lucas, Green	441
Ruth Johnson, Ch. P.	199
Vote Zero None of the Above, ND	172

C. majority 6,914 (14.31%)
Notional 6.37% swing Lab. to C.
(2005: C. majority 653 (1.58%))

§FINCHLEY & GOLDERS GREEN
E. 77,198 T. 47,157 (61.09%) C. hold

*Mike Freer, C.	21,688
Alison Moore, Lab.	15,879
Laura Edge, LD	8,036
Susan Cummins, UKIP	817
Donald Lyven, Green	737

C. majority 5,809 (12.32%)
Notional 5.81% swing Lab. to C.
(2005: C. majority 294 (0.70%))

§FOLKESTONE & HYTHE
E. 78,003 T. 52,800 (67.69%) C. hold

*Damian Collins, C.	26,109
Lynne Beaumont, LD	15,987
Donald Worsley, Lab.	5,719
Frank McKenna, UKIP	2,439
Harry Williams, BNP	1,662
Penny Kemp, Green	637
David Plumstead, Ind.	247

C. majority 10,122 (19.17%)
Notional 2.58% swing C. to LD
(2005: C. majority 12,446 (24.33%))

FOREST OF DEAN
E. 68,419 T. 48,763 (71.27%) C. hold

Mark Harper, C.	22,853
Bruce Hogan, Lab.	11,789
Chris Coleman, LD	10,676
Tim Congdon, UKIP	2,522
James Greenwood, Green	923

C. majority 11,064 (22.69%)
9.19% swing Lab. to C.
(2005: C. majority 2,049 (4.30%))

§FYLDE
E. 65,917 T. 43,690 (66.28%) C. hold

*Mark Menzies, C.	22,826
Bill Winlow, LD	9,641
Liam Robinson, Lab.	8,624
Martin Bleeker, UKIP	1,945
Philip Mitchell, Green	654

C. majority 13,185 (30.18%)
Notional 4.15% swing C. to LD
(2005: C. majority 11,117 (28.67%))

§GAINSBOROUGH
E. 72,144 T. 49,251 (68.27%) C. hold

Edward Leigh, C.	24,266
Pat O'Connor, LD	13,707
Jamie McMahon, Lab.	7,701
Steve Pearson, UKIP	2,065
Malcolm Porter, BNP	1,512

C. majority 10,559 (21.44%)
Notional 1.80% swing LD to C.
(2005: C. majority 7,895 (17.73%))

§GARSTON & HALEWOOD
E. 71,312 T. 42,825 (60.05%) Lab. hold

Maria Eagle, Lab.	25,493
Paula Keaveney, LD	8,616
Richard Downey, C.	6,908
Tony Hammond, UKIP	1,540
Diana Raby, Respect	268

Lab. majority 16,877 (39.41%)
Notional 5.74% swing LD to Lab.
(2005: Lab. majority 10,814 (27.92%))

§GATESHEAD
E. 66,492 T. 38,257 (57.54%) Lab. hold

*Ian Mearns, Lab.	20,712
Frank Hindle, LD	8,163
Hazel Anderson, C.	5,716
Kevin Scott, BNP	1,787
John Tennant, UKIP	1,103
Andy Redfern, Green	379
Elaine Brunskill, TUSC	266
David Walton, Ch. P.	131

Lab. majority 12,549 (32.80%)
Notional 3.94% swing Lab. to LD
(2005: Lab. majority 14,245 (40.68%))

§GEDLING
E. 70,590 T. 48,190 (68.27%) Lab. hold

Vernon Coaker, Lab.	19,821
Bruce Laughton, C.	17,962
Julia Bateman, LD	7,350
Stephen Adcock, BNP	1,598
Dave Marshall, UKIP	1,459

Lab. majority 1,859 (3.86%)
Notional 2.89% swing Lab. to C.
(2005: Lab. majority 4,335 (9.63%))

§GILLINGHAM & RAINHAM
E. 70,865 T. 46,786 (66.02%) C. gain

*Rehman Chishti, C.	21,624
Paul Clark, Lab.	12,944
Andrew Stamp, LD	8,484
Robert Oakley, UKIP	1,515
Brian Ravenscroft, BNP	1,149
Dean Lacey, Eng. Dem.	464
Trish Marchant, Green	356
Gordon Bryan, ND	141
George Meegan, Med. Ind.	109

C. majority 8,680 (18.55%)
Notional 9.29% swing Lab. to C.
(2005: Lab. majority 15 (0.03%))

§GLOUCESTER
E. 79,322 T. 50,764 (64.00%) C. gain

*Richard Graham, C.	20,267
Parmjit Dhanda, Lab.	17,847
Jeremy Hilton, LD	9,767
Mike Smith, UKIP	1,808
Alan Platt, Eng. Dem.	564
Bryan Meloy, Green	511

C. majority 2,420 (4.77%)
Notional 8.86% swing Lab. to C.
(2005: Lab. majority 6,063 (12.95%))

GOSPORT
E. 72,720 T. 46,939 (64.55%) C. hold

*Caroline Dinenage, C.	24,300
Rob Hylands, LD	9,887
Graham Giles, Lab.	7,944
Andrew Rice, UKIP	1,496
Barry Bennett, BNP	1,004
Bob Shaw, Eng. Dem.	622
Andrea Smith, Green	573
David Smith, Ind.	493
Charles Read, Ind.	331
Brian Hart, Ind.	289

C. majority 14,413 (30.71%)
1.27% swing LD to C.
(2005: C. majority 5,730 (13.32%))

§GRANTHAM & STAMFORD
E. 78,000 T. 52,799 (67.69%) C. hold

*Nicholas Boles, C.	26,552
Harrish Bisnauthsing, LD	11,726
Mark Bartlett, Lab.	9,503
Christopher Robinson, BNP	2,485
Tony Wells, UKIP	1,604
Mark Horn, Lincs Ind.	929

C. majority 14,826 (28.08%)
Notional 1.18% swing C. to LD
(2005: C. majority 7,308 (15.77%))

GRAVESHAM
E. 70,195 T. 47,303 (67.39%) C. hold

Adam Holloway, C.	22,956
Kathryn Smith, Lab. (Co-op)	13,644
Anna Arrowsmith, LD	6,293
Geoffrey Clark, UKIP	2,265
Steven Uncles, Eng. Dem.	1,005
Richard Crawford, Green	675
Alice Dartnell, Ind.	465

C. majority 9,312 (19.69%)
9.12% swing Lab. (Co-op) to C.
(2005: C. majority 654 (1.45%))

GREAT GRIMSBY
E. 61,229 T. 32,954 (53.82%) Lab. hold

Austin Mitchell, Lab.	10,777
Victoria Ayling, C.	10,063
Andrew de Freitas, LD	7,388
Henry Hudson, UKIP	2,043
Steve Fyfe, BNP	1,517
Ernie Brown, Ind.	835
Adrian Howe, PNPD	331

Lab. majority 714 (2.17%)
10.53% swing Lab. to C.
(2005: Lab. majority 7,654 (23.22%))

GREAT YARMOUTH
E. 70,315 T. 43,057 (61.23%) C. gain

*Brandon Lewis, C.	18,571
Tony Wright, Lab.	14,295
Simon Partridge, LD	6,188
Alan Baugh, UKIP	2,066
Bosco Tann, BNP	1,421
Laura Biggart, Green	416
Margaret McMahon-Morris, LTT	100

C. majority 4,276 (9.93%)
8.66% swing Lab. to C.
(2005: Lab. majority 3,055 (7.38%))

§GREENWICH & WOOLWICH
E. 65,489 T. 41,188 (62.89%) Lab. hold
Nick Raynsford, Lab.   20,262
Spencer Drury, C.   10,109
Joseph Lee, LD   7,498
Lawrence Rustem, BNP   1,151
Andy Hewett, Green   1,054
Edward Adeleye, Ch. P.   443
Topo Wresniwiro, Eng. Dem.   339
Onay Kasab, TUSC   267
Dr Tammy Alingham, Ind.   65
Lab. majority 10,153 (24.65%)
Notional 5.12% swing Lab. to C.
(2005: Lab. majority 11,638 (32.77%))

§GUILDFORD
E. 77,082 T. 55,567 (72.09%) C. hold
Anne Milton, C.   29,618
Sue Doughty, LD   21,836
Tim Shand, Lab.   2,812
Mazhar Manzoor, UKIP   1,021
John Morris, PPN-V   280
C. majority 7,782 (14.00%)
Notional 6.91% swing LD to C.
(2005: C. majority 89 (0.17%))

§HACKNEY NORTH & STOKE
NEWINGTON
E. 73,874 T. 46,488 (62.93%) Lab. hold
Diane Abbott, Lab.   25,553
Keith Angus, LD   11,092
Darren Caplan, C.   6,759
Matt Sellwood, Green   2,133
Maxine Hargreaves, Ch. P.   299
Suzanne Moore, ND   285
Knigel Knapp, Loony   182
Paul Shaer, Ind.   96
Alessandra Williams, Ind.   61
Dr Jack Pope-De-Locksley, Magna
Carta   28
Lab. majority 14,461 (31.11%)
Notional 2.61% swing LD to Lab.
(2005: Lab. majority 8,002 (25.88%))

§HACKNEY SOUTH & SHOREDITCH
E. 72,816 T. 42,858 (58.86%) Lab. hold
Meg Hillier, Lab.   23,888
Dave Raval, LD   9,600
Simon Nayyar, C.   5,800
Polly Lane, Green   1,493
Michael King, UKIP   651
Ben Rae, Lib.   539
John Williams, Ch. P.   434
Nusret Sen, DDP   202
Paul Davies, Comm. Lge   110
Denny De La Haye, Ind.   95
Jane Tuckett, Ind.   26
Michael Spinks, Ind.   20
Lab. majority 14,288 (33.34%)
Notional 0.99% swing Lab. to LD.
(2005: Lab. majority 9,629 (31.37%))

§HALESOWEN & ROWLEY REGIS
E. 63,693 T. 43,979 (69.05%) C. gain
*James Morris, C.   18,115
Sue Hayman, Lab.   16,092
Philip Tibbets, LD   6,515
Derek Baddeley, UKIP   2,824
Derek Thompson, Ind.   433
C. majority 2,023 (4.60%)
Notional 7.13% swing Lab. to C.
(2005: Lab. majority 4,010 (9.66%))

§HALIFAX
E. 70,380 T. 43,555 (61.89%) Lab. hold
Linda Riordan, Lab.   16,278
Philip Allott, C.   14,806
Elisabeth Wilson, LD   8,335
Tom Bates, BNP   2,760
Diane Park, Ind. Voice   722
Jay Sangha, UKIP   654
Lab. majority 1,472 (3.38%)
Notional 2.69% swing Lab. to C.
(2005: Lab. majority 3,481 (8.75%))

§HALTEMPRICE & HOWDEN
E. 70,403 T. 48,737 (69.23%) C. hold
David Davis, C.   24,486
Jon Neal, LD   12,884
Danny Marten, Lab.   7,630
James Cornell, BNP   1,583
Joanne Robinson, Eng. Dem.   1,485
Shan Oakes, Green   669
C. majority 11,602 (23.81%)
Notional 6.64% swing LD to C.
(2005: C. majority 5,080 (10.52%))

§HALTON
E. 68,884 T. 41,338 (60.01%) Lab. hold
Derek Twigg, Lab.   23,843
Ben Jones, C.   8,339
Frank Harasiwka, LD   5,718
Andrew Taylor, BNP   1,563
John Moore, UKIP   1,228
Jim Craig, Green   647
Lab. majority 15,504 (37.51%)
Notional 2.87% swing Lab. to C.
(2005: Lab. majority 16,060 (43.25%))

§HAMMERSMITH
E. 72,348 T. 47,452 (65.59%) Lab. hold
Andy Slaughter, Lab.   20,810
Shaun Bailey, C.   17,261
Merlene Emerson, LD   7,567
Rollo Miles, Green   696
Vanessa Crichton, UKIP   551
Lawrence Searle, BNP   432
Stephen Brennan, Ind.   135
Lab. majority 3,549 (7.48%)
Notional 0.48% swing Lab. to C.
(2005: Lab. majority 3,673 (8.44%))

§HAMPSHIRE EAST
E. 72,250 T. 51,317 (71.03%) C. hold
*Damian Hinds, C.   29,137
Adam Carew, LD   15,640
Jane Edbrooke, Lab.   4,043
Hugh McGuinness, UKIP   1,477
Matt Williams, Eng. Dem.   710
Don Jerrard, J & AC   310
C. majority 13,497 (26.30%)
Notional 6.61% swing LD to C.
(2005: C. majority 5,968 (13.09%))

§HAMPSHIRE NORTH EAST
E. 72,196 T. 52,939 (73.33%) C. hold
James Arbuthnot, C.   32,075
Denzil Coulson, LD   13,478
Barry Jones, Lab.   5,173
Ruth Duffin, UKIP   2,213
C. majority 18,597 (35.13%)
Notional 4.52% swing LD to C.
(2005: C. majority 11,189 (26.09%))

§HAMPSHIRE NORTH WEST
E. 76,040 T. 53,292 (70.08%) C. hold
Sir George Young, C.   31,072
Thomas McCann, LD   12,489
Sarah Evans, Lab.   6,980
Stan Oram, UKIP   2,751
C. majority 18,583 (34.87%)
Notional 4.67% swing LD to C.
(2005: C. majority 12,683 (25.53%))

§HAMPSTEAD & KILBURN
E. 79,713 T. 52,822 (66.27%) Lab. hold
Glenda Jackson, Lab.   17,332
Chris Philp, C.   17,290
Edward Fordham, LD   16,491
Bea Campbell, Green   759
Magnus Nielsen, UKIP   408
Victoria Moore, BNP   328
Tamsin Omond, TOC   123
Gene Alcantara, Ind.   91
Lab. majority 42 (0.08%)
Notional 6.65% swing Lab. to C.
(2005: Lab. majority 474 (1.14%))

§HARBOROUGH
E. 77,917 T. 54,945 (70.52%) C. hold
Edward Garnier, C.   26,894
Zuffar Haq, LD   17,097
Kevin McKeever, Lab.   6,981
Geoff Dickens, BNP   1,715
Marrietta King, UKIP   1,462
David Ball, Eng. Dem.   568
Jeff Stephenson, Ind.   228
C. majority 9,797 (17.83%)
Notional 4.73% swing LD to C.
(2005: C. majority 4,047 (8.38%))

§HARLOW
E. 67,439 T. 43,878 (65.06%) C. gain
*Robert Halfon, C.   19,691
Bill Rammell, Lab.   14,766
David White, LD   5,990
Eddy Butler, BNP   1,739
John Croft, UKIP   1,591
Oluyemi Adeeko, Ch. P.   101
C. majority 4,925 (11.22%)
Notional 5.90% swing Lab. to C.
(2005: Lab. majority 230 (0.58%))

§HARROGATE & KNARESBOROUGH
E. 75,269 T. 53,134 (70.59%) C. gain
*Andrew Jones, C.   24,305
Claire Kelley, LD   23,266
Kevin McNerney, Lab.   3,413
Steven Gill, BNP   1,094
John Upex, UKIP   1,056
C. majority 1,039 (1.96%)
Notional 9.09% swing LD to C.
(2005: LD majority 7,980 (16.22%))

§HARROW EAST
E. 68,554 T. 48,006 (70.03%) C. gain
*Bob Blackman, C.   21,435
Tony McNulty, Lab.   18,032
Nahid Boethe, LD   6,850
Abhijit Pandya, UKIP   896
Madeleine Atkins, Green   793
C. majority 3,403 (7.09%)
Notional 6.99% swing Lab. to C.
(2005: Lab. majority 2,934 (6.89%))

§HARROW WEST
E. 71,510 T. 46,116 (64.49%)
                    Lab. (Co-op) hold
Gareth Thomas, Lab. (Co-op)   20,111
Dr Rachel Joyce, C.   16,968
Christopher Noyce, LD   7,458
Herbert Crossman, UKIP   954
Rowan Langley, Green   625
Lab. (Co-op) majority 3,143 (6.82%)
Notional 5.72% swing Lab. (Co-op) to C.
(2005: Lab. (Co-op) majority 7,742
(18.26%))

HARTLEPOOL
E. 68,923 T. 38,242 (55.49%) Lab. hold
Iain Wright, Lab.   16,267
Alan Wright, C.   10,758
Reg Clark, LD   6,533
Stephen Allison, UKIP   2,682
Ronnie Bage, BNP   2,002
Lab. majority 5,509 (14.41%)
12.82% swing Lab. to C.
(2005: Lab. majority 7,478 (21.10%))

§HARWICH & ESSEX NORTH
E. 70,743 T. 49,000 (69.26%) C. hold
Bernard Jenkin, C.   23,001
James Raven, LD   11,554
Darren Barrenger, Lab.   9,774
Simon Anselmi, UKIP   2,527
Stephen Robey, BNP   1,065
Chris Fox, Green   909
Peter Thompson Bates, Ind.   170
C. majority 11,447 (23.36%)
Notional 0.00% swing C. to LD
(2005: C. majority 5,583 (11.73%))

§HASTINGS & RYE
E. 78,000 T. 49,814 (63.86%) C. gain
*Amber Rudd, C.   20,468
Michael Foster, Lab.   18,475
Nicholas Perry, LD   7,825
Anthony Smith, UKIP   1,397
Nicholas Prince, BNP   1,310
Rodney Bridger, Eng. Dem.   339
C. majority 1,993 (4.00%)
Notional 3.27% swing Lab. to C.
(2005: Lab. majority 1,156 (2.54%))

§HAVANT
E. 69,712 T. 43,903 (62.98%) C. hold
David Willetts, C.   22,433
Alex Payton, LD   10,273
Robert Smith, Lab.   7,777
Gary Kerrin, UKIP   2,611
Fungus Addams, Eng. Dem.   809
C. majority 12,160 (27.70%)
Notional 1.79% swing LD to C.
(2005: C. majority 6,395 (15.58%))

§HAYES & HARLINGTON
E. 70,233 T. 42,637 (60.71%) Lab. hold
John McDonnell, Lab.   23,377
Scott Seaman-Digby, C.   12,553
Satnam Kaur Khalsa, LD   3,726
Chris Forster, BNP   1,520
Andrew Cripps, NF   566
Cliff Dixon, Eng. Dem.   464
Jessica Lee, Green   348
Aneel Shahzad, Ch. P.   83
Lab. majority 10,824 (25.39%)
Notional 1.65% swing Lab. to C.
(2005: Lab. majority 10,594 (28.68%))

§HAZEL GROVE
E. 63,074 T. 41,981 (66.56%) LD hold
Andrew Stunell, LD   20,485
Annesley Abercorn, C.   14,114
Richard Scorer, Lab.   5,234
John Whittaker, UKIP   2,148
LD majority 6,371 (15.18%)
Notional 2.37% swing LD to C.
(2005: LD majority 7,694 (19.92%))

§HEMEL HEMPSTEAD
E. 72,754 T. 49,471 (68.00%) C. hold
Mike Penning, C.   24,721
Dr Richard Grayson, LD   11,315
Ayfer Orhan, Lab.   10,295
Janet Price, BNP   1,615
David Alexander, UKIP   1,254
Mick Young, Ind.   271
C. majority 13,406 (27.10%)
Notional 1.94% swing LD to C.
(2005: C. majority 168 (0.36%))

§HEMSWORTH
E. 72,552 T. 43,840 (60.43%) Lab. hold
Jon Trickett, Lab.   20,506
Ann Myatt, C.   10,662
Alan Belmore, LD   5,667
Ian Womersley, Ind.   3,946
Ian Kitchen, BNP   3,059
Lab. majority 9,844 (22.45%)
Notional 7.03% swing Lab. to C.
(2005: Lab. majority 14,026 (36.51%))

§HENDON
E. 78,923 T. 46,374 (58.76%) C. gain
*Matthew Offord, C.   19,635
Andrew Dismore, Lab.   19,529
Matthew Harris, LD   5,734
Robin Lambert, UKIP   958
Andrew Newby, Green   518
C. majority 106 (0.23%)
Notional 4.14% swing Lab. to C.
(2005: Lab. majority 3,231 (8.06%))

§HENLEY
E. 75,005 T. 53,520 (71.36%) C. hold
John Howell, C.   30,054
Andrew Crick, LD   13,466
Richard McKenzie, Lab.   5,835
Laurence Hughes, UKIP   1,817
Mark Stevenson, Green   1,328
John Bews, BNP   1,020
C. majority 16,588 (30.99%)
Notional 1.93% swing LD to C.
(2005: C. majority 13,366 (27.13%))

§HEREFORD & HEREFORDSHIRE
SOUTH
E. 71,435 T. 48,381 (67.73%) C. gain
*Jesse Norman, C.   22,366
Sarah Carr, LD   19,885
Philippa Roberts, Lab.   3,506
Valentine Smith, UKIP   1,638
John Oliver, BNP   986
C. majority 2,481 (5.13%)
Notional 3.76% swing LD to C.
(2005: LD majority 1,089 (2.39%))

§HEREFORDSHIRE NORTH
E. 66,525 T. 47,568 (71.50%) C. hold
Bill Wiggin, C.   24,631
Lucy Hurds, LD   14,744
Neil Sabharwal, Lab.   3,373
Jonathan Oakton, UKIP   2,701
Felicity Norman, Green   1,533
John King, Ind.   586
C. majority 9,887 (20.78%)
Notional 3.82% swing C. to LD
(2005: C. majority 12,688 (28.43%))

§HERTFORD & STORTFORD
E. 78,459 T. 55,377 (70.58%) C. hold
Mark Prisk, C.   29,810
Andrew Lewin, LD   14,373
Steve Terry, Lab.   7,620
David Sodey, UKIP   1,716
Roy Harris, BNP   1,297
Loucas Xenophontos, Ind.   325
Martin Adams, Ind.   236
C. majority 15,437 (27.88%)
Notional 1.95% swing C. to LD
(2005: C. majority 12,756 (25.95%))

§HERTFORDSHIRE NORTH EAST
E. 72,200 T. 50,425 (69.84%) C. hold
Oliver Heald, C.   26,995
Hugh Annand, LD   11,801
David Kirkman, Lab.   8,291
Adrianne Smyth, UKIP   2,075
Rosemary Bland, Green   875
Richard Campbell, Ind.   209
David Ralph, YRDPL   143
Philip Reichardt, Ind.   36
C. majority 15,194 (30.13%)
Notional 1.19% swing LD to C.
(2005: C. majority 9,510 (19.75%))

§HERTFORDSHIRE SOUTH WEST
E. 78,248 T. 56,750 (72.53%) C. hold
David Gauke, C.   30,773
Christopher Townsend, LD   15,853
Harry Mann, Lab.   6,526
Mark Benson, UKIP   1,450
Deirdre Gates, BNP   1,302
James Hannaway, Ind.   846
C. majority 14,920 (26.29%)
Notional 4.66% swing LD to C.
(2005: C. majority 8,640 (16.97%))

HERTSMERE
E. 73,062 T. 47,270 (64.70%) C. hold
James Clappison, C.   26,476
Sam Russell, Lab.   8,871
Anthony Rowlands, LD   8,210
David Rutter, UKIP   1,712
Daniel Seabrook, BNP   1,397
Arjuna Krishna-Das, Green   604
C. majority 17,605 (37.24%)
5.59% swing Lab. to C.
(2005: C. majority 11,093 (26.06%))

§HEXHAM
E. 61,375 T. 43,483 (70.85%) C. hold
*Guy Opperman, C.   18,795
Andrew Duffield, LD   13,007
Antoine Tinnion, Lab.   8,253
Steve Ford, Ind.   1,974
Quentin Hawkins, BNP   1,205
Colin Moss, Ind.   249
C. majority 5,788 (13.31%)
Notional 1.70% swing C. to LD
(2005: C. majority 4,957 (12.03%))

§HEYWOOD & MIDDLETON
E. 80,171 T. 46,125 (57.53%) Lab. hold
Jim Dobbin, Lab.   18,499
Michael Holly, C.   12,528
Wera Hobhouse, LD   10,474
Peter Greenwood, BNP   3,239
Victoria Cecil, UKIP   1,215
Chrissy Lee, Ind.   170
Lab. majority 5,971 (12.95%)
Notional 6.82% swing Lab. to C.
(2005: Lab. majority 11,034 (26.58%))

§HIGH PEAK
E. 71,973 T. 50,337 (69.94%) C. gain
*Andrew Bingham, C.   20,587
Caitlin Bisknell, Lab.   15,910
Alistair Stevens, LD   10,993
Sylvia Hall, UKIP   1,690
Peter Allen, Green   922
Lance Dowson, Ind.   161
Tony Alves, ND   74
C. majority 4,677 (9.29%)
Notional 6.54% swing Lab. to C.
(2005: Lab. majority 1,750 (3.80%))

§HITCHIN & HARPENDEN
E. 73,851 T. 54,707 (74.08%) C. hold
Peter Lilley, C.   29,869
Nigel Quinton, LD   14,598
Oliver de Botton, Lab.   7,413
Graham Wilkinson, UKIP   1,663
Richard Wise, Green   807
Margaret Henderson, Ind.   109
Simon Byron, R and E   108
Eric Hannah, YRDPL   90
Peter Rigby, Ind.   50
C. majority 15,271 (27.91%)
Notional 2.50% swing LD to C.
(2005: C. majority 11,064 (22.90%))

§HOLBORN & ST PANCRAS
E. 86,863 T. 54,649 (62.91%) Lab. hold
Frank Dobson, Lab.   25,198
Jo Shaw, LD   15,256
George Lee, C.   11,134
Natalie Bennett, Green   1,480
Robert Carlyle, BNP   779
Max Spencer, UKIP   587
John Chapman, Ind.   96
Mikel Susperregi, Eng. Dem.   75
Iain Meek, Ind.   44
Lab. majority 9,942 (18.19%)
Notional 0.38% swing Lab. to LD
(2005: Lab. majority 8,348 (18.95%))

§HORNCHURCH & UPMINSTER
E. 78,487 T. 53,390 (68.02%) C. hold
Angela Watkinson, C.   27,469
Kath McGuirk, Lab.   11,098
Karen Chilvers, LD   7,426
William Whelpley, BNP   3,421
Lawrence Webb, UKIP   2,848
Melanie Collins, Green   542
David Durant, Ind.   305
Johnson Olukotun, Ch. P.   281
C. majority 16,371 (30.66%)
Notional 7.14% swing Lab. to C.
(2005: C. majority 8,058 (16.38%))

HORNSEY & WOOD GREEN
E. 79,916 T. 55,042 (68.87%) LD hold
Lynne Featherstone, LD   25,595
Karen Jennings, Lab.   18,720
Richard Merrin, C.   9,174
Pete McAskie, Green   1,261
Stephane De Roche, Ind.   201
Rohen Kapur, Ind.   91
LD majority 6,875 (12.49%)
3.72% swing Lab. to LD
(2005: LD majority 2,395 (5.06%))

§HORSHAM
E. 76,835 T. 55,841 (72.68%) C. hold
Francis Maude, C.   29,447
Godfrey Newman, LD   17,987
Andrew Skudder, Lab.   4,189
Harry Aldridge, UKIP   2,839
Nick Fitter, Green   570
Steve Lyon, Ch. P.   469
Jim Duggan, PPN-V   253
Derek Kissach, Ind.   87
C. majority 11,460 (20.52%)
Notional 0.57% swing C. to LD
(2005: C. majority 10,780 (21.66%))

§HOUGHTON & SUNDERLAND
SOUTH
E. 68,729 T. 38,021 (55.32%) Lab. hold
*Bridget Phillipson, Lab.   19,137
Robert Oliver, C.   8,147
Chris Boyle, LD   5,292
Colin Wakefield, Ind.   2,462
Karen Allen, BNP   1,961
Richard Elvin, UKIP   1,022
Lab. majority 10,990 (28.91%)
Notional 8.44% swing Lab. to C.
(2005: Lab. majority 16,986 (45.78%))

§HOVE
E. 71,708 T. 49,819 (69.47%) C. gain
*Mike Weatherley, C.   18,294
Celia Barlow, Lab.   16,426
Paul Elgood, LD   11,240
Ian Davey, Green   2,568
Paul Perrin, UKIP   1,206
Brian Ralfe, Ind.   85
C. majority 1,868 (3.75%)
Notional 2.37% swing Lab. to C.
(2005: Lab. majority 448 (1.00%))

§HUDDERSFIELD
E. 66,316 T. 40,524 (61.11%) Lab. hold
Barry Sheerman, Lab.   15,725
Karen Tweed, C.   11,253
James Blanchard, LD   10,023
Andrew Cooper, Green   1,641
Rachel Firth, BNP   1,563
Paul Cooney, TUSC   319
Lab. majority 4,472 (11.04%)
Notional 7.14% swing Lab. to C.
(2005: Lab. majority 7,883 (22.29%))

§HULL EAST
E. 67,530 T. 34,184 (50.62%) Lab. hold
*Karl Turner, Lab.   16,387
Jeremy Wilcock, LD   7,790
Christine Mackay, C.   5,667
Mike Hookem, UKIP   2,745
Joe Uttley, NF   880
Mike Burton, Eng. Dem.   715
Lab. majority 8,597 (25.15%)
Notional 5.35% swing Lab. to LD
(2005: Lab. majority 11,740 (35.84%))

§HULL NORTH
E. 64,082 T. 33,291 (51.95%) Lab. hold
Diana Johnson, Lab.   13,044
Denis Healy, LD   12,403
Victoria Aitken, C.   4,365
John Mainprize, BNP   1,443
Paul Barlow, UKIP   1,358
Martin Deane, Green   478
Michael Cassidy, Eng. Dem.   200
Lab. majority 641 (1.93%)
Notional 12.18% swing Lab. to LD
(2005: Lab. majority 7,384 (26.29%))

§HULL WEST & HESSLE
E. 69,017 T. 31,505 (45.65%) Lab. hold
Alan Johnson, Lab.   13,378
Mike Ross, LD   7,636
Gary Shores, C.   6,361
Ken Hordon, UKIP   1,688
Edward Scott, BNP   1,416
Peter Mawer, Eng. Dem.   876
Keith Gibson, TUSC   150
Lab. majority 5,742 (18.23%)
Notional 7.92% swing Lab. to LD
(2005: Lab. majority 9,430 (34.06%))

§HUNTINGDON
E. 83,557 T. 54,266 (64.94%) C. hold
Jonathan Djanogly, C.   26,516
Martin Land, LD   15,697
Anthea Cox, Lab.   5,982
Ian Curtis, UKIP   3,258
Jonathan Salt, Ind.   1,432
John Clare, Green   652
Lord Toby Jug, Loony   548
Carrie Holliman, APP   181
C. majority 10,819 (19.94%)
Notional 2.08% swing C. to LD
(2005: C. majority 11,652 (24.10%))

§HYNDBURN
E. 67,221 T. 42,672 (63.48%) Lab. hold
*Graham Jones, Lab.   17,531
Karen Buckley, C.   14,441
Andrew Rankine, LD   5,033
David Shapcott, BNP   2,137
Granville Barker, UKIP   1,481
The Revd Kevin Logan, CPA   795
Kerry Gormley, Green   463
Christopher Reid, Eng. Dem.   413
Craig Hall, Ind.   378
Lab. majority 3,090 (7.24%)
Notional 3.28% swing Lab. to C.
(2005: Lab. majority 5,528 (13.80%))

§ILFORD NORTH
E. 71,995 T. 47,018 (65.31%) C. hold
Lee Scott, C.   21,506
Sonia Klein, Lab.   16,102
Alex Berhanu, LD   5,966
Danny Warville, BNP   1,545
Henri van der Stighelen, UKIP   871
Caroline Allen, Green   572
The Revd Robert Hampson, CPA   456
C. majority 5,404 (11.49%)
Notional 3.68% swing Lab. to C.
(2005: C. majority 1,735 (4.14%))

ILFORD SOUTH
E. 75,246 T. 51,191 (68.03%)
                      Lab. (Co-op) hold
Mike Gapes, Lab. (Co-op)   25,301
Toby Boutle, C.   14,014
Anood Al-Samerai, LD   8,679
Wilson Chowdhry, Green   1,319
Terry Murray, UKIP   1,132
John Jestico, King George   746
Lab. (Co-op) majority 11,287 (22.05%)
0.22% swing C. to Lab. (Co-op)
(2005: Lab. (Co-op) majority 9,228
(21.61%))

§IPSWICH
E. 78,371　T. 46,941 (59.90%)　C. gain
*Benedict Gummer, C.　　18,371
Chris Mole, Lab.　　16,292
Mark Dyson, LD　　8,556
Chris Streatfield, UKIP　　1,365
Dennis Boater, BNP　　1,270
Tim Glover, Green　　775
Kim Christofi, Ch. P.　　149
Peter Turtill, Ind.　　93
Sally Wainman, Ind.　　70
C. majority 2,079 (4.43%)
Notional 8.12% swing Lab. to C.
(2005: Lab. majority 5,235 (11.81%))

ISLE OF WIGHT
E. 109,966　T. 70,264 (63.90%)　C. hold
Andrew Turner, C.　　32,810
Jill Wareham, LD　　22,283
Mark Chiverton, Lab.　　8,169
Mike Tarrant, UKIP　　2,435
Geoff Clynch, BNP　　1,457
Ian Dunsire, Eng. Dem.　　1,233
Bob Keats, Green　　931
Paul Martin, Mid. England　　616
Pete Harris, Ind.　　175
Paul Randle-Jolliffe, Ind.　　89
Edward Corby, Ind.　　66
C. majority 10,527 (14.98%)
2.22% swing C. to LD
(2005: C. majority 12,978 (19.42%))

ISLINGTON NORTH
E. 68,120　T. 44,554 (65.41%)　Lab. hold
Jeremy Corbyn, Lab.　　24,276
Rhodri Jamieson-Ball, LD　　11,875
Adrian Berrill-Cox, C.　　6,339
Emma Dixon, Green　　1,348
Dominic Lennon, UKIP　　716
Lab. majority 12,401 (27.83%)
3.25% swing LD to Lab.
(2005: Lab. majority 6,716 (21.32%))

ISLINGTON SOUTH & FINSBURY
E. 67,649　T. 43,555 (64.38%)　Lab. hold
Emily Thornberry, Lab.　　18,407
Bridget Fox, LD　　14,838
Antonia Cox, C.　　8,449
James Humphreys, Green　　710
Rose-Marie McDonald, UKIP　　701
John Dodds, Eng. Dem.　　301
Richard Deboo, Animals　　149
Lab. majority 3,569 (8.19%)
3.32% swing LD to Lab.
(2005: Lab. majority 484 (1.56%))

§JARROW
E. 64,350　T. 38,784 (60.27%)　Lab. hold
Stephen Hepburn, Lab.　　20,910
Jeffrey Milburn, C.　　8,002
Tom Appleby, LD　　7,163
Andy Swaddle, BNP　　2,709
Lab. majority 12,908 (33.28%)
Notional 6.38% swing Lab. to C.
(2005: Lab. majority 12,749 (36.35%))

KEIGHLEY
E. 65,893　T. 47,692 (72.38%)　C. gain
*Kris Hopkins, C.　　20,003
Jane Thomas, Lab.　　17,063
Nader Fekri, LD　　7,059
Andrew Brons, BNP　　1,962
Paul Latham, UKIP　　1,470
Steven Smith, NF　　135
C. majority 2,940 (6.16%)
8.32% swing Lab. to C.
(2005: Lab. majority 4,852 (10.48%))

§KENILWORTH & SOUTHAM
E. 59,630　T. 48,431 (81.22%)　C. hold
Jeremy Wright, C.　　25,945
Nigel Rock, LD　　13,393
Nicholas Milton, Lab.　　6,949
John Moore, UKIP　　1,214
James Harrison, Green　　568
Joe Rukin, Ind.　　362
C. majority 12,552 (25.92%)
Notional 1.20% swing C. to LD
(2005: C. majority 10,956 (24.80%))

§KENSINGTON
E. 65,961　T. 35,150 (53.29%)　C. hold
Sir Malcolm Rifkind, C.　　17,595
Sam Gurney, Lab.　　8,979
Robin Meltzer, LD　　6,872
Lady Caroline Pearson, UKIP　　754
Zahra-Melan Ebrahimi-Fardouee,
　Green　　753
Eddie Adams, Green Soc.　　197
C. majority 8,616 (24.51%)
Notional 5.19% swing Lab. to C.
(2005: C. majority 4,540 (14.13%))

§KETTERING
E. 68,837　T. 47,328 (68.75%)　C. hold
Philip Hollobone, C.　　23,247
Phil Sawford, Lab.　　14,153
Chris Nelson, LD　　7,498
Clive Skinner, BNP　　1,366
Derek Hilling, Eng. Dem.　　952
Dave Bishop, BP Elvis　　112
C. majority 9,094 (19.21%)
Notional 9.41% swing Lab. to C.
(2005: C. majority 176 (0.39%))

§KINGSTON & SURBITON
E. 81,116　T. 57,111 (70.41%)　LD hold
Edward Davey, LD　　28,428
Helen Whately, C.　　20,868
Max Freedman, Lab.　　5,337
Jonathan Greensted, UKIP　　1,450
Chris Walker, Green　　555
Monkey the Drummer, Loony　　247
Anthony May, CPA　　226
LD majority 7,560 (13.24%)
Notional 2.43% swing LD to C.
(2005: LD majority 9,084 (18.11%))

§KINGSWOOD
E. 66,361　T. 47,906 (72.19%)　C. gain.
*Chris Skidmore, C.　　19,362
Roger Berry, Lab.　　16,917
Sally Fitzharris, LD　　8,072
Neil Dowdney, UKIP　　1,528
Michael Carey, BNP　　1,311
Nick Foster, Green　　383
Michael Blundell, Eng. Dem.　　333
C. majority 2,445 (5.10%)
Notional 9.43% swing Lab. to C.
(2005: Lab. majority 6,145 (13.76%))

§KNOWSLEY
E. 79,561　T. 44,658 (56.13%)　Lab. hold
George Howarth, Lab.　　31,650
Flo Clucas, LD　　5,964
David Dunne, C.　　4,004
Steven Greenhalgh, BNP　　1,895
Anthony Rundle, UKIP　　1,145
Lab. majority 25,686 (57.52%)
Notional 0.25% swing Lab. to LD
(2005: Lab. majority 24,333 (58.02%))

LANCASHIRE WEST
E. 75,975　T. 48,473 (63.80%) Lab. hold
Rosie Cooper, Lab.　　21,883
Adrian Owens, C.　　17,540
John Gibson, LD　　6,573
Damon Noone, UKIP　　1,775
Peter Cranie, Green　　485
David Braid, Clause 28　　217
Lab. majority 4,343 (8.96%)
2.57% swing Lab. to C.
(2005: Lab. majority 6,084 (14.10%))

§LANCASTER & FLEETWOOD
E. 69,908　T. 42,701 (61.08%)　C. gain
*Eric Ollerenshaw, C.　　15,404
Clive Grunshaw, Lab.　　15,071
Stuart Langhorn, LD　　8,167
Gina Dowding, Green　　1,888
Fred McGlade, UKIP　　1,020
Debra Kent, BNP　　938
Keith Riley, Ind.　　213
C. majority 333 (0.78%)
Notional 4.80% swing Lab. to C.
(2005: Lab. majority 3,428 (8.82%))

§LEEDS CENTRAL
E. 64,698　T. 37,394 (57.80%) Lab. hold
Hilary Benn, Lab.　　18,434
Michael Taylor, LD　　7,789
Alan Lamb, C.　　7,541
Kevin Meeson, BNP　　3,066
Dave Procter, Ind.　　409
We Beat The Scum One-Nil, ND　　155
Lab. majority 10,645 (28.47%)
Notional 4.76% swing Lab. to LD
(2005: Lab. majority 12,916 (37.98%))

§LEEDS EAST
E. 65,067　T. 37,813 (58.11%) Lab. hold
George Mudie, Lab.　　19,056
Barry Anderson, C.　　8,763
Andrew Tear, LD　　6,618
Trevor Brown, BNP　　2,947
Michael Davies, Green Soc.　　429
Lab. majority 10,293 (27.22%)
Notional 5.49% swing Lab. to C.
(2005: Lab. majority 13,689 (38.21%))

§LEEDS NORTH EAST
E. 67,899　T. 47,535 (70.01%) Lab. hold
Fabian Hamilton, Lab.　　20,287
Matthew Lobley, C.　　15,742
Aqila Choudhry, LD　　9,310
Warren Hendon, UKIP　　842
Tom Redmond, BNP　　758
Celia Foote, Green Soc.　　596
Lab. majority 4,545 (9.56%)
Notional 2.97% swing Lab. to C.
(2005: Lab. majority 6,762 (15.51%))

§LEEDS NORTH WEST
E. 65,399　T. 43,483 (66.49%) LD hold
Greg Mulholland, LD　　20,653
Julia Mulligan, C.　　11,550
Judith Blake, Lab.　　9,132
Geoffrey Bulmer, BNP　　766
Mark Thackray, UKIP　　600
Martin Hemingway, Green　　508
Alan Procter, Eng. Dem.　　153
Trevor Bavage, Green Soc.　　121
LD majority 9,103 (20.93%)
Notional 5.44% swing C. to LD
(2005: LD majority 2,064 (4.96%))

§LEEDS WEST
E. 67,453 T. 38,752 (57.45%) Lab. hold
*Rachel Reeves, Lab.   16,389
Ruth Coleman, LD   9,373
Joe Marjoram, C.   7,641
Joanna Beverley, BNP   2,377
David Blackburn, Green   1,832
Jeff Miles, UKIP   1,140
Lab. majority 7,016 (18.10%)
Notional 10.36% swing Lab. to LD
(2005: Lab. majority 13,699 (38.83%))

§LEICESTER EAST
E. 72,986 T. 47,995 (65.76%) Lab. hold
Keith Vaz, Lab.   25,804
Jane Hunt, C.   11,722
Ali Asghar, LD   6,817
Colin Gilmore, BNP   1,700
Mo Taylor, Green   733
Felicity Ransome, UKIP   725
Avtar Sadiq, UPS   494
Lab. majority 14,082 (29.34%)
Notional 4.77% swing Lab. to C.
(2005: Lab. majority 16,400 (38.89%))

§LEICESTER SOUTH
E. 77,175 T. 47,124 (61.06%) Lab. hold
Sir Peter Soulsby, Lab.   21,479
Parmjit Singh Gill, LD   12,671
Ross Grant, C.   10,066
Adrian Waudby, BNP   1,418
Dave Dixey, Green   770
Christopher Lucas, UKIP   720
Lab. majority 8,808 (18.69%)
Notional 4.96% swing LD to Lab.
(2005: Lab. majority 3,727 (8.78%))

§LEICESTER WEST
E. 64,900 T. 35,819 (55.19%) Lab. hold
*Elizabeth Kendall, Lab.   13,745
Celia Harvey, C.   9,728
Peter Coley, LD   8,107
Gary Reynolds, BNP   2,158
Stephen Ingall, UKIP   883
Geoff Forse, Green   639
Steven Huggins, Ind.   181
Steve Score, TUSC   157
Shaun Dyer, Pirate   113
David Bowley, Ind.   108
Lab. majority 4,017 (11.21%)
Notional 7.60% swing Lab. to C.
(2005: Lab. majority 8,539 (26.42%))

LEICESTERSHIRE NORTH WEST
E. 71,219 T. 51,952 (72.95%) C. gain
*Andrew Bridgen, C.   23,147
Ross Willmott, Lab. (Co-op)   15,636
Paul Reynolds, LD   8,639
Ian Meller, BNP   3,396
Martin Green, UKIP   1,134
C. majority 7,511 (14.46%)
11.98% swing Lab. (Co-op) to C.
(2005: Lab. (Co-op) majority 4,477
(9.50%))

§LEICESTERSHIRE SOUTH
E. 76,639 T. 54,577 (71.21%) C. hold
Andrew Robathan, C.   27,000
Aladdin Ayesh, LD   11,476
Sally Gimson, Lab.   11,392
Paul Preston, BNP   2,721
John Williams, UKIP   1,988
C. majority 15,524 (28.44%)
Notional 1.03% swing LD to C.
(2005: C. majority 7,704 (15.77%))

§LEIGH
E. 76,350 T. 44,332 (58.06%) Lab. hold
Andy Burnham, Lab.   21,295
Shazia Awan, C.   9,284
Chris Blackburn, LD   8,049
Gary Chadwick, BNP   2,724
Mary Lavelle, UKIP   1,535
Norman Bradbury, Ind.   988
Terry Dainty, Ind.   320
Ryan Hessell, Ch. P.   137
Lab. majority 12,011 (27.09%)
Notional 7.17% swing Lab. to C.
(2005: Lab. majority 15,098 (38.73%))

§LEWES
E. 68,708 T. 50,088 (72.90%) LD hold
Norman Baker, LD   26,048
Jason Sugarman, C.   18,401
Hratche Koundarjian, Lab.   2,508
Peter Charlton, UKIP   1,728
Susan Murray, Green   729
David Lloyd, BNP   594
Ondrej Soucek, Ind.   80
LD majority 7,647 (15.27%)
Notional 0.81% swing LD to C.
(2005: LD majority 7,889 (16.89%))

§LEWISHAM DEPTFORD
E. 67,058 T. 41,220 (61.47%) Lab. hold
Joan Ruddock, Lab.   22,132
Tam Langley, LD   9,633
Gemma Townsend, C.   5,551
Darren Johnson, Green   2,772
Ian Page, Soc. Alt.   645
Malcolm Martin, CPA   487
Lab. majority 12,499 (30.32%)
Notional 3.56% swing Lab. to LD
(2005: Lab. majority 13,012 (37.43%))

§LEWISHAM EAST
E. 65,926 T. 41,719 (63.28%) Lab. hold
*Heidi Alexander, Lab.   17,966
Pete Pattisson, LD   11,750
Jonathan Clamp, C.   9,850
Roderick Reed, UKIP   771
Priscilla Cotterell, Green   624
James Rose, Eng. Dem.   426
George Hallam, CNBPG   332
Lab. majority 6,216 (14.90%)
Notional 6.41% swing Lab. to LD
(2005: Lab. majority 8,758 (23.31%))

§LEWISHAM WEST & PENGE
E. 69,022 T. 45,028 (65.24%) Lab. hold
Jim Dowd, Lab.   18,501
Alex Feakes, LD   12,673
Chris Phillips, C.   11,489
Peter Staveley, UKIP   1,117
Romayne Phoenix, Green   931
Stephen Hammond, CPA   317
Lab. majority 5,828 (12.94%)
Notional 3.10% swing Lab. to LD
(2005: Lab. majority 7,779 (19.15%))

§LEYTON & WANSTEAD
E. 63,541 T. 40,159 (63.20%) Lab. hold
*John Cryer, Lab.   17,511
Farooq Qureshi, LD   11,095
Ed Northover, C.   8,928
Graham Wood, UKIP   1,080
Ashley Gunstock, Green   562
Jim Clift, BNP   561
Sonika Bhatti, Ch. P.   342
Martin Levin, Ind. Fed.   80
Lab. majority 6,416 (15.98%)
Notional 2.57% swing Lab. to LD
(2005: Lab. majority 7,253 (21.11%))

§LICHFIELD
E. 72,586 T. 51,563 (71.04%) C. hold
Michael Fabricant, C.   28,048
Ian Jackson, LD   10,365
Steve Hyden, Lab.   10,230
Karen Maunder, UKIP   2,920
C. majority 17,683 (34.29%)
Notional 0.74% swing LD to C.
(2005: C. majority 7,791 (16.49%))

§LINCOLN
E. 73,540 T. 45,721 (62.17%) C. gain
*Karl McCartney, C.   17,163
Gillian Merron, Lab.   16,105
Reg Shore, LD   9,256
Robert West, BNP   1,367
Nick Smith, UKIP   1,004
Ernest Coleman, Eng. Dem.   604
Gary Walker, Ind.   222
C. majority 1,058 (2.31%)
Notional 5.89% swing Lab. to C.
(2005: Lab. majority 3,806 (9.47%))

§LIVERPOOL RIVERSIDE
E. 74,539 T. 38,801 (52.05%) Lab. hold
Louise Ellman, Lab.   22,998
Richard Marbrow, LD   8,825
Kegang Wu, C.   4,243
Tom Crone, Green   1,355
Peter Stafford, BNP   706
Pat Gaskell, UKIP   674
Lab. majority 14,173 (36.53%)
Notional 0.30% swing LD to Lab.
(2005: Lab. majority 11,731 (35.93%))

§LIVERPOOL WALTON
E. 62,612 T. 34,335 (54.84%) Lab. hold
*Steve Rotheram, Lab.   24,709
Patrick Moloney, LD   4,891
Adam Marsden, C.   2,241
Peter Stafford, BNP   1,104
Joe Nugent, UKIP   898
John Manwell, CPA   297
Daren Ireland, TUSC   195
Lab. majority 19,818 (57.72%)
Notional 1.47% swing LD to Lab.
(2005: Lab. majority 17,611 (54.77%))

§LIVERPOOL WAVERTREE
E. 62,518 T. 37,914 (60.64%)
                  Lab. (Co-op) hold
*Luciana Berger, Lab. (Co-op)   20,132
Colin Eldridge, LD   12,965
Andrew Garnett, C.   2,830
Neil Miney, UKIP   890
Rebecca Lawson, Green   598
Kim Singleton, Soc. Lab.   200
Steven McEllenborough, BNP   150
Frank Dunne, Ind.   149
Lab. (Co-op) majority 7,167 (18.90%)
Notional 5.00% swing LD to Lab. (Co-op)
(2005: Lab. (Co-op) majority 2,911
(8.91%))

§LIVERPOOL WEST DERBY
E. 63,082 T. 35,784 (56.73%)
                  Lab. (Co-op) hold
*Stephen Twigg, Lab. (Co-op)   22,953
Paul Twigger, LD   4,486
Stephen Radford, Lib   3,327
Pamela Hall, C.   3,311
Hilary Jones, UKIP   1,093
Kai Andersen, Soc. Lab.   614
Lab. (Co-op) majority 18,467 (51.61%)
Notional 3.16% swing LD to Lab. (Co-op)
(2005: Lab. (Co-op) majority 13,874
(45.29%))

§LOUGHBOROUGH
E. 77,502 T. 52,838 (68.18%) C. gain
*Nicky Morgan, C. 21,971
Andy Reed, Lab. (Co-op) 18,227
Mike Willis, LD 9,675
Kevan Stafford, BNP 2,040
John Foden, UKIP 925
C. majority 3,744 (7.09%)
Notional 5.48% swing Lab. (Co-op) to C.
(2005: Lab. (Co-op) majority 1,816
(3.88%))

§LOUTH & HORNCASTLE
E. 77,650 T. 50,494 (65.03%) C. hold
Sir Peter Tapsell, C. 25,065
Fiona Martin, LD 11,194
Patrick Mountain, Lab. 8,760
Julia Green, BNP 2,199
Pat Nurse, UKIP 2,183
Daniel Simpson, Lincs Ind. 576
Colin Mair, Eng. Dem. 517
C. majority 13,871 (27.47%)
Notional 0.80% swing LD to C.
(2005: C. majority 9,813 (21.08%))

LUDLOW
E. 66,631 T. 48,732 (73.14%) C. hold
Philip Dunne, C. 25,720
Heather Kidd, LD 15,971
Anthony Hunt, Lab. 3,272
Christopher Gill, UKIP 2,127
Christina Evans, BNP 1,016
Jacqui Morrish, Green 447
Alan Powell, Loony 179
C. majority 9,749 (20.01%)
7.82% swing LD to C.
(2005: C. majority 2,027 (4.36%))

§LUTON NORTH
E. 65,062 T. 43,018 (66.12%) Lab. hold
Kelvin Hopkins, Lab. 21,192
Jeremy Brier, C. 13,672
Rabi Martins, LD 4,784
Colin Brown, UKIP 1,564
Shelley Rose, BNP 1,316
Simon Hall, Green 490
Lab. majority 7,520 (17.48%)
Notional 0.55% swing C. to Lab.
(2005: Lab. majority 6,439 (16.39%))

§LUTON SOUTH
E. 59,962 T. 42,216 (70.40%)
Lab. (Co-op) hold
*Gavin Shuker, Lab. (Co-op) 14,725
Nigel Huddleston, C. 12,396
Qurban Hussain, LD 9,567
Esther Rantzen, Ind. Rantzen 1,872
Tony Blakey, BNP 1,299
Charles Lawman, UKIP 975
Stephen Rhodes, Ind. 463
Marc Scheimann, Green 366
Joe Hall, Ind. 264
Faruk Choudhury, Ind. 130
Stephen Lathwell, Ind. 84
Frank Sweeney, WRP 75
Lab. (Co-op) majority 2,329 (5.52%)
Notional 4.59% swing Lab. (Co-op) to C.
(2005: Lab. (Co-op) majority 5,698
(14.71%))

§MACCLESFIELD
E. 73,417 T. 50,059 (68.18%) C. hold
*David Rutley, C. 23,503
Roger Barlow, LD 11,544
Adrian Heald, Lab. 10,164
Brendan Murphy, Macc. Ind. 2,590
Jacqueline Smith, UKIP 1,418
John Knight, Green 840
C. majority 11,959 (23.89%)
Notional 3.11% swing C. to LD
(2005: C. majority 9,464 (20.66%))

§MAIDENHEAD
E. 72,844 T. 53,720 (73.75%) C. hold
Theresa May, C. 31,937
Tony Hill, LD 15,168
Pat McDonald, Lab. 3,795
Kenneth Wight, UKIP 1,243
Tim Rait, BNP 825
Peter Forbes, Green 482
Peter Prior, F and R 270
C. majority 16,769 (31.22%)
Notional 7.82% swing LD to C.
(2005: C. majority 7,650 (15.58%))

§MAIDSTONE & THE WEALD
E. 71,041 T. 48,928 (68.87%) C. hold
*Helen Grant, C. 23,491
Peter Carroll, LD 17,602
Rav Seeruthun, Lab. 4,769
Gareth Kendall, UKIP 1,637
Stuart Jeffery, Green 655
Gary Butler, NF 643
Heidi Simmonds, Ch. P. 131
C. majority 5,889 (12.04%)
Notional 8.48% swing C. to LD
(2005: C. majority 12,922 (28.99%))

§MAKERFIELD
E. 73,641 T. 43,771 (59.44%) Lab. hold
*Yvonne Fovargue, Lab. 20,700
Itrat Ali, C. 8,210
David Crowther, LD 7,082
Bob Brierley, Ind. 3,424
Ken Haslam, BNP 3,229
John Mather, Ind. 1,126
Lab. majority 12,490 (28.53%)
Notional 9.98% swing Lab. to C.
(2005: Lab. majority 17,903 (48.49%))

§MALDON
E. 68,861 T. 47,895 (69.55%) C. hold
John Whittingdale, C. 28,661
Elfreda Tealby-Watson, LD 9,254
Swatantra Nandanwar, Lab. 6,070
Jesse Pryke, UKIP 2,446
Len Blaine, BNP 1,464
C. majority 19,407 (40.52%)
Notional 0.40% swing C. to LD
(2005: C. majority 13,641 (32.13%))

§MANCHESTER CENTRAL
E. 90,110 T. 39,927 (44.31%) Lab. hold
Tony Lloyd, Lab. 21,059
Marc Ramsbottom, LD 10,620
Suhail Rahuja, C. 4,704
Tony Trebilcock, BNP 1,636
Gayle O'Donovan, Green 915
Nicola Weatherill, UKIP 607
Ron Sinclair, Soc. Lab. 153
John Cartwright, Ind. 120
Jonty Leff, WRP 59
Robert Skelton, SEP 54
Lab. majority 10,439 (26.15%)
Notional 6.11% swing Lab. to LD
(2005: Lab. majority 11,636 (38.36%))

§MANCHESTER GORTON
E. 75,933 T. 38,235 (50.47%) Lab. hold
Gerald Kaufman, Lab. 19,211
Qassim Afzal, LD 12,508
Caroline Healy, C. 4,224
Justine Hall, Green 1,048
Karen Reissman, TUSC 507
Mohammed Zulfikar, Respect 337
Peter Harrison, Ch. P. 254
Tim Dobson, Pirate 236
Lab. majority 6,703 (17.49%)
Notional 1.06% swing Lab. to LD
(2005: Lab. majority 6,355 (19.61%))

§MANCHESTER WITHINGTON
E. 74,371 T. 45,031 (60.55%) LD hold
John Leech, LD 20,110
Lucy Powell, Lab. 18,216
Christopher Green, C. 5,005
Brian Candeland, Green 798
Bob Gutfreund-Walmsley, UKIP 698
Yasmin Zalzala, Ind. 147
Marcus Farmer, Ind. 57
LD majority 1,894 (4.21%)
Notional 1.41% swing Lab. to LD
(2005: LD majority 531 (1.39%))

§MANSFIELD
E. 80,069 T. 48,395 (60.44%) Lab. hold
Joseph Meale, Lab. 18,753
Tracy Critchlow, C. 12,741
Michael Wyatt, LD 7,469
Andre Camilleri, Mansfield Ind. 4,339
David Hamilton, UKIP 2,985
Rachel Hill, BNP 2,108
Lab. majority 6,012 (12.42%)
Notional 9.49% swing Lab. to C.
(2005: Lab. majority 13,776 (31.39%))

§MEON VALLEY
E. 70,488 T. 51,238 (72.69%) C. hold
*George Hollingbery, C. 28,818
Liz Leffman, LD 16,693
Howard Linsley, Lab. 3,266
Steve Harris, UKIP 1,490
Pat Harris, Eng. Dem. 582
Sarah Coats, APP 255
Graeme Quar, Ind. 134
C. majority 12,125 (23.66%)
Notional 9.38% swing LD to C.
(2005: C. majority 2,378 (4.91%))

§MERIDEN
E. 83,826 T. 52,162 (62.23%) C. hold
Caroline Spelman, C. 26,956
Ed Williams, Lab. 10,703
Simon Slater, LD 9,278
Frank O'Brien, BNP 2,511
Barry Allcock, UKIP 1,378
Elly Stanton, Green 678
Nikki Sinclaire, RA 658
C. majority 16,253 (31.16%)
Notional 7.90% swing Lab. to C.
(2005: C. majority 7,412 (15.37%))

§MIDDLESBROUGH
E. 65,148 T. 33,455 (51.35%) Lab. hold
Sir Stuart Bell, Lab. 15,351
Chris Foote-Wood, LD 6,662
John Walsh, C. 6,283
Joan McTigue, Ind. 1,969
Michael Ferguson, BNP 1,954
Robert Parker, UKIP 1,236
Lab. majority 8,689 (25.97%)
Notional 6.45% swing Lab. to LD
(2005: Lab. majority 12,476 (38.87%))

§MIDDLESBROUGH SOUTH &
CLEVELAND EAST
E. 72,664 T. 46,214 (63.60%) Lab. hold
*Tom Blenkinsop, Lab. 18,138
Paul Bristow, C. 16,461
Nick Emmerson, LD 7,340
Stuart Lightwing, UKIP 1,881
Shaun Gatley, BNP 1,576
Mike Allen, Ind. 818
Lab. majority 1,677 (3.63%)
Notional 7.44% swing Lab. to C.
(2005: Lab. majority 8,096 (18.51%))

§MILTON KEYNES NORTH
E. 85,841 T. 53,888 (62.78%) C. gain
Mark Lancaster, C.   23,419
Andrew Pakes, Lab.   14,458
Jill Hope, LD   11,894
Michael Phillips, UKIP   1,772
Richard Hamilton, BNP   1,154
Alan Francis, Green   733
Revd John Lennon, CPA   206
Matt Bananamatt Fensome, Loony   157
Anant Vyas, Ind.   95
C. majority 8,961 (16.63%)
Notional 9.17% swing Lab. to C.
(2005: Lab. majority 848 (1.71%))

§MILTON KEYNES SOUTH
E. 90,487 T. 55,333 (61.15%) C. gain
*Iain Stewart, C.   23,034
Phyllis Starkey, Lab.   17,833
Peter Jones, LD   9,787
Philip Pinto, UKIP   2,074
Matthew Tait, BNP   1,502
Katrina Deacon, Green   774
Suzanne Nti, CPA   245
Jonathan Worth, NFP   84
C. majority 5,201 (9.40%)
Notional 6.22% swing Lab. to C.
(2005: Lab. majority 1,497 (3.04%))

§MITCHAM & MORDEN
E. 65,939 T. 43,797 (66.42%) Lab. hold
Siobhain McDonagh, Lab.   24,722
Melanie Hampton, C.   11,056
Diana Coman, LD   5,202
Tony Martin, BNP   1,386
Andrew Mills, UKIP   857
Smarajit Roy, Green   381
Rathy Alagaratnam, Ind.   155
Ernest Redgrave, Ind.   38
Lab. majority 13,666 (31.20%)
Notional 0.44% swing Lab. to C.
(2005: Lab. majority 12,739 (32.08%))

MOLE VALLEY
E. 72,612 T. 54,324 (74.81%) C. hold
Sir Paul Beresford, C.   31,263
Alice Humphreys, LD   15,610
James Dove, Lab.   3,804
Leigh Jones, UKIP   2,752
Rob Sedgwick, Green   895
C. majority 15,653 (28.81%)
2.27% swing LD to C.
(2005: C. majority 11,997 (24.28%))

§MORECAMBE & LUNESDALE
E. 69,965 T. 43,616 (62.34%) C. gain
*David Morris, C.   18,035
Geraldine Smith, Lab.   17,169
Leslie Jones, LD   5,971
Mark Knight, UKIP   1,843
Chris Coates, Green   598
C. majority 866 (1.99%)
Notional 6.86% swing Lab. to C.
(2005: Lab. majority 4,849 (11.74%))

§MORLEY & OUTWOOD
E. 74,200 T. 48,856 (65.84%)
                          Lab. (Co-op) hold
Ed Balls, Lab. (Co-op)   18,365
Antony Calvert, C.   17,264
James Monaghan, LD   8,186
Chris Beverley, BNP   3,535
David Daniel, UKIP   1,506
Lab. (Co-op) majority 1,101 (2.25%)
Notional 9.35% swing Lab. (Co-op) to C.
(2005: Lab. (Co-op) majority 8,669
(20.95%))

§NEW FOREST EAST
E. 72,858 T. 50,036 (68.68%) C. hold
Julian Lewis, C.   26,443
Terry Scriven, LD   15,136
Peter Sopowski, Lab.   4,915
Peter Day, UKIP   2,518
Beverley Golden, Green   1,024
C. majority 11,307 (22.60%)
Notional 3.20% swing LD to C.
(2005: C. majority 7,653 (16.21%))

§NEW FOREST WEST
E. 68,332 T. 47,572 (69.62%) C. hold
Desmond Swayne, C.   27,980
Mike Plummer, LD   11,084
Janice Hurne, Lab.   4,666
Martin Lyon, UKIP   2,783
Janet Richards, Green   1,059
C. majority 16,896 (35.52%)
Notional 0.60% swing C. to LD
(2005: C. majority 16,183 (36.71%))

§NEWARK
E. 71,785 T. 51,228 (71.36%) C. hold
Patrick Mercer, C.   27,590
Dr Ian Campbell, Lab.   11,438
Pauline Jenkins, LD   10,246
Tom Irvine, UKIP   1,954
C. majority 16,152 (31.53%)
Notional 4.68% swing Lab. to C.
(2005: C. majority 10,077 (22.17%))

§NEWBURY
E. 83,411 T. 58,589 (70.24%) C. hold
Richard Benyon, C.   33,057
David Rendel, LD   20,809
Hannah Cooper, Lab.   2,505
David Black, UKIP   1,475
Adrian Hollister, Green   490
Brian Burgess, Ind.   158
David Yates, AD   95
C. majority 12,248 (20.90%)
Notional 7.24% swing LD to C.
(2005: C. majority 3,452 (6.42%))

NEWCASTLE-UNDER-LYME
E. 69,433 T. 43,191 (62.21%) Lab. hold
Paul Farrelly, Lab.   16,393
Robert Jenrick, C.   14,841
Nigel Jones, LD   8,466
David Nixon, UKIP   3,491
Lab. majority 1,552 (3.59%)
8.39% swing Lab. to C.
(2005: Lab. majority 8,108 (20.38%))

§NEWCASTLE UPON TYNE CENTRAL
E. 60,507 T. 34,157 (56.45%) Lab. hold
*Chinyelu Onwurah, Lab.   15,694
Gareth Kane, LD   8,228
Nick Holder, C.   6,611
Ken Booth, BNP   2,302
Martin Davies, UKIP   754
John Pearson, Green   568
Lab. majority 7,466 (21.86%)
Notional 0.60% swing Lab. to LD
(2005: Lab. majority 7,509 (23.07%))

§NEWCASTLE UPON TYNE EAST
E. 64,487 T. 37,840 (58.68%) Lab. hold
Nicholas Brown, Lab.   17,043
Wendy Taylor, LD   12,590
Dominic Llewellyn, C.   6,068
Alan Spence, BNP   1,342
Andrew Gray, Green   620
Martin Levy, Comm.   177
Lab. majority 4,453 (11.77%)
Notional 4.60% swing Lab. to LD
(2005: Lab. majority 6,987 (20.97%))

§NEWCASTLE UPON TYNE NORTH
E. 67,110 T. 43,946 (65.48%) Lab. hold
*Catherine McKinnell, Lab.   17,950
Ronald Beadle, LD   14,536
Stephen Parkinson, C.   7,966
Terry Gibson, BNP   1,890
Ian Proud, UKIP   1,285
Anna Heyman, Green   319
Lab. majority 3,414 (7.77%)
Notional 4.54% swing Lab. to LD
(2005: Lab. majority 6,878 (16.84%))

§NEWTON ABBOT
E. 69,343 T. 48,283 (69.63%) C. gain
*Anne-Marie Morris, C.   20,774
Richard Younger-Ross, LD   20,251
Patrick Canavan, Lab.   3,387
Jackie Hooper, UKIP   3,088
Corinne Lindsey, Green   701
Keith Sharp, Ind.   82
C. majority 523 (1.08%)
Notional 5.79% swing LD to C.
(2005: LD majority 4,830 (10.50%))

§NORFOLK MID
E. 74,260 T. 50,765 (68.36%) C. hold
*George Freeman, C.   25,123
David Newman, LD   11,267
Elizabeth Hughes, Lab.   8,857
Toby Coke, UKIP   2,800
Tim Birt, Green   1,457
Christine Kelly, BNP   1,261
C. majority 13,856 (27.29%)
Notional 0.02% swing C. to LD
(2005: C. majority 7,793 (16.29%))

§NORFOLK NORTH
E. 67,841 T. 49,661 (73.20%) LD hold
Norman Lamb, LD   27,554
Trevor Ivory, C.   15,928
Phil Harris, Lab.   2,896
Michael Baker, UKIP   2,680
Andrew Boswell, Green   508
Simon Mann, Ind.   95
LD majority 11,626 (23.41%)
Notional 3.06% swing C. to LD
(2005: LD majority 8,575 (17.28%))

§NORFOLK NORTH WEST
E. 73,207 T. 47,800 (65.29%) C. hold
Henry Bellingham, C.   25,916
William Summers, LD   11,106
Manish Sood, Lab.   6,353
John Gray, UKIP   1,841
David Fleming, BNP   1,839
Michael de Whalley, Green   745
C. majority 14,810 (30.98%)
Notional 2.09% swing C. to LD
(2005: C. majority 8,417 (18.34%))

§NORFOLK SOUTH
E. 76,165 T. 54,993 (72.20%) C. hold
Richard Bacon, C.   27,133
Jacky Howe, LD   16,193
Mick Castle, Lab.   7,252
Evan Heasley, UKIP   2,329
Helen Mitchell, BNP   1,086
Jo Willcott, Green   1,000
C. majority 10,940 (19.89%)
Notional 3.25% swing LD to C.
(2005: C. majority 6,719 (13.39%))

§NORFOLK SOUTH WEST
E. 74,298 T. 49,150 (66.15%) C. hold
*Elizabeth Truss, C.   23,753
Stephen Gordon, LD   10,613
Peter Smith, Lab.   9,119
Kay Hipsey, UKIP   3,061
Dennis Pearce, BNP   1,774
Lori Allen, Green   830
C. majority 13,140 (26.73%)
Notional 0.48% swing LD to C.
(2005: C. majority 6,817 (15.00%))

§NORMANTON, PONTEFRACT &
CASTLEFORD
E. 82,239 T. 46,239 (56.23%) Lab. hold
Yvette Cooper, Lab.   22,293
Nick Pickles, C.   11,314
Chris Rush, LD   7,585
Graham Thewlis-Hardy, BNP   3,864
Gareth Allen, Ind.   1,183
Lab. majority 10,979 (23.74%)
Notional 12.49% swing Lab. to C.
(2005: Lab. majority 20,608 (48.73%))

§NORTHAMPTON NORTH
E. 64,230 T. 40,271 (62.70%) C. gain
*Michael Ellis, C.   13,735
Sally Keeble, Lab.   11,799
Andrew Simpson, LD   11,250
Ray Beasley, BNP   1,316
Jim Macarthur, UKIP   1,238
Tony Lochmuller, Green   443
Eamonn Fitzpatrick, Ind.   334
Timothy Webb, Ch. P.   98
Malcolm Mildren, Ind.   58
C. majority 1,936 (4.81%)
Notional 6.90% swing Lab. to C.
(2005: Lab. majority 3,340 (9.00%))

§NORTHAMPTON SOUTH
E. 66,923 T. 38,978 (58.24%) C. gain
*Brian Binley, C.   15,917
Clyde Loakes, Lab.   9,913
Paul Varnsverry, LD   7,579
Tony Clarke, Ind.   2,242
Derek Clark, UKIP   1,897
Kevin Sills, Eng. Dem.   618
Julie Hawkins, Green   363
Dave Green, NSPS   325
Kevin Willsher, Ind.   65
Liam Costello, SMA   59
C. majority 6,004 (15.40%)
Notional 9.59% swing Lab. to C.
(2005: Lab. majority 1,445 (3.78%))

§NORTHAMPTONSHIRE SOUTH
E. 82,032 T. 59,890 (73.01%) C. hold
*Andrea Leadsom, C.   33,081
Scott Collins, LD   12,603
Matthew May, Lab.   10,380
Barry Mahoney, UKIP   2,406
Tony Tappy, Eng. Dem.   735
Marcus Rock, Green   685
C. majority 20,478 (34.19%)
Notional 0.12% swing C. to LD
(2005: C. majority 11,356 (22.85%))

§NORWICH NORTH
E. 65,258 T. 42,573 (65.24%) C. gain
Chloe Smith, C.   17,280
John Cook, Lab.   13,379
John Stephen, LD   7,783
Glenn Tingle, UKIP   1,878
Jessica Goldfinch, Green   1,245
Thomas Richardson, BNP   747
Bill Holden, Ind.   143
Andrew Holland, Ch. P.   118
C. majority 3,901 (9.16%)
Notional 12.88% swing Lab. to C.
(2005: Lab. majority 6,769 (16.60%))

§NORWICH SOUTH
E. 73,649 T. 47,551 (64.56%) LD gain
*Simon Wright, LD   13,960
Charles Clarke, Lab.   13,650
Antony Little, C.   10,902
Adrian Ramsay, Green   7,095
Steve Emmens, UKIP   1,145
Leonard Heather, BNP   697
Gabriel Polley, WRP   102
LD majority 310 (0.65%)
Notional 4.03% swing Lab. to LD
(2005: Lab. majority 3,023 (7.40%))

§NOTTINGHAM EAST
E. 58,707 T. 33,112 (56.40%)
                          Lab. (Co-op) hold
*Christopher Leslie, Lab. (Co-op) 15,022
Sam Boote, LD   8,053
Ewan Lamont, C.   7,846
Pat Wolfe, UKIP   1,138
Benjamin Hoare, Green   928
Parvaiz Sardar, Ch. P.   125
Lab. (Co-op) majority 6,969 (21.05%)
Notional 1.89% swing Lab. (Co-op) to LD
(2005: Lab. (Co-op) majority 7,083
(24.22%))

§NOTTINGHAM NORTH
E. 63,240 T. 34,285 (54.21%) Lab. hold
Graham Allen, Lab.   16,646
Martin Curtis, C.   8,508
Tim Ball, LD   5,849
Bob Brindley, BNP   1,944
Irenea Marriott, UKIP   1,338
Lab. majority 8,138 (23.74%)
Notional 8.65% swing Lab. to C.
(2005: Lab. majority 12,870 (41.04%))

§NOTTINGHAM SOUTH
E. 67,441 T. 40,789 (60.48%) Lab. hold
*Lilian Greenwood, Lab.   15,209
Rowena Holland, C.   13,437
Tony Sutton, LD   9,406
Tony Woodward, BNP   1,140
Ken Browne, UKIP   967
Matthew Butcher, Green   630
Lab. majority 1,772 (4.34%)
Notional 7.43% swing Lab. to C.
(2005: Lab. majority 6,665 (19.20%))

§NUNEATON
E. 67,837 T. 44,646 (65.81%) C. gain
*Marcus Jones, C.   18,536
Jayne Innes, Lab.   16,467
Christina Jebb, LD   6,846
Martyn Findley, BNP   2,797
C. majority 2,069 (4.63%)
Notional 7.19% swing Lab. to C.
(2005: Lab. majority 3,894 (9.74%))

§OLD BEXLEY & SIDCUP
E. 65,665 T. 45,492 (69.28%) C. hold
James Brokenshire, C.   24,625
Rick Everitt, Lab.   8,768
Duncan Borrowman, LD   6,996
John Brooks, BNP   2,132
David Coburn, UKIP   1,532
Elaine Cheeseman, Eng. Dem.   520
John Hemming-Clark, Save QM   393
Jonathan Rooks, Green   371
Napoleon Dynamite, Loony   155
C. majority 15,857 (34.86%)
Notional 6.43% swing Lab. to C.
(2005: C. majority 9,309 (22.00%))

§OLDHAM EAST & SADDLEWORTH
E. 72,765 T. 44,520 (61.18%) Lab. hold
Phil Woolas, Lab.   14,186
Elwyn Watkins, LD   14,083
Kashif Ali, C.   11,773
Alwyn Stott, BNP   2,546
David Bentley, UKIP   1,720
Gulzar Nazir, Ch. P.   212
Lab. majority 103 (0.23%)
Notional 5.08% swing Lab. to LD
(2005: Lab. majority 4,245 (10.39%))

§OLDHAM WEST & ROYTON
E. 72,651 T. 42,910 (59.06%) Lab. hold
Michael Meacher, Lab.   19,503
Kamran Ghafoor, C.   10,151
Mark Alcock, LD   8,193
David Joines, BNP   3,049
Helen Roberts, UKIP   1,387
Shahid Miah, Respect   627
Lab. majority 9,352 (21.79%)
Notional 2.74% swing Lab. to C.
(2005: Lab. majority 10,454 (27.13%))

§ORPINGTON
E. 67,732 T. 48,911 (72.21%) C. hold
*Joseph Johnson, C.   29,200
David McBride, LD   12,000
Stephen Morgan, Lab.   4,400
Mick Greenhough, UKIP   1,360
Tess Culnane, BNP   1,241
Tamara Galloway, Green   511
Chriss Snape, Eng. Dem.   199
C. majority 17,200 (35.17%)
Notional 12.19% swing LD to C.
(2005: C. majority 5,221 (10.79%))

§OXFORD EAST
E. 81,886 T. 51,651 (63.08%) Lab. hold
Andrew Smith, Lab.   21,938
Steve Goddard, LD   17,357
Edward Argar, C.   9,727
Sushila Dhall, Green   1,238
Julia Gasper, UKIP   1,202
David O'Sullivan, SEP   116
Roger Crawford, Parenting   73
Lab. majority 4,581 (8.87%)
Notional 4.07% swing LD to Lab.
(2005: Lab. majority 332 (0.73%))

§OXFORD WEST & ABINGDON
E. 86,458 T. 56,480 (65.33%) C. gain
*Nicola Blackwood, C.   23,906
Evan Harris, LD   23,730
Richard Stevens, Lab.   5,999
Paul Williams, UKIP   1,518
Chris Goodall, Green   1,184
Keith Mann, APP   143
C. majority 176 (0.31%)
Notional 6.87% swing LD to C.
(2005: LD majority 6,816 (13.43%))

PENDLE
E. 66,417   T. 45,045 (67.82%)   C. gain
*Andrew Stephenson, C.   17,512
Gordon Prentice, Lab.   13,927
Afzal Anwar, LD   9,095
James Jackman, BNP   2,894
Graham Cannon, UKIP   1,476
Richard Masih, Ch. P.   141
C. majority 3,585 (7.96%)
6.63% swing Lab. to C.
(2005: Lab. majority 2,180 (5.30%))

§PENISTONE & STOCKSBRIDGE
E. 68,501   T. 46,516 (67.91%) Lab. hold
Angela Smith, Lab.   17,565
Spencer Pitfield, C.   14,516
Ian Cuthbertson, LD   9,800
Paul James, BNP   2,207
Grant French, UKIP   1,936
Paul McEnhill, Eng. Dem.   492
Lab. majority 3,049 (6.55%)
Notional 7.45% swing Lab. to C.
(2005: Lab. majority 8,617 (20.43%))

§PENRITH & THE BORDER
E. 64,548   T. 45,087 (69.85%)   C. hold
*Rory Stewart, C.   24,071
Peter Thornton, LD   12,830
Barbara Cannon, Lab.   5,834
John Stanyer, UKIP   1,259
Chris Davidson, BNP   1,093
C. majority 11,241 (24.93%)
Notional 0.32% swing C. to LD
(2005: C. majority 10,795 (25.58%))

§PETERBOROUGH
E. 70,316   T. 44,927 (63.89%)   C. hold
Stewart Jackson, C.   18,133
Ed Murphy, Lab.   13,272
Nick Sandford, LD   8,816
Frances Fox, UKIP   3,007
Rob King, Eng. Dem.   770
Fiona Radic, Green   523
John Swallow, Ind.   406
C. majority 4,861 (10.82%)
Notional 0.94% swing Lab. to C.
(2005: C. majority 4,005 (8.93%))

§PLYMOUTH MOOR VIEW
E. 67,261   T. 41,526 (61.74%) Lab. hold
Alison Seabeck, Lab.   15,433
Matthew Groves, C.   13,845
Stuart Bonar, LD   7,016
Bill Wakeham, UKIP   3,188
Roy Cook, BNP   1,438
Wendy Miller, Green   398
David Marchesi, Soc. Lab.   208
Lab. majority 1,588 (3.82%)
Notional 7.77% swing Lab. to C.
(2005: Lab. majority 7,740 (19.37%))

§PLYMOUTH SUTTON &
DEVONPORT
E. 71,035   T. 43,894 (61.79%)   C. gain
*Oliver Colville, C.   15,050
Linda Gilroy, Lab. (Co-op)   13,901
Judy Evans, LD   10,829
Andrew Leigh, UKIP   2,854
Tony Brown, Green   904
Brian Gerrish, Ind.   233
Robert Hawkins, Soc. Lab.   123
C. majority 1,149 (2.62%)
Notional 6.86% swing Lab. (Co-op) to C.
(2005: Lab. (Co-op) majority 4,472
(11.11%))

§POOLE
E. 64,661   T. 47,436 (73.36%)   C. hold
Robert Syms, C.   22,532
Philip Eades, LD   14,991
Jason Sanderson, Lab.   6,041
Nick Wellstead, UKIP   2,507
David Holmes, BNP   1,188
Ian Northover, Ind.   177
C. majority 7,541 (15.90%)
Notional 0.79% swing LD to C.
(2005: C. majority 6,035 (14.32%))

§POPLAR & LIMEHOUSE
E. 74,956   T. 46,700 (62.30%) Lab. hold
Jim Fitzpatrick, Lab.   18,679
Tim Archer, C.   12,649
George Galloway, Respect   8,160
Jonathan Fryer, LD   5,209
Wayne Lochner, UKIP   565
Andrew Osborne, Eng. Dem.   470
Chris Smith, Green   449
Kabir Mahmud, Ind.   293
Mohammed Hoque, Ind.   167
Jim Thornton, Ind.   59
Lab. majority 6,030 (12.91%)
Notional 1.04% swing C. to Lab.
(2005: Lab. majority 3,823 (10.84%))

§PORTSMOUTH NORTH
E. 70,329   T. 44,118 (62.73%)   C. gain
*Penny Mordaunt, C.   19,533
Sarah McCarthy-Fry, Lab.
  (Co-op)   12,244
Darren Sanders, LD   8,874
Mike Fitzgerald, UKIP   1,812
David Knight, Eng. Dem.   1,040
Iain Maclennan, Green   461
Mick Tosh, TUSC   154
C. majority 7,289 (16.52%)
Notional 8.64% swing Lab. (Co-op) to C.
(2005: Lab. (Co-op) majority 315 (0.77%))

§PORTSMOUTH SOUTH
E. 70,242   T. 41,264 (58.75%)   LD hold
Mike Hancock, LD   18,921
Flick Drummond, C.   13,721
John Ferrett, Lab.   5,640
Christopher Martin, UKIP   876
Geoff Crompton, BNP   873
Tim Dawes, Green   716
Ian DuCane, Eng. Dem.   400
Les Cummings, J & AC   117
LD majority 5,200 (12.60%)
Notional 2.30% swing C. to LD
(2005: LD majority 2,955 (8.00%))

§PRESTON
E. 62,460   T. 32,505 (52.04%)
                        Lab. (Co-op) hold
Mark Hendrick, Lab. (Co-op)   15,668
Mark Jewell, LD   7,935
Nerissa Warner-O'Neill, C.   7,060
Richard Muirhead, UKIP   1,462
George Ambroze, Ch. P.   272
Krishna Tayya, Ind.   108
Lab. (Co-op) majority 7,733 (23.79%)
Notional 2.50% swing Lab. (Co-op) to LD
(2005: Lab. (Co-op) majority 8,338
(27.67%))

§PUDSEY
E. 69,257   T. 49,083 (70.87%)   C. gain
*Stuart Andrew, C.   18,874
Jamie Hanley, Lab.   17,215
Jamie Matthews, LD   10,224
Ian Gibson, BNP   1,549
David Dews, UKIP   1,221
C. majority 1,659 (3.38%)
Notional 7.56% swing Lab. to C.
(2005: Lab. majority 5,204 (11.74%))

§PUTNEY
E. 63,370   T. 40,785 (64.36%)   C. hold
Justine Greening, C.   21,223
Stuart King, Lab.   11,170
James Sandbach, LD   6,907
Bruce Mackenzie, Green   591
Peter Darby, BNP   459
Hugo Wareham, UKIP   435
C. majority 10,053 (24.65%)
Notional 9.92% swing Lab. to C.
(2005: C. majority 1,723 (4.80%))

§RAYLEIGH & WICKFORD
E. 75,905   T. 52,343 (68.96%)   C. hold
Mark Francois, C.   30,257
Susan Gaszczak, LD   7,919
Michael Le-Surf, Lab.   7,577
John Hayter, Eng. Dem.   2,219
Tino Callaghan, UKIP   2,211
Anthony Evennett, BNP   2,160
C. majority 22,338 (42.68%)
Notional 2.13% swing LD to C.
(2005: C. majority 12,983 (27.37%))

§READING EAST
E. 74,922   T. 49,985 (66.72%)   C. hold
Rob Wilson, C.   21,269
Gareth Epps, LD   13,664
Anneliese Dodds, Lab.   12,729
Adrian Pitfield, UKIP   1,086
Rob White, Green   1,069
Joan Lloyd, Ind.   111
Michael Turberville, Ind.   57
C. majority 7,605 (15.21%)
Notional 1.97% swing LD to C.
(2005: C. majority 739 (1.71%))

§READING WEST
E. 72,118   T. 47,530 (65.91%)   C. gain
*Alok Sharma, C.   20,523
Naz Sarkar, Lab.   14,519
Daisy Benson, LD   9,546
Bruce Hay, UKIP   1,508
Howard Thomas, CSP   852
Adrian Windisch, Green   582
C. majority 6,004 (12.63%)
Notional 12.05% swing Lab. to C.
(2005: Lab. majority 4,931 (11.47%))

REDCAR
E. 67,125   T. 41,963 (62.51%)   LD gain
*Ian Swales, LD   18,955
Vera Baird, Lab.   13,741
Steve Mastin, C.   5,790
Martin Bulmer, UKIP   1,875
Kevin Broughton, BNP   1,475
Hannah Walter, TUSC   127
LD majority 5,214 (12.43%)
21.80% swing Lab. to LD
(2005: Lab. majority 12,116 (31.18%))

§REDDITCH
E. 68,550   T. 44,018 (64.21%)   C. gain
*Karen Lumley, C.   19,138
Jacqui Smith, Lab.   13,317
Nicholas Lane, LD   7,750
Anne Davis, UKIP   1,497
Andy Ingram, BNP   1,394
Kevin White, Green   393
Vincent Schittone, Eng. Dem.   255
Scott Beverley, Ch. P.   101
Paul Swansborough, Ind.   100
Derek Fletcher, Nobody   73
C. majority 5,821 (13.22%)
Notional 9.21% swing Lab. to C.
(2005: Lab. majority 2,163 (5.20%))

§REIGATE
E. 71,604   T. 49,978 (69.80%)   C. hold
Crispin Blunt, C.   26,688
Jane Kulka, LD   13,097
Robert Hull, Lab.   5,672
Joe Fox, UKIP   2,089
Keith Brown, BNP   1,345
Jonathan Essex, Green   1,087
C. majority 13,591 (27.19%)
Notional 0.89% swing LD to C.
(2005: C. majority 11,093 (25.41%))

§RIBBLE VALLEY
E. 78,068   T. 52,287 (66.98%)   C. hold
Nigel Evans, C.   26,298
Paul Foster, Lab.   11,529
Allan Knox, LD   10,732
Stephen Rush, UKIP   3,496
Tony Johnson, ND   232
C. majority 14,769 (28.25%)
Notional 6.58% swing Lab. to C.
(2005: C. majority 6,953 (15.09%))

§RICHMOND (YORKS)
E. 79,478   T. 53,412 (67.20%)   C. hold
William Hague, C.   33,541
Lawrence Meredith, LD   10,205
Eileen Driver, Lab.   8,150
Leslie Rowe, Green   1,516
C. majority 23,336 (43.69%)
Notional 0.64% swing LD to C.
(2005: C. majority 19,450 (38.73%))

§RICHMOND PARK
E. 77,060   T. 59,268 (76.91%)   C. gain
*Zac Goldsmith, C.   29,461
Susan Kramer, LD   25,370
Eleanor Tunnicliffe, Lab.   2,979
Peter Dul, UKIP   669
James Page, Green   572
Susan May, CPA   133
Charles Hill, Ind.   84
C. majority 4,091 (6.90%)
Notional 7.00% swing LD to C.
(2005: LD majority 3,613 (7.09%))

§ROCHDALE
E. 78,952   T. 45,907 (58.15%) Lab. hold
*Simon Danczuk, Lab.   16,699
Paul Rowen, LD   15,810
Mudasir Dean, C.   8,305
Chris Jackson, NF   2,236
Colin Denby, UKIP   1,999
Mohammed Salim, IZB   545
John Whitehead, Ind.   313
Lab. majority 889 (1.94%)
Notional 0.79% swing LD to Lab.
(2005: Lab. majority 149 (0.35%))

§ROCHESTER & STROOD
E. 73,882   T. 47,971 (64.93%)   C. hold
*Mark Reckless, C.   23,604
Teresa Murray, Lab.   13,651
Geoffrey Juby, LD   7,800
Ron Sands, Eng. Dem.   2,182
Simon Marchant, Green   734
C. majority 9,953 (20.75%)
Notional 9.81% swing Lab. to C.
(2005: C. majority 503 (1.14%))

§ROCHFORD & SOUTHEND EAST
E. 71,080   T. 41,631 (58.57%)   C. hold
James Duddridge, C.   19,509
Kevin Bonavia, Lab.   8,459
Graham Longley, LD   8,084
James Moyies, UKIP   2,405
Geoff Strobridge, BNP   1,856
Andrew Vaughan, Green   707
Anthony Chytry, Ind.   611
C. majority 11,050 (26.54%)
Notional 6.37% swing Lab. to C.
(2005: C. majority 5,307 (13.80%))

§ROMFORD
E. 71,193   T. 46,481 (65.29%)   C. hold
Andrew Rosindell, C.   26,031
Rachel Voller, Lab.   9,077
Helen Duffett, LD   5,572
Robert Bailey, BNP   2,438
Gerard Batten, UKIP   2,050
Dr Peter Thorogood, Eng. Dem.   603
Gary Haines, Green   447
Philip Hyde, Ind.   151
David Sturman, Ind.   112
C. majority 16,954 (36.48%)
Notional 3.94% swing Lab. to C.
(2005: C. majority 12,120 (28.59%))

§ROMSEY & SOUTHAMPTON NORTH
E. 66,901   T. 48,939 (73.15%)   C. gain
*Caroline Nokes, C.   24,345
Sandra Gidley, LD   20,189
Aktar Beg, Lab.   3,116
John Meropoulos, UKIP   1,289
C. majority 4,156 (8.49%)
Notional 4.48% swing LD to C.
(2005: LD majority 204 (0.46%))

§ROSSENDALE & DARWEN
E. 73,003   T. 47,128 (64.56%)   C. gain
*Jake Berry, C.   19,691
Janet Anderson, Lab.   15,198
Robert Sheffield, LD   8,541
David Duthie, UKIP   1,617
Kevin Bryan, NF   1,062
Michael Johnson, Eng. Dem.   663
Tony Melia, Impact   243
Mike Sivieri, Ind.   113
C. majority 4,493 (9.53%)
Notional 8.94% swing Lab. to C.
(2005: Lab. majority 3,696 (8.35%))

§ROTHER VALLEY
E. 72,841   T. 46,758 (64.19%) Lab. hold
Kevin Barron, Lab.   19,147
Lynda Donaldson, C.   13,281
Wesley Paxton, LD   8,111
Will Blair, BNP   3,606
Tina Dowdall, UKIP   2,613
Lab. majority 5,866 (12.55%)
Notional 7.96% swing Lab. to C.
(2005: Lab. majority 11,558 (28.47%))

§ROTHERHAM
E. 63,565   T. 37,506 (59.00%) Lab. hold
Denis MacShane, Lab.   16,741
Jackie Whiteley, C.   6,279
Rebecca Taylor, LD   5,994
Marlene Guest, BNP   3,906
Peter Thirlwall, Ind.   2,366
Caven Vines, UKIP   2,220
Lab. majority 10,462 (27.89%)
Notional 8.27% swing Lab. to C.
(2005: Lab. majority 13,865 (41.33%))

§RUGBY
E. 68,914   T. 47,468 (68.88%)   C. gain
*Mark Pawsey, C.   20,901
Andy King, Lab.   14,901
Jerry Roodhouse, LD   9,434
Mark Badrick, BNP   1,375
Roy Sandison, Green   451
Barry Milford, UKIP   406
C. majority 6,000 (12.64%)
Notional 8.92% swing Lab. to C.
(2005: Lab. majority 2,397 (5.20%))

§RUISLIP, NORTHWOOD & PINNER
E. 70,873   T. 50,205 (70.84%)   C. hold
Nick Hurd, C.   28,866
Anita McDonald, Lab.   9,806
Thomas Papworth, LD   8,345
Jason Pontey, UKIP   1,351
Ian Edward, NF   899
Graham Lee, Green   740
Ruby Akhtar, Ch. P.   198
C. majority 19,060 (37.96%)
Notional 3.63% swing Lab. to C.
(2005: C. majority 13,274 (30.71%))

RUNNYMEDE & WEYBRIDGE
E. 72,566   T. 48,150 (66.35%)   C. hold
Philip Hammond, C.   26,915
Andrew Falconer, LD   10,406
Paul Greenwood, Lab.   6,446
Toby Micklethwait, UKIP   3,146
Jenny Gould, Green   696
David Sammons, Ind.   541
C. majority 16,509 (34.29%)
0.38% swing LD to C.
(2005: C. majority 12,349 (28.37%))

§RUSHCLIFFE
E. 72,955   T. 53,687 (73.59%)   C. hold
Kenneth Clarke, C.   27,470
Karrar Khan, LD   11,659
Andrew Clayworth, Lab.   11,128
Matthew Faithfull, UKIP   2,179
Richard Mallender, Green   1,251
C. majority 15,811 (29.45%)
Notional 0.63% swing C. to LD
(2005: C. majority 9,932 (20.60%))

§RUTLAND & MELTON
E. 77,185   T. 55,220 (71.54%)   C. hold
Alan Duncan, C.   28,228
Grahame Hudson, LD   14,228
John Morgan, Lab.   7,893
Peter Baker, UKIP   2,526
Keith Addison, BNP   1,757
Leigh Higgins, Ind.   588
C. majority 14,000 (25.35%)
Notional 3.65% swing C. to LD
(2005: C. majority 12,998 (26.29%))

§SAFFRON WALDEN
E. 76,035   T. 54,369 (71.51%)   C. hold
Sir Alan Haselhurst, C.   30,155
Peter Wilcock, LD   14,913
Barbara Light, Lab.   5,288
Roger Lord, UKIP   2,228
Christine Mitchell, BNP   1,050
Reza Hossain, Green   735
C. majority 15,242 (28.03%)
Notional 3.39% swing LD to C.
(2005: C. majority 10,483 (21.25%))

§ST ALBANS
E. 70,058 T. 52,835 (75.42%) C. hold
Anne Main, C.   21,533
Sandy Walkington, LD   19,228
Roma Mills, Lab.   9,288
John Stocker, UKIP   2,028
Jack Easton, Green   758
C. majority 2,305 (4.36%)
Notional 3.74% swing C. to LD
(2005: C. majority 1,334 (2.94%))

§ST AUSTELL & NEWQUAY
E. 76,346 T. 47,238 (61.87%) LD hold
*Stephen Gilbert, LD   20,189
Caroline Righton, C.   18,877
Lee Jameson, Lab.   3,386
Dick Cole, Meb. Ker.   2,007
Clive Medway, UKIP   1,757
James Fitton, BNP   1,022
LD majority 1,312 (2.78%)
Notional 4.83% swing LD to C.
(2005: LD majority 5,723 (12.44%))

§ST HELENS NORTH
E. 74,985 T. 44,556 (59.42%) Lab. hold
Dave Watts, Lab.   23,041
Paul Greenall, C.   9,940
John Beirne, LD   8,992
Gary Robinson, UKIP   2,100
Stephen Whatham, Soc. Lab.   483
Lab. majority 13,101 (29.40%)
Notional 4.55% swing Lab. to C.
(2005: Lab. majority 15,265 (36.49%))

§ST HELENS SOUTH & WHISTON
E. 77,975 T. 46,081 (59.10%) Lab. hold
Shaun Woodward, Lab.   24,364
Brian Spencer, LD   10,242
Val Allen, C.   8,209
James Winstanley, BNP   2,040
John Sumner, UKIP   1,226
Lab. majority 14,122 (30.65%)
Notional 1.94% swing LD to Lab.
(2005: Lab. majority 10,987 (26.76%))

§ST IVES
E. 66,930 T. 45,921 (68.61%) LD hold
Andrew George, LD   19,619
Derek Thomas, C.   17,900
Philippa Latimer, Lab.   3,751
Mick Faulkner, UKIP   2,560
Tim Andrewes, Green   1,308
Jonathan Rogers, Cornish D.   396
Simon Reed, Meb. Ker.   387
LD majority 1,719 (3.74%)
Notional 10.39% swing LD to C.
(2005: LD majority 10,711 (24.52%))

§SALFORD & ECCLES
E. 75,482 T. 41,533 (55.02%) Lab. hold
Hazel Blears, Lab.   16,655
Norman Owen, LD   10,930
Matthew Sephton, C.   8,497
Tina Wingfield, BNP   2,632
Duran O'Dwyer, UKIP   1,084
David Henry, TUSC   730
Stephen Morris, Eng. Dem.   621
Richard Carvath, Ind.   384
Lab. majority 5,725 (13.78%)
Notional 9.43% swing Lab. to LD
(2005: Lab. majority 10,707 (32.64%))

§SALISBURY
E. 67,429 T. 48,481 (71.90%) C. hold
*John Glen, C.   23,859
Nick Radford, LD   17,893
Tom Gann, Lab.   3,690
Frances Howard, UKIP   1,392
Sean Witheridge, BNP   765
Nick Startin, Green   506
King Arthur, Ind.   257
John Holme, Ind.   119
C. majority 5,966 (12.31%)
Notional 3.60% swing C. to LD
(2005: C. majority 8,860 (19.50%))

SCARBOROUGH & WHITBY
E. 75,443 T. 49,282 (65.32%) C. hold
Robert Goodwill, C.   21,108
Annajoy David, Lab.   12,978
Tania Exley-Moore, LD   11,093
Michael James, UKIP   1,484
Trisha Scott, BNP   1,445
Dilys Cluer, Green   734
Peter Popple, Ind.   329
Juliet Boddington, Green Soc.   111
C. majority 8,130 (16.50%)
6.92% swing Lab. to C.
(2005: C. majority 1,245 (2.65%))

§SCUNTHORPE
E. 63,089 T. 37,034 (58.70%) Lab. hold
*Nic Dakin, Lab.   14,640
Caroline Johnson, C.   12,091
Neil Poole, LD   6,774
Jane Collins, UKIP   1,686
Douglas Ward, BNP   1,447
Natalie Hurst, Green   396
Lab. majority 2,549 (6.88%)
Notional 9.18% swing Lab. to C.
(2005: Lab. majority 8,638 (25.24%))

§SEDGEFIELD
E. 64,727 T. 40,222 (62.14%) Lab. hold
Phil Wilson, Lab.   18,141
Neil Mahapatra, C.   9,445
Alan Thompson, LD   8,033
Mark Walker, BNP   2,075
Brian Gregory, UKIP   1,479
Paul Gittins, Ind.   1,049
Lab. majority 8,696 (21.62%)
Notional 11.60% swing Lab. to C.
(2005: Lab. majority 18,198 (44.82%))

§SEFTON CENTRAL
E. 67,512 T. 48,463 (71.78%) Lab. hold
*Bill Esterson, Lab.   20,307
Debi Jones, C.   16,445
Richard Clein, LD   9,656
Peter Harper, UKIP   2,055
Lab. majority 3,862 (7.97%)
Notional 2.03% swing Lab. to C.
(2005: Lab. majority 4,950 (12.02%))

§SELBY & AINSTY
E. 72,789 T. 51,728 (71.07%) C. hold
*Nigel Adams, C.   25,562
Jan Marshall, Lab.   13,297
Tom Holvey, LD   9,180
Darren Haley, UKIP   1,635
Duncan Lorriman, BNP   1,377
Graham Michael, Eng. Dem.   677
C. majority 12,265 (23.71%)
Notional 9.70% swing Lab. to C.
(2005: C. majority 2,060 (4.31%))

§SEVENOAKS
E. 69,591 T. 49,408 (71.00%) C. hold
Michael Fallon, C.   28,076
Alan Bullion, LD   10,561
Gareth Siddorn, Lab.   6,541
Chris Heath, UKIP   1,782
Paul Golding, BNP   1,384
Louise Uncles, Eng. Dem.   806
Mark Ellis, Ind.   258
C. majority 17,515 (35.45%)
Notional 3.13% swing LD to C.
(2005: C. majority 13,060 (29.19%))

§SHEFFIELD BRIGHTSIDE &
HILLSBOROUGH
E. 68,186 T. 38,914 (57.07%) Lab. hold
David Blunkett, Lab.   21,400
Jonathan Harston, LD   7,768
John Sharp, C.   4,468
John Sheldon, BNP   3,026
Pat Sullivan, UKIP   1,596
Maxine Bowler, TUSC   656
Lab. majority 13,632 (35.03%)
Notional 10.77% swing Lab. to LD
(2005: Lab. majority 18,801 (56.58%))

§SHEFFIELD CENTRAL
E. 69,519 T. 41,468 (59.65%) Lab. hold
*Paul Blomfield, Lab.   17,138
Paul Scriven, LD   16,973
Andrew Lee, C.   4,206
Jillian Creasy, Green   1,556
Tracey Smith, BNP   903
Jeffrey Shaw, UKIP   652
Rod Rodgers, Ind.   40
Lab. majority 165 (0.40%)
Notional 7.36% swing Lab. to LD
(2005: Lab. majority 5,025 (15.12%))

§SHEFFIELD HALLAM
E. 69,378 T. 51,135 (73.70%) LD hold
Nick Clegg, LD   27,324
Nicola Bates, C.   12,040
Jack Scott, Lab.   8,228
Nigel James, UKIP   1,195
Steve Barnard, Green   919
David Wildgoose, Eng. Dem.   586
Martin Fitzpatrick, Ind.   429
Ray Green, Ch. P.   250
Mark Adshead, Loony   164
LD majority 15,284 (29.89%)
Notional 6.86% swing C. to LD
(2005: LD majority 7,416 (16.17%))

§SHEFFIELD HEELEY
E. 65,869 T. 40,871 (62.05%) Lab. hold
Meg Munn, Lab.   17,409
Simon Clement-Jones, LD   11,602
Anne Crampton, C.   7,081
John Beatson, BNP   2,260
Charlotte Arnott, UKIP   1,530
Gareth Roberts, Green   989
Lab. majority 5,807 (14.21%)
Notional 9.23% swing Lab. to LD
(2005: Lab. majority 12,340 (32.67%))

§SHEFFIELD SOUTH EAST
E. 67,284 T. 41,408 (61.54%) Lab. hold
Clive Betts, Lab.   20,169
Gail Smith, LD   9,664
Nigel Bonson, C.   7,202
Christopher Hartigan, BNP   2,345
Jonathan Arnott, UKIP   1,889
Steven Andrew, Comm. Brit.   139
Lab. majority 10,505 (25.37%)
Notional 9.00% swing Lab. to LD
(2005: Lab. majority 15,843 (43.36%))

§SHERWOOD
E. 71,043 T. 48,954 (68.91%) C. gain
*Mark Spencer, C.   19,211
Emilie Oldknow, Lab.   18,997
Kevin Moore, LD   7,283
James North, BNP   1,754
Margot Parker, UKIP   1,490
Russ Swan, Ind.   219
C. majority 214 (0.44%)
Notional 8.17% swing Lab. to C.
(2005: Lab. majority 6,869 (15.90%))

§SHIPLEY
E. 67,689 T. 49,427 (73.02%) C. hold
Philip Davies, C.   24,002
Susan Hinchcliffe, Lab.   14,058
John Harris, LD   9,890
Kevin Warnes, Green   1,477
C. majority 9,944 (20.12%)
Notional 9.58% swing Lab. to C.
(2005: C. majority 450 (0.97%))

SHREWSBURY & ATCHAM
E. 75,438 T. 53,045 (70.32%) C. hold
Daniel Kawczynski, C.   23,313
Charles West, LD   15,369
Jon Tandy, Lab.   10,915
Peter Lewis, UKIP   1,627
James Whittall, BNP   1,168
Alan Whittaker, Green   565
James Gollings, Impact   88
C. majority 7,944 (14.98%)
0.06% swing LD to C.
(2005: C. majority 1,808 (3.59%))

SHROPSHIRE NORTH
E. 78,926 T. 51,869 (65.72%) C. hold
Owen Paterson, C.   26,692
Ian Croll, LD   10,864
Ian McLaughlan, Lab.   9,406
Sandra List, UKIP   2,432
Phil Reddall, BNP   1,667
Steve Boulding, Green   808
C. majority 15,828 (30.52%)
0.33% swing LD to C.
(2005: C. majority 11,020 (23.69%))

§SITTINGBOURNE & SHEPPEY
E. 75,354 T. 48,578 (64.47%) C. hold
*Gordon Henderson, C.   24,313
Angela Harrison, Lab.   11,930
Keith Nevols, LD   7,943
Ian Davison, UKIP   2,610
Lawrence Tames, BNP   1,305
Mad Mike Young, Loony   319
David Cassidy, Ind.   158
C. majority 12,383 (25.49%)
Notional 12.72% swing Lab. to C.
(2005: C. majority 22 (0.05%))

§SKIPTON & RIPON
E. 77,381 T. 54,724 (70.72%) C. hold
*Julian Smith, C.   27,685
Helen Flynn, LD   17,735
Claire Hazelgrove, Lab.   5,498
Rodney Mills, UKIP   1,909
Bernard Allen, BNP   1,403
Roger Bell, Ind.   315
Dylan Gilligan, Youth   95
Robert Leakey, Currency   84
C. majority 9,950 (18.18%)
Notional 2.63% swing C. to LD
(2005: C. majority 11,596 (23.43%))

§SLEAFORD & NORTH HYKEHAM
E. 85,550 T. 59,530 (69.59%) C. hold
*Stephen Phillips, C.   30,719
David Harding-Price, LD   10,814
James Normington, Lab.   10,051
Marianne Overton, Lincs Ind.   3,806
Rodger Doughty, UKIP   2,163
Mike Clayton, BNP   1,977
C. majority 19,905 (33.44%)
Notional 0.46% swing LD to C.
(2005: C. majority 12,687 (24.15%))

§SLOUGH
E. 77,068 T. 47,742 (61.95%) Lab. hold
Fiona Mactaggart, Lab.   21,884
Diana Coad, C.   16,361
Chris Tucker, LD   6,943
Peter Mason-Apps, UKIP   1,517
Miriam Kennet, Green   542
Sunil Chaudhary, Ch. P.   495
Lab. majority 5,523 (11.57%)
Notional 4.14% swing Lab. to C.
(2005: Lab. majority 7,924 (19.86%))

§SOLIHULL
E. 77,863 T. 55,129 (70.80%) LD gain
Lorely Burt, LD   23,635
Maggie Throup, C.   23,460
Sarah-Jayne Merrill, Lab.   4,891
Andrew Terry, BNP   1,624
John Ison, UKIP   1,200
Neill Watts, RA   319
LD majority 175 (0.32%)
Notional 0.28% swing C. to LD
(2005: C. majority 124 (0.25%))

§SOMERSET NORTH
E. 77,304 T. 57,941 (74.95%) C. hold
Dr Liam Fox, C.   28,549
Brian Mathew, LD   20,687
Steven Parry-Hearn, Lab.   6,448
Susan Taylor, UKIP   2,257
C. majority 7,862 (13.57%)
Notional 0.98% swing LD to C.
(2005: C. majority 6,007 (11.61%))

§SOMERSET NORTH EAST
E. 67,412 T. 51,203 (75.96%) C. hold
*Jacob Rees-Mogg, C.   21,130
Dan Norris, Lab.   16,216
Gail Coleshill, LD   11,433
Peter Sandell, UKIP   1,754
Michael Jay, Green   670
C. majority 4,914 (9.60%)
Notional 4.57% swing Lab. to C.
(2005: C. majority 212 (0.46%))

§SOMERTON & FROME
E. 81,548 T. 60,612 (74.33%) LD hold
David Heath, LD   28,793
Annunziata Rees-Mogg, C.   26,976
David Oakensen, Lab.   2,675
Barry Harding, UKIP   1,932
Niall Warry, Leave EU   236
LD majority 1,817 (3.00%)
Notional 0.94% swing C. to LD
(2005: LD majority 595 (1.12%))

§SOUTH HOLLAND & THE DEEPINGS
E. 76,243 T. 50,188 (65.83%) C. hold
John Hayes, C.   29,639
Jennifer Conroy, LD   7,759
Gareth Gould, Lab.   7,024
Richard Fairman, UKIP   3,246
Roy Harban, BNP   1,796
Ashley Baxter, Green   724
C. majority 21,880 (43.60%)
Notional 0.27% swing C. to LD
(2005: C. majority 15,127 (32.48%))

§SOUTH RIBBLE
E. 75,822 T. 51,458 (67.87%) C. gain
*Lorraine Fullbrook, C.   23,396
David Borrow, Lab.   17,842
Peter Fisher, LD   7,271
David Duxbury, UKIP   1,895
Rosalind Gauci, BNP   1,054
C. majority 5,554 (10.79%)
Notional 8.11% swing Lab. to C.
(2005: Lab. majority 2,528 (5.42%))

§SOUTH SHIELDS
E. 63,294 T. 36,518 (57.70%) Lab. hold
David Miliband, Lab.   18,995
Karen Allen, C.   7,886
Stephen Psallidas, LD   5,189
Donna Watson, BNP   2,382
Shirley Ford, Green   762
Siamak Kaikavoosi, Ind.   729
Victor Thompson, Ind.   316
Sam Navabi, Ind.   168
Roger Nettleship, Anti-War   91
Lab. majority 11,109 (30.42%)
Notional 6.36% swing Lab. to C.
(2005: Lab. majority 13,368 (41.61%))

§SOUTHAMPTON ITCHEN
E. 74,532 T. 44,412 (59.59%) Lab. hold
John Denham, Lab.   16,326
Royston Smith, C.   16,134
David Goodall, LD   9,256
Alan Kebbell, UKIP   1,928
John Spottiswoode, Green   600
Tim Cutter, TUSC   168
Lab. majority 192 (0.43%)
Notional 10.28% swing Lab. to C.
(2005: Lab. majority 8,479 (21.00%))

§SOUTHAMPTON TEST
E. 71,931 T. 44,187 (61.43%) Lab. hold
Alan Whitehead, Lab.   17,001
Jeremy Moulton, C.   14,588
David Callaghan, LD   9,865
Pearline Hingston, UKIP   1,726
Chris Bluemel, Green   881
Charles Sanderson, Ind.   126
Lab. majority 2,413 (5.46%)
Notional 6.86% swing Lab. to C.
(2005: Lab. majority 7,817 (19.17%))

§SOUTHEND WEST
E. 66,527 T. 43,606 (65.55%) C. hold
David Amess, C.   20,086
Peter Welch, LD   12,816
Thomas Flynn, Lab.   5,850
Garry Cockrill, UKIP   1,714
Tony Gladwin, BNP   1,333
Barry Bolton, Green   644
Dr Vel, Ind.   617
Terry Phillips, Eng. Dem.   546
C. majority 7,270 (16.67%)
Notional 2.77% swing C. to LD
(2005: C. majority 9,008 (22.20%))

SOUTHPORT
E. 67,202 T. 43,757 (65.11%) LD hold
John Pugh, LD   21,707
Brenda Porter, C.   15,683
Jim Conalty, Lab.   4,116
Terry Durrance, UKIP   2,251
LD majority 6,024 (13.77%)
2.23% swing C. to LD
(2005: LD majority 3,838 (9.32%))

SPELTHORNE
E. 70,479 T. 47,304 (67.12%) C. hold
*Kwasi Kwarteng, C.   22,261
Mark Chapman, LD   12,242
Adam Tyler-Moore, Lab.   7,789
Christopher Browne, UKIP   4,009
Ian Swinglehurst, Ind.   314
Rod Littlewood, Best   244
Paul Couchman, TUSC   176
John Gore, CIP   167
Grahame Leon-Smith, Ind. Fed.   102
C. majority 10,019 (21.18%)
6.11% swing C. to LD
(2005: C. majority 9,936 (23.20%))

§STAFFORD
E. 70,587 T. 50,239 (71.17%) C. gain
*Jeremy Lefroy, C.   22,047
David Kidney, Lab.   16,587
Barry Stamp, LD   8,211
Roy Goode, UKIP   1,727
Roland Hynd, BNP   1,103
Mike Shone, Green   564
C. majority 5,460 (10.87%)
Notional 7.44% swing Lab. to C.
(2005: Lab. majority 1,852 (4.01%))

§STAFFORDSHIRE MOORLANDS
E. 62,071 T. 43,815 (70.59%) C. hold
*Karen Bradley, C.   19,793
Charlotte Atkins, Lab.   13,104
Henry Jebb, LD   7,338
Steve Povey, UKIP   3,580
C. majority 6,689 (15.27%)
Notional 5.71% swing Lab. to C.
(2005: C. majority 1,618 (3.86%))

§STAFFORDSHIRE SOUTH
E. 73,390 T. 50,440 (68.73%) C. hold
*Gavin Williamson, C.   26,834
Kevin McElduff, Lab.   10,244
Sarah Fellows, LD   8,427
Mike Nattrass, UKIP   2,753
David Bradnock, BNP   1,928
Andrew Morris, Ind.   254
C. majority 16,590 (32.89%)
Notional 1.12% swing Lab. to C.
(2005: C. majority 8,346 (30.65%))

§STALYBRIDGE & HYDE
E. 69,037 T. 40,879 (59.21%) Lab. hold
*Jonathan Reynolds, Lab.   16,189
Rob Adlard, C.   13,445
John Potter, LD   6,965
Anthony Jones, BNP   2,259
John Cooke, UKIP   1,342
Ruth Bergan, Green   679
Lab. majority 2,744 (6.71%)
Notional 8.47% swing Lab. to C.
(2005: Lab. majority 8,455 (23.64%))

§STEVENAGE
E. 68,937 T. 44,651 (64.77%) C. gain
*Stephen McPartland, C.   18,491
Sharon Taylor, Lab. (Co-op)   14,913
Julia Davies, LD   7,432
Marion Mason, UKIP   2,004
Andrew Green, BNP   1,007
Charles Vickers, Eng. Dem.   366
Stephen Phillips, No Vote   327
David Cox, Ind.   80
Andrew Ralph, YRDPL   31
C. majority 3,578 (8.01%)
Notional 8.03% swing Lab. (Co-op) to C.
(2005: Lab. (Co-op) majority 3,288
(8.05%))

§STOCKPORT
E. 63,525 T. 39,128 (61.59%) Lab. hold
Ann Coffey, Lab.   16,697
Stephen Holland, C.   9,913
Stuart Bodsworth, LD   9,778
Duncan Warner, BNP   1,201
Mike Kelly, UKIP   862
Peter Barber, Green   677
Lab. majority 6,784 (17.34%)
Notional 5.74% swing Lab. to C.
(2005: Lab. majority 9,982 (28.82%))

§STOCKTON NORTH
E. 67,363 T. 39,498 (58.63%) Lab. hold
*Alex Cunningham, Lab.   16,923
Ian Galletley, C.   10,247
Philip Latham, LD   6,342
James Macpherson, BNP   1,724
Frank Cook, Ind.   1,577
Gordon Parkin, UKIP   1,556
Ian Saul, Eng. Dem.   1,129
Lab. majority 6,676 (16.90%)
Notional 8.35% swing Lab. to C.
(2005: Lab. majority 12,742 (33.60%))

§STOCKTON SOUTH
E. 74,552 T. 50,284 (67.45%) C. gain
*James Wharton, C.   19,577
Dari Taylor, Lab.   19,245
Jacquie Bell, LD   7,600
Neil Sinclair, BNP   1,553
Peter Braney, UKIP   1,471
Yvonne Hossack, Ind.   536
Ted Strike, Ch. P.   302
C. majority 332 (0.66%)
Notional 7.05% swing Lab. to C.
(2005: Lab. majority 5,834 (13.44%))

§STOKE-ON-TRENT CENTRAL
E. 60,995 T. 32,470 (53.23%) Lab. hold
*Tristram Hunt, Lab.   12,605
John Redfern, LD   7,039
Norsheen Bhatti, C.   6,833
Simon Darby, BNP   2,502
Carol Lovatt, UKIP   1,402
Paul Breeze, Ind.   959
Gary Elsby, Ind.   399
Brian Ward, City Ind.   303
Alby Walker, Ind.   295
Matthew Wright, TUSC   133
Lab. majority 5,566 (17.14%)
Notional 8.33% swing Lab. to LD
(2005: Lab. majority 9,717 (33.80%))

§STOKE-ON-TRENT NORTH
E. 72,052 T. 40,196 (55.79%) Lab. hold
Joan Walley, Lab.   17,815
Andy Large, C.   9,580
John Fisher, LD   7,120
Melanie Baddeley, BNP   3,196
Geoffrey Locke, UKIP   2,485
Lab. majority 8,235 (20.49%)
Notional 8.77% swing Lab. to C.
(2005: Lab. majority 13,666 (38.03%))

§STOKE-ON-TRENT SOUTH
E. 68,031 T. 39,852 (58.58%) Lab. hold
Rob Flello, Lab.   15,446
James Rushton, C.   11,316
Zulfiqar Ali, LD   6,323
Michael Coleman, BNP   3,762
Mark Barlow, UKIP   1,363
Terry Follows, Staffs Ind.   1,208
Mark Breeze, Ind.   434
Lab. majority 4,130 (10.36%)
Notional 6.15% swing Lab. to C.
(2005: Lab. majority 8,324 (22.67%))

§STONE
E. 66,979 T. 47,229 (70.51%) C. hold
Bill Cash, C.   23,890
Christine Tinker, LD   10,598
Jo Lewis, Lab.   9,770
Andrew Illsley, UKIP   2,481
Damon Hoppe, Green   490
C. majority 13,292 (28.14%)
Notional 0.81% swing C. to LD
(2005: C. majority 8,191 (18.72%))

§STOURBRIDGE
E. 69,637 T. 47,234 (67.83%) C. gain
*Margot James, C.   20,153
Lynda Waltho, Lab.   14,989
Christopher Bramall, LD   7,733
Maddy Westrop, UKIP   2,103
Robert Weale, BNP   1,696
Will Duckworth, Green   394
Alun Nicholas, Ind.   166
C. majority 5,164 (10.93%)
Notional 6.93% swing Lab. to C.
(2005: Lab. majority 1,280 (2.92%))

§STRATFORD-ON-AVON
E. 69,516 T. 50,542 (72.71%) C. hold
*Nadhim Zahawi, C.   26,052
Martin Turner, LD   14,706
Robert Johnston, Lab.   4,809
Brett Parsons, UKIP   1,846
George Jones, BNP   1,097
Neil Basnett, Ind.   1,032
Karen Varga, Green   527
Fred Bishop, Eng. Dem.   473
C. majority 11,346 (22.45%)
Notional 0.72% swing C. to LD
(2005: C. majority 10,928 (23.90%))

§STREATHAM
E. 74,531 T. 46,837 (62.84%) Lab. hold
*Chuka Umunna, Lab.   20,037
Chris Nicholson, LD   16,778
Rahoul Bhansali, C.   8,578
Rebecca Findlay, Green   861
Geoffrey Macharia, Ch. P.   237
Janus Polenceus, Eng. Dem.   229
Paul Lepper, WRP   117
Lab. majority 3,259 (6.96%)
Notional 5.25% swing Lab. to LD
(2005: Lab. majority 6,584 (17.47%))

§STRETFORD & URMSTON
E. 70,091 T. 44,910 (64.07%) Lab. hold
*Kate Green, Lab.   21,821
Alex Williams, C.   12,886
Steve Cooke, LD   7,601
David Owen, UKIP   1,508
Margaret Westbrook, Green   916
Samuel Jacob, Ch. P.   178
Lab. majority 8,935 (19.90%)
Notional 0.69% swing Lab. to C.
(2005: Lab. majority 8,310 (21.28%))

§STROUD
E. 78,305 T. 57,973 (74.03%) C. gain
*Neil Carmichael, C.   23,679
David Drew, Lab. (Co-op)   22,380
Dennis Andrewartha, LD   8,955
Martin Whiteside, Green   1,542
Steve Parker, UKIP   1,301
Alan Lomas, Ind.   116
C. majority 1,299 (2.24%)
Notional 2.05% swing Lab. (Co-op) to C.
(2005: Lab. (Co-op) majority 996
(1.85%))

§SUFFOLK CENTRAL & IPSWICH
NORTH
E. 75,848   T. 53,420 (70.43%)   C. hold
*Daniel Poulter, C.   27,125
Andrew Aalders-Dunthorne, LD   13,339
Bhavna Joshi, Lab.   8,636
Roy Philpot, UKIP   2,361
Andrew Stringer, Green   1,452
Mark Trevitt, Ind.   389
Richard Vass, New Party   118
C. majority 13,786 (25.81%)
Notional 0.76% swing LD to C.
(2005: C. majority 7,786 (16.07%))

§SUFFOLK COASTAL
E. 76,687   T. 54,893 (71.58%)   C. hold
*Therese Coffey, C.   25,475
Daisy Cooper, LD   16,347
Adam Leeder, Lab.   8,812
Prof. Stephen Bush, UKIP   3,156
Rachel Fulcher, Green   1,103
C. majority 9,128 (16.63%)
Notional 2.91% swing C. to LD
(2005: C. majority 9,674 (18.43%))

§SUFFOLK SOUTH
E. 72,498   T. 51,416 (70.92%)   C. hold
Tim Yeo, C.   24,550
Nigel Bennett, LD   15,861
Emma Bishton, Lab.   7,368
David Campbell Bannerman,
UKIP   3,637
C. majority 8,689 (16.90%)
Notional 1.63% swing LD to C.
(2005: C. majority 6,664 (13.64%))

§SUFFOLK WEST
E. 74,413   T. 48,089 (64.62%)   C. hold
*Matthew Hancock, C.   24,312
Belinda Brooks-Gordon, LD   11,262
Ohid Ahmed, Lab.   7,089
Ian Smith, UKIP   3,085
Ramon Johns, BNP   1,428
Andrew Appleby, Ind.   540
Colin Young, CPA   373
C. majority 13,050 (27.14%)
Notional 2.28% swing C. to LD
(2005: C. majority 8,735 (19.92%))

§SUNDERLAND CENTRAL
E. 74,485   T. 42,463 (57.01%)   Lab. hold
*Julie Elliott, Lab.   19,495
Lee Martin, C.   12,770
Paul Dixon, LD   7,191
John McCaffrey, BNP   1,913
Pauline Featonby-Warren, UKIP   1,094
Lab. majority 6,725 (15.84%)
Notional 4.85% swing Lab. to C.
(2005: Lab. majority 9,464 (25.53%))

SURREY EAST
E. 76,855   T. 54,640 (71.09%)   C. hold
*Sam Gyimah, C.   31,007
David Lee, LD   14,133
Mathew Rodda, Lab.   4,925
Helena Windsor, UKIP   3,770
Martin Hogbin, Loony   422
Sandy Pratt, Ind.   383
C. majority 16,874 (30.88%)
0.72% swing C. to LD
(2005: C. majority 15,921 (32.32%))

SURREY HEATH
E. 77,690   T. 54,347 (69.95%)   C. hold
Michael Gove, C.   31,326
Alan Hilliar, LD   14,037
Matthew Willey, Lab.   5,552
Mark Stroud, UKIP   3,432
C. majority 17,289 (31.81%)
4.58% swing LD to C.
(2005: C. majority 10,845 (22.66%))

§SURREY SOUTH WEST
E. 77,980   T. 57,259 (73.43%)   C. hold
Jeremy Hunt, C.   33,605
Mike Simpson, LD   17,287
Richard Mollet, Lab.   3,419
Roger Meekins, UKIP   1,486
Cherry Allan, Green   690
Helen Hamilton, BNP   644
Luke Leighton, Pirate   94
Arthur Price, Ind.   34
C. majority 16,318 (28.50%)
Notional 8.63% swing LD to C.
(2005: C. majority 5,969 (11.23%))

§SUSSEX MID
E. 77,182   T. 55,855 (72.37%)   C. hold
Nicholas Soames, C.   28,329
Serena Tierney, LD   20,927
David Boot, Lab.   3,689
Marc Montgomery, UKIP   1,423
Paul Brown, Green   645
Stuart Minihane, BNP   583
Baron Von Thunderclap, Loony   259
C. majority 7,402 (13.25%)
Notional 0.32% swing LD to C.
(2005: C. majority 6,462 (12.62%))

§SUTTON & CHEAM
E. 66,658   T. 48,508 (72.77%)   LD hold
Paul Burstow, LD   22,156
Philippa Stroud, C.   20,548
Kathy Allen, Lab.   3,376
John Clarke, BNP   1,014
David Pickles, UKIP   950
Peter Hickson, Green   246
John Dodds, Eng. Dem.   106
Matthew Connolly, CPA   52
Martin Cullip, Libertarian   41
Dr Brian Hammond, UK Integrity   19
LD majority 1,608 (3.31%)
Notional 1.45% swing LD to C.
(2005: LD majority 2,689 (6.22%))

§SUTTON COLDFIELD
E. 74,489   T. 50,589 (67.91%)   C. hold
Andrew Mitchell, C.   27,303
Robert Pocock, Lab.   10,298
Richard Brighton, LD   9,117
Robert Grierson, BNP   1,749
Edward Siddall-Jones, UKIP   1,587
Joe Rooney, Green   535
C. majority 17,005 (33.61%)
Notional 3.44% swing Lab. to C.
(2005: C. majority 12,318 (26.72%))

§SWINDON NORTH
E. 78,391   T. 50,295 (64.16%)   C. gain
*Justin Tomlinson, C.   22,408
Victor Agarwal, Lab.   15,348
Jane Lock, LD   8,668
Stephen Halden, UKIP   1,842
Reginald Bates, BNP   1,542
Bill Hughes, Green   487
C. majority 7,060 (14.04%)
Notional 10.14% swing Lab. to C.
(2005: Lab. majority 2,675 (6.25%))

§SWINDON SOUTH
E. 72,622   T. 47,119 (64.88%)   C. gain
*Robert Buckland, C.   19,687
Anne Snelgrove, Lab.   16,143
Damon Hooton, LD   8,305
Robin Tingey, UKIP   2,029
Jenni Miles, Green   619
Alastair Kirk, Ch. P.   176
Karsten Evans, Ind.   160
C. majority 3,544 (7.52%)
Notional 5.51% swing Lab. to C.
(2005: Lab. majority 1,493 (3.50%))

TAMWORTH
E. 72,693   T. 46,390 (63.82%)   C. gain
*Christopher Pincher, C.   21,238
Brian Jenkins, Lab.   15,148
Jenny Pinkett, LD   7,516
Paul Smith, UKIP   2,253
Charlene Detheridge, Ch. P.   235
C. majority 6,090 (13.13%)
9.50% swing Lab. to C.
(2005: Lab. majority 2,569 (5.87%))

§TATTON
E. 65,689   T. 45,231 (68.86%)   C. hold
George Osborne, C.   24,687
David Lomax, LD   10,200
Richard Jackson, Lab.   7,803
Sarah Flannery, Ind.   2,243
Michael Gibson, Poetry   298
C. majority 14,487 (32.03%)
Notional 1.17% swing LD to C.
(2005: C. majority 11,537 (27.73%))

§TAUNTON DEANE
E. 82,537   T. 58,150 (70.45%)   LD hold
Jeremy Browne, LD   28,531
Mark Formosa, C.   24,538
Martin Jevon, Lab.   2,967
Tony McIntyre, UKIP   2,114
LD majority 3,993 (6.87%)
Notional 1.78% swing C. to LD
(2005: LD majority 1,868 (3.30%))

§TELFORD
E. 65,061   T. 41,310 (63.49%)   Lab. hold
David Wright, Lab.   15,974
Tom Biggins, C.   14,996
Phil Bennion, LD   6,399
Denis Allen, UKIP   2,428
Phil Spencer, BNP   1,513
Lab. majority 978 (2.37%)
Notional 6.32% swing Lab. to C.
(2005: Lab. majority 5,651 (15.01%))

§TEWKESBURY
E. 76,655   T. 53,961 (70.39%)   C. hold
Laurence Robertson, C.   25,472
Alistair Cameron, LD   19,162
Stuart Emmerson, Lab.   6,253
Brian Jones, UKIP   2,230
Matthew Sidford, Green   525
George Ridgeon, Loony   319
C. majority 6,310 (11.69%)
Notional 4.04% swing C. to LD
(2005: C. majority 9,130 (19.78%))

§THANET NORTH
E. 69,432   T. 43,343 (62.43%)   C. hold
Roger Gale, C.   22,826
Michael Britton, Lab.   9,298
Laura Murphy, LD   8,400
Rosamund Parker, UKIP   2,819
C. majority 13,528 (31.21%)
Notional 7.94% swing Lab. to C.
(2005: C. majority 6,118 (15.33%))

§THANET SOUTH
E. 71,596 T. 45,933 (64.16%) C. hold
*Laura Sandys, C.	22,043
Dr Stephen Ladyman, Lab.	14,426
Peter Bucklitsch, LD	6,935
Trevor Shonk, UKIP	2,529
C. majority 7,617 (16.58%)
Notional 7.41% swing Lab. to C.
(2005: C. majority 810 (1.76%))

§THIRSK & MALTON
E. 76,231 T. 38,142 (50.03%) C. hold
Anne McIntosh, C.	20,167
Howard Keal, LD	8,886
Jonathan Roberts, Lab.	5,169
Toby Horton, UKIP	2,502
John Clark, Lib.	1,418
C. majority 11,281 (29.58%)
Notional 1.75% swing C. to LD
(2005: C. majority 14,117 (28.50%))

§THORNBURY & YATE
E. 64,092 T. 48,226 (75.24%) LD hold
Steve Webb, LD	25,032
Matthew Riddle, C.	17,916
Roxanne Egan, Lab.	3,385
Jenny Knight, UKIP	1,709
Thomas Beacham, Ind. Fed.	126
Anthony Clements, ND	58
LD majority 7,116 (14.76%)
Notional 4.35% swing LD to C.
(2005: LD majority 11,060 (23.45%))

§THURROCK
E. 92,390 T. 45,821 (49.60%) C. gain
*Jackie Doyle-Price, C.	16,869
Carl Morris, Lab.	16,777
Carys Davis, LD	4,901
Emma Colgate, BNP	3,618
Clive Broad, UKIP	3,390
Arinola Araba, Ch. P.	266
C. majority 92 (0.20%)
Notional 6.61% swing Lab. to C.
(2005: Lab. majority 5,358 (13.02%))

§TIVERTON & HONITON
E. 76,810 T. 54,894 (71.47%) C. hold
*Neil Parish, C.	27,614
Jon Underwood, LD	18,294
Vernon Whitlock, Lab.	4,907
Daryl Stanbury, UKIP	3,277
Cathy Connor, Green	802
C. majority 9,320 (16.98%)
Notional 0.28% swing C. to LD
(2005: C. majority 9,007 (17.55%))

TONBRIDGE & MALLING
E. 71,790 T. 51,314 (71.48%) C. hold
Sir John Stanley, C.	29,723
Elizabeth Simpson, LD	11,545
Daniel Griffiths, Lab.	6,476
David Waller, UKIP	1,911
Steve Dawe, Green	764
Mike Easter, NF	505
Lisa Rogers, Eng. Dem.	390
C. majority 18,178 (35.43%)
1.02% swing LD to C.
(2005: C. majority 13,352 (28.99%))

§TOOTING
E. 73,836 T. 50,655 (68.60%) Lab. hold
Sadiq Khan, Lab.	22,038
Mark Clarke, C.	19,514
Nasser Butt, LD	7,509
Strachan McDonald, UKIP	624
Roy Vickery, Green	609
Susan John-Richards, Ind.	190
Shereen Paul, Ch. P.	171
Lab. majority 2,524 (4.98%)
Notional 3.60% swing Lab. to C.
(2005: Lab. majority 5,169 (12.17%))

§TORBAY
E. 76,151 T. 49,210 (64.62%) LD hold
Adrian Sanders, LD	23,126
Marcus Wood, C.	19,048
David Pedrick-Friend, Lab.	3,231
Julien Parrott, UKIP	2,628
Ann Conway, BNP	709
Sam Moss, Green	468
LD majority 4,078 (8.29%)
Notional 1.14% swing C. to LD
(2005: LD majority 2,727 (6.01%))

§TOTNES
E. 67,937 T. 47,843 (70.42%) C. hold
*Dr Sarah Wollaston, C.	21,940
Julian Brazil, LD	17,013
Carole Whitty, Lab.	3,538
Jeff Beer, UKIP	2,890
Lydia Somerville, Green	1,181
Mike Turner, BNP	624
Simon Drew, Ind.	390
Dr Stephen Hopwood, Ind.	267
C. majority 4,927 (10.30%)
Notional 2.27% swing LD to C.
(2005: C. majority 2,693 (5.76%))

TOTTENHAM
E. 69,933 T. 40,687 (58.18%) Lab. hold
David Lammy, Lab.	24,128
David Schmitz, LD	7,197
Sean Sullivan, C.	6,064
Jenny Sutton, TUSC	1,057
Anne Gray, Green	980
Winston McKenzie, UKIP	466
Neville Watson, Ind. People	265
Abimbola Kadara, Ch. P.	262
Sheik Thompson, Ind.	143
Errol Carr, Ind.	125
Lab. majority 16,931 (41.61%)
0.22% swing LD to Lab.
(2005: Lab. majority 13,034 (41.16%))

§TRURO & FALMOUTH
E. 70,598 T. 48,768 (69.08%) C. gain
*Sarah Newton, C.	20,349
Terrye Teverson, LD	19,914
Charlotte Mackenzie, Lab.	4,697
Harry Blakeley, UKIP	1,911
Loic Rich, Meb. Ker.	1,039
Ian Wright, Green	858
C. majority 435 (0.89%)
Notional 5.07% swing LD to C.
(2005: LD majority 3,931 (9.25%))

§TUNBRIDGE WELLS
E. 72,042 T. 50,320 (69.85%) C. hold
Greg Clark, C.	28,302
David Hallas, LD	12,726
Gary Heather, Lab.	5,448
Victor Webb, UKIP	2,054
Hazel Dawe, Green	914
Andrew McBride, BNP	704
Farel Bradbury, Ind.	172
C. majority 15,576 (30.95%)
Notional 2.79% swing LD to C.
(2005: C. majority 11,572 (25.38%))

TWICKENHAM
E. 79,861 T. 59,721 (74.78%) LD hold
Vince Cable, LD	32,483
Deborah Thomas, C.	20,343
Brian Tomlinson, Lab.	4,583
Brian Gilbert, UKIP	868
Steve Roest, Green	674
Chris Hurst, BNP	654
Harry Cole, R and E	76
Paul Armstrong, Magna Carta	40
LD majority 12,140 (20.33%)
0.52% swing C. to LD
(2005: LD majority 9,965 (19.28%))

§TYNEMOUTH
E. 75,680 T. 52,668 (69.59%) Lab. hold
Alan Campbell, Lab.	23,860
Wendy Morton, C.	18,121
John Appleby, LD	7,845
Dorothy Brooke, BNP	1,404
Natasha Payne, UKIP	900
Julia Erskine, Green	538
Lab. majority 5,739 (10.90%)
Notional 0.38% swing Lab. to C.
(2005: Lab. majority 5,490 (11.65%))

§TYNESIDE NORTH
E. 77,690 T. 46,405 (59.73%) Lab. hold
*Mary Glindon, Lab.	23,505
David Ord, LD	10,621
Gagan Mohindra, C.	8,514
John Burrows, BNP	1,860
Claudia Blake, UKIP	1,306
Bob Batten, NF	599
Lab. majority 12,884 (27.76%)
Notional 4.81% swing Lab. to LD
(2005: Lab. majority 14,929 (37.38%))

§UXBRIDGE & RUISLIP SOUTH
E. 71,168 T. 45,076 (63.34%) C. hold
John Randall, C.	21,758
Sidharath Garg, Lab.	10,542
Michael Cox, LD	8,995
Dianne Neal, BNP	1,396
Mark Wadsworth, UKIP	1,234
Mike Harling, Green	477
Roger Cooper, Eng. Dem.	403
Francis Mcallister, NF	271
C. majority 11,216 (24.88%)
Notional 3.44% swing Lab. to C.
(2005: C. majority 7,178 (18.01%))

§VAUXHALL
E. 74,811 T. 43,191 (57.73%) Lab. hold
Kate Hoey, Lab.	21,498
Caroline Pidgeon, LD	10,847
Glyn Chambers, C.	9,301
Joseph Healy, Green	708
Jose Navarro, Eng. Dem.	289
Lana Martin, Ch. P.	200
Daniel Lambert, Soc.	143
Jeremy Drinkall, WP	109
James Kapetanos, APP	96
Lab. majority 10,651 (24.66%)
Notional 0.06% swing LD to Lab.
(2005: Lab. majority 8,503 (24.54%))

§WAKEFIELD
E. 70,834 T. 44,444 (62.74%) Lab. hold
Mary Creagh, Lab.   17,454
Alex Story, C.   15,841
David Smith, LD   7,256
Ian Senior, BNP   2,581
Miriam Hawkins, Green   873
Mark Harrop, Ind.   439
Lab. majority 1,613 (3.63%)
Notional 6.94% swing Lab. to C.
(2005: Lab. majority 7,349 (17.50%))

§WALLASEY
E. 65,915 T. 41,654 (63.19%) Lab. hold
Angela Eagle, Lab.   21,578
Leah Fraser, C.   13,071
Steve Pitt, LD   5,693
Derek Snowden, UKIP   1,205
Emmanuel Mwaba, Ind.   107
Lab. majority 8,507 (20.42%)
Notional 1.78% swing Lab. to C.
(2005: Lab. majority 9,130 (23.98%))

§WALSALL NORTH
E. 65,183 T. 36,187 (55.52%) Lab. hold
David Winnick, Lab.   13,385
Helyn Clack, C.   12,395
Nadia Fazal, LD   4,754
Christopher Woodall, BNP   2,930
Elizabeth Hazell, UKIP   1,737
Peter Smith, Dem. Lab.   842
Babar Shakir, Ch. P.   144
Lab. majority 990 (2.74%)
Notional 9.03% swing Lab. to C.
(2005: Lab. majority 6,901 (20.79%))

§WALSALL SOUTH
E. 64,830 T. 40,882 (63.06%) Lab. hold
*Valerie Vaz, Lab.   16,211
Richard Hunt, C.   14,456
Dr Murli Sinha, LD   5,880
Derek Bennett, UKIP   3,449
Gulzaman Khan, Ch. P.   482
Mohammed Mulia, ND   404
Lab. majority 1,755 (4.29%)
Notional 8.24% swing Lab. to C.
(2005: Lab. majority 7,910 (20.77%))

WALTHAMSTOW
E. 64,625 T. 40,994 (63.43%) Lab. hold
*Stella Creasy, Lab.   21,252
Farid Ahmed, LD   11,774
Andy Hemsted, C.   5,734
Judith Chisholm-Benli, UKIP   823
Daniel Perrett, Green   767
Nancy Taaffe, TUSC   279
Ashar Mall, Ch. P.   248
Paul Warburton, Ind.   117
Lab. majority 9,478 (23.12%)
0.04% swing Lab. to LD
(2005: Lab. majority 7,993 (23.21%))

WANSBECK
E. 63,045 T. 38,273 (60.71%) Lab. hold
*Ian Lavery, Lab.   17,548
Simon Reed, LD   10,517
Campbell Storey, C.   6,714
Stephen Finlay, BNP   1,418
Linda Lee-Stokoe, UKIP   974
Nic Best, Green   601
Malcolm Reid, Ind.   359
Michael Flynn, Ch. P.   142
Lab. majority 7,031 (18.37%)
5.19% swing Lab. to LD
(2005: Lab. majority 10,581 (28.75%))

§WANTAGE
E. 80,456 T. 56,341 (70.03%) C. hold
Ed Vaizey, C.   29,284
Alan Armitage, LD   15,737
Steven Mitchell, Lab.   7,855
Jacqueline Jones, UKIP   2,421
Adam Twine, Green   1,044
C. majority 13,547 (24.04%)
Notional 4.30% swing LD to C.
(2005: C. majority 8,039 (15.44%))

§WARLEY
E. 63,106 T. 38,270 (60.64%) Lab. hold
John Spellar, Lab.   20,240
Jasbir Parmar, C.   9,484
Edward Keating, LD   5,929
Nigel Harvey, UKIP   2,617
Lab. majority 10,756 (28.11%)
Notional 1.94% swing Lab. to C.
(2005: Lab. majority 11,206 (31.99%))

§WARRINGTON NORTH
E. 71,601 T. 44,211 (61.75%) Lab. hold
Helen Jones, Lab.   20,135
Paul Campbell, C.   13,364
David Eccles, LD   9,196
Albert Scott, Ind.   1,516
Lab. majority 6,771 (15.32%)
Notional 6.61% swing Lab. to C.
(2005: Lab. majority 11,382 (28.53%))

§WARRINGTON SOUTH
E. 80,506 T. 54,874 (68.16%) C. gain
*David Mowat, C.   19,641
Nick Bent, Lab.   18,088
Jo Crotty, LD   15,094
James Ashington, UKIP   1,624
Steph Davies, Green   427
C. majority 1,553 (2.83%)
Notional 6.00% swing Lab. to C.
(2005: Lab. majority 4,337 (9.17%))

§WARWICK & LEAMINGTON
E. 58,030 T. 49,032 (84.49%) C. gain
*Chris White, C.   20,876
James Plaskitt, Lab.   17,363
Alan Beddow, LD   8,977
Christopher Lenton, UKIP   926
Ian Davison, Green   693
Jim Cullinane, Ind.   197
C. majority 3,513 (7.16%)
Notional 8.76% swing Lab. to C.
(2005: Lab. majority 4,393 (10.35%))

§WARWICKSHIRE NORTH
E. 70,143 T. 47,265 (67.38%) C. gain
*Dan Byles, C.   18,993
Mike O'Brien, Lab.   18,939
Stephen Martin, LD   5,481
Jason Holmes, BNP   2,106
Steven Fowler, UKIP   1,335
David Lane, Eng. Dem.   411
C. majority 54 (0.11%)
Notional 7.69% swing Lab. to C.
(2005: Lab. majority 6,684 (15.27%))

§WASHINGTON & SUNDERLAND
WEST
E. 68,910 T. 37,334 (54.18%) Lab. hold
Sharon Hodgson, Lab.   19,615
Ian Cuthbert, C.   8,157
Peter Andras, LD   6,382
Ian McDonald, BNP   1,913
Linda Hudson, UKIP   1,267
Lab. majority 11,458 (30.69%)
Notional 11.56% swing Lab. to C.
(2005: Lab. majority 17,060 (52.56%))

§WATFORD
E. 80,798 T. 55,208 (68.33%) C. gain
*Richard Harrington, C.   19,291
Sal Brinton, LD   17,866
Claire Ward, Lab.   14,750
Andrew Emerson, BNP   1,217
Graham Eardley, UKIP   1,199
Ian Brandon, Green   885
C. majority 1,425 (2.58%)
Notional 6.08% swing Lab. to C.
(2005: Lab. majority 1,151 (2.33%))

§WAVENEY
E. 78,532 T. 51,141 (65.12%) C. gain
*Peter Aldous, C.   20,571
Bob Blizzard, Lab.   19,802
Alan Dean, LD   6,811
Jack Tyler, UKIP   2,684
Graham Elliott, Green   1,167
Louis Barfe, Ind.   106
C. majority 769 (1.50%)
Notional 6.75% swing Lab. to C.
(2005: Lab. majority 5,950 (12.00%))

§WEALDEN
E. 76,537 T. 54,969 (71.82%) C. hold
Charles Hendry, C.   31,090
Chris Bowers, LD   13,911
Lorna Blackmore, Lab.   5,266
Dan Docker, UKIP   3,319
David Jonas, Green   1,383
C. majority 17,179 (31.25%)
Notional 2.79% swing LD to C.
(2005: C. majority 12,812 (25.66%))

§WEAVER VALE
E. 66,538 T. 43,990 (66.11%) C. gain
*Graham Evans, C.   16,953
John Stockton, Lab.   15,962
Peter Hampson, LD   8,196
Colin Marsh, BNP   1,063
Paul Remfry, UKIP   1,018
Howard Thorp, Green   338
Mike Cooksley, Ind.   270
Tom Reynolds, Ind.   133
Will Charlton, Ind.   57
C. majority 991 (2.25%)
Notional 8.14% swing Lab. to C.
(2005: Lab. majority 5,277 (14.03%))

§WELLINGBOROUGH
E. 76,857 T. 51,661 (67.22%) C. hold
Peter Bone, C.   24,918
Jayne Buckland, Lab.   13,131
Kevin Barron, LD   8,848
Adrian Haynes, UKIP   1,636
Rob Walker, BNP   1,596
Terry Spencer, Eng. Dem.   530
Jonathan Hornett, Green   480
Paul Crofts, TUSC   249
Gary Donaldson, Ind.   240
Marcus Lavin, Ind.   33
C. majority 11,787 (22.82%)
Notional 10.78% swing Lab. to C.
(2005: C. majority 610 (1.25%))

WELLS
E. 79,432 T. 55,864 (70.33%) LD gain
*Tessa Munt, LD   24,560
David Heathcoat-Amory, C.   23,760
Andy Merryfield, Lab.   4,198
Jake Baynes, UKIP   1,711
Richard Boyce, BNP   1,004
Chris Briton, Green   631
LD majority 800 (1.43%)
3.59% swing C. to LD
(2005: C. majority 3,040 (5.74%))

WELWYN HATFIELD
E. 72,058   T. 48,972 (67.96%)   C. hold
Grant Shapps, C.   27,894
Mike Hobday, Lab.   10,471
Paul Zukowskyj, LD   8,010
David Platt, UKIP   1,643
Jill Weston, Green   796
Nigel Parker, Ind.   158
C. majority 17,423 (35.58%)
11.14% swing Lab. to C.
(2005: C. majority 5,946 (13.30%))

§WENTWORTH & DEARNE
E. 72,586   T. 42,106 (58.01%)   Lab. hold
John Healey, Lab.   21,316
Michelle Donelan, C.   7,396
Nick Love, LD   6,787
John Wilkinson, UKIP   3,418
George Baldwin, BNP   3,189
Lab. majority 13,920 (33.06%)
Notional 7.49% swing Lab. to C.
(2005: Lab. majority 17,551 (45.55%))

§WEST BROMWICH EAST
E. 62,824   T. 37,950 (60.41%)   Lab. hold
Tom Watson, Lab.   17,657
Alistair Thompson, C.   10,961
Ian Garrett, LD   4,993
Terry Lewin, BNP   2,205
Mark Cowles, Eng. Dem.   1,150
Steve Grey, UKIP   984
Lab. majority 6,696 (17.64%)
Notional 7.68% swing Lab. to C.
(2005: Lab. majority 11,947 (33.00%))

§WEST BROMWICH WEST
E. 65,013   T. 36,171 (55.64%)   Lab. hold
Adrian Bailey, Lab.   16,263
Andrew Hardie, C.   10,612
Sadie Smith, LD   4,336
Russ Green, BNP   3,394
Mac Ford, UKIP   1,566
Lab. majority 5,651 (15.62%)
Notional 7.64% swing Lab. to C.
(2005: Lab. majority 9,821 (30.90%))

§WEST HAM
E. 85,313   T. 46,951 (55.03%)   Lab. hold
Lyn Brown, Lab.   29,422
Virginia Morris, C.   6,888
Martin Pierce, LD   5,392
Stan Gain, CPA   1,327
Kamran Malik, Ind.   1,245
Michael Davidson, NF   1,089
Kim Gandy, UKIP   766
Jane Lithgow, Green   645
Grace Agbogun-Toko, Ind.   177
Lab. majority 22,534 (47.99%)
Notional 4.16% swing C. to Lab.
(2005: Lab. majority 12,274 (31.76%))

§WESTMINSTER NORTH
E. 66,739   T. 39,598 (59.33%)   Lab. hold
Karen Buck, Lab.   17,377
Joanne Cash, C.   15,251
Mark Blackburn, LD   5,513
Tristan Smith, Green   478
Stephen Curry, BNP   334
Jasna Badzak, UKIP   315
Dr Ali Bahaijoub, Ind.   101
Edward Roseman, Eng. Dem.   99
Gabriela Fajardo, Ch. P.   98
Abby Dharamsey, Ind.   32
Lab. majority 2,126 (5.37%)
Notional 0.61% swing Lab. to C.
(2005: Lab. majority 2,120 (6.59%))

§WESTMORLAND & LONSDALE
E. 67,881   T. 51,487 (75.85%)   LD hold
Tim Farron, LD   30,896
Gareth McKeever, C.   18,632
Jonathan Todd, Lab.   1,158
John Mander, UKIP   801
LD majority 12,264 (23.82%)
Notional 11.06% swing C. to LD
(2005: LD majority 806 (1.70%))

§WESTON-SUPER-MARE
E. 78,487   T. 52,716 (67.17%)   C. hold
John Penrose, C.   23,356
Mike Bell, LD   20,665
David Bradley, Lab.   5,772
Paul Spencer, UKIP   1,406
Peryn Parsons, BNP   1,098
John Peverelle, Eng. Dem.   275
Steve Satch, Ind.   144
C. majority 2,691 (5.10%)
Notional 0.42% swing LD to C.
(2005: C. majority 2,088 (4.26%))

§WIGAN
E. 75,564   T. 44,140 (58.41%)   Lab. hold
*Lisa Nandy, Lab.   21,404
Michael Winstanley, C.   10,917
Mark Clayton, LD   6,797
Alan Freeman, UKIP   2,516
Charles Mather, BNP   2,506
Lab. majority 10,487 (23.76%)
Notional 7.69% swing Lab. to C.
(2005: Lab. majority 15,501 (39.15%))

§WILTSHIRE NORTH
E. 66,313   T. 48,699 (73.44%)   C. hold
James Gray, C.   25,114
Mike Evemy, LD   17,631
Jason Hughes, Lab.   3,239
Charles Bennett, UKIP   1,908
Phil Chamberlain, Green   599
Philip Allnatt, Ind.   208
C. majority 7,483 (15.37%)
Notional 0.01% swing LD to C.
(2005: C. majority 6,888 (15.34%))

§WILTSHIRE SOUTH WEST
E. 71,645   T. 49,018 (68.42%)   C. hold
Andrew Murrison, C.   25,321
Trevor Carbin, LD   14,954
Rebecca Rennison, Lab.   5,613
Michael Cuthbert-Murray, UKIP   2,684
Crispin Black, Ind.   446
C. majority 10,367 (21.15%)
Notional 1.15% swing LD to C.
(2005: C. majority 8,568 (18.85%))

§WIMBLEDON
E. 65,723   T. 47,395 (72.11%)   C. hold
Stephen Hammond, C.   23,257
Shas Sheehan, LD   11,849
Andrew Judge, Lab.   10,550
Mark McAleer, UKIP   914
Rajeev Thacker, Green   590
David Martin, Ch. P.   235
C. majority 11,408 (24.07%)
Notional 0.42% swing LD to C.
(2005: C. majority 2,480 (5.69%))

§WINCHESTER
E. 73,806   T. 55,955 (75.81%)   C. gain
*Steve Brine, C.   27,155
Martin Tod, LD   24,107
Patrick Davies, Lab.   3,051
Jocelyn Penn-Bull, UKIP   1,139
Mark Lancaster, Eng. Dem.   503
C. majority 3,048 (5.45%)
Notional 9.09% swing LD to C.
(2005: LD majority 6,524 (12.74%))

§WINDSOR
E. 69,511   T. 49,588 (71.34%)   C. hold
Adam Afriyie, C.   30,172
Julian Tisi, LD   11,118
Amanjit Jhund, Lab.   4,910
John-Paul Rye, UKIP   1,612
Peter Phillips, BNP   950
Derek Wall, Green   628
Peter Hooper, Ind.   198
C. majority 19,054 (38.42%)
Notional 8.05% swing LD to C.
(2005: C. majority 9,605 (22.32%))

§WIRRAL SOUTH
E. 56,099   T. 39,906 (71.13%)   Lab. hold
*Alison McGovern, Lab.   16,276
Jeff Clarke, C.   15,745
Jamie Saddler, LD   6,611
David Scott, UKIP   1,274
Lab. majority 531 (1.33%)
Notional 3.98% swing Lab. to C.
(2005: Lab. majority 3,538 (9.30%))

§WIRRAL WEST
E. 55,050   T. 39,372 (71.52%)   C. hold
*Esther McVey, C.   16,726
Phillip Davies, Lab.   14,290
Peter Reisdorf, LD   6,630
Philip Griffiths, UKIP   899
David Kirwan, Ind.   506
David James, CSP   321
C. majority 2,436 (6.19%)
Notional 2.34% swing Lab. to C.
(2005: C. majority 569 (1.51%))

§WITHAM
E. 66,750   T. 46,835 (70.16%)   C. hold
*Priti Patel, C.   24,448
Margaret Phelps, LD   9,252
John Spademan, Lab.   8,656
David Hodges, UKIP   3,060
James Abbott, Green   1,419
C. majority 15,196 (32.45%)
Notional 1.06% swing C. to LD
(2005: C. majority 7,241 (17.29%))

§WITNEY
E. 78,766   T. 57,769 (73.34%)   C. hold
David Cameron, C.   33,973
Dawn Barnes, LD   11,233
Joe Goldberg, Lab.   7,511
Stuart Macdonald, Green   2,385
Nikolai Tolstoy, UKIP   2,001
Howling Hope, Loony   234
Paul Wesson, Ind.   166
Johnnie Cook, Ind.   151
Colin Bex, Wessex Reg.   62
Aaron Barschak, Ind.   53
C. majority 22,740 (39.36%)
Notional 6.29% swing LD to C.
(2005: C. majority 13,874 (26.78%))

WOKING
E. 73,838   T. 52,786 (71.49%)   C. hold
*Jonathan Lord, C.   26,551
Rosie Sharpley, LD   19,744
Tom Miller, Lab.   4,246
Rob Burberry, UKIP   1,997
Julie Roxburgh, PPN-V   204
Ruth Temple, Magna Carta   44
C. majority 6,807 (12.90%)
0.73% swing C. to LD
(2005: C. majority 6,612 (14.36%))

§WOKINGHAM
E. 76,219   T. 54,528 (71.54%)   C. hold
John Redwood, C.   28,754
Prue Bray, LD   15,262
George Davidson, Lab.   5,516
Mark Ashwell, Ind.   2,340
Ann Zebedee, UKIP   1,664
Marjory Bisset, Green   567
Top Cat Owen, Loony   329
Robin Smith, Ind.   96
C. majority 13,492 (24.74%)
Notional 4.65% swing LD to C.
(2005: C. majority 7,257 (15.44%))

§WOLVERHAMPTON NORTH EAST
E. 59,324   T. 34,894 (58.82%)   Lab. hold
*Emma Reynolds, Lab.   14,448
Julie Rook, C.   11,964
Colin Ross, LD   4,711
Simon Patten, BNP   2,296
Paul Valdmanis, UKIP   1,138
Shangara Bhatoe, Soc. Lab.   337
Lab. majority 2,484 (7.12%)
Notional 9.00% swing Lab. to C.
(2005: Lab. majority 8,628 (25.12%))

§WOLVERHAMPTON SOUTH EAST
E. 60,450   T. 34,707 (57.41%)   Lab. hold
Pat McFadden, Lab.   16,505
Ken Wood, C.   9,912
Richard Whitehouse, LD   5,277
Gordon Fanthom, UKIP   2,675
Sudhir Handa, Ind.   338
Lab. majority 6,593 (19.00%)
Notional 8.79% swing Lab. to C.
(2005: Lab. majority 12,309 (36.58%))

§WOLVERHAMPTON SOUTH WEST
E. 59,160   T. 40,160 (67.88%)   C. gain
*Paul Uppal, C.   16,344
Rob Marris, Lab.   15,653
Robin Lawrence, LD   6,430
Amanda Mobberley, UKIP   1,487
Raymond Barry, Parenting   246
C. majority 691 (1.72%)
Notional 3.52% swing Lab. to C.
(2005: Lab. majority 2,114 (5.31%))

WORCESTER
E. 72,831   T. 48,974 (67.24%)   C. gain
*Robin Walker, C.   19,358
Michael Foster, Lab.   16,376
Jackie Alderson, LD   9,525
Jack Bennett, UKIP   1,360
Spencer Lee Kirby, BNP   1,219
Louis Stephen, Green   735
Andrew Robinson, Pirate   173
Peter Nielsen, Ind.   129
Andrew Christian-Brookes, Ind.   99
C. majority 2,982 (6.09%)
6.43% swing Lab. to C.
(2005: Lab. majority 3,144 (6.78%))

§WORCESTERSHIRE MID
E. 72,171   T. 50,931 (70.57%)   C. hold
Peter Luff, C.   27,770
Margaret Rowley, LD   11,906
Robin Lunn, Lab.   7,613
John White, UKIP   3,049
Gordon Matthews, Green   593
C. majority 15,864 (31.15%)
Notional 0.04% swing LD to C.
(2005: C. majority 12,906 (27.33%))

§WORCESTERSHIRE WEST
E. 73,270   T. 54,093 (73.83%)   C. hold
*Harriett Baldwin, C.   27,213
Richard Burt, LD   20,459
Penelope Barber, Lab.   3,661
Caroline Bovey, UKIP   2,119
Malcolm Victory, Green   641
C. majority 6,754 (12.49%)
Notional 3.23% swing LD to C.
(2005: C. majority 3,053 (6.03%))

§WORKINGTON
E. 59,607   T. 39,259 (65.86%)   Lab. hold
Tony Cunningham, Lab.   17,865
Judith Pattinson, C.   13,290
Stan Collins, LD   5,318
Martin Wingfield, BNP   1,496
Stephen Lee, UKIP   876
Rob Logan, Eng. Dem.   414
Lab. majority 4,575 (11.65%)
Notional 5.66% swing Lab. to C.
(2005: Lab. majority 8,226 (22.97%))

§WORSLEY & ECCLES SOUTH
E. 72,473   T. 41,701 (57.54%)   Lab. hold
Barbara Keeley, Lab.   17,892
Iain Lindley, C.   13,555
Richard Gadsden, LD   6,883
Andrew Townsend, UKIP   2,037
Paul Whitelegg, Eng. Dem.   1,334
Lab. majority 4,337 (10.40%)
Notional 7.61% swing Lab. to C.
(2005: Lab. majority 10,001 (25.62%))

§WORTHING EAST & SHOREHAM
E. 74,001   T. 48,397 (65.40%)   C. hold
Tim Loughton, C.   23,458
James Doyle, LD   12,353
Emily Benn, Lab.   8,087
Mike Glennon, UKIP   2,984
Susan Board, Green   1,126
Clive Maltby, Eng. Dem.   389
C. majority 11,105 (22.95%)
Notional 1.70% swing LD to C.
(2005: C. majority 8,180 (18.37%))

§WORTHING WEST
E. 75,945   T. 49,123 (64.68%)   C. hold
Peter Bottomley, C.   25,416
Hazel Thorpe, LD   13,687
Ian Ross, Lab.   5,800
John Wallace, UKIP   2,924
David Aherne, Green   996
Stuart Dearsley, Christian   300
C. majority 11,729 (23.88%)
Notional 1.50% swing LD to C.
(2005: C. majority 9,383 (20.89%))

§WREKIN, THE
E. 65,544   T. 45,968 (70.13%)   C. hold
Mark Pritchard, C.   21,922
Paul Kalinauckas, Lab. (Co-op)   12,472
Ali Cameron-Daw, LD   8,019
Malcolm Hurst, UKIP   2,050
Susan Harwood, BNP   1,505
C. majority 9,450 (20.56%)
Notional 8.85% swing Lab. (Co-op) to C.
(2005: C. majority 1,187 (2.85%))

§WYCOMBE
E. 74,502   T. 48,151 (64.63%)   C. hold
*Steven Baker, C.   23,423
Steve Guy, LD   13,863
Andrew Lomas, Lab.   8,326
John Wiseman, UKIP   2,123
Madassar Khokar, Ind.   228
David Fitton, Ind.   188
C. majority 9,560 (19.85%)
Notional 4.83% swing C. to LD
(2005: C. majority 7,597 (17.29%))

§WYRE & PRESTON NORTH
E. 71,201   T. 51,308 (72.06%)   C. hold
*Ben Wallace, C.   26,877
Danny Gallagher, LD   11,033
Cat Smith, Lab.   10,932
Nigel Cecil, UKIP   2,466
C. majority 15,844 (30.88%)
Notional 3.86% swing C. to LD
(2005: C. majority 12,082 (27.51%))

§WYRE FOREST
E. 76,711   T. 50,899 (66.35%)   C. gain
*Mark Garnier, C.   18,793
Dr Richard Taylor, Ind. CHC   16,150
Nigel Knowles, Lab.   7,298
Neville Farmer, LD   6,040
Michael Wrench, UKIP   1,498
Gordon Howells, BNP   1,120
C. majority 2,643 (5.19%)
Notional 7.35% swing Ind. CHC to C.
(2005: Ind. CHC majority 4,613 (9.51%))

WYTHENSHAWE & SALE EAST
E. 79,923   T. 40,751 (50.99%)   Lab. hold
Paul Goggins, Lab.   17,987
Janet Clowes, C.   10,412
Martin Eakins, LD   9,107
Bernard Todd, BNP   1,572
Chris Cassidy, UKIP   1,405
Lynn Worthington, TUSC   268
Lab. majority 7,575 (18.59%)
5.67% swing Lab. to C.
(2005: Lab. majority 10,827 (29.92%))

§YEOVIL
E. 82,314   T. 57,160 (69.44%)   LD hold
David Laws, LD   31,843
Kevin Davis, C.   18,807
Lee Skevington, Lab.   2,991
Nigel Pearson, UKIP   2,357
Robert Baehr, BNP   1,162
LD majority 13,036 (22.81%)
Notional 2.74% swing C. to LD
(2005: LD majority 8,779 (17.33%))

§YORK CENTRAL
E. 74,908   T. 46,483 (62.05%)   Lab. hold
Hugh Bayley, Lab.   18,573
Susan Wade Weeks, C.   12,122
Christian Vassie, LD   11,694
Andy Chase, Green   1,669
Jeff Kelly, BNP   1,171
Paul Abbott, UKIP   1,100
Eddie Vee, Loony   154
Lab. majority 6,451 (13.88%)
Notional 6.02% swing Lab. to C.
(2005: Lab. majority 10,344 (25.92%))

§YORK OUTER
E. 74,965 T. 53,300 (71.10%) C. gain
*Julian Sturdy, C.   22,912
Madeleine Kirk, LD   19,224
James Alexander, Lab.   9,108
Judith Morris, UKIP   1,100
Cathy Smurthwaite, BNP   956
C. majority 3,688 (6.92%)
Notional 3.68% swing LD to C.
(2005: LD majority 203 (0.44%))

§YORKSHIRE EAST
E. 80,342 T. 51,254 (63.79%) C. hold
Greg Knight, C.   24,328
Robert Adamson, LD   10,842
Paul Rounding, Lab.   10,401
Chris Daniels, UKIP   2,142
Gary Pudsey, BNP   1,865
Ray Allerston, Soc. Dem.   914
Michael Jackson, Green   762
C. majority 13,486 (26.31%)
Notional 0.06% swing C. to LD
(2005: C. majority 6,284 (13.31%))

WALES

ABERAVON
E. 50,789 T. 30,958 (60.95%) Lab. hold
Hywel Francis, Lab.   16,073
Keith Davies, LD   5,034
Caroline Jones, C.   4,411
Paul Nicholls-Jones, PC   2,198
Kevin Edwards, BNP   1,276
Andrew Tutton, Ind.   919
Captain Beany, Bean   558
Joe Callan, UKIP   489
Lab. majority 11,039 (35.66%)
5.32% swing Lab. to LD
(2005: Lab. majority 13,937 (46.30%))

§ABERCONWY
E. 44,593 T. 29,966 (67.20%) C. gain
*Guto Bebb, C.   10,734
Ronald Hughes, Lab.   7,336
Mike Priestley, LD   5,786
Phil Edwards, PC   5,341
Mike Wieteska, UKIP   632
Louise Wynne-Jones, Ch. P.   137
C. majority 3,398 (11.34%)
Notional 7.63% swing Lab. to C.
(2005: Lab. majority 1,070 (3.93%))

ALYN & DEESIDE
E. 60,931 T. 39,923 (65.52%) Lab. hold
Mark Tami, Lab.   15,804
Will Gallagher, C.   12,885
Paul Brighton, LD   7,308
Maurice Jones, PC   1,549
John Walker, BNP   1,368
James Howson, UKIP   1,009
Lab. majority 2,919 (7.31%)
8.15% swing Lab. to C.
(2005: Lab. majority 8,378 (23.60%))

§ARFON
E. 41,198 T. 26,078 (63.30%) PC gain
Hywel Williams, PC   9,383
Alan Pugh, Lab.   7,928
Robin Millar, C.   4,416
Sarah Green, LD   3,666
Elwyn Williams, UKIP   685
PC majority 1,455 (5.58%)
Notional 3.70% swing Lab. to PC
(2005: Lab. majority 456 (1.82%))

BLAENAU GWENT
E. 52,438 T. 32,395 (61.78%) Lab. gain
*Nick Smith, Lab.   16,974
Dai Davies, Blaenau Voice   6,458
Matt Smith, LD   3,285
Liz Stevenson, C.   2,265
Rhodri Davies, PC   1,333
Anthony King, BNP   1,211
Mike Kocan, UKIP   488
Alyson O'Connell, Soc. Lab.   381
Lab. majority 10,516 (32.46%)
(2005: Ind. Law majority 9,121
(25.87%))(2006: Ind. Davies majority
2,484 (9.14%))

BRECON & RADNORSHIRE
E. 53,589 T. 38,845 (72.49%) LD hold
Roger Williams, LD   17,929
Suzy Davies, C.   14,182
Christopher Lloyd, Lab.   4,096
Janet Davies, PC   989
Clive Easton, UKIP   876
Dorienne Robinson, Green   341
Jeffrey Green, Ch. P.   222
Lord Offa, Loony   210
LD majority 3,747 (9.65%)
0.27% swing LD to C.
(2005: LD majority 3,905 (10.18%))

§BRIDGEND
E. 58,700 T. 38,347 (65.33%) Lab. hold
Madeleine Moon, Lab.   13,931
Helen Baker, C.   11,668
Wayne Morgan, LD   8,658
Nick Thomas, PC   2,269
Brian Urch, BNP   1,020
David Fulton, UKIP   801
Lab. majority 2,263 (5.90%)
Notional 5.98% swing Lab. to C.
(2005: Lab. majority 6,089 (17.87%))

§CAERPHILLY
E. 62,134 T. 38,992 (62.75%) Lab. hold
Wayne David, Lab.   17,377
Maria Caulfield, C.   6,622
Lindsay Whittle, PC   6,460
Kay David, LD   5,988
Laurence Reid, BNP   1,635
Tony Jenkins, UKIP   910
Lab. majority 10,755 (27.58%)
Notional 6.57% swing Lab. to C.
(2005: Lab. majority 13,517 (37.32%))

CARDIFF CENTRAL
E. 61,162 T. 36,151 (59.11%) LD hold
Jenny Willott, LD   14,976
Jenny Rathbone, Lab.   10,400
Karen Robson, C.   7,799
Chris Williams, PC   1,246
Susan Davies, UKIP   765
Sam Coates, Green   575
Ross Saunders, TUSC   162
Mark Beech, Loony   142
Alun Mathias, Ind.   86
LD majority 4,576 (12.66%)
1.41% swing LD to Lab.
(2005: LD majority 5,593 (15.48%))

CARDIFF NORTH
E. 65,553 T. 47,630 (72.66%) C. gain
*Jonathan Evans, C.   17,860
Julie Morgan, Lab.   17,666
John Dixon, LD   8,724
Llywelyn Rhys, PC   1,588
Lawrence Gwynn, UKIP   1,130
Christopher von Ruhland, Green   362
Derek Thomson, Ch. P.   300
C. majority 194 (0.41%)
1.47% swing Lab. to C.
(2005: Lab. majority 1,146 (2.53%))

§CARDIFF SOUTH & PENARTH
E. 73,704 T. 44,370 (60.20%)
                        Lab. (Co-op) hold
Alun Michael, Lab. (Co-op)   17,263
Simon Hoare, C.   12,553
Dominic Hannigan, LD   9,875
Farida Aslam, PC   1,851
Simon Zeigler, UKIP   1,145
George Burke, Ind.   648
Matt Townsend, Green   554
Clive Bate, Ch. P.   285
Robert Griffiths, Comm   196
Lab. (Co-op) majority 4,710 (10.62%)
Notional 6.03% swing Lab. (Co-op) to C.
(2005: Lab. (Co-op) majority 8,955
(22.68%))

§CARDIFF WEST
E. 62,787 T. 40,957 (65.23%) Lab. hold
Kevin Brennan, Lab.   16,893
Angela Jones-Evans, C.   12,143
Rachael Hitchinson, LD   7,186
Mohammed Sarul Islam, PC   2,868
Mike Henessey, UKIP   1,117
Jake Griffiths, Green   750
Lab. majority 4,750 (11.60%)
Notional 5.33% swing Lab. to C.
(2005: Lab. majority 8,361 (22.25%))

§CARMARTHEN EAST & DINEFWR
E. 52,385 T. 38,011 (72.56%) PC hold
*Jonathan Edwards, PC   13,546
Christine Gwyther, Lab.   10,065
Andrew Morgan, C.   8,506
Bill Powell, LD   4,609
John Atkinson, UKIP   1,285
PC majority 3,481 (9.16%)
Notional 4.19% swing PC to Lab.
(2005: PC majority 6,551 (17.54%))

§CARMARTHEN WEST &
PEMBROKESHIRE SOUTH
E. 57,519 T. 40,507 (70.42%) C. gain
*Simon Hart, C.   16,649
Nick Ainger, Lab.   13,226
John Gossage, LD   4,890
John Dixon, PC   4,232
Ray Clarke, UKIP   1,146
Henry Langen, Ind.   364
C. majority 3,423 (8.45%)
Notional 6.88% swing Lab. to C.
(2005: Lab. majority 2,043 (5.32%))

§CEREDIGION
E. 59,043 T. 38,258 (64.80%) LD hold
Mark Williams, LD   19,139
Penri James, PC   10,815
Luke Evetts, C.   4,421
Richard Boudier, Lab.   2,210
Elwyn Williams, UKIP   977
Leila Kiersch, Green   696
LD majority 8,324 (21.76%)
Notional 10.57% swing PC to LD
(2005: LD majority 218 (0.61%))

§CLWYD SOUTH
E. 53,748 T. 34,681 (64.53%) Lab. hold
*Susan Elan Jones, Lab.   13,311
John Bell, C.   10,477
Bruce Roberts, LD   5,965
Janet Ryder, PC   3,009
Sarah Hynes, BNP   1,100
Nick Powell, UKIP   819
Lab. majority 2,834 (8.17%)
Notional 5.83% swing Lab. to C.
(2005: Lab. majority 6,220 (19.84%))

§CLWYD WEST
E. 57,913 T. 38,111 (65.81%) C. hold
David Jones, C.   15,833
Donna Hutton, Lab.   9,414
Llyr Huws Gruffydd, PC   5,864
Michele Jones, LD   5,801
Warwick Nicholson, UKIP   864
Revd Dr David Griffiths, Ch. P.   239
Joe Blakesley, Ind.   96
C. majority 6,419 (16.84%)
Notional 8.35% swing Lab. to C.
(2005: C. majority 51 (0.14%))

§CYNON VALLEY
E. 50,656 T. 29,876 (58.98%) Lab. hold
Ann Clwyd, Lab.   15,681
Dafydd Trystan Davies, PC   6,064
Lee Thacker, LD   4,120
Juliette Ash, C.   3,010
Frank Hughes, UKIP   1,001
Lab. majority 9,617 (32.19%)
Notional 8.65% swing Lab. to PC
(2005: Lab. majority 14,390 (49.48%))

DELYN
E. 53,470 T. 36,984 (69.17%) Lab. hold
David Hanson, Lab.   15,083
Antoinette Sandbach, C.   12,811
Bill Brereton, LD   5,747
Peter Ryder, PC   1,844
Jennifer Matthys, BNP   844
Andrew Haigh, UKIP   655
Lab. majority 2,272 (6.14%)
6.70% swing Lab. to C.
(2005: Lab. majority 6,644 (19.54%))

§DWYFOR MEIRIONNYDD
E. 45,354 T. 28,906 (63.73%) PC hold
Elfyn Llwyd, PC   12,814
Simon Baynes, C.   6,447
Alwyn Humphreys, Lab.   4,021
Steve Churchman, LD   3,538
Louise Hughes, Ind.   1,310
Frank Wykes, UKIP   776
PC majority 6,367 (22.03%)
Notional 7.28% swing PC to C.
(2005: PC majority 8,706 (29.02%))

§GOWER
E. 61,696 T. 41,671 (67.54%) Lab. hold
Martin Caton, Lab.   16,016
Byron Davies, C.   13,333
Mike Day, LD   7,947
Darren Price, PC   2,760
Adrian Jones, BNP   963
Gordon Triggs, UKIP   652
Lab. majority 2,683 (6.44%)
Notional 5.26% swing Lab. to C.
(2005: Lab. majority 6,703 (16.95%))

§ISLWYN
E. 54,826 T. 34,690 (63.27%)
                    Lab. (Co-op) hold
*Christopher Evans, Lab. (Co-op) 17,069
Daniel Thomas, C.   4,854
Steffan Lewis, PC   4,518
Asghar Ali, LD   3,597
Dave Rees, Ind.   1,495
John Voisey, BNP   1,320
Jason Crew, UKIP   936
Paul Taylor, Ind.   901
Lab. (Co-op) majority 12,215 (35.21%)
Notional 9.05% swing Lab. (Co-op) to C.
(2005: Lab. (Co-op) majority 17,582
(51.91%))

LLANELLI
E. 55,637 T. 37,461 (67.33%) Lab. hold
Nia Griffith, Lab.   15,916
Myfanwy Davies, PC   11,215
Christopher Salmon, C.   5,381
Myrddin Edwards, LD   3,902
Andrew Marshall, UKIP   1,047
Lab. majority 4,701 (12.55%)
3.96% swing Lab. to PC
(2005: Lab. majority 7,234 (20.47%))

MERTHYR TYDFIL & RHYMNEY
E. 54,715 T. 32,076 (58.62%) Lab. hold
Dai Havard, Lab.   14,007
Amy Kitcher, LD   9,951
Maria Hill, C.   2,412
Clive Tovey, Ind.   1,845
Glyndwr Cennydd Jones, PC   1,621
Richard Barnes, BNP   1,173
Adam Brown, UKIP   872
Alan Cowdell, Soc. Lab.   195
Lab. majority 4,056 (12.64%)
16.92% swing Lab. to LD
(2005: Lab. majority 13,934 (46.48%))

MONMOUTH
E. 62,768 T. 46,519 (74.11%) C. hold
David Davies, C.   22,466
Hamish Sandison, Lab.   12,041
Martin Blakebrough, LD   9,026
Jonathan Clark, PC   1,273
Derek Rowe, UKIP   1,126
Steve Millson, Green   587
C. majority 10,425 (22.41%)
6.25% swing Lab. to C.
(2005: C. majority 4,527 (9.92%))

§MONTGOMERYSHIRE
E. 48,730 T. 33,813 (69.39%) C. gain
*Glyn Davies, C.   13,976
Lembit Opik, LD   12,792
Heledd Fychan, PC   2,802
Nick Colbourne, Lab.   2,407
David Rowlands, UKIP   1,128
Milton Ellis, NF   384
Bruce Lawson, Ind.   324
C. majority 1,184 (3.50%)
Notional 13.15% swing LD to C.
(2005: LD majority 7,048 (22.80%))

§NEATH
E. 57,186 T. 37,122 (64.91%) Lab. hold
Peter Hain, Lab.   17,172
Alun Llewelyn, PC   7,397
Frank Little, LD   5,535
Emmeline Owens, C.   4,847
Michael Green, BNP   1,342
James Bevan, UKIP   829
Lab. majority 9,775 (26.33%)
Notional 4.58% swing Lab. to PC
(2005: Lab. majority 12,710 (35.49%))

NEWPORT EAST
E. 54,437 T. 34,448 (63.28%) Lab. hold
Jessica Morden, Lab.   12,744
Ed Townsend, LD   11,094
Dawn Parry, C.   7,918
Keith Jones, BNP   1,168
Fiona Cross, PC   724
David Rowlands, UKIP   677
Liz Screen, Soc. Lab.   123
Lab. majority 1,650 (4.79%)
8.35% swing Lab. to LD
(2005: Lab. majority 6,838 (21.49%))

NEWPORT WEST
E. 62,111 T. 39,720 (63.95%) Lab. hold
Paul Flynn, Lab.   16,389
Matthew Williams, C.   12,845
Veronica German, LD   6,587
Timothy Windsor, BNP   1,183
Hugh Moelwyn Hughes, UKIP   1,144
Jeff Rees, PC   1,122
Pippa Bartolotti, Green   450
Lab. majority 3,544 (8.92%)
3.18% swing Lab. to C.
(2005: Lab. majority 5,458 (15.27%))

§OGMORE
E. 55,527 T. 34,650 (62.40%) Lab. hold
Huw Irranca-Davies, Lab.   18,644
Emma Moore, C.   5,398
Jackie Radford, LD   5,260
Danny Clark, PC   3,326
Kay Thomas, BNP   1,242
Carolyn Passey, UKIP   780
Lab. majority 13,246 (38.23%)
Notional 4.28% swing Lab. to C.
(2005: Lab. majority 14,839 (46.29%))

§PONTYPRIDD
E. 58,219 T. 36,671 (62.99%) Lab. hold
*Owen Smith, Lab.   14,220
Michael Powell, LD   11,435
Lee Gonzalez, C.   5,932
Ioan Bellin, PC   2,673
David Bevan, UKIP   1,229
Simon Parsons, Soc. Lab.   456
Donald Watson, Ch. P.   365
John Matthews, Green   361
Lab. majority 2,785 (7.59%)
Notional 13.31% swing Lab. to LD
(2005: Lab. majority 11,694 (34.21%))

§PRESELI PEMBROKESHIRE
E. 57,419 T. 39,602 (68.97%) C. hold
Stephen Crabb, C.   16,944
Mari Rees, Lab.   12,339
Nick Tregoning, LD   5,759
Henry Jones-Davies, PC   3,654
Richard Lawson, UKIP   906
C. majority 4,605 (11.63%)
Notional 5.05% swing Lab. to C.
(2005: C. majority 601 (1.53%))

RHONDDA
E. 51,554 T. 31,072 (60.27%) Lab. hold
Chris Bryant, Lab.   17,183
Geraint Davies, PC   5,630
Paul Wasley, LD   3,309
Philip Howe, Ind.   2,599
Juliet Henderson, C.   1,993
Taffy John, UKIP   358
Lab. majority 11,553 (37.18%)
7.48% swing Lab. to PC
(2005: Lab. majority 16,242 (52.14%))

SWANSEA EAST
E. 59,823 T. 32,676 (54.62%) Lab. hold
Sian James, Lab.   16,819
Robert Speht, LD   5,981
Christian Holliday, C.   4,823
Dic Jones, PC   2,181
Clive Bennett, BNP   1,715
David Rogers, UKIP   839
Tony Young, Green   318
Lab. majority 10,838 (33.17%)
1.66% swing Lab. to LD
(2005: Lab. majority 11,249 (36.48%))

SWANSEA WEST
E. 61,334 T. 35,593 (58.03%) Lab. hold
*Geraint Davies, Lab.   12,335
Peter May, LD   11,831
Rene Kinzett, C.   7,407
Harri Roberts, PC   1,437
Alan Bateman, BNP   910
Tim Jenkins, UKIP   716
Keith Ross, Green   404
Ian McCloy, Ind.   374
Rob Williams, TUSC   179
Lab. majority 504 (1.42%)
5.74% swing Lab. to LD
(2005: Lab. majority 4,269 (12.90%))

TORFAEN
E. 61,178 T. 37,640 (61.53%) Lab. hold
Paul Murphy, Lab.   16,847
Jonathan Burns, C.   7,541
David Morgan, LD   6,264
Rhys ab Elis, PC   2,005
Jennifer Noble, BNP   1,657
Fred Wildgust, Ind.   1,419
Gareth Dunn, UKIP   862
Richard Turner-Thomas, Ind.   607
Owen Clarke, Green   438
Lab. majority 9,306 (24.72%)
8.19% swing Lab. to C.
(2005: Lab. majority 14,791 (41.11%))

§VALE OF CLWYD
E. 55,781 T. 35,534 (63.70%) Lab. hold
Chris Ruane, Lab.   15,017
Matt Wright, C.   12,508
Paul Penlington, LD   4,472
Caryl Wyn Jones, PC   2,068
Ian Si'Ree, BNP   827
Tom Turner, UKIP   515
Mike Butler, Green Soc.   127
Lab. majority 2,509 (7.06%)
Notional 3.56% swing Lab. to C.
(2005: Lab. majority 4,629 (14.18%))

§VALE OF GLAMORGAN
E. 70,262 T. 48,667 (69.27%)   C. gain
*Alun Cairns, C.   20,341
Alana Davies, Lab.   16,034
Eluned Parrott, LD   7,403
Ian Johnson, PC   2,667
Kevin Mahoney, UKIP   1,529
Rhodri Thomas, Green   457
John Harrold, Ch. P.   236
C. majority 4,307 (8.85%)
Notional 6.11% swing Lab. to C.
(2005: Lab. majority 1,574 (3.37%))

WREXHAM
E. 50,872 T. 32,976 (64.82%) Lab. hold
Ian Lucas, Lab.   12,161
Tom Rippeth, LD   8,503
Gareth Hughes, C.   8,375
Arfon Jones, PC   2,029
Melvin Roberts, BNP   1,134
John Humberstone, UKIP   774
Lab. majority 3,658 (11.09%)
5.67% swing Lab. to LD
(2005: Lab. majority 6,819 (22.44%))

YNYS MON
E. 50,075 T. 34,444 (68.78%) Lab. hold
Albert Owen, Lab.   11,490
Dylan Rees, PC   9,029
Anthony Ridge-Newman, C.   7,744
Matt Wood, LD   2,592
Peter Rogers, Ind.   2,225
Elaine Gill, UKIP   1,201
The Rev David Owen, Ch. P.   163
Lab. majority 2,461 (7.14%)
1.82% swing PC to Lab.
(2005: Lab. majority 1,242 (3.50%))

SCOTLAND

ABERDEEN NORTH
E. 64,808 T. 37,701 (58.17%) Lab. hold
Frank Doran, Lab.   16,746
Joanna Strathdee, SNP   8,385
Kristian Chapman, LD   7,001
Stewart Whyte, C.   4,666
Roy Jones, BNP   635
Ewan Robertson, SSP   268
Lab. majority 8,361 (22.18%)
1.00% swing SNP to Lab.
(2005: Lab. majority 6,795 (18.55%))

ABERDEEN SOUTH
E. 64,031 T. 43,034 (67.21%) Lab. hold
Anne Begg, Lab.   15,722
John Sleigh, LD   12,216
Amanda Harvie, C.   8,914
Mark McDonald, SNP   5,102
Susan Ross, BNP   529
Rhonda Reekie, Green   413
Robert Green, SACL   138
Lab. majority 3,506 (8.15%)
2.45% swing LD to Lab.
(2005: Lab. majority 1,348 (3.24%))

ABERDEENSHIRE WEST &
KINCARDINE
E. 66,110 T. 45,195 (68.36%) LD hold
Sir Robert Smith, LD   17,362
Alex Johnstone, C.   13,678
Dennis Robertson, SNP   7,086
Greg Williams, Lab.   6,159
Gary Raikes, BNP   513
Anthony Atkinson, UKIP   397
LD majority 3,684 (8.15%)
4.89% swing LD to C.
(2005: LD majority 7,471 (17.94%))

AIRDRIE & SHOTTS
E. 62,364 T. 35,849 (57.48%) Lab. hold
*Pamela Nash, Lab.   20,849
Sophia Coyle, SNP   8,441
Ruth Whitfield, C.   3,133
John Love, LD   2,898
John McGeechan, Ind.   528
Lab. majority 12,408 (34.61%)
3.93% swing Lab. to SNP
(2005: Lab. majority 14,084 (42.48%))

ANGUS
E. 62,863 T. 37,960 (60.39%) SNP hold
Mike Weir, SNP   15,020
Alberto Costa, C.   11,738
Kevin Hutchens, Lab.   6,535
Sanjay Samani, LD   4,090
Martin Gray, UKIP   577
SNP majority 3,282 (8.65%)
2.22% swing C. to SNP
(2005: SNP majority 1,601 (4.20%))

ARGYLL & BUTE
E. 67,165 T. 45,207 (67.31%) LD hold
Alan Reid, LD   14,292
Gary Mulvaney, C.   10,861
David Graham, Lab.   10,274
Michael MacKenzie, SNP   8,563
Elaine Morrison, Green   789
George Doyle, Ind.   272
John Black, Jacobite   156
LD majority 3,431 (7.59%)
2.72% swing LD to C.
(2005: LD majority 5,636 (13.04%))

AYR, CARRICK & CUMNOCK
E. 73,320 T. 45,893 (62.59%) Lab. hold
Sandra Osborne, Lab.   21,632
William Grant, C.   11,721
Charles Brodie, SNP   8,276
James Taylor, LD   4,264
Lab. majority 9,911 (21.60%)
0.30% swing Lab. to C.
(2005: Lab. majority 9,997 (22.19%))

AYRSHIRE CENTRAL
E. 68,352 T. 43,915 (64.25%) Lab. hold
Brian Donohoe, Lab.   20,950
Maurice Golden, C.   8,943
John Mullen, SNP   8,364
Andrew Chamberlain, LD   5,236
James McDaid, Soc. Lab.   422
Lab. majority 12,007 (27.34%)
1.51% swing C. to Lab.
(2005: Lab. majority 10,423 (24.31%))

AYRSHIRE NORTH & ARRAN
E. 74,953 T. 46,116 (61.53%) Lab. hold
Katy Clark, Lab.	21,860
Patricia Gibson, SNP	11,965
Philip Lardner, C.	7,212
Gillian Cole-Hamilton, LD	4,630
Louise McDaid, Soc. Lab.	449

Lab. majority 9,895 (21.46%)
2.26% swing Lab. to SNP
(2005: Lab. majority 11,296 (25.55%))

BANFF & BUCHAN
E. 64,300 T. 38,466 (59.82%) SNP hold
*Eilidh Whiteford, SNP	15,868
Jimmy Buchan, C.	11,841
Glen Reynolds, Lab.	5,382
Galen Milne, LD	4,365
Richard Payne, BNP	1,010

SNP majority 4,027 (10.47%)
10.67% swing SNP to C.
(2005: SNP majority 11,837 (31.81%))

BERWICKSHIRE, ROXBURGH &
SELKIRK
E. 73,826 T. 49,014 (66.39%) LD hold
Michael Moore, LD	22,230
John Lamont, C.	16,555
Ian Miller, Lab.	5,003
Paul Wheelhouse, SNP	4,497
Sherry Fowler, UKIP	595
Chris Black, Jacobite	134

LD majority 5,675 (11.58%)
0.71% swing LD to C.
(2005: LD majority 5,901 (13.00%))

CAITHNESS, SUTHERLAND & EASTER
ROSS
E. 47,257 T. 28,768 (60.88%) LD hold
John Thurso, LD	11,907
John Mackay, Lab.	7,081
Jean Urquhart, SNP	5,516
Alastair Graham, C.	3,744
Gordon Campbell, Ind.	520

LD majority 4,826 (16.78%)
6.38% swing LD to Lab.
(2005: LD majority 8,168 (29.53%))

COATBRIDGE, CHRYSTON &
BELLSHILL
E. 70,067 T. 41,635 (59.42%) Lab. hold
Tom Clarke, Lab.	27,728
Frances McGlinchey, SNP	7,014
Kenneth Elder, LD	3,519
Fiona Houston, C.	3,374

Lab. majority 20,714 (49.75%)
0.58% swing Lab. to SNP
(2005: Lab. majority 19,519 (50.90%))

CUMBERNAULD, KILSYTH &
KIRKINTILLOCH EAST
E. 64,037 T. 41,150 (64.26%) Lab. hold
*Gregg McClymont, Lab.	23,549
Julie Hepburn, SNP	9,794
Rod Ackland, LD	3,924
Stephanie Fraser, C.	3,407
William O'Neill, SSP	476

Lab. majority 13,755 (33.43%)
1.92% swing SNP to Lab.
(2005: Lab. majority 11,562 (29.58%))

DUMFRIES & GALLOWAY
E. 74,581 T. 52,173 (69.95%) Lab. hold
Russell Brown, Lab.	23,950
Peter Duncan, C.	16,501
Andrew Wood, SNP	6,419
Richard Brodie, LD	4,608
William Wright, UKIP	695

Lab. majority 7,449 (14.28%)
4.27% swing C. to Lab.
(2005: Lab. majority 2,922 (5.74%))

DUMFRIESSHIRE, CLYDESDALE &
TWEEDDALE
E. 66,627 T. 45,892 (68.88%) C. hold
David Mundell, C.	17,457
Claudia Beamish, Lab.	13,263
Catriona Bhatia, LD	9,080
Aileen Orr, SNP	4,945
Steven McKeane, UKIP	637
Alis Ballance, Green	510

C. majority 4,194 (9.14%)
2.62% swing Lab. to C.
(2005: C. majority 1,738 (3.90%))

DUNBARTONSHIRE EAST
E. 63,795 T. 47,948 (75.16%) LD hold
Jo Swinson, LD	18,551
Mary Galbraith, Lab.	16,367
Mark Nolan, C.	7,431
Iain White, SNP	5,054
James Beeley, UKIP	545

LD majority 2,184 (4.55%)
2.07% swing LD to Lab.
(2005: LD majority 4,061 (8.69%))

DUNBARTONSHIRE WEST
E. 66,085 T. 42,266 (63.96%)
                       Lab. (Co-op) hold
*Gemma Doyle, Lab. (Co-op)	25,905
Graeme McCormick, SNP	8,497
Helen Watt, LD	3,434
Martyn McIntyre, C.	3,242
Mitch Sorbie, UKIP	683
Katharine McGavigan, Soc. Lab.	505

Lab. (Co-op) majority 17,408 (41.19%)
5.50% swing SNP to Lab. (Co-op)
(2005: Lab. (Co-op) majority 12,553
(30.18%))

DUNDEE EAST
E. 65,471 T. 40,568 (61.96%) SNP hold
Stewart Hosie, SNP	15,350
Katrina Murray, Lab.	13,529
Chris Bustin, C.	6,177
Clive Sneddon, LD	4,285
Shiona Baird, Green	542
Mike Arthur, UKIP	431
Angela Gorrie, SSP	254

SNP majority 1,821 (4.49%)
1.76% swing Lab. to SNP
(2005: SNP majority 383 (0.97%))

DUNDEE WEST
E. 63,013 T. 37,126 (58.92%) Lab. hold
Jim McGovern, Lab.	17,994
Jim Barrie, SNP	10,716
John Barnett, LD	4,233
Colin Stewart, C.	3,461
Andy McBride, Ind.	365
Jim McFarlane, TUSC	357

Lab. majority 7,278 (19.60%)
2.52% swing SNP to Lab.
(2005: Lab. majority 5,379 (14.56%))

DUNFERMLINE & FIFE WEST
E. 73,769 T. 48,947 (66.35%) Lab. gain
*Thomas Docherty, Lab.	22,639
Willie Rennie, LD	17,169
Joe McCall, SNP	5,201
Belinda Hacking, C.	3,305
Otto Inglis, UKIP	633

Lab. majority 5,470 (11.18%)
8.05% swing Lab. to LD
(2005: Lab. majority 11,562
(27.27%))(2006: LD majority 1,800
(5.21%))

EAST KILBRIDE, STRATHAVEN &
LESMAHAGOW
E. 76,534 T. 50,946 (66.57%) Lab. hold
*Michael McCann, Lab.	26,241
John McKenna, SNP	11,738
Graham Simpson, C.	6,613
John Loughton, LD	5,052
Kirsten Robb, Green	1,003
John Houston, Ind.	299

Lab. majority 14,503 (28.47%)
1.19% swing Lab. to SNP
(2005: Lab. majority 14,723 (30.84%))

EAST LOTHIAN
E. 73,438 T. 49,161 (66.94%) Lab. hold
*Fiona O'Donnell, Lab.	21,919
Michael Veitch, C.	9,661
Stuart Ritchie, LD	8,288
Andrew Sharp, SNP	7,883
James Mackenzie, Green	862
Jon Lloyd, UKIP	548

Lab. majority 12,258 (24.93%)
0.28% swing Lab. to C.
(2005: Lab. majority 7,620 (16.65%))

EDINBURGH EAST
E. 60,941 T. 39,865 (65.42%) Lab. hold
*Sheila Gilmore, Lab.	17,314
George Kerevan, SNP	8,133
Beverley Hope, LD	7,751
Martin Donald, C.	4,358
Robin Harper, Green	2,035
Gary Clark, TUSC	274

Lab. majority 9,181 (23.03%)
0.01% swing SNP to Lab.
(2005: Lab. majority 6,202 (15.62%))

EDINBURGH NORTH & LEITH
E. 69,204 T. 47,356 (68.43%)
                       Lab. (Co-op) hold
Mark Lazarowicz, Lab. (Co-op)	17,740
Kevin Lang, LD	16,016
Iain McGill, C.	7,079
Calum Cashley, SNP	4,568
Kate Joester, Green	1,062
John Hein, Lib.	389
Willie Black, TUSC	233
David Jacobsen, Soc. Lab.	141
Cameron MacIntyre, Ind.	128

Lab. majority 1,724 (3.64%)
0.70% swing Lab. (Co-op) to LD
(2005: Lab. (Co-op) majority 2,153
(5.05%))

EDINBURGH SOUTH
E. 59,354 T. 43,801 (73.80%) Lab. hold
*Ian Murray, Lab.	15,215
Fred Mackintosh, LD	14,899
Neil Hudson, C.	9,452
Sandy Howat, SNP	3,354
Steve Burgess, Green	881

Lab. majority 316 (0.72%)
0.11% swing Lab. to LD
(2005: Lab. majority 405 (0.95%))

EDINBURGH SOUTH WEST
E. 66,359 T. 45,462 (68.51%) Lab. hold
Alistair Darling, Lab.   19,473
Jason Rust, C.   11,026
Tim McKay, LD   8,194
Kaukab Stewart, SNP   5,530
Clare Cooney, Green   872
Colin Fox, SSP   319
Caroline Bellamy, Comm. Lge   48
Lab. majority 8,447 (18.58%)
1.05% swing C. to Lab.
(2005: Lab. majority 7,242 (16.49%))

EDINBURGH WEST
E. 65,161 T. 46,447 (71.28%) LD hold
*Michael Crockart, LD   16,684
Cameron Day, Lab.   12,881
Stewart Geddes, C.   10,767
Sheena Cleland, SNP   6,115
LD majority 3,803 (8.19%)
11.35% swing LD to Lab.
(2005: LD majority 13,600 (30.05%))

FALKIRK
E. 81,869 T. 50,777 (62.02%) Lab. hold
Eric Joyce, Lab.   23,207
John McNally, SNP   15,364
Katie Mackie, C.   5,698
Kieran Leach, LD   5,225
Brian Goldie, UKIP   1,283
Lab. majority 7,843 (15.45%)
7.00% swing Lab. to SNP
(2005: Lab. majority 13,475 (29.45%))

FIFE NORTH EAST
E. 62,969 T. 40,064 (63.62%) LD hold
Sir Menzies Campbell, LD   17,763
Miles Briggs, C.   8,715
Mark Hood, Lab.   6,869
Rod Campbell, SNP   5,685
Mike Scott-Hayward, UKIP   1,032
LD majority 9,048 (22.58%)
5.01% swing LD to C.
(2005: LD majority 12,571 (32.60%))

GLASGOW CENTRAL
E. 60,062 T. 30,580 (50.91%) Lab. hold
*Anas Sarwar, Lab.   15,908
Osama Saeed, SNP   5,357
Chris Young, LD   5,010
John Bradley, C.   2,158
Alastair Whitelaw, Green   800
Ian Holt, BNP   616
James Nesbitt, SSP   357
Ramsay Urquhart, UKIP   246
Finlay Archibald, Pirate   128
Lab. majority 10,551 (34.50%)
0.54% swing SNP to Lab.
(2005: Lab. majority 8,531 (30.43%))

GLASGOW EAST
E. 61,516 T. 32,164 (52.29%) Lab. gain
*Margaret Curran, Lab.   19,797
John Mason, SNP   7,957
Kevin Ward, LD   1,617
Hamira Khan, C.   1,453
Joseph Finnie, BNP   677
Frances Curran, SSP   454
Arthur Thackeray, UKIP   209
Lab. majority 11,840 (36.81%)
3.42% swing Lab. to SNP
(2005: Lab. majority 13,507
(43.66%))(2008: SNP majority 365
(1.39%))

GLASGOW NORTH
E. 51,416 T. 29,613 (57.59%) Lab. hold
Ann McKechin, Lab.   13,181
Katy Gordon, LD   9,283
Patrick Grady, SNP   3,530
Erin Boyle, C.   2,089
Martin Bartos, Green   947
Thomas Main, BNP   296
Angela McCormick, TUSC   287
Lab. majority 3,898 (13.16%)
0.60% swing LD to Lab.
(2005: Lab. majority 3,338 (11.96%))

GLASGOW NORTH EAST
E. 59,859 T. 29,409 (49.13%) Lab. hold
Willie Bain, Lab.   20,100
Billy McAllister, SNP   4,158
Eileen Baxendale, LD   2,262
Ruth Davidson, C.   1,569
Walter Hamilton, BNP   798
Graham Campbell, TUSC   187
Kevin McVey, SSP   179
Jim Berrington, Soc. Lab.   156
Lab. majority 15,942 (54.21%)
(2005: Speaker majority 10,134
(35.66%))(2009: Lab. majority 8,111
(39.38%))

GLASGOW NORTH WEST
E. 60,968 T. 35,582 (58.36%) Lab. hold
John Robertson, Lab.   19,233
Natalie McKee, LD   5,622
Mags Park, SNP   5,430
Richard Sullivan, C.   3,537
Moira Crawford, Green   882
Scott Mclean, BNP   699
Marc Livingstone, Comm.   179
Lab. majority 13,611 (38.25%)
4.31% swing LD to Lab.
(2005: Lab. majority 10,093 (29.63%))

GLASGOW SOUTH
E. 65,029 T. 40,094 (61.66%) Lab. hold
Tom Harris, Lab.   20,736
Malcolm Fleming, SNP   8,078
Shabnum Mustapha, LD   4,739
Davena Rankin, C.   4,592
Marie Campbell, Green   961
Mike Coyle, BNP   637
Brian Smith, TUSC   351
Lab. majority 12,658 (31.57%)
1.51% swing Lab. to SNP
(2005: Lab. majority 10,832 (28.19%))

GLASGOW SOUTH WEST
E. 58,182 T. 31,781 (54.62%)
                            Lab. (Co-op) hold
Ian Davidson, Lab. (Co-op)   19,863
Chris Stephens, SNP   5,192
Isabel Nelson, LD   2,870
Maya Henderson Forrest, C.   2,084
Tommy Sheridan, TUSC   931
David Orr, BNP   841
Lab. (Co-op) majority 14,671 (46.16%)
0.65% swing SNP to Lab. (Co-op)
(2005: Lab. (Co-op) majority 13,896
(44.86%))

GLENROTHES
E. 67,893 T. 40,501 (59.65%) Lab. hold
Lindsay Roy, Lab.   25,247
David Alexander, SNP   8,799
Harry Wills, LD   3,108
Sheila Low, C.   2,922
Kris Seunarine, UKIP   425
Lab. majority 16,448 (40.61%)
6.04% swing SNP to Lab.
(2005: Lab. majority 10,664
(28.54%))(2008: Lab. majority 6,737
(18.61%))

GORDON
E. 73,420 T. 48,775 (66.43%) LD hold
Malcolm Bruce, LD   17,575
Richard Thomson, SNP   10,827
Barney Crockett, Lab.   9,811
Ross Thomson, C.   9,111
Sue Edwards, Green   752
Elise Jones, BNP   699
LD majority 6,748 (13.83%)
7.61% swing LD to SNP
(2005: LD majority 11,026 (24.81%))

INVERCLYDE
E. 59,209 T. 37,502 (63.34%) Lab. hold
David Cairns, Lab.   20,993
Innes Nelson, SNP   6,567
Simon Hutton, LD   5,007
David Wilson, C.   4,502
Peter Campbell, UKIP   433
Lab. majority 14,426 (38.47%)
3.64% swing SNP to Lab.
(2005: Lab. majority 11,259 (31.19%))

INVERNESS, NAIRN, BADENOCH &
STRATHSPEY
E. 72,528 T. 47,086 (64.92%) LD hold
Danny Alexander, LD   19,172
Mike Robb, Lab.   10,407
John Finnie, SNP   8,803
Jim Ferguson, C.   6,278
Dr Donald Boyd, Ch. P.   835
Donnie MacLeod, Green   789
Ross Durance, UKIP   574
George MacDonald, TUSC   135
Kit Fraser, Joy   93
LD majority 8,765 (18.61%)
4.62% swing Lab. to LD
(2005: LD majority 4,148 (9.37%))

KILMARNOCK & LOUDOUN
E. 74,131 T. 46,553 (62.80%)
                            Lab. (Co-op) hold
*Cathy Jamieson, Lab. (Co-op)   24,460
George Leslie, SNP   12,082
Janette McAlpine, C.   6,592
Sebastian Tombs, LD   3,419
Lab. (Co-op) majority 12,378 (26.59%)
3.49% swing SNP to Lab. (Co-op)
(2005: Lab. (Co-op) majority 8,703
(19.61%))

KIRKCALDY & COWDENBEATH
E. 73,665 T. 45,802 (62.18%) Lab. hold
Gordon Brown, Lab.   29,559
Douglas Chapman, SNP   6,550
John Mainland, LD   4,269
Lindsay Paterson, C.   4,258
Peter Adams, UKIP   760
Susan Archibald, Ind.   184
Donald MacLaren of MacLaren, Ind. 165
Derek Jackson, Land   57
Lab. majority 23,009 (50.24%)
3.33% swing SNP to Lab.
(2005: Lab. majority 18,216 (43.58%))

LANARK & HAMILTON EAST
E. 74,773 T. 46,554 (62.26%) Lab. hold
Jim Hood, Lab.   23,258
Clare Adamson, SNP   9,780
Colin McGavigan, C.   6,981
Douglas Herbison, LD   5,249
Duncan McFarlane, Ind.   670
Rob Sale, UKIP   616
Lab. majority 13,478 (28.95%)
0.34% swing SNP to Lab.
(2005: Lab. majority 11,947 (27.41%))

LINLITHGOW & FALKIRK EAST
E. 80,907 T. 51,450 (63.59%) Lab. hold
Michael Connarty, Lab.   25,634
Tam Smith, SNP   13,081
Stephen Glenn, LD   6,589
Andrea Stephenson, C.   6,146
Lab. majority 12,553 (24.40%)
0.13% swing SNP to Lab.
(2005: Lab. majority 11,202 (24.15%))

LIVINGSTON
E. 75,924 T. 47,907 (63.10%) Lab. hold
*Graeme Morrice, Lab.   23,215
Lis Bardell, SNP   12,424
Charles Dundas, LD   5,316
Alison Adamson-Ross, C.   5,158
David Orr, BNP   960
Alistair Forrest, UKIP   443
Ally Hendry, SSP   242
Jim Slavin, Ind.   149
Lab. majority 10,791 (22.52%)
3.51% swing Lab. to SNP
(2005: Lab. majority 13,097
(29.54%))(2005: Lab. majority 2,680
(9.09%))

MIDLOTHIAN
E. 61,387 T. 39,242 (63.93%) Lab. hold
David Hamilton, Lab.   18,449
Colin Beattie, SNP   8,100
Ross Laird, LD   6,711
James Callander, C.   4,661
Ian Baxter, Green   595
Gordon Norrie, UKIP   364
George McCleery, Ind.   196
Willie Duncan, TUSC   166
Lab. majority 10,349 (26.37%)
1.07% swing Lab. to SNP
(2005: Lab. majority 7,265 (19.27%))

MORAY
E. 65,925 T. 41,004 (62.20%) SNP hold
Angus Robertson, SNP   16,273
Douglas Ross, C.   10,683
Kieron Green, Lab.   7,007
James Paterson, LD   5,956
Donald Gatt, UKIP   1,085
SNP majority 5,590 (13.63%)
0.50% swing SNP to C.
(2005: SNP majority 5,676 (14.63%))

MOTHERWELL & WISHAW
E. 66,918 T. 39,123 (58.46%) Lab. hold
Frank Roy, Lab.   23,910
Marion Fellows, SNP   7,104
Stuart Douglas, LD   3,840
Patsy Gilroy, C.   3,660
Ray Gunnion, TUSC   609
Lab. majority 16,806 (42.96%)
0.97% swing SNP to Lab.
(2005: Lab. majority 15,222 (41.02%))

NA H-EILEANAN AN IAR
E. 22,266 T. 14,717 (66.10%) SNP hold
Angus MacNeil, SNP   6,723
Donald John MacSween, Lab.   4,838
Murdo Murray, Ind.   1,412
Jean Davis, LD   1,097
Sheena Norquay, C.   647
SNP majority 1,885 (12.81%)
1.20% swing Lab. to SNP
(2005: SNP majority 1,441 (10.41%))

OCHIL & PERTHSHIRE SOUTH
E. 75,115 T. 50,469 (67.19%) Lab. hold
Gordon Banks, Lab.   19,131
Annabelle Ewing, SNP   13,944
Gerald Michaluk, C.   10,342
Graeme Littlejohn, LD   5,754
David Bushby, UKIP   689
Hilary Charles, Green   609
Lab. majority 5,187 (10.28%)
4.40% swing SNP to Lab.
(2005: Lab. majority 688 (1.47%))

ORKNEY & SHETLAND
E. 33,085 T. 19,346 (58.47%) LD hold
Alistair Carmichael, LD   11,989
Mark Cooper, Lab.   2,061
John Mowat, SNP   2,042
Frank Nairn, C.   2,032
Robert Smith, UKIP   1,222
LD majority 9,928 (51.32%)
6.98% swing Lab. to LD
(2005: LD majority 6,627 (37.35%))

PAISLEY & RENFREWSHIRE NORTH
E. 63,704 T. 43,707 (68.61%) Lab. hold
Jim Sheridan, Lab.   23,613
Mags MacLaren, SNP   8,333
Alistair Campbell, C.   6,381
Ruaraidh Dobson, LD   4,597
Gary Pearson, Ind.   550
Chris Rollo, SSP   233
Lab. majority 15,280 (34.96%)
4.03% swing SNP to Lab.
(2005: Lab. majority 11,001 (26.91%))

PAISLEY & RENFREWSHIRE SOUTH
E. 61,197 T. 39,998 (65.36%) Lab. hold
Douglas Alexander, Lab.   23,842
Andy Doig, SNP   7,228
Gordon McCaskill, C.   3,979
Ashay Ghai, LD   3,812
Paul Mack, Ind.   513
Jimmy Kerr, SSP   375
William Hendry, Ind.   249
Lab. majority 16,614 (41.54%)
3.27% swing SNP to Lab.
(2005: Lab. majority 13,232 (34.95%))

PERTH & PERTHSHIRE NORTH
E. 72,141 T. 48,268 (66.91%) SNP hold
Pete Wishart, SNP   19,118
Peter Lyburn, C.   14,739
Jamie Glackin, Lab.   7,923
Peter Barrett, LD   5,954
Douglas Taylor, Trust   534
SNP majority 4,379 (9.07%)
2.88% swing C. to SNP
(2005: SNP majority 1,521 (3.31%))

RENFREWSHIRE EAST
E. 66,249 T. 51,181 (77.26%) Lab. hold
Jim Murphy, Lab.   25,987
Richard Cook, C.   15,567
Gordon Macdonald, LD   4,720
Gordon Archer, SNP   4,535
Donald MacKay, UKIP   372
Lab. majority 10,420 (20.36%)
3.16% swing C. to Lab.
(2005: Lab. majority 6,657 (14.04%))

ROSS, SKYE & LOCHABER
E. 51,836 T. 34,838 (67.21%) LD hold
Charles Kennedy, LD   18,335
John McKendrick, Lab.   5,265
Alasdair Stephen, SNP   5,263
Donald Cameron, C.   4,260
Eleanor Scott, Green   777
Philip Anderson, UKIP   659
Ronnie Campbell, Ind.   279
LD majority 13,070 (37.52%)
3.14% swing LD to Lab.
(2005: LD majority 14,249 (43.79%))

RUTHERGLEN & HAMILTON WEST
E. 76,408 T. 46,981 (61.49%)
                          Lab. (Co-op) hold
*Tom Greatrex, Lab. (Co-op)   28,566
Graeme Horne, SNP   7,564
Ian Robertson, LD   5,636
Malcolm Macaskill, C.   4,540
Janice Mackintosh, UKIP   675
Lab. (Co-op) majority 21,002 (44.70%)
1.51% swing SNP to Lab. (Co-op)
(2005: Lab. (Co-op) majority 16,112
(37.24%))

STIRLING
E. 66,080 T. 46,791 (70.81%) Lab. hold
Anne McGuire, Lab.   19,558
Bob Dalrymple, C.   11,204
Alison Lindsay, SNP   8,091
Graham Reed, LD   6,797
Mark Ruskell, Green   746
Paul Henke, UKIP   395
Lab. majority 8,354 (17.85%)
3.47% swing C. to Lab.
(2005: Lab. majority 4,767 (10.91%))

NORTHERN IRELAND

§ANTRIM EAST
E. 60,204 T. 30,502 (50.66%)

		DUP hold
Sammy Wilson, DUP		13,993
Rodney McCune, UCUNF		7,223
Gerry Lynch, Alliance		3,377
Oliver McMullan, SF		2,064
Justin McCamphill, SDLP		2,019
Samuel Morrison, TUV		1,826

DUP majority 6,770 (22.20%)
Notional 0.2% swing UCUNF to DUP
(2005: DUP majority 6,996 (21.76%))

§ANTRIM NORTH
E. 73,338 T. 42,397 (57.81%)

		DUP hold
*Ian Paisley Junior, DUP		19,672
Jim Allister, TUV		7,114
Daithi McKay, SF		5,265
Irwin Armstrong, UCUNF		4,634
Declan O'Loan, SDLP		3,738
Jayne Dunlop, Alliance		1,368
Lyle Cubitt, ND		606

DUP majority 12,558 (29.62%)
(2005: DUP majority 18,486 (41.80%))

§ANTRIM SOUTH
E. 63,054 T. 34,009 (53.94%)

		DUP hold
Revd William McCrea, DUP		11,536
Sir Reg Empey, UCUNF		10,353
Mitchel McLaughlin, SF		4,729
Michelle Byrne, SDLP		2,955
Alan Lawther, Alliance		2,607
Melwyn Lucas, TUV		1,829

DUP majority 1,183 (3.48%)
Notional 3.6% swing DUP to UCUNF
(2005: DUP majority 3,778 (10.74%))

§BELFAST EAST
E. 59,007 T. 34,488 (58.45%)

		Alliance gain
*Naomi Long, Alliance		12,839
Peter Robinson, DUP		11,306
Trevor Ringland, UCUNF		7,305
David Vance, TUV		1,856
Niall Donnelly, SF		817
Mary Muldoon, SDLP		365

Alliance majority 1,533 (4.45%)
Notional 22.87% swing DUP to Alliance
(2005: DUP majority 7,900 (22.87%))

§BELFAST NORTH
E. 65,504 T. 36,993 (56.47%)

		DUP hold
Nigel Dodds, DUP		14,812
Gerry Kelly, SF		12,588
Alban Maginness, SDLP		4,544
Fred Cobain, UCUNF		2,837
William Webb, Alliance		1,809
Martin McAuley, Ind.		403

DUP majority 2,224 (6.01%)
Notional 5.00% swing DUP to SF
(2005: DUP majority 5,832 (16.02%))

§BELFAST SOUTH
E. 59,524 T. 34,186 (57.43%)

		SDLP hold
Dr Alasdair McDonnell, SDLP		14,026
Jimmy Spratt, DUP		8,100
Paula Bradshaw, UCUNF		5,910
Anna Lo, Alliance		5,114
Adam McGibbon, Green		1,036

SDLP majority 5,926 (17.33%)
Notional 8.41% swing DUP to SDLP
(2005: SDLP majority 188 (0.52%))

§BELFAST WEST
E. 59,522 T. 32,133 (53.99%) SF hold

Gerry Adams, SF		22,840
Alex Attwood, SDLP		5,261
William Humphrey, DUP		2,436
Bill Manwaring, UCUNF		1,000
Maire Hendron, Alliance		596

SF majority 17,579 (54.71%)
Notional 1.07% swing SDLP to SF
(2005: SF majority 19,527 (52.57%))

DOWN NORTH
E. 60,698 T. 33,481 (55.16%)

		Ind. hold
Lady Sylvia Hermon, Ind.		21,181
Ian Parsley, UCUNF		6,817
Stephen Farry, Alliance		1,876
Mary Kilpatrick, TUV		1,634
Steven Agnew, Green		1,043
Liam Logan, SDLP		680
Vincent Parker, SF		250

Ind. majority 14,364 (42.90%)
(2005: UUP majority 4,944 (15.31%))

§DOWN SOUTH
E. 70,784 T. 42,589 (60.17%)

		SDLP hold
*Margaret Ritchie, SDLP		20,648
Caitriona Ruane, SF		12,236
Jim Wells, DUP		3,645
John McCallister, UCUNF		3,093
Ivor McConnell, TUV		1,506
Cadogan Enright, Green		901
David Griffin, Alliance		560

SDLP majority 8,412 (19.75%)
Notional 0.06% swing SDLP to SF
(2005: SDLP majority 8,801 (19.87%))

FERMANAGH & SOUTH TYRONE
E. 67,908 T. 46,803 (68.92%) SF hold

Michelle Gildernew, SF		21,304
Rodney Connor, Ind.		21,300
Fearghal McKinney, SDLP		3,574
Vasundhara Kamble, Alliance		437
John Stevenson, Ind.		188

SF majority 4 (0.01%)
(2005: SF majority 4,582 (9.39%))

§FOYLE
E. 65,843 T. 37,889 (57.54%)

		SDLP hold
Mark Durkan, SDLP		16,922
Martina Anderson, SF		12,098
Maurice Devenney, DUP		4,489
Eammon McCann, PBP		2,936
David Harding, UCUNF		1,221
Keith McGrellis, Alliance		223

SDLP majority 4,824 (12.73%)
Notional 0.17% swing SDLP to SF
(2005: SDLP majority 5,570 (13.08%))

§LAGAN VALLEY
E. 65,257 T. 36,540 (55.99%)

		DUP hold
Jeffrey Donaldson, DUP		18,199
Daphne Trimble, UCUNF		7,713
Trevor Lunn, Alliance		4,174
Keith Harbinson, TUV		3,154
Brian Heading, SDLP		1,835
Paul Butler, SF		1,465

DUP majority 10,486 (28.70%)
Notional 3.3% swing DUP to UCUNF
(2005: DUP majority 13,493 (35.33%))

§LONDONDERRY EAST
E. 63,220 T. 34,950 (55.28%)

		DUP hold
Gregory Campbell, DUP		12,097
Cathal O hOisin, SF		6,742
Lesley Macaulay, UCUNF		6,218
Thomas Conway, SDLP		5,399
William Ross, TUV		2,572
Bernard Fitzpatrick, Alliance		1,922

DUP majority 5,355 (15.32%)
Notional 4.13% swing DUP to SF
(2005: DUP majority 8,192 (21.26%))

NEWRY & ARMAGH
E. 74,308 T. 44,906 (60.43%) SF hold

Conor Murphy, SF		18,857
Dominic Bradley, SDLP		10,526
Danny Kennedy, UCUNF		8,558
William Irwin, DUP		5,764
William Frazer, Ind.		656
Andrew Muir, Alliance		545

SF majority 8,331 (18.55%)
1.19% swing SDLP to SF
(2005: SF majority 8,195 (16.16%))

§STRANGFORD
E. 60,539 T. 32,505 (53.69%)

		DUP hold
*Jim Shannon, DUP		14,926
Mike Nesbitt, UCUNF		9,050
Deborah Girvan, Alliance		2,828
Claire Hanna, SDLP		2,164
Terry Williams, TUV		1,814
Michael Coogan, SF		1,161
Barbara Haig, Green		562

DUP majority 5,876 (18.08%)
Notional 7.6% swing DUP to UCUNF
(2005: DUP majority 10,934 (33.32%))

TYRONE WEST
E. 61,148 T. 37,275 (60.96%) SF hold

Pat Doherty, SF		18,050
Thomas Buchanan, DUP		7,365
Ross Hussey, UCUNF		5,281
Joe Byrne, SDLP		5,212
Michael Bower, Alliance		859
Ciaran McClean, Ind.		508

SF majority 10,685 (28.67%)
3.79% swing DUP to SF
(2005: SF majority 5,005 (11.51%))

ULSTER MID
E. 64,594 T. 40,842 (63.23%) SF hold

Martin McGuinness, SF		21,239
Ian McCrea, DUP		5,876
Tony Quinn, SDLP		5,826
Sandra Overend, UCUNF		4,509
Walter Millar, TUV		2,995
Ian Butler, Alliance		397

SF majority 15,363 (37.62%)
6.73% swing DUP to SF
(2005: SF majority 10,976 (24.16%))

UPPER BANN
E. 74,732 T. 41,383 (55.38%)

		DUP hold
David Simpson, DUP		14,000
Harry Hamilton, UCUNF		10,639
John O'Dowd, SF		10,237
Dolores Kelly, SDLP		5,276
Brendan Heading, Alliance		1,231

DUP majority 3,361 (8.12%)
Notional 1.9% swing DUP to UCUNF
(2005: DUP majority 5,298 (11.93%))

BY-ELECTIONS 2010–11

For abbreviations of parties standing in the 2010–11 by-elections see also General Election results:

PBPA   People Before Profit Alliance

BARNSLEY CENTRAL
3 March 2011
E. 65,471   T. 24,252 (37%)   Lab. hold
Dan Jarvis, Lab.   14,724
Jane Collins, UKIP   2,953
James Hockney, C.   1,999
Enis Dalton, BNP   1,463
Tony Devoy, Ind.   1,266
Dominic Carman, LD   1,012
Kevin Riddiough, Eng. Dem.   544
Alan Hope, Loony   198
Michael Val Davies, Ind.   60
Lab. maj. 11,771 (48%)
3% swing UKIP to Lab.
(2010: Lab. maj. 11,093 (29.98%))

BELFAST WEST
9 June 2011
E. 61,441   T. 23,048 (37%)   SF hold
Paul Maskey, SF   16,211
Alex Attwood, SDLP   3,088
Gerry Carroll, PBPA   1,751
Brian Kingston, DUP   1,393
Bill Manwaring, UUP   386
Aaron McIntyre, Alliance   122
SF maj. 13,123 (56%)
1% swing SDLP to SF
(2010: SF maj. 17,579 (54.71%))

INVERCLYDE
30 June 2011
E. 61,856   T. 28,163 (45%)   Lab. hold
Iain McKenzie, Lab.   15,118
Anne McLaughlin, SNP   9,280
David Wilson, C.   2,784
Sophie Bridger, LD   627
Mitch Sorbie, UKIP   288
Lab. maj. 5,838 (20%)
8% swing Lab. to SNP
(2010: Lab. maj. 14,426 (38.47%))

LEICESTER SOUTH
5 May 2011
E. 77,880   T. 34,707 (44%)   Lab. hold
Jon Ashwurth, Lab.   19,771
Zuffar Haq, LD   7,693
Jane Hunt, C.   5,169
Abhijit Pandya, UKIP   994
Alan Hope, Loony   553
Lab. maj.12,078 (34%)
8% swing LD to Lab.
(2010: Lab. maj. 8,808 (18.69%))

OLDHAM EAST & SADDLEWORTH
13 January 2011
E. 72,788   T. 34,930 (47.99%)   Lab. hold
Debbie Abrahams, Lab.   14,718
Elwyn Watkins, LD   11,160
Kashif Ali, C.   4,481
Paul Nuttall, UKIP   2,029
Derek Adams, BNP   1,560
Peter Allen, Green   530
The Flying Brick, Loony   145
Stephen Morris, Eng. Dem.   144
Loz Kaye, Pirate   96
David Bishop, Bus-Pass Elvis   67
Lab. maj. 3,558 (10.19%)
4.98% swing LD to Lab.
(2010: Lab. maj. 103 (0.23%))

GENERAL ELECTION FACTS AND FIGURES

TURNOUT

VOTER TURNOUT 1945 – 2010
per cent

'45 '50 '51 '55 '59 '64 '66 '70 '74*'79 '83 '87 '92 '97 '01 '05 '10
* Average turnout – two elections were held in 1974

The UK parliamentary electorate on 6 May 2010 was 45,533,536. Overall turnout was 29,643,522, or 65.1 per cent. This excludes the 77,000 electors in the Thirsk & Malton constituency, where the election was held on 27 May 2010 owing to the death of a candidate.

HIGHEST TURNOUT
East Renfrewshire	77.3%
Westmorland & Lonsdale	76.9%
Richmond Park	76.2%
Winchester	75.8%
Devon Central	75.7%

LOWEST TURNOUT
Manchester Central	44.3%
Leeds Central	46.0%
Birmingham Ladywood	48.7%
Glasgow North East	49.1%
Blackley & Broughton	49.2%

WOMEN MPS
by party

Labour	81 (31 per cent)
Conservative	48 (16 per cent)
Liberal Democrat	7 (12 per cent)
Alliance	1 (100 per cent)
Green	1 (100 per cent)
SDLP	1 (33 per cent)
Sinn Fein	1 (20 per cent)
SNP	1 (17 per cent)
Other	1 (50 per cent)
DUP	0
Plaid Cymru	0
SDLP	0
Total	142 (22 per cent)

MAJORITIES

SMALLEST MAJORITIES

	Majority	Majority (per cent)
Fermanagh & South Tyrone,		
Michelle Gildernew, SF	4	0.0
Hampstead & Kilburn,		
Glenda Jackson, Lab.	42	0.1
Warwickshire North, Dan Byles, C.	54	
Camborne & Redruth,		
George Eustice, C.	66	0.2
Bolton West, Julie Hilling, Lab.	92	0.2

LARGEST MAJORITIES

Liverpool Walton,		
Steve Rotherham, Lab.	19,818	57.7
Knowsley, George Howarth, Lab.	25,686	57.5
East Ham, Stephen Timms, Lab.	27,826	55.2
Belfast West, Gerry Adams, SF	17,579	54.7
Glasgow North East, Willie Bain,		
Lab.	15,942	54.2

VOTES CAST 2001, 2005 AND 2010

	2001	2005	2010
Conservative	8,357,615	8,784,915	10,683,577
Labour	10,724,953	9,552,436	8,601,349
Liberal Democrat	4,814,321	5,985,454	6,827,312
UKIP	390,563	605,973	917,581
BNP	47,129	192,745	564,003
SNP	464,314	412,267	491,386
Green	166,477	283,414	284,823
Sinn Fein	175,933	174,530	171,942
DUP	181,999	241,856	168,216
Plaid Cymru	195,893	174,838	165,394
SDLP	169,865	125,626	110,970
UUP/ UCUNF*	216,839	127,414	102,361
Other	461,482	487,042	554,608
Total	26,367,383	27,148,510	29,643,522

* For the 2010 general election the Ulster Unionist Party formed an alliance with the Conservative Party in Northern Ireland and appeared on ballot papers as Ulster Conservatives and Unionists – New Force

AVERAGE AGE OF MPS
by party

Conservative	48
Liberal Democrat	50
Other	51
Labour	52
All Parties	50

Youngest MP: Pamela Nash (Lab.), Airdrie & Shotts, 25
Oldest MP: Sir Peter Tapsell (C.), Louth & Horncastle, 80

THE GOVERNMENT

A coalition government formed of the Conservative Party and Liberal Democrat Party (since 12 May 2010)

as at 1 September 2011

* Liberal Democrats

THE CABINET

Prime Minister, First Lord of the Treasury and Minister for the Civil Service
Rt. Hon. David Cameron, MP
Deputy Prime Minister, Lord President of the Council (with special responsibility for political and constitutional reform)
*Rt. Hon. Nick Clegg, MP
Chancellor of the Exchequer
Rt. Hon. George Osborne, MP
First Secretary of State, Secretary of State for Foreign and Commonwealth Affairs
Rt. Hon. William Hague, MP
Secretary of State for the Home Department and Minister for Women and Equalities
Rt. Hon. Theresa May, MP
Secretary of State for Business, Innovation and Skills and President of the Board of Trade
*Rt. Hon. Dr Vincent Cable, MP
Secretary of State for Communities and Local Government
Rt. Hon. Eric Pickles, MP
Secretary of State for Culture, Olympics, Media and Sport
Rt. Hon. Jeremy Hunt, MP
Secretary of State for Defence
Rt. Hon. Dr Liam Fox, MP
Secretary of State for Education
Rt. Hon. Michael Gove, MP
Secretary of State for Energy and Climate Change
*Rt. Hon. Chris Huhne, MP
Secretary of State for Environment, Food and Rural Affairs
Rt. Hon. Caroline Spelman, MP
Secretary of State for Health
Rt. Hon. Andrew Lansley, CBE, MP
Secretary of State for International Development
Rt. Hon. Andrew Mitchell, MP
Secretary of State for Justice and Lord Chancellor
Rt. Hon. Kenneth Clarke, QC, MP
Secretary of State for Northern Ireland
Rt. Hon. Owen Paterson, MP
Secretary of State for Scotland
*Rt. Hon. Michael Moore, MP
Secretary of State for Transport
Rt. Hon. Philip Hammond, MP
Secretary of State for Wales
Rt. Hon. Cheryl Gillan, MP
Secretary of State for Work and Pensions
Rt. Hon. Iain Duncan Smith, MP
Chief Secretary to the Treasury
*Rt. Hon. Danny Alexander, MP
Leader of the House of Lords, Chancellor of the Duchy of Lancaster
Rt. Hon. Lord Strathclyde
Minister without Portfolio (Minister of State)
Rt. Hon. Baroness Warsi

ALSO ATTENDING CABINET MEETINGS
Attorney-General
†Rt. Hon. Dominic Grieve, QC, MP

Leader of the House of Commons and Lord Privy Seal
Rt. Hon. Sir George Young, Bt., MP
Minister for the Cabinet Office and Paymaster General
Rt. Hon. Francis Maude, MP
Minister for the Cabinet Office (providing policy advice to the prime minister)
Rt. Hon. Oliver Letwin, MP
Minister of State for Universities and Science
Rt. Hon. David Willetts, MP
Parliamentary Secretary to the Treasury and Chief Whip
Rt. Hon. Patrick McLoughlin, MP

† Only attends cabinet meetings when ministerial responsibilities are on the agenda

LAW OFFICERS

Attorney-General
Rt. Hon. Dominic Grieve, QC, MP
Solicitor-General
Edward Garnier, QC, MP
Advocate-General for Scotland
*Rt. Hon. Lord Wallace of Tankerness, QC

MINISTERS OF STATE

Business, Innovation and Skills
Rt. Hon. Greg Clark, MP
†Lord Green of Hurstpierpoint
John Hayes, MP
Mark Prisk, MP
Rt. Hon. David Willetts, MP
Cabinet Office
Rt. Hon. Oliver Letwin, MP
Communities and Local Government
Rt. Hon. Greg Clark, MP
Rt. Hon. Grant Shapps, MP
Defence
*Nick Harvey, MP
Education
Nick Gibb, MP
John Hayes, MP
*Sarah Teather, MP
Energy and Climate Change
Gregory Barker, MP
Charles Hendry, MP
Environment, Food and Rural Affairs
Rt. Hon. James Paice, MP
Equalities Office
Rt. Hon. Theresa May, MP
Foreign and Commonwealth Office
*Jeremy Browne, MP
Rt. Hon. Lord Howell of Guildford
Rt. Hon. David Lidington, MP
‡Lord Green of Hurstpierpoint

† position held jointly with the Foreign and Commonwealth Office
‡ position held jointly with the Department of Business, Innovation and Skills

Health
Rt. Hon. Simon Burns, MP
*Paul Burstow, MP
Home Office
Baroness Browning
Damian Green, MP
§Rt. Hon. Nick Herbert, MP
Rt. Hon. Baroness Neville-Jones
International Development
Rt. Hon. Alan Duncan, MP
Justice
¶Rt. Hon. Nick Herbert, MP
*Rt. Hon. Lord McNally
Northern Ireland Office
Rt. Hon. Hugo Swire, MP
Transport
Rt. Hon. Theresa Villiers, MP
Work and Pensions
Rt. Hon. Chris Grayling, MP
*Steve Webb, MP

§ position held jointly with the Ministry of Justice
¶ position held jointly with the Home Office

UNDER-SECRETARIES OF STATE

Business, Innovation and Skills
*Edward Davey, MP
Baroness Wilcox
Communities and Local Government
Baroness Hanham, CBE
Bob Neill, MP
*Andrew Stunell, OBE, MP
Culture, Media and Sport
John Penrose, MP
Hugh Robertson, MP
Hon. Ed Vaizey, MP
Defence
Lord Astor of Hever
Gerald Howarth, MP
Peter Luff, MP
Rt. Hon. Andrew Robathan, MP
Education
Lord Hill of Oareford, CBE
Tim Loughton, MP
Energy and Climate Change
Lord Marland
Environment, Food and Rural Affairs
Richard Benyon, MP
Lord Henley
Equalities Office
*Lynne Featherstone, MP
Foreign and Commonwealth Office
Henry Bellingham, MP
Alistair Burt, MP
Health
Earl Howe
Anne Milton, MP
Home Office
James Brokenshire, MP
International Development
Stephen O'Brien, MP
Justice
Crispin Blunt, MP
Jonathan Djanogly, MP
Scotland Office
Rt. Hon. David Mundell, MP

Transport
*Norman Baker, MP
Mike Penning, MP
Wales Office
David Jones, MP
Work and Pensions
Lord Freud
Maria Miller, MP

OTHER MINISTERS

Parliamentary Private Secretary to the Prime Minister
Desmond Swayne, MP
Cabinet Office
Mark Harper, MP *(Parliamentary Secretary)*
Nick Hurd, MP *(Parliamentary Secretary)*
Office of the Leader of the House of Commons
*David Heath, CBE, MP *(Parliamentary Secretary and Deputy Leader of the Commons)*
Treasury
Mark Hoban, MP *(Financial Secretary)*
Justine Greening, MP *(Economic Secretary)*
David Gauke, MP *(Exchequer Secretary)*
Lord Sassoon *(Commercial Secretary)*

GOVERNMENT WHIPS

HOUSE OF LORDS
Captain of the Honourable Corps of the Gentlemen-at-Arms (Chief Whip)
Rt. Hon. Baroness Anelay of St Johns, DBE
Captain of the Queen's Bodyguard of the Yeomen of the Guard (Deputy Chief Whip)
*Rt. Hon. Lord Shutt of Greetland, OBE
Lords-in-Waiting
Earl Attlee
Lord Astor of Hever
Lord De Mauley
Lord Taylor of Holbeach, CBE
*Lord Wallace of Saltaire
Baronesses-in-Waiting
*Baroness Northover
Baroness Rawlings
Baroness Verma
*Baroness Garden of Frognal

HOUSE OF COMMONS
Parliamentary Secretary to the Treasury (Chief Whip)
Rt. Hon. Patrick McLoughlin, MP
Treasurer of HM Household (Deputy Chief Whip)
Rt. Hon. John Randall, MP
Comptroller of HM Household (Deputy Chief Whip)
*Rt. Hon. Alistair Carmichael, MP
Vice-Chamberlain of HM Household
Rt. Hon. Mark Francois, MP
Lords Commissioners of HM Treasury
James Duddridge, MP; Michael Fabricant, MP; Brooks Newmark, MP; Angela Watkinson, MP; Jeremy Wright, MP
Assistant Whips
Stephen Crabb, MP; Philip Dunne, MP; Robert Goodwill, MP; *Mark Hunter, MP; *Norman Lamb, MP; Chloe Smith, MP; Shailesh Vara, MP; Bill Wiggin, MP

GOVERNMENT DEPARTMENTS

THE CIVIL SERVICE

Under the Next Steps programme, launched in 1988, many semi-autonomous executive agencies were established to carry out much of the work of the civil service. Executive agencies operate within a framework set by the responsible minister which specifies policies, objectives and available resources. All executive agencies are set annual performance targets by their minister. Each agency has a chief executive, who is responsible for the day-to-day operations of the agency and who is accountable to the minister for the use of resources and for meeting the agency's targets. The minister accounts to parliament for the work of the agency. Nearly 75 per cent of civil servants now work in executive agencies. In the first quarter of 2011 there were 471,000 permanent civil servants, down from about 537,000 in June 2005.

The Senior Civil Service was created in 1996 and comprises around 4,000 staff from permanent secretary to the former grade 5 level, including all agency chief executives. All government departments and executive agencies are now responsible for their own pay and grading systems for civil servants outside the Senior Civil Service.

SALARIES 2011–12

MINISTERIAL SALARIES *from 1 April 2011*

Ministers who are members of the House of Commons receive a parliamentary salary of £65,738 in addition to their ministerial salary.

Prime minister	£76,762
Cabinet minister (Commons)	£68,827
Cabinet minister (Lords)	£101,038
Minister of state (Commons)	£33,002
Minister of state (Lords)	£78,891
Parliamentary under-secretary (Commons)	£23,697
Parliamentary under-secretary (Lords)	£68,710

SPECIAL ADVISERS' SALARIES *from 1 April 2011*

Special advisers to government ministers are paid out of public funds; their salaries are negotiated individually, but are usually in the range of £40,352 to £106,864.

CIVIL SERVICE SALARIES *from 1 April 2011*

Senior Civil Servants	
Permanent secretary	£141,800–£277,300
Band 3	£101,500–£208,100
Band 2	£82,900–£162,500
Band 1A	£67,600–£128,900
Band 1	£58,200–£117,800

Staff are placed in pay bands according to their level of responsibility and taking account of other factors such as experience and marketability. Movement within and between bands is based on performance. Following the delegation of responsibility for pay and grading to government departments and agencies from 1 April 1996, it is no longer possible to show service-wide pay rates for staff outside the Senior Civil Service.

GOVERNMENT DEPARTMENTS

For more information on government departments, *see* W www.cabinetoffice.gov.uk/resource-library/government-ministers-and-responsibilities

ATTORNEY-GENERAL'S OFFICE

Attorney-General's Office, 20 Victoria Street, London SW1H 0NF
T 020-7271 2492
E correspondenceunit@attorneygeneral.gsi.gov.uk
W www.attorneygeneral.gov.uk

The law officers of the crown for England and Wales are the Attorney-General and the Solicitor-General. The Attorney-General, assisted by the Solicitor-General, is the chief legal adviser to the government and is also ultimately responsible for all crown litigation. He has overall responsibility for the work of the Law Officers' Departments (the Treasury Solicitor's Department, the Crown Prosecution Service incorporating the Revenue and Customs Prosecutions Office, the Serious Fraud Office, the Army Prosecuting Authority, HM Crown Prosecution Service Inspectorate and the Attorney-General's Office). He has a specific statutory duty to superintend the discharge of their duties by the Director of Public Prosecutions (who heads the Crown Prosecution Service) and the Director of the Serious Fraud Office. The Attorney-General has specific responsibilities for the enforcement of the criminal law and also performs certain public interest functions, eg protecting charities and appealing unduly lenient sentences. He also deals with questions of law arising in bills and with issues of legal policy.

Following the devolution of power to the Northern Ireland Assembly on 12 April 2010, the assembly now appoints the Attorney-General for Northern Ireland. The Attorney-General for England and Wales now holds the newly created office of Advocate-General for Northern Ireland, with significantly reduced responsibilities in Northern Ireland.

Attorney-General, Rt. Hon. Dominic Grieve, QC, MP
Private Secretary, D. Parish
Solicitor-General, Edward Garnier, QC, MP
Director-General, P. Fish
Director, Criminal Law, S. Patten

DEPARTMENT FOR BUSINESS, INNOVATION AND SKILLS

1 Victoria Street, London SW1H 0ET
T 020-7215 5000
W www.bis.gov.uk

The Department for Business, Innovation and Skills (BIS) was established in June 2009 by merging the Department for Business, Enterprise and Regulatory Reform and the Department for Innovation, Universities and Skills. It aims to build Britain's capabilities to compete in the global economy. The merger brought together expertise in enterprise, innovation, and world-class science and research. Among other roles, the department advocates the needs of business across government; promotes an enterprise environment; invests in the development of the

higher education system; invests in the UK's science base; invests in skills through the further education system, aims to expand the number of apprenticeships; collaborates with regional development agencies to build economic growth in England; and encourages innovation in the UK.

Secretary of State for Business, Innovation and Skills and President of the Board of Trade, Rt. Hon. Dr Vince Cable, MP
Principal Private Secretary, Joanna Crellin
Senior Private Secretary, Bryan Payne
Special Advisers, Katie Waring; Giles Wilkes
Minister of State, Rt. Hon. David Willetts, MP *(Universities and Science)*
Senior Private Secretary, Emma Payne
Special Adviser, Nick Hillman
Minister of State, John Hayes *(Further Education, Skills and Lifelong Learning)**
Private Secretary, Kellie Hurst
Minister of State, Lord Green *(Trade and Investement)*
Private Secretary, Nick Whittingham
Minister of State, Mark Prisk, MP *(Business and Enterprise)*
Senior Private Secretary, Helen Mitchell
Parliamentary Under-Secretary of of State, Edward Davey, MP *(Employment Relations, Consumer and Postal Affairs)*
Private Secretary, Sarah Barraclough
Parliamentary Under-Secretary of State, Baroness Wilcox *(Business, Innovation and Skills)*
Private Secretary, Rachael Bishop
Permanent Secretary, Martin Donnelly
Senior Private Secretary, Karis Hewitt
Head of Parliamentary Unit, Ian Webster

* Jointly with the Department of Education

DEPARTMENTAL BOARD
Chair, Rt. Hon Dr Vince Cable, MP *(Secretary of State)*
Members, Tera Allas *(Economics, Strategy and Better Regulation);* Nick Baird *(Chief Executive UK Trade and Investment);* Martin Donnelly *(Permanent Secretary);* Bernadette Kelly *(Market Framework);* Stephen Lovegrove *(Shareholder Executive);* Howard Orme *(Finance and Commercial);* Philip Rutnam *(Business and Skills);* Rachel Sandby-Thomas *(Legal, People and Communications);* Adrian Smith *(Knowledge and Innovation)*
Non-Executive Members, Prof. Julia King; Andrew Witty; Dr Brian Woods-Scawen

BETTER REGULATION EXECUTIVE
1 Victoria Street, London SW1 0ET
T 020-7215 5000 E breadmin@bis.gsi.gov.uk
W www.bis.gov.uk/betterregulation

The Better Regulation Executive (BRE) is part of the Department for Business, Innovation and Skills (BIS) and leads the regulatory reform agenda across government. Working with other departments and regulators, the BRE helps to improve the design of new regulations and how they are communicated; to simplify and modernise existing regulations; and to change attitudes and approaches to regulation to become more risk-based.
Non-Executive Chair, Sir Don Curry
Chief Executive, Graham Turnock

SHAREHOLDER EXECUTIVE
1 Victoria Street, London SW1H 0ET
T 020-7215 3909
W www.shareholderexecutive.gov.uk

The Shareholder Executive was set up in September 2003 to work with other departments in government to improve the government's capabilities and performance as a shareholder, and to offer corporate finance expertise and advice across government. Its goal is to create a climate of ownership that, while challenging, is genuinely supportive and provides the framework for the 28 businesses under its remit to be successful. In addition, the Shareholder Executive's Government Property Unit is responsible for maximising value from the state's property portfolio.
Chair, vacant
Chief Executive, Stephen Lovegrove

CABINET OFFICE
70 Whitehall, London SW1A 2AS
T 020-7276 1234; Switchboard 020-7276 3000
W www.cabinet-office.gov.uk

The Cabinet Office, alongside the Treasury, sits at the centre of the government, with an overarching purpose of making government work better. It supports the prime minister and the cabinet, helping to ensure effective development, coordination and implementation of policy and operations across all government departments. The Cabinet Office also leads work to ensure that the Civil Service provides the most effective and efficient support to the government to meet its objectives. The department is headed by the Minister for the Cabinet Office.

Prime Minister, First Lord of the Treasury and Minister for the Civil Service, Rt. Hon. David Cameron, MP
Principal Private Secretary to the Prime Minister, James Bowler
Deputy Prime Minister, Rt. Hon. Nick Clegg, MP
Principal Private Secretary to the Deputy Prime Minister, Calum Miller
Minister for the Cabinet Office and Paymaster General, Rt. Hon. Francis Maude, MP
Principal Private Secretary, Sue Pither
Private Secretaries, Kitty von Bertele, Richard Stirling, Vicky Woodbine
Minister for Government Policy, Rt. Hon. Oliver Letwin, MP
Assistant Private Secretaries, Nasira Ashraf; Rose Jefferies
Parliamentary Secretary (Minister for Civil Society), Nick Hurd, MP
Private Secretary, Cameron Smith
Parliamentary Secretary (Minister for Political and Constitutional Reform), Mark Harper, MP
Private Secretary, Joanne Trimble-Bruce
Leader of the House of Lords and Chancellor of the Duchy of Lancaster, Rt. Hon. Lord Strathclyde
Private Secretary, Phil Lloyd *(Head of Office)*
Assistant Private Secretary, Sarah Kerr
Minister without Portfolio, Rt. Hon. Baroness Warsi
Private Secretary, Anna Shotbolt
Secretary of the Cabinet and Head of the Home Civil Service, Sir Gus O'Donnell, GCB
Principal Private Secretary, Rachel Hopcroft
Private Secretary, Lynne Charles

MANAGEMENT BOARD
Chair, Sir Gus O'Donnell, GCB *(Cabinet Secretary and Principal Accounting Officer for the Cabinet Office)*
Board Members, Ruth Carnall; Alexis Cleveland *(Corporate Services Group);* Sir Jon Cunliffe, CB *(Prime Minister's Adviser);* Sue Gray *(Head of Propriety and Ethics Team and Director of Private Offices Group);* Jeremy Heywood, CB, CVO *(Permanent Secretary, Prime*

Minister's Office); Bruce Mann *(Finance Director and Board Secretary);* Ian Watmore *(Chief Operating Officer for the Efficiency and Reform Group);* Chris Wormald *(Director-General and Head of the Deputy Prime Minister's Office)*
Non-Executive Directors, Lord Browne; Dame Barbara Stocking; Ian Davis; Rona Fairhead

HONOURS AND APPOINTMENTS SECRETARIAT
Ground Floor, Admiralty Arch, The Mall, London SW1A 2WH
T 020-7276 2777
Permanent Secretary, Alex Allan
Prime Minister's Appointments Secretary, Sir Paul Britton, CB
Ceremonial Officer, Denis Brennan

DOMESTIC POLICY GROUP
Comprising Economic and Domestic Affairs, Economic Policy Coordination, the Strategy Unit, and European and Global Issues.
Director-General, Chris Wormald

ECONOMIC AND DOMESTIC AFFAIRS SECRETARIAT
Director, Robin Fellgett, CB
Deputy Directors, Scott McPherson *(MoJ, Home Office, Devolution);* Hannah Tooze *(Legislation, Home Affairs – Olympics);* Patrick White *(Health and Social Justice)*
Parliamentary Adviser, John Healey

ECONOMIC POLICY COORDINATION
Director of the National Economic Council Secretariat and Deputy Head, Economic and Domestic Affairs Secretariat, Jeremy Pocklington
Deputy Directors, Caleb Deeks *(Public Spending, Labour Market);* Debbie Gillat *(Business Banking and Reform)*

STRATEGY UNIT
Director, Gareth Davies
Deputy Directors, Miatta Fahnbulleh *(Localism);* Hugh Harris *(Welfare);* Axel Heitmueller *(Economy);* Halima Khan *(Value for Money);* Sophia Oliver *(Health and Social Care);* Harvey Redgrave *(Home Affairs);* Matt Robinson *(Strategic Challenges);* Chloe Ross *(Education and Family)*

EUROPEAN AND GLOBAL ISSUES SECRETARIAT
Director, Paul Rankin
Prime Minister's Adviser, Sir Jon Cunliffe, CB *(Europe and Global Issues)*
Senior Adviser, Jonathan Portes *(Economic Policy Issues)*
Deputy Directors, Harold Freeman *(International Economic Affairs);* Hermione Gough *(Economic Reform, Energy and Climate Change, Employment and Social Affairs);* Matthew Taylor *(EU Issues)*

NATIONAL SECURITY
Comprises the Joint Intelligence Organisation, National Security Secretariat, Foreign Policy and Intelligence, Security and Resilience

JOINT INTELLIGENCE ORGANISATION
Chair, Joint Intelligence Committee and Professional Head of Intelligence Analysis, Alex Allan
Chief of the Assessments Staff and Deputy Head of Intelligence, Paul Rimmer

NATIONAL SECURITY SECRETARIAT
70 Whitehall, London SW1A 2AS
Prime Minister's National Security Adviser, Sir Peter Ricketts, GCMG

Deputy National Security Adviser, Julian Miller, CB *(Foreign Policy)*
Directors, Philip Barton, CMG, OBE *(Afghanistan and Pakistan);* Julian Miller, CB *(Foreign and Defence Policy)*

INTELLIGENCE, SECURITY AND RESILIENCE
Director, Oliver Robbins
Directors, Ciaran Martin *(Security and Intelligence);* Willam Nye *(Strategy and Counter-Terrorism);* Christina Scott *(Civil Contingencies Secretariat);* Neil Thompson *(Office of Cyber Security)*

EFFICIENCY AND REFORM GROUP
Chief Operating Officer, Ian Watmore
Director, Ben Jupp
Deputy Director, Paula McDonald, CBE *(Pay and Workforce Reform)*

OFFICE OF GOVERNMENT COMMERCE (OGC)
Rosebery Court, St Andrews Business Park, Norwich, Norfolk NR7 0HS
T 0845-000 4999 E servicedesk@ogc.gsi.gov.uk
W www.ogc.gov.uk

The Office of Government Commerce was set up in April 2000, and became part of the Efficiency and Reform Group in the Cabinet Office in June 2010. It is responsible for increasing the government's value for money by improving standards and capability in procurement, for example by delivering major capital projects, and maximising the effective use of government spending and a £30bn property estate.

CIVIL SERVICE CAPABILITY GROUP
Admiralty Arch, The Mall, London SW1A 2WH

Comprises Civil Service Reform, Civil Service Workforce and Leadership and Talent Management
Head, Gill Rider

CIVIL SERVICE REFORM
Director, Brian Etheridge, CBE
Deputy Directors, Liz McKeown *(Analysis and Insight);* Adam Pemberton *(Strategy and Performance);* Ian Wood *(Capability Review)*

CIVIL SERVICE WORKFORCE
Director, Dusty Amroliwala
Deputy Directors, Jennifer Hutton *(Diversity, Health and Wellbeing Strategy);* John Whittaker, CBE *(Employment Policy);* Julia Wood *(Pay and Reward)*

LEADERSHIP AND TALENT MANAGEMENT
Director, Helen Dudley, CBE
Deputy Directors, Jacquie Heany *(HR Profession);* Joanne Peel *(Fast Stream);* Esther Wallington *(Senior Appointments and Talent Management)*

CABINET OFFICE/NO. 10 COMMUNICATIONS
22 Whitehall, London SW1A 2WH
T 020-7276 1234
Director, Jenny Grey *(Policy Communication)*
Deputy Directors, John Toker *(Security, Intelligence and Counter-Terrorism);* Rishi Saha *(Digital Communication);* James Sorene *(Deputy Prime Minister's Spokesperson/Head of Communications);* Michael Warren *(Cross-Government Campaigns);* Emily Tofield, *(Efficiency and Reform Communication)*

OFFICE OF THE GOVERNMENT CHIEF INFORMATION OFFICER
Admiralty Arch, The Mall, London SW1A 2AH
HM Government Chief Information Officer, John Suffolk
Private Secretary and Secretary to the CIO Council, Sue Bateman
Special Projects, Andy Bloyce
Director, Martin Bellamy *(IT Strategy and Policy)*
Heads, Jo Clift *(Shared Services);* Owen Pengelly *(Central Sponsor for Information Assurance Unit)*

GOVERNMENT CLOUD PROGRAMME
Director, Chris Chant
Deputy Director, Andrew Tait *(Data Centre Strategy, G-Cloud and Apps Store)*

ICT STRATEGY AND POLICY
Deputy Government Chief Information Officer and Director, Bill McCluggage
Deputy Director, Rachel Gentry

SHARED ICT INFRASTRUCTURE
Director, Lesley Hume
Deputy Directors, Claire Baker *(Government IT Profession);* Kevin Doherty *(Cabinet Office ICT Strategy, Policy and Security);* Neill Goulder *(ICT Service Delivery);* John Stubley *(Public Service Network Programme);* Chris Thirkell *(Reliable Delivery)*

OFFICE FOR CIVIL SOCIETY
The Office for Civil Society replaced the Office for the Third Sector in May 2010 and takes a key role in delivering the government's Big Society agenda.
Executive Director, Gareth Davies
Programme Director, Juliet Mountford
Deputy Directors, Sarah Benioff *(Social Action);* Rannia Leontaridi *(Public Services);* Liz Liston-Jones *(Charities and Sector Support);* Juliet Mountford *(Strategy and Communications);* Helen Stephenson *(Bank and Investment Funds);* Annabel Turpie *(Big Society Policy and Analysis)*

CORPORATE SERVICES GROUP
Comprises Finance and Human Resources
Deputy Director, Karen Cadman *(Head of Civil Service Pensions)*
Head of Knowledge and Information Management, Roger Smethurst

FINANCE
Director, Bruce Mann, CB
Deputy Director Jerry Page *(Finance and Estates)*

HUMAN RESOURCES
Director, Janette Durbin
Deputy Director, Simon Fryer

NATIONAL SCHOOL OF GOVERNMENT
Sunningdale Park, Larch Avenue, Ascot, Berks SL5 0QE
T 01344-634000
E customer.services@nationalschool.gsi.gov.uk
W www.nationalschool.gov.uk

Since 1 April 2011, the National School of Government re-joined the Cabinet Office, and ceased to be a non-ministerial government department. The learning and development partner of the UK Civil Service, it is run by public servants for public servants, and aims to improve services for citizens by using learning and development to raise the bar for public services. Among these services are e-learning solutions, a range of open courses and qualifications and bespoke learning packages.
Principal and Chief Executive, Rod Clark

PRIME MINISTER'S OFFICE
10 Downing Street, London SW1A 2AA
T 020-7930 4433 W www.number-10.gov.uk
Prime Minister, Rt. Hon David Cameron, MP
Parliamentary Private Secretary, Desmond Swayne, MP
Permanent Secretary, Jeremy Heywood, CB, CVO
Principal Private Secretary, James Bowler
Private Secretaries, John Casson; Simon King; Gila Sacks; Matthew Style
Speech Writer to the Prime Minister, Tim Kiddell
Chief Operating Officer, Eric Hepburn
Director of Communications, Craig Oliver
Prime Minister's Official Spokesman, Steve Field
Head of News and Deputy Spokesperson, Vickie Sheriff
Chief of Staff (Political), Ed Llewellyn
Deputy Chief of Staff (Political), Catherine Fall
Director of Policy, James O'Shaughnessy
Political Press Secretary to the Prime Minister, Gabby Bertin

POLICY AND IMPLEMENTATION UNIT
Head of Policy Unit, Paul Kirby
Head of Implementation Unit, Kris Murrin
Head of Analytics Team, Ivan Collister

DEPUTY PRIME MINISTER'S OFFICE AND CONSTITUTIONAL REFORM
Principal Private Secretary to the Deputy Prime Minister, Calum Miller

CONSTITUTIONAL GROUP
Director-General, Rowena Collins-Rice
Director, Vijay Rangarajan
Deputy Directors, Judith Simpson *(Constitutional Settlement and Clerk of the Privy Council);* Mark Sweeney *(Elections and Democracy)*

CROSS GOVERNMENT UNITS in the Cabinet Office comprises the Committee on Standards in Public Life (*see* Public Bodies), Independent Offices and the Office of the Parliamentary Counsel.

INDEPENDENT OFFICES

THE COMMISSIONER FOR PUBLIC APPOINTMENTS
3rd Floor, 35 Great Smith Street, London SW1P 3BQ
T 020-7276 2625
E enquiries@publicappointmentscommissioner.org
W http://publicappointmentscommissioner.independent.gov.uk

The Commissioner for Public Appointments is responsible for monitoring, regulating and reporting on ministerial appointments to public bodies. The commissioner can investigate complaints about the way in which appointments were made.
Commissioner for Public Appointments, Sir David Normington, GCB
Head of Office, Leila Brosnan

CIVIL SERVICE COMMISSION
35 Great Smith Street, London SW1P 3BQ
T 020-7276 2617
W http://civilservicecommission.independent.gov.uk

The Civil Service Commission regulates the principle that selection for appointment to the Civil Service must be on merit on the basis of fair and open competition; the commission publishes its recruitment principles and audit departments and agencies' performance against these. They personally chair competitions for the most senior jobs in the civil service. In addition, the commission hears complaints from civil servants under the Civil Service Code.

The commission was established as a statutory body in November 2010 under the provisions of the Constitutional Reform and Governance Act 2010.
First Commissioner, Sir David Normington, GCB
Commissioners (part-time), Sir Michael Aaronson, CBE; Mark Addison; Adele Biss; Peter Blausten; Prof. Christine Hallett; Eliza Hermann; Bernard Knight, CBE; Sir Neil McIntosh; Anthea Millett, CBE; Ranjit Sondhi; Libby Watkins

OFFICE OF THE PARLIAMENTARY COUNSEL
36 Whitehall, London SW1A 2AY
T 020-7210 2588
W www.cabinetoffice.co.uk/parliamentarycounsel
First Parliamentary Counsel, Sir Stephen Laws, KCB
Chief Executive, Jim Barron, CBE

DEPARTMENT FOR COMMUNITIES AND LOCAL GOVERNMENT
Eland House, Bressenden Place, London SW1E 5DU
T 0303-444 0000
W www.communities.gov.uk

The Department for Communities and Local Government (CLG) was formed in May 2006 with a remit to promote community cohesion and prevent extremism, as well as responsibility for housing, urban regeneration and planning. It unites the communities and civil renewal functions previously undertaken by the Home Office, with responsibility for regeneration, neighbourhood renewal and local government (previously held by the Office of the Deputy Prime Minister, which was abolished following a cabinet reshuffle in May 2006).

The DCLG also has responsibility for equality policy on race and faith (functions that were previously split between several government departments).
Secretary of State for Communities and Local Government, Rt. Hon. Eric Pickles, MP
Principal Private Secretary, David Hill
Parliamentary Private Secretary, Stephen Hammond, MP
Minister of State, Rt. Hon. Grant Shapps, MP *(Housing)*
Private Secretary, Mark Livesey
Minister of State, Rt. Hon. Greg Clark, MP
(Decentralisation and Cities)
Private Secretary, Fakruz Zaman
Parliamentary Under-Secretary of State, Bob Neill, MP
Private Secretary, Lee Burge
Parliamentary Under-Secretary of State, Andrew Stunell, OBE, MP
Private Secretary, Stella Michael-Sargeant
Parliamentary Under-Secretary of State, Baroness Hanham, CBE
Private Secretary, Elspeth Robinson
Permanent Secretary, Sir Bob Kerslake

Private Secretary, Caroline Winter
Chief Scientific Adviser, Jeremy Watson

MANAGEMENT BOARD
Chair, Rt. Hon. Eric Pickles, MP
Members, Andrew Campbell; Sue Higgins; Sir Bob Kerslake *(Permanent Secretary);* Richard McCarthy; David Prout
Non-Executive Members, Diana Brightmore-Armour; Stephen Hay; Sara Weller *(Lead)*

DEPARTMENT FOR CULTURE, MEDIA AND SPORT
2–4 Cockspur Street, London SW1Y 5DH
T 020-7211 6200
E enquiries@culture.gov.uk W www.culture.gov.uk

The Department for Culture, Media and Sport (DCMS) was established in July 1997 and aims to improve the quality of life for all those in the UK through cultural and sporting activities while championing the tourism, creative and leisure industries. It is responsible for government policy relating to the arts, sport, the National Lottery, tourism, libraries, museums and galleries, broadcasting, creative industries – including film and the music industry – press freedom and regulation, licensing, gambling and the historic environment.

The department is also responsible for 55 public bodies that help deliver the department's strategic aims and objectives, the 2012 Olympic Games and Paralympic Games, the listing of historic buildings and scheduling of ancient monuments, the export licensing of cultural goods, and the management of the Government Art Collection and the Royal Parks (its sole executive agency). It has the responsibility for humanitarian assistance in the event of a disaster, as well as for the organisation of the annual Remembrance Day ceremony at the Cenotaph. In May 2005 the DCMS assumed responsibility for fashion design, advertising and the arts market from the then Department for Trade and Industry – now the Department for Business, Innovation and Skills – which it also works jointly with on design issues (including sponsorship of the Design Council) and on relations with the computer games and publishing industries.
Secretary of State for Culture, Olympics, Media and Sport, Rt. Hon. Jeremy Hunt, MP
Principal Private Secretary, Paul Oldfield
Special Advisers, Sue Beeby; Adam Smith
Parliamentary Private Secretary, Rob Wilson, MP
Parliamentary Under-Secretary of State, John Penrose, MP *(Tourism and Heritage)*
Private Secretary, Leonie Phillips
Parliamentary Under-Secretary of State, Hugh Robertson, MP *(Sport and the Olympics)*
Private Secretary, Liz Wilson
Parliamentary Under-Secretary of State, Ed Vaizey, MP *(Culture, Communications and Creative Industries)*
Private Secretary, Craig Westwood
Permanent Secretary, Jonathan Stephens
Private Secretary, Helen Ewen

MANAGEMENT BOARD
Chair, Jonathan Stephens *(Permanent Secretary of State)*
Members, Jeremy Beeton *(Government Olympic Executive);* Simon Judge *(Finance)*

MINISTRY OF DEFENCE
see Defence section

DEPARTMENT FOR EDUCATION

Castle View House, East Lane, Runcorn, Cheshire WA7 2GJ
T 0870-001 2345 **Public Enquiries** 0370-000 2288
W www.education.gov.uk

The Department for Education (DfE) was established in May 2010 in place of the Department for Children, Schools and Families (DCSF), in order to refocus the department on its core purpose of supporting teaching and learning. The department is responsible for education and children's services, but the Department for Business, Innovation and Skills is responsible for higher education.

The department's objectives include the expansion of the academies programme, to allow schools to apply to become independent of their local authority, and the introduction of the free schools programme, to allow any suitable proposers, such as parents, businesses or charities, to set up their own school.

Secretary of State for Education, Rt. Hon. Michael Gove, MP
Principal Private Secretary, Hilary Spencer
Deputy Principal Private Secretary, Bernie Serieux
Private Secretary, Peter Walsh
Special Advisers, Dominic Cummings; Henry de Zoete
Parliamentary Private Secretary, David Evennett, MP
Minister of State, Sarah Teather, MP *(Children and Families)*
Private Secretary, Patrick Flack
Parliamentary Private Secretary, Duncan Hames, MP
Minister of State, Nick Gibb, MP *(Schools)*
Private Secretary, Camilla Frappell
Parliamentary Private Secretary, Nick Boles, MP
Minister of State, John Hayes, MP *(Further Education, Skills and Lifelong Learning)**
Private Secretary, Kellie Hurst
Parliamentary Under-Secretary of State, Lord Hill of Oareford, CBE *(Schools)*
Private Secretary, Jamie Weatherhead
Parliamentary Under-Secretary of State, Tim Loughton, MP *(Children and Families)*
Private Secretary, David Curtis
Parliamentary Clerk, Helen Heyden
Spokesperson in the House of Lords, Lord Hill of Oareford, CBE
Permanent Secretary, Sir David Bell, KCB
Private Secretary, Sophie Taylor

MANAGEMENT BOARD
Chair, David Bell *(Permanent Secretary of State)*
Members, Jon Coles; Sue Higgins; Tom Jeffery; Lesley Longstone
Non-Executive Members, Theodore Agnew; Sue John; John Nash; Anthony Saltz
*Jointly with the Department for Business, Innovation and Skills

DEPARTMENT OF ENERGY AND CLIMATE CHANGE

3 Whitehall Place, London SW1A 2AW
T 0300-060 4000 E correspondence@decc.gsi.gov.uk
W www.decc.gsi.gov.uk

The Department of Energy and Climate Change (DECC) was formed in 2008 to bring together energy policy, previously the responsibility of BERR (now the Department for Business, Innovation and Skills), and climate change mitigation policy, previously the responsibility of the Department for Environment, Food and Rural Affairs. DECC is responsible for tackling the threat of climate change by securing safe, clean and affordable energy in the UK, and by changing how we resource, manage and use our energy to create a low carbon and resource-efficient world.

Secretary of State for the Department for Energy and Climate Change, Rt. Hon. Chris Huhne, MP
Private Secretary, Ashley Ibbett
Parliamentary Private Secretary, Duncan Hames, MP
Minister of State, Charles Hendry, MP
Private Secretary, Emily Veitch
Parliamentary Private Secretary, Mark Menzies, MP
Minister of State, Gregory Barker, MP
Private Secretary, David Watson
Parliamentary Private Secretary, George Freeman, MP
Parliamentary Under-Secretary of State, Lord Marland
Private Secretary, Patrick Whitehead

EXECUTIVE TEAM
Private Secretary, Jen Goffin
Permanent Secretary, Moira Wallace
Members, Edmund Hosker *(Acting Chief Operating Officer);* Prof. David Mackay *(Chief Scientific Adviser);* Phil Wynn Owen *(Director General, International Climate Change and Energy Efficiency);* Simon Virley *(Director General, Energy Markets and Infrastructure)*

DEPARTMENT FOR ENVIRONMENT, FOOD AND RURAL AFFAIRS

Nobel House, 17 Smith Square, London SW1P 3JR
T 020-7238 3000 **Helpline** 0845-933 5577
E helpline@defra.gsi.gov.uk **W** www.defra.gov.uk

The Department for Environment, Food and Rural Affairs (DEFRA) is responsible for government policy on the environment, rural matters and farming and food production. In association with the agriculture departments of the Scottish government, the National Assembly for Wales and the Northern Ireland Office, and with the Intervention Board, the department is responsible for negotiations in the EU on the common agricultural and fisheries policies, and for single European market questions relating to its responsibilities. Its remit includes international agricultural and food trade policy.

The department's five strategic priorities are climate change; adaptation and mitigation; sustainable consumption and production; the protection of natural resources and the countryside; sustainable rural communities; and sustainable farming and food, including animal health and welfare. DEFRA is also the lead government department for emergencies in animal and plant diseases, flooding, food and water supply, dealing with the consequences of a chemical, biological, radiological or nuclear incident, and other threats to the environment.

Secretary of State for Environment, Food and Rural Affairs, Rt. Hon. Caroline Spelman, MP
Principal Private Secretary, Dr Jeremy Marlow
Private Secretaries, Alison Campbell; Mike Dowell; Emma Southard
Minister of State, Jim Paice, MP *(Agriculture and Food)*
Senior Private Secretary, Karen Morgan
Private Secretaries, Jaspreet Bassi; Ashwin Bolar; Caroline Jack;
Parliamentary Private Secretary, Mark Simmons, MP
Parliamentary Under-Secretary of State, Richard Benyon, MP *(Natural Environment and Fisheries)*
Senior Private Secretary, Simon Stannard
Private Secretaries, Emma Black; Sarah Nicholson; William Pryer

Parliamentary Under-Secretary of State, Lord Henley
Senior Private Secretary, Helena Busby
Private Secretaries, Samuel Evans; Helen Hazzledine; Darryl Pearson
Permanent Secretary, Ms Bronwyn Hill
Senior Private Secretary, David Read
Private Secretaries, Lisa Lewis, Julie Little, Stratos Ttofis

MANAGEMENT BOARD
Chair, Ms Bronwyn Hill *(Permanent Secretary)*
Members, Alexis Cleveland; Iain Ferguson; Bill Griffiths; Bill Stow *(Central Approvals Panel);* Peter Unwin *(Environment and Rural);* Prof. Robert Watson *(Chief Scientific Adviser);* Katrina Williams *(Food and Farming)*

FOREIGN AND COMMONWEALTH OFFICE
King Charles Street, London SW1A 2AH
T 020-7008 1500 W www.fco.gov.uk

The Foreign and Commonwealth Office (FCO) provides, through its staff in the UK and through its diplomatic missions abroad, the means of communication between the British government and other governments – and international governmental organisations – on all matters falling within the field of international relations.

It is responsible for alerting the British government to the implications of developments overseas; promoting British interests overseas; protecting British citizens abroad; explaining British policies to, and cultivating relationships with, governments overseas; the discharge of British responsibilities to the overseas territories; entry clearance UK visas (with the Home Office); and promoting British business overseas (jointly with the Department for Business, Innovation and Skills through UK Trade and Investment).

Secretary of State for Foreign and Commonwealth Affairs, Rt. Hon. William Hague, MP
Principal Private Secretary, Lindsay Appleby
Special Advisers, Denzil Davidson; Arminka Helic; Will Littlejohn
Parliamentary Private Secretary, Keith Simpson, MP
Minister of State, Rt. Hon. David Lidington, MP *(Europe and NATO)*
Private Secretary, Paul Heardman
Minister of State, Jeremy Browne, MP
Private Secretary, Rachel Lloyd
Parliamentary Under-Secretary of State, Alistair Burt, MP
Private Secretary, Russ Dixon
Parliamentary Under-Secretary of State, Henry Bellingham, MP
Private Secretary, Nick Heath
Minister of State, Rt. Hon. Lord Howell of Guildford *(House of Lords; the Commonwealth; International Energy Policy)*
Private Secretary, Ryder Thomas
Minister of State, Lord Green of Hurstpierpoint *(Trade and Investment and the FCO's relations with British business)*
Permanent Under-Secretary of State and Head of HM Diplomatic Service, Simon Fraser
Private Secretary, Anna Bradbury
Special Representatives, John Ashton *(Climate Change);* Sir Andrew Burns *(Post-Holocaust Issues);* Sir Brian Fall *(South Caucasus);* Michael Ryder *(Sudan);* Mark Sedwill *(Afghanistan and Pakistan)*

BOARD
Chair, Simon Fraser

Members, Sir Geoffrey Adams *(Political);* Nick Baird *(Europe and Globalisation);* Alison Currie *(Finance);* Susan Haird *(acting Chief Executive, UKTI);* Robert Hannigan *(Defence and Intelligence);* Susan le Jeune *(HR);* Shan Morgan *(HM Ambassador, Buenos Aires);* Matthew Rycroft *(Chief Operating Officer)*
Non-Executive Members, Julia Bond; Rudy Markham

DEPARTMENT OF HEALTH
Richmond House, 79 Whitehall, London SW1A 2NS
T 020-7210 4850 W www.dh.gov.uk

The Department of Health is responsible for the provision of the National Health Service (NHS) in England and for social care. The department's aims are to support, protect, promote and improve the nation's health; to secure the provision of comprehensive, high-quality care for all those who need it, regardless of their ability to pay, where they live or their age; and to provide responsive adult social care for those who lack the support they need.

The Department of Health is responsible for setting health and social care policy in England. The department's work sets standards and drives modernisation across all areas of the NHS, social care and public health.

Secretary of State for Health, Rt. Hon. Andrew Lansley, CBE, MP
Principal Private Secretary, Paul Macnaught
Parliamentary Private Secretary, Dr Andrew Murrison, MP
Minister of State, Simon Burns, MP *(Health)*
Private Secretary, Guy Mayou
Minister of State, Paul Burstow, MP *(Care Services)*
Private Secretary, Ben Pledger
Parliamentary Under-Secretary of State, Anne Milton, MP *(Public Health)*
Private Secretary, Giancarlo Laura
Parliamentary Under-Secretary, Lord Howe *(Quality)*
Parliamentary Clerk, Tim Elms

DEPARTMENTAL BOARD
Chair and Permanent Secretary, Una O'Brien
Members, David Behan, CBE *(Social Care, Local Government and Care Partnerships);* Prof. Dame Sally Davies *(Chief Medical Officer);* Richard Douglas, CB *(Principal Accounting Officer);* Sir David Nicholson, KCB, CBE *(Chief Executive, NHS);* Mike Wheeler *(Non-Executive Director)*

NATIONAL CLINICAL DIRECTORS
Cancer, Prof. Sir Mike Richards, CBE
Children, Young People and Maternity Services, Dr Sheila Shribman
Clinical Neurosciences (adviser), Dr Chris Clough
Dementia, Prof. Alistair Burns
Diabetes, Dr Rowan Hillson, MBE
Endoscopy, Roland Valori
Equality and Human Rights, Surinder Sharma
Health and Criminal Justice, Prof. Louis Appleby, CBE
Health and Work, Prof. Dame Carol Black
Imaging, Dr Erika Denton
Informatics, Dr Charles Gutteridge
Kidney Services, Dr Donal O'Donoghue
Learning Disabilities, Anne Williams, CBE
Liver Disease, Prof. Martin Lombard
Mental Health, Hugh Griffiths
Older People, Prof. David Oliver
Pathology, Dr Ian Barnes
Patient and Public Affairs, Joan Saddler, OBE
Pharmacy (Community), Jonathan Mason

Pharmacy (Hospitals), Martin Stephens
Respiratory Disease, Prof. Sue Hill; Robert Winter
Screening, Dr Anne Mackie
Transplantation, Chris J. Rudge
Trauma Care, Prof. Keith Willett
Urgent and Emergency Care, Prof. Matthew Cooke
Venous Thrombo-Embolism, Dr Mike Durkin

SOLICITOR'S OFFICE*
Solicitor, Gill Aitken
Director of DWP Legal Services, Greer Kerrigan
Director of DH Legal Services, Mark Wilson
* Also the solicitor's office for the Department for Work and Pensions

SPECIAL HEALTH AUTHORITIES
Health and Social Care Information Centre
W www.ic.nhs.uk
National Institute for Health and Clinical Excellence
W www.nice.org.uk
National Patient Safety Agency
W www.npsa.nhs.uk
National Treatment Agency for Substance Misuse
W www.nta.nhs.uk
NHS Blood and Transplant
W www.nhsbt.nhs.uk
NHS Business Services Authority
W www.nhsbsa.nhs.uk
NHS Institute for Innovation and Improvement
W www.institute.nhs.uk
NHS Litigation Authority
W www.nhsla.com

HOME OFFICE
2 Marsham Street, London SW1P 4DF
T 020-7035 4848 E public.enquiries@homeoffice.gsi.gov.uk
W www.homeoffice.gov.uk

The Home Office deals with those internal affairs in England and Wales which have not been assigned to other government departments. The Secretary of State for the Home Department is the link between the Queen and the public, and exercises certain powers on her behalf, including that of the royal pardon.

The Home Office aims to build a safe, just and tolerant society and to maintain and enhance public security and protection; to support and mobilise communities so that they are able to shape policy and improvement for their locality, overcome nuisance and anti-social behaviour, maintain and enhance social cohesion and enjoy their homes and public spaces peacefully; to deliver departmental policies and responsibilities fairly, effectively and efficiently; and to make the best use of resources. These objectives reflect the priorities of the government and the home secretary in areas of crime, citizenship and communities, namely to reduce crime and the fear of crime through visible, responsive and accountable policing; to reduce organised and international crime; to combat terrorism and other threats to national security; to ensure the effective delivery of justice; to reduce re-offending and protect the public; to reduce the availability and abuse of dangerous drugs; to regulate entry to, and settlement in, the UK in the interests of sustainable growth and social inclusion; and to support strong, active communities in which people of all races and backgrounds are valued and participate on equal terms.

The Home Office delivers these aims through the immigration services, its agencies and non-departmental public bodies, and by working with partners in private, public and voluntary sectors, individuals and communities. The home secretary is also the link between the UK government and the governments of the Channel Islands and the Isle of Man.

Secretary of State for the Home Department, Rt. Hon. Theresa May, MP
Principal Private Secretary, Gillian McGregor
Assistant Private Secretary, Alan Webster
Special Advisers, Fiona Cunningham; Nick Timothy
Minister of State, Rt. Hon. Baroness Browning *(Crime Prevention and Anti-Social Behaviour)*
Private Secretary, Nicola Payne
Minister of State, Damian Green, MP *(Immigration)*
Private Secretary, Benjamin Brown
Minister of State, Nick Herbert, MP *(Policing and Criminal Justice)*
Private Secretary, Christina Bankes
Parliamentary Under-Secretary of State, James Brokenshire, MP *(Crime and Security)*
Private Secretary, Katherine Richardson
Parliamentary Under-Secretary of State, Lynne Featherstone, MP *(Equalities and Criminal Information)*
Private Secretary, Mike Box
Permanent Secretary of State, Dame Helen Ghosh, DCB
Private Secretary, Rachel Hopcroft

MANAGEMENT BOARD
Chair, Sir David Normington, KCB *(Permanent Secretary of State)*
Members, Philip Augar; Val Gooding; Yasmin Diamond *(Communications);* Charles Farr *(Office for Security and Counter Terrorism);* Sarah Rapson *(Identity and Passport Service);* John Heywood; Lin Homer, CB *(UK Border Agency);* Helen Kilpatrick *(Financial and Commercial);* Peter Makeham, CB *(Strategy and International Group);* Stephen Rimmer *(Crime and Policing Group);* Kevin White, CB *(Human Resources)*

GOVERNMENT EQUALITIES OFFICE (GEO)
The GEO is responsible for the government's overall strategy on equality. Its work includes leading the development of a more integrated approach on equality across government with the aim of improving equality and reducing discrimination and disadvantage for all. The office is also responsible for leading policy on gender equality, sexual orientation and transgender equality matters.
Minister for Women and Equality, Rt. Hon. Theresa May, MP
Parliamentary Under-Secretary of State, Lynne Featherstone, MP *(Equalities)*

DEPARTMENT FOR INTERNATIONAL DEVELOPMENT
1 Palace Street, London SW1 5HE
T 020-7023 0000
Abercrombie House, Eaglesham Road, East Kilbride, Glasgow G75 8EA
T 01355-844000 Public Enquiries 0845-300 4100
E enquiry@dfid.gov.uk W www.dfid.gov.uk

The Department for International Development (DFID) is responsible for promoting sustainable development and reducing poverty. The central focus of the government's policy, based on the 1997, 2000 and 2006 white papers on international development, is a commitment to the internationally agreed Millennium Development Goals, to be achieved by 2015. These seek to eradicate extreme poverty and hunger; achieve universal primary education; promote gender equality and empower women; reduce child mortality; improve maternal health; combat HIV/AIDS, malaria and other diseases; ensure environmental sustainability; and encourage a global partnership for development.

DFID's assistance is concentrated in the poorest countries of sub-Saharan Africa and Asia, but also contributes to poverty reduction and sustainable development in middle-income countries, including those in Latin America and Eastern Europe. It also responds to overseas emergencies. The department works in partnership with governments of developing countries, charities, non-governmental organisations and businesses. It also works with multilateral institutions, including the World Bank, United Nations agencies and the European Commission. The department has headquarters in London and East Kilbride, offices in many developing countries, and staff based in British embassies and high commissions around the world.

Secretary of State for International Development, Rt. Hon. Andrew Mitchell, MP
Principal Private Secretary, Melanie Speight
Private Secretary, Mark Richardson
Special Advisers, Philippa Buckley; Richard Parr
Parliamentary Clerk, Jo Smith
Minister of State, Alan Duncan, MP
Private Secretary, Alice Mann
Parliamentary Under-Secretary of State, Stephen O'Brien, MP
Private Secretary, Greg Hicks
House of Lords Spokesperson, Baroness Verma
Whips, Chloe Smith, MP *(Commons);* Earl Attlee *(Lords)*
Permanent Secretary, Mark Lowcock

MANAGEMENT BOARD
Chair, Mark Lowcock
Members, Michael Anderson *(Policy and Global Issues);* Richard Calvert *(Finance and Corporate Performance);* Joy Hutcheon *(Country Programmes)*
Non-Executive Members, Vivienne Cox; Doreen Langston

CDC GROUP
Cardinal Place, 80 Victoria Street SW1E 5JL
T 020-7963 4700 E enquiries@cdcgroup.com
W www.cdcgroup.com

Founded in 1948, CDC is a government-owned Development Finance Institution that invests in the creation and growth of viable private businesses in poorer developing countries in order to contribute to economic growth and reduce poverty. In 2010 CDC invested £420m, with 44 per cent of new investments in Africa and 48 per cent in Asia. CDC is a public limited company with the Department for International Development as its 100 per cent shareholder.
Chair, Richard Gillingwater, CBE
Chief Executive (acting), Rod Evison

MINISTRY OF JUSTICE
102 Petty France, London SW1P 9AJ
T 020-3334 3555 E general.queries@justice.gsi.gov.uk
W www.justice.gov.uk

The Ministry of Justice (MoJ) was established in May 2007. MoJ is headed by the Lord Chancellor and Secretary of State for Justice who is responsible for improvements to the justice system so that it better serves

the public. He is also responsible for some areas of constitutional policy (those not covered by the Deputy Prime Minister).

The MoJ's priorities are to reduce reoffending and protect the public; provide access to justice; increase confidence in the justice system; and uphold people's civil liberties. The Lord Chancellor is the government minister responsible to parliament for the judiciary, the court system and prisons and probation. The Lord Chief Justice has been the head of the judiciary since 2006.

MoJ incorporates the National Offender Management Service, which includes HM Prison Service and the National Probation Service, and Her Majesty's Courts and Tribunals Service.

MoJ has several associated departments, non-departmental public bodies and executive agencies, including Her Majesty's Land Registry, the National Archives, the Legal Services Commission, and the Public Guardianship Office. The administrative functions of the Scotland Office and the Wales Office fall under the MoJ but these offices report to the respective Secretaries of State for Scotland and Wales.

Lord Chancellor and Secretary of State for Justice, Rt. Hon. Kenneth Clarke, QC, MP
Principal Private Secretary, Mark Sweeney
Special Advisers, David Hass; Kathryn Laing
Parliamentary Private Secretary, Ben Wallace, MP
Minister of State and Deputy Leader of the House of Lords, Rt. Hon. Lord McNally
Private Secretary, Emma Douglas
Minister of State, Nick Herbert*, MP
Private Secretary, Christina Bankes
Parliamentary Under-Secretary of State, Jonathan Djanogly, MP
Private Secretary, Sally Jones
Parliamentary Under-Secretary of State, Crispin Blunt, MP
Private Secretary, David Young
Permanent Secretary, Sir Suma Chakrabarti, KCB
Private Secretary, Ben Connah
Parliamentary Clerk, Ann Nixon
* Nick Herbert, MP, is responsible for criminal justice strategy and reports jointly to the Lord Chancellor and the home secretary

DEPARTMENTAL BOARD
Chair, Rt. Hon. Kenneth Clarke, QC, MP *(Lord Chancellor and Secretary of State for Justice)*
Members, Anne Beasley *(Director-General, Finance);* Crispin Blunt, MP; Sir Suma Chakrabarti, KCB *(Permanent Secretary);* Jonathan Djanogly, MP; Nick Herbert, MP; Rt. Hon. Lord McNally; Jonathan Slater *(Director-General, Transforming Justice)*
Non-Executive Members, Anne Bulford; James Leng; David MacLeod; Dame Sue Street, DCB

NORTHERN IRELAND OFFICE
11 Millbank, London SW1P 4PN
Stormont House, Stormont Estate, Belfast BT4 3SH
T 028-9052 0700
W www.nio.gov.uk

The Northern Ireland Office was established in 1972, when the Northern Ireland (Temporary Provisions) Act transferred the legislative and executive powers of the Northern Ireland parliament and government to the UK parliament and a secretary of state.

The Northern Ireland Office is responsible primarily for security issues, and for matters relating to the political and constitutional future of the province. It also deals with international issues as they affect Northern Ireland. In April 2010 the office transferred responsibility for policing and criminal justice to the Northern Ireland Assembly and Executive.

Under the terms of the 1998 Good Friday Agreement, power was devolved to the Northern Ireland Assembly in 1999. The assembly took on responsibility for the relevant areas of work previously undertaken by the departments of the Northern Ireland Office, covering agriculture and rural development, the environment, regional development, social development, education, higher education, training and employment, enterprise, trade and investment, culture, arts and leisure, health, social services, public safety and finance and personnel. In October 2002 the Northern Ireland Assembly was suspended and Northern Ireland returned to direct rule, but despite repeated setbacks, devolution was restored on 8 May 2007. For further details, *see* Regional Government section.

Secretary of State for Northern Ireland, Rt. Hon. Owen Paterson, MP
Minister of State, Rt. Hon. Hugo Swire, MP
Permanent Secretary and Head of the Northern Ireland Civil Service, Sir Bruce Robinson, KCB

OFFICE OF THE ADVOCATE-GENERAL FOR SCOTLAND
Dover House, Whitehall, London SW1A 2AU
T 020-7270 6770
Office of the Solicitor to the Advocate-General, Victoria Quay, Leith, Edinburgh EH6 6QQ
T 0131-244 1635
E privateoffice@advocategeneral.gsi.gov.uk
W www.oag.gov.uk

The Advocate-General for Scotland is one of the three law officers of the crown, alongside the Attorney-General and the Solicitor-General for England and Wales. He is the legal adviser to the UK government on Scottish law and is supported by staff in the Office of the Advocate-General for Scotland. The office is divided into the Legal Secretariat, based mainly in London, and the Office of the Solicitor to the Advocate-General, based in Edinburgh.

The post was created as a consequence of the constitutional changes set out in the Scotland Act 1998, which created a devolved Scottish parliament. The Lord Advocate and the Solicitor-General for Scotland then became part of the Scottish government and the Advocate-General took over their previous role as legal adviser to the government on Scots law. *See also* Regional Government section and Ministry of Justice.

Advocate-General for Scotland, Lord Wallace of Tankerness, QC
Private Secretary, Alice Adamson

OFFICE OF THE LEADER OF THE HOUSE OF COMMONS
26 Whitehall, London SW1A 2WH
T 020-7276 1005
E leader@commonsleader.x.gsi.gov.uk
W www.commonsleader.gov.uk

The Office of the Leader of the House of Commons is responsible for the arrangement of government business in the House of Commons and for planning and supervising the government's legislative programme. The Leader of the House of Commons upholds the rights and privileges of the house and acts as a spokesperson for the government as a whole.

The leader reports regularly to the cabinet on parliamentary business and the legislative programme. In his capacity as leader of the house, he is a member of the Public Accounts Commission and of the House of Commons Commission. He also chairs the cabinet committee on the legislative programme. As Lord Privy Seal, he is chair of the board of trustees of the Chevening Estate.

The Deputy Leader of the House of Commons supports the leader in handling the government's business in the house. He is responsible for monitoring MPs' and peers' correspondence.

Leader of the House of Commons and Lord Privy Seal, Rt. Hon. Sir George Young, Bt., MP
Head of Office, Mike Winter
Private Secretary, Christine Hill
Assistant Private Secretaries, Robert Foot *(Parliamentary Business);* Ben Sneddon *(Parliamentary Reform)*
Deputy Leader of the House of Commons, David Heath, CBE, MP
Private Secretary, Ben Sneddon

PRIVY COUNCIL OFFICE
2 Carlton Gardens, London SW1Y 5AA
T 020-7747 5310 E pcosecretariat@pco.x.gsi.gov.uk
W www.privy-council.gov.uk

The primary function of the office is to act as the secretariat to the Privy Council. It is responsible for the arrangements leading to the making of all royal proclamations and orders in council; for certain formalities connected with ministerial changes; for considering applications for the granting (or amendment) of royal charters; for the scrutiny and approval of by-laws and statutes of chartered institutions and of the governing instruments of universities and colleges; and for the appointment of high sheriffs and Privy Council appointments to governing bodies. Under the relevant acts, the office is responsible for the approval of certain regulations and rules made by the regulatory bodies of the medical and certain allied professions.

The Lord President of the Council is the ministerial head of the office and presides at meetings of the Privy Council. The Clerk of the Council is the administrative head of the Privy Council office.

Lord President of the Council and Deputy Prime Minister, Rt. Hon. Nick Clegg, MP
Clerk of the Council, Judith Simpson
Head of Secretariat and Senior Clerk, Ceri King
Senior Clerk, Christopher Berry

SCOTLAND OFFICE
Dover House, Whitehall, London SW1A 2AU
T 020-7270 6754
1 Melville Crescent, Edinburgh EH3 7HW
T 0131-244 9010
E scottish.secretary@scotland.gsi.gov.uk
W www.scotlandoffice.gov.uk

The Scotland Office is the department of the Secretary of State for Scotland which represents Scottish interests within the UK government in matters reserved to the UK parliament. The Secretary of State for Scotland also exercises certain specific functions in relation to devolution, including those provided for in the Scotland Act 1998; maintains the stability of the devolution settlement for Scotland; and pays grants to the Scottish Consolidated Fund and manages other financial transactions.

Reserved matters include the constitution, foreign affairs, defence, international development, the civil service, financial and economic matters, national security, immigration and nationality, misuse of drugs, trade and industry, various aspects of energy regulation (eg coal, electricity, oil, gas and nuclear energy), various aspects of transport, social security, employment, abortion, genetics, surrogacy, medicines, broadcasting and equal opportunities. Devolved matters include health and social work, education and training, local government and housing, justice and police, agriculture, forestry, fisheries, the environment, tourism, sports, heritage, economic development and internal transport. See also Regional Government section and Ministry of Justice.

Secretary of State for Scotland, Michael Moore, MP
Principal Private Secretary, Kate Richards
Parliamentary Under-Secretary of State, David Mundell, MP
Private Secretary, Jennifer Manton
Advocate-General and Spokesperson in the House of Lords, Rt. Hon. Lord Wallace of Tankerness, QC
Private Secretary, Alice Adamson

DEPARTMENT FOR TRANSPORT

Great Minster House, 33 Horseferry Road, London SW1P 4DR
T 020-7944 8300 W www.dft.gov.uk

The Department for Transport (DfT) works to deliver a transport system that balances the needs of the economy, the environment and society. Its main responsibilities include aviation, public transport, freight, regional and local transport, social inclusion, railways, roads and road safety, science and research, shipping and vehicles and sustainable travel.

The department provides leadership across the transport sector to achieve its objectives, working with regional, local and private-sector partners to deliver many of the services. Much of the department's work is delivered by seven executive agencies that employ around 90 per cent of its staff.

Secretary of State for Transport, Rt. Hon. Philip Hammond, MP
Principal Private Secretary, Natasha Robinson
Minister of State, Rt. Hon. Theresa Villiers, MP
Private Secretary, Rosa Estevez
Parliamentary Under-Secretary of State, Norman Baker, MP
Private Secretary, Joanna Guthrie
Parliamentary Under-Secretary of State, Mike Penning, MP
Private Secretary, Claire McAllister
Permanent Secretary, Lin Homer
Private Secretary, Natasha Coates

MANAGEMENT BOARD
Chair, Rt. Hon Philip Hammond, MP *(Secretary of State)*
Members, Lucy Chadwick *(Major Projects and London);* Steve Gooding *(Domestic);* Richard Hatfield *(International, Strategy and Environment);* Lin Homer *(Permanent Secretary);* Claire Moriarty *(Corporate);* Christopher Muttukumaru *(General Counsel);* Rt. Hon Theresa Villiers, MP
Non-Executive Members, Alan Cook, Sally Davis; Sam Laidlaw; Ed Smith

HM TREASURY

1 Horse Guards Road, London SW1A 2HQ
T 020-7270 4558
E public.enquiries@hm-treasury.gov.uk
W www.hm-treasury.gov.uk

HM Treasury is the country's economics and finance ministry, and is responsible for formulating and implementing the government's financial and economic policy. It aims to raise the rate of sustainable growth, boost prosperity, and provide the conditions necessary for universal economic and employment opportunities. The Office of the Lord High Treasurer has been continuously in commission for over 200 years. The Lord High Commissioners of HM Treasury are the First Lord of the Treasury (who is also the prime minister), the Chancellor of the Exchequer and five junior lords. This board of commissioners is assisted at present by the chief secretary, the parliamentary secretary (who is also the government chief whip in the House of Commons), the financial secretary, the economic secretary, the exchequer secretary and the commercial secretary. The prime minister as first lord is not primarily concerned with the day-to-day aspects of Treasury business; neither are the parliamentary secretary and the junior lords as government whips. Treasury business is managed by the Chancellor of the Exchequer and the other Treasury ministers, assisted by the permanent secretary.

The chief secretary is responsible for public expenditure, including spending reviews and strategic planning; in-year control; public-sector pay and pensions; Annually Managed Expenditure and welfare reform; efficiency in public services; procurement and capital investment. He also has responsibility for the Treasury's interest in devolution.

The financial secretary is the departmental minister for HM Revenue and Customs and the Valuation Office Agency and has responsibility for financial services policy including banking and financial services reform and regulation; financial stability; city competitiveness; wholesale and retail markets in the UK, Europe and internationally; and the Financial Services Authority. His other responsibilities include banking support; bank lending; UK Financial Investments; Equitable Life; and personal savings and pensions policy. He also provides support to the chancellor on EU and wider international finance issues.

The exchequer secretary is a title only used occasionally, normally when the post of paymaster-general is allocated to a minister outside of the Treasury (as it is at present; Francis Maude, MP was appointed paymaster-general and minister of the Cabinet Office in May 2010). The exchequer secretary's responsibilities include strategic oversight of the UK tax system; corporate and small business taxation, with input from the commercial secretary; departmental minister for HM Revenue and Customs and the Valuation Office Agency; lead minister on European and international tax issues; and has overall responsibility for the finance bill.

The economic secretary's responsibilities include environmental issues such as taxation of transport, international climate change and energy; North Sea oil taxation; tax credits and child poverty; assisting the chief secretary on welfare reform; charities and the voluntary sector; excise duties and gambling; stamp duty land tax; EU Budget; the Royal Mint; minister for HM Treasury Group; and working with the exchequer secretary on the finance bill.

The role of commercial secretary was created in 2010. Responsibilities include enterprise and productivity; corporate finance; assisting the financial secretary on financial services, banking policy promoting the government's financial services policies and the competitiveness of the UK; asset freezing and financial crime; foreign exchange reserves and debt management policy; National Savings and Investments; and the Debt Management Office. The commercial secretary is also the treasury spokesperson in the House of Lords.

Prime Minister and First Lord of the Treasury, Rt. Hon. David Cameron, MP

Chancellor of the Exchequer, Rt. Hon. George Osborne, MP

Principal Private Secretary, Beth Russell

Private Secretary, Sophie Dean

Special Advisers, Ramesh Chhabra; Poppy Mitchell-Rose

Council of Economic Advisers, Rupert Harrison; Eleanor Shawcross

Chief Secretary to the Treasury, Rt. Hon. Danny Alexander, MP

Private Secretary, David Silk

Financial Secretary to the Treasury, Mark Hoban, MP

Private Secretary, Josh Fleming

Exchequer Secretary to the Treasury, David Gauke, MP

Private Secretary, Oliver Hayden

Economic Secretary to the Treasury, Justine Greening, MP

Private Secretary, Robin Tasker

Commercial Secretary to the Treasury, Lord Sassoon

Permanent Secretary to the Treasury, Sir Nicholas Macpherson

Private Secretary and Speechwriter, Helen Chamberlain

Lords Commissioners of HM Treasury (Whips), James Duddridge, MP; Michael Fabricant, MP; Brooks Newmark, MP; Angela Watkinson, MP; Jeremy Wright, MP

Assistant Whips, Stephen Crabb, MP; Philip Dunne, MP; Robert Goodwill, MP; Mark Hunter, MP; Norman Lamb, MP*; Chloe Smith, MP; Shailesh Vera, MP; Bill Wiggin, MP

* Also Chief Parliamentary and Political Adviser to the Deputy Prime Minister

MANAGEMENT BOARD

Chair, Sir Nicholas Macpherson *(Permanent Secretary)*

Members, Mark Bowman *(Strategy, Planning and Budget);* Alison Cottrell *(Corporate Services);* Michael Ellam *(International and EU);* Andrew Hudson *(Public Services);* Julian Kelly *(Finance and Commercial);* Dave Ramsden *(Chief Economic Adviser);* Tom Scholar *(Second Permanent Secretary);* Jonathan Taylor *(Financial Services);* Edward Troup *(Tax and Welfare)*

WALES OFFICE
Gwydyr House, Whitehall, London SW1A 2NP
T 020-7270 0534
E walesoffice@walesoffice.gsi.gov.uk
W www.walesoffice.gov.uk

The Wales Office was established in 1999 when most of the powers of the Welsh Office were handed over to the National Assembly for Wales. It is the department of the Secretary of State for Wales, who is the key government figure liaising with the devolved government in Wales and who represents Welsh interests in the cabinet and parliament. The secretary of state has the right to attend and speak at sessions of the National Assembly (and must consult the assembly on the government's legislative programme). *See also* Regional Government section and Ministry of Justice.

Secretary of State for Wales, Rt. Hon. Cheryl Gillan, MP

Principal Private Secretary, Stephen Hillcoat

Parliamentary Under-Secretary, David Jones, MP

Director of Office, Fiona Adams-Jones

DEPARTMENT FOR WORK AND PENSIONS
Caxton House, Tothill Street, London SW1H 9NA
T 020-7962 8000 E enquiries@dwp.gsi.gov.uk
W www.dwp.gov.uk

The Department for Work and Pensions was formed in June 2001 from parts of the former Department of Social Security, the Department for Education and Employment and the Employment Service. The department helps unemployed people of working age into work, helps employers to fill their vacancies and provides financial support to people unable to help themselves, through back-to-work programmes. The department also administers the child support system, social security benefits and the social fund. In addition, the department has reciprocal social security arrangements with other countries.

Secretary of State for Work and Pensions, Rt. Hon. Iain Duncan Smith, MP

Principal Private Secretary, John-Paul Marks

Private Secretaries, Jennifer Bradley; Matt Davies; Mark Swindells

Minister of State, Rt. Hon. Chris Grayling, MP *(Employment)*

Private Secretary, Debbie McMahon

Assistant Private Secretaries, Pippa Knott; Ann Lyle; John Mazzeo

Minister of State, Steve Webb, MP *(Pensions)*

Private Secretary, Michael Dynan-Oakley

Assistant Private Secretaries, Polly Fortune; Biba Hussain; Mark Swindells

Parliamentary Under-Secretary and Minister of State, Maria Miller, MP *(Disabled People)*

Private Secretary, Rachael Hunter

Assistant Private Secretaries, James Frew; Alice Simpson; Vicky Smith

Minister of State, Lord Freud *(Welfare Reform)*

Private Secretary, Jessica Yuille

Assistant Private Secretaries, Aisling Fox; Manjula Pelpola; Billy Street

EXECUTIVE TEAM

Permanent Secretary and Head of Department, Robert Devereux

Directors-General, Gill Aitken *(Legal Group);* Joe Harley *(IT and Chief Information Officer);* Richard Heaton *(Strategy, Information and Pensions);* Chris Last *(Human Resources);* Terry Moran *(Universal Credit Programme);* Hunada Nouss *(Finance);* Sue Owen *(Welfare and Wellbeing);* Adam Sharples *(Employment)*

Agencies Chief Executives, Vivien Hopkins *(Pension, Disability and Carers Service (acting));* Darra Singh *(Jobcentre Plus)*

EXECUTIVE AGENCIES

Executive agencies are well-defined business units that carry out services with a clear focus on delivering specific outputs within a framework of accountability to ministers. They can be set up or disbanded without legislation, and they are organisationally independent from the department they are answerable to. In the following list the agencies are shown in the accounts of their sponsor departments. Legally they act on behalf of the relevant secretary of state. Their chief executives also perform the role of accounting officers, which means they are responsible for the money spent by their organisations. Staff employed by agencies are civil servants.

CABINET OFFICE

COI (CENTRAL OFFICE OF INFORMATION)
Hercules Road, London SE1 7DU
T 020-7928 2345 W www.coi.gov.uk

The COI was created to improve the effectiveness of and add value to government publicity programmes, through consultancy, procurement and project management services across all communication channels. Administrative responsibility for the COI rests with the minister for the Cabinet Office.

Following recommendations by the former Permanent Secretary of Government Communications, Matt Tee, the Minister for the Cabinet Office, Francis Maude, announced in June 2011 that the COI will close by April 2012.
Chief Executives (acting), Graham Hooper; Emma
  Lochhead

GOVERNMENT PROCUREMENT SERVICE
3rd Floor, Royal Liver Building, Pier Head, Liverpool L3 1PE
T 0345-410 2222 E info@buyingsolutions.gsi.gov.uk
W www.buyingsolutions.gov.uk

The Government Procurement Service is an executive agency of the Cabinet Office, providing a professional procurement service to the UK public sector. As a result of the Strategic Review of Buying Solutions, published in July 2011, it will play a key role in delivering centralised procurement of common goods and services for central government departments. It was originally known as The Buying Agency when it was launched in 1991, and was later renamed Buying Solutions.
Chief Procurement Officer, John Collington
Managing Director, David Shields

ATTORNEY-GENERAL'S OFFICE

TREASURY SOLICITOR'S DEPARTMENT
1 Kemble Street, London WC2B 4TS
T 020-7210 3000
E thetreasurysolicitor@tsol.gsi.gov.uk
W www.tsol.gov.uk

The Treasury Solicitor's Department, which became an executive agency in 1996, provides legal services for many government departments and other publicly funded bodies, and is answerable to the Attorney-General. Those departments and bodies without their own lawyers are provided with legal advice and litigation services. The Treasury Solicitor is also the Queen's Proctor, and is responsible for collecting ownerless goods *(bona vacantia)* on behalf of the crown.
*HM Procurator-General and Treasury Solicitor (Permanent
  Secretary)*, Paul Jenkins, QC
Deputy Treasury Solicitor, Jonathan Jones

BONA VACANTIA DIVISION
Head of Division, Zane Denton

CENTRAL ADVISORY DIVISION
Head of Division, Iain Macleod

EUROPEAN DIVISION
Head of Division, Paul Berman

LITIGATION AND EMPLOYMENT GROUP
Head of Division, Hugh Giles

DEPARTMENT FOR BUSINESS, INNOVATION AND SKILLS

COMPANIES HOUSE
Crown Way, Cardiff CF14 3UZ
T 0303-123 4500
E enquiries@companieshouse.gov.uk
W www.companieshouse.gov.uk

Companies House incorporates companies, registers company documents and provides company information.
Registrar of Companies for England and Wales, Gareth Jones
Registrar of Companies for Scotland, Dorothy Blair
Registrar of Companies for Northern Ireland, Helen
  Shilliday

THE INSOLVENCY SERVICE
21 Bloomsbury Street, London WC1B 3QW
Insolvency Enquiry Line 0845-602 9848
Redundancy Enquiry Line 0845-145 0004
E insolvency.enquiryline@insolvency.gsi.gov.uk
W www.bis.gov.uk/insolvency

The role of the service includes administration and investigation of the affairs of bankrupts, partners and companies in compulsory liquidation; dealing with the disqualification of directors in all corporate failures; authorising and regulating the insolvency profession; providing banking and investment services for bankruptcy and liquidation estate funds; assessing and paying statutory entitlement to redundancy payments when an employer cannot, or will not, pay its employees; and advising ministers on insolvency, redundancy and related issues. The service has around 2,100 staff, operating from 35 locations across Great Britain.
Inspector-General and Chief Executive, Stephen Speed
Deputy Chief Executive, Graham Horne
Deputy Inspector-General, Les Cramp, CBE
*Inspector of Companies and Head of Investigation and
  Enforcement Services*, Robert Burns

INTELLECTUAL PROPERTY OFFICE
Concept House, Cardiff Road, Newport NP10 8QQ
T 0300-300 2000 E information@ipo.gov.uk
W www.ipo.gov.uk

The Intellectual Property Office (an operating name of the Patent Office) was set up in 1852 to act as the UK's sole office for the granting of patents. It was established as an executive agency in 1990 and became a trading fund in 1991. The office is responsible for the granting of intellectual property (IP) rights which include patents, trade marks, designs and copyright.
Comptroller-General and Chief Executive, John Alty

NATIONAL MEASUREMENT OFFICE
Stanton Avenue, Teddington, Middx TW11 0JZ
T 020-8943 7272 E info@nmo.gov.uk
W www.bis.gov.uk/nmo

The National Measurement Office (NMO) was created in April 2009, merging the functions of the National Weights and Measures Laboratory and the National Measurement System. NMO is responsible for all aspects of the national measurement system and provides a legal metrology infrastructure necessary to facilitate fair competition, support innovation, promote international trade and protect consumers, health and the environment.
Chief Executive, Peter Mason

UK SPACE AGENCY
Polaris House, North Star Avenue, Swindon, Wiltshire
SN2 1SZ
T 020-7215 5000 E info@ukspaceagency.bis.gsi.gov.uk
W www.bis.gov.uk/ukspaceagency

The UK Space Agency was established on 23 March 2010 and became an executive agency on 1 April 2011. It was created to provide a single voice for UK space ambitions, and is responsible for all strategic decisions on the UK civil space programme. Responsibilities of the UK Space Agency include coordinating UK civil space activity; supporting academic research; nurturing the UK space industry; raising the profile of UK space activities at home and abroad; working to increase understanding of space science and its practical benefits; and inspiring the next generation of UK scientists and engineers.
Chief Executive, Dr David Williams

DEPARTMENT FOR COMMUNITIES AND LOCAL GOVERNMENT

FIRE SERVICE COLLEGE
Moreton-in-Marsh, Gloucestershire GL56 0RH
T 01608-650831 E enquiries@fireservicecollege.ac.uk
W www.fireservicecollege.ac.uk

The Fire Service College provides fire-related training, both practical and theoretical, consultancy, and library and information services to the UK fire and rescue service, other UK public sector organisations, the private sector, and the international market.
Chief Executive, Kim Robinson

ORDNANCE SURVEY
Adanac Drive, Southampton SO16 0AS
T 0845-605 0505
E customerservices@ordnancesurvey.co.uk
W www.ordnancesurvey.co.uk

Ordnance Survey is the national mapping agency for Great Britain. It is a government department and executive agency operating as a trading fund since 1999.
Director-General and Chief Executive, Vanessa Lawrence, CB

PLANNING INSPECTORATE
Temple Quay House, 2 The Square, Temple Quay, Bristol BS1 6PN
T 0117-372 6372
E enquiries@planning-inspectorate.gsi.gov.uk
Crown Buildings, Cathays Park, Cardiff CF10 3NQ
T 029-2082 3866 E wales@planning-inspectorate.gsi.gov.uk
W www.planning-inspectorate.gov.uk

The main work of the inspectorate consists of the processing of planning and enforcement appeals, and holding examinations into development plan documents. It also deals with advertisement appeals; rights of way cases; cases arising from the Environmental Protection and Water acts, the Transport and Works Act 1992 and other highways legislation; and reporting on planning applications called in for decision by the Department for Communities and Local Government and the Welsh government
Chief Executive, Katrine Sporle

THE QUEEN ELIZABETH II CONFERENCE CENTRE
Broad Sanctuary, London SW1P 3EE
T 020-7222 5000 F 020-7798 4200
E info@qeiicc.co.uk W www.qeiicc.co.uk

The centre provides secure conference facilities for national and international government and private sector use.
Chief Executive, Ernest Vincent

DEPARTMENT FOR CULTURE, MEDIA AND SPORT

THE ROYAL PARKS
The Old Police House, Hyde Park, London W2 2UH
T 0300-061 2000 E hq@royalparks.gsi.gov.uk
W www.royalparks.org.uk

Royal Parks is responsible for maintaining and developing over 2,000 hectares (5,000 acres) of urban parkland contained within the eight royal parks in London: Bushy Park (with the Longford river); Green Park; Greenwich Park; Hyde Park; Kensington Gardens; Regent's Park (with Primrose Hill); Richmond Park and St James's Park.
Chief Executive, Mark Camley

DEPARTMENT FOR ENVIRONMENT, FOOD AND RURAL AFFAIRS

ANIMAL HEALTH
Corporate Centre, Block C, Government Buildings, Whittington Road, Worcester WR5 2LQ
T 01905-763355
E corporate.centre@ahvla.gsi.gov.uk
W www.defra.gov.uk/ahvla

The Animal Health and Veterinary Laboratories Agency (AHVLA) is an executive agency of DEFRA. It was formed on 1 April 2011 following the merger of Animal Health and The Veterinary Laboratories Agency.

The agency is responsible, on behalf of DEFRA, the Welsh government and the Scottish government for protecting the health and welfare of farmed animals, including playing a key role in the prevention, detection and management of exotic and endemic diseases in animals. It is also responsible for delivering research and laboratory services for animal and public health and for advising DEFRA regarding the veterinary evidence base for policy development.

The AHVLA's services include a wide range of core functions covering veterinary research, disease surveillance and specialised testing. This includes protecting the welfare of farmed animals; the eradication of endemic disease; import and export certification; animal by-product regulation; and preparedness for managing exotic animal diseases. The AHVLA also has an emergency response capability.

Animal Health is also responsible for licensing the trade in endangered species for conservation purposes; for ensuring that eggs are correctly labelled and that marketing regulations are being complied with. It also monitors the standard of hygiene in dairies in relation to the nation's raw milk supply.
Chief Executive, Catherine Brown

CENTRE FOR ENVIRONMENT, FISHERIES AND AQUACULTURE SCIENCE (CEFAS)
Pakefield Road, Lowestoft, Suffolk NR33 0HT
T 01502-562244 W www.cefas.defra.gov.uk

Established in April 1997, the agency provides research and consultancy services in fisheries science and management, aquaculture, fish health and hygiene, environmental impact assessment, and environmental quality assessment.
Chief Executive, Dr Richard Judge

FOOD AND ENVIRONMENT RESEARCH AGENCY
Sand Hutton, York YO41 1LZ
T 01904-462000
E info@fera.gsi.gov.uk W wwwdefra.gov.uk/fera

The Food and Environment Research Agency was formed on 1 April 2009 from the merger of the Central Science Laboratory, the Government Decontamination Service, and DEFRA's Plant Health division and Plant Varieties office. The agency's purpose is to support and develop a sustainable food chain, a healthy natural environment, and to protect the community from biological and chemical risks. It does this by providing evidence, analysis and professional advice to the government, international organisations and the private sector. The agency brings together expertise in policy issues, particularly relating to seed, plant and bee health; inspection services necessary to ensure protection for seeds, crops and horticulture; multi-disciplinary science to rapidly diagnose threats, evaluate risk and inform policy in food and environmental areas; and in responding to and recovering from unforeseen or emergency situations.
Chief Executive, Adrian Belton

RURAL PAYMENTS AGENCY
PO Box 69, Reading RG1 3YD
T 0845-603 7777
E enquiries@rpa.gsi.gov.uk W http://rpa.defra.gov.uk

The RPA was established in 2001. It is the single paying agency responsible for Common Agricultural Policy (CAP) schemes in England and for certain other schemes throughout the UK; it is also responsible for operating cattle tracing services across Great Britain, conducting inspections of farms, processing plants and fresh produce markets in England, and managing the Rural Land Register.
Chief Executive, Mark Grimshaw

VETERINARY MEDICINES DIRECTORATE
Woodham Lane, New Haw, Addlestone, Surrey KT15 3LS
T 01932-336911 E postmaster@vmd.defra.gsi.gov.uk
W www.vmd.defra.gov.uk

The Veterinary Medicines Directorate is responsible for all aspects of the authorisation and control of veterinary medicines, including post-authorisation surveillance of residues in animals and animal products. It is also responsible for the development and enforcement of legislation concerning veterinary medicines and the provision of policy advice to ministers.
Chief Executive, Steve Dean

FOREIGN AND COMMONWEALTH OFFICE

FCO SERVICES
Hanslope Park, Milton Keynes MK19 7BH
T 020-7008 02959 E fco.services@fco.gov.uk
W www.fcoservices.gov.uk

FCO Services was established as an executive agency in April 2006 and became a trading fund in April 2008. It provides a range of bespoke, secure services worldwide to the FCO and other UK government departments. In addition to the FCO, existing customers include foreign governments and international organisations closely linked to the UK.
Chief Executive, Chris Moxey

WILTON PARK CONFERENCE CENTRE
Wiston House, Steyning, W. Sussex BN44 3DZ
T 01903-815020 E admin@wiltonpark.org.uk
W www.wiltonpark.org.uk

Wilton Park organises international affairs conferences and is hired out to government departments and commercial users.
Chief Executive, Richard Burge

DEPARTMENT OF HEALTH

MEDICINES AND HEALTHCARE PRODUCTS REGULATORY AGENCY (MHRA)
151 Buckingham Palace Road, London SW1W 9SS
E info@mhra.gsi.gov.uk
W www.mhra.gov.uk

The MHRA is responsible for protecting and promoting public and patient safety by ensuring that medicines, healthcare products and medical equipment meet appropriate standards of safety, quality, performance and effectiveness, and are used safely.
Chair, Prof. Sir Alasdair Breckenridge, CBE
Chief Executive, Prof. Kent Woods

HOME OFFICE

CRIMINAL RECORDS BUREAU
PO Box 110, Liverpool L69 3EF
T 0870-909 0811 E customerservices@crb.gov.uk
W www.homeoffice.gov.uk/crb

The Criminal Records Bureau was launched in March 2002 and provides access to criminal record information to enable organisations in the public, private and voluntary sectors to make safer recruitment decisions by identifying candidates who may be unsuitable for certain work – especially that which involves children or vulnerable adults.
Chief Executive, Steve Long

IDENTITY AND PASSPORT SERVICE
2 Marsham Street, London SW1V 1PN
Passport Advice Line 0300-222 0000
General Register Office 0845-603 7788
W http://www.homeoffice.gov.uk/agencies-public-bodies/ips/

Established in April 2006, the Identity and Passport Service (IPS) is an executive agency of the home office and incorporates the UK Passport Service and the General Register Office. The UK Passport Service issues, renews and amends passports for UK nationals both at home and abroad. The General Register Office is responsible for overseeing the system of civil registration in England and Wales, which involves administering the marriage laws; securing an effective system for the registration of births, adoptions, civil partnerships, marriages and deaths; maintaining an archive of births, civil partnerships, marriages and deaths; maintaining the adopted children's register, adoption contact register and other registers; and supplying certificates from the registers and the archives for research or family history purposes.

Chief Executive and Registrar-General for England and Wales, Sarah Rapson

NATIONAL FRAUD AUTHORITY
PO Box 64170, London WC1A 9BP
T 020-3356 1000 E NFAcontact@attorneygeneral.gsi.gov.uk
W www.attorneygeneral.gov.uk/nfa

The National Fraud Authority (NFA) was established on 1 October 2008 to increase protection for the UK economy from the harm caused by fraud. It works with private, public and third sector organisations to initiate, co-ordinate and communicate counter-fraud activity across the economy. The authority's priorities are to tackle the key fraud threats to the UK, to act effectively to pursue fraudsters and hold them to account, and to improve the nation's long-term capability to prevent fraud. The NFA is also working to improve the support available to fraud victims and to build the UK's capability to share and act on knowledge about fraud, both nationally and internationally.
Chief Executive, Dr Bernard Herdan, CB

UK BORDER AGENCY
11th Floor, Lunar House, 40 Wellesley Road, Croydon CR9 2BY
T 0870-606 7766 E UKBApublicenquiries@ukba.gsi.gov.uk
W www.ukba.homeoffice.gov.uk

The UK Border Agency was established in April 2008 and became an executive agency of the Home Office in April 2009. The agency brings together the work previously carried out by the Border and Immigration Agency, and, following Royal Assent to the Borders, Citizenship and Immigration Act in July 2009, customs detection work at the border from HM Revenue and Customs, and UK visa services from the Foreign and Commonwealth Office.
Chief Executive, Rob Whiteman
Board Members, Jonathan Sedgwick *(Deputy Chief Executive);* Zilla Bowell *(Chief Executive's Chief of Staff);* Martin Baker, QPM; James Bevan; Kathryn Bishop; Brodie Clark; Matthew Coats; Melanie Dawes; Joe Dugdale; Mike Hawker; Justin Holliday; Martin Peach; Graham Sims; Mark Thomson; David Wood; Barbara Woodward; Rob Yeldham

MINISTRY OF JUSTICE

HER MAJESTY'S COURTS AND TRIBUNALS SERVICE
see Law Courts and Offices section

LAND REGISTRY
Trafalgar House, 1 Bedford Park, Croydon CR0 2AQ
T 0300-006 0001 E customersupport@landregistry.gsi.gov.uk
W www.landregistry.gov.uk

The registration of title to land was first introduced in England and Wales by the Land Registry Act 1862. Land Registry maintains and develops the Land Register for England and Wales, and is an executive agency and trading fund responsible to the Lord Chancellor and Secretary of State for Justice. The Land Register has been open to public inspection since 1990.
Chief Land Registrar and Chief Executive, Malcolm Dawson, OBE

NATIONAL ARCHIVES
Kew, Richmond, Surrey TW9 4DU
T 020-8876 3444
W www.nationalarchives.gov.uk

The National Archives is a non-ministerial government department and an executive agency of the Ministry of Justice. It incorporates the Public Records Office, Historical Manuscripts Commission, Office of Public Sector Information and Her Majesty's Stationery Office. As the official archive of the UK government, it preserves, protects and makes accessible the historical collection of official records.
The National Archives also manages digital information including the UK government web archive which contains over one billion digital documents, and devises solutions for keeping government records readable now and in the future.
The organisation administers the UK's public records system under the Public Records Acts of 1958 and 1967. The records it holds span 1,000 years – from the Domesday Book to the latest government papers to be released – and fill more than 167km (104 miles) of shelving.
Chief Executive, Oliver Morley

NATIONAL OFFENDER MANAGEMENT SERVICE
see Prison Service section

OFFICE OF THE PUBLIC GUARDIAN
PO Box 15118, Birmingham B16 6GX
T 0300-456 0300
E customerservices@publicguardian.gsi.gov.uk

The Office of the Public Guardian supports and promotes decision making for those who lack capacity or would like to plan for their future, within the framework of the Mental Capacity Act 2005.
Chief Executive and Public Guardian, Martin John

TRIBUNALS SERVICE
see Tribunals section

DEPARTMENT FOR TRANSPORT

DRIVER AND VEHICLE LICENSING AGENCY (DVLA)
Longview Road, Swansea SA6 7JL
T 01792-782341 W www.dft.gov.uk/dvla

The DVLA was established as an executive agency in 1990. It became a trading fund in 2004, but relinquished this status on 1 April 2011. The DVLA is responsible for registering and licensing drivers and vehicles, and for collection and enforcement of vehicle excise duty (£5.78bn in 2010–11). The DVLA also maintains records of all those who are entitled to drive various types of vehicle (currently over 44 million people), all vehicles entitled to travel on public roads (currently 36 million), and drivers' endorsements, disqualifications and medical conditions.
Chief Executive, Simon Tse

DRIVING STANDARDS AGENCY

The Axis Building, 112 Upper Parliament Street, Nottingham NG1 6LP

T 0115-936 6666 E customer.services@dsa.gsi.gov.uk
W www.dft.gov.uk/dsa

The agency is responsible for carrying out theory and practical driving tests for car drivers, motorcyclists, bus and lorry drivers, and for maintaining the statutory register of approved driving instructors and the voluntary register of large goods vehicle instructors and fleet driver trainers. It also supervises Compulsory Basic Training (CBT) for learner motorcyclists. There are two area offices, which manage over 400 practical driving test centres across Britain and 158 theory test centres.
Chief Executive, Rosemary Thew

GOVERNMENT CAR AND DESPATCH AGENCY

46 Ponton Road, London SW8 5AX

T 020-7217 3837 E info@gcda.gsi.gov.uk
W www.dft.gov.uk/gcda

The agency provides secure transport and mail distribution to government and the public sector.
Chief Executive, Marian Duncan

HIGHWAYS AGENCY

3rd Floor, 157–197 Buckingham Palace Road, London SW1W 9HA

T 0300-123 5000
E ha_info@highways.gsi.gov.uk W www.highways.gov.uk

The Highways agency is responsible for operating, maintaining and improving England's 7,000km (4,300 miles) of motorways and trunk roads – known as the strategic road network – on behalf of the Secretary of State for Transport.
Chief Executive, Graham Dalton

MARITIME AND COASTGUARD AGENCY

Spring Place, 105 Commercial Road, Southampton SO15 1EG

T 023-8032 9100
W www.dft.gov.uk/mca

The agency's aims are to prevent loss of life, continuously improve maritime safety and protect the marine environment.
Chief Executive, Sir Alan Massey
Chief Coastguard, Rod Johnson

VEHICLE CERTIFICATION AGENCY

1 Eastgate Office Centre, Eastgate Road, Bristol BS5 6XX

T 0117-951 5151 E enquiries@vca.gov.uk
W www.vca.gov.uk/vca/

The agency is the UK authority responsible for ensuring that vehicles and vehicle parts have been designed and constructed to meet internationally agreed standards of safety and environmental protection.
Chief Executive, Paul Markwick

VEHICLE AND OPERATOR SERVICES AGENCY

Berkeley House, Croydon Street, Bristol BS5 0DA

T 0300-123 9000
E enquiries@vosa.gov.uk W www.vosa.gov.uk

The Vehicle and Operator Services Agency was formed in April 2003 from the merger of the Vehicle Inspectorate and the Traffic Area Network. The agency works with the independent traffic commissioners to improve road safety and the environment; safeguard fair competition by promoting and enforcing compliance with commercial operator licensing requirements; process applications for licences to operate lorries and buses; register bus services; operate and administer testing schemes for all vehicles, including the supervision of the MOT testing scheme; enforce the law on vehicles to ensure that they comply with legal standards and regulations; enforce drivers' hours and licensing requirements; provide training and advice for commercial operators; investigate vehicle defects and recalls; and provide support to the police by examining vehicles involved in accidents for contributory defects.
Chief Executive, Alastair Peoples

HM TREASURY

NATIONAL SAVINGS AND INVESTMENTS

1 Drummond Gate, Pimlico, London SW1V 2QX

T 0500-007007 W www.nsandi.com

NS&I (National Savings and Investments) came into being in 1861 when the Palmerston government set up the Post Office Savings Bank, a savings scheme which aimed to encourage ordinary wage earners 'to provide for themselves against adversity and ill health'. NS&I was established as a government department in 1969. It became an executive agency of the Treasury in 1996 and is responsible for the design, marketing and administration of savings and investment products for personal savers and investors. It has over 26 million customers and almost £100bn invested. *See also* Banking and Finance, National Savings.
Chief Executive, Jane Platt

ROYAL MINT

PO Box 500, Llantrisant, Pontyclun CF72 8YT

T 01443-222111
W www.royalmint.com

The Royal Mint has operated as a trading fund since 1975, and was established as an executive agency in 1990.

The prime responsibility of the Royal Mint is the provision of United Kingdom coinage, but it actively competes in world markets for a share of the available circulating coin business and about half of the coins and blanks it produces annually are exported. It also manufactures special proof and uncirculated quality coins in gold, silver and other metals; military and civil decorations and medals; commemorative and prize medals; and royal and official seals.
Master of the Mint, Chancellor of the Exchequer *(ex officio)*
Chief Executive, Adam Lawrence

UK DEBT MANAGEMENT OFFICE

Eastcheap Court, 11 Philpot Lane, London EC3M 8UD

T 0845-357 6500
W www.dmo.gov.uk

The UK Debt Management Office (DMO) was launched as an executive agency of HM Treasury in April 1998. The Chancellor of the Exchequer determines the policy and financial framework within which the DMO operates, but delegates operational decisions on debt and cash management and the day-to-day running of the office to the chief executive. The DMO's remit is to carry out the government's debt management policy of minimising financing costs over the long term, and to minimise the cost of offsetting the government's net cash flows over time, while operating at a level of risk approved by ministers in both cases. The DMO is also responsible for providing loans to local authorities through the Public Works Loan Board, for managing the assets of certain public-sector bodies through the Commissioners for the Reduction of the National Debt, and for administering the operational delivery of the government's Credit Guarantee Scheme.

Chief Executive, Robert Stheeman

DEPARTMENT FOR WORK AND PENSIONS

JOBCENTRE PLUS
Level 6, Caxton House, Tothill Street, London SW1H 9NQ
T 0845-606 0234 W www.dwp.gov.uk/jobcentreplus

Jobcentre Plus was formed in April 2002 following the merger of the Employment Service and some parts of the Benefits Agency. The agency administers claims for, and payment of, social security benefits to help people gain employment or improve their prospects for work, as well as helping employers to fill their vacancies.
Chief Executive, Darra Singh

THE PENSION, DISABILITY AND CARERS SERVICE
Room 111, Block 1, Norcross, Blackpool, Lancs FY5 3TA
T 020-7271 2601
W www.dwp.gov.uk/about-dwp/customer-delivery/disability-and-carers-service

The Pension, Disability and Carers Service was formed in 2008 from the Pension Service and the Disability and Carers Service (DCS). The agency serves 16 million customers in Great Britain and abroad. The service administers benefits including disability living allowance, attendance allowance, carers allowance, state pension, pension credit and winter fuel payments.
Chief Executive, Vivien Hopkins, OBE

NON-MINISTERIAL GOVERNMENT DEPARTMENTS

Non-ministerial government departments are part of central government but are not headed by a minister and are not funded by a sponsor department. They are created to implement specific legislation, but do not have the ability to change it. Departments may have links to a minister, but the minister is not responsible for the department's overall performance. Staff employed by non-ministerial departments are civil servants.

CROWN ESTATE

16 New Burlington Place, London W1S 2HX
T 020-7851 5000 E enquiries@thecrownestate.co.uk
W www.thecrownestate.co.uk

The Crown Estate is part of the hereditary possessions of the sovereign 'in right of the crown', managed under the provisions of the Crown Estate Act 1961. It is valued at £7.0bn, and includes substantial blocks of urban property, primarily in London, almost 106,000 hectares (263,000 acres) of rural land, over half of the foreshore, and the sea bed out to the 12 nautical mile territorial limit throughout the UK. The Crown Estate has a duty to maintain and enhance the capital value of estate and the income obtained from it. Under the terms of the act, the estate

pays its revenue surplus to the Treasury every year.
Chair, Sir Stuart Hampson
Chief Executive, Roger Bright

CROWN PROSECUTION SERVICE
Rose Court, 2 Southwark Bridge Road, London SE1 9HS
T 020-7796 8000 E enquiries@cps.gsi.gov.uk
W www.cps.gov.uk

The Crown Prosecution Service (CPS) is the independent body responsible for prosecuting people in England and Wales. The CPS was established as a result of the Prosecution of Offences Act 1985. It works closely with the police to advise on lines of inquiry and to decide on appropriate charges and other disposals in all but minor cases. *See also* Law Courts and Offices.

The Revenue and Customs Prosecutions Office, which prosecutes major drug trafficking and tax fraud cases in the UK, was incorporated into the CPS on 1 January 2010.
Director of Public Prosecutions, Keir Starmer, QC
Chief Executive, Peter Lewis

EXPORT CREDITS GUARANTEE DEPARTMENT (ECGD)
PO Box 2200, 2 Exchange Tower, Harbour Exchange Square,
London E14 9GS
T 020-7512 7887 E help@ecgd.gsi.gov.uk
W www.ecgd.gov.uk

ECGD is the UK export credit agency and was established in 1919. A separate government department reporting to the Secretary of State for Business, Innovation and Skills, it has more than 90 years' experience of working closely with exporters, project sponsors, banks and buyers to help UK exporters of capital equipment and project-related goods and services. ECGD does this by providing help in arranging finance packages for buyers of UK goods by guaranteeing bank loans; insurance against non-payment to UK exporters; and overseas investment insurance – a facility that gives UK investors up to 15 years' insurance against political risks such as war, expropriation and restrictions on remittances.
Chief Executive and Accounting Officer, Patrick Crawford
Non-Executive Chair, Guy Beringer, QC

FOOD STANDARDS AGENCY
Aviation House, 125 Kingsway, London WC2B 6NH
T 020-7276 8829
E helpline@foodstandards.gsi.gov.uk
W www.food.gov.uk

Established in April 2000, the FSA is a UK-wide non-ministerial government body responsible for food safety and hygiene. The agency has the general function of developing policy in these areas and provides information and advice to the government, other public bodies and consumers. It also sets standards for and monitors food safety and hygiene law enforcement by local authorities.
Chair, Lord Rooker
Chief Executive, Tim Smith
FOOD STANDARDS AGENCY NORTHERN
   IRELAND, 10C Clarendon Road, Belfast BT1 3BG
   T 028-9041 7700 E infosani@foodstandards.gsi.gov.uk
FOOD STANDARDS AGENCY SCOTLAND,
   St Magnus House, 6th Floor, 25 Guild Street, Aberdeen
   AB11 6NJ T 01224-285100
   E scotland@foodstandards.gsi.gov.uk

FOOD STANDARDS AGENCY WALES, 11th Floor,
Southgate House, Wood Street, Cardiff CF10 1EW
T 029-2067 8999 E wales@foodstandards.gsi.gov.uk

FORESTRY COMMISSION
Silvan House, 231 Corstorphine Road, Edinburgh
EH12 7AT
T 0131-334 0303 E enquiries@forestry.gsi.gov.uk
W www.forestry.gov.uk

The Forestry Commission is the government department
responsible for forestry policy in Great Britain. It reports
directly to forestry ministers (ie the Secretary of State for
Environment, Food and Rural Affairs, the Scottish
ministers and the National Assembly for Wales), to whom
it is responsible for advice on forestry policy and for the
implementation of that policy.

The commission's principal objectives are to protect
Britain's forests and woodlands; expand Britain's forest
area; enhance the economic value of forest resources;
conserve and improve the biodiversity, landscape and
cultural heritage of forests and woodlands; develop
opportunities for woodland recreation; and increase
public understanding of, and community participation in,
forestry.
Chair, Pamela Warhurst
Director-General and Deputy Chair, T. Rollinson

FORESTRY COMMISSION ENGLAND, 620 Bristol
Business Park, Coldharbour Lane, Bristol BS16 1EJ
T 0117-906 6000
FORESTRY COMMISSION SCOTLAND, Silvan House,
231 Corstorphine Road, Edinburgh EH12 7AT
T 0131-334 0303
FORESTRY COMMISSION WALES, Welsh Government,
Rhodfa Padarn, Llanbadarn Fawr, Aberystwyth SY23 3UR
T 0300-068 0300
NORTHERN RESEARCH STATION, Roslin, Midlothian
EH25 9SY T 0131-445 2176

FOREST ENTERPRISE
Forest Enterprise England, 620 Bristol Business Park,
Coldharbour Lane, Bristol BS16 1EJ
T 0117-906 6000
Forest Enterprise Scotland, 1 Highlander Way, Inverness Business
and Retail Park, Inverness IV2 7GB
T 01463-232811

Forest Enterprise was established as an executive agency
of the Forestry Commission in 1996 to manage the UK's
forest estate; it ceased to exist as a single executive agency
in March 2003, when three new agencies were created –
one each for England, Wales and Scotland. Forest
Enterprise Wales has since been wound up, with its
responsibilities reabsorbed by the Forestry Commission.
The agencies in England and Scotland take their
direction from their respective country governments but
their basic remit is to provide environmental, social and
economic benefits from the forests they manage.
Chief Executives, Simon Hodge *(Scotland);* Simon
Hodgson *(England)*

FOREST RESEARCH
Alice Holt Lodge, Farnham, Surrey GU10 4LH
T 01420-22255
E research.info@forestry.gsi.gov.uk
W www.forestresearch.gov.uk

Forest Research is also an executive agency of the Forestry
Commission. Its objectives are to inform and support
forestry's contribution to the development and delivery
of the policies of the government and devolved
administrations; to provide research, development and
monitoring services relevant to UK forestry interests; and
to transfer knowledge actively and appropriately.
Chief Executive, Dr James Pendlebury
Research Director, Dr Peter Freer-Smith

GOVERNMENT ACTUARY'S DEPARTMENT
Finlaison House, 15–17 Furnival Street, London EC4A 1AB
T 020-7211 2601
Abbey Business Centre, 83 Princes Street, Edinburgh EH2 2ER
T 0131-247 7510
E enquiries@gad.gov.uk W www.gad.gov.uk

The Government Actuary's Department was established in
1919 and provides actuarial advice to UK government
departments, the public sector, and overseas governments.
The actuaries provide valuations and advice for public-
service pensions and social security schemes, and advise
the government on occupational pension schemes and
private-sector pensions policy. They also provide advice
on the supervision of insurance companies, investment
and risk-related issues, demographic studies and
healthcare financing.
Government Actuary, T. J. Llanwarne
Deputy Government Actuary, G. Russell
Chief Actuaries (London), S. Bell; I. A. Boonin; H. Duckers;
    D. Grenham; A. Hale; S. R. Humphrey; A. Smith;
    N. Varma; S. Vivian
Chief Actuary (Edinburgh), K. Knelle

HM REVENUE AND CUSTOMS
Board of HM Revenue and Customs, 100 Parliament Street,
London SW1A 2BQ
T 020-7147 0000 W www.hmrc.gov.uk

HMRC was formed following the integration of the
Inland Revenue and HM Customs and Excise, which was
made formal by parliament in April 2005. It administers,
and advises the Chancellor of the Exchequer on, any
matters connected with the following areas: income,
corporation, capital gains, inheritance, insurance
premium, stamp, land and petroleum revenue taxes;
environmental taxes (climate change and aggregates levy;
landfill tax); value added tax (VAT); customs duties and
frontier protection; excise duties; National Insurance; tax
credits; child benefit and the Child Trust Fund;
enforcement of the minimum wage; and recovery of
student loan repayments.
Chair, Mike Clasper, CBE
Chief Executive and Permanent Secretary, Lesley Strathie

VALUATION OFFICE AGENCY
Wingate House, 93–107 Shaftesbury Avenue, London
W1D 5BU
T 0300-056 1700 E customerservices@voa.gsi.gov.uk
W www.voa.gov.uk

Established in 1991, the Valuation Office is an executive
agency of HM Revenue and Customs. It is responsible for
compiling and maintaining the business rating and
council tax valuation lists for England and Wales; valuing
property throughout Great Britain for the purposes of
taxes administered by the Inland Revenue; providing
statutory and non-statutory property valuation services in

England, Wales and Scotland; and giving policy advice to ministers on property valuation matters. In April 2009 the VOA assumed responsibility for the functions of The Rent Service, which provided a rental valuation service to local authorities in England, and fair rent determinations for landlords and tenants.
Chief Executive, Penny Ciniewicz

OFFICE OF FAIR TRADING (OFT)

Fleetbank House, 2–6 Salisbury Square, London EC4Y 8JX
T 020-7211 8000
E enquiries@oft.gsi.gov.uk W www.oft.gov.uk

The OFT is a non-ministerial government department established by statute in 1973, and it is the UK's consumer and competition authority. It encourages businesses to comply with competition and consumer law and to improve their trading practices through self-regulation. It acts decisively to stop serious or flagrant offenders, studies markets and recommends action where required, and empowers consumers with the knowledge and skills to make informed choices.
Chair, Philip Collins
Chief Executive Officer, John Fingleton

CHARITY COMMISSION

PO Box 1227, Liverpool L69 3UG
T 0845-300 0218
W www.charity-commission.gov.uk

The Charity Commission is established by law as the independent regulator and registrar of charities in England and Wales. Its aim is to provide the best possible regulation of these charities in order to ensure their legal compliance and increase their efficiency, accountability and effectiveness, as well as to encourage public trust and confidence in them. The commission maintains a register of over 160,000 charities. It is accountable to parliament and both the charity tribunal and the high court for decisions made in exercising its legal powers. The commission has offices in London, Liverpool, Taunton and Newport.
Chair, Dame Suzi Leather
Chief Executive, Sam Younger, CBE, FRSA

OFFICE OF GAS AND ELECTRICITY MARKETS (OFGEM)

9 Millbank, London SW1P 3GE
T 020-7901 7295 E consumeraffairs@ofgem.gov.uk
W www.ofgem.gov.uk

OFGEM is the regulator for Britain's gas and electricity industries. Its role is to protect and advance the interests of consumers by promoting competition where possible, and through regulation only where necessary. OFGEM operates under the direction and governance of the Gas and Electricity Markets Authority, which makes all major decisions and sets policy priorities for OFGEM. OFGEM's powers are provided for under the Gas Act 1986 and the Electricity Act 1989, as amended by the Utilities Act 2000. It also has enforcement powers under the Competition Act 1998 and the Enterprise Act 2002.
Chair, Lord Mogg, KCMG
Chief Executive, Alistair Buchanan

OFFICE OF RAIL REGULATION

1 Kemble Street, London WC2B 4AN
T 020-7282 2000 E contact.cct@orr.gsi.gov.uk
W www.rail-reg.gov.uk

The Office of the Rail Regulator was set up under the Railways Act 1993. It became the ORR in July 2004, under the provisions of the Railways and Transport Safety Act 2003. On 1 April 2006, in addition to its role as economic regulator, the ORR became the health and safety regulator for the rail industry. This transfer of responsibility from the Health and Safety Executive was given effect under the Railways Act 2005. The board and chair are appointed by the Secretary of State for Transport. The ORR's key roles are to ensure that Network Rail, the owner and operator of the national railway infrastructure (the track and signalling), manages the network efficiently and in a way that meets the needs of its users; to encourage continuous improvement in health and safety performance while securing compliance with relevant health and safety law, including taking enforcement action as necessary; and to develop policy and enhance relevant railway health and safety legislation. It is also responsible for licensing operators of railway assets, setting the terms for access by operators to the network and other railway facilities, and enforcing competition law in the rail sector.
Chair, Anna Walker
Chief Executive, Richard Price

OFFICE FOR STANDARDS IN EDUCATION, CHILDREN'S SERVICES AND SKILLS (OFSTED)

Royal Exchange Buildings, St Ann's Square, Manchester M2 7LA
T 0300-123 1231 E enquiries@ofsted.gov.uk
W www.ofsted.gov.uk

Ofsted was established under the Education (Schools Act) 1992 and was relaunched on 1 April 2007 with a wider remit, bringing together four formerly separate inspectorates. It works to raise standards in services through the inspection and regulation of care for children and young people, and inspects education and training for children of all ages. *See also* The Education System.
HM Chief Inspector, Miriam Rosen
Chair, Baroness Morgan of Huyton

SECURITY AND INTELLIGENCE SERVICES

GOVERNMENT COMMUNICATIONS HEADQUARTERS (GCHQ)

Hubble Road, Cheltenham GL51 0EX
T 01242-221491 E pressoffice@gchq.gsi.gov.uk
W www.gchq.gov.uk

GCHQ produces signals intelligence in support of national security and the UK's economic wellbeing, and in the prevention or detection of serious crime. Additionally, GCHQ's Information Assurance arm, CESG, is the national technical authority for information assurance, and provides advice and assistance to government departments, the armed forces and other national infrastructure bodies on the security of their communications and information systems. GCHQ was placed on a statutory footing by the Intelligence Services Act 1994 and is headed by a director who is directly accountable to the foreign secretary.
Director, Iain Lobban

SECRET INTELLIGENCE SERVICE (MI6)
PO Box 1300, London SE1 1BD
W www.sis.gov.uk

The Secret Intelligence Service produces secret intelligence in support of the government's security, defence, foreign and economic policies. It was placed on a statutory footing by the Intelligence Services Act 1994 and is headed by a chief, known as 'C', who is directly accountable to the foreign secretary.
Chief, Sir John Sawers

SECURITY SERVICE (MI5)
PO Box 3255, London SW1P 1AE
T 020-7930 9000
W www.mi5.gov.uk

The Security Service is responsible for security intelligence work against covertly organised threats to the UK. It is organised into seven branches, each with dedicated areas of responsibility, which include countering terrorism, espionage and the proliferation of weapons of mass destruction. The Security Service also provides security advice to a wide range of organisations to help reduce vulnerability to threats from individuals, groups or countries hostile to UK interests. The home secretary has parliamentary accountability for the Security Service.
Director-General, Jonathan Evans

SERIOUS FRAUD OFFICE
Elm House, 10–16 Elm Street, London WC1X 0BJ
T 020-7239 7272
E public.enquiries@sfo.gsi.gov.uk
W www.sfo.gov.uk

The Serious Fraud Office is an independent government department that investigates and prosecutes serious or complex fraud. It is part of the UK Criminal Justice System. The office is headed by a director who is appointed by and accountable to the Attorney-General, and has jurisdiction over England, Wales and Northern Ireland but not Scotland, the Isle of Man or the Channel Islands.
Director, Richard Alderman

UK STATISTICS AUTHORITY
Statistics House, Tredegar Park, Newport, Gwent NP10 8XG
T 0845-604 1857 E authority.enquiries@statistics.gov.uk
W www.statisticsauthority.gov.uk

The UK Statistics Authority was established on 1 April 2008 by the Statistics and Registration Service Act 2007 as an independent body operating at arm's length from government, reporting to the UK parliament and the devolved legislatures. Its overall objective is to promote and safeguard the production and publication of official statistics and ensure their quality and comprehensiveness. The authority's main functions are the oversight of the Office for National Statistics (ONS); monitoring and reporting on all UK official statistics; and independent assessment of official statistics.

BOARD
Chair, Sir Michael Scholar, KCB
Board Members, Richard Alldritt *(Head of Assessment);* Dr Colette Bowe; Partha Dasgupta; Moira Gibb, CBE; Prof. Sir Roger Jowell, CBE *(Deputy Chair, Statistical System);* Jil Matheson *(National Statistician);* Prof. Steve Nickell, FBA; Stephen Penneck *(Director-General, ONS);* Prof David Rhind, CBE, FRS, FBA; Lord Rowe-Beddoe *(Deputy Chair, ONS);* Sir John Shortridge, KCB

OFFICE FOR NATIONAL STATISTICS (ONS)
Cardiff Road, Newport NP10 8XG
T 0845-601 3034 E info@statistics.gov.uk
W www.statistics.gov.uk

The ONS was created in 1996 by the merger of the Central Statistical Office and the Office of Population Censuses and Surveys. On 1 April 2008 it became the executive office of the UK Statistics Authority. As part of these changes, the office's responsibility for the General Register Office transferred to the Identity and Passport Service of the Home Office.

The ONS is responsible for preparing, interpreting and publishing key statistics on the government, economy and society of the UK. Its key responsibilities include designing, managing and running the Census and providing statistics on health and other demographic matters in England and Wales; the production of the UK National Accounts and other economic indicators; the organisation of population censuses in England and Wales and surveys for government departments and public bodies.
National Statistician, Jil Matheson
Director-General, Stephen Penneck

UK TRADE AND INVESTMENT
Europa Building, 450 Argyle Street, Glasgow G2 8LH
T 020-7215 8000 W www.ukti.gov.uk

UK Trade and Investment is a government organisation that helps UK-based companies succeed in international markets. It assists overseas companies to bring high quality investment to the UK economy.
Chief Executive, Susan Haird

WATER SERVICES REGULATION AUTHORITY (OFWAT)
Centre City Tower, 7 Hill Street, Birmingham B5 4UA
T 0121-644 7500 E enquiries@ofwat.gsi.gov.uk
W www.ofwat.gov.uk

OFWAT is the independent economic regulator of the water and sewerage companies in England and Wales. It is responsible for ensuring that the water industry in England and Wales provides customers with a good quality service at a fair price. This is done by keeping bills for consumers as low as possible; monitoring and comparing the services that companies provide; scrutinising the companies' costs and investment; and encouraging competition where this benefits consumers.
Chair, Philip Fletcher
Chief Executive, Regina Finn

PUBLIC BODIES

The following section is a listing of public bodies and other civil service organisations: it is not a complete list of these organisations.

Whereas executive agencies are either part of a government department or are one in their own right (*see* Government Departments section), public bodies carry out their functions to a greater or lesser extent at arm's length from central government. Ministers are ultimately responsible to parliament for the activities of the public bodies sponsored by their department and in almost all cases (except where there is separate statutory provision) ministers make the appointments to their boards. Departments are responsible for funding and ensuring good governance of their public bodies.

The term 'public body' is a general one which includes public corporations, such as the BBC; NHS bodies; and non-departmental public bodies (NDPBs).

In October 2010, the government announced proposals to drastically reform public bodies or 'quangos' (quasi-autonomous non-governmental organisations, another term for NDPBs). In total, 901 bodies were reviewed – 679 NDPBs and 222 other statutory bodies. As a result of this review, 192 quangos were scheduled to be abolished, with a further 118 merged into exisiting NDPBs. While some of these have already disbanded, many others will only be abolished after the public bodies bill, due to be introduced to parliament on 28 October 2012, receives royal assent.

ADJUDICATOR'S OFFICE
8th Floor, Euston Tower, 286 Euston Road, London NW1 3US
T 0300-057 1111 W www.adjudicatorsoffice.gov.uk

The Adjudicator's Office investigates complaints about the way that HM Revenue and Customs, the Valuation Office Agency and the Insolvency Service have handled a person's affairs.
The Adjudicator, Judy Clements, OBE

ADMINISTRATIVE JUSTICE AND TRIBUNALS COUNCIL
81 Chancery Lane, London WC2A 1BQ
T 020-7855 5200 E enquiries@ajtc.gsi.gov.uk
W www.justice.gov.uk/ajtc

The Administrative Justice and Tribunals Council (AJTC) is a permanent standing advisory body set up under the Tribunals, Courts and Enforcement Act. It consists of 15 members appointed by the Lord Chancellor, Scottish and Welsh ministers. It has Scottish and Welsh Committees which discharge its responsibilities in their respective territories. The Parliamentary Ombudsman is an *ex officio* member of the council and of its Scottish and Welsh Committees.

The principal functions of the AJTC are to keep the administrative justice system under review; keep under review and report on the constitution and working of listed tribunals; and keep under review and report on the constitution and working of statutory inquiries. It is consulted by and advises government departments on a wide range of subjects relating to adjudicative procedures.

The public bodies bill introduced into the House of Lords in spring 2011 proposed that the ATJC be abolished. Subject to the bill's remaining stages in parliament and subsequent secondary legislation, the council may be abolished by spring 2012.
Chair, Richard Thomas, CBE
Members, The Parliamentary Ombudsman *(ex officio)*, Ann Abraham; Jodi Berg, OBE; Prof. Alice Brown, CBE; Prof. Andrew Coyle, CMG; Kate Dunlop; Richard Henderson, CB; Sukhvinder Kaur-Stubbs; Penny Letts, OBE; Bronwyn McKenna; Prof. Mary Seneviratne; Dr Jonathan Spencer, CB; Brian Thompson; Prof. Sir Adrian Webb

WELSH COMMITTEE OF THE ADMINISTRATIVE JUSTICE AND TRIBUNALS COUNCIL
81 Chancery Lane, London WC2A 1BQ
T 020-7855 5200 E enquiries@ajtc.gsi.gov.uk
W www.justice.gov.uk/ajtc/welsh/welsh.htm
Chair, Prof. Sir Adrian Webb
Members, The Parliamentary and Health Service Ombudsman *(ex officio);* The Public Services Ombudsman for Wales *(ex officio);* Bob Chapman; Gareth Lewis; Rhian Williams-Flew

SCOTTISH COMMITTEE OF THE ADMINISTRATIVE JUSTICE AND TRIBUNALS COUNCIL
George House, 126 George Street, Edinburgh EH2 4HH
T 0131-271 4300
W www.justice.gov.uk/ajtc/scottish/scottish.htm
Chair, Richard Henderson
Members, The Parliamentary Commissioner for Administration *(ex officio);* The Scottish Public Services Ombudsman *(ex officio);* Prof. Michael Adler; Prof. Andrew Coyle; Annabell Fowles; Michael Menlowe; Michael Scanlan

ADVISORY, CONCILIATION AND ARBITRATION SERVICE (ACAS)
22nd Floor, Euston Tower, 286 Euston Road, London NW1 3JJ
T 020-7396 0022 Helpline 0845-747 4747
W www.acas.org.uk

The Advisory, Conciliation and Arbitration Service was set up under the Employment Protection Act 1975 (the provisions now being found in the Trade Union and Labour Relations (Consolidation) Act 1992).

ACAS is largely funded by the Department for Business, Innovation and Skills. A council sets its strategic direction, policies and priorities, and ensures that the agreed strategic objectives and targets are met. It consists of a chair and 11 employer, trade union and independent members, appointed by the Secretary of State for Business, Innovation and Skills. ACAS aims to improve organisations and working life through better employment relations, to provide up-to-date information, independent advice and high-quality training, and to work with employers and employees to solve problems and improve performance.

ACAS has 13 regional offices, in Birmingham, Bristol, Bury St Edmonds, Cardiff, Fleet, Glasgow, Leeds, Liverpool, London, Manchester, Newcastle upon Tyne, Nottingham and Paddock Wood.
Chair, Ed Sweeney
Chief Executive, John Taylor

ADVISORY COUNCIL ON NATIONAL RECORDS AND ARCHIVES
The National Archives, Kew, Surrey TW9 4DU
T 020-8392 5377
W www.nationalarchives.gov.uk/advisorycouncil

The Advisory Council on National Records and Archives advises the Lord Chancellor on all matters relating to the preservation, use of and access to historical manuscripts, records and archives of all kinds. The council meets four times a year, and its main task is to consider requests for the extended closure of public records, or from departments that want to keep records. The council encompasses the statutory Advisory Council on Public Records and the Advisory Council on Historical Manuscripts.
Chair, Lord Neuberger of Abbotsbury, PC *(Master of the Rolls)*

AGRICULTURE AND HORTICULTURE DEVELOPMENT BOARD
Stoneleigh Park, Kenilworth, Warwickshire CV8 2TL
T 02476-692051 E info@ahdb.org.uk W www.ahdb.org.uk

The Agriculture and Horticulture Development Board (AHDB) is funded by the agriculture and horticulture industries through statutory levies, with the duty to improve efficiency and competitiveness within six sectors: pig meat in England; milk in Great Britain; beef and lamb in England; commercial horticulture in Great Britain; cereals and oilseeds in the UK; and potatoes in Great Britain. The AHDB represents about 75 per cent of total UK agricultural output. Levies raised from the six sectors are ring-fenced to ensure that they can only be used to the benefit of the sectors from which they were raised. The AHDB board consists of ten members: the chairs for each of the six sector organisations and four independent members.
Chair, John Godfrey, CBE
Independent members, Chris Bones; John Bridge; Lorraine Clinton; Clare Dodgson
Sector members, Tim Bennett (milk); Neil Bragg (horticulture); John Cross (beef and lamb); Stewart Houston (pig meat); Allan Stevenson (potatoes); Jonathan Tipples (cereals and oilseeds)
Chief Executive, Tom Taylor

ARCHITECTURE AND DESIGN SCOTLAND
Bakehouse Close, 146 Canongate, Edinburgh EH8 8DD
T 0131-556 6699 E info@ads.org.uk
W www.ads.org.uk

Architecture and Design Scotland (A+DS) was established in 2005 by the Scottish government as the national champion for good architecture, urban design and planning in the built environment; it works with a wide range of organisations at national, regional and local levels. A+DS also assumed the independent design review and advisory role of the Royal Fine Art Commission for Scotland.
Chair, Karen Anderson
Chief Executive, Jim MacDonald

ARMED FORCES' PAY REVIEW BODY
6th Floor, Victoria House, Southampton Row, London WC1B 4AD
T 020-7271 0469 W www.ome.uk.com

The Armed Forces' Pay Review Body was appointed in 1971. It advises the prime minister and the Secretary of State for Defence on the pay and allowances of members of naval, military and air forces of the Crown.
Chair, Prof. Alasdair Smith
Members, Mary Carter; Prof. Peter Dolton; Very Revd. Dr Graham Forbes, CBE; Vice-Adm. Sir Richard Ibbotson, KBE; Paul Kernaghan, CBE, QPM; Judy McKnight, CBE; John Steele

ARTS COUNCIL ENGLAND
14 Great Peter Street, London SW1P 3NQ
T 0845-300 6200 E enquiries@artscouncil.org.uk
W www.artscouncil.org.uk

Arts Council England is the national development agency for the arts in England. Using public money from government and the National Lottery, it supports a range of artistic activities, including theatre, music, literature, dance, photography, digital art, carnival and crafts. Between 2011 and 2015, Arts Council England will invest £1.4bn of public money from the government and a further £850m from the National Lottery.

In 2002, the Arts Council of England and nine regional arts boards joined together to form a single development organisation for the arts. The governing council's members and chair are appointed by the Secretary of State for Culture, Media, Olympics and Sport usually for a term of four years, and meet approximately five times a year.
Chair, Dame Liz Forgan
Members, Janet Barnes; Caroline Collier; Prof. Jon Cook; Joe Docherty; Ekow Eshun; Sheila Healy; Sir Nicholas Kenyon; Keith Khan; Francois Matarasso; Andrew Motion *(observer)*; Peter Phillips; Alice Rawsthorn; Anil Ruia, OBE; Alistair Spalding; Rosemary Squire, OBE; Veronica Wadley
Chief Executive, Alan Davey

ARTS COUNCIL OF NORTHERN IRELAND
77 Malone Road, Belfast BT9 6AQ
T 028-9038 5200 E info@artscouncil-ni.org
W www.artscouncil-ni.org

The Arts Council of Northern Ireland is the prime distributor of government funds in support of the arts in Northern Ireland. It is funded by the Department of Culture, Arts and Leisure and from National Lottery funds.
Chair, Rosemary Kelly
Members, Eithne Benson; Kate Bond; Damien Coyle *(Vice-Chair)*; Raymond Fullerton; David Irvine; Anthony Kennedy; Bill Montgomery; Prof. Ian Montgomery; Sharon O'Connor; Joseph Rice; Prof. Paul Seawright; Brian Sore; Peter Spratt; Janine Walker
Chief Executive, Roisin McDonough

ARTS COUNCIL OF WALES
Bute Place, Cardiff CF10 5AL
T 0845-873 4900 E feedback@artswales.org.uk
W www.artswales.org.uk

The Arts Council of Wales was established in 1994 by royal charter and is the development body for the arts

in Wales. It funds arts organisations with funding from the National Assembly for Wales and is the distributor of National Lottery funds to the arts in Wales. The grant-in-aid for 2011–12 was £30.6m from the National Assembly.
Chair, Prof. Dai Smith
Members, Emma Evans; John Geraint; Margaret Jervis, MBE; Robin Morrison; Osi Rhys Osmond; Ian Rees; Richard Turner; Alan Watkin; Gerwyn Wiliams; John Carey Williams; Dr Kate Woodward
Chief Executive, Nick Capaldi

AUDIT COMMISSION
1st Floor, Millbank Tower, London SW1P 4HQ
T 0844-798 1212
E public-enquiries@audit-commission.gov.uk
W www.audit-commission.gov.uk

The Audit Commission is a public corporation set up in 1983 to protect the public purse.

The commission appoints auditors to local authorities, NHS bodies (excluding NHS foundation trusts), police authorities and other local public services in England, and oversees their work. It also audits NHS foundation trusts under separate arrangements and helps public bodies to manage the financial challenges they face by providing authoritative, unbiased, evidence-based analysis and advice. The auditors are either Audit Commission employees or belong to one of the private audit firms

The commission has a chair, a deputy chair and a board of 10 commissioners who are appointed by the Department of Communities and Local Government following consultation with key stakeholders.

Following the public bodies' reform proposals, the Audit Commission will cease to exist as a public corporation, subject to legislation. The commission is working with the Department for Communities and Local Government to consider ways of transferring its in-house audit practice into the private sector.
Chair, Michael O'Higgins
Deputy Chair, Bahrat Shah
Commissioners, Lord Adebowale, CBE; Janet Baker; Cllr Sir Merrick Cockell; Dr Jennifer Dixon; Tony Harris; Cllr Stephen Houghton, CBE; Brian Landers; Cllr Chris White
Chief Executive, Eugene Sullivan

AUDIT SCOTLAND
110 George Street, Edinburgh EH2 4LH
T 0845-146 1010 E info@auditscotland.gov.uk
W www.audit-scotland.gov.uk

Audit Scotland was set up in 2000 to provide services to the Accounts Commission and the Auditor-General for Scotland. Together they help to ensure that public sector bodies in Scotland are held accountable for the proper, efficient and effective use of public funds.

Audit Scotland's work covers about 200 bodies including local authorities; police forces and fire rescue services; health boards; further education colleges; Scottish Water; the Scottish government; government agencies such as the Prison Service and non-departmental public bodies such as Scottish Enterprise.

Audit Scotland carries out financial and regularity audits to ensure that public sector bodies adhere to the highest standards of financial management and governance. It also performs audits to ensure that these bodies achieve the best value for money. All of Audit

Scotland's work in connection with local authorities, fire and police boards is carried out for the Accounts Commission; its other work is undertaken for the Auditor-General.
Auditor-General, R. W. Black
Chair of the Accounts Commission, J. Baillie

BANK OF ENGLAND
Threadneedle Street, London EC2R 8AH
T 020-7601 4444 E enquiries@bankofengland.co.uk
W www.bankofengland.co.uk

The Bank of England was incorporated in 1694 under royal charter. It was nationalised in 1946 under the Bank of England Act of that year which gave HM Treasury statutory powers over the bank. It is the banker of the government and it manages the issue of banknotes. Since 1998 it has been operationally independent and its Monetary Policy Committee has been responsible for setting short-term interest rates to meet the government's inflation target. Its responsibility for banking supervision was transferred to the Financial Services Authority in the same year. As the central reserve bank of the country, the Bank of England keeps the accounts of British banks, and of most overseas central banks; the larger banks and building societies are required to maintain with it a proportion of their cash resources. The bank's core purposes are monetary stability and financial stability. The Banking Act 2009 increased the responsibilities of the bank, including giving it a new financial stability objective and creating a special resolution regime for dealing with failing banks.
Governor, Sir Mervyn King, GBE
Deputy Governors, Charles Bean; Paul Tucker
Court of Directors, The Governor; the Deputy Governors; Brendan Barber; Roger Carr; Sir David Lees; Susan Rice; John Stewart; Mark Tucker; Lord Adair Turner; Harrison Young
Monetary Policy Committee, The Governor; the Deputy Governors; Ben Broadbent; Spencer Dale; Paul Fisher; David Miles; Adam Posen; Dr Martin Weale
Adviser to the Governor, Graham Nicholson
Chief Cashier and Executive Director, Banking Services, Andrew Bailey
The Auditor, Stephen Brown

BIG LOTTERY FUND
1 Plough Place, London EC4A 1DE
T 020-7211 1800 **Advice Line** 0845-410 2030
E general.enquiries@biglotteryfund.org.uk
W www.biglotteryfund.org.uk

The Big Lottery Fund was launched in 2004, merging the New Opportunities Fund and the Lottery Charities Board (Community Fund). The fund is responsible for giving out half of the money for good causes raised by the National Lottery. The money is distributed to charitable, benevolent and philanthropic organisations in the voluntary and community sectors, as well as health, education and environmental projects. The Big Lottery Fund also assumed the Millennium Commission's role of supporting large-scale regenerative projects.
Chair, Peter Ainsworth
Vice-Chair, Anna Southall
Regional Chairs, Nat Sloane *(England);* Frank Hewitt *(Northern Ireland);* Alison Magee *(Scotland);* Janet Reed, OBE *(Wales, acting)*
Chief Executive, Peter Wanless

BOUNDARY COMMISSIONS

ENGLAND
35 Great Smith Street, London SW1P 3BQ
T 020-7276 1102 E information@bcommengland.gsi.gov.uk
W www.boundarycommissionforengland.independent.gov.uk
Deputy Chair, Hon. Mr Justice Sales

WALES
1st Floor, Caradog House, 1–6 St Andrews Place, Cardiff
CF10 3BE
T 029-2039 5031 E bcomm.wales@wales.gsi.gov.uk
W www.bcomm-wales.gov.uk
Deputy Chair, Hon. Justice Lloyd Jones

SCOTLAND
Thistle House, 91 Haymarket Terrace, Edinburgh EH12 5HD
T 0131-538 7510 F 0131-538 7511
E secretariat@scottishboundaries.gov.uk
W www.bcomm-scotland.gov.uk
Deputy Chair, Hon. Lord Woolman

NORTHERN IRELAND
Forestview, Purdy's Lane, Newtownbreda, Belfast BT8 7AR
T 028-9069 4800 E bcni@belfast.org.uk
W www.boundarycommission.org.uk
Deputy Chair, Hon. Mr Justice McLaughlin

The commissions, established in 1944, are constituted under the Parliamentary Constituencies Act 1986 (as amended). The Speaker of the House of Commons is the *ex officio* chair of all four commissions in the UK. Each of the four commissions is required by law to keep the parliamentary constituencies in their part of the UK under review (in the case of the Scottish Commission this includes constituencies for the Scottish parliament).

The Boundary Commission for England completed its fifth general review of parliamentary constituencies in England in 2006. The commissions for Wales and Northern Ireland completed their reviews in 2005 and 2007 respectively. The Parliamentary Constituencies (England) Order 2007, the Parliamentary Constituencies and Assembly Electoral Regions (Wales) Order 2006 and the Parliamentary Constituencies (Northern Ireland) Order 2008 made provisions for the new constituencies which were first used at the 2010 general election. The Boundary Commission for Scotland submitted its final report in 2004 and the new constituencies came into force at the 2005 general election. The review of constituencies for the Scottish parliament was completed in May 2010 and the new constituencies were first used in the 2011 Scottish parliament election.

The 2013 (sixth) general reviews of parliamentary constituences in England, Wales, Scotland and Northern Ireland are currently underway and initial proposals are due to be published by each of the boundary commissions in October 2011.

BRITISH BROADCASTING CORPORATION (BBC)
Television Centre, Wood Lane, London W12 7RJ
T 020-8743 8000
W www.bbc.co.uk

The BBC was incorporated under royal charter in 1926 as successor to the British Broadcasting Company Ltd. The BBC's current charter, which came into force on 1 January 2007 and extends to 31 December 2016, recognises the BBC's editorial independence and sets out its public purposes. The BBC Trust was formed under the new charter and replaces the Board of Governors; it sets the strategic direction of the BBC and has a duty to represent the interests of licence fee payers. The chair, vice-chair and other trustees are appointed by the Queen-in-Council. The BBC is financed by revenue from receiving licences for the home services and by grant-in-aid from parliament for the World Service (radio). *See also* Broadcasting.

BBC TRUST MEMBERS
Chair, Lord Patten, CH, PC
Vice-Chair, Diane Coyle
National Trustees, Alison Hastings *(England);* Rotha Johnston *(Northern Ireland);* Bill Matthews *(Scotland);* Elan Closs Stephens *(Wales)*
Trustees, Richard Ayre; Anthony Fry; David Liddiment; Mehmuda Mian

EXECUTIVE BOARD
Director-General and Chair, Mark Thompson
Deputy Director-General, Mark Byford
Directors, Helen Boaden *(News);* Tim Davie *(Audio and Music);* George Entwistle *(Vision);* Zarin Patel *(Chief Financial Officer);* Ralph Rivera *(Future Media and Technology)*
Chief Executive, BBC Worldwide, John Smith
Chief Operating Officer, Caroline Thomson
Senior Non-Executive Director, Marcus Agius
Non-Executive Directors, Simon Burke; Val Gooding, CBE; Dr Mike Lynch, OBE; Robert Webb, QC

STATION CONTROLLERS
BBC1, Danny Cohen
BBC2, Janice Hadlow
BBC3, Zai Bennett
BBC4, Richard Klein
BBC News Channel, Kevin Bakhurst
BBC Parliament, Peter Knowles
BBC Northern Ireland, Peter Johnston
BBC Scotland, Ken MacQuarrie
BBC Wales, Menna Richards
CBBC, Damian Kavanagh
CBeebies, Kay Benbow
Radio 1, 1Xtra, Asian Network and Switch, Andy Parfitt
Radio 2 and 6 Music, Bob Shennan
Radio 3, Roger Wright
Radio 4, Gwyneth Williams
Radio 5 Live, Adrian Van Klaveren

BRITISH COUNCIL
Bridgewater House, 58 Whitworth Street, Manchester M1 6BB
T 0161-957 7755 E general.enquiries@britishcouncil.org
W www.britishcouncil.org

The British Council was established in 1934, incorporated by royal charter in 1940 and granted a supplemental charter in 1993. It is an independent, non-political organisation which promotes Britain abroad and is the UK's international organisation for educational and cultural relations. The British Council is represented in 216 towns and cities in 109 countries. Grant-in-aid received from the Foreign and Commonwealth Office in 2010-11 was £190m.
Chair, Vernon Ellis
Chief Executive, Martin Davidson, CMG

BRITISH FILM INSTITUTE (BFI)

21 Stephen Street, London W1T 1LN
T 020-7255 1444 W www.bfi.org.uk

The BFI, established in 1933, offers opportunities for people throughout the UK to experience, learn and discover more about the world of film and moving image culture. It incorporates the BFI National Archive, the BFI National Library, a range of DVD releases, publications and educational materials (including the monthly *Sight and Sound* magazine), BFI Southbank, BFI Distribution, the annual BFI London Film Festival as well as the BFI London Lesbian and Gay Film Festival, and the BFI IMAX cinema, and provides advice and support for regional cinemas and film festivals across the UK.

Following the closure of the UK Film Council in April 2011, the BFI has become the lead body for film in the UK. It is now in charge of allocating lottery money for the development and production of new British films, deciding which films should receive tax credits and overseeing support for the film in the English regions.
Chair, Greg Dyke
Director, Amanda Nevill

BRITISH LIBRARY

96 Euston Road, London NW1 2DB
T 0843-208 1144 E customer-services@bl.uk
W www.bl.uk

The British Library was established in 1973. It is the UK's national library and occupies a key position in the library and information network. It aims to serve scholarship, research, industry, commerce and all other major users of information. Its services are based on a collection of over 150 million separate items, including books, journals, manuscripts, maps, stamps, music, patents, newspapers and sound recordings in all written and spoken languages. The library is now based at three sites: London (St Pancras and Colindale) and Boston Spa, W. Yorks. The library's sponsoring department is the Department for Culture, Media and Sport.

Access to the reading rooms at St Pancras is limited to holders of a British Library reader's pass; information about eligibility is available from the reader admissions office. The exhibition galleries and public areas are open to all, free of charge.

BRITISH LIBRARY BOARD

Chair, Baroness Blackstone
Chief Executive and Deputy Chair, Dame L. Brindley, DBE
Members, Ms D. Airey; R. S. Broadhurst, CBE; Prof. R. Burgess; Sir K. Calman; Lord Fellowes; Ms S. Forbes, CBE; Prof. W. Hall, CBE; Ms E. Mackay, CB; Prof. K. McLuskie; Dr Stephen Page; M. Semple, OBE

SCHOLARSHIP AND COLLECTIONS

Americas Collections, T 020-7412 7743
Asia, Pacific and Africa Collections, T 020-7412 7873
British and Irish Collections, T 020-7412 7538
British Library Newspapers, Colindale Avenue, London NW9 5HE T 020-7412 7353
British Library Sound Archive, T 020-7412 7676
Early Printed Collections, T 020-7412 7564
Map Library, T 020-7412 7702
Music Library, T 020-7412 7772
Philatelic Collections, T 020-7412 7635
Reader Information, T 020-7412 7676
West European Collections, T 020-7412 7572/7569

OPERATIONS AND SERVICES

Permission Clearance, T 020-7412 7755
Research Services, T 020-7412 7903

SCIENCE, TECHNOLOGY AND INNOVATION

Business, T 020-7412 7454
National Preservation Office, T 020-7412 7612
Patents, T 020-7412 7454
Science and Technology, T 020-7412 7494/7288
Social Science, Law and Official Publications, T 020-7412 7536

BRITISH LIBRARY, BOSTON SPA

Boston Spa, Wetherby, W. Yorks LS23 7BQ
T 01937-546060

BRITISH MUSEUM

Great Russell Street, London WC1B 3DG
T 020-7323 8000
E information@britishmuseum.org
W www.britishmuseum.org

The British Museum houses the national collection of antiquities, ethnography, coins and paper money, medals, prints and drawings. The British Museum may be said to date from 1753, when parliament approved the holding of a public lottery to raise funds for the purchase of the collections of Sir Hans Sloane and the Harleian manuscripts, and for their proper housing and maintenance. The building (Montagu House) was opened in 1759. The existing buildings were erected between 1823 and the present day, and the original collection has increased to its current dimensions by gifts and purchases. Total government grant-in-aid for 2011–12 is £53.7m.

BOARD OF TRUSTEES

Appointed by the Sovereign, Chief Emeka Anyaoku
Appointed by the Prime Minister, Karen Armstrong; Prof. Sir Christopher Bayly; Sir Ronald Cohen; Francis Finlay; Val Gooding, CBE; Bonnie Greer; Penny Hughes; George Iacobescu, CBE; Baroness Kennedy, QC; Richard Lambert; David Norgrove; Lord Stern of Brentford, FBA; Baroness Wheatcroft of Blackheath
Appointed by the Trustees of the British Museum, Prof. Amartya Sen; Lord Broers of Cambridge, FRS, FRENG; Niall Fitzgerald *(Chair);* Edmee P. Leventis; Sir Martin Sorrell
Appointed by the Royal Society, Dr Olga Kennard, OBE
Appointed by the Royal Academy, Antony Gormley, OBE

OFFICERS

Director, Neil MacGregor
Deputy Director, Dr Andrew Burnett
Director of Public Engagement, Joanna Mackle
Director of Administration, Chris Yates
Director of Operations and Projects, Justin Morris
Heads of Departments, Carolyn Marsden-Smith
(Exhibitions); Xerxes Mazda *(Learning and Audience)*

KEEPERS

Keeper of Africa, Oceania and the Americas (acting), Vivian Davies
Keeper of Ancient Egypt and Sudan, Vivian Davies
Keeper of Asia, Jan Stuart
Keeper of Coins and Medals, Philip Attwood
Keeper of Greece and Rome, J. Lesley Fitton
Keeper of the Middle East, John Curtis
Keeper of Prehistory and Europe, Jonathan Williams

Keeper of Prints and Drawings, Antony Griffiths
Conservation and Scientific Research, David Saunders

BRITISH PHARMACOPOEIA COMMISSION

151 Buckingham Palace Road, London SW1W 9SZ
T 020-3080 6561 E bpcom@mhra.gsi.gov.uk
W www.pharmacopoeia.gov.uk

The British Pharmacopoeia Commission sets standards for medicinal products used in human and veterinary medicines and is responsible for publication of the *British Pharmacopoeia* (a publicly available statement of the standard that a product must meet throughout its shelf-life), the *British Pharmacopoeia (Veterinary)* and the *British Approved Names.* It has 15 members, including two lay members, who are appointed by the Appointments Commission (the body responsible for appointments to all of the Medicines Act advisory bodies).
Chair, Prof. A. D. Woolfson
Vice-Chair, V'lain Fenton-May
Secretary and Scientific Director, Dr M. G. Lee

BRITISH WATERWAYS

64 Clarendon Road, Watford WD17 1DA
T 01923-201120
E enquiries.hq@britishwaterways.co.uk
W www.britishwaterways.co.uk

British Waterways conserves and manages the network of over 3,540km (2,200 miles) of canals and rivers in England, Scotland and Wales. Its sponsoring departments are the Department for Environment, Food and Rural Affairs in England and Wales, and the Scottish Government Transport Directive.

Its responsibilities include maintaining the waterways and structures on and around them; looking after wildlife and the waterway environment; and ensuring that canals and rivers are safe and enjoyable places to visit.

As part of the public bodies' reform proposals announced in October 2010, management of the network of inland waterways in England and Wales will transfer to a new charitable body. The government intends to have this new body established by April 2012.
Chair, Tony Hales, CBE
Vice-Chair, John Bridgeman, CBE, TD
Chief Executive, Robin Evans, FRICS

CARE QUALITY COMMISSION

Finsbury Tower, 103–105 Bunhill Row, London EC1Y 8TG
T 0300-061 6161 E enquiries@cqc.org.uk
W www.cqc.org.uk

The Care Quality Commission (CQC) was established on 1 April 2009, bringing together the work of the Healthcare Commission, the Mental Health Act Commission and the Commission for Social Care Inspection. CQC is the independent regulator of health and adult social care services in England, including care provided by the NHS, local authorities, private companies and voluntary organisations.
Chair (acting), Jo Williams
Chief Executive, Cynthia Bower
Board, John Harwood; Prof. Deirdre Kelly; Martin Marshall; Olu Olasode; Kay Sheldon; Jo Williams

CENTRAL ARBITRATION COMMITTEE

22nd Floor, Euston Tower, 286 Euston Road, London NW1 3JJ
T 020-7904 2300 E enquiries@cac.gov.uk
W www.cac.gov.uk

The Central Arbitration Committee (CAC) is a permanent independent body with statutory powers whose main function is to adjudicate on applications relating to the statutory recognition and de-recognition of trade unions for collective bargaining purposes, where such recognition or de-recognition cannot be agreed voluntarily. In addition, the CAC has a statutory role in determining disputes between trade unions and employers over the disclosure of information for collective bargaining purposes, and in resolving applications and complaints under the information and consultation regulations, and performs a similar role in relation to the legislation on the European Works Council, European companies, European cooperative societies and cross-border mergers. The CAC also provides voluntary arbitration in industrial disputes.

The committee consists of a chair and 10 deputy chairs, 25 members experienced as representatives of employers and 22 members experienced as representatives of workers. Members of the committee are appointed by the Secretary of State for Business, Innovation and Skills after consultation with the Advisory, Conciliation and Arbitration Service (ACAS).

Following the public bodies' reform proposals of October 2010, the CAC will merge with the Certification Office, subject to legislation.
Chair, Sir Michael Burton
Chief Executive, Simon Gouldstone

CERTIFICATION OFFICE FOR TRADE UNIONS AND EMPLOYERS' ASSOCIATIONS

Euston Tower, 286 Euston Road, London NW1 3JJ
T 020-7210 3734 E info@certoffice.org
W www.certoffice.org

The Certification Office is an independent statutory authority. The Certification Officer is appointed by the Secretary of State for Business, Innovation and Skills and is responsible for maintaining a list of trade unions and employers' associations; ensuring compliance with statutory requirements and keeping available for public inspection annual returns from trade unions and employers' associations; determining complaints concerning trade union elections, certain ballots and certain breaches of trade union rules; ensuring observance of statutory requirements governing mergers between trade unions and employers' associations; overseeing political funds and finances of trade unions and employers' associations; and for certifying the independence of trade unions.

Following the public bodies' reform proposals of October 2010, the Certification Office will merge with the Central Arbitration Committee, subject to legislation.
Certification Officer, David Cockburn

SCOTLAND
69A George Street, Edinburgh EH2 2JG
T 0131-220 7660
Assistant Certification Officer for Scotland, Christine Stuart

CHURCH COMMISSIONERS

Church House, Great Smith Street, London SW1P 3AZ
T 020-7898 1000
E commissioners.enquiry@churchofengland.org
W www.churchofengland.org/about_us/structure/churchcommissioners

The Church Commissioners were established in 1948 by the amalgamation of Queen Anne's Bounty (established 1704) and the Ecclesiastical Commissioners (established 1836). They are responsible for the management of some of the Church of England's assets, the income from which is predominantly used to help pay for the stipend and pension of the clergy and to support the church's work throughout the country. The commissioners own UK and global company shares, over 43,000ha (106,000 acres) of agricultural land, a residential estate in central London, and commercial property across Great Britain, plus an interest in overseas property via managed funds. They also carry out administrative duties in connection with pastoral reorganisation and closed churches.

The commissioners are: the Archbishops of Canterbury and of York; four bishops, three clergy and four lay persons elected by the respective houses of the General Synod; two deans elected by all the deans; three persons nominated by the Queen; three persons nominated by the Archbishops of Canterbury and York; three persons nominated by the archbishops after consultation with others including the Lord Mayors of London and York and the vice-chancellors of the universities of Oxford and Cambridge; the First Lord of the Treasury; the Lord President of the Council; the home secretary; the Secretary of State for Culture, Olympics, Media and Sport; and the Speakers of the House of Commons and the House of Lords.

CHURCH ESTATES COMMISSIONERS
First, A. Whittam Smith
Second, T. Baldry, MP
Third, T. E. H. Walker

OFFICERS
Secretary, A. C. Brown
Director of Investments, T. Joy
Assistant Secretary, Pastoral and Redundant Churches,
  P. Lewis
Official Solicitor, S. Slack

COAL AUTHORITY
200 Lichfield Lane, Mansfield, Notts NG18 4RG
T 01623-637000 E thecoalauthority@coal.gov.uk
W http://coal.decc.gov.uk

The Coal Authority was established under the Coal Industry Act 1994 to manage certain functions previously undertaken by British Coal, including ownership of unworked coal. It is responsible for licensing coal mining operations and for providing information on coal reserves and past and future coal mining. It settles subsidence damage claims which are not the responsibility of licensed coal mining operators. It deals with the management and disposal of property, and with surface hazards such as abandoned coal mine entries.
Chair, Dr Helen Mounsey
Chief Executive, Philip Lawrence

COMMISSION FOR RURAL COMMUNITIES
Unit 1, Saw Mill End, Corinium Avenue, Gloucester GL4 3DE
T 0845-933 5577 E info@ruralcommunities.gov.uk
W www.defra.gov.uk/crc

The Commission for Rural Communities (CRC) was established in October 2006 to promote awareness of rural needs. It was announced in June 2010 that the CRC would be abolished, and that the Department for Environment, Food and Rural Affairs internal rural policy capacity would be expanded to create a Rural Communities Policy Unit (RCPU). It was later agreed that from 1 April 2011, the CRC would significantly reduce its staffing levels and the scale of its operation, with some of its work and staff transferring to a new unit. The attenuated CRC will carry out its statutory functions of advice, advocacy and watchdog activity through its chair, commissioners and a small support team.
Chair, Dr Stuart Burgess
Commissioners, Prof. Sheena Asthana; Richard Childs, QPM; Elinor Goodman; John Mills, CBE; Howard Petch, CBE; Sue Prince, OBE; Rachel Purchase; Prof. Mark Shucksmith, OBE; Prof. Michael Winter, OBE

COMMITTEE ON STANDARDS IN PUBLIC LIFE
35 Great Smith Street, London SW1P 3BQ
T 020-7276 2595 E public@standards.x.gsi.gov.uk
W www.public-standards.org.uk

The Committee on Standards in Public Life was set up in October 1994. It is formed of 10 people appointed by the prime minister, comprising the chair, three political members nominated by the leaders of the three main political parties and six independent members. The committee's remit is to examine concerns about standards of conduct of all holders of public office, including arrangements relating to financial and commercial activities, and to make recommendations as to any changes in present arrangements which might be required to ensure the highest standards of propriety in public life. It is also charged with reviewing issues in relation to the funding of political parties. The committee does not investigate individual allegations of misconduct.
Chair, Sir Christopher Kelly, KCB
Members, Lord Alderdice; Lloyd Clarke, QPM; Oliver Heald, MP; Rt. Hon. Margaret Beckett, MP; Sir Derek Morris; Dame Denise Platt, DBE; David Prince, CBE; Dr Elizabeth Vallance; Dr Brian Woods-Scawen, CBE

COMMONWEALTH WAR GRAVES COMMISSION
2 Marlow Road, Maidenhead, Berks SL6 7DX
T 01628-634221 E casualty.enq@cwgc.org
W www.cwgc.org

The Commonwealth War Graves Commission (formerly Imperial War Graves Commission) was founded by royal charter in 1917. It is responsible for the commemoration of around 1.7 million members of the forces of the Commonwealth who lost their lives in the two world wars. More than one million graves are maintained in 23,274 burial grounds throughout the world. Over three-quarters of a million men and women who have no known grave or who were cremated are commemorated by name on memorials built by the commission.

The funds of the commission are derived from the six participating governments, ie the UK, Canada, Australia, New Zealand, South Africa and India.
President, HRH The Duke of Kent, KG, GCMG, GCVO, ADC
Chair, Secretary of State for Defence (UK)
Vice-Chair, Lt.-Gen. Sir Alistair Irwin, KCB, CBE
Members, High Commissioners in London for Australia, Canada, South Africa, New Zealand and India; Air Chief Marshal Sir Joe French, KCB, CBE; Kevan Jones, MP; Sara Jones, CBE; Keith Simpson, MP; Prof. Hew

Strachan, FRSE; Vice-Adm. Tim Laurence, CB, MVO; Duke of Westminster, KG, CB, OBE; Sir Rob Young, GCMG

Director-General and Secretary to the Commission, Alan Pateman-Jones

Deputy Director-General, T. Reeves

Director of Legal Services, Gillian Stedman

COMPETITION COMMISSION

Victoria House, Southampton Row, London WC1B 4AD
T 020-7271 0100 E info@cc.gsi.gov.uk
W www.competition-commission.org.uk

The commission was established in 1948 as the Monopolies and Restrictive Practices Commission (later the Monopolies and Mergers Commission); it became the Competition Commission in April 1999 under the Competition Act 1998. The commission conducts in-depth inquiries into mergers, markets and the regulation of major industries. Every inquiry the commission undertakes is in response to a reference made to it by another authority, usually the Office of Fair Trading. The commission has no power to conduct inquiries on its own initiative. The Enterprise Act 2002 introduced a new regime for the assessment of mergers and markets in the UK – in most related investigations the commission is responsible for making decisions on the competition questions and for making and implementing decisions on appropriate remedies.

The commission has a full-time chair and three deputy chairs. There are usually around 40 part-time commission members, who usually carry out investigations in groups of four or five after appointment by the chair. All are appointed by the Secretary of State for Business, Innovation and Skills for eight-year terms.

As part of the public bodies' reform proposals of October 2010, it was announced that the Competition Commission would merge with the Office of Fair Trading to form a single agency – the Competition and Markets Authority (CMA), subject to legislation.

Chair, Roger Witcomb

Deputy Chairs, Laura Carstensen; Dr Peter Davis

Non-Executive Directors, Grey Denham; Dame Patricia Hodgson, DBE; Lesley Watkins

Chief Executive and Secretary, David Saunders

COMPETITION SERVICE

Victoria House, Bloomsbury Place, London WC1A 2EB
T 020-7979 7979 E info@catribunal.org.uk
W www.catribunal.org.uk

The Competition Service is the financial corporate body by which the Competition Appeal Tribunal is administered and through which it receives funding for the performance of its judicial functions.

Director, Operations, Jeremy Straker

President, Hon. Mr Justice Barling

Registrar, Charles Dhanowa, OBE

CONSUMER COUNCIL FOR WATER

Victoria Square House, Victoria Square, Birmingham B2 4AJ
T 0121-345 1000 E enquiries@ccwater.org.uk
W www.ccwater.org.uk

The Consumer Council for Water was established in 2005 under the Water Act 2003 to represent consumers' interests in respect of price, service and value for money from their water and sewerage services, and to investigate complaints from customers about their water company. There are four regional committees in England and one in Wales.

Chair, Dame Yve Buckland, DBE

CONSUMER FOCUS

Fleetbank House, 1 Salisbury Square, London EC4Y 8JX
T 020-7799 7900 E contact@consumerfocus.org.uk
W www.consumerfocus.org.uk

Consumer Focus was formed from the merger of Energywatch, Postwatch and the National Consumer Council, and began operations in October 2008. The organisation works for the interests of consumers in private and public sectors throughout England, Scotland and Wales (and for postal services in Northern Ireland). Consumer Focus has legislative powers, including the right to investigate any complaint if it is of wider interest; the right to open up information from providers; and the ability to make an official 'super-complaint' about failing services. Consumer Focus is not a complaints-handling body or a statutory regulator; consumer complaints or requests for advice should be directed to Consumer Direct or Citizens Advice.

Following the public bodies' reform proposals of October 2010, Consumer Focus will be abolished, subject to legislation, with some of its functions likely to be transferred to Citizens Advice, Citizens Advice Scotland and the General Consumer Council for Northern Ireland. This is likely to happen in spring 2013.

Chair, Christine Farnish

Chief Executive, Mike O'Connor

CORPORATION OF TRINITY HOUSE

Trinity House, Tower Hill, London EC3N 4DH
T 020-7481 6900 E enquiries@thls.org
W www.trinityhouse.co.uk

The Corporation of Trinity House is the General Lighthouse Authority for England, Wales and the Channel Islands, and was granted its first charter by Henry VIII in 1514. Its remit is to assist the safe passage of a variety of vessels through some of the busiest sea-lanes in the world; it does this by deploying and maintaining approximately 600 aids to navigation, ranging from lighthouses to a satellite navigation service. The corporation also has certain statutory jurisdiction over aids to navigation maintained by local harbour authorities and is responsible for marking or dispersing wrecks dangerous to navigation, except those occurring within port limits or wrecks of HM ships.

The statutory duties of Trinity House are funded by the General Lighthouse Fund, which is provided from light dues levied on ships calling at ports of the UK and the Republic of Ireland. The corporation is a deep-sea pilotage authority, authorised by the Secretary of State for Transport to license deep-sea pilots. In addition Trinity House is a charitable organisation that maintains a number of retirement homes for mariners and their dependants, funds a four-year training scheme for those seeking a career in the merchant navy, and also dispenses grants to a wide range of maritime charities. The charity work is wholly funded by its own activities.

The corporation is controlled by a board of Elder Brethren; a separate board controls the Lighthouse Service. The Elder Brethren also act as nautical assessors in marine cases in the Admiralty Division of the High Court.

ELDER BRETHREN

Master, HRH the Princess Royal, KG, KT, GCVO
Deputy Master, Capt. Ian McNaught
Wardens, Capt. Duncan Glass, OBE *(Rental);*
    Capt. Nigel Pryke *(Nether)*
Elder Brethren, HRH The Prince of Wales, KG, KT, GCB;
    HRH The Duke of York, KG, GCVO, ADC; HRH The
    Princess Royal, KG, KT, GCVO; Capt. Roger Barker;
    Adm. Lord Boyce, KG, GCB, OBE; Lord Browne of
    Madingley; Capt. John Burton-Hall, RD; Lord
    Carrington, KG, GCMG, CH, PC; Viscount Cobham;
    Capt. Sir Malcolm Edge, KCVO; Capt. Ian Gibb; Lord
    Greenway; Lord Mackay of Clashfern, KT, PC; Capt.
    Peter Mason, CBE; Cdre. Peter Melson, CVO, CBE,
    RN; Capt. David Orr; Sir John Parker, FRENG;
    Douglas Potter; Capt. Derek Richards, RD, RNR; Lord
    Robertson of Port Ellen, KT, GCMG, PC; Rear-Adm.
    Sir Patrick Rowe, KCVO, CBE; Cdre. Jim Scorer;
    Simon Sherrard; Adm. Sir Jock Slater, GCB, LVO; Capt.
    David Smith, OBE, RN; Cdre. David Squire, CBE,
    RFA; Cdre. Lord Sterling of Plaistow, CBE, GCVO,
    RNR; Capt. Colin Stewart, LVO; Sir Adrian Swire, AE;
    Capt. Sir Miles Wingate, KCVO; Capt. Thomas
    Woodfield, OBE; Capt. Richard Woodman

OFFICERS

Secretary, Cdr Graham Hockley
Director of Finance, Jerry Wedge
Director of Navigation, Capt. Roger Barker
Director of Operations, Cdre. Jim Scorer

COUNTRYSIDE COUNCIL FOR WALES/CYNGOR CEFN GWLAD CYMRU

Maes-y-Ffynnon, Penrhosgarnedd, Bangor, Gwynedd LL57 2DW
T 0845-130 6229 **E** enquiries@ccw.gov.uk
W www.ccw.gov.uk

The Countryside Council for Wales is the government's
statutory adviser on sustaining natural beauty, wildlife and
the opportunity for outdoor enjoyment in Wales and its
inshore waters. It is funded by the National Assembly for
Wales and accountable to the First Secretary, who
appoints its members.

Chair, Morgan Parry
Chief Executive, Roger Thomas

COVENT GARDEN MARKET AUTHORITY

Covent House, New Covent Garden Market, London SW8 5BH
T 020-7720 2211 **E** info@cgma.co.uk
W www.newcoventgardenmarket.com

The Covent Garden Market Authority is constituted under
the Covent Garden Market Acts 1961 to 1977, the board
being appointed by the Department of Environment,
Food and Rural Affairs. The authority owns and operates
the 22.7ha (56 acre) New Covent Garden Markets (fruit,
vegetables, flowers), which have been trading at the site
since 1974.

Chair (part-time), Baroness Dean of Thornton-le-Fylde,
    PC
Chief Executive, Jan Lloyd

CREATIVE SCOTLAND

Waverley Gate, 2–4 Waterloo Place, Edinburgh EH3 1EG
T 0330-333 2000 **E** enquiries@creativescotland.com
W www.creativescotland.com

Creative Scotland is the organisation tasked with leading
the development of the arts, creative and screen industries

across Scotland. It was created in 2010 as an
amalgamation of the Scottish Arts Council and Scottish
Screen, and it encourages and sustains the arts through
investment in the form of grants, bursaries, loans and
equity. It aims to invest in talent; artistic production;
audiences, access and participation; and the cultural
economy. The intelligence it gathers from practitioners,
partners and sector peers will be used to guide its future
investments – the money for which is inherited from the
grant-in-aid budgets of its two predecessor organisations.
The draft budget for 2010–11 was £57.5m.

Chair, Sir Sandy Crombie
Board, Peter Cabrelli; Gwilym Gibbons; Steve Grimmond;
    Robin MacPherson; Prof. Gayle McPherson; Barclay
    Price; Dr Gary West; Ruth Wishart
Chief Executive, Andrew Dixon

CRIMINAL CASES REVIEW COMMISSION

5 Philip's Place, Birmingham B3 2PW
T 0121-233 1473 **E** info@ccrc.gov.uk
W www.ccrc.gov.uk

The Criminal Cases Review Commission is the
independent body set up under the Criminal Appeal Act
1995. It is a non-departmental public body reporting to
parliament via the Lord Chancellor and Secretary of State
for Justice. It is responsible for investigating possible
miscarriages of justice in England, Wales and Northern
Ireland, and deciding whether or not to refer cases
back to an appeal court. Membership of the commission
is by royal appointment; the senior executive staff are
appointed by the commission.

Chair, Richard Foster, CBE
Members, M. Allen; Ms P. Barrett; J. England;
    Ms J. Goulding; A. MacGregor, QC; I. Nicholl;
    E. Smith; J. Weeden
Chief Executive, Claire Bassett

CRIMINAL INJURIES COMPENSATION AUTHORITY (CICA)

Tay House, 300 Bath Street, Glasgow G2 4LN
Helpline: 0300-003 3601
W www.justice.gov.uk/guidance/compensation-schemes/cica

CICA is the government body responsible for
administering the Criminal Injuries Compensation
Scheme in England, Scotland and Wales (separate
arrangements apply in Northern Ireland). CICA deals
with every aspect of applications for compensation
under the 1996, 2001 and 2008 Criminal Injuries
Compensation Schemes. There is a separate avenue of
appeal to the First-tier Tribunal (Criminal Injuries
Compensation) (*see* Tribunals).

Chief Executive, Carole Oatway

CROFTERS COMMISSION

Great Glen House, Leachkin Road, Inverness IV3 8NW
T 01463-663450 **E** info@croftersommission.org.uk
W www.croftersommission.org.uk

The Crofters Commission, established in 1955 under
the Crofters (Scotland) Act, is a government-funded
organisation tasked with overseeing crofting legislation. It
works with communities to regulate crofting and advises
Scottish ministers on crofting matters. The commission
administers the Croft House Grant Scheme and the
Crofters' Cattle Improvement Scheme. It also provides a
free enquiry service.

Convener, Drew Ratter
Chief Executive, Nick Reiter

ENGLISH HERITAGE (HISTORIC BUILDINGS AND MONUMENTS COMMISSION FOR ENGLAND)

1 Waterhouse Square, 138–142 Holborn, London EC1N 2ST
T 020-7973 3000 W www.english-heritage.org.uk

English Heritage was established under the National Heritage Act 1983. On 1 April 1999 it merged with the Royal Commission on the Historical Monuments of England to become the new lead body for England's historic environment. It is sponsored by the Department for Culture, Media and Sport and its duties are to carry out and sponsor archaeological, architectural and scientific surveys and research designed to increase the understanding of England's past and its changing condition; to identify buildings, monuments and landscapes for protection while also offering expert advice, skills and grants to conserve these sites; to encourage town planners to make imaginative re-use of historic buildings to aid regeneration of the centres of cities, towns and villages; to manage and curate selected sites; and to curate and make publicly accessible the National Monuments Record, whose records of over one million historic sites and buildings, and extensive collections of photographs, maps, drawings and reports, constitute the central database and archive of England's historic environment.

Chair, Baroness Andrews, OBE
Commissioners, Lynda Addison, OBE; Maria Adebowale; Joyce Bridges, CBE; Manish Chande; Prof. Sir Barry Cunliffe, CBE; David Fursdon; Prof. Ronald Hutton; Jane Kennedy; John Walker, CBE; Chris Wilkinson, OBE; Elizabeth Williamson, FSA
Chief Executive, Dr Simon Thurley

CUSTOMER SERVICES DEPARTMENT, PO Box 569, Swindon SN2 2YP
T 0870-333 1181 E customers@english-heritage.org.uk
NATIONAL MONUMENTS RECORD CENTRE, Kemble Drive, Swindon SN2 2GZ T 01793-414600

ENVIRONMENT AGENCY

National Customer Contact Centre, PO Box 544, Rotherham S60 1BY
T 0370-850 6506 E enquiries@environment-agency.gov.uk
W www.environment-agency.gov.uk

The Environment Agency was established in 1996 under the Environment Act 1995 and is a non-departmental public body sponsored by the Department for Environment, Food and Rural Affairs and the National Assembly for Wales – around 70 per cent of the agency's funding is from the government, with the rest raised from various charging schemes. The agency is responsible for pollution prevention and control in England and Wales and for the management and use of water resources, including flood defences, fisheries and navigation. Its remit also includes: scrutinising business operations which have the potential to be environmentally hazardous; helping businesses to use resources more efficiently; taking action against those who do not take environmental responsibilities seriously; looking after wildlife; and helping to improve the quality of inner city areas and parks.

The Environment Agency has head offices in London and Bristol, and seven regional offices.

THE BOARD

Chair, Lord Smith of Finsbury
Members, Andrew Brown; Prof. Ruth Hall; Julie Hill, MBE; Emma Howard Boyd; Robert Light; Dr Madeleine Harvard; John Varley; Jeremy Walker; Lady Warner, OBE; Lord Whitty
Chief Executive, Paul Leinster

EQUALITY AND HUMAN RIGHTS COMMISSION

Arndale House, The Arndale Centre, Manchester M4 3AQ
T 0161-829 8100 E info@equalityhumanrights.com
W www.equalityhumanrights.com

The Equality and Human Rights Commission (EHRC) is a statutory body, established under the Equality Act 2006 and launched in October 2007. It inherited the responsibilities of the Commission for Racial Equality, the Disability Rights Commission and the Equal Opportunities Commission. The EHRC's purpose is to reduce inequality, eliminate discrimination, strengthen relations between people, and promote and protect human rights. It enforces equality legislation on age, disability and health, gender, race, religion and belief, sexual orientation or transgender status, and encourages compliance with the Human Rights Act 1998 throughout England, Wales and Scotland. For information on how to contact the helpline, visit the EHRC website.

Chair, Trevor Phillips, OBE
Deputy Chair, Baroness Prosser, OBE
Commissioners, Stephen Alambritis; Ann Beynon, OBE; Prof. Geraldine Van Bueren; Kay Carberry, CBE; Meral Hussein Ece, OBE; Baroness Greengross, OBE; Dr Jean Irvine, OBE; Kaliani Lyle; Angela Mason; Michael Smith; Simon Woolley

EQUALITY COMMISSION FOR NORTHERN IRELAND

Equality House, 7–9 Shaftesbury Square, Belfast BT2 7DP
T 028-9089 0890 Textphone 028-9050 0589
E information@equalityni.org W www.equalityni.org

The Equality Commission was set up in 1999 under the Northern Ireland Act 1998 and is responsible for promoting equality, keeping the relevant legislation under review, eliminating discrimination on the grounds of race, disability, sexual orientation, gender (including marital and civil partner status, gender reassignment, pregnancy and maternity), age, religion and political opinion and for overseeing the statutory duty on public authorities to promote equality of opportunity.

Chief Commissioner, Bob Collins
Deputy Chief Commissioner, Jane Morrice
Chief Executive, Evelyn Collins, CBE, FRSA

GAMBLING COMMISSION

Victoria Square House, Victoria Square, Birmingham B2 4BP
T 0121-230 6666
E info@gamblingcommission.gov.uk
W www.gamblingcommission.gov.uk

The Gambling Commission was established under the Gambling Act 2005, and took over the role previously occupied by the Gaming Board for Great Britain in regulating and licensing all commercial gambling – apart from spread betting and the National Lottery – ie casinos, bingo, betting, remote gambling, gaming machines and lotteries. It also advises local and central government on related issues, and is responsible for the protection of children and the vulnerable from being exploited or harmed by gambling. The commission is sponsored by the Department for Culture, Media and Sport, with its work funded by licence fees paid by the gambling industry.

Following the public bodies' reform proposals of October 2010, the Gambling Commission will merge with the National Lottery Commission in 2012.

Chair, Philip Graf
Chief Executive, Jenny Williams

HEALTH AND SAFETY EXECUTIVE

Redgrave Court, Merton Road, Bootle, Merseyside L20 7HS
Incident Centre 0845-300 9923
W www.hse.gov.uk

The Health and Safety Commission (HSC) and the Health and Safety Executive (HSE) merged on 1 April 2008 to form a single national regulatory body responsible for promoting the cause of better health and safety at work.

HSE regulates all industrial and commercial sectors except operations in the air and at sea. This includes agriculture, construction, manufacturing, services, transport, mines, offshore oil and gas, nuclear, quarries and major hazard sites in chemicals and petrochemicals.

HSE is responsible for developing and enforcing health and safety law, providing guidance and advice, commissioning research, inspection including accident and ill-health investigation, developing standards and licensing or approving some work activities such as nuclear power and asbestos removal. HSE is sponsored by the Department for Work and Pensions.

Chair, Judith Hackitt, CBE
Board Members, Nick Baldwin; Sandy Blair; Robin Dahlberg; David Gartside; Paul Kenny; Frances Outram; Hugh Robertson; Elizabeth Snape; John Spanswick; Richard Taylor
Chief Executive, Geoffrey Podger

HEALTH PROTECTION AGENCY (HPA)

151 Buckingham Palace Road, London SW1W 9SZ
T 020-7811 7000 E hpa.enquiries@hpa.org.uk
W www.hpa.org.uk

The HPA was set up in 2003 and is responsible for providing an integrated approach to protecting public health through the provision of support and advice to the NHS, local authorities, emergency services, other non-departmental public bodies, the Department of Health and the devolved administrations.

The HPA works at local, regional, national and international levels to reduce the impact of infectious diseases and reduce exposure to chemicals, radiation and poisons, as well as ensure a rapid response when hazards occur. The HPA provides services in Northern Ireland and works closely with the devolved administrations, so that there is a coordinated response to incidents, trends and outbreaks on a national level. Research and development projects conducted by HPA scientists are primarily concerned with new methods of treating illness and assessing exposure to chemicals or radiation.

Following the public bodies' reform proposals of October 2010, the HPA will become part of Public Health England in April 2013.

Chair, Dr David Heymann
Board Members, Dr Barbara Bannister, FRCP; Michael Beaumont, CBE; James T. Brown; Michael Carroll; Prof. Charles Easmon, CBE, FMEDSCI *(Deputy Chair)*; Helen Froud; Prof. William Gelletly, OBE; Martin Hindle; Prof. Alan Maryon Davis, FRCP

(adviser); Dr Vanessa Mayatt; Deborah Oakley; Dr Dipti Patel; Prof. Debby Reynolds; John Wyn Owen, CB; Dr Timothy Wyatt
Chief Executive, Justin McCracken

HER MAJESTY'S OFFICERS OF ARMS

COLLEGE OF ARMS (HERALDS' COLLEGE)
Queen Victoria Street, London EC4V 4BT
T 020-7248 2762 E enquiries@college-of-arms.gov.uk
W www.college-of-arms.gov.uk

The Sovereign's Officers of Arms (Kings, Heralds and Pursuivants of Arms) were first incorporated by Richard III in 1484. The powers vested by the crown in the Earl Marshal (the Duke of Norfolk) with regard to state ceremonial are largely exercised through the college. The college is also the official repository of the arms and pedigrees of English, Welsh, Northern Irish and Commonwealth (except Canadian) families and their descendants, and its records include official copies of the records of the Ulster King of Arms, the originals of which remain in Dublin. The 13 officers of the college specialise in genealogical and heraldic work for their respective clients.

Arms have long been, and still are, granted by letters patent from the Kings of Arms. A right to arms can only be established by the registration in the official records of the College of Arms of a pedigree showing direct male line descent from an ancestor already appearing therein as being entitled to arms, or by making application through the College of Arms for a grant of arms. Grants are made to corporations as well as to individuals.

Earl Marshal, Duke of Norfolk

KINGS OF ARMS
Garter, T. Woodcock, LVO, FSA
Clarenceux (and Earl Marshal's Secretary), P. L. Dickinson, LVO
Norroy and Ulster, H. Paston-Bedingfeld

HERALDS
Chester, T. H. S. Duke
Lancaster, R. J. B. Noel
Windsor (and Registrar), W. G. Hunt, TD
Somerset, D. V. White
Richmond, C. E. A. Cheesman
York, vacant

PURSUIVANT
Bluemantle, M. P. D. O'Donoghue

COURT OF THE LORD LYON
HM New Register House, Edinburgh EH1 3YT
T 0131-556 7255
W www.lyon-court.com

Her Majesty's Officers of Arms in Scotland perform ceremonial duties and in addition may be consulted by members of the public on heraldic and genealogical matters in a professional capacity.

KING OF ARMS
Lord Lyon King of Arms, David Sellar, FSA SCOT, FRHISTS

HERALDS
Rothesay, Sir Crispin Agnew of Lochnaw, Bt., QC
Ross, C. J. Burnett, FSA SCOT
Snawdoun, Mrs C. G. W. Roads, MVO, FSA SCOT

PURSUIVANTS
Unicorn, The Hon. Adam Bruce, WS
Ormond, Mark D. Dennis

EXTRAORDINARY OFFICERS
Orkney Herald Extraordinary, Sir Malcolm Innes of
   Edingight, KCVO, WS
Angus Herald Extraordinary, R. O. Blair, CVO, WS
Islay Herald Extraordinary, Alastair Campbell of Airds
Ross Herald Extraordinary, C. J. Burnett, FSA SCOT

HERALD PAINTER
Herald Painter, Mrs Y. Holton

HIGHLANDS AND ISLANDS ENTERPRISE

Cowan House, Inverness Retail and Business Park,
Inverness IV2 7GF
T 01463-234171 E info@hient.co.uk
W www.hie.co.uk

Highlands and Islands Enterprise (HIE) was set up under
the Enterprise and New Towns (Scotland) Act 1991. Its
role is to deliver community and economic development
in line with the Scottish government economic strategy. It
focuses on helping high-growth businesses, improving
regional competitiveness and strengthening communities.
HIE's budget for 2010–11 was £83m.
Chair, William Roe, CBE
Chief Executive, Alex Paterson

HISTORIC ROYAL PALACES

Apartment 39, Hampton Court Palace, Surrey KT8 9AU
T 0844-482 7777 E operators@hrp.org.uk
W www.hrp.org.uk

Historic Royal Palaces was established in 1998 as a royal
charter body with charitable status and is contracted by
the Secretary of State for Culture, Olympics, Media and
Sport to manage the palaces on his behalf. The palaces –
the Tower of London, Hampton Court Palace, the
Banqueting House, Kensington Palace and Kew Palace –
are owned by the Queen on behalf of the nation.
   The organisation is governed by a board comprising a
chair and 11 non-executive trustees. The chief executive is
accountable to the board of trustees and ultimately to
parliament. Historic Royal Palaces receives no funding
from the government or the Crown.

TRUSTEES
Chair, Charles Mackay
Appointed by the Queen, Jonathan Marsden, LVO, FSA;
   Sir Trevor McDonald, OBE; Sir Adrian Montague,
   CBE; Sir Alan Reid, KCVO
Appointed by the Secretary of State, Sophie Andreae;
   Dawn Austwick, OBE; Ian Barlow; Sue Farr; John
   Hamer, OBE; Malcolm Reading
Ex officio, Gen. Lord Dannatt, GCB, CBE, MC *(Constable
   of the Tower of London)*

OFFICERS
Chief Executive, Michael Day

HOMES AND COMMUNITIES AGENCY

Maple House, 149 Tottenham Court Road, London W1T 7BN
T 0300-1234 500 E mail@homesandcommunities.co.uk
W www.homesandcommunities.co.uk

The Homes and Communities Agency (HCA) is the
national housing regeneration agency for England. With a
capital investment budget of nearly £7bn, the HCA
contributes to economic growth by delivering
high-quality affordable housing. The HCA also provides
investment to improve existing social housing as well as
identifying and regenerating surplus public sector land.
Chair, Robert Napier
Chief Executive, Pat Richie

HUMAN FERTILISATION AND EMBRYOLOGY AUTHORITY (HFEA)

Finsbury Tower, 103–105 Bunhill Row, London EC1Y 8HF
T 020-7291 8200 E admin@hfea.gov.uk
W www.hfea.gov.uk

The HFEA was established in 1991 under the Human
Fertilisation and Embryology Act 1990. It is the UK's
independent regulator tasked with overseeing safe and
appropriate practice in fertility treatment and embryo
research, including licensing and monitoring centres
carrying out IVF, artificial insemination and human
embryo research. The HFEA also provides a range of
detailed information for patients, professionals and
government, and maintains a formal register of
information about donors, fertility treatments and
children born as a result of those treatments.
   In July 2010, the government announced proposals to
transfer the functions of the HFEA to the Care Quality
Commission and, by the end of the current parliament,
to abolish the authority.
Chair, Prof. Lisa Jardine, CBE
Chief Executive, Alan Doran, CB

HUMAN GENETICS COMMISSION

Area 605, Wellington House, 133–155 Waterloo Road,
London SE1 8UG
T 020-7972 4351 E hgc@dh.gsi.gov.uk
W www.hgc.gov.uk

The Human Genetics Commission (HGC) was established
in 1999, subsuming three previous advisory committees.
Its remit is to give ministers strategic advice on how
developments in human genetics will impact on people
and healthcare, focusing in particular on the social and
ethical implications.
   Following the government's public bodies reform
proposals of October 2010, the HGC is due to be
abolished by the end of the current parliament, with some
of its functions transferred to other regulators.
Chair, Prof. Jonathan Montgomery
Members, Prof. Tim Aitman; Prof. Thomas Baldwin;
   Prof. Angus Clarke; Prof. Sarah Cunningham-Burley;
   Dr Paul Darragh; Dr Paul Debenham; Nicola Drury;
   Dr Frances Flinter; Ros Gardner; Prof. John Harris;
   Caroline Harrison; Alastair Kent; Dr Anneke Lucassen;
   Dr Duncan McHale; Dr Alice Maynard; Dr Lola Oni;
   Dr Rosalind Skinner; Dr Anita Thomas

HUMAN TISSUE AUTHORITY (HTA)

2nd Floor, 151 Buckingham Palace Road,
London SW1W 9SZ
T 020-7269 1900 E enquiries@hta.gov.uk
W www.hta.gov.uk

The Human Tissue Authority (HTA) was established on
1 April 2005 under the Human Tissue Act 2004, and is
sponsored and part-funded by the Department of Health.
It regulates organisations that remove, store and use
tissue for research, medical treatment, post-mortem
examination, teaching and display in public. The HTA
also gives approval for organ and bone marrow donations

from living people. The HTA is the competent authority for the UK under the EU organ donation directive (ODD).

Chair, Baroness Diana Warwick
Chief Executive, Craig Muir

IMPERIAL WAR MUSEUM

Lambeth Road, London SE1 6HZ
T 020-7416 5000 E mail@iwm.org.uk
W www.iwm.org.uk

The museum, founded in 1917, illustrates and records all aspects of the two world wars and other military operations involving Britain and the Commonwealth since 1914. It was opened in its present home, formerly Bethlem Royal Hospital, in 1936. The museum is a multi-branch organisation that also includes the Churchill War Rooms in Whitehall; HMS *Belfast* in the Pool of London; Imperial War Museum Duxford in Cambridgeshire; and Imperial War Museum North in Trafford, Manchester.

The total grant-in-aid (including grants for special projects) for 2011–12 was £21.7m.

OFFICERS

Chair of Trustees, Air Chief Marshal Sir Peter Squire, GCB, DFC, AFC
Director-General, Diane Lees
Directors, Richard Ashton *(Imperial War Museum Duxford);* Jon Card *(Secretary, Business and Governance);* Sue Coleman *(Marketing and Development);* Jim Forrester *(Imperial War Museum North);* Samantha Heywood *(Learning and Interpretation);* Phil Reed *(Churchill War Rooms and HMS Belfast);* Alan Stoneman *(Corporate Services);* Mark Whitmore *(Collections and Research)*

INDEPENDENT REVIEW SERVICE FOR THE SOCIAL FUND

4th Floor, Centre City Podium, 5 Hill Street, Birmingham B5 4UB
T 0800-096 1926 E sfc@irs-review.org.uk
W www.irs-review.org.uk

The Social Fund Commissioner is appointed by the Secretary of State for Work and Pensions. The commissioner appoints Social Fund Inspectors, who provide an independent review for customers dissatisfied with decisions made in Jobcentre Plus offices throughout England, Scotland and Wales regarding the grants and loans available from the Discretionary Social Fund.

Social Fund Commissioner, Karamjit Singh, CBE

INDEPENDENT SAFEGUARDING AUTHORITY

PO Box 181, Darlington DL1 9FA
T 0300-123 1111 E info@vbs-info.org.uk
W www.isa.homeoffice.gov.uk

The Independent Safeguarding Authority (ISA) is a non-departmental public body sponsored by the Home Office. It was created in 2008 to help prevent unsuitable people working with children and vulnerable adults in England, Wales and Northern Ireland. Its role is to make fair, consistent and thorough barring decisions on people who have caused harm and those who pose a risk of harm. The ISA also manages the vulnerable adults' barred list and the children's barred list. Employers, local authorities, professional regulators and inspection bodies are under a duty to refer to the ISA any information about an employee that they believe has harmed or poses a risk of harm to children or vulnerable adults.

As a result of the government's vetting and barring scheme review in February 2011, the ISA is due to merge with the Criminal Records Bureau, subject to the introduction of legislation.

Chair, Sir Roger Singleton, CBE
Chief Executive, Adrian McAllister

INDUSTRIAL INJURIES ADVISORY COUNCIL

Second Floor, Caxton House, Tothill Street, London SW1H 9NA
T 020-7449 5618 E iiac@dwp.gsi.gov.uk
W www.iiac.independent.gov.uk

The Industrial Injuries Advisory Council was established under the National Insurance (Industrial Injuries) Act 1946, which came into effect on 5 July 1948. Statutory provisions governing its work are set out in section 171–173 of the Social Security Administration Act 1992 and corresponding Northern Ireland legislation. The council usually consists of 16 independent members appointed by the Secretary of State for Work and Pensions, and has three roles: to consider and advise on matters relating to industrial injuries benefit or its administration referred to it by the Secretary of State for Work and Pensions or the Department for Social Development in Northern Ireland; to consider and provide advice on any draft regulations that the secretary of state proposes to make on industrial injuries benefit or its administration; and to advise on any other matter relating to industrial injuries benefit or its administration.

Chair, Prof. Keith Palmer

INFORMATION COMMISSIONER'S OFFICE

Wycliffe House, Water Lane, Wilmslow, Cheshire SK9 5AF
T 0303-123 1113 W www.ico.gov.uk

The Information Commissioner's Office (ICO) is sponsored by the Ministry of Justice and oversees and enforces the Freedom of Information Act 2000 and the Data Protection Act 1998, with the objective of promoting public access to official information and protecting personal information.

The Data Protection Act 1998 sets out rules for the processing of personal information and applies to records held on computers and some paper files. It works in two ways: it dictates that those who record and use personal information (data controllers) must be open about how the information is used and must follow the eight principles of 'good information handling', and it gives individuals certain rights to access their personal information.

The Freedom of Information Act 2000 is designed to help end the culture of unnecessary secrecy and open up the inner workings of the public sector to citizens and businesses. Under the Freedom of Information Act, public authorities must produce a publication scheme that sets out what information the public authority is obliged to publish by law.

The Information Commissioner's Office also enforces and oversees the environmental information regulations, and the privacy and electronic communications regulations.

The Information Commissioner reports annually to parliament on the performance of his functions under the acts and has obligations to assess breaches of the acts.

As of April 2010, the ICO has been able to fine organisations up to £500,000 for serious breaches of the Data Protection Act.

Information Commissioner, Christopher Graham

JOINT NATURE CONSERVATION COMMITTEE

Monkstone House, City Road, Peterborough PE1 1JY
T 01733-562626 E communications@jncc.gov.uk
W www.jncc.defra.gov.uk

The committee was established under the Environmental Protection Act 1990 and was reconstituted by the Natural Environment and Rural Communities Act 2006. It advises the government and devolved administrations on UK and international nature conservation issues. Its work contributes to maintaining and enriching biological diversity, conserving geological features and sustaining natural systems.

Chair, Dr Peter Bridgewater
Deputy Chair, Prof. Lynda Warren

LAW COMMISSION

Steel House, 11 Tothill Street, London SW1H 9LJ
T 020-3334 0200
E chief.executive@lawcommission.gsi.gov.uk
W www.lawcom.gov.uk

The Law Commission was set up under the Law Commissions Act 1965 to make proposals to the government for the examination of the law in England and Wales and for its revision where it is unsuited for modern requirements, obscure or otherwise unsatisfactory. It recommends to the lord chancellor programmes for the examination of different branches of the law and suggests whether the examination should be carried out by the commission itself or by some other body. The commission is also responsible for the preparation of Consolidation and Statute Law (Repeals) Bills.

Chair, Rt. Hon. Lord Justice Munby
Commissioners, E. J. Cooke; David Hertzell; Prof. David Ormerod; Frances Patterson, QC
Chief Executive, Mark Ormerod

LEGAL SERVICES COMMISSION

4 Abbey Orchard Street, London SW1P 2BS
T 020-7783 7000
W www.legalservices.gov.uk

The Legal Services Commission (LSC) was created under the Access to Justice Act 1999 and replaced the Legal Aid Board in April 2000. It is a non-departmental public body which is sponsored by the Ministry of Justice (MoJ).

The commission is responsible for two schemes. The Community Legal Service funds the delivery of civil legal and advice services, identifies priorities and unmet needs, and develops suppliers and services to meet those needs. The Criminal Defence Service provides free legal advice and representation for people involved in criminal investigations or proceedings.

As part of the MoJ legal aid reform programme, the LSC will be replaced by a new executive agency of the MoJ. The government introduced legislation to give effect to this reform in June 2011.

Chief Executive, Carolyn Downs
Chair, Sir Bill Callaghan

MUSEUM OF LONDON

150 London Wall, London EC2Y 5HN
T 020-7001 9844
E info@museumoflondon.org.uk
W www.museumoflondon.org.uk

The Museum of London illustrates the history of London from prehistoric times to the present day. It opened in 1976 and is based on the amalgamation of the former Guildhall Museum and London Museum. The museum is controlled by a board of governors, appointed (ten each) by the prime minister and the City of London. The museum is currently funded by grants from the Greater London Authority and the City of London. The total grant-in-aid for 2010–11 was £17m.

Chair of Board of Governors, Michael Cassidy, CBE
Director, Prof. Jack Lohman

MUSEUMS, LIBRARIES AND ARCHIVES COUNCIL (MLA)

1st Floor, Grosvenor House, 14 Bennetts Hill, Birmingham B2 5RS
T 0121-345 7300 E info@mla.gov.uk
W www.mla.gov.uk

The MLA was launched in April 2000 and is the lead strategic agency for museums, libraries and archives. It is a non-departmental public body sponsored by the Department for Culture, Media and Sport. The MLA replaced the Museums and Galleries Commission (MGC) and the Library and Information Commission (LIC).

It was announced in July 2010 that the MLA would be abolished; many of the key functions of the MLA are likely to transfer to Arts Council England by the end of Match 2012.

Chair, Sir Andrew Motion
Board Members, Geoffrey Bond, OBE; Patricia Cullen; Angela Dean; Yinnon Ezra, MBE; Helen Forde; Glen Lawes; Munira Mirza; Karen Tyerman; Robert Wand
Chief Executive (acting), Paul Lander

NATIONAL ARMY MUSEUM

Royal Hospital Road, London SW3 4HT
T 020-7730 0717 E info@nam.ac.uk
W www.nam.ac.uk

The National Army Museum was established by royal charter in 1960, and covers the history of five centuries of the British Army from the Middle Ages to the present. It chronicles the campaigns and battles fought over this time as well as the social history and development of the Army, and its impact on Britain, Europe and the world. The museum houses a wide array of artefacts, paintings, photographs, uniforms and equipment.

Chair, General Sir Jack Deverell, KCB, OBE
Council Members, Judith Anthony; Keith Baldwin; Mihir Bose; Patrick Bradley; Lord Freeman, PC, FCA; Richard Nunneley, MBE; Dr William Philpott; Maj.-Gen. C. Vyvyan, CB, CBE; Deborah Younger
Director, Janice Murray, FRSA

NATIONAL ENDOWMENT FOR SCIENCE, TECHNOLOGY AND THE ARTS (NESTA)

1 Plough Place, London EC4A 1DE
T 020-7438 2500 E information@nesta.org.uk
W www.nesta.org.uk

NESTA is an independent body helping to solve major economic and social challenges in the UK. It was established under the National Lottery Act 1998 with a £200m endowment from the proceeds of the National Lottery and operates at no cost to the taxpayer. NESTA carries out its work through experimental programmes, analytical research and investment in early-stage companies.

As part of the public bodies' reform proposals of October 2010, the government announced that, subject to legislation, NESTA will become a charitable company. It will continue to operate, as it has done since its creation, by virtue of its lottery endowment.

Chair, Sir John Chisholm
Chief Executive, Geoff Mulgan

NATIONAL GALLERIES OF SCOTLAND
The Dean Gallery, 73 Belford Road, Edinburgh EH4 3DS
T 0131-624 6200 E enquiries@nationalgalleries.org
W www.nationalgalleries.org

The National Galleries of Scotland comprise the National Gallery of Scotland, the Scottish National Portrait Gallery, the Scottish National Gallery of Modern Art, the Dean Gallery and the Royal Scottish Academy Building. There are also partner galleries at Paxton House, Berwickshire, and Duff House, Banffshire. Total government grant-in-aid for 2011–12 is £12m.

TRUSTEES
Chair, Ben Thomson
Trustees, Ian Barr; Richard Burns; Herbert Coutts, MBE; Prof. Ian Howard; James Knox; Lesley Knox; Ray Macfarlane; Alasdair Morton; Nicky Wilson

OFFICERS
Director-General, John Leighton
Directors, Nicola Caterall *(Chief Operating Officer);* Michael Clarke, CBE *(National Gallery of Scotland);* Dr Simon Groom *(Scottish National Gallery of Modern Art and Dean Gallery);* James Holloway *(Scottish National Portrait Gallery);* Jacqueline Ridge *(Keeper of Conservation);* Catrin Tilley *(Director of Development, Communications and Enterprise)*

NATIONAL GALLERY
Trafalgar Square, London WC2N 5DN
T 020-7747 2885 E information@ng-london.org.uk
W www.nationalgallery.org.uk

The National Gallery, which houses a permanent collection of western European painting from the 13th to the 20th century, was founded in 1824, following a parliamentary grant of £60,000 for the purchase and exhibition of the Angerstein collection of pictures. The present site was first occupied in 1838; an extension to the north of the building with a public entrance in Orange Street was opened in 1975; the Sainsbury Wing was opened in 1991; and the Getty Entrance opened off Trafalgar Square at the east end of the main building in 2004. Total government grant-in-aid for 2011–12 is £26.74m.

BOARD OF TRUSTEES
Chair, M. Getty
Trustees, L. Batchelor; G. Dalal; D. Dalwood; Prof. D. Ekserdjian; Lady Heseltine; M. Hintze; Prof. A. Hurlbert; P. Lankester; J. Nelson; Lady Normanby; H. Rothschild; C. Thomson

OFFICERS
Director, Dr N. Penny
Director of Collections and Deputy Director, Dr S. Foister
Director of Conservation, Larry Keith
Director of Education, Information and Access, Jillian Barker
Director of Operations and Administration, Greg Perry
Director of Public Affairs and Development, S. Ward
Director of Scientific Research, Dr A. Roy
Senior Curator, D. Jaffé

NATIONAL HERITAGE MEMORIAL FUND
7 Holbein Place, London SW1W 8NR
T 020-7591 6000 E enquire@hlf.org.uk
W www.nhmf.org.uk

The National Heritage Memorial Fund was set up under the National Heritage Act 1980 in memory of people who have given their lives for the United Kingdom. The fund provides grants to organisations based in the UK, mainly so that they can buy items of outstanding interest and of importance to the national heritage. These must either be at risk or have a memorial character. The fund is administered by a chair and 14 trustees who are appointed by the prime minister.

The National Heritage Memorial Fund receives an annual grant from the Department for Culture, Media and Sport. Under the National Lottery etc Act 1993, the trustees of the fund became responsible for the distribution of funds for both the National Heritage Memorial Fund and the Heritage Lottery Fund.

Chair, Jenny Abramsky
Chief Executive, Carole Souter

NATIONAL LIBRARY OF SCOTLAND
George IV Bridge, Edinburgh EH1 1EW
T 0131-623 3700 E enquiries@nls.uk
W www.nls.uk

The library, which was founded as the Advocates' Library in 1682, became the National Library of Scotland (NLS) in 1925. It is funded by the Scottish government. It contains about 14 million books and pamphlets, two million maps, 25,000 newspaper and magazine titles and 100,000 manuscripts, including the John Murray Archive. It has an unrivalled Scottish collection as well as online catalogues and digital resources which can be accessed through the NLS website.

Material can be consulted in the reading rooms, which are open to anyone with a valid library card.

Chair of the Trustees, Prof. Michael Anderson, OBE, FBA, FRSE
National Librarian and Chief Executive, Martyn Wade
Directors, Darryl Mead *(Collections and Research);* Duncan Campbell *(Corporate Services);* Alex Miller *(Customer Services)*

NATIONAL LIBRARY OF WALES/LLYFRGELL GENEDLAETHOL CYMRU
Aberystwyth, Ceredigion, Wales SY23 3BU
T 01970-632800
W www.llgc.org.uk

The National Library of Wales was founded by royal charter in 1907, and is funded by the National Assembly for Wales. It contains about five million printed books, 40,000 manuscripts, four million deeds and documents, numerous maps, prints and drawings, and a sound and moving image collection. It specialises in manuscripts and books relating to Wales and the Celtic peoples. It is the repository for pre-1858 Welsh probate records, manorial records and tithe documents, and certain legal records. Admission is by reader's ticket to the reading rooms but entry to the exhibition programme is free.

President, Rt. Hon. Dafydd Wigley

Trustees, David Barker *(Vice President);* Tricia Carter; Arwel Ellis Owen; Roy Evans; John E. Gittins; Aled Gruffydd Jones; Gareth Haulfryn Williams; Colin John *(Treasurer);* Elspeth Mitcheson; Enid Morgan; Wyn Penri Jones; Roy Roberts; Huw Williams

Heads of Departments, R. Arwel Jones *(Public Services);* Avril Jones *(Collection Services);* David Michael *(Finance)*

Librarian, A. M. W. Green

NATIONAL LOTTERY COMMISSION

101 Wigmore Street, London W1U 1QU
T 020-7016 3400 E publicaffairs@natlotcomm.gov.uk
W www.natlotcomm.gov.uk

The National Lottery Commission replaced the Office of the National Lottery (OFLOT) in 1999 under the National Lottery Act 1998. The commission is responsible for the granting, varying and enforcing of licences to run the National Lottery. It also runs the competition to award the next licence. Its duties are to ensure that the National Lottery is run with all due propriety, that the interests of players are protected and, subject to these two objectives, that returns to the good causes are maximised. The commission does not have a role in the distribution of funds to good causes: this is undertaken by 16 distributors; visit W www.lottery funding.org.uk for further information.

The Department for Culture, Media and Sport (DCMS) is responsible for gaming and lottery policy and laws. Empowered by the National Lottery Act 1993 (as amended), the DCMS directs the National Lottery Commission, which in turn regulates Camelot, the lottery operator. Camelot, a private company wholly owned by five shareholders, was granted a third licence to run the lottery from 1 February 2009 for ten years.

Following the government's public bodies' reform proposals of October 2010, the National Lottery Commission is due to merge with the Gambling Commission.

Chair, Dr Anne Wright, CBE
Chief Executive, Mark Harris

NATIONAL MARITIME MUSEUM

Romney Road, Greenwich, London SE10 9NF
T 020-8858 4422
W www.nmm.ac.uk

Established in 1934, the National Maritime Museum provides information on the maritime history of Great Britain and is the largest institution of its kind in the world, with over two million items in its collections related to seafaring, navigation and astronomy. The museum is in three groups of buildings in Greenwich Park: the main building, the Queen's House (built by Inigo Jones, 1616–35) and the Royal Observatory, Greenwich (including Christopher Wren's Flamsteed House). In 2007 a £16m project opened a new astronomy centre and planetarium (now the only public planetarium in London) at the Royal Observatory.

Director, Kevin Fewster, FRSA
Chair, Lord Sterling of Plaistow, GCVO, CBE

Trustees, Eleanor Boddington; Lord Boyce, GCB, OBE; Sir Robert Crawford, CBE; Prof. Geoffrey Crossick; Gilly Drummond, OBE; Sir John Guinness, CB; Linda Hutchinson; Jan Kopernicki; Dr Christopher Lintott; Nigel MacDonald; David Moorhouse, CBE; Dr David Quarmby, CBE

NATIONAL MUSEUM OF THE ROYAL NAVY

HM Naval Base (PP66), Portsmouth PO1 3NH
T 023-9272 7562 E info@nmrn.org.uk
W www.royalnavalmuseum.org

The National Museum of the Royal Navy and HMS *Victory* (formerly the Royal Naval Museum) is a subsidiary charity of the newly formed National Museum of the Royal Navy. It is located in Portsmouth Historic Dockyard alongside Nelson's flagship and is housed in three buildings offering exhibitions on the Navy from the 18th century onwards. The museum aims to provide an effective and accessible repository for the heritage of the Navy, and to raise public awareness of, and encourage scholarship and research into, the history and achievements of the Royal Navy.

Chair, Adm. Sir Peter Abbott, GBE, KCB

NATIONAL MUSEUMS AND GALLERIES NORTHERN IRELAND

Cultra, Holywood, Northern Ireland BT18 0EU
T 0845-608 0000 E info@nmni.com
W www.nmni.com

The organisation of National Museums and Galleries of Northern Ireland was established under the Museums and Galleries (Northern Ireland) Order in 1998 and comprises four sites: the Ulster Museum, the Armagh County Museum, the Ulster Folk and Transport Museum, the Ulster American Folk Park and W5 at the Odyssey compex in Belfast (a wholly owned subsidiary).

Legislation requires National Museums and Galleries of Northern Ireland's board of trustees to care for, preserve and add to the collections; ensure that the collections are exhibited to the public; ensure that the significance of the collections is interpreted; and promote the awareness, appreciation and understanding of the public in relation to art, history and science, to the culture and way of life of the people and to the migration and settlement of people.

Chair, Dan Harvey, OBE

Trustees, Linda Beers; Lt.-Col. Harvey Bicker, OBE, TD; Neil Bodger; Pat Carvill, CB; Dame Geraldine Keegan; Joe Kelly; Dr Richard Browne McMinn; David Moore; Wendy Osborne, OBE; Anne Peoples; Dr Brian Scott; Tom Shaw, CBE; Dr Alastair Walker

Chief Executive, Tim Cooke

NATIONAL MUSEUMS LIVERPOOL

127 Dale Street, Liverpool L2 2JH
T 0151-207 0001
W www.liverpoolmuseums.org.uk

The board of trustees of the National Museums Liverpool (formerly National Museums and Galleries on Merseyside) is responsible for World Museum, the Merseyside Maritime Museum (also home to the UK Border Agency National Museum, known as Seized! The Border and Customs Uncovered), the Lady Lever Art Gallery, the Walker Art Gallery, Sudley House, the International Slavery Museum and the Museum of Liverpool. Total government grant-in-aid for 2010–11 was £20.5m.

Chair of the Board of Trustees, Prof. P. Redmond, CBE
Director, Dr D. Fleming
Director of Art Galleries, R. King
Director, World Museum Liverpool, S. Judd
Director, Merseyside Maritime Museum, R. Mulhearn
Director, Museum of Liverpool, J. Dugdale
Director of Collections Management, Midland Railway Building, S. A. Yates
Head of International Slavery Museum, Dr R. Benjamin

NATIONAL MUSEUMS SCOTLAND

Chambers Street, Edinburgh EH1 1JF
T 0131-225 7534
E info@nms.ac.uk W www.nms.ac.uk

National Museums Scotland provides advice, expertise and support to the museums community across Scotland, and undertakes fieldwork that often involves collaboration at local, national and international levels. National Museums Scotland comprises the National Museum of Scotland, the National War Museum, the National Museum of Rural Life, the National Museum of Flight, the National Museum of Costume and the National Museums Collection Centre. Its collections represent more than two centuries of collecting and include Scottish and classical archaeology, decorative and applied arts, world cultures and social history and science, technology and the natural world. Total grant-in-aid funding from the Scottish government for 2011–12 was £20.4m.

Up to 15 trustees can be appointed by the Minister for Culture and External Affairs for a term of four years, and may serve a second term.

Chair, Sir Angus Grossart, CBE, LLD, DLITT, FRSE
Trustees, Dr Isabel Bruce, OBE; Dr Anna Gregor, CBE, FRCR, FRCP; Lesley Hart, MBE; Andrew Holmes; Michael Kirwan, FCA; Miller McLean, FCIBS, FIB; Prof. Malcolm McLeod, CBE, FRSE; Bruce Minto; Prof. Stuart Monro, OBE; James Troughton; Sir John Ward, CBE, FRSE, FRSA; Iain Watt, FCIBS
Director, Dr Gordon Rintoul

NATIONAL MUSEUM WALES – AMGUEDDFA CYMRU

Cathays Park, Cardiff CF10 3NP
T 029-2039 7951 E post@museumwales.ac.uk
W www.museumwales.ac.uk

National Museum Wales – Amgueddfa Cymru aims to provide a complete illustration of the geology, mineralogy, zoology, botany, ethnography, archaeology, art, history and special industries of Wales. It comprises the National Museum Cardiff; St Fagans National History Museum; Big Pit – National Coal Museum, Blaenafon; the National Roman Legion Museum, Caerleon; the National Slate Museum, Llanberis; the National Wool Museum, Dre-fach Felindre; the National Waterfront Museum, Swansea; and the National Collections Centre, Nantgarw. Total funding from the Welsh government for 2011–12 is £26.1m.

President, Elisabeth Elias
Director-General, David Anderson
Trustees, Prof. Anthony George Atkins; Carole-Anne Davies; Dr Haydn Edwards; Miriam Hazel Griffiths; Dr Iolo ap Gwynn; Emeritus Prof. Richard G. W. Jones, FLSW; Prof. J. W. Last, CBE; Christina Macaulay; W. Morgan, FCA *(Treasurer)*; Prof. Jonathan Osmond; J. Peter; Victoria Mary Provis; Dr Keshav Singhal; David Beresford Vokes; Gareth Williams

NATIONAL PORTRAIT GALLERY

St Martin's Place, London WC2H 0HE
T 020-7306 0055
W www.npg.org.uk

The National Portrait Gallery was formed after a grant was made in 1856 to form a gallery of the portraits of the most eminent persons in British history. The present building was opened in 1896 and the Ondaatje Wing (including a new Balcony Gallery, Tudor Gallery, IT Gallery, lecture theatre and roof-top restaurant) opened in May 2000. There are three regional partnerships displaying portraits at Montacute House, Beningbrough Hall and Bodelwyddan Castle. Total government grant-in-aid for 2011–12 is £7.4m.

BOARD OF TRUSTEES

Chair, Prof. David Cannadine, FBA, FRSL
Trustees, Zeinab Badawi; Prof. Dame Carol Black, DBE; Sir Nicholas Blake, QC; Dr Rosalind P. Blakesley; Dr Augustus Casely-Hayford; Marchioness of Douro, OBE; Rt. Hon. Nick Clegg, MP; Amelia Fawcett, DBE; Sir Nicholas Grimshaw, CBE, PRA; Rt. Hon. Lord Janvrin, GCB, GCVO, QSO; Mary McCartney; Sir William Proby Bt., CBE; David Ross; Marina Warner, CBE, FBA
Director, Sandy Nairne

NATURAL ENGLAND

1 East Parade, Sheffield S1 2ET
T 0845-600 3078 E enquiries@naturalengland.org.uk
W www.naturalengland.org.uk

Natural England was established on 1 October 2006 after the Natural Environment and Rural Communities Act received royal assent in March 2006. It is the government's advisor on the natural environment, providing practical advice, grounded in science, on how best to safeguard England's natural wealth. The organisation's remit is to ensure sustainable stewardship of the land and sea and to ensure that England's environment can adapt and survive for future generations. Natural England works with farmers and land managers; business and industry; planners and developers; national, regional and local government; interest groups and local communities to help them improve their local environment.

Chief Executive, Dr Helen Phillips

NATURAL HISTORY MUSEUM

Cromwell Road, London SW7 5BD
T 020-7942 5000 W www.nhm.ac.uk

The Natural History Museum originates from the natural history departments of the British Museum, which grew extensively during the 19th century; in 1860 it was agreed that the natural history collections should be separated from the British Museum's collections of books, manuscripts and antiquities. Part of the site of the 1862 International Exhibition in South Kensington was acquired for the new museum, and the museum opened to the public in 1881. In 1963 the Natural History Museum became completely independent with its own board of trustees. The Natural History Museum at Tring, bequeathed by the second Lord Rothschild, has formed part of the museum since 1937. The Geological Museum merged with the Natural History Museum in 1985. In September 2009 the Natural History Museum opened the Darwin Centre, which contains public galleries, a high-tech audio-visual area known as the Attenborough

Studio, scientific research areas and space for 22 million zoological specimens, 17 million insect specimens and three million botanical specimens. Total government grant-in-aid for 2011–12 is £46.48m.

BOARD OF TRUSTEES
Chair, Oliver Stocken
Trustees, Daniel Alexander, QC; Prof. Sir Roy Anderson, FRS, FMEDSCI; Louise Charlton; Prof. David Drewry; Prof. Christopher Gilligan; Prof. Alex Halliday, FRS; Ian J. Henderson, CBE, FRICS; Dr Derek Langslow, CBE; Prof. Georgina Mace, CBE, FRS; Sir David Omand, GCB

SENIOR STAFF
Director, Dr Michael Dixon
Director of Estates and Services, David Sanders
Director of Finance and Administration, Neil Greenwood
Director of Human Resources, Paul Brereton
Director, Policy and Planning and Director of the Natural History Museum at Tring, Teresa Wild
Director of Public Engagement, Sharon Ament
Director of Science, Prof. Ian Owens
Head of Risk and Assurance, David Thorpe
Head of Library and Information Services, Graham Higley
Keeper of Botany, Dr Johannes Vogel
Interim Keeper of Entomology, Dr Andrew Polaszek
Keeper of Mineralogy, Dr Andy Fleet
Keeper of Palaeontology, Prof. Norman MacLeod
Keeper of Zoology, Prof. Phil Rainbow
Museum Manager, Ian Jenkinson

NHS PAY REVIEW BODY
6th Floor, Victoria House, Southampton Row, London WC1B 4AD
T 020-7271 0490 W www.ome.uk.com

The NHS Pay Review Body (NHSPRB) makes recommendations to the prime minister, Secretary of State for Health and ministers in Scotland, Wales and Northern Ireland on the remuneration of all paid staff under agenda for change and employed in the NHS. The review body was established in 1983 for nurses and allied health professionals. Its remit has since expanded to cover over 1.8 million staff; ie almost all staff in the NHS, with the exception of dentists, doctors and very senior managers.
Chair, Jerry Cope
Members, Philip Ashmore; Prof. David Blackaby; Dame Denise Holt; Graham Jagger; Ian McKay; Maureen Scott; Prof. Anna Vignoles

NORTHERN IRELAND HUMAN RIGHTS COMMISSION
Temple Court, 39 North Street, Belfast BT1 1NA
T 028-9024 3987 **Textphone** 028-9024 9066
E information@nihrc.org W www.nihrc.org

The Northern Ireland Human Rights Commission is a non-departmental public body, established by the Northern Ireland Act 1998 and set up in March 1999. Its purpose is to protect and promote human rights in Northern Ireland. Its main functions include reviewing the law and practice relating to human rights in Northern Ireland, advising government and the Northern Ireland Assembly, and promoting an awareness of human rights in Northern Ireland. It can also investigate human rights violations and take cases to court. The members of the commission are appointed by the Secretary of State for Northern Ireland.

Chief Commissioner, Michael O'Flaherty
Commissioners, Christine Collins; John Corey; Milton Kerr; Grainia Long; Alan McBride; Marion Reynolds; Paul Yam
Director, Virginia McVea

NORTHERN LIGHTHOUSE BOARD
84 George Street, Edinburgh EH2 3DA
T 0131-473 3100 E enquiries@nlb.org.uk
W www.nlb.org.uk

The Northern Lighthouse Board is the general lighthouse authority for Scotland and the Isle of Man and owes its origin to an act of parliament passed in 1786. At present there are 19 commissioners who operate under the Merchant Shipping Act 1995.

The commissioners control 208 lighthouses, many lighted and unlighted buoys, a DGPS (differential global positioning system) station and an ELORAN (long-range navigation) system. *See also* Transport.
Chair, Sheriff Principal Alistair Dunlop, QC
Commissioners, Lord Advocate; Solicitor-General for Scotland; Lord Provosts of Edinburgh, Glasgow and Aberdeen; Convener of Highland Council; Convener of Argyll and Bute Council; Sheriffs-Principal of North Strathclyde, Tayside, Central and Fife, Grampian, Highlands and Islands, South Strathclyde, Dumfries and Galloway, Lothians and Borders and Glasgow and Strathkelvin; Capt. Mike Close; Alistair MacKenzie; Robert Quayle; John Ross, CBE; Alistair Whyte
Chief Executive, Roger Lockwood, CB

NUCLEAR DECOMMISSIONING AUTHORITY
Herdus House, Westlakes Science and Technology Park, Moor Row, Cumbria CA24 3HU
T 01925-802001 E enquiries@nda.gov.uk
W www.nda.gov.uk

The Nuclear Decommissioning Authority (NDA) was created under the Energy Act 2004. It is a strategic authority that owns 19 sites and associated civil nuclear liabilities and assets of the public sector, previously under the control of the UK Energy Authority and British Nuclear Fuels. The NDA decommissions and cleans up civil nuclear facilities; ensures the safe management of waste products, both radioactive and non-radioactive; implements government policy on the long-term management of nuclear waste; develops UK-wide nuclear low-level waste strategy and plans; and scrutinises the decommissioning plans of British Energy.

Total planned expenditure for 2011–12 is £2.9bn, with total grant-in-aid standing at £2bn. The remaining £0.9bn will come from commercial operations.
Chair, Stephen Henwood
Chief Executive, Tony Fountain

OFFICE FOR BUDGET RESPONSIBILITY
20 Victoria Street, London SW1H 0NF
T 020-7271 2442 E obrenquiries@obr.gsi.gov.uk
W http://budgetresponsibility.independent.gov.uk

The Office for Budget Responsibility (OBR) was created in 2010 to provide independent and authoritative analysis of the UK's public finances. It has four main roles: producing forecasts for the economy and public finances; judging progress towards the government's fiscal targets; assessing the long-term sustainability of the public finances; and scrutinising HM Treasury's costing of Budget measures.

In support of these activities, the OBR undertakes a variety of research projects through the year. It also answers parliamentary questions on its forecasts and gives evidence to parliamentary committees.

Chair, Robert Chote
Committee Members, Steve Nickell, CBE; Graham Parker, CBE

OFFICE OF COMMUNICATIONS (OFCOM)

Riverside House, 2A Southwark Bridge Road, London SE1 9HA
T 0300-123 3000
W www.ofcom.org.uk

OFCOM was established in 2003 under the Office of Communications Act 2002 as the independent regulator and competition authority for the UK communications industries with responsibility for television, radio, telecommunications and wireless communications services.

Following the passing of the Post Services Act 2011, OFCOM has assumed regulatory responsibility for postal services from Postcomm, the Postal Services Commission.

Chief Executive, Ed Richards
Chair, Colette Bowe
Deputy Chair, Philip Graf, CBE
Board Members, Norman Blackwell; Tim Gardam; Stuart McIntosh; Mike McTighe; Peter Phillips; Jill Ainscough

OFFICE OF MANPOWER ECONOMICS (OME)

6th Floor, Victoria House, Southampton Row, London WC1B 4AD
T 020-7271 0497 W www.ome.uk.com

The Office of Manpower Economics (OME) was established in 1971. It is an independent non-statutory organisation which is responsible for servicing independent review bodies that advise on the pay of various public sector groups, the Police Negotiating Board and the Police Advisory Board for England and Wales. The OME is also responsible for servicing *ad hoc* bodies of inquiry and for undertaking research into pay and associated matters as requested by the government.

The OME has been allocated a total of £2.58m by the Department for Business, Innovation and Skills for 2011–12.

OME Director, Geoff Dart
Director, Doctors' and Dentists' and NHS Pay Review Body Secretariats, Research and Analysis Group and OME
Deputy Director, Margaret McEvoy
Director, Armed Forces' and School Teachers' Secretariats, Jenny Eastabrook
Director, Senior Salaries', Prison Service and Police Board Secretariats, Keith Masson

OFFICE OF TAX SIMPLIFICATION

HM Treasury, 1 Horse Guards Road, London SW1A 2HQ
T 020-7270 4558 E ots@ots.gsi.gov.uk
W www.hm-treasury.gov.uk/ots.htm

The chancellor and exchequer secretary to HM Treasury launched the Office of Tax Simplification (OTS) on 20 July 2010 to provide the government with independent advice on simplifying the UK tax system. The chancellor has asked the OTS to carry out two initial reviews: a review of all tax reliefs, and a review of small business taxation.

The Office has been established as an independent office of HM Treasury for the life of the current parliament and draws together expertise from across the tax and legal professions, the business community and other interested parties.

Chair, Rt. Hon. Michael Jack
Tax Director, John Whiting

PARADES COMMISSION

Windsor House, 9–15 Bedford Street, Belfast BT2 7EL
T 028-9089 5900 E info@paradescommission.org
W www.paradescommission.org

The Parades Commission was set up under the Public Processions (Northern Ireland) Act 1998. Its function is to encourage and facilitate local accommodation of contentious parades; where this is not possible, the commission is empowered to make legal determinations about such parades, which may include imposing conditions on aspects of the notified parade (such as restrictions on routes/areas and exclusion of certain groups with a record of bad behaviour).

The chair and members are appointed by the Secretary of State for Northern Ireland; the membership must, as far as is practicable, be representative of the community in Northern Ireland.

Chair, Peter Osborne
Members, Douglas Bain; Delia Close; Revd Brian Kennaway; Dr Catriona King; Frances Nolan; Robin Percival

PAROLE BOARD FOR ENGLAND AND WALES

Grenadier House, 99–105 Horseferry Road, London SW1P 2DX
T 0845-251 2220 E info@paroleboard.gov.uk
W www.paroleboard.gov.uk

The Parole Board was established under the Criminal Justice Act 1967 and became an independent executive non-departmental public body under the Criminal Justice and Public Order Act 1994. It is the body that protects the public by making risk assessments about prisoners to decide who may safely be released into the community and who must remain in, or be returned to, custody. Board decisions are taken at two main types of panels of up to three members: 'paper panels' for the majority of cases, or oral hearings for decisions concerning prisoners serving life or indeterminate sentences for public protection.

Chair, Rt. Hon. Sir David Latham
Chief Executive, Linda Lennon, CBE

PAROLE BOARD FOR SCOTLAND

Saughton House, Broomhouse Drive, Edinburgh EH11 3XD
T 0131-244 8373
E paroleboardforscotlandexecutive@scotland.gsi.gov.uk
W www.scottishparoleboard.gov.uk

The board directs and advises the Scottish ministers on the release of prisoners on licence, and related matters.

Chair, Prof. A. Cameron
Vice-Chair, Ms H. Baillie

PENSION PROTECTION FUND (PPF)

Knollys House, 17 Addiscombe Road, Croydon CR0 6SR
T 0845-600 2541 E information@ppf.gsi.gov.uk
W www.pensionprotectionfund.org.uk

The PPF became operational in 2005. It was established to pay compensation to members of eligible defined-benefit

pension schemes where a qualifying insolvency event in relation to the employer occurs and where there is a lack of sufficient assets in the pension scheme. The PPF also administers the Financial Assistance Scheme, which helps members whose schemes wound-up before 2005. It is also responsible for the Fraud Compensation Fund (which provides compensation to occupational pension schemes that suffer a loss that can be attributed to dishonesty). The chair and board of the PPF are appointed by, and accountable to, the Secretary of State for Work and Pensions, and are responsible for paying compensation, calculating annual levies (which help fund the PPF), and setting and overseeing investment strategy.
Chair, Lady Barbara Judge
Chief Executive, Alan Rubenstein

PENSIONS REGULATOR

Napier House, Trafalgar Place, Brighton BN1 4DW
T 0870-606 3636
E customersupport@thepensionsregulator.gov.uk
W www.thepensionsregulator.gov.uk

The Pensions Regulator was established in 2005 as the regulator of work-based pension schemes in the UK, replacing the Occupational Pensions Regulatory Authority (OPRA). It aims to protect the benefits of occupational and personal pension scheme members by working with trustees, employers, pension providers and advisors. The regulator's work focuses on encouraging better management and administration of schemes, ensuring that final salary schemes have a sensible funding plan, and encouraging money purchase schemes to provide members with the information that they need to make informed choices about their pension fund. The pensions Acts of 2004 and 2008 gave the regulator a range of powers which can be used to protect scheme members, but a strong emphasis is placed on educating and enabling those responsible for managing pension schemes, and powers are used as a last resort. The regulator offers three free online resources to help trustees, employers, professionals and advisors understand their role, duties and obligations.
Chair, Michael O'Higgins
Chief Executive, Bill Galvin

POLICE ADVISORY BOARD FOR ENGLAND AND WALES

6th Floor, Victoria House, Southampton Row,
London WC1B 4AD
T 020-7271 0472 W www.ome.uk.com

The Police Advisory Board for England and Wales was established in 1965 and provides advice to the home secretary on general questions affecting the police in England and Wales. It also considers draft regulations which the secretary of state proposes to make with respect to matters other than hours of duty, leave, pay and allowances or the issue, use and return of police clothing, personal equipment and other effects.
Independent Chair, John Randall
Independent Deputy Chair, Prof. Gillian Morris

POLICE NEGOTIATING BOARD (PNB)

6th Floor, Victoria House, Southampton Row,
London WC1B 4AD
T 020-7271 0472 W www.ome.uk.com

The PNB was established in 1980 to negotiate pay; allowances; hours of duty; the issue, use and return of police clothing, personal equipment and accoutrements;

leave; and pensions of UK police officers, and to make recommendations on these matters to the home secretary, Northern Ireland secretary and Scottish ministers.
Independent Chair, John Randall
Independent Deputy Chair, Prof. Gillian Morris

PRISON SERVICE PAY REVIEW BODY

6th Floor, Victoria House, Southampton Row,
London WC1B 4AD
T 020-7215 8369 W www.ome.uk.com

The Prison Service Pay Review Body was set up in 2001. It makes independent recommendations on the pay of prison governors, operational managers, prison officers and related grades for the Prison Service in England and Wales and for the Northern Ireland Prison Service.
Chair, Dr Peter Knight, CBE
Members, Prof. John Beath; Richard J. N. Childs, QPM; Bronwen Mary Curtis, CBE; John Davies, OBE; Joseph Magee; Vilma Patterson; Trevor Spires

REGIONAL DEVELOPMENT AGENCIES

5th Floor, Oceanic House, 1A Cockspur Street,
London SW1Y 5BG
T 020-7968 0600 W www.englandsrdas.com

Regional Development Agencies (RDAs) were established to help the English regions improve their relative economic performance and reduce social and economic disparities within and between regions. Their five statutory objectives are to further economic development and regeneration; to promote business efficiency and competitiveness; to promote employment; to enhance the development and application of skills relevant to employment; and to contribute to sustainable development. There are nine RDAs in England, and they are financed through a single fund provided by contributing government departments (BIS, DCLG, DECC, DEFRA and DCMS). The RDA's budget for 2011–12 is £711m.

The government has announced that the RDAs will close at the end of March 2012. Some of the RDAs current functions will be taken over by newly created local enterprise partnerships, while other functions are likely to be carried out at national, rather than local, level.

RDA REGIONS
NORTH WEST: Renaissance House, Centre Park, Warrington
  WA1 1QN T 01925-400100 *Chair,* Robert Hough
YORKSHIRE: Victoria House, Victoria Place, Leeds LS11 5AE
  T 0113-394 9600 *Chair,* Julie Kenny
NORTH EAST: Stella House, Goldcrest Way, Newburn
  Riverside, Newcastle upon Tyne NE15 8NY T 0191-229 6200
  Chair, Paul Callaghan
WEST MIDLANDS: 3 Priestley Wharf, Holt Street, Aston
  Science Park, Birmingham B7 4BN T 0121-380 3500 *Chair,*
  Sir Roy McNulty
EAST MIDLANDS: Apex Court, City Link, Nottingham
  NG2 4LA T 0115-988 8300 *Chair,* Dr Bryan Jackson,
  OBE
EAST OF ENGLAND: Victory House, Vision Park, Chivers
  Way, Histon, Cambridgeshire CB24 9ZR T 01223-713900
  Chair, Will Pope
SOUTH WEST: Sterling House, Dix's Field, Exeter EX1 1QA
  T 01392-214747 *Chair,* Sir Harry Studholme
LONDON: Palestra, 197 Blackfriars Road, London SE1 8AA
  T 020-7593 8000 *Chair,* Harvey McGrath
SOUTH EAST: Cross Lanes, Guildford GU1 1YA
  T 01483-484200 *Chair,* Robert Douglas, CBE

REGISTRAR OF PUBLIC LENDING RIGHT

Richard House, Sorbonne Close, Stockton on Tees TS17 6DA
T 01642-604699 E authorservices@plr.uk.com
W www.plr.uk.com

Under the Public Lending Right (PLR) system, in operation since 1983, payment is made from public funds to authors whose books are lent out from public libraries. Payment is made once a year and the amount that each author receives is proportionate to the number of times (established from a sample) that each registered book has been lent out during the previous year. The registrar of PLR, who is appointed by the Secretary of State for Culture, Olympics, Media and Sport, compiles the register of authors and books. Authors resident in all European Economic Area countries are eligible to apply. (The term 'author' covers writers, illustrators, translators and some editors/compilers.)

A payment of 6.25 pence was made in 2010–11 for each estimated loan of a registered book, up to a top limit of £6,600 for the books of any one registered author; the money for loans above this level is used to augment the remaining PLR payments. In 2010–11 the sum of £6.7m was paid out to 23,366 registered authors and assignees as the annual payment of PLR.

In October 2010, the government announced that the PLR would be abolished, subject to legislation, and that responsibility for the PLR scheme would transfer to another public body.

Registrar, Dr J. G. Parker

REVIEW BODY ON DOCTORS' AND DENTISTS' REMUNERATION

6th Floor, Victoria House, Southampton Row, London WC1B 4AD
T 020-7271 0486 W www.ome.uk.com

The Review Body on Doctors' and Dentists' Remuneration was set up in 1971. It advises the prime minister, first ministers in Scotland, Wales and Northern Ireland, and the ministers for Health, in England, Scotland, Wales and Northern Ireland on the remuneration of doctors and dentists taking any part in the National Health Service.

Chair, Ron Amy, OBE
Members, Lucinda Bolton; Katrina Easterling; John Glennie; David Grafton; Sally Smedley; Prof. Steve Thompson; Prof. Ian Walker; David Williamson

ROYAL AIR FORCE MUSEUM

Grahame Park Way, London NW9 5LL
T 020-8205 2266 E london@rafmuseum.org
W www.rafmuseum.org.uk

The museum has two sites, one at the former airfield at Hendon and the second at Cosford, in the West Midlands, both of which illustrate the development of aviation from before the Wright brothers to the present-day RAF. The museum's collection across both sites consists of over 170 aircraft, as well as artefacts, aviation memorabilia, fine art and photographs. Total government grant-in-aid for 2011–12, provided by the Ministry of Defence, is £7.7m.

Director-General, Air Vice-Marshal Peter Dye, OBE

ROYAL BOTANIC GARDEN EDINBURGH

20A Inverleith Row, Edinburgh EH3 5LR
T 0131-552 7171 W www.rbge.org.uk

The Royal Botanic Garden Edinburgh (RBGE) originated as the Physic Garden, established in 1670 beside the Palace of Holyroodhouse. The garden moved to its present 28-hectare site at Inverleith, Edinburgh, in 1821. There are also three regional gardens: Benmore Botanic Garden, near Dunoon, Argyll; Logan Botanic Garden, near Stranraer, Wigtownshire; and Dawyck Botanic Garden, near Stobo, Peeblesshire. Since 1986 RBGE has been administered by a board of trustees established under the National Heritage (Scotland) Act 1985. It receives an annual grant from the Scottish government's Rural and Environmental Research and Analysis Directorate.

The RBGE is an international centre for scientific research on plant diversity and for horticulture education and conservation. It has an extensive library, a herbarium with almost three million preserved plant specimens, and over 15,000 species in the living collections.

Chair of the Board of Trustees, Sir George Mathewson, CBE, LLD, FRSE
Regius Keeper, Prof. Stephen Blackmore, FRSE

ROYAL BOTANIC GARDENS, KEW

Richmond, Surrey TW9 3AB
T 020-8332 5000
Wakehurst Place, Ardingly, W. Sussex RH17 6TN
T 01444-89000
E info@kew.org W www.kew.org

The Royal Botanic Gardens, Kew (RBG, Kew) were originally laid out as a private garden for the now demolished White House for George III's mother, Princess Augusta, in 1759. The gardens were much enlarged in the 19th century, notably by the inclusion of the grounds of the former Richmond Lodge. In 1965 Kew acquired the gardens at Wakehurst Place on a long lease from the National Trust. Under the National Heritage Act 1983 a board of trustees was set up to administer the gardens, which in 1984 became an independent body supported by grant-in-aid from the Department for Environment, Food and Rural Affairs.

The functions of RBG, Kew are to carry out research into plant sciences, to disseminate knowledge about plants and to provide the public with the opportunity to gain knowledge and enjoyment from the gardens' collections. There are extensive national reference collections of living and preserved plants and a comprehensive library and archive. The main emphasis is on plant conservation and biodiversity; Wakehurst Place houses the Millennium Seed Bank Partnership, which is the largest *ex situ* conservation project in the world – its aim is to save seed from 25 per cent of the earth's wild plant species by 2020.

BOARD OF TRUSTEES
Chair, Marcus Agius
Members, Prof. Michael Crawley; Prof. Jonathan Drori, CBE; Tessa Green; Dr Geoffrey Hawtin; Timothy Hornsby; Sir Henry Keswick; Mr George Loudon; Prof. Nicola Spence; Sir William Stewart, FRS; Ms Jennifer Ullman; Sir Ferrers Vyvyan
Director, Prof. Stephen D. Hopper

ROYAL COMMISSION ON THE ANCIENT AND HISTORICAL MONUMENTS OF SCOTLAND

John Sinclair House, 16 Bernard Terrace, Edinburgh EH8 9NX
T 0131-662 1456 E info@rcahms.gov.uk
W www.rcahms.gov.uk

The Royal Commission on the Ancient and Historical Monuments of Scotland (RCAHMS) was established by a royal warrant in 1908, which was revised in 1992, and is appointed to provide for the collecting, recording and interpretation of information on the architectural, industrial, archaeological and maritime heritage of Scotland, to give a picture of the human influence on Scotland's places from the earliest times to the present day. It is funded by the Scottish government. More than 15 million items, including photographs, maps, drawings and documents, are available through the search room, and online databases provide access to over 150,000 images and information on 300,000 buildings and sites. RCAHMS also holds Scotland's national collection of historical aerial photography as well as The Aerial Reconnaissance Archives (TARA) of international wartime photography.

Chair, Prof. John Hume, OBE, FSA SCOT

Commissioners, Kate Byrne, FRSA; Tom Dawson, FSA SCOT; Mark Hopton, FSA SCOT; Dr Jeremy Huggett, FSA, FSA SCOT; Prof. John Hunter, OBE, FSA, FSA SCOT; Paul Jardine; Dr Gordon Masterton, OBE; Jude Quartson-Mochrie; Elspeth Reid

Chief Executive, Diana Murray, FSA, FSA SCOT

ROYAL COMMISSION ON THE ANCIENT AND HISTORICAL MONUMENTS OF WALES

Crown Building, Plas Crug, Aberystwyth SY23 1NJ
T 01970-621200 E nmr.wales@rcahmw.gov.uk
W www.rcahmw.gov.uk

The Royal Commission on the Ancient and Historical Monuments of Wales, established in 1908, is responsible for developing and promoting understanding of the archaeological, built and maritime heritage of Wales. The Royal Commission holds a unique collection of photographs, maps, publications and reports within its archive, the National Monuments Record of Wales, which can be consulted via an online database or through the public enquiry service. The commission is funded by the National Assembly for Wales.

Chair, Dr Eurwyn William, FSA

Vice-Chair, Neil Harries, FCMI

Commissioners, Prof. Antony D. Carr, FRHISTS, FSA; Mrs Anne S. Eastham, FSA; Ms Catherine S. Hardman; Jonathan Hudson; John W. Lloyd, CB; Thomas O. S. Lloyd, OBE, FSA; John Newman, FSA; Henry Owen-John; Mark Redknap, FSA; Prof. C. M. Williams, FRHISTS

ROYAL MAIL GROUP

100 Victoria Embankment, London EC4Y 0HQ
T 020-7250 2888 W www.royalmailgroup.com

Crown services for the carriage of government dispatches were set up in about 1516. The conveyance of public correspondence began in 1635 and the mail service was made a parliamentary responsibility with the setting up of a Post Office in 1657. In 1840, Royal Mail launched the Penny Black, the world's first postage stamp. Telegraphs came under Post Office control in 1870 and the Post Office Telephone Service began in 1880. The National Girobank service of the Post Office began in 1968. The Post Office ceased to be a government department in 1969 when responsibility for the running of the postal, telecommunications, giro and remittance services was transferred to a public authority of the same name.

The British Telecommunications Act 1981 separated the functions of the Post Office, making it solely responsible for postal services and Girobank. Girobank was privatised in 1990. The Postal Services Act 2000 turned the Post Office into a wholly owned public limited company establishing a regulatory regime under the Postal Service Commission. The Post Office Group changed its name to Consignia plc in March 2001 when its new corporate structure took effect; in November 2002 the name was changed to Royal Mail Group plc. As of 1 January 2006 the UK postal service market was fully liberalised, and any licensed operator is now able to deliver mail to businesses and residential customers. Following the passing of the Postal Services Act 2011 on 13 June 2011, Royal Mail is now open to private ownership. A buyer will be able to own up to 90 per cent of the shares in the company, with Royal Mail staff offered the remaining 10 per cent.

Royal Mail processes and delivers around 62 million letters, packets and parcels to 28.8 million addresses every day; around 20 million customers are served in the 11,820 Post Office branches each week. The Royal Mail Group directly employs around 163,000 people in the UK.

The chair, chief executive and members of the board are appointed by the Secretary of State for Business, Innovation and Skills but responsibility for the running of Royal Mail Group as a whole rests with the board in its corporate capacity.

BOARD

Chair, Donald Brydon, CBE

Chief Executive, Moya Greene

Executive Directors, Mark Higson, Matthew Lester, David Smith, Paula Vannells

Non-Executive Directors, Lord Currie; Nick Horler; Cath Keers; Paul Murray; Orna Ni-Chionna; Les Owen

Company Secretary, Jon Millidge

SCHOOL TEACHERS' REVIEW BODY

6th Floor, Victoria House, Southampton Row,
London WC1B 4AD
T 020-7271 0474 W www.ome.uk.com

The School Teachers' Review Body was set up under the School Teachers' Pay and Conditions Act 1991. It is required to examine and report on such matters relating to the statutory conditions of employment of school teachers in England and Wales as may be referred to it by the education secretary.

Chair, vacant

Members, Dewi Jones; Elizabeth Kidd; Esmond Lindop; Stella Pantelides; Jill Pullen; Dr Patricia Rice; Anne Watts, CBE

SCIENCE MUSEUM

Exhibition Road, London SW7 2DD
T 0870-870 4868 E sciencem@sciencemuseum.org.uk
W www.sciencemuseum.org.uk

The Science Museum, part of the National Museum of Science & Industry (NMSI), houses the national collections of science, technology, industry and medicine. The museum began as the science collection of the South Kensington Museum and first opened in 1857. In 1883 it acquired the collections of the Patent Museum and in 1909 the science collections were transferred to the new Science Museum, leaving the art collections with the Victoria and Albert Museum. The Wellcome Wing was opened in July 2000.

The NMSI also incorporates the National Railway Museum, York; the National Media Museum, Bradford; and Locomotion: the National Railway Museum at Shildon.

Total government grant-in-aid for 2010–11 was £40m.

Chair, Dr Douglas Gurr
Trustees, Lady Chisholm; Howard Covington; Lord Faulkner of Worcester; Simon Linnett; Prof. Averil Macdonald; Sir Howard Newby, CBE; Dr Gill Samuels, CBE; Dr Maggie Semple, OBE; James Smith; Janet Street-Porter; Christopher Swinson, OBE; Michael G. Wilson, OBE
Director of NMSI, Ian Blatchford
Director of Science Museum, Ian Blatchford
Director of National Media Museum, Colin Philpott
Director of National Railway Museum, Steve Davies, MBE

SCOTTISH CRIMINAL CASES REVIEW COMMISSION
5th Floor, Portland House, 17 Renfield Street, Glasgow G2 5AH
T 0141-270 7030 E info@sccrc.org.uk
W www.sccrc.org.uk

The commission is a non-departmental public body, funded by the Scottish Government Criminal Justice Directorate, and established in April 1999. It assumed the role previously performed by the Secretary of State for Scotland to consider alleged miscarriages of justice in Scotland and refer cases meeting the relevant criteria to the high court for determination. Members are appointed by the Queen on the recommendation of the First Minister; senior executive staff are appointed by the commission.

Chair, Jean Couper, CBE
Members, Gerrard Bann; Graham Bell, QC; Prof. Brian Caddy; Stewart Campbell; Prof. George Irving, CBE; Gerard McClay; Francis McMenamin; Mhairi Richards, QC
Chief Executive, Gerard Sinclair

SCOTTISH ENTERPRISE
Atrium Court, 50 Waterloo Street, Glasgow G2 6HQ
T 0845-607 8787 E enquiries@scotent.co.uk
W www.scottish-enterprise.com

Scottish Enterprise was established in 1991 and its purpose is to stimulate the sustainable growth of Scotland's economy. It is mainly funded by the Scottish government and is responsible to the Scottish ministers. Working in partnership with the private and public sectors, Scottish Enterprise will invest £332m in 2011–12 to further the development of Scotland's economy by helping ambitious and innovative businesses grow and become more successful. Scottish Enterprise is particularly interested in supporting companies that provide renewable energy, encourage trade overseas, increase innovation, and those that will help Scotland become a low-carbon economy.

Chair, Crawford Gillies
Chief Executive, Lena C. Wilson

SCOTTISH ENVIRONMENT PROTECTION AGENCY (SEPA)
Erskine Court, Castle Business Park, Stirling FK9 4TR
T 01786-457700 **Hotline** 0800-807060
E info@sepa.org.uk W www.sepa.org.uk

SEPA was established in 1996 and is the public body responsible for environmental protection in Scotland. It regulates potential pollution to land, air and water; the storage, transport and disposal of controlled waste; and the safekeeping and disposal of radioactive materials. It does this within a complex legislative framework of acts of parliament, EU directives and regulations, granting licences to operations of industrial processes and waste disposal. SEPA also operates Floodline (T 0845-988 1188), a public service providing information on the possible risk of flooding 24 hours a day, 365 days a year.

Chair, David Sigsworth
Chief Executive, Campbell Gemmell
Directors, John Ford *(Finance and Corporate Services);* Calum MacDonald *(Operations);* James Curran *(Science and Strategy)*

SCOTTISH LAW COMMISSION
140 Causewayside, Edinburgh EH9 1PR
T 0131-668 2131 E info@scotlawcom.gsi.gov.uk
W www.scotlawcom.gov.uk

The Scottish Law Commission, established in 1965, keeps the law in Scotland under review and makes proposals for its development and reform. It is responsible to the Scottish ministers through the Scottish government law and courts directorate.

Chair (part-time), Hon. Lord Drummond Young
Chief Executive, M. McMillan
Commissioners, Ms L. Dunlop, QC; P. Layden, QC, TD; Prof. H. MacQueen

SCOTTISH LEGAL AID BOARD
44 Drumsheugh Gardens, Edinburgh EH3 7SW
T 0131-226 7061 **Helpline** 0845-122 8686
E general@slab.org.uk W www.slab.org.uk

The Scottish Legal Aid Board was set up under the Legal Aid (Scotland) Act 1986 to manage legal aid in Scotland. It reports to the Scottish government. Board members are appointed by Scottish ministers.

Chair, Iain A. Robertson, CBE
Members, Les Campbell; Joseph Hughes; Alastair Kinroy, QC; Denise Loney; Paul McBride, QC; Ray MacFarlane; Susan McPhee; Bill McQueen, CBE; Elaine Rosie; Sheriff Harry Small; Graham Watson
Chief Executive, Lindsay Montgomery, CBE

SCOTTISH NATURAL HERITAGE (SNH)
Great Glen House, Leachkin Road, Inverness IV3 8NW
T 01463-725000 E enquiries@snh.gov.uk
W www.snh.org.uk

SNH was established in 1992 under the Natural Heritage (Scotland) Act 1991. It is the government's adviser on all aspects of nature and landscape across Scotland and its role is to help the public understand, value and enjoy Scotland's nature.

Chair, Andrew Thin
Chief Executive, Ian Jardine
Director of Policy and Advice, Susan Davies
Directors of Operations, Andrew Bachell
Director of Corporate Services, Joe Moore

SEAFISH INDUSTRY AUTHORITY
18 Logie Mill, Logie Green Road, Edinburgh EH7 4HS
T 0131-558 3331 E seafish@seafish.co.uk
W www.seafish.org

Established under the Fisheries Act 1981, the authority on seafood works with all sectors of the UK seafood industry to satisfy consumers, raise standards, improve efficiency and secure a sustainable and profitable future. Services range from research and development, economic consulting, market research and training and accreditation through to legislative advice for the seafood industry. It is sponsored by the four UK fisheries departments, which appoint the board, and is funded by a levy on seafood.

Chair, John Whitehead, OBE

Chief Executive, Dr Paul Williams

SENIOR SALARIES REVIEW BODY

6th Floor, Victoria House, Southampton Row,
London WC1B 4AD
T 020-7271 0494 W www.ome.uk.com

The Senior Salaries Review Body (formerly the Top Salaries Review Body) was set up in 1971 to advise the prime minister on the remuneration of the judiciary, senior civil servants, senior officers of the armed forces and very senior managers in the NHS. In 1993 its remit was extended to cover the pay, pensions and allowances of MPs, ministers and others whose pay is determined by the Ministerial and Other Salaries Act 1975, and also the allowances of peers. If asked, it advises on the pay of officers and members of the devolved parliament and assemblies.

Chair, Bill Cockburn, CBE, TD

Members, Prof. Richard Disney; Martin Fish; Michael Langley; David Metcalf; Sir Peter North, CBE, QC; Alasdair Smith; Bruce Warman; Paul Williams

SERIOUS ORGANISED CRIME AGENCY (SOCA)

PO Box 8000, London SE11 5EN
T 0370-496 7622 W www.soca.gov.uk

SOCA was established in April 2006. It took over the functions of the National Criminal Intelligence Service and the National Crime Squad, as well as the role of HM Revenue and Customs in investigating drug trafficking and related criminal finance, and some of the functions of the UK Immigration Service in dealing with organised immigration crime. SOCA tackles serious organised crime affecting the UK and its citizens and is the custodian of a range of national and international capabilities. SOCA works to priorities set by the home secretary which currently include class A drugs, people smuggling and human trafficking, major gun crime, fraud, cyber crime and money laundering.

SOCA is due to become part of the new National Crime Agency in 2013.

Chair, Sir Ian Andrews, CBE, TD

Director-General, Trevor Pearce, QPM

Executive Directors, Malcolm Cornberg, OBE *(Capability and Service Delivery);* Brad Jones *(Operational Delivery);* Paul Evans *(Strategy and Prevention)*

Non-Executive Directors, Peter Clarke; Elizabeth France; Susan Garrard; Dame Janet Paraskeva, DBE; Francis Plowden

STUDENT LOANS COMPANY LTD

100 Bothwell Street, Glasgow G2 7JD
T 0141-306 2000 W www.slc.co.uk

The Student Loans Company (SLC) is wholly owned by the government. It processes and administers financial assistance for undergraduates who have secured a place at university or college, under the student loans scheme (established in 1990) and the income contingent student loans scheme (established in 1998). For 2010–11 support payments to students totalled £5.5bn, of which £3.6bn was in maintenance loans and £1.9bn was in maintenance grants and other non-repayable allowances. The SLC also paid £2.7bn in tuition fees to universities in 2010–11. At the end of 2010 the company had over 4 million borrowers.

Chair, Ed Smith

Chief Executive, Ed Lester

TATE BRITAIN

Millbank, London SW1P 4RG
T 020-7887 8888 E visiting.britain@tate.org.uk
W www.tate.org.uk/britain

Tate Britain displays the national collection of British art from 1500 to the present day – with special attention and dedicated space given to Blake, Turner and Constable. The gallery opened in 1897, the cost of building (£80,000) being defrayed by Sir Henry Tate, who also contributed the nucleus of the present collection. The Turner wing was opened in 1910, and further galleries and a new sculpture hall followed in 1937. In 1979 a further extension was built, and the Clore Gallery was opened in 1987. The Centenary Development was opened in 2001.

There are four Tate galleries: Tate Britain and Tate Modern in London, Tate Liverpool and Tate St Ives; the entire Tate collection is available to view online.

BOARD OF TRUSTEES

Chair, Lord Browne of Madingley

Trustees, Helen Alexander; Tom Bloxham; Howard Davies; Jeremy Deller; David Ekserdjian; Mala Gaonkar; Patricia Lankester; Elisabeth Murdoch; Franck Petitgas; Monisha Shah; Bob and Roberta Smith (Patrick Brill); Gareth Thomas; Wolfgang Tillmans

OFFICERS

Director, Sir Nicholas Serota

Director, Tate Britain, Dr Penelope Curtis

Director, Tate Liverpool, Dr Christoph Grunenberg

Director, Tate Modern, Chris Dercon

Artistic Director, Tate St Ives, Martin Clark

Executive Director, Tate St Ives, Mark Osterfield

TATE MODERN

Bankside, London SE1 9TG
T 020-7887 8888 E visiting.modern@tate.org.uk
W www.tate.org.uk/modern

Opened in May 2000, Tate Modern displays the Tate collection of international modern art dating from 1900 to the present day. It includes works by Dalí, Picasso, Matisse and Warhol as well as many contemporary works. It is housed in the former Bankside Power Station in London, which was redesigned by the Swiss architects Herzog and de Meuron.

Director, Chris Dercon

TENANT SERVICES AUTHORITY

Maple House, 149 Tottenham Court Road,
London W1T 7BN
T 0845-230 7000 E enquiries@tsa.gsi.gov.uk
W www.tenantservicesauthority.org

The Tenant Services Authority (TSA) was established on 1 December 2008 as the regulator for affordable housing.

It took over the regulatory powers of the Housing Corporation. The TSA's main aim is to raise the standards of services for tenants. In April 2010 the TSA became responsible for all affordable housing in England, whether it is provided by local authorities, housing associations or arm's-length management organisations.

The government announced in October 2010 that the TSA would be abolished by April 2012, and that its economic regulation and backstop consumer regulation functions would be transferred to the Homes and Communities Agency.

Chair, Anthony Mayer
Chief Executive, Claer Lloyd Jones

TOURISM BODIES
Visit Britain, Visit Scotland, Visit Wales and the Northern Ireland Tourist Board are responsible for developing and marketing the tourist industry in their respective regions. Visit Wales is not listed here as it is part of the Welsh government, within the Department for Heritage, and not a public body.

VISIT BRITAIN
1 Palace Street, Victoria SW1E 5HX T 020-7578 1000
W www.visitbritain.com
Chair, Christopher Rodrigues, CBE
Chief Executive, Sandie Dawe, MBE

VISIT SCOTLAND
Ocean Point One, 94 Ocean Drive, Leith, Edinburgh EH6 6JH
T 0131-472 2222
E info@visitscotland.com W www.visitscotland.com
Chair, Dr Mike Cantlay
Chief Executive, Malcolm Roughead, OBE

NORTHERN IRELAND TOURIST BOARD
St Anne's Court, 59 North Street, Belfast BT1 1NB
T 028-9023 1221
E info@nitb.com W www.discovernorthernireland.com
Chair, Howard Hastings
Chief Executive, Alan Clarke

TRAINING AND DEVELOPMENT AGENCY FOR SCHOOLS
Piccadilly Gate, Store Street, Manchester M1 2WD
T 0870-496 0123 E corporatecomms@tda.gov.uk
W www.tda.gov.uk

The Training and Development Agency for Schools (TDA) was launched in September 2005 and took on the role, and expanded the remit of, the Teacher Training Agency. The TDA aims to attract able and committed people to teaching, concentrating specifically on subjects where teachers are in short supply; provide schools and their staff with good information on training and development opportunities; and ensure that new teachers enter schools with appropriate skills and knowledge, through working closely with providers of initial teacher training. The government announced in November 2010 that from April 2012, the TDA will change in status from a non-departmental public body to an executive agency of the Department for Education.
Chief Executive, Stephen Hillier

TRANSPORT FOR LONDON (TFL)
Windsor House, 42–50 Victoria Street, London SW1H 0TL
T 020-7222 5600
E enquire@tfl.gov.uk W www.tfl.gov.uk

TfL was created in July 2000 and is the integrated body responsible for the capital's transport system. Its role is to implement the Mayor of London's transport strategy and manage the transport services across London for which the mayor has responsibility. These services include London's buses, London Underground, London Overground, the Docklands Light Railway (DLR), Tramlink, London River Services and Victoria Coach Station.

TfL is also responsible for managing the Congestion Charging scheme, maintaining 360 miles (580km) of main roads and all of London's traffic lights, regulating the city's taxis and private hire vehicles, promoting a range of walking and cycling initiatives and making London's transport system more accessible by coordinating schemes for people with impaired mobility and running Dial-a-ride alongside the London boroughs' Taxicard scheme.
Chair, Boris Johnson
Commissioner, Peter Hendy

UK ATOMIC ENERGY AUTHORITY
Culham Science Centre, Abingdon, Oxfordshire OX14 3DB
T 01235-528822
W www.uk-atomic-energy.org.uk

The UK Atomic Energy Authority (UKAEA) was established by the Atomic Energy Authority Act 1954 and took over responsibility for the research and development of the civil nuclear power programme. The authority reports to the Department for Business, Innovation and Skills and is responsible for managing UK fusion research, from its Culham Centre for Fusion Energy (CCFE). It also operates the Joint European Torus (JET) on behalf of the European Fusion Development Agency (EFDA) at its site in Culham, Oxfordshire, as well as managing the records service for the Nuclear Decommissioning Authority (NDA) at Harwell. In October 2009, as part of the government's Operation Efficiency Programme, the authority sold its commercial arm, UKAEA Limited; as a result, the UKAEA no longer provides nuclear decommissioning services.
Chair, Prof. Roger Cashmore
Chief Executive, Prof. Steven Cowley

UK SPORTS COUNCIL (UK SPORT)
40 Bernard Street, London WC1N 1ST
T 020-7211 5100
E info@uksport.gov.uk W www.uksport.gov.uk

UK Sport was established by royal charter in 1997 and is accountable to parliament through the Department for Culture, Media and Sport. Its mission is to lead sport in the UK to world-class success. This means working with partner organisations to deliver medals at the Olympic and Paralympic Games and organising, bidding for and staging major sporting events in the UK; increasing the UK's sporting activity and influence overseas; and promoting sporting conduct, ethics and diversity in society. UK Sport is funded by a mix of grant-in-aid and National Lottery income, as well as private investment through Team 2012. Projected government grant-in-aid for 2011–12 is £60.3m and National Lottery funding £60.45m.

As part of the public bodies' reform proposals, UK Sport and Sport England will merge into one body by 1 April 2013.
Chair, Baroness Sue Campbell, CBE

VICTORIA AND ALBERT MUSEUM

Cromwell Road, London SW7 2RL
T 020-7942 2000 W www.vam.ac.uk

The Victoria and Albert Museum (V&A) is the national museum of fine and applied art and design. It descends directly from the Museum of Manufactures, which opened in Marlborough House in 1852 after the Great Exhibition of 1851. The museum was moved in 1857 to become part of the South Kensington Museum. It was renamed the Victoria and Albert Museum in 1899. It also houses the National Art Library and Print Room.

The museum administers the V&A Museum of Childhood at Bethnal Green, which was opened in 1872; the building is the most important surviving example of the type of glass and iron construction used by Paxton for the Great Exhibition. Total government grant-in-aid for 2011–12 is £41.4m.

Chair, Paul Ruddock
Trustees, D. Adjaye, OBE; E. Davies, OBE; A. Hochhauser, QC; Ms B. Jackson, CBE; Prof. L. Jardine, CBE; S. McGuckin; Ms E. O' Connor; Ms M. Ogundehin; Rt. Hon. Sir T. Sainsbury; Dame M. Scardino, DBE; S. Shah, OBE; Sir John Sorrell; R. Stefanowski; Dr P. Thompson
Director of the V&A, Prof. M. Roth

WALLACE COLLECTION

Hertford House, Manchester Square, London W1U 3BN
T 020-7563 9500 E collections@wallacecollection.org
W www.wallacecollection.org

The Wallace Collection was bequeathed to the nation by the widow of Sir Richard Wallace, in 1897, and Hertford House was subsequently acquired by the government. The collection contains works by Titian and Rembrandt, and includes porcelain, furniture and an array of arms and armour. Total government grant-in-aid for 2010–11 was estimated at £4.21m.

Director, Dr Christoph Vogtherr

YOUNG PEOPLE'S LEARNING AGENCY

Cheylesmore House, Quinton Road, Coventry CV1 2WT
T 0845-377 2000 E enquiries@ypla.gov.uk
W www.ypla.gov.uk

The Young People's Learning Agency (YPLA) was launched in April 2010 with the mission of championing education and training for young people in England. It provides financial support to young learners, funds academies and supports local authorities to commission suitable education and training opportunities for all 16- to 19-year-olds.

The YPLA's board is made up of 12 members appointed by the Secretary of State for Education. Its budget for 2011 was £12.5bn. Subject to legislation, the YPLA will be replaced in April 2012 by the Education Funding Agency, an executive agency of the Department for Education.

Chair, Les Walton
Chief Executive, Peter Lauener

REGIONAL GOVERNMENT

LONDON

GREATER LONDON AUTHORITY (GLA)

City Hall, The Queen's Walk, London SE1 2AA
T 020-7983 4000 E mayor@london.gov.uk
W www.london.gov.uk

On 7 May 1998 London voted in favour of the formation of the Greater London Authority (GLA). The first elections to the GLA took place on 4 May 2000 and the new authority took over its responsibilities on 3 July 2000. In July 2002 the GLA moved to one of London's most spectacular buildings, newly built on a brownfield site on the south bank of the Thames, adjacent to Tower Bridge. The third and most recent election to the GLA took place on 1 May 2008.

The structure and objectives of the GLA stem from its main areas of responsibility: transport, policing, fire and emergency planning, economic development, planning, culture and health. There are four functional bodies that coordinate these functions and report to the GLA: the London Development Agency (LDA), the London Fire and Emergency Planning Authority (LFEPA), the Metropolitan Police Authority (MPA) and Transport for London (TfL).

The GLA consists of a directly elected mayor, the Mayor of London, and a separately elected assembly, the London Assembly. The mayor has the key role of decision making, with the assembly performing the tasks of regulating and scrutinising these decisions, and investigating issues of importance to Londoners. In addition, the GLA has around 600 permanent staff to support the activities of the mayor and the assembly, which are overseen by a head of paid service. The mayor may appoint two political advisers and not more than ten other members of staff, though he does not necessarily exercise this power, but he does not appoint the chief executive, the monitoring officer or the chief finance officer. These must be appointed jointly by the assembly and the mayor.

Every aspect of the assembly and its activities must be open to public scrutiny and therefore accountable. The assembly holds the mayor to account through scrutiny of his strategies, decisions and actions. This is carried out by direct questioning at assembly meetings and by conducting detailed investigations in committee.

People's Question Time and Mayor's Consultation Meetings give Londoners the chance to question the mayor and the London Assembly about plans, priorities and policies for London. Question time is held twice a year, and consultation meetings are held four times a year in different parts of London.

The role of the mayor can be broken down into a number of key areas:
- to represent and promote London at home and abroad and speak up for Londoners
- to devise strategies and plans to tackle London-wide issues, such as crime, transport, housing, planning, environment, accountability, business and skills, public services, society and culture, local government and the Olympic and Paralympic Games, sport and health; and

to set budgets for TfL, the LDA, the MPA and the LFEPA.
- the mayor is chair of TfL, and has the power to appoint the chair of the MPA and board members to TfL, the MPA and the LDA; he also makes appointments to the police and fire authorities
- with London's successful bid to host the 2012 Olympic and Paralympic Games, the previous mayor was the signatory to the contract with the International Olympic Committee undertaking that the games would be delivered

The role of the assembly can be broken down into a number of key areas:
- to check on and balance the mayor
- to scrutinise the mayor
- to have the power to amend the mayor's budget by a majority of two-thirds
- to have the power to summon the mayor, senior staff of the GLA and functional bodies
- to investigate issues of London-wide significance and make proposals to appropriate stakeholders
- to have representatives on the boards of the MPA, the LFEPA and the LDA

Mayor, Boris Johnson
Deputy Mayors, Richard Barnes (*Statutory Deputy Mayor*); Kit Malthouse (*Policing*); Sir Edward Lister (*Planning, and Chief of Staff*); Isabel Dedring (*Transport*)
Chair of the London Assembly, Jennette Arnold
Deputy Chair of the Assembly, Baroness Doocey

ELECTIONS AND VOTING SYSTEMS

The assembly is elected every four years at the same time as the mayor, and consists of 25 members. There is one member from each of the 14 GLA constituencies topped up with 11 London members who are either representatives of political parties or individuals standing as independent candidates. The last election was on 1 May 2008.

Two distinct voting systems are used to appoint the existing mayor and the assembly. The mayor is elected using the supplementary vote system (SVS). With SVS, electors have two votes: one to give a first choice for mayor and one to give a second choice. Electors can only have one effective vote and so cannot vote twice for the same candidate. If one candidate gets more than half of all the first-choice votes, he or she becomes mayor. If no candidate gets more than half of the first-choice votes, the two candidates with the most first-choice votes remain in the election and all the other candidates drop out. The second-choice votes on the ballot papers of the candidates who drop out are then counted. Where these second-choice votes are for the two remaining candidates they are added to the first-choice votes these candidates already have. The candidate with the most first- and second-choice votes combined becomes the Mayor of London.

The assembly is appointed using the additional member system (AMS). Under AMS, electors have two votes. The first vote is for a constituency candidate. The second vote is for a party list or individual candidate contesting the London-wide assembly seats. The

14 constituency members are elected under the first-past-the-post system, the same system used in general and local elections. Electors vote for one candidate and the candidate with the most votes wins. The additional (London) members are drawn from party lists or are independent candidates who stand as London members; they are chosen using a form of proportional representation.

The Greater London Returning Officer (GLRO) is the independent official responsible for running the election in London. He is supported in this by returning officers in each of the 14 London constituencies.

GLRO, John Bennett

TRANSPORT FOR LONDON (TFL)

TfL is the integrated body responsible for London's transport system. Its role is to implement the mayor's transport strategy for London and manage transport services across the capital for which the mayor has responsibility. TfL is directed by a management board whose members are chosen for their understanding of transport matters and are appointed by the mayor, who chairs the board. TfL's role is:

• to manage the London Underground, buses, Croydon Tramlink, London Overground and the Docklands Light Railway (DLR)
• to manage a network of main roads and all of London's traffic lights
• to regulate taxis and minicabs
• to run the London River Services, Victoria Coach Station and London Transport Museum
• to help to coordinate the Dial-a-Ride and Taxicard schemes for door-to-door services for transport users with mobility problems

The London Borough Councils maintain the role of highway and traffic authorities for 95 per cent of London's roads. A £5 congestion charge for motorists driving into central London between the hours of 7am and 6.30pm, Monday to Friday (excluding public holidays) was introduced on 17 February 2003, and was subsequently raised to £8 on 4 July 2005. On 19 February 2007, the charge zone roughly doubled in size after a westward expansion and the charging hours were shortened, to finish at 6pm. On 4 January 2011, the westward expansion was removed from the charging zone and the charge was increased to £10; an automated payment system was also introduced.

TfL introduced a low emission zone for London on 4 February 2008. It consisted of a £200 daily charge for polluting vehicles that entered the zone, which covered most of Greater London. Lorries over 12 tonnes that did not meet emissions standards were the first to be affected. Charges for vehicles exceeding three-and-a-half tonnes and buses and coaches exceeding five tonnes began on 7 July 2008; tougher emissions standards will be introduced in January 2012, which will extend to minibuses and vans.

Since 2 January 2009, Londoners over pensionable age (or over 60 if born before 1950) and those with eligible disabilities are entitled to free travel on the capital's transport network at any time. War veterans who are receiving ongoing payments under the war pensions scheme, or those receiving guaranteed income payments under the armed forces compensation scheme can travel free at any time on bus, underground, Docklands Light Railway, tram and London Overground services and at certain times on national rail services.

In the summer of 2010, the London cycle hire scheme launched with 6,000 new bicycles for hire from 400 docking stations across eight boroughs, the City and the Royal parks.

Transport Commissioner for London, Peter Hendy

METROPOLITAN POLICE AUTHORITY (MPA)

This body, which oversees the policing of London, consists of 23 members: 12 from the assembly and 11 independents. One of the independents is appointed directly by the home secretary. The role of the MPA is:

• to monitor and scrutinise the Metropolitan Police Service
• to maintain an efficient and effective police force
• to secure best value in the delivery of policing services
• to publish an annual policing plan
• to set police targets and monitor performance
• to be part of the appointment, discipline and removal of senior officers
• to be responsible for the police budget

The boundaries of the metropolitan police districts have been changed to be consistent with the 32 London boroughs. Areas beyond the GLA remit have been incorporated into the Surrey, Hertfordshire and Essex police areas. The City of London has its own police force.

Chair, Kit Malthouse

LONDON FIRE AND EMERGENCY PLANNING AUTHORITY (LFEPA)

In July 2000 the London Fire and Civil Defence Authority became the London Fire and Emergency Planning Authority. It consists of 17 members, eight drawn from the assembly, seven from the London boroughs and two mayoral appointees. The role of the LFEPA is:

• to set the strategy for the provision of fire services
• to ensure that the fire brigade can meet all the normal requirements efficiently
• to ensure that effective arrangements are made for the fire brigade to receive emergency calls and deal with them promptly
• to ensure members of the fire brigade are properly trained and equipped
• to ensure that information useful to the development of the fire brigades is gathered
• to ensure arrangements for advice and guidance on fire protection are made

Chair, Brian Coleman, FRSA

SALARIES *as at July 2011*	
Mayor	£143,911
Deputy Mayors	
Richard Barnes	£96,092
Kit Malthouse	£53,439
Sir Edward Lister	£127,784
Chair of the Assembly	£64,103
Assembly Members	£53,439

LONDON ASSEMBLY COMMITTEES

Chair, Audit Panel, Roger Evans
Chair, Budget and Performance Committee, John Biggs
Chair, Business Management and Administration Committee, Jennette Arnold
Chair, Confirmation Hearings Committee, various
Chair, Economy, Culture and Sport Committee, Baroness Doocey
Chair, Environment Committee, Murad Qureshi
Chair, Health and Public Services Committee, Victoria Borwick

Chair, Planning and Housing Committee, Jenny Jones
Chair, Standards Committee, Claer Lloyd-Jones
Chair, TIme for Action Panel, Joanne McCartney
Chair, Transport Committee, Caroline Pidgeon

LONDON ASSEMBLY MEMBERS
as at 1 July 2011

Arbour, Tony, *C., South West,* Maj. 26,928
Arnold, Jennette, *Lab. North East,* Maj. 28,437
Bacon, Gareth, *C., London List*
Barnbrook, Richard, *Ind., London List*
Barnes, Richard, *C., Ealing and Hillingdon,* Maj. 28,638
Biggs, John, *Lab., City and East,* Maj. 31,553
Boff, Andrew, *C., London List*
Borwick, Victoria, *C., London List*
Cleverly, James, *C., Bexley and Bromley,* Maj. 75,237
Coleman, Brian, *C., Barnet and Camden,* Maj. 19,693
Doocey, Baroness, *LD, London List*
Duvall, Len, *Lab., Greenwich and Lewisham,* Maj. 16,134
Evans, Roger, *C., Havering and Redbridge,* Maj. 43,025
Gavron, Nicky, *Lab., London List*
Johnson, Darren, *Green, London List*
Jones, Jenny, *Green, London List*
McCartney, Joanne, *Lab., Enfield and Haringey,* Maj. 1,402
Malthouse, Kit, *C., West Central,* Maj. 51,381
O'Connell, Steve, *C., Croydon and Sutton,* Maj. 42,665
Pidgeon, Caroline, *LD, London List*
Qureshi, Murad, *Lab., London List*
Shah, Navin, *Lab., Brent and Harrow,* Maj. 1,649
Shawcross, Valerie, *Lab., Lambeth and Southwark,* Maj. 23,648
Tracey, Richard, *C., Merton and Wandsworth,* Maj. 26,293
Tuffrey, Michael, *LD, London List*

STATE OF THE PARTIES *as at 1 July 2011*

Party	Seats
Conservative (C.)	11
Labour (Lab.)	8
Liberal Democrats (LD)	3
Green	2
Independent (Ind.)	1

MAYORAL ELECTION RESULTS
as at 1 May 2008

E. 5,419,913 T. 45.33%

Change in turnout from 2004: + 8.38%
Good votes: 1st choice 2,415,952 (98.32%); 2nd choice 2,004,078 (82.94%)
Rejected votes: 1st choice 41,032 (1.67%); 2nd choice 412,054 (17.05%)

First	Party	Votes	%
Boris Johnson	C.	1,043,761	42.48
Ken Livingstone	Lab.	893,877	36.38
Brian Paddick	LD	236,685	9.63
Sian Berry	Green	77,374	3.15
Richard Barnbrook	BNP	69,710	2.84
Alan Craig	CPA	39,249	1.60
Gerard Batten	UKIP	24,222	0.91
Lindsey German	Left List	16,796	0.68
Matt O'Connor	Eng. Dem.	10,695	0.44
Winston McKenzie	Ind.	5,389	0.22

Second	Party	Votes	%
Brian Paddick	LD	641,412	26.11
Sian Berry	Green	331,727	13.50
Ken Livingstone	Lab.	303,198	12.34
Boris Johnson	C.	257,792	10.49
Richard Barnbrook	BNP	128,609	5.23
Gerard Batten	UKIP	113,651	4.63
Alan Craig	CPA	80,140	3.26
Matt O'Connor	Eng. Dem.	73,538	2.99
Winston McKenzie	Ind.	38,954	1.59
Lindsey German	Left List	35,057	1.43

LONDON ASSEMBLY ELECTION RESULTS
as at 1 May 2008
E. Electorate T. Turnout
See General Election Results for a list of party abbreviations

CONSTITUENCIES
E. 5,419,913 T. 45.28%

BARNET AND CAMDEN
E. 376,818 T. 47.77%

Brian Coleman, C.	72,659
Nicky Gavron, Lab.	52,966
Nick Russell, LD	22,213
Miranda Dunn, Green	16,782
Magnus Nielsen, UKIP	3,678
Clement Adebayo, CPA	3,536
David Stevens, Eng. Dem.	2,146
Dave Hoefling, Left List	2,074
Graham Dare, Veritas	510
C. majority 19,693	

BEXLEY AND BROMLEY
E. 407,003 T. 49.85%

James Cleverly, C.	105,162
Alex Heslop, Lab.	29,925
Tom Papworth, LD,	21,244
Paul Winnett, NF	11,288
Ann Garrett, Green	9,261
Mick Greenhough, UKIP	8,021
John Hemming-Clark, Ind.	6,684
Miranda Suit, CPA	4,408
Steven Uncles, Eng. Dem.	2,907
David Davis, Left List	1,050
C. majority 75,237	

BRENT AND HARROW
E. 367,337 T. 43.10%

Navin Shah, Lab.	57,716
Bob Blackman, C.	56,067
James Allie, LD	19,299
Shahrar Ali, Green	10,129
Zena Sherman, CPA	4,180
Sunita Webb, UKIP	3,021
Pat McManus, Left List	2,287
Arvind Tailor, Eng. Dem.	2,150
Lab. majority 1,649	

CITY AND EAST
E. 470,863 T. 39.79%

John Biggs, Lab.	63,635
Philip Briscoe, C.	32,082
Hanif Abdulmuhit, Respect	26,760
Robert Bailey, BNP	18,020
Rajonuddin Jalal, LD	13,724
Heather Finlay, Green	11,478
Thomas Conquest, CPA	7,306
Michael McGough, UKIP	3,078
Graham Kemp, NF	2,350
Michael Gavan, Left List	2,274
John Griffiths, Eng. Dem.	2,048
Julie Crawford, Ind.	701

Lab. majority 31,553

CROYDON AND SUTTON
E. 360,221 T. 48.99%

Stephen O'Connell, C.	76,477
Shafi Khan, Lab.	33,812
Abigail Lock, LD	32,335
David Pickles, UKIP	9,440
Shasha Khan, Green	8,969
David Campanale, CPA	6,910
Richard Castle, Eng. Dem.	4,186
Zana Hussain, Left List	1,361

C. majority 42,665

EALING AND HILLINGDON
E. 401,671 T. 44.05%

Richard Barnes, C.	74,710
Ranjit Dheer, Lab.	46,072
Nigel Bakhai, LD	18,004
Sarah Edwards, Green	12,606
Ian Edward, NF	7,939
Mary Boyle, CPA	5,100
Lynnda Robson, UKIP	4,465
Salvinder Dhillon, Left List	2,390
Sati Chaggar, Eng. Dem.	1,853

C. majority 28,638

ENFIELD AND HARINGEY
E. 351,536 T. 46.04%

Joanne McCartney, Lab.	52,665
Matthew Laban, C.	51,263
Monica Whyte, LD	23,550
Pete McAskie, Green	12,473
Segun Johnson, CPA	5,779
Sait Akgul, Left List	5,639
Brian Hall, UKIP	4,682
Teresa Cannon, Eng. Dem.	2,282

Lab. majority 1,402

GREENWICH AND LEWISHAM
E. 347,252 T. 42.98%

Len Duvall, Lab.	53,174
Andy Jennings, C.	37,040
Brian Robson, LD	18,174
Susan Luxton, Green	15,607
Tess Culnane, NF	8,509
Stephen Hammond, CPA	5,079
Arnold Tarling, UKIP	3,910
Jennifer Jones, Left List	2,045
Johanna Munilla, Eng. Dem.	1,716
Chris Flood, Soc. Alt.	1,587

Lab. majority 16,134

HAVERING AND REDBRIDGE
E. 369,407 T. 45.46%

Roger Evans, C.	78,493
Balvinder Saund, Lab.	35,468
Farrukh Islam, LD	12,443
Lawrence Webb, UKIP	12,203
Ashley Gunstock, Green	9,126
Leo Brookes, Eng. Dem.	6,487
Paula Warren, CPA	5,533
Dr Peter Thorogood, Ind.	3,450
Carole Vincent, Left List	1,473

C. majority 43,025

LAMBETH AND SOUTHWARK
E. 395,202 T. 42.09%

Valerie Shawcross, Lab.	60,601
Caroline Pidgeon, LD	36,953
Shirley Houghton, C.	32,835
Shane Collins, Green	18,011
Geoffrey Macharia, CPA	4,432
Jens Winton, UKIP	3,012
Katt Young, Left List	1,956
Janus Polenceus, Eng. Dem.	1,867
Jasmijn De Boo, Animals Count	1,828
Daniel Lambert, Socialist	1,588

Lab. majority 23,648

MERTON AND WANDSWORTH
E. 362,542 T. 47.16%

Richard Tracey, C.	75,103
Leonie Cooper, Lab.	48,810
Shas Sheehan, LD	17,187
Roy Vickery, Green	14,124
Strachan McDonald, UKIP	4,286
Ellen Greco, CPA	4,053
Steve Scott, Eng. Dem.	2,160
Kris Stewart, Left List	1,714

C. majority 26,293

NORTH EAST
E. 451,787 T. 43.80%

Jennette Arnold, Lab.	73,551
Alexander Ellis, C.	45,114
Meral Ece, LD	28,973
Aled Fisher, Green	28,845
Unjum Mirza, Left List	6,019
Nicholas Jones, UKIP	5,349
Maxine Hargreaves, CPA	5,323
John Dodds, Eng. Dem.	3,637

Lab. majority 28,437

SOUTH WEST
E. 415,092 T. 46.15%

Tony Arbour, C.	76,913
Stephen Knight, LD	49,985
Ansuya Sodha, Lab.	30,190
John Hunt, Green	12,774
Andrew Cripps, NF	4,754
Peter Dul, UKIP	3,779
Sue May, CPA	3,718
Andrew Constantine, Free England Party	2,908
Roger Cooper, Eng. Dem.	1,874
Tansy Hoskins, Left List	1,526

C. majority 26,928

WEST CENTRAL
E. 343,182 T. 48.48%

Kit Malthouse, C.	86,651	
Murad Qureshi, Lab.	35,270	
Julia Stephenson, Green	16,874	
Merlene Emerson, LD	15,934	
Paul Wiffen, UKIP	3,060	
Alex Vaughan, Eng. Dem.	1,858	
Explo Nani-Kofi, Left List	1,630	
Abby Dharamsey, Ind.	962	

C. *majority* 51,381

TOP-UP MEMBERS

BRITISH NATIONAL PARTY
Richard Barnbrook

CONSERVATIVE
Andrew Boff
Victoria Borwick
Gareth Bacon

GREEN PARTY
Darren Johnson
Jenny Jones

LABOUR
Nicky Gavron
Murad Qureshi

LIBERAL DEMOCRAT
Baroness Doocey
Caroline Pidgeon
Michael Tuffrey

WALES

WELSH GOVERNMENT

Cathays Park, Cardiff CF10 3NQ
T 0845-010 3300 W http://wales.gov.uk

The Welsh government is the devolved government of Wales. It is accountable to the National Assembly for Wales, the Welsh legislature which represents the interests of the people of Wales, and makes laws for Wales. The Welsh government and the National Assembly for Wales were established as separate institutions under the Government of Wales Act 2006.

The Welsh government comprises the first minister, who is usually the leader of the largest party in the National Assembly for Wales; up to 12 ministers and deputy ministers; and a counsel general (the chief legal adviser).

Following the referendum on 3 March 2011 on granting further law-making powers to the national assembly, the Welsh government's functions now include the ability to propose bills to the national assembly on subjects within 20 set areas of policy. Subject to limitations prescribed by the Government of Wales Act 2006, acts of the National Assembly may make any provision that could be made by act of parliament. The 20 areas of responsibility devolved to the National Assembly for Wales (and within which Welsh ministers exercise executive functions) are: agriculture, fisheries, forestry and rural development; ancient monuments and historic buildings; culture; economic development; education and training; environment; fire and rescue services and promotion of fire safety; food; health and health services; highways and transport; housing; local government; the National Assembly for Wales; public administration; social welfare; sport and recreation; tourism; town and county planning; water and flood defence; and the Welsh language.

First Minister of Wales, Carwyn Jones, AM
Minister for Business, Enterprise, Technology and Science, Edwina Hart, MBE, AM
Minister for Education and Skills, Leighton Andrews, AM
Minister for Environment and Sustainable Development, John Griffiths, AM
Minister for Finance and Leader of the House, Jane Hutt, AM
Minister for Health and Social Services, Lesley Griffiths AM
Minister for Housing, Regeneration and Heritage, Huw Lewis, AM
Minister for Local Government and Communities, Carl Sargeant, AM
Deputy Minister for Agriculture, Food, Fisheries and European Programmes, Alun Davies, AM
Deputy Minister for Children and Social Services, Gwenda Thomas, AM
Deputy Minister for Skills, Jeff Cuthbert, AM
Counsel General, Theodore Huckle, QC
Chief Whip, Janice Gregory, AM

MANAGEMENT BOARD

Permanent Secretary, Dame Gillian Morgan
Director-General, Business, Enterprise, Technology and Science, James Price (acting)
Director-General, Education and Skills, Dr Emyr Roberts
Director-General, Health,Social Services and Children and Chief Executive of NHS Wales, David Sissling
Director-General, Local Government and Communities, Dr June Milligan
Director-General, People, Places and Corporate Services,, Bernard Galton
Director-General, Strategic Planning, Finance and Performance, Michael Hearty
Non-Executive Directors, Elan Cross Stephens; James Turner

DEPARTMENTS

Department for Education and Skills
Department for Health, Social Services and Children
Department for Business, Enterprise, Technology and Science
Department for Strategic Planning, Finance and Performance
People, Places and Corporate Services
Sustainable Futures
Local Government and Communities
Non-Directorate Services

ASSEMBLY COMMITTEES

Children and Young People
Communities, Equality and Local Government
Constitutional and Legislative Affairs
Enterprise and Business
Environment and Sustainability
Finance
Health and Social Care
Petitions
Public Accounts
Standards

ASSEMBLY COMMISSION

The Assembly Commission was created under the Government of Wales Act 2006 to ensure that the assembly is provided with the property, staff and services required for it to carry out its functions. The commission also sets the national assembly's strategic aims, objectives, standards and values. The Assembly Commission consists of the presiding officer, plus four other assembly members, one nominated by each of the four party groups. The five commissioners are accountable to the national assembly.

Presiding Officer, Rosemary Butler, AM
Commissioners, Peter Black, Angela Burns, Rhodri Glyn Thomas, Sandy Mewies
Chief Executive and Clerk to the Assembly, Claire Clancy

NATIONAL ASSEMBLY FOR WALES

Cardiff Bay, Cardiff CF99 1NA
T 0845-010 5500 W www.assemblywales.org

In July 1997 the government announced plans to establish a National Assembly for Wales. In a referendum in September 1997 about 50 per cent of the electorate voted, of whom 50.3 per cent voted in favour of a national assembly. Elections are held every four years and the first election took place on 6 May 1999. The fourth election took place on 5 May 2011.

National Assembly members are elected using the additional member system. Voters are given two votes: one for a constituency member and one for a regional member. The constituency members are elected under the first-past-the-post system, also used to elect constituency members to the London Assembly. Four regional members in each of the five constituencies are then chosen from party lists or independent candidates using a form of proportional representation.

Until 2007 the National Assembly for Wales was a corporate body comprising both the executive and legislative branches of government. It had no primary law-making powers and only had responsibility for exercising and implementing ministerial functions which had previously been vested in the Secretary of State for Wales.

The Government of Wales Act 2006 introduced a radical change to the functions and status of the National Assembly for Wales. With effect from 25 May 2007 the act formally separated the National Assembly for Wales (the legislature – made up of 60 elected assembly members) and the Welsh government (the executive – comprising the first minister, Welsh ministers, deputy Welsh ministers and the counsel general). It also made changes to the electoral process: candidates are no longer permitted to stand as both constituency and regional members. The act enabled the National Assembly for Wales to formulate its own legislation (assembly measures) on the 20 devolved areas for which it has responsibility (see Welsh government); the assembly was given legislative competence (the legal authority to pass measures) on a case-by-case basis by the UK parliament.

The act also included a mechanism that would allow for full transfer of legislative powers relating to all devolved matters to the National Assembly, provided that the people of Wales voted for such a proposal in a referendum. In a referendum held on 3 March 2011, 63.5 per cent voted in favour of giving the national assembly full legislative powers for all devolved matters. The National Assembly for Wales can now pass legislation (assembly acts) on the 20 devolved areas for which it has responsibility. An assembly act has the same powers as an act of the UK parliament and may be proposed by the Welsh government, assembly committees, an assembly member or the assembly commission.

The National Assembly for Wales also scrutinises and monitors the Welsh government. It meets in plenary in the Senedd debating chamber. The 60 assembly members examine and approve assembly bills and approve certain items of subordinate legislation; approve the Welsh government and assembly commssion's budget; hold Welsh ministers to account; and analyse and debate their decisions and policies.

Presiding Officer, Rosemary Butler AM

SALARIES 2010–11	
First Minister*	£80,870
Minister/Presiding Officer*	£41,949
Deputy Minister/Deputy Presiding Officer*	£26,385
Assembly Members (AM)†	£53,852

* Also receives the assembly member salary
† Reduced by two-thirds if the member is already an MP or an MEP

MEMBERS OF THE NATIONAL ASSEMBLY FOR WALES
as at 16 June 2011

Andrews, Leighton, *Lab., Rhondda,* Maj. 6,739
Antoniw, Mick, *Lab., Pontypridd,* Maj. 7,694
Asghar, Mohammad, *C., South Wales East region*
Black, Peter, *LD, South Wales West region*
Burns, Angela, *C., Carmarthen West and South Pembrokeshire,* Maj. 1,504
Butler, Rosemary, *Lab., Newport W.,* Maj. 4,220
Chapman, Christine, *Lab., Cynon Valley,* Maj. 6,515
Cuthbert, Jeff, *Lab., Caerphilly,* Maj. 4,924
Davies, Alun, *Lab., Blaenau Gwent,*Maj. 9,120
Davies, Andrew R.T., *C., South Wales Central region*
Davies, Byron, *C., South Wales West region*

Davies, Jocelyn, *PC, South Wales East region*
Davies, Keith, *Lab., Llanelli,* Maj. 80
Davies, Paul, *C., Preseli Pembrokeshire,* Maj. 2,175
Davies, Suzy, *C., South Wales West region*
Drakeford, Mark, *Lab., Cardiff West,* Maj. 5,901
Elis-Thomas, Lord Dafydd, *PC, Dwyfor Meirionnydd,* Maj. 5,417
Evans, Rebecca, *Lab., Mid and West Wales region*
Finch-Saunders, Janet, *C., Aberconwy,* Maj. 1,567
George, Russell, *C., Montgomeryshire,* Maj. 2,324
Gething, Vaughan, *Lab., Cardiff South and Penarth,* Maj. 6,259
Graham, William, *C., South Wales East region*
Gregory, Janice, *Lab., Ogmore,* Maj. 9,576
Griffiths, John, *Lab., Newport East,* Maj. 5,388
Griffiths, Lesley, *Lab., Wrexham,* Maj. 3,337
Hart, Edwina, *Lab., Gower,* Maj. 4,864
Hedges, Mike, *Lab., Swansea East,* Maj. 8,281
Hutt, Jane, *Lab., Vale of Glamorgan,* Maj. 3,775
Huws Gruffydd, Llyr, *PC, North Wales region*
Isherwood, Mark, *C., North Wales region*
James, Julie, *Lab., Swansea West,* Maj. 4,654
Jenkins, Bethan, *PC, South Wales West region*
Jones, Alun Ffred, *PC, Arfon,* Maj. 5,394
Jones, Ann, *Lab., Vale of Clwyd,* Maj. 4,011
Jones, Carwyn Howell, *Lab., Bridgend,* Maj. 6,775
Jones, Elin, *PC, Ceredigion,* Maj. 1,777
Lewis, Huw, *Lab., Merthyr Tydfil and Rhymney,* Maj. 7,051
Melding, David, *C., South Wales Central region*
Mewies, Sandra Elaine, *Lab., Delyn,* Maj. 2,881
Millar, Darren, *C., Clwyd West,* Maj. 4,248
Morgan, Julie, *Lab., Cardiff North,* Maj. 1,782
Neagle, Lynne, *Lab., Torfaen,* Maj. 6,088
Parrott, Eluned, *LD, South Wales Central region*
Powell, William, *LD, Mid and West Wales region*
Price, Gwyn, *Lab., Islwyn,* Maj. 7,589
Ramsay, Nicholas, *C., Monmouth,* Maj. 8,469
Rathbone, Jenny, *Lab., Cardiff Central,* Maj. 38
Rees, David, *Lab., Aberavon,* Maj. 9,311
Roberts, Aled, *LD, North Wales region*
Sandbach, Antoinette, *C., North Wales region*
Sargeant, Carl, *Lab., Alyn and Deeside,* Maj. 3,362
Skates, Ken, *Lab., Clwyd South,* Maj. 2,659
Thomas, Gwenda, *Lab., Neath,* Maj. 1,944
Thomas, Rhodri, *PC, Carmarthen East and Dinefwr,* Maj. 8,469
Thomas, Simon, *PC, Mid and West Wales region*
Watson, Joyce, *Lab., Mid and West Wales region*
Whittle, Lindsay, *PC, South Wales East region*
Williams, Kirsty, *LD, Brecon and Radnorshire,* Maj. 5,354
Wood, Leanne, *PC, South Wales Central region*
Wyn Jones, Ieuan, *PC, Ynys Mon,* Maj. 2,937

STATE OF THE PARTIES
as at 16 June 2011

	Constituency AMs	Regional AMs	AM total
Labour (Lab.)	28	2	30
Conservative (C.)	6	8	14
Plaid Cymru (PC)	5	6	11
Liberal Democrats (LD)	1	4	5
The Presiding Officer	1	0	1
The Deputy Presiding Officer	1	0	1
Total	40	18	60

NATIONAL ASSEMBLY ELECTION RESULTS

As at 5 May 2011
E. Electorate T. Turnout
See General Election Results for a list of party abbreviations

CONSTITUENCIES
E. 2,289,555 T. 41.5%

ABERAVON (S. WALES WEST)
E. 50,754 T. 18,879 (37.20%)

David Rees, Lab.	12,104
Paul Nicholls-Jones, PC	2,793
Tamojen Morgan, C.	2,704
Helen Ceri Clarke, LD	1,278

Lab. majority 9,311 (49.32%)
8.65% swing PC to Lab.

ABERCONWY (WALES N.)
E. 44,978 T. 20,288 (45.11%)

Janet Finch-Saunders, C.	6,888
Iwan Huws, PC	5,321
Eifion Wyn Williams, Lab.	5,206
Mike Priestley, LD	2,873

C. majority 1,567 (7.72%)
7.95% swing PC to C.

ALYN AND DEESIDE (WALES N.)
E. 61,751 T. 22,769 (36.87%)

Carl Sargeant, Lab.	11,978
John Bell, C.	6,397
Pete Williams, LD	1,725
Shane Brennan, PC	1,710
Michael Whitby, BNP	959

Lab. majority 5,581 (24.51%)
4.29% swing C. to Lab.

ARFON (WALES N.)
E. 41,093 T. 17,664 (42.99%)

Alun Ffred Jones, PC	10,024
Christina Rees, Lab.	4,630
Aled Davies, C.	2,209
Rhys Jones, LD	801

PC majority 5,394 (30.54%)
2.45% swing Lab. to PC

BLAENAU GWENT (S. WALES EAST)
E. 53,230 T. 20,211 (37.97%)

Alun Davies, Lab.	12,926
Jayne Sullivan, Ind.	3,806
Darren Jones, PC	1,098
Bob Hayward, C.	1,066
Brian Urch, BNP	948
Martin Blakebrough, LD	367

Lab. majority 9,120 (45.12%)
33.95% swing Ind. to Lab.

BRECON AND RADNORSHIRE (WALES MID AND W.)
E. 53,546 T. 28,348 (52.94%)

Kirsty Williams, LD	12,201
Chris Davies, C.	9,444
Christopher Lloyd, Lab.	4,797
Gary Price, PC	1,906

LD majority 2,757 (9.73%)
4.45% swing LD to C.

BRIDGEND (S. WALES WEST)
E. 59,104 T. 24,035 (40.67%)

Carwyn Jones, Lab.	13,499
Alex Williams,C.	6,724
Tim Thomas, PC	2,076
Briony Davies, LD	1,736

Lab. majority 6,775 (28.19%)
8.89% swing C. to Lab.

CAERPHILLY (S. WALES EAST)
E. 62,049 T. 25,570 (41.21%)

Jeff Cuthbert, Lab.	12,521
Ron Davies, PC	7,597
Owen Meredith, C.	3,368
Kay David, LD	1,062
Anthony King, BNP	1,022

Lab. majority 4,924 (19.26%)
5.25% swing PC to Lab.

CARDIFF CENTRAL (S. WALES CENTRAL)
E. 64,347 T. 23,628 (36.72%)

Jenny Rathbone, Lab.	8,954
Nigel Howells, LD	8,916
Matt Smith, C.	3,559
Chris Williams, PC	1,690
Mathab Khan, Ind.	509

Lab. majority 38 (0.16%)
14.74% swing LD to Lab.

CARDIFF NORTH (S. WALES CENTRAL)
E. 66,934 T. 34,431 (51.44%)

Julie Morgan, Lab.	16,384
Jonathan Morgan, C.	14,602
Ben Foday, PC	1,850
Matt Smith, LD	1,595

Lab. majority 1,782 (5.18%)
9.77% swing C. to Lab.

CARDIFF SOUTH AND PENARTH (S. WALES CENTRAL)
E. 75,038 T. 27,479 (36.62%)

Vaughan Gething, Lab.	13,814
Ben Gray, C.	7,555
Liz Musa, PC	3,324
Sian Cliff, LD	2,786

Lab. majority 6,259 (22.78%)
6.24% swing C. to Lab.

CARDIFF WEST (S. WALES CENTRAL)
E. 64,219 T. 27,726 (43.17%)

Mark Drakeford, Lab.	13,067
Craig Williams, C.	7,167
Neil McEvoy, PC	5,551
David Morgan, LD	1,942

Lab. majority 5,901 (21.28%)
3.77% C. to Lab.

CARMARTHEN EAST AND DINEFWR (WALES MID AND W.)
E. 54,243 T. 27,828 (51.30%)

Rhodri Glyn Thomas, PC	12,501
Anthony Jones, Lab.	8,353
Henrietta Hensher, C.	5,635
Will Griffiths, LD	1,339

PC majority 4,148 (14.91%)
7.01% swing PC to Lab.

CARMARTHEN WEST AND SOUTH PEMBROKESHIRE
(WALES MID AND W.)
E. 58,435 T. 28,156 (48.18%)

Angela Burns, C.	10,095
Christine Gwyther, Lab.	8,591
Nerys Evans, PC	8,373
Selwyn Runnett, LD	1,097

C. majority 1,504 (5.34%)
2.50% swing Lab. to C.

CEREDIGION (WALES MID AND W.)
E. 56,983 T. 29,076 (51.03%)

Elin Jones, PC	12,020
Liz Evans, LD	10,243
Luke Evetts, C.	2,755
Richard Boudier, Lab.	2,544
Chris Simpson, Green	1,514

PC majority 1,777 (6.11%)
3.51% swing PC to LD

CLWYD SOUTH (WALES N.)
E. 54,499 T. 19,498 (37.59%)

Ken Skates, Lab.	8,500
Paul Rogers, C.	5,841
Mabon ap Gwynfor, PC	3,719
Bruce Roberts, LD	1,977

Lab. majority 2,659 (13.27%)
3.77% swing C. to Lab.

CLWYD WEST (WALES N.)
E. 57,980 T. 25,153 (43.38%)

Darren Millar, C.	10,890
Crispin Jones, Lab.	6,642
Eifion Lloyd Jones, PC	5,775
Brian Cossey, LD	1,846

C. majority 4,248 (16.89%)
5.40% swing Lab. to C.

CYNON VALLEY (S. WALES CENTRAL)
E. 52,133 T. 18,760 (35.98%)

Christine Chapman, Lab.	11,626
Dafydd Trystan Davies, PC	5,111
Dan Saxton, C.	1,531
Ian Walton, LD	492

Lab. majority 6,515 (34.73%)
2.96% swing PC to Lab.

DELYN (WALES N.)
E. 53,996 T. 23,194 (42.96%)

Sandy Mewies, Lab.	10,695
Matt Wright, C.	7,814
Carrie Harper, PC	2,918
Michele Jones, LD	1,767

Lab. majority 2,881 (12.42%)
5.03% swing C. to Lab.

DWYFOR MEIRONNYDD (WALES MID
AND W.)
E. 44,669 T. 20,743 (46.44%)

Dafydd Elis-Thomas, PC	9,656
Simon Baynes, C.	4,239
Louise Hughes, Llais Gwynedd	3,225
Martyn Stuart Singleton, Lab.	2,623
Steven William Churchman, LD	1,000

PC majority 5,417 (26.11%)
6.99% swing PC to C.

GOWER (S. WALES WEST)
E. 61,909 T. 26,773 (43.25%)

Edwina Hart, Lab.	12,866
Caroline Jones, C.	8,002
Darren Price, PC	3,249
Peter May, LD	2,656

Lab. majority 4,864 (18.17%)
6.92% swing C. to Lab.

ISLWYN (S. WALES EAST)
E. 54,893 T. 20,908 (38.09%)

Gwyn Price, Lab.	12,116
Steffan Lewis, PC	4,527
David Chipp, C.	2,497
Peter Whalley, BNP	1,115
Tom Sullivan, LD	653

Lab. majority 7,589 (36.30%)
10.09% swing PC to Lab.

LLANELLI (WALES MID AND W.)
E. 58,838 T. 26,070 (44.31%)

Keith Davies, Lab.	10,359
Helen Mary Jones, PC	10,279
Andrew Morgan, C.	2,880
Sian Caiach, Putting Llanelli First	2,004
Cheryl Philpott, LD	548

Lab. majority 80 (0.31%)
7.19% swing PC to Lab.

MERTHYR TYDFIL AND RHYMNEY (S. WALES EAST)
E. 55,031 T. 19,320 (35.11%)

Huw Lewis, Lab.	10,483
Tony Rogers, Ind.	3,432
Amy Kitcher, LD	2,480
Noel Turner, PC	1,701
Chris O'Brien, C.	1,224

Lab. majority 7,051 (36.50%)
0.14% swing Ind. to Lab.

MONMOUTH (S. WALES EAST)
E. 64,857 T. 30,001 (46.26%)

Nick Ramsay, C.	15,087
Mark Whitcutt, Lab.	8,970
Janet Ellard, LD	2,937
Fiona Cross, PC	2,263
Steve Uncles, Eng. Dem.	744

C. majority 6,117 (20.39%)
4.13% swing C. to Lab.

MONTGOMERYSHIRE (WALES MID AND W.)
E. 48,675 T. 22,933 (47.11%)

Russell George, C.	10,026
Wyn Williams, LD	7,702
Nick Colbourne, Lab.	2,609
David Senior, PC	2,596

C. majority 2,324 (10.13%)
9.50% swing LD to C.

NEATH (S. WALES WEST)
E. 57,533 T. 23,849 (41.45%)

Gwenda Thomas, Lab.	12,736
Alun Llewelyn, PC	6,346
Alex Powell, C.	2,780
Michael Green, BNP	1,004
Mathew McCarthy, LD	983

Lab. majority 6,390 (26.79%)
9.54% swing PC to Lab.

NEWPORT EAST (S. WALES EAST)
E. 55,120 T. 19,460 (35.30%)

John Griffiths, Lab.	9,888
Nick Webb, C.	4,500
Ed Townsend, LD	3,703
Chris Paul, PC	1,369

Lab. majority 5,388 (27.69%)
9.11% swing C. to Lab.

NEWPORT WEST (S. WALES EAST)
E. 63,180 T. 23,014 (36.43%)

Rosemary Butler, Lab.	12,011
David Williams, C.	7,791
Lyndon Binding, PC	1,626
Liz Newton, LD	1,586

Lab. majority 4,220 (18.34%)
6.21% swing C. to Lab.

OGMORE (S. WALES WEST)
E. 55,442 T. 20,264 (36.55%)

Janice Gregory, Lab.	12,955
Danny Clark, PC	3,379
Martyn Hughes, C.	2,945
Gerald Francis, LD	985

Lab. majority 9,576 (47.26%)
6.28% swing PC to Lab.

PONTYPRIDD (S. WALES CENTRAL)
E. 60,028 T. 23,333 (38.87%)

Mick Antoniw, Lab.	11,864
Michael Powell, LD	4,170
Joel James, C.	3,659
Ioan Bellin, PC	3,139
Ken Owen, ND	501

Lab. majority 7,694 (32.97%)
9.28% swing LD to Lab.

PRESELI PEMBROKESHIRE (WALES MID AND W.)
E. 57,758 T. 27,218 (47.12%)

Paul Davies, C.	11,541
Terry Mills (Lab.)	9,366
Rhys Sinnett, PC	4,226
Rob Kilmister, LD	2,085

C. majority 2,175 (7.99%)
1.58% swing C. to Lab.

RHONDDA (S. WALES CENTRAL)
E. 52,532 T. 20,027 (38.12%)

Leighton Andrews, Lab.	12,650
Sarah Evans-Fear, PC	5,911
James Jeffreys, C.	969
George Summers, LD	497

Lab. majority 6,739 (33.65%)
2.77% swing PC to Lab.

SWANSEA EAST (S. WALES WEST)
E. 60,246 T. 18,910 (58.36%)

Mike Hedges, Lab.	11,035
Daniel Boucher, C.	2,754
Dic Jones, PC	2,346
Sam Samuel, LD.	1,673
Joanne Shannon, BNP	1,102

Lab. majority 8,281 (43.79%)
6.05% swing C. to Lab.

SWANSEA WEST (S. WALES WEST)
E. 62,345 T. 21,805 (34.97%)

Julie James, Lab.	9,885
Steve Jenkins, C.	5,231
Rob Speht, LD	3,654
Carl Harris, PC	3,035

Lab. majority 4,654 (21.34%)
4.09% swing C. to Lab.

TORFAEN (S. WALES EAST)
E. 61,126 T. 22,328 (36.53%)

Lynne Neagle, Lab.	10,318
Elizabeth Haynes, Ind.	4,230
Natasha Asghar, C.	3,306
Jeff Rees, PC	2,716
Susan Harwood, BNP	906
Will Griffiths, LD	852

Lab. majority 6,088 (27.27%)
0.52% swing Lab. to Ind.

VALE OF CLWYD (WALES N.)
E. 56,232 T. 23,056 (41.00%)

Ann Jones, Lab.	11,691
Ian Gunning, C.	7,680
Alun Lloyd Jones, PC	2,597
Heather Prydderch, LD	1,088

Lab. majority 4,011 (17.40%)
8.49% swing C. to Lab.

VALE OF GLAMORGAN (S. WALES CENTRAL)
E. 71,602 T. 33,254 (46.80%)

Jane Hutt, Lab.	15,746
Angela Jones-Evans, C.	11,971
Ian Johnson, PC	4,024
Damian Chick, LD	1,513

Lab. majority 3,775 (11.35%)
5.55% swing C. to Lab.

WREXHAM (WALES N.)
E. 53,516 T. 18,687 (34.92%)

Lesley Griffiths, Lab.	8,368
John Marek, C.	5,031
Bill Brereton	2,692
Marc Jones, PC	2,596

Lab. majority 3,337 (17.86%)
3.15% swing C. to Lab.

YNYS MON (WALES N.)
E. 49,431 T. 24,067 (48.69%)

Ieuan Wyn Jones, PC	9,969
Paul Williams, C.	7,032
Joe Lock, Lab.	6,307
Rhys Taylor, LD	759

PC majority 2,937 (12.20%)
7.27% swing PC to C.

REGIONS
E. 2,289,555 T. 41.4%

MID AND WEST WALES
E. 433,147 T. 210,352 (48.56%)

PC	56,384	(26.7%)
C.	52,905	(25.1%)
Lab.	47,348	(22.5%)
LD	26,847	(12.7%)
UKIP	9,211	(4.4%)
Green	8,660	(4.1%)
Soc. Lab.	3,951	(1.9%)
BNP	2,821	(1.3%)
Welsh Christian Party	1,630	(0.8%)
Comm. Brit.	595	(0.3%)

PC majority 3,479 (1.65%)
3.25% swing PC to C. (2007 PC majority 17,652)

ADDITIONAL MEMBERS
Rebecca Evans, *Lab.*   William Powell, *LD*
Joyce Watson, *Lab.*   Simon Thomas, *PC*

NORTH WALES
E. 473,296 T. 194,798 (41.16%)

Lab.	62,677	(32.2%)
C.	52,201	(26.8%)
PC	41,701	(21,104)
LD	11,507	(5.9%)
UKIP	9,608	(4.9%)
Soc. Lab.	4,895	(2.5%)
BNP	4,785	(2.5%)
Green	4,406	(2.3%)
Welsh Christian Party	1,401	(0.7%)
Ind.	1,094	(0.6%)
Comm. Brit.	523	(0.3%)

Lab. majority 10,476 (5.38%)
5.05% swing PC to Lab. (2007 Lab. majority 1,273)

ADDITIONAL MEMBERS
Mark Isherwood, *C.*   Aled Roberts, *LD*
Antoinette Sandbach, *C.*   Llyr Huws Griffiths, *PC*

SOUTH WALES CENTRAL
E. 506,293 T. 208,333 (41.15%)

Lab.	85,445	(41.0%)
C.	45,751	(22.0%)
PC	28,606	(13.7%)
LD	16,514	(7.9%)
Green	10,774	(5.2%)
UKIP	8,292	(4.0%)
Soc. Lab.	4,690	(2.3%)
BNP	3,805	(1.8%)
Welsh Christian Party	1,873	(0.9%)
Loony	1,237	(0.6%)
TUSC	830	(0.4%)
Comm. Brit.	516	(0.2%)

Lab. majority 39,694 (19.05%)
6.55% swing LD to C. (2007 Lab. majority 25,652)

ADDITIONAL MEMBERS
David Melding, *C.*   Leanne Wood, *PC*
Andrew Davies, *C.*   John Dixon, *LD*

SOUTH WALES EAST
E. 469,486 T. 181,024 (38.56%)

Lab.	82,699	(45.7%)
C.	35,459	(19.6%)
PC	21,851	(12.1%)
LD	10,798	(6.0%)
UKIP	9,526	(5.3%)
BNP	6,485	(3.6%)
Green	4,857	(2.7%)
Soc. Lab.	4,427	(2.4%)
Welsh Christian Party	2,441	(1.3%)
Eng. Dem.	1,904	(1.1%)
Comm. Brit.	578	(0.3%)

Lab. majority 47,240 (26.10%)
5.95% swing LD to Lab. (2007 Lab. majority 30,063)

ADDITIONAL MEMBERS
William Graham, *C.*   Jocelyn Davies, *PC*
Mohammad Asghar, *C.*   Lindsay Whittle, *PC*

SOUTH WALES WEST
E. 407,333 T. 154,381 (37.90%)

Lab.	71,766	(46.5%)
Con.	27,457	(17.8%)
PC	21,258	(13.8%)
LD	10,683	(6.9%)
UKIP	6,619	(4.3%)
Soc. Lab.	5,057	(3.3%)
BNP	4,714	(3.1%)
Green	3,952	(2.6%)
Welsh Christian Party	1,602	(1.0%)
TUSC	809	(0.5%)
Comm. Brit.	464	(0.3%)

Lab. majority 44,309 (28.70%)
8.10% swing LD to Lab. (2007 Lab. majority 29,528)

ADDITIONAL MEMBERS
Suzy Davies, *C.*   Peter Black, *LD*
Byron Davies, *C.*   Bethan Jenkins, *PC*

SCOTLAND

SCOTTISH GOVERNMENT

St Andrew's House, Regent Road, Edinburgh EH1 3DG
T 0845-774 1741 **Enquiry Line** 0131-556 840
E ceu@scotland.gsi.gov.uk **W** www.scotland.gov.uk

The devolved government for Scotland is responsible for most of the issues of day-to-day concern to the people of Scotland, including health, education, justice, rural affairs and transport.

The Scottish government was known as the Scottish executive when it was established in 1999, following the first elections to the Scottish parliament. The current administration was formed after elections in May 2007.

The government is led by a first minister who is nominated by the parliament and in turn appoints the other Scottish ministers who make up the cabinet.

Civil servants in Scotland are accountable to Scottish ministers, who are themselves accountable to the Scottish parliament.

CABINET

First Minister, Rt. Hon. Alex Salmond, MSP
Deputy First Minister and Cabinet Secretary for Health, Wellbeing and Cities Strategy, Nicola Sturgeon, MSP
Cabinet Secretary for Culture and External Affairs, Fiona Hyslop, MSP
Cabinet Secretary for Education and Lifelong Learning, Michael Russell, MSP
Cabinet Secretary for Finance, Employment and Sustainable Growth, John Swinney, MSP
Cabinet Secretary for Infrastructure and Capital Investment, Alex Neill, MSP
Cabinet Secretary for Justice, Kenny MacAskill, MSP
Cabinet Secretary for Parliamentary Business and Government Strategy, Bruce Crawford, MSP
Cabinet Secretary for Rural Affairs and the Environment, Richard Lochhead, MSP
Minister for Children and Young People, Angela Constance, MSP
Minister for Commonwealth Games and Sport, Shona Robison, MSP
Minister for Community Safety and Legal Affairs (with responsibility for tackling sectarianism), Roseanna Cunningham, MSP
Minister for Energy, Enterprise and Tourism, Fergus Ewing, MSP
Minister for Environment and Climate Change, Stewart Stevenson, MSP
Minister for Housing and Transport, Keith Brown, MSP
Minister for Learning and Skills (with responsibility for Gaelic and Scots), Alasdair Allan, MSP
Minister for Local Government and Planning, Aileen Campbell, MSP
Minister for Parliamentary Business and Chief Whip, Brian Adam, MSP
Minister for Public Health, Michael Matheson, MSP

LAW OFFICERS

Lord Advocate, Frank Mulholland, QC
Solicitor-General for Scotland, Lesley Thomson

STRATEGIC BOARD

Permanent Secretary, Peter Housden
Director-General, Enterprise and Environment, Mike Neilson
Director-General, Finance, Alyson Stafford
Director-General, Governance and Communities, Paul Gray
Director-General, Health and Social Care, Derek Feeley
Director-General, Learning and Justice, Leslie Evans

NON-DEPARTMENTAL AGENCIES

HISTORIC SCOTLAND
Longmore House, Salisbury Place, Edinburgh EH9 1SH
T 0131-668 8600 **W** www.historic-scotland.gov.uk
Chief Executive, Ruth Parsons

NATIONAL RECORDS FOR SCOTLAND
HM General Register House, 2 Princes Street, Edinburgh EH1 3YY
T 0131-535 1314 **E** enquiries@nas.gov.uk
W www.nas.gov.uk
Keeper of the Records of Scotland, George MacKenzie

GOVERNMENT DEPARTMENTS

DIRECTOR-GENERAL ENTERPRISE AND ENVIRONMENT

Victoria Quay, Edinburgh EH6 6QQ
Directorates: Business; Chief Scientific Adviser for Rural Affairs and the Environment; DG Coordination – Enterprise and Environment; Energy and Climate Change; Marine Scotland; Rural and Environment; Rural Payments and Inspections
Director-General, Mike Neilson

EXECUTIVE AGENCY
Transport Scotland

DIRECTOR-GENERAL FINANCE

Victoria Quay, Edinburgh EH6 6QQ
Directorates: CAP and Risk; Corporate Reporting; Financial Policy; Financial Programme Management; Financial Services Division; FISC Responsibility; Internal Audit; Scottish Procurement and Commercial Directorate
Director-General, Alyson Stafford

EXECUTIVE AGENCY
Scottish Public Pensions Agency

DIRECTOR-GENERAL GOVERNANCE AND COMMUNITIES

Saughton House, Broomhouse Drive, Edinburgh, EH11 3XD
Directorates: Built Environment; Culture and Digital; Housing, Regeneration and Commonwealth Games; HR and Organisational Development; International and Constitution; Legal Services; Local Government and the Third Sector; Strategy and Performance; Inspectorate of Prosecution in Scotland; Office of the Scottish Parliamentary Counsel
Director-General, Paul Gray

EXECUTIVE AGENCY
Scottish Housing Regulator

DIRECTOR-GENERAL HEALTH AND SOCIAL CARE

St Andrew's House, Regent Road, Edinburgh EH1 3DG
Directorates: Coordination – Health and Social Care; Chief Medical Officer, Public Health and Sport; Chief Nursing Officer, Patients, Public and Health Professions; Children and Families; Health and Healthcare Improvement; Health and Social Care Integration; Health Delivery; Health Finance and Information; Health Workforce
Director-General Health and Social Care and Chief Executive, Derek Feeley

EXECUTIVE AGENCY
Disclosure Scotland

DIRECTOR-GENERAL LEARNING AND JUSTICE
Victoria Quay, Edinburgh, EH6 6QQ
Directorates: Coordination – Learning and Justice;
Education Analytical Services; Employability, Skills and
Lifelong Learning; Justice; Learning; Office of the
Chief Scientific Adviser; Safer Communities
Director-General, Leslie Evans

EXECUTIVE AGENCIES
Accountant in Bankruptcy
HM Inspectorate of Education
Scottish Prison Service
Student Awards Agency for Scotland

ASSOCIATED BODY
Scottish Courts Service

NON-DEPARTMENTAL OFFICES

AUDIT SCOTLAND
110 George Street, Edinburgh EH2 4LH
T 0845-146 1010 E info@audit-scotland.gov.uk
W www.audit-scotland.gov.uk
Auditor-General, Robert W. Black
Accounts Commission Chair, Prof. John Baillie

CROWN OFFICE AND PROCURATOR FISCAL
SERVICE
25 Chambers Street, Edinburgh EH1 1LA
T 0131-226 2626
Chief Executive and Crown Agent, Catherine Dyer

OFFICE OF THE PERMANENT SECRETARY
St Andrew's House, Regent Road, Edinburgh EH1 3DG
T 0131-556 8400
Permanent Secretary, Sir Peter Housden

SCOTTISH PARLIAMENT
Edinburgh EH99 1SP
T 0131-348 5000 **Textphone** 0800-092 7100
E sp.info@scottish.parliament.uk
W www.scottish.parliament.uk

In July 1997 the government announced plans to
establish a Scottish parliament. In a referendum on 11
September 1997 about 60 per cent of the electorate
voted. Of those who voted, 74.3 per cent voted in favour
of the parliament and 63.5 per cent in favour of it having
tax-raising powers. Elections are held every four years.
The first elections were held on 6 May 1999, when
around 59 per cent of the electorate voted. The first
meeting was held on 12 May 1999 and the Scottish
parliament was officially opened on 1 July 1999 at the
Assembly Hall, Edinburgh. A new building to house
parliament was opened, in the presence of the Queen, at
Holyrood on 9 October 2004. On 5 May 2011 the
fourth elections to the Scottish parliament took place.

The Scottish parliament has 129 members (including
the presiding officer), comprising 73 constituency
members and 56 additional regional members, mainly
from party lists. It can introduce primary legislation and
has the power to raise or lower the basic rate of income
tax by up to three pence in the pound. Members of the
Scottish parliament are elected using the additional
member system, the same system used to elect London
Assembly and Welsh Assembly members.

The areas for which the Scottish parliament is
responsible include: education, health, law, environment,
economic development, local government, housing,
police, fire services, planning, financial assistance to
industry, tourism, some transport, heritage and the arts,
agriculture, social work, sports, public registers and
records, forestry and food standards.

SALARIES *as at 1 May 2011*	
First Minister*	£83,326
Cabinet Secretaries*	£43,227
Lord Advocate*	£56,473
Solicitor-General for Scotland*	£40,837
Ministers*	£27,077
MSPs†	£57,521
Presiding Officer*	£43,227
Deputy Presiding Officer*	£27,077

* In addition to the MSP salary
† Reduced by two-thirds if the member is already an MP or an
MEP

MEMBERS OF THE SCOTTISH PARLIAMENT
as at 5 May 2011
Adam, Brian, *SNP, Aberdeen Donside,* Maj. 7,175
Adam, George, *SNP, Paisley,* Maj. 248
Adamson, Clare, *SNP, Central Scotland region*
Allan, Alisdair, *SNP, Na h-Eileanan an Iar,* Maj. 4,772
Baillie, Jackie, *Lab., Dumbarton,* Maj. 1,639
Baker, Claire, *Lab., Mid Scotland and Fife region*
Baker, Richard, *Lab., North East Scotland region*
Beamish, Claudia, *Lab., South Scotland region*
Beattie, Colin, *SNP, Midlothian North and Musselburgh,*
  Maj. 2,996
Biagi, Marco, *SNP, Edinburgh Central,* Maj. 237
Bibby, Neil, *Lab., West Scotland region*
Boyack, Sarah, *Lab., Lothian region*
Brodie, Chic, *SNP, South Scotland region*
Brown, Gavin, *C., Lothian region*
Brown, Keith, *SNP, Clackmannanshire and Dunblane,*
  Maj. 3,609
Burgess, Margaret, *SNP, Cunninghame South,* Maj. 2,348
Campbell, Aileen, *SNP, Clydesdale,* Maj. 4,216
Campbell, Roderick, *SNP, North East Fife,* Maj. 2,592
Carlaw, Jackson, *C., West Scotland region*
Chisholm, Malcolm, *Lab., Edinburgh Northern and Leith,*
  Maj. 595
Coffey, Willie, *SNP, Kilmarnock and Irvine Valley,*
  Maj. 5,993
Constance, Angela, *SNP, Almond Valley,* Maj. 5,542
Crawford, Bruce, *SNP, Stirling,* Maj. 5,671
Cunningham, Roseanna, *SNP, Perthshire South and
  Kinross-shire,* Maj. 7,166
Davidson, Ruth, *C., Glasgow region*
Dey, Graeme, *SNP, Angus South,* Maj. 10,583
Don, Nigel, *SNP, Angus North and Mearns,* Maj. 7,286
Doris, Bob, *SNP, Glasgow region*
Dornan, James, *SNP, Glasgow Cathcart,* Maj. 1,592
Dugdale, Kezia, *Lab., Lothian region*
Eadie, Helen, *Lab., Cowdenbeath,* Maj. 1,247
Eadie, Jim, *SNP, Edinburgh Southern,* Maj. 693
Ewing, Annabelle, *SNP, Mid Scotland and Fife region*
Ewing, Fergus, *SNP, Inverness and Nairn,* Maj. 9,745
Fabiani, Linda, *SNP, East Kilbride,* Maj. 1,949
Fee, Mary, *Lab., West Scotland region*
Ferguson, Patricia, *Lab., Glasgow Maryhill and
  Springburn,* Maj. 1,252
Fergusson, Alex, *C., Galloway and West Dumfries,,*
  Maj. 862

Findlay, Neil, *Lab., Lothian region*
Finnie, John, *SNP, Highlands and Islands region*
FitzPatrick, Joe, *SNP, Dundee City West*, Maj. 6,405
Fraser, Murdo, *C., Mid Scotland and Fife region*
Gibson, Kenneth, *SNP, Cunninghame North*, Maj. 6,117
Gibson, Rob, *SNP, Caithness, Sutherland and Ross*, Maj. 7,458
Goldie, Annabel, *C., West Scotland region*
Grahame, Christine, *SNP, Midlothian South, Tweeddale and Lauderdale*, Maj. 4,924
Grant, Rhoda, *Lab., Highlands and Islands region*
Gray, Iain, *Lab., East Lothian*, Maj. 151
Griffin, Mark, *Lab., Central Scotland region*
Harvie, Patrick, *Green, Glasgow region*
Henry, Hugh, *Lab., Renfrewshire South*, Maj. 2,577
Hepburn, Jamie, *SNP, Cumbernauld and Kilsyth*, Maj. 3,459
Hume, Jim, *LD, South Scotland region*
Hyslop, Fiona, *SNP, Linlithgow*, Maj. 4,091
Ingram, Adam, *SNP, Carrick, Cumnock and Doon Valley*, Maj. 2,581
Johnstone, Alex, *C., North East Scotland region*
Johnstone, Alison, *Green, Lothian region*
Keir, Colin, *SNP, Edinburgh West*, Maj. 2,689
Kelly, James, *Lab., Rutherglen*, Maj. 1,779
Kidd, Bill, *SNP, Glasgow Anniesland*, Maj. 7
Lamont, Johann, *Lab., Glasgow Pollok*, Maj. 623
Lamont, John, *C., Ettrick, Roxburgh and Berwickshire*, Maj. 5,334
Lochhead, Richard, *SNP, Moray*, Maj. 10,944
Lyle, Richard, *SNP, Central Scotland region*
McAlpine, Joan, *SNP, South Scotland region*
McArthur, Liam, *LD, Orkney*, Maj. 860
MacAskill, Kenny, *SNP, Edinburgh Eastern*, Maj. 2,233
McCulloch, Margaret, *Lab., Central Scotland region*
MacDonald, Gordon, *SNP, Edinburgh Pentlands*, Maj. 1,758
Macdonald, Lewis, *Lab., North East Scotland region*
MacDonald, Margo, *Ind., Lothian region*
MacDonald, Angus, *SNP, Falkirk East*, Maj. 3,535
McDonald, Mark, *SNP, North East Scotland region*
McDougall, Margaret, *Lab., West Scotland region*
McGrigor, Jamie, *C., Highlands and Islands region*
McInnes, Alison, *LD, North East Scotland region*
Macintosh, Ken, *Lab., Eastwood*, Maj. 2,012
Mackay, Derek, *SNP Renfrewshire North and West*, Maj. 1,564
McKelvie, Christina, *SNP, Hamilton, Larkhall and Stonehouse*, Maj. 2,213
MacKenzie, Mike, *SNP, Highlands and Islands region*
McLeod, Aileen, *SNP, South Scotland region*
McLeod, Fiona, *SNP, Strathkelvin and Bearsden*, Maj. 1,802
McLetchie, David, *C., Lothian region*
McMahon, Michael, *Lab., Uddingston and Bellshill*, Maj. 714
McMahon, Siobhan, *Lab., Central Scotland region*
McMillan, Stuart, *SNP, West Scotland region*
McNeil, Duncan, *Lab., Greenock and Inverclyde*, Maj. 511
McTaggart, Anne, *Lab., Glasgow region*
Malik, Hanzala, *Lab., Glasgow region*
Marra, Jenny, *Lab., North East Scotland region*
Martin, Paul, *Lab., Glasgow Provan*, Maj. 2,079
Marwick, Tricia, *SNP, Mid Fife and Glenrothes*, Maj. 4,188
Mason, John, *SNP, Glasgow Shettleston*, Maj. 586
Matheson, Michael, *SNP, Falkirk West*, Maj. 5,745
Maxwell, Stewart, *SNP, West Scotland region*
Milne, Nanette, *C., North East Scotland region*

Mitchell, Margaret, *C., Central Scotland region*
Murray, Elaine, *Lab., Dumfriesshire*, Maj. 3,156
Neil, Alex, *SNP, Airdrie and Shotts*, Maj. 2,001
Park, John, *Lab., Mid Scotland and Fife region*
Paterson, Gil, *SNP, Clydebank and Milngavie*, Maj. 714
Pearson, Graeme, *Lab, South Scotland region*
Pentland, John, *Lab., Motherwell and Wishaw*, Maj. 587
Rennie, Willie, *LD, Mid Scotland and Fife region*
Robertson, Dennis, *SNP, Aberdeenshire West*, Maj. 4,112
Robison, Shona, *SNP, Dundee City East*, Maj. 10,679
Russell, Michael, *SNP, Argyll and Bute*, Maj. 8,543
Salmond, Alex, *SNP, Aberdeenshire East*, Maj. 15,295
Scanlon, Mary, *C., Highlands and Islands region*
Scott, John, *C., Ayr*, Maj. 1,113
Scott, Tavish, *LD, Shetland Islands*, Maj. 1,617
Simpson, Richard, *Lab., Mid Scotland and Fife region*
Smith, Drew, *Lab., Glasgow region*
Smith, Elaine, *Lab., Coatbridge and Chryston*, Maj. 2,741
Smith, Liz, *C., Mid Scotland and Fife region*
Stevenson, Stewart, *SNP, Banffshire and Buchan Coast*, Maj. 12,220
Stewart, David, *Lab., Highlands and Islands region*
Stewart, Kevin, *SNP, Aberdeen Central*, Maj. 617
Sturgeon, Nicola, *SNP, Glasgow Southside*, Maj. 4,349
Swinney, John, *SNP, Perthshire North*, Maj. 10,353
Thompson, Dave, *SNP, Skye, Lochaber and Badenoch* Maj. 4,995
Torrance, David, *SNP, Kirkcaldy*, Maj. 182
Urquhart, Jean, *SNP, Highlands and Islands region*
Walker, Bill, *SNP, Dunfermline*, Maj. 590
Watt, Maureen, *SNP, Aberdeen South and North Kincardine*, Maj. 6,323
Wheelhouse, Paul, *SNP, South Scotland region*
White, Sandra, *SNP, Glasgow Kelvin*, Maj. 882
Wilson, John, *SNP, Central Scotland region*
Yousaf, Humza, *SNP, Glasgow region*

STATE OF THE PARTIES
as at 5 May 2011

	Constituency MSPs	Regional MSPs	Total
Scottish National Party (SNP)	52	16	68
Scottish Labour Party (Lab.)	15	22	37
Scottish Conservative and Unionist Party (C.)	3	12	15
Scottish Liberal Democrats (LD)	2	3	5
Scottish Green Party (Green)	0	2	2
Independent (Ind.)	0	1	1
‡Presiding Officer	1	0	1
Total	73	56	129

‡The presiding officer was elected as a constituency member for the SNP but has no party allegiance while in post

The Presiding Officer, Tricia Marwick, MSP
Deputy Presiding Officers, John Scott, MSP *(C.)*; Elaine Smith, MSP *(Lab.)*

SCOTTISH PARLIAMENT ELECTION RESULTS
as at 5 May 2011
E. Electorate T. Turnout
See General Election Results for a list of party abbreviations

CONSTITUENCIES
E. 3,985,161 T. 50.4%

ABERDEEN CENTRAL
(Scotland North East Region)
E. 57,396 T. 25,149 (43.82%)
Kevin Stewart, SNP	10,058
Lewis Macdonald, Lab.	9,441
Sandy Wallace, C.	3,100
Sheila Thomson, LD	2,349
Mike Phillips, NF	201

SNP majority 617 (2.45%)
0.54% swing Lab. to SNP

ABERDEEN DONSIDE
(Scotland North East Region)
E. 56,145 T. 26,761 (47.66%)
Brian Adam, SNP	14,790
Barney Crockett, Lab.	7,615
Ross Thomson, C.	2,166
Millie McLeod, LD.	1,606
David Henderson, Ind.	371
Christopher Willett, NF	213

SNP majority 7,175 (26.81%)
6.87% swing Lab. to SNP

ABERDEEN SOUTH AND KINCARDINE NORTH
(Scotland North East Region)
E. 54,338 T. 28,697 (52.81%)
Maureen Watt, SNP	11,947
Greg Williams, Lab.	5,624
John Sleigh, LD	4,994
Stewart Whyte, C.	4,058

SNP majority 6,323 (22.03%)
15.77% swing LD to SNP

ABERDEENSHIRE EAST
(Scotland North East Region)
E. 57,591 T. 30,286 (52.59%)
Alex Salmond, SNP	19,533
Alison McInnes, LD	4,238
Geordie Burnett Stuart, C.	4,211
Peter Smyth, Lab.	2,304

SNP majority 15,295 (50.5%)
19.53% swing LD to SNP

ABERDEENSHIRE WEST
(Scotland North East Region)
E. 53,779 T. 28,636 (53.25%)
Dennis Robertson, SNP	12,186
Mike Rumbles, LD	8,074
Nanette Milne, C.	6,027
Jean Morrison, Lab.	2,349

SNP majority 4,112 (14.36%)
13.45% swing LD to SNP

AIRDRIE AND SHOTTS
(Scotland Central Region)
E. 51,336 T. 23,894 (46.54%)
Alex Neil, SNP	11,984
Karen Whitefield, Lab.	9,983
Robert Crozier, C.	1,396
John Love, LD	531

SNP majority 2,001 (8.37%)
5.50% swing Lab. to SNP

ALMOND VALLEY
(Lothian Region)
E. 59,896 T. 30,737 (51.32%)
Angela Constance, SNP	16,704
Lawrence Fitzpatrick, Lab.	11,162
Andrew Hardie, C.	1,886
Emma Sykes, LD	656
Neil McIvor, NF	329

SNP majority 5,542 (18.03%)
9.01% swing Lab. to SNP

ANGUS NORTH AND MEARNS
(Scotland North East Region)
E. 52,124 T. 24,920 (47.81%)
Nigel Don, SNP	13,660
Alex Johnstone, C.	6,374
Kevin Hutchens, Lab.	3,160
Sanjay Samani, LD	1,726

SNP majority 7,286 (29.24%)
4.15% swing C. to SNP

ANGUS SOUTH
(Scotland North East Region)
E. 54,922 T. 27,643 (50.33%)
Graeme Dey, SNP	16,164
Hughie Campbell Adamson, C.	5,581
William Campbell, Lab.	3,703
David Fairweather, AIR	1,321
Clive Sneddon, LD	874

SNP majority 10,583 (38.28%)
9.31% swing C. to SNP

ARGYLL AND BUTE
(Highlands and Islands Region)
E. 49,028 T. 26,476 (54.00%)
Michael Russell, SNP	13,390
Jamie McGrigor, C.	4,847
Mick Rice, Lab.	4,041
George Doyle, Ind.	542
George White, Lib.	436

SNP majority 8,543 (32.27%)
8.52% swing C. to SNP

AYR
(Scotland South Region)
E. 61,563 T. 33,373 (54.21%)
John Scott, C.	12,997
Chic Brodie, SNP	11,884
Gordon McKenzie, Lab.	7,779
Eileen Taylor, LD	713

C. majority 1,113 (3.34%)
5.16% swing C. to SNP

BANFFSHIRE AND BUCHAN COAST
(Scotland North East Region)
E. 53,698 T. 25,004 (46.56%)

Stewart Stevenson, SNP	16,812
Michael Watt, C.	4,592
Alan Duffill, Lab.	2,642
Galen Milne, LD	958

SNP majority 12,220 (48.87%)
3.48% swing C. to SNP

CAITHNESS, SUTHERLAND AND ROSS
(Highlands and Islands Region)
E. 55,116 T. 28,600 (51.89%)

Rob Gibson, SNP	13,843
Robbie Rowantree, LD	6,385
John MacKay, Lab.	5,438
Edward Mountain, C.	2,934

SNP majority 7,458 (26.08%)
17.32% swing LD to SNP

CARRICK, CUMNOCK AND DOON VALLEY
(Scotland South Region)
E. 59,368 T. 28,703 (48.35%)

Adam Ingram, SNP	13,250
Richard Leonard, Lab.	10,669
Peter Kennerley, C.	4,160
Andrew Chamberlain, LD	624

SNP majority 2,581 (8.99%)
11.77% Lab. to SNP

CLACKMANNANSHIRE & DUNBLANE
(Mid Scotland and Fife Region)
E. 49, 415 T. 27,416 (55.48%)

Keith Brown, SNP	13,253
Richard Simpson, Lab.	9,644
Callum Campbell, C.	3,501
Tim Brett, LD	1,018

SNP majority 3,609 (13.16%)
5.20% swing Lab. to SNP

CLYDEBANK AND MILNGAVIE
(Scotland West Region)
E. 53,018 T. 28,369 (53.51%)

Gils Paterson, SNP	12,278
Des McNulty, Lab.	11,564
Alice Struthers, C.	2,758
John Duncan, LD	1,769

SD majority 714 (2.52%)
6.56% swing Lab. to SNP

CLYDESDALE
(Scotland South Region)
E. 56,828 T. 29,937 (52.68%)

Aileen Campbell, SNP	14,931
Karen Gillon, Lab.	10,715
Colin McGavigan, C.	4,291

SNP majority 4,216 (14.08%)
8.89% swing Lab. to SNP

COATBRIDGE AND CHRYSTON
(Scotland Central Region)
E. 51,206 T. 23,279 (45.46%)

Elaine Smith, Lab.	12,161
John Wilson, SNP	9,420
Jason Lingiah, C.	1,317
Rod Ackland, LD	381

Lab. majority 2,741 (11.77%)
3.28% swing Lab. to SNP

COWDENBEATH
(Mid Scotland and Fife Region)
E. 54,284 T. 25,670 (47.29%)

Helen Eadie, Lab.	11,926
Ian Chisholm, SNP	10,679
Belinda Don, C.	1,792
Keith Legg, LD	997
Mike Heenan, Land Party	276

Lab. majority 1,247 (4.86%)
4.85% swing Lab. to SNP

CUMBERNAULD AND KILSYTH
(Scotland Central Region)
E. 48,006 T. 25,254 (52.61%)

Jamie Hepburn, SNP	13,595
Cathie Craigie, Lab.	10,136
James Boswell, C.	1,156
Martin Oliver, LD	367

SNP majority 3,459 (13.7%)
10.79% Lab. to SNP

CUNNINGHAME NORTH
(Scotland West Region)
E. 56,548 T. 29,536 (52.23%)

Kenneth Gibson, SNP	15,539
Allan Wilson, Lab.	9,422
Maurice Golden, C.	4,032
Mallika Punukollu, LD	543

SNP majority 6,117 (20.71%)
10.29% swing Lab. to SNP

CUNNINGHAME SOUTH
(Scotland South Region)
E. 50,926 T. 22,056 (43.31%)

Margaret Burgess, SNP	10,993
Irene Oldfather, Lab.	8,645
Alistair Haw, C.	1,871
Ruby Kirkwood, LD	547

SNP majority 2,348 (10.65%)
9.93% swing Lab. to SNP

DUMBARTON
(Scotland West Region)
E. 53,470 T. 28,508 (53.32%)

Jackie Baillie, Lab.	12,562
Iain Robertson, SNP	10,923
Graham Smith, C.	3,395
Helen Watt, LD	858
George Rice, Ind.	770

Lab. majority 1,639 (5.75%)
0.24% swing SNP to Lab.

DUMFRIESSHIRE
(Scotland South Region)
E. 59,716 T. 31,895 (53.41%)

Elaine Murray, Lab.	12,624
Gill Dykes, C.	9,468
Aileen Orr, SNP	8,384
Richard Brodie, LD	1,419

Lab. majority 3,156 (9.89%)
5.99% swing C. to Lab.

DUNDEE EAST
(Scotland North East Region)
E. 54,404 T. 25,753 (47.34%)

Shona Robison, SNP	16,541
Mohammed Asif, Lab.	5,862
Brian Docherty, C.	2,550
Allan Petrie, LD	800

SNP majority 10,679 (41.47%)
12.47% swing Lab. to SNP

DUNDEE WEST
(Scotland North East Region)
E. 53,841 T. 24,461 (45.43%)

Joe Fitzpatrick, SNP	14,089
Richard McCready, Lab.	7,684
Colin Stewart, C.	1,625
Alison Burns, LD	1,063

SNP majority 6,405 (26.18%)
8.88% swing Lab. to SNP

DUNFERMLINE
(Scotland Mid and Fife Region)
E. 55,479 T. 29,299 (52.81%)

Bill Walker, SNP	11,010
Alex Rowley, Lab.	10,420
Jim Tolson, LD	5,776
James Reekie, C.	2,093

SNP majority 599 (2.01%)
13.41% swing LD to SNP

EAST KILBRIDE
(Scotland Central Region)
E. 58,251 T. 29,911 (51.35%)

Linda Fabiani, SNP	14,359
Andy Kerr, Lab.	12,410
Graham Simpson, C.	2,260
Douglas Herbison, LD	468
John Houston, Ind.	414

SNP majority 1,949 (6.52%)
6.64% swing Lab. to SNP

EAST LOTHIAN
(Scotland South Region)
E. 56,333 T. 32,177 (57.12%)

Iain Gray, Lab.	12,536
David Berry, SNP	12,385
Derek Brownlee, C.	5,344
Ettie Spencer, LD	1,912

Lab. majority 151 (0.47%)
3.12% swing Lab to SNP

EASTWOOD
(Scotland West Region)
E. 50,476 T. 31,924 (63.25%)

Ken Macintosh, Lab.	12,662
Jackson Carlaw, C.	10,650
Stewart Maxwell, SNP	7,777
Gordon Cochrane, LD	835

Lab. majority 2,012 (6.3%)
8.74% swing C. to Lab.

EDINBURGH CENTRAL
(Lothian Region)
E. 53,606 T. 29,014 (54.12%)

Marco Biagi, SNP	9,480
Sarah Boyack, Lab.	9,243
Alex Cole-Hamilton, LD	5,937
Iain McGill, C.	4,354

SNP majority 237 (0.82%)
10.16% swing Lab. to SNP

EDINBURGH EASTERN
(Lothian Region)
E. 55,773 T. 30,728 (55.09%)

Kenny MacAskill, SNP	14,552
Ewan Aitken, Lab.	12,319
Cameron Buchanan, C.	2,630
Martin Veart, LD	1,227

SNP majority 2,233 (7.27%)
4.53% swing Lab. to SNP

EDINBURGH NORTHERN AND LEITH
(Lothian Region)
E. 59,138 T. 30,885 (52.23%)

Malcolm Chisholm, Lab.	12,858
Shirley-Anne Somerville, SNP	12,263
Sheila Low, C.	2,928
Don Farthing, LD	2,836

Lab. majority 595 (1.93%)
2.66% swing Lab. to SNP

EDINBURGH PENTLANDS
(Lothian Region)
E. 52,620 T. 30,049 (57.11%)

Gordon MacDonald, SNP	11,197
David McLetchie, C.	9,439
Ricky Henderson, Lab.	7,993
Simon Clark, LD	1,420

SNP majority 1,758 (5.85%)
7.42% swing C. to SNP

EDINBURGH SOUTHERN
(Lothian Region)
E. 54,868 T. 33,796 (61.60%)

Jim Eadie, SNP	9,947
Paul Godzik, Lab.	9,254
Mike Pringle, LD	8,297
Gavin Brown, C.	6,298

SNP majority 693 (2.05%)
12.06% swing LD to SNP

EDINBURGH WESTERN
(Lothian Region)
E. 56,338 T. 33,452 (59.38%)

Colin Keir, SNP	11,965
Margaret Smith, LD	9,276
Lesley Hinds, Lab.	7,164
Gordon Lindhurst, C.	5,047

SNP majority 2,689 (8.04%)
12.60% swing LD to SNP

ETTRICK, ROXBURGH AND BERWICKSHIRE
(Scotland South Region)
E. 54,327 T. 28,816 (53.04%)

John Lamont, C.	12,933
Paul Wheelhouse, SNP	7,599
Euan Robson, LD	4,990
Rab Stewart, Lab.	2,986
Jesse Rae, Ind.	308

C. majority 5,334 (18.51%)
1.39% swing C. to SNP

FALKIRK EAST
(Scotland Central Region)
E. 56,408 T. 28,168 (49.94%)

Angus MacDonald, SNP	14,302
Cathy Peattie, Lab.	10,767
Lynn Munro, C.	2,372
Ross Laird, LD	727

SNP majority 3,535 (12.55%)
9.33% swing Lab. to SNP

FALKIRK WEST
(Scotland Central Region)
E. 55,739 T. 28,199 (50.59%)

Michael Matheson, SNP	15,607
Dennis Goldie, Lab.	9,862
Allan Finnie, C.	2,086
Callum Chomczuk, LD	644

SNP majority 5,745 (20.37%)
8.91% swing Lab. to SNP

FIFE MID AND GLENROTHES
(Scotland Mid and Fife Region)
E. 53,701 T. 26,313 (49.0%)

Tricia Marwick, SNP	13,761
Claire Baker, Lab.	9,573
Allan Smith, C.	1,676
Jim Parker, ASPP	673
Callum Leslie, LD	630

SNP majority 4,188 (15.92%)
3.43% swing Lab. to SNP

FIFE NORTH EAST
(Scotland Mid and Fife Region)
E. 58,858 T. 29,676 (50.42%)

Roderick Campbell, SNP	11,029
Iain Smith, LD	8,437
Miles Briggs, C.	5,618
Colin Davidson, Lab.	3,613
Mike Scott-Hayward, UKIP	979

SNP majority 2,592 (8.73%)
15.02% swing LD to SNP

GALLOWAY AND WEST DUMFRIES
(Scotland South Region)
E. 56,611 T. 29,997 (52.99%)

Alex Fergusson, C.	11,071
Aileen McLeod, SNP	10,209
Willie Scobie, Lab.	7,954
Joe Rosiejak, LD	763

C. majority 862 (2.87%)
2.40% swing C. to SNP

GLASGOW ANNIESLAND
(Glasgow Region)
E. 55,411 T. 23,918 (43.16%)

Bill Kidd, SNP	10,329
Bill Butler, Lab.	10,322
Matthew Smith, C.	2,011
Paul McGarry, LD	1,000
Marc Livingstone, Comm. Brit.	256

SNP majority 7 (0.03%)
10.09% swing Lab. to SNP

GLASGOW CATHCART
(Glasgow Region)
E. 58,525 T. 26,222 (44.8%)

James Dornan, SNP	11,918
Charlie Gordon, Lab.	10,326
Richard Sullivan, C.	2,410
Eileen Baxendale, LD	1,118
John McKee, Ind.	450

SNP majority 1,592 (6.07%)
6.53% swing Lab. to SNP

GLASGOW KELVIN
(Glasgow Region)
E. 61,893 T. 24,548 (39.66%)

Sandra White, SNP	10,640
Pauline McNeil, Lab.	9,758
Natalie McKee, LD	1,900
Ruth Davidson, C.	1,845
Tom Muirhead, Ind.	405

SNP majority 882 (3.59%)
4.03% swing Lab. to SNP

GLASGOW MARYHILL AND SPRINGBURN
(Glasgow Region)
E. 56,622 T. 20,531 (36.26%)

Patricia Ferguson, Lab.	9,884
Bob Doris, SNP	8,592
Stephanie Murray, C.	1,222
Sophie Bridger, LD	833

Lab. majority 1,292 (6.29%)
5.43% swing Lab. to SNP

GLASGOW POLLOK
(Glasgow Region)
E. 58,429 T. 22,915 (39.22%)

Johann Lamont, Lab.	10,875
Chris Stephens, SNP	10,252
Andrew Morrison, C.	1,298
Isabel Nelson, LD	490

Lab. majority 623 (2.72%)
8.53% swing Lab. to SNP

GLASGOW PROVAN
(Glasgow Region)
E. 55,118 T. 19,185 (34.81%)

Paul Martin, Lab.	10,037
Anne McLaughlin, SNP	7,958
Majid Hussain, C.	777
Michael O'Donnell, LD	413

Lab. majority 2,079 (10.84%)
8.68% swing Lab. to SNP

GLASGOW SHETTLESTON
(Glasgow Region)
E. 55,874 T. 21,204 (37.95%)

John Mason, SNP	10,128
Frank McAveety, Lab.	9,542
David Wilson, C.	1,163
Ruaraidh Dobson, LD	371

SNP majority 586 (2.76%)
12.61% swing Lab. to SNP

GLASGOW SOUTHSIDE
(Glasgow Region)
E. 52,325 T. 22,608 (43.21%)

Nicola Sturgeon, SNP	12,306
Stephen Curran, Lab.	7,957
David Meikle, C.	1,733
Kenneth Elder, LD	612

SNP majority 4,349 (19.24%)
9.68% swing Lab. to SNP

GREENOCK AND INVERCLYDE
(Scotland West Region)
E. 56,989 T. 28,298 (49.50%)

Duncan McNeil, Lab.	12,387
Stuart McMillan, SNP	11,876
Graeme Brooks, C.	2,011
Ross Finnie, LD	1,934

Lab. majority 511 (1.81%)
6.90% swing Lab. to SNP

HAMILTON, LARKHALL AND STONEHOUSE
(Scotland Central Region)
E. 56,123 T. 25,354 (45.18%)

Christina McKelvie, SNP	12,202
Tom McCabe, Lab.	9,989
Margaret Mitchell, C.	2,547
Ewan Hoyle, LD	616

SNP majority 2,213 (8.73%)
10.99% swing Lab. to SNP

INVERNESS & NAIRN
(Highlands and Islands Region)
E. 62,168 T. 32,731 (52.65%)

Fergus Ewing, SNP	16,870
David Stewart, Lab.	7,125
Mary Scanlon, C.	3,797
Christine Jardine, LD	3,763
Donald Boyd, Christian Party	646
Ross Durance, UKIP	530

SNP majority 9,745 (29.77%)
4.85% swing Lab. to SNP

KILMARNOCK AND IRVINE VALLEY
(Scotland Central Region)
E. 63,257 T. 31,858 (50.36%)

Willie Coffey, SNP	16,964
Matt McLaughlin, Lab.	10,971
Grant Fergusson, C.	3,309
Robbie Simpson, LD	614

SNP majority 5,993 (18.81%)
7.40% swing Lab. to SNP

KIRKCALDY
(Scotland Mid and Fife Region)
E. 60,079 T. 27,803 (46.28%)

David Torance, SNP	12,579
Marilyn Livingstone, Lab.	12,397
Ian McFarlane, C.	2,007
John Mainland, LD	820

SNP majority 182 (0.65%)
6.19% swing Lab. to SNP

LINLITHGOW
(Lothian Region)
E. 65,025 T. 34,182 (52.57%)

Fiona Hyslop, SNP	17,027
Mary Mulligan, Lab.	12,936
Christopher Donnelly, C.	2,646
Jennifer Lang, LD	1,015
Mike Coyle, NF	558

SNP majority 4,091 (11.97%)
6.42% swing Lab. to SNP

MIDLOTHIAN NORTH AND MUSSELBURGH
(Lothian Region)
E. 58,246 T. 29,818 (51.19%)

Colin Beattie, SNP	14,079
Bernard Harkins, Lab.	11,083
Scott Douglas, C.	2,541
Ian Younger, LD	1,254
Alan Hay, Ind.	861

SNP majority 2,996 (10.05%)
7.61% swing Lab. to SNP

MIDLOTHIAN SOUTH, TWEEDDALE AND
LAUDERDALE
(Lothian Region)
E. 57,781 T. 31,841 (55.11%)

Christine Grahame, SNP	13,855
Jeremy Purvis, LD	8,931
Ian Miller, Lab.	5,312
Peter Duncan, C.	3,743

SNP majority 4,924 (15.46%)
5.87% swing LD to SNP

MORAY
(Highlands and Islands Region)
E. 56,215 T. 28,596 (50.87%)

Richard Lochhead, SNP	16,817
Douglas Ross, C.	5,873
Kieron Green, Lab.	3,580
Jamie Paterson, LD	1,327
Donald Gatt, UKIP	999

SNP majority 10,944 (38.27%)
6.19% swing C. to SNP

MOTHERWELL AND WISHAW
(Scotland Central Region)
E. 53,610 T. 24,451 (45.61%)

John Pentland, Lab.	10,713
Clare Adamson, SNP	10,126
Bob Burgess, C.	1,753
John Swinburne, ASPP	945
Tom Selfridge, Christian Party	547
Beverley Hope, LD	367

Lab. majority 587 (2.4%)
10.20% swing Lab. to SNP

NA H-EILEANAN AN IAR
(Highlands and Islands Region)
E. 21,834 T. 13,011 (59.59%)

Alasdair Allan, SNP	8,496
Donald Crichton, Lab.	3,724
Charlie McGrigor, C.	563
Peter Morrison, LD	228

SNP majority 4,772 (36.68%)
15.82% swing Lab. to SNP

ORKNEY
(Highlands and Islands Region)
E. 16,393 T. 8,152 (49.73%)

Liam McArthur, LD	2,912
James Stockan, Ind.	2,052
George Adam, SNP	2,044
Jamie Halcro Johnston, C.	686
William Sharkey, Lab.	458

LD majority 860 (10.55%)
17.70% swing LD to Ind.

PAISLEY
(Scotland West Region)
E. 52,066 T. 25,590 (49.15%)

George Adam, SNP	10,913
Evan Williams, Lab.	10,665
Malcolm MacAskill, C.	2,229
Eileen McCartin, LD	1,783

SNP majority 248 (0.97%)
7.80% swing Lab. to SNP

PERTHSHIRE NORTH
(Scotland and Mid Fife Region)
E. 53,412 T. 29,953 (56.08%)

John Swinney, SNP	18,219
Murdo Fraser, C.	7,866
Pete Cheema, Lab.	2,672
Victor Clements, LD	1,196

SNP majority 10,353 (34.56%)
6.53% swing C. to SNP

PERTHSHIRE SOUTH AND KINROSS-SHIRE
(Scotland and Mid Fife Region)
E. 58,093 T. 31,216 (53.73%)

Roseanna Cunningham, SNP	16,073
Liz Smith, C.	8,907
Tricia Duncan, Lab.	3,980
Willie Robertson, LD	2,256

SNP majority 7,166 (22.96%)
9.25% swing C. to SNP

RENFREWSHIRE NORTH AND WEST
(Scotland West Region)
E. 49,060 T. 27,495 (56.04%)

Derek Mackay, SNP	11,510
Stuart Clark, Lab.	9,946
Annabel Goldie, C.	5,489
Andrew Page, LD	550

SNP majority 1,564 (5.69%)
8.42% swing Lab. to SNP

RENFREWSHIRE SOUTH
(Scotland West Region)
E. 50,221 T. 26,908 (53.58%)

Hugh Henry, Lab.	12,933
Andrew Doig, SNP	10,356
Alistair Campbell, C.	2,917
Gordon Anderson, LD	702

Lab. majority 2,577 (9.58%)
5.41% swing Lab. to SNP

RUTHERGLEN
(Glasgow Region)
E. 57,777 T. 27,122 (46.94%)

James Kelly, Lab.	12,489
Jim McGuigan, SNP	10,710
Martyn McIntyre, C.	2,096
Lisa Strachan, LD	1,174
Caroline Johnstone, Ind.	633

Lab. majority 1,779 (6.56%)
7.43% swing Lab. to SNP

SHETLAND ISLANDS
(Highlands and Islands Region)
E. 17,505 T. 9,391 (53.65%)

Tavish Scott, LD	4,462
Billy Fox, Ind.	2,845
Jean Urquhart, SNP	1,134
Jamie Kerr, Lab.	620
Sandy Cross, C.	330

LD majority 1,617 (17.22%)
5.5% swing LD to Ind.

SKYE, LOCHABER AND BADENOCH
(Highlands and Islands Region)
E. 57,024 T. 31,915 (55.97%)

Dave Thompson, SNP	14,737
Alan MacRae, LD	9,742
Linda Stewart, Lab.	4,112
Kerensa Carr, C.	2,834
Ronnie Campbell, Ind.	490

SNP majority 4,995 (15.65%)
12.97% swing LD to SNP

STIRLING
(Scotland and Mid Fife Region)
E. 51,458 T. 30,406 (59.09%)

Bruce Crawford, SNP	14,858
John Hendry, Lab.	9,188
Neil Benny, C.	4,610
Graham Reed, LD	1,296
Jack Black, Ind.	454

SNP majority 5,670 (18.65%)
9.93% swing Lab. to SNP

STRATHKELVIN AND BEARSDEN
(Scotland West Region)
E. 59,323 T. 33,752 (56.90%)

Fiona McLeod, SNP	14,258
David Whitton, Lab.	12,456
Jean Turner, Ind.	6,742
Stephanie Fraser, C.	4,438
Gordon Macdonald, LD	2,600

SNP majority 1,802 (5.34%)
7.69% swing Lab. to SNP

UDDINGSTON AND BELLSHILL
(Central Scotland Region)
E. 55,584 T. 24,995 (44.97%)

Michael McMahon, Lab.	11,531
Richard Lyle, SNP	10,817
Mark Brown, C.	2,117
Fraser Macgregor, LD	530

Lab. majority 714 (2.86%)
9.04% swing Lab. to SNP

REGIONS
E. 3,985,161 T. 50.4%

GLASGOW
E. 514,393 T. 208,712 (40.57%)

SNP	83,109	(39.82%)
Lab.	73,031	(35.0%)
C.	12,749	(6.1%)
Green	12,454	(6.0%)
Respect	6,972	(3.3%)
LD	5,312	(2.5%)
ASPP	3,750	(1.8%)
BNP	2,424	(1.2%)
Socialist Labour	2,276	(1.1%)
Christian Party	1,501	(0.7%)
Scottish Unionist Party	1,447	(0.7%)
SSP	1,362	(0.7%)
UKIP	1,123	(0.5%)
Pirate	581	(0.3%)
Ind. Johnstone	338	(0.2%)
SHP	283	(0.1%)

Lab. majority 10,078 (4.3%)
8.04% swing Lab. to SNP (2007 Lab. majority 23,006)

ADDITIONAL MEMBERS
Humza Yousaf, SNP
Bob Doris, SNP
Hanzala Malik, Lab.
Drew Smith, Lab.
Anne McTaggert, Lab.
Ruth Davidson, C.
Patrick Harvie, Green

HIGHLANDS AND ISLANDS
E. 337,588 T. 179,010 (53.03%)

SNP	85,082	(47.5%)
Lab.	25,884	(14.5%)
C.	21,729	(12.1%)
LD	20,843	(11.6%)
Green	9,076	(5.1%)
Christian Party	3,541	(2%)
UKIP	3,372	(1.9%)
ASPP	2,770	(1.5%)
Ban Bankers Bonuses	1,764	(1%)
Lib.	1,696	(0.9%)
Soc. Lab.	1,406	(0.8%)
BNP	1,134	(0.6%)
SSP	509	(0.3%)
Solidarity	204	(0.1%)

SNP majority 59,198 (33.07%)
8.16% swing Lab. to SNP (2007 SNP majority 26,978)

ADDITIONAL MEMBERS
John Finnie, SNP
Jean Urquhart, SNP
Mike MacKenzie, SNP
Rhoda Grant, Lab.
David Stewart, Lab.
Jamie McGrigor, C.
Mary Scanlon, C.

LOTHIAN
E. 515,978 T. 283,203 (54.89%)

SNP	110,953	(39.2%)
Lab.	70,544	(24.9%)
C.	33,019	(11.7%)
Green	21,505	(7.6%)
LD	15,588	(5.5%)
ASPP	3,218	(1.1%)
BNP	1,978	(0.7%)
UKIP	1,822	(0.6%)
Soc. Lab.	1,681	(0.6%)
SSP	1,183	(0.4%)
Christian Party	914	(0.3%)
Lib.	697	(0.2%)
CPA	553	(0.2%)
Solidarity	327	(0.1%)
Ind. Hogg	294	(0.1%)
Ind. O'Neill	134	(0.1%)
Ind. Brown	61	(0.1%)

SNP majority 40,409 (14.27%)
7.03% swing Lab. to SNP (2007 SNP majority 524)

ADDITIONAL MEMBERS
Sarah Boyack, Lab.
Kezia Dugdale, Lab.
Neil Findlay, Lab.
David McLetchie, C.
Gavin Brown, C.
Alison Johnstone, Green
Margo MacDonald, Ind.

SCOTLAND CENTRAL
E. 497,737 T. 233,560 (46.92%)

SNP	108,261	(46.4%)
Lab.	82,459	(35.3%)
C.	14,870	(6.4%)
ASPP	5,793	(2.5%)
Green	5,634	(2.4%)
LD	3,318	(1.4%)
Christian Party	3,173	(1.4%)
Soci. Lab.	2,483	(1.1%)
BNP	2,214	(0.9%)
Scottish Unionist Party	1,555	(0.7%)
UKIP	1,263	(0.5%)
Ind. O'Donnell	821	(0.4%)
SSP	820	(0.4%)
Solidarity	559	(0.2%)
SHP	337	(0.1%)

Lab. majority 25,802 (11.05%)
10.08% swing Lab. to SNP (2007 Lab. majority 23,386)

ADDITIONAL MEMBERS
Richard Lyle, SNP
John Wilson, SNP
Claire Adamson, SNP
Siobhan McMahon, Lab.
Mark Griffin, Lab.
Margaret McCulloch, Lab.
Margaret Mitchell, C.

SCOTLAND MID AND FIFE
E. 503,559 T. 258,163 (51.27%)

SNP	116,691	(25.0%)
Lab.	64,623	(26.3%)
C.	36,458	(14.1%)
LD	15,103	(5.9%)
Green	10,914	(4.2%)
ASPP	4,113	(1.6%)
UKIP	2,838	(1.1%)
Soc. Lab.	1,771	(0.7%)
BNP	1,726	(0.7%)
Ind. Rodger	1,466	(0.6%)
SSP	834	(0.3%)
Christian Party	786	(0.3%)
CPA	638	(0.2%)
Solidarity	202	(0.1%)

SNP majority 52,068 (20.17%)
7.43% swing Lab. to SNP (2007 Lab. majority 18,168)

ADDITIONAL MEMBERS
Annabelle Ewing, SNP
John Park, Lab.
Claire Brennan-Baker, Lab.
Richard Simpson, Lab.
Murdo Fraser, C.
Elizabeth Smith, C.
Willie Rennie, LD

SCOTLAND NORTH EAST
E. 550,162 T. 267,045 (48.54%)

SNP	140,749	(52.7%)
Lab.	43,893	(16.4%)
C.	37,681	(14.1%)
LD	18,178	(6.8%)
Green	10,407	(3.9%)
ASPP	4,420	(1.7%)
UKIP	2,477	(0.9%)
Christian Party	2,159	(0.8%)
BNP	1,925	(0.7%)
Soc. Lab.	1,459	(0.5%)
Ind. Cox	758	(0.3%)
NF	640	(0.2%)
AIR	471	(0.2%)
Solidarity	286	(0.1%)
Ind. Henderson	237	(0.1%)
Ind. McBride	190	(0.1%)

SNP majority 96,856 (36.27%)
7.68% swing Lab. to SNP (2007 SNP majority 53,140)

ADDITIONAL MEMBERS
Mark McDonald, SNP
Richard Baker, Lab.
Jenny Marra, Lab.
Lewis McDonald, Lab.
Alex Johnstone, C.
Nanette Milne, C.
Alison McInnes, LD

SCOTLAND SOUTH
E. 529,682 T. 278,987 (52.67%)

SNP	114,270	(41.0%)
Lab.	70,595	(25.3%)
C.	54,352	(19.5%)
LD	15,096	(5.4%)
Green	8,656	(3.1%)
ASPP	4,418	(1.6%)
UKIP	3,243	(1.2%)
Soc. Lab.	2,906	(1.0%)
BNP	2,017	(0.7%)
Christian Party	1,924	(0.7%)
Solidarity	813	(0.3%)
SSP	697	(0.2%)

SNP majority 43,675 (15.66%)
7.95% swing Lab. to SNP (2007 Lab. majority 2,709)

ADDITIONAL MEMBERS
Joan McAlpine, SNP
Aileen McLeod, SNP
Paul Wheelhouse, SNP
Chic Brodie, SNP
Claudia Beamish, Lab.
Graeme Pearson, Lab.
Jim Hume, LD

SCOTLAND WEST
E. 536,062 T. 282,371 (52.68%)

SNP	117,306	(32.8%)
Lab.	92,530	(32.8%)
C.	35,995	(12.7%)
LD	9,148	(3.2%)
Green	8,414	(3.0%)
ASPP	4,771	(1.7%)
Soc. Lab.	2,865	(1.0%)
Christian Party	2,468	(0.9%)
BNP	2,162	(0.8%)
UKIP	2,000	(0.7%)
SSP	1,752	(0.6%)
Ban Bankers Bonuses	1,204	(0.4%)
Pirate	850	(0.3%)
Ind. Vassie	460	(0.2%)
Solidarity	446	(0.2%)

SNP majority 24,776 (8.77%)
7.4% swing Lab. to SNP (2007 Lab. majority 15,772)

ADDITIONAL MEMBERS
Stewart Maxwell, SNP
Stuart McMillan, SNP
Mary Fee, Lab.
Neil Bibby, Lab.
Margaret McDougall, Lab.
Annabel Goldie, C.
Jackson Carlaw, C.

NORTHERN IRELAND

NORTHERN IRELAND EXECUTIVE
Stormont Castle, Stormont, Belfast BT4 3TT
T 028-9052 0700
W www.northernireland.gov.uk

The first minister and deputy first minister head the executive committee of ministers and, acting jointly, determine the total number of ministers in the executive. First and deputy first ministers are elected by Northern Ireland assembly members through a formula of parallel consent that requires a majority of designated unionists, a majority of designated nationalists and a majority of the whole assembly to vote in favour. The parties elected to the assembly select ministerial portfolios in proportion to party strengths using the d'Hondt nominating procedure.

The executive committee includes five DUP ministers, four SF ministers, two Alliance members, one Social Democratic and Labour Party minister and one Ulster Unionist minister alongside the first minister Peter Robinson, MLA of the DUP and the deputy first minister, Martin McGuinness, MLA, of SF.

EXECUTIVE COMMITTEE
First Minister, Rt. Hon. Peter Robinson, MLA
Deputy First Minister, Martin McGuinness, MP, MLA
Junior Ministers, Martina Anderson, MLA; Jonathan Bell, MLA
Minister for Agriculture and Rural Development, Michelle O'Neill, MLA
Minister for Culture, Arts and Leisure, Carai ni Chuilin, MLA
Minister for Education, John O'Dowd, MLA
Minister for Employment and Learning, Dr Stephen Farry, MLA
Minister for Enterprise, Trade and Investment, Arlene Foster, MLA
Minister for Environment, Alex Atwood, MLA
Minister for Finance and Personnel, Sammy Wilson, MP, MLA
Minister for Health, Social Services and Public Safety, Edwin Poots, MLA
Minister for Justice, David Ford, MLA
Minister for Regional Development, Danny Kennedy, MLA
Minister for Social Development, Nelson McCausland, MLA

OFFICE OF THE FIRST MINISTER AND DEPUTY FIRST MINISTER
Stormont Castle, Stormont, Belfast BT4 3TT
T 028-9052 8400 W www.ofmdfmni.gov.uk

DEPARTMENT OF AGRICULTURE AND RURAL DEVELOPMENT
Dundonald House, Upper Newtownards Road, Belfast BT4 3SB
T 028-9052 4420 W www.dardni.gov.uk

EXECUTIVE AGENCIES
Forest Service
Rivers Agency

DEPARTMENT OF CULTURE, ARTS AND LEISURE
Causeway Exchange, 1–7 Bedford Street, Belfast BT1 7FB
T 028-9025 8825 W www.dcalni.gov.uk

DEPARTMENT OF EDUCATION
Rathgael House, Balloo Road, Bangor, Co. Down BT19 7PR
T 028-9127 9279 W www.deni.gov.uk

DEPARTMENT FOR EMPLOYMENT AND LEARNING
Adelaide House, 39–49 Adelaide Street, Belfast BT2 8FD
T 028-9025 7777 W www.delni.gov.uk

DEPARTMENT OF ENTERPRISE, TRADE AND INVESTMENT
Netherleigh, Massey Avenue, Belfast BT4 2JP T 028-9052 9900
W www.detini.gov.uk

EXECUTIVE AGENCIES
General Consumer Council for Northern Ireland
Health and Safety Executive
Invest Northern Ireland
Northern Ireland Tourist Board

DEPARTMENT OF THE ENVIRONMENT
Clarence Court, 10–18 Adelaide Street, Belfast BT2 8GB
T 028-9054 0540 W www.doeni.gov.uk

EXECUTIVE AGENCIES
Driver and Vehicle Agency (Northern Ireland)
NI Environment Agency
Planning Service

DEPARTMENT OF FINANCE AND PERSONNEL
Rathgael House, Balloo Road, Bangor BT19 7PR
T 028-9185 8111 W www.dfpni.gov.uk

EXECUTIVE AGENCIES
Land and Property Services
Northern Ireland Statistics and Research Agency (Incorporates Land Registers of Northern Ireland and Ordnance Survey of Northern Ireland)

DEPARTMENT OF HEALTH, SOCIAL SERVICES AND PUBLIC SAFETY
Castle Buildings, Stormont, Belfast BT4 3SJ T 028-9052 0500
W www.dhsspsni.gov.uk

DEPARTMENT FOR REGIONAL DEVELOPMENT
Clarence Court, 10–18 Adelaide Street, Belfast BT2 8GB
T 028-9054 0540 W www.drdni.gov.uk

EXECUTIVE AGENCY
Roads Agency

DEPARTMENT FOR SOCIAL DEVELOPMENT
Lighthouse Building, 1 Cromac Place, Gasworks Business Park, Ormeau Road, Belfast BT7 2JB T 028-9082 9028
W www.dsdni.gov.uk

EXECUTIVE AGENCIES
Northern Ireland Housing Executive
Social Security Agency

DEPARTMENT OF JUSTICE
Block B, Castle Buildings, Stormont Estate, Belfast BT4 3SG
T 028-9076 3000 W www.dojni.gov.uk

EXECUTIVE AGENCIES
Compensation Agency
Forensic Science Agency
Northern Ireland Courts and Tribunals Service
Northern Ireland Prison Service
Youth Justice Agency

NORTHERN IRELAND AUDIT OFFICE
106 University Street, Belfast BT7 1EU
T 028-9025 1000 E info@niauditoffice.gov.uk
W www.niauditoffice.gov.uk
Comptroller and Auditor-General, Kieran Donnelly

NORTHERN IRELAND AUTHORITY FOR UTILITY REGULATION
Queens House, 14 Queen Street, Belfast BT1 6ED
T 028-9031 1575 E info@uregni.gov.uk W www.uregni.gov.uk
Chair, Prof. Peter Matthews

NORTHERN IRELAND ASSEMBLY
Parliament Buildings, Stormont, Belfast BT4 3XX
T 028-9052 1137 E info@niassembly.gov.uk
W www.niassembly.gov.uk

The Northern Ireland Assembly was established as a result of the Belfast Agreement (also known as the Good Friday Agreement) in April 1998. The agreement was endorsed through a referendum held in May 1998 and subsequently given legal force through the Northern Ireland Act 1998.

The Northern Ireland Assembly has full legislative and executive authority for all matters that are the responsibility of the government's Northern Ireland departments – known as transferred matters. Excepted and reserved matters are defined in schedules 2 and 3 of the Northern Ireland Act 1998 and remain the responsibility of UK parliament.

The first assembly election occurred on 25 June 1998 and the 108 members elected met for the first time on 1 July 1998. Members of the Northern Ireland Assembly are elected by the single transferable vote system from 18 constituencies – six per constituency. Under the single transferable vote system every voter has a single vote that can be transferred from one candidate to another. Voters number their candidates in order of preference. Where candidates reach their quota of votes and are elected, surplus votes are transferred to other candidates according to the next preference on each voter's ballot slip. The candidate in each round with the fewest votes is eliminated and their surplus votes are redistributed according to the voter's next preference. The process is repeated until the required number of members are elected.

On 29 November 1999 the assembly appointed ten ministers as well as the chairs and deputy chairs for the ten statutory departmental committees. Devolution of powers to the Northern Ireland Assembly occurred on 2 December 1999, following several delays concerned with Sinn Fein's inclusion in the executive while Irish Republican Army (IRA) weapons were yet to be decommissioned.

Since the devolution of powers, the assembly has been suspended by the Secretary of State for Northern Ireland on four occasions. The first was between 11 February and 30 May 2000, with two 24-hour suspensions on 10 August and 22 September 2001 – all owing to a lack of progress in decommissioning. The final suspension took place on 14 October 2002 after unionists walked out of the executive following a police raid on Sinn Fein's office investigating alleged intelligence gathering.

The assembly was formally dissolved in April 2003 in anticipation of an election, which eventually took place on 26 November 2003. The results of the election changed the balance of power between the political parties, with an increase in the number of seats held by the Democratic Unionist Party (DUP) and Sinn Fein (SF), so that they became the largest parties. The assembly was restored to a state of suspension following the November election while political parties engaged in a review of the Belfast Agreement aimed at fully restoring the devolved institutions.

In July 2005 the leadership of the IRA formally ordered an end to its armed campaign; it authorised a representative to engage with the Independent International Commission on Decommissioning in order to verifiably put the arms beyond use. On 26 September 2005 General John de Chastelain, the chair of the commission, along with two independent church witnesses confirmed that the IRA's entire arsenal of weapons had been decommissioned.

Following the passing of the Northern Ireland Act 2006 the secretary of state created a non-legislative fixed-term assembly, whose membership consisted of the 108 members elected in the 2003 election. It first met on 15 May 2006 with the remit of making preparations for the restoration of devolved government; its discussions informed the next round of talks called by the British and Irish governments held at St Andrews. The St Andrews agreement of 13 October 2006 led to the establishment of the transitional assembly.

The Northern Ireland (St Andrews Agreement) Act 2006 set out a timetable to restore devolution, and also set the date for the third election to the assembly as 7 March 2007. The DUP and SF again had the largest number of Members of the Legislative Assembly (MLAs) elected, and although the initial restoration deadline of 26 March was missed, the leaders of the DUP and SF (Revd Dr Ian Paisley, MP, MLA and Gerry Adams, MLA, respectively) took part in a historic meeting and made a joint commitment to establish an executive committee in the assembly to which devolved powers were restored on 8 May 2007. After completing a full four-year mandate, new assembly elections took place on 5 May 2011 to elect the 108 members of the legislative assembly.

SALARIES *as at May 2011*	
Assembly Member	£43,101

NORTHERN IRELAND ASSEMBLY MEMBERS
as at May 2011
Agnew, Steven, *Green, North Down*
Allister, Jim, *TUV, North Antrim*
Anderson, Martina, *SF, Foyle*
Anderson, Sydney, *DUP, Upper Bann*
Attwood, Alex, *SDLP, Belfast West*
Beggs, Roy, *UUP, East Antrim*
Bell, Jonathan, *DUP, Strangford*
Boylan, Cathal, *SF, Newry and Armagh*
Boyle, Michaela, *SF, West Tyrone*
Bradley, Dominic, *SDLP, Newry and Armagh*
Bradley, Paula, *SDLP, South Down*
Brady, Mickey, *SF, Newry and Armagh*
Buchanan, Thomas, *DUP, West Tyrone*
Byrne, Joe, *SDLP, West Tyrone*
Campbell, Gregory, *DUP, East Londonderry*
Clarke, Trevor, *DUP, South Antrim*
Clarke, Willie, *SF, South Down*
Cochrane, Judith, *Alliance, Belfast East*
Copeland, Michael, *UUP, Belfast East*
Craig, Jonathan, *DUP, Lagan Valley*
Cree, Leslie, *UUP, North Down*
Dallat, John, *SDLP, East Londonderry*

Dickson, Stewart, *Alliance, East Antrim*
Dobson, Jo-Anne, *UUP, Upper Bann*
Doherty, Pat, *SF, West Tyrone*
Douglas, Sammy, *DUP, Belfast East*
Dunne, Gordon, *DUP, North Down*
Durkan, Mark, *SDLP, Foyle*
Easton, Alex, *DUP, North Down*
Eastwood, Colum, *SDLP, Foyle*
Elliot, Tom, *UUP, Fermanagh and South Tyrone*
Farry, Stephen, *Alliance, North Down*
Flanagan, Phil, *SF, Fermanagh and South Tyrone*
Ford, David, *Alliance, South Antrim*
Foster, Arlene, *DUP, Fermanagh and South Tyrone*
Frew, Paul, *DUP, North Antrim*
Gardiner, Samuel, *UUP, Upper Bann*
Gildernew, Michelle, *SF, Fermanagh and South Tyrone*
Girvan, Paul, *DUP, South Antrim*
Givan, Paul, *DUP, Lagan Valley*
Hale, Brenda, *DUP, Lagan Valley*
Hamilton, Simon, *DUP, Strangford*
Hay, William, *DUP, Foyle*
Hilditch, David, *DUP, East Antrim*
Humphrey, William, *DUP, Belfast North*
Hussey, Ross, *UUP, West Tyrone*
Irwin, William, *DUP, Newry and Armagh*
Kelly, Dolores, *SDLP, Upper Bann*
Kelly, Gerry, *SF, Belfast North*
Kennedy, Danny, *UUP, Newry and Armagh*
Kinahan, Danny, *UUP, South Antrim*
Lewis, Pam, *DUP, South Antrim*
Lo, Anna, *Alliance, Belfast South*
Lunn, Trevor, *Alliance, Lagan Valley*
Lyttle, Chris, *Alliance, Belfast East*
Lynch, Sean, *SDLP, Fermanagh and South Tyrone*
Maginness, Alban, *SDLP, Belfast North*
Maskey, Alex, *SF, Belfast South*
Maskey, Paul, *SF, Belfast West*
McCallister, John, *UUP, South Down*
McCann, Fra, *SF,Belfast West*
McCann, Jennifer, *SF, Belfast West*
McCarthy, Kieran, *Alliance, Strangford*
McCartney, Raymond, *SF, Foyle*
McCausland, Nelson, *DUP, Belfast North*
McClarty, David, *UUP, East Londonderry*
McCrea, Basil, *UUP, Lagan Valley*
McCrea, Ian, *DUP, Mid Ulster*
McDevitt, Conall, *SDLP, Belfast South*
McDonnell, Dr Alasdair, *SDLP, Belfast South*
McElduff, Barry, *SF, West Tyrone*
McGimpsey, Michael, *UUP, Belfast South*
McGlone, Patsy, *SDLP, Mid Ulster*
McGuinness, Martin, *SF, Mid Ulster*
McIlveen, David, *DUP, North Antrim*
McIlveen, Michelle, *DUP, Strangford*
McKay, Daithi, *SF, North Antrim*
McKevitt, Karen, *SDLP, South Down*
McLaughlin, Mitchel, *SF, South Antrim*
McMullan, Oliver, *SF, East Antrim*
McNarry, David, *UUP, Strangford*
McQuillan, Adrian, *DUP, East Londonderry*
Molloy, Francie, *SF, Mid Ulster*
Morrow, Lord, *DUP, Fermanagh and South Tyrone*
Moutray, Stephen, *DUP, Upper Bann*
Murphy, Conor, *SF, Newry and Armagh*
Nesbitt, Mike, *UUP, Strangford*
Newton, Robin, *DUP, Belfast East*
Ni Chuilin, Caral, *SF, Belfast North*
O'Dowd, John, *SF, Upper Bann*

O hOisin, Cathal, *SF, East Londonderry*
O'Neill, Michelle, *SF, Mid Ulster*
Overend, Sandra, *UUP, Mid Ulster*
Poots, Edwin, *DUP, Lagan Valley*
Ramsey, Pat, *SDLP, Foyle*
Ramsey, Sue, *SF, Belfast West*
Ritchie, Margaret, *SDLP, South Down*
Robinson, George, *DUP, East Londonderry*
Robinson, Peter, *DUP, Belfast East*
Ross, Alastair, *DUP, East Antrim*
Ruane, Caitriona, *SF, South Down*
Sheehan, Pat, *SF, Belfast West*
Spratt, Jimmy, *DUP, Belfast South*
Storey, Mervyn, *DUP, North Antrim*
Swann, Robin, *UUP, North Antrim*
Weir, Peter, *DUP, North Down*
Wells, Jim, *DUP, South Down*
Wilson, Sammy, *DUP, East Antrim*

STATE OF THE PARTIES *as at May 2011*

Party	Seats
Democratic Unionist Party (DUP)	38
Sinn Fein (SF)	29
Ulster Unionist Party (UUP)	16
Social Democratic and Labour Party (SDLP)	14
Alliance Party (Alliance)	8
Green Party	1
Independent (Ind.)	1
Traditional Unionist Voice (TUV)	1
Total	108

NORTHERN IRELAND ASSEMBLY ELECTION RESULTS

As at 5 May 2011
E. 1,210,009 T. 55.64%

E. Electorate T. Turnout
First = first-preference votes
Final = final total for that candidate, after all necessary transfers of lower-preference votes
R. = round
* = eliminated last
See General Election Results for a list of party abbreviations

ANTRIM EAST
E. 61,617 T. 29,430 (47.76%)

	First	Final	Elected (R.)
Sammy Wilson, DUP	7,181	7,181	First (1)
David Hilditch, DUP	3,288	4,219	Second (2)
Roy Beggs, UUP	3,042	4,194	Fifth (9)
Stewart Dickson, Alliance	2,889	4,777	Fourth (9)
Oliver McMullan, SF	2,369	3,389	Sixth (10)
*Rodney McCune, UUP	1,851	2,890	
Gerardine Mulvenna, Alliance	1,620		
Alastair Ross, DUP	1,608	4,267	Third (6)
Ruth Wilson, TUV	1,346		
Justin McCamphill, SDLP	1,333		
Gordon Lyons, DUP	1,321		
Daniel Donnelly, Green	664		
Steven Moore, BNP	511		

ANTRIM NORTH
E. 74,760 T. 40,983 (54.82%)

	First	Final	Elected (R.)
Paul Frew, DUP	6,581	6,581	First (1)
Daithi McKay, SF	6,152	6,152	Second (1)
Mervyn Storey, DUP	6,083	6,083	Third (1)
Jim Allister, TUV	4,061	5,430	Sixth (9)
*Declan O'Loan, SDLP	3,682	4,816	
David McIlveen, DUP	3,275	6,594	Fourth (8)
Evelyne Robinson, DUP	3,256		
Robin Swann, UUP	2,518	5,557	Fifth (9)
Bill Kennedy, UUP	2,189		
Jayne Dunlop, Alliance	1,848		
Audrey Patterson, TUV	668		

ANTRIM SOUTH
E. 65,231 T. 32,652 (50.06%)

	First	Final	Elected (R.)
Paul Girvan, DUP	4,844	4,844	First (1)
Mitchel McLaughlin, SF	4,662	4,662	Second (1)
Trevor Clarke, UUP	4,607	4,607	Third (1)
David Ford, Alliance	4,554	4,660	Fourth (2)
Danny Kinahan, UUP	3,445	5,585	Fifth (3)
*Thomas Burns, SDLP	3,406	3,591	
Pam Lewis, DUP	2,866	4,668	Sixth (4)
Adrian Cochrane-Watson, UUP	2,285		
Mel Lucas, TUV	1,091		
Stephen Parkes, BNP	404		

BELFAST EAST
E. 61,263 T. 32,828 (53.59%)

	First	Final	Elected (R.)
Peter Robinson, DUP	9,149	9,149	First (1)
Judith Cochrane, Alliance	4,329	4,755	Third (7)
Chris Lyttle, Alliance	4,183	4,696	Fourth (9)
Sammy Douglas, DUP	2,668	4,783	Fifth (11)
Robin Newton, DUP	2,436	4,801	Second (2)
Michael Copeland, UUP	2,194	3,723	Sixth (11)
*Dawn Purvis, Ind.	1,702	2,789	
Brian Ervine, PUP	1,493		
Niall O'Donnghaile, SF	1,030		
Philip Robinson, UUP	943		
Harry Toan, TUV	712		
Martin Gregg, Green	572		
Ann Cooper, BNP	337		
Magdalena Wolska, SDLP	250		
Tommy Black, SP	201		
Kevin McNally, WP	102		
Stephen Stewart, Ind.	46		

BELFAST NORTH
E. 68,119 T. 34,280 (50.32%)

	First	Final	Elected (R.)
Gerry Kelly, SF	6,674	6,674	First (1)
Nelson McCausland, DUP	5,200	5,200	Second (1)
Alban Maginness, SDLP	4,025	5,004	Fourth (6)
William Humphrey, DUP	3,724	4,332	Fifth (7)
Paula Bradley, DUP	3,488	4,065	Sixth (7)
Caral Ni Chuilin, SF	2,999	4,868	Third (6)
*Fred Cobain, UUP	2,758	3,623	
Billy Webb, Alliance	2,096		
Raymond McCord, Ind.	1,176		
JJ Magee, SF	998		
John Lavery, WP	332		

BELFAST SOUTH
E. 62,484 T. 32,752 (52.42%)

	First	Final	Elected (R.)
Anna Lo, Alliance	6,390	6,390	First (1)
Dr Alasdair McDonnell, SDLP	4,527	4,916	Second (2)
Jimmy Spratt, DUP	4,045	4,281	Sixth (5)
Alex Maskey, SF	4,038	4,452	Fourth (5)
*Ruth Patterson, DUP	3,800	4,163	
Connall McDevitt, SDLP	3,191	4,445	Fifth (5)
Michael McGimpsey, UUP	2,988	4,622	Third (5)
Mark Finlay, UUP	1,394		
Claire Bailey, Green	889		
Brian Faloon, PBP	414		
Paddy Meehan, SP	234		
Nico Torregrosa, UKIP	234		
Paddy Lynn, WP	135		
Charles Smyth, Pro-Capitalism	29		

BELFAST WEST
E. 61,520 T. 35,618 (57.89%)

	First	Final	Elected (R.)
Paul Maskey, SF	5,343	5,343	First (1)
Jennifer McCann, SF	5,239	5,239	Second (1)
Fra McCann, SF	4,481	5,167	Third (10)
Sue Ramsey, SF	4,116	4,823	Fifth (11)
Alex Atwood, SDLP	3,765	5,152	Fourth (10)
Pat Sheehan, SF	3,723	4,327	Sixth (11)
*Brian Kingston, DUP	2,587	3,867	
Gerry Carroll, PBP	1,661		
Bill Manwaring, UUP	1,471		
Colin Keenan, SDLP	802		
John Lowry, WP	586		
Pat Lawlor, SP	384		
Dan McGuinness, Alliance	365		
Brian Pelan, Ind.	122		

DOWN NORTH
E. 62,170 T. 28,528 (45.89%)

	First	Final	Elected (R.)
Alex Easton, DUP	5,175	5,175	First (1)
Gordon Dunne, DUP	3,741	4,121	Second (2)
Peter Weir, DUP	3,496	4,101	Third (2)
Stephen Farry, Alliance	3,131	4,078	Fourth (10)
Steven Agnew, Green	2,207	3,229	Sixth (11)
*Anne Wilson, Alliance	2,100	3,130	
Alan McFarland, Ind.	1,879		
Alan Chambers, Ind.	1,765		
Leslie Cree, UUP	1,585	4,015	Fifth (10)
Colin Breen, UUP	1,343		
Liam Logan, SDLP	768		
Fred McGlade, UKIP	615		
Conor Keenan, SF	293		

DOWN SOUTH
E. 73,240 T. 42,551 (58.10%)

	First	Final	Elected (R.)
Margaret Ritchie, SDLP	8,506	8,506	First (1)
Catriona Ruane, SF	5,955	6,192	Second (2)
Jim Wells, DUP	5,200	6,543	Third (5)
John McCallister, UUP	4,409	6,240	Fourth (6)
Willie Clarke, SF	3,882	6,777	Fifth (7)
Karen McKevitt, SDLP	3,758	5,347	Sixth (9)
Naomi Bailie, SF	3,050		
*Eamonn O'Neill, SDLP	2,663	4,883	
Henry Reilly, UKIP	2,332		
Cadogan Enright, Green	1,107		
David Griffin, Alliance	864		

FERMANAGH AND SOUTH TYRONE
E. 70,985 T. 48,949 (68.96%)

	First	Final	Elected (R.)
Michelle Gildernew, SF	9,110	9,110	First (1)
Tom Elliott, UUP	6,896	6,896	Second (1)
Arlene Foster, DUP	6,876	6,876	Third (3)
Sean Lynch, SF	5,146	6,476	Fifth (6)
Phil Flanagan, SF	5,082	6,137	Sixth (6)
Maurice Morrow, DUP	4,844	7,229	Fourth (5)
*Tommy Gallagher, SDLP	4,606	6,075	
Kenny Donaldson, UUP	2,366		
Alex Elliott, TUV	1,231		
Pat Cox, Ind.	997		
Hannah Su, Alliance	845		

FOYLE
E. 68,663 T. 39,686 (57.80%)

	First	Final	Elected (R.)
William Hay, DUP	7,154	7,154	First (1)
Martina Anderson, SF	6,950	6,950	Second (1)
Mark Durkan, SDLP	4,970	5,794	Third (4)
Raymond McCartney, SF	3,638	6,245	Fourth (7)
Pat Ramsey, SDLP	3,138	4,876	Sixth (7)
*Eamonn McCann (PBP)	3,120	3,916	
Colum Eastwood, SDLP	2,967	5,563	Fifth (7)
Pol Callaghan, SDLP	2,624		
Paul Fleming, SF	2,612		
Paul McFadden, Ind.	1,280		
Keith McGrellis, Alliance	334		
Terry Doherty, Ind.	60		

LAGAN VALLEY
E. 67,532 T. 35,842 (53.07%)

	First	Final	Elected (R.)
Edwin Poots, DUP	7,329	7,329	First (1)
Basil McCrea, UUP	5,771	5,771	Second (1)
Trevor Lunn, Alliance	4,389	5,120	Fourth (6)
Paul Givan, DUP	4,352	5,518	Fifth (7)
Jonathan Craig, DUP	4,263	5,081	Third (5)
Brenda Hale, DUP	2,910	4,791	Sixth (7)
*Pat Catney, SDLP	2,165	3,406	
Mark Hill, UUP	1,482		
Mary-Kate Quinn, SF	1,203		
Lyle Rea, TUV	1,031		
Conor Quinn, Green	592		

LONDONDERRY EAST
E. 65,226 T. 35,303 (54.12%)

	First	Final	Elected (R.)
Gregory Campbell, DUP	6,319	6,319	First (1)
Cathal O hOisin, SF	4,681	4,962	Third (6)
George Robinson, DUP	3,855	4,823	Fourth (7)
David McClarty (Ind.)	3,003	4,405	Fifth (7)
John Dallat, SDLP	2,967	5,207	Second (6)
Bernadette Archibald, SF	2,639		
Adrian McQuillan, DUP	2,633	3,782	Sixth (7)
Thomas Conway	2,222		
Barney Fitzpatrick, Alliance	1,905		
Boyd Douglas, TUV	1,568		
Lesley Macaulay, UUP	1,472		
*David Harding, UUP	1,458	3,460	

NEWRY AND ARMAGH
E. 77,544 T. 47,562 (61.34%)

	First	Final	Elected (R.)
Conor Murphy, SF	9,127	9,127	First (1)
Danny Kennedy, UUP	8,718	8,718	Second (1)
Dominic Bradley, SDLP	7,123	7,123	Third (1)
Cathal Boylan, SF	6,614	8,092	Fourth (2)
William Irwin, DUP	6,101	7,502	Fifth (3)
*Thomas O'Hanlon, SDLP	3,825	5,014	
Mickey Brady, SF	3,254	5,625	Sixth (6)
Barrie Halliday, TUV	830		
David Murphy, Alliance	734		
Robert Woods, UKIP	98		
James Malone, ND	90		

STRANGFORD
E. 62,178 T. 30,186 (48.55%)

	First	Final	Elected (R.)
Michelle McIlveen, DUP	4,573	4,573	First (1)
Kieran McCarthy, Alliance	4,284	4,284	Second (1)
Jonathan Bell, DUP	4,265	4,265	Third (1)
Simon Hamilton, DUP	3,456	5,745	Fourth (5)
Mike Nesbitt, UUP	3,273	4,072	Fifth (6)
David McNarry, UUP	2,733	3,767	Sixth (6)
*Joe Boyle, SDLP	2,525	3,308	
Billy Walker, DUP	2,175		
Mickey Coogan, SF	902		
Terry Williams, TUV	841		
Cecil Andrews, UKIP	601		

TYRONE WEST
E. 62,970 T. 40,323 (64.04%)

	First	Final	Elected (R.)
Barry McElduff, SF	6,008	6,008	First (1)
Pat Doherty, SF	5,630	5,630	Second (1)
Michaela Boyle, SF	5,053	7,792	Third (4)
Tom Buchanan, DUP	5,027	5,162	Fifth (5)
Ross Hussey, UUP	4,072	4,398	Sixth (5)
*Allan Bresland, DUP	4,059	4,124	
Joe Byrne, SDLP	3,353	5,321	Fourth (5)
Declan McAleer, SF	3,008		
Paddy McGowan, Ind.	1,145		
Eugene McMenamin, Ind.	1,096		
Eric Bullick, Ind.	852		

ULSTER MID
E. 66,602 T. 43,522 (65.35%)

	First	Final	Elected (R.)
Martin McGuinness, SF	8,957	8,957	First (1)
Ian McCrea, DUP	7,127	7,127	Second (1)
Michelle O'Neill, SF	5,178	5,735	Sixth (7)
Patsy McGlone, SDLP	5,065	6,110	Third (5)
Sandra Overend, UUP	4,409	7,130	Fourth (6)
Francie Molloy, SF	4,263	5,191	Fifth (7)
*Ian Milne, SF	2,635	4,412	
Walter Millar, TUV	2,075		
Austin Kelly, SDLP	1,214		
Hugh McCloy, Ind.	933		
Michael McDonald, Alliance	398		
Harry Hutchinson, PBP	243		
Gary McCann, Ind.	241		

UPPER BANN
E. 77,905 T. 43,113 (55.34%)

	First	Final	Elected (R.)
John O'Dowd, SF	6,649	6,649	First (1)
Sydney Anderson, DUP	5,584	6,163	Second (5)
Stephen Moutray, DUP	5,645	6,085	Third (5)
*Johnny McGibbon, SF	4,879	5,438	
Dolores Kelly, SDLP	4,846	5,787	Sixth (7)
Sam Gardiner, UUP	3,676	6,012	Fourth (7)
Colin McCusker, UUP	3,402		
Joanne Dobson, UUP	3,348	5,827	Fifth (7)
Harry Hamilton, Alliance	1,979		
David Vance, TUV	1,026		
Sheila McQuaid, Alliance	786		
Barbara Trotter, UKIP	272		

EUROPEAN PARLIAMENT

European parliament elections take place at five-yearly intervals; the first direct elections to the parliament were held in 1979. In mainland Britain, members of the European parliament (MEPs) were elected in all constituencies on a first-past-the-post basis until 1999, when a regional system of proportional representation was introduced; in Northern Ireland three MEPs have been elected by the single transferable vote system of proportional representation since 1979. From 1979 to 1994 the number of seats held by the UK in the European parliament was 81, which increased to 87 in the 1994 election, decreased to 78 following EU enlargement in 2004, and decreased to 72 (England 59, Wales 4, Scotland 6, Northern Ireland 3) for the 2009 election as a result of Bulgaria and Romania joining the EU in 2007. Under the Lisbon treaty, which came into force in December 2009, the UK will gain an extra seat. This seat will be added to the West Midlands region and will be filled by a Conservative MEP, based on the results from the 2009 European parliament elections; however, the earliest he/she could be installed is January 2012.

At the 2009 European parliament elections all UK MEPs were elected under a 'closed-list' regional system of proportional representation, with England being divided into nine regions* and Scotland, Wales and Northern Ireland each constituting a single region each. Parties submitted a list of candidates for each region in their own order of preference. Votes were cast for a party or an independent candidate, and the first seat in each region was allocated to the party or candidate with the highest number of votes. The rest of the seats in each region were then allocated broadly in proportion to each party's share of the vote. Each region returned the following number of members: East Midlands, 5; Eastern, 7; London, 8; North East, 3; North West, 8; South East, 10; South West, 6; West Midlands, 6; Yorkshire and the Humber, 6; Wales, 4; Northern Ireland, 3; Scotland, 6.

If a vacancy occurs due to the resignation or death of an MEP, it is filled by the next available person on that party's list. If an independent MEP resigns or dies, a by-election is held. Where an MEP leaves the party on whose list he/she was elected, there is no requirement to resign the post of MEP, and he/she can remain in office until the next election.

British subjects and nationals of member states of the European Union are eligible for election to the European parliament provided they are 18 or over and not subject to disqualification. Since 1994, eligible citizens have had the right to vote in elections to the European parliament in the UK as long as they are entered on the electoral register.

MEPs previously received a salary set at the level of the national parliamentary salary of their country. In July 2009 an MEP statute introduced a uniform salary for all MEPs, set at a rate of 38.5 per cent of the basic salary of a European court of justice judge. In 2011 this approximated an annual salary of €95,482 (£84,826).

The next elections to the European parliament will take place in 2014. For further information visit the UK's European parliament website (W www.europarl.org.uk).

* Since June 2004 residents of Gibraltar vote in the South West region.

UK MEMBERS *as at September 2011*

* Denotes membership of the last European parliament
† Previously sat as a member of the Conservative party
‡ Previously sat as a member of UUP

Agnew, John Stuart (*b.* 1949), *UKIP, Eastern*
Andreasen, Marta (*b.* 1954), *UKIP, South East*
***Ashworth**, Richard (*b.* 1947), *C., South East*
***Atkins**, Rt. Hon. Sir Robert (*b.* 1946), *C., North West*
***Batten**, Gerard (*b.* 1954), *UKIP, London*
Bearder, Catherine (*b.* 1949) *LD, South East*
***Bloom**, Godfrey (*b.* 1949), *UKIP, Yorkshire and the Humber*
***Bowles**, Sharon M. (*b.* 1953), *LD, South East*
***Bradbourn**, Philip, OBE (*b.* 1951), *C., West Midlands*
Brons, Andrew H. W. (*b.* 1947), *BNP, Yorkshire and the Humber*
Bufton, John (*b.* 1962), *UKIP, Wales*
***Callanan**, Martin (*b.* 1961), *C., North East*
Campbell Bannerman, David (*b.* 1960), *UKIP, Eastern*
***Cashman**, Michael (*b.* 1950), *Lab., West Midlands*
***Chichester**, Giles B. (*b.* 1946), *C., South West*
***Clark**, Derek Rowland (*b.* 1933), *UKIP, East Midlands*
Colman, Trevor (*b.* 1941), *UKIP, South West*
Dartmouth, Earl of (*b.* 1949), *UKIP, South West*
***Davies**, Chris G. (*b.* 1954), *LD, North West*
***de Brún**, Bairbre (*b.* 1954), *SF, Northern Ireland*
***Deva**, Nirj J. A. (*b.* 1948), *C., South East*
Dodds, Diane (*b.* 1958), *DUP, Northern Ireland*
***Duff**, Andrew N. (*b.* 1950), *LD, Eastern*
***Elles**, James E. M. (*b.* 1949), *C., South East*
***Evans**, Jill R. (*b.* 1959), *PC, Wales*
***Farage**, Nigel P. (*b.* 1964), *UKIP, South East*
Ford, Vicky (*b.* 1967), *C. Eastern*
Foster, Jacqueline (*b.* 1947), *C., North West*
Fox, Ashley (*b.* 1969), *C., South West*
Girling, Julie (*b.* 1956), *C., South West*
Griffin, Nick (*b.* 1959), *BNP, North West*
***Hall**, Fiona (*b.* 1955), *LD, North East*
***Hannan**, Daniel J. (*b.* 1971), *C., South East*
***Harbour**, Malcolm (*b.* 1947), *C., West Midlands*
***Helmer**, Roger (*b.* 1944), *C., East Midlands*
***Honeyball**, Mary (*b.* 1952), *Lab., London*
***Howitt**, Richard (*b.* 1961), *Lab., Eastern*
***Hudghton**, Ian (*b.* 1951), *SNP, Scotland*
***Hughes**, Stephen (*b.* 1952), *Lab., North East*
***Kamall**, Dr Syed S. (*b.* 1967), *C., London*
***Karim**, Sajjad (*b.* 1970), *C., North West*
***Kirkhope**, Timothy J. R. (*b.* 1945), *C., Yorkshire and the Humber*
***Lambert**, Jean D. (*b.* 1950), *Green, London*
***Ludford**, Baroness Sarah (*b.* 1951), *LD, London*
***Lynne**, Elizabeth (*b.* 1948), *LD, West Midlands*
Lyon, George (*b.* 1956), *LD, Scotland*
***McAvan**, Linda (*b.* 1962), *Lab., Yorkshire and the Humber*
***McCarthy**, Arlene (*b.* 1960), *Lab., North West*
McClarkin, Emma (*b.* 1978), *C., East Midlands*
*†**McMillan-Scott**, Edward H. C. (*b.* 1949), *LD, Yorkshire and the Humber*
***Martin**, David W. (*b.* 1954), *Lab., Scotland*
***Moraes**, Claude (*b.* 1965), *Lab., London*
***Nattrass**, Mike (*b.* 1945), *UKIP, West Midlands*
***Newton Dunn**, Bill F. (*b.* 1941), *LD, East Midlands*

*‡**Nicholson**, James (b. 1945), *UCUNF, Northern Ireland*
Nuttall, Paul (b. 1976), *UKIP, North West*
***Simpson**, Brian (b. 1953), *Lab., North West*
Sinclaire, Nikki (b. 1968), *Ind., West Midlands*
***Skinner**, Peter W. (b. 1959), *Lab., South East*
***Smith**, Alyn (b. 1973), *SNP, Scotland*
***Stevenson**, Struan (b. 1948), *C., Scotland*
***Stihler**, Catherine D. (b. 1973), *Lab., Scotland*
***Sturdy**, Robert W. (b. 1944), *C., Eastern*

Swinburne, Dr Kay (b. 1967), *C., Wales*
***Tannock**, Dr Charles (b. 1957), *C., London*
Taylor, Keith (b. 1953), *Green, South East*
***Van Orden**, Geoffrey (b. 1945), *C., Eastern*
Vaughan, Derek (b. 1961), *Lab., Wales*
***Wallis**, Diana (b. 1954), *LD, Yorkshire and the Humber*
***Watson**, Sir Graham R. (b. 1956), *LD, South West*
***Willmott**, Glenis (b. 1951), *Lab., East Midlands*
Yannakoudakis, Marina (b. 1956), *C., London*

UK REGIONS *as at 4 June 2009 election*

Abbreviations

AC	Animals Count
ChP	Christian Party
JT	Jury Team
Libertas	Libertas
No2EU	No2EU Yes to Democracy
Peace	Peace Party
Pensioners	Pensioners Party
Roman	Roman Party
SGB	Socialist Party of Great Britain
SLP	Socialist Labour Party
SSP	Scottish Socialist Party
TUV	Traditional Unionist Voice
UCUNF	Ulster Conservatives and Unionists – New Force
UKF	United Kingdom First
YD	Wai D (Your Decision)
Yes2EU	YES2EUROPE

For other abbreviations, *see* UK General Election Results. For detailed information on which areas of the country are covered by a particular region, please contact the Home Office.

E. 44,173,690　　T. 34.48%

EASTERN
(Bedfordshire, Cambridgeshire, Essex, Hertfordshire, Luton, Norfolk, Peterborough, Southend-on-Sea, Suffolk, Thurrock)

E. 4,252,669	T. 38.0%
C.	500,331 (31.2%)
UKIP	313,921 (19.6%)
LD	221,235 (13.8%)
Lab.	167,833 (10.5%)
Green	141,016 (8.8%)
BNP	97,013 (6.1%)
UKF	38,185 (2.4%)
Eng. Dem.	32,211 (2.0%)
CPA	24,646 (1.5%)
No2EU	13,939 (0.9%)
SLP	13,599 (0.8%)
AC	13,201 (0.8%)
Libertas	9,940 (0.6%)
Ind.	9,916 (0.6%)
JT	6,354 (0.4%)
C. majority	186,410

(June 2004, C. maj. 169,366)

MEMBERS ELECTED
1. *G. Van Orden, C. 2. D. Campbell Bannerman, *UKIP* 3. *R. Sturdy, C.

4. *A. Duff, *LD* 5. *R. Howitt, *Lab.*
6. V. Ford, *C.* 7. J. Agnew, *UKIP*

EAST MIDLANDS
(Derby, Derbyshire, Leicester, Leicestershire, Lincolnshire, Northamptonshire, Nottingham, Nottinghamshire, Rutland)

E. 3,312,944	T. 37.51%
C.	370,275 (30.2%)
Lab.	206,945 (16.9%)
UKIP	201,984 (16.4%)
LD	151,428 (12.3%)
BNP	106,319 (8.7%)
Green	83,939 (6.8%)
Eng. Dem.	28,498 (2.3%)
UKF	20,561 (1.7%)
CPA	17,907 (1.5%)
SLP	13,590 (1.1%)
No2EU	11,375 (0.9%)
Libertas	7,882 (0.6%)
JT	7,362 (0.6%)
C. majority	204,243

(June 2004, C. maj. 4,864)

MEMBERS ELECTED
1. *R. Helmer, C. 2.*G. Willmott, *Lab.* 3. *D. Clark, *UKIP*
4. E. McClarkin, C. 5. *W. Newton Dunn, *LD*

LONDON

E. 5,257,624	T. 33.53%
C.	479,037 (27.4%)
Lab.	372,590 (21.3%)
LD	240,156 (13.7%)
Green	190,589 (10.9%)
UKIP	188,440 (10.8%)
BNP	86,420 (4.9%)
CPA	51,336 (2.9%)
Ind.	50,014 (2.9%)
Eng. Dem.	24,477 (1.4%)
No2EU	17,758 (1.0%)
SLP	15,306 (0.9%)
Libertas	8,444 (0.5%)
JT	7,284 (0.4%)
Ind, SC	4,918 (0.3%)
SGB	4,050 (0.2%)
Yes2EU	3,384 (0.2%)
Ind.	3,248 (0.2%)
Ind.	1,972 (0.1%)
Ind.	1,603 (0.1%)
C. majority	106,447

(June 2004, C. maj. 38,357)

MEMBERS ELECTED
1. *C. Tannock, C. 2. *C. Moraes, *Lab.* 3. *Baroness Ludford, *LD*
4. *S. Kamall, C. 5. *J. Lambert, *Green* 6. *G. Batten, *UKIP* 7. *M. Honeyball, *Lab.* 8. M. Yannakoudakis, C.

NORTH EAST
(Co. Durham, Darlington, Hartlepool, Middlesbrough, Northumberland, Redcar and Cleveland, Stockton-on-Tees, Tyne and Wear)

E. 1,939,709	T. 30.50%
Lab.	147,338 (25.0%)
C.	116,911 (19.8%)
LD	103,644 (17.6%)
UKIP	90,700 (15.4%)
BNP	52,700 (8.9%)
Green	34,081 (5.8%)
Eng. Dem.	13,007 (2.2%)
SLP	10,238 (1.7%)
No2EU	8,066 (1.4%)
CPA	7,263 (1.2%)
Libertas	3,010 (0.5%)
JT	2,904 (0.5%)
Lab. majority	30,427

(June 2004, Lab. maj. 121,088)

MEMBERS ELECTED
1. *S. Hughes, *Lab.* 2. *M. Callanan, C. 3. *Ms F. Hall, *LD*

NORTHERN IRELAND
(Northern Ireland forms a three-member seat with a single transferable vote system)

E. 1,141,979	T. 42.81%
	1st Pref. Votes
Bairbre de Brún, *SF*	126,184 (26.0%)
Diane Dodds, *DUP*	88,346 (18.2%)
Jim Nicholson, *UCUNF*	82,893 (17.1%)
Alban Maginness, *SDLP*	78,489 (16.2%)
Jim Allister, *TUV*	66,197 (13.7%)
Ian James Parsley, *Alliance*	26,699 (5.5%)
Steven Agnew, *Green*	15,764 (3.3%)

MEMBERS ELECTED
1. *B. de Brún, *SF* 2. *†J. Nicholson, *UCUNF* 3. D. Dodds, *DUP*

NORTH WEST
(Blackburn-with-Darwen, Blackpool, Cheshire, Cumbria, Greater Manchester, Halton, Lancashire, Merseyside, Warrington)

E. 1,651,825   T. 31.90%

C.	423,174 (25.6%)
Lab.	336,831 (20.4%)
UKIP	261,740 (15.8%)
LD	235,639 (14.3%)
BNP	132,094 (8.0%)
Green	127,133 (7.7%)
Eng. Dem.	40,027 (2.4%)
SLP	26,224 (1.6%)
CPA	25,999 (1.6%)
No2EU	23,580 (1.4%)
JT	8,783 (0.5%)
Libertas	6,980 (0.4%)
Ind.	3,621 (0.2%)
C. majority	86,343

(June 2004, Lab. maj. 66,942)

MEMBERS ELECTED
1. *Sir R. Atkins, C. 2. A. McCarthy, Lab. 3. P. Nuttall, UKIP
4. *C. Davies, LD 5. *S. Karim, C.
6. *B. Simpson, Lab. 7. J. Foster, C.
8. N. Griffin, BNP

SCOTLAND
E. 3,873,163   T. 28.60%

SNP	321,007 (29.1%)
Lab.	229,853 (20.8%)
C.	185,794 (16.8%)
LD	127,038 (11.5%)
Green	80,442 (7.3%)
UKIP	57,788 (5.2%)
BNP	27,174 (2.5%)
SLP	22,135 (2.0%)
CPA	16,738 (1.5%)
SSP	10,404 (0.9%)
Ind.	10,189 (0.9%)
No2EU	9,693 (0.9%)
JT	6,257 (0.6%)
SNP majority	91,154

(June 2004, Lab. maj. 79,360)

MEMBERS ELECTED
1. *I. Hughton, SNP 2. *D. Martin, Lab. 3. *S. Stevenson, C. 4. *A. Smith, SNP 5. G. Lyon, LD 6. *C. Stihler, Lab.

SOUTH EAST
(Bracknell Forest, Brighton and Hove, Buckinghamshire, East Sussex, Hampshire, Isle of Wight, Kent, Medway, Milton Keynes, Newbury, Oxfordshire, Portsmouth, Reading, Slough, Southampton, Surrey, West Sussex, Windsor and Maidenhead, Wokingham)

E. 6,231,875   T. 38.19%

C.	812,288 (34.8%)
UKIP	440,002 (18.8%)
LD	330,340 (14.1%)
Green	271,506 (11.6%)

Lab.	192,592 (8.2%)
BNP	101,769 (4.4%)
Eng. Dem.	52,526 (2.2%)
CPA	35,712 (1.5%)
No2EU	21,455 (0.9%)
Libertas	16,767 (0.7%)
SLP	15,484 (0.7%)
UKF	15,261 (0.7%)
JT	14,172 (0.6%)
Peace Party	9,534 (0.4%)
Roman Party	5,450 (0.2%)
C. majority	372,286

(June 2004, C. maj. 345,259)

MEMBERS ELECTED
1. *D. Hannan, C. 2. *N. Farage, UKIP 3. *R. Ashworth, C.
4. *S. Bowles, LD 5. *Dr C. Lucas, Green 6. *N. Deva, C.
7. M. Andreasen, UKIP
8. *J. Elles, C. 9. *P. Skinner, Lab.
10. C. Bearder, LD

SOUTH WEST
(Bath and North East Somerset, Bournemouth, Bristol, Cornwall, Devon, Dorset, Gloucestershire, North Somerset, Plymouth, Poole, Somerset, South Gloucestershire, Swindon, Torbay, Wiltshire, Isles of Scilly, Gibraltar)

E. 3,998,479   T. 39.04%

C.	468,472 (30.2%)
UKIP	341,845 (22.1%)
LD	266,253 (17.2%)
Green	144,179 (9.3%)
Labour	118,716 (7.7%)
BNP	60,889 (3.9%)
Pensioners	37,785 (2.4%)
Eng. Dem.	25,313 (1.6%)
CPA	21,329 (1.4%)
Meb. Ker.	14,922 (1.0%)
SLP	10,033 (0.6%)
No2EU	9,741 (0.6%)
Ind.	8,971 (0.6%)
Libertas	7,292 (0.5%)
FPFT	7,151 (0.5%)
JT	5,758 (0.4%)
YD	789 (0.1%)
C. majority	126,627

(June 2004, C. maj. 130,587)

MEMBERS ELECTED
1. *G. Chichester, C. 2. T. Colman, UKIP 3. *G. Watson, LD
4. J. McCulloch Girling, C.
5. W. Dartmouth, UKIP 6. A. Fox, C.

WALES
E. 2,251,968   T. 30.50%

C.	145,193 (21.2%)
Lab.	138,852 (20.3%)
PC	126,702 (18.5%)
UKIP	87,585 (12.8%)
LD	73,082 (10.7%)
Green	38,160 (5.6%)
BNP	37,114 (5.4%)
ChP	13,037 (1.9%)

SLP	12,402 (1.8%)
No2EU	8,600 (1.3%)
JT	3,793 (0.6%)
C. majority	6,341

(June 2004, Lab. maj. 120,039)

MEMBERS ELECTED
1. K. Swinburne, C. 2. D. Vaughan. Lab. 3. *J. Evans, PC 4. J. Bufton, UKIP

WEST MIDLANDS
(Herefordshire, Shropshire, Staffordshire, Stoke-on-Trent, Telford and Wrekin, Warwickshire, West Midlands Metropolitan area, Worcestershire)

E. 4,056,370   T. 35.07%

C.	396,487 (28.1%)
UKIP	300,471 (21.3%)
Lab.	240,201 (17.0%)
LD	170,246 (12.0%)
BNP	121,967 (8.6%)
Green	88,244 (6.2%)
Eng. Dem.	32,455 (2.3%)
CPA	18,784 (1.3%)
SLP	14,724 (1.0%)
No2EU	13,415 (0.9%)
JT	8,721 (0.6%)
Libertas	6,961 (0.5%)
C. majority	96,016

(June 2004, C. maj. 56,324)

MEMBERS ELECTED
1. *P. Bradbourn, C. 2. *M. Nattrass, UKIP 3. *M. Cashman, Lab.
4. *M. Harbour, C. 5. *L. Lynne, LD
6. N. Sinclaire, UKIP

YORKSHIRE AND THE HUMBER
(East Riding of Yorkshire, Kingston-upon-Hull, North East Lincolnshire, North Lincolnshire, North Yorkshire, South Yorkshire, West Yorkshire, York)

E. 3,792,415   T. 32.51%

C.	299,802 (24.5%)
Lab.	230,009 (18.8%)
UKIP	213,750 (17.4%)
LD	161,552 (13.2%)
BNP	120,139 (9.8%)
Green	104,456 (8.5%)
Eng. Dem.	31,287 (2.6%)
SLP	19,380 (1.6%)
CPA	16,742 (1.4%)
No2EU	15,614 (1.3%)
JT	7,181 (0.6%)
Libertas	6,268 (0.5%)
C. majority	69,793

(June 1999, Lab. maj. 25,844)

MEMBERS ELECTED
1. *E. McMillan-Scott, C.
2. *L. McAvan, Lab. 3. *G. Bloom, UKIP 4. *D. Wallis, LD
5. *T. Kirkhope, C. 6. A. Brons, BNP

LOCAL GOVERNMENT

Major changes in local government were introduced in England and Wales in 1974 and in Scotland in 1975 by the Local Government Act 1972 and the Local Government (Scotland) Act 1973. Further significant alterations were made in England by the Local Government Acts of 1985, 1992 and 2000.

The structure in England was based on two tiers of local authorities (county councils and district councils) in the non-metropolitan areas; and a single tier of metropolitan councils in the six metropolitan areas of England and London borough councils in London.

Following reviews of the structure of local government in England by the Local Government Commission (now the Boundary Commission for England), 46 unitary (all-purpose) authorities were created between April 1995 and April 1998 to cover certain areas in the non-metropolitan counties. The remaining county areas continue to have two tiers of local authorities. The county and district councils in the Isle of Wight were replaced by a single unitary authority on 1 April 1995; the former counties of Avon, Cleveland, Humberside and Berkshire were replaced by unitary authorities; and Hereford and Worcester was replaced by a new county council for Worcestershire (with district councils) and a unitary authority for Herefordshire. On 1 April 2009 the county areas of Cornwall, Durham, Northumberland, Shropshire and Wiltshire were given unitary status and two new unitary authorities were created for Bedfordshire (Bedford and Central Bedfordshire) and Cheshire (Cheshire East and Cheshire West & Chester) replacing the two-tier county/district system in these areas.

The Local Government (Wales) Act 1994 and the Local Government etc (Scotland) Act 1994 abolished the two-tier structure in Wales and Scotland with effect from 1 April 1996, replacing it with a single tier of unitary authorities.

ELECTIONS

Local elections are normally held on the first Thursday in May. Generally, all British subjects, citizens of the Republic of Ireland, Commonwealth and other European Union citizens who are 18 years or over and resident on the qualifying date in the area for which the election is being held, are entitled to vote at local government elections. A register of electors is prepared and published annually by local electoral registration officers.

A returning officer has the overall responsibility for an election. Voting takes place at polling stations, arranged by the local authority and under the supervision of a presiding officer specially appointed for the purpose. Candidates, who are subject to various statutory qualifications and disqualifications designed to ensure that they are suitable to hold office, must be nominated by electors for the electoral area concerned.

In England, the Local Government Boundary Commission for England is responsible for carrying out periodic reviews of electoral arrangements, to consider whether the boundaries of wards or divisions within a local authority need to be altered to take account of changes in electorate; structural reviews, to consider whether a single, unitary authority should be established in an area instead of an existing two-tier system; and administrative boundary reviews of district or county authorities.

The Local Government Boundary Commission for Wales, the Local Government Boundary Commission for Scotland and the local government boundary commissioner for Northern Ireland (appointed when required by the Boundary Commission for Northern Ireland) are responsible for reviewing the electoral arrangements and boundaries of local authorities within their respective regions.

The Local Government Act 2000 provided for the secretary of state to change the frequency and phasing of elections in England and Wales.

LOCAL GOVERNMENT BOUNDARY COMMISSION FOR ENGLAND, Layden House, 76–86 Turnmill Street, London EC1M 5LG T 020-7664 8534
E reviews@lgbce.org.uk W www.lgbce.org.uk

LOCAL GOVERNMENT BOUNDARY COMMISSION FOR WALES, Caradog House, 1–6 St Andrew's Place, Cardiff CF10 3BE T 029-2039 5031
E lgbc.wales@wales.gsi.gov.uk W www.lgbc-wales.gov.uk

LOCAL GOVERNMENT BOUNDARY COMMISSION FOR SCOTLAND, Thistle House, 91 Haymarket Terrace, Edinburgh EH12 5HD T 0131-538 7510
E lgbcs@scottishboundaries.gov.uk
W www.lgbc-scotland.gov.uk

BOUNDARY COMMISSION FOR NORTHERN IRELAND, Forestview, Purdy's Lane, Newtownbreda, Belfast BT8 7AR T 028-9069 4800 E bcni@belfast.org.uk
W www.boundarycommission.org.uk

INTERNAL ORGANISATION

The council as a whole is the final decision-making body within any authority. Councils are free to a great extent to make their own internal organisational arrangements. The Local Government Act, given royal assent on 28 July 2000, allows councils to adopt one of three broad categories of constitution which include a separate executive:
• A directly elected mayor with a cabinet selected by that mayor
• A cabinet, either elected by the council or appointed by its leader
• A directly elected mayor and council manager
Normally, questions of policy are settled by the full council, while the administration of the various services is the responsibility of committees of councillors. Day-to-day decisions are delegated to the council's officers, who act within the policies laid down by the councillors.

FINANCE

Local government in England, Wales and Scotland is financed from four sources: council tax, non-domestic rates, government grants and income from fees and charges for services.

COUNCIL TAX

Under the Local Government Finance Act 1992, from 1 April 1993 council tax replaced the community charge (which had been introduced in April 1989 in Scotland and April 1990 in England and Wales in place of domestic rates).

Council tax is a local tax levied by each local council. Liability for the council tax bill usually falls on the owner-occupier or tenant of a dwelling which is their sole or main residence. Council tax bills may be reduced because of the personal circumstances of people resident in a property, and there are discounts in the case of dwellings occupied by fewer than two adults.

In England, unitary and metropolitan authorities are responsible for collecting their own council tax from which the police authorities claim their share. In areas where there are two tiers of local authority, each county, district and police authority sets its own council tax rate; the district authorities collect the combined council tax and the county councils and police authorities claim their share from the district councils' collection funds. In Wales, each unitary authority and each police authority sets its own council tax rate. The unitary authorities collect the combined council tax and the police authorities claim their share from the funds. In Scotland, each local authority sets its own rate of council tax.

The tax relates to the value of the dwelling. In England and Scotland each dwelling is placed in one of eight valuation bands, ranging from A to H, based on the property's estimated market value as at 1 April 1991. In Wales there are nine bands, ranging from A to I, based on the estimated market value of property as at 1 April 2003.

The valuation bands and ranges of values in England, Wales and Scotland are:

England

A	Up to £40,000	E	£88,001–£120,000
B	£40,001–£52,000	F	£120,001–£160,000
C	£52,001–£68,000	G	£160,001–£320,000
D	£68,001–£88,000	H	Over £320,001

Wales

A	Up to £44,000	F	£162,001–£223,000
B	£44,001–£65,000	G	£223,001–£324,000
C	£65,001–£91,000	H	£324,001–£424,000
D	£91,001–£123,000	I	Over £424,001
E	£123,001–£162,000		

Scotland

A	Up to £27,000	E	£58,001–£80,000
B	£27,001–£35,000	F	£80,001–£106,000
C	£35,001–£45,000	G	£106,001–£212,000
D	£45,001–£58,000	H	Over £212,001

The council tax within a local area varies between the different bands according to proportions laid down by law. The charge attributable to each band as a proportion of the Band D charge set by the council is approximately:

A	67%	F	144%
B	78%	G	167%
C	89%	H	200%
D	100%	I	233%*
E	122%		

* Wales only

The average Band D council tax bill for each authority area is given in the tables on the following pages. There may be variations from the given figure within each district council area because of different parish or community precepts being levied.

NON-DOMESTIC RATES

Non-domestic (business) rates are collected by billing authorities; these are the district councils in those areas of England with two tiers of local government and are unitary authorities in other parts of England, in Wales and in Scotland. In respect of England and Wales, the Local Government Finance Act 1988 provides for liability for rates to be assessed on the basis of a poundage (multiplier) tax on the rateable value of property (hereditaments). Separate multipliers are set by the Department for Communities and Local Government (CLG) in England, the Welsh government and the Scottish government. Rates are collected by the billing authority for the area where a property is located. Rate income collected by billing authorities is paid into a national non-domestic rating (NNDR) pool and redistributed to individual authorities on the basis of the adult population figure as prescribed by CLG, the Welsh government or the Scottish government. The rates pools are maintained separately in England, Wales and Scotland. Actual payment of rates in certain cases is subject to transitional arrangements, to phase in the larger increases and reductions in rates resulting from the effects of the latest revaluation.

Rateable values for the 2010 rating lists came into effect on 1 April 2010. They are derived from the rental value of property as at 1 April 2003 and determined on certain statutory assumptions by the Valuation Office Agency in England and Wales, and by local area assessors in Scotland. New property which is added to the list, and significant changes to existing property, necessitate amendments to the rateable value on the same basis. Rating lists (valuation rolls in Scotland) remain in force until the next general revaluation. Such revaluations take place every five years, the next being in 2015.

Certain types of property are exempt from rates, eg agricultural land and buildings, certain businesses and some places of public religious worship. Charities and other non-profit-making organisations may receive full or partial relief. Empty commercial property in England and Wales is exempt from business rates for the first three months that the property is vacant (six months for an industrial property), after which full business rates are normally payable. In Scotland an empty commercial property is exempt from business rates for the first three months and entitled to a 50 per cent discount thereafter, except for some types of premises, such as factories, which are entirely exempt.

GOVERNMENT GRANTS

In addition to specific grants in support of revenue expenditure on particular services, central government pays a revenue support grant to local authorities. This grant is paid to each local authority so that if each authority spends at the level of its standard spending assessment, all authorities in the same class can set broadly the same council tax.

COMPLAINTS

ENGLAND

In England the Local Government Ombudsman investigates complaints of injustice arising from maladministration by local authorities and certain other bodies. The Local Government Ombudsman will not usually consider a complaint unless the local authority concerned has had an opportunity to investigate and reply to a complainant.

The Local Government Act 2000 established a standards board and an independent tribunal known as the Adjudication Panel for England. Under the Localism bill introduced to parliament in December 2010 responsibility for standards has been passed back to the local authorities and the board is due to be abolished in 2012. In addition, the functions of the Adjudication Panel to determine references and appeals about the conduct of members of local authorities have been subsumed by First-tier Tribunal (Local Government Standards in England), part of the general regulatory chamber of HM Courts and Tribunals Service.

FIRST-TIER TRIBUNAL (LOCAL GOVERNMENT STANDARDS IN ENGLAND), York House, 31–36 York Place, Leeds LS1 2ED T 0113-389 6086
E AP-enquiries@tribunals.gsi.gov.uk

LOCAL GOVERNMENT OMBUDSMAN, PO Box 4771, Coventry CV4 0EH T 0300-061 0614 E advice@lgo.org.uk
W www.lgo.org.uk
Ombudsmen, Jane Martin, Anne Seex

WALES

The office of Public Services Ombudsman for Wales came into force on 1 April 2006, incorporating the functions of the Local Government Ombudsman for Wales.

PUBLIC SERVICES OMBUDSMAN FOR WALES, 1 Ffordd yr Hen Gae, Pencoed CF35 5LJ T 01656-641150
E ask@ombudsman-wales.org.uk
W www.ombudsman-wales.org.uk
Ombudsman, Peter Tyndall

SCOTLAND

The Scottish Public Services Ombudsman is responsible for complaints regarding the maladministration of local government in Scotland.

SCOTTISH PUBLIC SERVICES OMBUDSMAN, 4 Melville Street, Edinburgh EH3 7NS T 0800-377 7330
W www.spso.org.uk
Ombudsman, Jim Martin

NORTHERN IRELAND

The Northern Ireland Commissioner for Complaints fulfils a similar function in Northern Ireland, investigating complaints about local authorities and certain public bodies. Complaints are made to the relevant local authority in the first instance but may also be made directly to the commissioner.

NORTHERN IRELAND OMBUDSMAN COMMISSIONER FOR COMPLAINTS, Freepost BEL 1478, Belfast BT1 6BR
T 0800-343424 E ombudsman@ni-ombudsman.org.uk
W www.ni-ombudsman.org.uk
Northern Ireland Commissioner for Complaints, Tom Frawley, CBE

THE QUEEN'S REPRESENTATIVES

The lord-lieutenant of a county is the permanent local representative of the Crown in that county. The appointment of lord-lieutenants is now regulated by the Lieutenancies Act 1997. They are appointed by the sovereign on the recommendation of the prime minister. The retirement age is 75. The office of lord-lieutenant dates from 1551, and its holder was originally responsible for maintaining order and for local defence in the county. The duties of the post include attending on royalty during official visits to the county, performing certain duties in connection with the armed forces (and in particular the reserve forces), and making presentations of honours and awards on behalf of the Crown. In England, Wales and Northern Ireland, the lord-lieutenant also holds the office of *Custos Rotulorum.* As such, he or she acts as head of the county's commission of the peace (which recommends the appointment of magistrates).

The office of sheriff (from the Old English *shire-reeve*) of a county was created in the tenth century. The sheriff was the special nominee of the sovereign, and the office reached the peak of its influence under the Norman kings. The Provisions of Oxford (1258) laid down a yearly tenure of office. Since the mid-16th century the office has been purely civil, with military duties taken over by the lord-lieutenant of the county. The sheriff (commonly known as 'high sheriff') attends on royalty during official visits to the county, acts as the returning officer during parliamentary elections in county constituencies, attends the opening ceremony when a high court judge goes on circuit, executes high court writs, and appoints under-sheriffs to act as deputies. The appointments and duties of the sheriffs in England and Wales are laid down by the Sheriffs Act 1887.

The serving high sheriff submits a list of names of possible future sheriffs to a tribunal, which chooses three names to put to the sovereign. The tribunal nominates the high sheriff annually on 12 November and the sovereign picks the name of the sheriff to succeed in the following year. The term of office runs from 25 March to the following 24 March (the civil and legal year before 1752). No person may be chosen twice in three years if there is any other suitable person in the county.

CIVIC DIGNITIES

District councils in England and local councils in Wales may petition for a royal charter granting borough or 'city' status to the council.

In England and Wales the chair of a borough or county borough council may be called a mayor, and the chair of a city council may be called a lord mayor (if lord mayoralty has been conferred on that city). Parish councils in England and community councils in Wales may call themselves 'town councils', in which case their chair is the town mayor.

In Scotland the chair of a local council may be known as a convenor; a provost is the mayoral equivalent. The chair of the councils for the cities of Aberdeen, Dundee, Edinburgh and Glasgow are lord provosts.

ENGLAND

In April 2009 five county councils were given unitary status, abolishing the two-tier district/county system within these areas, and a further four unitary authorities were created from the division of the county areas of Bedfordshire and Cheshire. Plans to create unitary authorities at Exeter, Norwich and Suffolk were revoked by the coalition government in May 2010. There are 27 counties, divided into 201 districts, 55 unitary authorities (plus the Isles of Scilly) and 36 metropolitan boroughs. The populations of most of the unitary authorities are in the range of 100,000 to 300,000. The district councils have populations broadly in the range of 60,000 to 100,000; some, however, have larger populations, because of the need to avoid dividing large towns, and some in mainly rural areas have smaller populations.

The main conurbations outside Greater London – Tyne and Wear, West Midlands, Merseyside, Greater Manchester, West Yorkshire and South Yorkshire – are divided into 36 metropolitan boroughs, most of which have a population of over 200,000.

There are also about 8,700 town and parish councils with a population coverage of around 17 million.

ELECTIONS

For districts, counties and for around 8,700 parishes, there are elected councils, consisting of directly elected councillors. The councillors elect one of their number as chair annually.

In general, councils can have whole council elections, elections by thirds or elections by halves. However all metropolitan authorities must hold elections by thirds. The electoral cycle of any new unitary authority is specified in the appropriate statutory order under which it is established.

FUNCTIONS

In areas with a two-tier system of local governance, functions are divided between the district and county authorities, with those functions affecting the larger area or population generally being the responsibility of the county council. A few functions continue to be exercised over the larger area by joint bodies, made up of councillors from each authority within the area.

Generally the allocation of functions is as follows:

County councils: education; strategic planning; traffic, transport and highways; fire service; consumer protection; refuse disposal; smallholdings; social care; libraries

District councils: local planning; housing; highways (maintenance of certain urban roads and off-street car parks); building regulations; environmental health; refuse collection; cemeteries and crematoria; collection of council tax and non-domestic rates

Unitary and metropolitan councils: their functions are all those listed above, except that the fire service is exercised by a joint body

Concurrently by county and district councils: recreation (parks, playing fields, swimming pools); museums; encouragement of the arts, tourism and industry

PARISH COUNCILS

Parish or town councils are the most local tier of government in England. There are currently around 10,000 parishes in England, of which around 8,700 have councils served by approximately 70,000 councillors. Since 15 February 2008 local councils have been able to

create new parish councils without seeking approval from the government. Around 80 per cent of parish councils represent populations of less than 2,500; parishes with no parish council can be grouped with neighbouring parishes under a common parish council. A parish council comprises at least five members, the number being fixed by the district council. Elections are held every four years, at the time of the election of the district councillor for the ward including the parish. Full parish councils must be formed for those parishes with more than 999 electors – below this number, parish meetings comprising the electors of the parish must be held at least twice a year.

Parish council functions include: allotments; encouragement of arts and crafts; community halls, recreational facilities (eg open spaces, swimming pools), cemeteries and crematoria; and many minor functions. They must also be given an opportunity to comment on planning applications. They may, like county and district councils, spend limited sums for the general benefit of the parish. They levy a precept on the district councils for their funds. Parish precepts for 2011–12 totalled £367m, an increase of 2.8 per cent on 2010–11.

FINANCE

The local government budget requirement (including parish precepts) for 2011–12 is £56.7bn; of this £26.5bn is to be raised through council tax, £19bn from redistributed business rates, £5.9bn from revenue support grant and £4.5bn from police grant.

In England, the average council tax per dwelling for 2011–12 is £1,196, an increase of just £1 from £1,195 in 2010–11. The average council tax bill for a Band D dwelling (occupied by two adults, including parish precepts) for 2011–12 is £1,439, the same as for 2010–11 – with the exception of parishes, no local authority has increased its Band D council tax for 2011–12. The average Band D council tax is £1,484 in shire areas, £1,399 in metropolitan areas and £1,308 in London. Since 2006–7 the London figure has included a levy to fund the 2012 Olympic Games, which equates to a £20 a year increase on a Band D council tax.

The provisional amount estimated to be raised from national non-domestic rates from central and local lists is £19bn. The non-domestic rating multiplier for England for 2011–12 is 43.3p (42.6p for small businesses). The City of London is able to set a different multiplier from the rest of England; for 2011–12 this is 43.7p (43.0p for small businesses).

Under the Local Government and Housing Act 1989, local authorities have four main ways of paying for capital expenditure: borrowing and other forms of extended credit; capital grants from central government towards some types of capital expenditure; 'usable' capital receipts from the sale of land, houses and other assets; and revenue.

The amount of capital expenditure which a local authority can finance by borrowing (or other forms of credit) is effectively limited by the credit approvals issued to it by central government. Most credit approvals can be used for any kind of local authority capital expenditure; these are known as basic credit approvals. Others (supplementary credit approvals) can be used only for the kind of expenditure specified in the approval, and so are often given to fund particular projects or services.

Local authorities can use all capital receipts from the sale of property or assets for capital spending, except in the case of sales of council houses. Generally, the 'usable' part of a local authority's capital receipts consists of

25 per cent of receipts from the sale of council houses and 50 per cent of other housing assets such as shops or vacant land. The balance has to be set aside as provision for repaying debt and meeting other credit liabilities.

EXPENDITURE

Local authority budgeted net expenditure for 2011–12 is:

Service	£ million
Education	43,002
Highways and transport	5,602
Social care	21,201
Housing (excluding HRA)	2,339
Cultural, environment and planning	9,796
Police	11,840
Fire and rescue	2,224
Central services	3,525
Mandatory rent allowances	13,925
Mandatory rent rebates	488
Rent rebates granted to HRA tenants	4,035
Other services	82
Net current expenditure	118,059
Capital financing	4,202
Capital expenditure charged to revenue account	1,171
Council tax benefit	4,141
Discretionary non-domestic rate relief	29
Bad debt provision	45
Flood defence payments to Environment Agency	32
Private Finance Initiative schemes	46
Less interest receipts	(390)
Less specific grants outside AEF	(25,229)
Less Business Rates Supplement	(222)
Gross revenue expenditure	101,885
Less specific grants inside AEF	(44,649)
Less Local Services Support Grant	(189)
NET REVENUE EXPENDITURE	57,048

HRA = Housing Revenue Account
AEF = aggregate external finance

LONDON

The Greater London Council was abolished in 1986 and London was divided into 32 borough councils, which have a status similar to the metropolitan borough councils in the rest of England, and the City of London Corporation.

In March 1998 the government announced proposals for a Greater London Authority (GLA) covering the area of the 32 London boroughs and the City of London, which would comprise a directly elected mayor and a 25-member assembly. A referendum was held in London on 7 May 1998; the turnout was approximately 34 per cent and 72 per cent of electors voted in favour of the GLA. A London mayor was elected on 4 May 2000 and the authority assumed its responsibilities on 3 July 2000 (*see also* Regional Government).

The GLA is responsible for transport, economic development, strategic planning, culture, health, the environment, the police and fire and emergency planning. The separately elected assembly scrutinises the mayor's activities and approves plans and budgets. There are 14 constituency assembly members, each representing a separate area of London (each constituency is made up of two or three complete London boroughs). Eleven additional members, making up the total assembly complement of 25 members, are elected on a London-wide basis, either as independents or from party political lists on the basis of proportional representation.

LONDON BOROUGH COUNCILS

The London boroughs have whole council elections every four years, in the year immediately following the county council election year. The most recent elections took place on 6 May 2010.

The borough councils have responsibility for the following functions: building regulations, cemeteries and crematoria, consumer protection, education, youth employment, environmental health, electoral registration, food, drugs, housing, leisure services, libraries, local planning, local roads, museums, parking, recreation (parks, playing fields, swimming pools), refuse collection and street cleaning, social services, town planning and traffic management.

CITY OF LONDON CORPORATION

The City of London Corporation is the local authority for the City of London. Its legal definition is the 'Mayor and Commonalty and Citizens of the City of London'. It is governed by the court of common council, which consists of the lord mayor, 25 other aldermen and 100 common councilmen. The lord mayor and two sheriffs are nominated annually by the City guilds (the livery companies) and elected by the court of aldermen. Aldermen and councilmen are elected from the 25 wards into which the City is divided; councilmen must stand for re-election annually. The council is a legislative assembly, and there are no political parties.

The corporation has the same functions as the London borough councils. In addition, it runs the City of London Police; is the health authority for the Port of London; has health control of animal imports throughout Greater London, including at Heathrow airport; owns and manages public open spaces throughout Greater London; runs the central criminal court; and runs Billingsgate, Smithfield and Spitalfields markets.

THE CITY GUILDS (LIVERY COMPANIES)

The livery companies of the City of London grew out of early medieval religious fraternities and began to emerge as trade and craft guilds, retaining their religious aspect, in the 12th century. From the early 14th century, only members of the trade and craft guilds could call themselves citizens of the City of London. The guilds began to be called livery companies, because of the distinctive livery worn by the most prosperous guild members on ceremonial occasions, in the late 15th century.

By the early 19th century the power of the companies within their trades had begun to wane, but those wearing the livery of a company continued to play an important role in the government of the City of London. Liverymen still have the right to nominate the lord mayor and sheriffs, and most members of the court of common council are liverymen.

WALES

The Local Government (Wales) Act 1994 abolished the two-tier structure of eight county and 37 district councils which had existed since 1974, and replaced it, from 1 April 1996, with 22 unitary authorities. The new authorities were elected in May 1995. Each unitary authority inherited all the functions of the previous county and district councils, except fire services (which are provided by three combined fire authorities, composed of representatives from the unitary authorities) and national parks (which are the responsibility of three independent national park authorities).

COMMUNITY COUNCILS

In Wales community councils are the equivalent of parishes in England. Unlike England, where many areas are not in any parish, communities have been established for the whole of Wales, approximately 865 communities in all. Community meetings may be convened as and when desired.

Community or town councils exist in around 740 of the communities and further councils may be established at the request of a community meeting. Community councils have broadly the same range of powers as English parish councils. Community councillors are elected for a term of four years.

ELECTIONS

Elections take place every four years; the last elections took place in May 2008.

FINANCE

Total budgeted revenue expenditure for 2011–12 is £7.6bn, an increase of 0.9 per cent on 2010–11. Total budget requirement, which excludes expenditure financed by specific and special government grants and any use of reserves, is £5.8bn. This comprises revenue support grant of £3.4bn, support from the national non-domestic rate pool of £787m, police grant of £246m and £1.3bn to be raised through council tax. The non-domestic rating multiplier for Wales for 2011–12 is 42.8p. The average Band D council tax levied in Wales for 2011–12 is £1,162, comprising unitary authorities £954, police authorities £183 and community councils £25.

EXPENDITURE

Local authority budgeted net revenue expenditure for 2011–12 is:

Service	£ million
Education	2,576
Social services	1,440
Council fund housing, including housing benefit	965
Local environmental services	419
Roads and transport	316
Libraries, culture, heritage, sport and recreation	264
Planning, economic and community development	134
Council tax collection	30
Debt financing costs: counties	326
Central administrative and other revenue expenditure	303
Police	663
Fire	149
National parks	16
Gross revenue expenditure	7,602
Less specific and special government grants	(1,826)
Net revenue expenditure	5,777
Less appropriations from reserves	(22)
BUDGET REQUIREMENT	5,755

SCOTLAND

The Local Government etc (Scotland) Act 1994 abolished the two-tier structure of nine regional and 53 district councils which had existed since 1975 and replaced it, from 1 April 1996, with 29 unitary authorities on the mainland; the three islands councils remained. The new authorities were elected in April 1995.

In July 1999 the Scottish parliament assumed responsibility for legislation on local government. The government had established a commission on local government and the Scottish parliament (the McIntosh Commission) to make recommendations on the relationship between local authorities and the Scottish parliament and on increasing local authorities' accountability.

The local government in Scotland bill was introduced to the Scottish parliament in May 2002. The bill focused on three integrated core elements:

- A power for local authorities to promote and improve the well-being of their area and/or persons in it
- Statutory underpinning for community planning through the introduction of a duty on local authorities and key partners, including police, health boards and enterprise agencies
- A duty to secure best value

ELECTIONS

The unitary authorities consist of directly elected councillors. The Scottish Local Government (Elections) Act 2002 moved elections from a three-year to a four-year cycle, but to avoid the local authority elections coinciding with the Scottish parliament elections in May 2011, local authority elections are now due to take place in May 2012. The last elections took place in May 2007.

FUNCTIONS

The functions of the councils and islands councils are: education; social work; strategic planning; the provision of infrastructure such as roads; consumer protection; flood prevention; coast protection; valuation and rating; the police and fire services; civil defence; electoral registration; public transport; registration of births, deaths and marriages; housing; leisure and recreation; development and building control; environmental health; licensing; allotments; public conveniences; and the administration of district courts.

COMMUNITY COUNCILS

Scottish community councils differ from those in England and Wales. Their purpose as defined in statute is to ascertain and express the views of the communities they represent, and to take in the interests of their communities such action as appears to be expedient or practicable. Around 1,200 community councils have been established under schemes drawn up by local authorities in Scotland.

FINANCE

Budgeted total revenue support for 2011–12 is £10.4bn, comprising £7.7bn general revenue funding, non-domestic rate income of £2.2bn and ring-fenced grants of £503m. The non-domestic rate multiplier or poundage for 2011–12 is 42.6p. All non-domestic properties with a rateable value of £18,000 or less may be eligible for non-domestic rates relief of up to 100 per cent. The average Band D council tax for 2011–12 is £1,149.

EXPENDITURE

Local authority budgeted net revenue expenditure for 2011–12 is:

Service	£ million
Education	4,623
Cultural and related services	607
Social work services	2,859
Police	951
Roads and transport	475
Environmental services	693
Fire	264
Planning and development services	280
Other	2,006
TOTAL	12,759

NORTHERN IRELAND

For the purpose of local government, Northern Ireland has a system of 26 single-tier district councils.

ELECTIONS

Council members are elected for periods of four years at a time on the principle of proportional representation. The last elections took place in May 2011.

FUNCTIONS

The district councils have three main roles. These are:

Executive: responsibility for a wide range of local services including building regulations; community services; consumer protection; cultural facilities; environmental health; miscellaneous licensing and registration provisions, including dog control; litter prevention; recreational and social facilities; refuse collection and disposal; street cleaning; and tourist development

Representative: nominating representatives to sit as members of the various statutory bodies responsible for the administration of regional services such as drainage, education, fire, health and personal social services, housing, and libraries

Consultative: acting as the medium through which the views of local people are expressed on the operation in their area of other regional services – notably conservation (including water supply and sewerage services), planning and roads – provided by those departments of central government which have an obligation, statutory or otherwise, to consult the district councils about proposals affecting their areas

FINANCE

Government in Northern Ireland is part-funded by a system of rates, which supplement the Northern Ireland budget from the UK government. The ratepayer receives a combined tax bill consisting of the regional rate, set by the Northern Ireland executive, and the district rate, which is set by each district council. The regional and district rates are both collected by the Land and Property Services Agency (formerly the Rate Collection Agency). The product of the district rates is paid over to each council while the product of the regional rate supports expenditure by the departments of the executive and assembly.

Since April 2007 domestic rates bills have been based on the capital value of a property, rather than the rental value. The capital value is defined as the price the property might reasonably be expected to realise had it been sold on the open market on 1 January 2005. Non-domestic rates bills are based on 2001 rental values.

Rate bills are calculated by multiplying the property's net annual rental value (in the case of non-domestic property), or capital value (in the case of domestic property), by the regional and district rate poundages respectively.

For 2011–12 the overall average domestic poundage is 0.6888p compared to 0.6731p in 2010–11. The overall average non-domestic rate poundage in 2011–12 is 55.61p compared to 54.33p in 2010–11.

POLITICAL COMPOSITION OF LOCAL COUNCILS

as at May 2011

Abbreviations

All.	Alliance
BNP	British National Party
C.	Conservative
DUP	Democratic Unionist Party
Green	Green
Ind.	Independent
Ind. Un.	Independent Unionist
Lab.	Labour
LD	Liberal Democrat
Lib.	Liberal
O.	Other
PC	Plaid Cymru
R	Residents Associations/Ratepayers
SD	Social Democrat
SDLP	Social Democratic and Labour Party
SF	Sinn Fein
SNP	Scottish National Party
Soc.	Socialist
UUP	Ulster Unionist Party
v.	Vacant

Total number of seats is given in parentheses after council name.

ENGLAND

COUNTY COUNCILS

Buckinghamshire (57)	C. 46; LD 11
Cambridgeshire (69)	C. 41; LD 21; Lab. 3; Ind. 2; Green 1; O. 1
Cumbria (84)	C. 39; Lab. 24; LD 15; Ind. 4; O. 2
Derbyshire (64)	C. 33; Lab. 21; LD 8; v. 2
Devon (62)	C. 41; LD 13; Lab. 5; Ind. 2; Green 1
Dorset (45)	C. 28; LD 16; Ind. 1
East Sussex (49)	C. 29; LD 13; Lab. 4; O. 2; Ind. 1
Essex (75)	C. 59; LD 11; Lab. 2; Ind. 2; v. I
Gloucestershire (63)	C. 40; LD 14; Lab. 5; O. 2; Ind. 1; Green 1
Hampshire (78)	C. 51; LD 25; Lab. 1; O. 1
Hertfordshire (77)	C. 55; LD 17; Lab. 3; Green 1; O. 1
Kent (84)	C. 73; LD 7; Lab. 3; O. 1
Lancashire (84)	C. 51; Lab. 17; LD 9; Ind. 3; Green 2; BNP 1; O. 1
Leicestershire (55)	C. 36; LD 14; Lab. 4; Ind. 1
Lincolnshire (77)	C. 61; Ind. 7; LD 5; Lab. 4
Norfolk (84)	C. 60; LD 13; Green 7; Lab. 3; O. 1
North Yorkshire (72)	C. 47; LD 11; Ind. 9; Lib. 2; O. 2; Lab. 1
Northamptonshire (73)	C. 56; LD 9; Lab. 6; Ind. 2
Nottinghamshire (67)	C. 35; Lab. 15; LD 9; O. 6; Ind. 2
Oxfordshire (74)	C. 52; LD 10; Lab. 9; Green 2; Ind. 1
Somerset (58)	C. 34; LD 22; Lab. 2
Staffordshire (62)	C. 48; O. 10; Lab. 2; v. 2
Suffolk (75)	C. 55; LD 11; Lab. 4; Green 2; Ind. 2; O. 1
Surrey (80)	C. 56; LD. 13; Ind. 10; Lab. 1
Warwickshire (62)	C. 39; LD 11; Lab. 11; Ind. 1
West Sussex (71)	C. 49; LD 19; Lab. 2; Ind. 1
Worcestershire (57)	C. 41; LD 8; Lab. 3; O. 3; Lib. 1; Ind. 1

DISTRICT COUNCILS

Adur (29)	C. 25; Ind. 2; LD. 2
Allerdale (56)	Lab. 28; C. 12; Ind. 10; O. 6
Amber Valley (45)	C. 28; Lab. 15; BNP 2
Arun (56)	C. 48; LD 4; Lab. 3; Ind. 1
Ashfield (33)	Lab. 24; LD 6; Ind. 3
Ashford (43)	C. 30; Lab. 5; O. 5; LD 2; Ind. 1
Aylesbury Vale (59)	C. 37; LD 17; Lab. 2; O. 2; Ind. 1
Babergh (43)	C. 18; LD 12; Ind. 9; lab. 3; O. 1
Barrow-in-Furness (36)	Lab. 29; C. 7
Basildon (42)	C. 29; Lab. 11; LD 2
Basingstoke and Deane (60)	C. 34; LD 13; Lab. 11; Ind. 2
Bassetlaw (48)	Lab. 27; C. 18; Ind. 3
Blaby (39)	C. 28; Lab. 6; LD 5
Bolsover (37)	Lab. 31; Ind. 4; R 1; Green 1
Boston (32)	C. 19; O. 6; Ind. 4; Lab. 3
Braintree (60)	C. 47; Lab. 9; Green 2; R 1; Ind. 1
Breckland (54)	C. 47; Lab. 4; Ind. 3
Brentwood (37)	C. 28; LD 7; Ind. 1; Lab. 1
Broadland (47)	C. 34; LD 12; Lab. 1
Bromsgrove (39)	C. 27; Lab. 10; R 2
Broxbourne (38)	C. 34; Lab. 3; v. 1
Broxtowe (44)	C. 18; Lab. 17; LD 9
Burnley (45)	LD 21; Lab. 18; C. 5; BNP 1
Cambridge (42)	LD 25; Lab. 14; Green 2; Ind. 1
Cannock Chase (41)	Lab. 17; C. 13; LD 11
Canterbury (50)	C. 37; LD 10; Lab. 3
Carlisle (52)	Lab. 24; C. 22; LD 4; Ind. 2
Castle Point (41)	C. 25; Ind. 16
Charnwood (52)	C. 33; Lab. 16; LD 1; BNP 1; Ind. 1
Chelmsford (57)	C. 40; LD 15; Lab. 1; Ind. 1
Cheltenham (40)	LD 25; C. 12; O. 3
Cherwell (50)	C. 43; Lab. 4; LD 3
Chesterfield (48)	Lab. 34; LD 14
Chichester (48)	C. 38; LD 8; Ind. 2
Chiltern (40)	C. 33; LD 5; Ind. 2
Chorley (42)	C. 23; Lab. 20; LD 2; Ind. 2
Christchurch (24)	C. 21; Ind. 2; LD 1
Colchester (60)	LD 26; C. 24; Lab. 7; Ind. 3
Copeland (51)	Lab. 34; C. 15; Ind. 2
Corby (29)	Lab. 22; C. 4; LD 3
Cotswolds (44)	C. 27; LD 12; Ind. 5
Craven (30)	C. 18; Ind. 9; LD 3
Crawley (37)	C. 24; Lab. 13
Dacorum (51)	C. 43; LD 6; Lab. 2
Dartford (44)	C. 31; Lab. 9; R 4
Daventry (38)	C. 34; LD 2; Lab. 2
Derbyshire Dales (39)	C. 28; Lab. 5; LD 4; Ind. 1; v. 1
Dover (45)	C. 26; Lab. 19
East Cambridgeshire (39)	C. 25; LD 10; Ind. 4
East Devon (59)	C. 43; LD 10; Ind. 6
East Dorset (36)	C. 30; LD 6
East Hampshire (44)	C. 39; LD 5
East Hertfordshire (50)	C. 46; LD 2; Ind. 2
East Lindsey (60)	C. 30; Ind. 15; Lab. 10; O. 5

East Northamptonshire C. 35; Ind. 3; Lab. 2
(40)
East Staffordshire (39) C. 22; Lab. 16; LD 1
Eastbourne (27) LD 15; C. 12
Eastleigh (44) LD 38; C. 4; Ind. 2
Eden (38) C. 16; Ind. 10; LD 9; O. 3
Elmbridge (60) C. 35; R 18; LD 5; O. 2
Epping Forest (58) C. 37; R 10; LD 6; Ind. 3;
BNP 1; Lab. 1
Epsom and Ewell (38) R 26; LD 6; C. 3; Lab.3
Erewash (51) C. 26; Lab. 25
Exeter (40) Lab. 19; C. 11; LD 9; Lib. 1
Fareham (31) C. 23; LD 7; Ind. 1
Fenland (40) C. 34; Ind. 4; LD 2
Forest Heath (27) C. 23; LD 2; Ind. 1; Lab. 1
Forest of Dean (48) C. 19; Lab. 17; Ind. 9; O. 2; LD 1
Fylde (51) C. 28; Ind. 17; O. 3; LD 3
Gedling (50) Lab. 32; C. 15; LD 3
Gloucester (36) C. 19; LD 10; Lab. 7
Gosport (34) C. 22; LD 5; Lab. 3; Ind. 2; O. 2
Gravesham (44) Lab. 25; C. 19
Great Yarmouth (39) C. 24; Lab. 14; Ind. 1
Guildford (48) C. 34; LD 12; Lab. 2
Hambleton (44) C. 39; Ind. 3; LD 2
Harborough (37) C. 27; LD 10
Harlow (33) C. 17; Lab. 14; LD 2
Harrogate (54) C. 34; LD 17; Ind. 2; Lib. 1
Hart (35) C. 20; LD 10; O. 5
Hastings (32) Lab 17; C. 14; LD 1
Havant (38) C. 35; LD 2; Lab. 1
Hertsmere (39) C. 35; Lab. 4
High Peak (43) Lab. 21; C. 15; LD 3; Ind. 3; O. 1
Hinckley and
Bosworth (34) LD 18; C. 15; Lab. 1
Horsham (44) C. 34; LD 8; Ind. 2
Huntingdonshire (52) C. 41; LD 8; O. 2; Ind. 1
Hyndburn (35) Lab. 18; C. 14; Ind. 3
Ipswich (48) Lab. 28; C. 16; LD 4
Kettering (36) C. 26; Lab. 9; Ind. 1
King's Lynn and West C. 42; Lab. 13; LD 3; Ind. 3;
Norfolk (62) Green 1
Lancaster (60) Lab. 24; C. 16; Ind. 12; Green 8
Lewes (41) C. 22; LD 18; Ind. 1
Lichfield (56) C. 46; LD 10
Lincoln City (33) Lab. 17; C. 15; LD 1
Maidstone (55) C. 30; LD 21; Ind. 4
Maldon (31) C. 28; Ind. 3
Malvern Hills (38) C. 21; LD 11; Ind. 4; Green 2
Mansfield (46) Lab. 25; Ind. 10; v. 1
Melton (28) C. 20; Lab. 7; Ind. 1
Mendip (47) C. 31; LD 15; Ind. 1
Mid Devon (42) C. 24; Ind. 10; LD 6; Lib. 1; O. 1
Mid Suffolk (40) C. 22; LD 6; Ind. 5; Green 4;
O. 2; Lab. 1
Mid Sussex (54) C. 45; LD 8; Lab. 1
Mole Valley (41) C. 18; LD 17; Ind. 5; O. 1
New Forest (60) C. 54; LD 6
Newark and Sherwood C. 22; Lab. 15; Ind. 6; LD 3
(46)
Newcastle-under-Lyme Lab. 25; C. 21; LD 12;
(60) O. 2
North Devon (43) C. 18; LD 14; Ind. 11
North Dorset (33) C. 23; LD 6; Ind. 3; O. 1
North East Derbyshire Lab. 34; C. 17; Ind. 2
(53)
North Hertfordshire C. 34; LD 8; Lab. 7
(49)
North Kesteven (43) C. 27; O. 9; Ind. 4; LD 3

North Norfolk (48) C. 28; LD 18; Ind. 1; O. 1
North Warwickshire Lab. 18; C. 17
(35)
North West
Leicestershire (38) C. 21; Lab. 16; LD 1
Northampton (45) C. 26; Lab. 15; LD 4
Norwich (39) Lab. 18; Green 15; LD 4; C. 2
Nuneaton and Lab. 17; C. 14; Ind. 2; BNP 1
Bedworth (34)
Oadby and Wigston LD 23; C. 3
(26)
Oxford (48) Lab. 26; LD 16; Green 5; O. 1
Pendle (49) C. 18; Lab. 16; LD 12; BNP 2;
Ind. 1
Preston (57) Lab. 29; C. 21; LD 6; Ind. 1
Purbeck (24) C. 11; LD 10; Ind. 2; v. 1
Redditch (29) C. 17; Lab. 11; LD 1
Reigate and Banstead C. 35; R 7; LD 3; O. 3; Green 2;
(51) Ind. 1
Ribble Valley (40) C. 33; LD 6; Ind. 1
Richmondshire (34) Ind. 16; C. 14; LD 4
Rochford (39) C. 31; LD 4; Green 2; R 2
Rossendale (36) Lab. 17; C. 16 LD 2; O. 1
Rother (38) C. 27; LD 5; Ind. 3; Lab. 2; O. 1
Rugby (48) C. 29; Lab. 11; LD 8
Runnymede (42) C. 36; Ind. 6
Rushcliffe (50) C. 36; LD 6; Lab. 5; Green 2;
Ind. 1
Rushmoor (42) C. 32; Lab. 6; LD 4
Ryedale (30) C. 20; Lib. 4; Ind. 3; LD 2; O. 1
St Albans (58) C. 29; LD 24; Lab. 3; Ind. 1;
Green 1
St Edmundsbury (45) C. 38; Ind. 4; Lab. 3
Scarborough (50) C. 25; Ind. 12; Lab. 6; LD 3;
Green 2; O. 2
Sedgemoor (48) C. 31; Lab. 13; LD 2; Ind. 2
Selby (41) C. 29; Lab. 10; Ind. 2
Sevenoaks (54) C. 47; Lab. 4; LD 2; Ind. 1
Shepway (46) C. 44; O. 2
South Bucks (40) C. 38; Ind. 1; LD 1
South Cambridgeshire C. 31; LD 18; Ind. 7; Lab. 1
(57)
South Derbyshire (36) C. 19; Lab. 17
South Hams (40) C. 30; LD 5; Green 3; Ind. 1;
Lab. 1
South Holland (37) C. 25; Ind. 12
South Kesteven (58) C. 38; Ind. 12; Lab. 6; LD 1; O. 1
South Lakeland (51) LD 32; C. 18; Lab. 1
South Norfolk (46) C. 38; LD 8
South
Northamptonshire C. 33; Ind. 7; LD 2
(42)
South Oxfordshire (48) C. 33; LD 4; Ind. 4; Lab. 4; R 2;
O. 1
South Ribble (55) C. 33; Lab. 21; LD 1
South Somerset (60) LD 31; C. 25; Ind. 4
South Staffordshire C. 42; Ind. 5; Lab. 2
(49)
Spelthorne (39) C. 32; LD 6; Ind. 1
Stafford (59) C. 38; Lab. 17; LD 3
Staffordshire C. 25; Ind. 11; O. 9; Lab. 7;
Moorlands (56) LD 4
Stevenage (39) Lab. 27; C. 9; LD 3
Stratford-on-Avon (53) C. 34; LD 16; Ind. 2; O. 1
Stroud (51) C. 26; Lab. 11; LD 6; Green 6;
Ind. 1; O. 1
Suffolk Coastal (55) C. 44; LD 5; Lab. 4; Ind. 1; O. 1
Surrey Heath (40) C. 35; Lab. 2; Ind. 2; LD 1

Swale (47) | C. 32; Lab. 13; Ind. 2
Tamworth (30) | C. 23; Lab. 6; Ind. 1
Tandridge (42) | C. 34; LD 6; Ind. 2
Taunton Deane (56) | C. 28; LD 23; lab. 3; Ind. 2
Teignbridge (46) | C. 26; LD 13; Ind. 7
Tendring (60) | C. 33; Lab. 9; Ind. 8; O. 8; LD 2
Test Valley (48) | C. 36; LD 12
Tewkesbury (38) | C. 24; LD 11; O. 2; Ind. 1
Thanet (56) | C. 27; Lab. 26; Ind. 3
Three Rivers (48) | LD 29; C. 14; Lab. 4; Ind. 1
Tonbridge and Malling | C. 48; LD 4; Lab. 1
(53)
Torridge (36) | C. 18; Ind. 8; LD 6; O. 2; Lab. 1; Green 1

Tunbridge Wells (48) | C. 39; LD 6; Lab. 1; Ind. 1; O. 1
Uttlesford (44) | C. 34; LD 8; Ind. 2
Vale of White Horse | C. 31; LD 19; Lab. 1
(51)
Warwick (46) | C. 25; LD 9; Lab. 8; R 3; Ind. 4

Watford (37) | LD 25; Lab. 6; C. 3; Green 3
Waveney (48) | C. 23; Lab. 23; Green 1; Ind. 1

Waverley (57) | C. 56; Ind. 1
Wealden (55) | C. 47; Ind. 4; LD 3; O. 1
Wellingborough (36) | C. 27; Lab. 9
Welwyn and Hatfield | C. 37; Lab. 9; LD 2
(48)
West Devon (31) | C. 19; Ind. 8; LD 3; O. 1
West Dorset (48) | C. 32; LD 11; Ind. 5
West Lancashire (54) | C. 33; Lab. 21
West Lindsey (37) | C. 21; LD 11; Ind. 3; Lab. 2
West Oxfordshire (49) | C. 44; LD 4; Lab. 1
West Somerset (28) | C. 19; Ind. 7; Lab. 2
Weymouth and | C. 16; LD 10; Lab. 7; Ind. 3
Portland (36)
Winchester (57) | C. 27; LD 27; Ind. 2; Lab. 1
Woking (36) | C. 20; LD 16
Worcester (35) | C. 18; Lab. 12; LD 3; Ind. 2
Worthing (37) | C. 25; LD 11; Lib. 1
Wychavon (45) | C. 39; LD 5; Lab. 1
Wycombe (60) | C. 42; Lab. 7; LD 8; Ind. 2; O. 1

Wyre (55) | C. 40; Lab. 15
Wyre Forest (42) | C. 24; Lab. 7; O. 5; Lib. 4; Ind. 2

LONDON BOROUGH COUNCILS

Barking and Dagenham | Lab. 51
(51)
Barnet (63) | C. 39; Lab. 21; LD 3
Bexley (63) | C. 52; Lab. 11
Brent (63) | Lab. 40; LD 17; C. 6
Bromley (60) | C. 53; LD 4; Lab. 3
Camden (54) | Lab. 30; LD 13; C. 10; Green 1
Croydon (70) | C. 37; Lab. 33
Ealing (69) | Lab. 40; C. 24; LD 5
Enfield (63) | Lab. 36; C. 26; v. 1
Greenwich (51) | Lab. 40; C. 11
Hackney (57) | Lab. 49; C. 5; LD 3
Hammersmith and | Lab. 31; C. 15
Fulham (46)
Haringey (57) | Lab. 34; LD 23
Harrow (63) | Lab. 34; C. 26; Ind. 2; LD 1
Havering (54) | C. 33; R 12; Lab. 5; Ind. 4
Hillingdon (65) | C. 46; Lab. 19
Hounslow (60) | Lab. 35; C. 25
Islington (48) | Lab. 35; LD 13

Kensington and | C. 40; Lab. 9; LD 3; v. 2
Chelsea (54)
Kingston upon Thames | LD 27; C. 21
(48)
Lambeth (63) | Lab. 44; LD 15; C. 4
Lewisham (55) | Lab. 39; LD 12; C. 2; Green 1
Merton (60) | Lab. 28; C. 27; R 3; LD 2
Newham (60) | Lab. 60
Redbridge (63) | C. 29; Lab. 26; LD 7; Ind. 1
Richmond upon | C. 30; LD 24
Thames (54)
Southwark (63) | Lab. 35; LD 25; C. 3
Sutton (54) | LD 43; C. 11
Tower Hamlets (51) | Lab. 32; C. 8; Ind. 8; O. 2; LD 1
Waltham Forest (60) | Lab. 36; C. 18; LD 6
Wandsworth (60) | C. 47; Lab.13
Westminster (60) | C. 48; Lab. 12

METROPOLITAN BOROUGHS

Barnsley (63) | Lab. 43; Ind. 13; C. 6; O. 1
Birmingham (120) | Lab. 55; C. 39; LD 24; O. 2
Bolton (60) | Lab. 35; C. 20; LD 5
Bradford (90) | Lab. 44; C. 28; LD 11; Ind. 4; Green 3
Bury (51) | Lab. 26; C. 20 LD 8
Calderdale (51) | C. 21; LD 13; Lab. 13; Ind. 2; BNP 1; O. 1
Coventry (54) | Lab. 35; C. 17; LD 1; Soc. 1
Doncaster (64) | Lab. 43; C. 9; LD 6; O. 5; Ind. 1
Dudley (72) | C. 43; Lab. 28; O. 1
Gateshead (66) | Lab. 50; LD 15; Lib. 1
Kirklees (69) | Lab. 27; C. 22; LD 14; Green 4; Ind. 2
Knowsley (63) | Lab. 58; LD 4; v. 1
Leeds (99) | Lab. 55; C. 21; LD 16; O. 5; Green 2
Liverpool (90) | Lab. 62; LD 21; Lib. 3; Green 2; Ind. 1; O. 1
Manchester (96) | Lab. 75; LD 20; Ind. 1
Newcastle-upon-Tyne | Lab. 45; LD 32; Ind.1
(78)
North Tyneside (60) | Lab. 35; C. 19; LD 6
Oldham (60) | Lab. 34; LD 21; C. 5
Rochdale (60) | Lab. 31; C. 17; LD 12
Rotherham (63) | Lab. 54; C. 7; Ind. 1; BNP 1
St Helens (48) | Lab. 35; LD 9; C. 4
Salford (60) | Lab. 44; C. 11; LD 3; Ind. 2
Sandwell (72) | Lab. 60; C. 9; Ind. 1; LD 1
Sefton (66) | LD 28; Lab. 23; C. 11; Ind. 3; O. 1
Sheffield (84) | Lab. 49; LD 32; Green 2; Ind. 1
Solihull (51) | C. 29; LD 12; Lab. 6; Green 3; Ind. 1
South Tyneside (54) | Lab. 39; O. 9; Ind. 4; C. 1; LD 1
Stockport (63) | LD 31; Lab. 18; C. 11; Ind. 3
Sunderland (75) | Lab. 56; C. 14; Ind. 3; LD 1; O. 1
Tameside (57) | Lab. 48; C. 8; Ind. 1
Trafford (63) | C. 37; Lab. 22; LD 4
Wakefield (63) | Lab. 39; C. 21; Ind. 3
Walsall (60) | C. 28; Lab. 26; LD 5; Ind. 1
Wigan (75) | Lab. 58; Ind. 8; C. 5; O. 2; LD 2
Wirral (66) | Lab. 30; C. 27; LD 9
Wolverhampton (60) | Lab. 35; C. 22; LD 3

UNITARY COUNCILS

Bath and North East Somerset (65)	C. 29; LD 29; Lab. 5; Ind. 2
Bedford (40)	LD 12; C. 12; Lab. 12; Ind. 4
Blackburn with Darwen (64)	Lab. 38; C. 17; LD 6; O. 2; Ind. 1
Blackpool (42)	Lab. 27; C. 14; LD 1
Bournemouth (54)	C. 46; LD 3; Lab. 3; Ind. 2
Bracknell Forest (42)	C. 40; Lab. 2
Brighton and Hove (54)	Green 23; C. 18; Lab. 13
Bristol (70)	LD 33; Lab 21; C. 14; Green 2
Central Bedfordshire (59)	C. 49; LD 5; Ind. 3; Lab. 1; O. 1
Cheshire East (82)	C. 52; Lab. 14; Ind. 10; LD 4; v. 2
Cheshire West and Chester (75)	C. 42; Lab. 32; LD 1
Cornwall (123)	C. 47; LD 40; Ind. 31; O. 4; Lab. 1
Darlington (53)	Lab. 34; C. 14; LD 5
Derby (51)	Lab. 22; C. 16; LD 12; Ind. 1
Durham (126)	Lab. 69; LD 23; Ind. 21; C. 10; O. 3
East Riding of Yorkshire (67)	C. 53; Lab. 6; Ind. 4; LD 3; SD 1
Halton (56)	Lab. 44; LD 6; C. 3; O. 2; Ind. 1
Hartlepool (48)	Lab. 29; Ind. 13; C. 4; LD 2
Herefordshire (58)	C. 30; Ind. 14; O. 9; LD 3; Lab. 1; Green 1
Isles of Scilly (21)*	Ind. 21
Isle of Wight (40)	C. 24; Ind. 10; LD 4; Lab. 1; v. 1
Kingston-upon-Hull (59)	Lab. 34; LD 22; C. 2; O. 1
Leicester (54)	Lab. 52; C. 1; LD 1
Luton (48)	Lab. 36; LD 8; C. 4
Medway (55)	C. 35; Lab. 15; LD 3; Ind. 2
Middlesbrough (49)	Lab. 30; Ind. 7; O. 6; C. 4; LD 1; Green 1
Milton Keynes (51)	C. 21; LD 18; Lab. 9; Ind. 3
North East Lincolnshire (42)	Lab. 20; C. 14; LD 8
North Lincolnshire (43)	C. 23; Lab. 20
North Somerset (61)	C. 42; Ind. 7; LD 6; Lab. 5; Green 1
Northumberland (67)	LD 25; C. 17; Lab. 17; Ind. 5; O. 3
Nottingham (55)	Lab. 50; C. 5
Peterborough (57)	C. 38; Ind. 9; Lab. 6; LD 3; O. 1
Plymouth (57)	C. 32; Lab. 25
Poole (42)	C. 21; LD 18; Ind. 3
Portsmouth (42)	LD 23; C. 17; Lab. 2
Reading (46)	Lab. 22; C. 16; LD 5; Green 2; O. 1
Redcar and Cleveland (59)	Lab. 32; LD 16; C. 6; Ind. 5
Rutland (26)	C. 16; Ind. 8; LD 2
Shropshire (74)	C. 52; LD 13; Lab. 7; Ind. 2
Slough (41)	Lab. 27; C. 9; O. 5
South Gloucestershire (70)	C. 34; LD 21; Lab. 15
Southampton (48)	C. 26; Lab. 19; LD 3
Southend-on-Sea (51)	C. 28; LD 10; Ind. 9; Lab. 4
Stockton-on-Tees (56)	Lab. 27; O. 13; C. 12; LD 4
Stoke-on-Trent (44)	Lab. 34; Ind. 7; C. 2; O. 1
Swindon (59)	C. 38; Lab. 17; LD 4
Telford and Wrekin (54)	Lab. 33; C. 17; LD 3; Ind. 1
Thurrock (49)	Lab. 24; C. 22; Ind. 2; O. 1
Torbay (37)	C. 22; LD 10; Ind. 4; Lab. 1
Warrington (57)	Lab. 27; LD 24; C. 6
West Berkshire (52)	C. 39; LD 13
Wiltshire (98)	C. 61; LD 24; Ind. 8; O. 3; Lab. 2
Windsor and Maidenhead (57)	C. 51; Ind. 5; LD 1
Wokingham (54)	C. 45; LD 9
York (47)	Lab. 26; C. 10; LD 8; Green 2; Ind. 1

* Thirteen councillors are elected by the residents of the isle of St Mary's and two councillors each are elected by the residents of the four other islands (Bryher, St Agnes, St Martins and Tresco)

WALES

Blaenau Gwent (42)	Ind. 42; Lab. 15; O. 2
Bridgend (54)	Lab. 27; Ind. 14; C. 6; LD 6; PC 1
Caerphilly (73)	PC 32; Lab. 30; Ind. 8; O. 3
Cardiff (75)	LD 35; C. 17; Lab. 13; PC 7; Ind. 3
Carmarthenshire (74)	PC 30; Ind. 28; Lab. 11; O. 3; LD 1; v. 1
Ceredigion (42)	PC 20; Ind. 12; LD 9; Lab. 1
Conwy (59)	C. 19; PC 14; Ind. 13; Lab. 7; LD 5; v. 1
Denbighshire (47)	C. 18; Ind. 10; PC 8; Lab. 6; O. 4; LD 1
Flintshire (70)	Lab. 22; Ind. 19; O. 10; C. 9; LD 9; PC 1
Gwynedd (75)	PC 37; Ind. 16; O. 13; LD 4; Lab. 4; v. 1
Merthyr Tydfil (33)	Ind. 13; Lab. 10; O. 6; LD 4
Monmouthshire (43)	C. 27; Lab. 7; LD 4; O. 5
Neath Port Talbot (64)	Lab. 39; PC 11; Ind. 6; LD 3; SD 3; O. 2
Newport (50)	Lab. 21; C. 17; LD 9; Ind. 2; PC 1
Pembrokeshire (60)	Ind. 39; O. 6; C. 5; Lab. 5; PC 5
Powys (73)	O. 45; LD 14; C. 9; Lab. 4; O. 1
Rhondda Cynon Taff (75)	Lab. 48; PC 18; Ind. 5; LD 3; C. 1
Swansea (72)	Lab. 27; LD 22; O. 11; Ind. 6; C. 5; PC 1
Torfaen (44)	Lab. 20; Ind. 8; O. 7; C. 5; PC 2; LD 1; v. 1
Vale of Glamorgan (47)	C. 25; Lab. 12; PC 6; Ind. 4
Wrexham (52)	O. 27; Lab. 12; C. 5; Ind. 4; PC 4
Ynys Mon (Isle of Anglesey) (40)	Ind. 14; O. 13; PC 8; Lab. 5

SCOTLAND

NORTHERN IRELAND

Aberdeen (43)	LD 13; SNP 13; Lab. 10; C. 4; Ind. 1; v. 2
Aberdeenshire (68)	LD 21; SNP 20; C. 13; Ind. 9; O. 5
Angus (29)	SNP 13; Ind. 6; C. 5; LD 3; Lab. 2
Argyll and Bute (36)	Ind. ; SNP 10; LD 6; O. 6; C. 2
Clackmannanshire (18)	Lab. 8; SNP 7; C. 1; Ind. 1; LD 1
Dumfries and Galloway (47)	C. 18; Lab. 14; SNP 10; LD 3; Ind. 2; O. 1
Dundee (29)	SNP 14; Lab. 8; C. 3; Ind. 2; LD 2
East Ayrshire (32)	Lab. 15; SNP 14; C. 3
East Dunbartonshire (24)	SNP 8; Lab. 6; C. 4; LD 4; Ind. 2
East Lothian (23)	SNP 9; Lab. 7; LD 4; C. 2; Ind. 1
East Renfrewshire (20)	C. 7; Lab. 7; SNP 3; Ind. 2; LD 1
Edinburgh (58)	LD 17; Lab. 15; SNP 12; C. 11; Green 3
Eilean Siar (Western Isles) (31)	Ind. 25; SNP 4; Lab. 2
Falkirk (32)	Lab. 14; SNP 13; Ind. 2; C. 2; O. 1
Fife (78)	Lab. 24; SNP 22; LD 21; Ind. 7; C. 4
Glasgow (79)	Lab. 47; SNP 19; LD 6; Green 5; C. 1; Ind. 1
Highland (80)	Ind. 25; LD 20; SNP 18; O. 10; Lab. 7
Inverclyde (20)	Lab. 8; SNP 5; LD 3; Ind. 2; C. 1; Lib. 1
Midlothian (18)	Lab. 10; SNP 6; LD 2
Moray (26)	Ind. 12; SNP 10; C. 2; Lab. 2
North Ayrshire (30)	Lab. 12; SNP 8; Ind. 6; C. 2; LD 2
North Lanarkshire (70)	Lab. 41; SNP 22; Ind. 4; C. 1; LD 1; O. 1
Orkney Islands (21)	Ind. 21
Perth and Kinross (41)	SNP 18; C. 11; LD 7; Lab. 3; Ind. 2
Renfrewshire (40)	Lab. 19; SNP 18; LD 2; C. 1
Scottish Borders (34)	C. 11; LD 10; SNP 6; Ind. 5; O. 2
Shetland Islands (22)	Ind. 11; O. 11
South Ayrshire (30)	C. 12; SNP 9; Lab. 6; Ind. 3
South Lanarkshire (67)	Lab. 32; SNP 23; C. 8; Ind. 2; LD 2
Stirling (22)	Lab. 8; SNP 7; C. 4; LD 3
West Dunbartonshire (22)	SNP 9; Lab. 8; Ind. 4; O. 1
West Lothian (32)	Lab. 14; SNP 13; O. 3; C. 1; Ind. 1

Antrim (19)	DUP 5; UUP 5; SF 4; SDLP 3; All. 2
Ards (23)	DUP 11; UUP 6; All. 4; SDLP 1; Ind. 1
Armagh City (22)	Sf 6; UUP 6; SDLP 5; DUP 4; Ind. 1
Ballymena (24)	DUP 12; UUP 6; SDLP 2; SF 2; O. 2; All. 1; Ind. 1
Ballymoney (16)	DUP 8; SF 3; UUP 2; SDLP 1; Ind. 1; O. 1
Banbridge (17)	UUP 7; DUP 5; SDLP 2; SF 2; All. 1
Belfast (51)	SF 16; DUP 15; SDLP 8; All. 6; UUP 3; Green 3
Carrickfergus (17)	DUP 8; UUP 4; All. 3; Ind. 2
Castlereagh (23)	DUP 11; All. 6; UUP 3; SDLP 2; Green 1
Coleraine (22)	DUP 9; UUP 5; SDLP 3; All. 2; Ind. 2; SF 1
Cookstown (16)	SF 6; SDLP 4; DUP 3; UUP 3
Craigavon (26)	DUP 9; SF 8; UUP 6; SDLP 2; All. 1
Derry City (30)	SDLP 14; SF 10; DUP 5; UUP 1
Down (23)	SDLP 9; SF 5; DUP 3; UUP 3; All. 1; Green 1; Ind. 1s
Dungannon and South Tyrone (22)	SF 8; DUP 6; UUP 4; SDLP 3; Ind. 1
Fermanagh (23)	SF 9; UUP 6; DUP 4; SDLP 3; Ind. 1
Larne (15)	DUP 4; UUP 4; All. 2; Ind. 2; SDLP 2; O. 1
Limavady (15)	SF 6; SDLP 3; DUP 3; UUP 2; O. 1
Lisburn (30)	DUP 14; UUP 5; SF 5; All. 3; SDLP 3;
Magherafelt (16)	SF 9; DUP 3; SDLP 2; UUP 2
Moyle (15)	Ind. 4; DUP 3; SDLP 3; SF 3; UUP 2
Newry and Mourne (30)	SF 14; SDLP 10; UUP 3; Ind. 2; DUP 1
Newtownabbey (25)	DUP 12; UUP 5; All. 5; SF 2; SDLP 1
North Down (25)	DUP 11; All. 6; UUP 4; Ind. 3; Green 1
Omagh (21)	SF 10; DUP 3; SDLP 3; UUP 3; Ind. 2
Strabane (16)	SF 8; DUP 4; Ind. 2; SDLP 1; UUP 1

ENGLAND

The region of England lies between 55° 46' and 49° 57' 30" N. latitude (from a few miles north of the mouth of the Tweed to the Lizard), and between 1° 46' E. and 5° 43' W. longitude (from Lowestoft to Land's End). England is bounded on the north by the Cheviot Hills; on the south by the English Channel; on the east by the Straits of Dover (Pas de Calais) and the North Sea; and on the west by the Atlantic Ocean, Wales and the Irish Sea. It has a total area of 130,432 sq. km (50,360 sq. miles): land 130,279 sq. km (50,301 sq. miles); inland water 153 sq. km (59 sq. miles).

POPULATION
The population at the 2001 census was 49,138,831. The average density of the population in 2001 was 377 persons per sq. km (976 per sq. mile).

FLAG
The flag of England is the cross of St George, a red cross on a white field (cross gules in a field argent). The cross of St George, the patron saint of England, has been used since the 13th century.

RELIEF
There is a marked division between the upland and lowland areas of England. In the extreme north the Cheviot Hills (highest point, the Cheviot, 815m/2,674ft) form a natural boundary with Scotland. Running south from the Cheviots, though divided from them by the Tyne Gap, is the Pennine range (highest point, Cross Fell, 893m/2,930ft), the main orological feature of the country. The Pennines culminate in the Peak District of Derbyshire (Kinder Scout, 636m/2,088ft). West of the Pennines are the Cumbrian mountains, which include Scafell Pike (978m/3,210ft), the highest peak in England, and to the east are the Yorkshire Moors, their highest point being Urra Moor (454m/1,490ft).

In the west, the foothills of the Welsh mountains extend into the bordering English counties of Shropshire (the Wrekin, 407m/1,334ft; Long Mynd, 516m/1,694ft) and Hereford and Worcester (the Malvern Hills – Worcestershire Beacon, 425m/1,394ft). Extensive areas of highland and moorland are also to be found in the south-western peninsula formed by Somerset, Devon and Cornwall, principally Exmoor (Dunkery Beacon, 519m/1,704ft), Dartmoor (High Willhays, 621m/2,038ft) and Bodmin Moor (Brown Willy, 420m/1,377ft). Ranges of low, undulating hills run across the south of the country, including the Cotswolds in the Midlands and south-west, the Chilterns to the north of London, and the North (Kent) and South (Sussex) Downs of the south-east coastal areas.

The lowlands of England lie in the Vale of York, East Anglia and the area around the Wash. The lowest-lying are the Cambridgeshire Fens in the valleys of the Great Ouse and the river Nene, which are below sea-level in places. Since the 17th century extensive drainage has brought much of the Fens under cultivation. The North Sea coast between the Thames and the Humber, low-lying and formed of sand and shingle for the most part, is subject to erosion, and defences against further incursion have been built along many stretches.

HYDROGRAPHY
The Severn is the longest river in Great Britain, rising in the north-eastern slopes of Plynlimon (Wales) and entering England in Shropshire, with a total length of 354km (220 miles) from its source to its outflow into the Bristol Channel, where it receives the Bristol Avon on the east and the Wye on the west; its other tributaries are the Vyrnwy, Tern, Stour, Teme and Upper (or Warwickshire) Avon. The Severn is tidal below Gloucester, and a high bore or tidal wave sometimes reverses the flow as high as Tewkesbury (21.75km/13.5 miles above Gloucester). The scenery of the greater part of the river is very picturesque, and the Severn is a noted salmon river, with some of its tributaries being famous for trout. Navigation is assisted by the Gloucester and Berkeley Ship Canal (26km/16.25 miles), which admits vessels of 350 tons to Gloucester. The Severn Tunnel was begun in 1873 and completed in 1886 at a cost of £2m and after many difficulties caused by flooding. It is 7km (4 miles 628 yards) in length (of which 3.67km/2.25 miles are under the river). The Severn road bridge between Haysgate, Gwent, and Almondsbury, Glos, with a centre span of 988m (3,240ft), was opened in 1966.

The longest river wholly in England is the Thames, with a total length of 346km (215 miles) from its source in the Cotswold hills to the Nore, and is navigable by ocean-going ships to London Bridge. The Thames is tidal to Teddington (111km/69 miles from its mouth) and forms county boundaries almost throughout its course; on its banks are situated London, Windsor Castle, Eton College and Oxford University. Of the remaining English rivers, those flowing into the North Sea are the Tyne, Wear, Tees, Ouse and Trent from the Pennine Range, the Great Ouse (257km/160 miles), which rises in Northamptonshire, and the Orwell and Stour from the hills of East Anglia. Flowing into the English Channel are the Sussex Ouse from the Weald, the Itchen from the Hampshire Hills, and the Axe, Teign, Dart, Tamar and Exe from the Devonian hills. Flowing into the Irish Sea are the Mersey, Ribble and Eden from the western slopes of the Pennines and the Derwent from the Cumbrian mountains.

The English Lakes, notable for their picturesque scenery and poetic associations, lie in Cumbria's Lake District; the largest are Windermere (14.7 sq. km/5.7 sq. miles), Ullswater (8.8 sq. km/3.4 sq. miles) and Derwent Water (5.3 sq. km/2.0 sq. miles).

ISLANDS
The Isle of Wight is separated from Hampshire by the Solent. The capital, Newport, stands at the head of the estuary of the Medina, and Cowes (at the mouth) is the chief port. Other centres are Ryde, Sandown, Shanklin, Ventnor, Freshwater, Yarmouth, Totland Bay, Seaview and Bembridge.

Lundy (the name is derived from the Old Norse for 'puffin island'), 18km (11 miles) north-west of Hartland Point, Devon, is around 5km (3 miles) long and almost 1km (half a mile) wide on average, with a total area of around 452 hectares (1,116 acres), and a population of around 18. It became the property of the National Trust in 1969 and is now principally a bird sanctuary and the UK's first marine conservation zone.

The Isles of Scilly comprise around 140 islands and skerries (total area, 10 sq. km/6 sq. miles) situated 45 km (28 miles) south-west of Land's End in Cornwall. Only five are inhabited: St Mary's, St Agnes, Bryher, Tresco and St Martin's. The population at the 2001 census was 2,153. The entire group has been designated an Area of Outstanding Natural Beauty because of its unique flora and fauna. Tourism and the winter/spring flower trade for the home market form the basis of the economy of the islands. The island group is a recognised rural development area.

EARLY HISTORY

Archaeological evidence suggests that England has been inhabited since at least the Palaeolithic period, though the extent of the various Palaeolithic cultures was dependent upon the degree of glaciation. The succeeding Neolithic and Bronze Age cultures have left abundant remains throughout the country; the best-known of these are the henges and stone circles of Stonehenge (ten miles north of Salisbury, Wilts) and Avebury (Wilts), both of which are believed to have been of religious significance. In the latter part of the Bronze Age the Goidels, a people of the Celtic race, invaded the country and brought with them Celtic civilisation and dialects; as a result place names in England bear witness to the spread of the invasion across the whole region.

THE ROMAN CONQUEST
The Roman conquest of Gaul (57–50 BC) brought Britain into close contact with Roman civilisation, but although Julius Caesar raided the south of Britain in 55 and 54 BC, conquest was not undertaken until nearly 100 years later. In AD 43 the Emperor Claudius dispatched Aulus Plautius, with a well-equipped force of 40,000, and himself followed with reinforcements in the same year. Success was delayed by the resistance of Caratacus (Caractacus), the British leader from AD 48–51, who was finally captured and sent to Rome, and by a great revolt in AD 61 led by Boudicca (Boadicea), Queen of the Iceni, but the south of Britain was secured by AD 70, and Wales and the area north to the Tyne by about AD 80.

In AD 122, the Emperor Hadrian visited Britain and built a continuous rampart, since known as Hadrian's Wall, from Wallsend to Bowness (Tyne to Solway). The work was entrusted by the Emperor Hadrian to Aulus Platorius Nepos, legate of Britain from AD 122 to 126, and it was intended to form the northern frontier of the Roman Empire.

The Romans administered Britain as a province under a governor, with a well-defined system of local government, each Roman municipality ruling itself and its surrounding territory, while London was the centre of the road system and the seat of the financial officials of the Province of Britain. Colchester, Lincoln, York, Gloucester and St Albans stand on the sites of five Roman municipalities, and Wroxeter, Caerleon, Chester, Lincoln and York were at various times the sites of legionary fortresses. Well-preserved Roman towns have been uncovered at or near Silchester *(Calleva Atrebatum)*, ten miles south of Reading, Wroxeter *(Viroconium Cornoviorum)*, near Shrewsbury, and St Albans *(Verulamium)* in Hertfordshire. Four main groups of roads radiated from London, and a fifth (the Fosse) ran obliquely from Lincoln through Leicester, Cirencester and Bath to Exeter. Of the four groups radiating from London, one ran south-east to Canterbury and the coast of Kent, a second to Silchester and thence to parts of western Britain and south Wales, a third (later known as Watling Street) ran through St Albans to Chester, with various branches, and the fourth reached Colchester, Lincoln, York and the eastern counties.

In the fourth century Britain was subjected to raids along the east coast by Saxon pirates, which led to the establishment of a system of coastal defences from the Wash to Southampton Water, with forts at Brancaster, Burgh Castle (Yarmouth), Walton (Felixstowe), Bradwell, Reculver, Richborough, Dover, Lympne, Pevensey and Porchester (Portsmouth). The Irish (Scoti) and Picts in the north were also becoming more aggressive and from around AD 350 incursions became more frequent and more formidable. As the Roman Empire came increasingly under attack towards the end of the fourth century, many troops were removed from Britain for service in other parts of the empire. The island was eventually cut off from Rome by the Teutonic conquest of Gaul, and with the withdrawal of the last Roman garrison early in the fifth century, the Romano-British were left to themselves.

SAXON SETTLEMENT
According to legend, the British King Vortigern called in the Saxons to defend his lands against the Picts. The Saxon chieftains Hengist and Horsa landed at Ebbsfleet, Kent, and established themselves in the Isle of Thanet, but the events during the one-and-a-half centuries between the final break with Rome and the re-establishment of Christianity are unclear. However, it would appear that over the course of this period the raids turned into large-scale settlement by invaders traditionally known as Angles (England north of the Wash and East Anglia), Saxons (Essex and southern England) and Jutes (Kent and the Weald), which pushed the Romano-British into the mountainous areas of the north and west. Celtic culture outside Wales and Cornwall survives only in topographical names. Various kingdoms established at this time attempted to claim overlordship of the whole country, hegemony finally being achieved by Wessex (with the capital at Winchester) in the ninth century. This century also saw the beginning of raids by the Vikings (Danes), which were resisted by Alfred the Great (871–899), who fixed a limit on the advance of Danish settlement by the Treaty of Wedmore (878), giving them the area north and east of Watling Street on the condition that they adopt Christianity.

In the tenth century the kings of Wessex recovered the whole of England from the Danes, but subsequent rulers were unable to resist a second wave of invaders. England paid tribute *(Danegeld)* for many years, and was invaded in 1013 by the Danes and ruled by Danish kings (including Cnut) from 1016 until 1042, when Edward the Confessor was recalled from exile in Normandy. On Edward's death in 1066 Harold Godwinson (brother-in-law of Edward and son of Earl Godwin of Wessex) was chosen to be King of England. After defeating (at Stamford Bridge, Yorkshire, 25 September 1066) an invading army under Harald Hadraada, King of Norway (aided by the outlawed Earl Tostig of Northumbria, Harold's brother), Harold was himself defeated at the Battle of Hastings on 14 October 1066, and the Norman conquest secured the throne of England for Duke William of Normandy, a cousin of Edward the Confessor.

CHRISTIANITY
Christianity reached the Roman province of Britain from Gaul in the third century (or possibly earlier). Alban,

traditionally Britain's first martyr, was put to death as a Christian during the persecution of Diocletian (22 June 303) at his native town *Verulamium*, and the Bishops of *Londinium*, *Eboracum* (York), and *Lindum* (Lincoln) attended the Council of Arles in 314. However, the Anglo-Saxon invasions submerged the Christian religion in England until the sixth century: conversion was undertaken in the north from 563 by Celtic missionaries from Ireland led by St Columba, and in the south by a mission sent from Rome in 597 which was led by St Augustine, who became the first archbishop of Canterbury. England appears to have been converted again by the end of the seventh century and followed, after the Council of Whitby in 663, the practices of the Roman Church, which brought the kingdom into the mainstream of European thought and culture.

PRINCIPAL CITIES

There are 50 cities in England and space constraints prevent us from including profiles of them all. Below is a selection of England's principal cities with the date on which city status was conferred in parenthesis. Other cities are: Chichester (pre-1900), Derby (1977), Ely (pre-1900), Exeter (pre-1900), Gloucester (pre-1900), Hereford (pre-1900), Lancaster (1937), Lichfield (pre-1900), London (pre-1900), Peterborough (pre-1900), Plymouth (1928), Portsmouth (1926), Preston (2002), Ripon (pre-1900), Salford (1926), Sunderland (1992), Truro (pre-1900), Wakefield (pre-1900), Wells (pre-1900), Westminster (pre-1900), Wolverhampton (2000) and Worcester (pre-1900).

Certain cities have also been granted a lord mayoralty – this grant confers no additional powers or functions and is purely honorific. Cities with lord mayors are Birmingham, Bradford, Bristol, Canterbury, Chester, Coventry, Exeter, Kingston-upon-Hull, Leeds, Leicester, Liverpool, London, Manchester, Newcastle-upon-Tyne, Norwich, Nottingham, Oxford, Plymouth, Portsmouth, Sheffield, Stoke-on-Trent, Westminster and York.

BATH (PRE-1900)
Bath stands on the River Avon between the Cotswold Hills to the north and the Mendips to the south. In the early 18th century, Bath became England's premier spa town where the rich and celebrated members of fashionable society gathered to 'take the waters' and enjoy the town's theatres and concert rooms. During this period the architect John Wood laid the foundations for a new Georgian city to be built using the honey-coloured stone for which Bath is famous today.

Contemporary Bath is a thriving tourist destination and remains a leading cultural, religious and historical centre with many art galleries and historic sites including the Pump Room (1790); the Royal Crescent (1767); the Circus (1754); the 18th-century Assembly Rooms (housing the Museum of Costume); Pulteney Bridge (1771); the Guildhall and the Abbey, now over 500 years old, which is built on the site of a Saxon monastery. In 2006 the Bath Thermae Spa was completed and the hot springs re-opened to the public for the first time since 1978; combining five historic spa buildings with contemporary architecture, it is the only spa in the UK to utilise naturally occurring thermal waters.

BIRMINGHAM (PRE-1900)
Birmingham is Britain's second largest city, with a population of over one million. The generally accepted derivation of 'Birmingham' is the *ham* (dwelling-place) of the *ing* (family) of *Beorma*, presumed to have been Saxon. During the Industrial Revolution the town grew into a major manufacturing centre and in 1889 was granted city status.

Recent developments include Millennium Point, which houses Thinktank, the Birmingham science museum, and Brindleyplace, a development of shops, offices and leisure facilities on a former industrial site clustered around canals. In 2003 the Bullring shopping centre was officially opened as part of the city's urban regeneration programme.

The principal buildings are the Town Hall (1834–50), the Council House (1879), Victoria Law Courts (1891), the University of Birmingham (1906–9), the 13th-century Church of St Martin-in-the-Bull-Ring (rebuilt 1873), the cathedral (formerly St Philip's Church) (1711), the Roman Catholic cathedral of St Chad (1839–41), the Assay Office (1773), the Rotunda (1964) and the National Exhibition Centre (1976). There is also the Birmingham Museum and Art Gallery which was founded in 1885 and is home to a collection of Pre-Raphaelite paintings.

BRADFORD (PRE-1900)
During the Industrial Revolution of the 18th and 19th centuries Bradford expanded rapidly, largely as a result of the thriving wool industry.

Bradford city centre has a host of buildings with historical and cultural interest, including City Hall, with its 19th-century Lord Mayor's rooms and Victorian law court; Bradford Cathedral; the Priestley, a theatre and arts centre originally established as the Bradford Civic Playhouse by J. B. Priestley and friends; the National Media Museum which houses seven floors of interactive displays and three cinemas; Piece Hall Yard which incorporates the Bradford Club, a Victorian Gothic style building dating from 1837, and the Peace Museum.

BRIGHTON AND HOVE (2000)
Brighton and Hove is situated on the south coast of England, around 96 km (60 miles) south of London. Originally a fishing village called Brighthelmstone, it was transformed into a fashionable seaside resort in the 18th century when Dr Richard Russell popularised the benefits of his 'sea-water cure'; as one of the closest beaches to London, Brighton began to attract wealthy visitors. One of these was the Prince Regent (the future King George IV), who first visited in 1783 and became so fond of the city that in 1807 he bought the former farmhouse he had been renting, and gradually turned it into Brighton's most recognisable building, the Royal Pavilion. The Pavilion is renowned for its Indo-Saracenic exterior, featuring minarets and an enormous central dome designed by John Nash, combined with the lavish chinoiserie of Frederick Crace's and Robert Jones' interiors.

Brighton and Hove's Regency heritage can also be seen in the numerous elegant squares and crescents designed by Amon Wilds and Augustin Busby that dominate the seafront.

Brighton and Hove is once again a fashionable resort, known for its cafe culture, lively nightlife and thriving gay scene.

BRISTOL (PRE-1900)
Bristol was a royal borough before the Norman conquest. The earliest form of the name is *Bricgstow*.

The principal buildings include the 12th-century

Cathedral with Norman chapter house and gateway; the 14th-century Church of St Mary Redcliffe; Wesley's Chapel, Broadmead; the Merchant Venturers' Almshouses; the Council House (1956); the Guildhall; the Exchange (erected from the designs of John Wood in 1743); Cabot Tower; the University and Clifton College. The Roman Catholic cathedral at Clifton was opened in 1973.

The Clifton Suspension Bridge, with a span of 214m (702ft) over the Avon, was projected by Isambard Kingdom Brunel in 1836 but was not completed until 1864. Brunel's SS *Great Britain*, the first ocean-going propeller-driven ship, now forms a museum at the Western Dockyard, from where she was originally launched in 1843. The docks themselves have been extensively restored and redeveloped; the 19th-century two-storey former tea warehouse is now the Arnolfini centre for contemporary arts, and an 18th-century sail loft houses the Architecture Centre. Behind the baroque-domed facade of the former 'E' Shed are shops, cafes, restaurants and the Watershed Media Centre, and on Princes Wharf 1950s transit sheds, which formerly housed the Industrial Museum, have been renovated and converted into the new museum of Bristol, M Shed, which opened in June 2011.

CAMBRIDGE (1951)

Cambridge, a settlement far older than its ancient university, lies on the River Cam (or Granta). The city is a county town and regional headquarters. Its industries include technology research and development, and biotechnology. Among its open spaces are Jesus Green, Sheep's Green, Coe Fen, Parker's Piece, Christ's Pieces, the University Botanic Garden, and the 'Backs' – lawns and gardens through which the Cam winds behind the principal line of college buildings. Historical sites east of the Cam include King's Parade, Great St Mary's Church, Gibbs' Senate House and King's College Chapel.

University and college buildings provide the outstanding features of Cambridge's architecture but several churches (especially St Benet's, the oldest building in the city, and Holy Sepulchre or the Round Church) are also notable. The Guildhall (1937) stands on a site, of which at least part has held municipal buildings since 1224.

CANTERBURY (PRE-1900)

Canterbury, seat of the Archbishop of Canterbury, the primate of the Church of England, dates back to prehistoric times. It was the Roman *Durovernum Cantiacorum* and the Saxon *Cant-wara-byrig* (stronghold of the men of Kent). It was here in 597 that St Augustine began the conversion of the English to Christianity, when Ethelbert, King of Kent, was baptised.

Of the Benedictine St Augustine's Abbey, burial place of the Jutish Kings of Kent, only ruins remain. St Martin's Church, on the eastern outskirts of the city, is stated by Bede to have been the place of worship of Queen Bertha, the Christian wife of King Ethelbert, before the advent of St Augustine.

In 1170 the rivalry of Church and State culminated in the murder in Canterbury Cathedral, by Henry II's knights, of Archbishop Thomas Becket. His shrine became a great centre of pilgrimage, as described in Chaucer's *Canterbury Tales*. After the Reformation pilgrimages ceased, but the prosperity of the city was strengthened by an influx of Huguenot refugees, who introduced weaving. The poet and playwright Christopher Marlowe was born and raised in Canterbury (the city is home to the 1,000-seat Marlowe Theatre) and

there are also literary associations with Defoe, Dickens, Joseph Conrad and Somerset Maugham.

The cathedral, its architecture ranging from the 11th to the 15th centuries, is famous worldwide. Visitors are attracted particularly to the Martyrdom, the Black Prince's Tomb, the Warriors' Chapel and the many examples of medieval stained glass.

The medieval city walls are built on Roman foundations and the 14th-century West Gate is one of the finest buildings of its kind in the country.

The Canterbury Arts Festival takes place at a variety of venues throughout the city each autumn.

CARLISLE (PRE-1900)

Carlisle is situated at the confluence of the rivers Eden and Caldew, 497km (309 miles) north-west of London and around 16km (10 miles) from the Scottish border. It was granted a charter in 1158.

The city stands at the western end of Hadrian's Wall and dates from the original Roman settlement of *Luguvalium*. Granted to Scotland in the tenth century, Carlisle is not included in the Domesday Book. William Rufus reclaimed the area in 1092 and the castle and city walls were built to guard Carlisle and the western border; the citadel is a Tudor addition to protect the south of the city. Border disputes were common until the problem of the Debateable Lands was settled in 1552. During the Civil War the city remained Royalist; in 1745 Carlisle was besieged for the last time by the Young Pretender (Bonnie Prince Charlie).

The cathedral, originally a 12th-century Augustinian priory, was enlarged in the 13th and 14th centuries after the diocese was created in 1133. To the south is a restored tithe barn and nearby the 18th-century church of St Cuthbert, the third to stand on a site dating from the seventh century.

Carlisle is the major shopping, commercial and agricultural centre for the area, and industries include the manufacture of metal goods, biscuits and textiles. However, the largest employer is the services sector, most notably in central and local government, retailing and transport. The city occupies an important position at the centre of a network of major roads, as a stage on the main west coast rail services, and with its own airport at Crosby-on-Eden.

CHESTER (PRE-1900)

Chester is situated on the River Dee. Its recorded history dates from the first century when the Romans founded the fortress of *Deva*. The city's name is derived from the Latin *castra* (a camp or encampment). During the Middle Ages, Chester was the principal port of north-west England but declined with the silting of the Dee estuary and competition from Liverpool. The city was also an important military centre, notably during Edward I's Welsh campaigns and the Elizabethan Irish campaigns. During the Civil War, Chester supported the King and was besieged from 1643 to 1646. Chester's first charter was granted c.1175 and the city was incorporated in 1506. The office of sheriff is the earliest created in the country (1120s), and in 1992 the mayor was granted the title of Lord Mayor, who also enjoys the title 'Admiral of the Dee'.

The city's architectural features include the city walls (an almost complete two-mile circuit), the unique 13th-century Rows (covered galleries above the street-level shops), the Victorian Gothic Town Hall (1869), the castle (rebuilt 1788 and 1822) and numerous half-timbered buildings. The cathedral was a Benedictine abbey until the Dissolution of the Monasteries. Remaining monastic buildings include the chapter house, refectory and cloisters and there is a modern free-standing bell tower. The Norman church of St John the Baptist was a cathedral church in the early Middle Ages.

COVENTRY (PRE-1900)

Coventry is an important industrial centre, producing vehicles, machine tools, agricultural machinery, man-made fibres, aerospace components and telecommunications equipment. New investment has come from financial services, power transmission, professional services, leisure and education.

The city owes its beginning to Leofric, Earl of Mercia, and his wife Godiva who, in 1043, founded a Benedictine monastery. The guildhall of St Mary and three of the city's churches date from the 14th and 15th centuries, and 16th-century almshouses can still be seen. Coventry's first cathedral was destroyed during the Reformation, its second in the 1940 blitz (the walls and spire remain) and the new cathedral designed by Sir Basil Spence, consecrated in 1962, now draws numerous visitors.

Coventry is the home of the University of Warwick, Coventry University, Coventry Transport Museum, which specialises in British road transport, and the Skydome Arena.

DURHAM (PRE-1900)

The city of Durham is a major tourist attraction and its prominent Norman cathedral and castle are set high on a wooded peninsula overlooking the River Wear. The cathedral was founded as a shrine for the body of St Cuthbert in 995. The present building dates from 1093 and among its many treasures is the tomb of the Venerable Bede (673–735). Durham's prince bishops had unique powers up to 1836, being lay rulers as well as religious leaders. As a palatinate, Durham could have its own army, nobility, coinage and courts. The castle was the main seat of the prince bishops for nearly 800 years; it is now used as a college by the University of Durham. The university, founded in the early 19th century on the initiative of Bishop William Van Mildert, is England's third oldest.

Among other buildings of interest is the Guildhall in the Market Place which dates from the 14th century. Annual events include Durham's regatta in June (claimed to be the oldest rowing event in Britain) and the annual Gala (formerly Durham Miners' Gala) in July.

KINGSTON-UPON-HULL (PRE-1900)

Hull (officially Kingston-upon-Hull, so named by Edward I) lies at the junction of the River Hull with the Humber, 35km (22 miles) from the North Sea. It is one of the major seaports of the UK. The port provides a wide range of cargo services, including ro-ro and container traffic, and handles an estimated million passengers annually on daily sailings to Rotterdam and Zeebrugge. There is a variety of manufacturing and service industries. City status was accorded in 1897 and the office of mayor raised to the dignity of Lord Mayor in 1914.

The city, restored after heavy air raid damage during the Second World War, has good educational facilities with both the University of Hull and a campus of the University of Lincoln being within its boundaries. Hull is home to the world's only submarium, The Deep, which opened in 2002, and the state-of-the-art Truck Theatre, which opened in 2009.

Tourism is a growing industry; the old town area has been renovated and includes museums, a marina and a shopping complex. Just west of the city is the Humber Bridge, a suspension bridge, opened in 1981, which crosses the Humber Estuary.

LEEDS (PRE-1900)

Leeds, situated in the lower Aire Valley, is a junction for road, rail, canal and air services and an important commercial centre. It was first incorporated by Charles I in 1626. The earliest forms of the name are *Loidis* or *Ledes*, the origins of which are obscure.

The principal buildings are the Civic Hall (1933), the Town Hall (1858), the Municipal Buildings and Art Gallery (1884) with the Henry Moore Gallery (1982), the Corn Exchange (1863) and the University. The parish church (St Peter's) was rebuilt in 1841; the 17th-century St John's Church has a fine interior with a famous English Renaissance screen; the last remaining 18th-century church in the city is Holy Trinity in Boar Lane (1727). Kirkstall Abbey (about three miles from the centre of the city), founded by Henry de Lacy in 1152, is one of the most complete examples of a Cistercian house now remaining. Temple Newsam, birthplace of Lord Darnley and largely rebuilt by Sir Arthur Ingram c.1620, was acquired by the council in 1922. Adel Church, about five miles from the centre of the city, is a fine Norman structure. The Royal Armouries Museum forms part of a group of museums that house the national collection of antique arms and armour.

LEICESTER (1919)

Leicester is situated in central England. The city was an important Roman settlement and also one of the five Viking boroughs of Danelaw. In 1485 Richard III was buried in Leicester following his death at the nearby Battle of Bosworth. In 1589 Queen Elizabeth I granted a charter to the city and the ancient title was confirmed by letters patent in 1919.

The textile industry was responsible for Leicester's early expansion and the city still maintains a strong manufacturing base. Cotton mills and factories are now undergoing extensive regeneration and are being converted into offices, apartments, bars and restaurants. The principal buildings include the two universities (the University of Leicester and De Montfort University), as well as the Town Hall, the 13th-century Guildhall, De Montfort Hall, Leicester Cathedral, the Jewry Wall (the UK's highest standing Roman wall), St Nicholas Church and St Mary de Castro church. The motte and Great Hall of Leicester can be seen from the castle gardens, situated next to the River Soar.

Leicester is now one of the UK's most ethnically diverse cities – home to the only Jain temple in the West and hosting the country's second-largest Caribbean carnival.

LINCOLN (PRE-1900)

Situated 64km (40 miles) inland on the River Witham, Lincoln derives its name from a contraction of *Lindum Colonia,* the settlement founded in AD 48 by the Romans to command the crossing of Ermine Street and Fosse Way. Sections of the third-century Roman city wall can be seen, including an extant gateway (Newport Arch), and excavations have discovered traces of a sewerage system unique in Britain. The Romans also drained the surrounding fenland and created a canal system, laying the foundations of Lincoln's agricultural prosperity and also the city's importance in the medieval wool trade as a port and staple town.

As one of the five boroughs of Danelaw, Lincoln was an important trading centre in the ninth and tenth centuries and prosperity from the wool trade lasted until the 14th century. This wealth enabled local merchants to build parish churches, of which three survive, and there are also remains of a 12th-century Jewish community (Jew's House and Court, Aaron's House). However, the removal of the staple to Boston in 1369 heralded a decline, from which the city only recovered fully in the 19th century, when improved fen drainage made Lincoln agriculturally important. Improved canal and rail links led to industrial development, mainly in the manufacture of machinery, components and engineering products.

The castle was built shortly after the Norman Conquest and is unusual in having two mounds; on one motte stands a keep (Lucy's Tower) added in the 12th century. It currently houses one of the four surviving copies of the Magna Carta. The cathedral was begun c.1073 when the first Norman bishop moved the see of Lindsey to Lincoln, but was mostly destroyed by fire and earthquake in the 12th century. Rebuilding was begun by St Hugh and completed over a century later. Other notable architectural features are the 12th-century High Bridge, the oldest in Britain still to carry buildings, and the Guildhall, situated above the 15th-century Stonebow gateway.

LIVERPOOL (PRE-1900)

Liverpool, on the north bank of the river Mersey, 5km (3 miles) from the Irish Sea, is the United Kingdom's foremost port for Atlantic trade. Tunnels link Liverpool with Birkenhead and Wallasey.

There are 2,100 acres of dockland on both sides of the river and the Gladstone and Royal Seaforth Docks can accommodate tanker-sized vessels. Liverpool Free Port was opened in 1984.

Liverpool was created a free borough in 1207 and a city in 1880. From the early 18th century it expanded rapidly with the growth of industrialisation and the transatlantic slave trade. Surviving buildings from this period include the Bluecoat Chambers (1717, formerly the Bluecoat School), the Town Hall (1754, rebuilt to the original design 1795), and buildings in Rodney Street, Canning Street and the suburbs. Notable from the 19th and 20th centuries are the Anglican cathedral, built from the designs of Sir Giles Gilbert Scott (the foundation stone was laid in 1904, but the building was only completed in 1980); the Catholic Metropolitan Cathedral (designed by Sir Frederick Gibberd, consecrated 1967) and St George's Hall (1842), regarded as one of the finest modern examples of classical architecture. The refurbished Albert Dock (designed by Jesse Hartley) contains the Merseyside Maritime Museum, the International Slavery Museum and the Tate Liverpool art gallery.

In 1852 an act was passed establishing a public library, museum and art gallery; as a result Liverpool had one of the first public libraries in the country. The Brown, Picton and Hornby libraries form one of the country's major collections. The Victoria Building of Liverpool University; the Royal Liver, Cunard and Mersey Docks & Harbour Company buildings at the Pier Head; the Municipal Buildings and the Philharmonic Hall are other examples of the city's fine architecture.

Six areas of Liverpool's maritime mercantile city were designated as UNESCO World Heritage Sites in 2004.

MANCHESTER (PRE-1900)

Manchester (the *Mamucium* of the Romans, who occupied it in AD 79) is a commercial and industrial centre engaged in the engineering, chemical, clothing, food processing and textile industries and in education. Banking, insurance and a growing leisure industry are among its prime commercial activities. The city is connected with the sea by the Manchester Ship Canal, opened in 1894, 57km (35.5 miles) long, and accommodating ships up to 15,000 tons.

The principal buildings are the Town Hall, erected in 1877 from the designs of Alfred Waterhouse, with a large extension of 1938; the Royal Exchange (1869, enlarged 1921); the Central Library (1934); Heaton Hall; the 17th-century Chetham Library; the Rylands Library (1900), which includes the Althorp collection; the university precinct; the 15th-century cathedral (formerly the parish church); the Manchester Central conference and exhibition centre and the Bridgewater Hall (1996) concert venue. Manchester is the home of the Hallé Orchestra, the Royal Northern College of Music, the Royal Exchange Theatre and numerous public art galleries.

To accommodate the Commonwealth Games held in the city in 2002, new sports facilities were built including a stadium, swimming pool complex and the National Cycling Centre.

The town received its first charter of incorporation in 1838 and was created a city in 1853.

NEWCASTLE UPON TYNE (PRE-1900)

Newcastle upon Tyne, on the north bank of the River Tyne, is 13km (8 miles) from the North Sea. A cathedral and university city, it is the administrative, commercial and cultural centre for north-east England and the principal port. It is an important manufacturing centre with a wide variety of industries.

The principal buildings include the Castle Keep (12th century), Black Gate (13th century), Blackfriars (13th century), West Walls (13th century), St Nicholas's Cathedral (15th century, fine lantern tower), St Andrew's Church (12th–14th century), St John's (14th–15th century), All Saints (1786 by Stephenson), St Mary's Roman Catholic Cathedral (1844), Trinity House (17th century), Sandhill (16th-century houses), Guildhall (Georgian), Grey Street (1834–9), Central Station (1846–50), Laing Art Gallery (1904), University of Newcastle Physics Building (1962) and Medical Building (1985), Civic Centre (1963) and the Central Library (1969). Open spaces include the Town Moor (927 acres) and Jesmond Dene. Numerous bridges span the Tyne at Newcastle, including the Tyne Bridge (1928) and the tilting Millennium Bridge (2001) – which links the city with Gateshead to the south.

The city's name is derived from the 'new castle' (1080) erected as a defence against the Scots. In 1400 it was made a county, and in 1882 a city.

NORWICH (PRE-1900)

Norwich grew from an early Anglo-Saxon settlement near the confluence of the rivers Yare and Wensum, and now serves as the provincial capital for the predominantly agricultural region of East Anglia. The name is thought to relate to the most northerly of a group of Anglo-Saxon villages or *wics*. The city's first known charter was granted in 1158 by Henry II.

Norwich serves its surrounding area as a market town and commercial centre, with banking and insurance prominent among the city's businesses. From the 14th century until the Industrial Revolution, Norwich was the regional centre of the woollen industry, but now the biggest single industry is financial services and principal trades are engineering, printing, shoemaking, the production of chemicals and clothing, food processing and technology. Norwich is accessible to seagoing vessels by means of the River Yare, entered at Great Yarmouth, 32km (20 miles) to the east.

Among many historic buildings are the cathedral (completed in the 12th century and surmounted by a 15th-century spire 96m (315ft) in height); the keep of the Norman castle (now a museum and art gallery); the 15th-century flint-walled Guildhall; some thirty medieval parish churches; St Andrew's and Blackfriars' Halls; the Tudor houses preserved in Elm Hill and the Georgian Assembly House. The University of East Anglia is on the city's western boundary.

NOTTINGHAM (PRE-1900)

Nottingham stands on the River Trent. *Snotingaham* or *Notingeham*, literally the homestead of the people of Snot, is the Anglo-Saxon name for the Celtic settlement of *Tigguocobauc*, or the house of caves. In 878, Nottingham became one of the five boroughs of Danelaw. William the Conqueror ordered the construction of Nottingham Castle, while the town itself developed rapidly under Norman rule. Its laws and rights were later formally recognised by Henry II's charter in 1155. The castle became a favoured residence of King John. In 1642 King Charles I raised his personal standard at Nottingham Castle at the start of the Civil War.

Nottingham is home to Notts County FC (the world's oldest football league side), Nottingham Forest FC, Nottingham Racecourse, Trent Bridge cricket ground and the National Watersports Centre. The principal industries include textiles, pharmaceuticals, food manufacturing, engineering and telecommunications. There are two universities within the city boundaries.

Architecturally, Nottingham has a wealth of notable buildings, particularly those designed in the Victorian era by T. C. Hine and Watson Fothergill. The city council owns the castle, of Norman origin but restored in 1878, Wollaton Hall (1580–8), Newstead Abbey (once home of Lord Byron), the Guildhall (1888) and Council House (1929). St Mary's, St Peter's and St Nicholas' churches are of interest, as is the Roman Catholic cathedral (Pugin, 1842–4). Nottingham was granted city status in 1897.

OXFORD (PRE-1900)

Oxford is a university city, an important industrial centre and a market town. Industry played a minor part in Oxford until the motor industry was established in 1912.

Oxford is known for its architecture, its oldest specimens being the reputedly Saxon tower of St Michael's Church, the remains of the Norman castle and city walls, and the Norman church at Iffley. It also has many Gothic buildings, such as the Divinity Schools, the Old Library at Merton College, William of Wykeham's New College, Magdalen and Christ Church colleges and many other college buildings. Later centuries are represented by the Laudian quadrangle at St John's College, the Renaissance Sheldonian Theatre by Wren, Trinity College Chapel, All Saints Church, Hawksmoor's mock-Gothic at All Souls College, and the 18th-century Queen's College. In addition to individual buildings, High Street and Radcliffe Square both form interesting architectural compositions. Most of the colleges have gardens, those of Magdalen, New College, St John's and Worcester being the largest.

The Oxford University Museum of Natural History, renowned for its spectacular neo-gothic architecture, houses the university's scientific collections of zoological, entomological and geological specimens and is attached to the neighbouring Pitt Rivers Museum which houses ethnographic and archaeological objects from around the world. The Ashmolean is the city's museum of art and archaeology and Modern Art Oxford hosts a programme of contemporary art exhibitions.

ST ALBANS (PRE-1900)

The origins of St Albans, situated on the River Ver, stem from the Roman town of *Verulamium*. Named after the first Christian martyr in Britain, who was executed there, St Albans has developed around the Norman abbey and cathedral church (consecrated 1115), built partly of materials from the old Roman city. The museums house Iron Age and Roman artefacts and the Roman theatre, unique in Britain, has a stage as opposed to an amphitheatre. Archaeological excavations in the city centre have revealed evidence of pre-Roman, Saxon and medieval occupation.

The town's significance grew to the extent that it was a signatory and venue for the drafting of the Magna Carta. It was also the scene of riots during the Peasants' Revolt, the French King John was imprisoned there after the Battle of Poitiers, and heavy fighting took place there during the Wars of the Roses.

Previously controlled by the Abbot, the town achieved a charter in 1553 and city status in 1877. The street market, first established in 1553, is still an important feature of the city, as are many hotels and inns, surviving from the days when St Albans was an important coach stop. Tourist attractions include historic churches and houses and a 15th-century clock tower.

The city is now home to a wide range of businesses, with special emphasis on information and legal services, and is home to the Royal National Rose Society.

SALISBURY (PRE-1900)

The history of Salisbury centres around the cathedral and cathedral close. The city evolved from an Iron Age camp a mile to the north of its current position which was strengthened by the Romans and called *Serviodunum*. The Normans built a castle and cathedral on the site and renamed it Sarum. In 1220 Bishop Richard Poore and the architect Elias de Derham decided to build a new Gothic style cathedral. The cathedral was completed 38 years later and a community known as New Sarum, now called Salisbury, grew around it. Originally the cathedral had a squat tower; the 123m (404ft) spire that makes the cathedral the tallest medieval structure in the world was added *c*.1315. A walled close with houses for the clergy was built around the cathedral; the Medieval Hall still stands today, alongside buildings dating from the 13th to the 20th century, including some designed by Sir Christopher Wren.

A prosperous wool and cloth trade allowed Salisbury to flourish until the 17th century. When the wool trade declined new crafts were established including cutlery, leather and basket work, saddlery, lacemaking, joinery and malting. By 1750 it had become an important road junction and coaching centre and in the Victorian era the railways enabled a new age of expansion and prosperity. Today Salisbury is a thriving tourist centre.

SHEFFIELD (PRE-1900)

Sheffield is situated at the junction of the Sheaf, Porter, Rivelin and Loxley valleys with the River Don and was created a city in 1893. Though its cutlery, silverware and plate have long been famous, Sheffield has other and now more important industries: special and alloy steels, engineering, tool-making, medical equipment and media-related industries (in its new cultural industries quarter). Sheffield has two universities and is an important research centre.

The parish church of St Peter and St Paul, founded in the 12th century, became the cathedral church of the Diocese of Sheffield in 1914. The Roman Catholic Cathedral Church of St Marie (founded 1847) was created a cathedral for the new diocese of Hallam in 1980. Parts of the present building date from c.1435. The principal buildings are the Town Hall (1897), the Cutlers' Hall (1832), City Hall (1932), Graves Art Gallery (1934), Mappin Art Gallery, the Crucible Theatre and the restored Lyceum theatre, which dates from 1897 and was reopened in 1990. Three major sporting and entertainment venues were opened between 1990 and 1991: Sheffield Arena, Don Valley Stadium and Pond's Forge. The Millennium Galleries opened in 2001.

SOUTHAMPTON (1964)

Southampton is a major seaport on the south coast of England, situated between the mouths of the Test and Itchen rivers. Southampton's natural deep-water harbour has made the area an important settlement since the Romans built the first port (known as *Clausentum*) in the first century, and Southampton's port has witnessed several important departures, including those of King Henry V in 1415 for the Battle of Agincourt, RMS *Titanic* in 1912, and the *Mayflower* in 1620.

The city's strategic importance, not only as a seaport but also as a centre for aircraft production, meant that it was heavily bombed during the Second World War; however, many historically significant structures remain, including the Wool House, dating from 1417 and now used as the Maritime Museum; parts of the Norman city walls which are among the most complete in the UK; the Bargate, which was originally the main gateway into the city; God's House Tower, now the Museum of Archaeology; St Michael's, the city's oldest church; and the Tudor Merchants Hall.

Home to the National Oceanography Centre, the international Southampton Boat Show and some of the country's principal watersports venues, Southampton's coastal setting and maritime history remain its main focus, but it also features extensive parks and a thriving entertainment scene.

STOKE-ON-TRENT (1925)

Stoke-on-Trent, standing on the River Trent and familiarly known as 'the potteries', is the main centre of employment for the population of north Staffordshire. The city is the largest clayware producer in the world (china, earthenware, sanitary goods, refractories, bricks and tiles) and also has a wide range of other manufacturing industries, including steel, chemicals, engineering and tyres. Extensive reconstruction has been carried out in recent years.

The city was formed by the federation of the separate municipal authorities of Tunstall, Burslem, Hanley, Stoke, Fenton, and Longton in 1910 and received its city status in 1925.

WINCHESTER (PRE-1900)

Winchester, the ancient capital of England, is situated on the River Itchen. The city is rich in architecture of all types, especially notable is the cathedral. Built in 1079–93 the cathedral exhibits examples of Norman, early English and Perpendicular styles and is the burial place of author Jane Austen. Winchester College, founded in 1382, is one of the country's most famous public schools, and the original building (1393) remains largely unaltered. St Cross Hospital, another great medieval foundation, lies one mile south of the city. The almshouses were founded in 1136 by Bishop Henry de Blois, and Cardinal Henry Beaufort added a new almshouse of 'Noble Poverty' in 1446. The chapel and dwellings are of great architectural interest, and visitors may still receive the 'Wayfarer's Dole' of bread and ale.

Excavations have done much to clarify the origins and development of Winchester. Part of the forum and several of the streets from the Roman town have been discovered. Excavations in the Cathedral Close have uncovered the entire site of the Anglo-Saxon cathedral (known as the Old Minster) and parts of the New Minster which was built by Alfred's son, Edward the Elder, and is the burial place of the Alfredian dynasty. The original burial place of St Swithun, before his remains were translated to a site in the present cathedral, was also uncovered.

Excavations in other parts of the city have thrown much light on Norman Winchester, notably on the site of the Royal Castle (adjacent to which the new Law Courts have been built) and in the grounds of Wolvesey Castle, where the great house built by Bishops Giffard and Henry de Blois in the 12th century has been uncovered. The Great Hall, built by Henry III between 1222 and 1236, survives and houses the Arthurian Round Table.

YORK (PRE-1900)

The city of York is an archiepiscopal seat. Its recorded history dates from AD 71, when the Roman Ninth Legion established a base under Petilius Cerealis that would later become the fortress of *Eburacum*, or *Eboracum*. In Anglo-Saxon times the city was the royal and ecclesiastical centre of Northumbria, and after capture by a Viking army in AD 866 it became the capital of the Viking kingdom of Jorvik. By the 14th century the city had become a great mercantile centre, mainly because of its control of the wool trade, and was used as the chief base against the Scots. Under the Tudors its fortunes declined, although Henry VIII made it the headquarters of the Council of the North. Excavations on many sites, including Coppergate, have greatly expanded knowledge of Roman, Viking and medieval urban life.

With its development as a railway centre in the 19th century the commercial life of York expanded, and today the city is home to the award-winning National Railway Museum. The principal industries are the manufacture of chocolate, scientific instruments and sugar.

The city is rich in examples of architecture of all periods. The earliest church was built in AD 627 and, from the 12th to 15th centuries, the present Minster was built in a succession of styles. Other examples within the city are the medieval city walls and gateways, churches and guildhalls. Domestic architecture includes the Georgian mansions of The Mount, Micklegate and Bootham.

LORD-LIEUTENANTS AND HIGH SHERIFFS

Area	Lord-Lieutenant	High Sheriff (2011–12)
Bedfordshire	Sir Samuel Whitbread, KCVO	Andrew Slack
Berkshire	Hon. Mary Bayliss	Robert Woods, CBE
Bristol	Mary Prior, MBE	John Cottrell
Buckinghamshire	Sir Henry Aubrey-Fletcher	James Naylor
Cambridgeshire	Hugh Duberly, CBE	Richard Barnwell
Cheshire	David Briggs, MBE	John Lea
Cornwall	Lady Mary Holborow, DCVO	Col. Edward Bolitho, OBE
Cumbria	Sir James Cropper, KCVO	Iona Frost-Pennington
Derbyshire	William Tucker	David Coke-Steel
Devon	Eric Dancer, CBE	Hon. Sarah Lopes
Dorset	Valerie Pitt-Rivers	Alan Frost
Durham	Sir Paul Nicholson, KCVO	Roger Howell
East Riding of Yorkshire	Hon. Susan Cunliffe-Lister	John Holtby
East Sussex	Peter Field	Kathleen Gore
Essex	Lord Petre	Rosemary Ruggles-Brise
Gloucestershire	Dame Janet Trotter, DBE	Marcus Heywood
Greater London	Sir David Brewer, CMG	Lady Elizabeth Arnold
Greater Manchester	Warren Smith	Christine Lee-Jones
Hampshire	Dame Mary Fagan, DCVO	Nigel Scott
Herefordshire	Countess of Darnley	Simon Arbuthnott
Hertfordshire	Countess of Verulam	Lord Charles Cecil
Isle of Wight	Maj.-Gen. Martin White, CB, CBE	Susan Sheldon
Kent	Allan Willett, CMG	Georgie Warner
Lancashire	Lord Shuttleworth, KCVO	Peter Mileham
Leicestershire	Lady Gretton	Resham Sandhu, MBE
Lincolnshire	Anthony Worth	Robin Battle
Merseyside	Dame Lorna Fox Muirhead, DBE	Prof. Helen Carty
Norfolk	Richard Jewson	Georgina Holloway
North Yorkshire	Lord Crathorne	Alexandra Holford
Northamptonshire	Lady Juliet Townsend, LVO	Penelope Escombe, MBE
Northumberland	Duchess of Northumberland	Revd Fiona Sample
Nottinghamshire	Sir Andrew Buchanan, Bt., KCVO	John Peace
Oxfordshire	Tim Stevenson, OBE	Penelope Glen
Rutland	Dr Laurence Howard, OBE	Peter Lawson
Shropshire	A. Heber-Percy	Richard Burbidge, OBE
Somerset	Lady Gass	John Cullum
South Yorkshire	David Moody	Andrew Coombe
Staffordshire	Sir James Hawley, KCVO, TD	Simon Clarke
Suffolk	Lord Tollemache	Stephen Miles
Surrey	Mrs S. Goad	Prof. Michael Joy, OBE
Tyne and Wear	N. Sherlock, OBE	Geoffrey Hodgson
Warwickshire	M. Dunne	Timothy Cox
West Midlands	Paul Sabapathy, CBE	David Grove, OBE
West Sussex	Susan Pyper	David Tupper
West Yorkshire	Dr Ingrid Roscoe	Anthony Grant, OBE
Wiltshire	John Bush, OBE	Robert Hiscox
Worcestershire	M. Brinton	Hon. Lady Morrison

COUNTY COUNCILS

Council & Administrative Headquarters	Telephone	Population*	Council Tax†	Chief Executive
Buckinghamshire, Aylesbury	01296-395000	494,700	£1,078	Chris Williams
Cambridgeshire, Cambridge	0345-045 5200	607,000	£1,048	Mark Lloyd
Cumbria, Carlisle	01228-606060	495, 000	£1,162	Jill Stannard
Derbyshire, Matlock	01629-580000	760,200	£1,077	Nick Hodgson
Devon, Exeter	0845-155 1015	747,400	£1,116	Phil Norrey
Dorset, Dorchester	01305-221000	404,000	£1,168	David Jenkins
East Sussex, Lewes	01273-481000	512,100	£1,158	Becky Shaw
Essex, Chelmsford	0845-743 0430	1,399,000	£1,087	Joanna Killian
Gloucestershire, Gloucester	01452-425000	589,100	£1,091	Peter Bungard
Hampshire, Winchester	01962-841841	1,289,400	£1,038	Andrew Smith
Hertfordshire, Hertford	01992-555644	1,095,500	£1,119	Caroline Tapster
Kent, Maidstone	01622-671411	1,411,100	£1,048	Katherine Kerswell
Lancashire, Preston	0545-053 0000	1,165,800	£1,108	Phil Halsall
Leicestershire, Leicester	0116-232 3232	644,700	£1,063	John Sinnott
Lincolnshire, Lincoln	01522-552222	697,900	£1,066	Tony McArdle
Norfolk, Norwich	0844-800 8020	853,400	£1,145	David White
North Yorkshire, Northallerton	01609-780780	597,700	£1,057	Richard Flinton
Northamptonshire, Northampton	01604-236236	683,800	£1,028	Paul Blantern
Nottinghamshire, Nottingham	0115-982 3823	776,600	£1,193	Mick Burrows
Oxfordshire, Oxford	01865-792422	640,300	£1,162	Joanna Simons
Somerset, Taunton	0845-345 9166	523,500	£1,027	Sheila Wheeler
Staffordshire, Stafford	01785-223121	828,700	£1,029	Nick Bell
Suffolk, Ipswich	0845-606 6067	714,000	£1,127	Lucy Robinson (acting)
Surrey, Kingston upon Thames	0845-600 9009	1,113,100	£1,116	David McNulty
Warwickshire, Warwick	01926-410410	535,100	£1,155	Jim Graham
West Sussex, Chichester	01243-777100	792,900	£1,162	Kieran Stigant
Worcestershire, Worcester	01905-763763	556,500	£1,039	Trish Haines

* Source: The Office of National Statistics – Mid-2009 Population Estimates (Crown copyright)
† Average 2011–12 Band D council tax in the county area exclusive of precepts for fire and police authorities. County councils claim their share of the combined council tax from the collection funds of the district authorities into whose area they fall. Average Band D council tax bills for the billing authority are given on the following pages

DISTRICT COUNCILS

District Council	Telephone	Population*	Council Tax†	Chief Executive
Adur	01273-263000	61,300	£1,588	Peter Latham
Allerdale	01900-702702	94,300	£1,539	Harry Dyke
Amber Valley	01773-570222	121,000	£1,495	Peter Carney
Arun	01903-737500	149,900	£1,520	Ian Sumnall
Ashfield	01623-450000	116,400	£1,596	Philip Marshall
Ashford	01233-331111	114,100	£1,413	John Bunnett
Aylesbury Vale	01296-585858	173,500	£1,493	Andrew Grant
Babergh	01473-822801	85,800	£1,490	Charlie Adan
Barrow-in-Furness	01229-876300	70,900	£1,562	Tom Campbell
Basildon	01268-533333	174,100	£1,544	Bala Mahendran
Basingstoke and Deane	01256-844844	163,300	£1,366	Tony Curtis
Bassetlaw	01909-533533	111,600	£1,598	David Hunter
Blaby	0116-275 0555	93,600	£1,497	Sandra Whiles
Bolsover	01246-240000	74,200	£1,563	Wesley Lumley
Boston	01205-314200	59,000	£1,427	Richard Harbord
Braintree	01376-552525	142,700	£1,480	Allan Reid
Breckland	01362-656870	129,900	£1,455	Terry Huggins
Brentwood	01277-312500	73,800	£1,467	Joanna Killian
Broadland	01603-431133	123,000	£1,507	Colin Bland
Bromsgrove	01527-881288	93,400	£1,502	Kevin Dicks
Broxbourne	01992-785555	90,200	£1,380	Mike Walker
Broxtowe	0115-917 7777	111,500	£1,607	Ruth Hyde, OBE
Burnley	01282-425011	85,600	£1,577	Steve Rumbelow
CAMBRIDGE	01223-457000	121,100	£1,442	Antoinette Jackson
Cannock Chase	01543-462621	94,500	£1,490	Stephen Brown
CANTERBURY	01227-862000	149,100	£1,444	Colin Carmichael
CARLISLE	01228-817000	104,700	£1,561	Maggie Mooney
Castle Point	01268-882200	89,200	£1,523	David Marchant
Charnwood	01509-263151	165,000	£1,459	Geoff Parker
Chelmsford	01245-606606	167,800	£1,481	Steve Packham
Cheltenham	01242-262626	113,900	£1,481	Andrew North
Cherwell	01295-252535	139,200	£1,519	Sue Smith
Chesterfield	01246-345345	100,900	£1,460	Huw Bowen
Chichester	01243-785166	112,600	£1,475	John Marsland
Chiltern	01494-729000	90,900	£1,506	Alan Goodrum
Chorley	01257-515151	104,800	£1,514	Gary Hall
Christchurch	01202-495000	47,000	£1,584	David McIntosh
Colchester	01206-282222	177,100	£1,477	Adrian Pritchard
Copeland	0845-054 8600	69,700	£1,555	Paul Walker
Corby	01536-464000	55,200	£1,402	Chris Mallender
Cotswold	01285-623000	83,500	£1,488	David Neudegg
Craven	01756-700600	55,500	£1,525	Paul Shevlin
Crawley	01293-438000	105,300	£1,488	Lee Harris
Dacorum	01442-228000	141,600	£1,447	Daniel Zammit
Dartford	01322-343434	93,600	£1,443	Graham Harris
Daventry	01327-871100	78,900	£1,407	Ian Vincent
Derbyshire Dales	01629-761100	70,100	£1,538	David Wheatcroft
Dover	01304-821199	106,100	£1,461	Nadeem Aziz
East Cambridgeshire	01353-665555	83,900	£1,463	John Hill
East Devon	01395-516551	132,700	£1,501	Mark Williams
East Dorset	01202-886201	87,600	£1,639	David McIntosh
East Hampshire	01730-266551	111,900	£1,433	Sandy Hopkins
East Hertfordshire	01279-655261	137,100	£1,486	Anne Freimanis
East Lindsey	01507-601111	140,800	£1,388	Nigel Howells
East Northamptonshire	01832-742000	85,000	£1,411	David Oliver
East Staffordshire	01283-508000	108,800	£1,485	Andy O'Brien
Eastbourne	01323-410000	96,400	£1,603	Robert Cottrill
Eastleigh	023-8068 8000	120,800	£1,434	Bernie Topham
Eden	01768-817817	51,800	£1,551	Robin Hooper (acting)
Elmbridge	01372-474474	130,600	£1,515	Robert Moran
Epping Forest	01992-564000	124,000	£1,491	Derek Macnab (acting)

District Council	Telephone	Population*	Council Tax†	Chief Executive
Epsom and Ewell	01372-732000	72,700	£1,478	Frances Rutter
Erewash	0115-907 2244	110,900	£1,480	Jeremy Jaroszek
EXETER	01392-277888	118,800	£1,470	Philip Bostock
Fareham	01329-236100	111,500	£1,386	Peter Grimwood
Fenland	01354-654321	91,700	£1,541	Sandra Claxton
Forest Heath	01638-719000	62,200	£1,499	David Burnip
Forest of Dean	01594-810000	82,800	£1,505	Sue Pangbourne *(acting)*
Fylde	01253-658658	76,300	£1,523	Phillip Woodward
Gedling	0115-901 3901	112,700	£1,577	John Robinson
GLOUCESTER	01452-522232	117,300	£1,476	Julian Wain
Gosport	023-9258 4242	80,000	£1,448	Ian Lycett
Gravesham	01474-337000	98,800	£1,427	Glyn Thomson
Great Yarmouth	01493-856100	96,300	£1,492	Richard Packham
Guildford	01483-505050	135,700	£1,481	David Hill
Hambleton	0845-121 1555	87,300	£1,445	Peter Simpson
Harborough	01858-828282	83,400	£1,490	Anna Graves
Harlow	01279-446655	80,600	£1,537	Malcolm Morley
Harrogate	01423-500600	157,900	£1,553	Wallace Sampson
Hart	01252-622122	91,200	£1,456	Geoff Bonner
Hastings	01424 451066	86,900	£1,614	Roy Mawford
Havant	023-9247 4174	116,500	£1,438	Sandy Hopkins
Hertsmere	020-8207 2277	98,900	£1,447	Donald Graham
High Peak	0845-129 7777	92,400	£1,500	Simon Baker
Hinckley and Bosworth	01455-238141	104,800	£1,438	Steve Atkinson
Horsham	01403-215100	129,800	£1,479	Tom Crowley
Huntingdonshire	01480-388388	165,800	£1,476	David Monks
Hyndburn	01254-388111	81,100	£1,549	David Welsby
Ipswich	01473-432000	126,600	£1,597	Russell Williams
Kettering	01536-410333	90,100	£1,429	David Cook, MBE
King's Lynn and West Norfolk	01553-616200	143,000	£1,491	Ray Harding
LANCASTER	01524-582000	139,800	£1,523	Mark Cullinan
Lewes	01273-471600	96,400	£1,643	Jenny Rowlands
Lichfield	01543-308000	98,300	£1,453	Nina Dawes
LINCOLN	01522-881188	88,500	£1,481	Andrew Taylor
Maidstone	01622-602000	148,200	£1,494	Alison Broom
Maldon	01621-854477	62,900	£1,495	Fiona Marshall
Malvern Hills	01684-862151	75,000	£1,478	Chris Bocock
Mansfield	01623-463463	99,700	£1,610	Ruth Marlow
Melton	01664-502502	48,900	£1,487	Lynn Aisbett
Mendip	01749-648999	118,700	£1,466	Stuart Brown
Mid Devon	01884-255255	76,000	£1,560	Kevin Finan
Mid Suffolk	01449-720711	94,200	£1,492	Charlie Adan
Mid Sussex	01444-458166	131,600	£1,505	Kathryn Hall
Mole Valley	01306-885001	83,800	£1,470	Darren Mepham
New Forest	023-8028 5000	176,400	£1,466	David Yates
Newark and Sherwood	01636-650000	113,000	£1,646	Andrew Muter
Newcastle-under-Lyme	01782-717717	124,200	£1,460	Mark Barrow
North Devon	01271-327711	91,500	£1,554	M. Mansell
North Dorset	01258-454111	64,300	£1,588	Elizabeth Goodall
North East Derbyshire	01246-231111	98,000	£1,566	Wes Lumley
North Hertfordshire	01462-474000	124,700	£1,481	John Campbell
North Kesteven	01529-414155	105,700	£1,444	Ian Fytche
North Norfolk	01263-513811	101,200	£1,510	Philip Burton
North Warwickshire	01827-715341	61,900	£1,579	Jeremy Hutchinson
North West Leicestershire	01530-454545	90,600	£1,506	Christine Fisher
Northampton	01604-837837	210,500	£1,445	David Kennedy
NORWICH	0344-980 3333	140,100	£1,562	Laura McGillivray
Nuneaton and Bedworth	02476-376376	122,000	£1,533	Alan Franks & Gareth Owens
Oadby and Wigston	0116-288 8961	58,500	£1,489	Mark Hall
OXFORD	01865-249811	149,300	£1,583	Peter Sloman
Pendle	01282-661661	89,300	£1,572	Stephen Barnes
PRESTON	01772-906900	134,600	£1,581	Lorraine Norris
Purbeck	01929-556561	45,200	£1,627	Steve Mackenzie
Redditch	01527-64252	78,700	£1,501	Kevin Dicks
Reigate and Banstead	01737-276000	136,100	£1,514	John Jory
Ribble Valley	01200-425111	57,700	£1,476	Marshal Scott
Richmondshire	01748-829100	52,800	£1,539	Peter Simpson

District Council	Telephone	Population*	Council Tax†	Chief Executive
Rochford	01702-546366	83,100	£1,521	Paul Warren
Rossendale	01706-217777	67,100	£1,574	Helen Lockwood
Rother	01424-787999	89,200	£1,588	Derek Stevens
Rugby	01788-533533	93,300	£1,517	Ian David & Andrew Gabbitas
Runnymede	01932-838383	83,900	£1,452	Paul Turrell
Rushcliffe	0115-981 9911	111,700	£1,598	Allen Graham
Rushmoor	01252-398398	91,100	£1,430	Andrew Lloyd
Ryedale	01653-600666	53,600	£1,534	Janet Waggott
ST ALBANS	01727-866100	137,200	£1,472	Daniel Goodwin
St Edmundsbury	01284-763233	103,500	£1,505	Geoff Rivers
Scarborough	01723-232323	108,500	£1,552	Jim Dillon
Sedgemoor	0845-408 2540	112,100	£1,445	Mr Kerry Rickards
Selby	01757-705101	82,200	£1,530	Martin Connor
Sevenoaks	01732-227000	113,200	£1,503	Robin Hales
Shepway	01303-853000	100,300	£1,535	Alistair Stewart
South Bucks	01895-837200	66,600	£1,489	Chris Furness
South Cambridgeshire	0345-0450500	144,500	£1,456	Jean Hunter
South Derbyshire	01283-221000	92,800	£1,476	Frank McArdle
South Hams	01803-861234	83,500	£1,520	Richard Sheard
South Holland	01775-761161	84,100	£1,430	Terry Huggins
South Kesteven	01476-406080	131,200	£1,408	Beverly Agass
South Lakeland	01539-733333	103,800	£1,557	Lawrence Conway
South Norfolk	01508-533633	119,700	£1,528	Sandra Dinneen
South Northamptonshire	01327-322322	88,500	£1,449	Sue Smith
South Oxfordshire	01491-823000	130,600	£1,508	David Buckle
South Ribble	01772-421491	108,200	£1,528	Mike Nuttall
South Somerset	01935-462462	158,600	£1,481	Mark Williams
South Staffordshire	01902-696000	106,300	£1,418	Steve Winterflood
Spelthorne	01784-451499	92,600	£1,482	Roberto Tambini
Stafford	01785-619000	125,500	£1,441	Ian Thompson
Staffordshire Moorlands	01538-483483	95,400	£1,454	Simon Baker
Stevenage	01438-242242	81,000	£1,455	Nick Parry
Stratford-on-Avon	01789-267575	118,900	£1,510	Paul Lankester
Stroud	01453-766321	111,100	£1,535	David Hagg
Suffolk Coastal	01394-383789	124,100	£1,481	Stephen Baker
Surrey Heath	01276-707100	83,900	£1,518	Karen Whelan
Swale	01795-417330	131,900	£1,430	Abdool Kara
Tamworth	01827-709709	75,700	£1,424	Tony Goodwin
Tandridge	01883-722000	82,200	£1,523	Stephen Weigel
Taunton Deane	01823-356356	108,700	£1,415	Penny James
Teignbridge	01626-361101	126,900	£1,540	Nicola Bulbeck
Tendring	01255-686868	148,000	£1,462	Ian Davidson
Test Valley	01264-368000	113,400	£1,397	Roger Tetstall
Tewkesbury	01684-295010	80,600	£1,434	Michael Dawson
Thanet	01843-577000	130,900	£1,480	Dr Sue McGonigal
Three Rivers	01923-776611	88,100	£1,459	Dr Steven Halls
Tonbridge and Malling	01732-844522	117,400	£1,466	David Hughes
Torridge	01237-428700	65,300	£1,524	Nicola Bulbeck
Tunbridge Wells	01892-526121	107,600	£1,434	William Benson
Uttlesford	01799-510510	75,600	£1,496	John Mitchell
Vale of White Horse	01235-520202	118,700	£1,493	David Buckle
Warwick	01926-450000	139,000	£1,497	Chris Elliott
Watford	01923-226400	83,800	£1,516	Manny Lewis
Waveney	01502-562111	117,700	£1,448	Stephen Baker
Waverley	01483-523333	119,300	£1,519	Mary Orton
Wealden	01323-443322	143,100	£1,631	Charles Lant
Wellingborough	01933-229777	75,700	£1,369	Joe Hubbard
Welwyn & Hatfield	01707-357000	112,800	£1,498	Michel Saminaden
West Devon	01822-813600	52,700	£1,584	Richard Sheard
West Dorset	01305-251010	96,500	£1,599	David Clarke
West Lancashire	01695-577177	110,200	£1,515	William Taylor, MBE
West Lindsey	01427-676676	88,600	£1,484	Manjeet Gill
West Oxfordshire	01993-861000	102,500	£1,455	David Neudegg
West Somerset	01643-703704	35,400	£1,453	Adrian Dyer
Weymouth and Portland	01305-838000	63,600	£1,678	David Clarke
WINCHESTER	01962-840222	113,300	£1,436	Simon Eden
Woking	01483-755855	92,400	£1,520	Ray Morgan, OBE

District Council	Telephone	Population*	Council Tax†	Chief Executive
WORCESTER	01905-723471	94,700	£1,457	Duncan Sharkey
Worthing	01903-239999	102,400	£1,516	Peter Latham
Wychavon	01386-565000	116,700	£1,440	Jack Hegarty
Wycombe	01494-461000	163,600	£1,457	Karen Satterford
Wyre	01253-891000	111,100	£1,507	Garry Payne
Wyre Forest	01562-732928	98,100	£1,502	Ian Miller

* Source: ONS – Mid-2009 Population Estimates (Crown copyright)
† Average Band D council tax bill for 2011–12
Councils in CAPITAL LETTERS have city status

METROPOLITAN BOROUGH COUNCILS

Metropolitan Borough Councils	Telephone	Population*	Council Tax†	Chief Executive
Barnsley	01226-770770	226,300	£1,401	Philip Coppard, OBE
BIRMINGHAM	0121-303 9944	1,028,700	£1,261	Stephen Hughes
Bolton	01204-333333	265,100	£1,414	Sean Harriss
BRADFORD	01274-432001	506,800	£1,283	Tony Reeves
Bury	0161-253 5000	182,600	£1,457	Mike Kelly
Calderdale	01422-357257	201,600	£1,417	Owen Williams
COVENTRY	024-7683 3333	312,800	£1,471	Martin Reeves
Doncaster	01302-734444	290,100	£1,316	Robert Vincent
Dudley	0300-555 2345	306,600	£1,273	John Polychronakis
Gateshead	0191-433 3000	190,800	£1,600	Roger Kelly
Kirklees	01484-221000	406,800	£1,405	Adrian Lythgo
Knowsley	0151-489 6000	149,400	£1,484	Sheena Ramsey
LEEDS	0113-222 4444	787,700	£1,312	Tom Riordan
LIVERPOOL	0151-233 3000	442,300	£1,519	Ged Fitzgerald
MANCHESTER	0161-234 5000	483,800	£1,327	Sir Howard Bernstein
NEWCASTLE UPON TYNE	0191-232 8520	284,300	£1,512	Barry Rowland
North Tyneside	0191-643 5991	197,200	£1,485	John Marsden
Oldham	0161-911 3000	218,800	£1,547	Charlie Parker
Rochdale	01706-647474	204,700	£1,482	Roger Ellis
Rotherham	01709-382121	253,900	£1,451	Martin Kimber
St Helens	01744-676789	177,100	£1,366	Carole Hudson
SALFORD	0161-794 4711	225,100	£1,523	Barbara Spicer
Sandwell	0121-569 2200	291,000	£1,323	Jan Britton (acting)
Sefton	0151-922 4040	273,300	£1,488	Margaret Carney
SHEFFIELD	0114-272 6444	547,000	£1,478	John Mothersole
Solihull	0121-704 6000	205,200	£1,337	Mark Rogers
South Tyneside	0191-427 1717	152,400	£1,448	Martin Swales
Stockport	0161-480 4949	283,700	£1,560	Eamonn Boylan
SUNDERLAND	0191-520 5555	281,700	£1,343	Dave Smith
Tameside	0161-342 8355	215,400	£1,366	Steven Pleasant
Trafford	0161-912 2000	215,300	£1,303	Janet Callender
WAKEFIELD	0845-8506 506	323,900	£1,306	Joanne Roney, OBE
Walsall	01922-650000	255,900	£1,532	Paul Sheehan
Wigan	01942-244991	306,500	£1,369	Joyce Redfearn
Wirral	0151-606 2000	308,500	£1,464	James Wilkie
WOLVERHAMPTON	01902-556556	238,500	£1,464	Simon Warren

* Source: ONS – Mid-2009 Population Estimates (Crown copyright)
† Average Band D council tax bill for 2011–12
Councils in CAPITAL LETTERS have city status

UNITARY COUNCILS

Unitary Councils	Telephone	Population*	Council Tax†	Chief Executive
Bath and North East Somerset	01225-477000	177,700	£1,462	John Everitt
Bedford	01234-267422	158,000	£1,556	Philip Simpkins
Blackburn with Darwen	01254-585585	139,900	£1,481	Graham Burgess
Blackpool	01253-477477	140,000	£1,516	Steve Weaver
Bournemouth	01202-451451	164,900	£1,499	Pam Donnellan
Bracknell Forest	01344-352000	115,100	£1,366	Timothy Wheadon
BRIGHTON AND HOVE	01273-290000	256,300	£1,483	John Barradell, OBE
BRISTOL	0117-922 2000	433,100	£1,567	Jan Ormondroyd
Central Bedfordshire	0300-300 8000	252,900	£1,641	Richard Carr
Cheshire East	0300-123 5500	362,700	£1,451	Erika Wenzel
Cheshire West and Chester	0300-123 8123	326,600	£1,486	Steve Robinson
Cornwall	0300-123 4100	531,100	£1,460	Kevin Lavery
Darlington	01325-380651	100,400	£1,394	Ada Burns
DERBY	01332-293111	244,100	£1,358	Adam Wilkinson
DURHAM	0300-123 7070	506,400	£1,602	George Garlick
East Riding of Yorkshire	01482-887700	337,000	£1,500	Nigel Pearson
Halton	0151-907 8300	118,700	£1,350	David Parr
Hartlepool	01429-266522	90,900	£1,671	Paul Walker
Herefordshire	01432-260000	179,100	£1,493	Chris Bull
Isle of Wight	01983-821000	140,200	£1,466	Joe Duckworth
Isles of Scilly‡	01720-422537	2,200	£1,187	Philip Hygate
KINGSTON-UPON-HULL	01482-609100	262,400	£1,341	Nicola Yates
LEICESTER	0116-254 9922	304,700	£1,409	Sheila Lock
Luton	01582-546000	194,300	£1,371	Trevor Holden
Medway	01634-333333	254,800	£1,330	Neil Davies
Middlesbrough	01642-245432	140,500	£1,514	Ian Parker
Milton Keynes	01908-691691	236,700	£1,390	David Hill
North East Lincolnshire	01472-313131	157,100	£1,503	Tony Hunter
North Lincolnshire	01724-296296	161,000	£1,555	Simon Driver
North Somerset	01934-888888	209,100	£1,423	Graham Turner
Northumberland	01670-533000	311,100	£1,496	Steve Stewart
NOTTINGHAM	0115-915 5555	300,800	£1,562	Jane Todd
PETERBOROUGH	01733-747474	171,200	£1,330	Gillian Beasley
PLYMOUTH	01752-668000	256,700	£1,473	Barry Keel
Poole	01202-633633	141,200	£1,450	John McBride
PORTSMOUTH	023-9282 2251	203,500	£1,357	David Williams
Reading	0118-9373737	151,800	£1,499	Michael Coughlin
Redcar and Cleveland	0164-277 4774	137,500	£1,556	Amanda Skelton
Rutland	01572-722577	38,400	£1,691	Helen Briggs
Shropshire	0345-678 9000	291,800	£1,495	Kim Ryley
Slough	01753-475111	128,400	£1,368	Ruth Bagley
South Gloucestershire	01454-868686	262,200	£1,529	Amanda Deeks
SOUTHAMPTON	023-8022 3855	236,700	£1,447	Alistair Neill
Southend-on-Sea	01702-215000	164,200	£1,320	Robert Tinlin
Stockton-on-Tees	01642-393939	191,100	£1,483	Neil Schneider
STOKE-ON-TRENT	01782-234567	238,900	£1,389	John van de Laarschot
Swindon	01793-445500	198,800	£1,393	Gavin Jones
Telford and Wrekin	01952-380000	162,300	£1,419	Richard Partington (interim)
Thurrock	01375-652652	157,200	£1,301	Graham Farrant
Torbay	01803-201201	134,000	£1,493	Elizabeth Raikes
Warrington	01925-444400	197,800	£1,369	Diana Terris
West Berkshire	01635-42400	153,000	£1,500	Nick Carter
Wiltshire	0300-456 0100	456,100	£1,514	Andrew Kerr
Windsor and Maidenhead	01628-683800	143,800	£1,218	Ian Trenholm
Wokingham	0118-974 6000	161,900	£1,462	Susan Law
YORK	01904-613161	198,800	£1,366	Kersten England

* Source: ONS – Mid-2009 Population Estimates (Crown copyright)
† Average Band D council tax bill for 2011–12
‡ Under the Isles of Scilly Clause the council has additional functions to other unitary authorities
Councils in CAPITAL LETTERS have city status

MAP OF COUNCILS IN ENGLAND

1 Stockton-on-Tees
2 Middlesbrough
3 Blackpool
4 Blackburn
   with Darwen
5 Bolton
6 Bury
7 Rochdale
8 Salford
9 Oldham
10 Liverpool
11 Knowsley
12 St Helens
13 Halton
14 Warrington
15 Trafford
16 Manchester
17 Tameside
18 Stockport
19 Nottingham
20 Telford and
   Wrekin
21 Wolverhampton

22 Walsall
23 Sandwell
24 Dudley
25 Birmingham
26 Solihull
27 Coventry
28 Peterborough
29 South Glos
30 Bristol
31 Bath and
   NE Somerset
32 Windsor and
   Maidenhead
33 Slough
34 Reading
35 Wokingham
36 Bracknell Forest
37 Thurrock
38 Southend
39 Medway
40 Plymouth
41 Torbay
42 Bournemouth

LONDON

1 Hillingdon
2 Harrow
3 Barnet
4 Enfield
5 Waltham Forest
6 Redbridge
7 Barking and Dagenham
8 Havering
9 Ealing
10 Brent
11 Camden
12 Haringey
13 Islington
14 Hackney
15 Newham
16 Hounslow
17 Hammersmith and Fulham

18 Kensington and Chelsea
19 City of Westminster
20 City of London
21 Tower Hamlets
22 Richmond upon Thames
23 Wandsworth
24 Lambeth
25 Southwark
26 Lewisham
27 Greenwich
28 Bexley
29 Kingston upon Thames
30 Merton
31 Sutton
32 Croydon
33 Bromley

LONDON

THE CITY OF LONDON CORPORATION

The City of London is the historic centre at the heart of London known as 'the square mile' around which the vast metropolis has grown over the centuries. The City's residential population is roughly 8,000 and in addition, around a third of a million people work in the City. The civic government is carried on by the City of London Corporation through the court of Common Council.

The City is an international financial and business centre, generating about £30bn a year for the British economy. It includes the head offices of the principal banks, insurance companies and mercantile houses, in addition to buildings ranging from the historic Roman Wall and the 15th-century Guildhall, to the massive splendour of St Paul's Cathedral and the architectural beauty of Wren's spires.

The City of London was described by Tacitus in AD 62 as 'a busy emporium for trade and traders'. Under the Romans it became an important administration centre and hub of the road system. Little is known of London in Saxon times, when it formed part of the kingdom of the East Saxons. In 886 Alfred recovered London from the Danes and reconstituted it a burgh under his son-in-law. In 1066 the citizens submitted to William the Conqueror who in 1067 granted them a charter, which is still preserved, establishing them in the rights and privileges they had hitherto enjoyed.

THE MAYORALTY

The mayoralty was probably established about 1189, the first mayor being Henry Fitz Ailwyn who filled the office for 23 years and was succeeded by Fitz Alan (1212–14). A new charter was granted by King John in 1215, directing the mayor to be chosen annually, which has been done ever since, though in early times the same individual often held the office more than once. A familiar instance is that of 'Whittington, thrice Lord Mayor of London' (in reality four times: 1397, 1398, 1406 and 1419); and many modern cases have occurred. The earliest instance of the phrase 'lord mayor' in English is in 1414. It was used more generally in the latter part of the 15th century and became invariable from 1535 onwards. At Michaelmas the liverymen in Common Hall choose two aldermen who have served the office of sheriff for presentation to the Court of Aldermen, and one is chosen to be lord mayor for the following mayoral year.

LORD MAYOR'S DAY

The lord mayor of London was previously elected on the feast of St Simon and St Jude (28 October), and from the time of Edward I, at least, was presented to the King or to the Barons of the Exchequer on the following day, unless that day was a Sunday. The day of election was altered to 16 October in 1346, and after some further changes was fixed for Michaelmas Day in 1546, but the ceremonies of admittance and swearing-in of the lord mayor continued to take place on 28 and 29 October respectively until 1751. In 1752, at the reform of the calendar, the lord mayor was continued in office until 8 November, the 'new style' equivalent of 28 October. The lord mayor is now presented to the lord chief justice at the royal courts of justice on the second Saturday in November to make the final declaration of office, having been sworn in at Guildhall on the preceding day. The procession to the royal courts of justice is popularly known as the Lord Mayor's Show.

REPRESENTATIVES

Aldermen are mentioned in the 11th century and their office is of Saxon origin. They were elected annually between 1377 and 1394, when an act of parliament of Richard II directed them to be chosen for life. Aldermen now serve a six-year term of office before submitting themselves for re-election.

The Common Council was, at an early date, substituted for a popular assembly called the *Folkmote*. At first only two representatives were sent from each ward, but now each of the City's 25 wards is represented by an alderman and at least two Common Councilmen (the number depending on the size of the ward). Common Councilmen are elected every four years.

OFFICERS

Sheriffs were Saxon officers; their predecessors were the *wic-reeves* and *portreeves* of London and Middlesex. At first they were officers of the Crown, and were named by the Barons of the Exchequer; but Henry I (in 1132) gave the citizens permission to choose their own sheriffs, and the annual election of sheriffs became fully operative under King John's charter of 1199. The citizens lost this privilege, as far as the election of the sheriff of Middlesex was concerned, by the Local Government Act 1888; but the liverymen continue to choose two sheriffs of the City of London, who are appointed on Midsummer Day and take office at Michaelmas.

The office of chamberlain is an ancient one, the first contemporary record of which is 1237. The town clerk (or common clerk) is first mentioned in 1274.

ACTIVITIES

The work of the City of London Corporation is assigned to a number of committees which present reports to the Court of Common Council. These committees are: Administration of the Sir William Coxen Trust Fund; Audit and Risk Management; Barbican Centre; Barbican Residential; Board of Governors of the City of London Freeman's School, the City of London School, the City of London School for Girls, Emanuel Hospital Charitable Trust, the Guildhall School of Music and Drama and the Museum of London; Bridewell Royal Hospital; Christ's Hospital; City Bridge Trust; Community and Children's Services; Corporation Benevolent Association Management; Court of Aldermen; Court of Common Council; Culture, Heritage and Libraries; Epping Forest and Commons; Establishment; Finance; Freedom Applications; Gresham (city side); General Purposes; Guildhall Improvement; Hampstead Heath, Highgate Wood and Queen's Park Management; Joint Overview and Scrutiny; Joint Working Party of the Three Schools; Keats House Management; Licensing; Livery; London Drug Policy Forum; Markets; Open Spaces, City Gardens and West Ham Park; Planning and Transportation; Police;

Policy and Resources; Port Health and Environmental Services and Standards Committees.

The City's estate, in the possession of which the City of London Corporation differs from other municipalities, is managed by the City Lands and Bridge House Estates Committee, the chairmanship of which carries with it the title of chief commoner.

The Honourable the Irish Society, which manages the City Corporation's estates in Ulster, consists of a governor and five other aldermen, the recorder, and 19 common councilmen, of whom one is elected deputy governor.

THE LORD MAYOR 2011–12

The Rt. Hon. the Lord Mayor, David Wootton*
Private Secretary, William Chapman
* Provisional at time of going to press

THE SHERIFFS 2011–12

Wendy Mead (Farringdon Wt.); Alderman Alan Yarrow (Bridge & Bridge Wt.)

OFFICERS, ETC

Town Clerk, Chris Duffield
Chamberlain, Chris Bilsland
Chief Commoner (2011), Richard Regan
Clerk, The Honourable the Irish Society, C. Fisher

THE ALDERMEN

with office held and date of appointment to that office

Name and Ward	Common Councilman	Alderman	Sheriff	Lord Mayor
Lord Levene of Portsoken, KBE, Aldgate	1983	1984	1995	1998
Sir David Howard, Bt., Cornhill	1972	1986	1997	2000
Sir Robert Finch, Coleman Street	–	1992	1999	2003
Sir Michael Savory, Bread Street	1980	1996	2001	2004
Sir John Stuttard, Lime Street	–	2001	2005	2006
Sir David Lewis, Broad Street	–	2001	2006	2007
Ian Luder, Castle Baynard	1998	2005	2007	2008
Nicholas Anstee, Aldersgate	1987	1996	2003	2009
Michael Bear, Portsoken	2003	2005	2007	2010

All the above have passed the Civic Chair

Name and Ward	Common Councilman	Alderman	Sheriff	Lord Mayor
Simon Walsh, Farringdon Wt.	1989	2000		
Dr Andrew Parmley, Vintry	1992	2001		
Benjamin R. Hall, Farringdon Wn.	1995	2002		
Alison Gowman, Dowgate	1991	2002		
Gordon Haines, Queenhithe	–	2004		
Roger Gifford, Cordwainer	–	2004	2008	
David Wootton, Langbourn	2002	2005	2009	
Alan Yarrow, Bridge & Bridge Wt.	–	2007		
Jeffrey Evans, Cheap	–	2007		
Sir Paul Judge, Tower	–	2007		
Fiona Woolf, CBE, Candlewick	–	2007	2010	
John White, TD, Billingsgate	–	2008		
David Graves, Cripplegate	–	2008		
John Garbutt, Walbrook	–	2009		
Neil Redcliffe, Bishopsgate	–	2009		
Philip Remnant, CBE, Bassishaw	–	2010		

THE COMMON COUNCIL

Deputy: each common councilman so described serves as deputy to the alderman of her/his ward.

Name	Ward
Abrahams, G. C. (2000)	Farringdon Wt.
Absalom, J. D. (1994)	Farringdon Wt.
Ayers, Deputy K. E., MBE (1996)	Bassishaw
Bain-Stewart, A. (2005)	Farringdon Wn.
Barker, Deputy J. A., OBE (1981)	Cripplegate Wn.
Barrow, Deputy D. (2007)	Aldgate
Bennett, Deputy J. A. (2005)	Broad Street
Bird, J. L., OBE (1977)	Tower
Boleat, M. J. (2002)	Cordwainer
Bradshaw, D. J. (1991)	Cripplegate Wn.
Cassidy, Deputy M. J., CBE (1989)	Coleman Street
Catt, R. M. (2004)	Castle Baynard
Chadwick, R. A. H. (1994)	Tower
Challis, N. K. (2005)	Castle Baynard
Chapman, J. D. (2006)	Langbourn
Cotgrove, D. (1991)	Lime Street
Cressey, N. (2009)	Portsoken
Currie, Deputy Miss S. E. M. (1985)	Cripplegate Wt.
Davies, P. S. (2009)	Broad Street
Day, M. J. (2005)	Bishopsgate
Deane, A. J. (2011)	Farringdon Wt.
Dove, W. H., MBE (1993)	Bishopsgate
Duckworth, S. D. (2000)	Bishopsgate
Dudley, Revd Dr M. R. (2002)	Aldersgate
Duffield, R. W. (2004)	Farringdon Wn.
Dunphy, P. G. (2009)	Cornhill
Eskenzi, Deputy A. N., CBE (1970)	Farringdon Wn.
Eve, Deputy R. A. (1980)	Cheap
Everett, K. M. (1984)	Candlewick
Farr, M. C. (1998)	Walbrook
Fernandes, S. A. (2009)	Coleman Street
Fraser, S. J. (1993)	Coleman Street
Fraser, Deputy W. B., OBE (1981)	Vintry
Fredericks, M. B. (2008)	Tower
Galloway, A. D., OBE (1981)	Bishopsgate
Gillon, G. M. F. (1995)	Cordwainer
Ginsburg, Deputy S. (1990)	Bishopsgate
Graves, A. C. (1985)	Bishopsgate
Haines, Deputy Revd S. D. (2005)	Cornhill
Halliday, Deputy Mrs P. A., OBE (1992)	Walbrook
Hardwick, Dr P. B. (1987)	Aldgate
Harris, B. N. (2004)	Bridge
Henderson-Begg, M. (1977)	Coleman Street
Hoffman, T. D. D. (2002)	Vintry
Howard, R. P. (2011)	Lime Street

Hudson, M. (2007) — *Castle Baynard*
Hughes-Penney, R. C. (2004) — *Farringdon Wn.*
Hunt, W. G., TD (2004) — *Castle Baynard*
James, Clare (2008) — *Farringdon Wn.*
Jones, *Deputy* H. L. M. (2004) — *Portsoken*
King, *Deputy* A. J. N. (1999) — *Queenhithe*
Knowles, *Deputy* S. K., MBE (1984) — *Candlewick*
Lawrence, *Deputy* G. A. (2002) — *Farringdon Wt.*
Leck, P. (1998) — *Aldersgate*
Littlechild, V. (2009) — *Cripplegate Wn.*
Llewelyn-Davies, A. (2009) — *Billingsgate*
Lodge, O. A. W., TD (2009) — *Bread Street*
Lord, C. E. (2009) — *Farringdon Wt.*
McGuinness, *Deputy* C. S. (1997) — *Castle Baynard*
Malins, *Deputy* J. H., QC (1981) — *Farringdon Wt.*
Martinelli, P. J. (2009) — *Farringdon Wt.*
Mayhew, J. P. (1996) — *Aldersgate*
Mead, Mrs W. (1997) — *Farringdon Wt.*
Merrett, R. A. (2009) — *Bassishaw*
Mooney, B. D. F. (1998) — *Queenhithe*
Moore, G. W. (2009) — *Cripplegate Wn.*
Morris, H. F. (2008) — *Aldgate*
Moys, Mrs S. D. (2001) — *Aldgate*
Nash, *Deputy* Mrs J. C., OBE (1983) — *Aldersgate*
Newman, Mrs B. P., CBE (1989) — *Aldersgate*
Owen, *Deputy* Mrs J., MBE (1975) — *Langbourn*
Owen-Ward, *Deputy* J. R., MBE (1983) — *Bridge*
Page, M. (2002) — *Farringdon Wn.*
Pembroke, Mrs A. M. F. (1978) — *Cheap*
Pollard, J. H. G. (2002) — *Dowgate*
Priest, H. J. S. (2009) — *Castle Baynard*
Pulman, *Deputy* G. A. G. (1983) — *Tower*
Punter, C. (1993) — *Cripplegate Wn.*
Quilter, S. D. (1998) — *Cripplegate Wt.*
Regan, *Deputy* R. D. (1998) — *Farringdon Wn.*
Regis, D. (2009) — *Portsoken*
Richardson, M. C. (2009) — *Coleman Street*
Robinson, Mrs D. C. (1989) — *Bishopsgate*
Rogula, E. (2008) — *Lime Street*
Rounding, V. (2011) — *Farringdon Wn.*
Scott, J. G. S. (1999) — *Broad Street*
Seaton, I. (2009) — *Bassishaw*
Sherlock, *Deputy* M. R. C. (1992) — *Dowgate*
Shilson, *Deputy*, G. R. E., DPHIL (2009) — *Bread Street*
Simons, J. L. (2004) — *Castle Baynard*
Snyder, *Deputy* Sir Michael (1986) — *Cordwainer*
Spanner, J. H., TD (2001) — *Farringdon Wt.*
Starling, Mrs A. J. (2006) — *Cripplegate Wt.*
Thompson, D. J. (2004) — *Aldgate*
Tomlinson, J. (2004) — *Cripplegate Wt.*
Tumbridge, J. R. (2009) — *Tower*
Twogood, M. (2004) — *Farringdon Wt.*
Welbank, *Deputy* M. (2005) — *Billingsgate*
Willoughby, *Deputy* P. J. (1985) — *Bishopsgate*

THE CITY GUILDS (LIVERY COMPANIES)

The constitution of the livery companies has been unchanged for centuries. There are three ranks of membership: freemen, liverymen and assistants. A person can become a freeman by patrimony (through a parent having been a freeman); by servitude (through having served an apprenticeship to a freeman); or by redemption (by purchase).

Election to the livery is the prerogative of the company, who can elect any of its freemen as liverymen. Assistants are usually elected from the livery and form a Court of Assistants which is the governing body of the company. The master (in some companies called the prime warden) is elected annually from the assistants.

The register for 2011–12 lists 24,971 liverymen of the guilds entitled to vote at elections at Common Hall.

The order of precedence, omitting extinct companies, is given in parentheses after the name of each company in the list below. In certain companies the election of master or prime warden for the year does not take place until the autumn. In such cases the master or prime warden for 2010–11, rather than 2011–12, is given.

THE TWELVE GREAT COMPANIES
In order of civic precedence

MERCERS *(1)*. *Hall*, Mercers' Hall, Ironmonger Lane, London EC2V 8HE *Livery*, 233. *Clerk*, Menna McGregor *Master*, Thomas Clifford Sheldon

GROCERS *(2)*. *Hall*, Grocers' Hall, Princes Street, London EC2R 8AD *Livery*, 342. *Clerk*, Brig. Robert Pridham, OBE *Master*, T. Stubbs

DRAPERS *(3)*. *Hall*, Drapers' Hall, Throgmorton Avenue, London EC2N 2DQ *Livery*, 300. *Clerk*, Rear-Adm. A. B. Ross, CB, CBE *Master*, A. H. R. Walker

FISHMONGERS *(4)*. *Hall*, Fishmongers' Hall, London Bridge, London EC4R 9EL *Livery*, 388. *Clerk*, Nigel Cox *Prime Warden*, Thomas Boyd, OBE

GOLDSMITHS *(5)*. *Hall*, Goldsmiths' Hall, Foster Lane, London EC2V 6BN *Livery*, 313. *Clerk*, Richard Melly *Prime Warden*, H. J. Miller

MERCHANT TAYLORS *(6/7)*. *Hall*, Merchant Taylors' Hall, 30 Threadneedle Street, London EC2R 8JB *Livery*, 330. *Clerk*, Rear-Adm. Nicholas Harris, CB, MBE *Master*, Eddie Charlton

SKINNERS *(6/7)*. *Hall*, Skinners' Hall, 8 Dowgate Hill, London EC4R 2SP *Livery*, 400. *Clerk*, Maj.-Gen. Brian Plummer, CBE *Master*, Andrew Boggis

HABERDASHERS *(8)*. *Hall*, Haberdashers' Hall, 18 West Smithfield, London EC1A 9HQ *Livery*, 314. *Clerk*, Rear-Adm. Richard Phillips, CB *Master*, Deborah Knight

SALTERS *(9)*. *Hall*, Salters' Hall, 4 Fore Street, London EC2Y 5DE *Livery*, 163. *Clerk*, Capt. David Morris, RN *Master*, Rt. Hon. Lord Butler of Brockwell, KG, GCB, CVO

IRONMONGERS *(10)*. *Hall*, Ironmongers' Hall, 1 Shaftesbury Place, London EC2Y 8AA *Livery*, 98. *Clerk*, Col. Hamon Massey *Master*, M. A. Hudson

VINTNERS *(11)*. *Hall*, Vintners' Hall, Upper Thames Street, London EC4V 3BG *Livery*, 310. *Clerk*, Brig. Michael Smythe, OBE *Master*, Michael Turner

CLOTHWORKERS *(12)*. *Hall*, Clothworkers' Hall, Dunster Court, Mincing Lane, London EC3R 7AH *Livery*, 200. *Clerk*, Andrew Blessley *Master*, John Stoddart-Scott

OTHER CITY GUILDS
In alphabetical order

ACTUARIES *(91)*. 3rd Floor Cheapside House, 138 Cheapside, London EC2V 6BW *Livery*, 234. *Clerk*, David Johnson *Master*, John Lockyer

AIR PILOTS AND AIR NAVIGATORS *(81)*. *Hall*, Cobham House, 9 Warwick Court, Gray's Inn, London WC1R 5DJ *Livery*, 600. *Clerk*, Paul Tacon *Grand Master*, HRH the Duke of York, KG, GCVO, ADC(P) *Master*, O. W. Epton

APOTHECARIES *(58)*. *Hall*, Apothecaries' Hall, 14 Black Friars Lane, London EC4V 6EJ *Livery*, 1,250. *Clerk*, Ann Wallington-Smith *Master*, Dr T. L. Chambers

ARBITRATORS *(93)*. 13 Hall Gardens, Colney Heath, St Albans, Herts AL4 0QF *Livery*, 108. *Clerk*, Gaye Duffy *Master*, Kay Linnell

ARMOURERS AND BRASIERS *(22)*. *Hall*, Armourers' Hall, 81 Coleman Street, London EC2R 5BJ *Livery*, 128. *Clerk*, Cdre Christopher Waite *Master*, Sir Timothy Ruggles Brise Bt.

BAKERS *(19)*. *Hall*, Bakers' Hall, 9 Harp Lane, London EC3R 6DP *Livery*, 350. *Clerk*, John Tompkins *Master*, Alan Cornwell

BARBERS *(17)*. *Hall*, Barber-Surgeons' Hall, Monkwell Square, Wood Street, London EC2Y 5BL *Livery*, 220. *Clerk*, Col. Peter Durrant, MBE *Master*, H. Harris Hughes, CBE

BASKETMAKERS *(52)*. Doric House, 108 Garstang Road West, Poulton le Fylde, Lancs FY6 7SN *Livery*, 300. *Clerk*, Roger de Pilkyngton *Prime Warden*, John Barker, OBE

BLACKSMITHS *(40)*. 9 Little Trinity Lane, London EC4V 2AD *Livery*, 235. *Clerk*, Christopher Jeal *Prime Warden*, Donald Banner

BOWYERS *(38)*. 46 The Haydens, Tonbridge, Kent TN9 1NS, *Livery*, 86. *Clerk*, Richard Sawyer *Master*, A. H. Mundy

BREWERS *(14)*. *Hall*, Brewers' Hall, Aldermanbury Square, London EC2V 7HR *Livery*, 190. *Clerk*, Brig. D. J. Ross, CBE *Master*, D. G. F. Thompson

BRODERERS *(48)*. Ember House, 35–37 Creek Road, East Molesey, Surrey KT8 9BE *Livery*, 125. *Clerk*, Peter J. C. Crouch *Master*, Lt-Col. G. T. R. Birdwood

BUILDERS MERCHANTS *(88)*. 4 College Hill, London EC4R 2RB *Livery*, 187. *Clerk*, T. Statham *Master*, Graham Ballinger

BUTCHERS *(24)*. *Hall*, Butchers' Hall, 87 Bartholomew Close, London EC1A 7EB *Livery*, 638. *Clerk*, Cdre Anthony Morrow, CVO *Master*, Ray Woodhouse

CARMEN *(77)*. Five Kings House, 1 Queen Street Place, London EC4R 1QS *Livery*, 500. *Clerk*, Walter Gill *Master*, John Older

CARPENTERS *(26)*. *Hall*, Carpenters' Hall, 1 Throgmorton Avenue, London EC2N 2JJ *Livery*, 196. *Clerk*, Brig. Tim Gregson, MBE *Master*, Giles Downes, CVO

CHARTERED ACCOUNTANTS *(86)*. Larksfield, Kent Hatch Road, Crockham Hill, Edenbridge, Kent TN8 6SX *Livery*, 286. *Clerk*, Peter Dickinson *Master*, Alderman Sir John Stuttard

CHARTERED ARCHITECTS *(98)*. 82A Muswell Hill Road, London N10 3JR *Livery*, 165. *Clerk*, David Cole-Adams *Master*, Michael Wilkey

CHARTERED SECRETARIES AND ADMINISTRATORS *(87)*. 3rd Floor, Saddlers' House, 40 Gutter Lane, London EC2V 6BR *Livery*, 279. *Clerk*, Col. Michael Dudding, OBE, TD *Master*, Ian Richardson

CHARTERED SURVEYORS *(85)*. 75 Meadway Drive, Horsell, Woking, Surrey GU21 4TF *Livery*, 345. *Clerk*, Amanda Jackson *Master*, Mickola Wilson

CLOCKMAKERS *(61)*. Salters' Hall, 4 Fore Street, London EC2Y 5DE *Livery*, 285. *Clerk*, Joe Buxton *Master*, Mark Elliott

COACHMAKERS AND COACH-HARNESS MAKERS *(72)*. 48 Aldernay Street,London SW1V 4EX *Livery*, 400. *Clerk*, Lt.-Col. Peter Henderson, OBE *Master*, Vice-Adm. Timothy Laurence, CB, MVO

CONSTRUCTORS *(99)*. 5 Delft Close, Locks Heath, Southampton SO31 7TQ *Livery*, 170. *Clerk*, Kim Tyrrell *Master*, Doug Barrat

COOKS *(35)*. 18 Solent Drive, Warsash, Southampton SO31 9HB *Livery*, 75. *Clerk*, Vice-Adm. P. J. Wilkinson, CB, CVO *Master*, Geoffrey J. Osborne

COOPERS *(36)*. *Hall*, Coopers' Hall, 13 Devonshire Square, London EC2M 4TH *Livery*, 260. *Clerk*, Lt.-Col. Adrian Carroll *Master*, Peter Timms

CORDWAINERS *(27)*. Clothworkers' Hall, Dunster Court, Mincing Lane, London EC3R 7AH *Livery*, 172. *Clerk*, John Miller *Master*, Geoffrey Branford

CURRIERS *(29)*. Hedgerley, 10 The Leaze, Ashton Keynes, Wiltshire SN6 6PE *Livery*, 92. *Clerk*, Simon Bevan *Master*, Richard Stewart

CUTLERS *(18)*. *Hall*, Cutlers' Hall, Warwick Lane, London EC4M 7BR *Livery*, 100. *Clerk*, J. P. Allen *Master*, C. C. Fisher

DISTILLERS *(69)*. 1 The Sanctuary, Westminster, London SW1P 3JT *Livery*, 260. *Clerk*, Edward Macey-Dare *Master*, Terence Barr

DYERS *(13)*. *Hall*, Dyers' Hall, 10 Dowgate Hill, London EC4R 2ST *Livery*, 136. *Clerk*, J. R. Vaizey *Prime Warden*, L. S. Mackintosh

ENGINEERS *(94)*. Wax Chandlers' Hall, 6 Gresham Street, London EC2V 7AD *Livery*, 320. *Clerk*, Wg Cdr A. G. Willenbruch, FRSE *Master*, John Banyard, OBE, FRENG

ENVIRONMENTAL CLEANERS *(97)*. 121 Hacton Lane, Upminster, Essex RM14 2NL *Livery*, 280. *Clerk*, Neil Morley *Master*, Peter D. Holt

FAN MAKERS *(76)*. Skinners' Hall, 8 Dowgate Hill, London EC4R 2SP *Livery*, 202. *Clerk*, Martin Davies *Master*, James Moore

FARMERS *(80)*. *Hall*, The Farmers' and Fletchers' Hall, 3 Cloth Street, London EC1A 7LD *Livery*, 330. *Clerk*, Col. David King, OBE *Master*, Peter Faulkner

FARRIERS *(55)*. 19 Queen Street, Chipperfield, Kings Langley, Herts WD4 9BT *Livery*, 342. *Clerk*, Charlotte Clifford *Master*, Stephen J. W. Scott

FELTMAKERS *(63)*. Post Cottage,Greywell, Hook, Hants RG29 1DA *Livery*, 173. *Clerk*, Maj. J. T. H. Coombs *Master*, Mrs E. M. B. Rose-Lawson

FIREFIGHTERS *(103)*. The Insurance Hall, 20 Aldermanbury, London EC2V 7HY *Livery*, 103. *Clerk*, Sir Martin Bonham *Master*, Peter Cowland

FLETCHERS *(39)*. *Hall*, The Farmers' and Fletchers' Hall, 3 Cloth Street, London EC1A 7LD *Livery*, 143. *Clerk*, Georgina Butler *Master*, John Owen-Ward, MBE

FOUNDERS *(33)*. *Hall*, Founders' Hall, 1 Cloth Fair, London EC1A 7JQ *Livery*, 175. *Clerk*, A. Gillett *Master*, Dr D. Cogan

FRAMEWORK KNITTERS *(64)*. 86 Park Drive, Upminster, Essex RM14 3AS *Livery*, 200. *Clerk*, Alan Clark *Master*, Paul Bethel

FRUITERERS *(45)*. Chapelstones, 84 High Street, Codford St Mary, Warminster BA12 0ND *Livery*, 283. *Clerk*, Lt.-Col. L. French *Master*, E. Dawes

FUELLERS *(95)*. 26 Merrick Square, London SE1 4JB *Livery*, 135. *Clerk*, Sir Anthony Reardon Smith, Bt. *Master*, Stuart Goldsmith

FURNITURE MAKERS *(83)*. *Hall*, Furniture Makers' Hall, 12 Austin Friars, London EC2N 2HE *Livery*, 228. *Clerk*, Charles Kerrigan *Master*, Hugh Garforth-Bles

GARDENERS *(66)*. 25 Luke Street, London EC2A 4AR *Livery*, 298. *Clerk*, Cdr Robert Woolgar, OBE *Master*, Daniel Caspi

GIRDLERS *(23)*. *Hall*, Girdlers' Hall, Basinghall Avenue, London EC2V 5DD *Livery*, 80. *Clerk*, Brig. I. D. O. Rees *Master*, J. J. Meade

GLASS SELLERS *(71)*. 57 Witley Court, Coram Street, London WC1N 1HD *Livery*, 230. *Clerk*, Col. Audrey Smith *Master*, Richard Lawman

GLAZIERS AND PAINTERS OF GLASS *(53)*. Hall, Glaziers' Hall, 9 Montague Close, London SE1 9DD *Livery*, 292. *Clerk*, Alex Galloway, CVO *Master*, David Ingmire

GLOVERS *(62)*. London SW3 *Livery*, 250. *Clerk*, C. Blackshaw *Master*, K. Ebsworth

GOLD AND SILVER WYRE DRAWERS *(74)*. 9A Prince of Wales Mansions, Prince of Wales Drive, London SW11 4BG *Livery*, 300. *Clerk*, Cdr. R. House *Master*, E. M. V. Knapper

GUNMAKERS *(73)*. The Proof House, 48–50 Commercial Road, London E1 1LP *Livery*, 350. *Clerk*, Col. William Chesshyre *Master*, W. Richards, OBE

HACKNEY CARRIAGE DRIVERS *(104)*. 25 The Grove, Parkfield, Latimer, Bucks HP5 1UE *Livery*, 98. *Clerk*, Mary Whitworth *Master*, James Rainbird

HORNERS *(54)*. St. Stephen's House, Hide Place, London SW1P 4NJ *Livery*, 225. *Clerk*, Raymond Layard *Master*, Georgina Scott

INFORMATION TECHNOLOGISTS *(100)*. Hall, Information Technologists' Hall, 39A Bartholomew Close, London EC1A 7JN *Livery*, 750. *Clerk*, Mike Jenkins *Master*, Jonathan Soar

INNHOLDERS *(32)*. Hall, Innholders' Hall, 30 College Street, London EC4R 2RH *Livery*, 154. *Clerk*, Dougal Bulger *Master*, Ian White, FRICS

INSURERS *(92)*. The Hall, 20 Aldermanbury, London EC2V 7HY *Livery*, 380. *Clerk*, Leonard Walters *Master*, Timothy Ablett

INTERNATIONAL BANKERS *(106)*. 12 Austin Friars, London EC2N 2HE *Livery*, 183. *Clerk*, Wg Cdr Tim Woods, BEM *Master*, Joseph King

JOINERS AND CEILERS *(41)*. 75 Meadway Drive, Horsell, Woking, Surrey GU21 4TF *Livery*, 128. *Clerk*, Amanda Jackson *Master*, Clive Turrell

LAUNDERERS *(89)*. Hall, Launderers' Hall, 9 Montague Close, London Bridge, London SE1 9DD *Livery*, 215. *Clerk*, Mrs J. Polek *Master*, Martyn Lewis

LEATHERSELLERS *(15)*. Hall, 21 Garlick Hill, London EC4V 2AU *Livery*, 150. *Clerk*, David Santa-Olalla *Master*, Miles Emley

LIGHTMONGERS *(96)*. 5 Rokefield House, Westcott Street, Dorking, Surrey RH4 3NZ *Livery*, 168. *Clerk*, Stephen Thomas *Master*, John Harding

LORINERS *(57)*. Hampton House, High Street, East Grinstead, West Sussex RH19 3AW *Livery*, 435. *Clerk*, Peter Lusty *Master*, Lady Milnes Coates

MAKERS OF PLAYING CARDS *(75)*. 256 St David's Square, London E14 3WE *Livery*, 147. *Clerk*, David Barrett *Master*, Lance Whitehouse

MANAGEMENT CONSULTANTS *(105)*. Skinners' Hall, 8 Dowgate Hill, London EC4R 2SP *Livery*, 177. *Clerk*, Leslie Johnson *Master*, Vicky Pryce

MARKETORS *(90)*. Plaisterers' Hall, 1 London Wall, London EC2Y 5JU *Livery*, 267. *Clerk*, Adele Thorpe *Master*, John Flynn

MASONS *(30)*. 22 Cannon Hill, Southgate, London N14 6LG *Livery*, 150. *Clerk*, Heather Rowell *Master*, Derek Sayer

MASTER MARINERS *(78)*. Hall, HQS Wellington, Temple Stairs, Victoria Embankment, London WC2R 2PN *Livery*, 197. *Clerk*, Rear-Adm. Nick Harris, CB, MBE *Master*, R. W. E. Charlton

MUSICIANS *(50)*. 6th Floor, 2 London Wall Building, London EC2M 5PP *Livery*, 385. *Clerk*, Margaret Alford *Master*, Alderman Dr Andrew Parmley

NEEDLEMAKERS *(65)*. PO Box 3682, Windsor, Berkshire SL4 3WR *Livery*, 200. *Clerk*, Philip Grant *Master*, Roger Staines

PAINTER-STAINERS *(28)*. Hall, Painters' Hall, 9 Little Trinity Lane, London EC4V 2AD *Livery*, 320. *Clerk*, Christopher Twyman *Master*, M. Lawson

PATTENMAKERS *(70)*. 3 The High Street, Sutton Valence, Kent ME17 3AG *Livery*, 200. *Clerk*, Col. R. Murfin, TD *Master*, John Timpson, CBE

PAVIORS *(56)*. 3 Ridgemount Gardens, Enfield, Middx EN2 8QL *Livery*, 283. *Clerk*, John White *Master*, John Price

PEWTERERS *(16)*. Hall, Pewterers' Hall, Oat Lane, London EC2V 7DE *Livery*, 120. *Clerk*, Capt. Paddy Watson, RN *Master*, Richard Boggis-Rolfe

PLAISTERERS *(46)*. Hall, Plaisterers' Hall, 1 London Wall, London EC2Y 5JU *Livery*, 236. *Clerk*, Nigel Bamping *Master*, Peter Baker

PLUMBERS *(31)*. Wax Chandlers' Hall, 6 Gresham Street, London EC2V 7AD *Livery*, 360. *Clerk*, Air Cdre Paul Nash, OBE *Master*, Lt.-Col. Antony Paterson-Fox

POULTERS *(34)*. The Old Butchers, Station Road, Groombridge, Kent TN3 9QX *Livery*, 204. *Clerk*, Vernon Ashford *Master*, Brendan Tobin

SADDLERS *(25)*. Hall, Saddlers' Hall, 40 Gutter Lane, London EC2V 6BR *Livery*, 75. *Clerk*, Col. N. Lithgow, CBE *Master*, P. Laurie

SCIENTIFIC INSTRUMENT MAKERS *(84)*. 9 Montague Close, London SE1 9DD *Livery*, 185. *Clerk*, Neville Watson *Master*, B. D. Fishwick

SCRIVENERS *(44)*. HQS Wellington, Temple Stairs, Victoria Embankment, London WC2R 2PN *Livery*, 193. *Clerk*, Giles Cole *Master*, Peter Esslemont

SECURITY PROFESSIONALS *(108)*. 34 Tye Green, Glemsford, , Suffolk CO10 7RG *Livery*, 150. *Clerk*, Tricia Boswell *Master*, Nigel Churton, MBE

SHIPWRIGHTS *(59)*. Ironmongers Hall, Shaftesbury Place, London EC2Y 8AA *Livery*, 450. *Clerk*, Lt.-Col. Andy Milne, RN *Prime Warden*, HRH the Prince of Wales, KG, GCB, OM

SOLICITORS *(79)*. 4 College Hill, London EC4R 2RB *Livery*, 350. *Clerk*, Neil Cameron *Master*, Alderman John White, TD

SPECTACLE MAKERS *(60)*. Apothecaries' Hall, Black Friars Lane, London EC4V 6EL *Livery*, 390. *Clerk*, Lt.-Col. John Salmon, OBE *Master*, Prof. John Mardhall

STATIONERS AND NEWSPAPER MAKERS *(47)*. Hall, Stationers' Hall, Ave Maria Lane, London EC4M 7DD *Livery*, 476. *Clerk*, William Alden, MBE *Master*, Nigel Stapleton

TALLOW CHANDLERS *(21)*. Hall, Tallow Chandlers' Hall, 4 Dowgate Hill, London EC4R 2SH *Livery*, 180. *Clerk*, Brig. R. Wilde, CBE *Master*, Sir Christopher Pryke, Bt.

TAX ADVISERS *(107)*. 191 West End Road, Ruislip, Middx HA4 6LD *Freemen*, 142. *Clerk*, Paul Herbage *Master*, Peter Gravestock

TIN PLATE WORKERS (ALIAS WIRE WORKERS) *(67)*. Highbanks, Ferry Road, Surlingham, Norwich, Norfolk NR14 7AR *Livery*, 220. *Clerk*, Michael Henderson-Begg *Master*, Ian T. Chamberlain

TOBACCO PIPE MAKERS AND TOBACCO BLENDERS *(82)*. 108 Dorset Road, Bexhill on Sea, E. Sussex TN40 2HT *Livery*, 150. *Clerk*, Lt-Col. Peter Swanson *Master*, Fiona Adler

TURNERS *(51)*. Skinner's Hall, 8 Dowgate Hill, London EC4R 2SP *Livery*, 186. *Clerk*, Edward Windsor Clive *Master*, Ilan Krieger

TYLERS AND BRICKLAYERS *(37)*. 3 Farmers' Way, Seer Green, Bucks HP9 2YY *Livery*, 155. *Clerk*, John Brooks *Master*, Piers Nicholson

UPHOLDERS *(49)*. Hall in the Wood, 46 Quail Gardens, Selsdon Vale, Croydon CR2 8TF *Livery*, 209. *Clerk*, Jean Cody *Master*, James Kelly

WATER CONSERVATORS *(102)*. The Lark, 2 Bell Lane, Worlington, Bury St Edmunds, Suffolk IP28 8SE *Livery*, 210. *Clerk*, Ralph Riley *Master*, Barry Dennis

WAX CHANDLERS *(20)*. *Hall*, Wax Chandlers' Hall, 6 Gresham Street, London EC2V 7AD *Livery*, 120. *Clerk*, Georgina Brown *Master*, John Sleeman

WEAVERS *(42)*. Saddlers' House, Gutter Lane, London EC2V 6BR *Livery*, 125. *Clerk*, John Snowdon *Upper Bailiff*, His Honour Giles Forrester

WHEELWRIGHTS *(68)*. 7 Glengall Road, Bexleyheath, Kent DA7 4AL *Livery*, 220. *Clerk*, Brian François *Master*, Graham Westwell

WOOLMEN *(43)*. The Old Post Office, 56 Lower Way, Great Brickhill, Bucks MK17 9AG *Livery*, 150. *Clerk*, Gillian Wilson *Master*, William Wilson, CBE

WORLD TRADERS *(101)*. 13 Hall Gardens, Colney Heath, St. Albans, Herts AL4 0QF *Livery*, 240. *Clerk*, Mrs Gaye Duffy *Master*, Mei Sim Lai, OBE

PARISH CLERKS *(No Livery*)*. Acreholt, 33 Medstead Road, Beech, Alton, Hants GU34 4AD *Members*, 88. *Clerk*, Alana Coombes *Master*, Peter Maplestone

WATERMEN AND LIGHTERMEN *(No Livery*)*. *Hall*, Watermen's Hall, 16 St Mary-at-Hill, London EC3R 8EF *Craft Owning Freemen*, 600. *Clerk*, Colin Middlemiss *Master*, Paul Ludwig

* Parish Clerks and Watermen and Lightermen have requested to remain with no livery

LONDON BOROUGH COUNCILS

Council	Telephone	Population*	Council Tax†	Chief Executive
Barking and Dagenham	020-8592 4500	175,600	£1,326	Stella Manzie
Barnet	020-8359 2000	343,100	£1,423	Nick Walkley
Bexley	020-8303 7777	225,900	£1,438	Will Tuckley
Brent	020-8937 1234	255,500	£1,369	Gareth Daniel
Bromley	020-8464 3333	310,200	£1,301	Doug Patterson
Camden	020-7974 4444	231,200	£1,332	Moira Gibb, CBE
CITY OF LONDON CORPORATION	020-7606 3030	11,500	£939	Chris Duffield
Croydon	020-8726 6000	342,800	£1,460	Jon Rouse
Ealing	020-8825 5000	316,600	£1,370	Martin Smith
Enfield	020-8379 1000	291,200	£1,410	Rob Leak
Greenwich	020-8854 8888	226,100	£1,291	Mary Ney
Hackney	020-8356 5000	216,000	£1,308	Tim Shields
Hammersmith and Fulham	020-8748 3020	169,700	£1,122	Derek Myers
Haringey	020-8489 0000	225,500	£1,494	Kevin Crompton
Harrow	020-8863 5611	228,100	£1,496	Michael Lockwood
Havering	01708-434343	234,100	£1,505	Cheryl Coppell
Hillingdon	01895-250111	262,500	£1,423	Hugh Dunnachie
Hounslow	020-8583 2000	234,200	£1,400	Mary Harpley
Islington	020-7527 2000	191,800	£1,272	Lesley Seary
Kensington and Chelsea	020-7361 3000	169,900	£1,092	Derek Myers
Kingston upon Thames	020-8547 5757	166,700	£1,663	Bruce McDonald
Lambeth	020-7926 1000	283,300	£1,235	Derrick Anderson, CBE
Lewisham	020-8314 6000	264,500	£1,352	Barry Quirk, CBE
Merton	020-8543 2222	206,400	£1,416	Ged Curran
Newham	020-8430 2000	241,200	£1,255	Kim Bromley-Derry
Redbridge	020-8554 5000	267,700	£1,405	Roger Hampson
Richmond upon Thames	020-8891 1411	189,000	£1,597	Gillian Norton
Southwark	020-7525 5000	285,600	£1,222	Annie Shepperd
Sutton	020-8770 5000	192,200	£1,451	Niall Bolger
Tower Hamlets	020-7364 5000	234,800	£1,195	Dr. Kevan Collins
Waltham Forest	020-8496 3000	224,300	£1,462	Martin Esom
Wandsworth	020-8871 6000	286,600	£687	Paul Martin
WESTMINSTER	020-7641 6000	249,400	£688	Mike More

* *Source:* ONS – *Mid-2009 Population Estimates* (Crown copyright)
† Average Band D council tax bill for 2011–12
Councils in CAPITAL LETTERS have city status

WALES

Cymru

The principality of Wales (Cymru) occupies the extreme west of the central southern portion of the island of Great Britain, with a total area of 20,778 sq. km (8,022 sq. miles): land 20,733 sq. km (8,005 sq. miles); inland water 45 sq. km (17 sq. miles). It is bordered in the north by the Irish Sea, in the south by the Bristol Channel, in the east by the English counties of Cheshire West and Chester, Shropshire, Herefordshire and Gloucestershire, and in the west by St George's Channel.

Across the Menai Straits is Ynys Mon (Isle of Anglesey) (715 sq. km/276 sq. miles), communication with which is facilitated by the Menai Suspension Bridge (305m/1,000ft long) built by Telford in 1826, and by the Britannia Bridge (351m/1,151ft), a two-tier road and rail truss arch design, rebuilt in 1972 after a fire destroyed the original tubular railway bridge built by Stephenson in 1850. Holyhead harbour, on Holy Isle (north-west of Anglesey), provides ferry services to Dublin (113km/70 miles).

POPULATION
The population at the 2001 census was 2,903,085 (men 1,403,782; women 1,499,303). The average density of population in 2001 was 140 persons per sq. km (362 per sq. mile).

RELIEF
Wales is a country of extensive tracts of high plateau and shorter stretches of mountain ranges deeply dissected by river valleys. Lower-lying ground is largely confined to the coastal belt and the lower parts of the valleys. The highest mountains are those of Snowdonia in the north-west (Snowdon, 1,085m/3,559ft and Aran Fawddwy, 906m/2,971ft). Snowdonia is also home to Cader Idris (Pen y Gadair, 892m/2,928ft). Other high peaks are to be found in the Cambrian range (Plynlimon, 752m/2,467ft), and the Black Mountains, Brecon Beacons and Black Forest ranges in the south-east (Pen y Fan, 886m/2,906ft; Waun Fâch, 811m/2,660ft; Carmarthen Van, 802m/2,630ft).

HYDROGRAPHY
The principal river in Wales is the Severn, which flows from the slopes of Plynlimon to the English border. The Wye (209km/130 miles) also rises in the slopes of Plynlimon. The Usk (90km/56 miles) flows into the Bristol Channel through Gwent. The Dee (113km/70 miles) rises in Bala Lake and flows through the Vale of Llangollen, where an aqueduct (built by Telford in 1805) carries the Pontcysyllte branch of the Shropshire Union Canal across the valley. The estuary of the Dee is the navigable portion, it is 23km (14 miles) in length and about 8km (5 miles) in breadth. The Towy (109km/68 miles), Teifi (80km/50 miles), Taff (64km/40 miles), Dovey (48km/30 miles), Taf (40km/25 miles) and Conway (39km/24 miles) are wholly Welsh rivers.

The largest natural lake is Bala (Llyn Tegid) in Gwynedd, nearly 7km (4 miles) long and 1.6km (1 mile) wide. Lake Vyrnwy is an artificial reservoir, about the size of Bala, it forms the water supply of Liverpool;

Birmingham's water is supplied from reservoirs in the Elan and Claerwen valleys.

WELSH LANGUAGE
According to the 2001 census results, the percentage of people aged three years and over who are able to speak Welsh is:

Blaenau Gwent	9.1	Neath Port Talbot	17.8
Bridgend	10.6	Newport	9.6
Caerphilly	10.9	Pembrokeshire	21.5
Cardiff	10.9	Powys	20.8
Carmarthenshire	50.1	Rhondda Cynon Taf	12.3
Ceredigion	51.8	Swansea	13.2
Conwy	29.2	Torfaen	10.7
Denbighshire	26.1	Vale of Glamorgan	11.1
Flintshire	14.1	Wrexham	14.4
Gwynedd	67.8	Ynys Mon	
Merthyr Tydfil	10.0	(Isle of Anglesey)	59.8
Monmouthshire	9.0	*Total in Wales*	20.5

FLAG
The flag of Wales, the Red Dragon (*Y Ddraig Goch*), is a red dragon on a field divided white over green (per fess argent and vert a dragon passant gules). The flag was augmented in 1953 by a royal badge on a shield encircled with a riband bearing the words *Ddraig Goch Ddyry Cychwyn* and imperially crowned, but this augmented flag is rarely used.

EARLY HISTORY

The earliest inhabitants of whom there is any record appear to have been subdued or exterminated by the Goidels (a people of Celtic race) in the Bronze Age. A further invasion of Celtic Brythons and Belgae followed in the ensuing Iron Age. The Roman conquest of southern Britain and Wales was for some time successfully opposed by Caratacus (Caractacus or Caradog), chieftain of the Catuvellauni and son of Cunobelinus (Cymbeline). South-east Wales was subjugated and the legionary fortress at Caerleon-on-Usk established by around AD 75–7; the conquest of Wales was completed by Agricola around AD 78. Communications were opened up by the construction of military roads from Chester to Caerleon-on-Usk and Caerwent, and from Chester to Conwy (and thence to Carmarthen and Neath). Christianity was introduced in the fourth century, during the Roman occupation.

ANGLO-SAXON ATTACKS
The Anglo-Saxon invaders of southern Britain drove the Celts into the mountain stronghold of Wales, and into Strathclyde (Cumberland and south-west Scotland) and Cornwall, giving them the name of *Waelisc* (Welsh), meaning 'foreign'. The West Saxons' victory of Deorham (AD 577) isolated Wales from Cornwall and the battle of Chester (AD 613) cut off communication with Strathclyde and northern Britain. In the eighth century

the boundaries of the Welsh were further restricted by the annexations of Offa, King of Mercia, and counter-attacks were largely prevented by the construction of an artificial boundary from the Dee to the Wye (Offa's Dyke).

In the ninth century Rhodri Mawr (844–878) united the country and successfully resisted further incursions of the Saxons by land and raids of Norse and Danish pirates by sea, but at his death his three provinces of Gwynedd (north), Powys (central) and Deheubarth (south) were divided among his three sons, Anarawd, Mervyn and Cadell. Cadell's son Hywel Dda ruled a large part of Wales and codified its laws but the provinces were not united again until the rule of Llewelyn ap Seisyllt (husband of the heiress of Gwynedd) from 1018 to 1023.

THE NORMAN CONQUEST
After the Norman conquest of England, William I created palatine counties along the Welsh frontier, and the Norman barons began to make encroachments into Welsh territory. The Welsh princes recovered many of their losses during the civil wars of Stephen's reign (1135–54), and in the early 13th century Owen Gruffydd, prince of Gwynedd, was the dominant figure in Wales. Under Llywelyn ap Iorwerth (1194–1240) the Welsh united in powerful resistance to English incursions and Llywelyn's privileges and de facto independence were recognised in the Magna Carta. His grandson, Llywelyn ap Gruffydd, was the last native prince; he was killed in 1282 during hostilities between the Welsh and English, allowing Edward I of England to establish his authority over the country. On 7 February 1301, Edward of Caernarvon, son of Edward I, was created Prince of Wales, a title subsequently borne by the eldest son of the sovereign.

Strong Welsh national feeling continued, expressed in the early 15th century in the rising led by Owain Glyndwr, but the situation was altered by the accession to the English throne in 1485 of Henry VII of the Welsh House of Tudor. Wales was politically annexed to England under the Act of Union of 1535, which extended English laws to the principality and gave it parliamentary representation for the first time.

EISTEDDFOD
The Welsh are a distinct nation, with a language and literature of their own; the national bardic festival (Eisteddfod), instituted by Prince Rhys ap Griffith in 1176, is still held annually.

PRINCIPAL CITIES

There are five cities in Wales (with date city status conferred): Bangor (pre-1900), Cardiff (1905), Newport (2002), St David's (1994) and Swansea (1969).

Cardiff and Swansea have also been granted Lord Mayoralities.

CARDIFF
Cardiff (Caerdydd), at the mouth of the rivers Taff, Rhymney and Ely, is the capital city of Wales and at the 2001 census had a population of 305,353. The city has changed dramatically in recent years following the regeneration of Cardiff Bay and construction of a barrage, which has created a permanent freshwater lake and waterfront for the city. As the capital city, Cardiff is home to the National Assembly for Wales and is a major administrative, retail, business and cultural centre.

The city is home to many fine buildings including the City Hall, Cardiff Castle, Llandaff Cathedral, the National Museum of Wales, university buildings, law courts and the Temple of Peace and Health. The Millennium Stadium opened in 1999 and has hosted high-profile events since 2001.

SWANSEA
Swansea (Abertawe) is a seaport with a population of 223,293 at the 2001 census. The Gower peninsula was brought within the city boundary under local government reform in 1974.

The principal buildings are the Norman Castle (rebuilt c.1330), the Royal Institution of South Wales, founded in 1835 (including library), the University of Wales Swansea at Singleton and the Guildhall, containing Frank Brangwyn's British Empire panels. The Dylan Thomas Centre, formerly the old Guildhall, was restored in 1995. More recent buildings include the County Hall, the Maritime Quarter Marina, the Wales National Pool and the National Waterfront Museum.

Swansea was chartered by the Earl of Warwick (1158–84), and further charters were granted by King John, Henry III, Edward II, Edward III and James II, Oliver Cromwell and the Marcher Lord William de Breos. It was formally invested with city status in 1969 by HRH The Prince of Wales.

LORD-LIEUTENANTS AND HIGH SHERIFFS

Area	Lord-Lieutenant	High Sheriff (2011–12)
Clwyd	T. Jones, CBE	Edmund Fitzhugh, OBE
Dyfed	Hon. Robin Lewis, OBE	Thomas Lloyd, OBE
Gwent	S. Boyle	Lady Hayman-Joyce
Gwynedd	His Hon. Huw Daniel	Prof. Robin Grove-White
Mid Glamorgan	Kate Thomas, CVO	Dr Barbara Wilding, CBE, QPM
Powys	Hon. Mrs E. Legge-Bourke, LVO	Col. John Brunt, OBE, TD
South Glamorgan	Dr Peter Beck, MD, FRCP	Roger Thomas, OBE
West Glamorgan	D. Byron Lewis	Susan Thomas

LOCAL COUNCILS

Council	Administrative Headquarters	Telephone	Population*	Council Tax†	Chief Executive
Blaenau Gwent	Ebbw Vale	01495-350555	68,600	£1,426	David Waggett
Bridgend	Bridgend	01656-643643	134,200	£1,288	Dr Jo Farrar
Caerphilly	Hengoed	01443-815588	172,700	£1,095	Anthony O'Sullivan
CARDIFF	Cardiff	029-2087 2000	336,200	£1,086	Jonathan House
Carmarthenshire	Carmarthen	01267-234567	180,800	£1,188	Mark James
Ceredigion	Aberaeron	01545-570881	76,400	£1,133	Bronwen Morgan
Conwy	Conwy	01492-574000	111,400	£1,089	K. W. Finch *(acting)*
Denbighshire	Ruthin	01824-706000	96,700	£1,270	Dr Mohammed Mehmet
Flintshire	Mold	01352-752121	149,900	£1,151	Colin Everett
Gwynedd	Caernarfon	01766-771000	118,800	£1,237	Harry Thomas
Merthyr Tydfil	Merthyr Tydfil	01685-725000	55,700	£1,343	Gareth Chapman
Monmouthshire	Cwmbran	01633-644644	88,000	£1,225	Paul Matthews
Neath Port Talbot	Port Talbot	01639-763333	137,400	£1,384	Steven Phillips
NEWPORT	Newport	01633-656656	140,400	£995	Tracey Lee
Pembrokeshire	Haverfordwest	01437-764551	117,400	£923	Bryn Parry-Jones
Powys	Llandrindod Wells	01597-826000	131,700	£1,138	Jeremy Patterson
Rhondda Cynon Taff	Tonypandy	01443-424000	234,400	£1,303	Keith Griffiths
SWANSEA	Swansea	01792-636000	231,300	£1,162	Jack Straw
Torfaen	Pontypool	01495-762200	90,700	£1,180	Alison Ward
Vale of Glamorgan	Barry	01446-700111	124,600	£1,123	John Maitland-Evans
Wrexham	Wrexham	01978-292000	133,200	£1,135	Helen Paterson
Ynys Mon (Isle of Anglesey)	Ynys Mon	01248-750057	68,800	£1,094	Richard Parry Jones

* *Source:* ONS – *Mid-2009 Population Estimates* (Crown copyright)
† Average Band D council tax bill 2011–12
Councils in CAPITAL LETTERS have city status

Key	Council	Key	Council
1	Anglesey (Ynys Mon)	12	Merthyr Tydfil
2	Blaenau Gwent	13	Monmouthshire
3	Bridgend	14	Neath Port Talbot
4	Caerphilly	15	Newport
5	Cardiff	16	Pembrokeshire
6	Carmarthenshire	17	Powys
7	Ceredigion	18	Rhondda Cynon Taff
8	Conwy	19	Swansea
9	Denbighshire	20	Torfaen
10	Flintshire	21	Vale of Glamorgan
11	Gwynedd	22	Wrexham

SCOTLAND

Scotland occupies the northern portion of the main island of Great Britain and includes the Inner and Outer Hebrides, Orkney, Shetland and many other islands. It lies between 60° 51′ 30″ and 54° 38′ N. latitude and between 1° 45′ 32″ and 6° 14′ W. · longitude, with England to the south-east, the North Channel and the Irish Sea to the south-west, the Atlantic Ocean on the north and west, and the North Sea on the east.

The greatest length of the mainland (Cape Wrath to the Mull of Galloway) is 441km (274 miles), and the greatest breadth (Buchan Ness to Applecross) is 248km (154 miles). The customary measurement of the island of Great Britain is from the site of John o' Groats house, near Duncansby Head, Caithness, to Land's End, Cornwall, a total distance of 970km (603 miles) in a straight line and approximately 1,448km (900 miles) by road.

The total area of Scotland is 78,807 sq. km (30,427 sq. miles): land 77,907 sq. km (30,080 sq. miles), inland water 900 sq. km (347 sq. miles).

POPULATION
The population at the 2001 census was 5,062,011 (men 2,432,494; women 2,629,517). The average density of the population in 2001 was 64 persons per sq. km (166 per sq. mile).

RELIEF
There are three natural orographic divisions of Scotland. The southern uplands have their highest points in Merrick (843m/2,766ft), Rhinns of Kells (814m/2,669ft) and Cairnsmuir of Carsphairn (797m/2,614ft), in the west; and the Tweedsmuir Hills in the east (Broad Law 840m/2,756ft; Dollar Law 817m/2,682ft; Hartfell 808m/2,651ft).

The central lowlands, formed by the valleys of the Clyde, Forth and Tay, divide the southern uplands from the Highlands, which extend from close to the extreme north of the mainland to the central lowlands, and are divided into a northern and a southern system by the Great Glen.

The Grampian Mountains, the southern Highland system, include in the west Ben Nevis (1,343m/4,406ft), the highest point in the British Isles, and in the east the Cairngorm Mountains (Ben Macdui 1,309m/4,296ft; Braeriach 1,295m/4,248ft; Cairn Gorm 1,245m/4,084ft). The North West Highlands area contains the mountains of Wester and Easter Ross (Carn Eige 1,183m/3,880ft; Sgurr na Lapaich 1,151m/3,775ft).

Created, like the central lowlands, by a major geological fault, the Great Glen (97km/60 miles long) runs between Inverness and Fort William, and contains Loch Ness, Loch Oich and Loch Lochy. These are linked to each other and to the north-east and south-west coasts of Scotland by the Caledonian Canal, providing a navigable passage between the Moray Firth and the Inner Hebrides.

HYDROGRAPHY
The western coast is fragmented by peninsulas and islands, and indented by fjords (sea-lochs), the longest of which is Loch Fyne (68km/42 miles long) in Argyll. Although the east coast tends to be less fractured and lower, there are several great drowned inlets (firths), including the Firth of Forth, the Firth of Tay and the Moray Firth, as well as the Firth of Clyde in the west.

The lochs are the principal hydrographic feature. The largest in Scotland and in Britain is Loch Lomond (70 sq. km/27 sq. miles), in the Grampian valleys and the longest and deepest is Loch Ness (39km/24 miles long and 244m/800ft deep), in the Great Glen.

The longest river is the Tay (188km/117 miles), noted for its salmon. It flows into the North Sea, with Dundee on the estuary, which is spanned by the Tay Bridge (3,136m/10,289ft) opened in 1887 and the Tay Road Bridge (2,245m/7,365ft) opened in 1966. Other noted salmon rivers are the Dee (145km/90 miles) which flows into the North Sea at Aberdeen, and the Spey (177km/110 miles), the swiftest flowing river in the British Isles, which flows into Moray Firth. The Tweed, which gave its name to the woollen cloth produced along its banks, marks in the lower stretches of its 154km (96 mile) course the border between Scotland and England.

The most important river commercially is the Clyde (171km/106 miles), formed by the junction of the Daer and Portrail water, which flows through the city of Glasgow to the Firth of Clyde. During its course it passes over the picturesque Falls of Clyde, Bonnington Linn (9m/30ft), Corra Linn (26m/84ft), Dundaff Linn (3m/10ft) and Stonebyres Linn (24m/80ft), above and below Lanark. The Forth (106km/66 miles), upon which stands Edinburgh, the capital, is spanned by the Forth Railway Bridge (1890), which is 1,625m (5,330ft) long, and the Forth Road Bridge (1964), which has a total length of 1,876m (6,156ft) (over water) and a single span of 914m (3,000ft).

The highest waterfall in Scotland, and the British Isles, is Eas a'Chùal Aluinn with a total height of 201m (658ft), which falls from Glas Bheinn in Sutherland. The Falls of Glomach, on a head-stream of the Elchaig in Wester Ross, have a drop of 113m (370ft).

GAELIC LANGUAGE
According to the 2001 census, 1.2 per cent of the population of Scotland, mainly in Eilean Siar (Western Isles), were able to speak the Scottish form of Gaelic.

LOWLAND SCOTTISH LANGUAGE
Several regional lowland Scottish dialects, known variously as Scots, Lallans or Doric, are widely spoken. The General Register Office (Scotland) estimated in 1996 that 1.5 million people, or 30 per cent of the population, are Scots speakers. A question on Scots was not included in the 2001 census.

FLAG
The flag of Scotland is known as the Saltire. It is a white diagonal cross on a blue field (saltire argent in a field azure) and represents St Andrew, the patron saint of Scotland.

THE SCOTTISH ISLANDS

ORKNEY

The Orkney Islands (total area 972 sq. km/376 sq. miles) lie about 10km (six miles) north of the mainland, separated from it by the Pentland Firth. Of the 90 islands and islets (holms and skerries) in the group, about one-third are inhabited.

The total population at the 2001 census was 19,245; the 2001 populations of the islands shown here include those of smaller islands forming part of the same council district.

Mainland, 15,339	Rousay, 267
Burray, 357	Sanday, 478
Eday, 121	Shapinsay, 300
Flotta, 81	South Ronaldsay, 854
Hoy, 392	Stronsay, 358
North Ronaldsay, 70	Westray, 563
Papa Westray, 65	

The islands are rich in prehistoric and Scandinavian remains, the most notable being the Stone Age village of Skara Brae, the burial chamber of Maes Howe, the many brochs (towers) and the 12th-century St Magnus Cathedral. Scapa Flow, between the Mainland and Hoy, was the war station of the British Grand Fleet from 1914 to 1919 and the scene of the scuttling of the surrendered German High Seas Fleet (21 June 1919).

Most of the islands are low-lying and fertile, and farming (principally beef cattle) is the main industry. Flotta, to the south of Scapa Flow, is the site of the oil terminal for the Piper, Claymore and Tartan fields in the North Sea.

The capital is Kirkwall (population 6,206) situated on Mainland.

SHETLAND

The Shetland Islands have a total area of 1,427 sq. km (551 sq. miles) and a population at the 2001 census of 21,988. They lie about 80km (50 miles) north of the Orkneys, with Fair Isle about half way between the two groups. Out Stack, off Muckle Flugga, 1.6km (one mile) north of Unst, is the most northerly part of the British Isles (60° 51' 30" N. lat.).

There are over 100 islands, of which 16 are inhabited. Populations at the 2001 census were:

Mainland, 17,575	Muckle Roe, 104
Bressay, 384	Trondra, 133
East Burra, 66	Unst, 720
Fair Isle, 69	West Burra, 784
Fetlar, 86	Whalsay, 1,034
Housay, 76	Yell, 957

Shetland's many archaeological sites include Jarlshof, Mousa and Clickhimin, and its long connection with Scandinavia has resulted in a strong Norse influence on its place names and dialect.

Industries include fishing, knitwear and farming. In addition to the fishing fleet there are fish processing factories, and the traditional handknitting of Fair Isle and Unst is now supplemented with machine-knitted garments. Farming is mainly crofting, with sheep being raised on the moorland and hills of the islands. Latterly the islands have become a centre of the North Sea oil industry, with pipelines from the Brent and Ninian fields

running to the terminal at Sullom Voe, the largest of its kind in Europe.

The capital is Lerwick (population 6,830) situated on Mainland. Lerwick is the main centre for supply services for offshore oil exploration and development.

THE HEBRIDES

Until the late 13th century the Hebrides included other Scottish islands in the Firth of Clyde, the peninsula of Kintyre (Argyll), the Isle of Man, and the (Irish) Isle of Rathlin. The origin of the name is probably the Greek *Eboudai,* latinised as *Hebudes* by Pliny, and corrupted to its present form. The Norwegian name *Sudreyjar* (Southern Islands) was latinised as *Sodorenses,* a name that survives in the Anglican bishopric of Sodor and Man.

There are over 500 islands and islets, of which about 100 are inhabited, though mountainous terrain and extensive peat bogs mean that only a fraction of the total area is under cultivation. Stone, Bronze and Iron Age settlement has left many remains, including those at Callanish on Lewis, and Norse colonisation influenced language, customs and placenames. Occupations include farming (mostly crofting and stock-raising), fishing and the manufacture of tweeds and other woollens. Tourism is also an important part of the economy.

The Inner Hebrides lie off the west coast of Scotland and are relatively close to the mainland. The largest and best-known is Skye (area 1,665 sq. km/643 sq. miles; pop. 9,251; chief town, Portree), which contains the Cuillin Hills (Sgurr Alasdair 993m/3,257ft), Bla Bheinn (928m/3,046ft), the Storr (719m/2,358ft) and the Red Hills (Beinn na Caillich 732m/2,403ft). Other islands in the Highland council area include Raasay (pop. 194), Rum, Eigg (pop. 131) and Muck.

Further south the Inner Hebridean islands include Arran (pop. 5,058) containing Goat Fell (874m/2,868ft); Coll and Tiree (pop. 934); Colonsay and Oronsay (pop. 113); Easdale (pop. 58); Gigha (pop. 110); Islay (area 608 sq. km/235 sq. miles; pop. 3,457); Jura (area 414 sq. km/160 sq. miles; pop. 188) with a range of hills culminating in the Paps of Jura (Beinn-an-Oir, 785m/2,576ft, and Beinn Chaolais, 755m/2,477ft); Lismore (pop. 146); Luing (pop. 220); and Mull (area 950 sq. km/367 sq. miles; pop. 2,696; chief town Tobermory) containing Ben More (967m/3,171ft).

The Outer Hebrides, separated from the mainland by the Minch, now form the Eilean Siar (Western Isles) council area (area 2,897 sq. km/1,119 sq. miles; pop. 26,502). The main islands are Lewis with Harris (area 1,994 sq. km/770 sq. miles, pop. 19,918), whose chief town, Stornoway, is the administrative headquarters; North Uist (pop. 1,320); South Uist (pop. 1,818); Benbecula (pop. 1,249) and Barra (pop. 1,078). Other inhabited islands include Bernera (233), Berneray (136), Eriskay (133), Grimsay (201), Scalpay (322) and Vatersay (94).

EARLY HISTORY

There is evidence of human settlement in Scotland dating from the third millennium BC, the earliest settlers being Mesolithic hunters and fishermen. Early in the second millennium BC, Neolithic farmers began to cultivate crops and rear livestock; their settlements were on the west coast and in the north, and included Skara Brae and Maeshowe (Orkney). Settlement by the early Bronze Age 'Beaker Folk', so-called from the shape of their drinking vessels, in eastern Scotland dates from about 1800 BC. Further settlement is believed to have occurred from 700 BC onwards, as tribes were displaced from further south by new incursions from the Continent and the Roman invasions from AD 43.

Julius Agricola, the Roman governor of Britain AD 77–84, extended the Roman conquests in Britain by advancing into Caledonia, culminating with a victory at Mons Graupius, probably in AD 84; he was recalled to Rome shortly afterwards and his forward policy was not pursued. Hadrian's Wall, mostly completed by AD 30, marked the northern frontier of the Roman empire except for the period between about AD 144 and 190 when the frontier moved north to the Forth-Clyde isthmus and a turf wall, the Antonine Wall, was manned.

After the Roman withdrawal from Britain, there were centuries of warfare between the Picts, Scots, Britons, Angles and Vikings. The Picts, generally accepted to be descended from the indigenous Iron Age people of northern Scotland, occupied the area north of the Forth. The Scots, a Gaelic-speaking people of northern Ireland, colonised the area of Argyll and Bute (the kingdom of Dalriada) in the fifth century AD and then expanded eastwards and northwards. The Britons, speaking a Brythonic Celtic language, colonised Scotland from the south from the first century BC; they lost control of south-eastern Scotland (incorporated into the kingdom of Northumbria) to the Angles in the early seventh century but retained Strathclyde (south-western Scotland and Cumbria). Viking raids from the late eighth century were followed by Norse settlement in the western and northern isles, Argyll, Caithness and Sutherland from the mid-ninth century onwards.

UNIFICATION
The union of the areas which now comprise Scotland began in AD 843 when Kenneth mac Alpin, king of the Scots from c.834, also became king of the Picts, joining the two lands to form the kingdom of Alba (comprising Scotland north of a line between the Forth and Clyde rivers). Lothian, the eastern part of the area between the Forth and the Tweed, seems to have been leased to Kenneth II of Alba (reigned 971–995) by Edgar of England c.973, and Scottish possession was confirmed by Malcolm II's victory over a Northumbrian army at Carham c.1016. At about this time Malcolm II (reigned 1005–34) placed his grandson Duncan on the throne of the British kingdom of Strathclyde, bringing under Scots rule virtually all of what is now Scotland.

The Norse possessions were incorporated into the kingdom of Scotland from the 12th century onwards. An uprising in the mid-12th century drove the Norse from most of mainland Argyll. The Hebrides were ceded to Scotland by the treaty of Perth in 1266 after a Norwegian expedition in 1263 failed to maintain Norse authority over the islands. Orkney and Shetland fell to Scotland in 1468–9 as a pledge for the unpaid dowry of Margaret of Denmark, wife of James III, although Danish claims of suzerainty were relinquished only with the marriage of Anne of Denmark to James VI in 1590.

From the 11th century, there were frequent wars between Scotland and England over territory and the extent of England's political influence. The failure of the Scottish royal line with the death of Margaret of Norway in 1290 led to disputes over the throne which were resolved by the adjudication of Edward I of England. He awarded the throne to John Balliol in 1292 but Balliol's refusal to be a puppet king led to war. Balliol surrendered to Edward I in 1296 and Edward attempted to rule Scotland himself. Resistance to Scotland's loss of

independence was led by William Wallace, who defeated the English at Stirling Bridge (1297), and Robert Bruce, crowned in 1306, who held most of Scotland by 1311 and routed Edward II's army at Bannockburn (1314). England recognised the independence of Scotland in the treaty of Northampton in 1328. Subsequent clashes include the disastrous battle of Flodden (1513) in which James IV and many of his nobles fell.

THE UNION
In 1603 James VI of Scotland succeeded Elizabeth I on the throne of England (his mother, Mary Queen of Scots, was the great-granddaughter of Henry VII), his successors reigning as sovereigns of Great Britain. Political union of the two countries did not occur until 1707.

THE JACOBITE REVOLTS
After the abdication (by flight) in 1688 of James VII and II, the crown devolved upon William III (grandson of Charles I) and Mary II (elder daughter of James VII and II). In 1689 Graham of Claverhouse roused the Highlands on behalf of James VII and II, but died after a military success at Killiecrankie.

After the death of Anne (younger daughter of James VII and II), the throne devolved upon George I (great-grandson of James VI and I). In 1715, armed risings on behalf of James Stuart (the Old Pretender, son of James VII and II) led to the indecisive battle of Sheriffmuir, and the Jacobite movement died down until 1745, when Charles Stuart (the Young Pretender) defeated the Royalist troops at Prestonpans and advanced to Derby (1746). From Derby, the adherents of 'James VIII and III' (the title claimed for his father by Charles Stuart) fell back on the defensive and were finally crushed at Culloden (16 April 1746) by an army led by by the Duke of Cumberland, son of George II.

PRINCIPAL CITIES

ABERDEEN
Aberdeen, 209km (130 miles) north-east of Edinburgh, received its charter as a Royal Burgh in 1124. Scotland's third largest city, Aberdeen lies between two rivers, the Dee and the Don, facing the North Sea; the city has a strong maritime history and is today a major centre for offshore oil exploration and production. It is also an ancient university town and distinguished research centre. Other industries include engineering, food processing, textiles, paper manufacturing and chemicals.

Places of interest include King's College, St Machar's Cathedral, Brig o' Balgownie, Duthie Park and Winter Gardens, Hazlehead Park, the Kirk of St Nicholas, Mercat Cross, Marischal College and Marischal Museum, Provost Skene's House, Aberdeen Art Gallery, Gordon Highlanders Museum, Satrosphere Science Centre, and Aberdeen Maritime Museum.

DUNDEE
The Royal Burgh of Dundee is situated on the north bank of the Tay estuary. The city's port and dock installations are important to the offshore oil industry and the airport also provides servicing facilities. Principal industries include textiles, biotechnology and digital media, lasers, printing, tyre manufacture, food processing, engineering and tourism.

The unique City Churches – three churches under one roof, together with the 15th-century St Mary's Tower – are the most prominent architectural feature. Dundee is home to two historic ships: the Dundee-built RRS *Discovery* which took Capt. Scott to the Antarctic lies alongside Discovery Quay, and the frigate *Unicorn,* the only British-built wooden warship still afloat, is moored in Victoria Dock. Places of interest include Mills Public Observatory, the Tay road and rail bridges, Dundee Contemporary Arts centre, McManus Galleries, Claypotts Castle, Broughty Castle, Verdant Works (textile heritage centre) and the Sensation Science Centre.

EDINBURGH

Edinburgh is the capital city and seat of government in Scotland. The new Scottish parliament building designed by Enric Miralles was completed in 2004 and is open to visitors. The city is built on a group of hills and both the Old and New Towns are inscribed on the UNESCO World Cultural and Natural Heritage List for their cultural significance.

Other places of interest include the castle, which houses the Stone of Scone and also includes St Margaret's Chapel, the oldest building in Edinburgh, and near it, the Scottish National War Memorial; the Palace of Holyroodhouse, the Queen's official residence in Scotland; Parliament House, the present seat of the judicature; Princes Street; three universities (Edinburgh, Heriot-Watt, Napier); St Giles' Cathedral; St Mary's (Scottish Episcopal) Cathedral (Sir George Gilbert Scott); the General Register House (Robert Adam); the National and Signet libraries; the National Gallery of Scotland; the Royal Scottish Academy; the Scottish National Portrait Gallery and the Edinburgh International Conference Centre.

GLASGOW

Glasgow, a Royal Burgh, is Scotland's largest city and its principal commercial and industrial centre. The city occupies the north and south banks of the Clyde, formerly one of the chief commercial estuaries in the world. The main industries include engineering, electronics, finance, chemicals and printing. The city is also a key tourist and conference destination.

The chief buildings are the 13th-century Gothic cathedral, the university (Sir George Gilbert Scott), the City Chambers, the Royal Concert Hall, St Mungo Museum of Religious Life and Art, Pollok House, the School of Art (Charles Rennie Mackintosh), Kelvingrove Art Gallery and Museum, the Gallery of Modern Art, the Riverside Museum: Scotland's Museum of Transport and Travel (Zaha Hadid), the Burrell Collection museum and the Mitchell Library. The city is home to the Royal Scottish National Orchestra, Scottish Opera, Scottish Ballet and BBC Scotland and Scottish Television (STV).

INVERNESS

Inverness was granted city status in 2000. The city's name is derived from the Gaelic for 'the mouth of the Ness', referring to the river on which it lies. Inverness is recorded as being at the junction of the old trade routes since AD 565. Today the city is the main administrative centre for the north of Scotland and is the capital of the Highlands. Tourism is one of the city's main industries.

Among the city's most notable buildings is Abertarff House, built in 1593 and the oldest secular building remaining in Inverness. Balnain House, built as a town house in 1726, is a fine example of early Georgian architecture. The Old High Church, on St Michael's Mount, is the original parish church of Inverness and is built on the site of the earliest Christian church in the city. Parts of the church date back to the 14th century.

Stirling was granted city status in 2002. Aberdeen, Dundee, Edinburgh and Glasgow have also been granted Lord Mayoralty/Lord Provostship.

LORD-LIEUTENANTS

Title	Name
Aberdeen City*	Lord Provost Peter Stephen
Aberdeenshire	James Ingleby
Angus	Mrs G. Osborne
Argyll and Bute	Patrick Stewart, MBE
Ayrshire and Arran	John Duncan, QPM
Banffshire	Clare Russell
Berwickshire	Maj. A. Trotter
Caithness	Miss M. Dunnett
Clackmannanshire	Rt. Hon. George Reid
Dumfries	Jean Tulloch
Dunbartonshire	Rear-Adm. Alexander Gregory, OBE
Dundee City*	Lord Provost John Letford
East Lothian	W. Garth Morrison, CBE
Edinburgh City*	Rt. Hon. Lord Provost George Grubb
Eilean Siar (Western Isles)	A. Matheson, OBE
Fife	Mrs C. Dean
Glasgow City*	Rt. Hon. Lord Provost Robert Winter
Inverness	Donald Angus Cameron of Lochiel
Kincardineshire	Carol Kinghorn
Lanarkshire	Mushtaq Ahmad, OBE
Midlothian	Patrick Prenter, CBE
Moray	Grenville Shaw Johnston, OBE, TD
Nairn	Ewen Brodie of Lethan
Orkney	Dr Anthony Trickett, MBE
Perth and Kinross	Brig. Melville Jameson, CBE
Renfrewshire	Guy Clark
Ross and Cromarty	Janet Bowen
Roxburgh, Ettrick and Lauderdale	Hon. Capt. Gerald Maitland-Carew
Shetland	Sir John Scott, KCVO
Stirling and Falkirk	Mrs M. McLachlan
Sutherland	Dr Monica Maitland Main
The Stewartry of Kirkcudbright	Lt.-Col. Sir Malcolm Walter Hugh Ross, GCVO, OBE
Tweeddale	Capt. D. Younger
West Lothian	Mrs I. Brydie, MBE
Wigtown	Marion Brewis

* The Lord Provosts of the four cities of Aberdeen, Dundee, Edinburgh and Glasgow are Lord-Lieutenants *ex officio* for those districts

LOCAL COUNCILS

Council	Administrative Headquarters	Telephone	Population*	Council Tax†	Chief Executive
ABERDEEN	Aberdeen	08456 08 09 10	213,800	£1,230	Sue Bruce
Aberdeenshire	Aberdeen	01467-620981	243,500	£1,141	Colin Mackenzie
Angus	Forfar	0845-277 7778	110,300	£1,072	David Sawers
Argyll and Bute	Lochgilphead	01546-602127	90,000	£1,178	Sally Loudon
Clackmannanshire	Alloa	01259-452000	50,500	£1,148	Angela Leitch
Dumfries and Galloway	Dumfries	01387-260000	148,500	£1,049	Gavin Stevenson
DUNDEE	Dundee	01382-434000	143,400	£1,211	David Dorward
East Ayrshire	Kilmarnock	01563-576000	120,200	£1,189	Fiona Lees
East Dunbartonshire	Kirkintilloch	0845-045 4510	104,700	£1,142	Gerry Cornes
East Lothian	Haddington	01620-827827	96,800	£1,118	Alan Blackie
East Renfrewshire	Giffnock	0141-577 3000	89,200	£1,126	Lorraine McMillan
EDINBURGH	Edinburgh	0131-200 2000	477,700	£1,169	Tom Aitchison, CBE
Eilean Siar (Western Isles)	Stornoway	01851-703773	26,200	£1,024	Malcolm Burr
Falkirk	Falkirk	01324-506070	152,500	£1,070	Mary Pitcaithly, OBE
Fife	Glenrothes	0845-555555	363,500	£1,118	Ronnie Hinds
GLASGOW	Glasgow	0141-287 2000	588,500	£1,213	George Black
Highland	Inverness	01463-702000	220,500	£1,163	Alistair Dodds
Inverclyde	Greenock	01475-717171	80,200	£1,198	John Mundell
Midlothian	Dalkeith	0131-270 7500	80,800	£1,210	Kenneth Lawrie
Moray	Elgin	01343-543451	87,700	£1,135	Alastair Keddie
North Ayrshire	Irvine	0845-603 0590	135,500	£1,152	Elma Murray
North Lanarkshire	Motherwell	01698-302222	326,300	£1,098	Gavin Whitefield
Orkney	Kirkwall	01856-873535	20,000	£1,037	Albert Tait
Perth and Kinross	Perth	01738-475000	145,900	£1,158	Bernadette Malone
Renfrewshire	Paisley	0141-842 5000	169,900	£1,165	David Martin
Scottish Borders	Melrose	01835-824000	112,700	£1,084	David Hume
Shetland	Lerwick	01595-693535	22,200	£1,053	vacant
South Ayrshire	Ayr	01292-612000	111,400	£1,154	David Anderson
South Lanarkshire	Hamilton	01698-454444	310,900	£1,101	Archie Strang
STIRLING	Stirling	0845-277 7000	88,700	£1,209	Bob Jack
West Dunbartonshire	Dumbarton	01389-737000	90,900	£1,163	David McMillan
West Lothian	Livingston	01506-775000	171,000	£1,128	Alex Linkston

* Source: ONS – Mid-2009 Population Estimates (Crown copyright)
† Average Band D council tax bill 2011–12
Councils in CAPITAL LETTERS have city status

Key	Council	Key	Council
1	Aberdeen City	18	Midlothian
2	Aberdeenshire	19	Moray
3	Angus	20	North Ayrshire
4	Argyll and Bute	21	North Lanarkshire
5	City of Edinburgh	22	Orkney
6	Clackmannanshire	23	Perth and Kinross
7	Dumfries and Galloway	24	Renfrewshire
8	Dundee City	25	Scottish Borders
9	East Ayrshire	26	Shetland
10	East Dunbartonshire	27	South Ayrshire
11	East Lothian	28	South Lanarkshire
12	East Renfrewshire	29	Stirling
13	Falkirk	30	West Dunbartonshire
14	Fife	31	Western Isles (Eilean Siar)
15	Glasgow City	32	West Lothian
16	Highland		
17	Inverclyde		

NORTHERN IRELAND

Northern Ireland has a total area of 14,149 sq. km (5,463 sq. miles): land, 13,576 sq. km (5,242 sq. miles); inland water, 573 sq. km (221 sq. miles).

The population of Northern Ireland at the 2001 census was 1,685,267 (men 821,449; women 863,818). The average density of population in 2001 was 119 persons per sq. km (308 per sq. mile).

At the 2001 census, the number of persons in the various religious denominations (expressed as percentages of the total population) were: Catholic, 40.26%; Presbyterian, 20.69%; Church of Ireland, 15.30%; Methodist Church in Ireland, 3.51%; other Christian (including Christian related), 6.07%; other religions and philosophies, 0.3%; no religion or religion not stated, 13.88%.

FLAG
The official national flag of Northern Ireland is the Union Flag.

PRINCIPAL CITIES

In addition to Belfast and Londonderry, three other places in Northern Ireland have been granted city status: Armagh (1994), Lisburn (2002) and Newry (2002).

BELFAST
Belfast, the administrative centre of Northern Ireland, is situated at the mouth of the River Lagan at its entrance to Belfast Lough. The city grew to be a great industrial centre, owing to its easy access by sea to Scottish coal and iron.

The principal buildings are of a relatively young age and include the parliament buildings at Stormont, the City Hall, Waterfront Hall, the Law Courts, the Public Library and the Museum and Art Gallery.

Belfast received its first charter of incorporation in 1613 and was created a city in 1888; the title of lord mayor was conferred in 1892.

LONDONDERRY
Londonderry (originally Derry) is situated on the River Foyle, and has important associations with the City of London. The Irish Society was created by the City of London in 1610, and under its royal charter of 1613 it fortified the city and was for a long time closely associated with its administration. Because of this connection the city was incorporated in 1613 under the new name of Londonderry.

The city is famous for the great siege of 1688–9, when for 105 days the town held out against the forces of James II. The city walls are still intact and form a circuit of 1.6 km (one mile) around the old city.

Interesting buildings are the Protestant cathedral of St Columb's (1633) and the Guildhall, reconstructed in 1912 and containing a number of beautiful stained glass windows, many of which were presented by the livery companies of London.

CONSTITUTIONAL HISTORY

Northern Ireland is subject to the same fundamental constitutional provisions which apply to the rest of the

UK. It had its own parliament and government from 1921 to 1972, but after increasing civil unrest the Northern Ireland (Temporary Provisions) Act 1972 transferred the legislative and executive powers of the Northern Ireland parliament and government to the UK parliament and a secretary of state. The Northern Ireland Constitution Act 1973 provided for devolution in Northern Ireland through an assembly and executive, but a power-sharing executive formed by the Northern Ireland political parties in January 1974 collapsed in May 1974. Following the collapse of the power-sharing executive Northern Ireland returned to direct rule governance under the provisions of the Northern Ireland Act 1974, placing the Northern Ireland department under the direction and control of the Northern Ireland secretary.

In December 1993 the British and Irish governments published the Joint Declaration complementing their political talks, and making clear that any settlement would need to be founded on principles of democracy and consent.

On 12 January 1998 the British and Irish governments issued a joint document, *Propositions on Heads of Agreement*, proposing the establishment of various new cross-border bodies; further proposals were presented on 27 January. A draft peace settlement was issued by the talks' chairman, US Senator George Mitchell, on 6 April 1998 but was rejected by the Unionists the following day. On 10 April agreement was reached between the British and Irish governments and the eight Northern Ireland political parties still involved in the talks (the Good Friday Agreement). The agreement provided for an elected Northern Ireland Assembly, a North/South Ministerial Council, and a British-Irish Council comprising representatives of the British, Irish, Channel Islands and Isle of Man governments and members of the new assemblies for Scotland, Wales and Northern Ireland. Further points included the abandonment of the Republic of Ireland's constitutional claim to Northern Ireland; the decommissioning of weapons; the release of paramilitary prisoners and changes in policing.

The agreement was ratified in referendums held in Northern Ireland and the Republic of Ireland on 22 May 1998. In the UK, the Northern Ireland Act received royal assent in November 1998.

On 28 April 2003 the secretary of state again assumed responsibility for the direction of the Northern Ireland departments on the dissolution of the Northern Ireland Assembly, following its initial suspension from midnight on 14 October 2002. In 2006, following the passing of the Northern Ireland Act, the secretary of state created a non-legislative fixed-term assembly which would cease to operate either when the political parties agreed to restore devolution, or on 24 November 2006 (whichever occurred first). In October 2006 a timetable to restore devolution was drawn up (St Andrews Agreement) and a transitional Northern Ireland Assembly was formed on 24 November. The transitional assembly was dissolved in January 2007 in preparation for elections to be held on 7 March; following the elections a power-sharing executive was formed and the new 108-member Northern Ireland Assembly became operational on 8 May 2007.

See also Regional Government.

LORD-LIEUTENANTS AND HIGH SHERIFFS

County	Lord-Lieutenant	High Sheriff (2011)
Antrim	Joan Christie	David Traill
Armagh	The Earl of Caledon	Dr Peter Colvin
Belfast City	Dame Mary Peters, DBE	Cllr Ian Adamson, OBE
Down	David Lindsay	Ian Webb
Fermanagh	The Earl of Erne	Terence McCartney
Londonderry	Denis Desmond, CBE	John Burns
Londonderry City	Dr Donal Keegan, OBE	Steven Lindsay
Tyrone	Robert Scott, OBE	Gerard Broderick Francis Shields

LOCAL COUNCILS

Council	County Area	Map Key	Telephone	Population*	Chief Executive
Antrim	Down	1	028-9446 3113	54,000	David McCammick
Ards	Down	2	028-9182 4000	78,100	Ashley Boreland
ARMAGH	Armagh	3	028-3752 9600	58,800	John Briggs
Ballymena	Antrim	4	028-2566 0300	63,200	Anne Donaghy
Ballymoney	Antrim	5	028-2766 0200	30,400	John Dempsey
Banbridge	Down	6	028-4066 0600	47,600	Liam Hannaway
BELFAST	Antrim & Down	7	028-9032 0202	268,400	Peter McNaney
Carrickfergus	Antrim	8	028-9335 8000	40,100	Alan Cardwell
Castlereagh	Down	9	028-9046 4500	66,800	Stephen Reid
Coleraine	Londonderry	10	028-7034 7034	57,100	Roger Wilson
Cookstown	Tyrone	11	028-8676 2205	36,300	Michael McGuckin
Craigavon	Armagh	12	028-3831 2400	92,400	Dr Theresa Donaldson
DERRY	Londonderry	13	028-7136 5151	109,600	John Meehan (acting)
Down	Down	14	028-4461 0800	70,300	John Dumigan
Dungannon & South Tyrone	Tyrone	15	028-8772 0300	56,400	Alan Burke
Fermanagh	Fermanagh	16	028-6632 5050	62,400	Brendan Hegarty
Larne	Antrim	17	028-2827 2313	31,400	Geraldine McGahey
Limavady	Londonderry	18	028-7772 2226	34,000	Liam Flanigan
LISBURN	Antrim	19	028-9250 9250	116,500	Norman Davidson
Magherafelt	Londonderry	20	028-7939 7979	44,200	John McLaughlin
Moyle	Antrim	21	028-2076 2225	16,900	Richard Lewis
NEWRY & Mourne	Down & Armagh	22	028-3031 3031	98,700	Thomas McCall
Newtownabbey	Antrim	23	028-9034 0000	83,740	Jacqui Dixon
North Down	Down	24	028-9127 0371	79,600	Trevor Polley
Omagh	Tyrone	25	028 8224 5321	52,400	Daniel McSorley
Strabane	Tyrone	26	028-7138 2204	39,900	Philip Faithfull

* Source: ONS – Mid-2009 Population Estimates (Crown copyright)
Councils in CAPITAL LETTERS have city status

THE ISLE OF MAN

Ellan Vannin

The Isle of Man is an island situated in the Irish Sea, at latitude 54° 3'–54° 25' N. and longitude 4° 18'–4° 47' W., nearly equidistant from England, Scotland and Ireland. Although the early inhabitants were of Celtic origin, the Isle of Man was part of the Norwegian Kingdom of the Hebrides until 1266, when this was ceded to Scotland. Subsequently granted to the Stanleys (Earls of Derby) in the 15th century and later to the Dukes of Atholl, it was brought under the administration of the Crown in 1765. The island forms the bishopric of Sodor and Man.

The total land area is 572 sq. km (221 sq. miles). The 2006 census showed a resident population of 80,058 (men, 39,523; women, 40,535). The main language in use is English. Around 1,550 people are able to speak the Manx Gaelic language.

CAPITAL – ΨDouglas; population, 26,218 (2006). ΨCastletown (3,109) is the ancient capital; the other towns are ΨPeel (4,280) and ΨRamsey (7,309)

FLAG – A red flag charged with three conjoined armoured legs in white and gold

NATIONAL DAY – 5 July (Tynwald Day)

GOVERNMENT

The Isle of Man is a self-governing Crown dependency, with its own parliamentary, legal and administrative system. The British government is responsible for international relations and defence. Under the UK Act of Accession, Protocol 3, the island's relationship with the European Union is limited to trade alone and does not extend to financial aid. The Lieutenant-Governor is the Queen's personal representative on the island.

The legislature, Tynwald, is the oldest parliament in the world in continuous existence. It has two branches: the Legislative Council and the House of Keys. The council consists of the President of Tynwald, the Bishop of Sodor and Man, the Attorney-General (who does not have a vote) and eight members elected by the House of Keys. The House of Keys has 24 members, elected by universal adult suffrage. The branches sit separately to consider legislation and sit together, as Tynwald Court, for most other parliamentary purposes.

The presiding officer of Tynwald Court is the President of Tynwald, elected by the members, who also presides over sittings of the Legislative Council. The presiding officer of the House of Keys is the Speaker, who is elected by members of the house.

The principal members of the Manx government are the chief minister and nine departmental ministers, who comprise the Council of Ministers.

Lieutenant-Governor, HE Adam Wood
President of Tynwald, Hon. Clare Christian

Speaker, House of Keys, Hon. Steve Rodan, SHK
The First Deemster and Clerk of the Rolls, His Hon. David Doyle
Clerk of Tynwald, Secretary to the House of Keys and Counsel to the Speaker, Roger Phillips
Clerk of the Legislative Council and Deputy Clerk of Tynwald, Jonathan King
Attorney-General, Stephen Harding
Chief Minister, Hon. Tony Brown, MHK
Chief Secretary, Will Greenhow

ECONOMY

Most of the income generated in the island is earned in the services sector with financial and professional services accounting for just over half of the national income. Tourism and manufacturing are also major generators of income while the island's other traditional industries of agriculture and fishing now play a smaller role in the economy. Under the terms of protocol 3, the island has tariff-free access to EU markets for its goods.

In May 2011 the island's unemployment rate was 1.9 per cent and inflation (RPI) was 6.3 per cent.

FINANCE

The budget for 2011–12 provides for net revenue expenditure of £533m. The principal sources of government revenue are taxes on income and expenditure. Income tax is payable at a rate of 10 per cent on the first £10,500 of taxable income for single resident individuals and 20 per cent on the balance, after personal allowances of £9,300. These bands are doubled for married couples. The rate of income tax for trading companies is zero per cent except for income from banking and land and property, which is taxed at 10 per cent. By agreement with the British government, the island keeps most of its rates of indirect taxation (VAT and duties) the same as those in the UK. However, VAT on tourist accommodation, property, repairs and renovations is charged at 5 per cent. A reciprocal agreement on national insurance benefits and pensions exists between the governments of the Isle of Man and the UK. Taxes are also charged on property (rates), but these are comparatively low.

The major government expenditure items are health, social security, social care, which account for 67 per cent of the government budget. The island makes an annual contribution to the UK for defence and other external services.

The island has a special relationship with the European Union and neither contributes money to nor receives funds from the EU budget.

Ψ = sea port

THE CHANNEL ISLANDS

The Channel Islands, situated off the north-west coast of France (at a distance of 16km (10 miles) at their closest point), are the only portions of the Dukedom of Normandy still belonging to the Crown, to which they have been attached since the Norman Conquest of 1066. They were the only British territory to come under German occupation during the Second World War, following invasion on 30 June and 1 July 1940. The islands were relieved by British forces on 9 May 1945, and 9 May (Liberation Day) is now observed as a bank and public holiday.

The islands consist of Jersey (11,630ha/28,717 acres), Guernsey (6,340ha/15,654 acres), and the dependencies of Guernsey: Alderney (795ha/1,962 acres), Brecqhou (30ha/74 acres), Great Sark (419ha/1,035 acres), Little Sark (97ha/239 acres), Herm (130ha/320 acres), Jethou (18ha/44 acres) and Lihou (15ha/38 acres) – a total of 19,474ha/48,083 acres, or 195 sq. km/75 sq. miles.

The most recent estimate of the population of Jersey from the States of Jersey Statistics Unit was 92,500. The most recent official records for Guernsey and Alderney were estimated at 62,431 and 2,194 respectively. The 2001 census showed the population of Jersey as 87,186; Guernsey, 59,807 and Alderney, 2,294. Sark did not complete the same census but an informal census gave its population figure as 591. The official languages are English and French. In country districts of Jersey and Guernsey and throughout Sark a Norman-French *patois* is also in use, though to a lesser extent.

GOVERNMENT
The islands are Crown dependencies with their own legislative assemblies (the States in Jersey and Alderney, the States of Deliberation in Guernsey and the Chief Pleas in Sark), systems of local administration and law, and their own courts. *Projets de Loi* (Acts) passed by the States require the sanction of the Queen-in-council. The UK government is responsible for defence and international relations. The Channel Islands are not part of the European Union but, under protocol 3 of the UK's treaty of accession, have trading rights with the free movement of goods within the EU.

In both Jersey and Guernsey bailiwicks the Lieutenant-Governor and Commander-in-Chief, who is appointed by the Crown, is the personal representative of the Queen and the channel of communication between the Crown (via the Privy Council) and the island's government.

The head of government in both Jersey and Guernsey is the Chief Minister. Jersey has a ministerial system of government; the executive comprises the Council of Ministers and consists of a chief minister and nine other ministers. The ministers are assisted by up to 13 assistant ministers. Members of the States who are not in the executive are able to sit on a number of scrutiny panels and the Public Accounts Committee to examine the policy of the executive and hold ministers to account. Guernsey has a consensus form of government. There are ten States departments with mandated responsibilities, each department is constituted of a minister and four members of the States. Each of the ministers has a seat on the Policy Council which is presided over by the Chief Minister. The

States of Deliberation is the overarching executive. There are also five specialist committees, each led by a chair, responsible for scrutinising policy, finance and legislation, parliamentary procedural matters and public sector pay negotiations.

Justice is administered by the royal courts of Jersey and Guernsey, each consisting of the bailiff and 12 elected jurats. The bailiffs of Jersey and Guernsey, appointed by the Crown, are presidents of the states and of the royal courts of their respective islands.

Each bailiwick constitutes a deanery under the jurisdiction of the Bishop of Winchester.

ECONOMY
A mild climate and good soil have led to the development of intensive systems of agriculture and horticulture, which form a significant part of the economy. Equally important are earnings from tourism and banking and finance: the low rates of income and corporation tax and the absence of death duties make the islands an important offshore financial centre. The financial services sector contributes over 50 per cent of GDP in Jersey and around 40 per cent in Guernsey. In addition, there is no VAT or equivalent tax in Guernsey and only small goods and services tax in Jersey (set at 5 per cent from 1 June 2011). The Channel Islands stock exchange is located in Guernsey, which also has a thriving e-gaming sector.

Principal exports are agricultural produce and flowers; imports are chiefly machinery, manufactured goods, food, fuel and chemicals. Trade with the UK is regarded as internal.

British currency is legal tender in the Channel Islands but each bailiwick issues its own coins and notes (*see* Currency section). They also issue their own postage stamps; UK stamps are not valid.

JERSEY

Lieutenant-Governor and Commander-in-Chief of Jersey,
  HE Gen. Sir John McColl, KCB, CBE, DSO,
  apptd 2011
Secretary and ADC, Lt.-Col. A. Woodrow, OBE, MC
Bailiff of Jersey, Michael St J. Birt
Deputy Bailiff, W. Bailhache
Attorney-General, Timothy Le Cocq, QC
Receiver-General, P. Lewin
Solicitor-General, Howard Sharp, QC
Greffier of the States, M. de la Haye
States Treasurer, L. Rowley
Chief Minister, Senator T. Le Sueur

FINANCE
	2009	2010
Revenue income	£830,688,000	£745,741,000
Revenue expenditure	£784,603,000	£974,890,000
Capital expenditure	£123,531,000	£73,306,000

CHIEF TOWN – ΨSt Helier, on the south coast
FLAG – A white field charged with a red saltire cross, and the arms of Jersey in the upper centre

GUERNSEY AND DEPENDENCIES

Lieutenant-Governor and Commander-in-Chief of the Bailiwick of Guernsey and its Dependencies, HE Air Marshal Peter Walker, CB, CBE, *apptd* 2011

Presiding Officer of the Royal Court and of the States of Deliberation, Bailiff Sir Geoffrey Rowland

Deputy Presiding Officer of the Royal Court and States of Deliberation, Richard Collas

HM Procureur and Receiver-General (Attorney-General), Howard Roberts, QC

HM Comptroller (Solicitor-General), Richard McMahon, QC

GUERNSEY
Chief Minister, Deputy Lyndon Trott
Chief Executive, Mike Brown

FINANCE

	2009	2010
Revenue	£341m	£331m
Expenditure	£326m	£330m

CHIEF TOWNS – ΨSt Peter Port, on the east coast of Guernsey; St Anne on Alderney

FLAG – White, bearing a red cross of St George, with a gold cross of Normandy overall in the centre

ALDERNEY
President of the States, Stuart Trought
Chief Executive, Roy Burke
Greffier, Sarah Kelly

SARK

Sark was the last European territory to abolish feudal parliamentary representation. Elections for a democratic legislative assembly took place in December 2008, with the *conseillers* taking their seats in the newly constituted Chief Pleas in January 2009.

Seigneur of Sark, John Beaumont, OBE
Seneschal, Lt.-Col. R Guille, MBE
Greffier, Trevor Hamon

OTHER DEPENDENCIES

Herm and Lihou are owned by the States of Guernsey; Herm is leased, Lihou is uninhabited. Jethou is leased by the Crown to the States of Guernsey and is sub-let by the States. Brecqhou is within the legislative and judicial territory of Sark.

Ψ = seaport

LAW COURTS AND OFFICES

SUPREME COURT OF THE UNITED KINGDOM

The supreme court of the United Kingdom is the highest judicial authority; it replaced the House of Lords in its judicial capacity on 1 October 2009. It is the ultimate court of appeal for all courts in Great Britain and Northern Ireland (except criminal courts in Scotland) for all cases except those concerning the interpretation and application of European Union law, including preliminary rulings requested by British courts and tribunals, which are decided by the court of justice of the European Union (see European Union section). The UK supreme court also assumed jurisdiction in relation to devolution matters under the Scotland Act 1998, the Northern Ireland Act 1988 and the Government of Wales Act 2006; these powers were transferred from the Judicial Committee of the Privy Council. Ten of the 12 Lords of Appeal in Ordinary from the House of Lords transferred to the 12-member supreme court when it came into operation (at the same time one law lord retired and another was appointed Master of the Rolls). All new justices of the supreme court are now appointed by an independent UK Supreme Court Appointments Commission, and are not members of the House of Lords.

SUPREME COURT OF THE UNITED KINGDOM

President of the Supreme Court (£214,165), Rt. Hon. Lord Phillips of Worth Matravers, KG, *born* 1938, *apptd* 2008
Deputy President of the Supreme Court (£206,857), Rt. Hon. Lord Hope of Craighead, KT, *born* 1938, *apptd* 1996

JUSTICES OF THE SUPREME COURT *as at July 2011* (each £206,857)
Style, The Rt. Hon. Lord/Lady–

Rt. Hon. Lord Walker of Gestingthorpe, *born* 1938, *apptd* 2002
Rt. Hon. Lady Hale of Richmond, *born* 1945, *apptd* 2004
Rt. Hon. Lord Brown of Eaton-under-Heywood, *born* 1937, *apptd* 2004
Rt. Hon. Lord Mance, *born* 1943, *apptd* 2005
Rt. Hon. Lord Kerr of Tonaghmore, *born* 1948, *apptd* 2009
Rt. Hon. Lord Clarke of Stone-cum-Ebony, *born* 1943, *apptd* 2009
Rt. Hon. Lord Dyson, *born* 1943, *apptd* 2010
Rt. Hon. Lord Wilson of Culworth, *born* 1945, *apptd* 2011

UNITED KINGDOM SUPREME COURT
Parliament Square, London SW1P 3BD T 020-7960 1900
Chief Executive, Jenny Rowe

JUDICATURE OF ENGLAND AND WALES

The legal system in England and Wales is divided into criminal law and civil law. Criminal law is concerned with acts harmful to the community and the rules laid down by the state for the benefit of citizens, whereas civil law governs the relationships and transactions between individuals. Administrative law is a kind of civil law usually concerning the interaction of individuals and the state, and most cases are heard in tribunals specific to the subject (see Tribunals section). Scotland and Northern Ireland possess legal systems that differ from the system in England and Wales in law, judicial procedure and court structure, but retain the distinction between criminal and civil law.

Under the provisions of the Criminal Appeal Act 1995, a commission was set up to direct and supervise investigations into possible miscarriages of justice and to refer cases to the appeal courts on the grounds of conviction and sentence; these functions were formerly the responsibility of the home secretary.

SENIOR COURTS OF ENGLAND AND WALES
The senior courts of England and Wales (until September 2009 known as the supreme court of judicature of England and Wales) comprise the high court, the crown court and the court of appeal. The President of the Courts of England and Wales, a new title given to the Lord Chief Justice under the Constitutional Reform Act 2005, is the head of the judiciary.

The high court was created in 1875 and combined many previously separate courts. Sittings are held at the royal courts of justice in London and at around 120 district registries outside the capital. It is the superior civil court and is split into three divisions – the chancery division, the Queen's bench division and the family division – each of which is further divided. The chancery division is headed by the Chancellor of the High Court and is concerned mainly with equity, trusts, tax and bankruptcy, while also including two specialist courts, the patents court and the companies court. The Queen's bench division (QBD) is the largest of the three divisions, and is headed by its own president. It deals with common law (ie tort, contract, debt and personal injuries), some tax law, eg VAT tribunal appeals, and encompasses the admiralty court and the commercial court. The QBD also administers the technology and construction court. The family division was created in 1970 and is headed by its own president, who is also Head of Family Justice, and hears cases concerning divorce, access to and custody of children, and other family matters. The divisional court of the high court sits in the family and chancery divisions, and hears appeals from the magistrates' courts and county courts.

The crown court was set up in 1972 and sits at 77 centres throughout England and Wales. It deals with more serious (indictable) criminal offences, which are triable before a judge and jury, including treason, murder, rape, kidnapping, armed robbery and Official Secrets Act offences. It also handles cases transferred from the magistrates' courts where the magistrate decides his or her own power of sentence is inadequate, or where someone appeals against a magistrate's decision, or in a case that is triable 'either way' where the accused has chosen a jury trial. The crown court centres are divided into three tiers:

HIERARCHY OF ENGLISH COURTS

Court	Courts it binds	Courts it follows
European court of justice	The court making the preliminary reference	None
Supreme court	All English courts	None
Court of appeal	Divisional courts High court Crown court County courts Magistrates' courts	Supreme court
Divisional courts	High court Crown court County courts Magistrates' courts	Supreme court Court of appeal
High court	County courts Magistrates' courts	Supreme court Court of appeal Divisional courts
Crown court	None	Supreme court
County courts	None	Court of appeal
Magistrates' courts	None	Divisional courts High court

high court judges, circuit judges and sometimes recorders (part-time circuit judges), sit in first-tier centres, hearing the most serious criminal offences (eg murder, treason, rape, manslaughter) and some civil high court cases. The second-tier centres are presided over by high court judges, circuit judges or recorders and also deal with the most serious criminal cases. Third-tier courts deal with the remaining criminal offences, with circuit judges or recorders presiding.

The court of appeal hears appeals against both fact and law, and was last restructured in 1966 when it replaced the court of criminal appeal. It is split into the civil division (which hears appeals from the high court, tribunals and in certain cases, the county courts) and the criminal division (which hears appeals from the crown court). Cases are heard by Lords Justices of Appeal and high court judges if deemed suitable for reconsideration.

The Constitutional Reform Act 2005 instigated several key changes to the judiciary in England and Wales. These included the establishment of the independent supreme court, which opened in October 2009; the reform of the post of Lord Chancellor, transferring its judicial functions to the President of the Courts of England and Wales; a duty on government ministers to uphold the independence of the judiciary by barring them from trying to influence judicial decisions through any special access to judges; the formation of a fully transparent and independent Judicial Appointments Commission that is responsible for selecting candidates to recommend for judicial appointment to the Lord Chancellor and Secretary of State for Justice; and the creation of the post of Judicial Appointments and Conduct Ombudsman.

CRIMINAL CASES
In criminal matters the decision to prosecute (in the majority of cases) rests with the Crown Prosecution Service (CPS), which is the independent prosecuting body in England and Wales. The CPS is headed by the director of public prosecutions, who works under the superintendence of the Attorney-General. Certain categories of offence continue to require the Attorney-General's consent for prosecution.

Most minor criminal cases (summary offences) are dealt with in magistrates' courts, usually by a bench of three unpaid lay magistrates (justices of the peace) sitting without a jury and assisted on points of law and procedure by a legally trained clerk. There were 26,966 justices of the peace as at 1 April 2011. In some courts a full-time, salaried and legally qualified district judge (magistrates' court) – formerly known as a stipendiary judge – presides alone. There were 137 district judges (magistrates' courts) as at 1 April 2011. Magistrates' courts oversee the completion of 95 per cent of all criminal cases. Magistrates' courts also house some family proceedings courts (which deal with relationship breakdown and childcare cases) and youth courts. Cases of medium seriousness (known as 'offences triable either way') where the defendant pleads not guilty can be heard in the crown court for a trial by jury, if the defendant so chooses. Preliminary proceedings in a serious case to decide whether there is evidence to justify committal for trial in the crown court are dealt with in the magistrates' courts.

The 77 centres that the crown court sits in are divided into seven regions. There are 673 circuit judges and 1,221 recorders (part-time circuit judges); they must sit a minimum of 15 days per year and are usually subject to a maximum of 30. A jury is present in all trials that are contested.

Appeals from magistrates' courts against sentence or conviction are made to the crown court, and appeals upon a point of law are made to the high court, which may ultimately be appealed to the supreme court. Appeals from the crown court, either against sentence or conviction, are made to the court of appeal (criminal division). Again, these appeals may be brought to the supreme court if a point of law is contested, and if the house considers it is of sufficient importance.

CIVIL CASES
Most minor civil cases – including contract, tort (especially personal injuries), property, divorce and other family matters, bankruptcy etc – are dealt with by the county courts, of which there are 216 (see the Court

Service website, W www.justice.gov.uk, for further details). Cases are heard by circuit judges, recorders or district judges. For cases involving small claims (with certain exceptions, where the amount claimed is £5,000 or less) there are informal and simplified procedures designed to enable parties to present their cases themselves without recourse to lawyers. Where there are financial limits on county court jurisdiction, claims that exceed those limits may be tried in the county courts with the consent of the parties, subject to the court's agreement, or in certain circumstances on transfer from the high court. Outside London, bankruptcy proceedings can be heard in designated county courts. Magistrates' courts also deal with certain classes of civil case, and committees of magistrates license public houses, clubs and betting shops. For the implementation of the Children Act 1989, a new structure of hearing centres was set up in 1991 for family proceedings cases, involving magistrates' courts (family proceedings courts), divorce county courts, family hearing centres and care centres.

Appeals in certain family matters heard in the family proceedings courts go to the family division of the high court. Appeals from county courts may be heard in the court of appeal (civil division) or the high court, and may go on to the supreme court.

CORONERS' COURTS
The coroners' courts investigate violent and unnatural deaths or sudden deaths where the cause is unknown. Doctors, the police, various public authorities or members of the public may bring cases before a local coroner (a senior lawyer or doctor), in order to determine whether further criminal investigation is necessary. Where a death is sudden and the cause is unknown, the coroner may order a post-mortem examination to determine the cause of death rather than hold an inquest in court. An inquest must be held, however, if a person died in a violent or unnatural way, or died in prison or other unusual circumstances. If the coroner suspects murder, manslaughter or infanticide, he or she must summon a jury.

SENIOR JUDICIARY OF ENGLAND AND WALES
Lord Chief Justice of England and Wales (£239,845), Rt. Hon. Lord Judge, *born* 1941, *apptd* 2008
Master of the Rolls and Head of Civil Justice (£214,165), Rt. Hon. Lord Neuberger of Abbotsbury, *born* 1948, *apptd* 2009
President of the Queen's Bench Division (£206,857), Sir Anthony May, *born* 1940, *apptd* 2008
President of the Family Division and Head of Family Justice (£206,857), Rt. Hon. Sir Nicholas Wall, *born* 1945, *apptd* 2010
Chancellor of the High Court (£206,857), Rt. Hon. Sir Robert (Andrew) Morritt, CVO, *born* 1938, *apptd* 2000

SENIOR COURTS OF ENGLAND AND WALES
COURT OF APPEAL
Master of the Rolls (£214,165), Rt. Hon. Lord Neuberger of Abbotsbury, *born* 1948, *apptd* 2009
Secretary, Noella Roberts
Clerk, Graham Lister
Vice-President, Civil Division (£196,707), Rt. Hon. Sir Maurice Kay, *born* 1942, *apptd* 2010

Vice-President, Criminal Division (£196,707), Rt. Hon Sir Anthony Hughes, *born* 1948, *apptd* 2009

LORD JUSTICES OF APPEAL *as at July 2011* (each £196,707)
Style, The Rt. Hon. Lord/Lady Justice [surname]

Rt. Hon. Sir Malcolm Pill, *born* 1938, *apptd* 1995
Rt. Hon. Sir Alan Ward, *born* 1938, *apptd* 1995
Rt. Hon. Sir Mathew Thorpe, *born* 1938, *apptd* 1995
Rt. Hon. Sir John Mummery, *born* 1938, *apptd* 1996
Rt. Hon. Sir John Laws, *born* 1945, *apptd* 1999
Rt. Hon. Sir Bernard Rix, *born* 1944, *apptd* 2000
Rt. Hon. Dame Mary Arden, DBE, *born* 1947, *apptd* 2000
Rt. Hon. Sir Andrew Longmore, *born* 1944, *apptd* 2001
Rt. Hon. Sir Robert Carnwath, CVO, *born* 1945, *apptd* 2002
Rt. Hon. Sir Roger Thomas, *born* 1947, *apptd* 2003
Rt. Hon. Sir Maurice Kay, *born* 1942, *apptd* 2004
Rt. Hon. Sir Anthony Hooper, *born* 1937, *apptd* 2004
Rt. Hon. Sir Timothy Lloyd, *born* 1946, *apptd* 2005
Rt. Hon. Sir Martin Moore-Bick, *born* 1948, *apptd* 2005
Rt. Hon. Sir Alan Moses, *born* 1945, *apptd* 2005
Rt. Hon. Sir Stephen Richards, *born* 1950, *apptd* 2005
Rt. Hon. Dame Heather Hallett, DBE, *born* 1949, *apptd* 2005
Rt. Hon. Sir Anthony Hughes, *born* 1948, *apptd* 2006
Rt. Hon. Sir Brian Leveson, *born* 1949, *apptd* 2006
Rt. Hon. Sir Roger Toulson, *born* 1946, *apptd* 2007
Rt. Hon. Sir Colin Rimer, *born* 1944, *apptd* 2007
Rt. Hon. Sir Stanley Burnton, *born* 1942, *apptd* 2007
Rt. Hon. Sir Terence Etherton, *born* 1951, *apptd* 2008
Rt. Hon. Sir Rupert Jackson, *born* 1948, *apptd* 2008
Rt. Hon. Sir John Goldring, *born* 1944, *apptd* 2008
Rt. Hon. Sir Richard Aikens, *born* 1948, *apptd* 2008
Rt. Hon. Sir Jeremy Sullivan, *born* 1945, *apptd* 2009
Rt. Hon. Sir Patrick Elias, *born* 1947, *apptd* 2009
Rt. Hon. Sir Nicholas Patten, *born* 1950, *apptd* 2009
Rt. Hon. Sir James Munby, *born* 1948, *apptd* 2009
Rt. Hon. Sir Christopher Pitchford, *born* 1947, *apptd* 2010
Rt. Hon. Dame Jill Black, DBE, *born* 1954, *apptd* 2010
Rt. Hon. Sir Stephen Tomlinson, *born* 1952, *apptd* 2010
Rt. Hon. Sir Peter Gross, *born* 1952, *apptd* 2010
Rt. Hon. Dame Anne Rafferty, *born* 1950, *apptd* 2011
Rt. Hon. Sir Andrew McFarlane, *born* 1954, *apptd* 2011
Ex Officio Judges, Lord Chief Justice of England and Wales; Master of the Rolls; President of the Queen's Bench Division; President of the Family Division; and Chancellor of the High Court

COURTS-MARTIAL APPEAL COURT
Judges, Lord Chief Justice of England and Wales; Master of the Rolls; Lord Justices of Appeal; and Judges of the High Court of Justice

HIGH COURT OF JUSTICE
CHANCERY DIVISION
Chancellor of the High Court (£206,857), Rt. Hon. Sir Andrew Morritt, CVO, *born* 1938, *apptd* 2000
Secretary, Elaine Harbert
Clerk, Sheila Glasgow

JUDGES *as at July 2011* (each £172,753)
Style, The Hon. Mr/Mrs Justice [surname]

Hon. Sir Peter Smith, *born* 1952, *apptd* 2002
Hon. Sir Kim Lewison, *born* 1952, *apptd* 2003
Hon. Sir David Richards, *born* 1951, *apptd* 2003

Hon. Sir George Mann, *born* 1951, *apptd* 2004
Hon. Sir Nicholas Warren, *born* 1949, *apptd* 2005
Hon. Sir David Kitchin, *born* 1955, *apptd* 2005
Hon. Sir Michael Briggs, *born* 1954, *apptd* 2006
Hon. Sir Launcelot Henderson, *born* 1951, *apptd* 2006
Hon. Sir Paul Morgan, *born* 1952, *apptd* 2007
Hon. Sir Alastair Norris, *born* 1950, *apptd* 2007
Hon. Sir Gerald Barling, *born* 1949, *apptd* 2007
Hon. Sir Christopher Floyd, *born* 1951, *apptd* 2007
Hon. Sir Philip Sales, *born* 1962, *apptd* 2008
Hon. Dame Sonia Proudman, DBE, *born* 1949, *apptd* 2008
Hon. Sir Richard Arnold, *born* 1961, *apptd* 2008
Hon. Sir Peter Roth, *born* 1952, *apptd* 2009
Hon. Sir Geoffrey Vos, *born* 1955, *apptd* 2009
Hon. Sir Guy Newey, *born* 1959, *apptd* 2010

The Chancery Division also includes three specialist courts: the companies court, the patents court and the bankruptcy court.

QUEEN'S BENCH DIVISION
Lord Chief Justice of England and Wales (£239,845), Rt. Hon. Lord Judge, *born* 1941, *apptd* 2008
Secretary, Michèle Souris
Clerk, Linda Francis
President (£206,857), Rt. Hon. Sir Anthony May, *born* 1940, *apptd* 2008
Vice-President (£196,707), Rt. Hon. Sir Roger Thomas, *born* 1947, *apptd* 2008

JUDGES *as at July 2011* (each £172,753)
Style, The Hon. Mr/Mrs Justice [surname]

Hon. Sir Andrew Collins, *born* 1942, *apptd* 1994
Hon. Sir Alexander Butterfield, *born* 1942, *apptd* 1995
Hon. Sir David Eady, *born* 1943, *apptd* 1997
Hon. Sir David Steel, *born* 1943, *apptd* 1998
Hon. Sir Nicolas Bratza, *born* 1945, *apptd* 1998
Hon. Sir Michael Burton, *born* 1946, *apptd* 1998
Hon. Sir Stephen Silber, *born* 1944, *apptd* 1999
Hon. Sir Richard Henriques, *born* 1943, *apptd* 2000
Hon. Sir Andrew Smith, *born* 1947, *apptd* 2000
Hon. Sir Duncan Ouseley, *born* 1950, *apptd* 2000
Hon. Sir Richard McCombe, *born* 1952, *apptd* 2001
Hon. Sir Raymond Jack, *born* 1942, *apptd* 2001
Hon. Sir Robert Owen, *born* 1944, *apptd* 2001
Hon. Sir Colin Mackay, *born* 1943, *apptd* 2001
Hon. Sir John Mitting, *born* 1947, *apptd* 2001
Hon. Sir Roderick Evans, *born* 1946, *apptd* 2001
Hon. Sir Nigel Davis, *born* 1951, *apptd* 2001
Hon. Sir Brian Keith, *born* 1944, *apptd* 2001
Hon. Sir Jeremy Cooke, *born* 1949, *apptd* 2001
Hon. Sir Richard Field, *born* 1947, *apptd* 2002
Hon. Sir Colman Treacy, *born* 1949, *apptd* 2002
Hon. Sir Peregrine Simon, *born* 1950, *apptd* 2002
Hon. Sir Roger Royce, *born* 1944, *apptd* 2002
Hon. Dame Laura Cox, DBE, *born* 1951, *apptd* 2002
Hon. Sir Adrian Fulford, *born* 1953, *apptd* 2002
Hon. Sir Jack Beatson, *born* 1948, *apptd* 2003
Hon. Sir Michael Tugendhat, *born* 1944, *apptd* 2003
Hon. Dame Elizabeth Gloster, DBE, *born* 1949, *apptd* 2004
Hon. Sir David Bean, *born* 1954, *apptd* 2004
Hon. Sir Alan Wilkie, *born* 1947, *apptd* 2004
Hon. Dame Linda Dobbs, DBE, *born* 1951, *apptd* 2004
Hon. Sir Paul Walker, *born* 1954, *apptd* 2004
Hon. Sir David Calvert-Smith, *born* 1945, *apptd* 2005

Hon. Sir Christopher Clarke, *born* 1947, *apptd* 2005
Hon. Sir Charles Openshaw, *born* 1947, *apptd* 2005
Hon. Dame Caroline Swift, DBE, *born* 1955, *apptd* 2005
Hon. Sir Brian Langstaff, *born* 1948, *apptd* 2005
Hon. Sir David Lloyd Jones, *born* 1952, *apptd* 2005
Hon. Sir Vivian Ramsey, *born* 1950, *apptd* 2005
Hon. Sir Nicholas Underhill, *born* 1952, *apptd* 2006
Hon. Sir Stephen Irwin, *born* 1953, *apptd* 2006
Hon. Sir Nigel Teare, *born* 1952, *apptd* 2006
Hon. Sir Griffith Williams, *born* 1944, *apptd* 2007
Hon. Sir Wyn Williams, *born* 1951, *apptd* 2007
Hon. Sir Timothy King, *born* 1946, *apptd* 2007
Hon. Sir John Saunders, *born* 1959, *apptd* 2007
Hon. Sir Julian Flaux, *born* 1955, *apptd* 2007
Hon. Sir David Foskett, *born* 1949, *apptd* 2007
Hon. Sir Robert Akenhead, *born* 1949, *apptd* 2007
Hon. Sir Nicholas Stadlen, *born* 1950, *apptd* 2007
Hon. Sir Nicholas Blake, *born* 1949, *apptd* 2007
Hon. Sir Ross Cranston, *born* 1948, *apptd* 2007
Hon. Sir Peter Coulson, *born* 1958, *apptd* 2008
Hon. Sir David Maddison, *born* 1947, *apptd* 2008
Hon. Sir Richard Plender, *born* 1945, *apptd* 2008
Hon. Sir William Blair, *born* 1950, *apptd* 2008
Hon. Sir Alistair MacDuff, *born* 1945, *apptd* 2008
Hon. Sir Ian Burnett, *born* 1958, *apptd* 2008
Hon. Sir Nigel Sweeney, *born* 1954, *apptd* 2008
Hon. Dame Elizabeth Slade, DBE, *born* 1949, *apptd* 2008
Hon. Sir Nicholas Hamblen, *born* 1957, *apptd* 2008
Hon. Sir Gary Hickinbottom, *born* 1955, *apptd* 2009
Hon. Sir Timothy Holroyde, *born* 1955, *apptd* 2009
Hon. Dame Victoria Sharp, DBE, *born* 1956, *apptd* 2009
Hon. Sir Andrew Nicol, *born* 1951, *apptd* 2009
Hon. Sir Kenneth Parker, *born* 1945, *apptd* 2009
Hon. Sir Antony Edwards-Stuart, *born* 1946, *apptd* 2009
Hon. Dame Nicola Davies, DBE, *born* 1953, *apptd* 2010
Hon. Dame Kathryn Thirlwall, DBE, *born* 1957, *apptd* 2010
Hon. Sir Michael Supperstone, *born* 1950, *apptd* 2010
Hon. Sir Robin Spencer, *born* 1955, *apptd* 2010
Hon. Sir Keith Lindblom, *born* 1956, *apptd* 2010
Hon. Sir Henry Bernard Eder, *born* 1952, *apptd.* 2011

The Queen's Bench Division also includes three specialist courts – the commercial court, the admiralty court and the administration court – and administers the technology and construction court.

FAMILY DIVISION
President (£206,857), Rt. Hon. Sir Nicholas Wall, *born* 1945, *apptd* 2010
Secretary, Mrs Sarah Leung
Clerk, John Curtis

JUDGES *as at July 2011* (each £172,753)
Style, The Hon. Mr/Mrs Justice [surname]

Hon. Sir Jan Singer, *born* 1944, *apptd* 1993
Hon. Sir Edward Holman, *born* 1947, *apptd* 1995
Hon. Dame Mary Hogg, DBE, *born* 1947, *apptd* 1995
Hon. Sir Arthur Charles, *born* 1948, *apptd* 1998
Hon. Sir David Bodey, *born* 1947, *apptd* 1999
Hon. Sir Paul Coleridge, *born* 1949, *apptd* 2000
Hon. Sir Mark Hedley, *born* 1946, *apptd* 2002
Hon. Dame Anna Pauffley, DBE, *born* 1956, *apptd* 2003
Hon. Sir Roderic Wood, *born* 1951, *apptd* 2004
Hon. Dame Florence Baron, DBE, *born* 1952, *apptd* 2004
Hon. Sir Ernest Ryder, *born* 1957, *apptd* 2004
Hon. Dame Julia Macur, DBE, *born* 1957, *apptd* 2005

Hon. Sir Andrew Moylan, *born* 1953, *apptd* 2007
Hon. Dame Eleanor King, DBE, *born* 1957, *apptd* 2008
Hon. Dame Judith Parker, DBE, *born* 1950, *apptd* 2008
Hon. Sir Jonathan Baker, *born* 1955, *apptd* 2009
Hon. Sir Nicholas Mostyn, *born* 1957, *apptd* 2010
Hon. Sir Peter Arthur Jackson, *born* 1955, *apptd* 2010
Hon. Dame Lucy Theis, *born* 1960, *apptd* 2010

DEPARTMENTS AND OFFICES OF THE SENIOR
COURTS OF ENGLAND AND WALES
Royal Courts of Justice, London WC2A 2LL
T 020-7947 6000

ADMIRALTY, COMMERCIAL AND LONDON
MERCANTILE COURT
T 020-7947 6112
Registrar (£102,921), J. Kay, QC
Admiralty Marshal and Court Manager, K. Houghton

BANKRUPTCY AND COMPANIES COURT REGISTRY
T 020-7947 6441
Chief Registrar (£128,296), S. Baister
Bankruptcy Registrars (£102,921), S. Barber; C. Derrett;
G. W. Jaques; W. Nicholls; J. A. Simmonds
Court Manager, T. Pollen

CENTRAL OFFICE OF THE QUEEN'S BENCH DIVISION
Senior Master, and Queen's Remembrancer (£128,296),
S. D. Whitaker
Masters of the Queen's Bench Division (£102,921), D.
Cook; R. Eastman; P. G. A. Eyre; B. J. F. Fontaine;
I. H. Foster; R. Kay; H. J. Leslie; R. Roberts;
B. Yoxall
Court Manager, J. Ryan

CHANCERY CHAMBERS
T 020-7947 6148
Chief Master (£128,296), J. Winegarten
Masters of the Senior Courts (£102,921, T. J. Bowles;
N. W. Bragge; J. A. Moncaster; N. S. Price;
P. R. Teverson
Court Manager, T. Pollen

COURT OF APPEAL CIVIL DIVISION
T 020-7947 6916
Court Manager, Kim Langan

COURT OF APPEAL CRIMINAL DIVISION
T 020-7947 6011
Registrar (£102,921), R. A. Venne
Deputy Registrar, Mrs L. G. Knapman
Court Manager, Miss C. Brownbill

ADMINISTRATIVE COURT OFFICE
T 020-7947 6655
*Master of the Crown Office, and Queen's Coroner and
Attorney* (£102,921), R. A. Venne
Deputy Master of the Crown Office, Mrs L. G. Knapman
Court Manager, Dave Brupbacher

EXAMINERS OF THE COURT
Empowered to take examination of witnesses in all
divisions of the High Court.

Examiners, His Hon. M. W. M. Chism; A. G. Dyer; A. W.
Hughes; Mrs G. M. Keene; R. M. Planterose

COSTS OFFICE
T 020-7947 6423
Senior Costs Judge (£128,296), P. T. Hurst
Masters of the Senior Courts (£102,921), C. D. N.
Campbell; A. Gordon-Saker; P. Haworth; C. Leonard;
J. E. O'Hare; J. Simons; C. C. Wright
Court Manager, Helene Newman

COURT OF PROTECTION
11th Floor, Archway Tower, 2 Junction Road, London N19 5SZ
T 0300-456 4600
Senior Judge (£128,296), D. Lush

COURT OF PROTECTION VISITORS
Office of the Public Guardian, PO Box 15118, Birmingham
B16 6GX T 0845-330 2900

The Mental Capacity Act 2005 came into force on 1
October 2007, and it makes provision for two panels of
court of protection visitors (special visitors or general
visitors).

ELECTION PETITIONS OFFICE
Room E13, Royal Courts of Justice, London WC2A 2LL
T 020-7947 7529

The office accepts petitions and deals with all matters
relating to the questioning of parliamentary, European
parliament, local government and parish elections, and
with applications for relief under the 'representation of
the people' legislation.
Prescribed Officer (£128,296), Senior Master and Queen's
Remembrancer, S. D. Whitaker
Chief Clerks, Helene Newman; Stuart Pycock

OFFICIAL RECEIVERS' DEPARTMENT (THE
INSOLVENCY SERVICE)
21 Bloomsbury Street, London WC1B 3QW
T 020-7637 1110
Inspector General and Chief Executive, S. Speed
Deputy Inspector General, L. Cramp, CB

OFFICE OF COURT FUNDS
22 Kingsway, London WC2B 6LE
T 0845-223 8500
Head of Court Funds Office, E. Bloomfield

OFFICIAL SOLICITOR AND PUBLIC TRUSTEE
81 Chancery Lane, London WC2A 1DD
T 020-7911 7127
Official Solicitor to the Senior Courts, A. Pitblado
Public Trustee, E. Bloomfield

PRINCIPAL REGISTRY (FAMILY DIVISION)
First Avenue House, 42–49 High Holborn, London WC1V 6NP
T 020-7947 6000
Senior District Judge (£128,296), P. Waller
District Judges (£102,921), Mrs A. Aitken; A. R. S.
Bassett-Cross; M. C. Berry; Ms S. M. Bowman;
Ms H. C. Bradley; Ms P. Cushing; Ms Y. Gibson;
Mrs L. Gordon-Saker; P. Greene; R. Harper; E. Hess;
Ms H. MacGregor; K. Malik; C. Million; Ms C. Reid;
Ms L. D. Roberts; R. Robinson; C. Simmonds;
Ms S. Walker; K. J. White
Area Director, London Civil and Family, K. Launchbury
Head of Operations, London Family, J. Miller
Court Manager, J. Risk

PROBATE SERVICE
London Probate Department (Principal Registry)
7th Floor, PRFD, First Avenue House, 42–49 High Holborn,
London WC1V 6NP T 020-7947 6939
Registrar, H. Whitby (Ipswich District)
Probate Manager, Tina Constantinou

DISTRICT PROBATE REGISTRARS/MANAGERS
Birmingham District Registrar, P. Walbeoff
Brighton District Probate Manager, S. Catt
Bristol District Registrar, B. Phillips
Cardiff District (Wales) Registrar, F. Herdman
Ipswich District Registrar, H. Whitby
Leeds District Probate Manager, S. Holding
Liverpool District Probate Manager, D. Shone
Manchester District Registrar, K. Murphy
Newcastle District Registrar, M. C. Riley
Oxford District Registrar, F. Herdman
Winchester District Registrar, A. Butler

JUDGE ADVOCATES GENERAL
The Judge Advocate General is the judicial head of the
Service justice system, and the leader of the judges who
preside over trials in the court martial and other Service
courts. The defendants are service personnel from the
Royal Navy, the army and the Royal Air Force, and
civilians accompanying them overseas.

JUDGE ADVOCATE GENERAL OF THE FORCES
9th Floor, Thomas More Building, Royal Courts of Justice,
Strand, London WC2A 2LL
T 020-7218 8095
Judge Advocate General (£138,548), His Hon. Judge
Blackett
Vice Judge Advocate General (£120,785), Michael Hunter
Assistant Judge Advocates General (£106,921)*, J. P. Camp;
M. R. Elsom; R. D. Hill; A. M. Large; A. J. B. McGrigor;
E. Peters
Style, Judge [surname]

* Salary includes £2,000 London salary lead and a London
allowance of £2,000

HIGH COURT AND CROWN COURT CENTRES
First-tier centres deal with both civil and criminal cases
and are served by high court and circuit judges.
Second-tier centres deal with criminal cases only and are
served by high court and circuit judges. Third-tier centres
deal with criminal cases only and are served only by
circuit judges.

LONDON REGION
First-tier – None
Second-tier – Central Criminal Court
Third-tier – Blackfriars, Croydon, Harrow, Inner London,
Isleworth, Kingston upon Thames, Snaresbrook,
Southwark, Wood Green, Woolwich
Regional Director, Alan Eccles, 2nd Floor, Rose Court,
2 Southwark Bridge, London SE1 9HS T 020-7921 2006
Area Directors, Dave Weston *(Crime, Central and South);*
Sandra Aston *(Crime, North and West);* Kelvin
Launchbury *(Civil and Family)*

The high court (first-tier) in Greater London sits at the
Royal Courts of Justice.

MIDLANDS REGION
First-tier – Birmingham, Lincoln, Nottingham, Stafford,
Warwick
Second-tier – Leicester, Northampton, Shrewsbury,
Worcester, Wolverhampton
Third-tier – Coventry, Derby, Hereford, Stoke on Trent
Delivery Director, Lucy Garrod, PO Box 11772, 6th Floor,
Temple Court, Bull Street, Birmingham B4 6WF

NORTH-EAST REGION
First-tier – Leeds, Newcastle upon Tyne, Sheffield,
Teesside
Second-tier – Bradford, York
Third-tier – Doncaster, Durham, Kingston upon Hull,
Great Grimsby
Delivery Director, Sheila Proudlock, Old Elvet, Green Lane,
Durham DH1 3RG T 0191-375 1815
Head of Crime, Dave Foley

NORTH-WEST REGION
First-tier – Carlisle, Chester, Liverpool, Manchester
(Crown Square), Preston
Third-tier – Barrow in Furness, Bolton, Burnley,
Knutsford, Lancaster, Manchester (Minshull Street),
Warrington
Regional Director, Richard Knott, PO Box 4237, Manchester
Civil Justice Centre, 1 Bridge Street West, Manchester
M60 1TE T 0161-240 5000
Area Directors, Gill Hague *(Cumbria and Lancashire);*
John Foley *(Greater Manchester);* Paul McGladrigan
(Merseyside and Cheshire)

SOUTH-EAST REGION
First-tier – Cambridge, Chelmsford, Lewes, Norwich,
Oxford
Second-tier – Guildford, Ipswich, Luton, Maidstone,
Reading, St Albans
Third-tier – Aylesbury, Basildon, Canterbury, Chichester,
Croydon, King's Lynn, Peterborough, Southend
Regional Director, Keith Budgen, 3rd Floor, Rose Court,
2 Southwark Bridge, London SE1 9HS T 020-7332 1831
Area Directors, Pauline Cornford *(Cambridgeshire,
Norfolk and Suffolk);* Julia Eeles *(Surrey and Sussex);*
Dr Jonathan Lane *(Thames Valley);* Mike Littlewood,
OBE *(Bedfordshire, Essex and Hertfordshire);*
Dave Weston *(Kent)*

SOUTH-WEST REGION
First-tier – Bristol, Exeter, Truro, Winchester
Second-tier – Dorchester & Weymouth, Gloucester,
Plymouth
Third-tier – Barnstaple, Bournemouth, Newport (IoW),
Portsmouth, Salisbury, Southampton, Swindon,
Taunton
Regional Director, Peter Risk, Spectrum, 3rd Floor, Suite A,
Bond Street, Bristol BS1 3LG T 0117-300 6238
Area Directors, David Gentry *(West);* Simon Townley
(East)

WALES REGION
First-tier – Caernarfon, Cardiff, Merthyr Tydfil, Mold,
Swansea
Second-tier – Carmarthen, Newport, Welshpool
Third-tier – Dolgellau, Haverfordwest
Delivery Director, Mark Swales, Churchill House,
Churchill Way, Cardiff CF10 2HH T 029-2067 8311

CIRCUIT JUDGES

Circuit judges are barristers of at least seven years' standing or recorders of at least five years' standing. Circuit judges serve in the county courts and the crown court.

Style, His/Her Hon. Judge [surname]
Senior Presiding Judge, Rt. Hon. Lord Justice Goldring
Senior Circuit Judges, each £138,548
Circuit Judges at the Central Criminal Court, London (Old Bailey Judges), each £138,548
Circuit Judges, each £128,296

MIDLANDS CIRCUIT
Presiding Judges, Hon. Mr Justice Flaux; Hon. Mrs Justice Thirlwall

NORTH-EASTERN CIRCUIT
Presiding Judges, Hon. Mr Justice Coulson; Hon. Mr Justice Openshaw

NORTHERN CIRCUIT
Presiding Judges, Hon. Mr Justice Holroyde; Hon. Mr Justice Ryder

SOUTH-EASTERN CIRCUIT
Presiding Judges, Hon. Mr Justice Fulford; Hon. Mr Justice Nicol; Hon. Mr Justice Saunders; Mr Justice Sweeney

WALES CIRCUIT
Presiding Judges, Hon. Mr Justice Griffith Williams; Hon. Mr Justice Wyn Williams

WESTERN CIRCUIT
Presiding Judges, Hon. Mr Justice Burnett; Hon. Mr Justice Field

DISTRICT JUDGES

District judges, formerly known as registrars of the court, are solicitors of at least seven years' standing and serve in county courts.
District Judges, each £102,921

DISTRICT JUDGES (MAGISTRATES' COURTS)

District judges (magistrates' courts), formerly known as stipendiary magistrates, must be barristers or solicitors of at least seven years' standing (including at least two years' experience as a deputy district judge), and serve in magistrates' courts. All former provincial and metropolitan stipendiary magistrates can serve nationally within any district.
District Judges (Magistrates' Courts), each £102,921

CROWN PROSECUTION SERVICE
Rose Court, 2 Southwark Bridge Road, London SE1 9HS
T 020-7023 6539 E enquiries@cps.gsi.gov.uk
W www.cps.gov.uk

The Crown Prosecution Service (CPS) is responsible for prosecuting cases investigated by the police in England and Wales, with the exception of cases conducted by the Serious Fraud Office and certain minor offences.

The CPS is headed by the director of public prosecutions (DPP), who works under the superintendence of the attorney-general. The service is divided into 13 areas across England and Wales, with each area led by a chief crown prosecutor.
Director of Public Prosecutions, Keir Starmer, QC

Chief Executive, Peter Lewis
Chief Operating Officer, Mike Kennedy, CBE
Principal Legal Adviser, Alison Levitt
Directors, David Jones *(Business Information Systems);* Paul Staff *(Finance);* Sue Hemming, OBE *(Counter-Terrorism);* Simon Clements *(Special Crime);* Ros McCool *(Human Resources);* Roger Daw *(Policy);* Nick Hunt *(Strategy and Policy)*

CPS AREAS
WALES, 20th Floor, Capital Tower, Greyfriars Road, Cardiff CF10 3PL T 029-2080 3800
Chief Crown Prosecutor, Jim Brisbane
EAST MIDLANDS, 2 King Edward Court, King Edward Street, Nottingham NG1 1EL T 0115-852 3300
Chief Crown Prosecutor, Judith Walker
EASTERN, County House, 100 New London Road, Chelmsford, Essex CM2 0RG T 01245-455800
Chief Crown Prosecutor, Ken Caley
LONDON, 3rd Floor, New King's Beam House, 22 Upper Ground, London SE1 9BT T 020-3357 0000
Chief Crown Prosecutor, Alison Saunders
MERSEY/CHESHIRE, 7th Floor, Royal Liver Building, Pier Head, Liverpool L3 1HN T 0151-239 6400
Chief Crown Prosecutor, Paul Whittaker
NORTH EAST, St Ann's Quay, 112 Quayside, Newcastle Upon Tyne, NE1 3BD T 0191-260 4200
Chief Crown Prosecutor, Wendy Williams
NORTH WEST, 1st Floor, Stocklund House, Castle Street, Carlisle CA3 8SY T 01228-882900
Chief Crown Prosecutor, Nazir Afzal, OBE
SOUTH EAST, 29 Union Street, Maidstone, Kent ME14 1PT T 01622-356300
Chief Crown Prosecutor, Roger Coe-Salazar
SOUTH WEST, 2nd Floor, Froomsgate House, Rupert Street, Bristol BS1 2QJ T 0117-930 2800
Chief Crown Prosecutor, Barry Hughes
THAMES AND CHILTERN, Eaton Court, 112 Oxford Road, Reading, Berks RG1 7LL T 0118-951 3600
Chief Crown Prosecutor, Baljit Ubhey
WESSEX, 3rd Floor, Black Horse House, 8–10 Leigh Road, Eastleigh, Hants SO50 9FH T 02380-673 800
Chief Crown Prosecutor, Nick Hawkins
WEST MIDLANDS, Operations Centre, Colmore Gate, 2 Colmore Row, Birmingham B3 2QA T 0121-262 1300
Chief Crown Prosecutor, Harry Ireland
YORKSHIRE AND HUMBERSIDE, 27 Park Place, Leeds, LS1 2SZ T 0113-290 2700
Chief Crown Prosecutor, Martin Goldman

HER MAJESTY'S COURTS AND TRIBUNALS SERVICE
Zone C, 1st Floor, 102 Petty France, London SW1H 9AJ
T 0845-456 8770 W www.justice.gov.uk

Her Majesty's Courts Service and the Tribunals Service merged on 1 April 2011 to form HM Courts and Tribunals Service. It is an agency of the Ministry of Justice, operating as a partnership between the Lord Chancellor, the Lord Chief Justice and the Senior President of Tribunals. It is responsible for administering the criminal, civil and family courts and tribunals in England and Wales and non-devolved tribunals in Scotland and Northern Ireland.
Chief Executive, Peter Handcock

JUDICIAL APPOINTMENTS COMMISSION

Steel House, 11 Tothill Street, London SW1H 9LJ
T 020-3334 0453 E jaas@jac.gsi.gov.uk
W http://jac/judiciary.gov.uk

The Judicial Appointments Commission was established as an independent non-departmental public body in April 2006 by the Constitutional Reform Act 2005. Its role is to select judicial office holders independently of government (a responsibility previously held by the Lord Chancellor) for courts and tribunals in England and Wales, and for some tribunals whose jurisdiction extends to Scotland or Northern Ireland. It has a statutory duty to encourage diversity in the range of persons available for selection and is sponsored by the Ministry of Justice and accountable to parliament through the Lord Chancellor. It is made up of 15 commissioners, including a chair.
Chair, Christopher Stephens
Commissioners, Hon. Mr Justice Bean; Lady Justice Black, DBE; Dame Boreland-Kelly, DBE, FRSA; Dame Prof. Hazel Genn, DBE; Sir Geoffrey Inkin, OBE; Sara Nathan, OBE; Charles Newman; His Hon. Judge Pearl; Hon. Francis Plowden; Harriet Spicer; Jonathan Sumption, OBE, QC; Rt. Hon. Lord Justice Toulson
Chief Executive (interim), Nigel Reeder

DIRECTORATE OF JUDICIAL OFFICES

The Judicial Office was established in April 2006 to support the judiciary in discharging its responsibilities under the Constitutional Reform Act 2005. It is led by a chief executive, who reports to the Lord Chief Justice rather than to ministers, and its work is directed by the judiciary rather than by the administration of the day. The Judicial Office incorporates the Judicial College (formerly the Judicial Studies Board), the Judicial Communications Office, sponsorship of the Family and Civil Justice Councils, the Office for Judicial Complaints and the Tribunals Judicial Office.

CHIEF EXECUTIVE'S OFFICE
T 020-7947 7960
Chief Executive Officer, Anne Sharp
Personal Secretary, Maxine Fidler

HR FOR THE JUDICIARY
Head, Helen Wallace
Personal Secretary, Susan Holleran

JUDICIAL COLLEGE
T 020-3334 0700
Director of Studies, His Hon. Judge Phillips, CBE
Executive Director, Sheridan Greenland
Personal Secretary, Wendy Ford

OFFICE FOR JUDICIAL COMPLAINTS
T 020-3334 0145

STRATEGY, GOVERNANCE AND COMMUNICATIONS
Deputy Director, Jo Gordon
Personal Secretary, Susan Holleran
Head of News Stephen Ward

JUDICIAL COMMITTEE OF THE PRIVY COUNCIL

The Judicial Committee of the Privy Council is the final court of appeal for the United Kingdom overseas territories (*see* UK Overseas Territories section), crown dependencies and those independent Commonwealth countries which have retained this avenue of appeal (Antigua and Barbuda, Bahamas, Brunei, Cook Islands and Niue, Dominica, Grenada, Jamaica, Kiribati, Mauritius, St Christopher and Nevis, St Lucia, St Vincent and the Grenadines, Trinidad and Tobago, and Tuvalu) and the sovereign base areas of Akrotiri and Dhekelia in Cyprus. The committee also hears appeals against pastoral schemes under the Pastoral Measure 1983, and deals with appeals from veterinary disciplinary bodies.

Until October 2009, the Judicial Committee of the Privy Council was the final arbiter in disputes as to the legal competence of matters done or proposed by the devolved legislative and executive authorities in Scotland, Wales and Northern Ireland. This is now the responsibility of the new UK Supreme Court.

In 2010 the Judicial Committee dealt with a total of 33 appeals and 46 petitions for special leave to appeal.

The members of the Judicial Committee are the justices of the supreme court, and Privy Counsellors who hold or have held high judicial office in the United Kingdom or in certain designated courts of Commonwealth countries from which appeals are taken to committee.

JUDICIAL COMMITTEE OF THE PRIVY COUNCIL
Parliament Square, London SW1A 2AJ T 020-7960 1500
Registrar of the Privy Council, Louise di Mambro
Chief Clerk, Jackie Lindsay

SCOTTISH JUDICATURE

Scotland has a legal system separate from, and differing greatly from, the English legal system in enacted law, judicial procedure and the structure of courts.

In Scotland the system of public prosecution is headed by the Lord Advocate and is independent of the police, who have no say in the decision to prosecute. The Lord Advocate, discharging his functions through the Crown Office in Edinburgh, is responsible for prosecutions in the high court, sheriff courts and district courts. Prosecutions in the high court are prepared by the Crown Office and conducted in court by one of the law officers, by an advocate-depute, or by a solicitor advocate. In the inferior courts the decision to prosecute is made and prosecution is preferred by procurators fiscal, who are lawyers and full-time civil servants subject to the directions of the Crown Office. A permanent legally qualified civil servant, known as the crown agent, is responsible for the running of the Crown Office and the organisation of the Procurator Fiscal Service, of which he or she is the head.

Scotland is divided into six sheriffdoms, each with a full-time sheriff principal. The sheriffdoms are further divided into sheriff court districts, each of which has a legally qualified resident sheriff or sheriffs, who are judges of the court.

In criminal cases sheriffs principal and sheriffs have the same powers; sitting with a jury of 15 members, they may try more serious cases on indictment, or, sitting alone, may try lesser cases under summary procedure. Minor summary offences are dealt with in Justice of the Peace Courts, which replaced district courts formerly operated by local authorities, and presided over by lay justices of the peace (of whom some 500 regularly sit in court) and, in Glasgow only, by stipendiary magistrates. Juvenile offenders (children under 16) may be brought before an informal children's hearing comprising three local lay people. The superior criminal court is the high court of justiciary which is both a trial and an appeal court. Cases on indictment are tried by a high court judge, sitting with a jury of 15, in Edinburgh and on circuit in other towns. Appeals from the lower courts against conviction or sentence are also heard by the high court, which sits as an appeal court only in Edinburgh. There is no further appeal to the supreme court in criminal cases.

In civil cases the jurisdiction of the sheriff court extends to most kinds of action. Appeals against decisions of the sheriff may be made to the sheriff principal and thence to the court of session, or direct to the court of session, which sits only in Edinburgh. The court of session is divided into the inner and the outer house. The outer house is a court of first instance in which cases are heard by judges sitting singly, sometimes with a jury of 12. The inner house, itself subdivided into two divisions of equal status, is mainly an appeal court. Appeals may be made to the inner house from the outer house as well as from the sheriff court. An appeal may be made from the inner house to the supreme court.

The judges of the court of session are the same as those of the high court of justiciary, with the Lord President of the court of session also holding the office of Lord Justice General in the high court. Senators of the College of Justice are Lords Commissioners of Justiciary as well as judges of the court of session. On appointment, a senator takes a judicial title, which is retained for life. Although styled The Hon./Rt. Hon. Lord, the senator is not a peer, although some judges are peers in their own right.

The office of coroner does not exist in Scotland. The local procurator fiscal inquires privately into sudden or suspicious deaths and may report findings to the crown agent. In some cases a fatal accident inquiry may be held before the sheriff.

COURT OF SESSION AND HIGH COURT OF JUSTICIARY

The Lord President and Lord Justice General (£214,165), Rt. Hon. Lord Hamilton, *born* 1942, *apptd* 2005
Private Secretary, A. Maxwell

INNER HOUSE
Lords of Session (each £196,707)

FIRST DIVISION
The Lord President

Rt. Hon. Lord Eassie (Ronald Mackay), *born* 1945, *apptd* 2006
Rt. Hon. Lord Reed (Robert Reed), *born* 1956, *apptd* 2008
Rt. Hon. Lord Hardie (Andrew Hardie), *born* 1946, *apptd* 2009
Rt. Hon. Lord Bonomy (Iain Bonomy), *born* 1946, *apptd* 2010
Rt. Hon. Lord Emslie (George Emslie), *born* 1947, *apptd* 2010

SECOND DIVISION
Lord Justice Clerk (£206,857), Rt. Hon. Lord Gill (Brian Gill), *born* 1942, *apptd* 2001
Rt. Hon. Lady Paton (Ann Paton), *born* 1952, *apptd* 2007
Rt. Hon. Lord Carloway (Colin Sutherland), *born* 1954, *apptd* 2008
Rt. Hon. Lord Clarke (Matthew Clarke), *born* 1947, *apptd* 2008
Rt. Hon. Lord Mackay of Drumadoon (Donald Mackay), *born* 1946, *apptd* 2010

OUTER HOUSE
Lords of Session (each £172,753)
Hon. Lord Menzies (Duncan Menzies), *born* 1953, *apptd* 2001
Hon. Lord Drummond Young (James Drummond Young), *born* 1950, *apptd* 2001
Hon. Lady Smith (Anne Smith), *born* 1955, *apptd* 2001
Hon. Lord Brodie (Philip Brodie), *born* 1950, *apptd* 2002
Hon. Lord Bracadale (Alastair Campbell), *born* 1949, *apptd* 2003
Hon. Lady Dorrian (Leona Dorrian), *born* 1957, *apptd* 2005
Hon. Lord Hodge (Patrick Hodge), *born* 1953, *apptd* 2005
Hon. Lord Glennie (Angus Glennie), *born* 1950, *apptd* 2005
Hon. Lord Kinclaven (Alexander F. Wylie), *born* 1951, *apptd* 2005
Hon. Lord Turnbull (Alan Turnbull), *born* 1958, *apptd* 2006
Hon. Lady Clark of Calton (Lynda Clark), *born* 1949, *apptd* 2006
Hon. Lord Brailsford (Sidney Brailsford), *born* 1954, *apptd* 2006
Hon. Lord Uist (Roderick Macdonald), *born* 1951, *apptd* 2006
Hon. Lord Malcolm (Colin M. Campbell), *born* 1953, *apptd* 2007
Hon. Lord Matthews (Hugh Matthews), *born* 1953, *apptd* 2007
Hon. Lord Woolman (Stephen Woolman), *born* 1953, *apptd* 2008
Hon. Lord Pentland (Paul Cullen), *born* 1957, *apptd* 2008
Hon. Lord Bannatyne (Iain Peebles), *born* 1954, *apptd* 2008
Hon. Lady Stacey (Valerie E. Stacey), *born* 1954, *apptd* 2009
Hon. Lord Tyre (Colin Tyre), *born* 1956, *apptd* 2010
Hon. Lord Doherty (Raymond Doherty), *born* 1958, *apptd* 2010
Hon. Lord Stewart (Angus Stewart), *born* 1946, *apptd* 2010

COURT OF SESSION AND HIGH COURT OF JUSTICIARY
Parliament House, Parliament Square, Edinburgh EH1 1RQ
T 0131-225 2595
Principal Clerk of Session and Justiciary, G. Marwick
Deputy Principal Clerk of Justiciary, G. Prentice
Deputy Principal Clerk of Session and Principal Extractor, R. Cockburn
Depute in Charge of Offices of Court, Y. Anderson
Keeper of the Rolls, G. Combe
Division Clerks, D. Cullen; E. Dickson; R. Jenkins
Appeal Clerks, R. MacPherson; A. Mackay; R. Sinclair
Depute Clerks of Session and Justiciary Team Leaders, W. Dunn; A. McArdle; L. McLachlan; D. MacLeod; C. Reid
Depute Clerks of Session and Justiciary R. Broome; A. Corr; K. Cumming; L. Curran; H. Fraser; C. Fyffe; A. Galloway; T. Kell; K. Kier; A. Lynch; E. McLeod; L. McNamara; N. Marchant; I. Martin; R. Martin; D. Morrison; N. Newlands; C. Richardson; N. Roberts; C. Scott; G. Slater; K. Todd; C. Truby; P. Weir

SHERIFF COURT OF CHANCERY
27 Chambers Street, Edinburgh EH1 1LB
T 0131-225 2525

The court deals with service of heirs and completion of title in relation to heritable property.
Sheriff of Chancery, M. Stephen

EDINBURGH SHERIFF COURT AND JUSTICE OF THE PEACE COURT
27 Chambers Street, Edinburgh EH1 1LB
T 0131-225 2525

The work of the Sheriff Courts and Justice of the Peace Courts can be divided into three main categories: civil, criminal and commissary, and is administered by local sheriff clerks and their staff.

SCOTTISH LAND COURT
126 George Street, Edinburgh EH2 4HH
T 0131-271 4360

The court deals with disputes relating to agricultural and crofting land in Scotland.
Chair (£138,548), Hon. Lord McGhie (James McGhie), QC
Deputy Chair, R. J. Macleod
Members, D. J. Houston; A. Macdonald *(part-time)*; J. A. Smith *(part-time)*
Principal Clerk, B. A. Brown, WS

SCOTTISH GOVERNMENT JUSTICE DIRECTORATE
Legal System Division, Room 2W, St Andrew's House, Edinburgh EH1 3DG
T 0131-244 2698

The Justice Directorate is responsible for the appointment of judges and sheriffs to meet the needs of the business of the supreme and sheriffs court in Scotland. It is also responsible for providing resources for the efficient administration of certain specialist courts and tribunals.
Deputy Director, C. McKay

JUDICIAL APPOINTMENTS BOARD FOR SCOTLAND
38–39 Drumsheugh Gardens, Edinburgh EH3 7SW
T 0131-528 5101

The board's remit is to provide the first minister with the names of candidates recommended for appointment to the posts of judge of the court of session chair of the Scottish Land Court, temporary judge, sheriff principal, sheriff and part-time sheriff.
Chair, Sir Muir Russell, KCB, FRSE

SCOTTISH COURT SERVICE
Saughton House, Broomhouse Drive, Edinburgh EH11 3XD
T 0131-444 3300 W www.scotcourts.gov.uk

The Scottish Court Service is responsible for the provision of staff, buildings and technology to support Scotland's courts, the independent judiciary, the courts' Rules Councils and the Office of the Public Guardian. On 1 April 2010 it was established by the Judiciary and Courts (Scotland) Act 2008 as an independent body, governed by a corporate board and chaired by the Lord President.
Chief Executive, E. Emberson

JUDICIAL OFFICE FOR SCOTLAND
1A Parliament Square, Edinburgh EH1 1RQ
T 0131-240 6672 W www.scotland-judiciary.org.uk

The Judicial Office for Scotland came into being on 1 April 2010 as part of the changes introduced by the Judiciary and Courts (Scotland) Act 2008. It provides support for the Lord President in his role as head of the Scottish judiciary with responsibility for the training, welfare, deployment and conduct of judges and the efficient disposal of business in the courts.
Executive Director, Steve Humphreys

SHERIFFDOMS

SALARIES

Sheriff Principal	£138,548
Sheriff	£128,296

GLASGOW AND STRATHKELVIN
  Sheriff Principal, C. A. L. Scott
GRAMPIAN, HIGHLAND AND ISLANDS
  Sheriff Principal, Sir Stephen S. T. Young, Bt., QC
LOTHIAN AND BORDERS
  Sheriff Principal, M. M. Stephen
NORTH STRATHCLYDE
  Sheriff Principal, B. A. Kerr, QC
SOUTH STRATHCLYDE, DUMFRIES AND GALLOWAY
  Sheriff Principal, B. A. Lockhart
TAYSIDE, CENTRAL AND FIFE
  Sheriff Principal, R. A. Dunlop, QC

JUSTICE OF THE PEACE AND STIPENDIARY MAGISTRATES COURT
GLASGOW
R. B. Christie, *apptd* 1985; A. Findlay, *apptd* 2008; Ms J. Kerr, *apptd* 2008; Mrs J. A. M. MacLean, *apptd* 1990

CROWN OFFICE AND PROCURATOR FISCAL SERVICE
CROWN OFFICE
25 Chambers Street, Edinburgh EH1 1LA
T 0131-226 2626 W www.crownoffice.gov.uk
Crown Agent, Catherine Oyer
Deputy Crown Agent, John Dunn

PROCURATORS FISCAL

SALARIES

Area Fiscals	£58,200–£162,500
District Procurator Fiscal	£48,899–£128,900

GRAMPIAN AREA
  Area Procurator Fiscal, Mrs A. Currie *(Aberdeen)*
HIGHLAND AND ISLANDS AREA
  Area Procurator Fiscal, A. Laing *(Inverness)*
LANARKSHIRE AREA
  Area Procurator Fiscal, Ms J. Cameron *(Hamilton)*
CENTRAL AREA
  Area Procurator Fiscal, D. Harvie *(Stirling)*
TAYSIDE AREA
  Area Procurator Fiscal, J. Logue *(Dundee)*
FIFE AREA
  Area Procurator Fiscal, D. Green *(Kirkcaldy)*
LOTHIAN AND BORDERS AREA
  Area Procurator Fiscal, vacant *(Edinburgh)*
AYRSHIRE AREA
  Area Procurator Fiscal, T. Dysart *(Kilmarnock)*

ARGYLL AND CLYDE AREA
Area Procurator Fiscal, J. Watt *(Paisley)*
DUMFRIES AND GALLOWAY AREA
Area Procurator Fiscal, Ms R. McQuaid *(Dumfries)*
GLASGOW AREA
Area Procurator Fiscal, Ms L. Thomson *(Glasgow)*

COURT OF THE LORD LYON
HM New Register House, Edinburgh EH1 3YT
T 0131-556 7255
W www.lyon-court.com

The Court of the Lord Lyon is the Scottish Court of
Chivalry (including the genealogical jurisdiction of the
Ri-Sennachie of Scotland's Celtic kings). The Lord Lyon
King of Arms has jurisdiction, subject to appeal to the
Court of Session and the House of Lords, in questions of
heraldry and the right to bear arms. The court also
administers the Public Register of All Arms and Bearings
and the Public Register of All Genealogies in Scotland.
Pedigrees are established by decrees of Lyon Court and by
letters patent. As Royal Commissioner in Armory, the
Lord Lyon grants patents of arms to virtuous and
well-deserving Scots and to petitioners (personal or
corporate) in the Queen's overseas realms of Scottish
connection, and also issues birthbrieves. For information
on Her Majesty's Officers of Arms in Scotland, *see* the
Court of the Lord Lyon in the Public Bodies section.
Lord Lyon King of Arms, David Sellar, FSA SCOT,
FRHISTS
Lyon Clerk and Keeper of the Records, Mrs C. G. W. Roads,
MVO, FSA SCOT
Procurator Fiscal, Alexander M. S. Green
Macer, H. M. Love

NORTHERN IRELAND JUDICATURE

In Northern Ireland the legal system and the structure of
courts closely resemble those of England and Wales; there
are, however, often differences in enacted law.
The court of judicature of Northern Ireland comprises
the court of appeal, the high court of justice and the
crown court. The practice and procedure of these courts is
similar to that in England. The superior civil court is the
high court of justice, from which an appeal lies to the
Northern Ireland court of appeal; the UK supreme court is
the final civil appeal court.
The crown court, served by high court and county
court judges, deals with criminal trials on indictment.
Cases are heard before a judge and, except those certified
by the Director of Public Prosecutions under the Justice
and Security Act 2007, a jury. Appeals from the crown
court against conviction or sentence are heard by the
Northern Ireland court of appeal; the supreme court is the
final court of appeal.
The decision to prosecute in criminal cases in Northern
Ireland rests with the director of public prosecutions.
Minor criminal offences are dealt with in magistrates'
courts by a legally qualified district judge (magistrates'
courts) and, where an offender is under the age of 18,
by youth courts each consisting of a district judge
(magistrates' courts) and two lay magistrates (at least one
of whom must be a woman). Appeals from magistrates'
courts are heard by the county court, or by the court of
appeal on a point of law or an issue as to jurisdiction.
Magistrates' courts in Northern Ireland can deal with
certain classes of civil case but most minor civil cases
are dealt with in county courts. Judgments of all civil

courts are enforceable through a centralised procedure
administered by the Enforcement of Judgments Office.

COURT OF JUDICATURE
The Royal Courts of Justice, Belfast BT1 3JF
T 028-9023 5111
Lord Chief Justice of Northern Ireland (£214,165), Rt.
Hon. Sir Declan Morgan, *born* 1952, *apptd* 2009
Principal Secretary, Mrs Laurene McAlpine

LORD JUSTICES OF APPEAL (£196,707)
Style, The Rt. Hon. Lord Justice [surname]
Rt. Hon. Sir Malachy Higgins, *born* 1944, *apptd* 2007
Rt. Hon. Sir Paul Girvan, *born* 1948, *apptd* 2007
Rt. Hon. Sir Patrick Coghlin, *born* 1945, *apptd* 2008

PUISNE JUDGES (£172,753)
Style, The Hon. Mr Justice [surname]
Hon. Sir John Gillen, *born* 1947, *apptd* 1999
Hon. Sir Richard McLaughlin, *born* 1947, *apptd* 1999
Hon. Sir Ronald Weatherup, *born* 1947, *apptd* 2001
Hon. Sir Reginald Weir, *born* 1947, *apptd* 2003
Hon. Sir Donnell Deeny, *born* 1950, *apptd* 2004
Hon. Sir Anthony Hart, *born* 1946, *apptd* 2005
Hon. Sir Seamus Treacy, *born* 1956, *apptd* 2007
Hon. Sir William Stephens, *born* 1954, *apptd* 2007
Hon. Sir Bernard McCloskey, *born* 1956, *apptd* 2008

MASTERS OF THE SUPREME COURT (£102,921)
Master, Queen's Bench and Appeals, C. J. McCorry
Master, Office of Care and Protection, H. Wells
Master, Chancery and Probate, R. A. Ellison
Master, Matrimonial, C. W. G. Redpath
Master, Queen's Bench and Matrimonial, E. Bell
Master, Taxing Office, J. Baillie
Master, Bankruptcy, F. Kelly

OFFICIAL SOLICITOR
Official Solicitor to the Supreme Court of Northern Ireland,
Miss B. M. Donnelly

COUNTY COURTS

JUDGES (£138,548)
Style, His/Her Hon. Judge [surname]

Judge Babington; Judge Devlin; Judge Finnegan, QC;
Judge Fowler, QC; Her Hon. Judge Kennedy; Judge
Loughran; Judge Lynch, QC; Judge McFarland; Judge
McReynolds; Judge Marrinan, QC; Judge Miller, QC;
Judge Philpott, QC; Judge Rodgers; Judge Smyth, QC;
Her Hon. Judge Smyth

RECORDERS
Belfast (£149,631), Judge Burgess
Londonderry (£138,548), Judge Grant

MAGISTRATES' COURTS

DISTRICT JUDGES (MAGISTRATES' COURTS) (£102,921)
There are 21 district judges (magistrates' courts) in
Northern Ireland.

NORTHERN IRELAND COURTS AND TRIBUNALS
SERVICE
Laganside House, 23–25 Oxford Street, Belfast BT1 3LA
T 028-9032 8594 W www.courtsni.gov.uk
Director, D. A. Lavery

CROWN SOLICITOR'S OFFICE
Royal Courts of Justice, Chichester Street, Belfast BT1 3JE
T 028-9054 2555
Crown Solicitor, J. Conn

PUBLIC PROSECUTION SERVICE
93 Chichester Street, Belfast BT1 3JR
T 028-9054 2444 **W** www.ppsni.gov.uk
Director of Public Prosecutions (acting), Jim Scholes

TRIBUNALS

Information on all the tribunals listed here, with the exception of the independent tribunals and the tribunals based in Scotland, Wales and Northern Ireland can be found on the Ministry of Justice website (W www.justice.gov.uk).

HM COURTS AND TRIBUNALS SERVICE

5th Floor, 102 Petty France, London SW1H 9AJ
T 0845-600 0877 W www.justice.gov.uk

HM Courts Service and the Tribunals Service merged on 1 April 2011 to form HM Courts and Tribunals Service. This new service is an executive agency within the Ministry of Justice, operating as a partnership between the Lord Chancellor, the Lord Chief Justice and the Senior President of Tribunals. The agency provides common administrative support, including infrastructure and resources, to the non-devolved government tribunals in the UK for which the Lord Chancellor is responsible.

A two-tier tribunal system, comprising the First-tier Tribunal and Upper Tribunal, was established on 3 November 2008 as a result of radical reform under the Tribunals, Courts and Enforcement Act 2007. Both of these tiers are split into a number of separate chambers. These chambers group together individual tribunals (also known as 'jurisdictions') which deal with similar work or require similar skills. Cases start in the First-tier Tribunal and there is a right of appeal to the Upper Tribunal. Some tribunals transferred to the new two-tier system immediately, with many more transferring in 2010. The exception is employment tribunals, which remain outside this structure. The Act also allowed legally qualified tribunal chairs and adjudicators to swear the judicial oath and become judges.
Senior President, Lord Justice Carnwath, CVO
Chief Executive, Peter Handcock, CBE

FIRST-TIER TRIBUNAL

The main function of the First-tier Tribunal is to hear appeals by citizens against decisions of the government. In most cases appeals are heard by a panel made up of one judge and two specialists in their relevant field, known as 'members'. Both judges and members are appointed through the Independent Judicial Appointments Commission. Most of the tribunals administered by central government are part of the First-tier Tribunal, which is split into six separate chambers.

GENERAL REGULATORY CHAMBER
President (acting), Judge Warren

CHARITY
PO Box 9300, Leicester LE1 8DJ
T 0845-1234 504 E charitytribunal@tribunals.gsi.gov.uk

First-tier Tribunal (Charity) was established under the Charities Act 2006 to hear appeals against the decisions of the Charity Commission, applications for the review of decisions made by the Charity Commission and to consider references from the Attorney-General or the Charity Commission on points of law. It became part of the General Regulatory Chamber on 1 September 2009. The tribunal consists of the principal judge, five legal members and seven non-legal members. The tribunal currently only has jurisdiction in respect of Charity Commission decisions made on or after 18 March 2008.
Principal Judge, Alison McKenna

CLAIMS MANAGEMENT SERVICES
PO Box 9300, Leicester LE1 8DJ
T 0300-1234 504 E cmst@tribunals.gsi.gov.uk

First-tier Tribunal (Claims Management Services) was established under the Compensation Act 2006 to hear appeals pertaining to decisions made by the Claims Regulator in relation to personal injury; criminal injuries compensation; employment matters; housing disrepair; financial products and services; and industrial injury disablement benefits. It was formerly known as the Claims Management Services Tribunal until it became part of the General Regulatory Chamber in January 2010.
Principal Judge, Judge Warren

CONSUMER CREDIT
PO Box 9300, Leicester LE1 8DJ T 0300-1234 504
E consumercreditappeals@tribunals.gsi.gov.uk

First-tier Tribunal (Consumer Credit) replaced the Consumer Credit Appeals Tribunal on 1 September 2009. It hears appeals against licensing decisions made by the Office of Fair Trading under the Consumer Credit Act 1974 and the amended Consumer Credit Act 2006. The tribunal also hears appeals relating to the implementation of requirements or a civil penalty on licensees under the Act; and the refusal to register, cancellation of registration, or imposition of a penalty under the Money Laundering Regulations 2007.
Principal Judge, His Hon. Judge Wulwik

ENVIRONMENT
PO Box 9300, Leicester LE1 8DJ T 0845-600 0877
E RegulatoryAppeals@tribunals.gsi.gov.uk

First-tier Tribunal (Environment) was created to decide appeals regarding civil sanctions made by environmental regulators. It forms part of the General Regulatory Chamber and was established in April 2010. Panels usually consist of a tribunal judge and two members, all of whom are appointed by the Lord Chancellor. The jurisdiction of the tribunal extends to England and Wales.
Principal Judge, Judge Warren

ESTATE AGENTS
PO Box 9300, Leicester LE1 8DJ T 0845-600 0877
E RegulatoryAppeals@tribunals.gsi.gov.uk

First-tier Tribunal (Estate Agents) hears appeals against decisions made by the Office of Fair Trading pertaining to orders preventing a person from being employed as an estate agent when that person has been, for example, convicted of fraud or another offence involving dishonesty. The tribunal also hears appeals relating to decisions refusing to revoke or vary a prohibition order or warning order under the 1979 Estate Agents Act, as

well as appeals regarding the issuing of a warning order when a person has not fulfilled their obligations under the Act.
Principal Judge, His Hon. Judge Wulwik

GAMBLING APPEALS
PO Box 9300, Leicester LE1 8DJ
T 0845-600 0877 E RegulatoryAppeals@tribunals.gsi.gov.uk

First-tier Tribunal (Gambling) hears and decides appeals against decisions made by the Gambling Commission. The cases heard by the tribunal involve the provision and withdrawal of both operating and personal management licenses. The tribunal comprises 12 judges, and each appeal is heard by one judicial member or a panel of members, depending on the complexity of the specific case.
Principal Judge, Judge Warren

IMMIGRATION SERVICES
7th Floor, Victory House, 30–34 Kingsway, London WC2B 6EX
T 020-3077 5860 E imset@tribunals.gsi.gov.uk

First-tier tribunal (Immigration Services) is an independent judicial body established in 2000 to provide a forum in which appeals against decisions of the Immigration Services Commissioner and complaints made by the Immigration Services Commissioner can be heard and determined.

There is a principal judge, who is the judicial head; other judicial members, who must be legally qualified; lay members, who must have substantial experience in immigration services or in the law and procedure relating to immigration; and a secretary, who is responsible for administration. The tribunal can sit anywhere in the UK.
Principal Judge, Judge Hunter, QC

INFORMATION RIGHTS
Arnhem House Support Centre, PO Box 9300, Leicester LE1 8DJ
T 0300-1234 504 E informationtribunal@tribunals.gsi.gov.uk

First-tier Tribunal (Information Rights) determines appeals against notices issued by the Information Commissioner. The principal judge and other judges are appointed by the Lord Chancellor and must be legally qualified. Members are appointed by the Lord Chancellor to represent the interests of data users or data subjects. A tribunal consists of the principal judge and one other judge sitting with two of the members.
Principal Judge, Judge Angel

LOCAL GOVERNMENT STANDARDS IN ENGLAND
York House, 31–36 York Place, Leeds, West Yorkshire LS1 2ED
T 0113-389 6086 E AP-enquiries@tribunals.gsi.gov.uk

First-tier Tribunal (Local Government Standards in England) was formed on 18 January 2010. It replaces the tribunal created by the Local Government Act 2000 to decide references and appeals regarding the conduct of members of local authorities.
Principal Judge, Judge Laverick

TRANSPORT
7th Floor, Victory House, 30–34 Kingsway, London WC2B 6EX
T 020-3077 5860 E transport@tribunals.gsi.gov.uk

First-tier Tribunal (Transport) hears appeals against decisions of the Registrar of Approved Driving Instructors, hears and decides appeals for London service permits against decisions made by Transport for London

and is able to resolve disputes over postal charges under the Postal Services Act 2000. The tribunal consists of a legally qualified principal judge, other judicial members, and lay members. The principal judge and legal members are appointed by the Lord Chancellor and the lay members by the transport secretary.
Principal Judge, Judge Brodrick

HEALTH, EDUCATION AND SOCIAL CARE CHAMBER
President, His Hon. Judge Sycamore

CARE STANDARDS
Mowden Hall, Staindrop Road, Darlington, Co Durham DL3 9BG
T 01325-392712 E cst@tribunals.gsi.gov.uk

First-tier Tribunal (Care Standards) was established under the Protection of Children Act 1999 and considers appeals in relation to decisions made about the inclusion of individuals' names on the list of those considered unsuitable to work with children or vulnerable adults, restrictions from teaching and employment in schools/ further education institutions, and the registration of independent schools. It also deals with general registration decisions made about care homes, children's homes, childcare providers, nurses' agencies, social workers, residential family centres, independent hospitals and fostering agencies. The tribunal's principal judge appoints the panels for each case.
Deputy Chamber President, Judge Aitken

MENTAL HEALTH
Secretariat: PO Box 8793, 5th Floor, Leicester LE1 8BN
T 0300-123 2203

The First-tier Tribunal (Mental Health) hears applications and references for people detained under the Mental Health Act 1983 (as amended by the Mental Health Act 2007). The judiciary and members are appointed by the Lord Chancellor and the tribunal's jurisdiction covers the whole of England. There is a separate mental health tribunal for Wales, which is administered and based in Cardiff, and a separate mental health review tribunal for Scotland.
Deputy Chamber President, Judge Hinchliffe

PRIMARY HEALTH LISTS
Mowden Hall, Staindrop Road, Darlington DL3 9BG
T 01325-391 091

First-tier Tribunal (Primary Health Lists) took over the role of the Family Health Services Appeal Authority on 18 January 2010. The tribunal is independent of the Department of Health and considers appeals against the decisions of primary care trusts (PCTs), including appeals by GPs, dentists, pharmacists and opticians regarding action taken against them. The tribunal allocates appeals and applications to panels normally consisting of a tribunal judge, a specialist member and a lay member. All members are appointed by the Lord Chancellor following recommendation from the Judicial Appointments Commission, or may be assigned from other areas of the tribunal.
Deputy Chamber President, Judge Aitken

SPECIAL EDUCATIONAL NEEDS AND DISABILITY
Ground Floor, Mowden Hall, Staindrop Road DL3 9BG
T 01325-392760
E sendistqueries@tribunals.gsi.gov.uk

First-tier Tribunal (Special Educational Needs and Disability) considers parents' appeals against the decisions of local authorities (LAs) about children's special educational needs if parents cannot reach agreement with the LA. It also considers claims of disability discrimination in schools.

Deputy Chamber President, Judge Aitken

IMMIGRATION AND ASYLUM CHAMBER

Administrative Support Centre, Birmingham AIT, PO Box 14619, Birmingham B16 6FQ

T 0300-123 1711 E customer.service@tribunals.gsi.gov.uk

The Immigration and Asylum Chamber replaced the Asylum and Immigration Tribunal in February 2010. It is an independent tribunal dealing with appeals against decisions made by the Home Office, such as the decision to refuse a person asylum, or the decision to refuse a person leave to remain in the UK. Judges and non-legal members are appointed by the Lord Chancellor. Appeals are heard by one or more immigration judges, sometimes accompanied by non-legal members.

President (acting), Judge Arfon-Jones

SOCIAL ENTITLEMENT CHAMBER

President, His Hon. Judge Martin

ASYLUM SUPPORT

2nd Floor, Anchorage House, 2 Clove Crescent, London E14 2BE

T 020-7538 6171

First-tier Tribunal (Asylum Support) deals with appeals against decisions made by the UK Border Agency (UKBA). The UKBA decides whether asylum seekers, failed asylum seekers and/or their dependants are entitled to support and accommodation on the grounds of destitution, as provided by Section 4 and Part IV of the Immigration and Asylum Act 1999. The tribunal can only consider appeals against a refusal or termination of support. It can, if appropriate, require the Secretary of State for the Home Department to reconsider the original decision, substitute the original decision with the tribunal's own decision or dismiss the appeal.

Principal Judge, Sehba Storey

CRIMINAL INJURIES COMPENSATION

Head Office, Wellington House, 134–136 Wellington Street, Glasgow G2 2XL T 0141-354 8555

Judicial Review Enquiries, 5th Floor, Fox Court, 14 Gray's Inn Road, London WC1X 8HN T 020-3206 0664

E enquiries-cicap@tribunals.gsi.gov.uk

First-tier Tribunal (Criminal Injuries Compensation) determines appeals against review decisions made by the Criminal Injuries Compensation Authority on applications for compensation made by victims of violent crime. It only considers appeals on claims made on or after 1 April 1996 under the Criminal Injuries Compensation Scheme.

Principal Judge, Anthony Summers

SOCIAL SECURITY AND CHILD SUPPORT

Administrative Support Centre, PO Box 14620, Birmingham B16 6FR

T 0845-408 3500

First-tier Tribunal (Social Security and Child Support) arranges and hears appeals on a range of decisions made by the Department for Work and Pensions, HM Revenue and Customs, and local authorities. Appeals considered include those concerned with income support, jobseeker's allowance, child support, tax credits, retirement pensions, housing benefit, council tax benefit, disability living allowance, vaccine damage and compensation recovery. It is headed by the president of the Social Entitlement Chamber.

The tribunal also contains an executive agency responsible for the administration of appeals, headed by the chief executive of the HM Courts and Tribunals Service.

Judicial Lead, His Hon. Judge Martin

TAX CHAMBER

45 Bedford Square, London WC1B 3DN

T 0845-223 8080 E taxappeals@tribunals.gsi.gov.uk

The Tax Chamber, established on 1 April 2009, replaced four separate tax tribunals: the General Commissioners of Income Tax, the Special Commissioners, the VAT and Duties Tribunals, and section 706 tribunals. The chamber hears most appeals against decisions of HM Revenue and Customs in relation to tax. The chamber listens to appeals about income tax; corporation tax; capital gains tax; inheritance tax; national insurance contributions; and VAT or duties, and appeals can be made by individuals or organisations, single taxpayers or large multinational companies. Appeals are heard by legally qualified judges, non-legally qualified expert members or a mix of the two. The chamber has jurisdiction throughout the UK.

President, His Hon. Colin Bishopp, QC

WAR PENSIONS AND ARMED FORCES COMPENSATION CHAMBER

5th Floor, Fox Court, 14 Gray's Inn Road, London WC1X 8HN

T 020-3206 0705 E armedforces.chamber@hmcts.gsi.gov.uk

The War Pensions and Armed Forces Compensation Chamber of the First-tier Tribunal is the successor to the Pensions Appeal Tribunal which has existed in different forms since the War Pensions Act 1919. The tribunal hears appeals brought by ex-servicemen and women against decisions of the Secretary of State for Defence under the war pensions legislation for injuries sustained before 5th April 2005 and under the armed forces compensation scheme for injuries after that date. Under the war pensions legislation, the tribunal decides on entitlement to a war pension, the degree of disablement and entitlement to certain allowances (eg for mobility needs). Under the armed forces compensation scheme, the tribunal decides both the entitlement to an award and the tariff level of the award. The tribunal's jurisdiction covers England and Wales.

President, Judge Bano

PENSIONS APPEAL TRIBUNALS FOR SCOTLAND

George House, 126 George Street, Edinburgh EH2 4HH

T 0131-271 4340 E info@patscotland.org.uk

W www.patscotland.org.uk

President, C. M. McEachran, QC

UPPER TRIBUNAL

Comprising four separate chambers, the Upper Tribunal deals mostly with appeals from, and enforcement of, decisions taken by the First-tier Tribunal, but it also handles some cases that do not go through the First-tier Tribunal. Additionally, It has assumed some of the supervisory powers of the courts to deal with the actions of tribunals, government departments and some other public authorities. All the decision-makers of the Upper Tribunal are judges or expert members sitting in a panel chaired by a judge, and are specialists in the areas of law they handle. Over time their decisions are expected to build comprehensive case law for each area covered by the tribunals.

ADMINISTRATIVE APPEALS CHAMBER
5th Floor, Chichester Rents, 81 Chancery Lane, London WC2A 1DD
T 020-7911 7085 E adminappeals@tribunals.gsi.gov.uk

The Administrative Appeals Chamber deals with appeals from the Social Entitlement Chamber, the War Pensions and Armed Forces Compensation Chamber, the Health, Education and Social Care Chamber and the General Regulatory Chamber of the First-tier Tribunal, Forfeiture Act references and appeals in cases about safeguarding vulnerable groups. The Upper Tribunal in Northern Ireland deals with appeals from the Pensions Appeal Tribunal for Northern Ireland. There are 16 full-time judges and 17 deputy judges who sit part-time. Judges normally sit on their own and most of their cases are decided without oral hearings.
President, Mr Justice Walker

OFFICE OF THE SOCIAL SECURITY COMMISSIONERS AND CHILD SUPPORT COMMISSIONERS FOR NORTHERN IRELAND
Bedford House, 3rd Floor, 16–22 Bedford Street, Belfast BT2 7FD
T 028-9072 8731
E socialsecuritycommissioners@courtsni.gov.uk
W www.courtsni.gov.uk

The Social Security Commissioners and Child Support Commissioners in Northern Ireland are the specialised members of the judiciary appointed to determine appeals on points of law from appeal tribunals under the Social Security and Child Support legislation. They also have jurisdiction to deal with questions arising under the Forfeiture (NI) Order 1982. There are two Commissioners for Northern Ireland.
Chief Commissioner, Dr Kenneth Mullan

IMMIGRATION AND ASYLUM CHAMBER
Arnhem Support Centre, PO Box 6987, Leicester LE1 6ZX
T 0845-6000 877 E customer.service@tribunals.gsi.gov.uk

The Immigration and Asylum Chamber was created on 15 February 2010. It hears appeals against decisions made by the Immigration and Asylum Chamber in the First-tier Tribunal in matters of immigration, asylum and nationality. Appeals are heard by one or more senior or designated immigration judges, sometimes accompanied by non-legal members.
President, Mr Justice Blake

LANDS CHAMBER
45 Bedford Square, London WC1B 3AS
T 020-7612 9710 E lands@tribunals.gsi.gov.uk

The Lands Tribunal determines questions relating to the valuation of land, rating appeals from valuation tribunals, appeals from leasehold valuation tribunals and residential property tribunals, applications to discharge or modify restrictions on the use of land, and compulsory purchase compensation. The tribunal may also arbitrate under a reference by consent. Cases are usually heard by a single member of the tribunal but they may sometimes be heard by two or three members.
President, Judge Bartlett, QC

LANDS TRIBUNAL FOR SCOTLAND
George House, 126 George Street, Edinburgh EH2 4HH
T 0131-271 4350 E mailbox@lands-tribunal-scotland.org.uk
W www.lands-tribunal-scotland.org.uk

The Lands Tribunal for Scotland has much the same remit as the tribunal for England and Wales but also covers questions relating to tenants' rights to buy their homes under the Housing (Scotland) Act 1987 and appeals under the Land Registration (Scotland) Act 1979 and the Land Reform (Scotland) Act 2004. It is not part of HM Courts and Tribunals Service. The president is appointed by the Lord President of the Court of Session.
President, Hon. Lord McGhie, QC

TAX AND CHANCERY CHAMBER
45 Bedford Square, London WC1B 3DN
T 020-7612 9700 E financeandtaxappeals@tribunals.gsi.gov.uk

The Tax and Chancery Chamber decides applications for permission to appeal and appeals on point of law from decisions of the first-tier tribunal in tax or charity cases. The judiciary consists of high court judges and specialist tax judiciary, and the tribunal has jurisdiction throughout the UK. The jurisdiction of the former Financial Services and Markets tribunal transferred to the chamber in April 2010. As a result the chamber now hears appeals against decisions issued by the Financial Services Authority and from the Pensions Regulator.
President, Mr Justice Warren

EMPLOYMENT TRIBUNALS

ENGLAND AND WALES
Ground Floor, Victory House, 30–34 Kingsway, London WC2B 6EX
T 0845-795 9775

Employment Tribunals for England and Wales sit in 12 regions. The tribunals deal with matters of employment law, redundancy, dismissal, contract disputes, sexual, racial and disability discrimination and related areas of dispute which may arise in the workplace. A public register of judgments is held at 100 Southgate Street, Bury St Edmunds, Suffolk IP33 2AQ.
Chairs, who may be full-time or part-time, are legally qualified. They, along with the tribunal members, are appointed by the Ministry of Justice.
President, David John Latham

SCOTLAND
Central Office, Eagle Building, 215 Bothwell Street, Glasgow G2 7TS
T 0141-204 0730

Tribunals in Scotland have the same remit as those in England and Wales. Employment judges are appointed by the Lord President of the Court of Session and lay members by the Lord Chancellor.
President, Shona Simon

EMPLOYMENT APPEAL TRIBUNAL
London Office: Audit House, 58 Victoria Embankment, London EC4Y 0DS
T 020-7273 1041 E londoneat@tribunals.gsi.gov.uk
Edinburgh Office: 52 Melville Street, Edinburgh EH3 7HF
T 0131-225 3963 E edinburgheat@tribunals.gsi.gov.uk

The Employment Appeal Tribunal hears appeals (on points of law only) arising from decisions made by

employment tribunals. Hearings are conducted by a judge, either alone or accompanied by two lay members who have practical experience in employment relations.
President, Hon. Mr Justice Underhill
Registrar, Pauline Donleavy

SPECIAL IMMIGRATION APPEALS COMMISSION

PO Box 36469, London EC4A 1WR
T 0845-600 0877 **E** customer.service@tribunals.gsi.gov.uk

The commission was set up under the Special Immigration Appeals Commission Act 1997. It remains separate from the First-tier and Upper Tribunal structure but is part of HM Courts and Tribunals Service. Its main function is to consider appeals against orders for deportations in cases which involve, in the main, considerations of national security or the public interest. The commission also hears appeals against decisions to deprive persons of citizenship status. Members are appointed by the Lord Chancellor.
Chair, Hon. Mr Justice Mitting

INDEPENDENT TRIBUNALS

The following represents a selection of tribunals not administered by HM Courts and Tribunals Service.

AGRICULTURAL LAND TRIBUNALS

c/o DEFRA, Area 8E (Millbank), 17 Smith Square, London SW1P 3JR
T 0845-933 5577 **E** helpline@defra.gsi.gov.uk
W www.defra.gov.uk

Agricultural Land Tribunals settle disputes and other issues between landlords and tenants of agricultural holdings under the Agricultural Holdings Act 1986, mainly in relation to succession rights and notices to quit. The tribunals also settle drainage disputes between neighbours under the Land Drainage Act 1991.

There are seven tribunals covering England and one covering Wales. For each tribunal the Lord Chancellor appoints a chair and one or more deputies (barristers or solicitors of at least seven years' standing). The Lord Chancellor also appoints three panels of lay members: the 'landowners' panel, the 'farmers' panel and the 'drainage' panel.

Each tribunal is an independent statutory body with jurisdiction only within its own geographical area. A separate tribunal is constituted for each case, and consists of a chair and two lay members nominated by the chair.
Chairs (England), Shirley Evans; His Hon. John Machin; George Newsom; Paul de la Piquerie; His Hon. Robert Taylor; Nigel Thomas; Martin Wood
Chair (Wales), James Buxton

CIVIL AVIATION AUTHORITY

CAA House, 45–59 Kingsway, London WC2B 6TE
T 020-7453 6172 **E** legal@caa.co.uk
W www.caa.co.uk

The Civil Aviation Authority (CAA) does not have a separate tribunal department as such, but for certain purposes the CAA must conform to tribunal requirements. For example, to deal with appeals against the refusal or revocation of aviation licences and certificates issued by the CAA, and the allocation of routes outside of the EU to airlines.

The chair and four non-executive members who may sit on panels for tribunal purposes are appointed by the Secretary of State for Transport.
Chair, Dame Deirdre Hutton, DBE

COMPETITION APPEAL TRIBUNAL

Victoria House, Bloomsbury Place, London WC1A 2EB
T 020-7979 7979 **E** info@catribunal.org.uk
W www.catribunal.org.uk

The Competition Appeal Tribunal (CAT) is a specialist tribunal established to hear certain cases in the sphere of UK competition and economic regulatory law. It hears appeals against decisions of the Office of Fair Trading (OFT) and their sectoral regulators, and also decisions of the OFT, Secretary of State for Business, Innovation and Skills and the Competition Commission. The CAT also has jurisdiction to award damages in respect of infringements of EU or UK competition law and to hear appeals against decisions of OFCOM.

Cases are heard before a panel consisting of three members: either the president or a member of the panel of chairs and two ordinary members. The members of the panel of chairs are judges of the Chancery Division of the high court and other senior lawyers. The ordinary members have expertise in law and/or related fields. The president and chairs are appointed by the Lord Chancellor; the ordinary members are appointed by the secretary of state.
President, Hon. Mr Justice Barling

COPYRIGHT TRIBUNAL

21 Bloomsbury Street, London WC1B 3HF
T 020-7034 2836 **E** copyright.tribunal@ipo.gov.uk
W www.ipo.gov.uk/copy/tribunal

The Copyright Tribunal resolves disputes over the terms and conditions of licences offered by, or licensing schemes operated by, collective licensing bodies in the copyright and related rights area. Its decisions are appealable to the high court on points of law only.

The chair and two deputy chairs are appointed by the Lord Chancellor. Up to eight ordinary members are appointed by the Secretary of State for Business, Innovation and Skills. The tribunal operates on a panel basis and its members have wide expertise in copyright and rights, business and public administration.
Chair, His Hon. Judge Birss, QC

INDUSTRIAL TRIBUNALS AND THE FAIR EMPLOYMENT TRIBUNAL (NORTHERN IRELAND)

Killymeal House, 2 Cromac Quay, Ormeau Road, Belfast BT7 2JD
T 028-9032 7666 **E** mail@employmenttribunalsni.org
W www.employmenttribunalsni.co.uk

The industrial tribunal system in Northern Ireland was set up in 1965 and has a similar remit to the employment tribunals in the rest of the UK. There is also a Fair Employment Tribunal, which hears and determines individual cases of alleged religious or political discrimination in employment. Employers can appeal to the Fair Employment Tribunal if they consider the directions of the Equality Commission to be unreasonable, inappropriate or unnecessary, and the Equality Commission can make application to the tribunal for the enforcement of undertakings or directions with which an employer has not complied.

The president, vice-president and chairs of the Industrial Tribunal and the Fair Employment Tribunal are

appointed by the Lord Chancellor. The panel members to both the industrial tribunals and the Fair Employment Tribunal were appointed by the Department for Employment and Learning, but any future appointments will be made through a full public appointment process.
President of the Industrial Tribunals and the Fair Employment Tribunal, Eileen McBride

INVESTIGATORY POWERS TRIBUNAL
PO Box 33220, London SW1H 9ZQ
T 020-7035 3711 E info@ipt-uk.com W www.ipt-uk.com

The Investigatory Powers Tribunal replaced the Interception of Communications Tribunal, the Intelligence Services Tribunal, the Security Services Tribunal and the complaints function of the commissioner appointed under the Police Act 1997.

The Regulation of Investigatory Powers Act 2000 (RIPA) provides for a tribunal made up of senior members of the legal profession, independent of the government and appointed by the Queen, to consider all complaints against the intelligence services and those against public authorities in respect of powers covered by RIPA; and to consider proceedings brought under section 7 of the Human Rights Act 1998 against the intelligence services and law enforcement agencies in respect of these powers.
President, Rt. Hon. Lord Justice Mummery

NATIONAL HEALTH SERVICE TRIBUNAL (SCOTLAND)
Anderson Strathern LLP, 24 Blythswood Square, Glasgow G2 4BG
T 0141-242 6060 E nhstribunal@nhs.net

The Scottish National Health Service Tribunal considers representations that the continued inclusion of a family health service practitioner (eg a doctor, dentist, optometrist or pharmacist) on a health board's list would be prejudicial to the efficiency of the service concerned, by virtue either of fraudulent practices or unsatisfactory personal or professional conduct. If this is established, the tribunal has the power to disqualify practitioners from working in the NHS family health services. The tribunal sits when required and is composed of a chair, one lay member, and one practitioner member drawn from a representative professional panel. The chair is appointed by the Lord President of the Court of Session, and the lay member and the members of the professional panel are appointed by the Scottish ministers.
Chair, J. Michael D. Graham

RESIDENTIAL PROPERTY TRIBUNAL SERVICE
10 Alfred Place, London WC1E 7LR
T 0845-600 3178 E rptscorporateunit@communities.gsi.gov.uk
W www.rpts.gov.uk

The Residential Property Tribunal Service provides members to sit on panels for the Rent Assessment Committees, Residential Property Tribunals and Leasehold Valuation Tribunals, and serves the private-rented and leasehold property market in England by resolving disputes between leaseholders, tenants and landlords. The president and chair are appointed by the Lord Chancellor and other members are appointed by the Department for Communities and Local Government and the Ministry of Justice.
Senior President, Siobhan McGrath

SOLICITORS' DISCIPLINARY TRIBUNAL
3rd Floor, Gate House, 1 Farringdon Street, London EC4M 7NS
T 020-7329 4808 E enquiries@solicitorsdt.com
W www.solicitorstribunal.org.uk

The Solicitors' Disciplinary Tribunal is an independent statutory body whose members are appointed by the Master of the Rolls. The tribunal considers applications made to it alleging either professional misconduct and/or a breach of the statutory rules by which solicitors are bound against an individually named solicitor, former solicitor, registered foreign lawyer, or solicitor's clerk. The tribunal has around 60 members; two-thirds are solicitor members and one-third are lay members.
President, Jeremy Barnecutt

SOLICITORS' DISCIPLINE TRIBUNAL (SCOTTISH)
Unit 3.5, The Granary Business Centre, Coal Road, Cupar, Fife KY15 5YQ
T 01334-659088 W www.ssdt.org.uk

The Scottish Solicitors' Discipline Tribunal is an independent statutory body with a panel of 21 members, 11 of whom are solicitors; members are appointed by the Lord President of the Court of Session. Its principal function is to consider complaints of misconduct against solicitors in Scotland.
Chair, A. Cockburn

TRAFFIC PENALTY TRIBUNAL
Barlow House, Minshull Street, Manchester M1 3DZ
T 0161-242 5252 E info@trafficpenaltytribunal.gov.uk
W www.trafficpenaltytribunal.gov.uk

The Traffic Penalty Tribunal considers appeals from motorists against penalty charge notices issued by Civil Enforcement Authorities in England (outside London) and Wales under the Traffic Management Act 2004, and considers appeals against bus lane contraventions in England (outside London) under the Bus Lane Contraventions Regulations 2005. Parking adjudicators are appointed with the express consent of the Lord Chancellor and must be lawyers of five years' standing. Cases are decided by a single adjudicator, either in a postal, telephone or a personal hearing.
Head of Service, Louise Hutchinson

VALUATION TRIBUNAL SERVICE
2nd Floor, Black Lion House, 45 Whitechapel Road, London E1 1DU
T 0300-123 2035 W www.valuationtribunal.gov.uk

The Valuation Tribunal Service (VTS) was created as a corporate body by the Local Government Act 2003, and is responsible for providing or arranging the services required for the operation of the Valuation Tribunal for England. The VTS board consists of a chair and members appointed by the secretary of state. The VTS is funded by the Department for Communities and Local Government.
Chair, VTS Board, Anne Galbraith, CBE

VALUATION TRIBUNAL FOR ENGLAND
President's Office, 2nd Floor, Black Lion House, 45 Whitechapel Road, London E1 1DU
T 020-7246 3900 W www.valuationtribunal.gov.uk

The Valuation Tribunal for England (VTE) came into being on 1 October 2009, replacing 56 valuation tribunals in England. Provision for the VTE was made in the Local Government and Public Involvement in Health Act 2007. The Valuation Tribunal for England hears appeals concerning council tax and non-domestic rating and land drainage rates. A separate tribunal is constituted for each hearing, and consists of a chair and two or three other members. A clerk, who is a paid employee of the VTS, is present to advise on points of procedure and law. The national president is the judicial head of a volunteer membership. Members will in future be appointed by the Judicial Appointments Commission.

President, Prof. Graham Zellick CBE, QC

VALUATION TRIBUNAL SERVICE FOR WALES

Governing Council of VTW, 22 Gold Tops, Newport, South Wales NP20 4PG

T 01633-266367 **E** VTWaleseast@vtw.gsi.gov.uk

The Valuation Tribunal for Wales (VTW) was established by the Valuation Tribunal for Wales Regulations 2010, and hears and determines appeals concerning council tax, non-domestic rating and drainage rates in Wales. The governing council, comprising the president, four regional representatives and one member who is appointed by the Welsh government, performs the management functions on behalf of the tribunal. Individual tribunal hearings are conducted by three members of the tribunal, supported by a clerk. These hearings are arranged locally.

Chief Executive, Simon Hill

OMBUDSMAN SERVICES

The following section is a listing of selected ombudsman services. Ombudsmen are a free, independent and impartial means of resolving certain disputes outside of the courts. These disputes are, in the majority of cases, concerned with whether something has been badly or unfairly handled (for example owing to delay, neglect, inefficiency or failure to follow proper procedures). Most ombudsman schemes are established by statute; they cover various public and private bodies and generally examine matters only after the relevant body has been given a reasonable opportunity to deal with the complaint.

After conducting an investigation an ombudsman will usually issue a written report, which normally suggests a resolution to the dispute and often includes recommendations concerning the improvement of procedures.

BRITISH AND IRISH OMBUDSMAN ASSOCIATION (BIOA)

PO Box 308, Twickenham TW1 9BE
T 020-8894 9272 E secretary@bioa.org.uk
W www.bioa.org.uk

The BIOA was established in 1994 and exists to provide information to the government, public bodies, and the public about ombudsmen and other complaint-handling services. An ombudsman scheme must meet four criteria in order to attain full BIOA membership: independence from the organisations the ombudsman has the power to investigate, fairness, effectiveness and public accountability. Associate membership is open to complaint-handling bodies that do not meet these criteria in full. Ombudsmen schemes from the UK, Ireland, British crown dependencies and overseas territories may apply to BIOA for membership.
Secretary, Ian Pattison

The following is a selection of organisations that are members of the BIOA.

FINANCIAL OMBUDSMAN SERVICE

South Quay Plaza, 183 Marsh Wall, London E14 9SR
T 020-7964 1000
E complaint.info@financial-ombudsman.org.uk
W www.financial-ombudsman.org.uk

The Financial Ombudsman Service settles individual disputes between businesses providing financial services and their customers. The service deals with around a million enquiries every year and settles over 100,000 disputes. The service examines complaints about most financial matters, including banking, insurance, mortgages, pensions, savings, loans and credit cards. *See also* Banking and Finance.
Chief Ombudsman and Chief Executive, Natalie Ceeney

HOUSING OMBUDSMAN SERVICE

81 Aldwych, London WC2B 4HN
T 020-7421 3800 E ihol@housing-ombudsman.org.uk
W www.housing-ombudsman.org.uk

The Housing Ombudsman Service, established in 1997, deals with complaints and disputes involving tenants and housing associations and social landlords, certain private-sector landlords and managing agents. The ombudsman has a statutory jurisdiction over all registered social landlords in England. Private and other landlords can join the service on a voluntary basis. Complaints from council/local authority tenants have to be made to the Local Government Ombudsman.
Ombudsman, Dr Mike Biles
Deputy Ombudsman, Rafael Runco

INDEPENDENT POLICE COMPLAINTS COMMISSION (IPCC)

90 High Holborn, London WC1V 6BH
T 0845-300 2002 E enquiries@ipcc.gsi.gov.uk
W www.ipcc.gov.uk

The IPCC succeeded the Police Complaints Authority in 2004. It was established under the Police Reform Act 2002. The IPCC has teams of investigators headed by commissioners in each of its regions to assist with the supervision and management of some police investigations. They also carry out independent investigations into serious incidents or allegations of misconduct by persons serving with the police. The IPCC decides on appeals against complaints investigated by the police service. It also has responsibility for investigating complaints of serious incidents, including death or injury, made against staff of HM Revenue and Customs, the Serious Organised Crime Agency and the United Kingdom Border Agency. The 12 commissioners of the IPCC must not previously have worked for the police.
Chair (interim), Len Jackson
Deputy Chairs, Deborah Glass
Chief Executive, Jane Furniss

LEGAL OMBUDSMAN

2nd Floor, Baskerville House, Centenary Square, Broad Street, Birmingham B1 2ND
T 0121-245 3100 E enquiries@legalombudsman.org.uk
W www.legalombudsman.org.uk

The Legal Ombudsman was set up by the Office for Legal Complaints under the Legal Services Act 2007 and replaced the Office of the Legal Services Ombudsman in 2010. The Legal Ombudsman is the single body for all consumer legal complaints in England and Wales. It aims to resolve disputes between individuals and authorised legal practitioners, including barristers, law costs draftsmen, legal executives, licensed conveyancers, notaries, patent attorneys, probate practitioners, registered European lawyers, solicitors and trade mark attorneys.
Chief Ombudsman, Adam Sampson

LOCAL GOVERNMENT OMBUDSMAN

Advice Team, PO Box 4771, Coventry CV4 OEH
T 0300-061 0614 W www.lgo.org.uk

The Local Government Ombudsman deals with complaints about councils and some other authorities and organisations, including education admission appeal panels and adult social care providers.

There are three ombudsmen in England, each with responsibility for different regions; they aim to provide satisfactory redress for complainants and better administration for the authorities. The ombudsmen investigate complaints about most council matters, including housing, planning, education, social care, consumer protection, drainage and council tax. See also Local Government.

Local Government Ombudsmen, Anne Seex; Jane Martin

NORTHERN IRELAND OMBUDSMAN

Progressive House, 33 Wellington Place, Belfast BT1 6HN
T 028-9023 3821 E ombudsman@ni-ombudsman.org.uk
W www.ni-ombudsman.org.uk

The ombudsman (also known as the Assembly Ombudsman for Northern Ireland and the Northern Ireland Commissioner for Complaints) is appointed under legislation with powers to investigate complaints by people claiming to have sustained injustice arising from action taken by a Northern Ireland government department, or any other public body within his remit. The ombudsman can investigate all local councils, education and library boards, health and social services boards and trusts, as well as all government departments and their agencies. As commissioner for complaints, the ombudsman can investigate complaints about doctors, dentists, pharmacists, optometrists and other healthcare professionals.

Ombudsman, Dr Tom Frawley, CBE
Deputy Ombudsman, Marie Anderson

OFFICE OF THE PENSIONS OMBUDSMAN

6th Floor, 11 Belgrave Road, London SW1V 1RB
T 020-7630 2200 E enquiries@pensions-ombudsman.org.uk
W www.pensions-ombudsman.org.uk

The Pensions Ombudsman is appointed by the Secretary of State for Work and Pensions, under the Pension Schemes Act 1993 as amended by the Pensions Act 1995. He investigates and decides complaints and disputes about the way that personal and occupational pension schemes are run. As the Ombudsman for the Board of the Pension Protection Fund, he can deal with disputes about the decisions made by the board or the actions of their staff. He also deals with appeals against decisions made by the scheme manager under the Financial Assistance Scheme.

Pensions Ombudsman, Tony King
Deputy Pensions Ombudsman, Jane Irvine

OMBUDSMAN SERVICES

Brew House, Wilderspool Park, Greenalls Avenue, Warrington WA4 6HL
W www.ombudsman-services.org

Ombudsman Services provides independent dispute resolution for the communications, copyright licensing, energy and property sectors.

Ombudsman Services: Communications investigates complaints from consumers about companies which provide communication services to the public.

Ombudsman Services: Copyright Licensing helps to resolve complaints from consumers regarding PRS for Music (formerly the Performing Right Society), its members, and those who may require or who have obtained a licence for the public performance of copyright music.

Ombudsman Services: Energy helps to resolve complaints from consumers about energy (gas and electricity companies).

Ombudsman Services: Property investigates complaints from consumers about chartered surveying companies, surveyors, estate agents and other property professionals.

Chair, Dame Janet Finch
Chief Ombudsman, Lewis Shand Smith
Ombudsmen, Andrew Walker *(Communications)*; Richard Sills *(Energy)*; Gillian Fleming *(Property)*

OMBUDSMAN SERVICES: COMMUNICATIONS

PO Box 730, Warrington WA4 6WU
T 0300-440 1614
E enquiries@os-communications.org

OMBUDSMAN SERVICES: COPYRIGHT LICENSING

PO Box 1124, Warrington WA4 9GH
T 0300-440 1601
E enquiries@os-cpl.org

OMBUDSMAN SERVICES: ENERGY

PO Box 966, Warrington WA4 9DF
T 0330-440 1624
E enquiries@os-energy.org

OMBUDSMAN SERVICES: PROPERTY

PO Box 1021, Warrington WA4 9FE
T 0300-440 1634
E enquiries@os-property.org

PARLIAMENTARY AND HEALTH SERVICE OMBUDSMAN

Millbank Tower, Millbank, London SW1P 4QP
T 0345-015 4033 E phso.enquiries@ombudsman.org.uk
W www.ombudsman.org.uk

The Parliamentary Ombudsman (also known as the Parliamentary Commissioner for Administration) is independent of government and is an officer of parliament. She is responsible for investigating complaints referred to her by MPs from members of the public who claim to have sustained injustice in consequence of maladministration by or on behalf of government departments and certain non-departmental public bodies in the UK. Certain types of action by government departments or bodies are excluded from investigation.

The Health Service Ombudsman is responsible for investigating complaints against National Health Service authorities and trusts in England that are not dealt with by those authorities to the satisfaction of the complainant. Complaints can be referred directly by the member of the public who claims to have sustained injustice or hardship in consequence of the failure in a service provided by a relevant body. The ombudsman's jurisdiction also covers complaints about family doctors, dentists, pharmacists and opticians, and complaints about actions resulting from clinical judgement.

The parliamentary and the health offices are traditionally held by the same person.

Parliamentary Ombudsman and Health Service Ombudsman, Ms A. Abraham
Deputy Ombudsman, Ms K.Hudson

PROPERTY OMBUDSMAN

Milford House, 43–55 Milford Street, Salisbury, Wiltshire SP1 2BP
T 01722-333306 E admin@tpos.co.uk
W www.tpos.co.uk

The Property Ombudsman service was established in 1998 and provides a service for dealing with disputes between estate agents (or residential letting agents) and consumers who are actual or potential buyers or sellers of residential property in the UK.

Complaints that the ombudsman considers include allegations of unfair treatment, maladministration and infringement of legal rights. The ombudsman's role is to resolve these complaints in full and final settlement and, where appropriate, make an award of financial compensation.
Ombudsman, Christopher Hamer

PUBLIC SERVICES OMBUDSMAN FOR WALES

1 Ffordd yr Hen Gae, Pencoed CF35 5LJ
T 01656-641150 E ask@ombudsman-wales.org.uk
W www.ombudsman-wales.org.uk

The office of Public Services Ombudsman for Wales was established, with effect from 1 April 2006, by the Public Services Ombudsman (Wales) Act 2005. The ombudsman, who is appointed by the Queen, investigates complaints of injustice caused by maladministration or service failure by the Assembly Commission (and public bodies sponsored by the assembly); Welsh government; National Health Service bodies, including GPs, family health service providers and hospitals; registered social landlords; local authorities, including community councils; fire and rescue authorities; police authorities; national park authorities; and countryside and environmental organisations. Free leaflets explaining the process of making a complaint are available from the ombudsman's office.
Ombudsman, Peter Tyndall

REMOVALS INDUSTRY OMBUDSMAN SCHEME

PO Box 3862, Gerrards Cross, Bucks SL9 7WG
T 01753-888206 E ombudsman@removalsombudsman.co.uk
W www.removalsombudsman.org.uk

The Removals Industry Ombudsman Scheme was established to resolve disputes between removal companies that are members of the scheme and their clients, both domestic and commercial. The ombudsman investigates complaints such as breaches of contract, unprofessional conduct, delays, or breaches in the code of practice.
Ombudsman, Matti Alderson

SCOTTISH PUBLIC SERVICES OMBUDSMAN

Freepost EH641, Edinburgh EH3 0BR
T 0800-377 7330 E ask@spso.org.uk
W www.spso.org.uk

The Scottish Public Services Ombudsman (SPSO) was established in 2002. The SPSO is the final stage for complaints about public services in Scotland. Its service is free and independent. SPSO investigates complaints about the Scottish government, its agencies and departments; colleges and universities; councils; housing associations; NHS Scotland; prisons; and most other Scottish public bodies. The Ombudsman looks at complaints regarding poor service or administrative failure and can only look at complaints that have been through the formal complaints process of the organisation concerned.
Scottish Public Services Ombudsman, Jim Martin

WATERWAYS OMBUDSMAN

PO Box 35, York YO60 6WW
T 01347-879075 E enquiries@waterways-ombudsman.org
W www.waterways-ombudsman.org

The Waterways Ombudsman considers complaints of maladministration or unfairness made against British Waterways or its subsidiaries, including British Waterways Marinas Limited. Complaints concerning the waterways responsibilities of the Environment Agency should be directed to the Parliamentary and Health Service Ombudsman.
Ombudsman, Hilary Bainbridge

THE POLICE SERVICE

There are 52 police forces in the United Kingdom: 43 in England and Wales, including the Metropolitan Police and the City of London Police, eight in Scotland and the Police Service of Northern Ireland. Forces' areas are coterminous with one or more local authority areas. The Isle of Man, Jersey and Guernsey have their own forces responsible for policing in their respective islands and bailiwicks. The Serious Organised Crime Agency (SOCA) is responsible for the investigation of national and international serious organised crime.

Police authorities are independent bodies, responsible for the supervision of local policing. There are 43 police authorities in England and Wales, plus an additional one for British Transport Police. Most police authorities have 17 members, comprising nine local councillors and eight independent members, of whom at least one must be a magistrate. Authorities which are responsible for larger areas may have more members, such as the Metropolitan Police Authority, which has 23 members: 12 drawn from the London Assembly, 10 independent members and one magistrate. The Corporation of London acts as the police authority for the City of London Police. In Scotland, six of the forces are maintained by joint police boards, made up of local councillors from each council in the force area; the other two constabularies (Dumfries & Galloway and Fife) are directly administered by their respective councils. The Northern Ireland Policing Board is an independent public body consisting of 19 political and independent members.

Police forces in England, Scotland and Wales are financed by central and local government grants and a precept on the council tax. The Police Service of Northern Ireland is wholly funded by central government. The police authorities, subject to the approval of the home secretary (in England and Wales), the Northern Ireland Minister of Justice and to regulations, are responsible for appointing the Chief Constable. In England and Wales the latter are responsible for the force's budget, levying the precept on the council tax, publishing annual policing plans and reports, setting local objectives, monitoring performance targets and appointing or dismissing senior officers. In Scotland the police authorities are responsible for setting the force's budget, providing the resources necessary to police the area adequately and appointing officers of the rank of Assistant Chief Constable and above. In Northern Ireland, the Northern Ireland Policing Board exercises similar functions.

The home secretary, the Northern Ireland Minister of Justice and the Scottish government are responsible for the organisation, administration and operation of the police service. They regulate police ranks, discipline, hours of duty and pay and allowances. All police forces are subject to inspection by HM Inspectors of Constabulary, who report to the home secretary, Scottish government or the Northern Ireland Minister of Justice.

COMPLAINTS

The Independent Police Complaints Commission (IPCC) was established under the Police Reform Act 2002 and became operational on 1 April 2004. The IPCC is responsible for carrying out independent investigations into serious incidents or allegations of misconduct by those serving with the police in England and Wales, HM Revenue and Customs, SOCA and the UK Border Agency. It has the power to initiate, undertake and oversee investigations and is also responsible for the way in which complaints are handled by local police forces. Complaints regarding local operational issues or quality of service should be made directly to the Chief Constable of the police force concerned or to the local police authority.

If a complaint is relatively minor, the police force will attempt to resolve it internally and an official investigation might not be required. In more serious cases the IPCC or police force may refer the case to the Crown Prosecution Service, which will decide whether to bring criminal charges against the officer(s) involved. An officer who is dismissed, required to resign or reduced in rank, whether as a result of a complaint or not, can appeal to a police appeals tribunal established by the relevant police authority.

Under the Police, Public Order and Criminal Justice (Scotland) Act 2006, which came into force on 1 April 2007, the Police Complaints Commissioner for Scotland is responsible for providing independent scrutiny of the way in which Scottish police forces, authorities and policing agencies handle complaints from the public. The commissioner also has the power to direct police forces to re-examine any complaints which are not considered to have been dealt with satisfactorily. If there is a suggestion of criminal activity, the complaint is investigated by a procurator fiscal.

The Police Ombudsman for Northern Ireland provides an independent police complaints system for Northern Ireland, dealing with all stages of the complaints procedure. Complaints that cannot be resolved informally are investigated and the ombudsman recommends a suitable course of action to the Chief Constable of the Police Service of Northern Ireland or the Northern Ireland Policing Board based on the investigation's findings. The ombudsman may recommend that a police officer be prosecuted, but the decision to prosecute a police officer rests with the Director of Public Prosecutions.

INDEPENDENT POLICE COMPLAINTS COMMISSION, 90 High Holborn, London WC1V 6BH T 0845-300 2002 E enquiries@ipcc.gsi.gov.uk W www.ipcc.gov.uk

POLICE COMPLAINTS COMMISSIONER FOR SCOTLAND, Hamilton House, Hamilton Business Park, ML3 0QA T 0808-178 5577 E enquiries@pcc-scotland.org W www.pcc-scotland.org
Police Complaints Commissioner for Scotland, John McNeill

POLICE OMBUDSMAN FOR NORTHERN IRELAND, New Cathedral Buildings, St Anne's Square, 11 Church Street, Belfast BT1 1PG T 028-9082 8600 E info@policeombudsman.org W www.policeombudsman.org
Police Ombudsman, Al Hutchinson

POLICE SERVICES

FORENSIC SCIENCE SERVICE

Headquarters: Trident Court, 2920 Solihull Parkway,
Birmingham Business Park, Birmingham B37 7YN
T 0121-329 5200 W www.forensic.gov.uk

The Forensic Science Service (FSS) is a government-owned company which is independent from the police service. It provides forensic science and technology services to police forces in England and Wales and other law enforcement agencies such as the Crown Prosecution Service, SOCA, MoD Police and Guarding Agency, British Transport Police and HM Revenue and Customs. Services are also available to defence lawyers and commercial companies. The FSS primarily covers England and Wales but can provide services worldwide.
Chair, Bill Griffiths

NATIONAL EXTREMISM TACTICAL COORDINATION UNIT

PO Box 525, Huntingdon PE29 9AL
T 01480-425091 E mailbox@netcu.pnn.police.uk
W www.netcu.org.uk

The National Extremism Tactical Coordination Unit (NETCU) provides the police service of England and Wales and other law enforcement agencies with tactical advice and guidance on policing domestic extremism and associated criminality. The unit also supports organisations and companies that are the targets of domestic extremism campaigns. NETCU is funded by the Home Office, is accountable to the National Coordinator for Domestic Extremism and forms part of the Association of Chief Police Officers' Terrorism and Allied Matters business unit.
National Coordinator for Domestic Extremism,
Anton Setchell

NATIONAL POLICING IMPROVEMENT AGENCY

Fry Building, 2 Marsham Street, London SW1P 4DF
T 020-3113 6000 E enquiries@npia.pnn.police.uk
W www.npia.police.uk

The National Policing Improvement Agency (NPIA) was formed in April 2007 to make a unique contribution to improving public safety. The NPIA is owned and governed by the board which comprises representatives of the Association of Chief Police Officers, the Association of Police Authorities and the Home Office, in addition to the chair, chief executive and two independent members. The board is responsible for agreeing the budget and setting the objectives for the NPIA.

The NPIA's remit is to improve public safety through the provision of critical national services, building capability across the police service, and providing professional expertise to police forces and authorities. It is responsible for the procurement and deployment of information and communications technology systems to support and improve policing and works actively with police forces to develop a wide range of learning and professional development programmes. The NPIA is charged with improving policing in England and Wales but it is also connected to policing bodies in Scotland and Northern Ireland and collaborates with them on some initiatives.
Chief Executive, Nick Gargan
Chair, Peter Holland, CBE

NPIA MISSING PERSONS BUREAU

Foxley Hall, Bramshill, Hook, Hampshire RG27 0JW
T 01256-602979
E missingpersonsbureau@npia.pnn.police.uk
W www.npia.police.uk/en/10200.htm

The NPIA Missing Persons Bureau was launched in April 2008 within the National Policing Improvement Agency. The NPIA Missing Persons Bureau acts as the centre for the exchange of information connected with the search for missing persons nationally and internationally alongside the police and other related organisations. The unit focuses on cross-matching missing persons with unidentified persons or bodies by maintaining records, including a dental index of ante-mortem chartings of long-term missing persons and post-mortem chartings from unidentified bodies. The bureau also manages the missing children website (W www.missingkids.co.uk) and coordinates the child rescue alert services.

Information is supplied and collected for all persons who have been missing in the UK for over 72 hours (or fewer where police deem appropriate), foreign nationals reported missing in the UK, UK nationals reported missing abroad and all unidentified bodies and persons found within the UK.

SERIOUS ORGANISED CRIME AGENCY

PO Box 8000, London SE11 5EN T 0370-496 7622
W www.soca.gov.uk

The Serious Organised Crime Agency (SOCA) tackles serious organised crime affecting the UK and its citizens and is the custodian of a range of national and international capabilities. SOCA works to priorities set by the home secretary which currently include Class A drugs, people smuggling and human trafficking, major gun crime, fraud, cyber crime and money laundering. SOCA works to bring serious criminals to justice and uses many other tactics to disrupt crime and to make it harder to commit crime.

The National Crime Agency, to be established in 2013, will replace SOCA and the Child Exploitation and Online Protection Centre.
Chair, Sir Ian Andrews, CBE, TD
Director-General, Trevor Pearce, QPM

POLICE FORCES

ENGLAND*

Force	Telephone	Strength†	Chief Constable
Avon and Somerset	0845-456 7000	3,261	C. Port
Bedfordshire	01234-841212	1,260	Alfred Hitchcock, QPM
Cambridgeshire	0345-456 4564	1,421	Simon Parr
Cheshire	0845-458 0000	2,160	D. Whatton, QPM
Cleveland	01642-326326	1,695	Sean Price, QPM
Cumbria	0845-330 0247	1,236	Craig Mackey, QPM
Derbyshire	0345-123 3333	2,122	M. Creedon, QPM
Devon and Cornwall	0845-277 7444	3,469	Stephen Otter, QPM
Dorset	01202-222222	1,456	M. Baker, QPM
Durham	0345-606 0365	1,443	T. Stoddart, QPM
Essex	0300-333 4444	3,690	Jim Barker-McCardle, QPM
Gloucestershire	0845-090 1234	1,309	Tony Melville
Greater Manchester	0161-872 5050	7,849	Peter Fahy, QPM
Hampshire	0845-045 4545	3,615	Alex Marshall
Hertfordshire	0845-330 0222	2,055	Frank Whiteley, QPM
Humberside	0845-606 0222	2,011	Tim Hollis, QPM
Kent	01622-690690	3,766	Ian Learmonth
Lancashire	01772-614444	3,447	Stephen Finnigan, CBE, QPM
Leicestershire	0116-222 2222	2,216	Simon Cole
Lincolnshire	01522-532222	1,208	R. Crompton
Merseyside	0151-709 6010	4,461	J. Murphy, QPM
Norfolk	0845-456 4567	1,648	P. Gormley
North Yorkshire	0845-606 0247	1,547	Grahame Maxwell
Northamptonshire	03000-111222	1,279	Adrian Lee
Northumbria	01661-872555	4,145	S. Sim
Nottinghamshire	0115-967 0999	2,352	J. Hodson, QPM
South Yorkshire	0114-220 2020	2,979	M. Hughes, QPM
Staffordshire	0300-123 4455	2,150	Mike Cunningham
Suffolk	01473-613500	1,258	Simon Ash
Surrey	0845-125 2222	1,817	Mark Rowley, QPM
Sussex	0845-607 0999	3,167	Martin Richards
Thames Valley	0845-850 5505	4,257	Sara Thornton, CBE, QPM
Warwickshire	01926-415000	966	Keith Bristow, QPM
West Mercia	0300-333 3000	2,270	Paul West, QPM
West Midlands	0345-113 5000	8,567	C. Sims, OBE, QPM
West Yorkshire	01924-375222	5,670	Sir Norman Bettison
Wiltshire	0845-408 7000	1,169	Brian Moore, QPM

WALES

Force	Telephone	Strength†	Chief Constable
Dyfed-Powys	0845-330 2000	1,179	Ian Arundale, QPM
Gwent	01633-838111	1,531	Carmel Napier
North Wales	0845-607 1001	1,544	M. Polin, QPM
South Wales	01656-655555	3,105	Peter Vaughan

SCOTLAND

Force	Telephone	Strength†	Chief Constable
Central Scotland	01786-456000	840	Kevin Smith, QPM
Dumfries and Galloway	0845-600 5701	514	Patrick Shearer, QPM
Fife	0845-600 5702	1,099	Norma Graham, QPM
Grampian	0845-600 5700	1,535	Colin McKerracher, CBE, QPM
Lothian and Borders	0131-311 3131	3,053	David Strang, QPM
Northern	0845-603 3388	775	Ian Latimer
Strathclyde	0141-532 2000	7,949	Stephen House, QPM
Tayside	0300-111 2222	1,235	Justine Curran

NORTHERN IRELAND

Force	Telephone	Strength†	Chief Constable
Police Service of NI	0845-600 8000	7,172	Matt Baggott, CBE, QPM

ISLANDS

Force	Telephone	Strength†	Chief Constable
Isle of Man	01624-631212	236	Mike Langdon, QPM
States of Jersey	01534-612612	246	Mike Bowron
Guernsey	01481-725111	177	Patrick Rice

* For the City of London Police and the Metropolitan Police Service *see* London Forces
† Size of force *as at* February 2011
Source: R. Hazell & Co. *Police and Constabulary Almanac 2011*

LONDON FORCES

CITY OF LONDON POLICE

37 Wood Street, London EC2P 2NQ **T** 020-7601 2222
W www.cityoflondon.police.uk
Strength (February 2011), 823

Though small, the City of London has one of the most important financial centres in the world and the force has particular expertise in areas such as fraud investigation. The force has a wholly elected police authority, the police committee of the Corporation of London, which appoints the commissioner.
Commissioner, Adrian Leppard
Assistant Commissioner, Frank Armstrong
Commander, Ian Dyson

METROPOLITAN POLICE SERVICE

New Scotland Yard, 8–10 Broadway, London SW1H 0BG
T 020-7230 1212 **W** www.met.police.uk
Strength (February 2011), 31,865
Acting Commissioner, Tim Godwin, QPM
Acting Deputy Commissioner, Bernard Hogan-Howe, QPM

The Metropolitan Police Service is divided into four main areas for operational purposes:

TERRITORIAL POLICING
Most of the day-to-day policing of London is carried out by 33 borough operational command units; 32 command units operate within the same boundaries as the London borough councils, plus there is an additional unit which is responsible for policing Heathrow airport.
Assistant Commissioner, Ian McPherson, QPM

SPECIALIST CRIME DIRECTORATE
The Specialist Crime Directorate's main areas of focus are dismantling criminal networks of all levels, from neighbourhood street gangs to sophisticated international operations, and seizing their assets; safeguarding children and young people from physical, sexual and emotional abuse; and the investigation and prevention of homicide.
Assistant Commissioner, Cressida Dick, QPM

SPECIALIST OPERATIONS
Specialist Operations is divided into three commands:
• *Counter Terrorism Command* is responsible for the prevention and disruption of terrorist activity, domestic extremism and related offences both within London and nationally, providing an explosives disposal and chemical, biological, radiological and nuclear capability within London, assisting the security services in fulfilling their roles and providing a single point of contact for international partners in counter-terrorism matters.
• *Protection Command* is responsible for the protection and security of high-profile persons; key public figures, including the royal family; official delegations in the UK and overseas; and others where it is in the national interest or intelligence suggests that protection is necessary. It is also responsible for protecting royal residences and embassies, providing residential protection for visiting heads of state, heads of government and foreign ministers and advising the diplomatic community on security.
• *Protective Security Command* works in conjunction with authorities at the Houses of Parliament to provide security for peers, MPs, employees and visitors to the

palace of Westminster. It is also responsible for policing Heathrow and London City airports.
Assistant Commissioner, Cressida Dick, QPM

CENTRAL OPERATIONS
Central Operations consists of a number of specialised units with a broad range of policing functions which provide an integrated, community-focused service to London. Central Operations also has the remit for delivering the security arrangements for the 2012 London Olympic Games.
Assistant Commissioner, Lynne Owens

SPECIALIST FORCES

BRITISH TRANSPORT POLICE

25–27 Camden Road, London NW1 9LN **T** 020-7830 8800
W www.btp.police.uk
Strength (February 2011), 2,835

British Transport Police is the national police force for the railways in England, Wales and Scotland, including the London Underground system, Docklands Light Railway, Glasgow Subway, Midland Metro Tram system and Croydon Tramlink. The chief constable reports to the British Transport Police Authority. The members of the authority are appointed by the transport secretary and include representatives from the rail industry as well as independent members. Officers are paid the same as other police forces.
Chief Constable, Andrew Trotter, OBE, QPM
Deputy Chief Constable, Paul Crowther

CIVIL NUCLEAR CONSTABULARY

Building F6, Culham Science Centre, Abingdon,
Oxfordshire OX14 3DB **T** 01235-466606 **W** www.cnc.police.uk
Strength (March 2011), c.1,000

The Civil Nuclear Constabulary (CNC) operates under the strategic direction of the Department of Energy and Climate Change. The CNC is a specialised armed force that protects civil nuclear sites and nuclear materials. The constabulary is responsible for policing UK civil nuclear industry facilities and for escorting nuclear material between establishments within the UK and worldwide.
Chief Constable, Richard Thompson
Deputy Chief Constable, John Sampson

MINISTRY OF DEFENCE POLICE

Ministry of Defence Police and Guarding Agency, Wethersfield,
Braintree, Essex CM7 4AZ **T** 01371-854000
W www.mod.police.uk
Strength (March 2011), 3,302

Part of the Ministry of Defence Police and Guarding Agency, the Ministry of Defence Police is a statutory civil police force with particular responsibility for the security and policing of the MoD environment. It contributes to the physical protection of property and personnel within its jurisdiction and provides a comprehensive police service to the MoD as a whole.
Chief Constable / Chief Executive, Stephen Love, QPM
Deputy Chief Constable, G. McAuley

THE SPECIAL CONSTABULARY

The Special Constabulary is a force of trained volunteers who support and work with their local police force, usually for a minimum of four hours a week (the

Metropolitan Police Special Constabulary usually asks for a minimum commitment of eight hours a week). Special constables are thoroughly grounded in the basic aspects of police work, such as self-defence, powers of arrest, common crimes and preparing evidence for court, before they can begin to carry out any police duties. Once they have completed their training, they have the same powers as a regular officer and wear a similar uniform. Information on the Special Constabulary can be found at W www.policespecials.com.

RATES OF PAY

London weighting of £2,277 per annum (as at August 2011) is awarded to all police officers working in London irrespective of their ranks and in addition to the salaries listed below:

BASIC RATES OF PAY *as at August 2011*

Chief Constables of Greater Manchester, Strathclyde and West Midlands*	£178,431–£181,455
Chief Constable*	£127,017–£169,359
Deputy Chief Constable*	£108,873–£139,119
Assistant Chief Constable and Commanders*	£90,726–£105,849
Chief Superintendent	£74,394–£78,636
Superintendent Range 2†	£71,331–£75,909
Superintendent	£62,298–£72,585
Chief Inspector‡§	£51,789 (£53,853)–£53,919 (£55,980)
Inspector‡§	£46,788 (£48,840)–£50,751 (£52,818)
Sergeant‡	£36,519–£41,040
Constable‡	£23,259–£36,519

Metropolitan Police
Commissioner	£260,088
Deputy Commissioner	£214,722

City of London Police
Commissioner	£160,902
Assistant Commissioner	£132,714

Police Service of Northern Ireland
Chief Constable	£193,548
Deputy Chief Constable	£157,257

* Chief Officers may receive a bonus of at least 5 per cent of pensionable pay if their performance is deemed exceptional
† For Superintendents who were not given the rank of Chief Superintendent on its re-introduction on 1 January 2002
‡ Officers who have been on the highest available salary for one year have access to a competence-related threshold payment of £1,212 per annum
§ London salary in parentheses (applicable only to officers in the Metropolitan and City of London police forces)

STAFF ASSOCIATIONS

Police officers are not permitted to join a trade union or to take strike action. All ranks have their own staff associations.

ASSOCIATION OF CHIEF POLICE OFFICERS OF ENGLAND, WALES AND NORTHERN IRELAND, 10 Victoria Street, London SW1H 0NN T 020-7084 8950
Chief Executive, Thomas Flaherty

ENGLAND AND WALES
POLICE FEDERATION OF ENGLAND AND WALES, Federation House, Highbury Drive, Leatherhead, Surrey KT22 7UY T 01372-352000 W www.polfed.org E gensec@polfed.org
General Secretary, Ian Rennie
POLICE SUPERINTENDENTS' ASSOCIATION OF ENGLAND AND WALES, 67A Reading Road, Pangbourne, Reading RG8 7JD T 0118-984 4005 E enquiries@policesupers.com W www.policesupers.com
National Secretary, Chief Supt. Graham Cassidy

SCOTLAND
ASSOCIATION OF CHIEF POLICE OFFICERS IN SCOTLAND, 26 Holland Street, Glasgow G2 4NH T 0141-435 1230 W www.acpos.police.uk
General Secretary, Cliff Anderson
ASSOCIATION OF SCOTTISH POLICE SUPERINTENDENTS, *Secretariat,* 99 Main Street, Glasgow G62 6JM T 0141-532 4022 E secretariat@scottishpolicesupers.org.uk W www.scottishpolicesupers.org.uk
General Secretary, Carol Forfar
SCOTTISH POLICE FEDERATION, 5 Woodside Place, Glasgow G3 7QF T 0141-332 5234 W www.spf.org.uk
General Secretary and Treasurer, Calum Steele

NORTHERN IRELAND
POLICE FEDERATION FOR NORTHERN IRELAND, 77–79 Garnerville Road, Belfast BT4 2NX T 028-9076 4200 E office.pfni@btconnect.com W www.policefed-ni.org.uk
Secretary, Stevie McCann
SUPERINTENDENTS' ASSOCIATION OF NORTHERN IRELAND, PSNI College, Garnerville Road, Belfast BT4 2NX T 028-9092 2201 E mail@policesuperintendentsni.org W www.policesuperintendentsni.org
Joint Secretary (interim), Ray Phillips; Wesley Wilson, QPM

THE PRISON SERVICE

The prison services in the United Kingdom are the responsibility of the Secretary of State for Justice, the Scottish Justice Department and the Minister of Justice in Northern Ireland. The chief directors-general (chief executive in Scotland, director-general in Northern Ireland), officers of the Prison Service, the Scottish Prison Service and the Northern Ireland Prison Service are responsible for the day-to-day running of the system.

There are 133 prison establishments in England and Wales, 15 in Scotland and three in Northern Ireland. Convicted prisoners are classified according to their assessed security risk and are housed in establishments appropriate to that level of security. There are no open prisons in Northern Ireland. Female prisoners are housed in women's establishments or in separate wings of mixed prisons. Remand prisoners are, where possible, housed separately from convicted prisoners. Offenders under the age of 21 are usually detained in a Young Offender Institution, which may be a separate establishment or part of a prison. Appellant and failed asylum seekers are held in Immigration Removal Centres, or in separate units of other prisons.

Eleven prisons are now run by the private sector in England and Wales, and in England, Wales and Scotland all escort services have been contracted out to private companies. In Scotland, two prisons (Kilmarnock and Addiewell) were built and financed by the private sector and are being operated by private contractors.

There are independent prison inspectorates in England, Wales and Scotland which report annually on conditions and the treatment of prisoners. The Chief Inspector of Criminal Justice in Northern Ireland and HM Chief Inspector of Prisons for England and Wales perform an inspectorate role for prisons in Northern Ireland. Every prison establishment also has an independent monitoring board made up of local volunteers.

Any prisoner whose complaint is not satisfied by the internal complaints procedures may complain to the prisons and probation ombudsman for England and Wales, the Scottish public services ombudsman or the prisoner ombudsman for Northern Ireland.

The 11 private sector prisons in England and Wales are the direct responsibility of the chief executive of the National Offender Management Service (NOMS). NOMS was created in January 2004, in order to integrate prisons and probation into a system whereby end-to-end management of offenders is provided; this is expected to reduce re-offending and cut the growth rate of the prison population. In May 2007 NOMS was amalgamated into the Ministry of Justice; in 2008 it was restructured with responsibilities for running HM Prison Service, overseeing the contracts of privately run prisons, managing probation performance and creating probation trusts. The prisons and probation inspectors, the prisons ombudsman and the independent monitoring boards report to the home secretary and to the Minister of Justice in Northern Ireland.

PRISON STATISTICS

The projected 'high scenario' prison population for 2016 in England and Wales is 93,600; the 'low scenario' is 83,100.

PRISON POPULATION (UK) *as at April 2011*

	Remand	Sentenced	Other
ENGLAND AND WALES			
Male	11,517	68,718	913
Female	783	3,448	21
Total	12,300	72,166	934
SCOTLAND*			
Male	1,042	5,553	–
Female	55	329	–
Total	1,097	5,882	–
N. IRELAND			
Male	553	1,054	2
Female	18	29	–
Total	571	1,083	2
UK TOTAL	13,968	79,131	938

* Figures from August 2011
Sources: Home Office; Scottish Prison Service; Northern Ireland Prison Service

PRISON CAPACITY (ENGLAND AND WALES)
as at April 2011

Male prisoners	81,148
Female prisoners	4,252
Total	85,400
Useable operational capacity	88,093
Number under home detention curfew supervision	3,002

SENTENCED PRISON POPULATION BY SEX AND OFFENCE (ENGLAND AND WALES) *as at July 2011*

	Male	Female
Violence against the person	19,520	911
Sexual offences	9,767	83
Burglary	6,931	171
Robbery	8,840	301
Theft, handling	3,747	451
Fraud and forgery	1,202	174
Drugs offences	9,899	722
Motoring offences	824	17
Other offences	7,219	536
Offence not recorded	475	45
*Total**	68,424	3,411

* Figures do not include civil (non-criminal) prisoners or fine defaulters
Source: Ministry of Justice – *Offender Management Statistics*

SENTENCED POPULATION BY LENGTH OF SENTENCE
(ENGLAND AND WALES) *as at June 2011*

	Adults	Young offenders
Less than 12 months	6,394	1,420
12 months to less than 4 years	16,964	3,428
4 years to less than life	22,745	1,594
Indeterminate	13,286	358
*Total**	59,389	6,800

* Figures do not include civil (non-criminal) prisoners or fine defaulters
Source: Ministry of Justice – *Offender Management Statistics*

AVERAGE DAILY SENTENCED POPULATION BY LENGTH
OF SENTENCE 2010–11 (SCOTLAND)

	Adults	Young offenders
Less than 4 years	2,851	450
4 years or over (including life)	2,924	154
Total	5,775	604

Source: Scottish Prison Service – *Annual Report and Accounts 2010–11*

SUICIDES IN PRISON IN 2010 (ENGLAND AND WALES)

Men	57
Women	1
Total	58
Rate per 100,000 prisoners in custody	68

Source: www.justice.gov.uk

THE PRISON SERVICES

NATIONAL OFFENDER MANAGEMENT SERVICE

T 0300-047 6325 E public.enquiries@noms.gsi.gov.uk
W www.justice.gov.uk

HM Prison Service became part of the National Offender
Management Service (NOMS) on 1 April 2008 as part of
the reorganisation of the Ministry of Justice.

SALARIES *from 1 April 2011*

Senior manager A	£64,765–£82,892
Senior manager B	£60,980–£80,458
Senior manager C	£56,920–£72,451
Senior manager D	£45,700–£61,038
Manager E	£33,335–£46,024
Manager F	£29,685–£39,041
Manager G	£25,105–£32,140

THE NATIONAL OFFENDER MANAGEMENT
SERVICE BOARD
Chief Executive Officer (SCS), Michael Spurr
Director of High Security Prisons (SCS), Danny McAllister
Director of Probation and Contracted Services (SCS),
    Colin Allars
Director of National Operational Sevices (SCS), Phil Copple
Director of Human Resources (SCS), Robin Wilkinson
Director of Information and Communications Technology,
    Martin Bellamy
Director of Commissioning and Commercial (SCS), Ian Poree
Director of Offender Health (SCS), Richard Bradshaw
Board Secretary and Head of Secretariat (SMB), Ken
    Everett
Director of Public Sector Prisons (SCS), Steve Wagstaffe

DEPUTY DIRECTORS OF CUSTODY
Andrew Cross *(East Midlands)*; Adrian Smith *(East of
England)*; Paul Carroll *(Kent and Sussex)*; Nick Pascoe
(London); Alan Tallentire *(North-East)*; Alan Scott
(North-West); Claudia Sturt *(South-Central)*; Roger Hill
(South-East); Ferdie Parker *(South-West)*; Ian Mullholland
(Wales); Luke Serjeant *(West Midlands)*; Amy Rice
(Yorkshire and Humberside)

OPERATING COSTS OF PRISON SERVICE IN
ENGLAND AND WALES 2010–11

Staff costs	£2,563,863,000
Other operating costs	£2,036,743,000
Operating income	(£409,483,000)
Net operating costs for the year	£4,192,180,000

Source: NOMS – *Annual Report 2010–11*

SCOTTISH PRISON SERVICE (SPS)

Calton House, 5 Redheughs Rigg, Edinburgh EH12 9HW
T 0131-244 8747 E gaolinfo@sps.pnn.gov.uk
W www.sps.gov.uk

SALARIES 2011–12
Senior managers in the Scottish Prison Service, including
governors and deputy governors of prisons, are paid
across three pay bands depending on the size of the
establishment:

Band I	£54,930–£68,433
Band H	£43,601–£56,704
Band G	£34,333–£47,149

SPS BOARD
Chief Executive, John Ewing
Directors, Willie Pretswell *(Finance)*; Dr Andrew Fraser
    (Health and Care); Stephen Swan *(Human Resources)*;
    Eric Murch *(Partnerships and Commissioning)*; Rona
    Sweeney *(Prisons)*
Non-Executive Directors, Allan Burns; Harry McGuigan;
    Jane Martin; Susan Matheson; Bill Morton; Zoe Van
    Zwanenberg

OPERATING COSTS OF SCOTTISH PRISON
SERVICE 2010–11

Total income	£2,954,000
Total expenditure	£304,724,000
Staff costs	£139,374,000
Running costs	£130,550,000
Other current expenditure	£30,696,000
Operating cost	£301,770,000
Interest payable and similar charges	£8,254,000
Net operating cost	£310,024,000

Source: Scottish Prison Service – *Annual Report and Accounts
2010–11*

NORTHERN IRELAND PRISON SERVICE

Dundonald House, Upper Newtownards Road, Belfast BT4 3SU
T 028-9052 2922 E info@niprisonservice.gov.uk
W www.niprisonservice.gov.uk

SALARIES 2010–11

Governor 1	£74,747–£80,550
Governor 2	£67,983–£72,183
Governor 3	£58,824–£62,766
Governor 4	£51,156–£55,407
Governor 5	£44,934–£50,396

SENIOR STAFF
Director-General, Colin McConnell
Directors, Ronnie Armour (Human Resources and
   Organisation Development); Max Murray (Offender
   Policy and Regimes); Graeme Wilkinson (Finance,
   Planning and Corporate Compliance)

OPERATING COSTS OF NORTHERN IRELAND
PRISON SERVICE 2010–11

Staff costs	£91,154,000
Net running costs	£25,704,000
Depreciation and Amortisation	£13,333,000
Operating expenditure	£130,191,000
Net operating costs for the year	£128,774,000

Source: Northern Ireland Prison Service – Annual Report and
Accounts 2010–11

PRISON ESTABLISHMENTS

as at June 2011

ENGLAND AND WALES

Prison	Address	Prisoners	Governor/Director
ACKLINGTON	Northumberland NE65 9XF	823	Patrick Fox (acting)
ALTCOURSE (private prison)	Liverpool L9 7WU	1,162	John McLaughlin
†‡ASHFIELD (private prison)	Bristol BS16 9QJ	355	Wendy Sinclair
*‡ASKHAM GRANGE	York YO23 3FT	125	Marion Mahoney
‡AYLESBURY	Bucks HP20 1EH	420	Kevin Leggett
BEDFORD	Bedford MK40 1HG	480	Frank Flynn
BELMARSH	London SE28 0EB	842	Phil Wragg
BIRMINGHAM	Birmingham B18 4AS	1,459	James Shanley
BLANTYRE HOUSE	Kent TN17 2NH	121	Jim Carmichael
BLUNDESTON	Suffolk NR32 5BG	449	David Bamford
†‡BRINSFORD	Wolverhampton WV10 7PY	538	Steph Roberts-Bibby
‡BRISTOL	Bristol BS7 8PS	586	Kenny Brown
‡BRIXTON	London SW2 5XF	737	Edmond Tullett
*BRONZEFIELD (private prison)	Middlesex TW15 3JZ	499	Helga Swidenbank
BUCKLEY HALL	Lancs OL12 9DP	436	Susan Kennedy
BULLINGDON	Oxon OX25 1PZ	1,113	Andy Lattimore
‡BULLWOOD HALL	Essex SS5 4TE	223	Steve Bradford
BURE	Norfolk NR10 5GB	519	Sue Doolan
CANTERBURY	Kent CT1 1PJ	307	Chris Bartlett
†CARDIFF	Cardiff CF24 0UG	802	Richard Booty
‡CASTINGTON	Northumberland NE65 9XG	356	Patrick Fox
CHANNINGS WOOD	Devon TQ12 6DW	726	Jeannine Hendrick
‡CHELMSFORD	Essex CM2 6LQ	672	Rob Davis
COLDINGLEY	Surrey GU24 9EX	508	Glenn Knight
‡COOKHAM WOOD	Kent ME1 3LU	118	Emily Thomas
DARTMOOR	Devon PL20 6RR	504	Tony Corcoran
‡DEERBOLT	Co. Durham DL12 9BG	478	Jenny Mooney
‡DONCASTER (private prison)	Doncaster DN5 8UX	1,089	John Biggin
†DORCHESTER	Dorset DT1 1JD	199	Steve Hodson
DOVEGATE (private prison)	Staffs ST14 8XR	1,129	Wyn Jones
§DOVER	Kent CT17 9DR	270	Andy Bell
*DOWNVIEW	Surrey SM2 5PD	278	Louise Spencer
*‡DRAKE HALL	Staffs ST21 6LQ	309	Bridie Oakes-Richards
DURHAM	Durham DH1 3HU	881	Tim Allen (acting)
*‡EAST SUTTON PARK	Kent ME17 3DF	96	Jim Carmichael
*‡EASTWOOD PARK	Glos GL12 8DB	331	Andrea Albutt
ELMLEY	Kent ME12 4DZ	1,173	Nigel Foote
ERLESTOKE	Wilts SN10 5TU	369	Andy Rogers
EVERTHORPE	E. Yorks HU15 1RB	672	Alec McCrystal
†‡EXETER	Devon EX4 4EX	524	Jeannine Hendrick
FEATHERSTONE	Wolverhampton WV10 7PU	649	Deborah McGivern
†‡FELTHAM	Middx TW13 4ND	740	Cathy Robinson
FORD	W. Sussex BN18 0BX	505	Sharon Williams
‡FOREST BANK (private prison)	Manchester M27 8FB	1,340	Trevor Shortt
*FOSTON HALL	Derby DE65 5DN	271	Grey Riley-Smith
FRANKLAND	Durham DH1 5YD	813	Dave Thompson
FULL SUTTON	York YO41 1PS	608	Steve Tilley
GARTH	Preston PR26 8NE	829	Terry Williams
GARTREE	Leics LE16 7RP	672	Neil Richards
†‡GLEN PARVA	Leicester LE18 4TN	736	Michael Wood
†‡GLOUCESTER	Glos GL1 2JN	300	Mike Bolton

Prison	Address	Prisoners	Governor/Director
GRENDON/SPRING HILL	Bucks HP18 0TL	544	Dr Peter Bennett
‡GUYS MARSH	Dorset SP7 0AH	503	Duncan Burles
§HASLAR	Hampshire PO12 2AW	139	Vicky Baker
HAVERIGG	Cumbria LA18 4NA	639	Martin Farquhar
HEWELL	Worcs B97 6QS	1,399	Kieron Taylor
HIGH DOWN	Surrey SM2 5PJ	1,093	Peter Dawson
HIGHPOINT	Suffolk CB8 9YG	1,307	Michelle Jarman-Howe
†‡HINDLEY	Lancs WN2 5TH	338	Peter Francis
‡HOLLESLEY BAY	Suffolk IP12 3JW	365	Declan Moore
*‡HOLLOWAY	London N7 0NU	541	Julia Killick
HOLME HOUSE	Stockton-on-Tees TS18 2QU	1,053	Matt Spencer
‡HULL	Hull HU9 5LS	945	Paul Foweather
‡HUNTERCOMBE	Oxon RG9 5SB	367	Nigel Atkinson
ISIS	Thamesmead SE28 0NZ	424	Lisa Smitherman
ISLE OF WIGHT	Isle of Wight PO30 5RS	1,657	Barry Greenbury
KENNET	Merseyside L31 1HX	341	Derek Harrison
KINGSTON	Portsmouth PO3 6AS	197	Ian Telfer
KIRKHAM	Lancs PR4 2RN	590	John Hewitson
KIRKLEVINGTON GRANGE	Cleveland TS15 9PA	274	Gabrielle Lee *(acting)*
†‡LANCASTER FARMS	Lancaster LA1 3QZ	518	Steve Lawrence
LATCHMERE HOUSE	Surrey TW10 5HH	198	Phil Taylor
LEEDS	Leeds LS12 2TJ	1,018	Rob Kellett
LEICESTER	Leicester LE2 7AJ	335	Karen Head *(acting)*
‡LEWES	E. Sussex BN7 1EA	478	Robin Eldridge
LEYHILL	Glos GL12 8BT	476	Mick Bell
LINCOLN	Lincoln LN2 4BD	628	Ian Thomas
§LINDHOLME	Doncaster DN7 6EE	1,093	Bob Mullen
LITTLEHEY	Cambs PE28 0SR	1,132	Danny Spencer
LIVERPOOL	Liverpool L9 3DF	1,236	John Illingsworth
LONG LARTIN	Worcs WR11 8TZ	621	Simon Cartwright
*‡LOW NEWTON	Durham DH1 5YA	263	Alan Richer
LOWDHAM GRANGE (private prison)	Notts NG14 7DA	926	Gareth Sands
MAIDSTONE	Kent ME14 1UZ	593	Andy Hudson
MANCHESTER	Manchester M60 9AH	1,151	Richard Vince
‡MOORLAND/MOORLAND OPEN	Doncaster DN7 6BW	733	Rob Kellet
§MORTON HALL	Lincoln LN6 9PT	123	Jamie Bennett
THE MOUNT	Herts HP3 0NZ	758	Damian Evans
*‡NEW HALL	W. Yorks WF4 4XX	389	Marion Mahoney
NORTH SEA CAMP	Lincs PE22 0QX	367	Graham Batchford
‡NORTHALLERTON	N. Yorks DL6 1NW	189	Norman Griffin
‡NORWICH	Norfolk NR1 4LU	741	Will Styles
NOTTINGHAM	Notts NG5 3AG	993	Peter Wright
‡ONLEY	Warks CV23 8AP	697	Dave Harding
†‡PARC (private prison)	Bridgend CF35 6AP	1,446	Janet Wallsgrove
‡PENTONVILLE	London N7 8TT	1,213	Gary Monaghon
*†PETERBOROUGH (private prison)	Peterborough PE3 7PD	583	Nick Leader
‡PORTLAND	Dorset DT5 1DL	467	Steve Holland
PRESTON	Lancs PR1 5AB	759	Paul Holland
RANBY	Notts DN22 8EU	1,082	Louise Taylor
†‡READING	Berks RG1 3HY	231	Dave Rogers
RISLEY	Cheshire WA3 6BP	1,075	Bob McColm
‡ROCHESTER	Kent ME1 3QS	536	John Wilson
RYE HILL (private prison)	Warks CV23 8SZ	615	Tom Wheatley
*SEND	Surrey GU23 7LJ	282	Louise Spencer
SHEPTON MALLET	Somerset BA4 5LU	188	Nick Evans
‡SHREWSBURY	Shropshire SY1 2HR	331	Gerry Hendry
STAFFORD	Stafford ST16 3AW	736	Peter Small
STANDFORD HILL	Kent ME12 4AA	455	Nigel Foote
STOCKEN	Leics LE15 7RD	838	John O'Sullivan
‡STOKE HEATH	Shropshire TF9 2JL	247	John Huntington
*‡STYAL	Cheshire SK9 4HR	443	Clive Chatterton
SUDBURY	Derbys DE6 5HW	571	Ken Kan
SWALESIDE	Kent ME12 4AX	1,103	Jim Bourke
†‡SWANSEA	Swansea SA1 3SR	419	Neil Lavis
‡SWINFEN HALL	Staffs WS14 9QS	638	Tom Watson
‡THORN CROSS	Cheshire WA4 4RL	289	Bob McColm
USK/PRESCOED	Monmouthshire NP15 1XP	461	Steve Cross

Prison	Address	Prisoners	Governor/Director
VERNE	Dorset DT5 1EQ	591	James Lucas
WAKEFIELD	West Yorks WF2 9AG	738	Susan Howard
WANDSWORTH	London SW18 3HS	1,599	David Taylor
‡WARREN HILL	Suffolk IP12 3JW	116	Bev Bevan
WAYLAND	Norfolk IP25 6RL	1,015	Kevin Reilly
WEALSTUN	W. Yorks LS23 7AZ	820	Norma Harrington
WELLINGBOROUGH	Northants NN8 2NH	580	Peter Siddons
‡WERRINGTON	Stoke-on-Trent ST9 0DX	149	Carl Hardwick
‡WETHERBY	W. Yorks LS22 5ED	362	Will Styles
WHATTON	Nottingham NG13 9FQ	838	Lynn Saunders
WHITEMOOR	Cambs PE15 0PR	459	Paul Cawkwell
WINCHESTER	Winchester SO22 5DF	687	David Ward
WOLDS (private prison)	E. Yorks HU15 2JZ	351	Cathy James
WOODHILL	Bucks MK4 4DA	788	Nigel Smith
WORMWOOD SCRUBS	London W12 0AE	1,248	Phil Taylor
WYMOTT	Preston PR26 8LW	1,142	Paul Norbury

SCOTLAND *as at April 2011*

Prison	Address	Prisoners	Governor/Director
ABERDEEN	Aberdeen AB11 8FN	228	Audrey Mooney
ADDIEWELL(private prison)	West Lothian EH55 8QA	702	Audrey Park
†BARLINNIE	Glasgow G33 2QX	1,384	Derek McGill
*†‡CORNTON VALE	Stirling FK9 5NU	329	Teresa Medhurst
†DUMFRIES	Dumfries DG2 9AX	200	Martyn Bettel
†EDINBURGH	Edinburgh EH11 3LN	897	Sue Brookes
GLENOCHIL	Tullibody FK10 3AD	656	Dan Gunn
†‡GREENOCK	Greenock PA16 9AH	275	Jim Kerr
*†INVERNESS	Inverness IV2 3HH	139	Angus MacVicar
†‡KILMARNOCK (private prison)	Kilmarnock KA1 5AA	567	Sandy McEwan
OPEN ESTATE NORANSIDE	Angus DD8 3QY	256	Jim Farish
†PERTH	Perth PH2 8AT	640	Mike Inglis
PETERHEAD	Aberdeenshire AB42 2YY	245	Mike Hebden
†‡POLMONT	Falkirk FK2 0AB	732	Kate Donegan
SHOTTS	Lanarkshire ML7 4LE	536	Ian Whitehead

NORTHERN IRELAND *as at April 2011*

Prison	Address	Prisoners	Governor/Director
*†‡HYDEBANK WOOD	Belfast BT8 8NA	258	Gary Alcock
†§MAGHABERRY	Co. Antrim BT28 2NF	881	Pat Maguire
MAGILLIGAN	Co. Londonderry BT49 0LR	517	Alan Longwell

PRISON ESTABLISHMENTS KEY
* Women's establishment or establishment with units for women
† Remand Centre or establishment with units for remand prisoners
‡ Young Offender Institution or establishment with units for young offenders
§ Immigration Removal Centre or establishment with units for immigration detainees

DEFENCE

The armed forces of the United Kingdom comprise the Royal Navy, the Army and the Royal Air Force (RAF). The Queen is Commander-in-Chief of all the armed forces. The Secretary of State for Defence is responsible for the formulation and content of defence policy and for providing the means by which it is conducted. The formal legal basis for the conduct of defence in the UK rests on a range of powers vested by statute and letters patent in the Defence Council, chaired by the Secretary of State for Defence. Beneath the ministers lies the top management of the Ministry of Defence (MoD), headed jointly by the Permanent Secretary and the Chief of Defence Staff. The Permanent Secretary is the government's principal civilian adviser on defence and has the primary responsibility for policy, finance, management and administration. She is also personally accountable to parliament for the expenditure of all public money allocated to defence purposes. The Chief of the Defence Staff is the professional head of the armed forces in the UK and the principal military adviser to the secretary of state and the government.

The Defence Board is the executive of the Defence Council. Chaired by the Permanent Secretary, it acts as the main executive board of the Ministry of Defence, providing senior level leadership and strategic management of defence.

The Central Staff, headed by the Vice-Chief of the Defence Staff and the Second Permanent Under-Secretary of State, is the policy core of the department. Defence Equipment and Support, headed by the Chief of Defence Materiel, is responsible for purchasing defence equipment and providing logistical support to the armed forces.

A permanent Joint Headquarters for the conduct of joint operations was set up at Northwood in 1996. The Joint Headquarters connects the policy and strategic functions of the MoD head office with the conduct of operations and is intended to strengthen the policy/executive division.

The UK pursues its defence and security policies through its membership of NATO (to which most of its armed forces are committed), the European Union, the Organisation for Security and Cooperation in Europe and the UN (see International Organisations section).

STRENGTH OF THE ARMED FORCES

	Royal Navy	Army	RAF	All Services
1975 strength	76,200	167,100	95,000	338,300
2001 strength	42,420	109,530	53,700	205,650
2002 strength	41,630	110,050	53,000	204,680
2003 strength	41,550	112,130	53,240	206,920
2004 strength	40,880	112,750	53,390	207,020
2005 strength	39,940	109,290	51,870	201,100
2006 strength	39,390	107,730	48,730	195,850
2007 strength*	38,860	106,170	45,370	190,400
2008 strength*	38,570	105,090	43,390	187,060
2009 strength*	38,340	106,460	43,570	188,370
2010 strength*	38,730	108,870	44,050	191,660
2011 strength*	37,660	106,230	42,460	186,360

* Provisional figures apart from the 2007 Royal Navy data
Source: Defence Analytical Services and Advice (DASA) National Statistics (Crown copyright)

SERVICE PERSONNEL BY RANK AND GENDER

	Officers		Other ranks	
	Males	Females	Males	Females
All services	27,930	3,900	140,570	13,950
Royal Navy	6,690	720	27,430	2,810
Army	13,090	1,670	84,660	6,810
RAF	8,150	1,510	28,480	4,330

Source: DASA National Statistics (Crown copyright)

UK regular forces include trained and untrained personnel and nursing services, but exclude Gurkhas, full-time reserve service personnel, mobilised reservists and naval activated reservists. As at 1 April 2011 these groups provisionally numbered:

All Gurkhas	3,890
Full-time reserve service	2,050
Mobilised reservists	
Army	1,460
RAF	80
Naval activated reservists	140

Source: DASA National Statistics (Crown copyright)

CIVILIAN PERSONNEL

1993 level	159,600
2000 level	121,300
2001 level	118,200
2002 level	110,100
2003 level	107,600
2004 level	108,990
2005 level	107,680
2006 level	102,970
2007 level	95,790
2008 level	88,690
2009 level	85,730
2010 level	85,180
2011 level	83,100

Source: DASA National Statistics (Crown copyright)

UK REGULAR FORCES: DEATHS

In 2010 there were a total of 187 deaths among the UK regular armed forces, of which 30 were serving in the Royal Navy and Royal Marines, 136 in the Army and 21 in the RAF. The largest single cause of death was as a result of hostile action (killed in action and died of wounds), which accounted for 95 deaths (51 per cent of the total) in 2010. Land transport accidents accounted for 36 deaths (19 per cent) and other accidents accounted for a further 15 deaths (8 per cent). Suicides and open verdicts accounted for five deaths or 3 per cent of the total.

NUMBER OF DEATHS AND MORTALITY RATES

	2005	2007	2008	2009	2010
Total number	160	204	137	205	187
Royal Navy	27	27	40	23	30
Army	93	145	79	158	136
RAF	40	32	18	24	21
Mortality rates per thousand					
Tri-service rate	0.81	1.06	0.73	1.07	0.97
Navy	0.71	0.72	1.09	0.56	0.78
Army	0.87	1.29	0.73	1.34	1.16
RAF	0.72	0.71	0.36	0.53	0.49

Source: DASA *National Statistics* (Crown copyright)

NUCLEAR FORCES

The Vanguard Class SSBN (ship submersible ballistic nuclear) provides the UK's strategic nuclear deterrent. Each Vanguard Class submarine is capable of carrying 16 Trident D5 missiles equipped with nuclear warheads.

There is a ballistic missile early warning system station at RAF Fylingdales in North Yorkshire.

ARMS CONTROL

The 1990 Conventional Armed Forces in Europe (CFE) Treaty, which commits all NATO and former Warsaw Pact members to limiting their holdings of five major classes of conventional weapons, has been adapted to reflect the changed geo-strategic environment and negotiations continue for its implementation. The Open Skies Treaty, which the UK signed in 1992 and entered into force in 2002, allows for the overflight of states parties by other states parties using unarmed observation aircraft.

The UN Convention on Certain Conventional Weapons (as amended 2001), which bans or restricts the use of specific types of weapons that are considered to cause unnecessary or unjustifiable suffering to combatants, or to affect civilians indiscriminately, was ratified by the UK in 1995. In 1968 the UK signed and ratified the Nuclear Non-Proliferation Treaty, which came into force in 1970 and was indefinitely and unconditionally extended in 1995. In 1996 the UK signed the Comprehensive Nuclear Test Ban Treaty and ratified it in 1998. The UK is a party to the 1972 Biological and Toxin Weapons Convention, which provides for a worldwide ban on biological weapons, and the 1993 Chemical Weapons Convention, which came into force in 1997 and provides for a verifiable worldwide ban on chemical weapons.

DEFENCE BUDGET DEPARTMENTAL EXPENDITURE LIMITS (DEL) £ billion

	Resource budget	Capital budget	Total DEL
2010–11 (estimate)	28.4	9.6	38.0
2011–12 (plans)	27.3	10.0	37.3
2012–13 (plans)	25.2	9.1	34.3

Source: HM Treasury – *Budget 2011* (Crown copyright)

MINISTRY OF DEFENCE
Main Building, Whitehall, London SW1A 2HB
T 020-7218 9000 W www.mod.uk

Secretary of State for Defence, Rt. Hon. Liam Fox, MP
Private Secretary, Barry Burton
Special Advisers, Hayden Allen; Luke Coffey; Ollie Waghorn
Parliamentary Private Secretary, vacant
Minister of State, Nick Harvey, MP *(Armed Forces)*

Private Secretary, Gareth Martin
Parliamentary Under-Secretary of State, Gerald Howarth, MP *(International Security Strategy)*
Private Secretary, Austin Mitchell
Parliamentary Under-Secretary of State, Andrew Robathan, MP *(Defence Personnel, Welfare and Vetarans)*
Private Secretary, Alan Nisbett
Parliamentary Under-Secretary of State, Peter Luff, MP *(Defence Equipment, Support and Technology)*
Private Secretary, Anna Platt
Parliamentary Under-Secretary of State for Defence and Lords Spokesman on Defence, Lord Astor
Private Secretary, Natasha Foskett

CHIEFS OF STAFF

Chief of the Defence Staff, Gen. Sir David Richards, GCB, CBE, DSO, ADC
Vice Chief of the Defence Staff, Gen. Sir Nick Houghton, GCB, CBE
Chief of the Naval Staff and First Sea Lord, Adm. Sir Mark Stanhope, GCB, OBE, ADC
Assistant Chief of the Naval Staff, Rear-Adm. Philip Jones
Chief of the General Staff, Gen. Sir Peter Wall, KCB, CBE, ADC
Assistant Chief of the General Staff, Maj.-Gen. James Everard, CBE
Chief of the Air Staff, Air Chief Marshal Sir Stephen Dalton, KCB, ADC
Assistant Chief of the Air Staff, Air Vice-Marshal Barry North, OBE

SENIOR OFFICIALS

Permanent Under-Secretary of State, Ursula Brennan
Second Permanent Under-Secretary of State, Jon Day
Chief of Defence Materiel, Bernard Gray
Chief Scientific Adviser, Prof. Mark Welland, FRS, FRENG
Director-General Finance, Jon Thompson

THE DEFENCE COUNCIL

The Defence Council is the senior committee of the MoD, and was established by royal prerogative under letters patent in April 1964. The letters patent confer on the Defence Council the command over all of the armed forces and charge the council with such matters relating to the administration of the armed forces as the Secretary of State for Defence should direct them to execute. It is chaired by the Secretary of State for Defence and consists of the Secretary of State for Defence, the Minister of State for the Armed Forces, the Minister of State for International Security Strategy, the Minister of State for Defence Personnel, Welfare and Veterans, the Minister of State for Defence Equipment, Support and Technology, the Parliamentary Under-Secretary of State for Defence and Lords Spokesman on Defence, the Chief of Defence Staff, the Permanent Under-Secretary of State, the Chief of the Naval Staff and First Sea Lord, the Chief of the General Staff, the Chief of the Air Staff, the Vice-Chief of the Defence Staff, the Chief of Defence Materiel, the Chief Scientific Adviser, the Second Permanent Under-Secretary of State and the Director-General Finance.

CENTRAL STAFF

Vice-Chief of the Defence Staff, Gen. Sir Nick Houghton, GCB, CBE
Second Permanent Under-Secretary of State, Jon Day

PERMANENT JOINT HQ
Chief of Joint Operations, Air Marshal Sir Stuart Peach, KCB, CBE
Chief of Staff (Operations), Maj.-Gen. Gordon Messenger, DSO, OBE
Chief of Staff (Joint Warfare Development), Maj.-Gen. Roddy Porter, MBE

FLEET COMMAND
Commander-in-Chief Fleet, Adm. Sir Trevor Soar, KCB, OBE
Deputy Commander-in-Chief Fleet, Vice-Adm. George Zambellas, DSC

NAVAL HOME COMMAND
Second Sea Lord and Commander-in-Chief Naval Home Command, Vice-Adm. Charles Montgomery,
Naval Secretary and Chief of Staff (Personnel), Rear-Adm. David Steel, CBE

LAND FORCES
Commander-in-Chief Land Forces, Gen. Sir Nick Parker, KCB, CBE
Chief of Staff Land Forces, Maj.-Gen. Mark Poffley, OBE

AIR COMMAND
Commander-in-Chief Air Command, Air Chief Marshal Sir Simon Bryant, KCB, CBE, ADC
Deputy Commander-in-Chief Operations, Air Marshal R. Garwood, CB
Deputy Commander-in-Chief Personnel, Air Marshal A. Pulford, CBE

DEFENCE EQUIPMENT AND SUPPORT
Chief of Defence Materiel, Bernard Gray
Chief Operating Officer, Dr Andrew Tyler
Chief of Corporate Services, Trevor Woolley
Chief of Materiel (Fleet), Vice-Adm. Andy Matthews, OBE
Chief of Materiel (Land), Lt.-Gen. Gary Coward, CB, OBE
Chief of Materiel (Air), Air Marshal Kevin Leeson, CBE

EXECUTIVE AGENCIES
DEFENCE SCIENCE AND TECHNOLOGY LABORATORY
Porton Down, Salisbury, Wiltshire SP4 0JQ **T** 01980-613121
E centralenquiries@dstl.gov.uk **W** www.dstl.gov.uk
Chief Executive, Dr Frances Saunders

DEFENCE SUPPORT GROUP
Building 203, Monxton Road, Andover, Hampshire SP11 8HT
T 01264-383295 **E** info@dsg.mod.uk **W** www.dsg.mod.uk
Chief Executive, Archie Hughes

MET OFFICE
Fitzroy Road, Exeter, Devon EX1 3PB **T** 0870-900 0100
E enquiries@metoffice.gov.uk **W** www.metoffice.gov.uk
Chief Executive, John Hirst

UK HYDROGRAPHIC OFFICE
Admiralty Way, Taunton, Somerset TA1 2DN **T** 01823-337900
E customerservices@ukho.gov.uk **W** www.ukho.gov.uk
Chief Executive, Mike Robinson

ARMED FORCES TRAINING AND RECRUITMENT

In April 2006 the MoD removed agency status from the three armed forces training agencies which now function as an integral part of their respective service.

Flag Officer Sea Training (FOST) is responsible for all Royal Navy and Royal Fleet Auxiliary training. FOST's International Defence Training provides the focal point for all aspects of naval training. Training is divided into five streams: Naval Core Training (responsible for new entry, command, leadership and management training); Royal Marine; Submarine; Surface and Aviation.

The Army Recruiting and Training Division (ARTD) is responsible for the four key areas of army training: soldier initial training, at the School of Infantry or at one of the army's four other facilities; officer initial training at the Royal Military Academy Sandhurst; trade training at one of the army's specialist facilities; and resettlement training for those about to leave the army. Trade training facilities include: the Armour Centre; the Defence College of Logistics and Personnel Administration; the Royal School of Artillery; the Royal School of Military Engineering and the Army Aviation Centre.

The Royal Air Force No. 22 (Training) Group exists to recruit RAF personnel and provide trained specialist personnel to the armed forces as a whole, such as providing the army air corps with trained helicopter pilots. The group is split into eight areas: RAF College Cranwell and Inspectorate of Recruiting; the Directorate of Flying Training (DFT); the Directorate of Joint Technical Training (DJTT); the Air Cadet Organisation (ACO); Core Headquarters; the Defence College of Aeronautical Engineering (DCAE); the Defence College of Communications and Information Systems (DCCIS) and the Defence College of Electro-Mechanical Engineering (DCEME).

USEFUL WEBSITES
W www.royalnavy.mod.uk
W www.army.mod.uk
W www.raf.mod.uk

THE ROYAL NAVY

In Order of Seniority

LORD HIGH ADMIRAL OF THE UNITED KINGDOM
HRH The Prince Philip, Duke of Edinburgh, KG, KT, OM, GBE, AC, QSO, PC, *apptd* 2011

ADMIRALS OF THE FLEET
HRH The Prince Philip, Duke of Edinburgh, KG, KT, OM, GBE, AC, QSO, PC, *apptd* 1953
Sir Edward Ashmore, GCB, DSC, *apptd* 1977
Sir Julian Oswald, GCB, *apptd* 1993
Sir Benjamin Bathurst, GCB, *apptd* 1995

ADMIRALS
(Former Chiefs or Vice Chiefs of Defence Staff and First Sea Lords who remain on the active list)
Slater, Sir Jock, GCB, LVO, *apptd* 1991
Boyce, Lord, KG, GCB, OBE, *apptd* 1995
Abbott, Sir Peter, GBE, KCB, *apptd* 1995
Essenhigh, Sir Nigel, GCB, *apptd* 1998
West of Spithead, Lord, GCB, DSC, PC, *apptd* 2000
Band, Sir Jonathon, GCB, *apptd* 2002

ADMIRALS
HRH The Prince of Wales, KG, KT, GCB, OM, AK, QSO, PC, ADC
Stanhope, Sir Mark, KCB, OBE, ADC *(First Sea Lord and Chief of Naval Staff)*
Soar, Sir Trevor, KCB, OBE *(Commander-in-Chief Fleet)*

VICE-ADMIRALS
HRH The Princess Royal, KG, KT, GCVO, QSO *(Chief Commandant for Women in the Royal Navy)*
Lambert, Paul, CB *(Deputy Chief of Defence Staff (Capability))*
Matthews, Andrew, CB *(Chief of Materiel (Fleet) and Chief of Fleet Support to the Navy Board)*
Cooling, Robert, CB *(Chief of Staff to the Supreme Allied Commander Transformation)*
Montgomery, Charles, CBE, ADC *(Second Sea Lord and Commander-in-Chief Naval Home Command)*
Zambellas, George, DSC, *(Deputy Commander-in-Chief Fleet, Chief of Staff Navy Command HQ and Chief Naval Warfare Officer)*

REAR-ADMIRALS
HRH The Duke of York, KG, GCVO, ADC
Mosisetti, Neil, CB *(MoD and FCO Climate and Energy Security Envoy)*
Hussain, Amjad, CB *(Director (Precision Attack) and Controller of the Navy)*
Johnstone-Burt, (Charles) Anthony, OBE *(Head of British Defence Staff (USA) and Defence Attaché)*
Richards, Alan *(Assistant Chief of Defence Staff (Strategy and Plans))*
Charlier, Simon *(Military Aviation Authority Operational Director)*
Jones, Philip *(Assistant Chief of Naval Staff)*
Lister, Simon, OBE *(Director Submarines and Chief Naval Engineering Officer)*
Lloyd, Stephen *(Chief Strategic Systems Executive)*
Corder, Ian *(Cdr (Operations) and Rear-Adm. Submarines (Head of Fighting Arm))*
Williams, Simon, OBE *(Senior Directing Staff (Navy), Royal College of Defence Studies)*
Hudson, Peter, CBE *(Chief of Staff (Capability))*

Williams, Bruce, CBE *(Deputy Director-General EU Military Staff)*
Cunningham, Thomas *(Chief of Staff (Aviation) and Rear-Adm. Fleet Air Arm (Head of Fighting Arm))*
Rymer, Alan *(Director Training, Education and Skills)*
Steel, David, CBE *(Naval Secretary and Chief of Staff (Personnel) and Chief Naval Logistics Officer)*
Mathias, Philip, MBE *(Strategic Defence and Security Review Nuclear Director)*
Lambert, Nicholas *(National Hydrographer and Deputy Chief Executive (Hydrography))*
Potts, D. *(Cdr UK Maritime Forces and Rear-Adm. Surface Ships as Head of Fighting Arm)*
Westbrook, Jonathan, MBE *(Chief of Staff to the Maritime Component Command and Senior Naval Representative, Naples)*
Harding, Russell, OBE *(Deputy Cdr Strike Force NATO)*
Johnstone, Clive, CBE *(Flag Officer Sea Training)*
Hockley, Christopher *(Flag Officer Scotland, Northern England and Northern Ireland and Flag Officer Reserve Forces)*

MEDICAL
Raffaelli, Philip, QHP, FRCP *(Surgeon Vice-Adm., Surgeon General)*
Jarvis, Lionel, QHS *(Assistant Chief of Defence Staff (Health), Chief Naval Medical Officer and Medical Director-General (Naval))*

ROYAL MARINES

CAPTAIN-GENERAL
HRH The Prince Philip, Duke of Edinburgh, KG, KT, OM, GBE, AC, QSO, PC

MAJOR-GENERALS
Thomas, Jeremy, DSO *(Assistant Chief of Defence Staff (Intelligence Capability))*
Salmon, Andrew, OBE *(Deputy Chief of Staff Force Readiness, Supreme HQ Allied Powers Europe)*
Capewell, David, OBE *(Assistant Chief of Defence Staff (Operations))*
Mason, Jeffrey, MBE *(Assistant Chief of Defence Staff (Operations), Permanent Joint HQ)*
Messenger, Gordon, DSO, OBE *(Chief of Defence Staff (Operations), Permanent Joint HQ)*
Howes, F., OBE *(Cdr UK Amphibious Forces and Commandant General Royal Marines)*
Hook, David, CBE *(Director Force Reintegration, HQ International Security and Assistance Force, Afghanistan)*

The Royal Marines were formed in 1664 and are part of the Naval Service. Their primary purpose is to conduct amphibious and land warfare. The principal operational units are:

- Three Commando Brigade, an amphibious all-arms brigade trained to operate in arduous environments (a core element of the UK's Joint Rapid Reaction Force). The commando units each have a strength of around 700 and are based in Taunton (40 Commando), Plymouth (42 Commando) and Arbroath (45 Commando)
- Fleet Protection Group, responsible for a wide range of tasks worldwide in support of the Royal Navy. The group is over 500 strong and is based at HM Naval Base Clyde on the west coast of Scotland

- Assault Group, which has its headquarters located in Devonport, Plymouth is responsible for ten landing craft training squadron at Poole, Dorset and 11 amphibious trials and training squadron at Instow, Devon

The Royal Marines also provide detachments for warships and land-based naval parties as required.

ROYAL MARINES RESERVES (RMR)

The Royal Marines Reserve is a commando-trained volunteer force with the principal role, when mobilised, of supporting the Royal Marines. The RMR consists of approximately 600 trained ranks who are distributed between the five RMR centres in the UK. Approximately 10 per cent of the RMR are working with the regular corps on long-term attachments within all of the Royal Marines regular units.

OTHER PARTS OF THE NAVAL SERVICE

FLEET AIR ARM

The Fleet Air Arm (FAA) provides the Royal Navy with a multi-role aviation combat capability able to operate autonomously at short notice worldwide in all environments, over the sea and land. The FAA numbers some 6,200 people, which comprises 11.5 per cent of the total Royal Naval strength. It operates some 200 combat aircraft and more than 50 support/training aircraft.

ROYAL FLEET AUXILIARY SERVICE (RFA)

The Royal Fleet Auxiliary Service is a civilian-manned flotilla of 13 ships owned by the MoD. Its primary role is to supply the Royal Navy and host nations while at sea with fuel, ammunition, food and spares, enabling them to maintain operations away from their home ports. It also provides amphibious support and secure sea transport for military units and their equipment. The ships routinely support and embark Royal Naval Air Squadrons.

ROYAL NAVAL RESERVE (RNR)

The Royal Naval Reserve is an integral part of the Naval Service. It is a part-time force of 2,300 trained men and women who are deployed with the Royal Navy in times of tension, humanitarian crisis or conflict.

The Royal Naval Reserve has 22 units throughout the UK; 19 of these provide initial training while three other specialist units provide intelligence and aviation training. Basic training is provided at HMS *Raleigh*, Torpoint in Cornwall for ratings and at the Britannia Royal Naval College, Dartmouth in Devon for officers; both these and most other RNR courses are of two weeks' duration or less.

QUEEN ALEXANDRA'S ROYAL NAVAL NURSING SERVICE

The first nursing sisters were appointed to naval hospitals in 1884 and the Queen Alexandra's Royal Naval Nursing Service (QARNNS) gained its current title in 1902. Nursing ratings were introduced in 1960 and men were integrated into the service in 1982; QARNNS recruits qualified nurses as both officers and ratings, and student nurse training can be undertaken in the service.

Patron, HRH Princess Alexandra, the Hon. Lady Ogilvy, KG, GCVO

Director of Naval Nursing Services and Matron-in-Chief, Capt. Helen Allkins, QARNNS

HM FLEET

as at 1 June 2011

Submarines

Vanguard Class	Vanguard, Vengeance, Victorious, Vigilant
Trafalgar Class	Talent, Tireless, Torbay, Trafalgar, Trenchant, Triumph, Turbulent
Astute Class	Astute
Aircraft Carrier	Illustrious
Amphibious Assault Ships	Ocean, Albion, Bulwark
Destroyers	
Type 42 Batch 2	Liverpool
Type 42 Batch 3	Edinburgh, York
Type 45	Daring, Dauntless
Frigates	
Type 23	Argyll, Iron Duke, Kent, Lancaster, Monmouth, Montrose, Northumberland, Portland, Richmond, St Albans, Somerset, Sutherland, Westminster
Minehunters	
Hunt Class	Atherstone, Brocklesby, Cattistock, Chiddingfold, Hurworth, Ledbury, Middleton, Quorn
Sandown Class	Bangor, Blyth, Grimsby, Pembroke, Penzance, Ramsey, Shoreham
Patrol Class	
Archer Class P2000	Archer, Biter, Blazer,
Training Boats	Charger, Dasher, Example, Exploit, Explorer, Express, Puncher, Pursuer, Raider, Ranger, Smiter, Tracker, Trumpeter
Gibraltar Squadron 16m	
Fast Patrol Class	Sabre, Scimitar
River Class Patrol	
Vessels	Mersey, Severn, Tyne, Clyde
Survey Vessels	
Ice Patrol Ships	Endurance*, Protector
Ocean Survey Vessel	Scott
Coastal Survey Vessel	Gleaner
Multi-Role Survey	
Vessels	Echo, Enterprise

* HMS *Endurance* is currently non-operational

ROYAL FLEET AUXILIARY

Landing Ship Dock (Auxiliary)	RFA Cardigan Bay, RFA Mounts Bay, RFA Lyme Bay
Wave Class	RFA Wave Knight, RFA Wave Ruler
Rover Class	RFA Black Rover, RFA Gold Rover
Leaf Class	RFA Orangeleaf
Fort Class	RFA Fort Austin, RFA Fort Rosalie, RFA Fort Victoria
Forward Repair Ship	RFA Diligence
Joint Casualty Treatment Ship/Maritime Afloat Training Capability	RFA Argus

THE ARMY

In Order of Seniority

THE QUEEN

FIELD MARSHALS
HRH The Prince Philip, Duke of Edinburgh, KG, KT, OM, GBE, AC, QSO, PC, *apptd* 1953
Lord Bramall, KG, GCB, OBE, MC, *apptd* 1982
Lord Vincent of Coleshill, GBE, KCB, DSO, *apptd* 1991
Sir John Chapple, GCB, CBE, *apptd* 1992
HRH The Duke of Kent, KG, GCMG, GCVO, ADC, *apptd* 1993
Lord Inge, KG, GCB *apptd* 1994

FORMER CHIEFS OF STAFF
Gen. Lord Guthrie of Craigiebank, GCB, LVO, OBE, *apptd* 1994
Gen. Sir Roger Wheeler, GCB, CBE, *apptd* 1997
Gen. Lord Walker of Aldringham, GCB, CMG, CBE, *apptd* 2000
Gen. Sir Mike Jackson, GCB, CBE, DSO, *apptd* 2003
Gen. Lord Richard Dannatt, GCB, CBE, MC, *apptd* 2006

FORMER VICE-CHIEF OF STAFF
Gen. Sir Timothy Granville-Chapman, GBE, KCB, *apptd* 2005

GENERALS
HRH The Prince of Wales, KG, KT, GCB, OM, AK, QSO, PC, ADC
Richards, Sir David, GCB, CBE, DSO, ADC *(Chief of the Defence Staff)*
Houghton, Sir Nicholas, GCB, CBE, ADC *(Vice Chief of the Defence Staff)*
Wall, Sir Peter, KCB, CBE, ADC *(Chief of the General Staff)*
Parker, Sir Nick, KCB, CBE, ADC *(Commander-in-Chief Land Forces)*
Shirreff, Sir A., KCB, CBE *(Deputy Supreme Allied Cdr Europe)*

LIEUTENANT-GENERALS
Rollo, Sir William, KCB, CBE *(Deputy Chief of the Defence Staff (Personnel))*
Bill, Sir David, KCB *(UK Military Representative to NATO and the European Union)*
Brown, C., CBE *(Iraq Compendium Study Team Leader)*
Mayall, S., CB *(Defence Senior Adviser to the Middle East)*
White-Spunner, Sir Barney, KCB, CBE *(Cdr Field Army)*
Mans, M., CBE *(Adjutant-General)*
Coward, G., CB, OBE *(Chief of Materiel (Land), Defence Equipment and Support and Quartermaster General)*
Newton, P., CBE *(Cdr Force Development and Training, HQ Land Forces)*
Bucknall, J., CBE *(Cdr Allied Rapid Reaction Corps)*
Barrons, R., CBE *(Deputy Chief of the Defence Staff (Operations))*

MAJOR-GENERALS
Gregory, A., CB *(Military Secretary)*
Melvin, R., CB, OBE *(Royal College of Defence Studies)*
von Bertele, M., OBE, QHS *(Director-General Army Medical Services)*
Berragan, G., CB *(Director-General Personnel, HQ Land Forces)*

Shaw, J., CBE *(GOC 2nd Division)*
Page, J., CB, OBE *(MoD)*
Moore, W., CBE *(Director Battlespace Manoeuvre and Master General of the Ordnance)*
Rutledge, M., CB, OBE *(GOC 5th Division)*
Brealey, B., *(Director-General Reserves and Basing, HQ Land Forces)*
Bradshaw, A., CB, OBE *(Deputy Cdr International Security Assistance Force, Afghanistan)*
Inshaw, T., CB *(Director Information Systems and Services, Defence Equipment and Support)*
Boag, C., CBE *(GOC Support Command)*
Kennett, A., CBE *(Senior Directing Staff (Army), Royal College of Defence Studies)*
Caplin, N. *(GOC UK Support Command, Germany)*
Robbins, Ven. S., CB, QHC *(Chaplain-General to HM Land Forces)*
Dale, I., CBE *(Director Land Equipment, Defence Equipment and Support)*
Porter, R., MBE *(Chief of Staff (Joint Warfare Development), Permanent Joint HQ, UK)*
Gordon, J., CBE *(Senior British Loan Service Officer, Oman)*
Kirkland, R., CBE *(GOC 4th Division)*
Deverell, C., MBE *(Director Materiel Strategy, Defence Equipment and Support)*
Carter, N., CBE, DSO *(Director-General Land Warfare)*
Poffley, M., OBE *(Chief of Staff HQ Land Forces)*
Andrews, S., CBE *(Director Strategic Change, Defence Medical Services)*
Foster, A., MBE *(Deputy Force Cdr UN Mission, D. R. Congo)*
Everard, J., CBE *(Assistant Chief of the General Staff)*
Marriot, P., CBE *(Commandant Royal Military Academy Sandhurst)*
Evans, T., DSO, MBE *(Chief of Staff HQ International Security Assistance Force Joint Command, Afghanistan)*
Shaw, D. *(Assistant Chief of the Defence Staff (Global Issues))*
Smith, G. *(Assistant Chief of the Defence Staff (Reserves and Cadets))*
Jones, P., MBE *(Director Force Reintegration, HQ International Security Assistance Force, Afghanistan)*
Porter, S., CBE *(Supreme Allied Cdr Transformation Representative Europe)*
Beckett, T., CBE *(Deputy Cdr NATO Rapid Redeployment Corps, Italy)*
Chapman, C. *(Senior British Military Advisor, US Central Command)*
Conway, M. *(Director-General Army Legal Services)*
Lorimer, J., DSO, MBE *(GOC 3rd (UK) Division)*
Copeland, I. *(Director Joint Support Chain, Defence Equipment and Support)*
Davis, R., CBE *(Director-General Army Recruiting and Training)*
Jaques, P., *(Director-General Logistics, Support and Equipment, HQ Land Forces)*
Burley, S., MBE *(GOC Theatre Troops)*
Bashall, J., CBE *(GOC 1st (UK) Armoured Division)*
Wilks, C., CBE *(Director Land Equipment, Defence Equipment and Support)*
Pope, N., CBE *(Chief of the Defence Staff's Strategic Communications Officer)*
Norton, G., CBE *(GOC London District and Maj.-Gen. Commanding, The Household Division)*

CONSTITUTION OF THE ARMY

The army consists of the Regular Army, the Regular Reserve and the Territorial Army (TA). It is commanded by the Chief of the General Staff, who is the professional Head of Service and Chair of the Executive Committee of the Army Board, which provides overall strategic policy and direction to the Commander-in-Chief Land Forces. There are four subordinate commands that report to the Commander-in-Chief Land Forces: the Field Army; Personnel and Support Command, headed by the Adjutant-General; Force Development and Training Command and the Joint Helicopter Command. The army is divided into functional arms and services, subdivided into regiments and corps (listed below in order of precedence). During 2008, as part of the Future Army Structure (FAS) reform programme, the infantry was re-structured into large multi-battalion regiments, which involved amalgamations and changes in title for some regiments.

Members of the public can write for general information to Headquarters Adjutant General Secretariat, Trenchard Lines, Upavon, Wiltshire SN9 6BE. All enquiries with regard to records of serving personnel (Regular and Territorial Army) should be directed to The Army Personnel Centre Help Desk, Kentigern House, 65 Brown Street, Glasgow G2 8EX T 0141-224 2023/3303. Enquirers should note that the Army is governed in the release of personal information by various acts of parliament.

ORDER OF PRECEDENCE OF CORPS AND REGIMENTS OF THE BRITISH ARMY

ARMS

HOUSEHOLD CAVALRY
The Life Guards
The Blues and Royals (Royal Horse Guards and 1st Dragoons)

ROYAL HORSE ARTILLERY
(when on parade, the Royal Horse Artillery take precedence over the Household Cavalry)

ROYAL ARMOURED CORPS
1st the Queen's Dragoon Guards
The Royal Scots Dragoon Guards (Carabiniers and Greys)
The Royal Dragoon Guards
The Queen's Royal Hussars (The Queen's Own and Royal Irish)
9th/12th Royal Lancers (Prince of Wales')
The King's Royal Hussars
The Light Dragoons
The Queen's Royal Lancers
1st Royal Tank Regiment
2nd Royal Tank Regiment

ROYAL REGIMENT OF ARTILLERY
(with the exception of the Royal Horse Artillery *(see above)*)

CORPS OF ROYAL ENGINEERS

ROYAL CORPS OF SIGNALS

REGIMENTS OF FOOT GUARDS
Grenadier Guards
Coldstream Guards
Scots Guards
Irish Guards
Welsh Guards

REGIMENTS OF INFANTRY
The Royal Regiment of Scotland
The Princess of Wales' Royal Regiment (Queen and Royal Hampshire's)
The Duke of Lancaster's Regiment (King's, Lancashire and Border)
The Royal Regiment of Fusiliers
The Royal Anglian Regiment
The Rifles
The Yorkshire Regiment
The Mercian Regiment
The Royal Welsh
The Royal Irish Regiment
The Parachute Regiment
The Royal Gurkha Rifles

SPECIAL AIR SERVICE

ARMY AIR CORPS

SERVICES

ROYAL ARMY CHAPLAINS' DEPARTMENT
THE ROYAL LOGISTIC CORPS
ROYAL ARMY MEDICAL CORPS
CORPS OF ROYAL ELECTRICAL AND MECHANICAL ENGINEERS
ADJUTANT-GENERAL'S CORPS
ROYAL ARMY VETERINARY CORPS
SMALL ARMS SCHOOL CORPS
ROYAL ARMY DENTAL CORPS
INTELLIGENCE CORPS
ARMY PHYSICAL TRAINING CORPS
QUEEN ALEXANDRA'S ROYAL ARMY NURSING CORPS
CORPS OF ARMY MUSIC
THE ROYAL MONMOUTHSHIRE ROYAL ENGINEERS (MILITIA) (TA)
THE HONOURABLE ARTILLERY COMPANY (TA)
REST OF THE TERRITORIAL ARMY (TA)

ARMY EQUIPMENT

Tanks	325
Challenger 2	325
Reconnaissance vehicles	738
Fuchs	11
Jackal	400
Scimitar	327
Armoured Infantry Fighting Vehicle	526
Warrior	526
Armoured Personnel Carrier	2,059+
AFV432	646
Bulldog	380
Mastiff	277
Ridgeback	118
Saxon (Northern Ireland only)	109
Spartan	394
Warthog	115
Wolfhound	20+
Light Forces Vehicle (Panther)	401
Artillery pieces	670
Anti-tank missile†	800+
Aircraft	8*
Defender	4
King Air	4

Helicopters	298
Apache	66
Gazelle	133
Lynx	99
Unmanned aerial vehicle	450
Surface-to-air missile	338+
Land radar	157
Amphibious craft	6
Logistics and support vehicles	5

* Includes 3 King Air and 1 Defender on order
† 2009 figure

THE TERRITORIAL ARMY (TA)

The Territorial Army is part of the UK's reserve land forces and provides support to the regular army at home and overseas. The TA is divided into three types of unit: national, regional, and sponsored. TA soldiers serving in regional units complete a minimum of 27 days training a year, comprising some evenings, weekends and an annual two-week camp. National units normally specialise in a specific role or trade, such as logistics, IT, communications or medical services. Members of national units have a lower level of training commitment and complete 19 days training a year. Sponsored reserves are individuals who will serve, as members of the workforce of a company contracted to the MoD, in a military capacity and have agreed to accept a reserve liability to be called up for active service in a crisis. The TA's total strength is around 35,000.

QUEEN ALEXANDRA'S ROYAL ARMY NURSING CORPS

The Queen Alexandra's Royal Army Nursing Corps (QARANC) was founded in 1902 as Queen Alexandra's Imperial Military Nursing Service and gained its present title in 1949. The QARANC has trained nurses for the register since 1950 and also trains and employs health care assistants to Level 2 NVQ, with the option to train to Level 3. The corps recruits qualified nurses as officers and other ranks and in 1992 male nurses already serving in the army were transferred to the QARANC.

Colonel-in-Chief, HRH The Countess of Wessex
Colonels Commandant, Col. Rosemary Kennedy, TD;
    Col. Bridget McEvilly, CBE

THE ROYAL AIR FORCE

In Order of Seniority

THE QUEEN

MARSHAL OF THE ROYAL AIR FORCE
HRH The Prince Philip, Duke of Edinburgh, KG, KT, OM, GBE, AC, QSO, PC, *apptd* 1953

FORMER CHIEFS OF THE AIR STAFF

MARSHALS OF THE ROYAL AIR FORCE
Sir Michael Beetham, GCB, CBE, DFC, AFC, *apptd* 1982
Sir Keith Williamson, GCB, AFC, *apptd* 1985
Lord Craig of Radley, GCB, OBE, *apptd* 1988

AIR CHIEF MARSHALS
Sir Michael Graydon, GCB, CBE, *apptd* 1991
Sir Richard Johns, GCB, KCVO, OBE, *apptd* 1994
Sir Peter Squire, GCB, DFC, AFC *apptd* 1999
Sir Glenn Torpy, GCB, CBE, DSO *apptd* 2006

AIR RANK LIST

AIR CHIEF MARSHALS
HRH The Prince of Wales, KG, KT, GCB, OM, AK, QSO, PC, ADC
Dalton, Sir Stephen, KCB, ADC *(Chief of the Air Staff)*
Bryant, Sir Simon, KCB, CBE, ADC *(Commander-in-Chief, Air Command)*

AIR MARSHALS
Peach, Sir Stuart, KCB, CBE *(Chief of Joint Operations)*
Walker, D., CB, CBE, AFC *(Deputy Cdr Joint Force Command, Brunssum)*
Nickols, C., CB, CBE *(Chief of Defence Intelligence)*
Harper, Sir Christopher, KBE, *(UK Military Representative to NATO and the EU)*
Leeson, K., CBE *(Chief of Materiel (Air)/Air Member for Materiel)*
Pulford, A., CBE *(Deputy Commander-in-Chief Personnel and Air Member for Personnel, Air Command)*
Garwood, R., CB *(Deputy Commander-in-Chief Operations, Air Command)*
Hillier, S., CBE, DFC *(Deputy Chief of the Defence Staff (Capability))*

AIR VICE-MARSHALS
Ness, C., CB *(Director of Technical Airworthiness in the Military Aviation Authority)*
Walker, Sir David, KCVO, OBE, MVO *(Master of the Royal Household)*
Bollom, S., CB *(Director Combat (Air) Defence Equipment and Support)*
Wiles, M., CBE, *(Executive Officer, HQ Air Command)*
Dixon, C., CB, OBE *(Cdr Joint Helicopter Command)*
Evans, C., QHP *(Cdr Joint Medical Command)*
Harwood, M., CBE *(Head of the British Defence Staff, USA and Defence Attaché)*
Bagwell, G., CBE *(Chief of Staff, Joint Warfare Development, Permanent Joint HQ)*
Stacey, G., CB, MBE *(Cdr British Forces Cyprus)*
Lloyd, M., *(Chief of Staff Personnel and Air Secretary)*

North, B., OBE *(Assistant Chief of the Air Staff)*
Irvine, L., *(Director RAF Legal Services)*
Bates, B., CBE *(Senior Directing Staff (Air), Royal College of Defence Studies)*
Young, J., OBE *(Chief of Staff (Support))*
Morris, C., QHS *(Chief of Staff Health and Director-General Medical Services (RAF))*
Pentland, R., QHC *(Chaplain Chief (RAF))*
Bushell, C., *(Director of the Oman Typhoon Project Team, UK Trade and Investment Defence and Security Organisation)*
Colley, M., OBE *(Assistant Chief of the Defence Staff Concepts and Doctrine)*
Green, M., CBE *(Air Officer Commanding, No. 22 Group/Chief of Staff Training)*
Murray, D., OBE *(Assistant Chief of the Defence Staff (Personnel) and Defence Services Secretary)*
Lock, R., CBE *(Commandant Joint Services Command and Staff College)*
Osborn, P., CBE *(Air Officer Commanding No. 2 Group)*
Bell, S. *Director-General Saudi Armed Forces Project)*
Howard, G. *(Assistant Chief of the Defence Staff Logistics Operations)*
Atha, S., DSO *(Air Officer Commanding No. 1 Group)*

CONSTITUTION OF THE RAF

The RAF consists of a single command, Air Command, based at RAF High Wycombe. RAF Air Command was formed on 1 April 2007 from the amalgamation of Strike Command and Personnel and Training Command.

Air Command consists of three groups, each organised around specific operational duties. No. 1 Group is the coordinating organisation for the tactical fast-jet forces responsible for attack, offensive support and air defence operations. No. 2 Group provides air combat support including air transport and air to air refuelling; intelligence surveillance; targeting and reconnaissance; and force protection. No. 22 (Training) Group recruits personnel and provides trained specialist personnel to the RAF, as well as to the Royal Navy and the Army (*see also* Armed Forces Training and Recruitment).

RAF EQUIPMENT

Aircraft	
BAe 125	6
BAe 146	2
Dominie	9
Firefly	38
Globemaster	7
Hawk	145
Hercules	43
Islander	2
Nimrod	14
Sentinel	5
Sentry	6
Shadow	4
Super King Air (leased)	7
Tornado	105
Tristar	9
Tucano	95
Tutor	101
Typhoon	72
VC10	16

Helicopters

Chinook	41
Griffin	16
Merlin	28
Puma	34
Sea King	25
Squirrel	31

ROYAL AUXILIARY AIR FORCE

The Auxiliary Air Force was formed in 1924 to train an elite corps of civilians to serve their country in flying squadrons in their spare time. In 1947 the force was awarded the prefix 'royal' in recognition of its distinguished war service and the Sovereign's Colour for the Royal Auxiliary Air Force (RAuxAF) was presented in 1989. The RAuxAF continues to recruit civilians who undertake military training in their spare time to support the Royal Air Force in times of emergency or war.

Air Commodore-in-Chief, HM The Queen
Honorary Inspector-General Royal Auxiliary Air Force, Air Vice-Marshal Lord Beaverbrook
Inspector Royal Auxiliary Air Force, Gp Capt. Gary Bunkell, QVRM, AE, ADC

PRINCESS MARY'S ROYAL AIR FORCE NURSING SERVICE

The Princess Mary's Royal Air Force Nursing Service (PMRAFNS) was formed on 1 June 1918 as the Royal Air Force Nursing Service. In June 1923, His Majesty King George V gave his royal assent for the Royal Air Force Nursing Service to be known as the Princess Mary's Royal Air Force Nursing Service. Men were integrated into the PMRAFNS in 1980.

Patron and Air Chief Commandant, HRH Princess Alexandra, The Hon. Lady Ogilvy, KG, GCVO
Director of Nursing Services and Matron-in-Chief, Gp Capt. Jacqueline Gross

SERVICE SALARIES

In line with the announcement made in the June 2010 Budget, all public sector workers earning £21,000 a year or less, received a pay increase of £250 for 2011–12. Those earning over £21,000 had their pay frozen for two years.

The following rates of pay apply from 1 April 2011 and are rounded to the nearest pound.

The pay rates shown are for army personnel. The rates also apply to personnel of equivalent rank and pay band in the other services (*see* below for table of relative ranks).

Rank	Annual salary
SECOND LIEUTENANT	£24,615
LIEUTENANT	
On appointment	£29,587
After 1 year in rank	£30,369
After 2 years in rank	£31,147
After 3 years in rank	£31,921
After 4 years in rank	£32,703
CAPTAIN	
On appointment	£37,916
After 1 year in rank	£38,932
After 2 years in rank	£39,959
After 3 years in rank	£40,991
After 4 years in rank	£42,011
After 5 years in rank	£43,039
After 6 years in rank	£44,059
After 7 years in rank	£44,579
After 8 years in rank	£45,090
MAJOR	
On appointment	£47,760
After 1 year in rank	£48,940
After 2 years in rank	£50,111
After 3 years in rank	£51,298
After 4 years in rank	£52,474
After 5 years in rank	£53,661
After 6 years in rank	£54,841
After 7 years in rank	£56,016
After 8 years in rank	£57,199
LIEUTENANT-COLONEL	
On appointment	£67,032
After 1 year in rank	£67,920
After 2 years in rank	£68,801
After 3 years in rank	£69,681
After 4 years in rank	£70,562
After 5 years in rank	£74,614
After 6 years in rank	£75,609
After 7 years in rank	£76,613
After 8 years in rank	£77,617
COLONEL	
On appointment	£81,310
After 1 year in rank	£82,321
After 2 years in rank	£83,336
After 3 years in rank	£84,347
After 4 years in rank	£85,357
After 5 years in rank	£86,368
After 6 years in rank	£87,379
After 7 years in rank	£88,394
After 8 years in rank	£89,408
BRIGADIER	
On appointment	£97,030
After 1 year in rank	£98,013
After 2 years in rank	£98,995
After 3 years in rank	£99,973
After 4 years in rank	£100,964

PAY SYSTEM FOR SENIOR MILITARY OFFICERS

Pay rates effective from 1 April 2011 for all military officers of 2* rank and above (excluding medical and dental officers). All pay rates are rounded to the nearest pound.

Rank	Annual salary
MAJOR-GENERAL (2*)	
Scale 1	£108,201
Scale 2	£110,317
Scale 3	£112,476
Scale 4	£114,678
Scale 5	£116,924
Scale 6	£119,214
LIEUTENANT-GENERAL (3*)	
Scale 1	£125,908
Scale 2	£132,084
Scale 3	£138,569
Scale 4	£144,016
Scale 5	£148,265
Scale 6	£152,642
GENERAL (4*)	
Scale 1	£165,284
Scale 2	£169,416
Scale 3	£173,652
Scale 4	£177,993
Scale 5	£181,553
Scale 6	£185,184

Field Marshal – appointments to this rank will not usually be made in peacetime. The salary for holders of the rank is equivalent to the salary of a 5-star General, a salary created only in times of war. In peacetime, the equivalent rank to Field Marshal is the Chief of the Defence Staff. From 1 April 2011, the annual salary range for the Chief of the Defence Staff is £238,123–£252,698.

OFFICERS COMMISSIONED FROM THE SENIOR RANKS

Rank	Annual salary
Level 15	£50,680
Level 14	£50,349
Level 13	£50,000
Level 12	£49,325
Level 11	£48,653
Level 10	£47,973
Level 9	£47,298
Level 8	£46,622
Level 7*	£45,778
Level 6	£45,258
Level 5	£44,730
Level 4†	£43,686
Level 3	£43,166
Level 2	£42,633
Level 1‡	£41,593

* Officers commissioned from the ranks with more than 15 years' service enter on level 7
† Officers commissioned from the ranks with between 12 and 15 years' service enter on level 4
‡ Officers commissioned from the ranks with less than 12 years' service enter on level 1

SOLDIERS' SALARIES

Under the Pay 2000 scheme, personnel are paid in either a high or low band in accordance with how their trade has been allocated to those bands at each rank. Pay is based on trade and rank, not on individual appointment, or in response to temporary changes in role.

Rates of pay effective from 1 April 2011 (rounded to the nearest pound) are:

Rank	Lower band	Higher band
PRIVATE		
Level 1	£17,265	£17,265
Level 2	£17,736	£18,592
Level 3	£18,207	£20,500
Level 4	£19,779	£21,773
LANCE CORPORAL (levels 5–7 also applicable to Privates)		
Level 5	£20,832	£24,074
Level 6	£21,441	£25,245
Level 7	£22,358	£26,404
Level 8	£23,382	£27,592
Level 9	£24,230	£28,939
CORPORAL		
Level 1	£26,404	£27,592
Level 2	£27,592	£28,939
Level 3	£28,939	£30,356
Level 4	£29,160	£31,064
Level 5	£29,389	£31,814
Level 6	£29,623	£32,473
Level 7	£29,840	£33,182

Rank	Lower band	Higher band
SERGEANT		
Level 1	£30,012	£32,756
Level 2	£30,798	£33,603
Level 3	£31,592	£34,455
Level 4	£31,892	£34,889
Level 5	£32,723	£35,569
Level 6	£33,853	£36,249
Level 7	£34,111	£36,929
STAFF SERGEANT		
Level 1	£33,223	£36,953
Level 2	£33,657	£37,846
Level 3	£34,750	£38,751
Level 4	£35,565	£39,648
WARRANT OFFICER II (levels 5–7 also applicable to Staff Sergeants)		
Level 5	£36,048	£40,549
Level 6	£37,678	£41,445
Level 7	£38,255	£42,043
Level 8	£38,751	£42,641
Level 9	£39,627	£43,251
WARRANT OFFICER I		
Level 1	£38,599	£42,080
Level 2	£39,349	£42,907
Level 3	£40,143	£43,644
Level 4	£40,938	£44,447
Level 5	£41,737	£45,242
Level 6	£42,907	£46,048
Level 7	£44,119	£46,783

RELATIVE RANK – ARMED FORCES

Royal Navy	Army	Royal Air Force
1 Admiral of the Fleet	1 Field Marshal	1 Marshal of the RAF
2 Admiral (Adm.)	2 General (Gen.)	2 Air Chief Marshal
3 Vice-Admiral (Vice-Adm.)	3 Lieutenant-General (Lt.-Gen.)	3 Air Marshal
4 Rear-Admiral (Rear-Adm.)	4 Major-General (Maj.-Gen.)	4 Air Vice-Marshal
5 Commodore (Cdre)	5 Brigadier (Brig.)	5 Air Commodore (Air Cdre)
6 Captain (Capt.)	6 Colonel (Col.)	6 Group Captain (Gp Capt.)
7 Commander (Cdr)	7 Lieutenant-Colonel (Lt.-Col.)	7 Wing Commander (Wg Cdr)
8 Lieutenant-Commander (Lt.-Cdr)	8 Major (Maj.)	8 Squadron Leader (Sqn Ldr)
9 Lieutenant (Lt.)	9 Captain (Capt.)	9 Flight Lieutenant (Flt Lt)
10 Sub-Lieutenant (Sub-Lt.)	10 Lieutenant (Lt.)	10 Flying Officer (FO)
11 Midshipman	11 Second Lieutenant (2nd Lt.)	11 Pilot Officer (PO)

SERVICE RETIRED PAY
on compulsory retirement

Those who leave the services having served at least five years, but not long enough to qualify for the appropriate immediate pension, now qualify for a preserved pension and terminal grant, both of which are payable at age 60. The tax-free resettlement grants shown below are payable on release to those who qualify for a preserved pension and who have completed nine years' service from age 21 (officers) or 12 years from age 18 (other ranks).

The annual rates for army personnel are given. The rates also apply to personnel of equivalent rank in the other services, including the nursing services.

OFFICERS

Applicable to officers who give full pay service on the active list on or after 31 March 2011. Pensionable earnings for senior officers (*) is defined as the total amount of basic pay received during the year ending on the day prior to retirement, or the amount of basic pay received during any 12-month period within 3 years prior to retirement, whichever is the higher. Figures for senior officers are percentage rates of pensionable earnings on final salary arrangements on or after 31 March 2011.

No. of years reckonable service	Capt. and below	Major	Lt.-Col.	Colonel	Brigadier	Major-General*	Lieutenant-General*	General*
16	£12,557	£14,955	£19,608	£23,751	£28,214	—	—	—
17	£13,135	£15,665	£20,610	£24,840	£29,313	—	—	—
18	£13,714	£16,376	£21,612	£25,930	£30,413	—	—	—
19	£14,293	£17,086	£22,614	£27,019	£31,513	—	—	—
20	£14,872	£17,797	£23,616	£28,109	£32,613	—	—	—
21	£15,450	£18,507	£24,618	£29,199	£33,713	—	—	—
22	£16,029	£19,217	£25,620	£30,288	£34,813	—	—	—
23	£16,608	£19,928	£26,622	£31,378	£35,913	—	—	—
24	£17,187	£20,638	£27,624	£32,467	£37,013	38.5%	—	—
25	£17,765	£21,348	£28,626	£33,557	£38,113	39.7%	—	—
26	£18,344	£22,059	£29,628	£34,646	£39,213	40.8%	—	—
27	£18,923	£22,769	£30,630	£35,736	£40,313	42.0%	42.0%	—
28	£19,502	£23,480	£31,632	£36,826	£41,413	43.1%	43.1%	—
29	£20,080	£24,190	£32,634	£37,915	£42,513	44.3%	44.3%	—
30	£20,659	£24,900	£33,636	£39,005	£43,613	45.4%	45.4%	45.4%
31	£21,238	£25,611	£34,638	£40,094	£44,713	46.6%	46.6%	46.6%
32	£21,817	£26,321	£35,640	£41,184	£45,813	47.7%	47.7%	47.7%
33	£22,395	£27,031	£36,642	£42,273	£46,913	48.9%	48.9%	48.9%
34	£22,974	£27,742	£37,644	£43,363	£48,012	50.0%	50.0%	50.0%

WARRANT OFFICERS, NCOS AND PRIVATES
(Applicable to soldiers who give full pay service on or after 31 March 2011)

No. of years reckonable service	Below Corporal	Corporal	Sergeant	Staff Sergeant	Warrant Officer Level II	Warrant Officer Level I
22	£7,431	£9,586	£10,509	£11,971	£12,781	£13,590
23	£7,690	£9,920	£10,876	£12,389	£13,227	£14,065
24	£7,950	£10,255	£11,243	£12,807	£13,673	£14,539
25	£8,209	£10,590	£11,610	£13,225	£14,119	£15,014
26	£8,469	£10,924	£11,977	£13,643	£14,565	£15,488
27	£8,728	£11,259	£12,344	£14,061	£15,011	£15,962
28	£8,987	£11,593	£12,710	£14,479	£15,458	£16,437
29	£9,247	£11,928	£13,077	£14,896	£15,904	£16,911
30	£9,506	£12,263	£13,444	£15,314	£16,350	£17,385
31	£9,765	£12,597	£13,811	£15,732	£16,796	£17,860
32	£10,025	£12,932	£14,178	£16,150	£17,242	£18,334
33	£10,284	£13,266	£14,545	£16,568	£17,688	£18,809
34	£10,544	£13,601	£14,911	£16,986	£18,134	£19,283
35	£10,803	£13,935	£15,278	£17,404	£18,580	£19,757
36	£11,062	£14,270	£15,645	£17,821	£19,026	£20,232
37	£11,322	£14,605	£16,012	£18,239	£19,473	£20,706

GRANTS AND GRATUITIES

Terminal grants are in each case three times the rate of retired pay or pension. There are special rates of retired pay for certain other ranks not shown above. Lower rates are payable in cases of voluntary retirement.

A gratuity of £4,270 is payable for officers with short service commissions for each year completed. Resettlement grants are £14,686 for officers and £10,038 for other ranks.

EDUCATION

THE UK EDUCATION SYSTEM

The structure of the education system in the UK is a devolved matter with each of the countries of the UK having separate systems under separate governments. There are differences between the school systems in terms of the curriculum, examinations and final qualifications and, at university level, in terms of the nature of some degrees and the matter of tuition fees. The systems in England, Wales and Northern Ireland are similar and have more in common with one another than the Scottish system, which differs significantly.

Education in England is overseen by the Department for Education (DfE) (formed by the coalition government on 12 May 2010 to replace the former government's Department for Children, Schools and Families (DCSF)) and by the Department for Business, Innovation and Skills (BIS).

In Wales, responsibility for education lies with the Department for Children, Education, Lifelong Learning and Skills (DCELLS) within the Welsh government. Ministers in the Scottish government are responsible for education in Scotland, led by the directorates of Learning and Lifelong Learning, while in Northern Ireland responsibility lies with the Department of Education (DENI) and the Department for Employment and Learning (DELNI) within the Northern Ireland government.

DEPARTMENT FOR EDUCATION T 0370-000 2288
  W www.education.gov.uk
DEPARTMENT FOR BUSINESS, INNOVATION AND
  SKILLS T 020-7215 5000 W www.bis.gov.uk
DEPARTMENT FOR CHILDREN, EDUCATION,
  LIFELONG LEARNING AND SKILLS (DCELLS)
  T 0300-060 3300; 0845-010 3300
  W www.wales.gov.uk/topics/educationandskills
SCOTTISH GOVERNMENT – EDUCATION
  T 08457-741741; 0131-556 8400
  W www.scotland.gov.uk/Topics/Education
DEPARTMENT OF EDUCATION (NI) T 028-9127 9279
  W www.deni.gov.uk
DEPARTMENT FOR EMPLOYMENT AND
  LEARNING (NI) T 028-9025 7777 W www.delni.gov.uk

RECENT DEVELOPMENTS
Many changes affecting the education sector in England have been introduced or announced by the Conservative and Liberal Democrat coalition government that took office in May 2010. These include:

- introducing a 'pupil premium' to allocate more money directly to poorer pupils and free early years care for two-year-olds from disadvantaged families
- enabling more schools to become academies and parent/teacher groups to set up 'free schools'
- giving schools greater autonomy
- giving teachers more disciplinary powers and restricting public reporting of allegations against teachers
- changing school inspection to focus on four core areas of achievement: teaching, leadership and management, behaviour and safety

- abolishing five bodies – the Qualifications and Curriculum Development Agency, the General Teaching Council for England, the Training and Development Agency for Schools, the School Support Staff Negotiating Body and the Young People's Learning Agency
- replacing the Education Maintenance Allowance, which paid 16- to 19-year-olds from low income families up to £30 a week to carry on studying, with a new bursary scheme

Schools will also be affected by the final outcomes of reviews of: the primary and secondary National Curriculum and associated programmes of study; national testing at the end of primary school; the Early Years Foundation Stage; music education; and arrangements for pupils with special educational needs.

Changes have been announced in teacher recruitment and training. From September 2012 only graduates with a 2:2 degree or above will be eligible for funding and trainees' basic skills will be tested at the start of courses. The Teach First scheme will double its intake, more ex-armed forces personnel will be sponsored to become teachers and in-school training will be increased.

Changes affecting higher education have been the most controversial. Cuts in funding mean that universities and colleges will cease to receive grants for teaching students starting courses from September 2012 – with the exception of science, technology and engineering courses. The government's decision to allow universities to compensate by raising tuition fees to a maximum of £9,000 a year led to protests by students and university staff. Government hopes that only a few universities would charge the maximum rate proved optimistic when, in April 2011, most universities announced that they would be setting their fees at or near £9,000. The higher education white paper published in June 2011 made clear that, to avoid unaffordable calls on student loan funding, controls over the numbers of students allowed to start higher education courses will be implemented. However, these controls will not apply to the 65,000 or so students admitted with top A-level grades (A ,A, B or better); and 20,000 places will be reserved for universities and colleges charging average tuition fees of £7,500 or less. Universities will also only be allowed to charge fees over £6,000 if they ensure access for students from poorer families by offering fee discounts or other financial support. Students will not have to start repaying loans until their income reaches £21,000 a year (formerly £15,000) and part-time students will no longer have to pay their tuition fees up front. In addition, all students are promised better information before they apply, better teaching while at university, greater transparency in areas such as feedback on their work and better preparation for the job market.

STATE SCHOOL SYSTEM

PRE-SCHOOL
Pre-school education for children from 3 to 5 years of age is not compulsory. Parents may take as little or as much of

their entitlement as they choose, although a free place is available for every 3- and 4-year-old whose parents want one. All 3- and 4-year-olds in England are entitled to 15 hours a week of free early education over 38 weeks of the year until they reach compulsory school age (the term following their fifth birthday). This is delivered flexibly over a minimum of three days each week during normal term times. Free places are funded by local authorities and are delivered by a range of providers in the maintained and non-maintained sectors – nursery schools; nursery classes in primary schools; private schools; private day nurseries; voluntary playgroups; pre-schools; and registered childminders. In order to receive funding, providers must be working towards the early learning goals and other features of the Early Years Foundation Stage curriculum (though this curriculum is being reviewed and may change), must be inspected on a regular basis by Ofsted and must meet any conditions set by the local authority.

In Wales, every child is entitled to receive free Foundation Phase education for a minimum of two hours a day from the term following their third birthday.

In Scotland, councils have a duty to provide a pre-school education for all 3- and 4-year-olds whose parents request one. Education authorities must offer each child 475 hours of free pre-school education a year (less for children who start pre-school later in the year), although they may provide more if they choose. This is usually delivered as five 2.5 hour sessions a week.

In Northern Ireland, there are now free, part-time nursery places available for all 3- and 4-year-old children in their final pre-school year. Most places offer 2.5 hours a day, five days a week for 38 weeks a year.

PRIMARY AND SECONDARY SCHOOLS

By law, full-time education starts at the age of five for children in England, Scotland and Wales and at the age of four in Northern Ireland. In practice, most children in the UK start school before their fifth birthday: in England from 2011 all children will be entitled to a primary school place from the September after their fourth birthday. In all parts of the UK, compulsory schooling ends at age 16, but children born between certain dates may leave school before their 16th birthday. Most young people stay in some form of education until 17 or 18. From 2013, all pupils in England will be required to continue in education or training to 17 years and from 2015, to 18 years. Primary education consists mainly of infant schools for children aged 5 to 7, junior schools for those aged 7 to 11, and combined infant and junior schools for both age groups.

First schools in some parts of England cater for ages 5 to 10 as the first stage of a three-tier system of first (lower), middle and secondary (upper) schools. Scotland has only primary schools with no infant/junior division.

Children usually leave primary school and move on to secondary school at the age of 11 (or 12 in Scotland). In the few areas of England that have a three-tier system of schools, middle schools cater for children after they leave first schools for three to four years between the ages of 8 and 14, depending on the local authority.

Secondary schools cater for children aged 11 to 16 and, if they have a sixth form, for those who choose to stay on to age 17 or 18. From the age of 16, students may move instead to further education colleges or work-based training.

Most UK secondary schools are co-educational. The largest secondary schools have more than 1,500 pupils

and around 60 per cent of pupils in the UK are in schools that take more than 1,000 pupils.

Most state-maintained secondary schools in England, Wales and Scotland are comprehensive schools, whose admission arrangements are made without reference to ability or aptitude. In England there remain some areas with grammar schools, catering for pupils aged 11 to 18, which select pupils on the basis of high academic ability. Northern Ireland continues to have many grammar schools, though this is changing – see below.

More than 90 per cent of pupils in the UK attend publicly funded schools and receive free education. The rest attend privately funded 'independent' schools, which charge fees, or are educated at home. No fees are charged by any publicly maintained school in England, Wales or Scotland. In Northern Ireland, fees may be charged in the preparatory classes of grammar schools.

The bulk of the UK government's expenditure on school education is through local authorities (Education and Library Boards in Northern Ireland), who pass on state funding to schools and other educational institutions.

SPECIAL EDUCATION

Schools and local authorities in England and Wales, Education and Library Boards (ELBs) in Northern Ireland and education authorities in Scotland are required to identify and secure provision for children with special educational needs and to involve parents in decisions. Where appropriate, and taking parents' wishes into account, children with special educational needs are educated in ordinary mainstream schools, sometimes with supplementary help from outside specialists. Parents of children with special educational needs (referred to as additional support needs in Scotland) have a right of appeal to independent tribunals if their wishes are not met.

Special educational needs provision may be made in maintained special schools, special units attached to mainstream schools or in mainstream classes themselves, all funded by local authorities. There are also non-maintained special schools run by voluntary bodies, mainly charities, who may receive grants from central government for capital expenditure and equipment but whose other costs are met primarily from the fees charged to local authorities for pupils placed in the schools. Some independent schools also provide education wholly or mainly for children with special educational needs.

ADDITIONAL SUPPORT NEEDS TRIBUNALS FOR SCOTLAND T 0845-120 2906
W www.asntscotland.gov.uk
FIRST-TIER TRIBUNAL (SPECIAL EDUCATIONAL NEEDS AND DISABILITY) T 01325-392760
W www.justice.gov.uk/guidance/courts-and-tribunals/tribunals/send/index.htm
SPECIAL EDUCATIONAL NEEDS TRIBUNAL FOR WALES T 01597-829800 W http://wales.gov.uk/sentwsub

HOME EDUCATION

In England and Wales parents have the right to educate their children at home and do not have to be qualified teachers to do so. Home-educated children do not have to follow the National Curriculum or take national tests nor do they need a fixed timetable, formal lessons or to observe school hours, days or terms. However, by law parents must ensure that the home education provided is full-time and suitable for the child's age, ability and aptitude and, if appropriate, to any special educational needs. Parents have no legal obligation to notify the local authority that a child is being educated at home, but if they take a child out of school, they must notify the school in writing and the school must report this to the local authority. Local authorities can make informal enquiries of parents to establish that a suitable education is being provided. For children in special schools, parents must seek the consent of the local authority before taking steps to educate them at home.

In Northern Ireland, Education and Library Boards monitor the quality of home provision and provide general guidance on appropriate materials and exam types through regular home visits.

The home schooling law in Scotland is similar to that of England. One difference, however, is that if parents wish to take a child out of school they must have permission from the local education authority.

HOME EDUCATION ADVISORY SERVICE
T 01707-371854 W www.heas.org.uk
HOME EDUCATION IN NORTHERN IRELAND
W www.hedni.org
SCHOOLHOUSE HOME EDUCATION
ASSOCIATION (SCOTLAND) T 01307-463120
W www.schoolhouse.org.uk

FURTHER EDUCATION

In the UK, further education (FE) is generally understood as post-secondary education: ie any education undertaken after an individual leaves school that is below higher education level. FE therefore embraces a wide range of general and vocational study undertaken by people of all ages from 16 upwards, full-time or part-time, who may be self-funded, employer-funded or state-funded.

FE in the UK is often undertaken at further education colleges, although some takes place on employers' premises. Many of these colleges offer some courses at higher education level; some FE colleges teach certain subjects to 14- to 16-year-olds under collaborative arrangements with schools. Colleges' income comes from public funding, student fees and work for and with employers.

HIGHER EDUCATION

Higher education (HE) in the UK describes courses of study, provided in universities, specialist colleges of higher education and in some FE colleges, where the level of instruction is above that of A-level or equivalent exams.

All UK universities and colleges that provide HE are autonomous bodies with their own internal systems of governance. They are not owned by the state. However, most receive a portion of their income from state funds distributed by the separate HE funding councils for England, Scotland and Wales, and the Department for Employment and Learning in Northern Ireland. The rest of their income comes from a number of sources including fees from home and overseas students, government funding for research, endowments and work with or for business.

EXPENDITURE

UK-MANAGED EXPENDITURE ON EDUCATION
(Real terms) £bn

2001–2	61.8	2006–7	76.9
2002–3	64.0	2007–8	80.1
2003–4	69.4	2008–9	82.6
2004–5	72.0	2009–10	88.6
2005–6	75.7	2010–11 (est)	90.6

Source: Public Expenditure Statistical Analyses (PESA) 2011

SCHOOLS

ENGLAND AND WALES

In England and Wales, publicly funded schools are referred to as 'state schools'. The four main categories of state school – community, foundation, voluntary-aided and voluntary-controlled – are maintained by local authorities, which have a duty to ensure there is a suitable place for every school-age child resident in their area. Each school has a governing body, made up of volunteers elected or appointed by parents, staff, the community and the local authority, which is responsible for strategic management, ensuring accountability, monitoring school performance, setting budgets and appointing the headteacher and senior staff. The headteacher is responsible for the school's day-to-day management and operations and for decisions requiring professional teaching expertise.

In *Community schools*, which are non-denominational, local authorities are the employers of the staff, own the land and buildings and set the admissions criteria.

In *Foundation schools*, the governing body employs staff and sets the admissions criteria. The land and buildings are usually owned by the governing body or a charitable foundation. A foundation school may have a religious character, although most do not. A *trust school* is a distinct type of foundation school that forms a charitable trust with an outside partner – for example, a business, a university, an educational charity or simply another school – that shares the school's aspirations. The decision to become a trust school is taken by the governing body while taking account of parents' views. Community schools can take on foundation status and set up a trust in a single process.

Most *voluntary-aided schools* are religious schools founded by Christian denominations or other faiths. As with foundation schools, the governing body employs the staff and sets the admissions criteria, which may include priority for members of the faith or denomination. The school buildings and land are normally owned and provided by a charitable foundation, often a religious organisation, which appoints a majority of the school's governors and makes a small contribution to major building costs.

Voluntary-controlled schools are similar to voluntary-aided schools in that they often have a particular religious ethos, commonly Church of England, and the school land and buildings are normally owned by a charity. However, as with community schools, the local authority employs the school's staff, sets the admissions criteria and bears all the costs.

Among the local authority-maintained schools are some with particular characteristics:

- *Community and foundation special schools* cater for children with specific special educational needs, which may include physical disabilities or learning difficulties
- *Grammar schools* are secondary schools catering for pupils aged 11 to 18 that select all of their pupils based on academic ability. In England there are 164 grammar schools, concentrated in certain local authority areas. Wales has none
- *Maintained boarding schools* are state-funded and offer free tuition but charge fees for board and lodging

In Wales, Welsh-medium primary and secondary schools were first established in the 1950s and 1960s, originally in response to the wishes of Welsh-speaking parents who wanted their children to be educated through the medium of the Welsh language. Now, many children who are not from Welsh-speaking homes also attend Welsh-medium and bilingual schools throughout Wales. Welsh language education has become increasingly important following the Welsh government's vision of creating a bilingual Wales. The latest statistics show that Wales has 428 Welsh-medium primary schools, where the main or sole medium of instruction is in the Welsh language, and 34 Welsh-medium secondary schools, where more than half of foundation subjects (other than English and Welsh) and religious education are taught wholly or partly in Welsh.

England now has increasing numbers of schools that are publicly funded and charge no fees but are not local authority-maintained. Almost all of these are *Academies*, sometimes called 'independent state schools'. Academies are all-ability schools set up by sponsors from business, faith or voluntary groups in partnership with the Department for Education. Together they fund the land and buildings, with the government covering the running costs at a level comparable to other local schools. The new coalition government has introduced legislation to enable more schools, including primaries for the first time, to apply for academy status in order to leave local authority control and have greater freedom over what they teach, the pay and conditions of their teachers and how they organise schooling. As at June 2011 there were 704 academies, of which 100 were primaries and 10 were 'all-through' schools taking pupils aged 3 or 5 to 18.

SCOTLAND

Most schools in Scotland, known as 'publicly funded' schools, are state-funded and charge no fees. Funding is met from resources raised by the Scottish local authorities and from an annual grant from the Scottish government. Scotland does not have school governing bodies like the rest of the UK: local authorities retain greater responsibility for the management and performance of publicly funded schools. Headteachers manage at least 80 per cent of a school's budget, covering staffing, furnishings, repairs, supplies, services and energy costs. Expenditure on new buildings, modernisation projects and equipment is financed by the local authority within the limits set by the Scottish government.

Scotland has approaching 400 state-funded *faith schools*, the majority of which are Catholic. It has no grammar schools.

Integrated community schools form part of the Scottish government's strategy to promote social inclusion and to raise educational standards. They encourage closer and better joint working among education, health and social work agencies and professionals, greater pupil and parental involvement in schools, and improved support and service provision for vulnerable children and young people.

Scotland has a number of *grant-aided schools* that are independent of local authorities but supported financially by the Scottish government. These schools are managed by boards and most of them provide education for children and young people with special educational needs.

NORTHERN IRELAND

Most schools in Northern Ireland are maintained by the state and generally charge no fees, though fees may be charged in preparatory departments of some grammar schools. There are different types of state-funded schools,

each under the control of management committees, which also employ the teachers.

Controlled schools (nursery, primary, special, secondary and grammar schools) are managed by Northern Ireland's five ELBs through boards of governors which consist of teachers, parents, members of the ELB and transferor representatives (mainly from the Protestant churches).

Catholic maintained schools (nursery, primary, special and secondary) are under the management of boards of governors that consist of teachers, parents and members nominated by the employing authority, the Council for Catholic Maintained Schools (CCMS).

Other maintained schools (primary, special and secondary) are, in the main, Irish-medium schools that provide education in an Irish-speaking environment. The Department of Education has a duty to encourage and facilitate the development of Irish-medium education. Northern Ireland has more than 20 standalone Irish-medium schools, most of them primary schools, and around a dozen Irish-medium units attached to English-medium host schools.

Voluntary schools are mainly grammar schools, which select pupils according to academic ability. They are managed by boards of governors consisting of teachers, parents and, in most cases, representatives from the Department of Education and the ELB.

Integrated schools (primary and secondary) educate pupils from both the Protestant and Catholic communities as well as those of other faiths and no faith; each school is managed by a board of governors. There are at present 62 integrated schools maintained by the state, 24 of which are controlled schools.

In 2008 Northern Ireland's Minister for Education proposed a phased ending of grammar schools' academic selection over a three-year period, but these proposals did not attract the necessary level of support to become law. As a result, post-primary transfer arrangements for September 2010 admissions were unregulated, although informed by guidance from the Department of Education which did not recommend the use of academic admissions criteria. From 2013 new post-primary arrangements will guarantee all pupils access to a much wider range of courses, with a minimum of 24 courses at Key Stage 4, and 27 at post-16. At least one-third of the courses on offer will be academic and another third will be vocational. Legislation is already in place to give effect to these changes and to enable schools to enter into collaborative arrangements with other schools, FE colleges or other providers.

INDEPENDENT SCHOOLS

Around 7 per cent of the UK's schoolchildren are educated by privately funded 'independent' schools that charge fees and set their own admissions policies. Independent schools are required to meet certain minimum standards but need not teach the National Curriculum. *See also* Independent Schools.

UK SCHOOLS BY CATEGORY (2009–10)

	England	Wales
Maintained nursery schools	430	25
Maintained primary and secondary schools (total)	20,098	1,685
Community	12,024	1,415
Voluntary-aided	4,246	161
Voluntary-controlled	2,618	97
Foundation	1,210	12

Pupil referral units	443	42
Maintained special schools	979	43
*Non-maintained special schools	75	–
†Academies, including City Technology Colleges	205	–
Independent schools	2,375	64
Total	24,605	1,859

* Excludes voluntary and private pre-school education centres
† Figure includes two hospital schools
Source: DfE; Welsh government

Scotland

Publicly funded schools (total)	2,667
Primary	2,119
Secondary	372
Special	176
Independent schools (total)*	159
Primary	59
Secondary	55
Special	45
Total	2,867

* 2008–9 figures
Source: Scottish government

Northern Ireland

State-maintained nursery schools	98
State-maintained primary and secondary schools (total)	1,068
Controlled	460
Voluntary	52
Catholic maintained	470
Other maintained	25
Integrated	61
Special schools	41
Independent schools	14
Total	1,221

Source: DENI

INSPECTION

ENGLAND

The Office for Standards in Education, Children's Services and Skills (Ofsted) is the main body responsible for inspecting education in English schools. As well as inspecting all publicly funded and some independent schools, Ofsted inspects a range of other services in England, including childcare, children's homes, pupil referral units, local authority children's services, further education, initial teacher training and publicly funded adult skills training.

Ofsted is an independent, non-ministerial government department that reports directly to parliament, headed by Her Majesty's Chief Inspector (HMCI). Ofsted is required to promote improvement in the public services that it inspects; ensure that these services focus on the interests of their users – children, parents, learners and employers; and see that these services are efficient, effective and promote value for money. The education bill of January 2011 established that Ofsted will now focus only on four core elements of schools – pupil achievement, teaching, leadership, and behaviour and safety (*see* also Recent Developments).

Ofsted publishes the findings of its inspection reports, its recommendations and statistical information on its website.

OFFICE FOR STANDARDS IN EDUCATION, CHILDREN'S SERVICES AND SKILLS
T 0300-123 1231 W www.ofsted.gov.uk

WALES

Estyn is the office of Her Majesty's Inspectorate for Education and Training in Wales. It is independent of, but funded by, the Welsh government and is led by Her Majesty's Chief Inspector of Education and Training in Wales.

Estyn's role is to inspect quality and standards in education and training in Wales, including in primary, secondary, special and independent schools, and pupil referral units, publicly funded nursery schools and settings, further education, adult community-based and work-based learning, local authorities and teacher education and training.

Estyn also provides advice on quality and standards in education and training to the Welsh government and others and its remit includes making public good practice based on inspection evidence. Estyn publishes the findings of its inspection reports, its recommendations and statistical information on its website.

HER MAJESTY'S INSPECTORATE FOR EDUCATION AND TRAINING IN WALES
T 029-2044 6446 W www.estyn.gov.uk

SCOTLAND

HM Inspectorate of Education (HMIE) merged with Learning and Teaching Scotland in July 2011 to become Education Scotland, an executive agency of the Scottish government. Education Scotland operates independently and impartially while being directly accountable to Scottish ministers for the standards of its work. The new agency's core business will continue to be inspection and review. It is responsible for delivering measurable year-on-year improvements, with maximum efficiency, by promoting excellence, building on strengths, and identifying and addressing under-performance.

Education Scotland is also responsible for supporting learners and their parents or carers and all those working in education. It will contribute to and support policy development, working with Scottish ministers and government officials who will continue to set policy and strategy for the education system at a national level.

Services it is responsible for include inspecting or reviewing all schools, pre-school centres, further education colleges, local authorities, teacher education and publicly funded training programmes. The agency will also take over responsibility for the Curriculum for Excellence Management Board and Excellence Groups from October 2011 and support continuing professional development at a national level. It will publish the findings of its inspection reports and reviews, its recommendations, examples of good practice and statistical information on its website.

EDUCATION SCOTLAND T 0141 282 5000
W www.educationscotland.gov.uk

NORTHERN IRELAND

The Education and Training Inspectorate (ETINI) provides inspection services for the Department of Education Northern Ireland, the Department for Employment and Learning, the Department of Culture, Arts and Leisure and Criminal Justice Inspection Northern Ireland. Its role is to promote improvement in the interests of all learners, through inspections and the dissemination of its findings.

ETINI carries out inspections of all schools, pre-school services, special education, further education colleges, initial teacher training, training organisations, and curriculum advisory and support services.

The inspectorate provides evidence-based advice to ministers in order to assist in the formulation of policies. It publishes the findings of its inspection reports, its recommendations and statistical information on its website.

EDUCATION AND TRAINING INSPECTORATE
T 028-9127 9726 W www.etini.gov.uk

THE NATIONAL CURRICULUM

ENGLAND

The National Curriculum, first introduced in 1988, is mandatory in all state schools. It is organised into blocks of years called 'Key Stages' and sets out the core subjects that must be taught and the standards or attainment targets for each subject at each Key Stage. In addition, there is also a mandatory curriculum for the Early Years Foundation Stage (EYFS).

The National Curriculum has four Key Stages:

- The Early Years Foundation Stage covers children from birth to age 5, or the end of Reception Year in primary school
- Key Stage 1 covers Years 1 and 2 of primary school, for children aged 5–7
- Key Stage 2 covers Years 3 to 6 of primary school, for children aged 7–11
- Key Stage 3 covers Years 7 to 9 of secondary school, for children aged 11–14
- Key Stage 4 covers Years 10 and 11 of secondary school, for children aged 14–16

Within the framework of the National Curriculum, schools may plan and organise teaching and learning in the way that best meets the needs of their pupils. However, the government is reviewing both EYFS and the National Curriculum for 5- to 16-year-olds (*see* also Recent Developments).

The present EYFS learning and development requirement, which all schools, nurseries and other registered early years providers must deliver, has three elements: the early learning goals, educational programmes and assessment arrangements. It sets out six areas covered by the early learning goals and educational programmes: personal, social and emotional development; communication, language and literacy; problem-solving, reasoning and numeracy; knowledge and understanding of the world; physical development; and creative development.

KEY STAGES 1 AND 2 COMPULSORY SUBJECTS
English
Mathematics
Science
Design and technology
Information and communication technology (ICT)
History
Geography
Art and design
Music
Physical education

Schools must also provide religious education (RE), although parents have the right to withdraw children for all or part of the RE curriculum. Schools are also advised to teach personal, social and health education (PSHE) and citizenship, together with at least one modern foreign language.

The former Labour government intended to introduce, from September 2011, a new primary curriculum, which included a requirement for children to learn a modern foreign language from the age of seven. However, the new coalition government announced in June 2010 that it would not proceed with this. The existing primary curriculum will remain in force until 2012.

The government then intends to introduce a revised National Curriculum for 5- to 16-year-olds (*see* Recent Developments), the stated aims of which are to, ensure a focus on traditional, basic subjects and give teachers more freedom in what and how they teach.

New programmes of study for English, mathematics, science and physical education will be available to schools in September 2012 and become statutory in maintained schools in September 2013. Other subjects and programmes of study will be made available in September 2013 and become statutory in 2014. Until then, in Key Stage 3, compulsory subjects include those for Key Stages 1 and 2 plus modern foreign languages and citizenship. Sex and relationship education (SRE) and RE must also be provided, as must careers education and guidance during Year 9. Parents can choose to withdraw their children from all or part of the RE curriculum and from the non-statutory elements of SRE, but not from the statutory elements of SRE which form part of the National Curriculum for science.

Pupils in Key Stage 4 study a mix of compulsory and optional subjects in preparation for national examinations such as GCSEs.

KEY STAGE 4 COMPULSORY SUBJECTS
English
Mathematics
Science
ICT
Physical education
Citizenship

Pupils also have to undertake careers education and work-related learning. Schools must also offer RE, SRE and at least one subject from each of four 'entitlement' areas: arts subjects (art and design, music, dance, drama and media arts); design and technology; humanities (history and geography); and modern foreign languages. Other subjects such as classical languages are taught when school resources permit.

For each National Curriculum subject, there is a programme of study that describes the subject knowledge, skills and understanding that pupils are expected to develop during each Key Stage.

The programmes of study also map out a scale of attainment within the subject. In most subjects, these 'attainment targets' are split into eight levels plus an 'exceptional performance' level.

Schools inform parents what National Curriculum level their children have reached in any formal assessment. Parents can use these levels to get an idea of how their child is progressing compared to what is typical for their age. For example, by the end of Key Stage 2, most will be at level 4.

Statutory assessment takes place towards the end of the EYFS, when children's level of development is compared to and recorded against a Foundation Stage Profile. National tests and tasks take place in English and mathematics at the end of Key Stages 1 and 2; all pupils in publicly funded schools in the relevant years are expected to take these tests. At Key Stage 1 the results of tasks and tests are not reported, except to parents, but are used to underpin teachers' overall assessment of pupils. At Key Stages 2 and 3, separate teacher assessments of pupils' progress are made. In Key Stage 2 this is set alongside the test results. At Key Stage 4, national examinations are the main form of assessment.

Each year the DfE publishes on its website achievement and attainment tables, showing performance measures for every school and local authority. The tables for primary schools are based mainly on the results of the tests taken by children at the end of Key Stage 2 when they are usually aged 11; since 2010 the tables also include teacher assessment results. The tables for secondary schools and for attainment post-16 rely mainly on the results of national examinations. All tables include indicators of the progress that pupils have made since their last assessment.

DEPARTMENT FOR EDUCATION T 0370-000 2288
W www.education.gov.uk

WALES

Wales has introduced a Foundation Phase curriculum for 3- to 7-year-olds. Full implementation began for 3-year-olds from September 2008, for 4-year-olds from September 2009, for 5-year-olds from September 2010 and will begin for 6-year-olds from September 2011. The emphasis is on learning-by-doing and children's skills and knowledge are planned across seven areas of learning. They are:

- Personal and social development, well-being and cultural diversity
- Language, literacy and communication skills
- Mathematical development
- Welsh language development
- Knowledge and understanding of the world
- Physical development
- Creative development

Full details of the Foundation Phase can be found in *Framework for Children's Learning for 3- to 7-year-olds in Wales*, available on the Welsh government website (*see* below).

The National Curriculum exists for 7- to 16-year-olds. Originally it was broadly similar to that of England, with distinctive characteristics for Wales reflected in the programmes of study. From September 2008 a revised school curriculum was implemented, consisting of the National Curriculum subjects together with non-statutory frameworks for personal and social education, the world of work, religious education and skills.

The National Curriculum in Wales includes the following subjects:

- *Key Stage 2* – English, Welsh, mathematics, science, design and technology, ICT, history, geography, art and design, music, and physical education
- *Key Stage 3* – as Key Stage 2, plus a modern foreign language
- *Key Stage 4* – English, Welsh, mathematics, science and physical education

Welsh is compulsory for pupils at all key stages, either as a first or as a second language. The proportion of pupils

taught Welsh as a first language rose from 16 per cent in 2009 to 16.5 per cent in 2010.

Statutory testing was removed for pupils in Wales at the end of Key Stage 2 from 2004–5. Only statutory teacher assessment remains. It is also done at the end of Key Stage 1 (in future, the Foundation Phase) and Key Stage 3, and is being strengthened by moderation and accreditation arrangements.

THE WELSH GOVERNMENT – EDUCATION AND SKILLS
W http://wales.gov.uk/topics/educationandskills/
schoolshome/curriculuminwales

SCOTLAND

The curriculum in Scotland is not prescribed by statute but is the responsibility of education authorities and individual schools. However, schools and authorities are expected to follow the Scottish government's guidance on management and delivery of the curriculum.

Advice and guidance are provided by the Scottish government primarily through new executive agency Education Scotland, after Learning and Teaching Scotland, an executive non-departmental public body sponsored by the government, merged with HMIE in May 2011.

Scotland is pursuing its biggest education reform for a generation by introducing a new curriculum – Curriculum for Excellence – which aims to provide more autonomy for teachers, greater choice and opportunity for pupils and a single coherent curriculum for all children and young people aged 3 to 18.

The purpose of Curriculum for Excellence is encapsulated in 'the four capacities': to enable each child or young person to be a successful learner, a confident individual, a responsible citizen and an effective contributor. It focuses on providing a broad curriculum that develops skills for learning, skills for life and skills for work, with a sustained focus on literacy and numeracy. The period of education from pre-school through to the end of secondary stage 3, when pupils reach age 14, has the particular purpose of providing each young person in Scotland with this broad general education.

Curriculum for Excellence sets out 'experiences and outcomes', which describe broad areas of learning and what is to be achieved within them. They are:

- Expressive arts (including art and design, dance, drama, music)
- Health and wellbeing (including physical education, food and health, relationships and sexual health, and mental, physical and social wellbeing)
- Languages
- Mathematics
- Religious and moral education
- Sciences
- Social studies (including history, geography, society and economy)
- Technologies (including business, computing, food and textiles, craft, design, engineering and graphics)

The experiences and outcomes are written at five levels with progression to examinations and qualifications during the senior phase, which covers secondary stages 4 to 6 when students are generally aged 14 to 17. The framework is designed to be flexible so that pupils can progress at their own pace.

Level	Stage
Early	The pre-school years and primary 1 (ages 3–5), or later for some
First	To the end of primary 4 (age 8), but earlier or later for some
Second	To the end of primary 7 (age 11), but earlier or later for some
Third and Fourth	Secondary 1 to secondary 3 (ages 12–14), but earlier for some. The fourth level experiences and outcomes are intended to provide possibilities for choice and young people's programmes will not include all of the Fourth level outcomes
Senior phase	Secondary 4 to secondary 6 (ages 15–18), and college or other means of study

Under the new curriculum, assessment of students' progress and achievements from ages 3 to 15 is carried out by teachers who are required to base their assessment judgements on a range of evidence rather than single assessment instruments such as tests. Teachers have access to an online National Assessment Resource (NAR) set up in 2010, which provides a range of assessment material and national exemplars across the curriculum areas.

In the senior phase, young people aged 16 to 18, including those studying outside school, build up a portfolio of national qualifications, awarded by the Scottish Qualifications Authority (SQA).

Provision is made for teaching in Gaelic in many parts of Scotland and the number of pupils, from nursery to secondary, in Gaelic-medium education is growing.

EDUCATION SCOTLAND T 0141-282 5000
W www.educationscotland.gov.uk
SCOTTISH QUALIFICATIONS AUTHORITY
T 0845-279 1000 W www.sqa.org.uk

NORTHERN IRELAND

Since September 2007 Northern Ireland has been phasing in a revised statutory curriculum that places greater emphasis than before on developing skills and preparing young people for life and work. The new curriculum has now been in place across Years 1 to 12 since September 2009.

The revised curriculum includes a new Foundation Stage to cover years one and two of primary school. This is to allow a more appropriate learning style for the youngest pupils and to ease the transition from pre-school. Key Stage 1 now covers primary years 3 and 4, until children are 8, and Key Stage 2 covers primary years 5, 6 and 7, until children are 11. At post-primary, Key Stage 3 covers Years 8, 9 and 10 and Key Stage 4 Years 11 and 12.

The revised primary curriculum is made up of RE and the following areas of learning:

• Language and literacy
• Mathematics and numeracy
• The arts
• The world around us
• Personal development and mutual understanding
• Physical education

The revised post-primary curriculum includes a new area of learning for life and work, made up of employability, personal development, local and global citizenship and home economics (at Key Stage 3). In addition, it is made up of RE and the following areas of learning:

• Language and literacy
• Mathematics and numeracy
• Modern languages
• The arts
• Environment and society
• Physical education
• Science and technology

At Key Stage 4, the statutory requirements have been significantly reduced to learning for life and work, Physical education, RE and developing skills and capabilities. The aim is to provide greater choice and flexibility for pupils and allow them access to a wider range of academic and vocational courses provided under the revised curriculum's 'entitlement framework' (EF). This should be fully in place by 2013.

From 2013, schools will be required to provide pupils with access to at least 24 courses at Key Stage 4 and at least 27 courses post-16. In both cases at least one-third of the courses must be academic and at least one-third applied (vocational/professional/technical). The remaining third is at the discretion of each school. Individual pupils decide on the number and mix of courses they wish to follow.

RE is a compulsory part of the Northern Ireland curriculum, although parents have the right to withdraw their children from part or all of RE or collective worship. Schools have to provide RE in accordance with a core syllabus drawn up by the province's four main churches (Church of Ireland, Presbyterian, Methodist and Roman Catholic) and specified by the Department of Education.

Revised assessment and reporting arrangements, expected to be fully in place by June 2012, are being introduced to support the revised curriculum. The focus from Foundation to Key Stage 3 is on 'assessment for learning'. This programme includes classroom-based teacher assessment, computer-based assessment of literacy and numeracy and pupils deciding on their strengths and weaknesses and how they might progress to achieve their potential. Assessment information is reported to parents using a new pupil profile. Pupils at Key Stage 4 and beyond continue to be assessed through public examinations.

The Council for the Curriculum, Examinations and Assessment (CCEA), a non-departmental public body reporting to the Department of Education in Northern Ireland, is unique in the UK in combining the functions of a curriculum advisory body, an awarding body and a qualifications regulatory body. It advises the government on what should be taught in Northern Ireland's schools and colleges, ensures that qualifications and examinations offered by awarding bodies in Northern Ireland are of an appropriate quality and standard and, as the leading awarding body itself, offers a range of qualifications including GCSEs, A-levels and AS-levels.

The CCEA hosts a dedicated curriculum website covering all aspects of the revised curriculum, assessment and reporting – see below.

COUNCIL FOR THE CURRICULUM,
EXAMINATIONS AND ASSESSMENT
T 028-9026 1200 W www.ccea.org.uk
NORTHERN IRELAND CURRICULUM
T 028-9028 1200 W www.nicurriculum.org.uk

QUALIFICATIONS

ENGLAND, WALES AND NORTHERN IRELAND

There is a very wide range of public examinations and qualifications available, accredited by the Office of Qualifications and Examinations Regulation (OFQUAL) in England; the Department for Children, Education, Lifelong Learning and Skills (DCELLS) in Wales; and the Council for the Curriculum, Examinations and Assessment (CCEA) in Northern Ireland. Up-to-date information on all accredited qualifications and awarding bodies is available online at the Register of Regulated Qualifications website.

The National Qualifications Framework (NQF) establishes the level of all accredited qualifications in England, Wales and Northern Ireland. The NQF comprises nine levels (entry level to level 8) and, at each level, groups together qualifications that place similar demands on individuals as learners. Entry level, for example, covers basic knowledge and skills in English, maths and ICT not geared towards specific occupations, while level 3 includes qualifications such as A-levels which are appropriate for people who plan to go to university, and level 7 covers Masters' degrees and vocational qualifications appropriate for senior professionals and managers.

Young people aged 14 to 19 in schools or (post-16) colleges or apprenticeships may gain academic qualifications such as GCSEs, AS-levels and A-levels; qualifications linked to particular career fields, like Diplomas; vocational qualifications such as BTECs and NVQs; and functional, key or basic skills qualifications.

COUNCIL FOR THE CURRICULUM, EXAMINATIONS AND ASSESSMENT (NORTHERN IRELAND) T 028-9026 1200
W www.ccea.org.uk

DEPARTMENT FOR CHILDREN, EDUCATION, LIFELONG LEARNING AND SKILLS (DCELLS)
T 0300-0603300; 0845-010 3300
W http://wales.gov.uk/topics/educationandskills

DIRECTGOV W www.direct.gov.uk

REGISTER OF REGULATED QUALIFICATIONS
T 0300-303 3346 W http://register.ofqual.gov.uk

OFFICE OF QUALIFICATIONS AND EXAMINATIONS REGULATION (OFQUAL)
T 0300-303 3344 W www.ofqual.gov.uk

GCSE

The vast majority of pupils in their last year of compulsory schooling in England, Wales and Northern Ireland take at least one General Certificate of Secondary Education (GCSE) exam, though GCSEs may be taken at any age. GCSEs assess the performance of pupils on a subject-specific basis and are mostly taken after a two-year course. They are available in more than 50 subjects, most of them academic subjects, though some, known as vocational or applied GCSEs, involve the study of a particular area of employment and the development of work-related skills. Some subjects are also offered as short-course qualifications, equivalent to half a standard GCSE, or as double awards, equivalent to two GCSEs.

GCSEs have traditionally been assessed by exams at the end of the course and by coursework completed by students during the course. GCSE certificates are awarded on an eight-point scale from A* to G. In most subjects two different papers, foundation and higher, are provided for different ranges of ability with grades A*–D available

from the higher tier and C–G available from the foundation tier.

All GCSE specifications, assessments and grading procedures are monitored by OFQUAL, DCELLS and the CCEA (which is currently revising the qualification and subject criteria). A key change is that coursework is being replaced in nearly all subjects by 'controlled assessment': extended tasks sat in exam conditions. The new specifications for many GCSE subjects were introduced in schools in September 2009 and in September 2010 for English, ICT and mathematics.

Since September 2010 the government has allowed state schools to offer pupils International GCSE (iGCSE) exams in key subjects including English, mathematics, science and ICT. The iGCSEs do not include coursework and are viewed by some experts as more rigorous than traditional GCSEs.

GCE A-LEVEL AND AS-LEVEL

GCE (General Certificate of Education) advanced levels (A-levels) are the qualifications that the majority of young people in England, Wales and Northern Ireland use to gain entry to university.

A-levels are subject-based qualifications mostly taken by UK students aged 16 to 19 over a two-year course in school sixth forms or at college, but they can be taken at any age. They are available in more than 45, mostly academic, subjects, though there are some A-levels in vocational areas, often known as applied A-levels.

An A-level qualification consists of advanced subsidiary (AS) and A2 units. The AS is a standalone qualification and is worth half a full A-level qualification. It normally consists of two units, assessed at the standard expected for a learner half way through an A-level course, that together contribute 50 per cent towards the full A-level.

The A2 is the second half of a full A-level qualification. It normally consists of two units, assessed at the standard expected for a learner at the end of a full A-level course, that together are worth 50 per cent of the full A-level qualification. Most units are assessed by examination but some are by internal assessment. Each unit is graded A–E. Revised A-level specifications were introduced in September 2008, with a new A* grade awarded from 2010 to reward exceptional candidates.

An extended project was introduced in September 2008 as a separate qualification. It is a single piece of work on a topic of the student's own choosing that requires a high degree of planning, preparation, research and autonomous working. Awards are graded A–E and the extended project is accredited as half an A-level.

INTERNATIONAL BACCALAUREATE

The International Baccalaureate (IB) offers three educational programmes for students aged 3 to 19.

Some 219 schools and colleges in the UK, both state and independent, now offer the IB diploma programme for students aged 16 to 19. Based around detailed academic study of a wide range of subjects, including languages, the arts, science, maths, history and geography, this leads to a single qualification recognised by UK universities.

The IB diploma is made up of a compulsory 'core' plus six separate subjects where individuals have some choice over what they study. The compulsory core contains three elements: theory of knowledge; creativity, action and service; and a 4,000-word extended essay.

The diploma normally takes two years to complete and most of the assessment is done through externally marked examinations. Candidates are awarded points for each part of the programme, up to a maximum of 45. A candidate must score 24 points or more to achieve a full diploma.

Successfully completing the diploma earns points on the 'UCAS tariff', the UK system for allocating points to qualifications used for entry to higher education. An IB diploma total of 24 points is worth 260 UCAS points – the same as a B and two C grades at A-level. The maximum of 45 points earns 720 UCAS points – equivalent to six A-levels at grade A.

WELSH BACCALAUREATE

The Welsh Baccalaureate (WBQ), available for 14- to 19-year-olds in Wales, combines a compulsory core, which incorporates personal development skills, with options from existing qualifications such as A-levels, GCSEs and NVQs to make one broader award. The WBQ can be studied in English or Welsh, or a combination of the two. Following positive evaluation of pilots, the WBQ is being rolled out across the 14 to 19 age range at Advanced, Intermediate and Foundation levels. From September 2011 the qualification will be available to some 70,000 learners in a total of over 240 centres across Wales.

DIPLOMAS

The Diploma is a new qualification for 14- to 19-year-olds that combines practical, hands-on experience with academic learning. It was introduced by the former Labour government to increase the qualification choices available to young people and to help them to develop the knowledge and skills that employers and universities demand. Consequently, all Diplomas were developed in partnership with employers. The Diploma is a flexible 'umbrella' qualification that can be gained by accruing other qualifications at the relevant level, so young people studying for a Diploma can include GCSEs and A-levels within their Diploma programme.

Diplomas in ten subject areas were introduced in selected schools and colleges from September 2009:

- business administration and finance
- construction and the built environment
- creative and media
- engineering
- environmental and land-based studies
- hair and beauty studies
- hospitality
- information technology
- manufacturing and product design
- society, health and development

A further four Diplomas – travel and tourism; public services; retail business; and sport and active leisure – began in September 2010. However, the Diplomas that the previous government planned to introduce in science, languages and humanities, to be taught from September 2011, have been cancelled. There are three levels of Diploma, each taking two years to complete:

- Foundation Diploma – a level 1 qualification, equivalent to five GCSEs at grades D to G
- Higher Diploma – a level 2 qualification, equivalent to seven GCSEs at grades A* to C
- Advanced Diploma – a level 3 qualification for those over 16, equivalent to 3.5 A-levels

All Diploma students continue to study English, maths and ICT and have some work experience with an employer. Advanced Diplomas can lead either to university or to a career.

BTECS, OCR NATIONALS AND OTHER VOCATIONAL QUALIFICATIONS

Vocational qualifications can range from general qualifications where a person learns skills relevant to a variety of jobs, to specialist qualifications designed for a particular sector. They are available from several awarding bodies, such as City & Guilds, Edexcel and OCR, and can be taken at many different levels.

BTEC qualifications and OCR Nationals are particular types of work-related qualifications, available in a wide range of subjects, including: art and design, business, health and social care, information technology, media, public services, science and sport. The qualifications offer a mix of theory and practice, can include work experience and can take the form of (or be part of) a technical certificate, one of the key components of an Apprenticeship. They can be studied full-time at college or school, or part-time at college. BTEC qualifications are available at various levels on the National Qualifications Framework (NQF), including Higher National Certificates and Diplomas (HNCs and HNDs), at higher education level; OCR Nationals are achieved at levels 1 to 3.

Learners complete a range of assignments, case studies and practical activities, as well as a portfolio of evidence that shows what work has been completed. Assessment is usually done by the teacher or trainer, sometimes externally. BTEC and OCR Nationals are graded as pass, merit or distinction. BTEC and OCR Nationals at level 3 can qualify the learner for university entry.

All vocational and work-related qualifications fit into the Qualifications and Credit Framework (QCF). QCF qualifications are made up of units that can be studied at each individual's own pace and built up to full qualifications over time. Every qualification and unit on the QCF has a credit value, showing how long it takes to complete. One credit is equivalent to ten hours. When an individual takes QCF units or qualifications, their learning is 'banked' and stored on their personal learner record, showing what they have completed and how they can progress further.

There are more than 2,500 new vocational qualifications on the QCF, available in a broad range of subjects from a wide range of learning providers and some employers. Available in England, Northern Ireland and Wales, they are also recognised in Scotland.

NVQS

A National Vocational Qualification (NVQ) is a 'competence-based' qualification that is recognised by employers. Individuals learn practical, work-related tasks designed to help them develop the skills and knowledge to do a particular job effectively. NVQs can be taken in school, at college or by people already in work. There are more than 1,300 different NVQs available from the vast majority of business sectors. NVQs exist at levels 1 to 5 on the NQF and as new vocational qualifications on the QCF, though some will continue to be called NVQs. An NVQ qualification at level 2 or 3 can also be taken as part of an apprenticeship.

FUNCTIONAL SKILLS

Functional skills are a new set of qualifications launched across England during 2010, available for all learners aged 14 and above. They test the practical skills in English, mathematics and ICT that allow people to work confidently, effectively and independently in life. These skills are an integral part of the secondary school curriculum and of other qualifications including Diplomas and apprenticeships. Stand-alone functional skills qualifications are also available. These skills are assessed mainly by a set of practical tasks completed within a given time limit, though new ways of assessment such as electronic and online methods are being considered. Functional skills replace previous skills for life qualifications and the three main key skills qualifications in England. In Wales these new qualifications are known as 'essential skills'.

APPRENTICESHIPS

An apprenticeship combines on-the-job training with nationally recognised qualifications, allowing individuals to gain skills and qualifications while working and earning a wage. Apprenticeships are available in more than 190 job roles across a wide variety of industry sectors and take between one and four years to complete. There are three levels available:

> • Apprenticeships – at level 2 on the National Qualifications Framework (NQF), they are equivalent to five good GCSE passes
> • Advanced Apprenticeships – at level 3 on the NQF, they are equivalent to two A-level passes
> • Higher Apprenticeships – lead to qualifications at NVQ Level 4 or, in some cases, a foundation degree

In England, the National Apprenticeship Service (NAS), launched in 2009, has responsibility for the delivery of apprenticeships including the provision of an online vacancy matching system. Between April 2010 and March 2011, 257,000 young people started an apprenticeship in England. The Welsh government and the Department for Employment and Learning (DEL) are responsible for the apprenticeship programmes in Wales and Northern Ireland respectively.
NATIONAL APPRENTICESHIP SERVICE (NAS)
T 02476-826482 W www.apprenticeships.org.uk

SCOTLAND

Scotland has its own system of public examinations and qualifications. The Scottish Qualifications Authority (SQA) is Scotland's national body for qualifications, responsible for developing, accrediting, assessing and certificating all Scottish qualifications apart from university degrees and some professional body qualifications.

There are qualifications at all levels of attainment. Almost all school candidates gain SQA qualifications in the fourth year of secondary school and most obtain further qualifications in the fifth or sixth year or in further education colleges. Increasingly, people also take them in the workplace.

SQA, with partners such as Universities Scotland, has introduced the Scottish Credit and Qualifications Framework (SCQF) as a way of comparing and understanding Scottish qualifications. It includes qualifications across academic and vocational sectors and compares them by giving a level and credit points. There are 12 levels in the SCQF, level 1 being the least difficult and level 12 the most difficult. The number of SCQF credit points shows how much learning has to be done to achieve the qualification. For instance, one SCQF credit point equals about 10 hours of learning including assessment.

SQA is responsible for three main types of qualification: units, courses and group awards.

UNITS
NATIONAL UNITS

National Units can be taken at schools, colleges and in other training centres. There are more than 3,500 units available in a wide range of subjects such as science, engineering, agriculture and care. Most units are designed to take 40 hours of teaching time to complete. National Units can be built up into National Courses, National Progression Awards (NPAs) and National Certificates (NCs) – see below. The names for the National Units at the various SCQF levels are:

> • level 1 – Access 1
> • level 2 – Access 2
> • level 3 – Access 3
> • level 4 – Intermediate 1
> • level 5 – Intermediate 2
> • level 6 – Higher
> • level 7 – Advanced Higher

HIGHER NATIONAL UNITS

Higher National Units, which cover the skills and knowledge that people need in jobs at middle management and technician levels, are mainly taken at college. They are the building blocks of Higher National Certificates (HNCs) and Higher National Diplomas (HNDs) – see below, though they are also qualifications in their own right. These units can sit at various SCQF levels but are normally between levels 6 and 9 and are often used for progression to courses in higher education.

SVQ UNITS

Scottish Vocational Qualifications units (SVQs) are based on national 'standards of competence' drawn up by government-sponsored bodies called 'sector skills councils', which are made up of trade bodies, employers and specialists. There are sector skills councils for most industries. Each SVQ unit defines one aspect of a job or a work-role, and says what it is to be competent in that aspect of the job. These units can be built into SVQs, see below, and are sometimes used in wider schemes such as apprenticeships.

COURSES
STANDARD GRADES

Standard Grades are generally taken over two years of study in years 3 and 4 at secondary school. These courses are made up of different parts called 'elements', usually with an exam at the end. There are Standard Grades at SCQF levels 3, 4 and 5 called:

> • level 3 – Foundation
> • level 4 – General
> • level 5 – Credit

Candidates generally progress from Standard Grades to National Courses.

NATIONAL COURSES

National Courses are available at these levels:

- level 2 – Access 2
- level 3 – Access 3
- level 4 – Intermediate 1
- level 5 – Intermediate 2
- level 6 – Higher
- level 7 – Advanced Higher

Most National Courses are made up of three units plus an external assessment, usually an examination marked and checked by professional examiners appointed by the SQA. Candidates must pass all three units and are awarded grades A to D on the basis of how they did in their external assessment. Most young people who qualify for places at college and university do so on the basis of the Highers and Advanced Highers.

SKILLS FOR WORK COURSES

Skills for Work Courses are practical courses designed as an equivalent option to an existing qualification, such as Standard Grade, to help young people develop skills that are important to employment and life. These courses offer candidates practical experiences that are linked to particular careers and are normally delivered by a school and college working in partnership. They are assessed by the teacher or lecturer and have no final exam.

GROUP AWARDS

NATIONAL PROGRESSION AWARDS

National Progression Awards (NPAs) are designed to assess a defined set of skills and knowledge in specialist vocational areas and link to national occupational standards, the basis of SVQs. NPAs are at SCQF levels 2 to 6, and are mainly used in colleges for short programmes of study.

NATIONAL CERTIFICATES

National Certificates, also at SCQF levels 2 to 6, aim to develop a range of skills and knowledge, including transferable skills, such as core skills. Each National Certificate also has specific aims relating to a subject or occupational area and is designed to prepare candidates for further progression. They are primarily aimed at 16- to 18-year-olds and adults in full-time education, normally at a college. They prepare candidates for more advanced study at HNC/HND level or employment.

HNCS AND HNDS

HNCs and HNDs are qualifications introduced in the mid-1920s that provide the skills and knowledge needed for training towards jobs at middle management and technician level. They are made up of Higher National Units and cover a wide range of occupations. Many HNDs allow the holder entry to the second or third year of a degree course. HNCs are at SCQF level 7 and HNDs at level 8.

SVQS

SVQs are based on job competence, and recognise the skills and knowledge that people need in employment. There are SVQs in most occupations, and they are available for all types and levels of jobs. Primarily delivered to candidates in full-time employment, they are available at SCQF levels 4 to 12.

PDAS

Professional Development Awards (PDAs) are qualifications for people who are already in a career or vocation and who wish to extend or broaden their skills. People often take a PDA after completing a degree or vocational qualification. There are PDAs at SCQF levels 6 to 12. Customised Awards are vocational qualifications specially designed by SQA to meet an organisation's specific needs for skills and expertise.

THE SCOTTISH QUALIFICATIONS AUTHORITY (SQA) T 0845-279 1000 W www.sqa.org.uk

SCOTTISH CREDIT AND QUALIFICATIONS FRAMEWORK (SCQF) T 0845-270 7371 W www.scqf.org.uk

FURTHER EDUCATION AND LIFELONG LEARNING

ENGLAND

The further education (FE) system in England provides a wide range of education and training opportunities for young people and adults. From the age of 16, young people who wish to remain in education, but not in a school setting, can undertake further education (including skills training) in an FE college. There are two main types of college in the FE sector: sixth form colleges and general further education (GFE) colleges. Some FE colleges focus on a particular area, such as art and design or agriculture and horticulture. Each institution decides its own range of subjects and courses. Students at FE colleges can study for a wide and growing range of academic and/or work-related qualifications, from entry level to higher education level.

Though the Department for Business, Innovation and Skills is responsible for the FE sector and for funding FE for adults (19 or over), the Department for Education funds all education and training for 16- to 18-year-olds.

The proportion of 16- to 18-year-olds in education or training has risen steadily over recent years. In 2009–10 nearly 1.64 million 16- to 18-year-olds, 84.4 per cent of the age group, were in education or training, including 70.6 per cent in full-time education. By the time that England's education-leaving age rises to 18 in 2015, 100 per cent should be in education or training. It is assumed that most of the additional students will go into FE or work-based training rather than staying on at school.

The 'September Guarantee', introduced in 2007, offers a place in post-16 education or training to all 16- and 17-year-olds who want one. In 2010, 97 per cent of 16-year-olds and 91 per cent of 17-year-olds received an offer of a place.

Statutory responsibility for 16 to 19 education and training in England, formerly with the Learning and Skills Council (LSC), now rests with local authorities, supported by the Young People's Learning Agency (YPLA), a non-departmental public body. The agency's remit also includes funding and supporting academies and providing direct support for young learners.

The FE sector in England, as in other parts of the UK, also provides a range of opportunities for adults.

The Skills Funding Agency (SFA), part of the Department for Business, Innovation and Skills, is presently responsible for funding and regulating education and training for adults. It will invest government funding of £3.7bn in FE and skills training places for over 3 million adult learners (aged 19 or over) in the 2011/12 academic year.

In November 2010, the government announced a new strategy for FE, including more adult apprenticeships (provision for 200,000 adults by 2014–15 with £605m in funding in 2011–12); fully funded training for 19- to 24-year-olds undertaking their first full level 2 (GCSE equivalent) or first level 3 qualification when they do not already have one; and fully funded basic skills for people who left school without basic skills in reading, writing and mathematics. 'Train to Gain', the programme that funded trainees sponsored by employers, was replaced in July 2011 by a programme focused on helping small employers to train low-skilled staff.

There are currently 18 employer-led, funded and designed centres of training excellence called National Skills Academies in various stages of development. Each academy operates in a key sector of the economy, from financial services to construction, and operates in partnership with colleges, schools and independent training providers to offer specialist training within their sector.

Among the many voluntary bodies providing adult education, the Workers' Educational Association (WEA) is the UK's largest, operating throughout England and Scotland. It provides part-time courses to adults in response to local need in community centres, village halls, schools, pubs or workplaces. Similar but separate WEA organisations operate in Wales and Northern Ireland.

The National Institute of Adult Continuing Education (NIACE), a charitable non-governmental organisation, promotes lifelong learning opportunities for adults in England and Wales.

NATIONAL INSTITUTE OF ADULT CONTINUING EDUCATION (NIACE) T 0116-204 4200
W www.niace.org.uk
THE SKILLS FUNDING AGENCY T 0845-377 5000
W www.skillsfundingagency.bis.gov.uk
WORKERS' EDUCATIONAL ASSOCIATION (WEA)
T 020-7426 3450 W www.wea.org.uk
THE YOUNG PEOPLE'S LEARNING AGENCY
T 0845-337 2000 W www.ypla.gov.uk

WALES
In Wales, the aims and makeup of the FE system are similar to those outlined for England. The Welsh government funds a wide range of learning programmes for young people through colleges, local authorities and private organisations. Current thinking is outlined in *Skills That Work for Wales,* published in July 2008, which describes the 'one Wales' ambition for a highly educated, highly skilled and high-employment Wales, and *Transforming Education and Training Provision in Wales; Delivering Skills that Work for Wales,* published in November 2009. The Welsh government has set out plans to improve learning opportunities for all post-16 learners in the shortest possible time, to increase the engagement of disadvantaged young people in the learning process, and to transform the learning network to increase learner choice, reduce duplication of provision and encourage higher-quality learning and teaching in all post-16 provision. One goal is to ensure that, by 2015, 95 per cent of young people will be ready for high-skilled employment or higher education by the age of 25.

In Wales, responsibility for adult and continuing education lies with the Department for Children, Education, Lifelong Learning and Skills (DCELLS) within the Welsh government. Wales operates a range of programmes to support skills development, including subsidised work-based training courses for employees

and the Workforce Development Programme, where employers can use the free services of experienced skills advisers to develop staff training plans.
COLEG HARLECH WEA T 01248-353254
W www.harlech.ac.uk/en/
NIACE DYSGU CYMRU T 029-2037 0900
W www.niacedc.org.uk
WEA SOUTH WALES T 029-2023 5277
W www.swales.wea.org.uk

SCOTLAND
Scotland's 43 FE colleges (known simply as colleges) are at the forefront of lifelong learning, education, training and skills in Scotland. Colleges cater for the needs of learners both in and out of employment at all stages in their lives from middle secondary school and earlier to retirement. Colleges' courses span much of the range of learning needs, from specialised vocational education and training through to general educational programmes. The level of provision ranges from essential life skills and provision for students with learning difficulties to HNCs and HNDs. Some colleges, notably those in the Highlands and Islands, also deliver degrees and postgraduate qualifications.

The Scottish Funding Council (SFC) is the statutory body responsible for funding teaching and learning provision, research and other activities in Scotland's colleges. The 43 colleges were incorporated in 1993. Overall strategic direction for the sector is provided by the Lifelong Learning Directorate of the Scottish government, which provides annual guidance to the SFC and liaises closely with bodies such as Scotland's Colleges, the Scottish Qualifications Authority and the FE colleges themselves to ensure that its policies remain relevant and practical.

The Scottish government takes responsibility for community learning and development in Scotland while Skills Development Scotland, a non-departmental public body, is charged with improving Scotland's skills performance by linking skills supply and demand and helping people and organisations to learn, develop and make use of these skills to greater effect. ILA Scotland is a Scottish Government scheme delivered by Skills Development Scotland that provides funding for training to individuals over the age of 16 with an income of less than £22,000 a year.
ILA SCOTLAND T 0808-100 1090
W www.ilascotland.org.uk
SCOTLAND'S COLLEGES T 01786-892000
W www.scotlandscolleges.ac.uk
SCOTTISH FUNDING COUNCIL T 0131-313 6500
W www.sfc.ac.uk
SKILLS DEVELOPMENT SCOTLAND T 0141-285 6000
W www.skillsdevelopmentscotland.co.uk

NORTHERN IRELAND
FE in Northern Ireland is provided through six multi-campus colleges. Most secondary schools also provide a sixth form where students can choose to attend for two additional years to complete their AS-levels and A-levels.

Colleges Northern Ireland (CNI) acts as the representative body for the six FE colleges which, like their counterparts in the rest of the UK, are independent corporate bodies where management responsibility lies with each individual college's governing body. The range of courses that they offer spans essential skills, a wide choice of vocational and academic programmes and higher education programmes. The majority of full-time enrolments in the six colleges are in the 16 to 19 age group, while most part-time students are over 19.

The Department for Employment and Learning (DELNI) is responsible for the policy, strategic development and financing of the statutory FE sector and for lifelong learning, and also provides support to a small number of non-statutory FE providers. The Educational Guidance Service for Adults (EGSA), an independent, not-for-profit organisation, has a network of local offices based across Northern Ireland which provide services to adult learners, learning advisers, providers, employers and others interested in improving access to learning for adults.

COLLEGES NORTHERN IRELAND (CNI)
T 028-9068 2296 W www.anic.ac.uk
THE EDUCATIONAL GUIDANCE SERVICE FOR
ADULTS T 028-9024 4274 W www.egsa.org.uk
WEA NORTHERN IRELAND T 028-9032 9718
W www.wea-ni.com

FINANCIAL SUPPORT

The *Education Maintenance Allowance* (EMA) in England, a scheme that paid 16- to 19-year-olds from low income families a weekly allowance to continue in education, closed in January 2011 (*see* Recent Developments). From September 2011 it will be replaced by a bursary scheme for full-time 16- to 19-year-old students facing financial hardship. Those in care, leaving care, on income support or on certain disability benefits will be guaranteed a bursary of £1,200 a year.

There are similar EMA schemes in Scotland, Wales and Northern Ireland, but with slightly different eligibility conditions. Students must apply to the EMA scheme for the part of the UK where they intend to study.

The *Adult Learning Grant* (ALG), a similar scheme to the EMA but for those aged 19 and over, has also closed. From 2011/12 colleges and learning providers will award learner support funds directly to new students.

Care to Learn is available in England to help young parents under the age of 20 who are caring for their own child or children with the costs of childcare and travel while they are in some form of publicly funded learning (below higher education level). The scheme is not income assessed and pays up to £160 a week (£175 in London) to cover costs. The Sixth Form College Childcare Scheme is similar to Care to Learn, also for the under-20s, and pays the same rates, but is income-assessed and available only to those learning in a school sixth form or sixth-form college.

Dance and Drama Awards (DaDA) are state-funded scholarships for students over the age of 16 enrolled at one of 22 private dance and drama schools in England, who are taking specified courses at National Certificate or National Diploma level. Awards cover most of a student's tuition fees but students also need to make a personal contribution – £1,275 for the 2011–12 academic year. DaDA is not income-assessed. Students from England, Scotland or Wales may get extra help with living costs and childcare if their family's annual income is below £33,000.

Young people studying away from home because their chosen course is not available locally may qualify for the *Residential Support Scheme* or *Residential Bursaries*.

Information and advice on funding support and applications are available from the Learner Support helpline on the Directgov website.

Discretionary Support Funds (DSF) are available in colleges and school sixth forms to help students who have trouble meeting the costs of participating in further education.

In Wales, students aged 19 or over on FE courses may be eligible for the *Assembly Learning Grant for Further Education Scheme* (ALG (FE)). This is a means-tested payment of up to £1,500 for full-time students and up to £750 for those studying part-time. *Discretionary Financial Contingency Funds* are also available to all students in Wales suffering hardship and are administered by the institutions themselves. *Individual Learning Accounts in Wales* closed in March 2011.

In Scotland, FE students can apply to their college for discretionary support in the form of *Further Education Bursaries*. These can include allowances for maintenance, travel, study, childcare and additional support needs. *Individual Learning Accounts* provide up to £500 for those with incomes of less than £22,000.

In Northern Ireland, FE students may be eligible for *Further Education Awards,* non-refundable assistance administered on behalf of the five Education and Library Boards by the Western Education and Library Board.

UK FE students over 18 whose costs are not fully met from the grants described above may also be eligible for *Professional and Career Development Loans.* These loans – also available to HE students – cover up to 80 per cent of course fees (up to 100 per cent for those unemployed for three months); other course costs, such as books, travel and childcare; and living expenses, such as rent, food and clothing (for those who are unemployed or working fewer than 30 hours a week). The loans, of between £300 and £10,000, are available from participating high street banks – currently Barclays and the Co-operative. The Young People's Learning Agency (YPLA) pays the interest on the loan while the student is studying and for one month afterwards. Once students complete their courses, they must pay interest at the rate fixed when they took out the loan, which will be competitive with other commercially available 'unsecured' personal loans.

CAREERS SCOTLAND
W www.careers-scotland.org.uk/Education/Funding/
Funding.asp
DIRECTGOV W www.direct.gov.uk
STUDENT FINANCE WALES T 0845-602 8845
W www.studentfinancewales.co.uk
WESTERN EDUCATION AND LIBRARY BOARD
T 028-8241 1411 W www.welbni.org

HIGHER EDUCATION

Publicly funded higher education (HE) in the UK is provided in 115 universities; 50 higher education colleges and other specialist HE institutions; and a significant number of FE colleges which offer higher education courses.

The Higher Education Funding Council for England (HEFCE) funds teaching and research in 130 English higher education institutions (HEIs), of which 91 are universities, and also funds the HE courses in 124 FE colleges.

The Higher Education Funding Council for Wales (HEFCW) distributes funding for HE in Wales through Wales's 12 HEIs and some FE colleges.

The Scottish Funding Council (SFC) – which is also responsible for FE in Scotland – is the national, strategic body responsible for funding HE teaching and research in Scotland's 20 HEIs, of which 16 are universities, and 43 colleges.

In Northern Ireland HE is provided by two universities,

the Open University (OU) and two university colleges, and six regional institutes of further and higher education. Unlike other parts of the UK, Northern Ireland has no higher education funding council; the Department for Employment and Learning fulfils that role.

All UK universities and a number of HE colleges award their own degrees and other HE qualifications. HE providers who do not have their own degree-awarding powers offer degrees under 'validation arrangements' with other institutions that do have those powers. The OU, for example, runs a validation service which enables a number of other institutions to award OU degrees, after the OU has assured itself that the academic standards of their courses are as high as the OU's own standards.

Each HE institution is responsible for the standards of the awards it makes and the quality of the education it provides to its students, and each has its own internal quality assurance procedures. External quality assurance for HE institutions throughout the UK is provided by the Quality Assurance Agency for Higher Education (QAA). The QAA is independent of government, funded by subscriptions from all publicly funded UK universities and colleges of HE. Its main role is to safeguard the standards of HE qualifications. It does this by defining standards for HE through a framework known as the academic infrastructure. QAA also carries out reviews of the quality of UK HE institutions via a system known as 'institutional audits'. QAA also advises government on a range of HE quality issues, including applications for the grant of degree-awarding powers. It publishes reports on its review activities on its website.
DEPARTMENT FOR EMPLOYMENT AND
  LEARNING T 028-9025 7777 W www.delni.gov.uk
HIGHER EDUCATION FUNDING COUNCIL FOR
  ENGLAND T 0117-931 7317 W www.hefce.ac.uk
HIGHER EDUCATION FUNDING COUNCIL FOR
  WALES T 029-2076 1861 W www.hefcw.ac.uk
SCOTTISH FUNDING COUNCIL T 0131-313 6500
  W www.sfc.ac.uk
THE QUALITY ASSURANCE AGENCY FOR HIGHER
  EDUCATION T 01452-557000 W www.qaa.ac.uk
See also Universities for information on the Research Assessment Exercise (being replaced from 2011 by the Research Excellence Framework) and listings of universities in the UK.

STUDENTS IN HIGHER EDUCATION (2009–10)*			
	Full-time	Part-time	Total
HE students	–	–	2,493,415
Postgraduate students	298,255	284,450	578,705
Undergraduate students	1,333,900	580,810	1,914,710
*Includes UK, EU and non-EU students			
Source: Higher Education Statistics Agency 2010			

UK HIGHER EDUCATION QUALIFICATIONS AWARDED (2009–10)		
	Full-time	Part-time
First degrees	312,740	38,120
Other undergraduate qualifications	62,025	77,725
Postgraduate Certificate in Education (PGCE)	20,395	1,640
Other postgraduate qualifications	14,985	31,180
Total higher degrees including doctorates	118,235	39,900
Source: HESA 2010		

COURSES

HE institutions in the UK mainly offer courses leading to the following qualifications. These qualifications go from levels 4 to 8 on England's National Qualifications Framework, levels 7 to 12 on Scotland's Credit and Qualifications Framework (Scotland is reviewing its framework level descriptors until June 2012). Individual HEIs may not offer all of these.

Certificates of Higher Education (CertHE), awarded after one year's full-time study (or equivalent). If available to students on longer courses, they certify that students have reached a minimum standard in their first year.

Diplomas of Higher Education (DipHE) and other Higher Diplomas, awarded after two to three years' full-time study (or equivalent). They certify that a student has achieved a minimum standard in first- and second-year courses and, in the case of nursing, third-year courses. They can often be used for entry to the third year of a related degree course.

Foundation degrees, awarded after two years of full-time study (or equivalent). These degrees combine academic study with work-based learning, and have been designed jointly by universities, colleges and employers with a particular area of work in mind. They are usually accepted as a basis for entry to the third year of a related degree course.

Bachelor's degrees, also referred to as first degrees. There are different titles; Bachelor of Arts (BA) and Bachelor of Science (BSc) being the most common. In England, Wales and Northern Ireland most Bachelor's degree courses are typically 'with Honours' and awarded after three years of full-time study, although in some subjects the courses last longer. In Scotland, where young people often leave school and go to university a year younger, HE institutions typically offer Ordinary Bachelor's degrees after three years' study and Bachelor's degrees with Honours after four years. Honours degrees are graded as first, upper-second (2:1), lower second (2:2) or third. HEIs in England, Wales and Northern Ireland may allow students who fail the first year of an Honours degree by a small margin to transfer to an Ordinary degree course, if they have one. Ordinary degrees may also be awarded to Honours degree students who do not finish an Honours degree course but complete enough of it to earn a pass.

Postgraduate or Higher degrees. Graduates may go on to take Master's degrees, which involve one or two years' work and can be taught or research-based. They may also take one-year postgraduate diplomas and certificates, often linked to a specific profession, such as the Postgraduate Certificate in Education (PGCE) required to become a state school teacher. A doctorate, leading to a qualification such as a Doctor of Philosophy – a PHD or DPHIL – usually involves at least three years of full-time research.

The framework for HE qualifications in England, Wales and Northern Ireland (FHEQ) and the framework for qualifications of HE institutions in Scotland, can both be found on the QAA website (W www.qaa.ac.uk/ academicinfrastructure/FHEQ/SCQF/), which describes the achievement represented by HE qualifications.

ADMISSIONS

When preparing to apply to a university or other HE college, individuals can compare facts and figures on institutions and courses using the government's Unistats website. This includes details of students' views from the annual National Student Survey.

For the vast majority of full-time undergraduate courses, individuals need to apply online through UCAS, the organisation responsible for managing applications to HE courses in the UK. More than half a million people wanting to study at a university or college each year use this UCAS service, which has useful online tools to help students find the right course.

UCAS also provides two specialist applications services used by more than 50,000 people each year: the Conservatoires UK Admissions Service (CUKAS), for those applying to UK music conservatoires, and the Graduate Teacher Training Registry (GTTR), for postgraduate applications for initial teacher training courses in England and Wales and some in Scotland. Details of initial teacher training courses in Scotland can also be obtained from Universities Scotland and from Teach in Scotland, the website created by the Scottish government to promote teaching.

Each university or college sets its own entry requirements. These can be in terms of particular exam grades or total points on the 'UCAS tariff' (UCAS's system for allocating points to different qualifications on a common basis), or be non-academic, like having a health check. HEIs will make 'firm offers' to candidates who have already gained the qualifications they present for entry, and 'conditional offers' to those who have yet to take their exams or obtain their results. Conditional offers often require a minimum level of achievement in a specified subject, for example '300 points to include grade A at A-level Chemistry'. If candidates' achievements are lower than specified in their conditional offers, the university or college may not accept them; then, if they still wish to go into HE, they need to find another institution through the UCAS 'clearing' process.

The OU conducts its own admissions. It is the UK's only university dedicated to distance learning and the UK's largest for part-time HE. Because it is designed to be 'open' to all, no qualifications are needed for entry to the majority of its courses.

Individuals can search more than 58,000 UK postgraduate courses and research opportunities on UK graduate careers website Prospects. The application process for postgraduate places can vary between institutions. Most universities and colleges accept direct applications and many accept applications through UKPASS, a free, centralised online service run by UCAS that allows individuals to submit up to ten different applications, track their progress and attach supporting material, such as references. Applications for postgraduate social work courses must also be made through UCAS.

UNISTATS W http://unistats.direct.gov.uk
UCAS T 0871-468 0468 W www.ucas.com
UNIVERSITIES SCOTLAND T 0131-226 1111
 W www.universities-scotland.ac.uk
TEACH IN SCOTLAND T 0845-345 4745
 W www.teachinginscotland.com
PROSPECTS T 0161-277 5200 W www.prospects.ac.uk
UKPASS T 0871-334 4447 W http://ukpass.ac.uk

TUITION FEES AND STUDENT SUPPORT
TUITION FEES
HE institutions in England, Wales and Northern Ireland are allowed to charge variable tuition fees for full-time HE courses. Although students from outside the EU can be charged the full cost of their courses, the amount that HEIs may charge students from the UK and other EU countries has been capped since 2006 at £3,000 a year plus inflationary increases. The maximum that an

institution can charge new UK and EU students for the 2011–12 academic year is £3,375. From September 2012, universities will be able to charge up to £9,000 a year in tuition fees (see Recent Developments). The exact fee depends on the course studied and the institution attended. Full-time students do not have to pay their fees before or during their course, as tuition fee loans are available to cover the full cost; these do not have to be repaid until the student is working (see below).

In recent years, Scottish HE institutions have charged flat rate fees, set by the Scottish government, to undergraduate students classed as being ordinarily resident in England, Wales or Northern Ireland; though, as explained above, they can get repayable tuition fee loans to cover the cost. The fee for undergraduates starting courses in 2011–12 is £1,820 a year. However, the Scottish government has announced that it intends to allow universities to set their own fees, up to £9,000 a year, for these students from 2012–13. However, undergraduate students classed as being ordinarily resident in Scotland or another EU country do not have to pay tuition fees at Scottish HE institutions. All tuition fees are paid on their behalf by the Scottish government through the Student Awards Agency for Scotland (SAAS); students must apply for this funding every year.

STUDENT LOANS, GRANTS AND BURSARIES
ENGLAND
All students starting a full-time HE course in 2011–12 can apply through Student Finance England for financial support. Two student loans are available from the government: a *tuition fee loan* of up to £3,375 for 2011–12; and a *maintenance loan* to help with living expenses of up to £4,950 for those living away from home (£6,928 if studying away from home in London) and £3,838 for those living with their parents during term time.

The tuition fee loan is not affected by household income and is paid directly to the relevant HE institution. A proportion (currently 72 per cent) of the maximum maintenance loan is available irrespective of household income while the rest depends on an income assessment. Student Finance England usually pays the money into the student's own bank account in three instalments, one at the start of each term.

Repayment of both loans does not start until the April after the student has left university or college and is earning more than £15,000 a year. At this point the individual's employer will take 9 per cent of any salary above the £15,000 threshold through the Pay As You Earn (PAYE) system. The self-employed make repayments through their tax returns. Someone earning £20,000 a year, the average starting salary for graduates entering full-time employment, will have to pay back £8.65 a week. Student loans accrue interest from the date they are paid out, up until they are repaid in full. Generally, the interest rate for student loans is set in September each year. The latest rate can be found online (W www.studentloanrepayment.co.uk/interest).

Students can also apply for a *maintenance grant* towards living expenses which does not have to be repaid. The maximum grant available for 2011–12 is £2,906 for the academic year. This is available to full-time HE students with a household income of £25,000 or under. Those with a household income of £50,020 or under receive a partial grant. The exact amount paid depends upon income. Students eligible for help through the maintenance grant receive some of it instead of the maintenance loan. The amount they are eligible for through the maintenance loan is reduced by 50p for every £1 of maintenance grant that they are entitled to. This means that students from lower income households generally have less to repay when they finish studying and start work.

Certain groups of students who claim means-tested state benefits can get the *special support grant*, also worth up to £2,906, instead of the maintenance grant. Likely recipients include single parents and students with certain disabilities. If a student receives the special support grant, it does not affect the amount of maintenance loan that he or she receives.

Bursaries are an additional source of help available from universities and colleges. They do not have to be repaid. Institutions in England must offer at least a minimum bursary payment of £338 in 2011–12 to students paying maximum tuition fees and getting the full maintenance grant or special support grant.

Students can use the student finance calculator on the Student Finance England website to work out what financial support they may get.

PART-TIME HIGHER EDUCATION STUDENTS

Part-time HE students in England may be entitled to a grant towards their fees, and a grant towards their course costs. This help does not have to be repaid. Those with a household income of less than £28,066 may be able to get a maximum of £1,495 in 2011–12.

There are no regulations stating how much universities or colleges can charge in tuition fees for most part-time courses. The maximum *fee grant* is based on how 'intensive' the course is, or how long it takes to complete compared to the equivalent full-time course. Students on certain state benefits qualify for the maximum automatically. Otherwise the amount awarded depends on the student's household income. Separate applications for these grants must be made each academic year. Details are available on the Student Finance England website.

If the student's chosen HE institution runs the *additional fee support scheme*, it could provide extra financial help if the student is on a low income and in certain other circumstances. Help may also be available through the institution's *access to learning fund*, for students in financial difficulty.

STUDENT FINANCE ENGLAND T 0845-300 5090
    W www.direct.gov.uk/studentfinance

WALES

Welsh students starting a full-time HE course in 2011–12 can apply through Student Finance Wales for the forms of financial support described below.

A similar system of tuition fee loans and maintenance loans now operates in Wales as in England but with slightly lower maximum maintenance loans available: up to £4,715 for students living away from home (£6,618 if studying away from home in London) and £3,643 for those living with their parents during term time. Tuition fee loans of up to £3,375 are available to cover the exact amount that the institution charges for a course.

The Welsh government has made a commitment that all new Welsh-domiciled students who take out a maintenance loan from academic year 2011–12, irrespective of where they study in the UK, will receive up to £1,500 debt relief when they start repayment.

Welsh-domiciled students may apply for an *assembly learning grant* (ALG) of up to £5,600 to help meet general living costs. This is paid in three instalments, one at the start of each term, like the student maintenance loan. The amount that a student gets depends on household income. The maximum grant is available to those with a household income of £18,370 or under. Those with an income of £50,020 or under receive a partial grant.

Universities and colleges in Wales are committed to providing additional support for students under the *Welsh bursary scheme*. Every full-time HE student, regardless of where they live in the UK, may be considered for a means-tested bursary, which is paid in addition to other financial support received and is not offset by any reductions in other forms of support.

Institutions also hold *financial contingency funds* to provide discretionary assistance to students experiencing financial difficulties.

Students can use the student finance calculator on the Student Finance Wales website to work out what financial support they may be entitled to.

PART-TIME HIGHER EDUCATION STUDENTS

Part-time undergraduate students studying at least 50 per cent of an equivalent full-time course are entitled to receive a *fee grant*, depending on their household income (anyone earning over £28,181 will receive no support). The rate depends on how intensive the course is. For 2011–12, the maximum fee grant, which applies to students who study at a rate equivalent to 75 per cent of a full-time course, is £1,000 (less than 60 per cent is £670 and between 60 and 74 per cent is £800). Such students may also be entitled to receive *adult dependants' grant* (ADG), *childcare grant* (CCG) or *parents' learning allowance* (PLA). The amount received depends on the intensity of the course undertaken. The maximum grants paid to eligible students are £2,647 for ADG and £1,508 for PLA; CCG depends on the cost of childcare.

Part-time students can also apply for assistance with course-related costs worth up to £1,125. Students who already have a degree cannot normally apply for this support. Those on part-time teacher-training courses are not eligible for part-time grants but may qualify for full-time support.

STUDENT FINANCE WALES T 0845-602 8845
    W www.studentfinancewales.co.uk

SCOTLAND

All students starting a full-time HE course in 2011–12 can apply through the Student Awards Agency for Scotland for financial support. Living cost support is mainly provided through a *student loan*, the majority of which is income-assessed. The maximum loan for 2011–12 paid to students living away from home is £5,417 and for those living with their parents is £4,457 a year. If the family income is over approximately £62,000 a year, the student receives only the minimum loans of £915 and £605 respectively. Low-income students may also be eligible for an *additional loan* of up to £785 with the maximum lent to those whose household income is £18,000 or less a year.

The *young students' bursary* (YSB) is available to young students from low-income backgrounds and is non-repayable. Eligible students receive this bursary instead of part of the student loan, thus reducing their level of repayable debt. In 2011–12 the maximum annual support provided through YSB is £2,640 if household income is £18,000 or less a year.

The *independent students' bursary* (ISB) similarly replaces part of the loan and reduces repayable debt for low-income students classed as 'independent' of parental support. The maximum paid is £1,000 a year to those whose household income is £18,000 or less a year. From 2011–12 travel expenses will be included within the student loan. There are also *supplementary grants* available to certain categories of students such as lone parents and those with dependants. Extra help is also available to those who have a disability, learning difficulty or mental health problem.

STUDENT AWARDS AGENCY FOR SCOTLAND
T 0300-555 0505
W www.saas.gov.uk/student_support/index.htm

NORTHERN IRELAND
All students starting a full-time HE course in 2011–12 can apply through Student Finance Northern Ireland for financial support. The arrangements for both full-time and part-time students are similar to those for England. The main difference is that the income-assessed *maintenance grant* (or *special support grant* for students on certain income-assessed benefits) for new full-time students studying at UK universities and colleges is worth up to £3,475 while continuing students are eligible instead for a *higher education bursary* of up to £2,000.

STUDENT FINANCE NORTHERN IRELAND
T 0845-600 0662 W www.studentfinanceni.co.uk

DISABLED STUDENTS' ALLOWANCES
Disabled Students' Allowances (DSAs) are grants available throughout the UK to help meet the extra course costs that students can face as a direct result of a disability, ongoing health condition, mental health condition or specific learning difficulty. They help disabled people to study in HE on an equal basis with other students. They are paid on top of the standard student finance package and do not have to be repaid. The amount that an individual gets depends on the type of extra help needed, not on household income. This amounts to £5,161 for specialist equipment for the entire course, non-medical helper allowance of £20,520 a year and a general allowance of £1,724 a year. Eligible individuals should apply as early as possible to their relevant UK awarding authority.

POSTGRADUATE AWARDS
In general, postgraduate students do not qualify for mandatory support like student loans. An exception to this is students taking a Postgraduate Certificate in Education (PGCE), who can qualify for the finance package usually available only to undergraduates.

There is heavy competition for any postgraduate funding available. Individuals can search for postgraduate awards and scholarships on two websites: Hot Courses and Prospects. They can also search for grants available from educational trusts, often reserved for students from poorer backgrounds or for those who have achieved academic excellence, on the Educational Grants Advisory Service (EGAS) website. Otherwise they need to fund their own fees and living expenses.

Postgraduates from Scotland on certain full-time vocational courses can apply through the Student Awards Agency for Scotland for funding under the *postgraduate students' allowances scheme*. In Northern Ireland, the Department for Employment and Learning and the Education and Library Boards provide postgraduate funding for certain courses. Postgraduate students with an impairment, health condition or learning difficulty can apply for disabled students' allowances (*see* above) for both taught courses and research places.

DEPARTMENT FOR EMPLOYMENT AND
LEARNING (DELNI) T 028-9025 7777
W www.delni.gov.uk
EDUCATIONAL GRANTS ADVISORY SERVICE
(EGAS) T 020-7254 6251 W www.family-action.org.uk
HOT COURSES W www.scholarship-search.org.uk
PROSPECTS W www.prospects.ac.uk
STUDENT AWARDS AGENCY FOR SCOTLAND
(SAAS) T 0300-555 0505
W www.student-support-saas.gov.uk

TEACHER TRAINING

See Professional Education.

EMPLOYEES AND SALARIES

EMPLOYEES
QUALIFIED TEACHERS IN MAINTAINED SCHOOLS
(2009–10)
Full-time equivalent, thousands

	England	Wales	Scotland	NI	UK
Nursery and primary schools	200.9	13.6	24.7	8.1	247.3
Secondary schools	225.6*	13.2	24.8	10.1	273.7
Special schools	15.1	0.7	1.9	0.8	18.5
Education elsewhere†	6.5	–	–	–	6.5
Total	448.1	27.5	51.4	19.0	546.0

* Includes academies and city technology colleges in England
† Figure includes pupil referral units and is a separate statistic for England only

SUPPORT STAFF IN MAINTAINED SCHOOLS (2009–10)
Full-time equivalent, thousands

	England	Wales	Scotland	NI*
Teaching assistants	194.2	15.5	11.6	N/A
Other support staff	168.6†	5.0	10.5	N/A

* Figures are not collated centrally for Northern Ireland
† Includes academies and city technology colleges in England

ACADEMIC STAFF IN UK HIGHER EDUCATION
INSTITUTIONS (2009–10)

	Full-time	Part-time	Total
Professors	15,320	2,055	17,375
Non-professors	102,605	61,610	164,220
Teaching only	8,360	38,115	46,475
Teaching and research	75,220	18,665	93,885
Research only	33,700	6,770	40,470
Neither teaching or research	650	120	770

Source: HESA 2010

SALARIES
State school teachers in England and Wales are employed by local authorities or the governing bodies of their schools, but their pay and conditions are set nationally. Classroom teachers start on the main pay scale which has different rates for different areas. Each September teachers move one point up on the main pay scale until they reach the maximum basic rate of pay (M6). Qualified teachers who reach the top of the main pay scale are eligible to apply and be assessed against national standards to 'cross

the threshold' on to a three point upper pay scale. Progress along the upper pay scale is not automatic, but is based on performance recommendations made by the headteacher. Unqualified 'associate' teachers such as instructors are paid on a separate salary scale.

There are teaching and learning responsibility payments for specific posts, special needs work and recruitment and retention factors which may be awarded at the discretion of the school governing body or the local authority. An 'Excellent Teacher' scheme allows eligible teachers, who share their skills in classroom teaching for the benefit of professional development of other teachers within their own school, to access a higher salary. The Advanced Skills Teacher grade was introduced to enhance the prospects of the most able classroom teachers who disseminate good practice by working in other local schools. Advanced Skills Teachers have their own pay spine. Headteachers and other school leaders are paid on a separate leadership pay spine. All teachers are eligible for membership of the Teachers' Pension Scheme.

As at September 2010, salary scales for teachers in England and Wales were:

Headteacher	£42,379–£105,097
Excellent Teacher	£39,697–£52,090
Advanced Skills Teacher	£37,461–£56,950
Classroom teacher (upper pay scale)	£34,181–£36,755
Classroom teacher (main pay scale)	£21,588–£31,552
Associate teachers	£15,817–£25,016
Inner London	
Headteacher	£49,466–£112,181
Excellent Teacher	£48,600–£60,993
Advanced Skills Teacher	£44,540–£64,036
Classroom teacher (upper pay scale)	£41,497–£45,000
Classroom teacher (main pay scale)	£27,000–£36,387
Associate teachers	£19,893–£29,088

Pay structures for teachers in Scotland were agreed up until April 2011 when pay was frozen for two years until 2013. Teachers are paid on a seven-point scale where the entry point is for newly qualified teachers undertaking their probationary year. There is no equivalent in Scotland of the upper pay spine operated in England and Wales. Experienced, ambitious teachers who reach the top of the main pay scale are eligible to become chartered teachers

and earn more on a separate pay spine. However, to do so they must study for further professional qualifications and finance these studies. Headteachers and deputies have a separate pay spine as do 'principals' or heads of department. Additional allowances are payable to teachers under a range of circumstances, such as working in distant islands and remote schools.

As at September 2011, salary scales for teachers in Scotland were:

Headteacher/deputy headteacher	£42,288–£82,542
Principal teacher	£37,284–£48,120
Chartered teacher	£35,253–£41,925
Main grade	£21,438–£34,200

Teachers in Northern Ireland have broadly similar pay and working conditions to teachers in England and Wales, although there is neither an Advanced Skills Teacher grade nor an Excellent Teacher scheme. Classroom teachers who take on teaching and learning responsibilities outside their normal classroom duties may be awarded one of five teaching allowances.

As at September 2010, salary scales for teachers in Northern Ireland were:

Principal (headteacher)	£42,379–£105,379
Classroom teacher (upper pay scale)	£34,181–£36,756
Classroom teacher (main pay scale)	£21,588–£31,552
Associate teachers	£13,734
Teaching allowances	£1,847–£11,911

Since 2007, most academic staff in HE across the UK are paid on a single national pay scale as a result of a national framework agreement negotiated by the HE unions and HE institutions. The main features of the agreement are that all staff are paid according to rates on a 51-point national pay spine and that academic and academic-related staff are graded according to a national grading structure. Since August 2009 the pay spine has ranged from £13,150 to £55,535. As HE institutions are autonomous employers, precise job grades and salaries do vary to some extent from one institution to another but the following table gives a guide to the salaries that typically tally with certain job roles in HE.

Principal lecturer	£45,336–£52,556
Senior lecturer	£35,788–£44,016
Lecturer	£29,972–£34,745
Junior researcher	£23,661–£29,099

UNIVERSITIES

The following is a list of universities, which are those institutions that have been granted degree awarding powers by either a royal charter or an act of parliament, or have been permitted to use the word 'university' (or 'university college') by the Privy Council. There are other recognised bodies in the UK with degree awarding powers, as well as institutions offering courses leading to a degree from a recognised body. Further information is available at W www.bis.gov.uk

Student figures represent the number of undergraduate and postgraduate students based on information available at May 2011.

For information on tuition fees and student loans, *see* Education, Higher Education.

RESEARCH ASSESSMENT EXERCISE

The research assessment exercise (RAE) gives a rating to each university department or specialist college put forward for evaluation, based on the quality of its research. It enables the higher education funding bodies to distribute public funds for research selectively on the basis of quality. Institutions conducting the best research receive a larger proportion of the available grant so that the infrastructure for the top level of research in the UK is protected and developed. The table below shows the top five universities or specialist colleges for each discipline based on the mean average ranking of the overall quality of their research. The research excellence framework (REF) is the new system for assessing the quality of research in UK higher education institutions. It will replace the RAE and will be completed in 2014.

Subject	Universities or university colleges
Anthropology	LSE (1), SOAS (1), Cambridge (3), Roehampton (4), UCL (5)
Archaeology	Durham (1), Reading (2), Cambridge (3), Oxford (3), Liverpool (5)
Biological sciences	Institute of Cancer Research (1), Manchester (2), Oxford (2), Sheffield (2), Dundee (5), RHUL (5)
Business and management	London Business School (1), Imperial (2), Cambridge (3), Cardiff (4), Bath (5), King's (5), Lancaster (5), LSE (5), Oxford (5), Warwick (5)
Chemistry	Cambridge (1), Nottingham (2), Oxford (3), Bristol (4), Edinburgh (4), St Andrews (4)
Classics	Cambridge (1), Oxford (2), UCL (3), Durham (4), King's (4), Warwick (4)
Communication and media studies	Westminster (1), East Anglia (2), Goldsmiths (3), LSE (3), Cardiff (5)
Computer science	Cambridge (1), Edinburgh (2), Imperial (2), Southampton (2), Manchester (5), Oxford (5), UCL (5)
Dentistry	Manchester (1), Queen Mary (2), King's (3), Sheffield (4), Bristol (5), Cardiff (5)

Subject	Universities or university colleges
Drama and performing arts	Queen Mary (1), St Andrews (1), Manchester (3), Warwick (4), Bristol (5), King's (5)
Economics	LSE (1), UCL (2), Essex (3), Oxford (3), Warwick (3)
Engineering (electronic)	Leeds (1), Bangor (2), Manchester (2), Surrey (2), Imperial (5)
Engineering (general)	Cambridge (1), Oxford (2), Leeds (3), Nottingham (3), Imperial (5), Swansea (5)
English	York (1), Edinburgh (2), Manchester (2), Queen Mary (2), Exeter (5), Nottingham (5), Oxford (5)
French	Oxford (1), King's (2), Warwick (2), Aberdeen (4), Cambridge (4), St Andrews (4)
Geography	Bristol (1), Cambridge (1), Durham (1), Oxford (1), Queen Mary (1)
German, Dutch and Scandinavian	Oxford (1), Cambridge (2), Durham (2), King's (2), Leeds (2), RHUL (2), St Andrews (2)
History	Imperial (1), Essex (2), Kent (2), Liverpool (2), Oxford (2), Warwick (2)
Law	LSE (1), UCL (2), Oxford (3), Durham (4), Nottingham (4)
Mathematics (applied)	Cambridge (1), Oxford (1), Bristol (3), Bath (4), Portsmouth (4), St Andrews (4)
Mathematics (pure)	Imperial (1), Warwick (2), Oxford (3), Cambridge (4), Bristol (5), Edinburgh (5), Heriot-Watt (5)
Music	RHUL (1), Birmingham (2), Manchester (2), Cambridge (4), King's (4), Sheffield (4), Southampton (4)
Philosophy	UCL (1), St Andrews (1), King's (3), Reading (3), Sheffield (3)
Physics	Lancaster (1), Bath (2), Cambridge (2), Nottingham (2), St Andrews (2)
Politics	Essex (1), Sheffield (1), Aberystwyth (3), Oxford (4), LSE (5)
Psychology	Cambridge (1), Oxford (2), Birmingham (3), UCL (4), Birkbeck (5), Cardiff (5)
Sociology	Essex (1), Goldsmiths (1), Manchester (1), York (1), Lancaster (5)
Sports-related subjects	Birmingham (1), Loughborough (1), Bristol (3), Liverpool John Moores (4), Stirling (5)
Theology and religious studies	Durham (1), Aberdeen (2), Cambridge (3), Oxford (3), UCL (3)

UG= undergraduate   PG= postgraduate
UNIVERSITY OF ABERDEEN (1495)
King's College, Aberdeen AB24 3FX T 01224-272000
W www.abdn.ac.uk
Students: 11,610 UG; 3,925 PG
Chancellor, Lord Wilson of Tillyorn, KT, GCMG, FRSE
Vice-Chancellor and Principal, Prof. Ian Diamond
University Secretary, Dr Gillian Mackintosh

UNIVERSITY OF ABERTAY DUNDEE (1994)
Bell Street, Dundee DD1 1HG T 01382-308000
W www.abertay.ac.uk
Students: 3,719 UG; 463 PG
Chancellor, Lord Cullen of Whitekirk, KT, PC, FRSE
Vice-Chancellor, Prof. Bernard King, CBE, PHD
Registrar, Dr Colin Fraser, PHD

ANGLIA RUSKIN UNIVERSITY (1992)
Chelmsford Campus, Bishop Hall Lane, Chelmsford, Essex
CM1 1SQ T 0845-271 3333 W www.anglia.ac.uk
Students: 19,742 UG; 4,034 PG
Chancellor, Lord Ashcroft, KCMG
Vice-Chancellor, Prof. Michael Thorne, FRSA, PHD
Secretary and Clerk, Stephen Bennett

**UNIVERSITY OF THE ARTS LONDON (Formerly
The London Institute (1986), University of the Arts
London was formed in 2004)**
272 High Holborn, London WC1V 7EY T 020-7514 6000
W www.arts.ac.uk
Students: 13,161 UG; 2,774 PG
Chancellor, Lord Stevenson, CBE
Rector, Sir Michael Bichard, KCB
University Secretary, Martin Prince

COLLEGES
CAMBERWELL COLLEGE OF ARTS (1898)
Peckham Road, London SE5 8UF T 020-7514 6302
W www.camberwell.arts.ac.uk
Head of College, Chris Wainwright

CENTRAL SAINT MARTINS COLLEGE OF ART & DESIGN
(1854)
Southampton Row, London WC1B 4AP T 020-7514 7022
W www.csm.arts.ac.uk
Head of College, Jane Rapley, OBE

CHELSEA COLLEGE OF ART & DESIGN (1895)
Millbank, London SW1P 4RJ T 020-7514 7751
W www.chelsea.arts.ac.uk
Head of College, Chris Wainwright

LONDON COLLEGE OF COMMUNICATION (1894)
Elephant & Castle, London SE1 6SB T 020-7514 6500
W www.lcc.arts.ac.uk
Head of College, Sandra Kemp

LONDON COLLEGE OF FASHION (1963)
20 John Princes Street, London W1G 0BJ T 020-7514 7500
W www.fashion.arts.ac.uk
Head of College, Dr Frances Corner

WIMBLEDON COLLEGE OF ART (1930)
Merton Hall Road, London SW19 3QA T 020-7514 9641
W www.wimbledon.arts.ac.uk
Head of College, Chris Wainwright

ASTON UNIVERSITY (1966)
Aston Triangle, Birmingham B4 7ET T 0121-204 3000
W www.aston.ac.uk

Students: 7,718 UG; 1,945 PG
Chancellor, Sir John Sunderland
Vice-Chancellor, Prof. Julia King, CBE, FRENG, FRSA
Registrar, John Walter

UNIVERSITY OF BATH (1966)
Bath BA2 7AY T 01225-388388 W www.bath.ac.uk
Students: 9,913 UG; 4,005 PG
Chancellor, Lord Tugendhat
Vice-Chancellor, Prof. Glynis Breakwell, FRSA
University Secretary, Mark Humphriss

BATH SPA UNIVERSITY (2005)
Newton Park, Newton St Loe, Bath BA2 9BN T 01225-875875
W www.bathspa.ac.uk
Students: 5,290 UG; 2,099 PG
Vice-Chancellor, Prof. Frank Morgan
Academic Registrar, Christopher Ellicott

UNIVERSITY OF BEDFORDSHIRE (1993)
Park Square, Luton LU1 3JU T 01234-400400
W www.beds.ac.uk
Students: 14,410 UG; 4,780 PG
Chancellor, Baroness Howells of St Davids, OBE
Vice-Chancellor, Prof. Les Ebdon, CBE
Registrar, Alice Hynes

UNIVERSITY OF BIRMINGHAM (1900)
Edgbaston, Birmingham B15 2TT T 0121-414 3344
W www.bham.ac.uk
Students: 17,355 UG; 8,718 PG
Chancellor, Sir Dominic Cadbury
Vice-Chancellor and Principal, Prof. David Eastwood
Registrar and Secretary, Lee Sanders

BIRMINGHAM CITY UNIVERSITY (1992)
City North Campus, Birmingham B42 2SU T 0121-331 5000
W www.bcu.ac.uk
Students: 20,610 UG; 4,225 PG
Chancellor, Lord Mayor of Birmingham, Anita Ward
Vice-Chancellor, Prof. David H. Tidmarsh
University Secretary, Ms Christine Abbott

UNIVERSITY OF BOLTON (2005)
Deane Road, Bolton BL3 5AB T 01204-900600
W www.bolton.ac.uk
Students: 10,327 UG; 2,295 PG
Chancellor, Rt. Hon. Baroness Morris of Bolton, OBE,
DPHIL
Vice-Chancellor, Dr George Holmes

BOURNEMOUTH UNIVERSITY (1992)
Fern Barrow, Poole, Dorset BH12 5BB T 01202-524111
W www.bournemouth.ac.uk
Students: 15,670 UG; 2,645 PG
Chancellor, Rt. Hon. Lord Phillips of Worth Matravers,
PC, QC
Vice-Chancellor, Prof. John Vinney
Clerk, Noel Richardson

UNIVERSITY OF BRADFORD (1966)
Bradford, W. Yorks BD7 1DP T 01274-232323
W www.brad.ac.uk
Students: 10,045 UG; 3,135 PG
Chancellor, Imran Khan
Vice-Chancellor, Prof. Mark Cleary
University Secretary, Adrian Pearce

UNIVERSITY OF BRIGHTON (1992)
Mithras House, Lewes Road, Brighton BN2 4AT
T 01273-600900 **W** www.bton.ac.uk
Students: 17,003 UG; 4,006 PG
Chairman, Lord Mogg
Vice-Chancellor, Prof. Julian Crampton
Registrar, Mrs Carol Burns

UNIVERSITY OF BRISTOL (1909)
Senate House, Tyndall Avenue, Bristol BS8 1TH
T 0117-928 9000 **W** www.bristol.ac.uk
Students: 13,468 UG; 5,147 PG
Chancellor, Baroness Hale of Richmond, DBE, PC
Vice-Chancellor, Prof. Eric Thomas
Registrar, Derek Pretty

BRUNEL UNIVERSITY (1966)
Uxbridge, Middx UB8 3PH **T** 01895-274000
W www.brunel.ac.uk
Students: 10,549 UG; 4,213 PG
Chancellor, Lord Wakeham
Vice-Chancellor and Principal, Prof. Chris Jenkins, FRSA
Interim Academic Registrar, Bob Westaway

UNIVERSITY OF BUCKINGHAM (1983)
Buckingham MK18 1EG **T** 01280-814080
W www.buckingham.ac.uk
Students: 835 UG; 448 PG
Chancellor, Lord Tanlaw of Tanlaw Hill
Vice-Chancellor, Dr Terence Kealey, DPHIL
Registrar, Anne Miller

BUCKINGHAMSHIRE NEW UNIVERSITY (2007)
High Wycombe Campus, Queen Alexandra Road, High
Wycombe HP11 2JZ **T** 0800-0565 660 **W** www.bucks.ac.uk
Students: 6,017 UG; 527 PG
Vice-Chancellor, Prof. Ruth Farwell
Director of Academic Quality, Ellie Smith

UNIVERSITY OF CAMBRIDGE (1209)
The Old Schools, Trinity Lane, Cambridge CB2 1TN
T 01223-337733 **W** www.cam.ac.uk
Students: 12,192 UG; 5,795 PG
Chancellor, vacant
Vice-Chancellor, Prof. Sir Leszek Borysiewicz, FRS
(Wolfson)
High Steward, Lord Watson of Richmond, CBE (Jesus)
Deputy High Steward, Mrs A. Lonsdale, CBE (Murray
Edwards)
Commissary, Lord Mackay of Clashfern, KT, PC, FRSE
(Trinity)
Pro-Vice-Chancellors, Dr J. C. Barnes (Murray Edwards);
Prof. L. F. Gladden, CBE, FRS (Trinity); Prof. J. M.
Rallison (Trinity); Prof. I. H. White, FRENG (Jesus);
Prof. S. J. Young, FRENG (Emmanuel)
Proctors, Dr Oren Scherman (Jesus); Dr Alan Winter
(Christ's)
Orator, Dr R. J. E. Thompson (Selwyn)
Registrary, Dr J. W. Nicholls (Emmanuel)
Librarian, Mrs A. E. Jarvis (Wolfson)
Director of the Fitzwilliam Museum, Dr T. F. Potts (Clare)
Academic Secretary, G. P. Allen (Wolfson)
Director of Finance, A. M. Reid (Wolfson)

COLLEGES AND HALLS *with dates of foundation*
CHRIST'S (1505)
Master, Prof. F. P. Kelly, FRS

CHURCHILL (1960)
Master, Prof. Sir David Wallace, CBE, FRS
CLARE (1326)
Master, Prof. A. J. Badger
CLARE HALL (1966)
President, Prof. Sir Martin Harris, CBE
CORPUS CHRISTI (1352)
Master, Mr S. Laing
DARWIN (1964)
Master, Prof. W. A. Brown, CBE
DOWNING (1800)
Master, Prof. B. J. Everitt, FRS
EMMANUEL (1584)
Master, Lord Wilson of Dinton, GCB
FITZWILLIAM (1966)
Master, Prof. R. D. Lethbridge
GIRTON (1869)
Mistress, Prof. S. J. Smith, FBA
GONVILLE AND CAIUS (1348)
Master, Sir Christopher Hum, KCMG
HOMERTON (1824)
Principal, Dr K. B. Pretty, CBE
HUGHES HALL (1985)
President, Mrs S. L. Squire
JESUS (1496)
Master, Prof. R. Mair, CBE, FRS
KING'S (1441)
Provost, Prof. T. R. Harrison
LUCY CAVENDISH (1965)
President, Prof. J. M. Todd
MAGDALENE (1542)
Master, Mr D. D. Robinson, CBE
MURRAY EDWARDS (1954)
President, Dr J. C. Barnes
NEWNHAM (1871)
Principal, Dame Patricia Hodgson, DBE
PEMBROKE (1347)
Master, Sir Richard Dearlove, KCMG, OBE
PETERHOUSE (1284)
Master, Prof. A. K. Dixon, FRCP
QUEENS' (1448)
President, Prof. Lord Eatwell
ROBINSON (1977)
Warden, Prof. A. D. Yates
ST CATHARINE'S (1473)
Master, Prof. Dame Jean Thomas, DBE, FRS
ST EDMUND'S (1896)
Master, Prof. J. P. Luzio, FRCPATH
ST JOHN'S (1511)
Master, Prof. C. M. Dobson, FRS
SELWYN (1882)
Master, Prof. R. J. Bowring
SIDNEY SUSSEX (1596)
Master, Prof. A. F. Wallace-Hadrill, OBE
TRINITY (1546)
Master, Prof. Lord Rees of Ludlow, OM, PRS
TRINITY HALL (1350)
Master, Prof. M. J. Daunton, FBA
WOLFSON (1965)
President, Prof. R. J. Evans, FBA

CANTERBURY CHRIST CHURCH UNIVERSITY (2005)
North Holmes Road, Canterbury CT1 1QU **T** 01227-767700
W www.canterbury.ac.uk
Students: 4,407 UG; 13,571 PG
Chancellor, Most Revd Rowan Williams, PC, DPHIL
Vice-Chancellor and Principal, Prof. Robin Baker, CMG
Academic Registrar, Lorri Currie

CARDIFF UNIVERSITY (1883)
Cardiff CF10 3XQ **T** 029-2087 4000 **W** www.cardiff.ac.uk
Students: 21,243 UG; 7,597 PG
President, Prof. Sir Martin Evans, FRS
Vice-Chancellor, Dr David Grant, CBE
Chair of Council, Prof. Sir Keith Peters

UNIVERSITY OF CENTRAL LANCASHIRE
(1992)
Preston PR1 2HE **T** 01772-201201 **W** www.uclan.ac.uk
Students: 27,660 UG; 4,635 PG
Chancellor, Sir Richard Evans, CBE
Vice-Chancellor, Dr Malcolm McVicar

UNIVERSITY OF CHESTER (2005)
Parkgate Road, Chester CH1 4BJ **T** 01244-511000
W www.chester.ac.uk
Students: 12,013 UG; 3,582 PG
Chancellor, His Grace, the Duke of Westminster, KG,
   OBE, DL
Vice-Chancellor, Canon Prof. Tim Wheeler, DL
Director of Registry Services, Jonathan Moores

UNIVERSITY OF CHICHESTER (2005)
Bishop Otter Campus, College Lane, Chichester PO19 6PE
T 01243-816000 **W** www.chi.ac.uk
Students: 3,670 UG; 477 PG
Vice-Chancellor, Prof. Clive Behagg, PHD

CITY UNIVERSITY LONDON (1966)
Northampton Square, London EC1V 0HB **T** 020-7040 5060
W www.city.ac.uk
Students: 9,763 UG; 6,945 PG
Chancellor, Michael Bear
Vice-Chancellor, Prof. Paul Curran

COVENTRY UNIVERSITY (1992)
Priory Street, Coventry CV1 5FB **T** 024-7688 7688
W www.coventry.ac.uk
Students: 18,772 UG; 3,473 PG
Chancellor, Sir John Egan
Vice-Chancellor, Prof. Madeleine Atkins
Academic Registrar and Secretary, Kate Quantrell

CRANFIELD UNIVERSITY (1969)
Cranfield, Bedfordshire MK43 0AL **T** 01234-750111
W www.cranfield.ac.uk
Students: 4,300 PG (postgraduate only)
Chancellor, Baroness Young of Old Scone
Vice-Chancellor, Prof. Sir John O'Reilly
Registrar, Prof. William Stephens

UNIVERSITY FOR THE CREATIVE ARTS (2008)
Falkner Road, Farnham, Surrey GU9 7DS **T** 01252-892883
W www.ucreative.ac.uk
Students: 5,500 UG; 350 PG
Chancellor, Zandra Rhodes, CBE
Vice-Chancellor, Prof. Elaine Thomas
Registrar, David Burt

UNIVERSITY OF CUMBRIA (2007)
Fusehill Street, Carlisle CA1 2HH **T** 01228-616234
W www.cumbria.ac.uk
Students: 9,695 UG; 2,715 PG
Chancellor, Most Revd and Rt. Hon. Dr John Sentamu,
   Archbishop of York
Interim Vice-Chancellor, Prof. Peter Strike
University Secretary, Neil Harris

DE MONTFORT UNIVERSITY (1992)
The Gateway, Leicester LE1 9BH **T** 0845-945 4647
W www.dmu.ac.uk
Students: 18,452 UG; 4,076 PG
Chancellor, Lord Waheed Alli
Vice-Chancellor, Prof. Dominic Shellard
Registrar, Joanne Cooke

UNIVERSITY OF DERBY (1992)
Kedleston Road, Derby DE22 1GB **T** 01332-590500
W www.derby.ac.uk
Students: 14,390 UG; 3,085 PG
Chancellor, The Duke of Devonshire, KCVO, CBE,
   DL
Vice-Chancellor, Prof. John Coyne
Registrar, June Hughes

UNIVERSITY OF DUNDEE (1967)
Nethergate, Dundee DD1 4HN **T** 01382-383000
W www.dundee.ac.uk
Students: 10,730 UG; 5,465 PG
Chancellor, Lord Patel, KT, FRSE
Vice-Chancellor and Principal, Prof. Peter Downes, OBE,
   FRSE
Secretary, Dr Jim McGeorge

DURHAM UNIVERSITY (1832)
The University Office, Old Elvet, Durham DH1 3HP
T 0191-334 2000 **W** www.dur.ac.uk
Students: 11,350 UG; 4,625 PG
Chancellor, Dr Bill Bryson
Vice-Chancellor and Warden, Prof. Christopher Higgins,
   FRSE
Registrar, Carolyn Fowler

COLLEGES
COLLINGWOOD (1972)
Principal, Prof. E. Corrigan, FRS
GREY
Master, Prof. J. M. Chamberlain, DPHIL
HATFIELD (1846)
Master, Prof. T. P. Burt, DSC
JOHN SNOW (2001)
Principal, Prof. Carolyn Summerbell
JOSEPHINE BUTLER (2006)
Principal, A. Simpson
ST AIDAN'S
Principal (acting), Dr Susan F. Frenk
ST CHAD'S (1904)
Principal, Revd Dr J. P. M. Cassidy
ST CUTHBERT'S SOCIETY (1888)
Principal, Prof. A. Broderick
ST HILD AND ST BEDE (1975)
Principal, Prof. C. J. Hutchinson
ST JOHN'S (1909)
Principal, Revd Dr D. Wilkinson
ST MARY'S
Principal, Prof. P. Gilmartin
STEPHENSON (2001)
Principal, Prof. A. C. Darnell
TREVELYAN (1966)
Principal, Prof. H. M. Evans
UNIVERSITY (1832)
Master, Prof. M. E. Tucker
USHAW
President, Fr. J. Marsland

USTINOV
Principal, Penelope B. Wilson, DPHIL
VAN MILDERT (1965)
Master, Prof. P. O'Meara, DPHIL

UNIVERSITY OF EAST ANGLIA (1963)
Norwich NR4 7TJ T 01603-456161 W www.uea.ac.uk
Students: 11,804 UG; 2,509 PG
Chancellor, Sir Brandon Gough
Vice-Chancellor, Prof. Edward Acton
Registrar, Brian Summers

UNIVERSITY OF EAST LONDON (1898)
University Way, London E16 2RD T 020-8223 3000
W www.uel.ac.uk
Students: 18,700 UG; 8,230 PG
Chancellor, Lord Rix
Vice-Chancellor, Prof. Patrick McGhee
Clerk to the Governors, Jill Grinstead

EDGE HILL UNIVERSITY (2006)
St Helens Road, Ormskirk, Lancs L39 4QP T 01695-575171
W www.edgehill.ac.uk
Students: 10,575 UG; 14,745 PG
Chancellor, Prof. Tanya Byron
Vice-Chancellor, Dr John Cater
University Secretary, Lesley Munro

UNIVERSITY OF EDINBURGH (1583)
Old College, South Bridge, Edinburgh EH8 9YL
T 0131-650 1000 W www.ed.ac.uk
Students: 17,955 UG; 7,735 PG
Chancellor, HRH the Princess Royal, KG, KT, GCVO
Vice-Chancellor and Principal, Prof. Sir Timothy O'Shea, FRSE
University Secretary, Dr Kim Waldron

EDINBURGH NAPIER UNIVERSITY (1992)
Craighouse Road, Edinburgh EH10 5LG T 0845-260 6040
W www.napier.ac.uk
Students: 13,107 UG; 2,584 PG
Chancellor, Tim Waterstone
Vice-Chancellor, Prof. Dame Joan Stringer, CBE
Secretary, Dr Gerry Webber

UNIVERSITY OF ESSEX (1965)
Wivenhoe Park, Colchester CO4 3SQ T 01206-873333
W www.essex.ac.uk
Students: 7,590 UG; 2,690 PG
Chancellor, Lord Phillips of Sudbury, OBE
Vice-Chancellor, Prof. Colin Riordan
Academic Registrar, Dr Tony Rich

UNIVERSITY OF EXETER (1955)
The Queen's Drive, Exeter EX4 4QJ T 01392-661000
W www.exeter.ac.uk
Students: 12,855 UG; 4,355 PG
Chancellor, Baroness Floella Benjamin, OBE
Vice-Chancellor, Prof. Steve Smith
Registrar, David Allen

UNIVERSITY OF GLAMORGAN (1992)
Pontypridd CF37 1DL T 0845-6434 030 W www.glam.ac.uk
Students: 17,140 UG; 3,930 PG
Chancellor, Lord Morris of Aberavon, KG, PC, QC
Vice-Chancellor, Julie Lydon
Academic Registrar, William Callaway

UNIVERSITY OF GLASGOW (1451)
University Avenue, Glasgow G12 8QQ T 0141-330 2000
W www.gla.ac.uk
Students: 20,000 UG; 5,600 PG
Chancellor, Prof. Sir Kenneth Calman, KCB, MD, FRCS
Vice-Chancellor, Prof. Anton Muscatelli, FRSE
Secretary of Court, David Newall

GLASGOW CALEDONIAN UNIVERSITY (1993)
City Campus, Cowcaddens Road, Glasgow G4 0BA
T 0141-331 3000 W www.gcu.ac.uk
Students: 15,427 UG; 3,049 PG
Chancellor, Rt. Hon. Lord Macdonald of Tradeston, CBE
Vice-Chancellor and Principal, Prof. Pamela Gillies, FRSA
Registrar, Brendan Ferguson

UNIVERSITY OF GLOUCESTERSHIRE (2001)
The Park, Cheltenham GL50 2RH T 0844-801 0001
W www.glos.ac.uk
Students: 7,065 UG; 2,655 PG
Vice-Chancellor, Stephen Marston
Academic Registrar, Julie Thackray

UNIVERSITY OF GREENWICH (1992)
Old Royal Naval College, Park Row, Greenwich, London
SE10 9LS T 020-8331 8000 W www.gre.ac.uk
Students: 22,658 UG; 6,145 PG
Chancellor, Lord Hart of Chilton
Vice-Chancellor, David Maguire
Secretary and Registrar, Linda Cording

HERIOT-WATT UNIVERSITY (1966)
Edinburgh EH14 4AS T 0131-449 5111 W www.hw.ac.uk
Students: 6,280 UG; 5,020 PG
Chancellor, Baroness Susan Greenfield, CBE, FRCP
Vice-Chancellor and Principal, Prof. Steve Chapman, FRSE
Secretary, Ann Marie Dalton

UNIVERSITY OF HERTFORDSHIRE (1992)
College Lane, Hatfield, Herts AL10 9AB T 01707-284000
W www.herts.ac.uk
Students: 21,650 UG; 6,000 PG
Chancellor, Marquess of Salisbury, PC
Vice-Chancellor, Prof. Quintin Mckellar, CBE
Registrar, Philip Waters, FRSA

UNIVERSITY OF HUDDERSFIELD (1992)
Queensgate, Huddersfield HD1 3DH T 01484-422288
W www.hud.ac.uk
Students: 18,064 UG; 4,070 PG
Chancellor, Sir Patrick Stewart, OBE
Vice-Chancellor, Prof. Bob Cryan, PHD, DSC
Head of Registry, Kathy Sherlock

UNIVERSITY OF HULL (1927)
Cottingham Road, Hull HU6 7RX T 01482-346311
W www.hull.ac.uk
Students: 19,700 UG; 3,375 PG
Chancellor, Baroness Bottomley, PC
Vice-Chancellor, Prof. Calie Pistorius, FRSA
Registrar and Secretary, Mrs Frances Owen

IMPERIAL COLLEGE LONDON (1907)
South Kensington, London SW7 2AZ T 020-7589 5111
W www.imperial.ac.uk

Students: 8,608 UG; 5,959 PG
Rector, Sir Keith O'Nions
Deputy Rector, Prof. Stephen Richardson
Academic Registrar, Nigel Wheatley

KEELE UNIVERSITY (1962)
Keele, Staffs ST5 5BG T 01782-732000 W www.keele.ac.uk
Students: 8,255 UG; 2,215 PG
Chancellor, Prof. Sir David Weatherall, DSC, MD,
   FRCP
Vice-Chancellor, Prof. Nick Foskett
Registrar and Secretary, Simon Morris

UNIVERSITY OF KENT (1965)
Canterbury, Kent CT2 7NZ T 01227-764000
W www.kent.ac.uk
Students: 17,825 UG; 2,840 PG
Chancellor, Prof. Sir Robert Worcester, KBE
Vice-Chancellor, Prof. Dame Julia Goodfellow, CBE
Registrar, Jon Pink

KINGSTON UNIVERSITY (1992)
River House, 53–57 High Street, Kingston upon Thames,
Surrey KT1 1LQ T 020-8417 9000 W www.kingston.ac.uk
Students: 20,355 UG; 6,730 PG
Chancellor, Sir Peter Hall
Vice-Chancellor, Prof. Julius Weinberg
Acting Academic Registrar, Marie Sheehan

UNIVERSITY OF LANCASTER (1964)
Bailrigg, Lancaster LA1 4YW T 01524-65201
W www.lancs.ac.uk
Students: 8,780 UG; 3,345 PG
Chancellor, Sir Christian Bonington, CBE
Vice-Chancellor, Prof. Paul Wellings
University Secretary, Fiona Aiken

UNIVERSITY OF LEEDS (1904)
Leeds LS2 9JT T 0113-243 1751 W www.leeds.ac.uk
Students: 24,965 UG; 7,850 PG
Chancellor, Lord Bragg, LLD, DLITT, DCL
Vice-Chancellor, Prof. Michael Arthur, DM, FRCP
Registrar, Mr J. Roger Gair

LEEDS METROPOLITAN UNIVERSITY (1992)
Civic Quarter, Leeds LS1 3HE T 0113-812 0000
W www.leedsmet.ac.uk
Students: 23,628 UG; 4,796 PG
Chancellor, Lord Woolmer
Vice-Chancellor, Prof. Susan Price
Registrar, Steve Denton

UNIVERSITY OF LEICESTER (1957)
University Road, Leicester LE1 7RH T 0116-252 2522
W www.le.ac.uk
Students: 10,946 UG; 11,857 PG
Chancellor, vacant
Vice-Chancellor, Prof. Sir Robert Burgess
Registrar, Dave Hall

UNIVERSITY OF LINCOLN (1992)
Brayford Pool, Lincoln LN6 7TS T 01522-882000
W www.lincoln.ac.uk
Students: 9,597 UG; 1,085 PG
Chancellor, Lord Victor Adebowale
Vice-Chancellor, Prof. Mary Stuart
Registrar, Chris Spendlove

UNIVERSITY OF LIVERPOOL (1903)
Liverpool, Merseyside L69 7ZX T 0151-794 2000
W www.liv.ac.uk
Students: 14,049 UG; 3,036 PG
Chancellor, Prof. Sir David King, CH, PC, FRCP
Vice-Chancellor, Prof. Sir Howard Newby, FRSA
Chief Operating Officer, Patrick Hackett

LIVERPOOL HOPE UNIVERSITY (2005)
Hope Park, Liverpool L16 9JD T 0151-291 3000
W www.hope.ac.uk
Students: 4,674 UG; 1,774 PG
Chancellor, Baroness Cox of Queensbury, FRCN
Vice-Chancellor and Rector, Prof. Gerald Pillay, FRSA
Registrar, Neil McLaughlin-Cook

LIVERPOOL JOHN MOORES UNIVERSITY
(1992)
Kingsway House, 2nd Floor, Hatton Garden, Liverpool L3 2AJ
T 0151-231 2121 W www.ljmu.ac.uk
Students: 21,000 UG; 4,860 PG
Chancellor, Dr Brian May, CBE
Vice-Chancellor and Chief Executive, Prof. Michael Brown,
   CBE, DL
Secretary, Denise Tipping

UNIVERSITY OF LONDON (1836)
Senate House, Malet Street, London WC1E 7HU
T 020-7862 8000 W www.london.ac.uk
Chancellor, HRH the Princess Royal, KG, KT, GCVO
Vice-Chancellor, Prof. Geoffrey Crossick
Chair of the Board of Trustees, Dame Jenny Abramsky
Director of Administration, Catherine Swarbrick

COLLEGES
BIRKBECK COLLEGE
Malet Street, London WC1E 7HX
Students: 14,240 UG; 4,435 PG
President, Prof. Eric Hobsbawm
Master, Prof. David Latchman

CENTRAL SCHOOL OF SPEECH AND DRAMA
Embassy Theatre, Eton Avenue, London NW3 3HY
Students: 555 UG; 300 PG
President, Michael Grandage, CBE
Principal, Prof. Gavin Henderson, CBE

COURTAULD INSTITUTE OF ART
North Block, Somerset House, Strand, London WC2R 0RN
Students: 150 UG; 255 PG
Director, Prof. Deborah Swallow

GOLDSMITHS COLLEGE
Lewisham Way, New Cross, London SE14 6NW
Students, 5,510 UG; 2,460 PG
Warden, Pat Loughrey

HEYTHROP COLLEGE
Kensington Square, London W8 5HN
Students: 515 UG; 420 PG
Principal, Revd Dr John McDade, SJ, BD

INSTITUTE OF CANCER RESEARCH
15 Cotswold Road, Belmont, Surrey SM2 5NG
Students: 300 PG (postgraduate only)
Chief Executive, Prof. Alan Ashworth

INSTITUTE OF EDUCATION
20 Bedford Way, London WC1H 0AL
Students: 540 UG; 6,830 PG
Director, Prof. Geoff Whitty, CBE

KING'S COLLEGE LONDON (includes Guy's, King's and St Thomas's Schools of Medicine, Dentistry and Biomedical Sciences)
Strand, London WC2R 2LS
Students: 14,970 UG; 9,525 PG
Principal, Prof. Rick Trainor

LONDON BUSINESS SCHOOL
Regent's Park, London NW1 4SA
Students: 2,050 PG (postgraduate only)
Dean, Sir Andrew Likierman

LONDON SCHOOL OF ECONOMICS AND POLITICAL SCIENCE
Houghton Street, London WC2A 2AE
Students: 4,000 UG; 5,560 PG
Director, Prof. Judith Rees, CBE

LONDON SCHOOL OF HYGIENE AND TROPICAL MEDICINE
50 Bedford Square, London WC1B 3DP
Students: 1,270 PG (postgraduate only)
Director, Peter Piot

QUEEN MARY (incorporating St Bartholomew's and the Royal London School of Medicine and Dentistry)
Mile End Road, London E1 4NS
Students: 11,085 UG; 3,640 PG
Principal, Prof. Simon Gaskell

ROYAL ACADEMY OF MUSIC
Marylebone Road, London NW1 5HT
Students: 330 UG; 385 PG
Principal, Prof. Jonathan Freeman-Attwood

ROYAL HOLLOWAY
Egham Hill, Egham, Surrey TW20 0EX
Students: 7,295 UG; 2,240 PG
Principal, Prof. Paul Layzell

ROYAL VETERINARY COLLEGE
Royal College Street, London NW1 0TU
Students: 1,535 UG; 530 PG
Principal, Prof. Stuart Reid

ST GEORGE'S
Cranmer Terrace, London SW17 0RE
Students: 4,590 UG; 535 PG
Principal, Prof. Peter Kopelman, FRCGP

SCHOOL OF ORIENTAL AND AFRICAN STUDIES
Thornhaugh Street, Russell Square, London WC1H 0XG
Students: 2,970 UG; 2,255 PG
Director, Prof. Paul Webley

SCHOOL OF PHARMACY
29–39 Brunswick Square, London WC1N 1AX
Students: 735 UG; 675 PG
Principal and Dean, Prof. Anthony Smith

UNIVERSITY COLLEGE LONDON (including UCL Medical School)
Gower Street, London WC1E 6BT
Students: 12,765 UG; 10,460 PG
Provost and President, Prof. Malcolm Grant, CBE

INSTITUTES
UNIVERSITY OF LONDON INSTITUTE IN PARIS
9–11 rue de Constantine, 75340 Paris Cedex 07
Dean, Prof. Andrew Hussey

UNIVERSITY MARINE BIOLOGICAL STATION
Millport, Isle of Cumbrae KA28 0EG
Director, Prof. Jim Atkinson

SCHOOL OF ADVANCED STUDY
Senate House, Malet Street, London WC1E 7HU
Dean and Chief Executive, Prof. Roger Kain, CBE

INSTITUTE OF ADVANCED LEGAL STUDIES
Charles Clore House, 17 Russell Square, London WC1B 5DR
Dean and Chief Executive, Prof. Roger Kain, CBE

INSTITUTE OF CLASSICAL STUDIES
Senate House, Malet Street, London WC1E 7HU
Director, Prof. M. Edwards

INSTITUTE OF COMMONWEALTH STUDIES
Senate House, Malet Street, London WC1E 7HU
Director, Prof. Philip Murphy

INSTITUTE OF ENGLISH STUDIES
Senate House, Malet Street, London WC1E 7HU
Director, Prof. Warwick Gould

INSTITUTE OF GERMANIC AND ROMANCE STUDIES
Senate House, Malet Street, London WC1E 7HU
Director, Prof. Naomi Segal

INSTITUTE OF HISTORICAL RESEARCH
Senate House, Malet Street, London WC1E 7HU
Director, Prof. Miles Taylor

INSTITUTE OF MUSICAL RESEARCH
Senate House, Malet Street, London WC1E 7HU
Director, Prof. John Irving

INSTITUTE OF PHILOSOPHY
Senate House, Malet Street, London WC1E 7HU
Director, Prof. Barry Smith

INSTITUTE FOR THE STUDY OF THE AMERICAS
Senate House, Malet Street, London WC1E 7HU
Director, Prof. Maxine Molyneux

WARBURG INSTITUTE
Woburn Square, London WC1H 0AB
Director, Prof. Peter Mack

LONDON METROPOLITAN UNIVERSITY (2002)
166–220 Holloway Road, London N7 8D8 T 020-7423 0000
W www.londonmet.ac.uk
Students: 19,485 UG; 7,750 PG
Patron, HRH the Prince Philip, Duke of Edinburgh, KG, KT, OM
Vice-Chancellor, Prof. Malcolm Gillies
Interim Secretary, Sally Neocosmos

386   Education

LONDON SOUTH BANK UNIVERSITY (1992)
103 Borough Road, London SE1 0AA T 020-7815 7815
W www.lsbu.ac.uk
Students: 18,875 UG; 6,070 PG
Vice-Chancellor, Martin Earwicker

LOUGHBOROUGH UNIVERSITY (1966)
Ashby Road, Loughborough, Leics LE11 3TU T 01509-263171
W www.lboro.ac.uk
Students: 11,311 UG; 2,420 PG
Chancellor, Sir Nigel Rudd, CBE, FRSE, PHD
Vice-Chancellor, Prof. Shirley Pearce, CBE
Academic Registrar, Dr Jennifer Nutkins

UNIVERSITY OF MANCHESTER (2004)
Oxford Road, Manchester M13 9PL T 0161-306 6000
W www.manchester.ac.uk
Students: 28,313 UG; 11,125 PG
Chancellor, Tom Bloxham, MBE
Vice-Chancellor, Prof. Dame Nancy Rothwell, FRS
Registrar, Will Spinks

MANCHESTER METROPOLITAN UNIVERSITY
(1992)
All Saints, Manchester M15 6BH T 0161-247 2000
W www.mmu.ac.uk
Students: 27,904 UG; 7,822 PG
Chancellor, Dianne Thompson, CBE, FRSA
Vice-Chancellor, Prof. John Brooks, DSC
Registrar, Gwyn Arnold

MIDDLESEX UNIVERSITY (1992)
Hendon Campus, The Burroughs, London NW4 4BT
T 020-8411 5555 W www.mdx.ac.uk
Students: 13,867 UG; 7,955 PG
Chancellor, Lord Sheppard of Didgemere, KT, KCVO
Vice-Chancellor, Prof. Michael Driscoll
Academic Registrar, Colin Davies

NEWCASTLE UNIVERSITY (1963)
Newcastle upon Tyne NE1 7RU T 0191-222 6000
W www.ncl.ac.uk
Students: 14,383 UG; 5,284 PG
Chancellor, Sir Liam Donaldson
Vice-Chancellor, Prof. Chris Brink, FRS, DPHIL
Registrar, Dr John Hogan

UNIVERSITY OF NORTHAMPTON (2005)
Park Campus, Boughton Green Road, Northampton NN2 7AL
T 01604-735500 W www.northampton.ac.uk
Students: 11,415 UG; 2,510 PG
Chancellor, Baroness Falkner
Vice-Chancellor, Prof. Nick Petford
Registrar, Jane Bunce

NORTHUMBRIA UNIVERSITY AT
NEWCASTLE (1992)
Ellison Building, Ellison Place, Newcastle upon Tyne NE1 8ST
T 0191-232 6002 W www.northumbria.ac.uk
Students: 28,197 UG; 5,225 PG
Chancellor, Lord Stevens of Kirkwhelpington, QPM, DCL
Vice-Chancellor, Prof. Andrew Wathey, FRSA, DPHIL
Registrar, Prof. Jane Core

UNIVERSITY OF NOTTINGHAM (1948)
University Park, Nottingham NG7 2RD T 0115-951 5151
W www.nottingham.ac.uk
Students: 24,665 UG; 9,455 PG
Chancellor, Prof. Yang Fujia, LITTD

Vice-Chancellor, Prof. David Greenaway
Registrar, Dr Paul Greatrix

NOTTINGHAM TRENT UNIVERSITY (1992)
Burton Street, Nottingham NG1 4BU T 0115-941 8418
W www.ntu.ac.uk
Students: 21,365 UG; 5,090 PG
Chancellor, Sir Michael Parkinson, MBE
Vice-Chancellor, Prof. Neil Gorman
Registrar, David Samson

OPEN UNIVERSITY (1969)
Walton Hall, Milton Keynes MK7 6AA T 01908-274066
W www.open.ac.uk
Students: 190,272 UG; 16,300 PG
Chancellor, Lord Puttnam
Vice-Chancellor, Martin Bean
University Secretary, Fraser Woodburn

UNIVERSITY OF OXFORD (c.12th century)
University Offices, Wellington Square, Oxford OX1 2JD
T 01865-270000 W www.ox.ac.uk
Students: 11,723 UG; 9,327 PG
Chancellor, Lord Patten of Barnes, CH, PC (Balliol,
St Antony's)
Vice-Chancellor, Prof. Andrew Hamilton, FRS (Kellogg,
Harris Manchester, Wolfson)
High Steward, Lord Rodger of Earlsferry (Balliol, New,
St Hugh's)
Pro-Vice-Chancellors, Prof. S. J. Goss (Wadham); Prof.
W. James (Brasenose); Dr S. L. Mapstone (St Hilda's);
Prof. J. N. P. Rawlins (Wolfson); Prof. I. A. Walmsley
(St. Hugh's)
Registrar, Prof. E. G. McKendrick (Lady Margaret Hall)
Secretary of the Faculties and Academic Registrar, M. D.
Sibly (St Anne's)
Public Orator, R. H. A. Jenkyns (Lady Margaret Hall)
Director of University Library Services and Bodley's
Librarian, Dr S. E. Thomas (Balliol)
Director of the Ashmolean Museum, Dr C. Brown
(Worcester)
Keeper of Archives, S. Bailey (Linacre)
Acting Director of Estates, M. Wigg
Director of Finance, G. F. B. Kerr (Keble)

COLLEGES AND HALLS with dates of foundation
ALL SOULS (1438)
Warden, Prof. Sir John Vickers, FBA
BALLIOL (1263)
Master, Prof. Sir Drummond Bone
BLACKFRIARS (1221)
Regent, Revd Dr Richard Finn
BRASENOSE (1509)
Acting Principal, Prof. Alan K. Bowman, FBA, FSA
CAMPION HALL (1896)
Master, Revd Brendan Callaghan
CHRIST CHURCH (1546)
Dean, Very Revd Dr Christopher A. Lewis
CORPUS CHRISTI (1517)
President, Prof. Richard Carwardine, FBA
EXETER (1314)
Rector, Ms Frances Cairncross, CBE, FRSE
GREEN TEMPLETON (2008)
Principal, Prof. Sir David Watson
HARRIS MANCHESTER (1889)
Principal, Revd Dr Ralph Waller, FRSE
HERTFORD (1740)
Principal, Will Hutton

JESUS (1571)
Principal, Lord Krebs, FRS
KEBLE (1870)
Warden, Sir Jonathan Phillips
KELLOGG (1990)
President, Prof. Jonathan M. Michie
LADY MARGARET HALL (1878)
Principal, Dr Frances Lannon
LINACRE (1962)
Principal, Dr Nick Brown
LINCOLN (1427)
Rector, Prof. Paul Langford, FBA
MAGDALEN (1458)
President, Prof. David Clary, FRS
MANSFIELD (1886)
Principal, Baroness Helena Kennedy, QC
MERTON (1264)
Warden, Prof. Sir Martin Taylor
NEW COLLEGE (1379)
Warden, Prof. Sir Curtis Price
NUFFIELD (1958)
Warden, Prof. Stephen Nickell, CBE, FBA
ORIEL (1326)
Provost, Sir Derek Morris
PEMBROKE (1624)
Master, Giles Henderson, CBE
QUEEN'S (1341)
Provost, Prof. Paul Madden, FRS, FRSE
REGENT'S PARK (1810)
Principal, Revd Dr Robert Ellis
ST ANNE'S (1878)
Principal, Tim Gardam
ST ANTONY'S (1953)
Warden, Prof. Margaret MacMillan
ST BENET'S HALL (1897)
Master, Revd J. Felix Stephens
ST CATHERINE'S (1963)
Master, Prof. Roger Ainsworth
ST CROSS (1965)
Master, Sir Mark Jones
ST EDMUND HALL (c.1278)
Principal, Prof. Keith Gull, CBE, FRS
ST HILDA'S (1893)
Principal, Sheila Forbes, CBE
ST HUGH'S (1886)
Principal, Andrew Dilnot, CBE
ST JOHN'S (1555)
President, Sir Michael Scholar, KCB
ST PETER'S (1929)
Principal, Mark Damazer
ST STEPHEN'S HOUSE (1876)
Principal, Revd Dr Robin Ward
SOMERVILLE (1879)
Principal, Dr Alice Prochaska
TRINITY (1554)
President, Sir Ivor Roberts, KCMG
UNIVERSITY (1249)
Master, Sir Ivor Crewe
WADHAM (1610)
Warden, Sir Neil Chalmers
WOLFSON (1981)
President, Prof. Hermione Lee, FBA, FRSL, CBE
WORCESTER (1714)
Provost, Prof. Jonathan Bate
WYCLIFFE HALL (1877)
Principal, Revd Dr Richard Turnbull

OXFORD BROOKES UNIVERSITY (1992)
Gipsy Lane, Oxford OX3 0BP T 01865-741111
W www.brookes.ac.uk
Students: 14,255 UG; 4,075 PG
Chancellor, Shami Chakrabarti, CBE
Vice-Chancellor, Prof. Janet Beer
Registrar, Paul Large

UNIVERSITY OF PLYMOUTH (1992)
Drake Circus, Plymouth PL4 8AA T 01752-600600
W www.plymouth.ac.uk
Students: 27,865 UG; 4,340 PG
Vice-Chancellor and Chief Executive, Prof. Wendy Purcell
Academic Registrar and Secretary, Jane Hopkinson

UNIVERSITY OF PORTSMOUTH (1992)
University House, Winston Churchill Avenue, Portsmouth
PO1 2UP T 023-9284 8484 W www.port.ac.uk
Students: 18,219 UG; 3,385 PG
Chancellor, Sheila Hancock, OBE
Vice-Chancellor, Prof. John Craven
Academic Registrar, Andrew Rees

QUEEN MARGARET UNIVERSITY (2007)
Queen Margaret University Drive, Musselburgh, Edinburgh
EH21 6UU T 0131-474 0000 W www.qmu.ac.uk
Students: 4,632 UG; 1,722 PG
Chancellor, Sir Tom Farmer, CVO, CBE
Vice-Chancellor, Prof. Petra Wend, FRSA
Registrar, Irene Hynd

QUEEN'S UNIVERSITY BELFAST (1908)
University Road, Belfast BT7 1NN T 028-9024 5133
W www.qub.ac.uk
Students: 17,209 UG; 5,497 PG
Chancellor, His Excellency Kamalesh Sharma
Vice-Chancellor, Prof. Sir Peter Gregson, FRENG, MRIA
Registrar and Chief Operating Officer, James O'Kane

UNIVERSITY OF READING (1926)
Whiteknights, PO Box 217, Reading RG6 6AH T 0118-987 5123
W www.reading.ac.uk
Students: 9,330 UG; 5,145 PG
Chancellor, Sir John Madejski, OBE, DL
Vice-Chancellor, Prof. Gordon Marshall, CBE, FBA
University Secretary, Keith Hodgson

ROBERT GORDON UNIVERSITY (1992)
Schoolhill, Aberdeen AB10 1FR T 01224-262000
W www.rgu.ac.uk
Students: 10,425 UG; 5,980 PG
Chancellor, Sir Ian Wood, CBE
Vice-Chancellor, Prof. Ferdinand non Prondzynski
Registrar, Hilary Douglas

ROEHAMPTON UNIVERSITY (2004)
Erasmus House, Roehampton Lane, London SW15 5PU
T 020-8392 3000 W www.roehampton.ac.uk
Students: 6,285 UG; 2,535 PG
Chancellor, John Simpson, CBE
Vice-Chancellor, Prof. Paul O'Prey
University Secretary and Registrar, Robin Geller

ROYAL COLLEGE OF ART (1967)
Kensington Gore, London SW7 2EU T 020-7590 4444
W www.rca.ac.uk
Students: 939 PG (postgraduate only)
Chancellor, Sir James Dyson
Vice-Chancellor, Dr Paul Thompson
Registrar, Jane Alexander

ROYAL COLLEGE OF MUSIC (1882)
Prince Consort Road, London SW7 2BS **T** 020-7591 4300
W www.rcm.ac.uk
Students: 365 UG; 315 PG
President, HRH the Prince of Wales, KG, KT, GCB
Director, Prof. Colin Lawson, DMUS, FRCM
Deputy Director, Kevin Porter

UNIVERSITY OF ST ANDREWS (1413)
College Gate, St Andrews, Fife KY16 9AJ **T** 01334-476161
W www.st-andrews.ac.uk
Students: 7,155 UG; 1,980 PG
Chancellor, Sir Menzies Campbell, CBE, QC, MP
Vice-Chancellor and Principal, Prof. Louise Richardson

UNIVERSITY OF SALFORD (1967)
The Crescent, Salford, Greater Manchester M5 4WT
T 0161-295 5000 **W** www.salford.ac.uk
Students: 16,385 UG; 4,388 PG
Chancellor, Dr Irene Khan
Vice-Chancellor, Prof. Martin Hall
Registrar, Dr Adrian Graves

UNIVERSITY OF SHEFFIELD (1905)
Western Bank, Sheffield S10 2TN **T** 0114-222 2000
W www.sheffield.ac.uk
Students: 18,357 UG; 6,559 PG
Chancellor, Sir Peter Middleton, GCB
Vice-Chancellor, Prof. Keith Burnett, CBE, DPHIL, FRS
Registrar and Secretary, Philip Harvey

SHEFFIELD HALLAM UNIVERSITY (1992)
City Campus, Howard Street, Sheffield S1 1WB
T 0114-225 5555 **W** www.shu.ac.uk
Students: 27,377 UG; 8,034 PG
Chancellor, Prof. Lord Winston, DSC, FRCOG, FRCP
Vice-Chancellor, Prof. Philip Jones, LLB, LLM
Secretary and Registrar, Elizabeth Winders

UNIVERSITY OF SOUTHAMPTON (1952)
Building 37, Highfield, Southampton SO17 1BJ
T 023-8059 5000 **W** www.soton.ac.uk
Students: 16,124 UG; 6,145 PG
Chancellor, Helen Alexander, CBE
Vice-Chancellor, Prof. Don Nutbeam
Registrar and Chief Operating Officer, Malcolm Ace

SOUTHAMPTON SOLENT UNIVERSITY (2005)
East Park Terrace, Southampton SO14 0YN **T** 023-8031 9000
W www.solent.ac.uk
Students: 11,730 UG; 810 PG
Chancellor, Adm. Lord West of Spithead, GCB, DSC, PC
Vice-Chancellor, Prof. Van Gore

STAFFORDSHIRE UNIVERSITY (1992)
College Road, Stoke-on-Trent, Staffs ST4 2DE **T** 01782-294000
W www.staffs.ac.uk
Students: 17,390 UG; 3,835 PG
Chancellor, Lord Morris of Handsworth
Vice-Chancellor and Chief Executive, Prof. Michael Gunn
University Secretary, Ken Sproston

UNIVERSITY OF STIRLING (1967)
Stirling FK9 4LA **T** 01786-473171 **W** www.stir.ac.uk
Students: 8,452 UG; 2,961 PG
Chancellor, Dr James Naughtie, OBE
Vice-Chancellor, Prof. Gerry McCormac, FRSE
Registrar, Kevin Clarke

UNIVERSITY OF STRATHCLYDE (1964)
16 Richmond Street, Glasgow G1 1XQ **T** 0141-552 4400
W www.strath.ac.uk
Students: 12,063 UG; 4,480 PG
Chancellor, Rt. Hon. Lord Hope of Craighead, KT, PC,
FRSE
Vice-Chancellor and Principal, Prof. Jim McDonald,
FRENG, FRSE
Chief Operating Officer, Hugh Hall

UNIVERSITY OF SUNDERLAND (1992)
Edinburgh Building, Chester Road, Sunderland SR1 3SD
T 0191-515 2000 **W** www.sunderland.ac.uk
Students: 16,085 UG; 2,845 PG
Chancellor, Steve Cram, MBE
Vice-Chancellor and Chief Executive, Prof. Peter Fidler
Secretary, John Pacey

UNIVERSITY OF SURREY (1966)
Guildford, Surrey GU2 7XH **T** 01483-300800
W www.surrey.ac.uk
Students: 10,190 UG; 5,225 PG
Chancellor, HRH the Duke of Kent, KG, GCMG, GCVO
Vice-Chancellor and Chief Executive, Prof. Christopher
Snowden, FRS, FRENG
Registrar, Dr David Ashton

UNIVERSITY OF SUSSEX (1961)
Sussex House, Brighton BN1 9RH **T** 01273-606755
W www.sussex.ac.uk
Students: 8,362 UG; 3,479 PG
Chancellor, Sanjeev Bhaskar, OBE
Vice-Chancellor, Prof. Michael Farthing
Academic Registrar, John Duffy

UNIVERSITY OF TEESSIDE (1992)
Middlesbrough, Tees Valley TS1 3BA **T** 01642-218121
W www.tees.ac.uk
Students: 25,172 UG; 4,113 PG
Chancellor, Lord Sawyer
Vice-Chancellor, Prof. Graham Henderson, CBE
University Secretary, Morgan McClintock

UNIVERSITY OF ULSTER (1984)
Cromore Road, Coleraine, Co. Londonderry BT52 1SA
T 028-7012 3456 **W** www.ulster.ac.uk
Students: 20,610 UG; 5,420 PG
Chancellor, James Nesbitt
Vice-Chancellor, Prof. Richard Barnett
Registrar, Norma Cameron

UNIVERSITY OF WALES (1893)
King Edward VII Avenue, Cathays Park, Cardiff CF10 3NS
T 029-2037 6999 **W** www.wales.ac.uk
Chancellor, HRH the Prince of Wales, KG, KT, GCB
Vice-Chancellor and Chief Executive, Prof. Marc Clement

ACCREDITED INSTITUTIONS
ABERYSTWYTH UNIVERSITY
Old College, King Street, Aberystwyth SY23 2AX
T 01970-623111
Students: 9,030 UG; 1,775 PG
Vice-Chancellor, Prof. Noel G. Lloyd

BANGOR UNIVERSITY
Gwynedd LL57 2DG
T 01248-351151
Students: 8,685 UG; 2,770 PG
Vice-Chancellor, Prof. John Hughes

GLYNDWR UNIVERSITY
Mold Road, Wrexham LL11 2AW
T 01978-290666
Students: 6,865 UG; 1,135 PG
Vice-Chancellor, Prof. Michael Scott

UNIVERSITY OF WALES INSTITUTE, CARDIFF
Llandaff Campus, Western Avenue, Cardiff CF5 2YB
T 029-2041 6070
Students: 8,325 UG; 4,755 PG
Vice-Chancellor and Principal, Prof. Antony J. Chapman

UNIVERSITY OF WALES, NEWPORT
Caerleon Campus, Newport NP18 3QT
T 01633-432432
Students: 7,450 UG; 1,840 PG
Vice-Chancellor, Dr P. Noyes

UNIVERSITY OF WALES, TRINITY SAINT DAVID
Carmarthen SA31 3EP
T 01267-676767
Students: 4,775 UG; 1,335 PG
Vice-Chancellor, Prof. Medwin Hughes

SWANSEA UNIVERSITY
Singleton Park SA2 8PP
T 01792-205678
Students: 12,280 UG; 2,060 PG
Vice-Chancellor, Prof. Richard B. Davies

SWANSEA METROPOLITAN UNIVERSITY
Mount Pleasant, Swansea SA1 6ED
T 01792-481000
Students: 4,910 UG; 1,275 PG
Vice-Chancellor, Prof. David Warner

UNIVERSITY OF WARWICK (1965)
Coventry CV4 7AL T 024-7652 3523 W www.warwick.ac.uk
Students: 12,823 UG; 9,825 PG
Chancellor, Sir Richard Lambert
Vice-Chancellor, Prof. Nigel Thrift
Registrar, Jon Baldwin

UNIVERSITY OF WEST LONDON (1992)
St Mary's Road, Ealing, London W5 5RF T 020-8579 5000
W www.uwl.ac.uk
Students: 14,350 UG; 2,030 PG
Chancellor, Laurence Geller
Vice-Chancellor, Prof. Peter John
University Secretary, Maureen Skinner

UNIVERSITY OF WESTMINSTER (1992)
309 Regent Street, London W1B 2UW T 020-7911 5000
W www.westminster.ac.uk
Students: 17,175 UG; 6,785 PG
Chancellor, Lord Paul
Vice-Chancellor and Rector, Prof. Geoffrey Petts
Registrar and Secretary, Carole Mainstone

UNIVERSITY OF THE WEST OF ENGLAND
(1992)
Frenchay Campus, Coldharbour Lane, Bristol BS16 1QY
T 0117-965 6261 W www.uwe.ac.uk
Students: 21,826 UG; 6,411 PG
Chancellor, Rt. Hon. Baroness Butler-Sloss, GBE
Vice-Chancellor, Prof. Steven West, KB, CBE
Academic Registrar, Andrea Cheshire

UNIVERSITY OF THE WEST OF SCOTLAND
(1992)
Paisley PA1 2BE T 0141-848 3000 W www.uws.ac.uk
Students: 10,000 UG; 10,000 PG
Chancellor, Lord Smith of Kelvin
Vice-Chancellor and Principal, Prof. Seamus McDaid
Secretary, Kenneth Alexander

UNIVERSITY OF WINCHESTER (2005)
Winchester SO22 4NR T 01962-841515
W www.winchester.ac.uk
Students: 5,041 UG; 1,387 PG
Chancellor, Dame Mary Fagan
Vice-Chancellor, Prof. Joy Carter
Registrar, Malcolm Willis

UNIVERSITY OF WOLVERHAMPTON (1988)
Wulfruna Street, Wolverhampton WV1 1LY T 01902-321000
W www.wlv.ac.uk
Students: 18,740 UG; 3,870 PG
Chancellor, Rt. Hon. Lord Paul of Marylebone
Vice-Chancellor, Prof. Geoff Layer, OBE, FRSA

UNIVERSITY OF WORCESTER (2005)
Henwick Grove, Worcester WR2 6AJ T 01905-855000
W www.worcester.ac.uk
Students: 7,730 UG; 1,810 PG
Chancellor, HRH the Duke of Gloucester, KG, GCVO
Vice-Chancellor and Chief Executive, Prof. David Green
Registrar, John Ryan

UNIVERSITY OF YORK (1963)
Heslington, York YO10 5DD T 01904-320000
W www.york.ac.uk
Students: 10,383 UG; 2,881 PG
Chancellor, Greg Dyke
Vice-Chancellor, Prof. Brian Cantor, FRENG
Registrar, Dr David Duncan

YORK ST JOHN UNIVERSITY (2006)
Lord Mayor's Walk, York YO31 7EX T 01904-624624
W www.yorksj.ac.uk
Students: 4,449 UG; 887 PG
Chancellor, Most Revd Dr John Sentamu, Archbishop
  of York, PC
Vice-Chancellor, Prof. David Fleming
Registrar, vacant

PROFESSIONAL EDUCATION

The organisations selected below provide specialist training, conduct examinations or are responsible for maintaining a register of those with professional qualifications in their sector, thereby controlling entry into a profession.

EU RECOGNITION

It is possible for those with professional qualifications obtained in the UK to have these recognised in other European countries. Further information can be obtained from:

EUROPE OPEN UK NARIC, Oriel House, Oriel Road, Cheltenham, Glos GL50 1XP T 0871-226 2850 W www.europeopen.org.uk

ACCOUNTANCY

Salary range for chartered accountants:
Certified £14,500–£25,000 (starting) rising to £29,000–£52,000+ (qualified), £40,000–£100,000+ at senior levels
Management £23,000 (starting), £25,000–£57,000 (newly qualified), £62,000–£106,000+ at senior levels
Public finance £23,000–£50,000 (newly qualified) rising to £35,000–£100,000+ at senior levels

Most chartered accountancy trainees are graduates, although some contracts are available to school-leavers. The undergraduate degree is followed by a three-year training contract with an approved employer culminating in professional exams provided by the Institute of Chartered Accountants of England and Wales (ICAEW), the Institute of Chartered Accountants of Scotland (ICAS) or the Institute of Chartered Accountants in Ireland (ICAI). Success in the examination and membership of one of the institutes allows the use of the designation 'chartered accountant' and the letters ACA or CA.

The Association of Chartered Certified Accountants (ACCA) is the global body for professional accountants. The ACCA aims to offer business-relevant qualifications to students in a range of business sectors and countries seeking a career in accountancy, finance and management. The ACCA Qualification consists of up to 14 examinations, practical experiences and a professional ethics module. Chartered certified accountants can use the designatory letters ACCA.

Chartered management accountants focus on accounting for businesses, and most do not work in accountancy practices but in industry, commerce, not-for-profit and public sector organisations. Graduates who have not studied a business or accounting undergraduate degree must gain the Chartered Institute of Management Accountants (CIMA) Certificate in Business Accounting before studying for the CIMA Professional Qualification which requires three years of practical experience, nine examinations and a pass in the Institute's Test of Professional Competence in Management Accounting (TOPCIMA). In May 2011, CIMA and the American Institute of Certified Public Accountants agreed on the creation of a new professional designation, the Chartered Global Management Accountant (CGMA),

which will represent a worldwide standard of professional excellence in management accounting.

Chartered public finance accountants usually work for public bodies, but they can also work in the private sector. To gain chartered public finance accountant status (CPFA), trainees must complete the three parts of the Chartered Institute of Public Finance and Accountancy (CIPFA) Professional Accountancy Qualification (PAQ), which takes approximately three years. The first stage is the certificate level, which leads to affiliate membership of CIPFA, the second is the diploma level which leads to associate membership, and finally completion of the Final Test of Professional Competence leads to full membership of CIPFA.

ASSOCIATION OF CHARTERED CERTIFIED ACCOUNTANTS (ACCA) 29 Lincoln's Inn Fields, London WC2A 3EE T 020-7059 5000
E info@accaglobal.com W www.accaglobal.com
Chief Executive, Helen Brand
CHARTERED INSTITUTE OF MANAGEMENT ACCOUNTANTS (CIMA) 26 Chapter Street, London SW1P 4NP T 020-8849 2251
E cima.contact@cimaglobal.com W www.cimaglobal.com
Chief Executive, Charles Tilley
CHARTERED INSTITUTE OF PUBLIC FINANCE AND ACCOUNTANCY (CIPFA) 3 Robert Street, London WC2N 6RL T 020-7543 5600
E corporate@cipfa.org.uk W www.cipfa.org.uk
Chief Executive, Steve Freer
INSTITUTE OF CHARTERED ACCOUNTANTS IN ENGLAND AND WALES (ICAEW) Chartered Accountants' Hall, Moorgate Place, London EC2R 6EA T 020-7920 8100 W www.icaew.com
Chief Executive, Michael Izza
INSTITUTE OF CHARTERED ACCOUNTANTS IN IRELAND (ICAI) The Linenhall, 32–38 Linenhall Street, Belfast BT2 8BG T 028-9043 5840
E ca@charteredaccountants.ie
W www.charteredaccountants.ie
Chief Executive, Pat Costello
INSTITUTE OF CHARTERED ACCOUNTANTS OF SCOTLAND (ICAS) CA House, 21 Haymarket Yards, Edinburgh EH12 5BH T 0131-347 0100
E enquiries@icas.org.uk W www.icas.org.uk
Chief Executive, Anton Colella

ACTUARIAL SCIENCE

Salary range: £25,000–£35,000 for graduate trainees; £45,000–£55,000 after qualification; £60,000–£100,000+ for senior roles

Actuaries apply financial and statistical theories to solve business problems. These problems usually involve analysing future financial events in order to assess investment risks. Following a vote of their respective members, the Faculty of Actuaries in Edinburgh and the Institute of Actuaries in London merged in August 2010 to form one professional body in the UK: the Institute and Faculty of Actuaries (IFA). The IFA develops actuarial techniques and sets examinations, professional codes and disciplinary standards. UK qualified actuaries are fellows and bear the designations FIA or FFA. On average, it takes five years to qualify as an actuary; examinations are held twice a year, and applicants to the profession must also have completed three years of actuarial work experience before gaining fellowship.

The Financial Reporting Council (FRC) is the unified independent regulator for corporate reporting, auditing, actuarial practice, corporate governance and the professionalism of accountants and actuaries. The FRC's Board for Actuarial Standards sets and maintains technical actuarial standards independently of the profession while the Professional Oversight Board of the FRC oversees the regulation of the accountancy and actuarial professions by their respective professional bodies. The Accountancy and Actuarial Discipline Board operates an investigation and discipline scheme in relation to members of the profession who raise issues affecting UK public interest.

FINANCIAL REPORTING COUNCIL (FRC) 5th Floor, Aldwych House, 71–91 Aldwych, London WC2B 4HN T 020-7492 2300 W www.frc.org.uk
Chief Executive, Stephen Haddrill
INSTITUTE AND FACULTY OF ACTUARIES Staple Inn Hall, High Holborn, London WC1V 7QJ T 020-7632 2100 E info@actuaries.org.uk W www.actuaries.org.uk
Acting Chief Executive, Derek Cribb

ARCHITECTURE

Salary range: £17,000–£30,000 during training; newly registered £25,000–£35,000; project architect and senior roles £35,000–£80,000+

It takes a minimum of seven years to become an architect, involving three stages: a three-year first degree, a two-year second degree or diploma and two years of professional experience followed by the successful completion of a professional practice examination.

The Architects Registration Board (ARB) is the independent regulator for the profession. It was set up by an act of parliament in 1997 and is responsible for maintaining the register of UK architects, prescribing qualifications that lead to registration as an architect, investigating complaints about the conduct and competence of architects, and ensuring that only those who are registered with ARB offer their services as an architect. It is only following registration with ARB that an architect can apply for chartered membership of the Royal Institute of British Architects (RIBA). RIBA, the UK body for architecture and the architectural profession, received its royal charter in 1837 and validates courses at over 40 UK schools of architecture; it also validates overseas courses. RIBA provides support and guidance for its members in the form of training, technical services and events and sets standards for the education of architects.

The Chartered Institute of Architectural Technologists is the international qualifying body for chartered architectural technologists (MCIAT) and architectural technicians (TCIAT).

ARCHITECTS REGISTRATION BOARD (ARB) 8 Weymouth Street, London W1W 5BU T 020-7580 5861 E info@arb.org.uk W www.arb.org.uk
Registrar and Chief Executive, Alison Carr
CHARTERED INSTITUTE OF ARCHITECTURAL TECHNOLOGISTS 397 City Road, London EC1V 1NH T 020-7278 2206 E info@ciat.org.uk W www.ciat.org.uk
Chief Executive, Francesca Berriman
ROYAL INCORPORATION OF ARCHITECTS IN SCOTLAND 15 Rutland Square, Edinburgh EH1 2BE T 0131-229 7545 E info@rias.org.uk W www.rias.org.uk
Secretary and Treasurer, Neil Baxter

ROYAL INSTITUTE OF BRITISH ARCHITECTS (RIBA) 66 Portland Place, London W1B 1AD T 020-7580 5533 E info@inst.riba.org W www.riba.org
Chief Executive, Harry Rich

ENGINEERING

Salary range:
Civil/structural £27,000–£34,000 (graduate); £32,000–£48,000 with experience, rising to £80,000+ in senior posts
Chemical £26,000 average (graduate); £44,000–£72,000+ (chartered)
Electrical £20,000–£23,000 (graduate); £45,000+ with experience

The Engineering Council sets standards of professional competence and ethics for engineers, technologists and technicians, and regulates the profession through the 36 institutions (Licensed Members) listed below, which are licensed to put suitably qualified members on the Engineering Council's Register of Engineers. All candidates for registration as chartered engineer, incorporated engineer, engineering technician or information and communication technology technicians must satisfy the competence standards set by the Engineering Council and be members of the appropriate institution. Applicants must show that they have a satisfactory educational base, have undergone approved professional development and, at interview, must demonstrate their professional competence against specific criteria.

ENGINEERING COUNCIL 246 High Holborn, London WC1V 7EX T 020-3206 0500 E info@engc.org.uk W www.engc.org.uk
Chief Executive Officer, Jon Prichard

LICENSED MEMBERS
British Computer Society W www.bcs.org
British Institute of Non-destructive Testing W www.bindt.org
Chartered Institution of Building Services Engineers W www.cibse.org
Chartered Institution of Highways and Transportation W www.ciht.org.uk
Chartered Institute of Plumbing and Heating Engineers W www.ciphe.org.uk
Chartered Institution of Water and Environmental Management W www.ciwem.org
Energy Institute W www.energyinst.org.uk
Institute of Acoustics W www.ioa.org.uk
Institute of Cast Metals Engineers W www.icme.org.uk
Institute of Healthcare Engineering and Estate Management W www.iheem.org.uk
Institute of Highway Engineers W www.theihe.org
Institute of Marine Engineering, Science and Technology W www.imarest.org
Institute of Materials, Minerals and Mining W www.iom3.org
Institute of Measurement and Control W www.instmc.org.uk
Institute of Physics W www.iop.org
Institute of Physics and Engineering in Medicine W www.ipem.ac.uk
Institute of Water W www.instituteofwater.org.uk
Institution of Agricultural Engineers W www.iagre.org
Institution of Chemical Engineers W www.icheme.org
Institution of Civil Engineers W www.ice.org.uk
Institution of Diesel and Gas Turbine Engineers W www.idgte.org

Institution of Engineering Designers W www.ied.org.uk
Institution of Engineering and Technology
W www.theiet.org
Institution of Fire Engineers W www.ife.org.uk
Institution of Gas Engineers and Managers
W www.igem.org.uk
Institution of Lighting Professionals W www.theilp.org.uk
Institution of Mechanical Engineers W www.imeche.org
Institution of Railway Signal Engineers W www.irse.org
Institution of Royal Engineers W www.instre.org
Institution of Structural Engineers W www.istructe.org
Nuclear Institute W www.nuclearinst.com
Royal Aeronautical Society W www.aerosociety.com
Royal Institution of Naval Architects W www.rina.org.uk
Society of Environmental Engineers
W www.environmental.org.uk
Society of Operations Engineers W www.soe.org.uk
Welding Institute W www.twi.co.uk

HEALTHCARE

CHIROPRACTIC
Salary range: £22,000–£40,000 starting salary; with own practice up to £70,000

Chiropractors diagnose and treat conditions caused by problems with joints, ligaments, tendons and nerves of the body. The General Chiropractic Council (GCC) is the independent statutory regulatory body for chiropractors and its role and remit is defined in the Chiropractors Act 1994. The GCC sets the criteria for the recognition of chiropractic degrees and for standards of proficiency and conduct. Details of the institutions offering degree programmes are available on the GCC website (*see* below). It is illegal for anyone in the UK to use the title 'chiropractor' unless registered with the GCC.

The British Chiropractic Association and the Scottish Chiropractic Association are two representative bodies for the profession and are sources of further information.
BRITISH CHIROPRACTIC ASSOCIATION 59 Castle Street, Reading RG1 7SN T 0118-950 5950
E enquiries@chiropractic-uk.co.uk
W www.chiropractic-uk.co.uk
Executive Director, Sue Wakefield
GENERAL CHIROPRACTIC COUNCIL
44 Wicklow Street, London WC1X 9HL T 020-7713 5155
E enquiries@gcc-uk.org W www.gcc-uk.org
Chief Executive and Registrar, Satjit Singh
SCOTTISH CHIROPRACTIC ASSOCIATION
1 Chisholm Avenue, Bishopton, Renfrewshire PA7 5JH
T 0141-404 0260 E admin@sca-chiropractic.org
W www.sca-chiropractic.org
Administrator, Morag Cairns

DENTISTRY
Salary range: see Health: Employees and Salaries

The General Dental Council (GDC) is the organisation that regulates dental professionals in the UK. All dentists, dental hygienists, dental therapists, clinical dental technicians, dental nurses and orthodontic therapists must be registered with the GDC to work in the UK.

There are various different routes to qualify for registration as a dentist, including holding a degree from a UK university; completing the GDC's qualifying examination; or holding a relevant European Economic Area or overseas diploma. The GDC's purpose is to protect the public through the regulation of UK dental professionals. It keeps up-to-date registers of dental professionals, works to set standards of dental practice, behaviour and education, and helps to protect patients by hearing complaints and taking action against professionals where necessary.

The British Dental Association is a membership organisation that provides dentists with professional and educational services.
BRITISH DENTAL ASSOCIATION 64 Wimpole Street, London W1G 8YS T 020-7935 0875 E enquiries@bda.org
W www.bda.org
Chief Executive, Peter Ward
GENERAL DENTAL COUNCIL 37 Wimpole Street, London W1G 8DQ T 020-7887 3800
E information@gdc-uk.org W www.gdc-uk.org
Chief Executive, Evlynne Gilvarry

MEDICINE
Salary range: see Health: Employees and Salaries

The General Medical Council (GMC) regulates medical education and training in the UK. This covers undergraduate study (usually five years), the two-year foundation programme taken by doctors directly after graduation and all subsequent postgraduate study, including specialty and GP training.

All doctors must be registered with the GMC, which is responsible for protecting the public. It does this by setting standards for professional practice, overseeing medical education, keeping a register of qualified doctors and taking action where a doctor's fitness to practise is in doubt. Doctors are eligible for full registration upon successful completion of the first year of training after graduation.

Following the foundation programme, many doctors undertake specialist training (provided by the colleges and faculties listed below) to become either a consultant or a GP. Once specialist training has been completed, doctors are awarded the Certificate of Completion of Training (CCT) and are eligible to be placed on either the GMC's specialist register or its GP register.
GENERAL MEDICAL COUNCIL (GMC) 350 Euston Road, London NW1 3JN T 0161-923 6602
E gmc@gmc-uk.org W www.gmc-uk.org
Chief Executive, Niall Dickson
SOCIETY OF APOTHECARIES OF LONDON
Black Friars Lane, London EC4V 6EJ T 020-7236 1189
E clerk@apothecaries.org W www.apothecaries.org
Master, Dr T. Chambers

SPECIALIST TRAINING COLLEGES AND FACULTIES
College of Emergency Medicine
W www.collemergencymed.ac.uk
Faculty of Pharmaceutical Medicine W www.fpm.org.uk
Faculty of Public Health W www.fph.org.uk
Royal College of Anaesthetists W www.rcoa.ac.uk
Royal College of General Practitioners W www.rcgp.org.uk
Royal College of Obstetricians and Gynaecologists
W www.rcog.org.uk
Royal College of Opthalmologists W www.rcophth.ac.uk
Royal College of Paediatrics and Child Health
W www.rcpch.ac.uk
Royal College of Pathologists W www.rcpath.org
Royal College of Physicians, London W www.rcplondon.ac.uk
Royal College of Physicians and Surgeons of Glasgow
W www.rcpsg.ac.uk
Royal College of Physicians of Edinburgh W www.rcpe.ac.uk
Royal College of Psychiatrists W www.rcpsych.ac.uk

Royal College of Radiologists W www.rcr.ac.uk
Royal College of Surgeons of Edinburgh W www.rcsed.ac.uk
Royal College of Surgeons of England W www.rcseng.ac.uk

MEDICINE, SUPPLEMENTARY PROFESSIONS

The standard of professional education for arts therapists, biomedical scientists, chiropodists and podiatrists, clinical scientists, dietitians, occupational therapists, operating department practitioners, orthoptists, paramedics, physiotherapists, practitioner psychologists, prosthetists and orthotists, radiographers, and speech and language therapists is regulated by the Health Professions Council (HPC), which only registers those practitioners who meet certain standards of training, professional skills, behaviour and health. Other than biomedical science and clinical science, all the professions listed below are described by the NHS as 'allied health professions'. The HPC currently registers over 200,000 professionals.
HEALTH PROFESSIONS COUNCIL Park House, 184 Kennington Park Road, London SE11 4BU T 020-7582 0866 E registration@hpc-uk.org W www.hpc-uk.org
Chief Executive and Registrar, Marc Seale

ART, DRAMA AND MUSIC THERAPIES
Salary range: £25,000–£47,000

An art, drama or music therapist encourages people to express their feelings and emotions through art, such as painting and drawing, drama or music. A postgraduate qualification in the relevant therapy is required. Details of accredited training programmes in the UK can be obtained from the following organisations:
BRITISH ASSOCIATION FOR MUSIC THERAPY 24–27 White Lion Street, London N1 9PD T 020-7387 6100 E info@bamt.org W www.bamt.org
Chair, Angela Harrison
BRITISH ASSOCIATION OF ART THERAPISTS 24–27 White Lion Street, London N1 9PD T 020-7686 4216 E info@baat.org W www.baat.org
Chief Executive, Val Huet
BRITISH ASSOCIATION OF DRAMA THERAPISTS Waverley, Battledown Approach, Cheltenham, Gloucestershire GL52 6RE T 0124-2235 5155 E enquiries@badth.org.uk W www.badth.org.uk
Chair, Dr Bruce Bayley

BIOMEDICAL SCIENCES
Salary range: £21,000–£34,000, rising to £66,000+ in senior posts

Biomedical scientists analyse specimens from patients in order to help make diagnoses. Qualifications from higher education establishments and training in medical laboratories are required for membership of the Institute of Biomedical Science, which sets the professional standards of competence for those who practise biomedical science.
INSTITUTE OF BIOMEDICAL SCIENCE 12 Coldbath Square, London EC1R 5HL T 020-7713 0214 E mail@ibms.org W www.ibms.org
Chief Executive, Jill Rodney

CHIROPODY AND PODIATRY
Salary range: £21,000–£40,000

Chiropodists and podiatrists assess, diagnose and treat problems of the lower leg and foot. The Society of Chiropodists and Podiatrists is the professional body and trade union for the profession. Qualifications granted and degrees recognised by the society are approved by the Health Professions Council (HPC). HPC registration is required in order to use the titles chiropodist and podiatrist.
SOCIETY OF CHIROPODISTS AND PODIATRISTS 1 Fellmonger's Path, Tower Bridge Road, London SE1 3LY T 020-7234 8620 E enq@scpod.org W www.feetforlife.org
Chief Executive, Joanna Brown

CLINICAL SCIENCE
Salary range: £25,000–£95,000+

Clinical scientists conduct tests in laboratories in order to diagnose and manage disease. The Association of Clinical Scientists is responsible for setting the criteria for competence of applicants to the HPC's register and to present a Certificate of Attainment to candidates following a successful assessment. This certificate will allow direct registration with the HPC.
ASSOCIATION OF CLINICAL SCIENTISTS c/o Association for Clinical Biochemistry, 130–132 Tooley Street, London SE1 2TU T 020-7940 8960 E info@assclinsci.org W www.assclinsci.org
Chair, Dr Iain Chambers

DIETETICS
Salary range: £21,000–£40,000

Dietitians advise patients on how to improve their health and counter specific health problems through diet. The British Dietetic Association, established in 1936, is the professional association for dietitians. Full membership is open to UK-registered dietitians, who must also be registered with the HPC.
BRITISH DIETETIC ASSOCIATION 5th Floor, Charles House, 148–149 Great Charles Street Queensway, Birmingham B3 3HT T 0121-200 8080 E info@bda.uk.com W www.bda.uk.com
Chief Executive, Andy Burman

OCCUPATIONAL THERAPY
Salary range: £20,000–£40,000, rising to £55,000 in senior posts

Occupational therapists work with people who have physical, mental and/or social problems, either from birth or as a result of accident, illness or ageing, and aim to make them as independent as possible. The professional qualification and eligibility for registration may be obtained upon successful completion of a validated course in any of the educational institutions approved by the British Association of Occupational Therapists, which is the professional body for occupational therapy in the UK. The courses are normally degree-level courses based in higher education institutions.
BRITISH ASSOCIATION OF OCCUPATIONAL THERAPISTS 106–114 Borough High Street, London SE1 1LB T 020-7357 6480 W www.cot.org.uk
Chief Executive, Julia Scott

MENTAL HEALTH
Salary range:
Clinical psychologist £24,000, rising to £50,000–£80,000+ at senior levels
Counsellor £18,000–£27,000, rising to £40,000–£50,000 with experience
Educational psychologist £21,000, rising to £31,000 when chartered and up to £63,000 at senior levels
Psychotherapist £20,000–£26,000 (starting), rising to £77,000+ at senior levels

Psychologists are mental health professionals who can work in a range of settings including prisons, schools and hospitals as well as businesses. The UK psychological profession is represented by the British Psychological Society (BPS). It accredits qualifications in psychology, and offers support to members through continuing professional development. The Association of Educational Psychologists (AEP) represents the interests of educational psychologists, while the British Association for Counselling and Psychotherapy (BACP) sets educational standards and provides professional support to those psychologists working in psychotherapy or counselling-related roles. The BPS website provides more information on the different specialisations that may be pursued by psychologists.

ASSOCIATION OF EDUCATIONAL
PSYCHOLOGISTS (AEP) 4 The Riverside Centre, Frankland Lane, Durham DH1 5TA T 0191-384 9512
E enquiries@aep.org.uk W www.aep.org.uk
General Secretary, Kate Fallon
BRITISH ASSOCIATION FOR COUNSELLING AND PSYCHOTHERAPY (BACP) BACP House, 15 St John's Business Park, Lutterworth, Leicestershire LE17 4HB
T 01455-883300 E bacp@bacp.co.uk W www.bacp.co.uk
President, Laurie Clarke
BRITISH PSYCHOLOGICAL SOCIETY (BPS)
St Andrews House, 48 Princess Road East, Leicester LE1 7DR
T 0116-254 9568 E enquiries@bps.org.uk
W www.bps.org.uk
President, Dr Carole Allan

ORTHOPTICS
Salary range: £20,000–£38,000, rising to £38,000–£65,000 in senior posts

Orthoptists undertake the diagnosis and treatment of all types of squint and other anomalies of binocular vision, working in close collaboration with ophthalmologists. The all-graduate workforce comes from two universities: the University of Liverpool and University of Sheffield.

BRITISH AND IRISH ORTHOPTIC SOCIETY
62 Wilson Street, London EC2R 2BU T 01353-665541
W www.orthoptics.org.uk
Chair, Lesley-Anne Baxter

PARAMEDICAL SERVICES
Salary range: £21,000–£34,000

Paramedics deal with accidents and emergencies, assessing patients and carrying out any specialist treatment and care needed in the first instance. The body that represents ambulance professionals is the College of Paramedics.

COLLEGE OF PARAMEDICS The Exchange, Express Park, Bristol Road, Bridgwater TA6 4RR T 01278-420014
E help@collegeofparamedics.net
W www.collegeofparamedics.net
Chief Executive, Roland Furber

PHYSIOTHERAPY
Salary range: £19,000–£37,000, rising to £62,000 in senior posts

Physiotherapists are concerned with movement and function and deal with problems arising from injury, illness and ageing. Full-time three- or four-year degree courses are available at around 35 higher education institutions in the UK. Information about courses leading to state registration is available from the Chartered Society of Physiotherapy.

CHARTERED SOCIETY OF PHYSIOTHERAPY
14 Bedford Row, London WC1R 4ED T 020-7306 6666
E enquiries@csp.org.uk W www.csp.org.uk
Chief Executive, Phil Gray

PROSTHETICS AND ORTHOTICS
Salary range: £21,000 on qualification up to £67,000 as a consultant

Prosthetists provide artificial limbs, while orthotists provide devices to support or control a part of the body. It is necessary to obtain an honours degree to become a prosthetist or orthotist. Training is centred at the universities of Salford and Strathclyde.

BRITISH ASSOCIATION OF PROSTHETISTS AND
ORTHOTISTS Sir James Clark Building, Abbey Mill Business Centre, Paisley PA1 1TJ T 0141-561 7217
E enquiries@bapo.com W www.bapo.org
Chair, Peter Honeycombe

RADIOGRAPHY
Salary range: £20,000–£38,000, rising to £64,000 in senior posts

In order to practise both diagnostic and therapeutic radiography in the UK, it is necessary to have successfully completed a course of education and training recognised by the Health Professionals Council. Such courses are offered by universities throughout the UK and lead to the award of a degree in radiography. Further information is available from the Society and College of Radiographers.

SOCIETY AND COLLEGE OF RADIOGRAPHERS
207 Providence Square, Mill Street, London SE1 2EW
T 020-7740 7200 E info@sor.org W www.sor.org
Chief Executive, Richard Evans

SPEECH AND LANGUAGE THERAPY
Salary range: £20,000 rising upwards of £53,000 in senior roles

Speech and language therapists (SLTs) work with people with communication, swallowing, eating and drinking problems. The Royal College of Speech and Language Therapists is the professional body for speech and language therapists and support workers. Alongside the Health Professions Council, it accredits education and training courses leading to qualification.

ROYAL COLLEGE OF SPEECH AND LANGUAGE
THERAPISTS 2 White Hart Yard, London SE1 1NX
T 020-7378 1200 E info@rcslt.org W www.rcslt.org
Chief Executive, Kamini Gadhok, MBE

NURSING
Salary range: see Health: Employees and Salaries

In order to practise in the UK, all nurses and midwives must be registered with the Nursing and Midwifery Council (NMC). The NMC is a statutory regulatory body that establishes and maintains standards of education, training, conduct and performance for nursing and midwifery. Courses leading to registration are currently at a minimum of diploma in higher education, with some offered at degree level. All are a minimum of three years if undertaken full-time. From September 2011 diplomas will be phased out, and by 2013 all new entrants to the nursing profession will have to study a degree. The NMC approves programmes run jointly by higher education institutions with their healthcare service partners who offer clinical placements. The nursing part of the register has four fields of practice: adult, children's, learning disability and mental health nursing. During the first year of a nursing course, the common foundation programme, students are taught across all four fields of practice. In addition, those studying to become adult nurses gain experience of nursing in relation to medicine, surgery, maternity care and nursing in the home. The NMC also sets standards for programmes leading to registration as a midwife and a range of post-registration courses including specialist practice programmes, nurse prescribing and those for teachers of nursing and midwifery. The NMC has a part of the register for specialist community public health nurses and approves programmes for health visitors, occupational health nurses and school nurses.

The Royal College of Nursing is the largest professional union for nursing in the UK, representing qualified nurses, healthcare assistants and nursing students in the NHS and the independent sector.

NURSING AND MIDWIFERY COUNCIL 23 Portland Place, London W1B 1PZ T 020-7333 9333
E communications@nmc-uk.org W www.nmc-uk.org
Chief Executive and Registrar, Prof. Dickon Weir-Hughes
ROYAL COLLEGE OF NURSING 20 Cavendish Square, London W1G 0RN T 020-740 3333 W www.rcn.org.uk
Chief Executive and General Secretary, Dr Peter Carter

OPTOMETRY AND DISPENSING OPTICS
Salary range:
Optometrist £19,000–£53,000 (up to £80,000 for consultant posts)
Dispensing Optician £18,000–£30,000+

There are various routes to qualification as a dispensing optician. Qualification takes three years in total, and can be completed by combining a distance learning course or day release while working as a trainee under the supervision of a qualified and registered optician. Alternatively, students can do a two-year full-time course followed by one year of supervised practice with a qualified and registered optician. Training must be done at a training establishment approved by the regulatory body – the General Optical Council (GOC). There are five training establishments which are approved by the GOC: Association of British Dispensing Opticians College, Anglia Ruskin University, Bradford College, City and Islington College and Glasgow Caledonian University. All routes are concluded by professional qualifying examinations, successful completion of which leads to registration with the GOC, which is compulsory for all practising dispensing opticians. After two years post-qualifying experience and completing training to fit contact lenses, students have the option to take a career progression course at the University of Bradford that allows them to graduate with a degree in optometry in one calendar year.

Optometrists must obtain an undergraduate optometry degree from one of the eight institutions approved by the GOC (Anglia Ruskin University, Aston University, the University of Bradford, Cardiff University, City University, Glasgow Caledonian University, the University of Manchester or the University of Ulster). Following graduation, trainees must complete a year of supervised

salaried training with a registered optometrist after which they must pass a series of assessments set by the College of Optometrists. As with dispensing opticians, optometrists must be registered with the GOC in order to practise.

ASSOCIATION OF BRITISH DISPENSING OPTICIANS Godmersham Park, Godmersham, Canterbury, Kent CT4 7DT T 01227-738829
E membership@abdo.org.uk W www.abdo.org.uk
General Secretary, Sir Anthony Garrett, CBE
COLLEGE OF OPTOMETRISTS 42 Craven Street, London WC2N 5NG T 020-7839 6000
E optometry@college-optometrists.org
W www.college-optometrists.org
Chief Executive, Bryony Pawinska
GENERAL OPTICAL COUNCIL (GOC)
1 Harley Street, London W1G 8DJ T 020-7580 3898
E goc@optical.org W www.optical.org
Chief Executive, Samantha Peters

OSTEOPATHY
Salary Range: £16,000–£65,000

Osteopathy is a system of diagnosis and treatment for a wide range of medical conditions. It works with the structure and function of the body, and is based on the principle that the well-being of an individual depends on the skeleton, muscles, ligaments and connective tissues functioning smoothly together. The General Osteopathic Council (GOsC) regulates the practice of osteopathy in the UK and maintains a register of those entitled to practise. It is a criminal offence for anyone to describe themselves as an osteopath unless they are registered with the GOsC.

To gain entry to the register, applicants must hold a recognised qualification from an osteopathic education institute accredited by the GOsC; this involves a four- to five-year honours degree programme combined with clinical training.

GENERAL OSTEOPATHIC COUNCIL Osteopathy House, 176 Tower Bridge Road, London SE1 3LU
T 020-7357 6655 E info@osteopathy.org.uk
W www.osteopathy.org.uk
Chief Executive and Registrar, Evlynne Gilvarry

PHARMACY
Salary range: £23,000–£68,000+

Pharmacists are involved in the preparation and use of medicines, from the discovery of their active ingredients to their use by patients. Pharmacists also monitor the effects of medicines, both for patient care and for research purposes.

The General Pharmaceutical Council (GPhC) is the independent regulatory body for pharmacists in England, Scotland and Wales, having taken over the regulating function of the Royal Pharmaceutical Society in 2010. The GPhC maintains the register of pharmacists, pharmacy technicians and pharmacy premises; it also sets national standards for training, ethics, proficiency and continuing professional development. The Pharmaceutical Society of Northern Ireland (PSNI) performs the same role in Northern Ireland. In order to register, students must complete a four-year degree in pharmacy that is accredited by either the GPhC or the PSNI followed by one year of pre-registration training at an approved pharmacy, and must then pass an entrance examination.

GENERAL PHARMACEUTICAL COUNCIL (GPHC)
129 Lambeth Road, London SE1 7BT T 020-3365 3400
E info@pharmacyregulation.org
W www.pharmacyregulation.org
Chief Executive and Registrar, Duncan Rudkin
PHARMACEUTICAL SOCIETY OF NORTHERN
IRELAND 73 University Street, Belfast BT7 1HL
T 028-9032 6927 E info@psni.org.uk W www.psni.org.uk
Director, Trevor Patterson
ROYAL PHARMACEUTICAL SOCIETY 1 Lambeth High
Street, London SE1 7JN T 020-7572 2737
E support@rpharms.com W www.rpharms.com
Chief Executive, Helen Gordon

INFORMATION MANAGEMENT
Salary range:
Archivist   £21,000–£30,000   (starting);   £30,000–
£55,000+ in senior posts
Information   Officer   £19,000–£28,000   (starting);
£28,000–£55,000+ in senior posts
Librarian £19,000–£24,000 (newly qualified); £49,000+
in senior posts

The Chartered Institute of Library and Information
Professionals (CILIP) is the professional body for
librarians, information specialists and knowledge
managers. The Archives and Records Association is the
professional body for archivists and record managers.
The Association of Special Libraries and Information
Bureau (ASLIB) is a membership association serving
people who manage information and knowledge in
organisations across all sectors.
ARCHIVES AND RECORDS ASSOCIATION Prioryfield
House, 20 Canon Street, Taunton, Somerset TA1 1SW
T 01823-327077 E ara@archives.org.uk
W www.archives.org.uk
Chief Executive, John Chambers
ASLIB Howard House, Wagon Lane, Bingley, West Yorkshire,
BD16 1WA T 01274-777700 E support@aslib.com
W www.aslib.com
Chief Executive, John Peters
CHARTERED INSTITUTE OF LIBRARY AND
INFORMATION PROFESSIONALS (CILIP)
7 Ridgmount Street, London WC1E 7AE T 020-7255 0500
E info@cilip.org.uk W www.cilip.org.uk
President, Brian Hall

JOURNALISM
Salary range: starting salaries £12,000 (trainee)–£18,000;
£22,000+ for established journalists, rising to £39,000–
£85,000 for senior journalists/editors

The National Council for the Training of Journalists
(NCTJ) accredits 70 courses for journalists run by 42
education providers; it also provides professional support
to journalists.
The Broadcast Journalism Training Council (BJTC) is
an association of the UK's main broadcast journalism
employers and accredits courses in broadcast journalism.
BROADCAST JOURNALISM TRAINING COUNCIL
(BJTC) 18 Miller's Close, Rippingale Nr. Bourne,
Lincolnshire PE10 0TH T 01778-440025 E sec@bjtc.org.uk
W www.bjtc.org.uk
Secretary, Jim Latham
NATIONAL COUNCIL FOR THE TRAINING OF
JOURNALISTS (NCTJ) The New Granary, Station Road,
Newport, Saffron Walden, Essex CB11 3PL T 01799-544014
E info@nctj.com W www.nctj.com
Chief Executive, Joanne Butcher

LAW
There are three types of practising lawyers: barristers,
notaries and solicitors. Solicitors tend to work as a group
in firms, and can be approached directly by individuals.
They advise on a variety of legal issues and must decide
the most appropriate course of action, if any. Notaries
have all the powers of a solicitor other than the conduct
of litigation. Most of them are primarily concerned with
the preparation and authentication of documents for
use abroad. Barristers are usually self-employed. If a
solicitor believes that a barrister is required, he or she will
instruct one on behalf of the client; the client will not
have contact with the barrister without the solicitor being
present.
When specialist expertise is needed, barristers give
opinions on complex matters of law, and when clients
require representation in the higher courts (crown courts,
the high court, the court of appeal and the supreme
court), barristers provide a specialist advocacy service.
However, solicitors – who represent their clients in the
lower courts such as tribunals, magistrates' courts and
county courts – can also apply for advocacy rights in the
higher courts instead of briefing a barrister.

THE BAR
Salary range: £10,000–£200,000+

The governing body of the Bar of England and Wales is
the General Council of the Bar, also known as the Bar
Council. Since January 2006, the regulatory functions of
the Bar Council (including regulating the education and
training requirements for those wishing to enter the
profession) have been undertaken by the Bar Standards
Board.
In the first (or 'academic') stage of training, aspiring
barristers must obtain a law degree of a good standard
(at least second class). Alternatively, those with a non-
law degree (at least second class) may complete a
one-year full-time or two-year part-time Common
Professional Examination (CPE) or Graduate Diploma in
Law (GDL).
The second (vocational) stage is the completion of the
Bar Professional Training Course (BPTC), which is
available at nine validated institutions in the UK and
must be applied for around one year in advance
(W www.barprofessionaltraining.org.uk). All barristers must
join one of the four Inns of Court prior to commencing
the BPTC.
Students are 'called to the Bar' by their Inn after
completion of the vocational stage, but cannot practise as
a barrister until completion of the third stage, which is
called 'pupillage'. Call to the Bar does not entitle a person
to practise as a barrister – successful completion of
pupillage is now a pre-requisite. Pupillage lasts for two
six-month periods: the 'non-practising six' and the
'practising six'. The former consists of shadowing an
experienced barrister, while the latter involves appearing
in court as a barrister.
Admission to the Bar of Northern Ireland is controlled
by the General Council of the Bar of Northern Ireland;
admission as an Advocate to the Scottish Bar is through
the Faculty of Advocates.
BAR STANDARDS BOARD address as above
E contactus@barstandardsboard.org.uk
W www.barstandardsboard.org.uk
Chair of the Bar Council, Peter Lodder, QC
Director Bar Standards Board, Dr Vanessa Davies

FACULTY OF ADVOCATES Parliament House, Edinburgh
EH1 1RF T 0131-226 5071 W www.advocates.org.uk
Dean, Richard Keen, QC
GENERAL COUNCIL OF THE BAR (THE BAR
COUNCIL) 289–293 High Holborn, London WC1V 7HZ
T 020-7242 0082 E contactus@barcouncil.org.uk
W www.barcouncil.org.uk
GENERAL COUNCIL OF THE BAR OF NORTHERN
IRELAND The Bar Library, 91 Chichester Street, Belfast
BT1 3JQ T 028-9056 2349 W www.barlibrary.com
Chief Executive, Brendan Garland

THE INNS OF COURT
HONOURABLE SOCIETY OF GRAY'S INN
8 South Square, London WC1R 5ET T 020-7458 7800
W www.graysinn.org.uk
Under-Treasurer, Brig. Anthony Faith, CBE
HONOURABLE SOCIETY OF LINCOLN'S INN
Treasury Office, Lincoln's Inn, London WC2A 3TL
T 020-7405 1393 E mail@lincolnsinn.org.uk
W www.lincolnsinn.org.uk
Under-Treasurer, Col. D. Hills, MBE
HONOURABLE SOCIETY OF THE INNER TEMPLE
Inner Temple, London EC4Y 7HL T 020-7797 8250
E enquiries@innertemple.org.uk
W www.innertemple.org.uk
Sub-Treasurer, Patrick Maddams
HONOURABLE SOCIETY OF THE MIDDLE TEMPLE
Middle Temple Lane, London EC4Y 9AT T 020-7427 4800
E members@middletemple.org.uk
W www.middletemple.org.uk
Under-Treasurer, Catherine Quinn

NOTARIES PUBLIC
Notaries are qualified lawyers with a postgraduate
diploma in notarial practice. Once a potential notary has
passed the postgraduate diploma, they can petition the
Court of Faculties for a 'faculty'. After the faculty is
granted, the notary is able to practise; however, for the
first two years this must be under the supervision of an
experienced notary. The admission and regulation of
notaries in England and Wales is a statutory function of
the Faculty Office. This jurisdiction was confirmed by the
Courts and Legal Services Act 1990. The Notaries Society
of England and Wales is the representative body for
practising notaries.
THE FACULTY OFFICE 1 The Sanctuary, Westminster,
London SW1P 3JT T 020-7222 5381
E faculty.office@1thesanctuary.com
W www.facultyoffice.org.uk
Registrar, Peter Beesley
THE NOTARIES SOCIETY OF ENGLAND AND
WALES PO Box 226, Melton Woodbridge IP12 1WX
T 01394-380436 E admin@the notariessociety.org.uk
W www.thenotariessociety.org.uk
Secretary, Christopher Vaughan

SOLICITORS
Salary range: £15,000–£23,000 (trainee); £42,000–
£50,000 (associate or partner)

Graduates from any discipline can train to be a solicitor;
however, if the undergraduate degree is not in law, a
one-year conversion course – either the Common
Professional Examination (CPE) or the Graduate Diploma
in Law (GDL) – must be completed. The next stage, and
the beginning of the vocational phase, is the Legal
Practice Course (LPC), which takes one year and is
obligatory for both law and non-law graduates. The LPC

provides professional instruction for prospective solicitors
and can be completed on a full-time or part-time basis.
Trainee solicitors then enter the final stage, that is a paid
period of supervised work that lasts two years for full-time
contracts. The employer that provides the training contract
must be authorised by the Solicitors Regulation Authority
(SRA) (the regulatory body of the Law Society of England
and Wales), the Law Society of Scotland or the Law
Society of Northern Ireland. The SRA also monitors the
training contract to ensure that it provides the trainee with
the expertise to qualify as a solicitor.
Conveyancers are specialist property lawyers, dealing
with the legal processes involved in transferring buildings,
land and associated finances from one owner to another.
This was the sole responsibility of solicitors until 1987
but under current legislation it is now possible for others
to train as conveyancers.
COUNCIL FOR LICENSED CONVEYANCERS (CLC)
16 Glebe Road, Chelmsford, Essex CM1 1QG
T 01245-349599 W www.conveyancer.org.uk
Chief Executive, Victor Olowe
THE LAW SOCIETY OF ENGLAND AND WALES
The Law Society's Hall, 113 Chancery Lane, London
WC2A 1PL T 020-7242 1222 E enquiries@lawsociety.org.uk
W www.lawsociety.org.uk
Chief Executive, Des Hudson
LAW SOCIETY OF NORTHERN IRELAND
Law Society House, 96 Victoria Street, Belfast BT1 3GN
T 028-9023 1614 E info@lawsoc-ni.org
W www.lawsoc-ni.org
Chief Executive and Secretary, Alan Hunter
LAW SOCIETY OF SCOTLAND 26 Drumsheugh Gardens,
Edinburgh EH3 7YR T 0131-226 7411
E lawscot@lawscot.org.uk W www.lawscot.org.uk
Chief Executive, Lorna Jack
SOLICITORS REGULATION AUTHORITY Ipsley Court,
Berrington Close, Redditch, Worcs B98 0TD
T 0870-606 2555 E contactcentre@sra.org.uk
W www.sra.org.uk
Chief Executive, Antony Townsend

SOCIAL WORK
Salary range: £24,000–£30,000 (starting), rising to
£42,000 as an experienced manager; £57,000+ at senior
levels

Social workers tend to specialise in either adult or
children's services. The General Social Care Council is
responsible for setting standards of conduct and practice
for social care workers and their employers; regulating
the workforce and social work education and training.
A degree or postgraduate qualification is needed in order
to become a social worker. For more information *see* Social
Welfare.
GENERAL SOCIAL CARE COUNCIL (GSCC)
Goldings House, 2 Hay's Lane, London SE1 2HB
T 020-7397 5100 E customer.service@gscc.org.uk
W www.gscc.org.uk
Chief Executive, Penny Thompson

SURVEYING
Salary range: £20,000–£26,000 (starting); £32,000+
(senior); £70,000+ (partner)

The Royal Institution of Chartered Surveyors (RICS) is
the professional body that represents and regulates
property professionals including land surveyors, valuers,
auctioneers, quantity surveyors and project managers.
Entry to the institution, following completion of a
RICS-accredited degree, is through completion of the

Assessment of Professional Competence (APC), which involves a period of practical training concluded by a final assessment of competence. Entry as a technical surveyor requires completion of the Assessment of Technical Competence (ATC), which mirrors the format of the APC. The different levels of RICS membership are MRICS (member) or FRICS (fellow) for chartered surveyors, and AssocRICS for associate members.

Relevant courses can also be accredited by the Chartered Institute of Building (CIOB), which represents managers working in a range of construction disciplines. The CIOB offers four levels of membership to those who satisfy its requirements: FCIOB (fellow), MCIOB (member), ICIOB (incorporated) and ACIOB (associate).

CHARTERED INSTITUTE OF BUILDING Englemere, King's Ride, Ascot SL5 7TB T 01344-630700
E reception@ciob.org.uk W www.ciob.org.uk
Chief Executive, Chris Blythe
ROYAL INSTITUTION OF CHARTERED
SURVEYORS (RICS) RICS Contact Centre, Surveyor Court, Westwood Way, Coventry CV4 8JE T 0870-333 1600
E contactrics@rics.org W www.rics.org
Chief Executive, Sean Tompkins

TEACHING

Salary range: £21,000–£64,000; headteacher £42,000–£112,000 (for more detailed information *see* Education, Employees and Salaries)

The General Teaching Councils (GTCs) for England, Northern Ireland, Scotland and Wales maintain registers of qualified teachers in their respective countries, and registration is a legal requirement in order to teach in local authority schools. The Graduate Teacher Training Registry (GTTR) processes applications for entry to postgraduate teaching courses in England, Wales and Scotland. All new entrants to the UK teaching profession must have qualified teacher status (QTS), which requires completing an initial teacher training (ITT) period. In order to gain QTS, individuals must be graduates.

Teachers in Further Education (FE) need not have QTS, though new entrants to FE are required to work towards a specified FE qualification recognised by the Learning and Skills Improvement Service. Similarly, academic staff in Higher Education require no formal teaching qualification, but are expected to obtain a qualification that meets standards set by the Higher Education Academy.

Details of routes to gaining QTS and funding for ITT are available in England from the Training and Development Agency for Schools (TDA), in Wales from the Teacher Training & Education Recruitment Forum Wales, in Scotland from Teach in Scotland and in Northern Ireland from the Department of Education.

The College of Teachers, under the terms of its royal charter, provides professional qualifications and membership to teachers and those involved in education in the UK and overseas.

COLLEGE OF TEACHERS Institute of Education, 20 Bedford Way, London WC1H 0AL T 020-7911 5536
W www.cot.ac.uk
Chief Executive and Registrar, Matthew Martin
DEPARTMENT OF EDUCATION NORTHERN
IRELAND Rathgael House, Balloo Road, Bangor BT19 7PR
T 028-9127 9279 E mail@deni.gov.uk W www.deni.gov.uk
Permanent Secretary, Paul Sweeney
GENERAL TEACHING COUNCIL FOR ENGLAND
Whittington House, 19–30 Alfred Place, London WC1E 7EA
T 0370-001 0308 E info@gtce.org.uk W www.gtce.org.uk
Chief Executive, Alan Meyrick

GENERAL TEACHING COUNCIL FOR NORTHERN
IRELAND 4th Floor, Albany House, 73–75 Great Victoria
Street, Belfast BT2 7AF T 028-9033 3390
E info@gtcni.org.uk W www.gtcni.org.uk
Chair, Sally McKee
GENERAL TEACHING COUNCIL FOR SCOTLAND
Clerwood House, 96 Clermiston Road, Edinburgh EH12 6UT
T 0131-314 6000 E gtcs@gtcs.org.uk W www.gtcs.org.uk
Chief Executive, Anthony Finn
GENERAL TEACHING COUNCIL FOR WALES
9th Floor, Eastgate House, 35–43 Newport Road, Cardiff
CF24 0AB T 029-2046 0099 E information@gtcw.org.uk
W www.gtcw.org.uk
Chief Executive, Gary Brace
GRADUATE TEACHER TRAINING REGISTRY
Rosehill, New Barn Lane, Cheltenham GL52 3LZ
T 0871-468 0469 E enquiries@gttr.ac.uk W www.gttr.ac.uk
Chief Executive, Mary Curnock Cook
HIGHER EDUCATION ACADEMY Innovation Way, York
Science Park, Heslington, York YO10 5BR T 01904-717500
E enquiries@heacademy.ac.uk W www.heacademy.ac.uk
Chief Executive, Craig Mahoney
LEARNING AND SKILLS IMPROVEMENT SERVICE
Friars House, Manor House Drive, Coventry CV1 2TE
T 0247-662 7900 E enquiries@lsis.org.uk
W www.lsis.org.uk
Chief Executive, Rob Wye
TRAINING AND DEVELOPMENT AGENCY FOR
SCHOOLS Piccadilly Gate, Store Street, Manchester
M1 2WD T 0870-496 0123 W www.tda.gov.uk
Chief Executive, Stephen Hillier

VETERINARY MEDICINE

Salary range: £30,000–£48,000

The regulatory body for veterinary surgeons in the UK is the Royal College of Veterinary Surgeons (RCVS), which keeps the register of those entitled to practise veterinary medicine as well as the list of qualified veterinary nurses. Holders of recognised degrees from any of the six UK university veterinary schools or from certain EU or overseas universities are entitled to be registered, and holders of certain other degrees may take a statutory membership examination. The UK's veterinary schools are located at the University of Bristol, the University of Cambridge, the University of Edinburgh, the University of Glasgow, the University of Liverpool and the Royal Veterinary College in London; all veterinary degrees last for five years except that offered at Cambridge, which lasts for six. A new course at the University of Nottingham's School of Veterinary Medicine and Science produced its first veterinary graduates in 2011.

The British Veterinary Association is the professional body representing veterinary surgeons. The British Veterinary Nursing Association is the professional body representing veterinary nurses.

BRITISH VETERINARY ASSOCIATION 7 Mansfield
Street, London W1G 9NQ T 020-7636 6541
E bvahq@bva.co.uk W www.bva.co.uk
Secretary General, Henrietta Alderman
BRITISH VETERINARY NURSING ASSOCIATION
82 Greenway Business Centre, Harlow Business Park, Harlow
CM19 5QE T 01279-408644 E bvna@bvna.co.uk
W www.bvna.org.uk
Honorary Secretary, Kirstie Shield
ROYAL COLLEGE OF VETERINARY SURGEONS
Belgravia House, 62–64 Horseferry Road, London SW1P 2AF
T 020-7222 2001 E admin@rcvs.org.uk W www.rcvs.org.uk
Registrar, Jane Hern

INDEPENDENT SCHOOLS

Independent schools (non-maintained mainstream schools) charge fees and are owned and managed under special trusts, with profits being used for the benefit of the schools concerned. In 2009–10 there were 2,570 non-maintained mainstream schools in the UK, educating over 621,000 pupils, or around 6.4 per cent of the total school-age population. The approximate number of pupils at non-maintained mainstream schools in 2009–10 was:

UK	621,750
England	581,400
Wales	9,200
Scotland	30,500
Northern Ireland	650

The Independent Schools Council (ISC), formed in 1974, acts on behalf of the eight independent schools' associations which constitute it. These associations are:

Association of Governing Bodies of Independent Schools (AGBIS)
Council of British International Schools (COBIS)
Girls' Schools Association (GSA)
Headmasters' & Headmistresses' Conference (HMC)
Independent Association of Prep Schools (IAPS)
Independent Schools Association (ISA)
Independent Schools' Bursars Association (ISBA)
Society of Heads of Independent Schools (SHMIS)

In 2010–11 there were 506,500 pupils being educated in 1,234 schools in membership of associations within the Independent Schools Council (ISC). Most schools not in membership of an ISC association are likely to be privately owned. The Independent Schools Inspectorate (ISI) was demerged from ISC with effect from 1 January 2008 and is legally and operationally independent of ISC. ISI works as an accredited inspectorate of schools in membership of the ISC associations under a framework agreed with the Department for Education (DfE). A school must pass an ISI accreditation inspection to qualify for membership of an association within ISC.

In 2010 at GCSE 60.2 per cent of all exams taken by candidates in ISC associations' member schools achieved either an A* or A grade (compared to the national average of 22.6 per cent), and at A-level 18.2 per cent of entries were awarded the new A* grade (national average, 8.1 per cent). In 2010–11 a total of 164,105 pupils at schools in ISC associations received help with their fees, mainly in the form of bursaries and scholarships from the schools. These cost the schools more than £550m.

INDEPENDENT SCHOOLS COUNCIL
St Vincent House, 30 Orange Street, London WC2H 7HH
T 020-7766 7070 W www.isc.co.uk

The list of schools below was compiled from the Independent Schools Yearbook 2011–12 (ed. Judy Mott, published by A&C Black) which includes schools whose heads are members of one of the ISC's five Heads' Associations. Further details are available online (W www.isyb.co.uk).

The fees shown below represent the upper limits payable as at September 2011.

School	Web Address	Termly Fees Day	Board	Head
ENGLAND				
Abbey Gate College, Cheshire	www.abbeygatecollege.co.uk	£3,367	–	Mrs L. Horner
The Abbey School, Berks	www.theabbey.co.uk	£4,200	–	Mrs B. Stanley
Abbots Bromley School for Girls, Staffs	www.abbotsbromley.staffs.sch.uk	£4,775	£7,995	Mrs J. Dowling
Abbot's Hill School, Herts	www.abbotshill.herts.sch.uk	£4,880		Mrs K. Lewis
Abbotsholme School, Derbys	www.abbotsholme.com	£6,285	£9,225	S. Fairclough
Abingdon School, Oxon	www.abingdon.org.uk	£4,835	£9,915	Miss O. Lusk
Ackworth School, W. Yorks	www.ackworthschool.com	£3,920	£6,545	Mrs K. Bell
Aldenham School, Herts	www.aldenham.com	£6,083	£8,860	J. Fowler
Alderley Edge School for Girls, Cheshire	www.aesg.info	£3,067	–	Mrs S. Goff
Alleyn's School, London SE22	www.alleyns.org.uk	£4,867	–	Dr G. Savage
Amberfield School, Suffolk	www.amberfield.suffolk.sch.uk	£3,505	–	Mrs L. Ingram
Ampleforth College, N. Yorks	www.college.ampleforth.org.uk	£6,095	£9,472	Revd C. Everitt
Ardingly College, W. Sussex	www.ardingly.com	£6,880	£9,105	P. Green
Arnold School, Lancs	www.arnoldschool.com	£3,020	–	J. Keefe
Ashford School, Kent	www.ashfordschool.co.uk	£4,856	£9,401	M. Buchanan
Ashville College, N. Yorks	www.ashville.co.uk	£3,790	£7,420	D. Lauder
Austin Friars St Monica's Senior School, Cumbria	www.austinfriars.cumbria.sch.uk	£3,765	£3,765	C. Lumb
Bablake School, W. Midlands	www.bablake.com	£3,056	£3,056	J. Watson
Badminton School, Bristol	www.badminton.bristol.sch.uk	£5,270	£9,880	Mrs J. Scarrow
Bancroft's School, Essex	www.bancrofts.org	£4,396	£4,396	Mrs M. Ireland
Barnard Castle School, Durham	www.barnardcastleschool.org.uk	£3,660	£6,572	A. Stevens
Bearwood College, Berks	www.bearwoodcollege.co.uk	£5,455	£9,360	S. Aiano
Bedales School, Hants	www.bedales.org.uk	£7,850	£9,985	K. Budge

School	Website	Day Fee	Boarding Fee	Head
Bedford Girls' School, Beds	www.bedfordgirlsschool.co.uk	£3,561	–	Miss J. MacKenzie
Bedford Modern School, Beds	www.bedmod.co.uk	£3,561	–	M. Hall
Bedford School, Beds	www.bedfordschool.org.uk	£5,264	£8,649	J. Moule
Bedstone College, Shropshire	www.bedstone.org	£4,085	£7,410	M. Symonds
Beechwood Sacred Heart School, Kent	www.beechwood.org.uk	£4,835	£8,020	N. Beesley
Benenden School, Kent	www.benenden.kent.sch.uk	–	£9,980	Mrs C. Oulton
Berkhamsted School, Herts	www.berkhamstedschool.org	£5,600	£8,920	M. Steed
Bethany School, Kent	www.bethanyschool.org.uk	£5,040	£7,867	M. Healy
Birkdale School, S. Yorks	www.birkdaleschool.org.uk	£3,559	–	P. Owen
Birkenhead School, Merseyside	www.birkenheadschool.co.uk	£3,202	–	D. Clark
Bishop's Stortford College, Herts	www.bishops-stortford-college.herts.sch.uk	£3,999	£7,192	J. Gladwin
Blackheath High School, London SE3	www.blackheathhighschool.gdst.net	£4,171	–	Mrs E. Laws
Bloxham School, Oxon	www.bloxhamschool.com	£5,055	£9,255	M. Allbrook
Blundell's School, Devon	www.blundells.org	£5,830	£9,040	I. Davenport
Bolton School Boys' Division, Lancs	www.boltonschool.org/seniorboys	£3,290	–	P. Britton
Bolton School Girls' Division, Lancs	www.boltonschool.org/seniorgirls	£3,290	–	Miss S. Hincks
Bootham School, N. Yorks	www.boothamschool.com	£5,125	£8,600	J. Taylor
Bournemouth Collegiate School, Dorset	www.bournemouthcollegiateschool.co.uk	£4,070	£7,338	S. Duckitt
Box Hill School, Surrey	www.boxhillschool.com	£5,200	£8,750	M. Eagers
Bradfield College, Berks	www.bradfieldcollege.org.uk	£7,876	£9,845	S. Henderson
Bradfield Girls' Grammar School, W. Yorks	www.bggs.com	£3,722	–	K. Matthews
Bradford Grammar School, W. Yorks	www.bradfordgrammar.com	£3,497	–	S. Davidson
Brentwood School, Essex	www.brentwoodschool.co.uk	£4,724	£8,481	D. Davies
Brighton and Hove High School, E. Sussex	www.bhhs.gdst.net	£3,459	–	Mrs L. Duggleby
Brighton College, E Sussex	www.brightoncollege.net	£6,225	£10,782	R. Cairns
Brigidine School Windsor, Berks	www.brigidine.org.uk	£4,585	–	Mrs E. Robinson
Bristol Grammar School, Bristol	www.bristolgrammarschool.co.uk	£3,711	–	R. MacKinnon
Bromley High School, Kent	www.bromleyhigh.gdst.net	£4,202	–	Ms L. Simpson
Bromsgrove School, Worcs	www.bromsgrove-school.co.uk	£3,985	£8,395	C. Edwards
Bruton School for Girls, Somerset	www.brutonschool.co.uk	£4,325	£7,820	J. Burrough
Bryanston School, Dorset	www.bryanston.co.uk	£8,192	£9,990	Ms S. Thomas
Burgess Hill School for Girls, W. Sussex	www.burgesshill-school.com	£4,520	£7,970	Mrs A. Aughwane
Bury Grammar School Boys, Lancs	www.bgsboys.co.uk	£2,912	–	Revd S. Harvey
Bury Grammar School Girls, Lancs	www.bgsg.bury.sch.uk	£2,912	–	Mrs R. Georghiou
Canford School, Dorset	www.canford.com	£7,245	£9,305	J. Lever
Casterton School, Lancs	www.castertonschool.co.uk	£5,082	£8,520	Mrs M. Lucas
Caterham School, Surrey	www.caterhamschool.co.uk	£4,817	£8,988	J. Thomas
Central Newcastle High School, Tyne and Wear	www.newcastlehigh.gdst.net	£3,370	–	Mrs H. French
Channing School, London N6	www.channing.co.uk	£4,680	–	Mrs B. Elliott
Charterhouse, Surrey	www.charterhouse.org.uk	£8,414	£10,178	Revd J. Witheridge
Cheadle Hulme School, Cheshire	www.cheadlehulmeschool.co.uk	£3,158	£3,158	Miss L. Pearson
Cheltenham College, Glos	www.cheltenhamcollege.org	£7,425	£9,909	Dr A. Peterken
The Cheltenham Ladies' College, Glos	www.cheltladiescollege.org	£6,455	£9,615	Miss E. Jardine-Young
Chetham's School of Music, Greater Manchester	www.chethams.com	sliding scale		Mrs C. Hickman
Chetwynde School, Cumbria	www.chetwynde.co.uk	£2,800	–	R. Collier
Chigwell School, Essex	www.chigwell-school.org	£4,846	£7,665	M. Punt
Christ's Hospital, W. Sussex	www.christs-hospital.org.uk	£5,665	£8,335	J. Franklin
Churcher's College, Hants	www.churcherscollege.com	£3,850	–	S. Williams
City of London Freemen's School, Surrey	www.clfs.surrey.sch.uk	£4,866	£7,746	P. MacDonald
City of London School, London EC4	www.clsb.org.uk	£4,350	–	D. Levin
City of London School for Girls, London EC2	www.clsg.org.uk	£4,377	–	Miss D. Vernon
Claremont Fan Court School, Surrey	www.claremont-school.co.uk	£4,550	–	J. Insall-Reid
Clayesmore School, Dorset	www.clayesmore.com	£6,993	£9,558	M. Cooke
Clifton College, Bristol	www.cliftoncollegeuk.com	£6,790	£9,750	M. Moore

School	Website			Head
Clifton High School, Bristol	www.cliftonhigh.bristol.sch.uk	£3,780	£6,795	Dr A. Neill
Cobham Hall, Kent	www.cobhamhall.com	£5,950	£8,950	P. Mitchell
Cokethorpe School, Oxon	www.cokethorpe.org.uk	£4,975	–	D. Ettinger
Colfe's School, London SE12	www.colfes.com	£4,371	–	R. Russell
Colston's School, Bristol	www.colstons.bristol.sch.uk	£3,445	£6,580	P. Fraser
Combe Bank School, Kent	www.combebank.kent.sch.uk	£4,870	–	Mrs E. Abbotts
Concord College, Shropshire	www.concordcollegeuk.com	£3,900	£8,850	N. Hawkins
Cranford House School, Oxon	www.cranford-house.org	£4,475	–	Mrs C. Hamilton
Cranleigh School, Surrey	www.cranleigh.org	£7,990	£9,805	G. Waller
Croydon High School, Surrey	www.croydonhigh.gdst.net	£4,203	–	Mrs D. Leonard
Culford School, Suffolk	www.culford.co.uk	£5,285	£8,555	J. Johnson-Munday
Dame Allan's Boys' School, Tyne and Wear	www.dameallans.co.uk	£3,291	–	Dr J. Hind
Dame Allan's Girls' School, Tyne and Wear	www.dameallans.co.uk	£3,291	–	Dr J. Hind
Dauntsey's School, Wilts	www.dauntseys.org	£5,195	£8,755	S. Roberts
Dean Close School, Glos	www.deanclose.org.uk	£6,790	£9,615	J. Lancashire
Denstone College, Staffs	www.denstonecollege.org	£4,061	£7,072	D. Derbyshire
Derby High School, Derbyshire	www.derbyhigh.derby.sch.uk	£3,360	–	C. Callaghan
Dodderhill School, Worcs	www.dodderhill.co.uk	£3,125	–	Mrs C. Mawston
Dover College, Kent	www.dovercollege.org.uk	£4,330	£8,650	S. Jones
d'Overbroeck's College, Oxon	www.doverbroecks.com	£6,175	£9,350	S. Cohen
Downe House, Berks	www.downehouse.net	£7,245	£10,010	Mrs E. McKendrick
Dulwich College, London SE21	www.dulwich.org.uk	£4,964	£10,213	Dr J. Spence
Dunottar School, Surrey	www.dunottarschool.com	£4,200	–	Mrs N. Matthews
Durham High School for Girls, Durham	www.dhsfg.org.uk	£3,315	–	A. Whelpdale
Durham School, Durham	www.durhamschool.co.uk	£5,000	£7,425	E. George
Eastbourne College, E. Sussex	www.eastbourne-college.co.uk	£5,995	£9,105	S. Davies
Edgbaston High School, W. Midlands	www.edgbastonhigh.co.uk	£3,176	–	Dr R. Weeks
Ellesmere College, Shropshire	www.ellesmere.com	£5,145	£8,679	B. Wignall
Eltham College, London SE9	www.eltham-college.org.uk	£4,260	–	P. Henderson
Emanuel School, London SW11	www.emanuel.org.uk	£4,861	–	M. Hanley-Browne
Epsom College, Surrey	www.epsomcollege.org.uk	£6,650	£9,730	S. Borthwick
Eton College, Berks	www.etoncollege.com	–	£10,327	A. Little
Ewell Castle School, Surrey	www.ewellcastle.co.uk	£4,150	–	A. Tibble
Exeter School, Devon	www.exeterschool.org.uk	£3,470	–	R. Griffin
Farlington School, W. Sussex	www.farlingtonschool.net	£4,831	£7,885	Mrs J. Goyer
Farnborough Hill, Hants	www.farnborough-hill.org.uk	£3,725	–	Mrs S. Buckle
Farringtons School, Kent	www.farringtons.org.uk	£3,920	£7,500	Mrs C. James
Felsted School, Essex	www.felsted.org	£6,470	£8,645	Dr M. Walker
Forest School, London E17	www.forest.org.uk	£4,650	–	Mrs S. Kerr-Dineen
Framlingham College, Suffolk	www.framlinghamcollege.co.uk	£5,318	£8,274	P. Taylor
Francis Holland School, London NW1	www.francisholland.org.uk	£4,800	–	Mrs V. Durham
Francis Holland School, London SW1	www.francisholland.org.uk	£4,880	–	Miss S. Pattenden
Frensham Heights, Surrey	www.frenshamheights.org	£5,300	£7,990	A. Fisher
Friends' School, Essex	www.friends.org.uk	£4,895	£7,790	G. Wigley
Fulneck School, W. Yorks	www.fulneckschool.co.uk	£3,530	£6,620	T. Kernohan
Gateways School, W. Yorks	www.gatewaysschool.co.uk	£3,582	–	Y. Wilkinson
Giggleswick School, N. Yorks	www.giggleswickschool.co.uk	£6,150	£8,980	G. Boult
The Godolphin and Latymer School, London W6	www.godolphinandlatymer.com	£5,175	–	Mrs R. Mercer
The Godolphin School, Wilts	www.godolphin.org	£5,754	£8,273	Mrs S. Price
The Grange School, Cheshire	www.grange.org.uk	£3,040	–	C. Jeffery
Greenacre School for Girls, Surrey	www.greenacre.surrey.sch.uk	£4,100	–	Mrs L. Redding
Gresham's School, Norfolk	www.greshams.com	£6,975	£9,100	P. John
Guildford High School, Surrey	www.guildfordhigh.surrey.sch.uk	£4,434	–	Mrs F. Boulton
The Haberdashers' Aske's Boys' School, Herts	www.habsboys.org.uk	£4,889	–	P. Hamilton
Haberdashers' Aske's School for Girls, Herts	www.habsgirls.org.uk	£3,983	–	Miss B. O'Connor
Haileybury, Herts	www.haileybury.com	£6,855	£9,128	J. Davies
Halliford School, Middx	www.hallifordschool.co.uk	£3,807	–	P. Cottam

School	Website			Head
Hampshire Collegiate School, Hants	www.hampshirecs.org.uk	£4,438	£7,345	H. MacDonald
Hampton School, Middx	www.hamptonschool.org.uk	£4,870	–	B. Martin
Harrogate Ladies' College, N. Yorks	www.hlc.org.uk	£4,481	£7,825	Mrs R. Wilkinson
Harrow School, Middx	www.harrowschool.org.uk	–	£10,310	J. Hawkins
Headington School, Oxon	www.headington.org	£4,445	£8,606	Mrs C. Jordan
Heathfield School, Berks	www.heathfieldschool.net	–	£9,650	Mrs J. Heywood
Heathfield School, Middx	www.heathfield.gdst.net	£4,223	–	Mrs A. Stevens
Hereford Cathedral School, Herefordshire	www.herefordcs.com	£3,800	–	P. Smith
Hethersett Old Hall School, Norfolk	www.hohs.co.uk	£3,975	£7,400	S. Crump
Highgate School, London N6	www.highgateschool.org.uk	£5,290	–	A. Pettitt
Hipperholme Grammar School Foundation, W. Yorks	www.hgsf.org.uk	£3,150	–	J. Scarth
Hollygirt School, Notts	www.hollygirt.co.uk	£3,120	–	P. Hutley
Hull Collegiate School, E. Yorks	www.hullcollegiateschool.co.uk	£3,250	–	R. Haworth
Hurstpierpoint College, W. Sussex	www.hppc.co.uk	£6,345	£9,525	T. Manly
Hymers College, E. Yorks	www.hymerscollege.co.uk	£2,982	–	D. Elstone
Immanuel College, Herts	www.immanuelcollege.co.uk	£4,466	–	P. Skelker
Ipswich High School, Suffolk	www.ipswichhighschool.co.uk	£3,402	–	Ms E. Purves
Ipswich School, Suffolk	www.ipswich.suffolk.sch.uk	£3,895	£9,699	N. Weaver
James Allen's Girls' School (JAGS), London SE22	www.jags.org.uk	£4,520	–	Mrs M. Gibbs
The John Lyon School, Middx	www.johnlyon.org	£4,590	–	Miss K. Haynes
Kelly College, Devon	www.kellycollege.com	£4,875	£8,500	Dr G. Hawley
Kent College, Kent	www.kentcollege.com	£5,122	£9,109	D. Lamper
Kent College Pembury, Kent	www.kent-college.co.uk	£5,364	£8,648	Mrs S. Huang
Kimbolton School, Cambs	www.kimbolton.cambs.sch.uk	£4,215	£6,975	J. Belbin
King Edward VI High School for Girls, W. Midlands	www.kehs.org.uk	£3,405	–	Miss S. Evans
King Edward VI School, Hants	www.kes.hants.sch.uk	£3,870	–	A. Thould
King Edward VII and Queen Mary School, Lancs	www.keqms.co.uk	£2,900	–	R. Karling
King Edward's School, Somerset	www.kesbath.com	£3,775	–	M. Boden
King Edward's School, W. Midlands	www.kes.org.uk	£3,465	–	J. Claughton
King Edward's School, Surrey	www.kesw.org	£6,060	£8,660	J. Attwater
King Henry VIII School, W. Midlands	www.khviii.com	£3,056	–	J. Slack
King William's College, Isle of Man	www.kwc.im	£6,103	£8,888	M. Humphreys
Kingham Hill School, Oxon	www.kingham-hill.oxon.sch.uk	£5,145	£8,360	Revd N. Seward
King's College School, London SW19	www.kcs.org.uk	£5,840	–	A. Halls
King's College, Somerset	www.kings-taunton.co.uk	£5,910	£8,800	R. Biggs
King's High School, Warwicks	www.kingshighwarwick.co.uk	£3,252	–	Mrs E. Surber
King's School, Somerset	www.kingsbruton.com	£6,285	£8,782	I. Wilmshurst
The King's School, Canterbury, Kent	www.kings-school.co.uk	£7,470	£9,990	P. Roberts
The King's School, Chester, Cheshire	www.kingschester.co.uk	£3,544	–	C. Ramsey
The King's School, Cambs	www.kingsschoolely.co.uk	£5,615	£8,128	Mrs S. Freestone
The King's School, Glos	www.thekingsschool.co.uk	£5,320	–	A. Macnaughton
The King's School, Macclesfield, Cheshire	www.kingsmac.co.uk	£3,165	–	S. Hyde
King's Rochester, Kent	www.kings-rochester.co.uk	£5,270	£8,550	Dr I. Walker
The King's School, Tyne and Wear	www.kings-tynemouth.org.uk	£3,330	–	E. Wesson
The King's School, Worcs	www.ksw.org.uk	£3,697	–	T. Keyes
Kingsley School, Devon	www.kingsleyschoolbideford.co.uk	£3,880	£7,400	A. Waters
The Kingsley School, Warwicks	www.thekingsleyschool.com	£3,495	–	Ms H. Owens
Kingston Grammar School, Surrey	www.kgs.org.uk	£4,945	–	Mrs S. Fletcher
Kingswood School, Somerset	www.kingswood.bath.sch.uk	£3,853	£8,303	S. Morris
Kirkham Grammar School, Lancs	www.kirkhamgrammar.co.uk	£3,020	£5,726	D. Walker
The Lady Eleanor Holles School, Middx	www.lehs.org.uk	£4,900	–	Mrs G. Low
Lancing College, W. Sussex	www.lancingcollege.co.uk	£6,720	£9,615	J. Gillespie
Langley School, Norfolk	www.langleyschool.co.uk	£3,795	£7,715	D. Findlay

Latymer Upper School, London W6	www.latymer-upper.org	£4,985	–	P. Winter
Lavant House, W. Sussex	www.lavanthouse.org.uk	£4,470	£7,035	Mrs K. Bartholomew
The Grammar School at Leeds, W. Yorks	www.gsal.org.uk	£3,585	–	M. Gibbons
Leicester Grammar School, Leics	www.leicestergrammar.org.uk	£3,507	–	C. King
Leicester High School for Girls, Leics	www.leicesterhigh.co.uk	£3,175	–	Mrs J. Burns
Leighton Park School, Berks	www.leightonpark.com	£5,998	£9,154	A. McGrath
Leweston School, Dorset	www.leweston.co.uk	£5,295	£8,195	A. Aylward
The Leys School, Cambs	www.theleys.net	£5,750	£8,640	M. Slater
LVS Ascot (The Licensed Victuallers' School), Berks	www.lvs.ascot.sch.uk	£4,600	£8,080	Mrs C. Cunniffe
Lincoln Minster School, Lincs	www.lincolnminsterschool.co.uk	£3,749	£7,250	C. Rickart
Liverpool College, Merseyside	www.liverpoolcollege.org.uk	£3,225	–	H. van Mourik Broekman
Longridge Towers School, Northumberland	www.lts.org.uk	£3,653	£7,442	T. Manning
Lord Wandsworth College, Hants	www.lordwandsworth.org	£6,220	£8,770	F. Livingstone
Loughborough Grammar School, Leics	www.lesgrammar.org	£3,370	£6,182	P. Fisher
Loughborough High School, Leics	www.leshigh.org	£3,139	–	Mrs G. Byrom
Luckley-Oakfield School, Berks	www.luckley.wokingham.sch.uk	£4,492	£7,862	Miss V. Davis
Magdalen College School, Oxon	www.mcsoxford.org	£4,465	–	T. Hands
Malvern College, Worcs	www.malcol.org	£6,771	£10,572	A. Clark
Malvern St James, Worcs	www.malvernstjames.co.uk	£4,930	£9,645	Mrs P. Woodhouse
The Manchester Grammar School, Greater Manchester	www.mgs.org	£3,332	–	C. Ray
Manchester High School for Girls, Greater Manchester	www.manchesterhigh.co.uk	£3,214	–	Mrs A. Hewitt
Manor House School, Surrey	www.manorhouseschool.org	£4,420	–	Miss Z. Axton
The Marist Senior School, Berks	www.themaristschools.com	£3,565	–	K. McCloskey
Marlborough College, Wilts	www.marlboroughcollege.org	£8,150	£10,100	N. Sampson
Marymount International School, Surrey	www.marymountlondon.com	£6,320	£10,610	Ms S. Gallagher
The Maynard School, Devon	www.maynard.co.uk	£3,566	–	Ms B. Hughes
Merchant Taylors' Boys' School, Merseyside	www.merchanttaylors.com	£3,125	–	D. Cook
Merchant Taylors' Girls' School, Merseyside	www.merchanttaylors.com	£3,125	–	Mrs L. Robinson
Merchant Taylors' School, Middx	www.mtsn.org.uk	£5,340	–	S. Wright
Mill Hill School, London NW7	www.millhill.org.uk	£5,531	£8,739	Dr D. Luckett
Millfield, Somerset	www.millfieldschool.com	£6,500	£9,670	C. Considine
Milton Abbey School, Dorset	www.miltonabbey.co.uk	£7,350	£9,780	G. Doodes
Moira House Girls School, E. Sussex	www.moirahouse.co.uk	£4,765	£8,510	Mrs L. Watson
Monkton Combe School, Somerset	www.monktoncombeschool.com	£5,727	£9,045	R. Backhouse
More House School, London SW1	www.morehouse.org.uk	£4,685	–	R. Carlysle
Moreton Hall, Shropshire	www.moretonhall.org	£7,465	£9,115	J. Forster
Mount St Mary's College, Derbyshire	www.msmcollege.com	£3,705	£7,667	L. McKell
The Mount School, London NW7	www.mountschool.com	£3,775	–	Ms C. Cozens
The Mount School, N. Yorks	www.mountschoolyork.co.uk	£4,900	£7,625	Ms J. Lodrick
New Hall School, Essex	www.newhallschool.co.uk	£5,112	£7,901	Mrs K. Jeffrey
Newcastle School for Boys, Tyne and Wear	www.newcastleschool.co.uk	£3,495	–	L. Francis
Newcastle-under-Lyme School, Staffs	www.nuls.org.uk	£3,169	–	N. Rugg
The Newcastle upon Tyne Church High School, Tyne and Wear	www.churchhigh.com	£3,625	–	Mrs J. Gatenby
North Cestrian Grammar School, Cheshire	www.ncgs.co.uk	£2,767	–	D. Vanstone
North London Collegiate School, Middx	www.nlcs.org.uk	£4,841	–	Mrs B. McCabe
Northampton High School, Northants	www.gdst.net/northamptonhigh	£3,731	–	Mrs S. Dixon
Northwood College, Middx	www.northwoodcollege.co.uk	£4,350	–	Miss J. Pain
Norwich High School, Norfolk	www.norwichhigh.gdst.net	£3,420	–	J. Morrow
Norwich School, Norfolk	www.norwich-school.org.uk	£4,058	–	S. Griffiths

School	Website	Day	Boarding	Head
Notre Dame Senior School, Surrey	www.notredame.co.uk	£4,300	–	Mrs B. Williams
Notting Hill and Ealing High School, London W13	www.nhehs.gdst.net	£4,343	–	Ms L. Hunt
Nottingham Girls' High School, Notts	www.nottinghamgirlshigh.gdst.net	£3,370	–	Mrs S. Gorham
Nottingham High School, Notts	www.nottinghamhigh.co.uk	£3,724	–	K. Fear
Oakham School, Rutland	www.oakham.rutland.sch.uk	£5,450	£9,080	N. Lashbrook
Ockbrook School, Derbyshire	www.ockbrook.derby.sch.uk	£3,275	£6,220	Mrs A. Steele
Oldham Hulme Grammar Schools, Lancs	www.hulme-grammar.oldham.sch.uk	£2,940	–	Dr P. Neeson
The Oratory School, Berks	www.oratory.co.uk	£6,485	£8,980	C. Dytor
Oswestry School, Shropshire	www.oswestryschool.org.uk	£4,240	£7,380	D. Robb
Oundle School, Northants	www.oundleschool.org.uk	£6,160	£9,530	C. Bush
Our Lady of Sion School, W. Sussex	www.sionschool.org.uk	£3,345	–	M. Scullion
Our Lady's Abingdon Senior School, Oxon	www.olab.org.uk	£3,756	–	Mrs L. Renwick
Oxford High School, Oxon	www.oxfordhigh.gdst.net	£3,567	–	Mrs J. Carlisle
Padworth College, Berks	www.padworth.com	£3,950	£8,300	Mrs L. Melhuish
Palmers Green High School, London N21	www.pghs.co.uk	£3,945	–	Mrs C. Edmundson
Pangbourne College, Berks	www.pangbournecollege.com	£6,600	£9,330	T. Garnier
The Perse Upper School, Cambs	www.perse.co.uk	£4,549	–	E. Elliott
The Peterborough School, Cambs	www.thepeterboroughschool.co.uk	£3,986	£7,420	A. Meadows
Pipers Corner School, Bucks	www.piperscorner.co.uk	£4,490	£7,400	Mrs H. Ness-Gifford
Pitsford School, Northants	www.pitsfordschool.com	£3,927	–	N. Toone
Plymouth College, Devon	www.plymouthcollege.com	£4,070	£7,970	Dr S. Wormleighton
Pocklington School, E. Yorks	www.pocklingtonschool.com	£3,855	£6,898	M. Ronan
Polam Hall School, Durham	www.polamhall.com	£3,890	£7,475	J. Moreland
Portland Place School, London W1	www.portland-place.co.uk	£5,225	–	T. Cook
The Portsmouth Grammar School, Hants	www.pgs.org.uk	£4,186	–	J. Priory
Portsmouth High School, Hants	www.portsmouthhigh.co.uk	£3,467	–	Mrs J. Prescott
Princess Helena College, Herts	www.princesshelenacollege.co.uk	£5,680	£8,205	Mrs J. Duncan
Princethorpe College, Warwicks	www.princethorpe.co.uk	£3,118	–	E. Hester
Prior Park College, Somerset	www.thepriorfoundation.com	£4,061	£8,160	J. Murphy-O'Connor
Prior's Field, Surrey	www.priorsfieldschool.com	£4,995	£7,995	Mrs J. Roseblade
The Purcell School, Herts	www.purcell-school.org	£8,259	£10,562	P. Crook
Putney High School, London SW15	www.putneyhigh.gdst.net	£4,388	–	Dr D. Lodge
Queen Anne's School, Berks	www.qas.org.uk	£6,090	£8,975	Mrs J. Harrington
Queen Elizabeth Grammar School, W. Yorks	www.wgsf.org.uk	£3,332	–	D. Craig
Queen Elizabeth's Grammar School, Lancs	www.qegs.blackburn.sch.uk	£3,295	–	S. Corns
Queen Elizabeth's Hospital (QEH), Bristol	www.qehbristol.co.uk	£3,753	–	S. Holliday
Queen Margaret's School, N. Yorks	www.queenmargarets.com	£5,513	£8,700	Dr P. Silverwood
Queen Mary's School, N. Yorks	www.queenmarys.org	£4,640	£6,120	Mrs S. Lewis-Beckett
Queen's College, London, London W1	www.qcl.org.uk	£4,950	–	Dr F. Ramsey
Queen's College, Somerset	www.queenscollege.org.uk	£4,900	£7,800	C. Alcock
Queen's Gate School, London SW7	www.queensgate.org.uk	£5,100	–	Mrs R. Kamaryc
The Queen's School, Cheshire	www.queens.cheshire.sch.uk	£3,550	–	Mrs E. Clark
Queenswood, Herts	www.queenswood.org	£6,965	£9,165	Mrs P. Edgar
Radley College, Oxon	www.radley.org.uk	–	£9,875	A. McPhail
Ratcliffe College, Leics	www.ratcliffe-college.co.uk	£4,548	£6,954	G. Lloyd
The Read School, N. Yorks	www.readschool.co.uk	£3,060	£6,600	Mrs B. McCrea
Reading Blue Coat School, Berks	www.rbcs.org.uk	£4,320	–	M. Windsor
The Red Maids' School, Bristol	www.redmaids.co.uk	£3,480	–	Mrs I. Tobias
Redland High School for Girls, Bristol	www.redlandhigh.com	£3,400	–	Mrs C. Bateson
Reed's School, Surrey	www.reeds.surrey.sch.uk	£6,498	£8,595	D. Jarrett
Reigate Grammar School, Surrey	www.reigategrammar.org	£4,792	–	D. Thomas
Rendcomb College, Glos	www.rendcombcollege.org.uk	£6,180	£8,275	G. Holden

School	Website	Fee 1	Fee 2	Head
Repton School, Derbyshire	www.repton.org.uk	£6,980	£9,407	R. Holroyd
Rishworth School, W. Yorks	www.rishworth-school.co.uk	£3,480	£7,090	R. Baker
Roedean School, E. Sussex	www.roedean.co.uk	£5,820	£10,050	Mrs F. King
Rossall School, Lancs	www.rossallschool.org.uk	£3,900	£9,960	Dr S. Winkley
The Royal Grammar School, Surrey	www.rgs-guildford.co.uk	£4,540	–	J. Cox
Royal Grammar School, Tyne and Wear	www.rgs.newcastle.sch.uk	£3,332	–	B. Trafford
RGS Worcester, Worcs	www.rgsw.org.uk	£3,244	–	A. Rattue
The Royal High School, Bath, Somerset	www.royalhighbath.gdst.net	£3,419	£6,827	Mrs R. Dougall
The Royal Hospital School, Suffolk	www.royalhospitalschool.org	£4,153	£7,663	H. Blackett
The Royal Masonic School for Girls, Herts	www.royalmasonic.herts.sch.uk	£4,485	£7,480	Mrs D. Rose
Royal Russell School, Surrey	www.royalrussell.co.uk	£4,740	£9,370	C. Hutchinson
Royal School Hampstead, London NW3	www.royalschoolhampstead.net	£3,950	£7,850	Ms J. Ebner
The Royal Wolverhampton School, W. Midlands	www.theroyalschool.co.uk	£3,985	£8,540	M. Heywood
Rugby School, Warwicks	www.rugbyschool.net	£6,060	£9,725	P. Derham
Ryde School with Upper Chine, Isle of Wight	www.rydeschool.org.uk	£3,405	£7,000	Dr N. England
Rye St Antony, Oxon	www.ryestantony.co.uk	£4,100	£6,650	Miss A. Jones
St Albans High School for Girls, Herts	www.stahs.org.uk	£4,095	–	Mrs R. Martin
St Albans School, Herts	www.st-albans.herts.sch.uk	£4,598	–	A. Grant
St Andrew's School, Beds	www.standrewsschoolbedford.com	£3,492	–	S. Skehan
Saint Augustine's Priory School, London W5	www.saintaugustinespriory.org.uk	£3,730	–	Mrs F. Gumley-Mason
St Bede's College, Greater Manchester	www.stbedescollege.co.uk	£2,966	–	D. Kearney
St Bede's Senior School, E. Sussex	www.stbedesschool.org	£5,475	£9,115	Dr R. Maloney
St Bees School, Cumbria	www.st-bees-school.org	£4,998	£8,421	P. Capes
St Benedict's School, London W5	www.stbenedicts.org.uk	£4,120	–	C. Cleugh
St Catherine's School, Surrey	www.stcatherines.info	£4,780	£7,865	Mrs A. Phillips
St Catherine's School, Middx	www.stcatherineschool.co.uk	£3,705	–	Sister P. Thomas
St Christopher School, Herts	www.stchris.co.uk	£4,990	£8,830	R. Palmer
St Columba's College, Herts	www.stcolumbascollege.org	£3,770	–	D. Buxton
St Dominic's High School for Girls, Staffs	www.stdominicsschool.co.uk	£3,780	–	Mrs S. White
St Dominic's Priory School, Staffs	www.stdominicspriory.co.uk	£3,135	–	Mrs M. Adamson
St Dunstan's College, London SE6	www.stdunstans.org.ukintranet: www.sdonline.org.uk	£4,507	–	Mrs J. Davies
St Edmund's College & Prep School, Herts	www.stedmundscollege.org	£4,860	£8,010	C. Long
St Edmund's School, Kent	www.stedmunds.org.uk	£5,686	£8,849	Mrs L. Moelwyn-Hughes
St Edward's, Oxford, Oxon	www.stedwards.oxon.sch.uk	£7,948	£9,935	S. Jones
St Edward's School, Glos	www.stedwards.co.uk	£4,078	–	P. Harvey
Saint Felix School, Suffolk	www.stfelix.co.uk	£4,400	£7,775	S. Letman
St Francis' College, Herts	www.st-francis.herts.sch.uk	£3,925	£7,720	Mrs D. MacGinty
St Gabriel's School, Berks	www.stgabriels.co.uk	£4,410	–	A. Jones
St George's College, Surrey	www.st-georges-college.co.uk	£4,900	–	J. Peake
St George's School, W. Midlands	www.sgse.co.uk	£3,255	–	Sir Robert Dowling
St George's School, Berks	www.stgeorges-ascot.org.uk	£6,150	£9,460	Mrs R. Owens
St Helen & St Katharine, Oxon	www.shsk.org.uk	£3,945	–	Miss R. Edbrooke
St Helen's School, Middx	www.sthn.co.uk	£4,443	–	Dr M. Short
St James Senior Boys' School, Surrey	www.stjamesboys.co.uk	£4,220	–	D. Boddy
St James Senior Girls' School, London W14	www.stjamesgirls.co.uk	£4,360	–	Mrs L. Hyde
St John's College, Hants	www.stjohnscollege.co.uk	£3,100	£6,700	G. Best
St John's School, Surrey	www.stjohnsleatherhead.co.uk	£6,465	£8,865	M. Collier
St Joseph's College, Suffolk	www.stjos.co.uk	£4,075	£8,375	Mrs S. Grant
St Joseph's College, Berks	www.stjosephscollegereading.co.uk	£3,680	–	Mrs M. Sheridan
St Lawrence College, Kent	www.slcuk.com	£5,090	£8,835	Revd M. Aitken
St Leonards-Mayfield School, E. Sussex	www.mayfieldgirls.org	£5,540	£8,580	Miss A. Beary

School	Website	Day	Boarding	Head
St Margaret's School, Herts	www.stmargaretsbushey.org.uk	£4,500	£8,350	Mrs L. Crighton
St Margaret's School, Devon	www.stmargarets-school.co.uk	£3,395	–	Mrs S. Cooper
St Margaret's School, London NW3	www.st-margarets.co.uk	£3,542	–	M. Webster
St Martha's, Herts	www.st-marthas.co.uk	£3,720	–	J. Sheridan
Saint Martin's, W. Midlands	www.saintmartins-school.com	£3,485	–	Mrs J. Carwithen
St Mary's School Ascot, Berks	www.st-marys-ascot.co.uk	£6,930	£9,740	Mrs M. Breen
St Mary's Calne, Wilts	www.stmaryscalne.org	£7,350	£10,100	Mrs H. Wright
St Mary's School, Cambs	www.stmaryscambridge.co.uk	£4,230	£9,110	Miss C. Avery
St Mary's School, Essex	www.stmaryscolchester.org.uk	£3,255	–	Mrs H. Vipond
St Mary's College, Merseyside	www.stmarys.ac	£2,997	–	M. Kennedy
St Mary's School, Bucks	www.stmarysschool.co.uk	£4,260	–	Mrs J. Ross
St Mary's School, Dorset	www.st-marys-shaftesbury.co.uk	£5,450	£7,930	R. James
St Mary's, Worcs	www.stmarys.org.uk	£3,400	–	Mrs C. Jawaheer
St Nicholas' School, Hants	www.st-nicholas.hants.sch.uk	£3,701	–	Mrs A. Whatmough
St Paul's Girls' School, London W6	www.spgs.org	£5,842	–	Ms C. Farr
St Paul's School, London SW13	www.stpaulsschool.org.uk	£6,275	£9,297	M. Bailey
St Peter's School York, N. Yorks	www.st-peters.york.sch.uk	£4,839	£7,791	L. Winkley
St Swithun's School, Hants	www.stswithuns.com	£5,240	£8,640	Ms J. Gandee
St Teresa's School, Surrey	www.stteresasschool.com	£4,645	£3,360	Mrs J. Elburn
Scarborough College, N. Yorks	www.scarboroughcollege.co.uk	£3,743	£6,139	Mrs I. Nixon
Seaford College, W. Sussex	www.seaford.org	£5,355	£8,300	T. Mullins
Sedbergh School, Cumbria	www.sedberghschool.org	£6,675	£9,060	A. Fleck
Sevenoaks School, Kent	www.sevenoaksschool.org	£5,946	£9,537	Mrs C. Ricks
Shebbear College, Devon	www.shebbearcollege.co.uk	£3,495	£6,605	R. Barnes
Sheffield High School, S. Yorks	www.sheffieldhighschool.org.uk	£3,336	–	Mrs V. Dunsford
Sherborne Girls, Dorset	www.sherborne.com	£6,870	£9,450	Mrs J. Dwyer
Sherborne School, Dorset	www.sherborne.org	£7,875	£9,725	C. Davis
Shiplake College, Oxon	www.shiplake.org.uk	£5,740	£8,510	A. Davies
Shrewsbury High School, Shropshire	www.shrewsburyhigh.gdst.net	£3,434	–	Mrs M. Cass
Shrewsbury School, Shropshire	www.shrewsbury.org.uk	£6,595	£9,420	M. Turner
Sibford School, Oxon	www.sibford.oxon.sch.uk	£3,886	£7,550	M. Goodwin
Silcoates School, W. Yorks	www.silcoates.org.uk	£3,876	–	D. Wideman
Solihull School, W. Midlands	www.solsch.org.uk	£3,320	–	D. Lloyd
South Hampstead High School, London NW3	www.shhs.gdst.net	£4,343	–	Mrs J. Stephen
Stafford Grammar School, Staffs	www.stafford-grammar.co.uk	£3,249	–	M. Darley
Stamford High School, Lincs	www.ses.lincs.sch.uk	£4,084	£7,452	S. Roberts
Stamford School, Lincs	www.ses.lincs.sch.uk	£4,084	£7,452	S. Roberts
Stanbridge Earls School, Hants	www.stanbridgeearls.co.uk	£6,754	£8,920	P. Trythall
The Stephen Perse Foundation, Cambs	www.stephenperse.com	£4,675	–	Miss P. Kelleher
Stockport Grammar School, Cheshire	www.stockportgrammar.co.uk	£3,090	–	A. Chicken
Stonar School, Wilts	www.stonarschool.com	£4,455	£7,850	Mrs E. Thomas
Stonyhurst College, Lancs	www.stonyhurst.ac.uk	£5,151	£9,010	A. Johnson
Stover School, Devon	www.stover.co.uk	£3,497	£7,230	Mrs S. Bradley
Stowe School, Bucks	www.stowe.co.uk	£7,005	£9,655	A. Wallersteiner
Streatham & Clapham High School, London SW16	www.gdst.net/streathamhigh	£4,203	–	R. Hinton
Sunderland High School, Tyne and Wear	www.sunderlandhigh.co.uk	£2,778	–	Dr A. Slater
Surbiton High School, Surrey	www.surbitonhigh.com	£4,305	–	Ms E. Haydon
Sutton High School, Surrey	www.suttonhigh.gdst.net	£4,239	–	Mrs B. Goulding
Sutton Valence School, Kent	www.svs.org.uk	£5,800	£8,840	B. Grindlay
Sydenham High School, London SE26	www.sydenhamhighschool.gdst.net	£4,203	–	Mrs K. Pullen
Talbot Heath, Dorset	www.talbotheath.org	£3,555	£5,921	Mrs A. Holloway
Taunton School, Somerset	www.tauntonschool.co.uk	£5,150	£8,535	Dr J. Newton
Teesside High School, Cleveland	www.teessidehigh.co.uk	£3,545	–	M. Wilkinson
Tettenhall College, W. Midlands	www.tettenhallcollege.co.uk	£4,215	£7,680	M. Long
Thetford Grammar School, Norfolk	www.thetgram.norfolk.sch.uk	£3,516	–	G. Price
Thornton College, Bucks	www.thorntoncollege.com	£3,615	£5,925	Miss A. Williams
Tonbridge School, Kent	www.tonbridge-school.co.uk	£7,780	£10,421	T. Haynes
Tormead School, Surrey	www.tormeadschool.org.uk	£4,010	–	Mrs C. Foord
Trent College, Notts	www.trentcollege.net	£4,665	£7,905	Mrs G. Dixon

Tring Park School for the Performing Arts, Herts	www.tringpark.com	£6,105	£9,100	S. Anderson
Trinity School, Surrey	www.trinity-school.org	£4,154	–	M. Bishop
Truro High School for Girls, Cornwall	www.trurohigh.co.uk	£3,536	£6,721	Mrs C. Pascoe
Truro School, Cornwall	www.truroschool.com	£3,720	£7,120	P. Smith
Tudor Hall, Oxon	www.tudorhallschool.com	£5,725	£8,900	Miss W. Griffiths
University College School, London NW3	www.ucs.org.uk	£5,335	–	K. Durham
Uppingham School, Rutland	www.uppingham.co.uk	£6,860	£9,800	R. Harman
Wakefield Girls' High School, W. Yorks	www.wgsf.org.uk	£3,332	–	Mrs G. Wallwork
Walthamstow Hall, Kent	www.walthamstow-hall.co.uk	£5,080	–	Mrs J. Milner
Warminster School, Wilts	www.warminsterschool.org.uk	£4,340	£7,810	M. Priestley
Warwick School, Warwicks	www.warwickschool.org	£3,453	£7,369	E. Halse
Wellingborough School, Northants	www.wellingboroughschool.org	£4,202	–	G. Bowe
Wellington College, Berks	www.wellingtoncollege.org.uk	£7,515	£10,025	Dr A. Seldon
Wellington School, Somerset	www.wellington-school.org.uk	£4,010	£7,220	M. Reader
Wells Cathedral School, Somerset	www.wells-cathedral-school.com	£4,893	£8,218	Mrs E. Cairncross
West Buckland School, Devon	www.westbuckland.devon.sch.uk	£3,975	£7,510	J. Vick
Westfield School, Tyne and Wear	www.westfield.newcastle.sch.uk	£3,547	–	Mrs M. Farndale
Westholme School, Lancs	www.westholmeschool.com	£2,864	–	Mrs L. Croston
Westminster School, London SW1	www.westminster.org.uk	£7,026	£10,146	M. Spurr
Westonbirt, Glos	www.westonbirt.gloucs.sch.uk	£6,590	£9,990	Mrs M. Henderson
Whitgift School, Surrey	www.whitgift.co.uk	£4,808	–	C. Barnett
Wimbledon High School, London SW19	www.wimbledonhigh.gdst.net	£4,343	–	Mrs H. Hanbury
Winchester College, Hants	www.winchestercollege.org	–	£10,450	R. Townsend
Windermere School, Cumbria	www.windermereschool.co.uk	£4,589	£8,372	I. Lavender
Wisbech Grammar School, Cambs	www.wgs.cambs.sch.uk	£3,530	–	N. Hammond
Withington Girls' School, Greater Manchester	www.withington.manchester.sch.uk	£3,190	–	Mrs S. Marks
Woldingham School, Surrey	www.woldinghamschool.co.uk	£5,925	£9,470	Mrs J. Triffitt
Wolverhampton Grammar School, W Midlands	www.wgs.org.uk	£3,775	–	J. Darby
Woodbridge School, Suffolk	www.woodbridge.suffolk.sch.uk	£4,508	£8,050	S. Cole
Woodhouse Grove School, W. Yorks	www.woodhousegrove.co.uk	£3,520	£7,140	D. Humphreys
Worksop College, Notts	www.worksopcollege.notts.sch.uk	£5,115	£7,840	R. Collard
Worth School, W. Sussex	www.worthschool.co.uk	£6,517	£8,883	G. Carminati
Wrekin College, Shropshire	www.wrekincollege.com	£5,044	£8,325	R. Pleming
Wychwood School, Oxon	www.wychwood-school.org.uk	£3,840	£6,250	Mrs S. Wingfield Digby
Wycliffe College, Glos	www.wycliffe.co.uk	£5,600	£8,670	Mrs M. Burnet Ward
Wycombe Abbey School, Bucks	www.wycombeabbey.com	–	£10,200	Mrs C. Hall
Wykeham House School, Hants	www.wykehamhouse.com	£3,400	–	Mrs L. Clarke
Yarm School, Cleveland	www.yarmschool.org	£3,539	–	D. Dunn
The Yehudi Menuhin School, Surrey	www.yehudimenuhinschool.co.uk	sliding scale		Dr R. Hillier

WALES

Christ College, Brecon	www.christcollegebrecon.com	£4,725	£7,300	Mrs E. Taylor
Haberdashers' Monmouth School for Girls, Monmouth	www.habs-monmouth.org	£3,929	£7,381	Mrs H. Davy
Howell's School, Denbigh	www.howells.org	£3,900	£6,900	B. Routledge
Howell's School Llandaff, Cardiff	www.howells-cardiff.gdst.net	£3,404	–	Mrs S. Davis
Llandovery College, Llandovery	www.llandoverycollege.com	£4,695	£6,950	I. Hunt
Monmouth School, Monmouth	www.habs-monmouth.org	£4,238	£7,442	S. Connors
Rougemont School, Newport	www.rougemontschool.co.uk	£3,500	–	Dr J. Tribbick
Ruthin School, Ruthin	www.ruthinschool.co.uk	£3,917	£7,167	T. Belfield
Rydal Penrhos School, Colwyn Bay	www.rydal-penrhos.com	£4,500	£9,905	P. Lee-Browne

NORTHERN IRELAND

Bangor Grammar School, Bangor	www.bangorgrammarschool.org.uk	–	–	S. Connolly
Belfast Royal Academy, Belfast	www.belfastroyalacademy.com	£140	–	J. Dickson
Campbell College, Belfast	www.campbellcollege.co.uk	£2,200	£8,751	J. Piggot
Coleraine Academical Institution, Coleraine	www.coleraineai.com	£140	–	Dr D. Carruthers

Foyle and Londonderry College, Londonderry	www.foylenet.org	£135	–	W. Magill
Methodist College, Belfast	www.methody.org	£140	–	J. Naismith
The Royal Belfast Academical Institution, Belfast	www.rbai.org.uk	£795	–	Miss J. Williamson
The Royal School Dungannon, Dungannon	www.royaldungannon.com	£135	£7,335	D. Burnett

SCOTLAND

Dollar Academy, Dollar	www.dollaracademy.org.uk	£3,351	£4,296	D. Knapman
The High School of Dundee, Dundee	www.highschoolofdundee.org.uk	£3,350	–	Dr J. Halliday
The Edinburgh Academy, Edinburgh	www.edinburghacademy.org.uk	£3,012	–	M. Longmore
Fettes College, Edinburgh	www.fettes.com	£6,745	£9,050	M. Spens
George Heriot's School, Edinburgh	www.george-heriots.com	£3,233	–	A. Hector
George Watson's College, Edinburgh	www.gwc.org.uk	£3,202	–	G. Edwards
The Glasgow Academy, Glasgow	www.theglasgowacademy.org.uk	£3,360	–	P. Brodie
The High School of Glasgow, Glasgow	www.glasgowhigh.com	£2,957	–	C. Mair
Glenalmond College, Perth	www.glenalmondcollege.co.uk	£6,175	£9,054	G. Woods
Hutchesons' Grammar School, Glasgow	www.hutchesons.org	£3,153	–	Dr K. Greig
Kelvinside Academy, Glasgow	www.kelvinsideacademy.org.uk	£3,415	–	Mrs L. Douglas
Kilgraston, Bridge of Earn	www.kilgraston.com	£4,690	£7,995	M. Farmer
Lomond School, Helensburgh	www.lomond-school.org	£3,160	£6,760	S. Mills
Loretto School, Musselburgh	www.loretto.com	£6,100	£8,975	P. Hogan
The Mary Erskine School, Edinburgh	www.esms.edin.sch.uk	£3,032	£6,083	J. Gray
Merchiston Castle School, Edinburgh	www.merchiston.co.uk	£6,250	£8,585	A. Hunter
Morrison's Academy, Crieff	www.morrisonsacademy.org	£3,319	–	G. Pengelley
Robert Gordon's College, Aberdeen	www.rgc.aberdeen.sch.uk	£3,405	–	H. Ouston
St Aloysius' College, Glasgow	www.staloysius.org	£3,003	–	J. Stoer
St Columba's School, Kilmacolm	www.st-columbas.org	£3,147	–	D. Girdwood
St George's School for Girls, Edinburgh	www.st-georges.edin.sch.uk	£3,710	£7,530	Mrs A. Everest
St Leonards School, St Andrews	www.stleonards-fife.org	£3,650	£8,690	M. Carslaw
St Margaret's School for Girls, Aberdeen	www.st-margaret.aberdeen.sch.uk	£3,326	–	Dr J. Land
Stewart's Melville College, Edinburgh	www.esms.edin.sch.uk	£3,032	£6,083	J. Gray
Strathallan School, Perth	www.strathallan.co.uk	£5,955	£8,776	B. Thompson

CHANNEL ISLANDS

Elizabeth College, Guernsey	www.elizabethcollege.gg	£2,717	–	G. Hartley
The Ladies' College, Guernsey	www.ladiescollege.com	£2,110	–	Ms J. Riches
Victoria College, Jersey	www.victoriacollege.je	£1,482	–	A. Watkins

NATIONAL ACADEMIES OF SCHOLARSHIP

The national academies are self-governing bodies whose members are elected as a result of achievement and distinction in the academy's field. Within their discipline, the academies provide advice, support education and exceptional scholars, stimulate debate, promote UK research worldwide and collaborate with international counterparts.

Three of the national academies – the Royal Society, the British Academy and the Royal Academy of Engineering – receive grant-in-aid funding from the Department for Business, Innovation and Skills (BIS). The Academy for Medical Sciences receives core funding from the Department of Health, and the Royal Society of Edinburgh is aided by funds provided by the Scottish government. In addition to government funding, the national academies generate additional income from donations, membership contributions, trading and investments.

SCIENCE BUDGET ALLOCATIONS
£ thousands

Royal Society, British Academy, Royal Academy of Engineering

2005–6: 32,520; 14,050; 5,850
2011–12: 47,830; 27,001; 12,634

Source: BERR/DIUS *Science Budget Allocations*

ACADEMY OF MEDICAL SCIENCES (1998)
41 Portland Place, London W1B 1QH
T 020-3176 2150
W www.acmedsci.ac.uk

The Academy of Medical Sciences was established in 1998 to promote advances in medical science and to ensure these are converted into healthcare benefits for society. It campaigns for the development, protection and promotion of careers for academics in the biomedical sciences and encourages good practice in training and development.

The academy is independent and self-governing and receives funding from a variety of sources including the fellowship, charitable donations, government and industry.

Fellows are elected from a broad range of medical sciences: biomedical, clinical and population based. The academy includes in its remit veterinary medicine, dentistry, nursing, medical law, economics, sociology and ethics. Elections are from nominations put forward by existing fellows.

As at May 2011 there were 1,023 fellows and 29 honorary fellows.
President, Prof. Sir John Bell, FRS, PMEDSCI
Vice-Presidents, Prof. Patrick Sissons FMEDSCI; Prof. Ronald Laskey FRS, FMEDSCI
Executive Director, Dr Helen Munn

BRITISH ACADEMY (1902)
10–11 Carlton House Terrace, London SW1Y 5AH
T 020-7969 5200
W www.britac.ac.uk

The British Academy is an independent, self-governing learned society for the promotion of the humanities and social sciences. It was founded in 1901 and granted a royal charter in 1902. The British Academy supports advanced academic research and is a channel for the government's support of research in those disciplines.

The fellows are scholars who have attained distinction in one of the branches of study that the academy exists to promote. Candidates must be nominated by existing fellows. There are 902 fellows, 17 honorary fellows and 294 corresponding fellows overseas.
President, Prof. Sir Adam Roberts, KCMG
Chief Executive, Dr R. Jackson

ROYAL ACADEMY OF ENGINEERING (1976)
3 Carlton House Terrace, London SW1Y 5DG
T 020-7766 0600
W www.raeng.org.uk

The Royal Academy of Engineering was established as the Fellowship of Engineering in 1976. It was granted a royal charter in 1983 and its present title in 1992. It is an independent, self-governing body whose object is the pursuit, encouragement and maintenance of excellence in the whole field of engineering, in order to promote the advancement of science, art and practice of engineering for the benefit of the public.

Election to the fellowship is by invitation only, from nominations supported by the body of fellows. As at May 2011 there were 1,386 fellows. The Duke of Edinburgh is the senior fellow and the Duke of Kent is a royal fellow.
President, Lord Browne of Madingley, FRENG, FRS
Senior Vice-President, Prof. R. J. Mair, CBE, FRENG, FRS
Chief Executive, P. D. Greenish, CBE

ROYAL SOCIETY (1660)
6–9 Carlton House Terrace, London SW1Y 5AG
T 020-7451 2500
W www.royalsociety.org

The Royal Society is an independent academy promoting the natural and applied sciences. Founded in 1660 and granted a royal charter in 1662, the society has three roles, as the UK academy of science, as a learned society and as a funding agency. It is an independent, self-governing body under a royal charter, promoting and advancing all fields of physical and biological sciences, of mathematics and engineering, medical and agricultural sciences and their application.

Fellows are elected for their contributions to science, both in fundamental research resulting in greater understanding, and also in leading and directing scientific and technological progress in industry and research establishments. A maximum of 44 new fellows, who must be citizens or residents of the British Commonwealth countries or Ireland, may be elected annually.

Up to eight foreign members, who are selected from those not eligible to become fellows because of citizenship or residency, are elected annually for their contributions to science.

One honorary fellow may be elected each year from those not eligible for election as fellows or foreign members. There are approximately 1,400 fellows and foreign members covering all scientific disciplines.
President, Sir Paul Nurse, PRS
Executive Secretary, Dr Julie Maxton

ROYAL SOCIETY OF EDINBURGH (1783)
22–26 George Street, Edinburgh EH2 2PQ
T 0131-240 5000
W www.royalsoced.org.uk

The Royal Society of Edinburgh (RSE) is an educational charity and Scotland's National Academy. An independent body with charitable status, its multidisciplinary membership represents a knowledge resource for the people of Scotland. Granted its royal charter in 1783 for the 'advancement of learning and useful knowledge', the society organises conferences, debates and lectures; conducts independent inquiries; facilitates international collaboration and showcases the country's research and development capabilities; provides educational activities for primary and secondary school students and awards prizes and medals. The society also awards over £2m annually to Scotland's top researchers and entrepreneurs working in Scotland.

As at May 2011 there were 1,551 fellows.
President, Lord Wilson of Tillyorn, KT, GCMG, PRS
Vice-Presidents, Prof. Jean Beggs, CBE, FRSE;
Prof. Hector MacQueen, FRSE; John McClelland, CBE; Prof. Wilson Sibbett, CBE, FRS, FRSE
General Secretary, Prof. Geoffrey Boulton, OBE, FRS, FRSE

PRIVATELY FUNDED ARTS ACADEMIES

The Royal Academy and the Royal Scottish Academy support the visual arts community in the UK, hold educational events and promote interest in the arts. They are entirely privately funded through contributions by 'friends' (regular donors who receive benefits such as free entry, previews and magazines), bequests, corporate donations and exhibitions.

ROYAL ACADEMY OF ARTS (1768)
Burlington House, Piccadilly, London W1J 0BD
T 020-7300 8000
W www.royalacademy.org.uk

The Royal Academy of Arts is an independent, self-governing society devoted to the encouragement and promotion of the fine arts.

Membership of the academy is limited to 80 academicians, all of whom are either painters, engravers, sculptors or architects. Candidates are nominated and elected by the existing academicians. The members are known as royal academicians (RAs) and are responsible for both the governance and direction of the academy.

The title of honorary academician is awarded to a small number of distinguished artists who are not UK citizens; as at May 2011, there were 21 honorary academicians. Unlike the RAs, they do not take part in the governance of the academy and are unable to vote.
President, Sir Nicholas Grimshaw, CBE, PRA
Secretary & Chief Executive, Charles Saumarez Smith, CBE

ROYAL SCOTTISH ACADEMY (1838)
The Mound, Edinburgh EH2 2EL
T 0131-225 6671
W www.royalscottishacademy.org

Founded in 1826 and granted a Royal Charter in 1837, the Royal Scottish Academy is an independent institution led by prominent Scottish artists and architects. It promotes and supports the visual arts through an ongoing exhibitions programme, related educational events and through a series of awards, bursaries and scholarships for artists at all stages of their careers.

Academicians (members) have to be Scots by birth or domicile, and are elected from the disciplines of art and architecure following nominations put forward by the existing membership. There are also a small number of honorary academicians – distinguished artists and architects, writers, historians and musicians – who do not have to be Scottish. At mid 2011 there were 31 honorary academicians and 109 academicians.
President, Prof. Bill Scott, FRBS, PRSA
Secretary, Arthur Watson, RSA

RESEARCH COUNCILS

The government funds basic and applied civil science research, mostly through seven research councils, which are established under royal charter and supported by the Department for Business, Innovation and Skills (BIS). Research Councils UK is the strategic partnership of these seven councils* (for further information *see* W www.rcuk.ac.uk). The councils support research and training in universities and other higher education and research facilities.

The science budget, administered by BIS, is the main source of public sector funding for research councils, with further public funds provided through the Large Facilities Capital Fund and the Higher Education Innovation Fund. Additional funds may also be provided by other government departments, devolved administrations, the European Commission and other international bodies. The councils also receive income for research specifically commissioned by government departments and the private sector, and income from charitable sources.

GOVERNMENT SCIENCE BUDGET
£ thousand

	2010–11	2011–12
Arts and Humanities Research Council	103,867	100,051
Biotechnology and Biological Sciences Research Council	435,737	415,806
Economic and Social Research Council	179,048	174,637
Engineering and Physical Sciences Research Council	829,306	801,720
Medical Research Council	702,229	615,467
Natural Environment Research Council	355,450	368,800
Science and Technology Facilities Council*	467,860	538,009
Large Facilities Capital Fund†	103,380	115,279
Higher Education Innovation Fund	113,000	113,000

* Includes cross-council facilities and international subscriptions budgets, which are managed by STFC on behalf of all research councils

† Allocations for 2011–12 are as follows: BBSRC £30.0m; EPSRC £15.0m; MRC £31.1m; NERC £20.0m; STFC £13.5m
Source: BIS – The Allocation of Science and Research Funding 2011/12–2014/15

ALCOHOL EDUCATION AND RESEARCH COUNCIL
4th Floor, Willow House, 17–23 Willow Place, London SW1P 1JH
T 020-7821 7880 W www.aerc.org.uk

The AERC was established by act of parliament in 1982 to administer the Alcohol Education and Research Fund. The government fund is used in UK education and research projects to develop new ways to help those with drinking problems. Every year, the AERC funds a small number of research projects of around £50,000, although funding of up to £70,000 is available depending on the nature of the project. The council also awards a number of research grants up to a maximum of £5,000. The AERC aims to increase awareness of alcohol issues, to reduce alcohol-related harm and to encourage best practice.
Chief Executive, Mr Dave Roberts
Research Director, Prof. Ray Hodgson

ARTS AND HUMANITIES RESEARCH COUNCIL*
Polaris House, North Star Avenue, Swindon SN2 1FL
T 01793-416000 W www.ahrc.ac.uk

Launched in April 2005 as the successor organisation to the Arts and Humanities Research Board, the AHRC provides funding for postgraduate training and research in the arts and humanities. In any one year, the AHRC makes approximately 700 research awards and around 1,500 postgraduate awards. Awards are made after a rigorous peer review process, which ensures the quality of applications.
Chair, Prof. Sir Alan Wilson
Chief Executive, Prof. Rick Rylance

BIOTECHNOLOGY AND BIOLOGICAL SCIENCES RESEARCH COUNCIL*
Polaris House, North Star Avenue, Swindon SN2 1UH
T 01793-413200 W www.bbsrc.ac.uk

Established by royal charter in 1994, the BBSRC is the UK funding agency for research in the life sciences. It funds research into how all living organisms function and behave, benefiting the agriculture, food, health, pharmaceutical and chemical sectors. To deliver its mission, the BBSRC supports research and training in universities and research centres throughout the UK, including providing strategic research grants to the institutes listed below.
Chair, Prof. Sir Tom Blundell
Chief Executive, Prof. D. Kell

INSTITUTES
BABRAHAM INSTITUTE, Babraham Hall, Babraham, Cambridge CB22 3AT T 01223-496000
Director, Prof. M. Wakelam
GENOME ANALYSIS CENTRE , Norwich Research Park, Colney, Norwich NR4 7UH T 01603-450861
Director, Dr J. Rogers
INSTITUTE FOR ANIMAL HEALTH, Pirbright Laboratory, Ash Road, Pirbright, Surrey GU24 0NF T 01483-232 441
Director, Prof. J. Fazakerley
INSTITUTE FOR BIOLOGICAL, ENVIRONMENTAL AND RURAL SCIENCES (ABERYSTWYTH UNIVERSITY), Penglais, Aberystwyth, Ceredigion SY23 3DA
T 01970-622316
Director, Prof. W. Powell
INSTITUTE OF FOOD RESEARCH, Norwich Research Park, Colney Lane, Norwich NR4 7UA T 01603-255000
Director, Prof. D. Boxer
JOHN INNES CENTRE, Norwich Research Park, Colney, Norwich NR4 7UH T 01603-450000
Director, Prof. D. Sanders

ROSLIN INSTITUTE (UNIVERSITY OF EDINBURGH),
Roslin Biocentre, Roslin, Midlothian EH25 9PS
T 0131-651 9100
Director, Prof. D. Hume
ROTHAMSTED RESEARCH, Rothamsted, Harpenden,
Herts AL5 2JQ T 01582-763133
Director, Prof. M. Moloney

ECONOMIC AND SOCIAL RESEARCH COUNCIL*
Polaris House, North Star Avenue, Swindon SN2 1UJ
T 01793-413000 E comms@esrc.ac.uk
W www.esrc.ac.uk

The purpose of the ESRC is to promote and support research and postgraduate training in the social sciences. It also provides advice, disseminates knowledge and promotes public understanding in these areas. The ESRC provides core funding to the centres listed below. Further information can be obtained on the ESRC website, including details of centres it funds in collaboration with other research councils.
Chair, Dr Alan Gillespie
Chief Executive, Prof. Paul Boyle

RESEARCH CENTRES
CENTRE FOR BUSINESS RELATIONSHIPS, ACCOUNTABILITY, SUSTAINABILITY AND SOCIETY, University of Cardiff, 55 Park Place, Cardiff CF10 3AT
T 029-2087 6562
Director, Prof. K. Peattie
CENTRE FOR CHARITABLE GIVING AND PHILANTHROPY, Cass Business School, 106 Bunhill Row, London EC1Y 8TZ T 020-7040 0136
Directors, Prof. J. Harrow; Prof. C. Pharoah
CENTRE FOR CLIMATE CHANGE, ECONOMICS AND POLICY, LSE, Houghton Street, London WC2 2AE
T 020-7955 6228
Directors, Prof. J. Rees; Prof. A. Gouldson
CENTRE FOR COMPETITION POLICY, University of East Anglia, Norwich NR4 7TJ T 01603-593715
Director, Prof. C. Waddams
CENTRE FOR COMPETITIVE ADVANTAGE IN THE GLOBAL ECONOMY, Department of Economics, University of Warwick, Coventry, Warks CV4 7AL T 02476-523468
Director, Prof. Nick Crafts
CENTRE FOR ECONOMIC AND SOCIAL ASPECTS OF GENOMICS, Cardiff University, 6 Museum Place, Cardiff CF10 3BG
Director, Prof. Ruth Chadwick
CENTRE FOR ECONOMIC PERFORMANCE, London School of Economics and Political Science, Houghton Street, London WC2A 2AE T 020-7955 7048
Director, Prof. J. Van Reenen
CENTRE FOR GENOMICS IN SOCIETY, Egenis Office, University of Exeter, Byrne House, St German's Road, Exeter EX4 4PJ T 01392-269127
Director, Prof. John Dupré
CENTRE FOR MARKET AND PUBLIC ORGANISATION , Bristol Institute of Public Affairs, 2 Priory Road, Bristol BS8 1TX T 0117-928 8436
Director, Prof. S. Burgess
CENTRE FOR MICRODATA METHODS AND PRACTICE, Department of Economics, UCL, Gower Street, London WC1E 6BT T 020-7679 5857
Director, Prof. Andrew Chesher
CENTRE FOR MICROECONOMIC ANALYSIS OF PUBLIC POLICY, Institute for Fiscal Studies, 7 Ridgmount Street, London WC1E 7AE T 020-7291 4820
Director, Prof. R. Blundell

CENTRE FOR POPULATION CHANGE, School of Social Sciences, University of Southampton SO17 1BJ
T 023-8059 3192
Director, Prof. J. Falkingham
CENTRE FOR RESEARCH ON SOCIO-CULTURAL CHANGE, University of Manchester, 178 Waterloo Place, Oxford Road, Manchester M13 9PL T 0161-275 8985
Directors, Prof. M. Savage
CENTRE FOR SOCIAL AND ECONOMIC RESEARCH ON INNOVATION IN GENOMICS, Innogen Centre, University of Edinburgh, Old Surgeon's Hall, High School Yards, Edinburgh EH1 1LZ T 0131-650 6385
Director, Prof. D. Wield
CENTRE FOR SOCIAL, TECHNOLOGICAL AND ENVIRONMENTAL PATHWAYS TO SUSTAINABILITY, Institute of Development Studies, Brighton BN1 9RE
T 01273-606261
Director, Prof. M. Leach
CENTRE FOR SPATIAL ECONOMICS, LSE, Houghton Street, London WC2A 2AE T 020-7955 6581
Director, Dr Henry Overman
CENTRE FOR THIRD SECTOR RESEARCH, Park House, 40 Edgbaston Park Road, University of Birmingham B15 2RT
T 0121-414 3171
Director, Prof. Peter Alcock
CENTRE OF MICRO-SOCIAL CHANGE, University of Essex, Colchester, Essex CO4 3SQ T 01206-873789
Director, Prof. S. Pudney
CENTRE ON MIGRATION, POLICY AND SOCIETY, University of Oxford, 58 Banbury Road, Oxford OX2 6QS
T 01865-274711
Director, Prof. M. Keith
CENTRE ON SKILLS, KNOWLEDGE AND ORGANISATIONAL PERFORMANCE, Department of Education, University of Oxford, 15 Norham Gardens, Oxford OX2 6PY T 01865-611030
Director, Mr K. Mayhew
ELECTRICITY POLICY RESEARCH GROUP, University of Cambridge, Trumpington Street CB2 1AG
T 01223-335246
Director, Prof. D. Newbery
INNOVATION RESEARCH CENTRE, Judge Business School Building, Trumpington Street, Cambridge CB2 1AG
T 01223-765335
Director, Prof. Alan Hughes
INTERNATIONAL CENTRE FOR LIFECOURSE STUDIES IN SOCIETY AND HEALTH, UCL Research Department of Epidemiology and Public Health, 1–19 Torrington Place, London WC1E 7HB
T 020-7679 1708
Director, Prof. M. Bartley
LANGUAGE-BASED AREA STUDIES CENTRES
T 01793-413089
Directors, Dr Robin Aizlewood; Dr Richard Berry; Prof. Anoush Ehteshami; Prof. Victor King; Dr Frank Pieke
LEARNING AND LIFE CHANCES IN KNOWLEDGE ECONOMIES AND SOCIETIES, Institute of Education, University of London, 20 Bedford Way, London WC1H 0AL
T 020-7911 5464
Director, Prof. A. Green
RESEARCH GROUP ON LIFESTYLES, VALUES AND ENVIRONMENT, Centre for Environmental Strategy, University of Surrey, Guildford, Surrey GU2 7XH
T 01483-689072
Director, Prof. T. Jackson

ENGINEERING AND PHYSICAL SCIENCES RESEARCH COUNCIL*

Polaris House, North Star Avenue, Swindon SN2 1ET
T 01793-444000 W www.epsrc.ac.uk

The EPSRC is the UK government's main agency for funding research and training in engineering and the physical sciences in universities and other organisations throughout the UK. It also provides advice, disseminates knowledge and promotes public understanding in these areas.

Chair, John Armitt, CBE, FRENG
Chief Executive, Prof. David Delpy, FRS

HEALTH PROTECTION AGENCY

151 Buckingham Palace Road, London SW1W 9SZ
T 020-7811 7000 E webteam@hpa.org.uk
W www.hpa.org.uk

The Health Protection Agency was established as a special health authority in 2003 and became a non-departmental public body, incorporating the National Radiological Board in 2005. The HPA gives advice to the public, health authorities and the government. It works to reduce the impact of infectious diseases and exposure to chemicals, poisons and radiation at local, national and regional levels and in emergency situations. The agency researches new ways to combat illness and to assess exposure to chemicals and radiation to determine whether treatment is needed. The HPA will become part of Public Health England from April 2012.

Chair, Dr David Heymann
Chief Executive, Justin McCracken

RESEARCH CENTRES

CENTRE FOR INFECTIONS, 61 Colindale Avenue, London NW9 5EQ T 020-8200 4400
CENTRE FOR EMERGENCY PREPAREDNESS AND RESPONSE, Porton Down, Salisbury, SP4 0JG
    T 01980-612100
CENTRE FOR RADIATION, CHEMICAL AND ENVIRONMENTAL HAZARDS, Chilton, Didcot OX11 0RQ
    T 01235-831600

MEDICAL RESEARCH COUNCIL*

20 Park Crescent, London W1B 1AL T 020-7636 5422
W www.mrc.ac.uk

The MRC is a publicly funded organisation dedicated to improving human health. The MRC supports research across the entire spectrum of medical sciences, in universities, hospitals, centres and institutes.

Chair, Sir John Chisholm
Chief Executive, Sir John Savill
Chair, Neurosciences and Mental Health Board, Prof. Chris Kennard
Chair, Molecular and Cellular Medicine Board, Prof. Paul Luzio
Chair, Infections and Immunity Board, Prof. Doreen Cantrell
Chair, Population and Systems Medicine Board, Prof. Jill Pell

MRC UNITS, CENTRES AND INSTITUTES

Anatomical Neuropharmacology Unit
    W mrcanu.pharm.ox.ac.uk
Asthma UK Centre in Allergic Mechanisms of Asthma
    W www.asthma-allergy.ac.uk
Centre for Behavioural and Clinical Neuroscience Institute (BCNI)
    W www.psychol.cam.ac.uk/bcni
Biostatistics Unit
    W www.mrc-bsu.cam.ac.uk

Centre for Brain Ageing and Vitality
    W www.ncl.ac.uk/cbav
Cancer Cell Unit
    W www.hutchison-mrc.cam.ac.uk
Cancer Research UK / BHF Clinical Trial Service Unit & Epidemiological Studies Unit (CTSU)
    W www.ctsu.ox.ac.uk
Cancer Research UK Gray Institute for Radiation Oncology and Biology, University of Oxford
    W www.rob.ox.ac.uk
Centre for Causal Analyses in Translational Epidemiology
    W www.bristol.ac.uk/caite
Cell Biology Unit
    W www.ucl.ac.uk/lmcb
Clinical Trials Unit
    W www.ctu.mrc.ac.uk
Cognition and Brain Sciences Unit
    W www.mrc-cbu.cam.ac.uk
Centre for Cognitive Ageing and Cognitive Epidemiology
    W www.ccace.ed.ac.uk
The Crucible Centre
    W www.ucl.ac.uk/crucible
Centre for Developmental and Biomedical Genetics
    W cdbg.shef.ac.uk
Centre for Developmental Neurobiology at King's College London
    W www.kcl.ac.uk/depsta/biomedical/mrc
Centre for Drug Safety Science
    W www.liv.ac.uk/drug-safety/
Centre for Environment and Health
    W www.environment-health.ac.uk
Centre of Epidemiology for Child Health
    W www.ich.ucl.ac.uk
Epidemiology Unit
    W www.mrc-epid.cam.ac.uk
Functional Genomics Unit
    W www.mrcfgu.ox.ac.uk
General Practice Research Framework (GPRF)
    W www.gprf.mrc.ac.uk
Centre in Genome Damage and Stability
    W www.sussex.ac.uk/gdsc
Centre for Genomics and Global Health
    W www.cggh.ox.ac.uk
Institute of Hearing Research
    W www.ihr.mrc.ac.uk
Institute of Hearing Research (Glasgow)
    T 0141-211 4695
Human Genetics Unit
    W www.hgu.mrc.ac.uk
Human Immunology Unit
    W www.imm.ox.ac.uk
Human Nutrition Research
    W www.mrc-hnr.cam.ac.uk
Human Reproductive Sciences Unit
    W www.hrsu.mrc.ac.uk
Centre for Immune Regulation
    W www.mrcbcir.bham.ac.uk
Centre for Inflammation Research
    W www.cir.med.ed.ac.uk
International Nutrition Group
    T 020-7958 8140
Laboratory of Molecular Biology (LMB)
    W www2.mrc-lmb.cam.ac.uk
Lifecourse Epidemiology Unit
    W www.mrc.soton.ac.uk
Unit for Lifelong Health and Ageing
    W www.nhsd.mrc.ac.uk
Mammalian Genetics Unit
    W www.har.mrc.ac.uk

Centre for Medical Molecular Virology
W www.ucl.ac.uk/infection-immunity/mrc_ucl-centre
*National Institute for Medical Research (NIMR) including the
MRC Biomedical NMR Centre*
W www.nimr.mrc.ac.uk
Mitochondrial Biology Unit
W www.mrc-mbu.cam.ac.uk
Molecular Haemotology Unit
T 01865-222398
Centre for Neurodegeneration Research
W cnr.iop.kcl.ac.uk
Centre for Neuromuscular Diseases
W www.cnmd.ac.uk
Centre for Neuropsychiatric Genetics and Genomics
W http://medicine.cf.ac.uk/research/research-groups/cngg/
*Centre for Nutritional Epidemiology in Cancer Prevention and
Survival (CNC)*
W www.srl.cam.ac.uk
Centre for Obesity and Related Metabolic Diseases
W www.mrc-cord.org
Centre for Outbreak Analysis and Modelling
W www1.imperial.ac.uk
Prion Unit
W www.prion.ucl.ac.uk
Protein Phosphorylation Unit
W www.ppu.mrc.ac.uk
Centre for Regenerative Medicine
W www.scrm.ed.ac.uk
Research Complex at Hawell (RCaH)
W www.rc-harwell.ac.uk
Scottish Collaboration for Public Health Research and Policy
W www.scphrp.ac.uk
Social and Public Health Sciences Unit
W www.sphsumrc.ac.uk
Social, Genetic and Developmental Psychiatry Research Centre
W www.iop.kcl.ac.uk/index.aspx
Centre for Stem Cell Biology and Regenerative Medicine
W www.stemcells.cam.ac.uk
Centre for Synaptic Plasticity
W www.bris.ac.uk/depts/synaptic
Toxicology Unit
W www.mrctox.le.ac.uk
Centre for Transplantation
W http://transplantation.kcl.ac.uk
Centre for Virus Research
W www.cvr.ac.uk
MRC (UK), the Gambia
W www.mrc.gm
UVRI Uganda Research Unit on AIDS
W www.mrcuganda.org

NATIONAL PHYSICAL LABORATORY
Hampton Road, Teddington, Middx TW11 0LW
T 020-8977 3222 W www.npl.co.uk

The National Physical Laboratory (NPL) was established in 1900 and is the UK's national measurement institute. It develops, maintains and disseminates national measurement standards for physical quantities such as mass, length, time, temperature, voltage and force. It also conducts underpinning research on engineering materials and information technology, and disseminates good measurement practice. It is government-owned but contractor-operated.
Managing Director, B. Bowsher

NATURAL ENVIRONMENT RESEARCH COUNCIL*
Polaris House, North Star Avenue, Swindon SN2 1EU
T 01793-411500 W www.nerc.ac.uk

The NERC funds and carries out impartial scientific research in the sciences relating to the natural environment. Its work covers the full range of atmospheric, earth, biological, terrestrial and aquatic sciences, from the depths of the oceans to the upper atmosphere. Its mission is to gather and apply knowledge, create understanding and predict the behaviour of the natural environment and its resources.
Chair, Edmund Wallis
Chief Executive, Prof. Alan Thorpe

RESEARCH CENTRES
BRITISH ANTARCTIC SURVEY, High Cross, Madingley
Road, Cambridge CB3 OET T 01223-221400
Director, Prof. Nick Owens
BRITISH GEOLOGICAL SURVEY, Kingsley Dunham Centre,
Keyworth, Nottingham NG12 5GG T 0115-936 3100
Executive Director, Prof. John Ludden
CENTRE FOR ECOLOGY AND HYDROLOGY, Maclean
Building, Benson Lane, Crowmarsh Gifford, Wallingford
OX10 8BB T 01491-838800
Director, Prof. Patricia Nuttall, OBE
NATIONAL CENTRE FOR ATMOSPHERIC SCIENCE,
NERC, Polaris House, North Star Avenue, Swindon SN2 1EU
T 01793-442543
Director, Prof. Stephen Mobbs
NATIONAL CENTRE FOR EARTH OBSERVATION,
Department of Meteorology, University of Reading, Building
58, Earley Gate, Reading RG6 6BB T 0118-378 6728
Director, Prof. Alan O'Neill
NATIONAL OCEANOGRAPHY CENTRE, Joseph Proudman
Building, 6 Brownlow Street, Liverpool L3 5DA
T 0151-795 4800
Director, Prof. Edward Hill

SCIENCE AND TECHNOLOGY FACILITIES COUNCIL*
Polaris House, North Star Avenue, Swindon SN2 1SZ
T 01793-442000 W www.stfc.ac.uk

Formed by royal charter on 1 April 2007, through the merger of the Council for the Central Laboratory of the Research Councils and the Particle Physics and Astronomy Research Council, the STFC is a non-departmental public body reporting to the Department for Business, Innovation and Skills.

The STFC invests in large national and international research facilities, while delivering science, technology and expertise for the UK. The council is involved in research projects including the Diamond Light Source Synchrotron and the Large Hadron Collider, and develops new areas of science and technology. The EPSRC has transferred its responsibility for nuclear physics to the STFC.
Chair, Prof. Michael Sterling
Chief Executive, Prof. Keith Mason

CHILBOLTON OBSERVATORY, Chilbolton, Stockbridge,
Hampshire SO20 6BJ T 01264-860391
DARESBURY LABORATORY, Daresbury Science and
Innovation Campus, Warrington WA4 4AD T 01925-603000

RUTHERFORD APPLETON LABORATORY, Harwell Science and Innovation Campus, Didcot OX11 0QX
T 01235-445000
UK ASTRONOMY TECHNOLOGY CENTRE, Royal Observatory, Edinburgh, Blackford Hill, Edinburgh EH9 3HJ
T 0131-668 8100

RESEARCH AND TECHNOLOGY ORGANISATIONS

Over 30 industrial and technological research bodies are members of the Association of Independent Research and Technology Organisations Limited (AIRTO). Members'

activities span a wide range of disciplines from life sciences to engineering. Their work includes basic research, development and design of innovative products or processes, instrumentation testing and certification, and technology and management consultancy. AIRTO publishes a directory to help clients identify the organisations that might be able to assist them. For a full list of members, see AIRTO's website.

AIRTO LTD, c/o The National Physical Laboratory, Hampton Road, Teddington, Middlesex TW11 0LW
T 020-8943 6600 E enquiries@airto.co.uk
W www.airto.co.uk
President, Prof. R. Brook, OBE, FRENG

HEALTH

NATIONAL HEALTH SERVICE

The National Health Service (NHS) came into being on 5 July 1948 under the National Health Service Act 1946, covering England and Wales and, under separate legislation, Scotland and Northern Ireland. The NHS is now administered by the Secretary of State for Health (in England), the Welsh government, the Scottish government and the Secretary of State for Northern Ireland.

The function of the NHS is to provide a comprehensive health service designed to secure improvement in the physical and mental health of the people and to prevent, diagnose and treat illness. It was founded on the principle that treatment should be provided according to clinical need rather than ability to pay, and should be free at the point of delivery.

Hospital, mental, dental, nursing, ophthalmic and ambulance services and facilities for the care of expectant and nursing mothers and young children are provided by the NHS to meet all reasonable requirements. Rehabilitation services such as occupational therapy, physiotherapy, speech therapy and surgical and medical appliances are supplied where appropriate. Specialists and consultants who work in NHS hospitals can also engage in private practice, including the treatment of their private patients in NHS hospitals.

STRUCTURE

The structure of the NHS remained relatively stable for the first 30 years of its existence. In 1974, a three-tier management structure comprising regional health authorities, area health authorities and district management teams was introduced in England, and the NHS became responsible for community health services. In 1979 area health authorities were abolished and district management teams were replaced by district health authorities.

The National Health Service and Community Care Act 1990 provided for more streamlined regional health authorities and district health authorities, and for the establishment of family health services authorities (FHSAs) and NHS trusts. The concept of the 'internal market' was introduced into health care, whereby care was provided through NHS contracts where health authorities or boards and GP fundholders (the purchasers) were responsible for buying health care from hospitals, non-fundholding GPs, community services and ambulance services (the providers). The Act also paved the way for the community care reforms, which were introduced in April 1993, and changed the way care is administered for older people, the mentally ill, the physically disabled and people with learning disabilities.

ENGLAND

Regional health authorities in England were abolished in April 1996 and replaced by eight regional offices which, together with the headquarters in Leeds, formed the NHS executive (which has since been merged with the Department of Health). In April 2002, as an interim arrangement, the eight regional offices were replaced by four directorates of health and social care (DHSCs). In April 2003, the DHSCs were abolished.

HEALTH AUTHORITIES

In April 1996 the district health authorities and family health service authorities were merged to form 100 unified health authorities (HAs) in England. In April 2002, 28 new health authorities were formed from the existing HAs. In October 2002, as part of the new arrangements set out in the NHS Reform and Health Care Professions Act 2002, these new health authorities were renamed strategic health authorities (SHAs). The whole of England is now split into 10 strategic health authorities, each of which is divided into various types of trusts that take responsibilty for running different NHS services locally. The different types of trusts comprise acute trusts and foundation trusts (which are responsible for the management of NHS hospitals), ambulance trusts, care trusts, mental health trusts and primary care trusts. SHAs are charged with improving and monitoring the performance of the trusts in their area.

PRIMARY CARE TRUSTS

The first 17 primary care trusts (PCTs) became operational on 1 April 2000 and there are now around 150 PCTs in England. PCTs were created to give primary care professionals greater control over how resources are best used to benefit patients. PCTs are free-standing statutory bodies responsible for securing the provision of services and integrating health and social care locally. PCTs receive most of their funding directly from the Department of Health and can use this to purchase hospital and other services from NHS trusts and other healthcare providers. They are also responsible for making payments to independent primary care contractors such as GPs and dentists.

Each PCT is overseen by a board, typically comprising a chair; at least five non-executive directors who are appointed by the Appointments Commission; at least five executive members, including the chief executive, finance director and director of public health; and at least two members of the PCT's professional executive committee (PEC), which is made up of health professionals. Clinical expertise is provided by the PEC with representation from local GPs, nurses, other health professionals and social services. The board concentrates on the overall strategies for the trust and ensures that the trust meets its statutory, financial and legal obligations.

ACUTE TRUSTS AND FOUNDATION TRUSTS

Hospitals are managed by acute trusts that are responsible for the quality of hospital health care and for spending funds efficiently. There are 167 acute NHS trusts and 58 mental health NHS trusts which oversee around 1,600 NHS hospitals and specialist care centres.

First introduced in April 2004, there are now 129 foundation trusts in England. NHS foundation trusts are NHS hospitals, but have their own accountability and governance systems, which function outside of the Department of Health's framework, giving them greater freedom to run their own affairs. NHS foundation trusts treat patients according to NHS principles and standards and are regulated by the Care Quality Commission.

STRATEGIC HEALTH AUTHORITIES

EAST OF ENGLAND, Victoria House, Capital Park, Fulbourn, Cambridge CB21 5XB **T** 01223-597500 **W** www.eoe.nhs.uk
Chief Executive, Sir Neil McKay, CB

EAST MIDLANDS, Octavia House, Bostocks Lane, Sandiacre, Nottingham NG10 5QG **T** 0115-968 4444 **W** www.eastmidlands.nhs.uk
Chief Executive, Dame Barbara Hakin, DBE

LONDON, 4th Floor Southside, 105 Victoria Street, London SW1E 6QT **T** 020-7932 3700 **W** www.london.nhs.uk
Chief Executive, Ruth Carnall, CBE

NORTH EAST, Riverside House, Goldcrest Way, Newcastle upon Tyne NE15 8NY **T** 0191-210 6400 **W** www.northeast.nhs.uk
Chief Executive, Ian Dalton

NORTH WEST, 4th Floor, 3 Piccadilly Place, Manchester M1 3BN **T** 0845-050 0194 **W** www.northwest.nhs.uk
Chief Executive, Mike Farrar, CBE

SOUTH CENTRAL, Newbury Business Park, London Road, Newbury, Berks RG14 2PZ **T** 01635-275500 **W** www.southcentral.nhs.uk
Chief Executive, Andrea Young

SOUTH EAST, York House, 18–20 Masetts Road, Horley, Surrey RH6 7DE **T** 01293-778899 **W** www.southeastcoast.nhs.uk
Chief Executive, Candy Morris, CBE

SOUTH WEST, South West House, Blackbrook Park Avenue, Taunton, Somerset TA1 2PX **T** 01823-361000 **W** www.southwest.nhs.uk
Chief Executive, Sir Ian Carruthers, OBE

WEST MIDLANDS, St Chad's Court, 213 Hagley Road, Edgbaston, Birmingham B16 9RG **T** 0121-695 2222 **W** www.westmidlands.nhs.uk
Chief Executive, Ian Cumming, OBE

YORKSHIRE AND THE HUMBER, Blenheim House, Duncombe Street, Leeds LS1 4PL **T** 0113-295 2000 **W** www.yorksandhumber.nhs.uk
Chief Executive, Bill McCarthy

Contact details for PCTs and other NHS trusts in England can be found on the NHS Choices website (**W** www.nhs.uk).

WALES

The NHS Wales was reorganised according to Welsh Assembly commitments laid out in the *One Wales* strategy and came into effect in October 2009. There are now seven local health boards (LHBs) that are responsible for delivering all health care services within a geographical area, rather than the trust and local health board system that existed previously. Community health councils (CHCs) are statutory lay bodies that represent the public for the health service in their region. The number of CHCs is being reduced to seven, contiguous with the new LHBs. These seven CHCs are to be underpinned by 23 area associations with strong local links.

NHS TRUSTS

There are three NHS trusts in Wales. The Welsh Ambulance Services NHS Trust is for emergency services; the Velindre NHS Trust offers specialist services in cancer care and other national support services; while Public Health Wales serves as a unified public health organisation for Wales.

REGIONAL HEALTH BOARDS

The websites of the seven LHBs, and contact details for community health councils and NHS trusts, are available in the *NHS Wales Directory* on the NHS Wales website (**W** www.wales.nhs.uk).

ANEURIN BEVAN HEALTH BOARD, Mamhilad House, Block A, Mamhilad Park Estate, Pontypool, Torfaen NP4 0YP **T** 01873-732732
Chief Executive, Dr Andrew Goodall

ABERTAWE BRO MORGANNWG UNIVERSITY HEALTH BOARD, One Talbot Gateway, Baglan Energy Park, Baglan, Port Talbot SA12 7BR **T** 01639-683670
Chief Executive (acting), Alexandra Howells

BETSI CADWALADR UNIVERSITY HEALTH BOARD, Ysbyty Gwynedd, Penrhosgarnedd, Bangor, Gwynedd LL57 2PW **T** 01248-384384
Chief Executive, Mary Burrows

CARDIFF AND VALE UNIVERSITY HEALTH BOARD, Whitchurch Hospital, Park Road, Whitchurch, Cardiff CF14 7XB **T** 029-2074 7747
Chief Executive, Jan Williams

CWM TAF HEALTH BOARD, Ynysmeurig House, Navigation Park, Abercynon, Mid Glamorgan CF45 4SN **T** 01443-406834
Chief Executive, Allison Williams

HYWEL DDA HEALTH BOARD, Merlin's Court, Winch Lane, Haverfordwest, Pembrokeshire SA61 1SB **T** 01437-771220
Chief Executive, Trevor Purt

POWYS TEACHING HEALTH BOARD, Mansion House, Bronllys, Brecon, Powys LD3 0LS **T** 01874-771661
Chief Executive, Andrew Cottom

SCOTLAND

The Scottish government Health Directorate is responsible both for NHS Scotland and for the development and implementation of health and community care policy. The chief executive of NHS Scotland leads the central management of the NHS, is accountable to ministers for the efficiency and performance of the service and heads the Health Department which oversees the work of the 14 regional health boards. These boards provide strategic management for the entire local NHS system and are responsible for ensuring that services are delivered effectively and efficiently.

In addition to the 14 regional health boards there are a further eight special boards which provide national services, such as the Scottish ambulance service and NHS National Services Scotland, the latter of which provides national screening programmes, blood transfusion services and monitors communicable diseases. A new health body, Healthcare Improvement Scotland, was formed on 1 April 2011 by the Public Services Reform Act 2010 to improve the quality of Scottish healthcare.

REGIONAL HEALTH BOARDS

AYRSHIRE AND ARRAN, Eglinton House, Ailsa Hospital, Dalmellington Road, Ayr KA6 6AB **T** 0800-169 1441 **W** www.nhsayrshireandarran.com
Chief Executive, Dr Wai-yin Hatton

BORDERS, Newstead, Melrose TD6 9DA **T** 01896-826000 **W** www.nhsborders.org.uk
Chief Executive, Calum Campbell

DUMFRIES AND GALLOWAY, Ryan North, Crichton Hall, Dumfries DG1 4TG **T** 01387-246246 **W** www.nhsdg.scot.nhs.uk
Chief Executive, John Burns

FIFE, Hayfield House, Hayfield Road, Kirkcaldy, Fife KY2 5AH **T** 01592-643355 **W** www.nhsfife.scot.nhs.uk
Chief Executive, George Brechin

FORTH VALLEY, Carseview House, Castle Business Park, Stirling FK9 4SW T 01786-463031
W www.nhsforthvalley.com
Chief Executive, Prof. Fiona Mackenzie
GRAMPIAN, Summerfield House, 2 Eday Road, Aberdeen AB15 6RE T 0845-456 6000 W www.nhsgrampian.org
Chief Executive, Richard Carey
GREATER GLASGOW AND CLYDE, J B Russell House, Gartnavel Royal Hospital Campus, 1055 Great Western Road, Glasgow G12 0XH T 0141-201 4444
W www.nhsggc.org.uk
Chief Executive, Robert Calderwood
HIGHLAND, Assynt House, Beechwood Park, Inverness IV2 3BW T 01463-717123 W www.nhshighland.scot.nhs.uk
Chief Executive, Elaine Mead
LANARKSHIRE, Kirklands, Fallside Road, Bothwell G71 8BB T 0845-313 0130 W www.nhslanarkshire.org.uk
Chief Executive, Tim Davison
LOTHIAN, Waverley Gate, 2–4 Waterloo Place, Edinburgh EH1 3EG T 0131-536 9000 W www.nhslothian.scot.nhs.uk
Chief Executive, Prof. James Barbour, OBE
ORKNEY, Balfour Hospital, New Scapa Road, Kirkwall, Orkney KW15 1BH T 01856-888000 W www.ohb.scot.nhs.uk
Chief Executive, Cathie Cowan
SHETLAND, Brevik House, South Road, Lerwick ZE1 0TG T 01595-743060 W www.shb.scot.nhs.uk
Chief Executive, Ralph Roberts
TAYSIDE, Kings Cross, Clepington Road, Dundee DD3 8EA T 01382-818479 W www.nhstayside.scot.nhs.uk
Chief Executive, Gerry Marr
WESTERN ISLES, 37 South Beach Street, Stornoway, Isle of Lewis HS1 2BB T 01851-702997
W www.wihb.scot.nhs.uk
Chief Executive, Gordon Jamieson

NORTHERN IRELAND

On 1 April 2009 the four health and social services boards in Northern Ireland were replaced by a single health and social care board for the whole of Northern Ireland. The new board together with its local commissioning groups (whose boundaries are subject to review pending the outcome of local government reform) are responsible for improving the health and social wellbeing of people in the area for which they are responsible, planning and commissioning services, and coordinating the delivery of services in a cost-effective manner.

HEALTH AND SOCIAL CARE BOARD, 12–22 Linenhall Street, Belfast BT2 8BS T 028-9032 1313
W www.hscboard.hscni.net
Chief Executive, John Compton

NHS POLICY

In July 2000 the Labour government launched the NHS Plan, a ten-year strategy to modernise the health service. In June 2004 it also launched the NHS Improvement Plan, which set out the next stage of NHS reform, moving the focus from access to services towards the broader issues of public health and chronic disease management. The core aims were to sustain increased levels of investment in the NHS and to continue to focus on the improvements outlined in the NHS Plan, while delivering greater levels of choice and information to patients. In July 2004, the Department of Health published *National Standards, Local Action: Health and Social Care Standards and Planning Framework 2005/6–2007/8*, which cut the number of national targets from 62 to 20. The

national targets, which covered areas such as waiting times for accident and emergency treatment, became national core standards which all providers of care were required to maintain from April 2005. Alongside this, NHS providers were given power to set more locally relevant targets.

In June 2010 the coalition government published a white paper, *Liberating the NHS*, which set out its intentions for NHS reforms. In the lead up to 2013 it is proposed that GPs will be given increased control over budgets, which at present are controlled by the primary care trusts. The *Revision to the Operating Framework for the NHS in England 2010/11*, also published in June 2010, announced immediate changes to performance targets and plans for further changes to targets in 2011–12. The framework and further information on planned changes is available on the Department for Health website (W www.dh.gov.uk).

FINANCE

The NHS is still funded mainly through general taxation, although in recent years more reliance has been placed on the NHS element of national insurance contributions, patient charges and other sources of income.

The budgeted departmental expenditure limit for the NHS in England was set at £105.9bn for 2011–12. Expenditure for the NHS in Wales, Scotland and Northern Ireland is set by the devolved governments.

PRIVATE FINANCE INITIATIVE
The Private Finance Initiative (PFI) was launched in 1992, and involves the private sector in designing, building, financing and operating new hospitals and primary care premises, which are then leased to the NHS. Partnerships for Health, a public-private venture between the Department of Health and Partnerships UK plc was established in September 2001. Its role was to support the development of NHS Local Improvement Finance Trusts (LIFTs) by implementing a standard approach to procurement as well as providing some equity. LIFTs were set up as limited companies with the local NHS Partnerships for Health and the private sector as shareholders to build and refurbish primary care premises, which the schemes own and then rent to GPs on a lease basis (as well as other parties such as chemists, opticians, dentists etc).

EMPLOYEES AND SALARIES

NHS HEALTH SERVICE STAFF 2010 (ENGLAND)
Full-time equivalent

All hospital, community and dental staff	1,431,557
Consultants	37,752
Registrars	38,158
Qualified nursing and midwifery staff	410,615
General practitioners	39,409
Qualified scientific, therapeutic and technical staff	151,607

Source: NHS

SALARIES
Many general practitioners (GPs) are self-employed and hold contracts, either on their own or as part of a partnership, with their local PCT. The profit of GPs varies according to the services they provide for their patients and the way they choose to provide these services. The

pay range for salaried GPs employed directly by PCTs for 2011–12 is £53,781–£81,158, dependent on, among other factors, length of service and experience. Most NHS dentists are self-employed contractors. A contract for dentists was introduced on 1 April 2006 which provides dentists with an annual income in return for carrying out an agreed amount, or units, of work. A salaried dentist employed directly by a PCT earns between £37,714 and £80,674.

BASIC SALARIES FOR HOSPITAL MEDICAL AND DENTAL STAFF*
from 1 April 2011

Consultant (2003 contract)	£74,504–£100,446
Consultant (pre-2003 contract)	£61,859–£80,186
Specialist registrar	£30,992–£46,708
Speciality registrar (full)	£29,705–£46,708
Speciality registrar (fixed term)	£29,705–£39,300
Senior house officer	£27,798–£38,705
House officer	£22,412–£25,209

* These figures do not include merit awards, discretionary points or banding supplements

NURSES
From 1 December 2004 the *Agenda for Change* pay system was introduced throughout the UK for all NHS staff with the exception of medical and dental staff, doctors in public health medicine and the community health service. Nurses' salaries are incorporated in the *Agenda for Change* nine pay band structure, which provides additional payments for flexible working such as providing out-of-hours services, working weekends and nights and being 'on-call'.

SALARIES FOR NURSES AND MIDWIVES

Nurse/Midwife consultant	£38,851–£67,134
Modern matron	£38,851–£46,621
Nurse advanced/team manager	£30,460–£40,157
Midwife higher level	£30,460–£40,157
Nurse specialist/team leader	£25,528–£34,189
Hospital/community midwife	£25,528–£34,189
Registered nurse/entry level midwife	£21,176–£27,625

HEALTH SERVICES

PRIMARY CARE
Primary care comprises the services provided by general practitioners, community health centres, pharmacies, dental surgeries and opticians. Primary nursing care includes the work carried out by practice nurses, community nurses, community midwives and health visitors.

PRIMARY MEDICAL SERVICES
In England, primary medical services are the responsibility of PCTs who contract with health care providers – GPs, dentists, pharmacists etc – to provide the service to the NHS.
In Wales, responsibility for primary medical services rests with local health boards (LHBs), in Scotland with the 14 regional health boards and in Northern Ireland with the health and social care board.
Any vocationally trained doctor may provide general or personal medical services. GPs may also have private fee-paying patients, but not if that patient is already an NHS patient on that doctor's patient list.

A person who is ordinarily resident in the UK is eligible to register with a GP (or PMS provider) for free primary care treatment. Should a patient have difficulty in registering with a doctor, he or she should contact the local PCT for help. When a person is away from home he/she can still access primary care treatment from a GP if they ask to be treated as a temporary resident. In an emergency any doctor in the service will give treatment and advice.
GPs or PCTs are responsible for the care of their patients 24 hours a day, seven days a week, but can fulfil the terms of their contract by delegating or transferring responsibility for out-of-hours care to an accredited provider.
Increasingly, some secondary care services, such as minor operations and consultations, can be provided in a primary care setting. The number of such practitioners is growing.
In addition there are around 93 NHS walk-in centres throughout England. Usually open seven days a week, from early in the morning until late in the evening, they are nurse-led and provide treatment for minor ailments and injuries, health information and self-help advice.

HEALTH COSTS
Some people are exempt from, or entitled to help with, health costs such as prescription charges, ophthalmic and dental costs, and in some cases help towards travel costs to and from hospital.
The following list is intended as a general guide to those who may be entitled to help, or who are exempt from some of the charges relating to the above:
• children under 16 and young people in full-time education who are under 19
• people aged 60 or over
• pregnant women and women who have had a baby in the last 12 months and have a valid maternity exemption certificate (MatEx)
• people, or their partners, who are in receipt of income support, income-based jobseeker's allowance and/or income-based employment and support allowance
• people in receipt of the pension credit
• diagnosed glaucoma patients, people who have been advised by an ophthalmologist that they are at risk of glaucoma and people aged 40 or over who have an immediate family member who is a diagnosed glaucoma patient
• NHS in-patients
• NHS out-patients for all prescribed contraceptives, medication given at a hospital, NHS walk-in centre, personally administered by a GP or supplied at a hospital or primary care trust clinic for the treatment of tuberculosis or a sexually transmissable infection
• patients of the Community Dental Service or an out-patient of the NHS Hospital Dental Service
• people registered blind or partially sighted
• people who need complex lenses
• war pensioners whose treatment/prescription is for their accepted disablement and who have a valid exemption certificate
• people who are entitled to, or named on, a valid NHS tax credit exemption or HC2 certificate
• people who have a medical exemption (MedEx) certificate, including those with cancer or diabetes
People in other circumstances may also be eligible for help; *see* booklet HC12 (England) and HCS2 (Scotland) for further information.

WALES
On 1 April 2007 all prescription charges (including those for medical supports and appliances and wigs) for people living in Wales were abolished. The above guide still applies for NHS dental and optical charges although all people aged under 25 living in Wales are also entitled to free dental examinations.

SCOTLAND
On 1 April 2011 all prescription charges in Scotland were abolished. Those entitled to free prescriptions in Scotland include patients registered with a Scottish GP and receiving a prescription from a Scottish pharmacy, and Scottish patients who have an English GP and an entitlement card.

NORTHERN IRELAND
On 1 April 2010 all prescription charges in Northern Ireland were abolished. All prescriptions dispensed in Northern Ireland are free, even for patients visiting from England, Wales or Scotland.

PHARMACEUTICAL SERVICES
Patients may obtain medicines and appliances under the NHS from any pharmacy whose owner has entered into arrangements with the PCT to provide this service. There are also some suppliers who only provide special appliances. In rural areas, where access to a pharmacy may be difficult, patients may be able to obtain medicines, etc, from a dispensing doctor.

In England, a charge of £7.40 is payable for each item supplied (except for contraceptives for which there is no charge), unless the patient is exempt and the declaration on the back of the prescription form is completed. Prepayment certificates (£29.10 valid for three months, £104.00 valid for a year) may be purchased by those patients not entitled to exemption who require frequent prescriptions.

DENTAL SERVICES
Dentists, like doctors, may take part in the NHS and also have private patients. Dentists are responsible to the local health provider in whose areas they provide services. Patients may go to any dentist who is taking part in the NHS and is willing to accept them. On 1 April 2006 the charging system for NHS dentistry in England and Wales was changed. There is now a three-tier payment system based on the individual course of treatment required.

COURSE OF TREATMENT COSTS 2010–11

	England/Wales
Examination, diagnosis, preventive care (A)* (eg x-rays, scale and polish)	£17.00/£12.00
A+ basic additional treatment (eg fillings and extractions)	£47.00/£39.00
A+ all other treatment (eg more complex procedures such as crowns, dentures etc)	£204.00/£177.00

* Urgent and out-of-hours treatment is also charged at this payment tier

The cost of individual treatment plans should be known prior to treatment and some dental practices may require payment in advance. There is no charge for writing a prescription or removing stitches and only one charge is payable for each course of treatment even if more than one visit to the dentist is required. If additional treatment is required within two months of visiting the dentist and this is covered by the course of treatment most recently paid for (eg payment was made for the second tier of treatment but an additional filling is required) then this will be provided free of charge.

SCOTLAND AND NORTHERN IRELAND
Scotland and Northern Ireland have yet to simplify their charging systems. NHS dental patients pay 80 per cent of the cost of the individual items of treatment provided up to a maximum of £384. Patients in Scotland are entitled to free basic and extensive examinations.

GENERAL OPHTHALMIC SERVICES
General ophthalmic services are administered by local health providers. Testing of sight may be carried out by any ophthalmic medical practitioner or ophthalmic optician (optometrist). The optician must give the prescription to the patient, who can take this to any supplier of glasses to have them dispensed. Only registered opticians can supply glasses to children and to people registered as blind or partially sighted.

Free eyesight tests and help towards the cost are available to people in certain circumstances. Help is also available for the purchase of glasses or contact lenses (see Health Costs section). In Scotland eye examinations, which include a sight test, are free to all. Help is also available for the purchase of glasses or contact lenses to those entitled to help with health costs in the same way it is available to those in England and Wales.

CHILD HEALTH SERVICES
Pre-school services at GP surgeries or child health clinics provide regular monitoring of children's physical, mental and emotional health and development and advise parents on their children's health and welfare.

NHS DIRECT AND NHS 24
NHS Direct is a website and 24-hour nurse-led advice telephone service for England and Wales. It provides medical advice as well as directing people to the appropriate part of the NHS for treatment if necessary (W www.nhsdirect.nhs.uk T 0845-4647).

NHS 24 provides an equivalent service for Scotland (T 0845-424 2424).

SECONDARY CARE AND OTHER SERVICES

HOSPITALS
NHS hospitals provide acute and specialist care services, treating conditions which normally cannot be dealt with by primary care specialists, and provide for medical emergencies.

NUMBER OF BEDS 2010–11*

	Average daily	
	available beds	occupation of beds
England	141,019	121,614
Wales	12,868	10,449
Scotland	17,099	14,004
Northern Ireland	7,276	5,952

* Figures for Scotland, Wales and Northern Ireland are for 2009–10

Sources: Department of Health; Welsh government, NI Direct

HOSPITAL CHARGES

Acute or foundation trusts can provide hospital accommodation in single rooms or small wards, if not required for patients who need privacy for medical reasons. The patient is still an NHS patient, but there may be a charge for these additional facilities. Acute or foundation trusts can charge for certain patient services that are considered to be additional treatments over and above the normal hospital service provision. There is no blanket policy to cover this and each case is considered in the light of the patient's clinical need. However, if an item or service is considered to be an integral part of a patient's treatment by their clinician, then a charge should not be made.

In some NHS hospitals, accommodation and services are available for the treatment of private patients where it does not interfere with care for NHS patients. Income generated by treating private patients is then put back into local NHS services. Private patients undertake to pay the full costs of medical treatment, accommodation, medication and other related services. Charges for private patients are set locally.

WAITING LISTS

England

In July 2004 a target of an 18-week maximum wait, from start time (ie seeing a GP) to treatment, was introduced. For June 2011, 321,921 admitted patients and 937,205 non-admitted patients completed their referral to treatment. Of the admitted patients, 90.2 per cent were treated within 18 weeks, and for non-admitted patients 97.6 per cent were treated within 18 weeks. The *Revision to the Operating Framework for the NHS in England 2010/11*, published in June 2010, abolished the performance management of the 18-week waiting time target although referral-to-treatment data will continue to be published.

Wales

In Wales the main target is for referral to treatment to take no longer than 26 weeks. In February 2011, 87.3 per cent of patients were treated within 26 weeks and 97.4 per cent were treated within 36 weeks of the date the referral letter was received in the hospital. There are also operational standards for maximum waiting times for first outpatient appointments and inpatient or day-case treatment but these are not set targets. The standards are 14 weeks for inpatient or day case treatment, and ten weeks for a first outpatient appointment.

Scotland

An 18-week referral to treatment target, due to be delivered from December 2011, was set out in the publication *Better Health, Better Care*. In March 2011, 85.2 per cent of patients on an 18 week referral to treatment pathway were reported as being seen within 18 weeks, an increase from 83.7 per cent in February 2011.

Northern Ireland

From April 2009 the target is that no patient should wait more than nine weeks for a first out-patient appointment or 13 weeks for in-patient or day-case treatment. The total number of people waiting for a first out patient appointment at the end of 31 March 2011 was 106,227; of these, 31,909 had been waiting over nine weeks, an increase of 23,328 from the same quarter in 2010. The number of people waiting for in patient treatment during

the quarter ending 31 March 2011 was 52,880; of these, 17,630 had been waiting for more than 13 weeks.

AMBULANCE SERVICE

The NHS provides emergency ambulance services free of charge via the 999 emergency telephone service. Air ambulances, provided through local charities and partially funded by the NHS, are used throughout the UK. They assist with cases where access may be difficult or heavy traffic could hinder road progress. Non-emergency ambulance services are provided free to patients who are deemed to require them on medical grounds.

Since 1 April 2001 all services have had a system of call prioritisation. The prioritisation procedures require all emergency calls to be classified as either immediately life threatening (category A) or other emergency (category B). Services are expected to reach 75 per cent of Category A (life threatening) calls within eight minutes and 95 per cent of category B calls within 19 minutes.

AMBULANCE STAFF

	Total staff	Number of paramedics
England	32,284	10,089
Wales	1,413*	847*
Scotland	3,836	1,323
Northern Ireland	1,033	635†

* 2008 figures
† Includes emergency medical technicians
Source: ONS – *Annual Abstract of Statistics 2009* (Crown copyright)

BLOOD AND TRANSPLANT SERVICES

There are four national bodies which coordinate the blood donor programme and transplant and related services in the UK. Donors give blood at local centres on a voluntary basis.

NHS BLOOD AND TRANSPLANT, Oak House, Reeds Crescent, Watford, Herts WD24 4QN
T 01923-486800 W www.nhsbt.nhs.uk
WELSH BLOOD SERVICE, Ely Valley Road, Talbot Green, Pontyclun CF72 9WB T 01443-622000
W www.welsh-blood.org.uk
SCOTTISH NATIONAL BLOOD TRANSFUSION SERVICE, 21 Ellen's Glen Road, Edinburgh EH17 7QT
T 0845-909 0999 W www.scotblood.co.uk
NORTHERN IRELAND BLOOD TRANSFUSION SERVICE, Lisburn Road, Belfast BT9 7TS T 028-9032 1414
W www.nibts.org

HOSPICES

Hospice or palliative care may be available for patients with life-threatening illnesses. It may be provided at the patient's home or in a voluntary or NHS hospice or in hospital, and is intended to ensure the best possible quality of life for the patient during their illness, and to provide help and support to both the patient and the patient's family. The National Council for Palliative Care coordinates NHS and voluntary services in England, Wales and Northern Ireland; the Scottish Partnership for Palliative Care performs the same function in Scotland.

NATIONAL COUNCIL FOR PALLIATIVE CARE, The Fitzpatrick Building, 188–194 York Way, London N7 9AS
T 020-7697 1520 W www.ncpc.org.uk

SCOTTISH PARTNERSHIP FOR PALLIATIVE CARE,
1A Cambridge Street, Edinburgh EH1 2DY **T** 0131-229 0538
W www.palliativecarescotland.org.uk

COMPLAINTS

Firstly, an attempt must be made to resolve the complaint at a local level directly with the health care provider concerned. Patient advice and liaison services (PALS) have been established for every NHS and PCT in England. PALS are not part of the complaints procedure itself, but can give advice on local complaints procedure, or resolve concerns informally. For more information, *see* **W** www.pals.nhs.uk. If the case is not resolved locally or the complainant is not satisfied with the way a local NHS body or practice has dealt with their complaint, they may approach the Health Service Ombudsman in England, the Scottish Public Services Ombudsman, Public Services Ombudsman for Wales or the Northern Ireland Commissioner for Complaints.

RECIPROCAL ARRANGEMENTS

The European Health Insurance Card (EHIC) allows UK residents access to state-provided health care that may become necessary while temporarily travelling in all European Economic Area countries and Switzerland either free or at a reduced cost. A card is free, valid for up to five years and should be obtained before travelling. Applications can be made by telephone (**T** 0845-606 2030), online (**W** www.ehic.org.uk) or by post (a form is available from the post office).

The UK also has bilateral agreements with several other countries, including Australia and New Zealand, for the free provision of urgent medical treatment.

European Economic Area nationals visiting the UK and visitors from other countries with which the UK has bilateral health care agreements are entitled to receive emergency health care on the NHS on the same terms as it is available to UK residents. For further information regarding health care abroad, *see* Travel Overseas.

SOCIAL WELFARE

SOCIAL SERVICES

The Secretary of State for Health (in England), the Welsh government, the Scottish government and the Secretary of State for Northern Ireland are responsible, under the Local Authority Social Services Act 1970, for the provision of social services for older people, disabled people, families and children, and those with mental disorders. Personal social services are administered by local authorities according to policies, with standards set by central and devolved government. Each authority has a director and a committee responsible for the social services functions placed upon them. Local authorities provide, enable and commission care after assessing the needs of their population. The private and voluntary sectors also play an important role in the delivery of social services, and an estimated 6 million people in the UK provide substantial regular care for a member of their family.

The Care Quality Commission (CQC) was established in April 2009, bringing together the independent regulation of health, mental health and adult social care. Prior to 1 April 2009 this work was carried out by three separate organisations: the Healthcare Commission, the Mental Health Act Commission and the Commission for Social Care Inspection. The CQC is responsible for the registration of health and social care providers, the monitoring and inspection of all health and adult social care, issuing fines, public warnings or closures if standards are not met and for undertaking regular performance reviews. Since April 2007 the Office for Standards in Education, Children's Services and Skills (Ofsted) has been responsible for inspecting and regulating all care services for children and young people in England. Both Ofsted and CQC collate information on local care services and make this information available to the public.

The Care and Social Services Inspectorate Wales (CSSIW), an operationally independent part of the Welsh government, is reponsible for the regulation and inspection of all social care services in Wales. A new unified body, Social Care and Social Work Improvement Scotland, was established on 1 April 2011, replacing the Scottish Commission for the Regulation of Care (the Care Commission) and is now the independent care services regulator for Scotland.

The Department of Health, Social Services and Public Safety is responsible for social care services in Northern Ireland.

CARE QUALITY COMMISSION (CQC), Citygate, Gallowgate, Newcastle upon Tyne NE1 4PA
T 0300-061 6161 E enquiries@cqc.org.uk
W www.cqc.org.uk

OFFICE FOR STANDARDS IN EDUCATION, CHILDREN'S SERVICES AND SKILLS (Ofsted), Piccadilly Gate, Store Street, Manchester M1 2WD
T 0300-123 1231 E enquiries@ofsted.gov.uk
W www.ofsted.gov.uk

CARE AND SOCIAL SERVICES INSPECTORATE WALES (CSSIW), Cathays Park, Cardiff CF10 3NQ
T 01443-848450 E cssiw@wales.gsi.gov.uk
W www.cssiw.org.uk

SOCIAL CARE AND SOCIAL WORK IMPROVEMENT SCOTLAND, Compass House, 11 Riverside Drive, Dundee DD1 4NY T 0845-600 9527
E enquiries@scswis.com W www.scswis.com

DEPARTMENT OF HEALTH, SOCIAL SERVICES AND PUBLIC SAFETY, Castle Buildings, Stormont, Belfast BT4 3SJ T 028-9052 0500 E webmaster@dhsspsni.gov.uk
W www.dhsspsni.gov.uk

STAFF

Total Social Services Staff (England, full-time)	197,400
Area office/field work	110,700
Residential care staff	39,700
Day care staff	24,500
Central and strategic staff	20,200
Other staff	2,500

Source: Department of Health

OLDER PEOPLE

Services for older people are designed to enable them to remain living in their own homes for as long as possible. Local authority services include advice, domestic help, meals in the home, alterations to the home to aid mobility, emergency alarm systems, day and/or night attendants, laundry services and the provision of day centres and recreational facilities. Charges may be made for these services. Respite care may also be provided in order to allow carers temporary relief from their responsibilities.

Local authorities and the private sector also provide 'sheltered housing' for older people, sometimes with resident wardens.

If an older person is admitted to a residential home, charges are made according to a means test; if the person cannot afford to pay, the costs are met by the local authority.

DISABLED PEOPLE

Services for disabled people are designed to enable them to remain living in their own homes wherever possible. Local authority services include advice, adaptations to the home, meals in the home, help with personal care, occupational therapy, educational facilities and recreational facilities. Respite care may also be provided in order to allow carers temporary relief from their responsibilities.

Special housing may be available for disabled people who can live independently, and residential accommodation for those who cannot.

FAMILIES AND CHILDREN

Local authorities are required to provide services aimed at safeguarding the welfare of children in need and, wherever possible, allowing them to be brought up by their families. Services include advice, counselling, help in the home and the provision of family centres. Many authorities also provide short-term refuge accommodation for women and children.

DAY CARE

In allocating day care places to children, local authorities give priority to children with special needs, whether in

terms of their health, learning abilities or social needs. Since September 2001 Ofsted has been responsible for the regulation and registration of all early years childcare and education provision in England (previously the responsibility of the local authorities). All day care and childminding services that care for children under eight years of age for more than two hours a day must register with Ofsted and are inspected at least every two years. As at 30 June 2011 there were 95,774 registered childcare providers in England.

CHILD PROTECTION

Children considered to be at risk of physical injury, neglect or sexual abuse are placed on the local authority's child protection register. Local authority social services staff, schools, health visitors and other agencies work together to prevent and detect cases of abuse. As at 31 March 2010, there was a total of 46,705 children on child protection registers or subject to a child protection plan in the UK. In England, there were 39,100 children on child protection registers, of these, 17,200 were at risk of neglect, 4,700 of physical abuse, 2,200 of sexual abuse and 11,400 of emotional abuse. At 31 March 2010 there were 2,730 children on child protection registers in Wales, 2,518 in Scotland and 2,357 in Northern Ireland.

LOCAL AUTHORITY CARE

Local authorities are required to provide accommodation for children who have no parents or guardians or whose parents or guardians are unable or unwilling to care for them. A family proceedings court may also issue a care order where a child is being neglected or abused, or is not attending school; the court must be satisfied that this would positively contribute to the well-being of the child.

The welfare of children in local authority care must be properly safeguarded. Children may be placed with foster families, who receive payments to cover the expenses of caring for the child or children, or in residential care.

Children's homes may be run by the local authority or by the private or voluntary sectors; all homes are subject to inspection procedures. As at 31 March 2010, 64,400 children in the UK were in the care of local authorities, of these, 47,200 were in foster placements and 6,200 were in children's homes, hostels or secure units.

ADOPTION

Local authorities are required to provide an adoption service, either directly or via approved voluntary societies. In 2009–10, there were 2,300 children aged under 18 entered in the adopted children register in the UK.

PEOPLE WITH LEARNING DISABILITIES

Services for people with learning disabilities are designed to enable them to remain living in the community wherever possible. Local authority services include short-term care, support in the home, the provision of day care centres, and help with other activities outside the home. Residential care is provided for the severely or profoundly disabled.

MENTALLY ILL PEOPLE

Under the care programme approach, mentally ill people should be assessed by specialist services and receive a care plan, and a key worker should be appointed for each patient. Regular reviews of the person's progress should be conducted. Local authorities provide help and advice to mentally ill people and their families, and places in day centres and social centres. Social workers can apply for a mentally disturbed person to be compulsorily detained in hospital. Where appropriate, mentally ill people are provided with accommodation in special hospitals, local authority accommodation, or at homes run by private or voluntary organisations. Patients who have been discharged from hospitals may be placed on a supervision register.

NATIONAL INSURANCE

The National Insurance (NI) scheme operates under the Social Security Contributions and Benefits Act 1992 and the Social Security Administration Act 1992, and orders and regulations made thereunder. The scheme is financed by contributions payable by earners, employers and others (*see* below). Money collected under the scheme is used to finance the National Insurance Fund (from which contributory benefits are paid) and to contribute to the cost of the National Health Service.

NATIONAL INSURANCE FUND

Estimated receipts, payments and statement of balances of the National Insurance Fund for 2011–12:

Receipts	£ million
Net national insurance contributions	80,195
Compensation from the Consolidated Fund for statutory sick, maternity, paternity and adoption pay recoveries	2,106
Income from investments	358
State scheme premiums	77
Other receipts	49
TOTAL RECEIPTS	82,784

Payments	£ million
Benefits	
At present rates	79,062
Increase due to proposed rate changes	3,233
Personal and stakeholder pensions contracted-out rebates	2,011
Age-related rebates for contracted-out money purchase schemes	195
Administration costs	1,377
Redundancy fund payments	308
Transfer to Northern Ireland	157
Other payments	137
TOTAL PAYMENTS	86,480

Balances	£ million
Opening balance	44,089
Excess of receipts over payments	(3,696)
BALANCE AT END OF YEAR	40,394

CONTRIBUTIONS

There are six classes of National Insurance contributions (NICs):

Class 1	paid by employees and their employers
Class 1A	paid by employers who provide employees with certain benefits in kind for private use, such as company cars
Class 1B	paid by employers who enter into a pay as you earn (PAYE) settlement agreement with HM Revenue and Customs
Class 2	paid by self-employed people
Class 3	voluntary contributions paid to protect entitlement to the state pension for those who do not pay enough NI contributions in another class
Class 4	paid by the self-employed on their taxable profits over a set limit. These are normally paid by self-employed people in addition to class 2 contributions. Class 4 contributions do not count towards benefits.

The lower and upper earnings limits and the percentage rates referred to below apply from April 2011 to April 2012.

CLASS 1

Class 1 contributions are paid where a person:
- is an employed earner (employee), office holder (eg company director) or employed under a contract of service in Great Britain or Northern Ireland
- is 16 or over and under state pension age
- earns at or above the earnings threshold of £139 per week (including overtime pay, bonus, commission, etc, without deduction of superannuation contributions)

Class 1 contributions are made up of primary and secondary contributions. Primary contributions are those paid by the employee and these are deducted from earnings by the employer. Since 6 April 2001 the employee's and employer's earnings thresholds have been the same and are referred to as the earnings threshold. Primary contributions are not paid on earnings below the earnings threshold of £139.00 per week. However, between the lower earnings limit of £102.00 per week and the earnings threshold of £139.00 per week, NI contributions are treated as having been paid to protect the benefit entitlement position of lower earners. Contributions are payable at the rate of 12 per cent on earnings between the earnings threshold and the upper earnings limit of £817.00 per week (10.4 per cent for contracted-out employment). Above the upper earnings limit 2 per cent is payable.

Some married women or widows pay a reduced rate of 5.85 per cent on earnings between the earnings threshold and upper earnings limits and 2 per cent above this. It is no longer possible to elect to pay the reduced rate but those who had reduced liability before 12 May 1977 may retain it for as long as certain conditions are met.

Secondary contributions are paid by employers of employed earners at the rate of 13.8 per cent on all earnings above the earnings threshold of £139.00 per week. There is no upper earnings limit for employers' contributions. Employers operating contracted-out salary related schemes pay reduced contributions of 10.1 per cent; those with contracted-out money-purchase schemes pay 12.4 per cent. The contracted-out rate applies only to that portion of earnings between the earnings threshold and the upper earnings limit. Employers' contributions below and above those respective limits are assessed at the appropriate not contracted-out rate.

CLASS 2

Class 2 contributions are paid where a person is self-employed and is 16 or over and under state pension age. Contributions are paid at a flat rate of £2.50 per week regardless of the amount earned. However, those with earnings of less than £5,315 a year can apply for small earnings exception. Those granted exemption from class 2 contributions may pay class 2 or class 3 contributions voluntarily. Self-employed earners (whether or not they pay class 2 contributions) may also be liable to pay class 4 contributions based on profits. There are special rules for those who are concurrently employed and self-employed.

Married women and widows can no longer choose not to pay class 2 contributions but those who elected not to pay class 2 contributions before 12 May 1977 may retain the right for as long as certain conditions are met.

Class 2 contributions are collected by the national insurance contributions department of HM Revenue and Customs (HMRC), by direct debit or quarterly bills.

CLASS 3

Class 3 contributions are voluntary flat-rate contributions of £12.60 per week payable by persons over the age of 16 who would otherwise be unable to qualify for retirement pension and certain other benefits because they have an insufficient record of class 1 or class 2 contributions. This may include those who are not working, those not liable for class 1 or class 2 contributions, or those excepted from class 2 contributions. Married women and widows who on or before 11 May 1977 elected not to pay class 1 (full rate) or class 2 contributions cannot pay class 3 contributions while they retain this right. Class 3 contributions are collected by HMRC by quarterly bills or direct debit.

CLASS 4

Self-employed people whose profits and gains are over £7,225 a year pay class 4 contributions in addition to class 2 contributions. This applies to self-employed earners over 16 and under the state pension age. Class 4 contributions are calculated at 9 per cent of annual profits or gains between £7,225 and £42,475 and 2 per cent above. Class 4 contributions are assessed and collected by HMRC. It is possible, in some circumstances, to apply for exceptions from liability to pay class 4 contributions or to have the amount of contribution reduced.

PENSIONS

Many people will qualify for a state pension; however, there are further pension choices available, such as personal and stakeholder pensions. There are also other non-pension savings and investment options. The following section provides background information on existing pension schemes.

STATE PENSION SCHEME
The state pension scheme consists of:
* basic state pension
* additional state pension

People may be able to get both or either when they reach state pension age and meet the qualifying conditions.

The state pension does not have to be claimed at state pension age, people can delay claiming it to earn extra weekly state pension or a lump sum payment.

Basic State Pension
The amount of basic state pension paid is dependent on the number of 'qualifying years' a person has established during their working life. In 2011–12, the full basic state pension is £102.15 a week (*see also* Benefits, State Pension: Categories A and B).

Working Life
Generally a working life is counted from the start of the tax year (6 April) in which a person reaches 16 to the end of the tax year (5 April) before the one in which they reach state pension age (*see* State Pension Age).

Qualifying Years
A 'qualifying year' is a tax year in which a person has sufficient earnings upon which they have paid, are treated as having paid, or have been credited with national insurance (NI) contributions (*see* National Insurance Credits section).

Since 6 April 2010, a person who has 30 qualifying years will be entitled to a full basic state pension. Someone with less than 30 qualifying years will be entitled to a proportion of the full basic state pension based on the number of qualifying years they have. Just one qualifying year, achieved through paid or credited contributions, will give entitlement to the basic state pension worth one-thirtieth of the full basic state pension.

Until 6 April 2010, women normally needed 39 qualifying years for a full basic state pension (£102.15 in 2011–12) and men normally needed 44 qualifying years. A reduced-rate basic state pension was payable if the number of qualifying years was less than 90 per cent of the working life, but to receive any basic state pension at all, a person must have had enough qualifying years, normally 10 or 11, to receive a basic state pension of at least 25 per cent of the standard rate.

National Insurance Credits
Those in receipt of carer's allowance, working tax credit (with a disability element), jobseeker's allowance, incapacity benefit, employment support allowance, unemployability supplement, statutory sick pay, statutory maternity pay or statutory adoption pay may have class 1 NI contributions credited to them each week. People may also get credits if they are unemployed and looking for work or too sick to work, even if they have not paid enough contributions to receive benefit. Since April 2010, spouses and civil partners of members of HM forces may get credits if they are on an accompanied assignment

outside the UK. Persons undertaking certain training courses or jury service or who have been wrongly imprisoned for a conviction which is quashed on appeal may also get class 1 NI credits for each week they fulfil certain conditions. Class 1 credits may also be available to men approaching state pension age. Until 5 April 2010, these credits were awarded for the tax years in which they reached age 60 and continued until age 64, if they were not liable to pay contributions and were not absent from the UK for more than six months in any tax year. Since 6 April 2010 these credits are being phased out in line with the increase in women's state pension age. Since 6 April 2010, spouses and civil partners who are accompanying members of HM forces on an assignment outside the UK can also apply for class 1 credits. Class 1 NI credits count toward all future contributory benefits. A class 3 NI credit for basic state pension and bereavement benefit purposes is awarded, where required, for each week the working tax credit (without a disability element) has been received or child benefit, for a child under 12, has been received. Class 3 credits may also be awarded, on application, to approved foster carers and people caring for at least 20 hours a week. Before 6 April 2010 class 3 credits were automatically awarded to young people in the tax years of their 16th, 17th and 18th birthdays if they did not work or earn enough to pay NI contributions. Since 6 April 2010 these credits are no longer awarded.

State Pension Age
State pension age is currently 60 for men and between 60 and 65 for women. However, this is planned to increase to 66 in 2020. Further information can be obtained from the online state pension calculator (W www.direct.gov.uk/en/pensionsandretirementplanning/statepension).

Using the NI Contribution Record of Another Person to Claim a State Pension
Married people or civil partners whose own NI record is incomplete may get a lower-rate basic state pension calculated using their partner's NI contribution record. This can be up to £61.20 a week in April 2011–12. Married men and civil partners may only be able to qualify if their wife or civil partner was born on or after 6 April 1950. A state pension may also be payable to widows, widowers, surviving civil partners, and people who are divorced or whose civil partnership has been dissolved, based on their late or ex-spouse's/civil partner's NI contributions.

Non-contributory State Pensions
A non-contributory state pension may be payable to those aged 80 or over who live in England, Scotland or Wales, and have done so for a total of ten years or more for any continuous period in the 20 years after their 60th birthday, if they are not entitled to another category of state pension, or are entitled to one below the rate of £61.20 a week in 2011–12 (*see also* Benefits, State Pension for people aged 80 and over).

Graduated Retirement Benefit
Graduated Retirement Benefit (GRB) is based on the amount of graduated NI contributions paid into the GRB scheme between April 1961 and April 1975 (*see also* Benefits, Graduated Retirement Benefit).

Home Responsibilities Protection
From 6 April 1978 until 5 April 2010, it was possible for people who had low income or were unable to work because they cared for children or a sick or disabled

person at home to reduce the number of qualifying years required for basic state pension. This was called home responsibilities protection (HRP); the number of years for which HRP was given was deducted from the number of qualifying years needed. HRP could, in some cases, also qualify the recipient for additional state pension. From April 2003 to April 2010 HRP was also available to approved foster carers.

From 6 April 2010, HRP was replaced by weekly credits for parents and carers. A class 3 national insurance credit is given, where eligible, towards basic pension and bereavement benefits for spouses and civil partners. An earnings factor credit towards additional state pension is also awarded. Any years of HRP accrued before 6 April 2010 have been converted into qualifying years of credits for people reaching state pension age after that date, up to a maximum of 22 years for basic state pension purposes.

Additional State Pension
The amount of additional state pension paid depends on the amount of earnings a person has, or is treated as having, between the lower and upper earnings limits (from April 2009, the upper accruals point replaced the upper earnings limit for additional pension) for each complete tax year between 6 April 1978 (when the scheme started) and the tax year before they reach state pension age. The right to additional state pension does not depend on the person's right to basic state pension.

From 1978 to 2002, additional state pension was called the State Earnings-Related Pension Scheme (SERPS). SERPS covered all earnings by employees from 6 April 1978 to 5 April 1997 on which standard rate class 1 NI contributions had been paid, and earnings between 6 April 1997 and 5 April 2002 if the standard rate class 1 NI contributions had been contracted-in.

In 2002, SERPS was reformed through the state second pension, by improving the pension available to low and moderate earners and extending access to certain carers and people with long-term illness or disability. If earnings on which class 1 NI contributions have been paid or can be treated as paid are above the annual NI lower earnings limit (£5,304 for 2011–12) but below the statutory low earnings threshold (£14,400 for 2011–12), the state second pension regards this as earnings of £14,400 and it is treated as equivalent. Certain carers and people with long-term illness and disability will be considered as having earned at the low earnings threshold for each complete tax year since 2002–3 even if they do not work at all, or earn less than the annual NI lower earnings limit.

The amount of additional state pension paid also depends on when a person reaches state pension age; changes phased in from 6 April 1999 mean that pensions are calculated differently from that date.

Inheritance
Men or women widowed before 6 October 2002 can inherit all of their late spouse's SERPS pension. From 6 October 2002, the maximum percentage of SERPS pension that a person can inherit from a late spouse or civil partner depends on their late spouse or civil partner's date of birth:

Maximum SERPS entitlement	d.o.b (men)	d.o.b (women)
100%	5/10/37 or earlier	5/10/42 or earlier
90%	6/10/37 to 5/10/39	6/10/42 to 5/10/44
80%	6/10/39 to 5/10/41	6/10/44 to 5/10/46
70%	6/10/41 to 5/10/43	6/10/46 to 5/10/48
60%	6/10/43 to 5/10/45	6/10/48 to 5/7/50
50%	6/10/45 or later	6/7/50 or later

The maximum state second pension a person can inherit from a late spouse or civil partner is 50 per cent. If a person is bereaved before they have reached their state pension age, inherited SERPS or state second pension can be paid as part of widowed parents allowance (in the case of a person who has dependent children) or otherwise only from state pension age.

Pension Forecasts
The Pension Service provides a state pension forecasting service. A state pension forecast provides an estimate of the current value of an individual's state pension, based on information held on their NI record, and an estimate of what it may be worth when they reach state pension age. There is also an online state pension profiler which, based on information input by individuals, tells the user their state pension age, an estimate of their basic state pension and how they are affected by changes to the state pension (T 0845-300 0168 W www.direct.gov.uk/pensionsandretirementplanning).

CONTRACTED-OUT PENSIONS

'Contracting-out' means leaving the state second pension scheme. There are two main types of contracting-out:
• occupational pension scheme
• personal pension scheme or stakeholder pension scheme (also known as an appropriate scheme)

Contracting-Out with an Occupational Pension Scheme
An occupational pension scheme is an arrangement some employers set up to give the people who work for them a pension when they retire. There are two main types of occupational pension schemes:
• salary-related (also known as defined benefit)
• money purchase (also known as defined contribution)
In contracting-out with a money purchase scheme, both the scheme member and the employer pay a reduced rate of NI contributions (the contracted-out rebate) to compensate for the state pension given up. In addition, at the end of each tax year, HM Revenue and Customs (HMRC) pays an additional age-related rebate direct to the scheme for investment on behalf of the employee.

In contracting-out with personal pension scheme or stakeholder pension schemes, an individual pays standard NI contributions and at the end of the tax year, HMRC pays an age-related rebate, together with tax relief on the employee's share of the rebate, directly into the scheme to be invested on behalf of the employee. These payments are known as 'minimum contributions'.

Contracting-out of the state second pension through money purchase, personal pension scheme and stakeholder pension scheme arrangements is to be abolished from 6 April 2012. From this date, employees will not be able to contract-out of the state second pension on this basis. Anyone contracted-out on this basis at that time will automatically be contracted back into the additional state pension. However, those rights built up before the abolition date will be used to provide pension benefits. These changes will not affect contracting-out via a salary-related occupational pension scheme.

Contracted-Out Salary-Related (COSR) Scheme
• these schemes (also known as contracted-out defined benefit (DB) schemes) provide a pension related to earnings and the length of pensionable service

- any notional additional state pension built up from 6 April 1978 to 5 April 1997 will be reduced by the amount of guaranteed minimum pension (GMP) accrued during that period (the contracted-out deduction)
- since 6 April 1997 these schemes no longer provide a GMP. Instead, as a condition of contracting-out they have to satisfy a reference scheme test to ensure that the benefits provided are at least as good as a prescribed standard
- when someone contracts-out of the additional state pension through a COSR scheme, both the scheme member and the employer pay a reduced rate of NI contributions (known as the contracted-out rebate) to compensate for the additional state pension given up

Contracted-Out Mixed Benefit (COMB) Scheme
A mixed benefit scheme is a single scheme with both a salary-related section and a money purchase section. Scheme rules set out which section individual employees may join and the circumstances (if any), in which members may move between sections. Each section must satisfy the respective contracting-out conditions for COSR and COMP schemes.

For more information on contracted-out pension schemes *see* the Department for Work and Pensions' leaflet *Contracted-out Pensions* (PM7).

STAKEHOLDER PENSION SCHEMES
Introduced in 2001, stakeholder pensions are available to everyone but are principally for moderate earners who do not have access to a good value company pension scheme. Stakeholder pensions must meet a number of minimum standards to make sure they are flexible, portable and annual management charges are capped. The minimum contribution is £20.

As with personal pensions it is possible to invest up to £3,600 (including tax relief) into stakeholder pensions each year without evidence of earnings. Contributions can be made on someone else's behalf, for example a non-working partner.

Stakeholder pensions can also be used by employees to contract-out of the additional state pension. For more information *see* Contracted-Out Appropriate Personal Pension Schemes (including Appropriate Stakeholder Pension Schemes).

COMPLAINTS
The Pensions Advisory Service provides information and guidance to members of the public, on state, company, personal and stakeholder schemes. They also help any member of the public who has a problem, complaint or dispute with their occupational or personal pensions.

There are two bodies for pension complaints. The Financial Ombudsman Service deals with complaints which predominantly concern the sale and/or marketing of occupational, stakeholder and personal pensions. The Pensions Ombudsman deals with complaints which predominantly concern the management (after sale or marketing) of occupational, stakeholder and personal pensions.

The Pensions Regulator is the UK regulator for work-based pension schemes; it concentrates its resources on schemes where there is the greatest risk to the security of members' benefits, promotes good administration practice for all work-based schemes and works with trustees, employers and professional advisers to put things right when necessary.

WAR PENSIONS AND THE ARMED FORCES COMPENSATION SCHEME
The Service Personnel and Veterans Agency (SPVA) is part of the Ministry of Defence. SPVA was formed on 1 April 2007 from the former Armed Forces Personnel Administration Agency and the Veterans Agency to provide services to both serving personnel and veterans.

SPVA is responsible for the administration of the war pensions scheme and the armed forces compensation scheme (AFCS) to members of the armed forces in respect of disablement or death due to service. There is also a scheme for civilians and civil defence workers in respect of the Second World War, and other schemes for groups such as merchant seamen and Polish armed forces who served under British command during the Second World War. The agency is also responsible for the administration of the armed forces pension scheme, which provides occupational pensions for ex-service personnel *(see* Defence).

THE WAR PENSIONS SCHEME
War disablement pension is awarded for the disabling effects of any injury, wound or disease which was the result of, or was aggravated by, service in the armed forces prior to 6 April 2005. Claims are only considered once the person has left the armed forces. The amount of pension paid depends on the severity of disablement, which is assessed by comparing the health of the claimant with that of a healthy person of the same age and sex. The person's earning capacity or occupation are not taken into account in this assessment. A pension is awarded if the person has a disablement of 20 per cent or more and a lump sum is usually payable to those with a disablement of less than 20 per cent. No award is made for noise-induced sensorineural hearing loss where the assessment of disablement is less than 20 per cent.

A pension is payable to war widows, widowers and surviving civil partners where the spouse's or civil partner's death was due to, or hastened by, service in the armed forces prior to 6 April 2005 or where the spouse or civil partner was in receipt of a war disablement pension constant attendance allowance (or would have been if not in hospital) at the time of death. A pension is also payable to widows, widowers or surviving civil partners if the spouse or civil partner was receiving the war disablement pension at the 80 per cent rate or higher in conjunction with unemployability supplement at the time of death. War widows, widowers and surviving civil partners receive a standard rank-related rate, but a lower weekly rate is payable to war widows, widowers and surviving civil partners of personnel of the rank of Major or below who are under the age of 40, without children and capable of maintaining themselves. This is increased to the standard rate at age 40. Allowances are paid for children (in addition to child benefit) and adult dependants. An age allowance is automatically given when the widow, widower or surviving civil partner reaches 65 and increased at ages 70 and 80.

Pensioners living overseas receive the same pension rates as those living in the UK. All war disablement pensions and allowances and pensions for war widows, widowers and surviving civil partners are tax-free in the UK; this does not always apply in overseas countries due to different tax laws.

SUPPLEMENTARY ALLOWANCES
A number of supplementary allowances may be awarded to a war pensioner and are intended to meet various needs.

The principal supplementary allowances are unemployability supplement, allowance for lowered standard of occupation and constant attendance allowance. Others include exceptionally severe disablement allowance, severe disablement occupational allowance, treatment allowance, mobility supplement, comforts allowance, clothing allowance, age allowance and widow/widower/surviving civil partner's age allowance. Rent and children's allowances are also available on pensions for war widows, widowers and surviving civil partners.

ARMED FORCES COMPENSATION SCHEME

The armed forces compensation scheme (AFCS) became effective on 6 April 2005 and covers all regular (including Gurkhas) and reserve personnel whose injury, ill health or death is caused by service on or after 6 April 2005. Ex-members of the armed forces who served prior to this date or who are in receipt of any pension under the war pensions scheme will continue to receive their pension and any associated benefits in the normal way.

The AFCS provides compensation where service in the armed forces is the only or main cause of injury, illness or death. Compensation can also be paid in certain exceptional circumstances to off-duty personnel; for example, to victims of a terrorist attack targeted owing to their position in the armed forces. Under the terms of the scheme a lump sum is payable to service or ex-service personnel based on a 15-level tariff, graduated according to the seriousness of the condition. A guaranteed income payment (GIP), payable for life, is received by those who could be expected to experience a serious loss of earning capability. A survivors GIP (SGIP) will also be paid to surviving spouses, civil partners and unmarried partners who meet certain criteria. GIP is calculated by multiplying the pensionable pay of the service person by a factor that depends on the age at the person's last birthday. The younger the person, the higher the factor, because there are more years to normal retirement age.

DEPARTMENT FOR WORK AND PENSIONS BENEFITS

Most benefits are paid in addition to those in receipt of payments under the AFCS and the war pensions scheme, but may be affected by any supplementary allowances in payment. Any state pension for which a war widow, widower or surviving civil partner qualifies for on their own NI contribution record can be paid in addition to monies received under the war pensions scheme.

CLAIMS AND QUESTIONS

Further information on the war pensions scheme, the armed forces compensation scheme and the nearest Veterans' Welfare Office can be obtained from the Service Personnel and Veterans Agency by telephone (T 0800-169 2277, if calling from the UK or, if living overseas, T (+44) (125) 386-6043).

SERVICE PERSONNEL AND VETERANS AGENCY,
Norcross, Thornton-Cleveleys FY5 3WP
E veterans.help@spva.gsi.gov.uk W www.veterans-uk.info

TAX CREDITS

Tax credits are administered by HM Revenue and Customs (HMRC). They are based on an individual's or couple's household income and current circumstances. Adjustments can be made during the year to reflect changes in income and/or circumstances. Further information regarding the qualifying conditions for tax credits, how to claim and the rates payable is available online on the HMRC website (W www.hmrc.gov.uk/taxcredits).

WORKING TAX CREDIT

Working tax credit is a payment from the government to support people on low incomes. It may be claimed by:
- those aged 25 or over who work at least 30 hours a week
- both partners in a couple who are responsible for a child or young person, who work at least 16 hours a week
- those aged 16 or over who work at least 16 hours a week, who are responsible for a child or young person, or have a disability that puts them at a disadvantage of getting a job
- from April 2011, those aged 60 or over, who work at least 16 hours a week
- from April 2012, couples who are responsible for a child or young person, who must work at least 24 hours per week between them with one partner working at least 16 hours a week

The amount received depends on the circumstances and number of hours worked a week.

WORKING TAX CREDIT FOR INDIVIDUALS WITHOUT CHILDREN 2011–12

Annual Income/Status	Tax Credit per annum
£4,996*	
Single	–
Couple	–
Single adult with a disability	£4,575
£9,368†	
Single	£1,500
Couple	£3,450
Single adult with a disability	£4,155
£10,000	
Single	£1,240
Couple	£3,195
Single adult with a disability	£3,895
£15,000	
Single	–
Couple	£1,145
Single adult with a disability	£1,845

* An annual income of £4,996 represents the 2011–2012 income of an adult working 16 hours a week at the national minimum wage: six months at the 2010–2011 rate of £5.93 a hour and six months at the rate of £6.08 a hour (national minimum wage from October 2011)

† Income of £9,368 represents the income of an adult working 30 hours a week at the national minimum wage rate (*see* above for explanation). For families with an income of £10,000 or above, it is assumed that at least one individual works 30 hours. From April 2012, couples who are responsible for a child or a young person have to be working at least 24 hours a week between them, with one partner working at least 16 hours a week

CHILDCARE

In families with children where a lone parent works at least 16 hours a week or both partners in a couple work at least 16 hours a week (from April 2012 couples must work at least 24 hours a week between them, with one partner working at least 16 hours a week) or where one partner works and the other is disabled, an in-patient in hospital, or in prison, the family is entitled to the childcare element of working tax credit. This payment can contribute up to 70 per cent of childcare costs up to a maximum of £175 a week for one child and up to £300 a week for two or more children. Families can only claim if they use an approved or registered childcare provider.

CHILD TAX CREDIT

Child tax credit combines all income-related support for children and is paid direct to the main carer. The credit is made up of a main 'family' payment with additional payments for each extra child in the household, for children with a disability and an extra payment for children who are severely disabled. Child tax credit is available to households where:
- there is at least one dependant under 16
- there is at least one dependant between 16 and 20 who is in relevant education or training or is registered for work, education or training with an approved body

CHILD TAX CREDIT AND WORKING TAX CREDIT
2011–12 *(£ per annum)*

Annual Income	One Child No Childcare	One Child Maximum Childcare	Two Children No Childcare	Two Children Maximum Childcare
0	3,100	3,100	5,660	5,660
4.996*	6,975	13,345	9,530	20,450
9,368*	6,555	12,925	9,115	20,035
10,000†	6,295	12,665	8,855	19,775
15,000	4,245	10,615	6,805	17,725
20,000	2,195	8,565	4,755	15,675
25,000	545	6,515	2,705	13,625
30,000	545	4,465	655	11,575
35,000	545	2,415	545	9,525
40,000	545	545	545	7,475
45,000	–	–	–	5,425
50,000	–	–	–	5,015
60,000	–	–	–	4,605
65,000	–	–	–	4,195
70,000	–	–	–	3,785

* At income levels of £4,996 and £9,368 awards are shown for lone parents. At an income level of £4,996 the award is shown for a lone parent working part-time (between 16 and 30 hours a week). At an income level of £9,368 the award is shown for a lone parent working 30 hours a week

† At an income level of £10,000 and above awards are shown for a couple who are responsible for a child or young person, with both partners working at least 16 hours a week

BENEFITS

The following is intended as a general guide to the benefits system. Conditions of entitlement and benefit rates change annually and all prospective claimants should check exact entitlements and rates of benefit directly with their local Jobcentre Plus office, pension centre or online (W www.direct.gov.uk). Leaflets relating to the various benefits and contribution conditions for different benefits are available from local Jobcentre Plus offices.

CONTRIBUTORY BENEFITS

Entitlement to contributory benefits depends on national insurance contribution conditions being satisfied either by the claimant or by someone on the claimant's behalf (depending on the kind of benefit). The class or classes of national insurance contribution relevant to each benefit are:

Jobseeker's allowance (contribution-based)	Class 1
Incapacity benefit	Class 1 or 2
Employment and Support Allowance (contributory)	Class 1 or 2
Widow's benefit and bereavement benefit	Class 1, 2 or 3
State pensions, categories A and B	Class 1, 2 or 3

The system of contribution conditions relates to yearly levels of earnings on which national insurance (NI) contributions have been paid.

JOBSEEKER'S ALLOWANCE

Jobseeker's allowance (JSA) replaced unemployment benefit and income support for unemployed people under state pension age from 7 October 1996. There are two routes of entitlement. Contribution-based JSA is paid at a personal rate (ie additional benefit for dependants is not paid) to those who have made sufficient NI contributions in two particular tax years. Savings and partner's earnings are not taken into account and payment can be made for up to six months. Rates of JSA correspond to income support rates.

Claims are made through Jobcentre Plus. A person wishing to claim JSA must generally be unemployed or working on average less than 16 hours a week, capable of work and available for any work which he or she can reasonably be expected to do, usually for at least 40 hours a week. The claimant must agree and sign a 'jobseeker's agreement', which will set out his or her plans to find work, and must actively seek work. If the claimant refuses work or training the benefit may be sanctioned for between one and 26 weeks.

A person will be sanctioned from JSA for up to 26 weeks if he or she has left a job voluntarily without just cause or through misconduct. In these circumstances, it may be possible to receive hardship payments, particularly where the claimant or the claimant's family is vulnerable, eg if sick or pregnant, or with children or caring responsibilities.

Weekly Rates from April 2011

Person aged 16–24	£53.45
Person aged 25 to state pension age*	£67.50

* Since October 2003 people aged between 60 and state pension age can choose to claim pension credits instead of JSA

INCAPACITY BENEFIT

Since 31 January 2011 people can no longer make claims for incapacity benefit. Those seeking incapacity benefit should now claim employment and support allowance instead. Those claiming incapacity benefit prior to 31 January 2011 will continue to receive it for as long as they qualify, although it is intended that remaining recipients of incapacity benefit will be moved to employment and support allowance by 2014. There are three rates of incapacity benefit:

- short-term lower rate for the first 28 weeks of sickness
- short-term higher rate from weeks 29 to 52
- long-term rate from week 53 onwards

The terminally ill and those entitled to the highest rate care component of disability living allowance are paid the long-term rate after 28 weeks. Incapacity benefit is taxable after 28 weeks.

An age addition payment may be available where incapacity for work commenced before the age of 45. Increases are also available for adult dependants caring for children.

The 'personal capability' assessment is the main test for incapacity benefit claims. Claimants are assessed on their ability to carry out a range of work-related activities and may also be required to attend a medical examination. Incapacity benefit claimants (excluding people who are severely disabled and those who are terminally ill) are invited back for work-focused interviews at intervals of not longer than three years. The interviews do not include medical tests, but if the claimant is due for a medical test around the same time, their local office will aim to schedule both together.

Weekly Rates from April 2011

Short-term incapacity benefit lower rate

Person under state pension age	£71.10
Person over state pension age	£90.45

Short-term incapacity benefit higher rate

Person under state pension age	£84.15
Person over state pension age	£94.25

Long-term incapacity benefit

Person under state pension age	£94.25
Person over state pension age	–

EMPLOYMENT AND SUPPORT ALLOWANCE

From 27 October 2008, employment and support allowance (ESA) replaced incapacity benefit and income support paid on the grounds of incapacity or disability. The benefit consists of two strands, contribution-based benefit and income-related benefit, so that people no longer need to make two claims for benefit in order to gain their full entitlement. Contributory ESA is available to those who have limited capability for work but cannot get statutory sick pay from their employer. Those over pensionable age are not entitled to ESA. Apart from those who qualify under the special provisions for people incapacitated in youth, entitlement to contributory ESA is based on a person's NI contribution record. In order to qualify for contributory ESA, two contribution conditions, based on the last three years before the tax year in which benefit is claimed, must be satisfied. The amount of contributory ESA payable may be reduced where the person receives more than a specified amount of occupational or personal pension. Contributory ESA is paid only in respect of the person claiming the benefit – there are no additional amounts for dependants.

At the outset, new claimants are paid a basic allowance (the same rate as jobseeker's allowance) for 13 weeks while their medical condition is assessed and a work capability assessment is conducted. Following the completion of the assessment phase those claimants capable of engaging in work-related activities will receive a work-related activity component on top of the basic rate. The work-related activity component can be subject to sanctions if the claimant does not engage in the conditionality requirements without good reason. The maximum sanction is equal to the value of the work-related activity component of the benefit.

Those with the most severe health conditions or disabilities will receive the support component, which is more than the work-related activity component. Claimants in receipt of the support component are not required to engage in work-related activities, although they can volunteer to do so or undertake permitted work if their condition allows.

Weekly Rates from April 2011

ESA plus work-related activity component	up to £94.25
ESA plus support component	up to £99.85

BEREAVEMENT BENEFITS
Bereavement benefits replaced widow's benefit on 9 April 2001. Those claiming widow's benefit before this date will continue to receive it under the old scheme for as long as they qualify. The new system provides bereavement benefits for widows, widowers and, from 5 December 2005, surviving civil partners (providing that their deceased spouse or civil partner paid NI contributions). The new system offers benefits in three forms:

- *Bereavement payment* – may be received by a man or woman who is under the state pension age at the time of their spouse or civil partner's death, or whose husband, wife or civil partner was not entitled to a category A retirement pension when he or she died. It is a single tax-free lump sum of £2,000 payable immediately on widowhood or loss of a civil partner
- *Widowed parent's allowance* – a taxable benefit payable to the surviving partner if he or she is entitled or treated as entitled to child benefit, or to a widow if she is expecting her husband's baby at the time of his death
- *Bereavement allowance* – a taxable weekly benefit paid for 52 weeks after the spouse or civil partner's death. If aged over 55 and under state pension age the full allowance is payable, if aged between 45 and 54 a percentage of the full rate is paid. A widow, widower or surviving civil partner may receive this allowance if his or her widowed parent's allowance ends before 52 weeks

It is not possible to receive widowed parent's allowance and bereavement allowance at the same time. Bereavement benefits and widow's benefit, in any form, cease upon remarriage or a new civil partnership or are suspended during a period of cohabitation as partners without being legally married or in a civil partnership.

Weekly Rates from April 2011

Bereavement payment (lump sum)	£2,000
Widowed parent's allowance (or widowed mother's allowance)	£100.70
Bereavement allowance (or widow's pension), full entitlement (aged 55 and over at time of spouse's or civil partner's death)	£100.70

Amount of bereavement allowance (or widow's pension) by age of widow/widower or surviving civil partner at spouse's or civil partner's death:

aged 54	£93.65
aged 53	£86.60
aged 52	£79.55
aged 51	£72.50
aged 50	£65.46
aged 49	£58.41
aged 48	£51.36
aged 47	£44.31
aged 46	£37.26
aged 45	£30.21

STATE PENSION: CATEGORIES A AND B
Category A pension is payable for life to men and women who reach state pension age, who satisfy the contributions conditions and who claim for it. Category B pension may be payable to married women, married men and civil partners who are not entitled to a basic state pension on their own NI contributions or whose own basic state pension entitlement is less than £61.20 a week in 2011–12. It is based on their wife's, husband's or civil partner's NI contributions and is payable when both members of the couple have reached state pension age. Married men and civil partners may only be able to qualify for a category B pension if their wife or civil partner was born on or after 6 April 1950. Category B pension is also payable to widows, widowers and surviving civil partners who are bereaved before state pension age if they were previously entitled to widowed parent's allowance or bereavement allowance based on their late spouse's or civil partner's NI contributions. If they were receiving widowed parent's allowance on reaching state pension age, they could qualify for a category B pension payable at the same rate as their widowed parent's allowance comprising a basic pension, plus, if applicable, the appropriate share of their late spouse's or late civil partner's additional state pension. If their widowed parent's allowance had stopped before they reached state pension age, or they had been getting bereavement allowance at any time before state pension age, their category B pension will consist of inheritable additional state pension only. No basic state pension is included, although they may qualify for a basic state pension or have their own basic state pension improved by substituting their late spouse's or late civil partner's NI records for their own.

Widows who are bereaved when over state pension age can qualify for a category B pension regardless of the age of their husband when he died. This is payable at the same rate as the basic state pension the widow's late husband was entitled to (or would have been entitled to) at the time of his death. It can also be paid to widowers and civil partners who are bereaved when over state pension age if their wife or civil partner had reached state pension age when they died. Widowers and surviving civil partners who reached state pension age on or after 6 April 2010 and bereaved when over state pension age can qualify for a category B pension regardless of the age of their wife or civil partner when they died.

Where a person is entitled to both a category A and category B pension then they can be combined to give a composite pension, but this cannot be more than the full rate pension. Where a person is entitled to more than one category A or category B pension then only one can be paid. In such cases the person can choose which to get; if no choice is made, the most favourable one is paid.

A person may defer claiming their pension beyond state pension age. In doing so they may earn increments which will increase the weekly amount paid by 1 per cent per five weeks of deferral (equivalent to 10.4 per cent/year) when they claim their state pension. If a person delays claiming for at least 12 months they are given the option of a one-off taxable lump sum, instead of a pension increase, based on the weekly pension deferred, plus interest of at least 2 per cent above the Bank of England base rate. Historically, if a married man deferred his category A pension, his wife could not claim a category B pension on his contributions but could earn increments on her state pension during this time. Since 6 April 2010, a category B pension has been treated independently of the spouse's or partner's pension. It is possible to take a category B pension even if the spouse or partner has deferred theirs.

It is no longer possible to claim an increase on a state pension for another adult (known as adult dependency increase). Those who received the increase before April 2010 can keep receiving it until the conditions are no longer met or until 5 April 2020, whichever is first.

Provision for children is made through child tax credits. An age addition of 25p a week is payable with a state pension if a pensioner is aged 80 or over.

Since 1989 pensioners have been allowed to have unlimited earnings without affecting their state pension. *See also* Pensions.

Weekly Rates from April 2011

Category A or B pension for a single person	£102.15
Maximum category B pension (married women)	£61.20
Increase for adult dependant	£61.20
Age addition at age 80	£0.25

GRADUATED RETIREMENT BENEFIT

Graduated retirement benefit (GRB) is based on the amount of graduated NI contributions paid into the GRB scheme between April 1961 and April 1975; however, it is still paid in addition to any state pension to those who made the relevant contributions. A person will receive graduated retirement benefit based on their own contributions, even if not entitled to a basic state pension. Widows, widowers and surviving civil partners may inherit half of their deceased spouse's or civil partner's entitlement, but none that the deceased spouse or civil partner may have been eligible for from a former spouse or civil partner. If a person defers making a claim beyond state pension age, they may earn an increase or a one-off lump sum payment in respect of their deferred graduated retirement benefit; calculated in the same way as for category A or B state pension.

NON-CONTRIBUTORY BENEFITS

These benefits are paid from general taxation and are not dependent on NI contributions.

JOBSEEKER'S ALLOWANCE (INCOME-BASED)

Those who do not qualify for contribution-based jobseeker's allowance (JSA), those who have exhausted their entitlement to contribution-based JSA or those for whom contribution-based JSA provides insufficient income may qualify for income-based JSA. The amount paid depends on age, whether they are single or a couple, number of dependants and amount of income and savings. Income-based JSA comprises three parts:

- a personal allowance for the jobseeker and his/her partner*
- premiums for people with special needs
- amounts for housing costs

* Since April 2003, child dependants have been provided for through the child tax credit system

The rules of entitlement are the same as for contribution-based JSA.

If one person in a couple was born after 28 October 1957 and neither person in the couple has responsibility for a child or children, then the couple will have to make a joint claim for JSA if they wish to receive income-based JSA.

Weekly Rates from April 2011

Person aged 16–24	£53.45
Person aged 25 to state pension age	£67.50
Couple with one or both under 18*	£53.45
Couple aged 18 to state pension age	£105.95
Lone parent aged under 18	£53.45
Lone parent aged 18 to state pension age	£67.50

* depending on circumstances

MATERNITY ALLOWANCE

Maternity allowance (MA) is a benefit available for pregnant women who cannot get statutory maternity pay (SMP) from their employer or have been employed/self-employed during or close to their pregnancy. In order to qualify for payment, a woman must have been employed and/or self-employed for at least 26 weeks in the 66-week period up to and including the week before the baby is due (test period). These weeks do not have to be in a row and any part weeks worked will count towards the 26 weeks. She must also have an average weekly earning of at least £30 (maternity allowance threshold) over any 13 weeks of the woman's choice within the test period.

Self-employed women who pay class 2 NI contributions or who hold a small earnings exception certificate are deemed to have enough earnings to qualify for MA.

A woman can choose to start receiving MA from the 11th week before the week in which the baby is due (if she stops work before then) up to the day following the day of birth. The exact date MA starts will depend on when the woman stops work to have her baby or if the baby is born before she stops work. However, where the woman is absent from work wholly or partly due to her pregnancy in the four weeks before the week the baby is due to be born, MA will start the day following the first day of absence from work. MA is paid for a maximum of 39 weeks.

The woman may be entitled to get extra payments for her husband, civil partner or someone else who looks after her children.

Weekly Rate from April 2011

Standard rate	£128.73 or 90 per cent of the woman's average weekly earnings if less than £128.73

CHILD BENEFIT

Child benefit is payable for virtually all children aged under 16 and for those aged 16 and 17 if they are in relevant education or training or are registered for work, education or training with an approved body.

Weekly Rates from April 2011

Eldest/only child	£20.30
Each subsequent child	£13.40

GUARDIAN'S ALLOWANCE

Guardian's allowance is payable to a person who is bringing up a child or young person because the child's parents have died, or in some circumstances, where only one parent has died. To receive the allowance the person must be in receipt of child benefit for the child or young person, although they do not have to be the child's legal guardian.

Weekly Rate (in addition to child benefit) from April 2011

Each child	£14.75

CARER'S ALLOWANCE

Carer's allowance (CA) is a benefit payable to people who spend at least 35 hours a week caring for a severely disabled person. To qualify for CA a person must be caring for someone in receipt of one of the following benefits:

* attendance allowance
* disability living allowance care component at the middle or highest rate
* constant attendance allowance, paid at not less than the normal maximum rate with an industrial injuries disablement payment or basic (full-day) rate, under the industrial injuries or war pension schemes.

Weekly Rate from April 2011

Carer's allowance	£55.55

SEVERE DISABLEMENT ALLOWANCE

Since April 2001 severe disablement allowance (SDA) has not been available to new claimants. Those claiming SDA before that date will continue to receive it for as long as they qualify.

Weekly Rates from April 2011

Basic rate	£62.95
Age related addition*:	
Under 40	£13.80
40–49	£7.10
50–59	£5.60

* The age addition applies to the age when incapacity began

ATTENDANCE ALLOWANCE

This may be payable to people aged 65 or over who need help with personal care because they are physically or mentally disabled, and who have needed help for a period of at least six months. Attendance allowance has two rates: the lower rate is for day or night care, and the higher rate is for day and night care. People not expected to live for more than six months because of a progressive disease can receive the highest rate of attendance allowance straight away.

Weekly Rates from April 2011

Higher rate	£73.60
Lower rate	£49.30

DISABILITY LIVING ALLOWANCE

This may be payable to people aged under 65 who have had personal care and/or mobility needs because of an illness or disability for a period of at least three months and are likely to have those needs for a further six months or more. The allowance has two components: the care component, which has three rates, and the mobility component, which has two rates. The rates depend on the care and mobility needs of the claimant. People not expected to live for more than six months because of a progressive disease will automatically receive the highest rate of the care component.

Weekly Rates from April 2011

Care component	
Higher rate	£73.60
Middle rate	£49.30
Lowest rate	£19.55
Mobility component	
Higher rate	£51.40
Lower rate	£19.55

STATE PENSION FOR PEOPLE AGED 80 AND OVER

A state pension, also referred to as category D pension, is provided for people aged 80 and over if they are not entitled to another category of pension or are entitled to a state pension that is less than £58.50 a week. The person must also live in Great Britain and have done so for a period of ten years or more in any continuous 20-year period since their 60th birthday.

Weekly Rate from April 2010

Single person	£58.50

INCOME SUPPORT

Broadly speaking income support is a benefit for those between age 16 and the age they can receive pension credit, whose income is below a certain level, who work on average less than 16 hours a week and who are:

* bringing up children alone
* registered sick or disabled
* a student who is also a lone parent or disabled
* caring for someone who is sick or elderly

Income support is not payable if the claimant, or claimant and partner, have capital or savings in excess of £16,000 – and deductions are made for capital and savings in excess of £6,000. For people permanently in residential care and nursing homes deductions apply for capital in excess of £10,000.

Sums payable depend on fixed allowances laid down by law for people in different circumstances. If both partners are eligible for income support, either may claim it for the couple. People receiving income support may be able to receive housing benefit, help with mortgage or home loan interest and help with healthcare. They may also be eligible for help with exceptional expenses from the Social Fund. Special rates may apply to some people living in residential care or nursing homes.

INCOME SUPPORT PREMIUMS

Income support premiums are extra weekly payments for those with additional needs. People qualifying for more than one premium will normally only receive the highest single premium for which they qualify. However, family premium, disabled child premium, severe disability premium and carer premium are payable in addition to other premiums.

Child tax credit replaced premiums for people with children for all new income support claims from 6 April

2004. People with children who were already in receipt of income support in April 2004 and have not claimed child tax credit may qualify for:
- the family premium if they have at least one child
- the disabled child premium if they have a child who receives disability living allowance or is registered blind
- the enhanced disability child premium if they have a child in receipt of the higher rate disability living allowance care component

Carers may qualify for:
- the carer premium if they or their partner are in receipt of carer's allowance

Long-term sick or disabled people may qualify for:
- the disability premium if they or their partner are receiving certain benefits because they are disabled or cannot work; are registered blind; or if the claimant has been incapable of work or receiving statutory sick pay for at least 364 days (196 days if the person is terminally ill), including periods of incapacity separated by eight weeks or less
- the severe disability premium if the person lives alone and receives the middle or higher rate of disability living allowance care component and no one receives carer's allowance for caring for that person
- the enhanced disability premium if the person is in receipt of the higher rate disability living allowance care component

People with a partner aged over 60 may qualify for:
- the pensioner premium

WEEKLY RATES OF INCOME SUPPORT
from April 2011

Single person

aged 16–24	£53.45
aged 25+	£67.50
aged under 18 and a single parent	£53.45
aged 18+ and a single parent	£67.50

Couples

Both under 18	£53.45
Both under 18, in certain circumstances	£80.75
One under 18, one aged 18–24	£53.45
One under 18, one aged 25+	£67.50
Both aged 18+	£105.95

Premiums

Carer premium	£31.00
Severe disability premium	£55.30
Enhanced disability premium	
Single person	£14.05
Couples	£20.25
Pensioner premium (couple)	£103.75

PENSION CREDIT
Pension credit was introduced on 6 October 2003 and replaced income support for those aged 60 and over. Between April 2010 and April 2020 the pension credit qualifying age is increasing from 60 to 65 alongside the increase in women's state pension age.

There are two elements to pension credit:

THE GUARANTEE CREDIT
The guarantee credit guarantees a minimum income of £137.75 for single people and £209.70 for couples, with additional elements for people who have:

- eligible housing costs
- severe disabilities
- caring responsibilities

Income from state pension, private pensions, earnings, working tax credit and certain benefits are taken into account when calculating the pension credit. For savings and capital in excess of £10,000, £1 for every £500 or part of £500 held is taken into account as income when working out entitlement to pension credit.

People receiving the guarantee credit element of pension credit will be able to receive housing benefit, council tax benefit and help with healthcare costs.

Weekly Rates from April 2011

Additional amount for severe disability

Single person	£55.30
Couple (one qualifies)	£55.30
Couple (both qualify)	£110.60
Additional amount for carers	£31.00

THE SAVINGS CREDIT
Single people aged 65 or over (and couples where one member is 65 or over) may be entitled to a savings credit which provides additional support for pensioners who have made modest provision towards their retirement. The savings credit is calculated by taking into account any qualifying income above the savings credit threshold. For 2011–12 the threshold is £103.15 for single people and £164.55 for couples. The savings credit gives pensioners a cash addition calculated at 60p for every pound of qualifying income they have between the savings credit threshold and the guarantee credit. After this, the maximum savings credit will be reduced by 40p for every pound of income above the guarantee level. The maximum savings credit is £20.52 per week (£27.09 a week for couples).

Income that qualifies towards the savings credit includes state pensions, earnings, second pensions and income taken into account from capital above £10,000.

Some people will be entitled to the guarantee credit, some to the savings credit and some to both.

Where only the savings credit is in payment, people need to claim standard housing benefit or council tax benefit. Although local authorities take any savings credit into account in the housing benefit or council tax benefit assessment, for people aged 65 and over housing benefit or council tax benefit is enhanced to ensure that gains in pension credit are not depleted.

HOUSING BENEFIT
Housing benefit is designed to help people with rent (including rent for accommodation in guesthouses, lodgings or hostels). It does not cover mortgage payments. The amount of benefit paid depends on:
- the income of the claimant, and partner if there is one, including earned income, unearned income (any other income including some other benefits) and savings
- number of dependants
- certain extra needs of the claimant, partner or any dependants
- number and gross income of people sharing the home who are not dependent on the claimant
- how much rent is paid

Housing benefit is not payable if the claimant, or claimant and partner, have savings in excess of £16,000. The amount of benefit is affected if savings held exceed £6,000 (£10,000 for people living in residential care and nursing homes). Housing benefit is not paid for meals, fuel or certain service charges that may be included in the rent. Deductions are also made for most non-dependants who live in the same accommodation as the claimant (and their partner). If the claimant is living with a partner or civil partner there can only be one claim.

The maximum amount of benefit (which is not necessarily the same as the amount of rent paid) may be paid where the claimant is in receipt of income support, income-based jobseeker's allowance, the guarantee element of pension credit or where the claimant's income is less than the amount allowed for their needs. Any income over that allowed for their needs will mean that their benefit is reduced.

LOCAL HOUSING ALLOWANCE

Local housing allowance (LHA), which was rolled out nationally from 7 April 2008, is a way of calculating the rent element of housing benefit based on the area in which a person lives and household size. It affects people in the deregulated private rented sector who make a new claim for housing benefit or existing recipients who move address. LHA ensures that tenants in similar circumstances in the same area receive the same amount of financial support for their housing costs. It does not affect the way a person's income or capital is taken into account. LHA is paid to the tenant rather than the landlord in most circumstances. From 1 April 2011, the rates for LHA were reduced across England and the maximum £15 weekly excess was removed. A weekly limit on payments is now in place so LHA does not exceed:

- £250 for a one bedroom property
- £290 for a two bedroom property
- £340 for a three bedroom property
- £400 for a four bedroom property

COUNCIL TAX BENEFIT

Nearly all the rules that apply to housing benefit apply to council tax benefit, which helps people on low incomes to pay council tax bills. The amount payable depends on how much council tax is paid and who lives with the claimant. The benefit may be available to those receiving income support, income-based jobseeker's allowance, the guarantee element of pension credit or to those whose income is less than that allowed for their needs. Any income over that allowed for their needs will mean that their council tax benefit is reduced. Deductions are made for non-dependants.

The maximum amount that is payable for those living in properties in council tax bands A to E is 100 per cent of the claimant's council tax liability. This also applies to those living in properties in bands F to H who were in receipt of the benefit at 31 March 1998 if they have remained in the same property.

If a person shares a home with one or more adults (not their partner) who are on a low income, it may be possible to claim a second council tax rebate. Those who are entitled to both council tax benefit and second adult rebate will be awarded whichever is the greater. Second adult rebate may be claimed by those not in receipt of or eligible for council tax benefit.

THE SOCIAL FUND

REGULATED PAYMENTS

Sure Start Maternity Grant

Sure start maternity grant (SSMG) is a one-off payment of £500 to help people on low incomes pay for essential items for new babies that are expected, born, adopted, the subject of a parental order (following a surrogate birth) or, in certain circumstances, the subject of a residency order. SSMG can be claimed any time from within 11 weeks of the expected birth and up to three months after the birth, adoption or date of parental or residency order. Those eligible are people in receipt of income support, income-based jobseeker's allowance, pension credit, child tax credit at a rate higher than the family element or working tax credit where a disability or severe disability element is in payment. Since 11 April 2011, new rules have been applied for babies due, born or adopted on this date. These are that SSMG is only available if there are no other children under 16 in the family or in the case of a dependent child's new baby, SSMG is only available if the dependent is under the age of 20 and has no other children.

Funeral Payments

Payable to help cover the necessary cost of burial or cremation, a new burial plot with an exclusive right of burial (where burial is chosen), certain other expenses, and up to £700 for any other funeral expenses, such as the funeral director's fees, the coffin or flowers. Those eligible are people receiving income support, income-based jobseeker's allowance, pension credit, child tax credit at a higher rate than the family element, working tax credit where a disability or severe disability element is in payment, council tax benefit or housing benefit who have good reason for taking responsibility for the funeral expenses. These payments are recoverable from any estate of the deceased.

Cold Weather Payments

A payment of £25.00 per seven day period between 1 November and 31 March when the average temperature is recorded at or forecast to be 0°C or below over seven consecutive days in the qualifying person's area. Payments are made to people on pension credit or child tax credit with a disability element, those on income support whose benefit includes a pensioner or disability premium, and those on income-based jobseeker's allowance or employment and support allowance who have a child who is disabled or under the age of five. Payments are made automatically and do not have to be repaid.

Winter Fuel Payments

For 2011–12 the winter fuel payment has been decreased to £200 for households with someone aged 60–79 and down to £300 for households with someone aged 80 or over. The rate paid is based on the person's age and circumstances in the 'qualifying week' between 19 and 25 September 2011. The majority of eligible people are paid automatically before Christmas, although a few need to claim. Payments do not have to be repaid.

Christmas Bonus

The Christmas bonus is a one-off tax-free £10 payment made before Christmas to those people in receipt of a qualifying benefit in the qualifying week.

DISCRETIONARY PAYMENTS

Community Care Grants

These are intended to help people in receipt of income support, income-based jobseeker's allowance or employment and support allowance, pension credit, or payments on account of such benefits (or those likely to receive these benefits within the next six weeks because they are leaving residential or institutional accommodation) to live as independently as possible in the community; ease exceptional pressures on families; care for a prisoner or young offender released on temporary licence; help people set up home as part of a resettlement programme and/or assist with certain travelling expenses. They do not have to be repaid.

Budgeting Loans
These are interest-free loans to people who have been receiving income support, income-based jobseeker's allowance or employment and support allowance, pension credit or payments on account of such benefits for at least 26 weeks, for intermittent expenses that may be difficult to budget for.

Crisis Loans
These are interest-free loans to anyone aged 16 or over, whether receiving benefits or not, who is without resources in an emergency or due to a disaster, where there is no other means of preventing serious damage or serious risk to their or their family members' health or safety.

SAVINGS
Savings over £500 (£1,000 for people aged 60 or over) are taken into account for community care grants and savings of £1,000 (£2,000 for people aged 60 or over) are taken into account for budgeting loans. All savings are taken into account for crisis loans. Savings are not taken into account for sure start maternity grant, funeral payments, cold weather payments, winter fuel payments or the Christmas bonus.

INDUSTRIAL INJURIES AND DISABLEMENT BENEFITS
The Industrial Injuries Scheme, administered under the Social Security Contributions and Benefits Act 1992, provides a range of benefits designed to compensate for disablement resulting from an industrial accident (ie an accident arising out of and in the course of an earner's employment) or from a prescribed disease due to the nature of a person's employment. Those who are self-employed are not covered by this scheme.

INDUSTRIAL INJURIES DISABLEMENT BENEFIT
A person may be able to claim industrial injuries disablement benefit if they are ill or disabled due to an accident or incident that happened at work or in connection with work in England, Scotland or Wales. The amount of benefit awarded depends on the person's age and the degree of disability as assessed by a doctor.

The benefit is payable whether the person works or not and those who are incapable of work are entitled to draw other benefits, such as statutory sick pay or incapacity benefit, in addition to industrial injuries disablement benefit. It may also be possible to claim the following allowances:

- reduced earnings allowance for those who are unable to return to their regular work or work of the same standard and who had their accident (or whose disease started) before 1 October 1990. At state pension age this is converted to retirement allowance
- constant attendance allowance for those with a disablement of 100 per cent who need constant care. There are four rates of allowance depending on how much care the person needs
- exceptionally severe disablement allowance can be claimed in addition to constant care attendance allowance at one of the higher rates for those who need constant care permanently

Weekly Rates of Benefit from April 2011

Degree of disablement	Aged 18+ or with dependants	Aged under 18 with no dependants
100 per cent	£150.30	£92.10
90	£135.27	£82.89
80	£120.24	£73.68
70	£105.21	£64.47
60	£90.18	£55.26
50	£75.15	£46.05
40	£60.12	£36.84
30	£45.09	£27.63
20	£30.06	£18.42
Unemployability supplement		£92.90
Reduced earnings allowance (maximum)		£60.12
Retirement allowance (maximum)		£15.03
Constant attendance allowance (normal maximum rate)		£60.20
Exceptionally severe disablement allowance		£60.20

OTHER BENEFITS
People who are disabled because of an accident or disease that was the result of work that they did before 5 July 1948 are not entitled to industrial injuries disablement benefit. They may, however, be entitled to payment under the Workmen's Compensation Scheme or the Pneumoconiosis, Byssinosis and Miscellaneous Diseases Benefit Scheme. People who suffer from certain industrial diseases caused by dust, or their dependants, can make a claim for an additional payment under the Pneumoconiosis Act 1979 if they are unable to get damages from the employer who caused or contributed to the disease.

Diffuse Mesothelioma Payment
Since 1 October 2008 any person suffering from the asbestos-related disease, diffuse mesothelioma, who is unable to make a claim under the Pneumoconiosis Act 1979, have not received payment in respect of the disease from an employer, via a civil claim or elsewhere, and are not entitled to compensation from a MoD scheme, can claim a one-off lump sum payment. The scheme covers people whose exposure to asbestos occurred in the UK and was not as a result of their work as an employee (ie they lived near a factory using asbestos). The amount paid depends on the age of the person when the disease was diagnosed, or the date of the claim if the diagnosis date is not known. The current rate is £77,506 for those aged 37 and under to £12,040 for persons aged 77 and over. From 1 October 2009 claims must be received within 12 months of the date of diagnosis. If the sufferer has died, their dependants may be able to claim, but must do so within 12 months of the date of death.

CLAIMS AND QUESTIONS
Entitlement to benefit and regulated Social Fund payments is determined by a decision maker on behalf of the Secretary of State for the Department for Work and Pensions. A claimant who is dissatisfied with that decision can ask for an explanation. He or she can dispute the decision by applying to have it revised or, in particular circumstances, superseded. The claimant can go to the Appeals Service where the case will be heard by an independent tribunal. There is a further right of appeal to a social security commissioner against the tribunal's decision but this is on a point of law only and leave to appeal must first be obtained.

Decisions on claims and applications for housing benefit and council tax benefit are made by local authorities. The explanation, dispute and appeals process is the same as for other benefits.

All decisions on applications to the discretionary Social Fund are made by Jobcentre Plus Social Fund decision makers. Applicants can ask for a review of the decision within 28 days of the date on the decision letter. The Social Fund review officer will review the case and there is a further right of review by an independent Social Fund inspector.

EMPLOYER PAYMENTS

STATUTORY MATERNITY PAY

Employers pay statutory maternity pay (SMP) to pregnant women who have been employed by them full or part-time continuously for at least 26 weeks into the 15th week before the week the baby is due, and whose earnings on average at least equal the lower earnings limit applied to NI contributions (£102 a week from April 2011). SMP can be paid for a maximum period of up to 39 weeks. If the qualifying conditions are met women will receive a payment of 90 per cent of their average earnings for the first six weeks, followed by 33 weeks at £128.73 or 90 per cent of the woman's average weekly earnings if this is less than £128.73. SMP can be paid, at the earliest, 11 weeks before the week in which the baby is due, up to the day following the birth. Women can decide when they wish their maternity leave and pay to start and can work until the baby is born. However, where the woman is absent from work wholly or partly due to her pregnancy in the four weeks before the week the baby is due to be born, SMP will start the day following the first day of absence from work.

Employers are reimbursed for 92 per cent of the SMP they pay. Small employers with annual gross NI payments of £45,000 or less recover 103 per cent of the SMP paid out.

STATUTORY PATERNITY PAY

Employers pay statutory paternity pay (SPP) to employees who are taking leave when a child is born or placed for adoption. To qualify the employee must:

• have responsibility for the child's upbringing
• be the biological father of the child (or the child's adopter), or the spouse/civil partner/partner of the mother or adopter
• have been employed by the same employer for at least 26 weeks ending with the 15th week before the baby is due (or the week in which the adopter is notified of having been matched with a child)
• continue working for the employer up to the child's birth (or placement for adoption)
• have earnings on average at least equal to the lower earnings limit applied to NI contributions (£102 a week from April 2011)

Employees who meet these conditions receive payment of £128.73 or 90 per cent of the employee's average weekly earnings if this is less than £128.73. The employee can choose to be paid for one or two consecutive weeks. The earliest the SPP period can begin is the date of the child's birth or placement for adoption. The SPP period must be completed within eight weeks of that date. SPP is not payable for any week in which the employee works. Employers are reimbursed in the same way as for statutory maternity pay.

ADDITIONAL PATERNITY LEAVE

Regulations introduced on 6 April 2010 give parents greater flexibility in how they use their maternity and paternity provisions. For births from 3 April 2011, additional paternity leave (APL) entitles eligible fathers to take up to 26 weeks' additional paternity leave, allowing for up to a total of one year's leave to be shared between the couple. APL entitlement requires the mother to have returned to work; it must also be taken between 20 weeks and one year after the child is born. APL may be paid if taken during the mother's statutory maternity pay period or maternity allowance period.

The APL entitlement will also apply to husbands, partners or civil partners who are not the child's father but expect to have the main responsibility (apart from the mother) for the child's upbringing.

Statutory paternity pay (see above) is due to be renamed ordinary paternity leave (OPL) but otherwise remains unchanged.

STATUTORY ADOPTION PAY

Employers pay statutory adoption pay (SAP) to employees taking adoption leave from their employers. To qualify for SAP the employee must:

• be newly matched with a child by an adoption agency
• have been employed by the same employer for at least 26 weeks ending the week in which they have been notified of being matched with a child
• have earnings at least equal to the lower earnings limit applied to NI contributions (£102 a week from April 2011)

Employees who meet these conditions receive payment of £128.73 or 90 per cent of their average weekly earnings if this is less than £128.73 for up to 39 weeks. The earliest SAP can be paid from is two weeks before the expected date of placement; the latest it can start is the date of the child's placement. Where a couple adopt a child, only one of them may receive SAP, the other may be able to receive statutory paternity pay (SPP) if they meet the eligibility criteria. Employers are reimbursed in the same way as for statutory maternity pay.

The additional paternity leave entitlement (see above) will also apply to adoptions where adoptive parents are notified of a match on or after 3 April 2011.

STATUTORY SICK PAY

Employers pay statutory sick pay (SSP) for up to a maximum of 28 weeks to any employee incapable of work for four or more consecutive days. Employees must have done some work under their contract of service and have average weekly earnings of at least £102 from April 2011. SSP is a daily payment and is usually paid for the days that an employee would normally work, these days are known as qualifying days. SSP is not paid for the first three qualifying days in a period of sickness. SSP is paid at £81.60 per week and is subject to PAYE and NI contributions. Employees who cannot obtain SSP may be able to claim incapacity benefit. Employers may be able to recover some SSP costs.

THE WATER INDUSTRY

In the UK, the water industry provides services to over 54 million consumers each day and has an annual turnover of around £10bn. It supplies around 17 billion litres of water a day to domestic and commercial customers and collects and treats more than 16 billion litres of wastewater a day. It also manages assets that include around 1,400 water treatment and 9,350 wastewater treatment works, 550 impounding reservoirs, over 6,500 service reservoirs/water towers and 800,000km of water mains and sewers.

Water services in England and Wales are provided by private companies. In Scotland and Northern Ireland there are single authorities, Scottish Water and Northern Ireland Water, that are publicly owned companies answerable to their respective governments. In drinking water quality tests carried out in 2010, the water industry in England and Wales achieved 99.96 per cent compliance with the standards required by the EU Drinking Water Directive; Scotland achieved 99.78 per cent and Northern Ireland 99.69 per cent.

Water UK is the industry association that represents all UK water and wastewater service suppliers at national and European level and is funded directly by its members, who are the service suppliers for England, Scotland, Wales and Northern Ireland; every member has a seat on the Water UK Council.

WATER UK, 1 Queen Anne's Gate, London SW1H 9BT
T 020-7344 1844 W www.water.org.uk
Chief Executive, Pamela Taylor

ENGLAND AND WALES

In England and Wales, the Secretary of State for Environment, Food and Rural Affairs and the National Assembly for Wales have overall responsibility for water policy and oversee environmental standards for the water industry.

The statutory consumer representative body for water services is the Consumer Council for Water.

CONSUMER COUNCIL FOR WATER, 1st Floor, Victoria Square House, Victoria Square, Birmingham B2 4AJ
T 0845-039 2837 W www.ccwater.org.uk

REGULATORY BODIES

The Water Services Regulation Authority (OFWAT) was established in 1989 when the water and sewerage industry in England and Wales was privatised. Its statutory role and duties are laid out under the Water Industry Act 1991 and it is the independent economic regulator of the water and sewerage companies in England and Wales. Overall responsibility for water policy and overseeing environmental standards for the water industry lies with DEFRA and the Welsh government. OFWAT's main duties are to ensure that the companies can finance and carry out their statutory functions and to protect the interests of water customers. OFWAT is a non-ministerial government department headed by a board following a change in legislation introduced by the Water Act 2003.

Under the Competition Act 1998, from 1 March 2000 the Competition Appeal Tribunal has heard appeals against the regulator's decisions regarding anti-competitive agreements and abuse of a dominant position in the marketplace. The Water Act 2003 placed a new duty on OFWAT to contribute to the achievement of sustainable development.

The Environment Agency has statutory duties and powers in relation to water resources, pollution control, flood defence, fisheries, recreation, conservation and navigation in England and Wales. It is also responsible for issuing permits, licences, consents and registrations such as industrial licences to extract water and fishing licences.

The Drinking Water Inspectorate (DWI) is the drinking water quality regulator for England and Wales, responsible for assessing the quality of the drinking water supplied by the water companies and investigating any incidents affecting drinking water quality, initiating prosecution where necessary. The DWI also provides scientific advice on drinking water policy issues to DEFRA and the Welsh government.

OFWAT, Centre City Tower, 7 Hill Street, Birmingham B5 4UA
T 0121-644 7500 E enquiries@ofwat.gsi.gov.uk
W www.ofwat.gov.uk
Chair, Philip Fletcher, CBE
Chief Executive, Regina Finn

METHODS OF CHARGING

In England and Wales, most domestic customers still pay for domestic water supply and sewerage services through charges based on the rateable value of their property. OFWAT estimates that the proportion of household customers in England and Wales to have metered supplies will increase from 41.5 per cent in 2011–12 to around 50 per cent in 2014–15. Nearly all non-household customers are charged according to consumption.

Under the Water Industry Act 1999, water companies can continue basing their charges on the old rateable value of the property. Domestic customers can continue paying on an unmeasured basis unless they choose to pay according to consumption. After having a meter installed (which is free of charge), a customer can revert to unmeasured charging within 12 months. However, water companies may charge by meter for new homes, or homes where there is a high discretionary use of water. Domestic, school and hospital customers cannot be disconnected for non-payment.

Price limits for the period 2010–15 were set by OFWAT in November 2009.

On average, prices for 2011–12 will increase by an average of 4.6 per cent. This takes into account a reduction in the average bill of 0.1 per cent before inflation of 4.7 per cent. Average household water bills in 2011–12 range from £91 for Portsmouth Water to £218 for Wessex Water; the overall average is £174. The average household sewerage bill costs £182, ranging from £123 for Thames Water up to £300 for South West Water.

WATER SUPPLY AND CONSUMPTION 2009–10 (ENGLAND AND WALES)

	Supply		Consumption			
	Distribution Input (megalitres/day)	Total Leakage (megalitres/day)	Household (litres/head/day)		Non-household (litres/property/day)	
			Unmetered	Metered	Unmetered	Metered
WATER AND SEWERAGE COMPANIES						
Anglian	1,145.4	210	178.7	138.8	626.2	2,691.5
Dwr Cymru	816.3	195	168.6	127.4	503.6	1,916.5
Northumbrian (NE)	710.0	155	166.3	151.5	810.0	3,220.2
Northumbrian (Essex & Suffolk)	455.1	67	173.7	159.4	645.0	2,462.7
Severn Trent	1,826.9	495	142.1	122.6	852.1	1,986.9
South West	421.1	82	177.1	133.6	1,156.0	1,411.4
Southern	560.4	95	157.0	138.1	806.9	2,481.8
Thames	2,574.6	670	195.7	151.5	650.9	2,836.4
United Utilities	1,785.0	460	151.0	121.6	714.5	2,490.2
Wessex	344.0	74	169.5	142.5	3,347.4	1,822.8
Yorkshire	1,284.7	295	173.3	125.9	175.8	2,364.3
Total	11,923.2	2,800	—	—	—	—
Average	—	—	167.3	135.0	778.5	2,358.5
WATER ONLY COMPANIES						
Total	2,670.4	480	—	—	—	—
Average	—	—	182.0	150.4	951.8	2,373.1

Source: OFWAT

SCOTLAND

Overall responsibility for national water policy in Scotland rests with the Scottish ministers. Until the Local Government (Scotland) Act 1994, water supply and sewerage services were local authority responsibilities. The Central Scotland Water Development Board had the function of developing new sources of water supply for the purpose of providing water in bulk to water authorities whose limits of supply were within the board's area. Under the act, three new public water authorities, covering the north, east and west of Scotland respectively, took over the provision of water and sewerage services from April 1996. The Central Scotland Water Development Board was then abolished. The act also established the Scottish Water and Sewerage Customers Council, representing consumer interests. It monitored the performance of the authorities; approved charges schemes; investigated complaints; and advised the secretary of state. The Water Industry Act 1999, whose Scottish provisions were accepted by the Scottish government, abolished the Scottish Water and Sewerage Customers Council and replaced it in November 1999 with a Water Industry Commissioner.

The Water Industry (Scotland) Act 2002 resulted from the Scottish government's proposal that a single authority was better placed than three separate authorities to harmonise changes across the Scottish water industry. In 2002 the three existing water authorities (East of Scotland Water, North of Scotland Water and West of Scotland Water) merged to form Scottish Water. Scottish Water, which serves around 2.4 million households, is a public sector company, structured and managed like a private company, but remains answerable to the Scottish parliament. Scottish Water is regulated by the Water Industry Commission for Scotland (established under the Water Services (Scotland) Act 2005), the Scottish Environment Protection Agency (SEPA) and the Drinking Water Quality Regulator for Scotland. The Water Industry Commissioner is responsible for regulating all aspects of economic and customer service performance, including water and sewerage charges. SEPA, created under the Environment Act 1995, is responsible for environmental issues, including controlling pollution and promoting the cleanliness of Scotland's rivers, lochs and coastal waters. Waterwatch Scotland is the consumer representative body for the water industry and the national complaints handling authority for water customers in Scotland.

METHODS OF CHARGING
Scottish Water sets charges for domestic and non-domestic water and sewerage provision through charges schemes which are regulated by the Water Industry Commission for Scotland. In February 2004 the harmonisation of all household charges across the country was completed following the merger of the separate authorities under Scottish Water. In November 2009 the Water Industry Commission for Scotland published The Strategic Review of Charges 2010–2015, stating that annual price rises would be kept at 5 per cent below the rate of inflation during this five-year period and for the year 2011–12 there would be a freeze on charges. The average household bill for 2011–12 therefore remains around £324.

SCOTTISH ENVIRONMENT PROTECTION
  AGENCY, Erskine Court, Castle Business Park, Stirling
  FK9 4TR T 01786-457700 W www.sepa.org.uk
SCOTTISH WATER, PO Box 8855, Edinburgh EH10 6YQ
  T 0845-601 8855 W www.scottishwater.co.uk
WATER INDUSTRY COMMISSION FOR SCOTLAND,
  First Floor, Moray House, Forthside Way, Stirling FK8 1QZ
  T 01786-430200 W www.watercommission.co.uk

WATERWATCH SCOTLAND, Corporate Office, Forrester Lodge, Inglewood, Alloa FK10 2HU T 0845-850 3344 W www.waterwatchscotland.org

NORTHERN IRELAND

Formerly an executive agency of the Department for Regional Development, Northern Ireland Water is a government-owned company but with substantial independence from government. Northern Ireland Water was set up as a result of government reform of water and sewerage services in April 2007. It is responsible for policy and coordination with regard to the supply, distribution and cleanliness of water, and the provision and maintenance of sewerage services. The Northern Ireland Authority for Utility Regulation (known as the Utility Regulator) is responsible for regulating the water services provided by Northern Ireland Water. The Drinking Water Inspectorate, a unit in the Northern Ireland Environment Agency (NIEA), regulates drinking water quality. Another NIEA unit, the Water Management Unit, has responsibility for the protection of the aquatic environment. The Consumer Council for Northern Ireland is the consumer representative body for water services.

METHODS OF CHARGING
The water and sewerage used by domestic customers in Northern Ireland is currently paid for by the Department for Regional Development (DRD), a system which will continue during 2011–2012. In March 2010, the Northern Ireland Assembly passed the Water and Sewerage Services (Amendment) Act (Northern Ireland) 2010, which ensured that Northern Ireland Water would continue to receive DRD subsidy until 2013. Whether domestic billing will be introduced before this date is yet to be decided. Non-domestic customers in Northern Ireland became subject to water and sewerage charges and trade effluent charges where applicable in April 2008.

CONSUMER COUNCIL FOR NORTHERN IRELAND, 116 Holywood Road, Belfast BT4 1NY T 028-9067 2488 W www.consumercouncil.org.uk
NORTHERN IRELAND AUTHORITY FOR UTILITY REGULATION, Queens House, 14 Queen Street, Belfast BT1 6ED T 028-9031 1575 W www.uregni.gov.uk
NORTHERN IRELAND WATER, PO Box 1026, Belfast BT1 9DJ T 0845-744 0088 W www.niwater.com

WATER SERVICE COMPANIES

(* not a member of Water UK; † associate member of Water UK)

*ALBION WATER LTD, Harpenden Hall, Southdown Road, Harpenden, Herts AL5 1TE T 01582-767720 W www.albionwater.co.uk
ANGLIAN WATER SERVICES LTD, Customer Services, PO Box 10642, Harlow CM20 9HA T 0845-791 9155 W www.anglianwater.co.uk
BRISTOL WATER PLC, PO Box 218, Bridgwater Road, Bristol BS99 7AU T 0117-966 5881 W www.bristolwater.co.uk
CAMBRIDGE WATER PLC, 90 Fulbourn Road, Cambridge CB1 9JN T 01223-706050 W www.cambridge-water.co.uk
†CHOLDERTON & DISTRICT WATER COMPANY, Estate Office, Cholderton, Salisbury, Wiltshire SP4 0DR T 01980-629203 W www.choldertonwater.co.uk

DEE VALLEY WATER PLC, Packsaddle, Wrexham Road, Rhostyllen, Wrexham LL14 4EH T 01978-846946 W www.deevalleywater.co.uk
DWR CYMRU (WELSH WATER), PO Box 690, Cardiff CF3 5WL T 0800-052 0145 W www.dwrcymru.co.uk
ESSEX & SUFFOLK WATER PLC (subsidiary of Northumbrian Water Ltd), Customer Centre, PO Box 292, Durham DH1 9TX T 0845-782 0999 W www.eswater.co.uk
NORTHUMBRIAN WATER LTD, Customer Centre, PO Box 300, Durham DH1 9WQ T 0845-717 1100 W www.nwl.co.uk
PORTSMOUTH WATER LTD, PO Box 8, West Street, Havant, Hampshire PO9 1LG T 023-9249 9888 W www.portsmouthwater.co.uk
SEMBCORP BOURNEMOUTH WATER LTD, George Jessel House, Francis Avenue, Bournemouth, Dorset BH11 8NX T 01202-590059 W www.sembcorpbw.co.uk
SEVERN TRENT WATER LTD, PO Box 5310, Coventry CV3 9FJ T 0800-783 4444 W www.stwater.co.uk
SOUTH EAST WATER LTD, Rocfort Road, Snodland, Kent ME6 5AH T 0333-000 0002 W www.southeastwater.co.uk
SOUTH STAFFORDSHIRE WATER PLC, Green Lane, Walsall WS2 7PD T 0845-607 0456 W www.south-staffs-water.co.uk
SOUTH WEST WATER LTD, Peninsula House, Rydon Lane, Exeter EX2 7HR T 0800-169 1133 W www.southwestwater.co.uk
SOUTHERN WATER SERVICES LTD, Southern House, Yeoman Road, Worthing, W. Sussex BN13 3NX T 0845-278 0845 W www.southernwater.co.uk
SUTTON AND EAST SURREY WATER PLC, London Road, Redhill, Surrey RH1 1LJ T 01737-772000 W www.waterplc.com
THAMES WATER UTILITIES LTD, PO Box 286, Swindon SN38 2RA T 0845-920 0800 W www.thameswater.co.uk
UNITED UTILITIES WATER PLC, Haweswater House, Lingley Mere Business Park, Great Sankey, Warrington WA5 3LP T 01925-237000 W www.unitedutilities.com
VEOLIA WATER CENTRAL LTD, Tamblin Way, Hatfield, Herts AL10 9EZ T 0845-782 3333 W www.veoliawater.co.uk/central
VEOLIA WATER EAST LTD, Mill Hill, Manningtree, Essex CO11 2AZ T 0845-148 9288 W www.veoliawater.co.uk/east
VEOLIA WATER SOUTHEAST LTD, The Cherry Garden, Cherry Garden Lane, Folkestone, Kent CT19 4QB T 0845-888 5888 W www.veoliawater.co.uk/southeast
WESSEX WATER SERVICES LTD, Claverton Down, Bath BA2 7WW T 0845-600 3600 W www.wessexwater.co.uk
YORKSHIRE WATER SERVICES LTD, PO Box 52, Bradford BD3 7YD T 0845-124 2424 W www.yorkshirewater.com

ISLAND WATER AUTHORITIES
(not members of Water UK)

COUNCIL OF THE ISLES OF SCILLY, Town Hall, St Mary's, Isles of Scilly TR21 0LW T 01720-422537 W www.scilly.gov.uk
ISLE OF MAN WATER AND SEWERAGE AUTHORITY, Tromode Road, Douglas, Isle of Man IM2 5PA T 01624-695949 W www.gov.im/water
JERSEY WATER, PO Box 69, Mulcaster House, Westmount Road, St Helier, Jersey JE4 9PN T 01534-707301 W www.jerseywater.je
GUERNSEY WATER, PO Box 30, Brickfield House, St Andrew, Guernsey GY1 3AS T 01481-239500 W www.water.gg

ENERGY

The main primary sources of energy in Britain are coal, oil, natural gas, renewables and nuclear power. The main secondary sources (ie sources derived from the primary sources) are electricity, coke and smokeless fuels and petroleum products. The UK was a net importer of fuels in the 1970s, however as a result of growth in oil and gas production from the North Sea, the UK became a net exporter of energy for most of the 1980s. Output decreased in the late 1980s following the Piper Alpha disaster until the mid 1990s, after which the UK again became a net exporter. Since 2004, the UK reverted back to become a net importer of energy and has since continued to be so. In value terms, the total fuel deficit for 2010 was £7.5bn. The Department of Energy and Climate Change is responsible for promoting energy efficiency.

INDIGENOUS PRODUCTION OF PRIMARY FUELS
Million tonnes of oil equivalent

	2009	2010
Primary oils	74.7	69.0
Natural gas	59.7	57.2
Primary electricity	16.5	15.1
Coal	11.0	11.5
Renewable and waste	5.0	5.3
Total	167.0	158.1

Source: Department of Energy and Climate Change

INLAND ENERGY CONSUMPTION BY PRIMARY FUEL
Million tonnes of oil equivalent, seasonally adjusted

	2009	2010
Natural gas	86.0	93.2
Petroleum	71.1	70.7
Coal	31.5	32.2
Nuclear electricity	15.2	13.9
Renewables and waste	6.2	7.0
Wind and hydro electricity	1.3	1.2
Net Imports	0.2	0.2
Total	211.6	218.5

Source: Department of Energy and Climate Change

TRADE IN FUELS AND RELATED MATERIALS (2010)

	Quantity, million tonnes of oil equivalent	Value £m
Imports		
Crude oil	55.0	19,490
Petroleum products	28.9	12,291
Natural gas	50.7	6,849
Coal and other solid fuel	15.5	1,879
Electricity	0.6	326
Total	150.7	40,835
Exports		
Crude oil	45.2	15,744
Petroleum products	35.9	14,947
Natural gas	15.2	2,191
Coal and other solid fuel	1.0	220
Electricity	0.4	204
Total	97.6	33,306

Source: DECC/ONS

OIL

Until the 1960s Britain imported almost all its oil supplies. In 1969 oil was discovered in the Arbroath field in the North Sea. The first oilfield to be brought into production was Argyll in 1975, and since the mid-1970s Britain has been a major producer of crude oil.

At the end of 2009, there were a total of 317 offshore oil and gas fields in production. To date, the UK has produced around 3.5 billion tonnes of oil. It is estimated that there are 750 million tonnes remaining to be produced. Licences for exploration and production are granted to companies by the Department of Energy and Climate Change. At the end of 2004, 565 seaward production licences and 101 onshore petroleum exploration and development licenses had been awarded. At the end of 2009, there were a total of 317 offshore oil and gas fields in production. To date, the UK has produced around 26 billion barrels of oil. An estimated 4 to 12 billion barrels remain to be produced. Total UK oil production peaked in 1999 and is now declining. Profits from oil production are subject to a special tax regime with different taxes applying depending on the date of approval of each field.

DRILLING ACTIVITY (2010)
by number of wells started

	Offshore	Onshore
Exploration	28	8
Appraisal	34	1
Development	130	12

Source: Department of Energy and Climate Change

INDIGENOUS PRODUCTION AND REFINERY RECEIPTS
Thousand tonnes

	2009	2010
Indigenous production	68,199	62,962
Crude oil	62,820	58,047
NGLs*	5,378	4,915
Refinery receipts	79,078	77,335

* Natural Gas Liquids: condensates and petroleum gases derived at onshore treatment plants
Source: Department of Energy and Climate Change

DELIVERIES OF PETROLEUM PRODUCTS FOR INLAND CONSUMPTION BY ENERGY USE
Thousand tonnes

	2009	2010
Transport	49,601	49,087
Industry	4,505	4,529
Domestic	2,713	3,083
Other	1,145	1,155
Total	57,964	57,854

Source: Department of Energy and Climate Change

COAL

Mines were in private ownership until 1947 when they were nationalised and came under the management of the National Coal Board, later the British Coal Corporation. The corporation held a near monopoly on coal production until 1994 when the industry was restructured. Under the Coal Industry Act 1994, the Coal Authority was established to take over ownership of coal reserves and to issue licences to private mining companies. The Coal Authority is also responsible for the physical legacy of mining, eg subsidence damage claims, and for holding and making available all existing records. It also publishes current data on the coal industry.

The mines owned by the British Coal Corporation were sold as five separate businesses in 1994 and coal production is now undertaken entirely in the private sector. Coal output was around 50 million tonnes a year in 1994 but has since declined to just under 19 million tonnes. As at 31 March 2011 there were five large and twelve small underground mines as well as 34 surface mines in production or development in the UK.

The main consumer of coal in the UK is the electricity supply industry. Coal still supplies a third of the UK's electricity needs but as indigenous production has declined, imports have continued to make up the shortfall and now represent around 50 per cent of UK coal supply, 40 per cent of which is currently supplied from Russia.

UK government policy is to meet the long-term challenges posed by climate change while continuing to ensure secure, clean and affordable energy. Coal's availability, flexibility and reliability compared to other sources mean that it is expected to continue to play an important role in the future generating mix, but its carbon emissions will need to be managed through the introduction of abatement technologies including carbon capture and storage (CCS).

CCS attempts to mitigate the effects of global warming by capturing the carbon dioxide emissions from power stations that burn fossil fuels, preventing the gas from being released into the atmosphere, and storing it in underground geological formations. CCS is still in its infancy and only through its successful demonstration and development will it be possible for coal to remain a part of a low-carbon UK energy mix. The government is committed to public sector investment in CCS technology on four power stations and has made it clear that there can be no new coal power stations in England and Wales without CCS on a defined amount of capacity. As part of a wider package of reforms to the electricity market, the government will also be introducing an Emissions Performance Standard, which will limit the emissions from new fossil fuel power stations.

COAL PRODUCTION AND FOREIGN TRADE
Thousand tonnes

	2009	2010
Opencast	9,854	10,426
Deep-mined	7,520	7,390
Imports	38,167	26,521
Exports	(646)	(715)
Total supply	48,786*	51,429*
TOTAL	48,904	51,464

* Includes an estimate for slurry and stock change
Source: Department of Energy and Climate Change

INLAND COAL USE
Thousand tonnes

	2009	2010
Fuel producers		
Electricity generators	39,764	41,505
Coke manufacture	4,936	5,654
Blast furnaces	852	978
Heat generation	482	480
†Other conversion industries	341	351
Final consumption		
Industry	1,742	1,715
Domestic	689	718
Public administration	24	28
Commercial	49	4
Agriculture	–	1
Miscellaneous	3	6

† Mainly recycled products
Source: Department of Energy and Climate Change

GAS

From the late 18th century gas in Britain was produced from coal. In the 1960s town gas began to be produced from oil-based feedstocks using imported oil. In 1965 gas was discovered in the North Sea in the West Sole field, which became the first gasfield in production in 1967, and from the late 1960s natural gas began to replace town gas. From October 1998 Britain was connected to the continental European gas system via a pipeline from Bacton, Norfolk to Zeebrugge, Belgium. Gas is transported through 278,000km of mains pipeline including 7,600km of high-pressure gas pipelines owned and operated in the UK by National Grid Gas plc.

The gas industry in Britain was nationalised in 1949 and operated as the Gas Council. The Gas Council was replaced by the British Gas Corporation in 1972 and the industry became more centralised. The British Gas Corporation was privatised in 1986 as British Gas plc. In 1993 the Monopolies and Mergers Commission found that British Gas's integrated business in Great Britain as a gas trader and the owner of the gas transportation system could operate against the public interest. In February 1997, British Gas demerged its trading arm to become two separate companies, BG plc and Centrica plc. BG Group, as the company is now known, is an international natural gas company whose principal business is finding and developing gas reserves and building gas markets. Its core operations are located in the UK, South America, Egypt, Trinidad and Tobago, Kazakhstan and India. Centrica runs the trading and services operations under the British Gas brand name in Great Britain. In October 2000 BG demerged its pipeline business, Transco, which became part of Lattice Group, finally merging with the National Grid Group in 2002 to become National Grid Transco plc.

In July 2005 National Grid Transco plc changed its name to National Grid plc and Transco plc became National Grid Gas plc. In the same year National Grid Gas also completed the sale of four of its eight gas distribution networks. The distribution networks transport gas at lower pressures, which eventually supply the consumers such as domestic customers. The Scotland and south-east of England networks were sold to Scotia Gas Networks. The Wales and south-west network was sold to Wales

& West Utilities and the network in the north-east to Northern Gas Networks. This was the biggest change in the corporate structure of gas infrastructure since privatisation in 1986.

Competition was gradually introduced into the industrial gas market from 1986. Supply of gas to the domestic market was opened to companies other than British Gas, starting in April 1996 with a pilot project in the West Country and Wales, with the rest of the UK following soon after.

Declines in UK indigenous gas production and increasing demand led to the UK becoming a net importer of gas once more in 2004. In 2010, gross natural gas production was 4 per cent lower than in 2009 and 46 per cent lower than the record level seen in 2000. As part of the Energy Act 2008, the government planned to strengthen regulation of the offshore gas supply infrastructure, to allow private sector investment to help maintain UK energy supplies.

BG GROUP PLC, Thames Valley Park, Reading RG6 1PT
T 0118-935 3222 W www.bg-group.com
Chair, Sir Robert Wilson
Chief Executive, Sir Frank Chapman

CENTRICA PLC, Millstream, Maidenhead Road, Windsor, Berkshire SL4 5GD T 01753-494000 W www.centrica.com
Chair, Sir Roger Carr
Chief Executive, Sam Laidlaw

NATIONAL GRID PLC, Lakeside House, The Lakes, Northampton NN4 7HD T 0845-605 6677
W www.nationalgrid.com
Chair, Sir John Parker
Chief Executive, Steve Holliday

UK GAS CONSUMPTION BY INDUSTRY
GWh

	2009	2010
Domestic	332,499	389,595
Industry	116,409	121,963
Public administration	37,084	38,390
Commercial	29,305	31,758
Agriculture	1,860	1,969
Miscellaneous	15,485	16,507
Total gas consumption	540,643	608,683

Source: Department of Energy and Climate Change

ELECTRICITY

The first power station in Britain generating electricity for public supply began operating in 1882. In the 1930s a national transmission grid was developed and it was reconstructed and extended in the 1950s and 1960s. Power stations were operated by the Central Electricity Generating Board.

Under the Electricity Act 1989, 12 regional electricity companies, responsible for the distribution of electricity from the national grid to consumers, were formed from the former area electricity boards in England and Wales. Four companies were formed from the Central Electricity Generating Board: three generating companies (National Power plc, Nuclear Electric plc and Powergen plc) and the National Grid Company plc, which owned and operated the transmission system in England and Wales. National Power and Powergen were floated on the stock market in 1991.

National Power was demerged in October 2000 to form two separate companies: International Power plc and Innogy plc, which manages the bulk of National Power's UK assets. Nuclear Electric was split into two parts in 1996.

The National Grid Company was floated on the stock market in 1995 and formed a new holding company, National Grid Group. National Grid Group completed a merger with Lattice in 2002 to form National Grid Transco, a public limited company (*see* Gas).

Following privatisation, generators and suppliers in England and Wales traded via the Electricity Pool. A competitive wholesale trading market known as NETA (New Electricity Trading Arrangements) replaced the Electricity Pool in March 2001, and was extended to include Scotland via the British Electricity Transmissions and Trading Arrangements (BETTA) in 2005. As part of BETTA, National Grid became the system operator for all transmission. The introduction of competition into the domestic electricity market was completed in May 1999. Since competition was introduced, over 19 million of Britain's 28 million electricity customers have switched their supplier.

In Scotland, three new companies were formed under the Electricity Act 1989: Scottish Power plc and Scottish Hydro-Electric plc, which were responsible for generation, transmission, distribution and supply; and Scottish Nuclear Ltd. Scottish Power and Scottish Hydro-Electric were floated on the stock market in 1991. Scottish Hydro-Electric merged with Southern Electric in 1998 to become Scottish and Southern Energy plc. Scottish Nuclear was incorporated into British Energy in 1996. BETTA opened the Scottish market to the same competition that had applied in England and Wales.

In Northern Ireland, Northern Ireland Electricity plc (NIE) was set up in 1993 under a 1991 Order in Council. In 1993 it was floated on the stock market and in 1998 it became part of the Viridian Group and was responsible for distribution and supply until NIE was sold to ESB Independent Energy in December 2010. In June 2010, Airtricity became the first new electricity supplier since the Northern Ireland electricity market was opened to competition in 2007.

On 12 July 2011, the government published *Planning Our Electric Future: a White Paper for Secure, Affordable and Low-carbon Electricity* in response to the challenges set by increasing electricity demands. It has been agreed that over £110bn in investment is needed to update the grid and build new power stations.

On 30 September 2003 the Electricity Association, the industry's main trade association, was replaced with three separate trade bodies:

ASSOCIATION OF ELECTRICITY PRODUCERS, Charles House, 5–11 Regent Street, London SW1Y 4LR
T 020-7930 9390 W www.aepuk.com

ENERGY NETWORKS ASSOCIATION, 6th floor, Dean Bradley House, 52 Horseferry Road, London SW1P 2AF T 020-7706 5100
W www.energynetworks.org

ENERGY RETAIL ASSOCIATION, 1 Hobhouse Court, Suffolk Street, London SW1Y 4HH T 020-7104 4150
W www.energy-retail.org.uk

ELECTRICITY PRODUCTION, SUPPLY AND
CONSUMPTION
GWh

	2009	2010
Electricity produced		
Nuclear	69,098	62,140
Hydro	5,262	3,603
Wind	9,324	10,216
Coal	103,038	107,694
Oil	6,042	4,860
Gas	166,494	175,003
Renewables	11,470	12,837
Other	2,327	1,625
Total	373,055	377,977
Electricity supplied		
Production	373,055	377,977
Other sources*	3,685	3,150
Imports	6,609	7,144
Exports	(3,748)	(4,481)
Total	379,601	383,791
Electricity consumed		
Industry	100,841	104,499
Transport	3,906	3,899
Other	217,970	219,920
Domestic	118,541	118,681
Public administration	19,442	18,773
Commercial	76,187	78,437
Agriculture	3,801	4,029
Total	322,717	328,318

* Pumped storage production

Source: Department of Energy and Climate Change

GAS AND ELECTRICITY SUPPLIERS

With the gas and electricity markets open, most suppliers offer their customers both services. The majority of gas/electricity companies have become part of larger multi-utility companies, often operating internationally.

As part of measures to reduce the UK's carbon output, the government has outlined plans to introduce 'smart meters' to all UK homes. Smart meters perform the traditional meter function of measuring energy consumption, in addition to more advanced functions such as allowing energy suppliers to communicate directly with their customers and removing the need for meter readings and bill estimates. The meters also allow domestic customers to have direct access to energy consumption information.

The following list comprises a selection of suppliers offering gas and electricity. Organisations in italics are subsidiaries of the companies listed in capital letters directly above.

ENGLAND, SCOTLAND AND WALES

CE ELECTRIC UK, W www.ce-electricuk.com
Northern Electric Distribution Ltd, Manor House, Station Road, Penshaw, Houghton-le-Spring DH4 7LA
T 0800-668877
Yorkshire Electricity Distribution, 98 Aketon Road, Castleford WF10 9DS T 0800-375675
CENTRICA PLC, Millstream, Maidenhead Road, Windsor, Berkshire SL4 5GD T 01753-494000 W www.centrica.com
British Gas/Scottish Gas, PO Box 4805, Worthing BN11 9QW
T 0800-048 0202 W www.britishgas.co.uk
EDF ENERGY, Osprey House, Osprey Road, Exeter, EX2 7WN
T 0800-096 9000 W www.edfenergy.com

E.ON, 6th Floor, 100 Pall Mall, London SW1Y 5NQ
T 024-7642 4000 W www.eon-uk.com
NPOWER, PO Box 93, Peterlee SR8 2XX T 0845-070 4851
W www.npower.com
SCOTTISH AND SOUTHERN ENERGY PLC,
Inveralmond House, 200 Dunkeld Road, Perth PH1 3AQ
T 01738-456000 W www.scottish-southern.co.uk
Scottish Hydro, T 0845-026 0655 W www.hydro.co.uk
Southern Electric, T 0845-026 0654
W www.southern-electric.co.uk
SWALEC, T 0800-026 0656 W www.swalec.co.uk
SCOTTISHPOWER, PO Box 8729, Bellshill ML4 3YD
T 0845-273 4444 W www.scottishpower.com

NORTHERN IRELAND

AIRTRICITY (a member of Scottish and Southern Energy), Airtricity House, Ravenscourt Office Park, Sandyford, Dublin 18 T 1850-812220 W www.airtricity.com
VIRIDIAN GROUP LTD, Greenwood House, 64 Newforge Lane, Belfast BT9 5NF T 028-9066 8416
W www.viridiangroup.co.uk
Energia, PO Box 1275, Belfast BT9 5WH T 1850-363744
W www.energia.ie
ESB INDEPENDENT ENERGY LTD (ELECTRIC IRELAND), Woodford Business Park, Santry, Dublin 17
T 1850-372999 W www.esbie.ie
Northern Ireland Electricity, 120 Malone Road, Belfast BT9 5HT T 08457-643643 W www.nie.co.uk

REGULATION OF THE GAS AND ELECTRICITY INDUSTRIES

The Office of the Gas and Electricity Markets (OFGEM) regulates the gas and electricity industries in Great Britain. It was formed in 1999 by the merger of the Office of Gas Supply and the Office of Electricity Regulation. OFGEM's overriding aim is to protect and promote the interests of all gas and electricity customers by promoting competition and regulating monopolies. It is governed by an authority and its powers are provided for under the Gas Act 1986, the Electricity Act 1989, the Competition Act 1998, the Utilities Act 2000 and the Enterprise Act 2002. Energywatch is the independent gas and electricity watchdog, set up in November 2000 through the Utility Act to protect and promote the interests of gas and electricity consumers. In October 2008 Energywatch merged with Postwatch and the National Consumer Council to form a new advocacy body, Consumer Focus. In October 2010, the government announced that Consumer Focus would be abolished and some of its functions would transfer to Citizens Advice, Citizens Advice Scotland and the General Consumer Council for Northern Ireland. This transfer is due to take place in spring 2013.

CONSUMER FOCUS, Fleetbank House, Salisbury Square, London EC4Y 8JX T 020-7799 7900
W www.consumerfocus.org.uk
THE OFFICE OF THE GAS AND ELECTRCITY MARKETS (OFGEM), 9 Millbank, London SW1 3GE
T 020-7901 7000 W www.ofgem.gov.uk

NUCLEAR POWER

Nuclear reactors began to supply electricity to the national grid in 1956. Nuclear power is currently generated in the UK at ten sites: two magnox reactors (shutdown expected in late 2012), seven advanced gas-cooled reactors (AGR) and one pressurised water reactor (PWR), Sizewell 'B' in Suffolk. The AGRs and PWR are owned by a private company, British Energy, while the two magnox reactors are state-owned by the Nuclear Decommissioning Authority. The first of a series of new-generation plants is expected to come on-line around 2018; all but one of the current sites (Sizewell 'B') will be retired by 2023.

In April 2005 the responsibility for the decommissioning of civil nuclear reactors and other nuclear facilities used in research and development was handed to the Nuclear Decommissioning Authority (NDA). The NDA is a non-departmental public body, funded mainly by the Department of Energy and Climate Change (DECC). Until April 2007, UK Nirex was responsible for the disposal of intermediate and some low-level nuclear waste. After this date Nirex was integrated into the NDA and renamed the Radioactive Waste Management Directorate.

There are currently nine non-operational magnox power stations and four nuclear research facilities undergoing decommissioning by the NDA, including the world's first commercial power station at Calder Hall on the Sellafield site in Cumbria. The decommissioning of these sites is scheduled for completion within the next 15 to 20 years. In the case of the Dounreay research facility in Scotland, controls on access to contaminated land are expected to remain in place until around 2300.

In 2010 electricity supplied from nuclear sources accounted for 16.4 per cent of the total electricity supply. The 2008 Energy Bill paved the way for the construction of up to ten new nuclear power stations by 2020. A number of factors have led to government backing for nuclear power: domestic gas supplies are running low; oil and gas prices are high; carbon emissions must be cut to comply with EU legislation and meet global climate change targets; and a number of coal-fired power stations that fail to meet clean air requirements are due to be closed.

Nuclear power has its advantages: reactors emit virtually no carbon dioxide and uranium prices remain relatively steady. However, the advantages of low emissions are countered by the high costs of construction and difficulties in disposing of nuclear waste. Currently, the only method is to store it securely until it has slowly decayed to safe levels. Public distrust persists despite the advances in safety technology.

SAFETY AND REGULATION

The Office for Nuclear Regulation (OCR), an agency of the Health and Safety Executive is the nuclear industry's regulator. Operations at all UK nuclear power stations are governed by a site licence which is issued under the Nuclear Installations Act. The OCR monitors compliance and has the jurisdiction to close down a reactor if the terms of the licence are breached. The DECC is responsible for security at all the UK's nuclear power stations, which are policed by the Civil Nuclear Constabulary, a specialised armed force created in April 2005. In 2009 Magnox Electric Ltd was found guilty of breaking the Radioactive Substances Act 2003: it had left a radioactive leak on a holding tank at Bradwell power station, Essex, unchecked for 14 years.

RENEWABLE SOURCES

Renewable sources of energy principally include biofuels, hydro, wind and solar. Renewable sources produced over 7.6 million tonnes of oil equivalent for primary energy usage in 2010; of this, about 5.2 million tonnes was used to generate electricity, 1.2 million tonnes to generate heat and 1.2 million tonnes was used as transport fuels. In 2010, the UK generated 6.8 per cent of its total energy production from renewable sources, up by 0.1 per cent from 2009.

The government's principal mechanism for developing renewable energy sources is the Renewables Obligation (RO), which aims to increase the contribution of electricity from renewables in the UK. There are separate RO schemes for England and Wales, Scotland and Northern Ireland. For both England and Wales and Scotland, the RO is set so that 9.7 per cent of licensed electricity sales should be from renewable sources eligible for the RO by 2009/10, and 15.4 per cent should be eligible by 2015/16. For Northern Ireland, these figures are 3.5 per cent and 6.3 per cent. In 2010, renewable sources accounted for 7.0 per cent of sales on an RO basis, an increase of 6.7 per cent from 2009.

A renewables obligation has been in place in England and Wales since April 2002 to give incentives to generators to supply progressively higher levels of renewable energy over time. These measures included exempting renewable energy sources from the climate change levy, capital grants, enhanced research funding and regional planning to meet renewables targets.

In addition to the RO, in April 2010, the government launched a Feed-in Tariff (FIT) scheme in Great Britain to encourage the uptake of small-scale low carbon electricity generation technologies, principally renewables such as solar photovoltaics, wind and hydro-electricity.

The government approved an EU-wide agreement in March 2007 to generate 20 per cent of energy production from renewable sources by 2020. It has since negotiated down the national share in this target to 15 per cent of energy production by 2020. In July 2009 the government published a Renewable Energy Strategy in order to meet this target. Other impediments to the expansion of renewable energy production include planning restrictions, rising raw material prices, and the possible redirection of funds to develop CCS technology and nuclear energy sources. For further information on renewable energy *see* The Environment.

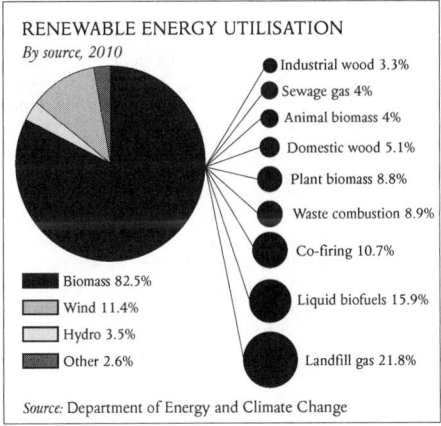

RENEWABLE ENERGY UTILISATION
By source, 2010

- Industrial wood 3.3%
- Sewage gas 4%
- Animal biomass 4%
- Domestic wood 5.1%
- Plant biomass 8.8%
- Waste combustion 8.9%
- Co-firing 10.7%
- Liquid biofuels 15.9%
- Landfill gas 21.8%

- Biomass 82.5%
- Wind 11.4%
- Hydro 3.5%
- Other 2.6%

Source: Department of Energy and Climate Change

TRANSPORT

CIVIL AVIATION

Since the privatisation of British Airways in 1987, UK airlines have been operated entirely by the private sector. In 2010, total capacity of British airlines amounted to 47 billion tonne-km, of which 38 billion tonne-km was on scheduled services. UK airlines carried around 124 million passengers; 103 million on scheduled services and 21 million on charter flights. Passenger traffic through UK airports decreased by 3.4 per cent; the third consecutive year traffic had decreased. Traffic at the six main London area airports (Gatwick, Heathrow, London City, Luton, Southend and Stansted) decreased by 5 per cent over 2010 and other UK regional airports saw a decrease of 6 per cent.

Leading British airlines include BMI, British Airways, EasyJet, Monarch, Thomas Cook Airlines, Thomson Airways and Virgin Atlantic. Irish airline Ryanair also operates frequent flights from the UK.

There are around 140 licensed civil aerodromes in Britain, with Heathrow and Gatwick handling the highest volume of passengers. BAA plc owns and operates six major airports: Heathrow, Stansted, Southampton, Glasgow, Edinburgh and Aberdeen. BAA sold Gatwick to an investment group in December 2009 for £1.5bn. Other airports are controlled by local authorities or private companies.

The Civil Aviation Authority (CAA), an independent statutory body, is responsible for the regulation of UK airlines. This includes economic and airspace regulation, air safety, consumer protection and environmental research and consultancy. All commercial airline companies must be granted an air operator's certificate, which is issued by the CAA to operators meeting the required safety standards. The CAA issues airport safety licences, which must be obtained by any airport used for public transport and training flights. All British-registered aircraft must be granted an airworthiness certificate, and the CAA issues professional licences to pilots, flight crew, ground engineers and air traffic controllers. The CAA also manages the Air Travel Organiser's Licence (ATOL), the UK's principal travel protection scheme. The CAA's costs are met entirely from charges on those whom it regulates; there is no direct government funding of the CAA's work.

The Transport Act, passed by parliament on 29 November 2000, separated the CAA from its subsidiary, National Air Traffic Services (NATS), which provides air traffic control services to aircraft flying in UK airspace and over the eastern part of the North Atlantic. NATS is a public-private partnership (PPP) between the Airline Group (a consortium of UK airlines), which holds 42 per cent of the shares; NATS staff, who hold 5 per cent; BAA, which holds 4 per cent, and the government, which holds 49 per cent and a golden share. In 2010 NATS handled a total of 2,106,689 flights, a decrease of 4.3 per cent compared with 2009 figures. The effect of the severe winter weather and the ash cloud resulting from the eruption of the Eyjafjallajokull volcano in Iceland in spring 2010 contributed to the decrease in the number of aircraft in UK controlled airspace in 2010.

AIR PASSENGERS 2010

All UK Airports: Total	211,830,788
Aberdeen (BAA)	2,763,708
Barra (HIAL)	10,192
Belfast City	2,740,341
Belfast International	4,016,170
Benbecula (HIAL)	30,406
Birmingham	8,572,398
Blackpool	235,340
Bournemouth	751,331
Bristol	5,747,604
Cambridge	916
Campbeltown (HIAL)	8,682
Cardiff	1,404,613
City of Derry (Eglinton)	339,432
Doncaster Sheffield	876,153
Dundee	70,398
Durham Tees Valley	226,209
East Midlands	4,113,501
Edinburgh (BAA)	8,596,715
Exeter	744,957
Gatwick (BAA)	31,375,290
Glasgow (BAA)	6,548,865
Gloucestershire	16,533
Heathrow (BAA)	65,881,660
Humberside	283,160
Inverness (HIAL)	530,213
Islay (HIAL)	25,009
Isle of Man	675,871
Isles of Scilly (St Mary's)	115,194
Isles of Scilly (Tresco)	34,310
Kent International	15,580
Kirkwall (HIAL)	141,399
Lands End (St Just)	30,214
Leeds Bradford	2,755,110
Lerwick (Tingwall)	4,609
Liverpool	5,013,940
London City	2,780,582
Luton	8,738,717
Lydd	485
Manchester	17,759,015
Newcastle	4,356,130
Newquay	315,107
Norwich	425,821
Oxford (Kidlington)	2,186
Penzance Heliport	89,469
Plymouth	128,603
Prestwick	1,662,744
Scatsta	279,482
Shoreham	886
Southampton (BAA)	1,733,690
Southend	3,583
Stansted (BAA)	18,573,803
Stornoway (HIAL)	113,680
Sumburgh (HIAL)	140,129
Tiree (HIAL)	7,943
Wick (HIAL)	22,710
Channel Islands Airports: Total	2,456,916
Alderney	70,012
Guernsey	923,683
Jersey	1,463,221

HIAL = Highlands and Islands Airports Ltd
Source: Civil Aviation Authority

CAA, CAA House, 45–59 Kingsway, London WC2B 6TE
T 020-7379 7311 **W** www.caa.co.uk
BAA, The Compass Centre, Nelson Road, London Heathrow
Airport, Hounslow TW6 2GW **T** 020-8745 9800
W www.baa.com

Heathrow Airport	**T** 0844-335 1801
Southampton Airport	**T** 0844-481 7777
Stansted Airport	**T** 0844-335 1803
Aberdeen Airport	**T** 0844-481 6666
Edinburgh Airport	**T** 0844 481 8989
Glasgow Airport	**T** 0844 481 5555

BMI, Donington Hall, Castle Donington, Derby DE74 2SB
T 01332-854000 **W** www.flybmi.com
BRITISH AIRWAYS, PO Box 365, Waterside,
Harmondsworth UB7 0GB **T** 01805-266522
W www.britishairways.com
EASYJET, Hangar 89, London Luton Airport LU2 9PF
T 0871-244 2366 **W** www.easyjet.com
MONARCH, Prospect House, Prospect Way, London Luton
Airport LU2 9NU **T** 0871-225 0250 **W** www.monarch.co.uk
THOMAS COOK AIRLINES, Thomas Cook Business Park,
Coningsby Road, Peterborough PE3 8SB **T** 0844-855 0515
W www.thomascookairlines.co.uk
THOMSON AIRWAYS, Wigmore House, Wigmore Place,
Wigmore Lane, Luton, Bedfordshire LU2 9TN
T 0844-871 1603 **W** www.thomson.co.uk
VIRGIN ATLANTIC, PO Box 747, Dunstable LU6 9AH
T 0844-811 0000 **W** www.virgin-atlantic.com

RAILWAYS

The railway network in Britain was developed by private companies in the 19th century. In 1948 the main railway companies were nationalised and were run by a public authority, the British Transport Commission. The commission was replaced by the British Railways Board in 1963, operating as British Rail. On 1 April 1994, responsibility for managing the track and railway infrastructure passed to a newly formed company, Railtrack plc. In October 2001 Railtrack was put into administration under the Railways Act 1993 and Ernst and Young was appointed as administrator. In October 2002 Railtrack was taken out of administration and replaced by the not-for-profit company Network Rail. The British Railways Board continued as operator of all train services until 1996–7, when they were sold or franchised to the private sector.

The Strategic Rail Authority (SRA) was created to provide strategic leadership to the rail industry and formally came into being on 1 February 2001 following the passing of the Transport Act 2000. In January 2002 it published its first strategic plan, setting out the strategic priorities for Britain's railways over the next ten years. In addition to its coordinating role, the SRA was responsible for allocating government funding to the railways and awarding and monitoring the franchises for operating rail services.

On 15 July 2004 the transport secretary announced a new structure for the rail industry in the white paper *The Future of Rail*. These proposals were implemented under the Railways Act 2005, which abolished the Strategic Rail Authority, passing most of its functions to the Department for Transport; established the Rail Passengers Council (RPC) as a single national body, dissolving the regional committees; and gave devolved governments in Scotland and Wales more say in decisions at a local level.

In addition, responsibility for railway safety regulation was transferred to the Office of Rail Regulation from the Health and Safety Executive.

OFFICE OF RAIL REGULATION

The Office of Rail Regulation (ORR) was established on 5 July 2004 by the Railways and Transport Safety Act 2003, replacing the Office of the Rail Regulator. As the railway industry's economic and safety regulator, the ORR's principal function is to regulate Network Rail's stewardship of the national network. The ORR also licenses operators of railway assets, approves agreements for access by operators to track, stations and light maintenance depots, and enforces domestic competition law. The ORR is led by a board appointed by the Secretary of State for Transport and chaired by Anna Walker.

SERVICES

For privatisation, under the Railways Act 1993, domestic passenger services were divided into 25 train operating units, which were franchised to private sector operators via a competitive tendering process. The train operators formed the Association of Train Operating Companies (ATOC) to act as the official voice of the passenger rail industry and provide its members with a range of services enabling them to comply with conditions imposed on them through their franchise agreements and operating licences.

As at July 2011 there were 23 passenger train operating companies: Arriva Trains Wales, c2c, Chiltern Railways, CrossCountry, East Coast, East Midlands Trains, Eurostar, First Capital Connect, First Great Western, First Hull Trains, First TransPennine Express, Grand Central, Heathrow Express, London Midland, London Overground, Merseyrail, National Express East Anglia, Northern Rail, ScotRail, South West Trains, Southeastern, Southern and Virgin Trains.

Network Rail publishes a national timetable which contains details of rail services operated over the UK network and sea ferry services which provide connections with Ireland, the Isle of Man, the Isle of Wight, the Channel Islands and some European destinations.

The national rail enquiries service offers information about train times and fares for any part of the country, Transport for London (TfL) provides London-specific travel information for all modes of travel and Eurostar provides information for international channel tunnel rail services:

NATIONAL RAIL ENQUIRIES
T 0845-748 4950 **W** www.nationalrail.co.uk
TRANSPORT FOR LONDON
T 0843-222 1234 **W** www.tfl.gov.uk
EUROSTAR
T 08432-186186 **W** www.eurostar.com

PASSENGER FOCUS AND LONDON TRAVELWATCH

Passenger Focus is the operating name of the Passengers' Council, a single national consumer body for rail, which is funded by the Department for Transport but whose independence is guaranteed by an act of parliament. Under the Passengers' Council (non-railway functions) Order of February 2010, Passenger Focus also represents bus passengers in England, outside London. Included in this remit are local bus services and scheduled domestic coach journeys.

Established in July 2000, London TravelWatch is the operating name of the official watchdog organisation representing the interests of transport users in and around the capital. Officially known as the London Transport Users' Committee, it is sponsored and funded by the London Assembly and is independent of the transport operators. London TravelWatch represents users of buses, the Underground, river and rail services in and around London, including Eurostar and Heathrow Express, Croydon Tramlink and the Docklands Light Railway. The interests of pedestrians, cyclists and motorists are also represented, as are those of taxi users.

FREIGHT

On privatisation in 1996, British Rail's bulk freight operations were sold to North and South Railways – subsequently called English, Welsh and Scottish Railways (EWS). In 2007, EWS was bought by Deutsche Bahn and in January 2009 was re-named DB Schenker. The other major companies in the rail freight sector are: Colas Rail, Direct Rail Services, Freightliner, Freight Europe and GB Railfreight (GBRf). In 2010–11 freight moved by rail amounted to 19.23 billion tonne-kilometres, a 0.9 per cent increase from 2009–10.

NETWORK RAIL

Network Rail is responsible for the tracks, bridges, tunnels, level crossings, viaducts and 18 main stations that form Britain's rail network. In addition to providing the timetables for the passenger and freight operators, Network Rail is also responsible for all the signalling and electrical control equipment needed to operate the rail network and for monitoring and reporting performance across the industry.

Network Rail is a private company run as a commercial business; it is directly accountable to its members and regulated by the ORR. The members have similar rights to those of shareholders in a public company except they do not receive dividends or share capital and thereby have no financial or economic interest in Network Rail. All of Network Rail's profits are reinvested into maintaining and upgrading the rail infrastructure.

ASSOCIATION OF TRAIN OPERATING
COMPANIES, 3rd Floor, 40 Bernard Street, London WC1N 1BY T 020-7841 8000 W www.atoc.org
LONDON TRAVELWATCH, 6 Middle Street, London EC1A 7JA T 020-7505 9000
W www.londontravelwatch.org.uk
NETWORK RAIL, Kings Place, 90 York Way, London N1 9AG T 020-7557 8000 W www.networkrail.co.uk
OFFICE OF RAIL REGULATION, 1 Kemble Street, London WC2B 4AN T 020-7282 2000
W www.rail-reg.gov.uk
PASSENGER FOCUS, Freepost (RRRE-ETTC-LEET), PO Box 4257, Manchester M60 3AR T 0300-123 2350
W www.passengerfocus.org.uk

RAIL SAFETY

On 1 April 2006 responsibility for health and safety policy and enforcement on the railways transferred from the Health and Safety Executive to the Office of Rail Regulation (ORR).

In 2010–11 a total of 40 passengers, railway staff and other members of the public were fatally injured in all rail incidents (excluding suicides), compared with 70 in 2009–10.

ACCIDENTS ON RAILWAYS

	2009–10	2010–11
Rail incident fatalities	70	40
Passengers	5	8
Railway employees	3	1
Public	62	31
Rail incident major injuries	396	395
Passengers	235	240
Railway employees	122	122
Public	39	33

SUICIDES AND ATTEMPTED SUICIDES 2010–11
Fatalities   208
Major Injuries   36
Source: ORR – National Rail Trends 2010–11 Yearbook

OTHER RAIL SYSTEMS

Responsibility for the London Underground passed from the government to the Mayor and Transport for London on 15 July 2003, with a public-private partnership already in place. Plans for a public-private partnership for London Underground were pushed through by the government in February 2002 despite opposition from the Mayor of London and a range of transport organisations. Under the PPP, long-term contracts with private companies were estimated to enable around £16bn to be invested in renewing and upgrading the London Underground's infrastructure over 15 years. In July 2007, Metronet, which was responsible for two of three PPP contracts, went into administration; TfL took over both contracts. Responsibility for stations, trains, operations, signalling and safety remains in the public sector. In 2008–9 there were 1,089 million passenger journeys on the London Underground.

In addition to Glasgow Subway, which is classified as an underground system, Britain has eight other light rail and tram systems: Blackpool Trams, Croydon Tramlink, Docklands Light Railway (DLR), Manchester Metrolink, Midland Metro, Nottingham Express Transit (NET), Sheffield Supertram and Tyne and Wear Metro.

In 2009–10 there were 186.2 million passenger light rail and tram journeys in Great Britain; a decrease of 1.3 per cent on 2008–9 figures, and the first year-on-year decrease in light rail passenger journeys since 1991–2.

THE CHANNEL TUNNEL

The earliest recorded scheme for a submarine transport connection between Britain and France was in 1802. Tunnelling began simultaneously on both sides of the Channel three times: in 1881, in the early 1970s, and on 1 December 1987, when construction workers bored the first of the three tunnels which form the Channel Tunnel. Engineers 'holed through' the first tunnel (the service tunnel) on 1 December 1990 and tunnelling was completed in June 1991. The tunnel was officially inaugurated by the Queen and President Mitterrand of France on 6 May 1994.

The submarine link comprises two rail tunnels, each carrying trains in one direction, which measure 7.6m (24.93ft) in diameter. Between them lies a smaller service tunnel, measuring 4.8m (15.75ft) in diameter. The service tunnel is linked to the rail tunnels by 130 cross-passages for maintenance and safety purposes. The tunnels are 50km (31 miles) long, 38km (24 miles) of which is under the seabed at an average depth of 40m (132ft). The rail terminals are situated at Folkestone and Calais, and the tunnels go underground at Shakespeare Cliff, Dover and Sangatte, west of Calais.

RAIL LINKS

The British Channel Tunnel Rail Link route runs from Folkestone to St Pancras station, London, with intermediate stations at Ashford and Ebbsfleet in Kent.

Construction of the rail link was financed by the private sector with a substantial government contribution. A private sector consortium, London and Continental Railways Ltd (LCR), comprising Union Railways and the UK operator of Eurostar, owns the rail link and was responsible for its design and construction. The rail link was constructed in two phases: phase one, from the Channel Tunnel to Fawkham Junction, Kent, began in October 1998 and opened to fare-paying passengers on 28 September 2003; phase two, from Southfleet Junction to St Pancras, was completed in November 2007.

There are direct services from the UK to Calais, Disneyland Paris, Lille and Paris in France and Brussels in Belgium. There are also direct services to Avignon in the south of France between July and September and during the winter months (December to April) to the French Alps. High-speed trains also run from Lille to the south of France.

Eurostar, the high-speed passenger train service, connects London with Paris in 2 hours 15 minutes, Brussels in 1 hour 51 minutes and Lille in 1 hour 20 minutes. There are Eurostar terminals at London St Pancras, Ashford and Ebbsfleet in Kent, Paris Gare Du Nord, Brussels-South and Lille in France, and Brussels-South in Belgium.

ROADS

HIGHWAY AUTHORITIES

The powers and responsibilities of highway authorities in England and Wales are set out in the Highways Act 1980; for Scotland there is separate legislation.

Responsibility for motorways and other trunk roads in Great Britain rests in England with the Secretary of State for Transport, in Scotland with the Scottish government, and in Wales with the Welsh government. The highway authority for non-trunk roads in England, Wales and Scotland is, in general, the local authority in whose area the roads lie. With the establishment of the Greater London Authority in July 2000, Transport for London became the highway authority for roads in London.

In Northern Ireland the Department of Regional Development is the statutory road authority responsible for public roads and their maintenance and construction; the Roads Service executive agency carries out these functions on behalf of the department.

FINANCE

In England all aspects of trunk road and motorway funding are provided directly by the government to the Highways Agency, which operates, maintains and improves a network of motorways and trunk roads around 7,050km (4,381 miles) long, on behalf of the secretary of state. Since 2001 the length of the network that the Highways Agency is responsible for has been decreasing owing to a policy of de-trunking, which transfers responsibility for non-core roads to local authorities. For the financial year 2011–12 the Highways Agency's total planned expenditure is £4,211m: £417m for maintenance, £797m for major schemes and the remainder for traffic management, technology improvements, other programmes and administration costs.

Government support for local authority capital expenditure on roads and other transport infrastructure is provided through grant and credit approvals as part of the Local Transport Plan (LTP). Local authorities bid for resources on the basis of a five-year programme built around delivering integrated transport strategies. As well as covering the structural maintenance of local roads and the construction of major new road schemes, LTP funding also includes smaller-scale safety and traffic management measures with associated improvements for public transport, cyclists and pedestrians.

For the financial year 2011–12, total allocated LTP funding amounted to £1,106m: £806m for maintenance and £300m for integrated transport measures.

Total budgeted expenditure by the Welsh government in 2010–11 to improve and maintain the trunk road network is £116m, a further £41m is allocated to improve and maintain local roads.

Since 1 July 1999 all decisions on Scottish transport expenditure have been devolved to the Scottish government. Total expenditure on motorways and trunk roads in Scotland during 2010–11 was £592m (including depreciation and other annually managed expenditure charges). Planned expenditure for 2011–12 is £560m. The cost of capital charges was abolished by HM Treasury during 2010–11; at the start of the year these had originally been forecast at £650m.

In Northern Ireland total expenditure by the Roads Service on all roads in 2010–11 was £284.5m, with £237.8m spent on trunk roads and motorways. Planned expenditure for 2011–12 is £122.5m, with £57.9m allocated for trunk roads and motorways.

The Transport Act 2000 gave English and Welsh local authorities (outside London) powers to introduce road-user charging or workplace parking levy schemes. The act requires that the net revenue raised is used to improve local transport services and facilities for at least ten years. The aim is to reduce congestion and encourage greater use of alternative modes of transport. Schemes developed by local authorities require government approval. The UK's first toll road, the M6 Toll, opened in December 2003 and runs for 43.5km (27 miles) around Birmingham from junction 3a to junction 11a on the M6.

Charging schemes in London are allowed under the 1999 Greater London Authority Act. The Central London Congestion Charge Scheme began on 17 February 2003 (see also Regional Government).

ROAD LENGTHS 2010
Miles

	England	Wales	Scotland	Great Britain
Major Roads	21,918.1	2,674.9	6,639.9	31,233.0
Motorways	1,870.1	87.8	252.6	2,210.6
Minor Roads	165,193.0	18,349.6	30,202.0	213,744.5
Total	187,111.1	21,024.5	36,841.9	244,977.5

Source: Department for Transport

FREIGHT TRANSPORT BY ROAD (GREAT BRITAIN) 2009
GOODS MOVED
By mode of working (billion tonne kilometres)

All modes	131.7
Own account	50.4
Public haulage	81.4

By gross weight of vehicle (billion tonne kilometres)

All vehicles	131.7
3.5–25 tonnes	13.8
Over 25 tonnes	117.9

GOODS LIFTED
By mode of working (million tonnes)

All modes	1,422
Own account	699
Public haulage	723

By gross weight of vehicle (million tonnes)

All vehicles	1,422
3.5–25 tonnes	207
Over 25 tonnes	1,215

Source: Department for Transport

ROAD TRAFFIC BY TYPE OF VEHICLE (GREAT BRITAIN) 2009
Million vehicle kilometres

All motor vehicles	504,000
Cars and taxis	400,700
Light vans	66,600
Goods vehicles	26,400
Buses and coaches	5,200
Motorcycles	5,200
Pedal cycles	5,000

Source: Department for Transport

BUSES
The majority of bus services outside London are provided on a commercial basis by private operators. Local authorities have powers to subsidise services where needs are not being met by a commercial service.

Since April 2008 people aged 60 and over and disabled people who qualify under the categories listed in the Transport Act 2000 have been able to travel for free on any local bus across England between 9.30am and 11pm Monday to Friday and all day on weekends and bank holidays. Local authorities recompense operators for the reduced fare revenue. A similar scheme operates in Wales and within London, although there is no time restriction. In Scotland, people aged 60 and over and disabled people have been able to travel for free on any local or long-distance bus since April 2006.

In London, Transport for London (TfL) has overall responsibility for setting routes, service standards and fares for the bus network. Almost all routes are competitively tendered to commercial operators.

In Northern Ireland, passenger transport services are provided by Ulsterbus and Metro (formerly Citybus), two wholly owned subsidiaries of the Northern Ireland Transport Holding Company. Along with Northern Ireland Railways, Ulsterbus and Metro operate under the brand name of Translink and are publicly owned. Ulsterbus is responsible for virtually all bus services in Northern Ireland except Belfast city services, which are operated by Metro. People living in Northern Ireland aged 65 and over can travel on buses and trains for free once they have obtained a Senior SmartPass from Translink.

LOCAL BUS PASSENGER JOURNEYS 2009–10
No. of journeys (millions)

England	4,604
London	2,238
Scotland	467
Wales	117
Total	5,188

Source: Department for Transport

TAXIS AND PRIVATE HIRE VEHICLES
A taxi is a public transport vehicle with fewer than nine passenger seats, which is licensed to 'ply for hire'. This distinguishes taxis from private hire vehicles which must be booked in advance through an operator. In London, taxis and private hire vehicles are licensed by the Public Carriage Office (PCO), part of TfL. Outside London, local authorities are responsible for the licensing of taxis and private hire vehicles operational in their respective administrative areas. At the end of March 2009 there were 71,000 licensed taxis in England.

ROAD SAFETY
In March 2000, the government published a new road safety strategy, *Tomorrow's Roads – Safer for Everyone,* which set casualty reduction targets for 2010. The targets included a 40 per cent reduction in the overall number of people killed or seriously injured in road accidents, a 50 per cent reduction in the number of children killed or seriously injured and a 10 per cent reduction in the slight casualty rate (per 100 million vehicle kilometres), all compared with the average for 1994–8.

There were 208,648 reported casualties on roads in Great Britain in 2010, 6 per cent fewer than in 2009. Child casualties (0–15 years) fell by 5 per cent to 19,569 in 2010, with 55 child fatalities: a 32 per cent reduction. Car user casualties decreased by 7 per cent on the 2009 level to 133,205 and fatalities decreased by 21 per cent to 835. Pedestrian casualties were 25,845 in 2010, 4 per cent less than 2009, while pedestrian deaths were 19 per cent lower compared to 2009 at 405. Compared to 2009, pedal cyclist casualties increased slightly by 1 per cent to 17,185 and the number of pedal cyclists killed on British roads increased by 7 per cent to 111.

ROAD ACCIDENT CASUALTIES 2010

	Fatal	Serious	Slight	All Severities
Average for 1994–8	3,578	44,078	272,272	319,928
England	1,553	19,702	164,114	185,369
Wales	89	998	8,868	9,955
Scotland	208	1,960	11,156	13,324
Great Britain	1,850	22,660	184,138	208,648

Source: Department for Transport

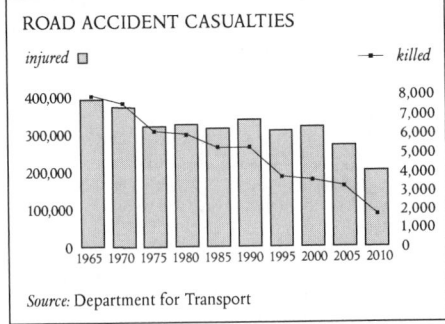

ROAD ACCIDENT CASUALTIES
injured ☐   ●— *killed*

Source: Department for Transport

DRIVING LICENCES
It is necessary to hold a valid full licence in order to drive unaccompanied on public roads in the UK. Learner drivers must obtain a provisional driving licence before starting to learn to drive and must then pass theory and practical tests to obtain a full driving licence.

There are separate tests for driving motorcycles, cars, passenger-carrying vehicles (PCVs) and large goods vehicles (LGVs). Drivers must hold full car entitlement before they can apply for PCV or LGV entitlements.

The Driver and Vehicle Licensing Agency (DVLA) ceased the issue of paper licences in March 2000, but those currently in circulation will remain valid until they expire or the details on them change. The photocard driving licence was introduced to comply with the second EC directive on driving licences. This requires a photograph of the driver to be included on all UK licences issued from July 2001.

To apply for a first photocard driving licence, individuals are required to complete the form *Application for a Driving Licence* (D1).

The minimum age for driving motor cars, light goods vehicles up to 3.5 tonnes and motorcycles is 17 (moped, 16). Since June 1997, drivers who collect six or more penalty points within two years of qualifying lose their licence and are required to take another test. All forms and leaflets including *What You Need to Know About Driving Licences* (D100), are available from post offices, DVLA local offices and online (W www.dvla.gov.uk or W www.direct.gov.uk).

The DVLA is responsible for issuing driving licences, registering and licensing vehicles, and collecting excise duty in Great Britain. Driver and Vehicle Licensing Northern Ireland (DVLNI), part of the Driver and Vehicle Agency (DVA), has similar responsibilities in Northern Ireland.

DRIVING LICENCE FEES
As at August 2011

Provisional licence

Car, motorcycle or moped	£50.00
Bus or lorry	Free
After disqualification until passing re-test	Free
Changing a provisional licence to a full licence	Free

Renewal

Renewing the photo on the licence (must be renewed every 10 years)	£20.00
At age 70 and over	Free
For medical reasons	Free
Bus or lorry licence	Free
After disqualification	£65.00
After disqualification for some drink driving offences*	£90.00
After revocation (under the New Drivers Act)	£50.00
Replacing a lost or stolen licence	£20.00
Adding an entitlement to a full licence	Free

Exchanging

a paper licence for a photocard licence†	£20.00
a photocard for a photocard licence†	£20.00
a full GB licence for a full Northern Ireland licence	Free
a full GB licence for a full EU/EEA or other foreign licence (including Channel Islands and Isle of Man)	Free
a full EU/EEA or other foreign licence (including Channel Islands and Isle of Man) for a full GB licence	£50.00
Change of name or address (existing licence must be surrendered)	Free

* For an alcohol-related offence where the DVLA needed to arrange medical enquiries
† Including removing expired endorsements

DRIVING TESTS

The Driving Standards Agency (DSA) is responsible for carrying out driving tests and approving driving instructors in Great Britain. Driver and Vehicle Testing, part of the Driver and Vehicle Agency, is responsible for testing drivers and vehicles in Northern Ireland.

DRIVING TESTS TAKEN AND PASSED
April 2010–March 2011

	Number Taken	Percentage Passed
Practical Test		
Car	1,605,599	46
Motorcycle Module 1	57,711	65
Motorcycle Module 2	49,644	67
Large goods vehicle	43,894	52
Passenger-carrying vehicle	8,546	54
Theory Test		
Car	1,346,192	63
Motorcycle	58,133	81
Large goods vehicle		
Multiple choice	26,606	80
Hazard perception	26,478	82
Driver CPC*	10,874	62
Passenger-carrying vehicle		
Multiple choice	7,421	77
Hazard perception	7,291	81
Driver CPC*	5,348	49

* Driver Certificate of Professional Competence – legal requirement for all professional bus, coach and lorry drivers
Source: DSA

The theory and practical driving tests can be booked with a postal application, online (W www.direct.gov.uk/drivingtest) or by phone (T 0300-200 1122).

DRIVING TEST FEES (WEEKDAY/EVENING* AND WEEKEND)
As at June 2010

Theory tests	
Car and motorcycle	£31.00
Bus and lorry	
Multiple choice test	£35.00
Hazard perception test	£15.00
Driver Certificate of Professional Competence (CPC)	£30.00
Practical tests	
Car	£62.00/£75.00
Tractor and other specialist vehicles	£62.00/£75.00
Motorcycle	
Module 1	£15.50/£15.50
Module 2	£75.00/£88.50
Lorry and bus	£115.00/£141.00
Driver Certificate of Professional Competence (CPC)	£55.00/£63.00
Car and trailer	£115.00/£141.00
Extended tests for disqualified drivers	
Car	£124.00/£150.00
Motorcycle	
Module 1	£15.50/£15.50
Module 2	£150.00/£177.00

* After 4.30pm

RATES OF DUTY
Cars registered on or after 1 March 2001 and first-year rates*

Band	CO_2 Emissions (g/km)	Petrol and Diesel Car		Alternative Fuel Car	
		6 months	12 months	6 months	12 months
A	Up to 100	–	–	–	–
B	101–110	£20.00	–	£10.00	–
C	111–120	£30.00	–	£20.00	–
D	121–130	£95.00	£52.25	£85.00	£46.75
E	131–140	£115.00	£63.25	£105.00	£57.75
F	141–150	£130.00	£71.50	£120.00	£66.00
G	151–165	£165.00	£90.75	£155.00	£85.25
H	166–175	£190.00 (£265.00)	£104.50	£180.00 (£255.00)	£99.00
I	176–185	£210.00 (£315.00)	£115.50	£200.00 (£305.00)	£110.00
J	186–200	£245.00 (£445.00)	£134.75	£233.00 (£435.00)	£129.25
K†	201–225	£260.00 (£580.00)	£143.00	£250.00 (£570.00)	£137.50
L	226–255	£445.00 (£790.00)	£244.75	£435.00 (£780.00)	£239.25
M	255+	£460.00 (£1,000.00)	£253.00	£450.00 (£990.00)	£247.50

* First-year rates (figures in parentheses) are payable for some vehicles' first tax disc taken out at first registration
† Includes cars that have a CO_2 emission figure over 225g/km but were registered before 23 March 2006

VEHICLE LICENCES

Registration and first licensing of vehicles is through local offices of the DVLA in Swansea. Local facilities for relicensing are available at any post office which deals with vehicle licensing. Applicants will need to take their vehicle registration document (V5C) or, if this is not available, the applicant must complete form V62. Postal applications can be made to the post offices shown in the V100 booklet, which also provides guidance on registering and licensing vehicles. All forms and booklets are available at post offices, DVLA local offices and online (W www.dvla.gov.uk or W www.direct.gov.uk)

MOTOR VEHICLES LICENSED 2010 (GREAT BRITAIN)

	Thousands
All cars	28,421
Light goods vehicles	3,208
Motorcycles	1,234
Heavy goods vehicles	470
Buses and coaches	171
Other vehicles*	616
Total	34,120

* Includes rear diggers, lift trucks, rollers, ambulances, Hackney Carriages, three-wheelers and agricultural vehicles
Source: Department for Transport

VEHICLE EXCISE DUTY

Details of the present duties chargeable on motor vehicles are available at DVLA local offices, post offices and online (W www.dvla.gov.uk or W www.direct.gov.uk). The Vehicle Excise and Registration Act 1994 provides *inter alia* that any vehicle kept on a public road but not used on roads is chargeable to excise duty as if it were in use. All non-commercial vehicles constructed before 1 January 1973 are exempt from vehicle excise duty. Any vehicle licensed on or after 31 January 1998, not in use and not kept on public roads must be registered as SORN (Statutory Off Road Notification) to be exempted from vehicle excise duty. From 1 January 2004 the registered keeper of a vehicle remains responsible for taxing a vehicle or making a SORN declaration until that liability is formally transferred to a new keeper.

RATES OF DUTY *from April 2011*

	12 months	6 months
Cars (private/light goods) registered before 1 March 2001		
Under 1,549cc	£130.00	£71.50
Over 1,549cc	£215.00	£118.25
Cars (private/light goods) registered on or after 1 March 2001	£210.00	£115.00
Euro 4 light goods vehicles registered between 1 March 2003 and 31 December 2006	£130.00	£71.50
Euro 5 light goods vehicles registered between 1 January 2009 and 31 December 2010	£130.00	£71.50
Motorcycles (with or without sidecar)		
Not over 150cc	£16.00	–
151–400cc	£35.00	–
401–600cc	£53.00	£29.15
600cc+	£74.00	£40.70
Tricycles		
Not over 150cc	£16.00	–
All others	£74.00	£40.70
Buses*		
Seating 10–17	£165.00	£90.75
Seating 18–36	£220.00	£121.00
Seating 37–61	£330.00	£181.50
Seating 62+	£500.00	£275.00

* Seating capacity includes driver. The 12-month rate for all reduced pollution buses is £165.00 and the 6-month rate is £90.75

MOT TESTING

Cars, motorcycles, motor caravans, light goods and dual-purpose vehicles more than three years old must be covered by a current MOT test certificate. However, some vehicles (ie minibuses, ambulances and taxis) may require a certificate at one year old. All certificates must be renewed annually. The MOT testing scheme is administered by the Vehicle and Operator Services Agency (VOSA) on behalf of the Secretary of State for Transport.

A fee is payable to MOT testing stations, which must be authorised to carry out tests. The current maximum fees are:

For cars, private hire and public
service vehicles, motor caravans,
dual purpose vehicles, ambulances
and taxis (all up to eight passenger
seats)   £54.85
For motorcycles   £29.65
For motorcycles with sidecar   £37.80
For three-wheeled vehicles (up to
450kg unladen weight)   £37.80
*Private passenger vehicles and
ambulances with:
9–12 passenger seats   £57.30 (£64.00)
13–16 passenger seats   £59.55 (£80.50)
16+ passenger seats   £80.65 (£124.50)
Goods vehicles (3,000–3,500kg)   £58.60

* Figures in parentheses include seatbelt installation check

SHIPPING AND PORTS

Sea trade has always played a central role in Britain's economy. By the 17th century Britain had built up a substantial merchant fleet and by the early 20th century it dominated the world shipping industry. Until the late 1990s the size and tonnage of the UK-registered trading fleet had been steadily declining. By the end of 2010* the number of ships in the UK-flagged merchant fleet had increased by 76 per cent while gross tonnage had more than quadrupled since 1999. The UK-flagged merchant fleet now constitutes 1.2 per cent of the world merchant fleet in terms of vessels and 1.8 per cent in terms of gross tonnage.

Freight is carried by liner and bulk services, almost all scheduled liner services being containerised. About 95 per cent by weight of Britain's overseas trade is carried by sea; this amounts to 75 per cent of its total value. Passengers and vehicles are carried by roll-on, roll-off ferries, hovercraft, hydrofoils and high-speed catamarans. There were around 44 million ferry passengers in 2010, of whom 22 million travelled internationally.

Lloyd's of London provides the most comprehensive shipping intelligence service in the world. *Lloyd's Shipping Index*, published daily, lists some 25,000 ocean-going vessels and gives the latest known report of each.

PORTS

There are more than 650 ports in Great Britain for which statutory harbour powers have been granted. Of these about 120 are commercially significant ports. In 2010* the largest ports in terms of freight tonnage were Grimsby and Immingham (54.0 million tonnes), London (48.1 million tonnes), Milford Haven (42.8 million tonnes), Southampton (39.4 million tonnes), Tees and Hartlepool (35.7 million tonnes), Forth (34.3 million tonnes), Liverpool (30.1 million tonnes), Felixstowe (25.8 million tonnes) and Dover (24.1 million tonnes). Belfast (12.8 million tonnes) is the principal freight port in Northern Ireland.

Broadly speaking, ports are owned and operated by private companies, local authorities or trusts. The largest operator is Associated British Ports which owns 21 ports. Provisional port traffic results show that 510 million tonnes were handled by UK ports in 2010, an increase of 2 per cent on the previous year's figure of 501 million tonnes.

* Provisional data

MARINE SAFETY

The Maritime and Coastguard Agency is an executive agency of the Department for Transport. Working closely with the shipping industry and the public, it aims to:
* reduce accidents and accident-related deaths within UK search and rescue waters and coastline
* reduce accidents and accident-related deaths from UK-registered merchant ships and fishing vessels
* reduce the number of incidents of pollution from shipping activities in the UK pollution control zone

HM Coastguard maintains a 24-hour search and rescue response and coordination capability for the whole of the UK coast and the internationally agreed search and rescue region. HM Coastguard is responsible for mobilising and organising resources in response to people in distress at sea, or at risk of injury or death on the UK's cliffs or shoreline.

Locations hazardous to shipping in coastal waters are marked by lighthouses and other lights and buoys. The lighthouse authorities are the Corporation of Trinity House (for England, Wales and the Channel Islands), the Northern Lighthouse Board (for Scotland and the Isle of Man), and the Commissioners of Irish Lights (for Northern Ireland and the Republic of Ireland). Trinity House maintains 69 lighthouses, 10 light vessels/floats, 412 buoys, 19 beacons, 48 radar beacons and seven DGPS (Differential Global Positioning System) stations*. The Northern Lighthouse Board maintains 208 lighthouses, 160 buoys, 31 beacons, 27 radar beacons, 26 AIS (automatic identification system) stations, four DGPS stations and one LORAN (long-range navigation) station; and Irish Lights looks after 80 lighthouses, 148 buoys, 45 beacons, 22 radar beacons, three DGPS stations, one LANBY (large automatic navigational buoy) with AIS in operation on ten lighthouses.

Harbour authorities are responsible for pilotage within their harbour areas; and the Ports Act 1991 provides for the transfer of lights and buoys to harbour authorities where these are used mainly for local navigation.

* DGPS is a satellite-based navigation system

UK-OWNED TRADING VESSELS
500 gross tons and over, as at end 2009

Type of vessel	No.	Gross tonnage
Tankers	153	6,374,000
Fully cellular container	108	5,341,000
Dry bulk carriers	65	3,185,000
Ro-Ro (passenger and cargo)	106	1,535,000
Passenger	25	1,207,000
Other general cargo	116	685,000
Specialised carriers	26	1,250,000
All vessels	599	19,577,000

Source: Department for Transport

UK SEA PASSENGER MOVEMENTS 2009

Type of journey	No. of passenger movements
International	
Ro-Ro Passengers on short sea routes	21,626,000
Passengers on cruises beginning or ending at UK ports*	1,347,000
Passengers on long sea journeys	55,000
Total	23,028,000

* Passengers are included at both departure and arrival if their journeys begin and end at a UK seaport
Source: Department for Transport

MARINECALL WEATHER FORECAST SERVICE

Marinecall offers a wide range of inshore, offshore and European forecasts from the Met Office which include gale and strong wind warnings, the general situation, wind speed and direction, probability and strength of gusts, developing weather conditions, visibility and sea state. Information is provided by various means including telephone, fax, SMS etc. Marinecall 10-day forecasts contain a 48-hour inshore waters forecast for the coastal area and up to 12 miles offshore, followed by a 1–5 day forecast for the local sea area, 6–10 day national forecast and an outlook for the month ahead. In addition fax forecasts provide an Atlantic surface pressure chart and 24-hour offshore forecast maps. Other services such as area specific, current weather reports and 48-hour forecasts are also available.

MARINECALL 10-DAY FORECAST

INSHORE AREA	By Phone 09068-500+	By Fax 09065-300+
Cape Wrath – Rattray Head	451	251
Rattray Head – Berwick	452	252
Berwick – Whitby	453	253
Whitby – Gibraltar Point	454	254
Gibraltar Point – North Foreland	455	255
North Foreland – Selsey Bill	456	256
Selsey Bill – Lyme Regis	457	257
Lyme Regis – Hartland Point	458	258
Hartland Point – St David's Head	459	259
St David's Head – Great Ormes Head	460	260
Great Ormes Head – Mull of Galloway	461	261
Mull of Galloway – Mull of Kintyre	462	262
Mull of Kintyre – Ardnamurchan	463	263
Ardnamurchan – Cape Wrath	464	264
Lough Foyle – Carlingford Lough	465	265
Channel Islands	432	–
OFFSHORE AREA		
English Channel	992	270
Southern North Sea	991	271
Irish Sea	954	273
Biscay	953	274
North-west Scotland	955	275
Northern North Sea	985	276

Marinecall by UK landline is charged at 60p per minute and Marinecall by fax at £1.50 per minute. Calls from mobiles may be subject to network operator surcharges. Subscription packages are available.

UK SHIPPING FORECAST AREAS

Weather bulletins for shipping are broadcast daily on BBC Radio 4 at 00h 48m, 05h 20m, 12h 01m and 17h 54m. All transmissions are broadcast on long wave at 1515m (198kHz) and the 00h 48m and 05h 20m transmissions are also broadcast on FM. The bulletins consist of a gale warning summary, general synopsis, sea-area forecasts and coastal station reports. In addition, gale warnings are broadcast at the first available programme break after receipt. If this does not coincide with a news bulletin, the warning is repeated after the next news bulletin. Shipping forecasts and gale warnings are also available on the Met Office and BBC Weather websites.

KEY
Br Bridlington
C   Channel Light-Vessel (automatic)
F   Fife Ness
G   Greenwich Light-Vessel (automatic)
J   Jersey
L   Lerwick
M   Malin Head
R   Ronaldsway
S   Sandettie Light-Vessel (automatic)
Sc Scilly (automatic)
St Stornoway
T   Tiree
V   Valentia

RELIGION IN THE UK

The 2001 census included a voluntary question on religion for the first time (although the question had been included in previous censuses in Northern Ireland); 92 per cent of people chose to answer the question. In the UK, 71.6 per cent of people in Britain identified themselves as Christian (42.1 million people). After Christianity, the next most prevalent faith was Islam with 2.7 per cent describing their religion as Muslim (1.6 million people). The next largest religious groups were Hindus (559,000), followed by Sikhs (336,000), Jews (267,000), Buddhists (152,000) and people from other religions (179,000). Together, these groups accounted for less than 3 per cent of the total UK population. People in Northern Ireland were most likely to say that they identified with a religion (86 per cent) compared with 77 per cent in England and Wales and 67 per cent in Scotland. The English counties with the highest proportion of Christians are Durham, Merseyside and Cumbria, each with 82 per cent or more; in Wales it is Ynys Mon (Isle of Anglesey) (79 per cent). London has the highest proportion of Muslims (8.5 per cent), Hindus (4.1 per cent), Jews (2.1 per cent), Buddhists (0.8 per cent) and people of other religions (0.5 per cent). Around 16 per cent of the UK population stated that they had no religion. The districts with the highest proportions of people with no religion were Norwich, Brighton and Hove and Cambridge, all with over 25 per cent. This category included those who identified themselves as agnostics, atheists, heathens and Jedi Knights.

CENSUS 2001 RESULTS – RELIGIONS IN THE UK

	thousands	per cent
Christian	42,079	71.6
Buddhist	152	0.3
Hindu	559	1.0
Jewish	267	0.5
Muslim	1,591	2.7
Sikh	336	0.6
Other religion	179	0.3
All religions	45,163	76.8
No religion	9,104	15.5
Not stated	4,289	7.3
All no religion / not stated	13,626	23.2
TOTAL	58,789	100

Source: Census 2001

INTER-CHURCH AND INTER-FAITH COOPERATION

The main umbrella body for the Christian churches in the UK is Churches Together in Britain and Ireland. There are also ecumenical bodies in each of the constituent countries of the UK: Churches Together in England, Action of Churches Together in Scotland, CYTUN (Churches Together in Wales), and the Irish Council of Churches. The Free Churches Group (formerly the Free Churches Council), which is closely associated with Churches Together in England, represents most of the free churches in England and Wales, and the Evangelical Alliance represents evangelical Christians.
The Inter Faith Network for the United Kingdom

promotes cooperation between faiths, and the Council of Christians and Jews works to improve relations between the two religions. Churches Together in Britain and Ireland also has a commission on inter-faith relations.

ACTION OF CHURCHES TOGETHER IN SCOTLAND, Inglewood House, Alloa, Clackmannanshire FK10 2HU T 01259-216980 W www.acts-scotland.org
General Secretary, Brother Stephen Smyth
CHURCHES TOGETHER IN BRITAIN AND IRELAND, 39 Ecclestone Square, London SW1V 1BX T 020-7901 4890 E info@ctbi.org.uk W www.ctbi.org.uk
General Secretary, Revd Bob Fyffe
CHURCHES TOGETHER IN ENGLAND, 27 Tavistock Square, London WC1H 9HH T 020-7529 8131 E office@cte.org.uk W www.churches-together.net
General Secretary, Revd Dr David Cornick
COUNCIL OF CHRISTIANS AND JEWS, 1st Floor, Camelford House, 87–89 Albert Embankment, London SE1 7TP T 020-7820 0090 E cjrelations@ccj.org.uk W www.ccj.org.uk
Chief Executive, David Gifford
CYTUN (CHURCHES TOGETHER IN WALES), 58 Richmond Road, Cardiff CF24 3UR T 029-2046 4204 E post@scytun.org.uk W www.cytun.org.uk
Chief Executive, Revd Aled Edwards, OBE
EVANGELICAL ALLIANCE, 186 Kennington Park Road, London SE11 4BT T 020-7207 2100 E info@eauk.org W www.eauk.org
General Director, Steve Clifford
FREE CHURCHES GROUP, 27 Tavistock Square, London WC1H 9HH T 020-7529 8131 E freechurch@cte.org.uk
Executive Secretary, Revd Mark Fisher
INTERFAITH NETWORK FOR THE UK, 8A Lower Grosvenor Place, London SW1W 0EN T 020-7931 7766 E ifnet@interfaith.org.uk W www.interfaith.org.uk
Director, Dr Harriet Crabtree
IRISH COUNCIL OF CHURCHES, Inter-Church Centre, 48 Elmwood Avenue, Belfast BT9 6AZ T 028-9066 3145 E info@irishchurches.org W www.irishchurches.org
Executive Officer, Mervyn McCullagh

RELIGIONS AND BELIEFS

BAHA'I FAITH

Mirza Husayn-'Ali, known as *Baha'u'llah* (Glory of God) was born in Iran in 1817 and became a follower of the *Bab,* a religious reformer and prophet who was imprisoned for his beliefs and executed on the grounds of heresy in 1850. Baha'u'llah was himself imprisoned in 1852, and in 1853 he had a vision that he was the 'promised one' foretold by the Bab. He was exiled after his release from prison and eventually arrived in Acre, now in Israel, where he continued to compose the Baha'i sacred scriptures. He died in 1892 and was succeeded by his son, Abdu'l-Baha, as spiritual leader, under whose guidance the faith spread to Europe and North America. He was followed by Shoghi Effendi, his grandson, who translated many of Baha'u'llah's works into English. Upon his death in 1957, a democratic system of leadership was brought into operation.

The Baha'i faith espouses the unity and relativity of religious truth and teaches that there is only one God, whose will has been revealed to mankind by a series of messengers, such as Zoroaster, Abraham, Moses, Buddha, Krishna, Christ, Muhammad, the Bab and Baha'u'llah, who were seen as the founders of separate religions, but whose common purpose was to bring God's message to mankind. It teaches that all races and both sexes are equal and deserving of equal opportunities and treatment, that education is a fundamental right and encourages a fair distribution of wealth. In addition, the faith exhorts mankind to establish a world federal system to promote peace and tolerance.

A feast is held every 19 days, which consists of prayer and readings of Baha'i scriptures, consultation on community business, and social activities. Music, food and beverages usually accompany the proceedings. There is no clergy; each local community elects a local assembly, which coordinates community activities (such as devotional gatherings, study circles and classes for children and young people), enrols new members, counsels and assists members in need, and conducts Baha'i marriages and funerals. A national assembly is elected annually by locally elected delegates, and every five years the national spiritual assemblies meet together to elect the Universal House of Justice, the supreme international governing body of the Baha'i Faith. Worldwide there are over 13,000 local spiritual assemblies; there are around five million members residing in about 235 countries, of which 179 have national organisations.

BAHA'I COMMUNITY OF THE UK,
27 Rutland Gate, London SW7 1PD T 020-7584 2566
E oea@bahai.org.uk W www.bahai.org.uk
Director, Office of External Affairs, Dr Kishan Manocha

BUDDHISM

Buddhism originated in what is now the Bihar area of northern India in the teachings of Siddhartha Gautama, who became the *Buddha* (Enlightened One). In the Thai or Suriyakati calendar the beginning of the Buddhist era is dated from death of Buddha; the year 2011 is therefore 2554 by the Thai Buddhist reckoning.

Fundamental to Buddhism is the concept of rebirth, whereby each life carries with it the consequences of the conduct of earlier lives (known as the law of *karma*) and this cycle of death and rebirth is broken only when the state of *nirvana* has been reached. Buddhism steers a middle path between belief in personal continuity and the belief that death results in total extinction.

While doctrine does not have a pivotal position in Buddhism, a statement of four 'Noble Truths' is common to all its schools and varieties. These are: suffering is inescapable in even the most fortunate of existences; craving is the root cause of suffering; abandonment of the selfish mindset is the way to end suffering; and bodily and mental discipline, accompanied by the cultivation of wisdom and compassion, provides the spiritual path ('Noble Eightfold Path') to accomplish this. Buddhists deny the idea of a creator and prefer to emphasise the practical aspects of moral and spiritual development.

The schools of Buddhism can be broadly divided into three: *Theravada,* the generally monastic-led tradition practised in Sri Lanka and South-East Asia; *Mahayana,* the philosophical and popular traditions of the Far East; and *Esoteric,* the Tantric-derived traditions found in Tibet and Mongolia and, to a lesser extent, China and Japan. The extensive Theravada scriptures are contained in the *Pali Canon,* which dates in its written form from the first century BC. Mahayana and Esoteric schools have Sanskrit-derived translations of these plus many more additional scriptures as well as exegetical material.

In the East the new and full moons and the lunar quarter days were (and to a certain extent, still are) significant in determining the religious calendar. Most private homes contain a shrine where offerings, worship and other spiritual practices (such as meditation, chanting or mantra recitation) take place on a daily basis. Buddhist festivals vary according to local traditions within the different schools and there is little uniformity – even in commemorating the birth, enlightenment and death of the Buddha.

There is no governing authority for Buddhism in the UK. Communities representing all schools of Buddhism operate independently. The Buddhist Society was established in 1924; it runs courses, lectures and meditation groups, and publishes books about Buddhism. The Network of Buddhist Organisations was founded in 1993 to promote fellowship and dialogue between Buddhist organisations and to facilitate cooperation in matters of common interest.

There are estimated to be at least 300 million Buddhists worldwide. Of the 152,000 Buddhists in the UK (according to the 2001 census), 60,000 are white British (the majority are converts), 36,000 Chinese, 15,000 Asian and 36,000 'other ethnic'.

THE BUDDHIST SOCIETY, 58 Eccleston Square, London
SW1V 1PH T 020-7834 5858 E info@thebuddhistsociety.org
W www.thebuddhistsociety.org
LONDON BUDDHIST CENTRE,
51 Roman Road, London E2 0HU T 0845-458 4716
E info@lbc.org.uk W www.lbc.org.uk
THE NETWORK OF BUDDHIST ORGANISATIONS,
PO Box 4147, Maidenhead SL60 1DN T 0845-345 8978
E secretary@nbo.org.uk W www.nbo.org.uk
THE OFFICE OF TIBET, Tibet House, 1 Culworth Street,
London NW8 7AF T 020-7722 5378 E samdup@tibet.com
W www.tibet.com
Representative of HH the Dalai Lama, Thubten Samdup
SOKA GAKKAI INTERNATIONAL (UK), Taplow Court
Grand Cultural Centre, Taplow, Berkshire SL6 0ER
T 01628-773163 W www.sgi-uk.org

CHRISTIANITY

Christianity is a monotheistic faith based on the person and teachings of Jesus Christ, and all Christian denominations claim his authority. Central to its teaching is the concept of God and his son Jesus Christ, who was crucified and resurrected in order to enable mankind to attain salvation.

The Jewish scriptures predicted the coming of a *Messiah,* an 'anointed one', who would bring salvation. To Christians, Jesus of Nazareth, a Jewish rabbi (teacher) who was born in Palestine, was the promised Messiah. Jesus' birth, teachings, crucifixion and subsequent resurrection are recorded in the *Gospels,* which, together with other scriptures that summarise Christian belief, form the *New Testament.* This, together with the Hebrew scriptures – entitled the *Old Testament* by Christians – makes up the Bible, the sacred texts of Christianity.

Christians believe that sin distanced mankind from God, and that Jesus was the son of God, sent to redeem mankind from sin by his death. In addition, many believe that Jesus will return again at some future date, triumph over evil and establish a kingdom on earth, thus inaugurating a new age. The Gospel assures Christians that those who believe in Jesus and obey his teachings will be forgiven their sins and will be resurrected from the dead.

The Apostles were Jesus' first converts and are recognised by Christians as the founders of the Christian community. Early Christianity spread rapidly throughout the eastern provinces of the Roman Empire but was subjected to great persecution until AD 313, when Emperor Constantine's Edict of Toleration confirmed its right to exist. Christianity was established as the religion of the Roman Empire in AD 381.

Between AD 325 and 787 there were seven Oecumenical Councils at which bishops from the entire Christian world assembled to resolve various doctrinal disputes. The estrangement between East and West began after Constantine moved the centre of the Roman Empire from Rome to Constantinople, and it grew after the division of the Roman Empire into eastern and western halves. Linguistic and cultural differences between Greek East and Latin West served to encourage separate ecclesiastical developments which became pronounced in the tenth and early 11th centuries. Administration of the church was divided between five ancient patriarchates: Rome and all the West, Constantinople (the imperial city – the 'New Rome'), Jerusalem and all of Palestine, Antioch and all the East, and Alexandria and all of Africa. Of these, only Rome was in the Latin West and after the schism in 1054, Rome developed a structure of authority centralised on the Papacy, while the Orthodox East maintained the style of localised administration. Papal authority over the doctrine and jurisdiction of the church in Western Europe was unrivalled after the split with the Eastern Orthodox Church until the Protestant Reformation in the 16th century.

Christian practices vary widely between different Christian churches, but prayer, charity and giving (for the maintenance of the church buildings, for the work of the church, and to those in need) are common to all. In addition, certain days of observance, ie the *Sabbath, Easter* and *Christmas,* are celebrated by most Christians. The Orthodox, Roman Catholic and Anglican churches celebrate many more days of observance, based on saints and significant events in the life of Jesus. The belief in sacraments, physical signs believed to have been ordained by Jesus Christ to symbolise and convey spiritual gifts, varies greatly between Christian denominations; *baptism* and the *Eucharist* are practised by most Christians. Baptism, symbolising repentance and faith in Jesus, is an act marking entry into the Christian community; the Eucharist, the ritual re-enactment of the Last Supper, Jesus' final meal with his disciples, is also practised by most denominations. Other sacraments, such as anointing the sick, the laying on of hands to symbolise the passing on of the office of priesthood or to heal the sick, and speaking in tongues, where it is believed that the person is possessed by the Holy Spirit, are less common. In denominations where infant baptism is practised, confirmation (where the person confirms the commitments made on their behalf in infancy) is common. Matrimony and the ordination of priests are also widely believed to be sacraments. Many Protestants regard only baptism and the Eucharist to be sacraments; the Quakers and the Salvation Army reject the use of sacraments.

See Churches for contact details of the Church of England, the Roman Catholic Church and other Christian churches in the UK.

HINDUISM

Hinduism has no historical founder but had become highly developed in India by c.2500 BC. Its adherents originally called themselves Aryans; Muslim invaders first called the Aryans 'Hindus' (derived from 'Sindhu', the name of the river Indus) in the eighth century.

Most Hindus hold that *satya* (truthfulness), honesty, sincerity and devotion to God are essential for good living. They believe in one supreme spirit *(Brahman),* and in the transmigration of *atman* (the soul). Most Hindus accept the doctrine of *karma* (consequences of actions), the concept of *samsara* (successive lives) and the possibility of all atmans achieving *moksha* (liberation from samsara) through *jnana* (knowledge), *yoga* (meditation), *karma* (work or action) and *bhakti* (devotion).

Most Hindus offer worship to *murtis* (images of deities) representing different incarnations or aspects of Brahman, and follow their *dharma* (religious and social duty) according to the traditions of their *varna* (social class), *ashrama* (stage in life), *jaiti* (caste) and *kula* (family).

Hinduism's sacred texts are divided into *shruti* ('that which is heard'), including the *Vedas,* and *smriti* ('that which is remembered'), including the *Ramayana,* the *Mahabharata,* the *Puranas* (ancient myths), and the sacred law books. Most Hindus recognise the authority of the *Vedas,* the oldest holy books, and accept the philosophical teachings of the *Upanishads,* the *Vedanta Sutras* and the *Bhagavad-Gita.*

Hindus believe Brahman to be omniscient, omnipotent, limitless and all-pervading. Brahman is usually worshipped in its deity form. Brahma, Vishnu and Shiva are the most important deities or aspects of Brahman worshipped by Hindus; their respective consorts are Saraswati, Lakshmi and Durga or Parvati, also known as Shakti. There are believed to have been ten *avatars* (incarnations) of Vishnu, of whom the most important are Rama and Krishna. Other popular gods are Ganesha, Hanuman and Subrahmanyam. All Hindu gods are seen as aspects of the supreme spirit (Brahman), not as competing deities.

Orthodox Hindus revere all gods and goddesses equally, but there are many denominations, including the Hare-Krishna movement (ISKCon), the Arya Samaj and the Swaminarayan Hindu mission, in which worship is concentrated on one deity. The *guru* (spiritual teacher) is seen as the source of spiritual guidance.

Hinduism does not have a centrally trained and ordained priesthood. The pronouncements of the *shankaracharyas* (heads of monasteries) of Shringeri, Puri, Dwarka and Badrinath are heeded by the orthodox but may be ignored by the various sects.

The commonest form of worship is *puja,* in which water, flowers, food, fruit, incense and light are offered to the deity. Puja may be done either in a home shrine or a *mandir* (temple). Many British Hindus celebrate *samskars* (purification rites), to name a baby, for the sacred thread (an initiation ceremony), marriage and cremation.

The largest communities of Hindus in Britain are in Leicester, London, Birmingham and Bradford, and developed as a result of immigration from India, eastern Africa and Sri Lanka.

There are an estimated 800 million Hindus worldwide; there are around 559,000 adherents, according to the 2001 UK census, and over 140 temples in the UK.

ARYA SAMAJ LONDON, 69A Argyle Road, London W13 0LY **T** 020-8991 1732
E aryasamajlondon@yahoo.co.uk
Vice President, Amrit Lal Bhardwaj

BHARATIYA VIDYA BHAVAN, Institute of Indian Art and Culture, 4A Castletown Road, London W14 9HE
T 020-7381 3086/4608 E info@bhavan.net
W www.bhavan.net
Executive Director, Dr M. N. Nandakumara
INTERNATIONAL SOCIETY FOR KRISHNA CONSCIOUSNESS (ISKCON), Bhaktivedanta Manor, Dharam Marg, Hilfield Lane, Aldenham, Watford, Herts WD25 8EZ T 01923-851000 E info@krishnatemple.com
W www.krishnatemple.com
Temple President, Sruti Dharma Das
NATIONAL COUNCIL OF HINDU TEMPLES (UK), 1 Hans Close, Stoke, Coventry CV2 4WA T 0780-505 4776
E sanjay.jagatia@ntlworld.com W www.nchtuk.org
General Secretary, Sanjay Jagatia
SWAMINARAYAN HINDU MISSION (SHRI SWAMINARAYAN MANDIR), 105–119 Brentfield Road, London NW10 8LD T 020-8965 2651 E info@mandir.org
W www.mandir.org

HUMANISM

Humanism traces its roots back to ancient times, with Indian, Chinese, Greek and Roman philosophers expressing Humanist ideas some 2,500 years ago. Confucius, the Chinese philosopher who lived c.500 BC, believed that religious observances should be replaced with moral values as the basis of social and political order and that 'the true way' is based on reason and humanity. He also stressed the importance of benevolence and respect for others, and believed that the individual situation should be considered rather than the global application of traditional rules.

Humanists believe that there is no God or other supernatural being, that humans have only one life (Humanists do not believe in an afterlife or reincarnation) and that humans can live ethical and fulfilling lives without religious beliefs through a moral code derived from a shared history, personal experience and thought. There are no sacred Humanist texts. Particular emphasis is placed on science as the only reliable source of knowledge of the universe. Many Humanists recognise a need for ceremonies to mark important occasions in life and the British Humanist Association has a network of celebrants who are trained and accredited to conduct baby namings, weddings and funerals. The British Humanist Association's campaigns for a secular society (a society based on freedom of religious or non-religious belief with no privileges for any particular set of beliefs) are based on equality and human rights. The association also campaigns for inclusive schools that meet the needs of all parents and pupils, regardless of their religious or non-religious beliefs.
BRITISH HUMANIST ASSOCIATION, 1 Gower Street, London WC1E 6HD T 020-7079 3580 F 020-7079 3588
E info@humanism.org.uk W www.humanism.org.uk
Chief Executive, Andrew Copson

ISLAM

Islam (which means 'peace arising from submission to the will of Allah' in Arabic) is a monotheistic religion which was taught in Arabia by the Prophet Muhammad, who was born in Mecca (Al-Makkah) in 570 AD. Islam spread to Egypt, north Africa, Spain and the borders of China in the century following the Prophet's death, and is now the predominant religion in Indonesia, the near and Middle East, northern and parts of western Africa, Pakistan, Bangladesh, Malaysia and some of the former Soviet republics. There are also large Muslim communities in other countries.

For Muslims (adherents of Islam), there is one God (*Allah*), who holds absolute power. Muslims believe that Allah's commands were revealed to mankind through the prophets, who include Abraham, Moses and Jesus, but that Allah's message was gradually corrupted until revealed finally and in perfect form to Muhammad through the angel *Jibril* (Gabriel) over a period of 23 years. This last, incorruptible message is said to have been recorded in the *Qur'an* (Koran), which contains 114 divisions called *surahs,* each made up of *ayahs* of various lengths, and is held to be the essence of all previous scriptures. The *Ahadith* are the records of the Prophet Muhammad's deeds and sayings (the *Sunnah*) as practised and recounted by his immediate followers. A culture and a system of law and theology gradually developed to form a distinctive Islamic civilisation. Islam makes no distinction between sacred and worldly affairs and provides rules for every aspect of human life. The *Shariah* is the sacred law of Islam based primarily upon prescriptions derived from the *Qur'an* and the *Sunnah* of the Prophet.

The 'five pillars of Islam' are *shahadah* (a declaration of faith in the oneness and supremacy of Allah and the messengership of Muhammad); *salat* (formal prayer, to be performed five times a day facing the *Ka'bah* (the most sacred shrine in the holy city of Mecca)); *zakat* (welfare due, paid annually on all savings at the rate of 2.5 per cent); *sawm* (fasting during the month of Ramadan from dawn until sunset); and *hajj* (pilgrimage to Mecca made once in a lifetime if the believer is financially and physically able). Some Muslims would add *jihad* as the sixth pillar (striving for the cause of good and resistance to evil).

Two main groups developed among Muslims. *Sunni* Muslims accept the legitimacy of Muhammad's first four *caliphs* (successors as head of the Muslim community) and of the authority of the Muslim community as a whole. About 90 per cent of Muslims are Sunni Muslims.

Shi'ites recognise only Muhammad's son-in-law Ali as his rightful successor and the *Imams* (descendants of Ali, not to be confused with *imams,* who are prayer leaders or religious teachers) as the principal legitimate religious authority. The largest group within Shi'ism is *Twelver Shi'ism,* which has been the official school of law and theology in Iran since the 16th century; other subsects include the *Ismailis,* the *Druze* and the *Alawis,* the latter two differing considerably from the main body of Muslims. The *Ibadis* of Oman are neither Sunni nor Shia, deriving from the strictly observant *Khariji* (Seceders). There is no organised priesthood, but learned men such as imams, *ulama,* and *ayatollahs* are accorded great respect. The *Sufis* are the mystics of Islam. Mosques are centres for worship and teaching and also for social and welfare activities.

Islam was first recorded in western Europe in the eighth century AD when 800 years of Muslim rule began in Spain. Later, Islam spread to eastern Europe. More recently, Muslims came to Europe from Africa, the Middle East and Asia in the late 19th century. Both the Sunni and Shi'a traditions are represented in Britain, but the majority of Muslims in Britain adhere to Sunni Islam. Efforts to establish a representative national body for Muslims in Britain resulted in the founding, in 1997, of the Muslim Council of Britain. In addition, there are many other Muslim organisations in the UK. There are around 1,200 million Muslims worldwide, with nearly two million adherents and about 1,650 mosques in the UK.

IMAMS AND MOSQUES COUNCIL, 20–22 Creffield Road, London W5 3RP T 020-8992 6636 E msraza@muslimcollege.ac.uk
Director, Moulana M. S. Raza
ISLAMIC CULTURAL CENTRE – THE LONDON CENTRAL MOSQUE, 146 Park Road, London NW8 7RG T 020-7725 2213 E info@iccuk.org W www.iccuk.org
Director, Dr Ahmad Al-Dubayan
MUSLIM WORLD LEAGUE LONDON, 46 Goodge Street, London W1T 4LU T 020-7636 7568
Director, Dr Ahmad Makhoodom
UNION OF MUSLIM ORGANISATIONS OF THE UK AND IRELAND, 109 Campden Hill Road, London W8 7TL T 020-7581 9236
Secretary-General, Dr Syed A. Pasha

JAINISM

Jainism traces its history to Vardhamana Jnatriputra, known as *Tirthankara Mahavira* (the Great Hero) whose traditional dates were 599–527 BC. Jains believe he was the last of a series of 24 *Jinas* (those who overcome all passions and desires) or *Tirthankaras* (those who show a way across the ocean of life) stretching back to remote antiquity. Born to a noble family in north-eastern India (the state of Bihar), he renounced the world for the life of a wandering ascetic and after 12 years of austerity and meditation he attained enlightenment. He then preached his message until, at the age of 72, he left the mortal world and achieved total liberation *(moksha)* from the cycle of death and rebirth.

Jains declare that the Hindu rituals of transferring merit are not acceptable as each living being is responsible for its own actions. They recognise some of the minor deities of the Hindu pantheon, but the supreme objects of worship are the Tirthankaras. The pious Jain does not ask favours from the Tirthankaras, but seeks to emulate their example in his or her own life.

Jains believe that the universe is eternal and self-subsisting, that there is no omnipotent creator God ruling it and the destiny of the individual is in his or her own hands. *Karma,* the fruit of past actions, is believed to determine the place of every living being and rebirth may be in the heavens, on earth as a human, an animal or other lower being, or in the hells. The ultimate goal of existence for Jains is *moksha,* a state of perfect knowledge and tranquility for each individual soul, which can be achieved only by gaining enlightenment.

The Jainist path to liberation is defined by the three jewels: *Samyak Darshan* (right perception), *Samyak Jnana* (right knowledge) and *Samyak Charitra* (right conduct). Of the five fundamental precepts of the Jains, *Ahimsa* (non-injury to any form of being, in any mode: thought, speech or action) is the first and foremost, and was popularised by Gandhi as *Ahimsa paramo dharma* (non-violence is the supreme religion).

The largest population of Jains can be found in India but there are approximately 30,000 Jains in Britain, sizeable communities in North America, East Africa, Australia and smaller groups in many other countries.
INSTITUTE OF JAINOLOGY, Unit 18, Silicon Business Centre, 28 Wadsworth Road, Perivale, Greenford, Middx UB6 7JZ T 020-8997 2300 E secretary@jainology.org W www.jainology.org
Hon. Secretary, Dr Harshad Sanghrajka

JUDAISM

Judaism is the oldest monotheistic faith. The primary text of Judaism is the Hebrew bible or *Tanakh,* which records

how the descendants of Abraham were led by Moses out of their slavery in Egypt to Mount Sinai where God's law *(Torah)* was revealed to them as the chosen people. The *Talmud,* which consists of commentaries on the *Mishnah* (the first text of rabbinical Judaism), is also held to be authoritative, and may be divided into two main categories: the *halakah* (dealing with legal and ritual matters) and the *aggadah* (dealing with theological and ethical matters not directly concerned with the regulation of conduct). The *midrash* comprises rabbinic writings containing biblical interpretations in the spirit of the aggadah. The halakah has become a source of division: orthodox Jews regard Jewish law as derived from God and therefore unalterable; progressive Jews seek to interpret it in the light of contemporary considerations; and conservative Jews aim to maintain most of the traditional rituals but to allow changes in accordance with tradition. Reconstructionist Judaism, a 20th-century movement, regards Judaism as a culture rather than a theological system and accepts all forms of Jewish practice.

The family is the basic unit of Jewish ritual, with the synagogue playing an important role as the centre for public worship and religious study. A synagogue is led by a group of laymen who are elected to office. The Rabbi is primarily a teacher and spiritual guide. The *Sabbath* is the central religious observance. Most British Jews are descendants of either the *Ashkenazim* of central and eastern Europe or the *Sephardim* of Spain, Portugal and the Middle East.

The Chief Rabbi of the United Hebrew Congregations of the Commonwealth is appointed by a Chief Rabbinate Conference, and is the rabbinical authority of the mainstream Orthodox sector of the Ashkenazi Jewish community, the largest body of which is the United Synagogue. His formal ecclesiastical authority is not recognised by the Reform Synagogues of Great Britain (the largest progressive group), the Union of Liberal and Progressive Synagogues, the Sephardi community or the Assembly of Masorti Synagogues. He is, however, generally recognised both outside the Jewish community and within it as the public religious representative of the totality of British Jewry. The Chief Rabbi is President of the London *Beth Din* (Court of Judgment), a rabbinic court. The *Dayanim* (Assessors) adjudicate in disputes or on matters of Jewish law and tradition; they also oversee dietary law administration, marriage, divorce and issues of personal status.

The Board of Deputies of British Jews, established in 1760, is the representative body of British Jewry. The basis of representation is through the election of deputies by synagogues and communal organisations. It protects and promotes the interests of British Jewry, acts as the central voice of the community and seeks to counter anti-Jewish discrimination and anti-Semitic activities.

There are over 12.5 million Jews worldwide; in the UK there are an estimated 300,000 adherents and over 400 synagogues.

OFFICE OF THE CHIEF RABBI, 305 Ballards Lane, London N12 8GB T 020-8343 6301 E info@chiefrabbi.org W www.chiefrabbi.org
Chief Rabbi, Lord Sacks
BETH DIN (COURT OF THE CHIEF RABBI), 305 Ballards Lane, London N12 8GB T 020-8343 6270 E info@bethdin.org.uk W www.theus.org.uk
Registrar, David Frei
Dayanim, Rabbi Chanoch Ehrentreu *(Consultant Dayan);* Menachem Gelley *(Senior Dayan);* Ivan Binstock; Yonason Abraham; Shmuel Simons

ASSEMBLY OF MASORTI SYNAGOGUES,
Alexander House, 3 Shakespeare Road, London N3 1XE
T 020-8349 6650 E enquiries@masorti.org.uk
W www.masorti.org.uk
Executive Director, Michael Gluckman
BOARD OF DEPUTIES OF BRITISH JEWS,
6 Bloomsbury Square, London WC1A 2LP T 020-7543 5400
F 020-7543 0010 E info@bod.org.uk W www.bod.org.uk
President, Vivian Wineman
FEDERATION OF SYNAGOGUES, 65 Watford Way,
London NW4 3AQ T 020-8202 2263
E info@federationofsynagogues.com
W www.federationofsynagogues.com
President, Alan Finlay
Chief Executive, Dr Eli Kienwald
LIBERAL JUDAISM, The Montagu Centre, 21 Maple Street,
London W1T 4BE T 020-7580 1663
E montagu@liberaljudaism.org W www.liberaljudaism.org
Chief Executive, Rabbi Danny Rich
THE MOVEMENT FOR REFORM JUDAISM, The
Sternberg Centre for Judaism, 80 East End Road, London
N3 2SY T 020-8349 5640 E admin@reformjudaism.org.uk
W www.reformjudaism.org.uk
Chief Executive, Ben Rich
SPANISH AND PORTUGUESE JEWS'
CONGREGATION, 2 Ashworth Road, London W9 1JY
T 020-7289 2573 E howardmiller@spsyn.org.uk
W www.sandp.org.uk
Chief Executive, Howard Miller
UNION OF ORTHODOX HEBREW
CONGREGATIONS, 140 Stamford Hill, London N16 6QT
T 020-8802 6226
Executive Coordinator, Chanoch Kesselman
Secretary, Chayim Schneck
UNITED SYNAGOGUE HEAD OFFICE, Adler House,
735 High Road, London N12 0US T 020-8343 8989
E info@theus.org.uk W www.theus.org.uk
Chief Executive, Jeremy Jacobs

PAGANISM

Paganism draws on the ideas of the Celtic people of
pre-Roman Europe and is closely linked to Druidism. The
first historical record of Druidry comes from classical
Greek and Roman writers of the third century BC, who
noted the existence of Druids among a people called the
Keltoi who inhabited central and southern Europe. The
word druid may derive from the Indo-European
'dreo-vid', meaning 'one who knows the truth'. In
practice it was probably understood to mean something
like 'wise-one' or 'philosopher-priest'.

Paganism is a pantheistic nature-worshipping religion
which incorporates beliefs and ritual practices from
ancient times. Pagans place much emphasis on the natural
world and the ongoing cycle of life and death is central to
their beliefs. Most Pagans believe that they are part of
nature and not separate from, or superior to it, and seek to
live in a way that minimises harm to the natural
environment (the word Pagan derives from the Latin
Paganus, meaning 'rural'). Paganism strongly emphasises
the equality of the sexes, with women playing a
prominent role in the modern Pagan movement and
goddess worship featuring in most ceremonies. Paganism
cannot be defined by any principal beliefs because it is
shaped by each individual's experiences.

The Pagan Federation was founded in 1971 to provide
information on Paganism, campaigns on issues which
affect Paganism and provides support to members of the
Pagan community. Within the UK the Pagan Federation is
divided into 13 districts each with a district manager,
regional and local coordinators. Local meetings are called
'moots' and take place in private homes, pubs or coffee
bars. The Pagan Federation publishes a quarterly journal,
Pagan Dawn, formerly *The Wiccan* (founded in 1968). The
federation also publishes other material, arranges
members-only and public events and maintains personal
contact by letter with individual members and the wider
Pagan community. Regional gatherings and conferences
are held throughout the year.
THE PAGAN FEDERATION, BM Box 7097, London
WC1N 3XX E secretary@paganfed.org
W www.paganfed.org
President, Chris Crowley
General Secretary, Lee-Anne Haye

SIKHISM

The Sikh religion dates from the birth of Guru Nanak in
the Punjab in 1469. 'Guru' means teacher but in Sikh
tradition has come to represent the divine presence of
God giving inner spiritual guidance. Nanak's role as the
human vessel of the divine guru was passed on to nine
successors, the last of whom (Guru Gobind Singh) died in
1708. The immortal guru is now held to reside in the
sacred scripture, Guru Granth Sahib, and so to be present
in all Sikh gatherings.

Guru Nanak taught that there is one God and that
different religions are like different roads leading to the
same destination. He condemned religious conflict,
ritualism and caste prejudices. The fifth Guru, Guru Arjan
Dev, largely compiled the Sikh Holy scripture, a
collection of hymns *(gurbani)* known as the *Adi Granth.*
It includes the writings of the first five gurus and the
ninth guru, and selected writings of Hindu and Muslim
saints whose views are in accord with the gurus'
teachings. Guru Arjan Dev also built the Golden Temple
at Amritsar, the centre of Sikhism. The tenth guru, Guru
Gobind Singh, passed on the guruship to the sacred
scripture, *Guru Granth Sahib* and founded the *Khalsa,*
an order intended to fight against tyranny and injustice.
Male initiates to the order added 'Singh' to their
given names and women added 'Kaur'. Guru Gobind
Singh also made the wearing of five symbols obligatory:
kaccha (a special undergarment), *kara* (a steel bangle),
kirpan (a small sword), *kesh* (long unshorn hair, and
consequently the wearing of a turban) and *kangha*
(a comb). These practices are still compulsory for
those Sikhs who are initiated into the Khalsa (the
Amritdharis). Those who do not seek initiation are known
as *Sehajdharis.*

There are no professional priests in Sikhism; anyone
with a reasonable proficiency in the Punjabi language can
conduct a service. Worship can be offered individually or
communally, and in a private house or a *gurdwara*
(temple). Sikhs are forbidden to eat meat prepared by
ritual slaughter; they are also asked to abstain from
smoking, alcohol and other intoxicants. Such abstention is
compulsory for the Amritdharis.

There are about 20 million Sikhs worldwide and,
according to the 2001 census, there are 336,000
adherents in the UK. Every gurdwara manages its own
affairs; there is no central body in the UK. The Sikh
Missionary Society provides an information service.
SIKH MISSIONARY SOCIETY UK, 10 Featherstone Road,
Southall, Middx UB2 5AA T 020-8574 1902
E info@sikhmissionarysociety.org
W www.sikhmissionarysociety.org
Hon. General Secretary, Teja Singh Manget

ZOROASTRIANISM

Zoroastrians are followers of the Iranian prophet Spitaman Zarathushtra (or Zoroaster in its hellenised form) who lived c.1200 BC. Zoroastrians were persecuted in Iran following the Arab invasion of Persia in the seventh century AD and a group (who are known as Parsis) migrated to India in the eighth century AD to avoid harassment and persecution. Zarathushtra's words are recorded in five poems called the *Gathas*, which, together with other scriptures, form the *Avesta*.

Zoroastrianism teaches that there is one God, *Ahura Mazda* (Wise Lord), and that all creation stems ultimately from God; the Gathas teach that human beings have free will, are responsible for their own actions and can choose between good and evil. It is believed that choosing *Asha* (truth or righteousness), with the aid of *Vohu Manah* (good mind), leads to happiness for the individual and society, whereas choosing evil leads to unhappiness and conflict. The *Gathas* also encourage hard work, good deeds and charitable acts. Zoroastrians believe that after death the immortal soul is judged by God, and is then sent to paradise or hell, where it will stay until the end of time to be resurrected for the final judgment.

In Zoroastrian places of worship, an urn containing fire is the central feature; the fire symbolises purity, light and truth and is a visible symbol of the *Fravashi* or *Farohar* (spirit), the presence of Ahura Mazda in every human being. Zoroastrians respect nature and much importance is attached to cultivating land and protecting air, earth and water.

The Zoroastrian Trust Funds of Europe is the main body for Zoroastrians in the UK. Founded in 1861 as the Religious Funds of the Zoroastrians of Europe, it disseminates information on the Zoroastrian faith, provides a place of worship and maintains separate burial grounds for Zoroastrians. It also holds religious and social functions and provides assistance to Zoroastrians as considered necessary, including the provision of loans and grants to students of Zoroastrianism.

There are approximately 140,000 Zoroastrians worldwide, of which around 7,000 reside in Britain, mainly in London and the South East.

ZOROASTRIAN TRUST FUNDS OF EUROPE, Zoroastrian Centre, 440 Alexandra Avenue, Harrow, Middx HA2 9TL T 020-8866 0765 E secretary@ztfe.com W www.ztfe.com
President, Malcolm Deboo

CHURCHES

There are two established (ie state) churches in the United Kingdom: the Church of England and the Church of Scotland. There are no established churches in Wales or Northern Ireland, though the Church in Wales, the Scottish Episcopal Church and the Church of Ireland are members of the Anglican Communion.

CHURCH OF ENGLAND

The Church of England is divided into the two provinces of Canterbury and York, each under an archbishop. The two provinces are subdivided into 44 dioceses.

Legislative provision for the Church of England is made by the General Synod, established in 1970. It also discusses and expresses opinion on any other matter of religious or public interest. The General Synod has 467 members in total, divided between three houses: the House of Bishops, the House of Clergy and the House of Laity. It is presided over jointly by the Archbishops of Canterbury and York and normally meets twice a year. The synod has the power, delegated by parliament, to frame statute law (known as a 'measure') on any matter concerning the Church of England. A measure must be laid before both houses of parliament, who may accept or reject it but cannot amend it. Once accepted the measure is submitted for royal assent and then has the full force of law. In addition to the General Synod, there are synods at diocesan level. The entire General Synod is re-elected once every five years. The ninth General Synod was inaugurated by the Queen on 23 November 2010.

The Archbishops' Council was established in January 1999. Its creation was the result of changes to the Church of England's national structure proposed in 1995 and subsequently approved by the synod and parliament. The council's purpose, set out in the National Institutions Measure 1998, is 'to coordinate, promote and further the work and mission of the Church of England'. It reports to the General Synod. The Archbishops' Council comprises the Archbishops of Canterbury and York, *ex officio,* the prolocutors elected by the convocations of Canterbury and York, the chair and vice-chair of the House of Laity, two bishops, two clergy and two lay persons elected by their respective houses of the General Synod, the Church Estates Commissioner, and up to six persons appointed jointly by the two archbishops.

There are also a number of national boards, councils and other bodies working on matters such as social responsibility, mission, Christian unity and education which report to the General Synod through the Archbishops' Council.

GENERAL SYNOD OF THE CHURCH OF ENGLAND/ ARCHBISHOPS' COUNCIL, Church House, Great Smith Street, London SW1P 3NZ T 020-7898 1000
Secretary-General, William Fittall

THE ORDINATION OF WOMEN
The canon making it possible for women to be ordained to the priesthood was promulgated in the General Synod in February 1994 and the first 32 women priests were ordained on 12 March 1994.

PORVOO DECLARATION
The Porvoo Declaration was approved by the General Synod of the Church of England in July 1995. Churches that approve the declaration regard baptised members of each other's churches as members of their own, and allow free interchange of episcopally ordained ministers within the rules of each church.

MEMBERSHIP
In 2009, 138,300 people were baptised, 52,700 people were married in parish churches, the Church of England had an electoral roll membership of 1.2 million, and each week over 1.1 million people attended services. As at December 2010 there were over 16,000 churches and places of worship; 118 dignitaries (including bishops, archdeacons and cathedral clergy); 7,296 full-time parochial stipendiary clergy; 340 full-time non parochial stipendiary clergy; 3,110 self-supporting ministers; 1,570 chaplains; 320 lay workers and Church Army evangelists; 7,090 licensed readers and 2,690 readers with permission to officiate and active emeriti; and approximately 5,670 active retired ordained clergy.

	Full-time Equivalent Diocesan Clergy 2010		Electoral Roll Membership
	Male	Female	2009
Bath and Wells	152	53	36,200
Birmingham	125	47	17,200
Blackburn	157	21	32,500
Bradford	83	18	11,700
Bristol	100	23	15,800
Canterbury	118	24	20,700
Carlisle	95	26	20,400
Chelmsford	289	85	46,500
Chester	188	55	44,900
Chichester	268	24	52,200
Coventry	100	22	16,800
Derby	107	37	18,300
Durham	147	43	23,200
Ely	96	44	18,900
Europe	–	–	10,900
Exeter	170	38	30,900
Gloucester	103	36	23,600
Guildford	139	36	29,500
Hereford	65	27	17,500
Leicester	100	41	16,800
Lichfield	246	60	43,700
Lincoln	135	36	25,800
Liverpool	154	55	28,000
London	456	81	74,100
Manchester	178	64	32,400
Newcastle	101	33	16,000
Norwich	156	37	19,300
Oxford	300	93	54,500
Peterborough	108	28	19,400
Portsmouth	83	22	17,000
Ripon and Leeds	90	36	16,500
Rochester	179	33	30,100
St Albans	174	81	37,600

St Edmundsbury	108	42	23,100
and Ipswich			
Salisbury	166	52	41,400
Sheffield	115	39	17,900
Sodor and Man	11	0	2,500
Southwark	261	88	47,600
Southwell and	102	45	18,900
Nottingham			
Truro	89	18	15,600
Wakefield	101	39	19,300
Winchester	170	26	38,000
Worcester	103	27	19,200
York	174	44	33,900
Total	6,354	1,774	1,197,000

STIPENDS*

	2011–12	*2012–13*
Archbishop of Canterbury	£71,870	£73,310
Archbishop of York	£61,600	£62,830
Bishop of London	£56,460	£57,590
Other diocesan bishops	£39,020	£39,800
Suffragan bishops	£31,830	£32,470
Assistant bishops (full-time)	£30,810	£31,430
Deans	£31,830	£32,470
Archdeacons (recommended)	£31,110	£31,730
Residentiary canons	£24,640†	£25,130†
Incumbents and clergy of	£22,810†	£23,270†
similar status		

* For those appointed on or after 1 April 2004; transitional arrangements are in place for those appointed prior to this date.
† Adjusted regionally to reflect variations in the cost of living

CANTERBURY
104TH ARCHBISHOP AND PRIMATE OF ALL ENGLAND
Most Revd and Rt. Hon. Rowan Williams, *cons.* 1992, *apptd* 2002; Lambeth Palace, London SE1 7JU
Signs Rowan Cantuar:

BISHOPS SUFFRAGAN
Dover, Rt. Revd Trevor Willmott, *cons.* 2002, *apptd* 2009; Upway, St Martin's Hill, Canterbury, Kent CT1 1PR
Ebbsfleet, vacant
Richborough, vacant

DEAN
Very Revd Robert Willis, *apptd* 2001

Organist, D. Flood, FRCO, *apptd* 1988

ARCHDEACONS
Ashford, Ven. Philip Down, *apptd* 2011
Canterbury, Ven. Sheila Watson *apptd* 2007
Maidstone, Ven. Stephen Taylor, *apptd* 2011

Vicar-General of Province and Diocese, Chancellor Sheila Cameron, QC
Commissary-General, Morag Ellis, QC
Joint Registrars of the Province, Canon John Rees; Stephen Slack
Diocesan Registrar and Legal Adviser, Owen Carew Jones
Diocesan Secretary, Julian Hills, Diocesan House, Lady Wootton's Green, Canterbury CT1 1NQ T 01227-459401

YORK
97TH ARCHBISHOP AND PRIMATE OF ENGLAND
Most Revd and Rt. Hon. Dr John Sentamu, *cons.* 1996, *trans.* 2005; Bishopthorpe, York YO23 2GE
Signs Sentamu Ebor:

BISHOPS SUFFRAGAN
Hull, Rt. Revd Richard Frith, *cons.* 1998, *apptd* 1998; Hullen House, Woodfield Lane, Hessle, Hull HU13 0ES
Selby, Rt. Revd Martin Wallace, *cons.* 2003, *apptd* 2003; Bishop's House, Barton le Street, Malton, York YO17 6PL
Whitby, Rt. Revd Martin Warner, PHD, *cons.* 2010, *apptd* 2009; 60 West Green, Stokesley, Middlesbrough TS9 5BD

PRINCIPAL EPISCOPAL VISITOR
Rt. Revd Martyn Jarrett (*Bishop Suffragan of Beverley*), *cons.* 1994, *apptd* 2000; 3 North Lane, Roundhay, Leeds LS8 2QJ

DEAN
Very Revd Keith Jones, *apptd* 2004

Director of Music, Robert Sharpe, *apptd* 2008

ARCHDEACONS
Cleveland, Ven. Paul Ferguson, *apptd* 2001
East Riding, Ven. David Butterfield, *apptd* 2006
York, Ven. Richard Seed, *apptd* 1999

Chancellor of the Diocese, His Hon. Judge Collier, QC, *apptd* 2006
Registrar and Legal Secretary, Lionel Lennox
Diocesan Secretary, Peter Warry, Diocesan House, Aviator Court, Clifton Moor, York YO30 4WJ T 01904-699500

LONDON (CANTERBURY)
132ND BISHOP
Rt. Revd and Rt. Hon. Richard Chartres, KCVO, *cons.* 1992, *apptd* 1995; The Old Deanery, Dean's Court, London EC4V 5AA
Signs Richard Londin:

AREA BISHOPS
Edmonton, Rt. Revd Peter Wheatley, *cons.* 1999, *apptd* 1999; 27 Thurlow Road, London NW3 5PP
Kensington, Rt. Revd Paul Williams, *cons.* 2009, *apptd* 2008; Dial House, Riverside, Twickenham, Middlesex TW1 3DT
Stepney, Rt. Revd Adrian Newman, *cons.* 2011, *apptd* 2011; 63 Coburn Road, London E3 2DB
Willesden, Rt. Revd Peter Broadbent, *cons.* 2001, *apptd* 2001; 173 Willesden Lane, London NW6 7YN

BISHOP SUFFRAGAN
Fulham, vacant

DEAN OF ST PAUL'S
Rt. Revd Graeme Knowles, *apptd* 2007

Director of Music, Andrew Carwood, *apptd* 2007

ARCHDEACONS
Charing Cross, Ven. Dr William Jacob, *apptd* 1996
Hackney, vacant
Hampstead, Ven. Luke Miller, *apptd* 2011
London, Ven. David Meara, *apptd* 2009
Middlesex, Ven. Stephan Welch, *apptd* 2006
Northolt, Ven. Rachel Treweek, *apptd* 2006

Chancellor, Nigel Seed, QC, *apptd* 2002
Registrar and Legal Secretary, Paul Morris
Diocesan Secretary, Andrew Brookes, London Diocesan House, 36 Causton Street, London SW1P 4AU T 020-7932 1100

DURHAM *(YORK)*
72ND BISHOP
Rt. Revd Justin Welby, *cons.* 2011, *apptd* 2011;
Auckland Castle, Bishop Auckland DL14 7NR
Signs Justin Dunelm:

BISHOP SUFFRAGAN
Jarrow, Rt. Revd Mark Bryant, *cons.* 2007, *apptd* 2007;
Bishop's House, 25 Ivy Lane, Low Fell, Gateshead NE9 6QD

DEAN
Very Revd Michael Sadgrove, *apptd* 2003

Organist, James Lancelot, FRCO, *apptd* 1985

ARCHDEACONS
Auckland, Ven. Nicholas Barker, *apptd* 2007
Durham, Ven. Ian Jagger, *apptd* 2006
Sunderland, Ven. Stuart Bain, *apptd* 2002

Chancellor, The Worshipful Revd Dr Rupert Bursell, QC, *apptd* 1989
Registrar and Legal Secretary, Hilary Monckton-Milnes
Diocesan Secretary, Ian Boothroyd, Diocesan Office, Auckland Castle, Bishop Auckland, Co. Durham DL14 7QJ T 01388-604515

WINCHESTER *(CANTERBURY)*
97TH BISHOP
vacant

BISHOPS SUFFRAGAN
Basingstoke, Rt. Revd Peter Hancock, *apptd* 2010, *cons.* 2010; Bishop's Lodge, Colden Lane, Old Alresford, Hants SO24 9DY
Southampton, Rt. Revd Jonathan Frost, *apptd* 2010; Old Alresford Place, Alresford, Hants SO24 9DH

DEAN
Very Revd James Atwell, *apptd* 2005
Dean of Jersey (A Peculiar), Very Revd Robert Key, *apptd* 2005
Dean of Guernsey (A Peculiar), Very Revd Paul Mellor, *apptd* 2003
Director of Music, Andrew Lumsden, *apptd* 2002

ARCHDEACONS
Bournemouth, vacant
Winchester, Ven. Michael Harley, *apptd* 2009

Chancellor, His Hon. Judge Clark, QC, *apptd* 1993
Registrar and Legal Secretary, Andrew Johnson
Diocesan Secretary, Andrew Robinson, Old Alresford Place, Alresford, Hants SO24 9DH T 01962-737300

BATH AND WELLS *(CANTERBURY)*
78TH BISHOP
Rt. Revd Peter Price, *cons.* 1997, *apptd* 2003; The Palace, Wells BA5 2PD
Signs Peter Bath & Wells

BISHOP SUFFRAGAN
Taunton, Rt. Revd Peter Maurice, *cons.* 2006, *apptd* 2006; The Palace, Wells BA5 2PD

DEAN
Very Revd John Clarke, *apptd* 2004

Organist, Matthew Owens, *apptd* 2005

ARCHDEACONS
Bath, Ven. Andrew Piggott, *apptd* 2005
Taunton, Ven. John Reed, *apptd* 1999
Wells, Ven. Nicola Sullivan, *apptd* 2006

Chancellor, Timothy Briden, *apptd* 1993
Registrar and Legal Secretary, Tim Berry
Diocesan Secretary, Nick Denison, The Old Deanery, Wells, Somerset BA5 2UG T 01749-670777

BIRMINGHAM *(CANTERBURY)*
8TH BISHOP
Rt. Revd David Urquhart, *cons.* 2000, *apptd* 2006;
Bishop's Croft, Old Church Road, Harborne, Birmingham B17 0BG
Signs David Birmingham:

BISHOP SUFFRAGAN
Aston, Rt. Revd Andrew Watson, *cons.* 2008, *apptd* 2008;
175 Harborne Park Road, Birmingham B17 0BH

DEAN
Very Revd Catherine Ogle, *apptd* 2010

Director of Music, Marcus Huxley, FRCO, *apptd* 1986

ARCHDEACONS
Aston, Ven. Dr Brian Russell, *apptd* 2005
Birmingham, Ven. Hayward Osborne, *apptd* 2001

Chancellor, His Hon. Judge Cardinal, *apptd* 2005
Registrar and Legal Secretary, Hugh Carslake
Diocesan Secretary, Andrew Halstead, 175 Harborne Park Road, Harborne, Birmingham B17 0BH T 0121-426 0400

BLACKBURN *(YORK)*
8TH BISHOP
Rt. Revd Nicholas Reade, *apptd* 2003, *cons.* March 2004;
Bishop's House, Ribchester Road, Blackburn BB1 9EF
Signs Nicholas Blackburn

BISHOPS SUFFRAGAN
Burnley, Rt. Revd John Goddard, *cons.* 2000, *apptd* 2000;
All Saints House, Padiham Road, Burnley BB12 6PA
Lancaster, Rt. Revd Geoffrey Pearson, *cons.* 2006, *apptd* 2006; The Vicarage, Whinney Brow Lane, Shireshead, Forton, Preston PR3 0AE

DEAN
Very Revd Christopher Armstrong, *apptd* 2001

Organist and Director of Music, vacant

ARCHDEACON
Blackburn, Ven. John Hawley, *apptd* 2002
Lancaster, Ven. Michael Everitt, *apptd* 2011

Chancellor, His Hon. Judge Bullimore, *apptd* 1990
Registrar and Legal Secretary, Thomas Hoyle
Diocesan Secretary, Graeme Pollard, Diocesan Office, Cathedral Close, Blackburn BB1 5AA T 01254-503070

BRADFORD *(YORK)*
10TH BISHOP
Rt. Revd Nicholas Baines, *cons.* 2003, *apptd* 2010;
Bishopscroft, Ashwell Road, Heaton, Bradford BD9 4AU
Signs Nicholas Bradford

DEAN
Very Revd Dr David Ison, *apptd* 2005

Organist, Andrew Teague, FRCO, *apptd* 2003

ARCHDEACONS
Bradford, Ven. David Lee, *apptd* 2004
Craven, Ven. Paul Slater, *apptd* 2005

Chancellor, His Hon. Judge Walford, *apptd* 1999
Registrar and Legal Secretary, Peter Foskett
Diocesan Secretary (acting), Debbie Child, Kadugli House, Elmsley Street, Steeton, Keighley BD20 6SE **T** 01535-650555

BRISTOL *(CANTERBURY)*
55TH BISHOP
Rt. Revd Michael Hill, *cons.* 1998, *apptd* 2003;
58A High Street, Winterbourne, Bristol BS36 1JQ
Signs Michael Bristol

BISHOP SUFFRAGAN
Swindon, Rt. Revd Dr Lee Rayfield, *cons.* 2005, *apptd* 2005; Mark House, Field Rise, Swindon, Wiltshire, SN1 4HP

DEAN
Very Revd David Hoyle, *apptd* 2010

Organist and Director of Music, Mark Lee, *apptd* 1998

ARCHDEACONS
Bristol, Ven. Tim McClure, *apptd* 1999
Malmesbury, Ven. Christine Froude, *apptd* 2011

Acting Chancellor, Timothy Briden
Registrar and Legal Secretary, Tim Berry
Diocesan Secretary, Lesley Farrall, Diocesan Church House, 23 Great George Street, Bristol BS1 5QZ **T** 0117-906 0100

CARLISLE *(YORK)*
67TH BISHOP
Rt. Revd James Newcome, *cons.* 2002, *apptd* 2009;
Bishop's House, Ambleside Road, Keswick CA12 4DD
Signs James Carliol

BISHOP SUFFRAGAN
Penrith, vacant; Holm Croft, Castle Road, Kendal, Cumbria LA9 7AU

DEAN
Very Revd Mark Boyling, *apptd* 2004

Organist, Jeremy Suter, FRCO, *apptd* 1991

ARCHDEACONS
Carlisle, Ven. Kevin Roberts, *apptd* 2009
West Cumberland, Ven. Dr Richard Pratt, *apptd* 2009
Westmorland and Furness, vacant

Chancellor, Geoffrey Tattersall, QC, *apptd* 2003
Registrar and Legal Secretary, Jane Lowdon
Diocesan Secretary, Derek Hurton, Church House, West Walls, Carlisle CA3 8UE **T** 01228-522573

CHELMSFORD *(CANTERBURY)*
10TH BISHOP
Rt. Revd Stephen Cottrell, *cons.* 2004, *apptd.* 2010;
Bishopscourt, Main Road, Margaretting, Ingatestone, Essex CM4 0HD
Signs Stephen Chelmsford

BISHOPS SUFFRAGAN
Barking, Rt. Revd David Hawkins, *cons.* 2002, *apptd* 2003; Barking Lodge, Verulam Avenue, London, E17 8ES
Bradwell, vacant
Colchester, Rt. Revd Christopher Morgan, *cons.* 2001, *apptd* 2001; 1 Fitzwalter Road, Colchester, Essex CO3 3SS

DEAN
Very Revd Peter S. M. Judd, *apptd* 1997

Master of Music, Peter Nardone, *apptd* 2000

ARCHDEACONS
Colchester, Ven. Annette Cooper, *apptd* 2004
Harlow, Ven. Martin Webster, *apptd* 2009
Southend, Ven. David Lowman, *apptd* 2001
West Ham, Ven. Elwin Cockett, *apptd* 2007

Chancellor, George Pulman QC, *apptd* 2001
Registrar and Legal Secretary, Brian Hood
Chief Executive, John Ball, 53 New Street, Chelmsford, Essex CM1 1AT **T** 01245-294400

CHESTER *(YORK)*
40TH BISHOP
Rt. Revd Peter Forster, PHD, *cons.* 1996, *apptd* 1996;
Bishop's House, Abbey Square, Chester CH1 2JD
Signs Peter Cestr:

BISHOPS SUFFRAGAN
Birkenhead, Rt. Revd Keith Sinclair, *cons.* 2007, *apptd* 2007; Bishop's Lodge, 67 Bidston Road, Prenton CH43 6TR
Stockport, Rt. Revd Robert Atwell, *cons.* 2008, *apptd* 2008; Bishop's Lodge, Back Lane, Dunham Town, Altrincham WA14 4SG

DEAN
Very Revd Dr Gordon McPhate, *apptd* 2002

Organist and Director of Music, Philip Rushforth, FRCO, *apptd* 2008

ARCHDEACONS
Chester, Ven. Dr Michael Gilbertson, *apptd* 2010
Macclesfield, Ven. Ian Bishop, *apptd* 2011

Chancellor, His Hon. Judge Turner, QC, *apptd* 1998
Registrar and Legal Secretary, Helen McFall
Diocesan Secretary, George Colville, Church House, Lower Lane, Aldford, Chester CH3 6HP **T** 01244-681973

CHICHESTER *(CANTERBURY)*
102ND BISHOP
Rt. Revd Dr John Hind, *cons.* 1991, *apptd* 2001;
The Palace, Chichester PO19 1PY
Signs John Cicestr:

BISHOPS SUFFRAGAN
Horsham, Rt. Revd Mark Sowerby, *cons.* 2009, *apptd* 2009
Lewes, Rt. Revd Wallace Benn, *cons.* 1997, *apptd* 1997; Bishop's Lodge, 16A Prideaux Road, Eastbourne, E. Sussex BN21 2NB

DEAN
Very Revd Nicholas Frayling, *apptd* 2002

Organist, Sarah Baldock, *apptd* 2007

ARCHDEACONS
Chichester, Ven. Douglas McKittrick, *apptd* 2002
Horsham, Ven. Roger Combes, *apptd* 2003
Lewes and Hastings, Ven. Philip Jones, *apptd* 2005

Chancellor, Mark Hill
Registrar and Legal Secretary, John Stapleton
Diocesan Secretary, Angela Sibson, OBE, Diocesan Church House, 211 New Church Road, Hove, E. Sussex BN3 4ED **T** 01273-421021

COVENTRY *(CANTERBURY)*
9TH BISHOP
Rt. Revd Dr Christopher Cocksworth, *cons.* 2008, *apptd* 2008; The Bishop's House, 23 Davenport Road, Coventry CV5 6PW
Signs Christopher Coventry

BISHOP SUFFRAGAN
Warwick, Rt. Revd John Stroyan, *cons.* 2005, *apptd* 2005; Warwick House, 139 Kenilworth Road, Coventry CV4 7AP

DEAN
Very Revd John Irvine, *apptd* 2001

Director of Music, Mr Kerry Beaumont, *apptd* 2006

ARCHDEACONS
Coventry, Ven. Ian Watson, *apptd* 2007
Warwick, Ven. Morris Rodham, *apptd* 2010

Chancellor, Stephen Eyre, *apptd* 2009
Registrar and Legal Secretary, Mary Allanson
Diocesan Secretary, Simon Lloyd, Cathedral & Diocesan Offices, 1 Hilltop, Coventry CV1 5AB T 024-7652 1200

DERBY *(CANTERBURY)*
7TH BISHOP
Rt. Revd Dr Alastair Redfern, *cons.* 1997, *apptd* 2005; The Bishop's House, 6 King Street, Duffield, Belper, Derbyshire DE56 4EU
Signs Alastair Derby

BISHOP SUFFRAGAN
Repton, Rt. Revd Humphrey Southern, *cons.* 2007, *apptd* 2007; Repton House, Lea, Matlock, Derbyshire DE4 5JP

DEAN
Very Revd Dr John Davies *apptd* 2010

Organist, Peter Gould, *apptd* 1982

ARCHDEACONS
Chesterfield, Ven. Christine Wilson, *apptd* 2010
Derby, Ven. Dr Christopher Cunliffe, *apptd* 2006

Chancellor, His Hon. Judge Bullimore, *apptd* 1981
Registrar and Legal Secretary, Mrs Nadine Waldron
Diocesan Secretary, Bob Carey, Derby Church House, Full Street, Derby DE1 3DR T 01332-388650

ELY *(CANTERBURY)*
69TH BISHOP
Rt. Revd Stephen Conway, *cons.* 2006, *apptd* 2011; The Bishop's House, Ely CB7 4DW
Signs Stephen Ely

BISHOP SUFFRAGAN
Huntingdon, Rt. Revd David Thomson, DPHIL, *cons.* 2008, *apptd* 2008; 14 Lynn Road, Ely, Cambs CB6 1DA

DEAN
Very Revd Dr Michael Chandler, *apptd* 2003

Director of Music, Paul Trepte, FRCO, *apptd* 1991

ARCHDEACONS
Cambridge, Ven. John Beer, *apptd* 2004
Huntingdon and Wisbech, Ven. Hugh McCurdy, *apptd* 2005

Chancellor, Rt. Hon. Sir William Gage, QC
Registrar, Peter Beesley

Diocesan Secretary, Graham Shorter, Bishop Woodford House, Barton Road, Ely, Cambs CB7 4DX T 01353-652700

EXETER *(CANTERBURY)*
70TH BISHOP
Rt. Revd Michael Langrish, *cons.* 1993, *apptd* 2000; The Palace, Exeter EX1 1HY
Signs Michael Exon:

BISHOPS SUFFRAGAN
Crediton, Rt. Revd Robert Evens, *cons.* 2004, *apptd* 2004; 32 The Avenue, Tiverton EX16 4HW
Plymouth, Rt. Revd John Ford, *cons.* 2006, *apptd* 2005; 31 Riverside Walk, Tamerton Foliot, Plymouth PL5 4AQ

DEAN
vacant

Director of Music, Andrew Millington, *apptd* 1999

ARCHDEACONS
Barnstaple, Ven. David Gunn-Johnson, *apptd* 2003
Exeter, Ven. Penny Driver, *apptd* 2006
Plymouth, Ven. Ian Chandler, *apptd* 2010
Totnes, Ven. John Rawlings, *apptd* 2006

Chancellor, Hon. Sir Andrew McFarlane
Registrar and Legal Secretary, M. Follett
Diocesan Secretary, Mark Beedell, The Old Deanery, The Cloisters, Exeter EX1 1HS T 01392-272686

GIBRALTAR IN EUROPE *(CANTERBURY)*
3RD BISHOP
Rt. Revd Dr Geoffrey Rowell, *cons.* 1994, *apptd* 2001; Bishop's Lodge, Church Road, Worth, Crawley, West Sussex RH10 7RT

BISHOP SUFFRAGAN
In Europe, Rt. Revd David Hamid, *cons.* 2002, *apptd* 2002; 14 Tufton Street, London SW1P 3QZ
Dean, Cathedral Church of the Holy Trinity, Gibraltar, Very Revd Dr John Paddock

Chancellor, Pro-Cathedral of St Paul, Valletta, Malta, Canon Simon Godfrey
Chancellor, Pro-Cathedral of the Holy Trinity, Brussels, Belgium, Canon Dr Robert Innes

ARCHDEACONS
Eastern, Ven. Patrick Curran
North-West Europe, Ven. John de Wit
France, Ven. Kenneth Letts
Gibraltar, Ven. David Sutch
Italy, Ven. Jonathan Boardman
Scandinavia and Germany, Ven. Jonathan Lloyd
Switzerland, Ven. Peter Potter

Chancellor, Mark Hill
Registrar and Legal Secretary, Aiden Hargreaves-Smith
Diocesan Secretary, Adrian Mumford, 14 Tufton Street, London SW1P 3QZ T 020-7898 1155

GLOUCESTER *(CANTERBURY)*
40TH BISHOP
Rt. Revd Michael Perham, *cons.* 2004, *apptd* 2004; 2 College Green, Gloucester GL1 2LR
Signs Michael Gloucestr

BISHOP SUFFRAGAN
Tewkesbury, Rt. Revd John Went, *cons.* 1995, *apptd* 1995; 2 College Green, Gloucester GL1 2LR

DEAN
Very Revd Stephen Lake, *apptd* 2011

Director of Music, Adrian Partington, *apptd* 2007

ARCHDEACONS
Cheltenham, Ven. Robert Springett, *apptd* 2010
Gloucester, Ven. Geoffrey Sidaway, *apptd* 2000

Chancellor and Vicar-General, June Rodgers, *apptd* 1990
Registrar and Legal Secretary, Chris Peak
Diocesan Secretary, Dr Kevin Brown, Church House,
College Green, Gloucester GL1 2LY **T** 01452-410022

GUILDFORD *(CANTERBURY)*
9TH BISHOP
Rt. Revd Christopher Hill, *cons.* 1996, *apptd* 2004;
Willow Grange, Woking Road, Guildford GU4 7QS
Signs Christopher Guildford

BISHOP SUFFRAGAN
Dorking, Rt. Revd Ian Brackley, *cons.* 1996, *apptd* 1995;
Dayspring, 13 Pilgrims Way, Guildford GU4 8AD

DEAN
Very Revd Victor Stock, *apptd* 2002

Organist, Katherine Dienes-Williams, *apptd* 2007

ARCHDEACONS
Dorking, Ven. Julian Henderson, *apptd* 2005
Surrey, Ven. Stuart Beake, *apptd* 2005

Chancellor, Andrew Jordan
Registrar and Legal Secretary, Peter Beesley
Diocesan Secretary, Stephen Marriott, Diocesan House,
Quarry Street, Guildford GU1 3AG **T** 01483-571826

HEREFORD *(CANTERBURY)*
104TH BISHOP
Rt. Revd Anthony Priddis, *cons.* 1996, *apptd* 2004;
The Bishop's House, Hereford HR4 9BN
Signs Anthony Hereford

BISHOP SUFFRAGAN
Ludlow, Rt. Revd Alistair Magowan, *cons.* 2009, *apptd*
2009; Bishop's House, Corvedale Road, Craven Arms,
Shropshire SY7 9BT

DEAN
Very Revd Michael Tavinor, *apptd* 2002

Organist and Director of Music, Geraint Bowen, FRCO,
apptd 2001

ARCHDEACONS
Hereford, Ven. Paddy Benson, *apptd* 2011
Ludlow, Rt. Revd Alistair Magowan, *apptd* 2009

Chancellor, His Hon. Judge Kaye, QC
Registrar and Legal Secretary, Peter Beesley
Diocesan Secretary, John Clark, The Palace, Hereford HR4 9BL
T 01432-373300

LEICESTER *(CANTERBURY)*
6TH BISHOP
Rt. Revd Timothy Stevens, *cons.* 1995, *apptd* 1999;
Bishop's Lodge, 10 Springfield Road, Leicester LE2 3BD
Signs Timothy Leicester

ASSISTANT BISHOP
Rt. Revd Christopher Boyle, *cons.* 2000, *apptd* 2009;
Church House, St Martin' East, Leicester LE1 5FX

DEAN
Very Revd Vivienne Faull, *apptd* 2000

Director of Music, Dr Christopher Johns

ARCHDEACONS
Leicester, Ven. Richard Atkinson, *apptd* 2002
Loughborough, Ven. David Newman, *apptd* 2009

Chancellor, Dr James Behrens
Registrar and Legal Secretary, Revd Trevor Kirkman
Diocesan Secretary, Jonathan Kerry, St Martin's House,
7 Peacock Lane, Leicester LE1 5PZ **T** 0116-261 5200

LICHFIELD *(CANTERBURY)*
98TH BISHOP
Rt. Revd Jonathan Gledhill *cons.* 1996, *apptd* 2003;
Bishop's House, The Close, Lichfield WS13 7LG
Signs Jonathan Lichfield

BISHOPS SUFFRAGAN
Shrewsbury, Rt. Revd Mark Rylands, *cons.* 2009, *apptd*
2009; Athlone House, 66 London Road, Shrewsbury
SY2 6PG
Stafford, Rt. Revd Geoffrey Annas, *cons.* 2010, *apptd*
2010; Ash Garth, Broughton Crescent, Barlaston,
Stoke-on-Trent ST12 9DD
Wolverhampton, Rt. Revd Clive Gregory, *cons.* 2007,
apptd 2007; 61 Richmond Road, Wolverhampton WV3 9JH

DEAN
Very Revd Adrian Dorber, *apptd* 2005

Directors of Music, Ben and Cathy Lamb, *apptd* 2010
Organist, Martyn Rawles, *apptd* 2010

ARCHDEACONS
Lichfield, Ven. Christopher Liley, *apptd* 2001
Salop, Ven. Paul Thomas, *apptd* 2011
Stoke-on-Trent, Ven. Godfrey Owen Stone, *apptd* 2002
Walsall, Ven. Christopher Sims, *apptd* 2009

Chancellor, vacant
Registrar and Legal Secretary, N. Blackie
Diocesan Secretary, Julie Jones, St Mary's House, The Close,
Lichfield, Staffs WS13 7LD **T** 01543-306030

LINCOLN *(CANTERBURY)*
72ND BISHOP
Rt. Revd Christopher Lowson *cons.* 2011, *apptd* 2011;
Bishop's House, Eastgate, Lincoln LN2 1QQ
Signs Christopher Lincoln

BISHOPS SUFFRAGAN
Grantham, Rt. Revd Dr Timothy Ellis, *cons.* 2006, *apptd*
2006; Saxonwell Vicarage, Church Street, Long
Bennington, Newark NG23 5ES
Grimsby, Rt. Revd David D. J. Rossdale, *cons.* 2000, *apptd*
2000; Bishop's House, Church Lane, Irby-upon-Humber,
Grimsby DN37 7JR

DEAN
Very Revd Philip Buckler, *apptd* 2007

Director of Music, A. Prentice, *apptd* 2003

ARCHDEACONS
Lincoln, Ven. Timothy Barker, *apptd* 2009
Lindsey and Stow, Ven. Jane Sinclair, *apptd* 2007

Chancellor, His Hon. Judge Mark Bishop, QC, *apptd* 2007
Registrar and Legal Secretary, Caroline Mockford, *apptd*
2008

Diocesan Secretary, Max Manin, The Old Palace, Lincoln LN2 1PU **T** 01522-504050

LIVERPOOL *(YORK)*
7TH BISHOP
Rt. Revd James Jones, *cons.* 1994, *apptd* 1998; Bishop's Lodge, Woolton Park, Liverpool L25 6DT
Signs James Liverpool

BISHOP SUFFRAGAN
Warrington, Rt. Revd Richard Blackburn, *cons.* 2009, *apptd* 2009; 34 Central Avenue, Eccleston Park, Liverpool L34 2QP

DEAN
vacant

Director of Music, David Poulter, *apptd* 2008

ARCHDEACONS
Liverpool, Ven. Richard Panter, *apptd* 2002
Warrington, Ven. Peter Bradley, *apptd* 2001

Chancellor, Hon. Sir Mark Hedley
Registrar and Legal Secretary, Howard Dellar
Diocesan Secretary, Mike Eastwood, St James House, 20 St James Street, Liverpool L1 7BY **T** 0151-709 9722

MANCHESTER *(YORK)*
11TH BISHOP
Rt. Revd Nigel McCulloch, *cons.* 1986, *apptd* 2002, *trans.* 2002; Bishopscourt, Bury New Road, Manchester M7 4LE
Signs Nigel Manchester

BISHOPS SUFFRAGAN
Bolton, Rt. Revd Christopher Edmondson, *cons.* 2008, *apptd* 2008; Bishop's Lodge, Walkden Road, Worsley, Manchester M28 2WH
Middleton, Rt. Revd Mark Davies, *cons.* 2008, *apptd* 2008; The Hollies, Manchester Road, Rochdale OL11 3QY

DEAN
Revd Rogers Govender, *apptd* 2006

Organist, Christopher Stokes, *apptd* 1992

ARCHDEACONS
Bolton, Ven. David Bailey, *apptd* 2008
Manchester, Ven. Mark Ashcroft, *apptd* 2009
Rochdale, Ven. Cherry Vann, *apptd* 2008
Salford, Ven. David Sharples, *apptd* 2009

Chancellor, Geoffrey Tattersall, QC
Registrar and Legal Secretary, Jane Monks
Diocesan Secretary, Martin Miller, Diocesan Church House, 90 Deansgate, Manchester M3 2GH **T** 0161-828 1400

NEWCASTLE *(YORK)*
11TH BISHOP
Rt. Revd J. Martin Wharton, CBE, *cons.* 1992, *apptd* 1997; Bishop's House, 29 Moor Road South, Gosforth, Newcastle upon Tyne NE3 1PA
Signs Martin Newcastle

ASSISTANT BISHOP
Rt. Revd Frank White, *cons.* 2002, *apptd* 2010

DEAN
Very Revd Christopher C. Dalliston, *apptd* 2003

Director of Music, Michael Stoddart, *apptd* 2009

ARCHDEACONS
Lindisfarne, Ven. Dr Peter Robinson, *apptd* 2008
Northumberland, Ven. Geoffrey Miller, *apptd* 2004

Chancellor, His Hon. Judge David Hodson, *apptd* 2009
Registrar and Legal Secretary, Jane Lowdon
Diocesan Secretary, Graham Barnard, Church House, St John's Terrace, North Shields NE29 6HS **T** 0191-270 4100

NORWICH *(CANTERBURY)*
71ST BISHOP
Rt. Revd Graham R. James, *cons.* 1993, *apptd* 2000; Bishop's House, Norwich NR3 1SB
Signs Graham Norvic:

BISHOPS SUFFRAGAN
Lynn, Rt. Revd Jonathan Meyrick, *cons.* 2011, *apptd* 2011; The Old Vicarage, Castle Acre, King's Lynn PE32 2AA
Thetford, Rt. Revd Alan Winton PHD, *cons.* 2009, *apptd* 2009; The Red House, 53 Norwich Road, Stoke Holy Cross, Norwich NR14 8AB

DEAN
Very Revd Graham Smith, *apptd* 2004

Master of Music, David Lowe, *apptd* 2007

ARCHDEACONS
Lynn, Ven. John Ashe, *apptd* 2009
Norfolk, Ven. David Hayden, *apptd* 2002
Norwich, Ven. Jan McFarlane, *apptd* 2008

Chancellor, His Hon. Judge Downes, *apptd* 2007
Registrar and Legal Secretary, Stuart Jones
Diocesan Secretary, Richard Butler, Diocesan House, 109 Dereham Road, Easton, Norwich, Norfolk NR9 5ES **T** 01603-880853

OXFORD *(CANTERBURY)*
42ND BISHOP
Rt. Revd John Pritchard *cons.* 2002, *apptd* 2007; Diocesan Church House, North Hinksey Lane, Oxford OX2 0NB
Signs John Oxon:

AREA BISHOPS
Buckingham, Rt. Revd Dr Alan Wilson *cons.* 2003, *apptd* 2003; Sheridan, Grimms Hill, Great Missenden, Bucks HP16 9BD
Dorchester, Rt. Revd Colin Fletcher, *cons.* 2000, *apptd* 2000; Arran House, Sandy Lane, Yarnton, Oxon OX5 1PB
Reading, Rt. Revd Andrew Proud, *cons.* 2011 *apptd* 2011; Bishop's House, Tidmarsh Lane, Tidmarsh, Reading RG8 8HA

DEAN OF CHRIST CHURCH
Very Revd Dr Christopher Lewis, *apptd* 2003

Organist, Dr Stephen Darlington, FRCO, *apptd* 1985

ARCHDEACONS
Berkshire, Ven. Norman Russell, *apptd* 1998
Buckingham, Ven. Karen Gorham, *apptd* 2007
Oxford, Ven. Julian Hubbard, *apptd* 2005

Chancellor, Revd Dr Rupert Bursell, *apptd* 2001
Registrar and Legal Secretary, Revd Canon John Rees
Diocesan Secretary, Rosemary Pearce, Diocesan Church House, North Hinksey, Oxford OX2 0NB **T** 01865-208202

PETERBOROUGH *(CANTERBURY)*
38TH BISHOP
Rt. Revd Donald Allister, *cons.* 2010, *apptd* 2009; Bishop's
Lodging, The Palace, Peterborough PE1 1YA
Signs Donald Petriburg:

BISHOP SUFFRAGAN
Brixworth, Rt. Revd John Holbrook, *cons.* 2011, *apptd*
2011; Orchard Acre, 11 North Street, Mears Ashby,
Northants NN6 0DW

DEAN
Very Revd Charles Taylor, *apptd* 2007

Director of Music, Andrew Reid, *apptd* 2004

ARCHDEACONS
Northampton, Ven. Christine Allsopp, *apptd* 2005
Oakham, Ven. David Painter, *apptd* 2000

Chancellor, David Pittaway, QC, *apptd* 2005
Registrar and Legal Secretary, Revd Raymond Hemingray
Diocesan Secretary, Canon Richard Pestell, Diocesan Office,
The Palace, Peterborough PE1 1YB T 01733-887000

PORTSMOUTH *(CANTERBURY)*
9TH BISHOP
Rt. Revd Christopher Foster, *cons.* 2010, *apptd* 2010;
Bishopsgrove, 26 Osborn Road, Fareham, Hants PO16 7DQ
Signs Christopher Portsmouth

DEAN
Very Revd David Brindley, *apptd* 2002

Organist, David Price, *apptd* 1996

ARCHDEACONS
Isle of Wight, Ven. Caroline Baston, *apptd* 2006
Portsdown, Ven. Trevor Reader, *apptd* 2006
The Meon, Ven. Gavin Collins, *apptd* 2011

Chancellor, C. Clark, QC
Registrar and Legal Secretary, Hilary Tyler
Diocesan Secretary, Wendy Kennedy, Diocesan Offices,
1st Floor, Peninsular House, Wharf Road, Portsmouth
PO2 8HB T 023-9289 9664

RIPON AND LEEDS *(YORK)*
12TH BISHOP
Rt. Revd John Packer, *cons.* 1996, *apptd* 2000;
Hollin House, Weetwood Avenue LS16 5NG
Signs John Ripon and Leeds

BISHOP SUFFRAGAN
Knaresborough, Rt. Revd James Bell, *cons.* 2004, *apptd*
2004; Thistledown, Main Street, Exelby, Bedale DL8 2HD

DEAN
Revd Keith Jukes, *apptd* 2007

Director of Music, Andrew Bryden, *apptd* 2003

ARCHDEACONS
Leeds, Ven. Peter Burrows, *apptd* 2005
Richmond, Ven. Janet Henderson, *apptd* 2007

Chancellor, His Hon. Judge Simon Grenfell, *apptd* 1992
Registrars and Legal Secretaries, Nicola Harding;
   Christopher Tunnard
Diocesan Secretary, Dr Sue Proctor, Diocesan Office,
St Mary's Street, Leeds LS9 7DP T 0113-200 0540

ROCHESTER *(CANTERBURY)*
107TH BISHOP
Rt. Revd James Langstaff, *cons.* 2004 *apptd* 2010;
Bishopscourt, 24 St Margaret's Street, Rochester ME1 1TS

BISHOP SUFFRAGAN
Tonbridge, Rt. Revd Dr Brian C. Castle, *cons.* 2002, *apptd*
2002; Bishop's Lodge, 48 St Botolph's Road, Sevenoaks
TN13 3AG

DEAN
Very Revd Adrian Newman, *apptd* 2004

Director of Music, Scott Farrell, *apptd* 2008

ARCHDEACONS
Bromley, Ven. Dr Paul Wright, *apptd* 2003
Rochester, Ven. Simon Burton-Jones, *apptd* 2010
Tonbridge, Ven. Clive Mansell, *apptd* 2002

Chancellor, John Gallagher, *apptd* 2006
Registrar and Legal Secretary, Owen Carew-Jones
Diocesan Secretary, Canon Louise Gilbert, St Nicholas
Church, Boley Hill, Rochester ME1 1SL T 01634-560000

ST ALBANS *(CANTERBURY)*
10TH BISHOP
Rt. Revd Dr Alan Smith, *cons.* 2001, *apptd* 2009, *trans.*
2009; Abbey Gate House, St Albans AL3 4HD
Signs Alan St Albans

BISHOPS SUFFRAGAN
Bedford, Rt. Revd Richard N. Inwood, *cons.* 2003,
   apptd 2003; Bishop's Lodge, Bedford Road, Cardington,
   Bedford MK44 3SS
Hertford, Rt. Revd Paul Bayes, *cons.* 2010, *apptd* 2010;
   Bishopswood, 3 Stobarts Close, Knebworth, Herts SG3 6ND

DEAN
Very Revd Dr Jeffrey John, *apptd* 2004

Organist, Andrew Lucas, *apptd* 1998

ARCHDEACONS
Bedford, Ven. Paul Hughes, *apptd* 2004
Hertford, Ven. Trevor Jones, *apptd* 1997
St Albans, Ven. Jonathan Smith, *apptd* 2008

Chancellor, Roger Kaye, *apptd* 2002
Registrar and Legal Secretary, Lee Coley
Diocesan Secretary, Susan Pope, Holywell Lodge,
41 Holywell Hill, St Albans AL1 1HE T 01727-854532

ST EDMUNDSBURY AND IPSWICH
(CANTERBURY)
10TH BISHOP
Rt. Revd Nigel Stock, *cons.* 2000, *apptd* 2007;
Bishop's House, 4 Park Road, Ipswich IP1 3ST
Signs Nigel St Edum and Ipswich

BISHOP SUFFRAGAN
Dunwich, Rt. Revd Clive Young, *cons.* 1999, *apptd* 1999;
28 Westerfield Road, Ipswich IP4 2UJ

DEAN
Very Revd Frances Ward, *apptd* 2010

Director of Music, James Thomas, *apptd* 1997

ARCHDEACONS
Sudbury, Ven. Dr David Jenkins, *apptd* 2010
Suffolk, Ven. Dr Judy Hunt, *apptd* 2009

Chancellor, David Etherington, QC
Registrar and Legal Secretary, James Hall
Diocesan Secretary, Nicholas Edgell, Diocesan Office,
St Nicholas Centre, 4 Cutler Street, Ipswich IP1 1UQ
T 01473-298500

SALISBURY *(CANTERBURY)*
78TH BISHOP
Rt. Revd Nicholas Holtam, *cons.* 2011, *apptd* 2011;
South Canonry, 71 The Close, Salisbury SP1 2ER

BISHOPS SUFFRAGAN
Ramsbury, vacant
Sherborne, Rt. Revd Graham Kings, PHD, *cons.* 2009,
apptd 2009; Sherborne Area Office, St Nicholas'
Church Centre, Wareham Road, Corfe Mullen BH21 3LE

DEAN
Very Revd June Osborne, *apptd* 2004

Organist, David Halls, *apptd* 2005

ARCHDEACONS
Dorset, Ven. Stephen Waine, *apptd* 2010
Sarum, Ven. Alan Jeans, *apptd* 2003
Sherborne, Ven. Paul Taylor, *apptd* 2004
Wilts, Ven. John Wraw, *apptd* 2004

Chancellor, His Hon. Judge Wiggs, *apptd* 1997
Registrar and Legal Secretary, Andrew Johnson
Diocesan Secretary, Lucinda Herklots, Church House,
Crane Street, Salisbury SP1 2QB T 01722-411922

SHEFFIELD *(YORK)*
7TH BISHOP
Rt. Revd Steven Croft, PHD, *cons.* 2009, *apptd* 2008;
Bishopscroft, Snaithing Lane, Sheffield S10 3LG
Signs Steven Sheffield

BISHOP SUFFRAGAN
Doncaster, vacant

DEAN
Very Revd Peter Bradley, *apptd* 2003

Master of Music, Neil Taylor, *apptd* 1997

ARCHDEACONS
Doncaster, Ven. Robert Fitzharris, *apptd* 2001
Sheffield and Rotherham, Ven. Martyn Snow, *apptd* 2010

Chancellor, Prof. David McClean, *apptd* 1992
Registrar and Legal Secretary, Andrew Vidler
Diocesan Secretary, Malcolm Fair, Diocesan Church House,
95–99 Effingham Street, Rotherham S65 1BL
T 01709-309100

SODOR AND MAN *(YORK)*
81ST BISHOP
Rt. Revd Robert Paterson, *cons.* 2008, *apptd* 2008;
The Bishop's House, The Falls, Tromode Road, Douglas,
Isle of Man IM4 4PZ
Signs Robert Sodor as Mannin

ARCHDEACON OF MAN
Ven. Brian Smith, *apptd* 2005
Vicar-General and Chancellor, Clare Faulds

Registrar, Timothy Mann
Diocesan Secretary, Mrs S. Lawrinson, 8 Hilary Wharf,
South Quay, Douglas, Isle of Man IM1 5BL
T 01624-673477

SOUTHWARK *(CANTERBURY)*
10TH BISHOP
Rt. Revd Christopher Chessun, *cons.* 2005, *apptd* 2011;
Trinity House, 4 Chapel Court, Borough High Street, London
SE1 1HW
Signs Christopher Southwark

AREA BISHOPS
Croydon, vacant
Kingston upon Thames, Rt. Revd Richard Cheetham, *cons.*
2002, *apptd* 2002 ; Kingston Episcopal Area Office,
620 Kingston Road, London SW20 8DN
Woolwich, vacant

DEAN (ACTING)
Revd Canon Andrew Nunn

Organist, Peter Wright, FRCO, *apptd* 1989

ARCHDEACONS
Croydon, Ven. Barry Goodwin, *apptd* 2011
Lambeth, Ven. Christopher Skilton, *apptd* 2003
Lewisham, Ven. Christine Hardman, *apptd* 2001
Reigate, Ven. Daniel Kajumba, *apptd* 2001
Southwark, Ven. Dr Michael Ipgrave, *apptd* 2004
Wandsworth, Ven. Stephen Roberts, *apptd* 2005

Chancellor, Philip Petchey
Registrar and Legal Secretary, Paul Morris
Diocesan Secretary, Simon Parton, Trinity House,
4 Chapel Court, Borough High Street, London SE1 1HW
T 020-7939 9400

SOUTHWELL AND NOTTINGHAM *(YORK)*
11TH BISHOP
Rt. Revd Paul Butler, *cons.* 2004, *apptd* 2009;
Bishop's Manor, Southwell NG25 0JR
Signs Paul Southwell and Nottingham

BISHOP SUFFRAGAN
Sherwood, Rt. Revd Anthony Porter, *cons.* 2006,
apptd 2006; Dunham House, 8 Westgate, Southwell
NG25 0JL

DEAN
Very Revd John Guille, *apptd* 2007

Organist, Paul Hale, *apptd* 1989

ARCHDEACONS
Newark, Ven. Nigel Peyton, *apptd* 1999
Nottingham, Ven. Peter Hill, *apptd* 2007

Chancellor, Linda Box, *apptd* 2005
Registrar and Legal Secretary, Christopher Hodson
Chief Executive, Nigel Spraggins, Dunham House,
8 Westgate, Southwell, Notts NG25 0JL T 01636-814331

TRURO *(CANTERBURY)*
15TH BISHOP
Rt. Revd Tim Thornton, *cons.* 2001, *apptd* 2008; Lis Escop,
Truro TR3 6QQ
Signs Tim Truro

BISHOP SUFFRAGAN
St Germans, Rt. Revd Royden Screech, *cons.* 2000, *apptd;*
2000 32 Falmouth Road, Truro, Cornwall TR1 2HX

DEAN
Very Revd Dr Christopher Hardwick, *apptd* 2005

Organist and Director of Music, Chris Gray, *apptd*
2008

ARCHDEACONS
Cornwall, Ven. Roger Bush, *apptd* 2006
Bodmin, Ven. Audrey Elkington, *apptd* 2011

Chancellor, Timothy Briden, *apptd* 1998
Registrar and Legal Secretary, Martin Follett
Deputy Diocesan Secretary, Esther Pollard, Diocesan House,
Kenwyn, Truro TR1 1JQ T 01872-274351

WAKEFIELD *(YORK)*
12TH BISHOP
Rt. Revd Stephen Platten, *cons.* 2003, *apptd* 2003;
Bishop's Lodge, Woodthorpe Lane, Wakefield WF2 6JL
Signs Stephen Wakefield

BISHOP SUFFRAGAN
Pontefract, Rt. Revd Tony Robinson, *cons.* 2003, *apptd*
2002; Pontefract House, Manygates Lane, Sandal,
Wakefield WF2 7DR

DEAN
Very Revd Jonathan Greener, *apptd* 2007

Organist, Thomas Moore, *apptd* 2010

ARCHDEACONS
Halifax, Ven. Robert Freeman, *apptd* 2003
Pontefract, Ven. Peter Townley, *apptd* 2008

Chancellor, His Hon. Judge Downes, *apptd* 2006
Registrars and Legal Secretaries, Julian Gill; Julia
Wilding
Diocesan Secretary, Ashley Ellis, Church House,
1 South Parade, Wakefield WF1 1LP T 01924-371802

WORCESTER *(CANTERBURY)*
113TH BISHOP
Rt. Revd Dr John Inge, *cons.* 2003, *apptd* 2007;
The Bishop's Office, The Old Palace, Deansway, Worcester
WR1 2JE
Signs John Wigorn

SUFFRAGAN BISHOP
Dudley, Rt. Revd David Walker, *cons.* 2000, *apptd*
2000; The Bishop's House, Bishop's Walk, Cradley Heath
B64 7JF

DEAN
Very Revd Peter Atkinson, *apptd* 2006

Organist, Dr Adrian Lucas, *apptd* 1996

ARCHDEACONS
Dudley, Ven. Fred Trethewey, *apptd* 2001
Worcester, Ven. Roger Morris, *apptd* 2008

Chancellor, Charles Mynors, *apptd* 1999
Registrar and Legal Secretary, Michael Huskinson
Diocesan Secretary, Robert Higham, The Old Palace,
Deansway, Worcester WR1 2JE T 01905-20537

ROYAL PECULIARS
WESTMINSTER
The Collegiate Church of St Peter
Dean, Very Revd Dr John Hall
Sub Dean, Revd Canon Robert Reiss
Archdeacon, Ven. Dr June Hedges
Chapter Clerk, Receiver-General and Registrar, Sir Stephen
Lamport, KCVO, Chapter Office, 20 Dean's Yard, London
SW1P 3PA
Organist, James O'Donnell, *apptd* 1999
Legal Secretary, Christopher Vyse, *apptd* 2000

WINDSOR
The Queen's Free Chapel of St George within Her Castle of
Windsor
Dean, Rt. Revd David Conner, KCVO, *apptd* 1998
Chapter Clerk, Charlotte Manley, LVO, OBE, *apptd* 2003;
Chapter Office, The Cloisters, Windsor Castle, Windsor,
Berks SL4 1NJ
Director of Music, Timothy Byram-Wigfield, *apptd* 2004

OTHER ANGLICAN CHURCHES

THE CHURCH IN WALES
The Anglican Church was the established church in Wales
from the 16th century until 1920, when the estrangement
of the majority of Welsh people from Anglicanism
resulted in disestablishment. Since then the Church in
Wales has been an autonomous province consisting of six
sees. The bishops are elected by an electoral college
comprising elected lay and clerical members, who also
elect one of the diocesan bishops as Archbishop of Wales.
The legislative body of the Church in Wales is the
Governing Body, which has 143 members divided
between the three orders of bishops, clergy and laity. Its
president is the Archbishop of Wales and it meets twice
annually. Its decisions are binding upon all members of
the church. The church's property and finances are the
responsibility of the Representative Body. There are
58,136 members of the Church in Wales, with 518
stipendiary clergy and 923 parishes.
THE REPRESENTATIVE BODY OF THE CHURCH IN
WALES, 39 Cathedral Road, Cardiff CF11 9XF
T 029-2034 8200 *Secretary,* John Shirley
12TH ARCHBISHOP OF WALES, Most Revd Dr Barry
Morgan (Bishop of Llandaff), *elected* 2003
Signs Barry Cambrensis

BISHOPS
Bangor (81st), Rt. Revd Andrew John, *b.* 1964 *cons.* 2008,
elected 2008; Ty'r Esgob, Upper Garth Road, Bangor,
Gwynedd LL57 2SS *Signs* Andrew Bangor. *Stipendiary*
clergy, 52
Llandaff (102nd), Most Revd Dr Barry Morgan (*also*
Archbishop of Wales), *b.* 1947, *cons.* 1993, *trans.* 1999;
Llys Esgob, The Cathedral Green, Llandaff, Cardiff CF5 2YE
Signs Barry Cambrensis. *Stipendiary clergy,* 118
Monmouth (9th), Rt. Revd Dominic Walker, *b.* 1948,
cons. 1997, *elected* 2003; Bishopstow, Stow Hill,
Newport NP20 4EA *Signs* Dominic Monmouth.
Stipendiary clergy, 87
St Asaph (76th), Rt. Revd Gregory Cameron, *b.* 1959,
cons. 2009, *elected* 2009; Esgobty, Upper Denbigh Road,
St Asaph, Denbighshire LL17 0TW *Signs* Gregory Llanelwy.
Stipendiary clergy, 92
St David's (128th), Rt. Revd (John) Wyn Evans, *b.* 1946,
cons. 2008, *elected* 2008; Llys Esgob, Abergwili,

Carmarthen SA31 2JG *Signs* Wyn St Davids. *Stipendiary clergy*, 98
Swansea and Brecon (9th), Rt. Revd John Davies, *b.* 1953, *cons.* 2008, *elected* 2008; Ely Tower, Castle Square, Brecon, Powys LD3 9DJ *Signs* John Swansea & Brecon. *Stipendiary clergy*, 71

The stipend for a diocesan bishop of the Church in Wales is £39,576 a year for 2011–12.

SCOTTISH EPISCOPAL CHURCH
The Scottish Episcopal Church was founded after the Act of Settlement (1690) established the presbyterian nature of the Church of Scotland. The Scottish Episcopal Church is a member of the worldwide Anglican Communion. The governing authority is the General Synod, an elected body of 140 members (70 from the clergy and 70 from the laity) which meets once a year. The bishop who convenes and presides at meetings of the General Synod is called the 'primus' and is elected by his fellow bishops.

There are 35,780 members of the Scottish Episcopal Church, seven bishops, 524 serving clergy and around 309 churches and places of worship.
THE GENERAL SYNOD OF THE SCOTTISH EPISCOPAL CHURCH, 21 Grosvenor Crescent, Edinburgh EH12 5EE T 0131-225 6357
W www.scotland.anglican.org
Secretary-General, John Stuart
PRIMUS OF THE SCOTTISH EPISCOPAL CHURCH, Most Revd David Chillingworth (Bishop of St Andrews, Dunkeld and Dunblane), *elected* 2009

BISHOPS
Aberdeen and Orkney, Rt. Revd Dr Bob Gillies, *b.* 1951, *cons.* 2007, *elected* 2007. *Clergy*, 50
Argyll and the Isles, Rt. Revd Kevin Pearson, *b.* 1954, *cons.* 2011, *elected* 2010. *Clergy* 27
Brechin, vacant. *Clergy*, 35
Edinburgh, Rt. Revd Brian Smith, *b.* 1943, *cons.* 1993, *elected* 2001. *Clergy*, 170
Glasgow and Galloway, Rt. Revd Dr Gregor Duncan, *b.* 1950, *cons.* 2010, *elected* 2010. *Clergy*, 113
Moray, Ross and Caithness, Rt. Revd Mark Strange, *b.* 1961, *cons.* 2007, *elected* 2007. *Clergy*, 56
St Andrews, Dunkeld and Dunblane, Most Revd David Chillingworth, *b.* 1951, *cons.* 2005, *elected* 2005. *Clergy*, 89

The minimum stipend of a diocesan bishop of the Scottish Episcopal Church for 2011 is £34,215 (ie 1.5 times the standard clergy stipend of £22,810).

CHURCH OF IRELAND

The Anglican Church was the established church in Ireland from the 16th century but never secured the allegiance of the majority and was disestablished in 1871. The Church of Ireland is divided into the provinces of Armagh and Dublin, each under an archbishop. The provinces are subdivided into 12 dioceses.

The legislative body is the General Synod, which has 660 members in total, divided between the House of Bishops (12 members) and the House of Representatives (216 clergy and 432 laity). The Archbishop of Armagh is elected by the House of Bishops; other episcopal elections are made by an electoral college.

There are around 390,000 members of the Church of Ireland, 275,000 in Northern Ireland and 115,000 in the Republic of Ireland. There are two archbishops, ten bishops and over 500 stipendiary clergy.
CENTRAL OFFICE, Church of Ireland House, Church Avenue, Rathmines, Dublin 6 T (+353) (1) 497 8422
Chief Officer and Secretary of the Representative Church Body, D. C. Reardon

PROVINCE OF ARMAGH
Archbishop of Armagh, Primate of all Ireland and Metropolitan, Most Revd Alan Harper, OBE, *b.* 1944, *cons.* 2002, *trans.* 2007. *Clergy*, 55

BISHOPS
Clogher, Rt. Revd John McDowell, *b.* 1956, *cons.* 2011, *apptd* 2011. *Clergy*, 32
Connor, Rt. Revd Alan Abernethy, *b.* 1957, *cons.* 2007, *apptd* 2007. *Clergy*, 106
Derry and Raphoe, Rt. Revd Kenneth Good, *b.* 1952, *cons.* 2002, *apptd* 2002. *Clergy*, 51
Down and Dromore, Rt. Revd Harold Miller, *b.* 1950, *cons.* 1997, *apptd* 1997. *Clergy*, 116
Kilmore, Elphin and Ardagh, Rt. Revd Kenneth Clarke, *b.* 1949, *cons.* 2001, *apptd* 2001. *Clergy*, 21
Tuam, Killala and Achonry, Rt. Revd Patrick Rooke, *b.* 1955, *cons.* 2011, *apptd* 2011. *Clergy*, 13

PROVINCE OF DUBLIN
Archbishop of Dublin, Bishop of Glendalough, Primate of Ireland and Metropolitan, Most Revd Michael Jackson, PHD, DPHIL, *b.* 1956, *apptd* 2011. *Clergy*, 86

BISHOPS
Cashel and Ossory, Most Revd Michael Burrows, *b.* 1961, *cons.* 2006, *apptd* 2006. *Clergy*, 42
Cork, Cloyne and Ross, Rt. Revd William Colton, *b.* 1960, *cons.* 1999, *apptd* 1999. *Clergy*, 30
Limerick, Killaloe and Ardfert, Rt. Revd Trevor Williams, *b.* 1948, *cons.* 2008. *Clergy*, 19
Meath and Kildare, Most Revd Richard Clarke, PHD, *b.* 1949, *cons.* 1996, *apptd* 1996. *Clergy*, 26

OVERSEAS

PRIMATES
Primate and Presiding Bishop of Aotearoa, New Zealand and Polynesia, Most Revd William Turei
Primate of Australia, Most Revd Phillip Aspinall
Primate of Brazil, Most Revd Maurício Araújo de Andrade
Archbishop of the Province of Burundi, Most Revd Bernard Ntahoturi
Archbishop and Primate of Canada, Most Revd Frederick Hiltz
Archbishop of the Province of Central Africa, Rt. Revd Albert Chama
Primate of the Central Region of America, Most Revd Armando Soria
Archbishop of the Province of Congo, Most Revd Henry Isingoma
Primate of the Province of Hong Kong Sheng Kung Hui, Most Revd Paul Kwong
Archbishop of the Province of the Indian Ocean, Most Revd Gerald Ernest
Primate of Japan (Nippon Sei Ko Kai), Most Revd Nathaniel Uematsu
President-Bishop of Jerusalem and the Middle East, Most Revd Dr Mouneer Anis
Archbishop of the Province of Kenya, Most Revd Eliud Wabukala

Archbishop of the Province of Korea, Rt. Revd Paul
Keun-Sang Kim
Archbishop of the Province of Melanesia, Most Revd David
Vunagi
Archbishop of Mexico, Most Revd Carlos Touche-Porter
Archbishop of the Province of Myanmar (Burma), Most
Revd Stephen Oo
Archbishop of the Province of Nigeria, Most Rt. Revd
Nicholas Okoh
Archbishop of Papua New Guinea, Most Revd Joseph
Kopapa
Prime Bishop of the Philippines, Rt. Revd Edward Malecdan
Archbishop of the Province of Rwanda, Most Revd
Onesphore Rwaje
Primate of the Province of South East Asia, Most Revd Dr
John Chew
Metropolitan of the Province of Southern Africa, Most Revd
Thabo Makgoba
Presiding Bishop of the Southern Cone of America, Most
Revd Hector Zavala
Archbishop of the Province of the Sudan, Most Revd Daniel
Yak
Archbishop of the Province of Tanzania, Most Revd
Valentino Mokiwa
Archbishop of the Province of Uganda, Most Revd Henry
Orombi
Presiding Bishop and Primate of the USA, Most Revd
Katharine Schori
Archbishop of the Province of West Africa, Most Revd
Justice Ofei Akrofi
Archbishop of the Province of the West Indies, Most Revd Dr
John Holder

OTHER CHURCHES AND EXTRA-PROVINCIAL DIOCESES

Anglican Church of Bermuda, extra-provincial to
Canterbury
Bishop, Rt. Revd Patrick White
Church of Ceylon, extra-provincial to Canterbury
Bishop of Colombo, Rt. Revd Duleep de Chickera
Bishop of Kurunagala, Rt. Revd Kumara Illangasinghe
Episcopal Church of Cuba, extra-provincial to Canterbury
(interim)
Falkland Islands, extra-provincial to Canterbury
Episcopal Commissary, Rt. Revd Stephen Venner (Bishop
to the Forces)
Lusitanian Church (Portuguese Episcopal Church),
extra-provincial to Canterbury
Bishop, Rt. Revd Fernando Soares
Reformed Episcopal Church of Spain, extra-provincial to
Canterbury
Bishop, Rt. Revd Carlos López-Lozano

MODERATION OF CHURCHES IN FULL COMMUNION WITH THE ANGLICAN COMMUNION

Church of Bangladesh, Rt. Revd Paul Sarkar
Church of North India, Most Revd Purely Lyngdoh
Church of South India, Most Revd Suputhrappa Kumar
Church of Pakistan, Rt. Revd Samuel Azariah

CHURCH OF SCOTLAND

The Church of Scotland is the national church of
Scotland. The church is reformed in doctrine, and
presbyterian in constitution; ie based on a hierarchy of
courts of ministers and elders and, since 1990, of
members of a diaconate. At local level the Kirk Session

consists of the parish minister and ruling elders. At district
level the presbyteries, of which there are 44 in Britain,
consist of all the ministers in the district, one ruling elder
from each congregation, and those members of the
diaconate who qualify for membership. The General
Assembly is the supreme authority, and is presided over by
a Moderator chosen annually by the Assembly. The
sovereign, if not present in person, is represented by a
Lord High Commissioner who is appointed each year by
the Crown.

The Church of Scotland has around 600,000 members,
1,200 parish ministers and 1,464 churches. There are
about 20 ministers and other personnel working overseas.
Lord High Commissioner (2011–12), Rt. Hon. Lord
Wilson of Tillyorn, KT, GCMG
Moderator of the General Assembly (2011–12), Rt. Revd
David Arnott
Principal Clerk, Revd John Chalmers
Depute Clerk, vacant
Procurator, Laura Dunlop
Law Agent and Solicitor of the Church, Janette Wilson
Parliamentary Officer, Chloe Clemmons
General Treasurer, Iain Grimmond
Secretary, Church and Society Council, Revd Ewan Aitken
CHURCH OFFICE, 121 George Street, Edinburgh EH2 4YN
T 0131-225 5722

PRESBYTERIES AND CLERKS
Aberdeen, Revd Dr Ian McLean
Abernethy, Revd James MacEwan
Annandale and Eskdale, Revd C. Haston
Angus, Revd Mike Goss
Ardrossan, Revd Johnston Mackay
Argyll, Ian MacLagan
Ayr, Revd Kenneth Elliott
Buchan, George Berstan
Caithness, Revd Ronald Johnstone
Dumbarton, Revd Colin Caskie
Dumfries and Kirkcudbright, Revd Gordon Savage
Dundee, Revd James Wilson
Dunfermline, Revd Elizabeth Kenny
Dunkeld and Meigle, Revd John Russell
Duns, Peter Johnson
Edinburgh, Revd George Whyte
England, Revd Dr P. Mills
Europe, Revd John Cowie
Falkirk, Revd Jerome O'Brien
Glasgow, Revd Dr Angus Kerr
Gordon, Gerald Moore
Greenock and Paisley, Revd Alastair Cherry
Hamilton, Revd Shaw Paterson
Inverness, Revd Alastair Younger
Irvine and Kilmarnock, Revd Colin Brockie
Jedburgh, Revd W. Frank Campbell
Kincardine and Deeside, Revd Hugh Conkey
Kirkcaldy, Revd Rosemary Frew
Lanark, Revd Helen Jamieson
Lewis, Revd Thomas Sinclair
Lochaber, Ella Gill
Lochcarron-Skye, Revd Allan MacArthur
Lothian, John McCulloch
Melrose and Peebles, Jack Stewart
Moray, Revd Hugh Smith
Orkney, Revd James Wishart
Perth, Revd Derek Lawson
Ross, Ronald Gunstone
St Andrews, Revd James Redpath
Shetland, Revd Charles Greig

Stirling, Dorothy Kinloch
Sutherland, Mrs Mary Stobo
Uist, Wilson McKinlay
West Lothian, Revd Duncan Shaw
Wigtown and Stranraer, Nicola Steel

The stipends for ministers in the Church of Scotland in 2011 range from £23,139–£30,426, depending on length of service.

ROMAN CATHOLIC CHURCH

The Roman Catholic Church is a worldwide Christian church acknowledging as its head the Bishop of Rome, known as the Pope (father). Despite its widespread usage, 'Pope' is actually an unofficial term, the *Annuario Pontificio,* (Pontifical Yearbook) lists eight official titles: Bishop of Rome, Vicar of Jesus Christ, Successor of the Prince of the Apostles, Supreme Pontiff of the Universal Church, Primate of Italy, Archbishop and Metropolitan of the Roman Province, Sovereign of the State of the Vatican City and Servant of the Servants of God.

The Pope leads a communion of followers of Christ, who believe they continue his presence in the world as servants of faith, hope and love to all society. The Pope is held to be the successor of St Peter and thus invested with the power which was entrusted to St Peter by Jesus Christ. A direct line of succession is therefore claimed from the earliest Christian communities. With the fall of the Roman Empire the Pope also became an important political leader. His territory is now limited to the 0.44 sq. km (0.17 sq. miles) of the Vatican City State, created to provide some independence to the Pope from Italy and other nations. The episcopal jurisdiction of the Roman Catholic Church is called the Holy See.

The Pope exercises spiritual authority over the church with the advice and assistance of the Sacred College of Cardinals, the supreme council of the church. The number of cardinals was fixed at 70 by Pope Sixtus V in 1586 but has been steadily increasing since the pontificate of John XXIII and in May 2011 stood at 198.

Following the death of the Pope, the members of the College of Cardinals under the age of 80 are called to the Vatican to elect a successor. They are known as cardinal electors and as at May 2011 numbered 115. The assembly of cardinal electors is known as the conclave, and, in complete seclusion, they vote by a secret ballot. A two-thirds majority is necessary before the vote can be accepted as final. When a cardinal receives the necessary number of votes, the Dean of the Sacred College formally asks him if he will accept election and the name by which he wishes to be known. On his acceptance of the office of Supreme Pontiff, the conclave is dissolved and the first Cardinal Deacon announces the election to the assembled crowd in St Peter's Square.

The Pope has full legislative, judicial and administrative power over the whole Roman Catholic Church. He is aided in his administration by the curia, which is made up of a number of departments. The Secretariat of State is the central office for carrying out the Pope's instructions and is presided over by the Cardinal Secretary of State. It maintains relations with the departments of the curia, with the episcopate, with the representatives of the Holy See in various countries, governments and private persons. The congregations and pontifical councils are the Pope's ministries and include departments such as the Congregation for the Doctrine of Faith, whose field of competence concerns faith and morals; the

Congregation for the Clergy and the Congregation for the Evangelisation of Peoples, the Pontifical Council for the Family and the Pontifical Council for the Promotion of Christian Unity.

The Holy See, composed of the Pope and those who help him in his mission for the church, is recognised by the Conventions of Vienna as an international moral body. Apostolic nuncios are the Pope's diplomatic representatives; in countries where no formal diplomatic relations exist between the Holy See and that country, the papal representative is known as an apostolic delegate.

The Roman Catholic Church has over one billion adherents under the care of around 5,000 diocesan bishops worldwide.

SUPREME PONTIFF
His Holiness Pope Benedict XVI (Joseph Ratzinger), *born* Bavaria, Germany, 16 April 1927; *ordained priest* 1951; *appointed Archbishop* (of Munich), March 1977; *created Cardinal* June 1977; *assumed pontificate* 19 April 2005

SECRETARIAT OF STATE
Secretary of State, HE Cardinal Tarcisio Bertone
First Section (General Affairs), Most Revd Fernando Filoni (Titular Archbishop of Volturno)
Second Section (Relations with Other States), Most Revd Dominique Mamberti (Titular Archbishop of Sagona)

BISHOPS' CONFERENCE
The Catholic Church in England and Wales consists of a total of 22 dioceses. The Bishops' Conference, which coordinates common activity, includes the diocesan bishops, the Personal Ordinary of the Ordinariate of Our Lady of Walsingham, the Apostolic Exarch of the Ukrainians, the Bishop of the Forces and the auxiliary bishops. The conference is headed by the president (the Most Revd Vincent Nichols, Archbishop of Westminster) and vice-president (the Most Revd Peter Smith, Archbishop of Southwark). There are six departments, each with an episcopal chair: the Department for Christian Life and Worship (the Bishop of Leeds), the Department for Dialogue and Unity (the Archbishop of Birmingham), the Department for Catholic Education and Formation (the Bishop of Nottingham), the Department for Christian Responsibility and Citizenship (the Archbishop of Southwark), the Department for International Affairs (the Bishop of Clifton) and the Department for Evangelisation and Catechesis (the Bishop of Arundel and Brighton).

The Bishops' Conference Standing Committee is made up of two directly elected bishops in addition to the Metropolitan Archbishops and chairs from each of the above departments. The committee has general responsibility for continuity of policy between the plenary sessions of the conference, preparing the conference agenda and implementing its decisions.

The administration of the Bishops' Conference is funded by a levy on each diocese, according to income. A general secretariat in London coordinates and supervises the Bishops' Conference administration activities. There are also other agencies and consultative bodies affiliated to the conference.

The Bishops' Conference of Scotland is the permanently constituted assembly of the bishops of Scotland. The conference is headed by the president (HE Cardinal Keith Patrick O'Brien, Archbishop of St. Andrews and Edinburgh). The conference establishes various agencies which perform advisory functions in relation to the conference. The more important of these agencies are called commissions; each one is headed by a bishop president who, with the other members of the commissions, are appointed by the conference.

The Irish Catholic Bishops' Conference (also known as the Irish Episcopal Conference) has as its president Cardinal Sean Brady of Armagh. Its membership comprises all 31 of the archbishops and bishops of Ireland. It appoints various commissions and agencies to assist with the work of the Catholic Church in Ireland.

The Catholic Church in the UK has over 900,000 mass attendees, 5,599 priests and 4,583 churches.

Bishops' Conferences secretariats:

ENGLAND AND WALES, 39 Eccleston Square, London SW1V 1BX T 020-7630 8220 E secretariat@cbcew.org.uk W www.catholicchurch.org.uk

General Secretary, Fr Marcus Stock

SCOTLAND, 64 Aitken Street, Airdrie ML6 6LT T 01236-764061 W www.bpsconfscot.com

General Secretary, Very Revd Mgr Paul Conroy

IRELAND, Columba Centre, Maynooth, County Kildare T (+353) (1) 505 3000 E info@catholicbishops.ie W www.catholicbishops.ie

Secretary, Most Revd William Lee (Bishop of Waterford and Lismore)

Executive Secretary, Revd Gearoid Dullea

GREAT BRITAIN
APOSTOLIC NUNCIO TO GREAT BRITAIN
Most Revd Antonio Mennini, 54 Parkside, London SW19 5NE T 020-8944 7189

ENGLAND AND WALES
THE MOST REVD ARCHBISHOPS
Westminster, Vincent Nichols, *cons.* 1992, *apptd* 2009 *Archbishop Emeritus,* Cardinal Cormac Murphy-O'Connor, *cons.* 1977, *elevated* 2001 *Auxiliaries,* Alan Hopes *cons.* 2003; John Arnold *cons.* 2006. *Clergy,* 690. *Archbishop's Residence,* Archbishop's House, Ambrosden Avenue, London SW1P 1QJ T 020-7798 9033

Birmingham, Bernard Longley, *cons.* 2003, *apptd* 2009 *Auxiliaries,* David McGough, *cons.* 2005; William Kenney, *cons.* 1987; Philip Pargeter (retd), *cons.* 1990. *Clergy,* 430. *Archbishop's Residence,* Archbishop's House, 8 Shadwell Street, Birmingham B4 6EY T 0121-236 9090 *Cardiff,* George Stack *cons.* 2001, *apptd* 2011. *Clergy,* 95. *Archbishop's Residence,* Archbishop's House, 41–43 Cathedral Road, Cardiff CF11 9HD T 029-2022 0411

Liverpool, Patrick Kelly, *cons.* 1984, *apptd* 1996 *Auxiliary,* Thomas Williams, *cons.* 2003. *Clergy,* 434. *Diocesan Curia,* Archdiocese of Liverpool, Centre for Evangelisation, Croxteth Drive, Sefton Park, Liverpool L17 1AA T 0151-522 1000

Southwark, Peter Smith, *cons.* 1995, *apptd* 2010 *Auxiliaries,* John Hine, *cons.* 2001; Patrick Lynch, *cons.* 2006; Paul Hendricks, *cons.* 2006. *Clergy,* 546. *Diocesan Curia,* Archbishop's House, 150 St George's Road, London SE1 6HX T 020-7928 5592

THE RT. REVD BISHOPS
Arundel and Brighton, Kieran Conry, *cons.* 2001, *apptd* 2001. *Clergy,* 96. *Diocesan Curia,* Bishop's House, The Upper Drive, Hove, E. Sussex BN3 6NB T 01273-506387

Brentwood, Thomas McMahon, *cons.* 1980, *apptd* 1980. *Clergy,* 121. *Bishop's Office,* Cathedral House, Ingrave Road, Brentwood, Essex CM15 8AT T 01277-232266

Clifton, Declan Lang, *cons.* 2001, *apptd* 2001. *Clergy,* 251. *Bishop's House,* St Ambrose, North Road, Leigh Woods, Bristol BS8 3PW T 0117-973 3072

East Anglia, Michael Evans, *cons* 2003, *apptd* 2003. *Clergy,* 129. *Diocesan Curia,* The White House, 21 Upgate, Poringland, Norwich NR14 7SH T 01508-492202

Hallam, John Rawsthorne, *cons.* 1981, *apptd* 1997. *Clergy,* 75. *Bishop's House,* 75 Norfolk Road, Sheffield S2 2SZ T 0114-278 7988

Hexham and Newcastle, Seamus Cunningham, *cons.* 2009, *apptd* 2009. *Clergy,* 185. *Diocesan Curia,* Bishop's House, East Denton Hall, 800 West Road, Newcastle upon Tyne NE5 2BJ T 0191-228 0003

Lancaster, Michael Campbell, *cons.* 2008, *apptd* 2009. *Clergy,* 170. *Bishop's Office,* The Pastoral Centre, Balmoral Road, Lancaster LA1 3BT T 01524-596050

Leeds, Arthur Roche, *cons.* 2001, *apptd* 2004. *Clergy,* 193. *Diocesan Curia,* Hinsley Hall, 62 Headingley Lane, Leeds LS6 2BX T 0113-261 8022

Menevia (Wales), Thomas Burns, *cons.* 2002, *apptd* 2008. *Clergy,* 60. *Diocesan Curia,* 27 Convent Street, Swansea SA1 2BX T 01792-644017

Middlesbrough, Terence Drainey, *cons.* 2008, *apptd* 2007. *Clergy,* 98. *Diocesan Curia,* 50A The Avenue, Linthorpe, Middlesbrough TS5 6QT T 01642-850505

Northampton, Peter Doyle, *cons.* 2005, *apptd* 2005. *Clergy,* 122. *Diocesan Curia,* Bishop's House, Marriott Street, Northampton NN2 6AW T 01604-715635

Nottingham, Malcolm McMahon, *cons.* 2000, *apptd* 2000. *Clergy,* 162. *Bishop's House,* 27 Cavendish Road East, The Park, Nottingham NG7 1BB T 0115-947 4786

Plymouth, Christopher Budd, *cons.* 1986, *apptd* 1985. *Clergy,* 130. *Bishop's Residence,* Bishop's House, 31 Wyndham Street West, Plymouth PL1 5RZ T 01752-224414

Portsmouth, Crispian Hollis, *cons.* 1987, *apptd* 1989. *Clergy,* 282. *Bishop's Residence,* Bishop's House, Bishop Crispian Way, Portsmouth, Hants PO1 3HG T 023-9282 0894

Salford, Terence Brain, *cons.* 1991, *apptd* 1997. *Clergy,* 254. *Diocesan Curia,* Wardley Hall, Worsley, Manchester M28 2ND T 0161-794 2825

Shrewsbury, Mark Davies, *cons.* 2010, *apptd* 2011. *Clergy,* 123. *Diocesan Curia,* 2 Park Road South, Prenton, Wirral CH43 4UX T 0151-652 9855

Wrexham (Wales), Edwin Regan, *cons.*1994, *apptd* 1994. *Clergy,* 45. *Diocesan Curia,* Bishop's House, Sontley Road, Wrexham LL13 7EW T 01978-262726

SCOTLAND
THE MOST REVD ARCHBISHOPS
St Andrews and Edinburgh, HE Cardinal Keith Patrick O'Brien, *cons.* 1985, *apptd* 1985, *elevated* 2003. *Clergy,* 170. *Diocesan Office,* 100 Strathearn Road, Edinburgh EH9 1BB T 0131-447 3377

Glasgow, Mario Joseph Conti, *cons.* 1977, *apptd* 2002. *Clergy,* 225. *Diocesan Curia,* 196 Clyde Street, Glasgow G1 4JY T 0141-226 5898

THE RT. REVD BISHOPS
Aberdeen, Peter Moran, *cons.* 2003, *apptd* 2003. *Clergy,* 43. *Diocesan Curia,* 3 Queen's Cross, Aberdeen AB15 4XU T 01224-319154

Argyll and the Isles, Joseph Toal, *cons.* 2008, *apptd* 2008. *Clergy,* 32. *Bishop's House,* Esplanade, Oban, Argyll PA34 5AB T 01631-567436

Dunkeld, Vincent Logan, *cons.* 1981. *Clergy,* 49. *Diocesan Curia,* 24–28 Lawside Road, Dundee DD3 6XY T 01382-225453

Galloway, John Cunningham, *cons.* 2004, *apptd* 2004. *Clergy* 56. *Diocesan Curia,* 8 Corsehill Road, Ayr KA7 2ST T 01292-266750

Motherwell, Joseph Devine, *cons.* 1977, *apptd* 1983. *Clergy,* 123. *Diocesan Curia,* Coursington Road, Motherwell ML1 1PP T 01698-269114

Paisley, Philip Tartaglia, *cons.* 2005, *apptd* 2005. *Clergy,* 83. *Diocesan Curia,* Diocesan Centre, Cathedral Precincts, Incle Street, Paisley PA1 1HR T 0141-847 6130

BISHOPRIC OF THE FORCES

Rt. Revd Richard Moth, *cons.* 2009, *apptd* 2009. *Administration,* RC Bishopric of the Forces, Wellington House, St Omer Barracks, Thornhill Road, Aldershot, Hants GU11 2BG T 01252-348234

IRELAND

There is one hierarchy for the whole of Ireland. Several of the dioceses have territory partly in the Republic of Ireland and partly in Northern Ireland.

APOSTOLIC NUNCIO TO IRELAND

HE Most Revd Giuseppe Leanza (Titular Archbishop of Lilybaeum), 183 Navan Road, Dublin 7 T (+353) (1) 838 0577 F (+353) (1) 838 0276

THE MOST REVD ARCHBISHOPS

Armagh, Cardinal Sean Brady (*also* Primate of all Ireland), *cons.* 1995, *apptd* 1996. *Auxiliary Bishop,* Most Revd Gerard Clifford, *cons.* 1991. *Clergy,* 156. *Bishop's Residence,* Ara Coeli, Armagh BT61 7QY T 028-3752 2045

Cashel and Emly, Dermot Clifford, *cons.* 1986, *apptd* 1988. *Clergy,* 95. *Archbishop's House,* Thurles, Co. Tipperary T (+353) (504) 21512

Dublin, Diarmuid Martin, *cons.* 1999, *apptd Coadjutor Archbishop* 2003, *succeeded as Archbishop* 2004. *Archbishop Emeritus,* HE Cardinal Desmond Connell, *cons.* 1988, *elevated* 2001. *Auxiliary,* vacant. *Clergy,* 994. *Archbishop's House,* Drumcondra, Dublin 9 T (+353) (1) 837 3732

Tuam, Dr Michael Neary, *cons.* 1992, *apptd* 1995. *Clergy,* 128. *Archbishop's House,* Tuam, Co. Galway T (+353) (93) 24166

THE MOST REVD BISHOPS

Achonry, Brendan Kelly, *cons.* 2008, *apptd* 2007. *Clergy,* 53. *Bishop's House,* Edmondstown, Ballaghaderreen, Co. Roscommon T (+353) (94) 986 0021

Ardagh and Clonmacnois, Colm O'Reilly, *cons.* 1983, *apptd* 1983. *Clergy,* 61. *Diocesan Office,* St Michael's, Longford, Co. Longford T (+353) (43) 46432

Clogher, Liam MacDaid *cons.* 2010, *apptd* 2010. *Clergy,* 74. *Bishop's House,* Monaghan T (+353) (47) 81019

Clonfert, John Kirby, *cons.* 1988 *apptd* 1988. *Clergy,* 39. *Bishop's Residence,* Coorheen, Loughrea, Co. Galway T (+353) (91) 841560

Cloyne, vacant. *Clergy,* 132. *Diocesan Office,* Cobh, Co. Cork T (+353) (21) 481 1430

Cork and Ross, John Buckley, *cons.* 1984, *apptd* 1998. *Clergy,* 136. *Diocesan Office,* Cork and Ross Offices, Redemption Road, Cork T (+353) (21) 430 1717

Derry, Seamus Hegarty, *cons.* 1982, *apptd* 1994. *Clergy,* 120. *Bishop's House,* St Eugene's Cathedral, Derry BT48 9YG T 028-7126 2302

Down and Connor, Noel Treanor, *cons.* 2008, *apptd* 2008. *Auxiliaries,* Anthony Farquhar, *cons.* 1983; Donal McKeown, *cons.* 2001. *Clergy,* 218. *Bishop's Residence,* Lisbreen, 73 Somerton Road, Belfast, Co. Antrim BT15 4DE T 028-9077 6185

Dromore, John McAreavey, *cons.* 1999, *apptd* 1999. *Clergy,* 43. *Bishop's House,* 44 Armagh Road, Newry, Co. Down BT35 6PN T 028-3026 2444

Elphin, Christopher Jones, *cons.* 1994, *apptd* 1994. *Clergy,* 70. *Bishop's Residence,* St Mary's, Sligo T (+353) (71) 916 2670

Ferns, Denis Brennan, *cons.* 2006, *apptd* 2006. *Clergy,* 92. *Bishop's House,* Summerhill, Wexford T (+353) (53) 912 2177

Galway, Kilmacduagh and Kilfenora, Martin Drennan, *cons.* 1997, *apptd* 2005. *Clergy,* 57. *Bishop's Residence,* Mount Saint Mary's, Taylor's Hill, Galway T (+353) (91) 563566

Kerry, William Murphy, *cons.* 1995, *apptd* 1995. *Clergy,* 104. *Bishop's House,* Killarney, Co. Kerry T (+353) (64) 663 1168

Kildare and Leighlin, vacant. *Clergy,* 110. *Bishop's House,* Carlow T (+353) (59) 917 6725

Killala, John Fleming, *cons.* 2002, *apptd* 2002. *Clergy,* 54. *Bishop's House,* Ballina, Co. Mayo T (+353) (96) 21518

Killaloe, Dr Keiran O'Reilly, *cons.* 2010, *apptd* 2010. *Clergy,* 118. *Diocesan Office,* Westbourne, Ennis, Co. Clare T (+353) (65) 682 8638

Kilmore, Leo O'Reilly, *cons.* 1997, *apptd* 1998. *Clergy,* 75. *Bishop's Residence,* Cullies, Co. Cavan T (+353) (49) 433 1496

Limerick, vacant. *Clergy,* 109. *Diocesan Office,* Social Service Centre, Henry Street, Limerick T (+353) (61) 315856

Meath, Michael Smith, *cons.* 1984, *apptd* 1990. *Clergy,* 131. *Bishop's House,* Dublin Road, Mullingar, Co. Westmeath T (+353) (44) 934 8841

Ossory, Seamus Freeman, *cons.* 2007, *apptd* 2007. *Clergy,* 65. *Bishop's Residence,* Sion House, Kilkenny T (+353) (56) 776 2448

Raphoe, Dr Philip Boyce, *cons.* 1995, *apptd* 1995. *Clergy,* 82. *Bishop's Residence,* Ard Adhamhnáin, Letterkenny, Co. Donegal T (+353) (74) 912 1208

Waterford and Lismore, William Lee, *cons.* 1993, *apptd* 1993. *Clergy,* 114. *Bishop's House,* John's Hill, Waterford T (+353) (51) 874463

OTHER CHURCHES IN THE UK

ASSOCIATED PRESBYTERIAN CHURCHES OF SCOTLAND

The Associated Presbyterian Churches came into being in 1989 as a result of a division within the Free Presbyterian Church of Scotland. The Associated Presbyterian Churches is reformed and evangelistic in nature and emphasises the importance of doctrine based primarily on the Bible and secondly on the Westminster Confession of Faith. There are an estimated 500 members, 8 ministers and 12 congregations in Scotland. There are also congregations in Canada.

ASSOCIATED PRESBYTERIAN CHURCHES OF SCOTLAND, APC Manse, Polvinster Road, Oban PA34 5TN T 01631-567076 E archibald.mcphail@virgin.net

W www.apchurches.org

Moderator of Presbytery, Revd Dr Wayne Pearce

Clerk of Presbytery, Revd Archibald McPhail

BAPTIST CHURCH

Baptists trace their origins to John Smyth, who in 1609 in Amsterdam reinstituted the baptism of conscious believers as the basis of the fellowship of a gathered church. Members of Smyth's church established the first Baptist church in England in 1612. They came to be known as 'General' Baptists and their theology was Arminian, whereas a later group of Calvinists who adopted the baptism of believers came to be known as 'Particular' Baptists. The two sections of the Baptists were united into one body, the Baptist Union of Great Britain and Ireland, in 1891. In 1988 the title was changed to the Baptist Union of Great Britain.

Baptists emphasise the complete autonomy of the local church, although individual churches are linked in various kinds of associations. There are international bodies (such as the Baptist World Alliance) and national bodies, but some Baptist churches belong to neither. However, in Great Britain the majority of churches and associations belong to the Baptist Union of Great Britain. There are also Baptist Unions in Wales, Scotland and Ireland, which are much smaller than the Baptist Union of Great Britain, and there is some overlap of membership.

There are currently around 140,000 members, 2,500 ministers and 2,000 churches associated with the Baptist Union of Great Britain. The Baptist Union of Great Britain is one of the founder members of the European Baptist Federation (1948) and the Baptist World Alliance (1905), which represents around 40 million members worldwide.

In the Baptist Union of Scotland there are 11,450 members, 140 pastors and 165 churches.

In the Baptist Union of Wales (Undeb Bedyddwyr Cymru) there are 13,326 members, 105 pastors and 417 churches, including those in England.

BAPTIST UNION OF GREAT BRITAIN, Baptist House, PO Box 44, 129 Broadway, Didcot, Oxon OX11 8RT

T 01235-517700 E info@baptist.org.uk

W www.baptist.org.uk

General Secretary, Revd Jonathan Edwards

BAPTIST UNION OF SCOTLAND, 14 Aytoun Road, Glasgow G41 5RT T 0141-423 6169

E director@scottishbaptist.org.uk

General Director, Revd A. J. Donaldson

BAPTIST UNION OF WALES, Y Llwyfan, Trinity Saint David University College, College Road, Carmarthen SA31 3EQ T 01267-245660

E peter@bedyddwyrcymru.co.uk W www.buw.org.uk

President of the English Assembly (2011–12), Revd John P. R. Davies

President of the Welsh Assembly (2011–12), Glyndwr Prideaux

General Secretary of the Baptist Union of Wales, Revd Peter Thomas

THE BRETHREN

The Brethren was founded in Dublin in 1827–8, basing itself on the structures and practices of the early church and rejecting denominationalism and clericalism. Many groups sprang up; the group at Plymouth became the best known, resulting in its designation by others as the 'Plymouth Brethren'. Early worship had a prescribed form but quickly assumed an unstructured, non-liturgical format.

There are services devoted to worship, usually involving the breaking of bread, and separate preaching meetings. There is no salaried ministry.

A theological dispute led in 1848 to schism between the Open Brethren and the Closed or Exclusive Brethren, each branch later suffering further divisions.

Open Brethren churches are run by appointed elders and are completely independent, but freely cooperate with each other. Exclusive Brethren churches believe in a universal fellowship between congregations. They do not have appointed elders, but use respected members of their congregation to perform certain administrative functions.

The Brethren are established throughout the UK, Ireland, Europe, India, Africa and Australasia. In the UK there are over 70,000 members, 1,250 assembly halls and over 200 full-time Bible teachers, evangelists and administrators. There are a number of publishing houses that publish Brethren-related literature. Chapter Two is the main supplier of such literature in the UK; it also has a Brethren history archive which is available for use by appointment.

CHAPTER TWO, Conduit Mews, London SE18 7AP

T 020-8316 5389 E info@chaptertwobooks.org.uk

W www.chaptertwobooks.org.uk

CONGREGATIONAL FEDERATION

The Congregational Federation was founded by members of Congregational churches in England and Wales who did not join the United Reformed Church in 1972. There are also churches in Scotland and France affiliated to the federation. The federation exists to encourage congregations of believers to worship in free assembly, but it has no authority over them and emphasises their right to independence and self-governance.

The federation has 8,325 members, 67 accredited ministers and 282 churches in England, Wales and Scotland.

CONGREGATIONAL FEDERATION, 6 Castle Gate, Nottingham NG1 7AS T 0115-911 1460

E admin@congregational.org.uk

W www.congregational.org.uk

President of the Federation (2011–12), Revd Brian Gist

General Secretary, Revd M. Heaney

FELLOWSHIP OF INDEPENDENT EVANGELICAL CHURCHES

The Fellowship of Independent Evangelical Churches was founded by Revd E. J. Poole-Connor (1872–1962) in 1922. In 1923 the fellowship published its first register of non-denominational pastors, evangelists and congregations who had accepted the doctrinal basis for the fellowship.

Members of the fellowship have two primary convictions: firstly to defend the evangelical faith, and secondly that evangelicalism is the bond that unites the fellowship, rather than forms of worship or church government.

The Fellowship of Independent Evangelical Churches exists to promote the welfare of non-denominational Bible churches and to give expression to the fundamental doctrines of evangelical Christianity. It supports individual churches by gathering and disseminating information and resources, advising churches on current theological, moral, social and practical issues and seeking to uphold the quality and integrity of church leaders through the Pastors' Association.

More than 500 churches throughout the UK are linked through the fellowship. There are more than 350 pastors, and approximately 38,000 people worship in fellowship churches every Sunday.

FELLOWSHIP OF INDEPENDENT EVANGELICAL CHURCHES, 39 The Point, Market Harborough, Leics LE16 7QU T 01858-434540 E admin@fiec.org.uk W www.fiec.org.uk
Director, John Stevens

FREE CHURCH OF ENGLAND

The Free Church of England, otherwise called the Reformed Episcopal Church, is an independent church, constituted according to the historic faith, tradition and practice of the Church of England. Its roots lie in the 18th century, but it started to grow significantly from the 1840s onwards, as clergy and congregations joined it from the established church in protest against the Oxford Movement. The historic episcopate was conferred on the English church in 1876 through bishops of the Reformed Episcopal Church (which had broken away from the Protestant Episcopal Church in the USA in 1873). A branch of the Reformed Episcopal Church was founded in the UK and this merged with the Free Church of England in 1927 to create the present church.

Worship is according to the *Book of Common Prayer* and some modern liturgy is permissable. Only men are ordained to the orders of deacon, presbyter and bishop.

The Free Church of England has 29 ministers, 17 congregations and around 1,150 members, now mainly confined to England with one congregation in St Petersburg, Russia.

THE FREE CHURCH OF ENGLAND, St Andrews Church, Wolverhampton Road West, Bentley, Walsall WV13 2RL T 01902-607335 W www.fcofe.org.uk
General Secretary, Rt. Revd Paul Hunt

FREE CHURCH OF SCOTLAND

The Free Church of Scotland was formed in 1843 when over 400 ministers withdrew from the Church of Scotland as a result of interference in the internal affairs of the church by the civil authorities. In 1900, all but 26 ministers joined with others to form the United Free Church (most of which rejoined the Church of Scotland in 1929). In 1904 the remaining 26 ministers were recognised by the House of Lords as continuing the Free Church of Scotland.

The church maintains strict adherence to the Westminster Confession of Faith (1648) and accepts the Bible as the sole rule of faith and conduct. Its general assembly meets annually. It also has links with reformed churches overseas. The Free Church of Scotland has about 12,000 members, 90 ministers and 100 congregations.

FREE CHURCH OF SCOTLAND, 15 North Bank Street, The Mound, Edinburgh EH1 2LS T 0131-226 5286 E offices@freechurchofscotland.org.uk W www.freechurch.org
Chief Administrative Officer, Rod Morrison

FREE PRESBYTERIAN CHURCH OF SCOTLAND

The Free Presbyterian Church of Scotland was formed in 1893 by two ministers of the Free Church of Scotland who refused to accept a Declaratory Act passed by the Free Church General Assembly in 1892. The Free Presbyterian Church of Scotland is Calvinistic in doctrine and emphasises observance of the Sabbath. It adheres strictly to the Westminster Confession of Faith (1648).

The church has about 1,000 members in Scotland and about 4,000 in overseas congregations. It has 20 ministers and 50 churches in the UK.

FREE PRESBYTERIAN CHURCH OF SCOTLAND, 133 Woodlands Road, Glasgow G3 6LE T 0141-332 9283 W www.fpchurch.org.uk
Moderator (2011–12), Revd Kenneth Macleod
Clerk of the Synod, Revd John MacLeod

HOLY APOSTOLIC CATHOLIC ASSYRIAN CHURCH OF THE EAST

The Holy Apostolic Catholic Assyrian Church of the East traces its beginnings to the middle of the first century. It spread from Upper Mesopotamia throughout the territories of the Persian Empire. The Assyrian Church of the East became theologically separated from the rest of the Christian community following the Council of Ephesus in 431. The church is headed by the Catholicos Patriarch and is episcopal in government. The liturgical language is Syriac (Aramaic). The Assyrian Church of the East and the Roman Catholic Church agreed a common Christological declaration in 1994, and a process of dialogue between the Assyrian Church of the East and the Chaldean Catholic Church, which is in communion with Rome but shares the Syriac liturgy, was instituted in 1996.

The church has about 400,000 members in the Middle East, India, Europe, North America and Australasia. In Great Britain there are three congregations, 15 priests and around 7,000 members. The church in Great Britain forms part of the diocese of Europe under Mar Odisho Oraham.

HOLY APOSTOLIC CATHOLIC ASSYRIAN CHURCH OF THE EAST, St Mary's Church, Westminster Road, Hanwell, London W7 3TU T 020-8567 1814
Representative in Great Britain, Revd Tony

INDEPENDENT METHODIST CHURCHES

The Independent Methodist Churches were formed in 1805 and remained independent when the Methodist Church in Great Britain was formed in 1932. They are mainly concentrated in the industrial areas of the north of England.

The churches are Methodist in doctrine but their organisation is congregational. All the churches are members of the Independent Methodist Connexion of Churches. The controlling body of the Connexion is the Annual Meeting, to which churches send delegates. The Connexional President is elected annually. Between annual meetings the affairs of the Connexion are handled by departmental committees. Ministers are appointed by the churches and trained through the Connexion.

The ministry is open to both men and women and is unpaid.

There are 1,700 members, 86 ministers and 82 churches in Great Britain.

INDEPENDENT METHODIST RESOURCE CENTRE, Fleet Street, Pemberton, Wigan WN5 0DS
T 01942-223526 E resourcecentre@imcgb.org.uk
W www.imcgb.org.uk
President, Eric Southwick
General Secretary, Brian Rowney

LUTHERAN CHURCH

Lutheranism is based on the teachings of Martin Luther, the German leader of the Protestant Reformation. The authority of the scriptures is held to be supreme over church tradition. The teachings of Lutheranism are explained in detail in 16th-century confessional writings, particularly the Augsburg Confession. Lutheranism is one of the largest Protestant denominations and it is particularly strong in northern Europe and the USA. Some Lutheran churches are episcopal, while others have a synodal form of organisation; unity is based on doctrine rather than structure. Most Lutheran churches are members of the Lutheran World Federation, based in Geneva.

Lutheran services in Great Britain are held in 18 languages to serve members of different nationalities. Services usually follow ancient liturgies. English-language congregations are members either of the Lutheran Church in Great Britain or of the Evangelical Lutheran Church of England. The Lutheran Church in Great Britain and other Lutheran churches in Britain are members of the Lutheran Council of Great Britain, which represents them and coordinates their common work.

There are over 70 million Lutherans worldwide; in Great Britain there are about 170,000 members, 45 clergy and 100 congregations.

THE LUTHERAN COUNCIL OF GREAT BRITAIN, 30 Thanet Street, London WC1H 9QH T 020-7554 2900
E enquiries@lutheran.org.uk W www.lutheran.org.uk
Acting General Secretary, Revd Timothy Fletcher

METHODIST CHURCH

The Methodist movement started in England in 1729 when the Revd John Wesley, an Anglican priest, and his brother Charles met with others in Oxford and resolved to conduct their lives and study by 'rule and method'. In 1739 the Wesleys began evangelistic preaching and the first Methodist chapel was founded in Bristol in the same year. In 1744 the first annual conference was held, at which the Articles of Religion were drawn up. Doctrinal emphases included repentance, faith, the assurance of salvation, social concern and the priesthood of all believers. After John Wesley's death in 1791 the Methodists withdrew from the established church to form the Methodist Church. Methodists gradually drifted into many groups, but in 1932 the Wesleyan Methodist Church, the United Methodist Church and the Primitive Methodist Church united to form the Methodist Church of Great Britain.

The governing body of the Methodist Church is the Conference. The Conference meets annually in June or July and consists of two parts: the ministerial and representative sessions. The Methodist Church is structured as a 'Connexion' of churches, circuits and districts. The local churches in a defined area form a circuit, and a number of these circuits make up each of the 31 districts. There are around 70 million Methodists worldwide; at the last count in 2007 there were 267,257

members, 3,509 ministers, 226 Deacons and 6,402 churches in Great Britain.

THE METHODIST CHURCH OF GREAT BRITAIN, Methodist Church House, 25 Marylebone Road, London NW1 5JR T 020-7486 5502
E helpdesk@methodistchurch.org.uk
W www.methodist.org.uk
President of the Conference (2011–12),
Revd Lionel E. Osborne
General Secretary and Secretary of the Conference,
Revd Dr Martyn Atkins

THE METHODIST CHURCH IN IRELAND
The Methodist Church in Ireland is autonomous but has close links with British Methodism. It has a community roll of 51,425 members, 126 ministers, 233 lay preachers and 230 churches.

1 Fountainville Avenue, Belfast BT9 6AN T 028-9032 4554
E secretary@irishmethodist.org W www.irishmethodist.org
President (2011–12), Revd Ian D. Henderson
Secretary (2011–12), Donald P. Ket

ORTHODOX CHURCHES

EASTERN ORTHODOX CHURCH
The Eastern (or Byzantine) Orthodox Church is a communion of self-governing Christian churches that recognises the honorary primacy of the Ecumenical Patriarch of Constantinople.

The position of Orthodox Christians is that the faith was fully defined during the period of the Oecumenical Councils. In doctrine it is strongly trinitarian, and stresses the mystery and importance of the sacraments. It is episcopal in government. The structure of the Orthodox Christian year differs from that of western churches.

Orthodox Christians throughout the world are estimated to number about 300 million; there are around 300,000 in the UK.

GREEK ORTHODOX CHURCH (PATRIARCHATE OF ANTIOCH)
The Archdiocese of Europe is led by HE Metropolitan John (Yazigi), based in Paris.

St George's Cathedral Church, 1A Redhill Street, London NW1 4BG T 020-7383 0403
E fr.samir@antiochianorth.co.uk
W www.antiochianorth.co.uk
Archpriest, Fr. Samir Gholam
Antiochian Orthodox Deanery of the United Kingdom and Ireland, St Aidan's Orthodox Church, Clare Road, Levenshulme, Manchester T 0161-476 4847
E orthodox@.clara.net W www.antiochian-orthodox.co.uk
Dean, Archpriest Fr. Gregory Hallam

GREEK ORTHODOX CHURCH (PATRIARCHATE OF CONSTANTINOPLE)
The presence of Greek Orthodox Christians in Britain dates back at least to 1677 when Archbishop Joseph Geogirenes of Samos fled from Turkish persecution and came to London. The present Greek cathedral in Moscow Road, Bayswater, was opened for public worship in 1879, and the Diocese of Thyateira and Great Britain was established in 1922. There are now 116 parishes and other communities (including monasteries) in the UK, served by four bishops, 106 clergy, nine cathedrals and 109 parishes. .

The Patriarchate Of Constantinople In Great Britain, Thyateira House, 5 Craven Hill, London W2 3EN
T 020-7723 4787 E mail@thyateira.org.uk
W www.thyateira.org.uk
Archbishop, Gregorios of Thyateira and Great Britain

THE RUSSIAN ORTHODOX CHURCH (PATRIARCHATE OF MOSCOW) AND THE RUSSIAN ORTHODOX CHURCH OUTSIDE RUSSIA
The records of Russian Orthodox Church activities in Britain date from the visit to England of Tsar Peter I in the early 18th century. Clergy were sent from Russia to serve the chapel established to minister to the staff of the Imperial Russian Embassy in London.

In 2007, after an 80-year division, the Russian Orthodox Church Outside Russia agreed to become an autonomous part of the Russian Orthodox Church, Patriarchate of Moscow. The reunification agreement was signed by Patriarch Alexy II, 15th Patriarch of Moscow and All Russia and Metropolitan Laurus, leader of the Russian Orthodox Church Outside Russia on 17 May at a ceremony at Christ the Saviour Cathedral in Moscow. Patriarch Alexy II died on 5 December 2008. Metropolitan Kirill of Smolensk and Kaliningrad was enthroned as the 16th Patriarch of Moscow and All Russia on 1 February 2009, having been elected by a secret ballot of clergy on 27 January 2009.

The diocese of Sourozh is the diocese of the Russian Orthodox Church in Great Britain and Ireland and is led by Archbishop Elisey of Sourozh.
Diocese of Sourozh, Diocesan Office, Cathedral of the Dormition, 67 Ennismore Gardens, London SW7 1NH
T 020-7584 0096 W www.sourozh.org
Diocesan Bishop, Most Revd Elisey (Ganaba) of Sourozh
Assistant Diocesan Bishop, Most Revd Anatoly (Kuznetsov) of Kerch

SERBIAN ORTHODOX CHURCH (PATRIARCHATE OF SERBIA)
There are seven parishes in Great Britain and around 4,000 members. Great Britain is part of the Diocese of Great Britain and Scandinavia, which is led by Bishop Dositej. The church can be contacted via the church of St Sava in London.
Serbian Orthodox Church in Great Britain, Church of Saint Sava, 89 Lancaster Road, London W11 1QQ
T 020-7727 8367 E crkva@spclondon.org
W www.spclondon.org
Priest, Very Revd Milun Kostic

OTHER NATIONALITIES
The Patriarchates of Romania and Bulgaria (Diocese of Western Europe) have memberships estimated at 20,000 and 2,000 respectively, while the Georgian Orthodox Church has around 500 members. The Belarusian (membership estimated at 2,400) and Latvian (membership of around 100) Orthodox churches are part of the Patriarchate of Constantinople.

ORIENTAL ORTHODOX CHURCHES
The term 'Oriental Orthodox Churches' is now generally used to describe a group of six ancient eastern churches (Armenian, Coptic, Eritrean, Ethiopian, Indian (Malankara) and Syrian) which rejected the Christological definition of the Council of Chalcedon (AD 451). There are around 50 million members worldwide of the Oriental Orthodox Churches and about 20,075 in the UK.

ARMENIAN ORTHODOX CHURCH (CATHOLICOSATE OF ETCHMIADZIN)
The Armenian Orthodox Church is led by HH Karekin II, Catholicos of All Armenians. The Very Revd Dr Vahan Hovhanessian is the Primate of the Armenian Church of Great Britain and President of the Armenian Community and Church Council.
Armenian Church of Great Britain, The Armenian Vicarage, Iverna Gardens, London W8 6TP T 020-7937 0152
E information@armenianchurch.org.uk
W www.armenianchurch.co.uk
Primate, Very Revd Dr Vahan Hovhanessian

COPTIC ORTHODOX CHURCH
The Coptic Orthodox Church is led by HH Pope Shenouda III and is represented in Great Britain by Bishop Angaelos at the Coptic Orthodox Cathedral of St George at the Coptic Orthodox Church Centre. The Coptic Orthodox Church is the largest Oriental Orthodox community in Great Britain.
Coptic Orthodox Church Centre, Shephalbury Manor, Broadhall Way, Stevenage, Herts SG2 8NP T 01438-745232
E admin@copticcentre.com W www.copticcentre.com
Bishop, HG Bishop Angaelos

BRITISH ORTHODOX CHURCH
The British Orthodox Church is canonically part of the Coptic Orthodox Patriarchate of Alexandria. As it ministers to British people, all of its services are in English.
The British Orthodox Church, 10 Heathwood Gardens, Charlton, London SE7 8EP T 020-8854 3090
E info@britishorthodox.org W www.britishorthodox.org
Metropolitan, Abba Seraphim

INDIAN ORTHODOX CHURCH
The Indian Orthodox Church, also known as the Malankara Orthodox Church, traces its origins to the first century. The UK is part of the Diocese of Europe, UK and Africa.
Indian Orthodox Church, St Gregorios Indian Orthodox Church, Cranfield Road, Brockley, London SE4 1UF
T 020-8691 9456 E vicar@indian-orthodox.co.uk
W www.indian-orthodox.co.uk
Diocesan Metropolitan, HG Dr Mathews Mar Thimotios
Vicar, Fr. John Samuel

SYRIAN ORTHODOX CHURCH
The Patriarchate Vicariate of the Syrian Orthodox Church in the United Kingdom is represented by HE Mor Athanasius Toma Dawood.
Syrian Orthodox Church in the UK, St Thomas Cathedral, 7–11 Armstrong Road, London W3 7JL T 020-8654 7531
E enquiry-uk@syrianorthodoxchurch.net
W www.syrianorthodoxchurch.net
Patriarchal Vicar, HE Mor Athanasius Toma Dawood

PENTECOSTAL CHURCHES
Pentecostalism is inspired by the descent of the Holy Spirit upon the apostles at Pentecost. The movement began in Los Angeles, USA, in 1906 and is characterised by baptism with the Holy Spirit, divine healing, speaking in tongues (glossolalia), and a literal interpretation of the scriptures.

The Pentecostal movement in Britain dates from 1907. Initially, groups of Pentecostalists were led by laymen and did not organise formally. However, in 1915 the Elim Foursquare Gospel Alliance (more commonly called the Elim Pentecostal Church) was founded in Ireland by George Jeffreys and currently has about 550 churches, 68,500 adherents and 650 accredited ministers. In 1924 about 70 independent assemblies formed a fellowship called the Assemblies of God in Great Britain and Ireland, which now incorporates 591 churches, around 70,000 adherents and 720 ministers.

The Apostolic Church grew out of the 1904–5 Christian revivals in South Wales and was established in 1916. The Apostolic Church has around 109 churches, 5,400 adherents and 103 ministers in the UK. The New Testament Church of God was established in England in 1953 and has around 125 congregations, 28,137 members and 320 ministers across England and Wales. The Church of God of Prophecy was founded in 1923 in Cleveland, Tennessee. The UK branch was established in 1953 and now incorporates around 90 churches, 100 ministers and 25,000 adherents.

In recent years many aspects of Pentecostalism have been adopted by the growing charismatic movement within the Roman Catholic, Protestant and Eastern Orthodox churches. There are about 105 million Pentecostalists worldwide, with over 350,000 adherents in the UK.

THE APOSTOLIC CHURCH, International Administration Offices, PO Box 51298, London SE11 9AJ T 020-7587 1802
E admin@apostolic-church.org
National Leader, Emmanuel Mbakwe
THE ASSEMBLIES OF GOD INCORPORATED,
PO Box 7634, Nottingham NG11 6ZY T 0115-921 7272
E info@aog.org.uk W www.aog.org.uk
National leader, John Partington
THE CHURCH OF GOD OF PROPHECY,
6 Beacon Court, Birmingham Road, Great Barr,
Birmingham B43 6NN T 0121-358 2231
E admin@cogop.org.uk
National Overseer, Bishop Wilton Powell, OBE
THE ELIM PENTECOSTAL CHURCH, Elim International Centre, De Walden Road, West Malvern, Worcestershire WR14 4DF T 0845-302 6750 E info@elimhq.net
W www.elim.org.uk
General Superintendent, Revd John Glass
THE NEW TESTAMENT CHURCH OF GOD,
3 Cheyne Walk, Northampton NN1 5PT T 01604-824222
W www.ntcg.org.uk
Administrative Bishop, Eric Brown

PRESBYTERIAN CHURCH IN IRELAND

Irish Presbyterianism traces its origins back to the Plantation of Ulster in 1606, when English and Scottish Protestants began to settle on the land confiscated from the Irish chieftains. The first presbytery was established in Ulster in 1642 by chaplains of a Scottish army that had been sent to crush a Catholic rebellion in 1641.

The Presbyterian Church in Ireland is reformed in doctrine and belongs to the World Alliance of Reformed Churches. Structurally, the 549 congregations are grouped in 19 presbyteries under the General Assembly. This body meets annually and is presided over by a moderator who is elected for one year. The ongoing work of the church is undertaken by 15 boards under which there are specialist committees.

There are around 250,000 members of Irish presbyterian churches in the UK and Ireland.

THE PRESBYTERIAN CHURCH IN IRELAND,
Church House, Belfast BT1 6DW T 028-9032 2284
E info@presbyterianireland.org
W www.presbyterianireland.org
Moderator (2011–12), Rt. Revd Dr Ivan Patterson
Clerk of Assembly and General Secretary,
Revd Dr Donald Watts

PRESBYTERIAN CHURCH OF WALES

The Presbyterian Church of Wales or Calvinistic Methodist Church of Wales is Calvinistic in doctrine and presbyterian in constitution. It was formed in 1811 when Welsh Calvinists severed the relationship with the established church by ordaining their own ministers. It secured its own confession of faith in 1823 and a Constitutional Deed in 1826, and since 1864 the General Assembly has met annually, presided over by a moderator elected for a year. The doctrine and constitutional structure of the Presbyterian Church of Wales was confirmed by act of parliament in 1931–2.

The Church has 28,687 members, 65 ministers and 676 congregations.

THE PRESBYTERIAN CHURCH OF WALES,
Tabernacle Chapel, 81 Merthyr Road, Whitchurch,
Cardiff CF14 1DD T 029-2062 7465
E swyddfa.office@ebcpcw.org.uk W www.ebcpcw.org.uk
Moderator (2011–12), Revd R. Roberts
General Secretary, Revd Bryn Williams

RELIGIOUS SOCIETY OF FRIENDS (QUAKERS)

Quakerism is a religious denomination which was founded in the 17th century by George Fox and others in an attempt to revive what they saw as the original 'primitive Christianity'. The movement, at first called Friends of the Truth, started in the Midlands, Yorkshire and north-west England, but there are now Quakers all over the UK and in 36 countries around the world. The colony of Pennsylvania, founded William Penn, was originally a Quaker settlement.

Quakers place an emphasis on the experience of God in daily life rather than on sacraments or religious occasions. There is no church calendar. Worship is largely silent and there are no appointed ministers; the responsibility for conducting a meeting is shared equally among those present. Religious tolerance and social reform have always been important to Quakers, together with a commitment to peace and non-violence in resolving disputes.

There are more than 23,000 'friends' or Quakers in Great Britain. There are about 470 places where Quaker meetings are held, many of them Quaker-owned Friends Meeting Houses. The Britain Yearly Meeting is the name given to the central organisation of Quakers in Britain.

THE RELIGIOUS SOCIETY OF FRIENDS (QUAKERS) IN BRITAIN, Friends House, 173–177 Euston Road, London NW1 2BJ T 020-7663 1000
E enquiries@quaker.org.uk W www.quaker.org.uk
Recording Clerk, Paul Parker

SALVATION ARMY

The Salvation Army is an international Christian organisation working in 124 countries worldwide. As a church and registered charity, the Salvation Army is funded through donations from its members, the general public and, where appropriate, government grants.

The Salvation Army was founded by a Methodist minister, William Booth, in the East End of London in 1865, and now has 709 local church and community centres, more than 70 residential support centres for homeless people, 17 care homes for older people and six substance-misuse centres. It also runs a clothing recycling programme, charity shops, a prison-visiting service and a family-tracing service. In 1878 it adopted a quasi-military command structure intended to inspire and regulate its endeavours and to reflect its view that the church was engaged in spiritual warfare. There are around 50,000 members and 1,350 Salvation Army officers (full-time ministers) in the UK. Salvationists emphasise evangelism and the provision of social welfare.

UK TERRITORIAL HEADQUARTERS,
101 Newington Causeway, London SE1 6BN
T 020-7367 4500 E info@salvationarmy.org.uk
W www.salvationarmy.org.uk
UK Territorial Commander, Commissioner John Matear

SEVENTH-DAY ADVENTIST CHURCH

The Seventh-day Adventist Church is a worldwide Christian church marked by its observance of Saturday as the Sabbath and by its emphasis on the imminent second coming of Jesus Christ. Adventists summarise their faith in '28 fundamental beliefs'.

The church grew out of the Millerite movement in the USA during the mid-19th century and was formally established in 1863. The church has an ethnically and culturally diverse worldwide membership of over 16 million, with a presence in more than 200 countries. In the UK and Ireland there are approximately 31,000 members worshipping in 299 churches and companies.

BRITISH UNION CONFERENCE OF SEVENTH-DAY ADVENTISTS, Stanborough Park, Watford WD25 9JZ
T 01923-672251 W www.adventist.org.uk
President, Pastor Ian Sweeney

THE (SWEDENBORGIAN) NEW CHURCH

The New Church is based on the teachings of the 18th-century Swedish scientist and theologian Emanuel Swedenborg (1688–1772), who believed that Jesus Christ appeared to him and instructed him to reveal the spiritual meaning of the Bible. He claimed to have visions of the spiritual world, including heaven and hell, and conversations with angels and spirits. He published several theological works, including descriptions of the spiritual world and a Bible commentary.

Swedenborgians believe that the second coming of Jesus Christ is taking place, being not an actual physical reappearance of Christ, but rather his return in spirit. It is also believed that concurrent with our life on earth is life in a parallel spiritual world, of which we are usually unconscious until death. There are around 30,000 Swedenborgians worldwide, with 8,470 members, 21 Churches and 20 ministers in the UK.

THE GENERAL CONFERENCE OF THE NEW CHURCH, Swedenborg House, 20 Bloomsbury Way, London WC1A 2TH T 0845-686 0086
E enquiries@generalconference.org.uk
W www.generalconference.org.uk
Chief Executive, Michael Hindley

UNDEB YR ANNIBYNWYR CYMRAEG

Undeb Yr Annibynwyr Cymraeg (the Union of Welsh Independents) was formed in 1872 and is a voluntary association of Welsh Congregational churches and personal members. It is mainly Welsh-speaking. Congregationalism in Wales dates back to 1639 when the first Welsh Congregational church was opened in Gwent.

Member churches are traditionally congregationalist in organisation and Calvinistic in doctrine, although a wide range of interpretations are permitted. Each church has complete independence in the governance and administration of its affairs.

The Union has 28,892 members, 98 ministers and 449 member churches.

UNDEB YR ANNIBYNWYR CYMRAEG, 5 Axis Court, Riverside Business Park, Swansea Vale, Swansea SA7 0AJ
T 01792-795888 E undeb@annibynwyr.org
W www.annibynwyr.org
President of the Union (2010–12), Revd Andrew Lenny
General Secretary, Revd Dr Geraint Tudur

UNITED REFORMED CHURCH

The United Reformed Church (URC) was first formed by the union of most of the Congregational churches in England and Wales with the Presbyterian Church of England in 1972. Congregationalism dates from the mid-16th century. It is Calvinistic in doctrine, and its followers form independent self-governing congregations bound under God by covenant, a principle laid down in the writings of Robert Browne (1550–1633). From the late 16th century the movement was driven underground by persecution, but the cause was defended at the Westminster Assembly in 1643 and the Savoy Declaration of 1658 laid down its principles. Congregational churches formed county associations for mutual support and in 1832 these associations merged to form the Congregational Union of England and Wales.

Presbyterianism in England also dates from the mid 16th century, and was Calvinistic and evangelical in its doctrine. It was governed by a hierarchy of courts.

In the 1960s there was close cooperation locally and nationally between congregational and presbyterian churches. This led to union negotiations and a Scheme of Union, supported by act of parliament in 1972. In 1981 a further unification took place, with the Reformed Association of Churches of Christ becoming part of the URC. In 2000 a third union took place, with the Congregational Union of Scotland. In its basis the United Reformed Church reflects local church initiative and responsibility with a conciliar pattern of oversight.

The United Reformed Church is divided into 13 synods, each with a synod moderator. There are around 1,550 congregations which serve around 67,000 adults and 54,000 children and young people. There are around 660 ministers in active service.

The General Assembly is the central body, and comprises around 400 representatives, mainly appointed by the synods, of which half are lay persons and half are ministers. From 2010 the General Assembly will meet biennially to elect two moderators, both lay and ordained, who will then become the public representatives of the URC. This will replace the current arrangement where one lay or ordained moderator is elected annually by the General Assembly. As a transitional arrangement the moderator will remain in office for two years from 2008.

UNITED REFORMED CHURCH, 86 Tavistock Place, London WC1H 9RT T 020-7916 2020 E info@urc.org.uk
W www.urc.org.uk
Moderators of the General Assembly (2010–12),
Val Morrison; Revd Dr Kirsty Thorpe
General Secretary, Revd Roberta Rominger

WESLEYAN REFORM UNION

The Wesleyan Reform Union was founded by Methodists who left or were expelled from Wesleyan Methodism in 1849 following a period of internal conflict. Its doctrine is conservative evangelical and its organisation is congregational, each church having complete independence in the government and administration of its affairs. The union has around 1,540 members, 20 ministers and 96 churches.

THE WESLEYAN REFORM UNION, Wesleyan Reform Church House, 123 Queen Street, Sheffield S1 2DU
T 0114-272 1938 E admin@thewru.co.uk
W www.thewru.com
President (2011–12), Graham Evans
General Secretary, Revd Colin Braithwaite

NON-TRINITARIAN CHURCHES

CHRISTADELPHIAN

Christadelphians believe that the Bible is the word of God and that it reveals both God's dealings with mankind in the past and his plans for the future. These plans centre on the work of Jesus Christ, who it is believed will return to Earth to establish God's kingdom. The Christadelphian group was founded in the USA in the 1850s by the Englishman, Dr John Thomas.

THE CHRISTADELPHIAN, 404 Shaftmoor Lane, Hall Green, Birmingham B28 8SZ T 0121-777 6328
E enquiries@thechristadelphian.com
W www.thechristadelphian.com

CHURCH OF CHRIST, SCIENTIST

The Church of Christ, Scientist was founded by Mary Baker Eddy in the USA in 1879 to 'reinstate primitive Christianity and its lost element of healing'. Christian Science teaches the need for spiritual regeneration and salvation from sin, but it is best known for its reliance on prayer alone in the healing of sickness. Adherents believe that such healing is the result of divine laws, or divine science, and is in direct line with that practised by Jesus Christ (revered, not as God, but as the son of God) and by the early Christian church.

The denomination consists of The First Church of Christ, Scientist, in Boston, Massachusetts, USA ('The Mother Church') and its branch churches in almost 80 countries worldwide. The Bible and Mary Baker Eddy's book, *Science and Health with Key to the Scriptures*, are used for daily spiritual guidance and healing by all members and are read at services. There are no clergy; those engaged in full-time healing are called Christian Science practitioners, of whom there are 1,500 worldwide. The church also publishes *The Christian Science Monitor*.

No membership figures are available, since Mary Baker Eddy felt that numbers are no measure of spiritual vitality and ruled that such statistics should not be published. There are almost 2,000 branch churches worldwide, including over 100 in the UK.

CHRISTIAN SCIENCE COMMITTEE ON PUBLICATION, Unit T10, Tideway Yard, 125 Mortlake High Street, London SW14 8SN
T 020-8150 0245 E londoncs@csps.com
W www.christianscience.com
District Manager for the UK and the Republic of Ireland, Tony Lobl

CHURCH OF JESUS CHRIST OF LATTER-DAY SAINTS

The Church of Jesus Christ of Latter-Day Saints (often referred to as 'Mormons') was founded in New York State, USA, in 1830, and came to Britain in 1837. The oldest continuous congregation of the church is in Preston, Lancashire.

Mormons are Christians who claim to belong to the 'restored church' of Jesus Christ. They believe that true Christianity died when the last original apostle died, but that it was given back to the world by God and Jesus Christ through Joseph Smith, the church's founder and first president. They accept and use the Bible as scripture, but believe in continuing revelation from God; Mormons also use additional scriptures, including *The Book of Mormon: Another Testament of Jesus Christ*. The importance of the family is central to the church's beliefs and practices. Church members set aside Monday evenings as family home evenings when Christian family values are taught. Polygamy was formally discontinued in 1890.

The church has no paid ministry: local congregations are headed by a leader chosen from among their number. The world governing body, based in Utah, USA, is led by a president, believed to be the chosen prophet, and his two counsellors. There are more than 14 million members worldwide, with over 190,000 adherents and 411 congregations in the UK.

THE CHURCH OF JESUS CHRIST OF LATTER-DAY SAINTS, British Headquarters, 751 Warwick Road, Solihull, W. Midlands B91 3DQ T 0121-712 1200
W www.lds.org.uk

JEHOVAH'S WITNESSES

The movement now known as Jehovah's Witnesses grew from a Bible study group formed by Charles Taze Russell in 1872 in Pennsylvania, USA. In 1896 it adopted the name of the Watch Tower Bible and Tract Society, and in 1931, its members became known as Jehovah's Witnesses.

Jehovah's (God's) Witnesses believe in the Bible as the word of God, and consider it to be inspired and historically accurate. They take the scriptures literally, except where there are obvious indications that they are figurative or symbolic, and reject the doctrine of the Trinity. Witnesses also believe that all those approved of by Jehovah will have eternal life on a cleansed and beautified earth; only 144,000 will go to heaven to rule with Jesus Christ. They believe that the second coming of Christ began in 1914, that his thousand-year reign over the earth is imminent, and that armageddon (a final battle in which evil will be defeated) will precede Christ's rule of peace. Jehovah's Witnesses refuse to take part in military service and do not accept blood transfusions.

The seven-member world governing body is based in New York, USA. There is no paid ministry, but each congregation has elders assigned to look after various duties and every Witness takes part in the public ministry in their neighbourhood. There are over 7.5 million Jehovah's Witnesses worldwide, with 134,000 Witnesses in the UK organised into more than 1,500 congregations.

BRITISH ISLES HEADQUARTERS, Watch Tower, The Ridgeway, London NW7 1RN T 020-8906 2211
E opi@uk.jw.org W www.watchtower.org

UNITARIAN AND FREE CHRISTIAN CHURCHES

Unitarianism has its historical roots in the Judaeo-Christian tradition but rejects the deity of Christ and the doctrine of the Trinity. It allows the individual to embrace insights from all of the world's faiths and philosophies, as there is no fixed creed. It is accepted that beliefs may evolve in the light of personal experience.

Unitarian communities first became established in Poland and Transylvania in the 16th century. The first avowedly Unitarian place of worship in the British Isles opened in London in 1774. The General Assembly of Unitarian and Free Christian Churches came into existence in 1928 as the result of the amalgamation of two earlier organisations.

There are around 5,000 Unitarians in Great Britain and about 76 Unitarian ministers. Nearly 200 self-governing congregations and fellowship groups, including a small number overseas, are members of the General Assembly.

GENERAL ASSEMBLY OF UNITARIAN AND FREE CHRISTIAN CHURCHES, Essex Hall, 1–6 Essex Street, London WC2R 3HY T 020-7240 2384 E ga@unitarian.org.uk W www.unitarian.org.uk
President (2011–12), Revd Dr Ann Peart
Vice-President (2011–12), Lis Dyson-Jones

COMMUNICATIONS

POSTAL SERVICES

The Royal Mail Group plc operates Parcelforce Worldwide, General Logistics Systems (GLS), the Post Office and Royal Mail. Each working day Royal Mail processes and delivers more than 71 million items to 28 million addresses. Following the passing of the Post Services Act 2011, OFCOM assumed regulatory responsibility for postal services from the Postal Services Commission (Postcomm). It is responsible for promoting effective competition between postal operators after the market was opened to full competition in 2006. All 54 of the UK's current operators, including Royal Mail, are licensed by Postcomm to ensure that the mail they handle is secure and that they maintain certain standards. In October 2008 Postwatch merged with Energywatch and the National Consumer Council to form Consumer Focus, a consumer representation and advocacy body. Consumer Focus is responsible for postal services and takes up complaints on behalf of consumers against any licensed provider of postal services. In October 2010 the government announced that Consumer Focus would be abolished, most likely by spring 2013.

CONSUMER FOCUS, Fleetbank House, Salisbury Square, London EC4Y 8JX T 020-7799 7900
W www.consumerfocus.org.uk
POSTCOMM, Hercules House, 6 Hercules Road, London SE1 7DB T 020-7593 2100 W www.psc.gov.uk

PRICING IN PROPORTION
Since August 2006 Royal Mail has priced mail according to its size as well as its weight. The system is intended to reflect the fact that larger, bulkier items cost more to handle than smaller, lighter ones. There are three basic categories of correspondence:

LETTER
Length up to 240mm, width up to 165mm, thickness up to 5mm, weight up to 100g; eg most cards, postcards and bills

LARGE LETTER
Length up to 353mm, width up to 250mm, thickness up to 25mm, weight up to 750g; eg most A4 documents, CDs and magazines

PACKET
Length over 353mm, width over 250mm, thickness over 25mm, weight over 750g; eg books, clothes, gifts, prints and posters in cylindrical packaging

INLAND POSTAL SERVICES
Following are details of a number of popular postal services along with prices correct as at April 2011.

FIRST AND SECOND CLASS
Format	Maximum weight	First class	Second class†
Letter*	100g	£0.46	£0.36
Large letter	100g	£0.75	£0.58
	250g	£1.09	£0.92
	500g	£1.46	£1.23
	750g	£2.07	£1.76
Packet	100g	£1.58	£1.33
	250g	£1.96	£1.72
	500g	£2.48	£2.16
	750g	£3.05	£2.61
	1,000g‡	£3.71	£3.15

* Includes postcards
† First class post is normally delivered on the following working day and second class within three working days
‡ Packets heavier than 1,000g must be sent first class. For a full list of prices see W www.royalmail.com

STANDARD PARCEL RATES*
Maximum weight	Standard tariff
2kg	£4.41
4kg	£7.62
6kg	£10.34
8kg	£12.67
10kg	£13.61
20kg	£15.86

* Standard parcels may be up to 1.5m long and 20kg in weight with a combined length and width of less than 3m. They are normally delivered within three to five working days

OVERSEAS POSTAL SERVICES
Royal Mail divides the world into two zones: **Europe** (Albania, Andorra, Armenia, Austria, Azerbaijan, Azores, Balearic Islands, Belarus, Belgium, Bosnia and Hercegovina, Bulgaria, Canary Islands, Corsica, Croatia, Cyprus, Czech Republic, Denmark, Estonia, Faroe Islands, Finland, France, Georgia, Germany, Gibraltar, Greece, Greenland, Hungary, Iceland, Rep. of Ireland, Italy, Kazakhstan, Kosovo, Kyrgyzstan, Latvia, Liechtenstein, Lithuania, Luxembourg, Macedonia, Madeira, Malta, Moldova, Monaco, Montenegro, Netherlands, Norway, Poland, Portugal, Romania, Russia, San Marino, Serbia, Slovakia, Slovenia, Spain, Sweden, Switzerland, Tajikistan, Turkey, Turkmenistan, Ukraine, Uzbekistan, Vatican City State) and **Rest of the World** (all countries that are not listed under Europe).

OVERSEAS SURFACE MAIL RATES*
Letters
Maximum weight	Standard tariff	Maximum weight	Standard tariff
20g†	£0.66	450g	£6.05
60g	£1.14	500g	£6.68
100g	£1.60	750g	£9.68
150g	£2.27	1,000g	£12.68
200g	£2.89	1,250g	£15.68
250g	£3.54	1,500g	£18.68
300g	£4.16	1,750g	£21.68
350g	£4.79	2,000g	£24.68
400g	£5.43		

* Letters and postcards to Europe are sent by Airmail
† Includes postcards

Small packets and printed papers

Maximum weight	Standard tariff	Maximum weight	Standard tariff
100g	£1.12	450g	£3.79
150g	£1.50	500g	£4.16
200g	£1.89	750g	£5.86
250g	£2.28	1,000g	£7.56
300g	£2.64	1,500g	£10.96
350g	£3.02	2,000g*	£14.36
400g	£3.42		

* Maximum weight. For printed papers only: add £0.28 for each additional 50g up to a maximum weight of 5,000g

AIRMAIL LETTERS

Europe:

Maximum weight	Standard tariff	Maximum weight	Standard tariff
20g*	£0.68	300g	£4.20
40g	£1.00	400g	£4.96
60g	£1.30	500g	£5.72
80g	£1.49	600g	£6.71
100g	£1.73	700g	£7.70
120g	£2.01	800g	£8.69
140g	£2.29	900g	£9.68
160g	£2.58	1,000g	£10.67
180g	£2.86	1,200g	£12.39
200g	£3.11	1,400g	£14.11
220g	£3.38	1,600g	£15.83
240g	£3.64	1,800g	£17.55
260g	£3.89	2,000g	£19.27
280g	£4.13		

* Includes postcards

Rest of the World:

Maximum weight	Standard tariff
Postcards	£0.76
20g	£1.10
40g	£1.65
60g	£2.07
80g	£2.51
100g	£3.19
500g	£10.80
1,000g	£18.70
2,000g	£32.90

Note that there are different rates for small packets and printed matter, and that the latter has a greater maximum weight allowance. *See* W www.royalmail.com for further details.

SPECIAL DELIVERY SERVICES

INTERNATIONAL SIGNED FOR AND AIRSURE

Express airmail services (maximum weight 2kg) that include £41 compensation in case of loss or damage. The fee for International Signed For is £4.95 plus airmail or surface mail postage. The fee for Airsure is £5.30 plus airmail postage.

RECORDED SIGNED FOR

Provides a record of posting and delivery of letters and ensures a signature on delivery. This service is recommended for items of little or no monetary value. All packets must be handed to the post office and a receipt issued as proof of posting. The charge is 77p plus the standard first or second class postage with up to £41 compensation in case of loss or damage.

SPECIAL DELIVERY NEXT DAY

A guaranteed next working day delivery service by 1pm to 99 per cent of the UK (maximum item weight is 10kg). Prices start at £5.45. There is also a service that guarantees delivery by 9am (maximum item weight is 2kg). Prices start at £15.25. There is also a Saturday guarantee for mail sent out on a Friday, which costs an additional £2.70 an item. Note that size restrictions apply on these services.

OTHER SERVICES

BUSINESS SERVICES

A range of postal services are available to businesses, including business collection, freepost, business reply services, secure mail opening, international bulk and sustainable mailing options. Smartstamp allows businesses to print postage directly from a computer using a pre-pay system.

COMPENSATION

Compensation for loss or damage to an item sent varies according to the service used to send the item.

KEEPSAFE

Mail is held for up to two months while the addressee is away, and is delivered when the addressee returns. Prices start at £11.25 for 17 days. Recorded items are held for a week before being returned to the sender, and special delivery items for three weeks beyond the Keepsafe expiry date.

PASSPORT APPLICATIONS

Many post offices process passport applications. To find your nearest post office offering this service and for further information *see* W www.postoffice.co.uk

POST OFFICE BOX

A PO Box provides a short and memorable alternative address. Mail is held at a local delivery office until the addressee is ready to collect it, or delivered to a street address for an extra fee. Prices start at £95 for six months or £170 for a year.

POSTCODE FINDER

Customers can search an online database to find UK postcodes and addresses. For more information *see* Royal Mail's postcode finder W http://postcode.royalmail.com

REDIRECTION

Customers may arrange the redirection of their mail via phone, post, at the Post Office or online, subject to verification of their identity. A fee is payable for each different surname on the application form, and the service may be renewed up to a maximum of two years. The charges are: one month, £8.00; three months, £17.62; six months, £27.20; 12 months, £40.85. Prices for redirection overseas vary depending on location, beginning at £27 for one month to a non-EU address, up to £150 for 12 months to an EU address.

TRACK AND TRACE

An online service for customers to track the progress of items sent using special delivery. It is accessible from W http://track.royalmail.com and W http://track.postoffice.co.uk.

CONTACTS

Parcelforce Worldwide
  T 08448-004466 W www.parcelforce.com
Post Office enquiries
  T 08457-223344 W www.postoffice.co.uk
Postcode enquiry line
  T 0906-302 1222 / 08457-111222
Royal Mail business enquiries
  T 08457-950950 W www.royalmail.com/business-customers
Royal Mail general enquiries
  T 08457-740740 W www.royalmail.com

TELECOMMUNICATIONS

The 1984 Telecommunications Act set the framework for a competitive market for telecommunications by abolishing British Telecom's (BT) exclusive right to provide services. The early 1990s saw the market open up and a number of new national public telecommunications operators (PTOs) received licences. This ended the duopoly that had existed in the 1980s when only BT and Mercury were licensed to provide fixed-line telecoms networks in the UK.

Four EU directives were agreed in March 2002 with the aim of further developing a pro-competitive regulatory structure. These directives were provided for in the Communications Act which came into force in July 2003. Under the act, licences are no longer required for providing communications networks or services in the UK. All persons providing such networks and services are subject to 'general conditions of entitlement', which constitute a set of rules they are obliged to observe.

Mobile network technology has improved dramatically since the launch in 1985 of the first-generation global system for mobile communications (GSM), which offered little or no data capability. In 1992 Vodafone launched a new GSM network, usually referred to as 2G or second generation, which used digital encoding and allowed voice and low-speed data communications. This technology has now been extended, via the enhanced data transfer rate of 2.5G, to 3G – a family of mobile standards that provide high bandwidth support to applications such as voice- and video-calling, high-speed data transfer, television streaming and full internet access.

RECENT DEVELOPMENTS

The four GSM operators, namely Orange, O2, T-Mobile and Vodafone, were joined in March 2003 by the first 3G operator, '3' (Hutchison 3UK). Orange, T-Mobile and Vodafone all launched their own 3G services in 2004, and O2 in February 2005. In 2009 the number of 3G subscriptions increased by 7.1 million, with 31.8 per cent of mobile users using 3G at the end of the year compared to 24 per cent in 2008.

In April 2010 T-Mobile and Orange merged their UK operations becoming the largest mobile phone network in Britain with 28.4 million customers, or 37 per cent of the market, overtaking both O2 and Vodafone. Both T-Mobile and Orange remain separate brands, but from October 2010 they began signal-sharing, allowing customers to 'roam' across both mobile networks.

In March 2011 OFCOM announced plans for the auction of additional spectrum (the airwaves on which all communications rely) to provide the necessary capacity for 4G technology in the UK. The auction will be for two spectrum bands – 800 MHz and 2.6 GHz – which lie within the 'sweetspot', the frequency in greatest demand. This combination of low and high frequencies provides

the potential to cope with high demand of 4G services. OFCOM aims to begin the auction in early 2012 and expects operators to start offering 4G services in 2013.

The use of Wi-Fi (wireless fidelity) expanded rapidly in 2010 as the UK overtook the USA and China as the largest provider of public Wi-Fi locations with over 143,000 active hotspots; 24,000 in London alone. Deregulation has allowed public network operators to use certain parts of the spectrum, which are exempt from licensing, for wireless LAN (Wi-Fi) type systems. Initially only personal use was permitted in these bands, but this has been expanded to a full commercial service. Twelve city centres offer continuous Wi-Fi coverage using a network, or 'mesh', of 300m-range Wi-Fi signals.

FIXED-LINE COMMUNICATIONS

In the year to December 2009 there was a decrease in both the total fixed-line telephony revenue, down by £0.3bn to £8.8bn, and the number of fixed-line connections, down by 1.1 million to 32.1 million. BT's share of the fixed-line market decreased to under 60 per cent for the first time. Fixed-line telephony, which accounted for 60 per cent of telecoms revenue in 1998, contributed less than 30 per cent in 2009 as a result of the rise in the use of mobiles phones, email and voice over internet protocol (VoIP) services, such as Skype.

The average headline speed of residential fixed broadband connections increased in 2009 to 8.2Mbit/s, an increase of 1.8Mbit/s from 2008 as the average monthly cost decreased by 2 per cent to £13.31. There were 31.5 fixed broadband connections per 100 people in the UK at the end of 2009.

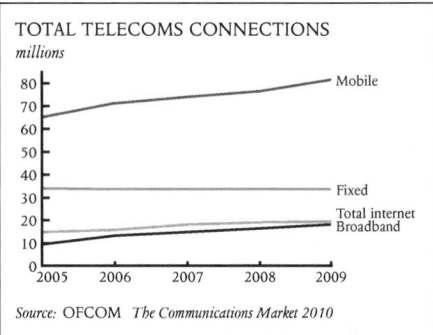

TOTAL TELECOMS CONNECTIONS
millions

Source: OFCOM *The Communications Market 2010*

MOBILE COMMUNICATIONS

In *The Communications Market 2010* report, revenue from mobile services declined sharply representing the first decrease since mobile telephony was established as a mass-market service in the late 1990's, falling to £14.9bn, a decrease of 3.5 per cent. OFCOM attributed the decline to falling prices, as a result of 'bundled' voice minutes and text messages being included within monthly rental fees. There was a rise in the amount of active mobile connections in the UK, with 132 connections per every 100 people, representing the increase in people using 3G dongles and multiple mobile phones for business purposes.

The number of people using the internet on mobile phones continued to grow – to 13.5 million – in the first quarter of 2010, due, in part, to the increase in the number of people using smartphones such as iPhones, Blackberrys and android operating systems.

MOBILE SUBSCRIPTIONS

There are two basic types of mobile subscription: contracts and pre-pay or 'pay as you go'. The proportion of contract to pay-as-you-go customers in the UK has remained relatively constant over the last few years. At the end of 2009 there were 33 million active contract subscribers and 47.3 million pre-pay customers.

MOBILE SUBSCRIPTIONS BY NETWORK
Active subscriptions, millions

■ 2006
▨ 2009

Orange: 15.3, 16.9
O2: 19.0, 22.4
T-Mobile: 16.9, 17.2
Vodafone: 15.0, 18.8
3UK: 3.8, 4.9

Source: OFCOM *The Communications Market 2010*

HEALTH

In 1999 the Independent Expert Group on Mobile Phones (IEGMP) was established to examine the possible effects on health of mobile phones, base stations and transmitters. The main findings of the IEGMP's report *Mobile Phones and Health*, published in May 2000, were:
• exposure to radio frequency radiation below guideline levels did not cause adverse health effects to the general population
• the use of mobile phones by drivers of any vehicle can increase the chance of accidents
• the widespread use of mobile phones by children for non-essential calls should be discouraged because if there are unrecognised adverse health effects children may be more vulnerable
• there is no general risk to the health of people living near to base stations on the basis that exposures are expected to be much lower than guidelines set by the International Commission on Non-Ionising Radiation Protection (ICNIRP)

As part of its response to the research recommendations contained in the IEGMP's report, the government set up the Mobile Telecommunications Health and Research (MTHR) programme in 2001 to undertake independent research into the possible health risks from mobile telephone technology. The MTHR programme published its report in September 2007 concluding that, in the short term, neither mobile phones nor base stations have been found to be associated with any biological or adverse health effects. An international cohort study into the possible long-term health effects of mobile phone use was launched by the MTHR in April 2010. The study is known as COSMOS and aims to follow the health of 250,000 mobile phone users from five countries over 20 to 30 years. The full 2007 report and details of COSMOS can be found on the MTHR website (W www.mthr.org.uk).

A national measurement programme, to ensure that emissions from mobile phone base stations do not exceed the ICNIRP guideline levels, is overseen by OFCOM and annual audits of these levels can be found on the sitefinder part of its website. The Health Protection Agency is responsible for providing information and advice in relation to the health effects of electromagnetic fields, including those emitted from mobile phones and base stations (W www.hpa.org.uk).

SAFETY WHILE DRIVING

Under legislation that came into effect in December 2003 it is illegal for drivers to use a hand-held mobile phone while driving. Since February 2007, under the Road Safety Act 2006, the fixed penalty for using a hand-held mobile device while driving is £60 and three penalty points. The same fixed penalty can also be issued to a driver for not having proper control of a vehicle while using a hands-free device. If the police or driver chooses to take the case to court rather than issue or accept a fixed penalty notice, the maximum fine is £1,000 for car drivers and £2,500 for drivers of buses, coaches or heavy goods vehicles.

REGULATION

Under the Communications Act 2003, OFCOM is the independent regulator and competition authority for the UK communications industries, with responsibilities across television, radio, telecommunications and wireless communications services. Competition in the communications market is also regulated by the Office of Fair Trading, although OFCOM takes the lead in competition investigations in the UK market. The Competition Appeal Tribunal hears appeals against OFCOM's decisions, and price-related appeals are referred to the Competition Commission.

CONTACTS

DEPARTMENT FOR BUSINESS, INNOVATION AND SKILLS, 1 Victoria Street, London SW1H 0ET
T 020-7215 5000 W www.bis.gov.uk

OFCOM, Riverside House, 2A Southwark Bridge Road, London SE1 9HA T 020-7981 3040 W www.ofcom.org.uk

INTERNATIONAL DIRECT DIALLING

When dialling add two zeros before the IDD code, followed by the area code and the telephone number. Also add two zeros before the IDD code when dialling into the UK unless otherwise indicated.

* No extra zeros should be added
† Varies depending on area and/or carrier
‡ used to dial between Ireland and Northern Ireland; cheaper than using the UK code

	IDD from UK	IDD to UK
Afghanistan	93	44
Albania	355	44
Algeria	213	44
American Samoa	1 684	011 44*
Andorra	376	44
Angola	244	44
Anguilla	1 264	011 44*
Antigua and Barbuda	1 268	011 44*
Argentina	54	44
Armenia	374	44
Aruba	297	44
Ascension Island	247	44
Australia	61	11 44
Austria	43	44
Azerbaijan	994	44
Azores	351	44
Bahamas	1 242	011 44*
Bahrain	973	44
Bangladesh	880	44
Barbados	1 246	011 44*
Belarus	375	810 44*
Belgium	32	44
Belize	501	44
Benin	229	44
Bermuda	1 441	011 44*
Bhutan	975	44
Bolivia	591	10 44†
		11 44†
		12 44†
		13 44†
Bosnia and Hercegovina	387	44
Botswana	267	44
Brazil	55	14 44†
		15 44†
		21 44†
		23 44†
		31 44†
British Virgin Islands	1 284	011 44*
Brunei	673	44
Bulgaria	359	44
Burkina Faso	226	44
Burundi	257	44
Cambodia	855	1 44
Cameroon	237	44
Canada	1	011 44*
Cape Verde	238	44
Cayman Islands	1 345	011 44*
Central African Republic	236	44
Chad	235	15 44*
Chile	56	44
China	86	44
Colombia	57	5 44†
		7 44†
		9 44†
The Comoros	269	44
Congo, Dem. Rep. of	243	44
Congo, Rep. of	242	44
Cook Islands	682	44
Costa Rica	506	44
Côte d'Ivoire	225	44
Croatia	385	44
Cuba	53	119 44*
Cyprus	357	44
Czech Rep.	420	44
Denmark	45	44
Djibouti	253	44
Dominica	1 767	011 44*
Dominican Rep.	1 809	011 44*
	1 829	
Ecuador	593	44
Egypt	20	44
El Salvador	503	44
Equatorial Guinea	240	44
Eritrea	291	44
Estonia	372	44
Ethiopia	251	44
Falkland Islands	500	44
Faeroe Islands	298	44
Fiji	679	44
Finland	358	44
France	33	44
French Guiana	594	44
French Polynesia	689	44
Gabon	241	44
The Gambia	220	44
Georgia	995	810 44*
Germany	49	44
Ghana	233	44
Gibraltar	350	44
Greece	30	44
Greenland	299	44
Grenada	1 473	011 44*
Guadeloupe	590	44
Guam	1 671	011 44*
Guatemala	502	44
Guinea	224	44
Guinea-Bissau	245	44
Guyana	592	1 44
Haiti	509	44
Honduras	504	44
Hong Kong	852	1 44
Hungary	36	44
Iceland	354	44
India	91	44
Indonesia	62	1 44†
		8 44†
Iran	98	44
Iraq	964	44
Ireland	353	44
		048*‡
Israel	972	44†
		012*†
		013*†
		014*†
Italy	39	44
Jamaica	1 876	011 44*
Japan	81	1 44†
		010 44*†
		41 44†
		61 44†
Jordan	962	44
Kazakhstan	7	810 44*
Kenya	254	0 44

Country	Code	Dialling
Kiribati	686	44
Korea, Dem. People's Rep. Of	850	44
Korea, Republic Of	82	1 44†
		2 44†
Kuwait	965	44
Kyrgyzstan	996	44
Laos	856	44
Latvia	371	44
Lebanon	961	44
Lesotho	266	44
Liberia	231	44
Libya	218	44
Liechtenstein	423	44
Lithuania	370	44
Luxembourg	352	44
Macao	853	44
Macedonia	389	44
Madagascar	261	44
Madeira	351	44
Malawi	265	44
Malaysia	60	44
Maldives	960	44
Mali	223	44
Malta	356	44
Marshall Islands	692	011 44*
Martinique	596	44
Mauritania	222	44
Mauritius	230	44
Mayotte	262	44
Mexico	52	44
Micronesia, Federated States of	691	011 44*
Midway Island	1 808	011 44*
Moldova	373	44
Monaco	377	44
Mongolia	976	1 44
Montenegro	382	44
Montserrat	1 664	011 44*
Morocco	212	44
Mozambique	258	44
Myanmar	95	44
Namibia	264	44
Nauru	674	44
Nepal	977	44
The Netherlands	31	44
Netherlands Antilles	599	44
New Caledonia	687	44
New Zealand	64	44
Nicaragua	505	44
Niger	227	44
Nigeria	234	9 44
Niue	683	44
Norfolk Island	672	44
Northern Mariana Islands	1 670	011 44*
Norway	47	44
Oman	968	44
Pakistan	92	44
Palau	680	011 44*
Palestinian Territories	970	44
Panama	507	44
Papua New Guinea	675	44
Paraguay	595	44
Peru	51	44
The Philippines	63	44
Poland	48	44
Portugal	351	44
Puerto Rico	1 787	011 44*
	1 939	
Qatar	974	44
Réunion	262	44
Romania	40	44
Russia	7	810 44*
Rwanda	250	44
St Christopher and Nevis	1 869	011 44*
St Helena	290	44
St Lucia	1 758	011 44*
St Pierre and Miquelon	508	44
St Vincent and the Grenadines	1 784	011 44*
Samoa	685	0 44*
San Marino	378	44
São Tomé and Príncipe	239	44
Saudi Arabia	966	44
Senegal	221	44
Serbia	381	44
Seychelles	248	44
Sierra Leone	232	44
Singapore	65	1 44†
		2 44†
		8 44†
Slovakia	421	44
Slovenia	386	44
Solomon Islands	677	44
Somalia	252	44
South Africa	27	44
Spain	34	44
Sri Lanka	94	44
Sudan	249	44
Suriname	597	44
Swaziland	268	44
Sweden	46	44
Switzerland	41	44
Syria	963	44
Taiwan	886	2 44
Tajikistan	992	810 44*
Tanzania	255	0 44
Thailand	66	1 44
Timor-Leste	670	44
Togo	228	44
Tokelau	690	44
Tonga	676	44
Trinidad and Tobago	1 868	011 44*
Tristan de Cunha	290	44
Tunisia	216	44
Turkey	90	44
Turkmenistan	993	810 44*
Turks and Caicos Islands	1 649	011 44*
Tuvalu	688	44
Uganda	256	0 44
Ukraine	380	44
United Arab Emirates	971	44
United States of America	1	011 44*
Uruguay	598	44
Uzbekistan	998	810 44*
Vanuatu	678	44
Vatican City State	39	44
Venezuela	58	44
Vietnam	84	44
Virgin Islands	1 340	011 44*
Yemen	967	44
Zambia	260	44
Zimbabwe	263	44

INTERNET DOMAIN NAMES

The domain name system (DNS) helps users to find their way around the internet. Just as a telephone line has an identifying number attached to it, each computer connected to the internet has a unique numerical address known as its IP address. The DNS means users seldom need to recall the string of numbers in an IP address, since they can instead access internet content via the more memorable domain names (for example, whitakersalmanack.com).

Top-level domains (TLDs) are the rightmost element of an internet domain name (in the above example .com is the website's TLD) and their management is delegated by the Internet Corporation for Assigned Names and Numbers (ICANN). There are two types of TLD: generic top-level domains (gTLDs) and country code top-level domains (ccTLDs).

Generic TLDs designate general categories of organisation, such as .org for public interest or .jobs for human resources. Some gTLDs, such as .com and .net, can be registered without restriction while others, such as .edu and .gov, have limited purposes.

Country code TLDs are usually two letters long and identify the website's country or territory of origin. In May 2010 the first ccTLDs using characters outside of the basic Latin alphabet were implemented by ICANN; as at March 2011, 17 territories had been granted permission to use a ccTLD composed of native script. The rules and policies for registering domain names within a ccTLD vary significantly, although registration of a ccTLD is always limited to citizens of the corresponding country.

The list below is of active two-letter domain names for countries only.

ad	Andorra	dz	Algeria	kz	Kazakhstan
ae	United Arab Emirates	ec	Ecuador	la	Laos
af	Afghanistan	ee	Estonia	lb	Lebanon
ag	Antigua and Barbuda	eg	Egypt	lc	St Lucia
al	Albania	er	Eritrea	li	Liechtenstein
am	Armenia	es	Spain	lk	Sri Lanka
ao	Angola	et	Ethiopia	lr	Liberia
ar	Argentina	fi	Finland	ls	Lesotho
at	Austria	fj	Fiji	lt	Lithuania
au	Australia	fm	Micronesia, Federated States	lu	Luxembourg
az	Azerbaijan		of	lv	Latvia
ba	Bosnia and Hercegovina	fr	France	ly	Libya
bb	Barbados	ga	Gabon	ma	Morocco
bd	Bangladesh	gd	Grenada	mc	Monaco
be	Belgium	ge	Georgia	md	Moldova
bf	Burkina Faso	gh	Ghana	me	Montenegro
bg	Bulgaria	gm	The Gambia	mg	Madagascar
bh	Bahrain	gn	Guinea	mh	Marshall Islands
bi	Burundi	gq	Equatorial Guinea	mk	Macedonia
bj	Benin	gr	Greece	ml	Mali
bn	Brunei	gt	Guatemala	mm	Myanmar
bo	Bolivia	gw	Guinea-Bissau	mn	Mongolia
br	Brazil	gy	Guyana	mr	Mauritania
bs	The Bahamas	hn	Honduras	mt	Malta
bt	Bhutan	hr	Croatia	mu	Mauritius
bw	Botswana	ht	Haiti	mv	Maldives
by	Belarus	hu	Hungary	mw	Malawi
bz	Belize	id	Indonesia	mx	Mexico
ca	Canada	ie	Ireland	my	Malaysia
cd	Congo, Dem. Rep. of	il	Israel	mz	Mozambique
cf	Central African Republic	in	India	na	Namibia
cg	Congo, Rep. of	iq	Iraq	ne	Niger
ch	Switzerland	ir	Iran	ng	Nigeria
ci	Côte d'Ivoire	is	Iceland	ni	Nicaragua
cl	Chile	it	Italy	nl	The Netherlands
cm	Cameroon	jm	Jamaica	no	Norway
cn	China	jo	Jordan	np	Nepal
co	Colombia	jp	Japan	nr	Nauru
cr	Costa Rica	ke	Kenya	nz	New Zealand
cu	Cuba	kg	Kyrgyzstan	om	Oman
cv	Cape Verde	kh	Cambodia	pa	Panama
cy	Cyprus	ki	Kiribati	pe	Peru
cz	Czech Republic	km	The Comoros	pg	Papua New Guinea
de	Germany	kn	St Christopher and Nevis	ph	The Philippines
dj	Djibouti	kp	Korea, Dem. People's	pk	Pakistan
dk	Denmark		Republic of	pl	Poland
dm	Dominica	kr	Korea, Republic of	pt	Portugal
do	Dominican Republic	kw	Kuwait	pw	Palau

py	Paraguay	sr	Suriname	tz	Tanzania
qa	Qatar	st	São Tomé and Príncipe	ua	Ukraine
ro	Romania	sv	El Salvador	ug	Uganda
rs	Serbia	sy	Syria	uk	United Kingdom
ru	Russian Federation	sz	Swaziland	us	United States of America
rw	Rwanda	td	Chad	uy	Uruguay
sa	Saudi Arabia	tg	Togo	uz	Uzbekistan
sb	Solomon Islands	th	Thailand	va	Vatican City State (Holy See)
sc	Seychelles	tj	Tajikistan	vc	St Vincent and the
sd	Sudan	tl	Timor-Leste		Grenadines
se	Sweden	tm	Turkmenistan	ve	Venezuela
sg	Singapore	tn	Tunisia	vn	Vietnam
si	Slovenia	to	Tonga	vu	Vanuatu
sk	Slovakia	tp	Timor-Leste*	ws	Samoa
sl	Sierra Leone	tr	Turkey	ye	Yemen
sm	San Marino	tt	Trinidad and Tobago	za	South Africa
sn	Senegal	tv	Tuvalu	zm	Zambia
so	Somalia	tw	Taiwan	zw	Zimbabwe

* No new registrations are being accepted for the code .tp, which is active but being phased out in favour of .tl

THE ENVIRONMENT

The past two decades have witnessed a reduction in the production of chemicals that damage the ozone layer by 95 per cent, the establishment of carbon trading and a greenhouse gas emissions reduction treaty, and the introduction of much legislation. However, there remain persistent and intractable problems.

The average temperature over the first decade of the 21st century was significantly warmer than any previous decade. There is a clear underlying trend of increasing global temperature from the late 1970s onwards at about 0.16°C per decade, although this rate of warming has decreased slightly in the last 10 years, according to the UK Met Office. A report by the US National Oceanic and Atmospheric Administration concluded that 2010 tied with 2005 as the warmest year on record for global surface temperature.

A best estimate for temperature rise in the 21st century is between 1.8°C and 4°C; with an increase of at least 0.6 per cent attributable to past emissions. A rise of more than 2°C above pre-industrial levels is the level at which major, irreversible damage becomes more likely. According to the European Environment Agency, past legislation has been effective. Water and air have been cleaned up, ozone-depleting substances have been phased out and more waste is recycled. However, this is potentially being undermined by changes in individual consumption patterns. Europeans are living longer and more of them live alone, increasing the demand on living space and associated resources. For example, consumption of electricity in a household of one is 55 per cent more than for an individual in a four-person household. Additionally, 75 per cent of Europe's population live in urban areas and this is expected to rise to 80 per cent by 2020. Cities emit 69 per cent of Europe's carbon dioxide.

Transport is the fastest-growing contributor to greenhouse gas emissions and is likely to be so for the foreseeable future; emissions from transport in Europe increased by 24 per cent between 1990 and 2008. Road transport produced 25 per cent of UK carbon dioxide emissions in 2010. The issue is being addressed both by legislation and the government's commitment to a national recharging network for electric and plug-in hybrid vehicles through the 'plugged-in places' programme. The programme offers funding to local consortia of businesses and public sector partners to install electric vehicle recharging infrastructure in key places across the UK. So far, London, Milton Keynes and the North East are installing recharging points in their areas and funding has been allocated for five additional 'plugged-in places' projects in Greater Manchester, the Midlands, the East of England, Scotland and Northern Ireland. In 2009 average CO_2 emissions from new cars in the UK decreased 5.4 per cent to 149g/km. However, an EU strategy to reduce this to 120g/km by 2012 looks unlikely to be met. Instead it is considering a target of 70g/km by 2025.

By 2020, 10 per cent of transport fuel must be from renewable sources. Biodiesel is the most common biofuel in Europe, while ethanol is the most common worldwide. The usage of biofuels helps to reduce fossil fuel use, decrease greenhouse gas emissions and promote rural development; the downside is that using farmland for biofuel production pushes up prices for food crops such as corn, reduces farmland biodiversity and contributes to soil erosion and deforestation. The challenge is to support biofuel production with policies to help ensure that biofuel commercialisation is sustainable. The government has a set of sustainability standards for biofuels, but currently just 31 per cent meet these standards, against a target of 50 per cent.

Attention is also on individuals and what they can do to reduce their carbon footprint. This is a measure of the amount of carbon dioxide emitted by the fossil fuels burned as part of a person's daily life or, in the case of an organisation, as part of its everyday operations. More than 40 per cent of the UK's carbon dioxide emissions come from people's homes and travel requirements, and 80 per cent of the energy used in homes is for heating.

The UK emitted 473.7 million tonnes of carbon dioxide in 2009 and has an average carbon footprint of 10 tonnes per person. To put this into context, the average American generates 20 tonnes of carbon dioxide a year, against a global average of around four tonnes per person.

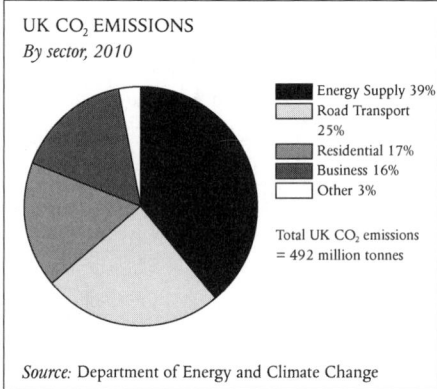

UK CO₂ EMISSIONS
By sector, 2010

- Energy Supply 39%
- Road Transport 25%
- Residential 17%
- Business 16%
- Other 3%

Total UK CO_2 emissions = 492 million tonnes

Source: Department of Energy and Climate Change

SELECTED UK TARGETS

AIR
- Reduce particulates (also referred to as fine particles or soot) in urban areas by 20 per cent by 2020

CLIMATE CHANGE
- Reduce carbon dioxide emissions to 20 per cent below 1990 levels by 2010, 34 per cent by 2020, and 80 per cent by 2050
- Reduce greenhouse gas emissions to 12.5 per cent below 1990 levels by 2008–12

ENERGY
- Provide 10 per cent of UK electricity from renewable sources by 2010 and 15 per cent by 2020
- Scotland to generate 80 per cent of electricity from renewable sources by 2020

- Around 40 per cent of UK electricity to be from low carbon sources (ie renewable, nuclear or clean coal) by 2020
- Produce 10 per cent of transport energy from renewable sources by 2020
- Improve energy efficiency by 20 per cent by 2020

WASTE

- Recycle 50 per cent of household waste by 2020
- Reduce amount of household waste not reused, recycled or composted from 22.2 million tonnes in 2000 to 12.2 million tonnes by 2020, a reduction of 45 per cent
- Reduce biodegradable municipal waste sent to landfill to 50 per cent by 2013 and 35 per cent by 2020
- Recycle or compost 50 per cent of municipal waste in Scotland by 2013, 60 per cent by 2020 and 70 per cent by 2025
- Recover 70 per cent of construction and demolition waste by 2020

EUROPEAN UNION MEASURES

Environmental legislation in the EU is based around the principle that the polluter pays and policies are formulated at the level of international conventions and protocols, European directives, and national legislation and strategies. The interlinked sixth environment action programme, the EU sustainable development strategy and the Cardiff process (which aims to integrate environmental concerns into other policies) are being developed as a framework for more detailed strategies.

The first environment action programme began in the 1970s and the EU adopted the sixth programme, Environment 2010: Our Future, Our Choice, in January 2001. Focusing on the topics of climate change, nature and biodiversity, environment and health, and natural resources and waste, it is the cornerstone of EU policy. Work has started on the seventh plan.

The European Commission (EC) is also using more diverse methods, in particular market-based instruments such as environmental taxes and voluntary measures. These are increasingly being adopted across Europe. Taxing energy consumption and selling the right to emit greenhouse gases are key ways of tackling climate change, and both follow the 'polluter pays' principle. Environmental taxes account for 2–6 per cent of GDP in most European countries. Items subject to environmental taxes in Europe include plastic bags (Belgium, Ireland and Italy), plastic mineral water bottles (Italy), milk and fruit juice cartons (Norway), tyres (Denmark and Finland), disposable cutlery (Belgium) and paper and cardboard (France).

SUSTAINABLE DEVELOPMENT

The environmental agenda is part of the wider issue of addressing sustainability that incorporates social, environmental and economic development. During the World Summit on Sustainable Development, held in Johannesburg in 2002, governments agreed on a series of commitments in five priority areas: water and sanitation, energy, health, agriculture and biodiversity. Targets and timetables included halving the number of people who lack access to clean water or proper sanitation by 2015, and reducing biodiversity loss by 2010. Following the summit, the United Nations Commission on Sustainable Development agreed its programme for the next 15 years.

In addition, 2005–15 has been named as the 'Water for Life' decade.

Countries have started to prepare for the next World Summit on Sustainable Development to be held in Brazil in 2012. Key themes emerging for the summit include concern about the potential toxicity of plastics when broken down in the sea, and phosphorus pollution. Phosphorus, a valuable fertiliser, is being lost to the oceans partly from a lack of recycling waste water. Sweden, for example, aims to recycle 60 per cent of phosphorus in municipal wastewater by 2015. The idea of a transition to a low-carbon resource efficient global economy will also be top of the agenda.

In June 2010, the EU committed to the Europe 2020 strategy that supports a shift to a resource efficient economy. It has set objectives on employment, innovation, education, social inclusion and climate/energy to be reached by 2020. Each member state will adopt its own national targets in each of these areas. In March 2011, as part of this framework, the EC published a roadmap for moving to a competitive low-carbon economy by 2050.

CLIMATE CHANGE AND AIR POLLUTION

Temperature in central England has risen by about 1°C since the 1970s, with 2010 being one of the warmest years on record. Sea levels around the UK rose by 1mm a year in the 20th century, although the rate for the 1990s and 2000s is higher.

The government's response to climate change has been driven by the UN framework convention on climate change. This is a binding agreement that aims to reduce the risks of global warming by limiting greenhouse gas emissions.

Annual global carbon dioxide emissions in 2009 were 1.3 per cent below 2008 figures, partly because of the global financial crisis. However, the concentration of carbon dioxide in the atmosphere rose to 387ppm (parts per million), up from 385ppm in 2008.

Progress towards the UN framework convention's targets is assessed at regular conferences. At Kyoto in 1997, the Kyoto protocol was adopted. It covers the six main greenhouse gases: carbon dioxide, methane, nitrous oxide, hydrofluorocarbons (HFCs), perfluorocarbons (PFCs) and sulphur hexafluoride. Under the protocol, industrialised countries agreed to a legally binding target of cutting emissions of greenhouse gases to 5.2 per cent below 1990 levels by 2008–12. The protocol came into force in February 2005 after it was ratified by Russia. The USA has not ratified the treaty, while the UK set its own target at a 12.5 per cent reduction on 1990.

A legally binding post-Kyoto agreement was expected at the Copenhagen climate change conference in December 2009, however, no consensus was reached. Instead, a political agreement was drawn up – known as the Copenhagen Accord – that recognises the objective to cap the global temperature rise to below 2°C (445–490ppm carbon dioxide equivalents). The accord also outlines developed countries' commitments to provide additional funding to help the developing world address climate change. Countries have made pledges to cut emissions, but the UN says these are unlikely to keep temperatures below the target of a 2°C temperature rise by 2050. At the UN climate change conference in Cancun, Mexico, in December 2010 an agreement was reached that builds on the decisions made at Copenhagen, but the UN says that there is still a gap between this and what is needed to cap temperature rises at 2°C. One of the major challenges for the next conference, to be held in Durban, South Africa, in November 2011 will be to bridge this gap.

To keep climate change below 2°C, the EU has an objective of reducing greenhouse gas emissions by 80–95 per cent by 2050 compared to 1990. In 2007, the EU heads of state and government agreed a firm target of cutting 20 per cent of the EU's greenhouse gas emissions by 2020, rising to 30 per cent if the USA, Canada and India make similar commitments. The UK, France and Germany are pushing for the EU to adopt a 30 per cent target.

Greenhouse gas emissions in the 27 EU member states are decreasing. Between 1990 and 2009, they decreased by 17 per cent with a particularly large decrease between 2008 and 2009, largely due to the economic crisis. The EU is currently on track to meet the 20 per cent target.

Scientists are also looking at ways to avoid global warming by reducing other emissions such as methane, black carbon (formed when fossil and biofuels are not completely combusted) and tropospheric ozone.

In 2008 the UK already had a goal to reduce its carbon dioxide emissions to 20 per cent below 1990 levels by 2010. However, the Climate Change Act proposed two further goals: an interim target of a 34 per cent reduction in carbon dioxide emissions below 1990 levels by 2020 and a legally binding target of an 80 per cent reduction by 2050. The government must also set binding limits on carbon dioxide emissions during five-year budget periods; budgets have been set until 2022 and the UK is on track to meet the first. Provisional figures show that UK greenhouse gas emissions rose by 2.8 per cent in 2010, with CO_2 emissions increasing by 3.8 per cent. Residential sector use contributed to this with an increase of 13 per cent, mainly attributable to the cold winter.

Measures to tackle climate change in the UK are also covered by the climate change programme, launched in March 2006. It targets every sector of the economy and includes: a stricter emissions cap for industry; measures to encourage the uptake of biofuels in petrol; tighter building regulations; measures to improve household energy efficiency; a renewed emphasis on encouraging and enabling the general public, businesses and public authorities to help achieve the government's targets; and increased levels of microgeneration.

The UK has a voluntary greenhouse gas emissions trading scheme that allows businesses to buy an emission allowance to meet emission targets, or to sell surplus emission allowances. The carbon reduction commitment (CRC) energy efficiency scheme, which came into force in April 2010, aims to improve energy efficiency and significantly reduce emissions from non-energy related businesses in the UK, such as supermarkets and banks.

A mandatory EU emissions trading scheme for carbon dioxide applies at a company level. The companies covered by the ruling account for around half of the EU's total carbon dioxide emissions. From 2012, airlines will be included in the scheme, covering emissions from all domestic and international flights arriving at, or departing from, an EU airport. Emissions of other pollutants are also regulated within the EU. Countries have legally binding targets for emissions of sulphur dioxide, nitrogen oxides, non-methane volatile organic compounds and ammonia, which harm both human health and the environment. These targets were due to be met by 2010, however, around half of the member states did not meet one or more of the targets, with emissions of nitrogen oxides, in particular, causing problems for most of the 27 EU countries. A revision of the limits is likely to introduce tougher targets for 2020.

WASTE

By 2020 the EU could be generating 45 per cent more waste than in 1995. In the UK the uncoupling of waste growth from economic growth is a key objective along with placing greater emphasis on prevention and reuse, putting less non-municipal waste into landfill and investing in the infrastructure necessary to divert waste from landfill.

In the year to June 2010, the UK generated about 456kg of municipal waste per person (a total of 23.6 million tonnes), a figure that has been decreasing each year since 2006–7. To put this into context, the average municipal waste generation in Europe is 524kg per person (ranging from 400kg to 800kg), while in the USA it is 750kg and in Japan 400kg. The majority of municipal waste across Europe went into landfill (41 per cent); the rest is recycled (22 per cent), incinerated (20 per cent) or composted (17 per cent). In the UK, the proportion of household waste recycled or composted has been increasing steadily, reaching 40 per cent in the year to June 2010 in contrast to 6 per cent in 1995–6. This meets the UK's 2010 waste recycling target. The UK is still behind countries such as Denmark, Belgium and Germany who recycle or compost around 60 per cent of their municipal waste. Others, such as Romania, Bulgaria, and Malta landfill over 80 per cent.

Meanwhile, 48 million tonnes of commercial and industrial waste was generated in 2009, a decrease of 29 per cent since the last survey in 2002–3. Of this, 52 per cent was recycled or reused.

A full review of waste policy is currently underway and is looking at what policies are needed to reduce the amount of waste generated and to maximise reuse and recycling. The review is also taking into consideration how waste policies affect local communities, individual households and businesses. It will also consider anaerobic digestion, and other energy from waste technologies, as part of the UK's long-term goal of becoming a zero-waste economy.

EU directives help to shape UK policy, particularly in relation to commercial and industrial waste. For instance, the EU's European Integrated Products Policy aims to

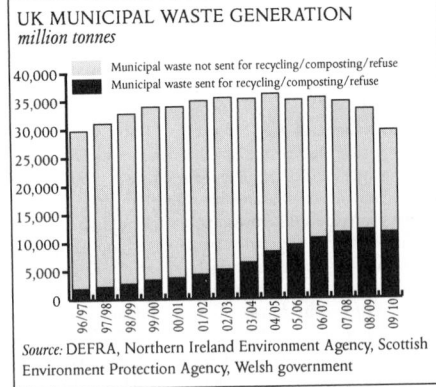

UK MUNICIPAL WASTE GENERATION
million tonnes

Municipal waste not sent for recycling/composting/refuse
Municipal waste sent for recycling/composting/refuse

Source: DEFRA, Northern Ireland Environment Agency, Scottish Environment Protection Agency, Welsh government minimise the environmental impact of a product by looking at all phases of its life-cycle and encouraging each one to improve its environmental performance. A series of directives on waste packaging, vehicles, electrical waste and electronic equipment and batteries is intended to promote greater responsibility for products at the end of their life. The EU is also examining the issue of bio-waste (ie biodegradable garden, kitchen and food waste) which accounts for around one third of municipal waste.

WATER

Climate change alters rainfall patterns in ways that can put pressure on water resources, resulting in certain regions having more droughts. The EU flagship water legislation, the Water Framework Directive, takes this into account. Among its policy suggestions is the pricing of water in ways that would encourage efficient water use, thereby addressing water scarcity and drought. A substantial proportion of Europe's freshwater (40 per cent of surface water and 30 per cent of groundwater) is at risk of not achieving 'good status' under the terms of the directive by 2015. Water strategy in the UK tackles similar issues: the sustainable delivery of secure water supplies; an improved and protected water environment; fair, affordable and cost-reflective water charges; reduced water industry greenhouse gas emissions; and more sustainable and effective management of surface water.

For drinking water, wastewater discharges, rivers, coastal water and bathing water, quality targets are set at both EU and UK level: the aim is again to achieve 'good status' throughout the EU by 2015. The EU has an interactive internet tool, WISE (Water Information System for Europe), which provides water data and allows users to monitor water quality in their neighbourhood. In 2010, nearly 98 per cent of bathing water in the UK met the EU directive's minimum requirements, compared to two-thirds in 1988, while over 72 per cent achieved a newer, tighter standard.

ENERGY

The Climate Change Act 2008 sets out four energy policy goals for the UK: cutting carbon dioxide emissions by 80 per cent by 2050, maintaining reliable energy supplies, promoting competitive energy markets, and ensuring homes are adequately and affordably heated. In terms of renewable energy, the UK target was to increase the contribution of renewables to 10 per cent of electricity by 2010, with a further target (set by the EU) of 15 per cent by 2020. In reality, renewables accounted for around 7 per cent of electricity generated in the UK in 2010.

The UK's Carbon Plan, launched in March 2011, sets out what the UK needs to do to meet carbon targets. It includes the changes needed as to how electricity is generated, how homes and businesses are heated and the way people need to change the way they travel. The UK also intends to turn more food waste into power; it produces more than 100 million tonnes of organic waste, which could be turned into heat and power for over 2 million homes.

The EU has also adopted a number of targets. These are to improve energy efficiency by 20 per cent by 2020; increase the level of renewables used in transport fuel to 10 per cent by 2020 (the target was originally just for biofuels); and for 20 per cent of the EU's energy consumption to come from renewables by 2020. If all member states keep on track, the EU will meet and slightly exceed the 20 per cent renewables target. In 2008, renewable energy accounted for 8.4 per cent of EU primary energy consumption, including nearly one third of energy consumed in Sweden and more than a quarter in Austria, Latvia and Finland. At the end of 2009, a quarter of global power capacity was renewables (1,230GW). Grid connected photovoltaic capacity rose 53 per cent, wind 32 per cent, solar water/heating 21 per cent and geothermal by 4 per cent. For the second year running more renewable capacity than traditional capacity was added in the USA and Europe. In 2010, renewables accounted for 60 per cent of new capacity in Europe.

ENVIRONMENT AND HEALTH

Particulate matter in the air (also known as fine particles or soot), noise and ground-level ozone damages the health of thousands of people each year. Environmental pollutants, including pesticides, endocrine disruptors, dioxins and PCBs persist in the environment and their long-term effect on health is not fully understood. Emerging evidence suggests that air pollution may not only damage lungs but might also contribute to diseases such as Type 1 diabetes and multiple sclerosis. There are concerns about the effects of electromagnetic fields on human health and whether the use of nanotechnology in food could be dangerous for the human body.

In 2008, the EU set binding limits on emissions of fine particles. Under the new law, which takes effect in 2011, countries will have to reduce exposure to fine particles in urban areas by an average of 20 per cent by 2020, based on 2010 levels.

A chemicals policy, under which industry has to provide information on the effects of chemicals on human health and the environment, as well as on safe ways of handling them, has also been established.

CONTACTS

DEPARTMENT FOR ENVIRONMENT, FOOD AND RURAL AFFAIRS (DEFRA), Nobel House, 17 Smith Square, London SW1P 3JR T 0845-933 5577 W www.defra.gov.uk

DEPARTMENT OF ENERGY AND CLIMATE CHANGE, 3 Whitehall Place, London SW1A 2AW T 0300-060 4000 W www.decc.gov.uk

ENVIRONMENT AGENCY, National Customer Contact Centre, PO Box 544, Rotherham S60 1BY T 0870-850 6506 W www.environment-agency.gov.uk

EUROPEAN ENVIRONMENT AGENCY, Kongens Nytorv 6, DK-1050 Copenhagen K, Denmark T +45 3336 7100 W www.eea.europa.eu

SCOTTISH GOVERNMENT, RURAL AND ENVIRONMENT DIRECTORATE, Victoria Quay, Edinburgh EH6 6QQ T 0131-556 8400 W www.scotland.gov.uk

CONSERVATION AND HERITAGE

NATIONAL PARKS

© Natural England – material is reproduced
with the permission of Natural England

ENGLAND AND WALES

There are nine national parks in England, and three in Wales. In addition, the Norfolk and Suffolk Broads are considered to have equivalent status to a national park. Under the provisions of the National Parks and Access to the Countryside Act 1949, as clarified by the Natural Environment and Rural Communities Act 2006, the two purposes of the national parks are to conserve and enhance the natural beauty, wildlife and cultural heritage, and to promote opportunities for the understanding and enjoyment of the special qualities of national parks by the public. If there is a conflict between the two purposes, then conservation takes precedence.

Natural England is the statutory body that has the power to designate national parks in England, and the Countryside Council for Wales is responsible for national parks in Wales. Designations in England are confirmed by the Secretary of State for Environment, Food and Rural Affairs and those in Wales by the Welsh government. The designation of a national park does not affect the ownership of the land or remove the rights of the local community. The majority of the land in the national parks is owned by private landowners (around 75 per cent) or by bodies such as the National Trust and the Forestry Commission. The national park authorities own only a small percentage of the land themselves.

The Environment Act 1995 replaced the existing national park boards and committees with free-standing national park authorities (NPAs). NPAs are the sole local planning authorities for their areas and as such influence land use and development, and deal with planning applications. NPAs are responsible for carrying out the statutory purposes of national parks stated above. In pursuing these purposes they have a statutory duty to seek to foster the economic and social well-being of the communities within national parks. The NPAs publish management plans setting out overarching policies for their area and appoint their own officers and staff.

The Broads Authority was established under the Norfolk and Suffolk Broads Act 1988 and meets the requirement for the authority to have a navigation function in addition to a regard for the needs of agriculture, forestry and the economic and social interests of those who live or work in the Broads.

MEMBERSHIP

Membership of English NPAs comprises local authority appointees, members directly appointed by the environment secretary of state and members appointed by her after a consultation with local parishes. Under the Natural Environment and Rural Communities Act 2006 every district, county or unitary authority with land in a national park is entitled to appoint at least one member unless it chooses to opt out. The total number of local authority and parish members must exceed the number of national members. The majority of the English NPAs currently have 22 members, except the Peak District which has 30 and the South Downs which has 27 members.

The Broads Authority has 21 members: nine appointed by the constituent local authorities, two appointed by the Navigation Committee and ten appointed by the secretary of state. The secretary of state's appointees include at least three which are appointed after consultation with representatives of boating interests and at least two which are appointed after consultation with representatives of landowning and farming interests.

In Wales, two-thirds of NPA members are appointed by the constituent local authorities and one-third by the Welsh government, advised by the Countryside Council for Wales.

FUNDING

The English NPAs and the Broads Authority are funded by central government. In the financial year 2011–12 a core grant totalling £55.2m was allocated between the authorities.

In Wales, national parks are funded via a grant from the Welsh government. The grant for 2011–12 amounted to £10.9m. The three NPAs in Wales receive further funding via a local authority levy.

All NPAs and the Broads Authority can take advantage of grants from other bodies including lottery and European grants.

The national parks (with date that designation was confirmed) are:

BRECON BEACONS (1957), Powys (66 per cent)/
Carmarthenshire/Rhondda, Cynon and Taff/Merthyr
Tydfil/Blaenau Gwent/Monmouthshire, 1,347
sq. km/520 sq. miles – The park is centred on the
Brecon Beacons mountain range, which includes the
three highest mountains in southern Britain (Pen y
Fan, Corn Du and Cribyn), but also includes the
valley of the rivers Usk and Wye, the Black
Mountains to the east and the Black Mountain
to the west. There are information centres at the
visitor centre at Libanus (near Brecon), Abergavenny
and Llandovery.
National Park Authority, Plas y Ffynnon, Cambrian Way,
Brecon, Powys LD3 7HP T 01874-624437
E enquiries@breconbeacons.org W www.breconbeacons.org
Chief Executive, John Cook

BROADS (1989), Norfolk/Suffolk, 303 sq. km/117 sq.
miles – The Broads are located between Norwich and
Great Yarmouth on the flood plains of the six rivers
flowing through the area to the sea. The area is one of
fens, winding waterways, woodland and marsh. The 60
or so broads are man-made, and many are connected to
the rivers by dykes, providing over 200km (124 miles)
of navigable waterways. There are information centres
at Hoveton, Whitlingham and Toad Hole Cottage at
How Hill.
Broads Authority, Dragonfly House, 2 Gilders Way, Norwich
NR3 1UB T 01603-610734
E broads@broads-authority.gov.uk
W www.broads-authority.gov.uk
Chief Executive, Dr John Packman

DARTMOOR (1951), Devon, 953 sq. km/368 sq. miles
– The park consists of moorland and rocky granite tors,
and is rich in prehistoric remains. There are information
centres at Haytor, Princetown (main visitor centre) and
Postbridge.
National Park Authority, Parke, Bovey Tracey, Devon
TQ13 9JQ T 01626-832093 E hq@dartmoor-npa.gov.uk
W www.dartmoor-npa.gov.uk
Chief Executive, Kevin Bishop

EXMOOR (1954), Somerset (71 per cent)/Devon,
692 sq. km/267 sq. miles – Exmoor is a moorland
plateau inhabited by wild Exmoor ponies and red deer.
There are many ancient remains and burial mounds.
There are national park centres at Dunster, Dulverton
and Lynmouth.
National Park Authority, Exmoor House, Dulverton,
Somerset TA22 9HL T 01398-323665
E info@exmoor-nationalpark.gov.uk
W www.exmoor-nationalpark.gov.uk
Chief Executive/National Park Officer, Dr Nigel Stone

LAKE DISTRICT (1951), Cumbria,
2,292 sq. km/885 sq. miles – The Lake District
includes England's highest mountains (Scafell Pike,
Helvellyn and Skiddaw) but it is most famous for its
glaciated lakes. There are national park information
centres at Bowness Bay, Keswick, Ullswater and a
visitor centre at Brockhole, Windermere.
National Park Authority, Murley Moss, Oxenholme Road,
Kendal, Cumbria LA9 7RL T 01539-724555
E hq@lakedistrict.gov.uk W www.lakedistrict.gov.uk
Chief Executive, Richard Leafe

NEW FOREST (2005), Hampshire, 570 sq. km/220 sq.
miles – The forest has been protected since 1079 when
it was declared a royal hunting forest. The area consists
of forest, ancient woodland and heathland. Much of
the forest is managed by the Forestry Commission,
which provides several campsites. The main villages

are Brockenhurst, Burley and Lyndhurst, which has a
visitor centre.
National Park Authority, Town Hall, Avenue Road,
Lymington, Hants SO41 9ZG T 01590-646600
E enquiries@newforestnpa.gov.uk
W www.newforestnpa.gov.uk
Chief Executive, Alison Barnes

NORTH YORK MOORS (1952), North Yorkshire
(96 per cent)/Redcar and Cleveland,
1,434 sq. km/554 sq. miles – The park consists of
woodland and moorland, and includes the Hambleton
Hills and the Cleveland Way. There are information
centres at Danby and Sutton Bank.
National Park Authority, The Old Vicarage, Bondgate,
Helmsley, York YO62 5BP T 01439-770657
E info@northyorkmoors-npa.gov.uk
W www.northyorkmoors.org.uk
Chief Executive, Andrew Wilson

NORTHUMBERLAND (1956), Northumberland,
1,049 sq. km/405 sq. miles – The park is an area of
hill country stretching from Hadrian's Wall to the
Scottish border. There are information centres at
Ingram, Once Brewed and Rothbury.
National Park Authority, Eastburn, South Park, Hexham,
Northumberland NE46 1BS T 01434-605555
E enquiries@nnpa.org.uk
W www.northumberlandnationalpark.org.uk
Chief Executive, Tony Gates

PEAK DISTRICT (1951), Derbyshire (64 per cent)/
Staffordshire/South Yorkshire/Cheshire/West
Yorkshire/Greater Manchester, 1,437 sq. km/555 sq.
miles – The Peak District includes the gritstone moors
of the 'Dark Peak' and the limestone dales of the
'White Peak'. There are information centres at
Bakewell, Castleton, Edale and Upper Derwent.
National Park Authority, Aldern House, Baslow Road,
Bakewell, Derbyshire DE45 1AE T 01629-816200
E customer.service@peakdistrict.gov.uk
W www.peakdistrict.gov.uk
Chief Executive, Jim Dixon

PEMBROKESHIRE COAST (1952 and 1995),
Pembrokeshire, 621 sq. km/240 sq. miles – The park
includes cliffs, moorland and a number of islands,
including Skomer and Ramsey. There are information
centres in Newport and Tenby and a gallery and
visitor centre, Oriel y Parc, in St Davids. The park
also manages sites at Castell Henllys and Carew Castle
and Tidal Mill.
National Park Authority, Llanion Park, Pembroke Dock,
Pembrokeshire SA72 6DY T 0845-345 7275
E info@pembrokeshirecoast.org.uk
W www.pembrokeshirecoast.org.uk
Chief Executive/National Park Officer, Tegryn Jones

SNOWDONIA/ERYRI (1951), Gwynedd/Conwy,
2,132 sq. km/823 sq. miles – Snowdonia, which
takes its name from Snowdon – the highest peak in
England and Wales – is an area of deep valleys and
rugged mountains. There are information centres at
Aberdyfi, Beddgelert, Betws y Coed, Dolgellau and
Harlech.
National Park Authority, Penrhyndeudraeth, Gwynedd
LL48 6LF T 01766-770274 E parc@snowdonia-npa.gov.uk
W www.snowdonia-npa.gov.uk
Chief Executive, Aneurin Phillips

THE SOUTH DOWNS (2010), West
Sussex/Hampshire, 1,648 sq. km/636 sq. miles – The
South Downs contains a diversity of natural habitats,
including flower-studded chalk grassland, ancient

woodland, flood meadow, lowland heath and rare chalk heathland. The South Downs National Park Authority acquired statutory powers on 1 April 2011 and is now responsible for planning the future of the park.

National Park Authority, Rosemary's Parlour, North Street, Midhurst, W. Sussex GU29 9SB

T 0300-303 1053 **E** info@southdowns.gov.uk
W www.southdowns.gov.uk
Chair, Margaret Paren

YORKSHIRE DALES (1954), North Yorkshire (88 per cent)/Cumbria, 1,762 sq. km/680 sq. miles – The Yorkshire Dales is composed primarily of limestone overlaid in places by millstone grit. The three peaks of Ingleborough, Whernside and Pen-y-ghent are within the park. There are information centres at Grassington, Hawes, Aysgarth Falls, Malham and Reeth.

National Park Authority, Yoredale, Bainbridge, Leyburn, N. Yorks DL8 3EL **T** 0300-456 0030

E info@yorkshiredales.org.uk **W** www.yorkshiredales.org.uk
Chief Executive, David Butterworth

SCOTLAND

On 9 August 2000 the national parks (Scotland) bill received royal assent, giving parliament the ability to create national parks in Scotland. The first two Scottish national parks became operational in 2002 and 2003 respectively. The Act gives Scottish parks wider powers than in England and Wales, including statutory responsibilities for the local economy and rural communities. The board of each Scottish NPA consists of 25 members, of which five are directly elected by a postal ballot of the local electorate. The remaining 20 members, ten of which are nominated by the constituent local authorities, are chosen by the Scottish ministers. In Scotland, the national parks are central government bodies and are wholly funded by the Scottish government. Funding for 2010–11 totals £12.9m.

CAIRNGORMS (2003), North-East Scotland, 4,528 sq. km/1,748 sq. miles – The Cairngorms national park is the largest in the UK. It displays a vast collection of landforms, including five of the six highest mountains in the UK. The near natural woodlands contain remnants of the original ancient Caledonian pine forest.

National Park Authority, 14 The Square, Grantown-on-Spey, Morayshire PH26 3HG **T** 01479-873535

E enquiries@cairngorms.co.uk **W** www.cairngorms.co.uk
Chief Executive, Jane Hope

LOCH LOMOND AND THE TROSSACHS (2002), Argyll and Bute/Perth and Kinross/Stirling/West Dunbartonshire, 1,865 sq. km/720 sq. miles – The park boundaries encompass lochs, rivers, forests, 20 mountains above 914m (3,000ft) including Ben More and a further 20 mountains between 762m (2,500ft) and 914m (3,000ft).

National Park Authority, Carrochan, Carrochan Road, Balloch G83 8EG **T** 01389-722600

E info@lochlomond-trossachs.org
W www.lochlomond-trossachs.org
Chief Executive, Fiona Logan

NORTHERN IRELAND

There is a power to designate national parks in Northern Ireland under the Nature Conservation and Amenity Lands Order (Northern Ireland) 1985, but there are currently no national parks in Northern Ireland.

AREAS OF OUTSTANDING NATURAL BEAUTY

ENGLAND AND WALES

Under the National Parks and Access to the Countryside Act 1949, provision was made for the designation of areas of outstanding natural beauty (AONBs). Natural England is responsible for AONBs in England and the Countryside Council for Wales for the Welsh AONBs. Designations in England are confirmed by the Secretary of State for Environment, Food and Rural Affairs and those in Wales by the National Assembly for Wales. The Countryside and Rights of Way (CROW) Act 2000 placed greater responsibility on local authorities to protect AONBs and made it a statutory duty for relevant authorities to produce a management plan for their AONB area. The CROW Act also provided for the creation of conservation boards for larger and more complex AONBs. The first two conservation boards for the Cotswolds and Chilterns AONBs were established in July 2004.

The primary objective of the AONB designation is to conserve and enhance the natural beauty of the area. Where an AONB has a conservation board, it has the additional purpose of increasing public understanding and enjoyment of the special qualities of the area; the board has greater weight should there be a conflict of interests between the two. In addition, the board is also required to foster the economic and social well-being of the local communities but without incurring significant expenditure in doing so. Overall responsibility for AONBs lies with the relevant local authorities or conservation board. To coordinate planning and management responsibilities between local authorities in whose area they fall, AONBs are overseen by a joint advisory committee (or similar body) which includes representatives from the local authorities, landowners, farmers, residents and conservation and recreation groups. Core funding for AONBs is provided by central government through Natural England and the Countryside Council for Wales.

The 40 AONBs (with date designation confirmed) are:

ARNSIDE AND SILVERDALE (1972),
    Cumbria/Lancashire, 75 sq. km/29 sq. miles
BLACKDOWN HILLS (1991), Devon/Somerset,
    370 sq. km/143 sq. miles
CANNOCK CHASE (1958), Staffordshire, 70 sq. km/
    27 sq. miles
CHICHESTER HARBOUR (1964), Hampshire/West
    Sussex, 73 sq. km/28 sq. miles
CHILTERNS (1965; extended 1990),
    Bedfordshire/Buckinghamshire/Herefordshire/
    Oxfordshire, 839 sq. km/324 sq. miles
CLWYDIAN RANGE (1985), Denbighshire/Flintshire,
    157 sq. km/61 sq. miles
CORNWALL (1959; Camel Estuary 1983), 963 sq. km/
    372 sq. miles
COTSWOLDS (1966; extended 1990), Gloucestershire/
    Oxfordshire/Warwickshire/Wiltshire/
    Worcestershire, 2,041 sq. km/788 sq. miles
CRANBORNE CHASE AND WEST WILTSHIRE
    DOWNS (1983), Dorset/Hampshire/
    Somerset/Wiltshire, 987 sq. km/381 sq. miles
DEDHAM VALE (1970; extended 1978, 1991),
    Essex/Suffolk, 90 sq. km/35 sq. miles
DORSET (1959), Dorset/Somerset, 1,129 sq. km/
    436 sq. miles
EAST DEVON (1963), 269 sq. km/104 sq. miles

EAST HAMPSHIRE (1962), 383 sq. km/148 sq. miles
FOREST OF BOWLAND (1964), Lancashire/North
Yorkshire, 805 sq. km/311 sq. miles
GOWER (1956), Swansea, 188 sq. km/73 sq. miles
HIGH WEALD (1983), East Sussex/Kent/Surrey/West
Sussex, 1,460 sq. km/564 sq. miles
HOWARDIAN HILLS (1987), North Yorkshire, 204 sq.
km/79 sq. miles
ISLE OF WIGHT (1963), 192 sq. km/74 sq. miles
ISLES OF SCILLY (1976), 16 sq. km/6 sq. miles
KENT DOWNS (1968), 878 sq. km/339 sq. miles
LINCOLNSHIRE WOLDS (1973), 559 sq. km/216 sq.
miles
LLYN (1957), Gwynedd, 161 sq. km/62 sq. miles
MALVERN HILLS (1959), Gloucestershire/
Worcestershire, 105 sq. km/41 sq. miles
MENDIP HILLS (1972; extended 1989), Somerset,
199 sq. km/77 sq. miles
NIDDERDALE (1994), North Yorkshire, 601 sq.
km/232 sq. miles
NORFOLK COAST (1968), 445 sq. km/172 sq. miles
NORTH DEVON (1960), 171 sq. km/66 sq. miles
NORTH PENNINES (1988), Cumbria/Durham/North
Yorkshire/Northumberland, 1,983 sq. km/766 sq.
miles
NORTH WESSEX DOWNS (1972), Hampshire/
Oxfordshire/Wiltshire, 1,730 sq. km/668 sq. miles
NORTHUMBERLAND COAST (1958), 132 sq. km/
51 sq. miles
QUANTOCK HILLS (1957), Somerset, 99 sq. km/38 sq.
miles
SHROPSHIRE HILLS (1959), 808 sq. km/
312 sq. miles
SOLWAY COAST (1964), Cumbria, 122 sq. km/47 sq.
miles
SOUTH DEVON (1960), 339 sq. km/131 sq. miles
SUFFOLK COAST AND HEATHS (1970), 403 sq. km/
156 sq. miles
SURREY HILLS (1958), 422 sq. km/163 sq. miles
SUSSEX DOWNS (1966), 983 sq. km/379 sq. miles
TAMAR VALLEY (1995), Cornwall/Devon, 197 sq. km/
76 sq. miles
WYE VALLEY (1971), Gloucestershire/Herefordshire/
Monmouthshire, 326 sq. km/126 sq. miles
YNYS MON (ISLE OF ANGLESEY) (1967), 221 sq. km/
85 sq. miles

NORTHERN IRELAND
The Department of the Environment for Northern
Ireland, with advice from the Council for Nature
Conservation and the Countryside, designates AONBs in
Northern Ireland. At present there are eight and these
cover a total area of 2,849 sq. km (1,100 sq. miles). Dates
given are those of designation.

ANTRIM COAST AND GLENS (1988), Co. Antrim,
706 sq. km/272 sq. miles
BINEVENAGH (2006), Co. Londonderry, 166 sq. km/
64 sq. miles
CAUSEWAY COAST (1989), Co. Antrim, 42 sq. km/
16 sq. miles
LAGAN VALLEY (1965), Co. Down, 39 sq. km/15 sq.
miles
MOURNE (1986), Co. Down, 570 sq. km/220 sq. miles
RING OF GULLION (1991), Co. Armagh, 154 sq. km/
59 sq. miles
SPERRIN (1968; extended 2008), Co. Tyrone/
Co. Londonderry, 1,182 sq. km/456 sq. miles

STRANGFORD LOUGH AND LECALE (2010)*, Co.
Down, 528 sq. km/204 sq. miles

*Strangford Lough (1972) and Lecale Coast (1967) merged in
2010

NATIONAL SCENIC AREAS

In Scotland, national scenic areas have a broadly
equivalent status to AONBs. Scottish Natural Heritage
recognises areas of national scenic significance. At the end
of May 2011 there were 40, covering a land area of
1,020,500 hectares (2,521,710 acres) and a marine area
of 357,900 hectares (884,390 acres).
   Development within national scenic areas is dealt with
by local authorities, who are required to consult Scottish
Natural Heritage concerning certain categories of
development. Disagreements between Scottish Natural
Heritage and local authorities are referred to the Scottish
government. Land management uses can also be modified
in the interest of scenic conservation.

ASSYNT-COIGACH, Highland, 90,200ha/222,884
acres
BEN NEVIS AND GLEN COE, Highland, 101,600ha/
251,053 acres
CAIRNGORM MOUNTAINS, Highland/
Aberdeenshire/Moray, 67,200ha/166,051 acres
CUILLIN HILLS, Highland, 21,900ha/54,115 acres
DEESIDE AND LOCHNAGAR, Aberdeenshire,
40,000ha/98,840 acres
DORNOCH FIRTH, Highland, 7,500ha/18,532 acres
EAST STEWARTRY COAST, Dumfries and Galloway,
4,500ha/11,119 acres
EILDON AND LEADERFOOT, Borders, 3,600ha/
8,896 acres
FLEET VALLEY, Dumfries and Galloway, 5,300ha/
13,096 acres
GLEN AFFRIC, Highland, 19,300ha/47,690 acres
GLEN STRATHFARRAR, Highland, 3,800ha/9,390
acres
HOY AND WEST MAINLAND, Orkney Islands,
14,800ha/36,571 acres
JURA, Argyll and Bute, 21,800ha/53,868 acres
KINTAIL, Highland, 15,500ha/38,300 acres
KNAPDALE, Argyll and Bute, 19,800ha/48,926 acres
KNOYDART, Highland, 39,500ha/97,604 acres
KYLE OF TONGUE, Highland, 18,500ha/45,713 acres
KYLES OF BUTE, Argyll and Bute, 4,400ha/10,872
acres
LOCH LOMOND, Argyll and Bute, 27,400ha/67,705
acres
LOCH NA KEAL, Mull, Argyll and Bute, 12,700ha/
31,382 acres
LOCH RANNOCH AND GLEN LYON, Perthshire and
Kinross, 48,400ha/119,596 acres
LOCH SHIEL, Highland, 13,400ha/33,111 acres
LOCH TUMMEL, Perthshire and Kinross, 9,200ha/
22,733 acres
LYNN OF LORN, Argyll and Bute, 4,800ha/11,861
acres
MORAR, MOIDART AND ARDNAMURCHAN,
Highland, 13,500ha/33,358 acres
NITH ESTUARY, Dumfries and Galloway, 9,300ha/
22,980 acres
NORTH ARRAN, North Ayrshire, 23,800ha/58,810
acres

NORTH-WEST SUTHERLAND, Highland, 20,500ha/ 50,655 acres

RIVER EARN, Perthshire and Kinross, 3,000ha/7,413 acres

RIVER TAY, Perthshire and Kinross, 5,600ha/13,838 acres

ST KILDA, Eilean Siar (Western Isles), 900ha/2,224 acres

SCARBA, LUNGA AND THE GARVELLACHS, Argyll and Bute, 1,900ha/4,695 acres

SHETLAND, Shetland Isles, 11,600ha/28,664 acres

SMALL ISLANDS, Highland, 15,500ha/38,300 acres

SOUTH LEWIS, HARRIS AND NORTH UIST, Eilean Siar (Western Isles), 109,600ha/270,822 acres

SOUTH UIST MACHAIR, Eilean Siar (Western Isles), 6,100ha/15,073 acres

THE TROSSACHS, Stirling, 4,600ha/11,367 acres

TROTTERNISH, Highland, 5,000ha/12,355 acres

UPPER TWEEDDALE, Borders, 10,500ha/25,945 acres

WESTER ROSS, Highland, 145,300ha/359,036 acres

THE NATIONAL FOREST

The National Forest is being planted across 517 sq. km (200 sq. miles) of Derbyshire, Leicestershire and Staffordshire. Nearly 8 million trees, of mixed species but mainly broadleaved, covering over 6,230ha (15,394 acres) have been planted. The aim is to eventually cover about one-third of the designated area.

The project was developed in 1992–5 by the Countryside Commission and is now run by the National Forest Company, which was established in April 1995. The National Forest Company is responsible for the delivery of the government-approved National Forest Strategy and is funded by DEFRA.

NATIONAL FOREST COMPANY, Bath Lane, Moira, Swadlincote, Derbyshire DE12 6BD T 01283-551211
E enquiries@nationalforest.org W www.nationalforest.org
Chief Executive, Sophie Churchill

SITES OF SPECIAL SCIENTIFIC INTEREST

Site of special scientific interest (SSSIs) is a legal notification applied to land in England, Scotland or Wales which Natural England (NE) (formerly English Nature), Scottish Natural Heritage (SNH) or the Countryside Council for Wales (CCW) identifies as being of special interest because of its flora, fauna, geological, geomorphological or physiographical features. In some cases, SSSIs are managed as nature reserves.

NE, SNH and CCW must notify the designation of an SSSI to the local planning authority, every owner/ occupier of the land, and the environment secretary, the Scottish ministers or the National Assembly for Wales. Forestry and agricultural departments and a number of other interested parties are also formally notified.

Objections to the notification of an SSSI can be made and ultimately considered at a full meeting of the Council of NE or CCW. In Scotland an objection will be dealt with by the main board of SNH or an appropriate subgroup, depending on the nature of the objection.

The protection of these sites depends on the cooperation of individual landowners and occupiers. Owner/occupiers must consult NE, SNH or CCW and gain written consent before they can undertake certain listed activities on the site. Funds are available through management agreements and grants to assist owners and occupiers in conserving sites' interests. Sites can also be protected by management schemes, management notices and other enforcement mechanisms. As a last resort a site can be purchased.

The number and area of SSSIs in Britain as at May 2011 was:

	Number	Hectares	Acres
England	4,118	1,077,168	2,661,740
Scotland	1,447	1,023,237	2,528,474
Wales	1,045	266,681	658,995

NORTHERN IRELAND
In Northern Ireland 305 areas of special scientific interest (ASSIs) have been declared by the Department of the Environment for Northern Ireland.

NATIONAL NATURE RESERVES

National nature reserves are defined in the National Parks and Access to the Countryside Act 1949 as modified by the Natural Environment and Rural Communities Act 2006. National nature reserves may be managed solely for the purpose of conservation, or for both the purposes of conservation and recreation, providing this does not compromise the conservation purpose.

NE, SNH or CCW can declare as a national nature reserve land which is held and managed as a nature reserve under an agreement; land held and managed by NE, SNH or CCW; or land held and managed as a nature reserve by an approved body. NE, SNH or CCW can make by-laws to protect reserves from undesirable activities; these are subject to confirmation by the Secretary of State for Environment, Food and Rural Affairs, the National Assembly for Wales or the Scottish ministers.

The number and area of national nature reserves in Britain as at May 2011 was:

	Number	Hectares	Acres
England	224	94,400	233,267
Scotland	62	133,736	330,469
Wales	72	25,623	63,316

NORTHERN IRELAND
Nature reserves are established and managed by the Department of the Environment for Northern Ireland, with advice from the Council for Nature Conservation and the Countryside. Nature reserves are declared under the Nature Conservation and Amenity Lands (Northern Ireland) Order 1985; to date, 49 nature reserves have been declared.

LOCAL NATURE RESERVES

Local nature reserves are defined in the National Parks and Access to the Countryside Act 1949 (as amended by the Natural Environment and Rural Communities Act 2006) as land designated for the study and preservation of flora and fauna, or of geological or physiographical features. Local nature reserves also have a statutory obligation to provide opportunities for the enjoyment of nature or open air recreation, providing this does not compromise the conservation purpose of the reserve. Local authorities in England, Scotland and Wales have the power to acquire, declare and manage reserves in consultation with NE, SNH and CCW. There is similar legislation in Northern Ireland, where the consulting organisation is the Environment Agency.

Any organisation, such as water companies, educational trusts, local amenity groups and charitable nature conservation bodies, such as wildlife trusts, may manage local nature reserves, provided that a local authority has a legal interest in the land. This means that the local authority must either own it, lease it or have a management agreement with the landowner.

The number and area of designated local nature reserves in Britain as at May 2011 was:

	Number	Hectares	Acres
England	1,475	35,527	87,751
Scotland	58	10,023	24,767
Wales	82	5,840	14,431

There are 11 local nature reserves in Northern Ireland.

FOREST RESERVES

The Forestry Commission is the government department responsible for forestry policy throughout Great Britain. Forestry is a devolved matter, with the separate Forestry Commissions for England, Scotland and Wales reporting directly to their appropriate minister. The equivalent body in Northern Ireland is the Forest Service, an agency of the Department of Agriculture and Rural Development for Northern Ireland. The Forestry Commission in each country is led by a director who is also a member of the GB Board of Commissioners. As at March 2011, UK woodland certified by the Forestry Commission (including Forestry Commission-managed woodland) amounted to around 1,325,000 hectares (3,274,146 acres): 335,000 hectares (827,803 acres) in England, 133,000 hectares (328,650 acres) in Wales, 793,000 hectares (1,959,545 acres) in Scotland and 63,000 hectares (155,676 acres) in Northern Ireland. For more information, see W www.forestry.gov.uk

There are 34 forest nature reserves in Northern Ireland, covering 1,512 hectares (3,736 acres), designated and administered by the Forest Service. There are also 16 national nature reserves on Forest Service-owned property.

MARINE NATURE RESERVES

Marine protected areas provide protection for marine flora and fauna, and geological and physiographical features on land covered by tidal waters or parts of the sea in or adjacent to the UK. These areas also provide opportunities for study and research.

The Marine and Coastal Access Act 2009 created a new kind of statutory protection for marine protected areas in England and Wales, marine conservation zones (MCZs), which are designed to increase the protection of species and habitats deemed to be of national importance. Individual MCZs can have varying levels of protection: some include specific activities that are appropriately managed, while others prohibit all damaging and disturbing activities. The act converted the waters around Lundy Island, a former marine protected area, to MCZ status and it is expected that further designations, including the waters around Skomer Island off the coast of Pembrokeshire, Wales, will be made in 2012.

The Secretary of State for Environment, Food and Rural Affairs and the National Assembly for Wales have the power to designate MCZs. Natural England and the Countryside Council for Wales have set up four regional projects covering the south-west, Irish Sea, North Sea and eastern channel to deliver recommendations for potential MCZ designations.

Under the Marine (Scotland) Act 2010 there are new statutory powers for the Scottish government to designate marine protected areas (MPAs) in the seas around Scotland; Scottish Natural Heritage is currently advising on potential MPA designations.

In Northern Ireland, marine nature reserves may be established under the Nature Conservation and Amenity Lands Order (Northern Ireland) 1985.

Marine Conservation Zone:
LUNDY (2010), Bristol Channel

Marine Nature Reserve:
STRANGFORD LOUGH (1995), Northern Ireland

CONSERVATION OF WILDLIFE AND HABITATS

The UK is party to a number of international conventions.

BERN CONVENTION

The 1979 Bern Convention on the Conservation of European Wildlife and Natural Habitats came into force in the UK in June 1982. Currently there are 50 contracting parties and a number of other states attend meetings as observers.

The aims are to conserve wild flora and fauna and their natural habitats, especially where this requires the cooperation of several countries, and to promote such cooperation. The convention gives particular emphasis to endangered and vulnerable species.

All parties to the convention must promote national conservation policies and take account of the conservation of wild flora and fauna when setting planning and development policies. Reports on contracting parties' conservation policies must be submitted to the standing committee every four years.

SECRETARIAT OF THE BERN CONVENTION
STANDING COMMITTEE, Council of Europe, 67075 Strasbourg-Cedex, France T (+33) (3) 8841 2000
W www.coe.int

BIODIVERSITY

The UK ratified the Convention on Biological Diversity in June 1994. As at June 2011 there were 193 parties to the convention.

The objectives are the conservation of biological diversity, the sustainable use of its components and the fair and equitable sharing of the benefits arising out of the use of genetic resources. There are seven thematic work programmes addressing agricultural biodiversity, marine and coastal biodiversity and the biodiversity of inland waters, dry and sub-humid lands, islands, mountains and forests. The Conference of the Parties to the Convention on Biological Diversity adopted a supplementary agreement to the convention known as the Cartagena Protocol on Biosafety on 29 January 2000. The protocol seeks to protect biological diversity from potential risks that may be posed by introducing modified living organisms, resulting from biotechnology, into the environment. As at June 2011, 160 countries were party to the protocol; the UK joined on 17 February 2004.

The UK Biodiversity Action Plan (UKBAP) is the UK government's response to the Convention on Biological Diversity and constitutes a record of UK biological resources and a detailed plan for their protection. The list of priority species and habitats under the UKBAP covers 1,150 species and 65 habitats. The UK Biodiversity Partnership Standing Committee guides and supports the UK Biodiversity Partnership in implementing UKBAP; it also coordinates between the four UK country groups which form the partnership and are responsible for implementing UKBAP at a national level. In addition, the UK Biodiversity Partnership includes two support groups: the Biodiversity Research Advisory Group and the Biodiversity Reporting and Information Group. Information on UKBAP is available from the Joint Nature Conservation Committee (JNCC).

JNCC, Monkstone House, City Road, Peterborough PE1 1JY
T 01733-562626 W www.jncc.defra.gov.uk

BONN CONVENTION

The 1979 Convention on Conservation of Migratory Species of Wild Animals (also known as the CMS or Bonn Convention) came into force in the UK in October 1985. As at 1 March 2011, 115 countries were party to the convention.

It requires the protection of listed endangered migratory species and encourages international agreements covering these and other threatened species. International agreements can range from legally binding treaties to less formal memoranda of understanding.

Seven agreements have been concluded to date under the convention. They aim to conserve seals in the Wadden Sea; bat populations in Europe; small cetaceans of the Baltic, north-east Atlantic, Irish and North Seas; African-Eurasian migratory waterbirds; cetaceans of the Mediterranean Sea, Black Sea and contiguous Atlantic area; albatrosses and petrels; and gorillas and their habitats. A further 19 memorandums of understanding have been agreed for the Siberian crane, slender-billed curlews, marine turtles of the Atlantic coast of Africa, Indian Ocean and South-East Asia, the middle-European population of the great bustard, bukhara deer, aquatic warblers, West-African populations of the African elephant, the saiga antelope, cetaceans of the Pacific Islands, dugongs (large marine mammals), Mediterranean monk seals, the ruddy-headed goose, grassland birds of southern South America, birds of prey of Africa and Eurasia, small cetaceans and manatees of West Africa, sharks, huemuls (Andean deer) and high Andean flamingoes.

UNEP/CMS SECRETARIAT, United Nations Premises, Hermann-Ehlers-Str. 10, 53113 Bonn, Germany
T (+49) (228) 815 2426 E secretariat@cms.int
W www.cms.int

CITES

The 1973 Convention on International Trade in Endangered Species of Wild Fauna and Flora (CITES) is an agreement between governments to ensure that international trade in specimens of wild animals and plants does not threaten their survival. The convention came into force in the UK in October 1976 and there are currently 175 member countries. Countries party to the convention ban commercial international trade in an agreed list of endangered species and regulate and monitor trade in other species that might become endangered. The convention accords varying degrees of protection to more than 30,000 species of animals and plants whether they are traded as live specimens or as products derived from them, such as fur coats and dried herbs.

The Conference of the Parties to CITES meets every two to three years to review the convention's implementation. The Animal Health agency at the Department for Environment, Food and Rural Affairs carries out the government's responsibilities under CITES.

CITES SECRETARIAT, International Environment House, 11 Chemin des Anémones, CH-1219 Châtelaine, Geneva, Switzerland T (+41) (22) 917 8139/8140 E info@cites.org
W www.cites.org

EUROPEAN WILDLIFE TRADE REGULATION

The Council (EC) Regulation on the Protection of Species of Wild Fauna and Flora by Regulating Trade Therein came into force in the UK on 1 June 1997. It is intended to standardise wildlife trade regulations across Europe and to improve the application of CITES.

RAMSAR CONVENTION

The 1971 Ramsar Convention on Wetlands of International Importance entered into force in the UK in May 1976. As at June 2011, 160 countries were party to the convention.

The aim of the convention is the conservation and wise use of wetlands and their resources. Governments that are party to the convention must designate wetlands and include wetland conservation considerations in their land-use planning; 1,933 wetland sites, totalling 189 million hectares, have been designated for inclusion in the list of wetlands of international importance. The UK currently has 168 designated sites covering 1,274,323 hectares. The member countries meet every three years to assess the progress of the convention and the next meeting is scheduled to be held in Bucharest in June 2012.

The UK has set targets under the Ramsar Strategic Plan, 2009–15. Progress towards these is monitored by the UK Ramsar Committee, known as the Joint Working Party. The UK and the Republic of Ireland have established a formal protocol to ensure common monitoring standards for waterbirds in the two countries.

RAMSAR CONVENTION SECRETARIAT,
Rue Mauverney 28, CH-1196 Gland, Switzerland
T (+41) (22) 999 0170 E ramsar@ramsar.org
W www.ramsar.org

UK LEGISLATION

The Wildlife and Countryside Act 1981 gives legal protection to a wide range of wild animals and plants. Every five years the statutory nature conservation agencies (Natural England, Countryside Council for Wales and Scottish Natural Heritage) are required to review schedules 5 (animals, other than birds) and 8 (plants) of the Wildlife and Countryside Act 1981. They make recommendations to the Secretary of State for Environment, Food and Rural Affairs, the National Assembly for Wales and the Scottish government for changes to these schedules. The most recent variation of schedule 5 for England came into effect in February 2008 (the fourth quinquennial review recommended no changes to schedule 8; the fifth is currently under way).

Under section 9 of the act it is an offence to kill, injure, take, possess or sell (whether alive or dead) any wild animal included in schedule 5 of the act and to disturb its place of shelter and protection or to destroy that place. However certain species listed on schedule 5 are protected against some, but not all, of these activities.

Under section 13 of the act it is illegal without a licence to pick, uproot, sell or destroy plants listed in schedule 8. Since January 2001, under the Countryside and Rights of Way Act 2000, persons found guilty of an offence under part 1 of the Wildlife and Countryside Act 1981 face a maximum penalty of up to £5,000 and/or up to a six-month custodial sentence per specimen.

BIRDS

The act lays down a close season for birds (listed on Schedule 2, part 1) from 1 February to 31 August inclusive, each year. Exceptions to these dates are made for:

Capercaillie and (except Scotland) Woodcock
– 1 February to 30 September
Snipe – 1 February to 11 August
Birds listed on schedule 2, part 1 (below high water mark) (*see* below) – 21 February to 31 August
Wild duck and wild geese, in or over any area below the high-water mark of ordinary spring tides – 21 February to 31 August
Birds listed on schedule 2, part 1, which may be killed or taken outside the close season are: capercaillie; coot; certain wild duck (gadwall, goldeneye, mallard, pintail, pochard, shoveler, teal, tufted duck, wigeon); certain wild geese (Canada, greylag, pink-footed, white-fronted (in England and Wales only); golden plover; moorhen; snipe; and woodcock.

Section 16 of the 1981 act allows licences to be issued on either an individual or general basis, to allow the killing, taking and sale of certain birds for specified reasons such as public health and safety. All other wild birds are fully protected by law throughout the year.

ANIMALS PROTECTED BY SCHEDULE 5

Adder *(Vipera berus)*
Allis Shad *(Alosa alosa)*
Anemone, Ivell's Sea *(Edwardsia ivelli)*
Anemone, Starlet Sea *(Nematostella vectensis)*
Bat, Horseshoe, all species *(Rhinolophidae)*
Bat, Typical, all species *(Vespertilionidae)*
Beetle *(Hypebaeus flavipes)*
Beetle, Bembridge Water *(Paracymus aeneus)*
Beetle, Lesser Silver Water *(Hydrochara caraboides)*
Beetle, Mire Pill *(Curimopsis nigrita)*
Beetle, Moccas *(Hypebaeus flavipes)*
Beetle, Rainbow Leaf *(Chrysolina cerealis)*
Beetle, Spangled Water *(Graphoderus zonatus)*
Beetle, Stag *(Lucanus cervus)*
Beetle, Violet Click *(Limoniscus violaceus)*
Beetle, Water *(Paracymus aeneus)*
Burbot *(Lota lota)*
Butterfly, Adonis Blue *(Lysandra bellargus)*
Butterfly, Black Hairstreak *(Strymonidia pruni)*
Butterfly, Brown Hairstreak *(Thecla betulae)*
Butterfly, Chalkhill Blue *(Lysandra coridon)*
Butterfly, Chequered Skipper *(Carterocephalus palaemon)*
Butterfly, Duke of Burgundy Fritillary *(Hamearis lucina)*
Butterfly, Glanville Fritillary *(Melitaea cinxia)*
Butterfly, Heath Fritillary *(Mellicta athalia* or *Melitaea athalia)*
Butterfly, High Brown Fritillary *(Argynnis adippe)*
Butterfly, Large Blue *(Maculinea arion)*
Butterfly, Large Copper *(Lycaena dispar)*
Butterfly, Large Heath *(Coenonympha tullia)*
Butterfly, Large Tortoiseshell *(Nymphalis polychloros)*
Butterfly, Lulworth Skipper *(Thymelicus acteon)*
Butterfly, Marsh Fritillary *(Eurodryas aurinia)*
Butterfly, Mountain Ringlet *(Erebia epiphron)*
Butterfly, Northern Brown Argus *(Aricia artaxerxes)*
Butterfly, Pearl-bordered Fritillary *(Boloria euphrosyne)*
Butterfly, Purple Emperor *(Apatura iris)*
Butterfly, Silver Spotted Skipper *(Hesperia comma)*
Butterfly, Silver-studded Blue *(Plebejus argus)*
Butterfly, Small Blue *(Cupido minimus)*
Butterfly, Swallowtail *(Papilio machaon)*

Butterfly, White Letter Hairstreak *(Stymonida w-album)*
Butterfly, Wood White *(Leptidea sinapis)*
Cat, Wild *(Felis silvestris)*
Cicada, New Forest *(Cicadetta montana)*
Crayfish, Atlantic Stream *(Austropotamobius pallipes)*
Cricket, Field *(Gryllus campestris)*
Cricket, Mole *(Gryllotalpa gryllotalpa)*
Cricket, Wart-biter *(Decticus verrucivorus)*
Damselfly, Southern *(Coenagrion mercuriale)*
Dolphin, all species *(Cetacea)*
Dormouse *(Muscardinus avellanarius)*
Dragonfly, Norfolk Aeshna *(Aeshna isosceles)*
Frog, Common *(Rana temporaria)*
Goby, Couch's *(Gobius couchii)*
Goby, Giant *(Gobius cobitis)*
Hatchet Shell, Northern *(Thyasira gouldi)*
Hydroid, Marine *(Clavopsella navis)*
Lagoon Snail *(Paludinella littorina)*
Lagoon Snail, De Folin's *(Caecum armoricum)*
Lagoon Worm, Tentacled *(Alkmaria romijni)*
Leech, Medicinal *(Hirudo medicinalis)*
Lizard, Sand *(Lacerta agilis)*
Lizard, Viviparous *(Lacerta vivipara)*
Marten, Pine *(Martes martes)*
Moth, Barberry Carpet *(Pareulype berberata)*
Moth, Black-veined *(Siona lineata* or *Idaea lineata)*
Moth, Essex Emerald *(Thetidia smaragdaria)*
Moth, Fiery Clearwing *(Bembecia chrysidiformis)*
Moth, Fisher's Estuarine *(Gortyna borelii)*
Moth, New Forest Burnet *(Zygaena viciae)*
Moth, Reddish Buff *(Acosmetia caliginosa)*
Moth, Sussex Emerald *(Thalera fimbrialis)*
Mussel, Fan *(Atrina fragilis)*
Mussel, Freshwater Pearl *(Margaritifera margaritifera)*
Newt, Great Crested (or Warty) *(Triturus cristatus)*
Newt, Palmate *(Triturus helveticus)*
Newt, Smooth *(Triturus vulgaris)*
Otter, Common *(Lutra lutra)*
Porpoise, all species *(Cetacea)*
Sandworm, Lagoon *(Armandia cirrhosa)*
Sea Fan, Pink *(Eunicella verrucosa)*
Sea Slug, Lagoon *(Tenellia adspersa)*
Sea-mat, Trembling *(Victorella pavida)*
Seahorse, Short Snouted (England only) *(Hippocampus hippocampus)*
Seahorse, Spiny (England only) *(Hippocampus guttulatus)*
Shad, Twaite *(Alosa fallax)*
Shark, Angel (England only) *(Squatina squatina)*
Shark, Basking *(Cetorhinus maximus)*
Shrimp, Fairy *(Chirocephalus diaphanus)*
Shrimp, Lagoon Sand *(Gammarus insensibilis)*
Shrimp, Tadpole (Apus) *(Triops cancriformis)*
Slow-worm *(Anguis fragilis)*
Snail, Glutinous *(Myxas glutinosa)*
Snail, Roman (England only) *(Helix pomatia)*
Snail, Sandbowl *(Catinella arenaria)*
Snake, Grass *(Natrix natrix* or *Natrix helvetica)*
Snake, Smooth *(Coronella austriaca)*
Spider, Fen Raft *(Dolomedes plantarius)*
Spider, Ladybird *(Eresus niger)*
Squirrel, Red *(Sciurus vulgaris)*
Sturgeon *(Acipenser sturio)*
Toad, Common *(Bufo bufo)*
Toad, Natterjack *(Bufo calamita)*
Turtle, Flatback *(Cheloniidae/Natator Depressus)*
Turtle, Green Sea *(Chelonia mydas)*
Turtle, Hawksbill *(Eretmochelys imbricate)*
Turtle, Kemp's Ridley Sea *(Lepidochelys kempii)*

Turtle, Leatherback Sea *(Dermochelys coriacea)*
Turtle, Loggerhead Sea *(Caretta caretta)*
Turtle, Olive Ridley *(Lepidochelys olivacea)*
Vendace *(Coregonus albula)*
Vole, Water *(Arvicola terrestris)*
Walrus *(Odobenus rosmarus)*
Whale, all species *(Cetacea)*
Whitefish *(Coregonus lavaretus)*

PLANTS PROTECTED BY SCHEDULE 8
Adder's Tongue, Least *(Ophioglossum lusitanicum)*
Alison, Small *(Alyssum alyssoides)*
Anomodon, Long-leaved *(Anomodon longifolius)*
Beech-lichen, New Forest *(Enterographa elaborata)*
Blackwort *(Southbya nigrella)*
Bluebell *(Hyacinthoides non-scripta)*
Bolete, Royal *(Boletus regius)*
Broomrape, Bedstraw *(Orobanche caryophyllacea)*
Broomrape, Oxtongue *(Orobanche loricata)*
Broomrape, Thistle *(Orobanche reticulata)*
Cabbage, Lundy *(Rhynchosinapis wrightii)*
Calamint, Wood *(Calamintha sylvatica)*
Caloplaca, Snow *(Caloplaca nivalis)*
Catapyrenium, Tree *(Catapyrenium psoromoides)*
Catchfly, Alpine *(Lychnis alpina)*
Catillaria, Laurer's *(Catellaria laureri)*
Centaury, Slender *(Centaurium tenuiflorum)*
Cinquefoil, Rock *(Potentilla rupestris)*
Cladonia, Convoluted *(Cladonia convoluta)*
Cladonia, Upright Mountain *(Cladonia stricta)*
Clary, Meadow *(Salvia pratensis)*
Club-rush, Triangular *(Scirpus triquetrus)*
Colt's-foot, Purple *(Homogyne alpina)*
Cotoneaster, Wild *(Cotoneaster integerrimus)*
Cottongrass, Slender *(Eriophorum gracile)*
Cow-wheat, Field *(Melampyrum arvense)*
Crocus, Sand *(Romulea columnae)*
Crystalwort, Lizard *(Riccia bifurca)*
Cudweed, Broad-leaved *(Filago pyramidata)*
Cudweed, Jersey *(Gnaphalium luteoalbum)*
Cudweed, Red-tipped *(Filago lutescens)*
Cut-grass *(Leersia oryzoides)*
Diapensia *(Diapensia lapponica)*
Dock, Shore *(Rumex rupestris)*
Earwort, Marsh *(Jamesoniella undulifolia)*
Eryngo, Field *(Eryngium campestre)*
Fern, Dickie's Bladder *(Cystopteris dickieana)*
Fern, Killarney *(Trichomanes speciosum)*
Flapwort, Norfolk *(Leiocolea rutheana)*
Fleabane, Alpine *(Erigeron borealis)*
Fleabane, Small *(Pulicaria vulgaris)*
Fleawort, South Stack *(Tephroseris integrifolia ssp maritima)*
Frostwort, Pointed *(Gymnomitrion apiculatum)*
Fungus, Hedgehog *(Hericium erinaceum)*
Galingale, Brown *(Cyperus fuscus)*
Gentian, Alpine *(Gentiana nivalis)*
Gentian, Dune *(Gentianella uliginosa)*
Gentian, Early *(Gentianella anglica)*
Gentian, Fringed *(Gentianella ciliata)*
Gentian, Spring *(Gentiana verna)*
Germander, Cut-leaved *(Teucrium botrys)*
Germander, Water *(Teucrium scordium)*
Gladiolus, Wild *(Gladiolus illyricus)*
Goblin Lights *(Catolechia wahlenbergii)*
Goosefoot, Stinking *(Chenopodium vulvaria)*
Grass-poly *(Lythrum hyssopifolia)*
Grimmia, Blunt-leaved *(Grimmia unicolor)*
Gyalecta, Elm *(Gyalecta ulmi)*

Hare's-ear, Sickle-leaved *(Bupleurum falcatum)*
Hare's-ear, Small *(Bupleurum baldense)*
Hawk's-beard, Stinking *(Crepis foetida)*
Hawkweed, Northroe *(Hieracium northroense)*
Hawkweed, Shetland *(Hieracium zetlandicum)*
Hawkweed, Weak-leaved *(Hieracium attenuatifolium)*
Heath, Blue *(Phyllodoce caerulea)*
Helleborine, Red *(Cephalanthera rubra)*
Helleborine, Young's *(Epipactis youngiana)*
Horsetail, Branched *(Equisetum ramosissimum)*
Hound's-tongue, Green *(Cynoglossum germanicum)*
Knawel, Perennial *(Scleranthus perennis)*
Knotgrass, Sea *(Polygonum maritimum)*
Lady's-slipper *(Cypripedium calceolus)*
Lecanactis, Churchyard *(Lecanactis hemisphaerica)*
Lecanora, Tarn *(Lecanora archariana)*
Lecidea, Copper *(Lecidea inops)*
Leek, Round-headed *(Allium sphaerocephalon)*
Lettuce, Least *(Lactuca saligna)*
Lichen, Arctic Kidney *(Nephroma arcticum)*
Lichen, Ciliate Strap *(Heterodermia leucomelos)*
Lichen, Coralloid Rosette *(Heterodermia propagulifera)*
Lichen, Ear-lobed Dog *(Peltigera lepidophora)*
Lichen, Forked Hair *(Bryoria furcellata)*
Lichen, Golden Hair *(Teloschistes flavicans)*
Lichen, Orange-fruited Elm *(Caloplaca luteoalba)*
Lichen, River Jelly *(Collema dichotomum)*
Lichen, Scaly Breck *(Squamarina lentigera)*
Lichen, Starry Breck *(Buellia asterella)*
Lily, Snowdon *(Lloydia serotina)*
Liverwort, Lindenberg's Leafy *(Adelanthus lindenbergianus)*
Marsh-mallow, Rough *(Althaea hirsuta)*
Marshwort, Creeping *(Apium repens)*
Milk-parsley, Cambridge *(Selinum carvifolia)*
Moss *(Drepanocladius vernicosus)*
Moss, Alpine Copper *(Mielichoferia mielichoferi)*
Moss, Baltic Bog *(Sphagnum balticum)*
Moss, Blue Dew *(Saelania glaucescens)*
Moss, Blunt-leaved Bristle *(Orthotrichum obtusifolium)*
Moss, Bright Green Cave *(Cyclodictyon laetevirens)*
Moss, Cordate Beard *(Barbula cordata)*
Moss, Cornish Path *(Ditrichum cornubicum)*
Moss, Derbyshire Feather *(Thamnobryum angustifolium)*
Moss, Dune Thread *(Bryum mamillatum)*
Moss, Flamingo *(Desmatodon cernuus)*
Moss, Glaucous Beard *(Barbula glauca)*
Moss, Green Shield *(Buxbaumia viridis)*
Moss, Hair Silk *(Plagiothecium piliferum)*
Moss, Knothole *(Zygodon forsteri)*
Moss, Large Yellow Feather *(Scorpidium turgescens)*
Moss, Millimetre *(Micromitrium tenerum)*
Moss, Multi-fruited River *(Cryphaea lamyana)*
Moss, Nowell's Limestone *(Zygodon gracilis)*
Moss, Polar Feather *(Hygrohypnum polare)*
Moss, Rigid Apple *(Bartramia stricta)*
Moss, Round-leaved Feather *(Rhyncostegium rotundifolium)*
Moss, Schleicher's Thread *(Bryum schleicheri)*
Moss, Slender Green Feather *(Drepanocladus vernicosus)*
Moss, Triangular Pygmy *(Acaulon triquetrum)*
Moss, Vaucher's Feather *(Hypnum vaucheri)*
Mudwort, Welsh *(Limosella australis)*
Naiad, Holly-leaved *(Najas marina)*
Naiad, Slender *(Najas flexilis)*
Orache, Stalked *(Halimione pedunculata)*

Orchid, Early Spider *(Ophrys sphegodes)*
Orchid, Fen *(Liparis loeselii)*
Orchid, Ghost *(Epipogium aphyllum)*
Orchid, Lapland Marsh *(Dactylorhiza lapponica)*
Orchid, Late Spider *(Ophrys fuciflora)*
Orchid, Lizard *(Himantoglossum hircinum)*
Orchid, Military *(Orchis militaris)*
Orchid, Monkey *(Orchis simia)*
Pannaria, Caledonia *(Panneria ignobilis)*
Parmelia, New Forest *(Parmelia minarum)*
Parmentaria, Oil Stain *(Parmentaria chilensis)*
Pear, Plymouth *(Pyrus cordata)*
Penny-cress, Perfoliate *(Thlaspi perfoliatum)*
Pennyroyal *(Mentha pulegium)*
Pertusaria, Alpine Moss *(Pertusaria bryontha)*
Petalwort *(Petallophyllum ralfsi)*
Physcia, Southern Grey *(Physcia tribacioides)*
Pigmyweed *(Crassula aquatica)*
Pine, Ground *(Ajuga chamaepitys)*
Pink, Cheddar *(Dianthus gratianopolitanus)*
Pink, Childing *(Petroraghia nanteuilii)*
Pink, Deptford (England and Wales only) *(Dianthus armeria)*
Polypore, Oak *(Buglossoporus pulvinus)*
Pseudocyphellaria, Ragged *(Pseudocyphellaria lacerata)*
Psora, Rusty Alpine *(Psora rubiformis)*
Puffball, Sandy Stilt *(Battarraea phalloides)*
Ragwort, Fen *(Senecio paludosus)*
Ramping-fumitory, Martin's *(Fumaria martinii)*
Rampion, Spiked *(Phyteuma spicatum)*
Restharrow, Small *(Ononis reclinata)*
Rock-cress, Alpine *(Arabis alpina)*
Rock-cress, Bristol *(Arabis stricta)*
Rustwort, Western *(Marsupella profunda)*
Sandwort, Norwegian *(Arenaria norvegica)*
Sandwort, Teesdale *(Minuartia stricta)*
Saxifrage, Drooping *(Saxifraga cernua)*
Saxifrage, Tufted *(Saxifraga cespitosa)*
Saxifrage, Yellow Marsh *(Saxifrage hirulus)*
Solenopsora, Serpentine *(Solenopsora liparina)*
Solomon's-seal, Whorled *(Polygonatum verticillatum)*
Sow-thistle, Alpine *(Cicerbita alpina)*
Spearwort, Adder's-tongue *(Ranunculus ophioglossifolius)*
Speedwell, Fingered *(Veronica triphyllos)*
Speedwell, Spiked *(Veronica spicata)*
Spike-rush, Dwarf *(Eleocharis parvula)*
Star-of-Bethlehem, Early *(Gagea bohemica)*
Starfruit *(Damasonium alisma)*
Stonewort, Bearded *(Chara canescens)*
Stonewort, Foxtail *(Lamprothamnium papulosum)*
Strapwort *(Corrigiola litoralis)*
Sulphur-tresses, Alpine *(Alectoria ochroleuca)*
Threadmoss, Long-leaved *(Bryum neodamense)*
Turpswort *(Geocalyx graveolens)*
Violet, Fen *(Viola persicifolia)*
Viper's-grass *(Scorzonera humilis)*
Water-plantain, Floating *(Luronium natans)*
Water-plantain, Ribbon-leaved *(Alisma gramineum)*
Wood-sedge, Starved *(Carex depauperata)*
Woodsia, Alpine *(Woodsia alpina)*
Woodsia, Oblong *(Woodsia ilvenis)*
Wormwood, Field *(Artemisia campestris)*
Woundwort, Downy *(Stachys germanica)*
Woundwort, Limestone *(Stachys alpina)*
Yellow-rattle, Greater *(Rhinanthus serotinus)*

WORLD HERITAGE SITES

The Convention Concerning the Protection of the World Cultural and Natural Heritage was adopted by the United Nations Educational, Scientific and Cultural Organization (UNESCO) in 1972 and ratified by the UK in 1984. As at June 2011, 187 states were party to the convention. The convention provides for the identification, protection and conservation of cultural and natural sites of outstanding universal value.

Cultural sites may be:
• sites representing architectural and technological innovation or cultural interchange
• sites of artistic, historic, aesthetic, archaeological, scientific, ethnologic or anthropologic value
• 'cultural landscapes', ie sites whose characteristics are marked by significant interactions between human populations and their natural environment
• exceptional examples of traditional settlement or land- or sea-use; especially those threatened by irreversible change.

Natural sites may be:
• those with remarkable physical, biological or geological formations
• those with outstanding universal value from the point of view of science, conservation or natural beauty
• the habitat of threatened species and plants.

Governments which are party to the convention nominate sites in their country for inclusion in the World Cultural and Natural Heritage List. Nominations are considered by the World Heritage Committee, an inter-governmental committee composed of 21 representatives of the parties to the convention. The committee is advised by the International Council on Monuments and Sites (ICOMOS), the International Centre for the Study of the Preservation and Restoration of Cultural Property (ICCROM) and the International Union for the Conservation of Nature (IUCN). ICOMOS evaluates and reports on proposed cultural and mixed sites, ICCROM provides expert advice and training on how to conserve and restore cultural property and IUCN provides technical evaluations of natural heritage sites and reports on the state of conservation of listed sites. The Department for Culture, Media and Sport represents the UK government in matters relating to the convention.

A prerequisite for inclusion in the World Heritage List is the existence of an effective legal protection system in the country in which the site is situated and a detailed management plan to ensure the conservation of the site. Inclusion in the list does not confer any greater degree of protection on the site than that offered by the national protection framework.

If a site is considered to be in serious danger of decay or damage, the committee may add it to the World Heritage in Danger List. Sites on this list may benefit from particular attention or emergency measures to allay threats and allow them to retain their world heritage status, or in extreme cases of damage or neglect they may lose their world heritage status completely.

Financial support for the conservation of sites on the World Cultural and Natural Heritage List is provided by the World Heritage Fund, administered by the World Heritage Committee. The fund's income is derived from compulsory and voluntary contributions from the states party to the convention and from private donations.

DESIGNATED SITES

As at 29 June 2011, following the 35th session of the World Heritage Committee, 936 sites were inscribed on the World Cultural and Natural Heritage List. Of these, 25 are in the UK and three in British overseas territories; 23 are listed for their cultural significance (†), four for their natural significance (*) and one for both cultural and natural significance. The year in which sites were designated appears in parentheses. In 2005 Hadrian's Wall, a World Heritage Site in its own right since 1987, was joined by the upper German-Raetian Limes to form the first section of a trans-national world heritage site, Frontiers of the Roman Empire.

UNITED KINGDOM

†Bath – the city (1987)
†Blaenarvon industrial landscape, Wales (2000)
†Blenheim Palace and Park, Oxfordshire (1987)
†Canterbury Cathedral, St Augustine's Abbey, St Martin's Church, Kent (1988)
†Castle and town walls of King Edward I, north Wales – Beaumaris, Caernarfon Castle, Conwy Castle, Harlech Castle, Ynys Mon (Isle of Anglesey) (1986)
†Cornwall and west Devon mining landscape (2006)
†Derwent Valley Mills, Derbyshire (2001)
*Dorset and east Devon coast (2001)
†Durham Cathedral and Castle (1986)
†Edinburgh old and new towns (1995)
†Frontiers of the Roman Empire, Hadrian's Wall, northern England (1987, 2005)
*Giant's Causeway and Causeway coast, Co. Antrim (1986)
†Greenwich, London – maritime Greenwich, including the Royal Naval College, Old Royal Observatory, Queen's House, town centre (1997)
†Heart of Neolithic Orkney (1999)
†Ironbridge Gorge, Shropshire – the world's first iron bridge and other early industrial sites (1986)
†Liverpool – six areas of the maritime mercantile city (2004)
†New Lanark, South Lanarkshire, Scotland (2001)
†Pontcysyllte Aqueduct and Canal, Wrexham, Wales (2009)
†Royal Botanic Gardens, Kew (2003)
†*St Kilda, Eilean Siar (Western Isles) (1986)
†Saltaire, West Yorkshire (2001)
†Stonehenge, Avebury and related megalithic sites, Wiltshire (1986)
†Studley Royal Park, Fountains Abbey, St Mary's Church, N. Yorkshire (1986)
†Tower of London (1988)
†Westminster Abbey, Palace of Westminster, St Margaret's Church, London (1987)

BRITISH OVERSEAS TERRITORIES

*Henderson Island, Pitcairn Islands, South Pacific Ocean (1988)
*Gough Island and Inaccessible Island (part of Tristan da Cunha), South Atlantic Ocean (1995)
†St George town and related fortifications, Bermuda (2000)

WORLD HERITAGE CENTRE, UNESCO, 7 Place de Fontenoy, 75352 Paris 07 SP, France
W http://whc.unesco.org

HISTORIC BUILDINGS AND MONUMENTS

ENGLAND

Under the Planning (Listed Buildings and Conservation Areas) Act 1990, the Secretary of State for Culture, Media and Sport has a statutory duty to approve lists of buildings or groups of buildings in England which are of special architectural or historic interest. In November 2009 responsibility for compiling the list of buildings was passed to English Heritage. Under the Ancient Monuments and Archaeological Areas Act 1979 as amended by the National Heritage Act 1983, the secretary of state is also responsible for compiling a schedule of ancient monuments. Decisions are taken on the advice of English Heritage. On 1 April 2005 responsibility for the administration of the listing system was transferred from the secretary of state to English Heritage. This marked the start of a programme of changes designed to increase the involvement and awareness of the property owner and make the listing process more straightforward and more accountable.

LISTED BUILDINGS

Listed buildings are classified into Grade I, Grade II* and Grade II. There are around 374,000 individual listed buildings in England, of which approximately 92 per cent are Grade II listed. Almost all pre-1700 buildings are listed, as are most buildings of 1700 to 1840. English Heritage carries out thematic surveys of particular types of buildings with a view to making recommendations for listing, and members of the public may propose a building for consideration. The main purpose of listing is to ensure that care is taken in deciding the future of a building. No changes which affect the architectural or historic character of a listed building can be made without listed building consent (in addition to planning permission where relevant). Applications for listed building consent are normally dealt with by the local planning authority, although English Heritage is always consulted about proposals affecting Grade I and Grade II* properties. It is a criminal offence to demolish a listed building, or alter it in such a way as to affect its character, without consent.

SCHEDULED MONUMENTS

There are around 19,700 scheduled monuments in England. English Heritage is carrying out a Monuments Protection Programme assessing archaeological sites with a view to making recommendations for scheduling, and members of the public may propose a monument for consideration. All monuments proposed for scheduling are considered to be of national importance. Where buildings are both scheduled and listed, ancient monuments legislation takes precedence. The main purpose of scheduling a monument is to preserve it for the future and to protect it from damage, destruction or any unnecessary interference. Once a monument has been scheduled, scheduled monument consent is required before any works can be carried out. The scope of the control is more extensive and more detailed than that applied to listed buildings, but certain minor works, as detailed in the Ancient Monuments (Class Consents) Order 1994, may be carried out without consent. It is a criminal offence to carry out unauthorised work to scheduled monuments.

WALES

Under the Planning (Listed Buildings and Conservation Areas) Act 1990 and the Ancient Monuments and Archaeological Areas Act 1979, the National Assembly for Wales is responsible for listing buildings and scheduling monuments in Wales on the advice of Cadw (the Welsh Assembly's historic environment division), the Historic Buildings Advisory Council for Wales, the Ancient Monuments Advisory Board for Wales and the Royal Commission on the Ancient and Historical Monuments of Wales (RCAHMW). The criteria for evaluating buildings are similar to those in England and the same listing system is used. There are approximately 29,900 listed buildings and 4,134 scheduled monuments in Wales.

SCOTLAND

Under the Planning (Listed Buildings and Conservation Areas) (Scotland) Act 1997 and the Ancient Monuments and Archaeological Areas Act 1979, Scottish ministers are responsible for listing buildings and scheduling monuments in Scotland on the advice of Historic Scotland, the Historic Environment Advisory Council for Scotland (HEACS) and the Royal Commission on the Ancient and Historical Monuments of Scotland (RCAHMS). The criteria for evaluating buildings are similar to those in England but an A, B, C(S) categorisation is used. As at March 2011 there were 47,643 listed buildings and 8,170 scheduled monuments in Scotland.

NORTHERN IRELAND

Under the Planning (Northern Ireland) Order 1991 and the Historic Monuments and Archaeological Objects (Northern Ireland) Order 1995, the Northern Ireland Environment Agency (part of the Department of the Environment of the Northern Ireland) is responsible for listing buildings and scheduling monuments. The Historic Buildings Council for Northern Ireland and the relevant district council must be consulted on listing proposals, and the Historic Monuments Council for Northern Ireland must be consulted on scheduling proposals. The criteria for evaluating buildings are similar to those in England but an A, B+, B1 and B2 categorisation is used. As at March 2011 there were 8,742 listed buildings and 1,897 scheduled monuments in Northern Ireland.

ENGLAND

For more information on English Heritage properties, including those listed below, the official website is www.english-heritage.org.uk
For more information on National Trust properties in England, including those listed below, the official website is www.nationaltrust.org.uk
(EH) English Heritage property
(NT) National Trust property

A LA RONDE (NT), Exmouth, Devon EX8 5BD
T 01395-265514
Unique 16-sided house completed c.1796
ALNWICK CASTLE, Alnwick, Northumberland NE66 1NQ
T 01665-510777 W www.alnwickcastle.com
Seat of the Dukes of Northumberland since 1309; Italian Renaissance-style interior; gardens with spectacular water features
ALTHORP, Northants NN7 4HQ T 01604-770107
W www.althorp.com
Spencer family seat; Diana, Princess of Wales memorabilia
ANGLESEY ABBEY (NT), Lode, Cambs CB25 9EJ
T 01223-810080
House built c.1600; houses many paintings and a unique clock collection; gardens and Lode Mill
APSLEY HOUSE (EH), London W1J 7NT T 020-7499 5676
Built by Robert Adam 1771–8, home of the Dukes of Wellington since 1817 and known as 'No. 1 London'; collection of fine and decorative arts
ARUNDEL CASTLE, Arundel, W. Sussex BN18 9AB
T 01903-882173 W www.arundelcastle.org
Castle dating from the Norman Conquest; seat of the Dukes of Norfolk
AVEBURY (EH/NT), Wilts SN8 1RF T 01672-539250
Remains of stone circles constructed 4,000 years ago surrounding the later village of Avebury
BANQUETING HOUSE, Whitehall, London SW1A 2ER
T 0844-482 7777 W www.hrp.org.uk
Designed by Inigo Jones; ceiling paintings by Rubens; site of the execution of Charles I
BASILDON PARK (NT), Reading, Berks RG8 9NR
T 0118-984 3040
Palladian mansion built in 1776–83 by John Carr
BATTLE ABBEY (EH), Battle, E. Sussex TN33 0AD
T 01424-775705
Remains of the abbey founded by William the Conqueror on the site of the Battle of Hastings
BEAULIEU, Brockenhurst, Hants SO42 7ZN T 01590-612345
W www.beaulieu.co.uk
House and gardens; Beaulieu Abbey and exhibition of monastic life; National Motor Museum
BEESTON CASTLE (EH), Cheshire CW6 9TX
T 01829-260464
Built in the 13th century by Ranulf, sixth Earl of Chester
BELTON HOUSE (NT), Grantham, Lincs NG32 2LS
T 01476-566116
17th-century house; formal gardens in landscaped park
BELVOIR CASTLE, Grantham, Lincs NG32 1PE
T 01476-871002 W www.belvoircastle.com
Seat of the Dukes of Rutland; 19th-century Gothic-style castle
BERKELEY CASTLE, Glos GL13 9BQ T 01453-810332
W www.berkeley-castle.com
Completed 1153; site of the murder of Edward II (1327)

BIRDOSWALD FORT (EH), Cumbria CA8 7DD
T 01697-747602
Stretch of Hadrian's Wall with Roman wall fort, turret and milecastle
BLENHEIM PALACE, Woodstock, Oxon OX20 1PX
T 01993-810500 W www.blenheimpalace.com
Seat of the Dukes of Marlborough and Winston Churchill's birthplace; designed by Vanbrugh
BLICKLING ESTATE (NT), Blickling, Norfolk NR11 6NF
T 01263-738030
Jacobean house with state rooms; extensive gardens, temple and 18th-century orangery
BODIAM CASTLE (NT), Bodiam, E. Sussex TN32 5UA
T 01580-830196
Well-preserved medieval moated castle built in 1385
BOLSOVER CASTLE (EH), Bolsover, Derbys S44 6PR
T 01246-822844
17th-century building on site of medieval castle
BOSCOBEL HOUSE (EH), Bishops Wood, Staffs ST19 9AR
T 01902-850244
Timber-framed 17th-century hunting lodge; refuge of fugitive Charles II
BOUGHTON HOUSE, Kettering, Northants NN14 1BJ
T 01536-515731 W www.boughtonhouse.org.uk
A 17th-century house with French-style additions; home of the Dukes of Buccleuch and Queensbury
BOWOOD HOUSE, Calne, Wilts SN11 0LZ
T 01249-812102 W www.bowood-house.co.uk
An 18th-century house in Capability Brown park, with lake, temple and arboretum
BRONTË PARSONAGE, Haworth, W. Yorks BD22 8DR
T 01535-642323 W www.bronte.org.uk
Home of the Brontë sisters; museum and memorabilia
BUCKFAST ABBEY, Buckfastleigh, Devon TQ11 0EE
T 01364-645500 W www.buckfast.org.uk
Benedictine monastery on medieval foundations
BUCKINGHAM PALACE, London SW1A 1AA
T 020-7766 7300 W www.royalcollection.org.uk
Purchased by George III in 1761, and the Sovereign's official London residence since 1837; 18 state rooms, including the Throne Room, and Picture Gallery
BUCKLAND ABBEY (NT), Yelverton, Devon PL20 6EY
T 01822-853607
13th-century Cistercian monastery; home of Sir Francis Drake
BURGHLEY HOUSE, Stamford, Lincs PE9 3JY
T 01780-752451 W www.burghley.co.uk
Late Elizabethan house built by William Cecil, first Lord Burghley
CALKE ABBEY (NT), Ticknall, Derbys DE73 7LE
T 01332-863822
Baroque 18th-century mansion
CARISBROOKE CASTLE (EH), Newport, Isle of Wight
PO30 1XY T 01983-522107
W www.carisbrookecastlemuseum.org.uk
Norman castle; museum; prison of Charles I 1647–8
CARLISLE CASTLE (EH), Carlisle, Cumbria CA3 8UR
T 01228-591922
Medieval castle; prison of Mary Queen of Scots
CARLYLE'S HOUSE (NT), Chelsea, London SW3 5HL
T 020-7352 7087
Home of Thomas and Jane Carlyle
CASTLE ACRE PRIORY (EH), Swaffham, Norfolk
PE32 2XD T 01760-755394
Remains include 12th-century church and prior's lodgings
CASTLE DROGO (NT), Drewsteignton, Devon EX6 6PB
T 01647-433306
Granite castle designed by Lutyens

CASTLE HOWARD, N. Yorks YO60 7DA T 01653-648333
W www.castlehoward.co.uk
Designed by Vanbrugh 1699–1726; mausoleum
designed by Hawksmoor

CASTLE RISING CASTLE (EH), King's Lynn, Norfolk
PE31 6AH T 01553-631330 W www.castlerising.co.uk
12th-century keep in a massive earthwork with
gatehouse and bridge

CHARLES DARWIN'S HOUSE (EH), Down House, Luxted
Road, Downe, Kent BR6 7JT T 01689-859119
The family home where Darwin wrote *On the Origin
of Species*

CHARTWELL (NT), Westerham, Kent TN16 1PS
T 01732-868381
Home of Sir Winston Churchill

CHATSWORTH, Bakewell, Derbys DE45 1PP
T 01246-565300 W www.chatsworth.org
Tudor mansion set in magnificent parkland

CHESTERS ROMAN FORT (EH), Chollerford,
Northumberland NE46 4EU T 01434-681379
Roman cavalry fort built to guard Hadrian's Wall

CHYSAUSTER ANCIENT VILLAGE (EH), Penzance,
Cornwall TR20 8XA T 07831-757934
Remains of Celtic settlement; eight stone-walled
homesteads

CLANDON PARK (NT), West Clandon, Guildford, Surrey
GU4 7RQ T 01483-222482 W www.clandonpark.co.uk
18th-century Palladian mansion and gardens, which
contain a Maori meeting house, removed from New
Zealand in 1892

CLIFFORD'S TOWER (EH), York YO1 9SA
T 01904-646940 W www.cliffordstower.com
13th-century tower built on a mound; remains of
a castle built by William the Conqueror

CLIVEDEN (NT), Taplow, Bucks SL6 0JA T 01494-755562
Former home of the Astors, now a hotel set in garden
and woodland

CORBRIDGE ROMAN SITE (EH), Corbridge,
Northumberland NE45 5NT T 01434-632349
Excavated central area of a Roman town and successive
military bases

CORFE CASTLE (NT), Wareham, Dorset BH20 5EZ
T 01929-481294
Ruined former royal castle dating from the 11th
century

CROFT CASTLE AND PARKLAND (NT), Yarpole,
Herefordshire HR6 9PW T 01568-780246
Pre-Conquest border castle with Georgian-Gothic
interior

DEAL CASTLE (EH), Deal, Kent CT14 7BA T 01304-372762
Largest of the coastal defence forts built by Henry VIII

DICKENS HOUSE, Doughty Street, London WC1N 2LX
T 020-7405 2127 W www.dickensmuseum.com
House occupied by Dickens 1837–9; manuscripts,
furniture and portraits

DOVE COTTAGE, Grasmere, Cumbria LA22 9SH
T 01539-435544 W www.wordsworth.org.uk
Wordsworth's home 1799–1808; museum

DOVER CASTLE (EH), Dover, Kent CT16 1HU
T 01304-211067
Castle with Roman, Saxon and Norman features;
wartime operations rooms

DR JOHNSON'S HOUSE, Gough Square, London
EC4A 3DE T 020-7353 3745 W www.drjohnsonshouse.org
Home of Samuel Johnson 1748–59

DUNSTANBURGH CASTLE (EH/NT), Craster,
nr Alnwick, Northumberland NE66 3TT T 01665-576231
14th-century castle ruins on a cliff with a substantial
gatehouse-keep

ELTHAM PALACE (EH), Eltham, London SE9 5QE
T 020-8294 2548
Combines an Art Deco country house and remains of
medieval palace set in moated gardens

FARLEIGH HUNGERFORD CASTLE (EH), Bath,
Somerset BA2 7RS T 01225-754026
Late 14th-century castle with two courts; chapel with
tomb of Sir Thomas Hungerford

FARNHAM CASTLE KEEP (EH), Farnham, Surrey
GA9 0AG T 01252-721194 W www.farnhamcastle.com
Large 12th-century castle keep with motte and
bailey wall

FISHBOURNE ROMAN PALACE, Salthill Road,
Fishbourne, Chichester, W. Sussex PO19 3QR
T 01243-789829 W www.sussexpast.co.uk
Excavated Roman palace with largest collection of
in-situ mosaics in Britain

FOUNTAINS ABBEY (NT), nr Ripon, N. Yorks HG4 3DY
T 01765-608888 W www.fountainsabbey.org.uk
Deer park; St Mary's Church; ruined Cistercian
monastery; Georgian water garden

FRAMLINGHAM CASTLE (EH), Woodbridge, Suffolk
IP13 9BP T 01728-724189
Castle (*c.*1200) with high curtain walls enclosing an
almshouse (1639)

FURNESS ABBEY (EH), Barrow-in-Furness, Cumbria
LA13 0PJ T 01229-823420
Remains of church and cloister buildings founded
in 1123

GLASTONBURY ABBEY, Glastonbury, Somerset BA6 9EL
T 01458-831631 W www.glastonburyabbey.com
Ruins of a 12th-century abbey rebuilt after fire; site of
an early Christian settlement

GOODRICH CASTLE (EH), Ross-on-Wye, Herefordshire
HR9 6HY T 01600-890538
Remains of 13th-century castle with 12th-century
keep

GREENWICH, London SE10 9NF
W www.visitgreenwich.org.uk
Former Royal Observatory (founded 1675) housing
the time ball and zero meridian of longitude; the
Queen's House, designed for Queen Anne, wife of
James I, by Inigo Jones; Painted Hall and Chapel (Old
Royal Naval College)

GRIMES GRAVES (EH), Brandon, Norfolk IP26 5DE
T 01842-810656
Neolithic flint mines; one shaft can be descended

GUILDHALL, London EC2P 2EJ T 020-7606 3030
W www.cityoflondon.gov.uk
Centre of civic government of the City built *c.* 1441;
facade built 1788–9

HADDON HALL, Bakewell, Derbys DE45 1LA
T 01629-812855 W www.haddonhall.co.uk
Well-preserved 12th-century manor house

HAILES ABBEY (EH), Cheltenham, Glos GL54 5PB
T 01242-602398
Ruins of a 13th-century Cistercian monastery

HAM HOUSE AND GARDEN (NT), Richmond-upon-
Thames, Surrey TW10 7RS T 020-8940 1950
Stuart house with lavish interiors and formal gardens

HAMPTON COURT PALACE, East Molesey, Surrey
KT8 9AU T 0844-482 7777 W www.hrp.org.uk
16th-century palace with additions by Wren

HARDWICK HALL (NT), Chesterfield, Derbys S44 5QJ
T 01246-850430
Built 1591–7 for Bess of Hardwick

HARDY'S BIRTHPLACE (NT), Higher Bockhampton,
Dorset DT2 8QJ T 01305-262366
Birthplace and home of Thomas Hardy

HAREWOOD HOUSE, Harewood, W. Yorks LS17 9LG
T 0113-218 1010 W www.harewood.org
18th-century house designed by John Carr and Robert Adam; park by Capability Brown

HATFIELD HOUSE, Hatfield, Herts AL9 5NQ
T 01707-287010 W www.hatfield-house.co.uk
Jacobean house built by Robert Cecil; surviving wing of Royal Palace of Hatfield (c.1485)

HELMSLEY CASTLE (EH), Helmsley, N. Yorks YO62 5AB
T 01439-770442
12th-century keep and curtain wall with 16th-century buildings; spectacular earthwork defences

HEVER CASTLE, nr Edenbridge, Kent TN8 7NG
T 01732-865224 W www.hevercastle.co.uk
13th-century double-moated castle; childhood home of Anne Boleyn

HOLKER HALL, Cumbria LA11 7PL T 01539-558328
W www.holker.co.uk
Former home of the Dukes of Devonshire; award-winning gardens

HOLKHAM HALL, Wells-next-the-Sea, Norfolk NR23 1AB
T 01328-710227 W www.holkham.co.uk
Palladian mansion; notable fine art collection

HOUSESTEADS ROMAN FORT (EH), Hexham, Northumberland NE47 6NN T 01434-344363
Excavated infantry fort on Hadrian's Wall with museum

HUGHENDEN MANOR (NT), High Wycombe, Bucks HP14 4LA T 01494-755565
Home of Disraeli; small formal garden

JANE AUSTEN'S HOUSE, Chawton, Hants GU34 1SD
T 01420-83262
W www.jane-austens-house-museum.org.uk
Jane Austen's home from 1809 to 1817

KEDLESTON HALL (NT), Derbys DE22 5JH
T 01332-842191
Classical Palladian mansion built 1759–65; complete Robert Adam interiors

KELMSCOTT MANOR, nr Lechlade, Glos GL7 3HJ
T 01367-252486 W www.kelmscottmanor.org.uk
Summer home of William Morris, with products of Morris and Co.

KENILWORTH CASTLE (EH), Kenilworth, Warks CV8 1NE
T 01926-852078
Largest castle ruin in England

KENSINGTON PALACE, Kensington Gardens, London W8 4PX T 0870-482 7777 W www.hrp.org.uk
Built in 1605 and enlarged by Wren; birthplace of Queen Victoria; 'Enchanted Palace' exhibition

KENWOOD HOUSE (EH), Hampstead Lane, London NW3 7JR T 020-8348 1286
Neo-classical villa housing the Iveagh bequest of paintings and furniture

KEW PALACE, Richmond-upon-Thames, Surrey TW9 3AB
T 0870-482 7777 W www.hrp.org.uk
Includes Queen Charlotte's Cottage, used by King George III and family as a summerhouse

KINGSTON LACY (NT), Wimborne Minster, Dorset BH21 4EA T 01202-883402
17th-century house with 19th-century alterations; important art collection

KNEBWORTH HOUSE, Knebworth, Herts SG3 6PY
T 01438-812661 W www.knebworthhouse.com
Tudor manor house concealed by 19th-century Gothic decoration; Lutyens gardens

KNOLE (NT), Sevenoaks, Kent TN15 0RP T 01732-450608
House dating from 1456 set in parkland; fine art collection; birthplace of Vita Sackville-West

LAMBETH PALACE, London SE1 7JU T 020-7898 1200
W www.archbishopofcanterbury.org
Official residence of the Archbishop of Canterbury since the 13th century

LANERCOST PRIORY (EH), Brampton, Cumbria CA8 2HQ
T 01697-73030
The nave of the Augustinian priory church, c.1166, is still used; remains of other claustral buildings

LANHYDROCK (NT), Bodmin, Cornwall PL30 5AD
T 01208-265950
House dating from the 17th century; 50 rooms, including kitchen and nursery

LEEDS CASTLE, nr Maidstone, Kent ME17 1PL
T 01622-765400 W www.leeds-castle.com
Castle dating from the 12th century, on two islands in lake

LEVENS HALL, Kendal, Cumbria LA8 0PD T 01539-560321
W www.levenshall.co.uk
Elizabethan house with unique topiary garden (1694); steam engine collection

LINCOLN CASTLE, Lincoln, Lincs LN1 3AA
T 01522-511068 W www.lincolnshire.gov.uk
Built by William the Conqueror in 1068

LINDISFARNE PRIORY (EH), Holy Island, Northumberland TD15 2RX T 01289-389200
Founded in AD 635; re-established in the 12th century as a Benedictine priory, now ruined

LITTLE MORETON HALL (NT), Congleton, Cheshire CW12 4SD T 01260-272018
Timber-framed moated Tudor manor house with knot garden

LONGLEAT HOUSE, Warminster, Wilts BA12 7NW
T 01985-844400 W www.longleat.co.uk
Elizabethan house in Italian Renaissance style; safari park

LULLINGSTONE ROMAN VILLA (EH), Eynsford, Kent DA4 0JA T 01322-863467
Large villa occupied for much of the Roman period; fine mosaics

MARBLE HILL HOUSE (EH), Twickenham, Middx TW1 2NL T 020-8892 5115
English Palladian villa with Georgian paintings and furniture

MICHELHAM PRIORY, Hailsham, E. Sussex BN27 3QS
T 01323-844224 W www.sussexpast.co.uk
Tudor house built onto an Augustinian priory

MIDDLEHAM CASTLE (EH), Leyburn, N. Yorks DL8 4QG
T 01969-623899
12th-century keep within later fortifications; childhood home of Richard III

MONTACUTE HOUSE (NT), Montacute, Somerset TA15 6XP T 01935-823289
Elizabethan house with National Portrait Gallery collection of portraits from the period

MOUNT GRACE PRIORY (EH), Northallerton, N. Yorks DL6 3JG T 01609-883494
Carthusian priory with remains of monastic buildings

OLD SARUM (EH), Salisbury, Wilts SP1 3SD
T 01722-335398
Earthworks enclosing remains of Norman castle and cathedral

ORFORD CASTLE (EH), Orford, Suffolk IP12 2ND
T 01394-450472
Polygonal tower keep of c.1170 and remains of coastal defence castle built by Henry II

OSBORNE HOUSE (EH), East Cowes, Isle of Wight PO32 6JX T 01983-200022
Queen Victoria's seaside residence

OSTERLEY PARK (NT), Isleworth, Middx TW7 4RB
T 020-8232 5050 W www.osterleypark.org.uk
Elizabethan mansion set in parkland

PENDENNIS CASTLE (EH), Falmouth, Cornwall TR11 4LP
T 01326-316594
Well-preserved 16th-century coastal defence castle

PENSHURST PLACE, Penshurst, Kent TN11 8DG
T 01892-870307 W www.penshurstplace.com
House with medieval Baron's Hall and 14th-century
gardens

PETWORTH HOUSE (NT), Petworth, W. Sussex GU28 0AE
T 01798-343929
Late 17th-century house set in Capability Brown
landscaped deer park

PEVENSEY CASTLE (EH), Pevensey, E. Sussex BN24 5LE
T 01323-762604
Walls of a fourth-century Roman fort; remains of an
11th-century castle

PEVERIL CASTLE (EH), Castleton, Derbys S33 8WQ
T 01433-620613
12th-century castle defended on two sides by
precipitous rocks

POLESDEN LACEY (NT), nr Dorking, Surrey RH5 6BD
T 01372-458203
Regency villa remodelled in the Edwardian era; fine
paintings and furnishings

PORTCHESTER CASTLE (EH), Portchester, Hants
PO16 9QW T 02392-378291
Walls of a late Roman fort enclosing a Norman keep
and an Augustinian priory church

POWDERHAM CASTLE, Kenton, Devon EX6 8JQ
T 01626-890243 W www.powderham.co.uk
Medieval castle with 18th- and 19th-century
alterations

RABY CASTLE, Staindrop, Co. Durham DL2 3AH
T 01833-660202 W www.rabycastle.com
14th-century castle with walled gardens

RAGLEY HALL, Alcester, Warks B49 5NJ T 01789-762090
W www.ragleyhall.com
17th-century house with gardens, park and lake

RICHBOROUGH ROMAN FORT (EH), Richborough,
Kent CT13 9JW T 01304-612013
Landing-site of the Claudian invasion in AD 43

RICHMOND CASTLE (EH), Richmond, N. Yorks
DL10 4QW T 01748-822493
12th-century keep with 11th-century curtain wall

RIEVAULX ABBEY (EH), nr Helmsley, N. Yorks YO62 5LB
T 01439-798228
Remains of a Cistercian abbey founded c.1132

ROCHESTER CASTLE (EH), Rochester, Kent ME1 1SW
T 01634-402276
11th-century castle partly on the Roman city wall, with
a square keep of c. 1127

ROCKINGHAM CASTLE, Market Harborough, Leics
LE16 8TH T 01536-770240 W www.rockinghamcastle.com
Built by William the Conqueror

ROYAL PAVILION, Brighton BN1 1EE T 03000-290900
W www.royalpavilion.org.uk
Palace of George IV, in Chinese style with Indian
exterior and Regency gardens

RUFFORD OLD HALL (NT), nr Ormskirk, Lancs L40 1SG
T 01704-821254
16th-century hall with unique screen

ST AUGUSTINE'S ABBEY (EH), Canterbury, Kent CT1 1PF
T 01227-378100
Remains of Benedictine monastery founded AD 597

ST MAWES CASTLE (EH), St Mawes, Cornwall TR2 5DE
T 01326-270526
Coastal defence castle built by Henry VIII

ST MICHAEL'S MOUNT (NT), Cornwall TR17 0HT
T 01736-710507 W www.stmichaelsmount.co.uk
12th-century castle with later additions, off the coast
at Marazion

SANDRINGHAM, Norfolk PE35 6EN T 01485-545408
W www.sandringhamestate.co.uk
The Queen's private residence; a neo-Jacobean house
built in 1870

SCARBOROUGH CASTLE (EH), Scarborough, N. Yorks
YO11 1HY T 01723-372451
Remains of 12th-century keep and curtain walls

SHERBORNE CASTLE, Sherborne, Dorset DT9 5NR
T 01935-812072 W www.sherbornecastle.com
16th-century castle built by Sir Walter Raleigh set in
landscaped gardens

SHUGBOROUGH ESTATE (NT), Milford, Staffs ST17 0XB
T 01889-881388 W www.shugborough.org.uk
House set in 18th-century park with monuments,
temples and pavilions in the Greek Revival style;
arboretum; seat of the Earls of Lichfield

SKIPTON CASTLE, Skipton, N. Yorks BD23 1AW
T 01756-792442 W www.skiptoncastle.co.uk
D-shaped castle with six round towers and inner
courtyard

SMALLHYTHE PLACE (NT), Tenterden, Kent TN30 7NG
T 01580-762334
Half-timbered 16th-century house; home of Ellen
Terry 1899–1928; the Barn Theatre

STONEHENGE (EH), nr Amesbury, Wilts SP4 7DE
T 0870-333 1181
Prehistoric monument consisting of concentric stone
circles surrounded by a ditch and bank

STONOR PARK, Henley-on-Thames, Oxon RG9 6HF
T 01491-638587 W www.stonor.com
Medieval house with Georgian facade; centre of
Roman Catholicism after the Reformation

STOURHEAD (NT), Stourton, Wilts BA12 6QD
T 01747-841152
English 18th-century Palladian mansion with
landscape gardens

STRATFIELD SAYE HOUSE, Hants RG7 2BT
T 01256-882694 W www.stratfield-saye.co.uk
House built 1630–40; home of the Dukes of
Wellington since 1817

STRATFORD-UPON-AVON, Warks T 01789-204016
W www.shakespeare.org.uk
Shakespeare's Birthplace Trust with Shakespeare
Centre; Anne Hathaway's Cottage, home of
Shakespeare's wife; Mary Arden's House, home of
Shakespeare's mother; grammar school attended by
Shakespeare; Holy Trinity Church, where Shakespeare
is buried; Royal Shakespeare Theatre (burnt down
1926, rebuilt 1932) and Swan Theatre (opened 1986)

SUDELEY CASTLE, Winchcombe, Glos GL54 5JD
T 01242-602308 W www.sudeleycastle.co.uk
Castle built in 1442; restored in the 19th century

SULGRAVE MANOR, nr Banbury, Oxon OX17 2SD
T 01295-760205 W www.sulgravemanor.org.uk
Home of George Washington's family

SUTTON HOUSE (NT), 2 & 4 Homerton High Street,
Hackney, London E9 6JQ T 020-8986 2264
Tudor house, built in 1535 by Sir Ralph Sadleir

SYON HOUSE, Brentford, Middx TW8 8JF T 020-8560 0882
W www.syonpark.co.uk
Built on the site of a former monastery; Robert Adam
interior; Capability Brown park

TILBURY FORT (EH), Tilbury, Essex RM18 7NR
T 01375-858489
16th-century coastal fort

TINTAGEL CASTLE (EH), Tintagel, Cornwall PL34 0HE
T 01840-770328
13th-century cliff-top castle and Dark Age settlement
site; linked with Arthurian legend
TOWER OF LONDON, London EC3N 4AB
T 0870-482 7777 W www.hrp.org.uk
Royal palace and fortress begun by William the
Conqueror in 1078; houses the Crown Jewels
TRERICE (NT), nr Newquay, Cornwall TR8 4PG
T 01637-875404
Elizabethan manor house
TYNEMOUTH PRIORY AND CASTLE (EH), Tyne and
Wear NE30 4BZ T 0191-257 1090
Remains of a Benedictine priory, founded c. 1090, on
Saxon monastic site
UPPARK (NT), South Harting, W. Sussex GU31 5QR
T 01730-825857
Late 17th-century house, completely restored after fire;
Fetherstonhaugh art collection
WALMER CASTLE (EH), Walmer, Kent CT14 7LJ
T 01304-364288
One of Henry VIII's coastal defence castles, now the
residence of the Lord Warden of the Cinque Ports
WARKWORTH CASTLE (EH), Warkworth,
Northumberland NE65 0UJ T 01665-711423
14th-century keep amid earlier ruins, with hermitage
upstream
WHITBY ABBEY (EH), Whitby, N. Yorks YO22 4JT
T 01947-603568
Remains of Norman church on the site of a monastery
founded in AD 657
WILTON HOUSE, nr Salisbury, Wilts SP2 0BJ
T 01722-746714 W www.wiltonhouse.co.uk
17th-century house on the site of a Tudor house and
ninth-century nunnery
WINDSOR CASTLE, Windsor, Berks SL4 1NJ
T 020-7766 7304 W www.royalcollection.org.uk
Official residence of the Queen; oldest royal residence
still in regular use; largest inhabited castle in the world.
Also St George's Chapel
WOBURN ABBEY, Woburn, Beds MK17 9WA
T 01525-290333 W www.woburn.co.uk
Built on the site of a Cistercian abbey; seat of the
Dukes of Bedford; art collection; antiques centre
WROXETER ROMAN CITY (EH), nr Shrewsbury,
Shropshire SY5 6PH T 01743-761330
Second-century public baths and part of the forum
of the Roman town of Viroconium; replica Roman
town house

WALES

For more information on Cadw properties, including
those listed below, the official website is
www.cadw.wales.gov.uk
For more information on National Trust properties in
Wales, including those listed below, the official website is
www.nationaltrust.org.uk
(C) Property of Cadw: Welsh Historic Monuments
(NT) National Trust property

BEAUMARIS CASTLE (C), Anglesey LL58 8AP
T 01248-810361
Concentrically planned castle, still virtually intact
CAERLEON ROMAN BATHS AND AMPHITHEATRE
(C), Newport NP18 1AE T 01633-422518
Rare example of a legionary bath-house and late
first-century arena surrounded by bank for spectators

CAERNARFON CASTLE (C), Gwynedd LL55 2AY
T 01286-677617
Castle built between 1283 and 1330, initially for King
Edward I of England; setting for the investiture of
Prince Charles in 1969
CAERPHILLY CASTLE (C), Caerphilly CF83 1JD
T 029-2088 3143
Concentrically planned castle (c. 1270) notable for its
scale and use of water defences
CARDIFF CASTLE, Cardiff CF10 3RB T 029-2087 8100
W www.cardiffcastle.com
Castle built on the site of a Roman fort
CASTELL COCH (C), Tongwynlais, Cardiff CF15 7JS
T 029-2081 0101
'Fairytale'-style castle, rebuilt 1875–90 on medieval
foundations
CHEPSTOW CASTLE (C), Monmouthshire NP16 5EZ
T 01291-624065
Rectangular keep amid extensive fortifications;
developed throughout the Middle Ages
CONWY CASTLE (C), Gwynedd LL32 8AY
T 01492-592358
Built for Edward I, 1283–7, on a narrow rocky
outcrop
CRICCIETH CASTLE (C), Gwynedd LL55 0DP
T 01766-522227
Native Welsh 13th-century castle, altered by Edward I
and Edward II
DENBIGH CASTLE (C), Denbighshire LL16 3NB
T 01745-813385
Remains of the castle (begun 1282), including
triple-towered gatehouse
HARLECH CASTLE (C), Gwynedd LL46 2YH
T 01766-780552
Well-preserved Edwardian castle, constructed
1283–9, on an outcrop above the former
shoreline
PEMBROKE CASTLE, Pembrokeshire SA71 4LA
T 01646-684585 W www.pembrokecastle.co.uk
Castle founded in 1093; Great Tower built in
late 12th century; birthplace of King Henry VII
PENRHYN CASTLE (NT), Bangor, Gwynedd LL57 4HN
T 01248-363219
Neo-Norman castle built in the 19th century; railway
museum; private art collection
PORTMEIRION, Gwynedd LL48 6ER T 01766-770000
W www.portmeirion-village.com
Village in Italianate style built by Clough Williams-Ellis
POWIS CASTLE (NT), Welshpool, Powys SY21 8RF
T 01938-551944
Medieval castle with interior in variety of styles;
17th-century gardens; Clive of India museum
RAGLAN CASTLE (C), Monmouthshire NP15 2BT
T 01291-690228
Remains of 15th-century castle with moated
hexagonal keep
ST DAVIDS BISHOP'S PALACE (C), Pembrokeshire
SA62 6PE T 01437-720517
Remains of residence of Bishops of St Davids built
1328–47
TINTERN ABBEY (C), nr Chepstow, Monmouthshire
NP16 6SE T 01291-689251
Remains of 13th-century church and conventual
buildings of a 12th-century Cistercian monastery
TRETOWER COURT AND CASTLE (C), nr Crickhowell,
Powys NP8 1RF T 01874-730279
Medieval house rebuilt in the 15th century, with
remains of 12th-century castle nearby

SCOTLAND

For more information on Historic Scotland properties, including those listed below, the official website is www.historic-scotland.gov.uk
For more information on National Trust for Scotland properties, including those listed below, the official website is www.nts.org.uk
(HS) Historic Scotland property
(NTS) National Trust for Scotland property

ABBOTSFORD HOUSE, Melrose, Roxburghshire TD6 9BQ
T 01896-752043 W www.scottsabbotsford.co.uk
Home of Sir Walter Scott
ANTONINE WALL, between the Clyde and the Forth
W www.antoninewall.org
Built around AD 142; consists of ditch, turf rampart, road and forts at regular intervals
BALMORAL CASTLE, Ballater, Aberdeenshire AB35 5TB
T 01339-742534 W www.balmoralcastle.com
Baronial-style castle built for Victoria and Albert; the Queen's private residence
BLACKHOUSE, ARNOL (HS), Lewis, Western Isles
HS2 9DB T 01851-710395
Traditional Lewis thatched house
BLAIR CASTLE, Blair Atholl, Perthshire PH18 5TL
T 01796-481207 W www.blair-castle.co.uk
Mid-18th-century mansion with 13th-century tower; seat of the Dukes and Earls of Atholl
BONAWE IRON FURNACE (HS), Taynuilt, Argyll
PA35 1JQ T 01866-822432
Charcoal-fuelled ironworks founded in 1753
BOWHILL, Selkirkshire TD7 5ET T 01750-22204
W www.bowhill.org
Seat of the Dukes of Buccleuch and Queensberry; fine collection of paintings
BROUGH OF BIRSAY (HS), Orkney KW17 2NH
T 01856-841815
Remains of Norse and Pictish village on the tidal island of Birsay
CAERLAVEROCK CASTLE (HS), Glencaple, Dumfriesshire
DG1 4RU T 01387-770244
Triangular 13th-century castle with classical Renaissance additions
CAIRNPAPPLE HILL (HS), Torphichen, West Lothian
T 01506-634622
Neolithic and Bronze Age ceremonial site and burial chambers
CALANAIS STANDING STONES (HS), Lewis, Western Isles HS2 9DY T 01851-621422
Standing stones in a cross-shaped setting, dating from c. 3000 BC
CATERTHUNS (BROWN AND WHITE) (HS), Menmuir, nr Brechin, Angus
Two large Iron Age hill forts
CAWDOR CASTLE, Nairn, Moray IV12 5RD
T 01667-404401 W www.cawdorcastle.com
14th-century keep with 15th- and 17th-century additions
CLAVA CAIRNS (HS), nr Inverness, Inverness-shire
T 01667-460232
Bronze Age cemetery complex of cairns and standing stones
CRATHES CASTLE (NTS), nr Banchory, Aberdeenshire
AB31 5QJ T 08444-932166
16th-century baronial castle in woodland, fields and gardens

CULZEAN CASTLE (NTS), Maybole, Ayrshire KA19 8LE
T 08444-932149 W www.culzeanexperience.org
18th-century Robert Adam castle with oval staircase and circular saloon
DRYBURGH ABBEY (HS), nr Melrose, Roxburghshire
TD6 0RQ T 01835-822381
12th-century abbey containing the tomb of Sir Walter Scott
DUNVEGAN CASTLE, Skye IV55 8WF T 01470-521206
W www.dunvegancastle.com
13th-century castle with later additions; home of the chiefs of the Clan MacLeod
EDINBURGH CASTLE (HS) EH1 2NG T 0131-225 9846
W www.edinburghcastle.gov.uk
Includes the Scottish Crown Jewels, Scottish National War Memorial, Scottish United Services Museum and historic apartments
EDZELL CASTLE (HS), nr Brechin, Angus DD9 7UE
T 01356-648631
16th-century tower house on medieval foundations; walled garden
EILEAN DONAN CASTLE, Dornie, Ross and Cromarty
IV40 8DX T 01599-555202 W www.eileandonancastle.com
13th-century castle with Jacobite relics at the meeting point of three sea lochs
ELGIN CATHEDRAL (HS), Moray IV30 1HU
T 01343-547171
13th-century cathedral and chapterhouse
FLOORS CASTLE, Kelso, Roxburghshire TD5 7SF
T 01573-223333 W www.floorscastle.com
Largest inhabited castle in Scotland; seat of the Dukes of Roxburghe; built 1721 by William Adam
FORT GEORGE (HS), Ardersier, Inverness-shire IV2 7TD
T 01667-460232
18th-century fort; still a working army barracks
GLAMIS CASTLE, Forfar, Angus DD8 1RJ T 01307-840393
W www.glamis-castle.co.uk
Seat of the Lyon family (later Earls of Strathmore and Kinghorne) since 1372
GLASGOW CATHEDRAL (HS), Lanarkshire G4 0QZ
T 0141-552 8198 W www.glasgowcathedral.org.uk
Medieval cathedral with elaborately vaulted crypt
GLENELG BROCHS (HS), Shielbridge, Ross and Cromarty
T 01667-460232
Two broch towers (Dun Telve and Dun Troddan) with well-preserved structural features
HOPETOUN HOUSE, South Queensferry, W. Lothian
EH30 9SL T 0131-331 2451 W www.hopetoun.co.uk
House designed by Sir William Bruce, enlarged by William Adam, built 1699
HUNTLY CASTLE (HS), Aberdeenshire AB54 4SH
T 01466-793191
Ruin of a 16th- and 17th-century baronial residence
INVERARAY CASTLE, Argyll PA32 8XE T 01499-302203
W www.inveraray-castle.com
Gothic-style 18th-century castle; seat of the Dukes of Argyll
IONA ABBEY (HS), Iona, Inner Hebrides PA76 6SQ
T 01681-700512
Monastery founded by St Columba in AD 563
JARLSHOF (HS), Sumburgh Head, Shetland ZE3 9JN
T 01950-460112
Prehistoric and Norse settlement
JEDBURGH ABBEY (HS), Scottish Borders TD8 6JQ
T 01835-863925
Romanesque and early Gothic church founded c.1138

KISIMUL CASTLE (HS), Castlebay, Barra, Western Isles HS9 5UZ T 01871-810313
Medieval home of the Clan MacNeil
LINLITHGOW PALACE (HS), Kirkgate, Linlithgow, W. Lothian EH49 7AL T 01506-842896
Ruin of royal palace in park setting; birthplace of James V and Mary, Queen of Scots
MAESHOWE (HS), Stenness, Orkney KW16 3HA
T 01856-761606
Neolithic chambered tomb
MEIGLE SCULPTURED STONES (HS), Meigle, Perthshire PH12 8SB T 01828-640612
Twenty-six carved stones dating from the 8th to the 10th centuries
MELROSE ABBEY (HS), Melrose, Roxburghshire TD6 9LG
T 01896-822562
Ruin of Cistercian abbey founded c.1136 by David I
MOUSA BROCH (HS), Island of Mousa, Shetland
T 01856-841815
Finest surviving Iron Age broch tower
NEW ABBEY CORN MILL (HS), Dumfriesshire DG2 8BX
T 01387-850260
Working water-powered mill; operates in summer months
PALACE OF HOLYROODHOUSE, Edinburgh EH8 8DX
T 0131-556 5100 W www.royalcollection.org.uk
The Queen's official Scottish residence; main part of the palace built 1671–9
RING O' BRODGAR (HS), nr Stromness, Orkney
T 01856-841815
Neolithic circle of upright stones with an enclosing ditch
ROBERT BURNS BIRTHPLACE MUSEUM (NTS), Alloway, Ayrshire KA7 4PQ T 0844-493 2601
W www.burnsmuseum.org.uk
Comprises Burns Cottage, birthplace of the poet, gardens and a museum
ROSSLYN CHAPEL, Roslin, Midlothian EH25 9PU
T 0131-440 2159 W www.rosslynchapel.org.uk
Historic church with unique stone carvings
RUTHWELL CROSS (HS), Ruthwell, Dumfriesshire
T 0131-550 7612
Seventh-century Anglo-Saxon cross, open by arrangement only
ST ANDREWS CASTLE AND CATHEDRAL (HS), Fife KY16 9QL T 01334-477196 (castle); 01334-472563 (cathedral)
Ruins of 13th-century castle and remains of the largest cathedral in Scotland
SCONE PALACE, Perth, Perthshire PH2 6BD
T 01738-552300 W www.scone-palace.net
House built 1802–13 on the site of a medieval palace
SKARA BRAE (HS), nr Stromness, Orkney KW16 3LR
T 01856-841815
Stone Age village with adjacent replica house
SMAILHOLM TOWER (HS), nr Kelso, Roxburghshire TD5 7PG T 01573-460365
Well-preserved 15th-century tower-house
STIRLING CASTLE (HS), Stirlingshire FK8 1EJ
T 01786-450000 W www.stirlingcastle.gov.uk
Great Hall and gatehouse of James IV, palace of James V, Chapel Royal remodelled by James VI
TANTALLON CASTLE (HS), North Berwick, E. Lothian EH39 5PN T 01620-892727
Fortification with earthwork defences; 14th-century curtain wall with towers

THREAVE CASTLE (HS), Castle Douglas, Kirkcudbrightshire DG7 1TJ T 07711-223101
Late 14th-century tower on an island; accessible only by boat
URQUHART CASTLE (HS), Drumnadrochit, Inverness-shire IV63 6XJ T 01456-450551
13th-century castle remains on the banks of Loch Ness

NORTHERN IRELAND

For the Northern Ireland Environment Agency, the official website is www.doeni.gov.uk/niea
For more information on National Trust properties in Northern Ireland, including those listed below, the official website is www.nationaltrust.org.uk
(NIEA) Property in the care of the Northern Ireland Environment Agency
(NT) National Trust property

CARRICKFERGUS CASTLE (NIEA), Carrickfergus, Co. Antrim BT38 7BG T 028-9335 1273
Castle begun in 1180 and garrisoned until 1928
CASTLE COOLE (NT), Enniskillen, Co. Fermanagh BT74 6JY T 028-6632 2690
18th-century neoclassical mansion in parkland; designed by James Wyatt
CASTLE WARD (NT), Strangford, Co. Down BT30 7LS
T 028-4488 1204
18th-century house with Classical and Gothic facades
DEVENISH MONASTIC SITE (NIEA), nr Enniskillen, Co. Fermanagh
Island monastery founded in the sixth century by St Molaise
DOWNHILL DEMESNE AND HEZLETT HOUSE (NT), Castlerock, Co. Londonderry BT51 4RP
T 028-7084 8728
Ruins of palatial house in landscaped estate including Mussenden Temple
DUNLUCE CASTLE (NIEA), Bushmills, Co. Antrim BT57 8UY T 028-2073 1938
Ruins of 16th-century stronghold of the McDonnells
FLORENCE COURT (NT), Enniskillen, Co. Fermanagh BT92 1DB T 028-6634 8249
Mid-18th-century house with Rococo decoration
GREY ABBEY (NIEA), Greyabbey, Co. Down BT22 2NQ
T 028-9181 1491
Substantial remains of a Cistercian abbey founded in 1193
HILLSBOROUGH COURTHOUSE (NIEA), Hillsborough, Co. Down BT26 6AG T 028-9054 3030
Built in the 18th century; Hillsborough Fort is nearby
MOUNT STEWART (NT), Newtownards, Co. Down BT22 2AD T 028-4278 8387
18th-century house; childhood home of Lord Castlereagh; estate includes Temple of the Winds
NENDRUM MONASTIC SITE (NIEA), Mahee Island, Co. Down T 028-9054 3037
Island monastery founded in the fifth century by St Machaoi
PATTERSON'S SPADE MILL (NT), Templepatrick, Co. Antrim BT39 0AP T 028-9443 3619
An authentic water-driven spade mill
TULLY CASTLE (NIEA), Co. Fermanagh T 028-6862 1588
Fortified house and bawn built in 1613

MUSEUMS AND GALLERIES

There are approximately 2,500 museums and galleries in the United Kingdom. Around 1,400 of these are accredited by the Museums, Libraries and Archives Council (MLA), which indicates that they have an appropriate constitution, are soundly financed, have adequate collection management standards and public services, and have access to professional curatorial advice. A further 400 museums and galleries have applied for, or are in the process of obtaining accreditation, and these applications are assessed by either the relevant regional agency in England; Museums, Archives and Libraries Wales (CyMAL); Museums Galleries Scotland or the Northern Ireland Museums Council.

The following is a selection of museums and art galleries in the UK. Opening hours and admission charges vary. Further information about museums and galleries in the UK is available from the Museums Association (W www.museumsassociation.org T 020-7426 6910)

W www.culture24.org.uk includes a database of all the museums and galleries in the UK.

ENGLAND

* England's national museums and galleries, which receive funding from a government department, such as the DCMS or MOD. These institutions are deemed to have collections of national importance, and the government is able to call upon their staff for expert advice

BARNARD CASTLE
The Bowes Museum, Co. Durham DL12 8NP T 01833-690606
  W www.thebowesmuseum.org.uk
  European art from the late medieval period to the 19th century; music and costume galleries; English period rooms from Elizabeth I to Victoria; local archaeology

BATH
American Museum, Claverton Manor BA2 7BD
  T 01225-460503 W www.americanmuseum.org
  American decorative arts from the 17th to 19th centuries; American heritage exhibition
Fashion Museum, Bennett Street BA1 2QH T 01225-477173
  W www.museumofcostume.co.uk
  Fashion from the 18th century to the present day
Roman Baths Museum, Pump Room, Stall Street BA1 1LZ
  T 01225-477785 W www.romanbaths.co.uk
  Museum adjoins the remains of a Roman baths and temple complex
Victoria Art Gallery, Bridge Street BA2 4AT T 01225-477233
  W www.victoriagal.org.uk
  European Old Masters and British art since the 15th century

BEAMISH
Beamish Museum, Co. Durham DH9 0RG T 0191-370 4000
  W www.beamish.org.uk
  Northern town recreated in 1825 and 1913

BEAULIEU
National Motor Museum, Hants SO42 7ZN T 01590-614650
  W www.nationalmotormuseum.org.uk
  Displays of over 250 vehicles dating from 1895 to the present day

BIRMINGHAM
Aston Hall, Trinity Road B6 6JD T 0121-675 4722
  W www.bmag.org.uk
  Jacobean House containing paintings, furniture and tapestries from the 17th to 19th centuries
Barber Institute of Fine Arts, University of Birmingham, Edgbaston B15 2TS T 0121-414 7333 W www.barber.org.uk
  Fine arts, including Old Masters
Birmingham Museum and Art Gallery, Chamberlain Square B3 3DH T 0121-303 1966 W www.bmag.org.uk
  Includes notable collection of Pre-Raphaelite art
Museum of the Jewellery Quarter, Vyse Street, Hockley B18 6HA T 0121-554 3598 W www.bmag.org.uk
  Built around a real jewellery workshop

BOVINGTON
Tank Museum, Dorset BH20 6JG T 01929-405096
  W www.tankmuseum.org
  Collection of 200 tanks from the earliest days of tank warfare to the present

BRADFORD
Bradford Industrial Museum and Horses at Work, Moorside Road, Eccleshill BD2 3HP T 01274-435900
  W www.bradfordmuseums.org
  Engineering, textiles, transport and social history exhibits
Cartwright Hall Art Gallery, Lister Park BD9 4NS
  T 01274-431212 W www.bradfordmuseums.org
  British 19th- and 20th-century fine art
**National Media Museum*, Princes Way BD1 1NQ
  T 0870-701 0200 W www.nationalmediamuseum.org.uk
  Photography, film and television interactive exhibits; features an IMAX cinema and the only public Cinerama screen in Europe

BRIGHTON
Booth Museum of Natural History, Dyke Road BN1 5AA
  T 03000-290900 W www.brighton-hove-rpml.org.uk/Museums/boothmuseum
  Zoology, botany and geology collections; British birds in recreated habitats
Brighton Museum and Art Gallery, Royal Pavilion Gardens BN1 1EE T 03000-290900
  W www.brighton-hove-rpml.org.uk/Museums/brightonmuseum
  Includes fine art and design, fashion, non-Western art; Brighton history

BRISTOL
Arnolfini, Narrow Quay BS1 4QA T 0117-917 2300
  W www.arnolfini.org.uk
  Contemporary visual arts, dance, performance, music, talks and workshops
Blaise Castle House Museum, Henbury BS10 7QS
  T 0117-903 9818 W www.bristol-city.gov.uk/museums
  Agricultural and social history collections in an 18th-century mansion
City Museum and Art Gallery, Queen's Road BS8 1RL
  T 0117-922 3571 W www.bristol-city.gov.uk/museums
  Includes fine and decorative art, oriental art, Egyptology and Bristol ceramics and paintings
M Shed, Prince's Wharf BS1 4RN T 0117-352 6600
  W www.mshed.org
  The story of Bristol's heritage of engineering, transport, music and industry

CAMBRIDGE

Fitzwilliam Museum, Trumpington Street CB2 1RB
T 01223-332900 W www.fitzmuseum.cam.ac.uk
Antiquities, fine and applied arts, clocks, ceramics,
manuscripts, furniture, sculpture, coins and medals

*Imperial War Museum Duxford, Duxford CB22 4QR
T 01223-835000 W duxford.iwm.org.uk
Displays of military and civil aircraft, tanks, guns and
naval exhibits

Sedgwick Museum of Earth Sciences, Downing Street CB2 3EQ
T 01223-333456 W www.sedgwickmuseum.org
Extensive geological collection

University Museum of Archaeology and Anthropology,
Downing Street CB2 3DZ T 01223-333516
W www.maa.cam.ac.uk
Due to reopen in 2012, extensive global archaeological
and anthropological collections

University Museum of Zoology, Downing Street CB2 3EJ
T 01223-336650 W www.museum.zoo.cam.ac.uk
Extensive zoological collection

Whipple Museum of the History of Science, Free School Lane
CB2 3RH T 01223-330906 W www.hps.cam.ac.uk/whipple
Scientific instruments from the 14th century to the
present

CARLISLE

Tullie House Museum and Art Gallery, Castle Street CA3 8TP
T 01228-618718 W www.tulliehouse.co.uk
Prehistoric archaeology, Hadrian's Wall, Viking and
medieval Cumbria, and the social history of Carlisle

CHATHAM

The Historic Dockyard, ME4 4TZ T 01634-823800
W www.thedockyard.co.uk
Maritime attractions including HMS *Cavalier*, the UK's
last Second World War destroyer

Royal Engineers Museum and Library, Prince Arthur Road,
Gillingham ME4 4UG T 01634-822839
W www.remuseum.org.uk
Regimental history, ethnography, decorative art and
photography

CHELTENHAM

Art Gallery and Museum, Clarence Street GL50 3JT
T 01242-237431 W www.cheltenhammuseum.org.uk
Paintings, arts and crafts

CHESTER

Grosvenor Museum, Grosvenor Street CH1 2DD
T 01244-402033 W www.cheshirewestandchester.gov.uk/
visiting
Roman collections, natural history, art, Chester silver,
local history and costume

CHICHESTER

Weald and Downland Open Air Museum, Singleton
PO18 0EU T 01243-811348 W www.wealddown.co.uk
Rebuilt vernacular buildings from south-east England;
includes medieval houses, agricultural and rural craft
buildings and a working watermill

COLCHESTER

Colchester Castle Museum, Castle Park CO1 1TJ
T 01206-282939 W www.colchestermuseums.org.uk
Largest Norman keep in Europe standing on
foundations of the Roman Temple of Claudius; tours
of the Roman vaults, castle walls and chapel

COVENTRY

Coventry Transport Museum, Hales Street CV1 1JD
T 024-7623 4270 W www.transport-museum.com
Hundreds of motor vehicles and bicycles

Herbert Art Gallery and Museum, Jordan Well CV1 5QP
T 024-7683 2386 W www.theherbert.org
Local history, archaeology and industry, and fine and
decorative art

DERBY

Derby Museum and Art Gallery, The Strand DE1 1BS
T 01332-641901 W www.derby.gov.uk/museums
Includes paintings by Joseph Wright of Derby and
Derby porcelain

Pickford's House Museum, Friar Gate DE1 1DA
T 01332-715181 W www.derby.gov.uk/museums
Georgian town house by architect Joseph Pickford;
museum of Georgian life and costume

The Silk Mill, Derby's Museum of Industry and History,
Silk Mill Lane DE1 3AF T 01332-642234
W www.derby.gov.uk/museums
Rolls-Royce aero engine collection and railway
engineering gallery; on the site of two silk mills built
in the early 1700s

DEVIZES

Wiltshire Heritage Museum, Long Street SN10 1NS
T 01380-727369 W www.wiltshireheritage.org.uk
Natural and local history; art gallery; archaeological
finds from prehistoric, Roman and Saxon sites

DORCHESTER

Dorset County Museum, High West Street DT1 1XA
T 01305-262735 W www.dorsetcountymuseum.org
Includes a collection of Thomas Hardy's manuscripts,
books, notebooks and drawings; local history, geology
and Roman mosaics

DOVER

Dover Museum, Market Square CT16 1PB T 01304-201066
W www.dover.gov.uk/museum
Contains the Dover Bronze Age Boat Gallery and
archaeological finds from Bronze Age, Roman and
Saxon sites

EXETER

Royal Albert Memorial Museum and Art Gallery,
Queen Street EX4 3RX T 01392-665858
W www.rammuseum.org.uk
Natural history, archaeology, worldwide fine and
decorative art including Exeter silver

GATESHEAD

Baltic Centre for Contemporary Art, South Shore Road
NE8 3BA T 0191-478 1810 W www.balticmill.com
Contemporary art exhibitions and events

Shipley Art Gallery, Prince Consort Road NE8 4JB
T 0191-477 1495 W www.twmuseums.org.uk/shipley
Contemporary crafts

GAYDON

Heritage Motor Centre, Banbury Road, Warks CV35 0BJ
T 01926-641188 W www.heritage-motor-centre.co.uk
History of British motor industry from 1895 to
present; classic vehicles; engineering gallery; Corgi
and Lucas collections

GLOUCESTER

Gloucester Waterways Museum, Gloucester Docks GL1 2EH
T 01452-318200
W www.gloucesterwaterwaysmuseum.org.uk
Two-hundred-year history of Britain's canals and
inland waterways

GOSPORT

Royal Navy Submarine Museum, Haslar Jetty Road, Hants
PO12 2AS T 023-9251 0354 W www.submarine-
museum.co.uk
Underwater warfare, including the submarine *Alliance*;
first Royal Navy submarine

GRASMERE

Dove Cottage and the *Wordsworth Museum*, Cumbria
LA22 9SH T 01539-435544 W www.wordsworth.org.uk
William Wordsworth's manuscripts, home and
garden

HULL
Ferens Art Gallery, Queen Victoria Square HU1 3RA
T 01482-300300 W www.hullcc.gov.uk
European art, especially Dutch 17th-century paintings, British portraits from 17th to 20th centuries, and marine paintings
Hull Maritime Museum, Queen Victoria Square HU1 3DX
T 01482-300300 W www.hullcc.gov.uk
Whaling, fishing and navigation exhibits
HUNTINGDON
The Cromwell Museum, Grammar School Walk PE29 3LF
T 01480-375830 W www.cambridgeshire.gov.uk/cromwell
Portraits and memorabilia relating to Oliver Cromwell
IPSWICH
Christchurch Mansion and *Wolsey Art Gallery*, Soane Street IP4 2BE T 01473-433554 W www.ipswich.gov.uk
Tudor house with paintings by Gainsborough, Constable and other Suffolk artists; furniture and 18th-century ceramics; temporary exhibitions
KESWICK
Pencil Museum, Southey Works CA12 5NG T 017687-73626
W www.pencilmuseum.co.uk
500-year history of the pencil; demonstration events and workshops throughout the year
LEEDS
Armley Mills, Leeds Industrial Museum, Canal Road, Armley LS12 2QF T 0113-263 7861
W www.leeds.gov.uk/armleymills
World's largest woollen mill, now a museum for textiles, clothing and engine manufacture
Leeds City Art Gallery, The Headrow LS1 3AA
T 0113-247 8256 W www.leeds.gov.uk/artgallery
Includes English watercolours; modern sculpture; Henry Moore gallery; print room
Lotherton Hall, Aberford LS25 3EB T 0113-281 3259
W www.leeds.gov.uk/lothertonhall
Costume, ceramics and furniture collections in furnished Edwardian house; deer park and bird garden
Royal Armouries Museum, Armouries Drive LS10 1LT
T 0113-220 1999 W www.royalarmouries.org
National collection of arms and armour from BC to present; demonstrations of foot combat in museum's five galleries; falconry and mounted combat in the tiltyard
Temple Newsam, LS15 0AE T 0113-264 5535
W www.leeds.gov.uk/templenewsam
Old Masters and 17th- and 18th-century decorative art in furnished Jacobean/Tudor house
LEICESTER
Jewry Wall Museum, St Nicholas Circle LE1 4LB
T 0116-225 4971 W www.leicester.gov.uk
Archaeology; Roman Jewry Wall and baths; mosaics
New Walk Museum and Art Gallery, 53 New Walk LE1 7EA
T 0116-255 4900 W www.leicester.gov.uk
Natural history and geology; ancient Egypt gallery; European art and decorative arts
LINCOLN
The Collection, Danes Terrace LN2 1LP T 01522-550990
W www.lincolnshire.gov.uk
Artefacts from the Stone Age to the Viking and Medieval eras; adjacent art gallery with decorative and contemporary visual arts
Museum of Lincolnshire Life, Burton Road LN1 3LY
T 01522-528448 W www.lincolnshire.gov.uk
Social history and agricultural collection
LIVERPOOL
International Slavery Museum, Albert Dock L3 4AX
T 0151-478 4499 W www.liverpoolmuseums.org.uk/ism

Explores historical and contemporary aspects of slavery
Lady Lever Art Gallery, Wirral CH62 5EQ T 0151-478 4136
W www.liverpoolmuseums.org.uk/ladylever
Paintings, furniture and porcelain
Merseyside Maritime Museum, Albert Dock L3 4AQ
T 0151-478 4499
W www.liverpoolmuseums.org.uk/maritime
Floating exhibits, working displays and craft demonstrations; incorporates *HM Customs and Excise National Museum*
Museum of Liverpool, Pier Head L3 1PZ
T 0151-478 4499 W www.liverpoolmuseums.org.uk/mol
Formerly the *Museum of Liverpool Life*; explores the significance of the city's geography, history and culture
Sudley House, Mossley Hill Road L18 8BX T 0151-724 3245
W www.liverpoolmuseums.org.uk/sudley
Late 18th- and 19th-century paintings in former shipowner's home
Tate Liverpool, Albert Dock L3 4BB T 0151-702 7400
W www.tate.org.uk/liverpool
Twentieth-century paintings and sculpture
Walker Art Gallery, William Brown Street L3 8EL
T 0151-478 4199 W www.liverpoolmuseums.org.uk/walker
Paintings from the 13th to 20th centuries
World Museum Liverpool, William Brown Street L3 8EN
T 0151-478 4393 W www.liverpoolmuseums.org.uk/wml
Includes Egyptian mummies, weapons and classical sculpture; planetarium, aquarium, vivarium and natural history centre
LONDON: GALLERIES
Barbican Art Gallery, Barbican Centre, Silk Street EC2Y 8DS
T 020-7638 4141 W www.barbican.org.uk
Temporary exhibitions
Courtauld Institute of Art Gallery, Somerset House, Strand WC2R 0RN T 020-7848 2526 W www.courtauld.ac.uk
Impressionist and post-impressionist paintings
Dulwich Picture Gallery, Gallery Road, Dulwich Village SE21 7AD T 020-8693 5254
W www.dulwichpicturegallery.org.uk
England's first public art gallery; designed by Sir John Soane to house 17th- and 18th-century paintings
Estorick Collection of Modern Italian Art, Canonbury Square N1 2AN T 020-7704 9522 W www.estorickcollection.com
Early 20th-century Italian drawings, paintings, sculptures and etchings, with an emphasis on Futurism
Hayward Gallery, Belvedere Road SE1 8XX T 020-7960 4200
W www.southbankcentre.co.uk
Temporary exhibitions
National Gallery, Trafalgar Square WC2N 5DN
T 020-7747 2885 W www.nationalgallery.org.uk
Western painting from the 13th to 19th centuries; early Renaissance collection in the Sainsbury Wing
National Portrait Gallery, St Martin's Place WC2H 0HE
T 020-7306 0055 W www.npg.org.uk
Portraits of eminent people in British history
Photographers' Gallery, Ramillies Street W1F 7LW
T 0845-262 1618 W www.photonet.org.uk
Temporary exhibitions
The Queen's Gallery, Buckingham Palace SW1A 1AA
T 020-7766 7301 W www.royalcollection.org.uk
Art from the Royal Collection
Royal Academy of Arts, Burlington House, Piccadilly W1J 0BD
T 020-7300 8000 W www.royalacademy.org.uk
British art since 1750 and temporary exhibitions; annual Summer Exhibition

Saatchi Gallery, Duke of York's HQ, King's Road, SW3 4SQ
T 020-7823 2363 W www.saatchi-gallery.co.uk
Contemporary art including paintings, photographs, sculpture and installations

Serpentine Gallery, Kensington Gardens W2 3XA
T 020-7402 6075 W www.serpentinegallery.org
Temporary exhibitions of British and international contemporary art

*Tate Britain, Millbank SW1P 4RG T 020-7887 8888
W www.tate.org.uk/britain
British painting and 20th-century painting and sculpture

*Tate Modern, Bankside SE1 9TG T 020-7887 8888
W www.tate.org.uk/modern
International modern art from 1900 to the present

*Wallace Collection, Manchester Square W1U 3BN
T 020-7563 9500 W www.wallacecollection.org
Paintings and drawings, French 18th-century furniture, armour, porcelain, clocks and sculpture

Whitechapel Art Gallery, Whitechapel High Street E1 7QX
T 020-7522 7888 W www.whitechapel.org
Temporary exhibitions of modern art

LONDON: MUSEUMS

Bank of England Museum, Threadneedle Street EC2R 8AH
(entrance on Bartholomew Lane) T 020-7601 5545
W www.bankofengland.co.uk/museum
History of the Bank of England since 1694

*British Museum, Great Russell Street WC1B 3DG
T 020-7323 8000 W www.thebritishmuseum.org
Antiquities, coins, medals, prints and drawings; temporary exhibitions; home of the Sir Percival David collection of Chinese ceramics

Brunel Museum, Rotherhithe SE16 4LF T 020-7231 3840
W www.brunel-museum.org.uk
Explores the engineering achievements of Isambard Kingdom Brunel and his father, Marc Brunel

*Churchill War Rooms, King Charles Street SW1A 2AQ
T 020-7930 6961 W cwr.iwm.org.uk
Underground rooms used by Churchill and the government during the Second World War

Cutty Sark, Greenwich SE10 9BG T 020-8858 2698
W www.cuttysark.org.uk
The world's last remaining tea clipper due to reopen in spring 2012 with new exhibitions

Design Museum, Shad Thames SE1 2YD T 020-7940 8790
W www.designmuseum.org
The development of design and the mass-production of consumer objects

Firepower, the Royal Artillery Museum, Royal Arsenal, Woolwich SE18 6ST T 020-8855 7755
W www.firepower.org.uk
The history and development of artillery over the last 700 years including the collections of the Royal Regiment of Artillery

Garden Museum, Lambeth Palace Road SE1 7LB
T 020-7401 8865 W www.gardenmuseum.org.uk
History and development of gardens and gardening; temporary exhibitions, symposia and events

Geffrye Museum, Kingsland Road E2 8EA T 020-7739 9893
W www.geffrye-museum.org.uk
English urban domestic interiors from 1600 to the present day; also paintings, furniture, decorative arts, walled herb garden and period garden rooms

*HMS Belfast, Morgan's Lane, Tooley Street SE1 2JH
T 020-7940 6300 W hmsbelfast.iwm.org.uk
Life on a Second World War cruiser

*Horniman Museum, London Road SE23 3PQ
T 020-8699 1872 W www.horniman.ac.uk
Museum of anthropology, musical instruments and natural history; aquarium; reference library; gardens

*Imperial War Museum, Lambeth Road SE1 6HZ
T 020-7416 5320 W www.iwm.org.uk
All aspects of the two World Wars and other military operations involving Britain and the Commonwealth since 1914

Jewish Museum, Albert Street NW1 7NB T 020-7284 7384
W www.jewishmuseum.org.uk
Jewish life, history and religion

London Metropolitan Archives , Northampton Road EC1R
OHB T 020-7332 3820 W www.cityoflondon.gov.uk/lma
Material on the history of London and its people dating 1067–2006

London Transport Museum, Covent Garden Piazza WC2E 7BB
T 020-7379 6344 W www.ltmuseum.co.uk
Vehicles, photographs and graphic art relating to the history of transport in London

MCC Museum, Lord's, St John's Wood NW8 8QN
T 020-7616 8656 W www.lords.org/mcc
Cricket museum; guided tours by appointment

Museum in Docklands, West India Quay, Hertsmere Road
E14 4AL T 020-7001 9844
W www.museumindocklands.org.uk
Explores the story of London's river, port and people over 2,000 years, from Roman times through to the recent regeneration of London's Docklands

*Museum of Childhood at Bethnal Green (V&A),
Cambridge Heath Road E2 9PA T 020-8983 5200
W www.vam.ac.uk/moc
Toys, games and exhibits relating to the social history of childhood

*Museum of London, London Wall EC2Y 5HN
T 020-7001 9844 W www.museumoflondon.org.uk
History of London from prehistoric times to the present day

National Archives Museum, Kew TW9 4DU T 020-8876 3444
W www.nationalarchives.gov.uk
Displays treasures from the archives, including the Domesday Book and Magna Carta

*National Army Museum, Royal Hospital Road SW3 4HT
T 020-7730 0717 W www.national-army-museum.ac.uk
Five-hundred-year history of the British soldier; exhibits include model of the Battle of Waterloo and recreated First World War trench

*National Maritime Museum, Greenwich SE10 9NF
T 020-8858 4422 W www.nmm.ac.uk
Maritime history of Britain; collections include globes, clocks, telescopes and paintings; comprises the main building, the Royal Observatory and the Queen's House

*Natural History Museum, Cromwell Road SW7 5BD
T 020-7942 5000 W www.nhm.ac.uk
Natural history collections and interactive Darwin Centre

Petrie Museum of Egyptian Archaeology, University College
London, Malet Place WC1E 6BT T 020-7679 2884
W www.ucl.ac.uk/museums/petrie
Egyptian archaeology collection

*Royal Air Force Museum, Hendon NW9 5LL
T 020-8205 2266 W www.rafmuseum.org.uk
Aviation from before the Wright brothers to the present-day RAF

Royal Mews, Buckingham Palace SW1A 1AA T 020-7766 7302
W www.royalcollection.org.uk
State vehicles, including the Queen's gold state coach; home to the Queen's horses

Science Museum, Exhibition Road SW7 2DD T 0870 870 4868
W www.sciencemuseum.org.uk

Science, technology, industry and medicine collections; children's interactive gallery; IMAX cinema

Shakespeare's Globe Exhibition, Bankside SE1 9DT
T 020-7902 1400 W www.shakespearesglobe.com

Recreation of Elizabethan theatre using 16th-century techniques; includes a tour of the theatre

Sir John Soane's Museum, Lincoln's Inn Fields WC2A 3BP
T 020-7405 2107 W www.soane.org

Art and antiquities collected by Soane throughout his lifetime; house designed by Soane

Tower Bridge Experience, SE1 2UP T 020-7403 3761
W www.towerbridge.org.uk

History of the bridge and display of Victorian steam machinery; panoramic views from walkways

Victoria and Albert Museum, Cromwell Road SW7 2RL
T 020-7942 2000 W www.vam.ac.uk

Includes National Art Library and Print Room; fine and applied art and design; furniture, glass, textiles, theatre and dress collections

Wellcome Collection, Euston Road NW1 2BE
T 020-7611 2222 W www.wellcomecollection.org

Contemporary and historic exhibitions and collections including the Wellcome Library

Wimbledon Lawn Tennis Museum, Church Road SW19 5AE
T 020-8946 6131 W www.wimbledon.com/visiting/museum

Tennis trophies, fashion and memorabilia; view of Centre Court

MALTON

Eden Camp, N. Yorks YO17 6RT T 01653-697777
W www.edencamp.co.uk

Restored POW camp and Second World War memorabilia

MANCHESTER

Gallery of Costume, Platt Hall, Rusholme M14 5LL
T 0161-245 7245 W www.manchestergalleries.org

Exhibits from the 17th century to the present day

Imperial War Museum North, Trafford Wharf Road M17 1TZ
T 0161-836 4000 W north.iwm.org.uk

History of war in the 20th and 21st centuries

Manchester Art Gallery, Mosley Street M2 3JL
T 0161-235 8888 W www.manchestergalleries.org

Six centuries of European fine and decorative art

Manchester Museum, Oxford Road M13 9PL T 0161-275 2634
W www.museum.manchester.ac.uk

Collections include archaeology, decorative arts, Egyptology, natural history and zoology

Museum of Science and Industry, Liverpool Road, Castlefield
M3 4FP T 0161-832 2244 W www.mosi.org.uk

On site of world's oldest passenger railway station; galleries relating to space, energy, power, transport, aviation, textiles and social history

National Football Museum, Cathedral Gardens M4 3BG
T 0161-870 9275 W www.nationalfootballmuseum.com

Home to the FIFA, FA and Football League collections including the 1966 World Cup final ball

People's History Museum, Left Bank, Spinningfields M3 3ER
T 0161-838 9190 W www.phm.org.uk

British political and working life history

Whitworth Art Gallery, Oxford Road M15 6ER
T 0161-275 7450 W www.whitworth.manchester.ac.uk

Watercolours, drawings, prints, textiles, wallpapers and British art

MILTON KEYNES

Bletchley Park National Codes Centre, Bucks MK3 6EB
T 01908-640404 W www.bletchleypark.org.uk

Home of British codebreaking during the Second World War; Enigma machine; computer museum; wartime toys and memorabilia

MONKWEARMOUTH

Monkwearmouth Station Museum, North Bridge Street, Sunderland SR5 1AP T 0191-567 7075
W www.twmuseums.org.uk/monkwearmouth

Victorian train station; interactive galleries

NEWCASTLE UPON TYNE

Discovery Museum, Blandford Square NE1 4JA
T 0191-232 6789 W www.twmuseums.org.uk/discovery

Science and industry, local history, fashion; Tyneside's maritime history; *Turbinia* (first steam-driven vessel) gallery

Great North Museum: Hancock, Barras Bridge NE2 4PT
T 0191-222 6765
W www.twmuseums.org.uk/greatnorthmuseum

Natural history and ancient history

Laing Art Gallery, New Bridge Street NE1 8AG
T 0191-232 7734 W www.twmuseums.org.uk/laing

18th- and 19th-century collection; watercolour gallery

NEWMARKET

National Horseracing Museum, High Street CB8 8JH
T 01638-667333 W www.nhrm.co.uk

The story of people and horses involved in racing; temporary exhibitions

NORTH SHIELDS

Stephenson Railway Museum, Middle Engine Lane NE29 8DX
T 0191-200 7146 W www.twmuseums.org.uk/stephenson

Locomotive engines and rolling stock

NOTTINGHAM

Castle Museum and Art Gallery, Friar Lane NG1 6EL
T 0115-915 3700 W www.nottinghamcity.gov.uk

Paintings, ceramics, silver and glass; history of Nottingham

Museum of Nottingham Life, Brewhouse Yard, Castle Boulevard NG7 1FB T 0115-915 3600
W www.nottinghamcity.gov.uk

Social history from the 17th to 20th centuries

Natural History Museum, Wollaton Hall, Wollaton NG8 2AE
T 0115-915 3900 W www.nottinghamcity.gov.uk

Local natural history and wildlife dioramas

OXFORD

Ashmolean Museum, Beaumont Street OX1 2PH
T 01865-278000 W www.ashmolean.org

European and Oriental fine and applied arts, archaeology, Egyptology and numismatics

Modern Art Oxford, Pembroke Street OX1 1BP
T 01865-722733 W www.modernartoxford.org.uk

Temporary exhibitions

Museum of the History of Science, Broad Street OX1 3AZ
T 01865-277280 W www.mhs.ox.ac.uk

Displays include early scientific instruments, chemical apparatus, clocks and watches

Oxford University Museum of Natural History, Parks Road
OX1 3PW T 01865-272950 W www.oum.ox.ac.uk

Entomology, geology, mineralogy and zoology

Pitt Rivers Museum, South Parks Road OX1 3PP
T 01865-270927 W www.prm.ox.ac.uk

Ethnographic and archaeological artefacts

PLYMOUTH

City Museum and Art Gallery, Drake Circus PL4 8AJ
T 01752-304774 W www.plymouthmuseum.gov.uk

Local and natural history; ceramics; silver; Old Masters; world artefacts; temporary exhibitions

PORTSMOUTH
Charles Dickens Birthplace, Old Commercial Road PO1 4QL
T 023-9282 7261 W www.charlesdickensbirthplace.co.uk
Dickens memorabilia
D-Day Museum, Clarence Esplanade, Southsea PO5 3NT
T 023-9282 7261 W www.ddaymuseum.co.uk
Includes the Overlord embroidery
Portsmouth Historic Dockyard, HM Naval Base PO1 3LJ
T 023-9283 9766 W www.historicdockyard.co.uk
Incorporates the *Royal Naval Museum* (PO1 3NH
T 023-9272 7562 W www.royalnavalmuseum.org), *HMS
Victory* (PO1 3NH T 023-9272 3111
W www.hms-victory.com), *HMS Warrior* (PO1 3QX
T 023-9277 8600 W www.hmswarrior.org), the *Mary Rose*
(PO1 3LX T 023-9281 2931 W www.maryrose.org) and
Action Stations (PO1 3LJ T 023-9289 3338
W www.actionstations.org)
History of the Royal Navy and of the dockyard;
warships and technology spanning 500 years
PRESTON
Harris Museum and Art Gallery, Market Square PR1 2PP
T 01772-258248 W www.harrismuseum.org.uk
British art since the 18th century; ceramics, glass,
costume and local history; contemporary exhibitions
ST ALBANS
Verulamium Museum, St Michael's Street AL3 4SW
T 01727-751810 W www.stalbansmuseums.org.uk
Remains of Iron Age settlement and the third-largest
city in Roman Britain; exhibits include Roman wall
plasters, jewellery, mosaics and room reconstructions
ST IVES
Tate St Ives, Porthmeor Beach, Cornwall TR26 1TG
T 01736-796226 W www.tate.org.uk/stives
Modern art, much by artists associated with St Ives;
includes the Barbara Hepworth Museum and Sculpture
Garden
SALISBURY
Salisbury & South Wiltshire Museum, The Close SP1 2EN
T 01722-332151 W www.salisburymuseum.org.uk
Archaeology collection
SHEFFIELD
Graves Art Gallery, Surrey Street S1 1XZ T 0114-278 2600
W www.museums-sheffield.org.uk
Twentieth-century British art, Grice Collection of
Chinese ivories
Millennium Galleries, Arundel Gate S1 2PP T 0114-278 2600
W www.museums-sheffield.org.uk
Incorporates four different galleries: the Special
Exhibition Gallery, the Craft and Design Gallery, the
Metalwork Gallery and the Ruskin Gallery, which
houses John Ruskin's collection of paintings, drawings,
books and medieval manuscripts
Weston Park Museum, Western Bank S10 2TP
T 0114-278 2600 W www.museums-sheffield.org.uk
World history for families
SOUTHAMPTON
City Art Gallery, Commercial Road SO14 7LP
T 023-8083 2277 W www.southampton.gov.uk/art
Fine art collection spanning six centuries of European
art
Maritime Museum, Town Quay Road SO14 2AR
T 023-8083 2706 W www.southampton.gov.uk
Southampton maritime history; Titanic exhibition
Museum of Archaeology (God's House Tower), Winkle Street
SO14 2NY T 023-8091 5732 W www.southampton.gov.uk
Roman, Saxon and medieval archaeology
Tudor House Museum and Garden, Bugle Street SO14 2AD
T 023-8063 5904 W www.southampton.gov.uk

Story of the 15th-century house and the people who
lived and worked in it
SOUTH SHIELDS
Arbeia Roman Fort, Baring Street NE33 2BB T 0191-456 1369
W www.twmuseums.org.uk/arbeia
Excavated ruins; reconstructions of original buildings
South Shields Museum and Art Gallery, Ocean Road
NE33 2JA T 0191-456 8740
W www.twmuseums.org.uk/southshields
South Tyneside history; interactive art gallery
STOKE-ON-TRENT
Etruria Industrial Museum, Lower Bedford Street ST4 7AF
T 01782-233144 W www.stokemuseums.org.uk/eim
Britain's sole surviving steam-powered potter's
mill
Gladstone Pottery Museum, Longton ST3 1PQ
T 01782-237777 W www.stokemuseums.org.uk/gpm
A working Victorian pottery
Potteries Museum and Art Gallery, Bethesda Street ST1 3DW
T 01782-232323 W www.stokemuseums.org.uk/pmag
Pottery, china and porcelain collections and a
Mark XVI Spitfire
The Wedgwood Museum, Barlaston ST12 9ER
T 01782-371900 W www.wedgwoodmuseum.org.uk
The story of Josiah Wedgwood and the company
he founded
SUNDERLAND
Sunderland Museum & Winter Gardens, Burdon Road
SR1 1PP T 0191-553 2323
W www.twmuseums.org.uk/sunderland
Fine and decorative art, local history and gardens
TELFORD
Ironbridge Gorge Museums, TF8 7DQ T 01952-433424
W www.ironbridge.org.uk
World's first iron bridge; Blists Hill (late Victorian
working town); Museum of Iron; Jackfield Tile
Museum; Coalport China Museum; Tar Tunnel;
Broseley Pipeworks
WAKEFIELD
Hepworth Wakefield, Gallery Walk WF1 5AW
T 01924-247360 W www.hepworthwakefield.org
Historic and modern art, temporary exhibitions of
contemporary art
National Coal Mining Museum for England, Overton
WF4 4RH T 01924-848806 W www.ncm.org.uk
Includes underground tours of one of Britain's oldest
working mines
Yorkshire Sculpture Park, West Bretton WF4 4LG
T 01924-832631 W www.ysp.co.uk
Open-air sculpture gallery including works by Moore,
Hepworth, Frink and others in 202 hectares
(500 acres) of parkland
WEYBRIDGE
Brooklands Museum, KT13 0QN T 01932-857381
W www.brooklandsmuseum.com
Birthplace of British motorsport; world's first
purpose-built motor racing circuit
WILMSLOW
Quarry Bank Mill, Styal SK9 4LA T 01625-527468
W www.quarrybankmill.org.uk
Working mill owned by the National Trust illustrating
history of cotton industry; costumed guides at restored
Apprentice House
WINCHESTER
INTECH, Telegraph Way, Hampshire SO21 1HZ
T 01962-863791 W www.intech-uk.com
Interactive science centre and planetarium

WORCESTER
City Art Gallery and Museum, Foregate Street WR1 1DT
  T 01905-25371 W www.worcestercitymuseums.org.uk
  Includes a military museum, 19th-century chemist
  shop and changing art exhibitions
Museum of Worcester Porcelain, Severn Street WR1 2ND
  T 01905-21247 W www.worcesterporcelainmuseum.org.uk
  Worcester porcelain from 1751 to the present day
YEOVIL
Fleet Air Arm Museum, Royal Naval Air Station, Yeovilton,
  Somerset BA22 8HT T 01935-840565
  W www.fleetairarm.com
  History of naval aviation; historic aircraft, including
  Concorde 002
YORK
Beningbrough Hall, Beningbrough YO30 1DD
  T 01904-472027 W www.nationaltrust.org.uk
  18th-century house with portraits from the National
  Portrait Gallery
JORVIK Viking Centre, Coppergate YO1 9WT
  T 01904-615505 W www.jorvik-viking-centre.co.uk
  Reconstruction of Viking York based on archaeological
  evidence
National Railway Museum, Leeman Road YO26 4XJ
  T 0844-815 3139 W www.nrm.org.uk
  Includes locomotives, rolling stock and carriages
York Art Gallery, Exhibition Square YO1 7EW
  T 01904-687687 W www.yorkartgallery.org.uk
  European and British painting spanning seven
  centuries; modern pottery; decorative arts
York Castle Museum, Eye of York YO1 9RY T 01904-687687
  W www.yorkcastlemuseum.org.uk
  Reconstructed streets and rooms; costume and military
  collections
Yorkshire Museum & Gardens, Museum Gardens YO1 7FR
  T 01904-687687 W www.yorkshiremuseum.org.uk
  Yorkshire life from Roman to medieval times; geology
  and biology; York observatory

WALES

* Members of National Museum Wales, a public body that
receives its funding through grant-in-aid from the Welsh
Assembly

ABERYSTWYTH
Ceredigion Museum, Terrace Road SY23 2AQ T 01970-633088
  W www.ceredigion.gov.uk
  Local history, housed in a restored Edwardian theatre
Llywernog Silver-Lead Mine, Ponterwyd
  SY23 3AB T 01970-890620 W www.silverminetours.co.uk
  Tours of an 18th-century silver mine, exhibitions
  containing artefacts used therein
BLAENAFON
Big Pit National Coal Museum, Torfaen NP4 9XP
  T 01495-790311 W www.museumwales.ac.uk
  Colliery with underground tour
BODELWYDDAN
Bodelwyddan Castle, Denbighshire LL18 5UY T 01745-584060
  W www.bodelwyddan-castle.co.uk
  Portraits from the National Portrait Gallery; furniture
  from the Victoria and Albert Museum; sculptures from
  the Royal Academy
CAERLEON
National Roman Legion Museum, NP18 1AE
  T 01633-423134 W www.museumwales.ac.uk
  Material from the site of the Roman fortress of Isca and
  its suburbs

CARDIFF
National Museum Cardiff, Cathays Park CF10 3NP
  T 029-2039 7951 W www.museumwales.ac.uk
  Includes natural sciences, archaeology and
  Impressionist paintings
St Fagans: National History Museum, St Fagans CF5 6XB
  T 029-2057 3500 W www.museumwales.ac.uk
  Open-air museum with re-erected buildings,
  agricultural equipment and costume
TECHNIQUEST, Stuart Street CF10 5BW T 029-2047 5475
  W www.techniquest.org
  Interactive science exhibits, planetarium and science
  theatre
CRICCIETH
Lloyd George Museum, Llanystumdwy LL52 0SH
  T 01766-522071 W www.gwynedd.gov.uk
  Childhood home of David Lloyd George; museum
  commemorates his life
DRE-FACH FELINDRE
National Wool Museum, nr Llandysul SA44 5UP
  T 01559-370929 W www.museumwales.ac.uk
  Exhibitions, a working woollen mill and craft
  workshops
LLANBERIS
National Slate Museum, Gwynedd LL55 4TY
  T 01286-870630 W www.museumwales.ac.uk
  Former slate quarry with original machinery and plant;
  slate crafts demonstrations; working waterwheel
LLANDRINDOD WELLS
National Cycle Collection, Automobile Palace, Temple Street
  LD1 5DL T 01597-825531 W www.cyclemuseum.org.uk
  Over 200 bicycles on display, from 1819–present
PRESTEIGNE
Judge's Lodging Museum, Broad Street LD8 2AD
  T 01544-260650 W www.judgeslodging.org.uk
  Restored apartments, courtroom, cells and servants'
  quarters
SWANSEA
Glynn Vivian Art Gallery, Alexandra Road SA1 5DZ
  T 01792-516900 W www.swansea.gov.uk/glynnvivian
  Paintings, ceramics, Swansea pottery and porcelain,
  clocks, glass and Welsh art
National Waterfront Museum, Oystermouth Road SA1 3RD
  T 01792-638950 W www.museumwales.ac.uk
  Wales during the Industrial Revolution
Swansea Museum, Victoria Road SA1 1SN T 01792-653763
  W www.swansea.gov.uk/swanseamuseum
  Archaeology, social history, Swansea pottery
TENBY
Tenby Museum and Art Gallery, Castle Hill SA70 7BP
  T 01834-842809 W www.tenbymuseum.org.uk
  Local archaeology, history, geology and art

SCOTLAND

* Members of National Museums of Scotland or National
Galleries of Scotland, which are non-departmental public bodies
funded by, and accountable to, the Scottish government

ABERDEEN
Aberdeen Art Gallery, Schoolhill AB10 1FQ T 01224-523700
  W www.aagm.co.uk
  Paintings, sculptures and graphics from the 15th
  century to the present day
Aberdeen Maritime Museum, Shiprow AB11 5BY
  T 01224-337700 W www.aagm.co.uk
  Maritime history, including shipbuilding and
  North Sea oil

DUMFRIES
*National Museum of Costume, New Abbey DG2 8HQ
T 0300-123 6789 W www.nms.ac.uk/costume
History of fashion from the 1850s to the 20th century
EDINBURGH
Britannia, Leith EH6 6JJ T 0131-555 5566
W www.royalyachtbritannia.co.uk
Former royal yacht with royal barge and royal family
picture gallery
City Art Centre, Market Street EH1 1DE T 0131-529 3993
W www.edinburghmuseums.org.uk
Scottish late 19th- and 20th-century art, worldwide
collections and temporary exhibitions
*Modern Art Galleries, 75 Belford Road EH4 3DR
T 0131-624 6200 W www.nationalgalleries.org
Includes the Gallery of Modern Art and the Dean Gallery
Museum of Childhood, High Street EH1 1TG T 0131-529 4142
W www.edinburghmuseums.org.uk
Toys, games, clothes and exhibits relating to the social
history of childhood
Museum of Edinburgh, Canongate EH8 8DD
T 0131-529 4143 W www.edinburghmuseums.org.uk
Local history, silver, glass and Scottish pottery
*Museum of Flight, East Fortune Airfield, East Lothian
EH39 5LF T 0300-123 6789 W www.nms.ac.uk/flight
Display of aircraft
*National Gallery Complex, The Mound EH2 2EL
T 0131-624 6200 W www.nationalgalleries.org
Paintings, drawings and prints from the early
Renaissance to the end of the 19th century
*National Museum of Scotland, Chambers Street EH1 1JF
T 0131-225 7534 W www.nms.ac.uk/scotland
Scottish history from prehistoric to present day
through 16 galleries
*National War Museum of Scotland, Edinburgh Castle
EH1 2NG T 0300-123 6789 W www.nms.ac.uk/war
History of Scottish military and conflicts
*Scottish National Portrait Gallery, Queen Street EH2 1JD
T 0131-624 6200 W www.nationalgalleries.org
Due to reopen in late 2011: portraits of eminent people
in Scottish history; the national collection of
photography
The Writers' Museum, Lawnmarket EH1 2PA
T 0131-529 4901 W www.edinburghmuseums.org.uk
Exhibitions relating to Robert Louis Stevenson, Walter
Scott and Robert Burns
FORT WILLIAM
West Highland Museum, Cameron Square PH33 6AJ
T 01397-702169 W www.westhighlandmuseum.org.uk
Includes tartan collections and exhibits relating to
1745 uprising
GLASGOW
Burrell Collection, Pollokshaws Road G43 1AT
T 0141-287 2550 W www.glasgowlife.org.uk/museums
Paintings, textiles, furniture, ceramics, stained glass and
silver from classical times to the 19th century
Gallery of Modern Art, Royal Exchange Square G1 3AH
T 0141-287 3005 W www.glasgowlife.org.uk/museums
Collection of contemporary Scottish and world art
Hunterian Museum & Art Gallery, University of Glasgow
G12 8QQ T 0141-330 4221 W www.hunterian.gla.ac.uk
Rennie Mackintosh and Whistler collections; Old
Masters; Scottish paintings; archaeology; medicine;
zoology
Kelvingrove Art Gallery & Museum, Argyle Street G3 8AG
T 0141-276 9599 W www.glasgowlife.org.uk/museums
Includes Old Masters, 19th-century French paintings
and armour collection

Museum of Piping, McPhater Street G4 0HW
T 0141-353 0220 W www.thepipingcentre.co.uk
The history and origins of bagpiping
*Museum of Rural Life, East Kilbride G76 9HR
T 0300-123 6789 W www.nms.ac.uk
History of rural life and work
People's Palace and Winter Gardens, Glasgow Green G40 1AT
T 0141-276 0788 W www.glasgowlife.org.uk/museums
Social history of Glasgow since 1750
*Riverside Museum, 100 Pointhouse Place G3 8RS
T 0141-287 2720 W www.glasgowlife.org.uk/museums
Scotland's museum of transport and travel; the Tall
Ship, a Clyde-built sailing ship, is berthed alongside
St Mungo Museum of Religious Life and Art, Castle Street
G4 0RH T 0141-276 1625 W www.glasgowlife.org.uk/
museums
Explores universal themes through objects from the
main world religions

NORTHERN IRELAND

* Members of National Museums Northern Ireland, a
non-departmental public body of the Northern Ireland Office

ARMAGH
*Armagh County Museum, The Mall East BT61 9BE
T 028-3752 3070 W www.nmni.com/acm
Local history; archaeology; crafts
BANGOR
North Down Museum, Town Hall BT20 4BT T 028-9127 1200
W www.northdown.gov.uk/heritage
Presents the history of North Down, including its
early-Christian monastery
BELFAST
*W5, Odyssey, Queen's Quay BT3 9QQ T 028-9046 7700
W www.w5online.co.uk
Interactive science and technology centre
HOLYWOOD
*Ulster Folk and Transport Museum, Cultra, Co. Down
BT18 0EU T 028-9042 8428 W www.nmni.com/uftm
Open-air museum with original buildings from Ulster
town and rural life c.1900; indoor galleries including
Irish rail and road transport
LONDONDERRY
The Tower Museum, Union Hall Place BT48 6LU
T 028-7137 2411 W www.derrycity.gov.uk/museums
Tells the story of Ireland through the history of
Londonderry
Workhouse Museum, Glendermott Road BT48 6BG
T 028-7131 8328 W www.derrycity.gov.uk/museums
Exhibitions on the Second World War, workhouse life,
19th-century poverty and the famine
NEWTOWNARDS
The Somme Heritage Centre, 233 Bangor Road BT23 7PH
T 01247-823202 W www.irishsoldier.org
Commemorates the part played by Irish forces in the
First World War
OMAGH
*Ulster American Folk Park, Castletown, Co. Tyrone
BT78 5QU T 028-8224 3292 W www.nmni.com/uafp
Open-air museum telling the story of Ulster's
emigrants to America; restored or recreated dwellings
and workshops; ship and dockside gallery
*Ulster Museum, Botanic Gardens BT9 5AB T 0845-608 0000
W www.nmni.com/um
Irish antiquities; natural and local history; fine and
applied arts

SIGHTS OF LONDON

For historic buildings, museums and galleries in London, *see* the Historic Buildings and Monuments, and Museums and Galleries sections.

BRIDGES

The bridges over the Thames in London, from east to west, are:

Queen Elizabeth II Bridge (2,872m/9,423ft), engineer: Sir William Halcrow and partners, opened 1991

Tower Bridge (268m/880ft by 18m/60ft), architect: Horace Jones, engineer: John Wolfe Barry, opened 1894

London Bridge (262m/860ft by 32m/105ft), original 13th-century stone bridge rebuilt and opened 1831 (engineer: John Rennie), reconstructed in Arizona when current London Bridge opened 1973 (architect: Lord Holford, engineer: Mott, Hay and Anderson)

Cannon Street Railway Bridge (261m/855ft), engineers: John Hawkshaw and John Wolfe Barry, originally named the Alexandra Bridge, opened 1866; renovated 1979–82

Southwark Bridge (244m/800ft by 17m/55ft), engineer: John Rennie, opened 1819; rebuilt 1912–21 (architect: Ernest George, engineer: Mott, Hay and Anderson)

Millennium Bridge (325m/1,066ft by 4m/13ft), architect: Foster and Partners, engineer: Ove Arup and Partners, opened 2000; reopened after modification 2002

Blackfriars Railway Bridge (284m/933ft), engineers: John Wolfe Barry and Henri Marc Brunel, opened 1886

London, Chatham and Dover Railway Bridge (234m/933ft), engineer: Joseph Cubitt, opened in 1864; only the columns remain, the rest of the structure was removed in 1985

Blackfriars Bridge (294m/963ft by 32m/105ft), engineer: Robert Mylne, opened 1769; rebuilt 1869 (engineer: Joseph Cubitt); widened 1909

Waterloo Bridge (366m/1,200ft by 24m/80ft), engineer: John Rennie, opened 1817; rebuilt 1945 (architect: Sir Giles Gilbert Scott, engineer: Rendel, Palmer and Triton)

Golden Jubilee Bridges (325m/1,066ft by 4.7m/15ft), architect: Lifschutz Davidson, engineer: WSP Group, opened 2002; commonly known as the Hungerford Footbridges

Hungerford Railway Bridge (366m/1,200ft), engineer: Isambard Kingdom Brunel, suspension bridge opened 1845; present railway bridge opened 1864 (engineer: John Hawkshaw); widened in 1886

Westminster Bridge (228m/748ft by 26m/85ft), engineer: Charles Labelye, opened 1750; rebuilt 1862 (architect: Charles Barry, engineer: Thomas Page)

Lambeth Bridge (237m/776ft by 18m/60ft), engineer: Peter W. Barlow, original suspension bridge opened 1862; current structure opened 1932 (architect: Reginald Blomfield, engineer: George W. Humphreys)

Vauxhall Bridge (231m/759ft by 24m/80ft), engineer: James Walker, opened 1816; redesigned and opened 1906 (architect: William Edward Riley, engineers: Alexander Binnie and Maurice Fitzmaurice)

Grosvenor Railway Bridge (213m/700ft), engineer: John Fowler, opened 1860; rebuilt 1965; also known as the Victoria Railway Bridge

Chelsea Bridge (213m/698ft by 25m/83ft), original suspension bridge opened 1858 (engineer: Thomas Page); rebuilt 1937 (architects: George Topham Forrest and E. P. Wheeler, engineer: Rendel, Palmer and Triton)

Albert Bridge (216m/710ft, by 12m/40ft), engineer: Rowland M. Ordish, opened 1873; restructured 1884 (engineer: Joseph Bazalgette); strengthened 1971–3

Battersea Bridge (204m/670ft by 17m/55ft), engineer: Henry Holland, opened 1771; rebuilt 1890 (engineer: Joseph Bazalgette)

Battersea Railway Bridge (204m/670ft), engineer: William Baker, opened 1863, also known as Cremorne Bridge

Wandsworth Bridge (189m/619ft by 18m/60ft), engineer: Julian Tolmé, opened 1873; rebuilt 1940 (architect: E. P. Wheeler, engineer: T. Peirson Frank)

Putney Railway Bridge (229m/750ft), engineers: W. H. Thomas and William Jacomb, opened 1889, also known as the Fulham Railway Bridge or the Iron Bridge – it has no official name

Putney Bridge (213m/700ft by 23m/74ft), architect: Jacob Ackworth, original wooden bridge opened 1729; current granite structure completed in 1886 (engineer: Joseph Bazalgette)

Hammersmith Bridge (210m/688ft by 10m/33ft), engineer: William Tierney Clarke; the first suspension bridge in London, originally built 1827; rebuilt 1887 (engineer: Joseph Bazalgette)

Barnes Railway Bridge (also footbridge, 110m/360ft), engineer: Joseph Locke, opened 1849; rebuilt 1895 (engineers: London and South Western Railway); the original structure stands unused

Chiswick Bridge (137m/450ft by 21m/70ft), architect: Herbert Baker, engineer: Alfred Dryland, opened 1933

Kew Railway Bridge (175m/575ft), engineer: W. R. Galbraith, opened 1869

Kew Bridge (110m/360ft by 17m/56ft), engineer: Robert Tunstall, original timber bridge built 1759; replaced by a Portland stone structure in 1789 (engineer: James Paine); current granite bridge renamed King Edward VII Bridge in 1903, but still known as Kew Bridge (engineers: John Wolfe Barry and Cuthbert Brereton)

Richmond Lock (91m/300ft by 11m/36ft), engineer: F. G. M. Stoney, lock and footbridge opened 1894

Twickenham Bridge (85m/280ft by 21m/70ft), architect: Maxwell Ayrton, engineer: Alfred Dryland, opened 1933

Richmond Railway Bridge (91m/300ft), engineer: Joseph Locke, opened 1848; rebuilt 1906–8 (engineer: J. W. Jacomb-Hood)

Richmond Bridge (85m/280ft by 10m/33ft), architect: James Paine, engineer: Kenton Couse, built 1777; widened 1939

Teddington Lock (198m/650ft), engineer: G. Pooley, two footbridges opened 1889; marks the end of the tidal reach of the Thames

Kingston Railway Bridge, architects: J. E. Errington and W. R. Galbraith, engineer: Thomas Brassey, opened 1863

Kingston Bridge (116m/382ft), engineer: Edward Lapidge, built 1825–8; widened 1911–14 (engineers: Basil Mott and David Hay) and 1999–2001

Hampton Court Bridge, engineers: Samuel Stevens and Benjamin Ludgator, built 1753; replaced by iron bridge 1865; present bridge opened 1933 (architect: Edwin Lutyens, engineer: W. P. Robinson)

CEMETERIES

In 1832, in response to the overcrowding of burial grounds in London, the government authorised the establishment of seven non-denominational cemeteries that would encircle the city. These large cemeteries, known as the 'magnificent seven', were seen by many Victorian families as places in which to demonstrate their wealth and stature, and as a result there are some highly ornate graves and tombs.

THE MAGNIFICENT SEVEN

Abney Park, Stamford Hill, N16 (13ha/32 acres), established 1840; tomb of General Booth, founder of the Salvation Army, and memorials to many nonconformists and dissenters

Brompton, Old Brompton Road, SW10 (16ha/40 acres), established 1840; graves of Sir Henry Cole, Emmeline Pankhurst, John Wisden. Managed by the Royal Parks, it is the only Crown cemetery

Highgate, Swains Lane, N6 (15ha/38 acres), established 1839; graves of Douglas Adams, George Eliot, Michael Faraday, Karl Marx, Christina Rossetti and Radclyffe Hall; western side only accessible as part of a guided tour

Kensal Green, Harrow Road, W10 (31.5ha/79 acres), established 1832; tombs of William Makepeace Thackeray, Anthony Trollope, Sydney Smith, Wilkie Collins, Tom Hood, George Cruikshank, Leigh Hunt, Isambard Kingdom Brunel and Charles Kemble

Nunhead, Linden Grove, SE15 (21ha/52 acres), established 1840; closed in 1969, subsequently restored and opened for burials

Tower Hamlets, Southern Grove, E3 (11ha/27 acres), established 1841; bombed heavily during the Second World War and closed to burials in 1966; now a nature reserve

West Norwood Cemetery and Crematorium, Norwood High Street, SE27 (17ha/42 acres), established 1837; tombs of Sir Henry Bessemer, Mrs Beeton, Sir Henry Tate and Joseph Whitaker *(Whitaker's Almanack)*

OTHER CEMETERIES

Bunhill Fields, City Road, EC1 (1.6ha/4 acres), 17th-century nonconformist burial ground containing the graves of William Blake, John Bunyan and Daniel Defoe

City of London Cemetery and Crematorium, Aldersbrook Road, E12 (81ha/200 acres), established 1856; grave of Bobby Moore

Golders Green Crematorium, Hoop Lane, NW11 (5ha/12 acres), established 1902; retains the ashes of Kingsley Amis, Peter Sellers, Marc Bolan, Sigmund Freud, Ivor Novello, Bram Stoker, H. G. Wells, Anna Pavlova and Joe Orton

Hampstead, Fortune Green Road, NW6 (10.5ha/26 acres), established 1876; graves of Kate Greenaway, Lord Lister and Marie Lloyd

MARKETS

Billingsgate (fish), a market site for over 1,000 years, with the Lower Thames Street site dating from 1876; moved to the Isle of Dogs (Trafalgar Way, E14) in 1982; owned and run by the Corporation of London

Borough, Southwark Street, SE1 (vegetables, fruit, gourmet food, flowers), established on present site in 1756; privately owned and run

Brick Lane, E1 (jewellery, vintage clothes, bric-a-brac, food), open Sunday

Brixton, SW8 (African-Caribbean food, music, clothes), open Monday to Saturday

Broadway, E8 (food, fashion, crafts), re-established in 2004, open Saturday

Camden Lock, NW1 (second-hand clothing, jewellery, alternative fashion, crafts), established in 1973

Columbia Road, E2 (flowers), dates from 19th century; became dedicated flower market in the 20th century

Covent Garden, WC2 (antiques, handicrafts, jewellery, clothing, food), originally a fruit and vegetable market (*see* New Covent Garden market), it has been trading in its current form since 1980

Grays, Davies Street, W1 (antiques), indoor market in listed building, established 1977

Greenwich, SE10 (crafts, fashion, food), market revived in the 1980s

Leadenhall, Leadenhall Street, EC3 (meat, poultry, cheese, etc), site of market since 14th century; present hall built 1881; owned and run by the Corporation of London

New Covent Garden Nine Elms, SW8 (wholesale vegetables, fruit and flowers) owned and run by the Covent Garden Market Authority, established in 1670 under a charter of Charles II; relocated from central London in 1974

Petticoat Lane, Middlesex Street, E1, a market has existed on the site for over 500 years, now a Sunday morning market selling almost anything

Portobello Road, W11, originally for herbs and horse-trading from 1870; became famous for antiques after the closure of the Caledonian Market in 1948

Smithfield, EC1 (meat, poultry), built 1866–8, refurbished 1993–4; the site of St Bartholomew's Fair from 12th to 19th century; owned and run by the Corporation of London

New Spitalfields, E10 (vegetables, fruit), established 1682, modernised 1928, moved out of the City to Leyton in 1991

Old Spitalfields, E1, continues to trade on the original Spitalfields site on Commercial Street, selling arts, crafts, books, clothes, organic food and antiques on Sundays

MONUMENTS

CENOTAPH

Whitehall, SW1. The Cenotaph (from the Greek meaning 'empty tomb') was built to commemorate 'The Glorious Dead' and is a memorial to all ranks of the sea, land and air forces who gave their lives in the service of the Empire during the First World War. Designed by Sir Edwin Lutyens and constructed in plaster as a temporary memorial in 1919, it was replaced by a permanent structure of Portland stone and unveiled by George V on 11 November 1920, Armistice Day. An additional inscription was made in 1946 to commemorate those who gave their lives in the Second World War

FOURTH PLINTH

Trafalgar Square, WC2. The fourth plinth (1841) was designed for an equestrian statue that was never built due to lack of funds. From 1999 temporary works have been displayed on the plinth including *Ecce Homo* (Mark Wallinger), *Regardless of History* (Bill Woodrow), *Monument* (Rachel Whiteread), *Alison Lapper Pregnant* (Marc Quinn) and *Model for a Hotel* (Thomas Schütte). Antony Gormley's project *One & Other* occupied the plinth from July–October 2009. This was followed in November 2009 by a memorial statue to Second World War hero Air Chief Marshal Sir Keith Park and from May 2010 by *Nelson's Ship in a Bottle* by Yinka Shonibare

LONDON MONUMENT

(Commonly called the Monument), Monument Street, EC3. Built to designs by Sir Christopher Wren and Robert Hooke between 1671 and 1677, the Monument commemorates the Great Fire of London, which broke out in Pudding Lane on 2 September 1666. The fluted Doric column is 36.6m (120ft) high, the moulded cylinder above the balcony supporting a flaming vase of gilt bronze is an additional 12.8 m (42ft), and the column is based on a square plinth 12.2m (40ft) high (with fine carvings on the west face), making a total height of 61.6m (202ft) – the tallest isolated stone column in the world, with views of London from a gallery at the top (311 steps)

OTHER MONUMENTS

(sculptor's name in parentheses):

7 July Memorial (Carmody Groarke), Hyde Park

Viscount Alanbrooke (Roberts-Jones), Whitehall

Albert Memorial (Scott), Kensington Gore

Battle of Britain (Day), Victoria Embankment

Beatty (Wheeler), Trafalgar Square

Belgian Gratitude (setting by Blomfield, statue by Rousseau), Victoria Embankment

Boadicea (or Boudicca), *Queen of the Iceni* (Thornycroft), Westminster Bridge

Brunel (Marochetti), Victoria Embankment

Burghers of Calais (Rodin), Victoria Tower Gardens, Westminster

Burns (Steell), Embankment Gardens

Canada Memorial (Granche), Green Park

Carlyle (Boehm), Chelsea Embankment

Cavalry (Jones), Hyde Park

Edith Cavell (Frampton), St Martin's Place

Charles I (Le Sueur), Trafalgar Square

Charles II (Gibbons), Royal Hospital, Chelsea

Churchill (Roberts-Jones), Parliament Square

Cleopatra's Needle (20.9m/68.5ft high, *c.*1500BC, erected in London in 1878; the sphinxes are Victorian), Thames Embankment

Clive (Tweed), King Charles Street

Captain Cook (Brock), The Mall

Oliver Cromwell (Thornycroft), outside Westminster Hall

Cunningham (Belsky), Trafalgar Square

Gen. Charles de Gaulle (Conner), Carlton Gardens

Diana, Princess of Wales Memorial Fountain (Gustafson Porter), Hyde Park

Disraeli, Earl of Beaconsfield (Raggi), Parliament Square

Lord Dowding (Winter), Strand

Duke of Cambridge (Jones), Whitehall

Duke of York (37.8m/124ft column, with statue by Westmacott), Carlton House Terrace

Edward VII (Mackennal), Waterloo Place

Elizabeth I (Kerwin, 1586, oldest outdoor statue in London; from Ludgate), Fleet Street

Eros (Shaftesbury Memorial) (Gilbert), Piccadilly Circus

Marechal/Marshall Foch (Mallisard, copy of one in Cassel, France), Grosvenor Gardens

Charles James Fox (Westmacott), Bloomsbury Square

Yuri Gagarin (Novikov, copy of the one in Russia), The Mall

George III (Cotes Wyatt), Cockspur Street

George IV (Chantrey), Trafalgar Square

George V (Reid Dick and Scott), Old Palace Yard

George VI (McMillan), Carlton Gardens

Gladstone (Thornycroft), Strand

Guards' (Crimea) (Bell), Waterloo Place

Guards Division (Ledward, figures, Bradshaw, cenotaph), Horse Guards' Parade

Haig (Hardiman), Whitehall

Sir Arthur (Bomber) Harris (Winter), Strand

Gen. Henry Havelock (Behnes), Trafalgar Square

International Brigades Memorial (Spanish Civil War) (Ian Walters), Jubilee Gardens, South Bank

Irving (Brock), north side of National Portrait Gallery

Isis (Gudgeon), Hyde Park

James II (Gibbons), Trafalgar Square

Jellicoe (McMillan), Trafalgar Square

Samuel Johnson (Fitzgerald), opposite St Clement Danes

Kitchener (Tweed), Horse Guards' Parade

Abraham Lincoln (Saint-Gaudens, copy of one in Chicago), Parliament Square

Mandela (Walters), Parliament Square

Milton (Montford), St Giles, Cripplegate

Mountbatten (Belsky), Foreign Office Green

Gen. Charles James Napier (Adams), Trafalgar Square

Nelson (Railton), Trafalgar Square, with Landseer's lions (cast from guns recovered from the wreck of the *Royal George*)

Florence Nightingale (Walker), Waterloo Place

Palmerston (Woolner), Parliament Square

Sir Keith Park (Johnson), Waterloo Place

Peel (Noble), Parliament Square

Pitt (Chantrey), Hanover Square

Portal (Nemon), Embankment Gardens

Prince Albert (Bacon), Holborn Circus

Queen Elizabeth Gate (Lund and Wynne), Hyde Park Corner

Queen Mother (Jackson), Carlton Gardens

Raleigh (McMillan), Greenwich

Richard I (Coeur de Lion) (Marochetti), Old Palace Yard

Roberts (Bates), Horse Guards' Parade

Royal Air Force (Blomfield), Victoria Embankment

Franklin D. Roosevelt (Reid Dick), Grosvenor Square

Royal Artillery (Great War) (Jagger and Pearson), Hyde Park Corner

Royal Artillery (South Africa) (Colton), The Mall; *Captain Scott* (Lady Scott), Waterloo Place; *Shackleton* (Jagger), Kensington Gore

Shakespeare (Fontana, copy of one by Scheemakers in Westminster Abbey), Leicester Square

Smuts (Epstein), Parliament Square

Sullivan (Goscombe John), Victoria Embankment

Trenchard (McMillan), Victoria Embankment

Victoria Memorial (Webb and Brock), in front of Buckingham Palace

Raoul Wallenberg (Jackson), Great Cumberland Place

George Washington (Houdon copy), Trafalgar Square

Wellington (Boehm), Hyde Park Corner

Wellington (Chantrey), outside Royal Exchange

John Wesley (Adams Acton), City Road

Westminster School (Crimea) (Scott), Broad Sanctuary

William III (Bacon), St James's Square

Wolseley (Goscombe John), Horse Guards' Parade

530   Conservation and Heritage

PARKS, GARDENS AND OPEN SPACES

CORPORATION OF LONDON OPEN SPACES
W www.cityoflondon.gov.uk
Ashtead Common (202ha/500 acres), Surrey
Burnham Beeches and *Fleet Wood* (219ha/540 acres), Bucks. Purchased by the Corporation for the benefit of the public in 1880, Fleet Wood (26ha/65 acres) being presented in 1921
Coulsdon Common (51ha/127 acres), Surrey
Epping Forest (2,476ha/6,118 acres), Essex. Purchased by the Corporation and opened to the public in 1882. The Queen Elizabeth Hunting Lodge, built for Henry VIII in the mid-16th century, lies at the edge of the forest. The present forest is 19.3km (12 miles) long by around 3km (2 miles) wide, approximately one-tenth of its original area
*Epping Forest Buffer Land (718ha/1,774 acres), Waltham Abbey/Epping
Farthing Downs and New Hill (95ha/235 acres), Surrey
Hampstead Heath (275ha/680 acres), NW3. Including Golders Hill (15ha/36 acres) and Parliament Hill (110ha/271 acres)
Highgate Wood (28ha/70 acres), N6/N10
Kenley Common (56ha/139 acres), Surrey
Queen's Park (12ha/30 acres), NW6
Riddlesdown (43ha/107 acres), Surrey
Spring Park (21ha/51 acres), Kent
Stoke Common (83ha/206 acres), Bucks. Ownership was transferred to the Corporation in 2007
West Ham Park (31ha/77 acres), E15
West Wickham Common (11ha/26 acres), Kent
Also over 150 smaller open spaces within the City of London, including *Finsbury Circus* and *St Dunstan-in-the-East*
* Includes Copped Hall Park, Woodredon Estate and Warlies Park

OTHER PARKS AND GARDENS
CHELSEA PHYSIC GARDEN, 66 Royal Hospital Road SW3 4HS T 020-7352 5646 W www.chelseaphysicgarden.co.uk
A garden of general botanical research and education, maintaining a wide range of rare and unusual plants; established in 1673 by the Society of Apothecaries
HAMPTON   COURT   PARK   AND   GARDENS (303.5ha/750 acres), Surrey KT8 9AU T 0844-482 7777 W www.hrp.org.uk Also known as Home Park, the park lies beyond the palace's formal gardens. It contains a herd of deer and a 1,000-year-old oak tree from the original park
KEW, ROYAL BOTANIC GARDENS (120ha/300 acres), Richmond, Surrey TW9 3AB T 020-8332 5655
W www.kew.org Officially inscribed on the UNESCO list of World Heritage Sites
THAMES   BARRIER   PARK   (9ha/22acres),   North Woolwich E16 2HP T 020-7476 3741
W www.thamesbarrierpark.org.uk Opened in 2000, landscaped gardens with spectacular views of the Thames Barrier

ROYAL PARKS
W www.royalparks.gov.uk
Bushy Park (450ha/1,099 acres), Middx. Adjoins Hampton Court; contains an avenue of horse-chestnuts enclosed in a fourfold avenue of limes planted by William III
Green Park (19ha/47 acres), W1. Between Piccadilly and St James's Park, with Constitution Hill leading to Hyde Park Corner

Greenwich Park (74ha/183 acres), SE10. Enclosed by Humphrey, Duke of Gloucester, and laid out by Charles II from the designs of Le Nôtre. On a hill in Greenwich Park is the Royal Observatory (founded 1675). Its buildings are now managed by the National Maritime Museum (T 020-8858 4422 W www.nmm.ac.uk) and the earliest building is named Flamsteed House, after John Flamsteed (1646–1719), the first astronomer royal
Hyde Park (142ha/350 acres), W1/W2. From Park Lane to Kensington Gardens and incorporating the Serpentine lake, Apsley House, the Achilles Statue, Rotten Row and the Ladies' Mile; fine gateway at Hyde Park Corner. To the north-east is Marble Arch, originally erected by George IV at the entrance to Buckingham Palace and re-erected in the present position in 1851
Kensington Gardens (111ha/275 acres), W2/W8. From the western boundary of Hyde Park to Kensington Palace; contains the Albert Memorial, Serpentine Gallery and Peter Pan statue
Regent's Park and *Primrose Hill* (197ha/487 acres), NW1. From Marylebone Road to Primrose Hill surrounded by the Outer Circle; divided by the Broad Walk leading to the Zoological Gardens
Richmond Park (1,000ha/2,500 acres), Surrey. Designated a National Nature Reserve, a Site of Special Scientific Interest and a Special Area of Conservation
St James's Park (23ha/58 acres), SW1. From Whitehall to Buckingham Palace; ornamental lake of 4.9ha (12 acres); the Mall leads from Admiralty Arch to Buckingham Palace, Birdcage Walk from Storey's Gate to Buckingham Palace

PLACES OF HISTORICAL AND CULTURAL INTEREST

1 Canada Square
Canary Wharf E14 5DY T 020-7418 2000
W www.canarywharf.com
Also known as 'Canary Wharf', the steel and glass skyscraper is designed to sway 35cm in the strongest winds
30 St Mary Axe
EC3A 8EP W www.30stmaryaxe.com
Completed in 2004 and commonly known as the 'Gherkin', each of the floors rotates five degrees from the one below
Alexandra Palace
Alexandra Palace Way, Wood Green N22 7AY
T 020-8365 2121 W www.alexandrapalace.com
The Victorian palace was severely damaged by fire in 1980 but was restored, and reopened in 1988. Alexandra Palace now provides modern facilities for exhibitions, conferences, banquets and leisure activities. There is a winter ice rink, a boating lake, the Phoenix Bar and a conservation area
Barbican Centre
Silk Street EC2Y 8DS T 020-7638 4141
W www.barbican.org.uk
Owned, funded and managed by the Corporation of London, the Barbican Centre opened in 1982 and houses the Barbican Theatre, a studio theatre called The Pit and the Barbican Hall; it is also home to the London Symphony Orchestra. There are three cinemas, seven conference rooms, two art galleries, a sculpture court, a lending library, trade and banqueting facilities, a conservatory, shops, restaurants, cafes and bars
British Library
St Pancras, 96 Euston Road NW1 2DB T 0843-208 1144
W www.bl.uk

The largest building constructed in the UK in the 20th century with basements extending 24.5m underground. Holdings include the *Magna Carta*, the *Lindisfarne Gospels*, Mozart manuscripts and the world's earliest dated printed book, the *Diamond Sutra*. Holds temporary exhibitions on a range of topics

Central Criminal Court
Old Bailey EC4M 7EH T 020-7248 3277
W www.cityoflondon.gov.uk
The highest criminal court in the UK, the 'Old Bailey' is located on the site of the old Newgate Prison. Trials held here have included those of Oscar Wilde, Dr Crippen and the Yorkshire Ripper. The courthouse has been rebuilt several times since 1674; Edward VII officially opened the current neo-baroque building in 1907

Charterhouse
Charterhouse Square EC1M 6AN T 020-7253 9503
W www.thecharterhouse.org
A Carthusian monastery from 1371 to 1538, purchased in 1611 by Thomas Sutton, who endowed it as a residence for aged men 'of gentle birth' and a school for poor scholars (removed to Godalming in 1872)

Downing Street SW1
Number 10 Downing Street is the official town residence of the prime minister, number 11 of the chancellor of the exchequer and number 12 is the office of the government whips. The street was named after Sir George Downing, Bt., soldier and diplomat, who was MP for Morpeth 1660–84

George Inn
Borough High Street SE1 1NH T 020-7407 2056
W www.nationaltrust.org.uk
The last galleried inn in London, built in 1677. Now owned by the National Trust and run as an ordinary public house

Horse Guards, Whitehall SW1
Archway and offices built about 1753. The changing of the guard takes place daily at 11am (10am on Sundays) and the inspection at 4pm. Only those with the Queen's permission may drive through the gates and archway into *Horse Guards' Parade*, where the colour is 'trooped' on the Queen's official birthday

HOUSES OF PARLIAMENT
House of Commons, Westminster SW1A 0AA T 020-7219 4272
W www.parliament.uk
House of Lords, Westminster SW1A 0PW T 020-7219 3107
W www.parliament.uk
The royal palace of Westminster, originally built by Edward the Confessor, was the normal meeting place of Parliament from about 1340. St Stephen's Chapel was used from about 1550 for the meetings of the House of Commons, which had previously been held in the Chapter House or Refectory of Westminster Abbey. The House of Lords met in an apartment of the royal palace. The fire of 1834 destroyed much of the palace, and the present Houses of Parliament were erected on the site from the designs of Sir Charles Barry and Augustus Welby Pugin between 1840 and 1867. The chamber of the House of Commons was destroyed by bombing in 1941, and a new chamber designed by Sir Giles Gilbert Scott was used for the first time in 1950. *Westminster Hall and the Crypt Chapel* was the only part of the old palace of Westminster to survive the fire of 1834. It was built by William II from 1097 to 1099 and altered by Richard II between 1394 and 1399. The hammerbeam roof of carved oak dates

from 1396–8. The Hall was the scene of the trial of Charles I. *The Victoria Tower* of the House of Lords is 98.5m (323ft) high, and *The Clock Tower* of the House of Commons is 96.3m (316ft) high and contains 'Big Ben', the hour bell said to be named after Sir Benjamin Hall, First Commissioner of Works when the original bell was cast in 1856. This bell, which weighed 16 tons 11 cwt, was found to be cracked in 1857. The present bell (13.5 tons) is a recasting of the original and was first brought into use in 1859. The dials of the clock are 7m (23ft) in diameter, the hands being 2.7m (9ft) and 4.3m (14ft) long (including balance piece).

During session, tours of the Houses of Parliament are only available to UK residents who have made advance arrangements through an MP or peer. Overseas visitors are no longer provided with permits to tour the Houses of Parliament during session, although they can tour on Saturdays and during the summer opening and attend debates for both houses in the Strangers' Galleries. During the summer recess, tickets for tours of the Houses of Parliament can be booked by telephone (T 0844-847 1672) or bought on site at the ticket office on Abingdon Green opposite Parliament and the Victoria Tower Gardens. The Strangers' Gallery of the House of Commons is open to the public when the house is sitting. To acquire tickets in advance, UK residents should write to their local MP and overseas visitors should apply to their embassy or high commission in the UK for a permit. If none of these arrangements has been made, visitors should join the public queue outside St Stephen's Entrance, where there is also a queue for entry to the House of Lords Gallery

INNS OF COURT
The Inns of Court are ancient unincorporated bodies of lawyers which for more than five centuries have had the power to call to the Bar those of their members who have qualified for the rank or degree of Barrister-at-Law. There are four Inns of Court as well as many lesser inns

Lincoln's Inn, Chancery Lane/Lincoln's Inn Fields WC2A 3TL T 020-7405 1393 W www.lincolnsinn.org.uk
The most ancient of the inns with records dating back to 1422. The hall and library buildings are from 1845, although the library is first mentioned in 1474; the old hall (late 15th century) and the chapel were rebuilt *c.*1619–23

Inner Temple, King's Bench Walk EC4Y 7HL
T 020-7797 8250 W www.innertemple.org.uk
Middle Temple, Middle Temple Lane EC4Y 9AT
T 020-7427 4800 W www.middletemple.org.uk
Records for the Middle and Inner Temple date back to the beginning of the 16th century. The site was originally occupied by the Order of Knights Templar *c.*1160–1312. The two inns have separate halls thought to have been formed *c.*1350. The division between the two societies was formalised in 1732 with Temple Church and the Masters House remaining in common. The Inner Temple Garden is normally open to the public on weekdays between 12.30pm and 3pm

Temple Church, EC4Y 7BB T 020-7353 8559
W www.templechurch.com
The nave forms one of five remaining round churches in England

Gray's Inn, South Square WC1R 5ET T 020-7458 7800
W www.graysinn.info
Founded early 14th century; hall 1556–8

No other 'Inns' are active, but there are remains of *Staple Inn*, a gabled front on Holborn (opposite Gray's Inn Road). *Clement's Inn* (near St Clement Danes Church), *Clifford's Inn*, Fleet Street, and *Thavies Inn*, Holborn Circus, are all rebuilt. *Serjeants' Inn*, Fleet Street, and another (demolished 1910) of the same name in Chancery Lane, were composed of Serjeants-at-Law, the last of whom died in 1922

Institute of Contemporary Arts
The Mall SW1Y 5AH T 020-7930 3647 W www.ica.org.uk
Exhibitions of modern art in the fields of film, theatre, new media and the visual arts

Lloyd's
Lime Street EC3M 7HA T 020-7327 1000
W www.lloyds.com
International insurance market which evolved during the 17th century from Lloyd's Coffee House. The present building was opened for business in May 1986, and houses the Lutine Bell. Underwriting is on three floors with a total area of 10,591 sq. m (114,000 sq. ft). The Lloyd's building is not open to the general public

London Central Mosque and the Islamic Cultural Centre
Park Road NW8 7RG T 020-7725 2213 W www.iccuk.org
The focus for London's Muslims; established in 1944 but not completed until 1977, the mosque can accommodate about 5,000 worshippers; guided tours are available

London Eye
South Bank SE1 7PB T 0870-990 8883
W www.londoneye.com
Opened in March 2000 as London's millennium landmark, this 450ft observation wheel is the tallest cantilevered observation wheel in the world. The wheel provides a 30-minute ride offering panoramic views of the capital

London Zoo
Regent's Park NW1 4RY T 020-7722 3333
W www.londonzoo.org

Madame Tussauds
Marylebone Road NW1 5LR T 0871-894 3000
W www.madametussauds.com
Waxwork exhibition

Marlborough House
Pall Mall SW1Y 5HX T 020-7747 6500
W www.thecommonwealth.org
Built by Sir Christopher Wren for the first Duke of Marlborough and completed in 1711, the house reverted to the Crown in 1835. In 1863 it became the London house of the Prince of Wales and was the London home of Queen Mary until her death in 1953. In 1959 Marlborough House was given by the Queen as the headquarters for the Commonwealth Secretariat and it was opened as such in 1965. The Queen's Chapel, Marlborough Gate, was begun in 1623 from the designs of Inigo Jones for the Infanta Maria of Spain, and completed for Queen Henrietta Maria. Marlborough House is not open to the public

Mansion House
Cannon Street EC4N 8BH T 020-7626 2500
W www.cityoflondon.gov.uk
The official residence of the Lord Mayor. Built in the 18th century in the Palladian style. Open to groups by appointment only

Neasden Temple
BAPS Shri Swaminarayan Mandir, 105–119 Brentfield Road, Neasden NW10 8LD T 020-8965 2651 W www.mandir.org
The first and largest traditional Hindu Mandir outside of India; opened in 1995

Olympic Park
Stratford E20 T 0845-267 2012 W www.london2012.com
The heart of the London 2012 Olympic Games, the purpose-built park comprises nine sporting venues including the Olympic Stadium, Velodrome and Aquatics Centre in addition to the Olympic Village

Port of London
Port of London Authority, Bakers' Hall, 7 Harp Lane EC3R 6LB T 01474-562200 W www.pla.co.uk
The Port of London covers the tidal section of the river Thames from Teddington to the seaward limit (the outer Tongue buoy and the Sunk light vessel), a distance of 150km. The governing body is the Port of London Authority (PLA). Cargo is handled at privately operated riverside terminals between Fulham and Canvey Island, including the enclosed dock at Tilbury, 40km below London Bridge. Passenger vessels and cruise liners can be handled at moorings at Greenwich, Tower Bridge and Tilbury

Roman Remains
The city wall of Roman *Londinium* was largely rebuilt during the medieval period but sections may be seen near the White Tower in the Tower of London; at Tower Hill; at Coopers' Row; at All Hallows, London Wall, its vestry being built on the remains of a semi-circular Roman bastion; at St Alphage, London Wall, showing a succession of building repairs from the Roman until the late medieval period; and at St Giles, Cripplegate. Sections of the great forum and basilica, more than 165 sq. m, have been encountered during excavations in the area of Leadenhall, Gracechurch Street and Lombard Street. Traces of Roman activity along the river include a massive riverside wall built in the late Roman period, and a succession of Roman timber quays along Lower and Upper Thames Street. Finds from these sites can be seen at the Museum of London.

Other major buildings are the amphitheatre at Guildhall, remains of bath-buildings in Upper and Lower Thames Street, and the temple of Mithras in Walbrook

Royal Albert Hall
Kensington Gore SW7 2AP T 020-7589 8212
W www.royalalberthall.com
The elliptical hall, one of the largest in the world, was completed in 1871; since 1941 it has been the venue each summer for the Promenade Concerts founded in 1895 by Sir Henry Wood. Other events include pop and classical music concerts, dance, opera, sporting events, conferences and banquets

Royal Courts of Justice
Strand WC2A 2LL T 020-7947 6000
W www.hmcourts-service.gov.uk
Victorian Gothic building that is home to the high court. Visitors are free to watch proceedings

Royal Hospital, Chelsea
Royal Hospital Road SW3 4SR T 020-7881 5200
W www.chelsea-pensioners.co.uk
Founded by Charles II in 1682 and built by Sir Christopher Wren; opened in 1692 for old and disabled soldiers. The extensive grounds include the former Ranelagh Gardens and are the venue for the Chelsea Flower Show each May

Royal Naval College
Greenwich SE10 9LW T 020-8269 4747
W www.oldroyalnavalcollege.org
The building was the Greenwich Hospital until 1869. It was built by Charles II, largely from designs by John

Webb, and by Queen Mary II and William III, from designs by Wren. It stands on the site of an ancient abbey, a royal house and Greenwich Palace, which was constructed by Henry VII. Henry VIII, Mary I and Elizabeth I were born in the royal palace and Edward VI died there

Royal Opera House

Covent Garden WC2E 9DD T 020-7240 1200
W www.roh.org.uk

Home of The Royal Ballet (1931) and The Royal Opera (1946). The Royal Opera House is the third theatre to be built on the site, opening 1858; the first was opened in 1732

St James's Palace

Pall Mall SW1A 1BQ T 020-7930 4832
W www.royal.gov.uk

Built by Henry VIII, only the Gatehouse and Presence Chamber remain; later alterations were made by Wren and Kent. Representatives of foreign powers are still accredited 'to the Court of St James's'. *Clarence House* (1825), the official London residence of the Prince of Wales and his sons, stands within the St James's Palace estate

St Paul's Cathedral

St Paul's Churchyard EC4M 8AD T 020-7236 4128
E chapter@stpaulscathedral.org.uk W www.stpauls.co.uk

Built 1675–1710. The cross on the dome is 111m (365ft) above ground level, the inner cupola 66.4m (218ft) above the floor. 'Great Paul' in the south-west tower weighs nearly 17 tons. The organ by Father Smith (enlarged by Willis and rebuilt by Mander) is in a case carved by Grinling Gibbons, who also carved the choir stalls

Shard

London Bridge SE1 T 020-7493 5311
W www.the-shard.com

Due to be completed in May 2012, the skyscraper standing at 310m (1,016ft) possesses a unique facade of 11,000 glass panels and a 360-degree viewing gallery

Somerset House

Strand WC2R 1LA T 020 7845 4600
W www.somersethouse.org.uk

The river facade (183m/600ft long) was built in 1776–1801 from the designs of Sir William Chambers; the eastern extension, which houses part of King's College, was built by Smirke in 1829–35. Somerset House was the property of Lord Protector Somerset, at whose attainder in 1552 the palace passed to the Crown, and it was a royal residence until 1692. Somerset House has recently undergone extensive renovation and is home to the Gilbert Collection, Embankment Galleries and the Courtauld Institute Gallery. Open-air concerts and ice-skating (Dec–Jan) are held in the courtyard

SOUTH BANK, SE1

Arts complex on the south bank of the river Thames which consists of:

The *Royal Festival Hall* T 020-7960 4200
W www.southbankcentre.co.uk

Opened in 1951 for the Festival of Britain, adjacent are the *Queen Elizabeth Hall*, the *Purcell Room* and the *Hayward Gallery*

BFI Southbank T 020-7633 0274 W www.bfi.org.uk

Opened in 1952 and is administered by the British Film Institute, has three auditoria and an IMAX cinema. The London Film Festival is held there every November

The *Royal National Theatre*, T 020-7452 3000
W www.nationaltheatre.org.uk

Opened in 1976; comprises the Olivier, the Lyttelton and the Cottesloe theatres

Southwark Cathedral

London Bridge SE1 9DA T 020-7367 6700
W www.cathedral.southwark.anglican.org

Mainly 13th century, but the nave is largely rebuilt. The tomb of John Gower (1330–1408) is between the Bunyan and Chaucer memorial windows in the north aisle; Shakespeare's effigy, backed by a view of Southwark and the Globe Theatre, is in the south aisle; the tomb of Bishop Andrewes (d.1626) is near the screen. The Lady Chapel was the scene of the consistory courts of the reign of Mary (Gardiner and Bonner) and is still used as a consistory court. John Harvard, after whom Harvard University is named, was baptised here in 1607, and the chapel by the north choir aisle is his memorial chapel

Thames Embankments

Sir Joseph Bazalgette (1819–91) constructed the *Victoria Embankment*, on the north side from Westminster to Blackfriars for the Metropolitan Board of Works, 1864–70; (the seats, of which the supports of some are a kneeling camel, laden with spicery, and of others a winged sphinx, were presented by the Grocers' Company and by W. H. Smith, MP, in 1874); the *Albert Embankment*, on the south side from Westminster Bridge to Vauxhall, 1866–9, and the Chelsea Embankment, 1871–4. The total cost exceeded £2m. Bazalgette also inaugurated the London main drainage system, 1858–65. A medallion *(Flumini vincula posuit)* has been placed on a pier of the *Victoria Embankment* to commemorate the engineer

Thames Flood Barrier

W www.environment-agency.gov.uk

Officially opened in May 1984, though first used in February 1983, the barrier consists of ten rising sector gates which span approximately 570 yards from bank to bank of the Thames at Woolwich Reach. When not in use the gates lie horizontally, allowing shipping to navigate the river normally; when the barrier is closed, the gates turn through 90 degrees to stand vertically more than 50 feet above the river bed. The barrier took eight years to complete and can be raised within about 30 minutes

Trafalgar Tavern

Park Row, Greenwich SE10 9NW T 020-8858 2909
W www.trafalgartavern.co.uk

Regency-period riverside public house built in 1837. Charles Dickens and William Gladstone were patrons

Westminster Abbey

Broad Sanctuary SW1P 3PA T 020-7222 5152
E info@westminster-abbey.org
W www.westminster-abbey.org

Founded as a Benedictine monastery over 1,000 years ago, the church was rebuilt by Edward the Confessor in 1065 and again by Henry III in the 13th century. The abbey is the resting place for monarchs including Edward I, Henry III, Henry V, Henry VII, Elizabeth I, Mary I and Mary Queen of Scots, and has been the setting of coronations since that of William the Conqueror in 1066. In Poets' Corner there are memorials to many literary figures, and many scientists and musicians are also remembered here. The grave of the Unknown Warrior is to be found in the nave

Westminster Cathedral

Francis Street SW1P 1QW T 020-7798 9055
W www.westminstercathedral.org.uk

Roman Catholic cathedral built 1895–1903 from the designs of J. F. Bentley. The campanile is 284ft high

LONDON 2012 OLYMPIC GAMES VENUES

Venue	*Event*
Olympic Park, Stratford E20	
Aquatics Centre	swimming, synchronised swimming, diving
Basketball Arena	basketball, handball
BMX Circuit	cycling (BMX)
Handball Arena	handball
Hockey Centre	hockey
Olympic Stadium	opening/closing ceremony, athletics
Velodrome	cycling (track)
Water Polo Arena	water polo
Greater London	
Earls Court, SW5 9TA	volleyball
ExCel Arena, E16 1XL	boxing, fencing, judo, table tennis, taekwondo, weightlifting, wrestling (freestyle/Greco-Roman)
Greenwich Park, SE10	equestrian (dressage/eventing/jumping)
Hampton Court Palace, KT8 9AU	cycling (road)
Horse Guards' Parade, SW1	beach volleyball
Hyde Park, W1/W2	swimming (marathon), triathlon
Lords Cricket Ground, NW8 8QN	archery
The Mall, SW1A	athletics (marathon/walk), cycling (road)
North Greenwich Arena, SE10 0DX	gymnastics (artistic/trampoline), basketball
The Royal Artillery Barracks, SE18	shooting
Wembley Arena, HA9 0AA	badminton, gymnastics (rhythmic)
Wembley Stadium, HA9 0WS	football
Wimbledon, SW19 5AE	tennis

Modern pentathlon takes place at the Handball Arena, Aquatics Centre and Greenwich Park

Rest of UK	
City of Coventry Stadium, W. Midlands CV6 6GE	football
Eton Dorney, Bucks SL4 6QP	rowing, canoe sprint
Hadleigh Farm, Essex SS7	cycling (mountain bike)
Hampden Park, Glasgow G42 9BA	football
Lee Valley White Water Centre, Herts E9 1AB	canoe slalom
Millennium Stadium, Cardiff CF10 1NS	football
Old Trafford, Manchester M16 0RA	football
St James' Park, Newcastle NE1 4ST	football
Weymouth and Portland, Dorset DT5 1SA	sailing

HALLMARKS

Hallmarks are the symbols stamped on gold, silver, palladium or platinum articles to indicate that they have been tested at an official Assay Office and that they conform to one of the legal standards. The marking of gold and silver articles to identify the maker was instituted in England in 1363 under a statute of Edward III. In 1478 the Assay Office in Goldsmiths' Hall was established and all gold and silversmiths were required to bring their wares to be date-marked by the Hall, hence the term 'hallmarked'.

With certain exceptions, all gold, silver, palladium or platinum articles are required by law to be hallmarked before they are offered for sale. Current hallmarking requirements come under the UK Hallmarking Act 1973 and subsequent amendments. The act is built around the principle of description, where it is an offence for any person to apply to an unhallmarked article a description indicating that it is wholly or partly made of gold, silver, palladium or platinum. There is an exemption by weight: compulsory hallmarks are not needed on gold and palladium under 1g, silver under 7.78g and platinum under 0.5g. Also, some descriptions, such as rolled gold and gold plate, are permissible. The British Hallmarking Council is a statutory body created as a result of the Hallmarking Act. It ensures adequate provision for assaying and hallmarking, supervises the assay offices and ensures the enforcement of hallmarking legislation. The four assay offices at London, Birmingham, Sheffield and Edinburgh operate under the act.

BRITISH HALLMARKING COUNCIL Secretariat, 1 Colmore Square, Birmingham B4 6AA **T** 0800-763 1414 **W** www.britishhallmarkingcouncil.gov.uk

COMPULSORY MARKS

Since January 1999 UK hallmarks have consisted of three compulsory symbols – the sponsor's mark, the millesimal fineness (purity) mark and the assay office mark. The distinction between UK and foreign articles has been removed, and more finenesses are now legal, reflecting the more common finenesses elsewhere in Europe.

SPONSOR'S MARK
Formerly known as the maker's mark, the sponsor's mark was instituted in England in 1363. Originally a device such as a bird or fleur-de-lis, now it consists of a combination of at least two initials (usually a shortened form of the manufacturer's name) and a shield design. The London Assay Office offers 45 standard shield designs but other designs are possible by arrangement.

MILLESIMAL FINENESS MARK
The millesimal fineness (purity) mark indicates the number of parts per thousand of pure metal in the alloy. The current finenesses allowed in the UK are:

Gold	999; 990; 916.6 (22 carat); 750 (18 carat); 585 (14 carat); 375 (9 carat)
Silver	999; 958.4 (Britannia); 925 (sterling); 800
Palladium	999; 950; 500
Platinum	999; 950; 900; 850

ASSAY OFFICE MARK
This mark identifies the particular assay office at which the article was tested and marked. The British assay offices are:

 LONDON, Goldsmiths' Hall, Gutter Lane, London EC2V 8AQ **T** 020-7606 8971 **W** www.thegoldsmiths.co.uk

 BIRMINGHAM, PO Box 151, Newhall Street, Birmingham B3 1SB **T** 0121-236 6951 **W** www.theassayoffice.co.uk

 SHEFFIELD, Guardians' Hall, Beulah Road, Hillsborough, Sheffield S6 2AN **T** 0114-231 2121 **W** www.assayoffice.co.uk

 EDINBURGH, Goldsmiths' Hall, 24 Broughton Street, Edinburgh EH1 3RH **T** 0131-556 1144 **W** www.assayofficescotland.com

Assay offices formerly existed in other towns, eg Chester, Exeter, Glasgow, Newcastle, Norwich and York, each having its own distinguishing mark.

OPTIONAL MARKS

Since 1999 traditional pictorial marks such as a crown for gold, the Britannia for 958 silver, the lion passant for 925 silver (lion rampant in Scotland) and the orb for 950 platinum may be added voluntarily to the millesimal mark. In 2010 a pictorial mark for 950 palladium was introduced.

 Gold – a crown

 Sterling silver (Scotland)

 Britannia silver

 Platinum – an orb

 Sterling silver (England)

 Palladium – the Greek goddess Pallas Athene

DATE LETTER

The date letter shows the year in which an article was assayed and hallmarked. Each alphabetical cycle has a distinctive style of lettering or shape of shield. The date letters were different at the various assay offices and the particular office must be established from the assay office mark before reference is made to tables of date letters. Date letter marks became voluntary from 1 January 1999.

The table which follows shows one specimen shield and letter used by the London Assay Office on silver articles for each alphabetical cycle from 1498. The same letters are found on gold articles but the surrounding shield may differ. Until 1 January 1975 two calendar years are given for each specimen date letter as the letter changed annually in May on St Dunstan's Day (the patron saint of silversmiths). Since 1 January 1975, each date letter has indicated a calendar year from January to December and each office has used the same style of date letter and shield for all articles:

LONDON (GOLDSMITHS' HALL) DATE LETTERS FROM 1498

	from	to		from	to
(symbol)	1498–9	1517–18	(symbol)	1756–7	1775–6
(symbol)	1518–19	1537–8	(symbol)	1776–7	1795–6
(symbol)	1538–9	1557–8	(symbol)	1796–7	1815–16
(symbol)	1558–9	1577–8	(symbol)	1816–17	1835–6
(symbol)	1578–9	1597–8	(symbol)	1836–7	1855–6
(symbol)	1598–9	1617–18	(symbol)	1856–7	1875–6
(symbol)	1618–19	1637–8	(symbol)	1876–7 (A to M square shield, N to Z as shown)	1895–6
(symbol)	1638–9	1657–8	(symbol)	1896–7	1915–16
(symbol)	1658–9	1677–8	(symbol)	1916–17	1935–6
(symbol)	1678–9	1696–7	(symbol)	1936–7	1955–6
(symbol)	1697	1715–16	(symbol)	1956–7	1974
(symbol)	1716–17	1735–6	(symbol)	1975	1999
(symbol)	1736–7	1738–9	(symbol)	2000	
(symbol)	1739–40	1755–6			

OTHER MARKS

FOREIGN GOODS

Foreign goods imported into the UK are required to be hallmarked before sale, unless they already bear a convention mark (*see* below) or a hallmark struck by an independent assay office in the European Economic Area which is deemed to be equivalent to a UK hallmark.

The following are the assay office marks used for gold imported articles until the end of 1998. For silver and platinum the symbols remain the same but the shields differ in shape.

 London

 Sheffield

 Birmingham

 Edinburgh

CONVENTION HALLMARKS

The UK has been a signatory to the International Convention on Hallmarks since 1972. A convention hallmark struck by the UK assay offices is recognised by all member countries in the convention and, similarly, convention marks from member countries are legally recognised in the UK. There are currently 19 members of the hallmarking convention: Austria, Cyprus, Czech Republic, Denmark, Finland, Hungary, Ireland, Israel, Latvia, Lithuania, the Netherlands, Norway, Poland, Portugal, Slovakia, Slovenia, Sweden, Switzerland, and the UK.

A convention hallmark comprises four marks: a sponsor's mark, a common control mark, a fineness mark, and an assay office mark.

Examples of common control marks (figures differ according to fineness, but the style of each mark remains the same for each article):

GOLD	SILVER	PALLADIUM	PLATINUM

(375) (800) (950) (850)

COMMEMORATIVE MARKS

There are other marks to commemorate special events: the silver jubilee of King George V and Queen Mary in 1935, the coronation of Queen Elizabeth II in 1953, her silver jubilee in 1977, and her golden jubilee in 2002. During 1999 and 2000 there was a voluntary additional Millennium Mark. A mark to commemorate the Queen's diamond jubilee in 2012 is available from July 2011 to October 2012:

 Diamond Jubilee Hallmark

BRITISH CURRENCY

The unit of currency is the pound sterling (£) of 100 pence. The decimal system was introduced on 15 February 1971.

COIN

Gold Coins
One hundred pounds £100*
Fifty pounds £50*
Twenty-five pounds £25*
Ten pounds £10*
Five pounds £5
Two pounds £2
Sovereign £1
Half-sovereign 50p

Silver Coins
(Britannia coins)*
Two pounds £2
One pound £1
50 pence 50p
Twenty pence 20p

Maundy Money†
Fourpence 4p
Threepence 3p
Twopence 2p
Penny 1p

Bi-colour Coins ‡
Two pounds £2

Nickel-Brass Coins
Two pounds £2 (pre-1997)§
One pound £1

Cupro-Nickel Coins
Crown £5 (since 1990)§
50 pence 50p
Crown 25p (pre-1990)§
20 pence 20p
10 pence 10p
5 pence 5p

Bronze Coins
2 pence 2p
1 penny 1p

Copper-plated Steel Coins ¶
2 pence 2p
1 penny 1p

* Britannia coins: gold bullion coins introduced 1987; silver coins introduced 1997
† Gifts of special money distributed by the sovereign annually on Maundy Thursday to the number of elderly men and women corresponding to the sovereign's own age
‡ Cupro-nickel centre and nickel-brass outer ring
§ Commemorative coins; not intended for general circulation
¶ Since September 1992, although in 1998 the 2p was struck in both copper-plated steel and bronze

GOLD COIN
Gold ceased to circulate during the First World War. Since then controls on buying, selling and holding gold coins have been imposed at various times but have subsequently been revoked. Under the Exchange Control (Gold Coins Exemption) Order 1979, gold coins may now be imported and exported without restriction, except gold coins which are more than 50 years old and valued at a sum in excess of £8,000; these cannot be exported without specific authorisation from the Department for Business, Innovation and Skills.

Value Added Taxation on the sale of gold coins was revoked in 2000.

SILVER COIN
Prior to 1920 silver coins were struck from sterling silver, an alloy of which 925 parts in 1,000 were silver. In 1920 the proportion of silver was reduced to 500 parts. Since 1947 all 'silver' coins, except Maundy money, have been struck from cupro-nickel, an alloy of 75 parts copper and 25 parts nickel, except for the 20p, composed of 84 parts copper, 16 parts nickel. Maundy coins continue to be struck from sterling silver.

BRONZE COIN
Bronze, introduced in 1860 to replace copper, is an alloy consisting mainly of copper with small amounts of zinc and tin. Bronze was replaced by copper-plated steel in September 1992 with the exception of 1998 when the 2p was made in both copper-plated steel and bronze.

LEGAL TENDER

Gold (dated 1838 onwards, if not below least current weight)	to any amount
£5 (Crown since 1990)*	to any amount
£2	to any amount
£1	to any amount
50p	up to £10
25p (Crown pre-1990)*	up to £10
20p	up to £10
10p	up to £5
5p	up to £5
2p	up to 20p
1p	up to 20p

* Only redeemable at the Post Office

The £1 coin was introduced in 1983 to replace the £1 note. The following coins have ceased to be legal tender:

Farthing	31 Dec 1960
Halfpenny (½d)	31 Jul 1969
Half-crown	31 Dec 1969
Threepence	31 Aug 1971
Penny (1d)	31 Aug 1971
Sixpence	30 Jun 1980
Halfpenny (½p)	31 Dec 1984
Old 5 pence	31 Dec 1990
Old 10 pence	30 Jun 1993
Old 50 pence	28 Feb 1998

The Channel Islands and the Isle of Man issue their own coinage, which is legal tender only in the island of issue.

COIN STANDARDS

	Metal	Standard weight (g)	Standard diameter (mm)
1p	bronze	3.56	20.3
1p	copper-plated steel	3.56	20.3
2p	bronze	7.13	25.9
2p	copper-plated steel	7.13	25.9
5p	cupro-nickel	3.25	18.0
10p	cupro-nickel	6.5	24.5
20p	cupro-nickel	5.0	21.4
25p Crown	cupro-nickel	28.28	38.6
50p	cupro-nickel	8.00	27.3
£1	nickel-brass	9.5	22.5
£2	nickel-brass	15.98	28.4
£2	cupro-nickel, nickel-brass	12.00	28.4
£5 Crown	cupro-nickel	28.28	38.6

The 'remedy' is the amount of variation from standard permitted in weight and fineness of coins when first issued from the Royal Mint.

THE TRIAL OF THE PYX

The Trial of the Pyx is the examination by a jury to ascertain that coins made by the Royal Mint, which have been set aside in the pyx (or box), are of the proper weight, diameter and composition required by law. The trial is held annually, presided over by the Queen's Remembrancer, with a jury of freemen of the Company of Goldsmiths.

BANKNOTES

Bank of England notes are issued in denominations of £5, £10, £20 and £50 for the amount of the fiduciary issue, and are legal tender in England and Wales. No £1 notes have been issued since 1984 and in March 1998 the outstanding notes were written off in accordance with the provision of the Currency Act 1983.

The current E series of notes was introduced from June 1990, replacing the D series (see below). A new-style £20 note, the first in series F, was introduced on 13 March 2007. The historical figures portrayed in these series are:

£5	May 2002–date	Elizabeth Fry
£5	Jun 1990–2003	George Stephenson*
£10	Nov 2000–date	Charles Darwin
£10	Apr 1992–2003	Charles Dickens*
£20	Mar 2007–date	Adam Smith
£20	Jun 1999–2010	Sir Edward Elgar*
£20	Jun 1991–2001	Michael Faraday*
£50	Apr 1994–date	Sir John Houblon

* These notes have been withdrawn from circulation

NOTE CIRCULATION

Note circulation is highest at the two peak spending periods of the year: around Christmas and during the summer holiday period.

The value of notes in circulation (£ million) at the end of February 2010 and 2011 was:

	2010	2011
£5	1,245	1,355
£10	6,399	6,493
£20	30,048	30,973
£50	9,248	9,940
Other notes*	3,280	3,433
TOTAL	50,220	52,194

* Includes higher value notes used internally in the Bank of England, eg as cover for the note issues of banks in Scotland and Northern Ireland in excess of their permitted issue

LEGAL TENDER

Banknotes which are no longer legal tender are payable when presented at the head office of the Bank of England in London.

The white notes for £10, £20, £50, £100, £500 and £1,000, which were issued until April 1943, ceased to be legal tender in May 1945, and the white £5 note in March 1946.

The white £5 note issued between October 1945 and September 1956, the £5 notes issued between 1957 and 1963 (bearing a portrait of Britannia) and the first series to bear a portrait of the Queen, issued between 1963 and 1971, ceased to be legal tender in March 1961, June 1967 and September 1973 respectively.

The series of £1 notes issued during the years 1928 to 1960 and the 10 shilling notes issued from 1928 to 1961 (those without the royal portrait) ceased to be legal tender in May and October 1962 respectively. The £1 note first issued in March 1960 (bearing on the back a representation of Britannia) and the £10 note first issued in February 1964 (bearing a lion on the back), both bearing a portrait of the Queen on the front, ceased to be legal tender in June 1979. The £1 note first issued in 1978 ceased to be legal tender on 11 March 1988. The 10 shilling note was replaced by the 50p coin in October 1969, and ceased to be legal tender on 21 November 1970.

The D series of banknotes was introduced from 1970 and ceased to be legal tender from the dates shown below. The predominant identifying feature of each note was the portrayal on the back of a prominent figure from British history:

£1	Feb 1978–Mar 1988	Sir Isaac Newton
£5	Nov 1971–Nov 1991	Duke of Wellington
£10	Feb 1975–May 1994	Florence Nightingale
£20	Jul 1970–Mar 1993	William Shakespeare
£50	Mar 1981–Sep 1996	Sir Christopher Wren

The £1 coin was introduced on 21 April 1983 to replace the £1 note.

OTHER BANKNOTES

Scotland – Banknotes are issued by three Scottish banks. The Royal Bank of Scotland issues notes for £1, £5, £10, £20, £50 and £100. Bank of Scotland and the Clydesdale Bank issue notes for £5, £10, £20, £50 and £100. Scottish notes are not legal tender in the UK but they are an authorised currency.

Northern Ireland – Banknotes are issued by four banks in Northern Ireland. The Bank of Ireland, the Northern Bank and the Ulster Bank issue notes for £5, £10, £20, £50 and £100. The First Trust Bank issues notes for £10, £20, £50 and £100. Northern Ireland notes are not legal tender in Northern Ireland but they circulate widely and enjoy a status comparable to that of Bank of England notes.

Channel Islands – The States of Guernsey issues its own currency notes and coinage. The notes are for £1, £5, £10, £20 and £50, and the coins are for 1p, 2p, 5p, 10p, 20p, 50p, £1 and £2. The States of Jersey issues its own currency notes and coinage. The notes are for £1, £5, £10, £20 and £50, and the coins are for 1p, 2p, 5p, 10p, 20p, 50p, £1 and £2.

The Isle of Man – The Isle of Man government issues notes for £1, £5, £10, £20 and £50. Although these notes are only legal tender in the Isle of Man, they are accepted at face value in branches of the clearing banks in the UK. The Isle of Man issues coins for 1p, 2p, 5p, 10p, 20p, 50p, £1, £2 and £5.

Although none of the series of notes specified above is legal tender in the UK, they are generally accepted by banks irrespective of their place of issue. At one time banks made a commission charge for handling Scottish and Irish notes but this was abolished some years ago.

BANK FAMILY TREE

Includes the major retail banks operating in the UK as at
April 2011. Financial results for these banks are given on
the following page. Building societies are only included in
instances where they demutualised to become a bank.

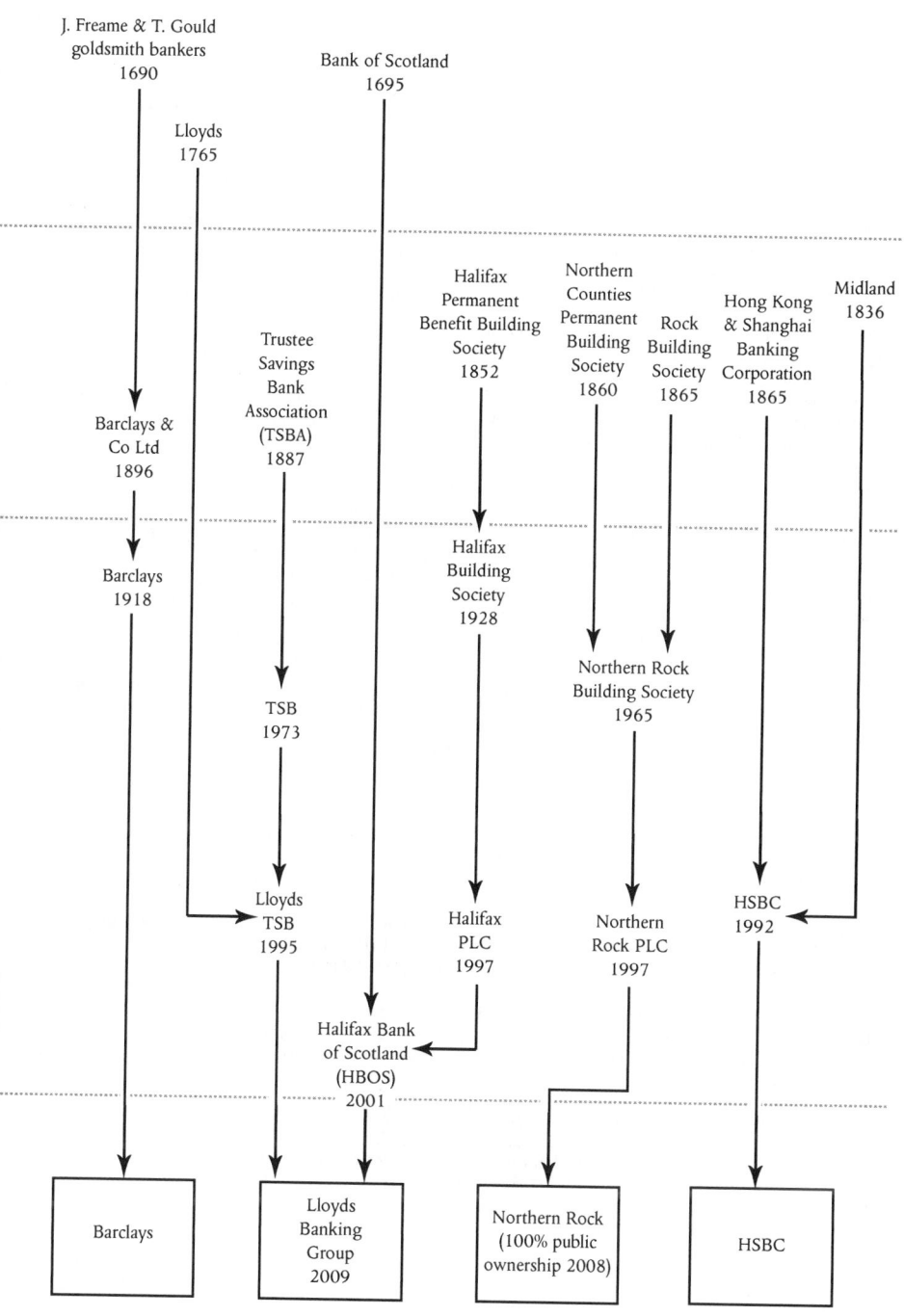

J. Freame & T. Gould
goldsmith bankers
1690

Bank of Scotland
1695

Lloyds
1765

Halifax
Permanent
Benefit Building
Society
1852

Northern
Counties
Permanent
Building
Society
1860

Rock
Building
Society
1865

Hong Kong
& Shanghai
Banking
Corporation
1865

Midland
1836

Trustee
Savings
Bank
Association
(TSBA)
1887

Barclays &
Co Ltd
1896

Barclays
1918

Halifax
Building
Society
1928

Northern Rock
Building Society
1965

TSB
1973

Lloyds
TSB
1995

Halifax
PLC
1997

Northern
Rock PLC
1997

HSBC
1992

Halifax Bank
of Scotland
(HBOS)
2001

Barclays

Lloyds
Banking
Group
2009

Northern Rock
(100% public
ownership 2008)

HSBC

BANKING AND PERSONAL FINANCE

There are two main types of deposit-taking institutions: banks and building societies, although National Savings and Investments also provides savings products. Banks and building societies are supervised by the Financial Services Authority (see Financial Services Regulation) and National Savings and Investments is accountable to the Treasury. As a result of the conversion of several building societies into banks in the 1990s, the size of the banking sector, which was already substantially greater than the non-bank deposit-taking sector, increased further.

The main institutions within the British banking system are the Bank of England (the central bank), retail banks, investment banks and overseas banks. In its role as the central bank, the Bank of England acts as banker to the government and as a note-issuing authority; it also oversees the efficient functioning of payment and settlement systems.

Since May 1997, the Bank of England has had operational responsibility for monetary policy. At monthly meetings of its monetary policy committee the Bank sets the interest rate at which it will lend to the money markets.

OFFICIAL INTEREST RATES 2005–11

4 August 2005	4.50%
3 August 2006	4.75%
9 November 2006	5.00%
11 January 2007	5.25%
10 May 2007	5.50%
5 July 2007	5.75%
6 December 2007	5.50%
7 February 2008	5.25%
10 April 2008	5.00%
8 October 2008	4.50%
6 November 2008	3.00%
4 December 2008	2.00%
8 January 2009	1.50%
5 February 2009	1.00%
5 March 2009	0.50%

RETAIL BANKING

Retail banks offer a wide variety of financial services to individuals and companies, including current and deposit accounts, loan and overdraft facilities, credit and debit cards, investment services, pensions, insurance and mortgages. All banks offer telephone and internet banking facilities in addition to traditional branch services.

The Financial Ombudsman Service provides independent and impartial arbitration in disputes between banks and their customers (see Financial Services Regulation).

PAYMENT CLEARINGS

The UK Payments Administration (UKPA) is a trade body that brings together the organisations responsible for delivering payment services. It also provides information on payment issues such as card fraud, cheques, plastic cards, electronic payments and cash. The Payments Council sets strategy for UK payments to ensure they meet the needs of users, payment service providers and the wider economy. Membership of the Payments Council is open to any member of a payment scheme that is widely used or significant in the UK. As at April 2011 the Payments Council had 30 members, comprising banks, financial services providers, one building society and the Post Office.

There are three organisations, overseen by UKPA, that manage the majority of payment clearings in the UK:

- BACS manages the schemes under which electronic payments are made, processing direct debits, direct credits and standing orders (W www.bacs.co.uk)
- CHAPS Clearing Company provides electronic same-day clearing and real-time settlement services for sterling payments (W www.chapsco.co.uk)
- The Cheque and Credit Clearing Company manages the cheque clearing system (W www.chequeandcredit.co.uk)

PAYMENTS COUNCIL/UKPA, 2 Thomas More Square, London E1W 1YN T 020-3217 8200
W www.ukpayments.org.uk

GLOSSARY OF FINANCIAL TERMS

AER (ANNUAL EQUIVALENT RATE) – A notional rate quoted on savings and investment products which demonstrates the return on interest, when compounded and paid annually.

APR (ANNUAL PERCENTAGE RATE) – Calculates the total amount of interest payable over the whole term of a product (such as investment or loan), allowing consumers to compare rival products on a like-for-like basis. Companies offering loans, credit cards

MAJOR RETAIL BANKS' FINANCIAL RESULTS 2010

Bank group	Profit/(loss) before taxation £ million	Profit/(loss) after taxation £ million	Total assets £ million
Banco Santander Group	10,681	7,251	1,079,341
Barclays	6,065	4,549	1,489,645
Cooperative Bank	109	79	45,581
HSBC	11,601	8,648	1,495,956
Lloyds Banking Group	281	(258)	991,574
Northern Rock*	(224)	(224)	18,562
RBS Group	(239)	(902)	1,452,634

* In February 2008 Northern Rock was taken into public ownership

mortgages or overdrafts are required by law to provide the APR rate. Where typical APR is shown, it refers to the company's typical borrower and so is given as a best example; rate and costs may vary depending on individual circumstances.

ANNUITY – A type of insurance policy that provides regular income in exchange for a lump sum. The annuity can be bought from a company other than the existing pension provider.

ASU – Accident, sickness and unemployment insurance taken out by a borrower to protect against being unable to work for these reasons. The policy will usually pay a percentage of the normal monthly mortgage repayment if the borrower is unable to work.

ATM (AUTOMATED TELLER MACHINES) – Commonly referred to as cash machines. Users can access their bank accounts using a card for simple transactions such as withdrawing and depositing cash. Some banks and independent ATM deployers charge for transactions.

BANKER'S DRAFT – A cheque drawn on a bank against a cash deposit. Considered to be a secure way of receiving money in instances where a cheque could 'bounce' or where it is not desirable to receive cash.

BASE RATE – The interest rate set by the Bank of England at which it will lend to financial institutions. This acts as a benchmark for all other interest rates.

BASIS POINT – Unit of measure (usually one-hundredth of a percentage point) used to express movements in interest rates, foreign rates or bond yields.

BUY-TO-LET – The purchase of a residential property for the sole purpose of letting to a tenant. Not all lenders provide mortgage finance for this purpose. Buy-to-let lenders assess projected rental income (typical expectations are between 125 and 130 per cent of the monthly interest payment) in addition to, or instead of, the borrower's income. Buy-to-let mortgages are available as either interest only or repayment.

CAPITAL GAIN/LOSS – Increase/decrease in the value of a capital asset when it is sold or transferred compared to its initial value.

CAPPED RATE MORTGAGE – The interest rate applied to a loan is guaranteed not to rise above a certain rate for a set period of time; the rate can therefore fall but will not rise above the capped rate. The level at which the cap is fixed is usually higher than for a fixed rate mortgage for a comparable period of time. The lender normally imposes early redemption penalties within the first few years.

CASH CARD – Issued by banks and building societies for withdrawing cash from ATMs.

CHARGE CARD – Charge cards, eg American Express and Diners Club, can be used in a similar way to credit cards but the debt must be settled in full each month.

CHIP AND PIN CARD – A credit/debit card which incorporates an embedded chip containing unique owner details. When used with a PIN, such cards offer greater security as they are less prone to fraud. Since 14 February 2006, most card transactions in the UK have required the use of a chip and pin card.

CREDIT CARD – Normally issued with a credit limit, credit cards can be used for purchases until the limit is reached. There is normally an interest-free period on the outstanding balance of up to 56 days. Charges can be avoided if the balance is paid off in full within the interest-free period. Alternatively part of the balance can be paid and in most cases there is a minimum

amount set by the issuer (normally a percentage of the outstanding balance) which must be paid on a monthly basis. Some card issuers charge an annual fee and most issuers belong to a least one major credit card network, eg Mastercard or Visa.

CREDIT RATING – Overall credit worthiness of a borrower based on information from a credit reference agency, such as Experian or Equifax, which holds details of credit agreements, payment records, county court judgements etc for all adults in the UK. This information is supplied to lenders who use it in their credit scoring or underwriting systems to calculate the risk of granting a loan to an individual and the probability that it will be repaid. Each lender sets their own criteria for credit worthiness and may accept or reject a credit application based on an individual's credit rating.

CRITICAL ILLNESS COVER – Insurance that covers borrowers against critical illnesses such as stroke, heart attack or cancer and is designed to protect mortgage or other loan payments.

DEBIT CARD – Debit cards were introduced on a large scale in the UK in the mid-1980s, replacing cash and cheques to purchase goods and services. They can be used to withdraw cash from ATMs in the UK and abroad and may also function as a cheque guarantee card. Funds are automatically withdrawn from an individual's bank account after making a purchase and no interest is charged.

DIRECT DEBIT – An instruction from a customer to their bank, which authorises the payee to charge costs to the customer's bank account.

DISCOUNTED MORTGAGE – Discounted mortgages guarantee an interest rate set at a margin below the standard variable rate for a period of time. The discounted rate will move up or down with the standard variable rate, but the payment rate will retain the agreed differential below the standard variable rate. The lender normally imposes early redemption penalties within the first few years.

EARLY REDEMPTION PENALTY – see Redemption Penalty

ENDOWMENT MORTGAGE – Only the interest on a property loan is paid back to the lender each month as long as an endowment life insurance policy is taken out for an agreed amount of time, typically 25 years. When the policy matures the lender will take repayment of the money owed on the property loan and any surplus goes to the policyholder. If the endowment policy shows a shortfall on projected returns, the policy holder must make further provision to pay off the mortgage.

EQUITY – When applied to real estate, equity is the difference between the value of a property and the amount outstanding on any loan secured against it. Negative equity occurs when the loan is greater than the market value of the property.

FIXED RATE MORTGAGE – A repayment mortgage where the interest rate on the loan is fixed for a set amount of time, normally a period of between one and ten years. The interest rate does not vary with changes to the base rate resulting in the monthly mortgage payment remaining the same for the duration of the fixed period. The lender normally imposes early redemption penalties within the first few years.

ISA (INDIVIDUAL SAVINGS ACCOUNT) – A means by which investors can save (in a cash ISA) and invest (in a stocks and shares ISA) without paying any tax on the proceeds. There are limits on the amount that can be invested during any given tax year (*see* Taxation).

INTEREST ONLY MORTGAGE – Only interest is paid by the borrower and capital remains constant for the term of the loan. The onus is on the borrower to make provision to repay the capital at the end of the term. This is usually achieved through an investment vehicle such as an endowment policy or pension.

LOAN TO VALUE (LTV) – This is the ratio between the size of a mortgage loan sought and the mortgage lender's valuation. On a loan of £55,000, for example, on a property valued at £100,000 the loan to value is 55 per cent. This means that there is sufficient equity in the property for the lender to be reassured that if interest or capital repayments were stopped, it could sell the property and recoup the money owed. Fewer options are available to borrowers requiring high LTV.

LONDON INTERBANK OFFERED RATE (LIBOR) – Is the interest rate that London banks charge when lending to one another on the wholesale money market. LIBOR is set by supply and demand of money as banks lend to each other in order to balance their books on a daily basis.

MIG (MORTGAGE INDEMNITY GUARANTEE) – An insurance for the lender paid by the borrower on high LTV mortgages (typically more than 90 per cent). It is a policy designed to protect the lender against loss in the event of the borrower defaulting or ceasing to repay a mortgage and is usually paid as a one-off premium or can be added to the value of the loan. It offers no protection to the borrower. Not all lenders charge MIG premiums.

OVERDRAFT – An 'authorised' overdraft is an arrangement made between customer and bank allowing the balance of the customer's account to go below zero; interest is normally charged at an agreed rate and sometimes an arrangement fee is charged. If the negative balance exceeds the agreed terms or a prior arrangement for an overdraft facility has not been made (an 'unauthorised' overdraft) then additional penalty fees can be charged and higher interest rates may apply. Interest-free overdrafts are availble for customers in certain circumstances, such as full-time higher education students and recent graduates.

PERSONAL PENSION PLAN (PPP) – Designed for the self-employed or those in non-pensionable employment. Contributions made to a PPP are exempt from tax and the retirement age may be selected at any time from age 50 to 75. Up to 25 per cent of the pension fund may be taken as a tax-free cash sum on retirement.

PHISHING – A fraudulent attempt to obtain bank account details and security codes through an email. The email purports to come from a *bona fide* bank or building society and attempts to steer the recipient, usually under the pretext that the banking institution is updating its security arrangements, to a website which requests personal details.

PIN (PERSONAL IDENTIFICATION NUMBER) – A PIN is issued alongside a cash card to allow the user to access a bank account via an ATM. PINs are also issued with smart, credit and debit cards and, since 14 February 2006, have been requested in the majority of shops and restaurants as a security measure when making a purchase.

PORTABLE MORTGAGE – A mortgage product that can be transferred to a different property in the event of a house move. Preferable where early redemption penalties are charged.

REDEMPTION PENALTY – A charge levied for paying off a loan, debt balance or mortgage before a date agreed with the lender.

REPAYMENT MORTGAGE – In contrast to the interest only mortgage, the monthly repayment includes an element of the capital sum borrowed in addition to the interest charged.

SELF-CERTIFICATION – Some lenders allow borrowers to self-certify their income. This type of scheme is useful to the self-employed who may not have accounts available or any other person who has difficulty proving their regular income.

SHARE – A share is a divided-up unit of the value of a company. If a company is worth £100m, and there are 50 million shares in issue, then each share is worth £2 (usually listed as pence). As the overall value of the company fluctuates so does the share price.

SMART CARD – *see* chip and pin card

STANDING ORDER – An instruction made by the customer to their bank, which allows the transfer of a set amount to a payee at regular intervals.

TELEPHONE BANKING – Banking facilities which can be accessed via the telephone.

UNIT TRUST – A 'pooled' fund of assets, usually shares, owned by a number of individuals. Managed by professional, authorised fund-management groups, unit trusts have traditionally delivered better returns than average cash deposits, but do rise and fall in value as their underlying investment varies in value.

VARIABLE RATE MORTGAGE – Repayment mortgages where the interest rate set by the lender increases or decreases in relation to the base interest rate which can result in fluctuating monthly repayments.

WITH-PROFITS – Usually applies to pensions, endowments, savings schemes or bonds. The intention is to smooth out the rises and falls in the stock market for the benefit of the investor. Actuaries working for the insurance company, or fund managers, hold back some profits in good years in order to make up the difference in years when shares perform badly.

FINANCIAL SERVICES REGULATION

FINANCIAL SERVICES AUTHORITY

The FSA has been the single regulator for financial services in the UK since 1 December 2001, when the Financial Services and Markets Act 2000 (FSMA) came into force. Under the FSMA the FSA has four main statutory objectives:

- maintaining market confidence
- contributing to financial stability
- protecting consumers
- reducing financial crime

In June 2010, the Chancellor of the Exchequer announced the government's intention to restructure the UK's financial regulatory framework and replace the FSA with two new regulatory bodies by 2013:

- The Prudential Regulation Authority (PRA), a subsidiary of the bank of England, will be responsible for promoting the stable and prudent operation of the financial system through the regulation of all deposit-taking institutions, insurers and investment banks
- The Financial Conduct Authority (FCA) will be responsible for regulation of conduct in retail, wholesale and financial markets and the infrastructure that supports these markets. The FCA will also have responsibility for the regulation of firms that do not fall under the PRA's scope.

On 4 April 2011, in order to ensure a smooth transition to the new regulatory framework, the FSA changed it's organisational structure, replacing the supervision and risk business units with a prudential business unit and a conduct business unit.

FUNDING

The FSA is a company limited by guarantee and financed by levies on the industry. It receives no funds from the public purse. It is accountable to treasury ministers and, through them, to parliament. The FSA must report annually on the achievement of its statutory objectives to the Treasury, which is required to lay the report before parliament. The FSA's budget for 2011–12 is £500.5m.

FSA REGISTER

The FSA register is a public record of financial services firms, individuals and other bodies who come under the FSA's regulatory jurisdiction as defined in the FSMA. The register has information on all authorised firms currently doing business in the UK. It includes firms that are UK registered as well as those authorised in other European economic area states that conduct business in the UK. Each entry outlines exactly what regulated activities the firm or individual is authorised to carry out.

FINANCIAL SERVICES AUTHORITY, 25 The North Colonnade, Canary Wharf, London E14 5HS **T** 020-7066 1000
W www.fsa.gov.uk
Chair, Lord Turner of Ecchinswell
Chief Executive, Hector Sants

COMPENSATION

Created under the FSMA, the Financial Services Compensation Scheme (FSCS) is the UK's statutory fund of last resort for customers of authorised financial services firms. It provides compensation if a firm authorised by the FSA is unable, or likely to be unable, to pay claims against it. In general this is when a firm has stopped trading and has insufficient assets to meet claims, or is in insolvency. The FSCS covers deposits, insurance policies, insurance broking, investment business and mortgage advice and arranging. The FSCS is independent of the FSA, with separate staff and premises. However, the FSA appoints the board of the FSCS and sets its guidelines. The FSCS is funded by levies on authorised firms.

The Pension Protection Fund (PPF) is a statutory fund established under the Pensions Act 2004 and became operational on 6 April 2005. The fund was set up to pay compensation to members of eligible defined benefit pension schemes, where there is a qualifying insolvency event in relation to the employer and where there are insufficient assets in the pension scheme to cover PPF levels of compensation. Compulsory annual levies are charged on all eligible schemes to help fund the PPF, in addition to investment of PPF assets.

FINANCIAL SERVICES COMPENSATION SCHEME, 7th Floor, Lloyds Chambers, Portsoken Street, London E1 8BN **T** 020-7741 4100/0800-678 1100 **E** enquiries@fscs.org.uk **W** www.fscs.org.uk
Chair, David Hall
Chief Executive, Mark Neale
PENSION PROTECTION FUND, Knollys House, 17 Addiscombe Road, Croydon, Surrey CR0 6SR **T** 0845-600 2541
E information@ppf.gsi.gov.uk
W www.pensionprotectionfund.org.uk
Chair, Lady Judge, CBE
Chief Executive, Alan Rubenstein

DESIGNATED PROFESSIONAL BODIES

Professional firms are exempt from requiring direct regulation by the FSA if they carry out only certain restricted activities that arise out of, or are complementary to, the provision of professional services, such as arranging the sale of shares on the instructions of executors or trustees, or providing services to small, private companies. These firms are, however, supervised by designated professional bodies (DPBs). There are a number of safeguards to protect consumers dealing with firms that do not require direct regulation. These arrangements include:

- the FSA's power to ban a specific firm from taking advantage of the exemption and to restrict the regulated activities permitted to the firms
- rules which require professional firms to ensure that their clients are aware that they are not authorised persons
- a requirement for the DPBs to supervise and regulate the firms and inform the FSA on how the professional firms carry on their regulated activities

See Professional Education section for contact details of the following DPBs:

Association of Chartered Certified Accountants
Council for Licensed Conveyancers
Institute and Faculty of Actuaries
Institute of Chartered Accountants in England and Wales
Institute of Chartered Accountants in Ireland
Institute of Chartered Accountants of Scotland
Law Society of England and Wales
Law Society of Northern Ireland
Law Society of Scotland
Royal Institution of Chartered Surveyors

RECOGNISED INVESTMENT EXCHANGES

The FSA currently supervises six recognised investment exchanges (RIEs) in the UK; under the FSMA, recognition confers an exemption from the need to be authorised to carry out regulated activities in the UK. The RIEs are organised markets on which member firms can trade investments such as equities and derivatives. As a regulator the FSA must focus on the impact of changes brought about by the continued growth in electronic trading by exchanges and other organisations. Issues such as how these changes affect market quality, reliability and access are important and the FSA works with the exchanges to ensure that new systems meet regulatory requirements. The RIEs are listed with their year of recognition in parentheses:

EUROPEAN DERIVATIVES EXCHANGE (EDX) LONDON (2003),
   10 Paternoster Square, London EC4M 7LS T 020-7797 4683
   W www.londonstockexchange.com/edx/
   home/homepage.htm
INTERCONTINENTAL EXCHANGE (ICE) FUTURES EUROPE (2001),
   5th Floor, Milton Gate, 60 Chiswell Street, London EC1Y 4SA
   T 020-7065 7700 W www.theice.com
LONDON INTERNATIONAL FINANCIAL FUTURES (LIFFE)
   ADMINISTRATION AND MANAGEMENT (2001), Cannon
   Bridge House, 1 Cousin Lane, London EC4R 3XX
   T 020-7623 0444 W www.liffe.com
LONDON METAL EXCHANGE (2001), 56 Leadenhall Street,
   London EC3A 2BJ T 020-7264 5555 W www.lme.co.uk
LONDON STOCK EXCHANGE (LSE) (2001), 10 Paternoster
   Square, London EC4M 7LS T 020-7797 1000
   W www.londonstockexchange.com
PLUS STOCK EXCHANGE (2007), 33 Queen Street, London
   EC4R 1AP T 020-7429 7800 W www.plusmarketsgroup.com

RECOGNISED CLEARING HOUSES

The FSA is also responsible for recognising and super-vising recognised clearing houses (RCHs), which organise the settlement of transactions on recognised investment exchanges. There are currently five RCHs in the UK:

CME CLEARING EUROPE (2010), Watling House, 33 Cannon
   Street, London EC4M 5SB T 020-7796 7150
   W www.cmeclearingeurope.co.uk
EUROCLEAR UK AND IRELAND (2001), Watling House, 33
   Cannon Street, London EC4M 5SB T 020-7849 0000
   W www.crestco.co.uk
EUROPEAN CENTRAL COUNTERPARTY (2008), Broadgate West,
   1 Snowdon Street, London EC2A 2DQ T 020-7650 1401
   W www.euroccp.co.uk
ICE CLEAR EUROPE (2008), 5th Floor, Milton Gate, 60 Chiswell
   Street, London EC1Y 4SA T 020-7265 3648
   W www.theice.com/clear_europe

LONDON CLEARING HOUSE (LCH) CLEARNET (2001), Aldgate
   House, 33 Aldgate High Street, London EC3N 1EA
   T 020-7426 7000 W www.lchclearnet.com

OMBUDSMAN SCHEMES

The Financial Ombudsman Service was set up by the Financial Services and Markets Act 2000 to provide consumers with a free, independent service for resolving disputes with authorised financial firms. The Financial Ombudsman Service can consider complaints about most financial matters including: banking; credit cards and store cards; financial advice; hire purchase and pawnbroking; insurance; loans and credit; money transfer; mortgages; pensions; savings and investments; stocks, shares, unit trusts and bonds.

Complainants must first complain to the firm involved. They do not have to accept the ombudsman's decision and are free to go to court if they wish, but if a decision is accepted, it is binding for both the complainant and the firm.

The Pensions Ombudsman can investigate and decide complaints and disputes about the way that occupational and personal pension schemes are administered and managed. The Pensions Ombudsman is also the Ombudsman for the Pension Protection Fund (PPF) and the Financial Assistance Scheme (which offers help to those who were a member of an under-funded defined benefit pension scheme that started to wind-up in specific financial circumstances between 1 January 1997 and 5 April 2005).

FINANCIAL OMBUDSMAN SERVICE, South Quay Plaza, 183
   Marsh Wall, London E14 9SR Helpline 0845-080 1800 T
   020-7964 1000 E
   complaint.info@financial-ombudsman.org.uk W
   www.financial-ombudsman.org.uk
   Chief Executive and Chief Ombudsman,
   Natalie Ceeney, CBE
   Principal Ombudsmen, Tony Boorman; David Thomas;
   Caroline Wayman
PENSIONS OMBUDSMAN, 11 Belgrave Road, London SW1V 1RB
   T 020-7630 2200 E enquiries@pensions-ombudsman.org.uk
   W www.pensions-ombudsman.org.uk
   Pensions Ombudsman, Tony King
   Deputy Pensions Ombudsman, Jane Irvine

PANEL ON TAKEOVERS AND MERGERS

The Panel on Takeovers and Mergers is an independent body, established in 1968, whose main functions are to issue and administer the City code and to ensure equality of treatment and opportunity for all shareholders in takeover bids and mergers. The panel's statutory functions are set out in the Companies Act 2006.

The panel comprises up to 35 members drawn from major financial and business institutions. The chair, deputy chair and up to 20 other members are nominated by the panel's own nomination committee. The remaining members are nominated by professional bodies representing the banking, insurance, investment, pension and accountancy industries and the CBI.

PANEL ON TAKEOVERS AND MERGERS, 10 Paternoster Square,
   London EC4M 7DY T 020-7382 9026
   W www.thetakeoverpanel.org.uk
   Chair, Sir Gordon Langley

NATIONAL SAVINGS AND INVESTMENTS

NS&I (National Savings and Investments) is an executive agency of HM Treasury and one of the UK's largest financial providers, with almost 27 million customers and over £98bn invested. NS&I offers savings and investment products to personal savers and investors and the money is used to manage the national debt. When people invest in NS&I they are lending money to the government which pays them interest or prizes in return. All products are financially secure because they are guaranteed by HM Treasury.

TAX-FREE PRODUCTS

SAVINGS CERTIFICATES

Index-linked Saving Certificates
Otherwise known as inflation-beating savings, index-inked saving certificates are fixed rate investments that pay tax-free returns guaranteed to be above inflation. They are sold in limited issues with a minimum and maximum investment.

Fixed Interest Saving Certificates
Fixed interest saving certificates are fixed rate investments that pay tax-free returns. They are sold in limited issues with a minimum and maximum investment.

PREMIUM BONDS
Introduced in 1956, premium bonds enable savers to enter a regular draw for tax-free prizes, while retaining the right to get their money back. A sum equivalent to interest on each bond is put into a prize fund and distributed by monthly prize draws. The prizes are drawn by ERNIE (electronic random number indicator equipment) and are free of all UK income tax and capital gains tax. A £1m jackpot is drawn each month in addition to other tax-free prizes ranging in value from £25 to £100,000.

Bonds are in units of £1, with a minimum purchase of £100; above this, purchases must be in multiples of £10, up to a maximum holding limit of £30,000 per person. Bonds become eligible for prizes once they have been held for one clear calendar month following the month of purchase. Each £1 unit can win only one prize per draw, but it will be awarded the highest for which it is drawn. Bonds remain eligible for prizes until they are repaid.

The scheme offers a facility to reinvest prize wins automatically. Upon completion of an automatic prize reinvestment mandate, holders receive new bonds which are immediately eligible for future prize draws. Bonds can only be held in the name of an individual and not by organisations.

As at April 2011, over 225 million prizes totalling £13bn had been distributed since the first prize draw in 1957.

CHILDREN'S BONUS BONDS
Children's bonus bonds were introduced in 1991. The bonds are sold in five-year issues at multiples of £25. For each issue the minimum holding is £25 and the maximum holding is £3,000 per child. They can be bought for any child under 16, but must be held by a parent or guardian.

All returns are totally exempt from UK income tax and a bonus is payable if the bond is held for the full five years.

OTHER PRODUCTS

GUARANTEED EQUITY BONDS
Guaranteed equity bonds are five-year investments where the returns are linked to the performance of the FTSE-100 index with a guarantee that the original capital invested will be returned even if the FTSE-100 index fell over the five years. They are sold in limited issues with a minimum investment of £1,000 and a maximum of £1m. The returns are subject to income tax on maturity, unless they are held in a self-invested pension plan (SIPP).

SAVINGS AND INVESTMENT ACCOUNTS
The direct saver account was launched in March 2010. Customers are able to invest between £1 and £2m per person. The account can be managed online or by telephone. Interest is paid without deduction of tax at source.

The easy access savings account offers access to savings via Post Office counters, an ATM card, telephone and online. It can be opened with a minimum balance of £100 and has a maximum limit of £2m (£4m jointly). The interest is paid without deduction of tax at source.

The investment account is a passbook account which pays tiered rates of interest. It can be opened with a minimum balance of £20 and has a maximum limit of £100,000. The interest is paid without deduction of tax at source.

Since April 1999 NS&I has offered cash individual savings accounts (ISAs). Its Direct ISA, launched in April 2006, can be opened and managed online and by telephone with a minimum investment of £100. Interest for the Direct ISA is calculated daily and is free of tax.

INCOME BONDS
NS&I income bonds were introduced in 1982. They are suitable for those who want to receive regular monthly payments of interest while preserving the full cash value of their capital. The bonds are sold in multiples of £500. The minimum holding is £500 and the maximum £1m (sole or joint holding). A variable rate of interest is calculated on a day-to-day basis and paid monthly. Interest is taxable but is paid without deduction of tax at source.

GUARANTEED INCOME BONDS
Guaranteed income bonds were introduced in February 2008. They are designed for those who want to receive regular monthly payments of interest while preserving the full cash value of their capital. The minimum holding is £500 and the maximum £1m, including any amount held in guaranteed growth bonds and fixed rate savings bonds. A fixed rate of interest is calculated on a day-to-day basis and paid monthly on these bonds. Interest is taxable and tax is deducted at source.

GUARANTEED GROWTH BONDS
Guaranteed growth bonds were introduced in February 2008. They are suitable for those who want to receive

regular monthly payments of interest while preserving the full cash value of their capital. The minimum holding is £500 and the maximum £1m, including any amount held in guaranteed income bonds and fixed rate savings bonds. A fixed rate of interest is calculated on a day-to-day basis and is paid annually on the anniversary of the date of investment. Interest is taxable and tax is deducted at source.

FURTHER INFORMATION
Further information regarding products and their current availability can be obtained online (W www.nsandi.com), by telephone (T 0500-007007) or at Post Office counters.

NATIONAL DEBT

The UK Debt Management Office (DMO), an executive agency of HM Treasury, was created in April 1998 following the transfer of operational responsibility for monetary policy from HM Treasury to the Bank of England. Initially the DMO was responsible only for the management of government marketable debt and for issuing gilts. In April 2000 responsibility for exchequer cash management and for issuing Treasury bills (short-dated securities with maturities of less than one year) was transferred from the Bank of England to the DMO. The national debt also includes the (non-marketable) liabilities of National Savings and Investments and other public sector and foreign currency debt.

In 2002 the operations of the long-standing statutory functions of the Public Works Loan Board, which lends capital to local authorities, and the Commissioners for the Reduction of the National Debt, which manages the investment portfolios of certain public funds, were integrated within the DMO (*see also* Government Departments).

Since 2008 the DMO has undertaken a range of activities at the request of HM Treasury to help stabilise the financial markets and support the UK banking sector. These include administering the credit guarantee scheme and the asset-backed securities guarantee scheme. Since November 2008, the DMO has also undertaken auctions of EU allowances on behalf of the Department of Energy and Climate Change as part of the emissions trading system.

UK NATIONAL DEBT

	£ billion	per cent of GDP
2009–10 (outturn)	741.1	52.7
2010–11 (forecast)	888.2	60.3
2011–12 (forecast)	1,020.6	66.1

Source: HM Treasury: *Budget 2011* (Crown copyright)

THE LONDON STOCK EXCHANGE

The London Stock Exchange serves the needs of companies and investors by providing facilities for raising capital and a central marketplace for securities trading. This marketplace covers UK and overseas company shares and other instruments such as: exchange traded funds (ETFs) and exchange traded commodities (ETCs), international equity derivative products (through EDX London) and both corporate and government bonds.

Over 400 member firms trading on the London Stock Exchange buy and sell securities on behalf of the public, as well as institutions such as pension funds or insurance companies.

The London Stock Exchange is a subsidiary, along with Borsa Italiana, of the London Stock Exchange Group (LSEG).

HISTORY

The London Stock Exchange is one of the world's oldest stock exchanges dating back more than 300 years when it began in the coffee houses of 17th-century London. It was formally established as a membership organisation in 1801.

RECENT DEVELOPMENTS

'BIG BANG'
What has come to be known as 'Big Bang' was a package of reforms in 1986 that transformed the Exchange and the City, liberalising the way in which banks and stock-broking firms operated and bringing in foreign investment. The Exchange ceased granting voting rights to individual members and became a private company. Big Bang also saw the start of a move towards fully electronic trading and the closure of the trading floor.

INTRODUCTION OF SETS
In October 1997, the Exchange introduced SETS, its electronic order book. The system enhanced the efficiency and transparency of trading on the Exchange, allowing trades to be executed automatically and anonymously rather than negotiated by telephone.

DEMUTALISATION AND LISTING
The London Stock Exchange became demutualised in 2000 and listed on its own main market in 2001 in order to allow further commercialisation.

EDX LONDON
In 2003 the London Stock Exchange created EDX London (European derivatives exchange), a recognised investment exchange for international equity derivatives.

MERGER WITH BORSA ITALIANA
On 1 October 2007 the Exchange merged with the Italian stock exchange Borsa Italiana and London Stock Exchange Group PLC replaced the London Stock Exchange as the listed entity.

PRIMARY MARKETS

The London Stock Exchange enables UK and overseas companies to raise capital for development and growth through the issue of securities. For a company entering the market the Exchange offers a choice of four differently regulated markets, depending upon the size, history and requirements of the company:

• the main market enables established companies to raise capital, widen their investor base and have their shares traded on a global stock market. The market is regulated by the FSA's UK Listing Authority (UKLA). The FTSE 100 index is based on main market stocks
• the Alternative Investment Market (AIM), established in June 1995, is specially designed to meet the needs of small, young and growing companies, enabling them to raise capital, broaden their investor base and benefit from being traded on an internationally recognised market. AIM is regulated by the London Stock Exchange and quoted companies must adhere to the AIM rules and retain a Nominated Adviser (or 'Nomad') at all times, who is responsible for ensuring the company's suitability for the market. The AIM model has been extended to AIM Italia, launched in Italy at the end of 2008, and AIM Tokyo, launched in collaboration with the Tokyo Stock Exchange in spring 2009
• the Professional Securities Market (PSM), established in July 2005 and regulated by the FSA, offers international companies that wish to access an exclusively institutional investor base an option to list equity and debt securities in London on a market that offers greater flexibility in accounting standards
• the Specialist Fund Market (SFM), established in November 2007, is the Exchange's market for highly specialised investment entities, such as hedge funds or private equity funds, that wish to target institutional investors. This market is regulated by the FSA in accordance with standards set out in EU directives

At April 2011 there were 2,612 companies quoted on the London Stock Exchange: 1,086 on the UK main market, with a combined market capitalisation of £2,007.1bn; 323 on the international main market, with a combined market capitalisation of £1,897.8bn; 1,164 on AIM, with a combined market capitalisation of £81.3bn; 31 on the PSM, with a combined market capitalisation of £10.2bn; and eight companies listed on the SFM.

LONDON STOCK EXCHANGE, 10 Paternoster Square, London EC4M 7LS T 020-7797 1000
W www.londonstockexchange.com
Chair, Chris Gibson-Smith, PHD
Chief Executive, Xavier Rolet

ECONOMIC STATISTICS

THE BUDGET (MARCH 2011)

GOVERNMENT EXPENDITURE
DEPARTMENTAL EXPENDITURE LIMITS
£ billion

	Estimate 2010–11	Projection 2011–12	Projection 2012–13
Resource DEL			
Education	51.3	51.2	52.1
Health	100	101.5	104.0
of which NHS England	98.4	101.5	104.0
Transport	5.2	5.3	5.0
Business, Innovation and Skills	17.2	16.5	15.7
Communities	3.6	2.0	1.7
Local Government	26.0	26.1	24.4
Home Office	8.9	8.9	8.5
Justice	8.6	8.2	7.8
Law Officers' Departments	0.7	0.6	0.6
Defence	28.4	27.3	25.2
Foreign and Commonwealth Office	2.1	1.5	1.5
International Development	5.9	6.7	7.2
Energy and Climate Change	1.3	1.5	1.4
Environment, Food and Rural Affairs	2.2	2.2	2.1
Culture, Media and Sport	1.5	1.4	1.9
Work and Pensions	8.7	7.6	7.4
Scotland	25.2	24.8	25.1
Wales	13.4	13.3	13.4
Northern Ireland	9.7	9.4	9.4
Chancellor's departments	3.8	3.8	3.7
Cabinet Office	2.0	2.1	2.1
Independent bodies	1.6	1.7	1.5
Reserve	0.0	0.0	0.2
Special reserve	0.0	2.4	2.5
Allowance for shortfall	(1.1)	0.0	0.0
TOTAL RESOURCE DEL	326.1	326.3	327.1
Capital DEL			
Education	7.3	5.1	4.2
Health	4.5	4.4	4.4
of which NHS England	4.5	4.4	4.4
Transport	7.1	7.7	8.1
Business, Innovation and Skills	2.1	1.3	1.1
Communities	6.4	3.5	2.3
Local Government	0.0	0.0	0.0
Home Office	0.8	0.5	0.5
Justice	0.6	0.4	0.3
Law Officers' Departments	0.0	0.0	0.0
Defence	9.6	10.0	9.1
Foreign and Commonwealth Office	0.2	0.1	0.1
International Development	1.6	1.4	1.6
Energy and Climate Change	2.0	1.5	2.0
Environment, Food and Rural Affairs	0.6	0.4	0.4
Culture, Media and Sport	0.6	1.3	0.4
Work and Pensions	0.3	0.2	0.3
Scotland	3.3	2.5	2.5
Wales	1.8	1.3	1.2
Northern Ireland	1.2	0.9	0.9
Chancellor's departments	0.2	0.3	0.2
Cabinet Office	0.4	0.4	0.4
Independent bodies	0.1	0.1	0.1
Reserve	0.0	0.9	1.0
Special reserve	0.0	0.2	0.8
Green investment bank	0.0	0.0	0.8
Allowance for shortfall	(0.6)	0.0	0.0
TOTAL CAPITAL DEL	50.0	44.5	42.6
TOTAL DEL	376.1	370.8	369.7

Source: HM Treasury – *Budget 2011* (Crown copyright)

TOTAL MANAGED EXPENDITURE
£ billion

	Estimate 2010–11	Projection 2011–12	Projection 2012–13
Current Expenditure			
Resource Annually Managed Expenditure	287.4	314.4	324.9
Implied Resource DELs	345.4	342.3	344.7
Capital Expenditure			
Capital Annually Managed Expenditure (AME)	11.5	9.2	8.0
Implied Capital DELs	50.0	44.5	42.6
TOTAL MANAGED EXPENDITURE	694.4	710.4	720.2

Source: HM Treasury – *Budget 2011* (Crown copyright)

GOVERNMENT RECEIPTS
£ billion

	Outturn 2009–10	Forecast 2010–11	Forecast 2011–12
HM Revenue and Customs (HMRC)			
Income tax (gross of tax credits)[1]	147.5	151.5	156.6
Income tax credits	(5.6)	(5.5)	(4.7)
National insurance contributions (NIC)	96.6	96.5	100.7
Value added tax	73.5	86.1	100.3
Corporation tax[2]	36.5	42.7	49.0
Corporation tax credits[3]	(0.7)	(0.9)	(0.9)
Petroleum revenue tax	0.9	1.5	2.0
Fuel duties	26.2	27.3	26.9

	Outturn 2009–10	Forecast 2010–11	Forecast 2011–12
Business rates	23.4	23.8	25.5
Council tax	25.3	25.7	26.1
VAT refunds	11.2	13.2	15.0
Capital gains tax	2.5	3.2	3.4
Inheritance tax	2.4	2.7	2.7
Stamp duties	7.9	9.0	9.1
Tobacco duties	8.8	9.1	9.3
Spirits duties	2.7	2.7	2.7
Wine duties	3.0	3.1	3.3
Beer and cider duties	3.5	3.7	3.7
Air passenger duty	1.9	2.2	2.5
Insurance premium tax	2.3	2.5	2.9
Climate change levy	0.7	0.7	0.7
Other HMRC taxes[4]	5.4	6.0	6.4
Vehicle excise duties	5.6	5.7	5.9
Temporary bank payroll tax	0.0	3.5	0.0
Bank levy	0.0	0.0	1.9
Licence fee recipts	3.0	3.1	3.1
Enviromental levies	0.5	0.6	1.8
EU ETS Auction recipts	0.0	0.4	0.3
Other taxes	5.3	5.3	5.3
National Accounts Taxes	490.3	525.3	562.4
Less own resources contribution to EU budget	(3.8)	(4.8)	(4.9)
Interest and dividends	3.4	3.3	5.2
Other receipts	23.4	24.7	25.9
CURRENT RECEIPTS	513.3	548.5	588.6
UK oil and gas revenues[5]	6.5	8.8	13.4

[1] Income tax includes PAYE and Self Assessment recipts, and also includes tax on savings income and other minor income tax components

[2] National Accounts measure, gross of enhanced and payable credits

[3] Includes enhanced company tax credits

[4] Consists of landfill tax, aggregates levy, betting and gaming duties, and customs duties and levies

[5] Consitis of offshore corporation tax and petroleum revenue tax

Source: HM Treasury – *Budget 2011* (Crown copyright)

TRADE

TRADE IN GOODS
£ million

	Exports	Imports	Balance
1999	166,166	195,217	(29,051)
2000	187,936	220,912	(32,976)
2001	189,093	230,305	(41,212)
2002	186,524	234,229	(47,705)
2003	188,320	236,927	(48,607)
2004	190,874	251,774	(60,900)
2005	211,608	280,197	(68,589)
2006	243,633	319,945	(76,312)
2007	220,858	310,612	(89,754)
2008	252,068	345,202	(93,116)
2009	227,645	310,010	(82,365)
2010	266,079	363,278	(97,199)

Source: ONS (Crown copyright)

BALANCE OF PAYMENTS, 2010
Current Account

	£ million
Trade in goods and services	
Trade in goods	(98,816)
Trade in services	49,515
Total trade in goods and services	(49,301)

Income

Compensation of employees	(360)
Investment income	23,218
Total income	22,858
Total current transfers	(19,823)
TOTAL (CURRENT BALANCE)	(46,266)

Source: ONS (Crown copyright)

UK GDP GROWTH
volume % change on previous quarter

Source: ONS

EMPLOYMENT

DISTRIBUTION OF THE WORKFORCE

	Mar 2009	Mar 2011
Workforce jobs	31,696,000	31,354,000
HM forces	196,000	193,000
Self-employment jobs	4,208,000	4,349,000
Employees jobs	27,247,000	26,780,000
Government-supported trainees	45,000	32,000

Source: ONS – *Labour Market Statistics 2011* (Crown copyright)

EMPLOYMENT, 2010–2011
thousands
Mar–May 2010

Age	Male	Female
16–17	175	214
18–24	1,175	1,629
25–34	3,448	2,848
35–49	5,684	5,119
50–64	3,931	3,346
65+	469	331
All aged 16+	15,483	13,487

Mar–May 2011

Age	Male	Female
16-17	161	194
18–24	1,789	1,605
25–34	3,573	2,943
35–49	5,691	5,040
50–64	3,966	3,422
65+	533	362
All aged 16+	15,713	13,566

Source: ONS – *Labour Market Statistics 2011* (Crown copyright)

UNEMPLOYMENT, 2009–10
per cent

Age	2009	2010
16–17	29.3	35.0
18–24	16.2	18.0
25–49	5.5	6.5
50+	4.2	4.6
All aged 16+	7.1	8.0

Source: ONS – *Social Trends 2011* (Crown copyright)

UNEMPLOYMENT RATES BY REGION
per cent
Mar–May 2011

North East	9.8
North West	8.6
Yorkshire and The Humber	8.6
East Midlands	7.9
West Midlands	8.5
East	6.5
London	9.3
South East	5.7
South West	6.4
England	7.8
Wales	7.9
Scotland	7.6
Northern Ireland	7.1

Source: ONS (Crown copyright)

DURATION OF UNEMPLOYMENT, APR–JUN 2011
thousands

All unemployed	2,494
Duration of unemployment	
Less than 6 months	1,228
6 months–1 year	428
1 year +	838
1 year + as percentage of total	33.6

Source: ONS – Labour Market Statistics 2011 (Crown copyright)

MEDIAN EARNINGS, 2010

	All	Male	Female
Median gross annual earnings (£, thousands)	25.9	28.1	22.5
Median gross weekly earnings (£)	498.8	538.21	439.0
Median hourly earnings, excluding overtime (£)	12.50	13.01	11.68

Source: ONS – Annual Survey of Hours and Earnings 2010 (Crown copyright)

NUMBER OF TAXPAYERS BY ANNUAL INCOME*, 2010–11

	Number of taxpayers (thousands)
£6,475†–£7,499	939
£7,500–£9,999	2,620
£10,000–£14,999	6,440
£15,000–£19,999	5,210
£20,000–£29,999	6,910
£30,000–£49,999	5,680
£50,000–£99,999	2,050
£100,000–£149,999	342
£150,000–£199,999	145
£200,000–£499,999	143
£500,000–£999,999	26
£1,000,000+	13
All incomes	30,500

* Includes investment income
† Basic personal tax-free allowance for 2010–11
Source: ONS – Social Trends 2011 (Crown copyright)

LABOUR STOPPAGES BY DURATION, 2009

Under 5 days	80
5–10 days	11
11–20 days	4
21–30 days	0
31–50 days	0
50+ days	3
All stoppages	98

Source: ONS – Economic and Labour Market Review 2010 (Crown copyright)

WORKING DAYS LOST THROUGH LABOUR DISPUTES BY INDUSTRY, 2009

Mining and energy	200
Manufacturing	1,100
Services	394,600
Sewage, waste management and water supply	86,100
Construction	59,200
Transport, storage, information and communication	296,200
Financial, insurance and other administrative activites	600
Public administration and defence	5,100
Education	6,700

Source: ONS – Economic & Labour Market Review 2010 (Crown copyright)

TRADE UNIONS

Year	No. of unions	Total membership
2000–1	237	7,897,519
2001–2	226	7,779,393
2002–3	216	7,750,990
2003–4	213	7,735,983
2004–5	206	7,559,062
2005–6	193	7,473,000
2006–7	192	7,602,842
2007–8	193	7,627,693
2008–9	185	7,656,156
2009–10	176	7,328,905

Source: Annual Report of the Certification Officer 2010–11

HOUSEHOLD INCOME AND EXPENDITURE

AVERAGE HOUSEHOLD INCOME, 2009–10

Income by source	£ per year	Percentage of total
Wages and Salaries	23,717	65.2
Imputed income from benefits in kind	325	0.9
Self-employment	2,937	8.1
Investments	910	2.5
Annuities and pensions	2,743	7.5
Social security benefits*	5,448	14.9
Other sources	293	0.8
Total	36,373	100

* Excluding council tax benefit
Source: ONS – The Effects of Taxes and Benefits on Household Income 2009–10 (Crown copyright)

WEEKLY HOUSEHOLD INCOME: BY ETHNIC GROUP OF HOUSEHOLD REFERENCE PERSON, 2006/7–8/9

	Wages and salaries	Self-employed income	Investments	Tax credits	State pension	Other pension	Social security	Other benefits
White	64	9	3	1	7	7	7	2
Mixed	71	8	1	2	2	2	9	4
Asian or Asian British	70	9	1	4	2	2	8	4
Indian	74	9	1	1	2	2	5	4
Pakistani and Bangladeshi	56	10	1	10	4	1	15	4
Black or Black British	69	7	0	3	3	1	11	4
Black Caribbean	70	5	1	3	5	2	12	2
Black non-Caribbean	69	8	0	4	1	1	12	5
Chinese or other	70	8	1	2	2	3	6	7
All households	64	9	3	2	6	7	7	2

Source: ONS – Social Trends 2011 (Crown copyright)

AVERAGE HOUSEHOLD EXPENDITURE, 2009

Commodity or service	£ per week	Percentage of total
Transport	58.40	12.8
Recreation and culture	57.90	12.7
Housing, fuel and power	57.30	12.6
Food and non-alcoholic drinks	52.20	11.5
Restaurants and hotels	38.40	8.4
Miscellaneous goods and services	35.00	7.7
Household goods and servies	27.90	6.1
Clothing and footwear	20.90	4.6
Communication	11.70	2.6
Alcoholic drinks, tobacco and narcotics	11.20	2.5
Education	7.00	1.5
Health	5.30	1.1
Other expenditure items	71.80	15.8
Total	455.00	100

Source: ONS – Family Spending 2009 (Crown copyright)

HOUSEHOLD OWNERSHIP OF SELECTED DURABLE GOODS

percentages

	2000–1	2009
Car/van	72	76
Central heating (full or partial)	91	95
Washing machine	93	96
Tumble dryer	53	58
Dishwasher	25	39
Microwave	84	93
Telephone	93	88
Mobile phone	47	81
Home computer	44	75
Video recorder	87	61
DVD player	–	90
CD player	77	84
Internet connection	32	71

Source: ONS – Family Spending 2009 (Crown copyright)

INDIVIDUAL INSOLVENCIES

	2000	2005	2009
England and Wales	29,528	67,584	134,142
Scotland	5,766	11,846	23,482
Northern Ireland	616	1,454	1,959
Total	35,910	80,884	159,583

Source: ONS – Annual Abstract of Statistics 2010 (Crown copyright)

COST OF LIVING AND INFLATION RATES

The first cost of living index to be calculated took July 1914 as 100 and was based on the pattern of expenditure of working-class families in 1914. The cost of living index was superseded in 1947 by the general index of retail prices (RPI), although the older term is still popularly applied.

The Harmonised Index of Consumer Prices (HICP) was introduced in 1997 to enable comparisons within the European Union using an agreed methodology. In 2003 the National Statistician renamed the HICP as the Consumer Prices Index (CPI) to reflect its role as the main target measure of inflation for macroeconomic purposes. The RPI and indices based on it continue to be published alongside the CPI. Some pensions, and index-linked gilts continue to be calculated with reference to RPI or its derivatives.

CPI AND RPI

The CPI and RPI measure the changes month by month in the average level of prices of goods and services purchased by households in the UK. The indices are compiled using a selection of around 650 goods and services, and the prices charged for these items are collected at regular intervals at about 150 locations throughout the country. The Office for National Statistics (ONS) reviews the components of the indices once every year to reflect changes in consumer preferences and the establishment of new products. The table below shows changes made by the ONS to the CPI 'shopping basket' in 2011.

CPI excludes a number of items that are included in RPI, mainly related to housing such as council tax and a range of owner-occupier housing costs, such as mortgage payments. The CPI covers all private households, whereas RPI excludes the top 4 per cent by income and pensioner households who derive at least three-quarters of their income from state benefits. The two indices use different methodologies to combine the prices of goods and services, which means that since 1996 the CPI inflation measure is less than the RPI inflation measure.

INFLATION RATE

The 12-monthly percentage change in the 'all items' index of the RPI or CPI is referred to as the rate of inflation. As the most familiar measure of inflation, RPI is often referred to as the 'headline rate of inflation'. CPI is the main measure of inflation for macroeconomic purposes and forms the basis for the government's inflation target, which is currently 2 per cent. The percentage change in prices between any two months/years can be obtained using the formula overleaf.

CHANGES TO THE 2011 'SHOPPING BASKET' OF GOODS AND SERVICES

The table below shows changes to the 2011 CPI* basket of goods and services made by the ONS in order to reflect changes in consumer preferences and the establishment of new products.

Goods and services group	Removed items	New items
Alcoholic beverages	canned lager (4-pack)	sparkling wine
Audio-visual equipment	flat panel TVs (14″–25″; 26″–42″)	flat panel TVs (14″–22″; 23″–32″; 33″+)
Books and newspapers	evening provincial newspaper; morning provincial newspaper	hardback book (fiction); provincial newspaper
Clothing	girls' summer jacket; girl's winter jacket; men's casual shirt (long-sleeved); women's casual outer jacket (eg fleece); women's premium branded dress	girl's jacket; men's casual shirt (long or short-sleeved); women's blouse/shirt;
Food	pork shoulder	oven-ready joint; dried fruit
Footwear	women's high-heeled party shoe; women's high-heeled sensible shoes	women's high heeled shoes
Maintenance and repair of dwelling	hardboard	medium density fibreboard (MDF)
Medical products, appliances and equipment	spectacle frames (without lenses)	spectacle frames with single-vision lens
Personal care	–	hair conditioner
Recreational items, gardens and pets	rosebush; vet fees for spaying a kitten	craft kit
Telephone equipment and services	mobile phone downloads	mobile phone applications; smart phone handsets
Tobacco	–	vending machine cigarettes
Other services (not elsewhere classified)	–	dating agency fees

* RPI goods and services are grouped together under different classifications

$$\frac{\text{Later date RPI/CPI} - \text{Earlier date RPI/CPI}}{\text{Earlier date RPI/CPI}} \times 100$$

eg to find the CPI rate of inflation for 2006, using the annual averages for 2005 and 2006:

$$\frac{102.3 - 100.0}{100.0} \times 100 = 2.3$$

From 14 February 2006 the reference year for CPI was re-based to 2005=100 to improve price comparison clarity across the EU. None of the underlying data, from which the re-referenced series was calculated, was revised. Historical rates of change (such as annual inflation figures), calculated from the re-based rounded index levels, were revised due to the effect of rounding. The CPI rate of inflation figure given in the table below may differ by plus or minus 0.1 percentage points from the figure calculated by the above equation. The change of reference period and revision due to rounding does not apply to the RPI which remains unchanged.

The RPI and CPI figures are published by the Office for National Statistics on either the second or third Tuesday of each month in an indices bulletin and electronically on the national statistics website (W www.statistics.gov.uk).

PURCHASING POWER OF THE POUND

Changes in the internal purchasing power of the pound may be defined as the 'inverse' of changes in the level of prices: when prices go up, the amount which can be purchased with a given sum of money goes down. To find the purchasing power of the pound in one month or year, given that it was 100p in a previous month or year, the calculation would be:

$$100p \times \frac{\text{Earlier month/year RPI}}{\text{Later month/year RPI}}$$

Thus, if the purchasing power of the pound is taken to be 100p in 1975, the comparable purchasing power in 2000 would be:

$$100p \times \frac{34.2}{170.3} = 20.1p$$

For longer term comparisons, it has been the practice to use an index which has been constructed by linking together the RPI for the period 1962 to date; an index derived from the consumers' expenditure deflator for the period from 1938 to 1962; and the pre-war 'cost of living' index for the period 1914 to 1938. This long-term index enables the internal purchasing power of the pound to be calculated for any year from 1914 onwards. It should be noted that these figures can only be approximate.

PLACEHOLDER

	Annual average RPI (1987 = 100)	Purchasing power of £ (1998 = 1.00)	Annual average CPI (2005 = 100)*	Rate of inflation (RPI/CPI)
1914	2.8	58.18		
1915	3.5	46.54		
1920	7.0	23.27		
1925	5.0	32.58		
1930	4.5	36.20		
1935	4.0	40.72		
1938	4.4	37.02		
There are no official figures for 1939–45				
1946	7.4	22.01		
1950	9.0	18.10		
1955	11.2	14.54		
1960	12.6	12.93		
1965	14.8	11.00		
1970	18.5	8.80		
1975	34.2	4.76		
1980	66.8	2.44	18.0	
1985	94.6	1.72	6.1	
1990	126.1	1.29	71.5	9.5/7.0
1995	149.1	1.09	86.0	3.5/2.6
1998	162.9	1.00	91.1	3.4/1.6
2000	170.3	0.96	93.1	3.0/0.8
2005	192.0	0.85	100.0	2.8/2.1
2006	198.1	0.82	102.3	3.2/2.3
2007	206.6	0.79	104.7	4.3/2.3
2008	214.8	0.76	108.5	4.0/3.6
2009	213.7	0.76	110.8	−0.5/2.2
2010	223.6	0.73	114.5	4.6/3.3

* In accordance with an EU Commission regulation all published CPI figures were re-based to 2005 = 100 with effect from 14 February 2006, replacing the 1996 = 100 series

INSURANCE

AUTHORISATION AND REGULATION OF INSURANCE COMPANIES

Since 2001, the Financial Services Authority (FSA) has been the authorising, enforcement, supervisory and rule-making body of insurers. Since 2005, this has also included insurance brokers and intermediaries.

The FSA's powers are primarily conferred by the Financial Services and Markets Act 2000, which unified the previous sectoral arrangements and regulators.

AUTHORISATION

The FSA's current role is to ensure that firms to which it grants authorisation satisfy the necessary financial criteria, that the senior management of the company are 'fit and proper persons' and that unauthorised firms are not permitted to trade. This part of the FSA's role was previously undertaken by HM Treasury under the Insurance Companies Act 1982, which was repealed when the Financial Services and Markets Act came fully into force. At the end of 2009 there were over 1,400 insurance organisations and friendly societies with authorisation from the FSA to transact one or more classes of insurance business in the UK. However, the single European insurance market, established in 1994, gave insurers authorised in any other European Union country automatic UK authorisation without further formality. This means a potential market of over 5,000 insurers.

In June 2010, the Chancellor of the Exchequer announced the government's intention to replace the FSA with two successor bodies, and to restructure the UK's financial regulatory framework by 2013 (*see* Financial Services Regulation).

REGULATION

All life insurers, general insurers, re-insurers, insurance and reinsurance brokers, financial advisers and composite firms are statutorily regulated. This is achieved through the formulation (after consultation) by the FSA of rules and guidance for regulated organisations. The FSA is also responsible for consumer education and the reduction of financial crime, particularly money laundering (*see also* Financial Services Regulation).

COMPLAINTS

Disputes between policyholders and insurers can be referred to the Financial Ombudsman Service (FOS). Policyholders with a complaint against their financial services provider must firstly take the matter to the highest level within the company. Thereafter, if it remains unresolved and it involves an amount below £100,000, they can refer, free of charge, to the FOS, which examines the facts of a complaint and delivers a decision binding on the provider (but not the policyholder). Small businesses with a turnover of up to €2m (£1.7m) and fewer than ten employees also have access to the scheme. The Financial Ombudsman Service also covers other areas of the financial services industry including banks, building societies and investment firms. In 2010 the FOS handled around 1 million enquires and around 150,000 complaints regarding financial services companies.

See also Financial Services Regulation.

ASSOCIATION OF BRITISH INSURERS

Over 90 per cent of the domestic business of UK insurance companies is transacted by the 300 members of the Association of British Insurers (ABI). ABI is a trade association which protects and promotes the interests of all its insurance company members. Only insurers authorised in the EU are eligible for membership. Brokers, intermediaries, financial advisers and claims handlers may not join ABI but may have their own trade associations.

ASSOCIATION OF BRITISH INSURERS (ABI),
51 Gresham Street, London EC2V 7HQ
T 020-7600 3333 W www.abi.org.uk
Chair, Tim Breedon
Director-General, Otto Thoresen

BALANCE OF PAYMENTS

The financial services industry contributes around 10 per cent to the UK's gross domestic product (GDP). In 2009 insurance companies' net exports rose to £8.3bn, a 10 per cent increase on 2008.

WORLDWIDE MARKET

The UK insurance industry is the largest in Europe and the third largest in the world behind the USA and Japan.

Market	Premium Income ($bn)	Percentage of total
United States	1,140	28
Japan	506	12
United Kingdom	309	8

TAKEOVERS AND MERGERS

Despite a few high profile attempts, such as the Prudential bid for the Asian operation of AIG and RSA's hostile bid for AVIVA, the only major activity in 2010 was the purchase of the UK life business of French insurer AXA by Resolution, the closed life fund specialist, for £2.75bn. The Royal Bank of Scotland also began the process of consolidating its UK insurance business to prepare it for sale by 2013, as mandated by the European Commission.

INDUSTRY ISSUES

Since 2002 the insurance industry has been negotiating with the European Commission (EC) on 'Solvency II' which aims to establish an EU-wide set of requirements for capital adequacy and management standards. The Solvency II directive is scheduled to come into force on 1 November 2012, although this is likely to be extended into 2013. The intention is that in all 27 European Union member states and in three European Economic Area countries a consistent standard will be established for insurers, which will reduce the possibility of company failures and consumer loss. In 2010 insurers spent a great deal of time convincing the EC that the financial problems suffered by the banks in 2009 were not a justification for increased capital adequacy requirements for insurers; this seems to have been accepted by the commission.

GENERAL INSURANCE

Extended periods of snow and freezing temperatures at the start and end of 2010 resulted in claims totalling £650m in January and £900m in November and December. In addition, £67m in travel cancellation claims resulted from the Eyjafjallajokull volcanic eruption in Iceland.

Motor insurance grabbed the headlines with claim costs rising 216 per cent to £1.6bn in the UK at a time when the competitive market meant UK premiums fell on average by around 7 per cent. Given that general insurers have also seen a fall in overall investment returns, motor premium increases in 2011–12 are inevitable, with rises of up to 40 per cent being suggested.

Personal injury claims under motor policies also contributed to these record claim levels; during 2010 insurers pressed for a reform of the legal system used for small claims of this kind. The average personal injury claim is around £2,430 but insurers point to the fact that they also have to pay a further £2,100 in legal fees to settle the claim. This could be drastically reduced if a simplified settlement system could be established to prevent small cases having to go to court. It is estimated that these legal costs add £40 a year to every UK driver's premium.

Fraud continues to be a problem for insurers but the number of fraudsters being caught continues to rise. It's impossible to accurately quantify the total cost of insurance fraud in the UK, but the number of bogus claims detected in 2010 increased to 335 a day (1.2 million a year) representing claims worth £2.3m a day. Fraudulent motor claims are the most costly, while bogus home insurance claims are the most common.

Government public spending cuts revived fears over the maintenance of flood and sea defences throughout the UK. In the past 10 years insurers have paid over £4.5bn in flood claims and although the UK insurance industry currently has an agreement with the government to offer flood cover to every home in the UK, this expires in 2013. It is estimated that one home in six is at risk of flooding and nearly 500,000 people face a significant flood risk.

Other general insurance areas, such as theft and fire, recorded a reduction in claims in 2010. Theft claims decreased by 4.5 per cent to £530m and fire claims totalled £1.07bn; a decrease of 10 per cent on 2009.

LONDON INSURANCE MARKET

The London Insurance Market is a unique wholesale marketplace and a distinct, separate sector of the UK insurance and reinsurance industry. It is the world's leading market for internationally traded insurance and reinsurance, its business comprising mainly overseas non-life large and high-exposure risks. It is the only place in the world where all 20 of the world's largest insurance companies have an office. The market is centred on the square mile of the City of London, which provides the required financial, banking, legal and other support services. Around 61 per cent of London market business is transacted at Lloyd's of London, 36 per cent through insurance companies and the remainder through protection and indemnity clubs. In 2009 the market had a written gross premium income of over £31.9bn. Around 170 Lloyd's brokers service the market.

The trade association for the international insurers and reinsurers writing primarily non-marine insurance and all classes of reinsurance business in the London market is the International Underwriting Association (IUA).

INTERNATIONAL UNDERWRITING ASSOCIATION, London Underwriting Centre, 3 Mincing Lane, London EC3R 7DD T 020-7617 4444 W www.iua.co.uk
Chair, Stephen Riley
Chief Executive, Dave Matcham

CLAIMS STATISTICS *(£m)*

	2006	2007	2008	2009	2010
Theft	517	525	531	555	530
Fire	1,139	1,102	1,273	1,205	1,073
Weather	475	2,459	904	662	706
Domestic subsidence	302	162	137	175	172
Business interruption	168	320	193	128	179
Total	2,601	4,568	3,038	2,725	2,660

WORLDWIDE GENERAL BUSINESS TRADING RESULTS *(£m)*

	2008	2009
Net written premiums	47,213	43,791
Underwriting results	1,115	(356)
Investment income	3,368	3,963
Overall trading profit	4,483	3,606
Profit as percentage of premium income	9.5	8.2

BRITISH INSURANCE COMPANIES

The following insurance company figures refer to members and certain non-members of the ABI.

WORLDWIDE GENERAL BUSINESS UNDERWRITING RESULTS *(£m)*

	2008			2009		
	UK	Overseas	Total	UK	Overseas	Total
Motor						
Premiums	10,676	4,086	14,783	9,894	4,447	14,341
Profit (loss)	(503)	264	(240)	(1,592)	123	(1,469)
Percentage of premiums	4.7	6.5	1.6	16	2.8	10.2
Non-motor						
Premiums	20,945	8,708	29,653	18,595	8,162	26,757
Profit (loss)	1,076	160	1,236	804	258	1,062
Percentage of premiums	5.1	1.8	4.2	4.3	4.2	4.0

NET PREMIUM INCOME BY SECTOR 2009 *(£m)*

	UK	Overseas
Motor	9,894	4,447
Non-motor	18,595	8,162
Marine, aviation and transport	665	128
Reinsurance	1,219	549
Total general business	30,373	13,286
Ordinary long-term	123,895	40,286
Total long-term business	123,895	40,286

LLOYD'S OF LONDON

Lloyd's of London is an international market for almost all types of general insurance. Lloyd's currently has a capacity to accept insurance premiums of around £23bn. Much of this business comes from outside the UK and makes a valuable contribution to the balance of payments.

A policy is underwritten at Lloyd's by a mixture of private and corporate members – corporate members having been admitted for the first time in 1992. Specialist underwriters accept insurance risks at Lloyd's on behalf of members (referred to as 'Names') grouped in syndicates. There are currently 86 syndicates of varying sizes, each managed by one of the 51 underwriting agents approved by the Council of Lloyd's.

Members divide into three categories: corporate organisations, individuals who have no limit to their liability for losses, and those who have an agreed limit (known as NameCos).

Lloyd's is incorporated by an act of parliament (Lloyd's Acts 1871 onwards) and is governed by an 18-person council, made up of six working, six external and six nominated members. The structure immediately below this changed when, in 2002, Lloyd's members voted at an extraordinary general meeting to implement a new franchise system for the market with the aim of improving profitability. The first move was the introduction of a new governance structure, replacing the Lloyd's Market Board and the Lloyd's Regulatory Board with an 11-person Lloyd's Franchise Board. Four main committees report to this board.

The corporation is a non-profit making body chiefly financed by its members' subscriptions. It provides the premises, administrative staff and services enabling Lloyd's underwriting syndicates to conduct their business. It does not, however, assume corporate liability for the risks accepted by its members. Individual members are responsible to the full extent of their personal means for their underwriting affairs unless they have converted to limited liability companies.

Lloyd's syndicates have no direct contact with the public. All business is transacted through insurance brokers accredited by the Corporation of Lloyd's. In addition, non-Lloyd's brokers in the UK, when guaranteed by Lloyd's brokers, are able to deal directly with Lloyd's motor syndicates, a facility that has made the Lloyd's market more accessible to the insuring public.

The FSA has ultimate responsibility for the regulation of the Lloyd's market. However, in situations where Lloyd's internal regulatory and compensation arrangements are more far-reaching – as for example with the Lloyd's Central Fund which safeguards claim payments to policyholders – the regulatory role is delegated to the Council of Lloyd's.

Lloyd's also provides the most comprehensive shipping intelligence service in the world. The shipping and other information received from Lloyd's agents, shipowners,

news agencies and other sources throughout the world is collated and distributed to the media as well as to the maritime and commercial sectors in general. *Lloyd's List* is London's oldest daily newspaper and contains news of general commercial interest as well as shipping information. It has been independent of Lloyd's since a management buy-out in 1992. *Lloyd's Shipping Index,* published weekly, lists some 23,000 ocean-going merchant vessels in alphabetical order and gives the latest known report of each.

DEVELOPMENTS IN 2010

It was a mixed year for Lloyd's in 2010, with natural disasters having a strong influence on the final result. None of the year's Atlantic storms made landfall, but three major earthquakes in Chile, Haiti and New Zealand, in addition to the Deepwater Horizon oil rig explosion and resulting spill in the Gulf of Mexico, did lead to substantial claims.

Overall the Lloyd's market recorded a profit before tax of £2.2bn; a 43 per cent decrease from the 2009 figure (£3.9bn). Despite this decrease, it still represented a healthy profit considering the market had seen a 29 per cent decrease in investment returns and a 16 per cent increase in net incurred claims.

LLOYD'S OF LONDON, One Lime Street, London EC3M 7HA T 020-7327 1000 W www.lloyds.com
Chair, John Nelson
Chief Executive, Richard Ward

LLOYD'S MEMBERSHIP

	2009	2010
Individual	773	700
Corporate	1,238	1,443

LLOYD'S SEGMENTAL RESULTS 2010 *(£m)*

	Gross premiums written	Net earned premium	Result
Reinsurance	8,388	6,112	590
Casualty	4,397	3,353	113
Property	4,908	3,786	283
Marine	1,671	1,408	128
Motor	1,103	1,009	(520)
Energy	1,419	983	164
Aviation	642	458	115
Life	63	51	3
Total from syndicate operations	22,591	17,111	1,143

LIFE AND LONG-TERM INSURANCE AND PENSIONS

The economic climate, low interest rates and poor investment returns continued to have an effect on life insurance sales. New business figures for regular premium investment and saving products decreased by 25 per cent in 2010, with single premium new business decreasing by 19 per cent.

Following an independent review, auto-enrolment for pensions is due to be phased-in (beginning with larger companies) over a four-year period from October 2012. This system will mean that all employers will have to automatically enrol their staff into a private pension scheme or the National Employment Savings Trust (NEST). Not surprisingly, this was warmly welcomed by the pensions industry but concerns were expressed elsewhere over the administration costs, particularly to small businesses. The Government estimated that for a small business employing four people the administrative cost would be £46 per person, but the Federation of Small Business (FSB) claimed the cost would be much higher at £2,550 per person. Although a number of issues remain to be fine-tuned, auto-enrolment is a reality and pension providers are updating their systems to cope with the workload it will bring.

After a consultation period lasting over two and a half years, the FSA's final proposals following their *Retail Distribution Review* were published in March 2010. When they are implemented in late 2012, the payment of commission to advisers will be replaced by a fee-paying structure. This is designed to eliminate fears that products have been recommended because of the commission rate rather than their suitability. It also provides remuneration for advisers who spend time and money researching for a client who subsequently decides not to go ahead with their purchase. The proposals from the review are designed to increase professional standards among advisers and re-establish consumer confidence in an industry harmed by scandals and mis-selling.

Regulatory changes, the introduction of Solvency II and automatic enrolment for workplace pensions combined with low consumer confidence and reduced disposable income present significant challenges for the UK life insurance and pensions market in 2012.

PAYMENTS TO POLICYHOLDERS *(£m)*

	2008	2009
Payments to UK policyholders	180,757	152,539
Payments to overseas policyholders	31,954	25,843
Total	212,108	178,382

WORLDWIDE LONG-TERM PREMIUM INCOME *(£m)*

	2005	2006	2007	2008	2009
UK Life Insurance					
Regular Premium	10,585	9,414	8,927	7,895	7,912
Single Premium	25,421	32,088	40,256	27,598	11,958
Total	36,032	41,502	49,183	35,493	19,870
Individual Pensions					
Regular Premium	8,548	8,628	8,714	9,547	9,629
Single Premium	12,311	24,906	24,368	18,721	15,177
Total	20,859	33,534	33,082	28,268	24,806
Other Pensions					
Regular Premium	4,577	5,752	5,687	5,863	5,695
Single Premium	54,383	59,410	93,020	57,013	64,032
Total	58,960	60,162	98,707	62,876	69,727
Other (eg income protection, annuities)	4,343	9,852	4,425	2,580	2,799
TOTAL UK PREMIUM INCOME	120,194	145,050	183,772	129,217	117,202
Overseas Premium Income					
Regular Premium	8,171	8,191	7,877	10,386	11,322
Single Premium	16,814	21,104	25,693	26,709	28,964
Total	24,985	29,295	33,571	37,095	40,286
TOTAL WORLDWIDE PREMIUM INCOME	145,178	174,345	218,968	166,312	157,488

PRIVATE MEDICAL INSURANCE

	2005	2006	2007	2008	2009
Number of people covered (thousand)	5,820	5,879	6,004	6,224	5,938
Corporate	4,125	4,188	4,341	4,571	4,384
Personal	1,695	1,691	1,663	1,653	1,554
Gross Earned Premiums (£m)	2,942	3,070	3,241	3,468	3,444
Corporate	1,493	1,561	1,696	1,831	1,838
Personal	1,449	1,509	1,545	1,637	1,606
Gross Claims Incurred (£m)	2,255	2,376	2,501	2,653	2,679

INVESTMENTS OF INSURANCE COMPANIES 2009

Investment of funds	Long-term business (£m)	General business (£m)
Index-linked British government securities	71,253	3,001
Non-index-linked British government securities	107,055	10,356
Other UK public sector debt securities	6,859	56
Overseas government, provincial and municipal securities	73,099	15,184
Debentures, loan shares, preference and guaranteed stocks and shares		
UK	157,789	14,585
Overseas	205,813	24,554
Ordinary stocks and shares UK	239,922	3,905
Overseas	236,014	8,400
Unit trusts		
Equities	160,272	6,167
Fixed interest	46,859	1,826
Loans secured on property	28,943	12,810
Real property and ground rents	52,490	2,680
Other invested assets	116,381	18,259
Total invested assets	1,495,750	109,450
NET INVESTMENT INCOME	61,588	3,963

NEW BUSINESS

	2006	2007	2008	2009	2010
New regular premiums					
Investment and savings	92	88	75	77	57
Individual protection	905	867	858	883	804
Group protection	311	318	290	313	256
Individual pension	3,024	3,273	3,363	2,805	3,184
Group pension	753	821	989	962	910
Offshore business	22	21	19	21	37
TOTAL REGULAR	5,107	5,388	5,594	5,060	5,248
New single premiums					
Investments and savings	30,540	38,903	23,769	12,444	10,034
Individual protection	1,634	1,266	1,019	236	225
Individual pensions	18,758	22,165	18,389	14,811	15,155
Retirement income products	12,157	14,061	13,916	12,673	13,183
Occupational pensions	10,796	10,986	12,097	10,039	12,802
Offshore business	7,150	7,594	7,777	4,267	6,404
TOTAL SINGLE	81,034	94,970	76,967	54,830	57,803

TAXATION

The government raises money to pay for public services such as education, health and the social security system through tax. Each year the Chancellor of the Exchequer's budget sets out how much it will cost to provide these services and how much tax is therefore needed to pay for them. HM Revenue and Customs (HMRC) is the government department that collects it. There are several different types of tax. The varieties that individuals may have to pay include income tax payable on earnings, pensions, state benefits, savings and investments; capital gains tax (CGT) payable on the disposal of certain assets; inheritance tax (IHT) payable on estates upon death and certain lifetime gifts; stamp duty payable when purchasing property and shares; and value added tax (VAT) payable on goods and services, plus certain other duties such as fuel duty on petrol and excise duty on alcohol and tobacco. Government funds are also raised from companies and small businesses through corporation tax.

In July 2010 the Chancellor of the Exchequer launched the Office of Tax Simplification (OTS), an independent office of the Treasury which draws together expertise from across the tax and legal professions to provide the government with independent advice on simplifying the UK tax system with the objective of reducing compliance burdens on both businesses and individual taxpayers. In March 2011 the OTS reported to the government on two initial reviews, one on all tax reliefs and one on small business taxation. As a result the government announced in the 2011 Budget that it will be abolishing 43 tax reliefs as their rationale is no longer valid. It will also consult on options for merging the operation of National Insurance and Income Tax. Details of the OTS and its work can be found on the Treasury website (W www.hm-treasury.gov.uk). The OTS welcomes views from individuals and can be contacted via email (E ots@ots.gsi.gov.uk).

HELP AND INFORMATION ON TAXATION

For detailed information on any aspect of taxation individuals may contact their local tax office or enquiry centre. The HMRC website (W www.hmrc.gov.uk) provides wide-ranging information online. All HMRC forms, leaflets and guides are listed on, and can be downloaded from, the website or ordered by telephone. A list of all HMRC telephone helplines and order lines is also on the website. Those most relevant to topics covered in this section on taxation are included at pertinent points throughout. Information on taxation is also available in the Money, Tax and Benefits section of the government's public information website for individuals (W www.direct.gov.uk), and the Tax, Payroll and Company Information section of the equivalent information website for companies (W www.businesslink.gov.uk).

INCOME TAX

Income tax is levied on different sorts of income. Not all types of income are taxable, however, and individuals are only taxed on their 'taxable income' above a certain level. Reliefs and allowances can also reduce or, in some cases, cancel out an individual's income tax bill.

An individual's taxable income is assessed each tax year, starting on 6 April and ending on 5 April the following year. The information below relates specifically to the year of assessment 2011–12, ending on 5 April 2012, and has only limited application to earlier years. Changes due to come into operation at a later date are briefly mentioned where information is available. Types of income that are taxable include:

- earnings from employment or self-employment
- most pensions income including state, company and personal pensions
- interest on most savings
- income (dividends) from shares
- income from property
- income received from a trust
- certain state benefits
- an individual's share of any joint income

There are certain sorts of income on which individuals never pay tax. These are ignored altogether when working out how much income tax an individual may need to pay. Types of income that are not taxable include:

- certain state benefits and tax credits such as child benefit, working tax credit, child tax credit, pension credit, attendance allowance, disability living allowance, housing benefit and the first 28 weeks of incapacity benefit
- winter fuel payments
- income from National Savings and Investments savings certificates
- interest, dividends and other income from various tax-free investments, notably individual savings accounts (ISAs)
- premium bond and national lottery prizes

PERSONAL ALLOWANCE

Every individual resident in the UK for tax purposes has a 'personal allowance'. This is the amount of taxable income that an individual can earn or receive each year tax-free. This tax year (2011–12) the basic personal allowance or tax-free amount is £7,475. Individuals may be entitled to a higher personal allowance if they are 65 or over. Income tax is only due on an individual's taxable income that is above his or her tax-free allowance. Husbands and wives are taxed separately, with each entitled to his or her personal allowance. Each spouse may obtain other allowances and reliefs where the required conditions are satisfied.

The amount of personal allowance depends on an individual's age on 5 April 2012 and, if he or she is 65 or over, the total income received from all taxable sources. There are three age-related levels of personal allowance – see table below. If an individual became 65 or 75 during the year to 5 April 2012, he or she is entitled to the allowance for that age group.

If an individual aged 65 or over has an income over the £24,000 'income limit' for age-related allowances but not more than £100,000, their age-related allowance reduces by half the amount (£1 for every £2) he or she has over the £24,000 limit, until the basic rate allowance for those aged under 65 is reached. For a 66-year-old with an income of £24,400 (£400 over the limit), for example, the age-related allowance would reduce by £200 to £9,740.

Since April 2010 all three levels of personal allowance have been subject to a single income limit of £100,000, meaning that the personal allowance is reduced for individuals with an 'adjusted net income' (*see* below) over £100,000. Those individuals with an 'adjusted net income' below or equal to the £100,000 limit are entitled to the full amount of personal allowance. However, where an individual's adjusted net income is above the £100,000 limit, their personal allowance is reduced by half the amount (£1 for every £2) they have over that limit, irrespective of age, until their personal allowance is reduced to nil.

'Adjusted net income' is the measure of an individual's income that is used for the calculation of the existing income-related reductions to personal allowances for those aged between 65 and 74 and for those 75 and over. It is calculated in a series of steps. The starting point is 'net income', which is the total of the individual's income subject to income tax less specified deductions such as payments made gross to pension schemes. This net income is then reduced by the grossed-up amount of the individual's Gift Aid contributions to charities and the grossed-up amount of the individual's pension contributions that have received tax relief at source. The final step is to add back any relief for payments to trade unions or police organisations deducted in arriving at the individual's net income. The result is the individual's adjusted net income.

LEVELS OF PERSONAL ALLOWANCE FOR 2011–12

	Personal allowance	Income limit
Age under 65	£7,475	£100,000
Age 65–74	£9,940	£24,000
Age 75 and over	£10,090	£24,000

BLIND PERSON'S ALLOWANCE

If an individual is registered blind or is unable to perform any work for which eyesight is essential, he or she can claim blind person's allowance, an extra amount of tax-free income added to the personal allowance. In 2011–12 the blind person's allowance is £1,980. It is the same for everyone who can claim it, whatever his or her age or level of income. If an individual is married or in a civil partnership and cannot use all of his or her blind person's allowance because of insufficient income, the unused part of the allowance can be passed to the spouse or civil partner.

Other deductible allowances and reliefs that have the effect of reducing an income tax bill are available to taxpayers in certain circumstances and will be explained in more detail later in this section.

CALCULATING INCOME TAX DUE

Individuals' liability to pay income tax is determined by establishing their level of taxable income for the year. For married couples and civil partners, income must be allocated between the couple by reference to the individual who is beneficially entitled to that income. Where income arises from jointly held assets, it is normally apportioned equally between the partners. If, however, the beneficial interests in jointly held assets are not equal, in most cases couples can make a special declaration to have income apportioned by reference to the actual interests in that income.

To work out an individual's liability for tax, his or her taxable income must be allocated between three different types: earned income (excluding income from savings and dividends); income from savings; and company dividends from shares and other equity-based investments.

After the tax-free allowance plus any deductible allowances and reliefs have been taken into account, the amount of tax an individual pays is calculated using different tax rates and a series of tax bands. The tax band applies to an individual's income after tax allowances and any reliefs have been taken into account. Individuals are not taxed on all of their income.

There were significant changes to income tax rates for 2008–9. The basic rate of income tax was reduced from 22 per cent to 20 per cent and a previous 10 per cent starting rate was removed for earned income and pensions. This created a simpler structure of two rates: 20 pence (in the pound) basic rate and a 40 pence (in the pound) higher rate. From 2010–11 an additional income tax rate of 50 per cent was introduced, which applies on both savings and non-savings income over £150,000.

The 10 per cent starting rate continues to be available for savings income only, with a limit of £2,560 for 2011–12. If an individual's taxable non-savings income is above £2,560, the 10 per cent savings rate is not applicable.

The personal allowance for people aged under 65 has been increased by £1,000 in cash terms to £7,475 for the tax year 2011–12. The basic rate band above which tax is payable at the higher rate of 40 per cent has been simultaneously reduced to ensure that higher rate taxpayers do not benefit from this change.

In the 2011 budget it was announced that the personal allowance for people aged under 65 will increase by £630 on 6 April 2012 to £8,105 for the 2012–13 tax year. The basic rate limit will simultaneously fall by £630, taking it down to £34,370 in 2012–13. All other income tax personal allowances and limits that are subject to indexation will be increased in line with the retail prices index (RPI) for the 2012–13 tax year.

INCOME TAX RATES (PER CENT) AND TAX BANDS FOR 2011–12

Band	Earned income	Band	Savings	Dividends
£0–£35,000	20%	£0–£2,560*	10%	10%
£35,000+	40%	£2,560–£35,000	20%	10%
£150,000+	50%	£35,000+	40%	32.5%
		£150,000+	50%	42.5%

* If an individual's taxable non-savings income is above £2,560 the 20 per cent tax band applies to savings income from £0–£35,000

The first calculation is applied to earned income which includes income from employment or self-employment, most pension income and rental income plus the value of a wide range of employee fringe benefits such as company cars, living accommodation and private medical insurance (for more information on fringe benefits, *see* later section on payment of income tax). In working out the amount of an individual's net taxable earnings, all expenses incurred 'wholly, exclusively and necessarily' in the performance of his or her work duties, together with the cost of business travel, may be deducted. Fees and subscriptions to certain professional bodies may also be deducted. Redundancy payments and other sums paid on the termination of an employment are assessable income, but the first £30,000 is normally tax-free provided the payment is not linked with the recipient's retirement or performance.

The first £35,000 of taxable income remaining after the tax-free allowance plus any deductible allowances and reliefs have been taken into account, is taxed at the basic rate of 20 per cent. Taxable income between £35,000 and £150,000 is taxed at the higher rate of 40 per cent. Taxable income above £150,000 is taxed at the additional rate of 50 per cent.

Savings and dividends income is added to an individual's other taxable income and taxed last. This means that tax on such sorts of income is based on an individual's highest income tax band.

SAVINGS INCOME
The second calculation is applied to any income from savings received by an individual. The appropriate rate at which it must be taxed is determined by adding income from savings to an individual's other taxable income, excluding dividends.

There is a 10 per cent starting rate for savings income only, with a limit of £2,560. If an individual's taxable non-savings income exceeds this limit, the 10 per cent savings rate is not applicable. Savings income above £2,560 and below the £35,000 basic rate limit is taxable at 20 per cent. Savings income between £35,000 and £150,000 is taxable at 40 per cent. Savings income over £150,000 is taxed at 50 per cent. If savings income falls on both sides of a tax band, the relevant amounts are taxed at the rates for each band.

Most savings income, such as interest paid on bank and building society accounts, already has tax at a rate of 20 per cent deducted from it 'at source' – that is, before it is paid out to individuals. This is confirmed by the entry 'net interest' on bank and building society statements.

Higher rate taxpayers whose income is sufficient to pay 40 or 50 per cent tax on their savings income must let their tax office know what savings income they have received so that the extra tax they owe can be collected.

Non taxpayers – ie individuals, including most children, whose taxable income is less than their tax allowances – can register to have their savings interest paid 'gross' without any tax being deducted from it at source. To do this, they must complete form R85, available at all banks and building societies. Parents or guardians need to fill in this form on behalf of those under 16. For individuals who are unsure whether they qualify as non-taxpayers and, therefore, whether they are able to register to have their savings interest paid gross, HMRC offers an 'R85 checker' on its website (W www.hmrc.gov.uk/calcs/r85/).

Non-taxpayers who have already had tax deducted from their savings interest can claim it back from HMRC by filling in form R40. For help or information about registering to get interest paid tax-free or to claim tax back on savings interest, individuals may visit W www.hmrc.gov.uk/taxon/bank.htm or call a dedicated savings helpline on T 0845-980 0645. Further information is available in the leaflet *IR111: Bank and building society interest – Are you paying tax when you don't need to?*

DIVIDEND INCOME
The third and final income tax calculation is on UK dividends, which means income from shares in UK companies and other share-based investments including unit trusts and open-ended investment companies (OEICs).

Dividend tax rates differ from those on savings income. The rate that an individual pays on his or her dividends depends on the amount of his or her overall taxable income (after allowances). Dividend income at or below the £35,000 basic rate tax limit is taxable at 10 per cent, between £35,000 and £150,000 at 32.5 per cent, and above £150,000 at 42.5 per cent.

When dividends are paid, a voucher is sent that shows the dividend paid and the amount of associated 'tax credit'. Companies pay dividends out of profits on which they have already paid or are due to pay tax. The tax credit takes account of this and is available to the shareholder to offset against any income tax that may be due on their dividend income. The dividend paid represents 90 per cent of their dividend income. The remaining 10 per cent is made up of the tax credit. In other words the tax credit represents 10 per cent of the dividend income.

Individuals who pay tax at the basic rate have no tax to pay on their dividend income because the tax liability is 10 per cent – the same amount as the tax credit. Higher rate taxpayers pay a total of 32.5 per cent tax on dividend income above the £35,000 basic rate income tax limit, but because the first 10 per cent of the tax due on their dividend income is already covered by the tax credit, in practice they owe only 22.5 per cent. For the same reason, additional rate taxpayers who pay a total of 42.5 per cent on dividend income above the £150,000 additional rate tax limit, owe only 32.5 per cent in practice.

Non-taxpayers cannot claim the 10 per cent tax credit. This is because income tax has not been deducted from the dividends paid to them. The view is that they have simply been given a 10 per cent credit against any income tax due.

If there is significant change to an individual's savings or other income, whatever his or her current tax bracket, it is the individual's responsibility to contact the relevant tax office immediately, even if he or she does not normally complete a tax return. This enables the tax office to work out whether extra or less tax should be paid.

INDIVIDUAL SAVINGS ACCOUNTS
There is a small selection of savings and investment products that are tax-free. This means that there is no tax to pay on any income generated in the form of interest or dividends nor on any increase in the value of the capital invested. Their tax-efficient status has been granted by the government in order to give people an incentive to save more. For this reason there are usually limits and restrictions on the amount of money an individual may invest in such savings and investments. Individual savings accounts (ISAs) are the best known among tax-efficient savings and investments. They were introduced in 1999 to replace other similar schemes called PEPs and TESSAs. Individuals can use an ISA to save cash, or invest in stocks and shares.

Changes were made to the ISA rules which took effect from April 2008. These reforms removed the distinction between what were previously known as maxi and mini ISAs and simplified an individual's options.

For the 2011–12 tax year individuals may save up to £10,680 each tax year in an ISA and receive all profits free of tax provided that they are UK residents and are over 18 (over 16 for cash ISAs). An ISA must be in an individual's name and cannot be held jointly with another person.

Individuals may invest in two separate ISAs each tax year: a cash ISA and a stocks and shares ISA (an umbrella term covering investments in unit trusts, company shares, bonds, investment-type life insurance and so on). Up to £5,340 of an individual's ISA allowance may be saved in one cash ISA with one provider. The remainder of the £10,680 can be invested in one stocks and shares ISA with either the same or a different provider. Alternatively an individual may open a single stocks and shares ISA and invest the full £10,680 into it. Various non-cash assets can be held in a stocks and shares ISA including unit trusts, company shares, bonds, investment-type life insurance and investment trusts.

The government has announced that annually, over the course of this parliament, the ISA limits will increase in line with the retail prices index (RPI). Each September's RPI figure will be used to set the ISA limits for the following tax year. The limits will be rounded each year to the nearest multiple of £120 to enable savers to plan monthly savings more easily.

Under the simplified ISA regime, what used to be known as mini cash ISAs, TESSA-only ISAs (TOISAs) and the cash component of a maxi ISA have become cash ISAs. Similarly, mini stocks and shares ISAs, the stocks and shares component of a maxi ISA and all Personal Equity Plans (PEPs) have become stocks and shares ISAs.

ISA savers have the option to transfer some or all of the money they have saved in previous tax years in cash ISAs to their stocks and shares ISA without affecting their annual ISA investment allowance. They may also choose to transfer all the money they have saved to date in a cash ISA in the current tax year to a stocks and shares ISA. However, the rules do not allow the reverse; that is, the transfer of monies saved in a stocks and shares ISA to a cash ISA.

Further details are available via HMRC's savings helpline (T 0845-604 1701).

DEDUCTIBLE ALLOWANCES AND RELIEF

Income taxpayers may be entitled to certain tax-deductible allowances and reliefs as well as their personal allowances. Examples include the married couple's allowance and maintenance payments relief, both of which are explained below. Unlike the tax-free allowances, these are not amounts of income that an individual can receive tax-free but amounts by which their tax bill can be reduced.

MARRIED COUPLE'S ALLOWANCE

A married couple's allowance (MCA) is available to taxpayers who are married or are in a civil partnership only where one or other partner was born before 6 April 1935. Eligible couples can start to claim the MCA from the year of marriage or civil partnership registration.

The MCA is restricted to give relief at a fixed rate of 10 per cent, which means that – unlike the personal allowance – it is not income that can be received without paying tax. Instead, it reduces an individual's tax bill up to a fixed amount calculated as 10 per cent of the amount of the allowance to which they are entitled.

In 2011–12, the MCA is £7,295 at 10 per cent, worth up to £729.50 off a couple's tax bill. The MCA is made up of two parts. There is a minimum amount (£2,800 in 2011–12) which will always be due. The remaining amount (£4,495 in 2011–12) can be reduced if the husband's income exceeds certain limits.

The husband will normally receive the allowance, but the couple can jointly decide which of them will get the minimum amount of the allowance. Alternatively, they can decide to have the minimum amount of the allowance split equally between them. They must inform their tax office of their decision before the start of the new tax year in which they want the decision to take effect. Once this is done, the change will apply until the couple decides to alter it. The remaining part of the allowance must go to the husband unless he lacks sufficient income to use it.

If an individual does not have enough income to use all his or her share of the married couple's allowance, the tax office can transfer the unused part of it to his or her spouse or civil partner.

Like the personal allowance, the MCA can be gradually reduced at the rate of £1 of the allowance for every £2 of income above the income limit (£24,000 in 2011–12). The amount of MCA can only be affected by the husband's income, and it only starts to be affected if his personal allowance has already been reduced back to the basic level for people under 65. The wife's income never affects the amount of MCA. It does not matter whether all or part of the minimum amount of the allowance has been transferred to her. Whatever the level of the husband's income, the MCA can never be reduced below the minimum amount: in 2011–12 this is £2,800 at 10 per cent.

The same system of allowance allocation applies to civil partners based on the income of the highest earner.

MAINTENANCE PAYMENTS RELIEF

An allowance is available to reduce an individual's tax bill for maintenance payments he or she makes to his or her ex spouse or former civil partner in certain circumstances. To be eligible one or other partner must have been born before 6 April 1935; the couple must be legally separated or divorced; the maintenance payments being made must be under a court order; and the payments must be for the maintenance of an ex-spouse or former civil partner (provided he or she is not now remarried or in a new civil partnership) or for children who are under 21. For the tax year 2011–12, this allowance can reduce an individual's tax bill by:

- 10 per cent of £2,800 (maximum £280) – this applies where an individual makes maintenance payments of £2,800 or more a year
- 10 per cent of the amount the individual has actually paid – this applies where an individual makes maintenance payments of less than £2,800 a year

An individual cannot claim a tax reduction for any voluntary payments he or she makes for a child, ex-spouse or former civil partner. To claim maintenance payments relief, individuals should contact their tax office.

CHARITABLE DONATION

A number of charitable donations qualify for tax relief. Individuals can increase the value of regular or one-off charitable gifts of money, however small, by using the Gift Aid scheme that allows charities or community amateur sports clubs (CASCs) to reclaim 20 per cent basic rate tax relief on donations they receive.

The way the scheme works means that if a taxpayer gives £10 using Gift Aid, for example, the donation is worth £12.50 to the charity or CASC.

Individuals who pay 40 per cent higher rate income tax can claim back the difference between the 40 per cent and the 20 per cent basic rate of income tax on the total (gross) value of their donations. For example, a 40 per cent tax payer donates £100. The total value of this donation to the charity or CASC is £125, of which the individual can claim back 20 per cent (£25) for themself. Similarly, those who pay 50 per cent additional rate income tax can claim back the difference between the 50 per cent and the 20 per cent basic rate on the total (gross) value of their donations. On a £100 donation, this means they can claim back £37.50.

Individuals who claim the age-related personal allowance, married couple's allowance or tax credits should tell HMRC about any Gift Aid donations they make because these can sometimes increase the amount of allowance or tax credit to which they are entitled.

In order to make a Gift Aid donation, individuals need to make a Gift Aid declaration. The charity or CASC will normally ask an individual to complete a simple form. One form can cover every gift made to the same charity or CASC for whatever period chosen, including both gifts made in the past and in the future. It was announced in the 2011 budget that the government intends to introduce a new scheme in April 2013 where charities will be able to claim Gift Aid on small donations, up to a total of £5,000 a year per charity, without the need for donors to fill in any forms at all. This will mean Gift Aid could be claimed on the contents of collecting tins, for example.

Individuals can use Gift Aid provided the amount of income tax and/or capital gains tax they have paid in the tax year in which their donations are made is at least equal to the amount of basic rate tax the charity or CASC is reclaiming on their gifts. It is the responsibility of the individual to make sure this is the case. If an individual makes Gift Aid donations and has not paid sufficient tax, they may have to pay the shortfall to HMRC. The Gift Aid scheme is not suitable for non-taxpayers.

Individuals who complete a tax return and are due a tax refund can ask HMRC to treat all or part of it as a Gift Aid donation.

For employees or those in receipt of an occupational pension, a tax-efficient way of making regular donations to charities is to use the Payroll Giving scheme. It allows the donations to be paid from a salary or pension before income tax is deducted. This effectively reduces the cost of giving for donors, which may allow them to give more. For example, it costs a basic-rate taxpayer only £8 in take-home pay to give £10 to charity from their pre-tax pay. Where a donor pays 40 per cent higher rate tax, that same £10 donation costs the taxpayer £6 and for donors who pay the additional 50 per cent rate tax, it costs £5.

Anyone who pays tax through the PAYE system can give to any charity of their choosing in this way, providing their employer or pension provider offers a payroll giving scheme. There is no limit to the amount individuals can donate.

It was announced in the 2011 budget that a reduced rate of inheritance tax (IHT) will apply where an individual, in their will, leaves 10 per cent or more of their net estate to charity. In such cases the current IHT 40 per cent rate will be reduced to 36 per cent. The new rate will apply where death occurs on or after 6 April 2012.

Details of tax-efficient charitable giving methods can be found at W www.direct.gov.uk/en/MoneyTaxAndBenefits/ManagingMoney and W www.hmrc.gov.uk/individuals/giving

TAX RELIEF ON PENSION CONTRIBUTIONS

Pensions are long-term investments designed to help ensure that people have enough income in retirement. The government encourages individuals to save towards a pension by offering tax relief on their contributions. Tax relief reduces an individual's tax bill or increases their pension fund.

The way tax relief is given on pension contributions depends on whether an individual pays into a company, public service or personal pension scheme.

For employees who pay into a company or public service pension scheme, most employers take the pension contributions from the employee's pay before deducting tax, which means that the individual – whether they pay income tax at the basic or higher rate – gets full tax relief straight away. Some employers, however, use the same method of paying pension contributions as that used by personal pension scheme payers described below.

Individuals who pay into a personal pension scheme make contributions from their net salary; that is, after tax has been deducted. For each pound that individuals contribute to their pension from net salary, the pension provider claims tax back from the government at the basic rate of 20 per cent and reinvests it on behalf of the individual into the scheme. In practice this means that for every £80 an individual pays into their pension, they receive £100 in their pension fund.

Higher rate taxpayers currently get 40 per cent tax relief on money they put into a pension. On contributions made from net salary, the first 20 per cent is claimed back from HMRC by the pension scheme in the same way as for a lower rate taxpayer. It is then up to individuals to claim back the other 20 per cent from their tax office, either when they fill in their annual tax return or by telephone or letter. In a similar fashion, individuals subject to the 50 per cent additional rate of income tax can get 50 per cent tax relief on their pension contributions.

Most providers of retirement annuities, which are a type of personal pension scheme set up before July 1988, do not offer a 'tax relief at source' scheme whereby they claim back tax at the basic rate as is the case with more modern personal pensions. In such cases, contributing individuals need to claim the tax relief they are due through their tax return or by telephoning or writing to HMRC.

Non taxpayers can still pay into a personal pension scheme and benefit from 20 per cent basic rate relief on the first £2,880 a year they contribute. In practice this means that the government tops up their £2,880 contribution to make it £3,600 which is the current universal pension allowance. Such pension contributions may be made on behalf of a non-taxpayer by another individual. An individual may, for example, contribute to a pension on behalf of a husband, wife, civil partner, child or grandchild. Tax relief will be added to their contribution at the basic rate, again on up to £2,880 a year benefiting the recipient, but their own tax bill will not be affected.

In any one tax year, individuals can get tax relief on pension contributions made into any number and type of registered pension schemes of 100 per cent of their annual earnings, irrespective of age, up to a maximum 'annual allowance'. For the tax year 2011–12 the annual allowance is £50,000, a dramatic reduction from the £255,000 allowance for tax-privileged pension saving in 2010–11. Individuals pay tax at 40 per cent on any contributions they make above the annual allowance. Everyone now also has a 'lifetime allowance' (£1.8m for 2011–12) which means taxpayers can save up to a total of

£1.8m in their pension fund and still get tax relief at their highest income tax rate on all their contributions. It was announced in the 2011 budget that the lifetime allowance will drop to £1.5 million in 2012–13.

For information on pensions and tax relief visit W www.direct.gov.uk/en/Pensionsandretirementplanning Another useful source of information and advice is The Pensions Advisory Service (TPAS), an independent voluntary organisation grant-aided by the Department for Work and Pensions at W www.pensionsadvisory service.org.uk; its Pensions Helpline is on T 0845-601 2923.

PAYMENT OF INCOME TAX
Employees have their income tax deducted from their wages throughout the year by their employer who sends it on to HMRC. Those in receipt of a company pension have their due tax deducted in the same way by their pension provider. This system of collecting income tax is known as 'pay as you earn' (PAYE).

BENEFITS IN KIND
The PAYE system is also used to collect tax on certain fringe benefits or 'benefits in kind' that employees or directors receive from their employer, but are not included in their salary cheque or wages. These include company cars, private medical insurance paid for by the employer or cheap or free loans from the employer. Some fringe benefits are tax-free, including employer-paid contributions into an employee's pension fund, cheap or free canteen meals, works buses, in-house sports facilities, reasonable relocation expenses, provision of a mobile phone and workplace nursery places provided for the children of employees. For taxable fringe benefits, tax is paid on the 'taxable value' of the benefit.

Employers submit returns for individual employees earning at or above the £8,500 per annum threshold (including the value of expenses and benefits) to the tax office on the form P11D, with details of any fringe benefits they have been given. For those earning less than the £8,500 threshold (part-time employees) a P9D form is submitted. Employees should get a copy of this form by 6 July following the end of the tax year and must enter the value of the fringe benefits they have received on their tax return for the relevant year, even if tax has already been paid on them under PAYE. Fringe benefits may be taxed under PAYE by being offset against personal tax allowances in an individual's PAYE code. Otherwise tax will be collected after the end of the tax year by the issue of an assessment on the fringe benefits.

SELF-ASSESSMENT
Individuals who are not on PAYE, notably the self-employed, need to complete a self-assessment tax return each year, in paper form or online at the HMRC website (W www.hmrc.gov.uk), and pay any income tax owed in twice-yearly instalments. Some individuals with more complex tax affairs such as those who earn money from rents or investments above a certain level may also need to fill out a self-assessment return, even if they are on PAYE. HMRC uses the figures supplied on the tax return to work out the individual's tax bill, or they can choose to work it out themselves. It is called 'self-assessment' because individuals are responsible for making sure the details they provide are correct.

Tax returns are usually sent out in early April, following the end of the tax year to which they apply. They may also go out at other times, for example if an individual wants to claim an allowance or repayment or to register for self-assessment for the first time.

Individuals with simple tax affairs may receive a short four-page return. Those with more complex affairs must fill out a full return that has 12 core pages plus extra pages, depending on the sorts of income received.

Central to the self-assessment system is the requirement for individuals to contact their tax office if they do not receive a self-assessment return but think they should or if their financial circumstances change. Individuals have six months from when the tax year ends to report any new income, for example. If an individual becomes self-employed, they have three months after the calendar month in which they began self-employed work to let HMRC know. This can be done by telephoning the helpline number for the newly self-employed on T 0845-915 4515.

TAX RETURN FILING AND PAYMENT DEADLINES
There are also key deadlines for filing (sending in) completed tax returns and paying the tax due. Failure to do so can incur penalties, interest charges and surcharges.

KEY FILING DATES FOR SELF-ASSESSMENT RETURNS

Date	Why the date is important
31 Oct*	Deadline for filing paper returns* for tax year ending the previous 5 April
30 Dec	Deadline for online filing where the amount owed for tax year ending the previous 5 April is less than £2,000 and the taxpayer wants HMRC to collect any tax due through their PAYE tax code
31 Jan†	Deadline for online filing of returns for tax year ending the previous 5 April

* Or three months from the date the return was requested if this was after 31 July
† Or three months from the date the return was requested if this was after 31 October

KEY SELF-ASSESSMENT PAYMENT DATES

Date	What payment is due?
31 Jan	Deadline for paying the balance of any tax owed – the 'balancing payment' – for the tax year ending the previous 5 April. It is also the date by which a taxpayer must make any first 'payment on account' (advance payment) for the current tax year. For example, on 31 January 2011 a taxpayer may have to pay both the balancing payment for the year 2010–11 and the first payment on account for 2011–12
31 Jul	Deadline for making a second payment on account for the current tax year

LATE FILING AND PAYMENT PENALTIES
Late filing of tax returns incurs an automatic £100 penalty although individuals may appeal against the penalty if they have a reasonable excuse. For late filing of 2010–11 tax returns the following additional penalties also apply:

- Over three months late – £10 each day, up to a maximum of £900
- Over six months late – an additional £300 or 5 per cent of the tax due, whichever is the higher
- Over 12 months late – a further £300 or 5 per cent of the tax due, whichever is the higher

Late payment of tax owing for 2010-11 incurs the following penalties:

• Over 30 days – 5 per cent of the tax unpaid at that date
• Over six months – an additional 5 per cent of the tax unpaid at that date
• Over 12 months – a further 5 per cent of the tax unpaid at that date

Interest is due on all outstanding amounts, including any unpaid penalties until payment is received in full.

TAX CREDITS
Child tax credit and working tax credit are paid to qualifying individuals. Although the title of both credits incorporates the word 'tax', neither affects the amount of income tax payable or repayable. Both are forms of social security benefits. *See* Social Welfare.

CAPITAL GAINS TAX

Capital gains tax (CGT) is a tax on the gain or profit that an individual makes when they sell, give away or otherwise dispose of an asset – that is, something they own such as shares, land or buildings. An individual potentially has to pay CGT on gains they make from any disposal of assets during a tax year. There is, however, a tax-free allowance and some additional reliefs that may reduce an individual's CGT bill. The following information relates to the tax year 2011–12 ending on 5 April 2012.

CGT is paid by individuals who are either resident or ordinarily resident in the UK for the tax year, executors or administrators – 'personal representatives' – responsible for a deceased person's financial affairs and trustees of a settlement. Non-residents are not usually liable to CGT unless they carry on a business in the UK through a branch or agency. Special CGT rules may apply to individuals who used to live and work in the UK but have since left the country.

CAPITAL GAINS CHARGEABLE TO CGT
Typically, individuals have made a gain if they sell an asset for more than they paid for it. It is the gain that is taxed, not the amount the individual receives for the asset. For example, a man buys shares for £1,000 and later sells them for £3,000. He has made a gain of £2,000 (£3,000 less £1,000). If someone gives an asset away, the gain will be based on the difference between what the asset was worth when originally acquired compared with its worth at the time of disposal. The same is true when an asset is sold for less than its full worth in order to give away part of the value. For example, a woman buys a property for £120,000 and three years later, when the property's market value has risen to £180,000, she gives it to her son. The son may pay nothing for the property or pay less than its true worth, eg £100,000. Either way, she has made a gain of £60,000 (£180,000 less £120,000).

If an individual disposes of an asset he or she received as a gift, the gain is worked out according to the market value of the asset when it was received. For example, a man gives his sister a painting worth £8,000. She pays nothing for it. Later she sells the painting for £10,000. For CGT purposes, she is treated as making a gain of £2,000 (£10,000 less £8,000). If an individual inherits an asset, the estate of the person who died does not pay CGT at the time. If the inheritor later disposes of the asset, the gain is worked out by looking at the market value at the time of the death. For example, a woman acquires some shares for £5,000 and leaves them to her niece when she dies. No CGT is payable at the time of death when the shares are worth £8,000. Later the niece sells the shares for £10,000. She has made a gain of £2,000 (£10,000 less £8,000).

Individuals may also have to pay CGT if they dispose of part of an asset or exchange one asset for another. Similarly, CGT may be payable if an individual receives a capital sum of money from an asset without disposing of it, for example where he or she receives compensation when an asset is damaged.

Assets that may lead to a CGT charge when they are disposed of include:

• shares in a company
• units in a unit trust
• land and buildings (though not normally an individual's main home – *see* 'disposal of a home' section for details)
• higher value jewellery, paintings, antiques and other personal effects assets used in business such as goodwill

EXEMPT GAINS
Certain kinds of assets do not give rise to a chargeable gain when they are disposed of. Assets exempt from CGT include:

• an individual's private car
• an individual's main home, provided certain conditions are met
• tax-free investments such as assets held in an individual savings account (ISA)
• UK government gilts or 'bonds'
• personal belongings including jewellery, paintings, antiques individually worth £6,000 or less
• cash in sterling or foreign currency held for an individual or his/her family's own personal use
• betting, lottery or pools winnings
• personal injury compensation

DISPOSAL OF A HOME: PRIVATE RESIDENCE RELIEF
Individuals do not have to pay CGT when they sell their main home if all the following conditions are met:

• they bought it and made any expenditure on it, primarily for use as their home rather than with a view to making a profit
• the property was their only home throughout the period they owned it (ignoring the last three years of ownership)
• the property was actually used as their home all the time that they owned it and, throughout the period, it was not used for any purpose other than as a home for the individual, his or her family and no more than one lodger
• the garden and area of grounds sold with the property does not exceed 5,000 sq. m (1.24 acres) including the site of the property

Even if all these conditions are not met, individuals may still be entitled to CGT relief when they sell the home. They may, for example, qualify for relief if they lived away from home temporarily while working abroad. Married couples or couples in a civil partnership may have relief from CGT on only one home. There is a special exception, however, where the spouse or partner each had a qualifying home before marriage or civil partnership and both live together in one of these homes after marriage or civil partnership and sell the other. Provided that it is sold within three years of marriage or the civil partnership, they may not have to pay any CGT (subject to the normal rules for this relief). If they sell it after more than three years it may qualify for partial relief. There are special rules on divorce and separation.

Certain other kinds of disposal similarly do not give rise to a chargeable gain. For example, individuals who are married or in a civil partnership and who live together may sell or give assets to their spouse or civil partner without having to pay CGT. Individuals may not, however, give or sell assets cheaply to their children without having to consider CGT. There is no CGT to pay on assets given to a registered charity.

CALCULATING CGT

CGT is worked out for each tax year and is charged on the total of an individual's taxable gains after taking into account certain costs and reliefs that can reduce or defer chargeable gains, allowable losses made on assets to which CGT normally applies and an annual exempt (tax-free) amount that applies to every individual. If the total of an individual's net gains in a tax year is less than the annual exempt amount (AEA), the individual will not have to pay CGT. For the tax year 2011–12 the AEA is £10,600. If an individual's net gains are more than the AEA, they pay CGT on the excess. Should any part of the exemption remain unused, this cannot be carried forward to a future year. A smaller exemption amount (£5,300 for 2011–12) applies to most trusts.

There are certain reliefs available that may eliminate, reduce or defer CGT. Some reliefs are available to many people while others are available only in special circumstances. Some reliefs are given automatically while others are given only if they are claimed. Some of the costs of buying, selling and improving assets may be deducted from total gains when working out an individual's chargeable gain.

RATES OF TAX

The net gains remaining, if any, calculated after subtracting the AEA, deducting costs and taking into account all CGT reliefs, incur liability to capital gains tax. There was a single rate of CGT of 18 per cent for individuals, trustees and personal representatives on taxable gains until the coalition government's budget on 22 June 2010 when it was announced that, from 23 June 2010, CGT would rise to 28 per cent for higher and additional rate taxpayers. Basic rate taxpayers continue to pay CGT at a rate of 18 per cent.

CGT for 2011–12 is due for payment in full on 31 January 2013. If payment is delayed, interest or surcharges may be imposed. A husband and wife or registered civil partners who live together are separately assessed to CGT. Each partner must independently calculate his or her gains and losses with each entitled to the AEA of £10,600 for 2011–12.

VALUATION OF ASSETS

The disposal proceeds – ie the amount received as consideration for the disposal of an asset – are the sum used to establish the gain or loss once certain allowable costs have been deducted. In most cases this is straightforward because the disposal proceeds are the amount actually received for disposing of the asset. This may include cash payable now or in the future and the value of any asset received in exchange for the asset

disposed of. However, in certain circumstances, the disposal proceeds may not accurately reflect the value of the asset and the individual may be treated as disposing of an asset for an amount other than the actual amount (if any) that they received. This applies, in particular, where an asset is transferred as a gift or sold for a price known to be below market value. Disposal proceeds in such transactions are deemed to be equal to the market value of the asset at the time it was disposed of rather than the actual amount (if any) received for it.

Market value represents the price that an asset might reasonably be expected to fetch upon sale in the open market. In the case of unquoted shares or securities, it is to be assumed that the hypothetical purchaser in the open market would have available all the information that a prudent prospective purchaser of shares or securities might reasonably require if that person were proposing to purchase them from a willing vendor by private treaty and at arm's length. The market value of unquoted shares or securities will often be established following negotiations with the specialist HMRC Shares & Assets Valuation department. The valuation of land and interests in land in the UK is dealt with by the Valuation Office Agency. Special rules apply to determine the market value of shares quoted on the London Stock Exchange.

ALLOWABLE COSTS

When working out a chargeable gain, once the actual or notional disposal proceeds have been determined, certain allowable costs may be deducted. There is a general rule that no costs that could be taken into account when working out income or losses for income tax purposes may be deducted. Subject to this, allowable costs are:

- acquisition costs – the actual amount spent on acquiring the asset or, in certain circumstances, the equivalent market value
- incidental costs of acquiring the asset such as fees paid for professional advice, valuation costs, stamp duty and advertising costs to find a seller
- enhancement costs – incurred for the purpose of enhancing the value of the asset (not including normal maintenance and repair costs)
- expenditure on defending or establishing a person's rights over the asset
- incidental costs of disposing of the asset such as fees paid for professional advice, valuation costs, stamp duty and advertising costs to find a buyer

If an individual disposes of part of his or her interest in an asset, or part of a holding of shares of the same class in the same company, or part of a holding of units in the same unit trust, he or she can deduct part of the allowable costs of the asset or holding when working out the chargeable gain. Allowable costs may also be reduced by some reliefs.

ENTREPRENEURS' RELIEF

Entrepreneurs' Relief allows individuals in business and some trustees to claim relief on the first £10m of gains (£5m prior to 6 April 2011) made on the disposal of any of the following: all or part of a business; the assets of a business after it has ceased; and shares in a company. The relief is available to taxpayers as individuals if they are in business, for example as a sole trader or as a partner in a trading business, or if they hold shares in their own personal trading company. This relief is not available for companies.

Depending on the type of disposal, certain qualifying conditions need to be met throughout a qualifying one-year period. For example, if an individual is selling all or part of their business, they must have owned the business during a one-year period that ends on the date of the disposal.

Where Entrepreneurs' Relief applies, qualifying gains liable to CGT on or after 23 June 2010, are charged at 10 per cent. An individual can make claims for this relief on more than one occasion as long as the lifetime total of all their claims does not exceed £10m of gains qualifying for relief.

BUSINESS ASSET ROLL-OVER RELIEF

When certain types of business asset are sold or disposed of and the proceeds reinvested in new qualifying trading assets, business asset roll-over relief makes it possible to 'roll-over' or postpone the payment of any CGT that would normally be due. The gain is deducted from the base cost of the new asset and only becomes chargeable to CGT on the eventual disposal of that replacement asset unless a further roll-over situation then develops. Full relief is available if all the proceeds from the original asset are reinvested in the qualifying replacement asset.

For example, a trader sells a freehold office for £75,000 and makes a gain of £30,000. All of the proceeds are reinvested in a new freehold business premises costing £90,000. The trader can postpone the whole of the £30,000 gain made on the sale of the old office, as all of the proceeds have been reinvested. When the trader eventually sells the new business premises and the CGT bill becomes payable, the cost of the new premises will be treated as £60,000 (£90,000 less the £30,000 gain).

If only part of the proceeds from the disposal of an old asset is reinvested in a new one, it may still be possible to postpone paying tax on part of the gain until the eventual disposal of the new asset.

Relief is only available if the acquisition of the new asset takes place within a period between 12 months before, and 36 months after, the disposal of the old asset. However, HMRC may extend this time limit at their discretion where there is a clear intention to acquire a replacement asset. The most common types of business assets that qualify for roll-over relief are land, buildings occupied and used for the purposes of trade, fixed plant and machinery. Assets used for the commercial letting of furnished holiday accommodation qualify if certain conditions are satisfied.

GIFTS HOLD-OVER RELIEF

The gift of an asset is treated as a disposal made for a consideration equal to market value, with a corresponding acquisition by the transferee at an identical value. In the case of gifts of business assets made by individuals and a limited range of trustees, a form of hold-over relief may be available. This relief, which must be claimed, in effect enables liability for CGT to be deferred and passed to the person to whom the gift is made. Relief is limited to the transfer of certain assets including the following:

- gifts of assets used for the purposes of a business carried on by the donor or his or her personal company
- gifts of shares in trading companies that are not listed on a stock exchange
- gifts of shares or securities in the donor's personal trading company

- gifts of agricultural land and buildings that would qualify for inheritance tax agricultural property relief
- gifts that are chargeable transfers for inheritance tax purposes
- certain types of gifts that are specifically exempted from inheritance tax

Hold-over relief is automatically due on certain sorts of gifts including gifts to charities and community amateur sports clubs, and gifts of works of art where certain undertakings have been given. There are certain rules to prevent gifts hold-over relief being used for tax-avoidance purposes. For example, restrictions may apply where an individual gifts assets to trustees administering a trust in which the individual retains an interest or the assets transferred comprise a dwelling-house. Subject to these exceptions, the effect of a valid claim for hold-over relief is similar to that following a claim for roll-over relief on the disposal of business assets.

OTHER CGT RELIEFS

There are certain other CGT reliefs available on the disposal of property, shares and business assets. For detailed information on all CGT reliefs and for more general guidance on CGT, see the capital gains tax pages on the HMRC website (W www.hmrc.gov.uk/cgt).

REPORTING AND PAYING CGT

Individuals are responsible for telling HMRC about capital gains on which they have to pay tax. Individuals who receive a self-assessment tax return may report capital gains by filling in the capital gains supplementary pages – the return explains how to obtain these pages if needed.

Individuals who do not normally complete a tax return but who need to report capital gains or losses should contact their local tax office. If an individual has CGT to pay, they must tell their tax office in writing by 5 October after the end of the tax year for which the CGT is due.

There is a time limit for claiming capital losses. The deadline is five years from 31 January after the end of the tax year in which the loss was made.

INHERITANCE TAX

Inheritance tax (IHT) is a tax on the value of a person's estate on death and on certain gifts made by an individual during his or her lifetime, usually payable within six months of death. Broadly speaking, a person's estate is everything he or she owned at the time of death including property, possessions, money and investments, less his or her debts. Not everyone pays IHT. It only applies if the taxable value of an estate is above the current inheritance tax threshold. If an estate, including any assets held in trust and gifts made within seven years of death, is less than the threshold, no IHT will be due. See table for the lower threshold limit, known as the nil rate band.

It was announced in the 2009 pre-Budget report that the nil rate band for 2010–11 would be frozen at £325,000 and it was further announced in the 2010 Budget that this freeze would extend until 2014–15.

2007–8	£300,000
2008–9	£312,000
2009–10	£325,000
2010–11	£325,000

A claim can be made to transfer any unused IHT nil-rate band on a person's death to the estate of their surviving spouse or civil partner. This applies where the IHT nil-rate band of the first deceased spouse or civil partner was not fully used in calculating the IHT liability of their estate. When the surviving spouse or civil partner dies, the unused amount may be added to their own nil-rate band (*see* below for details).

IHT used to be something only very wealthy individuals needed to consider. This is no longer the case. The fact that the IHT threshold has not kept pace with house price inflation in recent years means that the estates of some 'ordinary' taxpayers, who would not consider themselves wealthy, are now liable for IHT purely because of the value of their home. However, there are a number of ways that individuals – while still alive – can legally reduce the IHT bill that will apply to their estates on death. Several valuable IHT exemptions are available (explained further below) which allow individuals to pass on assets during their lifetime or in their will without any IHT being due. Detailed information on IHT is available on the HMRC website (W www.hmrc.gov.uk/inheritancetax/index.htm). Further help is also available from the IHT & Probate Helpline (T 0845-302 0900).

DOMICILE

Liability to IHT depends on an individual's domicile at the time of any gift or on death. Domicile is a complex legal concept and what follows explains some of the main issues. An individual is domiciled in the country where he or she has a permanent home. Domicile is different from nationality or residence, and an individual can only have one domicile at any given time.

A 'domicile of origin' is normally acquired from the individual's father on birth, though this may not be the country in which he or she is born. For example, a child born in Germany while his or her father is working there, but whose permanent home is in the UK, will have the UK as his or her domicile of origin. Until a person legally changes his or her domicile, it will be the same as that of the person on whom they are legally dependent.

Individuals can legally acquire a new domicile – a 'domicile of choice' – from the age of 16 by leaving the current country of domicile and settling in another country and providing strong evidence of intention to live there permanently or indefinitely. Women who were married before 1974 acquired their husband's domicile and still retain it until they legally acquire a new domicile.

For IHT purposes, there is a concept of 'deemed domicile'. This means that even if a person is not domiciled in the UK under general law, he or she is treated as domiciled in the UK at the time of a transfer (ie at the time of a lifetime gift or on death) if he or she (a) was domiciled in the UK within the three years immediately before the transfer, or (b) was 'resident' in the UK in at least 17 of the 20 income tax years of assessment ending with the year in which a transfer is made. Where a person is domiciled, or treated as domiciled, in the UK at the time of a gift or on death, the location of assets is immaterial and full liability to IHT arises. A non-UK domiciled individual is also liable to IHT but only on chargeable property in the UK.

The assets of husband and wife and registered civil partners are not merged for IHT purposes, except that the IHT value of assets owned by one spouse or civil partner may be affected if the other also owns similar assets (eg shares in the same company or a share in their jointly owned house). Each spouse or partner is treated as a separate individual entitled to receive the benefit of his or her exemptions, reliefs and rates of tax.

IHT EXEMPTIONS

There are some important exemptions that allow individuals to legally pass assets on to others, both before and after their death – without being subject to IHT.

Exempt Beneficiaries
Assets can be given away to certain people and organisations without any IHT having to be paid. These gifts, which are exempt whether individuals make them during their lifetime or in their will, include gifts to:

• a husband, wife or civil partner, even if the couple is legally separated (but not if they are divorced or the civil partnership has dissolved), as long as both partners have a permanent home in the UK. Note that gifts to an unmarried partner or a partner with whom the donor has not formed a civil partnership are not exempt
• UK charities
• some national institutions, including national museums, universities and the National Trust
• UK political parties

Annual Exemption
The first £3,000 of gifts made each tax year by each individual is exempt from IHT. If this exemption is not used, or not wholly used in any year, the balance may be carried forward to the following year only. A couple, therefore, may give away a total of £6,000 per tax year between them or £12,000 if they have not used their previous year's annual exemptions.

Wedding gifts/civil partnership ceremony gifts
Some gifts are exempt from IHT because of the type of gift or reason for making it. Wedding or civil partnership ceremony gifts made to either of the couple are exempt from IHT up to certain amounts:

• gifts by a parent, £5,000
• gifts by a grandparent or other relative, £2,500
• gifts by anyone else, £1,000

The gift must be made on or shortly before the date of the wedding or civil partnership ceremony. If the ceremony is called off but the gift is made, this exemption will not apply.

Small Gifts
An individual can make small gifts, up to the value of £250, to any number of people in any one tax year without them being liable for IHT. However, a larger sum such as £500 cannot be given and exemption claimed for the first £250. In addition, this exemption cannot be used with any other exemption when giving to the same person. For example, a parent cannot combine a 'small gifts exemption' with a 'wedding/civil partnership ceremony gift exemption' to give a child £5,250 when he or she gets married or forms a civil partnership. Neither may an individual combine a 'small gifts exemption' with the 'annual exemption' to give someone £3,250. Note that it is possible to use the 'annual exemption' with any other exemption, such as the 'wedding/civil partnership ceremony gift exemption'. For example, if a child marries or forms a civil partnership, the parent can give him or her a total IHT-free gift of £8,000 by combining £5,000

under the wedding/civil partnership gift exemption and £3,000 under the annual exemption.

Normal Expenditure

Any gifts made out of individuals' after-tax income (not capital) are exempt from IHT if they are part of their normal expenditure and do not result in a fall in their standard of living. These can include regular payments to someone, such as an allowance or gifts for Christmas or a birthday and regular premiums paid on a life insurance policy for someone else.

Maintenance Gifts

An individual can make IHT-free maintenance payments to his or her spouse or registered civil partner, ex-spouse or former civil partner, relatives dependent because of old age or infirmity, and children (including adopted children and step-children) who are under 18 or in full-time education.

POTENTIALLY EXEMPT TRANSFERS

If an individual makes a gift to either another individual or certain types of trust and it is not covered by one of the above exemptions, it is known as a 'potentially exempt transfer' (PET). A PET is only free of IHT on two strict conditions: (a) the gift must be made at least seven years before the donor's death. If the donor does not survive seven years after making the gift, it will be liable for IHT and (b) the gift must be made as a true gift with no strings attached (technically known as a 'gift with reservation of benefit'). This means that the donor must give up all rights to the gift and stop benefiting from it in any way.

If a gift is made and the donor does retain some benefit from it then it will still count as part of his or her estate no matter how long he or she lives after making it. For example, a father could make a lifetime gift of his home to his child. However, HMRC would not accept this as a true gift if the father continued to live in the home (unless he paid his child a full commercial rent to do so) because he would be considered to still have a material interest in the gifted home. Its value, therefore, would still be liable for IHT.

In some circumstances a gift with strings attached might give rise to an income tax charge on the donor based on the value of the benefit he or she retains. In this case the donor can choose whether to pay the income tax or have the gift treated as a gift with reservation.

CHARGEABLE TRANSFERS

Any remaining lifetime gifts that are not (potentially or otherwise) exempt transfers are chargeable transfers or 'chargeable gifts', meaning that they incur liability to IHT. Chargeable transfers comprise mainly gifts to or from companies and gifts to particular types of trust. There is an immediate claim for IHT on chargeable gifts, and additional tax may be payable if the donor dies within seven years of making a chargeable gift.

DEATH

Immediately before the time of death an individual is deemed to make a transfer of value. This transfer will comprise the value of assets forming part of the deceased's estate after subtracting most liabilities. Any exempt transfers may be excluded such as transfers for the benefit of a surviving spouse or civil partner, and charities. Death may also trigger three additional liabilities:

- a PET made within the seven years before the death loses its potential status and becomes chargeable to IHT
- the value of gifts made with reservation may incur liability if any benefit was enjoyed within the seven years before the death
- additional tax may become payable for chargeable lifetime transfers made within the seven years before the death

The 'personal representative' (the person nominated to handle the affairs of the deceased person) arranges to value the estate and pay any IHT that is due. One or more personal representatives can be nominated in a person's will, in which case they are known as the 'executors'. If a person dies without leaving a will a court can nominate the personal representative, who is then known as the 'administrator'. Valuing the deceased person's estate is one of the first things his or her personal representative needs to do. The representative will not normally be able to take over management of the estate (called 'applying for probate') until all or some of any IHT that is due has been paid.

VALUATIONS

When valuing a deceased person's estate all assets (property, possessions and money) owned at the time of death and certain assets given away during the seven years before death must be included. The valuation must accurately reflect what those assets would reasonably fetch in the open market at the date of death. The value of all of the assets that the deceased owned should include:

- his or her share of any assets owned jointly with someone else, for example a house owned with a partner
- any assets that are held in a trust, from which the deceased had the right to benefit
- any assets given away, but in which he or she kept an interest (gifts with reservation)
- PETs given away within the last seven years

Most estate assets can be valued quite easily, for example money in bank accounts or stocks and shares. In other instances the help of a professional valuer may be needed. Advice on how to value different assets including joint or trust assets is available at W www.hmrc.gov.uk. When valuing an estate, special relief is made available for certain assets. The two main reliefs are business relief and agricultural property relief outlined below. Once all assets have been valued, the next step is to deduct from the total assets everything that the deceased person owed such as unpaid bills, outstanding mortgages and other loans plus their funeral expenses. The value of all of the assets, less the deductible debts, is their estate. IHT is only payable on any value above £325,000 for the tax year 2011–12 at the current rate of 40 per cent.

RELIEF FOR SELECTED ASSETS

Agricultural Property

Relief from IHT is available on the agricultural value of agricultural property that is transferred. Agricultural property generally includes land or pasture used in the growing of crops or intensive rearing of animals for food consumption. It can also include farmhouses and farm cottages. The agricultural property can be owner-occupied or let. Relief is only due if the transferor has owned the property and it has been occupied for agricultural purposes for a minimum period.

The chargeable value transferred, either on a lifetime gift or on death, must be determined. This value may then be reduced by a percentage. Under current rates, a 100 per cent deduction will be available if the transferor retained vacant possession or could have obtained that possession within a period of 12 months following the transfer. In other cases, notably including land let to tenants, a lower deduction of 50 per cent is usually available. However, this lower deduction may be increased to 100 per cent if the letting was made after 31 August 1995.

To qualify for the relief, the agricultural property must either have been occupied by the transferor for the purposes of agriculture throughout a two-year period ending on the date of the transfer, or have been owned by the transferor throughout a period of seven years ending on that date and also occupied for agricultural purposes.

Business Relief

Business relief is available on transfers of certain types of business and of business assets if they qualify as relevant business property and the transferor has owned them for a minimum period. The relief can be claimed for transfers made during the person's lifetime and on death and on chargeable occasions arising on relevant business property held in trust. Where the chargeable value transferred is attributable to relevant business property, the business relief reduces that value by a percentage. Business relief may be claimed on relevant business property including:

• a business or an interest in a business such as a partnership
• unquoted shares and securities
• shares or securities of a quoted company which themselves or with other listed shares or securities give the transferor control of a company
• any land, buildings, plant or machinery owned by a partner or controlling shareholder and used wholly or mainly in the business of the partnership or company immediately before the transfer; this applies only if the partnership interest or shareholding would itself, if it were transferred, qualify for business relief
• any land, buildings, plant or machinery that were used wholly or mainly for the purpose of a business carried on by the transferor

If an asset qualifies for business relief, the rates at which it is currently allowed are as follows:

A business or interest in a business	100%
A holding of shares in an unquoted company	100%
Control holding of shares in a quoted company (more than 50 per cent of the voting rights)	50%
Land, buildings, plant or machinery used in a business of which the deceased was a partner at the date of death or used by a company controlled by the deceased	50%
Land, buildings, plant or machinery held in a trust where the deceased had the right to benefit from the trust and the asset was used in a business carried on by the deceased	50%

It is a general requirement that the property must have been retained for a period of two years before the transfer or death, and restrictions may be necessary if the property has not been used wholly for business purposes. The same property cannot obtain both business property relief and the relief available for agricultural property.

CALCULATION OF TAX PAYABLE

The calculation of IHT payable adopts the use of a cumulative or 'running' total. Looking back seven years from the death the chargeable value of gifts in that period is added to the total value of the estate at death. The gifts will use up all or part of the inheritance tax threshold (the 'nil-rate band' above which IHT becomes payable) first.

Lifetime Chargeable Transfers

The value transferred by lifetime chargeable transfers must be added to the seven-year running total to calculate whether any IHT is due. If the nil-rate band is exceeded, tax will be imposed on the excess at the rate of 20 per cent. However, if the donor dies within a period of seven years from the date of the chargeable lifetime transfer, additional tax may be due. This is calculated by applying tax at the full rate of 40 per cent in substitution for the rate of 20 per cent previously used. The amount of tax is then reduced to a percentage by applying tapering relief. This percentage is governed by the number of years from the date of the lifetime gift to the date of death, as follows:

PERIOD OF YEARS BEFORE DEATH

Not more than 3	100%
More than 3 but not more than 4	80%
More than 4 but not more than 5	60%
More than 5 but not more than 6	40%
More than 6 but not more than 7	20%

Should this exercise produce liability greater than that previously paid at the 20 per cent rate on the lifetime transfer, additional tax, representing the difference, must be paid. Where the calculation shows an amount falling below tax paid on the lifetime transfer, no additional liability can arise nor will the shortfall become repayable.

Tapering relief is, of course, only available if the calculation discloses a liability to IHT. There is no liability if the lifetime transfer falls within the nil-rate band.

Potentially Exempt Transfers

Where a PET loses immunity from liability to IHT because the donor dies within seven years of making the transfer, the value transferred enters into the running total. Any liability to IHT will be calculated by applying the full rate of 40 per cent, reduced to the percentage governed by tapering relief if the original transfer occurred more than three years before death. Again, liability to IHT can only arise if the nil-rate band is exceeded.

Death

On death, IHT is due on the value of the deceased's estate plus the running total of gifts made in the seven years before death if they come to more than the nil-rate band. IHT is then charged at the full rate of 40 per cent on the amount in excess of the nil-rate band.

Settled Property and Trusts

Trusts are special legal arrangements that can be used by individuals to control how their assets are distributed to their beneficiaries and minimise their IHT liability. Complex rules apply to establish IHT liability on settled property which includes property held in trust, and individuals are advised to take expert legal advice when setting up trusts.

RATES OF TAX

Since 1988 there have been three rates:

- a nil rate
- a lifetime rate of 20 per cent
- a full rate of 40 per cent

The nil-rate band usually changes on an annual basis, but has been frozen at £325,000 since 2009–10. Any excess over this level is taxable at 20 per cent or 40 per cent as the case may be.

The Government has announced that from April 2012 a reduced rate of IHT will apply where 10 per cent or more of a deceased's net estate (after deducting IHT exemptions, reliefs and the nil rate band) is left to charity. In those cases the current 40 per cent rate will be reduced to 36 per cent. The new rate will apply where death occurs on or after 6 April 2012.

TRANSFER OF NIL-RATE BAND

Transfers of property between spouses or civil partners are generally exempt from IHT. This means that someone who dies leaving some or all of their property to their spouse or civil partner may not have fully used up their nil-rate band. Under rules introduced in autumn 2007, any nil-rate band unused on the first death can be used when the surviving spouse or civil partner dies. A transfer of unused nil-rate band from a deceased spouse or civil partner (no matter what the date of their death) may be made to the estate of their surviving spouse or civil partner who dies on or after 9 October 2007.

Where a valid claim to transfer unused nil-rate band is made, the nil-rate band that is available when the surviving spouse or civil partner dies is increased by the proportion of the nil-rate band unused on the first death. For example, if on the first death the chargeable estate is £150,000 and the nil-rate band is £300,000, 50 per cent of the nil-rate band would be unused. If the nil-rate band when the survivor dies is £325,000, then that would be increased by 50 per cent to £487,500. The amount of the nil-rate band that can be transferred does not depend on the value of the first spouse or civil partner's estate. Whatever proportion of the nil-rate band is unused on the first death is available for transfer to the survivor.

The amount of additional nil-rate band that can be accumulated by any one surviving spouse or civil partner is limited to the value of the nil-rate band in force at the time of their death. This may be relevant, for example, where a person dies having survived more than one spouse or civil partner.

Where these rules have effect, personal representatives do not have to claim for the unused nil-rate band to be transferred at the time of the first death. Any claims for transfer of unused nil-rate band amounts are made by the personal representatives of the estate of the second spouse or civil partner to die when they make an IHT return.

Detailed guidance on how to transfer the nil-rate band can be found on the HMRC website (W www.hmrc.gov.uk).

PAYMENT OF TAX

IHT is normally due six months after the end of the month in which the death occurs or the chargeable transaction takes place. This is referred to as the 'due date'. Tax on some assets such as business property, certain shares and securities and land and buildings (including the deceased person's home) can be deferred and paid in equal instalments over ten years, though interest will be charged in most cases. If IHT is due on lifetime gifts and transfers, the person or transferee who received the gift or assets is normally liable to pay the IHT, though any IHT already paid at the time of a transfer into a trust or company will be taken into account. If tax owed is not paid by the due date, interest is charged on any unpaid IHT, no matter what caused the delay in payment.

CORPORATION TAX

Corporation tax is a tax on a company's profits, including all its income and gains. This tax is payable by UK resident companies and by non-resident companies carrying on a trade in the UK through a permanent establishment. The following comments are confined to companies resident in the UK. The word 'company' is also used to include:

- members' clubs, societies and associations
- trade associations
- housing associations
- groups of individuals carrying on a business but not as a partnership (for example, cooperatives)

A company's taxable income is charged by reference to income or gains arising in its 'accounting period', which is normally 12 months long. In some circumstances accounting periods can be shorter than 12 months, but never longer. The accounting period is also normally the period for which a company's accounts are drawn up, but the two periods do not have to coincide.

If a company is liable to pay corporation tax on its profits, several things must be done. HMRC must be informed that the company exists and is liable for tax. A self-assessment company tax return plus full accounts and calculation of tax liability must be filed by the statutory filing date, normally 12 months after the end of the accounting period. Companies have to work out their own tax liability and have to pay their tax without prior assessment by HMRC. Records of all company expenditure and income must be kept in order to work out the tax liability correctly. Companies are liable to penalties if they fail to carry out these obligations.

Extensive corporation tax information is available on the HMRC website (W www.hmrc.gov.uk/businesses) and companies may file their company tax returns online (W www.hmrc.gov.uk/ct/ct-online/file-return/online.htm).

RATE OF TAX

The rate of corporation tax is fixed for a financial year starting on 1 April and ending on the following 31 March. If a company's accounting period does not coincide with the financial year, its profits must be apportioned between the financial years and the tax rates for each financial year applied to those profits. The corporation tax liability is the total tax for both financial years.

The main rate of corporation tax for 2011–12 is 26 per cent, a decrease from 28 per cent in 2010–11. North Sea oil and gas ringfence activities but retain a main corporation tax rate of 30 per cent. The main rate of corporation tax applies when profits (including ringfence profits) are at a rate exceeding £1.5m, or where there is no claim to another rate, or where another rate does not apply.

It was announced in the 2011 March budget that the main rate of corporation tax will be reduced by one percentage point each forthcoming tax year until it reaches 23 per cent in 2014–15.

SMALL COMPANIES' RATE

Where the profits of a company do not exceed stated limits, corporation tax becomes payable at the small companies' rate. It is the amount of profits and not the size of the company that governs the application of the small companies' rate.

The small companies' rate for 2011–12 is 20 per cent, a decrease from 21 per cent in 2010–11. North Sea oil and gas ringfence activities retain a small companies' rate of 19 per cent.

A company can make profits of up to £300,000 without losing the benefit of the small companies' rate. If, however, its profits exceed £300,000 but fall below £1.5m, then marginal small companies' rate relief applies to ease the transition. The effect of marginal relief is that the average rate of corporation tax imposed on all profits steadily increases from the lower small companies' rate of 20 per cent to the main rate of 26 per cent, with tax being imposed on profits in the margin at an increased rate. HMRC has produced an easy-to-use corporation tax marginal relief rate calculator (W www.hmrc.gov.uk/calcs/mrr.htm).

Where a change in the rate of tax is introduced and the accounting period of a company overlaps 31 March, profits must be apportioned to establish the appropriate rate for each part of those profits.

The lower limit of £300,000 and the upper limit of £1.5m apply to a period of 12 months and must be proportionately reduced for shorter periods. Some restriction in the small companies' rate and the marginal rate may be necessary if there are two or more associated companies, namely companies under common control.

CORPORATION TAX ON PROFITS

£ per year	2010–11	2011–12
£0–£300,000	21%	20%
£300,001–£1,500,000	Marginal relief	Marginal relief
£1,500,001 or more	28%	26%

CAPITAL ALLOWANCES

Businesses can claim tax allowances, called capital allowances, on certain purchases or investments. This means that a proportion of these costs can be deducted from a business' taxable profits and reduce its tax bill. Capital allowances are currently available on plant and machinery, buildings and research and development. The amount of the allowance depends on what is being claimed for.

Detailed information on capital allowances is available from the Enhanced Capital Allowances website (W www.eca.gov.uk).

PAYMENT OF TAX

Corporation tax liabilities are normally due and payable in a single lump sum not later than nine months and one day after the end of the accounting period. For 'large' companies – those with profits over £1.5m which pay corporation tax at the main rate – there is a requirement to pay corporation tax in four quarterly instalments. Where a company is a member of a group, the profits of the entire group must be merged to establish whether the company is large.

In November 2008 HMRC launched a Business Payment Support Service (BPSS) which allows businesses facing temporary financial difficulties more time to pay their tax bills. Traders concerned about their ability to meet corporation tax, VAT or other payments owed to HMRC can call the Business Payment Support Line (T 0845-302 1435) seven days a week. This helpline is for new enquiries only, not for traders who have already been contacted by HMRC about an overdue payment. For details of the service visit W www.hmrc.gov.uk/pbr2008/business-payment.htm

CAPITAL GAINS

Chargeable gains arising to a company are calculated in a manner similar to that used for individuals. However, companies are not entitled to the CGT annual exemption. Companies do not suffer capital gains tax on chargeable gains but incur liability to corporation tax instead. Tax is due on the full chargeable gain of an accounting period after subtracting relief for any losses.

GROUPS OF COMPANIES

Each company within a group is separately charged to corporation tax on profits, gains and income. However, where one group member realises a loss for which special rules apply, other than a capital loss, a claim may be made to offset the deficiency against profits of some other member of the same group. The transfer of capital assets from one member of a group to a fellow member will usually incur no liability to tax on chargeable gains.

SPORTS CLUBS

Though corporation tax is payable by unincorporated associations including most clubs, a substantial exemption from liability to corporation tax, introduced in April 2002, is available to qualifying registered community amateur sports clubs (CASCs). Sports clubs that are registered as CASCs are exempt from liability to corporation tax on:

- profits from trading where the turnover of the trade is less than £30,000 in a 12-month period
- income from letting property where the gross rental income is less than £20,000 in a 12-month period
- bank and building society interest received
- chargeable gains

All of the exemptions depend upon the club having been a registered CASC for the whole of the relevant accounting period and the income or gains being used only for qualifying purposes. If the club has only been a registered CASC for part of an accounting period the exemption amounts of £30,000 (for trading) and £20,000 (for income from property) are reduced proportionately. Only interest and gains received after the club is registered are exempted.

Among other advantages available to registered clubs is that donations may be received under the Gift Aid arrangements. Charities are also generally exempt from corporation tax where they operate through a company structure.

VALUE ADDED TAX

Value added tax (VAT) is a tax on consumer expenditure charged when an individual buys goods and services in the European Union, including the UK. It is normally included in the sale price of goods and services and paid at the point of purchase. Each EU country has its own rate of VAT. From a business point of view, VAT is charged on most business transactions involving the supply of goods and services by a registered trader in the UK and Isle of

Man. It is also charged on goods and some services imported from places outside the EU and on goods and some services coming into the UK from the other EU countries. VAT is administered by HMRC. A wide range of information on VAT, including VAT forms, is available online at W www.hmrc.gov.uk/vat/index.htm. HMRC also runs a VAT and Excise helpline (T 0845-010 9000).

RATES OF TAX

There are three rates of VAT in the UK. The standard rate, payable on most goods and services in the UK, has been 20 per cent since 4 January 2011 when it was increased from 17.5 per cent.

The reduced rate – currently 5 per cent – is payable on certain goods and services including, for example, domestic fuel and power, children's car seats, women's sanitary products, contraceptive products and the installation of energy-saving materials such as wall insulation and solar panels. Since 1 January 2008 renovations and alterations to residential properties that have been empty for at least two years have been eligible for the 5 per cent rate.

A zero, or nil, rate applies to certain items including, for example, children's clothes, books, newspapers, most food and drink, and drugs and aids for disabled people. There are numerous exceptions to the zero-rated categories, however. While most food and drink is zero-rated, items including ice creams, chocolates, sweets, potato crisps and alcoholic drinks are not. Neither are drinks or items sold for consumption in a restaurant or cafe. Takeaway cold items such as sandwiches are zero-rated, while takeaway hot foods like fish and chips are not.

REGISTRATION

All traders, including professional persons and companies, must register for VAT if they are making 'taxable supplies' of a value exceeding stated limits. All goods and services that are VAT-rated are defined as 'taxable supplies' including zero-rated items which must be included when calculating the total value of a trader's taxable supplies – his or her 'taxable turnover'. The limits that govern mandatory registration are amended periodically.

An unregistered trader must register for VAT if:

- at the end of any month the total value of his or her taxable turnover (not just profit) for the past 12 months or less is more than the current VAT threshold of £70,000 – *and*
- at any time he or she has reasonable grounds to expect that his or her taxable turnover will be more than the current registration threshold of £70,000 in the next 30 days alone

To register for VAT, one or more forms must be completed and sent to HMRC within 30 days of any of the above. Basic VAT registration can currently be completed online (W https://online.hmrc.gov.uk/registration/). Traders who do not register at the correct time can be fined. Traders must charge VAT on their taxable supplies from the date they first need to be registered. Traders who only supply zero-rated goods may not have to register for VAT even if their taxable turnover goes above the registration threshold. However, a trader in this position must inform HMRC first and apply to be 'exempt from registration'. A trader whose taxable turnover does not reach the mandatory registration limit may choose to register for VAT voluntarily if what he or she does counts as a business for VAT purposes. This step may be thought

advisable to recover input tax (*see* below) or to compete with other registered traders. Registered traders may submit an application for deregistration if their taxable turnover subsequently falls. An application for deregistration can be made if the taxable turnover for the year beginning on the application date is not expected to exceed £71,000.

INPUT TAX

Registered traders suffer input tax when buying in goods or services for the purposes of their business. It is the VAT that traders pay out to their suppliers on goods and services coming *in* to their business. Relief can usually be obtained for input tax suffered, either by setting that tax against output tax due or by repayment. Most items of input tax can be relieved in this manner. Where a registered trader makes both exempt supplies and taxable supplies to his customers or clients, there may be some restriction in the amount of input tax that can be recovered.

OUTPUT TAX

When making a taxable supply of goods or services, registered traders must account for output tax, if any, on the value of that supply. Output tax is the term used to describe the VAT on the goods and services that they supply or sell – the VAT on supplies going *out* of the business and collected from customers on each sale made. Usually the price charged by the registered trader will be increased by adding VAT, but failure to make the required addition will not remove liability to account for output tax. The liability to account for output tax, and also relief for input tax, may be affected where a trader is using a special secondhand goods scheme.

EXEMPT SUPPLIES

VAT is not chargeable on certain goods and services because the law deems them 'exempt' from VAT. These include the provision of burial and cremation facilities, insurance, loans of money, certain types of education and training and some property transactions. The granting of a lease to occupy land or the sale of land will usually comprise an exempt supply, for example, but there are numerous exceptions. Exempt supplies do not enter into the calculation of taxable turnover that governs liability to mandatory registration (*see* above). Such supplies made by a registered trader may, however, limit the amount of input tax that can be relieved. It is for this reason that the exemption may be useful.

COLLECTION OF TAX

Registered traders submit VAT returns for accounting periods usually of three months in duration, but arrangements can be made to submit returns on a monthly basis. Very large traders must account for tax on a monthly basis, but this does not affect the three-monthly return. The return will show both the output tax due for supplies made by the trader in the accounting period and also the input tax for which relief is claimed. If the output tax exceeds input tax the balance must be remitted with the VAT return. Where input tax suffered exceeds the output tax due, the registered trader may claim the excess from HMRC.

This basis for collecting tax explains the structure of VAT. Where supplies are made between registered traders the supplier will account for an amount of tax that will usually be identical to the tax recovered by the person to whom the supply is made. However, where the supply is made to a person who is not a registered trader there can be no recovery of input tax and it is on this person that the final burden of VAT eventually falls. Where goods are acquired by a UK trader from a supplier within the EU, the trader must also account for the tax due on acquisition. There are a number of simplified arrangements to make VAT accounting easier for businesses, particularly small businesses, and there is advice on the HMRC website about how to choose the most appropriate scheme for a business:

Cash Accounting
This scheme allows businesses to only pay VAT on the basis of payments received from their customers rather than on invoice dates or time of supply. It can therefore be useful for businesses with cash flow problems that cannot pay their VAT as a result. Businesses may use the cash accounting scheme if taxable turnover is under £1.35m. There is no need to apply for the scheme – eligible businesses may start using it at the beginning of a new tax period. If a trader opts to use this scheme, he or she can do so until the taxable turnover reaches £1.6m.

Annual Accounting
If taxable turnover is under £1.35m a year, the trader may join the annual accounting scheme which allows them to make nine monthly or three quarterly instalments during the year based on an estimate of their total annual VAT bill. At the end of the year they submit a single return and any balance due. The advantages of this scheme for businesses are easier budgeting and cash flow planning because fixed payments are spread regularly throughout the year. Once a trader has joined the annual accounting scheme, membership may continue until the annual taxable turnover reaches £1.6m.

Flat Rate Scheme
First introduced in the 2002 budget, this scheme allows small businesses with an annual taxable turnover of less than £150,000 to save on administration by paying VAT as a set flat percentage of their annual turnover instead of accounting internally for VAT on each individual 'in and out'. The percentage rate used is governed by the trade sector into which the business falls. The scheme can no longer be used once annual income exceeds £230,000.

Retail Schemes
There are special schemes that offer retailers an alternative if it is impractical for them to issue invoices for a large number of supplies direct to the public. These schemes include a provision to claim relief from VAT on bad debts where goods or services are supplied to a customer who does not pay for them.

VAT FACT SUMMARY
from 1 April 2011

Standard rate	20%
Reduced rate	5%
Registration (last 12 months or next 30 days)	£73,000
Deregistration (next 12 months under)	£71,000
Cash accounting scheme – up to	£1,350,000
Flat rate scheme – up to	£150,000
Annual accounting scheme – up to	£1,350,000

STAMP DUTY

For the majority of people, contact with stamp duty arises when they buy a property. Stamp duty is payable by the buyer as a way of raising revenue for the government based on the purchase price of a property, stocks and shares. This section aims to provide a broad overview of stamp duty as it may affect the average person.

STAMP DUTY LAND TAX
Stamp duty land tax was introduced on 1 December 2003 and covers the purchase of houses, flats and other land, buildings and certain leases in the UK.

Before 1 December 2003 property purchasers had to submit documents providing all details of the purchase to the Stamp Office for 'stamping'. The purchaser's solicitor or licensed conveyancer would then send the stamped documentation to the appropriate land registry to register ownership of the property. Under stamp duty land tax, purchasers do not have to send documents for stamping. Instead, a land transaction return form SDLT1, which contains all information regarding the purchase that is relevant to HMRC, is signed by the purchaser. Buyers of property are responsible for completing the land transaction return and payment of stamp duty, though the solicitor or licensed conveyancer acting for them in a land transaction will normally complete the relevant paperwork. Once HMRC has received the completed land transaction return and the payment of any stamp duty due, a certificate will be issued that enables a solicitor or licensed conveyancer to register the property in the new owner's name at the Land Registry.

The threshold for notification of residential property is currently £40,000. This means that taxpayers entering into a transaction involving residential or non-residential property where the chargeable consideration is less than £40,000 do not need to notify HMRC about the transaction.

RATES OF STAMP DUTY LAND TAX
Stamp duty is charged at different rates and has thresholds for different types of property and different values of transaction. The tax rate and payment threshold can vary according to whether the property is in residential or non-residential use and whether it is freehold or leasehold.

Below a certain threshold, currently £125,000, no stamp duty is payable on residential property purchases. A two-year holiday period from stamp duty for first-time property buyers was announced by the Labour government in its 2010 budget. The relief is equivalent to a reduction in the average deposit for first-time buyers of £1,500 and is available where:

• an individual or individuals jointly purchase a major interest in land which is wholly residential, and
• the consideration is more than £125,000 but not more than £250,000, and
• that individual (or all of them) intends to occupy the property as their only or main residence, and
• that individual (or all of them) has not previously purchased such an interest, or its equivalent, anywhere in the world, and
• the effective date of the transaction is on or after 25 March 2010 and before 25 March 2012

In order to fund this first-time buyer stamp duty holiday, it was also announced in the 2010 budget that a new 5 per cent rate of stamp duty would apply to purchases of residential property over £1m from April 2011. The current coalition government has so far stuck with these plans and made no changes to the main rates and thresholds for stamp duty in its March 2011 budget.

The following table shows the rates of stamp duty and payment thresholds that apply on residential property purchase prices during 2011–12:

Purchase price	Rate of tax (% of purchase price)
up to £125,000*	0%
over £125,000 to £250,000**	1%
over £250,000 to £500,000	3%
over £500,000 to £1,000,000	4%
over £1,000,000	5%

* Up to £150,000 for residential property transactions in certain designated disadvantaged areas, a full list of which can be found at W www.hmrc.gov.uk. For transactions of non-residential land and property, the zero per cent rate applies for purchases up to £150,000; a 1 per cent rate is payable for transactions of £150,001 to £250,000; thereafter, rates are as per residential property transactions except there is no higher 5 per cent rate.

** First-time buyers can claim relief from stamp duty on residential transactions up to £250,000 between 25 March 2010 and 25 March 2012

When assessing how much stamp duty is payable, the entire purchase price must be taken into account so the relevant stamp duty rate is paid on the whole sum, not just on the amount over each tax threshold. For example, on a property bought for £250,000, 1 per cent (£2,500) is payable in stamp duty. On a property bought for £250,001, however, 3 per cent of the whole price (£7,500) is payable.

RELIEF FOR NEW ZERO CARBON HOMES
A relief from stamp duty land tax was introduced on 1 October 2007 for the vast majority of new-build 'zero carbon' homes in the UK. The relief was time limited for five years and is due to expire on 30 September 2012. Qualifying criteria for the relief require zero carbon emissions from all energy use in the home over a year. To achieve this, the fabric of the home is required to reach a very high energy efficiency standard and to be able to provide onsite renewable heat and power. New homes which are liable to stamp duty land tax on the first sale are eligible to qualify. The relief provides complete removal of stamp duty liabilities for all homes up to a purchase price of £500,000. Where the purchase price is in excess of £500,000 then the stamp duty liability is reduced by £15,000. The balance of the stamp duty is due in the normal way. Relief is not available on second and subsequent sales of new-build zero carbon homes.

FIXTURES AND CHATTELS
As well as buying a property a purchaser may buy items inside the property. Some things inside a property are, in law, part of the land. These are called 'fixtures'. Examples are fitted kitchen units and bathroom suites. Because these fixtures are part of the land, any price paid for them must be taken into account for stamp duty purposes. Other things inside a property are not part of the land. These are called 'chattels'. Examples are free-standing cookers, curtains and fitted carpets. The purchase of chattels is not chargeable to stamp duty. However, where both a property and chattels are purchased, the amount shown on the land transaction return as the purchase price of the property must be a 'just and reasonable' apportionment of the total amount paid. As with other entries on the form, the purchaser is responsible for the accuracy of this information. HMRC pays especial attention to residential property purchases just below stamp duty thresholds to prevent arrangements between buyer and seller to hand over cash so that the purchase price on paper looks lower, or where the buyer has paid an unreasonably high amount to buy chattels.

STAMP DUTY RESERVE TAX
Stamp duty or stamp duty reserve tax (SDRT) is payable at the rate of 0.5 per cent when shares are purchased. Stamp duty is payable when the shares are transferred using a stock transfer form, whereas SDRT is payable on 'paperless' share transactions where the shares are transferred electronically without using a stock transfer form. Most share transactions nowadays are paperless and settled by stockbrokers through CREST (the electronic settlement and registration system). SDRT therefore now accounts for the majority of taxation collected on share transactions effected through the London Stock Exchange.

The flat rate of 0.5 per cent is based on the amount paid for the shares, not what they are worth. If, for example, shares are bought for £2,000, £10 SDRT is payable, whatever the value of the shares themselves. If shares are transferred for free, no SDRT is payable.

A higher rate of 1.5 per cent is payable where shares are transferred into a 'depositary receipt scheme' or a 'clearance service'. These are special arrangements where the shares are held by a third party.

CREST automatically deducts the SDRT and sends it to the HMRC. A stockbroker will settle up with CREST for the cost of the shares and the SDRT and then bill the purchaser for these and the broker's fees. If shares are not purchased through CREST, the stamp duty must be paid by the purchaser to HMRC.

UK stamp duty or SDRT is not payable on the purchase of foreign shares, though there may be foreign taxes to pay. SDRT is already accounted for in the price paid for units in unit trusts or shares in open-ended investment companies.

HELP AND INFORMATION
Further information on stamp duty land tax is available via the stamp taxes helpline on T 0845-603 0135 (open 8.30am to 5pm Monday to Friday) or the HMRC website (W www.hmrc.gov.uk), where a stamp duty calculator for both shares and land and property can be found.

LEGAL NOTES

These notes outline certain aspects of the law as they might affect the average person. They are intended only as a broad guideline and are by no means definitive. The law is constantly changing so expert advice should always be taken. In some cases, sources of further information are given in these notes.

It is always advisable to consult a solicitor without delay. Anyone who does not have a solicitor can contact the following for assistance in finding one: Citizens Advice (W www.citizensadvice.org.uk), the Community Legal Service (W www.direct.gov.uk) or the Law Society of England and Wales. For assistance in Scotland, contact Citizens Advice Scotland (W www.cas.org.uk) or the Law Society of Scotland.

Legal aid schemes exist to make the help of a lawyer available to those who would not otherwise be able to afford one. Entitlement for most types of legal aid depends on an individual's means but a solicitor or Citizens Advice will be able to advise on this.

LAW SOCIETY OF ENGLAND AND WALES
113 Chancery Lane, London WC2A 1PL T 020-7242 1222
W www.lawsociety.org.uk
LAW SOCIETY OF SCOTLAND
26 Drumsheugh Gardens, Edinburgh EH3 7YR
T 0131-226 7411 W www.lawscot.org.uk

ABORTION

Abortion is governed by the Abortion Act 1967. Under its provisions, a legally induced abortion must be:
- performed by a registered medical practitioner
- carried out in an NHS hospital or other approved premises
- certified by two registered medical practitioners as justified on one or more of the following grounds:
  - (a) that the pregnancy has not exceeded its 24th week and that the continuance of the pregnancy would involve risk, greater than if the pregnancy were terminated, of injury to the physical or mental health of the pregnant woman or any existing children of her family
  - (b) that the termination is necessary to prevent grave permanent injury to the physical or mental health of the pregnant woman
  - (c) that the continuance of the pregnancy would involve risk to the life of the pregnant woman, greater than if the pregnancy were terminated
  - (d) that there is a substantial risk that if the child were born it would suffer from such physical or mental abnormalities as to be seriously handicapped.

In determining whether the continuance of a pregnancy would involve such risk of injury to health as is mentioned in grounds (a) or (b), account may be taken of the pregnant woman's actual or reasonably foreseeable environment.

The requirements relating to the opinion of two registered medical practitioners and to the performance of the abortion at an NHS hospital or other approved place cease to apply in circumstances where a registered medical practitioner is of the opinion, formed in good faith, that a termination is immediately necessary to save the life, or to prevent grave permanent injury to the physical or mental health, of the pregnant woman.

The Abortion Act 1967 does not apply to Northern Ireland, where abortion is not legal.

FAMILY PLANNING ASSOCIATION (UK)
50 Featherstone Street, London EC1Y 8QU T 020-7608 5240
W www.fpa.org.uk
BRITISH PREGNANCY ADVISORY SERVICE (BPAS)
T 0845-730 4030 W www.bpas.org

ADOPTION OF CHILDREN

The Adoption and Children Act 2002 reformed the framework for domestic and intercountry adoption in England and Wales and some parts of it extend to Scotland and Northern Ireland. The Children and Adoption Act 2006 introduces further provisions for adoptions involving a foreign element.

WHO MAY APPLY FOR AN ADOPTION ORDER
A couple (whether married or two people living as partners in an enduring family relationship) may apply for an adoption order where both of them are over 21 or where one is only 18 but the natural parent and the other is 21. An adoption order may be made for one applicant where that person is 21 and: a) the court is satisfied that person is the partner of a parent of the person to be adopted; or b) they are not married and are not civil partners; or c) married or in a civil partnership but they are separated from their spouse or civil partner and living apart with the separation likely to be permanent; or d) their spouse/civil partner is either unable to be found, or their spouse/civil partner is incapable by reason of ill-health of making an application. There are certain qualifying conditions an applicant must meet eg residency in the British Isles.

ARRANGING AN ADOPTION
Adoptions may generally only be arranged by an adoption agency or by way of an order from the high court; breach of the restrictions on who may arrange an adoption would constitute a criminal offence. When deciding whether a child should be placed for adoption, the court or adoption agency must consider all the factors set out in the 'welfare checklist' – the paramount consideration being the child's welfare, throughout his or her life. These factors include the child's wishes, needs, age, sex, background and any harm which the child has suffered or is likely to suffer. At all times, the court or adoption agency must bear in mind that delay is likely to prejudice a child's welfare.

ADOPTION ORDER
Once an adoption has been arranged, a court order is necessary to make it legal; this may be obtained from the high court, county court or magistrates' court (including the family proceedings court). An adoption order may not be given unless the court is satisfied that the consent of the child's natural parents (or guardians) has been given correctly. Consent can be dispensed with on two grounds: where the parent or guardian cannot be found or is incapable of giving consent, or where the welfare of the child so demands.

An adoption order extinguishes the parental responsibility that a person other than the adopters (or adopter) has for the child. Where an order is made on the application of the partner of the parent, that parent keeps parental responsibility. Once adopted the child has the same status as a child born to the adoptive parents, but may lose rights to the estates of those losing their parental responsibility.

REGISTRATION AND CERTIFICATES

All adoption orders made in England and Wales are required to be registered in the Adopted Children Register which also contains particulars of children adopted under registrable foreign adoptions. The General Register Office keeps this register from which certificates may be obtained in a similar way to birth certificates. The General Register Office also has equivalents in Scotland and Northern Ireland.

TRACING NATURAL PARENTS OR CHILDREN WHO HAVE BEEN ADOPTED

An adult adopted person may apply to the Registrar-General to obtain a certified copy of his/her birth certificate. Adoption agencies and adoption support agencies should provide services to adopted persons to assist them in obtaining information about their adoption and facilitate contact with their relatives. There is an Adoption Contact Register which provides a safe and confidential way for birth parents and other relatives to assure an adopted person that contact would be welcome. The BAAF (*see* below) can provide addresses of organisations which offer advice, information and counselling to adopted people, adoptive parents and people who have had their children adopted.

BRITISH ASSOCIATION FOR ADOPTION AND FOSTERING (BAAF)
Saffron House, 6–10 Kirkby Street, London EC1N 8TS
T 020-7421 2600 W www.baaf.org.uk

SCOTLAND

The relevant legislation is the Adoption and Children (Scotland) Act 2007. Previously adoption was governed in Scotland by the Adoption (Scotland) Act 1978, as amended by the Children (Scotland) Act 1995. In September 2009, the 2007 act made further amendments to the 1995 act and repealed the 1978 act – but for Part IV – when its final provisions took effect. The provisions of the 2007 act are similar to those described above. In Scotland, petitions for adoption are made to the sheriff court or the court of session.

BRITISH ASSOCIATION FOR ADOPTION AND FOSTERING (BAAF)
BAAF Scottish Centre, 113 Rose Street, Edinburgh EH2 3DT
T 0131-226 9270

BIRTHS (REGISTRATION)

It is the duty of the parents of a child born in England or Wales to register the birth within 42 days of the date of birth at the register office in the district in which the baby was born. If it is inconvenient to go to the district where the birth took place, the information for the registration may be given to a registrar in another district, who will send your details to the appropriate register office. Failure to register the birth within 42 days without reasonable cause may leave the parents liable to a penalty. If a birth

has not been registered within 12 months of its occurrence it is possible for the late registration of the birth to be authorised by the Registrar-General, provided certain requirements can be met.

Births that take place in England may only be registered in English, but births that take place in Wales may be registered bilingually in Welsh and English. In order to do this, the details must be given in Welsh and the registrar must be able to understand and write in Welsh.

If the parents of the child were married to each other at the time of the birth (or conception), either the mother or the father may register the birth. If the parents were not married to each other at the time of the child's birth (or conception), the father's particulars may be entered in the register only where he attends the register office with the mother and they sign the birth register together. Where an unmarried parent is unable to attend the register office either parent may submit to the registrar a statutory declaration on Form 16 (or Form 16W for births which took place in Wales) acknowledging the father's paternity (this form may be obtained from any registrar in England or Wales or online at W www.gro.gov.uk); alternatively a parental responsibility agreement or appropriate court order may be produced to the registrar.

If the father's details are not included in the birth register, it may be possible to re-register the birth at a later date. If the parents do not register the birth of their child the following people may do so:

- the occupier of the house or hospital where the child was born
- a person who was present at the birth
- a person who is responsible for the child

Upon registration of the birth a short certificate is issued. It may be possible to register the birth while still at hospital. Hospitals will advise individually whether this is possible.

BIRTHS ABROAD

There are certain countries where birth registrations may be made for British citizens overseas (for more details on British citizenship *see* below). The British consul or high commission may register the births and issue certificates which are then sent to the General Register Office. If a birth is registered by the British consul or high commission, the registration would show the person's claim to British citizenship, British overseas territories citizenship or British overseas citizenship.

SCOTLAND

In Scotland the birth of a child must be registered within 21 days at the registration office of any registration district in Scotland.

If the child is born, either in or out of Scotland, on a ship, aircraft or land vehicle that ends its journey at any place in Scotland, the child, in most cases, will be registered as if born in that place.

CERTIFICATES OF BIRTHS, DEATHS OR MARRIAGES

Certificates of births, marriages and deaths that have taken place in England and Wales since 1837 can be obtained from the General Register Office (GRO).

Marriage or death certificates may also be obtained from the minister of the church in which the marriage or funeral took place. Any register office can advise about the best way to obtain certificates.

The fees for certificates are:

Online application:
- full certificate of birth, marriage, death or adoption, £9.25
- full certificate of birth, marriage, death or adoption with GRO reference supplied, £9.25

By postal/phone/fax application:
- full certificate of birth, marriage, death or adoption, £9.25
- full certificate of birth, marriage, death or adoption with GRO reference supplied, £9.25
- extra copies of the same birth, marriage or death certificate issued at the same time, £9.25

A priority service is available for an additional fee.

A complete set of the GRO indexes including births, deaths and marriages, civil partnerships, adoptions and provisional indexes for births and deaths from January 2010 to March 2011 are available at the British Library, City of Westminster Archives Centre, London Metropolitan Archives, Manchester City Library, Birmingham Central Library, Bridgend Reference and Information Library and Plymouth Central Library. Copies of GRO indexes may also be held at some libraries, family history societies, local records offices and The Church of Jesus Christ of Latter Day Saints family history centres. Some organisations may not hold a complete record of indexes and a small fee may be charged by some of them. GRO indexes are also available online.

The Society of Genealogists has many records of baptisms, marriages and deaths prior to 1837.

SCOTLAND

Certificates of births, deaths or marriages that have taken place in Scotland since 1855 can be obtained from the National Records of Scotland (formerly the General Register Office for Scotland) or from the appropriate local registrar.

Applicable fees – local registrar:
- each extract or abbreviated certificate of birth, death, marriage, civil partnership or adoption within the year of registration, £10.00
- each extract or abbreviated certificate of birth, death, marriage, civil partnership or adoption outwith the current year of registration, £15.00

A priority service is available for an additional fee.

The National Records of Scotland also keeps the Register of Divorces (including decrees of declaration of nullity of marriage), and holds parish registers dating from before 1855.

Applicable fees – National Records of Scotland:
- personal application, or postal, telephone or fax order: £15.00

A priority service for a response within 24 hours is available for an additional fee of £15.00.

General search in the indexes to the statutory registers and parochial registers, per day or part thereof:
- full or part-day search pass: £15.00
- Quarterly search pass: £490.00
- annual search pass: £1,450.00

Online searching is also available. For more information, visit W www.scotlandspeople.gov.uk.

THE GENERAL REGISTER OFFICE

General Register Office, Certificate Services Section, PO Box 2, Southport PR8 2JD **T** 0845-603 7788
W www.gro.gov.uk/gro/content/certificates

THE NATIONAL RECORDS OF SCOTLAND

New Register House, 3 West Register Street, Edinburgh EH1 3YT **T** 0131-334 0380 **W** www.gro-scotland.gov.uk

THE SOCIETY OF GENEALOGISTS

14 Charterhouse Buildings, Goswell Road, London EC1M 7BA **T** 020-7251 8799 **W** www.sog.org.uk

BRITISH NATIONALITY

There are different types of British nationality status: British citizenship; British overseas citizenship; British overseas territories citizenship; British protected persons; and British subjects. The most widely held of these is British citizenship. Everyone born in the UK before 1 January 1983 became a British citizen when the British Nationality Act 1981 came into force, with the exception of children born to certain diplomatic staff working in the UK at the time. Individuals born outside the UK before 1 January 1983 but who at that date were citizens of the UK and colonies and had a right of abode in the UK also became British citizens. British citizens have the right to live permanently in the UK and are free to leave and re-enter the UK at any time.

A person born on or after 1 January 1983 in the UK (including, for this purpose, the Channel Islands and the Isle of Man) is entitled to British citizenship if he/she falls into one of the following categories:
- he/she has a parent who is a British citizen
- he/she has a parent who is settled in the UK
- he/she is a newborn infant found abandoned in the UK
- his/her parents subsequently settle in the UK or become British citizens and an application is made before he/she is 18
- he/she lives in the UK for the first ten years of his/her life and is not absent for more than 90 days in each of those years
- he/she is adopted in the UK and one of the adopters is a British citizen
- the home secretary consents to his/her registration while he/she is a minor
- if he/she has always been stateless and lives in the UK for a period of five years before his/her 22nd birthday

A person born outside the UK may acquire British citizenship if he/she falls into one of the following categories:
- he/she has a parent who is a British citizen otherwise than by descent, eg a parent who was born in the UK
- he/she has a parent who is a British citizen serving the crown or a European community institution overseas and was recruited to that service in the UK (including qualifying territories for those born on or after 21 May 2002) or in the European Community (for services within an EU institution)
- the home secretary consents to his/her registration while he/she is a minor
- he/she is a British overseas territories citizen, a British overseas citizen, a British subject or a British protected person and has been lawfully resident in the UK for five years
- he/she is a British overseas territories citizen who acquired that citizenship from a connection with Gibraltar
- he/she is adopted or naturalised

Where parents are married, the status of either may confer citizenship on their child. Since July 2006, both parents are able to pass on nationality even if they are not married, provided that there is satisfactory evidence of paternity. For children born before July 2006, it must be shown that there is parental consent and that the child would have an automatic claim to citizenship or entitlement to registration had the parents been married. Where parents are not married, the status of the mother determines the child's citizenship.

Under the 1981 act, Commonwealth citizens and citizens of the Republic of Ireland were entitled to registration as British citizens before 1 January 1983. In 1983, citizens of the Falkland Islands were granted British citizenship.

Renunciation of British citizenship must be registered with the home secretary and will be revoked if no new citizenship or nationality is acquired within six months. If the renunciation was required in order to retain or acquire another citizenship or nationality, the citizenship may be reacquired only once. If the renunciation was for another reason, the home secretary may allow reacquisition more than once, depending on the circumstances. The secretary of state may deprive a person of a citizenship status if he or she is satisfied that the person has done anything seriously prejudicial to the vital interests of the UK, or a British overseas territory, unless making the order would have the effect of rendering such a person stateless. A person may also be deprived of a citizenship status which results from his registration or naturalisation if the secretary of state is satisfied that the registration or naturalisation was obtained by fraud, false representation or concealment of a material fact.

BRITISH DEPENDENT TERRITORIES CITIZENSHIP
Since 26 February 2006, this category of nationality no longer exists and has been replaced by British overseas territory citizenship.

If a person had this class of nationality only by reason of a connection to the territory of Hong Kong, they lost it automatically when Hong Kong was returned to the People's Republic of China. However, if after 30 June 1997, they had no other nationality and would have become stateless, or were born after 30 June 1997 and would have been born stateless (but had a parent who was a British national (overseas) or a British overseas citizen), they became a British overseas citizen.

BRITISH OVERSEAS CITIZENSHIP
Under the 1981 act, as amended by the British Overseas Territories Act 2002, this type of citizenship was conferred on any UK and colonies citizens who did not become either a British citizen or a British overseas territories citizen on 1 January 1983 and as such is now, for most purposes, only acquired by persons who would otherwise be stateless.

BRITISH OVERSEAS TERRITORIES CITIZENSHIP
This category of nationality replaced British dependent territories citizenship. Most commonly, this form of nationality is acquired where, after 31 December 1982, a person was a citizen of the UK and colonies and did not become a British citizen, and that person, and their parents or grandparents, were born, registered or naturalised in the specified British overseas territory. However, on 21 May 2002, people became British citizens if they had British overseas territories citizenship by connection with any British overseas territory except for the sovereign base areas of Akrotiri and Dhekelia in Cyprus.

RESIDUAL CATEGORIES
British subjects, British protected persons and British nationals (overseas) may be entitled to registration as British citizens on completion of five years' legal residence in the UK.

Citizens of the Republic of Ireland who were also British subjects before 1 January 1949 can retain that status if they fulfil certain conditions.

EUROPEAN UNION CITIZENSHIP
British citizens (including Gibraltarians who are registered for this purpose) are also EU citizens and are entitled to travel freely to other EU countries to work, study, reside and set up a business. EU citizens have the same rights with respect to the UK.

NATURALISATION
Naturalisation is granted at the discretion of the home secretary. The basic requirements are five years' residence (three years if the applicant is married to, or is the civil partner of a British citizen), good character, adequate knowledge of the English, Welsh or Scottish Gaelic language, passing the UK citizenship test (if the applicant is not married to, or is the civil partner of a British citizen) and an intention to reside permanently in the UK.

STATUS OF ALIENS
Aliens, being persons without any of the above forms of British nationality, may not hold public office or vote in Britain and they may not own a British ship or aircraft. Citizens of the Republic of Ireland are not deemed to be aliens. Certain provisions of the Immigration and Asylum Act 1999 make provision about immigration and asylum and about procedures in connection with marriage by superintendent registrar's certificate.

CONSUMER LAW

SALE OF GOODS
A sale of goods contract is the most common type of contract. It is governed by the Sale of Goods Act 1979 (as amended by the Sale and Supply of Goods Act 1994). The act provides protection for buyers by implying terms into every sale of goods contract. These terms include:
- an implied term that the seller will pass good title to the buyer (unless it appears from the contract or is to be inferred from the circumstances that there is an intention that the seller should transfer only such title as he has)
- where the seller sells goods by reference to a description, an implied term that the goods will match that description and, where the sale is by sample and description, it will not be sufficient that the bulk of the goods correspond with the sample if the goods do not also correspond with the description
- where goods are sold by a business seller, an implied term that the goods will be of satisfactory quality ie they meet the standard that a reasonable person would regard as satisfactory, taking into account any description of the goods, the price, and all other relevant circumstances. The quality of the goods includes their state and condition, relevant aspects being whether they are fit for all the purposes for which such goods are commonly supplied, their appearance and finish, freedom from minor defects and their safety and durability. This term will not be implied, however, if a buyer has examined the goods (including in a sale by sample) and should have noticed the defect or if the

seller specifically drew the buyer's attention to the defect

- where goods are sold by a business seller, an implied term that the goods are reasonably fit for any purpose made known to the seller by the buyer (either expressly or by implication), unless it is shown that the buyer does not rely on the seller's judgment, or it is not reasonable for him/her to do so
- where goods are sold by sample, implied terms that the bulk of the sample will correspond with the sample in quality, and that the goods are free from any defect rendering them unsatisfactory which would not have been apparent on a reasonable examination of the sample

Some of the above terms can be excluded from contracts by the seller. The seller's right to do this is, however, restricted by the Unfair Contract Terms Act 1977. The act offers more protection to a buyer who 'deals as a consumer' (that is where the seller is selling in the course of a business, the goods are of a type ordinarily bought for private use and the goods are bought by a buyer who is not a business buyer) and does not allow for the implied terms described above to be excluded. In a sale of secondhand goods by auction (at which individuals have the opportunity of attending the sale in person), a buyer does not deal as a consumer.

HIRE-PURCHASE AGREEMENTS

Terms similar to those implied in contracts of sales of goods are implied into contracts of hire-purchase, under the Supply of Goods (Implied Terms) Act 1973. The 1977 act limits the exclusion of these implied terms as before.

SUPPLY OF GOODS AND SERVICES

Under the Supply of Goods and Services Act 1982, similar terms are also implied in other types of contract under which ownership of goods passes, and contracts for the hire of goods (though not hire-purchase agreements). These types of contracts have additional implied terms:

- that the supplier will use reasonable care and skill in carrying out the service
- that the supplier will carry out the service in a reasonable time (unless the time has been agreed)
- that the supplier will make a reasonable charge (unless the charge has already been agreed)

The 1977 act limits the exclusion of these implied terms in a similar manner as before.

UNFAIR TERMS

The Unfair Terms in Consumer Contracts Regulations 1999 apply to contracts between business sellers (or suppliers of goods and services) and consumers. Where the terms have not been individually negotiated (ie where the terms were drafted in advance so that the consumer was unable to influence those terms), a term will be deemed unfair if it operates to the detriment of the consumer (ie causes a significant imbalance in the parties' rights and obligations arising under the contract). An unfair term does not bind the consumer but the contract may continue to bind the parties if it is capable of existing without the unfair term. The regulations contain a non-exhaustive list of terms that are regarded as potentially unfair. When a term does not fall into such a category, whether it will be regarded as fair or not will depend on many factors, including the nature of the goods or services, the surrounding circumstances (such as the bargaining strength of both parties) and the other terms in the contract.

CONSUMER PROTECTION

The Consumer Protection from Unfair Trading Regulations 2008 (CPRs) replaced much previous consumer protection regulation including the majority of the Trade Descriptions Act 1968. CPRs prohibit 31 specific practices, including pyramid schemes. In addition CPRs prohibit business sellers from making misleading actions and misleading omissions, which cause, or are likely to cause, the average consumer to take a different transactional decision. There is also a general duty not to trade unfairly.

Under the Consumer Protection Act 1987, producers of goods are liable for any injury, death or damage to any property exceeding £275 caused by a defect in their product (subject to certain defences).

Consumers are also afforded protection under the Consumer Protection (Distance Selling) Regulations 2000 and the Cancellation of Contracts made in a Consumer's Home or Place of Work etc Regulations 2008 in relation to cancellation rights.

CONSUMER CREDIT

In matters relating to the provision of credit (or the supply of goods on hire or hire-purchase), consumers are also protected by the Consumer Credit Act 1974 (as amended by the Consumer Credit Act 2006). Under this act, a licence, issued by the Office of Fair Trading, is required in order to conduct a consumer credit or consumer hire business or an ancillary credit business, subject to certain exemptions. Any 'fit' person as defined within the act may apply to the Office of Fair Trading for a licence. The provisions of the act only apply to 'regulated' agreements; there are a number of exemptions under which consumer credit agreements are not regulated by the act (such as first charge mortgages which are regulated instead by the FSA). Provisions include:

- in order for a creditor to enforce a regulated agreement, the agreement must comply with certain formalities and must be properly executed. An improperly executed regulated agreement is enforceable only on an order of the court. The debtor must also be given specified information by the creditor or his/her broker or agent during the negotiations which take place before the signing of the agreement. The agreement must also state certain information to ensure that the debtor or hirer is aware of the rights and duties conferred or imposed on him/her and the protection and remedies available to him/her under the act
- the right to withdraw from or cancel some contracts depending on the circumstances. For example, subject to certain exceptions, a borrower may withdraw from a regulated credit agreement within 14 days without giving any reason. The exceptions include agreements for credit exceeding £60,260 and agreements secured on land. The right to withdraw applies only to the credit agreement itself and not to goods or services purchased with it. The borrower must also repay the credit and any interest
- if the debtor is in breach of the agreement, the creditor must serve a default notice before taking any action such as repossessing the goods
- if the agreement is a hire-purchase or conditional sale agreement, the creditor cannot repossess the goods without a court order if the debtor has paid one third of the total price of the goods
- in agreements where the relationship between the creditor and the debtor is unfair to the debtor, the court

may alter or set aside some of the terms of the agreement

Where a credit reference agency has been used to check the debtor's financial standing, the creditor may be required to give the agency's name to the debtor, who is entitled to see the agency's file on him. A fee of £2 is payable to the agency.

SCOTLAND

The legislation governing the sale and supply of goods applies to Scotland as follows:

- the Sale of Goods Act 1979 applies with some modifications and it has been amended by the Sale and Supply of Goods Act 1994
- the Supply of Goods (Implied Terms) Act 1973 applies
- the Supply of Goods and Services Act 1982 does not extend to Scotland but some of its provisions were introduced by the Sale and Supply of Goods Act 1994
- only Parts II and III of the Unfair Contract Terms Act 1977 apply
- the Trade Descriptions Act 1968 applies with minor modifications
- the Consumer Credit Act 1974 applies
- the Consumer Credit Act 2006 applies
- the Consumer Protection Act 1987 applies
- the General Product Safety Regulations 2005 apply
- the Unfair Terms in Consumer Contracts Regulations 1999 apply
- the Unfair Terms in Consumer Contracts (Amendment) Regulations 2001 apply
- the Consumer Protection (Distance Selling) Regulations 2000 apply
- the Sale and Supply of Goods to Consumers Regulations 2002 apply
- the Consumer Protection from Unfair Trading Regulations 2008 apply

PROCEEDINGS AGAINST THE CROWN

Until 1947, proceedings against the Crown were generally possible only by a procedure known as a petition of right, which put the private litigant at a considerable disadvantage. The Crown Proceedings Act 1947 placed the Crown (not the sovereign in his/her private capacity, but as the embodiment of the state) largely in the same position as a private individual and made proceedings in the high court involving the Crown subject to the same rules as any other case. The act did not, however, extinguish or limit the Crown's prerogative or statutory powers, and it continued the immunity of HM ships and aircraft. It also left certain Crown privileges unaffected. The act largely abolished the special procedures which previously applied to civil proceedings by and against the Crown. Civil proceedings may be initiated against the appropriate government department or if there is doubt regarding which is the appropriate department, against the attorney-general.

In Scotland proceedings against the Crown founded on breach of contract could be taken before the 1947 act and no special procedures applied. The Crown could, however, claim certain special pleas. The 1947 act applies in part to Scotland and brings the practice of the two countries as closely together as the different legal systems permit. As a result of the Scotland Act 1998 actions against government departments should be raised against the Lord Advocate or the advocate-general. Actions should be raised against the Lord Advocate where the

department involved administers a devolved matter. Devolved matters include agriculture, education, housing, local government, health and justice. Actions should be raised against the advocate-general where the department is dealing with a reserved matter. Reserved matters include defence, foreign affairs and social security.

DEATHS

WHEN A DEATH OCCURS

If the death (including stillbirth) was expected, the doctor who attended the deceased during their final illness should be contacted. If the death was sudden or unexpected, the family doctor (if known) and police should be contacted. If the cause of death is quite clear the doctor will provide:

- a medical certificate that shows the cause of death
- a formal notice that states that the doctor has signed the medical certificate and that explains how to get the death registered
- if the death was known to be caused by a natural illness but the doctor wishes to know more about the cause of death, he/she may ask the relatives for permission to carry out a post-mortem examination

In England and Wales a coroner is responsible for investigating deaths occurring:

- when there is no doctor who can issue a medical certificate of cause of death
- no doctor has treated the deceased during his or her last illness or when the doctor attending the patient did not see him or her within 14 days before death, or after death
- the death occurred during an operation or before recovery from the effect of an anaesthetic
- the death was sudden and unexplained or attended by suspicious circumstances
- the death might be due to an industrial injury or disease, or to accident, violence, neglect or abortion
- the death occurred in prison or in police custody

The doctor will write on the formal notice that the death has been referred to the coroner; if the post-mortem shows that death was due to natural causes, the coroner may issue a notification which gives the cause of death so that the death can be registered. If the cause of death was violent or unnatural, is still undetermined after a post-mortem, or took place in prison or police custody, the coroner must hold an inquest. The coroner must hold an inquest in these circumstances even if the death occurred abroad (and the body has been returned to England or Wales).

In Scotland the office of coroner does not exist. The local procurator fiscal inquires into sudden or suspicious deaths. A fatal accident inquiry will be held before the sheriff where the death has resulted from an accident during the course of the employment of the person who has died, or where the person who has died was in legal custody, or where the Lord Advocate deems it in the public interest that an inquiry be held.

REGISTERING A DEATH

In England and Wales the death must be registered by the registrar of births and deaths for the district in which it occurred. A death which occurs in Scotland can be registered in any registration district in Scotland. Information concerning a death can be given before any registrar of births and deaths in England and Wales. The registrar will pass the relevant details to the registrar for the district where the death occurred, who will then register the death.

In England and Wales the death must normally be registered within five days (unless the registrar says this period can be extended); in Scotland within eight days. If the death has been referred to the coroner/local procurator fiscal it cannot be registered until the registrar has received authority from the coroner/local procurator fiscal to do so. Failure to register a death involves a penalty in England and Wales and may lead to a court decree being granted by a sheriff in Scotland.

If the death occurred at a house or hospital, the death may be registered by:

- any relative of the deceased
- any person present at the death
- the occupier or any inmate of the house or hospital if he/she knew of the occurrence of the death
- any person making the funeral arrangements (but not the funeral director)
- an official from the hospital
- in Scotland, the deceased's executor or legal representative

For deaths that took place elsewhere, the death may be registered by:

- any relative of the deceased
- someone present at the death
- someone who found the body
- a person in charge of the body
- any person making the funeral arrangements

The majority of deaths are registered by a relative of the deceased. The registrar would normally allow one of the other listed persons to register the death only if there were no relatives available.

The person registering the death should take the medical certificate of the cause of death with them; it is also useful, though not essential, to take the deceased's birth and marriage/civil partnership certificates, NHS medical card, pension documentation and life assurance details. The details given to the registrar must be absolutely correct, otherwise it may be difficult to change them later. The person registering the death should check the entry carefully before it is signed. The registrar will issue a certificate for burial or cremation, and a certificate of registration of death (commonly known as a 'death certificate' which is issued for social security purposes if the deceased received a state pension or benefits) – both free of charge. A death certificate is a certified copy of the entry in the death register; copies can be provided on payment of a fee and may be required for the following purposes, in particular by the executor or administrator when sorting out the deceased's affairs:

- the will
- bank and building society accounts
- savings bank certificates and premium bonds
- insurance policies
- pension claims

If the death occurred abroad or on a foreign ship or aircraft, the death should be registered according to the local regulations of the relevant country and a death certificate should be obtained. In many countries the death can also be registered with the British consulate in that country and a record will be kept at the General Register Office. This avoids the expense of bringing the body back.

After 12 months (three months in Scotland) of death or the finding of a dead body, no death can be registered without the consent of the registrar-general.

BURIAL AND CREMATION

In most circumstances in England and Wales a certificate for burial or cremation must be obtained from the registrar before the burial or cremation can take place. If the death has been referred to the coroner, an order for burial or a certificate for cremation must be obtained. In Scotland a body may be buried (but not cremated) before the death is registered.

Funeral costs can normally be repaid out of the deceased's estate and will be given priority over any other claims. If the deceased has left a will it may contain directions concerning the funeral; however, these directions need not be followed by the executor.

The deceased's papers should also indicate whether a grave space had already been arranged. This information will be contained in a document known as a 'Deed of Grant'. Most town churchyards and many suburban churchyards are no longer open for burial because they are full. Most cemeteries are non-denominational and may be owned by local authorities or private companies; fees vary. If the body is to be cremated, an application form, two cremation certificates (for which there is a charge) or a certificate for cremation if the death was referred to the coroner, and a certificate signed by the medical referee must be completed in addition to the certificate for burial or cremation (the form is not required if the coroner has issued a certificate for cremation). All the forms are available from the funeral director or crematorium. Most crematoria are run by local authorities; the fees usually include the medical referee's fee and the use of the chapel. Ashes may be scattered, buried in a churchyard or cemetery, or kept.

The registrar must be notified of the date, place and means of disposal of the body within 96 hours (England and Wales) or three days (Scotland).

If the death occurred abroad or on a foreign ship or aircraft, a local burial or cremation may be arranged. If the body is to be brought back to England or Wales, a death certificate from the relevant country or an authorisation for the removal of the body from the country of death from the coroner or relevant authority, together with a certificate of embalming will be required. The British consulate can help to arrange this documentation. To arrange a funeral in England or Wales, an authenticated translation of a foreign death certificate or a death certificate issued in Scotland or Northern Ireland which must show the cause of death, is needed, together with a certificate of no liability to register from the registrar in England and Wales in whose sub-district it is intended to bury or cremate the body. If it is intended to cremate the body, a cremation order will be required from the Home Office or a certificate for cremation. If the body is to be cremated in Scotland, an order from the Scottish government Health Department must be obtained.

THE GENERAL REGISTER OFFICE
General Register Office, PO Box 2, Southport PR8 2JD
T 0845-603 7788
W www.gro.gov.uk/gro/content/certificates
THE NATIONAL RECORDS OF SCOTLAND
New Register House, 3 West Register Street, Edinburgh
EH1 3YT T 0131-334 0380 W www.gro-scotland.gov.uk

DIVORCE, DISSOLUTION AND RELATED MATTERS

Divorce is a legal process carried out by the civil courts to end the marriage of an opposite sex couple whilst dissolution is a similar process which ends a civil partnership. Divorce should be distinguished from judicial separation which is a court order confirming that the parties have separated but it does not legally dissolve the marriage/civil partnership. It is often applied for due to moral, religious or ethical grounds but it does allow for financial provision to be made as divorce does.

DIVORCE

The process for divorce begins with a petition and ends with what is known as a 'decree absolute' which dissolves the marriage.

The process begins with the lodging of a standard court form (known as an application for a matrimonial order) at any divorce county court or at the principal registry in London. This must be accompanied by a court form outlining the current and proposed arrangements for any children of the family under 16 or between 16 and 18 and in full-time education.

An application for a matrimonial order for divorce may only be presented to the court after one year of marriage and it must be based on matters which occurred within that time. The spouse who lodges this document is known as the 'petitioner' throughout the divorce proceedings and the other spouse is the 'respondent'.

The issue of where the petitioner normally lives or the connections the parties have abroad may have to be considered by the court to determine whether a court has authority to deal with a particular divorce (whether the court has jurisdiction). These matters concern the law relating to domicile and habitual residence and can be complex.

There is only one ground for divorce, namely that the marriage has broken down irretrievably. This ground must be 'proved' by one of the following facts:
- the respondent has committed adultery and the petitioner finds it intolerable to live with him/her
- the respondent has behaved in such a way that the petitioner cannot reasonably be expected to live with him/her
- the respondent has deserted the petitioner for a continuous period of at least two years
- the two spouses have lived apart for at least two years and the respondent agrees to a divorce
- the two spouses have lived apart for at least five years
If the court is satisfied that the petitioner has proved one of those facts then it must grant a decree nisi (*see* below) unless it is satisfied that the marriage has not broken down.

The procedure is more complex if the divorce is defended, although this is very rare.

DECREE NISI

If the judge is satisfied that the petitioner has proved the contents of the divorce petition, a date will be set for the pronouncement of the decree nisi in open court. The decree nisi is a preliminary decree of divorce which must be obtained but the marriage will not be legally dissolved until the decree absolute. Neither party needs to attend and all the proceedings up to this point are usually carried out on paper.

DECREE ABSOLUTE

The final step in the divorce procedure is to obtain a decree absolute which formally ends the marriage. The petitioner can apply for this six weeks and one day after the date of the decree nisi. If the petitioner does not apply the respondent can apply, but only after three months

from the earliest date on which the petitioner could have applied.

A decree absolute will not normally be granted until the parties have agreed, or the court has dealt with, the parties' financial situation (*see* below for details of financial provision).

DISSOLUTION OF CIVIL PARTNERSHIPS

The legal process for dissolution of a civil partnership follows a model closely based on divorce. Irretrievable breakdown of the partnership is the sole ground for dissolution. The facts to be proved to establish this are the same as for divorce, with the exception of adultery which, due to its legal definition, can only apply to opposite sex couples. Adultery can, however, be used as an example of unreasonable behaviour.

FINANCIAL RELIEF ANCILLARY TO DIVORCE, NULLITY AND JUDICIAL SEPARATION

Following a petition for divorce, nullity or judicial separation, it is open to either spouse or former spouse to make a claim for financial provision provided they have not remarried. It is common practice for such an application to be made at the same time, or shortly after, a divorce petition has been issued. The courts have wide powers to make financial provision where a marriage breaks down. Orders can be made for:
- spousal maintenance (periodical payments) which can be capitalised into a lump sum
- lump sum payments
- payments of school fees
- adjustment or transfer of interests in property
- adjustment of interests in trusts and settlements
- orders relating to pensions

EXERCISE OF THE COURT'S POWERS TO ORDER FINANCIAL PROVISION

The court must exercise its powers so as to achieve an outcome which is fair between the parties, although it has a wide discretion in determining what is a fair financial outcome. It will consider the worldwide assets of both parties, whether liquid or illiquid. In exercising its discretion, the court has to consider a range of statutory factors including:
- the income, earning capacity, property and other financial resources which either party has or is likely to have in the foreseeable future
- the financial needs, obligations and responsibilities which each of the parties to the marriage has or is likely to have in the foreseeable future
- the standard of living enjoyed by the family
- the age of each party and the duration of the marriage
- any physical or mental disability of either party
- the contribution which each of the parties has made or is likely to make in the foreseeable future to the welfare of the family, including any contribution by looking after the home or caring for the family
- the conduct of parties
- loss of benefits
When considering the above factors, however, the court must give paramount consideration to the welfare of any child of the family.

The court has a wide discretion in considering these factors in order to achieve an outcome it considers to be fair. However, the court has emphasised that a 50:50 division of assets is frequently the correct result unless there are compelling reasons to the contrary. It is important to bear in mind that the House of Lords (now the supreme court) in *White v White* said that if each spouse contributed equally in their different sphere it does not matter in principle which of them earned the money and built up the assets. The contributions of the 'breadwinner' and 'homemaker' are considered equal.

The Law Commission's Marital Property Agreements project began in October 2009 and a consultation paper was published on 11 January 2011. The project is examining the status and enforceability of agreements made between spouses or civil partners (or those contemplating marriage or civil partnership) concerning their property or finances.

In October 2010, the supreme court gave judgement in *Radmacher v Granatino* and made it clear that a person now entering into a pre-nuptial agreement will be considered to have intended to be held to that agreement. However, the court will still be able to decide as to whether the agreement is fair and whether it should govern all the financial results of divorce. The supreme court did not give clear guidelines on when a pre-nuptial agreement would be considered 'fair' and it is likely to depend on the facts of an individual case.

In *Miller v Miller* and *MacFarlane v MacFarlane*, the House of Lords said that fairness required the court to consider three strands:
• the needs of the parties going forwards
• compensation for any economic disparity between the parties (such as where one party has sacrificed their career to become a full-time parent)
• sharing
The court also has a duty to consider making an order which will settle once and for all the parties' financial responsibilities towards each other, known as a 'clean break'.

FINANCIAL PROVISION ON DISSOLUTION OF A CIVIL PARTNERSHIP

The Civil Partnership Act 2004 makes provisions for financial relief for civil partners generally and extends the same rights and responsibilities invoked by marriage. Again the court must consider a number of factors when exercising its discretion and must take into account all of the circumstances of the case while giving first consideration to the welfare of any child of the family who is under 18. The list of statutory factors the court must consider resemble those for marriage and it is likely that the interpretation of these factors will be based on the courts' interpretation of the factors relating to marriage.

COHABITING COUPLES

Rights of unmarried couples are not the same as for married couples. Agreements, whether express or inferred by conduct, often determine interest in money and property. Reliance upon inferences is problematic, therefore it is advisable to consider entering into a contract, or 'cohabitation agreement', which establishes how money and property should be divided in the event of a relationship breakdown.

This area of law is still developing. In July 2007, the Law Commission published its report to parliament, recommending a scheme to provide remedies for eligible candidates. The Cohabitation Bill was subsequently introduced to parliament in December 2008 and the first day of the committee stage took place in April 2009. The next day of the committee stage is yet to be determined. In the meantime, cohabitation agreements continue to be governed by the general principles of contract law.

FINANCIAL PROVISION FOR CHILDREN

All parents are under a legal obligation to support their children financially and the live-in parent with care of the child can make claims against the non-resident parent for maintenance for the child.

The Child Maintenance and Other Payments Act 2008 changed the law with regard to child maintenance and set up the Child Maintenance and Enforcement Commission ('CMEC') which took over responsibility from the Child Support Agency. Since October 2008, all parents have been able to choose either a private or statutory maintenance arrangement, thereby removing the compulsion for benefit claimants to use the Child Support Agency.

If a parent chooses a statutory maintenance calculation, the CMEC will assess the amount that the non-resident parent must pay based on a new gross income scheme. This bases the amount payable on the gross income as per the latest available tax information held by HMRC. Parents using the old scheme (based on a percentage formula relating to net income) are to be encouraged to move to the new scheme or to come to their own arrangements privately.

If a non-resident parent does not make the payments due, CMEC has a wide variety of enforcement powers which include the power to seize a passport or driving licence, without the need to refer to the court.

An application can be made to the court for child maintenance only in certain circumstances as the court's jurisdiction in this area has been limited by the statute. The circumstances include where the income of the non-resident parent exceeds the limit dealt with by CMEC or the parents have already come to a written agreement about child support; or where one parent is seeking additional maintenance to cover, for example, school fees.

Provision is also made under Schedule 1 of the Children Act 1989 for unmarried parents to apply to the court for lump sum and property adjustment orders and, in limited circumstances, orders for child maintenance.

SCOTLAND

Although some provisions are similar to those for England and Wales, there is separate legislation for Scotland covering nullity of marriage, judicial separation, divorce and ancillary matters. The principal legislation in relation to family law in Scotland is the Family Law (Scotland) Act 1985. The Family Law (Scotland) Act 2006 came in to force on 4 May 2006, and introduced reforms to various aspects of Scottish family law. The following is confined to major points on which the law in Scotland differs from that of England and Wales.

An action for judicial separation or divorce may be raised in the court of session; it may also be raised in the sheriff court if either party was resident in the sheriffdom for 40 days immediately before the date of the action or for 40 days ending not more than 40 days before the date of the action. The fee for starting a divorce petition in the sheriff court is £140.

The grounds for raising an action of divorce in Scotland have been subject to reform in terms of the 2006 act. The current grounds for divorce are:
• the defender has committed adultery. When adultery is cited as proof that the marriage has broken down irretrievably, it is not necessary in Scotland to prove that it is also intolerable for the pursuer to live with the defender

- the defender's behaviour is such that the pursuer cannot reasonably be expected to cohabit with the defender
- there has been no cohabitation between the parties for one year prior to the raising of the action for divorce, and the defender consents to the granting of decree of divorce
- there has been no cohabitation between the parties for two years prior to the raising of the action for divorce
- an interim gender recognition certificate under the Gender Recognition Act 2004 has, after the date of marriage, been issued to either party to the marriage

The previously available ground of desertion was abolished by the 2006 act.

A simplified procedure for 'do-it-yourself divorce' was introduced in 1983 for certain divorces. If the action is based on one or two years' separation and will not be opposed, and if there are no children under 16 and no financial claims, and there is no sign that the applicant's spouse is unable to manage his or her affairs through mental illness or handicap, the applicant can write directly to the local sheriff court or to the court of session for the appropriate forms to enable him or her to proceed. The fee is £105, unless the applicant receives income support or legal advice and assistance, in which case there may be no fee.

Where a divorce action has been raised, it may be put on hold for a variety of reasons. In all actions for divorce an extract decree, which brings the marriage to an end, will be made available 14 days after the divorce has been granted. Unlike in England, there is no decree nisi, only a final decree of divorce. Parties must ensure that all financial issues have been resolved prior to divorce, as it is not possible to seek further financial provision after divorce has been granted.

FINANCIAL PROVISION

In relation to financial provision on divorce, the first, and most important, principle is fair sharing of the matrimonial property. In terms of Scots law matrimonial property is defined as all property acquired by either spouse from the date of marriage up to the date of separation. Property acquired before the marriage is not deemed to be matrimonial unless it was acquired for use by the parties as a family home or as furniture for that home. Property acquired after the date of separation is not matrimonial property. Any property acquired by either of the parties by way of gift or inheritance during the marriage is excluded and does not form part of the matrimonial property.

When considering whether to make an award of financial provision a court shall also take account of any economic advantage derived by either party to the marriage as a result of contributions, financial or otherwise, by the other, and of any economic disadvantage suffered by either party for the benefit of the other party. The court must also ensure that the economic burden of caring for a child under the age of 16 is shared fairly between the parties.

A court can also consider making an order requiring one party to pay the other party a periodical allowance for a certain period of time following divorce. Such an order may be appropriate in cases where there is insufficient capital to effect a fair sharing of the matrimonial property. Orders for periodical allowance are uncommon, as courts will favour a 'clean break' where possible.

CHILDREN

The court has the power to award a residence order in respect of any children of the marriage or to make an order regulating the child's contact with the non-resident parent. The court will only make such orders if it is deemed better for the child to do so than to make no order at all, and the welfare of the children is of paramount importance. The fact that a spouse has caused the breakdown of the marriage does not in itself preclude him/her from being awarded residence.

NULLITY

An action for 'declaration of nullity' can be brought if someone with a legitimate interest is able to show that the marriage is void or voidable. The action can only be brought in the court of session. Although the grounds on which a marriage may be void or voidable are similar to those on which a marriage can be declared invalid in England, there are some differences. Where a spouse is capable of sexual intercourse but refuses to consummate the marriage, this is not a ground for nullity in Scots law, though it could be a ground for divorce. Where a spouse was suffering from venereal disease at the time of marriage and the other spouse did not know, this is not a ground for nullity in Scots law, neither is the fact that a wife was pregnant by another man at the time of marriage without the knowledge of her husband.

COHABITING COUPLES

The law in Scotland now provides certain financial and property rights for cohabiting couples in terms of the Family Law (Scotland) Act 2006, or 'the 2006 Act'. The relevant 2006 act provisions do not place cohabitants in Scotland on an equal footing with married couples or civil partners, but provide some rights for cohabitants in the event that the relationship is terminated by separation or death. The provisions relate to couples who cease to cohabit after 4 May 2006.

The legislation provides for a presumption that any contents of the home shared by the cohabitants are owned in equal shares. A former cohabitant can also seek financial provision on termination of the relationship in the form of a capital payment if they can successfully demonstrate that they have been financially disadvantaged, and that conversely the other cohabitant has been financially advantaged, as a consequence of contributions made (financial or otherwise). Such a claim must be made no later than one year after the day on which the cohabitants cease to cohabit.

The 2006 act also provides that a cohabitant may make a claim on their partner's estate in the event of that partner's death, providing that there is no will. A claim of this nature must be made no later than six months after the the date of the partner's death.

THE PRINCIPAL REGISTRY
First Avenue House, 42–49 High Holborn, London WC1 6NP
THE COURT OF SESSION
Parliament House, Parliament Square, Edinburgh EH1 1RQ
T 0131-225 2595 W www.scotcourts.gov.uk
THE CHILD SUPPORT AGENCY
T08457-133133 W www.csa.gov.uk

EMPLOYMENT LAW

EMPLOYEES

A fundamental distinction in UK employment law is that drawn between an employee and someone who is self-employed. Further, there is an important, intermediate category introduced by legislation: 'workers' covers all employees but also catches some of those who are self-employed. An 'employee' is someone who has entered into or works under a contract of employment, while a 'worker' has entered into or works under a contract whereby he undertakes to do or perform personally any work or services for another party whose status is not that of a client or customer. Whether or not someone is an employee or a worker as opposed to being genuinely self-employed is an important and complex question, for it determines that person's statutory rights and protections.

The greater the level of control that the employer has over the work carried out, the greater the depth of integration of the employee in the employer's business, and the closer the obligations to provide and perform work between the parties, the more likely it is that the parties will be employer and employee.

PAY AND CONDITIONS

The Employment Rights Act 1996 consolidated the statutory provisions relating to employees' rights. Employers must give each employee employed for one month or more a written statement containing the following information:

- names of employer and employee
- date when employment began and the date on which the employee's period of *continuous* employment began (taking into account any employment with a previous employer which counts towards that period)
- the scale, rate or other method of calculating remuneration and intervals at which it will be paid
- job title or description of job
- hours and the permitted place(s) of work and, where there are several such places, the address of the employer
- holiday entitlement and holiday pay
- provisions concerning incapacity for work due to sickness and injury, including provisions for sick pay
- details of pension scheme(s)
- length of notice period that employer and employee need to give to terminate employment
- if the employment is not intended to be permanent, the period for which it is expected to continue or, if it is for a fixed term, the end date of the contract
- details of any collective agreement (including the parties to the agreement) which affects the terms of employment
- details of disciplinary and grievance procedures (including the individual to whom a complaint should be made and the process of making that complaint)
- if the employee is to work outside the UK for more than one month, the period of such work and the currency in which payment is made
- a note stating whether a contracting-out certificate is in force

This must be given to the employee within two months of the start of their employment.

If the employer does not provide the written statement within two months (or a statement of any changes to these particulars within one month of the changes being made) then the employee can complain to an employment tribunal, which can specify the information that the employer should have given. When, in the context of an employee's successful tribunal claim, the employer is also found to have been in breach of the duty to provide the written statement at the time proceedings were commenced, the tribunal must award the employee two weeks' pay, and may award four weeks' pay, unless it would be unjust or inequitable to do so.

The Working Time Regulations 1998, the National Minimum Wage Act 1998, the Employment Rights (Dispute Resolution) Act 1998, Employment Relations Act 1999, the Employment Act 2002 and the Employment Act 2008 now supplement the 1996 act.

FLEXIBLE WORKING

The Employment Act 2002 (and regulations made under it) gives employees who are responsible for the upbringing of a child the right to apply for flexible working for the purpose of caring for that child. The right has been extended to carers of adults. Whether or not an employee has this right depends on both the employee and the child/adult cared for meeting a number of criteria. If an application under the act is rejected, the employee may complain to an employment tribunal.

SICK PAY

Employees absent from work through illness or injury are entitled to receive Statutory Sick Pay (SSP) from the employer for a maximum period of 28 weeks in any three-year period.

MATERNITY AND PARENTAL RIGHTS

Under the Employment Relations Act 1999, the Employment Act 2002, the Maternity and Parental Leave Regulations 1999 (as amended in 2002 and 2006) and the Paternity and Adoption Leave Regulations 2002 and 2003, both men and women are entitled to take leave when they become a parent. Women are protected from discrimination, detriment or dismissal by reason of their pregnancy or maternity, including discrimination by association and by perception. Men are protected from suffering a detriment or dismissal for taking paternity or parental leave.

Any woman who needs to attend an antenatal appointment on the advice of a registered medical professional is entitled to paid leave from work to attend the appointment. All pregnant women are entitled to a maximum period of maternity leave of 52 weeks. This comprises 26 weeks' ordinary maternity leave, followed immediately by 26 weeks' additional maternity leave. A woman who takes ordinary maternity leave normally has the right to return to the job in which she was employed before her absence. If she takes additional maternity leave, she is entitled to return to the same job or, if that is not reasonably practicable, to another job that is suitable and appropriate for her to do. There is a two-week period of compulsory maternity leave, immediately following the birth of the child, wherein the employer is not permitted to allow the mother to work.

A woman will qualify for Statutory Maternity Pay (SMP), which is payable for up to 39 weeks, if she has been continuously employed for not less than 26 weeks prior to the 15th week before the expected week of childbirth. For further information *see* Social Welfare, Employer Payments.

Employees are entitled to adoption leave and adoption pay (at the same rates as SMP) subject to fulfilment of similar criteria to those in relation to maternity leave and pay, but note that there is a 26-week qualifying period for adoption leave. Where a couple is adopting a child, either one (but not both) of the parents may take adoption leave, and the other may take paternity leave.

Certain employees are entitled to paternity leave on the birth or adoption of a child. To be eligible, the employee must be the child's father, or the partner of the mother or adopter, and meet other conditions. These conditions are, firstly, that they must have been continuously employed for not less than 26 weeks prior to the 15th week before the expected week of childbirth (or, in the case of adoptions, 26 weeks ending with the week in which notification of the adoption match is given) and, secondly, that the employee must have or expect to have responsibility for the upbringing of the child. The employee may take either one week's leave, or two consecutive weeks' leave. This leave may be taken at any time between the date of the child's birth (or placement for adoption) and 56 days later.

For births and adoptions from 3 April 2011, an eligible employee may take additional paternity leave at the end of the mother's or adopter's leave period. For more information *see* Social Welfare, Employer Payments.

Any employee with one year's service who has, or expects to have, responsibility for a child may take parental leave to care for the child. Each parent is entitled to a total of 13 weeks' parental leave for each of their children (or 18 weeks if the child is disabled). This leave must be taken (at the rate of no more than four weeks a year, and in blocks of whole weeks only) before the child's fifth birthday (18th birthday if the child is disabled) or before the fifth anniversary of the date of placement of an adopted child.

SUNDAY TRADING

The Sunday Trading Act 1994 allows shops to open on Sunday for serving retail customers. The Employment Rights Act 1996 gives shop workers and betting workers the right not to be dismissed, selected for redundancy or to suffer any detriment (such as the denial of overtime, promotion or training) if they refuse to work on Sundays. This does not apply to those who, under their contracts, are employed to work on Sundays.

TERMINATION OF EMPLOYMENT

An employee may be dismissed without notice if guilty of gross misconduct but in other cases a period of notice must be given by the employer. The minimum periods of notice specified in the Employment Rights Act 1996 are:
* one week if the employee has been continuously employed for one month or more but for less than two years
* an additional week for each complete year of continuous employment from and including two to 12 years (making the maximum statutory notice period 12 weeks after 12 years' continuous employment)
* longer periods apply if these are specified in the contract of employment

If an employee is dismissed with less notice than he/she is entitled to by statute, or under their contract if longer, he/she will have a wrongful dismissal claim (unless the employer paid the employee in lieu of notice in accordance with a contractual provision entitling it to do so). This claim for wrongful dismissal can be brought by the employee either in the civil courts or the employment tribunal, but if brought in the tribunal the maximum amount that can be awarded is £25,000.

REDUNDANCY

An employee dismissed because of redundancy may be entitled to redundancy pay. This applies if:
* the employee has at least two years' continuous service

* the employee is dismissed by the employer (this can include cases of voluntary redundancy)
* dismissal is due to redundancy.

Redundancy can mean closure of the entire business, closure of a particular site of the business, or a reduction in the need for employees to carry out work of a particular kind.

An employee may not be entitled to a redundancy payment if offered a suitable alternative job by the same employer. The amount of statutory redundancy pay depends on the length of service, age, and their earnings, subject to a weekly maximum of (currently) £400. The maximum payment that can be awarded is £12,000. The redundancy payment is guaranteed by the government in cases where the employer becomes insolvent.

UNFAIR DISMISSAL

Complaints of unfair dismissal are dealt with by an employment tribunal. Any employee with one year's continuous service (subject to exceptions, including in relation to whistleblowers – *see* below) can make a complaint to the tribunal. At the tribunal, it is for the employer to prove that the dismissal was due to one or more potentially fair reasons: a legal restriction preventing the continuation of the employee's contract; the employee's capability or qualifications for the job he/she was employed to do; the employee's conduct; redundancy; or some other substantial reason.

If the employer succeeds in showing this, the tribunal must then decide whether the employer acted reasonably in dismissing the employee for that reason. If the employee is found to have been unfairly dismissed, the tribunal can order that he/she be reinstated, re-engaged or compensated. Any person believing that they may have been unfairly dismissed should contact their local Citizens Advice bureau or seek legal advice. A claim must be brought within three months of the date of termination of employment.

The normal maximum compensatory award for unfair dismissal is £68,400 (as at 1 February 2011). If the dismissal occurred after 6 April 2009 and the employer unreasonably failed to follow the ACAS Code of Practice on Disciplinary and Grievance Procedures in carrying out the dismissal, the tribunal may increase the employee's compensation by up to 25 per cent.

WHISTLEBLOWING

Under the whistleblowing legislation (Public Interest Disclosure Act 1998, which inserted provisions into the Employment Rights Act 1996) dismissal of an employee is automatically unfair if the reason or principal reason for the dismissal is that the employee has made a protected disclosure. The legislation also makes it unlawful to subject workers (a broad category that includes employees and certain other individuals, such as agency workers) who have made a protected disclosure to any detriment on the ground that they have done so.

For a disclosure to qualify for protection, the claimant must show that he has disclosed information, which in his reasonable belief tends to show one or more of the following six categories of wrongdoing: criminal offences; breach of any legal obligation; miscarriages of justice; danger to the health and safety of any individual; damage to the environment; or the deliberate concealing of information about any of the other categories. The malpractices can be past, present, prospective or merely alleged.

A qualifying disclosure will only be protected if the manner of the disclosure fulfills certain conditions, including being made in good faith and being made to a defined category of persons, which varies according to the type of disclosure.

Any whistleblower claim in the employment tribunal must normally be brought within three months of the date of dismissal or other act leading to a detriment.

An individual does not need to have been working with the employer for any particular period of time to be able to bring such a claim and compensation is uncapped (and can include an amount for injury to feelings).

DISCRIMINATION

Discrimination in employment on the grounds of sex (including gender reassignment), sexual orientation, race, colour, nationality or national origins, religion or belief, marital or civil partnership status, age or disability is unlawful. Discrimination legislation generally covers direct discrimination, indirect discrimination, harassment and victimisation. Only in limited circumstances can such discrimination be justified (rendering it lawful).

An individual does not need to be employed for any particular period of time to be able to claim discrimination (discrimination can be alleged at the recruitment phase), and discrimination compensation is uncapped (and can include an amount for injury to feelings). These features distinguish the discrimination laws from, for example, the unfair dismissal laws.

The Equality Act 2010 was passed on 8 April 2010 and the main provisions came into force on 1 October 2010. The Act unifies several pieces of discrimination legislation, providing one definition of direct discrimination, indirect discrimination, harassment and victimisation. The Equality Act applies to those employed in Great Britain but not to employees in Northern Ireland or (subject to EC exceptions) to those who work mainly abroad, and provides that:

- it is unlawful to discriminate on the grounds of sex, gender reassignment or marital/civil partner status, including discrimination by association and by perception. This covers all aspects of employment (including advertising for jobs), but there are some limited exceptions, such as where the essential nature of the job requires it to be given to someone of a particular sex, or where decency and privacy requires it. The act entitles men and women to equality of remuneration for equivalent work or work of the same value
- individuals have the right not to be discriminated against on the grounds of race, colour, nationality, or ethnic or national origins and this applies to all aspects of employment. Employers may also take lawful positive action, including in relation to recruitment and promotion
- discrimination against a disabled person in all aspects of employment is unlawful. This includes protecting carers from discrimination by association with the disabled persons that they look after. In certain circumstances, the employer may show that the less favourable treatment is justified and so does not constitute discrimination. The act also imposes a duty on employers to make 'reasonable adjustments' to the arrangements and physical features of the workplace if these place disabled people at a substantial disadvantage compared with those who are not disabled. The definition of a 'disabled person' is wide and includes people diagnosed with HIV, cancer and multiple sclerosis

- discrimination against a person on the grounds of religion or belief (or lack of belief) including discrimination by association and by perception, in all aspects of employment, is unlawful
- discrimination against an individual on the grounds of sexual orientation, including discrimination by association and by perception, in all aspects of employment, is unlawful
- age discrimination in the workplace is unlawful, and an employer may no longer dismiss an employee by reason of retirement once they have reached a certain age

The responsibility for monitoring equality in society rests with the Equality and Human Rights Commission.

In Northern Ireland similar provisions exist to those that were in force in Great Britain prior to the coming into force of the Equality Act but are contained in separate legislation (although the Disability Discrimination Act does extend to Northern Ireland). As such, there is a general perception that Northern Ireland now offers less protection to individuals against discrimination than Great Britain.

In Northern Ireland there is one combined body working towards equality and eliminating discrimination, the Equality Commission for Northern Ireland.

WORKING TIME

The Working Time Regulations 1998 impose rules that limit working hours and provide for rest breaks and holidays. The regulations apply to workers and so cover not only employees but also other individuals who undertake to perform personally any work or services (eg freelancers). The regulations are complex and subject to various exceptions and qualifications but the basic provisions relating to adult day workers are as follows:

- No worker is permitted to work more than an average of 48 hours per week (unless they have made a genuine voluntary opt-out of this limit – it is not sufficient to make it a term of the contract that the worker opts out), and a worker is entitled to, but is not required to take, the following breaks:
- 11 consecutive hours' rest in every 24-hour period
- an uninterrupted rest period of at least 24 hours in each 7-day period or 48 hours in each fortnight (in addition to the daily rest period)
- 20 minutes' rest break provided that the working day is longer than 6 hours
- 5.6 weeks' paid annual leave (28 days full-time). This equates to 4 weeks plus public holidays

There are specific provisions relating to night work, young workers (ie those over school leaving age but under 18) and a variety of workers in specialised sectors (such as off-shore oil rig workers).

HUMAN RIGHTS

On 2 October 2000 the Human Rights Act 1998 came into force. This act incorporates the European Convention on Human Rights into the law of the UK. The main principles of the act are as follows:

- all legislation must be interpreted and given effect by the courts as compatible with the Convention so far as it is possible to do so. Before the second reading of a new bill the minister responsible for the bill must provide a statement regarding its compatibility with the Human Rights Act
- subordinate legislation (eg statutory instruments) which are incompatible with the Convention can be struck down by the courts

- primary legislation (eg an act of parliament) which is incompatible with the Convention cannot be struck down by a court, but the higher courts can make a declaration of incompatibility which is a signal to parliament to change the law
- all public authorities (including courts and tribunals) must not act in a way which is incompatible with the Convention
- individuals whose Convention rights have been infringed by a public authority may bring proceedings against that authority, but the act is not intended to create new rights as between individuals

The main human rights protected by the Convention are the right to life (article 2); protection from torture and inhuman or degrading treatment (article 3); protection from slavery or forced labour (article 4); the right to liberty and security of the person (article 5); the right to a fair trial (article 6); the right not to be subject to retrospective criminal offences (article 7); the right to respect for private and family life (article 8); freedom of thought, conscience and religion (article 9); freedom of expression (article 10); freedom of peaceful association and assembly (article 11); the right to marry and found a family (article 12); protection from discrimination (article 14); the right to property (article 1 protocol No.1); the right to education (article 2 protocol No.1); and the right to free elections (article 3 protocol No.1). Most of the Convention rights are subject to limitations which deem the breach of the right acceptable on the basis it is 'necessary in a democratic society'.

Human rights are also enshrined in the common law (of tort). Although this is of historical significance, the common law (for example the duty of confidentiality) remains especially important regarding violations of human rights that occur between private parties, where the Human Rights Act 1998 does not apply.

PARENTAL RESPONSIBILITY

The Children Act 1989 gives both the mother and father parental responsibility for the child if the parents are married to each other at the time of the child's birth. If the parents are not married, only the mother has parental responsibility. The father may acquire it in accordance with the provisions of section 4 of the Children Act 1989. He can do this in one of four ways: a) by being registered as the father on the child's birth certificate with the consent of the mother (only for fathers of children born after 1 December 2003, following changes to the Adoption and Children Act 2002); b) by applying to the court for a parental responsibility order; c) by entering into a parental responsibility agreement with the mother which must be in the prescribed form; or d) by obtaining a residence order from the court. Otherwise, a father can gain parental responsibility by marrying the mother of the child.

Where a child's parent, who has parental responsibility, marries a person who is not the child's parent, the child's parent(s) with parental responsibility can agree for the step-parent to have parental responsibility or, the step-parent may acquire parental responsibility by order of the court (section 4A(1) Children Act 1989).

Where a child is adopted, parental responsibility will be given to the adopter of the child. However, before an order for adoption can be made, the court must be satisfied that every parent or guardian consents. The consent of a father without parental responsibility is not required, although adoption agencies and local authorities must be careful to establish, if possible, the identity of the father and satisfy themselves that any person claiming to be the father either has no intention to apply for parental responsibility or that if he did apply, the application would be likely to be refused.

In Scotland, the relevant legislation is the Children (Scotland) Act 1995, which also gives the mother parental responsibility for her child whether or not she is married to the child's father. A father who is married to the mother, either at the time of the child's conception or subsequently, will also have automatic parental rights. Section 23 of the 2006 act provides that an unmarried father will obtain automatic parental responsibilities and rights if he is registered as the father on the child's birth certificate. For unmarried fathers who are not named on the birth certificate, or whose children were born before the 2006 act came into force, it is possible to acquire parental responsibilities and rights by applying to the court or by entering into a parental responsibilities and rights agreement with the mother. The father of any child, regardless of parental rights, has a duty to aliment that child until he/she is 18 (25 if the child is still at an educational establishment).

LEGITIMATION

Under the Legitimacy Act 1976, an illegitimate person automatically becomes legitimate when his/her parents marry. This applies even where one of the parents was married to a third person at the time of the birth. In such cases it is necessary to re-register the birth of the child. In Scotland, the status of illegitimacy has been abolished by section 21 of the 2006 act. The Law Reform Act 1987 reformed the law so as to remove so far as possible the legal disadvantages of illegitimacy.

JURY SERVICE

In England and Wales, the law concerning juries is largely consolidated in the Juries Act 1974. In England and Wales a person charged with a serious criminal offence is entitled to have their trial heard by a jury in a crown court, except in some complex fraud cases where the evidence is too complex to be usefully considered by a jury, or where there is a real risk of jury tampering. In such cases a judge may be entitled to order a trial by judge alone.

In civil cases, there is a right to a jury in the Queen's Bench Division of the high court in cases where the person applying for a jury has been accused of fraud, as well as in cases of libel, slander, malicious prosecution or false imprisonment. The same applies to the county court. In all other cases in the Queen's Bench Division only the judge has discretion to order trial with a jury, though such an order is seldom made. In the chancery division of the high court a jury is never used. The same is true in the family division of the high court.

No right to a jury trial exists in Scotland, although more serious offences are heard before a jury. In England and Wales there must be at least nine, and no more than 12 members of a jury in a criminal case. Civil cases held in the county court must have eight members but those held in the high court may have any number of members up to a maximum of 12. At an inquest, there must be at least seven and no more than 11 members. In Scotland there are 12 members of a jury in a civil case in the court of session (the civil jury being confined to the court of session and a restricted number of actions), and 15 in a criminal trial in the high court of justiciary. Jurors are normally asked to serve for ten working days, during which time they could sit on more than one case. Jurors selected for longer cases are expected to sit for the duration of the trial.

Every 'registered' parliamentary or local government elector between the ages of 18 and 70 who has lived in the UK (including, for this purpose, the Channel Islands and the Isle of Man) for any period of at least five years since reaching the age of 13 is qualified to serve on a jury unless he/she is 'mentally disordered' or disqualified.

Those disqualified from jury service include:

• those who have at any time been sentenced by a court in the UK (including, for this purpose, the Channel Islands and the Isle of Man) to a term of imprisonment or youth custody of five years or more
• those who have been imprisoned for life, detained at Her Majesty's, or the Secretary of State's pleasure, detained for a period of at least five years, imprisoned or detained for public protection, or received an 'extended sentence' under the relevant provisions of the Criminal Justice Act 2003 or the Criminal Procedure (Scotland) Act 1995
• those who have within the previous ten years served any part of a sentence of imprisonment, youth custody or detention, been detained in a young offenders' institution, received a suspended sentence of imprisonment or order for detention, or received a community order
• those who are on bail in criminal proceedings

The court has the discretion to excuse a juror from service, or defer the date of service, if the juror can show there is good reason why he/she should be excused from attending or good reason why his attendance should be deferred. It is an offence (punishable by a fine) to fail to attend when summoned, to serve knowing that you are disqualified from service, or to make false representations in an attempt to evade service. If a juror fails to turn up for service, or attends but cannot serve due to being under the influence of drink or drugs, this is punishable as contempt of court. Any party can object to any juror if he/she can show cause to the trial judge.

It may be appropriate for a judge to excuse a juror from a particular case if he is personally concerned in the facts of the particular case, or closely connected with a party to the proceedings or with a prospective witness. The judge may also discharge any juror who, from a mental or physical incapacity, temporary or permanent, cannot pay proper attention to the evidence.

An individual juror (or the entire jury) can be discharged if it is shown that they or any of their number have, among other things, separated from the rest of the jury without the leave of the court; talked to any person out of court who is not a member of the jury; determined the verdict of the trial by drawing lots; come to a compromise on the verdict; been drunk, or otherwise incapacitated, while carrying out their duties as a juror; exerted improper pressure on the other members of the jury (eg harassment or bullying); declined to take part in the jury's functions; displayed actual or apparent bias (eg racism, sexism or other discriminatory or deliberate hostility); or inadvertently possessed knowledge of the bad character of a party to the proceedings which has not been adduced as evidence in the proceedings. The factual situations that arise are many, and include consulting an ouija board in the course of deliberations, making telephone calls after retirement, and lunching with a barrister not connected with the proceedings.

A jury's verdict need not be unanimous. In criminal proceedings the agreement of 10 jurors will suffice when there are not fewer than 11 people on the jury (or 9 in a jury of 10). In civil proceedings in the county court the agreement of seven or eight jurors will suffice. However, where a majority verdict is given, the court must be satisfied that the jury had reasonable time to consider its verdict based on the nature and complexity of the case. In criminal proceedings this must be no less than two hours.

A juror is immune from prosecution or civil claim in respect of anything said or done by him or her in the discharge of their office. It is a contempt of court for a juror to disclose what happened in the jury room even after the trial is over. A juror may claim travelling expenses, a subsistence allowance and an allowance for other financial loss (eg loss of earnings or benefits, fees paid to carers or child-minders) up to a stated limit. For more information on jury service, visit W www.direct.gov.uk/en/crimejusticeandthelaw/juryservice

SCOTLAND

Qualification criteria for jury service in Scotland are similar to those in England and Wales, except that members of the judiciary are ineligible for ten years after ceasing to hold their post, and others concerned with the administration of justice are only eligible for service five years after ceasing to hold office. Certain persons who have the right to be excused include full-time members of the medical, dental, nursing, veterinary and pharmaceutical professions, full-time members of the armed forces, ministers of religion, persons who have served on a jury within the previous five years, members of the Scottish parliament, members of the Scottish government, junior Scottish ministers, those who have recently served on a jury and those aged over 71 years. For civil trials there is an age limit of 65 years. Those convicted of a serious crime are automatically disqualified. Those who are incapable by reason of a mental disorder may also be excused. The maximum fine for a person serving on a jury knowing himself/herself to be ineligible is £1,000. The maximum fine for failing to attend without good cause is also £1,000.

HER MAJESTY'S COURTS AND TRIBUNALS SERVICE
102 Petty France, London SW1H 9AJ T 0845-456 8770
JURY CENTRAL SUMMONING BUREAU
T 0845-803 8003 E jurysummoning@hmcts.gsi.gov.uk
SCOTTISH COURTS SERVICE
Courts of Session, Parliament House, Parliament Square, Edinburgh EH1 1RQ T 0131-225 2595
W www.scotcourts.gov.uk
THE CLERK OF JUSTICIARY
High Court of Justiciary, Lawnmarket, Edinburgh EH2 2NS
T 0131-240 6900

LANDLORD AND TENANT

RESIDENTIAL LETTINGS

The provisions outlined here apply only where the tenant lives in a separate dwelling from the landlord and where the dwelling is the tenant's only or main home. It does not apply to licensees such as lodgers, guests or service occupiers.

The 1996 Housing Act radically changed certain aspects of the legislation referred to below; in particular, the grant of assured and assured shorthold tenancies under the Housing Act 1988.

ASSURED SHORTHOLD TENANCIES

If a tenancy was granted on or after 15 January 1989 and before 28 February 1997, the tenant would have an assured tenancy unless the landlord served notice under section 20 in the prescribed form prior to the commencement of the tenancy, stating that the tenancy is to be an assured shorthold tenancy and the tenancy is for a minimum fixed term period of six months (*see* below). An assured tenancy gives that tenant greater security. The tenant could, for example, stay in possession of the dwelling for as long as the tenant observed the terms of the tenancy. The landlord cannot obtain possession from such a tenant unless the landlord can establish a specific ground for possession (set out in the Housing Act 1988) and obtains a court order. The rent payable is that agreed with the landlord at the start of the tenancy. The landlord has the right to increase the rent annually by serving a notice. If that happens the tenant can apply to have the rent fixed by the rent assessment committee of the local authority. The tenant or the landlord may request that the committee sets the rent in line with open market rents for that type of property.

Under the Housing Act 1996, all new lettings (below an annual rent threshold of £100,000 since October 2010) entered into on or after 28 February 1997 (for whatever term) will be assured shorthold tenancies unless the landlord serves a notice stating that the tenancy is not to be an assured shorthold tenancy. This means that the landlord is entitled to possession at the end of the tenancy provided he serves a notice under section 21 Housing Act 1988 and commences the proceedings in accordance with the correct procedure. The landlord must obtain a court order, however, to obtain possession if the tenant refuses to vacate at the end of the tenancy. If the tenancy is an assured shorthold tenancy, the court must grant the order. For both assured and assured shorthold tenancies, if the tenant is more than eight weeks in arrears, the landlord can serve notice and, if the tenant is still in arrears at the date of the hearing, the court must make an order for possession.

REGULATED TENANCIES

Before the Housing Act 1988 came into force on 15 January 1989 there were regulated tenancies; some are still in existence and are protected by the Rent Act 1977. Under this act it is possible for the landlord or the tenant to apply to the local rent officer to have a 'fair' rent registered. The fair rent is then the maximum rent payable.

SECURE TENANCIES

Secure tenancies are generally given to tenants of local authorities, housing associations (before 15 January 1989) and certain other bodies. This gives the tenant security of tenure unless the terms of the agreement are broken by the tenant and it is reasonable to make an order for possession. Those with secure tenancies may have the right to buy their property. In practice this right is generally only available to council tenants.

AGRICULTURAL PROPERTY

Tenancies in agricultural properties are governed by the Agricultural Holdings Act 1986, the Agricultural Tenancies Act 1995 (both amended by the Regulatory Reform (Agricultural Tenancies) (England and Wales) Order 2006), the Tribunals, Courts and Enforcement Act 2007, the Legal Services Act 2007 and the Rent (Agriculture) Act 1976, which give similar protections to those described above, eg security of tenure, right to

compensation for disturbance, etc. The Agricultural Holdings (Scotland) Act 1991 along with Agricultural Holdings (Scotland) Act 2003 and the Housing (Scotland) Act 2006 apply similar provisions to Scotland.

EVICTION

The Protection from Eviction Act 1977 (as amended by the Housing Act 1988 and Nationality, Immigration and Asylum Act 2002) sets out the procedure a landlord must follow in order to obtain possession of property. It is unlawful for a landlord to evict a tenant otherwise than in accordance with the law. For common law tenancies and for Rent Act tenants a notice to quit in the prescribed form giving 28 days notice is required. For secure and assured tenancies a notice seeking possession must be served. It is unlawful for the landlord to evict a person by putting their belongings on to the street, by changing the locks and so on. It is also unlawful for a landlord to harass a tenant in any way in order to persuade him/her to give up the tenancy. The tenant may be able to obtain an injunction to restrain the actions of the landlord and get back into the property and be awarded damages.

LANDLORD RESPONSIBILITIES

Under the Landlord and Tenant Act 1985, where the term of the lease is less than seven years, the landlord is responsible for maintaining the structure and exterior of the property, for sanitation, for heating and hot water, and all installations for the supply of water, gas and electricity.

LEASEHOLDERS

Strictly speaking, leaseholders have bought a long lease rather than a property and in certain limited circumstances the landlord can end the tenancy. Under the Leasehold Reform Act 1967 (as amended by the Housing Acts 1969, 1974, 1980 and 1985), leaseholders of houses may have the right to buy the freehold or to take an extended lease for a term of 50 years. This applies to leases where the term of the lease is over 21 years, at a low rent, and where the leaseholder has occupied the house as his/her only or main residence for the last two years, or for a total of two years over the last ten. The tenant must give the landlord written notice of his desire to acquire the freehold or extend the leasehold.

The Leasehold Reform, Housing and Urban Development Act came into force in 1993 and allows the leaseholders of flats in certain circumstances to buy the freehold of the building in which they live.

Responsibility for maintenance of the structure, exterior and interior of the building should be set out in the lease. Usually the upkeep of the interior of his/her part of the property is the responsibility of the leaseholder, and responsibility for the structure, exterior and common interior areas is shared between the freeholder and the leaseholder(s).

If leaseholders are dissatisfied with charges made in respect of lease extensions, they are entitled to have their situation evaluated by the Leasehold Valuation Tribunal.

The Commonhold and Leasehold Reform Act 2002 makes provision for the freehold estate in land to be registered as commonhold land and for the legal interest in the land to be vested in a 'commonhold association' ie a private limited company.

BUSINESS LETTINGS

The Landlord and Tenant Acts 1927 and 1954 (as amended) give security of tenure to the tenants of most business premises. The landlord can only evict the tenant on one of the grounds laid down in the 1954 act, and in some cases where the landlord repossesses the property the tenant may be entitled to compensation.

SCOTLAND

In Scotland assured and short assured tenancies exist for lettings after 2 January 1989 and are similar to assured tenancies in England and Wales. The relevant legislation is the Housing (Scotland) Act 1988.

Most tenancies created before 2 January 1989 were regulated tenancies and the Rent (Scotland) Act 1984 still applies where these exist. The act defines, among other things, the circumstances in which a landlord can increase the rent when improvements are made to the property. The provisions of the Rent Act do not apply to tenancies where the landlord is the Crown, a local authority or a housing corporation.

The Housing (Scotland) Acts of 1987 and 2001 relate to local authority responsibilities for housing, the right to buy, and local authority secured tenancies. The provisions are broadly similar to England and Wales. The Housing (Scotland) Act 2010 is expected to come fully into force by April 2012. When fully in force, the act will reform the existing right-to-buy provisions, modernise social housing regulation and replace the regulatory framework established by the 1988 and 2001 acts.

In Scotland, business premises are not controlled by statute to the same extent as in England and Wales, although the Tenancy of Shops (Scotland) Act 1949 gives some security to tenants of shops. Tenants of shops can apply to the sheriff, within 21 days of being served a notice to quit, for a renewal of tenancy if threatened with eviction. This application may be dismissed on various grounds including where the landlord has offered to sell the property to the tenant at an agreed price or, in the absence of agreement as to price, at a price fixed by a single arbiter appointed by the parties or the sheriff. The act extends to properties where the Crown or government departments are the landlords or the tenants.

Under the Leases Act 1449 the landlord's successors (either purchasers or creditors) are bound by the agreement made with any tenants so long as the following conditions are met:
• the lease, if for more than one year, must be in writing
• there must be a rent
• there must be a term of expiry
• the tenant must have entered into possession
• the subjects of the lease must be land
• the landlord, if owner, must be the proprietor with a recorded title, ie the title deeds recorded in the Register of Sasines or registered in the Land Register

The Antisocial Behaviour etc (Scotland) Act 2004 provides that all landlords letting property in Scotland must register with the local authority in which the let property is situated. Exceptions apply to holiday lets, owner-occupied accommodation and agricultural holdings. The act applies to partnerships, trusts and companies as well as to individuals.

LEGAL AID

The Access to Justice Act 1999 has transformed what used to be known as the Legal Aid system. The Legal Aid Board has been replaced by the Legal Services Commission, which is responsible for the development and administration of two legal funding schemes in England and Wales, namely the Criminal Defence Service and the Community Legal Service. The Criminal Defence

Service assists people who are under police investigation or facing criminal charges. The Community Legal Service is designed to increase access to legal information and advice by involving a much wider network of funders and providers in giving publicly funded legal services. In Scotland, provision of legal aid is governed by the Legal Aid (Scotland) Act 1986 and the Legal Profession and Legal Aid (Scotland) Act 2007 and administered by the Scottish Legal Aid Board.

LEGAL SERVICES COMMISSION
4 Abbey Orchard Street, London SW1P 2BS T 020-7783 7000
W www.legalservices.gov.uk

CIVIL LEGAL AID

From 1 January 2000, only organisations (such as solicitors or Citizens Advice) with a contract with the Legal Services Commission have been able to give initial help in any civil matter. Moreover, from that date decisions about funding were devolved from the Legal Services Commission to contracted organisations in relation to any level of publicly funded service in family and immigration cases. For other types of case, applications for public funding are made through a solicitor (or other contracted legal services providers) in much the same way as the former Legal Aid. On 1 April 2001 the so-called civil contracting scheme was extended to cover all levels of service for all types of cases.

Under the civil funding scheme there are broadly six levels of service available:
• legal help
• help at court
• family help – either family help (lower) or family help (higher)
• legal representation – either investigative help or full representation
• family mediation
• such other services as authorised by specific orders

ELIGIBILITY
Eligibility for funding from the Community Legal Service depends broadly on five factors:
• the level of service sought (see above)
• whether the applicant qualifies financially
• the merits of the applicant's case
• a costs-benefits analysis (if the costs are likely to outweigh any benefit that might be gained from the proceedings, funding may be refused)
• whether there is any public interest in the case being litigated (ie whether the case has a wider public interest beyond that of the parties involved, eg a human rights case)

The limits on capital and income above which a person is not entitled to public funding vary with the type of service sought.

CONTRIBUTIONS
Some of those who qualify for Community Legal Service funding will have to contribute towards their legal costs. Contributions must be paid by anyone who has a disposable income or disposable capital exceeding a prescribed amount. The rules relating to applicable contributions are complex and detailed information can be obtained from the Legal Services Commission.

STATUTORY CHARGE
A statutory charge is made if a person keeps or gains money or property in a case for which they have received

legal aid. This means that the amount paid by the Community Legal Service fund on their behalf is deducted from the amount that the person receives. This does not apply if the court has ordered that the costs be paid by the other party (unless the amount paid by the other party does not cover all of the costs). In certain circumstances, the Legal Services Commission may waive or postpone payment.

CONTINGENCY OR CONDITIONAL FEES

This system was introduced by the Courts and Legal Services Act 1990. It can offer legal representation on a 'no win, no fee' basis. It provides an alternative form of assistance, especially for those cases which are ineligible for funding by the Community Legal Service. The main area for such work is in the field of personal injuries.

Not all solicitors offer such a scheme and different solicitors may well have different terms. The effect of the agreement is that solicitors may not make any charges, or may waive some of their charges, until the case is concluded successfully. If a case is won then the losing party will usually have to pay towards costs, with the winning party contributing around one third.

SCOTLAND

Civil legal aid is available for cases in the following:
- the sheriff courts
- the court of session
- the House of Lords
- the lands valuation appeal court
- the Scottish land court
- the Lands Tribunal for Scotland
- the Employment Appeal Tribunals
- the Judicial Committee of the Privy Council
- the Proscribed Organisations Appeal Commissioner
- proceedings before the Social Security Commissioners
- proceedings before the Child Support Commissioners

Civil legal aid is not available for defamation actions, small claims or simplified divorce procedures or petitions by a debtor for his own sequestration.

Eligibility for civil legal aid is assessed in a similar way to that in England and Wales, though the financial limits differ in some respects. A person shall be eligible for civil legal aid if their disposable income does not exceed £26,239 a year. A person may be refused civil aid if their disposable capital exceeds £13,017 and it appears to the Legal Aid board that they can afford to pay without legal aid. Additionally:
- if disposable income is between £3,521 and £11,540, a contribution of one third of the difference between £3,521 and the disposable income may be payable
- if disposable income is between £11,541 and £15,743, one third of the difference between £3,521 and £11,540 plus half the difference between £11,541 and the disposable income may be payable
- if disposable income is between £15,743 and £26,239, a contribution of the following: one third of the difference between £3,521 and £11,540, plus half the difference between £11,541 and £15,743, plus all the remaining disposable income between £15,744 and £26,239 – will be payable

CRIMINAL LEGAL AID

The Legal Services Commission provides defendants facing criminal charges with free legal representation if they pass a merits test and a means test.

Criminal legal aid covers the cost of preparing a case and legal representation in criminal proceedings. It is also available for appeals against verdicts or sentences in magistrates' courts, the crown court or the court of appeal. It is not available for bringing a private prosecution in a criminal court.

If granted criminal legal aid, either the person may choose their own solicitor or the court will assign one. Contributions to the legal costs may be required. The rules relating to applicable contributions are complex and detailed information can be obtained from the Legal Services Commission.

DUTY SOLICITORS

The Legal Aid Act 1988 also provides free advice and assistance to anyone questioned by the police (whether under arrest or helping the police with their enquiries). No means test or contributions are required for this.

SCOTLAND

Legal advice and assistance operates in a similar way in Scotland. A person is eligible:
- if disposable income does not exceed £245 a week. If disposable income is between £105 and £245 a week, contributions are payable
- if disposable capital does not exceed £1,716 (if the person has dependent relatives, the savings allowance is higher)
- if receiving income support or income-related job seeker's allowance they qualify automatically provided they have no savings over the limit

The procedure for application for criminal legal aid depends on the circumstances of each case. In solemn cases (more serious cases, such as murder) heard before a jury, a person is automatically entitled to criminal legal aid until they are given bail or placed in custody. Thereafter, it is for the court to decide whether to grant legal aid. The court will do this if the person accused cannot meet the expenses of the case without undue hardship on him or his dependants. In less serious cases the procedure depends on whether the person is in custody:
- anyone taken into custody has the right to free legal aid from the duty solicitor up to and including the first court appearance
- if the person is not in custody and wishes to plead guilty, they are not entitled to criminal legal aid but may be entitled to legal advice and assistance, including assistance by way of representation
- if the person is not in custody and wishes to plead not guilty, they can apply for criminal legal aid. This must be done within 14 days of the first court appearance at which they made the plea

The criteria used to assess whether or not criminal legal aid should be granted is similar to the criteria for England and Wales. When meeting with your solicitor, take evidence of your financial position such as details of savings, bank statements, pay slips, pension book or benefits book.

THE SCOTTISH LEGAL AID BOARD
44 Drumsheugh Gardens, Edinburgh EH3 7SW
T 0131-226 7061 W www.slab.org.uk

MARRIAGE

Any two persons may marry provided that:
- they are at least 16 years old on the day of the marriage (in England and Wales persons under the age of 18 must generally obtain the consent of their parents or guardian; if consent is refused an appeal may be made

to the high court, the county court or a court of summary jurisdiction)
• they are not related to one another in a way which would prevent their marrying
• they are unmarried (a person who has already been married must produce documentary evidence that the previous marriage has been ended by death, divorce or annulment)
• they are not of the same sex (though same sex couples can register a civil partnership instead)
• they are capable of understanding the nature of a marriage ceremony and of consenting to marriage

The parties should check the marriage will be recognised as valid in their home country if either is not a British citizen.

DEGREES OF RELATIONSHIP

A marriage between persons within the prohibited degrees of consanguinity, affinity or adoption is void.

A man may not marry his mother, daughter, grandmother, granddaughter, sister, aunt, niece, adoptive mother, former adoptive mother, adopted daughter or former adopted daughter.

A woman may not marry her father, son, grandfather, grandson, brother, uncle, nephew, adoptive father, former adoptive father, adopted son or former adopted son. Under the Marriage (Prohibited Degrees of Relationship) Act 1986, some exceptions to the law permit a man or a woman to marry certain step-relatives or in-laws.

In addition to the above, a person may not marry a child of their former civil partner, a child of a former spouse, the former civil partner of a grandparent, former civil partner of a parent, the former spouse of a grandparent, the former spouse of a parent, the grandchild of a former civil partner or the grandchild of a former spouse, unless the only reason they cannot marry is the affinity mentioned above and both persons are over 21 and the younger party has not at any time before attaining the age of 18 been a child of the family in relation to the other party. All references to brothers/sisters include half-brothers/sisters.

ENGLAND AND WALES

TYPES OF MARRIAGE CEREMONY

It is possible to marry by either religious or civil ceremony. A religious ceremony can take place at a church or chapel of the Church of England or the Church in Wales, or at any other place of worship which has been formally registered by the Registrar-General.

A civil ceremony can take place at a register office, a registered building or any other premises approved by the local authority.

An application for an approved premises licence must be made by the owners or trustees of the building concerned; it cannot be made by the prospective marriage couple. Approved premises must be regularly open to the public so that the marriage can be witnessed; the venue must be deemed to be a permanent and immovable structure. Open-air ceremonies are prohibited.

Non-Anglican marriages may also be solemnised following the issue of a Registrar-General's licence in unregistered premises where one of the parties is seriously ill, is not expected to recover, and cannot be moved to registered premises. Detained and housebound persons may be married at their place of residence.

MARRIAGE IN THE CHURCH OF ENGLAND OR THE CHURCH IN WALES

Marriage by banns

The marriage can take place in a parish in which one of the parties lives, or in a church in another parish if it is the usual place of worship of either or both of the parties. New regulations introduced in October 2008 also allow marriages to take place in a parish where one of the parties was baptised or prepared for confirmation (but not if combined rite); a parish where one of the parties lived or attended worship for six months or more; a parish where one of the parents of either of the parties lived for six months or more; a parish where one of the parents of either of the parties has attended public worship for six months or more in the child's lifetime; or a parish where the parents or grandparents of either of the parties were married. The banns (ie the announcement of the marriage ceremony) must be called in the parish in which the marriage is to take place on three Sundays before the day of the ceremony; if either or both of the parties lives in a different parish the banns must also be called there. After three months the banns are no longer valid. The minister will not perform the marriage unless satisfied that the banns have been properly called.

Marriage by common licence

The vicar who is to conduct the marriage will arrange for a common licence to be issued by the diocesan bishop; this dispenses with the necessity for banns. One of the parties must have lived in the parish for 15 days immediately before the issuing of the licence or must usually worship at the church. Eligibility requirements vary from diocese to diocese, but it is not normally required that the parties should have been baptised. The licence is valid for three months.

Marriage by special licence

A special licence is granted by the Archbishop of Canterbury in special circumstances for the marriage to take place at any place, with or without previous residence in the parish, or at any time. It is usually required that at least one of the parties has been baptised. The special licence will expire after three months. Application must be made to the registrar of the Faculty Office: 1 The Sanctuary, London SW1P 3JT T 020-7222 5381.

Marriage by certificate

The marriage can be conducted on the authority of the superintendent registrar's certificate, provided that the vicar's consent is obtained (the vicar is not obliged to accept the certificate). One of the parties must live in the parish or must usually worship at the church.

MARRIAGE BY OTHER RELIGIOUS CEREMONY

One of the parties must normally live in the registration district where the marriage is to take place. If the building where the parties wish to be married has not been registered, the couple can still have a religious ceremony there, but will also need to have a separate civil ceremony for the marriage to be valid. If the building is registered, in addition to giving notice to the superintendent registrar it may also be necessary to book a registrar, or authorised person to be present at the ceremony.

CIVIL MARRIAGE

A marriage may be solemnised at any register office, registered building or approved premises in England and Wales, without either of the parties being resident in the same district. The superintendent registrar of the district should be contacted, and, if the marriage is to take place at approved premises, the necessary arrangements at the venue must also be made.

NOTICE OF MARRIAGE
Unless it is to take place by banns or under common or special licence in the Church of England or the Church in Wales, a notice of the marriage must be given in person to the superintendent registrar. Notice of marriage may be given in the following ways:

- by certificate. Both parties must have lived in a registration district in England or Wales for at least seven days immediately before giving notice personally at the local register office. If they live in different registration districts, notice must be given in both districts by the respective party in person. The marriage can take place in any register office or other approved premises in England and Wales no sooner than 16 days after notice has been given, when the superintendent registrar issues a certificate
- by licence. One of the parties must have lived in a registration district in England or Wales for at least 15 days before giving notice at the register office; the other party need only be a resident of, or be physically in, England and Wales on the day notice is given

A notice of marriage is valid for 12 months, unless it is for the marriage of a detained or housebound person, when it will usually only be accepted within three months of publication. Notice for marriages taking place within the Church of England or Church of Wales are also only valid for three months following publication. It should be possible to make an advance (provisional) booking 12 months before the ceremony. In this case it is still necessary to give formal notice three months before the marriage. When giving notice of the marriage it is necessary to produce official proof, if relevant, that any previous marriage has ended in divorce or death by producing a decree absolute or death certificate; it is also necessary to provide proof of age, identity and nationality for each of the parties, for example, with a passport. If either party is under 18 years old, evidence of consent by their parent or guardian is required. There are special procedures for those wishing to get married in the UK that are subject to immigration control; the register office will be able to advise on these.

SOLEMNISATION OF THE MARRIAGE
On the day of the wedding there must be at least two other people present who are prepared to act as witnesses and sign the marriage register. A registrar of marriages must be present at a marriage in a register office or at approved premises, but an authorised person may act in the capacity of registrar in a registered building.

If the marriage takes place at approved premises, the room must be separate from any other activity on the premises at the time of the ceremony, and no food or drink can be sold or consumed in the room during the ceremony or for one hour beforehand.

The marriage must be solemnised between 8am and 6pm, with open doors. At some time during the ceremony the parties must make a declaration that they know of no legal impediment to the marriage and they must also say the contracting words; the declaratory and contracting words may vary according to the form of service. A civil marriage cannot contain any religious aspects, but it may be possible for non-religious music and/or readings to be

included. It may also be possible to embellish the marriage vows taken by the couple.

CIVIL FEES
Notice and registration of Marriage at a Register Office
By superintendent registrar's certificate, £33.50 per person for the notice of the marriage (which is not refundable if the marriage does not in fact take place) and £40 for the registration of the marriage.

Marriage at a Register Office / Approved Premises
Fees for marriage at a register office are set by the local authority responsible. An additional fee will also be payable for the superintendent registrar's and registrar's attendance at the marriage on an approved premises. This is also set locally by the local authority responsible. A further charge is likely to be made by the owners of the building for the use of the premises. For marriages taking place in a religious building other than the Church of England or Church of Wales, an additional fee of £80 is payable for the registrar's attendance at the marriage unless an 'Authorised Person' appointed by the trustees of the building has agreed to register the marriage. Additional fees may be charged by the trustees of the building for the wedding and by the person who performs the ceremony.

ECCLESIASTICAL FEES
(Church of England and Church in Wales)
Marriage by banns
For publication of banns, £22*
For certificate of banns issued at time of publication, £12.00*
For marriage service, £262*
For marriage certificate at registration if required £3.50**
* These fees are revised from 1 January each calendar year. Some may not apply to the Church in Wales
** This fee is revised from 1 April each calendar year

SCOTLAND
REGULAR MARRIAGES
A regular marriage is one which is celebrated by a minister of religion or authorised registrar or other celebrant. Each of the parties must complete a marriage notice form and return it to the district registrar for the area in which they are to be married, irrespective of where they live, within the three month period prior to the date of the marriage and not later than 15 days prior to that date. The district registrar must then enter the date of receipt and certain details in a marriage book kept for this purpose, and must also enter the names of the parties and the proposed date of marriage in a list which is displayed in a conspicuous place at the registration office until the date of the marriage has passed. All persons wishing to enter into a regular marriage in Scotland must follow the same preliminary procedure regardless of whether they intend to have a religious or civil ceremony. Before the marriage ceremony takes place any person may submit an objection in writing to the district registrar.

A marriage schedule, which is prepared by the registrar, will be issued to one or both of the parties in person up to seven days before a religious marriage; for a civil marriage the schedule will be available at the ceremony. The schedule must be handed to the celebrant before the ceremony starts; it must be signed immediately after the wedding and the marriage must be registered within three days.

The authority to conduct a religious marriage is deemed to be vested in the authorised celebrant rather than the building in which it takes place; open-air religious ceremonies are therefore permissible in Scotland.

From 10 June 2002 it has been possible, under the Marriage (Scotland) Act 2002, for venues or couples to apply to the local council for a licence to allow a civil ceremony to take place at a venue other than a registration office. To obtain further information, a venue or couple should contact the district registrar in the area they wish to marry. A list of licensed venues is also available on the National Records of Scotland website.

MARRIAGE BY COHABITATION WITH HABIT AND REPUTE

Prior to the enactment of the 2006 act, if two people had lived together constantly as husband and wife and were generally held to be such by the neighbourhood and among their friends and relations, a presumption could arise from which marriage could be inferred. Before such a marriage could be registered, however, a decree of declarator of marriage had to be obtained from the court of session. Section 3 of the 2006 act provides that it will no longer be possible for a marriage to be constituted by cohabitation with habit and repute, but it will still be possible for couples whose period of cohabitation began before commencement of the 2006 act to seek a declarator under the old rule of law.

CIVIL FEES

The fee for submitting a notice of marriage to the district registrar is £30.00 a person. Solemnisation of a civil marriage costs £55.00, while the extract of the entry in the register of marriages attracts a fee of £10.00. The costs of religious marriage ceremonies can vary.

THE GENERAL REGISTER OFFICE
  PO Box 2, Southport PR8 2JD **T** 0845-603 7788
  W www.gro.gov.uk/gro/content/certificates
THE NATIONAL RECORDS OF SCOTLAND
  New Register House, 3 West Register Street, Edinburgh
  EH1 3YT **T** 0131-314 4452 **W** www.gro-scotland.gov.uk

TOWN AND COUNTRY PLANNING

The planning system can help to protect the environment and assist individuals in assessing their land rights. There are a number of acts governing the development of land and buildings in England and Wales and advice should always be sought from Citizens Advice or the local planning authority before undertaking building works on any land or property. If development takes place which requires planning permission without permission being given, enforcement action may take place and the situation may need to be rectified. Planning law in Scotland is similar but certain Scotland-specific legislation applies so advice should always be sought.

PLANNING PERMISSION

Planning permission is needed if the work involves:

- making a material change in use, such as dividing off part of the house or garden so that it can be used as a separate home or dividing off part of the house for commercial use, eg for a workshop
- going against the terms of the original planning permission, eg there may be a restriction on fences in front gardens on an open-plan estate
- building, engineering or mining, except for the permitted developments below
- new or wider access to a main road

- additions or extensions to flats or maisonettes
- work which might obstruct the view of road users

Planning permission is not needed to carry out internal alterations or work which does not affect the external appearance of the building, and are not works for making good war damage or works begun after 5 December 1968 for the alteration of a building by providing additional space in it underground.

Under regulations which came into effect on 1 October 2008, there are certain types of development for which the Secretary of State for the Environment, Food and Rural Affairs has granted general permissions (permitted development rights). These include house extensions and additions, outbuildings and garages, other ancillary garden buildings such as swimming pools or ponds, and laying patios, paths or driveways for domestic use. All developments are subject to a number of conditions.

Before carrying out any of the above permitted developments you should contact your local planning authority to find out whether the general permission has been modified in your area. For more information, visit **W** www.planningportal.gov.uk

OTHER RESTRICTIONS

It may be necessary to obtain other types of permissions before carrying out any development. These permissions are separate from planning permission and apply regardless of whether or not planning permission is needed, eg:

- building regulations will probably apply if a new building is to be erected, if an existing one is to be altered or extended, or if the work involves building over a drain or sewer. The building control department of the local authority will advise on this
- any alterations to a listed building or the grounds of a listed building must be approved by the local authority. Listing will include not only the main building but everything in the curtilage of the building
- local authority approval is necessary if a building (or, in some circumstances, gates, walls, fences or railings) in a conservation area is to be demolished; each local authority keeps a register of all local buildings that are in conservation areas
- a council order is required if your proposed development would obstruct a public path which crosses your property, and you should discuss any such proposals with the council at an early stage
- many trees are protected by tree preservation orders and must not be pruned or taken down without local authority consent
- bats and many other species are protected, and Natural England, the Countryside Council for Wales or Scottish Natural Heritage must be notified before any work is carried out that will affect the habitat of protected species, eg timber treatment, renovation or extensions of lofts
- developments in areas with special designations, such as National Parks, Areas of Outstanding Natural Beauty, National Scenic Areas or in the Norfolk or Suffolk Broads, are subject to greater restrictions. The local planning authority will advise or refer enquirers to the relevant authority

There may also be restrictions contained in the title to the property which require you to get someone else's agreement before carrying out certain developments, and which should be considered when works are planned.

VOTERS' QUALIFICATIONS

Those entitled to vote at parliamentary, and local government elections are those who, at the date of taking the poll, are:
- on the electoral roll
- aged 18 years or older
- British citizens, Commonwealth citizens or citizens of the Irish Republic who are resident in the UK
- those who suffer from no other legal bar to voting (eg prisoners). It should be noted that following a decision taken by the European Court of Human Rights, prisoners' voting rights are currently under review by the government
- in Northern Ireland electors must have been resident in Northern Ireland during the whole of the three-month period prior to the relevant date
- citizens of any EU member state may vote in local elections if they meet the criteria listed above (save for the nationality requirements)

British citizens resident abroad are entitled to vote for 15 years after leaving Britain, as overseas electors in domestic parliamentary elections in the constituency in which they were last resident if they are on the electoral roll of the relevant constituency. Members of the armed forces, Crown servants and employees of the British Council who are overseas and their spouses are entitled to vote regardless of how long they have been abroad. British citizens who had never been registered as an elector in the UK are not eligible to register as an overseas voter unless they left the UK before they were 18, providing they left the country no more than 15 years ago. Overseas electors may opt to vote by proxy or by postal vote. Overseas voters may not vote in local government elections.

The main categories of people who are not entitled to vote at general elections are:
- sitting peers in the House of Lords
- convicted persons detained in pursuance of their sentences (though remand prisoners, unconvicted prisoners and civil prisoners can vote if on the electoral register). This is currently subject to review, as detailed above
- those convicted within the previous five years of corrupt or illegal election practices
- EU citizens (who may only vote in EU and local government elections)

Under the Representation of the Peoples Act 2000, several new groups of people are permitted to vote for the first time. These include: people who live on barges; people in mental health hospitals (other than those with criminal convictions) and homeless people who have made a 'declaration of local connection'.

REGISTERING TO VOTE

Voters must be entered on an electoral register. The Electoral Registration Officer (ERO) for each council area is responsible for preparing and publishing the register for his area by 1 December each year. Names may be added to the register to reflect changes in people's circumstances as they occur and each month during December to August, the ERO publishes a list of alterations to the published register.

A registration form is sent to all households in the autumn of each year and the householder is required to provide details of all occupants who are eligible to vote, including ones who will reach their 18th birthday in the year covered by the register. Anyone failing to

supply information to the ERO when requested, or supplying false information, may be fined by up to £1,000. Application forms and more information are available from the Electoral Commission (W www.aboutmyvote.co.uk).

VOTING

Voting is not compulsory in the UK. Those who wish to vote do so in person at the allotted polling station. Postal votes are now available to anyone on request and you do not need to give a reason for using a postal vote.

A proxy (whereby the voter nominates someone to vote in person on their behalf) can be appointed to act in a specific election, for a specified period of time or indefinitely. For the appointment of an indefinite or long-term proxy, the voter needs to specify physical employment or study reasons as to why they are making an application. With proxy votes where a particular election is specified, the voter needs to provide details of the circumstances by which they cannot reasonably be expected to go to the polling station.

Further information can be obtained from the local authority's ERO in England and Wales or the electoral registration office in Scotland, or the Chief Electoral Officer in Northern Ireland.

WILLS

A will is used to appoint executors (who will administer the estate), give directions as to the disposal of the body, appoint guardians for children, and determine how and to whom property is to be passed. A well-drafted will can operate to reduce the level of inheritance tax which the estate pays. It is best to have a will drawn up by a solicitor, but if a solicitor is not employed the following points must be taken into account:
- if possible the will must not be prepared on behalf of another person by someone who is to benefit from it or who is a close relative of a major beneficiary
- the language used must be clear and unambiguous and it is better to avoid the use of legal terms where the same thing can be expressed in plain language
- it is better to rewrite the whole document if a mistake is made. If necessary, alterations can be made by striking through the words with a pen, and the signature or initials of the testator and the witnesses must be put in the margin opposite the alteration. No alteration of any kind should be made after the will has been executed
- if the person later wishes to change the will or part of it, it is better to write a new will revoking the old. The use of codicils (documents written as supplements or containing modifications to the will) should be left to a solicitor
- the will should be typed or printed, or if handwritten be legible and preferably in ink

The form of a will varies to suit different cases – a solicitor will be able to advise as to wording, however, 'DIY' will-writing kits can be purchased from good stationery shops and many banks offer a will-writing service.

LAPSED LEGATEES

If a person who has been left property in a will dies before the person who made the will, the gift fails and will pass to the person entitled to everything not otherwise disposed of (the residuary estate).

If the person left the residuary estate dies before the person who made the will, their share will pass to the closest relative(s) of the testator under the intestacy rules.

It is always better to draw up a new will if a beneficiary predeceases the person who made the will.

EXECUTORS

It is usual to appoint two executors, although one is sufficient. No more than four persons can deal with the estate of the person who has died. The name and address of each executor should be given in full (the addresses are not essential but including them adds clarity to the document). Executors should be 18 years of age or over. An executor may be a beneficiary of the will.

WITNESSES

A person who is a beneficiary of a will, or the spouse or civil partner of a beneficiary at the time the will is signed, must not act as a witness or else he/she will be unable to take his/her gift except in some limited circumstances. Husband and wife can both act as witnesses provided neither benefits from the will.

It is better that a person does not act as an executor and as a witness, as he/she can take no benefit under a will to which he/she is witness. The identity of the witnesses should be made as explicit as possible.

EXECUTION OF A WILL

The person making the will should sign his/her name in the presence of the two witnesses. It is advisable to sign at the foot of the document, so as to avoid uncertainty about the testator's intention. The witnesses must then sign their names while the person making the will looks on. If this procedure is not adhered to, the will may be considered invalid. There are certain exceptional circumstances where these rules are relaxed, eg where the person may be too ill to sign.

CAPACITY TO MAKE A WILL

Anyone aged 18 or over can make a will. However, if there is any suspicion that the person making the will is not, through reasons of infirmity or age, fully in command of his/her faculties, it is advisable to arrange for a medical practitioner to examine the person making the will at the time it is to be executed (to verify his/her mental capacity and to record that medical opinion in writing), and to ask the examining practitioner to act as a witness. If a person is not mentally able to make a will, the court may do this for him/her by virtue of the Mental Health Act 2005.

REVOCATION

A will may be revoked or cancelled in a number of ways:
• a later will revokes an earlier one if it says so; otherwise the earlier will is by implication revoked by the later one to the extent that it contradicts or repeats the earlier one
• a will is revoked if the physical document on which it is written is destroyed by the person whose will it is. There must be an intention to revoke the will and an act of destruction. It may not be sufficient to obliterate the will with a pen
• a will is revoked by the testator making a written declaration to this effect executed in the same way as a will
• a will is also revoked when the person marries or forms a civil partnership, unless it is clear from the will that the person intended the will to stand after that particular marriage or civil partnership
• where a marriage or civil partnership ends in divorce or dissolution or is annulled or declared void, gifts to the spouse or civil partner and the appointment of the

spouse or civil partner as executor fail unless the will says that this is not to happen. A former spouse or civil partner is treated as having predeceased the testator. A separation does not change the effect of a married person's will.

PROBATE AND LETTERS OF ADMINISTRATION

Probate is granted to the executors named in a will and once granted, the executors are obliged to carry out the instructions of the will. Letters of administration are granted where no executor is named in a will or is willing or able to act or where there is no will or no valid will; this gives a person, often the next of kin, similar powers and duties to those of an executor.

Applications for probate or for letters of administration can be made to the Principal Registry of the Family Division, to a district probate registry or to a probate sub-registry. Applicants will need the following documents: the Probate Application Form; the original will and codicils (if any); a certificate of death; oath for executors or administrators; and the appropriate tax form (an 'IHT 205' if no inheritance tax is owed; otherwise an 'IHT 400' and 'IHT 421'), in addition to a cheque for the relevant probate fee. Certain property, up to the value of £5,000, may be disposed of without a grant of probate or letters of administration, as can assets that do not pass under the will such as jointly owned assets which pass automatically on the death of one of the joint holders to the survivor.

WHERE TO FIND A PROVED WILL

Since 1858 wills which have been proved, that is wills on which probate or letters of administration have been granted, must have been proved at the Principal Registry of the Family Division or at a district probate registry. The Lord Chancellor has power to direct where the original documents are kept but most are filed where they were proved and may be inspected there and a copy obtained. The Principal Registry also holds copies of all wills proved at district probate registries and these may be inspected at First Avenue House, High Holborn, London. An index of all grants, both of probate and of letters of administration, is compiled by the Principal Registry and may be seen either at the Principal Registry or at a district probate registry.

It is also possible to discover when a grant of probate or letters of administration is issued by requesting a standing search. In response to a request and for a small fee, a district probate registry will supply the names and addresses of executors or administrators and the registry in which the grant was made, of any grant in the estate of a specified person made in the previous 12 months or following six months. This is useful for creditors of the deceased and for applicants who may be beneficiaries to a will but who have lost contact with the deceased.

INTESTACY

Intestacy occurs when someone dies without leaving a will or leaves a will which is invalid or which does not take effect for some reason. Intestacy can be partial, for instance, if there is a will which disposes of some but not all of the testator's property. In such cases the person's estate (property, possessions, other assets following the payment of debts) passes to certain members of the family. If a will has been written that disposes of only part of a person's property, these rules apply to the part which is undisposed of.

Some types of property do not follow the intestacy rules, for example, property held as joint tenants, insurance policies taken out for specified individuals or assigned into trust during the testator's lifetime and death benefits under a pension scheme.

If the person (intestate) leaves a spouse or a civil partner who survives for 28 days and children (legitimate, illegitimate and adopted children and other descendants), the estate is divided as follows:

- if the estate is worth more than £250,000, the spouse or civil partner takes the 'personal chattels' (household articles, including cars, but nothing used for business purposes), £250,000 and a life interest in half of the rest of the estate (which can be capitalised by the spouse or civil partner if he/she wishes)
- the rest of the estate goes to the children*

If the person leaves a spouse or civil partner who survives for 28 days but no children:

- if the estate is worth less than £450,000, the surviving spouse or civil partner takes it in its entirety
- if the estate is worth more than £450,000, the spouse or civil partner takes the personal chattels, £450,000 tax-free (interest payable as before) and full ownership of half of the rest of the estate
- the other half of the rest of the estate goes to the parents (equally, if both alive) or, if none, to the brothers and sisters of the whole blood*
- if there are no parents or brothers or sisters of the whole blood or their children, the spouse or civil partner takes the whole estate
- if the estate is worth less than £250,000, the surviving spouse or civil partner takes it in its entirety

If there is no surviving spouse or civil partner, the estate is distributed among those who survive the intestate as follows:

- to surviving children*, but if none to
- parents (equally, if both alive), but if none to
- brothers and sisters of the whole blood* (including issue of deceased ones), but if none to
- brothers and sisters of the half blood* (including issue of deceased ones), but if none to
- grandparents (equally, if more than one), but if none to
- aunts and uncles of the whole blood*, but if none to
- aunts and uncles of the half blood*, but if none to
- the Crown, Duchy of Lancaster or the Duke of Cornwall (*bona vacantia*)

* To inherit, a member of these groups must survive the intestate and attain the age of 18, or marry under that age. If they die under the age of 18 (unless married under that age), their share goes to others, if any, in the same group. If any member of these groups predeceases the intestate leaving children, their share is divided equally among their children.

In England and Wales the provisions of the Inheritance (Provision for Family and Dependants) Act 1975 may allow other people to claim provision from the deceased's assets. This act also applies to cases where a will has been made and allows a person to apply to the court if they feel that the will or rules of intestacy (or both) do not make adequate provision for them. The court can order payment from the deceased's assets or the transfer of property from them if the applicant's claim is accepted. The application must be made within six months of the grant of probate or letters of administration and the following people can make an application:

- the spouse or civil partner
- a former spouse or civil partner who has not remarried or formed a subsequent civil partnership
- a child of the deceased
- someone treated as a child of the deceased's family
- someone maintained by the deceased
- someone who has cohabited for two years before the death in the same household as the deceased and as the husband or wife or civil partner of the deceased

SCOTLAND

In Scotland any person over 12 and of sound mind can make a will. The person making the will can only freely dispose of the heritage and what is known as the 'dead's part' of the estate because:

- the spouse or civil partner has the right to inherit one-third of the moveable estate if there are children or other descendants, and one-half of it if there are not
- children are entitled to one-third of the moveable estate if there is a surviving spouse or civil partner, and one-half of it if there is not

The remaining portion of the moveable estate is the dead's part, and legacies and bequests are payable from this. Debts are payable out of the whole estate before any division.

From August 1995, wills no longer needed to be 'holographed' and it is now only necessary to have one witness. The person making the will still needs to sign each page. It is better that the will is not witnessed by a beneficiary although the attestation would still be sound and the beneficiary would not have to relinquish the gift.

Subsequent marriage or civil partnership does not revoke a will but the birth of a child who is not provided for may do so. A will may be revoked by a subsequent will, either expressly or by implication, but in so far as the two can be read together both have effect. If a subsequent will is revoked, the earlier will is revived.

Wills may be registered in the sheriff court Books of the Sheriffdom in which the deceased lived or in the Books of Council and Session at the Registers of Scotland.

CONFIRMATION

Confirmation (the Scottish equivalent of probate) is obtained in the sheriff court of the sheriffdom in which the deceased was resident at the time of death. Executors are either 'nominate' (named by the deceased in the will) or 'dative' (appointed by the court in cases where no executor is named in a will or in cases of intestacy). Applicants for confirmation must first provide an inventory of the deceased's estate and a schedule of debts, with an affidavit. In estates under £30,000 gross, confirmation can be obtained under a simplified procedure at reduced fees, with no need for a solicitor. The local sheriff clerk's office can provide assistance.

PRINCIPAL REGISTRY (FAMILY DIVISION)
First Avenue House, 42–49 High Holborn, London WC1 6NP
T 020-7947 6000
REGISTERS OF SCOTLAND
Erskine House, 68 Queen Street, Edinburgh, EH2 4NF
T 0845-607 0161

INTESTACY

The rules of distribution are contained in the Succession (Scotland) Act 1964 and are extended to include civil partners by the Civil Partnership Act 2004.

A surviving spouse or civil partner is entitled to 'prior rights'. This means that the spouse or civil partner has the right to inherit:

- the matrimonial or family home up to a value of £300,000, or one matrimonial or family home if there is more than one, or, in certain circumstances, the value of the home

- the furnishings and contents of that home, up to the value of £24,000
- a cash sum of £42,000 if the deceased left children or other descendants, or £75,000 if not

These figures are increased from time to time by regulations.

Once prior rights have been satisfied legal rights are settled. Legal rights are:

- *Jus relicti(ae) and rights under the section 131 of the Civil Partnership Act 2004* – the right of a surviving spouse or civil partner to one-half of the net moveable estate, after satisfaction of prior rights, if there are no surviving children; if there are surviving children, the spouse or civil partner is entitled to one-third of the net moveable estate
- *Legitim and rights under the section 131 of the Civil Partnership Act 2004* – the right of surviving children to one-half of the net moveable estate if there is no surviving spouse or civil partner; if there is a surviving spouse or civil partner, the children are entitled to one-third of the net moveable estate after the satisfaction of prior rights

Where there is no surviving spouse, civil partner or children, half of the estate is taken by the parents and half by the brothers and sisters. Failing that, the lines of succession, in general, are:

- to descendants
- if no descendants, then to collaterals (ie brothers and sisters) and parents
- surviving spouse or civil partner
- if no collaterals, parents, spouse or civil partner, then to ascendants collaterals (ie aunts and uncles), and so on in an ascending scale
- if all lines of succession fail, the estate passes to the Crown. Relatives of the whole blood are preferred to relatives of the half blood. The right of representation, ie the right of the issue of a person who would have succeeded if he/she had survived the intestate, also applies

INTELLECTUAL PROPERTY

Intellectual property is a broad term covering a number of legal rights provided by the government to help people protect their creative works and encourage further innovation. By using these legal rights people can own the things they create and control the way in which others use their innovations. Intellectual property owners can take legal action to stop others using their intellectual property, they can license their intellectual property to others or they can sell it on. Different types of intellectual property utilise different forms of protection including copyright, designs, patents and trade marks, which are all covered below in more detail.

COPYRIGHT

Copyright protects all original literary, dramatic, musical and artistic works, as well as sound and film recordings and broadcasts. Among the works covered by copyright are novels, computer programs, newspaper articles, sculptures, technical drawings, websites, maps and photographs. Under copyright the creators of these works can control the various ways in which their material may be exploited, the rights broadly covering copying, adapting, issuing (including renting and lending) copies to the public, performing in public, and broadcasting the material. The transfer of copyright works to formats accessible to visually impaired persons without infringement of copyright was enacted in 2002.

Copyright protection in the United Kingdom is automatic and there is no official registration system. The creator of a work can help to protect it by including the copyright symbol (©), the name of the copyright owner, and the year in which the work was created. In addition, steps can be taken by the work's creator to provide evidence that he/she had the work at a particular time (eg by depositing a copy with a bank or solicitor). The main legislation is the Copyright, Designs and Patents Act 1988 (as amended). As a result of an EU directive effective from January 1996, the term of copyright protection for literary, dramatic, musical (including song lyrics and musical compositions) and artistic works lasts for 70 years after the death of the creator. For film, copyright lasts for 70 years after the director, authors of the screenplay and dialogue, or the composer of any music specially created for the film have all died. Sound recordings are protected for 50 years after their publication (or their first performance if they are not published), and broadcasts for 50 years from the end of the year in which the broadcast/transmission was made. The typographical arrangement of published editions remains under copyright protection for 25 years from the end of the year in which the particular edition was published.

The main international treaties protecting copyright are the Berne Convention for the Protection of Literary and Artistic Works (administered by the World Intellectual Property Organisation (WIPO)), the Rome Convention for the Protection of Performers, Producers of Phonograms and Broadcasting Organisations (administered by UNESCO, the International Labour Organisation and WIPO), the Geneva Phonograms Convention (administered by WIPO), and the Universal Copyright Convention (developed by UNESCO); the UK is a signatory to these conventions. Copyright material created by UK nationals or residents is protected in the countries that have signed one of the above-named conventions by the national law of that country. A list of participating countries may be obtained from the UK Intellectual Property Office. The World Trade Organisation's Trade-Related Aspects of Intellectual Property Rights (TRIPS) agreement, signed in 1995, may also provide copyright protection abroad.

Two treaties which strengthen and update international standards of protection, particularly in relation to new technologies, were agreed in December 1996: the WIPO copyright treaty, and the WIPO performances and phonograms treaty. In May 2001 the European Union passed a new directive (which in 2003 became law in the UK) aimed at harmonising copyright law throughout the EU to take account of the internet and other technologies. More information can be found online (W www.ipo.gov.uk).

The government commissioned a major independent review of intellectual property laws in November 2010 to tackle the concern that the current framework does not adequately promote growth and innovation in the UK economy. The review was published in May 2011.

LICENSING

Use of copyright material without seeking permission in each instance may be permitted under 'blanket' licences available from national copyright licensing agencies. The International Federation of Reproduction Rights Organisations facilitates agreements between its member licensing agencies and on behalf of its members with organisations such as WIPO, UNESCO, the European Union and the Council of Europe. More information can be found online (W www.ifrro.org).

DESIGN PROTECTION

Design protection covers the outward appearance of an article and in the UK takes two forms: registered design and design right, which are not mutually exclusive. Registered design protects the aesthetic appearance of an article, including shape, configuration, pattern or ornament, although artistic works such as sculptures are excluded, being generally protected by copyright. To achieve design protection the owner of the design must apply to the Intellectual Property Office. In order to qualify for protection, a design must be new and materially different from earlier UK published designs. Initial registration lasts for five years and can be extended in five-year increments to a maximum of 25 years. The current legislation is the Registered Designs Act 1949 which has been amended several times, most recently by the Regulatory Reform Order 2006.

UK applicants wishing to protect their designs in the EU can do so by applying for a Registered Community Design with the Office for Harmonisation in the Internal Market. Outside the EU separate applications must be made in each country in which protection is sought.

Design right is an automatic right which applies to the shape or configuration of articles and does not require registration. Unlike registered design, two-dimensional designs do not qualify for protection but designs of electronic circuits are protected by design right. Designs must be original and non-commonplace. The term of design right is ten years from first marketing of the design, or 15 years after the creation of the design, whichever is earlier. This right is effective only in the UK. After five years anyone is entitled to apply for a licence of right, which allows others to make and sell products copying the design. The current legislation is Part 3 of the Copyright, Designs and Patents Act 1988, amended on 9 December 2001 to incorporate the European designs directive, and again in 2006.

PATENTS

A patent is a document issued by the UK Intellectual Property Office relating to an invention. It gives the proprietor the right for a limited period to stop others from making, using, importing or selling the invention without the inventor's permission. In return the patentee pays a fee to cover the costs of processing the patent and publicly discloses details of the invention.

To qualify for a patent an invention must be new, must be functional or technical, must exhibit an inventive step, and must be capable of industrial application. The patent is valid for a maximum of 20 years from the date on which the application was filed, subject to payment of annual fees from the end of the fifth year.

The UK Intellectual Property Office, established in 1852, is responsible for ensuring that all stages of an application comply with the Patents Act 1977, and that the invention meets the criteria for a patent.

WIPO is responsible for administering many of the international conventions on intellectual property. The Patent Cooperation Treaty allows inventors to file a single application for patent rights in some or all of the contracting states. This application is searched by an International Searching Authority to confirm the invention is novel and that the same concept has not already been made publicly available. The application and search report are then published by the International Bureau of WIPO. It may also be the subject of an (optional) international preliminary examination. Applicants must then deal directly with the patent offices in the countries where they are seeking patent rights. The European Patent Convention allows inventors to obtain patent rights in all the contracting states by filing a single application with the European Patent Office. More information can be found online (W www.ipo.gov.uk).

RESEARCH DISCLOSURES

Research disclosures are publicly disclosed details of inventions. Once published, an invention is considered no longer novel and becomes 'prior art'. Publishing a disclosure is significantly cheaper than applying for a patent; however, unlike a patent, it does not entitle the author to exclusive rights to use or license the invention. Instead, research disclosures are primarily published to ensure the inventor the freedom to use the invention. This works because publishing legally prevents other parties from patenting the disclosed innovation and in the UK, patent law dictates that by disclosing details of an invention, even the inventor relinquishes their right to a patent.

In theory, publishing details of an invention anywhere should be enough to constitute a research disclosure. However, to be effective, a research disclosure needs to be published in a location which patent examiners will include in their prior art searches. To ensure global legal precedent it must be included in a publication with a recognised date stamp and made publicly available throughout the world.

The *Research Disclosure* journal, established in 1960 and published by KMP Ltd, is the primary publisher of research disclosures. It is the only disclosure service recognised by the Patent Cooperation Treaty as a mandatory search resource which must be consulted by the international search authorities. More information can be found online (W www.researchdisclosure.com).

TRADE MARKS

Trade marks are a means of identification, which enable traders to make their goods and services readily distinguishable from those supplied by others. Trade marks can take the form of words, a logo or a combination of both. Registration prevents other traders using the same or similar trade marks for similar products or services for which the mark is registered.

In the UK trade marks are registered at the UK Intellectual Property Office. In order to qualify for registration a trade mark must be capable of distinguishing its proprietor's goods or services from those of other undertakings; it should be non-deceptive, should not describe the goods and services or any characteristics of them, should not be contrary to law or morality and should not be similar or identical to any earlier trade marks for the same or similar goods or services. The owner of a registered trade mark may include an ® symbol next to it, and must renew their registration every ten years to keep it in force. The relevant current legislation is the Trade Marks Act 1994 (as amended).

It is possible to obtain an international trade mark registration, effective in 81 countries, under the Madrid system for the international registration of marks, to which the UK is party. British companies can obtain international trade mark registration in those countries party to the system through a single application to WIPO.

EU trade mark regulation is administered by the Office for Harmonisation in the Internal Market (Trade Marks and Designs) in Alicante, Spain. The office registers Community trade marks, which are valid throughout the European Union. The registration of trade marks in individual member states continues in parallel with EU trade mark standards.

DOMAIN NAMES
An internet domain name (eg www.whitakersalmanack.com) has to be registered separately from a trade mark, and this can be done through a number of registrars which charge varying rates and compete for business. For each top-level domain name (eg .uk, .com), there is a central registry to store the unique internet names and addresses using that suffix. A list of accredited registrars can be found online (W www.icann.org).

CONTACTS

COPYRIGHT LICENSING AGENCY LTD,
Saffron House, 6–10 Kirby Street, London EC1N 8TS
T 020-7400 3100 W www.cla.co.uk
EUROPEAN PATENT OFFICE, 80298 Munich, Germany
T (+49) 89 2399-0 W www.epo.org
THE UK INTELLECTUAL PROPERTY OFFICE,
Concept House, Cardiff Road, Newport NP10 8QQ
T 0300-300 2000 W www.ipo.gov.uk
WORLD INTELLECTUAL PROPERTY
ORGANISATION, 34 chemin des Colombettes,
CH-1211 Geneva 20, Switzerland T (+41) 22 338 9111
W www.wipo.int

THE MEDIA

CROSS-MEDIA OWNERSHIP

The rules surrounding cross-media ownership were overhauled as part of the 2003 Communications Act. The act simplified and relaxed existing rules to encourage dispersion of ownership and new market entry while preventing the most influential media in any community being controlled by too narrow a range of interests. However, transfers and mergers are not solely subject to examination on competition grounds by the competition authorities. The Secretary of State for Culture, Olympics, Media and Sport has a broad remit to decide if a transaction is permissible and can intervene on public interest grounds (relating both to newspapers and cross-media criteria, if broadcasting interests are also involved). The Office of Communications (OFCOM) has an advisory role in this context. Government and parliamentary assurances were given that any intervention into local newspaper transfers would be rare and exceptional. Following a request from the Secretary of State for Culture, Olympics, Media and Sport in June 2010 for a removal of all restrictions from the ownership of local media, OFCOM recommended the liberalisation of local cross-media regulations to enable a single owner to control newspapers, a TV licence and radio stations in one area.

REGULATION

OFCOM is the regulator for the communication industries in the UK and has responsibility for television, radio, telecommunications and wireless communications services. It replaced the Broadcasting Standards Commission, the Independent Television Commission, the Radio Authority, the Radio Communications Agency and OFTEL. OFCOM is required to report annually to parliament and exists to further the interests of consumers by balancing choice and competition with the duty to foster plurality; protect viewers and listeners and promote cultural diversity in the media; and to ensure full and fair competition between communications providers.

OFFICE OF COMMUNICATIONS (OFCOM)
Riverside House, 2A Southwark Bridge Road, London SE1 9HA
T 020-7981 3000 W www.ofcom.org.uk
Chief Executive, Ed Richards

COMPLAINTS

Under the Communications Act 2003 OFCOM's licensees are obliged to adhere to the provisions of its codes (including advertising, programme standards, fairness, privacy and sponsorship). Complainants should contact the broadcaster in the first instance (details can be found on OFCOM's website); however, if the complainant wishes the complaint to be considered by OFCOM, it will do so. Complaints should be made within a reasonable time, as broadcasters are only required to keep recordings for the following periods: radio, 42 days; television, 90 days; and cable and satellite, 60 days. OFCOM can fine a broadcaster, revoke a licence or take programmes

off the air. Since November 2004 complaints relating to individual advertisements on TV or radio have been dealt with by the Advertising Standards Authority.

ADVERTISING STANDARDS AUTHORITY
Mid City Place, 71 High Holborn, London WC1V 6QT
T 020-7492 2222 W www.asa.org.uk
Chief Executive, Guy Parker

TELEVISION

There are six major television broadcasters operating in the UK. Four of these – the BBC, ITV, Channel 4 and Channel 5 – launched as free-to-air analogue terrestrial networks. BSkyB and Virgin Media Television provide satellite television services.

The BBC is the oldest broadcaster in the world. The corporation began a London-only television service from Alexandra Palace in 1936 and achieved nationwide coverage 15 years later. A second station, BBC Two, was launched in 1964. The BBC's digital services comprise BBC Three, BBC Four, BBC News, BBC Parliament and the children's channels, CBeebies and CBBC. The services are funded by the licence fee. The corporation also has a commercial arm, BBC Worldwide, which was formed in 1994 and exists to maximise the value of the BBC's programme and publishing assets for the benefit of the licence payer. Its businesses include international programming distribution, magazines, other licensed products, live events and media monitoring.

The ITV (Independent Television) network was set up on a regional basis in 1955 to provide competition for the BBC. ITV began broadcasting on Channel 3 in the London area, following the Television Act of 1954 which made commercial television possible. It comprised a number of independent licensees, the majority of which have now merged to form ITV plc. The network generates funds through broadcasting television advertisements. Its flagship analogue channel was renamed ITV1 in 2001 as part of a rebranding exercise to coincide with the creation of a number of digital-only channels. These now include ITV2, ITV3, ITV4 and CiTV. ITV Network Centre is wholly owned by the ITV companies and undertakes commissioning and scheduling of programmes shown across the ITV network and, as with the other terrestrial channels, 25 per cent of programmes must come from independent producers.

Channel 4 and S4C were launched in 1982 to provide programmes with a distinctive character that appeal to interests not catered for by ITV. Although publicly owned, Channel 4 receives no public funding and is financed by commercial activities, including advertising. It has expanded to create the digital stations E4, More4, Film4 and 4Music. S4C receives annual funding from the Department for Culture, Olympics, Media and Sport. In March 2010 the S4C analogue service was closed and its digital service, S4C Digidol, became the default S4C channel across Wales, broadcasting entirely in the Welsh language.

Channel 5 began broadcasting in 1997. It was rebranded Five in 2002 but reverted to its original name, Channel 5, after the station was acquired by Northern &

Shell in July 2010. Digital stations 5USA and 5* (formerly Five Life, then Fiver) were launched in October 2006.

BSkyB was formed after the merger in 1990 of Sky Television and British Sky Broadcasting. The company operates a satellite television service and has around 40 television channels, including Sky One and the Sky Sports and Sky Movies ranges. It is part-owned by Rupert Murdoch's News Corporation. Sky Digital was launched in 1998 and offers access to over 500 channels. With the 2005 acquisition of Easynet, an internet access provider and network operator, BSkyB now offers voice over IP (VoIP) telephony, video on demand and internet-based TV. With a special box, Sky+ allows viewers to pause and rewind live TV and record up to 40 hours of programming. In July 2010 BSkyB acquired Virgin Media Television, including its portfolio of channels such as Bravo, Challenge and Virgin1. It was subsequently rebranded as the Living TV Group.

VIEWING TRENDS, TERRESTRIAL TELEVISION
• National news and weather accounts for 22 per cent of viewing on BBC One
• Sport makes up 19 per cent of television watched on BBC Two
• 24 per cent of viewing on ITV1 is entertainment programmes
• 65 per cent of viewing on Channel 4 is factual and entertainment programming
• Drama accounts for 21 per cent of viewing on Channel 5
Source: OFCOM Public Service Broadcasting Annual Report 2011

THE TELEVISION LICENCE
In the UK and its dependencies, a television licence is required to receive any publicly broadcast television service, regardless of its source, including commercial, satellite and cable programming.

The TV licence is classified as a tax, therefore non-payment is a criminal offence. A fine of up to £1,000 can be imposed on those successfully prosecuted. The TV licence is issued on behalf of the BBC as the licensing authority under the Communications Act 2003. TV Licensing is the name of the agent contracted to collect the licence fee on behalf of the BBC. An additional 142,000 licence fees were collected in the year 2010–11 increasing the number of licences in force in the UK to over 25 million. In 2011 an annual colour television licence cost £145.50 and a black and white licence £49. Concessions are available for the elderly and people with disabilities. Further details can be found at W www.tvlicensing.co.uk/information

BBC EXPENDITURE
By medium, 2010–11

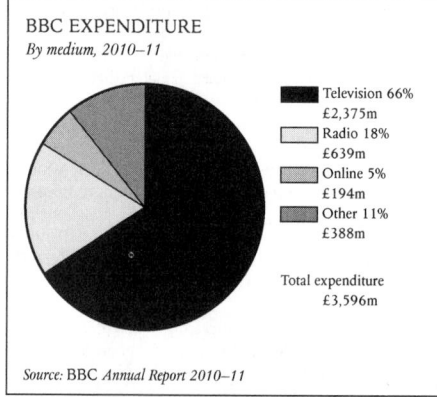

Television 66%
£2,375m
Radio 18%
£639m
Online 5%
£194m
Other 11%
£388m

Total expenditure
£3,596m

Source: BBC Annual Report 2010–11

DIGITAL TELEVISION
Digital broadcasting has dramatically increased the number and reception quality of television channels. Sound and pictures are converted into a digital format and compressed, using as few bits as possible to convey the information on a digital signal. This technique enables several television channels to be carried in the space used by the current analogue signals to carry one channel. Digital signals can be received by standard aerials using Freeview (see below), satellite dishes or cable. The signals are decoded and turned back into sound and pictures by either a set-top box or a decoder built into the television set (iDTV). A basic package of channels is available without charge and services are also offered by cable and satellite companies.

The Broadcasting Act 1996 provided for the licensing of 20 or more digital terrestrial television channels (on six frequency channels or 'multiplexes'). The first digital services went on air in autumn 1998.

In June 2002, following the collapse of ITV Digital, the digital terrestrial television licence was awarded to a consortium made up of the BBC, BSkyB and transmitter company Crown Castle by the Independent Television Commission. Freeview was launched on 30 October 2002: it offers around 50 digital channels and requires the purchase of a set-top box, but is subsequently free of charge.

As at March 2011, 93 per cent of British homes had access to digital TV. The digital channels combined have a greater share of viewing than any of the five main channels and continue to increase this lead.

DIGITAL SWITCHOVER
The digital switchover involves the turning off of the analogue terrestrial transmissions network that has been in place since the 1930s and replacing it with an all-digital terrestrial network. Viewers who receive television through an aerial will need to upgrade their sets with a set-top box (typically costing between £20 and £100) or use integrated digital television (iDTV), cable or satellite digital services. A Switchover Help Scheme is available for those who have difficulty in making the switch to digital TV such as people aged 75 or over, those on disability living allowance and people registered blind. The switchover has started and is due to be completed in 2012. For more information, see W www.digitaluk.co.uk.

Region	Expected switchover date
Border, West Country, Granada	Complete
Wales, West, STV North	Complete
STV Central	Complete
Central, Yorkshire, Anglia	2011
London, Meridian, Tyne Tees, UTV	2012

Source: Digital UK

RECENT DEVELOPMENTS
The advent of digital television has coincided with the emergence of the internet as a viable alternative means of watching TV. Channel 4's 4oD (4 On Demand) service allows viewers to revisit and download programmes from the previous 28 days and access an archive of older footage using their PC. The BBC launched its iPlayer on Christmas Day 2007, enabling viewers to watch programmes broadcast in the previous seven days via the streaming option or download and store programmes for up to 30 days on their computer. An integrated service, launched in June 2008, allows viewers to access BBC

radio programmes in addition to televisual output. The iPlayer service also allows viewers to watch live TV using the On Now facility. In 2009 iPlayer was extended to more than 20 devices, including mobile phones, televisions and games consoles. A high definition (HD) service was launched in the same year. ITV has a similar service called ITV Player, and Channel 5's service is called Demand Five. Online streaming of TV has been a major success, especially with a younger demographic. BBC iPlayer averaged over 100 million programme requests each month for the year 2010–11 and more than 1.6 billion programmes were viewed during the year, boosted by the iPlayer app released on smartphones and tablets.

HD TV is the latest development in TV picture quality, providing more vibrant colours, greater detail and picture clarity in addition to improved sound quality. While a standard television picture is made up of 576 lines of 720 pixels, an HD television screen uses 1,280 by 720 pixels up to 1,920 by 1,080 pixels. Sky Digital, ITV and the BBC all provide HD channels, with a growing number becoming available. To access HD channels, viewers need an 'HD ready' TV set and HD TV decoder, available through satellite services or a cable connection. It is expected that four HD channels will become nationally available through Freeview by 2012. In April 2010 Samsung released the first consumer 3D TV; in the same month Sky launched the UK's first dedicated 3D channel. Several sporting events have been broadcast in 3D including the Wimbledon men's final in July 2011.

In June 2010 the BBC Trust gave permission for the BBC to participate in the development of Project Canvas, now known as YouView, a proposed standard for internet protocol television (IPTV) in partnership with ITV, BT, Channel 4, TalkTalk and Arqiva. Through the IPTV platform, viewers will be able to watch programmes (including on-demand), browse the internet and listen to digital radio via a special set-top box connected to a broadband connection. The subscription-free service is due to begin in 2012.

In February 2011, a new version of OFCOM's Broadcasting Code came into force, permitting product placement for the first time in UK-produced television programmes. A large 'P' logo designed by OFCOM and broadcasters is displayed at the beginning and end of each programme containing product placement. The first instance of product placement occurred on 28 February 2011.

CONTACTS

THE BRITISH BROADCASTING CORPORATION
BBC TV Centre, Wood Lane, London W12 7RJ
T 020-8743 8000 W www.bbc.co.uk

BBC North, Media City UK, Salford Quays, Manchester
M50 2BH T 0161-886 5300
W www.bbc.co.uk/aboutthebbc/bbcnorth
Chair, Lord Patten of Barnes

BBC Worldwide, 201 Wood Lane, London W12 7TQ
W www.bbcworldwide.com

INDEPENDENT TELEVISION NETWORK
ITV Network Centre, 200 Gray's Inn Road, London WC1X 8HF
T 020-7156 6000 W www.itv.com
Chair, Archie Norman

INDEPENDENT TELEVISION NETWORK REGIONS AND COMPANIES
Anglia (eastern England), Anglia House, Norwich NR1 3JG
  T 0844-881 6900 W www.itv.com/anglia
Border (Borders and the Isle of Man), Television House,
  The Watermark, Gateshead NE11 9SZ T 0844-881 51000
  W www.itv.com/border
Central (east, west and south Midlands), Gas Street,
  Birmingham B1 2JT T 0844-881 4121
  W www.itv.com/central
Channel (Channel Islands), The Television Centre, St Helier,
  Jersey JE1 3ZD T 01534-816816 W www.channelonline.tv
Granada (north-west England), Quay Street, Manchester
  M60 9EA T 0161-952 6018 W www.itv.com/granada
London, 200 Gray's Inn Road, London WC1X 8XZ
  T 020-7430 4000 W www.itv.com/london
Meridian (south and south-east England), Parkway Solent
  Business Park, Whiteley, Hants PO15 7PA T 0844-881 2000
  W www.itv.com/meridian
STV (Scotland), Pacific Quay, Glasgow G51 1PQ
  T 0141-300 3704 W www.stv.tv
Tyne Tees (north-east England), Television House,
  The Watermark, Gateshead, Tyne and Wear NE11 9SZ
  T 0844-881 51000 W www.itv.com/tynetees
Ulster (Northern Ireland), Ormeau Road, Belfast BT7 1EB
  T 028-9032 8122 W www.u.tv
Wales, Media Centre, Culverhouse Cross, Cardiff CF5 6XJ
  T 0844-881 0100 W www.itv.com/wales
West, Television Centre, Bath Road, Bristol BS4 3HG
  T 0808-101 0185 W www.itv.com/westcountry
Yorkshire, 104 Kirkstall Road, Leeds LS3 1JS T 0113-222 8885
  W www.itv.com/yorkshire

OTHER TELEVISION COMPANIES
Channel 4 Television, 124 Horseferry Road, London
  SW1P 2TX T 020-7396 4444 W www.channel4.com
Channel 5 Broadcasting Ltd, 22 Long Acre, London WC2E 9LY
  T 020-7421 7270 W www.channel5.com
Independent Television News (ITN), 200 Gray's Inn Road,
  London WC1X 8XZ T 020-7833 3000 W www.itn.co.uk
  Provides news programming for ITV and Channel 4.
Sianel Pedwar Cymru (S4C), Parc Ty Glas, Llanishen, Cardiff
  CF14 5DU T 0870-600 4141 W www.s4c.co.uk
Teletext Ltd, 10 Chiswick Park, 566 Chiswick High Road,
  London W4 5TS T 020-8323 5000 W www.teletext.co.uk
  Its analogue news service closed in 2009, but Teletext Ltd continues to offer holiday and other commercial services on digital channels.

ESTIMATED AUDIENCE SHARE
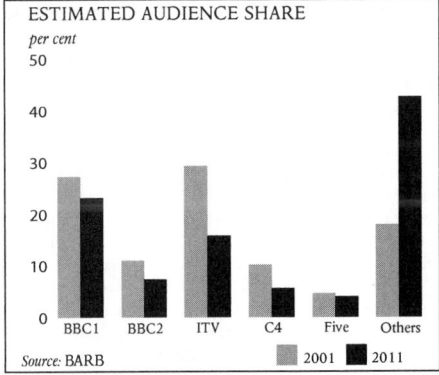
per cent
Source: BARB
■ 2001 ■ 2011

DIRECT BROADCASTING BY SATELLITE

TELEVISION

British Sky Broadcasting Ltd, Grant Way, Isleworth, Middx
TW7 5QD **T** 020-7705 3000 **W** www.sky.com
Chair, James Murdoch

RADIO

UK domestic radio services are broadcast across three wavebands: FM, medium wave and long wave (used by BBC Radio 4). In the UK the FM waveband extends in frequency from 87.5MHz to 108MHz and the medium waveband from 531kHz to 1602kHz. A number of radio stations are broadcast in both analogue and digital as well as a growing number in digital alone. As at March 2011, the BBC Radio network controlled 55 per cent of the listening market (*see* BBC Radio section), and the independent sector (*see* Independent Radio section) just over 42 per cent.

ESTIMATED AUDIENCE SHARE

		Percentage	
	Jan–Mar	*Jan–Mar*	*Jan–Mar*
	2009	2010	2011
BBC Radio 1	10.3	9.5	8.7
BBC Radio 2	15.9	17.2	16.0
BBC Radio 3	1.1	1.2	1.3
BBC Radio 4	12.5	12.2	12.3
BBC Radio Five Live	4.7	4.6	4.5
Five Live Sports Extra	0.1	0.2	0.2
6 Music	0.4	0.8	1.0
BBC Radio 7	0.5	0.6	0.6
Asian Network	0.2	0.2	0.3
1Xtra	0.3	0.3	0.4
BBC Local/Regional	9.4	9.3	8.8
BBC World Service	0.8	0.6	0.9
All BBC	56.3	56.5	55.0
All independent	41.6	41.3	42.6
All national independent	10.2	10.3	11.6
All local independent	31.3	31.1	31.0
Other	2.1	2.2	2.4

Source: RAJAR

DIGITAL RADIO

DAB (digital audio broadcasting) allows more services to be broadcast to a higher technical quality and provides the data facility for text and pictures. It improves the robustness of high fidelity radio services, especially compared with current FM and AM radio transmissions. It was developed in a collaborative research project under the pan-European Eureka 147 initiative and has been adopted as a world standard by the International Telecommunication Union for new digital radio systems. The frequencies allocated for terrestrial digital radio in the UK are 174 to 239MHz. Additional spectrum (in the 'L-Band' range: 1452–1478MHz) was introduced in 2007. Digital radios are available as standalone portable units, hi-fi stacks, car radios and PC cards, or inbuilt within a mobile phone. Newer DAB radios allow the listener to rewind, pause and record broadcasts and then upload them to a computer using a USB cable. Some portable sets now combine MP3 playback with DAB. An alternative method is to listen to digital radio through television sets via Freeview, cable or satellite.

The possibility of a switchover to entirely digital radio services remains uncertain as takeup is still proportionately low. Over 26 per cent of listening is now on a digital platform. DAB accounts for 63 per cent of total digital listening, 14 per cent is on the internet and 15 per cent on digital TV. In June 2009 the government published the white paper *Digital Britain*, which recommended that most services carried on the national and local DAB multiplexes should cease broadcasting on analogue radio by 2015. Ultra-local radio, consisting of small independent and community stations, would continue to broadcast on FM. There are two criteria that must be met for digital migration to occur:

- at least 50 per cent of radio listening is digital
- national DAB coverage is comparable to FM coverage, and local DAB reaches 90 per cent of the population and all major roads

LICENSING

The Broadcasting Act 1996 provided for the licensing of digital radio services (on multiplexes, where a number of stations share one frequency to transmit their services). To allocate the multiplexes, OFCOM advertises licences for which interested parties can bid. Once the licence has been awarded, the new owner seeks out services to broadcast on the multiplex. The BBC has a separate national multiplex for its services. There are local multiplexes around the country, each broadcasting an average of seven services, plus the local BBC station. There are also several regional multiplexes covering a wider area and broadcasting up to 11 services each.

INNOVATIONS

As with television, the opportunities offered by digital services and the internet have made important changes to radio. The internet offers a number of advantages compared to other digital platforms such as DAB including higher sound quality, a greater range of channel availability and flexibility in listening opportunity. Listeners can tune in to the majority of radio stations live on the internet or listen again online for seven days after broadcast. DAB radio does not allow the same interactivity: the data is only able to travel one-way from broadcaster to listener whereas the internet allows a two-way flow of information.

Since 2005 increasing numbers of radio stations offer all or part of their programmes as downloadable files, known as podcasts, to listen to on computers or mobile devices such as mp3 players or phones. Podcasting technology allows listeners to subscribe in order to receive automatically the latest episodes of regularly transmitted programmes as soon as they become available.

The relationship between radio stations and their audiences is also undergoing change. The quantity and availability of music on the internet has led to the creation of shows dedicated entirely to music sent in by listeners. Another new development in internet-based radio has been personalised radio stations, such as last.fm and Spotify. Last.fm 'recommends' songs based on the favourite artists and previous choices of the user. Spotify allows listeners access to the track, artist or genre of their choice, or to share and create playlists; either advertisements are played at set intervals or there is a subscription charge. Radioplayer, a joint-venture between the BBC and UK commercial radio allows audiences to listen to live and on demand radio from one place. The service attracted 5.7 million listeners in May 2011 after its launch eight weeks previously. WiFi technology is also making changes to radio-listening behaviour. WiFi internet radios and media adaptors (which plug into a hi-fi) mean that people are not limited to listening to internet radio stations, podcasts or on demand programmes solely when using their computer.

BBC RADIO

BBC Radio broadcasts network services to the UK, Isle of Man and the Channel Islands. There is also a tier of national services in Wales, Scotland and Northern Ireland and 40 local radio stations in England and the Channel Islands. In Wales and Scotland there are also dedicated language services in Welsh and Gaelic respectively. The frequency allocated for digital BBC broadcasts is 225.648MHz.

BBC Radio, Broadcasting House, Portland Place, London W1A 1AA T 020-7580 4468 W www.bbc.co.uk/radio

BBC NETWORK RADIO STATIONS

Radio 1 (contemporary pop music and entertainment news) – 24 hours a day, *Frequencies:* 97–99 FM and digital

Radio 2 (popular music, entertainment, comedy and the arts) – 24 hours a day, *Frequencies:* 88–91 FM and digital

Radio 3 (classical music, classic drama, documentaries and features) – 24 hours a day, *Frequencies:* 90–93 FM and digital

Radio 4 (news, documentaries, drama, entertainment and cricket on long wave in season) – 5.20am–1am daily, with BBC World Service overnight, *Frequencies:* 92–95 FM and 198 LW and digital

Radio Five Live (news and sport) – 24 hours a day, *Frequencies:* 693/909 MW and digital

Five Live Sports Extra (live sport) – schedule varies, digital only

6 Music (contemporary and classic pop and rock music) – 24 hours a day, digital only

Radio 7 (comedy, drama and children's) – 24 hours a day, digital only

Asian Network (news, music and sport) – 5am–1am, with Radio Five Live overnight, *Frequencies:* various MW frequencies in Midlands and digital

1Xtra (urban music: drum & bass, garage, hip hop, R&B) – 24 hours a day, digital only

BBC NATIONAL RADIO STATIONS

Radio Cymru (Welsh-language), *Frequencies:* 92–105 FM and digital

Radio Foyle, *Frequencies:* 93.1 FM and 792 MW and digital

Radio Nan Gaidheal (Gaelic service), *Frequencies:* 103.5–105 FM and digital

Radio Scotland, *Frequencies:* 92–95 FM and 810 MW and digital. Local programmes for Orkney and Shetland

Radio Ulster, *Frequencies:* 1341 MW and 92–95 FM and digital. Local programmes on Radio Foyle

Radio Wales, *Frequencies:* 657/882 MW and 93–104 FM and digital

BBC LOCAL RADIO STATIONS

In England, BBC local radio has an average weekly reach of 7.7 million listeners. There are 40 local stations serving England and the Channel Islands, all of which are available via the internet:

Berkshire, PO Box 104.4, Reading RG4 8FH
T 0118-946 4200 *Frequencies:* 95.4/104.1 FM and digital

Bristol, Broadcasting House, Whiteladies Road, Bristol, BS8 2LR
T 0117-974 1111 *Frequencies:* 94.9/104.6 and digital

Cambridgeshire, 104 Hills Road, Cambridge CB2 1LQ
T 01223-259696 *Frequencies:* 95.7/96 FM and digital

Cornwall, Phoenix Wharf, Truro TR1 1UA
T 01872-275421 *Frequencies:* 95.2/103.9 FM and digital

Coventry and Warwickshire, Priory Place, Coventry CV1 5SQ
T 024-7655 1000 *Frequencies:* 94.8/103.7 FM and digital

Cumbria, Annetwell Street, Carlisle CA3 8BB
T 01228-592444 *Frequencies:* 95.6/96.1 FM

Derby, PO Box 269, Derby DE1 3HL
T 01332-361111 *Frequencies:* 95.3/96.0/104.5 FM

Devon, PO Box 5, Broadcasting House, Seymour Road, Plymouth PL3 5YQ
T 01752-260323 *Frequencies:* 95.7/103.4 FM and digital

Essex, 198 New London Road, Chelmsford CM2 9XB
T 01245-616000 *Frequencies:* 95.3/103.5 FM, 765 AM and digital

Gloucestershire, London Road, Gloucester GL1 1SW
T 01452-308585 *Frequencies:* 95.0/95.8/104.7 FM, 1413 AM

Guernsey, Broadcasting House, Bulwer Avenue, St Sampson's GY2 4LA
T 01481-200373 *Frequencies:* 93.2/99.0 FM, 1116 AM

Hereford and Worcester, Hylton Road, Worcester WR2 5WW
T 01905-748485 *Frequencies:* 94.7/104.0/104.4, 738 AM

Humberside, Queen's Court, Hull HU1 3RH
T 01482-323232 *Frequencies:* 95.9 FM, 1485 AM and digital

Jersey, 18 Parade Road, St Helier JE2 3PL
T 01534-720255 *Frequencies:* 88.8 FM, 1026 AM

Kent, The Great Hall, Mount Pleasant Road, Tunbridge Wells TN1 1QQ
T 01892-670000 *Frequencies:* 96.7/104.2 FM, 774 AM and digital

Lancashire, 26 Darwen Street, Blackburn BB2 2EA
T 01254-583583 *Frequencies:* 95.5/103.9/104.5 FM, 1557 AM and digital

Leeds, 2 St Peter's Square, Leeds LS9 8AH
T 0113-244 2131 *Frequencies:* 92.4/95.3 FM, 774 AM and digital

Leicester, 9 St Nicholas Place, Leicester LE1 5LB
T 0116-251 1049 *Frequency:* 104.9 FM and digital

Lincolnshire, PO Box 219, Newport, Lincoln LN1 3XY
T 01522-511411 *Frequencies:* 94.9/104.7 FM

London, 2nd Floor, Egton Wing, BBC Broadcasting House, Portland Place, London W1A 1AA
T 020-7224 2424 *Frequency:* 94.9 FM and digital

Manchester, New Broadcasting House, Oxford Road, Manchester M60 1SJ
T 0161-200 2000 *Frequency:* 95.1 FM and digital

Merseyside, PO Box 95.8, Liverpool L69 1ZJ
T 0151-708 5500 *Frequencies:* 95.8 FM, 1485 AM and digital

Newcastle, Broadcasting Centre, Barrack Road, Newcastle upon Tyne NE99 1RN
T 0191-232 4141 *Frequencies:* 95.4/96.0/103.7/104.4 FM, 1458 AM and digital

Norfolk, The Forum, Millennium Plain, Norwich NR2 1BH
T 01603-617321 *Frequencies:* 95.1/95.6/104.4 FM, 855 AM and digital

Northampton, Broadcasting House, Abington Street, Northampton NN1 2BH
T 01604-239100 *Frequencies:* 103.6/104.2 FM

Nottingham, London Road, Nottingham NG2 4UU
T 0115-955 0500 *Frequencies:* 95.1/95.5/103.8 FM, 1584 AM and digital

Oxford, PO Box 95.2, Oxford OX2 7YL
T 0845-931 1444 *Frequency:* 95.2 FM

Sheffield, 54 Shoreham Street, Sheffield S1 4RS
   T 0114-273 1177 *Frequencies:* 88.6/104.1 FM, 1035 AM
   and digital
Shropshire, 2–4 Boscobel Drive, Shrewsbury SY1 3TT
   T 01743-248484 *Frequencies:* 90.0/95.0/96.0/104.1 FM
   and digital
Solent, Havelock Road, Southampton SO14 7PW
   T 023-8063 1311 *Frequencies:* 96.1/103.8 FM, 999 AM
   and digital
Somerset, Broadcasting House, Park Street, Taunton TA1 4DA
   T 01823-323956 *Frequencies:* 95.5 FM,1566 AM
Stoke, Cheapside, Hanley, Stoke-on-Trent ST1 1JJ
   T 01782-208080 *Frequencies:* 94.6/104.1 FM and digital
Suffolk, Broadcasting House, St Matthew's Street, Ipswich
   IP1 3EP
   T 01473-250000 *Frequencies:* 95.5/95.9/103.9/104.6 FM
Surrey, Broadcasting Centre, Guildford, Surrey GU2 7AP
   T 01483-306306 *Frequencies:* 104/104.6 FM, 1368 AM
Sussex, 40–42 Queens Road, Brighton, East Sussex BN1 3XB
   T 01273-320428 *Frequencies:* 95.3/104.5/104.8 FM,
   1161 AM and digital
Tees, PO Box 95FM, Broadcasting House, Newport Road,
   Middlesborough TS1 5DG
   T 01642-225211 *Frequency:* 95 FM and digital
Three Counties, PO Box 3CR, Luton LU1 5XL
   T 01582-637400 *Frequencies:* 95.5/103.8/104.5 FM,
   630/1161 AM
Wiltshire, PO Box 1234, Swindon SN1 3RW
   T 01793-513626 *Frequencies:* 103.5/104.3/104.9 FM, 1332
   AM and digital
WM (West Midlands), The Mailbox, Birmingham B1 1RF
   T 0121-567 6000 *Frequency:* 95.6 FM and digital
York, 20 Bootham Row, York YO3 7BR
   T 01904-641351 *Frequencies:* 95.5/103.7/104.3 FM,
   666/1260 AM

BBC WORLD SERVICE

The BBC World Service broadcasts to an estimated weekly audience of 180 million worldwide, in 28 languages including English, and is now available in 154 capital cities. It no longer broadcasts in Dutch, French for Europe, German, Hebrew, Italian, Japanese or Malay because it was found that most speakers of these languages preferred to listen to the English broadcasts. In 2006 services in ten languages (Bulgarian, Croatian, Czech, Greek, Hungarian, Kazakh, Polish, Slovak, Slovene and Thai) were terminated to provide funding for a new Arabic television channel, which was launched in March 2008. In August 2008 the BBC's Romanian World Service broadcasts were discontinued after 68 years. In January 2011 the BBC announced five more language services would be terminated: Albanian, Caribbean English, Macedonian, Portuguese for Africa and Serbian. The BBC World Service website offers interactive news services in English, Arabic, Chinese, Hindi, Persian, Portuguese for Brazil, Russian, Spanish and Urdu with audiostreaming available in 27 languages.

LANGUAGES
Arabic, Azeri, Bangla, Burmese, Chinese, English, French, Hausa, Hindi, Indonesian, Kinyarwanda, Kirundi, Kyrgyz, Nepali, Pashto, Persian, Portuguese, Russian, Sinhala, Somali, Spanish, Swahili, Tamil, Turkish, Ukrainian, Urdu, Uzbek and Vietnamese.

UK frequencies: digital; overnight on BBC Radio 4.
BBC Learning English teaches English worldwide through radio, television and a wide range of published and online courses.

BBC Monitoring tracks the global media for the latest news reports emerging around the world.
BBC World Service Trust is a registered charity established in 1999 by BBC World Service. It promotes development through the innovative use of the media in the developing world. The trust presently works in over 40 countries worldwide and focuses on health, education and good governance.
BBC WORLD SERVICE, Bush House, Strand, London WC2B 4PH T 020-7240 3456

INDEPENDENT RADIO

Until 1973, the BBC had a legal monopoly on radio broadcasting in the UK. During this time, the corporation's only competition came from pirate stations located abroad, such as Radio Luxembourg. Christopher Chataway, Minister for Post and Telecommunications in Edward Heath's government, changed this by creating the first licences for commercial radio stations. The Independent Broadcasting Authority (IBA) awarded the first of these licences to the London Broadcasting Company (LBC) to provide London's news and information service. LBC was followed by Capital Radio, to offer the city's entertainment service, Radio Clyde in Glasgow and BRMB in Birmingham.

The IBA was dissolved when the Broadcasting Act of 1990 de-regulated broadcasting, to be succeeded by the less rigid Radio Authority (RA). The RA began advertising new licences for the development of independent radio in January 1991. It awarded national and local radio, satellite and cable services licences, and long-term restricted service licences for stations serving non-commercial establishments such as hospitals and universities. The first national commercial digital multiplex licence was awarded in October 1998 and a number of local digital multiplex licences followed.

At the end of 2003 the RA was replaced by OFCOM, which now carries out the licensing administration.

The RadioCentre was formed in July 2006 as a result of the merger between the Radio Advertising Bureau (RAB) and the Commercial Radio Companies Association (CRCA), the former non-profit trade body for commercial radio companies in the UK, to operate essentially as a union for commercial radio stations. According to a 2008 audit, it is possible to listen to 93 per cent of independent radio stations online, while 48 per cent can be listened to on DAB radios.
THE RADIOCENTRE, 4th Floor, 5 Golden Square, London W1F 9BS T 020-3206 7800 W www.radiocentre.org
Chief Executive, Andrew Harrison

INDEPENDENT NATIONAL RADIO STATIONS
Absolute Radio, 1 Golden Square, London W1F 9DJ
   T 020-7434 1215 – 24 hours a day, *Frequencies:* 105.8 FM,
   1197/1215/1233/1242/1260 AM and digital
Amazing Radio, Church Street, Gateshead NE8 2AT –
   24 hours a day, *Frequencies:* digital only
BFBS Radio UK, Chalfont Grove, Narcot Lane, Chalfont St
   Peter, Bucks SL9 8TN T 01494-878354 *Frequency:* digital
   only
Classic FM, 30 Leicester Square, London WC2H 7LA
   T 020-7343 9000 – 24 hours a day, *Frequencies:*
   100–102 FM and digital
Planet Rock, 54 Lisson Street, London NW1 5DF
   T 020-7453 1600 – 24 hours a day, *Frequency:* digital
   only

Talk Sport, 18 Hatfields, London SE1 8DJ T 020-7959 7800 – 24 hours a day, *Frequencies:* 1053/1089 AM and digital

INDEPENDENT LOCAL RADIO STATIONS ENGLAND

2BR, 2A Petre Court, Accrington, Lancs BB5 5HY
T 01282-690000 *Frequency:* 99.8 FM

96.2 The Revolution, Sarah Moor Studios, Henshaw Street, Oldham OL1 3EN T 0161-621 6500 *Frequency:* 96.2 FM

96.2 Touch FM, Holly Farm Business Park, Honiley, Kenilworth, Warks CV8 1NP T 01926-485600 *Frequency:* 96.2 FM

96.3 Radio Aire, 51 Burley Road, Leeds LS3 1LR
T 0113-283 5500 *Frequency:* 96.3 FM and digital

96.4 Eagle Radio, Dolphin House, North Street, Guildford, Surrey GU1 4AA T 01483-300964 *Frequency:* 96.4 FM

96.4 FM BRMB, Nine Brindleyplace, 4 Oozells Square, Birmingham B1 2DJ T 0121-566 5200 *Frequency:* 96.4 FM

96.9 Viking FM, The Boathouse, Commercial Road, Hull, E. Yorks HU1 2SG T 01482-325141 *Frequency:* 96.9 FM and digital

97.2 Stray FM, The Hamlet, Hornbeam Park Avenue, Harrogate HG2 8RE T 01423-522972 *Frequency:* 97.2 FM

97.4 Rock FM, St. Paul's Square, Preston, Lancs PR1 1XA
T 01772-477700 *Frequency:* 97.4 FM and digital

99.9 Radio Norwich, Stanton House, 29 Yarmouth Road, Norwich NR7 0EE T 01603-703300 *Frequency:* 99.9 FM

102 Touch FM, Holly Farm Business Park, Honiley, Kenilworth, Warks CV8 1NP T 01926-485600 *Frequency:* 102 FM

102.4 Wish FM, Orrell Lodge, Orrell Road, Wigan, Lancs WN5 8HJ T 01942-761024 *Frequency:* 102.4 FM

103.4 Sun FM, PO Box 1034, Sunderland, Tyne and Wear SR5 2YL T 0191-548 6767 *Frequency:* 103.4 FM

107 The Bee, 2A Petre Court, Petre Road, Clayton-le-Moors BB5 5HY T 01254-350350 *Frequency:* 107 FM

107.2 The Wyre, 13 Oxford Street, Kidderminster DY10 1BQ
T 03331-231072 *Frequency:* 107.2 FM

107.5 Sovereign Radio, 14 St Mary's Walk, Hailsham, E. Sussex BN27 1AF T 01323-442700 *Frequency:* 107.5 FM

107.6 Banbury Sound, Holly Farm Business Park, Honiley, Kenilworth, Warks CV8 1NP T 01295-661076 *Frequency:* 107.6 FM

107.6 FM Juice Liverpool, 27 Fleet Street, Liverpool L1 4AR
T 0151-707 3107 *Frequency:* 107.6 FM

107.6 Touch Banbury, Unit 9A, Manor Park, Banbury, Oxfordshire OX16 3TB T 0129-566 1076 *Frequency:* 107.6 FM

107.7 Splash FM, Guildbourne Centre, Worthing, W. Sussex BN11 1LZ T 01903-233005 *Frequency:* 107.7 FM

107.7 The Wolf, 2nd Floor, Mander House, Wolverhampton WV1 3NB T 01902-571070 *Frequency:* 107.7 FM

107.8 Arrow FM, Priory Meadow Shopping Centre, Hastings, E. Sussex TN34 1PJ T 01424-461177 *Frequency:* 107.8 FM

107.8 Radio Jackie, 110 Tolworth Broadway, Surbiton, Surrey KT6 7JD T 020-8288 1300 *Frequency:* 107.8 FM

107.9 Dune FM, The Power Station, Victoria Way, Southport, Merseyside PR8 1RR T 01704-502500 *Frequency:* 107.9 FM

Absolute Radio 80s, 1 Golden Square, London W1F 9DJ
T 020-7434 1215 *Frequency:* digital only

Absolute Radio 90s, 1 Golden Square, London W1F 9DJ
T 020-7434 1215 *Frequency:* digital only

Absolute Radio 00s, 1 Golden Square, London W1F 9DJ T 020-7434 1215 *Frequency:* digital only

Absolute Radio Classic Rock, 1 Golden Square, London W1F 9DJ T 020-7434 1215 *Frequency:* digital only

Absolute Radio London, 1 Golden Square, London W1F 9DJ
T 020-7434 1215 *Frequency:* 105.8 FM, 1215 AM (nationwide) and digital

The Arrow , 30 Leicester Square, London WC2H 7LA
T 020-7766 6000 *Frequency:* digital only

Asian Sound Radio, Globe House, Southall Street, Manchester M3 1LG T 0161-288 1000 *Frequencies:* 963/1377 AM and digital

Atlantic FM, Unit 10, Wheal Kitty Workshops, St Agnes, Cornwall TR5 0RD T 01872-554400 *Frequencies:* 105.1/107 FM

The Bay, PO Box 969, St George's Quay, Lancaster LA1 3LD
T 01524-848747 *Frequencies:* 96.9/102.3/103.2 FM

The Beach, 10 Oulton Road, Lowestoft, Suffolk NR32 4QP
T 0845-345 1035 *Frequencies:* 97.4/103.4 FM and digital

Beacon Radio, 267 Tettenhall Road, Wolverhampton WV6 0DE
T 01902-461300 *Frequencies:* 97.2/103.1 FM and digital

Big L, 8 Manchester Park, Tewkesbury Road, Cheltenham GL51 9EJ T 01242-699555 *Frequency:* 1395 AM and digital

The Breeze, Roman Landing, Kingsway, Soton S014 1BN
T 0845-466 1107 *Frequencies:* 107.2/107.4/107.8 FM

Bright 106.4, 11A The Market Place Shopping Centre, Burgess Hill, W. Sussex RH15 9NP T 01444-248127 *Frequency:* 106.4 FM

Buzz Asia, Radio House, Southall, Middx UB2 4AT
T 020-8574 6666 *Frequencies:* 963/972 AM

Capital FM: Birmingham, 1 The Square, 111 Broad Street, Birmingham B15 1AS T 0121-695 0000 *Frequency:* 102.2 FM and digital

Capital FM: East Midlands, Level 6, Chapel Quarter, Maid Marian Way, Nottingham NG1 6JR T 0115-873 1500 *Frequencies:* 96.2/96.5/102.8/105.4 FM and digital

Capital FM: London, 30 Leicester Square, London WC2H 7LA
T 020-7766 6000 *Frequency:* 95.8 FM and digital

Capital FM: Manchester, Suite 1.1, 4 Exchange Way, Salford, Manchester M5 3EE T 0161-662 4700 *Frequency:* 102 FM and digital

Capital FM: North East, Kingfisher Way, Silverlink Business Park, Tyne & Wear NE28 9NX T 0191-206 8000 *Frequencies:* 105.3/105.6/105.8/106.4 FM and digital

Capital FM: South Coast, Radio House, Whittle Avenue, Segensworth West, Fareham PO15 5SH T 01489-589911 *Frequency:* 103.2 FM and digital

Capital FM: Yorkshire, Joseph's Well, Westgate, Leeds LS3 1AB T 0113-308 5100 *Frequencies:* 105.1/105.6/105.8 FM and digital

CFM (Carlisle and West Cumbria), PO Box 964, Carlisle, Cumbria CA1 3NG T 01228-818964 *Frequencies:* 96.4/102.5 FM (Carlisle); 102.2/103.4 FM (West Cumbria)

Chelmsford Radio 107.7, Icon Building, Western Esplanade, Southend-on-Sea, Essex SS1 1EE T 01702-455344 *Frequency:* 107.7 FM

Cheshire's Silk 106.9, 140 Moss Lane, Macclesfield, Cheshire SK11 7XE T 01625 268000 *Frequency:* 106.9 FM

Choice 96.9/107.1 FM, 30 Leicester Square, London WC2H 7LA T 020-7766 6000 *Frequency:* 96.9/107.1 FM and digital

Compass FM, 26A Wellowgate, Grimsby, Lincs DN32 0RA
T 01472-346666 *Frequency:* 96.4 FM

Connect FM, 55 Headlands, Kettering, Northants NN15 7EY
T 01733-704106 *Frequencies:* 97.2/106.8/107.4 FM

County Sound Radio 1566 AM, Dolphin House, North Street, Guildford, Surrey GU1 4AA T 01483-300964 *Frequency:* 1566 AM

Dearne FM, Unit 7, Network Centre, Zenith Park, Whaley Road, Barnsley S75 1HT T 01226-321733 *Frequencies:* 97.1/102 FM

Dee 106.3, 2 Chantry Court, Chester CH1 4QN
T 01244-391000 *Frequency:* 106.3 FM

Dream 100 FM, Northgate House, St Peter's Street, Colchester, Essex CO1 1HT T 01206-764466 *Frequency:* 100.2 FM

Fire 107.6 FM, 307 Holdenhurst Road, Bournemouth, Dorset BH8 8BX T 01202-835107 *Frequency:* 107.6 FM

Fresh Radio, The Watermill, Broughton Hall, Skipton, N. Yorks BD23 3AG T 0845-224 2052 *Frequencies:* 936/1413/1431 AM; 102.6/107.1 FM

Gaydar Radio, PO Box 113, Twickenham, Middx TW1 4WY T 020-8744 1287 *Frequency:* digital only

Gem 106, City Link, Nottingham NG2 4NG T 0115-910 6100 *Frequency:* 106 FM

Glide FM, 270 Woodstock Road, Oxford OX2 7NW T 01865-315980 *Frequency:* 107.9 FM

Gold, 30 Leicester Square, London WC2H 7LA T 020-7776 6000 *Frequencies:* 603 AM (East Kent); 774 AM (Gloucester); 792 AM (Bedford); 828 AM (Bournemouth, Luton); 936 AM (West Wiltshire); 945 AM (Eastbourne, Derby); 999 AM (Nottingham); 1152 AM (Norfolk, Plymouth); 1161 AM (Swindon); 1170 AM (Portsmouth, Ipswich); 1242 AM (West Kent); 1251 AM (Bury St. Edmunds); 1260 AM (Bristol, Bath); 1323 AM (Brighton); 1332 AM (Peterborough); 1359 AM (Chelmsford); 1431 AM (Southend, Reading); 1458 AM (Manchester); 1485 AM (Newbury); 1548 AM (London); 1557 AM (Northampton) and digital

Gold: Midlands, Nine Brindleyplace, 4 Oozells Square, Birmingham B1 2DJ T 0121-566 5200 *Frequencies:* 990 AM (Wolverhampton); 1017 AM (Shrewsbury & Telford); 1152 AM (Birmingham); 1359 AM (Coventry & Warwickshire) and digital

Hallam FM, Radio House, 900 Herries Road, Sheffield S6 1RH T 0114-209 1000 *Frequencies:* 97.4/102.9/103.4 FM and digital

Heart (Cambridgeshire), PO Box 225, Queensgate Centre, Peterborough PE1 1XJ T 01733-460460 *Frequencies:* 97.4/102.7/103 FM and digital

Heart (Devon), Exeter Business Park, Exeter, Devon EX1 3QS T 01392-444444 *Frequency:* 96.2/96.4/96.6/97/97.3/100.5/ 100.8/101.2/101.9/103 FM and digital

Heart (East Anglia), 47–49 Colegate, Norwich, Norfolk NR3 1DB T 01603-671180 *Frequencies:* 96.4/97.1/102.4 FM and digital

Heart (Essex), Radio House, 31 Glebe Road, Chelmsford, Essex CM1 1QG T 01245-524500 *Frequencies:* 96.1/96.3/97.5/101.7/102.6 FM and digital

Heart (Four Counties), Broadcast Centre, 14 Vincent Avenue, Milton Keynes MK8 0AB T 01908-269111 *Frequencies:* 96.6/96.9/97.6/103.3 FM and digital

Heart (Gloucestershire), Bridge Studios, Eastgate Centre, Gloucester, Gloucestershire GL1 1SS T 01452-313200 *Frequencies:* 102.4/103 FM

Heart (Hertfordshire), Unit 5, The Metro Centre, Dwight Road, Watford WD18 9UD T 01923-205470 *Frequency:* 96.6 FM

Heart (Kent), Radio House, John Wilson Business Park, Whitstable, Kent CT5 3QX T 01227-772004 *Frequencies:* 95.9/96.1/97/102.8/103.1 FM and digital

Heart (London), 30 Leicester Square, London WC2H 7LA T 020-7468 1062 *Frequency:* 106.2 FM and digital

Heart (South Coast), Radio House, Whittle Avenue, Segensworth West, Fareham PO15 5SH T 01489-589911 *Frequencies:* 96.7/97.5/102.3 FM

Heart (Sussex), Radio House, PO Box 2000, Brighton BN41 2SS T 01273-430111 *Frequencies:* 96.9/97.5/102/102.4/102.7/103.5 FM and digital

Heart (Thames Valley), PO Box 2020, The Chase, Reading, Berks RG31 7FG T 0118-945 4400 *Frequencies:* 97/97.4/102.6/102.9/103.4 FM

Heart (West Country), One Passage Street, Bristol BS2 0JF T 0117-984 3200 *Frequencies:* 96.3/96.5/97.1/102.6/103 FM and digital

Heart (West Midlands), 1 The Square, 111 Broad Street, Birmingham B15 1AS T 0121-695 0000 *Frequency:* 100.7 and digital

Heart (Wiltshire), PO Box 2000, Swindon SN4 7EX T 01793-842600 *Frequencies:* 96.5/97.2/102.2 FM and digital

High Peak Radio, PO Box 106, High Peak, Derbys SK23 0QD T 01298-813144 *Frequencies:* 103.3/106.4 FM

Imagine FM, Waterloo Place, Watson Square, Stockport SK1 3AZ T 0161-476 7340 *Frequency:* 104.9 FM

Isle Of Wight Radio, Dodnor Park, Newport, IOW PO30 5XE T 01983-822557 *Frequencies:* 102/107 FM

Jack FM (Bristol), County Gates, Ashton Road, Bristol BS3 2JH T 0117-966 1065 *Frequency:* 106.5 FM

Jack FM (Hertfordshire), The Pump House, Knebworth Park, Hertfordshire SG3 6HQ T 01438-810900 *Frequency:* 106 FM

Jack FM (Oxfordshire), 270 Woodstock Road, Oxford, Oxfordshire OX2 7NW T 01865-315980 *Frequency:* 106.8/106.4 FM

Jack FM (South Coast), Roman Landing, Kingsway, Soton SO14 1BN T 023-8038 4100 *Frequencies:* 106/106.6 FM

Juice 107.2, 170 North Street, Brighton BN1 1EA T 01273-386107 *Frequency:* 107.2 FM and digital

Kerrang! 105.2 FM , Kerrang! House, 20 Lionel Street, Birmingham B3 1AQ T 0845-053 1052 *Frequency:* 105.2 FM and digital

Kestrel FM, Suite 2, Paddington House, Festival Place, Basingstoke, Hants RG21 7LJ T 01256-694000 *Frequency:* 107.6 FM

Key 103, Castle Quay, Castlefield, Manchester M15 4PR T 0161-288 5000 *Frequency:* 103 FM and digital

Kismat, Radio House, Southall, Middx UB2 4AT T 020-8574 6666 *Frequency:* 1035 AM and digital

Kiss, Mappin House, 4 Winsley Street, London W1W 8HF T 020-7436 1515 *Frequencies:* 97.2/100/101/105.6/106.1/106.4/107.7 FM and digital

KL.FM 96.7, 18 Blackfriars Street, King's Lynn, Norfolk PE30 1NN T 01553-772777 *Frequency:* 96.7 FM

KMFM (Ashford), 34–36 North Street, Ashford, Kent TN24 8JR T 01233-623232 *Frequency:* 107.6 FM

KMFM (Canterbury), 183 Northdown Road, Cliftonville, Margate, Kent CT9 2PA T 01227-475950 *Frequency:* 106 FM

KMFM (Maidstone), Medway House, Ginsbury Close, Sir Thomas Longley Road, Medway City Estate, Strood, Rochester, Kent ME2 4DU T 01622-662500 *Frequency:* 105.6 FM

KMFM (Medway), Medway House, Ginsbury Close, Sir Thomas Longley Road, Medway City Estate, Strood, Rochester, Kent ME2 4DU T 01634-227808 *Frequencies:* 100.4/107.9 FM

KMFM (Shepway and White Cliffs Country), 34–36 North Street, Ashford, Kent TN24 8JR T 01303-220303 *Frequencies:* 96.4/106.8 FM

KMFM (Thanet), 2–14 High Street, Margate, Kent CT9 1DH T 01843-220222 *Frequency:* 107.2 FM

KMFM (West Kent), Medway House, Ginsbury Close, Sir Thomas Langley Road, Medway City Estate, Strood, Rochester, Kent ME2 4DU T 01732-369200 *Frequencies:* 96.2/101.6 FM

KMFM extra, Medway House, Ginsbury Close, Sir Thomas Langley Road, Medway City Estate, Strood, Rochester, Kent ME2 4DU T 0844-967 1000 *Frequency:* digital only

Lakeland Radio, Plumgarths, Crook Road, Kendal, Cumbria LA8 8QJ **T** 01539-737380 *Frequencies:* 100.1/100.8 FM

LBC 97.3 FM, 30 Leicester Square, London WC2H 7LA **T** 020-7766 6000 *Frequency:* 97.3 FM and digital

LBC News 1152, 30 Leicester Square, London WC2H 7LA **T** 020-7766 6000 *Frequency:* 1152 AM and digital

Lincs FM, Witham Park, Waterside South, Lincoln LN5 7JN **T** 01522-549900 *Frequencies:* 96.7/97.6/102.2 FM and digital

London Greek Radio, LGR House, 437 High Road, London N12 0AP **T** 0871-288 1000 *Frequency:* 103.3 FM

London Turkish Radio, 185B High Road, Wood Green, London N22 6BA **T** 020-8881 0606 *Frequency:* 1584 AM

Magic 105.4, Mappin House, 4 Winsley Street, London W1W 8HF **T** 020-7975 8100 *Frequency:* 105.4 FM and digital

Magic 828, 51 Burley Road, Leeds LS3 1LR **T** 0113-283 5500 *Frequency:* 828 AM and digital

Magic 999, St Paul's Square, Preston, Lancs PR1 1XS **T** 01772-477700 *Frequency:* 999 AM and digital

Magic 1152 (Manchester), Castle Quay, Castlefield, Manchester M15 4PR **T** 0161-288 5000 *Frequency:* 1152 AM and digital

Magic 1152 (Tyne & Wear), 55 Degrees North, Pilgrim Street, Newcastle upon Tyne NE1 6BF **T** 0191-230 6100 *Frequency:* 1152 AM and digital

Magic 1161 AM, Commercial Road, Hull, E. Yorks HU1 2SG **T** 01482-325141 *Frequency:* 1161 AM and digital

Magic 1170, Radio House, Yale Crescent, Thornaby, Stockton-on-Tees TS17 6AA **T** 01642-888222 *Frequency:* 1170 AM and digital

Magic 1548 AM, St John's Beacon, 1 Houghton Street, Liverpool L1 1RL **T** 0151-472 6800 *Frequency:* 1548 AM and digital

Magic AM (South Yorkshire), Radio House, 900 Herries Road, Sheffield S6 1RH **T** 0114-285 2121 *Frequencies:* 990/1305/1548 AM and digital

Mansfield 103.2 FM, The Media Suite, Brunts Business Centre, Samuel Brunts Way, Mansfield, Notts NG18 2AH **T** 01623-646666 *Frequency:* 103.2 FM

Mercia, Hertford Place, Coventry CV1 3TT **T** 024-7686 8200 *Frequencies:* 97/102.9 FM and digital

Metro Radio, 55 Degrees North, Pilgrim Street, Newcastle upon Tyne NE1 6BF **T** 0191-230 6100 *Frequencies:* 97.1/102.6/103/103.2 FM and digital

Midwest Radio (Blandford & The Vale) Longmead, Shaftesbury, Dorset SP7 8QQ **T** 01747-855711 *Frequencies:* 96.6/97.4 FM

Midwest Radio (Somerset & West Dorset), The Studios, Middle Street, Yeovil, Somerset BA20 1DJ **T** 01935-848488 *Frequencies:* 105.6/106.6 FM

Minster FM, PO Box 123, Dunnington, York YO19 5ZX **T** 01904-488888 *Frequencies:* 102.3/104.7 FM

Mix 96, Friars Square Studios, 11 Bourbon Street, Aylesbury, Bucks HP20 2PZ **T** 01296-399396 *Frequency:* 96.2 FM

Newbury Sound, 42 Bone Lane, Newbury, Berks RG14 5SD **T** 01635-841600 *Frequencies:* 105.6/107.4 FM

North Norfolk Radio, PO Box 962, Norfolk NR24 2ER **T** 01263-860808 *Frequencies:* 96.2/103.2 FM

Oak FM, Unit 3 Martins Court, Telford Way, Coalville LE67 3HD **T** 01530-835107 *Frequencies:* 107.9 FM

Palm 105.5, Marble Court, Lymington Road, Torquay TQ1 4FB **T** 01803-321 055 *Frequency:* 105.5 FM

Passion Radio, PO Box 4738, Worthing, West Sussex BN11 9LR **T** 01903-685555 *Frequency:* digital only

Peak FM, Radio House, Foxwood Road, Chesterfield, Derbys S41 9RF **T** 01246-269107 *Frequencies:* 102/107.4 FM

Pirate FM, Carn Brea Studios, Wilson Way, Redruth, Cornwall TR15 3XX **T** 0870-800 0007 *Frequencies:* 102.2/102.8 FM and digital

Polish Radio London, Unit 6, King Street Cloisters, Clifton Walk, London W6 0GY **T** 0870-041 3636 *Frequency:* digital only

Premier Christian Radio, 22 Chapter Street, London SW1P 4NP **T** 020-7316 1300 *Frequencies:* 1305/1332/1413 AM and digital

The Pulse of West Yorkshire, Forster Square, Bradford, W. Yorks BD1 5NE **T** 01274-203040 *Frequencies:* 97.5/102.5 FM and digital

Pulse 2, Forster Square, Bradford, W. Yorks BD1 5NE **T** 01274-203040 *Frequencies:* 1278/1530 AM and digital

Radio City 96.7, St John's Beacon, 1 Houghton Street, Liverpool L1 1RL **T** 0151-472 6800 *Frequency:* 96.7 FM and digital

Radio Wave 96.5, 965 Mowbray Drive, Blackpool, Lancs FY3 7JR **T** 01253-304965 *Frequency:* 96.5 FM

Radio XL 1296 AM, KMS House, Bradford Street, Birmingham B12 0JD **T** 0121-753 5353 *Frequency:* 1296 AM and digital

Ram FM, 35/36 Irongate, Derby DE1 3GA **T** 01332-324000 *Frequency:* 102.8 FM

Reading 107 FM, Radio House, Madejski Stadium, Reading, Berks RG2 0FN **T** 0118-986 2555 *Frequency:* 107 FM

Real Radio (Northeast), Marquis Court, Team Valley, Trading Estate, Gateshead NE11 0RU **T** 0191-440 7500 *Frequencies* 96.2/96.4/100.7/101.8 FM and digital

Real Radio (Northwest), Laser House, Waterfront Quay, Manchester M50 3XW **T** 0161-886 8800 *Frequency:* 105.4 FM and digital

Real Radio (Yorkshire), 1 Sterling Court, Tingley, Wakefield WF3 1EL **T** 0113-238 1114 *Frequencies:* 106.2/107.6/107.7 FM and digital

Ridings FM, PO Box 333, Wakefield WF2 7YQ **T** 01924-367177 *Frequency:* 106.8 FM and digital

Rother FM, Aspen Court, Bessemer Way, Rotherham S60 1FB **T** 01709-369994 *Frequency:* 96.1 FM

Rugby FM, Holly Farm Business Park, Honiley, Kenilworth CV8 1NP **T** 0845-094 9780 *Frequency:* 107.1 FM

Rutland Radio, 40 Melton Road, Oakham, Rutland, Leics LE15 6AY **T** 01572-757868 *Frequencies:* 97.4/107.2 FM

Sabras Radio, Radio House, 63 Melton Road, Leicester LE4 6PN **T** 0116-261 0666 *Frequency:* 1260 AM and digital

The Severn, Shropshire Star Building, Waterloo Road, Ketley, Telford TF1 5HU **T** 0333-456 0777 *Frequencies:* 106.5/107.1/107.4 FM

Signal 1, Stoke Road, Stoke-on-Trent ST4 2SR **T** 01782-441300 *Frequencies:* 96.4/96.9/102.6 FM and digital

Signal 2, Stoke Road, Stoke-on-Trent ST4 2SR **T** 01782-441300 *Frequency:* 1170 AM and digital

Smooth Radio Northwest, Laser House, Waterfront Quay, Salford Quays, Manchester M50 3XW **T** 0845-050 1004 *Frequencies:* 100.4 FM (North West); 101.4 FM (Derby); 102.2 FM (London); 105.7 FM (West Midlands); 106.6 FM (East Midlands) and digital

Southend Radio 105.1, The Icon Building, Western Esplanade, Southend-on-Sea, Essex SS1 1EE **T** 01702-455060, *Frequency:* 105.1 FM and digital

Spectrum Radio, 4 Ingate Place, Battersea, London SW8 3NS **T** 020-7627 4433 *Frequency:* 558 AM and digital

Spire FM, City Hall Studios, Malthouse Lane, Salisbury, Wilts SP2 7QQ **T** 01722-416644 *Frequency:* 102 FM

Spirit FM, 9 Dukes Court, Bognor Road, Chichester, W. Sussex PO19 8FX **T** 01243-773600 *Frequencies:* 96.6/102.3/106.6 FM

Star Radio (Cambridge and Ely), 20 Mercers Row, Cambridge CB5 8HY T 01223-305107 *Frequencies:* 107.1/107.9 FM

Star Radio (North East), Radio House, 11 Woodland Road, Darlington, Co. Durham DL3 7BJ T 01325-341810 *Frequencies:* 102.3/102.8/103.2/103.5/106.8 FM

Sunshine Radio, Penn House, Broad Street, Hereford HR4 9AP T 01432-360246 *Frequencies:* 106.2/107/107.8 FM

Sunrise Radio (London), Sunrise House, Sunrise Road, Southall, Middx UB2 4AT T 020-8574 6666 *Frequency:* 1458 AM and digital

Sunrise Radio (Yorkshire), Sunrise House, 55 Leeds Road, Little Germany, Bradford BD1 5AF T 01274-735043 *Frequency:* 103.2 FM and digital

Telford FM, MNA Broadcasting, Shropshire Newspapers, Waterloo Road, Ketley TF1 5HU T 01952-280011 *Frequency:* 107.4 FM

TFM, Radio House, Yale Crescent, Thornaby, Stockton-on-Tees TS17 6AA T 01642-888222 *Frequency:* 96.6 FM and digital

Time 106.6, Radio House, Southall, Middlesex UB2 4AT T 0845-194 1066 *Frequency:* 106.6 FM

Time 107.5, 7th Floor, Lambourne House, 7 Western Road, Romford, Essex RM1 3LD T 0870-607 1075 *Frequency:* 107.5 FM

Total Star Gloucestershire, 8 Manchester Park, Tewkesbury Road, Cheltenham GL51 9EJ T 01242-252333 *Frequency:* 107.5 FM

Total Star Somerset, 8 Manchester Park, Tewkesbury Road, Cheltenham GL51 9EJ T 01242-252333 *Frequencies:* 100.8/102.4/107.4 FM

Tower FM, The Mill, Brownlow Way, Bolton BL1 2RA T 01204-387000 *Frequency:* 107.4 FM

Town FM, First Floor, Radio House, Orion Court, Great Blakenham, Ipswich, Suffolk IP6 0LW T 01473-836102 *Frequency:* 102 FM

Touch FM, 5–6 Aldergate, Tamworth, Staffordshire B79 7DJ T 01827-318000 *Frequencies:* 101.6/102.4 FM and digital

Trax FM, 5 Sidings Court, White Rose Way, Doncaster DN4 5NU T 01302-341166 *Frequencies:* 107.1/107.9 FM and digital

Wave 105 FM, 5 Manor Court, Barnes Wallis Road, Fareham, Hampshire PO15 5TH T 01489-481057 *Frequencies:* 105.2/105.8 FM and digital

Wessex FM, Radio House, Trinity Street, Dorchester, Dorset DT1 1DJ T 01305-250333 *Frequencies:* 96/97.2 FM

Wire FM, Warrington Business Park, Long Lane, Warrington WA2 8TX T 01925-445545 *Frequency:* 107.2 FM

Wyvern FM, First Floor, Kirkham House, John Comyn Drive, Worcester WR3 7NS T 01905-545510 *Frequencies:* 96.7/97.6/102.8 FM

XFM Manchester, Suite 1.1, 4 Exchange Quay, Manchester M5 3EE T 0161-662 4700 *Frequency:* 97.7 FM and digital

XFM UK, 30 Leicester Square, London WC2H 7LA T 020-7766 6000 *Frequency:* 104.9 FM and digital

Yorkshire Coast Radio, Unit 2B, Newchase Business Centre, Hopper Hill Road, Scarborough, N. Yorks YO11 3YS T 01723-500962 *Frequencies:* 96.2/102.4/103.1 FM

Yorkshire Radio, PO Box 197 Elland Road, Leeds LS11 1AZ T 0871-521 2288 *Frequency:* digital only

WALES

96.4 The Wave, PO Box 964, Victoria Road, Gowerton, Swansea SA4 3AB T 01792-511964 *Frequency:* 96.4 FM and digital

97.1 Radio Carmarthenshire, PO Box 971, Llanelli, Carmarthenshire SA15 1YH T 0845-890 7000 *Frequencies:* 97.1/97.5 FM

97.5 Scarlet FM, PO Box 971, Llanelli, Carmarthenshire SA15 1YH T 0845-890 7000 *Frequency:* 97.5 FM

102.1 Bay Radio, Newby House, Neath Abbey Business Park, Neath SA10 7DR T 0845-890 4000 *Frequency:* 102.1 FM

102.5 Radio Pembrokeshire, Unit 14, Old School Estate, Station Road, Narberth, Pembrokeshire SA67 7DU T 01834-869384 *Frequencies:* 102.5/107.5 FM

106.3 Bridge FM, PO Box 1063, Bridgend CF35 6WY T 0845-890 4000 *Frequency:* 106.3 FM

Capital FM: South Wales, The Red Dragon Centre, Cardiff CF10 4DJ T 029-2066 2066 *Frequencies:* 97.4/103.2 FM and digital

Gold (Wales), Red Dragon Centre, Atlantic Wharf, Cardiff CF10 4DJ T 029-2066 2066 *Frequencies:* 1305/1359 AM and digital

Heart (North West and Wales), The Studios, Mold Road, Wrexham LL11 4AF T 01978-722 200 *Frequencies:* 96.3/97.1/103/103.4 FM

Nation Radio, Newby House, Neath Abbey Business Park, Neath SA10 7DR T 0845-025 1000 *Frequencies:* 106.8/107.3 FM and digital

NME, The Media Centre, Culverhouse Cross, Cardiff CF5 6XJ T 029-2141 4100 *Frequency:* digital only

Radio Ceredigion, Glan Yr Afon Industrial Estate, Aberystwyth, Ceredigion SY23 3FF T 01970-229113 *Frequencies:* 96.6/97.4/103.3 FM

Radio Hafren, The Studios, The Park, Newtown, Powys SY16 2NZ T 01686-623777 *Frequency:* 756 AM

Real Radio (Wales), Ty-Nant Court, Ty-Nant Road, Morganstown, Cardiff CF15 8LW T 029-2031 5100 *Frequencies:* 88/102.3/102.8/105.2/105.4/105.6/105.7/105.9/106/106.1/ 106.2/106.9/107.2/107.3/107.7 FM and digital

Red Dragon FM, Atlantic Wharf, Cardiff CF10 4DJ T 029-2066 2066 *Frequencies:* 97.4/103.2 FM and digital

Swansea Sound, Victoria Road, Gowerton, Swansea SA4 3AB T 01792-511170 *Frequency:* 1170 AM and digital

XS Wales, Unit 5, Water Street Business Centre, Water Street, Port Talbot SA12 6LF T 01639-262025 *Frequency:* 97.4/107.9 FM

SCOTLAND

Argyll FM, 27–29 Longrow, Campbelltown, Argyll PA28 6ER T 01586-551800 *Frequencies:* 106.5/107.1/107.7 FM

Central 103.1 FM, 201 High Street, Falkirk FK1 1DU T 01324-611164 *Frequency:* 103.1 FM

Clyde 1, Clydebank Business Park, Clydebank, Glasgow G81 2RX T 0141-565 2200 *Frequencies:* 97/102.3/102.5/103.3 FM and digital

Clyde 2, Clydebank Business Park, Clydebank, Glasgow G81 2RX T 0141-565 2200 *Frequency:* 1152 AM and digital

Cuillin FM, Stormyhill Road, Portree, Isle of Skye IV51 9DY T 01478-611797 *Frequencies:* 102.7/106.2 FM

Forth One, Forth House, Forth Street, Edinburgh EH1 3LE T 0131-556 9255 *Frequencies:* 97.3/97.6/102.2 FM and digital

Forth 2, Forth House, Forth Street, Edinburgh EH1 3LE T 0131-556 9255 *Frequency:* 1548 AM and digital

Heartland FM, 9 Alba Place, Pitlochry, Perthshire PH16 5BU T 01796-474040 *Frequency:* 97.5 FM

Isles FM, PO Box 333, Stornoway, Isle of Lewis HS1 2PU T 01851-703333 *Frequency:* 103 FM

Kingdom FM, Haig House, Haig Business Park, Balgonie Road, Markinch, Fife KY7 6AQ T 01592-753753 *Frequencies:* 95.2/96.1/96.6/105.4/106.3 FM

Lanarkshire's L107, Radio House, 69 Bothwell Road, Hamilton, Lanarkshire ML3 0DW T 01698-303420 *Frequencies:* 107.5/107.9 FM

Lochbroom FM, Radio House, Mill Street, Ullapool, Ross-shire IV26 2UN T 01854-613131 *Frequencies:* 96.8/102.2 FM

Moray Firth Radio (MFR), PO Box 271, Scorguie Place, Inverness IV3 8UJ T 01463-224433 *Frequencies:* 97.4 FM, 1107 AM and digital

NECR, The Shed, School Road, Kintore, Inverurie, Aberdeenshire AB51 0UX T 01467-632909 *Frequencies:* 97.1/101.9/102.1/102.6/103.2/106.4 FM and digital

Nevis Radio, Ben Nevis Estate, Claggan, Fort William PH33 6PR T 01397-700007 *Frequencies:* 96.6/97/102.3/102.4 FM

Northsound 1, Abbotswell Road, West Tullos, Aberdeen AB12 3AJ T 01224-337000 *Frequencies:* 96.9/97.6/103 FM and digital

Northsound 2, Abbotswell Road, West Tullos, Aberdeen AB12 3AJ T 01224-337000 *Frequency:* 1035 AM and digital

Oban FM, 132 George Street, Oban, Argyll PA34 5NT T 01631-570057 *Frequency:* 103.3 FM

Original 106, Craigshaw Road, West Tullos, Aberdeen AB12 3AR T 01224-294860 *Frequency:* 106.3/106.8 FM

Radio Borders, Tweedside Park, Galashiels TD1 3TD T 01896-759444 *Frequencies:* 96.8/97.5/103.1/103.4 FM

Real Radio (Scotland), Parkway Court, Glasgow Business Park, Glasgow G69 6GA T 0141-781 1011 *Frequencies:* 100.3/101.1 FM and digital

RNA (Radio North Angus), Rosemount Road, Arbroath, Angus DD11 2AT T 01241-879660 *Frequencies:* 96.6/87.7 FM and digital

Rock Radio, Glasgow Business Park, Glasgow G69 6GA T 0141-781 1011 *Frequency:* 96.3 FM and digital

SIBC, Market Street, Lerwick, Shetland ZE1 0JN T 01595-695299 *Frequencies:* 96.2/102.2 FM

Smooth 105.2, PO Box 105, Glasgow G69 1AQ T 0141-781 1011 *Frequency:* 105.2 FM and digital

Tay AM, 6 North Isla Street, Dundee DD3 7JQ T 01382-200800 *Frequencies:* 1161/1584 AM and digital

Tay FM, 6 North Isla Street, Dundee DD3 7JQ T 01382-200800 *Frequencies:* 96.4/102.8 FM and digital

Two Lochs Radio, Gairloch, Ross-shire IV21 2LR T 01445-712106 *Frequencies:* 106/106.6 FM

Wave 102, 8 South Tay Street, Dundee DD1 1PA T 01382-901000 *Frequency:* 102 FM and digital

Waves Radio, 7 Blackhouse Circle, Blackhouse Industrial Estate, Peterhead, Aberdeenshire AB42 1BN T 01779-491012 *Frequency:* 101.2 FM and digital

West FM, Radio House, 54A Holmston Road, Ayr KA7 3BE T 01292-283662 *Frequencies:* 96.7/97.5/106.7 FM and digital

West Sound AM, Radio House, 54A Holmston Road, Ayr KA7 3BE T 01292-283662 *Frequency:* 1035 AM and digital

West Sound FM, Unit 40, Loreburn Centre, Dumfries DG1 2BD T 01387-250999 *Frequencies:* 96.5/97/103 FM

Your Radio, Unit 3, 80 Castlegreen Street, Dumbarton G82 1JB T 01389-734411 *Frequencies:* 103 FM (Dumbarton), 106.9 FM (Helensburgh)

NORTHERN IRELAND

Citybeat 96.7 FM, 2nd Floor, Arena Building, 85 Ormeau Road, Belfast, Antrim BT7 1SH T 028-9023 4967 *Frequency:* 96.7/102.5 FM and digital

Cool FM, Kiltonga Industrial Estate, Newtownards, Belfast BT23 4ES T 028-9181 7181 *Frequency:* 97.4 FM and digital

Downtown Radio, Newtownards, Co. Down BT23 4ES T 028-9181 5555 *Frequencies:* 96.4 FM (Limavady); 96.6 FM (Enniskillen); 97.1 FM (Larne); 102.3 FM (Ballymena); 102.4 FM (Londonderry); 103.1 FM (South Newry); 103.4 FM (Newcastle), 1026 AM and digital

Q97.2 FM , 24 Cloyfin Road, Coleraine, Co. Londonderry BT52 2NU T 028-7035 9100 *Frequency:* 97.2 FM

Q101.2 West FM, 42 Market Street, Omagh, Co. Tyrone BT78 1EH T 028-8224 5777 *Frequency:* 101.2 FM

Q102.9 FM (Londonderry), The Riverview Suite, 87 Rossdowney Road, Waterside, Londonderry BT47 5SU T 028-7134 4449 *Frequency:* 102.9 FM and digital

Seven FM, 1 Millennium Park, Woodside Industrial Estate, Woodside Road, Ballymena, Co. Antrim BT42 4PT T 028-2564 8777 *Frequency:* 107 FM

Six FM, 2C Park Avenue, Cookstown, Co. Tyrone BT80 8AH T 028-8675 8696 *Frequencies:* 106/107.2 FM

U105, UTV, Ormeau Road, Belfast BT7 1EB T 028-9032 8122 *Frequency:* 105.8 FM

CHANNEL ISLANDS AND ISLE OF MAN

3FM, 45 Victoria Street, Douglas, Isle of Man IM1 3RS T 01624-616333 *Frequencies:* 104–106 FM

Channel 103 FM, 6 Tunnell Street, St Helier, Jersey JE2 4LU T 01534-888103 *Frequency:* 103.7 FM

Energy FM, 100 Market Street, Douglas, Isle of Man IM1 2PH T 01624-611936 *Frequencies:* 91.2 FM (Laxey); 93.4 FM (north Isle of Man); 98.4 FM (Ramsey); 98.6 FM

Island FM, 12 Westerbrook, St Sampsons, Guernsey GY2 4QQ T 01481-242000 *Frequencies:* 93.7/104.7 FM

Manx Radio, Broadcasting House, Douglas, Isle of Man IM99 1SW T 01624-682600 *Frequencies:* 89.0/97.2/103.7 FM, 1368 AM

THE PRESS

The newspaper and periodical press in the UK is large and diverse, catering for a wide variety of views and interests. There is no state control or censorship of the press; however, it is subject to the laws on publication, and the Press Complaints Commission (PCC) was set up by the industry as a means of self-regulation.

The press is not state-subsidised and receives few tax concessions. The income of most newspapers and periodicals is derived largely from sales and from advertising; the press remains one of the largest advertising mediums in the UK with around 18 per cent of the market share.

SELF-REGULATION

The PCC was founded by the newspaper and magazine industry in January 1991 to replace the Press Council (established in 1953). It is a voluntary, non-statutory body set up to operate the press' self-regulation system following the Calcutt report in 1990 on privacy and related matters, when the industry feared that failure to regulate itself might lead to statutory regulation of the press. The performance of the PCC was reviewed in February 2010 by the Culture, Media and Sport Select Committee, which concluded in favour of continuing self-regulation. In July 2010 an independent review into the commission's governance made 75 recommendations for enhancing the system of press self-regulation. In July 2011, following the News of the World phone-hacking scandal, prime minister David Cameron announced that an inquiry would be held regarding the regulation of the press.

The commission is funded by the industry through the Press Standards Board of Finance.

COMPLAINTS

The PCC's aims are to consider, adjudicate, conciliate, and resolve complaints of unfair treatment by the press; and to ensure that the press maintains the highest professional standards and shows respect for generally recognised freedoms, including freedom of expression, the public's right to know, and the right of the press to operate free from improper pressure. The commission judges newspaper and magazine conduct by a code of practice drafted by editors, agreed by the industry and ratified by the commission.

The PCC has three classes of members: the chair, public members and press members. Although a number of the commision's members are newspaper or magazine editors, the majority of the 17 members have no connection with the press in order to ensure that the PCC maintains independence from the newspaper industry. In 2010 the PCC processed 750 'complaints with merit', an increase of just 1.6 per cent from 2009, and received around 7,000 complaints in total, including multiple complaints about the same article. The PCC successfully mediated or ruled on 557 cases that related to privacy in 2010.

PRESS COMPLAINTS COMMISSION
Halton House, 20–23 Holborn, London EC1N 2JD
T 020-7831 0022 E complaints@pcc.org.uk
W www.pcc.org.uk
Chair, Baroness Peta Buscombe

NEWSPAPERS

Newspapers are mostly financially independent of any political party, though most adopt a political stance in their editorial comments, usually reflecting proprietorial influence. Ownership of the national and regional daily newspapers is concentrated in the hands of large corporations whose interests cover publishing and communications, although *The Guardian* and *The Observer* are owned by the Scott Trust, formed in 1936 to protect the financial and editorial independence of *The Guardian* in perpetuity. The rules on cross-media ownership, as amended by the Broadcasting Act 1996, which limited the extent to which newspaper organisations may become involved in broadcasting, have been relaxed by the Communications Act 2003: newspapers with over a 20 per cent share of national circulation may own national and/or local radio licences.

In October 2010, *The Independent* launched a concise newspaper, *i*, the first new daily newspaper since 1986. In July 2011, *News of the World* was closed by its parent company, News International, following accusations of phone-hacking (*see* Events of the Year: Arts and Media). There are around 14 daily and 13 Sunday national papers and several hundred local papers that are published daily, weekly or twice-weekly. Scotland, Wales and Northern Ireland all have at least one daily and one Sunday national paper.

UK CIRCULATION

National Daily Newspapers	June 2010	June 2011
The Sun	2,797,972	2,806,746
Daily Mail	1,924,051	2,047,206
Daily Mirror	1,119,135	1,170,541
Daily Star	703,365	708,163
The Daily Telegraph	635,719	622,719
Daily Express	624,288	621,871
The Times	463,177	440,581
Financial Times	110,684	356,194
Daily Record	307,574	305,840
The Guardian	261,738	256,283
The Independent	162,232	176,681
i	–	173,165
The Herald	53,228	48,465
The Scotsman	44,315	40,390

National Sunday Newspapers	June 2010	June 2011
News of the World	2,610,900	2,667,428
The Mail on Sunday	1,676,088	1,927,791
Sunday Mirror	1,052,230	1,087,796
The Sunday Times	920,681	1,000,848
Sunday Express	524,699	539,478
The Sunday Telegraph	475,995	474,722
The People	471,681	474,549
Sunday Mail	368,978	360,475
Daily Star Sunday	287,478	305,978
Sunday Post	323,742	302,420
The Observer	299,492	288,928
The Independent on Sunday	127,730	151,229
Scotland on Sunday	55,657	51,053
Sunday Herald	40,715	29,233

Source: Audit Bureau of Circulations Ltd

Newspapers are usually published in either broadsheet or smaller, tabloid format. The 'quality' daily papers – ie those providing detailed coverage of a wide range of public matters – have traditionally been broadsheets, the more populist newspapers tabloid. In 2004 this correlation between format and content was redefined when three traditionally broadsheet newspapers, *The Times*, *The Independent* and *The Scotsman*, switched to tabloid-sized editions, while *The Guardian* launched a 'Berliner' format in September 2005. In October 2005 *The Independent on Sunday* became the first Sunday broadsheet to be published in the tabloid (or 'compact') size, and *The Observer*, like its daily counterpart *The Guardian*, began publishing in the Berliner format in January 2006.

NATIONAL DAILY NEWSPAPERS
DAILY EXPRESS
Northern & Shell Building, 10 Lower Thames Street, London
    EC3R 6EN **T** 020-8612 7000 **W** www.express.co.uk
    Editor, Peter Hill
DAILY MAIL
Northcliffe House, 2 Derry Street, London W8 5TT
    T 020-7938 6000 **W** www.dailymail.co.uk
    Editor, Paul Dacre
DAILY MIRROR
1 Canada Square, Canary Wharf, London E14 5AP
    T 020-7293 3000 **W** www.mirror.co.uk
    Editor, Richard Wallace
DAILY RECORD
1 Central Quay, Glasgow G3 8DA **T** 0141-309 3000
    W www.dailyrecord.co.uk
    Editor, Bruce Waddell
DAILY STAR
Express Newspapers, Northern & Shell Building, 10 Lower
    Thames Street, London EC3R 6EN **T** 020-8612 7000
    W www.dailystar.co.uk
    Editor, Dawn Neesom
THE DAILY TELEGRAPH
111 Buckingham Palace Road, London SW1W 0DT
    T 020-7931 2000 **W** www.telegraph.co.uk
    Editor, Tony Gallagher
FINANCIAL TIMES
1 Southwark Bridge, London SE1 9HL **T** 020-7873 3000
    W www.ft.com
    Editor, Lionel Barber
THE GUARDIAN
King's Place, 90 York Way, London N1 9GU
    T 020-3353 2000 **W** www.guardian.co.uk
    Editor, Alan Rusbridger
THE HERALD
Herald & Times Group, 200 Renfield Street, Glasgow G2 3QB
    T 0141-302 7000 **W** www.heraldscotland.com
    Editor, Jonathan Russell
THE INDEPENDENT AND I
2 Derry Street, London W8 5HF **T** 020-7005 2000
    W www.independent.co.uk
    Editor-in-Chief, Simon Kelner
MORNING STAR
People's Press Printing Society Ltd, William Rust House, 52
    Beachey Road, London E3 2NS **T** 020-8510 0815
    W www.morningstaronline.co.uk
    Editor, John Haylett
THE SCOTSMAN
Barclay House, 108 Holyrood Road, Edinburgh EH8 8AS
    T 0131-620 8620 **W** www.scotsman.com
    Editor, John McLellan

THE SUN
News Group Newspapers Ltd, 1 Virginia Street, London E1 9XP
    T 020-7782 4000 **W** www.the-sun.co.uk
    Editor, Dominic Mohan
THE TIMES
1 Pennington Street, London E98 1TT **T** 020-7782 5000
    W www.thetimes.co.uk
    Editor, James Harding

WEEKLY NEWSPAPERS
DAILY STAR SUNDAY
Express Newspapers, The Northern and Shell Building,
    10 Lower Thames Street, London EC3R 6EN
    T 0871-520 7424 **W** www.dailystarsunday.co.uk
    Editor, Gareth Morgan
INDEPENDENT ON SUNDAY
2 Derry Street, London W8 5HF **T** 020-7005 2000
    W www.independent.co.uk
    Executive Editor, Lisa Markwell
MAIL ON SUNDAY
Northcliffe House, 2 Derry Street, London W8 5TT
    T 020-7938 6000 **W** www.mailonsunday.co.uk
    Editor, Peter Wright
THE OBSERVER
Kings Place, 90 York Way, London N1 9GU **T** 020-3353 2000
    W www.observer.co.uk
    Editor, John Mulholland
THE PEOPLE
1 Canada Square, Canary Wharf, London E14 5AP
    T 020-7293 3000 **W** www.people.co.uk
    Editor, Lloyd Embley
SCOTLAND ON SUNDAY
108 Holyrood Road, Edinburgh EH8 8AS **T** 0131-620 8620
    W www.scotlandonsunday.co.uk
    Editor, Ian Stewart
SUNDAY EXPRESS
Northern & Shell Building, 10 Lower Thames Street,
    London EC4R 6EN **T** 020-8612 7000
    W www.express.co.uk/sunday
    Editor, Martin Townsend
SUNDAY HERALD
200 Renfield Street, Glasgow G2 3QB **T** 0141-302 7800
    W www.sundayherald.com
    Editor, Richard Walker
SUNDAY MAIL
1 Central Quay, Glasgow G3 8DA **T** 0141-309 3000
    W www.sundaymail.com
    Editor, Allan Rennie
SUNDAY MIRROR
1 Canada Square, Canary Wharf, London E14 5AP
    T 020-7293 3000 **W** www.sundaymirror.co.uk
    Editor, Tina Weaver
SUNDAY POST
D.C. Thomson & Co. Ltd, 144 Port Dundas Road, Glasgow
    G4 0HZ **T** 0141-332 9933 **W** www.sundaypost.com
    Editor, Donald Martin
SUNDAY TELEGRAPH
111 Buckingham Palace Road, London SW1W 0DT
    T 020-7931 2000 **W** www.telegraph.co.uk
    Editor, Ian MacGregor
THE SUNDAY TIMES
3 Thomas More Square, London E98 1XY **T** 020-7782 5000
    W www.thesundaytimes.co.uk
    Editor, John Witherow
THE SUNDAY TIMES SCOTLAND
6th Floor, Guildhall, 57 Queen Street, Glasgow G1 3EN
    T 0141-420 5100 **W** www.timesonline.co.uk
    Editor, Carlos Alba

WALES ON SUNDAY
6 Park Street, Cardiff CF10 1XR **T** 029-2024 3600
  W www.icwales.co.uk
  Editor, Alison Gow

REGIONAL DAILY NEWSPAPERS

EAST ANGLIA
CAMBRIDGE EVENING NEWS
Winship Road, Milton, Cambs. CB24 6PP **T** 01223-434437
  W www.cambridge-news.co.uk
  Group Editor-in-Chief, Colin Grant
EAST ANGLIAN DAILY TIMES
30 Lower Brook Street, Ipswich, Suffolk IP4 1AN
  T 01473-230023 **W** www.eadt.co.uk
  Editor, Terry Hunt
EASTERN DAILY PRESS
Prospect House, Rouen Road, Norwich NR1 1RE
  T 01603-628311 **W** www.edp24.co.uk
  Editor, Peter Waters
EVENING STAR
Archant Regional, Press House, 30 Lower Brook Street, Ipswich,
  Suffolk IP4 1AN **T** 01473-230023 **W** www.eveningstar.co.uk
  Editor, Nigel Pickover
NORWICH EVENING NEWS
Prospect House, Rouen Road, Norwich NR1 1RE
  T 01603-628311 **W** www.eveningnews24.co.uk
  Editor, Tim Williams

EAST MIDLANDS
BURTON MAIL
Burton Daily Mail Ltd, 65–68 High Street, Burton on Trent
  DE14 1LE **T** 01283-524855 **W** www.burtonmail.co.uk
  Editor, Andy Parker
CHRONICLE & ECHO, NORTHAMPTON
Northamptonshire Newspapers Ltd, Upper Mounts,
  Northampton NN1 3HR **T** 01604-467000
  Editor, David Summers
DERBY EVENING TELEGRAPH
Northcliffe House, Meadow Road, Derby DE1 2BH
  T 01332-291111 **W** www.thisisderbyshire.co.uk
  Editor, Steve Hall
THE LEICESTER MERCURY
St George Street, Leicester LE1 9FQ **T** 0116-251 2512
  W www.thisisleicestershire.co.uk
  Editor, Keith Perch
LINCOLNSHIRE ECHO
Brayford Wharf East, Lincoln LN5 7AT **T** 01522-820000
  W www.thisislincolnshire.co.uk
  Editor, Jon Grubb
NOTTINGHAM POST
Castle Wharf House, Nottingham NG1 7EU **T** 0115-948 2000
  W www.thisisnottingham.co.uk
  Editor, Malcolm Pheby

LONDON
EVENING STANDARD
Northcliffe House, 2 Derry Street, London W8 5EE
  T 020-3367 7000 **W** www.thisislondon.com
  Editor, Geordie Greig
METRO
Northcliffe House, 2 Derry Street, London W8 5TT
  T 020-7651 5200 **W** www.metro.co.uk
  Editor, Sarah Getty

NORTH EAST
EVENING CHRONICLE
ncjMedia Ltd, Groat Market, Newcastle upon Tyne NE1 1ED
  T 0191-232 7500 **W** www.chroniclelive.co.uk
  Editor, Paul Robertson
EVENING GAZETTE
Gazette Media Company Ltd, 105–111 Borough Road,
  Middlesbrough TS1 3AZ **T** 01642-245401
  W www.gazettelive.co.uk
  Editor, Darren Thwaites
HARTLEPOOL MAIL
Northeast Press Ltd, New Clarence House, Wesley Square,
  Hartlepool TS24 8BX **T** 01429-239333
  W www.hartlepoolmail.co.uk, www.peterleemail.co.uk
  Editor, Joy Yates
THE JOURNAL
Groat Market, Newcastle upon Tyne NE1 1ED **T** 0191-232 7500
  W www.journallive.co.uk
  Editor, Brian Aitken
THE NORTHERN ECHO
Priestgate, Darlington, Co. Durham DL1 1NF **T** 01325-381313
  W www.thenorthernecho.co.uk
  Editor, Peter Barron
THE SHIELDS GAZETTE
Chapter Row, South Shields, Tyne & Wear NE33 1BL
  T 0191-427 4800 **W** www.shieldsgazette.com
  Editor, John Szymanski
THE SUNDAY SUN
Groat Market, Newcastle upon Tyne NE1 1ED **T** 0191-201 6201
  W www.sundaysun.co.uk
  Editor, Matt McKenzie
SUNDERLAND ECHO
Echo House, Pennywell, Sunderland, Tyne & Wear SR4 9ER
  T 0191-501 5800 **W** www.sunderlandecho.com
  Editor, Rob Lawson

NORTH WEST
THE BLACKPOOL GAZETTE
Blackpool Gazette & Herald Ltd, Avroe House, Avroe Crescent,
  Blackpool Business Park, Squires Gate, Blackpool FY4 2DP
  T 01253-400888 **W** www.blackpoolgazette.co.uk
  Editor, David Helliwell
THE BOLTON NEWS
Newspaper House, Churchgate, Bolton, Lancs. BL1 1DE
  T 01204-537270 **W** www.thisisbolton.co.uk
  Editor-in-Chief, Ian Savage
CARLISLE NEWS AND STAR
CN Group, Newspaper House, Dalston Road, Carlisle CA2 5UA
  T 01228-612600 **W** www.newsandstar.co.uk
  Editorial Director, Neil Hodgkinson
LANCASHIRE EVENING POST
Oliver's Place, Preston PR2 9ZA **T** 01772-254841
  W www.lep.co.uk
  Editor, Simon Reynolds
LANCASHIRE TELEGRAPH
Newspaper House, High Street, Blackburn, Lancs. BB1 1HT
  T 01254-678678 **W** www.lancashiretelegraph.co.uk
  Editor, Kevin Young
LIVERPOOL DAILY POST
PO Box 48, Old Hall Street, Liverpool L69 3EB **T** 0151-227 2000
  W www.liverpooldailypost.co.uk
  Editor, Mark Thomas
LIVERPOOL ECHO
PO Box 48, Old Hall Street, Liverpool L69 3EB **T** 0151-227 2000
  W www.liverpoolecho.co.uk
  Editor, Alastair Machray

MANCHESTER EVENING NEWS
MEN Media, Mitchell Henry House, Hollinwood Avenue,
    Chadderton OL9 8EF **T** 0161-832 7200
    W www.manchestereveningnews.co.uk
    Editor, Maria McGeoghan
NORTH-WEST EVENING MAIL
Newspaper House, Abbey Road, Barrow-in-Furness, Cumbria
    LA14 5QS **T** 01229-840150 **W** www.nwemail.co.uk
    Editor, Jonathan Lee
OLDHAM EVENING CHRONICLE
PO Box 47, 172 Union Street, Oldham, Lancs. OL1 1EQ
    T 0161-633 2121 **W** www.oldham-chronicle.co.uk
    Editor, David Whaley

SOUTH EAST
THE ARGUS
Argus House, Crowhurst Road, Hollingbury, Brighton BN1 8AR
    T 01273-544544 **W** www.theargus.co.uk
    Group Editor, Michael Beard
ECHO
Newspaper House, Chester Hall Lane, Basildon, Essex SS14 3BL
    T 01268-522792 **W** www.echo-news.co.uk
    Editor, Martin McNeill
MEDWAY MESSENGER
Medway House, Ginsbury Close, Sir Thomas Longley Road,
    Medway City Estate, Strood, Kent ME2 4DU
    T 01634-227800 **W** www.kentonline.co.uk
    Editor, Bob Bounds
THE NEWS, PORTSMOUTH
The News Centre, London Road, Hilsea, Portsmouth PO2 9SX
    T 023-9266 4488 **W** www.portsmouth.co.uk
    Editor, Mark Waldron
OXFORD MAIL
Newspaper House, Osney Mead, Oxford OX2 0EJ
    T 01865-425262 **W** www.oxfordmail.co.uk
    Editor, Simon O'Neill
READING EVENING POST
8 Tessa Road, Reading, Berks. RG1 8NS **T** 0118-918 3000
    W www.getreading.co.uk
    Editor, Andy Murrill
THE SOUTHERN DAILY ECHO
Newspaper House, Test Lane, Redbridge, Southampton
    SO16 9JX **T** 023-8042 4777 **W** www.dailyecho.co.uk
    Editor, Ian Murray

SOUTH WEST
BRISTOL EVENING POST
Temple Way, Old Market, Bristol BS99 7HD **T** 0117-934 3000
    W www.thisisbristol.co.uk
    Editor-in-Chief, Mike Norton
THE CITIZEN
1 Clarence Parade, Cheltenham GL50 3NY **T** 01452-420621
    W www.thisisgloucestershire.co.uk
    Editor, Ian Mean
DAILY ECHO
Richmond Hill, Bournemouth BH2 6HH **T** 01202-554601
    W www.bournemouthecho.co.uk
    Editor, Neal Butterworth
DORSET ECHO
Fleet House, Hampshire Road, Weymouth, Dorset DT4 9XD
    T 01305-830930 **W** www.dorsetecho.co.uk
    Editor, Toby Granville
EXPRESS & ECHO
Express & Echo News & Media, Heron Road, Sowton, Exeter
    EX2 7NF **T** 01392-442211 **W** www.thisisexeter.co.uk
    Editor, Marc Astley

GLOUCESTERSHIRE ECHO
Third Floor, St James's House, St James's Square, Cheltenham,
    Glos. GL50 3PR **T** 01242-278000
    W www.thisisgloucestershire.co.uk
    Editor, Kevan Blackadder
THE HERALD
17 Brest Road, Derriford Business Park, Plymouth PL6 5AA
    T 01752-765500 **W** www.thisisplymouth.co.uk
    Editor, Bill Martin
HERALD EXPRESS
Harmsworth House, Barton Hill Road, Torquay, Devon TQ2 8JN
    T 01803-676000 **W** www.thisissouthdevon.co.uk
    Editor, Andy Phelan
SUNDAY INDEPENDENT
The Sunday Independent Newspapers Ltd, Webbs House,
    Tindle Suite, Liskeard, Cornwall PL14 6AH **T** 01579-342174
    Editor, John Noble
SWINDON ADVERTISER
100 Victoria Road, Old Town, Swindon SN1 3BE
    T 01793-528144 **W** www.swindonadvertiser.co.uk
    Editor, Dave King
WESTERN DAILY PRESS
Bristol Evening Post and Press Ltd, Temple Way, Bristol
    BS99 7HD **T** 0117-934 3000
    W www.westerndailypress.co.uk
    Editor, Tim Dixon
THE WESTERN MORNING NEWS
17 Brest Road, Derriford, Plymouth PL6 5AA **T** 01752-765500
    W www.thisiswesternmorningnews.co.uk
    Editor, Alan Qualtrough

WEST MIDLANDS
BIRMINGHAM MAIL
6th Floor, Fort Dunlop, Fort Parkway, Birmingham B24 9FF
    T 0121-236 3366 **W** www.birminghammail.net
    Editor, David Brookes
THE BIRMINGHAM POST
6th Floor, Fort Dunlop, Fort Parkway, Birmingham B24 9FF
    T 0121-234 5301 **W** www.birminghampost.net
    Editor, David Brookes
COVENTRY TELEGRAPH
Corporation Street, Coventry CV1 1FP **T** 024-7663 3633
    W www.coventrytelegraph.net
    Editor, Darren Parkin
EXPRESS & STAR
51–53 Queen Street, Wolverhampton WV1 1ES
    T 01902-313131 **W** www.expressandstar.com
    Editor, Adrian Faber
THE SENTINEL
Staffordshire Sentinel News & Media Ltd, Sentinel House,
    Etruria, Stoke-on-Trent ST1 5SS **T** 01782-602525
    W www.thisisthesentinel.co.uk
    Editor, Michael Sassi
SHROPSHIRE STAR
Waterloo Road, Ketley, Telford TF1 5HU **T** 01952-242424
    W www.shropshirestar.com
    Editor, Sarah Jane Smith
WORCESTER NEWS
Berrows House, Hylton Road, Worcester WR2 5JX
    T 01905-748200 **W** www.worcesternews.co.uk
    Editor, Kevin Ward

YORKSHIRE AND HUMBERSIDE
EVENING COURIER
PO Box 19, King Cross Street, Halifax HX1 2SF **T** 01422-260200
    W www.halifaxcourier.co.uk
    Editor, Tim Robinson

EVENING NEWS
17–23 Aberdeen Walk, Scarborough, North Yorkshire YO11 1BB
T 01723-363636 W www.scarborougheveningnews.co.uk
Editor, Ed Asquith
GRIMSBY TELEGRAPH
80 Cleethorpe Road, Grimsby, North East Lincolnshire
DN31 3EH T 01472-360360 W www.thisisgrimsby.co.uk
Editor, Michelle Lalor
THE HUDDERSFIELD DAILY EXAMINER
Trinity Mirror Huddersfield Ltd, Queen Street South,
Huddersfield HD1 3DU T 01484-430000
W www.examiner.co.uk
Editor, Roy Wright
HULL DAILY MAIL
Blundell's Corner, Beverley Road, Hull HU3 1XS
T 01482-327111 W www.thisishullandeastriding.co.uk
Editor, John Meehan
THE PRESS
Newsquest York, PO Box 29, 76–86 Walmgate, York YO1 9YN
T 01904-653051 W www.yorkpress.co.uk
Managing Editor, Steve Hughes
SHEFFIELD STAR
York Street, Sheffield S1 1PU T 0114-276 7676
W www.thestar.co.uk
Editor, Alan Powell
TELEGRAPH & ARGUS
Hall Ings, Bradford BD1 1JR T 01274-729511
W www.telegraphandargus.co.uk
Editor, Perry Austin-Clarke
YORKSHIRE EVENING POST
PO Box 168, Wellington Street, Leeds LS1 1RF T 0113-2432701
W www.yorkshireeveningpost.co.uk
Editor, Paul Napier
YORKSHIRE POST
Wellington Street, Leeds LS1 1RF T 0113-243 2701
W www.yorkshirepost.co.uk
Editor, Peter Charlton

SCOTLAND
THE COURIER AND ADVERTISER
D.C. Thomson & Co. Ltd, 80 Kingsway East, Dundee DD4 8SL
T 01382-223131 W www.thecourier.co.uk
Editor, Mike Alexander
DUNDEE EVENING TELEGRAPH AND POST
80 Kingsway East, Dundee DD4 8SL T 01382-223131
W www.eveningtelegraph.co.uk
EVENING EXPRESS
Aberdeen Journals Ltd, PO Box 43, Lang Stracht, Mastrick,
Aberdeen AB15 6DF T 01224-690222
W www.eveningexpress.co.uk
Editor, Alan McCabe
EVENING NEWS
108 Holyrood Road, Edinburgh EH8 8AS T 0131-620 8620
W www.edinburghnews.com
Editor, Tom Little
GLASGOW EVENING TIMES
200 Renfield Street, Glasgow G2 3QB T 0141-302 7000
W www.eveningtimes.co.uk
Editor, Tony Carlin
INVERNESS COURIER
New Century House, Stadium Road, Inverness IV1 1FG
T 01463-233059 W www.inverness-courier.co.uk
Editor, Robert Taylor
PAISLEY DAILY EXPRESS
Scottish and Universal Newspapers Ltd, 14 New Street, Paisley,
Renfrewshire PA1 1YA T 0141-887 7911
W www.paisleydailyexpress.co.uk
Editor, Anne Dalrymple

THE PRESS AND JOURNAL
Lang Stracht, Aberdeen AB15 6DF T 01224-690222
W www.pressandjournal.co.uk
Editor, Damian Bates

WALES
THE LEADER
NWN Media Ltd, Mold Business Park, Wrexham Road, Mold,
Flintshire CH7 1XY T 01352-707707
W www.leaderlive.co.uk
Editor, Barrie Jones
SOUTH WALES ARGUS
South Wales Argus, Cardiff Road, Maesglas, Newport, Gwent
NP20 3QN T 01633-810000
W www.southwalesargus.co.uk
Editor, Gerry Keighley
SOUTH WALES ECHO
6 Park Street, Cardiff CF10 1XR T 02920-223333
W www.walesonline.co.uk
Editor, Tim Gordon
SOUTH WALES EVENING POST
PO Box 14, Adelaide Street, Swansea SA1 1QT
T 01792-510000 W www.thisissouthwales.co.uk
Editor-in-Chief, Spencer Feeney
WESTERN MAIL
6 Park Street, Cardiff CF10 1XR T 029-2022 3333
W www.walesonline.co.uk
Editor, Alan Edmunds

NORTHERN IRELAND
BELFAST TELEGRAPH
124–144 Royal Avenue, Belfast BT1 1EB T 028-9026 4000
W www.belfasttelegraph.co.uk
Editor, Mike Gilson
IRISH NEWS
113–117 Donegall Street, Belfast BT1 2GE T 028-9032 2226
W www.irishnews.com
Editor, Noel Doran
NEWS LETTER
2 Esky Drive, Portadown, Craigavon, Belfast BT63 5YY
T 028-9089 7720 W www.newsletter.co.uk
Editor, Darwin Templeton
SUNDAY LIFE
124–144 Royal Avenue, Belfast BT1 1EB T 028-9026 4000
W www.sundaylife.co.uk
Editor, Martin Breen

CHANNEL ISLANDS
GUERNSEY PRESS AND STAR
PO Box 57, Braye Road, Vale, Guernsey GY1 3BW
T 01481-240240 W www.guernseypress.com
Editor, Richard Digard
JERSEY EVENING POST
PO Box 582, Five Oaks, St Saviour, Jersey JE4 8XQ
T 01534-611611 W www.thisisjersey.com
Editor, Chris Bright

PERIODICALS

ACCOUNTANCY AGE
Incisive Media, 32–34 Broadwick Street, London W1A 2HG
T 020-7316 9000 W www.accountancyage.com
Editor, Gavin Hinks
ACCOUNTING & BUSINESS
Association of Chartered Certified Accountants, 29 Lincolns Inn
Fields, London WC2A 3EE T 020-7059 5000
W www.accaglobal.com
Editor, Chris Quick

AEROPLANE MONTHLY
IPC Media Ltd, The Blue Fin Building, 110 Southwark Street, London SE1 0SU **T** 020-3148 4100
W www.aeroplanemonthly.com
Editor, Michael Oakey

AESTHETICA MAGAZINE
PO Box 371, York YO23 1WL **T** 01904-479168
W www.aestheticamagazine.com
Editor, Cherie Federico

AFRICA CONFIDENTIAL
Asempa Ltd, 73 Farringdon Road, London EC1M 3JQ
T 020-7831 3511 **W** www.africa-confidential.com
Editor, Patrick Smith

ALL OUT CRICKET
Unit 3–23 Kennington Court, 1–3 Brixton Road, London SW9 6DE **T** 020-3176 0187 **W** www.alloutcricket.com
Editor, Andy Afford

AMATEUR GARDENING
IPC Media Ltd, Westover House, West Quay Road, Poole, Dorset BH15 1JG **T** 01202-440840
W www.amateurgardening.com
Editor, Tim Rumball

AMATEUR PHOTOGRAPHER
IPC Media, The Blue Fin Building, 110 Southwark Street, London SE1 0SU **T** 020-3148 5000
W www.amateurphotographer.co.uk
Editor, Damien Demolder

AMBIT
17 Priory Gardens, London N6 5QY **T** 020-8340 3566
W www.ambitmagazine.co.uk
Editor, Martin Bax

ANGLING TIMES
Bauer Consumer Media, Bushfield House, Orton Centre, Peterborough PE2 5UW **T** 01733-395106
W www.gofishing.co.uk/Angling-Times
Editor, Richard Lee

APOLLO
22 Old Queen Street, London SW1H 9HP **T** 020-7961 0150
W www.apollo-magazine.com
Editor, Oscar Humphries

THE ARCHITECTS' JOURNAL
EMAP Construct, Greater London House, Hampstead Road, London NW1 7EJ **T** 020-7728 5000
W www.architectsjournal.co.uk
Editor, Kieran Long

ART MONTHLY
4th Floor, 28 Charing Cross Road, London WC2H 0DB
T 020-7240 0389 **W** www.artmonthly.co.uk
Editor, Patricia Bickers

THE ART NEWSPAPER
70 South Lambeth Road, London SW8 1RL **T** 020-7735 3331
W www.theartnewspaper.com
Editor, Jane Morris

ART QUARTERLY
The Art Fund, Millais House, 7 Cromwell Place, London SW7 2JN
T 020-7225 4800 **W** www.artfund.org
Editor, Caroline Bugler

ASTRONOMY NOW
Pole Star Publications, PO Box 175, Tonbridge, Kent TN10 4ZY
T 01732-446110 **W** www.astronomynow.com
Editor, Keith Cooper

ATTITUDE
Ground Floor, 211 Old Street, London EC1V 9NR
T 020-7608 6446 **W** www.attitude.co.uk
Editor, Matthew Todd

BBC HISTORY MAGAZINE
Bristol Magazines Ltd, Tower House, Fairfax Street, Bristol BS1 3BN **T** 0117-927 9009 **W** www.historyextra.com
Editor, Dave Musgrove

THE BEANO
D.C. Thomson & Co. Ltd, 2 Albert Square, Dundee DD1 9QJ
W www.beano.com
Editor, Alan Digby

THE BIG ISSUE
1–5 Wandsworth Road, London SW8 2LN **T** 020-7526 3200
W www.bigissue.com
Editor-in-Chief, Charles Howgego

BIKE
Bauer Consumer Media, Media House, Lynchwood, Peterborough PE2 6EA **T** 01733-468181
W www.bikemagazine.co.uk
Editor, Tim Thompson

BIRDWATCH
Solo Publishing Ltd, The Chocolate Factory, 5 Clarendon Road, London N22 6XJ **T** 020-8881 0550
W www.birdwatch.co.uk
Editor, Dominic Mitchell

BIZARRE
Dennis Publishing, 30 Cleveland Street, London W1T 4JD
T 020-7907 6000 **W** www.bizarremag.com
Editor, David McComb

THE BOOKSELLER
Endeavour House, 189 Shaftesbury Avenue, London WC2H 8TJ
T 020-7420 6006 **W** www.thebookseller.com
Editor-in-Chief, Neill Denny

BRITISH CHESS MAGAZINE
44 Baker Street, London W1U 7RT **T** 020-7486 8222
W www.bcmchess.co.uk
Editor, John Saunders

BRITISH DEAF NEWS
British Deaf Association, Bushell Street Mill, Bushell Street, Preston, Lancs PR1 2SP **T** 01772-259725
W www.bda.org.uk
Editor, Alison Gudgeon

THE BRITISH JOURNAL OF PHOTOGRAPHY
32–34 Broadwick Street, London W1A 2HG **T** 020-7316 9000
W www.bjp-online.com
Editor, Simon Bainbridge

BRITISH JOURNALISM REVIEW
Sage Publications, 1 Oliver's Yard, 55 City Road, London EC1Y 1SP **T** 020-7324 8500 **W** www.bjr.org.uk
Editor, Bill Hagerty

BRITISH MEDICAL JOURNAL
BMJ Publishing Group, BMA House, Tavistock Square, London WC1H 9JR **T** 020-7387 4499 **W** www.bmj.com
Editor, Dr Fiona Godlee

BRITISH PHILATELIC BULLETIN
Royal Mail, 35–50 Rathbone Place, London W1T 1HQ
W www.royalmail.com/stamps
Editor, J.R. Holman

BUILDING DESIGN
UBM Information Ltd, Ludgate House, 245 Blackfriars Road, London SE1 9UY **T** 020-7921 5000
W www.bdonline.co.uk
Editor, Amanda Baillieu

CANALS & RIVERS
PO Box 618, Norwich NR7 0QT **T** 01603-708930
W www.canalsandrivers.co.uk
Editor, Chris Cattrall

CAR
Bauer Consumer Media, 3rd Floor, Media House, Lynchwood, Peterborough PE2 6EA **T** 01733-468379
Editor, Phil McNamara

CARAVAN MAGAZINE
IPC Inspire, Leon House, 233 High Street, Croydon CR9 1HZ
T 020-8726 8000 **W** www.caravanmagazine.co.uk
Editor, Victoria Bentley

CHURCH TIMES
13–17 Long Lane, London EC1A 9DJ **T** 020-7776 1060
  W www.churchtimes.co.uk
  Editor, Paul Handley
CLASSIC CARS
Bauer Consumer Media, Media House, Lynchwood,
  Peterborough Business Park, Peterborough PE2 6EA
  T 01733-468000 **W** www.classiccarsmagazine.co.uk
  Editor, Phil Bell
CLASSIC ROCK
Future Publishing Ltd, 2 Balcombe Street, London NW1 6NW
  T 020-7042 4000 **W** www.classicrockmagazine.com
  Editor-in-Chief, Scott Rowley
CLASSICAL MUSIC
Rhinegold Publishing Ltd, 241 Shaftesbury Avenue,
  London WC2H 8TF **T** 020-7333 1742
  W www.rhinegold.co.uk
  Editor, Keith Clarke
CLIMB MAGAZINE
160–164 Barkby Road, Leicester LE16 8FZ **T** 0116-202 2600
  W www.climbmagazine.com
  Editor, David Pickford
COIN NEWS
Token Publishing Ltd, Orchard House, Duchy Road, Heathpark,
  Honiton, Devon EX14 1YD **T** 01404-46972
  Editor, John Mussell
COMMUNITY CARE
Reed Business Information Ltd, Quadrant House, The Quadrant,
  Sutton, Surrey SM2 5AS **T** 020-8652 3500
  W www.communitycare.co.uk
  Editor, Bronagh Miskelly
COMPUTER WEEKLY
Marble Arch Tower, 55 Bryanston Street, London W1H 7AA
  T 020-7868 4282 **W** www.computerweekly.com
  Editor, Brian McKenna
CONDÉ NAST TRAVELLER
Vogue House, Hanover Square, London W1S 1JU
  T 020-7499 9080 **W** www.cntraveller.com
  Editor, Sarah Miller
CONTEMPORARY
Studio 56, 4 Montpelier Street, London SW7 1EE
  T 020-7019 6205 **W** www.contemporary-magazines.com
  Editor, Brian Muller
CONTEMPORARY REVIEW
Contemporary Review Co. Ltd, PO Box 1242, Oxford OX1 4FJ
  T 01865-201529 **W** www.contemporaryreview.co.uk
  Editor, Dr Richard Mullen
COSMOPOLITAN
National Magazine House, 72 Broadwick Street, London
  W1F 9EP **T** 020-7439 5000
  Editor-in-Chief, Louise Court
COUNTRYFILE
9th Floor, Tower House, Fairfax Street, Bristol BS1 3BN
  T 0117-927 9009 **W** www.countryfile.com
  Editor, Fergus Collins
COUNTRY LIFE
IPC Media Ltd, The Blue Fin Building, 110 Southwark Street,
  London SE1 0SU **T** 020-3148 4444
  W www.countrylife.co.uk
  Editor, Mark Hedges
CYCLING WEEKLY
IPC Media, Leon House, 233 High Street, Croydon CR9 1HZ
  T 020-8726 8462 **W** www.cyclingweekly.co.uk
  Editor, Robert Garbutt
DARTS WORLD
MB Graphics, 25 Orlestone View, Ham Street, Ashford, Kent
  TN26 2LB **T** 01233-733558 **W** www.dartsworld.com
  Editor, Michael Beeken

DIGITAL CAMERA
Future Publishing Ltd, 30 Monmouth Street, Bath BA1 2BW
  W www.magazine.photoradar.com
  Editor, Geoff Harris
DISABILITY NOW
6 Market Road, London N7 9PW **T** 020-7619 7323
  W www.disabilitynow.org.uk
  Editor, Ian Macrae
THE ECOLOGIST
Unit 102, Lana House Studios, 116–118 Commercial Street,
  London E1 6NF **T** 020-7422 8100 **W** www.theecologist.org
  Editor, Mark Anslow
THE ECONOMIST
25 St James's Street, London SW1A 1HG **T** 020-7830 7000
  W www.economist.com
  Editor, John Micklethwait
ELLE
Hachette Filipacchi UK, 64 North Row, London W1K 7LL
  T 020-7150 7000 **W** www.elleuk.com
  Editor, Lorraine Candy
EMPIRE
Bauer Consumer Media, Mappin House, 4 Winsley Street,
  London W1W 8HF **T** 020-7182 8000
  W www.empireonline.com
  Editor, Mark Dinning
THE ENGINEER
Centaur Communications Ltd, St Giles House, 50 Poland Street,
  London W1F 7AX **T** 020-7970 4437
  W www.theengineer.com
  Editor, Jon Excell
ESQUIRE
National Magazine House, 72 Broadwick Street, London
  W1F 9EP **T** 020-7439 5000 **W** www.esquire.co.uk
  Editor, Alex Bilmes
ESSENTIALS
IPC Media, The Blue Fin Building, 110 Southwark Street,
  London SE1 0SU **T** 020-3148 7211
  Editor, Jules Barton-Breck
FAMILY TREE
61 Great Whyte, Ramsey, Huntingdon, Cambs PE26 1HJ
  T 01487-814050 **W** www.family-tree.co.uk
  Editor, Helen Tovey
FARMERS WEEKLY
Reed Business Information, Quadrant House, The Quadrant,
  Sutton, Surrey SM2 5AS **T** 020-8652 4911 **W** www.fwi.co.uk
  Editor, Jane King
FHM
Bauer Consumer Media, Endeavour House, 189 Shaftesbury
  Avenue, London WC2H 8JG **T** 020-7182 8000
  W www.fhm.com
  Editor, Joe Barnes
FOCUS
Bristol Magazines Ltd, Tower House, Fairfax Street, Bristol
  BS1 3BN **T** 0117-927 9009 **W** www.sciencefocus.com
  Editor, Jheni Osman
FOLIO
2nd Floor, Bristol News and Media, Temple Way, Bristol
  BS99 7HD **T** 0117-942 8491 **W** www.foliomagazine.co.uk
  Editor, Mike Gartside
FORTEAN TIMES
Box 2409, London NW5 4NP **T** 020-7907 6235
  W www.forteantimes.com
  Editor, David Sutton
FOURFOURTWO
Haymarket, Teddington Studios, Broom Road, Teddington,
  Middlesex TW11 9BE **T** 020-8267 5848
  W www.fourfourtwo.magazine.co.uk
  Editor, David Hall

FRANCE
Archant House, Oriel Road, Cheltenham, Glos. GL50 1BB
T 01242-216050 W www.francemag.com
Editor, Carolyn Boyd

GAMESMASTER
Future Publishing Ltd, 30 Monmouth Street, Bath BA1 2BW
T 01225-442244
Editor-in-Chief, Robin Alway

GARDEN NEWS
Bauer Consumer Media Ltd, Lincoln Road, Peterborough
PE1 2RF T 01733-237111
W www.gardennewsmagazine.co.uk
Editor, Clare Foggett

GAY TIMES – GT
Spectrum House, 32–34 Gordon House Road, London
NW5 1LP T 020-7424 7400 W www.gaytimes.co.uk
Editor, Tris Reid-Smith

GEOGRAPHICAL JOURNAL
1 Kensington Gore, London SW7 2AR T 020-7591 3026
Editor, Prof. Klaus Dodds

GLAMOUR
6–8 Old Bond Street, London W1S 4PH T 020-7499 9080
W www.glamourmagazine.com
Editor, Jo Elvin

GOLF WORLD
Bauer Media, Media House, Lynchwood, Peterborough
Business Park, Peterborough PE2 6EA T 01733-468000
W www.golf-world.co.uk
Editor, Chris Jones

GOOD HOUSEKEEPING
National Magazine House, 72 Broadwick Street, London W1F 9EP
T 020-7439 5000 W www.goodhousekeeping.co.uk
Editorial Director, Lindsay Nicholson

GQ
Condé Nast Publications, Vogue House, Hanover Square,
London W1S 1JU T 020-7499 9080
W www.gq-magazine.co.uk
Editor, Dylan Jones

GRANTA
12 Addison Avenue, London W11 4QR T 020-7605 1360
W www.granta.com
Editor, John Freeman

GRAZIA
BauerConsumer Media, Endeavour House, 189 Shaftesbury
Avenue, London WC2H 8JG T 020-7437 9011
W www.graziadaily.co.uk
Editor-in-Chief, Jane Bruton

THE GROCER
William Reed Publishing Ltd, Broadfield Park, Crawley, West
Sussex RH11 9RT T 01293-613400 W www.thegrocer.co.uk
Editor, Adam Leyland

GUITARIST
Future Publishing UK, 30 Monmouth Street, Bath BA1 2BW
T 01225-442244 W www.guitarist.co.uk
Editor, Mick Taylor

HARPER'S BAZAAR
National Magazine House, 72 Broadwick Street, London
W1F 9EP T 020-7439 5000 W www.harpersbazaar.co.uk
Editor, Lucy Yeomans

HEAT
Bauer Consumer Media, Endeavour House, 189 Shaftesbury
Avenue, London WC2H 8JG T 020-7437 9011
W www.heatworld.com
Editor, Sam Delaney

HELLO!
Wellington House, 69–71 Upper Ground, London SE1 9PQ
T 020-7667 8700 W www.hellomagazine.com
Editor-in-Chief, Eduardo Sanchez Perez

HISTORY TODAY
25 Bedford Avenue, London WC1B 3AT T 020-3219 7810
W www.historytoday.com
Editor, Paul Lay

HORSE & HOUND
IPC Inspire, 9th Floor, The Blue Fin Building, 110 Southwark
Street, London SE1 0SU T 020-3148 4562
W www.horseandhound.co.uk
Editor, Lucy Higginson

HOUSE & GARDEN
Vogue House, 1 Hanover Square, London W1S 1JU
T 020-7499 9080
Editor, Susan Crewe

ICON MAGAZINE
Media 10, National House, High Street, Epping, Essex
CM16 4BD T 01992-570030 W www.iconeye.com
Editor, Justin McGuirk

IN STYLE
IPC Southbank, The Blue Fin Building, 110 Southwark Street,
London SE1 0SU T 020-3148 5000
Editor, Eilidh MacAskill

INTERNATIONAL AFFAIRS
The Royal Institute of International Affairs, Chatham
House, 10 St James's Square, London SW1Y 4LE
T 020-7957 5728
Editor, Caroline Soper

JEWISH CHRONICLE
25 Furnival Street, London EC4A 1JT T 020-7415 1500
W www.thejc.com
Editor, Stephen Pollard

KERRANG!
Endeavour House, Shaftesbury Avenue, London WC2H 8JG
T 020-7182 8406 W www.kerrang.com
Editor, Nichola Browne

THE LADY
39–40 Bedford Street, London WC2E 9ER T 020-7379 4717
W www.lady.co.uk
Editor, Rachel Johnson

LANCET
32 Jamestown Road, London NW1 7BY T 020-7424 4910
W www.thelancet.com
Editor, Dr Richard Horton

THE LAWYER
Centaur Communications Group, St Giles House, 50 Poland
Street, London W1F 7AX T 020-7970 4000
W www.thelawyer.com
Editor, Catrin Griffiths

LEGAL WEEK
32–34 Broadwick Street, London W1A 2HG T 020-7316 9000
W www.legalweek.com
Editor, Alex Novarese

THE LIST
14 High Street, Edinburgh EH1 1TE T 0131-550 3050
W www.list.co.uk
Editor, Jonathan Ensall

THE LITERARY REVIEW
44 Lexington Street, London W1F 0LW T 020-7437 9392
W www.literaryreview.co.uk
Editor, Nancy Sladek

LOADED
IPC Ignite, The Blue Fin Building, 110 Southwark Street, London
SE1 0SU T 020-3148 5000 W www.loaded.co.uk
Editor, Andy Sherwood

THE LONDON MAGAZINE: A REVIEW OF LITERATURE
AND THE ARTS
Administration Flat 5, 11 Queen's Gate, London SW7 5EL
W www.thelondonmagazine.net
Editor, Steven O'Brien

LONDON REVIEW OF BOOKS
28 Little Russell Street, London WC1A 2HN **T** 020-7209 1101
  W www.lrb.co.uk
  Editor, Mary-Kay Wilmers
MACWORLD
101 Euston Road, London NW1 2RA **T** 020-7756 2877
  W www.macworld.co.uk
  Editor, Karen Haslam
MARIE CLAIRE
European Magazines Ltd, 7th Floor, The Blue Fin Building,
  110 Southwark Street, London SE1 0SU **T** 020-3148 7513
  W www.marieclaire.co.uk
  Editor, Trish Halpin
MEDIA WEEK
Haymarket Publishing Ltd, 174 Hammersmith Road, London
  W6 7JP **T** 020-8267 8034 **W** www.mediaweek.co.uk
  Editor, Harriet Dennys
MEN'S HEALTH
Natmag Rodale Ltd, 33 Broadwick Street, London W1F 0DQ
  T 020-7339 4400 **W** www.menshealth.co.uk
  Editor, Morgan Rees
MODEL ENGINEER
MyHobbyStore Ltd, PO Box 718, Orpington, Kent BR6 1AP
  T 01847-821136
  Editor, David Clark
MOJO
Bauer Consumer Media, Mappin House, 4 Winsley Street,
  London W1W 8HF **T** 020-7182 8616
  W www.mojo4music.com
  Editor, Phil Alexander
MOTOR BOAT AND YACHTING
IPC Media Ltd, The Blue Fin Building, 110 Southwark Street,
  London SE1 0SU **T** 020-3148 4651 **W** www.mby.com
  Editor, Hugo Andreae
MUSCLE & FITNESS
Weider Publishing, 10 Windsor Court, Clarence Drive,
  Harrogate, North Yorkshire HG1 2PE **T** 01423-504516
  W www.muscle-fitness-europe.com
  Editor, Chris Lund
MUSIC WEEK
CMPi, 1st Floor, Ludgate House, 245 Blackfriars Road, London
  SE1 9UY **W** www.musicweek.com
  Editor, Paul Williams
THE NATIONAL TRUST MAGAZINE
The National Trust, Heelis, Kemble Drive, Swindon SN2 2NA
  T 01793-817400 **W** www.nationaltrust.org.uk
  Editor, Sue Herdman
NATURE
Macmillan Magazines Ltd, The Macmillan Building, 4 Crinan
  Street, London N1 9XW **T** 020-7833 4000
  W www.nature.com/nature
  Editor, Philip Campbell
NB MAGAZINE
RNIB, 105 Judd Street, London WC1H 9NE **T** 020-7391 2070
  Editor, Ann Lee
NEW HUMANIST
1 Gower Street, London WC1E 6HD **T** 020-7436 1171
  W www.newhumanist.org.uk
  Editor, Caspar Melville
NEW MUSICAL EXPRESS (NME)
IPC Ignite, The Blue Fin Building, 110 Southwark Street,
  London SE1 0SU **T** 020-3148 5000
  W www.nme.com/magazine
  Editor, Krissi Murison
NEW SCIENTIST
Lacon House, 84 Theobalds Road, London WC1X 8NS
  T 020-7611 1200 **W** www.newscientist.com
  Editor, Jeremy Webb

NEW STATESMAN
7th Floor, John Carpenter House, John Carpenter Street,
  London EC4Y 0AN **T** 020-7730 3444
  W www.newstatesman.co.uk
  Editor, Jason Cowley
THE NEWSPAPER
Young Media Holdings Ltd, PO Box 400, Bridgwater TA6 9DT
  T 0845-094 0646 **W** www.thenewspaper.org.uk
  Managing Editor, Phil Wood
NOW
IPC Connect, The Blue Fin Building, 110 Southwark Street,
  London SE1 0SU **T** 020-3148 5000
  W www.nowmagazine.co.uk
  Editor, Sally Eyden
OK!
Northern & Shell Building, 10 Lower Thames Street, London
  EC3R 6EN **T** 0871-434 1010 **W** www.ok-magazine.com
  Editor, Lisa Byrne
THE OLDIE
65 Newman Street, London W1T 3EG **T** 020-7436 8801
  W www.theoldie.co.uk
  Editor, Richard Ingrams
OPERA
36 Black Lion Lane, London W6 9BE **T** 020-8563 8893
  W www.opera.co.uk
  Editor, John Allison
OPERA NOW
241 Shaftesbury Avenue, London WC2H 8TF **T** 020-7333 1740
  W www.rhinegold.co.uk
  Editor, Ashutosh Khandekar
PC PRO
Dennis Publishing Ltd, 30 Cleveland Street, London W1T 4JD
  T 020-7907 6000 **W** www.pcpro.co.uk
  Editor, Barry Collins
PEACE NEWS
5 Caledonian Road, London N1 9DY **T** 020-7278 3344
  W www.peacenews.info
  Editors, Emily Johns and Milan Rai
THE PHOTOGRAPHER
PO Box 9337, Witham, Essex CM8 2UT **T** 01279-503871
  W www.bipp.com
  Editor, Jonathan Briggs
PICK ME UP
IPC Connect Ltd, The Blue Fin Building, 110 Southwark Street,
  London SE1 0SU **T** 020-3148 5000
  W www.pickmeupmagazine.co.uk
  Editor, Rachel Tompkins
POETRY LONDON
81 Lambeth Walk, London SE11 6DX **T** 020-7735 8880
  W www.poetrylondon.co.uk
  Editor, Colette Bryce
POETRY REVIEW
22 Betterton Street, London WC2H 9BX **T** 020-7420 9883
  W www.poetrysociety.org.uk
  Editor, Fiona Sampson
THE POLITICAL QUARTERLY
Wiley-Blackwell, 9600 Garsington Road, Oxford OX4 2DQ
  T 01865-776868 **W** www.wiley.com
  Editor, Andrew Gamble
PRACTICAL PARENTING
Magicalia Limited, 15–18 White Lion Street, Islington,
  London N1 9PD **T** 020-7843 8800
  W www.practicalparenting.co.uk
  Editor, Daniella Delaney
PRACTICAL PHOTOGRAPHY
Bauer, Media House, Lynchwood, Peterborough PE2 6EA
  T 01733-468000 **W** www.practicalphotography.co.uk
  Editor-in-Chief, Andrew James

PRESS GAZETTE
John Carpenter House, John Carpenter Street, London
EC4Y 0AN T 020-7936 6432 W www.pressgazette.co.uk
Editor, Dominic Ponsford
PRIDE
Pride House, 55 Battersea Bridge Road, London SW11 3AX
T 020-7228 3110 W www.pridemagazine.com
Publisher, C. Cushnie
PRIVATE EYE
6 Carlisle Street, London W1D 3BN T 020-7437 4017
W www.private-eye.co.uk
Editor, Ian Hislop
PROSPECT MAGAZINE
Prospect Publishing Ltd, 2 Bloomsbury Place, London
WC1A 2QA T 020-7255 1281
W www.prospect-magazine.co.uk
Editor, Bronwen Maddox
PSYCHOLOGIES
Hachette Filipacchi UK Ltd, 64 North Row, London W1K 7LL
T 020-7150 7000 W www.psychologies.co.uk
Editor, Louise Chunn
PULSE
CMP Medica Ltd, Ludgate House, 245 Blackfriars Road, London
SE1 9UY T 020-7921 8102 W www.pulsetoday.co.uk
Editor, Jo Haynes
Q MAGAZINE
Endeavour House, 189 Shaftesbury Avenue, London
WC2H 8JG T 020-7182 8000 W www.qthemusic.com
Editor, Paul Rees
RA MAGAZINE
Royal Academy of Arts, Burlington House, Piccadilly, London
W1J 0BD T 020-7300 5820 W www.ramagazine.org.uk
Acting Editor, Sarah Greenberg
RADIO TIMES
BBC Worldwide Ltd, 201 Wood Lane, London W12 7TQ
T 020-8433 3400 W www.radiotimes.com
Editor, Ben Preston
RAILWAY MAGAZINE
Media Centre, Morton Way, Horncastle, Lincs LN9 6JR
T 01507-529589 W www.railwaymagazine.co.uk
Editor, Nick Pigott
READER'S DIGEST
The Reader's Digest Association Ltd, 11 Westferry Circus,
Canary Wharf, London E14 4HE T 020-7715 8000
W www.readersdigest.co.uk
Editor-in-Chief, Gill Hudson
RED
Hachette Filipacchi UK Ltd, 64 North Row, London W1K 7LL
T 020-7150 7600 W www.redonline.co.uk
Editor-in-Chief, Sam Baker
RUGBY WORLD
IPC Media Ltd, 9th Floor, The Blue Fin Building, 110 Southwark
Street, London SE1 0SU T 020-3148 5000
Editor, Paul Morgan
RUNNER'S WORLD
Natmag Rodale Ltd, 33 Broadwick Street, London W1F 0DG
T 020-7339 4400 W www.runnersworld.co.uk
Editor, Andy Dixon
SAGA MAGAZINE
Saga Publishing Ltd, The Saga Building, Enbrook Park,
Sandgate, Folkestone, Kent CT20 3SE T 01303-771523
W www.saga.co.uk/saga-magazine
Editor, Katy Bravery
SCREEN INTERNATIONAL
EMAP Media, Greater London House, 1 Hampstead Road,
London NW1 7EJ T 020-7728 5000
W www.screendaily.com
Editor, Conor Dignam

SFX MAGAZINE
Future Publishing Ltd, 30 Monmouth Street, Bath BA1 2BW
T 01225-442244 W www.sfx.co.uk
Editor, Dave Bradley
SHOOTING TIMES AND COUNTRY MAGAZINE
IPC Inspire, The Blue Fin Building, 110 Southwark Street,
London SE1 0SU T 020-3148 4741
W www.shootingtimes.co.uk
Editor, Camilla Clark
SIGHT AND SOUND
BFI, 21 Stephen Street, London W1T 1LN T 020-7255 1444
W www.bfi.org.uk/sightandsound
Editor, Nick James
SKI + BOARD
The Ski Club of Great Britain, The White House, 57–63 Church
Road, London SW19 5SB T 020-8410 2010
W www.skiclub.co.uk
Editor, Arnie Wilson
SMARTPHONE ESSENTIALS
Imagine Publishing Ltd, Richmond House, 33 Richmond Hill,
Bournemouth BH2 6EZ W www.smartphonedaily.co.uk
Editor, Andy Betts
SNOOKER SCENE
Hayley Green Court, 130 Hagley Road, Halesowen, West
Midlands B63 1DY T 0121-585 9188
W www.snookerscene.com
Editor, Clive Everton
THE SPECTATOR
22 Old Queen Street, London SW1H 9HP T 020-7961 0200
W www.spectator.co.uk
Editor, Fraser Nelson
SPECTATOR BUSINESS
22 Old Queen Street, London SW1H 9HP T 020-7961 0200
W www.spectator.co.uk/business
Editor, Martin Vander Weyer
SPIRIT & DESTINY
H. Bauer Publishing, Academic House, 24–28 Oval Road,
London NW1 7DT T 020-7241 8000
Editor, Rhiannon Powell
THE STAGE
Stage House, 47 Bermondsey Street, London SE1 3XT
T 020-7403 1818 W www.thestage.co.uk
Editor, Brian Attwood
THE TABLET
1 King Street Cloisters, Clifton Walk, London W6 0GY
T 020-8748 8484 W www.thetablet.co.uk
Editor, Catherine Pepinster
TAKE A BREAK
H. Bauer Publishing, Academic House, 24–28 Oval Road,
London NW1 7DT T 020-7241 8000
W www.takeabreak.co.uk
Editor, Rebecca Fleming
TATE ETC
20 John Islip Street, London SW1P 4RG T 020-7887 8724
W www.tate.org.uk/tateetc
Editor, Simon Grant
TATLER
Vogue House, Hanover Square, London W1S 1JU
T 020-7499 9080 W www.tatler.co.uk
Editor, Catherine Ostler
THE TEACHER
National Union of Teachers, Hamilton House, Mabledon Place,
London WC1H 9BD T 020-7380 4708
Editor, Elyssa Campbell-Barr
THE TES
26 Red Lion Square, Holborn WC1R 4HQ T 020-3194 3000
W www.tes.co.uk
Editor, Gerard Kelly

TGO (THE GREAT OUTDOORS) MAGAZINE
Newsquest, 200 Renfield Street, Glasgow G2 3QB
T 0141-302 7736 W www.tgomagazine.co.uk
Editor, Emily Rodway

TIME OUT LONDON
Time Out Group Ltd, Universal House, 251 Tottenham Court
Road, London W1T 7AB T 020-7813 3000
W www.timeout.com
Acting Editor, Mark Frith

TLS (THE TIMES LITERARY SUPPLEMENT)
3 Thomas More Square, London E98 1BS T 020-7782 5000
W www.the-tls.co.uk
Editor, Peter Stothard

TOTAL FILM
2 Balcombe Street, London NW1 6NW T 020-7042 4000
W www.totalfilm.com
Editor, Aubrey Day

TRIBUNE
9 Arkwright Road, London NW3 6AN T 020-7433 6410
Editor, Chris McLaughlin

VANITY FAIR
The Condé Nast Publications Ltd, Vogue House, Hanover
Square, London W1S 1JU T 020-7499 9080
W www.vanityfair.com
Editor-in-Chief, Graydon Carter

VENUE
Bristol News & Media, Temple Way, Bristol BS99 7HD
T 0117-942 8491 W www.venue.co.uk
Editor, Joe Spurgeon

VIZ
Dennis Publishing, 30 Cleveland Street, London W1T 4JD
T 020-7907 6000 W www.viz.co.uk
Editor, Hampton Doubleday

VOGUE
Vogue House, 1 Hanover Square, London W1S 1JU
T 020-7499 9080 W www.vogue.co.uk
Editor, Alexandra Shulman

THE VOICE
6th Floor, Northern & Shell Tower, 4 Selsdon Way,
London E14 9GL T 020-7510 0340
W www.voice-online.co.uk
Editor, Steve Pope

WALK
The Ramblers' Association, 2nd Floor, Camelford House, 87–90
Albert Embankment, London SE1 7TW T 020-7339 8540
W www.walkmag.co.uk
Editor, Dominic Bates

WALLPAPER
IPC Media, The Blue Fin Building, 110 Southwark Street,
London SE1 0SU T 020-3148 5000 W www.wallpaper.com
Editor-in-Chief, Tony Chambers

WATERSTONE'S BOOKS QUARTERLY
Seven Squared, Sea Containers House, 20 Upper Ground,
London SE1 9PD T 020-7775 5777
W www.subscribeonline.com/wbq
Editor, Keeley Young

WEDDING MAGAZINE
Hubert Burda Media Ltd, Swan House, 37–39 High Holborn,
London WC1V 6AA T 020-7421 5000
W www.weddingmagazine.co.uk
Editor, Catherine Westwood

THE WEEK
The Week Ltd, 6th Floor, Compass House, 22 Redan Place,
London W2 4SA T 020-7907 6180 W www.theweek.co.uk
Editor, Caroline Law

WEIGHT WATCHERS MAGAZINE
River Publishing Ltd, 1 Neal Street, London WC2H 9QL
T 020-7306 0304
Editor, Mary Frances

WHAT CAR?
Haymarket Motoring Magazines Ltd, Teddington Studios,
Broom Road, Teddington, Middlesex TW11 9BE
T 020-8267 5688 W www.whatcar.com
Group Editor, Steve Fowler

WHO DO YOU THINK YOU ARE?
BBC Magazines Bristol, 9th Floor, Tower House, Fairfax Street,
Bristol BS1 3BN T 0117-314 7400
W www.whodoyouthinkyouaremagazine.com
Editor, Sarah Williams

THE WISDEN CRICKETER
2nd Floor, 123 Buckingham Palace Road, London SW1W 9SL
T 020-7705 4911 W www.wisdencricketer.com
Editor, John Stern

WOMAN'S OWN
IPC Connect Ltd, The Blue Fin Building, 110 Southwark Street,
London SE1 0SU T 020-3148 5000
Editor, Vicky Mayer

WOMAN'S WEEKLY
IPC Connect Ltd, The Blue Fin Building, 110 Southwark Street,
London SE1 0SU T 020-3148 5000
Editor, Diane Kenwood

THE WORD
Development Hell Ltd, 90–92 Pentonville Road, London N1 9HS
T 020-7078 8400 W www.wordmagazine.co.uk
Editor, Mark Ellen

WORLD SOCCER
IPC Inspire, The Blue Fin Building, 110 Southwark Street,
London SE1 0SU T 020-3148 5000
W www.worldsoccer.com
Editor, Gavin Hamilton

THE WORLD TODAY
Chatham House, 10 St James's Square, London SW1Y 4LE
T 020-7957 5712 W www.theworldtoday.org
Editor, Graham Walker

WRITING MAGAZINE
5th Floor, 31–32 Park Row, Leeds LS1 5JD T 0113-200 2929
W www.writersnews.co.uk
Editor, Jonathan Telfer

YACHTING MONTHLY
IPC Media, The Blue Fin Building, 110 Southwark Street,
London SE1 0SU T 020-3148 5000
W www.yachtingmonthly.com
Editor, Paul Gelder

YOGA & HEALTH
Yoga Today Ltd, PO Box 2130, Seaford, Sussex BN25 9BF
T 01323-872466 W www.yogaandhealthmag.co.uk
Editor, Jane Sill

YOUNG WRITER MAGAZINE
5th Floor, 31–32 Park Row, Leeds LS1 5JD T 0113-200 2929
W www.youngwriter.org
Editor, Matthew Hill

YOUR CAT MAGAZINE
BPG (Stamford) Ltd, Roebuck House, 33 Broad Street, Stamford,
Lincs. PE9 1RB T 01780-766199 W www.yourcat.co.uk
Editor, Sue Parslow

YOUR DOG MAGAZINE
BPG (Stamford) Ltd, Roebuck House, 33 Broad Street, Stamford,
Lincs. PE9 1RB T 01780-766199 W www.yourdog.co.uk
Editor, Sarah Wright

YOURS
Bauer Publishing, Media House, Peterborough Business Park,
Peterborough PE2 6EA T 01733-468000
W www.yours.co.uk
Editor, Valery McConnell

ZEST
National Magazine House, 72 Broadwick Street, London
W1F 9EP T 020-7439 5000 W www.zest.co.uk
Editor, Mandie Gower

INTERNET

INTERNET TRENDS

The number of UK households with an internet connection continued to increase in 2010, with 900,000 connecting since 2009. This brought the UK's total up to 73 per cent – some 19.2 million households. Of the total number of new internet users in 2010, over half (around 1 million people) were 50 years or older. However, 60 per cent of over 65 year-olds had still never used the internet.

The steady increase in home-based internet has coincided with a drop in the use of internet cafes: only 3 per cent of users had accessed the internet this way in 2010, down by half since 2009. Conversely, the number of users connecting via wifi hotspots had quadrupled since 2007, while the number of UK adults going online on their mobile phone went from one quarter in 2009 to nearly one third.

TOP 10 BROADBAND SUBSCRIBERS BY COUNTRY

Country (2009 position)	2010
1. China (all territories) (1)	136,496,883
2. USA (2)	87,172,827
3. Japan (3)	34,467,000
4. Germany (4)	26,715,350
5. France (5)	19,887,530
6. UK (6)	19,607,600
7. South Korea (7)	17,202,641
8. Italy (8)	14,257,650
9. Brazil (9)	12,656,200
10. Russia (13)	11,619,000

Source: www.point-topic.com

With the proliferation of connection methods came the ability to log on more frequently, and for longer periods. The number of UK adults connecting to the internet at least once a day has increased steadily over the two years since 2008, from 69 per cent to 78 per cent in 2010.

The year also saw an increase in average broadband speeds, which in turn precipitated a shift in usage trends. With the average UK speed increasing by over 25 per cent, more users could take advantage of bandwidth-hungry services, such as watching TV and films, downloading music or uploading images. Of all online media consumption, it was gaming that proved most popular, usurping film- and music-downloading on the top spot. Being more immersive than web-browsing or email, these activities, in addition to the time spent on social networking sites and blogs, added significantly to the time users spent connected: the average UK user was online for over 22 hours a month in 2010.

Despite these various media applications, it was communication that once again proved most popular among users: 90 per cent of all users had sent or received email, and the most popular internet application was Microsoft's instant messenger programme, Windows Live Messenger. Social networking also showed no sign of losing its appeal: nearly a quarter of all web time was spent browsing these sites.

• The internet's second most popular use in 2010 was

information gathering: three quarters of users had searched the web to find information on goods and services
• 56 per cent of the total UK population visited Google during May 2010
• One fifth of internet users believed that, by virtue of its inclusion on a search engine, information found online was accurate and unbiased

Sources: ONS, *Statistical Bulletin: Internet Access 2010*; Ofcom, *The Communications Market 2010*

GLOSSARY OF TERMS

The following is a list of selected internet terms. It is by no means exhaustive but is intended to cover those that the average computer user might encounter.

BANNER AD: An advertisement on a web page that links to a corresponding website when clicked.

BLOG: Short for 'web log' – an online personal journal that is frequently updated and intended to be read by the public. Blogs are kept by 'bloggers' and are commonly available as RSS feeds.

BROWSER: Typically refers to a 'web browser' program that allows a computer user to view web page content on their computer, eg Firefox, Internet Explorer or Safari.

CLICK-THROUGH: The number of times a web user 'clicks through' a paid advertisement link to the corresponding website.

CLOUD COMPUTING: The use of IT resources as an on-demand service across a network; through cloud computing, software, advanced computation and archived information can be accessed remotely, without the user needing local dedicated hardware.

COOKIE: A piece of information placed on a user's hard disk by a web server. Cookies contain data about the user's activity on a website, and are returned to the server whenever a browser makes further requests. They are important for remembering information such as login and registration details, 'shopping cart' data, user preferences etc, and are often set to expire after a fixed period.

CSS: Cascading Style Sheet – a standard for specifying the appearance of text. It provides a single 'library' of styles that are used throughout a large number of related documents.

DOMAIN: A set of words or letters, separated by dots, used to identify an internet server, eg www.whitakersalmanack.co.uk, where 'www' denotes a web (http) server, 'whitakersalmanack' denotes the organisation name, 'co' denotes that the organisation is a company and 'uk' indicates United Kingdom. (For a complete list of country suffixes see Internet Domain Names).

FTP: File Transfer Protocol – a set of network rules enabling a user to exchange files with a remote server.

HACKER: A person who attempts to break or 'hack' into websites. Motives typically involve the desire to procure personal information such as addresses, passwords or credit card details. Hackers may also delete code or incorporate traces of malicious code to damage the functionality of a website. The malicious activities of a hacker might be simulated by a 'penetration tester', someone legitimately employed to test the security of information systems.

HIT: A single request from a web browser for a single item from a web server. In order for a web browser to display a page that contains three graphics, four 'hits' would occur at the server: one for the HTML page and one for each of the three graphics. Therefore the number of hits on a website is not synonymous with the number of visitors.

HTML: HyperText Mark-up Language – a programming language used to denote or mark up how an internet page should be presented to a user from an HTTP server via a web browser.

HTTP: HyperText Transfer Protocol – an internet protocol whereby a web server sends web pages, images and files to a web browser.

HYPERLINK: A piece of specially coded text that users can click on to navigate to the web page, or element of a web page, associated with that link's code. Links are typically distinguished through the use of bold, underlined, or differently coloured text.

MALWARE: A combination of the words 'malicious' and 'software'. Malware is software designed with the specific intention of infiltrating a computer and damaging its system.

META TAG: A type of HTML tag that contains information not normally displayed to the user. Meta tags are typically used to include information for search engines to help them categorise a page.

MP3: A popular audio compression format allowing quicker transmission of files for later playback on personal computers and music players.

MPEG: Motion Picture Encoding Group – a popular format standard for compressing video and audio information for transmission over the internet and later playback on personal computers and hand-held devices.

OPEN CONTENT: Copyrighted information that is made available by the owner to the general public under licence terms that allow reuse of the material, often with the requirement that the reuser grant the public the same rights to the modified version. Information that is in the 'public domain' might also be considered a form of open content.

OPEN-SOURCE: Describes a computer program that has its source code (the instructions that make up a program) freely available for viewing and modification.

P2P: Peer to peer – the act of a computer on one network communicating to a computer on a different network. The communication usually involves the sharing of files between computers.

PAGERANK: A link analysis algorithm used by search engines that assigns a numerical value based on a website's relevance and reputation. In general, a site with a higher pagerank has more traffic than a site with a lower one.

PODCASTING: A form of audio and video broadcasting using the internet. Although the word is a portmanteau of 'iPod' and broadcasting, podcasting does not require the use of an iPod. A podcaster creates a list of files and makes it available in the RSS 2.0 format. The list can then be obtained using podcast 'retriever' software which makes the files available to digital devices (including, but not limited to, iPods); users may then listen or watch at their convenience.

RSS FEED: Rich Site Summary or RDF Site Summary or Real Simple Syndication – a commonly used protocol for syndication and sharing of content, originally developed to facilitate the syndication of news articles, now widely used to share the content of blogs.

SEO: Search engine optimisation – the process of optimising the content of a web page to ensure that a website is properly set up and structured to be indexed by search engines.

SERVER: A node on a network that provides service to the terminals on the network. These computers have higher hardware specifications, ie more resources and greater speed, in order to handle large amounts of data.

SOCIAL NETWORKING: The practice of using a web-hosted service such as Facebook or MySpace to upload and share content and build friendship networks.

SPAM: A term used for unsolicited, generally junk, email. Junk email is becoming a major issue, with some estimates suggesting that spam is becoming more prevalent than legitimate email. Many legislatures around the globe are taking steps to ban or regulate spam.

SPOTIFY: A peer-to-peer music streaming service that allows users to share songs and playlists.

TRAFFIC: The number of visitors to a website.

TROLL: Someone who posts controversial, inflammatory or irrelevant messages on a blog or other online discussion forum in order to disrupt on-topic discussion or provoke other users into an emotional response.

TWITTER: An online microblogging service that allows users to stay connected through the exchange of 140-character posts, known as 'tweets'.

URL: Uniform Resource Locator – address of a file accessible on the internet, eg http://www.whitakersalmanack.com

USER-GENERATED CONTENT (UGC): Refers to various media content produced or primarily influenced by end-users, as opposed to traditional media producers such as licensed broadcasters and production companies. These forms of media include digital video, blogging, podcasting, mobile phone photography and wikis.

VISIBILITY: How visible a website is to search engines and browsers.

VOIP: Voice Over Internet Protocol – various technologies used to make telephone calls over computer networks, especially the internet. Just as modems allow computers to connect to the internet over regular telephone lines, VOIP technology allows telephone calls to take place over internet connections. Costs for VOIP calls are usually much lower than for traditional telephone calls.

WEB 2.0: Generally refers to a second generation of services available on the web that lets people collaborate and share information online. In contrast to the static web pages of the first generation, Web 2.0 gives users an experience closer to that of desktop applications.

WIDGET: A piece of software that provides access to online information items or to functions which the user accesses on a regular basis.

WIKI: Software that allows users to freely create and edit web page content using any web browser. Theoretically this encourages the democratic use of the internet and promotes content composition by non-technical users.

BOOK PUBLISHERS

This is a selection of UK publishers and is not an exhaustive list. For more information refer to the *Writers' & Artists' Yearbook*, published by Bloomsbury Publishing Plc.

ANDERSEN PRESS LTD
20 Vauxhall Bridge Road, London SW1V 2SA T 020-7840 8701
W www.andersenpress.co.uk
Children's books: picture books, junior and teenage fiction. Founded 1976

ANOVA BOOKS
The Old Magistrate's Court, 10 Southcombe Street, London W14 0RA T 020-7605 1400 W www.anovabooks.com
Illustrated books. Founded 2005

ANVIL PRESS POETRY
Neptune House, 70 Royal Hill, London SE10 8RF
T 020-8469 3033 W www.anvilpresspoetry.com
Poetry. Founded 1968

ARCADIA BOOKS LTD
15–16 Nassau Street, London W1W 7AB T 020-7436 9898
W www.arcadiabooks.co.uk
Fiction, fiction in translation, autobiography, biography, travel, gay and gender studies. Founded 1996

ATLANTIC BOOKS
Ormond House, 26–27 Boswell Street, London WC1N 3JZ
T 020-7269 1610 W www.atlantic-books.co.uk
Literary fiction, history, current affairs, politics, reference, biography and memoir. Founded 2000

BERG PUBLISHERS
50 Bedford Square, London WC1B 3DP T 020-7631 5600
W www.bergpublishers.com
Fashion studies, design studies, food studies, cultural studies, visual culture, social anthropology and film studies. Founded 1983

BLACK DOG PUBLISHING LTD
10A Acton Street, London WC1X 9NG T 020-7713 5097
W www.blackdogonline.com
Contemporary art, architecture, design and photography

JOHN BLAKE PUBLISHING LTD
3 Bramber Court, 2 Bramber Road, London W14 9PB
T 020-7381 0666 W www.johnblakepublishing.co.uk
Popular non-fiction, biographies, food and drink, true crime and health. Founded 1991

BLOODAXE BOOKS LTD
Highgreen, Tarset, Northumberland NE48 1RP T 01434-240500
W www.bloodaxebooks.com
Poetry. Founded 1978

BLOOMSBURY PUBLISHING PLC
50 Bedford Square, London WC1B 3DP T 020-7631 5600
W www.bloomsbury.com
Fiction, biography, illustrated, travel, children's, trade paperbacks, mass market paperbacks, art and craft, drama, reference, sport and theatre. Founded 1986

BRITISH MUSEUM COMPANY LTD
38 Russell Square, London WC1B 3QQ T 020-7323 1234
W www.britishmuseum.co.uk
Adult and children's books on art history, archaeology, history and world cultures. Founded 1973

CAMBRIDGE UNIVERSITY PRESS
The Edinburgh Building, Shaftesbury Road, Cambridge CB2 8RU
T 01223-312393 W www.cambridge.org
Academic books. Founded 1534

CANONGATE BOOKS LTD
14 High Street, Edinburgh EH1 1TE T 0131-557 5111
W www.canongate.net
Adult general non-fiction and fiction, literary fiction, translated fiction, memoir, politics, pop science, humour, travel, popular culture, history and biography. Founded 1973

CONSTABLE & ROBINSON LTD
3 The Lanchesters, 162 Fulham Palace Road, London W6 9ER
T 020-8741 3663 W www.constablerobinson.com
Literary and crime fiction, current affairs, health, history and self-help. Founded 1795 (Constable); 1983 (Robinson)

THE CONTINUUM INTERNATIONAL PUBLISHING GROUP LTD
The Tower Building, 11 York Road, London SE1 7NX
T 020-7922 0880 W www.continuumbooks.com
Serious non-fiction, academic and professional

GERALD DUCKWORTH & CO. LTD
First Floor, 90–93 Cowcross Street, London EC1M 6BF
T 020-7490 7300 W www.ducknet.co.uk
General trade publishers; strong academic division. Founded 1898

EARTHSCAN
Dunston House, 14A St Cross Street, London EC1N 8XA
T 020-7841 1930 W www.earthscan.co.uk
Academic and professional: sustainable development, climate and energy, natural resource management, cities and built environment, business, economics and design and technology

EDINBURGH UNIVERSITY PRESS
22 George Square, Edinburgh EH8 9LF T 0131-650 4218
W www.euppublishing.com
Academic publishers of scholarly books and journals

EGMONT UK LTD
239 Kensington High Street, London W8 6SA T 020-7761 3500
W www.egmont.co.uk
Children's books. Founded 1878

ENCYCLOPAEDIA BRITANNICA (UK) LTD
2nd Floor, Unity Wharf, 13 Mill Street, London SE1 2BH
T 020-7500 7800 W www.britannica.co.uk

PUBLISHERS' FAMILY TREE

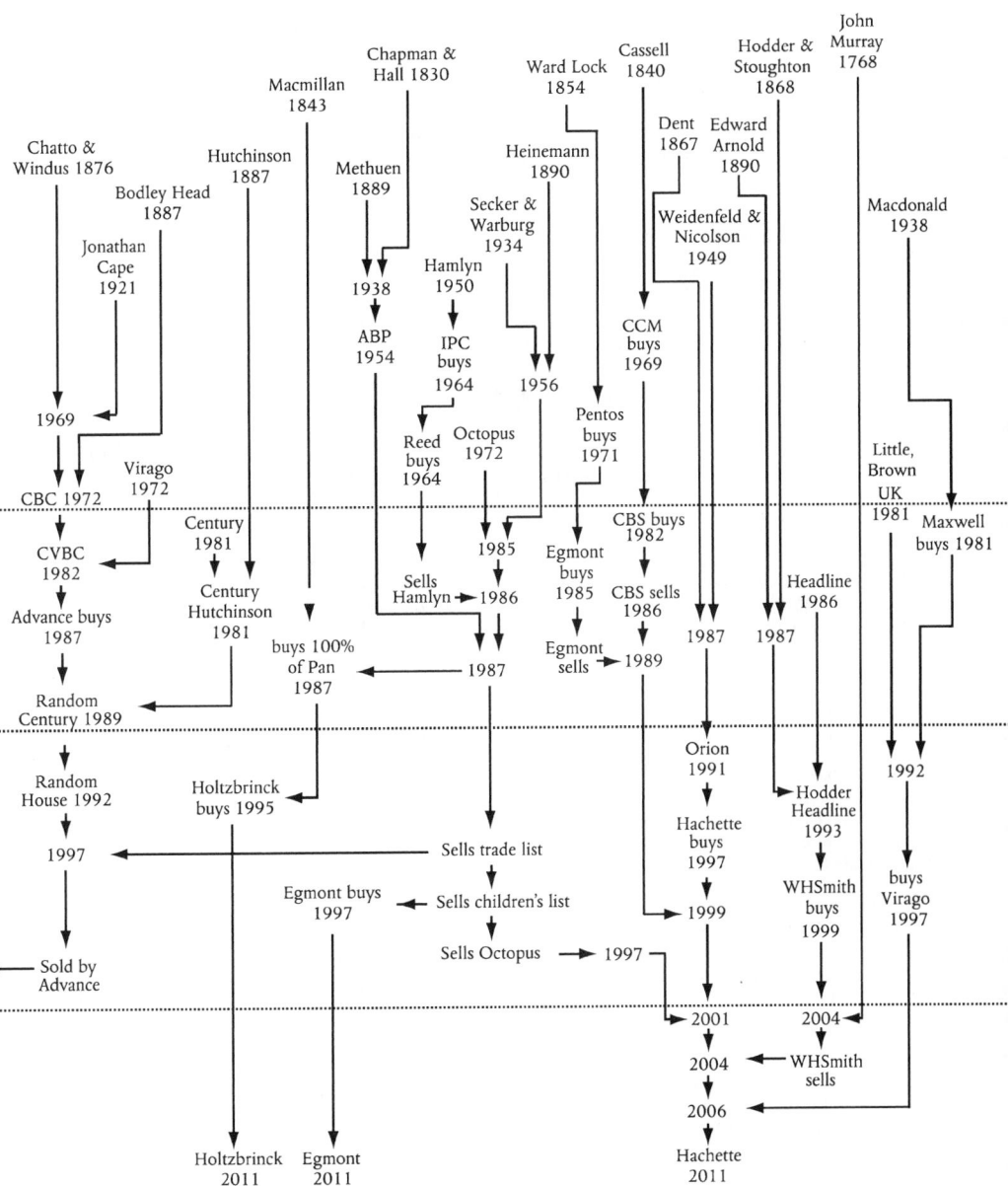

© **Bertoli Mitchell**

FABER AND FABER LTD
Bloomsbury House, 74–77 Great Russell Street, London
WC1B 3DA **T** 020-7927 3800 **W** www.faber.co.uk
High-quality general fiction and non-fiction, children's
fiction and non-fiction, drama, film, music and poetry

FABIAN SOCIETY
11 Dartmouth Street, London SW1H 9BN **T** 020-7227 4900
W www.fabians.org.uk
Current affairs, political thought, economics, education,
environment, foreign affairs and social policy. Founded
1884

SAMUEL FRENCH LTD
52 Fitzroy Street, London W1T 5JR **T** 020-7387 9373
W www.samuelfrench-london.co.uk
Plays. Founded 1830

GRANTA BOOKS
12 Addison Avenue, London W11 4QR **T** 020-7605 1360
W www.grantabooks.com
Literary fiction, memoir, nature writing, travel and history.
Founded 1982

HACHETTE UK
338 Euston Road, London NW1 3BH **T** 020-7873 6000
W www.hachette.co.uk
Fiction and non-fiction

HARLEQUIN MILLS & BOON LTD
Eton House, 18–24 Paradise Road, Richmond, Surrey TW9 1SR
T 020-8288 2800 **W** www.millsandboon.co.uk
Romance fiction. Founded 1908

HARPERCOLLINS PUBLISHERS
77–85 Fulham Palace Road, London W6 8JB **T** 020-8741 7070
W www.harpercollins.co.uk
Popular fiction and non-fiction. Founded 1819

THE HISTORY PRESS LTD
The Mill, Brimscombe Port, Stroud, Glos. GL5 2QG
T 01453-883300 **W** www.thehistorypress.co.uk
History, transport, biography, archaeology, sport, heritage,
leisure and walking

HODDER & STOUGHTON
338 Euston Road, London NW1 3BH **T** 020-7873 6000
W www.hodder.co.uk
Fiction, autobiography, biography, history, humour,
lifestyle and cookery. Founded 1868

ICON BOOKS LTD
The Omnibus Business Centre, 39–41 North Road, London
N7 9DP **T** 020-7697 9695 **W** www.iconbooks.co.uk
Popular non-fiction: *Introducing* series, literature, history,
philosophy, politics, psychology, sociology and cultural
studies. Founded 1991

LAURENCE KING PUBLISHING LTD
361–373 City Road, London EC1V 1LR **T** 020-7841 6900
W www.laurenceking.co.uk
Illustrated books: design, contemporary architecture, art,
interiors and fashion. Founded 1976

KOGAN PAGE LTD
120 Pentonville Road, London N1 9JN **T** 020-7278 0433
W www.koganpage.com
Training, business and management, finance and
accounting, human resource management and directories.
Founded 1967

FRANCES LINCOLN LTD
4 Torriano Mews, Torriano Avenue, London NW5 2RZ
T 020-7284 4009 **W** www.frances-lincoln.com
Illustrated,   international   co-editions: gardening,
architecture, environment, interiors, art, walking and
climbing, gift and children's books. Founded 1977

LITTLE, BROWN BOOK GROUP
100 Victoria Embankment, London EC4Y 0DY
T 020-7911 8000 **W** www.littlebrown.co.uk
Fiction and general non-fiction. Founded 1988

LONELY PLANET
2nd Floor, 186 City Road, London EC1V 2NT **T** 020-7106 2100
W www.lonelyplanet.com
Country, regional and city guidebooks

MCGRAW-HILL EDUCATION
McGraw-Hill House, Shoppenhangers Road, Maidenhead,
Berks. SL6 2QL **T** 01628-502500 **W** www.mcgraw-hill.co.uk
Higher education and professional

MACMILLAN PUBLISHERS LTD
The Macmillan Building, 4 Crinan Street, London N1 9XW
T 020-7833 4000 **W** www.macmillan.com
Academic, education, fiction and non-fiction and
reference

METHUEN PUBLISHING LTD
8 Artillery Row, London SW1P 1RZ **T** 020-7802 0018
W www.methuen.co.uk
Literary fiction and non-fiction

JOHN MURRAY (PUBLISHERS)
338 Euston Road, London NW1 3BH **T** 020-7873 6000
W www.johnmurray.co.uk
Commercial fiction and non-fiction: travel, history,
entertainment, reference, biography and memoir. Founded
1768

W.W. NORTON & COMPANY
Castle House, 75–76 Wells Street, London W1T 3QT
T 020-7323 1579 **W** www.wwnorton.co.uk
English and American literature, economics, music,
psychology and science. Founded 1980

OBERON BOOKS
521 Caledonian Road, London N7 9RH **T** 020-7607 3637
W www.oberonbooks.com
New and classic play texts, programme texts and general
theatre and performing arts books. Founded 1986

OMNIBUS PRESS
14–15 Berners Street, London W1T 3LJ **T** 020-7612 7400
W www.omnibuspress.com
Rock music biographies and general music. Founded
1976

ONEWORLD PUBLICATIONS
185 Banbury Road, Oxford OX2 7AR **T** 01865-310597
W www.oneworld-publications.com
Fiction and non-fiction, current affairs, politics, history,
popular science and green issues. Founded 1986

THE ORION PUBLISHING GROUP LTD
Orion House, 5 Upper St Martin's Lane, London WC2H 9EA
T 020-7240 3444 **W** www.orionbooks.co.uk
Fiction and non-fiction and audio. Founded 1992

OSPREY PUBLISHING LTD
Midland House, West Way, Botley, Oxford OX2 0PH
T 01865-727022 **W** www.ospreypublishing.com
Illustrated history of war and warfare. Founded 1968

OXFORD UNIVERSITY PRESS
Great Clarendon Street, Oxford OX2 6DP **T** 01865-556767
W www.oup.com
Academic, literature and reference. Founded 1478

PEARSON UK
Edinburgh Gate, Harlow, Essex CM20 2JE **T** 0845-313 6666
W www.pearsoned.co.uk
Education: business, technology, science, law and
humanities

PENGUIN GROUP
80 Strand, London WC2R 0RL **T** 020-7010 3000
W www.penguin.co.uk
Books for adults and children. Adult subjects include
biography, fiction, current affairs, general leisure, health,
history, humour, literature, politics, sports, travel and
TV/film tie-ins. Founded 1935

PROFILE BOOKS LTD
3A Exmouth House, Pine Street, London EC1R 0JH
T 020-7841 6300 **W** www.profilebooks.com
Non-fiction: history, biography, current affairs, popular
science and politics. Founded 1996

PUSHKIN PRESS
12 Chester Terrace, London NW1 4ND **T** 020-7730 0750
W www.pushkinpress.com
Continental European literature in translation. Founded
1997

THE QUARTO GROUP, INC.
226 City Road, London, EC1V 2TT **T** 020-7700 9000
W www.quarto.com
Independent publishing group encompassing traditional
and co-edition publishing

QUERCUS PUBLISHING PLC
21 Bloomsbury Square, London WC1A 2NS **T** 020-7291 7200
W www.quercusbooks.co.uk
Fiction and non-fiction. Founded 2005

THE RANDOM HOUSE GROUP LTD
20 Vauxhall Bridge Road, London SW1V 2SA **T** 020-7840 8400
W www.randomhouse.co.uk
Fiction and non-fiction

SCHOLASTIC LTD
Euston House, 24 Eversholt Street, London NW1 1DB
T 020-7756 7761 **W** www.scholastic.co.uk
Children's fiction and non-fiction and education
resources. Founded 1964

SIMON & SCHUSTER UK LTD
222 Gray's Inn Road, London WC1X 8HB **T** 020-7316 1900
W www.simonandschuster.co.uk
Commercial and literary fiction, general and serious
non-fiction and children's. Founded 1986

TASCHEN UK LTD
5th Floor, 1 Heathcock Court, 415 Strand, London WC2R 0NS
T 020-7845 8585 **W** www.taschen.com
Art, architecture, design, film, lifestyle, photography and
popular culture. Founded 1980

THAMES & HUDSON LTD
181A High Holborn, London WC1V 7QX **T** 020-7845 5000
W www.thamesandhudson.com
Illustrated non-fiction: art, architecture, graphic design,
garden and landscape design, archaeology, history,
fashion, photography, mythology and religion. Founded
1949

TITAN BOOKS
144 Southwark Street, London SE1 0UP **T** 020-7620 0200
W www.titanbooks.com
Graphic novels, film and TV tie-ins and cinema reference
books. Founded 1981

USBORNE PUBLISHING LTD
Usborne House, 83–85 Saffron Hill, London EC1N 8RT
T 020-7430 2800 **W** www.usborne.com
Children's books: fiction, reference, practical, craft,
natural history, science, languages, history, geography and
preschool. Founded 1973

V&A PUBLISHING
Victoria and Albert Museum, South Kensington, London
SW7 2RL **T** 020-7942 2964 **W** www.vandashop.com
Popular and scholarly books on fine and decorative
arts, architecture, contemporary design, fashion and
photography. Founded 1980

VERSO LTD
6 Meard Street, London W1V 3HR **T** 020-7437 3546
W www.verso.com
Current affairs, politics, sociology, economics, history,
philosophy and cultural studies. Founded 1970

WALKER BOOKS LTD
87 Vauxhall Walk, London SE11 5HJ **T** 020-7793 0909
W www.walker.co.uk
Children's: picture books, non-fiction and novelty titles,
junior and teenage fiction. Founded 1980

WILEY-BLACKWELL
9600 Garsington Road, Oxford OX4 2DQ **T** 01865-776868
W www.wiley.com
Books and journals in medicine, science, social sciences,
business and humanities

THE WOMEN'S PRESS
27 Goodge Street, London W1T 2LD **T** 020-7636 3992
W www.the-womens-press.com
Books by women in the areas of literary and crime fiction,
biography and autobiography, health, culture and politics.
Founded 1978

WORDSWORTH EDITIONS LTD
8B East Street, Ware, Herts. SG12 9HJ **T** 01920-465167
W www.wordsworth-editions.com
Reprints of classic books: literary, children's, poetry and
reference. Founded 1987

YALE UNIVERSITY PRESS LONDON
47 Bedford Square, London WC1B 3DP **T** 020-7079 4900
W www.yalebooks.co.uk
Art, architecture, history, economics, political science,
religion, history of science, biography, current affairs and
music. Founded 1961

ZED BOOKS LTD
7 Cynthia Street, London N1 9JF **T** 020-7837 4014
W www.zedbooks.co.uk
Social sciences on international issues. Founded 1976

TRADE AND PROFESSIONAL BODIES

The following is a list of employers' and trade associations and other professional bodies in the UK. It does not represent a comprehensive list. For further professional bodies *see* Professional Education.

ASSOCIATIONS

ADVERTISING ASSOCIATION 7th Floor North, Artillery House, 11–19 Artillery Row, London SW1P 1RT T 020-7340 1100 E aa@adassoc.org.uk W www.adassoc.org.uk
Chief Executive, Tim Lefroy

AEROSPACE DEFENCE SECURITY Salamanca Square, 9 Albert Embankment, London SE1 7SP T 020-7091 4500 E enquiries@adsgroup.org.uk W www.adsgroup.org.uk
Chief Executive, Rees Ward

AGRICULTURAL ENGINEERS ASSOCIATION Samuelson House, 62 Forder Way, Hampton, Peterborough PE7 8JB T 08456-448748 E ab@aea.uk.com W www.aea.uk.com
Chief Executive, Roger Lane-Nott

ASBESTOS REMOVAL CONTRACTORS ASSOCIATION ARCA House, 237 Branston Road, Burton upon Trent DE14 3BT T 01283-531126 E info@arca.org.uk W www.arca.org.uk
Chair, Mark Roberts

ASSOCIATION FOR CONSULTANCY AND ENGINEERING Alliance House, 12 Caxton Street, London SW1H 0QL T 020-7222 6557 E consult@acenet.co.uk W www.acenet.co.uk
Chief Executive, Nelson Ogunshakin, OBE

ASSOCIATION OF ACCOUNTING TECHNICIANS 140 Aldersgate Street, London EC1A 4HY T 020-7397 3000 E aat@aat.org.uk W www.aat.org.uk
Chief Executive, Jane Scott Paul

ASSOCIATION OF ANAESTHETISTS OF GREAT BRITAIN AND IRELAND 21 Portland Place, London W1B 1PY T 020-7631 1650 E info@aagbi.org W www.aagbi.org
President, Dr Iain H. Wilson

ASSOCIATION OF BRITISH INSURERS 51 Gresham Street, London EC2V 7HQ T 020-7600 3333 E info@abi.org.uk W www.abi.org.uk
Acting Director-General, Maggie Craig

ASSOCIATION OF BRITISH TRAVEL AGENTS (ABTA) 30 Park Street, London SE1 9EQ T 020-3117 0500 E abta@abta.co.uk W www.abta.com
Chief Executive, Mark Tanzer

ASSOCIATION OF BUILDING ENGINEERS Lutyens House, Billing Brook Road, Weston Favell, Northampton NN3 8NW T 01604-404121 E building.engineers@abe.org.uk W www.abe.org.uk
Chief Executive, John Hooper

ASSOCIATION OF BUSINESS RECOVERY PROFESSIONALS 8th Floor, 120 Aldersgate Street, London EC1A 4JQ T 020-7566 4200 E association@r3.org.uk W www.r3.org.uk
Chief Executive, Graham Rumney

ASSOCIATION OF CONSULTING SCIENTISTS 5 Willow Heights, Cradley Heath B64 7PL T 0121-602 3515 E secretary@consultingscientists.co.uk W www.consultingscientists.co.uk
Director, Dr Stuart Guy

ASSOCIATION OF CONVENIENCE STORES LTD Federation House, 17 Farnborough Street, Farnborough GU14 8AG T 01252-515001 E acs@acs.org.uk W www.acs.org.uk
Chief Executive, James Lowman

ASSOCIATION OF CORPORATE TREASURERS 51 Moorgate, London EC2R 6BH T 020-7847 2540 E enquiries@treasurers.org W www.treasurers.org
Chief Executive, Stuart Siddall

ASSOCIATION OF COUNCIL SECRETARIES AND SOLICITORS Afon Building, Worthing Road, Horsham RH12 1TL T 01483-788249 E admin@acses.org.uk W www.acses.org.uk
President, Susan Tovey

ASSOCIATION OF DRAINAGE AUTHORITIES 12 Cranes Drive, Surbiton KT5 8AL T 020-8399 7350 E admin@ada.org.uk W www.ada.org.uk
Chief Executive, Jean Venables, CBE FRENG

ASSOCIATION OF ELECTRICITY PRODUCERS Charles House, 5–11 Regent Street, London SW1Y 4LR T 020-7930 9390 E enquiries@aepuk.com W www.aepuk.com
Chief Executive, David Porter

BAR ASSOCIATION FOR LOCAL GOVERNMENT AND THE PUBLIC SERVICE c/o Birmingham City Council, Ingleby House, 11–14 Cannon Street, Birmingham B2 5EN T 0121-303 9991 E chairman@balgps.org.uk W www.balgps.org.uk
Chair, Dr Mirza Ahmad

BOOKSELLERS ASSOCIATION OF THE UK & IRELAND LTD Minster House, 272 Vauxhall Bridge Road, London SW1V 1BA T 020-7802 0802 E mail@booksellers.org.uk W www.booksellers.org.uk
Chief Executive, T. E. Godfray

BRITISH ANTIQUE DEALERS' ASSOCIATION 20 Rutland Gate, London SW7 1BD T 020-7589 4128 E info@bada.org W www.bada.org
Chair, Ian H. Walker

BRITISH ASSOCIATION OF SOCIAL WORKERS 16 Kent Street, Birmingham B5 6RD T 0121-622 3911 E info@basw.co.uk W www.basw.co.uk
Chief Executive, Hilton Dawson

BRITISH BANKERS' ASSOCIATION Pinners Hall, 105–108 Old Broad Street, London EC2N 1EX T 020-7216 8800 E info@bba.org.uk W www.bba.org.uk
Chief Executive, Angela Knight, CBE

BRITISH BEER AND PUB ASSOCIATION Market Towers, 1 Nine Elms Lane, London SW8 5NQ T 020-7627 9191 E web@beerandpub.com W www.beerandpub.com
Chief Executive, Brigid Simmonds, OBE

BRITISH CHAMBERS OF COMMERCE 65 Petty France, St James Park, London SW1H 9EU T 020-7654 5800 E info@britishchambers.org.uk W www.britishchambers.org.uk
Director-General, David Frost

BRITISH ELECTROTECHNICAL AND ALLIED MANUFACTURERS ASSOCIATION (BEAMA) Westminster Tower, 3 Albert Embankment, London SE1 7SL T 020-7793 3000 E info@beama.org.uk W www.beama.org.uk
Chief Executive, Dr Howard Porter

BRITISH HOROLOGICAL INSTITUTE Upton Hall, Upton, Newark NG23 5TE T 01636-813795 E clocks@bhi.co.uk W www.bhi.co.uk
Chair, Richard Thomas

BRITISH HOSPITALITY ASSOCIATION Queens House, 55–56 Lincoln's Inn Fields, London WC2A 3BH T 020-7404 7744 E bha@bha.org.uk W www.bha.org.uk
Chief Executive, Ufi Ibrahim

BRITISH INSTITUTE OF PROFESSIONAL PHOTOGRAPHY 1 Prebendal Court, Oxford Road, Aylesbury HP19 8EY T 01296-718530 E info@bipp.com W www.bipp.com
Chief Executive, Chris Harper, FBIPP

BRITISH INSURANCE BROKERS' ASSOCIATION 8th Floor, John Stow House, 18 Bevis Marks, London EC3A 7JB T 0870-950 1790 E enquiries@biba.org.uk W www.biba.org.uk
Chief Executive, Eric Galbraith

BRITISH MARINE FEDERATION Marine House, Thorpe Lea Road, Egham TW20 8BF T 01784-473377 E info@britishmarine.co.uk W www.britishmarine.co.uk
Chief Executive, Rob Stevens

BRITISH MEDICAL ASSOCIATION BMA House, Tavistock Square, London WC1H 9JP T 020-7387 4499 W www.bma.org.uk
Chief Executive, Tony Bourne

BRITISH OFFICE SUPPLIES AND SERVICES (BOSS) FEDERATION Farringdon Point, 29–35 Farringdon Road, EC1M 3JF T 0845-450 1565 E info@bossfederation.co.uk W www.bossfederation.co.uk
Chief Executive, Michael Gardner

BRITISH PHONOGRAPHIC INDUSTRY Riverside Building, County Hall, Westminster Bridge Road, London SE1 7JA T 020-7803 1390 E general@bpi.co.uk W www.bpi.co.uk
Chief Executive, Geoff Taylor

BRITISH PLASTICS FEDERATION 5–6 Bath Place, Rivington Street, London EC2A 3JE T 020-7457 5000 E reception@bpf.co.uk W www.bpf.co.uk
Director-General, Peter Davis, OBE

BRITISH PORTS ASSOCIATION 4th Floor Carthusian Court, 12 Carthusian Street, London EC1M 6EZ T 020-7260 1780 E info@britishports.org.uk W www.britishports.org.uk
Director, David Whitehead

BRITISH PRINTING INDUSTRIES FEDERATION Farringdon Point, 29–35 Farringdon Road, London EC1M 3JF T 020-7915 8300 W www.britishprint.com
Chief Executive, Michael Johnson

BRITISH PROPERTY FEDERATION 5th Floor, St Albans house, 57–59 Haymarket, London SW1Y 4QX T 020-7828 0111 E info@bpf.org.uk W www.bpf.org.uk
Chief Executive, Liz Peace

BRITISH RETAIL CONSORTIUM 2nd Floor, 21 Dartmouth Street, London SW1H 9BP T 020-7854 8900 E info@brc.org.uk W www.brc.org.uk
Director-General, Stephen Robertson

BRITISH TYRE MANUFACTURERS' ASSOCIATION LTD 5 Berewyk Hall Court, White Colne, Colchester CO6 2QD T 01787-226995 E mail@btmauk.com W www.btmauk.com
Chief Executive, Graham Willson

BUILDING SOCIETIES ASSOCIATION York House, 23 Kingsway, London WC2B 6UJ T 020-7520 5900 E simon.rex@bsa.org.uk W www.bsa.org.uk
Director-General, Adrian Coles

CHAMBER OF SHIPPING LTD Carthusian Court, 12 Carthusian Street, London EC1M 6EZ T 020-7417 2800 E postmaster@british-shipping.org W www.british-shipping.org
Director-General, Mark Brownrigg

CHARTERED INSTITUTE OF ENVIRONMENTAL HEALTH Chadwick Court, 15 Hatfields, London SE1 8DJ T 020-7928 6006 E information@cieh.org W www.cieh.org
Chief Executive, Graham Jukes

CHARTERED INSTITUTE OF JOURNALISTS 2 Dock Offices, Surrey Quays Road, London SE16 2XU T 020-7252 1187 E memberservices@cioj.co.uk W www.cioj.co.uk
General Secretary, Dominic Cooper

CHARTERED INSTITUTE OF PURCHASING AND SUPPLY Easton House, Easton on the Hill, Stamford PE9 3NZ T 01780-756777 E info@cips.org W www.cips.org
Chief Executive, David Noble

CHARTERED INSTITUTE OF TAXATION 1st Floor Artillery House, 11–19 Artillery Row, London SW1P 1RT T 020-7340 0550 E post@ciot.org.uk W www.tax.org.uk
Chief Executive, Peter Fanning

CHARTERED INSURANCE INSTITUTE 42–48 High Road, South Woodford, London E18 2JP T 020-8989 8464 E customer.serv@cii.co.uk W www.cii.co.uk
Chief Executive, Dr Alexander Scott

CHARTERED MANAGEMENT INSTITUTE Management House, Cottingham Road, Corby NN17 1TT T 01536-204222 E enquiries@managers.org.uk W www.managers.org.uk
Chief Executive, Ruth Spellman, OBE

CHARTERED QUALITY INSTITUTE 12 Grosvenor Crescent, London SW1X 7EE T 020-7245 6722 E info@thecqi.org W www.thecqi.org
Chair, Peter Bennett

CHEMICAL INDUSTRIES ASSOCIATION Kings Buildings, Smith Square, London SW1P 3JJ T 020-7834 3399 E enquiries@cia.org.uk W www.cia.org.uk
Chief Executive, Steve Elliott

CONFEDERATION OF PAPER INDUSTRIES 1 Rivenhall Road, Swindon SN5 7BD T 01793-889600 E cpi@paper.org.uk W www.paper.org.uk
Director-General, David Workman

CONFEDERATION OF PASSENGER TRANSPORT UK Drury House, 34–43 Russell Street, London WC2B 5HA T 020-7240 3131 E admin@cpt-uk.org W www.cpt-uk.org
Chief Executive, Simon Posner

CONSTRUCTION PRODUCTS ASSOCIATION The Building Centre, 26 Store Street, London WC1E 7BT T 020-7323 3770 E enquiries@constructionproducts.org.uk W www.constructionproducts.org.uk
Chief Executive, Michael Ankers, OBE

DAIRY UK 93 Baker Street, London W1U 6QQ T 020-7486 7244 E info@dairyuk.org W www.dairyuk.org
Chair, Robert Wiseman

EEF, THE MANUFACTURERS' ORGANISATION Broadway House, Tothill Street, London SW1H 9NQ T 020-7222 7777 E enquiries@eef.org.uk W www.eef.org.uk
Chief Executive, Terry Scuoler

FEDERATION OF BAKERS 6 Catherine Street, London WC2B 5JW T 020-7420 7190 E info@bakersfederation.org.uk W www.bakersfederation.org.uk
Director, Gordon Polson

FEDERATION OF MASTER BUILDERS Gordon Fisher House, 14–15 Great James Street, London WC1N 3DP T 020-7242 7583 E central@fmb.org.uk W www.fmb.org.uk
Director-General, Richard Diment

FEDERATION OF SPORTS AND PLAY ASSOCIATIONS Federation House, Stoneleigh Park, CV8 2RF T 024-7641 4999 E info@sportsandplay.com W www.sportsandplay.com
Managing Director, Jane Montgomery

FINANCE AND LEASING ASSOCIATION 2nd Floor, Imperial House, 15–19 Kingsway, London WC2B 6UN T 020-7836 6511 E info@fla.org.uk W www.fla.org.uk
Director-General, Stephen Sklaroff

FOOD AND DRINK FEDERATION 6 Catherine Street, London WC2B 5JJ T 020-7836 2460 E generalenquiries@fdf.org.uk W www.fdf.org.uk
Director-General, Melanie Leech

FREIGHT TRANSPORT ASSOCIATION LTD Hermes House, St John's Road, Tunbridge Wells TN4 9UZ T 01892-526171 E enquiries@fta.co.uk W www.fta.co.uk
Chief Executive, Theo de Pencier

GLASGOW CHAMBER OF COMMERCE 30 George Square, Glasgow G2 1EQ T 0141-204 2121 E chamber@glasgowchamber.org W www.glasgowchamber.org
President, James Andrew

INSTITUTE FOR ARCHAEOLOGISTS School of Human and Environmental Science, Whiteknights, University of Reading, PO Box 227 RG6 6AB T 0118-378 6446 E admin@archaeologists.net W www.archaeologists.net
Hon. Chair, Gerry Wait

INSTITUTE OF ADMINISTRATIVE MANAGEMENT 6 Graphite Square, Vauxhall Walk, London SE11 5EE T 020-7091 2600 E info@instam.org W www.instam.org
Chief Executive, Jenny Hewell

INSTITUTE OF BREWING AND DISTILLING 33 Clarges Street, London W1J 7EE T 020-7499 8144 E enquiries@ibd.org.uk W www.ibd.org.uk
Executive Director, Simon Jackson

INSTITUTE OF BRITISH ORGAN BUILDING 13 Ryefields, Thurston, Bury St Edmunds IP31 3TD T 01359-233433 E administrator@ibo.co.uk W www.ibo.co.uk
President, Martin Goetze

INSTITUTE OF CHARTERED FORESTERS 59 George Street, Edinburgh EH2 2JG T 0131-240 1425 E icf@charteredforesters.org W www.charteredforesters.org
Executive Director, Shireen Chambers

INSTITUTE OF CHARTERED SECRETARIES AND ADMINISTRATORS 16 Park Crescent, London W1B 1AH T 020-7580 4741 E info@icsa.org.uk W www.icsa.org.uk
Chief Executive, David Wilson

INSTITUTE OF CHARTERED SHIPBROKERS 85 Gracechurch Street, London EC3V 0AT T 020-7623 1111 E enquiries@ics.org.uk W www.ics.org.uk
President, Alan Marsh

INSTITUTE OF DIRECTORS 116 Pall Mall, London SW1Y 5ED T 020-7766 8866 E enquiries@iod.com W www.iod.com
Chief Operating Officer, Andrew Main Wilson

INSTITUTE OF EXPORT Export House, Minerva Business Park, Lynch Wood, Peterborough PE2 6FT T 01733-404400 E institute@export.org.uk W www.export.org.uk
Director General, Lesley Batchelor

INSTITUTE OF FINANCIAL ACCOUNTANTS Burford House, 44 London Road, Sevenoaks TN13 1AS T 01732-458080 E mail@ifa.org.uk W www.ifa.org.uk
Chief Executive, David Woodgate

INSTITUTE OF HEALTHCARE MANAGEMENT 18–21 Morley Street, London SE1 7QZ T 020-7620 1030 E enquiries@ihm.org.uk W www.ihm.org.uk
Chief Executive, Susan Hodgetts

INSTITUTE OF HOSPITALITY Trinity Court, 34 West Street, Sutton, Surrey SM1 1SH T 020-8661 4900 E info@instituteofhospitality.org W www.instituteofhospitality.org
Chief Executive, Philippe Rossiter

INSTITUTE OF INTERNAL COMMUNICATION Suite GA2, Oak House, Woodlands Business Park, Breckland, Linford Wood West MK14 6EY T 01908-313755 E enquiries@cib.uk.com W www.cib.uk.com
Chief Executive, Steve Doswell

INSTITUTE OF MANAGEMENT SERVICES Brooke House, 24 Dam Street, Lichfield WS13 6AA T 01543-266 909 E admin@ims-stowe.fsnet.co.uk W www.ims-productivity.com
Chair, David Blanchflower

INSTITUTE OF QUARRYING 7 Regent Street, Nottingham NG1 5BS T 0115-945 3880 E mail@quarrying.org W www.quarrying.org
Executive Director, Jack Berridge

INSTITUTE OF ROAD SAFETY OFFICERS 12 Haddon Close, Wellingborough, Northants NN8 5ZB T 0870-010 4442 E irso@live.co.uk W www.irso.org.uk
Acting Chair, Darren Divall

INSTITUTE OF THE MOTOR INDUSTRY Fanshaws, Brickendon, Hertford SG13 8PQ T 01992-511521 E imi@motor.org.uk W www.motor.org.uk
Executive Chair, Sarah Sillars, OBE

INSTITUTION OF OCCUPATIONAL SAFETY AND HEALTH The Grange, Highfield Drive, Wigston LE18 1NN T 0116-257 3100 E techinfo@iosh.co.uk W www.iosh.co.uk
Chief Executive, Rob Strange, OBE

IP FEDERATION 5th Floor, 63–66 Hatton Garden, London EC1N 8LE T 020-7242 3923 E admin@ipfederation.com W www.ipfederation.com
President, James R. Hayles

MAGISTRATES' ASSOCIATION 28 Fitzroy Square, London W1T 6DD T 020-7387 2353 E information@magistrates-association.org.uk W www.magistrates-association.org.uk
Executive Director, Patrick Cracroft-Brennan

MANAGEMENT CONSULTANCIES ASSOCIATION 60 Trafalgar Square, London WC2N 5DS T 020-7321 3990 E info@mca.org.uk W www.mca.org.uk
Chief Executive, Alan Leaman, OBE

MASTER LOCKSMITHS ASSOCIATION 5D Great Central Way, Wood Halse, Daventry, Northants NN11 3PZ T 01327-262 255 E enquiries@locksmiths.co.uk W www.locksmiths.co.uk
Chair, Roger Barratt

NATIONAL ASSOCIATION OF BRITISH MARKET AUTHORITIES The Guildhall, Oswestry, Shrops SY11 1PZ T 01691-680713 E nabma@nabma.com W www.nabma.com
Chief Executive, Graham Wilson

NATIONAL ASSOCIATION OF ESTATE AGENTS Arbon House, 6 Tournament Court, Edgehill Drive, Warwick CV34 6LG T 01926-496800 E info@nfopp.co.uk W www.naea.co.uk
President, Peter Bolton King

NATIONAL CATTLE ASSOCIATION (DAIRY) Brick House, Risbury, Leominster HR6 0NQ T 01568-760632 E timbrigstocke@hotmail.com
Executive Secretary, Tim Brigstocke, MBE

NATIONAL FARMERS' UNION (NFU) Agriculture House, Stoneleigh Park, Stoneleigh CV8 2TZ T 024-7685 8500 E tom.sales@nfu.org.uk W www.nfuonline.com
President, Peter Kendall

NATIONAL FEDERATION OF RETAIL NEWSAGENTS Yeoman House, Sekforde Street, London EC1R 0HF T 020-7253 4225 E service@nfrnonline.com W www.nfrnonline.com
President, Kieran McDonnell

NATIONAL LANDLORDS ASSOCIATION 22–26 Albert Embankment, London SE1 7TJ T 020-7840 8900 E info@landlords.org.uk W www.landlords.org.uk
Chair, David Salusbury

NATIONAL MARKET TRADERS FEDERATION Hampton House, Hawshaw Lane, Hoyland, Barnsley S74 0HA T 01226-749021 E genoffice@nmtf.co.uk W www.nmtf.co.uk
Chief Executive, Joe Harrison

NATIONAL PHARMACY ASSOCIATION Mallinson House, 38–42 St Peter's Street, St Albans, Herts AL1 3NP T 01727-858687 E npa@npa.co.uk W www.npa.co.uk
Chief Executive, Mike Holden

NEWSPAPER SOCIETY St Andrew's House, 18–20 St Andrew Street, London EC4A 3AY T 020-7632 7400 E ns@newspapersoc.org.uk W www.newspapersoc.org.uk
Director, David Newell

OIL AND GAS UK 6th Floor East, Portland House, Bressenden Place, London SW1E 5BH T 020-7802 2400 E info@oilandgasuk.co.uk W www.oilandgasuk.co.uk
Chief Executive, Malcolm Webb

PROPERTY CARE ASSOCIATION Lakeview Court, Ermine Business Park, Huntingdon PE29 6XR T 0844-375 4301 E pca@property-care.org W www.property-care.org
General Manager, Stephen Hodgson

PUBLISHERS ASSOCIATION 29B Montague Street, London WC1B 5BW T 020-7691 9191 E mail@publishers.org.uk W www.publishers.org.uk
Chief Executive, Richard Mollet

RADIOCENTRE 4th Floor, 5 Golden Square, London W1F 9BS T 020-3206 7800 E info@radiocentre.org W www.radiocentre.org
Chief Executive, Andrew Harrison

ROAD HAULAGE ASSOCIATION LTD Roadway House, Bretton PE3 8DD T 01733-261131 E southern-eastern@rha.uk.net W www.rha.uk.net
Chief Executive, Geoff Dunning

ROYAL ASSOCIATION OF BRITISH DAIRY FARMERS Dairy House, Unit 31, Abbey Park, Stareton, Kenilworth CV8 2LY T 0845-458 2711 E office@rabdf.co.uk W www.rabdf.co.uk
Chief Executive, Nick Everington

ROYAL FACULTY OF PROCURATORS IN GLASGOW 12 Nelson Mandela Place, Glasgow G2 1BT T 0141-332 3593 E library@rfpg.org W www.rfpg.org
Chief Executive, John McKenzie

SHELLFISH ASSOCIATION OF GREAT BRITAIN Fishmongers' Hall, London Bridge, London EC4R 9EL T 020-7283 8305 E tom@shellfish.org.uk W www.shellfish.org.uk
Director, Dr Tom Pickerell

SOCIETY OF LOCAL AUTHORITY CHIEF EXECUTIVES AND SENIOR MANAGERS Hope House, 45 Great Peter Street, London SW1P 3LT T 020-7233 0081 E hope.house@solace.org.uk W www.solace.org.uk
Director-General, David Clark

SOCIETY OF MOTOR MANUFACTURERS AND TRADERS LTD Forbes House, Halkin Street, London SW1X 7DS T 020-7235 7000 W www.smmt.co.uk
Chief Executive, Paul Everitt

TIMBER TRADE FEDERATION The Building Centre, 26 Store Street, London WC1E 7BT T 020-3205 0067 E ttf@ttf.co.uk W www.ttf.co.uk
Chief Executive, John White

TRADING STANDARDS INSTITUTE 1 Sylvan Court, Sylvan Way, Southfields Business Park, Basildon SS15 6TH T 0845-608 9400 E institute@tsi.org.uk W www.tradingstandards.gov.uk
Chief Executive, Ron Gainsford

UK FASHION AND TEXTILE INDUSTRY 3 Queen Square, Bloomsbury, London WC1N 3AR T 020-7843 9460 E info@ukft.org W www.ukft.org
Chair, Peter Lucas

UK LEATHER FEDERATION Leather Trade House, Kings Park Road, Moulton Park, Northampton NN3 6JD T 01604-679917 E info@uklf.org W www.ukleather.org
Director, Paul Pearson

UK PETROLEUM INDUSTRY ASSOCIATION LTD Quality House, Quality Court, London WC2A 1HP T 020-7269 7600 E info@ukpia.com W www.ukpia.com
Director-General, Chris Hunt

ULSTER FARMERS' UNION 475 Antrim Road, Belfast BT15 3DA T 028-9037 0222 E info@ufuhq.com W www.ufuni.org
Chief Executive, Clarke Black

WINE AND SPIRIT TRADE ASSOCIATION International Wine and Spirit Centre, 39–45 Bermondsey Street, London SE1 3XF T 020-7089 3877 E info@wsta.co.uk W www.wsta.co.uk
Chief Executive, Jeremy Beadles

CBI

Centre Point, 103 New Oxford Street, London WC1A 1DU T 020-7379 7400 W www.cbi.org.uk

The CBI was founded in 1965 and is an independent non-party political body financed by industry and commerce. It works with the UK government, international legislators and policymakers to help UK businesses compete effectively. It is the recognised spokesman for the business viewpoint and is consulted as such by the government.

The CBI speaks for some 240,000 businesses that together employ approximately one-third of the private sector workforce. Member companies, which decide all policy positions, include 80 of the FTSE 100 index, some 200,000 small and medium-size firms, more than 20,000 manufacturers and over 150 sectoral associations.

The CBI board meets four times a year in London under the chairmanship of the president. It is assisted by 16 expert standing committees which advise on the main aspects of policy. There are 13 regional councils and offices, covering the administrative regions of England, Wales, Scotland and Northern Ireland. There are also offices in Beijing, Brussels, Delhi and Washington.
Director-General, John Cridland

WALES: 2 Caspian Point, Caspian Way, Cardiff Bay, Cardiff CF10 4DQ T 029-2097 7600
Regional Director, David Rosser

SCOTLAND: 16 Robertson Street, Glasgow G2 8DS T 0141-222 2184
Regional Director, Iain McMillan

NORTHERN IRELAND: Scottish Amicable Building, 11 Donegall Square, Belfast BT1 5JE T 028-9010 1100
Regional Director, Nigel Smyth

TRADE UNIONS

A trade union is an organisation of workers formed (historically) for the purpose of collective bargaining over pay and working conditions. Today, trade unions may also provide legal and financial advice, sickness benefits and education facilities to their members. Legally any employee has the right to join a trade union, but not all employers recognise all or any trade unions. Conversely an employee also has the right not to join a trade union, in particular since the practice of a 'closed shop' system, where all employees have to join the employer's preferred union, is no longer permitted. Below is a list of key dates in the development of the British trade unionist movement.

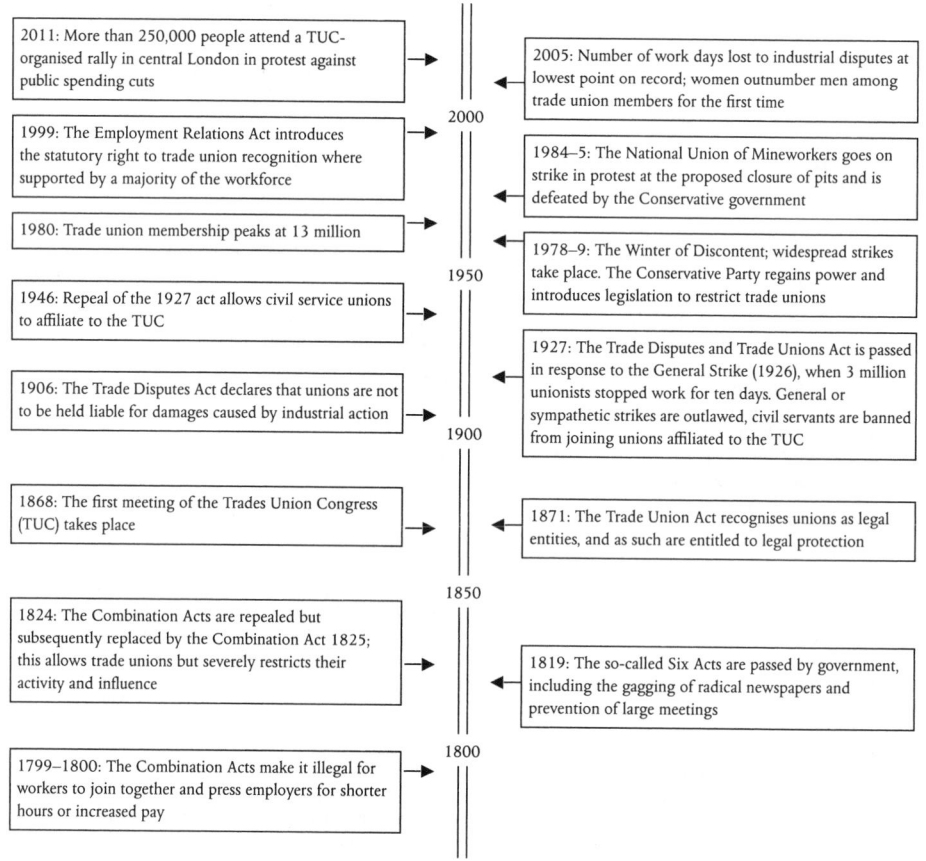

2011: More than 250,000 people attend a TUC-organised rally in central London in protest against public spending cuts

1999: The Employment Relations Act introduces the statutory right to trade union recognition where supported by a majority of the workforce

1980: Trade union membership peaks at 13 million

1946: Repeal of the 1927 act allows civil service unions to affiliate to the TUC

1906: The Trade Disputes Act declares that unions are not to be held liable for damages caused by industrial action

1868: The first meeting of the Trades Union Congress (TUC) takes place

1824: The Combination Acts are repealed but subsequently replaced by the Combination Act 1825; this allows trade unions but severely restricts their activity and influence

1799–1800: The Combination Acts make it illegal for workers to join together and press employers for shorter hours or increased pay

2005: Number of work days lost to industrial disputes at lowest point on record; women outnumber men among trade union members for the first time

1984–5: The National Union of Mineworkers goes on strike in protest at the proposed closure of pits and is defeated by the Conservative government

1978–9: The Winter of Discontent; widespread strikes take place. The Conservative Party regains power and introduces legislation to restrict trade unions

1927: The Trade Disputes and Trade Unions Act is passed in response to the General Strike (1926), when 3 million unionists stopped work for ten days. General or sympathetic strikes are outlawed, civil servants are banned from joining unions affiliated to the TUC

1871: The Trade Union Act recognises unions as legal entities, and as such are entitled to legal protection

1819: The so-called Six Acts are passed by government, including the gagging of radical newspapers and prevention of large meetings

2000

1950

1900

1850

1800

THE CENTRAL ARBITRATION COMMITTEE

22nd Floor, Euston Tower, 286 Euston Road, London NW1 3JJ
T 020-7904 2300 E enquiries@cac.gov.uk W www.cac.gov.uk
The Central Arbitration Committee's main role is concerned with requests for trade union recognition and de-recognition under the statutory procedures of Schedule A1 of the Employment Rights Act 1999. It also determines disclosure of information complaints under the Trade Union and Labour Relations (Consolidation) Act 1992, considers applications and complaints under the Information and Consultation Regulations 2004, and performs a similar role in relation to European works councils, European companies, European cooperative societies and cross-border mergers. It also provides voluntary arbitration in industrial disputes.
Chair, Sir Michael Burton
Chief Executive, Simon Gouldstone

TRADES UNION CONGRESS (TUC)

Congress House, 23–28 Great Russell Street, London WC1B 3LS T 020-7636 4030
E info@tuc.org.uk W www.tuc.org.uk
The Trades Union Congress, founded in 1868, is an independent association of trade unions. The TUC promotes the rights and welfare of those in work and helps the unemployed. It helps its member unions promote membership in new areas and industries, and

campaigns for rights at work for all employees, including part-time and temporary workers, whether union members or not. TUC representatives sit on many public bodies at national and international level such as government, political parties, employers and the European Union.

The governing body of the TUC is the annual congress. Between congresses, business is conducted by a general council, which meets five times a year, and an executive committee, which meets monthly. The full-time staff is headed by the general secretary who is elected by congress and is a permanent member of the general council.

There are 58 affiliated unions, with a total membership of nearly 6,300,000.

President (2010–11), Michael Leahy
General Secretary, Brendan Barber

SCOTTISH TRADES UNION CONGRESS (STUC)

333 Woodlands Road, Glasgow G3 6NG T 0141-337 8100 E info@stuc.org.uk W www.stuc.org.uk

The congress was formed in 1897 and acts as a national centre for the trade union movement in Scotland. The STUC promotes the rights to welfare of those in work and helps the unemployed. It helps its member unions to promote membership in new areas and industries, and campaigns for rights at work for all employees, including part-time temporary workers, whether union members or not. It also makes representations to government and employers. In April 2011 it consisted of 37 affiliated unions with a membership of more than 650,000 and 24 trades union councils.

The annual congress in April elects a 36-member general council on the basis of six sections.

President, Mike Kirby
General Secretary, Grahame Smith

WALES TUC

1 Cathedral Road, Cardiff CF11 9SD T 029-2034 7010 E wtuc@tuc.org.uk
W www.tuc.org.uk/tuc/regions_info_wales.cfm

The Wales TUC was established in 1974 to ensure that the role of the TUC was effectively undertaken in Wales. Its structure reflects the four economic regions of Wales and matches the regional committee areas of the National Assembly of Wales. The regional committees oversee the implementation of Wales TUC policy and campaigns in the relevant regions, and liaise with local government, training organisations and regional economic development bodies. The Wales TUC seeks to reduce unemployment, increase the levels of skill and pay, and eliminate discrimination.

The governing body of Wales TUC is the conference, which meets annually in May and elects a general council (usually of around 50 people) which oversees the work of the TUC throughout the year.

There are over 50 affiliated unions, with a total membership of around 500,000.

President, Sian Wiblin
General Secretary, Martin Mansfield

TUC-AFFILIATED UNIONS

As at April 2011

ACCORD Simmons House, 46 Old Bath Road, Charvil RG10 9QR T 0118-934 1808 E info@accordhq.org
W www.accord-myunion.org
General Secretary, Ged Nichols *Membership:* 29,027

ADVANCE (FORMERLY ANGU) 2nd Floor, 16–17 High Street, Tring HP23 5AH T 01442-891122
E info@advance-union.org W www.advance-union.org
General Secretary, Linda Rolph *Membership:* 6,800

AEGIS THE UNION AEGON UK Plc, Lochside Crescent, Edinburgh Park, Edinburgh EH12 9SE T 0131-549 5474
E aegismb@aegon.co.uk W www.aegistheunion.co.uk
General Secretary, Brian Linn *Membership:* 2,400

AEP (ASSOCIATION OF EDUCATIONAL PSYCHOLOGISTS) Unit 4, The Riverside Centre, Frankland Lane, Durham DH1 5TA T 0191-384 9512
E enquiries@aep.org.uk W www.aep.org.uk
General Secretary, Kate Fallon *Membership:* 3,287

AFA COUNCIL 7 (ASSOCIATION OF FLIGHT ATTENDANTS) United Airlines Cargo Centre, Shoreham Road East, Heathrow Airport TW6 3UA
T 020-8276 6723 E afalhr@unitedafa.org
W www.unitedafa.org/afa/mec/councils/7
President, Ronald Brunelle *Membership:* 600

ASLEF (ASSOCIATED SOCIETY OF LOCOMOTIVE ENGINEERS AND FIREMEN) 9 Arkwright Road, Hampstead, London NW3 6AB T 020-7317 8600
E info@aslef.org.uk W www.aslef.org.uk
General Secretary, Keith Norman *Membership:* 18,532

ASPECT Woolley Hall, Woolley WF4 2JR
T 01226-383428 E info@aspect.org.uk
W www.aspect.org.uk
General Secretary, John Chowcat *Membership:* 4,161

ATL (ASSOCIATION OF TEACHERS AND LECTURERS) 7 Northumberland Street, London WC2N 5RD T 020-7930 6441 E info@atl.org.uk
W www.atl.org.uk
General Secretary, Mary Bousted
Membership: 160,000

BACM-TEAM (BRITISH ASSOCIATION OF COLLIERY MANAGEMENT – TECHNICAL, ENERGY AND ADMINISTRATIVE MANAGEMENT) Danum House, 6A South Parade, Doncaster DN1 2DY T 01302-815551
E enquiries@bacmteam.org.uk W www.bacmteam.org.uk
General Secretary, Patrick Carragher
Membership: 2,537

BALPA (BRITISH AIRLINE PILOTS ASSOCIATION) BALPA House, 5 Heathrow Boulevard, 278 Bath Road, West Drayton UB7 0DQ T 020-8476 4000
E balpa@balpa.org W www.balpa.org
General Secretary, Jim McAuslan *Membership:* 10,000

BDA (BRITISH DIETETIC ASSOCIATION) 5th Floor, Charles House, 148–149 Great Charles Street, Birmingham B3 3HT T 0121-200 8080 E info@bda.uk.com
W www.bda.uk.com
Chief Executive, Andy Burman *Membership:* 6,700

BECTU (BROADCASTING, ENTERTAINMENT, CINEMATOGRAPH AND THEATRE UNION) 373–377 Clapham Road, London SW9 9BT
T 020-7346 0900 E info@bectu.org.uk W www.bectu.org.uk
General Secretary, Gerry Morrissey
Membership: 25,375

BFAWU (BAKERS, FOOD AND ALLIED WORKERS' UNION) Stanborough House, Great North Road, Stanborough, Welwyn Garden City AL8 7TA
T 01707-260150 E info@bfawu.org W www.bfawu.org
General Secretary, Ronnie Draper *Membership:* 22,000

BOS (BRITISH ORTHOPTIC SOCIETY)
14 Bedford Row, London WC1R 4ED T 020-7306 1135
E bos@orthoptics.org.uk W www.orthoptics.org.uk
Employment Relations Officer, Lesley-Anne Baxter
Membership: 913

BSU (BRITANNIA STAFF UNION) Court Lodge, Leonard Street, Leek ST13 5JP T 01538-399627 E staff.union@britannia.co.uk W www.britanniasu.org.uk *General Secretary,* John Stoddard *Membership:* 3,328

COMMUNITY 67–68 Long Acre, Covent Garden, London WC2E 9FA T 020-7420 4000 E info@community-tu.org W www.community-tu.org *General Secretary,* Michael Leahy, OBE *Membership:* 67,488

CSP (CHARTERED SOCIETY OF PHYSIOTHERAPY) 14 Bedford Row, London WC1R 4ED T 020-7306 6666 E enquiries@csp.org.uk W www.csp.org.uk *Chief Executive,* Phil Gray *Membership:* 50,000

CWU (COMMUNICATION WORKERS UNION) 150 The Broadway, Wimbledon, London SW19 1RX T 020-8971 7200 E info@cwu.org W www.cwu.org *General Secretary,* W. Hayes *Membership:* 211,208

EIS (EDUCATIONAL INSTITUTE OF SCOTLAND) 46 Moray Place, Edinburgh EH3 6BH T 0131-225 6244 E enquiries@eis.org.uk W www.eis.org.uk *General Secretary,* Ronald A. Smith *Membership:* 59,215

EQUITY Guild House, Upper St Martin's Lane, London WC2H 9EG T 020-7379 6000 E info@equity.org.uk W www.equity.org.uk *General Secretary,* Christine Payne *Membership:* 36,5253

FBU (FIRE BRIGADES UNION) Bradley House, 68 Coombe Road, Kingston upon Thames KT2 7AE T 020-8541 1765 E office@fbu.org.uk W www.fbu.org.uk *General Secretary,* Matt Wrack *Membership:* 43,000

FDA 8 Leake Street, London SE1 7NN T 020-7401 5555 E info@fda.org.uk W www.fda.org.uk *General Secretary,* Jonathan Baume *Membership:* 19,622

GMB 22–24 Worple Road, London SW19 4DD T 020-8947 3131 E info@gmb.org.uk W www.gmb.org.uk *General Secretary,* Paul Kenny *Membership:* 611,000

HCSA (HOSPITAL CONSULTANTS' AND SPECIALISTS' ASSOCIATION) 1 Kingsclere Road, Overton, Basingstoke RG25 3JA T 01256-771777 E conspec@hcsa.com W www.hcsa.com *Chief Executive,* Stephen Campion *Membership:* 3,450

MU (MUSICIANS' UNION) 60–62 Clapham Road, London SW9 0JJ T 020-7582 5503 E info@theMU.org W www.theMU.org *General Secretary,* John F. Smith *Membership:* 30,000

NACODS (NATIONAL ASSOCIATION OF COLLIERY OVERMEN, DEPUTIES AND SHOTFIRERS) Wadsworth House, 130–132 Doncaster Road, Barnsley S70 1TP T 01226-203743 E natnacods@googlemail.com W www.nacods.org.uk *General Secretary,* Rowland Soar *Membership:* 315

NACO (NATIONAL ASSOCIATION OF COOPERATIVE OFFICIALS) 6A Clarendon Place, Hyde SK14 2QZ T 0161-351 7900 E info@nacoco-op.org W www.naco.coop *President,* Karen Froggatt *Membership:* 2,196

NAPO (TRADE UNION AND PROFESSIONAL ASSOCIATION FOR FAMILY COURT AND PROBATION STAFF) 4 Chivalry Road, London SW11 1HT T 020-7223 4887 E info@napo.org.uk W www.napo.org.uk *General Secretary,* Jonathan Ledger *Membership:* 9,225

NASS (NATIONAL ASSOCIATION OF STABLE STAFF) 74A High Street, Swadlincote DE11 8HS T 01283-211522 E office@naoss.co.uk W www.naoss.co.uk *Chief Executive,* Jim Cornelius *Membership:* 1,703

NASUWT (NATIONAL ASSOCIATION OF SCHOOLMASTERS/UNION OF WOMEN TEACHERS) Hillscourt Education Centre, Rose Hill, Rednal, Birmingham B45 8RS T 0121-453 6150 E nasuwt@mail.nasuwt.org.uk W www.nasuwt.org.uk *General Secretary,* Ms Chris Keates *Membership:* 279,145

NAUTILUS INTERNATIONAL 1–2 The Shrubberies, George Lane, South Woodford, London E18 1BD T 020-8989 6677 E enquiries@nautilusint.org W www.nautilusint.org *General Secretary,* Mark Dickinson *Membership:* 22,000

NGSU (NATIONWIDE GROUP STAFF UNION) Middleton Farmhouse, 37 Main Road, Middleton Cheney OX17 2QT T 01295-710767 E ngsu@ngsu.org.uk W www.ngsu.org.uk *President,* Bill Blumsom *Membership:* 11,802

NUJ (NATIONAL UNION OF JOURNALISTS) Headland House, 308–312 Gray's Inn Road, London WC1X 8DP T 020-7843 3700 E info@nuj.org.uk W www.nuj.org.uk *General Secretary,* Michelle Stanistreet *Membership:* 35,000

NUM (NATIONAL UNION OF MINEWORKERS) Miners' Offices, 2 Huddersfield Road, Barnsley S70 2LS T 01226-215555 E chris.kitchen@num.org.uk W www.num.org.uk *President,* C. Kitchen *Membership:* 1,600

NUT (NATIONAL UNION OF TEACHERS) Hamilton House, Mabledon Place, London WC1H 9BD T 020-7388 6191 E enquiries@nut.org.uk W www.teachers.org.uk *General Secretary,* Christine Blower *Membership:* 375,042

OURS (ONE UNION FOR REGIONAL STAFF) 26 High Street, Mold, Flintshire CH7 1AZ T 01352-751512 *General Secretary,* Karen Hughes *Membership:* 656

PCS (PUBLIC AND COMMERCIAL SERVICES UNION) 160 Falcon Road, London SW11 2LN T 020-7924 2727 E editor@pcs.org.uk W www.pcs.org.uk *General Secretary,* Mark Serwotka *Membership:* 289,606

PFA (PROFESSIONAL FOOTBALLERS' ASSOCIATION) 20 Oxford Court, Bishopsgate, Manchester M2 3WQ T 0161-236 0575 E info@thepfa.co.uk W www.givemefootball.com *Chief Executive,* Gordon Taylor, OBE *Membership:* 2,713

POA (PROFESSIONAL TRADE UNION FOR PRISON, CORRECTIONAL AND SECURE PSYCHIATRIC WORKERS) Cronin House, 245 Church Street, London N9 9HW T 020-8803 0255 E general@poauk.org.uk W www.poauk.org.uk *General Secretary,* Steve Gillan *Membership:* 35,972

PROSPECT New Prospect House, 8 Leake Street, London SE1 7NN T 020-7902 6600 E enquiries@prospect.org.uk W www.prospect.org.uk *President,* Nigel Titchen *Membership:* 120,617

RMT (NATIONAL UNION OF RAIL, MARITIME AND TRANSPORT WORKERS) Unity House, 39 Chalton Street, London NW1 1JD T 020-7387 4771 E info@rmt.org.uk W www.rmt.org.uk *General Secretary,* Bob Crow *Membership:* 77,031

SCP (SOCIETY OF CHIROPODISTS AND PODIATRISTS) 1 Fellmonger's Path, Tower Bridge Road, London SE1 3LY T 0845-450 3720 E enq@scpod.org W www.feetforlife.org *General Secretary,* Joanna Brown *Membership:* 10,000

SOR (SOCIETY OF RADIOGRAPHERS) 207 Providence Square, Mill Street, London SE1 2EW **T** 020-7740 7200 **E** info@sor.org **W** www.sor.org
Chief Executive, Richard Evans *Membership:* 20,500

SURGE The Bailey, Harrogate Road, Skipton BD23 1DN **T** 0175-670 5826 **E** Brian.McDaid@skiptonunion.co.uk **W** www.skiptonunion.co.uk
General Secretary, Brian McDaid *Membership:* 1,890

TSSA (TRANSPORT SALARIED STAFFS' ASSOCIATION) Walkden House, 10 Melton Street, London NW1 2EJ **T** 020-7387 2101 **E** enquiries@tssa.org.uk **W** www.tssa.org.uk
General Secretary, Gerry Doherty *Membership:* 28,298

UCAC (UNDEB CENEDLAETHOL ATHRAWON CYMRU) (NATIONAL UNION OF THE TEACHERS OF WALES) Prif Swyddfa UCAC, Ffordd Penglais, Aberystwyth SY23 2EU **T** 01970-639950 **E** ucac@athrawon.com **W** www.athrawon.com
General Secretary, Elaine Edwards *Membership:* 4,477

UCATT (UNION OF CONSTRUCTION, ALLIED TRADES AND TECHNICIANS) UCATT House, 177 Abbeville Road, London SW4 9RL **T** 020-7622 2442 **E** info@ucatt.org.uk **W** www.ucatt.org.uk
Acting General Secretary, George Guy
Membership: 125,000

UCU (UNIVERSITY AND COLLEGE UNION) Carlow Street, London NW1 7LH **T** 020-7756 2500 **E** hq@ucu.org.uk **W** www.ucu.org.uk
General Secretary, Sally Hunt *Membership:* 120,000

UNISON 130 Euston Road, London NW1 2AY **T** 0845-355 0845 **W** www.unison.org.uk
General Secretary, Dave Prentis
Membership: 1,400,000

UNITE 128 Theobald's Road, London WC1Y 8TN **T** 020-7611 2500 **W** www.unitetheunion.org
General Secretary, Len McCluskey
Membership: 1,500,000

UNITY Hillcrest House, Garth Street, Hanley, Stoke-on-Trent ST1 2AB **T** 01782-272755 **E** geoffbagnall@unitytheunion.org.uk **W** www.unitytheunion.org.uk
General Secretary, Geoff Bagnall
Membership: 4,953

URTU (UNITED ROAD TRANSPORT UNION) Almond House, Oak Green, Stanley Green Business Park, Cheadle Hulme SK8 6QL **T** 0800-526639 **E** info@urtu.com **W** www.urtu.com
General Secretary, Robert Monks *Membership:* 16,000

USDAW (UNION OF SHOP, DISTRIBUTIVE AND ALLIED WORKERS) 188 Wilmslow Road, Manchester M14 6LJ **T** 0161-224 2804 **E** enquiries@usdaw.org.uk **W** www.usdaw.org.uk
General Secretary, John Hannett
Membership: 399,820

WRITERS' GUILD OF GREAT BRITAIN (WGGB) 40 Rosebery Avenue, London EC1R 4RX **T** 020-7833 0777 **E** admin@writersguild.org.uk **W** www.writersguild.org.uk
President, David Edgar *Membership:* 1,803

YORKSHIRE INDEPENDENT STAFF ASSOCIATION (YISA) c/o Yorkshire Building Society, Yorkshire House, Yorkshire Drive, Rooley Lane, Bradford BD5 8LJ **T** 01274-472453 **E** kmwatson@ybs.co.uk
Chair, Karen Watson *Membership:* 1,500

NON-AFFILIATED UNIONS

As at April 2011

ASCL (ASSOCIATION OF SCHOOL AND COLLEGE LEADERS) 130 Regent Road, Leicester LE1 7PG **T** 0116-299 1122 **E** info@ascl.org.uk **W** www.ascl.org.uk
General Secretary, Brian Lightman *Membership:* 15,300

BDA (BRITISH DENTAL ASSOCIATION) 64 Wimpole Street, London W1G 8YS **T** 020-7935 0875 **E** enquiries@bda.org **W** www.bda.org
Chief Executive, Peter Ward *Membership:* 23,349

CIOJ (CHARTERED INSTITUTE OF JOURNALISTS) 2 Dock Offices, Surrey Quays Road, London SE16 2XU **T** 020-7252 1187 **E** memberservices@cioj.co.uk **W** www.cioj.co.uk
General Secretary, Dominic Cooper *Membership:* 2,000

NAHT (NATIONAL ASSOCIATION OF HEAD TEACHERS) 1 Heath Square, Boltro Road, Haywards Heath RH16 1BL **T** 01444-472472 **E** info@naht.org.uk **W** www.naht.org.uk
General Secretary, Russell Hobby *Membership:* 27,500

NSEAD (NATIONAL SOCIETY FOR EDUCATION IN ART AND DESIGN) 3 Mason's Wharf, Potley Lane, Corsham SN13 9FY **T** 01225-810134 **E** info@nsead.org **W** www.nsead.org
General Secretary, Dr John Steers *Membership:* 2,057

RBA (RETAIL BOOK ASSOCIATION) 8–9 Commercial Road, Swindon SN1 5NF **T** 01793-864 848 **E** sarah@the-rba.org **W** www.the-rba.org
President, David Pickles *Membership:* 2,900

RCM (ROYAL COLLEGE OF MIDWIVES) 15 Mansfield Street, London W1G 9NH **T** 020-7312 3535 **E** info@rcm.org.uk **W** www.rcm.org.uk
General Secretary, Prof. Cathy Warwick, CBE
Membership: 38,000

SOCIETY OF AUTHORS 84 Drayton Gardens, London SW10 9SB **T** 020-7373 6642 **E** info@societyofauthors.org **W** www.societyofauthors.org
General Secretary, Nicola Solomon *Membership:* 8,980

SSTA (SCOTTISH SECONDARY TEACHERS' ASSOCIATION) West End House, 14 West End Place, Edinburgh EH11 2ED **T** 0131-313 7300 **E** info@ssta.org.uk **W** www.ssta.org.uk
General Secretary, Ann Ballinger *Membership:* 8,500

SPORTS BODIES

SPORTS COUNCILS

SPORT AND RECREATION ALLIANCE
Burwood House, 14 Caxton Street, London SW1H 0QT
T 020-7976 3900 E info@sportandrecreation.org.uk
W www.sportandrecreation.org.uk
Chief Executive, Tim Lamb
SPORT ENGLAND 3rd Floor, Victoria House, Bloomsbury
Square, London WC1B 4SE T 0845-850 8508
E info@sportengland.org W www.sportengland.org
Chief Executive, Jennie Price
SPORT NORTHERN IRELAND House of Sport,
2A Upper Malone Road, Belfast BT9 5LA T 028-9038 1222
E info@sportni.net W www.sportni.net
Chair, Dominic Walsh
SPORTSCOTLAND Doges, Templeton on the Green,
62 Templeton Street, Glasgow G40 1DA T 0141-534 6500
E sportscotland.enquiries@sportscotland.org.uk
W www.sportscotland.org.uk
Chief Executive, Stewart Harris
SPORTS COUNCIL FOR WALES Sophia Gardens,
Cardiff CF11 9SW T 0845-045 0904
E info@sportwales.org.uk
W www.sportswales.org.uk
Chief Executive, Dr Huw Jones
UK SPORT 40 Bernard Street, London WC1N 1ST
T 020-7211 5100 E info@uksport.gov.uk
W www.uksport.gov.uk
Chief Executive, Liz Nicholl, OBE

AMERICAN FOOTBALL

BRITISH AMERICAN FOOTBALL ASSOCIATION
West House, Hedley on the Hill, Stocksfield NE43 7SW
T 01661-843179 E bafachairman@gmail.com
W www.bafa.org.uk
Chair, Gary Marshall

ANGLING

ANGLING TRUST Eastwood House, 6 Rainbow Street,
Leominster, Herefordshire HR6 8DQ T 0844-770 0616
E admin@anglingtrust.net W www.anglingtrust.net
Chief Executive, Mark Lloyd

ARCHERY

GRAND NATIONAL ARCHERY SOCIETY Lilleshall
National Sports Centre, Newport TF10 9AT T 01952-677888
E enquiries@archerygb.org W www.archerygb.org
Chief Executive, David Sherratt

ASSOCIATION FOOTBALL

FOOTBALL ASSOCIATION Wembley Stadium, PO Box
1966, SW1P 9EQ T 020-7745 4545 W www.thefa.com
Chair, David Bernstein
FOOTBALL ASSOCIATION OF WALES
11–12 Neptune Court, Vanguard Way, Cardiff CF24 5PJ
T 029-2043 5830 E info@faw.org.uk W www.faw.org.uk
Chief Executive, Jonathan Ford
FOOTBALL LEAGUE Edward VII Quay, Navigation
Way, Preston PR2 2YF T 0844-463 1888
E enquiries@football-league.co.uk
W www.football-league.co.uk
Chief Operating Officer, A. G. Williamson
IRISH FOOTBALL ASSOCIATION 20 Windsor
Avenue, Belfast BT9 6EG T 028-9066 9458
E info@irishfa.com W www.irishfa.com
Chief Executive, Patrick Nelson

IRISH PREMIER LEAGUE 20 Windsor Avenue, Belfast
BT9 6EG T 028-9066 9458 E website@ifapremiership.com
W www.ifapremiership.com
General Secretary, Craig Stanfield
PREMIER LEAGUE 30 Gloucester Place, London W1U 8PL
T 020-7864 9000 E info@premierleague.com
W www.premierleague.com
Chief Executive, Richard Scudamore
SCOTTISH FOOTBALL ASSOCIATION
Hampden Park, Glasgow G42 9AY T 0141-616 6000
E info@scottishfa.co.uk W www.scottishfa.co.uk
Chief Executive, Stewart Regan
SCOTTISH FOOTBALL LEAGUE The National
Stadium, Hampden Park, Glasgow G42 9EB T 0141-620
4160 E info@scottishfootballleague.com
W www.scottishfootballleague.com
Chief Executive, David A. Longmuir

ATHLETICS

ATHLETICS NORTHERN IRELAND Athletics
House, Old Coach Road, Belfast BT9 5PR T 028-9060 2707
E info@niathletics.org W www.niathletics.org
General Secretary, John Allen
SCOTTISH ATHLETICS Caledonia House, South Gyle,
Edinburgh EH12 9DQ T 0131-539 7320
E admin@scottishathletics.org.uk
W www.scottishathletics.org.uk
Chief Executive, Nigel Holl
UK ATHLETICS Athletics House, Central Boulevard,
Blythe Valley Park, Solihull B90 8AJ T 0121-713 8400
W www.uka.org.uk
Chief Executive, Niels de Vos
WELSH ATHLETICS Cardiff International Sports
Stadium, Leckwith Road, Cardiff CF11 8AZ
T 029-2064 4870 E office@welshathletics.org
W www.welshathletics.org
Chief Executive Officer, Matt Newman

BADMINTON

BADMINTON ENGLAND National Badminton Centre,
Milton Keynes MK8 9LA T 01908-268400
E enquiries@badmintonengland.co.uk
W www.badmintonengland.co.uk
Chief Executive, Adrian Christy
BADMINTON SCOTLAND Cockburn Centre,
40 Bogmoor Place, Glasgow G51 4TQ T 0141-445 1218
E enquiries@badmintonscotland.org.uk
W www.badmintonscotland.org.uk
Chief Executive, Anne Smillie
WELSH BADMINTON UNION Sport Wales National
Centre, Sophia Gardens, Cardiff CF11 9SW T 0845-045
4301 E wbu@badmintonwales.net
W www.badmintonwales.net
Chief Executive, Eddie O'Neill

BASEBALL

BASEBALLSOFTBALL UK Ariel House, 74A Charlotte
Street, London W1T 4QJ T 020-7453 7055
W www.baseballsoftballuk.com
Head of Operations, Jenny Fromer

BASKETBALL

BASKETBALL SCOTLAND Caledonia House,
South Gyle, Edinburgh EH12 9DQ **T** 0131-317 7260
E enquiries@basketball-scotland.com
W www.basketballscotland.co.uk
Chair, Colin Pearson
ENGLAND BASKETBALL PO Box 3971, Sheffield
S9 9AZ **T** 0114-284 1060 **E** info@englandbasketball.co.uk
W www.englandbasketball.co.uk
Chief Executive, Keith Mair

BILLIARDS AND SNOOKER

WORLD LADIES BILLIARDS AND SNOOKER
ASSOCIATION 231 Ramnoth Road, Wisbech, PE13 2SN
T 01945-589589 **E** worldladiessnooker@ntlworld.com
W www.worldladiessnooker.co.uk
Chair, Mandy Fisher
WORLD SNOOKER 2nd Floor, Albert House, 111–117
Victoria Street, Bristol BS1 6AX **T** 0117-317 8200
E info@worldsnooker.com **W** www.worldsnooker.com
Chair, Barry Hearn

BOBSLEIGH

BRITISH BOBSLEIGH AND SKELETON
ASSOCIATION 9 Looke Lane, Puncknowle, Dorchester
DP2 9BD **T** 0845-901 447 **E** enquiries@bobteamgb.org
W www.bobteamgb.org
Chair, Andrew Ridgway

BOWLS

BOWLS ENGLAND Lyndhurst Road, Worthing
BN11 2AZ **T** 01903-820222 **E** enquiries@bowlsengland.com
W www.bowlsengland.com
Chief Executive, A. Allcock, MBE
BRITISH ISLES BOWLS COUNCIL 12/1 Oxgangs
Avenue, Edinburgh EH13 9JB **T** 01314-455838
E bibcsecretary@aol.co.uk **W** www.britishislesbowls.com
Hon. Secretary, Duncan Mclaren
ENGLISH INDOOR BOWLING ASSOCIATION
LIMITED David Cornwell House, Bowling Green, Melton
Mowbray LE13 0FA **T** 01664-481900
E enquiries@eiba.co.uk **W** www.eiba.co.uk
Chief Operating Executive, Peter Thompson

BOXING

AMATEUR BOXING ASSOCIATION OF
ENGLAND English Institute of Sport, Coleridge Road,
Sheffield S9 5DA **T** 0114-223 5654
E membership@abae.org.uk **W** www.abae.org.uk
Chief Executive, Mark Abberley
BRITISH BOXING BOARD OF CONTROL
14 North Road, Trinity Street, Cardiff CF10 3DY
T 029-2036 7000 **E** admin@bbbofc.com
W www.bbbofc.com
General Secretary, Robert Smith

CANOEING

BRITISH CANOE UNION 18 Market Place, Bingham,
Nottingham NG13 8AP **T** 0845-370 9500
E info@bcu.org.uk **W** www.bcu.org.uk
Chief Executive, Paul Owen

CHESS

ENGLISH CHESS FEDERATION The Watch Oak,
Chain Lane, Battle TN33 0YD **T** 01424-775222
E office@englishchess.org.uk **W** www.englishchess.org.uk
Chief Executive, Chris Majer

CRICKET

ENGLAND AND WALES CRICKET BOARD
Lord's Cricket Ground, London NW8 8QZ **T** 020-7432 1200
E feedback@ecb.co.uk **W** www.ecb.co.uk
Chief Executive, David Collier
MCC Lord's Cricket Ground, St John's Wood, London
NW8 8QN **T** 020-7616 8500 **E** reception@mcc.org.uk
W www.lords.org
Chief Executive, Keith Bradshaw

CROQUET

CROQUET ASSOCIATION Old Bath Road,
Cheltenham GL53 7DF **T** 01242-242318
E caoffice@croquet.org.uk **W** www.croquet.org.uk
President, Quiller Barrett

CURLING

BRITISH CURLING ASSOCIATION 51 Atholl Road,
Pitlochry, Perthshire PH16 5BU **T** 01463-242922
E info@britishcurling.co.uk **W** www.britishcurling.org.uk
Chair, Chris L. Hildrey
ROYAL CALEDONIAN CURLING CLUB Cairnie
House, Ingliston, Newbridge EH28 8NB **T** 0131-333 3003
E office@royalcaledoniancurlingclub.org
W www.royalcaledoniancurlingclub.org
Chief Executive Officer, Bruce Crawford

CYCLING

BRITISH CYCLING FEDERATION
National Cycling Centre, Stuart Street, Manchester
M11 4DQ **T** 0161-274 2000 **E** info@britishcycling.org.uk
W www.britishcycling.org.uk
Chief Executive, Ian Drake

DARTS

BRITISH DARTS ORGANISATION 2 Pages Lane,
Muswell Hill, London N10 1PS **T** 020-8883 5544
E britishdartsorg@btconnect.com **W** www.bdodarts.com
Chair, Dave Alderman

EQUESTRIANISM

BRITISH EQUESTRIAN FEDERATION Stoneleigh
Park, Kenilworth CV8 2RH **T** 024-7669 8871
E info@bef.co.uk **W** www.bef.co.uk
Chief Executive, Andrew Finding
BRITISH EVENTING Stoneleigh Park, Kenilworth
CV8 2RN **T** 0845-262 3344 **E** info@britisheventing.com
W www.britisheventing.com
Chief Executive, Mike Etherington-Smith

ETON FIVES

ETON FIVES ASSOCIATION 45 Sandhills Crescent,
Hillfield, Solihull B91 3UE **T** 07833-600230
E efa@etonfives.co.uk **W** www.fivesonline.net
Chair, Richard Barber, OBE

FENCING

BRITISH FENCING ASSOCIATION 1 Baron's Gate,
33–35 Rothschild Road, London W4 5HT **T** 020-8742 3032
E headoffice@britishfencing.com
W www.britishfencing.com
Chief Executive Officer, Piers Martin

GLIDING

BRITISH GLIDING ASSOCIATION 3rd Floor,
Kimberley House, Vaughan Way, Leicester LE1 4SE
T 0116-289-2956 **E** office@gliding.co.uk
W www.gliding.co.uk
Chief Executive, Pete Stratten

GOLF

ENGLISH GOLF UNION The National Golf Centre,
Woodhall Spa LN10 6PU **T** 01526-354500
E info@englishgolfunion.org
W www.englishgolfunion.org
Chief Executive, John Petrie
LADIES' GOLF UNION The Scores, St Andrews KY16 9AT
T 01334-475811 **E** info@lgu.org **W** www.lgu.org
Chief Executive, Shona Malcolm
THE ROYAL AND ANCIENT GOLF CLUB Golf
Place, St Andrews KY16 9JD **T** 01334-460000
E thesecretary@randagc.org **W** www.randa.org
Secretary, Peter Dawson

GYMNASTICS

BRITISH GYMNASTICS Ford Hall, Lilleshall National
Sports Centre, Newport TF10 9NB **T** 0845-129 7129
E information@british-gymnastics.org
W www.british-gymnastics.org
Chief Executive, Jane Allen

HANDBALL

BRITISH HANDBALL ASSOCIATION Elwick Club,
Church Road, Ashford TN23 1RD **T** 01233-878099
E office@britishhandball.com **W** www.britishhandball.com
Chief Executive, Paul Goodwin

HOCKEY

ENGLAND HOCKEY Bisham Abbey National Sports
Centre, Marlow SL7 1RR **T** 01628-897500
E info@englandhockey.org
W www.englandhockey.co.uk
Chief Executive, Sally Munday
SCOTTISH HOCKEY UNION 589 Lanark Road,
Edinburgh EH14 5DA **T** 0131-453 9070
E info@scottish-hockey.org.uk
W www.scottish-hockey.org.uk
Chief Executive, Brent Deans
WELSH HOCKEY UNION Sport Wales National
Centre, Sophie Gardens, Cardiff CF11 9SW **T** 029-2078
0730 **E** info@welsh-hockey.co.uk
W www.welsh-hockey.co.uk
Chief Executive, Helen Bushell

HORSERACING

BRITISH HORSERACING AUTHORITY
75 High Holborn, London WC1V 6LS **T** 020-7152 0000
E info@britishhorseracing.com
W www.britishhorseracing.com
Acting Chief Executive, Chris Brand
THE JOCKEY CLUB 75 High Holborn, London
WC1V 6LS **T** 020-7611 1800 **E** info@thejockeyclub.co.uk
W www.thejockeyclub.co.uk
Chief Executive, Simon Bazalgette

ICE SKATING

NATIONAL ICE SKATING ASSOCIATION OF
THE UK Grains Building, High Cross Street, Hockley,
Nottingham NG1 3AX **T** 0115-988 8060
E info@iceskating.org.uk **W** www.iceskating.org.uk
Chief Executive, Keith Horton

LACROSSE

ENGLISH LACROSSE ASSOCIATION Belle Vue
Athletics Centre, Pink Bank Lane, Manchester M12 5GL
T 0161-227 3626 **E** info@englishlacrosse.co.uk
W www.englishlacrosse.co.uk
Chief Executive Officer, David Shuttleworth

LAWN TENNIS

LAWN TENNIS ASSOCIATION National Tennis
Centre, 100 Priory Lane, London SW15 5JQ
T 020-8487 7000 **E** info@lta.org.uk **W** www.lta.org.uk
Chief Executive, Roger Draper

MARTIAL ARTS

BRITISH JUDO ASSOCIATION Suite B,
Loughborough Technology Park, Epinal Way, Loughborough
LE11 3GE **T** 01509-631670 **E** bja@britishjudo.org.uk
W www.britishjudo.org.uk
Chief Executive, Scott McCarthy
BRITISH JU JITSU ASSOCIATION 5 Avenue Parade,
Accrington BB5 6PN **T** 01254-396 806
E chairman@bjjagb.com **W** www.bjjagb.com
Chair, Martin Dixon
BRITISH TAEKWONDO COUNCIL TKD Centre,
192 High Street, West Drayton UB7 7PE **T** 01895-427359
E admin@tkdcouncil.com **W** www.tkdcouncil.com
Chair, M. Prewett

MODERN PENTATHLON

PENTATHLON GB Wessex House, University of Bath,
Claverton Down, Bath BA2 7AY **T** 01225-386808
E admin@pentathlongb.org **W** www.pentathlongb.org
Chief Executive, Jon Austin

MOTOR SPORTS

AUTO-CYCLE UNION ACU House, Wood Street,
Rugby CV21 2YX **T** 01788-566400 **E** admin@acu.org.uk
W www.acu.org.uk
General Secretary, Gary Thompson, MBE
MOTOR SPORTS ASSOCIATION Motor Sports
House, Riverside Park, Colnbrook, SL3 0HG
T 01753-765000 **W** www.msauk.org
Chief Executive, Colin Hilton
SCOTTISH AUTO CYCLE UNION 28 West Main
Street, Uphall EH52 5DW **T** 01506-858354
E office@sacu.co.uk **W** www.sacu.co.uk
President, Andy Russell

MOUNTAINEERING

BRITISH MOUNTAINEERING COUNCIL The Old
Church, 177–179 Burton Road, Manchester M20 2BB
T 0161-445 6111 **E** office@thebmc.co.uk
W www.thebmc.co.uk
Chief Executive, Dave Turnbull

MULTI-SPORTS BODIES

BRITISH OLYMPIC ASSOCIATION 60 Charlotte
Street, London W1T 2NU **T** 020-7842 5700
E boa@boa.org.uk **W** www.olympics.org.uk
Chief Executive, Andy Hunt

BRITISH PARALYMPIC ASSOCIATION 60
Charlotte Street, London W1T 2NU **T** 020-7842 5789
E info@paralympics.org.uk **W** www.paralympics.org.uk
Chair, Tim Reddish, OBE
BRITISH UNIVERSITIES AND COLLEGES
SPORT 20–24 Kings Bench Street, London SE1 0QX
T 020-7633 5080 **E** info@bucs.org.uk **W** www.bucs.org.uk
Chief Executive, Karen Rothery
COMMONWEALTH GAMES COUNCIL FOR
ENGLAND Jubilee Stand, Crystal Palace, National Sports
Centre, London SE19 2YY **T** 020-8676 3543
E info@weareengland.org **W** www.weareengland.org
Chief Executive, Ann Hogbin, CBE

COMMONWEALTH GAMES FEDERATION
2nd Floor, 138 Piccadilly, London W1J 7NR
T 020-7491 8801 E info@thecgf.com W www.thecgf.com
Chief Executive Officer, Michael Hooper

ENGLISH FEDERATION OF DISABILITY SPORT
Loughborough University, 3 Oakwood Drive,
Loughborough, LE11 3QF T 01509-227750
E federation@efds.co.uk W www.efds.co.uk
Chief Executive, Barry Horne

NETBALL

ALL ENGLAND NETBALL ASSOCIATION Netball
House, 9 Paynes Park, Hitchin SG5 1EH T 01462-442344
E info@englandnetball.co.uk W www.englandnetball.co.uk
Chief Executive, Paul Clark

NETBALL NI City of Lisburn Racquets Club, Belfast Road,
Lisburn BT27 4AF T 028-9266 8412 W www.netballni.org
Honorary President, Lorraine Lindsay

NETBALL SCOTLAND Suite 296, 3rd Floor, Central
Chambers, 93 Hope Street, Glasgow G2 6LD T 0141-572
0114 E membership@netballscotland.com
W www.netballscotland.com
Chair, Patricia Osborne

WELSH NETBALL ASSOCIATION Sport Wales
National Centre, Sophia Gardens, Cardiff CF11 9SW
T 0845-045 4302 E welshnetball@welshnetball.com
W www.welshnetball.co.uk
Chief Executive Officer, M. Fatkin

ORIENTEERING

BRITISH ORIENTEERING 8A Stancliffe House,
Whitworth Road, Darley Dale, Matlock DE4 2HJ
T 01629-734042 E info@britishorienteering.org.uk
W www.britishorienteering.org.uk
Chief Executive, Mike Hamilton

POLO

THE HURLINGHAM POLO ASSOCIATION Manor
Farm, Little Coxwell, Faringdon SN7 7LW T 01367-242828
E enquiries@hpa-polo.co.uk W www.hpa-polo.co.uk
Chief Executive, David Woodd

RACKETS AND REAL TENNIS

TENNIS AND RACKETS ASSOCIATION
c/o The Queen's Club, Palliser Road, London W14 9EQ
T 020-7835 6937 E office@tennisandrackets.com
W www.tennisandrackets.com
Chief Executive, C. S. Davies

ROWING

BRITISH ROWING 6 Lower Mall, Hammersmith,
London W6 9DJ T 020-8237 6700 E info@britishrowing.org
W www.britishrowing.org
National Manager, Rosemary Napp

HENLEY ROYAL REGATTA Regatta Headquarters,
Henley-on-Thames RG9 2LY T 01491-572153
W www.hrr.co.uk
Secretary, D. G. M. Grist

RUGBY LEAGUE

BRITISH AMATEUR RUGBY LEAGUE
ASSOCIATION West Yorkshire House,
4 New North Parade, Huddersfield HD1 5JP
T 01484-510682 E info@barla.org.uk
W www.barla.org.uk
Chair, Spen Allison

RUGBY FOOTBALL LEAGUE Red Hall,
Red Hall Lane, Leeds LS17 8NB T 0844-477 7113
E enquiries@rfl.uk.com W www.therfl.co.uk
Chair, Richard Lewis

RUGBY UNION

IRISH RUGBY FOOTBALL UNION 10–12
Lansdowne Road, Ballsbridge, Dublin 4T (+353) 1647 3800
E info@irishrugby.ie W www.irishrugby.ie
Chief Executive, Philip Browne

RUGBY FOOTBALL UNION Rugby House,
Twickenham Stadium, 200 Whitton Road, Twickenham
TW2 7BA T 0871-222 2120 E enquiries@therfu.com
W www.rfu.com
Chief Executive, Martyn Thomas

RUGBY FOOTBALL UNION FOR WOMEN
Rugby House, Rugby Road, Twickenham TW1 1DS
T 020-8831 7996 E rfuw@therfu.com
W www.rfu.com
Chair, Deborah Griffin

SCOTTISH RUGBY UNION Murrayfield,
Edinburgh EH12 5PJ T 0131-346 5000
E feedback@sru.org.uk
W www.scottishrugby.org
Chief Executive, Jock Millican

SCOTTISH WOMEN'S RUGBY UNION
Scottish Rugby Union, Murrayfield, Edinburgh EH12 5PJ
T 0131-346 5000 W www.swru.org.uk
Chair, Kath Vass

WELSH RUGBY UNION Westgate Terrace,
Millennium Stadium, Westgate Street, Cardiff
CF10 1NS T 0844-249 1999 E info@wru.co.uk
W www.wru.co.uk
Chief Executive, Roger Lewis

SHOOTING

BRITISH SHOOTING 40 Bernard Street,
London WC1N 1ST T 020-7211 5189
E admin@britishshooting.org.uk
W www.britishshooting.org.uk
Chair, David Parish

CLAY PIGEON SHOOTING ASSOCIATION
Edmonton House, National Shooting Centre,
Brookwood, Woking GU24 0NP T 01483-485400
E info@cpsa.co.uk W www.cpsa.co.uk
Chief Executive, Nick Fellows

NATIONAL RIFLE ASSOCIATION Bisley,
Brookwood, GU24 0PB T 01483-797777
E webadmin@nra.org.uk W www.nra.org.uk
Chair, Robin Pizer

NATIONAL SMALL-BORE RIFLE ASSOCIATION
Lord Roberts Centre, Bisley Camp, Brookwood,
Woking GU24 0NP T 01483-485505
W www.nsra.co.uk
Chief Executive, Allan Boosey

SNOWBOARDING

BRITISH SNOWBOARDING ASSOCIATION
3 Chandos House, 26 North Street, Brighton BN1 1EB
T 01273-358048 E info@snowboardclub.co.uk
W www.snowboardclub.co.uk/bsa
Chair, John O'Grady

SPEEDWAY

BRITISH SPEEDWAY ACU Headquarters,
Wood Street, Rugby CV21 2YX T 01788-560648
E office@speedwaygb.co W www.speedwaygb.co
Chair, Alex Harkess

SQUASH

ENGLAND SQUASH AND RACKETBALL
National Squash Centre, Sportcity, Manchester M11 3FF
T 0161-231 4499
E enquiries@englandsquashandracketball.com
W www.englandsquashandracketball.com
Chief Executive, Nick Rider

SCOTTISH SQUASH AND RACKETBALL
LIMITED Caledonia House, South Gyle, Edinburgh
EH12 9DQ T 0131-625 4425 E info@scottishsquash.org
W www.scottishsquash.org
Chief Executive Officer, John Dunlop
SQUASH WALES Sport Wales National Centre,
Sophia Gardens, Cardiff CF11 9SW T 0845-846 0027
E squashwales@squashwales.co.uk
W www.squashwales.co.uk
Chair, Phil Brailey

SUB-AQUA

BRITISH SUB-AQUA CLUB Telford's Quay, South
Pier Road, Ellesmere Port CH65 4FL T 0151-350 6200
E info@bsac.com W www.bsac.com
Chief Executive, Mary Tetley

SWIMMING

AMATEUR SWIMMING ASSOCIATION Pavilion 3,
Sport Park, 3 Oakwood Drive, Loughborough LE11 3QF
T 01509-618700 E customerservices@swimming.org
W www.swimming.org
Chief Executive, D. Sparkes
SCOTTISH SWIMMING National Swimming
Academy, University of Stirling, Stirling, FK9 4LA
T 01786-466520 E info@scottishswimming.com
W www.scottishswimming.com
Chief Executive, Ashley Howard
SWIM WALES Wales National Pool, Sketty Lane,
Swansea SA2 8QG T 01792-513636
W www.welshasa.co.uk
Chief Executive, Robert James

TABLE TENNIS

ENGLISH TABLE TENNIS ASSOCIATION
Queensbury House, 3rd Floor, Havelock Road, Hastings
TN34 1HF T 01424-722525 E admin@etta.co.uk
W www.englishtabletennis.org.uk
Chief Executive, Richard Yule
TABLE TENNIS ASSOCIATION OF WALES
8 Petit Close, Cefn-y-Bedd, Wrexham LL12 9YE
T 01978-760791 E admin@ttaw.co.uk W www.ttaw.co.uk
Chair, John Fraser

TABLE TENNIS SCOTLAND Caledonia House,
South Gyle, Edinburgh EH12 9DQ T 0131-317 8077
E admin@ttscotland.com W www.ttscotland.com
Chair, Jonathan Whitaker

TRIATHLON

BRITISH TRIATHLON PO Box 25, Loughborough
LE11 3WX T 01509-226161 E info@britishtriathlon.org
W www.britishtriathlon.org
Chief Executive, Zara Hyde Peters

VOLLEYBALL

ENGLISH VOLLEYBALL ASSOCIATION Sport Park,
Loughborough University, 3 Oakwood Drive, Loughborough
LE11 3QF T 01509-227722 E info@volleyballengland.org
W www.volleyballengland.org
President, Richard Callicott
NORTHERN IRELAND VOLLEYBALL ASSOCIATION
University of Ulster, Shore Road, Newtownabbey BT37 0QB
T 028-9036 6373 E mark@nivb.com W www.nivb.com
General Secretary, Mark Fulton
SCOTTISH VOLLEYBALL ASSOCIATION
48 The Pleasance, Edinburgh EH8 9TJ T 0131-556 4633
E info@scottishvolleyball.org W www.scottishvolleyball.org
Chief Executive, Margaret Ann Fleming
VOLLEYBALL WALES 13 Beckgrove Close, Pengam
Green, Cardiff CF24 2SE T 029-2041 6537
E mail@volleyballwales.org W www.volleyballwales.org
Chair, Yvonne Saker

WALKING

RACE WALKING ASSOCIATION Hufflers,
Heard's Lane, Shenfield, Brentwood CM15 0SF
T 01277-220687 E racewalkingassociation@btinternet.com
W www.racewalkingassociation.btinternet.co.uk
Hon. General Secretary, Peter Cassidy

WATER SKIING

BRITISH WATER SKI FEDERATION The Forum,
Hanworth Lane, Chertsey, KT16 9JX T 01932-560007
E info@bwsf.co.uk W www.britishwaterski.org.uk
Chief Executive Officer, Patrick Donovan

WEIGHTLIFTING

BRITISH WEIGHTLIFTERS ASSOCIATION
(BWLA) 110 Cavendish, Leeds Metropolitan University
Headingley Campus, Leeds LS6 3QS T 0113-812 7098
E support@bwla.co.uk W www.britishweightlifting.org
Chief Executive, Steve Cannon

WRESTLING

BRITISH WRESTLING ASSOCIATION
12 Westwood Lane, Chesterfield S43 1PA T 01246-236443
E admin@britishwrestling.org W www.britishwrestling.org
Chief Executive, Colin Nicholson

YACHTING

ROYAL YACHTING ASSOCIATION RYA House,
Ensign Way, Hamble, Southampton SO31 4YA
T 023-8060 4100 W www.rya.org.uk
Chief Executive, Sarah Treseder

CLUBS

Originally called gentlemen's clubs, these organisations are permanent institutions with a fixed clubhouse, which usually includes restaurants, bars, a library and overnight accommodation. Members are fee-paying and typically vetted for their suitability.

Gentlemen's clubs were created for males of the English upper class and grew out of the 17th-century fashion for coffee houses which enjoyed enormous popularity, despite opposition from Charles II, who believed they encouraged the spreading of royal disaffection. The first of the London clubs – White's – was founded in 1693 by Francesco Bianco in St James's Street, in the area that quickly became known as 'clubland'. Membership to the first of the clubs was a matter of hereditary privilege or special favour, a deliberately exclusionary measure which prompted an enormous growth in the number of clubs throughout the 19th century, fed by a burgeoning and aspirational middle class.

At the turn of the 20th century, there were more than 200 gentlemen's clubs in London alone, half of which had been founded since 1870. Inevitably, this level of competition could not be sustained, particularly given the number of men killed in two world wars. Financial restrictions necessitated greater provision for women and the relaxation of the social qualifications needed for membership. Nevertheless, waiting lists still exist for the leading clubs and a recommendation from at least one current member is almost always required to join.

* Men only   † Women only

ARMY AND NAVY CLUB (1837), 36 Pall Mall, London SW1Y 5JN T 020-7930 9721
E secretary@therag.co.uk W www.armynavyclub.co.uk
Chief Executive and Secretary, Cdr. R. W. W. Craig, RN
Former member: The Duke of Wellington
ARTS CLUB (1863), 40 Dover Street, London W1S 4NP
T 020-7499 8581 E secretary@theartsclub.co.uk
W www.theartsclub.co.uk
Managing Director, Brian Clivaz
Former members: Charles Dickens, Algernon Charles Swinburne, Ivan Turgenev
ATHENAEUM (1824), 107 Pall Mall, London SW1Y 5ER
T 020-7930 4843 E library@hellenist.org.uk
W www.athenaeumclub.co.uk
Secretary, J. H. Ford
Former members: Matthew Arnold, Michael Faraday, Anthony Trollope
ATHENAEUM (1797), Church Alley, Liverpool L1 3DD
T 0151-709 7770 E reception@theathenaeum.org.uk
W www.theathenaeum.org.uk
Honorary Secretary, Geoffrey Appleton
Former members: William Roscoe, William H. Duncan
AUTHORS' CLUB (1891), c/o Black's, 67 Dean Street, London W1D 4QH T 020-7287 3381
W www.theauthorsclub.co.uk
Chair, Chris Schuler
Former members: E. M. Forster, Jerome K. Jerome, George Meredith
BATH AND COUNTY CLUB (1858), Queen's Parade, Bath BA1 2NJ T 01225-423732

E secretary@bathandcountyclub.com
W www.bathandcountyclub.com
President, Sir Alec Morris, KBE, CB
BEEFSTEAK CLUB* (1876), 9 Irving Street, London WC2H 7AH T 020-7930 5722 E beefsteakclub@tiscali.co.uk
Secretary, Maria Hibbert
Former members: John Betjeman, Rudyard Kipling, Harold Macmillan
BOODLE'S* (1762), 28 St James's Street, London SW1A 1HJ T 020-7930 7166 E secretary@boodles.org
Secretary, Andrew Phillips
Former members: Winston Churchill, Ian Fleming
BROOKS'S* (1764), St James's Street, London SW1A 1LN T 020-7493 4411 E secretary@brooksclub.org
Secretary, Graham Snell
Former members: Edward Gibbon, Roy Jenkins, William Pitt
BUCK'S CLUB* (1919), 18 Clifford Street, London W1S 3RF T 020-7734 2337 E secretary@bucksclub.co.uk
Secretary, Maj. Rupert Lendrum
CALEDONIAN CLUB (1891), 9 Halkin Street, London SW1X 7DR T 020-7235 5162 E admin@caledonianclub.com
W www.caledonianclub.com
Secretary, Ian Campbell
CARLTON CLUB (1832), 69 St James's Street, London SW1A 1PJ T 020-7493 1164 E info@carltonclub.co.uk
W www.carltonclub.co.uk
Secretary, Jonathan Orr-Ewing
Former members: Stanley Baldwin, Benjamin Disraeli, Harold Macmillan, Margaret Thatcher, John Major
CAVALRY AND GUARDS CLUB (1890), 127 Piccadilly, London W1J 7PX T 020-7499 1261
E secretary@cavgds.co.uk W www.cavgds.co.uk
Secretary, David J Cowdery
Former member: Lawrence Oates
CHELSEA ARTS CLUB (1891), 143 Old Church Street, London SW3 6EB T 020-7376 3311
W www.chelseaartsclub.com
Secretary, D. Winterbottom
CITY LIVERY CLUB (1914), 38 St. Mary Axe, London EC3A 8EX T 020-7248 0620 E clerk@cityliveryclub.com
W www.cityliveryclub.com
Hon. Secretary, Roger T. Hacker, FCCA
CITY OF LONDON CLUB* (1832), 19 Old Broad Street, London EC2N 1DS T 020-7588 7991
E secretary@cityoflondonclub.com
W www.cityoflondonclub.com
Secretary, Ian Faul
Former member: Robert Peel
CITY UNIVERSITY CLUB (1895), 50 Cornhill, London EC3V 3PD T 020-7626 8571
E secretary@cityuniversityclub.co.uk
W www.cityuniversityclub.co.uk
Secretary, Miss R. C. Graham
CLUB LS1 (1849), 3 Albion Place, Leeds LS1 6JL T 0113-388 2820 E members@club-ls1.com
W www.club-ls1.com
General Manager, Clare Vidler
THE COBDEN CLUB (1996), 170–172 Kensal Road, London W10 5BN T 020-8960 4222
E info@thecobden.co.uk W www.thecobden.co.uk
Membership Secretary, Lesley Young

THE COMMONWEALTH CLUB (1868),
25 Northumberland Avenue, London WC2N 5AP
T 020-7766 9200 E info@thercs.org W www.thercs.org
Membership Manager, Kerrie Fuller
DEN NORSKE KLUB LTD (1887), In & Out,
4 St James's Square, London SW1Y 4JU T 020-7839 6242
E secretary@dennorskeklub.co.uk
W www.dennorskeklub.co.uk
Secretary, Elin Sandal
DISTRICT AND UNION CLUB* (1849), Northwood,
1 West Park Road, Blackburn BB2 6DE T 01254-51474
Secretary, John Dean
DURHAM COUNTY CLUB (1890), 52 Old Elvet,
Durham DH1 3HN T 0191-384 8156
Hon. Secretary, S. Smith
EAST INDIA CLUB* (1849), 16 St James's Square,
London SW1Y 4LH T 020-7930 1000
E secretary@eastindiaclub.co.uk
W www.eastindiaclub.co.uk
Secretary, A. Bray
FARMERS CLUB (1842), 3 Whitehall Court, London
SW1A 2EL T 020-7930 3557
E reception@thefarmersclub.com
W www.thefarmersclub.com
Secretary, Air Cdre Stephen Skinner
FOX CLUB, 46 Clarges Street, London W1J 7ER
T 020-7495 3656 E essi@foxclublondon.com
W www.foxclublondon.com
General Manager, Bethan Seaton
FREWEN CLUB* (1869), 98 St Aldate's, Oxford
OX1 1BT T 01865-243816
Hon. General Secretary, Tony Munsey
GARRICK CLUB* (1831), 15 Garrick Street, London
WC2E 9AY T 020-7379 6478 E office@garrickclub.co.uk
W www.garrickclub.co.uk
Secretary, Olaf Born
Former members: Charles Dickens, Henry Irving,
William Thackeray
GROUCHO CLUB (1985), 45 Dean Street, London
W1D 4QB T 020-7439 4685 E info@thegrouchoclub.com
W www.thegrouchoclub.com
Secretary, Miriam Brown
THE HURLINGHAM CLUB (1869), Ranelagh Gardens,
London SW6 3PR T 020-7610 7400
E membership@hurlinghamclub.org.uk
W www.hurlinghamclub.org.uk
Chief Executive, Rear-Adm. Niall Kilgour, CB
Former member: King Edward VII
LONDON PRESS CLUB (1882), 7–10 Adam Street,
The Strand, London WC2N 6AA T 020-7520 9082
E info@londonpressclub.co.uk
W www.londonpressclub.co.uk
Secretary, Peter Durrant
Former members: Lord Astor, Lord Rothermere,
Edgar Wallace
NATIONAL CLUB (1845), c/o The Carlton Club,
69 St James's Street, London SW1A 1PJ T 01225-480606
E secretary@thenationalclub.org.uk
W www.thenationalclub.org.uk
Hon. Secretary, Revd R. J. R. Paice
Former member: Lord Coggan
NATIONAL LIBERAL CLUB (1882), Whitehall Place,
London SW1A 2HE T 020-7930 9871
E secretary@nlc.org.uk W www.nlc.org.uk
Secretary, S. J. Roberts
Former members: Ramsay MacDonald, George Bernard
Shaw, H. G. Wells, William Gladstone, Winston
Churchill

NAVAL AND MILITARY CLUB (1862), 4 St James's
Square, London SW1Y 4JU T 020-7827 5757
E club@navalandmilitaryclub.co.uk
W www.navalandmilitaryclub.co.uk
Secretary, Ian Gregory
THE NEW CLUB (1874), 2 Montpellier Parade,
Cheltenham GL50 1UD T 01242-541121
E secretary@thenewclub.co.uk
W www.thenewclub.co.uk
Hon. Secretary, Peter Walsh
THE NEW CLUB (1787), 86 Princes Street, Edinburgh
EH2 2BB T 0131-226 4881 E info@newclub.co.uk
W www.newclub.co.uk
Secretary, Col. A. P. W. Campbell
Former members: Alec Douglas-Home, Walter Scott
NEW CAVENDISH CLUB (1920), 44 Great
Cumberland Place, London W1H 8BS T 020-7723 0391
E info@newcavendishclub.co.uk
W www.newcavendishclub.co.uk
Chair, Sue Ann Dowle
NORFOLK CLUB (1770), 17 Upper King Street,
Norwich NR3 1RB T 01603-626767
E generalmanager@thenorfolkclub.co.uk
W www.thenorfolkclub.co.uk
General Manager, George A. Wortley
NORTHERN COUNTIES CLUB (1829), 11 Hood Street,
Newcastle upon Tyne NE1 6LH T 0191-232 2744
E secretary@northerncountiesclub.co.uk
W www.northerncountiesclub.co.uk
General Manager, D. J. Devennie
ORIENTAL CLUB (1824), Stratford House, Stratford Place,
London W1C 1ES T 020-7629 5126
W www.orientalclub.org.uk
Secretary, D. M. Swain
OXFORD AND CAMBRIDGE CLUB (1830),
71 Pall Mall, London SW1Y 5HD T 020-7930 5151
E club@oandc.uk.com
W www.oxfordandcambridgeclub.co.uk
Secretary, Alistair E. Telfer
Former members: Clement Attlee, William Gladstone,
The Duke of Wellington
PORTLAND CLUB (1816), 69 Brook Street, London
W1Y 4ER T 020-7499 1523
Secretary, J. Burns, CBE
PRATT'S CLUB* (1841), 14 Park Place, London
SW1A 1LP T 020-7493 0397 E secretary@prattsclub.org
Secretary, Graham Snell
Former member: Winston Churchill
REFORM CLUB (1836), 104–105 Pall Mall, London
SW1Y 5EW T 020-7930 9374
E generaloffice@reformclub.com W www.reformclub.com
Secretary, M. D. B. McKerchar
Former members: Isambard Kingdom Brunel,
Guy Burgess, Arthur Conan Doyle, Henry James,
David Lloyd George
ROYAL AIR FORCE CLUB (1918), 128 Piccadilly,
London W1J 7PY T 020-7399 1000 E sales@rafclub.org.uk
W www.rafclub.org.uk
Secretary, P. N. Owen
ROYAL ANGLO-BELGIAN CLUB (1945), 8
Northumberland Avenue, London WC2N 5BY
T 020-7127 5139 E secretary@ra-bc.com
W www.ra-bc.com
Chair, Michel Vanhoonacker
ROYAL AUTOMOBILE CLUB (1897), Pall Mall
Clubhouse, 89 Pall Mall, London SW1Y 5HS
T 020-7930 2345 E members@royalautomobileclub.co.uk
W www.royalautomobileclub.co.uk

Secretary, David Wilkinson
Former members: Winston Churchill, Charles Rolls, Rudyard Kipling
ROYAL NORTHERN & UNIVERSITY CLUB* (1854), 9 Albyn Place, Aberdeen AB10 1YE T 01224-583292 E secretary@rnuc.org.uk W www.rnuc.org.uk
Secretary, Rosemary Black
ROYAL OVER-SEAS LEAGUE (1910), Over-Seas House, Park Place, St James's Street, London SW1A 1LR T 020-7408 0214 E info@rosl.org.uk W www.rosl.org.uk
Director-General, Robert F. Newell, CVO
ST STEPHEN'S CLUB (1870), 34 Queen Anne's Gate, London SW1H 9AB T 020-7222 1382 E info@ststephensclub.co.uk W www.ststephensclub.co.uk
General Manager, Bernard Moray
Former member: Benjamin Disraeli
SAVAGE CLUB* (1857), 1 Whitehall Place, London SW1A 2HD T 020-7930 8118 E info@savageclub.com W www.savageclub.com
Hon. Secretary, Adrian MacIntosh
Former members: Edward Elgar, Alexander Fleming, Harry Secombe, Dylan Thomas, Mark Twain, Peter Ustinov
SAVILE CLUB* (1868), 69 Brook Street, London W1K 4ER T 020-7629 5462 W www.savileclub.co.uk
Secretary, Julian Malone-Lee
Former members: Max Beerbohm, Thomas Hardy, Robert Louis Stevenson
SCOTTISH ARTS CLUB (1872), 24 Rutland Square, Edinburgh EH1 2BW T 0131-229 8157 E manager@scottishartsclub.co.uk W www.scottishartsclub.co.uk
House Convenor, Hilary Mounfield
SLOANE CLUB (1976), Lower Sloane Street, London SW1W 8BS T 020-7730 9131 E reservations@sloaneclub.co.uk W www.sloaneclub.co.uk
Membership Secretary, Fran Bremner
SOHO HOUSE (1995), 40 Greek Street, London W1D 4EB T 020-7734 5188 W www.sohohouselondon.com

THE CANNING CLUB (1910), 4 St James's Square, London SW1Y 4JU T 020-7827 5730 E canningclub@navalandmilitaryclub.co.uk
Secretary, Fiona Sedgwick
TRAVELLERS CLUB* (1819), 106 Pall Mall, London SW1Y 5EP T 020-7930 8688 E secretary@thetravellersclub.org.uk W www.thetravellersclub.org.uk
Secretary, David Broadhead
Former members: Arthur Balfour, Alec Douglas-Home, Anthony Powell
TURF CLUB (1868), 5 Carlton House Terrace, London SW1Y 5AQ T 020-7930 8555 E mail@turfclub.co.uk
Secretary, Lt.-Col. O. R. StJ. Breakwell, MBE
ULSTER REFORM CLUB (1885), 4 Royal Avenue, Belfast BT1 1DA T 028-9032 3411 E info@ulsterreformclub.com W www.ulsterreformclub.com
Chief Executive, A. W. Graham
UNIVERSITY WOMEN'S CLUB† (1883), 2 Audley Square, London W1K 1DB T 020-7499 2268 E uwc@uwc-london.com W www.universitywomensclub.com
Secretary, Ms S. McCue
VINCENT'S* (1863), 1A King Edward Street, Oxford OX1 4HS T 01865-722984 E secretary@vincents.org W www.vincents.org
Secretary, Calum Slowther
Former members: Roger Bannister, King Edward VIII
WESTERN CLUB (1825), 32 Royal Exchange Square, Glasgow G1 3AB T 0141-221 2016 E secretary@westernclub.co.uk W www.westernclub.co.uk
Secretary, Douglas H. Gifford
WHITE'S* (1693), 37–38 St James's Street, London SW1A 1JG T 020-7493 6671
Secretary, D. A. Anderson
Former members: Beau Brummel, Horace Walpole, Evelyn Waugh

CHARITIES AND SOCIETIES

The following is a selection of charities, societies and non-profit organisations in the UK and does not represent a comprehensive list. For professional and employment-related organisations, *see* Professional Education and Trade and Professional Bodies.

4CHILDREN City Reach, 5 Greenwich View Place, London E14 9NN **T** 020-7512 2112 **E** info@4children.org.uk
W www.4children.org.uk
Chief Executive, Anne Longfield, OBE

ABBEYFIELD SOCIETY (1956), Abbeyfield House, 53 Victoria Street, St Albans AL1 3UW **T** 01727-857536
E post@abbeyfield.com **W** www.abbeyfield.com
Chief Executive, Paul Allen

ACE CULTURAL TOURS (1958), Babraham, Cambridge CB22 3AP **T** 01223-835055 **E** ace@aceculturaltours.co.uk
W www.aceculturaltours.co.uk
General Secretary, Paul Barnes

ACTIONAID (1972), 33–39 Bowling Green Lane, London EC1R 0BJ **T** 020-3122 0561 **E** mail@actionaid.org.uk
W www.actionaid.org.uk
Executive Director, Richard Miller

ACTION FOR BLIND PEOPLE (1857), 14–16 Verney Road, London SE16 3DZ **T** 020-7635 4800
E helpline@rnib.org.uk **W** www.actionforblindpeople.org.uk
Chief Executive, Stephen Remington

ACTION FOR CHILDREN (1869), 3 The Boulevard, Ascot Road, Watford WD18 8AG **T** 0300-123 2112
E ask.us@actionforchildren.org.uk
W www.actionforchildren.org.uk
Chief Executive, Clare Tickell, DBE

ACTION MEDICAL RESEARCH (1952), Vincent House, Horsham RH12 2DP **T** 01403-210406 **E** info@action.org.uk
W www.action.org.uk
Chief Executive, Julie Buckler

ACTORS' BENEVOLENT FUND (1882), 6 Adam Street, London WC2N 6AD **T** 020-7836 6378 **E** office@abf.org.uk
W www.actorsbenevolentfund.co.uk
General Secretary, Willie Bicket

ACTORS' CHARITABLE TRUST (1896), 58 Bloomsbury Street, London WC1B 3QT **T** 020-7636 7868
E robert@tactactors.org **W** www.tactactors.org
General Secretary, Robert Ashby

ADAM SMITH INSTITUTE (1977), 23 Great Smith Street, London SW1P 3BL **T** 020-7222 4995 **E** info@adamsmith.org
W www.adamsmith.org
Director, Dr Eamonn Butler

ADDACTION (1967), 67–69 Cowcross Street, London EC1M 6PU **T** 020-7251 5860 **E** info@addaction.org.uk
W www.addaction.org.uk
Chief Executive, Simon Antrobus

ADVERTISING STANDARDS AUTHORITY (1962), Mid City Place, 71 High Holborn, London WC1V 6QT
T 020-7492 2222 **E** enquiries@asa.org.uk
W www.asa.org.uk
Chief Executive, Guy Parker

AFASIC (1968), 1st Floor, Olive House, 20 Bowling Green Lane, London EC1R 0BD **T** 020-7490 9410
E info@afasic.org.uk **W** www.afasic.org.uk
Chief Executive, Linda Lascelles

AGE UK (2010), 207–221 Pentonville Road, London N1 9UZ **T** 0800-169 6565 **E** contact@ageuk.org.uk
W www.ageuk.org.uk
Chief Executive, Tom Wright, CBE

ALCOHOLICS ANONYMOUS (1947), PO Box 1, 10 Toft Green, York YO1 7NJ **T** 01904-644026,
Helpline 0845-769 7555
E help@alcoholics-anonymous.org.uk
W www.alcoholics-anonymous.org.uk
General Secretary, Ann Napier

ALZHEIMER'S SOCIETY (1979), Devon House, 58 St Katharine's Way, London E1W 1LB **T** 020-7423 3500
E enquiries@alzheimers.org.uk **W** www.alzheimers.org.uk
Acting Chief Executive, Jeremy Hughes

AMNESTY INTERNATIONAL UNITED KINGDOM (1961), The Human Rights Action Centre, 17–25 New Inn Yard, London EC2A 3EA **T** 020-7033 1500
E sct@ammnesty.org.uk **W** www.amnesty.org.uk
UK Director, Kate Allen

ANCIENT MONUMENTS SOCIETY (1924), St Ann's Vestry Hall, 2 Church Entry, London EC4V 5HB
T 020-7236 3934
E office@ancientmonumentssociety.org.uk
W www.ancientmonumentssociety.org.uk
Secretary, M. J. Saunders, MBE

ANGLO-BELGIAN SOCIETY (1982), 5 Hartley Close, Bickley BR1 2TP **T** 020-8467 8442
E secretary@anglo-belgiansoc.co.uk
W www.anglo-belgiansoc.co.uk
Chair, David Colvin, CMG

ANGLO-NORSE SOCIETY (1918), 25 Belgrave Square, London SW1X 8QD **T** 020-7235 9529
E secretariat@anglo-norse.org.uk
W www.anglo-norse.org.uk
Chair, Sir Richard Dales

ANIMAL CONCERN (1876), PO Box 5178, Dumbarton G82 5YJ **T** 01389-841639 **E** animals@jfrobins.force9.co.uk
W www.animalconcern.com
Secretary, John F. Robins

ANIMAL HEALTH TRUST (1942), Lanwades Park, Kentford, Newmarket CB8 7UU **T** 01638-751000
E info@aht.org.uk **W** www.aht.org.uk
Chief Executive, Dr Peter Webbon

ANTHONY NOLAN TRUST (1974), 2–3 Heathgate Place, 75–87 Agincourt Road, London NW3 2NU **T** 0303-303 0303
E info@anthonynolan.org **W** www.anthonynolan.org
Chief Executive, Henny Braund

ANTI-SLAVERY INTERNATIONAL (1839),
Thomas Clarkson House, The Stableyard, Broomgrove Road,
London SW9 9TL T 020-7501 8920 E info@antislavery.org
W www.antislavery.org
Director, Aidan McQuade

ARCHITECTS BENEVOLENT SOCIETY (1850),
43 Portland Place, London W1B 1QH T 020-7580 2823
E help@absnet.org.uk W www.absnet.org.uk
Company Secretary, Keith Robinson

ARCHITECTURAL HERITAGE FUND (1976),
Alhambra House, 27–31 Charing Cross Road, London
WC2H 0AU T 020-7925 0199 E ahf@ahfund.org.uk
W www.ahfund.org.uk
Chief Executive, Ian Lush

ARLIS/UK AND IRELAND (1969), The National Art
Library, Word & Image Department, Victoria & Albert
Museum, Cromwell Road, London SW7 2RL
T 020-7942 2317 E arlis@vam.ac.uk W www.arlis.org.uk
Chair, Pat Christie

ASSOCIATION FOR LANGUAGE LEARNING (1990),
University of Leicester, University Road, Leicester LE1 7RH
T 0116-229 7602 E info@all-languages.org.uk
W www.all-languages.org.uk
Director, Linda Parker

ASSOCIATION FOR SCIENCE EDUCATION (1901),
College Lane, Hatfield AL10 9AA T 01707-283000
E info@ase.org.uk W www.ase.org.uk
Chief Executive, Annette Smith

ASSOCIATION OF GENEALOGISTS AND
RESEARCHERS IN ARCHIVES (1968), 43 Bowes
Wood, New Ash Green DA3 8QL E info@agra.org.uk
W www.agra.org.uk
Company Secretary, Craig Nimmo

ASSOCIATION OF ROYAL NAVY OFFICERS (1920),
70 Porchester Terrace, London W2 3TP T 020-7402 5231
E osec@arno.org.uk W www.arno.org.uk
Director, Cdr W. K. Ridley, OBE

ASTHMA UK (1927), Summit House, 70 Wilson Street,
London EC2A 2DB T 020-7786 4900 E info@asthma.org.uk
W www.asthma.org.uk
Chief Executive, Neil Churchill

AUDIT BUREAU OF CIRCULATIONS LTD (1931),
Saxon House, 211 High Street, Berkhamsted HP4 1AD
T 01442-870800 E info@abc.co.uk W www.abc.org.uk
Chair, Sally Cartwright, OBE

AUTISM INITIATIVES (1971), 7 Chesterfield Road,
Liverpool L23 9XL T 0151-330 9500
E info@autisminitiatives.org W www.autisminitiatives.org
Chair, Brian Williams

BALTIC EXCHANGE (1744), 38 St Mary Axe,
London EC3A 8BH T 020-7623 5501
E enquiries@balticexchange.com
W www.balticexchange.com
Chief Executive, Jeremy Penn

BALTIC EXCHANGE CHARITABLE SOCIETY (1978),
20 St Dunstans Hill, London EC3R 8HL T 020-7283 6090
E enquiries@balticexchange.com
W www.balticexchange.com
Secretary, R. J. M. Butler

BARNARDO'S (1866), Tanners Lane, Barkingside, Ilford
IG6 1QG T 020-8550 8822 E info@barnardos.org.uk
W www.barnardos.org.uk
Chief Executive, Anne Marie Carey

BARRISTERS' BENEVOLENT ASSOCIATION (1873),
14 Gray's Inn Square, London WC1R 5JP
T 020-7242 4761 E enquiries@the-bba.com
W www.the-bba.com
Chair, Terence Mowschenson, QC

BBC WORLD SERVICE TRUST (1999), Bush House,
PO Box 76, Strand, London WC2B 4PH T 020-7557 2462
E ws.trust@bbc.co.uk W www.bbc.co.uk/worldservice/trust
Executive Director, Caroline Nursey

BEAT, Wensum House, 103 Prince of Wales Road, Norwich
NR1 1DW T 0300-123 3355, **Helpline** 0845-634 1414,
Youthline 0845-634 7650 E info@b-eat.co.uk
W www.b-eat.co.uk (1989),
Chief Executive, Susan Ringwood

BEVIN BOYS ASSOCIATION (1989),
23 Great Cranford Street, Poundbury, Dorchester DT1 3SQ
T 01305-261269
Vice President & Chair, Warwick Taylor, MBE

BIBLE SOCIETY (1804), Stonehill Green, Westlea, Swindon
SN5 7DG T 01793-418222 E contactus@biblesociety.org.uk
W www.biblesociety.org.uk
Chief Executive, James Catford

BIBLIOGRAPHICAL SOCIETY (1892), c/o University of
London, Institute of English Studies, Senate House, Malet
Street, London WC1E 7HU T 020-7862 8679
E secretary@bibsoc.org.uk W www.bibsoc.org.uk
Hon. Secretary, Margaret Ford

BIRMINGHAM AND WARWICKSHIRE
ARCHAEOLOGICAL SOCIETY (1870),
c/o Birmingham and Midland Institute, 9 Margaret Street,
Birmingham B3 3BS W www.birminghamandwarwickshire
archaeologicalsociety.co.uk
President, Dr Della Hooke

BLISS (1979), 9 Holyrood Street, London SE1 2EL
T 020-7378 1122, **Helpline** 0500-618140
E information@bliss.org.uk W www.bliss.org.uk
Chief Executive, Andy Cole

BLUE CROSS (1897), Shilton Road, Burford OX18 4PF
T 01993-822651 E info@bluecross.org.uk
W www.bluecross.org.uk
Chief Executive, Kim Hamilton

BOOK AID INTERNATIONAL (1954), 39–41
Coldharbour Lane, London SE5 9NR T 020-7733 3577
E info@bookaid.org W www.bookaid.org
Director, Clive Nettleton

BOOK TRADE CHARITY (BTBS) (1837),
The Foyle Centre, The Retreat, Kings Langley WD4 8LT
T 01923-263128 E david@btbs.org
W www.booktradecharity.org
Chief Executive, David Hicks

BOOKTRUST (1926), Book House, 45 East Hill, London
SW18 2QZ T 020-8516 2977 E query@booktrust.org.uk
W www.booktrust.org.uk
Chief Executive, Viv Bird

BOYS' BRIGADE (1883), Felden Lodge, Felden, Hemel
Hempstead HP3 0BL T 01442-231681
E enquiries@boys-brigade.org.uk
W www.boys-brigade.org.uk
Brigade Secretary, Steven Dickinson

BRISTOL AND GLOUCESTERSHIRE
ARCHAEOLOGICAL SOCIETY (1876), Stonehatch,
Oakridge Lynch, Stroud GL6 7NR T 01285-760460
E john@loosleyj.freeserve.co.uk W www.bgas.org.uk
Hon. General Secretary, John Loosley

BRITISH ACADEMY OF FORENSIC SCIENCES
(1960), Academic Haematology, BICMS, Pathology Group,
4 Newark Street, London E1 2AT T 020-7882 2276
E y.d.syndercombe-court@qmul.ac.uk W www.bafs.org.uk
Secretary-General, Dr Denise Syndercombe Court

BRITISH ASSOCIATION FOR EARLY CHILDHOOD
EDUCATION (1923), 136 Cavell Street, London E1 2JA
T 020-7539 5400 E office@early-education.org.uk
W www.early-education.org.uk
Chief Executive, Megan Pacey

BRITISH ASTRONOMICAL ASSOCIATION (1890),
Burlington House, Piccadilly, London W1J 0DU
T 020-7734 4145 E office@britastro.org
W www.britastro.org
President, Prof. Bill Leatherbarrow

BRITISH BOARD OF FILM CLASSIFICATION (1912),
3 Soho Square, London W1D 3HD T 020-7440 1570
E contact_the_bbfc@bbfc.co.uk W www.bbfc.co.uk
Director, David Cooke

BRITISH CATTLE BREEDERS CLUB (1946),
Lake Villa, Bradworthy, Holsworthy, Devon EX22 7SQ
T 01409-241579 E lesley.lewin@cattlebreeders.org.uk
W www.cattlebreeders.org.uk
Chair, Lucy Andrews

BRITISH COPYRIGHT COUNCIL (1965),
29–33 Berners Street, London W1T 3AB T 01986-788122
E info@britishcopyright.org W www.britishcopyright.org
Secretary, Janet Ibbotson

BRITISH DEAF ASSOCIATION (1890), 10th Floor,
Coventry Point, Market Way, Coventry CV1 1EA
T 02476-550936 E bda@bda.org.uk W www.bda.org.uk
Chair, Terry Riley

BRITISH DRIVING SOCIETY LTD (1957),
83 New Road, Helmingham, Stowmarket IP14 6EA
T 01473-892001 E email@britishdrivingsociety.co.uk
W www.britishdrivingsociety.co.uk
Chair, John Parker

BRITISH ECOLOGICAL SOCIETY (1913),
Charles Darwin House, 12 Roger Street, London WC1N 2JU
T 020-7685 2500 E info@britishecologicalsociety.org
W www.britishecologicalsociety.org
Executive Director, Dr Hazel Norman

BRITISH FALSE MEMORY SOCIETY (1993),
Bradford on Avon BA15 1NF T 01225-868682
E bfms@bfms.org.uk W www.bfms.org.uk
Director, M. Greenhalgh

BRITISH FEDERATION OF WOMEN GRADUATES
(1907), 4 Mandeville Courtyard, 142 Battersea Park Road,
London SW11 4NB T 020-7498 8037 E office@bfwg.org.uk
W www.bfwg.org.uk
President, Marianne Haslegrave

BRITISH HEALTH CARE ASSOCIATION (1930),
PO Box 6752, Elgin IV30 9BN T 01343-544841
E info@bhcaservices.co.uk W www.bhca.org.uk
Chief Executive, Stephen Fritz

BRITISH HEART FOUNDATION (1961), Greater
London House, 180 Hampstead Road, London NW1 7AW
T 020-7554 0000 E supporterservices@bhf.org.uk
W www.bhf.org.uk
Chief Executive, Peter Hollins

BRITISH HEDGEHOG PRESERVATION SOCIETY
(1982), Hedgehog House, Dhustone, Ludlow SY8 3PL
T 01584-890801 E info@britishhedgehogs.org.uk
W www.britishhedgehogs.org.uk
Chief Executive, Fay Vass

BRITISH HERPETOLOGICAL SOCIETY (1947),
11 Strathmore Place, Montrose DD10 8LQ T 01674-671676
E info@thebhs.org W www.thebhs.org
President, Prof. Trevor J. C. Beebee

BRITISH HORSE SOCIETY (1947), Abbey Park, Stareton,
Kenilworth CV8 2XZ T 0844-848 1666
E enquiries@bhs.org.uk W www.bhs.org.uk
Chief Executive, Graham Cory

BRITISH HUMANIST ASSOCIATION (1896),
1 Gower Street, London WC1E 6HD T 020-7079 3580
E info@humanism.org.uk W www.humanism.org.uk
Chief Executive, Andrew Copson

BRITISH INSTITUTE IN EASTERN AFRICA
(1959), 10 Carlton House Terrace, London SW1Y 5AH
T 020-7969 5201 E biea@britac.ac.uk W www.biea.ac.uk
Director, Dr Ambreena Manji

BRITISH INTERPLANETARY SOCIETY (1933), 27–29
South Lambeth Road, London SW8 1SZ T 020-7735 3160
E mail@bis-spaceflight.com W www.bis-spaceflight.com
Executive Secretary, Suszann Parry

BRITISH-ISRAEL-WORLD FEDERATION (1919),
121 Low Etherley, Bishop Auckland, Co Durham DL14 0HA
T 01388-834395 E admin@britishisrael.co.uk
W www.britishisrael.co.uk
President, M. A. Clark

BRITISH MANAGEMENT DATA FOUNDATION
(1979), 24 Hawkhead Crescent, Edinburgh EH16 6LR
T 0131-664 1129 E bmdfmail@aol.co.uk
W www.bmdf.co.uk; www.eurotreaties.com
Director, Andrew Cowgill

BRITISH MENSA LTD (1946), St John's House, St John's Square, Wolverhampton WV2 4AH T 01902-772771 E enquiries@mensa.org.uk W www.mensa.org.uk
Chief Executive, John Stevenage

BRITISH MUSIC HALL SOCIETY (1963), 45 Mayflower Road, Park Street, St Albans AL2 2QN T 01727-768878 W www.music-hall-society.com
President, Roy Hudd

BRITISH NUTRITION FOUNDATION (1967), High Holborn House, 52–54 High Holborn, London WC1V 6RQ T 020-7404 6504 E postbox@nutrition.org.uk W www.nutrition.org.uk
Director-General, Prof. Judith Buttriss

BRITISH PHARMACOLOGICAL SOCIETY (1931), 16 Angel Gate, City Road, London EC1V 2PT T 020-7417 0110 E info@bps.ac.uk W www.bps.ac.uk
President, Prof. Ray Hill

BRITISH PIG ASSOCIATION (1884), Trumpington Mews, 40B High Street, Trumpington, Cambridge CB2 9LS T 01223-845100 E bpa@britishpigs.org W www.britishpigs.org.uk
Chief Executive, Marcus Bates

BRITISH RED CROSS (1870), 44 Moorfields, London EC2Y 9AL T 0844-871 1111, Textphone 020-7562 2000 E information@redcross.org.uk W www.redcross.org.uk
Chief Executive, Sir Nicholas Young

BRITISH SUNDIAL SOCIETY (1989), c/o The Royal Astronomical Society, Burlington House, London W1J 0BQ T 01233-712550 E secretary@sundialsoc.org.uk W www.sundialsoc.org.uk
President, Christopher St J. H. Daniel, FSA

BTCV (1959), Sedum House, Mallard Way, Doncaster DN4 8DB T 01302-388888 E information@btcv.org.uk W www.btcv.org
Chief Executive, Tom Flood, CBE

BUCKINGHAMSHIRE ARCHAEOLOGICAL SOCIETY (1847), County Museum, Church Street, Aylesbury HP20 2QP T 01296-387341 E bucksas@buckscc.gov.uk W www.bucksas.org.uk
Hon. Secretary, Sue Fox

BUILD AFRICA (1978), Second Floor, Vale House, Clarence Road, Tunbridge Wells TN1 1HE T 0800-652 6294 E hello@build-africa.org.uk W www.build-africa.org
Chief Executive, Oliver Kemp

BUSINESS AND PROFESSIONAL WOMEN UK LTD (1938), 74 Fairfield Rise, Billericay CM12 9NU T 01277-623867 E hq@bpwuk.co.uk W www.bpwuk.co.uk
President, Elizabeth Burden

CAMBRIAN ARCHAEOLOGICAL ASSOCIATION (1847), Braemar, Llangunnor Road, SA31 2PB T 01248-364865 E h.james443@btinternet.com W www.cambrians.org.uk
General Secretary, Heather James

CAMPAIGN FOR NUCLEAR DISARMAMENT (1958), 162 Holloway Road, London N7 8DQ T 020-7700 2393 E enquiries@cnduk.org W www.cnduk.org
General Secretary, Kate Hudson

CAMPAIGN FOR THE PROTECTION OF RURAL WALES (1928), Ty Gwyn, 31 High Street, Welshpool SY21 7YD T 01938-552525 E info@cprwmail.org.uk W www.cprw.org.uk
Director, Peter Ogden

CANCER RESEARCH UK (2002), Angel Building, 407 St John Street, London EC1V 4AD T 020-7242 0200 W www.cancerresearchuk.org
Chief Executive, Harpal S. Kumar

CARNEGIE UNITED KINGDOM TRUST (1913), Andrew Carnegie House, Pittencrieff Street, Dunfermline KY12 8AW T 01383-721445 E info@carnegieuk.org W www.carnegieuktrust.org.uk
Chief Executive, Martyn Evans

CATHOLIC TRUTH SOCIETY (1868), 40–46 Harleyford Road, London SE11 5AY T 020-7640 0042 E info@cts-online.org.uk W www.cts-online.org.uk
General Secretary, Fergal Martin

CENTRAL COUNCIL OF CHURCH BELL RINGERS (1891), 11 Bullfields, Sawbridgeworth, CM21 9DB T 01279-726159 E secretary@cccbr.org.uk W www.cccbr.org.uk
Hon. Secretary, Mary Bone

CENTREPOINT (1969), Central House, 25 Camperdown Street, London E1 8DZ T 0845-466 3400 E info@centrepoint.org W www.centrepoint.org.uk
Chief Executive, Seyi Obakin

CHANGING FACES (1992), The Squire Centre, 33–37 University Street, London WC1E 6JN T 0845-450 0275 E info@changingfaces.org.uk W www.changingfaces.org.uk
Chief Executive, James Partridge

CHARTERED INSTITUTE OF LINGUISTS (1910), Saxon House, 48 Southwark Street, London SE1 1UN T 020-7940 3100 E info@iol.org.uk W www.iol.org.uk
Chief Executive, Alexandra Jones

CHATHAM HOUSE (1920), Chatham House, 10 St James's Square, London SW1Y 4LE T 020-7957 5700 E contact@chathamhouse.org.uk W www.chathamhouse.org.uk
Director, Dr Robin Niblett

CHILDREN 1ST (1884), 83 Whitehouse Loan, Edinburgh EH9 1AT T 0131-446 2300 E info@children1st.org.uk W www.children1st.org.uk
Chief Executive, Anne Houston

CHRISTIAN AID (1945), 35 Lower Marsh, London SE1 7RL T 020-7620 4444 E info@christian-aid.org W www.christianaid.org.uk
Director, Loretta Minghella

CHRISTIAN AID SCOTLAND (1945), The Pentagon Centre, 36 Washington Street, Glasgow G3 8AZ T 0141-221 7475 E glasgow@christian-aid.org W www.christianaid.org.uk/scotland
Head of Team for Scotland, Kathy Galloway

CHRISTIAN EDUCATION (2001), 1020 Bristol Road, Selly Oak, Birmingham B29 6LB T 0121-472 4242 E admin@christianeducation.org.uk W www.christianeducation.org.uk
Chief Executive, Peter Fishpool

CHURCH BUILDINGS COUNCIL (1921),
Church House, Great Smith Street, London SW1P 3NZ
T 020-7898 1000 E enquiries.ccb@churchofengland.org
W www.churchcare.co.uk
Secretary, Janet Gough

CHURCHILL CENTRE UK (1968), PO Box 1915, Quarley,
Andover, Hants SP10 9EE T 01223-336175
E allen.packwood@chu.cam.ac.uk
W www.winstonchurchill.org
Executive Director, Allen Packwood

CHURCHILL SOCIETY – LONDON (1990), Ivy House,
18 Grove Lane, Ipswich IP4 1NR T 01473-413533
E dutysecretary@churchill-society-london.org.uk
W www.churchill-society-london.org.uk
General Secretary, J. H. Rogers

CHURCH LADS' AND CHURCH GIRLS' BRIGADE
(1891), 2 Barnsley Road, Wath-upon-Dearne, Rotherham
S63 6PY T 01709-876535 E brigadesecretary@clcgb.org.uk
W www.clcgb.org.uk
Brigade Secretary, A. Millward

CHURCH MISSION SOCIETY (1799), Watlington Road,
Oxford OX4 6BZ T 01865-787 400 E info@cms-uk.org
W www.cms-uk.org
Executive Director, Revd Canon Tim Dakin

CHURCH MONUMENTS SOCIETY (1979), Moor View,
Exbourne EX20 3SA T 01837-851483
E churchmonuments@aol.com
W www.churchmonumentssociety.org
Hon Secretary, Barbara Tomlinson, BA

CHURCH UNION (1859), 2A, The Cloisters, Gordon Square,
London WC1H 0AG E secretary@churchunion.co.uk
W www.churchunion.co.uk
Chair, David Morgan

CITIZENS ADVICE (1939), Myddelton House,
115–123 Pentonville Road, London N1 9LZ
T 020-7833 2181 W www.citizensadvice.org.uk
Chief Executive, Gillian Guy

CITY BUSINESS LIBRARY (1970), City Business Library,
Aldermanbury, London EC2V 7HH T 020-7332 1812
E cbl@cityoflondon.gov.uk
W www.cityoflondon.gov.uk/citybusinesslibrary
Business Librarian, Goretti Considine

CITY OF COVENTRY FREEMEN'S GUILD (1946),
1 Trossachs Road, Coventry CV5 7BJ T 024-7646 3203
W www.coventryfreemensguild.co.uk
Hon. Clerk, George Wilkinson

CITY OF STOKE-ON-TRENT MUSEUM
ARCHAEOLOGICAL SOCIETY (1959),
c/o The Potteries Museum and Art Gallery, Hanley,
Stoke-on-Trent ST1 3DW T 01782-513589
E info@stokearchaeologysociety.org.uk
W www.stokearchaeologysociety.org.uk
Chair, Paul Klinczak

CLASSICAL ASSOCIATION (1903), Senate House,
Malet Street, London WC1E 7HU T 020-7862 8706
E office@classicalassociation.org
W www.classicalassociation.org
Secretary, Claire Davenport

COMBAT STRESS (1919), Tyrwhitt House, Oaklawn Road,
Leatherhead, KT22 0BX T 01372-841600
E contactus@combatstress.org.uk
W www.combatstress.org.uk
Chair, Maj.-Gen. Peter Currie, CB

COMMONWEALTH SOCIETY FOR THE DEAF
'SOUND SEEKERS' (1959), 34 Buckingham Palace
Road, London SW1W 0RE T 020-7233 5700
E sound.seekers@btinternet.com
W www.sound-seekers.org.uk
Chief Executive, Gary Williams

CONTEMPORARY APPLIED ARTS (1948),
2 Percy Street, London W1T 1DD T 020-7436 2344
E sales@caa.org.uk W www.caa.org.uk
Joint Directors, Clare Maddison and Flora Bhattachary

CO-OPERATIVE PARTY (1917), 77 Weston Street,
London SE1 3SD T 020-7367 4150 E mail@party.coop
W www.party.coop
General Secretary, Michael Stephenson

CORAM FAMILY (1739), 49 Mecklenburgh Square,
London WC1N 2QA T 020-7520 0300
E reception@coram.org.uk W www.coram.org.uk
Chief Executive, Dr Carol Homden

CORONERS' SOCIETY OF ENGLAND AND WALES
(1846), HM Coroner's Court, The Cotton Exchange,
Old Hall Street, Liverpool L3 9UF T 0151-233 4708
W www.coronersociety.org.uk
Hon. Secretary, André Joseph Anthony Rebello, OBE

CORPORATION OF THE CHURCH HOUSE (1888),
Church House, Great Smith Street, London SW1P 3AZ
T 020-7898 1000 E info@churchhouse.org.uk
W www.churchhouse.org.uk
Secretary, Christopher Palmer, CBE

COUNCIL FOR AWARDS OF ROYAL
AGRICULTURAL SOCIETIES (1970), Springvale,
Orchard Close, Shaldon, TQ14 0HF T 01626-873234
E ejwibberley@btinternet.com
Hon. Secretary, Prof. John Wibberley, PHD, FRAGS

COUNCIL FOR WORLD MISSION (1977), Ipalo House,
32–34 Great Peter Street, London SW1P 2DB
T 020-7222 4214 E council@cwmission.org.uk
W www.cwmission.org.uk
General Secretary, Revd Dr Collin Cowan

COUNCIL OF CHRISTIANS AND JEWS (1942),
Godliman House, 21 Godliman Street, London EC4V 5BD
T 020-7015 5160 E cjrelations@ccj.org.uk
W www.ccj.org.uk
Chief Executive, David Gifford

COUNCIL OF UNIVERSITY CLASSICAL
DEPARTMENTS (1972), Faculty of Classics,
Sidgwick Avenue, Cambridge CB3 9DA T 01223-335158
E ro225@cam.ac.uk W www.rhul.ac.uk/classics/cucd
Chair, Prof. Robin G. Osborne, FBA

COUNSEL AND CARE (1954), Twyman House,
16 Bonny Street, London NW1 9PG T 020-7241 8555
E advice@counselandcare.org.uk
W www.counselandcare.org.uk
Chief Executive, Peter Watt

COUNTRY LAND & BUSINESS ASSOCIATION
(1907), 16 Belgrave Square, London SW1X 8PQ
T 020-7235 0511 E mail@cla.org.uk W www.cla.org.uk
President, William Worsely

COUNTRYSIDE ALLIANCE (1997), Old Town Hall,
367 Kennington Road, London SE11 4PT T 020-7840 9200
W www.countryside-alliance.org.uk
Chief Executive, Alice Barnard

CRISIS UK (1967), 66 Commercial Street, London E1 6LT
T 0300-636 1967 E enquiries@crisis.org.uk
W www.crisis.org.uk
Chief Executive, Leslie Morphy

CRUSE BEREAVEMENT CARE (1959), Unit 01,
One Victoria Villas, Richmond TW9 2GW T 020-8939 9530,
Helpline 0844-477 9400 E info@cruse.org.uk
W www.cruse.org.uk
Chief Executive, Debbie Kerslake

CSV (1962), 237 Pentonville Road, London N1 9NJ
T 020-7278 6601 E information@csv.org.uk
W www.csv.org.uk
Chief Executive, Lucy de Groot, CBE

CUMBERLAND AND WESTMORLAND
ANTIQUARIAN AND ARCHAEOLOGICAL
SOCIETY (1866), Westlands, Westbourne Drive,
Lancaster LA1 5EE T 01524-67523 E info@cwaas.org.uk
W www.cwaas.org.uk
General Secretary, Marion E. M. McClintock

CYSTIC FIBROSIS TRUST (1964), 11 London Road,
Bromley BR1 1BY T 020-8464 7211
E enquiries@cftrust.org.uk W www.cftrust.org.uk
Chief Executive, Matthew Reed

DAY ONE CHRISTIAN MINISTRIES (1831),
Ryelands Road, Leominster HR6 8NZ T 01568-613740
E sales@dayone.co.uk W www.dayone.co.uk
Managing Director, Mark Roberts

DEMOS, Third Floor, Magdalen House, 136 Tooley Street,
London SE1 2TU T 0845-458 5949 E hello@demos.co.uk
W www.demos.co.uk
Chair, Philip Collins

DESIGN AND TECHNOLOGY ASSOCIATION (1989),
16 Wellesbourne House, Walton Road, Wellesbourne
CV35 9JB T 01789-470007 E info@data.org.uk
W www.data.org.uk
Chief Executive, Richard Green

DEVON ARCHAEOLOGICAL SOCIETY (1929), Royal
Albert Memorial Museum, Queen Street, Exeter EX4 3RX
E dashonsec@btinternet.com W www.ex.ac.uk/das
Hon. Secretary, Amanda Eversett

DIABETES UK (1934), Macleod House, 10 Parkway,
London NW1 7AA T 020-7424 1000 E info@diabetes.org.uk
W www.diabetes.org.uk
Chief Executive, Barbara Young

DITCHLEY FOUNDATION (1958), Ditchley Park,
Enstone, Chipping Norton OX7 4ER T 01608-677346
E mail@ditchley.co.uk W www.ditchley.co.uk
Director, Sir John Holmes, GCVO, KBE, CMG

DOWN'S SYNDROME ASSOCIATION (1970),
The Langdon Down Centre, 2A Langdon Park, Teddington
TW11 9PS T 0845-230 0372
E info@downs-syndrome.org.uk
W www.downs-syndrome.org.uk
Chief Executive, Carol Boys

DUKE OF EDINBURGH'S AWARD (1956),
Gulliver House, Madeira Walk, Windsor SL4 1EU
T 01753-727400 E info@DofE.org W www.DofE.org
Chief Executive, Peter Westgarth

DYSLEXIA ACTION (2006), Park House, Wick Road,
Egham TW20 0HH T 01784-222300
E info@dyslexiaaction.org.uk W www.dyslexiaaction.org.uk
Chief Executive, Kevin Geeson

EAST HERTFORDSHIRE ARCHAEOLOGICAL
SOCIETY (1898), 41 St Leonard's Road, Bengeo, Hertford
SG14 3JW T 01992-423725 E EHASoc@googlemail.com
W www.ehas.org.uk
Hon. Secretary, S. G. Horner

EAST OF ENGLAND AGRICULTURAL SOCIETY
(1797), East of England Showground, Peterborough
PE2 6XE T 01733-234451 E info@eastofengland.org.uk
W www.eastofengland.org.uk
Chief Executive, Paul Wallwork

ECCLESIOLOGICAL SOCIETY (1879), 38 Rosebery
Avenue, New Malden KT3 4JS E info@ecclsoc.org
W www.ecclsoc.org
Chair, Trevor Cooper

EDUCATION OTHERWISE (1976), 125 Queen Street,
Sheffield S1 2DU T 0845-478 6345
E enquiries@education-otherwise.net
W www.education-otherwise.net
Chair, Shena Deuchars

EGYPT EXPLORATION SOCIETY (1882),
3 Doughty Mews, London WC1N 2PG T 020-7242 1880
W www.ees.ac.uk
Director, Dr Patricia Spencer

ELECTORAL REFORM SOCIETY (1884),
6 Chancel Street, London SE1 0UU T 020-7928 1622
E ers@electoral-reform.org.uk
W www.electoral-reform.org.uk
Chief Executive, Katie Ghose

ELGAR BIRTHPLACE MUSEUM (1935), The Elgar
Birthplace Museum, Lower Broadheath, Worcester WR2 6RH
T 01905-333224 E birthplace@elgarmuseum.org
W www.elgarmuseum.org
Museum Director, Catherine Sloan

ELGAR SOCIETY (1951), 12 Monkhams Drive,
Woodford Green IG8 0LQ T 020-8504 0295
E info@elgar.org W www.elgar.org
Chair, Steven Halls

EMERGENCY PLANNING SOCIETY (1993), The Media
Centre, Culverhouse Cross, Cardiff CF5 6XJ
T 0845-600 9587 E manager@the-eps.org
W www.the-eps.org
Chair, Marc Beveridge

ENGLISH ASSOCIATION (1906), University of Leicester, University Road, Leicester LE1 7RH **T** 0116-229 7622 **E** engassoc@le.ac.uk **W** www.le.ac.uk/engassoc
Chief Executive, Ms H. Lucas

ENGLISH CHESS FEDERATION (1904), The Watch Oak, Chain Lane, Battle TN33 0YD **T** 01424-775222 **E** office@englishchess.org.uk **W** www.englishchess.org.uk
Chief Executive, Andrew Farthing

ENGLISH FOLK DANCE AND SONG SOCIETY (1932), Cecil Sharp House, 2 Regent's Park Road, London NW1 7AY **T** 020-7485 2206 **E** info@efdss.org
W www.efdss.org
Chief Executive, K. Spicer

ENGLISH-SPEAKING UNION OF THE COMMONWEALTH (1918), Dartmouth House, 37 Charles Street, London W1J 5ED **T** 020-7529 1550 **E** esu@esu.org **W** www.esu.org
Director-General, Michael Lake, CBE

EPILEPSY ACTION (1950), New Anstey House, Gate Way Drive, Yeadon, Leeds LS19 7XY **T** 0113-210 8800, **Helpline** 0808-800 5050 **E** helpline@epilepsy.org.uk
W www.epilepsy.org.uk
Chief Executive, Philip Lee

EPILEPSY SOCIETY (1892), Chesham Lane, Chalfont St Peter SL9 0RJ **T** 01494-601300, **Helpline** 01494-601400
W www.epilepsysociety.org.uk
Chief Executive, Graham Faulkner

ESPERANTO ASSOCIATION OF BRITAIN (1976), Esperanto House, Station Road, Barlaston, Stoke-on-Trent ST12 9DE **T** 0845-230 1887 **E** eab@esperanto-gb.org
W www.esperanto-gb.org
President, Prof. John Wells

EVANGELICAL LIBRARY, Units 5 & 6 Gateway Mews, Ring Way, Bounds Green, London N11 2UT
T 020-8362 0868 **E** elenquire@gmail.com
W www.evangelical-library.org.uk
Librarian, S. J. Taylor

FABIAN SOCIETY (1884), 11 Dartmouth Street, London SW1H 9BN **T** 020-7227 4900 **E** info@fabian-society.org.uk
W www.fabian-society.org.uk
General Secretary, S. Katwala

FACULTY OF ROYAL DESIGNERS FOR INDUSTRY (1936), RSA, 8 John Adam Street, London WC2N 6EZ **T** 020-7451 6892 **E** rdi@rsa.org.uk **W** www.rsa.org.uk
Master, Robin Levien

FAIR ISLE BIRD OBSERVATORY TRUST (1948), Fair Isle Bird Observatory, Fair Isle ZE2 9JU **T** 01595-760258 **E** fairisle.birdobs@zetnet.co.uk **W** www.fairislebirdobs.co.uk
Administrator, H. Shaw

FAITH AND THOUGHT (1865), 15 The Drive, Harlow CM20 3QD **E** revjdbuxton@sky.com
W www.faithandthought.org.uk
President, Sir John Houghton, FRS

FEDERATION OF BRITISH ARTISTS (1961), 17 Carlton House Terrace, London SW1Y 5BD **T** 020-7930 6844 **E** info@mallgalleries.com
W www.mallgalleries.org.uk
Director, Lewis McNaught

FEDERATION OF FAMILY HISTORY SOCIETIES (1974), PO Box 8857, Lutterworth LE17 9BJ **T** 01455-293133 **E** info@ffhs.org.uk **W** www.ffhs.org.uk
Administrator, Philippa McCray

FEDERATION OF SMALL BUSINESSES (1974), 2 Catherine Place, Westminster, London SW1E 6HF **T** 020-7592 8100 **E** press@fsb.org.uk **W** www.fsb.org.uk
Head of Policy, Andrew Cave

FIELDS IN TRUST (1925), Ground Floor South, 100 Christian Street, London E1 1RS **T** 020-7427 2110 **E** info@fieldsintrust.org **W** www.fieldsintrust.org
Chief Executive, Alison Moore-Gwyn

FIELD STUDIES COUNCIL (1943), Preston Montford, Montford Bridge, Shrewsbury SY4 1HW **T** 0845-345 4071 **E** enquiries@field-studies-council.org
W www.field-studies-council.org
Chief Executive, Rob Lucas

FIGHT FOR SIGHT (1965), 36–38 Botolph Lane, London EC3R 8DE **T** 020-7929 7755 **E** info@fightforsight.org.uk
W www.fightforsight.org.uk
Chief Executive, Michele Acton

FIRE FIGHTERS CHARITY (1943), Level 6, Belvedere House, Basing View, Basingstoke RG21 4HG **T** 01256-366566 **E** info@firefighterscharity.org.uk
W www.firefighterscharity.org.uk
Chief Executive, John Parry

FLAG INSTITUTE (1971), 38 Hill Street, Mayfair, London W1J 5NS **E** membership@flaginstitute.org
W www.flaginstitute.org
President, Capt. Malcolm Farrow, OBE, FFI, RN

FLEET AIR ARM OFFICERS' ASSOCIATION (1957), 4 St James's Square, London SW1Y 4JU **T** 020-7930 7722 **E** faaoa@fleetairarmoa.org **W** www.fleetairarmoa.org
Chair, Rear-Adm. S. Lidbetter

FOREIGN PRESS ASSOCIATION IN LONDON (1888), 25 Northumberland Avenue, London WC2N 5AP **T** 020-7930 0445 **E** christopherwyld@fpalondon.org
W www.foreign-press.org.uk
Director, Christopher Wyld

FORENSIC SCIENCE SOCIETY (1959), Clarke House, 18A Mount Parade, Harrogate HG1 1BX **T** 01423-506068 **E** info@forensic-science-society.org
W www.forensic-science-society.org.uk
Chief Executive, Dr Carol Ostell

FOUNDATION FOR THE STUDY OF INFANT DEATHS (1971), 11 Belgrave Road, London SW1V 1RB **T** 020-7802 3200 **E** office@fsid.org.uk
W www.fsid.org.uk
Director, Mrs J. Epstein

FPA (1930), 50 Featherstone Street, London EC1Y 8QU **T** 0845-122 8600 **E** fpadirect@fpa.org.uk
W www.fpa.org.uk
Chief Executive, Julie Bentley

FRANCO-BRITISH SOCIETY (1924), 3 Dovedale Studios, 465 Battersea Park Road, London SW11 4LR
E execsec@francobritishsociety.org.uk
W www.francobritishsociety.org.uk
Executive Secretary, Kate Brayn

FRIENDS OF CATHEDRAL MUSIC (1956),
21 Bradford Road, Trowbridge BA14 9AL T 0845-644 3721
E info@fcm.org.uk W www.fcm.org.uk
Secretary, Roger Bishton

FRIENDS OF FRIENDLESS CHURCHES (1957),
St Ann's Vestry Hall, 2 Church Entry, London EC4V 5HB
T 020-7236 3934
E office@friendsoffriendlesschurches.org.uk
W www.friendsoffriendlesschurches.org.uk
Director, Matthew Saunders, MBE

FRIENDS OF THE BODLEIAN (1925), Bodleian Library,
Oxford OX1 3BG T 01865-277234 E fob@bodleian.ox.ac.uk
W www.bodleian.ox.ac.uk/bodley/friends
Chair, Prof. Richard McCabe

FRIENDS OF THE EARTH SCOTLAND (1978), Thorn House, 5 Rose Street, Edinburgh EH2 2PR T 0131-243 2700
E info@foe-scotland.org.uk W www.foe-scotland.org.uk
Chief Executive, Stan Blackley

FRIENDS OF THE NATIONAL LIBRARIES (1931),
c/o Department of Manuscripts, The British Library,
96 Euston Road, London NW1 2DB T 020-7412 7559
W www.friendsofnationallibraries.org.uk
Chair, Lord Egremont, FRSL

FURNITURE HISTORY SOCIETY (1964), 1 Mercedes Cottages, St John's Road, Haywards Heath RH16 4EH
T 01444-413845 E furniturehistorysociety@hotmail.com
W www.furniturehistorysociety.org
Membership Secretary, Dr Brian Austen

GALLIPOLI ASSOCIATION (1969), Earleydene Orchard,
Earleydene, Ascot SL5 9JY T 01344-626523
E webmaster@gallipoli-association.org
W www.gallipoli-association.org
Hon. Secretary, J. C. Watson Smith

GAME AND WILDLIFE CONSERVATION TRUST
(1969), Fordingbridge SP6 1EF T 01425-652381
E info@gwct.org.uk W www.gwct.org.uk
Chief Executive, Teresa Dent

GENERAL MEDICAL COUNCIL (1858), Regent's Place,
350 Euston Road, London NW1 3JN T 0161-923 6602
E gmc@gmc-uk.org W www.gmc-uk.org
Chief Executive, Niall Dickson

GENERAL OPTICAL COUNCIL (1958), 41 Harley Street,
London W1G 8DJ T 020-7580 3898 E goc@optical.org
W www.optical.org
Chief Executive & Registrar, Samantha Peters

GEOGRAPHICAL ASSOCIATION (1893),
160 Solly Street, Sheffield S1 4BF T 0114-296 0088
E info@geography.org.uk W www.geography.org.uk
Chief Executive, David Lambert

GIRLS' BRIGADE ENGLAND AND WALES (1965),
PO Box 196, 129 The Broadway, Didcot OX11 8XN
T 01235-510425 E gbco@girlsbrigadeew.org.uk
W www.girlsb.org
National Director, Ruth Gilson

GIRLS' VENTURE CORPS AIR CADETS (1964),
1 Bawtry Gate, Sheffield, S9 1UD T 0114-2448405
E gvcac@toucansurf.com W www.gvcac.org.uk
Corps Director, Brenda Layne, MBE

GLADSTONE'S LIBRARY (1894), Church Lane, Hawarden
CH5 3DF T 01244-532350 E enquiries@gladlib.org
W www.st-deniols.com
Warden Chief Librarian, Revd Peter Francis

GREENPEACE UK (1979), Canonbury Villas, London
N1 2PN T 020-7865 8100 E info@uk.greenpeace.org
W www.greenpeace.org.uk
Executive Director, John Sauven

GUIDE DOGS FOR THE BLIND ASSOCIATION
(1934), Hillfields, Burghfield Common, Reading RG7 3YG
T 0118-983 5555 E guidedogs@guidedogs.org.uk
W www.guidedogs.org.uk
Chief Executive, Richard Leaman

GUILD OF FREEMEN OF THE CITY OF LONDON
(1908), 4 Dowgate Hill, London EC4R 2SH
T 020-8541 1435 E clerk@guild-freemen-london.co.uk
W www.guild-freemen-london.co.uk
Clerk to the Guild, Brig. M. I. Keun

GURKHA WELFARE TRUST (1969), PO Box 2170,
22 Queen Street, Salisbury SP2 2EX T 01722-323955
E staffassistant@gwt.org.uk W www.gwt.org.uk
Chief Executive, Col. William Shuttlewood, OBE

GUY'S AND ST THOMAS' CHARITY (1553), West Wing, Counting House, Guy's Hospital, Great Maze Pond,
London SE1 9RT T 020-7188 7700 E info@gsttcharity.org.uk
W www.gsttcharity.org.uk
Chief Executive, Peter Hewitt

HAEMOPHILIA SOCIETY (1950), First Floor, Petersham House, 57A Hatton Garden, London EC1N 8JG
T 020-7831 1020, **Freephone Information and Support**
0800-018 6068 E info@haemophilia.org.uk
W www.haemophilia.org.uk
Chief Executive, Chris James

HAIG HOUSING TRUST (2009), Alban Dobson House,
Green Lane, Morden SM4 5NS T 020-8685 5777
E enquiries@haighousingtrust.org.uk
W www.haighousingtrust.org.uk
Chief Executive, Maj.-Gen. P. V. R. Besgrove, CBE

HAKLUYT SOCIETY (1846), c/o Map Library, The British Library, 96 Euston Road, London NW1 2DB
T 01428-641850 E office@hakluyt.com
W www.hakluyt.com
President, Prof. W. F. Ryan

HALIFAX ANTIQUARIAN SOCIETY (1900),
356 Oldham Road, Sowerby Bridge, Halifax HX6 4QU
T 01422-823966 E mail@halifaxhistory.org.uk
W www.halifaxhistory.org.uk
Hon. Secretary, Anne Kirker

HANSARD SOCIETY FOR PARLIAMENTARY GOVERNMENT (1944), 40–43 Chancery Lane, London WC2A 1JA **T** 020-7438 1222 **E** hansard@hansard.lse.ac.uk **W** www.hansardsociety.org.uk
Chief Executive, Fiona Booth

HARVEIAN SOCIETY OF LONDON (1831), Lettsom House, 11 Chandos Street, London W1G 9EB **T** 020-7580 1043 **E** harveiansoclondon@btconnect.com **W** www.harveiansocietyoflondon.btck.co.uk
Executive Secretary, Cdr R. C. Ireland, MBE

HAWICK ARCHAEOLOGICAL SOCIETY (1856), 8 Melgund Place, Hawick TD9 9HY **T** 01450-376220 **E** info@airchieoliver.co.uk **W** www.airchieoliver.co.uk
Hon. Secretary, Gerald M. Graham

HEARING LINK (1947), 27-28 The Waterfront, Eastbourne BN23 5UZ **T** 03001-111113 **E** enquiries@hearinglink.org **W** www.hearinglink.org
Chief Executive, Dr Lorraine Gailey

HELP FOR HEROES (2007), Unit 6, Aspire Business Centre, Ordnance Road, Tidworth SP9 7QD **T** 0845-673 1760 **E** info@helpforheroes.org.uk **W** www.helpforheroes.org.uk
Chair, Hadyn Parry

HERALDRY SOCIETY (1947), PO Box 772, Guildford GU3 3ZX **T** 01483-237373 **E** memsec@theheraldrysociety.com **W** www.theheraldrysociety.com
Hon. Secretary, John Tunesi of Liongam

HISPANIC AND LUSO BRAZILIAN COUNCIL (1943), Canning House, 2 Belgrave Square, London SW1X 8PJ **T** 020-7235 2303 **E** enquiries@canninghouse.org **W** www.canninghouse.org
Chief Executive, Dr Charles Goodson-Wickes

HISTORICAL ASSOCIATION (1906), 59A Kennington Park Road, London SE11 4JH **T** 020-7735 3901 **E** enquiry@history.org.uk **W** www.history.org.uk
Chief Executive, Rebecca Sullivan

HISTORIC HOUSES ASSOCIATION (1973), 2 Chester Street, London SW1X 7BB **T** 020-7259 5688 **E** info@hha.org.uk **W** www.hha.org.uk
Director-General, Nick Way

HONG KONG ASSOCIATION (1961), Swire House, 59 Buckingham Gate, London SW1E 6AJ **T** 020-7963 9447 **E** communications@hkas.org.uk **W** www.hkas.org.uk
Executive Director, Robert Guy

HONOURABLE SOCIETY OF CYMMRODORION (1751), PO Box 55178, London N12 2AY **T** 01582-832 971 **E** aelodau1751we@yahoo.co.uk **W** www.cymmrodorion1751.org.uk
Hon. Secretary, Peter Jeffreys

HOUSING JUSTICE (1956), 22–25 Finsbury Square, London EC2A 1DX **T** 020-7920 6600 **E** info@housingjustice.org.uk **W** www.housingjustice.org.uk
Director, Alison Gelder

HR SOCIETY LTD (1970), The Old Stables, Redenham Park, Redenham, Andover SP11 9AQ **T** 01264-774004 **E** info@hrsociety.co.uk **W** www.hrsociety.co.uk
President, Andrew Mayo

HUMANE RESEARCH TRUST (1962), Brook House, 29 Bramhall Lane South, Bramhall, Stockport SK7 2DN **T** 0161-439 8041 **E** info@humaneresearch.org.uk **W** www.humaneresearch.org.uk
Chair, K. Cholerton

HYMN SOCIETY OF GREAT BRITAIN AND IRELAND (1936), 99 Barton Road, Lancaster LA1 4EN **T** 01524-66740 **E** robcanham@haystacks.fsnet.co.uk **W** www.hymnsocietygbi.org.uk
Hon. Secretary, Revd Robert A. Canham

I CAN (1888), 8 Wakely Street, London EC1V 7QE **T** 0845-225 4073 **E** info@ican.org.uk **W** www.ican.org.uk
Chief Executive, Virginia Beardshaw

IFS SCHOOL OF FINANCE (1879), 8th Floor, Peninsular House, 36 Monument Street, London, EC3R 8LJ **T** 01227-818609 **E** customerservices@ifslearning.ac.uk **W** www.ifslearning.ac.uk
Principle, Gavin Shreeve

INDEPENDENTAGE (1863), 6 Avonmore Road, London W14 8RL **T** 020-7605 4200 **E** charity@independentage.org.uk **W** www.independentage.org.uk
Chief Executive, Janet Morrison

INDEPENDENT SCHOOLS' BURSARS ASSOCIATION (1932), Unit 11–12, Manor Farm, Cliddesden RG25 2JB **T** 01256-330369 **E** office@theisba.org.uk **W** www.theisba.org.uk
General Secretary, Mike Lower

INDUSTRY AND PARLIAMENT TRUST (1977), Suite 101, 3 Whitehall Court, London SW1A 2EL **T** 020-7839 9400 **E** industryandparliamenttrust@ipt.org.uk **W** www.ipt.org.uk
Acting Chief Executive, Monica Harding

INSTITUTE FOR PUBLIC POLICY RESEARCH (1988), 13–14 Buckingham Street, London WC2N 6DF **T** 020-7470 6100 **W** www.ippr.org **E** info@ippr.org
Director, Nick Pearce

INSTITUTE OF CANCER RESEARCH (1909), 237 Fulham Road, London SW3 6JB **T** 020-7352 8133 **W** www.icr.ac.uk
Chief Executive, Prof. Alan Ashworth

INSTITUTE OF ECONOMIC AFFAIRS (1955), 2 Lord North Street, London SW1P 3LB **T** 020-7799 8900 **E** iea@iea.org.uk **W** www.iea.org.uk
Director-General, Mark Littlewood

INSTITUTE OF HEALTH PROMOTION AND EDUCATION, School of Dentistry, University of Manchester, Coupland 3, Oxford Road, Manchester M13 9PL **T** 0161-275 6610 **E** honsec@ihpe.org.uk **W** www.ihpe.org.uk
Hon. Secretary, Kathy Lewis

INSTITUTE OF HERALDIC AND GENEALOGICAL STUDIES (1961), 79–82 Northgate, Canterbury CT1 1BA **T** 01227-768664 **E** ihgs@ihgs.ac.uk **W** www.ihgs.ac.uk
Principal, Dr Richard Baker

INSTITUTE OF MATHEMATICS AND ITS APPLICATIONS (1964), Catherine Richards House, 16 Nelson Street, Southend-on-Sea SS1 1EF T 01702-354020 E post@ima.org.uk W www.ima.org.uk *Executive Director,* David Youdan

INSTITUTE OF PHYSICS AND ENGINEERING IN MEDICINE, Fairmount House, 230 Tadcaster Road, York YO24 1ES T 01904-610821 E office@ipem.ac.uk W www.ipem.ac.uk *General Secretary,* R. W. Neilson

INSTITUTION OF ENGINEERING AND TECHNOLOGY (1871), 2 Savoy Place, London WC2R 0BL T 020-7240 1871 E postmaster@theiet.org W www.theiet.org *Chief Executive & Secretary,* Nigel Fine

INTERCONTINENTAL CHURCH SOCIETY (1823), 1 Athena Drive, Tachbrook Park CV34 6NL T 01926-430347 E enquiries@ics-uk.org W www.ics-uk.org *General Manager,* David Healey

INTERNATIONAL AFRICAN INSTITUTE (1926), SOAS, Thornhaugh Street, Russell Square, London WC1H 0XG T 020-7898 4420 E iai@soas.ac.uk W www.internationalafricaninstitute.org *Hon. Director,* Prof. Philip Burnham

INTERNATIONAL INSTITUTE FOR CONSERVATION OF HISTORIC AND ARTISTIC WORKS (1950), 6 Buckingham Street, London WC2N 6BA T 020-7839 5975 E iic@iiconservation.org W www.iiconservation.org *Secretary-General,* Josephine Kirby Atkinson

INTERNATIONAL RESCUE COMMITTEE UK (1997), 11 Gower Street, London WC1E 6HB T 020-7692 2727 E ircuk@.rescue-uk.org W www.rescue-uk.org *Executive Director,* Carolyn Makinson

INTERNATIONAL STUDENTS HOUSE (1962), 229 Great Portland Street, Regent's Park, London W1W 5PN T 020-7631 8300 E info@ish.org.uk W www.ish.org.uk *Executive Director,* Peter Anwyl

INTERNATIONAL TREE FOUNDATION (1924), Sandy Lane, Crawley Down RH10 4HS T 01342-717300 E info@internationaltreefoundation.org W www.internationaltreefoundation.org *Director,* Lorraine Dunk

INTERSERVE (1852), 5–6 Walker Avenue, Wolverton Hill MK12 5TW T 01908-552700 E enquiries@isewi.org W www.interserve.org.uk *National Director,* Steve Bell

IRAN SOCIETY (1911), 2 Belgrave Square, London SW1X 8PJ T 020-7235 5122 E info@iransociety.org W www.iransociety.org *Chair,* Antony Wynn

ISLE OF WIGHT NATURAL HISTORY AND ARCHAEOLOGICAL SOCIETY (1919), Unit 16, Prospect Business Centre, Prospect Road, Cowes PO31 7AD T 01983-282596 W www.iwnhas.org *President,* Mrs D. Backhouse Fry

JACQUELINE DU PRÉ MUSIC BUILDING LTD (1995), St Hilda's College, Oxford OX4 1DY T 01865-276821 E jdp@st-hildas.ox.ac.uk W www.st-hildas.ox.ac.uk/jdp *Administrator,* Tanya Smith

JAPAN SOCIETY (1891), Swire House, 59 Buckingham Gate, London SW1E 6AJ T 020-7828 6330 E info@japansociety.org.uk W www.japansociety.org.uk *Chief Executive,* Heidi Potter

JERUSALEM AND THE MIDDLE EAST CHURCH ASSOCIATION (1929), 1 Hart House, The Hart, Farnham GU9 7HJ T 01252-726994 E secretary@jmeca.eclipse.co.uk W www.jmeca.org.uk *Chair,* John Clark

JEWISH CARE (1990), 221 Golders Green Road, London NW11 9DQ T 020-8922 2000 E jcdirect@jcare.org W www.jewishcare.org *Chair,* Stephen Zimmerman

JOHN STUART MILL INSTITUTE (1992), 1 Whitehall Place, London SW1A 2HE T 07973-752473 E jsmi@cyberstar.uk.com W www.jsmillinstitute.org.uk *Convenor,* Dr Alan Butt Philip

JOURNALISTS' CHARITY (1864), Dickens House, 35 Wathen Road, Dorking RH4 1JY T 01306-887511 E enquiries@journalistscharity.org.uk W www.journalistscharity.org.uk *Director,* David Ilott

JUSTICE (1957), 59 Carter Lane, London EC4V 5AQ T 020-7329 5100 E admin@justice.org.uk W www.justice.org.uk *Director,* Roger Smith, OBE

KIPLING SOCIETY (1927), 6 Clifton Road, London W9 1SS T 020-7286 0194 E jmkeskar@btinternet.com W www.kipling.org.uk *Hon. Secretary,* Jane Keskar

LCIA (LONDON COURT OF INTERNATIONAL ARBITRATION) (1892), 70 Fleet Street, London EC4Y 1EU T 020-7936 7007 E lcia@lcia.org W www.lcia.org *Director-General,* Adrian Winstanley

LEAGUE OF THE HELPING HAND (1908), PO Box 342, Burgess Hill, RH15 5AQ T 01444-236099 E secretary@lhh.org.uk W www.lhh.org.uk *Executive Secretary,* Moira Parrott

LEPROSY MISSION, ENGLAND, WALES, THE CHANNEL ISLANDS AND THE ISLE OF MAN (1874), Goldhay Way, Orton Goldhay, Peterborough PE2 5GZ T 01733-370505 E post@tlmew.org.uk W www.leprosymission.org.uk *National Director,* Peter A. Walker

LEUKAEMIA AND LYMPHOMA RESEARCH (1960), 39–40 Eagle Street, London WC1R 4TH T 020-7405 0101 E info@beatbloodcancers.org W www.beatbloodcancers.org *Chief Executive,* Cathy Gilman

LIBERTY (NATIONAL COUNCIL FOR CIVIL LIBERTIES) (1934), 21 Tabard Street, London SE1 4LA T 020-7403 3888 W www.liberty-human-rights.org.uk *Chair,* Frances Butler

LINNEAN SOCIETY OF LONDON (1788),
Burlington House, Piccadilly, London W1J 0BF
T 020-7434 4479 **E** info@linnean.org **W** www.linnean.org
Executive Secretary, Dr Ruth Temple

LIONS CLUBS INTERNATIONAL (BRITISH ISLES
AND IRELAND) (1950), 257 Alcester Road South, Kings
Heath, Birmingham B14 6DT **T** 0121-441 4544
E mdhq@lions.org.uk **W** www.lionsmd105.org
Office Manager, Brigitte Waterfield

LISTENING BOOKS (1959), 12 Lant Street, London
SE1 1QH **T** 020-7407 9417 **E** info@listening-books.org.uk
W www.listening-books.org.uk
Director, Bill Dee

LOCAL GOVERNMENT ASSOCIATION (1997),
Local Government House, Smith Square, London SW1P 3HZ
T 020-7664 3000 **E** info@local.gov.uk **W** www.lga.gov.uk
Chief Executive, John Ransford

LONDON AND MIDDLESEX ARCHAEOLOGICAL
SOCIETY (1855), c/o Museum of London, 150 London
Wall, London EC2Y 5HN **T** 020-7814 5734
W www.lamas.org.uk
Hon. Secretary, Jackie Keily

LONDON CATALYST (1873), 45 Westminster Bridge
Road, London SE1 7JB **T** 020-7021 4204
E london.catalyst@peabody.org.uk
W www.londoncatalyst.org.uk
Director, Victor Willmott

LONDON CITY MISSION (1835), 175 Tower Bridge
Road, London SE1 2AH **T** 020-7407 7585
E enquiries@lcm.org.uk **W** www.lcm.org.uk
Chief Executive, Revd Dr John Nicholls

LONDON COUNCILS (2000), 59½ Southwark Street,
London SE1 0AL **T** 020-7934 9999
E info@londoncouncils.gov.uk
W www.londoncouncils.gov.uk
Chief Executive, John O'Brien

LONDON LIBRARY (1841), 14 St James's Square, London
SW1Y 4LG **T** 020-7930 7705
E enquiries@londonlibrary.co.uk
W www.londonlibrary.co.uk
Librarian, Inez Lynn

LONDON PLAYING FIELDS FOUNDATION (1890),
73 Collier Street, London N1 9BE **T** 0845-026 2292
E enquiries@lpff.org.uk **W** www.lpff.org.uk
Chief Executive, Alex Welsh

LONDON SOCIETY (1912), Mortimer Wheeler House,
46 Eagle Wharf Road, London N1 7ED **T** 020-7253 9400
E info@londonsociety.org.uk **W** www.londonsociety.org.uk
Chair, Frank Kelsall

MACMILLAN CANCER SUPPORT (1911),
89 Albert Embankment, London SE1 7UQ **T** 020-7840 7840
E contactus@macmillan.org.uk **W** www.macmillan.org.uk
Chief Executive, Ciarán Devane

MAKING MUSIC, THE NATIONAL FEDERATION OF
MUSIC SOCIETIES (1935), 2–4 Great Eastern Street,
London EC2A 3NW **T** 020-7422 8280
E info@makingmusic.org.uk **W** www.makingmusic.org.uk
Chief Executive, Robin Osterley

MANORIAL SOCIETY OF GREAT BRITAIN (1906),
104 Kennington Road, London SE11 6RE **T** 020-7735 6633
E manorial@msgb.co.uk **W** www.msgb.co.uk
Chair, Robert Smith

MARIE CURIE CANCER CARE (1948), 89 Albert
Embankment, London SE1 7TP **T** 0800-716 146
E supporter.services@mariecurie.org.uk
W www.mariecurie.org.uk
Chief Executive, Thomas Hughes-Hallett

MARINE BIOLOGICAL ASSOCIATION OF THE UK
(1884), Citadel Hill, Plymouth PL1 2BP **T** 01752-633207
E sec@mba.ac.uk **W** www.mba.ac.uk
President, Sir Geoffrey Holland, KCB

MARINE SOCIETY AND SEA CADETS (1756),
202 Lambeth Road, London SE1 7JW **T** 020-7654 7000
E info@ms-sc.org **W** www.ms-sc.org
Chief Executive, Martin Coles

MATERNITY ACTION (2008), Third Floor West,
52–54 Featherstone Street, London EC1Y 8RT
T 020-7253 2288 **W** www.maternityaction.org.uk
Chair, Moyra Rushby

MDF THE BIPOLAR ORGANISATION (1983),
Castle Works, 21 St George's Road, London SE1 6ES
T 020-7793 2600 **E** mdf@mdf.org.uk **W** www.mdf.org.uk
Chief Executive, Suzanne Hudson

ME ASSOCIATION (1976), 7 Apollo Office Court,
Radclive Road, Gawcott MK18 4DF **T** 0844-576 5326
E meconnect@meassociation.org.uk
W www.meassociation.org.uk
Chair, Neil Riley

MEDIAWATCH-UK (1965), 3 Willow House,
Kennington Road, Ashford TN24 0NR **T** 01233-633936
E info@mediawatchuk.org **W** www.mediawatchuk.org
Director, Vivienne Pattison

MEDICAL SOCIETY OF LONDON (1773),
Lettsom House, 11 Chandos Street, London W1G 9EB
T 020-7580 1043 **E** medicalsoclondon@btconnect.com
W www.medsoclondon.org
Registrar, Cdr Roger Ireland, MBE

MEDICAL WOMEN'S FEDERATION (1917), Tavistock
House North, Tavistock Square, London WC1H 9HX
T 020-7387 7765 **E** admin.mwf@btconnect.com
W www.medicalwomensfederation.org.uk
President, Dr Clarissa Fabre

MENCAP (ROYAL MENCAP SOCIETY) (1946),
123 Golden Lane, London EC1Y 0RT **T** 020-7454 0454
E information@mencap.org.uk **W** www.mencap.org.uk
Chief Executive, Mark Goldring, CBE

MENTAL HEALTH FOUNDATION (1972),
Sea Containers House, 20 Upper Ground, London SE1 9QB
T 020-7803 1100 **E** mhf@mhf.org.uk
W www.mentalhealth.org.uk
Chief Executive, Andrew McCulloch

MERCHANT NAVY WELFARE BOARD (1948),
8 Cumberland Place, Southampton SO15 2BH
T 023-8033 7799 **E** enquiries@mnwb.org.uk
W www.mnwb.org
Chief Executive, Capt. D. A. Parsons

MHA CARE GROUP (1943), Epworth House,
3 Stuart Street, Derby DE1 2EQ T 01332-296200
E enquiries@mha.org.uk W www.mha.org.uk
Chief Executive, Roger Davies

MIDDLE EAST ASSOCIATION (1961), Bury House,
33 Bury Street, London SW1Y 6AX T 020-7839 2137
E info@the-mea.co.uk W www.the-mea.co.uk
Director-General, Charles Hollis

MIGRAINE ACTION ASSOCIATION (1958),
27 East Street, LE1 6NB T 0116-275 8317
E info@migraine.org.uk W www.migraine.org.uk
Director, Joanna Hamilton Colclough

MILITARY HISTORICAL SOCIETY (1948), National
Army Museum, Royal Hospital Road, London SW3 4HT
T 01252-621056 E mhsqm.mt@btinternet.com
W www.militaryhistsoc.plus.com
Chair, Tim Wright

MIND (NATIONAL ASSOCIATION FOR MENTAL
HEALTH) (1946), 15–19 Broadway, London E15 4BQ
T 020-8519 2122, **Infoline** 0300-123 3393
E contact@mind.org.uk W www.mind.org.uk
Chief Executive, Paul Farmer

MISSING PEOPLE (1993), 284 Upper Richmond Road
West, London SW17 7JE T 020-8392 4590
E info@missingpeople.org.uk W www.missingpeople.org.uk
Chief Executive, Martin Houghton-Brown

MISSION TO SEAFARERS (1856), St Michael
Paternoster Royal, College Hill, London EC4R 2RL
T 020-7248 5202 E info@missiontoseafarers.org
W www.missiontoseafarers.org
Secretary General, Revd Tom Heffer

MULTIPLE SCLEROSIS SOCIETY (1953), MS National
Centre, 372 Edgware Road, Staples Corner, London
NW2 6ND T 020-8438 0700 W www.mssociety.org.uk
Chief Executive, Simon Gillespie

MUSEUMS ASSOCIATION (1889), 24 Calvin Street,
London E1 6NW T 020-7426 6910
E info@museumsassociation.org
W www.museumsassociation.org
Director, Mark Taylor

MUSICIANS BENEVOLENT FUND (1921), 7–11
Britannia Street, London WC1X 9JS T 020-7239 9100
E info@helpmusicians.org.uk W www.helpmusicians.org.uk
Chief Executive, David Sulkin

NACRO, THE CRIME REDUCTION CHARITY (1966),
Park Place, 10–12 Lawn Lane, London SW8 1UD
T 020-7840 7200 E debbie.john@nacro.org.uk
W www.nacro.org.uk
Chief Executive, Paul McDowell

NATIONAL ASSOCIATION FOR CROHN'S AND
COLITIS DISEASE, 4 Beaumont House, Sutton Road,
St Albans AL1 5HH T 0845-130 2233
E info@chronsandcolitis.org.uk W www.nacc.org.uk
Chief Executive, Richard Driscoll

NATIONAL ASSOCIATION FOR GIFTED CHILDREN
(1967), Suite 1.2, Challenge House, Bletchley, Milton
Keynes MK3 6DP T 01908-646433
E amazingchildren@nagcbritain.org.uk
W www.nagcbritain.org.uk
Chief Executive, Denise Yates

NATIONAL ASSOCIATION OF CLUBS FOR YOUNG
PEOPLE (1925), 371 Kennington Lane, London SE11 5QY
T 020-7793 0787 E office@clubsforyoungpeople.org.uk
W www.clubsforyoungpeople.org.uk
Chair, Peter Birch

NATIONAL BENEVOLENT INSTITUTION (1812),
Peter Herve House, Eccles Court, Tetbury GL8 8EH
T 01666-505500 E office@nbi.org.uk
W www.nbicharity.org.uk
Chief Executive, Paul Rossi

NATIONAL CAMPAIGN FOR COURTESY (1986),
240 Tolworth Rise South, Surbiton, Surrey KT5 9NB
T 020-8330 3707 E peter.foot1@btinternet.com
W www.campaignforcourtesy.org
Chair, Peter G. Foot

NATIONAL CHILDBIRTH TRUST (1956),
Alexandra House, Oldham Terrace, London W3 6NH
T 0300-330 0770 E enquiries@nct.org.uk W www.nct.co.uk
Chief Executive, Ms B. Phipps

NATIONAL CHILDMINDING ASSOCIATION (1971),
Royal Court, 81 Tweedy Road, Bromley BR1 1TG
T 0845 880 0044 E info@ncma.org.uk
W www.ncma.org.uk
Chief Executives, Liz Bayram and Catherine Farrell

NATIONAL COUNCIL OF WOMEN OF GREAT
BRITAIN (1895), 72 Victoria Road, Darlington DL1 5JG
T 01325-367375 E info@ncwgb.org W www.ncwgb.org
President, Sheila Eaton

NATIONAL EXTENSION COLLEGE (1963),
Michael Young Centre, Purbeck Road, Cambridge CB2 8HN
T 01223-400200 E info@nec.ac.uk W www.nec.ac.uk
Chief Executive, Chris Glennie

NATIONAL FEDERATION OF WOMEN'S
INSTITUTES (1915), 104 New Kings Road, London
SW6 4LY T 020-7371 9300 E hq@nfwi.org.uk
W www.thewi.org.uk
General Secretary, Mrs J. Osborne

NATIONAL FOUNDATION FOR EDUCATIONAL
RESEARCH IN ENGLAND AND WALES (1946),
The Mere, Upton Park, Slough SL1 2DQ T 01753-574123
E enquiries@nfer.ac.uk W www.nfer.ac.uk
Chief Executive, Sue Rossiter

NATIONAL HEALTH SERVICE CONFEDERATION
(1997), 29 Bressenden Place, London SW1E 5DD
T 020-7074 3200 E enquiries@nhsconfed.org
W www.nhsconfed.or
Chief Executive, Mike Farrar

NATIONAL OPERATIC AND DRAMATIC
ASSOCIATION (1899), NODA House,
58–60 Lincoln Road, Peterborough PE1 2RZ
T 01733-865790 E info@noda.org.uk W www.noda.org.uk
Chief Executive, Tony Gibbs

NATIONAL OSTEOPOROSIS SOCIETY (1986), Camerton, Bath BA2 0PJ T 01761-471771, **Helpline** 0845-450 0230 E info@nos.org.uk W www.nos.org.uk *Chief Executive,* Claire Severgnini

NATIONAL SECULAR SOCIETY (1866), 25 Red Lion Square, London WC1R 4RL T 020-7404 3126 E enquiries@secularism.org.uk W www.secularism.org.uk *Executive Director,* K. P. Wood

NATIONAL TRUST (1895), Heelis, Kemble Drive, Swindon SN2 2NA T 0844-800 1895 E enquiries@thenationaltrust.org.uk W www.nationaltrust.org.uk *Director-General,* Fiona Reynolds

NATIONAL TRUST FOR SCOTLAND (1931), Hermiston Quay, 5 Cultins Road, Edinburgh EH11 4DF T 0844-493 2100 E information@nts.org.uk W www.nts.org.uk *Chief Executive,* Kate Mavor

NATIONAL UNION OF STUDENTS (NUS) (1922), 4th Floor, 184-192 Drummond Street, London NW1 3HP T 0871-221 8221 E nusuk@nus.org.uk W www.nus.org.uk *Chief Executive,* Matt Hyde

NATIONAL WOMEN'S REGISTER (1966), 23 Vulcan House, Vulcan Road North, Norwich NR6 6AQ T 01603-406767 E office@nwr.org.uk W www.nwr.org.uk *Chair of Trustees,* Kathleen Tanner

NAT (NATIONAL AIDS TRUST) (1987), New City Cloisters, 196 Old Street, London EC1V 9FR T 020-7814 6767 E info@nat.org.uk W www.nat.org.uk *Chief Executive,* Deborah Jack

NAVY RECORDS SOCIETY (1893), c/o Pangbourne College, Pangbourne, Berks RG8 8LA T 01189-842101 E honsec@navyrecords.org.uk W www.navyrecords.org.uk *Hon. Secretary,* Robin Brodhurst

NOISE ABATEMENT SOCIETY (1959), Suite 2, 26 Brunswick Terrace, Hove BN3 1HJ T 01273-823850 E info@noise-abatement.org W www.noiseabatementsociety.com *Chief Executive,* Gloria Elliott

NSPCC (1884), Weston House, 42 Curtain Road, London EC2A 3NH T 020-7825 2500 E info@nspcc.org.uk W www.nspcc.org.uk *Chief Executive,* Andrew Flanagan

NUFFIELD FOUNDATION (1943), 28 Bedford Square, London WC1B 3JS T 020-7631 0566 E info@nuffieldfoundation.org W www.nuffieldfoundation.org *Director,* Anthony Tomei

NUFFIELD TRUST (1940), 59 New Cavendish Street, London W1G 7LP T 020-7631 8450 E info@nuffieldtrust.org.uk W www.nuffieldtrust.org.uk *Director,* Dr Jennifer Dixon

NURSE AID (1917), Grosvenor House, Prospect Hill, Worcestershire, B97 4DL T 01527-595999 E admin@nurseaid.org.uk W www.nurseaid.org.uk *Director,* Peter Farrall, CEO

NUTRITION SOCIETY (1941), 10 Cambridge Court, 210 Shepherds Bush Road, London W6 7NJ T 020-7602 0228 E office@nutsoc.org.uk W www.nutritionsociety.org *Chief Executive,* Frederick Wentworth-Bowyer

OFFICERS' ASSOCIATION (1919), Mountbarrow House, 6–20 Elizabeth Street, London SW1W 9RB T 020-7808 4160 E info@officersassociation.org.uk W www.officersassociation.org.uk *General Secretary,* Maj.-Gen. J. C. B. Sutherell, CBE

OPEN-AIR MISSION (1853), 4 Harrier Court, Woodside Road, Slip End, Luton LU1 4DQ T 01582-841141 E info@oamission.com W www.oamission.com *General Secretary,* Andy Banton

OPEN SPACES SOCIETY (1865), 25A Bell Street, Henley-on-Thames RG9 2BA T 01491-573535 E hq@oss.org.uk W www.oss.org.uk *General Secretary,* Kate Ashbrook

ORDERS AND MEDALS RESEARCH SOCIETY (1942), PO Box 1233, High Wycombe HP11 9BW T 01494-441207 E generalsecretary@omrs.org W www.omrs.org.uk *General Secretary,* P. M. R. Helmore

OVERSEAS DEVELOPMENT INSTITUTE (1960), 111 Westminster Bridge Road, London SE1 7JD T 020-7922 0300 E odi@odi.org.uk W www.odi.org.uk *Director,* Dr Alison Evans

OVERSEAS SERVICE PENSIONERS' ASSOCIATION (1960), 138 High Street, Tonbridge TN9 1AX T 01732-363836 E mail@ospa.org.uk W www.ospa.org.uk *Secretary,* D. F. B. Le Breton, CBE

OXFAM GREAT BRITAIN (1942), Oxfam House, John Smith Drive, Cowley, Oxford OX4 2JY T 0300-200 1300 W www.oxfam.org.uk *Chief Executive,* Barbara Stocking, CBE

OXFORD PRESERVATION TRUST (1927), 10 Turn Again Lane, St Ebbes, Oxford OX1 1QL T 01865-242918 E info@oxfordpreservation.org.uk W www.oxfordpreservation.org.uk *Director,* Debbie Dance

PALAEONTOLOGICAL ASSOCIATION (1957), c/o Institute of Geography & Earth Sciences, University of Aberystwyth, Ceredigion, SY23 3BD E palass@palass.org W www.palass.org *Chief Executive,* Dr T. J. Palmer

PARLIAMENTARY AND SCIENTIFIC COMMITTEE (1939), 3 Birdcage Walk, Westminster, London SW1H 9JJ T 020-7222 7085 E secretariat@pandsctte.demon.co.uk W www.scienceinparliament.org.uk *Scientific Secretary,* Prof. Peter Simpson

PEABODY TRUST (1862), Minster Court, 45 Westminster Bridge Road, London SE1 7JB T 020-7021 4000 E info@peabody.org.uk W www.peabody.org.uk *Chief Executive,* Steve Howlett

PEN INTERNATIONAL (1921), Brownlow House, 50–51 High Holborn, London WC1V 6ER T 020-7405 0338 E info@internationalpen.org.uk W www.internationalpen.org.uk *Interim Executive Directors,* Frank Geary and Sara Whyatt

PENSIONS ADVISORY SERVICE (1983),
11 Belgrave Road, London SW1V 1RB **T** 0845-601 2923
E enquiries@pensionsadvisoryservice.org.uk
W www.pensionsadvisoryservice.org.uk
Chief Executive, M. Phillips, OBE

PHILOLOGICAL SOCIETY (1842), Department of the
Languages and Cultures of Africa, School of Oriental and
African Studies, Thornhaugh Street, London WC1H 0XG
T 020-7898 4376 **E** secretary@philsoc.org.uk
W www.philsoc.org.uk
Hon. Secretary, Dr Martin Orwin

PHYSIOLOGICAL SOCIETY (1876), 8–14 Verulam
Street, 3rd Floor, Peer House, London WC1X 8LZ
T 020-7269 5710 **E** admin@physoc.org **W** www.physoc.org
Chief Executive, Dr Philip Wright

PILGRIMS OF GREAT BRITAIN (1902), PO Box 1289,
Maidstone ME18 SW9 **T** 01622-817780
E sec@pilgrimsociety.org **W** www.pilgrimsociety.org
Chair, Ronald M. Freeman

PLAIN ENGLISH CAMPAIGN (1979), PO Box 3,
New Mills, High Peak SK22 4QP **T** 01663-744409
E info@plainenglish.co.uk **W** www.plainenglish.co.uk
Director, Ms C. Maher

PLATFORM 51 (1855), Clarendon House,
52 Cornmarket Street, Oxford OX1 3EJ **T** 01865-304200
E info@platform51.org **W** www.platform51.org
Chief Executive, Penny Newman

POETRY SOCIETY (1909), 22 Betterton Street, London
WC2H 9BX **T** 020-7420 9880 **E** info@poetrysociety.org.uk
W www.poetrysociety.org.uk
Director, Judith Palmer

POWYSLAND CLUB (1867), Cartref, 14 Berriew Road,
Welshpool SY21 7SS **T** 01938-552161
E info@powyslandclub.co.uk **W** www.powyslandclub.co.uk
Hon. Secretary, Dr Roger L. Brown

PRAYER BOOK SOCIETY (1975), The Studio, Copyhold
Farm, Goring Heath, Reading RG8 7RT **T** 0118-984 2582
E pbs.admin@pbs.org.uk **W** www.pbs.org.uk
Chair, Prudence Dailey

PRE-SCHOOL LEARNING ALLIANCE (1961), The
Fitzpatrick Building, 188 York Way, London N7 9AD
T 020-7697 2500 **E** info@pre-school.org.uk
W www.pre-school.org.uk
Chief Executive, Neil Leitch

PRINCE'S TRUST (1976), 18 Park Square East, London
NW1 4LH **T** 020-7543 1234
E webinfops@princes-trust.org.uk
W www.princes-trust.org.uk
Chief Executive, Martina Milburn

PRINCESS ROYAL TRUST FOR CARERS (1991),
Unit 14, Bourne Court, Southend Road, Woodford Green
IG8 8HD **T** 0844-800 4361 **E** info@carers.org
W www.carers.org
Chair, Ray Robertson

PRISONERS ABROAD (1978), 89–93 Fonthill Road,
London N4 3JH **T** 020-7561 6820
E info@prisonersabroad.org.uk
W www.prisonersabroad.org.uk
Chief Executive, Pauline Crowe

PRIVATE LIBRARIES ASSOCIATION (1956), Ravelston,
South View Road, Pinner HA5 3YD **E** dchambrs@aol.com
W www.plabooks.org
Chair, David Chambers

PROSTATE ACTION (1994), 6 Crescent Stables,
139 Upper Richmond Road, London SW15 2TN
T 020-8788 7720 **E** info@prostateaction.org.uk
W www.prostateaction.org.uk
Chief Executive, Emma Malcolm

PSORIASIS ASSOCIATION (1968), Dick Coles House,
2 Queensbridge, Northampton NN4 7BF **T** 08456-760076
E mail@psoriasis-association.org.uk
W www.psoriasis-association.org.uk
Chief Executive, Helen McAteer

QUAKER PEACE AND SOCIAL WITNESS (2000),
Friends House, 173–177 Euston Road, London NW1 2BJ
T 020-7663 1000 **E** qpsw@quaker.org.uk
W www.quaker.org.uk
General Secretary, Helen Drewery

QUEEN ELIZABETH'S FOUNDATION FOR
DISABLED PEOPLE (1934), Leatherhead Court,
Woodlands Road, Leatherhead KT22 0BN **T** 01372-841100
E info@qef.org.uk **W** www.qef.org.uk
Chief Executive, Jonathan Powell

QUEEN'S NURSING INSTITUTE (1887),
3 Albemarle Way, London EC1V 4RQ **T** 020-7549 1400
E mail@qni.org.uk **W** www.qni.org.uk
Director, Rosemary Cook, CBE

QUEEN VICTORIA CLERGY FUND (1897),
Church House, Great Smith Street, London SW1P 3AZ
T 020-7898 1000 **E** info@churchhouse.org.uk
Chief Executive, Christopher Palmer, CBE

QUIT (1926), 63 St Marys Axe, London EC3A 8AA
T 020-7469 0400, **Quitline** 0800-002 200
E info@quit.org.uk **W** www.quit.org.uk
Chief Executive, Steve Crone

RAILWAY AND CANAL HISTORICAL SOCIETY
(1954), 17 Lovelace Road, Oxford OX2 8LP
T 01865-240514 **E** secretary@rchs.org.uk
W www.rchs.org.uk
Hon. Secretary, M. Searle

RAMBLERS' ASSOCIATION (1935), 2nd Floor,
Camelford House, 87–90 Albert Embankment, London
SE1 7TW **T** 020-7339 8500 **E** ramblers@ramblers.org.uk
W www.ramblers.org.uk
Chief Executive, Tom Franklin

RARE BREEDS SURVIVAL TRUST (1973),
Stoneleigh Park, Nr. Kenilworth CV8 2LG **T** 024-7669 6551
E enquiries@rbst.org.uk **W** www.rbst.org.uk
Executive Chair, Tim Brigstocke

REFUGEE COUNCIL (1981), 240–250 Ferndale Road,
London SW9 8BB **T** 020-7346 6700
E info@refugeecouncil.org.uk
W www.refugeecouncil.org.uk
Chief Executive, Donna Covey

REGIONAL STUDIES ASSOCIATION (1965),
PO Box 2058, Seaford BN25 4QU **T** 01323-899698
E info@rsa-ls.ac.uk **W** www.regional-studies-assoc.ac.uk
Chief Executive, Sally Hardy

REGULAR FORCES EMPLOYMENT ASSOCIATION
LTD (1885), 1st Floor, Mountbarrow House, 6–20
Elizabeth Street, London SW1W 9RB **T** 0845-873 7162
E adminrfea@ctp.org.uk **W** www.rfea.org.uk
Chief Executive, Brig. Stephen Gledhill

RELATE (1938), Premier House, Carolina Court, Lakeside,
Doncaster DN4 5RA **T** 0300-100 1234
E enquiries@relate.org.uk **W** www.relate.org.uk
Chief Executive, Claire Tyler

RETHINK (1972), 89 Albert Embankment, London SE1 7TP
T 0845-456 0455 **E** info@rethink.org **W** www.rethink.org
Chief Executive, Paul Jenkins

RETIRED NURSES' NATIONAL HOME (1934),
Riverside Avenue, Bournemouth BH7 7EE **T** 01202-396418
E office@rnnh.co.uk **W** www.rnnh.co.uk
Chair, Mrs S. Young

RICHARD III SOCIETY (1924), 23 Ash Rise, Halstead,
Essex CO9 1RD **E** wells4r3@btinternet.com
W www.richardiii.net
Chair, Dr P. T. Stone

RNIB NATIONAL LIBRARY SERVICE (1868),
Far Cromwell Road, Bredbury, Stockport SK6 2SG
T 0303-123 9999 **E** helpline@rnib.org.uk
W www.rnib.org.uk/reading
Head of National Library Service, Helen Brazier

RNID (ROYAL NATIONAL INSTITUTE FOR DEAF
PEOPLE) (1911), 19–23 Featherstone Street, London
EC1Y 8SL **T** 0808-808 0123, **Textphone** 0808-808 9000
E informationline@rnid.org.uk **W** www.rnid.org.uk
Chief Executive, Jackie Ballard

ROADS AND ROAD TRANSPORT HISTORY
ASSOCIATION (1992), c/o Kithead Trust, De Salis Drive,
Hampton Lovett, Droitwich WR9 0QE
E enquiries@rrtha.org.uk **W** www.rrtha.org.uk
Chair, Roy Larkin

ROTARY INTERNATIONAL IN GREAT BRITAIN
AND IRELAND (1922), Kinwarton Road, Alcester
B49 6PB **T** 01789-765411 **E** secretary@ribi.org
W www.rotary-ribi.org
Chief Executive, Annemarie Harte

ROYAL AERONAUTICAL SOCIETY (1866),
4 Hamilton Place, London W1J 7BQ **T** 020-7670 4300
E jean.wright@aerosociety.com **W** www.aerosociety.com
Chief Executive, Simon Luxmoore

ROYAL AGRICULTURAL SOCIETY OF THE
COMMONWEALTH (1957), c/o Royal Highland Centre,
Ingliston, Edinburgh EH28 8NF **T** 0131-335 6200
E rasc@commagshow.org **W** www.commagshow.org
Hon. Secretary, Michael Lambert

ROYAL AIR FORCES ASSOCIATION (1943),
117½ Loughborough Road, Leicester LE4 5ND
T 0116-266 5224 **E** enquiries@rafa.org.uk
W www.rafa.org.uk
Secretary General, Jane Easton

ROYAL ARTILLERY ASSOCIATION (1920), Artillery
House, Royal Artillery Barracks, Larkhill, Salisbury SP4 8QT
T 01980-845895
E ARTYCEN-RHQRA-RACF-RAA-GenSecPA@mod.uk
W www.theraa.co.uk
General Secretary, Lt.-Col. I. A. Vere Nicoll, MBE

ROYAL ASIATIC SOCIETY (1823), 14 Stephenson Way,
London NW1 2HD **T** 020-7388 4539
E info@royalasiaticsociety.org
W www.royalasiaticsociety.org
Curator, Alison Ohta

ROYAL ASSOCIATION FOR DEAF PEOPLE (1841),
18 Westside Centre, London Road, Stanway CO3 8PH
T 0845-688 2525 **E** info@royaldeaf.org.uk
W www.royaldeaf.org.uk
Chief Executive, Jan Sheldon

ROYAL ASSOCIATION FOR DISABILITY AND
REHABILITATION (1977), 12 City Forum,
250 City Road, London EC1V 8AF **T** 020-7250 3222
E radar@radar.org.uk **W** www.radar.org.uk
Chair, Phil Friend, OBE

ROYAL BIRMINGHAM SOCIETY OF ARTISTS (1814),
4 Brook Street, Birmingham B3 1SA **T** 0121-236 4353
E secretary@rbsa.org.uk **W** www.rbsa.org.uk
Gallery Director, Marie Considine

ROYAL BRITISH LEGION (1921), 199 Borough High
Street, London SE1 1AA **T** 020-3207 2100
E info@britishlegion.org.uk **W** www.britishlegion.org.uk
Director-General, Chris Simpkins

ROYAL BRITISH LEGION SCOTLAND (1921),
New Haig House, Logie Green Road, Edinburgh EH7 4HR
E lao@rblscotland.org **W** www.rblscotland.org
General Secretary, George Ross

ROYAL CALEDONIAN SCHOOLS TRUST (1815),
Unit 75, WENTA Business Park, Colne Way, Watford
WD24 7ND **T** 01923-215350 **E** admin@rcst.org.uk
W www.rcst.org.uk
Chief Executive, James MacBain

ROYAL CAMBRIAN ACADEMY (1882), Crown Lane,
Conwy LL32 8AN **T** 01492-593413 **E** rca@rcaconwy.org
W www.rcaconwy.org
President, Maurice Cockrill

ROYAL CELTIC SOCIETY (1820), 25 Rutland Street,
Edinburgh EH1 2RN **T** 0131-228 6449
E gcameron@stuartandstuart.co.uk
W www.royalcelticsociety.org.uk
Secretary, J. Gordon Cameron, WS

ROYAL COMMISSION FOR THE EXHIBITION OF
1851 (1850), 453 Sherfield Building, Imperial College
SW7 2AZ **T** 020-7594 8790 **E** royalcom1851@imperial.ac.uk
W www.royalcommission1851.org.uk
Chair, Sir Alan Rudge, CBE, FRE, FRS

ROYAL COMMONWEALTH EX-SERVICES LEAGUE
(1921), Haig House, 199 Borough High Street, London
SE1 1AA T 020-3207 2413
E mgordon-roe@commonwealthveterans.org.uk
W www.commonwealthveterans.org.uk
Secretary General, Col. P. A. Davis, CBE

ROYAL GEOGRAPHICAL SOCIETY (WITH THE
INSTITUTE OF BRITISH GEOGRAPHERS) (1830),
1 Kensington Gore, London SW7 2AR T 020-7591 3000
E enquiries@rgs.org W www.rgs.org
Director, Dr R. Gardner, CBE

ROYAL HIGHLAND AND AGRICULTURAL SOCIETY
OF SCOTLAND (1784), Royal Highland Centre,
Ingliston, Edinburgh EH28 8NB T 0131-335 6200
E info@rhass.org.uk W www.rhass.org.uk
Chief Executive, S. Hutt

ROYAL HISTORICAL SOCIETY (1868), University
College London, Gower Street, London WC1E 6BT
T 020-7387 7532 E royalhistsoc@ucl.ac.uk
W www.royalhistoricalsociety.org
President, Prof. Colin Jones

ROYAL HORTICULTURAL SOCIETY (1804),
80 Vincent Square, London SW1P 2PE T 0845-260 5000
E info@rhs.org.uk W www.rhs.org.uk
Director-General, Sue Biggs

ROYAL INSTITUTE OF NAVIGATION (1947),
1 Kensington Gore, London SW7 2AT T 020-7591 3130
E admin@rin.org.uk W www.rin.org.uk
Director, Capt. P. Chapman-Andrews

ROYAL INSTITUTE OF OIL PAINTERS (1882),
17 Carlton House Terrace, London SW1Y 5BD
T 020-7930 6844 E enquiries@theroi.org.uk
W www.theroi.co.uk
President, Peter Wileman

ROYAL INSTITUTION OF GREAT BRITAIN (1799),
21 Albemarle Street, London W1S 4BS T 020-7409 2992
E ri@ri.ac.uk W www.rigb.org
Chief Executive, Chris Rofe

ROYAL LIFE SAVING SOCIETY UK (1891), River House,
High Street, Broom B50 4HN T 01789-773994
E lifesavers@rlss.org.uk W www.rlss.org.uk
Chief Executive, D. Standley

ROYAL LITERARY FUND (1790), 3 Johnson's Court,
off Fleet Street, London EC4A 3EA T 020-7353 7160
E rlitfund@btconnect.com W www.rlf.org.uk
Chief Executive, Eileen Gunn

ROYAL LONDON SOCIETY FOR THE BLIND (1838),
Dorton House, Seal, Sevenoaks TN15 0ED T 01732-592500
E tom.pey@rlsb.org.uk W www.rlsb.org.uk
Chief Executive, Dr Thomas Pey

ROYAL MASONIC BENEVOLENT INSTITUTION
(1842), 20 Great Queen Street, London WC2B 5BG
T 020-7596 2400 E enquiries@rmbi.org.uk
W www.rmbi.org.uk
Chief Executive, David Innes

ROYAL MASONIC TRUST FOR GIRLS AND BOYS
(1982), 60 Great Queen Street, London WC2B 5AZ
T 020-7405 2644 E info@rmtgb.org W www.rmtgb.org
Chief Executive, Les Hutchinson

ROYAL MICROSCOPICAL SOCIETY (1839),
37–38 St Clements, Oxford OX4 1AJ T 01865-254760
E info@rms.org.uk W www.rms.org.uk
Administrator, Karen Lonsdale

ROYAL MUSICAL ASSOCIATION (1874), 4 Chandos
Road, Chorlton-cum-Hardy, Manchester M21 0ST
T 0161-861 7542 E jeffrey.dean@stingrayoffice.com
W www.rma.ac.uk
President, Philip Olleson

ROYAL NATIONAL COLLEGE FOR THE BLIND
(1872), College Road, Hereford HR1 1EB T 01432-265725
E info@rncb.ac.uk W www.rncb.ac.uk
Principal, Geoff Draper

ROYAL NATIONAL INSTITUTE OF BLIND PEOPLE
(1868), 105 Judd Street, London WC1H 9NE
T 020-7388 1266, **Helpline** 0303-123 9999
E helpline@rnib.org.uk W www.rnib.org.uk
Chief Executive, Lesley-Anne Alexander

ROYAL NATIONAL LIFEBOAT INSTITUTION (1824),
West Quay Road, Poole BH15 1HZ T 0845-122 6999
E info@rnli.org.uk W www.rnli.org.uk
Chief Executive, Paul Boissier

ROYAL NAVAL ASSOCIATION (1949), Room 209,
Royal Semaphore Tower, PP70, HM Naval Base, Portsmouth
PO1 3LT T 02392-723747
W www.royal-naval-association.co.uk
President, Vice-Adm. John McAnally, CB, LVO

ROYAL NAVY OFFICERS' CHARITY (1739),
70 Porchester Terrace, London W2 3TP T 020-7402 5231
E rnoc@arno.org.uk
Chief Executive, Cdr W. K. Ridley, OBE

ROYAL PHILHARMONIC SOCIETY (1813),
10 Stratford Place, London W1C 1BA T 020-7491 8110
E admin@royalphilharmonicsociety.org.uk
W www.royalphilharmonicsociety.org.uk
Executive Director, Rosemary Johnson

ROYAL PHOTOGRAPHIC SOCIETY (1853),
Fenton House, 122 Wells Road, Bath BA2 3AH
T 01225-325733 E reception@rps.org W www.rps.org
Director-General, Stuart Blake

ROYAL SCHOOL OF CHURCH MUSIC (1927),
19 The Close, Salisbury SP1 2EB T 01722-424848
E enquiries@rscm.com W www.rscm.com
Director, Lindsay Gray

ROYAL SCHOOL OF NEEDLEWORK (1872),
Apartment 12A, Hampton Court Palace KT8 9AU
T 020-3166 6932 E enquiries@royal-needlework.org.uk
W www.royal-needlework.org.uk
Chief Executive, Dr Susan Kay-Williams

ROYAL SOCIETY FOR ASIAN AFFAIRS (1901),
2 Belgrave Square, London SW1X 8PJ T 020-7235 5122
E sec@rsaa.org.uk W www.rsaa.org.uk
Chair of Council, Sir David John, KCMG

ROYAL SOCIETY FOR THE ENCOURAGEMENT OF ARTS, MANUFACTURES AND COMMERCE (RSA) (1754), 8 John Adam Street, London WC2N 6EZ
T 020-7930 5115 E general@rsa.org.uk W www.thersa.org
Chief Executive, Matthew Taylor

ROYAL SOCIETY FOR THE PREVENTION OF ACCIDENTS (1917), 28 Calthorpe Road, Edgbaston, Birmingham B15 1RP T 0121-248 2000 E help@rospa.com
W www.rospa.com
Chief Executive, Tom Mullarkey, MBE

ROYAL SOCIETY FOR THE PREVENTION OF CRUELTY TO ANIMALS (1824), Wilberforce Way, Horsham RH13 9RS T 0300-123 4555 W www.rspca.org.uk
Chief Executive, Mark Watts

ROYAL SOCIETY FOR THE PROTECTION OF BIRDS (1889), The Lodge, Sandy SG19 2DL
T 01767-680551 W www.rspb.org.uk
Chief Executive, Mike Clarke

ROYAL SOCIETY OF LITERATURE (1820),
Somerset House, Strand, London WC2R 1LA
T 020-7845 4676 E info@rslit.org W www.rslit.org
President, Colin Thubron

ROYAL SOCIETY OF MEDICINE (1805),
1 Wimpole Street, London W1G 0AE T 020-7290 2900
E membership@rsm.ac.uk W www.rsm.ac.uk
Chief Executive, Ian Balmer

ROYAL SOCIETY OF MINIATURE PAINTERS, SCULPTORS AND GRAVERS (1895), 3 Briar Walk, London SW15 6UD T 01983-866 970
E elizabethmeek@msn.com
W www.royal-miniature-society.org.uk
Executive Secretary, Elizabeth R. Meek

ROYAL SOCIETY OF MUSICIANS OF GREAT BRITAIN (1738), 10 Stratford Place, London W1C 1BA
T 020-7629 6137 W www.royalsocietyofmusicians.co.uk
Secretary, Mrs M. Gibb

ROYAL SOCIETY OF PAINTER-PRINTMAKERS (1880), Bankside Gallery, 48 Hopton Street, London SE1 9JH T 020-7928 7521 E info@banksidegallery.com
W www.re-printmakers.co.uk
President, Hilary Paynter

ROYAL SOCIETY OF PORTRAIT PAINTERS (1891),
17 Carlton House Terrace, London SW1Y 5BD
T 020-7930 6844 E enquiries@therp.co.uk
W www.therp.co.uk
President, Alastair Adams

ROYAL SOCIETY OF ST GEORGE (1894),
127 Sandgate Road, Folkstone CT20 2BH T 01303-241795
E info@royalsocietyofstgeorge.com
W www.royalsocietyofstgeorge.com
Chair, Cliff Trowse

ROYAL SOCIETY OF TROPICAL MEDICINE AND HYGIENE (1907), Northumberland House,
303–306 High Holborn, London WC1V 7JZ
T 020-7405 2628 E info@rstmh.org W www.rstmh.org
Chief Executive, Ms. G. McHugh

ROYAL THEATRICAL FUND (1839), 11 Garrick Street, London WC2E 9AR T 020-7836 3322 E admin@trtf.com
W www.trtf.com
President, Sir Donald Sinden, CBE, FRSA

ROYAL ULSTER AGRICULTURAL SOCIETY (1896),
King's Hall Complex, Balmoral, Belfast BT9 6GW
T 028-9066 5225 E general@kingshall.co.uk
W www.balmoralshow.co.uk
Chief Executive, Colin McDonald

ROYAL WATERCOLOUR SOCIETY (1804),
Bankside Gallery, 48 Hopton Street, London SE1 9JH
T 020-7928 7521 E info@banksidegallery.com
W www.royalwatercoloursociety.co.uk
President, David Paskett

RSABI (1897), The Rural Centre, West Mains of Ingliston, Newbridge, Edinburgh EH28 8LT T 0131-472 4166
E rsabi@rsabi.org.uk W www.rsabi.org.uk
Chief Executive, Dr Maurice S. Hankey

ST ALBANS AND HERTFORDSHIRE ARCHITECTURAL AND ARCHAEOLOGICAL SOCIETY (1845), 24 Monks Horton Way, St Albans AL1 4HA T 01727-851734 E admin@stalbanshistory.org
W www.stalbanshistory.org
Secretary, B. R. Hanlon

ST JOHN AMBULANCE (1877), 27 St John's Lane, London EC1M 4BU T 0870-010 4950 E info@sja.org.uk
W www.sja.org.uk
Chief Executive, Sue Killen

SALTIRE SOCIETY (1936), 9 Fountain Close,
22 High Street, Edinburgh EH1 1TF T 0131-556 1836
E saltire@saltiresociety.org.uk W www.saltiresociety.org.uk
Chair, Lorimer Mackenzie

SANE (1986), 1st Floor, Cityside House, 40 Adler Street, London E1 1EE T 020-7375 1002, **Helpline** 0845-767 8000
E info@sane.org.uk W www.sane.org.uk
Chief Executive, Ms M. Wallace, MBE

SAVE BRITAIN'S HERITAGE (1975), 70 Cowcross Street, London EC1M 6EJ T 020-7253 3500
E office@savebritainsheritage.org
W www.savebritainsheritage.org
President, Marcus Binney, OBE

SAVE THE CHILDREN UK (1919), 1 St John's Lane, London EC1M 4AR T 020-7012 6400
E supporter.care@savethechildren.org.uk
W www.savethechildren.org.uk
Chief Executive, Justin Forsyth

SCHOOL LIBRARY ASSOCIATION (1937), Unit 2, Lotmead Business Village, Lotmead Farm, Wanborough, Swindon SN4 0UY T 01793-791787 E info@sla.org.uk
W www.sla.org.uk
Chief Executive, Mrs T. Adams

SCOTTISH ASSOCIATION FOR MARINE SCIENCE (1884), Scottish Marine Institute, Oban, Argyll PA37 1QA
T 01631-559000 E info@sams.ac.uk W www.sams.ac.uk
Director, Prof. Laurence Mee

SCOTTISH CHAMBERS OF COMMERCE (1948),
30 George Square, Glasgow G2 1EQ **T** 0141-204 8316
E admin@scottishchambers.org.uk
W www.scottishchambers.org.uk
Chief Executive, Liz Cameron

SCOTTISH COUNCIL FOR VOLUNTARY
ORGANISATIONS (1943), Mansfield Traquair Centre,
15 Mansfield Place, Edinburgh EH3 6BB **T** 0131-556 3882
E enquiries@scvo.org.uk **W** www.scvo.org.uk
Chief Executive, M. Sime

SCOTTISH NATIONAL WAR MEMORIAL (1927),
The Castle, Edinburgh EH1 2YT **T** 0131-226 7393
E info@snwm.org **W** www.snwm.org
Secretary to the Trustees, Lt.-Col. R. J. Binks

SCOTTISH SOCIETY FOR THE PREVENTION OF
CRUELTY TO ANIMALS (1839), Kingseat Road,
Halbeath, Dunfermline KY11 8RY **T** 03000-999999
E info@scottishspca.org **W** www.scottishspca.org
Chief Executive, Stuart Earley

SCOUT ASSOCIATION (1907), Gilwell Park, Chingford,
London E4 7QW **T** 020-8443 7100
E scout.association@scouts.org.uk **W** www.scouts.org.uk
Chief Executive, D. M. Twine, CBE

SEEABILITY (1799), SeeAbility House, Hook Road, Epsom
KT19 8SQ **T** 01372-755000 **E** enquiries@seeability.org
W www.seeability.org
Chief Executive, D. Scott-Ralphs

SELDEN SOCIETY (1887), School of Law, Queen Mary,
Mile End Road, London E1 4NS **T** 020-7882 3968
E selden-society@qmul.ac.uk
W www.selden-society.qmul.ac.uk
Secretary, V. Tunkel

SENSE (THE NATIONAL DEAFBLIND AND RUBELLA
ASSOCIATION) (1955), 101 Pentonville Road, London
N1 9LG **T** 0845-127 0060 **E** info@sense.org.uk
W www.sense.org.uk
Chief Executive, Gill Morbey, OBE

SHELTER (NATIONAL CAMPAIGN FOR HOMELESS
PEOPLE) (1966), 88 Old Street, London EC1V 9HU
T 0300-330 1234, **Helpline** 0808-800 4444
E info@shelter.org.uk **W** www.shelter.org.uk
Chief Executive, Campbell Robb

SHIRE HORSE SOCIETY (1878), East of England
Showground, Peterborough PE2 6XE **T** 01733-234451
E info@shire-horse.org.uk **W** www.shire-horse.org.uk
Secretary, David Ralley-Davies

SIMPLIFIED SPELLING SOCIETY (1908),
20 Silhill Hall Road, Solihull, B91 1JU **T** 02476-712 119
E membership@spellingsociety.org
W www.spellingsociety.org
Membership Secretary, Stephen Linstead

SOCIALIST PARTY OF GREAT BRITAIN (1904),
52 Clapham High Street, London SW4 7UN
T 020-7622 3811 **E** spgb@worldsocialism.org
W www.worldsocialism.org
General Secretary, Tristan Miller

SOCIÉTÉ JERSIAISE (1873), 7 Pier Road, St Helier
JE2 4XW **T** 01534-758314 **E** societe@societe-jersiaise.org
W www.societe-jersiaise.org
Executive Director, Mrs P. Syvret

SOCIETY FOR NAUTICAL RESEARCH (1910),
6 Ashmeadow Road, Arnside, via Carnforth LA5 0AE
T 01524-761616 **E** honsec@snr.org.uk **W** www.snr.org.uk
Hon. Secretary, Peter Winterbottom

SOCIETY FOR PROMOTING CHRISTIAN
KNOWLEDGE (1698), 36 Causton Street, London
SW1P 4ST **T** 020-7592 3900 **E** spck@spck.org.uk
W www.spck.org.uk
General Secretary, Simon Kingston

SOCIETY FOR THE PROMOTION OF ROMAN
STUDIES (1910), Senate House, Malet Street, London
WC1E 7HU **T** 020-7862 8727 **E** office@romansociety.org
W www.romansociety.org
Secretary, Dr Fiona Haarer

SOCIETY FOR THE PROTECTION OF ANCIENT
BUILDINGS (1877), 37 Spital Square, London E1 6DY
T 020-7377 1644 **E** info@spab.org.uk **W** www.spab.org.uk
Secretary, Philip Venning

SOCIETY FOR THE PROTECTION OF UNBORN
CHILDREN (1967), 3 Whitacre Mews, London SE11 4AB
T 020-7091 7091 **E** information@spuc.org.uk
W www.spuc.org.uk
National Director, John Smeaton

SOCIETY OF ANTIQUARIES OF LONDON
(1707), Burlington House, Piccadilly, London W1J 0BE
T 020-7479 7080 **E** admin@sal.org.uk **W** www.sal.org.uk
General-Secretary, John S. C. Lewis, FSA

SOCIETY OF ANTIQUARIES OF NEWCASTLE UPON
TYNE (1813), Great North Museum: Hancock,
Barras Bridge, Newcastle upon Tyne NE2 4PT
T 0191-231 2700 **E** admin@newcastle-antiquaries.org.uk
W www.newcastle-antiquaries.org.uk
Hon. Secretary, Dr N. Hodgson

SOCIETY OF ANTIQUARIES OF SCOTLAND (1780),
National Museums Scotland, Chambers Street, Edinburgh
EH1 1JF **T** 0131-247 4115/4133 **E** director@socantscot.org
W www.socantscot.org
Director, Simon Gilmour, PHD, FSA, FSA SCOT

SOCIETY OF BIOLOGY (2009), 9 Red Lion Court,
London EC4A 3EF **T** 020-7685 2550
E info@societyofbiology.org **W** www.societyofbiology.org
Chief Executive, Dr Mark Downs

SOCIETY OF BOTANICAL ARTISTS (1985),
1 Knapp Cottages, Wyke, Gillingham SP8 4NQ
T 01747-825718 **E** pam@soc-botanical-artists.org
W www.soc-botanical-artists.org
Executive Secretary, Pam Henderson

SOCIETY OF EDITORS (1999), University Centre,
Granta Place, Mill Lane, Cambridge CB2 1RU
T 01223-304080 **E** info@societyofeditors.org
W www.societyofeditors.co.uk
Executive Director, Bob Satchwell

SOCIETY OF GENEALOGISTS (1911),
14 Charterhouse Buildings, Goswell Road, London
EC1M 7BA **T** 020-7251 8799 **E** librarian@sog.org.uk
W www.sog.org.uk
Chief Executive, June Perrin

SOCIETY OF GLASS TECHNOLOGY (1917),
9 Churchill Way, Chapeltown S35 2PY
T 0114-263 4455 **E** info@sgt.org **W** www.sgt.org
Managing Editor, David Moore

SOCIETY OF INDEXERS (1957), Woodbourn
Business Centre, 10 Jessell Street, Sheffield S9 3HY
T 0114-244 9561 **E** info@indexers.org.uk
W www.indexers.org.uk
Chair, Ann Kingdom

SOCIETY OF LEGAL SCHOLARS (1908), School of Law,
Southampton University, Southampton SO17 1BJ
T 023-8059 4039 **E** s.j.thomson@soton.ac.uk
W www.legalscholars.ac.uk
Hon. Secretary, Richard Taylor

SOCIETY OF SCHOOLMASTERS AND
SCHOOLMISTRESSES (1798), c/o L. I. Baggott,
SGBI Office, Queen Mary House, Manor Park Road,
Chistlehurst BR7 5PY **T** 020-8468 7997
E sgbi@fsmail.net
Secretary (acting), Sarah Brydon, CQSW

SOCIETY OF SCRIBES AND ILLUMINATORS (1921),
6 Queen Square, London WC1N 3AT **T** 01524-251534
E scribe@calligraphyonline.org
W www.calligraphyonline.org
Chair, Sylvie Gokulsing

SOCIETY OF SOLICITORS IN THE SUPREME
COURT OF SCOTLAND (1784), SSC Library,
Parliament House, 11 Parliament Square, Edinburgh EH1 1RF
T 0131-225 6268 **E** enquiries@ssclibrary.co.uk
W www.ssclibrary.co.uk
Secretary, I. L. S. Balfour

SOCIETY OF WOMEN ARTISTS (1855), 1 Knapp
Cottages, Wyke, Gillingham SP8 4NQ **T** 01747-825718
E pamhenderson@dsl.pipex.com
W www.society-women-artists.org.uk
Executive Secretary, Pam Henderson

SOCIETY OF WRITERS TO HM SIGNET (1594),
The Signet Library, Parliament Square, Edinburgh EH1 1RF
T 0131-220 3249 **E** enquiries@wssociety.co.uk
W www.wssociety.co.uk
Chief Executive, Robert Pirrie

SOIL ASSOCIATION (1946), South Plaza,
Marlborough Street, Bristol BS1 3NX **T** 0117-314 5000
E memb@soilassociation.org **W** www.soilassociation.org
Director, Helen Browning

SOMERSET ARCHAEOLOGICAL AND NATURAL
HISTORY SOCIETY (1849), Somerset Heritage Centre,
Brunel Way TA2 6SF **T** 01823-272429 **E** office@sanhs.org
W www.sanhs.org
Chair, Chris Sidaway

SOUTH WALES INSTITUTE OF ENGINEERS
(1857/2007), Suite 2, Bay Chambers, West Bute Street,
Cardiff CF10 5BB **T** 0292-063 0561
E sandra.chapman@swieet2007.org.uk
W www.swieet2007.org.uk
Hon. Secretary, D. M. Morgan

SPORT HORSE BREEDING OF GREAT BRITAIN
(1886), 96 High Street, Edenbridge TN8 5AR
T 01732-866277 **E** office@sporthorsegb.co.uk
W www.sporthorsegb.co.uk
General Secretary, Catherine Burdock

STANDING COUNCIL OF SCOTTISH CHIEFS,
Hope Chambers, 52 Leith Walk, Edinburgh EH6 5HW
T 0131-553 2232 **E** romilly.squire@virgin.net
W www.clanchiefs.org
Hon. Secretary, Romilly Squire of Rubislaw

STANDING COUNCIL OF THE BARONETAGE
(1903), Forestside, Martin's Corner, Hambledon,
Waterlooville PO7 4RA **T** 023-9263 2672
E secretary@baronetage.org **W** www.baronetage.org
Chair, Sir Ian Lowson, BT, OSTJ

SUFFOLK INSTITUTE OF ARCHAEOLOGY AND
HISTORY (1848), 116 Hardwick Lane, Bury St Edmunds,
IP33 2LE **T** 01284-753228
E generalsecretary@suffolkarch.org.uk
W www.suffolkarch.org.uk
Hon. Secretary, Jane Carr

SUNDERLAND ANTIQUARIAN SOCIETY (1900),
Sunderland Minster, High Sreet West, Sunderland SR1 3ET
T 0191-510 8183
President, D. W. Smith

SURREY ARCHAEOLOGICAL SOCIETY (1854),
Castle Arch, Guildford GU1 3SX **T** 01483-532454
E info@surreyarchaeology.org.uk
W www.surreyarchaeology.org.uk
Hon. Secretary, David Calow

SUSSEX ARCHAEOLOGICAL SOCIETY (1846),
Bull House, 92 High Street, Lewes BN7 1XH
T 01273-486260 **E** lamo@sussexpast.co.uk
W www.sussexpast.co.uk
Chief Executive, J. Manley

SWEDENBORG SOCIETY (1810),
20–21 Bloomsbury Way, London WC1A 2TH
T 020-7405 7986 **E** richard@swedenborg.org.uk
W www.swedenborg.org.uk
Secretary, Richard Lines

TAVISTOCK INSTITUTE (1947), 30 Tabernacle Street,
London EC2A 4UE **T** 020-7417 0407
W www.tavinstitute.org **E** hello@tavinstitute.org
Chief Executive, Eliat Aram

TEACHER SUPPORT NETWORK (1870),
40A Drayton Park, London N5 1EW **T** 0800-056 2561
E enquiries@teachersupport.info
W www.teachersupport.info
Chief Executive, Julian Stanley

THEATRES TRUST (1976), 22 Charing Cross Road, London WC2H 0QL **T** 020-7836 8591 **E** info@theatrestrust.org.uk **W** www.theatrestrust.org.uk *Director,* Mhora Samuel

THORESBY SOCIETY (1889), Claremont, 23 Clarendon Road, Leeds LS2 9NZ **T** 0113-247 0704 **E** secretary@thoresby.org.uk **W** www.thoresby.org.uk *President,* Revd Dr R. Yates

TOWN AND COUNTRY PLANNING ASSOCIATION, 17 Carlton House Terrace, London SW1Y 5AS **T** 020-7930 8903, **W** www.tcpa.org.uk **E** tcpa@tcpa.org.uk *Chief Executive,* Kate Henderson

TREE COUNCIL (1974), 71 Newcomen Street, London SE1 1YT **T** 020-7407 9992 **E** info@treecouncil.org.uk **W** www.treecouncil.org.uk *Director-General,* Pauline Buchanan Black

TURNER SOCIETY (1975), BCM Box Turner, London WC1N 3XX **W** www.turnersociety.org.uk *Chair,* Andrew Wilton

UK YOUTH (1911), Avon Tyrrell Activity Centre, Braggers Lane, Bransgore BH23 8EE **T** 01425-672347 **E** info@ukyouth.org.uk **W** www.ukyouth.org.uk *Chief Executive,* Charlotte Hill

UNDERSTANDING ANIMAL RESEARCH (2008), 25 Shaftesbury Avenue, London W1D 7EG **T** 020-7287 2818 **E** office@uar.org.uk **W** www.uar.org.uk *Chief Executive,* Dr S. Festing

UNITED GRAND LODGE OF ENGLAND (1717), Freemasons' Hall, Great Queen Street, London WC2B 5AZ **T** 020-7831 9811 **E** enquiries@ugle.org.uk **W** www.ugle.org.uk *Grand Master,* HRH the Duke of Kent, KG, GCMG, GCVO

UNITED KINGDOM RESERVE FORCES ASSOCIATION (1972), Holderness House, 51–61 Clifton Street, London EC2A 4EY **T** 020-7426 8358 **E** co-rfa@co.rfca.mod.uk **W** www.ukrfa.org *President,* Air Vice-Marshal B. H. Newton, CB, CVO, OBE

UNITED REFORMED CHURCH HISTORY SOCIETY (1972), Westminster College, Madingley Road, Cambridge CB3 0AA **T** 01223-741300 **E** hw374@cam.ac.uk *Hon. Secretary,* Revd E. J. Brown

UNIVERSITIES FEDERATION FOR ANIMAL WELFARE (1926), The Old School, Brewhouse Hill, Wheathampstead AL4 8AN **T** 01582-831818 **E** ufaw@ufaw.org.uk **W** www.ufaw.org.uk *Chief Executive & Scientific Director,* Dr J. K. Kirkwood

UNIVERSITIES UK (2000), Woburn House, 20 Tavistock Square, London WC1H 9HQ **T** 020-7419 4111 **E** info@universitiesuk.ac.uk **W** www.universitiesuk.ac.uk *Chief Executive,* Nicola Dandridge

VEGAN SOCIETY (1944), Donald Watson House, 21 Hylton Street, Hockley B18 6HJ **T** 0845-458 8244 **E** info@vegansociety.com **W** www.vegansociety.com *Chief Executive,* Nigel Winter

VEGETARIAN SOCIETY OF THE UNITED KINGDOM LTD (1847), Parkdale, Dunham Road, Altrincham, Cheshire WA14 4QG **T** 0161-925 2000 **E** info@vegsoc.org **W** www.vegsoc.org *Chief Executive,* Dr Jon Green

VERNACULAR ARCHITECTURE GROUP (1952), 21 Walton Street, OXford OX1 2HQ **T** 01633-889019 **E** lindajhall@googlemail.com **W** www.vag.org.uk *President,* David Clark

VICTIM SUPPORT (1979), Hallam House, 56–60 Hallam Street, London W1W 6JL **T** 020-7268 0200, **Helpline** 0845-303 0900 **W** www.victimsupport.org.uk *Chief Executive,* Javed Khan

VICTIM SUPPORT SCOTLAND (1985), 15–23 Hardwell Close, Edinburgh EH8 9RX **T** 0131-668 4486 **E** info@victimsupportsco.org.uk **W** www.victimsupport.org *Chief Executive,* D. McKenna

VICTORIA CROSS AND GEORGE CROSS ASSOCIATION (1956), Horse Guards, Whitehall, London SW1A 2AX **T** 020-7930 3506 *Secretary,* Mrs D. Grahame, OBE, MVO

VICTORIAN SOCIETY (1958), 1 Priory Gardens, Bedford Park, London W4 1TT **T** 020-8994 1019 **E** admin@victoriansociety.org.uk **W** www.victoriansociety.org.uk *Director,* Dr Ian Dungavell

VSO (VOLUNTARY SERVICE OVERSEAS) (1958), 27A Carlton Drive, Putney, London SW15 2BS **T** 020-8780 7500 **E** enquiry@vso.org.uk **W** www.vso.org.uk *Chair,* Sir Andrew Cubie

WAR WIDOWS ASSOCIATION OF GREAT BRITAIN (1971), 199 Borough High Street SE1 1AA **T** 0845-241 2189 **E** info@warwidowsassociation.org.uk **W** www.warwidowsassociation.org.uk *Chair,* Rosalind Campbell

WELLBEING OF WOMEN (1965), 27 Sussex Place, Regent's Park, London NW1 4SP **T** 020-7772 6400 **E** wellbeingofwomen@rcog.org.uk **W** www.wellbeingofwomen.org.uk *Director,* Liz Campbell

WESLEY HISTORICAL SOCIETY (1893), 7 Haugh Shaw Road, Halifax, West Yorkshire HX1 3AH **T** 01422-250780 **E** johnahargreaves@blueyonder.co.uk **W** www.wesleyhistoricalsociety.org.uk *General Secretary,* Dr John A. Hargreaves, FSA, FHA, FRHISTS

WESTMINSTER FOUNDATION FOR DEMOCRACY (1992), Artillery House, 11–19 Artillery Row, London SW1P 1RT **T** 020-7799 1311 **E** wfd@wfd.org **W** www.wfd.org *Chief Executive,* Linda Duffield

WHICH? (1957), 2 Marylebone Road, London NW1 4DF
T 020-7770 7000 E which@which.co.uk
W www.which.co.uk
Chair, Patrick Barwise

WILDFOWL AND WETLANDS TRUST (1946),
Slimbridge GL2 7BT T 01453-891900
E enquiries@wwt.org.uk W www.wwt.org.uk
Chief Executive, Martin Spray

WILTSHIRE ARCHAEOLOGICAL AND NATURAL
HISTORY SOCIETY (1853), Wiltshire Heritage
Museum, 41 Long Street, Devizes SN10 1NS
T 01380-727369 E wanhs@wiltshireheritage.org.uk
W www.wiltshireheritage.org.uk
Director, David Dawson

WOMEN'S ENGINEERING SOCIETY (1919),
c/o The IET, Michael Faraday House, Six Hills Way, Stevenage
SG1 2AY T 01438-765506 E info@wes.org.uk
W www.wes.org.uk
President, Dr Jan Peters

WOMEN'S ROYAL NAVAL SERVICE BENEVOLENT
TRUST (1941), 311 Twyford Avenue, Portsmouth
PO2 8RN T 023-9265 5301
E generalsecretary@wrnsbt.org.uk W www.wrnsbt.org.uk
General Secretary, Sarah Ayton

WOODLAND TRUST (1972), Kempton Way, Grantham
NG31 6LL T 01476-581111
E enquiries@woodlandtrust.org.uk
W www.woodlandtrust.org.uk
Chief Executive, Sue Holden

WORCESTERSHIRE ARCHAEOLOGICAL SOCIETY
(1854), 26 Albert Park Road, Malvern WR14 1HN
T 01299-250416
E secretary@worcestershirearchaeologicalsociety.org.uk
W www.worcestershirearchaeologicalsociety.org.uk
Hon. Secretary, Dr J. W. Dunleavey

WORKING FAMILIES (2003), 1–3 Berry Street, London
EC1V 0AA T 020-7253 7243
E office@workingfamilies.org.uk
W www.workingfamilies.org.uk
Chief Executive, Sarah Jackson

WRVS (1938), Beck Court, Cardiff Gate Business Park, Cardiff
CF23 8RP T 02920-739 000 E enquiries@wrvs.org.uk
W www.wrvs.org.uk
Chief Executive, Lynne Berry

YMCA (1844), 45 Beech Street, London EC2Y 8AD
T 020-7070 2160 E enquiries@ymca.org.uk
W www.ymca.org.uk
Chief Executive, Ian Green

YOUTH HOSTELS ASSOCIATION (ENGLAND &
WALES) (1930), Trevelyan House, Dimple Road, Matlock
DE4 3YH T 01629-592600 E customerservices@yha.org.uk
W www.yha.org.uk
Chief Executive, Caroline White

ZOOLOGICAL SOCIETY OF LONDON (1826),
Regent's Park, London NW1 4RY T 0844-225 1826
W www.zsl.org
President, Prof. Sir Patrick Bateson, FRS

THE WORLD

THE WORLD IN FIGURES

THE EARTH

The shape of the Earth is that of an oblate spheroid or solid of revolution whose meridian sections are ellipses, while the sections at right angles are circles.

DIMENSIONS

Equatorial diameter = 12,742.01km (7,917.51 miles)
Polar diameter = 12,713.50km (7,899.80 miles)
Equatorial circumference = 40,030.20km (24,873.6 miles)
Polar circumference = 40,007.86km (24,859.73 miles)
Mass = 5,972,190,000,000,000,000,000,000kg (5.972×10^{24}kg)

The equatorial circumference is divided into 360 degrees of longitude, which is measured in degrees, minutes and seconds east or west of the Greenwich (or 'prime') meridian (0°) to 180°; the meridian 180° E coinciding with 180° W. This was internationally ratified in 1884.

Distance north and south of the equator is measured in degrees, minutes and seconds of latitude. The equator is 0°, the North Pole is 90°N. and the South Pole is 90°S. The tropics lie at 23° 27′ N. (tropic of cancer) and 23° 27′ S. (tropic of capricorn). The Arctic Circle lies at 66° 33′ N. and the Antarctic Circle at 66° 33′ S. (Note the tropics and the Arctic and Antarctic circles are affected by the slow decrease in obliquity of the ecliptic, of about 0.47 arcseconds per year. The effect of this is that the Arctic and Antarctic circles are currently moving towards their respective poles by about 14m per annum, while the tropics move towards the equator by the same amount.)

AREA ETC

The surface area of the Earth is 510,064,472km² (196,936,994 miles²), of which the water area is 70.92 per cent and the land area is 29.08 per cent.

The radial velocity on the Earth's surface at the equator is 1,669.79km per hour (1,037.56mph). The Earth's mean velocity in its orbit around the Sun is 107,218km per hour (66,622mph). The Earth's mean distance from the Sun is 149,598,262km (92,956,050 miles).

OCEANS

AREA

	Km²	miles²
Pacific	165,250,000	63,800,000
Atlantic	82,440,000	31,830,000
Indian	73,440,000	28,360,000
Southern	20,327,000	7,848,300
Arctic	14,090,000	5,440,000

The equator divides the Pacific into the North and South Pacific and the Atlantic into the North and South Atlantic. In 2000 the International Hydrographic Organisation approved the description of the 20,327,000km² (7,848,300 miles²) of circum-Antarctic waters up to 60°S. as the Southern Ocean.

GREATEST KNOWN OCEAN DEPTHS

Greatest depth	Location	metres	feet
Mariana Trench*	Pacific	10,911	35,798
Puerto Rico Trench	Atlantic	8,380	27,493
Diamantina Trench	Indian	8,047	26,401
South Sandwich Trench	Southern	7,235	23,737
Molloy Deep	Arctic	5,607	18,397

* On 23 January 1960, Jacques Piccard (Swiss) and Don Walsh (USA) descended in the bathyscaphe *Trieste* to the floor of the Mariana Trench, a depth later calculated as 10,916m (35,814ft). The current depth was calculated by the Japanese remote-controlled probe *Kaiko* on 24 March 1995. On 1 June 2009, sonar mapping of the Challenger Deep in the Mariana Trench by the US oceanographic research vessel *Kilo Moana* indicated a possible depth of 10,971m (35,994ft).

SEAS

LARGEST BY AREA

	km²	miles²
South China	3,685,000	1,423,000
Caribbean	2,753,000	1,063,000
Mediterranean	2,509,900	969,100
Bering	2,304,000	890,000
Okhotsk	1,580,000	611,000
Gulf of Mexico	1,550,000	600,000
Japan	978,000	377,600
Hudson Bay	819,000	316,000
Andaman	798,000	308,000
East China	750,000	290,000
North Sea	570,000	220,000
Red Sea	453,000	174,900
Black Sea	422,000	163,000

GREATEST KNOWN DEPTHS

	metres	feet
Caribbean (Cayman Trench)	7,686	5,126
Philippine Sea (Ryu Kyu Trench)	7,507	24,629
Mediterranean (Calypso Deep)	5,267	17,280
South China	5,016	16,457
Andaman	4,400	14,500
Bering (Bowers Basin)	4,097	13,442
Gulf of Mexico (Sigsbee Deep)	5,203	17,070
Okhotsk	3,372	11,063
Japan	3,742	12,276
Red Sea	3,040	9,974
Black Sea	2,212	7,257
North Sea	700	2,300

THE CONTINENTS

There are generally considered to be seven continents: Africa, North America, South America, Antarctica, Asia, Australia and Europe. Europe and Asia are sometimes considered a single continent: Eurasia, and North and South America are sometimes referred to together as: the Americas.

AFRICA is surrounded by sea except for the narrow isthmus of Suez in the north-east, through which was cut the Suez Canal (opened 17 November 1869). Its extreme longitudes are 17° 20′ W. at Cape Verde, Senegal, and 51° 24′ E. at Raas Xaafunn, Somalia. The extreme latitudes are 37° 20′ N. at Cape Blanc, Tunisia, and 34° 50′ S. at Cape Agulhas, South Africa, about 7,081km (4,400 miles) apart. The Equator passes across Gabon, Republic of the Congo, Uganda, Kenya and Somalia in the middle of the continent.

NORTH AMERICA, including Mexico, is surrounded by ocean except in the south, where the isthmian states of Central America link North America with South America. Its extreme longitudes are 168° 5′ W. at Cape Prince of Wales, Alaska, and 55° 40′ W. at Cape Charles, Newfoundland. The extreme continental latitudes are the tip of the Boothia peninsula, NW Territories, Canada (71° 51′ N.) and 14° 22′ N. in southern Mexico near La Victoria, Guatemala.

SOUTH AMERICA lies mostly in the southern hemisphere, the equator passing across Ecuador, Colombia and Brazil in the north of the continent. It is surrounded by ocean except where it is joined to Central America in the north by the narrow isthmus through which was cut the Panama Canal (opened 15 August 1914). Its extreme longitudes are 34° 47′ W. at Cape Branco in Brazil and 81° 20′ W. at Punta Pariña, Peru. The extreme continental latitudes are 12° 25′ N. at Punta Gallinas, Colombia, and 53° 54′ S. at the southernmost tip of Peninsula de Brunswick, Chile. Cape Horn, on Cape Island, Chile, lies in 55° 59′ S.

ANTARCTICA lies almost entirely within the Antarctic Circle (66° 33′ S.) and is the largest of the world's glaciated areas. Ninety-eight per cent of the continent is permanently covered in ice. The ice amounts to some 30 million km³ (7.2 million miles³) and represents more than 70 per cent of the world's fresh water. The ice sheet is on average 1.6km (1 mile) thick; if it were to melt, the world's seas would rise by more than 60m (197ft). The environment is too hostile for unsupported human habitation.

ASIA is the largest continent and occupies 29.6 per cent of the world's land surface. The extreme longitudes are 26° 05′ E. at Baba Buran, Turkey, and 169° 40′ W. at Mys Dezhneva, Russia, a distance of about 9,656km (6,000 miles). Its extreme northern latitude is 77° 45′ N. at Mys Chelyuskin, Russia, and it extends over 8,046km (5,000 miles) south to Tanjong Piai, Malaysia.

AUSTRALIA is the smallest of the continents and lies in the southern hemisphere. It is entirely surrounded by ocean. Its extreme longitudes are 113° 11′ E. at Steep Point, Western Australia, and 153° 11′ E. at Cape Byron, New South Wales. The extreme latitudes are 10° 42′ S. at Cape York, Queensland, and 39°S. at South East Point, Tasmania. Australia, together with New Zealand (Australasia), Papua New Guinea and the Pacific Islands, comprises Oceania.

EUROPE, including European Russia, is the smallest continent in the northern hemisphere. Its extreme latitudes are 71° 11′ N. at Nord Kapp in Norway, and 36° 23′ N. at Akra Tainaron (Matapas) in southern Greece, a distance of about 3,862km (2,400 miles). Its breadth from Cabo Carvoeiro in Portugal (9° 34′ W.) in the west to the Kara River, north of the Urals (66° 30′ E.) in the east is about 5,310km (3,300 miles). The division between Europe and Asia is generally regarded as the watershed of the Ural Mountains; down the Ural river to Atyrau, Kazakhstan; across the Caspian Sea to Apsheronskiy Poluostrov, near Baku; along the watershed of the Caucasus Mountains to Anapa and then across the Black Sea to the Bosporus in Turkey; across the Sea of Marmara to Canakkale Bogazi (Dardanelles).

Continent	Area	
	km²	miles²
Asia	44,614,000	17,226,000
North America	24,247,039	9,361,791
South America	17,824,370	6,882,027
Africa	30,348.110	11,717,370
Antarctica	14,200,000	5,500,000
Europe*	9,699,000	3,745,000
Australia	7,702,501	2,973,952

* Includes 5,571,000km² (2,151,000 miles²) of former USSR territory, including the Baltic states, Belarus, Moldova, Ukraine and the part of Russia west of the Ural Mountains and Kazakhstan west of the Ural river. European Turkey (24,378km²/9,412 miles²) comprises territory to the west and north of the Bosporus and the Dardanelles

GLACIATED AREAS

It is estimated that around 14,800,000km² (5,712,800 miles²) or 10 per cent of the world's land surface is permanently covered with ice. Glacial retreat and thinning occurs where glaciers melt faster than they are created. The phenomenon has been observed since the mid-19th century but has accelerated since about 1980 as a result of global warming. It is most notable in the Antarctic: a 2005 report by the American Association for the Advancement of Science indicated that 87 per cent of the continent's 244 marine glaciers have retreated over the past 50 years. The largest glacier is the 515km (320 miles) long Lambert-Fisher Ice Passage, Mac Robertson Land, Eastern Antarctica.

Location	Area	
	km²	miles²
South Polar regions	13,829,000	5,340,000
North Polar regions (incl. Greenland)	1,965,000	758,500

PENINSULAS

Peninsula	Area	
	km²	miles²
Arabian	2,590,000	1,000,000
Southern Indian	2,072,000	800,000
Alaskan	1,500,000	580,000
Labradorian	1,300,000	500,000
Scandinavian	750,000	289,500
Iberian	584,000	225,500

LARGEST ISLANDS

Island and ocean	Area	
	km²	miles²
Greenland (Kalaallit Nunaat), Arctic	2,166,000	836,330
New Guinea, Pacific	800,000	309,000
Borneo, Pacific	743,330	287,000
Madagascar, Indian	587,051	226,662
Baffin Island, Arctic	507,451	195,928
Sumatra, Indian	473,606	182,860
Honshu, Pacific	227,898	87,992
Great Britain, Atlantic	218,077	84,200
Victoria Island, Arctic	217,291	83,896
Ellesmere Island, Arctic	196,236	75,767

LARGEST DESERTS

Desert and location	Area (approx)	
	km²	miles²
Sahara, N. Africa	8,600,000	3,300,000
Arabian, Middle East	2,330,000	900,000
Gobi, Mongolia/China	1,300,000	500,000
Kalahari, Botswana/Namibia/ S. Africa	930,000	360,000
Great Victoria, Australia	424,400	163,900
Taklimakan Shamo, Mongolia/China	320,000	123,550
Kara Kum, Turkmenistan	350,000	135,000
Kyzylkum, Kazakhstan/ Uzbekistan	300,000	115,000
Great Sandy, Australia	284,993	110,036
Thar, India/Pakistan	200,000	77,000

DEEPEST DEPRESSIONS

Depression and location	Maximum depth below sea level	
	metres	feet
Dead Sea, Jordan/Israel	408	1,338
Lake Assal, Djibouti	157	515
Turfan Depression, Sinkiang, China	155	508
Qattara Depression, Egypt	133	435
Batyr Depression, Kazakhstan	130	425
Kobar Sink, Ethiopia	116	381
Death Valley, California, USA	86	282
Salton Sea, California, USA	69	227
Caspian Depression, Russia/Kazakhstan	27	90

The world's largest exposed depression is the Caspian Depression covering the hinterland of the northern third of the Caspian Sea, which is itself 27m (90ft) below sea level.

Western Antarctica and central Greenland largely comprise crypto-depressions under ice burdens. The Antarctic Bentley subglacial trench has a bedrock 2,538m (8,326ft) below sea level. In Greenland (lat. 73° N., long. 39° W.) the bedrock is 365m (1,197ft) below sea level.

Around 26 per cent of the area of the Netherlands lies marginally below sea level, an area of more than 10,000km² (3,860 miles²).

No part of the Maldives is higher than 1.8m (6ft) above sea level and nowhere in Lesotho is lower than 1,381m (4,531ft).

CAVES

DEEPEST CAVES
The world's deepest cave was discovered in January 2001 by a team of Ukrainian cave explorers in the Arabikskaya system in the western Caucasus mountains of Georgia. It is a branch of the Voronya or 'Crow's Cave'.

Cave system/location	Depth	
	metres	feet
Krubera (Voronya), Georgia	2,191	7,188
Illyuzia-Mezhonnogo-Snezhnaya, Georgia	1,753	5,751
Lamprechtsofen Vogelschacht, Austria	1,632	5,354
Gouffre Mirolda, France	1,626	5,335
Réseau Jean Bernard, France	1,602	5,256
Torca del Cerro del Cuevon/Torca de las Saxifragas, Spain	1,589	5,213
Sarma, Georgia	1,543	5,062
Shakta Vyacheslav, Georgia	1,508	4,947
Sima de la Cornisa (Torca Magali), Spain	1,507	4,944
Cehi 2, Slovenia	1,502	4,928
Sistema Cheve (Cuicateco), Mexico	1,484	4,868
Sistema Huautla, Mexico	1,475	4,839

LONGEST CAVE SYSTEMS

Cave system/location	Total known length	
	km	miles
Mammoth Cave System, Kentucky, USA	627.6	390
Jewel Cave, South Dakota, USA	241.6	150
Optymistychna, Ukraine	232.0	144
Wind Cave, South Dakota, USA	218.4	136
Sistema Sac Actun, Mexico (submerged, but dry)	217.4	135
Lechuguilla Cave, New Mexico, USA	209.6	130
Hölloch, Switzerland	195.9	122
Fisher Ridge System, Kentucky, USA	183.6	114
Sistema Ox Bel Ha, Mexico (submerged)	182.2	113
Gua Air Jernih, Malaysia	175.7	109
Siebenhengste-hohgant, Switzerland	156.0	97
Schoenbergsystem, Austria	130.2	81

LONGEST MOUNTAIN RANGES

Range and location	Length	
	km	miles
Cordillera de Los Andes, South America	8,900	5,500
Rocky Mountains, North America	4,800	3,000
Great Dividing Range, Australia	3,700	2,300
Transantarctic Mountains, Antarctica	3,200	2,000
West Sumatran-Javan Range, Indonesia	2,900	1,800
Serra do Mar	2,600	1,600
Himalaya, Central Asia	2,500	1,550
Tien Shan, Central Asia	2,400	1,500
Central New Guinea Range, New Guinea	2,010	1,250

HIGHEST MOUNTAINS

Mountain (first ascent)	Height	
	metres	feet
Mt Everest* [Qomolangma] (29 May 1953)	8,850	29,035
K2 [Qogir]† (31 July 1954)	8,611	28,251
Kangchenjunga (25 May 1955)	8,586	28,169
Lhotse (18 May 1956)	8,501	27,890
Makalu (15 May 1955)	8,463	27,766
Cho Oyu (19 October 1954)	8,201	26,906
Dhaulagiri I (13 May 1960)	8,167	26,795
Manaslu I [Kutang I] (9 May 1956)	8,163	26,781
Nanga Parbat [Diamir] (3 July 1953)	8,125	26,660

* Named after Sir George Everest (1790–1866), Surveyor-General of India 1830–43, in 1863. He pronounced his name 'Eve-rest'.

† Formerly named after Col. Henry Haversham Godwin-Austen (1834–1923), who worked on the Trigonometrical Survey of India, which established the heights of the Himalayan peaks, including Everest

The culminating summits in the other major mountain ranges are:

Mountain, by range or country	Height	
	metres	feet
Victory Peak [Pik Pobedy], Tien Shan	7,439	24,406
Mt Aconcagua, Cordillera de Los Andes	6,959	22,831
Mt McKinley (S. Peak), Alaska Range	6,194	20,320
Kilimanjaro (Kibo), Tanzania	5,895	19,340
Hkakabo Razi, Myanmar	5,881	19,296
Mt Elbrus, (W. Peak), Caucasus	5,642	18,510
Citlaltépetl [Orizaba], Mexico	5,610	18,406
Jaya Peak, Central New Guinea Range	5,030	16,500
Vinson Massif, Antarctica	4,892	16,050
Mt Blanc, Alps	4,807	15,771

HIGHEST ACTIVE VOLCANOES

Although it displays fumarolic activity, emitting steam and gas, no major eruption has ever been observed of the world's highest volcano and second highest peak in the western hemisphere, the 6,893m (22,615ft) Ojos del Salado, in the Andes on the Argentina/Chile border. For comparison, Eyjafjallajokull, the Icelandic volcano which erupted in 2010 causing air transport chaos, has an elevation of 1,666m (5,466ft).

The volcanoes listed below include only those that have had activity recorded since 1960.

Volcano and location (most recent activity)	Height	
	metres	feet
San Pedro, Andes, Chile (1960)	6,145	20,161
Aracar, Andes, Argentina (1993)	6,082	19,954
Volcan Guallatiri, Andes, Chile (1960)	6,071	19,918
Tupungatito, Andes, Chile (1987)	6,000	19,685
Sabancaya, Andes, Peru (2003)	5,967	19,577
San José, Andes, Argentina/Chile (1960)	5,856	19,213
Lascar, Andes, Chile (2007)	5,591	18,346
Popocatepetl, Mexico (2010)	5,426	17,802
Nevado del Ruiz, Colombia (1991)	5,321	17,457
Sangay, Andes, Ecuador (2010)	5,230	17,159
Irruputuncu, Chile (1995)	5,163	16,939
Tungurahua, Ecuador (2010)	5,023	16,479
Kliochevskoi, Kamchatka peninsula, Russia (2010)	4,835	15,863

LAKES

LARGEST LAKES

The areas of some of the lakes listed are subject to seasonal variation. The most voluminous lakes are the Caspian Sea (saline) with 78,200km³ (18,800 miles³) and Baikal (fresh water) with 23,000km³ (5,518 miles³). Baikal is also the world's deepest lake (see below). It is estimated that it contains as much water as the entire Great Lakes system in North America – more than 20 per cent of the world's fresh water and some 90 per cent of all the fresh water in Russia.

The Aral was once the fifth largest in the world, with an area of 68,000km² (26,255 miles²), but since the 1960s many of its feeder rivers have been diverted for irrigation, as a result of which its area shrank to 17,160km² (6,626 miles²). Its salinity was almost three times that of seawater, and pollution led to the extinction of many aquatic species. Since the construction of the Kok-Aral dam (2005), water levels are rising again, especially in the north.

Lake and location	Area		Length	
	km²	miles²	km	miles
Caspian Sea, Iran/ Azerbaijan/Russia/ Turkmenistan/ Kazakhstan	386,400	149,200	1,200	750
Michigan–Huron, USA/Canada*	117,610	45,300	1,010	627
Superior, Canada/USA	82,100	31,700	563	350
Victoria, Uganda/ Tanzania/Kenya	69,484	26,828	337	210
Tanganyika, Dem. Rep. of Congo/Tanzania/ Zambia/Burundi	32,900	12,700	660	410
Baikal, Russia	31,500	12,200	636	395
Great Bear, Canada	31,328	12,096	309	192
Malawi [Nyasa], Tanzania/Malawi/ Mozambique	29,600	11,430	584	363
Great Slave, Canada	28,568	11,030	480	298
Erie, Canada/USA	25,670	9,910	388	241

* Lakes Michigan and Huron may be regarded as lobes of the same lake. The Michigan lobe has an area of 57,750km² (22,300 miles²) and the Huron lobe an area of 59,570km² (23,000 miles²)

UNITED KINGDOM (BY COUNTRY)

Lake and location	Area		Length	
	km²	miles²	km	miles
Lough Neagh, Northern Ireland	396.00	153.00	28.90	18.00
Loch Lomond, Scotland	71.12	27.46	36.44	22.64
Windermere, England	14.74	5.69	16.90	10.50
Lake Vyrnwy, Wales (artificial)	4.53	1.75	7.56	4.70
Llyn Tegid [Bala], Wales	4.38	1.69	5.80	3.65

LARGEST MANMADE LAKES

Dam/lake* (year of completion)	Volume	
	km³	miles³
Nalubaale dam [Owen Falls], Uganda/Kenya/Tanzania (1954)	204.80	49.13
Kariba, Zimbabwe/Zambia (1959)	180.60	43.33
Bratsk, Russia (1967)	169.27	40.61
Nasser, Egypt (1970)	168.90	40.52
Volta, Ghana (1965)	153.00	36.71
Manicouagan [Daniel Johnson dam], Canada (1968)	141.85	34.03
Guri [Raul Leoni], Venezuela (1986)	138.00	33.11
Krasnoyarskoye, Russia (1967)	73.30	17.58
Wadi-Tatar, Iraq (1967)	72.80	17.46
Williston (W. A. C. Bennett dam), Canada (1967)	70.31	16.87

* Formed as a result of dam construction

The UK's largest reservoir is Kielder Water, Northumberland (1982) with a volume of 0.2km³ (0.048 miles³)

DEEPEST LAKES

Lake and location	Greatest depth	
	metres	feet
Baikal, Russia	1,637	5,371
Tanganyika, Burundi/Tanzania/Dem. Rep. of Congo/Zambia	1,436	4,710

Caspian Sea, Azerbaijan/Iran/ Kazakhstan/Russia/Turkmenistan	1,025	3,363	
O'Higgins [San Martin], Chile/Argentina	836	2,743	
Malawi [Nyasa], Malawi/Mozambique/ Tanzania	704	2,310	
Ysyk, Kyrgyzstan	668	2,192	
Great Slave, Canada	614	2,015	
Quesnel, Canada	610	2,001	
Crater, Oregon, USA	592	1,943	
Matano, South Sulawesi, Indonesia	590	1,936	
Buenos Aires [General Carrera], Argentina/Chile	586	1,923	
Hornindalsvastnet, Norway	514	1,686	
Sarez, Tajikistan	505	1,657	
Toba, Sumatra, Indonesia	505	1,657	
Argentino, Argentina	500	1,640	
Tahoe, California/Nevada, USA	500	1,640	

Loch Morar, Highland, Scotland is the UK's deepest lake at 310m (1,017ft).

LONGEST RIVERS

River, source–outflow	Length	
	km	miles
Nile [Bahr-el-Nil], R. Luvironza, Burundi–E. Mediterranean Sea	6,650	4,132
Amazon [Amazonas], Lago Villafro, Peru–S. Atlantic Ocean	6,448	4,007
Yangtze [Chang Jiang], Kunlun Mts, W. China–Yellow Sea	6,300	3,915
Mississippi-Missouri-Red Rock, Montana–Gulf of Mexico	5,970	3,710
Yenisey-Selenga, W. Mongolia–Kara Sea	5,539	3,442
Huang He [Yellow River], Bayan Har Shan range, Central China–Yellow Sea	5,463	3,395
Ob'-Irtysh, W. Mongolia–Kara Sea	5,410	3,362
Congo [Zambia], R. Lualaba, Dem. Rep. of Congo-Zambia–S. Atlantic Ocean	4,665	2,900
Amur-Argun, R. Argun, Khingan Mts, N. China–Sea of Okhotsk	4,416	2,744
Lena, R. Kirenga, W. of Lake Baikal– Laptev Sea, Arctic Ocean	4,400	2,734

BRITISH ISLES

River, source and outflow	Length	
	km	miles
Shannon, Co. Cavan, Rep. of Ireland– Atlantic Ocean	372	231
Severn, Powys, Wales–Bristol Channel	354	220
Thames, Gloucestershire, England– North Sea	330	205
Tay, Perthshire, Scotland–North Sea	193	120
Clyde, Lanarkshire, Scotland–Firth of Clyde	170	106
Tweed, Scottish Borders–North Sea	155	96.5
Bann (Upper and Lower), Co. Down, N. Ireland–Atlantic Ocean	129	80

WATERFALLS

GREATEST BY HEIGHT

Waterfall, river and location	Total drop		Greatest single leap	
	metres	feet	metres	feet
Angel, Carrao Auyan Tepui, Venezuela	979	3,212	807	2,648
Tugela, Tugela, S. Africa (5 leaps)	947	3,110	411	1,350
Ramnefjellsfossen, Jostedal Glacier, Norway	800	2,625	600	1,970
Mongefossen, Monge, Norway	773	2,535	—	—
Gocta, Cocahuayco, Peru	771	2,531	—	—
Mutarazi, Mutarazi, Zimbabwe	762	2,499	479	1,572
Yosemite, Yosemite Creek, USA	740	2,425	436	1,430
Ostre Mardola Foss, Mardals, Norway*	655	2,149	296	974
Tyssestrengene, Tysso, Norway*	646	2,120	289	948
Kukenaam, Arabopo, Venezuela	610	2,000	—	—

* Volume much affected by hydroelectric harnessing

BRITISH ISLES, BY HEIGHT

Waterfall, river and location	Total drop	
	metres	feet
Eas a' Chual Aluinn, Glas Bheinn, Sutherland, Scotland	200	656
Powerscourt Falls, Dargle, Co. Wicklow, Rep. of Ireland	121	398
Pistyll-y-Llyn, Powys/Dyfed border, Wales (cascades)	91	300
Pistyll Rhaeadr, Clwyd/Powys border, Wales (single leap)	74	240
Cauldron Snout, Tees, Cumbria/Durham, England (cascades)	61	200

GREATEST BY VOLUME

Waterfall, river and location*	Mean annual flow (m³/sec)
Khone, Mekong, Laos	9,500
Para, Caura, Venezuela	3,540
Paulo Afonso, Sao Francisco, Brazil	2,832
Niagara (Horseshoe), Niagara/Lake Erie– Lake Ontario, Canada	2,407
Salto de Iguaçu, Parana, Argentina/Brazil	1,746
Victoria (Mosi-oa-Tunya), Zambezi, Zimbabwe/Zambia	1,088
Virginia, Nahanni, Canada	1,000
Sivasamudram, Kaveri (Cauvery), India	934
Kongou, Ivindo, Gabon	900
Willamette, Willamette, Oregon, USA	874

* Excludes waterfalls that have been submerged as a result of dam construction or consist of rapids or cascades with individual vertical drops of less than 6m (20ft)

DAMS

TALLEST DAMS

Dam and location (year of completion)	Height	
	metres	feet
Jinping-I, China (2014*)	305	1,001
Nurek, Tajikistan (1980)	300	984
Xiaowan, China (2013*)	292	960
Grande Dixence, Switzerland (1961)	285	935
Inguri, Georgia (1980)	272	892
Vaiont, Italy (1961)†	262	859
Manuel Moreno Torres, Mexico (1981)	261	856
Tehri, India (2006)	261	856

* Scheduled completion date
† Disused

TALLEST

All heights are in accordance with the Council on Tall Buildings and Urban Habitat's regulations, which measure from the ground level of the main entrance to the architectural tip of the building and include spires but not antennae, signage or flag poles.

INHABITED BUILDINGS

Building and location (year of completion)	Height	
	metres	feet
Burj Khalifa, Dubai, UAE (2010)	828	2,717
Abraj Al-Bait Tower, Mecca, Saudi Arabia (2011)	600	1,970
Taipei 101, Taipei, Taiwan (2003)	508	1,667
Federation Tower, Moscow, Russia (2016*)	506	1,660
Shanghai World Finance Centre, Shanghai, China (2008)	492	1,614
International Commerce Centre, Hong Kong, China (2010)	484	1,588
Petronas Towers I and II, Kuala Lumpur, Malaysia (1998)	452	1,482
Nangjing Greenland Financial Centre, Nanjing, China (2010)	450	1,475
Kingkey Finance Tower, Shenzhen, China	442	1,450
Willis Tower, Chicago, USA (1974)†	442	1,450
Guangzhou International Finance Centre, China (2010)	440	1,444
Trump International Hotel and Tower, Chicago, USA (2009)	423	1,388
Jin Mao Tower, Shanghai, China (1998)	421	1,380
Two International Finance Centre, Hong Kong, China (2003)	416	1,362
Princess Tower, Dubai, UAE (2011)	414	1,358
Al Hamra Tower, Kuwait (2011)	412	1,352

* Scheduled completion date
† With TV antennae, 520m (1,707ft)

STRUCTURES

Structure and location (year of completion)	Height	
	metres	feet
Tokyo Skytree, Tokyo, Japan (2012*)	634	2,080
KVLY (formerly KTHI)-TV Mast, North Dakota (guyed), USA (1963)†	629	2,063
Canton, Guangzhou, China (2010)	600	1,968
CN Tower, Toronto, Canada (1976)	553	1,815
Ostankino Tower, Moscow, Russia (1967)	540	1,772

* Scheduled completion date
† The USA has numerous other guyed TV towers above 600m (1,969ft)

TWIN TOWERS

Structure and location (year of completion)	Floors	Height	
		metres	feet
Petronas Towers, Kuala Lumpur, Malaysia (1998)	88	452	1,483
Emirates Park Towers, Dubai, UAE (2011)	54	355	1,163
The Cullinan, Hong Kong, China (2008)	68	270	886
Al Kazim Towers, Dubai, UAE (2008)	53	265	869

	Floors	metres	feet
Grand Gateway, Shanghai, China (2005)	54	262	859
Dual Towers, Manama, Bahrain (2007)	53	260	853
The Imperial, Mumbai, India (2009)	60	249	816
Al Fattan Towers, Dubai, UAE (2006)	51	245	804
Abraj Al Bait Towers, Mecca, Saudi Arabia (2012)	42	240	787

Destroyed 2001

	Floors	metres	feet
World Trade Center One, New York City, USA (1972)	110	417	1,368
World Trade Center Two, New York City, USA (1973)	110	415	1,362

CHURCHES

Structure and location (year of completion)	Height	
	metres	feet
Sagrada Família, Barcelona, Spain (2026*)	172	564
Ulm Cathedral, Ulm, Germany (1890)	162	530
Our Lady of Peace Basilica, Yamoussoukro, Côte d'Ivoire (1990)	158	518
Cologne Cathedral, Cologne, Germany (1880)	157	516
Notre-Dame Cathedral, Rouen, France (1876)	151	495
St Nicholas Church, Hamburg, Germany (1874)	148	485
Notre-Dame Cathedral, Strasbourg, France (1439)	144	472
Queen of Peace Shrine and Basilica, Lichen, Poland (2004)	140	459
St Stephen's Cathedral, Vienna, Austria (1570)	137	448
Basilica of St Peter, Rome, Italy (1626)	133	435

* Scheduled completion date, the 100th anniversary of the death of its architect, Antoni Gaudí; open for worship following its consecration by Pope Benedict XVI in 2010

The Chicago Methodist Temple, Chicago, USA (completed 1924) is 173m (568ft) high, but is sited atop a 25-storey, 100m (328ft) building. Salisbury Cathedral (1521), at 123m (404ft), is the UK's tallest religious building. St Paul's Cathedral, London, and Liverpool Anglican Cathedral are the only others in the UK over 100m (328ft) tall. At 94m (309ft) the Church of St Walburge, Preston, Lancashire is the tallest church in Britain that is not a cathedral.

TALLEST STRUCTURES — A CHRONOLOGY

Structure and location	Year	Height	
		metres	feet
Djoser's Step Pyramid, Saqqara, Egypt	c.2650 BC	61	200
Pyramid of Meidum, Egypt	c.2600 BC	92	302
Snefru's Bent Pyramid, Dahshur, Egypt	c.2600 BC	102	336
Red Pyramid, Dahshur, Egypt	c.2590 BC	105	345
Great Pyramid, Giza, Egypt*	c.2580 BC	146	479

		metres	feet
Liuhe (Six Harmonies) Pagoda, Hangzhou, China†	AD 970	150	492
Lincoln Cathedral, Lincoln, England‡	1311–1400	160	525
St Paul's Cathedral, London, England§	1315	149	489
St Olaf's Church, Tallinn, Estonia₵	1438–1519	159	522
St Mary's Church, Stralsund, Germany	1384–1478	151	495
Notre-Dame Cathedral, Strasbourg, France	1439	144	472
St Nicholas Church, Hamburg, Germany	1874	148	485
Notre-Dame Cathedral, Rouen, France	1876	151	495
Cologne Cathedral, Cologne, Germany	1880	157	516
Washington Monument, Washington DC, USA	1884	169	555
Eiffel Tower, Paris, France	1889	300	984
Chrysler Building, New York, USA	1930	319	1,046
Empire State Building, New York, USA	1931	381	1,250
KWTV Mast, Oklahoma City, USA	1954	481	1,577
KOBR-TV Tower, Caprock, USA	1960	490	1,608
KFVS TV Mast, Egypt Mills, USA	1960	511	1,677
KVLY (formerly KTHI)-TV Mast, Blanchard, USA	1963	629	2,063
Warszawa Radio Mast, Konstantynow, Poland**	1974	646	2,118
Burj Khalifa, Dubai, UAE	2010	828	2,717

* Later reduced through loss of topstone to 137m (449ft)
† Destroyed in 1121
‡ Destroyed in 1549
§ Destroyed in 1561
₵ Spire burned down in 1625; renovated in 1931 to present height of 123m (403ft)
** Collapsed in 1991 during renovation

BRIDGES

The longest stretch of bridging of any kind is the Danyang–Kunshan Grand Bridge (2010) in China at 164km (102 miles). The 'floating' bridging at Evergreen Point, Seattle, Washington, USA (1963), is 3,839m (12,596ft) long, of which 2,310m (7,578ft) floats.

LONGEST SUSPENSION SPANS

Bridge and location (year of completion)	Length	
	metres	feet
Akashi-Kaikyo, Japan (1998)	1,991	6,532
Xihoumen, China (2008)	1,650	5,413
Great Belt Bridge, Denmark (1998)	1,624	5,328
Gwangyang, South Korea (2012*)	1,545	5,069
Runyang, China (2005)	1,490	4,888
Nanjing Fourth Yangtze, China (2013*)	1,418	4,652
Humber Estuary, England (1981)	1,410	4,626
Jiangyin, China (1999)	1,385	4,544
Tsing Ma, Hong Kong, China (1997)	1,377	4,518
Hardanger, Norway (2013*)	1,310	4,298

* Scheduled completion date

LONGEST CANTILEVER SPANS

Bridge and location (year of completion)	Length	
	metres	feet
Pont de Québec, St Lawrence, Canada (1917)	548.6	1,800
Firth of Forth, Scotland (two spans of 1,710ft each) (1890)	521.2	1,710
Minato, Japan (1974)	510.0	1,673
Commodore Barry, New Jersey/Pennsylvania, USA (1974)	501.1	1,644
Greater New Orleans, Louisiana, USA (I 1958, II 1988)*	480.0	1,575
Howrah, India (1943)	457.2	1,500
Veterans Memorial, Louisiana, USA (1995)	445.0	1,460
San Francisco Oakland Bay, California, USA (1936)	426.7	1,400
Horace Wilkinson, Louisiana, USA (1969)	376.0	1,235
Tappan Zee, New York, USA (1955)	369.0	1,212

* Also known as Crescent City Connection

LONGEST STEEL ARCH SPANS

Bridge and location (year of completion)	Length	
	metres	feet
Sheikh Rashid bin Saeed Crossing, Dubai, UAE (2012)	667.0	2,188
Chaotianmen, China (2009)	552.0	1,811
Lupu, China (2003)	550.0	1,804
New River Gorge, West Virginia, USA (1977)	518.0	1,700
Bayonne [Kill van Kull], New Jersey/New York, USA (1931)	504.0	1,654
Sydney Harbour, Australia (1932)	502.9	1,650
Chenab, India (2015*)	460.0	1,509
Yongjiang, China (2011*)	464.0	1,522
Wushan, China (2005)	460.0	1,509
Zhijinghe, China (2009)	430.0	1,410

* Scheduled completion date

TALLEST BRIDGE TOWERS

Bridge and location (year of completion)	Height	
	metres	feet
Millau, France (2004)	343	1,125
Russky Island, Russia (2012*)	320	1,050
Sutong, China (2008)	306	1,004
Akashi-Kaikyo, Japan (1998)	298	978
Stonecutters, Hong Kong, China (2009)	298	978
Gwangan, South Korea (2002)	270	886
Jingsha, China (2009)	267	876
East Bridge, Great Belt Fixed Link, Denmark (1997)	254	833
Edong, China (2010)	243	797
Mezcala, Mexico (1993)	242	794

* Scheduled completion date

LONGEST VEHICULAR TUNNELS

Tunnel and location (year of completion)	Length	
	km	miles
*Seikan (rail), Tsugaru Channel, Japan (1988)	53.85	33.46
*Channel tunnel (rail), Cheriton, Kent, UK–Sangatte, Calais, France (1994)	50.45	31.35
Seoul subway (line 5), South Korea (1995)	47.60	29.58
Moscow metro, Serpukhovsko–Timiryazevskaya line, Moscow, Russia (2002)	41.50	25.79
Tokyo subway (Toei Oedo line), Japan (2000)	40.70	25.29
Lötschberg (rail), Switzerland (2007)	34.58	21.49
Berlin U-Bahn (U7 line) (rail), Germany (1984)	31.76	19.74
Guadarrama (rail), Spain (2007)	28.38	17.63
Taihang (rail), China (2008)	27.85	17.31
London Underground Northern Line, East Finchley–Morden (1939)	27.84	17.30

* Sub-aqueous

The longest non-vehicular tunnelling in the world is the Delaware Aqueduct in New York State, USA, constructed in 1937–44 to a length of 168.9km (105 miles).

St Gotthard (rail) tunnel in Switzerland will be 57.07km (35.46 miles) long when completed in 2018.

BRITISH RAIL TUNNELS

	Length	
	km	miles
Severn, Bristol–Newport	6.88	4.28
Totley, Manchester–Sheffield	5.70	3.54
Standedge, Manchester–Huddersfield	4.89	3.04
Sodbury, Swindon–Bristol	4.06	2.53
Strood, Medway, Kent	3.61	2.24
Disley, Stockport–Sheffield	3.54	2.20
Ffestiniog, Llandudno–Blaenau Ffestiniog	3.53	2.19
Bramhope, Leeds–Harrogate	3.44	2.14
Cowburn, Manchester–Sheffield	3.39	2.10

The longest road tunnel in Britain is the Mersey Queensway Tunnel (1934), 3.24km (2.01 miles) long. The longest canal tunnel, at Standedge, W. Yorks, is 5.03km (3.13 miles) long; it was completed in 1811, closed in 1944 and reopened in 2001.

LONGEST SHIP CANALS

Canal	Length		Min. depth	
	km	miles	metres	feet
White Sea–Baltic [formerly Stalin] (1933), of which canalised river 51.5km (32 miles)	227	141.00	5.0	16.5
Rhine–Main–Danube, Germany (1992)	171	106.25	4.0	13.1
*Suez (1869), links Red and Mediterranean Seas	162	100.60	12.9	42.3
V. I. Lenin Volga–Don, Russia (1952), links Black and Caspian Seas	100	62.20	3.6	11.8
Kiel (or North Sea), Germany (1895), links North and Baltic Seas	98	60.90	11.0	37.0
*Houston, USA (1940), links inland city with Gulf of Mexico	81	50.50	11.0	36.0
Alphonse XIII, Spain (1926), gives Seville access to Atlantic Ocean	85	53.00	7.6	25.0
Panama (1914), links Pacific Ocean and Caribbean Sea; lake chain, 78.9km (49 miles) dug	82	50.71	13.0	43.0
Danube–Black Sea, Romania (1984)	64.4	40.02	7.0	23.0
Manchester Ship, UK (1894), links city with Irish Channel	58	36.00	8.5	28.0

* Has no locks

The first section of China's Grand Canal, running 1,782km (1,107 miles) from Beijing to Hangzhou, was opened in AD 610 and completed in 1283. Today it is limited to 2,000-tonne vessels.

The St Lawrence Seaway comprises the Beauharnois, Welland and Welland Bypass and Seaway 54–59 canals, and allows access to Duluth, Minnesota, USA via the Great Lakes from the Atlantic end of Canada's Gulf of St Lawrence, a distance of 3,769km (2,342 miles). The St Lawrence Canal, completed in 1959, is 293km (182 miles) long.

AIR DISTANCES

	London (LHR)	Paris (CDG)	Madrid (MAD)	Rome (FCO)	Moscow (DME)	Dubai (DXB)	New York (JFK)	Delhi (DEL)	Beijing (PEK)	Los Angeles (LAX)	Durban (DUR)	Bangkok (BKK)	Tokyo (HND)	Hong Kong (HKG)	Singapore (SIN)	Buenos Aires (BHI)	Sydney (SYD)
London (LHR)		216 / 348km	773 / 1,244km	899 / 1,446km	1,587 / 2,553km	3,421 / 5,505km	3,452 / 5,554km	4,191 / 6,744km	5,081 / 8,175km	5,457 / 8,780km	5,904 / 9,499km	5,959 / 9,588km	5,975 / 9,614km	5,996 / 9,647km	6,767 / 10,888km	7,241 / 11,651km	10,575 / 17,016km
Paris (CDG)	216 / 348km		660 / 1,063km	685 / 1,102km	1,547 / 2,489km	3,260 / 5,245km	3,635 / 5,849km	4,088 / 6,578km	5,103 / 8,211km	5,671 / 9,124km	5,692 / 9,159km	5,879 / 9,459km	6,047 / 9,730km	5,971 / 9,607km	6,668 / 10,729km	7,220 / 11,617km	10,529 / 16,941km
Madrid (MAD)	773 / 1,244km	660 / 1,063km		829 / 1,334km	2,140 / 3,444km	3,517 / 5,659km	3,589 / 5,775km	4,518 / 7,269km	5,734 / 9,226km	5,846 / 9,406km	5,312 / 8,546km	6,343 / 10,206km	6,706 / 10,790km	6,541 / 10,524km	7,079 / 11,390km	6,589 / 10,602km	10,986 / 17,676km
Rome (FCO)	899 / 1,446km	685 / 1,102km	829 / 1,334km		1,491 / 2,398km	2,703 / 4,349km	4,278 / 6,884km	3,694 / 5,944km	5,076 / 8,167km	6,356 / 10,226km	5,059 / 8,140km	5,523 / 8,886km	6,162 / 9,915km	5,779 / 9,298km	6,250 / 10,057km	7,252 / 11,668km	10,157 / 16,342km
Moscow (DME)	1,587 / 2,553km	1,547 / 2,489km	2,140 / 3,444km	1,491 / 2,398km		2,262 / 3,639km	4,702 / 7,566km	2,679 / 4,311km	3,605 / 5,800km	6,122 / 9,851km	5,868 / 9,441km	4,388 / 7,060km	4,672 / 7,518km	4,424 / 7,118km	5,218 / 8,396km	8,720 / 14,031km	8,992 / 14,468km
Dubai (DXB)	3,421 / 5,505km	3,260 / 5,245km	3,517 / 5,659km	2,703 / 4,349km	2,262 / 3,639km		6,850 / 11,022km	1,359 / 2,187km	3,639 / 5,855km	8,340 / 13,420km	4,102 / 6,600km	3,051 / 4,909km	4,941 / 7,949km	3,685 / 5,929km	3,634 / 5,847km	8,733 / 14,051km	7,482 / 12,039km
New York (JFK)	3,452 / 5,554km	3,635 / 5,849km	3,589 / 5,775km	4,278 / 6,884km	4,702 / 7,566km	6,850 / 11,022km		7,319 / 11,777km	6,839 / 11,004km	2,475 / 3,983km	8,249 / 13,273km	8,678 / 13,963km	6,774 / 10,899km	8,074 / 12,990km	9,539 / 15,349km	5,511 / 8,868km	9,952 / 16,013km
Delhi (DEL)	4,191 / 6,744km	4,088 / 6,578km	4,518 / 7,269km	3,694 / 5,944km	2,679 / 4,311km	1,359 / 2,187km	7,319 / 11,777km		2,371 / 3,815km	8,015 / 12,896km	5,024 / 8,083km	1,831 / 2,947km	3,649 / 5,871km	2,332 / 3,752km	2,580 / 4,152km	10,017 / 16,117km	6,477 / 10,422km
Beijing (PEK)	5,081 / 8,175km	5,103 / 8,211km	5,734 / 9,226km	5,076 / 8,167km	3,605 / 5,800km	3,639 / 5,855km	6,839 / 11,004km	2,371 / 3,815km		6,252 / 10,059km	7,276 / 11,707km	2,057 / 3,309km	1,303 / 2,097km	1,235 / 1,987km	2,781 / 4,474km	12,321 / 19,825km	5,553 / 8,934km
Los Angeles (LAX)	5,457 / 8,780km	5,671 / 9,124km	5,846 / 9,406km	6,356 / 10,226km	6,122 / 9,851km	8,340 / 13,420km	2,475 / 3,983km	8,015 / 12,896km	6,252 / 10,059km		10,635 / 17,111km	8,271 / 13,308km	5,489 / 8,831km	7,261 / 11,684km	8,772 / 14,114km	6,164 / 9,918km	7,490 / 12,051km
Durban (DUR)	5,904 / 9,499km	5,692 / 9,159km	5,312 / 8,546km	5,059 / 8,140km	5,868 / 9,441km	4,102 / 6,600km	8,249 / 13,273km	5,024 / 8,083km	7,276 / 11,707km	10,635 / 17,111km		5,511 / 8,868km	8,353 / 13,440km	6,560 / 10,555km	5,244 / 8,438km	5,147 / 8,282km	6,571 / 10,573km
Bangkok (BKK)	5,959 / 9,588km	5,879 / 9,459km	6,343 / 10,206km	5,523 / 8,886km	4,388 / 7,060km	3,051 / 4,909km	8,678 / 13,963km	1,831 / 2,947km	2,057 / 3,309km	8,271 / 13,308km	5,511 / 8,868km		2,853 / 4,590km	1,049 / 1,688km	877 / 1,411km	10,420 / 16,766km	4,663 / 7,503km
Tokyo (HND)	5,975 / 9,614km	6,047 / 9,730km	6,706 / 10,790km	6,162 / 9,915km	4,672 / 7,518km	4,941 / 7,949km	6,774 / 10,899km	3,649 / 5,871km	1,303 / 2,097km	5,489 / 8,831km	8,353 / 13,440km	2,853 / 4,590km		1,805 / 2,904km	3,289 / 5,292km	11,217 / 18,048km	4,838 / 7,785km
Hong Kong (HKG)	5,996 / 9,647km	5,971 / 9,607km	6,541 / 10,524km	5,779 / 9,298km	4,424 / 7,118km	3,685 / 5,929km	8,074 / 12,990km	2,332 / 3,752km	1,235 / 1,987km	7,261 / 11,684km	6,560 / 10,555km	1,049 / 1,688km	1,805 / 2,904km		1,588 / 2,555km	11,278 / 18,147km	4,582 / 7,372km
Singapore (SIN)	6,767 / 10,888km	6,668 / 10,729km	7,079 / 11,390km	6,250 / 10,057km	5,218 / 8,396km	3,634 / 5,847km	9,539 / 15,349km	2,580 / 4,152km	2,781 / 4,474km	8,772 / 14,114km	5,244 / 8,438km	877 / 1,411km	3,289 / 5,292km	1,588 / 2,555km		9,717 / 15,634km	3,908 / 6,288km
Buenos Aires (BHI)	7,241 / 11,651km	7,220 / 11,617km	6,589 / 10,602km	7,252 / 11,668km	8,720 / 14,031km	8,733 / 14,051km	5,511 / 8,868km	10,017 / 16,117km	12,321 / 19,825km	6,164 / 9,918km	5,147 / 8,282km	10,420 / 16,766km	11,217 / 18,048km	11,278 / 18,147km	9,717 / 15,634km		6,996 / 11,257km
Sydney (SYD)	10,575 / 17,016km	10,529 / 16,941km	10,986 / 17,676km	10,157 / 16,342km	8,992 / 14,468km	7,482 / 12,039km	9,952 / 16,013km	6,477 / 10,422km	5,553 / 8,934km	7,490 / 12,051km	6,571 / 10,573km	4,663 / 7,503km	4,838 / 7,785km	4,582 / 7,372km	3,908 / 6,288km	6,996 / 11,257km	

Figures are in miles, and represent the great circle distance (the shortest distance between two points on the surface of the earth)

TIME ZONES

See colour plates for Time Zones world map.

Standard time differences from the Greenwich meridian

+ hours ahead of GMT
− hours behind GMT
* may vary from standard time at some part of the year (Summer Time or Daylight Saving Time)
† some areas may keep another time zone
‡ unofficial time zone
h hours
m minutes

	h	*m*
Afghanistan	+ 4	30
*Albania	+ 1	
Algeria	+ 1	
*Andorra	+ 1	
Angola	+ 1	
Antigua and Barbuda	− 4	
*†Argentina	− 3	
*Armenia	+ 4	
*Australia		
*ACT, NSW (except Broken Hill area and Lord Howe Island), Tas, Vic, Whitsunday Islands	+ 10	
Northern Territory	+ 9	30
Queensland	+ 10	
*South Australia	+ 9	30
*†Western Australia	+ 8	
Christmas Island (Indian Ocean)	+ 7	
Cocos (Keeling) Islands	+ 6	30
Norfolk Island	+ 11	30
*Austria	+ 1	
*Azerbaijan	+ 4	
*Bahamas	− 5	
Bahrain	+ 3	
*Bangladesh	+ 6	
Barbados	− 4	
*Belarus	+ 2	
*Belgium	+ 1	
Belize	− 6	
Benin	+ 1	
Bhutan	+ 6	
Bolivia	− 4	
*Bosnia and Hercegovina	+ 1	
Botswana	+ 2	
*Brazil		
†*central states	− 4	
*N. and N. E. coastal states	− 2	
*S. and E. coastal states, including Brasilia	− 3	
*Fernando de Noronha Island	− 2	
Brunei	+ 8	

	h	*m*
*Bulgaria	+ 2	
Burkina Faso	0	
Burundi	+ 2	
Cambodia	+ 7	
Cameroon	+ 1	
*Canada		
*Alberta	− 7	
*†British Columbia	− 8	
*Manitoba	− 6	
*New Brunswick	− 4	
*†Newfoundland and Labrador	− 3	30
*†Northwest Territories	− 7	
*Nova Scotia	− 4	
*Nunavut		
central	− 6	
eastern	− 5	
mountain	− 7	
*Ontario		
east of 90° W.	− 5	
west of 90° W.	− 6	
*Prince Edward Island	− 4	
*Québec		
east of 63° W.	− 4	
*west of 63° W.	− 5	
*†Saskatchewan	− 6	
*Yukon	− 8	
Cape Verde	− 1	
Central African Republic	+ 1	
Chad	+ 1	
*Chile	− 4	
*Easter Island	− 6	
China (inc. Hong Kong and Macau)	+ 8	
Colombia	− 5	
The Comoros	+ 3	
Congo, Dem. Rep. of		
eastern	+ 2	
western	+ 1	
Congo, Republic of	+ 1	
Costa Rica	− 6	
Côte d'Ivoire	0	
*Croatia	+ 1	
*Cuba	− 5	
*Cyprus	+ 2	
*Czech Republic	+ 1	
*Denmark	+ 1	
*Faeroe Islands	0	
*Greenland	− 3	
Danmarks Havn, Mesters Vig	0	
*Scoresby Sund	− 1	
Thule area	− 4	
Djibouti	+ 3	
Dominica	− 4	
Dominican Republic	− 4	
Ecuador	− 5	
Galápagos Islands	− 6	
*Egypt	+ 2	
El Salvador	− 6	

	h	*m*
Equatorial Guinea	+ 1	
Eritrea	+ 3	
*Estonia	+ 2	
Ethiopia	+ 3	
Fiji	+ 12	
*Finland	+ 2	
*France	+ 1	
French Guiana	− 3	
†French Polynesia	− 10	
Guadeloupe	− 4	
Martinique	− 4	
Mayotte	+ 3	
New Caledonia	+ 11	
St Barthélemy	− 4	
Réunion	+ 4	
*St Pierre and Miquelon	− 3	
Wallis and Futuna	+ 12	
Gabon	+ 1	
The Gambia	0	
Georgia	+ 4	
*Germany	+ 1	
Ghana	0	
*Greece	+ 2	
Grenada	− 4	
Guatemala	− 6	
Guinea	0	
Guinea-Bissau	0	
Guyana	− 4	
Haiti	− 5	
Honduras	− 6	
*Hungary	+ 1	
Iceland	0	
India	+ 5	30
Indonesia		
Java, Kalimantan (west and central), Madura, Sumatra	+ 7	
Bali, Flores, Kalimantan (south and east), Lombok, Sulawesi, Sumbawa, West Timor	+ 8	
Irian Jaya, Maluku	+ 9	
*Iran	+ 3	30
Iraq	+ 3	
*Ireland, Republic of	0	
*Israel	+ 2	
*Italy	+ 1	
Jamaica	− 5	
Japan	+ 9	
*Jordan	+ 2	
Kazakhstan		
western	+ 5	
eastern	+ 6	
Kenya	+ 3	
Kiribati	+ 12	
Line Islands	+ 14	
Phoenix Islands	+ 13	
Korea, Dem. People's Rep. of	+ 9	

	h	m
Korea, Republic of	+ 9	
Kosovo	+ 1	
Kuwait	+ 3	
Kyrgyzstan	+ 6	
Laos	+ 7	
*Latvia	+ 2	
*Lebanon	+ 2	
Lesotho	+ 2	
Liberia	0	
Libya	+ 2	
*Liechtenstein	+ 1	
*Lithuania	+ 2	
*Luxembourg	+ 1	
*Macedonia	+ 1	
Madagascar	+ 3	
Malawi	+ 2	
Malaysia	+ 8	
Maldives	+ 5	
Mali	0	
*Malta	+ 1	
Marshall Islands	+ 12	
Mauritania	0	
*Mauritius	+ 4	
*Mexico	− 6	
*Chihuahua, Nayarit,		
Sinaloa, S. Baja		
California	− 7	
*N. Baja California	− 8	
Sonora	− 7	
Micronesia, Fed. States of		
Chuuk, Yap	+ 10	
Kosrae, Pingelap,		
Pohnpei	+ 11	
*Moldova	+ 2	
*Monaco	+ 1	
†Mongolia	+ 8	
*Montenegro	+ 1	
Morocco	0	
Mozambique	+ 2	
Myanmar	+ 6	30
*Namibia	+ 1	
Nauru	+ 12	
Nepal	+ 5	45
*The Netherlands	+ 1	
Aruba	− 4	
Netherlands Antilles	− 4	
*New Zealand	+ 12	
*Chatham Islands	+ 12	45
Cook Islands	− 10	
Niue	− 11	
Tokelau Island	− 10	
Nicaragua	− 6	
Niger	+ 1	
Nigeria	+ 1	
*Norway	+ 1	
*Svalbard, Jan Mayen	+ 1	
Oman	+ 4	
Pakistan	+ 5	
Palau	+ 9	
*Palestinian Autonomous		
Areas	+ 2	
Panama	− 5	
Papua New Guinea	+ 10	
*Paraguay	− 4	
Peru	− 5	
The Philippines	+ 8	
*Poland	+ 1	

	h	m
*Portugal	0	
*Azores	− 1	
*Madeira	0	
Qatar	+ 3	
*Romania	+ 2	
Russia		
Zone 1	+ 3	
Zone 2	+ 4	
Zone 3	+ 6	
Zone 4	+ 7	
Zone 5	+ 8	
Zone 6	+ 9	
Zone 7	+ 10	
Zone 8	+ 11	
Zone 9	+ 12	
Rwanda	+ 2	
St Kitts and Nevis	− 4	
St Lucia	− 4	
St Vincent and the		
Grenadines	− 4	
*Samoa	− 11	
*San Marino	+ 1	
Sao Tome and Príncipe	0	
Saudi Arabia	+ 3	
Senegal	0	
*Serbia	+ 1	
Seychelles	+ 4	
Sierra Leone	0	
Singapore	+ 8	
*Slovakia	+ 1	
*Slovenia	+ 1	
Solomon Islands	+ 11	
Somalia	+ 3	
South Africa	+ 2	
*Spain	+ 1	
*Canary Islands	0	
Sri Lanka	+ 5	30
Sudan	+ 3	
Suriname	− 3	
Swaziland	+ 2	
*Sweden	+ 1	
*Switzerland	+ 1	
*Syria	+ 2	
Taiwan	+ 8	
Tajikistan	+ 5	
Tanzania	+ 3	
Thailand	+ 7	
Timor–Leste	+ 9	
Togo	0	
Tonga	+ 13	
Trinidad and Tobago	− 4	
Tunisia	+ 1	
*Turkey	+ 2	
Turkmenistan	+ 5	
Tuvalu	+ 12	
Uganda	+ 3	
*Ukraine	+ 2	
United Arab Emirates	+ 4	
*United Kingdom	0	
Anguilla	− 4	
*Bermuda	− 4	
††British Antarctic		
Territory	− 3	
British Indian Ocean		
Territory	+ 6	
British Virgin Islands	− 4	
Cayman Islands	− 5	

	h	m
*Channel Islands	0	
*Falkland Islands	− 4	
*Gibraltar	+ 1	
Montserrat	− 4	
Pitcairn Islands	− 8	
St Helena and		
Dependencies	0	
South Georgia and		
South Sandwich		
Islands	− 2	
*Turks and Caicos		
Islands	− 5	
*United States of America		
*Alaska	− 9	
Aleutian Islands, east		
of 169′ 30′ W.	− 9	
Aleutian Islands, west		
of 169′ 30′ W.	− 10	
*central time	− 6	
*eastern time	− 5	
Guam	+ 10	
Hawaii	− 10	
*mountain time	− 7	
Northern Mariana		
Islands	+ 10	
*Pacific time	− 8	
Puerto Rico	− 4	
Samoa, American	− 11	
Virgin Islands	− 4	
*Uruguay	− 3	
Uzbekistan	+ 5	
Vanuatu	+ 11	
*Vatican City State	+ 1	
Venezuela	− 4	30
Vietnam	+ 7	
Western Sahara	0	
Yemen	+ 3	
Zambia	+ 2	

CURRENCIES AND EXCHANGE RATES

Average rate against £1 sterling on 29 April 2011

COUNTRY/TERRITORY	CURRENCY	VALUE
Albania	Lek (Lk) of 100 qindarka	Lk 160.29
Algeria	Algerian dinar (DA) of 100 centimes	DA 119.51
American Samoa	Currency is that of the USA	US$1.67
Andorra	Euro (€) of 100 cents	€1.12
Angola	Kwanza (Krz) of 100 centimos	Kzrl 155.58
Anguilla	East Caribbean dollar (EC$) of 100 cents	EC$4.50
Antigua and Barbuda	East Caribbean dollar (EC$) of 100 cents	EC$4.50
Argentina	Peso of 100 centavos	Pesos 6.81
Aruba	Aruban guilder	Guilder 2.99
Ascension Island	Currency is that of St Helena	£1.00
Australia	Australian dollar ($A) of 100 cents	$A1.52
Austria	Euro (€) of 100 cents	€1.12
Azerbaijan	New manat of 100 gopik	New manat 1.33
The Bahamas	Bahamian dollar (B$) of 100 cents	B$1.67
Bahrain	Bahraini dinar (BD) of 1,000 fils	BD 0.63
Bangladesh	Taka (Tk) of 100 poisha	Tk 121.60
Barbados	Barbados dollar (BD$) of 100 cents	BD$3.34
Belarus	Belarusian rouble of 100 kopeks	BYR 5,027.20
Belgium	Euro (€) of 100 cents	€1.12
Belize	Belize dollar (BZ$) of 100 cents	BZ$3.31
Benin	Franc CFA of 100 centimes	Francs 737.47
Bermuda	Bermuda dollar of 100 cents	$1.67
Bhutan	Ngultrum of 100 chetrum (Indian currency is also legal tender)	Ngultrum 73.75
Bolivia	Boliviano ($b) of 100 centavos	$b11.58
Bosnia and Hercegovina	Convertible marka of 100 fenings	Mark 2.20
Botswana	Pula (P) of 100 thebe	P 10.60
Brazil	Real of 100 centavos	Real 2.62
Brunei	Brunei dollar (B$) of 100 sen	B$2.04
Bulgaria	Lev of 100 stotinki	Leva 2.20
Burkina Faso	Franc CFA of 100 centimes	Francs 737.47
Burundi	Burundi franc of 100 centimes	Francs 2,065.59
Cameroon	Franc CFA of 100 centimes	Francs 737.47
Canada	Canadian dollar (C$) 100 cents	C$1.58
Cayman Islands	Cayman Islands dollar (CI$) of 100 cents	CI$1.37
Central African Republic	Franc CFA of 100 centimes	Francs 737.47
Chad	Franc CFA of 100 centimes	Francs 737.47
Chile	Chilean peso of 100 centavos	Pesos 767.17
China	Renminbi yuan of 10 jiao or 100 fen	Yuan 10.83
Colombia	Colombian peso of 100 centavos	Pesos 2,954.27
The Comoros	Comorian franc (KMF) of 100 centimes	Francs 553.10
Congo, Rep. of	Franc CFA of 100 centimes	Francs 737.47
Congo, Dem. Rep. of	Congolese franc (CFr) of 100 cents	CFr 1,536.23
Cook Islands	Currency is that of New Zealand	NZ$2.07
Costa Rica	Costa Rican colón (C) of 100 céntimos	C834.58
Côte d'Ivoire	Franc CFA of 100 centimes	Francs 737.47
Croatia	Kuna of 100 lipa	Kuna 8.28
Cuba	Cuban peso of 100 centavos	Pesos 1.67
Cyprus	Euro (€) of 100 cents	€1.12
Czech Republic	Koruna (Kcs) of 100 haleru	Kcs 27.21
Denmark	Danish krone of 100 ore	Kroner 8.38
Dominica	East Caribbean dollar (EC$) of 100 cents	EC$4.50
Dominican Republic	Dominican Republic peso (RD$) of 100 centavos	RD$63.11
Ecuador	Currency is that of the USA (formerly sucre of 100 centavos)	US$1.67
Egypt	Egyptian pound (£E) of 100 piastres or 1,000 millièmes	£E9.92
El Salvador	Currency is that of the USA	US$1.67
Equatorial Guinea	Franc CFA of 100 centimes	Francs 737.47
Estonia	Euro (€) of 100 cents (since January 2011)	€1.12

Ethiopia	Ethiopian birr (EB) of 100 cents	EB 28.12
Faeroe Islands	Currency is that of Denmark	Kroner 8.38
Falkland Islands	Falkland pound of 100 pence	£1.00
Fiji	Fiji dollar (F$) of 100 cents	F$2.91
Finland	Euro (€) of 100 cents	€1.12
France	Euro (€) of 100 cents	€1.12
French Guiana	Euro (€) of 100 cents	€1.12
French Polynesia	Franc CFP of 100 centimes	Francs 134.16
Gabon	Franc CFA of 100 centimes	Francs 737.47
Gambia	Dalasi (D) of 100 butut	D 46.74
Georgia	Lari of 100 tetri	Lari 2.73
Germany	Euro (€) of 100 cents	€1.12
Ghana	Cedi of 100 pesewas	Cedi 2.51
Gibraltar	Gibraltar pound of 100 pence	£1.00
Greece	Euro (€) of 100 cents	€1.12
Greenland	Currency is that of Denmark	Kroner 8.38
Grenada	East Caribbean dollar (EC$) of 100 cents	EC$4.50
Guadeloupe	Euro (€) of 100 cents	€1.12
Guam	Currency is that of the USA	US$1.67
Guatemala	Quetzal (Q) of 100 centavos	Q 12.64
Guinea	Guinea franc of 100 centimes	Francs 11,050.23
Guinea-Bissau	Franc CFA of 100 centimes	Francs 737.47
Haiti	Gourde of 100 centimes	Gourdes 67.30
Honduras	Lempira of 100 centavos	Lempiras 31.52
Hong Kong	Hong Kong (HK$) of 100 cents	HK$12.96
Hungary	Forint of 100 filler	Forints 297.45
Iceland	Icelandic krona (Kr) of 100 aurar	Kr 185.05
India	Indian rupee (Rs) of 100 paise	Rs 73.75
Indonesia	Rupiah (Rp) of 100 sen	Rp 14,284.32
Ireland, Republic of	Euro (€) of 100 cents	€1.12
Israel	Shekel of 100 agora	Shekels 5.62
Italy	Euro (€) of 100 cents	€1.12
Jamaica	Jamaican dollar (J$) of 100 cents	J$142.15
Japan	Yen of 100 sen	Yen 135.34
Jordan	Jordanian dinar (JD) of 10 dirhams	JD 1.18
Kazakhstan	Tenge of 100 tiyn	Tenge 243.25
Kenya	Kenyan shilling (Ksh) of 100 cents	Ksh 139.02
Kiribati	Currency is that of Australia	$A1.52
Korea, Republic of	Won of 100 jeon	Won 1,787.46
Kuwait	Kuwaiti dinar (KD) of 1,000 fils	KD 0.46
Kyrgyzstan	Som of 100 tyiyn	Som 78.02
Latvia	Lats of 100 santims	Lats 0.80
Lebanon	Lebanese pound (L£) of of 100 piastres	L£2,506.10
Lesotho	Loti (M) of 100 lisente	M 10.99
Liechtenstein	Currency is that of Switzerland	Francs 1.45
Lithuania	Litas of 100 centas	Litas 3.88
Luxembourg	Euro (€) of 100 cents	€1.12
Macao	Pataca of 100 avos	Pataca 13.34
Macedonia	Denar of 100 deni	Den 69.17
Madagascar	Ariary of 5 iraimbilanja	MGA 3,240.00
Malawi	Kwacha (K) of 100 tambala	MK 251.53
Malaysia	Malaysian ringgit (dollar) (RM) of 100 sen	RM 4.91
Maldives	Rufiyaa of 100 laaris	Rufiyaa 21.35
Mali	Franc CFA of 100 centimes	Francs 737.47
Malta	Euro (€) of 100 cents	€1.12
Marshall Islands	Currency is that of the USA	US$1.67
Martinique	Currency is that of France	€1.12
Mauritania	Ouguiya (UM) of 5 khoums	UM 454.52
Mauritius	Mauritius rupee of 100 cents	Rs 45.79
Mayotte	Currency is that of France	€1.12
Mexico	Peso of 100 centavos	Pesos 19.23
Micronesia, Federated States of	Currency is that of the USA	US$1.67
Moldova	Moldovan leu of 100 bani	MDL 19.08
Monaco	Euro (€) of 100 cents	€1.12
Mongolia	Tugrik of 100 mongo	Tugriks 2,101.62
Montenegro	Euro (€) of 100 cents	€1.12
Montserrat	East Caribbean dollar (EC$) of 100 cents	EC$4.50
Morocco	Dirham (DH) of 100 centimes	DH 12.80

Mozambique	New metical (MT) of 100 centavos	MT 52.12
Namibia	Namibian dollar of 100 cents	$10.99
Nauru	Currency is that of Australia	$A1.52
Nepal	Nepalese rupee of 100 paisa	Rs 118.00
The Netherlands	Euro (€) of 100 cents	€1.12
Netherlands Antilles	Netherlands Antilles guilder of 100 cents	Guilders 2.99
New Caledonia	Franc CFP of 100 centimes	Francs 134.16
New Zealand	New Zealand dollar (NZ$) of 100 cents	NZ$2.07
Nicaragua	Córdoba (C$) of 100 centavos	C$37.08
Niger	Franc CFA of 100 centimes	Francs 737.47
Nigeria	Naira (N) of 100 kobo	N 257.95
Niue	Currency is that of New Zealand	NZ$2.07
Norfolk Island	Currency is that of Australia	$A1.52
Northern Mariana Islands	Currency is that of the USA	US$1.67
Norway	Krone of 100 ore	Kroner 8.74
Oman	Rial Omani (OR) of 1,000 baisas	OR 0.64
Pakistan	Pakistan rupee of 100 paisa	Rs 141.40
Palau	Currency is that of the USA	US$1.67
Panama	Balboa of 100 centésimos (US notes are in circulation)	Balboa 1.67
Papua New Guinea	Kina (K) of 100 toea	K 4.08
Paraguay	Guaraní (Gs) of 100 céntimos	Gs 6,571.73
Peru	New Sol of 100 céntimos	New Sol 4.70
The Philippines	Philippine peso (P) of 100 centavos	P 71.40
Pitcairn Islands	Currency is that of New Zealand	NZ$2.07
Poland	Zloty of 100 groszy	Zlotych 4.42
Portugal	Euro (€) of 100 cents	€1.12
Puerto Rico	Currency is that of the USA	US$1.67
Qatar	Qatar riyal of 100 dirhams	Riyals 6.07
Réunion	Currency is that of France	€1.12
Romania	New leu of 100 bani	Lei 4.58
Russian Federation	Rouble of 100 kopeks	Rbl 45.66
Rwanda	Rwanda franc of 100 centimes	Francs 1,003.68
St Helena	St Helena pound (£) of 100 pence	£1.00
St Kitts and Nevis	East Caribbean dollar (EC$) of 100 cents	EC$4.50
St Lucia	East Caribbean dollar (EC$) of 100 cents	EC$4.50
St Pierre and Miquelon	Currency is that of France	€1.12
St Vincent and the Grenadines	East Caribbean dollar (EC$) of 100 cents	EC$4.50
Samoa	Tala (S$) of 100 sene	S$3.78
San Marino	Euro (€) of 100 cents	€1.12
Saudi Arabia	Saudi riyal (SR) of 100 halala	SR 6.25
Senegal	Franc CFA of 100 centimes	Francs 737.47
Serbia	New dinar of 100 paras	New dinars 111.37
Seychelles	Seychelles rupee of 100 cents	Rs 20.42
Sierra Leone	Leone (Le) of 100 cents	Le 7,263.06
Singapore	Singapore dollar (S$) of 100 cents (fully interchangeable with Brunei currency)	S$2.04
Slovakia	Euro (€) of 100 cents	€1.12
Slovenia	Euro (€) of 100 cents	€1.12
Solomon Islands	Solomon Islands dollar (SI$) of 100 cents	SI$12.71
South Africa	Rand (R) of 100 cents	R 10.99
Spain	Euro (€) of 100 cents	€1.12
Sri Lanka	Sri Lankan rupee of 100 cents	Rs 183.31
Suriname	Surinamese dollar of 100 cents	Dollar 5.50
Swaziland	Lilangeni (E) of 100 cents (South African currency is also in circulation)	E 10.99
Sweden	Swedish krona of 100 ore	Kronor 10.05
Switzerland	Swiss franc of 100 rappen (or centimes)	Francs 1.45
Taiwan	New Taiwan dollar (NT$) of 100 cents	NT$47.77
Tanzania	Tanzanian shilling of 100 cents	Shillings 2,519.44
Thailand	Baht of 100 satang	Baht 49.79
Timor–Leste	Currency is that of the USA	US$1.67
Togo	Franc CFA of 100 centimes	Francs 737.47
Tokelau	Currency is that of New Zealand	NZ$2.07
Tonga	Pa'anga (T$) of 100 seniti	T$2.92
Trinidad and Tobago	Trinidad and Tobago dollar (TT$) of 100 cents	TT$10.68
Tristan da Cunha	Currency is that of the UK	£1.00
Tunisia	Tunisian dinar of 1,000 millimes	Dinars 2.25
Turkey	New Turkish lira (TL) of 100 kurus	TL 2.53

Turks and Caicos Islands	Currency is that of the USA	US$1.67
Tuvalu	Currency is that of Australia	$A1.52
Uganda	Uganda shilling of 100 cents	Shillings 3,969.72
Ukraine	Hryvna of 100 kopiykas	UAH 13.29
United Arab Emirates	UAE dirham (Dh) of 100 fils	Dirham 6.13
United States of America	US dollar (US$) of 100 cents	US$1.67
Uruguay	Uruguayan peso of 100 centésimos	Pesos 31.44
Uzbekistan	Sum of 100 tiyin	Sum 2,821,45
Vanuatu	Vatu	Vatu 150.73
Vatican City State	Euro (€) of 100 cents	€1.12
Venezuela	Bolívar fuerte (Bs. F) of 100 céntimos	Bs. F 7.16
Vietnam	Dong of 10 hao or 100 xu	Dong 34,434.85
Virgin Islands, British	Currency is that of the USA (£ sterling and EC$ also circulate)	US$1.67
Virgin Islands, US	Currency is that of the USA	US$1.67
Wallis and Futuna Islands	Franc CFP of 100 centimes	Francs 134.16
Yemen	Riyal of 100 fils	Riyals 356.61
Zambia	Kwacha (K) of 100 ngwee	K 7,847.71
Zimbabwe	Zimbabwe dollar (Z$) suspended April 2009; US dollar now base currency	US$1.67

Source: WM/Reuters Closing Spot Rates

TRAVEL OVERSEAS

PASSPORT REGULATIONS

Application forms for United Kingdom passports can be obtained from the UK Identity and Passport Service's (IPS) telephone advice line or website, regional passport offices, or from main post offices.

UK IDENTITY AND PASSPORT SERVICE

T 0300-222 0000

W www.direct.gov.uk/en/travelandtransport/passports

REGIONAL OFFICES

- Law Society House, 90–106 Victoria Street, Belfast BT1 3GN
- Millburngate House, Durham DH97 1PA
- 3 Northgate, 96 Milton Street, Cowcaddens, Glasgow G4 0BT
- 101 Old Hall Street, Liverpool L3 9BD
- Globe House, 89 Eccleston Square, London SW1V 1PN
- Olympia House, Upper Dock Street, Newport, Gwent NP20 1XA*
- Aragon Court, Northminster Road, Peterborough PE1 1QG

* The Newport Passport Office will stop processing passport applications from March 2012. It will then operate as a customer support centre

The passport offices are open Monday to Saturday on an appointment-only basis (appointments should be arranged by calling the central telephone number listed above). For an additional fee, passport offices provide either a guaranteed same-day service (not available for a first adult or child passport, extending a limited passport, replacing a lost, stolen or damaged passport or for complex amendments) or a one-week fast-track service (except for first adult passports).

Standard postal applications are processed within three weeks. The completed application form should be posted, with the appropriate supporting documents and fee, to the regional passport office indicated on the addressed envelope which is provided with each application form. Accompanying cheques and postal orders should be made payable to 'Identity and Passport Service', or to 'Post Office Ltd' when using the Check & Send service. For online applications, the completed online form will be printed out by the Passport Office and posted to the applicant for them to sign and return. After the paper copy has been received, online applications are also returned within three weeks.

Applications can also be submitted through Check & Send outlets at selected main post offices, who, for a small handling charge of £8.17, will forward the application form to the relevant regional passport office after having checked that it has been completed correctly and has the appropriate documents attached. These applications take a minimum of two weeks (first adult passport applications may take six weeks including passport interview).

A passport cannot be issued or extended on behalf of a person already abroad; such persons should apply to the nearest British High Commission or Consulate.

UK passports are granted to:
- British citizens
- British nationals (overseas)
- British overseas territories citizens
- British subjects
- British protected persons

UK passports are generally available for travel to all countries. The possession of a passport does not exempt the holder from compliance with any immigration regulations in force in British or foreign countries, or from the necessity of obtaining a visa where required (see below for a list of countries for which UK citizens do not require a visa).

Biometric passports were introduced in 2006. The design and security features, including a chip containing the biometrics (the facial image and biographical data of the holder), render the passport more secure against forgery and aid border controls.

ADULTS

A passport granted to a person over 16 will normally be valid for ten years. Thereafter, or if at any time the passport contains no further space for visas, a new passport must be obtained.

The issue of passports including details of the holder's spouse was discontinued in 1988.

British nationals born on or before 2 September 1929 are eligible for a free standard passport.

CHILDREN

Since 5 October 1998 all children under the age of 16 are required to have their own passport. This is primarily to help prevent child abductions. The passports are initially valid for five years, but can be renewed for a further five years at the end of this period. Any adult passport which includes children will have expired in or before 2008: the parent will need to renew their passport and apply for a separate first child passport for any children.

COUNTERSIGNATURES

A countersignature is needed if the application is for a first passport, to replace a lost, stolen or damaged passport, or to renew a passport for a child aged 11 or under. A countersignature is also needed for renewals if the applicant's appearance has significantly changed and the photograph in their previous passport is unrecognisable. The signatory must be willing to enter their own passport number on to the form. The list of acceptable countersignatories includes: MP; justice of the peace; minister of religion; a professionally qualified person (eg doctor, engineer, lawyer, teacher); bank officer; military officer; civil servant; police officer; or a person of similar standing who has known the applicant for at least two years, who lives in the UK and who holds a British or Irish passport. A relative or partner, someone living at the same address as the applicant, or an employee of the IPS must not countersign the application.

If the application is for a child under the age of 16, the countersignature should be by someone of relevant standing who has known the parent or person with parental responsibility who signs the declaration of consent, rather than the child.

PHOTOGRAPHS

Two identical, unmounted, recent colour photographs of the applicant must be sent. These photographs should measure 45mm by 35mm, be printed on plain white photographic paper and should be taken full face against a plain cream or light grey background. The photo must show the applicant's full face, looking straight at the camera, with a neutral expression and with their mouth closed. If a countersignature is required for the application, the person who countersigned the form should also certify one photograph as a true likeness of the applicant.

DOCUMENTATION
In addition to two photographs, the applicant's current or previous British passport, and other documents in support of the statements made in the application, must be produced at the time of applying. Details of which documents are required are set out in the notes accompanying the application form.

If the passport applicant is a British national by naturalisation or registration, the certificate proving this must be produced with the application, unless the applicant holds a previous British passport issued after registration or naturalisation.

INTERVIEWS
Interviews for adults applying for their first passport (not including those who held their own passport as a child) were introduced on 1 June 2007 to combat passport fraud and forgery. After applying for a passport, applicants will be sent a letter asking them to book an interview at one of the 66 offices in the UK. Interviews last for approximately 30 minutes and applicants are asked to confirm facts about themselves that someone attempting to steal their identity would not know. The IPS recommends that new applicants now allow six weeks to receive their passport. There is no one-week fast-track service for first adult passports.

48-PAGE PASSPORTS
The 48-page 'jumbo' passport is intended to meet the needs of frequent travellers who fill standard passports well before the validity has expired. It is valid for ten years but is not available for children.

PASSPORT FEES*	
First adult passport	£77.50
First child passport	£49
Renewal or amendment of adult passport	£77.50
Renewal or amendment of child passport	£49
48-page passport	£90.50

* Standard postal applications only. Applications made at UK regional offices have a higher fee

HEALTH ADVICE

The NHS Choices website provides health advice for those travelling abroad, including information on immunisations and reciprocal health agreements with other countries. *See* W www.nhs.uk/livewell/travelhealth

IMMUNISATION
In very general terms immunisation against typhoid, polio and hepatitis A should be considered for all countries with lower standards of hygiene and sanitation. Protection against malaria, in the form of tablets, as well as care to avoid mosquito bites, is advised for visits to malarious areas.

Immunisation against yellow fever is compulsory for entry into some countries, either for all travellers or for those arriving from a yellow fever-infected area, and is recommended for all travellers to infected areas.

A doctor should be consulted, preferably at least eight weeks before departure, and will advise travellers and arrange vaccinations. Most doctors will charge a fee for a course of vaccinations. If children will be travelling outside Europe, North America, Australia and New Zealand, the doctor should be informed, especially if they have not completed their full course of childhood immunisation. As a precaution, it is also recommended that all travellers are up to date with their tetanus and diphtheria inoculations.

Country-by-country guidance is set out on the website W www.fitfortravel.nhs.uk. Health care professionals can obtain information about immunisation recommendations from the Department of Health publication *Health Information for Overseas Travel* (the 'Yellow Book') or from:

HEALTH PROTECTION AGENCY, 151 Buckingham Palace Road, London SW1W 9SZ T 020-7811 7000
W www.hpa.org.uk

SCOTTISH GOVERNMENT HEALTH DEPARTMENT, St Andrew's House, Edinburgh EH1 3DG T 0131-556 8400 E ceu@scotland.gsi.gov.uk W www.scotland.gov.uk

HEALTH PROTECTION SCOTLAND, Meridian Court, 5 Cadogan Street, Glasgow G2 6QE T 0141-300 1100 E nss.hpsenquiries@nhs.net W www.hps.scot.nhs.uk

DEPARTMENT OF HEALTH, SOCIAL SERVICES AND PUBLIC SAFETY, Castle Buildings, Stormont, Belfast BT4 3SJ T 028-9052 0500 E webmaster@dhsspsni.gov.uk W www.dhsspsni.gov.uk

NATIONAL TRAVEL HEALTH NETWORK AND CENTRE (NaTHNaC), UCLH NHS Foundation Trust, 5th Floor West, 250 Euston Road, London NW1 2PG T 0845-155 5000 E nathnac@uclh.nhs.uk
W www.nathnac.org/travel

MEDICAL TREATMENT ABROAD
Details of free or reduced-cost emergency medical treatment when visiting European countries, and countries with which the UK has reciprocal health arrangements, are set out in *Health Advice for Travellers* and on the NHS Healthcare Abroad website (W www.nhs.uk/Healthcareabroad). They also contain guidance on applying for the free European Health Insurance Card (EHIC), which was introduced in September 2005 as a replacement for the E111 form. An EHIC entitles people to urgent medical treatment in the European Economic Area (EEA) and Switzerland. The booklet and website also explain changes to entitlement and the claims process. An EHIC is not an alternative to travel insurance and does not cover private medical healthcare.

For countries where the UK has no health care agreements, including Canada, the USA, India, the Far East, Africa and Latin America, it is advisable to take out medical insurance. A certain amount of insurance is also needed in countries with which the UK has health care agreements.

VISA REQUIREMENTS

The countries listed below do not require British citizens to hold a valid visa or tourist card before arrival on short visits. For longer visits – or for countries not listed – it is advisable to check specific visa requirements with the appropriate embassy before making final travel arrangements (*see* Countries of the World section for foreign embassy contact details or W www.fco.gov.uk/travel).

All EU member states and their overseas territories (*see* The European Union) except Ascension Island and Tristan da Cunha; Albania, Andorra, Antigua and Barbuda, Argentina, Barbados, Belize, Bolivia, Bosnia and Hercegovina, Botswana, Brazil, Brunei, Canada, Chile, Colombia, Costa Rica, Cyprus, Dominica, Ecuador, El Salvador, Fiji, Gambia, Georgia, Grenada, Guatemala, Haiti, Hong Kong, Iceland, Israel, Jamaica, Japan, Kiribati, Kosovo, Republic of Korea (South Korea), Lebanon*, Liechtenstein, Macao, Macedonia, Malawi*, Malaysia, Mauritius, Mexico, Micronesia (Federated States of)*, Moldova, Monaco, Montenegro, Morocco, Namibia, Nicaragua, New Zealand, Norway, Palau, Panama, Paraguay, Peru, Philippines, Rwanda, Saint Lucia, Samoa, San Marino, Senegal, Serbia, Seychelles, Singapore, Solomon Islands, South Africa, St Kitts and Nevis, St Vincent and the Grenadines, Swaziland, Switzerland, Taiwan, Thailand†, Tonga, Trinidad and Tobago, Tunisia, Tuvalu, United Arab Emirates*, Uruguay, USA‡, Vanuatu, Vatican City, Venezuela†, Western Sahara.

* Upon entry to these countries a visa or tourist card will be issued at no extra charge

† Only applicable when arriving by air; those arriving at overland crossings or by sea should arrange documentation in advance

‡ Those travelling to the USA under the Visa Waiver Programme must provide details online (the Electronic System for Travel Authorisation) at least 72 hours in advance of travel

The following countries bar entry to travellers with HIV or AIDS:

The Bahamas, Brunei, Equatorial Guinea, Iraq, Jordan, Papua New Guinea, Qatar, Russia, Singapore, Solomon Islands, Sudan, UAE and Yemen.

Residents of the following countries must hold a valid visa for every entry to the UK:

Afghanistan, Albania, Algeria, Angola, Armenia, Azerbaijan, Bahrain, Bangladesh, Belarus, Benin, Bhutan, Bolivia, Bosnia-Hercegovina, Burkina Faso, Burundi, Cambodia, Cameroon, Cape Verde, Central African Republic, Chad, China, Colombia, Comoros, Dem. Rep. of Congo, Rep. of Congo, Côte d'Ivoire, Cuba, Djibouti, Dominican Republic, Ecuador, Egypt, Equatorial Guinea, Eritrea, Ethiopia, Fiji, Gabon, Gambia, Georgia, Ghana, Guinea, Guinea-Bissau, Guyana, Haiti, India, Indonesia, Iran, Iraq, Jamaica, Jordan, Kazakhstan, Kenya, Dem. People's Republic of Korea, Kuwait, Kyrgyzstan, Laos, Lebanon, Lesotho, Liberia, Libya, Macedonia, Madagascar, Malawi, Mali, Mauritania, Moldova, Mongolia, Morocco, Mozambique, Myanmar, Nepal, Niger, Nigeria, Oman, Pakistan, Palestinian Authority,

Peru, Philippines, Qatar, Russian Federation, Rwanda, Sao Tome and Príncipe, Saudi Arabia, Senegal, Serbia, Sierra Leone, Somalia, South Africa, Sri Lanka, Sudan, Suriname, Swaziland, Syria, Tajikistan, Tanzania, Thailand, Togo, Tunisia, Turkey (including northern Cyprus), Turkmenistan, Uganda, Ukraine, United Arab Emirates, Uzbekistan, Vatican City (holders of Holy See Service and Emergency Passports), Venezuela, Vietnam, Yemen, Zambia, Zimbabwe.

BAGGAGE RESTRICTIONS

As of April 2010, the Department for Transport no longer sets a maximum size for items of hand baggage. Individual airlines may set their own limits, and travellers should check these before arriving at the airport: oversize baggage may have to be checked in as hold luggage, which often incurs a fee. Since January 2008, some airports have allowed passengers to take more than one item into the aircraft cabin. Other airports in the UK still have a one-bag restriction in place, and individual airlines may operate their own policies.

Passengers are allowed to carry small amounts of liquids as cabin baggage. These must be in containers not greater then 100ml, and placed in a single, transparent resealable bag which must not exceed one litre in capacity. Liquids are classified as drinks, make-up such as mascara or lipstick, sprays, pastes and gels. Medicines that are larger than 100ml must be accompanied by relevant documentation, such as a doctor's letter, and prior approval should be sought from the airline and departure airport. Liquid baby food or milk can be taken on board but may have to be tasted by the adult. One lighter is permitted as cabin baggage; this must be carried in the clear bag or separately for the duration of the flight and not placed in the main hand luggage bag.

Sharp items must not be carried in hand luggage; any essential items should be placed in a bag in the hold. Prohibited sharp items include knives, scissors, razor blades, cutlery, tools, hiking poles and hypodermic needles. Other prohibited items include baseball bats, golf clubs, snooker and pool cues and similar sports equipment, party poppers, crackers and non-safety matches.

Electrical equipment such as laptops, MP3 players, mobile phones and cameras are allowed in hand luggage but they must be removed and screened seperately prior to boarding.

The amount passengers can check in to the hold is determined by each airline. The airline will usually set a 'free baggage allowance' according to the number of items and the weight of each item; if this is exceeded there is normally an excess baggage charge. *See* W www.direct.gov.uk for more information on baggage restrictions.

THE EUROPEAN UNION

MEMBER STATE	ACCESSION DATE	POPULATION (2010)	COUNCIL VOTES	EP SEATS†
Austria	1 Jan 1995	8,375,290	10	17
Belgium	1 Jan 1958	10,839,905*	12	22
Bulgaria	1 Jan 2007	7,563,710	10	17
Cyprus	1 May 2004	803,147	4	6
Czech Republic	1 May 2004	10,506,813	12	22
Denmark	1 Jan 1973	5,534,738	7	13
Estonia	1 May 2004	1,340,127	4	6
Finland	1 Jan 1995	5,351,427	7	13
France	1 Jan 1958	64,716,310*	29	72
Germany	1 Jan 1958	81,802,257*	29	99
Greece	1 Jan 1981	11,305,118	12	22
Hungary	1 May 2004	10,014,324	12	22
Ireland	1 Jan 1973	4,467,854	7	12
Italy	1 Jan 1958	60,340,328	29	72
Latvia	1 May 2004	2,248,374	4	8
Lithuania	1 May 2004	3,329,039	7	12
Luxembourg	1 Jan 1958	502,066	4	6
Malta	1 May 2004	412,970	3	5
The Netherlands	1 Jan 1958	16,574,989	13	25
Poland	1 May 2004	38,167,329	27	50
Portugal	1 Jan 1986	10,637,713*	12	22
Romania	1 Jan 2007	21,462,186	14	33
Slovakia	1 May 2004	5,424,925	7	13
Slovenia	1 May 2004	2,046,976	4	7
Spain	1 Jan 1986	45,989,016	27	50
Sweden	1 Jan 1995	9,340,682	10	18
United Kingdom	1 Jan 1973	62,008,048*	29	72

* Provisional figures

† The treaty of Lisbon allows for 18 additional MEPs distributed among 12 member states, but they cannot take their seats until all member states have ratified the change.

Sources: Eurostat; www.europa.eu

CHRONOLOGY

1950   Robert Schuman (French foreign minister) proposes that France and West Germany pool their coal and steel industries under a supranational authority (Schuman Plan)

1951   Paris treaty, signed by France, West Germany, Belgium, Italy, Luxembourg and the Netherlands, establishes the European Coal and Steel Community (ECSC)

1952   ECSC treaty enters into force

1957   Treaty of Rome, signed by the six ECSC member countries, establishes the European Economic Community (EEC) and the European Atomic Energy Authority (EURATOM). Treaty aims to create a customs union; remove obstacles to free movement of capital, goods, people and services; establish common external trade policy and common agricultural and fisheries policies; coordinate economic policies; harmonise social policies; and promote cooperation in nuclear research

1958   EEC and EURATOM begin operation. Joint parliament and Court of Justice established for all three communities, and the Commission, Council of the European Union, Economic and Social Committee and Investment Bank for the EEC established

1962   Common Agricultural Policy (CAP) agreed

1967   EEC, ECSC and EURATOM merge to form the European Communities (EC), with a single Council of the European Union and Commission

1968   EEC customs union completed
       Implementation of CAP completed

1973   UK joins the European Communities

1974   Regular heads-of-governments' summits begin

1975   'Own resources' funding of EC budget introduced
       UK renegotiates its terms of accession
       European Regional Development Fund created

1979   European Monetary System (EMS) comes into operation
       First direct elections to European parliament

1984   Fontainebleau summit settles UK annual budget rebate and agrees first major CAP reform

1986   Single European Act (SEA) signed
       European Political Cooperation (EPC) established

1991   Maastricht treaty agreed

1992   Single internal market programme completed

1993   The exchange rate mechanism (ERM) of the EMS effectively suspended
       Maastricht treaty enters into force, establishing the European Union (EU)

1994   European Economic Area (EEA) agreement comes into operation
       Norway rejects EU membership in referendum

1997   Amsterdam treaty agreed

1998   Eleven states chosen to enter first round of European Monetary Union (EMU)

1999   Euro launched
       Amsterdam treaty enters into force

2000   Treaty of Nice agreed
       ECSC treaty expires following transfer of coal and steel sectors to the treaty of Rome

2004   Cyprus, Czech Republic, Estonia, Hungary, Latvia, Lithuania, Malta, Poland, Slovakia and Slovenia become members of the EU
       The European constitution is signed in Rome

2005   France and the Netherlands reject the European constitution

2007   Bulgaria and Romania join the EU
       The EU celebrates its 50th birthday
       EU leaders agree to the Lisbon treaty to replace the 2004 constitution

2008   Ireland votes against the treaty of Lisbon

2009   Ireland holds a second referendum in October – 67 per cent vote for the Lisbon treaty. The treaty enters into force on 1 December

LEGISLATIVE PROCESS

The core of the EU policy-making process is a dialogue between the European Commission, which initiates and implements policy, and the Council of the European Union and the European parliament, which take policy decisions.

The original legislative process is known as the consultation procedure. The commission drafts a proposal which it submits to the council and to the parliament. The council then consults the Economic and Social Committee, the parliament and the Committee of the Regions; the parliament may request that amendments are made. With or without these amendments, the proposal is then adopted by the council and becomes law. The consultation procedure now only applies to cases not specifically subject to one of the other procedures.

The Single European Act introduced the assent procedure (now the consent procedure), whereby an absolute majority of the parliament must vote to approve laws in certain fields before they are passed. Issues covered by the procedure include uniform procedure for elections, some international agreements, violation of human rights and the accession of new member states.

The Maastricht treaty introduced the co-decision procedure as an extension of the cooperation procedure; if, after the parliament's second reading of a proposal, the council and parliament fail to agree, a conciliation committee of the two will aim to reach a compromise. If a compromise is not reached, the parliament can reject the legislation by the vote of an absolute majority of its members. The Amsterdam treaty extended the co-decision procedure to all areas covered by qualified majority voting, with the exception of measures related to European Monetary Union.

The Lisbon treaty extended the use of the co-decision procedure to several new fields, and renamed it the ordinary legislative procedure. The treaty strengthens the role of the European parliament so that it is involved in almost all new legislation. The changes give the European parliament equal powers in areas such as legal immigration, crime prevention and police cooperation. As a result of the Lisbon treaty, the Council of the European Union must now vote in public on any new legislation, and if one-third of national parliaments disagree with a proposal then it can be sent back to be reviewed.

The council, commission and parliament can issue the following legislation:

• regulations, which are binding in their entirety and directly applicable to all member states; they do not need to be incorporated into national law to come into effect

- directives, which are less specific, binding as to the result to be achieved but leaving the method of implementation open to member states; a directive thus has no force until it is incorporated into national law
- decisions, which are also binding but are addressed solely to one or more member states or individuals in a member state
- recommendations or opinions, which are merely persuasive

The council and parliament also have certain budgetary powers and determine all expenditure together. The final decision on whether the budget should be adopted or rejected lies with the parliament.

The European Central Bank has legislative powers within its field of competence. The commission also has limited legislative powers, where it has been delegated the power to implement or revise legislation by the council.

RECENT LEGISLATION

SCHENGEN AGREEMENT

The Schengen agreement was signed by France, Germany, Belgium, Luxembourg and the Netherlands in 1985. The agreement committed the five states to abolishing internal border controls, erecting external frontiers against illegal immigrants, drug traffickers, terrorists and organised crime, and implementing the Schengen Information System to enable police stations and consular agents from Schengen member states to access data on specific individuals or vehicles and objects which are lost or stolen.

Subsequently signed by Spain and Portugal, the agreement was ratified by the seven signatory states and entered into force in March 1995 with the removal of internal frontier, passport, customs and immigration controls. Italy and Austria became full members of the agreement in 1997; Greece in 2000; and Denmark, Sweden and Finland in 2001. The Czech Republic, Estonia, Hungary, Latvia, Lithuania, Malta, Poland, Slovakia and Slovenia joined in 2007. Although not members of the EU, Norway and Iceland joined the agreement in 2001 and Switzerland in 2008. The UK and the Republic of Ireland have not signed the agreement and are only partial participants, since their border controls have been maintained. In May 2009 Sweden blocked Liechtenstein's accession to the Schengen agreement on financial grounds, but the European Council finally took the decision to allow Liechtenstein to join on 7 March 2011. There is no date set for Cyprus, Bulgaria or Romania to join.

The Schengen agreement originated as an intergovernmental agreement but became part of the EU following the signing of the Amsterdam treaty. A second generation Schengen Information System (SIS II), which will cater for the newest member states, is under development, but with delays due to legal and technical problems.

MAASTRICHT TREATY

Agreed in Maastricht, the Netherlands, in 1991, the treaty came into effect in November 1993 following ratification by the member states. Three pillars formed its basis:

- the European Community (EC) (removing Economic from its name) with its established institutions and decision-making processes
- a common foreign and security policy (see below) with the Western European Union as the potential defence component of the EU

- cooperation in justice and home affairs, with the Council of the European Union coordinating policies on asylum, immigration, conditions of entry, cross-border crime, drug trafficking and terrorism

The treaty established a common European citizenship for nationals of all member states and introduced the principle of subsidiarity, whereby decisions are taken at the most appropriate level (national, regional or local). It extended EC competency into the areas of environmental and industrial policies, consumer affairs, health, and education and training, and extended qualified majority voting in the Council of the European Union to some areas which had previously required a unanimous vote. The powers of the European parliament over the budget and over the European Commission were also enhanced, and a co-decision procedure enabled the parliament to override decisions made by the council in certain policy areas. A separate protocol to the Maastricht treaty on social policy was agreed by 11 states and was incorporated into the Amsterdam treaty in 1997 following adoption by the UK.

COMMON FOREIGN AND SECURITY POLICY

The common foreign and security policy (CFSP) was created as a pillar of the EU by the Maastricht treaty (see above). It adopted the machinery of the European political cooperation framework, which it replaced, and was charged with providing a forum for member states and EU institutions to consult on foreign affairs.

The CFSP system is headed by the European Council, which provides general lines of policy. Specific policy decisions are taken by the General Affairs and External Relations Council, which meets at least once a month to determine areas for joint action. The high representative of the CFSP initiates action, manages the CFSP and represents it abroad. The Council of the European Union is supported by the Political and Security Committee, which meets monthly, or within 48 hours if there is a crisis, to prepare for ministerial discussions. A group of correspondents, designated diplomats in each member's foreign ministry, provides day-to-day contact.

As part of the CFSP the EU also created the common security and defence policy (CSDP), originally named the European security and defence policy, with the potential, if agreed later on, for creating a common defence structure. In the recent past, missions have been deployed in Kosovo, Georgia and the Democratic Republic of the Congo. The member states agreed at the Helsinki summit in 1999 to establish a capability for military crisis-management operations, known as the rapid reaction force, which would have a credible intervention capability and be able to undertake peacemaking missions independently of NATO. The force was declared operational at the Laeken summit in 2001.

The Amsterdam treaty introduced qualified majority voting for foreign affairs and created a high representative of CFSP to act as a spokesperson. It also established a new planning and early warning unit to monitor international developments and provide the opportunity for the EU to react to these developments with a cohesive response. The Lisbon treaty merged the three pillars of the EU. It created a high representative of the union for foreign affairs and security policy to replace the high representative of CFSP and led to the dissolution of the Western European Union in June 2011.

AMSTERDAM TREATY

The treaties of Rome and Maastricht were amended through the Amsterdam treaty, which was signed in 1997 and came into effect on 1 May 1999. It extended the scope of qualified majority voting and the powers of the European parliament. It also included a formal commitment to fundamental human rights, gave additional powers to the European Court of Justice and provided for the reform of the CFSP.

LISBON TREATY

The treaty of Lisbon was drawn up to replace the original European constitution, which was rejected in referendums in France and the Netherlands in 2005. It amends, rather than replaces, existing European Union and European Community treaties. Ireland, the only country to hold a referendum on the Lisbon treaty, voted against ratification on 12 June 2008. It held a second referendum on 2 October 2009 where 67 per cent voted in favour, and – as a result of all EU countries approving the treaty – it came into force on 1 December 2009.

The Lisbon treaty granted 'legal personality' (the right under international law to adopt laws and treaties) to the European Union. The three pillars created by the Maastricht treaty (see above) merged to make the European Union a single legal entity, replacing the European Community. The Lisbon treaty introduced a number of changes to the EU: a new president was appointed to the European Council for a two-and-a-half year term to replace the previous system of a six-month rotating presidency (this still exists in a reduced capacity for the Council of the European Union). The position of High Representative of the Union for Foreign Affairs and Security Policy was created, to enhance the EU's relations with other countries. The European parliament was strengthened and given more legislative and budgetary powers, and the number of MEPs was set at 751 from the 2014 election onwards. The system of qualified majority voting was extended to new policy areas and from 2014 will be based on a double majority of member states and people; a decision must be agreed by 55 per cent of member states representing at least 65 per cent of the EU population. The treaty establishes the principle of 'mutual recognition', where each member state acknowledges that legal decisions by other member states are valid; the UK has an opt-out clause with regard to some policies such as external borders, asylum and immigration.

ENLARGEMENT AND EXTERNAL RELATIONS

The procedure for accession to the EU is laid down in the treaty of Rome; states must be stable European democracies governed by the rule of law with free-market economies. A membership application is studied by the European Commission, which produces an 'opinion'. If the opinion is positive, negotiations may be opened leading to an accession treaty that must be approved by all member state governments and parliaments, the European parliament, and the applicant state's government and parliament.

Cyprus, the Czech Republic, Estonia, Hungary, Latvia, Lithuania, Malta, Poland, Slovakia and Slovenia became full members of the EU on 1 May 2004. Bulgaria and Romania joined the EU on 1 January 2007. The European Council recalled the offer of an accession partnership to Turkey in 2002, following the commission's conclusion that Turkey did not yet fully meet the required political criteria. However, at its December 2004 meeting in Brussels, the council decided that Turkey sufficiently met the Copenhagen political criteria, and accession negotiations began in October 2005. Accession talks with Croatia, scheduled to start in March 2005 but postponed due to the lack of full cooperation with the UN war crimes tribunal, began in October 2005. Macedonia was granted candidate status in December 2005, but accession negotiations have not yet begun. Iceland applied for membership in July 2009 and accession negotiations started in June 2010. There are currently five potential candidates for membership of the EU: Montenegro, Albania, Serbia, Bosnia and Hercegovina, and Kosovo. Of these countries, only Bosnia and Hercegovina and Kosovo have not yet applied for membership.

The EU has several types of agreements with other European and non-European states. Association agreements can include commitments to reforming the country's trade, human rights, economy or political system in exchange for financial assistance or trade agreements. Countries that have signed agreements include Algeria, Egypt, Israel, Morocco and Turkey. Partnership and cooperation agreements (PCAs) are legal frameworks, based on the respect of democratic principles and human rights, setting out the political, economic and trade relationship between the EU and its partner countries. Each PCA is a ten-year bilateral treaty signed and ratified by the EU and the individual state. After the ten-year period expires the agreements are automatically renewed annually unless one of the parties objects. Agreements have been implemented with Russia (1997), Ukraine and Moldova (1998), Armenia, Azerbaijan, Georgia, Kazakhstan, Kyrgyzstan and Uzbekistan (1999). PCAs have also been signed with Belarus (1995), Turkmenistan (1998) and Tajikistan (2004) but stalled before or during the ratification process. In 2003 the PCA council summit decreed to strengthen EU cooperation with the Russian Federation by establishing a permanent partnership council (PPC). At the council's first meeting in April 2004 a protocol was signed, extending the PCA with the Russian Federation to the ten new member states of the EU; the agreement currently in place also covers Romania and Bulgaria.

Trade and cooperation agreements are intended to foster trade and economic relations, and include a commitment to respect the human rights and democratic principles of both parties. The European Commission has negotiated around 120 agreements worldwide. The European neighbourhood policy was developed in 2004 and applies to the enlarged EU's immediate neighbours. It aims to strengthen stability and security through economic integration and deeper political relationships based on a mutual commitment to common values (democracy, human rights, rule of law, good governance and market economy).

A stabilisation and association agreement (SAA) – which is tailored towards the western Balkan states and is similar to the earlier Europe agreements held with previous candidate countries, in that it provides the contractual framework for relations that will lead to accession to the EU – entered into force with Macedonia in April 2004, Croatia in February 2005, Albania in April 2009, and with Montenegro in May 2010. SAA negotiations were launched with Kosovo in November 2006 and are still ongoing; SAA agreements were signed by Serbia in April 2008 and Bosnia and Hercegovina in June 2008, which will enter into force following ratification.

TREATY OF NICE

The treaty of Nice was signed in 2001 and came into effect in 2003. It enabled the EU to accommodate up to 13 new member states, and extended qualified majority voting to 30 further articles of the treaties that previously required unanimity. The weighting of votes in the EU Council was altered from 1 January 2005 for the new member states. To obtain a qualified majority, a decision requires a specified number of votes (to be reviewed following each accession); the decision has to be approved by a majority of member states and represent at least 62 per cent of the total population of the EU. The treaty also set the number of MEPs that both existing and new member states would have following enlargement.

The Maastricht treaty established the right of groups of member states to work together without requiring the participation of all members (enhanced cooperation); the treaty of Nice removed the right of individual member states to veto the launch of enhanced cooperation.

The European Commission has been limited to one member per member state since 2005, with a maximum of 27 commissioners; a rotation system is to be introduced once EU membership exceeds 27 states. The treaty also added to the powers of the president of the commission and amended the rules of operation of the Court of Justice.

ECONOMY

BUDGET OF THE EUROPEAN UNION

The principles of funding the European Union budget (formerly known as the European Community budget) were established by the treaty of Rome and remain, with modifications, to this day. There is a legally binding limit on the overall level of resources (known as 'own resources') that the EU can raise from its member states; this limit is defined as a percentage of gross national income (GNI). Budget revenue and expenditure must balance, and there is therefore no deficit financing. The 'own resources' decision, which came into effect in 1975 and has been regularly updated, states that there are four sources of funding under which each member state makes contributions: duties charged on agricultural imports into the EU from non-member states; customs duties on imports from non-member states; contributions based on member states' shares of a notional EU-harmonised VAT base; and contributions based on member states' shares of total GNI. The latter is the budget-balancing item and covers the difference between total expenditure and the revenue from the other three sources.

EU BUDGET 2011

	Billion euro*
Sustainable growth	64.5
Natural resources	58.7
Global activities	8.8
Citizenship, freedom, security and justice	1.8
Administration	8.2
Total	141.9

* 1 euro = £0.87 as at 6 May 2011
Source: Publications Office of the European Union

The framework budget for 2007–13 (formally known as the Financial Perspective) was completed at the end of the UK's presidency of the EU in December 2005. A figure of €862.36bn (£682.21bn) was agreed, which is equal to 1.045 per cent of the EU's combined gross national income.

From 1984 up until 2005, the UK had received an annual rebate equivalent to 66 per cent of the difference between UK contributions to the budget and its receipts. This was introduced to compensate the UK for disproportionate contributions caused by its high share of agricultural and non-agricultural imports from non-member states and its relatively small receipts from the Common Agricultural Policy, the most important portion of EU expenditure. Before the budget for 2007–13 was finalised, the UK conceded €10.5bn (£8.3bn) (approximately 20 per cent) of its rebate over the six-year period, in return for a wide-ranging review of EU spending.

SINGLE MARKET

Even after the removal of tariffs and quotas between member states in the 1970s and 1980s, the European Community (EC) was still separated into a number of national markets by a series of non-tariff barriers. It was to overcome these internal barriers to trade that the concept of the single market was developed. The measures to be undertaken were codified in the commission's 1985 white paper on completing the internal market.

The white paper included articles removing obstacles distorting the internal market: the elimination of frontier controls; the mutual recognition of professional qualifications; the harmonisation of product specifications, largely by the mutual recognition of national standards; open tendering for public procurement contracts; the free movement of capital; the harmonisation of VAT and excise duties; and the reduction of state aid to particular industries. The Single European Act (SEA) aided the completion of the single market by changing the legislative process within the EC, particularly with the introduction of qualified majority voting in the Council of the European Union for some policy areas, and the introduction of the assent procedure in the European parliament. The SEA also extended EC competence into the fields of technology, the environment, regional policy, monetary policy and external policy. The single market came into effect on 1 January 1993, though full implementation of the elimination of frontier controls and the harmonisation of taxes have been repeatedly delayed. A fundamental review of the single market was completed in 2007, which resulted in an operational set of initiatives intended to modernise single market policy. Following the abolition of the EC in 2009 as a result of the Lisbon treaty, the single market policy now applies to the EU.

EUROPEAN ECONOMIC AREA

The single market programme spurred European non-member states to open negotiations with the EC on preferential access for their goods, services, labour and capital to the single market. Principal among these states were European Free Trade Association (EFTA) members who opened negotiations on extending the single market to EFTA by the formation of the European Economic Area (EEA), encompassing all 19 EC and EFTA states. Agreement was reached in 1992, but the operation of the EEA was delayed by its rejection in a Swiss referendum, necessitating an additional protocol agreed by the remaining 18 states. The EEA came into effect in 1994 after ratification by 17 member states (Liechtenstein joined in 1995 after adapting its customs union with Switzerland).

Austria, Finland and Sweden joined the EU on 1 January 1995, leaving only Norway, Iceland and Liechtenstein as the non-EU EEA members. Under the EEA agreement, the three states are to adopt the EU's *acquis communautaire*, apart from in the fields of agriculture, fisheries, and coal and steel.

The EEA is controlled by regular ministerial meetings and by a joint EU-EFTA committee which extends relevant EU legislation to EEA states. Apart from single market measures, there is cooperation in several areas, including education, civil protection, research and development, consumer policy and tourism. An EFTA Court has been established in Luxembourg and an EFTA surveillance authority in Brussels to supervise the implementation of the EEA Agreement.

The EEA Enlargement Agreement came into force on 1 May 2004, which allowed the simultaneous expansion of both the EU and the EEA without disruption of the internal market. A similar process took place to ensure that Bulgaria and Romania could become contracting parties to the EEA upon joining the EU in 2007.

EUROPEAN MONETARY SYSTEM AND THE SINGLE CURRENCY

The European Monetary System (EMS) began operation in March 1979 with three main purposes. The first was to establish monetary stability in Europe, initially in exchange rates between EC member state currencies through the Exchange Rate Mechanism (ERM), and in the longer term to be part of a wider stabilisation process, overcoming inflation and budget and trade deficits. The second purpose was to overcome the constraints resulting from the interdependence of EC economies, and the third was to aid the long-term process of European monetary integration.

The Maastricht treaty set in motion timetables for achieving economic and monetary union (EMU) and a single currency (the euro). At the Brussels summit in May 1998, 11 member states were judged to fulfil or be close to fulfilling the necessary convergence criteria for participation in the first stage of EMU: Austria, Belgium, Finland, France, Germany, Ireland, Italy, Luxembourg, the Netherlands, Portugal and Spain. The criteria were that:

- the budget deficit should be 3 per cent or less of gross domestic product (GDP)
- total national debt must not exceed 60 per cent of GDP
- inflation should be no more than 1.5 per cent above the average rate of the three best performing economies in the EU
- long-term interest rates should be no more than 2 per cent above the average of the three best performing economies in the EU in the previous 12 months
- applicants must have been members of the ERM for two years without having realigned or devalued their currency

Under the terms of a stability and growth pact agreed in Dublin in December 1996 and revised in 2005, penalties may be imposed on EMU members with high budget deficits. Governments with deficits exceeding 3 per cent of GDP will receive a warning and will be obliged to pay up to 0.5 per cent of their GDP into a fund after ten months. This will become a fine if the budget deficit is not rectified within two years. A member state with negative growth will be allowed to apply for an exemption from the fine by referring to a number of relevant factors outlined in the pact.

As a result of the global economic downturn, by May 2010, 24 out of 27 countries in the European Union had a deficit exceeding 3 per cent of GDP. The European Commission revised its existing recommendations in November 2009 and proposed extended deadlines for each country to correct its budget deficit. In the case of the UK, a deadline of 2014–5 was proposed, the longest deadline given to any of the EMU nations.

On 1 January 1999 the qualifying member states adopted the euro at irrevocably fixed exchange rates, the European Central Bank (ECB) took charge of the single monetary policy, and the euro replaced the ECU (an artificial currency adopted by European Community member states in 1979 as an internal accounting unit for the EMS) on a one-for-one basis.

In 2000 Greece was judged to have fulfilled the criteria for participation and adopted the euro on 1 January 2001. Referendums on the adoption of the euro have been held in Denmark and Sweden, but participation was rejected. In June 2003 Britain announced that the euro would not be adopted at present on the grounds that the country was not economically ready to join the single currency, though a future joining of the eurozone was not ruled out.

The euro is now the legal currency in the participating states. Euro notes and coins were introduced on 1 January 2002 and circulated alongside national currencies for a period of up to two months, after which time national notes and coins ceased to be legal tender. The new EU member states are expected to adopt the euro when the necessary economic conditions have been met; Slovenia joined the eurozone on 1 January 2007, Cyprus and Malta on 1 January 2008, Slovakia on 1 January 2009 and Estonia on 1 January 2011.

The ECB meets twice a month to set the following month's monetary policy applicable to the countries participating in the euro. Its governing council has 23 members, being the six members of the ECB's executive board and the 17 governors of the national central banks of the participating states.

THE EURO CRISIS OF 2010–11

Early in 2010, Greece's soaring budget deficit and the escalating cost of servicing the country's debt brought it to the verge of economic meltdown. In May 2010 a rescue package totalling €110bn (£95bn) was agreed following negotiations with the European Commission, the IMF and the ECB. The near collapse of the banking system in Ireland in November 2010 led to the approval of an €85bn (£72bn) rescue package by the EU and the IMF. On 6 April 2011 Portugal became the third country to request financial assistance from the EU after rising borrowing costs left the government unable to pay its debts. On 17 May 2011, European finance ministers finalised the terms of a three-year bailout agreement worth €78bn (£69bn).

COMMON AGRICULTURAL POLICY

The Common Agricultural Policy (CAP) was established to increase agricultural production, provide a fair standard of living for farmers and ensure the availability of food at reasonable prices. This aim was achieved by a number of mechanisms, including import levies, intervention purchase and export subsidies.

These measures stimulated production but also placed increasing demands on the European Community (EC) budget, which were exacerbated by the increase in EC members and yields enlarged by technological innovation; CAP now accounts for over 40 per cent of EC expenditure. To surmount these problems reforms were agreed in 1984, 1988, 1992, 1997, 1999, 2003 and 2008.

REFORMS

The 1984 reforms created the system of co-responsibility levies: farm payments to the EC by volume of product sold. This system was supplemented by national quotas for particular products, such as milk. The 1988 reforms emphasised 'set-aside', whereby farmers are given direct grants to take land out of production as a means of reducing surpluses. The set-aside reforms were extended in 1993 for another five years and to every farm in the EC. The 1999 reforms further reduced surpluses of cereals, beef and milk by cutting the intervention prices by up to 20 per cent and compensating producers by making area payments. Under the reforms, CAP rules were also simplified, eliminating inconsistencies between policies.

In June 2003, EU farm ministers adopted a fundamental reform of the CAP, which included the following provisions:

- a single farm payment for EU farmers, independent of production (begun in 2005)
- payment to be linked to the respect of environmental, food safety, animal and plant health and animal welfare standards, and the requirement to keep all farmland in good condition
- a strengthened rural development policy with more EU money to help farmers meet EU production standards (begun in 2005)
- a reduction in direct payments for bigger farms
- a mechanism for financial discipline to ensure that the farm budget fixed until 2013 is not exceeded

The ten EU members that joined in 2004 were also given access to a special €5.8bn (£3.9bn) three-year funding package. The 2007–13 EU budget stipulated that no extra money would be made available to pay farm subsidies to Romania and Bulgaria.

A CAP 'health check' was carried out in 2008 and resulted in a set of proposals intended to further modernise and streamline EU agricultural policy, and to allow farmers to follow market signals by breaking the link between direct payments and production. These include abolishing the requirement for farmers to leave 10 per cent of their arable land fallow; a gradual increase in milk quotas before their abolition in 2015 and a general reduction in market intervention.

THE UK AND THE EU IN 2011

- European Union Act (2011): the act came into force in the UK on 19 July; under the act the government legally requires the consent of the UK electorate via a national referendum on any future changes to EU treaties that would result in the transfer of legislative powers or an area of policy from the UK to the EU.
- EU bailout fund: in December 2010 the UK was obliged to contribute £3.75bn (€4.15bn) to the EU bailout fund to support the Irish economy. A separate, direct loan to the Irish government was set at £3.25bn (€3.6bn), which was also announced in December; on May 17 2011 the UK contributed £4.3bn (€4.9bn) to the £68bn (€78.5bn) EU financial rescue package agreed with the Portuguese government.

- EU budget: chancellor of the exchequer, George Osborne, labelled the proposed 4.9 per cent increase to the EU's annual budget for 2012 'completely unacceptable'. This increase equates to £680m more than the UK contributed in 2011. France and Germany joined the UK in condemning the proposed increase, suggesting that the EU budget should only increase in line with inflation, in light of the austerity measures imposed throughout many EU member states.
- Lisbon treaty: The European Union Act (2011) also provides parliamentary approval for the transitional MEPs protocol, which, when ratified by all member states, will enable 18 additional MEPs provided for under the treaty to take their seats during the current European parliamentary term rather than after the next European parliamentary elections in 2014.

INSTITUTIONS

EUROPEAN PARLIAMENT

E eplondon@europarl.europa.eu W www.europarl.europa.eu; www.europarl.org.uk

The European parliament (EP) originated as the common assembly of the ECSC, acquiring its present name in 1962. The parliament now comprises 736 seats. Members (MEPs), initially appointed from the membership of national parliaments, have been directly elected at five-year intervals since 1979. Elections to the parliament are held on differing bases throughout the EU; British MEPs have been elected by a regional list system of proportional representation since June 1999. The most recent elections were held in June 2009.

MEPs serve on committees which scrutinise draft EU legislation and the activities of the European Commission. A minimum of 12 plenary sessions a year are held in Strasbourg and six additional shorter plenary sessions a year are held in Brussels; committees meet in Brussels, and the secretariat's headquarters is in Luxembourg.

The influence of the EP has gradually expanded within the EU since the Single European Act of 1985, which introduced the cooperation procedure; the Maastricht treaty, which extended the cooperation procedure and introduced the co-decision (now ordinary legislative) procedure (see Legislative Process); the Amsterdam treaty, which effectively extended the ordinary legislative procedure to all areas except economic and monetary union, and taxation; and the Lisbon treaty, which gave parliament legislative powers comparable with the Council of the European Union. Parliament has general powers of supervision over the European Commission, and powers of consultation and co-decision with the Council of the European Union; it votes to approve a newly appointed commission and can dismiss it at any time by a two-thirds majority. Under the Maastricht treaty it has the right to be consulted on the appointment of the new commission, and can also veto its appointment. Under the Lisbon treaty, parliament elects the president of the commission on the proposal of the European Council. The EP has equal right to decide on budgetary matters as the Council of the European Union, and they work together to approve and adopt the entire annual budget. In accordance with the Maastricht treaty the EP appoints the European Ombudsman, to provide citizens with redress against maladministration by EU institutions.

The EP's organisation is deliberately biased in favour of multinational political groupings; recognition of a political grouping in the parliament entitles it to offices, funding, representation on committees and influence in debates and legislation. A political group must be composed of a minimum of 25 MEPs elected in at least seven member states. For a list of UK MEPs, *see* European Parliament section.

PARLIAMENT, Allée du Printemps, BP 1024/F, F-67070 Strasbourg Cedex, France
T (+33) (3) 8817 4001 F (+33) (3) 8817 5184
Wiertzstraat, Postbus 1047, B-1047 Brussels, Belgium
T (+32) (2) 284 2111 F (+32) (2) 284 6974
SECRETARIAT, Centre Européen, Plateau du Kirchberg, BP 1601, L-2929 Luxembourg
T (+352) 43001 F (+352) 4300 29393/29292
President, Jerzy Buzek (Poland)
OMBUDSMAN, 1 Avenue du Président Robert Schuman, CS 30403, F-67001 Strasbourg Cedex, France
E euro-ombudsman@europarl.europa.eu
W www.euro-ombudsman.europa.eu
Ombudsman, Nikiforos Diamandouros (Greece)

EUROPEAN PARLIAMENT UK OFFICE
Europe House, 32 Smith Square, London, SW1P 3EU
E eplondon@europarl.europa.eu W www.europarl.org.uk

EUROPEAN PARLIAMENT OFFICE IN SCOTLAND
The Tun, Holyrood Road, Edinburgh EH8 8PJ
E epedinburgh@europarl.europa.eu W www.europarl.org.uk

COUNCIL OF THE EUROPEAN UNION
Rue de la Loi, 175 B-1048 Brussels, Belgium
W www.consilium.europa.eu

The Council of the European Union (Council of Ministers) is the main decision-making body of the European Union, and formally comprises the ministers of the member states. Depending on the issue on the agenda, each country will be represented by the minister responsible for that subject. It passes laws, usually legislating jointly with the European parliament; coordinates the broad economic policies of the member states; approves the EU's budget jointly with the European parliament; defines and implements the EU's common foreign and security policy; concludes agreements between the EU and other states or international organisations; and coordinates the actions of member states and adopts measures in the area of police and judicial cooperation.

Council decisions are taken using one of three methods: by qualified majority vote (in which members' votes are weighted), by a simple majority, or by unanimity. The treaties define which one of the three methods should be used in each subject area. Unanimity votes are taken on sensitive issues such as taxation and defence, but the qualified majority vote (QMV) is now used for the majority of council decisions. Under the QMV system member states have weighted votes in the council loosely proportional to their relative population sizes (*see* introductory table), with a total of 345 votes. A qualified majority will be reached if the following two conditions are met:

- a majority of member states approve (in some cases a two-thirds majority)
- a minimum of 255 votes is cast in favour of the proposal, ie 73.9 per cent of the total

In addition, a member state may ask for confirmation that the votes in favour represent at least 62 per cent of the total population of the EU. If this is found not to be the case, the decision will not be adopted.

The presidency of the Council of the European Union is held in rotation for six-month periods, setting the agenda for and chairing council meetings in all policy areas except foreign affairs. The holders of the presidency for the years 2011–12 are:

2011 Jan–Jun, Hungary
2011 Jul–Dec, Poland
2012 Jan–Jun, Denmark
2012 Jul–Dec, Cyprus

In the area of foreign affairs, council meetings are chaired by the High Representative of the Union for Foreign Affairs and Security Policy.
High Representative of the Union for Foreign Affairs and Security Policy, Baroness Ashton of Upholland (UK)

GENERAL SECRETARIAT OF THE COUNCIL OF THE EUROPEAN UNION
Wetstraat, rue de la Loi, 175 B-1048 Brussels, Belgium
W www.consilium.europa.eu
Secretary-General of the Council of the European Union, Pierre de Boissieu (France)

EUROPEAN COUNCIL
The European Council, formed in 1974, was given formal recognition by the Single European Act in 1987; under the treaty of Lisbon it has become a fully fledged institution of the EU with a permanent president. It normally meets four times a year and comprises the heads of state or government of each EU member state and the president of the European Commission. Meetings are chaired by the president of the council.

The primary function of the European Council is to give political guidance in all areas of EU activity at both European and national levels. The European Council can issue declarations and resolutions expressing the opinions of the heads of state and governments, but its decisions are not legally binding.
President of the European Council, Herman Van Rompuy (Belgium)

EUROPEAN COMMISSION
Wetstraat 200, rue de la Loi, B-1049 Brussels, Belgium

The European Commission consists of 27 commissioners, one per member state. The members of the commission are appointed for five-year renewable terms by the agreement of the member states; the terms run concurrently with the terms of the European parliament. The president and the other commissioners are nominated by the governments of the member states, and, under the terms of the Lisbon treaty, the appointments are approved by the European parliament. The commissioners pledge sole allegiance to the EU. The commission initiates and implements EU legislation and is the guardian of the EU treaties. It is the exponent of community-wide interests rather than the national preoccupations of the council. Each commissioner is supported by advisers and oversees the departments assigned to them, known as directorates-general and services.

President Jose Manuel Barroso was re-elected for a second mandate by the European parliament on 16 September 2009. He announced the new commission on 27 November 2009, which officially took office on 10 February 2010.

The commission has a total staff of around 26,000 permanent civil servants.

COMMISSIONERS *as at September 2011*
President, Jose Manuel Barroso (Portugal)
Vice-President, High Representative of the Union for Foreign Affairs and Security Policy, Baroness Ashton of Upholland (United Kingdom)
Vice-President, Competition, Joaquín Almunia (Spain)
Vice-President, Digital Agenda, Neelie Kroes (The Netherlands)
Vice-President, Industry and Entrepreneurship, Antonio Tajani (Italy)
Vice-President, Inter-Institutional Relations and Administration, Marcos Sefcovic (Slovakia)
Vice-President, Justice, Fundamental Rights and Citizenship, Viviane Reding (Luxembourg)
Vice-President, Transport, Siim Kallas (Estonia)
Agriculture and Rural Development, Dacian Ciolos (Romania)
Climate Action, Connie Hedegaard (Denmark)
Development, Andris Piebalgs (Latvia)
Economic and Monetary Affairs, Olli Rehn (Finland)
Education, Culture, Multilingualism and Youth, Androulla Vassiliou (Cyprus)
Employment, Social Affairs and Inclusion, Laszlo Andor (Hungary)
Energy, Günther Oettinger (Germany)
Enlargement and European Neighbourhood Policy, Stefan Fule (Czech Republic)
Environment, Janez Potocnik (Slovenia)
Financial Programming and Budget, Janusz Lewandowski (Poland)
Health and Consumer Policy, John Dalli (Malta)
Home Affairs, Cecilia Malmstrom (Sweden)
Internal Market and Services, Michel Barnier (France)
International Cooperation, Humanitarian Aid and Crisis Response, Kristalina Giorgieva (Bulgaria)
Maritime Affairs and Fisheries, Maria Damanaki (Greece)
Regional Policy, Johannes Hahn (Austria)
Research, Innovation and Science Maire Geoghegan-Quinn (Ireland)
Taxation and Customs Union, Audit and Anti-Fraud, Algirdas Semeta (Lithuania)
Trade, Karel De Gucht (Belgium)

COURT OF JUSTICE OF THE EUROPEAN UNION

Palais de la Cour de Justice, Boulevard Konrad Adenauer, Kirchberg, L–2925 Luxembourg
W www.curia.europa.eu

The treaty of Lisbon gave a new framework to the EU court system. The court of justice of the European Union is now composed of three courts: the court of justice, the general court and the civil service tribunal.

COURT OF JUSTICE
Rue du Fort Niedergrunewald, L-2925 Luxembourg

The court of justice exists to safeguard the law in the interpretation and application of European Union treaties, to decide on the legality of decisions of the Council of the European Union or the European Commission, and to determine infringements of the treaties. Cases may be brought to it by the member states, EU institutions, firms or individuals. The decisions of the court are directly binding in the member countries. The court's powers are extended by the Maastricht treaty, allowing it to impose fines on member states who breach EU law. The court comprises 27 judges – one from each member state – and eight advocates-general. These positions are appointed simultaneously for renewable six-year terms by the member governments.
President, Vassilios Skouris (Greece)

GENERAL COURT
Rue du Fort Niedergrunewald, L-2925 Luxembourg

Established under powers conferred by the Single European Act, the general court (known as the Court of First Instance until 1 December 2009) has jurisdiction to hear and determine direct actions brought by natural persons (ie human beings) or legal persons (ie an entity with a legal personality, such as a company, association etc) against any of the institutions, bodies, agencies or offices of the EU, except those cases reserved for the court of justice. It also has jurisdiction to hear actions brought by member states against the European Commission and actions relating to community trade marks. The court is composed of 27 judges, one from each member state, appointed for renewable six-year terms by the individual national governments.
President, Marc Jaeger (Luxembourg)

CIVIL SERVICE TRIBUNAL
35A, Avenue J. F. Kennedy, L-1855 Luxembourg

Established in 2005, the civil service tribunal has jurisdiction to hear disputes between civil servants and the European Union in matters such as pay, disciplinary measures and accidents at work. It does not deal with disputes between national governments and their employees. There are seven judges, appointed for renewable six-year terms.
President, Paul J. Mahoney (United Kingdom)

EUROPEAN COURT OF AUDITORS
12 rue Alcide de Gasperi, L–1615 Luxembourg
E euraud@eca.europa.eu W www.eca.europa.eu

The European Court of Auditors, established in 1977, examines the accounts of all revenue and expenditure of the EU. It evaluates whether all revenue has been received and all expenditure incurred in a lawful and regular manner and in accordance with the principles of sound financial management. The court issues an annual report and a statement of assurance as to the reliability of the accounts and the legality and regularity of the underlying transactions. It also publishes special reports on specific topics and delivers opinions on financial matters. The court has one member from each member state appointed for a six-year term by the Council of the European Union following consultation with the European parliament.
President, Vitor Caldeira (Portugal)

FINANCIAL BODIES

EUROPEAN CENTRAL BANK
Kaiserstrasse 29, D-60311 Frankfurt am Main, Germany
E info@ecb.europa.eu W www.ecb.europa.eu

The European Central Bank (ECB), which superseded the European Monetary Institute, became fully operational on 1 January 1999 and defines and implements the single monetary policy for the euro area. The ECB's main task is to maintain the euro's purchasing power and price stability in the 17 EU countries that have introduced the currency since 1999. Its decision-making bodies are the executive board, the governing council and the general council. The executive board consists of the president, the vice-president and four other members. All members are appointed by the governments of the states participating in the single currency, at the level of heads of state and government. The governing council, the main decision-making body of the ECB, comprises the six members of the executive board and the governors of the national central banks of the 17 euro area states. The general council comprises the president and vice-president and the 27 governors of the national central banks of all the member states of the European Union, the other members of the executive board being entitled to participate but not to vote. The ECB is independent of national governments and of all other EU institutions.

President, Jean-Claude Trichet (France)
Vice-President, Vitor Constancio (Portugal)

EUROPEAN INVESTMENT BANK
100 Boulevard Konrad Adenauer, L-2950 Luxembourg
E info@eib.org W www.eib.org

The European Investment Bank (EIB) was set up in 1958 under the terms of the treaty of Rome and is the financing arm of the European Union. The EIB's main activity is to provide long-term loans in support of investments undertaken by private or public promoters, for projects furthering European integration.

The EIB also operates outside the EU, in support of EU development and cooperation policies in partner countries including the enlargement area of Europe (both candidate and potential candidate countries), the Mediterranean, Russia and the Southern Caucasus, Africa, the Caribbean and the Pacific, Asia and Latin America.

The EIB assesses and selects the projects it finances independently and usually only finances up to 50 per cent of the total cost of a project.

The bank is not dependent on the EU budget, and raises its own resources on the capital markets. It is the biggest supranational bond issuer and lender in the world with an AAA credit rating. In 2010 it raised €67bn (£59bn) and lent a total of €72bn (£64bn), of which 87.5 per cent (€63bn) (£54bn) was lent within the EU.

The shareholders of the EIB are the 27 member states, whose ministers of economy and finance constitute its board of governors. This body lays down general directives on the credit policy of the bank and appoints members to the board of directors. The board of directors consists of 27 members nominated by the member states, and one by the European Commission. It takes decisions on the granting and raising of loans and the fixing of interest rates. The management committee, composed of the bank's president and eight vice-presidents and also appointed by the board of governors, is responsible for the day-to-day operations of the bank.

President, Philippe Maystadt (Belgium)

ADVISORY BODIES

COMMITTEE OF THE REGIONS
Bâtiment Jacques Delors, rue Belliard 99–101, B-1040 Brussels, Belgium
E pressecdr@cor.europa.eu W www.cor.europa.eu

The Committee of the Regions (CoR) was established in 1994 and is the political assembly which provides local and regional authorities with a voice within the European Union. The Lisbon treaty obligates the European Commission, the Council of the European Union and the European Parliament to consult the CoR whenever new legislative proposals are made in areas which have repercussions at regional or local level. The CoR then issues opinions on these proposals for EU laws, and also has the right to comment on any amendments to proposed legislation by MEPs. The CoR has the right to challenge new EU laws in the European court of justice if it believes it has not been correctly consulted by the commission, parliament or council.

The committee has 344 full members and the same number of alternate members. They are proposed by the member states to the Council of the European Union, which appoints them for a five-year renewable term of office. Members must hold a regional or local authority electoral mandate or be politically accountable to an elected assembly. They participate in the work of six specialist commissions which are responsible for drafting the CoR's opinions and resolutions on a wide range of topics.

President, Mercedes Bresso (Italy)
Secretary-General, Gerhard Stahl (Germany)

EUROPEAN ECONOMIC AND SOCIAL COMMITTEE
Rue Belliard 99, B-1040 Brussels, Belgium
W www.eesc.europa.eu

The European Economic and Social Committee (EESC) is a consultative body of the European Union. It comprises 344 members drawn from economic and social interest groups in Europe; these members are appointed by the governments of the 27 member states for a five-year renewable term. The EESC is divided into three groups: employers, employees, and other interest groups such as consumers, farmers and the self-employed. Every two-and-a-half years the EESC elects a bureau made up of 39 members, including a president and two vice-presidents chosen from each of the three groups in rotation. The EESC issues opinions on draft EU legislation, which are forwarded to the larger institutions – the commission, council and parliament. The EESC's competencies have increased as a result of revisions to the treaty of Rome, and the treaty of Lisbon strengthens the committee's role.

President, Staffan Nilsson (Sweden)

AGENCIES

EUROPEAN ENVIRONMENT AGENCY
Kongens Nytorv 6, DK–1050 Copenhagen K, Denmark
T (+45) 3336 7100 W www.eea.europa.eu

The European Environment Agency (EEA) aims to support sustainable development and to help achieve significant and measurable improvement in Europe's environment, through the provision of information to policy-making agents and the public. The EEA has been operational since 1994, and now has 32 member countries. It is a European Union body but is open to non-EU countries that share its objectives. The management board consists of representatives of the member countries, two representatives of the European Commission and two representatives designated by the European parliament.

Chair, Karsten Sach (Germany)

EUROPEAN JUDICIAL COOPERATION UNIT (EUROJUST)

Maanweg 174, 2516 AB The Hague, The Netherlands
E info@eurojust.europa.eu W www.eurojust.europa.eu

The European Union's Judicial Cooperation Unit (Eurojust) was established in 2002 with the aim of developing Europe-wide cooperation in cases involving serious crime committed across more than one member state's jurisdiction. Eurojust also facilitates the provision of international mutual legal assistance and helps to implement extradition requests. It is a key interlocutor with the European parliament, the Council of the European Union and the European Commission.

The college of Eurojust is composed of 27 national members, one nominated by each member state. These members are experienced prosecutors, judges or police officers.

President of the College, Aled Williams (UK)

EUROPEAN POLICE OFFICE (EUROPOL)

Eisenhowelaan 73, 2517 KK The Hague, The Netherlands
W www.europol.europa.eu

The European Police Office (Europol) came into being on 1 October 1998 and assumed its full powers on 1 July 1999. It superseded the Europol Drugs Unit and exists to improve police cooperation between member states and to combat terrorism, illicit traffic in drugs and other serious forms of organised international crime. It is ultimately responsible to the Council of the European Union. Each member state has a national unit to liaise with Europol, and the units send at least one liaison officer to represent its interests at Europol headquarters. Europol maintains a computerised information system, designed to facilitate the exchange of information between member states, and has a management board comprising one senior representative from each member state.

Director, Rob Wainwright (United Kingdom)

EUROPEAN PARLIAMENT

POLITICAL GROUPINGS
as at September 2011

	EPP	S&D	ALDE	Greens/EFA	ECR	GUE/NGL	EFD	NA	Total
Austria	6	4	–	2	–	–	–	5	17
Belgium	5	5	5	4	1	–	–	2	22
Bulgaria	6	4	5	–	–	–	–	2	17
Cyprus	2	2	–	–	–	2	–	–	6
Czech Republic	2	7	–	–	9	4	–	–	22
Denmark	1	4	3	2	1	1	1	–	13
Estonia	1	1	3	1	–	–	–	–	6
Finland	4	2	4	2	–	–	1	–	13
France	29	14	6	14	–	5	1	3	72
Germany	42	23	12	14	–	8	–	–	99
Greece	7	8	1	1	–	3	2	–	22
Hungary	14	4	–	–	1	–	–	3	22
Ireland	4	3	4	–	–	1	–	–	12
Italy	35	22	6	–	–	–	9	–	72
Latvia	3	1	1	1	1	1	–	–	8
Lithuania	4	3	2	–	1	–	2	–	12
Luxembourg	3	1	1	1	–	–	–	–	6
Malta	2	3	–	–	–	–	–	–	5
The Netherlands	5	3	6	3	1	2	1	4	25
Poland	28	7	–	–	15	–	–	–	50
Portugal	10	7	–	1	–	4	–	–	22
Romania	14	11	5	–	–	–	–	3	33
Slovakia	6	5	1	–	–	–	1	–	13
Slovenia	3	2	2	–	–	–	–	–	7
Spain	23	21	2	2	–	1	–	1	50
Sweden	5	5	4	3	–	1	–	–	18
UK	–	13	12	5	26	1	9	6	72
Total	264	185	85	56	56	34	27	29	736

EPP – European People's Party (Christian Democrats)
W www.eppgroup.eu

S&D – Progressive Alliance of Socialists and Democrats in the European Parliament
W www.socialistsanddemocrats.eu

ALDE – Alliance of Liberals and Democrats for Europe
W www.alde.eu

Greens/EFA – Greens/European Free Alliance
W www.greens-efa.org

ECR – European Conservatives and Reformists
W www.ecrgroup.eu

GUE/NGL – Confederal Group of the European United Left/Nordic Green Left
W www.guengl.eu

EFD – Europe of Freedom and Democracy
W www.efdgroup.eu

NA – Non-Attached

EUROPEAN UNION INFORMATION

EUROPEAN COMMISSION REPRESENTATION OFFICES

UK, Europe House, 32 Smith Square, London SW1P 3EU
T 020-7973 1992
WALES, 2 Caspian Point, Caspian Way, Cardiff CF10 4QQ
T 029-2089 5020
SCOTLAND, 9 Alva Street, Edinburgh EH2 4PH
T 0131-225 2058
NORTHERN IRELAND, 74–76 Dublin Road, Belfast
BT2 7HP T 028-9024 0708

EUROPEAN COMMISSION DELEGATIONS

AUSTRALIA AND NEW ZEALAND, 18 Arkana Street,
Yarralumla, ACT 2600, Canberra

CANADA, 150 Metcalfe Street, Suite 1900, Ottawa,
Ontario K2P 1P1

UK OFFICE OF THE EUROPEAN PARLIAMENT,

Europe House, 32 Smith Square, London SW1P 3EU
T 020-7227 4300
USA, 2300 M Street, NW Washington DC 20037

UK PERMANENT REPRESENTATIVE TO THE EU

10 Ave d'Auderghem, Oudergemselaan, 1040 Brussels,
Belgium
T (+32) 2287 8211 W http://ukeu.fco.gov.uk
UK Permanent Representative to the EU, Sir Kim Darroch,
KCMG, *apptd* 2007

INTERNATIONAL ORGANISATIONS

International organisations are intergovernmental organisations, whose membership can only include either sovereign states or other international organisations. They are subject to international law and are capable of entering into agreements among themselves or with states. They do not include private non-governmental organisations with an international scope. International organisations are usually established by a treaty providing them with legal recognition, which distinguishes them from collections of states such as the G8.

AFRICAN UNION

PO Box 3243, Addis Ababa, Ethiopia
T (+251) (1) 1551 7700 E webmaster@africa-union.org
W www.africa-union.org

The African Union (AU) was launched in 2002 as a successor to the amalgamated Organisation of African Unity (OAU) and the African Economic Community. It currently has 53 members, representing every African country except Morocco, which left the OAU in 1984 in protest at the admission of Saharan Arab Democratic Republic, representing Western Sahara, as a member. The AU aims to further African unity and solidarity, to co-ordinate political, economic, social and defence policies, and eventually to create an African single currency.

Chief AU governing organs include the assembly of heads of state or government, the ultimate decision-making body; the executive council, composed of foreign ministers from member states and which advises the assembly; the African Commission, which is the AU secretariat and consists of eight commissioners, each with a separate portfolio, who elect a chair to a four-year term; the peace and security council, modelled on that of the UN and capable of military intervention; and the pan-African parliament, established in 2004 to debate and advise heads of state.

Substantial budgetary arrears due to delays in the payment of national contributions have presented the AU with difficulties in achieving its objectives. Since 2004, the AU has deployed a peacekeeping force in the Darfur region of Sudan which, in December 2007, amalgamated into a joint UN-AU operation (UNAMID). In February 2011 UNAMID had a strength of 23,055 uniformed personnel.

Chair, Bingu wa Mutharika (Malawi)

ANDEAN COMMUNITY

General Secretariat, Paseo de la República 3895, esq. Aramburú, San Isidro, Lima 27, Peru
T (+51) (1) 411 1400 E contacto@comunidadandina.org
W www.comunidadandina.org

The Andean Community, known as the Andean Pact until 1996, began operating formally on 21 November 1969 when its commission was established. It comprises four member states – Bolivia, Colombia, Ecuador and Peru – and the organisations and institutions of the Andean Integration System (AIS). Argentina, Brazil, Chile, Paraguay and Uruguay are associated states.

The community's objectives are to facilitate economic growth, create jobs and facilitate regional integration towards the goal of a Latin American common market.

It also aims to reduce the inequalities in development between member states. It pursues its objectives through a programme of trade liberalisation, a common external tariff, the relaxation of border controls, coordination between national legislatures and the promotion of industrial, agricultural and technological development.

The general secretariat of the Andean Community is its executive body, responsible for administration and dispute resolution. The general secretariat operates under the direction of the secretary-general, who is elected by the Andean council of foreign ministers (ACFM). It can propose decisions or suggestions to the ACFM; it also manages the integration process, ensures that community commitments are fulfilled, and maintains relations with the member countries and the executive bodies of other international organisations.

The Andean presidential council is the highest-level body of the AIS and comprises the presidents of the member states. Its responsibilities include setting new policies, evaluating the integration process and communicating with other bodies. The chairmanship is rotated among the members of the council each calendar year.

In 2001 the organisation introduced Andean passports for member states and since 2005 a policy of free flow of persons has enabled citizens to travel throughout the area without a visa.

Secretary-General, Adalid Contreras Baspineiro (Bolivia)

ARAB MAGHREB UNION

14 rue Tensift, Agdal, Rabat, Morocco
T (+212) (5) 376 81371 E sg.uma@maghrebarabe.org
W www.maghrebarabe.org

The treaty establishing the Arab Maghreb Union (AMU) was signed on 17 February 1989 by the heads of state of the five member states: Algeria, Libya, Mauritania, Morocco and Tunisia. The AMU aims to strengthen ties between the member countries by developing agriculture and commerce, working towards a customs union and economic common market, and establishing joint projects and economic cooperation programmes.

Decisions must be unanimous and are made by a council of heads of state, which is briefed by a council of foreign affairs ministers. The council of heads of state has not assembled since 1994 because of a dispute over the status of Western Sahara. A consultative assembly – consisting of 30 representatives from each member state – is based in Algiers; the secretariat is in Rabat; and the court of justice, with two judges from each country, operates in Nouakchott, Mauritania.

Secretary-General, Habib Ben Yahia (Tunisia)

ARCTIC COUNCIL

Framsenteret, NO-9296 Tromso, Norway
T (+47) 7775 0140 E ac-chair@arctic-council.org
W www.arctic-council.org

The Arctic Council was founded in 1996 in Ottawa, Canada, and is a regional forum for socio-economic development and scientific research within the Arctic region. It comprises eight states: Canada, Denmark (including Greenland and the Faeroe Islands), Finland,

Iceland, Norway, Russia, Sweden and the USA. A further six organisations representing indigenous peoples are granted permanent participatory status and include the Saami Council, Inuit Circumpolar Conference and the Arctic Athabaskan Council. Six states (France, Germany, the Netherlands, Poland, Spain and the UK) have observer status.

Decisions within the Arctic Council are made at biennial ministerial meetings attended by foreign ministers or designates of the member states. The chairmanship of the council and secretariat also rotate on a biennial basis. Between these meetings, the operation of the council is administered by the Committee of Senior Arctic Officials, which meets biannually.

The main scientific work of the Arctic Council is carried out by six working groups, each focusing on specific issues such as the monitoring and prevention of pollution; climate change; biodiversity; and public health.
Chair, Sweden (2011–13)

ASIA COOPERATION DIALOGUE
E acd@mfa.go.th W www.acddialogue.com

The Asia Cooperation Dialogue (ACD) was initiated by the former prime minister of Thailand, Thaksin Shinawatra, and inaugurated in June 2002. It currently has 31 members, with Morocco granted development partner status.

Its purpose is to provide a continent-wide forum to assist development in every Asian nation, with the ultimate goal to create an Asian community capable of equal interaction with the rest of the world. It aims to achieve these objectives through promoting interdependence among Asian countries, improving quality of life and expanding the continent's trade and financial markets.

Representatives from each of the member states (typically foreign ministers) meet annually to discuss ACD developments, issues of regional cooperation and methods of enhancing Asian unity. In addition, ministers also meet during the annual UN general assembly to discuss the implementation of policy and a common approach to international issues.

ASIAN-AFRICAN LEGAL CONSULTATIVE ORGANISATION
29-C, Rizal Marg, Diplomatic Enclave, Chanakyapuri, New Delhi 110021, India
T (+91) (11) 2419 7000
E mail@aalco.int W www.aalco.int

The Asian-African Legal Consultative Organisation (AALCO), founded as a result of the Bandung Conference of 1955, was previously known as both the Asian Legal Consultative Committee and the Asian-African Legal Consultative Committee before its name was changed again in 2001. It was initially established as a non-permanent committee for a five-year term which was repeatedly extended until 1981, when it was granted permanent status. It has 47 member states.

The functions of the AALCO include serving as an advisory body to its member states in the field of international law, operating as a forum for common concerns among its members and making recommendations to governments and other international organisations.

Representatives from member states meet for the annual session which is hosted on a rotational basis and is attended by members of government, observers from other organisations and members of the International Court of Justice and International Law Commission.

The secretariat is located in New Delhi and is responsible for the day-to-day functioning of the organisation. It is headed by a secretary-general, who is elected to a four-year term. Other infrastructure includes four regional arbitration centres, located in Egypt, Iran, Malaysia and Nigeria; plans have been agreed for a fifth centre to be established in Kenya.
Secretary-General, Prof Dr Ramat bin Mohamad (Malaysia)

ASIAN DEVELOPMENT BANK
6 ADB Avenue, Mandaluyong City 1550, The Philippines
T (+632) 632 4444 W www.adb.org

The Asian Development Bank (ADB) was founded in 1966 and is a multilateral financial institution dedicated to reducing poverty in Asia and the Pacific. It has 67 member countries from across the world. The ADB extends loans, equity investments and technical assistance to governments and public and private enterprises in its member countries, and promotes the investment of public and private capital for development. The bank's programmes prioritise economic growth, human development, good governance, environmental protection, private sector growth and regional cooperation.

The ADB is controlled by its board of governors, which meets annually and consists of a representative from each of the member states. It elects and delegates its powers to a board of directors which is responsible for administration and policy review.

The ADB raises funds through members' contributions and issuing bonds on the world's capital markets. In 2010, the ADB provided loans totalling US$11,460m (£7,032m) and technical assistance costing US$176m (£108m).
President, Haruhiko Kuroda (Japan)

ASIA-PACIFIC ECONOMIC COOPERATION
35 Heng Mui Keng Terrace, Singapore 119616
T (+65) 6891 9600 E info@apec.org W www.apec.org

Asia-Pacific Economic Cooperation (APEC) is an economic forum for Pacific Rim countries to discuss regional economy, cooperation, trade and investment. APEC was founded in 1989 in response to the growing interdependence among Asia-Pacific economies. The 1994 Declaration of Common Resolve envisaged free and open trade between member states with industrialised economies by 2010, extending to members with developing economies by 2020. At a summit in Japan in 2010, leaders of APEC concluded that more work remains to be done to meet these goals. Its 21 members define and fund work programmes for APEC's four committees, 11 working groups and other task forces.

APEC's chairmanship rotates annually among member states and the chair is responsible for hosting the annual leaders' meeting, as well as meetings of foreign affairs and trade ministers. The permanent secretariat, based in Singapore, is responsible for implementing policy, and is headed by an executive director selected by member states to serve a three-year term.
Executive Director, HE Muhamad Noor Yacob (Malaysia)

ASSOCIATION OF SOUTH-EAST ASIAN NATIONS
Jalan Sisingamangaraja 70a, Jakarta 12110, Indonesia
T (+62) (21) 726 2991/724 3372 E public@aseansec.org
W www.aseansec.org

The Association of South-East Asian Nations (ASEAN) is a geo-political and economic organisation formed in

1967 with the aim of accelerating economic growth, social progress and cultural development, and ensuring regional stability. It currently has ten member states.

The ASEAN summit, a biannual meeting of the heads of government, is the organisation's highest authority. The biannual ASEAN foreign ministers' meeting is responsible for preparing summit meetings, implementing their policies, and coordinating ASEAN's activities. The ASEAN economic ministers meet annually to coordinate economic policy.

An ASEAN free trade area was implemented in 2003, while a common preferential tariff was introduced in 1993. At the ASEAN summit in 1995, a south-east Asia nuclear-weapon-free zone was declared. In December 2008 a new charter came into force which gave ASEAN legal status and a new institutional framework, committed it to the promotion of democracy, and provided for the establishment of the intergovernmental commission on human rights – in October 2009.

The secretary-general of ASEAN is appointed on merit by the heads of government and can initiate, advise on, coordinate and implement ASEAN activities. In addition to the ASEAN secretariat based in Jakarta, each member state has a national secretariat in its foreign ministry which organises and implements activities at a national level.

Secretary-General, Dr Surin Pitsuwan (Thailand)

BALTIC ASSEMBLY
Room 616, 2 Citadeles Street, Riga, LV-1010, Latvia
T (+371) 6722 5178 E silga.lejasmeiere@baltasam.org
W www.baltasam.org

Established in November 1991, the Baltic Assembly (BA) is an international organisation for cooperation between the parliaments of Estonia, Latvia and Lithuania. Each member state appoints between 12 and 20 parliamentarians to the assembly, including a head and deputy head of the national delegation. The political allegiances of the appointees reflect party proportions in each of the domestic parliaments. The BA holds an annual session in each of the member states in rotation. Several permanent and *ad hoc* committees also meet at least three times a year. The Baltic council of ministers, which comprises the heads of government and ministers of the member states, meets with the BA once a year and promotes intergovernmental and regional cooperation between the Baltic states; the joint sessions are known as the Baltic council.

President, Trivimi Velliste (Estonia)

CAB INTERNATIONAL
Nosworthy Way, Wallingford, Oxon OX10 8DE
T 01491-832111 E enquiries@cabi.org W www.cabi.org

Founded in 1910, CAB International (CABI) (formerly the Commonwealth Agricultural Bureau) is a non-profit organisation that provides scientific expertise to assist sustainable development and environmental protection. The organisation consists of 40 countries and five British overseas territories; each is represented on both the executive council, which meets biannually, and the review conference, held every five years to appraise policy and set future goals. A governing board provides guidance on policy issues.

CABI has three divisions: publishing, development projects and research, and microbial services. Each division undertakes research and provides consultancy aimed at raising agricultural productivity, conserving biological resources, protecting the environment and controlling disease. Any country is eligible to apply for membership.

Chief Executive Officer, Dr Trevor Nicholls (UK)

CARIBBEAN COMMUNITY AND COMMON MARKET
Turkeyen, Greater Georgetown, Guyana
T (+592) 222 0001/ 0075 E registry@caricom.org
W www.caricom.org

The Caribbean Community and Common Market (CARICOM) was established in 1973 with the signing of the Treaty of Chaguaramas. The objectives of CARICOM are to improve member states' working and living standards, boost employment levels, promote economic development and competitiveness, coordinate foreign and economic policies and enhance cooperation in the delivery of services such as health and education.

The supreme organ is the conference of heads of government, which determines policy and resolves conflict. The community council of ministers consists of ministers of government assigned to CARICOM affairs and is responsible for economic and strategic planning. The principal administrative arm is the secretariat, based in Guyana. The bureau of the conference of heads of government is the executive body; it comprises the chair of the conference, the outgoing chair and the secretary-general, who are all authorised to initiate proposals and to secure the implementation of decisions. In addition, there are five ministerial councils dealing with trade and economic development, foreign and community relations, human and social development, finance and planning, and national security and law enforcement.

Thirteen member states are committed to the CARICOM single market and economy, agreed in 2006. Twelve member states now issue CARICOM passports.

CARICOM has 15 member states and five associate members.

Secretary-General, Lolita Applewhaite (Barbados)

THE COMMONWEALTH
The Commonwealth is a voluntary association of 54 sovereign and independent states together with their associated states and dependencies. All of the states were formerly parts of the British Empire or League of Nations (later the UN) mandated territories, except for Mozambique and Rwanda which were admitted because of their history of cooperation with neighbouring Commonwealth nations.

The status and relationship of member nations were first defined by the inter-imperial relations committee of the 1926 Imperial Conference, when the six existing dominions (Australia, Canada, the Irish Free State, Newfoundland, New Zealand and South Africa) were described as 'autonomous communities within the British Empire, equal in status, in no way subordinate one to another in any aspect of their domestic or external affairs, though united by a common allegiance to the Crown and freely associated as members of the British Commonwealth of Nations'. This formula was given legal substance by the statute of Westminster in 1931.

This concept of a group of countries owing allegiance to a single crown changed in 1949 when India decided to become a republic. Her continued membership of the Commonwealth was agreed by the other members on the basis of her 'acceptance of the monarch as the symbol of the free association of its independent member nations and as such the head of the Commonwealth'. This enabled subsequent new republics to join the association. Member nations agreed at the time of the accession of Queen Elizabeth II to recognise Her Majesty as the new head of the Commonwealth. However, the position is not vested in the British Crown.

THE MODERN COMMONWEALTH

As the UK's former colonies joined, after India and Pakistan in 1947, the Commonwealth was transformed from a grouping of all-white dominions into a multiracial association of equal nations. It increasingly focused on promoting development and racial equality. South Africa withdrew in 1961 when it became clear that its reapplication for membership on becoming a republic would be rejected over its policy of apartheid.

The new goals of advocating democracy, the rule of law, good government and social justice were enshrined in the Harare Commonwealth Declaration (1991), which formed the basis of new membership guidelines agreed in Cyprus in 1993. Following the adoption of measures at the New Zealand summit in 1995 against serious or persistent violations of these principles, Nigeria was suspended in 1995 and Sierra Leone was suspended in 1997 for anti-democratic behaviour. Sierra Leone's suspension was revoked the following year when a legitimate government was returned to power. Similarly, Nigeria's suspension was lifted in 1999, the day a newly elected civilian president took office. A heads of government meeting in 1997 established a set of economic principles for the Commonwealth, promoting economic growth while protecting smaller member states from the negative effects of globalisation. Zimbabwe was suspended from the councils of the Commonwealth in March 2002, and in 2003 the Zimbabwean government officially confirmed its departure from the association. Following President Pervez Musharraf's imposition of emergency rule in Pakistan in November 2007, the country was briefly suspended from the Commonwealth's councils. The suspension was lifted after successful democratic elections in February 2008. Fiji's Commonwealth membership was suspended in September 2009 after its military government refused to commit to elections in 2010.

MEMBERSHIP

Membership of the Commonwealth involves acceptance of the association's basic principles and is subject to the approval of existing members. There are 54 members at present, of which 16 have Queen Elizabeth II as head of state, 32 are republics and six have national monarchies. (The date of joining the Commonwealth is shown in parentheses.)

*Antigua and Barbuda (1981)	Dominica (1978)
*Australia (1931)	‡Fiji (1970)
*The Bahamas (1973)	The Gambia (1965)
Bangladesh (1972)	Ghana (1957)
*Barbados (1966)	*Grenada (1974)
*Belize (1981)	Guyana (1966)
Botswana (1966)	India (1947)
Brunei (1984)	*Jamaica (1962)
Cameroon (1995)	Kenya (1963)
*Canada (1931)	Kiribati (1979)
Cyprus (1961)	Lesotho (1966)
	Malawi (1964)

Malaysia (1957)	Seychelles (1976)
Maldives (1982)	Sierra Leone (1961)
Malta (1964)	Singapore (1965)
Mauritius (1968)	*Solomon Islands (1978)
Mozambique (1995)	South Africa
Namibia (1990)	(1931)
†Nauru (1968)	Sri Lanka (1948)
*New Zealand (1931)	Swaziland (1968)
Nigeria (1960)	Tanzania (1961)
Pakistan (1947)	Tonga (1970)
*Papua New Guinea (1975)	Trinidad and Tobago
Rwanda (2009)	(1962)
*St Kitts and Nevis (1983)	*Tuvalu (1978)
*St Lucia (1979)	Uganda (1962)
*St Vincent and the	*United Kingdom
Grenadines (1979)	Vanuatu (1980)
Samoa (1970)	Zambia (1964)

* Realms of Queen Elizabeth II
† Nauru is a member in arrears
‡ Currently suspended from the Commonwealth

COUNTRIES THAT HAVE LEFT THE COMMONWEALTH

Republic of Ireland (1949)
South Africa (1961, rejoined 1994)
Pakistan (1972, rejoined 1989; suspended 1999, suspension lifted 2004; suspended 2007, suspension lifted 2008)
Zimbabwe (2003)

In each of the realms where Queen Elizabeth II is head of state (except for the UK), she is personally represented by a governor-general, who holds in all essential respects the same position in relation to the administration of public affairs in the realm as is held by Her Majesty in the UK. The governor-general is appointed by the Queen on the advice of the government of the state concerned.

INTERGOVERNMENTAL AND OTHER LINKS

The main forum for consultation is the Commonwealth heads of government meetings, held biennially to discuss international developments and to consider cooperation among members. Decisions are reached by consensus, and the views of the meeting are set out in a communiqué. There are also annual meetings of finance ministers and frequent meetings of ministers and officials in other fields, such as education, health, gender and youth affairs. Intergovernmental links are complemented by the activities of some 90 Commonwealth non-governmental organisations linking professionals, sportsmen and sportswomen, and interest groups. The Commonwealth Games take place every four years.

COMMONWEALTH SECRETARIAT

The Commonwealth has a secretariat, established in 1965 in London, which is funded by member governments. This is the main agency for multilateral communication between member governments on issues relating to the Commonwealth as a whole. It promotes consultation and cooperation, disseminates information on matters of common concern, organises meetings including the biennial summits, coordinates Commonwealth activities and provides technical assistance for economic and social development through the Commonwealth fund for technical cooperation.

The Commonwealth Foundation was established by Commonwealth governments in 1965 as an autonomous body with a board of governors representing

Commonwealth governments that fund the foundation. It promotes and funds exchanges and other activities aimed at strengthening the skills and effectiveness of professionals and non-governmental organisations. It also promotes culture, rural development, social welfare, human rights and gender equality.

COMMONWEALTH SECRETARIAT, Marlborough House, Pall Mall, London SW1Y 5HX **T** 020-7747 6500
E info@commonwealth.int **W** www.thecommonwealth.org
Secretary-General, Kamalesh Sharma (India)
COMMONWEALTH FOUNDATION, Marlborough House, Pall Mall, London SW1Y 5HY **T** 020-7930 3783
E geninfo@commonwealth.int
W www.commonwealthfoundation.com
Chair, Prof. Guido de Marco (Malta)
COMMONWEALTH EDUCATION TRUST, New Zealand House, 80 Haymarket, London SW1Y 4TQ
T 020-7024 9822 **E** information@cet1886.org
W www.cet1886.org

COMMONWEALTH OF INDEPENDENT STATES
Ulitsa Kirova 17, Minsk 220030, Belarus
T (+375) (17) 222 35 17 **E** postmaster@cis.minsk.by
W www.cis.minsk.by

The Commonwealth of Independent States (CIS) is a multilateral grouping of 11 former Soviet republics. It was formed in 1991 and its charter was signed by ten states in 1993–4. The CIS acts as a coordinating mechanism for foreign, defence and economic policies and as a forum for addressing problems arising from the break-up of the USSR. These matters are addressed in more than 70 inter-state, intergovernmental coordinating and consultative statutory bodies.

The two supreme CIS organs are the council of heads of state, which meets twice a year, and the council of heads of government. The executive committee, based in Minsk and Moscow, provides administrative support. There are also numerous ministerial, parliamentary, economic and security councils.

On becoming members of the CIS, the member states agreed to recognise their existing borders, respect one another's territorial integrity and reject the use of military force or coercion to settle disputes. A treaty on collective security was signed in 1992 by six states, and a joint peacemaking force, to intervene in CIS conflicts, was agreed upon by nine states. Russia concluded bilateral and multilateral agreements with other CIS states under the supervision of the council of heads of collective security (established 1993). These agreements became the collective security treaty, enabling Russia to station troops in eight of the CIS states, and giving Russian forces *de facto* control of virtually all of the former USSR's external borders. Only Ukraine and Moldova remained outside the defence cooperation framework and did not sign the treaty. In 1999, Azerbaijan, Georgia and Uzbekistan withdrew from the treaty and formed a new defensive (GUAM) with Moldova and Ukraine. Georgia withdrew from the organisation entirely effective from August 2009, following the country's war with Russia in 2008.

In 1991, 11 republics signed a treaty forming an economic community. Members agreed to refrain from economic actions that would damage each other and to coordinate economic and monetary policies. A coordinating consultative committee, an economic arbitration court and an inter-state bank were established. Members also affirmed the principles of private ownership, free enterprise and competition as the basis for economic recovery.

The 11 CIS members who signed the Establishment of an Economic Union treaty in September 1993 (of which Ukraine remains an associate member) committed themselves to a common economic space with free movement of goods, services, capital and labour. Belarus, Kazakhstan, Kyrgyzstan and Russia signed a treaty on the establishment of a customs union in 1996; the treaty was later signed by Tajikistan. In 2000 the presidents of the five countries approved a treaty establishing the Eurasian Economic Community, and in 2010 Russia, Belarus and Kazakhstan formed a customs union. In April 2011 the economic council approved a draft agreement for the development of a free trade zone that would include all of the CIS member states.

Executive Secretary, Sergey Lebedev (Russian Federation)

COOPERATION COUNCIL FOR THE ARAB STATES OF THE GULF
PO Box 7153, Riyadh 11-462, Saudi Arabia
T (+966) (1) 482 7777 **W** www.gcc-sg.org

The Cooperation Council for the Arab States of the Gulf, or Gulf Cooperation Council (GCC), was established on 25 May 1981. Its main objectives are increasing coordination and integration, harmonising economic, commercial, educational and social policies and promoting scientific and technical innovation among its member states. It established a common market in 2008, and set up a customs union in 2003 which is yet to be fully enforced. The GCC has six members: Oman, the United Arab Emirates, Bahrain, Kuwait, Qatar, and Saudi Arabia; the latter four plan to adopt a common currency with a central bank based in Riyadh.

The highest authority of the GCC is the supreme council, whose presidency rotates among members' heads of states. It holds one regular session every year, but extraordinary sessions may be convened if necessary.

The ministerial council, which ordinarily meets every three months, consists of the foreign ministers of the member states or other delegated ministers. It is authorised to propose policies and recommendations and ensure that resolutions are implemented.

Secretary-General, Abdul Latif bin Rashid Al Zayani (Bahrain)

COUNCIL OF EUROPE
Avenue de l'Europe, F-67075 Strasbourg-Cedex, France
T (+33) (3) 8841 2000 **W** www.coe.int

The Council of Europe was founded in 1949. Its aim is to achieve greater unity between its members, to safeguard their European heritage and to facilitate their progress in economic, social, cultural, educational, scientific, legal and administrative matters, and to further pluralist democracy, human rights and fundamental freedoms. It has 47 member states.

The organs are the committee of ministers, consisting of the foreign ministers of member countries, and the parliamentary assembly of 318 members (and 318 substitutes), elected or chosen by the national parliaments of member countries in proportion to the relative strength of political parties.

The committee of ministers is the executive organ. The majority of its conclusions take the form of international agreements (known as European conventions) or recommendations to governments. Decisions of the ministers may also be embodied in partial agreements to which a limited number of member governments are party.

One of the principal achievements of the Council of Europe is the European Convention on Human Rights (1950) under which the European Commission of Human Rights and the European Court of Human Rights were established; the two merged in 1998. The reorganised European Court of Human Rights sits in chambers of seven judges or, exceptionally, as a grand chamber of 17 judges. Litigants must exhaust legal processes in their own country prior to bringing cases before the court.

Among other conventions and agreements are the European Social Charter, the European Cultural Convention, the European Code of Social Security, the European Convention on the Protection of National Minorities, and conventions on extradition, the legal status of migrant workers, torture prevention, conservation and the transfer of sentenced prisoners. In 1990 the Venice Commission, an independent legal advisory body, was set up to assist in developing legislative, administrative and constitutional reforms in both European and non-European countries; it currently has 57 member states.

Non-member states take part in certain Council of Europe activities, such as educational, cultural and sports activities on a regular or *ad hoc* basis. The council's ordinary budget for 2011 totalled €217m (£190.4m).

Secretary-General, Thorbjørn Jagland (Norway)

COUNCIL OF THE BALTIC SEA STATES

PO Box 2010, Slussplan 9, Gamla Stan, S-103 11 Stockholm, Sweden
T (+46) 8440 1920 E cbss@cbss.org W www.cbss.org

The Council of the Baltic Sea States was established in 1992 with the aim of creating a regional forum to increase cooperation and coordination among the states that border on the Baltic Sea. The organisation focuses mainly on the environment, economic development, energy, education, civil security and education and culture; members also cooperate on health, humanitarian aid, tourism, transportation and communication issues, and in assisting new democratic institutions. It currently has 12 members (11 countries and the European Commission) while a further ten countries (including the UK and the USA) hold observer status.

The council consists of the foreign ministers of each member state and a member of the European Commission. Chairmanship of the council rotates on an annual basis, and the annual session is held in the country currently in the chair. The foreign minister of the presiding country is responsible for coordinating activities between the sessions. Since 1998 a permanent international secretariat has been established in Stockholm, Sweden.

Chair, Germany (2011–12)

ECONOMIC COMMUNITY OF WEST AFRICAN STATES

101 Yakubu Gowon Crescent, Asokoro District, PMB 401, Abuja, Nigeria
T (+234) (9) 314 76479 E info@ecowas.int W www.ecowas.int

The Economic Community of West African States (ECOWAS) was founded in 1975 and came into operation in 1977. It aims to promote the economic, social and cultural development of West Africa through mutual cooperation, and to prevent and control regional conflicts.

The supreme authority of ECOWAS is vested in the annual summit of heads of government of all 15 member states. A council of ministers meets biannually to monitor the organisation and make recommendations to the summit. Since restructuring in 2007, ECOWAS has been managed by a commission, headed by the president. The ECOWAS parliament was inaugurated in November 2000 and judges for the court of justice were appointed in January 2001. Chad currently holds observer status.

Five member states of ECOWAS (The Gambia, Ghana, Guinea, Nigeria and Sierra Leone) plan to introduce the eco as a single common currency in January 2015. Eight other states currently use the CFA franc – it is planned eventually to amalgamate the two currencies. An ECOWAS travel certificate is issued allowing free movement within the community, and nine countries have a common passport.

An ECOWAS peacekeeping force has been involved in attempts to restore peace in Liberia (1990–6), Sierra Leone (1997–9) and in Guinea-Bissau (1998–9). In December 2010 the Côte d'Ivoire was suspended from ECOWAS following the failure of its *de facto* president, Laurent Gbagbo, to step down after a presidential election. In March 2011 both Guinea and Niger were reinstated to the organisation; their memberships had been suspended, for failure to hold satisfactory democratic elections, in January and December 2009 respectively.

President, Victor Gbeho (Ghana)

EUROPEAN BANK FOR RECONSTRUCTION AND DEVELOPMENT

One Exchange Square, London EC2A 2JN
T 020-7338 6000 W www.ebrd.com

The European Bank for Reconstruction and Development (EBRD), established in 1991, is an international institution whose membership comprises 61 member states, the European Union and the European Investment Bank.

Currently operating in 29 countries from central Europe to central Asia, the EBRD aims to aid the development of market economies and democracies. It provides project financing for banks, industries and businesses. It also works with publicly owned companies to support privatisation, the restructuring of state-owned firms and the improvement of public services.

The main forms of EBRD financing are loans, equity investments and guarantees, and its charter stipulates that at least 60 per cent of lending must contribute to the privatisation of state-owned enterprises. The EBRD pays particular attention to strengthening the financial sector and to promoting small and medium-sized businesses. It works in cooperation with national governments, private companies and international organisations such as the OECD, the IMF, the World Bank and the UN specialised agencies. The EBRD is also able to borrow on world capital markets.

The EBRD's strategic priority in 2010 was to support nascent recovery in the region after the global economic crisis. The bank reported €9.0bn (£7.9bn) in annual business volume – the highest investment level in its history and an increase of 15 per cent on 2009. After two years of losses, the EBRD recorded a net profit of €1.3bn (£1.1bn) in 2010 (before transfers of net income approved by the board of governors). This included unrealised amounts and compared with a net loss of €746m (£652m) for 2009.

The EBRD's highest authority is the board of governors; each member appoints one governor and one alternate. The governors delegate most powers to a 23-member board of directors; the directors are responsible for the EBRD's operations and budget, and are elected by the governors for three-year terms. The governors also elect the president of the board of directors, who acts as the bank's president for a four-year term.

President, Dr Thomas Mirow (Germany)

EUROPEAN FREE TRADE ASSOCIATION
9–11 rue de Varembé, CH-1211 Geneva 20, Switzerland
T (+41) (22) 332 2626 E mail.gva@efta.int W www.efta.int

The European Free Trade Association (EFTA) was established in 1960 by Austria, Denmark, Norway, Portugal, Sweden, Switzerland and the UK, and was subsequently joined by Finland, Iceland and Liechtenstein. Six members have left to join what is now the European Union: Denmark and the UK (1972), Portugal (1985), Austria, Finland and Sweden (1995). EFTA's remaining members are Iceland, Liechtenstein, Norway and Switzerland.

The first objective of EFTA was to establish free trade in industrial products between members; this was achieved in 1966. Its second goal was the creation of a single market in Western Europe and in 1972 EFTA signed free trade agreements with the EC covering trade in industrial goods. The remaining tariffs on industrial products were abolished in 1977, and the Luxembourg Declaration on broader cooperation between EFTA and the EC was signed in 1984.

An agreement on the creation of the European Economic Area (EEA), an extension of the EC single market to the EFTA states, was signed in 1992 and entered into force in January 1994. Switzerland rejected EEA membership in a referendum in 1992 and Liechtenstein joined in May 1995 after adapting its customs union with Switzerland.

Since 2002, free trade area agreements have been signed between the EFTA states and Albania, Canada, Chile, Colombia, Egypt, the Gulf Cooperation Council, Lebanon, the Republic of Korea, Peru, Serbia, Singapore, the Southern African Customs Union (SACU), Tunisia and Ukraine. Negotiations on free trade agreements with Algeria, Bosnia and Hercegovina, Hong Kong, India, Indonesia, Montenegro, Thailand and the customs union of Russia, Belarus and Kazakhstan are ongoing.

The EFTA council is the principal organ. Member states' permanent delegations to the EFTA hold monthly meetings in Geneva.

Secretary-General, Kare Bryn (Norway)

EUROPEAN ORGANISATION FOR NUCLEAR RESEARCH (CERN)
CH-1211 Geneva 23, Switzerland
T (+41) (22) 767 6111 E cern.reception@cern.ch
W www.cern.ch

The convention establishing the European Organisation for Nuclear Research (CERN) came into force in 1954. CERN promotes European collaboration in high-energy physics with scientific goals and no military implication. It has 20 member states and eight members with observer status, including the European Commission and UNESCO.

The council, which is the highest policy-making body,

comprises two delegates from each member state and is chaired by the president, who is elected by the council in session. The council also elects a director-general, who is responsible for the internal organisation of CERN. The director-general heads a workforce of approximately 2,400, including physicists, craftsmen, technicians and administrative staff. At present more than 10,000 physicists use CERN's facilities.

Tim Berners-Lee developed the World Wide Web while working at CERN in 1990, and in 2008 CERN completed construction work on the Large Hadron Collider, the world's largest and most powerful particle accelerator.

Director-General, Dr Rolf-Dieter Heuer (Germany)

EUROPEAN SPACE AGENCY
8–10 rue Mario Nikis, 75738 Paris Cedex 15, France
T (+33) (1) 5369 7654 E contactesa@esa.int W www.esa.int

The European Space Agency (ESA) was created in 1975 by the merger of the European Space Research Organisation and the European Launcher Development Organisation. Its aims include the advancement of space research and technology and the implementation of European space policy. ESA has 19 member states and one cooperating state, with four other nations participating in the Plan for European Cooperating States. ESA's mandatory activities are funded by contributions from all member states and calculated in accordance with each country's gross national income. In 2011, ESA's budget amounted to around €3,984m (£3,480m).

The agency is directed by a council composed of the representatives of its member states; its chief officer is the director-general who is elected by the council every four years. ESA has liaison offices in Belgium (for the EU), the United States of America and Russia, while a launch base is stationed in French Guiana.

Director-General, Jean-Jacques Dordain (France)

EUROPEAN UNION
See European Union section

FOOD AND AGRICULTURE ORGANISATION OF THE UNITED NATIONS
Viale delle Terme di Caracalla, 00153 Rome, Italy
T (+39) (06) 57051 E fao-hq@fao.org W www.fao.org

The Food and Agriculture Organisation (FAO) is a specialised UN agency, established in 1945. It assists rural populations by raising levels of nutrition and living standards, and by encouraging greater efficiency in food production and distribution. It analyses and publishes information on agriculture and natural resources. The FAO also advises governments on national agricultural policy and planning through its investment centre and collaboration with the World Bank and other financial institutions. The FAO's field programme covers a range of activities, including strengthening crop production, rural and livestock development and conservation.

The FAO's priorities are sustainable agriculture, rural development and food security. The organisation monitors potential famine areas, channels emergency aid from governments and other agencies, assists in rehabilitation, and responds to urgent or unforeseen requests for technical assistance.

The FAO has 192 members (191 states plus the European Union), and one associate member (the Faroe Islands). It is governed by a biennial conference of its members which sets a programme and budget. The budget for 2010–11 was US$1bn (£615m), funded by member countries in proportion to their gross national income. The FAO is also funded by donor governments and other institutions.

The conference elects a director-general and a 49-member council which governs between conferences. The regular and field programmes are administered by a secretariat, headed by the director-general. Five regional, nine sub-regional and 74 national offices help administer the field programme.

Director-General, Jacques Diouf (Senegal)

INTERNATIONAL ATOMIC ENERGY AGENCY

PO Box 100, Wagramer Strasse 5, A-1400 Vienna, Austria
T (+43) (1) 26000 E official.mail@iaea.org W www.iaea.org

The International Atomic Energy Agency (IAEA) was established in 1957. It is an intergovernmental organisation that reports to, but is not a specialised agency of, the UN.

The IAEA aims to enhance the contribution of atomic energy to peace, health and prosperity. It does not advocate the use of atomic energy for military purposes. It establishes atomic energy safety standards and offers services to its member states to upgrade safety and security measures for their nuclear installations and material, and for radioactive sources, material and waste. It is the focal point for international conventions on the early notification of a nuclear accident, accident assistance, civil liability for nuclear damage, physical protection of nuclear material, and the safety of spent fuel and radioactive waste management. The IAEA also encourages research and training in nuclear power. It is additionally charged with drawing up safeguards and verifying their enforcement in accordance with several international nuclear weapons treaties.

The IAEA has 151 members that meet annually in a general conference. The conference decides policy, a programme and a budget – €315.4m (£278.5m) in 2010 – as well as electing a director-general and a 35-member board of governors. The board meets five times a year to review and formulate policy, which is implemented by the secretariat.

Director-General, Yukiya Amano (Japan)

INTERNATIONAL CIVIL AVIATION ORGANISATION

999 University Street, Montréal, Québec, Canada H3C 5H7
T (+1) (514) 954 8219 E icaohq@icao.int W www.icao.int

The International Civil Aviation Organisation (ICAO) was founded with the signing of the Chicago Convention on International Civil Aviation in 1944 and became a specialised agency of the UN in 1947. It sets international technical standards and regulations for aviation safety, security and efficiency, as well as environmental protection.

ICAO has 190 members and is governed by an assembly, which convenes triennially. A council of 36 members is elected, which represents leading air transport nations as well as less developed countries. The council elects the president, appoints the secretary-general and supervises the organisation through subsidiary committees, serviced by a secretariat.

President of the Council, Roberto Kobeh González (Mexico)

INTERNATIONAL CRIMINAL POLICE ORGANISATION (INTERPOL)

200 Quai Charles de Gaulle, F-69006 Lyon, France
E compr@interpol.int W www.interpol.int

Interpol was set up in 1923 to establish an international criminal records office and to harmonise extradition procedures. In 2011, the organisation comprised 188 member states. Interpol's aims are to promote cooperation between criminal police authorities and to support government agencies concerned with combating crime, while respecting national sovereignty. It is financed by annual contributions from the governments of member states.

Interpol policy is formulated by the general assembly which meets annually and is composed of delegates appointed by the member states. The 13-member executive committee is elected by the general assembly from the member states' delegates and is chaired by the president, who serves a four-year term of office. The permanent administrative organ is the general secretariat, headed by the secretary-general, who is appointed by the general assembly.

The UK Interpol National Central Bureau is operated by the Serious Organised Crime Agency (SOCA).

Secretary-General, Ronald K. Noble (USA)

INTERNATIONAL ENERGY AGENCY

9 rue de la Fédération, F-75739 Paris, France
T (+33) (1) 4057 6500/01 E info@iea.org W www.iea.org

The International Energy Agency (IEA), founded in 1974, is an autonomous agency within the framework of the Organisation for Economic Cooperation and Development (OECD). The IEA's objectives include the improvement of energy cooperation worldwide, development of alternative energy sources and the promotion of relations between oil-producing and oil-consuming countries. The IEA also maintains an emergency system to alleviate the effects of severe oil supply disruptions.

The main decision-making body is the governing board, composed of senior energy officials from member countries. The IEA secretariat, with a staff of energy experts, carries out the work of the governing board and its subordinate bodies. The executive director is appointed by the board. The IEA has 28 member states; the European Commission also participates in its work.

Executive Director, Maria van der Hoeven (Netherlands)

INTERNATIONAL FRANCOPHONE ORGANISATION

Cabinet du Secrétaire général, 19–21 avenue Bosquet, 75007 Paris, France
T (+33) (1) 4411 1250 W www.francophonie.org

The International Francophone Organisation (known as La Francophonie) is an intergovernmental organisation founded in 1970 by 21 French-speaking countries. It aims to prevent conflict and promote development and cooperation, represent its member states internationally and promote French culture and language.

The conference of heads of state and government of countries with French as a common language – also known as the Francophone summit – takes place biennially. Other institutions include the ministerial conference, the permanent council and the secretariat.

The ministerial conference, which consists of the foreign ministers or the ministers responsible for

Francophone affairs of each member state, implements decisions made at the summits and puts forward prospective new members. The permanent council, which is chaired by the secretary-general and consists of representatives of the member states, oversees the execution of decisions made by the ministerial conference, allocates funds, and reviews and approves projects.

La Francophonie has 56 members, three associate member states and 14 observers.

Secretary-General, Abdou Diouf (Senegal)

INTERNATIONAL FUND FOR AGRICULTURAL DEVELOPMENT
44 Via Paolo di Dono, 00142 Rome, Italy
T (+39) (06) 54591 E ifad@ifad.org W www.ifad.org

The International Fund for Agricultural Development (IFAD) began operations as a UN specialised agency in 1978. It develops and finances agricultural and rural projects in developing countries and aims to promote employment and additional income for poor farmers, reduce malnutrition and improve food security systems.

IFAD has 166 members and membership is divided into three lists: List A (primarily OECD countries), List B (primarily OPEC countries), and List C (developing countries) which is subdivided into C1 (Africa), C2 (Europe, Asia and the Pacific) and C3 (Latin America and the Caribbean). All powers are vested in a governing council of all member countries, which meets annually. It elects an executive board composed of 18 members and 18 alternate members, and a president who chairs the executive board. The president serves a four-year term that can be renewed once.

Since its establishment, IFAD has committed $12bn (£7.4bn) in loans and grants for 860 approved projects and programmes. It has also mobilised around $19.6bn (£12bn) in cofinancing and funding for rural development from domestic sources.

President, Kanayo F. Nwanze (Nigeria)

INTERNATIONAL HYDROGRAPHIC ORGANISATION
4 Quai Antoine 1er, B.P. 445, 98011, Monaco
T (+377) 9310 8100 E info@ihb.mc W www.iho.int

The International Hydrographic Organisation began operating in 1921 with 19 member states and headquarters in the Principality of Monaco. In 1970 its name was changed from the International Hydrographic Bureau. The IHO is an intergovernmental organisation that has a purely consultative role and aims to support safety in international navigation, set policy for marine conservation and improve coordination between national hydrographic institutions. The IHO has a membership of 80 states that meet at five-yearly conferences to set policy, approve budget, review progress and adopt programmes of work. Each member is represented at these conferences by their most senior hydrographer. All member states have an opportunity to initiate new proposals for IHO consideration. Outside of its membership, the IHO acts to promote hydrography and facilitate the exchange of technology with developing countries. It is also the source that defines the boundaries between seas and oceans.

President, Vice-Adm. Alexandros Maratos (Greece)

INTERNATIONAL LABOUR ORGANISATION
4 route des Morillons, CH-1211 Geneva 22, Switzerland
T (+41) (22) 799 6111 E ilo@ilo.org W www.ilo.org

The International Labour Organisation (ILO) was established in 1919 as an autonomous body of the League of Nations and became the UN's first specialised agency in 1946. The ILO aims to increase employment, improve working conditions, extend social protection and promote dialogue between government, workers' and employers' organisations.

It sets minimum international labour standards through the drafting of international conventions. Member countries are obliged to submit these to their domestic authorities for ratification, and thus undertake to bring their domestic legislation in line with the conventions. Members must report to the ILO periodically on how these regulations are being implemented. The ILO is also a principal resource centre for information, analysis and guidance on labour and employment.

The ILO has 183 member states and is composed of the International Labour Conference, the governing body and the International Labour Office. The conference of members meets annually, and is attended by national delegations. It adopts international labour conventions and recommendations, provides a forum for discussion of world employment and social issues and approves the ILO's programme and budget.

The 56-member governing body is composed of 28 government, 14 worker and 14 employer members and acts as the ILO's executive council. It convenes triannually. Ten governments, including the UK, hold permanent seats on the governing body because of their industrial importance. There are also various regional conferences and advisory committees. The ILO acts as a secretariat and as a centre for operations, publishing and research.

Director-General, Juan Somavia (Chile)

INTERNATIONAL MARITIME ORGANISATION
4 Albert Embankment, London SE1 7SR
T 020-7735 7611 E info@imo.org W www.imo.org

Originally named the Inter-Governmental Maritime Consultative Organisation, the International Maritime Organisation (IMO) was established as a UN specialised agency in 1948. Owing to delays in treaty ratification it did not commence operations until 1958.

The IMO fosters intergovernmental cooperation in technical matters relating to international shipping, particularly regarding safety and security at sea, efficiency in navigation and protecting the marine environment from pollution caused by shipping. The IMO is responsible for convening maritime conferences and drafting marine conventions. It also provides technical aid to countries wishing to develop their activities at sea.

In 2010, the IMO had 169 members and three associate members. It is governed by an assembly comprising delegates of all its members. It meets biennially to formulate policy, set a budget (£61.2m for 2010–11), to vote on specific recommendations on pollution, maritime safety and security, and to elect the council. The council, which meets twice a year, fulfils the functions of the assembly between sessions and appoints a secretary-general. It consists of 40 members: ten from the world's largest shipping nations, ten from the nations most dependent on seaborne trade and 20 other members

to ensure a fair geographical representation. The IMO acts as the secretariat for the London convention (1972) which regulates the disposal of land-generated waste at sea.
Secretary-General, Efthimios E. Mitropoulos (Greece)

INTERNATIONAL MONETARY FUND
700 19th Street NW, Washington DC 20431, USA
T (+1) (202) 623 7000 E publicaffairs@imf.org W www.imf.org

The International Monetary Fund (IMF) was established at the UN Monetary and Financial Conference at Bretton Woods, New Hampshire, in 1944. Its articles of agreement entered into force in 1945 and it began operations in 1947.

The IMF exists to promote international monetary cooperation, the expansion of world trade and exchange stability. It advises members on their economic and financial policies; promotes policy coordination among the major industrial countries; and gives technical assistance in central banking, balance of payments accounting, taxation and other financial matters. The IMF serves as a forum for members to discuss monetary policy issues and seeks the balanced growth of international trade. It has 187 members; Kosovo joined in June 2009, and Tuvalu in June 2010.

Upon joining the IMF, a member is assigned a quota based on that member's relative standing in the world economy and its balance of payments position. The quota determines the size of the member's capital subscription to the fund, access to IMF resources, voting power and share in the allocation of special drawing rights (SDRs). Quotas are reviewed every five years and adjusted accordingly. After the 13th general review in 2008 the IMF board of governors adopted a reform package which would grant *ad hoc* quota increases to 54 countries found to be underrepresented, and allocate triple the number of basic votes to all members. These reforms became effective in March 2011. In December 2010 the board of governors approved recommendations of the 14th general review – namely the doubling of all available quotas, a shift in 6 per cent of quotas from over- to under-represented countries, and an overall realignment in quota shares to reflect emerging markets and developing countries (EDMCs). Under these reforms, China will become the 3rd largest member country and three further EDMCs (Brazil, India and Russia) will be among the top ten shareholders. These reforms will become effective upon their acceptance by three-fifths of members having 85 per cent of total voting power.

The SDR, the reserve currency created by the IMF in 1969, is calculated daily on a basket of usable currencies and is the IMF's unit of account; on 27 April 2011, 1 SDR equalled US$1.61 (£1.00). SDRs are allocated at intervals to supplement members' reserves and thereby improve international financial liquidity. Total quotas as at March 2011 stood at SDR238.4bn, or around US$384bn (£235.8bn).

The IMF is not a bank and does not lend money; it provides temporary financial assistance by selling a member's SDRs or other members' currencies in exchange for the member's own currency. The member can then use the purchased currency to alleviate its balance of payments difficulties. IMF financial resources derive primarily from members' capital subscriptions, which are equivalent to their quotas. In addition, the IMF is authorised to borrow from official lenders. It may also draw on a line of credit of SDR18.5bn from 12 countries under the so-called general arrangements

to borrow (GAB); the ten-fold expansion of another set of credit arrangements, the new arrangements to borrow (NAB), totalling SDR367.5bn, became effective in March 2011. A further 13 countries are expected to be added to the 26 currently participating in the NAB.

Benign market conditions between 2004 and 2008 prompted many countries to start repaying their outstanding loans, and demand for the fund's resources dropped dramatically; however, in 2008 the IMF increased its lending in response to the global financial crisis. In March 2009 the IMF announced a number of reforms to its lending framework, intended to provide greater speed and flexibility in lending arrangements, double access limits on loans and more closely tailor the conditionality of loans to fit the recipient state's needs and strengths. In February 2010 a defined poverty line (a gross national income of $1,135 per capita) was introduced under which countries would qualify to access low-cost concessional loans under the poverty reduction and growth trust. On 31 March 2011 total outstanding IMF credits amounted to SDR70.4bn, or US$70.2bn (£45.3bn).

The IMF supports long-term efforts at economic reform and transformation as well as medium-term programmes under the extended fund facility, which runs for three to four years and is aimed at overcoming balance of payments difficulties stemming from macroeconomic and structural problems. Typically, measures are introduced to reform taxation and the financial sector, to privatise state-owned enterprises and to make labour markets more flexible.

The IMF is headed by a board of governors, comprising representatives of each member state, which meets annually. The governors delegate powers to 24 executive directors, who are appointed or elected by member countries. The executive directors operate the fund on a daily basis under a managing director, whom they elect.
Managing Director, Christine Lagarde

INTERNATIONAL ORGANISATION FOR MIGRATION
17 route des Morillons, CH-1211 Geneva 19, Switzerland
T (+41) 22717 9111 E hq@iom.int W www.iom.int

The International Organisation for Migration (IOM) was founded in 1951 to resettle European displaced persons and refugees. During the 1960s and 1970s the IOM developed links with the United Nations High Commissioner for Refugees and began a programme of assistance and reintegration outside of Europe.

The role of the IOM is to help ensure the orderly and humane management of migration; its remit includes migration health services, international migration law, counter-trafficking measures, emergency and post-crisis management and assisted voluntary returns. It employs more than 7,000 staff and is present in over 420 field locations. There are 132 member states and 17 observer countries.

Internally, the IOM is led by a director-general who is elected for a five-year term. The director-general's office has the constitutional authority to manage the organisation, carry out the activities within its mandate and develop current policies, procedures and strategies. The office of the inspector-general (OIG) incorporates the functions of evaluation, internal audit and assessment of projects.
Director-General, William Lacy Swing (USA)

INTERNATIONAL RED CROSS AND RED CRESCENT MOVEMENT

19 avenue de la Paix, CH-1202 Geneva, Switzerland
T (+41) 2273 46001 W www.icrc.org

The International Red Cross and Red Crescent Movement is composed of three elements – the International Committee of the Red Cross, the International Federation of Red Cross and Red Crescent Societies, and the National Red Cross and Red Crescent Societies.

The International Committee of the Red Cross (ICRC), the organisation's founding body, was formed in 1863. It aims to protect and assist victims of armed conflict. It also seeks to ensure the application of the Geneva Conventions regarding prisoners of war and detainees.

The International Federation of Red Cross and Red Crescent Societies was founded in 1919 to assist the humanitarian activities of national societies, coordinate their relief operations for victims of natural disasters and care for refugees outside areas of conflict. There are Red Cross and Red Crescent societies in 186 countries; it has 63 field delegations internationally and runs over 80 relief operations a year.

The international conference of the Red Cross and Red Crescent meets every four years, bringing together delegates of the ICRC, the International Federation and the national societies, as well as representatives of all 194 states party to the Geneva Conventions.

President, Jakob Kellenberger (Switzerland)

INTERNATIONAL TELECOMMUNICATION UNION

Place des Nations, CH-1211 Geneva 20, Switzerland
T (+41) (22) 730 5111 E itumail@itu.int W www.itu.int

The International Telecommunication Union (ITU) was founded in Paris in 1865 as the International Telegraph Union and became a UN specialised agency in 1947.

ITU is an intergovernmental organisation for the development of telecommunications and the harmonisation of national telecommunication policies. It comprises 192 member states, 534 sector members and 151 associates who represent public and private organisations involved in telecommunications. Its mission is to promote the development of information and communication technologies, and to offer technical assistance to developing countries.

ITU operates initiatives aimed at promoting the growth and expansion of electronic commerce. These include a programme of strategic workshops; the adoption of international regulations, treaties and technical standards to foster global interactivity; and the provision of policy advice and technical assistance. ITU also organises worldwide and regional exhibitions and forums to exchange ideas, knowledge and technology.

Secretary-General, Dr Hamadoun Touré (Mali)

INTERNATIONAL TRADE UNION CONFEDERATION

5 Boulevard du Roi Albert II, 5 B 1, B-1210 Brussels, Belgium
T (+32) (2) 224 0211 E info@ituc-csi.org W www.ituc-csi.org

The International Trade Union Confederation (ITUC) was created in 2006 by the merger between the International Confederation of Free Trade Unions (ICFTU), the World Confederation of Labour (WCL) and other independent unions. Through public and industrial advocacy work it seeks to assert and defend the rights and interests of workers, and to foster international cooperation between

trade unions. In February 2011 the ITUC represented 175 million workers in 151 countries and territories and had 305 national affiliates.

The congress, the supreme authority of the ITUC, meets once every four years to review and propose policy and to elect the 78-member general council. Council members are apportioned according to population-weighted geographical regions, with six seats reserved for nomination by the women's committee, and two by the youth committee. The council, and the general secretary elected at each congress, govern the organisation. It also elects a 27-member executive bureau from among its members which deals with urgent issues and those delegated to it by the council; it also makes decisions on finances and formulates the annual budget for council approval.

The ITUC has regional organisations for Asia-Pacific (ITUC-AP), Africa (ITUC-AF), the Americas (TUCA) and Europe (the pan-European regional council, or PERC). It also cooperates closely with the Global Union Federations, the Trade Union Advisory Committee to the Organisation for Economic Cooperation and Development (OECD), the European Trade Union Confederation, the International Labour Organisation, a number of other UN specialised agencies, and national and regional unions and organisations.

General Secretary, Sharan Burrow (Australia)

INTERNATIONAL WHALING COMMISSION

The Red House, 135 Station Road, Impington, Cambridge CB24 9NP
T 01223-233971 E secretariat@iwcoffice.org
W www.iwcoffice.org

The International Whaling Commission (IWC) was set up under the International Convention for the Regulation of Whaling, signed in Washington DC in 1946. It has 89 member states as of April 2011. The purpose of the IWC is to provide for the conservation of whale stocks, enabling the development of the whaling industry. The organisation reviews and revises the schedule to the convention that decrees the complete protection of certain species, sets limits for when and where whaling can take place, coordinates and funds whale research, and publishes and promotes scientific studies.

The IWC has four main committees, responsible for scientific, technical, conservation and finance matters. There are further sub-committees and working groups concerned with aboriginal subsistence whaling, infractions, small cetaceans, whalewatching, whale-killing methods and animal welfare issues.

Chair, HE Cristián Maquieira (Chile)

LATIN UNION

131 rue du Bac, F-75007 Paris, France
T (+33) (1) 4549 6060 E ulsg@unilat.org W www.unilat.org

The Latin Union is an international organisation whose member states use a Romance language. It was created in 1954 with the signing of a constituent agreement in Madrid and has existed as a functioning institution since 1983. The aims of the organisation are to protect, project and promote the common heritage and to unify identities of the Latin and Latin-influenced world. It has 36 member states and four members with observer status.

The senior body of the organisation, the congress, consists of representatives from each of the member states and meets every two years. It is responsible for approving the budget and setting the agenda for the Union's activities. The executive council is made up of representatives from 12 member states who are elected for a four-year term by congress, as is the secretary-general who is responsible for the implementation of policy through the general secretariat.

The official languages of the Latin Union are Catalan, French, Italian, Portuguese, Castillian (Spanish) and Romanian, although Catalan and Romanian are not used as working languages.

Secretary-General, José Luis Dicenta (Spain)

LEAGUE OF ARAB STATES

Al-Tahrir Square, PO Box 11642, Cairo, Egypt
T (+20) (2) 2575 0511 W www.arableagueonline.org

The League of Arab States was founded in 1945 to protect the independence and sovereignty of its member states, supervise the affairs and interests of Arab countries and promote coordination among them. The organisation has 22 member states. The League itself has observer status at the United Nations.

The heads of member states meet annually at the Arab League summit, while foreign ministers convene every six months as part of the Arab League council. Member states participate in various specialised agencies which develop specific areas of cooperation between Arab states. These include the Arab Monetary Fund; the Arab Satellite Communications Organisation; the Arab Academy for Science, Technology and Maritime Transport; the Arab Bank for Economic Development in Africa; the Arab League Educational, Cultural and Scientific Organisation; and the Council of Arab Economic Unity.

Secretary-General, Amr Moussa (Egypt)

MERCOSUR

Luis Piera 1992, piso 1, 11200-Montevideo, Uruguay
T (+598) (2) 412 9024 E divulgacion@mercosur.org.uy
W www.mercosur.int

MERCOSUR (the Southern Common Market) was created by the treaty of Asunción, signed by Argentina, Brazil, Paraguay and Uruguay on 26 March 1991. Venezuela signed an adhesion protocol in 2006, but its full incorporation into MERCOSUR has yet to receive final ratification from the Paraguayan parliament. Five other countries have associate member status.

The Common Market Council (CMC) is the highest-level agency of MERCOSUR, with authority to formulate policy and enforce member states' compliance with the treaty of Asunción. The CMC comprises ministers of foreign affairs and economic ministers of the member states; it meets at least once a year.

The Common Market Group is the executive body of MERCOSUR and is coordinated by the foreign ministries of the member states. Its function is to implement decisions made by the CMC and resolve disputes. It can establish subgroups to work on particular issues and comprises four permanent members and four substitutes from each country. Other bodies include a joint parliamentary committee, a trade commission and a socio-economic advisory forum. The presidency of MERCOSUR rotates between member states every six months.

In 2005, Argentina, Brazil, Paraguay and Uruguay became associate members of the Andean Community, reciprocating MERCOSUR's action to grant associate membership to all Andean Community nations. In December 2005, the Colombian president ratified a free trade agreement (FTA) with MERCOSUR giving Colombian products preferential access to MERCOSUR countries. MERCOSUR signed an FTA with Israel in December 2007, the bloc's first such agreement outside Latin America. An FTA with Egypt was signed in August 2010. After stalling in 2004, negotiations with the EU over a possible FTA were relaunched in May 2010.

Presidency, Uruguay (July–December 2011)

NORDIC COUNCIL

Ven Stranden 18, 1061 Copenhagen K, Denmark
T (+45) 3396 0400 E nordisk-rad@norden.org
W www.norden.org

The Nordic Council was established in March 1952 as an advisory body on economic and social cooperation, comprising parliamentary delegates from Denmark, Iceland, Norway and Sweden. It was subsequently joined by Finland (1955), and representatives from the Faroes (1970), the Aland Islands (1970), and Greenland (1984).

Cooperation is regulated by the Helsinki agreement, signed in 1962. This was amended in 1971 to create a Nordic council of ministers, which discusses all matters except defence and foreign affairs. Decisions of the council of ministers, which are taken by consensus, are binding, although if ratification by member parliaments is required, decisions only become effective following parliamentary approval. The council of ministers is advised by the Nordic Council, to which it reports annually. There are ministers for Nordic cooperation in every member government.

The Nordic Council comprises 87 voting delegates nominated from member parliaments and about 80 non-voting government representatives. It meets at least once a year in plenary sessions. The full council chooses a 13-member presidium, which conducts business between sessions. A secretariat, headed by a secretary-general, provides administrative support. The presidency of the Nordic Council rotates between the five countries, and the presiding country always hosts the annual council session.

President, Jan-Erik Enestam (Finland)

NORTH AMERICAN FREE TRADE AGREEMENT

NAFTA SECRETARIAT, CANADIAN SECTION,
    111 Sussex Drive, 5th Floor, Ottawa, Ontario K1N 1J1,
    Canada
    T (+1) (613) 992 9388 E canada@nafta-sec-alena.org
NAFTA SECRETARIAT, MEXICAN SECTION, Blvd.
    Adolfo López Mateos 3025, 2° Piso, Col. Héroes de
    Padierna, C.P. 10700, Mexico, D.F.
    T (+52) (55) 5629 9630 E naftamexico@nafta-sec-alena.org
NAFTA SECRETARIAT, US SECTION, Room 2061,
    14th Street and Constitution Avenue, NW, Washington DC,
    20230, USA
    T (+1) (202) 482 5438 E usa@nafta-sec-alena.org
    W www.nafta-sec-alena.org

The leaders of Canada, Mexico and the USA signed the North American Free Trade Agreement (NAFTA) on 17 December 1992 in their respective capitals; it came into force in January 1994 after being ratified by the legislatures of the three member states.

NAFTA aims to eliminate barriers to trade in goods and services, promote fair competition within the free trade area, protect and enforce intellectual property rights and create a framework for further cooperation. To achieve these aims, import tariffs, quotas and limits on cross-border investment are being removed.

The NAFTA secretariat is composed of Canadian, Mexican and US sections. It is responsible for administering the dispute-settlement provisions of the agreement, providing assistance to the Free Trade Commission and support for various committees and working groups, and facilitating the operation of the agreement.

NORTH ATLANTIC TREATY ORGANISATION

Bvld Leopold III, Brussels B-1110, Belgium

T (+32) (2) 707 4111 E natodoc@hq.nato.int W www.nato.int

The North Atlantic Treaty Organisation (NATO) is a political and military alliance designed to provide common security for its members through cooperation and consultation in political, military and economic as well as scientific and other non-military fields.

The North Atlantic treaty (treaty of Washington) was signed in 1949 by Belgium, Canada, Denmark, France, Iceland, Italy, Luxembourg, the Netherlands, Norway, Portugal, the UK and the USA. Greece and Turkey acceded to the treaty in 1952, the Federal Republic of Germany in 1955 (the reunited Germany acceded in October 1990), Spain in 1982, and the Czech Republic, Hungary and Poland in 1999. Bulgaria, Estonia, Latvia, Lithuania, Romania, Slovakia and Slovenia signed membership protocols in March 2003 and officially joined NATO in March 2004. Albania and Croatia became official members in April 2009, having signed membership accords in September 2008.

STRUCTURE

The North Atlantic council (NAC), chaired by the secretary-general, is the highest authority of the alliance and is composed of permanent representatives of the 28 member countries. It meets weekly, but also holds meetings at higher levels involving foreign and defence ministers and heads of government. The permanent representatives (ambassadors) head national delegations of advisers and experts. The defence planning committee (DPC) is composed of all member countries, as is the nuclear planning group (NPG), with the exception of France. Both the DPC and the NPG also meet at ministerial level at least twice a year. The NATO secretary-general chairs the council, the DPC and the NPG. Much of the NAC policy is prepared and drafted by the senior political committee, a group of deputy permanent representatives and policy advisers.

The senior military authority in NATO, which advises the council and DPC, is the military committee, composed of the chief of defence staffs of each member country except Iceland, which has no military forces and is represented by a civilian. The military committee, which is assisted by an integrated international military staff, also meets in permanent session with permanent military representatives and is responsible for making recommendations to the council and DPC on measures considered necessary for the common defence of the NATO area and for supplying guidance on military matters to the NATO strategic commanders. The chair of the military committee, elected for a period of two to three years, represents the committee on the council.

The alliance's military command structure is divided between two functional strategic commands: Allied Command Operations (ACO) is responsible for all NATO military operations, whereas Allied Command Transformation (ACT) is charged with training and restructuring NATO military forces and capabilities. The headquarters of ACO is at the Supreme Headquarters of the Allied Powers Europe (SHAPE) at Mons, Belgium, and comes under the command of the Supreme Allied Commander Europe (SACEUR). The headquarters of ACT is at Norfolk, Virginia, USA, and is under the command of the Supreme Allied Commander, Transformation (SACT). There is also a regional planning group for Canada and the USA. At the Lisbon summit in November 2010, NATO leaders approved a plan to streamline the ACO while maintaining its military capability; the plans will result in a reduction of personnel within the military command structure from 13,000 to 8,950.

POST COLD WAR DEVELOPMENTS

The Euro-Atlantic partnership council (EAPC) was established in 1997 to develop closer security links with Eastern European and former Soviet states. Replacing the North Atlantic cooperation council (NACC) as the first institutional framework for cooperation between NATO member countries and former adversaries from Central and Eastern Europe, the EAPC focuses on defence planning, defence industry conversion, defence management and force structuring. Its membership comprises the 28 NATO members and Armenia, Austria, Azerbaijan, Belarus, Bosnia and Hercegovina, Finland, Georgia, Ireland, Kazakhstan, Kyrgyzstan, Macedonia, Malta, Moldova, Montenegro, Russia, Serbia, Sweden, Switzerland, Tajikistan, Turkmenistan, Ukraine and Uzbekistan. The EAPC provides the multilateral, political framework for the partnership for peace programme (PFP). The PFP is the basis for practical, bilateral security cooperation between NATO and all partner countries in the fields of defence planning and budgeting, military exercises and civil emergency operations. It also works to improve the interoperability between the forces of partner and member countries to enable them to undertake joint operations and has provided the context for cooperation by many of the partner countries in NATO-led peacekeeping and peace-support operations in Bosnia and Hercegovina, Kosovo and Afghanistan.

NATO and Russia committed themselves to helping build a stable, secure and undivided continent on the basis of partnership and mutual interest when they signed the 1997 Founding Act on mutual relations, cooperation and security, which provided for the creation of a NATO-Russia permanent joint council (PJC). In 2002 it was replaced by the NATO-Russia council (NRC). The NRC usually meets every month at ambassadorial level and twice each year at ministerial level to address issues of joint concern such as terrorist threats and the narcotics trade, and to pursue bilateral programmes in defence reform, search and rescue, and civil emergency planning. NATO suspended formal NRC meetings, and cooperation in many areas, in response to Russia's military action in Georgia in August 2008, and its subsequent recognition of South Ossetia and Abkhazia as independent states. Although the two sides resumed normal relations in April 2009, the status of these areas remains in dispute.

The establishment of the NATO-Ukraine commission (NUC) in 1997 committed both parties to developing their relationship under a programme of consultation and cooperation on political and security issues. The NUC meets at least twice a year. The NATO-Georgia commission (NGC), created in 2008, is pursuing political dialogue between NATO and Georgia, and helping to supervise Georgia's progress towards membership of

NATO. The NGC is also co-ordinating support to help the country recover from the summer 2008 conflict.

NATO's Mediterranean dialogue, launched in 1994, aims to improve trust and understanding of NATO's goals and objectives among the countries of the southern Mediterranean area: Algeria, Egypt, Israel, Jordan, Mauritania, Morocco and Tunisia. At its summit meeting in 2004, the alliance launched the Istanbul cooperation initiative (ICI), promoting practical cooperation with the Gulf cooperation council (GCC) and other interested countries in the Middle East. To date Bahrain, Qatar, Kuwait and the United Arab Emirates have joined the ICI.

The development of a European security and defence identity, which would strengthen NATO's European pillar, was agreed at the 1999 NATO summit meeting in Washington. Subsequent developments have served to strengthen cooperation between NATO and the European Union and to establish a strategic partnership.

At the 2002 Prague summit, further measures to improve defence capabilities were taken on the basis of a new capabilities commitment, in which member countries agreed to specific targets and time frames for improvements. A military concept for defence against terrorism was also agreed, and additional initiatives taken in the areas of nuclear, biological and chemical weapons defence, and protection against cyber attacks. The NATO response force, a rapid-reaction unit comprising land, sea and air special forces, was officially launched at the Prague summit and became fully operational in 2006. The Lisbon summit in 2010 saw the publication of NATO's strategic concept, a statement of core principles that emphasized the importance of international cooperation in defence, security and crisis management, with particular reference to strengthening NATO's relationships with the EU and UN. Cyber attacks, terrorism and nuclear proliferation were among the current threats considered most immediate, and the document asserted the continuing importance of both nuclear and conventional weapons as a core element of the organisation's defence and deterrence policy.

AFGHANISTAN
From January 2001, following the establishment of the Afghan Transitional Authority, an international security assistance force (ISAF) was created on the basis of a UN mandate to provide the security required to allow infrastructure reconstruction and create a stable democratic government. In 2002, NATO began providing support for ISAF at the request of the lead nations and, in August 2003, assumed full responsibility for the leadership of ISAF. In accordance with an October 2003 UN security council mandate, ISAF gradually extended its authority from the capital, Kabul, to assume responsibility for the security, reconstruction and development of the entire country in October 2006. ISAF is responsible for provincial reconstruction teams, which provide security for aid workers and help with reconstruction work across the country; it also provides training and mentoring for the Afghan National Army and support for the Afghan National Police. In March 2011 there were 132,203 ISAF troops serving in Afghanistan from 48 NATO and non-NATO countries.

IRAQ
Following a summit meeting in Istanbul in 2004, NATO agreed to establish an Iraq training mission. This included the foundation of a joint staff college, tasked with the training of mid- to senior-level Iraqi military officers,

which opened at Ar-Rustamiyah, near Baghdad, in September 2005. In 2007, NATO also initiated a programme of Gendarmerie-type training for the Iraqi police, and introduced further training schemes for the navy, airforce and other areas of national security in December 2008; training for Iraqi customs and border police was introduced in 2010.

AFRICA
NATO counter-piracy operations were active between October and December 2008, and again between March and July 2009, in response to the growing threat presented by piracy in the Horn of Africa region. Currently, Operation Ocean Shield – approved by the North Atlantic council in August 2009 – is focused on at-sea operations, but also offers assistance to regional states in developing their capacity to combat piracy.

Following the popular uprising in Benghazi in February 2011, NATO took on military operations in Libya under UN security council resolution 1973. The purpose of NATO's involvement was primarily to protect civilians from attack, and included deploying surveillance aircraft and ships; enforcing a national arms embargo and no-fly-zone; freezing the assets of Libyan leaders; and imposing a travel ban on all senior government figures.

Secretary-General and Chair of the North Atlantic Council, of the DPC and of the NPG, Anders Fogh Rasmussen (Denmark)

ORGANISATION FOR ECONOMIC COOPERATION AND DEVELOPMENT
2 rue André-Pascal, F-75775 Paris, France
T (+33) (1) 4524 8200 E webmaster@oecd.org
W www.oecd.org

The Organisation for Economic Cooperation and Development (OECD) was formed in 1961 to replace the Organisation for European Economic Cooperation. It is the instrument for international cooperation among industrialised member countries on economic and social policies. Its objectives are to assist its member governments in creating policies designed to achieve high, sustained economic growth and maintain financial stability, to contribute to world trade on a multilateral basis and to stimulate members' aid to developing countries. OECD has 34 members, most of which have developed, high-income economies. The European Commission is involved in the work of the OECD but is not a member of the organisation.

The council is the supreme body of the organisation. It is composed of one representative for each member country and meets at permanent representative level under the chairmanship of the secretary-general, and at ministerial level (usually once a year) under the chair of a minister, elected annually. Decisions and recommendations are adopted by unanimous agreement. Most of the OECD's work is undertaken by around 250 specialised committees and working parties. These are serviced by an international secretariat headed by a secretary-general.

In 2010 Chile, Estonia, Israel and Slovenia acceded to the OECD. As at April 2011, accession negotiations with the Russian Federation were ongoing, with a meeting between the OECD and Russian delegates scheduled for 2012. The organisation has links to many other non-member states and in 2007 launched a programme of enhanced engagement with Brazil, China, India, Indonesia and South Africa. The funding of the OECD is divided according to a member state's economy and population size; the USA, the largest contributor, supplies almost 24 per cent of the organisation's budget.

Secretary-General, Angel Gurría (Mexico)

ORGANISATION FOR SECURITY AND COOPERATION IN EUROPE

6 Wallnerstrasse, 1010 Vienna, Austria
T (+43) (1) 51436 6000 E info@osce.org W www.osce.org

The Organisation for Security and Cooperation in Europe (OSCE) was launched in 1975 as the Conference on Security and Cooperation in Europe (CSCE) under the Helsinki Final Act. This established agreements between NATO members, Warsaw Pact members, and neutral and non-aligned European countries covering security, cooperation and human rights. It was renamed in 1995.

The Charter of Paris for a New Europe, signed in November 1990, committed members to support multiparty democracy, free-market economics, the rule of law and human rights. The signatories also agreed to regular meetings of heads of government, ministers and officials. The first CSCE summit was held in Helsinki in July 1992, at which the Helsinki Document was adopted. This declared the CSCE to be a regional organisation under the UN charter and defined the structures of the organisation.

Three structures have been established: the ministerial council, which comprises the foreign ministers of participating states and meets at least once a year; the permanent council, which is the main regular body for political consulation, meeting weekly in Vienna; and the forum for security cooperation, also meeting weekly. The chairmanship of the OSCE rotates annually and the post of chair-in-office is held by the foreign minister of a participating state.

The OSCE is also underpinned by four permanent institutions: a secretariat (Vienna); an office for democratic institutions and human rights (Warsaw), which is charged with furthering human rights, democracy and the rule of law; an office of the high commissioner on national minorities (The Hague), which identifies ethnic tensions that might endanger peace and promotes their resolution; and a representative on freedom of the media (Vienna), which is responsible for assisting governments in the furthering of free, independent and pluralistic media.

The OSCE has 17 field operations in Europe, the Caucasus and Central Asia. Since 1996, the OSCE has observed more than 150 elections and supervised all elections in Bosnia and Hercegovina between 1996 and 2000 and in Kosovo between 2000 and 2004. In 1999, the charter on European security committed the OSCE to cooperating with other organisations and institutions concerned with the promotion of security within the OSCE area. The OSCE has 56 participating states and in 2011 its budget was €150.8m (£132.3m).

Chair, Lithuania (2011)
Chair-in-office, Audronius Azubalis (Lithuania)

ORGANISATION OF AMERICAN STATES

17th Street and Constitution Avenue, NW, Washington DC 20006, USA
T (+1) (202) 458 3000 W www.oas.org

Originally founded in 1890 for largely commercial purposes, the Organisation of American States (OAS) adopted its present name and charter in 1948. The charter entered into force in 1951 and was amended in 1970, 1988, 1996 and 1997. OAS has 35 member states, though the membership of Honduras was suspended in July 2009 following a coup against President Jose Zelaya. The European Union and 64 non-American states have permanent observer status.

The OAS aims to strengthen the peace and security of the Americas; to promote and consolidate representative democracy; to prevent or resolve any political, judicial or economic issues which may arise among member states; to promote their economic, social and cultural development; and to achieve an effective limitation of conventional weapons.

Policy is determined by the annual general assembly, the organisation's supreme authority, which elects the secretary-general for a five-year term. The meeting of consultation of ministers of foreign affairs considers urgent problems on an *ad hoc* basis. The permanent council, comprising one ambassador from each member state, implements the policies approved by the general assembly, acts as an intermediary in cases of disputes arising between states and oversees the general secretariat, the main administrative body. The inter-American council for integral development was created in 1996 by the ratification of the protocol of Managua to promote sustainable development and eliminate poverty.

Secretary-General, José Miguel Insulza (Chile)

ORGANISATION OF ARAB PETROLEUM EXPORTING COUNTRIES

PO Box 20501, Safat 13066, Kuwait
T (+965) 2495 9000 E oapec@oapecorg.org
W www.oapecorg.org

The Organisation of Arab Petroleum Exporting Countries (OAPEC) was founded in 1968. Its objectives are to promote cooperation in economic activities, unite efforts to ensure the flow of oil to consumer markets, and create a favourable climate for capital investment and the development of the petroleum industry. OAPEC has 11 member states, although Tunisia's membership has been inactive since 1987.

The ministerial council is composed of oil ministers from the member countries and meets twice a year to determine policy and approve the budgets and accounts of the general secretariat and the judicial tribunal. The judicial tribunal is composed of between seven and 11 judges who rule on disputes between member countries and between countries and oil companies. The executive organ of OAPEC is the general secretariat.

The active members are Algeria, Bahrain, Egypt, Iraq, Kuwait, Libya, Qatar, Saudi Arabia, Syria and the United Arab Emirates.

Secretary-General, Abbas Ali Naqi (Kuwait)

ORGANISATION OF THE BLACK SEA ECONOMIC COOPERATION

Sakip Sabanci Caddesi, Musir Fuad Pasa Yalisi, Eski Tersane, 34467 Istanbul, Turkey
T (+90) (212) 229 6330/6335 E info@bsec-organization.org
W www.bsec-organization.org

The Black Sea Economic Cooperation (BSEC) resulted from the Istanbul Summit Declaration and the adoption of the Bosphorus statement on 25 June 1992; it acquired a permanent secretariat in 1994. A charter was inaugurated to found the Organisation of the Black Sea Economic Cooperation in May 1999 following the Yalta Summit of the heads of state or government in June 1998. It has 12 member states.

The organisation aims to promote closer political and economic cooperation between the countries in the Black Sea region and to foster greater security, foreign investment, and good governance.

The council of the ministers of foreign affairs is the highest decision-making authority; it elects the organisation's secretary-general and meets twice-yearly. The meetings rotate among the member states and the chair is the foreign minister of the state in which the meeting is held. There is also a committee of senior officials, and a number of working groups which deal with specific areas of cooperation. BSEC has a permanent secretariat based in Istanbul.

Secretary-General, Leonidas Chrysanthopoulos (Greece)

ORGANISATION OF THE ISLAMIC CONFERENCE
PO Box 178, Jeddah 21411, Saudi Arabia
T (+966) (2) 651 5222 W www.oic-oci.org

The Organisation of the Islamic Conference (OIC) was established in 1969 with the purpose of promoting solidarity and cooperation between its member states. It also has the specific aims of supporting the formation of a Palestinian state, coordinating the views of member states in international forums such as the UN, and improving cooperation in the fields of economics, culture and science.

The OIC has three main bodies: the Islamic summit, the organisation's supreme authority composed of the heads of member states, which meets triennially; the annual conference of foreign ministers; and the general secretariat, which implements policy and is headed by a secretary-general elected by the conference of foreign ministers for a once-renewable five-year term.

In addition to this structure, the OIC has several subsidiary bodies, institutions, and standing committees. These include the international Islamic court of justice; the Islamic Solidarity Fund, to aid Islamic institutions in member countries; the Islamic Development Bank, to finance development projects in member states and the Islamic Educational, Scientific and Cultural Organisation.

Since 1991, the OIC has spoken out in protest of violence against Muslims in India, the Occupied Territories and Bosnia-Hercegovina. From 1993 to 1995 the OIC coordinated the offering of troops to the UN by Muslim states to protect Muslim areas of Bosnia-Hercegovina.

The organisation has 57 members (27 states in Africa; 24 in the Middle East, central and south-east Asia plus the Palestinian Authority; three in Europe, and two in South America) and five observer states.

Secretary-General, Prof. Ekmeleddin Ihsanoglu (Turkey)

ORGANISATION OF THE PETROLEUM EXPORTING COUNTRIES
Helferstorferstrasse 17, A-1010 Vienna, Austria
T (+43) (1) 2111 20 W www.opec.org

The Organisation of the Petroleum Exporting Countries (OPEC) was created in 1960 as a permanent intergovernmental organisation with the principal aims of unifying and coordinating the petroleum policies of its members, and stabilising prices and supply in international oil markets. Since 1982 OPEC has attempted, with mixed success, to impose overall production limits and production quotas to maintain stable oil prices.

The supreme authority is the conference of ministers of oil, mining and energy of member countries, which meets at least twice a year. The board of governors, nominated by member countries, directs the management of OPEC and implements conference resolutions. The secretariat carries out executive functions under the direction of the board of governors.

According to BP's annual statistical review, OPEC's 12 member countries held 77.2 per cent of the world's oil reserves at the end of 2009, and that year accounted for 41.2 per cent of the world's oil production. Indonesia suspended its membership of OPEC from January 2009, after declining production caused it to become a net importer of oil.

Secretary-General, Abdalla Salem El-Badri (Libya)

PACIFIC ISLANDS FORUM
Secretariat, Private Mail Bag, Suva, Fiji
T (+679) 331 2600 E info@forumsec.org.fj
W www.forumsec.org

The Pacific Islands Forum (PIF), formerly the South Pacific Forum, was established in 1971 and represents heads of governments of 16 independent and self-governing Pacific island countries. It aims to foster cooperation between its governments and to represent the interests of the region in international organisations. The PIF meets annually, after which a dialogue is conducted at ministerial level with 13 forum partner states and the European Union.

The PIF secretariat is governed by the forum officials committee (FOC), composed of senior figures from each member country. It comprises divisions dealing with development and economic policy, trade and investment, political and international affairs and services, and is responsible for implementing the forum's decisions.

In 2006, French Polynesia and New Caledonia became associate members. Tokelau, Wallis and Futuna, the Commonwealth, the Asia Development Bank, the United Nations and the World Bank currently hold observer status, with Timor–Leste as a special observer. Fiji's membership was suspended in May 2009 over the failure of its military government to commit to a timeframe for a return to democratic government.

Secretary-General, Gregory Tuiloma Neroni Slade (Samoa)

PARTNERS IN POPULATION AND DEVELOPMENT
IPH Building, Mohakhali, Dhaka-1212, Bangladesh
T (+88) (2) 988 1882 E partners@popdev.org
W www.partners-popdev.org

Partners in Population and Development (PPD) is an intergovernmental organisation launched at the UN International Conference on Population and Development in Cairo in 1994. It has 25 member states. PPD is dedicated to forming partnerships between and among individuals, organisations and the governments of developing countries. It provides a platform for its members to share successful experiences in education, migration, sexual health and combating infant mortality.

PPD is controlled by a board of directors consisting of ministers or other high-ranking officials in the field of population and development from member countries.. The responsibilities of the board include setting policy, promoting cooperation among members and providing advice to the secretariat. The secretariat is based in Dhaka, Bangladesh, and is mandated to serve as the administrative centre of the organisation. It ensures policies are implemented and identifies new areas for collaboration. PPD also has an international advisory committee consisting of specialists who advise the board and secretariat on current trends in population, development and reproductive health.

PPD is a permanent observer at the United Nations.

Chair, HE Ghulam Nabi Azad (India)

SECRETARIAT OF THE PACIFIC COMMUNITY

BP D5, Nouméa Cedex, 98848, New Caledonia
T (+687) 262 000 E spc@spc.int W www.spc.int

The Secretariat of the Pacific Community (SPC) (formerly the South Pacific Commission) was established in 1947 by Australia, France, the Netherlands, New Zealand, the UK and the USA with the aim of promoting the economic and social stability of the islands in the region. The community now numbers 26 member states and territories: the four remaining founder states (the Netherlands and the UK have withdrawn) and the other 22 states and territories of Melanesia, Micronesia and Polynesia.

The SPC is a technical assistance agency with programmes in marine and land development and health and social policy. The governing body is the conference of the Pacific community, which meets every two years.

Director-General, Dr Jimmie Rodgers (Solomon Islands)

SHANGHAI COOPERATION ORGANISATION

41 Liangmaqiao Road, Chaoyang District, 100600 Beijing, China
T (+86) (10) 6532 9807 E sco@sectsco.org W www.sectsco.org

The Shanghai Cooperation Organisation (SCO) is a permanent intergovernmental organisation. It was established in 1996 as the Shanghai Five, when China, Kazakhstan, Kyrgyzstan, Russia and Tajikistan signed an agreement on cooperating to resolve disputes along the former Sino-Soviet border. It was renamed in 2001 when Uzbekistan became an official member.

The main principle of the SCO is strengthening cooperation among member states across a range of fields, including politics, economics, science, culture, energy, transport, environmental protection and tourism.

The heads of state council is the organisation's supreme body and meets annually to formulate SCO policy. The heads of government council also holds annual meetings to discuss cooperation strategies and approve budgets. The SCO has two permanent bodies: a secretariat based in Beijing and a regional anti-terrorist structure in Tashkent. The secretary-general and the director of the executive committee are appointed by the council of heads of state for a period of three years.

Secretary-General, Muratbek Imanaliev (Kyrgyzstan)

SOUTH ASIAN ASSOCIATION FOR REGIONAL COOPERATION

PO Box 4222, Tridevi Marg, Kathmandu, Nepal
T (+977) (1) 422 1785/ 6350 E saarc@saarc-sec.org
W www.saarc-sec.org

The South Asian Association for Regional Cooperation (SAARC) was established in 1985 by Bangladesh, Bhutan, India, the Maldives, Nepal, Pakistan and Sri Lanka; Afghanistan was admitted as its eighth member in 2007. Its primary objective is the acceleration of economic and social development in member states through collective action in agreed areas of cooperation.

These include agricultural development, climate change, science and technology, health, education and communications.

A SAARC preferential trading arrangement, designed to reduce tariffs on trade between SAARC member states, was signed in 1993 and entered into force in 1995. The South Asian free trade area (SAFTA) was agreed in 2004, and came into effect in 2006, with the aim of abolishing practically all trade tarriffs by the end of 2016. The Convention on Cooperation on the Environment and an Agreement on Trade in Services were signed at the sixteenth SAARC summit in 2010, the theme for which was climate change.

The highest authority rests with the heads of state or government of each member state. The council of ministers, which meets twice a year, is made up of the foreign ministers of the member states and is responsible for formulating policy. The standing committee is composed of the foreign secretaries of the member states and monitors and coordinates SAARC programmes; it meets twice a year. Technical committees are assigned to individual areas of SAARC's activities. Its secretariat monitors, facilitates and promotes SAARC's activities and serves as a channel of communication between the association and other regional and intergovernmental institutions.

In 2005, as the only country in South Asia not to be a member of SAARC, Iran declared its wish to join and has since become an observer member, along with seven other states and the European Union.

Secretary-General, HE Fathimath Dhiyana Saeed (Maldives)

SOUTHERN AFRICAN DEVELOPMENT COMMUNITY

Private Bag 0095, Gaborone, Botswana
T (+267) 395 1863 E registry@sadc.int W www.sadc.int

The Southern African Development Community (SADC) was formed in 1992 by the members of its predecessor, the Southern African Development Coordination Conference. The latter was founded in 1980 to harmonise economic development among southern Africa's 'majority ruled' countries and reduce their dependence on then apartheid South Africa. The SADC now comprises 15 countries, including South Africa, though Madagascar's membership remains suspended following a coup in March 2009.

The SADC aims to evolve common political values, promote economic growth, regional security, sustainable development and the interdependence of member states. An annual summit attended by members' heads of state is the SADC's supreme authority, and its policies are implemented by a secretariat.

Executive Secretary, Tomaz Augusto Salomao (Mozambique)

UNITED NATIONS

UN Plaza, New York, NY 10017, USA
T (+1) (212) 963 1234 W www.un.org

The United Nations (UN) is an intergovernmental organisation dedicated, through signature of the UN charter, to the maintenance of international peace and security and the solution of economic, social and political problems through international cooperation.

The UN was founded as a successor to the League of Nations and inherited many of its procedures and institutions. The name United Nations was first used in the Washington Declaration of 1942 to describe the 26 states that had allied to fight the Axis powers. The UN charter developed from discussions at the Moscow conference of the foreign ministers of China, the Soviet Union, the UK and the USA in 1943. Further progress was made at Dumbarton Oaks, Washington, in 1944 during talks involving the same states. The role of the security council was formulated at the Yalta conference in 1945. The charter was formally drawn up by 50 allied nations at the San Francisco conference between April and June 1945, when it was signed. Following ratification, the UN came into effect on 24 October 1945, which is celebrated annually as United Nations Day. The UN flag is light blue with the UN emblem centred in white.

The principal organs of the UN are the general assembly, the security council, the economic and social council, the secretariat and the international court of justice. The economic and social council is an auxiliary, charged with assisting and advising the general assembly, security council and member states, and coordinating the economic and social aspects of the work of UN agencies and commissions. The official languages used are Arabic, Chinese, English, French, Russian and Spanish; the working languages of the secretariat and the international court of justice are English and French.

MEMBERSHIP
Membership is open to all countries that accept the charter and its principle of peaceful co-existence. New members are admitted by the general assembly on the recommendation of the security council. The original membership of 51 states has grown to 192 (see below).

Members of the UN

Afghanistan	Dominican Republic*	Lesotho	St Lucia
Albania	East Timor	Liberia*	St Vincent and the
Algeria	Ecuador*	Libya	Grenadines
Andorra	Egypt*	Liechtenstein	Samoa
Angola	El Salvador*	Lithuania	San Marino
Antigua and Barbuda	Equatorial Guinea	Luxembourg*	Sao Tom and Principe
Argentina*	Eritrea	Madagascar	Saudi Arabia*
Armenia	Estonia	Malawi	Senegal
Australia*	Ethiopia*	Malaysia	Serbia
Austria	Fiji	Maldives	Seychelles
Azerbaijan	Finland	Mali	Sierra Leone
Bahamas	France*	Malta	Singapore
Bahrain	FYR Macedonia	Marshall Islands	Slovakia
Bangladesh	Gabon	Mauritania	Slovenia
Barbados	The Gambia	Mauritius	Solomon Islands
Belarus*	Georgia	Mexico*	Somalia
Belgium*	Germany	Micronesia, Federated	South Africa*
Belize	Ghana	States of	Spain
Benin	Greece*	Moldova	Sri Lanka
Bhutan	Grenada	Monaco	Sudan
Bolivia*	Guatemala*	Mongolia	Suriname
Bosnia and Hercegovina	Guinea	Montenegro	Swaziland
Botswana	Guinea-Bissau	Morocco	Sweden
Brazil*	Guyana	Mozambique	Switzerland
Brunei	Haiti*	Myanmar	Syria*
Bulgaria	Honduras*	Namibia	Tajikistan
Burkina Faso	Hungary	Nauru	Tanzania
Burundi	Iceland	Nepal	Thailand
Cambodia	India*	The Netherlands*	Togo
Cameroon	Indonesia	New Zealand*	Tonga
Canada*	Iran*	Nicaragua*	Trinidad and Tobago
Cape Verde	Iraq*	Niger	Tunisia
Central African Republic	Ireland	Nigeria	Turkey*
Chad	Israel	Norway*	Turkmenistan
Chile*	Italy	Oman	Tuvalu
China*	Jamaica	Pakistan	Uganda
Colombia*	Japan	Palau	Ukraine*
Comoros	Jordan	Panama*	United Arab Emirates
Congo, Dem. Rep of the	Kazakhstan	Papua New Guinea	United Kingdom*
Congo, Republic of the	Kenya	Paraguay*	United States of America*
Costa Rica*	Kiribati	Peru*	Uruguay*
Côte d'Ivoire	Korea, Dem. People's Rep.	The Philippines*	Uzbekistan
Croatia	of	Poland*	Vanuatu
Cuba*	Korea, Rep. of	Portugal*	Venezuela*
Cyprus	Kuwait	Qatar	Vietnam
Czech Republic	Kyrgyzstan	Romania	Yemen
Denmark*	Laos	Russian Federation*	Zambia
Djibouti	Latvia	Rwanda	Zimbabwe
Dominica	Lebanon*	St Kitts and Nevis	

* Original member (ie from 1945). Czechoslovakia, Yugoslavia and the USSR were all original members until their dissolution.

OBSERVERS

Permanent observer status is held by the Holy See. The Palestinian Authority has special observer status.

THE GENERAL ASSEMBLY

UN Plaza, New York, NY 10017, USA

The general assembly is the main deliberative organ of the UN. It consists of all members, each entitled to five representatives but having only one vote. The annual session begins on the third Tuesday of September, when the president is elected, and usually continues until mid-December. Special sessions are held on specific issues and emergency special sessions can be called within 24 hours.

The assembly is empowered to discuss any matter within the scope of the charter – except when it is under consideration by the security council – and to make recommendations. Under the peace resolution, adopted in 1950, the assembly may also take action to maintain international peace and security when the security council fails to do so because of a lack of unanimity of its permanent members. Important decisions (such as those on peace and security, the election of officers, the budget, etc) need a two-thirds majority. Others need a simple majority. The assembly has effective power only over the internal operations of the UN itself; external recommendations are not legally binding.

The work of the general assembly is divided among a number of committees, on each of which every member has the right to be represented. Subjects include human rights, the use of torture, peacekeeping, assistance to developing countries and discrimination. In addition, the general assembly appoints *ad hoc* committees to consider more specific issues. All committees consider items referred to them by the assembly and recommend draft resolutions to its plenary meeting.

The assembly is assisted by a number of functional committees. The general committee coordinates its proceedings and operations, while the credentials committee verifies the representatives.

President of the General Assembly, Joseph Deiss (Switzerland)

SPECIALISED BODIES

The assembly has created a large number of specialised bodies, some of which are supervised jointly with the economic and social council. They are supported by UN and voluntary contributions from governments, non-governmental organisations and individuals. These organisations include:

CONFERENCE ON DISARMAMENT

Palais des Nations, CH-1211 Geneva 10, Switzerland

The Conference on Disarmament (CD) was established in 1979 as the international community's multilateral disarmament negotiating forum. Originally comprising 40 member states, the CD has expanded to 65 members. The non-proliferation of nuclear weapons treaty entered into force on 5 March 1970 and has so far been ratified by 190 states. A chemical weapons convention was agreed in Paris in 1993 and came into force in April 1997 after being ratified by 87 countries. Currently 135 states participate in the convention, which bans the use, production, stockpiling and transfer of all chemical weapons. A convention prohibiting the use of cluster munitions, agreed in Dublin in 2008 and currently ratified by 57 states, entered into force on 1 August 2010.

UNITED NATIONS CHILDREN'S FUND (UNICEF)

3 UN Plaza, New York, NY 10017, USA **T** (+1) 212 326 7000 **W** www.unicef.org

Established in 1946 to assist children and mothers in the immediate post-war period, UNICEF now concentrates on developing countries. It provides primary healthcare and health education, and conducts programmes in oral hydration, immunisation against common diseases, HIV/AIDS treatment and prevention and child growth monitoring. It also works to provide children with equal access to quality education.

UNITED NATIONS DEVELOPMENT PROGRAMME (UNDP)

1 UN Plaza, New York, NY 10017, USA **T** (+1) 212 906 5000 **W** www.undp.org

Established in 1965 from the merger of the UN expanded programme of technical assistance and the UN special fund, UNDP is the central funding agency for economic and social development projects around the world. Much of its annual expenditure is channelled through UN specialised agencies, governments and non-governmental organisations.

UNITED NATIONS HIGH COMMISSIONER FOR REFUGEES (UNHCR)

Case Postale 2500, CH-1211 Geneva 2 Depot, Switzerland **T** (+41) 22 739 8111 **W** www.unhcr.org

Established in 1950 to protect the rights and interests of refugees, UNHCR organises emergency relief and longer-term solutions, such as voluntary repatriation, local integration or resettlement.

UNITED NATIONS RELIEF AND WORKS AGENCY FOR PALESTINE REFUGEES IN THE NEAR EAST (UNRWA)

HQ Gaza, PO Box 61, Gaza City **T** (+972) 8 288 7333 **W** www.unrwa.org

The UNRWA was established in 1949 to bring relief to the Palestinians displaced by the Arab-Israeli conflict. The UN general assembly has repeatedly voted every three years to extend its mandate, most recently until June 2014.

UNITED NATIONS HUMAN RIGHTS COUNCIL (UNHRC)

Palais des Nations, CH-1211 Geneva 10, Switzerland **T** (+22) 917 9000 **E** infodesk@ohchr.org **W** www.ohchr.org

The UNHRC is a 47-member council, established in 2006, replacing the United Nations Commission on Human Rights (UNCHR). The UNHRC has a mandate to promote (and prevent violations of) human rights by engaging in dialogue with governments and international organisations. It is also responsible for the coordination of all UN human rights activities and reports to, and is directly elected by, the general assembly.

THE SECURITY COUNCIL

UN Plaza, New York, NY 10017, USA **T** (+41) (22) 917 9000 **W** www.un.org/docs/sc

The security council is the senior arm of the UN and has the primary responsibility for maintaining world peace and security. It consists of 15 members, each with one representative and one vote. There are five permanent members – China, France, Russia, the UK and the USA – and ten non-permanent members. Each of the non-permanent members is elected for a two-year term by a two-thirds majority of the general assembly and is ineligible for immediate re-election. Five of the elective seats are allocated to Africa and Asia, one to eastern Europe, two to Latin America and two to western Europe and remaining countries. Decisions on procedural matters require affirmative votes from at least nine of the 15 members. Other matters require the same, but must include the affirmative votes of the permanent members; they thus have a right of veto. The abstention of a permanent member does not constitute a veto. The presidency rotates each month by state in (English) alphabetical order. Parties in a dispute, other non-members and individuals can be invited to participate in security council debates but are not permitted to vote.

The security council is empowered to settle or adjudicate in disputes or situations which threaten international peace and security. It can adopt political, economic and military measures to achieve this end. Any matter considered to be a threat to or breach of the peace or an act of aggression can be brought to the security council's attention by any member state or by the secretary-general. The charter envisaged members placing at the disposal of the security council armed forces and other facilities which would be coordinated by the military staff committee, composed of military representatives of the five permanent members. The security council is also supported by a committee of experts, to advise on procedural and technical matters, and a committee on admission of new members.

Owing to superpower disunity, the security council has rarely played the decisive role set out in the charter; the military staff committee was effectively suspended from 1948 until 1990, when a meeting was convened during the Gulf crisis on the formation and control of UN-supervised armed forces. In 1992, heads of government laid plans to transform the UN in light of the changed post-Cold War world. The secretary-general produced *An Agenda for Peace*, a report which centred on the establishment of a UN army composed of national contingents on permanent standby, as envisaged at the time of the UN's formation. However, enthusiasm for UN intervention waned during the rest of the decade after a problematic mission in Somalia during which 42 UN personnel were killed. The security council has since been criticised for its failure to intervene in subsequent conflicts, including the genocide in Rwanda and the ongoing situation in Darfur. More recently it has applied sanctions to Iran, North Korea, the Pakistani militant group Lashkar-e-Taiba, and figures within Libya and the Côte d'Ivoire.

The security council also has the power to elect judges to the international court of justice and to recommend to the general assembly the election of a secretary-general.

PEACEKEEPING FORCES

The security council has established a number of peacekeeping forces since its foundation, comprising contingents provided mainly by neutral and non-aligned UN members. As at 31 March 2011, current operations were:

Continent	UN Code	Year implemented	Personnel deployed
Africa			
Western Sahara	MINURSO	1991	233
Democratic Republic of the Congo	MONUSCO (formerly MONUC)	1999	19,173
Liberia	UNMIL	2003	9,221
Côte d'Ivoire	UNOCI	2004	9,077
Sudan	UNMIS	2005	10,445
Darfur, Sudan	UNAMID	2007	23,026
The Americas			
Haiti	MINUSTAH	2004	12,318
Asia			
India and Pakistan	UNMOGIP	1949	44
Timor–Leste	UNMIT	2006	1,397
Europe			
Cyprus	UNFICYP	1964	922
Kosovo	UNMIK	1999	16
Middle East			
Egypt, Israel, Jordan, Lebanon and Syria	UNTSO	1948	152
Israel and Syria	UNDOF	1978	1,047
Lebanon	UNIFIL	1974	11,888

TOP FIVE CONTRIBUTORS TO UN PEACEKEEPING MISSIONS (*as at* February 2011)	
Country	Number of Troops
Pakistan	10,621
Bangladesh	10,450
India	8,665
Nigeria	5,860
Egypt	5,395

Source: www.un.org/en/peacekeeping/

INTERNATIONAL CRIMINAL TRIBUNAL FOR THE FORMER YUGOSLAVIA

Churchillplein 1, 2517 JW The Hague, The Netherlands
T (+31) 7051 28752 W www.icty.org

In February 1993, the security council voted to establish the International Criminal Tribunal for the Former Yugoslavia (ICTY) a war crimes tribunal to hear cases covering breaches of the Geneva Conventions and crimes against humanity during the Balkans conflict of the 1990s. The court was inaugurated in November 1993 in The Hague with 11 judges elected by the UN general assembly from 11 states. There are currently 16 permanent judges, divided into three trial chambers of three judges each and an appeal chamber of the remaining seven. As well as running and managing a detention unit based at The Hague and a witness protection and assistance programme, the ICTY also has powers to interview witnesses and seize evidence. The total biannual budget for 2010–11 is US$279.8m (£171.7m). Over 1,100 staff representing around 80 nations are currently employed by the tribunal. In December 2010 the UN security council approved the creation of the International Residual Mechanism for Criminal Tribunals (IRMCT), which will oversee the completion of the ICTY and ICTR (*see* below) by December 2014. The IRMCT will take over the functions of the ICTY on 1 July 2013 with a reduced staff and budget, and will not be able to raise new indictments.

President, Patrick L. Robinson (Jamaica)

INTERNATIONAL CRIMINAL TRIBUNAL FOR RWANDA
Churchillplein 1, 2517 JW The Hague, The Netherlands
T (+31) 7051 25027 **E** ictr-press@un.org **W** www.ictr.org

Following serious violations of humanitarian law in Rwanda, the UN security council created the International Criminal Tribunal for Rwanda on 8 November 1994 in order to contribute to the process of national reconciliation and the maintenance of peace in the region. Its remit is to prosecute persons responsible for genocide and other serious international humanitarian law violations committed in the territory of Rwanda between 1 January 1994 and 31 December 1994, and by Rwandan citizens in the territory of neighbouring states during the same period. The biannual budget for 2010–11 is US$245.3m (£158.2m). The IRMCT (*see* above) will take over the functions of the ICTR on 1 July 2012 with a reduced staff and budget, and will not be able to raise new indictments.
President, Judge Charles Michael Dennis Byron (St Kitts and Nevis)

THE ECONOMIC AND SOCIAL COUNCIL
UN Plaza, New York, NY 10017, USA
E ecosocinfo@un.org **W** www.un.org/ecosoc

The economic and social council is responsible under the general assembly for the economic and social work of the UN and for the coordination of the activities of the 14 specialised agencies and other UN bodies. It makes reports and recommendations on economic, social, cultural, educational, health and related matters, often in consultation with non-governmental organisations, passing the reports to the general assembly and other UN bodies. It also drafts conventions for submission to the assembly and calls conferences on matters within its remit.

The council consists of 54 members, 18 of whom are elected annually by the general assembly for overlapping three-year terms. Each member has one vote and can be immediately re-elected. The council elects a president and four vice-presidents each year: this five-member bureau proposes the council's agenda, draws up a programme of work and organises the substantive session. This session is held each July, and decisions are reached by a simple majority vote of those present.

The council has established a number of functional commissions and standing committees on particular issues. These include commissions on social development, sustainable development, population and development, the status of women, crime prevention and criminal justice, narcotic drugs, science and technology for development and the status of women, as well as five regional economic commissions.
President, HE Lazarous Kapambwe (Zambia)

THE SECRETARIAT
UN Plaza, New York, NY 10017, USA

The secretariat services the other principle UN organs and administers their programmes and policies. It is headed by a secretary-general elected by a majority vote of the general assembly on the recommendation of the security council. He is assisted by 44,134 staff worldwide, who represent all 192 member nationalities (as at May 2011). The secretary-general is charged with bringing to the attention of the security council any matter which he considers poses a threat to international peace and security. He may also bring other matters to the attention of the general assembly and other UN bodies and may be entrusted by them with additional duties. As chief administrator to the UN, the secretary-general is present in person or via representatives at all meetings of the other five main organs of the UN. He may also act as a mediator in disputes between member states.

The power and influence of the secretary-general has been determined largely by the character of the office-holder and by the state of relations between the superpowers. The thaw in these relations since the mid-1980s has increased the effectiveness of the UN, particularly in its attempts to intervene in international disputes. It helped to end the Iran-Iraq War and sponsored peace in Central America. Following Iraq's invasion of Kuwait in 1990, the UN took its first collective security action since the Korean War. Conflicts in Cyprus, Timor–Leste, Libya, Nigeria and Western Sahara were successfully prevented from escalating or spreading during the administration of Kofi Annan. However, the UN was heavily criticised for its failure to act in the Rwandan genocide of 1994 and its inability to halt the continuing conflict in Darfur, while the invasion of Iraq by the USA and UK in 2003 without a UN mandate, illegal under the organisation's charter, seriously undermined its authority.
Secretary-General, Ban Ki-moon (South Korea)
Deputy Secretary-General, Dr Asha-Rose Migiro (Tanzania)

FORMER SECRETARIES-GENERAL	
1946–52	Trygve Lie (Norway)
1953–61	Dag Hammarskjöld (Sweden)
1961–71	U Thant (Myanmar)
1972–81	Kurt Waldheim (Austria)
1982–91	Javier Pérez de Cuéllar (Peru)
1992–96	Boutros Boutros-Ghali (Egypt)
1997–2006	Kofi Annan (Ghana)

UK MISSION TO THE UN
1 Dag Hammarskjld Plaza, 885 Second Avenue, New York, NY 10017, USA
T (+1) (212) 745 9200 **E** uk@un.int **W** www.ukun.fco.gov.uk
Permanent Representative to the United Nations and Representative on the Security Council, Sir Mark Lyall Grant, *apptd* 2009

UK MISSION TO THE UN AND OTHER INTERNATIONAL ORGANISATIONS IN GENEVA
58 Avenue Louis Casai, 1216 Cointrin GE Geneva, Switzerland
T (+41) (22) 918 2300 **E** geneva_un@fco.gov.uk
Permanent UK Representative, Peter Gooderham, *apptd* 2008

UK MISSION TO THE UN IN VIENNA
Jaurèsgasse 12, A-1030 Vienna, Austria
T (+43) (1) 716 130 **E** ukmis.vienna@fco.gov.uk
W ukinaustria.fco.gov.uk
Permanent UK Representative, HE Simon Smith, *apptd* 2007

REGIONAL UN INFORMATION CENTRE
Block C2, Level 7, 155 rue de la Loi, Brussels 1040, Belgium
T (+32) 2788 8484 **E** info@unric.org **W** www.unric.org

THE INTERNATIONAL COURT OF JUSTICE
The Peace Palace, NL-2517 KJ, The Hague, The Netherlands
T (+31) 7030 22323 **W** www.icj-cij.org

The international court of justice is the principal judicial organ of the UN, and its statute is an integral part of the

UN charter; all members of the UN are *ipso facto* parties to it. The court is composed of 15 judges, elected by both the general assembly and the security council for nine-year terms, which are renewable. Judges may deliberate over cases in which their country is involved. If no judge on the bench is from a country that is a party to a dispute under consideration, that party may designate a judge to participate *ad hoc* in that particular deliberation. If any party to a case fails to adhere to the judgment of the court, the other party may have recourse to the security council.

President, Hisashi Owada (Japan)

Vice-President, Peter Tomka (Slovakia)

Judges, Antonio A. Cancado Trindade (Brazil); Xue Hanquin (China); Ronny Abraham (France); Bruno Simma (Germany); Awn Shawkat al-Khasawneh (Jordan); Bernardo Sepúlveda-Amor (Mexico); Mohamed Bennouna (Morocco); Kenneth Keith (New Zealand); Leonid Skotnikov (Russian Federation); Abdul G. Koroma (Sierra Leone); Abdulqawi Ahmed Yusuf (Somalia); Christopher Greenwood (UK); Joan Donoghue (USA)

UNITED NATIONS EDUCATIONAL, SCIENTIFIC AND CULTURAL ORGANISATION

7 place de Fontenoy, F-75352 Paris, France
T (+33) (01) 4568 1000 E bpi@unesco.org W www.unesco.org

The United Nations Educational, Scientific and Cultural Organisation (UNESCO) was established in 1945. It promotes collaboration among its member states in education, science, culture and communication. It aims to promote a universal respect for human rights, justice and the rule of law, without distinction of race, sex, language or religion, in accordance with the UN charter.

UNESCO runs a number of programmes to improve education and extend access to it. It provides assistance to ensure the free flow of information and its wider dissemination without any barriers to freedom of expression, to safeguard cultural heritages and encourage sustainable development. It fosters research and study in the social and environmental sciences. The UNESCO world heritage list, decided upon by a 21-member committee of state representatives, includes 911 cultural and natural sites of 'outstanding universal value'.

UNESCO has 193 member states and seven associate members. The general conference, consisting of representatives of all the members, meets biennially to decide the programme and the budget. It elects the 58-member executive board, which supervises operations, and appoints a director-general who heads a secretariat responsible for carrying out the organisation's programmes. In most member states national commissions liaise with UNESCO to execute its policies.

Director-General, Irina Bokova (Bulgaria)

UNITED NATIONS INDUSTRIAL DEVELOPMENT ORGANISATION

Vienna International Centre, Wagramerstrasse 5, PO Box 300, A-1400 Vienna, Austria
T (+43) (1) 260 260 E unido@unido.org W www.unido.org

The United Nations Industrial Development Organisation (UNIDO) was established in 1966 by the UN general assembly to act as the central coordinating body for industrial activities within the UN. It became a UN specialised agency in 1985. UNIDO aims to help countries with developing and transitional economies by increasing the productivity and competitiveness of their agricultural industries.

UNIDO has 172 members. It is funded by regular and operational budgets, together with contributions for technical cooperation activities. The regular budget is derived from member states' contributions. Technical cooperation is funded mainly through voluntary contributions from donor countries and institutions and by intergovernmental and non-governmental organisations. A general conference of all the members meets biennially to discuss strategy and policy, approve the budget – €381.6m (£308m) in 2008–9 – and elect the director-general. The industrial development board is composed of representatives from 53 member states and reviews the work programme and the budget, which is prepared by the programme and budget committee of 27 member states.

Director-General, Kandeh K. Yumkella (Sierra Leone)

UNIVERSAL POSTAL UNION

4 Weltpoststrasse, CH-3000 Bern 15, Switzerland
T (+41) (31) 350 3111 E info@upu.int W www.upu.int

The Universal Postal Union (UPU) was established by the treaty of Bern 1874, taking effect from 1875, and became a UN specialised agency in 1948. The UPU exists to form and regulate a single postal territory of all member countries for the reciprocal exchange of correspondence without discrimination. With a total of 191 members, it also assists and advises on the improvement of postal services.

The universal postal congress is the UPU's supreme authority and meets every four years. The council of administration meets annually to supervise the union's work between congresses, to investigate regulatory developments and policy issues, to approve the budget and to examine proposed treaty changes. The consultative committee was set up in 2004 to further the interests of the wider postal sector. It brings together representative bodies of customers, service providers, manufacturers and suppliers, and provides a forum for dialogue between postal industry stakeholders. The three UPU bodies are served by the international bureau, a secretariat headed by a director-general.

Funding is provided by members according to a scale of contributions drawn up by the congress. The council of administration sets the budget which amounts to approximately SFr37m (£25.2m) a year.

Director-General, Edouard Dayan (France)

UNREPRESENTED NATIONS AND PEOPLES ORGANISATION

Laan van Meerdervoort 70, 2517 AN, The Hague, The Netherlands
T (+31) (0) 70 364 6504 E unpo@unpo.org W www.unpo.org

The Unrepresented Nations and Peoples Organisation (UNPO) was founded in 1991 to offer an international forum for occupied nations, indigenous peoples and national minorities who are not represented in other international organisations.

The UNPO does not aim to represent these nations and peoples, but rather to assist and empower them to represent themselves more effectively, and provides professional services and facilities as well as education and training in the fields of diplomacy, international and human rights law, democratic processes, institution building, conflict management and resolution, and environmental protection.

Participation is open to all nations and peoples who are inadequately represented at the UN and who declare allegiance to five principles relating to the right of self-determination of all peoples: human rights, democracy, tolerance, non-violence and protection of the natural environment. Applicants must show that they constitute a nation or people and that the organisation applying for membership is representative of that nation or people.

As at May 2011, UNPO had 50 full members.

General Secretary, Marino Busdachin (Italy)

WESTERN EUROPEAN UNION

15 rue de l'Association, 1000 Brussels, Belgium
T (+32) (2) 500 4412 E secretariatgeneral@weu.int
W www.weu.int

Western European Union (WEU) is a defence and security organisation. It began as the Brussels Treaty Organisation (BTO), based on the Brussels treaty signed in 1948 by Belgium, France, Luxembourg, the Netherlands and the UK. The BTO was designed to provide collective self-defence and economic and social collaboration among its signatories. The treaty was modified to become the WEU in 1954 with the admission of West Germany and Italy.

In 1991, the EU Maastricht treaty committed the European Community to the establishment of a common foreign and security policy. The WEU was designated as the future defence component of the European Union, and member states of the EU who were not already members of the WEU were invited to join or become observers. In 1992, the WEU's role as the common security dimension of the EU was enhanced when WEU ministers signed a declaration with remaining European NATO members to give them various forms of WEU membership.

In 1999, NATO and the EU decided to establish a direct relationship; the EU committed itself to ensuring that it was able to take decisions on conflict prevention and crisis management and NATO agreed to give the EU access to its collective assets and capabilities for operations in which NATO as a whole was not engaged. The WEU's crisis management functions were transferred to the EU in 2001, and the Lisbon Treaty which entered into force in December 2009 introduced provisions for the collective self-defence of all EU member states, and the creation of *ad hoc* interparliamentary groups. Thus superseded, in March 2010 the Brussels treaty was terminated and the WEU announced that it would cease operations by June 2011.

The WEU currently has ten member states, six associate members, and five observers, and a further seven countries are associate partners.

Presidency, Italy, Luxembourg (2011); Netherlands, Portugal (2012)

Acting Secretary-General, Arnaud Jacomet (France)

WORLD BANK GROUP

1818 H Street NW, Washington DC 20433, USA
T (+1) (202) 473 1000 E pic@worldbank.org
W www.worldbank.org

The World Bank Group was founded in 1944 and is one of the world's largest sources of development assistance. It has 187 member states. Originally directed towards post-war reconstruction in Europe, the bank subsequently turned towards assisting less-developed countries worldwide, and in 2010 supported 51 projects across the developing world. It works with government agencies, non-governmental organisations and the private sector to formulate assistance strategies. Its local offices implement the bank's programme in each country.

The World Bank is owned by the governments of member countries and its capital is subscribed by its members. It finances its lending primarily from borrowing in world capital markets, and derives a substantial contribution to its resources from its retained earnings and the repayment of loans.

The World Bank Group consists of two institutions and three affiliates. The International Bank for Reconstruction and Development (IBRD) provides loans and development assistance to middle-income countries and creditworthy poorer countries (total loans for 2010 US$44.2bn (£27.12bn)). The International Development Association (IDA) performs the same function as the IBRD but primarily to less-developed countries and on terms that bear less heavily on their balance of payments than IBRD loans (total loans for 2010 US$14.5bn (£8.9bn)).

The three affiliates are the International Finance Corporation (IFC), which has 182 members and promotes private sector investment in developing countries by mobilising domestic and foreign capital; the Multilateral Investment Guarantee Agency (MIGA), which has 175 members and promotes foreign direct investment in developing states by insuring investors against political risk and helping member countries to improve their investment climates; and the International Centre for Settlement of Investment Disputes, which has 146 full members (known as contracting states) and provides facilities for resolving disputes between foreign investors and their host countries.

The IBRD, IDA and the affiliates are financially and legally distinct but share headquarters. The IBRD is headed by a board of governors, which meets annually and consists of one governor and one alternate governor appointed by each member country; most IBRD governors also serve on the separate boards of the IDA, IFC and MIGA. Twenty-five executive directors exercise all powers of the World Bank (except those reserved to the board of governors). The president, elected by the board of governors, conducts the business of the bank, assisted by an international staff. Membership in both the IFC and the IDA is open to all IBRD countries. The IDA is administered by the same staff as the bank; the IFC has its own personnel but can draw on the IBRD for administrative and other support. All share the same president.

President, Robert B. Zoellick (USA)

WORLD CUSTOMS ORGANISATION

30 rue de Marché, B-1210, Brussels, Belgium
T (+32) 2209 9211 E information@wcoomd.org
W www.wcoomd.org

The World Customs Organisation (WCO) is an international intergovernmental body that works to enhance the effectiveness and efficiency of customs administrations worldwide. By developing a harmonised commodity description and coding system, the WCO introduced a universal goods classification and revenue collection method. The WCO also administers the WTO agreements on customs valuation and rules of origin, as well as promoting standards for secure cross-border trade.

Comprising 177 customs administrations, its members process around 98 per cent of international trade. The WCO is governed by a council which meets annually and in which each member is represented and has one vote.

The council elects and is assisted by a 30-member policy commission, a 17-member finance committee, and a permanent secretariat which implements the council's policies.

Secretary-General, Kuniyo Mikuriya (Japan)

WORLD HEALTH ORGANISATION

Avenue Appia 20, 1211 Geneva 27, Switzerland
T (+41) (22) 791 2111 E info@who.int W www.who.int

The UN International Health Conference, held in 1946, established the World Health Organisation (WHO) as a UN specialised agency, with effect from 1948. It is dedicated to attaining the highest possible level of health for all. It collaborates with member governments, UN agencies and other bodies to improve health standards, control communicable diseases and promote all aspects of family and environmental health. It seeks to raise the standards of health teaching and training, and promotes research through collaboration with research centres worldwide.

WHO has 193 members and is governed by an annual assembly of members. This sets policy, approves the budget, appoints a director-general, and adopts health conventions and regulations. It also elects 34 member states to designate one expert each to serve on the executive board. The board sets the assembly's agenda and implements its policies, suggests initiatives, and is empowered to deal with emergencies. A secretariat, headed by the director-general, supervises the activities of six regional offices.

Director-General, Dr Margaret Chan (China)

WORLD INTELLECTUAL PROPERTY ORGANISATION

34 chemin des Colombettes, CH-1211, Geneva 20, Switzerland
T (+41) (22) 338 9111 W www.wipo.int

The World Intellectual Property Organisation (WIPO) was established in Stockholm in 1967 by the signing of the WIPO Convention, which entered into force in 1970. WIPO administers 24 treaties that deal with different legal and administrative aspects of intellectual property, notably the Paris Convention for the protection of industrial property and the Bern Convention for the protection of literary and artistic works. WIPO became a UN specialised agency in 1974.

Intellectual property falls into two main branches: industrial property (inventions, trademarks, industrial designs and geographical indications) and copyright (literary, musical, photographic, audiovisual and artistic works, etc). WIPO helps ensure that creative intellectual activity is rewarded, and facilitates technology transfer, particularly to developing countries.

WIPO's mission is to promote the protection of intellectual property rights worldwide. The organisation's activities fall into three broad categories: the progressive development of international intellectual property law, assistance to developing countries, and the provision of services which facilitate the process of obtaining intellectual property rights in multiple countries.

WIPO had 184 members as at May 2011. The biennial session of the general assembly, the conference and the coordination committee set policy, a programme and a budget. A separate agency, the International Union for the Protection of New Varieties of Plants, established by convention in 1961, is linked to WIPO and has 69 members.

Director-General, Francis Gurry (Australia)

WORLD METEOROLOGICAL ORGANISATION

7 bis, avenue de la Paix, PO Box 2300, CH-1211 Geneva 2, Switzerland
T (+41) (22) 730 8111 E wmo@wmo.int W www.wmo.int

The World Meteorological Organisation (WMO) was established in 1950 and became a UN specialised agency in 1951, succeeding the International Meteorological Organisation founded in 1873. It facilitates cooperation in the establishment of networks for making, processing and exchanging meteorological, climatological, hydrological and geophysical observations. It also fosters collaboration between meteorological and hydrological services, and furthers the application of meteorology to aviation, shipping, environment, water problems, agriculture and the mitigation of natural disasters.

In May 2011, the WMO had 183 member states and six member territories. Six regional associations are responsible for the coordination of activities within their own regions. There are also eight technical commissions, which study meteorological and hydrological problems, establish methodology and procedures, and make recommendations to the executive council and the congress. The supreme authority is the world meteorological congress, which meets every four years to determine general policy and set the budget (SFr457m (£312m) proposed for 2012–15). It also elects 27 members of the 37-member executive council which supervises the implementation of congress decisions, initiates studies and makes recommendations on matters requiring international action. The secretariat is headed by a secretary-general, appointed by the congress.

Secretary-General, Michel Jarraud (France)

WORLD TOURISM ORGANISATION

Capitán Haya 42, 28020 Madrid, Spain
T (+34) 9156 78100 E omt@unwto.org W www.unwto.org

The World Tourism Organisation (UNWTO) was officially launched in 1975 to act as an executing agency of the United Nations Development Programme. Primarily concerned with developing public and private sector partnerships, the UNWTO also promotes the global code of ethics for tourism, a framework of policy aimed at tour operators, governments, labour organisations and travellers. There are 154 member states and seven associate member states.

The general assembly is the principal gathering of the UNWTO and meets every two years in order to approve policy and budget. Every four years, the assembly elects a secretary-general. The executive council is UNWTO's governing board and meets at least twice a year to ensure the organisation adheres to policy and budget. It is composed of 31 members of the general assembly. As host country of UNWTO's headquarters, Spain has a permanent seat on the executive council.

Secretary-General, Taleb Rifai (Jordan)

WORLD TRADE ORGANISATION

Centre William Rappard, 154 rue de Lausanne, CH-1211 Geneva 21, Switzerland
T (+41) (22) 739 5111 E enquiries@wto.org W www.wto.org

The World Trade Organisation was established on 1 January 1995 as the successor to the General Agreement on Tariffs and Trade (GATT).

GATT was dedicated to the expansion of non-discriminatory international trade and progressively extended free trade via 'rounds' of multilateral negotiations. The final act of the comprehensive Uruguay round of negotiations was signed by trade ministers from the 128 GATT negotiating states and the EU in Marrakesh, Morocco, in 1994. New talks on agriculture and services began in 2000 and were incorporated into a broader agenda launched at the 2001 ministerial conference in Doha, Qatar.

The WTO is the legal and institutional foundation of the multilateral trading system. It provides the contractual obligations determining how governments frame and implement trade policy, and provides the forum for the debate, negotiation and adjudication of trade issues. The WTO's principal aims are to liberalise world trade and place it on a secure basis; it seeks to achieve this through the combination of an agreed set of trade rules and market-access agreements and further trade liberalisation negotiations. The WTO also administers and implements multilateral agreements in fields such as agriculture, industrial goods, services, government procurement, rules of origin and intellectual property.

The highest authority of the WTO is the ministerial conference composed of all members, which usually meets once every two years. The general council meets as required and acts on behalf of the ministerial conference in regard to the regular working of the WTO. The general council also convenes in two particular forms: as the dispute-settlement body, dealing with disagreements between members arising from WTO agreements or commitments; and as the trade policy review body, conducting regular reviews of the trade policies of members. A secretariat of 629 staff, headed by a director-general, services WTO bodies and provides trade performance and trade policy analysis.

As at May 2011, there were 153 WTO members and 31 observers. The WTO budget for 2010 was SFr194m (£132.4m), with members' contributions calculated on the basis of their share of international trade. The official languages of the WTO are English, French and Spanish.

Director-General, Pascal Lamy (France)

COUNTRIES OF THE WORLD A–Z

DEFINITIONS AND ABBREVIATIONS

est = estimate
(m) = male; (f) = female
BIRTH RATE – figures are per 1,000 population. The birth rate is usually the dominant factor in determining the rate of population growth.
CORRUPTION PERCEPTIONS INDEX (CPI) SCORE – the perception of the degree of public sector corruption as seen by business people and country analysts; ranging between 10 (very clean) and 0 (highly corrupt). © Transparency International
DEATH PENALTY:
Retained (not used) – countries that retain the death penalty for ordinary crimes such as murder but can be considered to have abolished it in practice, as they have not executed anyone during the last decade, are believed to have a policy against carrying out executions, or have made a commitment not to use the death penalty
Retained for certain crimes – countries whose laws provide for the death penalty only for exceptional crimes such as those committed under military law or in exceptional circumstances. ('Last used' = date of last execution.)
Retained – countries that retain the death penalty for ordinary crimes
GROSS ENROLMENT RATIO – the ratio of total enrolment, regardless of age, to the total population of the relevant age group expressed as a percentage; this figure can be above 100 per cent where, for example, a greater number of children are attending classes designed for six-year-olds than there are six-year-olds in the country, owing to some children starting school late or skipping a year
GROSS NATIONAL INCOME (GNI) – the total income earned by a country's residents, regardless of where the assets are located; the second figure is GNI divided by the population to give a per capita figure
HIV/AIDS ADULT PREVALENCE – estimate of the percentage of the total adult population (aged 15–49) infected with HIV/AIDS. A year-on-year percentage rise may indicate a higher survival rate due to advances in treatment, or the provision of treatment, rather than an increased rate of infection
INFANT MORTALITY RATE – averages for male and female infants under one year old and per 1,000 live births
LIFE EXPECTANCY – averages, at birth, for males and females
MORTALITY RATE – figures are per 1,000 population. This indicator is significantly affected by age distribution, and most countries will eventually show a rise in the overall death rate, in spite of continued decline in mortality at all ages, as declining fertility results in an ageing population
POPULATION BELOW POVERTY LINE – although strict definitions of poverty vary considerably between nations, this figure most commonly represents the percentage of the adult population whose income is less than US$1 per day
TOTAL EXTERNAL DEBT – the total public and private debt owed to non-residents repayable in foreign currency, goods or services

AFGHANISTAN

Jomhuri-ye Eslami-ye Afghanestan – Islamic Republic of Afghanistan

Area – 652,230 sq. km
Capital – Kabul; population, 3,572,960 (2009 est)
Major cities – Herat, Jalalabad, Kandahar, Mazar-e-Sharif
Currency – Afghani (Af) of 100 puls
Population – 29,121,286 rising at 2.47 per cent a year (2010 est); Pashtun (42 per cent), Tajik (27 per cent), Hazara (9 per cent), Uzbek (9 per cent), Aimak (4 per cent), Turkmen (3 per cent), Baloch (2 per cent) (est)
Religion – Muslim (Sunni 80 per cent, Shia 19 per cent) (est); Islam is the state religion
Language – Dari (a dialect of Persian), Pashto (both official), Uzbek, Turkmen
Population density – 46 per sq. km (2009 est)
Urban population – 24 per cent (2008 est)
Median age (years) – 18 (2010 est)
National anthem – 'Milli Tharana' ['National Anthem']
National day – 19 August (Independence Day)
Life expectancy (years) – 44.65 (2010 est)
Mortality rate – 17.65 (2010 est)
Birth rate – 38.11 (2010 est)
Infant mortality rate – 151.5 (2010 est)
Death penalty – Retained
CPI score – 1.4 (2010)

CLIMATE AND TERRAIN

Mountains, chief among which are the Hindu Kush, cover three-quarters of the landlocked country, with plains in the north and south-west. Elevation extremes range from 7,485m at the highest point (Nowshak, a peak in the Hindu Kush) to 258m at the lowest (Amu Dar'ya). There are three great river basins: the Amu Dar'ya (Oxus), Helmand and Kabul. Natural hazards are flooding, drought and earthquakes. The climate is arid to semi-arid, with extreme temperatures. Summers are hot and dry, and the winters cold with heavy snowfalls, particularly in the mountains. Average annual rainfall is around 240mm per year. Temperatures in Kabul average −8°C to 2°C in January and 16°C to 33°C in July.

HISTORY AND POLITICS

Afghanistan first became a nation in 1747 under Ahmad Shah Durrani. Britain and Russia vied for influence over the region in the 19th and early 20th centuries, but the country remained independent. The monarchy was overthrown in 1973 and a republic was declared. After a coup in 1978 a communist government took power, and armed resistance by conservative Muslim elements began. The government was overthrown in a further coup in 1979 that prompted an invasion by the Soviet Union, which installed a pro-Soviet government. The guerrilla resistance (mujahidin), with foreign backing, fought against Soviet forces, which withdrew in 1989, and against Afghan government forces until the government collapsed in 1992. Factionalism led to ongoing civil conflict until the rise of the Taliban which, between 1994–8, extended its power across more than 90 per cent of the country and imposed strict Shariah law.

The Taliban allowed the al-Qaida network to base terrorist training camps in Afghanistan, and its refusal to hand over al-Qaida leaders after the 11 September 2001 terrorist attacks on the USA led to the regime's overthrow by a US-led international coalition and the Northern Alliance, a grouping of the four main mujahidin factions. A multi-ethnic interim government under Hamid Karzai was installed in December 2001 and, following a *Loya Jirga* (tribal council) in 2002, a transitional government was installed until presidential and parliamentary elections were held in 2004 and 2005.

The government's authority, although still tenuous in the provinces and largely dependent on the presence of foreign troops, is increasingly being asserted by the Afghan army and police. However, the power vacuum after 2001 allowed corruption and local infighting to become endemic, while conflict has escalated owing to the resurgence of the Taliban since 2005, particularly in the south and east, and to opposition to NATO-led drug-eradication programmes.

Hamid Karzai was elected president in 2004, and was re-elected in 2009 in controversial circumstances; the first round of voting was marred by widespread electoral fraud, and the second-placed candidate withdrew from the second round as too little had been done to prevent a recurrence of fraud in the run-off. President Karzai took control of the Electoral Complaints Commission in February 2010, causing international concern about the management of the 2010 legislative elections. These were postponed from May to September 2010 and took place amid Taliban violence and widespread fraud, which caused the electoral commission to disqualify 21 candidates.

POLITICAL SYSTEM

Under the 2004 constitution, the executive president, who is directly elected for a five-year term, appoints the government, subject to the approval of the lower house of the legislature. The bicameral National Assembly, the *Jirga*, comprises the House of the People *(Wolesi Jirga)*, the lower house, and the House of Elders *(Meshrano Jirga)*. The House of the People has 249 members directly elected for a five-year term; ten seats are reserved for the Kuchi ethnic group and at least 65 seats for women. The House of Elders has 102 members: 34 elected by provincial councils for a three-year term, 34 elected by district councils for a four-year term, and 34 appointed by the president for a five-year term. There are no formal political parties at present.

HEAD OF STATE

President, Hamid Karzai, *elected* 9 October 2004, *sworn in* 7 December 2004, *re-elected* 2009
First Vice-President, Mohammad Qasim Fahim
Vice-President, Karim Khalili

SELECTED GOVERNMENT MEMBERS *as at May 2011*
Defence, Gen. Abdul Raheem Wardak
Foreign Affairs, Zalmai Rasul
Finance, Omar Zakhailwal
Interior (acting), Gen. Besmillah Mohammadi

EMBASSY OF THE ISLAMIC REPUBLIC OF AFGHANISTAN
31 Prince's Gate, London SW7 1QQ
T 020-7589 8891
Ambassador Extraordinary and Plenipotentiary,
    HE Mohammad Homayoun Tandar, *apptd* 2009

BRITISH EMBASSY
PO Box 334, 15th Street, Roundabout Wazir Akbar Khan, Kabul
T (+93) (0) 700 102 000 E britishembassy.kabul@fco.gov.uk
W http://ukinafghanistan.fco.gov.uk
Ambassador Extraordinary and Plenipotentiary,
    HE Sir William Patey, KCMG, *apptd* 2010

BRITISH COUNCIL
House 15–17, Kart-e-Parwan, Kabul
T (+93) (79) 000 0130 E info.afghanistan@britishcouncil.org
W www.britishcouncil.org/afghanistan
Director, Tony Jones

DEFENCE

The Afghan government and the international community aim to bolster security by developing the national army and police force, with the intention of handing over responsibility for security by the end of 2014. NATO's International Security Assistance Force has approximately 132,203 troops in Afghanistan.
Military expenditure – US$252m (2009)
Military personnel – 136,106: army 131,906, air force 4,200; paramilitary 119,639

ECONOMY AND TRADE

The economy, devastated by 30 years of conflict, has improved significantly since 2001 owing to international assistance, agricultural recovery and service sector growth. Economic growth has been sustained over the decade despite drought in 2006–7 and the global downturn in 2008–9, although security problems, weak governance, corruption and inadequate infrastructure continue to hamper reconstruction. Poverty is being reduced, although over a third of the population still lives below the poverty line. The illegal drug trade and smuggling underpin a large black economy. Eradication of the opium trade (which constitutes about 60 per cent of the economy) and exploration for oil and gas in the north are two major long-term policy objectives.

Nearly 80 per cent of the workforce is engaged in agriculture, both subsistence and commercial, which accounts for 31 per cent of GDP. The main agricultural products are opium, wheat, fruit, nuts, wool, meat, sheepskins and lambskins. Natural gas, coal, copper and gemstones are extracted. The main trading partners are the USA, Pakistan and India. Principal exports are agricultural products, handwoven carpets and gemstones. Imports are chiefly machinery and other capital goods, food, textiles and petroleum products.
GNI – US$10,644m; US$310 per capita (2008)
Annual average growth of GDP – 8.9 per cent (2010 est)
Inflation rate – 13.3 per cent (2009 est)
Population below poverty line – 36 per cent (2008–9)
Unemployment – 35 per cent (2008 est)
Total external debt – US$2,700m (2008–9)

BALANCE OF PAYMENTS
Trade – US$6,906m deficit (2010)
Current Account – US$188m deficit (2008)

Trade with UK	2009	2010
Imports from UK	£132,932,668	£195,669,976
Exports to UK	£1,134,183	£1,674,613

COMMUNICATIONS

There are two international airports, at Kabul and Kandahar, and a further four major and 16 smaller regional airports servicing internal flights. The Amu Dar'ya river makes up most of the 1,200km of inland waterways and carries barge traffic; the main river ports are Kheyrabad and Shir Khan. There is no railway system, although there are railheads on the Pakistan border, and a railway is under construction from Mashhad, in Iran, to Herat. Plans for a 2,000km national railway were set out by the minister of mines in May 2010. Much of the road system is in disrepair, although many of the main highways between Kabul, Kandahar and Herat have been reconstructed. The fixed-line telephone network is limited in extent (129,300 fixed lines in 2009), and mobile phone distribution has grown rapidly (12 million subscribers in 2009). Internet access is scarce, even in urban areas; there were 1 million subscribers in 2009.

EDUCATION AND HEALTH

Education is free and nominally compulsory, elementary schools having been established in most centres. In 2002, schools reopened to 1.5 million children, many of whom had not received schooling under the Taliban. However, militants have targeted education facilities for girls.
Literacy rate – 28.0 per cent (2008 est)
Gross enrolment ratio (percentage of relevant age group) –
   primary 104 per cent; secondary 44 per cent; tertiary 4 per cent (2009 est)
Health expenditure (per capita) – US$51 (2009)
Hospital beds (per 1,000 people) – 0.4 (2004–9)

MEDIA AND CULTURE

The media was severely restricted under the Taliban, which banned television broadcasting. Since 2001, radio and television stations and newspapers, both state-run and privately owned, have proliferated. National Radio-TV Afghanistan is the state broadcaster. Private TV stations are popular in urban areas, and provide imported Indian and Western-style programming. Relays of foreign radio stations, and stations funded by foreign governments and NGOs, are available in Kabul. The press enjoys freedom of expression and a growing readership. However, media laws prohibit content which offends Islamic law.

Much of Afghanistan's cultural heritage has been lost during its decades of conflict. The Kabul Museum was looted during the early 1990s, and treasures such as the Kunduz Hoard (silver Greek-style coins) were stolen. Its collection was further depleted by the Taliban's systematic iconoclasm, which included the demolition in 2001 of the giant Bamiyan Buddhas, carved in the fourth to sixth centuries. In 2008, adjacent caves in Bamiyan were found by scientists to contain the oldest known examples of oil painting in the world, dating from the seventh century.

ALBANIA

Republika e Shqiperise – Republic of Albania

Area – 28,748 sq. km
Capital – Tirana; population, 432,652 (2009 est)
Major towns – Durres, Elbasan, Shkoder, Vlore
Currency – Lek (Lk) of 100 qindarka
Population – 2,986,952 rising at 0.25 per cent a year (2010 est); Albanian (95 per cent), Greek (3 per cent) (est)
Religion – Muslim 70 per cent (Sunni, and Bektashi form of Shia Sufism), Christian 30 per cent (Albanian Orthodox and Roman Catholic) (est). Religious observance was banned in 1967; private religious practice has been permitted since 1990
Language – Albanian (official), Greek, Vlach, Romani, Slavic dialects
Population density – 115 per sq. km (2009)
Urban population – 47 per cent (2008 est)
Median age (years) – 30 (2010 est)
National anthem – 'Hymni i Flamurit' ['Hymn to the Flag']
National day – 28 November (Independence Day)
Life expectancy (years) – 77.22 (2010 est)
Mortality rate – 6.04 (2010 est)
Birth rate – 11.88 (2010 est)
Infant mortality rate – 15.11 (2010 est)
Death penalty – Abolished for all crimes (since 2007)
CPI score – 3.3 (2010)

CLIMATE AND TERRAIN

About two-thirds of the country is mountainous, and almost 40 per cent is covered by forest. The plain that runs the length of the Adriatic coastline is home to most of the population. The highest point of elevation is 2,764m (Maja e Korabit, a peak on the Macedonian border) and the lowest is 0m (Adriatic Sea). Albania shares Lake Scutari with Montenegro, and lakes Ohrid and Prespa with Macedonia. The climate is Mediterranean on the coast and continental in the interior. The average daily temperature in Tirana ranges between 2°C to 12°C in January and 17°C to 31°C in July.

HISTORY AND POLITICS

Albania was under Ottoman rule from 1468 until 1912, when independence was declared after the first Balkan War. After a period of unrest, a republic was declared in 1925 and a monarchy formed in 1928. The country was occupied by the Italians in 1939 and by the Germans in 1943. Albania was liberated by mostly communist partisans led by Enver Hoxha in 1944. Elections in 1945 resulted in a communist-controlled assembly; the king was deposed *in absentia* and a republic declared in 1946.

From 1946 to 1990 Albania was a one-party communist state. Aligned with the USSR until 1961 and with China from 1961 to 1978, it pursued an isolationist policy from 1978 until Hoxha's death in 1985. Gradual moves towards democratisation and westernisation began in the late 1980s, and in 1991 and 1992 democratic elections took place, the Communists losing power in 1992.

Anti-government protests following the collapse of several 'pyramid' investment schemes in early 1997 resulted in near-anarchy for some months, the government losing control of large areas of the country until a change of government and an EU peacekeeping force restored order. The country remained stable in 1999 despite the pressures caused by the influx of 480,000 refugees fleeing from Serbian attacks on ethnic Albanians in Kosovo; the government supported NATO's moves to deal with the crisis and by the end of 1999 nearly all the refugees had left Albania.

Talks with the EU began in 2003 and, following progress on political and economic reform, a stabilisation and association agreement was signed in 2006. Albania became a member of NATO in 2009.

Bamir Topi, of the Democratic Party (PD), was elected president in 2007 in the fourth round of voting. The incumbent PD and its allies remained the largest parliamentary bloc after the 2009 legislative election, and formed a new coalition with a minor party to secure an overall majority.

POLITICAL SYSTEM

Under the 1998 constitution, the president is elected by the legislature for a five-year term, renewable only once. The unicameral legislature, the People's Assembly, has 140 members directly elected for four-year terms. The president appoints the prime minister, who must be approved by the People's Assembly. The assembly elects the council of ministers.

HEAD OF STATE

President, Bamir Topi, *elected* 20 July 2007, *took office* 24 July 2007

SELECTED GOVERNMENT MEMBERS *as at May 2011*

Prime Minister, Sali Berisha

Deputy Prime Minister, Foreign Affairs, Edmond Haxhinasto

Defence, Arben Imami

Interior, Bujar Nishani

Finance, Ritvan Bode

EMBASSY OF THE REPUBLIC OF ALBANIA

33 St George's Drive, London SW1V 4DG

T 020-7828 8897 E embassy.london@mfa.gov.al

W www.albanianembassy.co.uk

Ambassador Extraordinary and Plenipotentiary, HE Zef Mazi, *apptd* 2007

BRITISH EMBASSY

Rruga Skenderbeg 12, Tirana

T (+355) (4) 223 4973 W http://ukinalbania.fco.gov.uk

Ambassador Extraordinary and Plenipotentiary, HE Fiona McIlwham, MBE, *apptd* 2009

BRITISH COUNCIL

Rruga Skenderbeg 12, Tirana

T (+355) (4) 224 0856/7 W www.britishcouncil.org/albania

Director, Clare Sears

DEFENCE

The Albanian Armed Forces (AAF) is a joint force. The land element has 3 main battle tanks and 6 armoured personnel carriers. The navy element has 3 patrol and coastal combatant vessels at two bases, Durres and Vlore. The air element has 16 helicopters.

Military budget – US$195m (2010)

Military personnel – 14,245: joint force command 8,150, support command 4,300, training and doctrine command 1,000, MoD and general staff 795; paramilitary 500

Conscription duration – 12 months

ECONOMY AND TRADE

Albania is one of the poorest countries in Europe. Communist isolationism resulted in dilapidated infrastructure and antiquated equipment and practices. Liberalisation measures have resulted in sustained growth since 2004, and inflation is under control. Nevertheless, the economy is still heavily dependent on remittances from expatriate workers, worth about 9 per cent of GDP, and overseas aid, primarily from the EU. Infrastructure and energy supply inadequacies, organised crime and corruption have deterred foreign investment, and tackling these are government priorities. A new thermal power plant and improved transmission lines from neighbouring countries should relieve energy shortages.

Agriculture accounts for 48 per cent of employment but only 18.9 per cent of GDP. The main crops are wheat, maize, vegetables, fruit, sugar beet and livestock products. The principal industries are food processing, textiles and clothing, timber, oil, cement, chemicals, mining (base metals) and hydro-electric power.

Trade is mainly with Italy, Greece and China. Exports include textiles and footwear, asphalt, metals and metal ores, crude oil, tobacco, fruit and vegetables. Imports include machinery and equipment, foodstuffs, textiles and chemicals.

GNI – US$11,906m; US$4,000 per capita (2009)

Annual average growth of GDP – 3.1 per cent (2010 est)

Inflation rate – 3.4 per cent (2010 est)

Population below poverty line – 25 per cent (2004 est)

Unemployment – 12.7 per cent (2010 est)

Total external debt – US$1,550m (2004)

Imports – US$4,500m (2009)

Exports – US$1,100m (2009)

BALANCE OF PAYMENTS

Trade – US$3,033m deficit (2010)

Current Account – US$1,975m deficit (2008)

Trade with UK	2009	2010
Imports from UK	£17,667,897	£20,447,099
Exports to UK	£1,776,531	£1,696,508

EDUCATION AND HEALTH

Literacy rate – 99.1 per cent (2008 est)

Gross enrolment ratio (percentage of relevant age group) – primary 118 per cent; secondary 72 per cent (2009 est)

Health expenditure (per capita) – US$265 (2009)

Hospital beds (per 1,000 people) – 2.9 (2004–9)

MEDIA

The public broadcaster Albanian Radio and TV (RTSh) faces increasing competition from dozens of private television channels and radio stations. Political parties, trade unions, religious groups and state bodies are prohibited from owning private television and radio stations, but many publish their own newspapers.

ALGERIA

Al-Jumhuriyah al-Jaza'iriyah ad Dimuqratiyah ash Sha'biyah – People's Democratic Republic of Algeria

Area – 2,381,741 sq. km
Capital – Algiers (El Djazair, Al Jaza'ir); population, 2,740,070 (2009 est)
Major cities – El Djelfa, Batna, Constantine (Qacentina), Oran (Wahran)
Currency – Algerian dinar (DA) of 100 centimes
Population – 34,586,184 rising at 1.18 per cent a year (2010 est); Arab-Berber (99 per cent) (est)
Religion – Muslim (Sunni 99 per cent) (est)
Language – Arabic (official), French, Berber dialects
Population density – 15 per sq. km (2009)
Urban population – 65 per cent (2008 est)
Median age (years) – 27.1 (2010 est)
National anthem – 'Kassaman' ['We Pledge']
National day – 1 November (Revolution Day)
Life expectancy (years) – 74.26 (2010 est)
Mortality rate – 4.66 (2010 est)
Birth rate – 16.71 (2010 est)
Infant mortality rate – 26.75 (2010 est)
Death penalty – Retained (not used since 1993)
CPI score – 2.9 (2010)

CLIMATE AND TERRAIN

Algeria, the second-largest country in Africa after Sudan, is dominated by the Sahara desert, which covers over 80 per cent of its territory. The eastern part of the Atlas mountain range crosses the north of the country, separating the coastal plain, where the majority of the population lives, from the desert plateaux of the interior. The highest point of elevation is 3,003m (Mt Tahat) and the lowest is –40m (Chott Melrhir, a salt lake). The mountains are subject to earthquakes, and to flooding and mudslides during the rainy season (November–March). The temperate northern coastal areas receive the greatest and most frequent rainfall, whereas the interior plateaux are drier and experience cold winters and hot summers.

HISTORY AND POLITICS

Algeria was a Roman province with a Berber population that was conquered by Arabs in the seventh century and converted to Islam. It was part of the Ottoman Empire from the 16th century until its annexation by France in 1830. It gained independence in 1962, following an eight-year guerrilla war by the socialist Front de Libération Nationale (FLN). The FLN was the only permitted political party for many years until political pluralism was introduced in 1989.

The 1991–2 legislative elections were abandoned after the first round in anticipation of a victory by the opposition Islamic Salvation Front (FIS), which had campaigned on a radical Islamist platform. The FIS was banned in 1992, triggering civil unrest and conflict between Islamic groups (the FIS-backed Islamic Salvation Army and the more extreme Armed Islamic Group) and the military. A state of emergency was declared in 1992, and the country suffered an insurgency that claimed an estimated 100,000 lives. The level of violence started to fall in 1999, when the newly elected president Abdelaziz Bouteflika initiated a policy of reconciliation with the Islamists, and his 'civil concord' was approved by referendum in 1999. In 2005 a referendum approved a second amnesty for militants and the military, but since 2006 a group aligning itself with al-Qaida has carried out a series of bombings.

Another divisive issue is the ethnic Berbers' campaign since 2001 for greater political and cultural recognition. Following occasionally violent demonstrations and a Berber boycott of the 2002 and 2004 elections, negotiations led to an agreement in 2005 that promised greater government investment in the Berber-populated Kabylie region and greater recognition for the Berber language. The Berber protests also reflected the wider population's discontent with social conditions and living standards. High food prices, unemployment and a lack of political freedom were the main reasons behind demonstrations in early 2011, and the government responded in February by ordering cuts in the prices of basic foodstuffs and lifting the 19-year state of emergency.

In the 2007 legislative election, the ruling FLN-led coalition won the most seats; the elections were blighted by violence, a low turnout and a high number of spoilt ballots. In 2009, President Bouteflika was re-elected for a third term with 90.2 per cent of the vote.

POLITICAL SYSTEM

The 1976 constitution was amended in 1989 to reintroduce political pluralism, and was revised in 2008, most notably to remove the limit on presidential terms. The president is directly elected for a five-year term, which may be renewed. The bicameral *Barlaman* comprises the National People's Assembly, the lower house, and the National Council. The assembly has 389 members, directly elected for a five-year term. The National Council has 144 members; 48 are appointed by the president, and 96 are indirectly elected for a six-year term by electoral colleges formed by local councils; half of these elected members are re-elected every three years. Although Algeria is no longer a one-party state, parties based on religion, including the FIS, or on race, language, gender or region, are banned under the constitution.

HEAD OF STATE
President, Defence, Abdelaziz Bouteflika, *elected* 15 April 1999, *re-elected* 2004, 2009

SELECTED GOVERMENT MEMBERS *as at June 2011*
Prime Minister, Ahmed Ouyahia
Deputy Prime Minister, Noureddine Yazid Zerhouni
Finance, Karim Djoudi
Foreign Affairs, Mourad Medelci
Interior, Dahou Ould Kablia

ALGERIAN EMBASSY
54 Holland Park, London W11 3RS
T 020-7221 7800 E info@algerianembassy.org.uk
W www.algerianembassy.org.uk
Ambassador Extraordinary and Plenipotentiary, HE Amar Abba, *apptd* 2010

BRITISH EMBASSY
3 Chemin Capitaine Hocine Slimane, Ex Chemin des Glycines, Algiers
T (+213) (770) 085 000 E britishembassy.algiers@fco.gov.uk
W http://ukinalgeria.fco.gov.uk
Ambassador Extraordinary and Plenipotentiary, HE Martyn Roper, *apptd* 2010

BRITISH COUNCIL
BP 452 Ben Aknoun RP, Algiers 16028
T (+213) (21) 916 891 W www.britishcouncil.org/algeria
Director, Jeremy Jacobson

DEFENCE
The army has 1,082 main battle tanks, 1,040 armoured infantry fighting vehicles and 750 armoured personnel carriers. The navy has 3 submarines, 3 frigates, 6 corvettes and 20 patrol and coastal vessels. There are bases at Mers el Kebir, Algiers, Annaba and Jijel. The air force has 163 combat aircraft and 33 armed helicopters.

Military budget – US$5,670m (2010)
Military personnel – 147,000: army 127,000, navy 6,000, air force 14,000; paramilitary 187,200
Conscription duration – 18 months

ECONOMY AND TRADE
In 1994 the government embarked on the liberalisation of the centrally planned economy, and in 1997 initiated a privatisation programme. These reforms, combined with high oil prices, resulted in trade surpluses, record foreign exchange reserves and the reduction of foreign debt, but greater economic buoyancy has had little impact on the high levels of poverty and unemployment. Diversification away from the energy sector and development of the financial system and infrastructure is slow because of difficulty in attracting investment, inefficiency and corruption.

Algeria has substantial oil and gas reserves and the hydrocarbon industry accounts for 30 per cent of GDP, nearly 60 per cent of government revenue and over 95 per cent of export earnings. Services provide 30.2 per cent of GDP, industry 61.5 per cent and agriculture 8.3 per cent. Industries other than oil and gas production and processing include mining, electrical goods, food processing and light industries.

Algeria's main trading partners are the USA, France, Italy, other EU countries and China. The chief imports are capital goods, foodstuffs and consumer goods.

GNI – US$139,577m; US$4,420 per capita (2009)
Annual average growth of GDP – 4.1 per cent (2010 est)
Inflation rate – 5 per cent (2010 est)
Population below poverty line – 23 per cent (2006 est)
Unemployment – 9.9 per cent (2010 est)
Total external debt – US$4,138m (2010 est)
Imports – US$39,100m (2009)
Exports – US$43,700m (2009)

BALANCE OF PAYMENTS
Trade – US$17,483m surplus (2010)
Current Account – US$34,452m surplus (2008)

Trade with UK	2009	2010
Imports from UK	£327,251,377	£345,666,316
Exports to UK	£511,253,376	£592,122,932

EDUCATION AND HEALTH
Literacy rate – 76.2 per cent (2008 est)
Gross enrolment ratio (percentage of relevant age group) – primary 108 per cent; tertiary 31 per cent (2009 est)

Health expenditure (per capita) – US$268 (2009)
Hospital beds (per 1,000 people) – 1.7 (2004–9)

MEDIA
The television (Entreprise Nationale de Télévision) and radio stations (Radio-Télévision Algérienne) are state-controlled. Their output is supplemented by satellite television received on domestic dishes; French and European channels are popular, and some actively target Algerian viewers. There are several main daily newspapers, some published in Arabic and some in French. There is no direct censorship but defamation laws are used to rein in press criticism. There have been infrequent instances of online censorship, but political commentators are generally able to make use of blogs and Twitter feeds; some political websites are blocked.

ANDORRA

Principat d'Andorra – Principality of Andorra

Area – 468 sq. km
Capital – Andorra la Vella; population, 24,864 (2009 est)
Major cities – Encamp, Les Escaldes
Currency – Euro (€) of 100 cents
Population – 84,525 rising at 0.38 per cent a year (2010 est); Spanish (43 per cent), Andorran (33 per cent), Portuguese (11 per cent), French (7 per cent) (est)
Religion – Christian (Roman Catholic 90 per cent) (est)
Language – Catalan (official), French, Spanish (Castilian), Portuguese
Population density – 181 per sq. km (2009)
Urban population – 89 per cent (2008 est)
Median age (years) – 39.9 (2010 est)
National anthem – 'El Gran Carlemany' ['The Great Charlemagne']
National day – 8 September (Our Lady of Meritxell Day)
Life expectancy (years) – 82.36 (2010 est)
Mortality rate – 6.21 (2010 est)
Birth rate – 10.03 (2010 est)
Infant mortality rate – 3.84 (2010 est)
Death penalty – Abolished for all crimes (since 1990)

CLIMATE AND TERRAIN
Located in the Pyrenees, on the border between France and Spain, Andorra is a landlocked country of dramatic mountains interspersed by narrow valleys. Over a third of the country is forested. The highest point of elevation is 2,946m (Coma Pedrosa) and the lowest is 840m (Riu Runer). The climate is alpine, with heavy snowfall in winter and warm summers. Average temperature ranges from −1°C to 6°C in January and 12°C to 26°C in July.

HISTORY AND POLITICS

Liberated from Moorish rule by Charlemagne in 803, Andorra is a small, neutral principality that was formed by a *paréage* (a type of feudal treaty) in 1278 and since then has owed dual allegiance to two co-princes, the Spanish Bishop of Urgell and the head of state of France. Andorra became an independent democratic parliamentary co-principality in 1993. The country subsequently formalised its links with the EU and joined the UN and the Council of Europe.

In the 2009 legislative election, the opposition Social Democratic Party won half of the 28 seats and formed a government, but found it difficult to enact legislation because of the balance in parliament. Early elections were called for April 2011, and these were won by the Democrats for Andorra party with 21 seats. It took office under Antoni Martí in May.

POLITICAL SYSTEM
Under the 1993 constitution, the heads of state are two co-princes, the President of France and the Bishop of Urgel, Spain. They are represented in Andorra by the permanent delegates (the Spanish vicar-general of the diocese of Urgell and the French prefect of the Pyrénées Orientales department), but their powers now relate solely to relations with France and Spain. The constitution established an independent judiciary and allows Andorra to conduct its own foreign policy, while its people may now join political parties and trade unions.

Andorra has a unicameral legislature, the General Council of the Valleys *(Consell General de las Valls)*, whose 28 members are directly elected for a four-year term by proportional representation. The council appoints the president of the executive council, who nominates government members.

HEADS OF STATE
The President of France, Nicolas Sarkozy
The Bishop of Urgell, Joan Enric Vives i Sicília
Permanent French Delegate, Christian Frémont
Permanent Episcopal Delegate, Nemesi Marqués Oste

SELECTED GOVERNMENT MEMBERS *as at May 2011*
President of the Executive Council, Culture, Antoni Martí
Economy and Territory, Jordi Alcobé
Foreign Affairs, Gilbert Saboya
Interior and Justice, Marc Vila

BRITISH CONSULATE-GENERAL
Ambassador, HE Giles Paxman, *apptd* 2009, resident at Madrid, Spain

ECONOMY AND TRADE

The economy is largely based on tourism (especially skiing), banking and commerce, which together account for over 75 per cent of GDP. Other activities include manufacturing tobacco products, forestry, furniture-making and sheep-farming. Most of Andorra's food and electricity has to be imported. Andorra has been a member of the EU customs union since 1991.
GNI – US$3,712m; US$41,130 per capita (2008)
Annual average growth of GDP – 2.6 per cent (2008 est)
Inflation rate – 2.3 per cent (2008)
Population below poverty line – 8 per cent (2008)
Unemployment – 7 per cent (2008)

BALANCE OF PAYMENTS
Trade – US$1,609m deficit (2010)

Trade with UK	2009	2010
Imports from UK	£17,477,363	£6,270,997
Exports to UK	£51,597	£402,284

COMMUNICATIONS

There are 320km of roads but no railways, airports or waterways. A road into Andorra from Spain is open all year round, and one from France is closed only occasionally in winter. Mobile telephones are nearly twice as widespread as fixed-line connections.

MEDIA

The media is influenced by France and Spain, and Andorrans have access to broadcasts from both countries. There is a state-owned radio station and a number of privately owned stations, as well as a state-owned television channel and two major daily newspapers *(Diari d'Andorra* and *El Periodic)*.

ANGOLA

Republica de Angola – Republic of Angola

Area – 1,246,700 sq. km; includes the exclave of Cabinda
Capital – Luanda; population, 4,510,690 (2009 est)
Major cities – Cabinda, Huambo, Lubango
Currency – Kwanza (Kzrl) of 100 centimos
Population – 13,068,161 rising at 2.06 per cent a year (2010 est); Ovimbundu (37 per cent), Kimbundu (25 per cent), Bakongo (13 per cent), other African, including Lunda-Chokwe and Ngangela (22 per cent), mestico (2 per cent) (est)
Religion – Christian (predominantly Roman Catholic; indigenous African Christian denominations 25 per cent, Protestant 10 per cent) (est). Some of the rural population practises animism or indigenous religions
Language – Portuguese (official), Bantu and other African languages
Population density – 15 per sq. km (2009)
Urban population – 57 per cent (2008 est)
Median age (years) – 18 (2010 est)
National anthem – 'Angola Avante' ['Forward Angola']
National day – 11 November (Independence Day)
Life expectancy (years) – 38.48 (2010 est)
Mortality rate – 23.74 (2010 est)
Birth rate – 43.33 (2010 est)
Infant mortality rate – 178.13 (2010 est)
HIV/AIDS adult prevalence – 2 per cent (2009 est)
Death penalty – Abolished for all crimes (since 1992)
CPI score – 1.9 (2010)
Literacy rate – 67.4 per cent (2008 est)
Gross enrolment ratio (percentage of relevant age group) – primary 128 per cent (2009 est)

Health expenditure (per capita) – US$204 (2009)
Hospital beds (per 1,000 people) – 0.8 (2004–9)

CLIMATE AND TERRAIN
The land rises from a narrow coastal plain to a vast interior plateau. On the plateau rise the Cunene, Cubango and Cuanza rivers, and further east are the sources of the Zambezi and several tributaries of the Congo river. Some of these are dry except in the rainy season, when flooding may occur. The south is desert. The highest point of elevation is 2,620m (Morro do Moco) and the lowest is 0m (Atlantic Ocean). The climate is tropical in the north – with a cool, dry season from April to September and a hot, rainy season from October to March – and sub-tropical in the south and along the coast to Luanda.

HISTORY AND POLITICS
A Portuguese colony was established in the region in the 15th century and its territory expanded over the centuries, the current boundaries being defined in the 19th century. An anti-colonial war began in 1961, which developed into a civil war between three independence movements shortly before Angola became independent on 11 November 1975. At this point, the Popular Movement for the Liberation of Angola (MPLA) declared itself the government and introduced a one-party Marxist-Leninist regime, establishing its control over the towns. The National Union for the Total Independence of Angola (UNITA), led by Jonas Savimbi, and the Front for the Liberation of Angola (FNLA) conducted a guerrilla war in rural areas. The FNLA ceased operations in the 1980s and foreign support for the MPLA and UNITA was withdrawn after 1988, but the civil war between the government and UNITA continued until 2002. Following the death of Jonas Savimbi in February of that year, UNITA and the government signed a formal ceasefire agreement in April and pledged to adhere to the 1994 peace agreement. UNITA gradually demobilised its forces and transformed itself into a political party.

Political pluralism was introduced under the 1991 peace agreement and multiparty elections were held in 1992, though UNITA refused to accept the results. The first legislative elections since 1992 were held in 2008; the MPLA won, with 191 seats to UNITA's 16 seats, and formed a new government. A presidential election has not been held since 1992; the new constitution introduced in 2010 ended direct election of the president, created the office of vice-president and abolished the post of prime minister.

SECESSION
In the oil-rich northern exclave of Cabinda, separatists have conducted a low-level guerrilla war since the mid-1970s. The government has been unable to end the fighting either through negotiation or by military means. A ceasefire and peace agreement reached in 2006 has not been observed by all parties.

POLITICAL SYSTEM
Under the 2010 constitution, the president is chosen by the party with the largest number of seats in the legislature. The unicameral National Assembly has 223 members, elected by proportional representation for a five-year term.

HEAD OF STATE
President, Jose Eduardo dos Santos, *re-elected*
  30 September 1992
Vice-President, Fernando da Piedade dos Santos

SELECTED GOVERNMENT MEMBERS *as at June 2011*
Defence, Candido Pereira dos Santos Van-Dunem
Finance, Carlos Alberto Lopes
Foreign Affairs, George Rebelo Pinto Chicoty
Interior, Sebastiao Jose Antonio Martins

EMBASSY OF THE REPUBLIC OF ANGOLA
22 Dorset Street, London W1U 6QY
T 020-7299 9850 E embassy@angola.org.uk
W www.angola.org.uk
Ambassador Extraordinary and Plenipotentiary, HE Ana Maria Teles Carreira, *apptd* 2005

BRITISH EMBASSY
Rua 17 de Setembro (Caixa Postal 1244), Luanda
T (+244) (22) 233 4583 W http://ukinangola.fco.gov.uk
Ambassador Extraordinary and Plenipotentiary, HE Richard Wildash, *apptd* 2010

DEFENCE
The army has an estimated 300 main battle tanks, 250 armoured infantry fighting vehicles and 170 armoured personnel carriers. The navy is based at Luanda and has 5 patrol and coastal combatant vessels. The air force has 103 combat aircraft and 14 armed helicopters.
Military budget – US$2,740m (2010)
Military personnel – 107,000: army 100,000, navy 1,000, air force 6,000; paramilitary 10,000

ECONOMY AND TRADE
The economy is still recovering from decades of mismanagement, corruption and war, but liberalisation and stabilisation are being achieved. Post-war increases in oil, diamond and agricultural production have driven strong economic growth, although the economy contracted in 2009 as the global downturn reduced demand for exports. The extractive industries and infrastructure projects have attracted foreign investment despite the corruption and stifling bureaucracy that have deterred investors in other sectors.

Angola, especially Cabinda, is rich in natural resources. The main industries involve extracting and processing oil (oil production and related activities account for around 85 per cent of GDP), diamonds, metals and other minerals, forestry, fishing, food processing and the manufacture of cement, metal products, tobacco products and textiles, and ship repair. Angola has large areas of good farmland, but the prevalence of unexploded landmines has reduced the area under cultivation and forced many areas back to subsistence agriculture, although coffee, sisal and cotton are produced for export. Despite rising production, the country still imports half of its food.

The main trading partners are China, the USA and Portugal. The principal exports are crude oil, diamonds, refined petroleum products, coffee, sisal, fish, timber and cotton. The main imports are machinery and electrical equipment, vehicles and spare parts, medicines, food, textiles and military goods.
GNI – US$67,478m; US$3,750 per capita (2009)
Annual average growth of GDP – 5.9 per cent (2010 est)
Inflation rate – 13.3 per cent (2010 est)
Population below poverty line – 40.5 per cent (2006 est)
Total external debt – US$17,980m (2010 est)
Exports – US$40,100m (2009)

BALANCE OF PAYMENTS
Trade – US$20,361m surplus (2010)
Current Account – US$6,408m surplus (2008)

Trade with UK	2009	2010
Imports from UK	£332,609,518	£534,742,729
Exports to UK	£270,034,371	£43,142,776

COMMUNICATIONS

Land transport difficulties, caused by war damage to road and rail infrastructure, are compounded by uncleared landmines and security problems. Reconstruction began in 2005 with foreign aid, provided largely by China, and several projects have been completed. There are 51,429km of roads and 2,764km of railway. Most internal travel takes place by air between the country's 193 airports and airfields. The main ports are Luanda, Lobito and Namibe. The fixed-line telephone system is poor, with about two fixed lines for 100 people; mobile phone use is growing rapidly, reaching about 65 per cent of people in 2009.

MEDIA

The only national daily newspaper and most television and radio broadcasters are state-owned and rarely critical. There are several commercial radio stations and private newspapers, one private television station, and some subscription services that include Brazilian and Portuguese channels; their coverage is confined to urban areas. One state-owned radio station offers programmes in the Bantu language. Although freedom of speech is enshrined in the constitution, the private media is liable to harassment.

ANTIGUA AND BARBUDA

Antigua and Barbuda

Area – 442.6 sq. km; Antigua 280 sq. km; Barbuda 161 sq. km; Redonda 1.6 sq. km
Capital – St John's; population, 26,580 (2009 est)
Currency – East Caribbean dollar (EC$) of 100 cents
Population – 86,754; rising at 1.3 per cent a year (2010 est)
Religion – Christian 74 per cent (Anglican 26 per cent, Catholic, Methodist and Moravian each less than 10 per cent, Evangelical 25 per cent, Jehovah's Witness 1 per cent), Rastafarian 1 per cent (2001)
Language – English (official)
Population density – 199 per sq. km (2009)
Urban population – 30 per cent (2008 est)
Median age (years) – 30 (2010 est)
National anthem – 'Fair Antigua, We Salute Thee'
National day – 1 November (Independence Day)
Life expectancy (years) – 75.26 (2010 est)
Mortality rate – 5.77 (2010 est)
Birth rate – 16.43 (2010 est)

Infant mortality rate – 15.1 (2010 est)
Death penalty – Retained
Literacy rate – 99.0 per cent (2008 est)

CLIMATE AND TERRAIN

Antigua is part of the Leeward Islands in the eastern Caribbean. Unlike most other Leeward Islands, it has few high hills and little forest cover. Its elevation extremes range from 402m (Boggy Peak) to 0m (Caribbean Sea). Barbuda, 48km north of Antigua, is a flat coral island with a large lagoon.

Both islands are tropical, but drier than most of the West Indies. They lie within the hurricane belt and are subject to tropical storms and hurricanes between August and October.

HISTORY AND POLITICS

Prehistoric settlers were succeeded by the Arawaks, then the Caribs. Although the islands were discovered by Columbus in 1493, the European (English) settlement of Antigua began only in 1632. Barbuda was colonised from Antigua in 1661. Administered as part of the Leeward Islands Federation from 1871 to 1956, it became internally self-governing in 1967 and fully independent on 1 November 1981.

The United Progressive Party defeated the Antigua Labour Party, which had been in office since 1976, in the 2004 election and was re-elected in 2009.

POLITICAL SYSTEM
The head of state is Queen Elizabeth II, represented by the governor-general. The bicameral parliament comprises a senate of 17 members, appointed by the governor-general on the advice of the prime minister and opposition leader, and a House of Representatives of 17 directly elected members; both chambers serve a five-year term.
Governor-General, HE Dame Louise Lake-Tack, GCMG, apptd 2007

SELECTED GOVERNMENT MEMBERS *as at June 2011*
Prime Minister, Foreign Affairs, Baldwin Spencer
Minister of Finance and Economy, Harold Lovell
National Security, Leon Errol Cort

HIGH COMMISSION FOR ANTIGUA AND BARBUDA
2nd Floor, 45 Crawford Place, London W1H 4LP
T 020-7258 0070 E enquiries@antigua-barbuda.com
W www.antigua-barbuda.com
High Commissioner, HE Dr Carl Roberts, apptd 2004

BRITISH HIGH COMMISSION
HE Paul Brummell, apptd 2009, resident at Bridgetown, Barbados

DEFENCE

The navy has 2 patrol and coastal combatant vessels at a base at St John's.
Military budget – US$33m (2010)
Military personnel – 170: army 125, navy 45 (combined Antigua and Barbuda Defence Force)

ECONOMY AND TRADE

The economy is largely based on tourism and related services (contributing over half of GDP), with light manufacturing (bedding, handicrafts, electronic components) for export, and agriculture (livestock, sea island cotton, market gardening, fishing) for local consumption. Economic growth and fiscal reform between 2004–7 enabled the government to reduce public debt. However, from 2008, a decline in tourism caused by the global economic downturn and the collapse of Alan Stanford's Antigua-based financial group (which included Antigua's major financial institution) hit the economy badly and public debt is rising again.

GNI – US$1,065m; US$12,130 per capita (2009)
Annual average growth of GDP – −4.1 per cent (2010 est)
Inflation rate – 1.5 per cent (2007 est)
Total external debt – US$359.8m (2006)

BALANCE OF PAYMENTS
Trade – US$505m deficit (2010)
Current Account – US$354m deficit (2008)

Trade with UK	2009	2010
Imports from UK	£24,019,586	£10,727,437
Exports to UK	£281,994	£2,261,243

MEDIA AND CULTURE
The Antigua Labour Party and the Bird family owns or controls many of the country's television and radio stations. Antigua's first independent radio station, Observer Radio, began broadcasting in 2001.

Antiguan culture is dominated by cricket and the country has produced several illustrious players, including former West Indies captains Viv Richards (*b.* 1952) and Richie Richardson (*b.* 1962) and bowler Curtly Ambrose (*b.* 1963).

ARGENTINA

República Argentina – Argentine Republic

Area – 2,780,400 sq. km
Capital – Buenos Aires; population, 12,987,800 (2009)
Major cities – Córdoba, La Plata, Mar del Plata, Mendoza, Rosario, Salta, San Miguel de Tucumán, Santa Fé
Currency – Peso of 100 centavos
Population – 41,343,201 rising at 1.04 per cent a year (2010 est)
Religion – Christian (Roman Catholic 76 per cent, Pentecostal 8 per cent), Muslim 1 per cent (of which Sunni 60 per cent, Shia 40 per cent) (est)
Language – Spanish (official), Italian, English, German, French
Population density – 15 per sq. km (2009)
Urban population – 92 per cent (2008 est)
Median age (years) – 30 (2010 est)
National anthem – 'Marcha de la Patria' ['March of the Fatherland']

National day – 25 May (Revolution Day)
Life expectancy (years) – 76.76 (2010 est)
Mortality rate – 7.39 (2010 est)
Birth rate – 17.75 (2010 est)
Infant mortality rate – 11.11 (2010 est)
Death penalty – Abolished for all crimes (since 2008)
CPI score – 2.9 (2010)

CLIMATE AND TERRAIN
The Andes mountain range runs the full length of the country, along its western border with Chile, and the area is prone to earthquakes. East of the Andes, the north is mostly subtropical rainforest, the centre contains the vast grasslands of the pampas (which experienced extreme drought in 2008–9), and the southern Patagonian plateau is arid and desolate, with glaciers in the far south. The highest point of elevation is 6,960m (Cerro Aconcagua) and the lowest is −105m (Laguna del Carbon). Temperatures range from subtropical in the north to subantarctic in the south. In Buenos Aires temperatures are between 19°C and 30°C in January and between 7°C and 15°C in June.

HISTORY AND POLITICS
The estuary of La Plata was discovered in 1515 by Juan Díaz de Solís and the region was subsequently colonised by the Spanish. Spain ruled the territory, which formed part of the United Provinces of the Rio Plata, from the 16th century until a revolution began in 1810. Independence was declared in 1816. During the following century power swung, often violently, between conservative and liberal factions, and between civil and military regimes.

A 1943 coup introduced a period of military rule before Juan Perón became president in 1946, establishing an authoritarian regime. His overthrow in 1955 instigated 18 years of political instability until 1973, when he was recalled from exile. Perón died within a year and was succeeded by the vice-president, his widow María ('Isabelita'), but she was overthrown in a coup in 1976 that established a military junta. The junta conducted a campaign known as the 'dirty war' in which over 8,000 people were allegedly murdered. The failure of Argentina's attempt to annex the Falkland Islands in 1982 discredited the junta and led to the restoration of civilian rule in 1983. In 2009 Argentina submitted to the UN a formal claim to an area of the South Atlantic Ocean that includes several island groups governed by Britain.

The 2007 presidential election was won in the first round by Cristina Fernández de Kirchner, wife of the outgoing president Néstor Kirchner. The Front for Victory, the pro-presidential wing of the internally divided Judicialist Party, a Peronist grouping, lost its absolute majorities in both chambers in the 2009 legislative elections, but remained in power. The next presidential and legislative elections are scheduled for 23 October 2011.

POLITICAL SYSTEM
After the constitutional amendments agreed in 1994, the executive president is directly elected for a four-year term, renewable only once. The bicameral National Congress consists of a 72-member senate (three members for each province and three for Buenos Aires) and a 257-member Chamber of Deputies. Deputies are directly elected for a four-year term, with half of the seats renewable every two years. Senators are directly elected for a six-year term, with one-third of seats renewable every two years.

The Argentine Republic is a federation of 23 provinces, each with an elected governor and legislature, plus the federal district of Buenos Aires, which has an elected mayor and autonomous government.

HEAD OF STATE
President, Cristina Fernández de Kirchner, *sworn in* 10 December 2007
Vice-President, Julio Cobos

SELECTED GOVERNMENT MEMBERS *as at June 2011*
Cabinet Chief, Anibal Fernandez
Defence, Arturo Puricelli
Economy, Amado Boudou
Foreign Relations, Héctor Timerman
Interior, Anibal Randazzo

EMBASSY OF THE ARGENTINE REPUBLIC
65 Brook Street, London W1K 4AH
T 020-7318 1300 E info@argentine-embassy-uk.org
W www.argentine-embassy-uk.org
Ambassador Extraordinary and Plenipotentiary, vacant

BRITISH EMBASSY
Dr Luis Agote 2412, 1425 Buenos Aires
T (+54) (11) 4808 2200 W http://ukinargentina.fco.gov.uk
Ambassador Extraordinary and Plenipotentiary, HE Shan Morgan, *apptd* 2008

BRITISH COUNCIL
4th Floor, Marcelo T. de Alvear 590, C1058AAF Buenos Aires
T (+54) (11) 4114 8600 W www.britishcouncil.org/argentina
Director, Huw Jones

DEFENCE
The army has 213 main battle tanks, 263 armoured infantry fighting vehicles and 294 armoured personnel carriers. The navy has 3 submarines, 5 destroyers, 6 frigates, 17 patrol and coastal vessels and 24 combat aircraft. There are bases at Ushuaia, Mar del Plata, Buenos Aires, Puerto Belgrano and Zarate. The air force has 121 combat aircraft.
Military budget – US$2,600m (2010)
Military personnel – 73,100: army 38,500, navy 20,000, air force 14,600; paramilitary 31,240

ECONOMY AND TRADE
The economy recovered rapidly from the economic collapse of 2001–2, experiencing strong growth from 2003. Argentina restructured its defaulted debt in 2005 and repaid its IMF loan in 2006. Inflation rose sharply in 2007–8 and remains high, pushing up prices, although the economy has recovered rapidly from a recession in 2008–9 caused by the global downturn. A shortfall in energy supplies remains a problem.

The country is rich in natural resources, particularly lead, zinc, tin, copper, iron ore, manganese, uranium, oil and coal. The fertile pampas supports a strong and export-orientated agricultural sector; the main crops are cereals, oil-bearing seeds, fruit, tea, tobacco and livestock products, especially beef, mutton and wool.

The main industrial activities are food processing (meat-packing, flour-milling, sugar-refining, wine production) and the production of motor vehicles, consumer durables, textiles, chemicals, petrochemicals, printing, metallurgy and steel.

The main trading partners are Brazil, China and the USA. The principal exports include soya beans and derivatives, petroleum and gas, motor vehicles and cereals.

The major imports are machinery, motor vehicles, petroleum and natural gas, chemicals and plastics.
GNI – US$297,710m; US$7,550 per capita (2009)
Annual average growth of GDP – 7.5 per cent (2010 est)
Inflation rate – 22 per cent (2010 est)
Population below poverty line – 30 per cent (2010)
Unemployment – 7.9 per cent (2010 est)
Total external debt – US$128,600m (2010)
Imports – US$39,100m (2009)
Exports – US$56,100m (2009)

BALANCE OF PAYMENTS
Trade – US$12,057m surplus (2010)
Current Account – US$8,651m surplus (2009)

Trade with UK	2009	2010
Imports from UK	£235,064,496	£329,605,990
Exports to UK	£588,187,659	£601,594,040

COMMUNICATIONS
The road and rail networks are extensive in the north and centre of the country; in Patagonia, there are fewer roads and no railways. All 36,966km of railway is state owned. The combined national and provincial road network totals 231,374km, of which 69,412km is surfaced. Internal long-distance travel is mainly by air and there are over 1,000 airports and airfields; the principal airports are at Buenos Aires, Córdoba, Salta and Rio Gallegos. There are many ports on the long coastline and the 11,000km of inland waterways formed by the major rivers; Buenos Aires, Ensenada (La Plata) and Bahía Blanca are the main seaports. The telecommunications system has been modernised and extended since the late 1990s. There were about 9.7 million fixed telephone lines in use and 51.9 million mobile phone subscriptions in 2009.

EDUCATION AND HEALTH
Education is compulsory until the age of 14.
Literacy rate – 97.7 per cent (2008 est)
Gross enrolment ratio (percentage of relevant age group) – primary 116 per cent; secondary 85 per cent; tertiary 68 per cent (2007 est)
Health expenditure (per capita) – US$730 (2009)
Hospital beds (per 1,000 people) – 4.0 (2004–9)

MEDIA AND CULTURE
Argentina's media is prolific, with over 150 daily newspapers (mainly in Spanish, with some in English and German), including seven major dailies published in Buenos Aires. There are hundreds of commercial radio stations (many unlicensed), over 40 television stations and widespread access to cable television.

Most Argentines are of European origin, particularly from Spain and Italy, and Patagonia also has a Welsh-speaking Argentine-Welsh community. The short-story writer, poet and essayist Jorge Luis Borges (1899–1986) is one of Latin America's most eminent literary figures, and the world's first animated films were made in Argentina by Quirino Cristiani (1896–1984). The tango, an African-influenced dance style set to music of diverse European origins, first became popular among European immigrants in Buenos Aires in the late 19th century.

Argentina has a vibrant sporting culture, with successes in football, motor racing and polo. Its football team is a double World Cup winner and has held the Copa America trophy 14 times; noted Argentine players include Alfredo di Stéfano (*b.* 1926), Diego Maradona (*b.* 1960) and Lionel Messi (*b.* 1987).

ARGENTINE ANTARCTIC TERRITORY

The Argentine Antarctic Territory consists of the Antarctic Peninsula and a triangular section extending to the South Pole, defined as the area between 25°W and 74° W and 60°S. This overlaps with both Britain's and Chile's claimed areas (*see also* The North and South Poles). Administratively, the territory is a department of the province of Tierra del Fuego, Antarctica and South Atlantic Islands. The population varies seasonally between approximately 150 and 300 people, all of whom are scientific researchers and their dependents.

ARMENIA

Hayastani Hanrapetut'yun – Republic of Armenia

Area – 29,743 sq. km
Capital – Yerevan; population, 1,110,190 (2009 est)
Major cities – Gyumri, Vanadzor
Currency – Dram of 100 luma
Population – 2,966,802 rising at 0.02 per cent a year (2010 est); Armenian (97.9 per cent), Yezidi (1.3 per cent) (2001). The Armenian diaspora numbers at least 4,700,000
Religion – Christian (Armenian Apostolic 90 per cent) (est). The kingdom of Armenia was the first state to adopt Christianity as its official religion, in AD 301
Language – Armenian, Yezidi, Russian
Population density – 108 per sq. km (2009)
Urban population – 64 per cent (2008 est)
Median age (years) – 31.9 (2010 est)
National anthem – 'Mer Hayrenik' ['Our Fatherland']
National day – 21 September (Independence Day)
Life expectancy (years) – 72.96 (2010 est)
Mortality rate – 8.42 (2010 est)
Birth rate – 12.74 (2010 est)
Infant mortality rate – 19.5 (2010 est)
Death penalty – Abolished for all crimes (since 2003)
CPI score – 2.6 (2010)

CLIMATE AND TERRAIN

Landlocked Armenia is situated in the south-western part of the Caucasus region between the Black and Caspian seas. It lies at a high altitude and consists of vast plateaux surrounded by mountain ranges. The elevation extremes range from 4,090m (the highest peak of Mt Aragats) to 400m at the lowest (Debed river). The climate is continental, with hot summers, cold winters and low rainfall. Armenia experiences occasional droughts and severe earthquakes.

HISTORY AND POLITICS

The first Armenian state was founded c.190 BC and became part of the Roman Empire in 64 BC.

It subsequently experienced short periods of autonomy interspersed with rule by successive empires and invasion by the Seljuk Turks, Mongols and other Central Asian tribes. In the 16th century most of Armenia was incorporated into the Ottoman Empire. The remaining eastern areas fell under the Persian Empire; these were later forcibly incorporated into the Russian Empire, which concluded wars with the Persians in 1813 and 1828. The part of Armenia that remained under Ottoman rule experienced pogroms from 1894 onwards, and from 1915 to 1918 over 1.5 million Armenians were deported, starved or killed.

Armenia declared its independence on 28 May 1918, but was invaded in 1920 by Soviet forces and declared a Soviet Socialist Republic. The Soviet government was overthrown by a nationalist revolt in 1921, but reinstated by the Red Army a few months later. In early 1922 Armenia acceded to the USSR.

An Armenian nationalist movement gained power in national elections in 1990. In a referendum in 1991, 99 per cent of the electorate voted for independence, which was declared on 21 September 1991.

In the 2007 legislative election, the Republican Party of Armenia (HHK) remained the largest party in the legislature, with 65 seats, and its leader, Serzh Sargsyan, continued in office at the head of a four-party coalition government. Sargsyan won the 2008 presidential election in the first round with 52.9 per cent of the vote; his victory led to several weeks of violent protests by opposition supporters. After his inauguration President Sargsyan nominated Tigran Sargsyan as prime minister.

FOREIGN RELATIONS

There is a longstanding dispute with Azerbaijan over the predominantly Armenian-populated Azeri region of Nagorny-Karabakh; Armenia claims this territory as historically native land arbitrarily granted to Soviet Azerbaijan by Stalin in 1921–2. The territory's government voted to transfer to Armenia in 1988 but this was rejected by the USSR. When the USSR collapsed in 1991, the territory declared independence. Azeri attempts to reassert control were met with resistance which escalated into a war that lasted from 1992 until a ceasefire was agreed between Armenia, Azerbaijan and Nagorny-Karabakh in 1994. By this time, Nagorno-Karabakh forces, supported by Armenia, had captured all of Nagorno-Karabakh, all Azeri territory that separated Nagorny-Karabakh from Armenia and all mountainous Azeri territory around the enclave. Talks mediated by the Organisation for Security and Cooperation in Europe failed to make any progress towards a peaceful resolution until 2008, when Azerbaijan and Armenia agreed to intensify efforts.

POLITICAL SYSTEM

The 1995 constitution was amended by referendum in 2005. The president is directly elected for a five-year term, renewable only once. The unicameral National Assembly (*Azgayin Joghov*) has 131 members who are directly elected for a four-year term.

HEAD OF STATE
President, Serzh Sargsyan, *elected* 19 February 2008,
    inaugurated 9 April 2008

SELECTED GOVERNMENT MEMBERS *as at May 2011*
Prime Minister, Tigran Sargsyan
Deputy Prime Minister, Armen Gevorgyan

Defence, Seyran Ohanyan
Economy, Tigran Davtyan
Foreign Affairs, Eduard Nalbandyan

EMBASSY OF THE REPUBLIC OF ARMENIA
25A Cheniston Gardens, London W8 6TG
T 020-7938 5435 E armemb@armenianembassyuk.com
W www.armenianembassy.org.uk
Ambassador Extraordinary and Plenipotentiary, vacant

BRITISH EMBASSY
34 Baghramyan Avenue, Yerevan 0019
T (+374) (10) 264 301 E Enquiries.Yerevan@fco.gov.uk
W http://ukinarmenia.fco.gov.uk
Ambassador Extraordinary and Plenipotentiary, HE Charles
    Lonsdale, *apptd* 2008

BRITISH COUNCIL
24 Baghramyan Avenue, Yerevan 0019
T (+374) (56) 9923 W www.britishcouncil.org/armenia
Director, Arevik Saribekyan

DEFENCE
The army has 110 main battle tanks, 104 armoured
infantry fighting vehicles and 136 armoured personnel
carriers. The air force has 16 combat aircraft and 8 armed
helicopters.

Russia maintains 3,214 army personnel in Armenia,
and in 2010 its lease on a military base was extended to
2044. An agreement on military cooperation with Russia
was signed in 1996 which paved the way for joint
military exercises. A protocol was also signed on the
establishment of coalition troops in Transcaucasia and the
planned use of Russian and Armenian armed forces as part
of coalition troops in cases of mutual interest. In 2001
President Putin of Russia signed a federal law relating to
an agreement between Russia and Armenia on the joint
planning of the use of troops in the interests of joint
security provision. This stipulates measures to prevent the
use by third countries of the territory of Armenia for
purposes that may inflict damage on Russian national
interests.

Military budget – US$434m (2010)
Military personnel – 48,570: army 45,393, air and air
    defence forces 3,177; paramilitary 7,163
Conscription duration – 24 months

ECONOMY AND TRADE
The economy experienced a severe decline following the
break-up of the USSR in 1991, adding to existing
problems arising from the 1988 earthquake and
subsequently exacerbated by the Nagorny-Karabakh
conflict and the consequent trade embargos imposed by
Azerbaijan and Turkey, both of which are still in place.
Economic liberalisation from 1994 brought sustained
high growth and falls in inflation and poverty levels until
the global economic crisis. This triggered a severe
recession in 2009, largely owing to declines in
construction and remittances, despite loans from Russia
and international institutions; a recovery began in
2010.

The agricultural sector produces fruit, vegetables and
livestock as cash crops, and grain; it contributes 22 per
cent of GDP and employs 46 per cent of the workforce.
There are large mineral deposits, including iron and
copper ore and non-ferrous metals. Industry, which
contributes 47 per cent of GDP, is diversified and most
small- and medium-sized enterprises are now privatised.

The main activities are diamond-processing, the
production of industrial machinery, vehicles and parts,
textiles and clothing, chemicals, instruments,
microelectronics, jewellery, and software development and
food processing. The severe energy shortages of the
mid-1990s were overcome by the reopening of the
nuclear power plant at Metsamor in 1995. This has
enabled Armenia to become an electricity exporter, but
there is international pressure to close the plant because of
the earthquake risks in the area.

The main trading partners are Russia, EU countries,
other former Soviet bloc states, China and the USA.
Principal exports are pig iron, copper, non-ferrous metals,
diamonds, mineral products, food and energy. The main
imports are natural gas, petrol, tobacco products,
foodstuffs and diamonds.

GNI – US$8,926m; US$3,100 per capita (2009)
Annual average growth of GDP – 4.7 per cent (2010 est)
Inflation rate – 6.9 per cent (2010 est)
Population below poverty line – 26.5 per cent (2006 est)
Unemployment – 7.1 per cent (2007 est)
Total external debt – US$5,227m (2010)
Imports – US$3,300m (2009)
Exports – US$700m (2009)

BALANCE OF PAYMENTS
Trade – US$2,772m deficit (2010)
Current Account – US$1,205m deficit (2009)

Trade with UK	2009	2010
Imports from UK	£8,503,500	£12,009,208
Exports to UK	£1,690,476	£4,732,347

EDUCATION AND HEALTH
State education is free and compulsory for all children
aged seven to 14. Children attend primary school until
the age of nine, then secondary school until the age of 14.
At the end of intermediate school a certificate of basic
education is awarded. Senior secondary school may be
attended from the ages of 14 to 16.

Literacy rate – 99.5 per cent (2008 est)
Gross enrolment ratio (percentage of relevant age group) –
    primary 99 per cent; secondary 93 per cent; tertiary
    50 per cent (2009 est)
Health expenditure (per capita) – US$129 (2009)
Hospital beds (per 1,000 people) – 4.1 (2004–9)

MEDIA
Armenia has more than 40 private television stations,
which operate alongside two public networks. The main
Russian television channels are also available. Censorship
is banned under a 2004 media law, but journalists have
been imprisoned for libel and defamation offences.
Newspapers have limited influence, often owing to small
print runs, and tend to be owned by wealthy individuals
and political parties.

AUSTRALIA

Commonwealth of Australia

Area – 7,692,024 sq. km (excluding overseas territories)
Capital – Canberra, in the Australian Capital Territory; population, 384,091 (2009 est)
Major cities – Adelaide, Brisbane, Melbourne, Perth, Sydney
Currency – Australian dollar ($A) of 100 cents
Population – 21,515,754 rising at 1.17 per cent a year (2010 est)
Religion – Christian (Roman Catholic 26 per cent, Anglican 19 per cent, other 19 per cent), Buddhist 2 per cent, Muslim 2 per cent, Hindu 1 per cent (est)
Language – English, Chinese, Italian, Aboriginal languages
Population density – 3 per sq. km (2009)
Urban population – 89 per cent (2008 est)
Median age (years) – 37.5 (2010 est)
National anthem – 'Advance Australia Fair'
National day – 26 January (Australia Day)
Life expectancy (years) – 81.72 (2010 est)
Mortality rate – 6.81 (2010 est)
Birth rate – 12.39 (2010 est)
Infant mortality rate – 4.67 (2010 est)
Death penalty – Abolished for all crimes (since 1985)
CPI score – 8.7 (2010)

CLIMATE AND TERRAIN

Australia is the world's sixth-largest country and home to a wide variety of landscapes and weather conditions. Most of the country is a plateau, with hills, low mountain ranges and sparsely populated deserts in the interior, and tropical wetlands and rainforest in the north-east. Mountain ranges running down the east coast are the source of the Murray and Darling river systems, which flow across the densely populated fertile plain in the south-east. Off the north-east coast is the Great Barrier Reef, the world's largest coral reef. The highest point of elevation is 2,229m (Mt Kosciuszko) and the lowest is −15m (Lake Eyre). The climate is arid or semi-arid in the interior, tropical in the north and temperate in the south and east. The summer begins in December and the winter in June.

HISTORY AND POLITICS

The Aboriginals are thought to have arrived in Australia from south-east Asia *c.*40,000 years ago. Europeans first discovered Australia in the 17th century. Its eastern coast was claimed by Captain James Cook on behalf of Britain in 1770 and became a penal colony from 1788. The discovery of gold sparked several gold rushes in the 1850s that helped to attract free settlers, and the population trebled in a decade. The colonies of Tasmania, Western Australia, South Australia, Victoria and Queensland were established between 1825 and 1859, and became self-governing from the 1850s onwards. They were federated as the Commonwealth of Australia on 1 January 1901, and Australia was granted dominion status within the British Empire. Australia became independent within the British Commonwealth under the 1931 Statute of Westminster. Following a referendum in 1967, the Aboriginal population was granted full political rights. In 1986, the Australia Act abolished the remaining legislative, executive and judicial links to the UK while retaining the British monarch as head of state. In a national referendum in 1999, the proposal to make Australia a republic was defeated, with 45.3 per cent voting in favour and 54.7 per cent against.

The Australian Labor Party's resounding victory in the 2007 general election ended 11 years of government by a Liberal Party–National Party coalition. Under Kevin Rudd, the ALP reversed many of the previous government's policies, signing the Kyoto protocol on climate change, apologising for past abuses of Aborigines and promising an end to the detention of asylum seekers on small Pacific island states. In June 2010 Mr Rudd was replaced as ALP party leader by deputy prime minister Julia Gillard, who became Australia's first female prime minister. In a general election in August 2010 the ALP won only 72 seats, and Ms Gillard formed a minority government with the support of independents.

POLITICAL SYSTEM

Under the 1901 constitution, the Commonwealth of Australia is a federation of six states. The constitution defines the powers of the federal government, and residuary legislative power remains with the states. A degree of self-government was granted to the Northern Territory in 1978 and the Australian Capital Territory in 1988, and both tend to be treated as states.

The head of state is Queen Elizabeth II, represented by the governor-general, who is appointed on the advice of the Australian prime minister. The bicameral parliament consists of the senate and the House of Representatives. The constitution provides that the number of members of the House of Representatives shall be proportionate to the population of each state, with a minimum of five members for each state, and that the number of senators shall be, as nearly as is practicable, half the number of representatives. There are currently 150 members, including two members for the Northern Territory and two for the Australian Capital Territory; they are directly elected for a three-year term. There are 76 senators; each state returns 12 senators, who are directly elected for a six-year term, with half retiring every third year. The Australian Capital Territory and the Northern Territory each return two senators, who are directly elected for a three-year term.

Each of the six states has its own constitution, executive, legislature and judicature. Executive authority is vested in a governor (appointed by the Crown), assisted by a council of ministers or executive council headed by a state premier. There are ten territories, and three – the Australian Capital Territory, Northern Territory and Norfolk Island – have limited self-government, with an executive authority headed by an administrator (appointed by the governor-general), and legislative assembly led by a chief minister. The other territories are directly administered by the federal government.

Governor-General, Quentin Bryce, *apptd* 2008

SELECTED GOVERNMENT MEMBERS *as at May 2011*
Prime Minister, Julia Gillard
Deputy Prime Minister, Treasurer, Wayne Swan
Defence, Stephen Smith
Foreign Affairs, Kevin Rudd

AUSTRALIAN HIGH COMMISSION
Australia House, Strand, London WC2B 4LA
T 020-7379 4334 W www.uk.embassy.gov.au
High Commissioner, HE John Dauth, LVO, *apptd* 2008

BRITISH HIGH COMMISSION
Commonwealth Avenue, Yarralumla, Canberra, ACT 2600
T (+61) (2) 6270 6666 E ukinaustralia@fco.gov.uk
W http://ukinaustralia.fco.gov.uk
High Commissioner, HE Paul Madden, *apptd* 2011

BRITISH COUNCIL
PO Box 88, Edgecliff, NSW 2027
T (+61) (2) 9326 2022 W www.britishcouncil.org/au
Director, Nick Marchand

DEFENCE
The army has 59 main battle tanks, 257 armoured infantry fighting vehicles, 606 armoured personnel carriers and 16 armed helicopters. The navy has 6 submarines, 12 frigates, 14 patrol and coastal vessels and 24 armed helicopters. There are bases at Sydney, Cairns, Darwin, Garden Island, Flinders, Jervis Bay and Nowra. The air force has 138 combat aircraft.
Military expenditure – US$24,500m (2010)
Military personnel – 56,552: army 28,246, navy 14,250, air force 14,056

ECONOMY AND TRADE
Australia has a highly diversified and internationally competitive market economy that saw sustained strong growth from the early 1990s until 2008. It weathered the global downturn better than most developed countries, avoiding recession through a government fiscal stimulus package and low interest rates. Recent problems have been climate related, with agricultural output, a key export sector, down by about 20 per cent in 2006 owing to the worst drought in a century, and agriculture, mining and infrastructure hit badly by extensive flooding in Queensland, the eastern seaboard and Victoria in 2010–11. The service sector contributes 71.2 per cent of GDP and employs 75 per cent of the workforce; industry accounts for 24.8 per cent of GDP and 21.1 per cent of labour; and agriculture contributes 4 per cent of GDP and employs 3.6 per cent of the workforce.

The diversity of Australia's climate and soil conditions means that a wide range of crops can be grown, although most are confined to specific regions. Scant or erratic rainfall, limited scope for irrigation and unsuitable soils or topography have restricted intensive agriculture, although wheat is a major export and sugar cane and fruit are important crops. Cattle and sheep ranching is widespread, providing meat, meat derivatives, wool and dairy products.

Significant natural resources include bauxite, coal, copper, diamonds, gold, iron ore, lead, mineral salts, nickel, silver, tin, tungsten, uranium, zinc, oil and natural gas. The main industrial activities are mining, the production of industrial and transport equipment, chemicals and steel, and food processing. Production and processing of hydrocarbons are expected to increase once the oil and gas fields in the Timor Sea begin production.

Over the past 20 years, the focus of Australia's trade, like its foreign policy, has shifted from Europe to Asia and the Pacific region. It is a leading member of the Asia-Pacific Economic Cooperation forum, and a free-trade agreement (FTA) between Australia and the ASEAN countries entered into force in 2010; it is also negotiating for FTAs with China, Japan, South Korea and Malaysia. Major trading partners include China, Japan, South Korea, India, Thailand, Singapore and Germany. The chief exports are coal, iron ore, gold, meat, wool, alumina, wheat, machinery and transport equipment. The main imports are machinery and transport equipment, computers, office and telecommunications equipment, crude oil and petroleum products.

GNI – US$900,676m; US$43,770 per capita (2009)
Annual average growth of GDP – 3.3 per cent (2010 est)
Inflation rate – 2.9 per cent (2010 est)
Unemployment – 5.1 per cent (2010 est)
Total external debt – US$1,169,000m (2010)
Imports – US$165,500m (2009)
Exports – US$153,900m (2009)

BALANCE OF PAYMENTS
Trade – US$19,111m surplus (2010)
Current Account – US$46,683m deficit (2008)

Trade with UK	2009	2010
Imports from UK	£2,948,910,238	£3,328,979,042
Exports to UK	£3,676,666,367	£4,305,486,888

COMMUNICATIONS
Most long-distance internal travel is by air or road. There are 465 airports and airfields. Road and rail networks are concentrated in the more densely populated areas of the east and south, and around Perth in the west. Elsewhere, roads are more widespread than railways, and both skirt the deserts of the interior, apart from a few transcontinental routes. There are six government-owned

STATES AND TERRITORIES

	Area (sq. km)	Population (2010 est)	Capital	Premier (2011)
Australian Capital Territory (ACT)	2,358	359,700	Canberra	Jon Stanhope†
New South Wales (NSW)	800,642	7,253,400	Sydney	Barry O'Farrell
Northern Territory (NT)	1,349,129	230,200	Darwin*	Paul Henderson†
Queensland (Qld)	1,730,648	4,532,300	Brisbane	Anna Bligh
South Australia (SA)	983,482	1,647,800	Adelaide	Mike Rann
Tasmania (Tas.)	68,401	508,500	Hobart	Lara Giddings
Victoria (Vic.)	227,416	5,567,100	Melbourne	Ted Baillieu
Western Australia (WA)	2,529,875	2,306,200	Perth	Colin Barnett

* Seat of administration † Chief Minister

railway systems, and 38,445km of railway track. Most heavy freight is moved by road trains (trucks hauling two or three trailers) which measure up to 45m in length. There are 813,000km of roads. The 11 major ports and terminals include all the state capitals except Hobart, and there are private mining ports at Gove and Groote Eylandt in the Northern Territory. Mobile telephone distribution has grown rapidly to about 24.2 million in 2009, a density exceeding 100 per 100 people.

EDUCATION AND HEALTH

Education is administered by each state and territory, and is compulsory between the ages of five and 16 (15 in New South Wales and the Northern Territory, 17 in Western Australia). It is available at government schools and at private or independent schools, some of which are denominational.

Gross enrolment ratio (percentage of relevant age group) – primary 106 per cent; secondary 149 per cent; tertiary 77 per cent (2008 est)
Health expenditure (per capita) – US$3,867 (2009)
Hospital beds (per 1,000 people) – 3.8 (2004–9)

MEDIA

The ownership of print and broadcast media is highly concentrated: 80 per cent of newspaper titles are in the hands of four privately owned groups, including Fairfax Media and Rupert Murdoch's News Corporation. Australia's leading newspapers are *The Sydney Morning Herald*, *Herald Sun*, *The Australian* and *The Daily Telegraph*. The Australian Broadcasting Corporation and the Special Broadcasting Service provide public service radio and television broadcasting, while the Seven, Nine and Ten networks dominate commercial television. Commercial broadcasters are required to transmit a minimum percentage of Australian programming and some of these home-made programmes are sold overseas.

CULTURE

Australia's diverse indigenous communities continue to practise traditional music and art forms, which for thousands of years have been used as the media for relating a community's history and folklore. In recent years these have also been adapted to modern materials and technology, and influenced by western cultural forms. Painting, carvings and sculpture are sources of income for many communities. Influential artists include Johnny Warangkula Tjupurrula (c. 1925–2001), pioneer of the commercially successful Aboriginal dot painting technique, and Rover Thomas (1926–98).

Since the colonial era, Australia has been dominated by European, and latterly US, culture. Prominent literary figures include T.S. Eliot Prize-winning poet Les Murray (b. 1938), Nobel Prize winner Patrick White (1912–90), and double Booker Prize-winner Peter Carey (b. 1943). Germaine Greer (b. 1939) and Clive James (b. 1939) are internationally respected cultural commentators.

The country's cinema industry enjoyed a renaissance in the 1980s with success for both art-house films and mass-market franchises such as *Mad Max* and *Crocodile Dundee*. Director Baz Luhrmann (b. 1962) and actors Russell Crowe (b. 1964) and Nicole Kidman (b. 1967) are established figures in Hollywood.

Sport is an integral part of the culture. Cricket and Australian rules football are the most popular sports; cricketer Don Bradman (1908–2001) is widely considered the country's sporting hero. Australia is successful at international level in most major team sports, as well as producing individual participants such as swimmer Ian Thorpe (b. 1982), athlete Cathy Freeman (b. 1973) and tennis players Rod Laver (b. 1938) and Roy Emerson (b. 1936).

EXTERNAL TERRITORIES

Most of the territories are administered by the federal government through the Department of Regional Australia, Regional Development and Local Government; the Australian Antarctic Territory and the Territory of Heard Island and McDonald Islands are administered through the Australian Antarctic Division of the Department of Sustainability, Environment, Water, Population and Communities.

ASHMORE AND CARTIER ISLANDS

The Ashmore Islands (comprising Middle, East and West Islands) and Cartier Island are situated in the Indian Ocean 320km off Australia's north-west coast. The islands became an Australian territory in 1933. A nature reserve was established on Ashmore Reef in 1983 and a marine reserve around Cartier Island in 2000.

THE AUSTRALIAN ANTARCTIC TERRITORY

The Australian Antarctic Territory was established in 1933 and is 5,896,500 sq. km. It comprises all the islands and territories, other than Adélie Land, that are situated south of latitude 60° S. and lying between 160° E. longitude and 45° E. longitude. (*See also* The North and South Poles).

CHRISTMAS ISLAND

Area – 135 sq. km
Population – 1,402 (2010 est)

Christmas Island is situated in the Indian Ocean about 1,565km north-west of Northwest Cape in Western Australia. The island was annexed by Britain in 1888. Sovereignty was transferred to Australia in 1958. The Shire of Christmas Island (SOCI) is responsible for local government services on the island; its council has nine members directly elected for a four-year term. The main activities are phosphate mining, tourism and the government sector.

Administrator, Brian Lacy

COCOS (KEELING) ISLANDS

Area – 14 sq. km
Population – 596 (2010 est)

The Cocos (Keeling) Islands are two separate atolls (North Keeling Island and, 24km to the south, the main atoll) comprising 27 small coral islands, situated in the Indian Ocean, about 2,950km north-west of Perth. The two inhabited islands of the southern atoll are West Island and Home Island, where around 80 per cent of the population lives, including most of the Cocos Malay community.

The islands were declared a British possession in 1857. In 1886 Queen Victoria granted all land in the islands to George Clunies-Ross and his heirs, who established coconut plantations worked by imported Malay labour. Sovereignty was transferred to Australia in 1955, and the government purchased the Clunies-Ross land and property in 1978, 1984 and 1993. The land is held in trust for the residents, with the local government body, the Shire of the Cocos (Keeling) Islands, as trustee.

In 1984 the Cocos community, in a UN-supervised Act of Self-Determination, voted to integrate with Australia. The seven-member Shire Council of Cocos (Keeling) Islands is responsible for local government services. The public sector is the main employer and there is a little tourism; coconuts are the only cash crop.
Administrator, Brian Lacy

CORAL SEA ISLANDS TERRITORY
The Coral Sea Islands Territory lies east of Queensland between the Great Barrier Reef and longitude 156° 06′ E., and between latitudes 12° and 24° S. It comprises scattered islands, spread over a sea area of 780,000 sq. km. The islands are formed mainly of coral and sand, and most are extremely small. There is a manned meteorological station on Willis Island but otherwise the islands are uninhabited. The territory was established in 1969. Much of it is nature reserve, administered jointly by the Department of Sustainability, Environment, Water, Population and Communities and the Department of Agriculture, Fisheries and Forestry.

HEARD ISLAND AND MCDONALD ISLANDS
The Territory of Heard Island and the McDonald Islands, about 4,100km south-west of Perth, comprises all the islands and rocks lying between 52° 30′ and 53° 30′ S. latitude and 72° and 74° 30′ E. longitude. The subantarctic islands, which have active volcanoes, were discovered in the 1850s and sovereignty was transferred from Britain to Australia in 1947. The islands are now part of a marine reserve established in 2002.

JERVIS BAY TERRITORY
Area – 73 sq. km
Population – 611 (2001 census)

The territory consists of 65 sq. km of land on the southern shore of Jervis Bay, 8 sq. km of marine waters and Bowen Island (0.5 sq. km), and lies about 200km south of Sydney. Originally part of New South Wales, the territory was acquired by the federal government in 1915 to provide Canberra with access to the sea. Much of the land and water now comprises Booderee National Park, leased from the Wreck Bay Aboriginal Community who since the 1980s have been granted 90 per cent of the land. The main economic activity is tourism.

NORFOLK ISLAND
Area – 36 sq. km
Population – 2,155 rising at 0.01 per cent per year (2010 est)
Seat of government – Kingston
National day – 8 June (Bounty Day)

Norfolk Island is situated in the South Pacific Ocean, about 1,600km north-east of Sydney. It is around 8km long by 5km wide. The climate is mild and subtropical. Discovered by Captain Cook in 1774, the island served as a penal colony from 1788 to 1814 and from 1825 to 1855. In 1856, 194 descendants of the *Bounty* mutineers accepted an invitation to leave Pitcairn and settle on Norfolk Island.
  The island became a territory in 1914 and has been internally self-governing since 1979. The nine-member legislative assembly is directly elected for a three-year term, and elects the five-member executive council. This advises the Administrator, who represents the federal government. The economy is dependent on tourism; other economic activities include the sale of postage stamps and pine and palm seeds, livestock-rearing and agriculture.
Administrator, Owen Walsh

AUSTRIA

Republik Österreich – Republic of Austria

Area – 83,871 sq. km
Capital – Vienna (Wien); population, 1,693,430 (2009 est)
Major cities – Graz, Innsbruck, Klagenfurt, Linz, Salzburg
Currency – Euro (€) of 100 cents
Population – 8,214,160 rising at 0.04 per cent a year (2010 est); Austrian (91.1 per cent), former Yugoslav (4 per cent), Turkish (1.6 per cent) (2001)
Religion – Christian (Roman Catholic 66 per cent, Protestant 4 per cent, Eastern Orthodox 2 per cent), Muslim 4 per cent (est)
Language – German (official), Croatian and Hungarian (official in Burgenland), Slovene (official in Carinthia), Turkish, Serbian
Population density – 101 per sq. km (2009)
Urban population – 67 per cent (2008 est)
Median age (years) – 42.6 (2010 est)
National anthem – 'Land der Berge, Land am Strome' ['Land of Mountains, Land on the River']
National day – 26 October (date law of neutrality passed, 1955)
Life expectancy (years) – 79.65 (2010 est)
Mortality rate – 10.05 (2010 est)
Birth rate – 8.65 (2010 est)
Infant mortality rate – 4.37 (2010 est)
Death penalty – Abolished for all crimes (since 1968)
CPI score – 7.9 (2010)

CLIMATE AND TERRAIN
The north and east of the landlocked country feature rolling hills in the river Danube basin, while the west and south contain the eastern Alps, which cover nearly two-thirds of the country. The highest peak is 3,798m (Grossglockner) and the lowest point of elevation is 115m (Lake Neusiedl). Around 47 per cent of the land area is forested. The climate is continental in the lowlands, and alpine in the mountains, with temperature averages ranging from −1°C in January to 20°C in July.

HISTORY AND POLITICS
The Austrian state dates back to the eighth century AD when Charlemagne conquered the territory, which had been settled from the sixth century onwards by Germanic tribes, and founded the *Ostmark*, the eastern march of the Holy Roman Empire. It became a duchy and in 1282

passed to the Habsburg dynasty, which established an empire that united much of central Europe, including present-day Austria and Hungary. Hegemony was lost to Prussia in the 19th century, when growing Hungarian nationalism also led to the establishment of the dual monarchy of Austria–Hungary. The assassination of the heir to the throne in 1914 triggered the First World War, towards the end of which the Austro-Hungarian Empire collapsed; most of the German-speaking lands became the Republic of Austria in November 1918. In March 1938, Austria was incorporated into Nazi Germany (the *Anschluss*) under the name *Ostmark*. After the Second World War, the Republic of Austria was reconstituted within its 1937 frontiers and a freely elected government took office in December 1945. The country was divided into four zones, occupied by the UK, USA, USSR and France, while Vienna was jointly occupied by the four powers.

In 1955 the occupying powers withdrew, recognising Austria as a sovereign, independent and democratic state with the same frontiers as on 1 January 1938. Austria joined the EU in 1995.

The 2004 presidential election was won by Heinz Fischer of the Social Democrats (SPÖ), who was re-elected in 2010. A snap legislative election was held in 2008 after the SPÖ-led coalition collapsed. The SPÖ and the Austrian People's Party (ÖVP) remained the largest parties after this election, but both lost ground to far-right parties. No party had an outright majority, and a new SPÖ–ÖVP coalition was formed under the new SPÖ leader, Werner Faymann.

POLITICAL SYSTEM

Under the 1955 constitution, the federal president is directly elected for a six-year term, renewable only once. There is a bicameral legislature, the *Parlament*, consisting of the National Council *(Nationalrat)*, which has 183 members directly elected for a four-year term, and the Federal Council *(Bundesrat)*, which has 62 members elected for terms of five to six years by the provincial assemblies. Some powers may only be exercised by both houses acting together as the Federal Assembly *(Bundesversammlung)*. The executive is headed by the federal chancellor, who is appointed by the president.

HEAD OF STATE

Federal President, Heinz Fischer, *took office* 8 July 2004, *re-elected* 2010

SELECTED GOVERNMENT MEMBERS *as at May 2011*
Chancellor, Werner Faymann
Vice-Chancellor, Foreign Affairs, Michael Spindelegger
Defence, Norbert Darabos
Finance, Maria Fekter
Interior, Johanna Mikl-Leitner

EMBASSY OF AUSTRIA
18 Belgrave Mews West, London SW1X 8HU
T 020-7344 3250 E london-ob@bmeia.gv.at
W www.bmeia.gv.at//london
Ambassador Extraordinary and Plenipotentiary, HE Emil Brix, *apptd* 2010

BRITISH EMBASSY
Jaurèsgasse 12, 1030 Vienna
T (+43) (1) 716 130 E viennaconsularenquiries@fco.gov.uk
W http://ukinaustria.fco.gov.uk
Ambassador Extraordinary and Plenipotentiary, HE Simon Smith, *apptd* 2007

BRITISH COUNCIL
Siebensterngasse 21, 1070 Vienna
T (+43) (1) 533 2616 W www.britishcouncil.org/austria
Regional Director, Michael Bird, OBE

FEDERAL STRUCTURE
There are nine provinces *(Länder)*: Burgenland, Carinthia, Lower Austria, Salzburg, Styria, Tyrol, Upper Austria, Vienna and Vorarlberg. Each has its own assembly and government.

DEFENCE
The army has 114 main battle tanks, 112 armoured infantry fighting vehicles and 282 armoured personnel carriers. The air force has 37 combat aircraft.
Military budget – US$2,810m (2010)
Military personnel – 25,900: army 12,800, air force 2,900, support 10,200
Conscription duration – 6 months (9–10 months for officers, NCOs and specialists)

ECONOMY AND TRADE
Austria has a well-developed market economy which is closely linked to other EU states. Its strong commercial links with central, eastern and south-eastern Europe, an attraction for foreign investors in the past, increased its vulnerability in the global economic downturn, and its financial sector required state support. The economy went into recession in 2008 but started to recover from late 2009.

The services sector contributes most to GDP (69.1 per cent in 2010), followed by industry (29.4 per cent) and the small but highly developed agricultural sector (1.5 per cent). The main industries include tourism (about 16 per cent of GDP), construction, manufacturing of machinery, vehicles and parts, food processing, timber and wood processing, production of metals and metal goods, chemicals, paper and cardboard, and communications equipment.

Austria's main trading partners are Germany, Italy and Switzerland. Principal exports include the goods produced by the main industries, iron and steel, and textiles. The main imports are machinery and equipment, vehicles, chemical products, metal goods, oil and oil products, and foodstuffs.
GNI – US$377,109m; US$46,450 per capita (2009)
Annual average growth of GDP – 2 per cent (2010 est)
Inflation rate – 1.5 per cent (2010 est)
Population below poverty line – 6 per cent (2008)
Unemployment – 4.6 per cent (2010 est)
Total external debt – US$755,000m (2010)
Imports – US$136,400m (2009)
Exports – US$131,400m (2009)

BALANCE OF PAYMENTS
Trade – US$5,679m deficit (2010)
Current Account – US$5,332m surplus (2009)

Trade with UK	2009	2010
Imports from UK	£1,235,724,751	£1,428,060,153
Exports to UK	£2,245,891,818	£2,585,566,519

COMMUNICATIONS
Although landlocked, Austria is strategically located in central Europe because of the navigability of the river Danube and the presence of traversable passes over the Alps. Of the 425km of waterways, 358km are navigable and there is considerable trade through the Danube ports

(Vienna, Krems, Enns, Linz) from both local and foreign shipping. There are 107,262km of roads and a network of 1,696km of *autobahn* between major cities that also links up with German and Italian networks. The railways are state-owned and comprise 6,399km of track. The main airports are at Vienna, Graz, Innsbruck, Klagenfurt, Linz and Salzburg. Mobile telephone subscriptions overtook fixed-line in the 1990s and totalled 11.8 million in 2009, and there are 6.1 million internet users.

EDUCATION AND HEALTH
Education is free and compulsory from six to 15.
Gross enrolment ratio (percentage of relevant age group) – primary 100 per cent; secondary 100 per cent; tertiary 55 per cent (2008 est)
Health expenditure (per capita) – US$5,037 (2009)
Hospital beds (per 1,000 people) – 7.7 (2004–9)

MEDIA
The public broadcaster Österreichischer Rundfunk (ÖRF) has dominated Austrian television and radio for many years, but the number of private broadcasters is now increasing. Austria's print media is largely privately owned, and there are five main daily titles, including *Der Standard* and *Neue Kronen Zeitung*.

CULTURE
From the 18th to the 20th centuries Vienna was one of Europe's greatest cultural centres. Musicians included Haydn (1732–1809), Mozart (1756–91), Beethoven (1770–1827), the Strauss family, Mahler (1860–1911) and Schoenberg (1874–1951). The late 19th century produced the writers Rainer Maria Rilke (1875–1926) and Robert Musil (1880–1942), the pioneering psychoanalyst Sigmund Freud (1856–1939), and the notable scientists Gregor Mendel (1822–84), whose research laid the foundations of modern genetics, and Erwin Schrödinger (1887–1961), who contributed to the development of quantum mechanics.

In art, the symbolist paintings of Gustav Klimt (1862–1918) are among the most recognisable of the Art Nouveau period. Film director Fritz Lang (1890–1976) produced two of cinema's earliest classics: *Metropolis* (1927) and *M* (1931).

AZERBAIJAN

Azarbaycan Respublikasi – Republic of Azerbaijan

Area – 86,600 sq. km
Capital – Baku (Baki); population, 1,950,030 (2009 est)
Major cities – Ganca, Sumqayit
Currency – New Manat of 100 gopik

Population – 8,303,512 rising at 0.81 per cent a year (2010 est); Azeri (90.6 per cent), Dagestani (2.2 per cent), Russian (1.8 per cent), Armenian (1.5 per cent). There are more Azeris in Iran than in Azerbaijan. Almost all of the Armenian population lives in the Nagorny-Karabakh enclave
Religion – Muslim 96 per cent (of which Shia 65 per cent, Sunni 35 per cent) (est)
Language – Azeri (official), Lezgi, Russian, Armenian
Population density – 106 per sq. km (2009)
Urban population – 52 per cent (2008 est)
Median age – 28.5 years (2010 est)
National anthem – 'Azerbaijan Marsi' ['March of Azerbaijan']
National day – 28 May (founding of the republic, 1918)
Life expectancy – 67.01 (2010 est)
Mortality rate – 8.28 (2010 est)
Birth rate – 17.75 (2010 est)
Infant mortality rate – 52.84 (2010 est)
Death penalty – Abolished for all crimes (since 1998)
CPI score – 2.4 (2010)

CLIMATE AND TERRAIN
Azerbaijan lies on the western shore of the Caspian Sea, in the eastern part of the Caucasus region. It includes the exclave of Nakhichevan, separated from it by Armenia. The north-east of Azerbaijan rises to the south-eastern end of the main Great Caucasus mountain range; to the country's south-west lie the lower Caucasus hills, and in its south-eastern corner the spurs of the Talysh Ridge. Central Azerbaijan lies in a low plain irrigated by the river Kura and the lower reaches of its tributary the Araks. The highest point of elevation is 4,485m (Mt Bazarduzu) while the lowest is −28m (Caspian Sea). The climate and landscape vary greatly, but rainfall is generally low.

HISTORY AND POLITICS
The Turkic Azeri people formed an independent state in the first century BC. This was invaded in the seventh century AD by Muslim Arabs, who introduced Islam and secured the region as a province of the Muslim caliphate. Azerbaijan was invaded by Persia in the 16th century. The country was divided in 1828, the north (present-day Azerbaijan) becoming part of the Russian Empire and the south remaining Persian and subsequently Iranian.

In 1918 an independent Azerbaijani republic was established, which was overthrown in 1920 by a Soviet Red Army invasion supported by Azeri communist sympathisers. Azerbaijan acceded to the USSR in 1922.

In 1990, the Azeri Popular Front took power from the local communist party and declared independence from the Soviet Union. Soviet troops restored the communist regime, which declared Azerbaijan's independence in August 1991 after the failed coup in Moscow. The president elected in 1992 was overthrown in a coup in 1993 and replaced by Heydar Aliyev, the former communist party leader, who retained power despite a number of coup attempts in the mid-1990s. Aliyev won the presidential elections in 1993 and 1998, but withdrew from the 2003 race owing to health problems, endorsing the campaign of his son, Ilham, who was successfully elected; as with all presidential and legislative elections since independence, external monitors judged that the poll failed to meet international democratic standards. Ilham Aliyev's regime has been as authoritarian as that of his father.

President Aliyev was re-elected in 2008. In the 2010 legislative election, the New Azerbaijan Party, which is aligned with President Aliyev, increased its number of seats, achieving an overall majority.

SECESSION

There is a longstanding dispute with Armenia over the predominantly Armenian-populated Azeri region of Nagorny-Karabakh, which was transferred to Azerbaijan by Stalin in 1921–2. The territory's government voted to transfer to Armenia in 1988 but this was rejected by the USSR. When the USSR collapsed in 1991, the territory declared independence. Azeri attempts to reassert control were met with fierce resistance which escalated into a war that lasted from 1992 until a ceasefire was agreed between Azerbaijan, Armenia and Nagorno-Karabakh in 1994. By this time, Nagorno-Karabakh forces, supported by Armenia, had captured all of Nagorny-Karabakh, all Azeri territory that separated Nagorny-Karabakh from Armenia and all mountainous Azeri territory around the territory. Around 16 per cent of Azeri territory remains under separatist control and Azerbaijan has had to absorb nearly a million Azeris displaced from the territory. Talks mediated by the OSCE failed to make any progress towards a peaceful resolution until 2008, when Azerbaijan and Armenia agreed to intensify efforts.

POLITICAL SYSTEM

The 1995 constitution was amended in 2002 and 2009, when the limit on presidential terms was amended to two terms (2002) and then abolished (2009). The executive president is directly elected for a five-year term, which is renewable. The unicameral National Assembly *(Milli Majlis)* has 125 members directly elected for a five-year term. The president appoints the prime minister and the cabinet.

HEAD OF STATE

President, Ilham Aliyev, *sworn in* 31 October 2003, *re-elected* 15 October 2008

SELECTED GOVERNMENT MEMBERS *as at May 2011*
Prime Minister, Artur Rasizade
First Deputy Prime Minister, Yagub Abdulla Eyyubov
Deputy Prime Ministers, Elchin Efendiyev; Ali Hasanov; Abid Sarifov
Defence, Col.-Gen. Safar Abiyev
Finance, Samir Sharifov
Foreign Affairs, Elmar Muharram Mammadyarov

EMBASSY OF THE REPUBLIC OF AZERBAIJAN
4 Kensington Court, London W8 5DL
T 020-7938 3412 E london@mission.mfa.gov.az
W www.azembassy.org.uk
Ambassador Extraordinary and Plenipotentiary, HE Fakhraddin Gurbanov, *apptd* 2007

BRITISH EMBASSY
45 Khagani Street, Baku AZ 1010
T (+994) (12) 497 51 88 E generalenquiries.baku@fco.gov.uk
W http://ukinazerbaijan.fco.gov.uk
Ambassador Extraordinary and Plentipotentiary, HE Peter Bateman, *apptd* 2011

BRITISH COUNCIL
8th Floor, Landmark III Building, 96 Nizami Street, Baku AZ1010
T (+994) (12) 497 1593 W www.britishcouncil.org/azerbaijan
Regional Director, Paul Clementson

DEFENCE

The army has 339 main battle tanks, 111 armoured infantry fighting vehicles and 357 armoured personnel carriers. The navy is based at Baku, with a share of the former Soviet Caspian Fleet Flotilla, comprising 8 patrol and coastal vessels. The air force has 41 combat aircraft and 15 armed helicopters.
Military budget – US$1,590m (2010)
Military personnel – 66,940: army 56,840, navy 2,200, air force 7,900; paramilitary 15,000
Conscription duration – 17 months, but can be extended for ground forces

ECONOMY AND TRADE

Azerbaijan's transition from a command to a market economy is slow. This has been exacerbated by its failure to attract foreign investment in sectors other than energy, widespread corruption and systemic inefficiencies. The economy is dominated by oil and natural gas extraction and related industries, centred in Baku and Sumqayit, and exploited through co-production deals with foreign companies. Oil pipelines (1,424km) link the Azeri oilfields to Black Sea ports in Russia, Georgia and Turkey. The economy avoided recession in the global economic downturn, but contracted owing to the fall in world oil prices, and transfers from the State Oil Fund were needed to make up the 2009 budget shortfall.

Although agriculture contributes only 5.5 per cent of GDP, it employs nearly 40 per cent of the workforce. The main crops are cotton, cereals, rice, fruit, vegetables, tea, tobacco and livestock. Industry, which contributes 61.4 per cent of GDP, produces oil, natural gas, petroleum products, oilfield equipment, steel, iron ore, cement, chemicals, petrochemicals and textiles.

Russia and other former Soviet republics are increasingly being replaced as trade partners by Turkey, India, the USA, and various European countries. Oil and gas constitute 90 per cent of exports, which also include machinery, cotton and foodstuffs. Principal imports are machinery and equipment, oil products, foodstuffs, metals and chemicals.

GNI – US$40,255m; US$4,840 per capita (2009)
Annual average growth of GDP – 3.7 per cent (2010 est)
Inflation rate – 5.1 per cent (2010 est)
Population below poverty line – 11 per cent (2009 est)
Unemployment – 0.9 per cent (2010 est)
Total external debt – US$3,221m (2010 est)
Imports – US$6,100m (2009)
Exports – US$14,700m (2009)

BALANCE OF PAYMENTS
Trade – US$14,726m surplus (2010)
Current Account – US$10,173m surplus (2009)

Trade with UK	2009	2010
Imports from UK	£271,289,551	£461,559,044
Exports to UK	£397,690,847	£77,910,045

COMMUNICATIONS

There are 2,900km of railway track, about 1,300km of it electrified, and over 59,000km of roads, although only half are paved. Azerbaijan is one of 12 participants in the Transport Corridor Europe–Caucasus–Asia (TRACECA) programme, which aims to construct an integrated multimodal transport system through the region by 2015. There are 35 airports, of which four (at Baku, Ganca, Nakhichevan and Lankaran) accept international flights. There are ferry links to Turkmenistan.

The telephone system is run by a state-owned monopoly so modernisation is slow. Greater competition in the mobile telephone market has led to rapid growth and by 2009 density was about 100 per 100 people, compared to 17 fixed lines per 100 people. There were 2.4 million internet users in 2009.

EDUCATION AND HEALTH

Education up to university level is free.
Literacy rate – 99.5 per cent (2008 est)
Gross enrolment ratio (percentage of relevant age group) – primary 95 per cent; secondary 99 per cent; tertiary 19 per cent (2009 est)
Health expenditure (per capita) – US$285 (2009)
Hospital beds (per 1,000 people) – 7.9 (2004–9)

MEDIA

There are state-run and public press, television and radio outlets, competing with a growing private sector. Media outlets critical of the government have been subjected to harassment, despite the guarantee of freedom of speech in the constitution. As a requirement of the country's membership of the Council of Europe, editorially independent public television and radio services were launched in 2005.

THE BAHAMAS

Commonwealth of the Bahamas

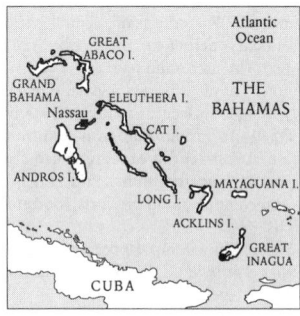

Area – 13,880 sq. km
Capital – Nassau, on New Providence; population, 247,659 (2009 est)
Major city – Freeport, on Grand Bahama
Currency – Bahamian dollar (B$) of 100 cents
Population – 310,426 rising at 0.94 per cent a year (2010 est)
Religion – Christian (Baptist 35 per cent, Anglican 15 per cent, Roman Catholic 14 per cent, Pentecostal 8 per cent, Church of God 5 per cent, Seventh-day Adventist 5 per cent, Methodist 4 per cent) (est)
Language – English (official), Creole
Population density – 34 per sq. km (2009)
Urban population – 84 per cent (2008 est)
Median age (years) – 29.9 (2010 est)
National anthem – 'March on, Bahamaland'
National day – 10 July (Independence Day)
Life expectancy (years) – 70.84 (2010 est)
Mortality rate – 6.89 (2010 est)
Birth rate – 16.25 (2010 est)
Infant mortality rate – 13.68 (2010 est)
HIV/AIDS adult prevalence – 3.1 per cent (2009 est)
Death penalty – Retained

CLIMATE AND TERRAIN

The Bahamas extend in a chain running from the coast of Florida in the north-west almost to Hispaniola in the south-east. The group consists of more than 700 islands and 2,400 cays, all low-lying. The highest point is 63m (Mt Alvernia, on Cat Island) and the lowest 0m (Atlantic Ocean). The principal islands include: Abaco Islands, Acklins, Andros, Berry Islands, Bimini, Cat Island, Crooked Island, Eleuthera, Exuma, Grand Bahama, Harbour Island, Great Inagua, Long Island, Mayaguana, New Providence, Ragged Island, Rum Cay, San Salvador and Spanish Wells. The 14 major islands are inhabited, as are a few of the smaller islands. The climate is semitropical. The hurricane season is June to November.

HISTORY AND POLITICS

The islands were discovered by Columbus in 1492, settled by the British from the 17th century and became a crown colony in 1717. The Bahamas became internally self-governing in 1964 and gained independence on 10 July 1973.

The Progressive Liberal Party (PLP) held power for 25 years until the Free National Movement (FNM) won an absolute majority in the 1992 general election. Power has subsequently alternated between the two parties. The PLP was defeated in the 2007 legislative election, which the FNM won with 23 seats.

POLITICAL SYSTEM
The head of state is Queen Elizabeth II, who is represented by a governor-general. The bicameral parliament has a senate of 16 appointed members and a House of Assembly of 41 members; both chambers serve a five-year term. A proposal that the country should become a republic is under consideration.
Governor-General, HE Sir Arthur Foulkes, *apptd* 2010

SELECTED GOVERNMENT MEMBERS *as at June 2011*
Prime Minister, Finance, Hubert Ingraham
Deputy Prime Minister, Foreign Affairs, Brent Symonette
National Security, Tommy Turnquest
Attorney-General, John Delaney

HIGH COMMISSION OF THE COMMONWEALTH OF THE BAHAMAS
10 Chesterfield Street, London W1J 5JL
T 020-7408 4488 E information@bahamashclondon.net
W www.bahamashclondon.net
High Commissioner, HE Paul Farquharson, *apptd* 2008

BRITISH HIGH COMMISSION
High Commissioner, Howard Drake, *apptd* 2010, resident in Kingston, Jamaica

DEFENCE

The Royal Bahamian Defence Force has 9 patrol and coastal combatant vessels based at Coral Harbour, New Providence Island.
Military budget – US$46m (2010)
Military personnel – 860 (Royal Bahamian Defence Force)

ECONOMY AND TRADE

The economy is dominated by tourism and offshore financial services, which together contribute about 90 per cent of GDP. A tightening of financial regulations in 2000 caused a number of international businesses to relocate elsewhere, and visitor numbers from the USA (over 80 per cent of all visitors) have declined since 2006.

The effects of the global economic downturn have caused the economy to contract further.

Manufacturing and agriculture account for 10 per cent of GDP and employment. Agriculture produces mainly fresh vegetables, fruit, meat and eggs. Mineral reserves produce aragonite and salt for export. Other activities include cement, rum, pharmaceuticals and steel pipe production, and the provision of oil trans-shipment services.

The main trading partners are the USA, Singapore, South Korea, Japan and Poland. The chief exports are mineral products and salt, animal products, rum, chemicals, fruit and vegetables. Imports are chiefly machinery and transport equipment, manufactured articles, chemicals, fuel, foodstuffs and livestock.

GNI – US$7,042m; US$21,390 per capita (2007)
Annual average growth of GDP – –0.5 per cent (2010 est)
Inflation rate – 2.4 per cent (2007 est)
Population below poverty line – 9.3 per cent (2004)
Unemployment – 7.6 per cent (2006 est)
Total external debt – US$342.6m (2004 est)
Imports – US$2,200m (2009)
Exports – US$500m (2009)

BALANCE OF PAYMENTS
Trade – US$1,663m deficit (2010)
Current Account – US$1,165m deficit (2008)

Trade with UK	2009	2010
Imports from UK	£18,797,494	£32,881,433
Exports to UK	£6,228,025	£2,476,742

COMMUNICATIONS
The main ports are Nassau (New Providence), Freeport and South Riding Point (Grand Bahama). The Bahamas is a major ship registry, and 1,080 of the 1,170 ships registered in 2010 were foreign-owned. International air services are operated from Andros, Chubb Cay, Eleuthera, Exuma, Grand Bahama and New Providence. Nearly 60 smaller airports and landing strips facilitate services between the islands, mainly provided by Bahamasair, the national carrier. The Bahamas have some 2,717km of roads, 1,560km of which are paved. There are no railways.

BAHRAIN

Mamlakat al-Bahrayn – Kingdom of Bahrain

Area – 760 sq. km
Capital – Manama; population, 163,311 (2009 est)
Major towns – Al Muharraq, Ar Rifa
Currency – Bahraini dinar (BD) of 1,000 fils

Population – 1,214,705 (including 235,108 non-nationals) rising at 1.24 per cent a year (2010 est); Bahraini (62.4 per cent) (2001). The non-Bahraini population includes large numbers of Europeans and South Asians
Religion – Muslim 99 per cent (of which Shia 60 per cent, Sunni 40 per cent) (est); Islam is the state religion
Language – Arabic (official), English, Farsi, Urdu
Population density – 1,041 per sq. km (2009)
Urban population – 89 per cent (2008 est)
Median age (years) – 30.4 (2010 est)
National anthem – 'Bahrainona' ['Our Bahrain']
National day – 16 December (date of independence from British protection, 1971)
Life expectancy (years) – 75.4 (2010 est)
Mortality rate – 4.37 (2010 est)
Birth rate – 16.81 (2010 est)
Infant mortality rate – 14.76 (2010 est)
Death penalty – Retained
CPI score – 4.9 (2010)
Literacy rate – 89.2 per cent (2008 est)

CLIMATE AND TERRAIN
Bahrain consists of an archipelago of 36 low-lying islands situated approximately halfway down the Persian Gulf, some 32km off the east coast of Saudi Arabia. The largest of these, Bahrain Island, is about 48km long and 16km wide at its broadest. The population is concentrated around the capital, Manama, on the north shore. The elevation extremes range from 122m (Jabal ad Dukhan) at the highest point to 0m at sea level. The climate is arid, hot and humid, with maximum average temperatures ranging from 20°C to 38°C.

HISTORY AND POLITICS
Bahrain was ruled by Persia (Iran) from 1602 until it was ousted in 1783 by the al-Khalifa family, who remain in power. The emirate was a British protectorate from 1820 until 1971, when it became independent. In 1975 the legislature was suspended and the emir assumed virtually absolute power after clashes between Sunni and Shia factions. Moves to return to democratic rule were made only in response to civil agitation in the 1990s, until Shaikh Hamad succeeded to the throne and initiated the transition to a constitutional monarchy. The 2002 constitution established Bahrain as a kingdom and a constitutional monarchy, and legalised elections. There has been ongoing agitation for further democratisation, particularly by the Shia majority against the predominantly Sunni authorities. This flared up in February 2011 into mass demonstrations that were repressed brutally by the government from March, when martial law was declared and the Pearl monument, the focal point of the demonstrations in Manama, was demolished.

In the 2010 legislative election, the radical Shia group al-Wefaq remained the largest bloc, with 18 seats. Although some Shia ministers were appointed, the majority are Sunnis. A number of ministers resigned in spring 2011 after protesting at the treatment of demonstrators.

POLITICAL SYSTEM
Under the 2002 constitution, the country is a hereditary constitutional monarchy with the king as head of state. The king appoints the cabinet. The bicameral National Assembly consists of a lower house, the Council of Representatives, and an upper house, the

Consultative Council. The lower house has 40 members directly elected for a four-year term, and the upper house has 40 members appointed by the king for a four-year term. The 2002 constitution granted women the right to vote and to stand for election.

HEAD OF STATE

HH The King of Bahrain, Shaikh Hamad bin Isa al-Khalifa, KCMG *succeeded as emir* 6 March 1999, *proclaimed king* 14 February 2002
Crown Prince, Chair of the National Economic Development Council, Shaikh Salman bin Hamad al-Khalifa

SELECTED GOVERNMENT MEMBERS *as at May 2011*
Prime Minister, HH Shaikh Khalifa bin Salman al-Khalifa
Deputy Prime Ministers, Shaikh Mohammed bin Mubarak al-Khalifa; Shaikh Ali bin Khalifa al-Khalifa; Jawad bin Salem al Oraied; Shaikh Khalid bin Abdullah al-Khalifa
Foreign Affairs, Shaikh Khalid bin Ahmed bin Mohammed al-Khalifa
Defence, Shaikh Mohammad bin Abdullah al-Khalifa
Finance, Shaikh Ahmed bin Mohammed al-Khalifa
Interior, Lt.-Gen. Shaikh Rashid bin Abdulla bin Ahmed al-Khalifa

EMBASSY OF THE KINGDOM OF BAHRAIN
30 Belgrave Square, London SW1X 8QB
T 020-7201 9170 E information@bahrainembassy.co.uk
W www.bahrainembassy.co.uk
Ambassador Extraordinary and Plenipotentiary, HE Shaikh Khalifa bin Ali bin Rashid al-Khalifa, *apptd* 2008

BRITISH EMBASSY
PO Box 114, 21 Government Avenue, Manama 306
T (+973) 1757 4100 E british.embassy@batelco.com.bh
W http://ukinbahrain.fco.gov.uk
Ambassador Extraordinary and Plenipotentiary, HE Iain Lindsay, OBE, *apptd* 2011

BRITISH COUNCIL
PO Box 452, AMA Centre, 146 Shaikh Salman Highway, Manama 356
T (+973) 17 261 555 W www.britishcouncil.org/me-bahrain
Director, Brendan McSharry

DEFENCE

The army has 180 main battle tanks, 25 armoured infantry fighting vehicles and over 235 armoured personnel carriers. The navy, based at Mina Salman, has 1 frigate and 10 patrol and coastal vessels. The air force has 39 combat aircraft and 2 armed helicopters.
Military budget – US$742m (2010)
Military personnel – 8,200: army 6,000, navy 700, air force 1,500; paramilitary 11,260

ECONOMY AND TRADE

Bahrain was one of the first Gulf states to discover oil, in the 1930s, but reserves and production are lower than in neighbouring countries. It has diversified its economy, developing particularly as a regional financial and business centre, and as a tourist destination. Petroleum production and refining still accounts for an estimated 11 per cent of GDP, 70 per cent of government revenue and 60 per cent of total exports. Other industries include petrochemicals, aluminium smelting, and shipbuilding and repair. Bahrain's main trading partners are Saudi Arabia, the EU, Far Eastern countries and the USA.

GNI – US$20,979m; US$25,420 per capita (2008)
Annual average growth of GDP – 3.9 per cent (2010 est)
Inflation rate – 3.3 per cent (2010 est)
Unemployment – 15 per cent (2005 est)
Total external debt – US$14,680m (2010 est)
Imports – US$6,100m (2009)
Exports – US$12,100m (2009)

BALANCE OF PAYMENTS
Trade – US$5,142m surplus (2010)
Current Account – US$2,256m surplus (2008)

Trade with UK	2009	2010
Imports from UK	£241,271,444	£228,848,890
Exports to UK	£11,960,822	£61,080,729

COMMUNICATIONS

Bahrain International Airport is one of the main air traffic centres of the Gulf and is the headquarters of Gulf Air and the main base of Bahrain Air; it also acts as a stopover point for other airlines on routes between Europe and Australia and the Far East. The four main islands are connected by causeways, and a 25km causeway links Bahrain Island to Saudi Arabia; the construction of an extension linking Bahrain to Qatar was approved in 2005 and is expected to conclude in 2015. Of the 3,850km of road, 3,120km is paved. There are no railways. Khalifa bin Salman Port, opened in 2009, is the main terminal. There are modern telecommunications systems and there has been rapid growth in mobile telephone distribution, to 1.6 million subscribers in 2009.

MEDIA

Most domestic television and radio services are provided by the state-run Bahrain Radio and Television Corporation. Most households also have a satellite receiver. Bahrain has a free press but self-censorship is widely practised. There are five main daily newspapers, including two published in English.

BANGLADESH

Gana Prajatantri Bangladesh – People's Republic of Bangladesh

Area – 143,998 sq. km
Capital – Dhaka; population, 14,251,300 (2009 est)
Major cities – Chittagong, Khulna, Narayanganj
Currency – Taka (Tk) of 100 paisa
Population – 156,118,464 rising at 1.55 per cent a year (2010 est); Bengali (98 per cent) (1998 est)
Religion – Muslim (Sunni 90 per cent), Hindu 9 per cent (est); Islam is the state religion

Language – Bengali (official), English
Population density – 1,246 per sq. km (2009)
Urban population – 27 per cent (2008 est)
Median age (years) – 22.9 (2010 est)
National anthem – 'Amar Shonar Bangla' ['My Golden Bengal']
National day – 26 March (Independence Day)
Life expectancy (years) – 69.44 (2010 est)
Mortality rate – 5.81 (2010 est)
Birth rate – 23.43 (2010 est)
Infant mortality rate – 52.54 (2010 est)
Death penalty – Retained
CPI score – 2.4 (2010)

CLIMATE AND TERRAIN

Although hilly in the south-east and north-east, over 75 per cent of the country is less than 3m above sea-level, situated on the alluvial plain and delta of the Ganges (Padma)–Brahmaputra (Jamuna)–Meghna river system, which empties into the Bay of Bengal, the largest estuarine delta in the world. The highest elevation is 1,230m (Keokradong) and the lowest 0m at the Indian Ocean. The climate is tropical, with a monsoon season (June–September) during which heavy rainfall causes flooding in around one-third of the country each year; annual rainfall in most of the country is up to 2,500mm.

HISTORY AND POLITICS

Bangladesh consists of what was the eastern part of Bengal province and the Sylhet district of Assam province in British India. On independence in 1947, these territories acceded to Pakistan, forming the province of East Bengal (renamed East Pakistan in 1955). Tensions between East and West Pakistan (separated by over 1,600km) caused the East to secede in 1971. After months of civil war, and following the intervention of India, Bangladesh achieved independence from Pakistan on 16 December 1971.

Since independence, Bangladesh has experienced periods of political instability, with a number of coups and attempted coups, the assassinations of President Mujibar Rahman (1975) and President Zia (1981), and periods of government under martial law (1975–8, 1982–6) or a state of emergency (1987–8, 2007–8).

Parliamentary government has remained in place since 1991, despite occasional boycotts of parliament. Governments have been formed, or coalition governments led, by one of the two main parties: the Bangladesh Nationalist Party (BNP), led by Khaleda Zia (widow of President Zia), in 1991–6 and 2001–6; and the Awami League, led by Sheikh Hasina Wajed (daughter of President Mujibar Rahman), in 1996–2001 and since January 2009.

The BNP-led coalition government headed by Khaleda Zia stepped down in 2006 when its term of office expired. Following violent protests over the choice of an interim government and the impartiality of election preparations, the president declared a state of emergency and appointed a caretaker administration until a new parliament was convened after the December 2008 legislative election. The election was won by the Awami League, with 230 of the 345 seats. Zillur Rahman was elected president in February 2009.

POLITICAL SYSTEM

The head of state is the president, elected by the legislature for a five-year term. The unicameral parliament, *Jatiya Sangsad,* has 345 members directly elected for a five-year term; under a 2004 constitutional amendment, 45 seats are reserved for women. The president appoints the prime minister, and the cabinet on the advice of the prime minister.

HEAD OF STATE
President, Zillur Rahman, *elected* 11 February 2009

SELECTED GOVERNMENT MEMBERS *as at May 2011*
Prime Minister, Defence, Sheikh Hasina Wajed
Finance, Abu Maal Abdul Muhith
Foreign Affairs, Dipu Moni
Law, Justice and Parliamentary Affairs, Shafiq Ahmed

HIGH COMMISSION FOR THE PEOPLE'S REPUBLIC OF BANGLADESH
28 Queen's Gate, London SW7 5JA
T 020-7584 0081 E info@bhclondon.org.uk
W www.bhclondon.org.uk
High Commissioner, HE Dr Mohammad Sayeedur Rahman Khan, *apptd* 2009

BRITISH HIGH COMMISSION
PO Box 6079, United Nations Road, Baridhara, Dhaka 1212
T (+880) (2) 882 2705
E consular.bangladesh@fconet.fco.gov.uk
W http://ukinbangladesh.fco.gov.uk
High Commissioner, HE Robert Winnington Gibson, CMG, *apptd* 2011

BRITISH COUNCIL
PO Box 161, 5 Fuller Road, Dhaka 1000
T (+880) (2) 861 8905 W www.britishcouncil.org/bangladesh
Director, Charles Nuttall

DEFENCE

The army has 232 main battle tanks and 226 armoured personnel carriers. The navy has 5 frigates and 40 patrol and coastal vessels. There are bases at Chittagong, Dhaka, Kaptai, Khulna and Mangla. The air force has 74 combat aircraft.
Military budget – US$1,320m (2010)
Military personnel – 157,053: army 126,153, navy 16,900, air force 14,000; paramilitary 63,900

ECONOMY AND TRADE

Bangladesh is a poor country, highly dependent on foreign aid. Although poverty has been reduced by 1–2 per cent a year since 1990, over a third of the population lives below the poverty line. Many migrate to the Gulf states and south-east Asia to find work, and their remittances and garment manufacturing are the mainstay of the economy. These have fuelled the steady growth of 5–6 per cent a year since the mid-1990s, which has continued throughout the global downturn. However, inefficient state-owned enterprises, slow implementation of economic reforms, corruption and unreliable power supplies are obstacles to greater growth.

The service and industrial sectors account for 52.9 per cent and 28.7 per cent of GDP respectively. Although the smallest contributor to GDP (18.4 per cent), agriculture is the primary occupation of 45 per cent of the workforce. The chief industries are based on processing agricultural and fisheries products such as cotton, jute, tea, sugar, fish and seafood, the manufacture of textiles, garments, newsprint, cement and fertiliser, and light engineering.

Most exports are to the USA and EU countries; imports come mainly from China, India and other Asian countries.

GNI – US$97,485m; US$580 per capita (2009)
Annual average growth of GDP – 6 per cent (2010 est)
Inflation rate – 8.1 per cent (2010 est)
Population below poverty line – 36.3 per cent (2008 est)
Unemployment – 5.1 per cent (2010 est)
Total external debt – US$24,460m (2010 est)
Imports – US$20,600m (2009)
Exports – US$12,400m (2009)

BALANCE OF PAYMENTS
Trade – US$11,740m deficit (2010)
Current Account – US$1,619m surplus (2008)

Trade with UK	2009	2010
Imports from UK	£68,076,584	£114,292,581
Exports to UK	£1,052,185,943	£1,182,581,509

COMMUNICATIONS
The principal seaports are Chittagong and Mongla. A state enterprise, the Bangladesh Shipping Corporation, operates the Bangladesh merchant fleet. Armed robbery of shipping in Bangladesh's territorial waters is growing. The 8,370km of internal waterways are a key element of the transport infrastructure, although reduced to 5,200km in the dry season. There are three international airports (at Dhaka, Chittagong and Sylhet) and 14 other airports and airfields. The international airline, Bangladesh Biman, provides international and internal flights. There are 2,622km of rail track, and rail links with India. The country's 239,226km of roads include only 22,726km that are surfaced. The telephone network is limited, with about 1 fixed line per 100 people, and has been overtaken by mobile-telephone distribution, which had a density of 30 per 100 people in 2009.

EDUCATION AND HEALTH
Education is compulsory and free for children aged 6 to 10, but drop-out rates are high.
Literacy rate – 54.5 per cent (2008 est)
Gross enrolment ratio (percentage of relevant age group) – primary 94 per cent; secondary 44 per cent; tertiary 7 per cent (2007 est)
Health expenditure (per capita) – US$18 (2009)
Hospital beds (per 1,000 people) – 0.4 (2004–9)

MEDIA
The main broadcasters (Radio Bangladesh and Bangladesh Television) are state-owned and pro-government. Television is the most popular medium, especially in urban areas, and foreign stations as well as domestic broadcasters have large audiences. Newspapers are privately owned and editorially independent, but journalists are liable to harassment despite the constitution guaranteeing press freedom. The four main daily newspapers are the Bengali-language *Dainik Ittefaq* and *Daily Prothom Alo,* and English-language publications *The Daily Star* and *The New Nation.*

BARBADOS

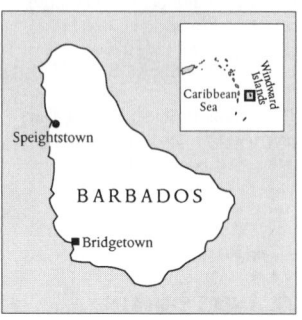

Area – 430 sq. km
Capital – Bridgetown, in the parish of St Michael; population, 112,154 (2009)
Currency – Barbados dollar (BD$) of 100 cents
Population – 285,653 rising at 0.37 per cent a year (2010 est)
Religion – Christian 75 per cent (Protestant 63 per cent, of which the largest denomination is Anglican), Muslim 1 per cent (2008 est)
Language – English (official)
Population density – 595 per sq. km (2009)
Urban population – 40 per cent (2008)
Median age (years) – 36.2 (2010 est)
National anthem – 'In Plenty and in Time of Need'
National day – 30 November (Independence Day)
Life expectancy (years) – 74.14 (2010 est)
Mortality rate – 8.39 (2010 est)
Birth rate – 12.43 (2010 est)
Infant mortality rate – 12.09 (2010 est)
HIV / AIDS adult prevalence – 1.4 per cent (2009 est)
Death penalty – Retained
CPI score – 7.8 (2010)

CLIMATE AND TERRAIN
Barbados is the most easterly of the Caribbean islands. The land rises gently to central highlands, and elevation extremes range from 336m (Mt Hillaby) at the highest point to 0m (Atlantic Ocean) at the lowest. The climate is tropical with a wet season from July to November, when the island is subject to occasional hurricanes.

HISTORY AND POLITICS
Early settlers were succeeded by the Arawaks and then the Caribs. The island was uninhabited when settled by the English in 1627 and was a crown colony from 1652, achieving self-government in 1961. It became an independent state on 30 November 1966.

Since independence, power has alternated between the two main political parties, the Barbados Labour Party (BLP) and the Democratic Labour Party (DLP). In the 2008 general election the BLP was defeated by the DLP, which won 20 of the 30 seats and took office under David Thompson. He died in October 2010 and was succeeded as prime minister by his deputy, Freundel Stuart.

POLITICAL SYSTEM
The head of state is Queen Elizabeth II, represented by the governor-general. The bicameral parliament consists of a senate of 21 appointed members and a House of Assembly of 30 directly elected members; both chambers serve a five-year term.

There are 11 administrative areas (parishes): St Michael, Christ Church, St Andrew, St George, St James, St John, St Joseph, St Lucy, St Peter, St Philip and St Thomas.
Governor-General, HE Sir Clifford Husbands, GCMG, *apptd* June 1996

SELECTED GOVERNMENT MEMBERS *as at June 2011*
Prime Minister, Freundel Stuart
Attorney-General, Home Affairs, Adriel Brathwaite
Finance, Christopher Sinckler
Foreign Affairs, Maxine McClean

BARBADOS HIGH COMMISSION
1 Great Russell Street, London WC1B 3ND
T 020-7631 4975 E london@foreign.gov.bb
High Commissioner, HE Hugh Arthur, *apptd* 2008

BRITISH HIGH COMMISSION
PO Box 676, Lower Collymore Rock, Bridgetown
T (+1) (246) 430 7800 W http://ukinbarbados.fco.gov.uk
High Commissioner, HE Paul Brummell, *apptd* 2009

DEFENCE
The navy has 6 patrol and coastal combatant vessels located at 2 bases.
Military budget – US$34m (2010)
Military personnel – 610: army 500, navy 110

ECONOMY AND TRADE
Historically, Barbados's chief products were sugar, rum and molasses. Since independence, tourism, offshore finance and information services, and light industry (especially the assembly of components for re-export) have become more significant. The global economic downturn affected tourism in particular, causing the economy to contract in 2009.

The main trading partners are Trinidad and Tobago, the USA and Jamaica. Chief exports are manufactured goods, sugar and molasses, rum, other food and beverages, chemicals and electronic components.
GNI – US$2,500m (2003); US$9,270 per capita (2003)
Annual average growth of GDP – –0.7 per cent (2010 est)
Inflation rate – 5.5 per cent (2007 est)
Unemployment – 10.7 per cent (2003 est)
Total external debt – US$668m (2003)
Imports – US$1,500m (2009)
Exports – US$400m (2009)

BALANCE OF PAYMENTS
Trade – US$1,089m deficit (2010)
Current Account – US$184m deficit (2008)

Trade with UK	2009	2010
Imports from UK	£40,813,526	£40,467,489
Exports to UK	£15,146,150	£19,506,750

COMMUNICATIONS
Barbados has around 1,600km of roads, all of which are surfaced. The Grantley Adams International airport near Bridgetown is a hub for connections to other Caribbean islands and the USA. Bridgetown, the only port of entry, has a deep-water harbour with berths for seven; there are also five tanker terminals. Mobile phone ownership is high, at nearly 125 per 100 persons.

EDUCATION
Education is free in government schools at primary (ages four to 11), secondary (ages 11 to 18) and tertiary levels, and is compulsory until the age of 15.
Literacy rate – 99.7 per cent (2004 est)

MEDIA
Barbados has two daily newspapers, both privately owned. The sole television station is run by the state-owned Caribbean Broadcasting Corporation. There are both public and privately owned radio stations. The media broadcast a range of opinions and are free to criticise the authorities.

BELARUS

Respublika Byelarus' – Republic of Belarus

Area – 207,600 sq. km
Capital – Minsk (the administrative centre of the CIS); population, 1,836,880 (2009 est)
Major cities – Brest, Homyel, Hrodna, Mahilyow, Vitsyebsk
Currency – Belarusian rouble of 100 kopeks
Population – 9,612,632 falling at 0.37 per cent a year (2010 est); Belarusian (81.2 per cent), Russian (11.4 per cent), Polish (3.9 per cent), Ukrainian (2.4 per cent) (est)
Religion – Christian (Belarusian Orthodox 48 per cent, Roman Catholic 7 per cent, Protestant 1 per cent) (est)
Language – Belarusian, Russian (both official)
Population density – 48 per sq. km (2009)
Urban population – 73 per cent (2008 est)
Median age (years) – 38.8 (2010 est)
National anthem – 'My Belarusy' ['We, the Belarusians']
National day – 3 July (Independence Day)
Life expectancy (years) – 70.92 (2010 est)
Mortality rate – 13.81 (2010 est)
Birth rate – 9.76 (2010 est)
Infant mortality rate – 6.34 (2010 est)
Death penalty – Retained
CPI score – 2.5 (2010)

CLIMATE AND TERRAIN
Belarus is a landlocked country in eastern Europe, and was formerly part of the USSR. Much of the land is a plain, with many lakes, swamps and marshes, and forest cover is around 39 per cent. Its main rivers are the upper reaches of the Dnieper, the Nyoman and the Western Dvina. Elevation extremes range from 346m (Dzyarzhynskaya Hara) at the highest point to 90m (Nyoman river) at the lowest. The climate is continental, with cold winters and warm, humid summers.

HISTORY AND POLITICS
In the 13th century the area was absorbed into the grand duchy of Lithuania, which entered into the Polish Commonwealth from the 16th until the 18th centuries. Following the partitions of Poland in the late 18th century it became part of the expanding Russian Empire. It was the site of fierce fighting during the First World War, but its brief period of independence in 1918 ended, after a war over the territory, in partition between Poland and the USSR. The Polish territory was largely regained by the USSR after the Second World War, which devastated Belarus; over a quarter of the population was killed.

Belarus declared its independence from the USSR after a failed coup in Moscow in 1991. Stanislav Shuskevich became Belarusian leader at the head of a coalition of communists and democrats, but he was forced to resign in 1994. He was replaced by Gen. Mecheslav Grib, who pursued closer political, economic and trade relations with Russia.

Alexander Lukashenko was elected to the newly created post of president in 1994. Since coming to power, President Lukashenko has opposed privatisation and economic liberalisation (precipitating economic collapse), subverted political processes and repressed opposition and the media, creating a virtual dictatorship. Elections since 2000 have been condemned as neither free nor fair by opposition groups and international observers. The EU and USA have imposed sanctions several times because of the regime's poor human rights record and obstructiveness towards international election monitors. In the 2010 presidential election, President Lukashenko was returned with 79.7 per cent of the vote. Popular protests at the outcome of these polls, and other public expressions of opposition to the regime, were suppressed by force. In the 2010 legislative elections, all the seats were won by the president's supporters.

FOREIGN RELATIONS
Belarus was a founder member of the Commonwealth of Independent States (CIS) in 1991. President Lukashenko, who opposed the break-up of the Soviet Union, has sought closer relations with Russia. In 1997 a treaty was signed with Russia providing for closer political and economic integration, and in 1999 the two countries signed a treaty that committed them to becoming a confederal state. However, there has been little progress towards integration, and Russia has increasingly condemned Belarus's poor economic development; relations have also been strained over energy supplies and transshipment fees. In 2010 Belarus formed a customs union with Kazakhstan and Russia despite Russia's refusal to abolish export taxes on oil and oil products within the union.

POLITICAL SYSTEM
Under the 1994 constitution, the president is directly elected for a five-year term; this was renewable only once until a 2004 constitutional amendment removed the two-term limit. The legislature is the bicameral National Assembly, comprising a 110-member House of Representatives (lower chamber), directly elected for a four-year term, and a Council of the Republic, with 56 members elected by regional soviets (councils) and eight members appointed by the president, for a four-year term.

The president may appoint half the members of the constitutional court and the electoral commission.

HEAD OF STATE
President, Alexander Lukashenko, elected 10 July 1994, re-elected 2001, 2006, 2010

SELECTED GOVERNMENT MEMBERS as at May 2011
Prime Minister, Mikhail Myasnikovich
First Deputy Prime Minister, Vladimir Semashko
Deputy Prime Ministers, Valery Ivanov; Anatoly Kalinin; Sergei Rumas; Anatoly Tozik
Finance, Andrei Kharkovets
Economy, Nikolay Snopkov
Foreign Affairs, Sergei Martynov

EMBASSY OF THE REPUBLIC OF BELARUS
6 Kensington Court, London W8 5DL
T 020-7937 3288 E uk@belembassy.org
W www.uk.belembassy.org
Ambassador Extraordinary and Plenipotentiary, HE Aleksandr Mikhnevich, apptd 2006

BRITISH EMBASSY
37 Karl Marx Street, 220030 Minsk
T (+375) (172) 298 200 W http://ukinbelarus.fco.gov.uk
Ambassador Extraordinary and Plenipotentiary, HE Rosemary Thomas, apptd 2009

DEFENCE
The army has 515 main battle tanks, 1,078 armoured infantry fighting vehicles and 280 armoured personnel carriers. The air force has 133 combat aircraft and 50 armed helicopters.
Military budget – US$716m (2010)
Military personnel – 72,940: army 29,600, air force 18,170, joint staff 25,170; paramilitary 110,000
Conscription duration – 9–12 months

ECONOMY AND TRADE
Although prosperous under the Soviet regime, the country experienced a dramatic decline after independence and over a quarter of the population now lives below the poverty line. Since 1994 President Lukashenko has resisted structural reform of the economy and reimposed state control of prices and currency exchange rates. Some privatised businesses have been renationalised, and the small private sector is subject to pressure and intervention by the state, circumstances that continue to discourage foreign investment. The country is highly dependent on Russia for its energy needs, and economic growth in recent years was largely based on the re-export at market prices of heavily discounted oil and natural gas from Russia. This revenue stream has been reduced by sharp increases in oil and gas prices from 2007 (increasing to world prices by 2011), Russia's introduction of an export duty on oil shipped to Belarus, and Belarus's obligation to share with Russia its duties on re-exported oil. The drop in revenue and the global downturn pushed the economy into recession in 2009, leading to a devaluation of the rouble.

The main economic activities are oil-refining and the manufacture of heavy machinery and equipment, vehicles, domestic appliances, chemicals and textiles. These commodities, along with oil, mineral products, metals and foodstuffs, constitute the main exports and the main imports. The main trading partner is Russia.
GNI – US$47,927m; US$5,560 per capita (2009)
Average annual growth of GDP – 4.8 per cent (2010 est)
Inflation rate – 7 per cent (2010 est)
Population below poverty line – 27.1 per cent (2003 est)

Unemployment – 1 per cent (2009)
Total external debt – US$24,800m (2010)
Imports – US$28,600m (2009)
Exports – US$21,300m (2009)

BALANCE OF PAYMENTS
Trade – US$9,432m deficit (2010)
Current Account – US$6,326m deficit (2009)

Trade with UK	2009	2010
Imports from UK	£76,366,405	£112,709,911
Exports to UK	£29,928,297	£32,286,768

COMMUNICATIONS
Belarus has an extensive 2,500km canal and river system, but its use is limited by shallowness or remoteness. There is an international airport at Minsk and six other major domestic airports, plus 60 smaller airports and airfields. Most of the 94,797km of roads are surfaced but many are in bad repair. There are 5,537km of railways. The telephone system is state-operated; the network is being modernised but is not extensive in rural areas, and fixed-line density is about 35 per 100 people. Mobile phone density reached 100 per 100 people in 2009. There were 2.6 million internet users in 2009.

EDUCATION AND HEALTH
The education system comprises pre-school, general secondary, out-of-school, vocational training and trade schools, secondary specialised and higher education. Education is compulsory between the ages of six and 15.
Literacy rate – 99.7 per cent (2008 est)
Gross enrolment ratio (percentage of relevant age group) – primary 97 per cent; secondary 95 per cent; tertiary 68 per cent (2007 est)
Health expenditure (per capita) – US$295 (2009)
Hospital beds (per 1,000 people) – 11.2 (2004–9)

MEDIA
A Soviet-era attitude towards press freedom remains; the government controls media content and the appointment of senior editors in the print and broadcast media. State-run newspapers and television channels receive large subsidies and support government policies, while opposition publications are subject to charges and harassment. The state operates domestic radio and TV channels; a few private broadcasters target Belarusian audiences but operate from outside the country. A resolution passed in 2010 forces owners of internet cafes to keep records of their customers' personal details and browsing history.

BELGIUM

Koninkrijk Belgie / Royaume de Belgique / Königreich Belgien – Kingdom of Belgium

Area – 30,528 sq. km
Capital – Brussels; population, 1,892,000 (2009 est)
Major cities – Antwerp, Bruges, Charleroi, Ghent, Liège
Currency – Euro (€) of 100 cents
Population – 10,423,493 rising at 0.08 per cent a year (2010 est); Fleming (58 per cent), Walloon (31 per cent) (est)
Religion – Christian (Roman Catholic 45 per cent, Protestant 1 per cent), Muslim 4 per cent (est).
Language – Dutch (Flemish), French, German (all official)
Population density – 356 per sq. km (2009)
Urban population – 97 per cent (2008 est)
Median age (years) – 42 (2010 est)
National anthem – 'La Brabançonne' ['The Song of Brabant']
National day – 21 July (Accession of King Leopold I, 1831)
Life expectancy (years) – 79.37 (2010 est)
Mortality rate – 10.5 (2010 est)
Birth rate – 10.1 (2010 est)
Infant mortality rate – 4.38 (2010 est)
Death penalty – Abolished for all crimes (since 1996)
CPI score – 7.1 (2010)

CLIMATE AND TERRAIN
There are two distinct regions: the west is generally low-lying and fertile, while in the east the forested hills of the Ardennes are more rugged with poorer soil. Elevation extremes range from 0m on the North Sea coast to 694m at the highest point (Signal de Botrange). The polders near the coast, which are protected against floods by dykes, cover an area of around 500 sq. km. The principal rivers are the Schelde and the Meuse (Maas). The climate is temperate. Average temperatures range from 2°C in January to 18°C in July.

HISTORY AND POLITICS
Part of the Roman Empire until the second century, the area was invaded by Germanic tribes and then became part of the Frankish Empire until much of the area was absorbed by the duchy of Burgundy from 1385. It was under the rule of the Spanish Habsburgs from 1477 until 1713 and the Austrian Habsburgs until 1794, when the area was conquered and held by Revolutionary France. After the collapse of the Napoleonic regime in 1814, it united with the kingdom of the Netherlands. The Belgian Revolution in 1830 led to the declaration of independence on 14 October 1830 and in 1831 the country became a constitutional monarchy. In the 20th

century Belgium was invaded and occupied by Germany in both world wars; Eupen and Malmédy were ceded to Belgium by Germany under the treaty of Versailles in 1919.

Tensions between the Flemings (Flemish speakers in the north of the country) and the Walloons (French speakers in the south) have caused political instability throughout the post-war period. Inter-communal disputes led in 1980 to the establishment of regional assemblies, and in 1989 the country adopted a federal constitution. Belgium was a founder member of the EU in 1957 and joined the eurozone in 2002.

In the 2007 election, the Christian Democrats won the most seats but not an outright majority. After months of negotiations a five-party government led by the Christian Democrats took office in March 2008, but this collapsed with the withdrawal of one of the Flemish parties in April 2010. Early elections were held in June 2010 and the New Flemish Alliance, a Flemish separatist party, emerged as the largest party in the Chamber of Representatives. Coalition negotiations have continued since the election but have failed to break the deadlock over the formation of a new coalition government. The outgoing government remains in office in a caretaker capacity.

POLITICAL SYSTEM

Belgium is a constitutional monarchy with a hereditary monarch as head of state. The bicameral legislature, the Federal Chambers, consists of a senate and a Chamber of Representatives. The latter has 150 members, directly elected by proportional representation for a four-year term. The senate has 71 members, who serve a four-year term; 40 are directly elected, the Flemish and French communities receive ten members each and the German community one, with the remaining ten co-opted by the elected members.

Amendments to the constitution since 1968 have devolved power to the regions. The national government retains competence only in foreign and defence policies, the national budget and monetary policy, social security, and the judicial, legal and penal systems.

There are three language communities: Flemish, Francophone and Germanophone. Each community has its own assembly, which elects the community government. At this level, Flanders is covered by the Flemish community assembly; most of Wallonia is covered by the Francophone community assembly, and areas of Wallonia lying in the German-speaking communities of Eupen and Malmédy are covered by the Germanophone community assembly; Brussels is covered by a joint community commission of the Flemish and Francophone community assemblies.

At regional level, Belgium is divided into the three regions of Wallonia, Brussels and Flanders. Each region has its own directly elected assembly and government.

The ten provinces of Belgium are: Antwerp, East Flanders, Flemish Brabant, Hainaut, Liège, Limburg, Luxembourg, Namur, Walloon Brabant and West Flanders. In addition, 589 communes form the lowest level of local government.

Minister-President of the Brussels Capital Government,
Charles Picqué
Minister-President of the Flemish Community and Flemish Region, Kris Peeters
Minister-President of the French Community and Walloon Region, Rudy Demotte
Minister-President of the German-speaking Community, Karl-Heinz Lambertz

HEAD OF STATE

HM The King of the Belgians, King Albert II, *born* 6 June 1934; *acceded* 9 August 1993
Heir, HRH Prince Philippe Léopold Louis Marie, *born* 15 April 1960

SELECTED GOVERNMENT MEMBERS *as at May 2011*
Prime Minister, Yves Leterme
Deputy Prime Ministers, Joëlle Milquet; Laurette Onkelinx; Didier Reynders *(Finance);* Steven Vanackere *(Foreign Affairs);* Guy Vanhengel
Defence, Pieter De Crem
Interior, Annemie Turtelboom

EMBASSY OF BELGIUM
17 Grosvenor Crescent, London SW1X 7EE
T 020-7470 3700 E london@diplobel.fed.be
W www.diplomatie.be/london
Ambassador Extraordinary and Plenipotentiary, HE Johan Verbeke, *apptd* 2010

BRITISH EMBASSY
Avenue d'Auderghem 10, Oudergemlaan, 1040 Brussels
T (+32) (2) 287 6211 E info@britain.be
W http://ukinbelgium.fco.gov.uk
Ambassador Extraordinary and Plenipotentiary, HE Jonathan Brenton, *apptd* 2010

BRITISH COUNCIL
Leopold Plaza, Rue de Trône 108/Troonstraat 108, 1050 Brussels
T (+32) (2) 227 0840 W www.britishcouncil.org/brussels
Director, Martin Hope

DEFENCE

The army has 40 main battle tanks, 37 armoured infantry fighting vehicles and 340 armoured personnel carriers. The navy is based at Zeebrugge and has 2 frigates and 1 patrol and coastal vessel. The air force has 88 combat aircraft and 5 air bases.

The headquarters of NATO, and of its Supreme Headquarters Allied Powers Europe, are in Belgium; 1,261 US personnel (EUCOM) are stationed in the country.
Military budget – US$3,640m (2010)
Military personnel – 37,882: army 13,601, navy 1,590, air force 6,814, medical and joint services 15,887

ECONOMY AND TRADE

Belgium has a free-market economy with highly diversified industrial and commercial sectors. With few natural resources, industry is based largely on processing imported raw materials for export. This makes the economy dependent on the state of world markets; rates of growth have been low in recent years and GDP contracted sharply in 2009. The banking sector was severely affected by the international banking crisis and government bail-outs caused the budget deficit to worsen, although the deficit has since been reduced.

Principal industries are engineering and metal products, vehicle assembly, transport equipment, scientific instruments, food processing and beverages, chemicals, base metals, textiles, glass, petroleum and diamonds. Industry accounts for 22.1 per cent of GDP and 25 per cent of employment. There is a large service sector, partly owing to the location in Brussels of EU institutions, NATO headquarters and a number of other international organisations. The service sector accounts for 77.2 per cent of GDP. There is a small agricultural sector (0.7 per cent of GDP).

Around three-quarters of trade is with other EU states, especially Germany, France and the Netherlands. External trade statistics relate to Luxembourg as well as Belgium, as the two countries formed an economic union in 1921.
GNI – US$475,015m; US$45,270 per capita (2009)
Annual average growth of GDP – 1.6 per cent (2010 est)
Inflation rate – 2.3 per cent (2010 est)
Population below poverty line – 15.2 per cent (2007 est)
Unemployment – 8.1 per cent (2010 est)
Total external debt – US$1,241,000m (2010)
Imports – US$351,000m (2009)
Exports – US$369,900m (2009)

BALANCE OF PAYMENTS
Trade – US$21,419m surplus (2010)
Current Account – US$12,855m deficit (2008)

Trade with UK	2009	2010
Imports from UK	£10,456,785,304	£12,940,306,643
Exports to UK	£14,783,451,915	£16,981,334,281

COMMUNICATIONS
There are 2,043km of inland waterways, of which 1,528km are in regular commercial use; ship canals link Ostend and Zeebrugge with Bruges and Ghent, Ghent with Terneuzen in the Netherlands, Brussels with Charleroi and Willebroek Rupel, and Liège with Antwerp. The Meuse (Maas), Sambre and Schelde rivers form an integral part of the network. The main seaports are Antwerp, Ghent, Ostend and Zeebrugge, with major inland ports at Brussels and Liège. The main airports are at Antwerp, Brussels, Liège and Ostend. The rail system is run by Belgian National Railways and, at 3,233km, the network is one of the densest in the world. There are 152,256km of roads, including 1,763km of motorways. Mobile phone ownership was 12.4 million in 2009, and there were 8.1 million internet users.

EDUCATION AND HEALTH
Nursery schools provide free education for children from two-and-a-half to six years of age. The official school-leaving age is 18.
Gross enrolment ratio (percentage of relevant age group) – primary 103 per cent; secondary 108 per cent; tertiary 63 per cent (2008 est)
Health expenditure (per capita) – US$5,104 (2009)
Hospital beds (per 1,000 people) – 6.6 (2004–9)

MEDIA AND CULTURE
The media reflects the multilingual nature of the population, with the community governments responsible for regulating broadcasting. There are two public broadcasters, each providing radio, TV and external broadcasting in a different language: RTBF in French, and VRT in Flemish. There are also French and Flemish commercial television channels and a German-language radio broadcaster. Cable television is popular, with 95 per cent of the population subscribing to domestic and foreign channels. A small number of media groups own and run the main news publications.

Belgium has produced some significant artists, including Pieter Bruegel, the Elder (c.1525–69) and key figures of the Baroque period, such as Peter Paul Rubens (1577–1640) and Anthony van Dyck (1599–1641); notable later artists include James Ensor (1860–1949) and surrealist René Magritte (1898–1967). During the 20th century a rich comic-strip culture took root in Belgium, producing popular characters such as Tintin (Hergé, 1907–81) and the Smurfs (Peyo, 1928–92). The prolific and critically lauded detective novelist Georges Simenon (1903–89) is widely translated from his original French. The country's chocolate and beer are considered to be among the world's finest. Six of the world's seven Trappist breweries are based in Belgium.

BELIZE

Area – 22,966 sq. km
Capital – Belmopan; population, 19,717 (2009 est)
Major towns – Belize City (the former capital), Orange Walk, San Ignacio
Currency – Belize dollar (BZ$) of 100 cents. The Belize dollar is tied to the US dollar
Population – 314,522 rising at 2.1 per cent a year (2010 est); mestizo (48.7 per cent), Creole (24.9 per cent), Maya (10.6 per cent), Garifuna (6.1 per cent) (2000)
Religion – Christian (Roman Catholic 50 per cent, Protestant 27 per cent) (2000)
Language – English (official), Spanish, Creole, Mayan dialects, Garifuna, German
Population density – 15 per sq. km (2009)
Urban population – 52 per cent (2008 est)
Median age (years) – 20.7 (2010 est)
National anthem – 'Land of the Free'
National day – 21 September (Independence Day)
Life expectancy (years) – 68.23 (2010 est)
Mortality rate – 5.82 (2010 est)
Birth rate – 26.84 (2010 est)
Infant mortality rate – 22.52 (2010 est)
HIV/AIDS adult prevalence rate – 2.3 per cent (2009 est)
Death penalty – Retained
CPI score – 2.9 (2008)

CLIMATE AND TERRAIN
Belize comprises a large coastal plain, swamps in the north, fertile land in the south, and the Maya Mountains in the south-west. The highest point of elevation is 1,160m (Doyle's Delight), the lowest is 0m (Caribbean Sea). Part of the Mesoamerican barrier reef system, the western hemisphere's longest, runs nearly the entire length of the coastline. The climate is subtropical but is cooled by trade winds. The hurricane season is from May to November.

HISTORY AND POLITICS
Numerous ruins in the area indicate that Belize was heavily populated by the Maya. The first British settlement was established in 1638 but was subject to repeated attacks by the Spanish, who claimed sovereignty

until their defeat by the British navy and settlers in 1798. In 1862 the settlement was given colonial status as British Honduras. The colony became self-governing in 1964. In 1973 it was renamed Belize and it was granted independence on 21 September 1981.

Since independence, power has alternated between the two main politicial parties, the People's United Party (PUP) and the United Democratic Party (UDP). The PUP, in power since 1998, lost the 2008 election to the UDP, which won 25 seats and took office under Dean Barrow.

FOREIGN RELATIONS
There is a longstanding territorial dispute with Guatemala, which claims the southern part of Belize. Following years of negotiations under the auspices of the Organisation of American States, both countries agreed in 2008 to refer the dispute to the International Court of Justice, subject to the outcome of referendums in each country.

POLITICAL SYSTEM
Under the 1981 constitution, the head of state is Queen Elizabeth II, represented by a governor-general. There is a bicameral National Assembly, comprising a House of Representatives with 31 members directly elected for a five-year term, and a senate of 13 members appointed by the governor-general, including six on the advice of the prime minister, three on the advice of the opposition leader, and three representing various sectors of society; a referendum in 2008 approved the reform of the senate into an elected chamber effective from the next elections, due in 2013. The prime minister is appointed by the governor-general and is responsible to the legislature.
Governor-General, HE Sir Colville Young, GCMG, *apptd* 17 November 1993

SELECTED GOVERNMENT MEMBERS *as at June 2011*
Prime Minister, Finance, Dean Barrow
Deputy Prime Minister, Gaspar Vega
Foreign Affairs, Wilfred Elrington
Attorney-General, Bernard Pitts

BELIZE HIGH COMMISSION
3rd Floor, 45 Crawford Place, London W1H 4LP
T 020-7723 3603 **E** bzhc-lon@btconnect.com
W www.belizehighcommission.com
High Commissioner, HE Kamela Palma, *apptd* 2008

BRITISH HIGH COMMISSION
PO Box 91, Belmopan
T (+501) 822 2146 **E** brithicom@btl.net
W http://ukinbelize.fco.gov.uk
High Commissioner, HE Patrick Ashworth, *apptd* 2009

DEFENCE
Military budget – US$19m (2010)
Military personnel – 1,050 (all army) (est)

ECONOMY AND TRADE
The economy grew steadily from 1999 to 2007, bolstered from 2006 by commercial exploitation of oil reserves. It contracted sharply in 2009 owing to the global downturn, natural disasters and the drop in international oil prices but started to recover in 2010. There is a high level of foreign debt, which was restructured in 2007. About one-third of the population lives below the poverty line.

The services sector has grown as tourism has developed, and accounts for around 54 per cent of GDP; industry contributes around 17 per cent, and agriculture and fisheries around 29 per cent. The main industries apart from tourism are garment manufacturing, food processing, construction and oil production. The chief trading partners are the USA, the UK and Mexico. The major exports are sugar, bananas, citrus fruits and juice, garments, shrimp, fish products, molasses, timber and crude oil. Imports are primarily machinery and transport equipment, manufactured goods, fuel, chemicals, pharmaceuticals, food, beverages and tobacco.
GNI – US$1,197m; US$3,740 per capita (2008)
Annual average growth of GDP – 1.5 per cent (2010)
Inflation rate – 4.1 per cent (2010 est)
Unemployment – 13.1 per cent (2009)
Total external debt – US$1,010m (2009 est)
Imports – US$600m (2009)
Exports – US$300m (2009)

BALANCE OF PAYMENTS
Trade – US$400m deficit (2010)
Current Account – US$137m deficit (2008)

Trade with UK	2009	2010
Imports from UK	£7,566,079	£7,500,829
Exports to UK	£67,120,553	£58,443,947

COMMUNICATIONS
Although there are 825km of waterways, these are only accessible by small craft. The main port is Belize City, which has deep-water quays. There are around 40 airports and airfields, including the international airport at Belize City. There are 3,007 km of roads, 575 km of which are surfaced, but no railway system. Mobile phone distribution has reached a density of about 55 per 100 people, exceeding fixed-line connections of 10 per 100 people.

EDUCATION
Education is free and compulsory for ten years. The government maintains some schools but most are run by churches. The government is the main provider of health services.
Literacy rate – 75.1 per cent (2008 est)
Gross enrolment ratio (percentage of relevant age group) – primary 122 per cent; secondary 76 per cent; tertiary 11 per cent (2009 est)

MEDIA
The state-run radio service was privatised in 1998 and broadcasts are now provided by a number of commercial radio stations. There is one regional daily newspaper and a number of privately owned weekly news publications. There are three main television stations (Channels 5, 7 and 9), all of which are commercial.

BENIN

République du Bénin – Republic of Benin

Area – 112,622 sq. km
Capital – Porto Novo; population, 275,993 (2009 est).
Cotonou is the seat of government; population
815,041 (2009 est)
Major cities – Abomey-Calavi, Djougou, Parakou
Currency – Franc CFA of 100 centimes
Population – 9,056,010 rising at 2.94 per cent a year
(2010 est); Fon (39.2 per cent), Adja (15.2 per cent),
Yoruba (12.3 per cent), Bariba (9.2 per cent), Fulani
(7 per cent), Ottamari (6.1 per cent), Yoa-Lokpa
(4 per cent), Dendi (2.5 per cent) (2002)
Religion – Christian 43 per cent (Roman Catholic
27 per cent, Celestial 5 per cent, Protestant 5 per cent),
Muslim 24 per cent (predominantly Sunni), Vodun
(voodoo) 17 per cent, other indigenous religions
6 per cent. Many Christians and Muslims also practise
voodoo, which originated in this region of Africa, or
other indigenous religions
Language – French (official), Fon, Yoruba and other
African languages
Population density – 81 per sq. km (2009)
Urban population – 41 per cent (2008 est)
Median age (years) – 17.3 (2010 est)
National anthem – 'L'Aube Nouvelle' ['The Dawn of a
New Day']
National day – 1 August (Independence Day)
Life expectancy – 59.42 (2010 est)
Mortality rate – 9.23 (2010 est)
Birth rate – 38.67 (2010 est)
Infant mortality rate – 63.13 (2010 est)
HIV/AIDS adult prevalence – 1.2 per cent (2009 est)
Death penalty – Retained (not used since 1987)
CPI score – 2.8 (2010)
Literacy rate – 41.4 per cent (2008 est)
Gross enrolment ratio (percentage of relevant age group) –
primary 122 per cent (2009 est)
Health expenditure (per capita) – US$32 (2007)
Hospital beds (per 1,000 people) – 0.5 (2004–9)

CLIMATE AND TERRAIN

Benin has a short coastline of 121km on the Gulf of
Guinea, but extends northwards inland for over 700km.
The coast is a sandbar backed by lagoons that are fed by
rivers. The land rises to a central plateau with the Atacora
massif in the north-west, and falls to plains in the Niger
basin in the north-east. Elevation extremes range from
658m (Mt Sokbaro) at the highest point to 0m (Atlantic
Ocean) at the lowest. The climate is tropical in the south
and semi-arid in the north.

HISTORY AND POLITICS

Dahomey, on the site of modern-day Benin, was a west
African kingdom founded in the 11th to 12th centuries
that rose to prominence during the 15th and 16th
centuries. The first Europeans to visit the country were the
Portuguese in 1472. Slavery became the region's primary
trade, hence the area's historical name of the Slave Coast.

After a war between the French and the Dahomey
kingdom, the French established a protectorate over the
south in 1893 and gradually extended this to include the
north by 1898. Dahomey was incorporated into French
West Africa in 1904. It became an independent republic
within the French Community in 1958 and independence
was proclaimed on 1 August 1960.

Between 1960 and 1972 there was acute political
instability, with frequent switches from civil to military
rule and regional ethnic conflicts, until a military coup in
1972 brought to power Lt.-Col. Mathieu Kérékou, who
declared the country a Marxist-Leninist state and in 1975
changed its name to Benin.

Civil rule was restored in 1977 (though Kérékou
remained president) and, in response to popular
discontent, Marxism-Leninism was abandoned in 1989 for
economic liberalisation, and a pluralistic constitution was
adopted in 1990. The transition to fully democratic
government was effected smoothly in 1991 and has
operated successfully, making Benin one of the most
stable countries in Africa.

The 2006 presidential election was won in the second
round by Yayi Boni, an independent candidate, and he
was re-elected in March 2011. In the 2011 legislative
election, the Cauri Forces for an Emerging Benin, which
supports the president, remained the largest group in the
National Assembly, winning 41 seats.

POLITICAL SYSTEM

Under the 1990 constitution, the executive president is
directly elected for a five-year term, renewable only once.
The unicameral National Assembly has 83 members,
directly elected for a four-year term. The president
appoints and chairs the council of ministers.

HEAD OF STATE

President and Head of the Armed Forces, Boni Yayi, *elected*
19 March 2006, *re-elected* 2011

SELECTED GOVERNMENT MEMBERS *as at June 2011*
Foreign Affairs, Nassirou Arifari Bako
Defence, Issifou Kogui N'douro
Economy, Finance, Adidjatou Mathys
Interior, Security, Benoêt Assouan Degla

EMBASSY OF THE REPUBLIC OF BENIN
87 Avenue Victor Hugo, 75116 Paris, France
T (+33) 1 4500 9882 E ambassade.benin@gofornet.com
Ambassador Extraordinary and Plenipotentiary, HE Albert
Agossou, *apptd* 2009

BRITISH AMBASSADOR
HE Robert Dewar, CMG, *apptd* 2007, resident at Abuja,
Nigeria

DEFENCE

The army has 18 light tanks. The navy has 2 patrol and
coastal combatant vessels.
Military budget – US$53m (2010)
Military personnel – 4,750: army 4,300, navy 200, air
force 250; paramilitary 2,500
Conscription duration – 18 months (selective)

ECONOMY AND TRADE

Although the economy is underdeveloped and still burdened by foreign debt, Benin has benefited from increased competitiveness and debt reduction or relief since its economic restructuring began. Privatisation of industries, including utilities, began in 2001 and economic growth has been steady since 2000. However, this has been outweighed by rapid population growth and over a third of the population remains below the poverty line. The economy is based on agriculture, particularly cotton production, and re-export trade with neighbouring countries; customs receipts provide about half of government revenue, but much of the re-export trade operates outside the official economy and is unrecorded.

Agriculture is mostly at subsistence level and contributes 33.2 per cent to GDP, declining recently as industry (14.5 per cent) and services (52.3 per cent) have developed. The main cash crops are cotton, cashew nuts, shea butter, palm products and seafood, and the principal industrial activities are textiles and food processing. The main trading partners are China (13 per cent of exports; 36 per cent of imports) and India, to which textiles and some of the cash crops are exported. The principal imports are food, capital goods and fuel.

GNI – US$6,646m; US$750 per capita (2009)
Annual average growth of GDP – 3 per cent (2010 est)
Inflation rate – 1.6 per cent (2010 est)
Population below poverty line – 37.4 per cent (2007 est)
Total external debt – US$2,894m (2009)
Imports – US$1,800m (2009)
Exports – US$1,000m (2009)

BALANCE OF PAYMENTS
Trade – US$1,714m deficit (2010)
Current Account – US$430m deficit (2008)

Trade with UK	2009	2010
Imports from UK	£76,754,972	£205,698,641
Exports to UK	£461,364	£16,117

MEDIA

Free speech is guaranteed by the constitution and the media enjoy a large degree of freedom, although journalists are wary of stringent libel laws. There are over 50 newspapers and periodicals, including six daily newspapers, five of which are privately owned. The state runs a television channel and a radio network, and there are a handful of other commercial TV broadcasters. Radio is the main information medium, especially in rural areas, and there are scores of independent local stations, many broadcasting in local languages.

BHUTAN

Druk Gyalkhap – Kingdom of Bhutan

Area – 38,394 sq. km
Capital – Thimphu; population, 89,454 (2009 est)
Major towns – Geylegphug, Paro, Phuentsholing
Currency – Ngultrum of 100 chetrum (Indian currency is also legal tender)
Population – 699,847 rising at 1.24 per cent a year (2010 est); Bhote (50 per cent), ethnic Nepalese (35 per cent), indigenous or migrant tribes (15 per cent) (est)
Religion – Buddhist 66 per cent (predominantly Tibetan school of Mahayana), Hindu 25 per cent (est)
Language – Dzongkha (official), English, Nepali, Tibetan
Population density – 18 per sq. km (2009)
Urban population – 35 per cent (2008 est)
Median age (years) – 24.3 (2010 est)
National anthem – 'Druk Tsendhen' ['The Thunder Dragon Kingdom']
National day – 17 December (inauguration of first hereditary monarch, 1907)
Life expectancy (years) – 66.71 (2010 est)
Mortality rate – 7.25 (2010 est)
Birth rate – 19.62 (2010 est)
Infant mortality rate – 46.92 (2010 est)
Death penalty – Abolished for all crimes (since 2004)
CPI score – 5.7 (2010)
Literacy rate – 52.8 per cent (2008 est)

CLIMATE AND TERRAIN

Bhutan is a landlocked Himalayan country lying between China and India. There is a mountainous northern region that is infertile and sparsely populated, central highlands, and densely forested foothills in the south, which are mainly inhabited by Nepalese settlers and indigenous tribespeople. The country is crossed by numerous rivers, and most of the population and cultivated land is found in the deep, fertile valleys of the highlands. Around 70 per cent of the land is forested. Extremes of elevation range from 7,570m (Gangkar Puensum) at the highest point to 97m (Drangme Chhu) at the lowest. The climate is determined by altitude, varying from subtropical in the south to alpine in the north. There is heavy annual rainfall of up to 1,000mm in the central valleys and 5,000mm in the south, which experiences monsoons from June to September.

HISTORY AND POLITICS

Bhutan's remoteness limited outside contact until modern times, although it signed a treaty of cooperation with Britain in 1774. Another treaty was signed with Britain in 1865 after Britain had annexed the south of the country. Bhutan's external relations were under the guidance of

Britain from the 19th century until 1947, and of India from 1947 until 2007; a 2007 revision of the friendship treaty between the two countries left Bhutan free to manage its external relations without India's advice.

Although the country has opened up since the 1970s, the monarchy has taken measures to preserve its indigenous culture and the environment, including the compulsory wearing of national dress and restrictions on tourism. The emphasis on the majority culture has caused tension with the sizeable Nepali minority. Many were denied citizenship in the 1990s and obliged to leave, which resulted in over 100,000 becoming refugees in Nepal, where most remain, living in refugee camps.

Bhutan's transition from an absolute monarchy to a democracy began in the 1950s, with the establishment of an elected legislature in 1953, and the transfer of powers from the king to the legislature in 1969 and 1989. The 2008 constitution formally established Bhutan as a parliamentary democracy with a constitutional monarchy, and provided for universal suffrage. King Jigme Singye Wangchuk abdicated in 2006 in favour of the Crown Prince.

The elections to the National Assembly resulted in an overwhelming majority for the pro-monarchy Bhutan Harmony Party (DPT), which won 45 of the 47 seats; the DPT leader, Jigme Thinley, was appointed prime minister and formed a government.

POLITICAL SYSTEM

Under the 2008 constitution, the head of state is a hereditary constitutional monarch, who must retire at the age of 65 and who may be required to abdicate by a two-thirds majority of the legislature. The bicameral parliament comprises a National Assembly with 47 directly elected members and a National Council with 25 members: 20 directly elected and five appointed by the king. Both chambers serve a fixed five-year term. The cabinet is appointed by the king on the recommendation of the prime minister, who may serve two parliamentary terms.

HEAD OF STATE
HM The King of Bhutan, Jigme Khesar Namgyal
  Wangchuk, *born* 21 February 1980, *acceded* 14
  December 2006, *crowned* 6 November 2008

SELECTED GOVERNMENT MEMBERS *as at May 2011*
Prime Minister, Jigme Thinley
Finance, Wangdi Norbu
Foreign Affairs, Ugyen Tshering
Home and Cultural Affairs, Minjur Dorji

HONORARY CONSULATE
2 Windacres, Warren Road, Guildford GU1 2HG
T 01483-538189 **E** rutland.michael@gmail.com
Honorary Consul, Michael R. Rutland

BRITISH DEPUTY HIGH COMMISSION
Vice Consul, Sanjay Wadvani, OBE, resident at Kolkata, India

ECONOMY AND TRADE

The economy is being cautiously modernised but is still based on agriculture (17.6 per cent of GDP in 2009) in what is largely a self-sufficient rural society. Industry (45 per cent of GDP) is on a small scale, and the growing services sector (37.4 per cent of GDP) is mostly the result of increased tourism. Agriculture and animal husbandry,

much at subsistence level, engage over 40 per cent of the workforce, although the mountainous terrain and heavy forest cover limit the area under cultivation. The principal food crops are rice, cereals, vegetables and fruit, especially oranges. Industries include forestry, mining (limestone, gypsum, dolomite, graphite, coal), cement and calcium carbide production, food processing, distilling, hydro-electric power generation and tourism.

The main trading partner is India, which also provides most of Bhutan's development funding. The principal exports are electricity (to India), ferrosilicon, cement, calcium carbide, copper wire, manganese and vegetable oil. The main imports are fuel and lubricants, passenger vehicles, machinery and parts, fabrics and rice.

GNI – US$1,322m; US$2,020 per capita (2009)
Annual average growth of GDP – 6.8 per cent (2010 est)
Inflation rate – 4.3 per cent (2008 est)
Population below poverty line – 23.2 per cent (2008)
Unemployment – 4 per cent (2009)
Total external debt – US$836m (2009)
Imports – US$600m (2009)
Exports – US$300m (2009)

BALANCE OF PAYMENTS
Trade – US$45m surplus (2010)
Current Account – US$132m surplus (2007)

Trade with UK	2009	2010
Imports from UK	£806,802	£620,578
Exports to UK	£49,597	£67,510

MEDIA

Fear that outside influences would undermine Bhutanese culture meant that radio broadcasting began only in 1973, and television broadcasting and internet access in 1999; the country's first daily newspaper, *Bhutan Today,* privately owned and published in English, was launched in 2008. Radio and television services are provided by the state-owned Bhutan Broadcasting Service (BBS). Media freedom is restricted by the government and there are no private broadcasters, although cable TV relays from India are very popular.

BOLIVIA

Estado Plurinacional de Bolivia – Plurinational State of Bolivia

Area – 1,098,581 sq. km
Capital – La Paz, the seat of government; population, 1,641,950 (2009 est); Sucre, the legal capital and seat of the judiciary; population, 280,925 (2009 est)

Major cities – Cochabamba, El Alto, Oruro, Potosí, Santa Cruz
Currency – Boliviano ($b) of 100 centavos
Population – 9,947,418 rising at 1.72 per cent a year (2010 est); Quechua (30 per cent), mestizo (30 per cent), Aymara (25 per cent) (est)
Religion – Christian (Roman Catholic 78 per cent, Protestant 16 per cent, other 3 per cent) (est)
Language – Spanish, 36 indigenous languages (all official); Quechua and Aymara are the main indigenous languages
Population density – 9 per sq. km (2009)
Urban population – 66 per cent (2008 est)
Median age (years) – 22.2 (2010 est)
National anthem – 'Himno Nacional de la República de Bolivia' ['National Anthem of the Republic of Bolivia']
National day – 6 August (Independence Day)
Life expectancy (years) – 67.23 (2010 est)
Mortality rate – 6.95 (2010 est)
Birth rate – 25.16 (2010 est)
Infant mortality rate – 43.41 (2010 est)
Death penalty – Retained for certain crimes (last used 1974)
CPI score – 2.8 (2010)

CLIMATE AND TERRAIN

Landlocked Bolivia's main topographical feature is its great central plateau, the Altiplano. Over 800km in length and at an average altitude of 3,750m above sea level, this plateau lies between two great chains of the Andes that traverse the country from north to south. Lake Titicaca, shared with Peru, lies on the Antiplano. Elevation extremes range from 6,542m (Nevado Sajama) at the highest point to 90m (Rio Paraguay) at the lowest. The low-lying north and eastern plains are drained by the principal rivers, the Itenez, Beni, Mamoré and Madre de Dios. The climate varies dramatically between regions: on the lowlands of the Amazon basin, temperatures average around 25°C; above 500m on the Altiplano, conditions are subpolar. The south is prone to droughts. The wet season is November to April.

HISTORY AND POLITICS

The area of present-day Bolivia was assimilated into the Inca Empire c.1450, and was then conquered by the Spanish in 1525. Bolivia won its independence in 1825 after a war of liberation led by Simón Bolívar (1783–1830), from whom the country takes its name. Much of its territory was lost after wars with neighbouring countries, including a devastating defeat in the Chaco War (1932–5) against Paraguay.

Bolivia was ruled by military juntas from 1936 to 1952 and from 1964 to 1982, when civilian rule was restored amid worsening economic conditions as the tin market collapsed and inflation rose dramatically. Austerity measures introduced in 1983 succeeded over the next decade in curbing inflation and attracting foreign investment, but the measures widened social divisions and created great social unrest. Protests centred on coca crop eradication programmes, which were essential to attract overseas aid but also caused economic hardship among the poor. The civil unrest also reflected the frustration of the mainly indigenous poor at their exclusion from political decision-making and failure to benefit from natural gas revenues. This led to a swing away from the traditional parties towards newer, more left-wing groupings.

Evo Morales, the country's first indigenous president and a former coca growers' leader, dealt with these issues by renationalising the energy industry and promising to relax restrictions on coca cultivation. He also sought to give greater political power to the indigenous population through constitutional changes. These were strongly opposed by many Bolivians, especially those in the wealthier regions in the east of the country which are seeking greater autonomy, provoking a political crisis in 2008, when President Morales faced a recall referendum. The president won that vote and the draft constitution was approved in a referendum in 2009.

President Morales, leader of the Movement Towards Socialism (MAS), took office in 2006 after winning the 2005 presidential elections, and was re-elected in 2009. After the 2005 legislative elections, the MAS had an outright majority in the lower chamber of the legislature but the Social and Democratic Power party was the largest party in the upper chamber. The MAS won a majority in both chambers in the 2009 legislative elections.

POLITICAL SYSTEM

The 1967 constitution was revised in 1994 and 2009. It provides for an executive president who is directly elected for a five-year term, which may be renewed once. The bicameral Plurinational Legislative Assembly, or National Congress, consists of a 36-member Chamber of Senators and a 130-member Chamber of Deputies; members of both chambers are directly elected for a five-year term.

HEAD OF STATE
President, Evo Morales Ayma, *elected* 18 December 2005, *sworn in* 22 January 2006, *re-elected* 2009
President of the Senate, Vice-President, Alvaro Garcia Linera

SELECTED GOVERNMENT MEMBERS *as at June 2011*
Defence, Maria Cecilia Chacon
Economy and Public Finance, Luis Alberto Arce Catacora
Foreign Affairs, David Choquehuanca Cespedes
Interior, Sacha Sergio Llorenti Soliz

BOLIVIAN EMBASSY
106 Eaton Square, London SW1W 9AD
T 020-7235 2257 E info@embassyofbolivia.co.uk
Ambassador Extraordinary and Plenipotentiary, HE Maria Beatriz Souviron, *apptd* 2006

BRITISH EMBASSY
PO Box 694, Avenida Arce 2732, La Paz
T (+591) (2) 243 3424 E ukinbolivia@gmail.com
W http://ukinbolivia.fco.gov.uk
Ambassador Extraordinary and Plenipotentiary, HE Nigel Baker, MVO, *apptd* 2007

DEFENCE

The army has 54 light tanks and over 152 armoured personnel carriers. The navy has 54 patrol and coastal vessels at 12 bases. The air force has 33 combat aircraft and 2 multi-role helicopters.
Military budget – US$357m (2010)
Military personnel – 46,100: army 34,800, navy 4,800, air force 6,500; paramilitary 37,100

ECONOMY AND TRADE

The country is one of the poorest and least developed in South America, although steady growth since the 1990s has lowered the proportion of the population living below the poverty line from over half to under one-third. Economic growth slowed in the 2000s owing to lower commodity prices and political instability, and the economy contracted in 2009 because of the global downturn, recovering strongly in 2010 as commodity prices rose. The renationalised energy industry is the mainstay of the economy but development is hampered by lack of investment. There are plans, some already implemented, to nationalise other key industries and utilities.

Mining (principally for zinc, tin and gold) and smelting, natural gas and oil production, agriculture and textiles are the principal industries. Industry contributes 38 per cent of GDP, agriculture 12 per cent and services 50 per cent.

The main trading partners are Brazil, the USA, Argentina and Peru. Principal exports are natural gas, soya beans and soya products, crude oil, zinc ore and tin. The main imports are petroleum products, plastics, paper, aircraft and aircraft parts, processed food, vehicles and insecticides.

GNI – US$16,666m; US$1,630 per capita (2009)
Annual average growth of GDP – 3.8 per cent (2010 est)
Inflation rate – 2.1 per cent (2010 est)
Population below poverty line – 30.3 per cent (2009 est; defined as living on less than US$2 a day)
Unemployment – 8.3 per cent (2010)
Total external debt – US$6,130m (2010 est)
Imports – US$4,400m (2009)
Exports – US$4,800m (2009)

BALANCE OF PAYMENTS
Trade – US$975m surplus (2010)
Current Account – US$2,015m surplus (2008)

Trade with UK	2009	2010
Imports from UK	£14,575,941	£15,514,489
Exports to UK	£17,063,308	£27,580,655

COMMUNICATIONS

Although landlocked, Bolivia has 10,000km of commercially navigable waterways, with an inland port on the river Paraguay at the border with Brazil. It has free port privileges at seaports in Argentina, Brazil, Chile and Paraguay, and a lease on a free-trade zone at the Peruvian port of Ilo. Bolivia has 881 airports and airfields, including four international airports serving the major cities. The 3,652km of railways form an eastern network and an Andean network; plans to link the two were initiated in 2004 (the link would complete a transcontinental railway line between the Brazilian and Chilean coasts). Of the 13,600km of roads, fewer than 5,000km are surfaced. The fixed-line telephone system is largely confined to the cities. Mobile phone use is growing rapidly, exceeding 75 per 100 people by 2009.

EDUCATION AND HEALTH

Elementary education is compulsory and free from the ages of five to 17.
Literacy rate – 90.7 per cent (2008 est)
Gross enrolment ratio (percentage of relevant age group) – primary 108 per cent; secondary 82 per cent; tertiary 38 per cent (2007 est)
Health expenditure (per capita) – US$85 (2009)
Hospital beds (per 1,000 people) – 1.1 (2004–9)

MEDIA

Owing to low literacy levels, radio is the most important news medium, particularly in rural areas. The media is largely privately owned and operated. Journalists enjoy greater freedoms than in many neighbouring countries, but still practise a degree of self-censorship, avoiding sensitive topics such as drug-trafficking and political corruption. There are six daily newspapers. Television is mostly commercial, with one government-run channel.

BOSNIA AND HERCEGOVINA

Bosna i Hercegovina – Bosnia and Hercegovina

Area – 51,197 sq. km
Capital – Sarajevo; population, 391,870 (2009 est)
Major towns – Banja Luka, Bijeljina, Bosanski Samac, Mostar, Tuzla, Zenica
Currency – Convertible mark of 100 fenings
Population – 4,621,598 rising at 0.02 per cent a year (2010 est); Bosniak (48 per cent), Serb (37.1 per cent), Croat (14.3 per cent) (2000 est)
Religion – Muslim 45 per cent (predominantly Sunni), Christian (Serb Orthodox 36 per cent, Roman Catholic 15 per cent, Protestant 1 per cent) (est)
Language – Bosnian, Croatian, Serbian (all official)
Population density – 74 per sq. km (2009)
Urban population – 47 per cent (2008 est)
Median age (years) – 40.3 (2010 est)
National anthem – 'Drzavna Himna Bosne i Hercegovine' ['National Anthem of Bosnia and Hercegovina']
National day – 25 November (formation of the anti-fascist resistance council, 1943)
Life expectancy (years) – 78.66 (2010 est)
Mortality rate – 8.71 (2010 est)
Birth rate – 8.87 (2010 est)
Infant mortality rate – 8.88 (2010 est)
Death penalty – Abolished for all crimes (since 2001)
CPI score – 3.2 (2010)
Literacy rate – 96.7 per cent (2008 est)
Gross enrolment ratio (percentage of relevant age group) – primary 109 per cent; secondary 91 per cent; tertiary 27 per cent (2009 est)
Health expenditure (per capita) – US$495 (2009)
Hospital beds (per 1,000 people) – 3.0 (2004–9)

CLIMATE AND TERRAIN

The country is nearly landlocked, apart from a 20km coastline on the Adriatic. The Dinaric Alps lie along the western border. The mountainous centre is split by deep valleys, while the north is lower-lying, falling to the basin of the river Sava, which forms the northern border with Croatia. The highest point of elevation is 2,386m (Maglic), the lowest point is 0m (Adriatic Sea). Average temperatures in Sarajevo range from −1°C in January to 20°C in July.

HISTORY AND POLITICS

The area was settled by Slavs in the seventh century and conquered by the Ottoman Turks in 1463. Ruled by the Turks for over 400 years, the country came under Austro-Hungarian control in 1878. The assassination of the heir to the Austro-Hungarian throne in Sarajevo in 1914 precipitated the First World War, after which Bosnia-Hercegovina became part of the Kingdom of Serbs, Croats and Slovenes (renamed Yugoslavia in 1929). It was occupied by Axis forces between 1941 and 1945. After the end of the Second World War, Bosnia-Hercegovina formed part of the Socialist Federal Republic of Yugoslavia. This collapsed in 1991–2 following the secession of Slovenia, Croatia and Macedonia in 1991 and Bosnia-Hercegovina on 5 March 1992. Bosnia-Hercegovina's independence was recognised internationally in May 1992.

Federal attempts to prevent the secession of the various republics resulted in a number of mainly short-lived conflicts with nationalist paramilitary groups. But in Bosnia-Hercegovina the conflict quickly developed into a three-sided civil war in which predominantly Muslim Bosnians (Bosniaks) loyal to the government attempted to resist first Bosnian Serbs (in the east) and later Bosnian Croats (in the west and north) who had declared independence and were fighting to partition the country along ethnic lines. The Bosniak–Croat conflict continued until 1994, when the two forces then united against the Serbs. All sides, but particularly the Serbs, expelled people of different ethnicity from the areas they seized ('ethnic cleansing'). UN forces, deployed from 1992, were unable to prevent ethnic cleansing or the many atrocities, such as the Srebrenica massacre (1995). In August 1995, NATO intervention against Serb forces forced their leaders to participate in negotiations. These produced the Dayton Accord, which brought the war to an end in December 1995. An estimated 100,000 people died between 1992 and 1995, and a further two million were displaced.

The Dayton Accord preserved Bosnia as a single state with an almost equal division of territory between two self-governing entities, the Federation of Bosnia-Hercegovina (Bosniak/Croat) and the Republika Srpska (Bosnian Serbs), with a national government, presidency and democratically elected institutions. The Office of the High Representative was created to oversee the implementation of the civil aspects of the accord, and remains the state's highest authority. Since 1995 international peacekeeping duties have been undertaken by, successively, the UN (1995), NATO (1995–2005) and the EU (2005–).

Although stable under international administration, the country's ethnic divisions remain strong and hamper political and economic development. Constitutional reforms intended to strengthen central government and end ethnic separatism, under negotiation since 2005, have made little progress despite the incentive of eventual EU and NATO membership.

The latest legislative elections were held in October 2010. In the federal legislature, the Bosniak-dominated Social Democratic Party (SDP) and the Serb-dominated Party of Independent Social Democrats (SNSD) won an equal number of seats; a coalition government was still being negotiated at the time of going to press. The SDP won a narrow majority in the Bosniak–Croat legislature and formed a coalition government under Nermin Niksic. In the Republika Srpska, the SNSD retained its majority and formed a new coalition government under Aleksandar Dzombic.

In the presidential elections in October 2010, Nebojsa Radmanovic and Zeljko Komsic were re-elected to the collective federal presidency and Bakir Izetbegovic was elected as the Bosniak member. Milorad Dodik, previously the prime minister, was elected president of Republika Srpska. The presidential election in the Bosniak–Croat Federation in March 2011 was won by Zivko Budimir.

POLITICAL SYSTEM

Under the Dayton Peace Accord, the Bosnian republican (national) government is responsible for foreign affairs, currency, citizenship and immigration. The head of state is a collective presidency comprising a representative from each of the three main ethnic groups, all directly elected for a four-year term; the chair of the presidency rotates among its members every eight months. Legislative authority is vested in the bicameral Parliamentary Assembly, comprising a House of Peoples and a House of Representatives. Both houses have four-year terms. The House of Peoples has 15 members – ten from the Federation and five from the Republika Srpska – who are appointed from the House of Representatives. The House of Representatives has 42 members who are directly elected to the two constituent chambers: the Chamber of Deputies of the Federation, which has 28 members, and the Chamber of Deputies of the Republika Srpska, which has 14 members.

In the Bosniak–Croat Federation, the president and vice-president are elected by the Bosniak and Croat members of the House of Peoples for a four-year term; a second vice-president is elected to represent the Serb population. There is a bicameral Assembly comprising a 58-member House of Peoples elected on an ethnic basis and a House of Representatives with 98 directly elected members.

In the Republika Srpska, the president is directly elected for a four-year term. There is a unicameral People's Assembly with 83 members directly elected for a four-year term.

There is a national council of ministers and each of the entities also has its own executive. All appointments to the executives are in consultation with the UN High Representative, who has the power of veto.

REPUBLIC OF BOSNIA AND HERCEGOVINA
HEADS OF STATE
Presidency Members, Nebojsa Radmanovic *(Serb)*, Zeljko Komsic *(Croat)*, Bakir Izetbegovic *(Bosniak)*

SELECTED GOVERNMENT MEMBERS *as at June 2011*
Chair of the Council of Ministers, Nikola Spiric
Finance, Dragan Vrankic
Foreign Affairs, Sven Alkalaj
Defence, Selmo Cikotic

FEDERATION OF BOSNIA AND HERCEGOVINA
President, Zivko Budimir
Vice-Presidents, Mirsad Kebo; Svetozar Pudaric

SELECTED GOVERNMENT MEMBERS *as at June 2011*
Prime Minister, Nermin Niksic
Deputy Prime Ministers, Jerko Ivankovic-Lijanovic;
    Desnica Radivojevic
Interior, Predrag Kurtes

REPUBLIKA SRPSKA
President, Milorad Dodik
Vice-Presidents, Enes Suljkanovic; Emil Vlajki

SELECTED GOVERNMENT MEMBERS *as at June 2011*
Prime Minister, Aleksandar Dzombic
Deputy Prime Minister, Anton Kasipovic
Interior, Stanislav Cadjo

OFFICE OF THE UN HIGH REPRESENTATIVE / EU
SPECIAL REPRESENTATIVE
UN High Representative, Dr Valentin Inzko, *apptd* 2009

EMBASSY OF BOSNIA AND HERCEGOVINA
5–7 Lexham Gardens, London W8 5JJ
T 020-7373 0867 E embassy@bhembassy.co.uk
W www.bhembassy.co.uk
Ambassador Extraordinary and Plenipotentiary, HE
   Jadranka Negodic, *apptd* 2008

BRITISH EMBASSY
Tina Ujevica 8, 71000 Sarajevo
T (+387) (33) 282 200 E britemb@bih.net.ba
W http://ukinbih.fco.gov.uk
Ambassador Extraordinary and Plenipotentiary, HE Nigel
   Casey, MVO, *apptd* 2011

BRITISH COUNCIL
Ljubljanska 9, 71000 Sarajevo
T (+387) (33) 250 220 W www.britishcouncil.org/bih
Director, Michael Moore

DEFENCE
A reform process completed in 2006 united the separate armies of the Republika Sprska and the Federation of Bosnia Hercegovina into a single entity. The armed forces have 334 main battle tanks, 137 armoured infantry fighting vehicles and 127 armoured personnel carriers. The air wing has 19 combat capable aircraft and 18 multi-role helicopters.
Military budget – US$227m (2010)
Military personnel – 10,577: armed forces 9,205, Joint
   Operational Command and Joint Staff 500, air and air
   defence 872

ECONOMY AND TRADE
When the civil war broke out, the structure of the economy – dominated by state-owned industries, mainly of a military nature – still reflected the central planning of the communist era. Since the war, growth has been largely generated by reconstruction, funded by external aid, but the private sector is increasingly significant. Economic restructuring, such as privatisation, has been slow and uneven, although the financial sector is now largely privatised and stable. The difficulties inherent in tackling problems such as the large public sector, large deficits and high unemployment are exacerbated by the duplication of administrative functions and reluctant cooperation between the different national and local political and administrative entities. There is a large unofficial economy, but undeclared activity has declined since the introduction of VAT in 2006.

Most agricultural products are for domestic consumption and foodstuffs also have to be imported. The main industrial activities include mining (metals, minerals and coal), production of steel, textiles, tobacco products, wooden furniture, ammunition and domestic appliances, assembly of vehicles, tanks and aircraft, and oil refining. The country produces enough hydroelectric power for its needs, and exports electricity. The main trading partners are Croatia, Slovenia and EU states, particularly Germany, Austria and Italy. Principal exports are metals, clothing and wood products, and the main imports are machinery and equipment, chemicals, fuels and foodstuffs.
GNI – US$17,422m; US$4,700 per capita (2009)
Annual average growth of GDP – 1.1 per cent (2010 est)
Inflation rate – 1.9 per cent (2010 est)
Population below poverty line – 25 per cent (2004 est)
Unemployment – 27.2 per cent (2010 est)
Total external debt – US$7,996m (2010 est)

BALANCE OF PAYMENTS
Trade – US$5,275m deficit (2010)
Current Account – US$2,765m deficit (2008)

Trade with UK	2009	2010
Imports from UK	£19,779,817	£21,909,228
Exports to UK	£11,220,188	£12,060,249

COMMUNICATIONS
Although the country has 20km of coastline on the Adriatic Sea, there are no seaports. There are four river ports on the river Sava, which is navigable by shipping but its use is limited. The 25 airports and airfields include international airports at Sarajevo, Banja Luka, Mostar and Tuzla. There are 601km of railways and 22,926km of roads, 19,426km of which are paved. Reconstruction of the telephone network has resulted in a rapid growth in fixed lines, to 22 per 100 people, while mobile phone subscriptions increased to 70 per 100 people in 2009.

MEDIA
During the war most media outlets became, to various degrees, propagandists for particular factions or centres of power; efforts since 1995 to develop multi-ethnic outlets have had limited success. There is a national broadcaster, BHRT, which operates alongside two separate-entity broadcasters. The public radio and television stations of these two entities are the most influential broadcasters but are not wholly independent, being subject to both government and party political pressure. There are more than 200 commercial television and radio stations, but a weak advertising market has limited their development.

BOTSWANA

Republic of Botswana

Area – 581,730 sq. km
Capital – Gaborone; population, 195,894 (2009 est)
Major cities – Francistown, Molepolole, Selebi-Phikwe
Currency – Pula (P) of 100 thebe
Population – 2,029,307 rising at 1.84 per cent a year
   (2010 est); Tswana (79 per cent), Kalanga (11 per cent),
   Basarwa (3 per cent) (est)

Religion – Christian 70 per cent (predominantly Protestant) (est)

Language – English (official), Setswana, Kalanga, Sekgalagadi

Population density – 3 per sq. km (2009)

Urban population – 60 per cent (2008 est)

Median age (years) – 22 (2010 est)

National anthem – 'Fatshe Leno La Rona' ['Blessed Be This Noble Land']

National day – 30 September (Botswana Day)

Life expectancy (years) – 60.93 (2010 est)

Mortality rate – 9.02 (2010 est)

Birth rate – 22.54 (2010 est)

Infant mortality rate – 11.79 (2010 est)

HIV/AIDS adult prevalence – 24.8 per cent (2009)

Death penalty – Retained

CPI score – 5.8 (2010)

CLIMATE AND TERRAIN

A landlocked country in southern Africa, Botswana lies on an undulating plateau. The Kalahari desert covers about three-quarters of the country, in the south and west. To the east, streams run into the Marico, Notwani and Limpopo rivers. In the north lies a flat region comprising the Makgadikgadi salt pans and the swampland of the Okavango delta. Elevation extremes range from 1,489m (Tsodilo Hills) at the highest point to 513m (junction of the Limpopo and Shashe rivers) at the lowest. The climate is subtropical in the north, arid in the south and west, and more temperate in the east, which has regular rain. Average temperatures range from 14°C in July to 25°C in January.

HISTORY AND POLITICS

The Tswana people were predominant in the area from the 17th century. In 1885, at the request of indigenous chiefs fearing invasion by the Boers, Britain formally took control of Bechuanaland, and the northern part of the territory was declared the Bechuanaland Protectorate, while land to the south of the Molopo river became British Bechuanaland, which was later incorporated into the Cape Colony and eventually South Africa. In 1964, the Bechuanaland Protectorate became self-governing, and on 30 September 1966 it became an independent republic under the name Botswana. Since independence, Botswana has been stable and relatively prosperous owing to the diamond mining industry. There is a high level of HIV/AIDS among the population, and although an advanced treatment programme in place since 2001 is reducing the level of infection, the country faces serious demographic and social problems.

President Festus Mogae stood down in 2008, having completed two terms of office, and was succeeded by the vice-president, Lt.-Gen. Ian Khama, son of the country's first president. The 2009 legislative election was won by the Botswana Democratic Party (BDP), with 45 seats. President Khama, of the BDP, was elected president two days later.

POLITICAL SYSTEM

Under the 1966 constitution, the executive president is elected by the legislature for a five-year term, renewable only once. He appoints the vice-president and the cabinet. The unicameral National Assembly has 57 members directly elected for a five-year term, plus a variable number of members (currently four) nominated by the president and elected by the assembly. A 15-member House of Chiefs advises on tribal matters and constitutional changes.

HEAD OF STATE

President, Lt.-Gen. (retd) Ian Khama, *sworn in* 1 April 2008, *elected* 18 October 2009

Vice-President (acting), Ponatshego Kedikilwe

SELECTED GOVERNMENT MEMBERS *as at June 2011*

Finance and Development Planning, Kenneth Matambo

Foreign Affairs, Phandu Skelemani

Defence (acting), Edwin Batshu

BOTSWANA HIGH COMMISSION

6 Stratford Place, London W1C 1AY

T 020-7499 0031 E bohico@govbw.com

High Commissioner, HE Roy Blackbeard, *apptd* 1998

BRITISH HIGH COMMISSION

Private Bag 0023, Plot 1079-1084 Main Mall, off Queens Road, Gaborone

T (+267) 395 2841 W http://ukinbotswana.fco.gov.uk

High Commissioner, HE Jennifer Anderson, *apptd* 2010

BRITISH COUNCIL

PO Box 439, British High Commission Building, 1079–1084 Main Mall, Gaborone

T (+267) 395 3602 W www.britishcouncil.org/africa

Director, Nobantu Kalake

DEFENCE

The army has 55 light tanks and 156 armoured personnel carriers. The air wing has 31 combat capable aircraft.

Military budget – US$628m (2010)

Military personnel – 9,000: army 8,500, air force 500; paramilitary 1,500

ECONOMY AND TRADE

Botswana has been relatively prosperous since independence because of its mining industry, political stability and sound economic management. Despite this, about 30 per cent of the population lives below the poverty line. Longer-term problems are the impact of the high levels of HIV/AIDS among the workforce and the levelling off of diamond production, which usually accounts for 70 to 80 per cent of export earnings; diamond exports declined owing to the global downturn, causing the economy to contract sharply in 2009. The government has sought to reduce the economy's dependence on the diamond industry by diversifying; safari tourism and financial services in particular have grown in recent years, and the services sector now contributes 51.9 per cent of GDP. The industrial sector contributes 45.8 per cent of GDP, mainly from mining diamonds, copper, nickel, salt, soda ash, potash, coal, iron ore and silver. Agriculture is predominantly pastoral and accounts for 2.3 per cent of GDP. Cattle-rearing represents over 80 per cent of agricultural production.

The main trading partners are EU and southern African countries. Principal exports are diamonds, copper, nickel, soda ash, meat and textiles. The main imports are foodstuffs, machinery, electrical goods, transport equipment, textiles, fuel and petroleum products.

GNI – US$11,341m; US$6,260 per capita (2009)

Annual average growth of GDP – 3.1 per cent (2010 est)

Inflation rate – 7.1 per cent (2010 est)

Population below poverty line – 30.3 per cent (2003)

Unemployment – 7.5 per cent (2007)

Total external debt – US$2,222m (2010 est)
Imports – US$4,700m (2009)
Exports – US$3,600m (2009)

BALANCE OF PAYMENTS
Trade – US$990m deficit (2010)
Current Account – US$664m surplus (2008)

Trade with UK	2009	2010
Imports from UK	£11,574,345	£11,023,942
Exports to UK	£227,663,305	£561,035,901

COMMUNICATIONS
Because of its landlocked position, Botswana's trade is dependent on its international rail and road links. The only railway is the 888km line from Zimbabwe to South Africa, which passes through eastern Botswana. There are 25,798km of roads, of which 8,410km are paved. These include a highway connecting all the main towns and district capitals. The network links at the borders with the road networks of South Africa and Namibia. A major link is the 595km Trans-Kalahari Highway which connects Botswana with Namibia's capital (Windhoek) and its port at Walvis Bay. There are 78 airports and airfields, including the international airport at Gaborone. Telecommunications systems are being expanded, although fixed-line connections have declined in recent years. Mobile phone distribution is growing rapidly, with nearly 100 mobile phones per 100 people by 2009.

EDUCATION AND HEALTH
Botswana does not have a compulsory education policy. Many children receive ten years of education, though the government announced in 2004 that efforts would be made to increase this to 12 years (seven years of primary education, three years of junior secondary and two years of senior secondary). In 2006 fees were reintroduced for state secondary schools, which had been free of charge for over 20 years.
Literacy rate – 83.5 per cent (2008 est)
Gross enrolment ratio (percentage of relevant age group) –
   primary 109 per cent; secondary 82 per cent (2007 est)
Health expenditure (per capita) – US$612 (2009)
Hospital beds (per 1,000 people) – 1.8 (2004–9)

MEDIA
Botswana has a good record on press transparency and respect for freedom of expression. Newspaper circulation is almost entirely limited to urban areas, and there are two daily newspapers, one private and one government-owned. Radio is the most important news medium; there are state-run and private commercial radio stations, and programmes are broadcast in both English and Setswana. State-run television (Botswana Television) was established in 2000, and commercial and satellite services are also available.

BRAZIL

Republica Federativa do Brasil – Federative Republic of Brazil

Area – 8,514,877 sq. km
Capital – Brasilia; population, 3,788,820 (2009 est)
Major cities – Belo Horizonte, Fortaleza, Porto Alegre, Recife, Rio de Janeiro (the former capital), Salvador, Sao Paulo
Currency – Real of 100 centavos
Population – 201,103,330 rising at 1.17 per cent a year (2010 est)
Religion – Christian (Roman Catholic 74 per cent, Protestant 15 per cent) (est)
Language – Portuguese (official), Spanish, German, Italian, Japanese, English, Amerindian languages
Population density – 23 per sq. km (2009)
Urban population – 86 per cent (2008 est)
Median age (years) – 28.9 (2010 est)
National anthem – 'Hino Nacional Brasileiro' ['Brazilian National Anthem']
National day – 7 September (Independence Day)
Life expectancy (years) – 72.26 (2010 est)
Mortality rate – 6.35 (2010 est)
Birth rate – 18.11 (2010 est)
Infant mortality rate – 21.86 (2010 est)
Death penalty – Retained for certain crimes (last used 1855)
CPI score – 3.7 (2010)

CLIMATE AND TERRAIN
Brazil is South America's biggest country, taking up almost half of the continent. It has six distinct topographical areas: the Amazon basin (north and west of the country), the Parana-Paraguay river basin (south; the Parana drains the Pantanal, the world's largest freshwater wetland), the Guiana Highlands (north of the Amazon), the Mato Grosso plateau (centre), the Brazilian Highlands (south of the Amazon) and the coastal strip. Elevation extremes range from 2,994m (Pico da Neblina) at the highest point to 0m (Atlantic Ocean) at the lowest. Brazil has the world's largest rainforest, as well as large expanses of savannah *(cerrado)*. The climate is mostly tropical, with the equator passing through the north and the Tropic of Capricorn through the south-east. The Amazon basin sees annual rainfall of up to 2,000mm a year and there is no dry season (average temperature 30°C). The north-east is the driest area of the country and can experience long periods of drought (maximum average temperature 38°C). The southern states have a seasonal temperate climate (average temperatures between 17°C and 19°C).

HISTORY AND POLITICS

Brazil was claimed by the Portuguese navigator Pedro Cabral in 1500 and colonised by Portugal in the early 16th century, becoming a viceroyalty in 1572. During the Napoleonic Wars the Portuguese court took refuge in Brazil. In 1822 Pedro I, son of King Joao VI of Portugal, declared Brazil an independent monarchy. In 1889, Pedro II was overthrown in a coup, and a federal republic was proclaimed. Brazil was a dictatorship from 1930 to 1945 and under military rule from 1964 to 1985, when civilian rule was restored after several years of gradual democratisation. Governments since then have faced difficult economic conditions, and exploitation of the Amazon basin has attracted controversy because it threatens the environmentally important rainforest.

Dilma Rousseff of the Workers' Party (PT) was elected in 2010, becoming Brazil's first female president. In the 2010 legislative election, the PBSM alliance led by the PT and the Brazilian Democratic Movement Party (PMDB) won a majority in both houses of Congress. President Rousseff appointed a coalition government dominated by the PT and including the PMDB, five other parties and independents.

POLITICAL SYSTEM

Under the 1988 constitution (amended in 1997), the executive president is directly elected for a four-year term, which is renewable once. The National Congress consists of an 81-member federal senate (three senators per state, directly elected for an eight-year term) and a 513-member Chamber of Deputies which is directly elected every four years; the number of deputies per state depends upon the state's population.

The Federative Republic of Brazil is composed of the Federal District of Brasilia in which the capital lies, and 26 states: Acre, Alagoas, Amapa, Amazonas, Bahia, Ceara, Espirito Santo, Goias, Maranhao, Mato Grosso, Mato Grosso do Sul, Minas Gerais, Para, Paraiba, Parana, Pernambuco, Piaui, Rio de Janeiro, Rio Grande do Norte, Rio Grande do Sul, Rondonia, Roraima, Santa Catarina, Sao Paulo, Sergipe and Tocantins. Each state has its own governor and legislative assembly.

HEAD OF STATE
President, Dilma Rousseff, *sworn in* 1 January 2011
Vice-President, Michel Temer

SELECTED GOVERNMENT MEMBERS *as at July 2011*
Defence, Celso Amorim
Foreign Affairs, Antonio Patriota
Finance, Guido Mantega
Attorney-General, Luis Inacio Lucena Adams

EMBASSY OF BRAZIL
32 Green Street, London W1K 7AT
T 020-7399 9000 E info@brazil.org.uk W www.brazil.org.uk
Ambassador Extraordinary and Plenipotentiary, HE Roberto Jaguaribe, *apptd* 2010

BRITISH EMBASSY
Setor de Embaixadas Sul, Quadra 801, Lote 8, CEP 70408-900, Brasilia DF
T (+55) (61) 3329 2300 W http://ukinbrazil.fco.gov.uk
Ambassador Extraordinary and Plenipotentiary, HE Alan Charlton, CMG, *apptd* 2008

BRITISH COUNCIL
Edificio Centro Empresarial Varig, SCN Quadra 04, Bloco B, Torre Oeste Conjunto 202, 70714-900 Brasilia DF
T (+55) (61) 2106 7500 W www.britishcouncil.org/brazil
Director, Jim Scarth

DEFENCE

The army has 267 main battle tanks, 807 armoured personnel carriers and 51 multi-role helicopters. The navy is equipped with 5 submarines, 1 aircraft carrier, 3 destroyers, 11 frigates and 42 patrol and coastal vessels. Naval aviation consists of 12 combat aircraft and 16 armed helicopters; the Marines have 18 light tanks and 42 armoured personnel carriers. The air force has 256 combat aircraft.

Military expenditure – US$34,700m (2010)
Military personnel – 318,480: army 190,000, navy 59,000, air force 69,480; paramilitary 395,000
Conscription duration – 12 months (can be extended to 18)

ECONOMY AND TRADE

Historically subject to boom and bust cycles, the economy was stabilised by reforms in the 1990s. Tight fiscal management, IMF programmes, a growth in output and an expanding export base have produced steady growth since 2003, although poverty is still widespread. Brazil's economy, based on well-developed agriculture, mining, manufacturing and service sectors, is now the tenth largest in the world, giving the country growing global influence. Although the economy contracted in the global downturn, it weathered the crisis better than many other countries and is recovering quickly.

The country is rich in mineral deposits, including iron ore (haematite), bauxite, gold, manganese, nickel, platinum and uranium. It produces oil, gas and hydroelectricity, and is close to self-sufficiency in oil. Brazil is the world's largest producer of coffee; the other main agricultural products are soya beans, wheat, rice, maize, sugar cane, cocoa, citrus fruit and beef. The expansion of agriculture and forestry threaten the rainforest, although recent governments' attempts to prevent further depredations by loggers and farmers have slowed the rate of deforestation considerably. Tourism is a growing industry. In 2010, services generated 67.5 per cent of GDP, industry 26.4 per cent and agriculture 6.1 per cent.

Brazil's main trading partners are the USA, China, Argentina and Germany. Principal exports are transport equipment, iron ore, soya beans, footwear, coffee and vehicles. The main imports are machinery, electrical and transport equipment, chemical products, oil, vehicle parts and electronics.

GNI – US$1,562,412m; US$8,070 per capita (2009)
Annual average growth of GDP – 7.5 per cent (2010)
Inflation rate – 4.9 per cent (2010 est)
Population below poverty line – 26 per cent (2008)
Unemployment – 7 per cent (2010 est)
Total external debt – US$310,800m (2010)
Imports – US$133,600m (2009)
Exports – US$153,000m (2009)

BALANCE OF PAYMENTS
Trade – US$20,299m surplus (2010)
Current Account – US$24,344m deficit (2009)

Trade with UK	2009	2010
Imports from UK	£1,727,355,122	£2,128,960,731
Exports to UK	£3,028,158,395	£3,694,788,983

COMMUNICATIONS

The 1,751,868km road network and 28,538km rail network are concentrated in the more densely populated south and east of the country. The railways are used primarily for transporting minerals to the ports; most passenger and freight traffic is on the roads. The Trans-Amazonian Highway connects the Amazon region with the rest of the country, although it is mostly unpaved and often becomes impassable in the rainy season. In remote regions, transport is primarily by air or water, utilising the 50,000km of navigable waterways, although a severe drought in 2010 left water levels so low that ferries and other craft were unable to operate. There are 4,072 airports and airfields; international flights operate to the major cities. Rio de Janeiro and Santos are the two leading seaports but there are also another 14 fully equipped ports. Piracy and armed robbery against ships in territorial and offshore waters is a growing problem. The fixed-line telephone system is extensive. Mobile phone distribution has grown rapidly, reaching a density of 90 per 100 people by 2009. There were 75.9 million internet users in 2009.

EDUCATION AND HEALTH

The education system includes both public and private institutions. Public education is free at all levels, and is compulsory between the ages of seven and 14.

Literacy rate – 90.0 per cent (2008 est)

Gross enrolment ratio (percentage of relevant age group) – primary 120 per cent; secondary 90 per cent; tertiary 38 per cent (2009 est)

Health expenditure (per capita) – US$734 (2009)

Hospital beds (per 1,000 people) – 2.4 (2004–9)

MEDIA AND CULTURE

Brazil has South America's biggest media industry, with Brazilian-made soap operas, game shows and dramas exported all over the world. There are thousands of radio stations and hundreds of television channels. Domestic conglomerates, most notably Globo, dominate the market and run television and radio networks, newspapers and subscription television stations. The constitution guarantees a free press and media debate is vigorous.

The country is a melting pot of races, cultures, religious traditions, music and dance (the samba, bossa nova and lambada are world-famous). Luis de Camoes (1525–80) is widely regarded as Brazil's national poet, while Paulo Coelho (*b.* 1947) is its most commercially successful author. The film industry is thriving, with two directors, Walter Salles *(The Motorcycle Diaries)* and Fernando Meirelles *(City of God)*, achieving international recognition in recent years.

Football is central to contemporary culture and Brazil has won a record five World Cups as well as producing some of the world's most gifted players, including Pele (*b.* 1940) and Ronaldo (*b.* 1976).

BRUNEI

Negara Brunei Darussalam – Brunei Darussalam

Area – 5,765 sq. km

Capital – Bandar Seri Begawan; population, 22,228 (2009 est)

Major towns – Kuala Belait, Seria, Tutong

Currency – Brunei dollar (B$) of 100 sen (fully interchangeable with Singapore currency)

Population – 395,027 rising at 1.73 per cent a year (2010 est); Malay (66.3 per cent), Chinese (11.2 per cent) (2004 est)

Religion – Muslim 82 per cent (predominantly Shafi'i, a school of Sunni Islam), Buddhist 7 per cent, Christian 3 per cent (est); Islam is the state religion

Language – Malay (official), English, Chinese

Population density – 76 per sq. km (2009)

Urban population – 75 per cent (2008 est)

Median age (years) – 28.1 (2010 est)

National anthem – 'Allah Peliharakan Sultan' ['God Bless the Sultan']

National day – 23 February (date of independence from British protection, 1984)

Life expectancy (years) – 75.96 (2010 est)

Mortality rate – 3.32 (2010 est)

Birth rate – 18 (2010 est)

Infant mortality rate – 11.87 (2010 est)

Death penalty – Retained (no known use since 1992)

CPI score – 5.5 (2010)

CLIMATE AND TERRAIN

The country lies on the north-west coast of the island of Borneo. It is surrounded and divided in two by the Malaysian state of Sarawak. The terrain is around 70 per cent rainforest (although current estimates vary), with extensive mangrove swamps along the coastal plain. There are mountains on the border with Sarawak. Elevation extremes range from 1,850m (Bukit Pagon) at the highest point to 0m (South China Sea) at the lowest. The climate is tropical, with high humidity, an annual average daily temperature of 27°C and about 2,722mm of rain per year.

HISTORY AND POLITICS

Formerly a powerful Muslim sultanate that controlled Borneo and parts of the Philippines, Brunei was reduced to its present size by the mid-19th century and came under British protection in 1889. It chose to remain a British dependency in 1963 rather than joining the Federation of Malaysia. Internally self-governing from 1959, Brunei gained full independence on 1 January 1984.

In 1962 the legislative election was annulled after it was won by a party that sought to remove the sultan;

a state of emergency was declared and the sultan has ruled by decree ever since. A ministerial system of government was introduced in 1984. Some political liberalisation and modernisation has taken place since 2004, when the legislature was reconvened after 20 years.

POLITICAL SYSTEM

Parts of the 1959 constitution have been suspended since the state of emergency began in 1962. Supreme executive authority is vested in the sultan, a hereditary monarch who presides over and is advised by a privy council, a religious council and the council of cabinet ministers. The legislative council was reconvened in 2004 with 21 members appointed by the sultan; it has passed constitutional amendments to increase its size to 45 members, 15 of whom will be directly elected. No date has been set for an election.

HEAD OF STATE

HM The Sultan of Brunei, Prime Minister, Defence, Finance, HM Hassanal Bolkiah, GCB, *acceded 5 October* 1967, *crowned* 1 August 1968

HM Crown Prince, Senior Minister in the Prime Minister's Office, Prince Al-Muhtadee Billah

SELECTED GOVERNMENT MEMBERS *as at May 2011*
Foreign Affairs, Prince Mohamed Bolkiah
Home Affairs, Pehin Dato Ustaz Badaruddin bin Pengarah Othman

BRUNEI DARUSSALAM HIGH COMMISSION
19–20 Belgrave Square, London SW1X 8PG
T 020-7581 0521 E info@bdhcl.co.uk
High Commissioner, HE Mohd Aziyan Del Abdullah, *apptd* 2010

BRITISH HIGH COMMISSION
2.01, 2nd Floor, Block D, Kompleks Yayasan Sultan Haji Hassanal Bolkiah, Bandar Seri Begawan, BS 8711
T (+673) (2) 222 231 E brithc@brunet.bn
W http://ukinbrunei.fco.gov.uk
High Commissioner, Robert Fenn, *apptd* 2009

DEFENCE

The army has 20 light tanks and 45 armoured personnel carriers. The navy has 12 patrol and coastal vessels. The air force has 5 support helicopters. There are 550 UK troops currently stationed in Brunei.
Military budget – US$372m (2010)
Military personnel – 7,000: army 4,900, navy 1,000, air force 1,100; paramilitary 2,250

ECONOMY AND TRADE

The economy is based on the production of oil and natural gas and the income from overseas investments. Royalties and taxes from these operations form the bulk of government revenue and have enabled the construction of free health, education and welfare services. However, oil and gas reserves are declining and Brunei is now trying to diversify its economy, developing financial services and tourism.

Agriculture accounts for 0.7 per cent of GDP, industry 74.1 per cent and services 25.3 per cent. The main trading partners are Japan, Singapore, Indonesia, Malaysia and South Korea. Principal exports are crude oil, natural gas and clothing. The main imports are machinery and transport equipment, manufactured goods, food (over 80 per cent of domestic requirements is imported) and chemicals.

GNI – US$10,287m; US$26,930 per capita (2007)
Annual average growth of GDP – 1 per cent (2010 est)
Inflation rate – 2.7 per cent (2008)
Unemployment – 3.7 per cent (2008)

BALANCE OF PAYMENTS
Trade – US$5,601m surplus (2010)
Current Account – US$8,346m surplus (2008)

Trade with UK	2009	2010
Imports from UK	£61,023,110	£151,419,603
Exports to UK	£22,819,339	£14,151,157

COMMUNICATIONS

There are ports at Kuala Belait, Muara and Tanjong Salirong, and terminals at Lumut and Seria. Seria is the location of one of Brunei's two airports, the other being the international airport at Bandar Seri Begawan. The 209km of internal waterways are navigable only by shallow craft. There is a road network of 2,971km, most of which is paved, but no railway. The telephone system is extensive and modern. Mobile phone distribution is very high, at 425,000 in 2009.

EDUCATION

All levels of education are free. Children undertake six years of primary education, three of lower secondary and two to three years of upper secondary, which can be in a secondary school, vocational school or technical college.
Literacy rate – 95.1 per cent (2008 est)
Gross enrolment ratio (percentage of relevant age group) – primary 107 per cent; secondary 98 per cent; tertiary 17 per cent (2009 est)

MEDIA

The media is mostly privately owned, but tightly controlled; laws against reporting 'false news' carry heavy punishments, therefore criticism of the government is rare. The only broadcast media organisation, Radio Television Brunei (RTB), is state-owned. It broadcasts television in Malay and English and radio in Malay, English, Mandarin Chinese and Gurkhali. Foreign television channels are available via cable. Internet access is unrestricted, and there were nearly 319,000 users in 2010.

BULGARIA

Republika Balgariya – Republic of Bulgaria

Area – 110,879 sq. km
Capital – Sofia; population, 1,191,890 (2009 est)
Major cities – Burgas, Plovdiv, Varna
Currency – Lev of 100 stotinki

Population – 7,148,785 falling at 0.77 per cent a year
(2010 est); Bulgarian (83.9 per cent), Turkish
(9.4 per cent), Roma (4.7 per cent) (2001)
Religion – Christian 85 per cent (Bulgarian Orthodox
84 per cent), Muslim 13 per cent (predominantly
Sunni) (est)
Language – Bulgarian (official), Turkish, Romani
Population density – 70 per sq. km (2009)
Urban population – 71 per cent (2008 est)
Median age (years) – 41.6 (2010 est)
National anthem – 'Mila Rodino' ['Dear Motherland']
National day – 3 March (Liberation Day)
Life expectancy (years) – 73.35 (2010 est)
Mortality rate – 14.31 (2010 est)
Birth rate – 9.43 (2010 est)
Infant mortality rate – 17.26 (2010 est)
Death penalty – Abolished for all crimes (since 1998)
CPI score – 3.6 (2010)

CLIMATE AND TERRAIN

The country is dominated by mountains: the Balkan
Mountains cross the country from west to east, averaging
2,000m in height; and the Rhodope Mountains in the
south-west climb to almost 3,000m. Elevation extremes
range from 2,925m (Musala) at the highest point to 0m
(Black Sea) at the lowest. The lowland plains of the north
and south-east are in the basins of the main rivers: the
Danube in the north, which forms much of the border
with Romania, and the Maritsa, which divides the Balkan
and Rhodope ranges. The climate is temperate, with cold,
damp winters and hot, dry summers. Average temperatures
in Sofia range from −2°C in January to 21°C in July.

HISTORY AND POLITICS

Bulgarians are descended from Slavs and Bulgars, who
migrated into the Balkans in the fifth century and the
seventh century AD respectively. The first Bulgarian
kingdom was founded in 681 but fell to the Ottoman
Empire in the 1390s. The treaty of San Stefano, which
concluded the Russo-Turkish war of 1877–8, envisaged
Bulgaria as an independent principality; however, this
agreement was revised by the treaty of Berlin in 1878,
under which Bulgaria's territory was substantially reduced
and part remained subject to Ottoman suzerainty. In 1908
the country regained its lost territory and was declared a
kingdom.

Bulgaria was allied with Germany in both world wars
but switched sides in September 1944 after a coup
brought to power the Fatherland Front, a left-wing
coalition that came to be dominated by the communists.
A referendum in 1946 led to the abolition of the monarchy
and the establishment of a republic. The Communist Party
(BCP), which had won the 1946 election, in 1947
established a one-party state and a centralised economy.

From the mid-1980s cautious reforms were introduced
in line with the Soviet policies of *perestroika* and *glasnost*,
and Bulgaria became a multiparty democracy in 1990.
Political and economic liberalisation progressed slowly in
the early 1990s, causing economic difficulties and
political unrest. This volatility had calmed by the late
1990s, when more radical economic reforms were
introduced. Bulgaria joined NATO in 2006 and the EU in
2007.

Georgi Parvanov, president since 2002, was re-elected
in 2006. In the 2009 legislative election, the new
centre-right party Citizens for European Development of
Bulgaria (GERB) won the most seats, but without an
overall majority, and formed a minority government with
support from small right-wing parties. A presidential
election is due in November 2011.

POLITICAL SYSTEM

Under the 1991 constitution, the president is directly
elected for a five-year term, renewable once. The head of
government is the prime minister, who is appointed by the
president, and is usually the leader of the largest party in
the legislature. There is a unicameral National Assembly
of 240 members who are directly elected for a four-year
term.

HEAD OF STATE

President, Georgi Parvanov, *elected* 18 November 2001,
re-elected 2006
Vice-President, Angel Marin

SELECTED GOVERNMENT MEMBERS *as at May 2011*

Prime Minister, Boiko Borisov
Deputy Prime Ministers, Simeon Djankov *(Finance)*,
Tsvetan Tsvetanov *(Interior)*
Defence, Anyu Angelov
Foreign Affairs, Nikolay Mladenov

EMBASSY OF THE REPUBLIC OF BULGARIA

186–188 Queen's Gate, London SW7 5HL
T 020-7584 9400 E info@bulgarianembassy.org.uk
W www.bulgarianembassy-london.org
Ambassador Extraordinary and Plenipotentiary, HE
Lyubomir Kyuchukov, *apptd* 2009

BRITISH EMBASSY

9 Moskovska Street, Sofia 1000
T (+359) (2) 933 9222 E britembsof@mbox.cit.bg
W http://ukinbulgaria.fco.gov.uk
Ambassador Extraordinary and Plenipotentiary, HE
Jonathan Allen, *apptd* 2011

BRITISH COUNCIL

7 Krakra Street, 1504 Sofia
T (+359) 2942 4344 E bc.sofia@britishcouncil.bg
W www.britishcouncil.org/bulgaria
Director, Tony Buckby

DEFENCE

The army has 301 main battle tanks, 160 armoured
infantry fighting vehicles and 1,084 armoured personnel
carriers. The navy has 1 submarine, 4 frigates, 6 patrol and
coastal vessels, and 6 armed helicopters. There are bases at
Burgas and Varna. The air force has 62 combat aircraft
and 18 armed helicopters.

Military budget – US$609m (2010)
Military personnel – 31,315: army 16,304, navy 3,471,
air force 6,706, central staff 4,834; paramilitary
34,000

ECONOMY AND TRADE

The government adopted radical economic reforms in
1996 and the economy achieved stability and attracted
significant foreign investment, although administrative
corruption and organised crime remain potential
deterrents. Despite steady economic growth in 2004–8
and responsible fiscal management, the economy
contracted in the global economic downturn as industrial
production and exports declined. Recovery has been slow.

Natural resources include copper, lead, zinc, other
minerals, coal and timber. Fertile arable land produces
vegetables, fruit, tobacco, wine, wheat, barley, sunflowers

and livestock. Agriculture employs 7.1 per cent of the workforce and accounts for 6 per cent of GDP. Industries include energy generation, food processing, beverages, tobacco, machinery and equipment, base metals, chemicals, mining and oil refining. Tourism is growing. One of the main exports is electricity generated at the controversial Kozloduy nuclear power plant. Bulgaria has decommissioned two reactors in response to EU concerns about safety.

The main trading partners are EU countries, Russia and Turkey. Principal exports are clothing and footwear, iron and steel, machinery and equipment, and fuels. The main imports are predominantly machinery and raw materials for the industrial sector.

GNI – US$46,591m; US$6,060 per capita (2009)
Annual average growth of GDP – 0 per cent (2010 est)
Inflation rate – 2.1 per cent (2010 est)
Population below poverty line – 14 per cent (2008 est)
Unemployment – 9.5 per cent (2010 est)
Total external debt – US$36,150m (2010)
Imports – US$23,300m (2009)
Exports – US$16,500m (2009)

BALANCE OF PAYMENTS
Trade – US$4,753m deficit (2010)
Current Account – US$4,458m deficit (2009)

Trade with UK	2009	2010
Imports from UK	£194,015,598	£238,895,611
Exports to UK	£177,906,639	£227,822,635

COMMUNICATIONS
The main ports are Burgas and Varna on the Black Sea. There are 470km of waterways, and inland ports include Vidin, Lom and Ruse on the river Danube. The main airports are at Sofia, Plovdiv, Burgas and Varna. There are 4,151km of railways and 40,231km of roads, including 418km of motorways. The telephone system is extensive and quality has improved since services were privatised in 2005. Mobile phone distribution is high, at 10.6 million in 2009. There were 2.2 million fixed lines in use in 2009, and 3.4 million internet users.

EDUCATION AND HEALTH
Education is free and compulsory from seven to 14 years.
Literacy rate – 98.3 per cent (2008 est)
Gross enrolment ratio (percentage of relevant age group) – primary 101 per cent; secondary 89 per cent; tertiary 51 per cent (2008 est)
Health expenditure (per capita) – US$475 (2009)
Hospital beds (per 1,000 people) – 6.5 (2004–9)

MEDIA AND CULTURE
Public service broadcasters Bulgarian National Radio and Bulgarian National Television share the market with a vigorous commercial sector that provides national and regional broadcasting. However, pressure from organised crime and political and business interests causes many journalists to self-censor; those who do not often risk harassment or even violence. Some media outlets are also known to accept money in return for favourable coverage, or the suppression of negative stories.

Bulgaria's Roman and Byzantine ruins are culturally significant, as are its churches and monasteries. Notable Bulgarian writers include Iordan Iovkov (1884–1938) and the Nobel laureate Elias Canetti (1905–1994).

BURKINA FASO

Area – 274,200 sq. km
Capital – Ouagadougou; population, 1,776,910 (2009 est)
Major city – Bobo-Dioulasso
Currency – Franc CFA of 100 centimes
Population – 16,241,811 rising at 3.1 per cent a year (2010 est); 63 ethnic groups, of which Mossi (40 per cent) (est) is the largest
Religion – Muslim 61 per cent (predominantly Sunni), Christian (Roman Catholic 19 per cent, Protestant denominations 4 per cent), traditional indigenous religions 15 per cent (est); many Christians and Muslims also practise indigenous religious beliefs
Language – French (official), various African languages (spoken by 90 per cent of the population)
Population density – 58 per sq. km (2009)
Urban population – 20 per cent (2008 est)
Median age (years) – 16.8 (2010 est)
National anthem – 'Une Seule Nuit' ['One Single Night']
National day – 11 December (Republic Day)
Life expectancy – 53.32 (2010 est)
Mortality rate – 13.02 (2010 est)
Birth rate – 43.98 (2010 est)
Infant mortality rate – 82.98 (2010 est)
HIV/AIDS adult prevalence – 1.2 per cent (2009 est)
Death penalty – Retained (not used since 1988)
CPI score – 3.1 (2010)

CLIMATE AND TERRAIN
The landlocked state occupies a plateau dissected by the White, Black and Red Volta rivers. There are tropical savannahs in the south and the north is semi-desert. Elevation extremes range from 749m (Tena Kourou) at the highest point to 200m (Mouhoun, or Black Volta, river) at the lowest. The climate is tropical, with a wet season from May to September; there are recurring droughts. Average temperatures in Ouagadougou range from 24°C to 33°C.

HISTORY AND POLITICS
Burkina Faso (Upper Volta until 1983) was part of the Mossi Empire in the 18th and 19th centuries. It was annexed by France in 1896 and between 1932 and 1947 was administered as part of other French colonies. In 1947 its original borders were reconstituted, and in 1958 it became autonomous within the French Community; independence was achieved on 5 August 1960.

In the three decades after independence there was a succession of military regimes; the last military coup, in 1987, brought to power Capt. Blaise Compaoré. Military rule ended in 1991 when a new constitution was adopted and multiparty elections were held in 1992. Despite the constitutional restriction on the number of terms that a president may serve, President Compaoré was re-elected for a fourth term in 2010. The 2007 legislative election was won by the governing Congress for Democracy and Progress (CDP) with a large overall majority. The government was dissolved in April 2011 following protests over food prices and an army mutiny, and a new government was appointed.

POLITICAL SYSTEM
The 1991 constitution was amended in 2000 to reduce the presidential term from seven years. The president is directly elected for a five-year term, renewable once, although this limit has been ignored by President Compaoré. The unicameral National Assembly has 111 deputies, who are directly elected for a five-year term. Executive power is vested jointly in the president and the council of ministers, both responsible to the legislature.

HEAD OF STATE
President, Minister for Defence, Capt. Blaise Compaoré, *assumed office* 1987, *elected* 1991, *re-elected* 1998, 2005, 2010

SELECTED GOVERNMENT MEMBERS *as at May 2011*
Prime Minister, Luc Adolphe Tiao
Economy and Finance, Lucien Marie Noël Bembamba
Foreign Affairs, Yipènè Djibril Bassolet

EMBASSY OF THE REPUBLIC OF BURKINA FASO
16 Place Guy d'Arezzo, 1180 Brussels, Belgium
T (+32) (2) 345 9912 E ambassade.burkina@skynet.be
W www.ambassadeduburkina.be
Ambassador Extraordinary and Plenipotentiary, HE Kadré Désiré Ouedraogo, *apptd* 2001

BRITISH AMBASSADOR
HE Peter Jones, *apptd* 2011, resident at Accra, Ghana

DEFENCE
The army has 13 armoured personnel carriers. The air force has 2 armed helicopters.
Military budget – US$97m (2010)
Military personnel – 11,200: army 6,400, air force 600, gendarmerie 4,200; paramilitary 250

ECONOMY AND TRADE
The country is one of the poorest in the world, with around 90 per cent of the population engaged in subsistence agriculture and animal husbandry, which are vulnerable to periodic droughts. The economy is heavily dependent on cotton and gold exports and therefore exposed also to the vagaries of global price fluctuations. The civil war in neighbouring Côte d'Ivoire harmed trade by cutting off transport routes, and caused many expatriate Burkinabes to return home, adding to the unemployment problem and depriving the economy of their remittances.

Agriculture contributes 30.1 per cent of GDP; the main product apart from cotton is livestock. Although there are few natural resources, a growing quantity of gold is mined and exploration for other minerals has begun. The processing of cotton and other agricultural products, gold mining and the manufacturing of beverages, soap, cigarettes and textiles are the main industries, contributing 20.7 per cent to GDP. Services account for 49.2 per cent of GDP.

The main export markets are Singapore, Belgium, China and Ghana. Principal exports are cotton, livestock

and gold. The chief import providers are Côte d'Ivoire and France, supplying capital goods, foodstuffs and fuel.

GNI – US$8,019m; US$510 per capita (2009)
Annual average growth of GDP – 5.2 per cent (2010 est)
Inflation rate – 1.4 per cent (2010 est)
Population below poverty line – 46.4 per cent (2004)
Unemployment – 77 per cent (2004)
Total external debt – US$2,002m (2010)
Imports – US$1,900m (2009)
Exports – US$800m (2009)

BALANCE OF PAYMENTS
Trade – US$997m deficit (2010)
Current Account – US$972m deficit (2008)

Trade with UK	2009	2010
Imports from UK	£6,395,809	£15,266,043
Exports to UK	£46,875	£211,667

COMMUNICATIONS
There are over 20 airports and airfields; the two main airports are at Ouagadougou, which receives international flights, and Bobo-Dioulasso. There are 92,495km of roads, of which 3,857km are surfaced; unpaved roads are often impassable during the wet season. There is 622km of railway track in operation. Fixed-line telephone connections are fewer than one per 100 people; mobile phone distribution is growing rapidly, with 3.2 million subscribers in 2009.

EDUCATION AND HEALTH
Literacy rate – 28.7 per cent (2008 est)
Gross enrolment ratio (percentage of relevant age group) –
  primary 78 per cent; secondary 20 per cent; tertiary
  3 per cent (2009 est)
Health expenditure (per capita) – US$38 (2009)
Hospital beds (per 1,000 people) – 0.9 (2004–9)

MEDIA
Radio is the country's most popular medium, with dozens of private and community radio stations and several private television channels operating alongside state-run broadcasters. State regulation of the media has created a culture of self-censorship, although private outlets are often critical of the government despite a risk of threats or arrest.

BURUNDI

Republika y'u Burundi/République du Burundi – Republic of Burundi

TANZANIA

Area – 27,830 sq. km

Capital – Bujumbura; population, 454,866 (2009 est)

Major towns – Muyinga, Ruyigi

Currency – Burundi franc of 100 centimes

Population – 9,863,117 rising at 3.56 per cent a year (2010 est); Hutu (85 per cent), Tutsi (14 per cent), Twa (1 per cent) (est)

Religion – Christian (Roman Catholic 60 per cent, Protestant denominations 15 per cent), traditional indigenous beliefs 20 per cent, Muslim 5 per cent (predominantly Sunni) (est)

Language – Kirundi, French (both official), Swahili

Population density – 323 per sq. km (2009)

Urban population – 10 per cent (2008 est)

Median age (years) – 16.8 (2010 est)

National anthem – 'Burundi Bwacu' ['Our Burundi']

National day – 1 July (Independence Day)

Life expectancy – 58.29 (2010 est)

Mortality rate – 9.87 (2010 est)

Birth rate – 41.43 (2010 est)

Infant mortality rate – 63.38 (2010 est)

HIV/AIDS adult prevalence – 3.3 per cent (2009 est)

Death penalty – Abolished for all crimes (since 2009)

CPI score – 1.8 (2010)

Literacy rate – 59.3 per cent (2008 est)

Gross enrolment ratio (percentage of relevant age group) – primary 147 per cent; secondary 21 per cent; tertiary 3 per cent (2009 est)

Health expenditure (per capita) – US$20 (2009)

Hospital beds (per 1,000 people) – 0.7 (2004–9)

CLIMATE AND TERRAIN

The landlocked country lies across the Nile–Congo watershed in central Africa. A hilly interior rises from an average altitude of 1,700m to the country's highest point at 2,670m (Heha) and falls to a plateau in the east. The river Ruzizi forms part of the north-western border with the Democratic Republic of the Congo, along with Lake Tanganyika (the lowest elevation in the country at 772m) in the south-west. The climate is equatorial, moderated by altitude; the average temperature in the lower regions is 29°C, and in the higher regions is 20°C. There are two rainy seasons: February to April and October to December.

HISTORY AND POLITICS

From the 16th century the area was ruled by Tutsi kings who dominated a majority Hutu population. Germany annexed the area in 1890 and included it in German East Africa. After the First World War it was part of the League of Nations-mandated territory (later UN trusteeship) of Ruanda-Urundi, administered by Belgium. Burundi broke the union with Rwanda in 1962, and became independent as a constitutional monarchy on 1 July 1962. The monarchy was overthrown in 1966, when the country became a republic and a one-party state under a series of brutal regimes dominated by the Tutsi minority. This led to intercommunal tensions that often resulted in ethnic conflict.

The first multiparty elections in 1993 ended Tutsi political dominance with the election of a Hutu president, Melchior Ndadaye, and a Hutu majority in the legislature. The assassination of President Ndadaye in October 1993 and of his successor, Cyprien Ntaryamira, in April 1994 sparked successive waves of ethnic conflict that degenerated into civil war. Most of the belligerents signed a peace accord at Arusha (Tanzania) in 2000, and the remaining rebel groups signed ceasefire agreements with

the government in 2003, 2006 and 2008. After a period of transitional government, legislative elections took place in 2005.

Pierre Nkurunziza of the National Council for the Defence of Democracy–Forces for the Defence of Democracy (CNDD-FDD), a Hutu party, was elected president by the newly elected legislature in 2005. He was re-elected unopposed in the country's first direct presidential election in June 2010, after opposition candidates boycotted the poll in protest at the alleged rigging of local elections held the previous month. Most opposition parties also boycotted the legislative elections in July 2010, in which the CNDD-FDD retained large majorities in both chambers.

POLITICAL SYSTEM

Under the 2005 constitution, the executive president is directly elected for a five-year term, renewable only once. The bicameral *Parlement* comprises the National Assembly and the senate; members of both serve a five-year term. The National Assembly has 100 directly elected members, three co-opted members from the Twa ethnic group, and up to 21 members (currently 15) co-opted to ensure a 60 per cent Hutu and 40 per cent Tutsi split and that 30 per cent of the total are women. The senate has 49 members: 34 directly elected members (one Hutu and one Tutsi from each province); three co-opted Twa members; all former presidents (currently four); and enough women (currently eight) to make the number of women senators up to 30 per cent of the total. The constitution also specifies the proportion of Hutu, Tutsi and female members of the council of ministers.

HEAD OF STATE

President, Pierre Nkurunziza, *sworn in* 26 August 2005, *re-elected* 2010

First Vice-President, Therence Sinunguruza

Second Vice-President, Gervais Rufyikiri

SELECTED GOVERNMENT MEMBERS *as at June 2011*

Defence, Maj.-Gen. Pontien Gaciyubwenge

Finance, Clotilde Nizigama

Interior, Edouard Nduwimana

EMBASSY OF THE REPUBLIC OF BURUNDI

46 Sq. Marie Louise, 1000 Brussels, Belgium

T (+32) (2) 230 4535 E ambassade.burundi@skynet.be

W www.ambassade-burundi.be

Ambassador Extraordinary and Plenipotentiary, HE Laurent Kavakure, *apptd* 2006

BRITISH AMBASSADOR

HE Benedict Llewellyn-Jones, OBE, *apptd* 2011, resident at Kigali, Rwanda

DEFENCE

The army has 57 armoured personnel carriers. The (reserve) air wing has 2 combat capable aircraft and 2 armed helicopters.

Military budget – US$57m (2010)

Military personnel – army 20,000; paramilitary 31,050

ECONOMY AND TRADE

Economic activity has increased since the civil war ended, but reform and reconstruction are hampered by a lack of administrative capacity, a poorly educated workforce, corruption and poor law enforcement. Agriculture is the mainstay of the economy, contributing 31.6 per cent of GDP. Subsistence agriculture has contracted recently owing to continued insecurity, population growth and soil erosion. Exports of coffee and tea account for over 90 per cent of foreign exchange earnings, leaving the economy vulnerable to the effects of global price fluctuations and weather conditions. Industry is relatively small-scale and employs around 2 per cent of the workforce but contributes 21.4 per cent of GDP. The main activities are light manufacturing, food processing, the assembly of imported components and public sector construction.

Most trade is with Germany, Belgium, Saudi Arabia and Switzerland, but it is constrained by the poor transport infrastructure and landlocked location. The main exports are coffee, tea, sugar, cotton and hides. The principal imports are capital goods, petroleum products and food.

GNI – US$1,331m; US$150 per capita (2009)
Annual average growth of GDP – 3.9 per cent (2010 est)
Inflation rate – 7.2 per cent (2010 est)
Total external debt – US$1,200m (2003)
Imports – US$400m (2009)
Exports – US$100m (2009)

BALANCE OF PAYMENTS
Trade – US$419m deficit (2010)
Current Account – US$153m deficit (2007)

Trade with UK	2009	2010
Imports from UK	£2,213,264	£3,371,402
Exports to UK	£191,502	£48,863

COMMUNICATIONS
There are no railways at present but the East African railways master plan, a project designed to expand the rail network in this region of Africa, is in its planning stage. Movement is currently either by water, on Lake Tanganyika, by road or by air. Bujumbura is the only port, the location of the only airport with a surfaced runway, and the main focus of the limited road network of 12,322km, only 1,286km of which is paved. The telephone system is rudimentary and limited. Mobile phone distribution is growing but was still only 10 per 100 people in 2009.

MEDIA
Low literacy levels mean that radio is the dominant news medium. The government-controlled *Radiodiffusion et Television Nationale de Burundi* (RTNB) runs the only television station and the only radio station with national coverage; the only newspaper to publish regularly is also government owned. Several radio stations are funded by international agencies or civil groups. Self-censorship is common because of the political climate, and occasional official censorship means that publication of opposition newspapers can be sporadic.

CAMBODIA

Preahreacheanachakr Kampuchea – Kingdom of Cambodia

Area – 181,035 sq. km
Capital – Phnom Penh; population, 1,519,330 (2009 est)
Major towns – Battambang, Siem Reap, Sihanoukville (Kompong Saom)
Currency – Riel of 100 sen; the US dollar is widely used
Population – 14,453,680 rising at 1.71 per cent a year (2010 est); Khmer (90 per cent), Vietnamese (5 per cent), Chinese (1 per cent) (est)
Religion – Buddhist (Theravada) 93 per cent, Muslim 4 per cent (predominantly Shafi'i, a school of Sunni Islam), Christian 2 per cent (predominantly Protestant) (est)
Language – Khmer (official), French, English
Population density – 84 per sq. km (2009)
Urban population – 22 per cent (2008 est)
Median age (years) – 22.6 (2010 est)
National anthem – 'Nokoreach' ['Royal Kingdom']
National day – 9 November (Independence Day)
Life expectancy (years) – 62.28 (2010 est)
Mortality rate – 8.19 (2010 est)
Birth rate – 25.58 (2010 est)
Infant mortality rate – 56.94 (2010 est)
Death penalty – Abolished for all crimes (since 1989)
CPI score – 2.1 (2010)
Literacy rate – 77.0 per cent (2008 est)
Gross enrolment ratio (percentage of relevant age group) – primary 120 per cent; secondary 40 per cent; tertiary 5 per cent (2007 est)
Health expenditure (per capita) – US$42 (2009)
Hospital beds (per 1,000 people) – 0.1 (2004–9)

CLIMATE AND TERRAIN
Cambodia is a mostly flat country, apart from the Cardamom Mountains in the south-west and the uplands of the north-east. The fertile central plains are drained by rivers that run into Tonle Sap, the largest lake in south-east Asia, and into the Mekong river, which flows through the country from north to south. The highest point of elevation is at 1,810m (Phnum Aoral) while the lowest is 0m (Gulf of Thailand). The climate is tropical, with a monsoon season from May to November.

HISTORY AND POLITICS
Although the Khmer people have inhabited the region for almost 2,000 years, the Khmer kingdom was at its strongest in the 10th and 11th centuries, its territory covering modern-day Laos, Thailand and Vietnam. The kingdom lost power and territory from 1432 onwards. Cambodia became a French protectorate in 1863 and part of French Indochina in 1887. It became an associate state

within the French Union in 1949, and gained full independence in 1953 as the Kingdom of Cambodia.

From the late 1960s there was a growing insurgency led by the left-wing Khmer Rouge. In 1970 the monarchy was overthrown in a right-wing coup and the country was renamed the Khmer Republic. Fighting throughout the country involved forces from North and South Vietnam and the USA. In 1975, the regime was overthrown by the North Vietnamese-backed Khmer Rouge. During Khmer Rouge rule under Pol Pot (1975–9), extreme Marxist policies were brutally implemented and famine, disease and maltreatment caused the deaths of an estimated 1.7 million people. In 1978, Vietnamese troops invaded Cambodia, ousting Pol Pot, and in 1979 established a government in Phnom Penh. Guerrilla warfare between the Vietnamese-backed government, the Khmer Rouge and Prince Sihanouk's nationalist forces continued until Vietnamese forces withdrew from Cambodia in 1987–9.

Under a UN peace plan agreed in 1991, multiparty elections were held in 1993, a new constitution was adopted and Prince Sihanouk was elected king. The premiership was shared between the two main parties, the Cambodian People's Party (CPP), headed by Hun Sen and other former leaders of the Vietnamese-backed regime, and Funcinpec, formed by supporters of the king and led by Prince Ranariddh. Ranariddh was ousted as co-prime minister in 1997 in an effective coup by Hun Sen, who became the sole prime minister.

King Sihanouk abdicated in 2004 and was succeeded by one of his sons, Prince Norodom Sihamoni. In the 2008 election, the CPP won 90 seats – a large enough majority to form a government without a coalition for the first time (although the arrangement with Funcinpec, reduced to only two seats, continued).

SECURITY PROBLEMS

The Khmer Rouge continued to fight a guerrilla war until 1996, when it was weakened by internal divisions. Pol Pot was tried by the Khmer Rouge in 1997 and died in captivity in 1998. The remaining Khmer Rouge soldiers surrendered in 1999. A UN-backed tribunal was established in 2007 to try former leaders of the Khmer Rouge regime for atrocities committed during its rule.

Relations with Thailand have deteriorated since 2008 because of a long-running dispute over the border in the area of the Preah Vihear temple, with sporadic exchanges of fire and occasional fighting between the two countries' forces there.

POLITICAL SYSTEM

Under the 1993 constitution, Cambodia is a pluralist liberal democracy with a hereditary constitutional monarchy. The monarch is chosen from eligible royal males by a Council of the Throne elected by parliament. Executive power rests with the government, which is responsible to parliament. The bicameral parliament comprises the National Assembly, which has 123 members directly elected for a five-year term, and the senate, which has 61 members, 57 of whom are elected for a six-year term by the National Assembly and commune councils, with two members appointed by the king and two appointed by the National Assembly.

HEAD OF STATE

HM The King of Cambodia, Norodom Sihamoni, *crowned* 29 October 2004
President of the National Assembly, Heng Samrin

SELECTED GOVERNMENT MEMBERS *as at May 2011*
Prime Minister, Hun Sen
Deputy Prime Ministers, Hor Namhong *(Foreign Affairs);* Sar Kheng *(Interior);* Gen. Tea Banh *(Defence);* Keat Chhon *(Economy and Finance);* Sok An; Gen. Nhoek Bunchhai; Yim Chhai Ly; Bin Chhin; Men Sam-On; Ke Kim Yan

ROYAL EMBASSY OF CAMBODIA
64 Brondesbury Park, London NW6 7AT
T 020-8451 7850 E cambodianembassy@btconnect.com
W www.cambodianembassy.org.uk
Ambassador Extraordinary and Plenipotentiary, HE Hor Nambora, *apptd* 2004

BRITISH EMBASSY
27–29 Street 75, Sangat Srah Chak, Khan Daun Penh, Phnom Penh
T (+855) (23) 427 124 E britemb@online.com.kh
W http://ukincambodia.fco.gov.uk
Ambassador Extraordinary and Plenipotentiary, HE Andrew Mace, *apptd* 2008

DEFENCE

The army has 150 main battle tanks, 70 armoured infantry fighting vehicles and over 190 armoured personnel carriers. The navy has 11 patrol and coastal vessels with bases at Phnom Penh and Ream. The air force has 24 combat aircraft.

Military budget – US$274m (2009)
Military personnel – 124,300: army 75,000, navy 2,800, air force 1,500, provincial forces 45,000; paramilitary 67,000

ECONOMY AND TRADE

Since 1999 the government has made progress with economic reform and development but the country remains very poor, with nearly a third of the population living below the poverty line and an absence of basic infrastructure in rural areas. The demographic imbalance (over half the population is under 25) and lack of education and skills also pose serious problems. Economic growth has been driven by the expansion of garment manufacturing, construction, agriculture and tourism, and mining is attracting foreign investment, but the benefits are largely limited to urban areas. The discovery of oil and gas deposits in territorial waters promises additional revenue once exploitation begins. Recent international aid has been made conditional on the government tackling widespread corruption.

The service sector contributes 45.2 per cent of GDP, industry 21.4 per cent and agriculture 33.4 per cent. Agriculture still engages 58 per cent of the workforce; the main crops are rice, rubber, maize, vegetables, cashew nuts and tapioca. The main industrial activities are tourism, garment and textiles manufacturing, processing of agricultural and forestry products, fishing and mining gemstones. The main trading partners are the USA (45 per cent of exports), Thailand (25 per cent of imports), Vietnam, Singapore and China.

GNI – US$9,952m; US$650 per capita (2009)
Annual average growth of GDP – 4.1 per cent (2010 est)
Inflation rate – 4.1 per cent (2010 est)
Population below poverty line – 31 per cent (2007)
Unemployment – 3.5 per cent (2007)
Total external debt – US$4,338m (2010 est)
Imports – US$5,400m (2009)
Exports – US$4,600m (2009)

BALANCE OF PAYMENTS
Trade – US$1,379m deficit (2010)
Current Account – US$1,149m deficit (2008)

Trade with UK	2009	2010
Imports from UK	£4,028,420	£7,104,793
Exports to UK	£205,852,501	£266,354,228

COMMUNICATIONS

There are 2,400km of navigable waterways, mostly on the Mekong river, and ships of up to 2,500 tonnes can sail as far as Phnom Penh all year round. The deep-water port at Sihanoukville (Kompong Saom) on the Gulf of Thailand is linked to Phnom Penh by a modern highway. The main airports are at Phnom Penh, Siem Reap and Sihanoukville, the latter two having been upgraded to accommodate increasing tourist traffic. Of the country's 38,100km of roads only 3,000km are surfaced and many are in a state of disrepair, although improvements are ongoing. There are 690km of railway lines, mostly still under repair. Rail services are infrequent; in response, improvised and unofficial 'bamboo trains' have arisen as a major mode of passenger and freight transport in some parts of the country.

With fixed-line connections scarce outside the cities, and connections at fewer than 1 per 100 people, mobile phone distribution continues to expand rapidly, having reached a density of about 40 per 100 people in 2009.

MEDIA

Despite public government support for press freedoms, the suppression of dissident media through fines and imprisonment remains common. Many media outlets are reliant on political parties. There are state television and radio broadcasters, as well as six other major commercial and privately owned television channels and three commercial radio stations. There are no restrictions on the ownership and use of private satellite dishes, and foreign radio is also easily received and widely accessed.

CAMEROON

République du Cameroun – Republic of Cameroon

Area – 475,440 sq. km
Capital – Yaoundé; population, 1,739,010 (2009 est)
Major cities – Bamenda, Douala, Garoua, Maroua
Currency – Franc CFA of 100 centimes
Population – 19,294,149 rising at 2.16 per cent a year (2010 est); Cameroon Highlanders (31 per cent), Equatorial Bantu (19 per cent), Kirdi (11 per cent), Fulani (10 per cent), Northwestern Bantu (8 per cent), Eastern Nigritic (7 per cent) (est)

Religion – Christian 69 per cent (Roman Catholic 38 per cent, Protestant 26 per cent), Muslim 21 per cent, animist 6 per cent (est)
Language – English, French (both official), about 250 African languages from 24 major language groups
Population density – 41 per sq. km (2009)
Urban population – 57 per cent (2008 est)
Median age (years) – 19.3 (2010 est)
National anthem – 'Chant de Ralliement' ['Rallying Song']
National day – 20 May (Republic Day)
Life expectancy (years) – 54.04 (2010 est)
Mortality rate – 12.01 (2010 est)
Birth rate – 33.58 (2010 est)
Infant mortality rate – 62.15 (2010 est)
HIV/AIDS adult prevalence – 5.3 per cent (2009 est)
Death penalty – Retained (not used since 1997)
CPI score – 2.2 (2010)
Literacy rate – 67.9 per cent (2008 est)
Gross enrolment ratio (percentage of relevant age group) – primary 114 per cent; secondary 42 per cent; tertiary 9 per cent (2009 est)
Health expenditure (per capita) – US$61 (2009)
Hospital beds (per 1,000 people) – 1.5 (2004–9)

CLIMATE AND TERRAIN

There are three main geographic zones: desert plains and savannah in the north (the Lake Chad basin), mountains and plateaux in the central region and tropical rainforests in the south and east. Elevation extremes range from 4,095m (Mt Cameroon, an active volcano) at the highest point to 0m (Atlantic Ocean) at the lowest. The climate varies from tropical in the south to arid in the north. There is a wet season from April to September in the north, while there is low rain from March to June and heavy rain from September to November in the south.

HISTORY AND POLITICS

The Bakas (Pygmies) and Bantu speakers of the Cameroonian highlands were probably the area's earliest inhabitants. Cameroon was explored by the Portuguese from 1472 and later by Spanish, Dutch and English traders. The Fulani people of the western Sahel conquered northern Cameroon between the 1770s and early 1800s.

The German protectorate of Kamerun was established in 1884. After the First World War it was divided into the League of Nations-mandated territories (later UN trusteeships) of East Cameroon (French-administered), and North and South Cameroons (British-administered). On 1 January 1960 East Cameroon became independent as the Republic of Cameroon. This was joined on 1 October 1961 by South Cameroon after a plebiscite held under the auspices of the UN; North Cameroon voted to join Nigeria. Cameroon became a federal republic comprising East Cameroon and West (formerly South) Cameroon; the federal system was abolished in 1972. From 1966 to 1990, the country was ruled by one party, the National Union of Cameroon (renamed the Cameroon People's Democratic Movement (RDPC) in 1984), with Paul Biya as president from 1982.

Sharp economic decline in 1990 provoked widespread civil unrest and agitation for political pluralism. In the 1992 multiparty elections, the ruling RDPC won the legislative election, and Paul Biya the presidential. The result was challenged by the opposition, which alleged vote-rigging; similar allegations have been made after all subsequent elections, and in 1997 the opposition boycotted the presidential election altogether.

In 2004 President Biya was returned to office with 70.8 per cent of the vote. In the 2007 legislative election, the RDPC retained its overwhelming majority in the legislature, although elections were re-run in a number of seats where the original results were annulled because of suspected fraud. A presidential election is due in October 2011.

INTERNATIONAL RELATIONS

A long-running dispute with Nigeria over their joint border, including the oil-rich Bakassi peninsula, was settled in Cameroon's favour in 2002 after being referred to the International Court of Justice. Nigeria's phased withdrawal from Bakassi was completed in 2008.

Cameroon joined the Commonwealth in 1995, becoming the first member to have been only partially under British rule in colonial times.

POLITICAL SYSTEM

The 1972 constitution was amended in 1990 to enable a return to multiparty rule, in 1996 to extend the presidential term and to provide for the establishment of a second legislative chamber (yet to be implemented), and in 2008 to remove the limit on the number of presidential terms.

The president is directly elected for a seven-year term, and appoints the prime minister and cabinet. The unicameral National Assembly has 180 members, directly elected for a five-year term.

HEAD OF STATE

President, Paul Biya, *took power* 6 November 1982, *elected* 14 January 1984, *re-elected* 1988, 1992, 1997, 2004

SELECTED GOVERNMENT MEMBERS *as at June 2011*
Prime Minister, Philemon Yang
Deputy Prime Ministers, Amadou Ali; Jean Nkuete
Economy, Louis Paul Motaze
Foreign Affairs, Henri Ayissi Eyebe

HIGH COMMISSION FOR THE REPUBLIC OF CAMEROON
84 Holland Park, London W11 3SB
T 020-7727 0771 E info@cameroonhighcommission.co.uk
W www.cameroonhighcommission.co.uk
High Commissioner, HE Nkwelle Ekaney, *apptd* 2008

BRITISH HIGH COMMISSION
PO Box 547, Avenue Winston Churchill, Yaoundé
T (+237) (2) 2220 545
E constance.njike-honcon@fconet.fco.gov.uk
W http://ukincameroon.fco.gov.uk
High Commissioner, HE Bharat Joshi, *apptd* 2009

BRITISH COUNCIL
Immeuble Christo, Avenue Charles de Gaulle, BP 818, Yaoundé
T (+237) (2) 2211 696/203 172
W www.britishcouncil.org/africa
Director, Paul Norton

DEFENCE

The army has 22 armoured infantry fighting vehicles and 33 armoured personnel carriers. The navy has 11 patrol and coastal combatant vessels at 3 bases. The air force has 15 combat capable aircraft and 22 helicopters.
Military budget – US$346m (2010)
Military personnel – 14,100: army 12,500, navy 1,300, air force 300; paramilitary 9,000

ECONOMY AND TRADE

Political stability and natural resources such as oil and timber have enabled agricultural, industrial and infrastructure development, although the economy is vulnerable to commodity price fluctuations and so contracted briefly in the global downturn. Cameroon also has a large and top-heavy public sector and endemic corruption, and recent IMF funding and debt relief have been conditional on progress towards privatisation and greater financial transparency.

Agriculture contributes 20 per cent to GDP, industry 30.9 per cent and services 49.1 per cent. Around 70 per cent of the workforce is engaged in agriculture. The main industrial activity is oil production and refining. Revenue is also earned from the oil pipeline passing through the country from Chad.

The main trading partners are EU countries, China, Nigeria and the USA. Principal exports are crude oil and petroleum products, timber, cocoa, aluminium, coffee and cotton. Imports are chiefly machinery, electrical and transport equipment, fuel and food.
GNI – US$22,059m; US$1,190 per capita (2009)
Annual average growth of GDP – 2.8 per cent (2010 est)
Inflation rate – 1.9 per cent (2010 est)
Total external debt – US$3,344m (2010 est)
Imports – US$3,800m (2009)
Exports – US$3,100m (2009)

BALANCE OF PAYMENTS
Trade – US$344m deficit (2010)
Current Account – US$427m deficit (2007)

Trade with UK	2009	2010
Imports from UK	£29,671,662	£40,468,828
Exports to UK	£108,555,035	£104,165,917

COMMUNICATIONS

The main seaports are at Douala and the Limboh terminal. The river Benue is navigable up to Garoua in the rainy season. There are 34 airports and airfields; the main ones are at Yaoundé, Douala and Garoua. The 50,000km of roads include 5,000km of surfaced roads linking the main population centres. A rail network of 987km links the coast with the capital and the central highlands.

The fixed-line telephone network is antiquated and unreliable, with around one line per 100 people. Mobile phone distribution has grown rapidly since 2002 and there were 40 per 100 people by 2009.

MEDIA

The state-run Cameroon Radio-Television Corporation (CRTV), which operates national television and radio networks as well as provincial stations, held a monopoly on broadcast media until liberalisation in 2000 allowed a commercial television station and several radio stations to be established. Commercial services have proliferated since, and in most parts of the country these command a larger audience share than state-owned broadcasts. Newspapers, the main source of news, are subject to government restrictions, and stringent libel laws are used against critics of the government.

CANADA

Area – 9,984,670 sq. km
Capital – Ottawa; population, 1,170,310 (2009 est; includes Gatineau)
Major cities – Calgary, Edmonton, Hamilton, Montréal, Québec, Toronto, Vancouver, Winnipeg
Currency – Canadian dollar (C$) of 100 cents
Population – 33,759,742 rising at 0.8 per cent a year (2010 est)
Religion – Christian (Roman Catholic 44 per cent, Protestant 29 per cent, other 4 per cent), Muslim 2 per cent, Jewish 1 per cent, Buddhist 1 per cent, Hindu 1 per cent, Sikh 1 per cent (2001)
Language – English, French (both official)
Population density – 4 per sq. km (2009)
Urban population – 80 per cent (2008 est)
Median age (years) – 40.7 (2010 est)
National anthem – 'O Canada'
National day – 1 July (Canada Day)
Life expectancy (years) – 81.29 (2010 est)
Mortality rate – 7.87 (2010 est)
Birth rate – 10.28 (2010 est)
Infant mortality rate – 4.99 (2010 est)
Death penalty – Abolished for all crimes (since 1998)
CPI score – 8.9 (2010)

CLIMATE AND TERRAIN

Canada occupies the entire northern part of the North American continent except for Alaska. The most southerly point is Middle Island in Lake Erie. The six main geographic divisions are: the Appalachian-Acadian region; the Canadian Shield, which comprises more than half the country; the St Lawrence-Great Lakes lowland; the interior plains; the Cordilleran region; and the Arctic archipelago, which lies under continuous permafrost. Elevation extremes range from 5,959m (Mt Logan) at the highest point to 0m (Atlantic Ocean) at the lowest. The climate varies from temperate in the south to subarctic and arctic in the north. The east and centre experience greater extremes than in corresponding latitudes in Europe, but the climate is milder in the south-western part of the prairie region and the southern parts of the Pacific slope. The tornado season is April to September, peaking in June and early July in southern Ontario, Alberta and Québec, Saskatchewan and Manitoba through to Thunder Bay. The interior of British Columbia and western New Brunswick are also tornado zones.

HISTORY AND POLITICS

The land was settled by peoples from Asia, who spread throughout the continent, including the Arctic regions. The first European contact was probably from Greenland c.1000, but the first recorded landing was by John Cabot in 1497. St John's, Newfoundland, was established as a shore base for English fisheries in 1504 and claimed for

England in 1583. The French explored the St Lawrence Seaway from the 1530s, and founded Québec in 1608. The Hudson's Bay Company, founded in 1670, was significant in exploring and opening up the interior. From the 17th century the territory was a pawn in the power struggles of the main colonial powers. Britain gained large areas of the country under the treaty of Utrecht (1713), and after the Seven Years' War, the treaty of Paris (1763) awarded almost all of France's North American possessions to Britain. The American War of Independence caused many British loyalists to migrate to southern Canada, exacerbating existing tensions between British and French colonists. In the mid-19th century, Canadian territory still under Hudson's Bay Company control was brought under government control.

The British North America Act of 1867 formed a dominion under the name of Canada, comprising four provinces: Ontario, Québec, New Brunswick and Nova Scotia. Other provinces and territories were subsequently admitted to this federation: Manitoba and Northwest Territories (1870), British Columbia (1871), Prince Edward Island (1873), Yukon (1898), Alberta and Saskatchewan (1905) and Newfoundland (1949). The territory of Nunavut ('our land') was created for the Inuit peoples in 1999 by partitioning the Northwest Territories.

The constitution was patriated (severed from the British parliament) in 1982. In 1985, following years of French-Canadian separatist agitation, the federal and the provincial governments concluded the Meech Lake accord, which provided for Québec to be recognised as a distinct society within Canada. However, two provincial legislatures withheld approval and the accord did not come into force. A referendum in Québec calling for sovereignty and a new political and economic partnership was defeated in 1995, and support for independence has declined. In 1997, Québec was recognised as having a 'unique character' by the other provinces and territories, and in 2006 the federal parliament passed a motion recognising the Québecois as a nation within a united Canada.

A parliamentary vote of no confidence ended 12 years of Liberal government in 2005. In snap general elections in 2006 and 2008, the Conservative Party won the most seats, but not a majority, and formed minority governments under Stephen Harper. His government won a snap general election in May 2011, increasing its seats to achieve an overall majority.

POLITICAL SYSTEM

Under the 1982 constitution, the head of state is Queen Elizabeth II, represented by a governor-general appointed on the advice of the Canadian prime minister.

The bicameral parliament consists of a senate and a House of Commons. The senate comprises 105 members, who serve until the age of 75, appointed by the governor-general on the recommendation of the prime minister; seats are assigned on a regional basis. The House of Commons has 308 members, directly elected for a four-year term. Representation is proportional to the population of each province.

Each province is largely self-governing, with its own lieutenant-governor and unicameral legislative assembly. The territories are administered by the federal government.

GOVERNOR-GENERAL
Governor-General, HE David Johnston, *apptd* 2010

SELECTED GOVERNMENT MEMBERS *as at June 2011*
Prime Minister, Stephen Harper
Finance, James Flaherty
Foreign Affairs, John Baird
Defence, Peter MacKay

CANADIAN HIGH COMMISSION
Macdonald House, 1 Grosvenor Square, London W1K 4AB
T 020-7258 6600 E 1dn@international.gc.ca
W www.unitedkingdom.gc.ca
High Commissioner, HE James R. Wright, *apptd* 2006

BRITISH HIGH COMMISSION
80 Elgin Street, Ottawa, Ontario K1P 5K7
T (+1) (613) 237 1530 W http://ukincanada.fco.gov.uk
High Commissioner, HE Andrew Pocock, CMG, *apptd* 2011

BRITISH COUNCIL
c/o British High Commission
T (+1) (613) 364 6233/6236 W www.britishcouncil.org/canada
Director, Liliana Biglou

DEFENCE

The Canadian armed forces are unified and organised into three functional commands: land force command, maritime command and air command.

The army (land forces) has 121 main battle tanks and 1,220 armoured personnel carriers. The navy (maritime command) has 4 submarines, 3 destroyers, and 12 frigates. There are bases at Esquimalt, Halifax, Ottawa and Québec City. The air force has 95 combat aircraft.
Military expenditure – US$19,600m (2009)
Military personnel – 65,722: army 34,775, navy 11,025, air force 19,922

ECONOMY AND TRADE

Canada has a highly developed, industrialised and diversified market economy, which was transformed from a predominantly rural to an industrial economy in the second half of the 20th century by the growth of mining, manufacturing and services. Tight management of government finances resulted in balanced budgets from the late 1990s until 2007, and free-trade agreements with the USA in 1989 and 1994 (NAFTA) stimulated trade. The economy went into recession in 2008 owing to the global downturn, although the financial sector proved more stable than that of many other major economies; recovery began in 2010.

Canada's wealth of natural resources make it the world's largest exporter of timber, pulp and newsprint (over half the land is tree-covered), and it is one of the world's largest exporters of minerals, particularly uranium (of which it is the world's second largest single producer) and diamonds (of which it is the world's third largest producer). About 5 per cent of the land area is farmed, of which 4.6 per cent is under cultivation, mostly in the prairie region of western Canada. The country is one of the world's leading food producers, particularly of wheat, barley, oilseed, tobacco, fruit, vegetables and dairy products. The fishing industry is also significant but has declined in recent years because of restrictions introduced to protect stocks after decades of overfishing. Oil, natural gas and hydroelectricity production is high enough for Canada to be a net exporter of energy. The shrinking of the Arctic ice cap is opening up access to offshore oil and gas reserves, new fishing grounds and shipping routes in the region. The government has plans to develop the area but the assertion of its sovereignty has attracted criticism from other Arctic countries and is complicated by the lack of international agreement on countries' territorial claims.

In 2010, the services sector contributed 78 per cent of GDP, industry 20 per cent and agriculture 2 per cent.

The USA is Canada's main trading partner, taking 75 per cent of exports and providing 51 per cent of imports. The main exports are motor vehicles and parts, industrial machinery, aircraft, telecommunications equipment, chemicals, plastics, fertilisers, forestry products, energy products (including crude oil, natural gas and electricity) and aluminium.
GNI – US$1,317,310m; US$41,980 per capita (2009)
Annual average growth of GDP – 3 per cent (2010 est)
Inflation rate – 1.6 per cent (2010 est)
Unemployment – 8 per cent (2010 est)
Total external debt – US$1,009,000m (2010)
Imports – US$329,900m (2009)
Exports – US$314,000m (2009)

BALANCE OF PAYMENTS
Trade – US$4,024m deficit (2010)
Current Account – US$36,132m deficit (2009)

Trade with UK	2009	2010
Imports from UK	£3,957,008,681	£4,868,802,524
Exports to UK	£8,076,735,617	£12,151,704,468

FEDERAL STRUCTURE

Provinces or Territories (with official contractions)	Population (2010)	Area (sq. km)	Capital	Premier
Alberta (AB)	3,720,946	661,848	Edmonton	Ed Stelmach
British Columbia (BC)	4,530,960	944,735	Victoria	Christy Clark
Manitoba (MB)	1,235,412	747,797	Winnipeg	Greg Selinger
New Brunswick (NB)	751,755	72,908	Fredericton	David Alward
Newfoundland and Labrador (NL)	509,739	405,212	St John's	Kathy Dunderdale
Northwest Territories (NT)	43,759	1,346,106	Yellowknife	Floyd Roland
Nova Scotia (NS)	942,506	55,284	Halifax	Darrell Dexter
Nunavut (NU)	33,220	2,093,190	Iqaluit	Eva Aariak
Ontario (ON)	13,210,667	1,076,395	Toronto	Dalton McGuinty
Prince Edward Island (PE)	142,266	5,660	Charlottetown	Robert Ghiz
Québec (QC)	7,907,375	1,542,056	Québec City	Jean Charest
Saskatchewan (SK)	1,045,622	651,036	Regina	Brad Wall
Yukon Territory (YT)	34,525	482,443	Whitehorse	Dennis Fentie

COMMUNICATIONS

Canada has a coastline on three oceans: the Atlantic, the Arctic and the Pacific. In addition, the Great Lakes/St Lawrence Seaway system, the world's longest inland waterway for ocean-going shipping, provides access to the North American interior. There are over 300 ports, the most significant of which are Vancouver and Prince Rupert on the Pacific coast and Montréal, Halifax, Port Cartier, Sept-Iles/Pointe Noire, Saint John and Québec in the east. Most deep-water ports are open all year, and Churchill, on Hudson's Bay, is ice-free for longer periods as a result of climate change.

There are over 1,400 airports and airstrips, of which 26 serve national and provincial capitals and other major cities. The national carriers are Air Canada and Canadian Airlines International. The 46,700km railway network transports over 270 million tonnes of freight a year; the main service providers are Canadian National Railways and Canadian Pacific Railways, which also own several US lines. There are 1.04 million kilometres of roads. The 7,800km Trans-Canadian Highway links all ten provinces.

The usage of fixed telephone lines has declined as mobile phone distribution has grown. There were 18 million fixed lines in use, 23 million mobile phone subscribers and 27 million internet users in 2009.

EDUCATION AND HEALTH

Education is under the control of the provincial governments, the cost of the publicly controlled schools being met by local taxation and aided by provincial grants. Education is compulsory from ages six to 16 (18 in Ontario and New Brunswick).
Gross enrolment ratio (percentage of relevant age group) – primary 98 per cent (2007 est)
Health expenditure (per capita) – US\$4,380 (2009)
Hospital beds (per 1,000 people) – 3.4 (2004–9)

MEDIA

The public broadcaster, the Canadian Broadcasting Corporation (CBC), was established in the 1930s and operates two television and four radio networks, transmitting programmes in English and French. It also operates television channels and radio services for indigenous peoples in the north of the country. Société Radio-Canada is the French-language public broadcasting service. There are several commercial television channels and around 2,000 licensed radio stations. The broadcasting regulator enforces quotas of Canadian material (30–35 per cent) on Canadian radio and television.

CULTURE

Canadian culture was originally influenced by the British and French heritage of its settlers, but is now dominated by the USA. Canada has produced a number of successful actors, directors and comedians, including Jim Carrey (b. 1962), David Cronenberg (b. 1943), Mike Myers (b. 1963) and Donald (b. 1935) and Kiefer (b. 1966) Sutherland.

The country is also one of the world's largest exporters of popular music. Leonard Cohen (b. 1934), Joni Mitchell (b. 1943) and Neil Young (b. 1945) are all internationally successful, as were the Band (1967–76), while the Montreal International Jazz Festival is the largest of its kind in the world. Writers include the Nobel laureate Saul Bellow (1915–2005), International Booker prize winner Alice Munro (b. 1931), Carol Shields (1935–2003), who won the Pulitzer prize, and the Booker prize winner Margaret Atwood (b. 1939).

CAPE VERDE

Republica de Cabo Verde – Republic of Cape Verde

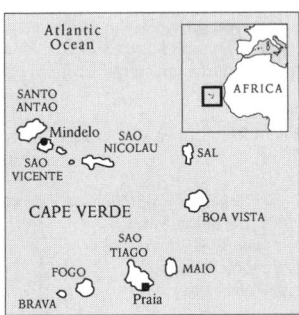

Area – 4,033 sq. km; comprises the Windward Islands (Santo Antao, Sao Vicente, Santa Luzia, Sao Nicolau, Boa Vista and Sal) and Leeward Islands (Maio, Sao Tiago, Fogo and Brava)
Capital – Praia, on Sao Tiago; population, 125,148 (2009)
Major town – Mindelo
Currency – Escudo Caboverdiano of 100 centavos
Population – 508,659 rising at 1.46 per cent a year (2010 est)
Religion – Christian (Roman Catholic 85 per cent) (est)
Language – Portuguese (official), Creole
Population density – 125 per sq. km (2009)
Urban population – 60 per cent (2008 est)
Median age (years) – 22.3 (2010 est)
National anthem – 'Cantico da Liberdade' ['Song of Liberty']
National day – 5 July (Independence Day)
Life expectancy – 70.41 (2010 est)
Mortality rate – 6.41 (2010 est)
Birth rate – 21.67 (2010 est)
Infant mortality rate – 27.89 (2010 est)
Death penalty – Abolished for all crimes (since 1981)
CPI score – 5.1 (2010)
Literacy rate – 84.5 per cent (2008)

CLIMATE AND TERRAIN

The archipelago of ten islands of volcanic origin lies 600km off the west African coast. Elevation extremes range from 2,829m (Mt Fogo, an active volcano on Fogo island) at the highest point to 0m (Atlantic Ocean) at the lowest. The climate is hot and dry, with periodic droughts.

HISTORY AND POLITICS

The islands were first discovered and colonised c.1460 by Portugal. Administered with Portuguese Guinea until 1879, they became an overseas province in 1951. The country achieved independence on 5 July 1975 after a campaign by the African Party for the Independence of Guinea Bissau and Cape Verde (PAIGC).

The republic was a one-party state under the African Party for the Independence of Cape Verde (PAICV) until 1990. Multiparty elections in 1991 were won by the opposition Movement for Democracy (MPD), and the MPD candidate was elected president. The 2001 legislative elections returned the PAICV to power, and its candidate, Pedro Pires, narrowly won the second round of the presidential election. The PAICV retained its overall majority in the 2006 and 2011 legislative elections. President Pires was re-elected in 2006 in the first round of voting. The presidential election was due in July 2011.

POLITICAL SYSTEM
Under the 1992 constitution, the president is directly elected for a five-year term. There is a unicameral National Assembly with 72 members directly elected for a five-year term. The prime minister appoints the council of ministers.

HEAD OF STATE
President, Pedro Pires, *elected* 25 February 2001, *re-elected* 2006, 2011

SELECTED GOVERNMENT MEMBERS *as at June 2011*
Prime Minister, Jose Maria Neves
Finance and Planning, Cristina Duarte
Foreign Affairs, Jorge Borges
Defence, Jorge Tolentino

EMBASSY OF THE REPUBLIC OF CAPE VERDE
Avenue Jeanne 29, 1050 Brussels, Belgium
T (+32) (2) 643 6270
Ambassador Extraordinary and Plenipotentiary, HE
    Fernando Jorge Wahnon Ferreira, *apptd* 2007

BRITISH AMBASSADOR
HE Christopher Trott, *apptd* 2007, resident at Dakar, Senegal

DEFENCE
The coastguard has 3 patrol and coastal combatant vessels.
Military budget – US$8m (2010)
Military personnel – 1,200: army 1,000, coastguard 100, air force 100
Conscription duration – 14 months

ECONOMY AND TRADE
The islands have few natural resources, little fresh water and are subject to periods of prolonged drought. A well-managed economy has produced steady growth, and further reforms are intended to attract foreign investment to aid diversification and development of the private sector. However, a large trade deficit leaves the government dependent on foreign aid and remittances; owing to large-scale emigration the expatriate population is larger than the resident one, and remittances are equivalent to over 20 per cent of GDP. The service sector dominates, with commerce, tourism, transport and public services accounting for 74.8 per cent of GDP. Industry contributed 16.2 per cent and agriculture 9 per cent; fishing resources are not fully exploited. The main industries are the production of food, beverages, garments and footwear, fishing and fish processing, salt mining and ship repair.
    The main trading partners are Portugal, Spain and the Netherlands. Exports are fuel, footwear, garments, fish and hides. Imports include foodstuffs (over 80 per cent of food is imported), industrial products, transport equipment and fuel.
GNI – US$1,499m; US$3,010 per capita (2009)
Annual average growth of GDP – 4.5 per cent (2010 est)
Inflation rate – 2.5 per cent (2010 est)
Total external debt – US$325m (2002)
Imports – US$700m (2009)
Exports – US$20m (2007)

BALANCE OF PAYMENTS
Trade – US$708m deficit (2010)
Current Account – US$216m deficit (2008)

Trade with UK	2009	2010
Imports from UK	£4,950,194	£5,133,771
Exports to UK	£141,923	£117,641

COMMUNICATIONS
The main ports are Praia and Mindelo. Ferry services operate between the islands. There are ten airports, including international airports at Praia and on Sal, and regular internal flights between the islands. The national carrier, Cape Verde Airlines, is being privatised. The islands have no railways. There are 1,350km of roads; most of these are cobbled but a programme to resurface the roads with asphalt is ongoing.
    The telephone system extends to all the islands, providing internet access and broadband services. Mobile phone services, introduced in 1998, had 392,000 subscribers in 2009.

MEDIA
Freedom of the media is guaranteed in the constitution, and this is generally upheld. There are growing private print and broadcast sectors, but much of the media remains state-run. Portuguese African services and Radio France Internationale are both available, as are a range of Portuguese and Brazilian newspapers.

CENTRAL AFRICAN REPUBLIC

République Centrafricaine – Central African Republic

Area – 622,984 sq. km
Capital – Bangui; population, 701,597 (2009 est)
Major cities – Berbérati, Bimbo, Mbaiki
Currency – Franc CFA of 100 centimes
Population – 4,844,927 rising at 2.15 per cent a year
    (2010 est); Baya (33 per cent), Banda (27 per cent),
    Mandja (13 per cent), Sara (10 per cent), Mboum (7 per
    cent), M'Baka (4 per cent), Yakoma (4 per cent) (est)
Religion – Christian (Protestant denominations 51 per
    cent, Roman Catholic 29 per cent), Muslim 15 per cent
    (est). Some also practise animism, although these
    beliefs are often integrated into Christian and Muslim
    worship
Language – French (official), Sangho
Population density – 7 per sq. km (2009)
Urban population – 39 per cent (2008 est)
Median age (years) – 19.1 (2010 est)
National anthem – 'La Renaissance' ['The Rebirth']
National day – 1 December (Republic Day)

Life expectancy – 49.68 (2010 est)
Mortality rate – 15.3 (2010 est)
Birth rate – 36.79 (2010 est)
Infant mortality rate – 101.6 (2010 est)
HIV/AIDS adult prevalence – 4.7 per cent (2009 est)
Death penalty – Retained (not used since 1981)
CPI score – 2.1 (2010)
Literacy rate – 48.6 per cent (2008 est)
Gross enrolment ratio (percentage of relevant age group) –
    primary 89 per cent; secondary 14 per cent; tertiary
    2 per cent (2009 est)
Health expenditure (per capita) – US$19 (2009)
Hospital beds (per 1,000 people) – 1.2 (2004–9)

CLIMATE AND TERRAIN
This landlocked state lies on a plateau between the Chad
and Congo river basins, with hills in the north-east and
the north-west. It is mostly savannah in the north and
rainforest in the south. The main river is the Oubangui,
which is the lowest point of elevation (335m). The
highest point is Mt Ngaoui (1,420m). The climate is
tropical, with a wet season in the north from May to
September and in the south from May to October. The
north can experience temperatures of up to 40°C between
February and May, and the humidity can be extreme. The
south has a more equatorial climate.

HISTORY AND POLITICS
The area was annexed by France in the 1880s and, as the
territory of Oubangui-Chari, became part of French
Equatorial Africa. In 1958 it elected to remain within the
French Community and adopted the title of the Central
African Republic. The country became fully independent
on 17 August 1960. Since independence it has been
politically unstable, experiencing several coups. The 1966
coup brought to power the despotic Jean-Bedel Bokassa,
who proclaimed himself emperor in 1976 and renamed
the country the Central African Empire. Bokassa was
deposed in a bloodless coup in 1979 and the country
reverted to a republic. After a period under military rule
(1981–5) and as a one-party state (1986–93), political
pluralism and a civilian government were restored in
1993. This government was undermined by mutinies,
financial crises and unrest in some neighbouring
countries, which caused large influxes of refugees and
border incursions. It was overthrown in 2003 in a coup
led by Gen. François Bozizé, who declared himself
president and appointed a transitional government until
elections were held in 2005.
    Gen. Bozizé's government has struggled to maintain
control outside the capital, faced with lawlessness,
banditry and an insurgency in the north (2005–8) as well
as the problems that beset previous administrations.
Although a peace agreement in 2008 brought the main
rebel groups into a national unity government, clashes
with the remaining northern insurgents continue, while
the south-east has been subject to attacks by the
Uganda-based Lord's Resistance Army (LRA) since 2008.
The government has been supported by a central African
peacekeeping force since 2007, and since 2009 Ugandan
troops have, with its approval, patrolled areas subject to
LRA attacks. The EU/UN mission deployed in 2008 to
protect Chadian and Sudanese refugees in the north-east
was withdrawn in 2010.
    President Bozizé was re-elected in January 2011.
Legislative elections in January and March 2011 were
won by the *Kwa Na Kwa* (KNK) coalition, a group loyal to
the president.

POLITICAL SYSTEM
Under the 2004 constitution, the president is elected for
a five-year term, renewable once. The unicameral National
Assembly has 105 members, directly elected for a
five-year term. The prime minister is appointed by the
president and appoints the ministers.

HEAD OF STATE
President, Defence, Gen. François Bozizé, *took power*
    15 March 2003, *elected* May 2005, *re-elected*
    January 2011

SELECTED GOVERNMENT MEMBERS *as at June 2011*
Prime Minister, Faustin Archange Touadera
Finance and Budget, Lt.-Col. Sylvain Ndoutingai
Foreign Affairs, Brig.-Gen. Antoine Gambi

EMBASSY OF THE CENTRAL AFRICAN REPUBLIC
30 Rue des Perchamps, 75016 Paris, France
(+33) (1) 4224 4256
Ambassador Extraordinary and Plenipotentiary, Jean
    Willybiro Sako, *apptd* 2009

BRITISH AMBASSADOR
HE Bharat Joshi, *apptd* 2009, resident at Yaoundé,
Cameroon

DEFENCE
The army has 3 main battle tanks, 18 armoured infantry
fighting vehicles, 39 armoured personnel carriers and
9 patrol and coastal combatant vessels.
Military budget – US$52m (2010)
Military personnel – 2,150: army 2,000, air force 150;
    paramilitary 1,000
Conscription duration – 24 months

ECONOMY AND TRADE
The economy is largely undeveloped owing to decades of
instability and misrule. Development is still hindered by
political factionalism, the landlocked location, poor
transport infrastructure, an unskilled workforce and
corruption. The country is dependent on international
aid. Natural resources include diamonds, gold, uranium
and timber; diamond and gold mining and forestry are
among the main industrial activities but the economy still
depends mostly on agriculture, which accounts for over
50 per cent of GDP. Most production is at subsistence
level but cotton, coffee and tobacco form the main
exports along with diamonds and timber. The main
imports are food, textiles, fuels and machinery. Trade is
mainly with Belgium, South Korea, France and China.
GNI – US$1,983m; US$450 per capita (2009)
Annual average growth of GDP – 3.7 per cent (2010 est)
Inflation rate – 0.9 per cent (2007 est)
Total external debt – US$1,153m (2007 est)
Imports – US$300m (2009)
Exports – US$100m (2009)

BALANCE OF PAYMENTS
Trade – US$243m deficit (2010)
Current Account – US$106m deficit (2007 est)

Trade with UK	2009	2010
Imports from UK	£796,679	£713,246
Exports to UK	£108,315	£97,003

COMMUNICATIONS
The infrastructure is poor: little of the 24,307km road
network is surfaced, making many roads unusable in the

wet season, and there is no railway system. There are 2,800km of waterways, mostly on the Oubangui and Sangha rivers, that are navigable all year and are important passenger and freight transport routes. The principal airport is at Bangui, and there are 36 other airports and airfields. Fixed-line and mobile telephone networks are largely limited to the Bangui area, with density fewer than one per 100 people for fixed lines and three per 100 people for mobile phones, although use of mobile phones in increasing.

MEDIA

Only state-run radio and television stations have a national reach, and these provide scant coverage of opposition parties. There are a number of private radio and television stations, of which the UN-sponsored Radio Ndeke Luka provides the most balanced output, regularly rebroadcasting international news. There are a number of privately owned newspapers which freely criticise the government, but low literacy levels mean that they have little influence. Legislation passed in 2004 abolished prison terms for press offences.

CHAD

République du Tchad/Jumhuriyat Tshad – Republic of Chad

Area – 1,284,000 sq. km

Capital – N'Djamena; population, 808,442 (2009 est)

Major cities – Abéché, Moundou, Sarh

Currency – Franc CFA of 100 centimes

Population – 10,543,464 rising at 2.04 per cent a year (2010 est); the population is made up of around 200 ethnic groups

Religion – Muslim 53 per cent (predominantly Tijaniyah, a local order of Sufism), Christian 34 per cent (est), traditional indigenous religions

Language – French, Arabic (both official), Sara (in the south), Ouadi, Toubon (in the north)

Population density – 9 per sq. km (2009)

Urban population – 27 per cent (2008 est)

Median age (years) – 16.6 (2010 est)

National anthem – 'La Tchadienne' ['Song of Chad']

National day – 11 August (Independence Day)

Life expectancy – 47.99 (2010 est)

Mortality rate – 15.79 (2010 est)

Birth rate – 40.12 (2010 est)

Infant mortality rate – 97.05 (2010 est)

HIV/AIDS adult prevalence – 3.4 per cent (2009 est)

Death penalty – Retained

CPI score – 1.7 (2010)

Literacy rate – 31.8 per cent (2008 est)

Gross enrolment ratio (percentage of relevant age group) – primary 90 per cent; secondary 24 per cent; tertiary 2 per cent (2008 est)

Health expenditure (per capita) – US$42 (2009)

Hospital beds (per 1,000 people) – 0.4 (2004–9)

CLIMATE AND TERRAIN

The population of this landlocked country is concentrated in the fertile lowlands of the south, away from the arid central and northern desert areas. The highest point of elevation is 3,415m (Emi Koussi) and the lowest is 160m (the Djourab depression). The climate is desert in the north and tropical in the south, with a wet season from July to September.

HISTORY AND POLITICS

Chad was colonised by France from the 1890s and became part of French Equatorial Africa. It became self-governing after the Second World War and independent on 11 August 1960. A one-party state was declared in 1963 by the president, a southerner, which in 1965 prompted a rebellion in the north against a perceived pro-southern bias in the government. Regional and ethnic tensions, most notably between the Muslim Arab north and the Christian and animist African south, underlie the series of rebellions and coups that have made the country politically unstable since independence. Chad's instability was exacerbated from the 1970s to the 1990s by Libya's support for some rebels and its annexation of territory in northern Chad, and since 2004 by the overspill of the Darfur conflict in Sudan.

Idriss Déby seized power in 1990 after leading a rebellion in eastern Chad, and initiated a transition to democracy. A new constitution was introduced in 1996, and the first multiparty elections were held.

Déby won the first multiparty presidential election in 1996 and was re-elected in 2001, 2006 and 2011, despite doubts over the integrity of the polls. The 2011 legislative election was won by Déby's Patriotic Salvation Movement (MPS) and its allies, with 133 seats.

INSURGENCIES

The series of insurgencies over the decades since independence means that no government has ever controlled the whole of the country. There are currently insurgencies in the north and east; rebels hold large areas of northern Chad, and rebel offensives reached the capital in 2006 and 2008 before being repulsed. In 2009, eight rebel groups united to form the Union of Resistance Forces alliance.

From 2004, the east and south-east were further destabilised by the overspill of fighting from Sudan's Darfur region, with some militias mounting cross-border incursions to attack the estimated 250,000 Sudanese refugees in Chad. The EU/UN mission deployed in 2008 to protect Sudanese refugees in Chad was withdrawn in 2010, and relations with Sudan have now been normalised and the border reopened. An estimated 185,000 Chadians have also been displaced by the incursions, the insurgencies and Chadian ethnic violence.

POLITICAL SYSTEM

The 1996 constitution was amended in 2005 to remove the limit on the number of terms a president may serve. The president is directly elected for a five-year term. The unicameral National Assembly of 188 members is directly elected for a four-year term. The prime minister is appointed by the president.

HEAD OF STATE
President, Idriss Déby, *took power* December 1990, *elected* 3 July 1996, *re-elected* 2001, 2006, 2011

SELECTED GOVERNMENT MEMBERS *as at June 2011*
Prime Minister, Emmanuel Nadingar
Economy, Mahamat Ali Hassan
Finance, Gata Ngoulou
Foreign Affairs, Moussa Faki Mahamat
Interior, Ahmat Mahamat Bachir
Defence, Gen. Kamougue Wadal Abdelkader

EMBASSY OF THE REPUBLIC OF CHAD
Boulevard Lambermont 52, 1030 Brussels, Belgium
T (+32) (2) 215 1975 E ambassade.tchad@chello.be
Ambassador Extraordinary and Plenipotentiary, HE Ahmat Abderaman Hagger, *apptd* 2006

BRITISH AMBASSADOR
HE Bharat Joshi, *apptd* 2009, resident at Yaoundé, Cameroon

DEFENCE
The army has 60 main battle tanks, 89 armoured infantry fighting vehicles and 52 armoured personnel carriers. The air force has 7 combat-capable aircraft and 7 armed helicopters.
Military budget – US$129m (2010)
Military personnel – 25,350: army 17,000–20,000, air force 350, Republican Guard 5,000; paramilitary 9,500

ECONOMY AND TRADE
Economic development has been limited by political instability, the landlocked location and poor transport infrastructure. About 80 per cent of the workforce is occupied in subsistence agriculture, herding and fishing, which contributes 50.5 per cent of GDP. The main focus of development, funded by foreign investment and international aid, is the exploitation of oil deposits in the Doba basin in the south, which came into production in 2003; the oil is exported via a pipeline through Cameroon, and a refinery is under construction. Other industries include processing cotton (the main industry before oil) and other agricultural products, and light manufacturing. Industry generates 7 per cent of GDP.

Chad's main trading partners are the USA (90 per cent of exports), France, China and Cameroon. Principal exports are oil, cattle, cotton and gum arabic. The main imports are machinery and transport equipment, industrial goods, food and textiles.
GNI – US$6,124m; US$600 per capita (2009)
Annual average growth of GDP – 2 per cent (2010 est)
Inflation rate – 4 per cent (2010 est)
Total external debt – US$1,749m (2008 est)
Imports – US$1,600m (2009)
Exports – US$3,500m (2009)

BALANCE OF PAYMENTS
Trade – US$1,799m surplus (2010)
Current Account – US$568m deficit (2006)

Trade with UK	2009	2010
Imports from UK	£14,503,525	£13,343,846
Exports to UK	£565,512	£739,858

COMMUNICATIONS
There are 4,800km of waterways, although only 2,000km are navigable all year round. Of the 33,400km of roads, only 267km are surfaced, so many are unusable in the wet season. The principal airport is at N'Djamena and there are more than 50 other airports and airfields. There are no railways. The fixed-line telephone system is primitive; mobile phone distribution is growing rapidly but was only about 25 per 100 people in 2009.

MEDIA
Low levels of literacy make radio the most important news medium. Radiodiffusion Nationale Tchadienne is the state-controlled radio station; private radio stations are closely monitored by the government. There is only one television station, Télétchad, and it is state-owned and controlled. Privately owned newspapers circulate in the capital and are often critical of the government.

CHILE

República de Chile – Republic of Chile

Area – 756,102 sq. km
Capital – Santiago; population, 5,883,040 (2009 est)
Major cities – Antofagasta, Arica, Concepción, Iquique, Punta Arenas, Temuco, Valparaíso
Currency – Chilean peso of 100 centavos
Population – 16,746,491 rising at 0.86 per cent a year (2010 est)
Religion – Christian (Roman Catholic 70 per cent, Protestant 15 per cent) (est)
Language – Spanish (official), Mapudungun, German, English
Population density – 23 per sq. km (2009)
Urban population – 88 per cent (2008 est)
Median age (years) – 31.7 (2010 est)
National anthem – 'Himno Nacional de Chile' ['National Anthem of Chile']
National day – 18 September (Independence Day)
Life expectancy (years) – 77.53 (2010 est)
Mortality rate – 5.9 (2010 est)
Birth rate – 14.46 (2010 est)
Infant mortality rate – 7.52 (2010 est)
Death penalty – Retained for certain crimes (last used 1985)
CPI score – 7.2 (2010)
Literacy rate – 96.5 per cent (2007 est)

CLIMATE AND TERRAIN
Chile lies between the shores of the South Pacific Ocean and the Andes to the east, extending over 4,600km from the arid north around Arica to Cape Horn; the average breadth is 180km. The Atacama desert lies in the north. In the central zone there is a fertile valley between the Andes and the low coastal range of mountains, with a

Mediterranean climate; two-thirds of the population live here. Chilean Patagonia, in the south, extends into subantarctic terrain, with glaciers and icefields; the climate is cool with high precipitation. Elevation extremes range from 6,880m (Nevado Ojos del Salado) at the highest point to 0m (Pacific Ocean) at the lowest. Its Pacific island possessions include the Juan Fernández group and Easter Island.

HISTORY AND POLITICS
Chile was conquered in the 16th century by the Spanish, who subjugated the indigenous population. It remained under Spanish rule until 1810, when the first autonomous government was established. Independence was achieved in 1818 after a revolutionary war.

A military coup in 1973 overthrew the Marxist president Salvador Allende. General Augusto Pinochet, the coup leader, assumed the presidency and retained the office until elections were held in 1989, beginning the transition to full democracy. Between 1998 and his death in 2006, a number of unsuccessful attempts were made to bring Gen. Pinochet to trial for human rights atrocities committed during his time in office. A massive earthquake, registering 8.8 in magnitude, hit central Chile in 2010, killing about 500 people and causing widespread devastation.

In the 2009 legislative elections, the right-wing Coalition for Change (APC) won one more seat than the incumbent Coalition of Parties for Democracy (CPD) in the lower chamber, and each grouping won half the seats in the senate. Sebastián Piñera, the candidate of the National Renewal party (part of the APC), won the 2010 presidential election and formed a government consisting of members of the APC and independents.

POLITICAL SYSTEM
The 1981 constitution was amended in 1989 and 2005. The executive president is directly elected for a four-year term that is not renewable. The bicameral National Congress comprises a senate of 38 members elected for an eight-year term (half renewed every four years) and a Chamber of Deputies of 120 members directly elected for a four-year term.

HEAD OF STATE
President, Sebastián Piñera, *elected* 17 January 2010, *sworn in* 11 March 2010

SELECTED GOVERNMENT MEMBERS *as at June 2011*
Defence, Andrés Allamand
Economy, Juan Andrés Fontaine Talavera
Finance, Felipe Larrain Bascunan
Foreign Affairs, Alfredo Moreno Charme
Interior, Rodrigo Hinzpeter Kirberg

EMBASSY OF CHILE
37–41 Old Queen Street, London SW1H 9JA
T 020-7222 2361 E embachile@embachile.co.uk
W www.chileabroad.gov.cl/reino-unido
Ambassador Extraordinary and Plenipotentiary, HE Tomás E. Müller Sproat, *apptd* 2010

BRITISH EMBASSY
Avda. El Bosque Norte 0125, Las Condes, Santiago
T (+56) (2) 370 4100 E embsan@britemb.cl
W http://ukinchile.fco.gov.uk/en
Ambassador Extraordinary and Plenipotentiary, HE Jon Benjamin, *apptd* 2009

BRITISH COUNCIL
Avenue Ricardo Lyon 222, Of 2001, Providencia, Santiago
T (+56) (2) 410 6900 W www.britishcouncil.org/chile
Manager, Andrew Chadwick

DEFENCE
The army has 262 main battle tanks, 191 armoured infantry fighting vehicles and 436 armoured personnel carriers. The navy has 4 submarines, 1 destroyer, 7 frigates, 13 patrol and coastal vessels and 20 combat aircraft. There are bases at Valparaíso, Talcahuano, Puerto Montt, Puerto Williams, Iquique and Punta Arenas. The marines have 15 light tanks and 25 armoured personnel carriers. The air force has 59 combat aircraft.
Military expenditure – US$2,070m (2010)
Military personnel – 59,059: army 35,000, navy 16,299, air force 7,760; paramilitary 44,712

ECONOMY AND TRADE
Economic reforms in the late 1970s and the 1980s and sound financial management have made Chile one of the most successful economies in Latin America; in 2010 it became the first South American country to join the OECD. Growth is based on high copper prices, a strong export base and growing domestic demand. Although the economy contracted slightly in 2009 owing to the global downturn, it began to recover later that year.

Chile is the world's largest producer of copper, and the world's only commercial producer of nitrate of soda (Chile saltpetre) from natural resources. The chief industries are mining, forestry, fishing, food and fish processing, and wine-making. Agriculture, which contributes 5.6 per cent of GDP, produces fruit, vegetables, cereals, meat and wool.

The main trading partners are the USA, China, Brazil, Argentina and Japan. Principal exports are copper, fruit, fish products, paper and pulp, chemicals and wine. The main imports are petrol and petroleum products, chemicals, electrical and telecommunications equipment, industrial machinery, vehicles and natural gas.
GNI – US$153,446m; US$9,470 per capita (2009)
Annual average growth of GDP – 5.3 per cent (2010 est)
Inflation rate – 1.7 per cent (2010 est)
Population living below poverty line – 18.2 per cent (2005)
Unemployment – 8.7 per cent (2010 est)
Total external debt – US$84,510m (2010 est)
Imports – US$41,400m (2009)
Exports – US$52,000m (2009)

BALANCE OF PAYMENTS
Trade – US$9,882m surplus (2010)
Current Account – US$2,522m deficit (2009)

Trade with UK	2009	2010
Imports from UK	£478,163,896	£584,394,080
Exports to UK	£535,933,078	£509,366,459

COMMUNICATIONS
The main ports are San Antonio, Valparaíso, San Vicente, Antofagasta and Iquique. There is a 7,082km railway system, but lines in some areas are not in use as rail travel is increasingly superseded by road and air travel; services are run by a state-owned company. The road network is about 80,505km in length, of which 16,745km is surfaced. There are over 360 airports and airfields; the principal airport is at Santiago. The national air carrier is LAN Airlines, with Sky Airline and PAL Airlines also

providing domestic flights. Mobile phone distribution is growing rapidly, reaching 100 per 100 people in 2009, and fixed-line connections are decreasing as a result.

EDUCATION AND HEALTH
Education is free and compulsory for 12 years, although the education system has suffered from underinvestment and mismanagement. In response to massive student demonstrations and strikes in 2006, the government introduced a limited education reform package in 2009. Student protests have continued, however, focusing on inequality in education provision and regulation of the private sector.

Literacy rate – 96.7 per cent (2008 est)

Gross enrolment ratio (percentage of relevant age group) – primary 106 per cent; secondary 90 per cent; tertiary 55 per cent (2008 est)

Health expenditure (per capita) – US$787 (2009)

Hospital beds (per 1,000 people) – 2.1 (2004–9)

MEDIA AND CULTURE
Television is a combination of national and local, private and state-owned, cable and terrestrial channels. Radio is an important news medium, with hundreds of stations nationwide. Chile's constitution provides for press freedom, and the last remaining media restrictions from the Pinochet era were lifted in 2001.

Chile has a vibrant arts culture and is considered the most European of the Latin American countries. Chilean Nobel Prize winners for literature include the writers Gabriela Mistral (1889–1957) in 1945, and poet Pablo Neruda (1904–73) in 1971.

One of the islands in the Juan Fernández group, about 576km from Valparaíso, was reputedly the scene of Alexander Selkirk's shipwreck in 1704, which inspired Daniel Defoe's novel *Robinson Crusoe*. Easter Island, about 3,200km away in the South Pacific Ocean, contains stone platforms and hundreds of mysterious stone figures, *moai*, thought to be carved from volcanic ash by Polynesian colonisers between 1100 and 1600.

CHILEAN ANTARCTIC TERRITORY
The Chilean Antarctic Territory covers the Antarctic peninsula and an area of the landmass that extends from 53°W to 90°W along a latitude of 60°S. This area is also claimed by the UK and Argentina, although the Antarctic treaty has frozen all disputes over territory. (*See also* The North and South Poles.)

CHINA

Zhonghua Renmin Gongheguo – People's Republic of China

Area – 9,596,961 sq. km

Capital – Beijing; population, 12,213,900 (2009 est)

Major cities – Changchun, Chengdu, Chongqing, Guangzhou, Harbin, Nanjing, Shanghai, Shenyang, Tianjin, Taiyuan, Wuhan, Xi'an

Currency – Renminbi (RMB) or yuan (Y) of 10 jiao or 100 fen

Population – 1,330,141,295 rising at 0.49 per cent a year (2010 est); Han Chinese (91.5 per cent), around 55 ethnic minorities 8.5 per cent (2000)

Religion – officially atheist, but permits four state-registered religions: Buddhism, Taoism, Islam, and Catholic and Protestant Christianity. It is difficult to estimate numbers, as many congregations worship in private; Mahayana Buddhism and Taoism are the predominant faiths but Christianity is growing rapidly

Language – Mandarin (official), Cantonese, Shanghainese, Fuzhou, Xiang, Gan, Taiwanese

Population density – 143 per sq. km (2009)

Urban population – 43 per cent (2008 est)

Median age (years) – 35.2 (2010 est)

National anthem – 'Yiyongjun Jinxingqu' ['The March of the Volunteers']

National day – 1 October (Founding of People's Republic)

Life expectancy (years) – 74.51 (2010 est)

Mortality rate – 6.89 (2010 est)

Birth rate – 12.17 (2010 est)

Infant mortality rate – 16.51 (2010 est)

Death penalty – Retained

CPI score – 3.5 (2010)

CLIMATE AND TERRAIN
China is twice the size of western Europe and contains a vast range of landscapes and climates. Two-thirds of the country is hilly or mountainous. The highest mountains are on the Tibetan plateau, in the west of the country, where the highest elevation is 8,850m (Mt Everest). To the north of the Tibetan plateau, the land drops to the arid, semi-desert steppes bisected by the Tian Shan mountains; the country's lowest elevation is −154m at Turpan Pendi. The southern plains and east coast have the most fertile land, irrigated by the Huang He (Yellow), Chang Jiang (Yangtze) and Xi Jiang (West) rivers, and are the most heavily populated areas.

There are seven climate zones. The north-east has cold winters, fierce winds, warm and humid summers and erratic rainfall. The mountainous south-west has mild winters and warm summers. Inner Mongolia has cold winters and hot summers. Central China has warm and humid summers with occasional tropical cyclones. South China is partly tropical with heavy rainfall. The high Tibet plateau is subject to harsh winters. Xinjiang and the west have a desert climate, with cold winters and little rain.

HISTORY AND POLITICS
China was ruled by imperial dynasties from the second millennium BC. The last emperor of the Qing dynasty abdicated in 1912 after a revolution broke out in 1911. Central authority collapsed, leading to a period of chaos and regional warlord domination, as neither the Guomindang (KMT), led by Sun Yat-sen, nor the Chinese Communist Party (CCP), founded in 1921, were able to unify the whole country. The KMT established a government in Nanjing in 1927 but the CCP broke with it in the mid-1930s and fled into the interior (the Long March, 1934–5). The conflict between them also hindered their individual and joint efforts to resist

Japanese encroachment; Japan occupied Manchuria in 1932, and most northern and coastal areas of China by 1939. Japan's occupation was ended by its defeat by the Allies in 1945. Despite Allied support after 1941 for the KMT, then led by Chiang Kai-shek, the Communists established control over large areas of China in the early 1940s, seizing the territory abandoned by Japan in 1945. Following a civil war (1946–9) won by the Communists, the CCP inaugurated the People's Republic of China (PRC), and the KMT went into exile in Taiwan. The USA continued to recognise the Chiang Kai-shek regime as the rightful government of China until 1971, when the PRC took over China's membership of the UN from Taiwan.

Under Mao Zedong (b. 1893 d. 1976), political and economic restructuring was undertaken, including the collectivisation of agriculture and industry, the establishment of communes and the redistribution of land. Mao's 'Great Leap Forward' (1958–61), an attempt to industrialise rural areas, resulted in a famine in which 30–40 million people died. China was plunged into chaos during the Cultural Revolution (1966–70), when the Red Guards were formed to rid the country of 'rightist elements'.

Following Mao's death, the ousted Deng Xiaoping (b. 1904 d. 1997) was recalled and he became the dominant force within the party; from 1978 he promoted an 'open door' policy in foreign relations, economic modernisation and social liberalisation. The party congresses of 1982 and 1987 reaffirmed Deng's policies, and in 1987 most of the revolutionary generation was replaced in the most senior posts by younger, more liberal supporters of reform.

Liberalisation suffered a setback in April–May 1989, when student-led pro-democracy demonstrations, centred on Tiananmen Square in Beijing, were brutally repressed by the army; some estimate that over 3,000 protesters died. The events strengthened the position of conservatives within the leadership, who readopted policies of centralisation based on Marxist ideology.

Although Deng retired from his last official post in 1989, he retained effective control until late 1994 and, at his instigation, the emphasis shifted back to economic reform in 1992. The 1992 party congress endorsed faster, bolder economic reforms and a socialist market economy. Following Deng's death the government continued to promote economic growth, and also sought to improve China's standing in the international community.

In 2003 Hu Jintao was elected by the National People's Congress as the new state president and Wen Jaibao was elected as premier; both were re-elected to their posts at the 2008 party congress. Hu is pursuing policies in health, education, the environment and other areas which are intended to address the social inequalities created by the economic growth of recent years.

HUMAN RIGHTS
Liberalisation has allowed ordinary people greater personal choice: they can now travel freely, for example, or change professions. However, freedom of expression, religion and association are still tightly controlled, and the regime firmly suppresses dissent by ethnic minorities or other groups that it perceives as a threat to its authority. This has led to moves against separatists from the Uygur Muslim minority group in Xinjiang Autonomous Region since the 1990s, the banning of the Falun Gong spiritual movement in 1999 and the violent suppression of demonstrations in Tibet in 2008. Religious gatherings that have not been approved by the state-sanctioned religious bodies are broken up by the authorities and their leaders harassed; despite this, all religions are experiencing a revival throughout China, and underground Protestant churches in particular are growing rapidly.

POLITICAL SYSTEM
The Communist Party of China is the dominant political party, and all elements of the political system are subordinate to it. A party congress is held every five years and elects the Politburo and its standing committee. This standing committee is the policy- and decision-making body and the *de facto* government.

Under the 1982 constitution, the National People's Congress is the highest organ of state power. It has 2,987 members, indirectly elected for a five-year term, and holds only one full session a year; between sessions, its work is delegated to its standing committee. The congress elects the premier and, on his nomination, the State Council. The head of state is the president, also elected by the congress, who serves a five-year term, renewable once.

Deputies to people's congresses at the primary level are directly elected by the voters from a list of approved candidates. These congresses elect the deputies to the congress at the next highest level. Deputies to the National People's Congress are elected by the provincial and municipal people's congresses, and by the armed forces.

Local government is conducted through people's governments at provincial/municipal, prefecture/city, county/district, township and village levels. There are 22 provinces (Taiwan is claimed as a 23rd province), four municipalities directly under the central government, five autonomous regions, and two special administrative areas; provinces may contain autonomous counties or towns for ethnic minorities.

HEAD OF STATE
President, Hu Jintao, *elected* 15 March 2003, *re-elected* March 2008
Vice-President, Xi Jinping

STATE COUNCIL *as at May 2011*
Premier, Wen Jiabao
Vice-Premiers, Zhang Dejiang; Li Keqiang; Hui Liangyu; Wang Qishan
State Councillors, Dai Bingguo; Liang Guanglie *(National Defence);* Meng Jianzhu *(Public Security);* Ma Kai *(Secretary-General of the State Council);* Liu Yandong

SELECTED GOVERNMENT MEMBERS *as at May 2011*
Civil Affairs, Li Liguo
Finance, Xie Xuren
Foreign Affairs, Yang Jiechi
State Security, Geng Huichang

EMBASSY OF THE PEOPLE'S REPUBLIC OF CHINA
49–51 Portland Place, London W1B 1JL
T 020-7299 4049 W www.chinese-embassy.org.uk
Ambassador Extraordinary and Plenipotentiary, HE Liu Xiaoming, *apptd* 2010

BRITISH EMBASSY
11 Guang Hua Lu, Jian Guo Men Wai, Beijing 100600
T (+86) (10) 5192 4000 E consular.beijing@fco.gov.uk
W http://ukinchina.fco.gov.uk
Ambassador, HE Sebastian Wood, *apptd* 2010

BRITISH COUNCIL
Cultural and Education Section, British Embassy, 4th Floor
Landmark Building Tower 1, 8 North Dongsanhuan Road,
Chaoyang District, Beijing 100004
T (+86) (10) 6590 6903 W www.britishcouncil.org/china
Director, Joanna Burke

DEFENCE

All three military arms are parts of the People's Liberation Army (PLA). China has at least 66 intercontinental, 204 short range and 118 intermediate ballistic missiles, and 3 nuclear-capable strategic submarines. The army has over 7,050 main battle tanks, 800 light tanks, 2,390 armoured infantry fighting vehicles, 2,700 armoured personnel carriers and 248 multi-role helicopters.

The navy has 71 submarines (3 strategic), 13 destroyers, 65 frigates, over 211 patrol and coastal vessels and 311 combat aircraft. The marines have 124 light tanks and 248 armoured personnel carriers. The air force has 1,687 combat aircraft.

Military budget – US$76,400m (2010)
Military personnel – 2,285,000: army 1,600,000, navy 255,000, air force 300,000, Strategic Missile Forces 100,000; paramilitary 660,000
Conscription duration – 24 months (selective)

ECONOMY AND TRADE

Liberalisation since the 1980s has transformed the economy, developing a more autonomous state sector, a rapidly expanding private sector and a leading presence in global trade and investment. A massive industrial base and transport infrastructure have been constructed, especially in the coastal regions, and the economy has become a free market in all but name, with several stock markets and Shanghai's emergence as a financial centre. China attracts considerable foreign investment and has become a major investor overseas. GDP has grown more than tenfold since 1978, and by some measures China's economy is now the second-largest in the world.

Although some 200 million people who migrated to urban areas have been lifted out of poverty in the past two decades, the effects of the rapid transformation have been unevenly distributed. There are wide income differences between urban and rural areas, poor healthcare provision, lack of access to public services for migrant workers, rampant official corruption and environmental degradation of land, water and air; officials estimate that pollution costs China between 8 and 15 per cent of GDP, and the 2006–11 five-year plan made environmental protection a priority. The government is also keen to increase domestic consumption (a priority of the 2011–16 five-year plan), and so reduce the economy's reliance on exports for growth, especially as foreign demand slowed in 2008 and plummeted in 2009 owing to the global economic downturn. The drop in production caused a sharp rise in unemployment (over 10 million jobs were lost in 2008), but the government used subsidies, stimulus packages, training and infrastructure projects to cushion the impact until growth resumed in late 2009. It is now struggling to contain inflation, which has pushed up prices of basic goods.

China's expansion boosted its need for oil and coal, met initially by imports but increasingly by domestic production. However, to achieve its aim of reducing environmental degradation, China is looking more to nuclear power (the government has contracted to buy five nuclear power generators) and alternative energy generation, such as hydroelectric power from the Three Gorges Dam.

Although rural areas have seen few benefits from the economic transformation and are suffering the effects of rural depopulation and pollution, agriculture remains important; it contributes 9.6 per cent of GDP but employs 38.1 per cent of the workforce. The size of the country, and the variations in terrain and climate, allow a wide variety of produce to be grown. The main crops are rice, cereals, vegetables, peanuts, tea, fruit, cotton and oilseed crops. Livestock is raised in large numbers. Silk farming is one of the oldest industries. Cotton, woollen and silk textiles are manufactured in large quantities.

The highly diversified industrial sector, encompassing heavy industry, manufacturing and construction, contributes 46.8 per cent of GDP and employs 27.8 per cent of the workforce. The services sector accounts for 43.6 per cent of GDP and 34.1 per cent of employment. Tourism is now a major industry.

Exports include machinery, electrical equipment, data processing equipment, garments, textiles, iron and steel, and optical and medical equipment. The principal imports are electrical and other machinery, oil and mineral fuels, optical and medical equipment, metal ores, plastics and organic chemicals. The main trading partners are the USA, Hong Kong, Japan, South Korea, Germany and Taiwan, although trade with Latin America and Africa is growing.

GNI – US$5,028,761m; US$3,650 per capita (2009)
Annual average growth of GDP – 10.3 per cent (2010 est)
Inflation rate – 5 per cent (2010 est)
Population below poverty line – 15.9 per cent (2005 est; based on a poverty line of US$1.25 per day)
Unemployment – 9 per cent (2009 est)
Total external debt – US$406,600m (2010 est)
Imports – US$1,004,200m (2009)
Exports – US$1,201,800m (2009)

BALANCE OF PAYMENTS
Trade – US$184,540m surplus (2010)
Current Account – US$426,107m surplus (2008)

Trade with UK	2009	2010
Imports from UK	£5,130,435,040	£7,305,572,838
Exports to UK	£27,790,721,887	£33,886,950,033

COMMUNICATIONS

The infrastructure created after the civil war has been greatly expanded and modernised since the 1980s. In the past, the principal means of internal communication was by river, the most important of which are the Huang He (Yellow), Chang Jiang (Yangtze) and Xi Jiang (West). These, together with the network of canals connecting them, are still much used, but their overall importance has declined. Coastal port facilities are being improved and the merchant fleet expanded. The main seaports are Shanghai and Dalian in the north, and Guangzhou in the south; Nanjing is the largest river port.

Long-distance internal travel is mostly by air and rail. The length of civil air routes has more than tripled in the past two decades. There are over 500 airports and airfields and several national air carriers. The rail system has 86,000km of track, although only 36,000km is electrified; extension of the Qinghai–Tibet railway is opening up the remote western provinces. The road network has been expanded to over 3.8 million km, making all towns and villages accessible, and the major cities are linked by 65,000km of modern highways.

Motor vehicle ownership is growing rapidly, creating congestion, road safety and pollution problems.

The telecommunications infrastructure is also expanding, although facilities for personal subscribers are unevenly distributed and concentrated in the cities, industrial centres and major towns. Mobile phone distribution is growing rapidly and, at 747 million in 2009, is more than double fixed-line subscriptions. There were 389 million internet users in 2009.

EDUCATION AND HEALTH

Primary education lasts six years and secondary education six years (three years in junior middle school and three optional years in senior middle school).

Literacy rate – 93.63 per cent (2008 est)
Gross enrolment ratio (percentage of relevant age group) – primary 113 per cent; secondary 78 per cent; tertiary 25 per cent (2009 est)
Health expenditure (per capita) – US$177 (2009)
Hospital beds (per 1,000 people) – 4.1 (2004–9)

MEDIA

The Communist Party maintains a firm grip on the media and the internet through surveillance and censorship. It restricts access to foreign news media by blocking websites, radio broadcasts and satellite receivers, limiting rebroadcasting of foreign programming and the distribution of overseas newspapers, and curtailing blogs. Foreign journalists were allowed greater freedom to travel and interview before the 2008 Olympic Games and this has been retained in new regulations issued since. However, Chinese journalists exercise self-censorship; official corruption may be criticised but not the party's monopoly on power.

China's media industry is huge, with television a particularly popular medium: state-run stations offer around 2,100 channels, and in 2010 over 175m households had cable subscription services. Every city has its own newspaper, as well as a local Communist Party publication.

CULTURE

The Chinese language has many dialects, notably Cantonese, Hakka, Amoy, Foochow, Changsha, Nanchang, Wu (Shanghai) and the northern dialect. The common speech, or *putonghua* (often referred to as Mandarin), is based on the northern dialect. The Communists have promoted it as the national language and it is taught throughout the country. Because *putonghua* encourages the use of the spoken language in writing, the old literary style and ideographic form of writing has fallen into disuse. Since 1956, simplified characters have been introduced to make reading and writing easier. In 1958 the National People's Congress adopted a system of romanisation known as *pinyin*.

Chinese literature is one of the oldest in the world. Paper has been used for writing and printing for nearly 2,000 years. The Confucian classics, which formed the basis of traditional Chinese culture, date from the Warring States period (fourth to third centuries BC), as do the earliest texts of Taoism. Histories, philosophical and scientific works, poetry, literary and art criticism, novels and romances survive from most periods.

TIBET

Area – 1,199,164 sq. km
Population – 2,610,000 (2001 est)
Capital – Lhasa

Tibet is a plateau, seldom lower than 3,000m, in south-west China. It forms the frontier with India (boundary imperfectly demarcated), from which it is separated by the Himalayas from Kashmir to Myanmar; Nepal and Bhutan also border it to the south. The Indus, Brahmaputra, Mekong and Yangtze rivers all rise on the Tibet plateau.

Tibet was under Mongol rule almost continuously from the 13th to the 17th centuries. Chinese control grew from the 18th century and direct rule began in 1910, but with the collapse of the Chinese Empire in 1911, Tibet declared its independence and the Dalai Lama ruled undisturbed until Communist rule was established in China. In 1950 Chinese Communist forces invaded Tibet, and in 1951 the Tibetan authorities signed a treaty agreeing joint Chinese-Tibetan rule. A series of revolts against Chinese rule culminated in a 1959 uprising in the capital, which was crushed following several days of fighting after which military rule was imposed. The Dalai Lama fled to India where he and his followers were granted political asylum and established a government in exile. Tibet became an Autonomous Region of China in 1965. Martial law was declared in Tibet in 1989.

The Panchen Lama, the second-highest Lama, remained in Lhasa after 1959; when he died in 1989, China rejected the Dalai Lama's choice of successor and enthroned its own candidate. Subsequent appointments have been handled in a similar manner. Despite occasional talks between the Chinese government and representatives of the Dalai Lama, relations remain poor. In March 2011, the Dalai Lama announced his intention to withdraw from political life, transferring leadership to the prime minister of the Tibetan parliament.

Another source of tension is the large number of Chinese migrants who have settled in Tibet since the 1970s, a development that the Tibetan government-in-exile regards as an attempt to eradicate the culture of the Tibetan people. Chinese now considerably outnumber Tibetans and have benefited disproportionately from the economic development of recent years.

Peaceful anti-Chinese demonstrations in Tibet increased in early 2008 as the imminence of the Beijing Olympics put China's human rights record under greater international scrutiny. The violence of the Chinese crackdown was condemned worldwide, and pro-Tibet activists abroad disrupted the Olympic torch relay in several countries. Resistance and unrest continue: in 2009, in a show of passive resistance, farmers in Tibet and neighbouring provinces refused to till the fields or plant crops; in 2011, demonstrations sparked by the self-immolation of a Tibetan monk in the Sechuan province led to hundreds of arrests.

SPECIAL ADMINISTRATIVE REGIONS

HONG KONG

Xianggang Tebie Xingzhengqu – Hong Kong Special Administrative Region
Area – 1,104 sq. km
Currency – Hong Kong dollar (HK$) of 100 cents
Population – 7,089,705, rising at 0.48 per cent a year (2010 est)
Population density – 6,721 per sq. km (2009)
Flag – Red, with a white bauhinia flower of five petals each containing a red star
National day – 1 July (Establishment Day)
Life expectancy (years) – 81.96 (2010 est)
Birth rate – 7.45 (2010 est)

Mortality rate – 6.91 (2010 est)
Infant mortality rate – 2.91 (2010 est)
Death penalty – Abolished for all crimes (since 2003)
CPI score – 8.4 (2010)

CLIMATE AND TERRAIN
Hong Kong consists of Hong Kong Island, Kowloon and the New Territories (on a peninsula of the mainland in Guangdong province) and over 260 islands, including Lantau Island. It is situated on the south-east coast of China, on the eastern side of the mouth of the Pearl river. Hong Kong Island is about 18km long and 3–8km wide. It is separated from the mainland by a narrow strait. The highest point is Tai Mo Shan (958m). The climate is subtropical, with hot, wet summers and cool, dry winters. Mean monthly temperatures range from 14°C to 31°C. Tropical cyclones occur between May and November, and over 75 per cent of the average annual rainfall of 2,383mm falls between May and September.

HISTORY AND POLITICS
Hong Kong developed as a major regional trading port because of its location on the main Far Eastern trade routes. Hong Kong Island was first occupied by Britain in 1841 and formally ceded to Britain in 1842. Kowloon was acquired in 1860, and the New Territories by a 99-year lease signed in 1898.

In 1984, the UK and China agreed that China would resume sovereignty over Hong Kong in 1997, and on 1 July 1997, Hong Kong became a Special Administrative Region (SAR) of the People's Republic of China. The 1984 joint declaration and the Basic Law (1990) guarantee that the SAR's social and economic systems will remain unchanged for 50 years and grant it a high degree of autonomy.

Although the Basic Law provides for the development of democratic processes, political reform has been slow, prompting frequent demonstrations to demand full democracy or to oppose measures perceived to be repressive. In 2007 the Chinese government said that the chief executive could be directly elected from 2017 and the legislature members from 2020.

Tung Chee-hwa resigned as chief executive in 2005 and Donald Tsang was elected to serve out the rest of his term of office; Tsang was re-elected in 2007. In the 2008 legislative elections, pro-China parties won 35 seats and pro-democracy parties won 23, sufficient for the pro-democracy parties to veto constitutional changes.

POLITICAL SYSTEM
The Basic Law, approved in 1990, has served as Hong Kong's constitution since 1997. Its government is headed by the chief executive, who is elected by a 800-member electoral committee and serves a five-year term. The chief executive is aided by an executive council consisting of 15 principal officials, who are the heads of administrative departments, and 14 non-official members. The legislative council consists of 60 members, 30 directly elected by geographic constituencies, and 30 elected by functional, occupation-based constituencies; they serve a four-year term. At the 2012 elections, the legislative council will be increased to 70 members (an additional five members each for the geographic and functional constituencies) and the electoral committee that elects the chief executive will be increased to 1,200 members.

Chief Executive, Donald Tsang, *elected* 16 June 2005, *sworn in* 24 June 2005, *re-elected* 2007

SELECTED GOVERNMENT MEMBERS *as at May 2011*
Chief Secretary for Administration, Henry Tang
Financial Secretary, John Tsang Chun-wah
Secretary for Security, Ambrose Lee

BRITISH CONSULATE-GENERAL
PO Box 528, 1 Supreme Court Road, Central Hong Kong
T (+852) 2901 3000 E consular@bcg.org.hk
W http://ukinhongkong.fco.gov.uk
Consul-General, Andrew Seaton, *apptd* 2008

BRITISH COUNCIL
3 Supreme Court Road, Admiralty, Hong Kong
T (+852) 2913 5100 W www.britishcouncil.org/hongkong
Director, Peter Upton

ECONOMY AND TRADE
The economy has moved away from manufacturing (which has mostly relocated to mainland China) and is now service-based, with a high reliance on international trade and re-exports. It has developed into a regional corporate and banking centre, and has benefited in recent years from closer integration with China through increased trade, tourism and financial links. Although badly affected by the global economic downturn in 2008–9, the strength of the Chinese economy helped it to recover quickly.

The economy is dominated by the service sector, which accounts for 92 per cent of GDP. The main contributors to this are tourism, financial services and shipping. Industry contributes 8 per cent of GDP. Principal products are textiles, clothing, electronics, plastics, toys, clocks and watches.

The principal export markets are China (51 per cent), the USA and Japan. China is Hong Kong's principal supplier of imported goods (46 per cent).
GNI – US$216,940m; US$31,570 per capita (2009)
Annual average growth of GDP – 5.7 per cent (2010 est)
Inflation rate – 2.2 per cent (2010 est)
Unemployment – 4.6 per cent (2010 est)
Imports – US$347,300m (2009)
Exports – US$318,500m (2009)

BALANCE OF PAYMENTS
Trade – US$43,136m deficit (2010)
Current Account – US$23,373m surplus (2009)

Trade with UK	2009	2010
Imports from UK	£3,558,215,474	£4,463,649,783
Exports to UK	£5,710,218,660	£5,377,455,132

EDUCATION
Education is free and compulsory for children up to the age of 15.
Gross enrolment ratio (percentage of age group) – primary 104 per cent; secondary 82 per cent; tertiary 57 per cent (2009 est)

COMMUNICATIONS
Hong Kong has one of the world's finest natural harbours, and is the third-busiest container port in the world. Dockyard facilities include eight floating drydocks; the largest is capable of docking vessels of up to 150,000 tonnes deadweight. There are two airports, one accommodating international flights. Modern telecommunications systems supported 4.2 million fixed lines, 12.2 million mobile phone subscribers and 4.8 million internet users in 2009.

MACAU (AOMEN)

Aomen Tebie Xingzhengqu – Macau Special Administrative Region

Area – 28.2 sq. km
Currency – Pataca of 100 avos
Population – 567,957 rising at 0.89 per cent a year (2010 est)
Population density – 19,213 per sq. km (2009)
Flag – Green, with a white lotus flower above a white stylised bridge and water, under a large gold five-point star and four gold stars in crescent
National day – 20 December (Establishment Day)
CPI score – 5.0 (2010)

CLIMATE AND TERRAIN
Macau consists of the Macau peninsula and the islands of Coloane and Taipa. It is situated at the western side of the mouth of the Pearl river, bordering Guangdong province in south-east China. It is 64km from Hong Kong. Its area has nearly doubled since the 19th century due to land reclamation. The highest point is Coloane Alto (172m). The climate is subtropical.

HISTORY AND POLITICS
The first Portuguese ship arrived at Macau in 1513 and trade with China commenced in 1553. Macau became a Portuguese colony in 1557; China recognised Portugal's sovereignty over Macau by treaty in 1887. An agreement to transfer the administration of Macau to China was signed in 1987, and Macau became the Macau Special Administrative Region (MSAR) of China on 20 December 1999. Fernando Chui was elected unopposed as chief executive in 2009, and the most recent legislative election was held in September 2009.

The Basic Law (1993) has served as Macao's constitution since 1999. The chief executive is elected by a 300-member election committee and serves a five-year term of office, which may be renewed once. The chief executive is assisted by the ten-member executive council. The legislative assembly has 29 members, who serve for four years; 12 are directly elected in geographic constituencies, ten are indirectly elected in functional constituencies and seven are appointed by the chief executive.

Chief Executive, Fernando Chui Sai On, *elected* July 2009, *sworn in* 20 December 2009

SELECTED GOVERNMENT MEMBERS *as at May 2011*
Economy and Finance, Francis Tam Pak Yuen
Secretary for Administration and Justice, Florinda Rosa Silva Chan

CONSUL-GENERAL
Andrew Seaton, *apptd* 2008, resident at Hong Kong

ECONOMY AND TRADE
The economy is based on tourism and gambling, which have grown rapidly since 2001, and garment and textile manufacturing, which is in decline. Visitors totalled nearly 25 million in 2010, the majority coming from mainland China, where gambling is illegal. The service sector contributes about 97 per cent of GDP and industry 3 per cent. The principal products and exports are clothing, textiles, footwear, toys, electronics, machinery and parts. The main trading partners are Hong Kong, China and the USA.

GNI – US$20,738m; US$39,550 per capita (2009)
Annual average growth of GDP – 1 per cent (2009 est)

Inflation rate – 1.2 per cent (2009)
Imports – US$4,600m (2009)
Exports – US$1,000m (2009)

BALANCE OF PAYMENTS
Trade – US$4,644m deficit (2010)
Current Account – US$4,163m surplus (2004)

Trade with UK	2009	2010
Imports from UK	£25,556,719	£31,516,776
Exports to UK	£18,486,074	£12,898,778

COLOMBIA

República de Colombia – Republic of Colombia

Area – 1,138,910 sq. km
Capital – Bogotá; population, 8,261,650 (2009 est)
Major cities – Barranquilla, Cali, Cartagena, Medellín
Currency – Colombian peso of 100 centavos
Population – 44,205,293 rising at 1.18 per cent a year (2010 est)
Religion – Christian (Roman Catholic 80 per cent, other denominations 14 per cent) (est)
Language – Spanish (official)
Population density – 41 per sq. km (2009)
Urban population – 74 per cent (2008 est)
Median age (years) – 27.6 (2010 est)
National anthem – 'Himno Nacional de la República de Colombia' ['National Anthem of the Republic of Colombia']
National day – 20 July (Independence Day)
Life expectancy (years) – 74.31 (2010 est)
Mortality rate – 5.24 (2010 est)
Birth rate – 17.76 (2010 est)
Infant mortality rate – 16.87 (2010 est)
Death penalty – Abolished for all crimes (since 1910)
CPI score – 3.5 (2010)

CLIMATE AND TERRAIN
Colombia has a coastline on both the Caribbean Sea and the Pacific Ocean. The western, central and eastern ranges of the Andes run from south-west to north-east, separating the arid north-eastern peninsula and the tropical coastal regions in the north and west from the densely forested south-eastern lowlands and the vast tablelands in the east. This last region, having a temperate climate, is the most densely populated part of the country. Elevation extremes range from 5,775m (Pico Cristobal Colon) at the highest point to 0m (Pacific Ocean) at the lowest. The principal rivers are the Magdalena, which flows into the Caribbean; the Guaviare and Meta, tributaries of the Orinocco; and the Caquetá and

Putumayo, which drain into the Amazon basin. The predominantly tropical climate is moderated by altitude in the interior.

HISTORY AND POLITICS

Spanish settlement of the region began in 1525, and Colombia was ruled as part of a vice-royalty until 1810, when independence was declared. In 1819, Simón Bolivar established the Republic of Gran Colombia, consisting of the territories now known as Colombia, Panama, Venezuela and Ecuador, after finally defeating the Spanish. In 1829–30 Venezuela and Ecuador withdrew, and in 1831 the remaining territories formed a separate state, which adopted the name of Colombia in 1866; Panama seceded in 1903.

Power alternated between the Conservative and Liberal parties from the mid-19th century. In 1949, a civil war broke out which lasted until 1957, when the Conservative and Liberal parties formed a coalition government known as the National Front. This arrangement continued until 1974 and was revived in 1978 in an attempt to maintain the rule of law in the face of violence by drugs cartels, a left-wing insurgency and counter-attacks by right-wing paramilitaries. Despite foreign assistance and increased military spending, drug trafficking continues to be widespread, although less of a threat to civil order than hitherto, but the government has been unable to suppress or reach a negotiated settlement with insurgents' leaders despite sporadic peace talks.

In the 2010 legislative elections, parties that supported President Uribe won the majority of seats in both chambers. The 2010 presidential election was won in the second round by former defence minister Juan Manuel Santos Calderón.

INSURGENCIES

Colombia has been dogged by violence since the 1960s, initially from insurgency by left-wing guerrilla groups, mainly the Revolutionary Armed Forces of Colombia (FARC) and the National Liberation Army (ELN), countered by right-wing paramilitaries affiliated with the United Self-Defence Forces of Colombia (AUC), which was suspected of having links with the security forces. In the 1980s, lawlessness increased with the rise of drug-producing and -trafficking cartels. The guerrillas and paramilitaries became involved in these and other crimes, including kidnapping, and often act to protect these sources of funding as much as to further their political aims.

Action against the insurgents and drug cartels since 2002 has extended state control so that the government now has a presence in every municipality. Talks between the government and the FARC and ELN have made little headway, but talks with the AUC from 2004 led to demobilisation of most units in 2006. The level of violence has dropped but drug-eradication programmes are aggressively resisted.

Neighbouring countries are affected by the overspill from the violence in Colombia, and cross-border incursions by Colombian forces in pursuit of the FARC, ELN or AUC have affected relations with both Ecuador and Venezuela in recent years. Venezuela also strongly opposes the USA's military presence in Colombia to counter drug-trafficking.

POLITICAL SYSTEM

Under the 1991 constitution, amended in 2005, the executive president is directly elected for a four-year term, which is renewable once. The bicameral congress comprises the 166-member House of Representatives, and the 102-member senate. All members are directly elected for a four-year term. Two senate seats are reserved for representatives of indigenous people.

HEAD OF STATE
President, Juan Manuel Santos Calderón, *elected* 20 June 2010, *sworn in* 7 August 2010
Vice-President, Angelino Garzón

SELECTED GOVERNMENT MEMBERS *as at June 2011*
Defence, Rodrigo Rivera
Finance, Juan Carlos Echeverry
Foreign Affairs, Maria Angela Holguin
Interior, Justice, German Vargas Lleras

EMBASSY OF COLOMBIA
3 Hans Crescent, London SW1X 0LN
T 020-7589 9177 E elondres@cancilleria.gov.co
W www.colombianembassy.co.uk
Ambassador Extraordinary and Plenipotentiary, HE Mauricio Rodriguez Munera, *apptd* 2009

BRITISH EMBASSY
Carrera 9, No 76–49, Piso 8, Edificio ING Barings, Bogotá D.C.
T (+57) (1) 326 8300 E inquiries.bogota@fco.gov.uk
W http://ukincolombia.fco.gov.uk
Ambassador Extraordinary and Plenipotentiary, HE John Dew, *apptd* 2008

BRITISH COUNCIL
c/o British Embassy
T (+57) (1) 325 9090 W www.britishcouncil.org/colombia
Director, Robert Ness

DEFENCE

The army has 194 armoured personnel carriers. The navy has 4 submarines, 4 frigates and 48 patrol and coastal vessels at 9 bases. The air force has 86 combat aircraft and 41 armed helicopters.
Military expenditure – US$6,180m (2010)
Military personnel – 283,004: army 235,798, navy 33,138, air force 13,758; paramilitary 158,824

ECONOMY AND TRADE

An improving security situation, economic liberalisation and international investment aided economic growth from 2002 to 2008. Although the economy contracted in 2009 owing to the global downturn, it recovered strongly in 2010. The government has encouraged diversification to reduce dependence on a limited range of commodities and markets, and this has led to the growth of new export-orientated industries (particularly textiles, clothing and footwear), and a broader range of export markets.

Services account for around 52.7 per cent of GDP, industry 38 per cent and agriculture 9.3 per cent. Coal, oil, natural gas and hydroelectricity resources are exploited, and hydrocarbons account for about half of mining output; iron ore, nickel, gold, emeralds, copper and other minerals account for the remainder. Major cash crops are coffee, bananas and cut flowers. Cattle are raised in large numbers, and forestry is also important.

The principal trading partners are the USA, China and the EU. Main exports are oil, coffee, coal, nickel, emeralds, garments, bananas and cut flowers. Imports include industrial and transport equipment, consumer goods, chemicals, paper products and fuels.

GNI – US$224,542m; US$4,990 per capita (2009)
Annual average growth of GDP – 4.4 per cent (2010 est)
Inflation rate – 2.6 per cent (2010 est)
Population below poverty line – 46.8 per cent (2008)
Unemployment – 11.2 per cent (2010 est)
Total external debt – US$57,740m (2010 est)
Imports – US$32,900m (2009)
Exports – US$32,800m (2009)

BALANCE OF PAYMENTS
Trade – US$863m deficit (2010)
Current Account – US$4,232m deficit (2009)

Trade with UK	2009	2010
Imports from UK	£165,772,165	£217,847,335
Exports to UK	£527,676,582	£618,806,284

COMMUNICATIONS

The terrain has always hampered internal transport, and historically travel was largely along the rivers, especially the Magdalena. This is still used for some bulk cargo but most long-distance internal travel is now by air. The road network (141,374km) is the main means of freight transport, superseding the 18,000km of waterways as well as the 874km rail system. There are 990 airports and airstrips, although only 116 have surfaced runways. The principal airports are at Bogotá, Barranquilla and Cali. The main seaports are Barranquilla, Cartagena and Santa Marta on the Caribbean Sea and Buenaventura on the Pacific coast. A modern telephone system covers the entire country, but falling mobile phone costs have seen fixed-line density decline to 15 per 100 people, while mobile phone density has risen to 90 per 100 people.

EDUCATION AND HEALTH

Elementary education is free and compulsory for ten years. Most primary schools are run by the Roman Catholic Church and courses in Roman Catholicism are compulsory. There are some Protestant church schools (mainly in the capital). The government finances secondary and university level education. Health care is provided through a mixture of contributory and subsidised health schemes by both the private and the public sector.
Literacy rate – 92.7 per cent (2008 est)
Gross enrolment ratio (percentage of relevant age group) –
    primary 120 per cent; secondary 95 per cent; tertiary
    37 per cent (2009 est)
Health expenditure (per capita) – US$323 (2009)
Hospital beds (per 1,000 people) – 1.0 (2004–9)

MEDIA

There are both state-run television and radio stations and private commercial networks. There are seven main daily newspapers, but television remains the most popular medium. Colombia is one of the most dangerous countries in the world for journalists, who are often targeted by drug traffickers, guerrillas and paramilitary groups. More than 120 Colombian journalists were killed in the 1990s.

THE COMOROS

*Udzima wa Komori / Jumhuriyat al-Qamar al-Muttahidah /
    Union des Comores – Union of the Comoros*

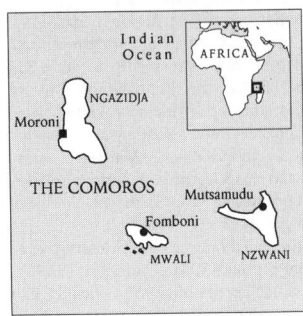

Area – 1,862 sq. km (excluding Mayotte). The Comoros includes the islands of Ngazidja (formerly Grande Comore), Nzwani (Anjouan), Mwali (Moheli) and certain islets in the Indian Ocean. Mayotte, the easternmost island of the archipelago, is a French dependency
Capital – Moroni, on Ngazidja; population, 48,629 (2009 est)
Major towns – Domoni, Fomboni, Mutsamudu
Currency – Comoran franc (KMF) of 100 centimes. The Franc CFA of 100 centimes is also used
Population – 773,407 rising at 2.73 per cent a year (2010 est)
Religion – Muslim (Sunni 99 per cent) (est); Islam is the state religion
Language – Comoran (Shikomoro, a blend of Swahili and Arabic), Arabic, French (all official)
Population density – 354 per sq. km (2009)
Urban population – 28 per cent (2008 est)
Median age (years) – 18.9 (2010 est)
National anthem – 'Udzima wa ya Masiwa' ['The Union of the Great Islands']
National day – 6 July (Independence Day)
Life expectancy (years) – 63.83 (2010 est)
Mortality rate – 7.4 (2010 est)
Birth rate – 34.71 (2010 est)
Infant mortality rate – 64.61 (2010 est)
Death penalty – Retained
CPI score – 2.1 (2010)
Literacy rate – 75.9 per cent (2008 est)

CLIMATE AND TERRAIN

Located in the Mozambique Channel between Africa and Madagascar, Njazidja, Nzwani and Mwali are mountainous volcanic islands in the Comoros archipelago. The highest point is Karthala (2,360m) on Njazidja, an active volcano that last erupted in 2007, and the lowest is 0m (Indian Ocean). The climate is tropical, with a hot, rainy season from November to April. The average temperature ranges from 25°C on the coasts to 22°C in the highlands. The islands are prone to cyclones during the rainy season.

HISTORY AND POLITICS

The islands were settled by a variety of peoples before becoming part of the trading empire of the Shirazis of Persia, who established sultanates in the 15th to 16th centuries. In 1886, France established protectorates over the islands, making them a colony in 1912. They achieved internal self-government in 1961. In a 1974 referendum, the residents of three of the main islands voted in favour of independence, which was declared on 6 July 1975; Mayotte voted to remain part of France.

The republic experienced about 18 coups or attempted coups between 1975 and 1999. Nzwani and Mwani seceded in 1997 but, after a coup in 1999, the military took control of all the islands' governments and reunited the state. Talks on the secessionist crisis produced a new constitution, introducing a federal structure with greater autonomy for the individual islands. Another constitutional crisis arose in June 2007 when the incumbent president of Nzwani, Mohamed Bacar, refused to stand down and then held elections which he claimed to have won. The federal government declared the elections null and void, and in March 2008 federal troops, supported by African Union forces, ousted Bacar.

Elections to the union parliament and the islands' legislatures were held in December 2009; in the union elections, supporters of President Sambi won 20 of the 24 seats. The federal president and island governors were elected in December 2010 and took office in May 2011; the federal presidency election was won by Ikililou Dhoinine, of Mwali.

POLITICAL SYSTEM

The 2002 constitution created a federal structure. Constitutional amendments approved in 2009 downgraded the islands' presidents to governors, ended the rotation of the federal presidency among the islands, and harmonised presidential and legislative terms by extending those of the president and governors.

Under the amended constitution, the union president is elected for a five-year term. The executive president appoints the union ministers. The unicameral Assembly of the Union has 33 members; three are appointed by each of the three island parliaments and 24 are directly elected for a five-year term.

Each island has its own governor and legislative assembly, and each island governor may appoint eight ministers to form a government. Governors serve a five-year term. The islands' governments deal with local issues; foreign affairs, finance, defence, judicial and religious matters remain the responsibility of the union government. There are still areas of dispute, principally over security, budget control and customs revenue.

HEAD OF STATE

President of the Union, Ikililou Dhoinine, *elected* 26 December 2010, *sworn in* 26 May 2011

SELECTED GOVERNMENT MEMBERS *as at June 2011*

Vice-Presidents, Nourdine Bourhane; Fouad Ben Mohadji; Mohamed Ali Soilihi *(Finance, Economy)*
Foreign Relations and Cooperation, Francophone and Arab Affairs, Mohamed Bakri ben Abdoulfatah Charif
Interior, Hamada Abdallah

HONORARY CONSULATE

Flat 6, 24–26 Avenue Road, London, NW8 6BU
T 020 7491 2098 E comorosuk@googlemail.com
Honorary Consul, Khaleb Chehabi

BRITISH AMBASSADOR

HE Nick Leake, *apptd* 2010, resident at Port Louis, Mauritius

ECONOMY AND TRADE

The Comoros is very poor and heavily dependent on foreign aid and technical assistance. It has few natural resources, an uneducated workforce and poor transport infrastructure. Although continuing political tensions hinder government attempts to reform and develop the economy and social welfare provision, progress is sufficient to attract further international aid and debt relief. Unemployment is high and over 20 per cent of the workforce is employed abroad; remittances are a valuable contribution to the economy. Agriculture, fishing and forestry account for about 40 per cent of GDP and employ 80 per cent of the population; service industries account for 56 per cent and the manufacturing industry 4 per cent. The main industries are fishing, tourism and perfume distillation. The main trading partners are France, Turkey, Singapore and China. Principal exports are vanilla, perfume essence, copra and cloves; coconuts, bananas and cassava are also cultivated.

GNI – US$535m; US$810 per capita (2009)
Annual average growth of GDP – 1.7 per cent (2010 est)
Inflation rate – 3 per cent (2007 est)

BALANCE OF PAYMENTS

Trade – US$144m deficit (2010)
Current Account – US$62m deficit (2008)

Trade with UK	2009	2010
Imports from UK	£177,260	£529,380
Exports to UK	£28,120	£36,172

MEDIA

Radio is the primary source of information. National radio and television broadcasting is provided by state-run networks, and some island governments run radio and television stations. There are also privately owned stations, and some areas receive programmes broadcast in Mayotte. Most newspapers are published weekly and have small circulations owing to a weak advertising market and poor distribution. These and other outlets practise self-censorship to avoid harsh government sanctions over material deemed offensive.

DEMOCRATIC REPUBLIC OF THE CONGO

République Démocratique du Congo – Democratic Republic of the Congo

Area – 2,344,858 sq. km
Capital – Kinshasa; population, 8,401,390 (2009 est)
Major cities – Boma, Kananga, Kisangani, Kolwezi, Likasi, Lubumbashi, Mbuji-Mayi

Currency – Congolese franc of 100 centimes
Population – 70,916,439 rising at 3.17 per cent a year
(2010 est). The population is composed of over 200
ethnic groups, including Bantu, Hamitic, Nilotic,
Sudanese and Pygmoid; the four largest tribes, Mongo,
Luba, Kongo (all Bantu) and Mangbtu-Azande
(Hamitic), make up around 45 per cent of the
population
Religion – Christian 79 per cent (Roman Catholic 50 per
cent, Protestant 20 per cent, Kimbanguist 9 per cent),
Muslim 10 per cent (est)
Language – French (official), Lingala, Kingwana (a Swahili
dialect), Kikongo, Tshiluba
Population density – 29 per sq. km (2009)
Urban population – 34 per cent (2008 est)
Median age (years) – 16.5 (2010 est)
National anthem – 'Debout Congolais' ['Stand Up,
Congolese']
National day – 30 June (Independence Day)
Life expectancy (years) – 54.73 (2010 est)
Mortality rate – 11.39 (2010 est)
Birth rate – 42.26 (2010 est)
Infant mortality rate – 79.36 (2010 est)
HIV/AIDS adult prevalence – 1.4 per cent (2009 est)
Death penalty – Retained
CPI score – 2.0 (2010)
Literacy rate – 67.2 per cent (2008 est)
Gross enrolment ratio (percentage of relevant age group) –
primary 90 per cent; secondary 37 per cent; tertiary
6 per cent (2009 est)
Health expenditure (per capita) – US$16 (2009)
Hospital beds (per 1,000 people) – 0.8 (2004–9)

CLIMATE AND TERRAIN

The Democratic Republic of the Congo is Africa's third-
largest country. The state lies on the equator, most of it in
the basin of the river Congo and its principal tributaries,
the Lualaba and the Kasai. A chain of mountains and lakes
(Albert, Edward, Kivu and Tanganyika) runs along the
eastern border. Elevation extremes range from 5,110m
(Mt Ngaliema, also known as Mt Stanley) at the highest
point to 0m (Atlantic Ocean) at the lowest. The climate is
tropical, though cooler in the eastern and southern
highlands. There are different climatic cycles either side
of the equator, which passes through the north of the
country, with a wet season in the north from April to
November and in the south from October to May.

HISTORY AND POLITICS

The state of the Congo, founded in 1885 by King
Leopold II of Belgium, became a Belgian colony in 1908
and gained its independence in 1960. Mobutu Sésé Seko
came to power in a military coup in 1965 and was elected
president in 1970. The *Mouvement Populaire de la
Révolution* (MPR) was the sole legal political party until
the late 1980s, when the regime began moves towards a
multiparty system, but progress was hindered by army
revolts and political disagreements.

In 1996 ethnic conflict in the country's east, largely the
aftermath of the Rwandan genocide in 1994, sparked a
civil war in which the army found itself outgunned by
anti-Mobutu rebels, who were backed by the Rwandan
and Ugandan governments. Under the leadership of
Laurent Kabila, the Alliance of Democratic Forces for the
Liberation of Congo-Zaire (AFDL) captured Kinshasa in
May 1997 and President Mobutu fled. The country,
which had been known as Zaire since 1971, was renamed
the Democratic Republic of the Congo.

In 1998 a rebellion against Kabila's government began
in the east, initiating years of fighting between
government forces and a shifting alliance of rebel groups,
with neighbouring countries lending support to either the
government (Angola, Chad, Kenya, Namibia, Zimbabwe)
or the rebels (Rwanda, Uganda). All parties to the conflict
plundered the country's rich natural resources and the
five-year civil war left an estimated 4 million dead from
violence, famine and disease. A disengagement agreement
was implemented in early 2001, and a power-sharing
agreement between the government and the main rebel
groups was concluded in 2002.

Despite a number of coup attempts and occasional
clashes with errant rebels, a fragile peace has held in much
of the country, apart from the eastern provinces. These
remain unstable, with continuing conflict between rebel
militias and the army. The civilian population of these
provinces have suffered atrocities by both sides, and are
also the victims of Rwandan and Ugandan insurgents.
A UN peacekeeping operation, established in 1999, was
replaced in mid-2010 by a stabilisation mission with a
mandate due to expire in June 2012.

Joseph Kabila succeeded his father Laurent
(assassinated in 2001) as president. After a period of
transitional government, a new constitution came into
effect in 2006 and presidential and legislative elections
were held. The presidential election was won in the
second round in October 2006 by Joseph Kabila. His
People's Party for Reconstruction and Development
(PPRD) won the largest number of seats in both
legislative chambers. The PPRD became the major
partner in a coalition government formed in February
2007. The next presidential and legislative elections are
scheduled for 27 November 2011.

POLITICAL SYSTEM

Under the 2006 constitution, the executive president is
directly elected for a five-year term, renewable once.
The bicameral *Parlement* consists of the National Assembly,
which has 500 members directly elected for a five-year
term, and the senate, which has 108 members elected by
the provincial assemblies to serve a five-year term, plus
former elected presidents, who are senators for life.

HEAD OF STATE
President, Maj.-Gen. Joseph Kabila, *sworn in* 26 January
2001, *sworn in as president of the transitional government*
7 April 2003, *elected* 29 October 2006

SELECTED GOVERNMENT MEMBERS *as at June 2011*
Prime Minister, Adolphe Muzito
Deputy Prime Ministers, Simon Buluphy Galati, Adolphe
Bwana N'sefu *(Interior)*
Finance, Matata Ponyo Mapon
Foreign Affairs and International Cooperation, Alexis
Thambwe Mwamba

EMBASSY OF THE DEMOCRATIC REPUBLIC OF THE
CONGO
45–47 Great Portland Street, London W1W 7LT
T 020-7580 3931
Ambassador Extraordinary and Plenipotentiary, HE Barnabé
Kikaya Bin Karubi, *apptd* 2009

BRITISH EMBASSY
83 Avenue du Roi Baudouin, Gombe, Kinshasa
T (+243) 81 330 0252/3/4 W http://ukindrc.fco.gov.uk
Ambassador Extraordinary and Plenipotentiary, HE Neil
Wigan, *apptd* 2010

DEFENCE

The army has 49 main battle tanks, 20 armoured infantry fighting vehicles and 138 armoured personnel carriers. The navy has 3 patrol and coastal combatant vessels. The air force has 5 combat-capable aircraft and 4 armed helicopters.

Military budget – US$197m (2010)
Military personnel – 144,000–159,000 (est): Central Staffs: 14,000 (est), army 110,000–120,000, navy 6,703, air force 2,548, Republican Guard 6,000–8,000

ECONOMY AND TRADE

A decade of civil war left the country with a huge external debt, little infrastructure, widespread corruption and an environment that discourages foreign investment. Improved stability since 2003 has allowed some economic growth, although the global downturn caused the economy to contract in 2008–9. Government reforms, international aid and debt relief are helping the economy in its slow recovery.

The country has great potential wealth in the form of immense natural resources, including copper, cobalt, diamonds, gold, silver, uranium, other minerals, coal, oil, timber and hydroelectric power; mining is the largest source of export income. Agriculture contributes 37.4 per cent of GDP, the services sector 36.6 per cent and industry 26 per cent. Apart from mining and mineral processing, the main industrial activities are the production of textiles, plastics, footwear, cigarettes, metal products, processed food, beverages, timber and cement, and ship repair. Oil deposits are exploited off the Congo estuary, and hydroelectric schemes on the river Congo supply power to the major cities.

The main trading partners are China, South Africa, Belgium, Zambia and the USA. Principal exports are diamonds, gold, copper, cobalt, wood products, crude oil and coffee. The main imports are foodstuffs, mining and other machinery, transport equipment and fuels.

GNI – US$9,831m; US$160 per capita (2009)
Annual average growth of GDP – 3 per cent (2010 est)
Inflation rate – 26.2 per cent (2010 est)
Total external debt – US$4,300m (2009 est)

BALANCE OF PAYMENTS
Trade – US$1,307m surplus (2010)
Current Account – US$1,839m deficit (2008)

Trade with UK	2009	2010
Imports from UK	£12,925,732	£14,913,224
Exports to UK	£17,885,141	£22,940,042

COMMUNICATIONS

The transport infrastructure is undeveloped owing to the terrain, poverty and warfare. The river Congo and its main tributaries provide 15,000km of waterways, and the 4,000km rail system links the interior to the rivers and to the great lakes in the east. The system also connects with neighbouring states, through which east and south African ports can be accessed. There are approximately 153,497km of roads, of which 2,794km are surfaced. The country has nearly 200 airports and airfields, the principal airports being at Kinshasa, Kananga, Goma, Gemena and Mbandaka. The principal seaports are at Matadi and Boma. Under a 2009 trade agreement, China is building roads and railways in the country in return for mineral concessions.

The telecommunications infrastructure is poor, with limited coverage in and between urban areas. Fixed-line connections are fewer than one per 1,000, but mobile phone distribution is growing rapidly, with a density exceeding 15 per 100 people in 2009.

MEDIA

The state-controlled Radio-Télévision Nationale Congolaise (RTNC) and La Voix du Congo have the greatest influence and broadcast reach. There are dozens of private and commercial television stations and over 100 radio stations; the UN- and Swiss-sponsored Radio Okapi has become one of the most popular. Around 15 newspapers are published regularly in Kinshasa. Dissident media workers can face threats, violence and arrest; despite this, there remains a culture of critical journalism and some publications openly endorse opposition parties.

REPUBLIC OF THE CONGO

République du Congo – Republic of the Congo

Area – 342,000 sq. km
Capital – Brazzaville; population, 1,292,390 (2009 est)
Major cities – Loubomo, Pointe-Noire
Currency – Franc CFA of 100 centimes
Population – 4,125,916 rising at 2.81 per cent a year (2010 est); Kongo (48 per cent), Sangha (20 per cent), Teke (17 per cent) and M'Bochi (12 per cent) (est) are the largest of the 15 main Bantu groups
Religion – Christian 50 per cent (Roman Catholic 45 per cent), indigenous religions (predominantly animist) 48 per cent, Muslim 2 per cent (est)
Language – French (official), Lingala, Monokutuba, Kikongo
Population density – 11 per sq. km (2009)
Urban population – 61 per cent (2008 est)
Median age (years) – 16.9 (2010 est)
National anthem – 'La Congolaise' ['The Congolese']
National day – 15 August (Independence Day)
Life expectancy (years) – 54.54 (2010 est)
Mortality rate – 11.75 (2010 est)
Birth rate – 41.01 (2010 est)
Infant mortality rate – 77.93 (2010 est)
HIV/AIDS adult prevalence – 3.4 per cent (2009 est)
Death penalty – Retained (not used since 1982)
CPI score – 2.1 (2010)

CLIMATE AND TERRAIN

The republic, which lies on the equator, is covered by grassland, mangrove and dense rainforest. The land rises from the narrow Atlantic coastal plain to a central plateau; in the north and east it falls to the northern part of the basin of the river Congo, which forms part of the border with the Democratic Republic of the Congo, and to the valleys of the Sangha and Alima rivers in the north. Elevation extremes range from 903m (Mt Berongou) at the highest point to 0m at the lowest (Atlantic Ocean). The climate is tropical. The annual daily temperature in Brazzaville is between 28°C and 33°C and humidity is high. Outside of the main dry season between June and September, the country is prone to flooding.

HISTORY AND POLITICS

The first European visitors to the area were the Portuguese, who established slave trading in the 16th century. The French established a colonial presence in the area in the 1880s and, as Middle Congo, it was part of French Equatorial Africa from 1910. It became independent as the Republic of the Congo on 17 August 1960.

One-party socialism was introduced in 1964; the Congolese Labour Party (PCT) was set up shortly after a military coup in 1968 and continued to rule until 1990, when Marxism was renounced and, after popular pressure, the PCT abandoned its monopoly of power. Elections in 1993 left the PCT a minority party, and the power shift destabilised the country, with factional fighting after the 1993 election, a civil war between 1997 and 1999 following Denis Sassou-Nguesso's deposition of the elected president, and a renewed insurgency by opponents of the PCT over the manipulation of the 2002 elections. A peace accord ended the insurgency in 2003 but the peace remains fragile and remnants of the rebel militias are still active in the south of the country, where many have turned to banditry.

Sassou-Nguesso was elected president in 2002, and was re-elected in 2009; the legitimacy of both victories was suspect after the barring or withdrawal of opponents, fraud and other irregularities. In the 2007 legislative election, which was boycotted by about 40 opposition parties, the PCT and its allies retained their large majority.

POLITICAL SYSTEM

Under the 2002 constitution, parties organised on regional, ethnic or religious lines are banned. The executive president is directly elected for a seven-year term, renewable once, and appoints the cabinet. The bicameral *Parlement* comprises the National Assembly, with 137 members directly elected for a five-year term, and the senate, which has 72 members indirectly elected for a six-term term, half of the members retiring every three years.

HEAD OF STATE

President, Denis Sassou-Nguesso, *took power* October 1997, *elected* 10 March 2002, *re-elected* 2009

SELECTED GOVERNMENT MEMBERS *as at June 2011*
Economy, Pierre Moussa
Finance, Gilbert Ondongo
Foreign Affairs, Basil Ikouebe
Defence, Charles Zacharie Bowao

EMBASSY OF THE REPUBLIC OF THE CONGO
37 bis Rue Paul Valéry, 75116 Paris, France
T (+33) (1) 4500 6057
Ambassador Extraordinary and Plenipotentiary, HE Henri Lopes, *apptd* 1999

BRITISH AMBASSADOR
HE Neil Wigan, *apptd* 2010, resident at Kinshasa, DR of the Congo

DEFENCE

The army has over 40 main battle tanks and 68 armoured personnel carriers. The navy has 3 patrol and coastal combatant vessels at a base at Pointe-Noire. The air force has 2 armed helicopters.

Military budget – US$218m (2010)
Military personnel – 10,000: army 8,000, navy 800, air force 1,200; paramilitary 2,000

ECONOMY AND TRADE

A decade of civil conflict left the country with a high external debt, a devastated infrastructure and widespread poverty. Since 2003 the government has made efforts to address these problems and has benefited from debt relief in 2006, 2007 and 2010.

Oil production is the backbone of the economy and the recent recovery in oil prices has boosted GDP. Mining (particularly of diamonds), forestry, brewing, agricultural processing and cement production are the other main industries. Agriculture, which is mostly at subsistence level, accounts for 4.4 per cent of GDP, industry for 63.7 per cent and services for 32 per cent.

The main trading partners are China, the USA and France. Principal exports are oil, timber, plywood, sugar, cocoa, coffee and diamonds. Imports are mainly capital equipment, construction materials and foodstuffs.

GNI – US$6,869m; US$2,080 per capita (2009)
Annual average growth of GDP – 10.5 per cent (2010 est)
Inflation rate – 5.2 per cent (2010 est)
Imports – US$2,700m (2009)
Exports – US$5,700m (2009)

BALANCE OF PAYMENTS
Trade – US$6,042m surplus (2010)
Current Account – US$148m deficit (2008)

Trade with UK	2009	2010
Imports from UK	£76,447,225	£72,969,155
Exports to UK	£7,774,670	£45,732,522

COMMUNICATIONS

Pointe-Noire is the main seaport and also the centre of the offshore oil industry. It is linked to Brazzaville by rail and road. Brazzaville is the main river port, lying on the river Congo which, with the river Oubangui, provides 1,120km of commercially navigable waterways. There are 886km of railways and 17,289km of roads, 864km of which are surfaced. Six of the 25 airports and airfields have surfaced runways. The fixed-line telephone network is limited and unreliable. Mobile phone distribution has grown rapidly, reaching a density of over 50 per 100 people by 2008.

EDUCATION AND HEALTH

Literacy rate – 81.1 per cent (2008 est)
Gross enrolment ratio (percentage of relevant age group) – primary 120 per cent; tertiary 6 per cent (2009 est)
Health expenditure (per capita) – US$70 (2009)
Hospital beds (per 1,000 people) – 1.6 (2004–9)
HIV/AIDS adult prevalence – 3.3 per cent (2007 est)

MEDIA

Brazzaville is the centre of the country's print media, with five privately owned newspapers regularly published there. These are free to criticise the government. TV Congo is the only television station and is controlled by the state. Two government radio stations, Radio Congo and Radio Brazzaville, exist alongside commercial and community stations. International news broadcasts from the Democratic Republic of the Congo can be received in the capital. Prison sentences for libel and insult were abolished in 2001.

COSTA RICA

República de Costa Rica – Republic of Costa Rica

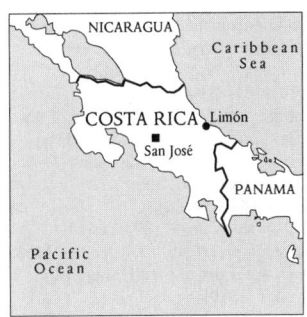

Area – 51,100 sq. km
Capital – San José; population, 1,415,510 (2009 est)
Major towns – Alajuela, Liberia, Limón, Paraíso, San Francisco
Currency – Costa Rican colón of 100 céntimos
Population – 4,516,220 rising at 1.35 per cent a year (2010 est)
Religion – Christian (Roman Catholic 70 per cent, Evangelical Protestant 17 per cent) (est)
Language – Spanish (official), English
Population density – 90 per sq. km (2009)
Urban population – 63 per cent (2008 est)
Median age (years) – 28.4 (2010 est)
National anthem – 'Noble Patria, Tu Hermosa Bandera' ['Noble Fatherland, Your Beautiful Flag']
National day – 15 September (Independence Day)
Life expectancy (years) – 77.54 (2010 est)
Mortality rate – 4.29 (2010 est)
Birth rate – 16.65 (2010 est)
Infant mortality rate – 9.72 (2010 est)
Death penalty – Abolished for all crimes (since 1877)
CPI score – 5.3 (2010)
Literacy rate – 96.1 per cent (2008 est)
Gross enrolment ratio (percentage of relevant age group) – primary 110 per cent; secondary 96 per cent (2009 est)
Health expenditure (per capita) – US$668 (2009)
Hospital beds (per 1,000 people) – 1.32 (2004–9)

CLIMATE AND TERRAIN

The Cordillera de Guanacaste (north-west), Cordillera de Talamanca and Cordillera Central (south-east) form a chain of volcanic mountain ranges that traverse the country from north to south. A central valley lies between the ranges, and the land slopes to plains on the Pacific and Caribbean coasts. Elevation extremes range from 3,810m (Cerro Chirripó Grande) to 0m (Pacific Ocean) at the lowest. The climate is tropical, with an average annual temperature of 24°C, and a wet season from May to November. The area is subject to occasional earthquakes, hurricanes, flooding and landslides.

HISTORY AND POLITICS

Visited by Columbus in 1502, Costa Rica was colonised by the Spanish from the 1560s and remained under Spanish rule until Central America gained its independence in 1821. Costa Rica was part of a Central American federation of former Spanish provinces from 1823 until its secession in 1838. Political unrest in the mid-20th century led to a brief civil war in 1948, after which the army was abolished and replaced with a national guard. Subsequently power alternated between the two main political parties, the National Liberation Party (PLN) and the Social Christian Unity Party (PUSC), but in recent years the scandal-ridden PUSC has lost ground to emerging new parties.

In the 2010 legislative elections, the PLN remained the largest party with 24 seats but failed to win an outright majority. The simultaneous presidential election was won by the PLN candidate, Laura Chinchilla, who became the country's first female president.

POLITICAL SYSTEM
Under the 1949 constitution, the executive president is directly elected for a four-year term. The unicameral legislative assembly has 57 members directly elected for a four-year term.

HEAD OF STATE
President, Laura Chinchilla, *elected* 7 February 2010, *sworn in* 8 May 2010
First Vice-President, Alfio Piva
Second Vice-President, Luis Liberman

SELECTED GOVERNMENT MEMBERS *as at June 2011*
Finance, Fernando Herrero
Foreign Affairs, René Castro
Economy, Mayi Antillón

EMBASSY OF COSTA RICA
14 Lancaster Gate, London W2 3LH
T 020-7706 8844 E embassy@costaricanembassy.co.uk
Ambassador Extraordinary and Plenipotentiary, HE Pilar Saborío de Rocafort, *apptd* 2007

BRITISH EMBASSY
Apartado 815–1007, Edificio Centro Colón (11th Floor), San José 1007
T (+506) 2258 2025 E consular.costarica@fco.gov.uk
W http://ukincostarica.fco.gov.uk
Ambassador Extraordinary and Plenipotentiary, HE Tom Kennedy, LVO, *apptd* 2006

DEFENCE

Costa Rica maintains a national guard of 9,800 paramilitaries. The coastguard unit has 8 patrol and coastal vessels at 6 bases.
Security Budget – US$215m (2010)
Military Personnel – 9,800 (all paramilitary)

ECONOMY AND TRADE

Sixty years of political stability have allowed steady economic growth, the creation of a social welfare system and a reduction in poverty to less than 20 per cent of the population. Although the economy contracted in 2008 owing to the global downturn, the impact of this on government spending was tempered by reductions in the internal and external debt since 2006.

Tourism is the largest single industry, and with one-third of the country now national parkland or nature reserve, eco-tourism is on the increase. The manufacturing industry accounts for 22.9 per cent of GDP, the principal products being microprocessors, foodstuffs, medical equipment, textiles, clothing, construction materials, fertiliser and plastic goods. The agricultural sector contributes 6.3 per cent of GDP; the principal products are tropical fruit, coffee, ornamental plants, sugar, rice, vegetables, meat and timber.

The main trading partners are the USA, China, the Netherlands and Mexico. The chief exports are tropical fruit, coffee, plants, sugar, beef, seafood, electrical components and medical equipment. The chief imports are raw materials, consumer goods, capital equipment, petrol and construction materials.

GNI – US$28,767m; US$6,260 per capita (2009)
Annual average growth of GDP – 3.5 per cent (2010 est)
Inflation rate – 5.8 per cent (2010 est)
Population below poverty line – 16 per cent (2006 est)
Unemployment – 6.6 per cent (2010 est)
Total external debt – US$9,126m (2010 est)
Imports – US$11,500m (2009)
Exports – US$8,700m (2009)

BALANCE OF PAYMENTS
Trade – US$4,229m deficit (2010)
Current Account – US$2,754m deficit (2008)

Trade with UK	2009	2010
Imports from UK	£24,779,401	£35,378,915
Exports to UK	£250,523,715	£213,149,918

COMMUNICATIONS
The chief seaports are Limón on the Atlantic coast, through which the majority of exported coffee passes, and Puntarenas on the Pacific coast. There are 151 airports and airfields, 39 of which have surfaced runways; the principal ones are at San José and Limón. The national air carrier is LACSA. There are 278km of railways, none of which is in use, and 35,330km of roads, 8,621km of which are surfaced. The telephone system is modern and efficient, although mobile phone subscriptions are only slightly higher than fixed-line subscriptions.

CÔTE D'IVOIRE

République de Côte d'Ivoire – Republic of the Ivory Coast

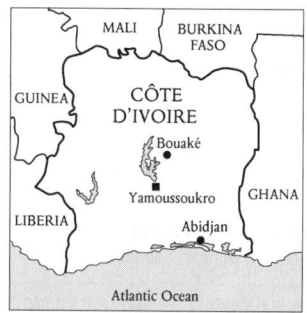

Area – 322,463 sq. km
Capital – Yamoussoukro (since 1983); population, 808,093 (2009 est); slow progress in transferring functions means that the former capital, Abidjan (population 4,008,990; 2009 est), remains the seat of government at present
Major cities – Abidjan, Bouaké, Daloa, Korhogo
Currency – Franc CFA of 100 centimes

Population – 21,058,798 rising at 2.11 per cent a year (2010 est); over 60 ethnic groups, including the Akan (42.1 per cent), Voltaiques or Gur (17.6 per cent), Northern Mandes (16.5 per cent), Krous (11 per cent), Southern Mandes (10 per cent) (est)
Religion – Christian 35 per cent, Muslim 35 per cent, indigenous religions 25 per cent (est). Many Christians and Muslims incorporate indigenous beliefs into their worship
Language – French (official), around 60 African languages of which Dioula is the most widely spoken
Population density – 66 per sq. km (2009)
Urban population – 49 per cent (2008 est)
Median age (years) – 19.4 (2010 est)
National anthem – 'L'Abidjanaise' ['Song of Abidjan']
National day – 7 August (Independence Day)
Life expectancy (years) – 56.19 (2010 est)
Mortality rate – 10.43 (2010 est)
Birth rate – 31.48 (2010 est)
Infant mortality rate – 66.43 (2010 est)
HIV/AIDS adult prevalence – 3.4 per cent (2009 est)
Death penalty – Abolished for all crimes (since 2000)
CPI score – 2.2 (2010)
Literacy rate – 48.7 per cent (2008 est)
Gross enrolment ratio (percentage of relevant age group) – primary 70 per cent; tertiary 8 per cent (2007 est)
Health expenditure (per capita) – US$55 (2009)
Hospital beds (per 1,000 people) – 0.4 (2004–9)

CLIMATE AND TERRAIN
The land rises from a coastal plain to a large interior plateau with mountains in the north and west. Coastal lagoons give way to tropical rainforest in the centre and savannah in the north; deforestation means that the area of savannah is increasing. The country is dissected by the Sassandra, Bandama and Komoé rivers, the first two forming large central lakes. Elevation extremes range from 1,752m (Mt Nimba) at the highest point to 0m (Gulf of Guinea) at the lowest. The climate is tropical in the south and semi-arid in the north. The south has two rainy seasons (May to July, October to November) and the north one (June to September). Average temperatures range from 24°C in August to 27°C in March.

HISTORY AND POLITICS
The first European visitors were Portuguese navigators in the 1460s, and Europeans established the ivory trade and some slave trading in the 16th century. The area came under French influence from 1842, and Côte d'Ivoire became a protectorate in 1889 and a colony in 1893, although it was not entirely pacified until 1912. It achieved self-government in 1958, and became independent on 7 August 1960 as a one-party state with Felix Houphouët-Boigny as president. A multiparty system was introduced in 1990.

The post-independence period of stability ended after President Houphouët-Boigny's death in 1993. The adoption of xenophobia as a political tool in the late 1990s opened up religious and ethnic divisions, particularly between the Muslim north and the Christian south and west of the country. These emerged in factional violence following the 2000 presidential election, won by Laurent Gbagbo. Reconciliation moves were progressing when a mutiny in 2002 developed into a rebellion that plunged the country into civil war.

The civil war ended in 2003 with a ceasefire that left the country divided between the government-controlled south and the rebel-held north, with international peacekeeping troops deployed to maintain a buffer zone between the two. Despite the ceasefire, clashes continued, drawing in UN peacekeepers in late 2004. The government of national unity formed in 2003 collapsed in 2004, but further talks in 2006–7 resulted in a new power-sharing agreement in March 2007, with rebel leader Guillaume Soro becoming prime minister of the transitional government. Although the country was officially reunited in April 2007, difficulties in preparing electoral registers continued to delay elections originally scheduled for 2005.

President Gbagbo and Alassane Ouattara both claimed victory in the 2010 presidential election. Ouattara's victory was endorsed by the Independent Electoral Commission and internationally, but Gbagbo refused to cede power, leading to four months of political stalemate and escalating violence in Abidjan until April 2011, when Ouattara's militia took control of most of the country and, supported by UN and French troops, captured Gbagbo.

POLITICAL SYSTEM
Under the 2000 constitution, the executive president is directly elected for a five-year term, renewable once. The president appoints the prime minister and the other ministers, who are nominated by the prime minister. The unicameral National Assembly has 225 members, directly elected for a five-year term.

HEAD OF STATE
President, Alassane Ouattara, *elected* 28 November 2010, *sworn in* 6 May 2011

SELECTED GOVERNMENT MEMBERS *as at June 2011*
Prime Minister, Defence, Guillaume Soro
Interior, Hamed Bakayoko
Foreign Affairs, Jean-Marie Kacou
Finance and Economy, Charles Koffi Diby

EMBASSY OF THE REPUBLIC OF CÔTE D'IVOIRE
2 Upper Belgrave Street, London SW1X 8BJ
T 020-7235 6991
Ambassador Extraordinary and Plenipotentiary, HE
   Philippe Djangoné-Bi, *apptd* 2007

BRITISH AMBASSADOR
HE Peter Jones, *apptd* 2011, resident at Accra, Ghana

DEFENCE
The army has 10 main battle tanks, 10 armoured infantry fighting vehicles and 41 armoured personnel carriers. The navy has 3 patrol and coastal combatant vessels. Little of the air force is combat capable; it may have 1 armed helicopter.
Military expenditure – US$330m (2009 est)
Military personnel – 17,050: army 6,500, navy 900, air force 700, Presidential Guard 1,350, gendarmerie 7,600; paramilitary 1,500

ECONOMY AND TRADE
The country was one of the most prosperous in the region, attracting large numbers of migrant workers from neighbouring countries, until the political turbulence of the late 1990s caused many to return home. The civil war particularly damaged the economy in the north (the cotton-growing area), although recovery is beginning, and continuing political instability has hampered

diversification away from agriculture, which makes the economy vulnerable to price fluctuations in its key exports. However, since 2006, revenue from oil, gas and refined products has outstripped earnings from cocoa, and offshore exploration for other deposits continues.

Agriculture accounts for 28.2 per cent of GDP, industry for 21.3 per cent and services for 50.6 per cent. Agriculture employs around 68 per cent of the workforce, producing cocoa (of which Côte d'Ivoire is the world's largest producer and exporter), coffee, cotton, bananas, pineapples and palm oil for export. The principal industries are food processing, forestry, oil refining, vehicle assembly, textiles, fishing and the production of oil, natural gas and hydroelectric power; the country is a net exporter of electricity. The main trading partners are Nigeria, France, other EU and west African states, and the USA.

GNI – US$22,406m; US$1,070 per capita (2009)
Annual average growth of GDP – 3.6 per cent (2010 est)
Inflation rate – 1.4 per cent (2010 est)
Population below poverty line – 42 per cent (2006 est)
Total external debt – US$11,600m (2010 est)
Imports – US$6,500m (2009)
Exports – US$9,300m (2009)

BALANCE OF PAYMENTS
Trade – US$2,597m surplus (2010)
Current Account – US$135m deficit (2007)

Trade	2009	2010
Imports from UK	£55,486,550	£52,727,942
Exports to UK	£168,874,087	£176,176,886

COMMUNICATIONS
Côte d'Ivoire has 660km of railways and 80,000km of roads, 6,500km of which are surfaced. There are 980km of navigable rivers, canals and lagoons. The main seaports are Abidjan and San Pedro. There are 27 airports and airfields, the principal international airport being at Abidjan. The telephone system is well developed, and fixed-line density has quadrupled since the late 1990s. Mobile phone distribution has risen rapidly, reaching 65 per 100 people in 2009.

MEDIA
The state broadcaster, Radiodiffusion Télévision Ivoirienne (RTI), operates two national radio stations and two television channels; all were used as propaganda tools during the civil war. There are no private terrestrial television stations but subscription services are available.

Radio is the most popular medium for news, provided by dozens of non-commercial community radio stations and a UN radio station, Onuci FM, set up in 2004 and now nationally available.

During the post-election stalemate in early 2011, nine independent or pro-Ouattara newspapers suspended printing, claiming their staff had been threatened by agents loyal to Laurent Gbagbo. Since his arrest most outlets have recommenced production.

CROATIA

Republika Hrvatska – Republic of Croatia

Area – 56,594 sq. km
Capital – Zagreb; population, 685,128 (2009 est)
Major cities – Dubrovnik, Osijek, Rijeka (Fiume), Split
Currency – Kuna of 100 lipa
Population – 4,486,881 falling at 0.06 per cent a year
(2010 est); Croat (89.6 per cent), Serb (4.5 per cent)
(2001)
Religion – Christian (Roman Catholic 85 per cent, Serbian
Orthodox 6 per cent), Muslim and Jewish minorities
(est)
Language – Croatian (official), Serbian
Population density – 79 per sq. km (2009)
Urban population – 57 per cent (2008 est)
Median age (years) – 41.2 (2010 est)
National anthem – 'Lijepa Nasa Domovino' ['Our
Beautiful Homeland']
National day – 8 October (Independence Day)
Life expectancy (years) – 75.58 (2010 est)
Mortality rate – 11.83 (2010 est)
Birth rate – 9.63 (2010 est)
Infant mortality rate – 6.26 (2010 est)
Death penalty – Abolished for all crimes (since 1990)
CPI score – 4.1 (2010)

CLIMATE AND TERRAIN

There are three major geographic areas: the plains of the
Pannonian region in the north, the central mountain belt,
and the Adriatic coast region of Istria and Dalmatia,
which has 1,185 islands and islets and 1,777km of
coastline. Elevation extremes range from 1,831m (Dinara)
at the highest point to 0m (Adriatic Sea) at the lowest. The
climate varies significantly between the Dalmatian coast,
where the winters are mild and the summers hot, and
inland areas, which have colder temperatures and rain in
the summer. Average temperatures in Zagreb range from
0°C in January to 22°C in July.

HISTORY AND POLITICS

The area was part of the Roman provinces of Pannonia
and Dalmatia, and was occupied by Croats in the sixth and
seventh centuries. By the 16th century the area was under
the rule of the Hapsburgs (Pannonia), the Ottomans
(Slavonia) and Venice (Dalmatia). Slavonia was restored to
the Hapsburgs in 1699 and Dalmatia passed to Austria in
1815; the whole area was part of the Austro-Hungarian
Empire until its collapse in 1918. Croatia declared its
independence in October 1918 but soon after joined with
Slovenia, Bosnia-Hercegovina, Serbia and Montenegro to
form the Kingdom of Serbs, Croats and Slovenes
(renamed Yugoslavia in 1929). From 1941 to 1945,

Yugoslavia was occupied by the Axis powers; Italy and
Hungary annexed parts of Croatia and a pro-Nazi puppet
state was established in the remainder of Croatia and
Bosnia-Hercegovina. At the end of the Second World
War, Croatia became a republic within the Socialist
Federal Republic of Yugoslavia.

In October 1991 Croatia declared its independence
from the disintegrating Yugoslav federation. The efforts of
the Federal Yugoslav Army (JNA) and ethnic Serbs in
Croatia to prevent Croatia's secession led to civil war until
January 1992, when a ceasefire was declared. Fighting
restarted the following year as Croatian forces set out to
retake the ethnic Serb areas of the country that had
seceded; Krajina and Western Slavonia were recaptured in
1995, and Eastern Slavonia agreed in 1995 to
reintegration by 1998. From 1992 to 1995 Croatian
forces were also involved in the war in Bosnia-
Hercegovina. Croatia signed the Dayton Accord in 1995.

Post-independence politics was dominated by the
authoritarian President Franjo Tudjman, who was first
elected president in 1990. After Tudjman's death in 1999,
Croatia became more outward-looking; it normalised
relations with its neighbours, began EU accession
negotiations in 2005 and joined NATO in 2009.

In the 2007 legislative election, the Croatian
Democratic Union (HDZ) remained the largest party in
the legislature but without an overall majority. It formed a
coalition government with the Croatian Social Liberal
Party, the Independent Democratic Serb Party and the
Croatian Peasant Party under Ivo Sanader. He resigned in
2009 and was replaced by Jadranka Kosor. The 2010
presidential election was won by Ivo Josipovic.

POLITICAL SYSTEM

The 1990 constitution was amended in 2000 to increase
the powers of the legislature, making the presidency a
largely ceremonial role, and in 2001 to abolish the upper
house of the legislature. The head of state is a president,
who is directly elected for a five-year term. The
legislature, the Croatian Assembly, has one chamber, the
House of Representatives, which has 153 members
directly elected for a four-year term. The prime minister is
appointed by the legislature and appoints the cabinet.

HEAD OF STATE
President, Ivo Josipovic, *elected* 10 January 2010, *sworn in*
18 February 2010

SELECTED GOVERNMENT MEMBERS *as at May 2011*
Prime Minister, Jadranka Kosor
Deputy Prime Ministers, Djurdja Adlesic;
Martina Dalic *(Finance);* Darko Milinovic;
Bozidar Pankretic; Slobodan Uzelac
Defence, Davor Bozinovic
Foreign Affairs, Gordan Jandrokovic
Interior, Tomislav Karamarko

EMBASSY OF THE REPUBLIC OF CROATIA
21 Conway Street, London W1T 6BN
T 020-7387 2022 **E** vrhlon@mvpei.hr **W** uk.mfa.hr
Ambassador Extraordinary and Plenipotentiary, HE Dr Ivica
Tomic, *apptd* 2009

BRITISH EMBASSY
Ivana Lucica 4, 10000 Zagreb
T (+385) 600 9100 **E** british.embassyzagreb@fco.gov.uk
W http://ukincroatia.fco.gov.uk
Ambassador Extraordinary and Plenipotentiary, HE David
Blunt, *apptd* 2008

BRITISH COUNCIL
Illica 12, PP 55, 10001 Zagreb
T (+385) 1489 9500 W www.britishcouncil.org/croatia
Director, Les Dangerfield

DEFENCE
The armed forces are subject to an arms limitation regime established under the Dayton Accord. The army has 261 main battle tanks, 103 armoured infantry fighting vehicles and 38 armoured personnel carriers. The navy has 3 submarines and 6 patrol and coastal combatant vessels at five bases. The air force has 10 combat aircraft.
Military budget – US$863m (2010)
Military personnel – 18,600: army 11,390, navy 1,850, air force 3,500, joint staff 1,860; paramilitary 3,000

ECONOMY AND TRADE
As part of Yugoslavia, Croatia was a prosperous and industrialised area, but the conflict in 1991–5 damaged its infrastructure, large areas of farmland, industrial productivity and the tourist industry. From 2000 to 2007 there was steady economic growth, led by a recovery in tourism, banking and public investment. However, a growing trade deficit, high unemployment, the size of the public sector, and the economy's over-reliance on tourism are longer-term problems that left the economy vulnerable in the global economic downturn and slow to recover. There is a seeming lack of political will to address these issues.

The service sector accounts for 66 per cent of GDP, industry for 27.2 per cent, and agriculture for 6.8 per cent. Tourism is a major contributor to GDP. Industry produces chemicals and plastics, machine tools, metals and metal products, electronics, wood products, construction materials and textiles, and includes food processing, shipbuilding and oil refining. Agricultural production includes cereals, pulses, fruit and vegetables, livestock and dairy products. Most trade is with EU and neighbouring countries.
GNI – US$60,543m; US$13,770 per capita (2009)
Annual average growth of GDP – –1.4 per cent (2010 est)
Inflation rate – 1.3 per cent (2010 est)
Population below poverty line – 17 per cent (2008)
Unemployment – 17.6 per cent (2010 est)
Total external debt – US$59,700m (2010 est)
Imports – US$21,200m (2009)
Exports – US$10,500m (2009)

BALANCE OF PAYMENTS
Trade – US$8,247m deficit (2010)
Current Account – US$6,397m deficit (2008)

Trade with UK	2009	2010
Imports from UK	£205,952,270	£165,949,905
Exports to UK	£76,375,229	£95,200,061

COMMUNICATIONS
Those parts of the transport infrastructure destroyed in fighting in the 1990s have mostly been reconstructed, and parts of the rail and road networks have been modernised and expanded. There are 2,722km of railways and 29,343km of roads, including 1,047km of motorway. The principal airports are at Zagreb and Split. The national carrier is Croatia Airlines. There are 785km of inland waterways, including a stretch of the river Danube, and frequent ferry services to the many Adriatic islands. The main seaports are Rijeka, Ploce, Omisalj,

Sibenik and Kraljevica. The telephone system is being modernised and extended. There were 6 million mobile phone subscribers in 2009, compared to 1.9 million fixed-line users.

EDUCATION AND HEALTH
Literacy rate – 98.8 per cent (2008 est)
Gross enrolment ratio (percentage of relevant age group) – primary 94 per cent; secondary 90 per cent; tertiary 51 per cent (2009 est)
Health expenditure (per capita) – US$1,120 (2009)
Hospital beds (per 1,000 people) – 5.5 (2004–9)

MEDIA
The constitution guarantees freedom of the press, although certain topics – such as Serbo-Croat relations – are considered off-limits. Croatian Radio-Television (HRT) is the national state-owned public service broadcaster and is the main source of news. There are a number of private national radio and television networks and three main news publications: *Vecernji List* (daily), *Jutarnji List* (daily) and *Nacional* (weekly).

CUBA

República de Cuba – Republic of Cuba

Area – 110,860 sq. km
Capital – Havana; population, 2,139,800 (2009 est)
Major cities – Camagüey, Guantánamo, Holguín, Santa Clara, Santiago de Cuba
Currency – Cuban peso of 100 centavos
Population – 11,477,459 rising at 0.22 per cent a year (2010 est)
Religion – Christian (Roman Catholic 60 per cent, Protestant 5 per cent) (est); many practise Santería (African religions syncretised with Christianity). Religious activity is tightly controlled; house churches must be state-registered
Language – Spanish (official)
Population density – 105 per sq. km (2009)
Urban population – 76 per cent (2008 est)
Median age (years) – 37.8 (2010 est)
National anthem – 'El Himno de Bayamo' ['The Anthem of Bayamo']
National day – 1 January (Triumph of the Revolution)
Life expectancy (years) – 77.64 (2010 est)
Mortality rate – 7.29 (2010 est)
Birth rate – 11.02 (2010 est)
Infant mortality rate – 5.72 (2010 est)
Death penalty – Retained
CPI score – 3.7 (2010)

CLIMATE AND TERRAIN

Cuba, the largest island in the Caribbean, is part of an archipelago that also includes Isla de la Juventud and around 1,600 other islets and cays. The island of Cuba has three mountainous ranges running from east to west. Elevation extremes range from 2,005m (Pico Turquino) at the highest point to 0m (Caribbean Sea) at the lowest. The climate is subtropical, with an average annual temperature of 25°C.

HISTORY AND POLITICS

The island was visited by Columbus in 1492. In the early 16th century the island was settled by the Spanish and remained under Spanish rule until a war of independence was won in 1898. Spain's defeat in Cuba coincided with its defeat in the Spanish–American War, and it ceded Cuba to the USA, which occupied the island in 1899. Cuba became independent in 1902, albeit with a condition allowing the USA to retain naval bases on the island.

The dictatorship of Gen. Batista (1933–44, 1952–9) was overthrown in 1959 in a revolution led by Fidel Castro. A communist state was established in 1961 which quickly became allied with the USSR. The regime's policies and its alignment with the Soviet bloc on the one hand, and the USA's support of exiled Cuban dissidents on the other, created great friction in US–Cuban relations; the USA has maintained an economic and trade embargo since 1961, although some restrictions were lifted after President Obama took office.

When the USSR collapsed in 1991, Cuba lost the economic, commercial and military support it had enjoyed since 1960. Faced with severe economic deterioration, the government introduced rationing and relaxed state controls on economic activity. The latter resulted in increased overseas investment and a growth in tourism, although state control has been reasserted in recent years. Between 2003–8, the EU restricted its political and cultural contacts with Cuba over its poor human rights record.

Fidel Castro, who had been president since 1959, announced in February 2008 that he would not accept another term of office owing to ill-health. His brother, Raúl Castro, who had been acting president since July 2006, was elected head of state and head of government later that month by the National Assembly. The most recent legislative election was in January 2008.

POLITICAL SYSTEM

The Communist Party of Cuba (PCC) is the only authorised political party. The 1976 constitution was amended in 1991 to allow direct election of the National Assembly by secret ballot, and in 2002 to enshrine socialism in the constitution. The president is elected by the legislature for a five-year term. The unicameral National Assembly of the People's Power has 614 members directly elected for a five-year term; all candidates are approved by the PCC and stand unopposed. Between its sessions, the assembly is represented by the Council of State, whose members are elected by the assembly.

HEAD OF STATE

President of Council of State and Council of Ministers, Gen. Raúl Castro Ruz, *elected* 24 February 2008
First Vice-President of Council of State, José Ramón Machado Ventura

SELECTED GOVERNMENT MEMBERS *as at June 2011*

Vice Presidents of Council of Ministers, José Ramón Machado Ventura; José Ramón Fernández Álvarez; Osmany Cienfugos Gorriarán; Ricardo Cabrisas Ruiz; Div.-Gen. Ulises Rosales del Toro; Ramiro Valdés Menéndez; Marino Murillo Jorge; Antonio Enrique Lusson Batlle
Economy and Planning, Abel Izquierdo Rodriguez
Finance and Prices, Lina Pedraza Rodriguez
Foreign Relations, Bruno Rodriguez Parrilla
Interior, Gen. Abelardo Colome Ibarra

EMBASSY OF THE REPUBLIC OF CUBA
167 High Holborn, London WC1V 6PA
T 020-7240 2488 E embacuba@cubaldn.com
W www.cubaldn.com
Ambassador Extraordinary and Plenipotentiary, HE Esther G. Armenteros Cárdenas, *apptd* 2010

BRITISH EMBASSY
Calle 34, No 702, Miramar, Playa, Havana
T (+53) (0) 7214 2200 W http://ukincuba.fco.gov.uk
Ambassador Extraordinary and Plenipotentiary, HE Dianna Melrose, *apptd* 2008

BRITISH COUNCIL
c/o British Embassy
T (+53) (0) 7214 2200 W www.britishcouncil.org/cuba
Director, Frank Fitzpatrick

DEFENCE

The army has around 900 main battle tanks, 50 armoured infantry fighting vehicles and 500 armoured personnel carriers. The navy has 7 patrol and coastal vessels and 7 bases. The air force has 45 combat aircraft and 4 armed helicopters.

The USA has 886 joint task force personnel at Guantánamo Bay Naval Base, which has been leased since 1902.

Military expenditure – US$1,960m (2009 est)
Military personnel – 49,000: army 38,000, navy 3,000, air force 8,000; paramilitary 26,500
Conscription duration – 24 months

ECONOMY AND TRADE

After the revolution virtually all land and industrial and commercial enterprises were nationalised. With the collapse of communism in Europe in 1989–91, the economy deteriorated sharply, necessitating rationing of energy, food and consumer goods, and obliging the government to introduce reforms. Since 1993, liberalisation has gradually opened up the economy to limited private enterprise and foreign ownership of property and business enterprises, and introduced price rises for some goods and services and income tax. The reforms resulted in steady growth, in particular stimulating tourism and the oil and mining industries, but the standard of living for most Cubans is still below the pre-1991 level. Further economic difficulties arising from the global economic downturn, which precipitated a marked fall in tourism and nickel prices, led to a further easing of restrictions on private enterprise in 2010 and plans to reduce public sector employment.

State farms have been transformed into privately run cooperatives and are permitted to sell 20 per cent of their produce on the open market. However, production of cash crops for export means that food production is insufficient for domestic needs, and Cuba imports over 80 per cent of its food. Agriculture contributes 4.2 per cent of GDP and employs about 20 per cent of the workforce. Industrial activities include sugar refining, oil production, tobacco processing, construction, nickel mining and production of steel, cement, agricultural machinery and pharmaceuticals. Industry contributes 22.7 per cent of GDP, and the service sector 72.9 per cent. About 78 per cent of the workforce is employed in the state sector.

The main trading partners are China, Canada, Venezuela and Spain; Venezuela provides oil on preferential terms. Principal exports are sugar, nickel, tobacco, fish, medical products, citrus fruits and coffee. The main imports are oil, food, machinery and equipment, and chemicals.

GNI – US$61,758m; US$5,550 per capita (2008)
Annual average growth of GDP – 1.5 per cent (2010 est)
Inflation rate – 0.7 per cent (2010 est)
Unemployment – 2 per cent (2010 est)
Total external debt – US$19,750m (2009 est)

BALANCE OF PAYMENTS
Trade – US$6,573m deficit (2010)

Trade with UK	2009	2010
Imports from UK	£8,886,817	£14,952,207
Exports to UK	£9,763,553	£13,873,908

COMMUNICATIONS
The transport system has suffered as a result of recent economic difficulties, although the growth in tourism has stimulated and paid for some remedies. Even so, public transport is poor, and car ownership and freedom to travel are very limited. There are 4,065km of railways, with an additional 4,533km of track used exclusively by the sugar plantations. There are 60,858km of roads, 29,820km of which are surfaced, including 638km of motorway. Air services link the major cities and offshore islands; the islands are also served by ferries. There are 136 airports and airfields, of which 65 are surfaced; the main international airport is at Havana. The main ports are Havana, Cienfuegos and Matanzas.

The telephone system has been improved since 2000 but fixed-line density is low, with fewer than 10 lines per 100 residents. Mobile phone ownership has been permitted since 2008 but the cost is prohibitive. Ownership of computers and other electrical consumer goods has also been permitted since 2008, but internet access is largely restricted to foreigners and the government elite.

EDUCATION AND HEALTH
Education is free of charge and compulsory between ages six and 14. In some rural areas children attend boarding schools where agricultural tasks are compulsory in addition to schoolwork. After basic education, students can choose to go to a pre-collegiate school or a technical school. The pre-collegiate school is free to graduates. Health care is free.

Literacy rate – 99.8 per cent (2008 est)
Gross enrolment ratio (percentage of relevant age group) – primary 104 per cent; secondary 90 per cent; tertiary 118 per cent (2009 est)
Health expenditure (per capita) – US$707 (2009)
Hospital beds (per 1,000 people) – 5.9 (2004–9)

MEDIA
The media is tightly controlled by the government; criticism of the government or its officials can be punished by a prison term of up to three years. Private ownership of electronic media is prohibited, and foreign news agencies are permitted to hire local journalists only through government offices. The official Communist Party newspaper is *Granma*. The main television stations are Cubavision, Tele-Rebelde and CHTV. The main radio stations are Radio Rebelde and Radio Reloj. Radio-TV Marti, a US government-backed station, transmits from Florida.

CULTURE
Cuba is known for its music, a vibrant mix of Spanish traditional guitar melodies and African rhythms. Rumba, mambo, bolero, salsa and cha-cha-cha all evolved from *son*, a type of Cuban music that originated in the hills of Oriente at the turn of the 20th century. Cuban music returned to the world stage with the success of the Buena Vista Social Club (publicised by the film of the same name) in the late 1990s. Writers of international standing include Cirilo Villaverde y de la Paz (1812–94), José Martí (1853–95), Nicolás Guillén (1902–89), Alejo Carpentier (1904–80) and Guillermo Cabrera Infante (1929–2005).

CYPRUS

Kypriaki Dimokratia / Kibris Cumhuriyeti – Republic of Cyprus

Area – 9,251 sq. km, of which 3,355 sq. km are in the Turkish Cypriot-administered area
Capital – Nicosia; population 239,859 (2009 est)
Major cities – Larnaca, Limassol, Paphos (south of the partition); Famagusta, Kyrenia (north)
Currency – Euro (€) of 100 cents (south), Turkish lira (north)
Population – 1,102,677 rising at 1.66 per cent a year (2010 est); Greek (77 per cent), Turkish (18 per cent) (2001 est)
Religion – Christian (Greek Orthodox 95 per cent) south of the partition; Sunni Muslim (98 per cent) in the north
Language – Greek, Turkish (both official), English
Population density – 94 per sq. km (2009)
Urban population – 70 per cent (2008 est)
Median age (years) – 34.5 (2010 est)
National anthem – 'Imnos eis tin Eleftherian' ['Hymn to Freedom']
National day – 1 October (Independence Day)
Life expectancy (years) – 77.66 (2010 est)
Mortality rate – 6.42 (2010 est)
Birth rate – 11.38 (2010 est)
Infant mortality rate – 9.57 (2010 est)

Death penalty – Abolished for all crimes (since 2002)
CPI score – 6.3 (2010)
Literacy rate – 97.9 per cent (2008 est)

CLIMATE AND TERRAIN

Cyprus is the third-largest island in the Mediterranean. It has two mountain ranges, the Pentadaktylos along the north coast, and the Troodos in the centre and west. Plains lie between the two ranges and on parts of the south coast. Elevation extremes range from 1,951m (Mt Olympus, Troodos range) at the highest point to 0m (Mediterranean Sea) at the lowest. The climate is Mediterranean, with very warm summers.

HISTORY AND POLITICS

Cyprus has a recorded history of over 4,000 years, and its rulers have included the Greeks, Phoenicians, Ptolemaic Egyptians, Romans, Byzantines, Arabs, Franks, Venetians, Turks and British. Administration of Cyprus was taken over by Britain from Turkey in 1878, then Cyprus was formally annexed by Britain in 1914, and became a crown colony in 1925. Greek Cypriot demands for union with Greece *(enosis)* led to guerrilla warfare against the British administration in the 1950s and a four-year state of emergency (1955–9). An agreement was signed in 1959 between Britain, Greece, Turkey and the Greek and Turkish Cypriots which stipulated that Cyprus would become an independent republic; the island became independent on 16 August 1960, with Britain retaining sovereignty over two military bases *(see* below).

Tensions between the Greek and Turkish Cypriots caused power-sharing to break down and led to intercommunal conflict throughout the 1960s and in 1971. The UN Peacekeeping Force in Cyprus was deployed in 1964. In 1974, a Greece-backed coup against the Cypriot government led Turkey, which feared *enosis,* to invade. It occupied the northern third of the island, partitioning the island and displacing over 160,000 Greek Cypriots. Talks on reunification in the 1980s and 1990s were unsuccessful, and a UN-sponsored reunification plan, put to simultaneous referendums in the north and south in April 2004, was rejected by Greek Cypriots; only the southern part of the island joined the EU in May 2004. Relations improved markedly after the 2008 presidential election, and UN-facilitated talks began in 2008.

Demetris Christofias, the candidate of the Progressive Party of the Working People (AKEL), was elected president in 2008. The legislative elections held in May 2011 resulted in gains for both AKEL and the opposition Democratic Rally (DISY) party; AKEL maintained its majority in the House of Representatives through a coalition with the Democratic Party (DIKO).

POLITICAL SYSTEM

The 1960 constitution provides for power-sharing between the Greek and Turkish Cypriots but some of these provisions have been in abeyance since 1963, when the Turkish Cypriots withdrew from the power-sharing arrangements. The executive president is directly elected for a five-year term. The unicameral legislature, the House of Representatives, has 80 members, directly elected for a five-year term; elections to the 24 seats reserved for Turkish Cypriots have not taken place since 1963.

HEAD OF STATE

President, Demetris Christofias, *elected* 24 February 2008, *sworn in* 28 February 2008

SELECTED GOVERNMENT MEMBERS *as at May 2011*
Defence, Costas Papacostas
Finance, Charilaos Stavrakis
Foreign Affairs, Markos Kyprianou
Interior, Neoclis Sylikiotis

HIGH COMMISSION FOR THE REPUBLIC OF CYPRUS
13 St James's Square, London SW1Y 4LB
T 020-7321 4100 E cyphclondon@btconnect.com
High Commissioner, HE Alexandros Zenon, *apptd* 2008

BRITISH HIGH COMMISSION
PO Box 21978, Alexander Pallis Street, 1587 Nicosia
T (+357) 2286 1100 W http://ukincyprus.fco.gov.uk
High Commissioner, HE Matthew Kidd, apptd 2010

BRITISH COUNCIL
1–3 Aristotelous Street, 1011 Nicosia
T (+357) 2258 5000 W www.britishcouncil.org/cyprus
Director, Heather Forbes

BRITISH SOVEREIGN BASE AREAS
The Sovereign Base Areas (SBAs) of Akrotiri and Dhekelia are those parts of Cyprus that remained under British sovereignty and jurisdiction after independence, and have the status of a UK overseas territory. They are around 254 sq. km in size. There are approximately 15,700 residents: 7,700 Cypriots and 8,000 military and UK-based civilian personnel and their dependants.
Administrator of the British Sovereign Base Areas, Air Vice-Marshal Graham Stacey, *apptd* 2010

DEFENCE

The National Guard has 147 main battle tanks, 43 armoured infantry fighting vehicles and 294 armoured personnel carriers. Turkey has around 36,000 troops in northern Cyprus.

A military airfield in Paphos provides a base for Greek military aircraft, as Cyprus does not possess its own air force.

Military budget – US$498m (2010)
Military personnel – national guard 10,000; paramilitary 750; Northern Cyprus Army around 5,000, paramilitary 150
Conscription duration – 24 months

ECONOMY AND TRADE

The Greek Cypriot economy is dominated by the service sector, which accounted for 79.3 per cent of GDP in 2010; this was derived mainly from tourism and financial services. Tourism represents around 20 per cent of GDP, making the economy vulnerable to fluctuations; reduced visitor numbers due to the global economic downturn contributed to the economy entering recession in 2009, and recovery is slow. Shipping services are also important; about 20 per cent of the world's shipping is Cypriot-registered. Industry contributes 18.6 per cent of GDP and agriculture 2.1 per cent. The main products for export are citrus fruits, potatoes, pharmaceuticals, cement and garments. Imports are primarily consumer goods, fuel and lubricants, machinery and transport equipment. Over half of trade is with other EU countries.

The Turkish Cypriot economy suffers from a small domestic market, international isolation and a bloated public sector. It is heavily dependent on financial support from the Turkish government. Services accounted for about 69 per cent of GDP in 2006, industry for 22 per cent and agriculture for 9 per cent. The main products for export are citrus fruits, dairy products, potatoes and textiles. The main imports are vehicles, fuel, cigarettes, food, minerals, chemicals and machinery. The tourist industry is small because the only international transport links are via Turkey, but a drop in tourist numbers and the global downturn had a serious impact on the economy in 2009.

GNI – US$24,590m; US$30,480 per capita (2009)
Annual average growth of GDP – 0.6 per cent (2010 est)
Inflation rate – 2.2 per cent (2010 est)
Unemployment – 6 per cent (2010 est)
Total external debt – US$32,610m (2008 est)
Imports – US$7,900m (2009)
Exports – US$1,300m (2009)

BALANCE OF PAYMENTS
Trade – US$7,065m deficit (2010)
Current Account – US$4,484m deficit (2008)

Trade with UK	2009	2010
Imports from UK	£581,141,711	£540,913,187
Exports to UK	£72,467,280	£105,631,055

COMMUNICATIONS
There are no railways. The road network (12,321km in the Greek part of the island and 2,350km in the Turkish part) serves the main population centres; crossings between the Greek and Turkish areas have all reopened or had some restrictions eased in recent years. In the Greek area, the main airports are at Larnaca and Paphos, and the principal ports are Limassol, Larnaca and Paphos. In the Turkish area, the main ports are Famagusta and Kyrenia; there is an airport but flight connections are with Turkey only.

MEDIA
The state-run Cyprus Broadcasting Corporation competes with a number of privately owned television and radio stations. The Turkish north operates its own services and broadcasts, and relays of mainland Greek and Turkish stations are available throughout the island. Newspapers on both sides of the divide are free to criticise the authorities.

TURKISH REPUBLIC OF NORTHERN CYPRUS
In 1974, a Greece-backed coup against the Cypriot government led Turkey, fearing the coup was a precursor to the union of Cyprus with Greece, to invade northern Cyprus and occupy over a third of the island. The following year, a Turkish Federated State of Cyprus was declared, and in 1983 a declaration of statehood was issued which purported to establish the Turkish Republic of Northern Cyprus. The declaration was condemned by the UN security council and only Turkey has recognised the republic. A constitution was adopted in 1985, and election have been held at regular intervals since.

Reunification talks were unsuccessful in the 1980s and 1990s, and although Turkish Cypriots approved a UN-sponsored reunification plan put to simultaneous referendums in 2004, it was rejected by Greek Cypriots. Since 2004, the EU has given aid to the area to promote and ease reunification, and UN-facilitated talks began in 2008.

The 2009 legislative election was won by the National Unity Party, which favours unification with Turkey. Dervis Eroglu won the 2010 presidential election, replacing Mehmet Ali Talat.

DE FACTO HEAD OF STATE
President, Dervis Eroglu, *elected* 18 April 2010, *sworn in* 23 April 2010
Prime Minister, Irsen Kucuk

CZECH REPUBLIC

Ceska Republika – Czech Republic

Area – 78,867 sq. km
Capital – Prague (Praha); population, 1,161,770 (2009 est)
Major cities – Brno (Brünn), Ostrava, Plzen (Pilsen)
Currency – Koruna (Kcs) of 100 haleru
Population – 10,201,707 falling at 0.11 per cent a year (2010 est); Czech (90.4 per cent), Moravian (3.7 per cent), Slovak (1.9 per cent) (2001)
Religion – Christian (Roman Catholic 27 per cent, Protestant 3 per cent, Czech Hussite 1 per cent)
Language – Czech (official), Slovak
Population density – 136 per sq. km (2009)
Urban population – 73 per cent (2008 est)
Median age (years) – 40.4 (2010 est)
National anthem – 'Kde Domov Muj?' ['Where is My Homeland?']
National day – 28 October (Founding Day)
Life expectancy (years) – 77.01 (2010 est)
Mortality rate – 10.79 (2010 est)
Birth rate – 8.76 (2010 est)
Infant mortality rate – 3.76 (2010 est)
Death penalty – Abolished for all crimes (since 1990)
CPI score – 4.6 (2010)

CLIMATE AND TERRAIN
The landlocked republic is composed of Bohemia (the west and centre) and Moravia (the east). Bohemia contains the fertile plains of the river Elbe and the surrounding low mountains, while the hilly region of Moravia extends towards the basin of the river Danube. Roughly a third of the country is covered by forest. Elevation extremes range from 1,602m (Snezka) at the highest point to 115m (river Elbe) at the lowest. The climate is continental, with warm, humid summers and cold, dry winters. The average temperature in Prague ranges from −3°C in January to 18°C in July.

HISTORY AND POLITICS
The medieval kingdom of Bohemia (which included Moravia) came under the rule of the Habsburg dynasty in 1526 and, despite the rise of Czech nationalism in the 19th century, remained part of the Austro-Hungarian Empire until 1918. The collapse of the empire led to the creation of Czechoslovakia, an amalgamation of Bohemia,

Moravia, Slovakia and Ruthenia. Its independence was declared on 28 October 1918 and confirmed at the Versailles Peace Conference of 1919.

Czechoslovakia was forced to cede the ethnic German Sudetenland to Nazi Germany in 1938 after the Munich agreement. German forces invaded the Czech lands in 1939 and incorporated them into Germany, while Slovakia became a puppet state. The republic was liberated by Soviet and US forces in 1945. The pre-war democratic Czechoslovak state was re-established in 1945, having ceded Ruthenia to the Soviet Union, but communists took power in a coup in 1948.

In 1968, the Communist Party under Alexander Dubcek embarked on a political and economic reform programme (the Prague Spring). The reforms were suppressed following an invasion by Soviet and Eastern bloc troops on 20 August 1968, and were abandoned when Gustav Husak became leader of the Communist Party in 1969.

After mass protests in November 1989, the Communist Party was forced to concede its monopoly on power. Free elections were held in 1990 in which the Communist Party was defeated.

In late 1992, the leaders of the Czech and Slovak republics agreed to dissolve the federation and form two sovereign states; this took effect on 1 January 1993. The Czech Republic joined NATO in 1999 and the EU in 2004.

Vaclav Klaus of the Civic Democrat Party (ODS) was elected president at the third attempt in 2003; he was narrowly re-elected in 2008. Legislative elections in May 2010 gave a combined majority to three centre-right parties – the ODS, Top09 and the Public Affairs party – which formed a coalition government under ODS leader Petr Necas. The partial senate elections in autumn 2010 resulted in a slight majority for the opposition, enabling it to disrupt the government's austerity programme.

POLITICAL SYSTEM
The 1992 constitution provided for the separation of the Czech Republic and Slovakia; federal laws remain in place unless superseded by Czech ones. The president is elected by a joint session of both chambers of the legislature for a five-year term, renewable once. The bicameral *Parlament* comprises a 200-member Chamber of Deputies, directly elected for a four-year term, and an 81-member senate directly elected for a six-year term, one-third being elected every two years. The council of ministers is appointed by the president on the recommendation of the prime minister.

HEAD OF STATE
President, Vaclav Klaus, *elected* 28 February 2003, *sworn in* 7 March 2003, *re-elected* 2008

SELECTED GOVERNMENT MEMBERS *as at June 2011*
Prime Minister, Petr Necas
Foreign Affairs, Karel Schwarzenburg
Defence, Alexandr Vondra
Interior, Jan Kubice
Finance, Miroslav Kalousek

EMBASSY OF THE CZECH REPUBLIC
26–30 Kensington Palace Gardens, London W8 4QY
T 020-7243 1115 E london@embassy.mzv.cz
W www.czechembassy.org.uk
Ambassador Extraordinary and Plenipotentiary, HE Michael Zantovsky, *apptd* 2009

BRITISH EMBASSY
Thunovska 14, 11800 Prague 1
T (+420) (2) 5740 2111 W http://ukinczechrepublic.fco.gov.uk
Ambassador Extraordinary and Plenipotentiary, HE Sian MacLeod, *apptd* 2009

BRITISH COUNCIL
Bredovsky dvur, Politickych veznu 13, 11000 Prague 1
T (+420) 221 991 160 W www.britishcouncil.org/czechrepublic
Director, Nigel Bellingham

DEFENCE
The army has 169 main battle tanks, 435 armoured infantry fighting vehicles and 78 armoured personnel carriers. The air force has 48 combat aircraft and 24 armed helicopters.
Military budget – US$2,550m (2010)
Military personnel – 23,441: army 7,0261, air force 4,567; paramilitary 3,100

ECONOMY AND TRADE
Economic reforms since 1990 have produced a stable and prosperous market economy. Accession to the EU encouraged further reform and restructuring, as well as contributing to steady growth by expanding export markets and encouraging foreign investment. The global economic downturn caused the economy to contract in 2009, largely because of a reduced demand for the country's major exports. A slow recovery began in late 2009.

Services account for 59.5 per cent of GDP, industry for 38.3 per cent and agriculture for 2.2 per cent. The principal agricultural products are cereal crops, sugar beet and potatoes; the timber industry is also important. The country has been industrialised since the 19th century, and motor vehicles, metals, machinery, glass and armaments are major products. Electricity is also exported. The principal trading partners are EU countries – especially Germany – and China and Russia.
GNI – US$178,078m; US$17,310 per capita (2009)
Annual average growth of GDP – 1.8 per cent (2010 est)
Inflation rate – 1.6 per cent (2010 est)
Unemployment – 9.3 per cent (2010 est)
Total external debt – US$86,790m (2010 est)
Imports – US$104,900m (2009)
Exports – US$146,100m (2008)

BALANCE OF PAYMENTS
Trade – US$6,511m surplus (2010)
Current Account – US$1,942m deficit (2009)

Trade with UK	2009	2010
Imports from UK	£1,395,477,771	£1,751,657,135
Exports to UK	£3,331,378,324	£3,948,048,160

COMMUNICATIONS
Extensive road (127,719km) and rail (9,632km) networks link the main population centres. Navigable inland waterways include 664km on the Elbe, Vltava, and Oder and other rivers, lakes and canals. The principal airport is at Prague and the national carrier is Czech Airlines, which operates international and domestic services. The telecommunications system is being modernised. Mobile phone distribution has grown rapidly, to 14.3 million subscriptions in 2009.

EDUCATION AND HEALTH
Education is free and compulsory for all children from the age of six to 15. Primary education lasts for nine years,

divided into two stages of five and four years respectively. Secondary education comprises three main types of school: academic, artistic and vocational.
Gross enrolment ratio (percentage of relevant age group) – primary 103 per cent; secondary 98 per cent; tertiary 43 per cent (2008 est)
Health expenditure (per capita) – US$1,384 (2009)
Hospital beds (per 1,000 people) – 7.2 (2004–9)

MEDIA AND CULTURE
The public broadcaster Ceska Televize (CT) runs two networks and a 24-hour news channel. Two major private television stations broadcast nationally. Czech public radio, Cesky Rozhlas (CRo), operates three national networks and local services, and there are scores of private radio stations throughout the country.

Prague is famous for its Art Nouveau architecture, cobbled streets and squares and thriving cultural life (particularly its contemporary jazz scene). Well-known Czech composers include Bedrich Smetana (1824–84), Antonin Dvorak (1841–1904) and Leos Janacek (1854–1928). Among its important writers are Franz Kafka (1883–1924), Karel Capek (1890–1938), Milan Kundera (b. 1929), Ivan Klima (b. 1931) and Vaclav Havel (b. 1936).

DENMARK

Kongeriget Danmark – Kingdom of Denmark

Area – 43,094 sq. km (excluding the Faeroe Islands and Greenland)
Capital – Copenhagen; population, 1,173,680 (2009 est)
Major cities – Aalborg, Aarhus, Esbjerg, Odense
Currency – Danish krone (DKr) of 100 ore
Population – 5,515,575 rising at 0.27 per cent a year (2010 est)
Religion – Christian (Lutheran 81 per cent, Roman Catholic 1 per cent), Muslim 4 per cent (est). The Evangelical Lutheran Church is the state church
Language – Danish (official), Faroese, Greenlandic, German. English is widely spoken as a second language
Population density – 130 per sq. km (2009)
Urban population – 87 per cent (2008 est)
Median age (years) – 40.7 (2010 est)
National anthem – 'Det er et Yndigt Land' ['There is a Lovely Land']
National day – 5 June (Constitution Day)
Life expectancy (years) – 78.47 (2010 est)
Mortality rate – 10.19 (2010 est)
Birth rate – 10.4 (2010 est)
Infant mortality rate – 4.29 (2010 est)
Death penalty – Abolished for all crimes (since 1978)
CPI score – 9.3 (2010)

CLIMATE AND TERRAIN
Denmark consists of most of the Jutland peninsula and 406 islands, mainly in the Baltic Sea or among the northern Frisian Islands in the North Sea. The largest islands are Sjaelland (Zealand), Fyn, Lolland, Faister and Bornholm. It is a low-lying country, indented by fjords on its east coast and with lagoons and sand dunes along the west coast; Lim Fjord nearly bisects the north of Jutland. Elevation extremes range from 171m (Mollehoj) at the highest point to −7m (Lammefjord) at the lowest. The climate is temperate, with cold winters and warm summers. Average temperatures range from 0°C in January to 17°C in July.

HISTORY AND POLITICS
The Danes were at the forefront of Viking expansionism from the eighth century. Denmark was unified in the tenth century and was the centre of a short-lived empire, also including Norway and England, created by Cnut (Canute) in the 11th century. The Union of Kalmar (1397) brought Norway and Sweden (including Finland) under Danish rule. Danish power waned during the 16th century, enabling Sweden to re-establish its independence in 1523. In 1814 Norway was ceded to Sweden under the treaty of Kiel, and in 1864 Schleswig and Holstein, which had been subsumed in 1460, were lost to Germany; northern Schleswig was returned in 1920 after a plebiscite. Denmark was neutral during the First World War, but in the Second World War it was invaded and occupied by Germany until May 1945.

Denmark joined the European Community in 1973. In a 2000 referendum, it rejected adopting the euro.

Social Democrat-led coalitions held office in the post-war era until the 1982 election, but were in power again from 1993 to 2001. In the 2001 legislative election, the Liberal Party became the largest party in parliament, and formed a coalition government with the Conservative People's Party. This coalition retained power in the 2005 and 2007 general elections. In 2009, Anders Fogh Rasmussen resigned as prime minister following his appointment as NATO secretary-general; he was replaced by Lars Loekke Rasmussen. A legislative election is due in late 2011.

POLITICAL SYSTEM
The country is a constitutional monarchy, with a hereditary monarch as head of state. The head of government is the prime minister, who appoints the cabinet. The unicameral legislature, the *Folketing*, has 179 members, including two for the Faeroes and two for Greenland; members are elected for a four-year term by proportional representation.

HEAD OF STATE
HM The Queen of Denmark, Queen Margrethe II, KG, *born* 16 April 1940, *acceded* 14 January 1972
Heir, HRH Crown Prince Frederik, *born* 26 May 1968

SELECTED GOVERNMENT MEMBERS *as at May 2011*
Prime Minister, Lars Loekke Rasmussen
Deputy Prime Minister, Lene Espersen *(Foreign Affairs)*
Defence, Gitte Lillelund Bech
Finance, Claus Hjort Frederiksen
Interior, Bertel Haarder

ROYAL DANISH EMBASSY
55 Sloane Street, London SW1X 9SR
T 020-7333 0200 E lonamb@um.dk W www.denmark.org.uk

Ambassador Extraordinary and Plenipotentiary, HE Birger Riis-Jorgensen, *apptd* 2006

BRITISH EMBASSY
Kastelsvej 36–40, 2100 Copenhagen O
T (+45) 3544 5200 W http://ukindenmark.fco.gov.uk
Ambassador Extraordinary and Plenipotentiary, Nick Archer, MVO, *apptd* 2008

BRITISH COUNCIL
Gammel Mont 12, 1117 Copenhagen K
T (+45) (33) 369 400 W www.britishcouncil.org/denmark
Director, Hans Meir Anderson

DEFENCE

The army has 117 main battle tanks, 45 armed infantry fighting vehicles and 403 armoured personnel carriers. The navy has 1 destroyer, 4 frigates and 11 patrol and coastal vessels at 2 bases. The air force has 48 combat aircraft.

Military budget – US$3,660m (2010)
Military personnel – 18,707: army 9,925, navy 2,959, air force 3,358, joint staff 2,465
Conscription duration – 4–12 months

ECONOMY AND TRADE

Denmark has a diversified and industrialised market economy with a high dependence on exports. It is a net exporter of food and energy (oil and natural gas). Slowing growth from 2007 and then the global downturn pushed the economy into recession in 2009; a modest recovery began in 2010. The service sector contributes 76.1 per cent of GDP, industry 22.8 per cent and the highly efficient agricultural sector 1.1 per cent. Metals, pharmaceuticals, shipping and renewable energy are key industries.

The main trading partners are other EU countries, especially Germany and Sweden. Principal exports are machinery and instruments, meat and meat products, dairy products, fish, pharmaceuticals, furniture and windmills. The main imports are machinery and equipment, industrial raw materials and semi-manufactures, chemicals, grain and foodstuffs, and consumer goods.

GNI – US$318,307m; US$59,060 per capita (2009)
Annual average growth of GDP – 1.8 per cent (2010 est)
Inflation rate – 2.2 per cent (2010 est)
Population below poverty line – 12.1 per cent (2007)
Unemployment – 4.2 per cent (2010 est)
Total external debt – US$559,500m (2010)
Imports – US$82,000m (2009)
Exports – US$92,500m (2009)

BALANCE OF PAYMENTS
Trade – US$12,308m surplus (2010)
Current Account – US$12,363m surplus (2009)

Trade with UK	2009	2010
Imports from UK	£2,396,508,316	£2,667,281,654
Exports to UK	£3,690,195,469	£4,023,222,364

COMMUNICATIONS

The main ports are Aarhus, Odense, Copenhagen, Aalborg and Esbjerg. The principal airports are at Copenhagen, Aarhus, Aalborg and near Vejle. There are 2,667km of railway, of which 640km is electrified, and 73,197km of roads, including 1,111km of motorways. A rail tunnel and a bridge link the islands of Sjaelland

(Zealand) and Fyn, and a road and rail tunnel and a bridge across the Oresund link Copenhagen with Malmo, Sweden. A tunnel from Lolland to Fehman, Germany, will be built in 2014–20. The telecommunications network is modern and extensive; mobile phone distribution is over 100 per cent.

EDUCATION AND HEALTH

Education is free and compulsory for nine years. Vocational educational programmes are numerous, with commercial, technical and agricultural training predominating.

Gross enrolment ratio (percentage of relevant age group) – primary 98 per cent; secondary 119 per cent; tertiary 78 per cent (2008 est)
Health expenditure (per capita) – US$6,273 (2009)
Hospital beds (per 1,000 people) – 3.6 (2004–9)

MEDIA

The public broadcaster is Danmarks Radio, which operates two television networks and national and regional radio stations. Private television stations can be obtained via satellite and cable. There are around 250 local commercial and community radio stations in operation.

CULTURE

Denmark has made significant contributions to science and its Nobel laureates include atomic physicist Niels Bohr (1885–1962), who helped to develop the first atomic bomb, and medical researcher Niels Finsen (1860–1904). Notable contributions have been made in music by Carl Nielsen (1865–1931), in design by Georg Jensen (1866–1935) and Arne Jacobsen (1902–71), in philosophy by Soren Kierkegaard (1813–55), and in literature by Hans Christian Andersen (1805–75) and Karen Blixen (1885–1962). Eminent film directors Lars von Trier (b. 1956) and Thomas Vinterburg (b. 1969) co-founded the avant-garde filmmaking movement Dogme 95 in the 1990s.

THE FAEROE ISLANDS

Area – 1,393 sq. km
Capital – Torshavn; population, 20,082 (2009 est)
Population – 49,057 rising at 0.4 per cent per year (2010 est)
National day – 29 July (Olaifest)

The Faeroe (Sheep) Islands are a group of 18 rugged islands (17 inhabited) and a few islets in the North Atlantic Ocean, between the Shetland Islands and Iceland. First settled in the ninth century, the islands were a Norwegian province and, with Norway, came under Danish rule in the 14th century. Since 1948 the Faeroes have been self-governing; they are not part of the EU.

The sovereign is represented in the islands by a high commissioner, and the islands elect two representatives to the Danish legislature. The Faroese government *(Landsstyri)* is responsible for internal affairs. The parliament *(Loegting)* has 33 members, elected for a four-year term. In the 2008 election, the Republican Party won the most seats but the coalition government of the Social Democrats, Union Party and People's Party formed in 2004 retained its overall majority and continued in office.

Prime Minister, Kaj Leo Johannesen

ECONOMY AND TRADE

The economy has grown steadily in recent years, although it slowed during the global downturn. It remains highly dependent on fishing and fish processing; fish and fish products account for 95 per cent of exports. Offshore oil discoveries raise the possibility of future diversification and less dependence on Danish government subsidies.

BALANCE OF PAYMENTS

Trade – US$90m deficit (2003)
Current Account – US$7m deficit (2003)

Trade with UK	2009	2010
Imports from UK	£13,816,524	£20,127,655
Exports to UK	£102,341,731	£119,085,555

BRITISH CONSULATE

P/F Damfar, PO Box 1154, Niels Finsengota 5, FR-110 Torshavn
T (+298) 35 00 77
Honorary Consul, Tummas H. Dam

GREENLAND (KALAALLIT NUNAAT)

Area – 2,166,086 sq. km
Capital – Nuuk (Godthab); population 15,182 (2009 est)
Population – 57,600 rising at 0.06 per cent per year (2009 est)
National day – 21 June (longest day)

Greenland, the world's largest island, lies between the Atlantic and Arctic oceans, to the east of Canada and to the west of Iceland. Most of Greenland is within the Arctic Circle, with permafrost covering about 80 per cent of the island, although this ice cap is beginning to melt (*see* North and South Poles). Elevation extremes range from 3,700m (Gunnbjorn) at the highest point to 0m (Atlantic Ocean) at the lowest.

Greenland was first discovered by small groups of hunters and nomadic groups who migrated from Canada *c.*500 BC. In the late tenth century Icelanders established settlements along the south-eastern coast, but these colonies had died out by the 16th century. Danish colonisation began in the 18th century. Greenland was integrated into Denmark in 1953 and was granted internal autonomy in 1979; greater autonomy was granted in 2009. Greenland negotiated its withdrawal from the EU, without discontinuing relations with Denmark, and left in 1985. The USA maintains air bases on the island.

The sovereign is represented by a high commissioner, and Greenland elects two representatives to the Danish legislature. The Greenlandic government *(Landsstyre)* is elected by the parliament *(Landsting)*, which has 31 members, elected for a four-year term. In the 2009 election to the *Landsting*, the Siumut (Forward) party, in power since the 1970s, was defeated by the Inuit Ataqatigiit (Brotherhood of the People) party, which won 14 seats.
Prime Minister, Kuupik Kleist

ECONOMY AND TRADE

The economy is dependent on Danish subsidies (nearly 60 per cent of government revenue) and fishing; fish and fish products comprise 82 per cent of exports. Natural resources include zinc, iron ore, lead, coal, molybdenum, gold, platinum and uranium, some of which are mined. Mineral exploration and mining operations are being extended as the ice cap shrinks. This is also benefiting offshore oil exploration, and global warming is extending the growing season. Tourism is being encouraged.

Trade with UK	2009	2010
Imports from UK	£997,106	£39,430,761
Exports to UK	£4,103,882	£7,347,501

DJIBOUTI

Jumhuriyat Jibuti / République de Djibouti – Republic of Djibouti

Area – 23,200 sq. km
Capital – Djibouti; population, 566,681
Currency – Djibouti franc of 100 centimes
Population – 740,528 rising at 2.18 per cent a year (2010 est); Somali (Issa) 60 per cent, Afar 35 per cent (est)
Religion – Sunni Muslim 99 per cent (est). This number may be inflated as citizens are officially presumed to be Muslim if they do not specifically identify with another faith
Language – French, Arabic (both official), Somali, Afar
Population density – 37 per sq. km (2009)
Urban population – 87 per cent (2008 est)
Median age (years) – 21.4 (2010 est)
National anthem – 'Djibouti'
National day – 27 June (Independence Day)
Life expectancy – 60.73 (2010 est)
Mortality rate – 8.37 (2010 est)
Birth rate – 25.58 (2010 est)
Infant mortality rate – 56.65 (2010 est)
HIV / AIDS adult prevalence – 2.5 per cent (2009 est)
Death penalty – Abolished for all crimes (since 1995)
CPI score – 3.2 (2010)

CLIMATE AND TERRAIN

Djibouti is situated on the strait linking the Gulf of Aden with the Red Sea, close to busy shipping lanes. The coastal plain is separated from an inland plateau by the central mountains. Elevation extremes range from 2,028m (Moussa Ali) at the highest point to −155m (Lake Assal) at the lowest. Although the climate is semi-arid with a hot season between April and October, occasional heavy rains can cause flash floods. The country is also prone to cyclones, drought and earthquakes.

HISTORY AND POLITICS

Settled by the Afars (Ethiopian) and Issas (Somali) about 2,000 years ago, the area was annexed by the French in 1888 and became French Somaliland; in 1967 it was renamed the French Territory of the Afars and the

Issas. The territory became independent as Djibouti on 27 June 1977, under President Hassan Gouled Aptidon (an Issa), the leader of *Rassemblement Populaire pour le Progrès* (RPP), which became the only legal political party in 1981.

In 1991, Afar discontent with the Issa domination of government under one-party rule led to civil war between the government and the *Front pour la Restauration de l'Unité et de la Démocratie* (FRUD), an alliance of rebel groups. A multiparty constitution was introduced and multiparty elections were held in 1992, but fighting continued until a power-sharing agreement was reached in 1994. The civil war ended with the signing of a peace accord in 1996, although a breakaway faction of the FRUD continued its armed opposition to the government until 2001.

Djibouti has a long-running dispute with Eritrea over an area of their common border. There were clashes between their troops in 2008, but in June 2010 both countries agreed to resolve the dispute peacefully.

In the 2008 legislative elections, which were boycotted by the opposition, the Union for a Presidential Majority (UMP) – an alliance of the RPP, FRUD and two other parties supporting President Guelleh – retained all 65 seats in the legislature. The 2011 presidential election, held a few months after mass demonstrations against the president, was boycotted by the opposition, and President Guellah won a third term in office.

POLITICAL SYSTEM
Under the 1992 constitution, amended in 2010, the president is directly elected for a five-year term, renewable without limit. The president appoints the council of ministers. The unicameral National Assembly has 65 members, directly elected for a five-year term. The 2010 constitutional amendments provided for the establishment of a senate.

HEAD OF STATE
President, Ismail Omar Guelleh, *elected* 9 April 1999, *re-elected* 2005, 2011

SELECTED GOVERNMENT MEMBERS *as at June 2011*
Prime Minister, Dileita Muhammad Dileita
Defence, Mohamed Kamil Abdoulkader
Interior, Hassan Darar Houffaneh
Economy and Finance, Ilyas Moussa Dawaleh
Foreign Affairs, Mahamoud Ali Youssouf

EMBASSY OF THE REPUBLIC OF DJIBOUTI
26 Rue Emile Ménier, 75116 Paris, France
T (+33) (1) 4727 4922 E webmaster@ambdjibouti.org
Ambassador Extraordinary and Plenipotentiary, HE Rachad Farah, *apptd* 2005

BRITISH AMBASSADOR
HE Norman Ling, *apptd* 2008, resident at Addis Ababa, Ethiopia

DEFENCE
The army has 20 armoured personnel carriers. The navy has 10 patrol and coastal combatant vessels. The gendarmerie has 1 patrol and coastal combatant vessel.
Military budget – US$10m (2010)
Military personnel – 10,450: army 8,000, navy 200, air force 250, gendarmerie 2,000; National Security Force 2,500

ECONOMY AND TRADE
A barren country with few natural resources and little industry, Djibouti's chief asset is its location on major shipping lanes. It is a transit port for neighbouring landlocked countries (especially Ethiopia, 70 per cent of whose trade passes through Djibouti), an international trans-shipment and refuelling centre, and a military base for US and EU forces because of its strategic position. The country is dependent on foreign aid, has a very high level of unemployment and has to import nearly all its food. The service sector accounts for 81.9 per cent of GDP, agriculture for 3.2 per cent, and industry for 14.9 per cent.

The main trading partners are Somalia (which takes 77 per cent of exports), Ethiopia, Saudi Arabia, India and China. Principal exports are re-exports, hides and skins, and coffee (in transit). The main imports are food, beverages, transport equipment, chemicals and petroleum products.
GNI – US$1,120m; US$1,280 per capita (2009)
Annual average growth of GDP – 4.8 per cent (2010 est)
Inflation rate – 6 per cent (2009 est)
Population below poverty line – 42 per cent (2007 est)
Unemployment – 59 per cent (2007 est)
Total external debt – US$428m (2006 est)
Imports – US$400m (2009)
Exports – US$100m (2009)

BALANCE OF PAYMENTS
Trade – US$391m deficit (2010)
Current Account – US$205m deficit (2007)

Trade with UK	2009	2010
Imports from UK	£6,270,592	£6,217,361
Exports to UK	£437,256	£56,275

COMMUNICATIONS
Djibouti city is the hub of the transport system, the location of the main port and the principal airport. The 100km Djibouti section of the Addis Ababa–Djibouti railway is controlled by both Djibouti and Ethiopia but is largely inoperable. The government is keen to expand the rail network into neighbouring countries to improve trade. Of the 3,065km of roads, 1,226km are now surfaced. There is a high risk of piracy and kidnapping for ransom in territorial waters.

The telecommunications system operates throughout the country, although mobile phone networks are largely confined to the capital city and its environs.

MEDIA
The main newspaper, *La Nation,* and the national radio and television stations, operated by Radiodiffusion-Télévision de Djibouti, are government-owned. There are no private broadcasters, and the government exercises tight control of electronic media. A number of privately owned newspapers circulate freely, but journalists practise self-censorship.

DOMINICA

Commonwealth of Dominica

Area – 751 sq. km
Capital – Roseau; population, 14,266 (2009 est)
Currency – East Caribbean dollar (EC$) of 100 cents
Population – 72,813 rising at 0.21 per cent a year (2010 est)
Religion – Christian (Roman Catholic 61 per cent, Pentecostal 6 per cent, Seventh-day Adventist 6 per cent, Baptist 4 per cent, Methodist 4 per cent) (est)
Language – English (official), Creole
Population density – 98 per sq. km (2009)
Urban population – 74 per cent (2008 est)
Median age (years) – 30.3 (2010 est)
National anthem – 'Isle of Beauty, Isle of Splendour'
National day – 3 November (Independence Day)
Life expectancy – 75.77 (2010 est)
Mortality rate – 8.12 (2010 est)
Birth rate – 15.68 (2010 est)
Infant mortality rate – 13.2 (2010 est)
Death penalty – Retained
CPI score – 5.2 (2010)
Literacy rate – 88.0 per cent (2008 est)

CLIMATE AND TERRAIN

Dominica, the most northerly of the Windward Islands, is 46km long and 25km wide, with a mountainous and forested centre. Its peaks include volcanic craters, one of which contains Boiling Lake, the world's second-largest thermally active lake. Elevation extremes range from 1,447m (Morne Diablotins) at the highest point to 0m (Caribbean Sea) at the lowest. The climate is tropical, with average daily temperatures around 26°C. The island is located within the hurricane zone.

HISTORY AND POLITICS

Dominica was discovered by Columbus in 1493, when it was a stronghold of the Caribs, the sole inhabitants of the island until the French founded settlements in the 18th century. It was ceded to the British in 1763 but passed back and forth between France and Britain until 1805, after which British possession was unchallenged. From 1871 until the 1960s Dominica was administered by Britain as part of various federations of West Indian islands. Internal self-government from 1967 was followed on 3 November 1978 by independence as a republic.

President Nicholas Liverpool was the sole candidate nominated in the 2008 presidential election and was returned for a second term. The Dominica Labour Party (DLP), in power since 2000, won the legislative election in 2009 and continued in government.

POLITICAL SYSTEM

Under the 1978 constitution, the president is elected by the legislature for a five-year term, renewable once. The unicameral House of Assembly has 30 members, 21 directly elected, and nine appointed senators; all members serve a five-year term.

HEAD OF STATE
President, Nicholas Liverpool, *elected* 2003, *re-elected* 26 July 2008

SELECTED GOVERNMENT MEMBERS *as at June 2011*
Prime Minister, Finance, Foreign Affairs, Roosevelt Skerrit
National Security, Charles Savarin
Attorney-General, Levi Peter

OFFICE OF THE HIGH COMMISSIONER FOR THE COMMONWEALTH OF DOMINICA
1 Collingham Gardens, London SW5 0HW
T 020-7370 5194 E info@dominicahighcommission.co.uk
W www.dominicahighcommission.co.uk
High Commissioner (acting), Janet Charles

BRITISH HIGH COMMISSIONER
HE Paul Brummell, *apptd* 2009, resident at Bridgetown, Barbados

ECONOMY AND TRADE

The economy, traditionally dependent on banana exports, struggled in the early 2000s as EU preferential access for the fruit was phased out; the industry also suffered serious hurricane damage in 2007. Economic restructuring from 2003 led to steady growth, with an emphasis on eco-agriculture and eco-tourism, until the global downturn caused the economy to contract in 2009. Diversification into offshore financial services and light industry is also being encouraged, and exploitation of geothermal energy, fishing and forestry resources is planned.

Agriculture is the principal occupation, employing 40 per cent of the workforce but producing only 17.7 per cent of GDP. Services contribute 49.5 per cent of GDP and industry 32.8 per cent. The main trading partners are Japan, the UK, the USA, other Caribbean countries and China. Principal exports are bananas, soap, bay oil, vegetables and citrus fruits. The main imports are manufactured goods, machinery and equipment, food and chemicals.

GNI – US$359m; US$4,900 per capita (2009)
Annual average growth of GDP – 1.4 per cent (2010 est)
Inflation rate – 0.1 per cent (2009 est)
Total external debt – US$213m (2004)
Imports – US$200m (2009)

BALANCE OF PAYMENTS
Trade – US$205m deficit (2010)
Current Account – US$116m deficit (2008)

Trade with UK	2009	2010
Imports from UK	£7,879,014	£5,789,611
Exports to UK	£20,554,225	£3,993,404

MEDIA

Although there is no national television service, a private cable network covers part of the island. There are no daily newspapers but there are several weekly publications. Private and public radio stations are in operation throughout the country. All media are free from government censorship and interference.

DOMINICAN REPUBLIC

República Dominicana – Dominican Republic

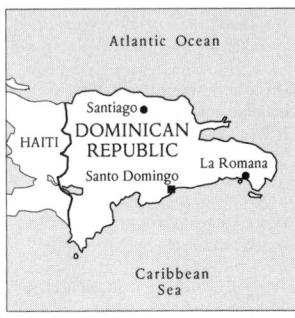

Area – 48,670 sq. km

Capital – Santo Domingo; population, 2,138,420 (2009 est)

Major cities – La Romana, San Pedro de Macorís, Santiago de los Caballeros

Currency – Dominican Republic peso (RD$) of 100 centavos

Population – 9,823,821 rising at 1.36 per cent a year (2010 est)

Religion – Christian (Roman Catholic 69 per cent, Protestant 18 per cent) (est). Many also practise Santería (a syncretisation of Christianity and African religions), brujería (witchcraft) or Vodou (voodoo)

Language – Spanish (official)

Population density – 209 per sq. km (2009)

Urban population – 69 per cent (2008 est)

Median age (years) – 25.8 (2010 est)

National anthem – 'Quisqueyanos Valientes' ['Valiant Quisqueyans']

National day – 27 February (Independence Day)

Life expectancy (years) – 77.15 (2010 est)

Mortality rate – 4.3 (2010 est)

Birth rate – 19.9 (2010 est)

Infant mortality rate – 23.1 (2010 est)

Death penalty – Abolished for all crimes (since 1966)

CPI score – 3 (2010)

Literacy rate – 89.5 per cent (2008 est)

Gross enrolment ratio (percentage of relevant age group) – primary 106 per cent; secondary 77 per cent (2009 est)

Health expenditure (per capita) – US$271 (2009)

Hospital beds (per 1,000 people) – 1.0 (2004–9)

CLIMATE AND TERRAIN

The republic forms the eastern two-thirds of the island of Hispaniola and is crossed from the north-west to the south-east by the Cordillera Central mountain range, which has a number of peaks over 3,000m. Elevation extremes range from 3,175m (Pico Duarte) at the highest point to −46m (Lake Enriquillo) at the lowest. The climate is maritime tropical, with an average temperature of 25°C.

HISTORY AND POLITICS

The island was discovered by Columbus in 1492, and a Spanish colony was established in 1496. The eastern province of Santo Domingo remained under Spanish rule after the partition of Hispaniola in 1697, but was ceded to France in 1795. It was restored to Spain in 1809, but rebelled in 1821 and achieved independence briefly before being annexed by Haiti in 1822. Haitian rule ended in 1844 when independence was declared as the Dominican Republic, although the country was

voluntarily under Spanish rule again from 1861 to 1865. A long dictatorship at the end of the 19th century was followed by revolution and bankruptcy, which led to occupation by US forces from 1916 until 1924. A military coup in 1930 established the dictatorship of Gen. Rafael Trujillo, whose corrupt rule continued until his assassination in 1961. After a period of political instability, a new constitution was adopted in 1966 and democracy was restored.

The 2004 presidential election was won by Leonel Fernández (president 1996–2000) of the Dominican Liberation Party (PLD), and he was re-elected in 2008. In legislative elections held in May 2010 the ruling PLD increased its majority in both houses.

POLITICAL SYSTEM

Under the 2010 constitution, the executive president is directly elected for a four-year term, which is not renewable. The bicameral National Congress comprises the Chamber of Deputies, which has 183 members, and the senate, with 32 members, one for each province and one for Santo Domingo. Both chambers are directly elected for a four-year term, but the current members will serve until 2016 so that presidential and legislative elections can be held simultaneously.

HEAD OF STATE

President, Leonel Fernández, *elected* 2004, *sworn in* August 2004, *re-elected* 17 May 2008, *sworn in* 16 August 2008

Vice-President, Rafael Alburquerque

SELECTED GOVERNMENT MEMBERS *as at June 2011*

Foreign Affairs, Carlos Morales

Armed Forces, Maj.-Gen. Joaquin Virgilio Perez Feliz

Finance, Vicente Bengoa

Interior, Franklin Almeyda

EMBASSY OF THE DOMINICAN REPUBLIC

139 Inverness Terrace, London W2 6JF

T 020-7727 7091 E info@dominicanembassy.org.uk

W www.dominicanembassy.org.uk

Ambassador Extraordinary and Plenipotentiary, HE Anibal de Castro, *apptd* 2005

BRITISH EMBASSY

Edificio Corominas Pepín, 7th–8th Floor, Ave 27 de Febrero No 233, Santo Domingo

T (+1) (829) 472 7111 E brit.emb.sadom@codetel.net.do

W http://ukindominicanrepublic.fco.gov.uk

Ambassador Extraordinary and Plenipotentiary, HE Steven Fisher, *apptd* 2009

DEFENCE

The army has 12 light tanks and 8 armoured personnel carriers. The navy has 16 patrol and coastal combatant vessels at two bases.

Military budget – US$335m (2010)

Military personnel – 24,500: army 15,000, navy 4,000, air force 5,500; paramilitary 15,000

ECONOMY AND TRADE

In recent years, tourism and the free trade zones have overtaken agriculture as the mainstay of the economy, and services now account for 67.5 per cent of GDP. Agriculture accounts for 11.5 per cent of GDP, industry for 21 per cent. The main crops are sugar, coffee, cotton, cocoa, tobacco, rice, vegetables and bananas, and the main industrial activities are tourism, sugar processing, mining and the production of textiles, cement and tobacco products. Remittances from expatriate workers represent nearly 10 per cent of GDP but, like tourism, were affected by the global economic downturn. A free-trade agreement with Central American states in 2007 has boosted trade, but unemployment and fluctuations in nickel prices remain problematic.

The main trading partner is the USA, which takes 54 per cent of exports and provides 43 per cent of imports. Principal exports are ferro-nickel, sugar, gold, silver, coffee, cocoa, tobacco, meats and consumer goods. The chief imports are foodstuffs, fuel, cotton and fabrics, chemicals and pharmaceuticals.

GNI – US$45,019m; US$4,550 per capita (2009)
Annual average growth of GDP – 4.2 per cent (2010 est)
Inflation rate – 6.3 per cent (2010 est)
Population below poverty line – 42.2 per cent (2004)
Unemployment – 14.2 per cent (2010 est)
Total external debt – US$13,090m (2010 est)
Imports – US$11,500m (2009)
Exports – US$1,700m (2009)

BALANCE OF PAYMENTS
Trade – US$9,009m deficit (2010)
Current Account – US$2,337m deficit (2009)

Trade with UK	2009	2010
Imports from UK	£80,202,598	£108,477,477
Exports to UK	£101,987,984	£120,680,833

COMMUNICATIONS
Santo Domingo and Rio Haina are the main seaports. There are 35 airports and airfields, seven of which handle international flights; the principal airport is at Santo Domingo. There are 19,705km of roads, 9,872km of which are surfaced. There are 142km of railway. Santo Domingo's metro system was inaugurated in 2009.

Mobile phone distribution has risen rapidly, reaching 75 per 100 people in 2008, while fixed-line density is 10 per 100 people. There are over 2.7 million internet users.

MEDIA
There are several terrestrial commercial broadcasting stations and many multi-channel cable TV operators. The state-owned broadcaster is Corporacion Estatal de Radio y Television (CERTV). There are more than 200 commercial radio stations. Four main daily newspapers publish in Spanish. Press freedom is guaranteed by law, although some sensitive subjects are avoided.

ECUADOR

República del Ecuador – Republic of Ecuador

Area – 283,561 sq. km
Capital – Quito; population, 1,800,850 (2009 est)
Major cities – Cuenca, Guayaquil, Machala, Manta, Santo Domingo de los Colorados
Currency – US dollar (US$) of 100 cents
Population – 14,790,608 rising at 1.47 per cent a year (2010 est)
Religion – Christian (Roman Catholic 85 per cent) (est)
Language – Spanish (official), Quechua, other Amerindian languages
Population density – 55 per sq. km (2009)
Urban population – 66 per cent (2008 est)
Median age (years) – 25.3 (2010 est)
National anthem – 'Salve, Oh Patria' ['We Salute You, Our Homeland']
National day – 10 August (Independence Day)
Life expectancy (years) – 75.52 (2010 est)
Mortality rate – 5 (2010 est)
Birth rate – 20.32 (2010 est)
Infant mortality rate – 20.26 (2010 est)
Death penalty – Abolished for all crimes (since 1906)
CPI score – 2.5 (2010)

CLIMATE AND TERRAIN
Ecuador is an equatorial state lying on the north-west coast of South America. Its territory includes the Galápagos Islands in the Pacific Ocean. The Andes run north to south through the centre of the country, dividing the coastal plain in the west from the low-lying rainforest in the east, and between two local Andean chains lie the central highlands. Elevation extremes range from 0m (Pacific Ocean) at the lowest point to 6,267m (Chimborazo) at the highest. Other Andean peaks include Cotopaxi (5,896m) and Cayambe (5,790m) in the Eastern Cordillera. Ecuador is located in an earthquake zone and five of its volcanoes have erupted since 2000 – most recently Tungurahua in April 2011. The country has four different climatic zones, and is one of the most bio-diverse countries on earth. The average annual temperature in Quito is 15°C.

HISTORY AND POLITICS
The kingdom of the Caras, around Quito, was conquered by the Incas of Peru in the 15th century. After the Spanish defeated the Incas in Peru, Ecuador was conquered in 1534 and added to the Spanish viceroyalty of Peru. Independence from Spain was achieved in a revolutionary war that culminated in the battle of Mt Pichincha (1822). Ecuador then formed part of Gran Colombia with Colombia, Panama and Venezuela, but left this union to become a fully independent state in 1830. After independence, the country experienced periods of political instability interspersed with dictatorships and military rule. Democratic rule under civilian government was restored in 1979.

The exploitation of oil reserves funded economic and social transformation from the 1970s onwards but also caused rapid inflation and increased foreign debt. In recent years, these problems have worsened because of economic recession, leading to strikes and demonstrations. The most notable of these were by indigenous people, who have benefited least from the oil boom but been hardest hit by the economic downturn. Civil unrest forced three presidents from office between 1997 and 2003.

Presidential and legislative elections were held in 2009 after a new constitution was approved by a national referendum in 2008. President Correa was re-elected in the first round of voting and his party, the left-wing PAIS Alliance, won the most seats in the new legislature.

POLITICAL SYSTEM
The 2008 constitution provides for an executive president who is directly elected for a four-year term, renewable once. The unicameral National Assembly has 124 members elected on a party-list proportional representation basis for a four-year term. The republic is divided into 24 provinces.

HEAD OF STATE
President, Rafael Correa, *took office* 15 January 2007, *re-elected* April 2009
Vice-President, Lenin Moreno

SELECTED GOVERNMENT MEMBERS *as at June 2011*
Finance, Patricio Rivera Yanez
Foreign Affairs, Ricardo Patino
National Defence, Javier Ponce Cevallos

EMBASSY OF ECUADOR
Flat 3B, 3 Hans Crescent, London SW1X 0LS
T 020-7584 1367 E eecugranbretania@mmrree.gov.ec
W www.consuladoecuador.org.uk
Ambassador Extraordinary and Plenipotentiary, HE Ana Alban Mora, *apptd* 2010

BRITISH EMBASSY
PO Box 17-17-830, Citiplaza Building, Av. Naciones Unidas y Republica de El Salvador, Piso 14, Quito
T (+593) (2) 2970 800 E britembq@interactive.net.ec
W http://ukinecuador.fco.gov.uk
Ambassador Extraordinary and Plenipotentiary, HE Linda Cross, *apptd* 2008

DEFENCE
The army has 24 light tanks, 123 armoured personnel carriers and 29 multi-role helicopters. The navy has 2 submarines, 2 frigates and 9 patrol and coastal combatant vessels at two bases. The air force has over 80 combat aircraft.
Military budget – US$1,470m (2010)
Military personnel – 58,483: army 46,500, navy 7,283, air force 4,200; paramilitary 500
Conscription duration – 12 months (selective)

ECONOMY AND TRADE
Structural reforms in 2000, including the adoption of the US dollar, in response to the severe economic crisis of 1999 paved the way for strong growth from 2002 to 2006. Growth has slowed since owing to the uncertainty created by windfall taxes imposed on foreign oil companies, a fall in oil production since 2007, the government defaulting on 80 per cent of private external debt in 2008, and the cancellation of a number of bilateral investment treaties in 2009. The global downturn further reduced oil revenue, remittances from expatriate workers (who number nearly one million) and export earnings, although the economy started to recover in 2010.

Oil is Ecuador's principal export, accounting for over half of export earnings and a third of government revenue in recent years. After oil, agriculture, fishing and forestry are the most important activities, providing products both for export and for the food- and wood-processing industries. The main exports are oil, bananas, cut flowers, fish, cacao, coffee, hemp and timber. The main imports are industrial materials, fuels and lubricants, and consumer goods. Principal trading partners are the USA and other South American countries.
GNI – US$56,091m; US$3,970 per capita (2009)
Annual average growth of GDP – 2.4 per cent (2010 est)
Inflation rate – 3.6 per cent (2010 est)
Population below poverty line – 35.1 per cent (2008)
Unemployment – 7.6 per cent (2010 est)
Total external debt – US$14,710m (2009)
Imports – US$15,100m (2009)
Exports – US$13,800m (2009)

BALANCE OF PAYMENTS
Trade – US$2,913m deficit (2010)
Current Account – US$1,205m surplus (2008)

Trade with UK	2009	2010
Imports from UK	£54,346,174	£54,453,817
Exports to UK	£86,549,384	£69,170,088

COMMUNICATIONS
There are 43,670km of roads, 6,472km of which are surfaced, and there are 965km of railways. The road and rail networks are largely to the west of the Andes. Travel to the east is mostly by air, with internal services between all major towns. There are 428 airports and airfields, of which 105 have surfaced runways, and international flights operate to Quito and Guayaquil. The main ports are Guayaquil and Esmeraldas. The fixed-line telephone system is being expanded but the service is limited. Mobile phone distribution has grown quickly, and in 2009 stood at 95 per 100 people.

EDUCATION AND HEALTH
Elementary education is free and compulsory until age 14.
Literacy rate – 91.0 per cent (2008 est)
Gross enrolment ratio (percentage of relevant age group) – primary 118 per cent; secondary 70 per cent; tertiary 35 per cent (2007 est)
Health expenditure (per capita) – US$255 (2009)
Hospital beds (per 1,000 people) – 1.5 (2004–9)

MEDIA AND CULTURE
The government owns around 20 media outlets but claims editorial distance from their output. Private media outlets include six daily newspapers and a number of television and radio stations. The offices of publications critical of the state have been raided by police, and journalists exercise a degree of self-censorship, especially on sensitive issues. By law, the media must provide the government with free space or air time on demand.

Quito has been a UNESCO World Heritage Site since 1978. South America's oldest market, which predates the Inca period, can be found in the small town of Otavalo.

GALÁPAGOS ISLANDS
The Galápagos (Giant Tortoise) Islands, about 960km from the mainland, were annexed by Ecuador in 1832. The 12 large and several hundred smaller islands lie on the equator, and most form part of a national park where unique marine birds, iguanas and the giant tortoises are conserved. This wildlife provided naturalist Charles Darwin (1809–82) with inspiration and research material for his theory of evolution by natural selection, expounded in *On the Origin of Species* (1859). The islands were declared a UNESCO World Heritage Site in 1978.

EGYPT

Jumhuriyat Misr al-Arabiyah – Arab Republic of Egypt

Area – 1,001,450 sq. km
Capital – Cairo; population, 10,902,500 (2009 est); stands on the Nile about 22km from the head of the delta
Major cities – Alexandria (founded 332 BC by Alexander the Great; the capital for over 1,000 years), Giza, Port Said, Suez
Currency – Egyptian pound (£E) of 100 piastres or 1,000 millièmes
Population – 80,471,869 rising at 2 per cent a year (2010 est); Egyptian (including Berber and Bedouin) 99.6 per cent (2006). The Bedouin of the Western and Eastern deserts are traditionally semi-sedentary tent-dwellers. The Nubians of the Nile Valley are of mixed Arab and African descent
Religion – Muslim 90 per cent (almost all Sunni), Christian 10 per cent (Coptic 9 per cent) (est)
Language – Arabic (official), English, French
Population density – 83 per sq. km (2009)
Urban population – 43 per cent (2008 est)
Median age (years) – 24 (2010 est)
National anthem – 'Biladi, Biladi, Biladi' ['My Homeland, My Homeland, My Homeland']
National day – 23 July (Revolution Day)
Life expectancy (years) – 72.4 (2010 est)
Mortality rate – 4.85 (2010 est)
Birth rate – 25.02 (2010 est)
Infant mortality rate – 26.2 (2010 est)
Death penalty – Retained
CPI score – 3.1 (2010)

CLIMATE AND TERRAIN

There are four broad regions: the Western Desert, which covers nearly two-thirds of the country to the west of the Nile valley; the Eastern Desert, which lies between the Nile and the mountains along the Red Sea coast; the fertile Nile valley and delta, where most of the population lives; and the Sinai peninsula, where a coastal plain on the Mediterranean rises to mountains in the south. The deserts are arid plateaux, with depressions in the Western Desert whose springs irrigate oases, while the Eastern Desert is dissected by wadis (dry watercourses). Elevation extremes range from 2,629m (Mt Catherine, Sinai) at the highest point to −133m (Qattara depression) at the lowest. The country has a desert climate, with hot, dry summers and mild winters. Temperatures increase further south, and rainfall increases nearer the coast. Average daily temperatures range from 18°C to 30°C.

HISTORY AND POLITICS

The unification of the kingdoms of Lower Egypt and Upper Egypt *c.*3100 BC marked the establishment of the Egyptian state, with Memphis as its capital. Egypt was ruled for nearly 2,800 years by a succession of 31 pharaonic dynasties, which built the pyramids at Giza. Egypt's independence was lost to the Assyrians in *c.*669 BC, and it was conquered by the Persians in 525 BC and then by Alexander the Great in 332 BC. Subsequently ruled by Alexander's general Ptolemy and his descendants, it was conquered and ruled by Rome (30 BC to AD 324) and then by the Byzantine Empire. In AD 640 Egypt was subjugated by Arab Muslim invaders. In 1517 the country was incorporated into the Ottoman Empire, under which it remained, nominally, until the early 20th century. Britain occupied Egypt in 1882, and a British protectorate over Egypt lasted from 1914 to 1922, when Sultan Ahmed Fuad was proclaimed King of Egypt and the country became independent. In 1952 the monarchy was deposed and in 1953 Egypt was declared a republic. Egypt joined with Syria to form a short-lived single state, the United Arab Republic (UAR), between 1958 and 1961, when Syria seceded.

Egypt was involved in the Arab-Israeli wars in 1948, 1967 and 1973. In the 1967 war (the Six Day War), the Sinai peninsula was lost to Israel. Sinai was returned to Egypt in 1982 under the 1979 treaty that resulted from the Camp David talks (1978–9) and formally terminated the 31-year-old state of war between the two countries. The treaty led to strained relations with other Arab nations until the mid-1980s.

President Hosni Mubarak, who took office after the assassination of President Sadat in 1981, played an active part in the Middle East peace process in the 1990s but was unable to suppress internal terrorism by Islamic fundamentalists. A state of emergency has been in force continuously since 1981 and was extended in June 2010 for a further two years. Frustration and resentment at the lack of political freedom found expression in public demonstrations in recent years, including during 2010 when vote-rigging was alleged after the 2010 legislative elections, which returned fewer opposition and independent candidates than previously. These grievances, fuelled by the success of the Tunisian revolution, inspired several weeks of mass anti-government demonstrations in early 2011 that eventually made President Mubarak's position untenable. His announcement that he would not stand in the 2011 presidential election failed to placate the demonstrators and he resigned on 11 February, handing over power to the high command of the army, which dissolved the legislature and suspended the constitution until presidential and legislative elections in autumn 2011. See also Events of the Year.

INSURGENCIES

Militant Islamic fundamentalists emerged in the 1980s. Their campaign against the government became increasingly violent from the early 1990s, and was eventually directed against foreign tourists as well as domestic targets. Although the largest fundamentalist organisation, Gamaat-i-Islamiya, renounced violence in 1999, attacks continue, often targeting foreigners.

POLITICAL SYSTEM

The 1971 constitution was suspended after President Mubarak's resignation, and substantial changes to it were approved by referendum in March 2011. It now provides for an executive president who is directly elected for a four-year term, which is renewable once. The unicameral People's Assembly, suspended in February 2011, has 518 members, who serve a five-year term; 508 members are directly elected (with 64 seats reserved for women) and ten are appointed by the president. The Consultative Council has an advisory role; its 264 members include 176 who are directly elected and 88 presidential appointees, all serving a six-year term. Religious political parties are banned.

HEAD OF STATE
Leader of the Supreme Council of the Armed Forces, Minister of Defence, Field Marshal Mohammed Tantawi, *assumed power* 11 February 2011
Vice-president, vacant

SELECTED GOVERNMENT MEMBERS *as at May 2011*
Prime Minister, Essam Sharaf
Deputy Prime Minister, Legal Affairs, Dr Yahia al-Gamal
Finance, Dr Samir Radwan
Foreign Affairs, Nabil al-Araby
Interior, Gen. Mansour al-Essawy

EMBASSY OF THE ARAB REPUBLIC OF EGYPT
26 South Street, London W1K 1DW
T 020-7499 3304 E eg.emb_london@mfa.gov.eg
W www.egyptembassyuk.org
Ambassador Extraordinary and Plenipotentiary, HE Hatem Seif el-Nasr, *apptd* 2008

BRITISH EMBASSY
7 Ahmed Ragheb Street, Garden City, Cairo
T (+20) (2) 2791 6000 E info@britishembassy.org.eg
W http://ukinegypt.fco.gov.uk
Ambassador Extraordinary and Plenipotentiary, HE Dominic Asquith, CMG, *apptd* 2007

BRITISH COUNCIL
192 El Nil Street, Agouza, Cairo
T (+20) (2) 219 789 W www.britishcouncil.org/egypt
Director, Paul Smith

DEFENCE
The army has 2,383 main battle tanks, 390 armoured infantry fighting vehicles and 4,160 armoured personnel carriers. The navy has 4 submarines, 8 frigates, 50 patrol and coastal vessels and 5 armed helicopters at 8 bases. The air force has 565 combat aircraft and 105 armed helicopters.
Military budget – US$6,240m (2010)
Military personnel – 468,500: army 340,000, navy 18,500, air force 30,000, Air Defence Command 80,000; paramilitary 397,000
Conscription duration – 12–36 months

ECONOMY AND TRADE
Economic liberalisation in recent years has attracted foreign investment and promoted exports, producing strong growth in GDP. However living standards for most of the population remain low, with a fifth living below the poverty line. There is a growing budget deficit, partly owing to price subsidies for basic necessities, and high public debt. Although the dams on the Nile have expanded the area of land under cultivation, other factors, such as population growth, put resources under pressure.

The services sector contributes 48.6 per cent to GDP and employs 51 per cent of the workforce. Tourism is the largest component of this sector (visitor numbers have increased by over 50 per cent since the late 1990s), along with Suez Canal revenues and expatriate remittances. Industry accounts for 37.9 per cent of GDP and 17 per cent of employment, but despite increasing industrialisation, agriculture still employs 32 per cent of the workforce, contributing 13.5 per cent of GDP. Egypt is a net importer of foodstuffs, especially grain, and a food security programme has been set up with the aim of achieving self-sufficiency.

The main cash crop is cotton, of which Egypt is one of the world's main producers. Other important crops are rice, maize, wheat, vegetables, fruit and livestock. Industry is centred on oil and gas extraction, processing hydrocarbons, cotton and other agricultural products, producing textiles, chemicals and pharmaceuticals. Oil is the backbone of the economy and helps, alongside considerable reserves of natural gas and the hydroelectric power produced by the Aswan and High dams, to make Egypt self-sufficient in energy.

The main trading partners are the USA, Italy, China and Germany. Principal exports are crude oil and petroleum products, cotton, textiles, metal products, chemicals and processed food. The main imports are machinery and equipment, foodstuffs, chemicals, wood products and fuels.
GNI – US$188,575m; US$2,070 per capita (2009)
Annual average growth of GDP – 5.3 per cent (2010 est)
Inflation rate – 12.8 per cent (2010 est)
Population below poverty line – 20 per cent (2005 est)
Unemployment – 9.7 per cent (2010 est)
Total external debt – US$30,610m (2010)
Imports – US$44,900m (2009)
Exports – US$23,100m (2009)

BALANCE OF PAYMENTS
Trade – US$26,505m deficit (2010)
Current Account – US$888m surplus (2008)

Trade with UK	2009	2010
Imports from UK	£945,413,153	£1,134,696,883
Exports to UK	£562,674,292	£600,616,526

COMMUNICATIONS
Egypt has 3,500km of waterways, including the River Nile and Lake Nasser, the Alexandria–Cairo waterway, numerous small canals in the Nile delta and the Suez Canal (opened 1869; closed 1967–75). The main seaports are Alexandria, Damietta and Port Said on the Mediterranean Sea and Suez on the Red Sea. A road network of 65,000km and a rail network of 5,500km link the Nile valley and delta with the main development areas east and west of the river, but there are few routes in the interior. There are 86 airports and airfields; the principal airports are at Cairo, Sharm el-Sheikh, Luxor, Alexandria and Hurgadah. The telephone system was modernised in the 1990s; there were 10.3 million fixed-line, 55.4 million mobile phone and 20.1 million internet subscribers in 2009.

EDUCATION AND HEALTH
Education is free between the ages of six and 15.
Literacy rate – 66.4 per cent (2008 est)
Gross enrolment ratio (percentage of relevant age group) – primary 100 per cent; tertiary 29 per cent (2007 est)
Health expenditure (per capita) – US$113 (2009)
Hospital beds (per 1,000 people) – 1.7 (2004–9)

MEDIA

Egyptian media play a central role in the Arab world; its newspapers are some of the most influential in the region, and the products of its film and television studios are shown in most Arab-speaking countries. Two state-run national television channels and six regional channels compete with the country's thriving satellite television industry, which is watched throughout the Arab-speaking world. The state's monopoly on radio broadcasting ended in 2003. The government has actively encouraged foreign media to base themselves in Egypt by establishing a free media zone in 2000 that offers economic incentives and access to its media infrastructure. The media are frequently critical of public figures, although in recent years defamation laws and provisions of the emergency law have been used to harass and detain bloggers, who are increasingly instrumental in mobilising political opposition. Social networking sites played a major role in organising the mass demonstrations that overthrew President Mubarak in 2011.

CULTURE

Egyptian culture dates back 5,000 years to one of the earliest-known civilisations on Earth; ancient Egyptian hieroglyphic scripts provide some of the world's oldest records of written communication. The country has experienced periods of Hellene, Christian, Arab and Islamic culture, and remains most famous for the pyramids of Giza, the library of Alexandria and the art and architecture of its ancient periods (beginning in the fourth millennium BC and waning around 31 BC). Modern Egypt has the highest number of Nobel laureates in Africa, including author Naguib Mahfouz (1911–2006) and diplomat Mohamed ElBaradei (b. 1942); actor Omar Sharif (b. 1932) is an Academy Award winner, while Cairo is home to Al-Ahly, the most widely supported football club in Africa.

EL SALVADOR

República de El Salvador – Republic of El Salvador

Area – 21,041 sq. km
Capital – San Salvador; population, 1,533,960 (2009 est)
Major cities – Apopo, San Miguel, Santa Ana
Currency – US dollar (US$) of 100 cents
Population – 6,052,064 rising at 0.33 per cent a year
   (2010 est)
Religion – Christian (Roman Catholic 50 per cent,
   Protestant 38 per cent) (est)
Language – Spanish (official), Nahua
Population density – 297 per sq. km (2009)
Urban population – 61 per cent (2008 est)

Median age (years) – 23.9 (2010 est)
National anthem – 'Himno Nacional de El Salvador'
   ['National Anthem of El Salvador']
National day – 15 September (Independence Day)
Life expectancy (years) – 73.18 (2010 est)
Mortality rate – 5.61 (2010 est)
Birth rate – 18.06 (2010 est)
Infant mortality rate – 20.97 (2010 est)
Death penalty – Retained for certain crimes (last known
   use 1973)
CPI score – 3.6 (2010)

CLIMATE AND TERRAIN

El Salvador lies on the west coast of Central America. The country is mountainous (much of the interior has an average altitude of 600m), with narrow coastal plains and a central plateau. Many of its peaks are volcanoes; most are extinct, but Ilamatepec (or Santa Ana) erupted in 2005. There are also numerous volcanic lakes. Elevation extremes range from 2,730m (Cerro El Pital) at the highest point to 0m (Pacific Ocean) at the lowest. The climate is tropical on the coast but more temperate at higher altitudes. The average annual temperature in San Salvador is 23°C. Earthquakes and volcanic activity are common, and the country is also susceptible to hurricanes and tropical storms.

HISTORY AND POLITICS

El Salvador was part of the Aztec kingdom conquered in 1524 by Pedro de Alvarado, and formed part of the Spanish viceroyalty of Guatemala until 1821. It was part of a Central American federation of former Spanish provinces from 1823 until the federation's dissolution in 1838, becoming fully independent in 1840.

There was political unrest in the 1970s, and guerrilla activity by the left-wing Farabundo Martí National Liberation Front (FMLN), which intensified from 1977 amid reports of human rights abuses by government troops and right-wing death squads. Decades of military rule ended in 1979, but elections in 1982 were boycotted by left-wing parties and the right-wing National Republican Alliance (ARENA) took office. The civil war between the FMLN and the US-backed government lasted throughout the 1980s, until a UN-sponsored peace agreement was signed in 1992. The FMLN was recognised as a political party, and it won a few seats in the 1994 election, steadily increasing its share of the vote in subsequent elections. Although the FMLN has often been the largest party in parliament, ARENA remained in office continuously until 2009 as it held the presidency and formed coalition governments with smaller right-wing parties.

In the 2009 legislative elections, the FMLN won the most seats in the legislature, although without a majority. The 2009 presidential election was won by FMLN candidate Mauricio Funes.

POLITICAL SYSTEM

Under the 1983 constitution, the executive president is directly elected for a five-year term, which is not renewable. The unicameral legislative assembly has 84 members, who are directly elected for a three-year term. The president appoints the Council of State. The country is divided into 14 departments.

HEAD OF STATE

President, Mauricio Funes, *elected* 15 March 2009, *took office* 1 June 2009
Vice-President, Sánchez Cerén

SELECTED GOVERNMENT MEMBERS *as at June 2011*
Defence, Col. David Munguía
Economy, Héctor Dada
Foreign Affairs, Hugo Martínez

EMBASSY OF EL SALVADOR
8 Dorset Square, 1st & 2nd Floors, London NW1 6PU
T 020-7224 9800 E embajadalondres@rree.gob.sv
Ambassador Extraordinary and Plenipotentiary, HE Werner
Matías Romero, *apptd* 2009

BRITISH AMBASSADOR
HE Julie Chappell, OBE, *apptd* 2009, resident at
Guatemala City, Guatemala

DEFENCE

The army has 38 armoured personnel carriers. The navy
has 11 patrol and coastal combatant vessels. The air force
has 14 combat aircraft.
Military budget – US$127m (2010)
Military personnel – 15,500: army 13,850, navy 700, air
force 771; paramilitary 17,000

ECONOMY AND TRADE

The country is one of the most industrialised in Central
America and has the region's third-largest economy
despite being its smallest country and having few natural
resources. Recovery after the civil war was set back by
a series of natural disasters, but the economy has been
transformed from a mainly agricultural to a service-based
economy with a growing manufacturing sector.
Government diversification efforts have promoted textile
production, international port services and tourism. Even
so, the value of expatriates' remittances is equivalent to
nearly double that of export earnings, and around 30 per
cent of the population live below the poverty line. The
economy contracted in 2009, with both exports and
remittances adversely affected by the global downturn,
but recovery began in 2010.

Agriculture contributes 11 per cent to GDP and
employs 19 per cent of the workforce. The principal
agricultural products are coffee, sugar, maize, rice, beans,
oilseed, cotton, sorghum, beef and dairy products.
Industry contributes 29.1 per cent of GDP, mostly
through assembly for re-export, food processing,
beverages, oil, chemicals, fertiliser, textiles, furniture and
light metals. Services, through tourism, commerce and
financial services, contribute 59.9 per cent of GDP.

The main trading partners are the USA and other
Central American states. Principal exports are offshore
assembly products, coffee, sugar, textiles, garments, gold,
ethanol, chemicals and electricity. The chief imports are
raw materials, consumer goods, capital goods, fuels,
foodstuffs, oil and electricity.
GNI – US$20,437m; US$3,370 per capita (2009)
Annual average growth of GDP – −1.2 per cent (2010 est)
Inflation rate – 0.8 per cent (2010 est)
Population below poverty line – 30.7 per cent (2006 est)
Unemployment – 7 per cent (2010 est)
Total external debt – US$11,450m (2010)
Imports – US$7,300m (2009)
Exports – US$3,800m (2009)

BALANCE OF PAYMENTS
Trade – US$4,051m deficit (2010)
Current Account – US$373m deficit (2009)

Trade with UK	2009	2010
Imports from UK	£8,220,360	£12,623,632
Exports to UK	£4,811,137	£8,435,432

COMMUNICATIONS

The principal ports are Cutuco and Acajutla, and ports in
Honduras and Guatemala are also used. There are
10,886km of roads, of which 2,827km are surfaced. The
Pan-American Highway from the Guatemalan frontier
passes through Santa Ana and San Salvador, continuing
to the Honduran frontier. The 283km rail network has
not been in operation since 2005 because of lack of
maintenance. There are 65 airports and airfields, although
only four have surfaced runways. There is an international
airport at San Salvador. Mobile phone density has grown
rapidly, exceeding 100 per 100 people in 2009; this
growth has slowed demand for fixed-line services.

EDUCATION AND HEALTH

Primary education is state-run, compulsory and free.
Literacy rate – 82.0 per cent (2008 est)
Gross enrolment ratio (percentage of relevant age group) –
primary 115 per cent; secondary 64 per cent; tertiary
25 per cent (2008 est)
Health expenditure (per capita) – US$229 (2009)
Hospital beds (per 1,000 people) – 1.1 (2004–9)

MEDIA

Television is dominated by a small number of large private
broadcasters, but there are hundreds of private radio
stations. Press freedom is guaranteed by the country's
constitution.

EQUATORIAL GUINEA

*República de Guinea Ecuatorial/République de Guinée
Equatoriale – Republic of Equatorial Guinea*

Area – 28,051 sq. km
Capital – Malabo, on Bioko; population, 127,743 (2009
est)
Major towns – Bata, the principal town and port of Río
Muni; Ebebiyín
Currency – Franc CFA of 100 centimes
Population – 650,702 rising at 2.67 per cent a year (2010
est); predominantly Fang; indigenous Bubi now a
minority on Bioko
Religion – Christian (Roman Catholic 87 per cent, other
denominations 6 per cent), traditional indigenous
religions 5 per cent (est). Many Catholics also follow
traditional beliefs
Language – Spanish, French (both official), Fang, Bubi
Population density – 24 per sq. km (2009)
Urban population – 39 per cent (2008 est)
Median age (years) – 19 (2010 est)
National anthem – 'Caminemos Pisando la Senda' ['Let Us
Tread the Path']

National day – 12 October (Independence Day)
Life expectancy – 61.98 (2010 est)
Mortality rate – 9.26 (2010 est)
Birth rate – 36 (2010 est)
Infant mortality rate – 79.47 (2010 est)
HIV/AIDS adult prevalence – 5 per cent (2009 est)
Death penalty – Retained
CPI score – 1.9 (2010)
Literacy rate – 87.0 per cent (2008 est)

CLIMATE AND TERRAIN
The country consists of several islands off the Cameroon coast and a small area on the mainland, Río Muni, where 80 per cent of the population lives. The islands, of which Bioko is the largest, are of volcanic origin. The mainland rises from a narrow coastal plain to a mountainous interior plateau, and is covered in dense vegetation. Elevation extremes range from 3,008m (Pico Basile) at the highest point to 0m (Atlantic Ocean) at the lowest. The climate is tropical, with a rainy season from July to January on Bioko, and from April to May and October to December on the mainland.

HISTORY AND POLITICS
The island of Fernando Po (Bioko) was claimed by the Portuguese in 1494 and held until 1777, when it was ceded to Spain. The mainland territory of Río Muni came under Spanish rule in 1844, and the two territories became one colony, subsequently known as Spanish Guinea, in 1904. The colony became autonomous in 1963, and independent in 1968 under its present name.

The first president, Francisco Macías Nguema, established a one-party state in 1970. His brutal regime was overthrown in 1979 in a military coup led by his nephew, Col. Obiang Nguema. A military regime was established after the coup, and only presidential nominees were allowed to stand in the 1983 and 1988 elections. Constitutional amendments were introduced in 1991 to allow multiparty elections, but President Nguema and the Democratic Party of Equatorial Guinea (PDGE) have retained power since 1992; most elections have been boycotted by the opposition parties because of election irregularities and intimidation. The regime has been accused of human rights abuses and the suppression of political opposition, and in 2003 opposition leaders set up a 'government-in-exile' in Spain. There is also a separatist movement on Bioko.

In the 2008 legislative election, the PDGE retained its overwhelming majority in parliament. President Nguema won the 2009 presidential election with 95 per cent of the vote.

POLITICAL SYSTEM
The 1991 constitution introduced a multiparty system. The president is directly elected for a seven-year term. The unicameral House of Representatives of the People has 100 members, who are directly elected for a five-year term.

HEAD OF STATE
President, Brig.-Gen. Teodoro Obiang Nguema Mbasogo, took power August 1979, re-elected 1989, 1996, 2002, 2009

SELECTED GOVERNMENT MEMBERS as at June 2011
Prime Minister, Ignacio Milam Tang
Economy, Francisca Tatchoup Belope

Foreign Affairs, Pastor Micha Ondo Bile
Defence, Gen. Antonio Mba Nguema Mikwe

EMBASSY OF THE REPUBLIC OF EQUATORIAL GUINEA
13 Park Place, St James' London SW1A 1LP
T 020-7499 6867 E embarege-londres@embarege-londres.org
W www.embarege-londres.org
Ambassador Extraordinary and Plenipotentiary, HE Agustin Nze Nfumu, apptd 2005

BRITISH AMBASSADOR
HE Robert Dewar, CMG, apptd 2007, resident at Abuja, Nigeria

DEFENCE
The army has 10 armoured personnel carriers and 20 armoured infantry fighting vehicles. The navy has 6 patrol and coastal combatant vessels at 2 bases. The coastguard has 6 patrol and coastal combatant vessel. The air force has 4 combat-capable aircraft and 3 armed helicopters.
Military expenditure – US$8m (2009 est)
Military personnel – 1,320: army 1,100, navy 120, air force 100

ECONOMY AND TRADE
Large oil and natural gas deposits discovered off Bioko in the 1990s have transformed the economy, which has grown dramatically since production began in 1996, despite contracting in 2009–10 during the global downturn. The country has the reputation of being one of the most corrupt in the world; oil exploitation has not benefited much of the population as most businesses are owned by government officials or their families. Despite the oil revenues, the country has a large external debt.

Industry contributes 93.9 per cent of GDP, agriculture 2.2 per cent and services 3.8 per cent. The oil-driven growth in the GDP masks stagnation in other sectors; agriculture, once the mainstay of the economy, has declined to subsistence level owing to neglect and lack of investment. The main crops are coffee, cocoa, rice, fruit, nuts, livestock and timber. Industrial activities other than oil and natural gas production include fishing and timber processing.

The main trading partners are the USA, China and Spain. Principal exports are petroleum and timber. The main imports are oil industry and other industrial equipment.
GNI – US$6,332m; US$12,420 per capita (2009)
Annual average growth of GDP – 2 per cent (2010 est)
Inflation rate – 8.2 per cent (2010 est)
Total external debt – US$832m (2010 est)
Imports – US$4,300m (2009)
Exports – US$9,200m (2009)

BALANCE OF PAYMENTS
Trade – US$4,544m surplus (2010)
Current Account – US$1,684m deficit (2008)

Trade with UK	2009	2010
Imports from UK	£43,598,988	£113,417,265
Exports to UK	£41,989,285	£10,749,130

MEDIA
Television and radio broadcasts are state-controlled; the government owns the only television station and, other than a private station owned by President Nguema's son, the only radio station. The main newspaper, Ebano, is also

state-owned; there are few privately owned publications. Criticism of the authorities is extremely rare as the government has legal powers of censorship.

ERITREA

Hagere Ertra – State of Eritrea

Area – 117,600 sq. km
Capital – Asmara; population, 648,961 (2009 est)
Major towns – Assab, Keren, Massawa
Currency – Nakfa of 100 cents
Population – 5,792,984 rising at 2.52 per cent a year (2010 est); Tigrinya (55 per cent), Tigre (30 per cent), Saho (4 per cent), Kunama (2 per cent), Rashaida (2 per cent), Bilen (2 per cent) (2010 est)
Religion – Sunni Muslim 50 per cent, Christian (Eritrean Orthodox 30 per cent, Roman Catholic 13 per cent), indigenous religions 2 per cent (est). Only Christians of the Eritrean Orthodox, Catholic and Lutheran churches and Muslims may marry freely
Language – Arabic, English, Tigrinya (all official), Tigre, Afar, Kunama
Population density – 50 per sq. km (2009)
Urban population – 21 per cent (2008 est)
Median age (years) – 18.5 (2010 est)
National anthem – 'Ertra, Ertra, Ertra' ['Eritrea, Eritrea, Eritrea']
National day – 24 May (Independence Day)
Life expectancy – 62.15 (2010 est)
Mortality rate – 8.25 (2010 est)
Birth rate – 33.48 (2010 est)
Infant mortality rate – 42.33 (2010 est)
HIV/AIDS adult prevalence – 1.3 per cent (2007 est)
Death penalty – Retained (not used since 1989)
CPI score – 2.6 (2010)
Literacy rate – 65.5 per cent (2008 est)
Gross enrolment ratio (percentage of relevant age group) – primary 48 per cent; secondary 32 per cent (2008 est); tertiary 2 per cent (2009 est)
Health expenditure (per capita) – US$10 (2009)
Hospital beds (per 1,000 people) – 1.2 (2004–9)

CLIMATE AND TERRAIN

The northern end of the Ethiopian Highlands extends into central Eritrea, where the average altitude is over 2,000m. The mountains fall in the west to a plateau, which then rises to the hills on the Sudanese border. To the east of the mountains, the land falls to the narrow coastal plain. The coastal strip extending to the Djibouti border is low-lying, the border with Ethiopia running along the edge of the Danakil desert. Elevation extremes range from 3,018m (Soira) at the highest point to −75m

(Danakil depression) at the lowest. The climate varies according to altitude, with temperatures averaging 16°C in the mountains, which are also wetter, and 30°C on the arid coastal plain.

HISTORY AND POLITICS

Part of the Axum empire from the first century AD, the area came under the control of the Ottoman Empire in the mid-16th century. It was occupied by Italy in the late 19th century and was the base for Italy's 1936 invasion of Abyssinia (now Ethiopia). After the Italian defeat in North Africa in 1941, Eritrea became a British protectorate until 15 September 1952, when a federation with Ethiopia was established by the UN. In 1962, Ethiopia annexed Eritrea outright.

The Eritrean Liberation Front (ELF) fought a guerrilla war for independence from 1961, and the Eritrean People's Liberation Front (EPLF) – a breakaway faction of the ELF – emerged in the 1970s, becoming the dominant rebel group in the 1980s. The EPLF joined with Ethiopian resistance groups to fight the Mengistu regime, which was overthrown in 1991. The EPLF secured the whole of Eritrea and formed an autonomous provisional government. The new Ethiopian government agreed to an Eritrean referendum on independence, held in April 1993, which recorded a 99.89 per cent vote in favour. Independence was declared on 24 May 1993.

Following independence, a transitional government for a four-year period was formed under Issaias Afwerki, and the EPLF became the ruling political party, renaming itself the People's Front for Democracy and Justice (PFDJ) in 1994. The post-independence regime has become increasingly authoritarian, and since 2001 has dealt harshly with anyone openly critical of the government. Although a new constitution was adopted in 1997, no presidential election has taken place since independence, and legislative elections scheduled for 2001 were postponed indefinitely. Opposition groups have plans to set up a parliament-in-exile.

FOREIGN RELATIONS

Since independence, Eritrea has been involved in disputes with Yemen, Ethiopia and Djibouti over territory, while Sudan has accused Eritrea of supporting rebels in eastern Sudan. The dispute with Yemen was over the Hanish and Mohabaka islands in the Red Sea; possession was divided between Yemen and Eritrea by international arbitration.

There has been fighting with Ethiopia in disputes over border territory, especially in the Tigray region, since 1998. Though usually sporadic, fighting escalated in 1999–2000 into a war that left thousands of people dead. An independent boundary commission defined the international border between the two countries in 2002, but both countries have failed to abide by the original demarcation or a revised ruling in 2006, and Ethiopia rejected the 2007 virtual demarcation. The UN peacekeeping mission deployed in 2000 was withdrawn in 2008, largely owing to the obstructiveness of the Eritrean government.

Fighting broke out on the part of the border disputed with Djibouti in 2008 after alleged incursions by Eritrean troops. Eritrea has repulsed international efforts to monitor a withdrawal or negotiate a settlement, denying that it has any troops in Djibouti territory, but agreed to seek a peaceful settlement in 2010.

In 2009, the UN imposed sanctions on Eritrea owing to its alleged support for Islamist insurgents in Somalia.

POLITICAL SYSTEM

Few of the provisions outlined in the 1997 constitution have been enacted and no presidential or legislative elections have been held, so the transitional president, state council (cabinet) and legislature remain in place. Under the constitution, the president is elected for a five-year term by the legislature, and the 150-member unicameral National Assembly is directly elected for a four-year term. The People's Front for Democracy and Justice (PFDJ) is the only legal political party.

HEAD OF STATE

President, Chairman of the State Council and of the National Assembly, Issaias Afewerki, *elected by the National Assembly* 22 May 1993

SELECTED GOVERNMENT MEMBERS *as at June 2011*
Defence, Gen. Sebhat Ephrem
Foreign Affairs, Osman Saleh
Finance, Berhane Abrehe

EMBASSY OF THE STATE OF ERITREA

96 White Lion Street, London N1 9PF
T 020-7713 0096 E eriemba@eriembauk.com
Ambassador Extraordinary and Plenipotentiary, HE
  Tesfamicael Gerahtu Ogbaghiorghis, *apptd* 2007

BRITISH EMBASSY

PO Box 5584, 66–68 Mariam Ghimbi Street, Asmara
T (+291) (1) 120 145 W http://ukineritrea.fco.gov.uk
Ambassador Extraordinary and Plenipotentiary, HE Sandra
  Tyler-Haywood, *apptd* 2010

BRITISH COUNCIL

PO Box 997, 175-11 Street No 23, Asmara
T (+291) (1) 123 415/120 529 W www.britishcouncil.org/africa
Director, Angus Bjarnason

DEFENCE

The army has 270 main battle tanks, 15 armoured infantry fighting vehicles and 25 armoured personnel carriers. The navy has 12 patrol and coastal combatant vessels at 3 bases. The air force has 31 combat aircraft and 1 armed helicopter.
Military expenditure – US$78m (2009 est)
Military personnel – 201,750: army 200,000, navy 1,400, air force 350
Conscription duration – 16 months

ECONOMY AND TRADE

Over 30 years of conflict left the country's economy devastated, and the restrictive policies of the post-independent regime have hampered recovery. The command economy has concentrated business ownership in military and party hands. Agricultural output is restricted by lack of labour owing to the failure to demobilise the large army, the conflict with Ethiopia and the frequent droughts and ensuing famines. Currently, agriculture and herding are the means of subsistence of around 80 per cent of the population, but food production is insufficient and emergency food aid is needed for two-thirds of the people. The industrial sector has contracted since trade with Ethiopia halted in 1998, and the principal ports have suffered from the loss of this transit trade.

Mineral reserves include zinc, potash, gold, copper and possibly oil; these are not fully exploited at present, although mining production began in 2010. Industries include food processing, beverages, clothing and textiles, salt, cement and light manufacturing. The opening of a free trade zone at Massawa in 2008 may boost revenues, currently heavily dependent on remittances from expatriates.

The main trade partners are India, Italy, Saudi Arabia, China and Sudan. Principal exports are livestock, sorghum, textiles, food and light manufactures. The main imports are machinery, petroleum products, food and manufactured goods.
GNI – US$1,856m; US$320 per capita (2009)
Annual average growth of GDP – 4 per cent (2010 est)
Inflation rate – 20 per cent (2010 est)
Population below poverty line – 50 per cent (2004 est)
Total external debt – $962m (2008 est)

BALANCE OF PAYMENTS

Trade – US$418m deficit (2010)
Current Account – US$75m deficit (2008)

Trade with UK	2009	2010
Imports from UK	£2,942,251	£2,597,526
Exports to UK	£91,165	£123,567

COMMUNICATIONS

Infrastructure reconstruction has focused on the ports of Massawa and Assab, the roads from these ports to Ethiopia, and the railway from Massawa to Sudan via Asmara. There are 306km of railways and 4,010km of roads, of which 874km are surfaced. There are 13 airports and airfields, of which four have surfaced runways; the main international airport is at Asmara. The fixed-line telephone system is poor and largely confined to Asmara; mobile phone subscriptions are nearly three times the number of fixed-line subscribers, at 141,100 in 2009, but the combined density of both types of subscriber is only three per 100 people.

MEDIA

Eritrea is the only country in Africa without any privately owned news media. Existing organisations were closed down by the government in 2001, helping Eritrea to supplant North Korea as the worst country in the world for press freedom in 2007, 2009 and 2010 according to Reporters Without Borders. Journalists have been detained without charge for publishing views critical of the government.

ESTONIA

Eesti Vabariik – Republic of Estonia

Area – 45,228 sq. km
Capital – Tallinn; population, 399,027 (2009 est)
Major towns – Kohtla-Jarve, Narva, Parnu, Tartu

Currency – Euro (€) of 100 cents
Population – 1,291,170 falling at 0.64 per cent a year
  (2010 est); Estonian (68.7 per cent), Russian (25.6 per
  cent), Ukrainian (2.1 per cent), Belarusian (1.2 per
  cent), Finn (0.8 per cent) (2008)
Religion – Christian (Lutheran 14 per cent, Orthodox
  13 per cent) (est)
Language – Estonian (official), Russian
Population density – 32 per sq. km (2009)
Urban population – 69 per cent (2008 est)
Median age (years) – 40.2 (2010 est)
National anthem – 'Mu Isamaa, Mu Onn Ja Room' ['My
  Native Land, My Joy and Delight']
National day – 24 February (Independence Day)
Life expectancy (years) – 73.08 (2010 est)
Mortality rate – 13.48 (2010 est)
Birth rate – 10.42 (2010 est)
Infant mortality rate – 7.19 (2010 est)
HIV/AIDS adult prevalence – 1.2 per cent (2009 est)
Death penalty – Abolished for all crimes (since 1998)
CPI score – 6.5 (2010)

CLIMATE AND TERRAIN

The country is mostly a plain of lakes, marshes and
forests, with a range of low hills in the south-east.
Elevation extremes range from 318m (Suur Munamagi) at
the highest point to 0m (Baltic Sea) at the lowest. Part of
the border with Russia runs through the large Lake Peipsi.
The climate is maritime, with average temperatures
ranging from −6°C in February to 16°C in July.

HISTORY AND POLITICS

The area came under Swedish control between 1561 and
1629, and was ceded to the Russian Empire in 1721. An
Estonian nationalist movement developed in the late
19th century and fought against occupying German
forces during the First World War. Estonia declared its
independence in February 1918 and defended it against
Soviet forces until 1920, when independence was
recognised by the USSR. However, the USSR annexed
Estonia in 1940, and the country was subsequently
occupied by German forces when they invaded the USSR
in 1941. In 1944 the USSR expelled the Germans and
reannexed the country, beginning a process of
'Sovietisation'.

There was a resurgence of nationalist sentiment in the
1980s, and in 1989 the Estonian Supreme Soviet declared
the republic to be sovereign and its 1940 annexation by
the USSR to be illegal. In 1990, the Communist Party's
monopoly of power was abolished and, following
multiparty elections in which pro-independence
candidates won the majority of seats, a period of
transition to independence was inaugurated, culminating
in its declaration on 20 August 1991. The last Russian
troops withdrew in 1994. Since independence, Estonia
has pursued pro-Western policies. It joined NATO and the
EU in 2004.

In 2006 Toomas Hendrik Ilves was elected president
by an electoral assembly. In the 2011 legislative election,
the Reform Party (ER), the main partner in the coalition
government since 2005, remained the largest party and
formed a coalition with the Union of Pro Patria and Res
Publica (IRL).

POLITICAL SYSTEM

Under the 1992 constitution, the president is elected
for a five-year term by the legislature by a two-thirds

majority or, if no candidate receives this majority after
three rounds of voting, by an electoral assembly
composed of the legislature members and 266 local
government representatives. The unicameral legislature,
the *Riigikogu,* has 101 members, directly elected
for a four-year term. The prime minister is appointed by
the president and nominates the government.
Members of the government need not be members of the
Riigikogu.

HEAD OF STATE

President, Toomas Hendrik Ilves, *elected by electoral
  assembly* 23 September 2006, *sworn in* 9 October
  2006

SELECTED GOVERNMENT MEMBERS *as at June 2011*
Prime Minister, Andrus Ansip
Defence, Mart Laar
Finance, Jurgen Ligi
Foreign Affairs, Urmas Paet
Internal Affairs, Ken-Marti Vaher

EMBASSY OF THE REPUBLIC OF ESTONIA
16 Hyde Park Gate, London SW7 5DG
T 020-7589 3428 E london@mfa.ee W www.estonia.gov.uk
Ambassador Extraordinary and Plenipotentiary, HE Aino
  Lepik von Wiren, *apptd* 2010

BRITISH EMBASSY
Wismari 6, Tallinn 10136
T (+372) 667 4700 W http://ukinestonia.fco.gov.uk
Ambassador Extraordinary and Plenipotentiary, HE Peter
  Carter, *apptd* 2007

BRITISH COUNCIL
Vana–Posti 7, Tallinn 10146
T (+372) 625 7788 W www.britishcouncil.org/estonia
Country Manager, Hede Kerstin Luik

DEFENCE

The army has 88 armoured personnel carriers. The navy
has 1 patrol and coastal combatant vessel. The
paramilitary Border Guard has 20 patrol and coastal
combatant vessels. Operates joint naval unit BALTRON
(*see* Latvia: Defence).
Military budget – US$330m (2010)
Military personnel – 5,450: army 4,800, navy 400, air
  force 250
Conscription duration – 8–11 months

ECONOMY AND TRADE

Economic reforms and restructuring since 1992 have
resulted in a market economy, the growth of which was
boosted by the country's accession to the EU. Estonia
entered recession in 2008 after an investment and
consumption slump and a drop in demand for
exports. Prudent financial management has enabled the
economy to recover slowly, and it met the accession
criteria for the eurozone, which Estonia joined in January
2011.

Agriculture engages 2.8 per cent of the workforce and
accounts for 2.5 per cent of GDP, the main products
being cereals, vegetables, livestock, dairy products
and fish. Industry accounts for 22.7 per cent of
employment and 28.7 per cent of GDP, concentrating on
engineering, electronics, wood and wood products,
textiles, information technology and telecommunications;
electronics and telecommunications are particularly

strong. The services sector accounts for 74.5 per cent of employment and 68.8 per cent of GDP.

The main trading partners are other EU countries, particularly Finland, and Russia. Principal exports are machinery and electrical equipment, wood and wood products, metals, furniture, vehicles and parts, food products and textiles. The main imports are machinery and electrical equipment, fuels, foodstuffs, plastics and textiles. Estonia remains dependent on Russian natural gas supplies.

GNI – US$18,531m; US$14,060 per capita (2009)
Annual average growth of GDP – 1.9 per cent (2010 est)
Inflation rate – 2.4 per cent (2010 est)
Population below poverty line – 19.5 per cent (2007)
Unemployment – 13.5 per cent (2010 est)
Total external debt – US$25,130m (2010 est)
Imports – US$10,200m (2009)
Exports – US$9,100m (2009)

BALANCE OF PAYMENTS
Trade – US$2,595m deficit (2010)
Current Account – US$880m surplus (2009)

Trade with UK	2009	2010
Imports from UK	£146,180,808	£185,109,178
Exports to UK	£123,472,598	£162,221,871

EDUCATION AND HEALTH

Primary and secondary level education is compulsory between the ages of seven and 15. The country's best known university is Tartu, founded in 1632.

Literacy rate – 99.8 per cent (2008 est)
Gross enrolment ratio (percentage of relevant age group) – primary 100 per cent; secondary 99 per cent; tertiary 64 per cent (2008 est)
Health expenditure (per capita) – US$1,004 (2009)
Hospital beds (per 1,000 people) – 5.7 (2004–9)

MEDIA AND CULTURE

Freedom of the press is guaranteed in the constitution, and the state monopoly on television and radio ended soon after independence. All newspapers are privately owned, and public broadcasting channels compete with private-sector companies. Russian-language news and programmes are provided on Estonian television, as are channels in Swedish, Finnish and Latvian.

The old town area of Tallinn is a UNESCO World Heritage Site. The city has suffered many occupations but, apart from a Soviet bombing raid in 1944, its medieval and 18th-century architecture has never been harmed. Estonia's heritage is rich in traditional folk songs and poetry, which influences much of its contemporary culture. Novelist and poet Jaan Kross (1920–2007) has been the country's most eminent fiction writer of modern times. Well-known names in modern classical music include conductors Neeme Jarvi (*b.* 1937) and Tonu Kaljuste (*b.* 1953), and composers Veljo Tormis (*b.* 1930) and Arvo Part (*b.* 1935).

ETHIOPIA

Ityop'iya Federalawi Demokrasiyawi Ripeblik – Federal Democratic Republic of Ethiopia

Area – 1,104,300 sq. km
Capital – Addis Ababa; population, 2,863,150 (2009 est)
Major cities – Bahir Dar, Dese, Dire Dawa, Gonder, Mek'ele, Nazret
Currency – Birr (EB) of 100 cents
Population – 88,013,491 rising at 3.2 per cent a year (2010 est); Oromo (34.5 per cent), Amhara (26.9 per cent), Somali (6.2 per cent), Tigray (6.1 per cent), Sidama (4 per cent), Guragie (2.5 per cent), Welaita (2.3 per cent) (2007)
Religion – Christian 63 per cent (Ethiopian Orthodox 44 per cent, Protestant 19 per cent), Muslim 34 per cent (mostly Sunni) (est)
Language – Amharic, English, Arabic (all official), Oromigna, Tigrinya, Somali, Guaragigna, Sidamo
Population density – 83 per sq. km (2009)
Urban population – 17 per cent (2008 est)
Median age (years) – 16.8 (2010 est)
National anthem – 'Wodefit Gesgeshi Widd Innat Ityopp'ya' ['March Forward, Dear Mother Ethiopia']
National day – 28 May (defeat of Mengistu government, 1991)
Life expectancy (years) – 55.8 (2010 est)
Mortality rate – 11.29 (2010 est)
Birth rate – 43.34 (2010 est)
Infant mortality rate – 78.99 (2010 est)
HIV/AIDS adult prevalence – 1.9 per cent (2007 est)
Death penalty – Retained
CPI score – 2.7 (2010)

CLIMATE AND TERRAIN

Ethiopia is a landlocked country dominated by a central plateau, rising to the mountains of the Ethiopian Highlands, which are divided by the Great Rift Valley. The western mountains are the source of the Blue Nile. The land drops to desert plains in the east (Ogaden) and north-east (Danakil desert). Elevation extremes range from 4,533m (Ras Dejen) at the highest point to −125m (Danakil depression) at the lowest. There is a tropical monsoon climate, with variations according to altitude. The wet season is from April to September.

HISTORY AND POLITICS

The area's Hamitic culture was influenced by Semitic immigration in the centuries before the time of Christ. The coastal trading empire based at Axum was established in the first century AD and reached its zenith in the sixth century. Coptic Christianity was introduced in the fourth century. The independent kingdom of Abyssinia emerged in the 11th century. Modern Ethiopia dates from 1855 when Theodros established supremacy over the various tribes. Menelik II repulsed an Italian invasion in 1896, but Italy conquered Abyssinia in 1936 and occupied the country until its liberation in 1941. Ethiopia was federated with Eritrea by the UN in 1952 and annexed the area in 1962.

Emperor Haile Selassie was deposed in a military coup in 1974 and a military government was installed. By 1977 Lt.-Col. Mengistu Haile Mariam had become head of state and his single-party Marxist regime initiated reforms based on the Soviet model, brutally suppressing opposition. War with Somalia over the predominantly ethnic Somali and Muslim territory of Ogaden (1977–8), internal conflict with Ethiopian resistance and Eritrean separatist forces, drought and famine (1984–5), and government mismanagement and corruption undermined the regime, and it was overthrown in 1991. A transitional administration comprising the Ethiopian People's Revolutionary Democratic Front (EPRDF) and other opposition groups governed until a new federal constitution was adopted in 1994. The Federal Democratic Republic of Ethiopia was proclaimed on 22 August 1995.

There is a continuing low-level insurgency by separatists in the predominantly Somali regions.

Since disputed elections in 2005 there has been a decline in respect for human rights, which has attracted international criticism and caused foreign donors to cut aid. Foreign agencies engaged in human rights or conflict resolution work were banned in 2009, and the activities of local agencies were restricted.

Lt. Girma Wolde Giorgis, the EPRDF candidate, was elected president in 2001 and re-elected in 2007. Meles Zenawi, prime minister since 1994, was re-appointed for a third term in 2005. In the 2010 legislative election, the EPRDF won an overwhelming majority of seats; observers considered the polls flawed and opposition leaders called for a rerun, alleging government intimidation.

FOREIGN RELATIONS
There has been fighting with Eritrea in disputes over border territory, especially in Tigray, since 1998. Though usually sporadic, fighting escalated in 1999–2000 into a war in which thousands of people died. An independent boundary commission defined the international border between the two countries in 2002 but both countries have failed to abide by the original demarcation or a revised ruling in 2006, and Ethiopia rejected a 2007 virtual demarcation.

Ethiopia intervened in Somalia in 2006 in support of the Somali transitional government. Ethiopia formally withdrew its forces in January 2009, in accordance with a 2008 peace agreement between the Somali government and rebels. However, Ethiopian forces appear to have been in action in Somalia since the withdrawal.

POLITICAL SYSTEM
The 1994 constitution provides for a federal government responsible for foreign affairs, defence and economic policy, and nine ethnically based states. The president is elected by both houses of the legislature for a six-year term, renewable once. The prime minister is appointed by the lower chamber of the legislature and appoints the government. The Federal Parliamentary Assembly is bicameral. The lower chamber, the House of People's Representatives, has 547 members, directly elected for a five-year term. The House of the Federation has 110 members, elected for a five-year term by the government councils of the nine states in the federation. These regional administrations have considerable autonomy and the right to secede.

HEAD OF STATE
President, Lt. Girma Wolde Giorgis, *elected* 8 October 2001, *re-elected* 2007

SELECTED GOVERNMENT MEMBERS *as at June 2011*
Prime Minister, C.-in-C. of the National Armed Forces, Meles Zenawi
Deputy Prime Minister, Foreign Affairs, Hailemariam Desalegn
Finance and Economic Development, Sufian Ahmed
Defence, Siraj Fegesa

EMBASSY OF THE FEDERAL DEMOCRATIC REPUBLIC OF ETHIOPIA
17 Princes Gate, London SW7 1PZ
T 020-7589 7212 E info@ethioembassy.org.uk
W www.ethioembassy.org.uk
Ambassador Extraordinary and Plenipotentiary, HE Berhanu Kebede, *apptd* 2006

BRITISH EMBASSY
PO Box 858, Comoros Street, Addis Ababa
T (+251) (11) 661 2354 W http://ukinethiopia.fco.gov.uk
Ambassador Extraordinary and Plenipotentiary, HE Norman Ling, *apptd* 2008

BRITISH COUNCIL
PO Box 1043, Comoros Street, Addis Ababa
T (+251) (11) 662 0338 W www.britishcouncil.org/africa
Director, Barbara Wickham

DEFENCE
The army has over 246 main battle tanks and around 450 armoured infantry fighting vehicles and armoured personnel carriers. The air force has 42 combat aircraft and 18 armed helicopters.
Military budget – US$311m (2010)
Military personnel – 138,000: army 135,000, air force 3,000

ECONOMY AND TRADE
The economy is highly dependent on agriculture, and therefore reliant on the rains; recurring droughts led to famine conditions in 1984–5, 1992, 1997, 2000, 2002 and 2009. In 2004, the government began to move more than two million people from the drought-stricken and overworked highlands to the east of the country, claiming that this would be a long-term solution to food shortages, but food aid is still required at times of drought. Although most foreign debt was cancelled in 2005 and economic growth has been steady, emergency IMF funding was needed to cushion the country from the effects of the global downturn.

Agriculture and herding account for approximately 42.9 per cent of GDP, and 85 per cent of the population is dependent upon the land for a living. The main crops are cereals, pulses, coffee, oilseed, cotton, sugar, potatoes, qat (or khat, a flowering plant chewed for its stimulant properties), cut flowers, livestock products and fish. Natural resources, including gold, platinum, copper, potash, oil and natural gas, are largely unexploited; most industrial activity involves the processing of agricultural products, gold mining and metalworking, and textiles.

The main trade partners are China, Saudi Arabia, the USA and Germany. Principal exports are coffee (which normally provides over 20 per cent of foreign exchange earnings), qat, gold, leather products, livestock and oilseeds. The main imports are food, livestock, petroleum and petroleum products, chemicals, machinery, vehicles, cereals and textiles.

GNI – US$28,489m; US$330 per capita (2009)
Annual average growth of GDP – 7 per cent (2010 est)
Inflation rate – 7 per cent (2010 est)
Population below poverty line – 38.7 per cent (2005/6 est)
Total external debt – US$4,289m (2010 est)
Imports – US$7,300m (2009)
Exports – US$1,500m (2009)

BALANCE OF PAYMENTS
Trade – US$6,719m deficit (2010)
Current Account – US$1,620m deficit (2009)

Trade with UK	2009	2010
Imports from UK	£77,243,170	£80,496,913
Exports to UK	£25,980,607	£24,574,960

COMMUNICATIONS
Since Eritrea became independent, Ethiopia has been landlocked. Most trade is via Djibouti, although Ethiopia also uses the port of Berbera in northern Somalia. A network of roads links the major cities with each other and with neighbouring countries; there are 36,469km of roads, 6,980km of which are surfaced. The only railway line, 681km in length, links Addis Ababa to Djibouti but is largely inoperable. There are over 60 airports and airfields, including the international airport at Addis Ababa. Ethiopian Airlines maintains regular services throughout Africa and to Europe. A number of infrastructure construction projects are being undertaken with foreign assistance and funding. There is a limited telephone service, and although access is growing, especially for mobile phones, only about five per 100 people have access to either type of telephone.

EDUCATION AND HEALTH
Non-compulsory elementary and secondary education are provided by government schools in the main centres of population; there are also mission schools. The National University at Addis Ababa (founded 1961) coordinates the institutions of higher education.

Literacy rate – 35.9 per cent (2008 est)
Gross enrolment ratio (percentage of relevant age group) – primary 103 per cent; secondary 33 per cent; tertiary 4 per cent (2009 est)
Health expenditure (per capita) – US$15 (2009)
Hospital beds (per 1,000 people) – 0.2 (2004–9)

MEDIA
Radio is the most popular medium and although state-owned Radio Ethiopia is the main broadcaster, two private stations were granted licences in 2006. State-owned Ethiopian Television is the only television station. Over 50 privately owned newspapers are published in addition to the state-owned daily *Addis Zemen* and *Ethiopian Herald*, which publishes in English. The media has experienced harassment and repression since 2005. In 2010, Voice of America's Amharic service was jammed; according to prime minister Meles Zenawi, it was engaging in destabilising propaganda.

FIJI

Matanitu ko Viti – Republic of the Fiji Islands

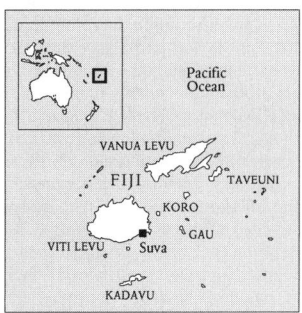

Area – 18,274 sq. km
Capital – Suva, on Viti Levu; population, 174,066 (2009 est)
Major towns – Lautoka, Nasinu, Nausori
Currency – Fiji dollar (F$) of 100 cents
Population – 875,983 rising at 0.83 per cent a year (2010 est); Fijian (57.3 per cent), Indian (37.6 per cent), Rotuman (1.2 per cent) (2007)
Religion – Christian 52 per cent (predominantly Methodist), Hindu 30 per cent, Muslim 7 per cent (predominantly Sunni) (est)
Language – English, Fijian, Hindustani (all official)
Population density – 46 per sq. km (2009)
Urban population – 52 per cent (2008 est)
Median age (years) – 26.6 (2010 est)
National anthem – 'Meda Dau Doka' ['God Bless Fiji']
National day – second Monday of October (Independence Day)
Life expectancy (years) – 71.03 (2010 est)
Mortality rate – 5.88 (2010 est)
Birth rate – 21.52 (2010 est)
Infant mortality rate – 11.28 (2010 est)
Death penalty – Retained for certain crimes (last used 1964)

CLIMATE AND TERRAIN
Fiji comprises a group of about 330 islands (around 110 are permanently inhabited) and over 500 islets in the South Pacific, about 1,770km north of New Zealand. The group extends 480km from east to west and 480km north to south. The International Date Line has been diverted to the east of the island group. The largest islands are Viti Levu and Vanua Levu. The terrain is mountainous and volcanic, with tropical rainforest and grassland, and most islands are surrounded by coral reefs. Elevation extremes range from 1,324m (Tomanivi, on Viti Levu) at the highest point to 0m (Pacific Ocean) at the lowest. Fiji has a tropical maritime climate with high humidity and an average annual temperature of 27°C.

HISTORY AND POLITICS
The islands were settled by Melanesian peoples. European contact began with the visit of the Dutch explorer Abel Tasman in 1643; later visitors included Captain Cook in 1774. The islands became a British colony in 1874, and sugar plantations, employing more than 60,000 indentured Indian labourers, were established. Fiji became independent as a constitutional monarchy on 10 October 1970, and became a republic after the 1987 coups.

The growing size and political strength of the ethnic Indian population caused political instability in the late 1980s. There were two coups in 1987 and one in 2000 as indigenous Fijians attempted to reassert their political dominance and entrench this in the constitution. A fourth coup occurred in 2006 over the government's proposed amnesty for those involved in the 2000 coup.

Since the 2006 coup a military regime headed by the coup leader, Commodore Frank Bainimarama, has held power. Although President Iloilo was reinstated in 2007, when Bainimarama became prime minister, the regime has become increasingly authoritarian, suppressing dissent and resisting calls to restore democratic government. In response to a court of appeal ruling in April 2009 that the military government was illegal, President Iloilo suspended the constitution, dismissed the judiciary, reappointed Bainimarama as interim prime minister and declared a state of emergency. The prime minister has said that a new constitution will be introduced in 2013, followed by elections in 2014.

President Iloilo retired in 2009 and was replaced by the vice-president, Ratu Epeli Nailatikau.

POLITICAL SYSTEM

Under the 1997 constitution, suspended in 2006, the head of state is the president, appointed for a five-year term by the Great Council of Chiefs. The lower house of the bicameral parliament, which was dissolved in 2006, is the House of Representatives, with 71 members directly elected for a five-year term; 25 seats are open to all races and elected in single-member constituencies, while the other 46 are allocated for election by the country's various ethnic communities. The upper house, the senate, has 32 members, who are appointed for a five-year term by the president on the recommendation of the political parties (in proportion to their representation in the lower house) and the Great Council of Chiefs.

HEAD OF STATE
President, Ratu Epeli Nailatikau, *sworn in* 5 November 2009

SELECTED GOVERNMENT MEMBERS *as at May 2011*
Prime Minister, Finance, Commodore Voreqe ('Frank') Bainimarama
Attorney-General, Aiyaz Sayed-Khaiyum
Defence (acting), Joketani Cokanasiga
Foreign Affairs, Ratu Inoke Kubuabola

HIGH COMMISSION OF THE REPUBLIC OF THE FIJI ISLANDS
34 Hyde Park Gate, London SW7 5DN
T 020-7584 3661 E mail@fijihighcommission.org.uk
W www.fijihighcommission.org.uk
High Commissioner, HE Pio Bosco Tikoisuva, apptd 2008

BRITISH HIGH COMMISSION
PO Box 1355, Victoria House, 47 Gladstone Road, Suva
T (+679) 322 9100 E publicdiplomacysuva@fco.gov.uk
W http://ukinfiji.fco.gov.uk
High Commissioner, HE Mac McLachlan, MBE, apptd 2009

DEFENCE
The navy has 7 patrol and coastal combatant vessels at 2 bases.
Military budget – US$55m (2010)
Military personnel – 3,500: army 3,200, navy 300

ECONOMY AND TRADE

Fiji has abundant natural resources and one of the more developed economies in the region. However, the economy suffered after the 1987 coups because of the mass emigration of Indian Fijians, and is now contracting owing to structural problems, inefficiency and continuing political instability. Tourism, the mainstay of the economy, has declined since 2006; in addition, remittances from expatriate Fijians have decreased significantly, and development aid has largely been reduced or suspended until the interim government moves to restore democracy.

Agriculture, much of it at subsistence level, accounts for 8.9 per cent of GDP and employs 70 per cent of the workforce. The principal cash crop is sugar cane, but revenue has been affected by a recent cut in EU subsidies. The other main crops are coconuts, cassava, rice, sweet potatoes, bananas, livestock and fish. The main industries are tourism, sugar processing, garment manufacturing, copra production, gold and silver mining, forestry and small cottage industries. The main trade partners are Australia, Singapore, New Zealand, the USA and the UK. Principal exports are sugar, garments, gold, timber, fish, molasses and coconut oil. The chief imports are manufactured goods, machinery and transport equipment, petroleum products, food and chemicals.

GNI – US$2,829m; US$3,840 per capita (2009)
Annual average growth of GDP – 1.8 per cent (2010 est)
Inflation rate – 4.8 per cent (2007)
Total external debt – US$127m (2004 est)
Imports – US$1,500m (2009)
Exports – US$700m (2009)

BALANCE OF PAYMENTS
Trade – US$903m deficit (2010)
Current Account – US$584m deficit (2007)

Trade with UK	2009	2010
Imports from UK	£6,168,515	£5,119,238
Exports to UK	£79,152,775	£30,840,120

COMMUNICATIONS

Fiji is one of the main aerial crossroads in the Pacific, providing services to New Zealand, Australia and other Pacific states; the 28 airports and airfields include international airports at Suva and Nadi. The main seaports are Suva and Lautoka. There are 3,440km of roads, 1,692km of which are surfaced. There are 597km of railway track, principally used by the sugar industry. The telephone system is modern and covers most of the inhabited islands.

MEDIA

Strict media censorship preventing the publication of any material critical of the government was imposed in April 2009. Fiji's privately owned newspapers are published in English, Fijian and Hindi; government-owned newspapers are also multilingual. Radio (both public and private) is a key source of news, particularly on the more remote outer islands. There are two main television networks, operated by Fiji Television Ltd: Fiji 1, a national channel, and Sky Fiji, accessed via subscription.

FINLAND

Suomen tasavalta / Republiken Finland – Republic of Finland

Area – 338,145 sq. km
Capital – Helsinki (Helsingfors); population, 1,106,910 (2009 est)
Major cities – Espoo (Esbo), Oulu (Uleaborg), Tampere (Tammerfors), Turku (Aabo), Vantaa (Vanda)
Currency – Euro (€) of 100 cents
Population – 5,255,068 rising at 0.08 per cent a year (2010 est); Finnish (93.4 per cent), Swedish (5.6 per cent), Sami (0.1 per cent) (2006 est)
Religion – Christian (Lutheran 81 per cent, Orthodox 1 per cent), Muslim 1 per cent (predominantly Sunni) (est)
Language – Finnish, Swedish (both official)
Population density – 18 per sq. km (2009)
Urban population – 63 per cent (2008 est)
Median age (years) – 42.3 (2010 est)
National anthem – 'Maamme'/'Vart Land' ['Our Land']
National day – 6 December (Independence Day)
Life expectancy (years) – 79.13 (2010 est)
Mortality rate – 10.15 (2010 est)
Birth rate – 10.37 (2010 est)
Infant mortality rate – 3.45 (2010 est)
Death penalty – Abolished for all crimes (since 1972)
CPI score – 9.2 (2010)

CLIMATE AND TERRAIN

Much of the centre of the country is a glaciated plateau of forests and lakes, with low hills along the eastern border with Russia and in the far north. Forests cover around 70 per cent of the country, including those of the coastal peatlands in the south west. There are over 60,000 lakes, with an average depth of 7m. Elevation extremes range from 1,328m (Haltiatunturi, or Halti) at the highest point to 0m (Baltic Sea) at the lowest. A quarter of the country lies north of the Arctic Circle; temperatures there can range from −50°C in January to 17°C in July. Average temperatures in Helsinki range from −6°C in January to 17°C in July.

Owing to isostatic uplift (the rise of land mass no longer depressed by the weight of glaciers), the surface area of Finland is growing by around 7 sq. km a year.

HISTORY AND POLITICS

Finland was part of the Swedish Empire from the 12th century until it was ceded to Russia in 1809, when it became an autonomous grand duchy of the Russian Empire. After the Russian Revolution in 1917, Finland declared its independence. An attempted coup by Finnish Bolsheviks led to a short civil war that ended in their defeat in 1918, and in 1919 a republic was established.

It resisted the 1939 invasion by the USSR but was defeated in 1940 and forced to cede territory; in the hope of recovering this territory it joined Germany's attack on the USSR in 1941. After agreeing an armistice with the USSR in 1944, Finland concluded a peace treaty in 1947 that conceded further territory to the USSR and obliged it to pay reparations. A Soviet-Finnish cooperation treaty in 1948 forced Finland to demilitarise its Soviet border and to adopt a stance of neutrality; these terms lasted until the demise of the USSR in 1991.

Since the mid-1960s the majority of Finnish governments have been coalitions of centre and moderate left-wing parties, usually led by the Social Democratic Party (SDP) or the Centre Party (KESK). Finland joined the EU in 1995 and the European Monetary Union in 1998.

Tarja Halonen of the SDP became Finland's first female president in 2000 and was re-elected in 2006. The results of the legislative election in April 2011 were inconclusive, with the four leading parties winning similar numbers of seats. After two months of negotiations, a six-party coalition government, comprising the National Coalition Party (KOK), the Social Democratic Party (SDP) and four smaller parties, took office under the SDP leader Jyrki Katainen.

POLITICAL SYSTEM

Under the 2000 constitution, the president is directly elected for a six-year term. There is a unicameral legislature, the *Eduskunta*, with 200 members directly elected for a four-year term. The prime minister is elected by the *Eduskunta* and appointed by the president.

HEAD OF STATE

President, Tarja Halonen, *elected* 6 February 2000, *inaugurated* 1 March 2000, *re-elected* 2006

SELECTED GOVERNMENT MEMBERS *as at June 2011*
Prime Minister, Jyrki Katainen
Deputy Prime Minister; Finance, Jutta Urpilainen
Defence, Stefan Wallin
Foreign Affairs, Erkki Tuomioja
Interior, Paivi Rasanen

EMBASSY OF FINLAND
38 Chesham Place, London SW1X 8HW
T 020-7838 6200 E sanomat.lon@formin.fi
W www.finemb.org.uk
Ambassador Extraordinary and Plenipotentiary, HE Pekka Huhtaniemi, *apptd* 2010

BRITISH EMBASSY
Itainen Puistotie 17, 00140 Helsinki
T (+358) (9) 2286 5100 W http://ukinfinland.fco.gov.uk
Ambassador Extraordinary and Plenipotentiary, HE Matthew Lodge, *apptd* 2010

BRITISH COUNCIL
Urho Kekkosen Katu 2 C, 00100 Helsinki
T (+358) (9) 774 3330 W www.britishcouncil.fi
Country Manager (acting), Monika Meling-Tynkkynen

DEFENCE

The army has 100 main battle tanks, 194 armoured infantry fighting vehicles and 613 armoured personnel carriers. The navy has 10 patrol and coastal vessels. The air force has 121 combat aircraft.

Military budget – US$3,590m (2010)
Military personnel – 22,250: army 16,000, navy 3,500, air force 2,750; paramilitary 2,800
Conscription duration – 6–12 months

ECONOMY AND TRADE

The country has a highly industrialised market economy which has thrived as a result of its telecommunications and electronics industries, particularly the manufacture of mobile phones, as well as its traditional timber and metals industries. The drop in exports and domestic demand due to the global economic downturn pushed the economy into recession in 2009, but recovery began in 2010. The economy is particularly vulnerable to fluctuations in trade with Russia, both its own trade (Russia is its leading supplier of imports and a major export market) and foreign trade, for which Finland is a major transit point.

The main trade partners are Russia, Germany and Sweden. Principal exports are electrical and optical equipment, machinery, transport equipment, paper and pulp, chemicals, base metals and timber. The main imports are foodstuffs (especially grain), petroleum and petroleum products, chemicals, transport equipment, iron and steel, machinery, textile yarn and fabrics, and components for manufactured goods. Finland is a net importer of energy.

GNI – US$238,084m; US$45,940 per capita (2009)
Annual average growth of GDP – 2.1 per cent (2010 est)
Inflation rate – 1.1 per cent (2010 est)
Unemployment – 7.9 per cent (2010 est)
Total external debt – US$370,800m (2010)
Imports – US$60,700m (2009)
Exports – US$62,800m (2009)

BALANCE OF PAYMENTS
Trade – US$1,154m surplus (2010)
Current Account – US$3,297m surplus (2009)

Trade with UK	2009	2010
Imports from UK	£1,322,505,684	£1,447,999,568
Exports to UK	£2,460,085,158	£2,162,791,050

COMMUNICATIONS

The road and rail networks are concentrated in the southern half of the country, where most of the population and industry are located. There are 78,141km of roads, 50,914km of which are surfaced. There are 5,919km of railways. The main seaports are Helsinki, Kotka, Rauma and Turku, and there are passenger services to Sweden, Estonia and Germany as well as countries outside the Baltic. The principal airports are at Helsinki, Turku and Tampere. Mobile phone distribution, at 7.7 million subscribers in 2009, is over 100 per cent.

EDUCATION AND HEALTH

The Finnish education system regularly features in the top three of the OECD's secondary education rankings. Basic education is free and compulsory for children from seven to 16 years.
Gross enrolment ratio (percentage of relevant age group) – primary 97 per cent; secondary 110 per cent; tertiary 94 per cent (2008 est)
Health expenditure (per capita) – US$4,310 (2009)
Hospital beds (per 1,000 people) – 6.5 (2004–9)

MEDIA

Finland is highly rated for press freedom by Reporters Without Borders; every citizen has the right to publish

and is guaranteed a right of reply. Newspapers are privately owned and offer a wide spectrum of political views. There are both commercial and state-owned broadcasters; the state broadcaster, Yleisradio Oy (YLE), is funded by licence fees and provides radio and television services in Swedish and Finnish, with radio in Sami (Lappish). Newspapers, books, plays and films appear in both Finnish and Swedish.

FRANCE

République française – French Republic

Area – 551,500 sq. km (excluding overseas territories)
Capital – Paris; population, 10,410,000 (2009 est)
Major cities – Bordeaux, Lille, Lyon, Marseille, Montpellier, Nantes, Nice, Reims, Rennes, Strasbourg, Toulouse. The chief towns of Corsica are Ajaccio and Bastia
Currency – Euro (€) of 100 cents
Population – 62,814,233 (excluding overseas territories), rising at 0.53 per cent a year (2010 est)
Religion – Christian (Roman Catholic 64 per cent, Protestant 2 per cent, Muslim 8 per cent, Jewish 1 per cent, Buddhist 1 per cent (est)
Language – French (official)
Population density – 114 per sq. km (2009) (excluding overseas territories)
Urban population – 77 per cent (2008 est)
Median age (years) – 39.7 (2010 est)
National anthem – 'La Marseillaise' ['Song of Marseille']
National day – 14 July (Fête de la Fédération/Fête Nationale)
Life expectancy (years) – 81.09 (2010 est)
Mortality rate – 8.65 (2010 est)
Birth rate – 12.43 (2010 est)
Infant mortality rate – 3.31 (2010 est)
Death penalty – Abolished for all crimes (since 1981)
CPI score – 6.8 (2010)

CLIMATE AND TERRAIN

The north and west consist of flat plains, particularly in the basins of the Somme, Seine, Loire and Garonne rivers, with some low hills. The centre of the south is occupied by the Massif Central plateau, which is divided by the valley of the Rhone and Soane rivers from the mountains – the French Alps, the Jura and the Vosges – on the eastern border. The Pyrenees range lies along the southern border with Spain. Elevation extremes range from 4,807m (Mt Blanc, Alps) at the highest point to −2m (Rhône delta) at the lowest. The climate is generally temperate, though the south has a Mediterranean climate and the east a continental climate.

HISTORY AND POLITICS

The area that is now France was conquered by the Romans in the first century BC and, as the province of Gaul, remained part of the Roman Empire until the Frankish invasions of the fifth and sixth centuries. The treaty of Verdun (AD 843) divided the Frankish Empire created by Charlemagne into three parts, of which the western part, *Francia Occidentalis,* became the basis of modern France. Weak central government allowed the great nobles to form virtually independent duchies, and the assertion of royal power over these nobles was not completed until the 16th century. France's attempts to establish itself as the supreme European power from the 16th century were hindered by civil and religious wars (1562–98), but by the early 18th century this ambition was attained, along with a large overseas empire.

The *ancien régime* was overthrown in the French Revolution (1789), a republic was declared in 1792 and the king, Louis XVI, was executed. The republic was overthrown by Napoléon Bonaparte, who established the first French Empire (1804–14). After Bonaparte's defeat, the congress of Vienna restored the monarchy, but in 1848 the Second Republic was declared, which lasted only until 1852, when the Second Empire was proclaimed under Napoléon III. He was forced to abdicate following the defeat of France in the Franco-Prussian war (1870–71), after which the Third Republic (1870–1940) was established.

France was one of the victors in the First World War (1914–18), when German offensives in the north and east of the country were held and eventually defeated. However, the country was invaded in the Second World War and the north was occupied by Germany from 1940 until 1944, with a pro-German government in the south. The Fourth Republic was declared in 1946, but collapsed in 1958, when a new constitution was adopted and the Fifth Republic was proclaimed. France granted most of its colonies independence between 1954 and 1962.

France was a founder member of the EEC in 1958, and joined the European Monetary Union in 1999. In a 2005 referendum, the population rejected the EU constitution; the French parliament signed the Lisbon Treaty in 2008.

The 2007 presidential election was won in the second round by Nicolas Sarkozy, the Rally for the Republic (RPR) candidate. In the 2007 legislative elections, the RPR-led Union for a Popular Movement (UMP) won 313 seats in the National Assembly, and the UMP-dominated coalition government continued in office after a reshuffle. The UMP has also held a majority of senate seats since the 2008 elections, but was heavily defeated in the 2010 regional elections.

INSURGENCIES

Corsican separatists have pursued a campaign of bombings and shootings since the 1970s apart from a ceasefire in 2003–5 observed by the main separatist faction. The French government's proposals to combine the island's two departments and to give the Corsican regional parliament greater autonomy were narrowly rejected in a 2003 referendum.

POLITICAL SYSTEM

Under the 1958 constitution, the head of state is a president directly elected for a five-year term, which is renewable once. The legislature, the *Parlement,* consists of the National Assembly and the senate. The National Assembly has 577 deputies, 555 for metropolitan France

and 22 for the overseas departments and territories; members are directly elected for a five-year term. The senate has been enlarged gradually over the past decade; from the September 2011 elections there will be 348 senators (328 for metropolitan France and the overseas departments, eight for overseas collectivities and territories, and 12 for French nationals abroad) elected by an electoral college to serve a six-year term, with half elected every three years.

The prime minister is nominated by the National Assembly and appointed by the president, as is the council of ministers. They are responsible to the legislature, but as the executive is constitutionally separate from the legislature, ministers may not sit in the legislature and must hand over their seats to a substitute.

The constitution was amended in 2003 to pave the way for the devolution to the 22 metropolitan regions and 96 metropolitan departments of powers over economic development, transport, tourism, culture and further education.

HEAD OF STATE
President of the French Republic, Nicolas Sarkozy, *elected*
6 May 2007

SELECTED GOVERNMENT MEMBERS *as at June 2011*
Prime Minister, François Fillon
Defence, Gérard Longuet
Economy, Christine Lagarde
Foreign Affairs, Alain Juppé
Interior, Claude Guéant

EMBASSY OF FRANCE
58 Knightsbridge, London SW1X 7JT
T 020-7073 1000 E presse.londres-amba@diplomatie.gouv.fr
W www.ambafrance-uk.org
Ambassador Extraordinary and Plenipotentiary, HE Bernard Emié, *apptd* 2011

BRITISH EMBASSY
35 rue du Faubourg St Honoré, 75363 Paris Cédex 08
T (+33) (1) 4451 3100 W http://ukinfrance.fco.gov.uk
Ambassador Extraordinary and Plenipotentiary, HE Sir Peter Westmacott, KCMG, LVO, *apptd* 2007

BRITISH COUNCIL
9 rue de Constantine, 75340 Paris Cédex 07
T (+33) (1) 4955 7300 W www.britishcouncil.org/france
Director, Chris Hickey

DEFENCE

The army has 254 main battle tanks, over 563 armoured infantry fighting vehicles, 3,586 armoured personnel carriers and 298 armed helicopters.

The navy has 9 submarines, 1 aircraft carrier, 13 destroyers, 11 frigates, 24 patrol and coastal vessels, 86 combat aircraft and 52 multi-role helicopters. The navy has 4 domestic and 6 overseas bases. The air force has 328 combat aircraft. There are currently 3 military satellites in service.
Military budget – US$42,600m (2010)
Military personnel – 238,591: army 130,600, navy 40,353, air force 52,669, other staff 14,969; paramilitary 103,376

ECONOMY AND TRADE

The economy is in transition from extensive government ownership and intervention to a more liberal and market-oriented form; reform was initiated in response to poor economic growth and high unemployment. Implementation has been slow because of the constraints of eurozone membership, and strong resistance to the government's plans for privatisation and reform of labour, pensions and welfare, which have provoked demonstrations and strikes. The government increased public investment in 2009 to alleviate the effects of the global downturn on the economy, but introduced public spending cuts in 2010 to deal with a growing budget deficit and public debt.

Over one-third of the land area of metropolitan France is utilised for agricultural production and a further quarter is covered by forests. Viniculture is extensive, although France has lost market share to other countries in recent years. Cognac, liqueurs and cider are also produced. Other important agricultural products include cereals, sugar beet, potatoes, beef, dairy products and fish. Agriculture employs 3.8 per cent of the workforce and contributes 1.8 per cent of GDP.

Oil is produced from fields in the Landes area, but France is a net importer of crude oil, for processing by its oil-refining industry. Natural gas is produced in the foothills of the Pyrenees.

Industry contributes 19.2 per cent of GDP, employing 24.3 per cent of the workforce. The sector is highly diversified and includes the production of machinery, iron, steel, aluminium, chemicals, vehicles, aircraft, electronic goods, textiles and processed food. The service sector contributes 79 per cent of GDP and employs 71.8 per cent of the workforce. Tourism is an important contributor to GDP.

The main trading partners are other EU countries, especially Germany. Principal exports are machinery, vehicles, aircraft, plastics, chemicals, pharmaceutical products, iron and steel, and beverages. The main imports are raw materials for industry (eg crude oil, chemicals, plastics), machinery and equipment, vehicles and aircraft.

GNI – US$2,671,201m; US$42,620 per capita (2009)
Annual average growth of GDP – 1.6 per cent (2010 est)
Inflation rate – 1.5 per cent (2010 est)
Population below poverty line – 6.2 per cent (2004)
Unemployment – 9.5 per cent (2010 est)
Total external debt – US$4,698,000m (2010)
Imports – US$706,000m (2008)
Exports – US$606,000m (2008)

BALANCE OF PAYMENTS
Trade – US$67,749m deficit (2010)
Current Account – US$38,841m deficit (2009)

Trade with UK	2009	2010
Imports from UK	£17,881,656,406	£20,183,783,626
Exports to UK	£21,140,965,776	£23,352,365,811

COMMUNICATIONS

There are extensive road and rail networks covering the whole country, with approximately 1 million km of roads, including 11,000km of motorways, and 29,640km of railways. The world's tallest road bridge was opened at Millau in 2004.

The principal seaports are Marseille on the Mediterranean Sea, Bordeaux and Nantes on the Atlantic coast, and Le Havre, Calais and Dunkirk on the Channel coast. There are 8,501km of navigable inland waterways, 1,621km navigable by large vessels, and Paris, Rouen and Strasbourg are significant river ports. The French

mercantile marine consisted in 2010 of 167 ships of 1,000 gross tonnage or over, 146 of which are registered overseas. There are two international airports serving Paris, and many regional airports capable of accepting international flights.

In 2009, there were 36 million fixed telephone lines in use, 61 million mobile phone users and 45 million internet users.

EDUCATION AND HEALTH

Education is compulsory and free between the ages of six and 16. Schools may be single-sex or co-educational. Primary education is given in nursery schools and elementary schools. Lower secondary education is provided at *collèges* (four-years), and higher secondary education in *lycées* (three years). There are three types of *lycée* – *général, technique* and *professionel* – and each leads to its own *baccalauéat* qualification. Specialist schools are numerous.

There are many *grandes écoles* in France which award diplomas in subjects not taught at university, especially applied science and engineering. Most of these are state institutions but have a competitive system of entry, unlike the universities.

Gross enrolment ratio (percentage of relevant age group) – primary 110 per cent; secondary 113 per cent; tertiary 55 per cent (2008 est)
Health expenditure (per capita) – US$4,797 (2009)
Hospital beds (per 1,000 people) – 7.1 (2004–9)

MEDIA

France has over 100 daily newspapers, including *Le Monde, Le Figaro* and *Libération*. The press is mostly privately owned and not linked to political parties. State radio broadcasting caters for both domestic (Radio France) and overseas (Radio France Internationale) audiences. TV5 is an international French-language television channel co-financed by Belgium, Canada, France and Switzerland. The main domestic channel, TF1, was privatised in 1987. A global news channel, France 24, was launched in 2006 and broadcasts in French, English and Arabic.

CULTURE

Two of the earliest masterpieces of French literature are the medieval *Song of Roland* and *The Romance of the Rose*. Literature flowered particularly in the 19th century with the novels of Victor Hugo (1802–85), Alexandre Dumas (1802–70), Gustave Flaubert (1821–80), Jules Verne (1828–1905) and Émile Zola (1840–1902). Marcel Proust's (1871–1922) seven-volume *A la recherche du temps perdu* (1913–27) was one of the most influential works of modernist literature. Philosophers Voltaire (1694–1778) and Rousseau (1712–78) also used fiction to illustrate their thought, in *Candide* (1759) and *Julie* (1761), respectively. French contributions to philosophy and critical theory in the 20th century included the works of Henri Bergson (1859–1941), Jean-Paul Sartre (1905–80), Simone de Beauvoir (1908–86), Albert Camus (1913–60), Michel Foucault (1926–84) and Jacques Derrida (1930–2004).

France's artistic movements range from the classicism of Nicholas Poussin (1594–1665) and the Romanticism typified by Eugène Delacroix (1798–1863) to Impressionism, one of France's most productive artistic movements, whose prominent figures include Édouard Manet (1832–83), Edgar Degas (1834–1917), Claude Monet (1840–1924), Pierre-Auguste Renoir

(1841–1919) and Mary Cassatt (1844–1926). The work of Post-Impressionists Paul Cézanne (1839–1906) and Paul Gauguin (1848–1903) informed later movements such as Fauvism, which includes the early work of Henri Matisse (1869–1954), and Cubism, developed by Georges Braque (1882–1963) in collaboration with Picasso. Eminent French sculptors include Auguste Rodin (1840–1917) and Marcel Duchamp (1887–1968).

French cinema is characterised by experimental auteurs such as Jean-Luc Godard (b. 1930) and François Truffaut (1932–1984), while actors such as Brigitte Bardot (b. 1934), Catherine Deneuve (b. 1943) and Juliette Binoche (b. 1964) succeeded in Hollywood as well as France. In music, Edith Piaf (1915–63) and Serge Gainsbourg (1928–91) are the best-known proponents of the French musical form *chanson*. In classical music, Hector Berlioz (1803–69), Georges Bizet (1838–75) and Claude Debussy (1862–1918) are among the country's best-known composers.

OVERSEAS DEPARTMENTS/REGIONS

French Guiana, Guadeloupe, Martinique and Réunion have had departmental status since 1946. They were given regional status with greater powers of self-government and elected assemblies in 1982, and were redesignated as Overseas Regions in 2003. Their regional and departmental status is identical to that of regions and departments of metropolitan France, and they can choose to replace these with a single structure by merging their regional and departmental assemblies. The French government is represented by a *prefect* in each. In referendums in 2010, French Guiana and Martinique rejected proposals for granting greater autonomy to their local governments.

FRENCH GUIANA
Area – 83,534 sq. km
Capital – Cayenne; population, 62,437 (2009 est)
Population – 225,751 (2009 est)

Situated on the north-eastern coast of South America, French Guiana is flanked by Suriname to the west and by Brazil to the south and east. Under the administration of French Guiana are the Îles du Salut group of islands (St Joseph, Île Royal and Île du Diable). The European Space Agency rocket launch site is situated at Kourou, and accounts for 25 per cent of GDP. Fishing, forestry and mining are the main activities, and the economy is dependent on government subsidies. The main exports are timber, shrimp and gold. Tourism is restricted by the lack of infrastructure, as much of the interior is only accessible by river.
Prefect, Denis Labbé, *apptd* 2011

GUADELOUPE
Area – 1,628 sq. km
Capital – Basse-Terre; population 12,000 (2007 est), on Guadeloupe
Population – 403,257 (2009 est)

The Guadeloupe archipelago consists of a number of islands in the Leeward Islands group in the West Indies, including Guadeloupe (or Basse-Terre), Grande-Terre, Marie-Galante, La Désirade and the Îles des Saintes. The main towns are Les Abymes, Pointe-à-Pitre (Grande-Terre) and Grand Bourg (Marie-Galante). The main industries are tourism, agriculture, sugar refining and rum distilling. Bananas, sugar, rum and vanilla are the main exports.
Prefect, Jean-Luc Fabre, *apptd* 2009

MARTINIQUE
Area – 1,100 sq. km
Capital – Fort-de-France; population, 87,787 (2009 est)
Population – 398,733 (2009 est)

An island in the Windward Islands group in the West Indies, Martinique lies between Dominica in the north and St Lucia in the south. It is dominated by Mt Pelée (1,397m), an active volcano that last erupted in 1902. Tourism is a major industry. The main exports are bananas, rum and petroleum products.
Prefect, Laurent Prevost, *apptd* 2011

MAYOTTE
Area – 374 sq. km
Capital – Mamoudzou; population, 53,022 (2007 est)
Population – 223,765 (2009 est)

Part of the Comoros archipelago, Mayotte remained a French dependency when the other three islands became independent as the Comoros Republic in 1975. It became a *collectivité territoriale* in 1976, and an overseas department/region in 2011. The main products are vanilla, ylang-ylang (perfume essence), coffee, copra, lobster and shrimp. The economy is dependent on French subsidies.
Prefect, Hubert Derache, *apptd* 2009

RÉUNION
Area – 2,513 sq. km
Capital – St-Denis; population 140,906 (2009 est)
Population – 821,168 (2009 est)

A French possession since 1638, Réunion lies in the Indian Ocean, about 650km east of Madagascar and 180km south-west of Mauritius. The main industries are tourism and sugar and rum production.
Prefect, Michel Lalande, *apptd* 2010

TERRITORIAL COLLECTIVITIES

Overseas *collectivités* are administrative divisions with a degree of autonomy but without the status of a similar administrative division in metropolitan France; each has its own laws and an elected assembly and president. The French government is represented by a *prefect* or high commissioner in each. Constitutional changes in 2003 redesignated most of the former overseas territories as *collectivités;* New Caledonia is treated in this category because this is its *de facto* status at present, but its official designation depends upon the outcome of independence referendums to be held between 2014 and 2019.

FRENCH POLYNESIA
Area – 4,167 sq. km
Capital – Papeete, on Tahiti; population, 132,980 (2009 est)
Population – 294,935; rising at 1.33 per cent per year (2011 est)

French Polynesia consists of over 118 volcanic or coral islands and atolls in the South Pacific. There are five archipelagos: the Society Islands (Windward Islands group includes Tahiti, Moorea, Makatea, Mehetia, Tetiaroa, Tubuai Manu; Leeward Islands group includes Huahine, Raiatea, Tahaa, Bora-Bora, Maupiti), the Tuamotu Islands (Rangiroa, Hao, Turéia etc), the Gambier Islands (Mangareva etc), the Tubuai Islands (Rimatara, Rurutu, Tubuai, Raivavae, Rapa etc) and the Marquesas Islands (Nuku-Hiva, Hiva-Oa, Fatu-Hiva, Tahuata, Ua Huka etc). Some of the atolls were used by France for testing nuclear weapons between 1966 and 1996. The main industries are tourism, pearl-farming, deep-sea fishing, coconut products and vanilla production.

High Commissioner, Richard Didier, *apptd* 2010

NEW CALEDONIA
Area – 18,575 sq. km
Capital – Nouméa; population, 143,577 (2009 est)
Population – 256,275 rising at 1.52 per cent per year (2011 est)

New Caledonia is a large island in the western Pacific, 1,120km off the eastern coast of Australia. Its dependencies are the Isle of Pines, the Loyalty Islands (Mahé, Lifou, Urea, etc), the Bélep Archipelago, the Chesterfield Islands, the Huon Islands and Walpole. New Caledonia was discovered in 1774 and annexed by France in 1853. Agitation for independence from the 1980s ended with the Nouméa accord in 1998, under which an increasing degree of autonomy will be transferred to the territory up to 2018, with a referendum on independence to be held between 2014 and 2018. The territory is divided into three provinces, each with a provincial assembly; these combine to form the territorial assembly.

A quarter of the world's nickel deposits are found in the territory, and nickel mining and smelting are the main industries, along with tourism and fishing. Ferronickel, nickel ore and fish are the main exports. About 20 per cent of food has to be imported.

High Commissioner, Albert Dupuy, *apptd* 2010

ST BARTHÉLEMY
Area – 21 sq. km
Capital – Gustavia
Population – 7,367 (2011 est)

The island lies in the Caribbean Sea about 240km north-west of Guadeloupe. It was settled by the French from 1648. France sold the island to Sweden in 1784 but bought it back again in 1878 and it was under the administration of Guadeloupe until 2007, when it became a *collectivité territoriale.* The economy is based on luxury tourism and duty-free commerce in luxury goods. Freshwater sources are limited, so all food and energy and most manufactured goods are imported.

Prefect, Jacques Simonnet, *apptd* 2009

ST MARTIN
Area – 54.4 sq. km
Capital – Marigot
Population – 30,615 (2011 est)

The territory occupies the northern part of the island of St Martin, 250km to the north-west of Guadeloupe; the southern part (Sint Maarten) is a territory of the Netherlands. The island was claimed for Spain by Columbus in 1493 but the Spanish relinquished it in 1648 to the Dutch and French, who divided the island between them. The French part was administered from

Guadeloupe until it was made a *collectivité territoriale* in 2007. The economy is dependent on tourism, which employs 85 per cent of the workforce. Nearly all food, energy and manufactured goods are imported.

Deputy Prefect, Jacques Simonnet, *apptd* 2009

ST PIERRE AND MIQUELON
Area – 242 sq. km
Capital – St-Pierre; population, 5,888 (2011 est)
Population – 7,051 rising at 0.09 per cent a year (2009 est)

These two small groups of eight islands off the south coast of Newfoundland became a *collectivité territoriale* in 1985. The main industry of fishing and servicing fishing fleets has declined in step with the decline in cod stocks, and fish farming, crab fishing and agriculture are being developed. Tourism is of growing importance, but the economy is dependent on government subsidies.

Prefect, Jean-Régis Borius, *apptd* 2009

WALLIS AND FUTUNA ISLANDS
Area – 142 sq. km
Capital – Mata-Utu, on Uvea, the main island of the Wallis group; population, 1,112 (2009 est)
Population – 15,398 (2011 est)

The two groups of islands (the Wallis Archipelago and the Îles de Horne) lie in the South Pacific, north-east of Fiji. They became a French protectorate from the 1840s and were administered from New Caledonia until 1961. The main products are copra, vegetables, bananas, livestock products, fish and timber.

Administrator, Michel Jeanjean, *apptd* 2010

OVERSEAS TERRITORIES

TERRITORY OF THE FRENCH SOUTHERN AND ANTARCTIC LANDS
Created in 1955 from former Réunion dependencies, the territory comprises the islands of Amsterdam (55 sq. km) and St Paul (7 sq. km), the Kerguelen Islands (7,215 sq. km) and Crozet Islands (352 sq. km) archipelagos, Adélie Land (302,500 sq. km) in the Antarctic continent and, since 2007, the islands of Bassas da India (80 sq. km), Europa (28 sq. km), les Glorieuses (5 sq. km), Juan de Nova (4.4 sq. km) and Tromelin (1 sq. km). The population consists only of staff of the meteorological and scientific research stations.

Administrator, Christian Gaudin, *apptd* 2010

THE FRENCH COMMUNITY OF STATES
The 1958 constitution envisaged the establishment of a French Community of States. A number of former French colonies in Africa have seceded from the community but for all practical purposes continue to enjoy the same close links with France as do those that remain formal members. Most former French African colonies are closely linked to France by financial, technical and economic agreements.

GABON

République Gabonaise – Gabonese Republic

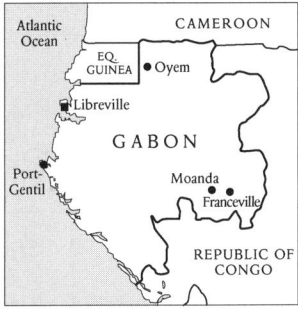

Area – 267,667 sq. km
Capital – Libreville; population, 618,957 (2009 est)
Major towns – Franceville (Masuku), Moanda, Oyem, Port-Gentil
Currency – Franc CFA of 100 centimes
Population – 1,545,255 rising at 2.03 per cent a year (2010 est); over 40 predominantly Bantu tribes, of which the Fang, Bapounou, Nzebi and Obamba are the largest tribal groupings
Religion – Christian 73 per cent (predominantly Roman Catholic), Muslim 5 per cent (mostly non-Gabonese), animism 10 per cent (est); many people combine elements of Christian and indigenous beliefs
Language – French (official), Fang, Myene, Nzebi, Bapounou, Bandjabi
Population density – 6 per sq. km (2009)
Urban population – 85 per cent (2008 est)
Median age (years) – 18.6 (2010 est)
National anthem – 'La Concorde' ['The Concord']
National day – 17 August (Independence Day)
Life expectancy (years) – 52.75 (2010 est)
Mortality rate – 12.9 (2010 est)
Birth rate – 35.39 (2010 est)
Infant mortality rate – 50.88 (2010 est)
HIV/AIDS adult prevalence – 5.2 per cent (2009 est)
Death penalty – Abolished for all crimes (since 2010)
CPI score – 2.8 (2010)
Literacy rate – 86.9 per cent (2008 est)
Gross enrolment ratio (percentage of relevant age group) – primary 152 per cent (2006 est)
Health expenditure (per capita) – US$266 (2009)
Hospital beds (per 1,000 people) – 1.3 (2004–9)

CLIMATE AND TERRAIN

The country lies on the equator. It rises from a narrow coastal plain to a hilly interior; approximately 85 per cent of the land is rainforest, with savannah in the east and south, although by 2006 as much as half of the country's forest was being leased for timber. In 2002, 10 per cent of the country was designated as national park. Elevation extremes range from 1,575m (Mt Iboundji) at the highest point to 0m (Atlantic Ocean) at the lowest. The climate is tropical, with an average temperature of 27°C. There are two wet seasons each year, from January to June and from September to December.

HISTORY AND POLITICS

The first Europeans to visit the region were the Portuguese in the 15th century; Dutch, French and English traders arrived soon after. Sovereignty was signed over to the French in 1839 by a local Mpongwe ruler. In 1849, slaves freed by the French formed a settlement which they called Libreville, now the capital. The country was occupied by the French in 1885 and became part of French Equatorial Africa in 1910. Gabon became autonomous within the French Community in 1958 and gained independence on 17 August 1960.

Omar Bongo succeeded to the presidency in 1967 after the death of the first president, and in 1968 he established a one-party state with the *Parti Démocratique Gabonais* (PDG) as the only party. By the late 1980s, the deteriorating economy was provoking unrest and demands for greater democracy, and in 1991 a multiparty system was reintroduced.

Under the multiparty system, the PDG has remained in power (amid allegations of electoral fraud) although it has included opposition party members in coalition governments since 1994. The 2006 legislative elections were again won by the PDG, which formed a coalition government with two smaller parties. President Bongo was re-elected for a sixth term of office in 2005; he died in June 2009, and was succeeded by his son, Ali-Ben Bongo, who was elected president in August 2009 amid allegations of vote-rigging.

POLITICAL SYSTEM

The 1991 constitution, amended in 1995, 1997 and 2003, provides for a president who is directly elected for a seven-year term; since 2003, there has been no limit on the number of terms a president may serve. The president appoints the prime minister, who then appoints the council of ministers. There is a bicameral *Parlement*, comprising the 120-member National Assembly (111 directly elected and nine appointed by the president, all for a five-year term) and the senate, which has 102 members elected for a six-year term by municipal and regional councillors.

HEAD OF STATE
President, Ali-Ben Bongo, *elected* 30 August 2009, *sworn in* 16 October 2009

SELECTED GOVERNMENT MEMBERS *as at June 2011*
Prime Minister, Paul Biyoghe-Mba
Defence, Pacome Rufin Ondzounga
Finance, Emmauel Issozet Ngondet
Economy, Magloire Ngambia
Interior, Jean-François Ndongou
Foreign Affairs, Paul Toungui

EMBASSY OF THE GABONESE REPUBLIC
27 Elvaston Place, London SW7 5NL
T 020-7823 9986
Ambassador Extraordinary and Plenipotentiary, Omer Piankali, *apptd* 2009

BRITISH AMBASSADOR
HE Bharat Joshi, *apptd* 2009, resident at Yaoundé, Cameroon

DEFENCE

The army has 12 armoured infantry fighting vehicles and over 28 armoured personnel carriers. The navy has 3 patrol and coastal combatant vessels at a base at Port-Gentil. The air force has 20 combat-capable aircraft and 10 multi-role helicopters.
Military budget – US$250m (2010)
Military personnel – 4,700: army 3,200, navy 500, air force 1,000; paramilitary 2,000

ECONOMY AND TRADE

Gabon is one of the most prosperous countries in Africa, largely owing to its small population and abundance of oil and mineral resources. The economy is heavily dependent on oil (which contributes over 50 per cent of GDP) and other mineral resources, including manganese and uranium, and timber, but the government is investing in diversification to reduce vulnerability to fluctuating commodity prices and the gradual decline in oil production as reserves become exhausted. Despite the country's wealth, a large proportion of the population remains poor, and weak fiscal management has resulted in a high foreign debt which has had to be rescheduled several times.

Agriculture is largely at subsistence level, employing 60 per cent of the workforce but contributing only 4.5 per cent of GDP. It is restricted by the forest cover and lack of suitable land. The main products include cocoa, coffee, sugar, palm oil, rubber, cattle, timber and fish. Industry contributes 62.7 per cent of GDP and employs 15 per cent of the workforce, mainly in oil and mineral extraction, oil refining, chemicals, ship repair, textiles, and processing agricultural and forestry products.

The main trading partners are France, Russia, the USA and China. Principal exports are crude oil (70 per cent), timber, manganese and uranium. The main imports are machinery and equipment, food, chemicals and construction materials.

GNI – US$9,549m; US$7,370 per capita (2009)
Annual average growth of GDP – 5.4 per cent (2010 est)
Inflation rate – −1.3 per cent (2010 est)
Unemployment – 21 per cent (2006 est)
Total external debt – US$2,374m (2010 est)
Imports – US$2,200m (2009)
Exports – US$5,100m (2009)

BALANCE OF PAYMENTS
Trade – US$4,407m surplus (2010)
Current Account – US$1,283m surplus (2009 est)

Trade with UK	2009	2010
Imports from UK	£43,511,082	£44,702,969
Exports to UK	£2,691,438	£3,387,144

MEDIA

The state-controlled broadcaster, Radiodiffusion-Télévision Gabonaise, operates two television channels and two radio networks; the only daily newspaper, *L'Union,* is also government-run. There are two other television channels and several privately owned newspapers that usually publish on a weekly basis. Radio is an important news medium because of low literacy rates in rural areas. Africa No1, a pan-African radio broadcaster, is based in Gabon.

THE GAMBIA

Republic of The Gambia

Area – 11,295 sq. km
Capital – Banjul; population, 436,447 (2009 est)
Major towns – Bakau, Brikama, Farafenni, Serekunda
Currency – Dalasi (D) of 100 butut
Population – 1,824,158 rising at 2.53 per cent a year (2010 est); Mandinka (42 per cent), Fulani (18 per cent), Wolof (16 per cent), Jola (10 per cent), Serahuli (Soninke) (9 per cent) (2003)
Religion – Sunni Muslim 90 per cent (majority Malikite Sufi), Christian 9 per cent (predominantly Roman Catholic), animist 1 per cent (est)
Language – English (official), Mandinka, Wolof, Fula
Population density – 171 per sq. km (2009)
Urban population – 57 per cent (2008 est)
Median age (years) – 18 (2010 est)
National anthem – 'For The Gambia Our Homeland'
National day – 18 February (Independence Day)
Life expectancy (years) – 54.07 (2010 est)
Mortality rate – 12.03 (2010 est)
Birth rate – 37.31 (2010 est)
Infant mortality rate – 67.49 (2010 est)
HIV / AIDS adult prevalence – 2 per cent (2009 est)
Death penalty – Retained (not used since 1981)
CPI score – 3.2 (2010)

CLIMATE AND TERRAIN

The Gambia consists of a narrow strip of land along the river Gambia, mostly comprising the basin and flood plain of the river, flanked by savannah and low hills. Elevation extremes range from 53m at the highest point to 0m (Atlantic Ocean) at the lowest. The climate is tropical, with a wet season from June to November.

HISTORY AND POLITICS

The Gambia river basin was part of an area dominated from the 10th to 16th centuries by the Mali and Songhai kingdoms. The Portuguese reached the river Gambia in 1447 and, followed later by other European merchants, established trading posts along the river. In 1816 a British garrison was stationed on an island at the river mouth; this became the capital of a small British colony, and a crown colony in 1843. The boundaries of the country were agreed by France and Britain in 1889; British territory would extend ten kilometres from the upper river on either bank. The Gambia became independent on 18 February 1965 and a republic in 1970.

The post-independence prime minister, Sir Dawda Jawara, was president from 1970 until 1994, when he was overthrown in a military coup. The coup leader, Lt. (later Col.) Yahya Jammeh, assumed the presidency and a civilian-military government was formed to govern in conjunction with the ruling military council. Civilian government was restored after elections in 1996 and 1997 following the approval of a new constitution. Jammeh was elected president and his Alliance for Patriotic Reorientation and Construction (APRC) won an overall majority of the legislative seats. Jammeh and the APRC have won all subsequent elections; the opposition and media are subject to harassment and detention without charge.

In the 2006 presidential election, Jammeh was re-elected with 67 per cent of the vote. The 2007 legislative election was won by the APRC, with 42 of the 48 elected seats. A presidential election is scheduled for 24 November 2011.

POLITICAL SYSTEM
Under the 1997 constitution, the executive president is directly elected for a five-year term; there is no limit on re-election. The unicameral National Assembly has 53 members, of whom 48 are directly elected and five are appointed by the president, for a five-year term.

HEAD OF STATE
President, Defence, Agriculture, Col. Yahya Jammeh, *took power* July 1994, *elected* September 1996, *re-elected* 2001, 2006
Vice-President, Women and Social Affairs, Ajaratou Isatou Njie-Saidy

SELECTED GOVERNMENT MEMBERS *as at June 2011*
Foreign Affairs, Mamadou Tangara
Finance and Economic Affairs, Mambury Njie
Interior, Ousman Sonko
Justice, Attorney-General, Edward Gomez

THE GAMBIA HIGH COMMISSION
57 Kensington Court, London W8 5DG
T 020-7937 6316 E gambiahighcomuk@btconnect.com
High Commissioner, HE Elizabeth Ya Eli Harding, *apptd* 2007

BRITISH HIGH COMMISSION
PO Box 507, 48 Atlantic Road, Fajara, Banjul
T (+220) 449 5133 W http://ukingambia.fco.gov.uk
High Commissioner, HE David Morley, *apptd* 2011

DEFENCE
The Marine Unit has 7 patrol and coastal combatant vessels at a base at Banjul.
Military budget – US$7m (2009 est)
Military personnel – Army 800

ECONOMY AND TRADE
The country has limited natural resources and agricultural land. Historically, the mainstay of the economy was re-export trade with neighbouring countries, but this has declined since the late 1990s, owing to the vagaries of government policies and trade and transport disputes with Senegal. There are high levels of public and foreign debt and the country is dependent on financial and technical aid from foreign donors. Remittances from Gambians working abroad and tourism are vital revenue sources.

About 75 per cent of the population is dependent on subsistence agriculture, which contributes 30.1 per cent of GDP. The chief product, peanuts, is also the main export and the basis of the main industrial activity, leaving the economy vulnerable to market fluctuations

and the weather. Industry contributes 16.3 per cent to GDP, chiefly through processing peanuts, fish and hides, assembling agricultural machinery, metalworking, woodworking and the production of beverages and clothing. The services sector employs only 6 per cent of the workforce but contributes 53.6 per cent of GDP, largely owing to the growing tourism and banking sectors.

The main trade partners are India (42 per cent of exports), China (20 per cent of imports), EU countries and Senegal. Principal exports are peanut products, fish, cotton lint and palm kernels. The main imports are foodstuffs, manufactures, fuel, machinery and transport equipment.
GNI – US$690m; US$440 per capita (2009)
Annual average growth of GDP – 5 per cent (2010 est)
Inflation rate – 5.5 per cent (2010 est)
Total external debt – US$530m (2010 est)
Imports – US$300m (2009)
Exports – US$13m (2007)

BALANCE OF PAYMENTS
Trade – US$305m deficit (2010)
Current Account – US$131m deficit (2008)

Trade with UK	2009	2010
Imports from UK	£15,586,743	£15,941,153
Exports to UK	£2,888,868	£3,955,733

EDUCATION AND HEALTH
Education is compulsory between the ages of seven and 12.
Gross enrolment ratio (percentage of relevant age group) – primary 86 per cent; secondary 51 per cent; tertiary 5 per cent (2008 est)
Health expenditure (per capita) – US$26 (2009)
Hospital beds (per 1,000 people) – 1.1 (2004–9)

MEDIA
Since 2002, private newspapers and radio stations have been tightly regulated by a government-run commission that has the power to imprison journalists and suspend publication or transmission licences, which are expensive to obtain; a 2004 law introduced jail terms for journalists convicted of libel or sedition. The state operates the only national television station, although there is also a private satellite channel. State-run Radio Gambia produces carefully controlled news broadcasts, which are relayed by private radio stations.

GEORGIA

Sak'art'velo – Georgia

Area – 69,700 sq. km
Capital – Tbilisi; population, 1,114,960 (2009 est)
Major cities – Batumi, Kutaisi, Poti, Rustavi
Currency – Lari of 100 tetri
Population – 4,600,825 falling at 0.33 per cent a year
  (2010 est); Georgian (83.8 per cent), Azeri (6.5 per
  cent), Armenian (5.7 per cent), Russian (1.5 per cent)
  (2002)
Religion – Christian 90 per cent (Orthodox 84 per cent,
  Armenian Apostolic 5 per cent, Catholic 1 per cent),
  Muslim 10 per cent (est)
Language – Georgian (official), Russian, Armenian, Azeri,
  Abkhaz (official in Abkhazia)
Population density – 61 per sq. km (2009)
Urban population – 53 per cent (2008 est)
Median age (years) – 38.8 (2010 est)
National anthem – 'Tavisupleba' ['Freedom']
National day – 26 May (Independence Day, 1918)
Life expectancy (years) – 76.93 (2010 est)
Mortality rate – 9.79 (2010 est)
Birth rate – 10.7 (2010 est)
Infant mortality rate – 15.67 (2010 est)
Death penalty – Abolished for all crimes (since 1997)
CPI score – 3.8 (2010)
Literacy rate – 100.0 per cent (2008 est)
Gross enrolment ratio (percentage of relevant age group) –
  primary 108 per cent; secondary 108 per cent; tertiary
  25 per cent (2009 est)
Health expenditure (per capita) – US$256 (2009)
Hospital beds (per 1,000 people) – 3.3 (2004–9)

CLIMATE AND TERRAIN

Georgia lies in the western part of the Caucasus region, on the eastern shore of the Black Sea. It is mountainous, with the Great Caucasus mountain range along the northern border with Russia, and the Lesser Caucasus in the south. These are divided by the Kolkhida lowland in the west and the Mtkvari (Kura) river basin in the east, between which runs the valley of the Mtkvari river. Elevation extremes range from 5,201m (Mt Shkhara) at the highest point to 0m (Black Sea) at the lowest. The climate is almost tropical in summer, while cold winters affect both the mountains and valleys. Average temperatures in Tbilisi range from 2°C in January to 25°C in July.

HISTORY AND POLITICS

The ancient kingdoms of the Georgian region came under Roman influence in the first century AD and converted to Christianity in the fourth century. After domination by Persians, Arabs and Turks, an independent kingdom was established that experienced a golden age from the 11th century until the Mongols invaded in 1236. The Ottoman and Persian empires competed for influence from the 16th to the 18th centuries; the Georgians increasingly turned to Russia for protection and were absorbed into the Russian Empire in 1801–4.

In the late 19th century, nationalist and Marxist movements competed for limited political influence under autocratic Russian rule; one of the most prominent Marxist activists was Iosif Dzhugashvili (Joseph Stalin). After the Russian Revolution of 1917, an independent nationalist government came to power in Georgia that was recognised by Soviet Russia shortly before Russian forces invaded and occupied the country in 1921. Georgia joined the USSR as part of the Transcaucasian Soviet Socialist Republic in 1922, becoming a separate republic in 1936.

Resurgent nationalism in the 1980s led to growing demands for autonomy, and in 1990 the Communist Party's monopoly on power was abolished and multiparty elections were held. Georgia declared its independence from the USSR in May 1991.

A coup in 1992 overthrew the increasingly authoritarian President Zviad Gamsakhurdia, who was replaced by Eduard Shevardnadze. A pro-Gamsakhurdia uprising in 1993, when most government forces were engaged in Abkhazia, forced Georgia to accept Russian armaments and troops to defeat the rebels; in return Georgia agreed to join the Commonwealth of Independent States, and remained a member until 2009.

President Shevardnadze was forced out of office in 2003 by mass demonstrations over alleged electoral fraud in the parliamentary elections. Mikheil Saakashvili, leader of the National Movement, was elected president in 2004, and re-elected in 2008 with 53 per cent of the vote in the first round; despite opposition allegations of fraud, international monitors considered the election democratic. The United National Movement for a Victorious Georgia won 119 seats in the 2008 legislative elections.

Relations between Russia and Georgia have been fraught since the 1990s owing to Russia's support for the secessionists in South Ossetia and Abkhazia (*see below*), Georgia's increasingly pro-Western stance, and Russia's use of trade embargos and disruption of energy supplies. After a series of clashes with secessionist forces, Georgia tried to retake South Ossetia by force in August 2008 and was repulsed by counter-attacking Russian troops. Russia expelled Georgian troops from South Ossetia and Abkhazia, and started to move further into Georgia before the EU brokered a ceasefire and a withdrawal to the positions held before fighting began. Russia has not fully complied with the ceasefire agreement, maintaining a considerable military presence in the secessionist areas and in a 'buffer zone' around them. It has also recognised both South Ossetia and Abkhazia as independent republics, attracting international condemnation for doing so.

SECESSION

Fears that Georgian independence would deprive them of their own autonomy led to unilateral declarations of independence by the central region of South Ossetia (1991) and the north-western region of Abkhazia (1992). The Georgian government resisted these moves and there was conflict with South Ossetia until 1992, while in Abkhazia, Georgian forces were forced to withdraw in 1993. In August 2008, clashes between Georgian troops and South Ossetian separatists escalated into a brief war between Georgia and Russia, in which Georgian forces were expelled from both separatist areas. Both regions remain outside Georgian control; their unilateral declarations of independence in August 2008 were recognised only by Russia. In both regions the economy and infrastructure are in ruins and the secessionists are dependent on Russia, which maintains peacekeeping forces in both and has stepped up its economic support. The UN operated a military observer mission in Abkhazia from 1993 to 2009, when Russia vetoed the renewal of its mandate.

Relations between Georgia and Ajaria, a semi-autonomous region in the south-west and a key trade hub, deteriorated briefly in 2004 when Aslan Abashidze, Ajaria's leader since 1991, refused to recognise the authority of the newly elected President Saakashvili, and accused Georgia of planning to invade Ajaria. Public demonstrations against Abashidze forced him to resign. The Georgian parliament granted the Ajarian assembly powers over local affairs but the Georgian president retains the power to nominate the region's head of government and to dissolve its government and assembly.

POLITICAL SYSTEM

The 1995 constitution provides for a federal republic with a unicameral legislature, to become bicameral 'following the creation of appropriate conditions'. It was amended in 2010 to transfer some of the president's powers to the legislature and prime minister. The president is directly elected for a five-year term, renewable once. The unicameral parliament has 150 members, 75 elected in single-member constituencies and 75 by proportional representation, who serve for a five-year term.

HEAD OF STATE
President, Mikheil Saakashvili, *elected* 4 January 2004, *sworn in* 25 January 2004, *re-elected* 2008

SELECTED GOVERNMENT MEMBERS *as at June 2011*
Prime Minister, Nika Gilauri
First Deputy Prime Minister, David Tkeshelashvili
Deputy Prime Ministers, Giorgi Baramidze, Eka Tkeshelashvili
Defence, Bachana Akhalaia
Finance, Kakha Baindurashvili
Foreign Affairs, Grigol Vashadze

EMBASSY OF GEORGIA
4 Russell Gardens, London W14 8EZ
T 020-7348 1941 E embassy@geoemb.plus.com
W www.uk.mfa.gov.ge
Ambassador Extraordinary and Plenipotentiary, HE Giorgi Badridze, *apptd* 2009

BRITISH EMBASSY
51 Krtsanisi Street, 0114 Tbilisi
T (+995) (32) 274 747 W http://ukingeorgia.fco.gov.uk
Ambassador Extraordinary and Plenipotentiary, HE Judith Gough, *apptd* 2010

BRITISH COUNCIL
34 Rustaveli Avenue, 0108 Tbilisi
T (+995) (32) 250 407/ 988 014 W www.britishcouncil.ge
Director, Dr Lloyd Anderson

DEFENCE
The army has 93 main battle tanks, 63 armoured infantry fighting vehicles and 137 armoured personnel carriers. The coastguard has 17 patrol and coastal combatant vessels located at Poti and Batumi. The air force has 12 combat aircraft.

Russia has 7,000 troops posted in Abkhazia and South Ossetia.

Military budget – US$420m (2010)
Military personnel – 20,655: army 17,767, air force 1,310, National Guard 1,578; paramilitary 11,700
Conscription duration – 18 months

ECONOMY AND TRADE
The economy grew rapidly from 2003, making good progress towards recovery following the near-collapse of the 1990s. Reform of the tax system nearly quadrupled government revenue, while added impetus in privatisation and anti-corruption programmes attracted foreign investment. However, the economy slowed in 2008 following the war with Russia and contracted in 2009 as the global economic downturn affected the regional economy and led to a decline in foreign investment and expatriates' remittances. The fuel crises in 2005–6 prompted the renovation of hydroelectric power plants and the repair of a pipeline from Azerbaijan which now brings in gas supplies. The government is also looking to diversify its export markets since Russia imposed an embargo on key exports, and it hopes Georgia's position as a transit state for oil and gas pipelines and for trade between central Asia and Europe will stimulate economic growth.

Agriculture employs 55.6 per cent of the workforce and generates 11 per cent of GDP, with a concentration on grapes for winemaking, tea, citrus fruits and hazelnuts. Industry, which contributes 27.1 per cent of GDP, produces steel, aircraft, machine tools, electrical appliances, manganese, copper, chemicals, wood products and wine.

The main trading partners are Turkey, Azerbaijan and Ukraine. Principal exports are scrap metal, wine, mineral water, mineral ores, vehicles, fruit and nuts. The main imports are fuels, vehicles, machinery and parts, food (especially grain) and pharmaceuticals.

GNI – US$10,586m; US$2,530 per capita (2009)
Annual average growth of GDP – 5.5 per cent (2010 est)
Inflation rate – 5.7 per cent (2010 est)
Population below poverty line – 31 per cent (2006)
Unemployment – 16.4 per cent (2009 est)
Total external debt – US$3,381m (2009)
Imports – US$4,400m (2009)
Exports – US$1,100m (2009)

BALANCE OF PAYMENTS
Trade – US$3,516m deficit (2010)
Current Account – US$1,312m deficit (2009)

Trade with UK	2009	2010
Imports from UK	£25,558,806	£38,340,686
Exports to UK	£83,156,383	£122,628,554

MEDIA
A law on broadcasting adopted in 2004 transformed the state-owned Television-Radio Corporation into a public broadcaster, Georgian Public Broadcasting, which provides television and radio services and is government funded. The state has also given up control of other media outlets, including newspapers and news agencies; there are many privately owned newspapers, publishing in Georgian, Russian and English, although readership is generally low. Slander and libel were decriminalised in 2004, but the suspension of several private media sources during a state of emergency in 2007 cast doubt on the government's commitment to media freedom.

GERMANY

Bundesrepublik Deutschland – Federal Republic of Germany

Area – 357,022 sq. km
Capital – Berlin; population, 3,437,780 (2009 est)
Major cities – Bremen, Cologne, Dortmund, Dresden, Düsseldorf, Essen, Frankfurt, Hamburg, Hannover, Leipzig, Munich, Nuremberg, Stuttgart
Currency – Euro (€) of 100 cents
Population – 82,282,988 falling at 0.06 per cent a year (2010 est); German (91.5 per cent), Turkish (2.4 per cent) (est)
Religion – Christian 63 per cent (Protestant 32 per cent, Roman Catholic 31 per cent), Muslim 5 per cent (predominantly Sunni) (est)
Language – German (official)
Population density – 235 per sq. km (2009)
Urban population – 74 per cent (2008 est)
Median age (years) – 44.3 (2010 est)
National anthem – 'Das Deutschlandlied' ['The Song of Germany']
National day – 3 October (Unity Day)
Life expectancy (years) – 79.41 (2010 est)
Mortality rate – 11 (2010 est)
Birth rate – 8.21 (2010 est)
Infant mortality rate – 3.95 (2010 est)
Death penalty – Abolished for all crimes (since 1949 in FRG and 1987 in GDR)
CPI score – 7.9 (2010)

CLIMATE AND TERRAIN

The north of the country is low-lying, rising in the centre to uplands and Alpine foothills, then to the Bavarian Alps in the south. Elevation extremes range from 2,963m (Zugspitze, Bavaria) at the highest point to −3.54m (Neuendorf bei Wilster) at the lowest. The Rhine, Weser and Elbe rivers flow from the south to the North Sea, the Oder and Neisse rivers flow north to the Baltic Sea, and the Danube flows east from its source in the south of the country to the Austrian border. Nearly a third of the land is covered by forest or woodland. The climate is temperate, with average temperatures in Berlin ranging from −1°C in January to 19°C in July.

HISTORY AND POLITICS

Charlemagne extended Frankish authority over the Germanic tribes in the eighth century, and took the title of Holy Roman Emperor. The treaty of Verdun (843) divided this empire into three, the eastern part (corresponding to modern Germany) comprising hundreds of small dukedoms and principalities that enjoyed virtual independence under the hegemony of a nominally elective Holy Roman Emperor. Although a number of dynasties succeeded at times in centralising power between 962 and 1806, shifting allegiances and alliances enabled the states to challenge the authority of the emperor, which was never sufficient to achieve unification into a single nation state.

The Holy Roman Empire was replaced in 1806 by a loose association of sovereign states known as the German Confederation. This was dissolved in 1866 and replaced by the Prussian-dominated North German Federation. The south German principalities united with the northern federation to form a second German Empire in 1871 and the King of Prussia was proclaimed emperor.

Defeat in the First World War led to the abdication of the emperor, and the country became a republic. The treaty of Versailles (1919) ceded Alsace-Lorraine to France, and large areas in the east were lost to Poland. The world economic crisis of 1929 contributed to the collapse of the Weimar Republic and the subsequent rise to power of the National Socialist movement led by Adolf Hitler, who became chancellor in 1933.

After concluding a treaty of non-aggression with the Soviet Union in August 1939, Germany invaded Poland (1 September 1939), precipitating the Second World War, which lasted until 1945. Hitler committed suicide on 30 April 1945. On 8 May 1945, Germany unconditionally surrendered.

Germany was divided into American, French, British and Soviet zones of occupation. The Federal Republic of Germany (FRG) was created out of the three Western zones in 1949. A Communist government was established in the Soviet zone, known as the German Democratic Republic (GDR). In 1961 the Soviet zone of Berlin was sealed off, and the Berlin Wall was built along the zonal boundary, partitioning the city.

Following the collapse of the Communist government in the GDR in 1989, Germany was reunified as a single sovereign state with effect from 3 October 1990. Berlin was declared the capital of the unified Germany, and the legislature and government departments were transferred from Bonn.

West Germany was a founder member of the EEC in 1958 and Germany joined the eurozone in 1999.

Angela Merkel, leader of the Christian Democratic Union of Germany and the Christian Social Union of Bavaria (CDU/CSU), became Germany's first female chancellor in 2005 at the head of a CDU/CSU and Social Democratic Party (SPD) coalition following inconclusive legislative elections. At the 2009 elections, the CDU increased its number of seats, while the SPD lost ground, and Angela Merkel was re-elected Chancellor at the head of a CDU/CSU coalition with the Free Democrats (FDP). Christian Wulff was elected president in June 2010 after his predecessor, Horst Köhler, resigned over a controversial speech linking military deployments overseas and economic benefit.

POLITICAL SYSTEM

The Basic Law was adopted in 1949 as the constitution of West Germany; at unification in 1990, Berlin and the five reformed *Länder* (states) of East Germany acceded to the Federal Republic. The president is elected for a five-year term by the *Bundesversammlung*, an electoral college comprising the members of the *Bundestag* (see below) and an equal number of representatives elected by the state legislatures. The bicameral legislature comprises a lower house, the Federal Assembly *(Bundestag)*, with 622 members elected by a mixed constituency and proportional representation system for a four-year term.

The Federal Council *(Bundesrat)* has 69 members appointed by the governments of the *Länder* in proportion to their populations; their term of office is determined by their *Land's* constitution. The head of government is the chancellor, who is proposed by the president and elected by the *Bundestag*.

HEAD OF STATE
Federal President, Christian Wulff, *elected and sworn in* 30 June 2010

SELECTED GOVERNMENT MEMBERS *as at June 2011*
Federal Chancellor, Angela Merkel
Foreign Affairs, Guido Westerwelle
Defence, Thomas de Maizière
Interior, Hans-Peter Friedrich
Finance, Wolfgang Schäuble

EMBASSY OF THE FEDERAL REPUBLIC OF GERMANY
23 Belgrave Square, London SW1X 8PZ
T 020-7824 1300 W www.london.diplo.de
Ambassador Extraordinary and Plenipotentiary, HE Georg Boomgaarden, *apptd* 2008

BRITISH EMBASSY
Wilhelmstrasse 70, 10117 Berlin
T (+49) (30) 204 570 W http://ukingermany.fco.gov.uk
Ambassador Extraordinary and Plenipotentiary, HE Simon McDonald, CMG, *apptd* 2010

BRITISH COUNCIL
Alexanderplatz 1, 10178 Berlin
T (+49) (30) 311 0990 W www.britishcouncil.de
Director, John Whitehead

FEDERAL STRUCTURE
Germany is a federal republic composed of 16 states *(Länder)* (ten from the former FRG, five from the former GDR, and Berlin). Each *Land* has its own directly elected legislature and government led by a minister-president (prime minister) or equivalent. The 1949 Basic Law vests executive power in the *Länder* governments except in those areas reserved for the federal government.

State	Capital	Population (millions) (2005 est)
Baden-Württemberg	Stuttgart	10.7
Bavaria	Munich	12.5
Berlin	—	3.4
Brandenburg	Potsdam	2.6
Bremen	—	0.7
Hamburg	—	1.7
Hesse	Wiesbaden	6.1
Lower Saxony	Hannover	8.0
Mecklenburg-West Pomerania	Schwerin	1.7
North Rhine-Westphalia	Düsseldorf	18.1
Rhineland-Palatinate	Mainz	4.1
Saarland	Saarbrücken	1.1
Saxony	Dresden	4.3
Saxony-Anhalt	Magdeburg	2.5
Schleswig-Holstein	Kiel	2.8
Thuringia	Erfurt	2.3

DEFENCE
The army has 768 main battle tanks, 2,157 armoured personnel carriers, 2,044 armoured infantry fighting vehicles and 150 multi-role helicopters. The navy has 4 submarines, 13 frigates, 10 patrol and coastal vessels, 8 combat aircraft and 22 armed helicopters at 6 bases. The air force has 318 combat aircraft.

Military budget – US$41,200m (2010)
Military personnel – 251,465: army 105,291, navy 19,179, air force 44,565, joint medical and support services 82,430
Conscription duration – 9 months. Conscription was due to be phased out from mid-2011

ECONOMY AND TRADE
Germany has one of the world's largest economies but decades of strong economic performance gave way in the 1990s to a severe recession, largely an aftermath of reunification and of macroeconomic stagnation. Although the economy as a whole began to grow again in 2006, in the east it remains weak despite costly modernisation and integration measures. However, the revival was largely export-led and a decline in demand due to the global economic downturn caused a recession in 2008–9. The government's economic stimulus measures pushed the budget deficit slightly beyond the eurozone's 3 per cent threshold in 2010.

The country has a modern, diverse, highly industrialised and technologically advanced market economy. The services sector contributes 71.3 per cent of GDP, industry 27.9 per cent and agriculture 0.8 per cent. The industrial sector is among the world's largest producers of iron, steel, coal, cement, chemicals, machinery, vehicles, machine tools, electronics, food and beverages, ships and textiles. Germany depends on imports to meet its oil and natural gas needs, but it remains a net exporter of electricity; in the wake of Japan's Fukushima crisis in March 2011, the German government revoked a decision to extend the life of the country's 17 nuclear power stations (which supply about 25 per cent of its electricity). All stations are expected to close by 2022.

The main trading partners are other EU countries, the USA and China. Machinery, vehicles, chemicals, metals and manufactures, foodstuffs and textiles are the principal imports and exports.

GNI – US$3,377,042m; US$42,450 per capita (2009)
Annual average growth of GDP – 3.3 per cent (2010 est)
Inflation rate – 1 per cent (2010 est)
Unemployment – 7.1 per cent (2010 est)
Total external debt – US$4,713,000m (2010)
Imports – US$939,000m (2009)
Exports – US$1,127,600m (2009)

BALANCE OF PAYMENTS
Trade – US$204,774m surplus (2010)
Current Account – US$160,627m surplus (2009)

Trade with UK	2009	2010
Imports from UK	£24,802,785,867	£28,520,245,056
Exports to UK	£39,654,119,835	£45,733,533,350

COMMUNICATIONS
There is an extensive road network of 644,480km, including 12,800km of motorways *(autobahn)*. There are 41,981km of railways. Around 20 per cent of domestic freight is carried on the 7,467km of inland waterways. The Rhine and the Danube are linked by the Rhine-Maine-Danube canal, creating a through route from the North Sea to the Black Sea. The Kiel canal links the North Sea and the Baltic Sea. The main river ports are Duisburg, Frankfurt, Karlsruhe and Mainz; the main

seaports are Hamburg, Bremen, Bremerhaven, Lübeck, Rostock and Wilhemshaven. The busiest airport is at Frankfurt; other major airports include Berlin, Munich and Bonn.

The telephone system in the east has been modernised and integrated with the rest of the country. Mobile phone distribution is widespread, with 105 million subscribers in 2009. There were 65.1 million internet users in 2009.

EDUCATION AND HEALTH

Education is free and compulsory between the ages of six and 18. It comprises nine years of full-time education at primary and secondary schools and three years of vocational education on a part-time basis. The secondary school leaving examination *(Abitur)* entitles the holder to a place at a university or another institution of higher education.

Children below the age of 18 who are not attending a general secondary or a full-time vocational school have compulsory day-release at a vocational school.

The largest universities are in Munich, Berlin, Hamburg, Bonn, Frankfurt and Cologne. Germany's oldest university is Heidelberg, founded in 1386.

Gross enrolment ratio (percentage of relevant age group) – primary 105 per cent; secondary 102 per cent (2008 est)
Health expenditure (per capita) – US$4,629 (2009)
Hospital beds (per 1,000 people) – 8.2 (2004–9)

MEDIA

Each of the country's 16 states regulates broadcasting, both private and public, in its own area. National and regional public television competes with a large private sector, with about 90 per cent of households having access to cable or satellite stations. Germany also has a considerable press industry, though this is stronger at regional than national level, and is home to many international media companies.

CULTURE

Germany has produced a wealth of composers, including Johann Sebastian Bach (1685–1750), Beethoven (1770–1827), Schubert (1797–1828), Wagner (1813–83) and Brahms (1833–97). Philosophers include Immanuel Kant (1724–1804), Karl Marx (1818–83), Friedrich Engels (1820–95) and Friedrich Nietzsche (1844–1900). The works of playwrights Goethe (1749–1832) and Schiller (1759–1805) had a Europe-wide influence. Novelists Thomas Mann (1875–1955), Hermann Hesse (1877–1962) and Günter Grass (*b.* 1927) have all received the Nobel prize for literature.

Key figures in the visual arts are Albrecht Dürer (1471–1528), Hans Holbein the Younger (1497–1543), surrealist Max Ernst (1891–1976) and Joseph Beuys (1921–86). Film directors Friedrich Murnau (1888–1931), Leni Riefenstahl (1902–2003), Werner Herzog (*b.* 1942) and Wim Wenders (*b.* 1945), and actor Klaus Kinski (1926–91), all gained Hollywood recognition.

Physicist Albert Einstein (1879–1955) is perhaps the world's best-known modern scientist, having introduced his theory of special relativity to the wider world in 1905. Other notable German scientists include Wilhelm Röntgen (1845–1923), Max Planck (1858–1947), Hans Geiger (1882–1945) and Werner Heisenberg (1901–1976).

GHANA

Republic of Ghana

Area – 238,533 sq. km
Capital – Accra; population, 2,268,500 (2009 est)
Major cities – Kumasi, Sekondi-Takoradi, Tamale
Currency – Cedi of 100 pesewas
Population – 24,339,838 rising at 1.86 per cent a year (2010 est); Akan (45.3 per cent), Mole-Dagbon (15.2 per cent), Ewe (11.7 per cent), Ga-Dangme (7.3 per cent), Guan (4 per cent), Gurma (3.6 per cent), Grusi (2.6 per cent) (2000)
Religion – Christian 69 per cent (including Pentecostal/Charismatic 24 per cent, Protestant 19 per cent), Muslim 16 per cent (predominantly Sunni), indigenous and other religions 9 per cent (est)
Language – English (official), Asante, Ewe, Fante, Boron, Dagomba, Dangme, Dagarte, Akyem, Ga, Akuapem
Population density – 105 per sq. km (2009)
Urban population – 50 per cent (2008 est)
Median age (years) – 21.1 (2010 est)
National anthem – 'God Bless Our Homeland Ghana'
National day – 6 March (Independence Day)
Life expectancy (years) – 60.55 (2010 est)
Mortality rate – 8.93 (2010 est)
Birth rate – 28.09 (2010 est)
Infant mortality rate – 49.89 (2010 est)
HIV/AIDS adult prevalence – 1.8 per cent (2009 est)
Death penalty – Retained (not used since 1993)
CPI score – 4.1 (2010)

CLIMATE AND TERRAIN

Ghana consists mostly of plains dissected by the Volta river basin and the great central Lake Volta, rising to the Ashanti plateau in the west. There is dense rainforest in the south and west and forested hills in the north, with savannah in the east and far north. Elevation extremes range from 880m (Mt Afadjato) at the highest point to 0m (Atlantic Ocean) at the lowest. The climate is tropical but with cooler temperatures on the south-east coast, and less rainfall in the south-east and north. Temperatures in Accra average between 23°C and 31°C.

HISTORY AND POLITICS

First reached by Europeans in the 15th century, after which it became a centre for gold and slave trading, the constituent parts of Ghana came under British administration at various times. The original Gold Coast colony was constituted in 1874 and Ashanti and the Northern Territories Protectorate in 1901. Trans-Volta-Togoland, part of the former German colony of Togo, was mandated to Britain by the League of Nations after the First World War and was integrated with the

Gold Coast colony in 1956 following a plebiscite. The colony became independent as Ghana on 6 March 1957. It was proclaimed a republic in 1960.

Ghana became a one-party state in 1964 and from 1966 experienced long periods of military rule (1966–9, 1972–9, 1981–91) interspersed with short-lived civilian governments (1969–72, 1979–81). Flt. Lt. Jerry Rawlings, who had ousted the military regime in 1979 and deposed the civilian government in 1981, was elected president in 1992 when the country returned to multiparty politics after a referendum approved a new constitution.

Since the mid-1990s there have been intermittent clashes over land ownership between ethnic groups in the north; a state of emergency was in place there for two years after the last major outbreak of ethnic violence in 2002.

In the 2008 elections, John Atta Mills, the candidate of the National Democratic Congress (NDC), was elected president, and the NDC became the largest party in the legislature, winning half of the seats.

POLITICAL SYSTEM

Under the 1993 constitution, the executive president is directly elected for a four-year term, renewable once. The president appoints members of the council of ministers subject to approval by the legislature. The unicameral parliament has 230 members who are directly elected for a four-year term.

HEAD OF STATE

President, National Security, John Atta Mills, *elected* 28 December 2008, *sworn in* 7 January 2009
Vice-President, John Dramani Mahama

SELECTED GOVERNMENT MEMBERS *as at June 2011*
Defence, Joseph Smith
Finance, Kabwena Duffuor
Foreign Affairs, Mohammed Mumuni
Interior, Benjamin Kumbour

OFFICE OF THE HIGH COMMISSION FOR GHANA
13 Belgrave Square, London SW1X 8PN
T 020-7201 5900 **E** ghmfa31@yahoo.com
W www.ghanahighcommissionuk.com
High Commissioner, Prof. Kwaku Danso-Boafo, *apptd* 2009

BRITISH HIGH COMMISSION
PO Box 296, Osu Link, off Gamel Abdul Nasser Avenue, Accra
T (+233) (302) 213 250 **E** high.commission.accra@fco.gov.uk
W http://ukinghana.fco.gov.uk
High Commissioner, HE Peter Jones, *apptd* 2011

BRITISH COUNCIL
PO Box GP 771, Liberia Road, Accra
T (+233) (21) 610 090 **W** www.britishcouncil.org/ghana
Director, Moses Anibaba

DEFENCE

The army has 39 armoured infantry fighting vehicles and 50 armoured personnel carriers. The navy has 7 patrol and coastal combatant vessels at 2 bases. The air force has 11 combat-capable aircraft.
Military budget – US$126m (2010)
Military personnel – 15,500: army 11,500, navy 2,000, air force 2,000

ECONOMY AND TRADE

Ghana has abundant natural resources, but high foreign debt and budget and trade deficits make it dependent on international financial and technical aid to fund its economic and social development programmes. It has benefited from tighter government management of the economy since 2001, and from debt relief in 2002 and 2006.

Gold, cocoa and expatriate remittances are the main foreign exchange earners. Agriculture, mostly at subsistence level, forms the basis of the economy, along with forestry and fishing. The sector employs 56 per cent of the workforce and generates 33.7 per cent of GDP. The main cash crops are cocoa, timber and tuna. Industry employs 15 per cent of the workforce and contributes 24.7 per cent of GDP, mainly from mining (gold, manganese, bauxite, diamonds), forestry, light manufacturing, aluminium smelting, food processing and shipbuilding. Services employ 29 per cent and account for 41.6 per cent of GDP. Hydroelectric power is generated at dams on Lake Volta and is transmitted to most of Ghana, and to Togo and Benin. Oil was discovered offshore in 2007 and production began in 2010.

The main export markets are EU countries, Ukraine and Malaysia. Principal exports are gold, cocoa, timber, tuna, metals, minerals and diamonds. Imports are provided mainly by China, Nigeria, the USA, Côte d'Ivoire, India and the EU. The main imports are capital equipment, fuel and foodstuffs.
GNI – US$25,871m; US$1,190 per capita (2009)
Annual average growth of GDP – 4.7 per cent (2010 est)
Inflation rate – 10.9 per cent (2010 est)
Population below poverty line – 28.5 per cent (2007 est)
Total external debt – US$6,483m (2010 est)
Imports – US$8,100m (2009)
Exports – US$5,500m (2009)

BALANCE OF PAYMENTS
Trade – US$2,878m deficit (2010)
Current Account – US$791m deficit (2008)

Trade with UK	2009	2010
Imports from UK	£259,140,634	£353,686,641
Exports to UK	£186,391,219	£219,473,671

EDUCATION AND HEALTH

The government provides ten years of compulsory basic education for all children free of charge. Ghana has one of Africa's oldest universities, at Legon in Accra (established in 1948).
Literacy rate – 65.8 per cent (2008 est)
Gross enrolment ratio (percentage of relevant age group) – primary 105 per cent; secondary 57 per cent; tertiary 9 per cent (2009 est)
Health expenditure (per capita) – US$45 (2009)
Hospital beds (per 1,000 people) – 0.9 (2004–9)

MEDIA

The Ghana Broadcasting Corporation (GBC), the state-run broadcaster, operates national radio and television networks alongside many private broadcasters. Despite a growing television industry, radio remains the country's most popular medium; there are scores of private stations available, including international broadcasts in Accra. Ghana's private press and broadcasters operate without significant restrictions.

GREECE

Elliniki Dhimokratia – Hellenic Republic

Area – 131,957 sq. km
Capital – Athens; population, 3,252,250 (2009 est)
Major cities – Iraklion (Heraklion) on Crete, Larisa, Patrai (Patras), Piraeus, Thessaloniki (Salonika)
Currency – Euro (€) of 100 cents
Population – 10,749,943 rising at 0.11 per cent a year (2010 est)
Religion – Christian (Greek Orthodox 95 per cent) (est)
Language – Greek (official)
Population density – 88 per sq. km (2009)
Urban population – 61 per cent (2008 est)
Median age (years) – 42.2 (2010 est)
National anthem – 'Imnos eis tin Eleftherian' ['Hymn to Freedom']
National day – 25 March (Independence Day)
Life expectancy (years) – 79.8 (2010 est)
Mortality rate – 10.6 (2010 est)
Birth rate – 9.34 (2010 est)
Infant mortality rate – 5.08 (2010 est)
Death penalty – Abolished for all crimes (since 2004)
CPI score – 3.5 (2010)

CLIMATE AND TERRAIN

The main areas of Greece are: Macedonia, Thrace, Epirus, Thessaly, Continental Greece, the Peloponnese and Attica on the mainland and the island of Crete. The main island groups are the Sporades, the Dodecanese or Southern Sporades and the Cyclades in the Aegean Sea, and the Ionian islands, including Corfu, to the west of the mainland. Low-lying coastal areas rise to a hilly or mountainous interior on the mainland and the islands. The Pindos mountains form a spine down the centre of the mainland, continuing down the Peloponnese, which is divided from the mainland by the Gulf of Corinth, the largest of the gulfs and bays indenting the coast. Elevation extremes range from 2,917m (Mt Olympus) at the highest point to 0m (Mediterranean Sea) at the lowest. The climate is temperate; the coastline and islands have a Mediterranean climate but the weather is cooler at higher altitudes. The average temperature in Athens ranges from 9°C in January to 28°C in July and August.

HISTORY AND POLITICS

Successive civilisations flourished in ancient Greece from the second millennium BC until it was conquered by Philip II of Macedon in the fourth century BC and then by the Romans in 146 BC. When the western Roman Empire fell, the eastern part continued as the Byzantine Empire until it was conquered by the Turks in the

mid-15th century. Turkish rule was overthrown in a war of independence (1821–7) that led to the establishment of a Greek kingdom in the Peloponnese and the south in 1829. Other islands and territories were added gradually over the next century, but the country's political and economic stability was precarious.

After the German occupation of 1941–4 ended, a civil war broke out between monarchist and communist groups that lasted from 1944 to 1949, and although it resulted in the restoration of democracy, tension between right- and left-wing groups continued. In 1967, a right-wing faction of the army seized power and established a military regime (the Greek Colonels), and the king went into exile. The Colonels' regime was toppled following its involvement in an unsuccessful coup against President Makarios of Cyprus in 1974 and democratic rule was restored, although the restoration of the monarchy was rejected in a referendum and Greece became a republic. Political life since has been dominated by the conservative New Democracy (ND) party and the left-wing Panhellenic Socialist Party (PASOK).

Greece joined the European Community in 1981 and adopted the euro in 2001.

Karolos Papoulias was elected president in 2005, and was re-elected in 2010. A legislative election was held in October 2009, nearly two years early, and PASOK returned to government after winning an outright majority of seats. In 2010 the PASOK government pushed through unpopular austerity measures to address the severe financial crisis, and agreed a three-year programme of economic reforms with the IMF and other EU countries in return for financial help to avoid defaulting on its debt.

POLITICAL SYSTEM

Under the 1975 constitution, the head of state is the president, elected by the legislature for a five-year term, renewable once. The unicameral legislature, the *Vouli*, has 300 members directly elected for a four-year term.

HEAD OF STATE

President of the Hellenic Republic, Karolos Papoulias, *elected* 8 February 2005, *sworn in* 12 March 2005, *re-elected* 2010

SELECTED GOVERNMENT MEMBERS *as at June 2011*
Prime Minister, George Papandreou
Interior, Yiannis Ragoussis
Defence, Evangelos Venizelos
Finance, Georgios Papaconstantinou

EMBASSY OF GREECE
1A Holland Park, London W11 3TP
T 020-7727 3071 W www.greekembassy.org.uk
Ambassador Extraordinary and Plenipotentiary, Aristidis Sandis, *apptd* 2010

BRITISH EMBASSY
1 Ploutarchou Street, 106 75 Athens
T (+30) (210) 727 2600 E information.athens@fco.gov.uk
W http://ukingreece.fco.gov.uk
Ambassador Extraordinary and Plenipotentiary, HE Dr David Landsman, OBE, *apptd* 2009

BRITISH COUNCIL
17 Kolonaki Square (Plateia Philikis Etairias), 106 73, Athens
T (+30) (210) 369 2333 W www.britishcouncil.org/greece
Director, Richard Walker

DEFENCE

The army has 1,590 main battle tanks, 1,778 armoured personnel carriers, 401 armoured infantry fighting vehicles and 30 armed helicopters. The navy has 9 submarines, 14 frigates, 32 patrol and coastal vessels and 21 helicopters, with bases at Salamis, Patras and Soudha Bay. The air force has 303 combat aircraft.

Greece maintains 950 army personnel in Cyprus.

Military budget – US$9,660m (2010)

Military personnel – 138,936: army 78,836, navy 20,000, air force 28,500, joint staff 11,600; paramilitary 4,000

Conscription duration – Up to 9 months

ECONOMY AND TRADE

Greece has a capitalist economy, with a large public sector which currently accounts for 40 per cent of GDP, although several state enterprises are being privatised as part of the government's economic reforms. It experienced rapid economic growth in the final quarter of the 20th century, owing largely to increased tourism and its accession to the EC. But in the 2000s, high government spending, low fiscal revenue and recession contributed to a growing budget deficit, which soared to over 15 per cent of GDP in 2009 and left the country particularly vulnerable in the global economic downturn. The New Democracy government's persistent failure to address the public finances crisis contributed to Greece's international debt rating being downgraded in late 2009, amid fears of an imminent default on its debt. The PASOK government's austerity measures, and financial assistance from the IMF and other EU countries, saw the budget deficit reduced to 9.4 per cent of GDP in 2010 but unemployment and inflation both rose by over 3 per cent.

Despite substantial industrialisation in the 20th century, agriculture still employs 12 per cent of the workforce, contributing 4 per cent of GDP. The most important agricultural products are cereals, vegetables, fruit, tobacco, beef and dairy products. Industrial activities, which contribute 17.6 per cent of GDP, include food and tobacco processing, textiles, chemicals, metal products, mining and petroleum production. The service sector employs 65 per cent of the workforce and generates 78.5 per cent of GDP; much of this is derived from tourism, which accounts for about 15 per cent of GDP, and shipping. Greece is a net importer of energy, including oil for refining and re-export.

The main trading partners are other EU countries (especially Germany and Italy) and China. Principal exports are food and drink, manufactured goods, petroleum products, chemicals and textiles. The main imports are machinery, transport equipment, fuels and chemicals.

GNI – US$320,818m; US$29,040 per capita (2009)

Annual average growth of GDP – –4.8 per cent (2010 est)

Inflation rate – 4.5 per cent (2010 est)

Population below poverty line – 20 per cent (2009 est)

Unemployment – 12 per cent (2010 est)

Total external debt – US$532,900m (2010)

Imports – US$59,300m (2009)

Exports – US$19,900m (2009)

BALANCE OF PAYMENTS

Trade – US$29,542m deficit (2010)

Current Account – US$37,104m deficit (2009)

Trade with UK	2009	2010
Imports from UK	£1,568,037,397	£1,337,325,672
Exports to UK	£537,898,962	£671,070,949

COMMUNICATIONS

There are extensive rail and road networks. The 2,500km of railways are state-owned (with the exception of the Athens–Piraeus Electric Railway) but the loss-making state-controlled rail network operator TrainOSE is being privatised. There are 117,533km of roads, including 880km of motorways. The main seaports are Piraeus, Thessaloniki and Patrai on the mainland and Iraklion on Crete. An extensive ferry system connects the islands to one another and to the mainland. The 6km Corinth canal across the Corinth isthmus shortens the sea journey by 325km. There are 81 airports and airfields, of which 67 have surfaced runways; the main airports are at Athens, Thessaloniki, Iraklion (Crete) and Corfu town (Corfu), although several other islands, especially tourist destinations, have airports. In 2009 there were 6 million fixed-line and 13.3 million mobile telephone subscribers, and 4.9 million internet users.

EDUCATION AND HEALTH

Education is free and compulsory between the ages of six and 14, and is maintained by state grants.

Literacy rate – 97.2 per cent (2008 est)

Gross enrolment ratio (percentage of relevant age group) – primary 101 per cent; secondary 102 per cent; tertiary 91 per cent (2007 est)

Health expenditure (per capita) – US$3,041 (2009)

Hospital beds (per 1,000 people) – 4.8 (2004–9)

MEDIA

The Greek media is largely free from regulation, although there have been reports of violence and threats against journalists, especially from anarchist groups. The state-run broadcasters had a near-monopoly of the market until the late 1980s, but have since lost the majority of market share to commercial services. A sizeable proportion of the country's roughly 1,700 private radio and television stations are unlicensed.

CULTURE

Greek civilisation emerged c.1300 BC and underpins the philosophy, politics, literature, art and mathematics of the Western world. The epic poems of Homer, the *Iliad* and the *Odyssey,* are thought to date from c.800 BC, making them the earliest recorded works in Western literature. Dramatists whose work has survived include Aeschylus (c.525–c.456 BC), who is credited with inventing modern drama, Euripedes (480–406 BC) and Aristophanes (446–388 BC), author of the earliest known comedies. Socrates (470–399 BC), Plato (c.428–c.348 BC) and Aristotle (384–322 BC), whose *Poetics* is the earliest work of literary criticism, are considered the founders of western philosophy. Hippocrates (c.460 –370 BC) was the first to separate medicine from philosophy and religion.

The spoken language of modern Greece is descended from the common Greek of Alexander the Great's empire. *Katharevousa,* a conservative literary dialect evolved by Adamantios Korais (1748–1833), which was used for official and technical matters, has been phased out. Novels and poetry are mostly written in *dimotiki,* a progressive literary dialect that owes much to Yannis Psycharis (1854–1929). Poets Giorgos Seferis (1900–71) and Odysseus Elytis (1911–96) won the Nobel prize for literature, in 1963 and 1979 respectively.

GRENADA

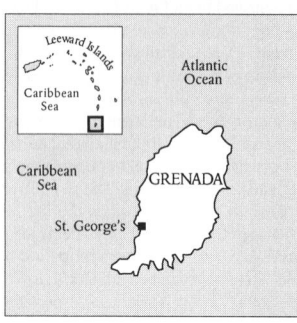

Area – 344 sq. km
Capital – St George's; population, 40,400 (2009 est)
Currency – East Caribbean dollar (EC$) of 100 cents
Population – 107,818 rising at 0.56 per cent a year (2010 est)
Religion – Christian (Roman Catholic 44 per cent, Anglican 12 per cent, Pentecostal 11 per cent, Seventh-day Adventist 11 per cent) (est)
Language – English (official), Creole (small minority)
Population density – 306 per sq. km (2009)
Urban population – 31 per cent (2008 est)
Median age (years) – 28.2 (2010 est)
National anthem – 'Hail Grenada'
National day – 7 February (Independence Day)
Life expectancy (years) – 72.79 (2010 est)
Mortality rate – 7.9 (2010 est)
Birth rate – 17.2 (2010 est)
Infant mortality rate – 11.76 (2010 est)
Death penalty – Retained (not used since 1978)
CPI score – 3.4 (2007)
Literacy rate – 96.0 per cent (2008 est)

CLIMATE AND TERRAIN
The most southerly of the Windward Islands, Grenada comprises three islands: Grenada (the largest at 18km in length and 34km in width), Carriacou and Petite Martinique. Elevation extremes range from 840m (Mt St Catherine) at the highest point to 0m (Caribbean Sea) at the lowest. The climate is subtropical, with the wettest weather from July to November. Grenada lies in a hurricane zone.

HISTORY AND POLITICS
Discovered by Columbus in 1498 and named Concepción, Grenada was colonised from the mid-17th century by the French, who subdued the native Caribs; the island was ceded to Britain in 1763. It became a crown colony in 1877, a self-governing associated state in 1967 and an independent nation on 7 February 1974.

The government was overthrown in 1979 by the New Jewel Movement led by Maurice Bishop, and the People's Revolutionary Government (PRG) was set up with Bishop as prime minister. In 1983, disagreements within the PRG led to the deposition and execution of Bishop, whose government was replaced by a revolutionary military council. These events prompted the intervention of Caribbean and US forces. After a period of interim government, democracy was restored and a general election held in 1984. Since the restoration of democracy, power has alternated between the New National Party (NNP) and the National Democratic Congress (NDC).

In the 2008 general election the NDC defeated the NNP, which had held power since 1995.

POLITICAL SYSTEM
Under the 1974 constitution, reinstated in 1984, the head of state is Queen Elizabeth II, represented locally by a governor-general. The bicameral parliament consists of the House of Representatives, with 15 directly elected members, and a senate with 13 appointed members, ten of whom are appointed by the government and three by the opposition; both chambers serve a five-year term.
Governor-General, HE Sir Carlyle Glean, GCMG, *apptd* 2008

SELECTED GOVERNMENT MEMBERS *as at June 2011*
Prime Minister, National Security, Tillman Thomas
Finance, Nazim Burke
Foreign Affairs, Karl Hood

HIGH COMMISSION FOR GRENADA
The Chapel, Archel Road, London W14 9QH
T 020-7385 4415 E office@grenada-highcommission.co.uk
High Commissioner, HE Ruth Rouse, *apptd* 2008

BRITISH HIGH COMMISSIONER
HE Paul Brummell, *apptd* 2009, resident at Bridgetown, Barbados

ECONOMY AND TRADE
The economy has grown considerably in recent decades owing to diversification into tourism, offshore financial services and other service industries. Tourism and agriculture have recovered from severe hurricane damage in 2004 and 2005, but reconstruction has burdened the country with considerable debt and the global downturn's effect on tourism and remittances caused the economy to contract in 2009.

Agriculture now employs only 24 per cent of the workforce and produces 5.4 per cent of GDP. Industry consists of processing agricultural products, textile manufacturing, light assembly operations and construction, and contributes 18 per cent of GDP. The service sector, including tourism and financial services, accounts for 62 per cent of employment and 76.6 per cent of GDP.

The main trading partners are Trinidad and Tobago (40 per cent of imports), the USA and other Caribbean states. Principal exports are bananas, cocoa, nutmeg, fruit, vegetables, clothing and mace. Imports include food, manufactured goods, machinery, chemicals and fuels.
GNI – US$578m; US$5,580 per capita (2009)
Annual average growth of GDP – 0.8 per cent (2010 est)
Inflation rate – 3.7 per cent (2007 est)
Total external debt – US$347m (2004)
Imports – US$300m (2009)
Exports – US$20m (2006)

BALANCE OF PAYMENTS
Trade – US$297m deficit (2010)
Current Account – US$263m deficit (2008)

Trade with UK	2009	2010
Imports from UK	£5,285,737	£5,610,921
Exports to UK	£321,720	£331,844

MEDIA
Grenadian law guarantees a free media. Of the two available television stations, GBN TV is operated by the public broadcaster Grenada Broadcasting Network, and MTV is US-owned. There are several radio stations, both public and private. There are no daily newspapers but several private weekly publications.

GUATEMALA

República de Guatemala – Republic of Guatemala

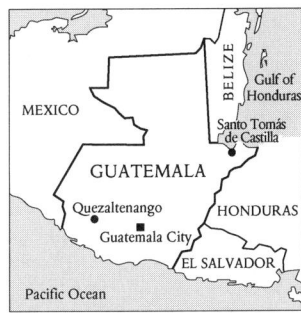

Area – 108,889 sq. km
Capital – Guatemala City; population, 1,074,870 (2009 est)
Major cities – Mixco, Quezaltenango, Villa Nueva
Currency – Quetzal (Q) of 100 centavos
Population – 13,550,440 rising at 2.02 per cent a year (2010 est); mestizo and European (59.4 per cent), Mayan (40.3 per cent), indigenous non-Mayan 0.2 per cent (2001)
Religion – Christian (Roman Catholic 65 per cent, Evangelical Protestant 35 per cent) (est)
Language – Spanish, 23 Amerindian languages (all official)
Population density – 131 per sq. km (2009)
Urban population – 49 per cent (2008 est)
Median age (years) – 19.7 (2010 est)
National anthem – 'Himno Nacional de Guatemala' ['National Anthem of Guatemala']
National day – 15 September (Independence Day)
Life expectancy (years) – 70.59 (2010 est)
Mortality rate – 5.04 (2010 est)
Birth rate – 27.4 (2010 est)
Infant mortality rate – 26.91 (2010 est)
Death penalty – Retained
CPI score – 3.2 (2010)

CLIMATE AND TERRAIN
Narrow tropical plains on both the north (Caribbean) and south (Pacific) coasts rise to a mountainous interior in the centre and south. The mountains fall in the north to lowlands covered in tropical jungle. Elevation extremes range from 4,211m (Tajumulco volcano) at the highest point to 0m (Pacific Ocean) at the lowest. There are 37 volcanoes, three active, in the central plateau. The climate is tropical but is cooler in the highlands. The wet season runs from May to September, when mudslides and hurricanes can occur. There are also frequent minor earth tremors and some earthquakes.

HISTORY AND POLITICS
Mayan and Aztec civilisations flourished in the area until the Spanish conquest in 1523–4, after which the area became a Spanish colony. It gained independence in 1821, and formed part of a Central American federation of former Spanish provinces from 1823 to 1839. After independence, the country was ruled by a series of dictatorships and military regimes, interspersed with periods of democratic government. In 1960 a civil war between military governments, right-wing vigilantes and left-wing guerrillas began, lasting 36 years and during which over 200,000 people died or disappeared.

In 1996 the democratically elected civilian government concluded a peace agreement with the left-wing Guatemalan Revolutionary National Unity guerrillas that ended the civil war and began a reduction in the size and political influence of the army; this has been continued by its successors. In 1999, an independent commission found that 93 per cent of human rights abuses during the war had been instigated by the security forces, and in 2000 and 2004 the state formally admitted guilt in several human rights cases, paying damages to the victims. At present, only a small number of the military personnel found to be responsible for the atrocities have been prosecuted.

In the 2007 legislative election, the National Unity of Hope party (UNE) won the most seats, but without an overall majority. The 2007 presidential election was won in the second round by the UNE candidate Alvaro Colom. The next legislative and presidential elections are due in September 2011.

POLITICAL SYSTEM
Under the 1986 constitution, the executive president is directly elected for a four-year term, which is not renewable. He or she is responsible to the congress and appoints the cabinet. The unicameral Congress of the Republic has 158 members, who are directly elected for a four-year term.

HEAD OF STATE
President, Alvaro Colom Caballeros, *elected* 4 November 2007, *sworn in* 14 January 2008
Vice-President, Rafael Espada

SELECTED GOVERNMENT MEMBERS *as at June 2011*
Defence, Abraham Valenzuela González
Economy, Erick Coyoy Echeverría
Foreign Affairs, Haroldo Rodas Melgar
Interior, Carlos Menocal

EMBASSY OF GUATEMALA
13A Fawcett Street, London SW10 9HN
T 020-7351 3042 E inglaterra@minex.gob.gt
Ambassador Extraordinary and Plenipotentiary, HE Acisclo Valladares Molina, *apptd* 2010

BRITISH EMBASSY
Edificio Torre Internacional, Nivel 11, 16 Calle 0-55, Zona 10, Guatemala City
T (+502) 2380 7300 E embassy@intelnett.com
W http://ukinguatemala.fco.gov.uk
Ambassador Extraordinary and Plenipotentiary, Julie Chappel, OBE, *apptd* 2009

DEFENCE
The army has 52 armoured personnel carriers. The navy has 10 patrol and coastal combatant vessels at 2 bases. The air force has 9 combat-capable aircraft.
Military budget – US$169m (2010)
Military personnel – 15,212: army 13,444, navy 897, air force 871; paramilitary 19,000

ECONOMY AND TRADE
IMF funding and foreign aid have underpinned the government's economic reforms and stabilisation programmes, but the trade deficit, poor infrastructure, security problems and high levels of corruption still deter foreign investment. The country suffers from a huge imbalance in wealth, and over half the population lives

below the poverty line. Remittances from expatriates, equivalent to nearly 10 per cent of GDP, are vital to the economy, which began to recover from the global downturn in 2010.

Half of the population is dependent on agriculture, which contributes 13.3 per cent of GDP and accounts for a high proportion of exports. Industry accounts for 24.4 per cent of GDP, and the services sector, which includes tourism, for 62.3 per cent of GDP.

The main trading partners are the USA, El Salvador and Mexico. The principal exports are coffee, sugar, petroleum, garments, bananas, fruit, vegetables and cardamom. The chief imports are fuels, machinery and transport equipment, construction materials, grain, fertilisers and electricity.

GNI – US$36,121m; US$2,650 per capita (2009)
Annual average growth of GDP – 2.2 per cent (2010 est)
Inflation rate – 3.9 per cent (2010 est)
Population below poverty line – 56.2 per cent (2004 est)
Unemployment – 3.2 per cent (2005 est)
Total external debt – US$17,470m (2010 est)
Imports – US$10,100m (2009)
Exports – US$3,800m (2009)

BALANCE OF PAYMENTS
Trade – US$6,231m deficit (2010)
Current Account – US$1,773m deficit (2008)

Trade with UK	2009	2010
Imports from UK	£24,524,502	£26,854,888
Exports to UK	£25,956,118	£39,778,846

EDUCATION AND HEALTH
There are nine years of compulsory education.
Literacy rate – 73.9 per cent (2008 est)
Gross enrolment ratio (percentage of relevant age group) – primary 113 per cent; secondary 56 per cent; tertiary 18 per cent (2007 est)
Health expenditure (per capita) – US$186 (2009)
Hospital beds (per 1,000 people) – 0.6 (2004–9)

MEDIA AND CULTURE
Freedom of the press is enshrined in the constitution, but journalists who pursue controversial stories are often subjected to threats. There are four major daily newspapers, including *Prensa Libre* and *El Periodico*. Four privately run television channels under the same ownership monopolise Guatemalan television.

The ruins of the Mayan civilisation dot the country, while the influence of African culture is evident along the Caribbean coast. Distinguished Guatemalans include the writers Miguel Ángel Asturias (1899–1974), who won the Nobel prize for literature in 1967; Luis Cardoza y Aragón (1901–92), who edited the influential periodical *Revista de Guatemala* after the 1944 revolution; and Rigoberta Menchú (*b.* 1959), who won the Nobel peace prize in 1992.

GUINEA

République de Guinée – Republic of Guinea

Area – 245,857 sq. km
Capital – Conakry; population, 1,597,420 (2009 est)
Major cities – Guéckédou, Kankan, Nzérékoré
Currency – Guinea franc of 100 centimes
Population – 10,324,025 rising at 2.65 per cent a year (2010 est); Fulani (40 per cent), Malinke (30 per cent), Susu (20 per cent) (est)
Religion – Muslim 85 per cent (predominantly Sunni), Christian 10 per cent, traditional indigenous religions 5 per cent (est); some combine Islam or Christianity with indigenous beliefs
Language – French (official), eight African languages
Population density – 41 per sq. km (2009)
Urban population – 34 per cent (2008 est)
Median age (years) – 18.5 (2010 est)
National anthem – 'Liberté' ['Liberty']
National day – 2 October (Independence Day)
Life expectancy – 57.6 (2010 est)
Mortality rate – 10.72 (2010 est)
Birth rate – 37.21 (2010 est)
Infant mortality rate – 63.09 (2010 est)
HIV/AIDS adult prevalence – 1.3 per cent (2009 est)
Death penalty – Retained
CPI score – 2 (2010)
Literacy rate – 29.5 per cent (2008 est)
Gross enrolment ratio (percentage of relevant age group) – primary 90 per cent; secondary 36 per cent; tertiary 9 per cent (2008 est)
Health expenditure (per capita) – US$19 (2009)
Hospital beds (per 1,000 people) – 0.3 (2004–9)

CLIMATE AND TERRAIN
Guinea has a flat coastal plain that rises to the hilly Fouta Djallon plateau in the north-west, where the Gambia and Senegal rivers rise. East of the plateau is the central savannah, the source of the Niger river, with rainforest in the south-east. Elevation extremes range from 1,752m (Mt Nimba) at the highest point to 0m at the lowest (Atlantic Ocean). The climate is tropical, with a wet season from April to November; the average daily temperature is 26°C.

HISTORY AND POLITICS
Susi kingdoms were established in the area by the 13th century, and in the 16th century the north-east of the country was part of the Mali Empire. The Portuguese established ivory and slave trading in the region from the mid-15th century. In 1849 the French established a protectorate over the coastal areas, and the country was governed with Senegal until the 1890s, when it was

renamed French Guinea, becoming part of French West Africa in 1904.

Guinea became independent on 2 October 1958 under President Ahmed Sekou Touré, who established a one-party socialist state. Touré's death in 1984 was followed by a military coup that brought Lansana Conté to power. Conté introduced greater economic liberalisation and, following strikes and mass protests in 1991, reintroduced a multiparty system. President Conté and his Party of Unity and Progress (PUP) won all subsequent elections, amid allegations of electoral fraud and intimidation of opponents.

The civil wars in neighbouring Sierra Leone, Liberia and Côte d'Ivoire caused an influx of refugees (about 700,000 over 15 years) that strained the economy, exacerbating already poor conditions. Low pay, poor living standards and price rises contributed to the growing unpopularity of Conté's government and led to strikes and violent protests, including by the army, between 2006 and 2008.

A military junta seized power the day after President Conté's death in December 2008, but its tenure was unstable, with rapidly rising inflation and debt. After a massacre of pro-democracy demonstrators and an assassination attempt on the junta president in late 2009, Vice President Sékouba Konaté became acting president, negotiating a power-sharing transitional government in January 2010. A presidential election in 2010, the first democratic election since independence, was won by Alpha Condé, in a second round delayed by allegations of fraud in the first round; his victory sparked off several weeks of intercommunal violence. A legislative election has yet to be scheduled.

POLITICAL SYSTEM
Under the 2010 constitution, the executive president is directly elected for a five-year term, renewable once. The unicameral National Assembly has 114 members, who are directly elected for a five-year term. The president appoints the council of ministers.

HEAD OF STATE
President, Defence, Alpha Condé, *elected* 7 November 2010, *sworn in* 21 December

SELECTED GOVERNMENT MEMBERS *as at June 2011*
Prime Minister, Mohamed Said Fofana
Economy and Finance, Kerfalla Yansane
Foreign Affairs, Edouard Gnankoye Lama
Security, Maj.-Gen. Mamadou Ba Toto Camara

EMBASSY OF THE REPUBLIC OF GUINEA
258 Belsize Road, London NW6 4BT
T 020-7316 1861 E ambaguineeuk@yahoo.co.uk
Ambassador Extraordinary and Plenipotentiary, HE Lansana Keita, *apptd* 2005

BRITISH EMBASSY
BP 6729, Conakry
T (+224) 6335 5329 E britembconakry@hotmail.com
Ambassador Extraordinary and Plenipotentiary, HE Graham Trayton Styles, *apptd* 2011

DEFENCE
The army has 38 main battle tanks and 40 armoured personnel carriers. The navy has 2 patrol and coastal combatant vessels at 2 bases. The air force has 7 combat-capable aircraft and 5 attack helicopters.

Military expenditure – US$75m (2009 est)
Military personnel – 12,300: army 8,500, navy 400, air force 800, gendarmerie 1,000, Republican Guard 1,600; paramilitary 7,000
Conscription duration – 24 months

ECONOMY AND TRADE
Despite an abundance of natural resources, including 30 per cent of the world's known bauxite reserves, decades of mismanagement and corruption have left the economy undeveloped, and nearly half the population live below the poverty line; some basic necessities are now unaffordable for many. There is a large foreign debt, and budget and trade deficits, but little foreign aid as most was suspended after the 2008 coup, although mining is attracting foreign direct investment. Agriculture, much of it at subsistence level, employs 76 per cent of the population and contributes 25.8 per cent of GDP. Industry accounts for 45.7 per cent of GDP, mostly through mining and the processing of minerals and agricultural produce.

The main trading partners are India, China and EU countries, especially Spain. Principal exports are bauxite, alumina, gold, diamonds, coffee, fish and other agricultural products. The main imports are petroleum products, metals, machinery, transport equipment, textiles, grain and other foodstuffs.
GNI – US$3,692m; US$370 per capita (2009)
Annual average growth of GDP – 3 per cent (2010 est)
Inflation rate – 15 per cent (2010 est)
Population below poverty line – 47 per cent (2006 est)
Total external debt – US$3,072m (2009 est)
Imports – US$1,400m (2009)
Exports – US$1,000m (2009)

BALANCE OF PAYMENTS
Trade – US$196m deficit (2010)
Current Account – US$517m deficit (2008)

Trade with UK	2009	2010
Imports from UK	£85,418,006	£35,499,155
Exports to UK	£478,579	£2,125,967

COMMUNICATIONS
Guinea has almost 1,185km of railways, 44,348km of roads (only 10 per cent of which are surfaced) and 1,300km of inland waterways navigable by shallow-draught craft. The major seaports are Conakry and Kamsar. Guinea has 16 airports, including four with surfaced runways; the principal airport is at Conakry. The fixed-line telephone system is limited in extent, with density of less than one per 100 people. Mobile phone distribution is growing more quickly, with over 50 per 100 people. There were 95,000 internet users in 2009.

MEDIA
The state-run Radiodiffusion-Television Guineenne provides national radio and television broadcasting. The only daily national newspaper is also state-run. Private radio station licences became available in 2006, but the civil unrest of 2007 caused the government to tighten its control of the media, closing some radio stations and cybercafes. Although publishing is stifled by strict censorship laws and prohibitive printing costs, around a dozen private publications are printed on a weekly basis.

GUINEA-BISSAU

Republica da Guine-Bissau – Republic of Guinea-Bissau

Area – 36,125 sq. km
Capital – Bissau; population, 301,839 (2009 est)
Currency – Franc CFA of 100 centimes
Population – 1,565,126 rising at 2 per cent a year (2010 est); Balanta (30 per cent), Fulani (20 per cent), Manjaca (14 per cent), Mandinga (13 per cent), Papel (7 per cent) (est)
Religion – Muslim 50 per cent (predominantly Sunni), indigenous beliefs 40 per cent, Christian 10 per cent (est)
Language – Portuguese (official), Creole
Population density – 57 per sq. km (2009)
Urban population – 30 per cent (2008 est)
Median age (years) – 19.4 (2010 est)
National anthem – 'Esta e a Nossa Patria Bem Amada' ['This is Our Beloved Country']
National day – 24 September (Independence Day)
Life expectancy (years) – 48.3 (2010 est)
Mortality rate – 15.52 (2010 est)
Birth rate – 35.56 (2010 est)
Infant mortality rate – 98.05 (2010 est)
HIV/AIDS adult prevalence – 2.5 per cent (2009 est)
Death penalty – Abolished for all crimes (since 1993)
CPI score – 2.1 (2010)
Literacy rate – 66.2 per cent (2008 est)
Gross enrolment ratio (percentage of relevant age group) – primary 120 per cent; secondary 36 per cent; tertiary 3 per cent (2008)
Health expenditure (per capita) – US$18 (2009)
Hospital beds (per 1,000 people) – 1.0 (2004–9)

CLIMATE AND TERRAIN

Guinea-Bissau has a low coastal plain that rises to savannah in the east. The coast is heavily indented and covered with mangrove swamps. Elevation extremes range from 300m (in the north-east) at the highest point to 0m (Atlantic Ocean) at the lowest. The climate is tropical, with a wet season from July to September.

HISTORY AND POLITICS

A part of the ancient African empire of Mali, Guinea-Bissau was once the kingdom of Gabu, which became independent of the empire in 1546 and survived until 1867. In 1446, Portuguese traders discovered the coast and established slave trading there, subsequently administering Guinea-Bissau with the Cape Verde islands; it became a separate colony in 1879. After a guerrilla war led by the left-wing African Party for the Independence of Guinea and Cape Verde (PAIGC), Guinea-Bissau declared independence unilaterally in 1973 and Portugal recognised this in 1974.

After independence Guinea-Bissau became a one-party socialist state under the PAIGC, led by Luis Cabral. He was deposed in 1980, in a military coup led by General Joao Vieira, and the country was under military rule until 1994. A multiparty system was introduced in 1991 after popular agitation, but the following 15 years saw a short civil war (1998–9) and two more military coups (1999, 2003); democratic government was restored in 2004–5. Guinea-Bissau's political turbulence has been exacerbated by the unrest in Senegal's Casamance region since the 1990s, and the country's increasing use as a staging post by drug-smugglers and people-traffickers; the latter's political influence is fostering a culture of impunity and petty corruption.

The November 2008 legislative election was won by the PAIGC, which formed a government in January 2009. The PAIGC candidate, Malam Bacai Sanha, was elected president in July 2009, succeeding Joao Vieira (president 1980–99, 2005–9), who had been assassinated in March.

POLITICAL SYSTEM

Under the 1999 constitution, the executive president is directly elected for a five-year term, which is renewable once. The president appoints the council of ministers. The unicameral National People's Assembly has 102 members, who are directly elected for a four-year term.

HEAD OF STATE

President, Malam Bacai Sanha, *elected* July 2009, *sworn in* 8 September 2009

SELECTED GOVERNMENT MEMBERS *as at June 2011*
Prime Minister, Carlos Gomes Jr
Economy, Helena Nosolini Embalo
Foreign Affairs, Adelino Mano Queita
Defence, Aristides Ocante da Silva
Interior, Dinis Cablol Na Fantchamna

EMBASSY OF THE REPUBLIC OF GUINEA-BISSAU
94 Rue St Lazare, 75009 Paris, France
T (+33) (1) 4526 1851
Ambassador Extraordinary and Plenipotentiary, vacant

BRITISH CONSULATE
Ambassador Extraordinary and Plenipotentiary, HE Christopher Trott, *apptd* 2007, resident in Dakar, Senegal

DEFENCE

The army has 10 main battle tanks and 55 armoured personnel carriers. The navy has 2 patrol and coastal combatant vessels at a base at Bissau. The air force has 2 combat-capable aircraft.
Military expenditure – US$14m (2009 est)
Military personnel – 4,458 (est): army 4,000 (est), navy 350, air force 100; gendarmerie 2,000

ECONOMY AND TRADE

The economy is in a poor state owing to decades of mismanagement and corruption, the devastating effects of the 1998–9 civil war and ongoing political instability. There is massive foreign debt and the country is heavily dependent on foreign aid; emergency aid provided over 80 per cent of the national budget in 2004.

Although Guinea-Bissau has mineral resources, including oil, the high cost of exploiting these inhibits development and the economy is based almost exclusively on agriculture and fishing. This sector employs 82 per cent of the population and contributes 62 per cent of GDP. The small industrial sector generates 12 per cent of GDP, mainly through processing agricultural products and beer and soft drink production.

The main trading partners are India (64 per cent of exports), Nigeria, Portugal and Senegal. Principal exports include fish, cashew nuts, peanuts, palm kernels and timber. The main imports are foodstuffs, machinery and transport equipment, and fuels.

GNI – US$826m; US$510 per capita (2009)
Annual average growth of GDP – 1.8 per cent (2010 est)
Inflation rate – 3.8 per cent (2007 est)
Imports – US$200m (2009)
Exports – US$100m (2009)

BALANCE OF PAYMENTS
Trade – US$66m deficit (2010)
Current Account – US$20m surplus (2008)

Trade with UK	2009	2010
Imports from UK	£510,846	£656,894
Exports to UK	£12,795	£6,601

COMMUNICATIONS

The infrastructure, already rudimentary, was badly damaged in the civil war. Guinea-Bissau has 3,455km of roads, of which 965km are surfaced, and no railways. There are nine airports and airfields, two of which have surfaced runways; the principal airport is at Bissau. The main rivers are navigable for part of their lengths, and shallow-draught craft can access much of the interior via creeks and inlets. Bissau is the main seaport. The fixed-line telephone system is limited, with fewer than one per 100 people in 2009, while mobile phone density is 35 per 100 people. There are around 37,100 internet users.

MEDIA

Since the 2003 military coup, media organisations have been able to operate with greater freedom; government interference is often less of a concern now than reliable power supplies. Guinea-Bissau's principal television station and national radio broadcaster are state-run, and there are a number of commercial radio stations. One state-owned and three privately owned national newspapers are published, although the sector is limited by financial restraints.

GUYANA

Cooperative Republic of Guyana

Area – 214,969 sq. km
Capital – Georgetown; population, 131,660 (2009 est)
Major towns – Linden, New Amsterdam
Currency – Guyana dollar (G$) of 100 cents
Population – 748,486 falling at 0.55 per cent a year (2010 est); East Indian 43.5 per cent, African 30.2 per cent, mixed 16.7 per cent, Amerindian 9.1 per cent (2002)
Religion – Christian 57 per cent (predominantly Protestant), Hindu 28 per cent, Muslim 7 per cent (predominantly Sunni) (2002)
Language – English (official), Amerindian dialects, Creole, Caribbean Hindustani (a dialect of Hindi), Urdu
Population density – 4 per sq. km (2009)
Urban population – 28 per cent (2008 est)
Median age (years) – 23.6 (2010 est)
National anthem – 'Dear Land of Guyana, of Rivers and Plains'
National day – 23 February (Republic Day)
Life expectancy (years) – 66.74 (2010 est)
Mortality rate – 7.24 (2010 est)
Birth rate – 17.61 (2010 est)
Infant mortality rate – 37.89 (2010 est)
HIV/AIDS adult prevalence – 1.2 per cent (2009 est)
Death penalty – Retained
CPI score – 2.7 (2010)

CLIMATE AND TERRAIN

The land rises from a narrow coastal plain to forested highlands in the west and savannah on the southern border; about 90 per cent of the population lives on the coastal plain, which constitutes 5 per cent of the land area. Around 79 per cent of the country is covered by rainforest. Elevation extremes range from 2,835m (Mt Roraima) at the highest point to 0m (Atlantic Ocean) at the lowest. The climate is tropical, with an average daily temperature of 27°C, and two wet seasons, from April to July and from November to January.

HISTORY AND POLITICS

Carib and Arawak peoples inhabited the coastal region of Guyana when Dutch merchants founded the first European settlement in the late 16th century. Guyana became an important producer of sugar, grown on plantations worked first by African slaves and then, after the abolition of slavery in 1834, by indentured labourers, mostly from India. Several areas were ceded to Britain in 1815, and consolidated as British Guiana in 1831. The country became independent, as Guyana, on 26 May 1966, and became a republic in 1970.

Guyana's first political party, the People's Progressive Party (PPP), split along ethnic lines in the 1950s; the PPP continued as a predominantly Indian party under Cheddi Jagan, while those of African descent formed the People's National Congress (PNC), led by Forbes Burnham. Burnham dominated political life after independence, first as prime minister (1966–80) and then as executive president until his death in 1985. Under his autocratic rule, politics became characterised by suspect elections and a disregard for civil liberties and human rights. The PPP's electoral victory in 1992 ended the PNC's monopoly of power but persistent ethnic tensions continue to destabilise politics.

Bharrat Jagdeo of the PPP, interim president from 1999 to 2001, was elected president in 2001. His presidency has seen attempts to encourage joint action between the government and the private sector, and reconciliation between the PPP and Guyana's other political parties.

The 2006 legislative election was won by the PPP, securing its fourth consecutive term of office and the re-election of President Jagdeo for a second term. A legislative election was scheduled for 12 August 2011.

POLITICAL SYSTEM

Under the 1980 constitution, the executive president is nominated by the majority party in the legislature after each legislative election, and serves a five-year term, renewable once. The unicameral National Assembly has 65 members, of whom 53 are elected by proportional representation and 12 are regional representatives; they serve a five-year term.

HEAD OF STATE
President, Bharrat Jagdeo, *succeeded* 11 August 1999, *elected* 2001, *re-elected* 28 August 2006

SELECTED GOVERNMENT MEMBERS *as at June 2011*
Prime Minister, Samuel Hinds
Finance, Ashni Kumar Singh
Foreign Affairs, Carolyn Rodrigues-Burkett
Home Affairs, Clement Rohee

HIGH COMMISSION FOR GUYANA
3 Palace Court, Bayswater Road, London W2 4LP
T 020-7229 7684 E guyanahc1@btconnect.com
W www.guyanahclondon.co.uk
High Commissioner, HE Laleshwar Singh, *apptd* 1993

BRITISH HIGH COMMISSION
PO Box 10849, 44 Main Street, Georgetown
T (+592) 226 5881 E bhcguyana@networksgy.com
W http://ukinguyana.fco.gov.uk
High Commissioner (acting), HE Simon Bond, *apptd* 2010

DEFENCE

The navy has 5 patrol and coastal combatant vessels at 3 bases. The air force has 1 multi-role helicopter.
Military budget – US$128m (2010)
Military personnel – 1,100: army 900, navy 100, air force 100; paramilitary 1,500

ECONOMY AND TRADE

The economy grew from 2001 to 2008 owing to expansion in agriculture and mining, the cancellation of over one-third of Guyana's external debt, and increases in foreign direct investment and remittances from expatriate workers. Following contraction in 2009 due to the global downturn and lower commodity prices, recovery began in 2010. In the longer term, poor infrastructure and skills shortages inhibit growth, especially attempts to develop tourism.

Agriculture accounts for 24.3 per cent of GDP and provides the raw materials for the major industries of sugar processing and rice milling. Non-agricultural activities include bauxite and gold mining, forestry, fishing and textile manufacturing; industry accounts for 24.7 per cent of GDP.

The main trading partners are the USA, Trinidad and Tobago, Canada and the UK. Principal exports include sugar, gold, bauxite, alumina, rice, shrimp, molasses, rum and timber. The main imports are manufactured goods, machinery, fuel and food.

GNI – US$2,042m; US$2,660 per capita (2009)
Annual average growth of GDP – 2.5 per cent (2010 est)
Inflation rate – 6.8 per cent (2010 est)
Unemployment – 11 per cent (2007 est)
Total external debt – US$804.3m (2008)
Imports – US$1,200m (2009)
Exports – US$800m (2009)

BALANCE OF PAYMENTS
Trade – US$523m deficit (2010)
Current Account – US$254m deficit (2008)

Trade with UK	2009	2010
Imports from UK	£24,906,039	£51,831,405
Exports to UK	£72,293,260	£33,727,633

COMMUNICATIONS

Roads and navigable waterways (the Berbice, Demerara and Essequibo rivers) form the main arteries of communication, though only 590km of roads, out of a total of 7,970km, are surfaced. Georgetown is the main seaport and the location of the principal airport. There are 96 airports and airfields in total, though only ten have surfaced runways. The Takutu bridge, completed in 2009, has opened up cross-border transport and trade links with Brazil, bringing economic benefits to the south. Many areas lack fixed-line telephone services; density was about 15 per 100 people in 2005. Mobile phone distribution has grown quickly and density was 35 per 100 people in 2005.

MEDIA

The government operates one television and two radio stations, and there are numerous private competitors. There are three daily newspapers, one of which is state-owned. Journalists operate freely but often practise self-censorship.

HAITI

République d'Haïti/Repiblik d'Ayiti – Republic of Haiti

Area – 27,750 sq. km
Capital – Port-au-Prince; population, 2,642,760 (2009 est)
Major cities – Cap-Haïtien, Gonaïves, Pétionville
Currency – Gourde of 100 centimes
Population – 9,648,924 falling at 1.72 per cent a year (2010 est)
Religion – Christian (Roman Catholic 55 per cent, Baptist 15 per cent, Pentecostal 8 per cent, Seventh-day Adventist 3 per cent); many Christians also practise Voodoo, recognised as an official religion in 2003

Language – French, Creole (both official)
Population density – 364 per sq. km (2009)
Urban population – 47 per cent (2008 est)
Median age (years) – 21.1 (2010 est)
National anthem – 'La Dessalinienne' ['Song of
    Dessalines']
National day – 1 January (Independence Day)
Life expectancy (years) – 29.93 (2010 est)
Mortality rate – 32.31 (2010 est)
Birth rate – 24.92 (2010 est)
Infant mortality rate – 77.26 (2010 est)
HIV/AIDS adult prevalence – 1.9 per cent (2009 est)
Death penalty – Abolished for all crimes (since 1987)
CPI score – 2.2 (2010)
Literacy rate – 63.2 per cent (2008 est)
Health expenditure (per capita) – US$40 (2009)
Hospital beds (per 1,000 people) – 1.3 (2004–9)

CLIMATE AND TERRAIN
The country occupies the western third of the island of
Hispaniola. The terrain is mountainous, with coastal
plains and a large central plateau. Elevation extremes
range from 2,680m (Châine de la Selle) at the highest
point to 0m (Caribbean Sea) at the lowest. The climate
is tropical, and semi-arid where the eastern mountains
block the trade winds, with two wet seasons (April–June,
August–November) and a hurricane season from June to
November.

HISTORY AND POLITICS
Columbus landed on Hispaniola in 1492 and it was
colonised by the Spanish from the late 1490s. In 1697
the western part of Hispaniola was ceded to France
and named Saint Domingue. It became the richest
colony in the French Empire through its sugar-cane and
coffee plantations, worked by African slaves. In 1791,
a slave rebellion expelled the French from the northern
part of the colony and instigated a long war between
freed slaves and colonists. By 1804 the Republic of
Haiti was founded, marking the inception of the
world's first black republic and, after the USA, the
oldest republic in the western hemisphere. Separate
post-independence regimes in the north and south were
united in 1820.
    Haiti has experienced very little stability since. The
country endured 22 changes of government between
1843 and 1915. The resultant disorder led the USA to
intervene in 1915, the beginning of 19 years of US
occupation. Sovereign rule was restored in 1934.
    In 1956, the Duvalier family gained control of the
country and began a dictatorial rule that lasted 29 years.
A series of transitional governments followed before
Jean-Bertrand Aristide won the 1990 presidential
election. Aristide was deposed in a military coup in 1991,
but was restored in 1994 after the severity of the
military's rule prompted the UN to authorise international
intervention. Flawed elections in 1997 and 2000 led to
several years of political turmoil until an armed rebellion
in 2004 ousted Aristide, who had been re-elected in
2000. An interim government was sworn in and a UN-led
multinational stabilisation force was deployed. By 2010,
UN peacekeepers' joint operations with the national
police force were slowly having an impact on the
widespread violence, lawlessness and corruption, but
these increased in the aftermath of the massive earthquake
in January 2010. This left 230,000 dead, 300,000
injured and 1.2 million homeless, and caused severe
damage to the country's infrastructure; thousands more
died in subsequent cholera outbreaks.
    The presidential and legislative elections due in 2010
were postponed because of the earthquake. The
presidential election was won in the second round of
voting in March 2011 by Michel Martelly of the Repons
Peyizan party. Following the second round of voting in
the legislative election in March 2011, the Inite party
held the most seats.

POLITICAL SYSTEM
Under the 1987 constitution, the president is directly
elected for a five-year term that may not be renewed
immediately. The bicameral National Assembly comprises
a lower house, the Chamber of Deputies, with 99
members directly elected for a four-year term, and the
senate, with 30 members directly elected for a six-year
term; one-third of the senators is elected every two years.
The president appoints the prime minister, who must be
approved by the legislature.

HEAD OF STATE
President, Michel Martelly, *elected* 20 March 2011, *sworn
in* 14 May 2011

SELECTED GOVERNMENT MEMBERS *as at June 2011*
Prime Minister, Jean-Max Bellerive
Foreign Affairs, Marie Michèle Rey
Economy and Finance, Ronald Baudin
Interior, Paul Antoine Bien-Aime

BRITISH AMBASSADOR
HE Steven Fisher, *apptd* 2009, resident at Santo Domingo,
Dominican Republic

ECONOMY AND TRADE
The country is the poorest in the western hemisphere,
with most of the population living below the poverty line
and over half in abject poverty. Its economy, damaged by
years of political instability, violence and corruption as
well as the natural disasters to which it is vulnerable,
experienced moderate growth from 2005 and Haiti had
its foreign debt written off in 2009 and 2010. But the
2010 earthquake reversed these gains, devastating the
infrastructure and continuing the government's complete
dependence on foreign aid. Remittances from the
estimated one in six Haitians who live abroad, principally
in the USA, are the main source of foreign revenue, worth
nearly 20 per cent of GDP. Two-thirds of the population
depend on agriculture – predominantly small-scale
subsistence farming – which contributes 25 per cent of
GDP. Industrial activities include production of textiles
and garments, sugar refining, flour milling and assembly
of goods, especially vehicle parts, for re-export.
    The main trading partners are the USA and Dominican
Republic. Principal exports are garments (three-quarters
of exports), manufactured goods, essential oils, cocoa,
mangoes and coffee. The main imports are food,
manufactured goods, machinery and transport equipment,
fuels and raw materials.
GNI – US$5,000m; US$520 per capita (2007)
Annual average growth of GDP – –8 per cent (2010 est)
Inflation rate – 4.6 per cent (2010 est)
Population below poverty line – 80 per cent (2003 est)
Total external debt – US$494m (2010 est)
Imports – US$2,100m (2009)
Exports – US$600m (2009)

BALANCE OF PAYMENTS
Trade – US$2,452m deficit (2010)
Current Account – US$296m deficit (2008)

Trade with UK	2009	2010
Imports from UK	£6,339,379	£16,483,018
Exports to UK	£4,041,794	£2,609,284

COMMUNICATIONS
Less than a quarter of the country's 4,160km of highways are surfaced. There are 14 airports, four of which have surfaced runways; the international airports are at Port-au-Prince and Cap-Haitien. Cap-Haitien is the main port. The international airports and the main port are operable again following earthquake damage, but many roads remain impassable.

The telephone system is poor, with only 108,000 fixed lines in use. Mobile phone distribution has grown rapidly, with 40 per 100 people in 2009.

MEDIA
Low literacy levels mean that radio is Haiti's most important medium, with more than 250 radio stations broadcasting in French and Creole. A single state-broadcaster, Télévision Nationale d'Haiti, operates alongside two privately owned French-language stations. The media represent a wide spectrum of political views, although journalists often exercise a degree of self-censorship.

HONDURAS

República de Honduras – Republic of Honduras

Area – 112,090 sq. km
Capital – Tegucigalpa; population, 1,000,080 (2009 est)
Major cities – Choloma, La Ceiba, El Progreso, San Pedro Sula
Currency – Lempira of 100 centavos
Population – 7,989,415 rising at 1.94 per cent a year (2010 est); mainly mestizo, with Amerindian and black minorities
Religion – Christian (Roman Catholic 47 per cent, Protestant 36 per cent) (est)
Language – Spanish (official), Amerindian dialects
Population density – 67 per sq. km (2009)
Urban population – 48 per cent (2008 est)
Median age (years) – 20.7 (2010 est)
National anthem – 'Himno Nacional de Honduras' ['National Anthem of Honduras']
National day – 15 September (Independence Day)
Life expectancy – 70.51 (2010 est)
Mortality rate – 4.99 (2010 est)

Birth rate – 25.61 (2010 est)
Infant mortality rate – 21.04 (2010 est)
Death penalty – Abolished for all crimes (since 1956)
CPI score – 2.4 (2010)

CLIMATE AND TERRAIN
Honduras has a mountainous interior, falling to narrow coastal plains. Elevation extremes range from 2,870m (Cerro Las Minas) at the highest point to 0m (Caribbean Sea) at the lowest. The climate is subtropical in the lowlands and temperate in the mountains. The average temperature in Tegucigalpa is 22°C.

HISTORY AND POLITICS
Honduras was home to part of the Mayan civilisation between the fourth and ninth centuries AD. Christopher Columbus first set foot on the American mainland at Trujillo in Honduras in 1502, but it was 1525 before Spanish colonisation began. In 1821, the country gained independence from Spain, and it was part of a Central American federation of former Spanish colonies from 1823 until it became fully independent in 1839. Thereafter the country underwent periods of political instability interspersed with military rule until 1982, when a civilian government took office. During the civil wars in Nicaragua and El Salvador, Honduras acted as a base for US forces and anti-Sandinista Contras, and there was a marked decline in its respect for human rights. The end of the civil wars led to a decline in the power of the army, which was brought under civilian control in 1999, but there are still very high levels of violent crime.

President Manuel Zelaya of the Liberal Party (PLH), elected in 2005, was deposed in June 2009 after his planned constitutional referendum was declared illegal. There was international condemnation of Zelaya's deposition and several months of mass protests within the country by his supporters, but the interim government, upheld by the courts, rejected his reinstatement. In November 2009, the National Party of Honduras (PNH) candidate, Porfirio Lobo, defeated the PLH candidate in the presidential election, and the PLH also lost the legislative election to the PNH, which won 71 of the 128 seats. President Lobo formed a PNH-dominated government of national unity.

POLITICAL SYSTEM
Under the 1982 constitution, the executive president is directly elected for a four-year term, which is not renewable, and appoints the government. The unicameral National Congress has 128 members, directly elected for a four-year term.

HEAD OF STATE
President, Porfirio Lobo, elected 29 November 2009, took office 27 January 2010
Vice-Presidents, Victor Barnica; Maria Antonieta Guillen de Bogran; Samuel Reyes

SELECTED GOVERNMENT MEMBERS as at June 2011
Defence, Marlon Pascua
Finance, William Chong Wong
Foreign Relations, Mario Canahuati
Interior; Justice, Africo Madrid

EMBASSY OF HONDURAS
115 Gloucester Place, London W1U 6JT
T 020-7486 4880 E hondurasuk@lineone.net
Ambassador Extraordinary and Plenipotentiary, HE Ivan Romero-Martinez, apptd 2008

BRITISH AMBASSADOR
HE Julie Chappell, OBE, *apptd* 2009, resident at Guatemala City, Guatemala

DEFENCE

The army has 12 light tanks. The navy has 15 patrol and coastal combatant vessels at 3 bases. The air force has 16 combat-capable aircraft.

Military budget – US$138m (2010)
Military personnel – 12,000: army 8,300, navy 1,400, air force 2,300; paramilitary 8,000

ECONOMY AND TRADE

The country has a huge imbalance in wealth and high levels of corruption and violent crime, often connected with drug-trafficking. Its narrow range of exports is vulnerable to natural disasters and commodity price changes. Economic activity is heavily dependent on the USA; a drop in exports and remittances due to the global economic downturn contributed to the economy's contraction in 2009. Remittances from expatriate workers are equivalent to a fifth of GDP.

Although still dependent on agriculture, fishing and forestry, whose products form the basis of industrial activity and are the main exports, the economy is gradually diversifying into offshore assembly for re-export and tourism. Agriculture employs 39.2 per cent of the workforce and contributes 12.4 per cent of GDP. Industry accounts for 26.9 per cent of GDP and 20.9 per cent of employment, and the services sector for 60.8 per cent of GDP and 39.8 per cent of employment.

The main trading partner is the USA, which takes 60 per cent of exports and provides 47 per cent of imports. Principal exports are garments, coffee, shrimp, wire harnessing, cigars, bananas, gold, palm oil, fruit, lobster and timber. The main imports are machinery and transport equipment, industrial raw materials, chemical products, fuels and foodstuffs.

GNI – US$13,827m; US$1,800 per capita (2009)
Annual average growth of GDP – 2.5 per cent (2010 est)
Inflation rate – 4.6 per cent (2010 est)
Unemployment – 5.1 per cent (2010 est)
Population below poverty line – 65 per cent (2010)
Total external debt – US$3,540m (2010 est)
Imports – US$6,200m (2009)
Exports – US$2,400m (2009)

BALANCE OF PAYMENTS
Trade – US$4,599m deficit (2010)
Current Account – US$457m deficit (2009)

Trade with UK	2009	2010
Imports from UK	£7,811,797	£10,835,148
Exports to UK	£70,685,611	£77,684,707

COMMUNICATIONS

Honduras has ports on its Caribbean (Puerto Castilla, Puerto Cortes, Tela) and Pacific (San Lorenzo) coasts. There are 75km of railway and 14,200km of roads, 3,150km of which are surfaced. The mountainous interior has led to the development of a large number of airports, though only 12 of the 104 have surfaced runways; the principal airports are at Tegucigalpa, La Ceiba and San Pedro Sula. The fixed-line telephone system is expanding but density is only about 10 per 100 people. Mobile phone distribution has grown rapidly and reached 100 per 100 people in 2009.

EDUCATION AND HEALTH

Primary and secondary education is free of charge and primary education is compulsory between the ages of six and 11.

Literacy rate – 83.6 per cent (2008 est)
Gross enrolment ratio (percentage of relevant age group) – primary 116 per cent; secondary 65 per cent; tertiary 19 per cent (2008 est)
Health expenditure (per capita) – US$117 (2009)
Hospital beds (per 1,000 people) – 0.8 (2004–9)

MEDIA

Honduras has a state-owned radio station as well as several privately run broadcasters and newspapers. Televicentro operates several television channels. Harsh defamation laws are in place and journalists, who are often the target of threats and assault, tend to practise self-censorship. The interim government of 2009–10 reportedly censored and sabotaged numerous media outlets critical of its policies.

HUNGARY

Magyar Koztarsasag – Republic of Hungary

Area – 93,028 sq. km
Capital – Budapest; population, 1,704,710 (2009 est)
Major cities – Debrecen, Gyor, Miskolc, Pecs, Szeged
Currency – Forint of 100 filler
Population – 9,992,339 falling at 0.16 per cent a year (2010 est); Hungarian (92.3 per cent), Roma (1.9 per cent) (2001). There are also smaller groups of ethnic Germans, Serbs, Romanians and Slovaks
Religion – Christian (Roman Catholic 55 per cent, Protestant 18 per cent, Jewish (1 per cent) (est)
Language – Hungarian (official)
Population density – 112 per sq. km (2009)
Urban population – 68 per cent (2008 est)
Median age (years) – 40 (2010 est)
National anthem – 'Himnusz' ['Hymn']
National day – 20 August (St Stephen's Day)
Life expectancy (years) – 74.57 (2010 est)
Mortality rate – 12.67 (2010 est)
Birth rate – 9.7 (2010 est)
Infant mortality rate – 5.38 (2010 est)
Death penalty – Abolished for all crimes (since 1990)
CPI score – 4.7 (2010)

CLIMATE AND TERRAIN

Landlocked Hungary lies mostly on the vast plain created by the Danube and Tisza rivers, with hills and mountains along the northern border. Elevation extremes range from 1,014m (Mt Kekes) at the highest point to 78m (river

Tisza) at the lowest. Lake Balaton lies in the west. The climate is temperate, with average temperatures ranging from −1°C in January to 21°C in July.

HISTORY AND POLITICS

Magyar tribes (the ancestors of modern Hungarians) settled on the Hungarian plains in the ninth century and became a Christian kingdom under St Stephen in 1000. Most of the kingdom was conquered by Ottoman Turks in 1526, but the Turks were expelled in 1699 by the Habsburgs and Hungary became a province of the dynasty's central European empire. Following years of Hungarian agitation, a dual monarchy was created in 1867, giving Hungary control of its internal affairs in return for the continued union of the Austrian and Hungarian crowns. This period is remembered as a time of cultural achievement and economic success. An ally of Germany in the First World War, the defeated Austro-Hungarian Empire collapsed in 1918.

Initially a communist republic after the war, in 1920 the country became a kingdom, with Admiral Horthy as regent. Hungary remained neutral when the Second World War began, but joined the conflict in 1941 on the side of the Axis powers. Horthy was deposed in 1944 after seeking an armistice with advancing Soviet troops, who drove out German forces in 1945.

The Communists came to power in the 1947 elections, and in 1949 Hungary became a communist state aligned with the Soviet Union. A national uprising broke out in 1956, with protesters demanding the withdrawal of Soviet forces from the country, but this was brutally suppressed. In the 1960s Janos Kadar introduced limited liberalisation, which encouraged the development of the most prosperous and permissive regime in the Soviet bloc.

The opening of Hungary's border with Austria in 1989 triggered the developments that led to the fall of communism throughout eastern Europe. Communist rule ended shortly afterwards in Hungary, which began the transition to a free-market democracy. The country joined NATO in 1999 and the EU in 2004.

The 2010 legislative election was won by the opposition Fidesz and Christian Democratic People's Party bloc with an overwhelming majority and it formed a government under Viktor Orban (prime minister 1998-2002). The 2010 presidential election was won outright at the first vote by Pal Schmitt of the Fidesz party.

POLITICAL SYSTEM

The 1949 constitution will be superseded in 2012 by a new constitution approved by the legislature in April 2011. Under the 1949 constitution, the president is elected by the legislature for a five-year term, renewable once; he or she appoints the prime minister. The unicameral National Assembly has 386 members directly elected for a four-year term.

HEAD OF STATE

President, Pal Schmitt, *elected* 29 June 2010, *sworn in* 6 August 2010

SELECTED GOVERNMENT MEMBERS *as at June 2011*
Prime Minister, Viktor Orban
Deputy Prime Ministers, Tibor Navracsics; Zsolt Semjen
Economy, Gyorgy Matolcsy
Foreign Affairs, Janos Martonyi
Defence, Csaba Hende

EMBASSY OF THE REPUBLIC OF HUNGARY
35 Eaton Place, London SW1X 8BY
T 020-7201 3440 E office.lon@kum.hu
W www.mfa.gov.hu/emb/london
Ambassador Extraordinary and Plenipotentiary, Janos Csak, *apptd* 2011

BRITISH EMBASSY
Harmincad Utca 6, 1051 Budapest
T (+36) (1) 266 2888 E info@britemb.hu
W http://ukinhungary.fco.gov.uk
Ambassador Extraordinary and Plenipotentiary, HE Greg Dorey, *apptd* 2007

BRITISH COUNCIL
Madach Trade Center, Madach Imre ut 13–14, Building B, Floor 4, 1075 Budapest
T (+36) (1) 478 2020 W www.britishcouncil.org/hungary
Director, Simon Ingram-Hill

DEFENCE

Hungary's armed forces have been reorganised into a joint force. The land component has 29 main battle tanks, and 380 armoured infantry fighting vehicles and personnel carriers. The air component has 14 combat aircraft and 12 armed helicopters.

Military budget – US$1,350m (2010)
Military personnel – 29,626: army 10,100, air force 5,806, joint staff 13,720; paramilitary 12,000

ECONOMY AND TRADE

Hungary made a successful transition to a market economy after 1989, attracting high levels of foreign direct investment, and over 80 per cent of GDP is now generated by the private sector. This strong economic growth started to slow in 2006–7, partly as a result of a government austerity programme intended to reduce the budget deficit and public debt. The global economic downturn left Hungary struggling to service both state and private debt in the face of rising interest rates and falling export demand, and the government had to obtain international assistance in 2008. The economy went into recession in 2009 but began to recover in 2010.

Nearly half the land is under cultivation, but agriculture accounts for only 3.3 per cent of GDP; the main crops are cereals, sunflower seeds, vegetables, livestock and dairy products. Industry contributes 30.8 per cent of GDP; the main activities include mining, metallurgy, food processing, and the production of construction materials, textiles, chemicals (especially pharmaceuticals) and motor vehicles. The main trading partners are Germany, other EU countries, Russia and China. Machinery and manufactured goods account for 90 per cent of exports and 50 per cent of imports. The country is a net importer of fuels and electricity.

GNI – US$121,189m; US$12,980 per capita (2009)
Annual average growth of GDP – 0.8 per cent (2010 est)
Inflation rate – 4.5 per cent (2010 est)
Unemployment – 11.5 per cent (2010 est)
Population below poverty line – 12 per cent (2010 est)
Total external debt – US$340,600m (2010 est)
Imports – US$78,000m (2009)
Exports – US$84,600m (2009)

BALANCE OF PAYMENTS
Trade – US$7,815m surplus (2010)
Current Account – US$11,172m deficit (2008)

Trade with UK	2009	2010
Imports from UK	£822,619,289	£1,047,387,553
Exports to UK	£2,122,988,188	£3,242,161,824

COMMUNICATIONS

Hungary has 197,519km of roads, 74,993km of which are surfaced, and 9,208km of railways (including a cross-border line to Austria jointly managed by the two countries). There are 1,622km of permanently navigable waterways, mainly on the river Danube, which has several major river ports and harbours, including Budapest. There are 43 airports and airfields, 22 of which have surfaced runways; the principal airport is at Budapest. Since 2000, fixed-line telephone subscriptions have declined as mobile phone use has risen; there were 11.8 million mobile phone subscribers and 6.2 million internet users in 2009.

EDUCATION AND HEALTH

Hungarians have ten years of compulsory education until age 16; a further two years at secondary level is optional.

Literacy rate – 98.9 per cent (2008 est)
Gross enrolment ratio (percentage of relevant age group) – primary 99 per cent; secondary 97 per cent; tertiary 65 per cent (2008 est)
Health expenditure (per capita) – US$938 (2009)
Hospital beds (per 1,000 people) – 7.0 (2004–9)

MEDIA AND CULTURE

The state-run broadcasters, Magyar Televizio and Hungarian Radio, compete with a number of privately owned television and radio stations. In 2011, a proposed law was amended following claims that it would tighten the government's control over the media. Hungary has a wide range of weekly and daily newspapers, some of which are owned by foreign investors.

The strong folk music tradition has influenced many native composers of classical music, including Franz Liszt (1811–86), Bela Bartok (1881–1945), Zoltan Kodaly (1882–1967) and Gyorgy Ligeti (1923–2006). Hungary's best known author is Imre Kertesz (*b.* 1929), who won the Nobel prize for literature in 2002.

ICELAND

Lydveldid Island – Republic of Iceland

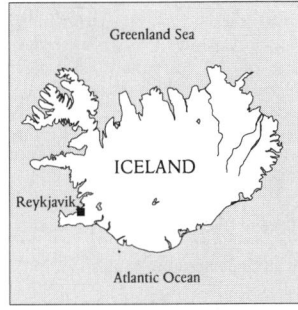

Area – 103,000 sq. km
Capital – Reykjavik; population, 198,093 (2009 est)
Major towns – Hafnarfjordur, Kopavogur
Currency – Icelandic krona (Kr) of 100 aurar
Population – 308,910 rising at 0.7 per cent a year (2010 est)

Religion – Christian (Lutheran 84 per cent, Roman Catholic 3 per cent) (est)
Language – Icelandic (official), English, German
Population density – 3 per sq. km (2009)
Urban population – 92 per cent (2008 est)
Median age (years) – 35.4 (2010 est)
National anthem – 'Lofsongur' ['Hymn']
National day – 17 June (Independence Day)
Life expectancy (years) – 80.79 (2010 est)
Mortality rate – 6.9 (2010 est)
Birth rate – 13.36 (2010 est)
Infant mortality rate – 3.21 (2010 est)
Death penalty – Abolished for all crimes (since 1928)
CPI score – 8.5 (2010)
Security budget – US$32m (2009)
Security personnel – none active; paramilitary (coastguard) 130

CLIMATE AND TERRAIN

Iceland is a volcanic island in the North Atlantic Ocean, to the east of Greenland and to the west of Norway, and its northernmost point reaches the Arctic Circle. Some parts of the coastline have narrow strips of low-lying land, others are sheer cliffs. An inland plateau of glaciers, lakes and lava fields covers most of the interior, with mountainous areas in the north and at the four glaciers in the centre and south. Elevation extremes range from 2,110m (Hvannadalshnukur, on the Oraefajokull volcano) at the highest point to 0m (North Atlantic Ocean) at the lowest. There are geysers and hot springs owing to the numerous active volcanoes, which can create new islands, such as Surtsey in 1963; the volcano under the Eyjafjallajokull glacier has been active since March 2010. It is estimated that over the past 500 years, Iceland has emitted a third of the earth's total lava flow. The climate is influenced by the Gulf Stream and is therefore temperate in spite of the country's location. Average temperatures range from −3°C in January to 11°C in July.

HISTORY AND POLITICS

The first major settlement occurred from around AD 870 onwards, as turmoil in Scandinavia drove migrants to seek new homelands. Iceland hosted a flourishing Viking culture in the ninth and tenth centuries, becoming a fully Christian country in 1000. Iceland recognised Norwegian sovereignty in 1263 and, with Norway, came under Danish rule in 1397. When Norway was ceded to Sweden in 1814, Iceland remained Danish territory, achieving autonomy in domestic affairs in 1874. Although it became an independent state with the same sovereign as Denmark in 1918, Copenhagen continued to control its foreign policy and defence. The treaty of union with Denmark expired in 1943, while Denmark was under German occupation, and in a referendum Icelanders voted to become a fully independent republic, proclaimed on 17 June 1944.

The country's dependence on the fishing industry has led occasionally to fraught foreign relations. The introduction and extensions of an exclusive fishing limit around Iceland in 1958, 1972 and 1975 caused the so-called 'Cod War' disputes with the UK. Subsequent restrictions on fishing in Icelandic waters in the 1990s were less controversial.

Post-independence politics was dominated by the conservative Independence Party (SSF) until January 2009, when the country's economic crisis forced the government first to call an early election, then to resign with immediate effect. The Social Democratic Alliance, the junior party in the outgoing coalition, formed a new coalition with the Left-Green Movement (VGF) which then won the legislative election in April. Iceland applied for EU membership in 2009, and formal accession talks began in July 2010.

POLITICAL SYSTEM
Under the 1944 constitution, the head of state is the president, who is directly elected for a four-year term, which is renewable. The unicameral legislature, the *Althing*, has 63 members, who are directly elected for a four-year term. Founded in AD 930, the *Althing* is the world's oldest functioning parliament.

HEAD OF STATE
President, Olafur Ragnar Grimsson, *elected* 29 June 1996, *re-elected* 2000, 2004, 2008

SELECTED GOVERNMENT MEMBERS *as at June 2011*
Prime Minister, Johanna Sigurdardottir
Economic Affairs, Arni Pall Arnason
Finance, Steingrimur Sigfusson
Foreign Affairs, Ossur Skarphedinsson
Interior, Ogmundur Jonasson

EMBASSY OF ICELAND
2A Hans Street, London SW1X 0JE
T 020-7259 3999 E icemb.london@utn.stjr.is
W www.iceland.is/iceland-abroad/uk/
Ambassador Extraordinary and Plenipotentiary, HE Benedikt Jonsson, *apptd* 2009

BRITISH EMBASSY
Laufasvegur 31, 101 Reykjavik
T (+354) 550 5100 E britemb@centrum.is
W http://ukiniceland.fco.gov.uk
Ambassador Extraordinary and Plenipotentiary and Consul-General, HE Ian Whitting, *apptd* 2008

ECONOMY AND TRADE
Iceland has a market economy with an extensive welfare system. While it remains heavily dependent on the fishing industry, which accounts for 12 per cent of GDP and 40 per cent of export earnings, there has been recent diversification into aluminium smelting, ferrosilicon production, software production, biotechnology and tourism, encouraged by the plentiful supply of geothermal power. A major area of diversification was into banking, but aggressive expansion in the 2000s led to over-exposure in foreign markets. In the 2008 global financial crisis, the three largest banks collapsed and the government required over US$10bn in loans to stabilise its currency and financial system. The economy contracted sharply, causing widespread unemployment and rapid inflation, and has been in recession since 2009.

The main trading partners are EU countries, Norway and the USA. Principal exports are fish and fish products, aluminium, animal products, ferrosilicon and diatomite. The main imports are machinery, petroleum products, foodstuffs and textiles.

GNI – US$10,829m; US$43,430 per capita (2009)
Annual average growth of GDP – –3.4 per cent (2010 est)
Inflation rate – 5.5 per cent (2010 est)
Unemployment – 8.6 per cent (2010 est)
Total external debt – US$119,051m (2010 est)
Imports – US$3,600m (2009)
Exports – US$4,000m (2009)

BALANCE OF PAYMENTS
Trade – US$669m surplus (2010)
Current Account – US$460m surplus (2009)

Trade with UK	2009	2010
Imports from UK	£124,501,001	£127,241,888
Exports to UK	£409,675,556	£353,323,319

COMMUNICATIONS
Iceland has no railways and no navigable waterways. Although the country has 12,869km of roads, about two-thirds are unsurfaced. Consequently much internal travel is by air or sea. Iceland has 99 airports and airfields, the principal ones being at Keflavik, near Reykjavik, in the south and Akureyri in the north. The national carrier is Icelandair. There are 57 ice-free ports including 15 with appreciable cargo activity; Reykjavik receives over 70 per cent of imports and operates shipping services to the USA and Europe. There were 185,000 fixed-line telephone connections in use, 349,000 mobile phone subscribers and 301,600 internet users in 2009.

MEDIA AND CULTURE
The state provides public service broadcasting on television and radio via the Icelandic National Broadcasting Service (RUV). There are several commercial stations and a variety of newspapers. Reporters Without Borders ranked the country the joint highest for press freedom in 2010.

Iceland enjoys a rich literary tradition. The Icelandic sagas, dating from the 12th to 14th centuries, are among the major works of medieval European literature. One of Iceland's best-known modern writers is Halldor Laxness (1902–98), winner of the Nobel prize for literature in 1955. The country is also known for popular music groups the Sugarcubes (whose singer Bjork has enjoyed worldwide success) and Sigur Ros.

INDIA

Bharatiya Ganarajya – Republic of India

Area – 3,287,263 sq. km
Capital – New Delhi; population, 294,783 (2001 est). Delhi urban agglomeration; population, 21,719,700 (2009 est)
Major cities – Ahmadabad, Bengaluru (Bangalore), Chennai (Madras), Hyderabad, Jaipur, Kanpur, Kolkata (Calcutta), Mumbai (Bombay), Pune, Surat
Currency – Indian rupee (Rs) of 100 paise
Population – 1,173,108,018 rising at 1.38 per cent a year (2010 est); Indo-Aryan (72 per cent), Dravidian (25 per cent) (2000 est)

Religion – Hindu 81 per cent, Muslim 13 per cent (of
which Sunni 85 per cent, Shia 15 per cent), Christian
2 per cent, Sikh 2 per cent (est)
Language – Hindi (official national language), English,
Assamese, Bengali, Bodo, Dogri, Gujurati, Kannada,
Kashmiri, Konkani, Maithili, Malayalam, Manipuri,
Marathi, Nepali, Oriya, Punjabi, Sanskrit, Santhali,
Sindhi, Tamil, Telugu, Urdu (all official)
Population density – 389 per sq. km (2009)
Urban population – 29 per cent (2008 est)
Median age (years) – 25.9 (2010 est)
National anthem – 'Jana Gana Mana' ['Thou Art the Ruler
of the Minds of all People']
National day – 26 January (Republic Day)
Life expectancy (years) – 66.46 (2010 est)
Mortality rate – 7.53 (2010 est)
Birth rate – 21.34 (2010 est)
Infant mortality rate – 49.13 (2010 est)
Death penalty – Retained
CPI score – 3.3 (2010)

CLIMATE AND TERRAIN

India has three well-defined regions: the mountain range
of the Himalayas, the Indo-Gangetic plain and the
southern peninsula. The Himalayas along the northern
border reach 8,598m (Kanchenjunga) at the highest point
of elevation, then drop to the northern plains formed
by the basins of the Indus, Ganges and Brahmaputra
rivers before rising to low hills running east to west
that mark the division with the southern Deccan
peninsula. The peninsula has narrow coastal plains
rising to a central plateau, with the Western Ghats and
Eastern Ghats ranges of hills lying along the west
and east coasts respectively. The Thar Desert lies in
the north-west. The climate varies from tropical in the
south to temperate in the north. It is influenced by the
south-west monsoon; the main rainy season is June to
October. During the drier season from December to May,
the weather is cooler until February and then becomes
increasingly hot until the monsoon breaks. The average
temperature in New Delhi ranges from 14°C in January
to 34°C in June.

HISTORY AND POLITICS

The Indus civilisation emerged in the Indus valley region
c.2500 BC, and the beginnings of Hinduism date from
this period. This civilisation was destroyed by Aryan
tribes from central Asia between 1500 and 200 BC.
Buddhism emerged in India from c.500 BC and was
embraced by the Emperor Ashoka; it spread to the rest of
eastern Asia via trade routes, but a Hindu revival from
AD 40 onwards caused Buddhism to decline in the
subcontinent.

The first Muslim advances into India occurred in the
10th and 11th centuries. Incursions swept across the
north of the subcontinent, where large Muslim
communities were established. Europeans arrived in India
in the 15th century and had established territorial
holdings by the 18th century, though it was not until
1803, when the British East India Company consolidated
its influence, that a single power came to dominate the
subcontinent. In 1857, rule passed from the company to
the British government. From the late 19th century,
opposition to British rule, led by the Indian National
Congress (INC), latterly under the leadership of Mahatma
Gandhi, became a concerted nationwide movement, and
India achieved its independence in 1947. Against a
backdrop of intercommunal violence, its predominantly

Muslim regions were partitioned off to become the
separate state of Pakistan. India became a republic in
1950. Small French and Portuguese enclaves on the west
coast were integrated into the union in 1954 and 1961
respectively.

The INC has been the dominant party in Indian
politics since independence, holding power almost
continuously for four decades. Jawaharlal Nehru's
appointment as prime minister at independence began
the rise of the Gandhi family, which has dominated the
INC. Nehru was succeeded by his daughter, Indira
Gandhi, who was succeeded after her assassination in
1984 by her son Rajiv until he too was assassinated
in 1991; Rajiv's widow Sonia became president of the
party in 1998. The INC's dominance was challenged
in the early 1990s by the Hindu nationalist Bharatiya
Janata Party (BJP), which formed a series of coalition
governments between 1998 and 2004. The INC returned
to power with a surprise victory in the 2004
parliamentary election and formed a coalition government
called the United Progressive Alliance. The 2007
presidential election was won by Pratibha Patil, who
became the country's first female head of state. In the
2009 legislative elections, the INC and its coalition
partners won the most seats in the *Lok Sabha* (*see* below),
and were only ten seats short of an outright majority. A
new INC-led coalition government was formed under
Manmohan Singh, prime minister since 2004.

INTERNAL UNREST

Tensions between India's Hindu majority and large
Muslim minority have never been fully resolved. Violence
between the two at the time of partition in 1947 is
thought to have cost up to one million lives. The rise of
Hindu nationalism in the 1990s accompanied a rise in
communal clashes. In 1992, a mosque in the town of
Ayodhya was destroyed by Hindus who claimed it was
built on the birthplace of the Hindu god Rama.
Anti-Muslim mobs rampaged through many parts of
India and the army was called upon to restore order.
Intercommunal violence flared up again in 2002 when the
massacre of pilgrims returning from Ayodhya prompted
revenge killings.

There have been separatist campaigns or insurgencies
in Manipur, Meghalaya, Mizoram, Nagaland and Tripura
since 1947; in Assam since 1979; by Islamists in Kashmir
since 1989; and by ethnic Gurkhas in Darjeeling since
1986–8 and since 2008. Sikh separatist agitation for an
independent state in the Punjab became increasingly
violent in the 1980s. The suppression of Sikh militants,
and in particular the Indian army assault on the
militant-occupied Golden Temple at Amritsar in 1984,
led to the assassination of Indira Gandhi by her Sikh
bodyguards later that year.

A peasant uprising in Naxalbari, West Bengal, in 1967
has developed into a Maoist uprising with the declared
aim of overthrowing the government by 2050. By 2010
the insurgency affected 223 districts in 20 states, and the
Maoists controlled a 'red corridor' between the east coast
and the Nepalese border. Nationwide federal operations
to tackle the insurgents in 2009 and 2010 have been met
by a series of attacks by the Maoists.

FOREIGN RELATIONS

Since partition, sovereignty over the predominantly
Muslim state of Jammu and Kashmir has been disputed by
India and Pakistan. A short war in 1947–8 resulted in
the state being partitioned between the two countries;

its status remains unresolved, despite further outbreaks of war in 1965 and 1971, low-level conflict for control of the Siachen glacier since 1985 and occasional increases in military exchanges, most recently in 1999–2002 and 2003. Tension was exacerbated by Pakistan's support of the Muslim insurgency in the Indian part of the state, which began in the late 1980s and has included terrorist attacks in Indian cities, and by both countries' acquisition of nuclear weapons. Moves towards a peaceful settlement began in 2003, when diplomatic missions were reopened and the resumption of transport links was initiated. Formal diplomatic talks began in 2004 and have achieved several accords intended to reduce tension between the two countries, although the status of Kashmir has yet to be addressed. Talks were temporarily suspended by the Indian government after the Mumbai attacks in 2008 but resumed in 2010.

In the Sino-Indian war in 1962, India lost territory to China. In addition, China claims Arunachal Pradesh and does not recognise Indian sovereignty over Sikkim. Talks between India and China in 2003 resulted in India's formal recognition of the Tibetan Autonomous Region as a part of China and a cross-border trade agreement on Sikkim.

POLITICAL SYSTEM

Under the 1950 constitution, the president is elected for a five-year term by an electoral college consisting of members of both chambers of the legislature. The president appoints the prime minister, who is responsible to the legislature. The vice-president, who is elected by both chambers for a five-year term, is *ex-officio* chair of the upper chamber. The legislature, the *Sansad,* consists of two chambers. The upper chamber, the Council of States *(Rajya Sabha),* has up to 250 members, who serve a six-year term; up to 238 members are elected by the state legislative assemblies as individual terms expire, and the rest are nominated by the president. The House of the People *(Lok Sabha)* has 545 members; 543 are directly elected for a five-year term, and two representatives of the Anglo-Indian community are nominated by the president.

There are 28 states and seven union territories (including the national capital territory). Each state has its own executive, comprising a governor, who is appointed by the president for a five-year term, and a council of ministers. All states have a legislative assembly, and some also have a legislative council, elected directly for a maximum period of five years. The states have considerable autonomy, although the union government controls such matters as foreign policy, defence and external trade.

The union territories are administered, except where otherwise provided by parliament, by a lieutenant-governor or an administrator appointed by the president.

HEAD OF STATE
President, Pratibha Patil, *elected* 19 July 2007, *took office* 25 July 2007
Vice-President, Hamid Ansari

SELECTED GOVERNMENT MEMBERS *as at June 2011*
Prime Minister, Manmohan Singh
Defence, A. K. Antony
Finance, Pranab Mukherjee
Home Affairs, Palaniappan Chidambaram
External Affairs, S. M. Krishna

OFFICE OF THE HIGH COMMISSIONER FOR INDIA
India House, Aldwych, London WC2B 4NA
T 020-7836 8484 E administration@hcilondon.in
W www.hcilondon.in
High Commissioner, HE Nalin Surie, *apptd* 2009

BRITISH HIGH COMMISSION
Chanakyapuri, New Delhi 110021
T (+91) (11) 2419 2100 E web.newdelhi@fco.gov.uk
W www.ukinindia.fco.gov.uk
High Commissioner, Sir Richard Stagg, KCMG, *apptd* 2007

BRITISH COUNCIL
17 Kasturba Gandhi Marg, New Delhi 110001
T (+91) (11) 2371 1401/2371 0111
W www.britishcouncil.org/india
Director, Rob Lynes

DEFENCE

The army has over 4,117 main battle tanks, 1,455 armoured infantry fighting vehicles, 222 multi-role helicopters and more than 331 armoured personnel carriers. The navy has 16 submarines, 1 aircraft carrier, 10 destroyers, 12 frigates, 49 patrol and coastal vessels, 26 combat aircraft and 54 armed helicopters. The air force has 665 combat aircraft and 20 armed helicopters.

India has had nuclear weapon technology since the mid-1970s, and by the mid-1990s had also successfully developed intermediate-range ballistic missiles.
Military budget – US$38,400m (2010)
Military personnel – 1,325,000: army 1,129,900, navy 58,350, air force 127,200, coastguard 9,550; paramilitary 1,300,586

ECONOMY AND TRADE

The economy was closed for several decades after independence, with high import tariffs and limits on foreign investment to stimulate domestic growth. Since 1991, economic liberalisation and increased foreign investment have generated rapid expansion, with GDP growing by an average 7 per cent a year since 1997, apart from a brief contraction in 2008–9 during the global economic downturn.

India's large skilled workforce has enabled it to develop knowledge-based industries, and become a global centre for manufacturing and services. Other areas of growth are pharmaceuticals, tourism and the provision of services to the burgeoning urban middle class. The service sector now accounts for 55.3 per cent of GDP and industry for 28.6 per cent, employing 34 per cent and 14 per cent of the workforce respectively.

Although about 1 per cent of the population has been lifted out of poverty each year since 1997, rural areas have benefited disproportionately little from the economic growth. Since 2004 the government has initiated schemes intended to reduce rural poverty, which has been exacerbated by prolonged drought in some areas and the effects of the Indian Ocean tsunami of 2004. Agriculture, forestry and fishing support 52 per cent of the population and contribute 16.1 per cent of GDP. The main food crops are rice, cereals (principally wheat) and pulses. The major cash crops include cotton, jute, tea and sugar cane. Agriculture and forestry are threatened by deforestation, soil erosion, over-grazing and desertification.

Despite recent advances, the economy faces a number of problems, chief among which is population growth.

Economic constraints on continued growth include underinvestment in infrastructure (especially transport and power supply), shortfalls in energy generation, excessive regulation and corruption.

The main trading partners are the USA, the UAE, China and Saudi Arabia. Principal exports include petroleum products, precious stones, machinery, iron and steel, chemicals, vehicles and garments. Its main imports are crude oil, precious stones, machinery, fertiliser, iron and steel, and chemicals.

GNI – US$1,369,275m; US$1,220 per capita (2009)
Annual average growth of GDP – 8.3 per cent (2010 est)
Inflation rate – 11.7 per cent (2010 est)
Population below poverty line – 25 per cent (2007 est)
Unemployment – 10.8 per cent (2010 est)
Total external debt – US$237,100m (2010 est)
Imports – US$249,600m (2009)
Exports – US$162,600m (2009)

BALANCE OF PAYMENTS
Trade – US$117,792m deficit (2010)
Current Account – US$26,621m deficit (2009)

Trade with UK	2009	2010
Imports from UK	£2,943,446,125	£4,017,261,290
Exports to UK	£4,181,713,411	£5,380,470,481

COMMUNICATIONS
India has 63,974km of railways and 3.3 million km of roads. There are 352 airports and airfields, principally at Delhi, Mumbai, Chennai and Kolkata. The chief seaports are Mumbai, Kolkata, Haldia, Chennai, Cochin, Visakhapatnam, Mangalore and Tuticorin. The merchant fleet includes over 300 ships of over 1,000 tonnes. There are 485km of canals and the great rivers provide around 5,200km of navigable waterways.

There were 670 million mobile phone subscribers in 2010, compared to 166 million in 2006. This has caused a decline in fixed-line use, to 35.8 million lines in 2010. There were 61.3 million internet users in 2009, and 4.5 million internet hosts in 2010.

EDUCATION AND HEALTH
Education is free and became compulsory for children aged six to 14 years in April 2010.
Literacy rate – 66.8 per cent (2008 est)
Gross enrolment ratio (percentage of relevant age group) – primary 113 per cent; secondary 57 per cent; tertiary 13 per cent (2007 est)
Health expenditure (per capita) – US$45 (2009)
Hospital beds (per 1,000 people) – 0.9 (2004–9)

MEDIA
The state's monopoly of television broadcasting ended in 1992, since when the number of channels has increased rapidly. The satellite and cable television market is one of the biggest in the world and includes popular 24-hour news channels. Commercial radio has expanded in recent years, but stations tend to aim programming at urban audiences, and only the public broadcaster All India Radio can broadcast the news. The private press is a thriving and diverse industry, often outspoken and critical of the government; circulations have grown in step with the growth of the urban middle class.

CULTURE
Bengali writer, polymath and social reformist Rabindranath Tagore (1861–1941) won the Nobel prize for literature in 1913, becoming Asia's first Nobel laureate. Contemporary writers of international standing include Vikram Seth (*b.* 1952), Salman Rushdie (*b.* 1947) and Arundhati Roy (*b.* 1961); Kiran Desai (*b.* 1971) and Aravind Adiga (*b.* 1974) won the 2006 and 2008 Booker prizes respectively. The Indian film industry – which includes the Mumbai-based studios known as Bollywood – produces nearly 1,300 films a year. The influence of Bollywood in the West is growing, as shown by the success of films such as *Bride and Prejudice* (2004) and eight-time Oscar-winner *Slumdog Millionaire* (2008).

Cricket, the most popular sport in India, was introduced by the British and matches have been played in the country since 1721. Notable players include spin bowlers Bishan Singh Bedi (*b.* 1946) and Anil Kumble (*b.* 1970), batsman Sachin Tendulkar (*b.* 1973) and *Wisden's* Indian Cricketer of the Century Kapil Dev (*b.* 1959).

INDONESIA

Republik Indonesia – Republic of Indonesia

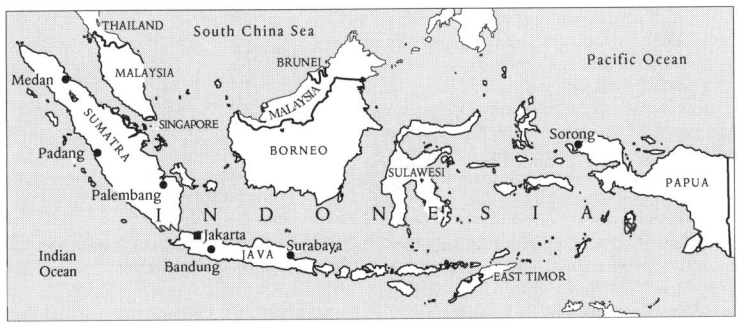

Area – 1,904,569 sq. km
Capital – Jakarta; population, 9,120,730 (2009 est)
Major cities – Bandung, Bekasi, Depok, Makasar, Medan, Palembang, Semarang, Surabaya, Tangerang

Currency – Rupiah (Rp) of 100 sen
Population – 242,968,342 rising at 1.1 per cent a year (2010 est); Javanese (40.6 per cent), Sundanese (15 per cent), Madurese (3.3 per cent), Minangkabau (2.7 per

cent), Betawi (2.4 per cent), Bugis (2.4 per cent), Banten (2 per cent), Banjar (1.7 per cent) (2000)
Religion – Muslim 88 per cent (predominantly Sunni), Christian 9 per cent, Hindu 2 per cent (est)
Language – Bahasa Indonesia (official), English, Dutch, Javanese, over 580 languages and dialects
Population density – 127 per sq. km (2009)
Urban population – 52 per cent (2008 est)
Median age (years) – 27.9 (2010 est)
National anthem – 'Indonesia Raya' ['Great Indonesia']
National day – 17 August (Independence Day)
Life expectancy (years) – 71.05 (2010 est)
Mortality rate – 6.25 (2010 est)
Birth rate – 18.45 (2010 est)
Infant mortality rate – 28.94 (2010 est)
Death penalty – Retained
CPI score – 2.8 (2010)
Literacy rate – 92.0 per cent (2008 est)
Gross enrolment ratio (percentage of relevant age group) – primary 121 per cent; secondary 79 per cent; tertiary 24 per cent (2009 est)
Health expenditure (per capita) – US$55 (2009)

CLIMATE AND TERRAIN

Indonesia is an archipelago of over 17,500 islands, of which about 6,000 are inhabited. They include the islands of Sumatra, Java, Madura, Bali, Lombok, Sumbawa, Sumba, Flores, the Riouw-Lingga archipelago, Bangka and Billiton, part of the island of Borneo (Kalimantan), Sulawesi (formerly Celebes), the Maluku (formerly Moluccas) archipelago and others comprising the provinces of East and West Nusa Tenggara, and the western halves of the islands of New Guinea (Papua; formerly Irian Jaya) and Timor. Many of the islands have narrow coastal plains with hilly or mountainous interiors, and around half of the country is covered by tropical rainforest. Elevation extremes range from 5,030m (Puncak Jaya, in Papua) at the highest point to 0m (Indian Ocean) at the lowest. The climate is tropical; the average temperature is 28°C, but rainfall peaks in January and February and is lowest in August.

The country is located near to an intersection of tectonic plates, making it susceptible to seismic activity such as earthquakes and volcanic eruptions. Its weather patterns are being affected by climate change.

HISTORY AND POLITICS

Hindu and Buddhist kingdoms existed in some parts of the Indonesian islands until the 14th century. Islam was introduced in the 13th century and spread over the next three centuries. Trading by the Portuguese began in the 16th century, but the Portuguese were displaced by the Dutch who, lured by the rich spice trade, came to dominate Indonesia by the early 20th century. Opposition to Dutch rule grew in the 1920s and the Japanese occupation of Indonesia during the Second World War strengthened nationalism, leading to a declaration of independence after liberation in 1945. This was not recognised by the Dutch, who attempted to reassert control, but after four years of guerrilla warfare they granted independence to the Netherlands Indies in 1949. Irian Jaya (now Papua) was annexed in 1963. Timor-Leste was invaded and annexed in 1975 but gained its independence in 2002.

Achmed Soekarno, the foremost proponent of self-rule since the 1920s, became president in 1949 but was deposed in 1966 in a military coup suppressed by General Suharto, who subsequently became president. Suharto remained in power until 1998 when, amid economic and social upheaval, he was succeeded by his deputy B. J. Habibie. Habibie's cautious introduction of social and economic reforms led to him being defeated in 1999 by Abdurrahman Wahid, in the first democratic elections for 44 years. President Wahid was impeached for alleged financial corruption and in 2001 the legislature appointed Megawati Soekarnoputri (daughter of Achmed Soekarno) to replace him.

Susilo Bambang Yudhoyono, of the Democratic Party, was elected president in 2004, and he was re-elected in 2009. In the 2009 legislative elections, the Democratic Party won the greatest number of seats but without an overall majority, and a coalition government was appointed by the president.

INSURGENCIES

Separatist movements developed in several parts of Indonesia after independence, including Maluku, which fought an unsuccessful separatist war in the 1950s; Irian Jaya (now Papua), which was granted greater autonomy in 2002, although separatist agitation continues; Timor-Leste, from its annexation in 1975 until independence in 2002; and Aceh province in Sumatra, which was granted a degree of autonomy in 2005.

Since the fall of Suharto in 1998, tensions between different ethnic and religious groups have surfaced, and there has been intercommunal violence in Kalimantan (1996–7, 1999, 2001), Sulawesi (1998–2000, 2001, 2005) and Maluku (1999–2002, 2004).

At least two Muslim extremist groups are based in Indonesia and claim links with al-Qaida. They have been held responsible for bombings in Bali in 2002 and 2005 and Jakarta in 2003, 2004 and 2009.

POLITICAL SYSTEM

The 1959 constitution was amended in 2001 to provide for the establishment of the upper chamber of the legislature, and in 2002 to provide for the direct election of the president and the abolition of parliamentary seats reserved for the armed forces.

The executive president is directly elected for a five-year term, renewable once, and appoints the cabinet. The bicameral People's Consultative Assembly comprises the House of Representatives, which has 560 members directly elected for a five-year term, and the House of Representatives of the Regions, which has 132 members, four for each province, directly elected on a non-partisan basis for a five-year term.

HEAD OF STATE
President, Susilo Bambang Yudhoyono, *sworn in* 20 October 2004, *re-elected* 2009
Vice-President, Boediono

SELECTED GOVERNMENT MEMBERS *as at June 2011*
Defence, Purnomo Yusgiantoro
Finance, Agus Martowardojo
Foreign Affairs, Marty Muliana Natalegawa
Home Affairs, Gamawan Fauzi

EMBASSY OF THE REPUBLIC OF INDONESIA
38 Grosvenor Square, London W1K 2HW
T 020-7499 7661 E kbri@btconnect.com
W www.indonesianembassy.org.uk
Ambassador Extraordinary and Plenipotentiary, Yuri Octavian Thamrin, *apptd* 2008

BRITISH EMBASSY
Jalan M. H. Thamrin 75, Jakarta 10310
T (+62) (21) 2356 5200 W http://ukinindonesia.fco.gov.uk
Ambassador Extraordinary and Plenipotentiary, HE Martin
Hatfull, *apptd* 2008

BRITISH COUNCIL
Jakarta Stock Exchange, Tower II, 16th Floor, Jalan Jenderal
Sudirman Kav. 52–53, Jakarta 12190
T (+62) (021) 515 5561 W www.britishcouncil.org/indonesia
Director, Keith Davies

DEFENCE
The army has 356 armoured personnel carriers, 11
armoured infantry fighting vehicles and 6 armed
helicopters. The navy has 2 submarines, 11 frigates, 66
patrol and coastal vessels and 9 armed helicopters. There
are 5 principal naval bases. The air force has 100 combat
aircraft.
Military budget – US$4,470m (2010)
Military personnel – 302,000: army 233,000, navy
45,000, air force 24,000; paramilitary 280,000
Conscription duration – 24 months (selective)

ECONOMY AND TRADE
The economy struggled from the late 1990s until recent
years, hit in succession by the Asian financial crisis, the
political turmoil following the fall of Suharto, a downturn
in tourism following the Bali bombings and a number of
natural disasters since 2004. President Yudhoyono's
government introduced significant economic reforms
which reduced debt, unemployment and inflation and
boosted growth in 2004–8. Although growth slowed
owing to the rises in global food and fuel prices in 2008,
government stimulus measures countered the effect of the
global downturn in 2009. Poverty, poor infrastructure,
corruption, a complex regulatory regime and inequitable
resource distribution among Indonesia's regions continue
to present problems.
   Natural resources include oil, tin, natural gas, nickel,
timber, bauxite, copper, coal, gold and silver. However, a
lack of investment in prospecting for new sources has led
to a decline in oil production and Indonesia has been a net
importer since 2004. The exploitation and processing of
mineral assets, production of textiles, clothing, cement,
fertilisers, plywood and rubber, and tourism are the main
industrial activities; industry accounts for 46.4 per cent of
GDP and services 37.1 per cent, employing 13 per cent
and 49 per cent of the workforce respectively. Agriculture
contributes only 16.5 per cent of GDP but employs 38
per cent of the workforce. The main crops are rice,
cassava, peanuts, rubber, cocoa, coffee, palm oil, copra and
livestock products.
   The main trading partners are Singapore, Japan, China,
the USA, South Korea and other Pacific Rim nations.
Principal exports are oil and natural gas, electrical
appliances, plywood, textiles and rubber. The main
imports are machinery and equipment, chemicals, fuel and
foodstuffs.
GNI – US$478,394m; US$2,050 per capita (2009)
Annual average growth of GDP – 6 per cent (2010 est)
Inflation rate – 5.2 per cent (2010 est)
Population below poverty line – 13.3 per cent (2010)
Unemployment – 7.1 per cent (2010 est)
Total external debt – US$155,900m (2010 est)
Imports – US$92,700m (2009)
Exports – US$119,500m (2009)

BALANCE OF PAYMENTS
Trade – US$26,510m surplus (2010)
Current Account – US$10,581m surplus (2009)

Trade with UK	2009	2010
Imports from UK	£350,183,691	£438,877,161
Exports to UK	£1,196,969,843	£1,373,289,047

COMMUNICATIONS
Indonesia has 437,759km of roads, 5,042km of railways
and 21,579km of navigable waterways. An extensive
network of ferry services links the islands. There are
684 airports and airfields, of which 171 have surfaced
runways; each of the main islands has a major airport,
with most capable of accepting international flights.
There are nine major ports, usually the chief towns of the
major islands, and the merchant fleet contains 1,244 ships
of over 1,000 tonnes. The Strait of Malacca and the South
China Sea are busy shipping lanes, although the latter has
high risks of piracy.
   The telephone system covers the whole country, and
access has improved with the installation of over 200,000
kiosks, many in remote areas. Mobile phone distribution is
growing quickly and, at 159 million subscribers in 2009,
exceeds fixed-line use at 34 million lines. There were
20 million internet users in 2009.

MEDIA
Media freedom has grown since the end of the Suharto
regime, although defamation laws are used to deter media
criticism. The dominant medium is television; the
public-service broadcaster, Televisi Republik Indonesia,
competes with several major commercial stations.
A public-service radio broadcaster operates six networks,
and there are scores of commercial radio stations. There
are many daily newspapers, including two
English-language publications in the capital.

IRAN

Jomhuri-ye Eslami-ye Iran – Islamic Republic of Iran

Area – 1,648,195 sq. km
Capital – Tehran; population 7,190,400 (2009 est)
Major cities – Ahvaz, Esfahan, Karaj, Mashhad, Qom,
   Shiraz, Tabriz
Currency – Iranian rial of 100 dinar
Population – 76,923,300 rising at 1.25 per cent a year
   (2010 est); Persian (51 per cent), Azeri (24 per cent),
   Gilaki and Mazandarani (8 per cent), Kurdish (7 per
   cent), Arab (3 per cent), Lur (2 per cent), Baloch (2 per
   cent), Turkmen (2 per cent) (est)

Religion – Muslim (Shia 89 per cent, Sunni 9 per cent)
(est); small Zoroastrian, Jewish, Christian and Baha'i
minorities; Sufism is growing, but Shia orders of Sufism
are being persecuted by the state
Language – Persian (official), Turkic, Kurdish, Luri,
Balochi, Arabic, Turkish
Population density – 45 per sq. km (2009)
Urban population – 68 per cent (2008 est)
Median age (years) – 26.3 (2010 est)
National anthem – 'Sorud-e Melli-e Jomhuri-ye Eslami-ye
Iran' ['Anthem of the Islamic Republic of Iran']
National day – 1 April (Republic Day)
Life expectancy (years) – 69.77 (2010 est)
Mortality rate – 5.94 (2010 est)
Birth rate – 18.52 (2010 est)
Infant mortality rate – 43.45 (2010 est)
Death penalty – Retained
CPI score – 2.2 (2010)

CLIMATE AND TERRAIN

Apart from narrow coastal plains on the Gulf coasts and
the shores of the Caspian Sea, the interior is a plateau
consisting of barren desert in the centre and east. This is
enclosed by high mountains in the west and north, with
smaller ranges on the eastern border and the southern
coast. Elevation extremes range from 5,671m (Kuh-e
Damavand) at the highest point to −28m (Caspian Sea) at
the lowest. Earthquakes are frequent. The climate is arid
or semi-arid in the interior, and subtropical on the
Caspian shores. Average temperatures in Tehran are 3°C
in January and 30°C in July.

HISTORY AND POLITICS

Iran is part of the Middle East's so-called fertile crescent,
an area associated with the development of sophisticated
agriculture in prehistoric times. In the sixth century BC,
the Achaemenian king Cyrus the Great gained control
of the area. His dynasty founded the Persian Empire,
in which Zoroastrianism was the main religion. Two
hundred years later, Persia was conquered by Alexander
the Great. Alexander's death led to a period of economic
turbulence, civil conflict and foreign invasion until the
Sassanian Persian Empire was founded in the second
century AD. This was destroyed in AD 637 by Arab
conquerors who introduced Islam, converting the
majority of the population and initiating a cultural
revolution. The area was ruled by Arabs, Turks and
Mongols until the accession of the Safavid dynasty,
which ruled between the 16th and 18th centuries, a time
recognised as a cultural golden age; it was followed by the
Qajar dynasty in the 19th and 20th centuries.

The Qajar dynasty was overthrown in 1921 by Reza
Khan, who became prime minister in 1923 and was
crowned Shah in 1925. He was succeeded in 1941 by
his son, Mohammad Reza Shah Pahlavi, who began a
programme of economic modernisation, Westernisation
and secularisation in the 1960s. Opposition to reform and
popular protests against the Shah's regime in the 1970s
led to a revolution in 1978. The Shah went into exile and
in 1979 a non-party theocratic Islamic republic was
proclaimed under Ayatollah Khomeini.

Since Ayatollah Khomeini's death in 1989, there has
been a struggle for political dominance between
conservatives and more liberal reformers. Although the
reformers were generally in the ascendancy until 2004,
liberalisation has been blocked by the religious authorities
and the conservative judiciary, which also constitute the
membership of the Council of Guardians and so are able

to influence the selection of parliamentary candidates.
There is a vocal, popular pro-democracy movement.

At the 2008 legislative election, many pro-reform
candidates were disqualified from standing by the Council
of Guardians; conservatives won more than two-thirds
of the seats. The incumbent president Mahmoud
Ahmadinejad was declared the outright winner after the
first round of voting in the 2009 presidential election, but
the result was challenged by the other candidates, who
alleged electoral fraud. Following massive protest rallies,
the Council of Guardians confirmed Ahmadinejad's
victory and ruled out an annulment; further popular
protests were suppressed. Since the protests in summer
2009, the regime has ruthlessly suppressed opposition
(the Green Movement) and purged liberals from official
positions.

FOREIGN RELATIONS

Between 1980 and 1988, Iran was engaged in a bitter
war with Iraq; ostensibly a boundary dispute over the
Shatt-al-Arab waterway, it was fuelled by Iran's fear that
Iraq was encouraging demands for autonomy by Arabs in
its westernmost province. Fighting ended in 1988 and
a peace settlement was agreed in 1990. Iran remained
neutral in the Gulf War (1991) and the Iraq War (2003),
but it has been accused since of subverting reconstruction
in Iraq by arming Shia insurgents.

Since the 1978 revolution, Iran's relations with the
West, and especially the USA, have been strained. It
has not cooperated with international efforts to achieve
peace in the Middle East, and has long been suspected
of sponsoring terrorism by Islamic fundamentalists,
especially in Lebanon and Palestine, and now is believed
to be supplying arms to the Taliban.

Since 2002 international relations have deteriorated
further because of concerns over Iran's nuclear and
ballistic missile programmes, especially its acquisition of
the ability to enrich uranium. Iran insists that this is for
power generation and is not a precursor to developing
nuclear weapons, but refuses to halt the programme
or cooperate with the IAEA. The UN has passed six
resolutions since 2006 calling on Iran to suspend uranium
enrichment and reprocessing and to comply with its IAEA
obligations and responsibilities; four of the resolutions
imposed or extended sanctions on trade and travel.

POLITICAL SYSTEM

Under the 1979 constitution, overall authority rests with
the spiritual leader of the republic, who is appointed for
life by the Assembly of Experts; this consists of 86 clerics
who are directly elected and decide religious and spiritual
matters. The executive president is directly elected for
a four-year term, renewable once. Ministers are nominated
by the president but must be approved by the legislature.
The unicameral Consultative Council *(Majlis al-Shoura)*
has 290 members who are directly elected for a four-year
term on a non-party basis; five seats are reserved for
religious minorities. Laws passed by the legislature
must be approved by the Council of Guardians of the
Constitution, six theologians appointed by the spiritual
leader and six jurists nominated by the judiciary and
approved by the legislature; it also has a supervisory
role in elections. In 1997, the Constitutional Surveillance
Council, a five-member body, was established to supervise
the proper application of constitutional laws.

*Spiritual Leader of the Islamic Republic and C.-in-C. of
Armed Forces,* Ayatollah Seyed Ali Khamenei, *appointed*
June 1989

President, Mahmoud Ahmadinejad, *elected* 24 June 2005,
  re-elected 2009
First Vice-President, Mohammad Reza Rahimi

SELECTED GOVERNMENT MEMBERS *as at June 2011*
Defence, Ahmad Vahidi
Economic Affairs and Finance, Shamseddin Hosseini
Foreign Affairs, Ali Akbar Salehi
Interior, Mostafa Mohammad Najjar

EMBASSY OF THE ISLAMIC REPUBLIC OF IRAN
16 Prince's Gate, London SW7 1PT
T 020-7225 3000 E info@iran-embassy.org.uk
W www.iran-embassy.org.uk
Ambassador Extraordinary and Plenipotentiary, vacant

BRITISH EMBASSY
198 Ferdowsi Avenue, 113116–91144 Tehran
T (+98) (21) 6405 2000 W http://ukiniran.fco.gov.uk
Ambassador Extraordinary and Plenipotentiary, vacant

BRITISH COUNCIL
Operations suspended indefinitely from 31 January 2009.
W www.britishcouncil.org/iran

DEFENCE
The army has over 1,613 main battle tanks, 640 armoured
personnel carriers, 640 armoured infantry fighting
vehicles and 50 armed helicopters. The navy has 23
submarines, over 100 patrol and coastal vessels, 3 combat
aircraft and 10 armed helicopters. There are 8 naval bases.
The air force has 336 combat aircraft.
Military budget – US$9,020m (2010)
Military personnel – 523,000: army 350,000, Islamic
  Revolutionary Guard Corps 125,000, navy 18,000, air
  force 30,000; paramilitary 40,000

ECONOMY AND TRADE
Iran was one of the best-performing economies in the
Middle East owing to its vast reserves of oil and natural
gas, but its performance has been deteriorating; the
predominantly state-controlled economy is inefficient
and inflexible, with little diversification and only a
limited, small-scale private sector. Unemployment and
underemployment are serious problems, and there is a
flourishing unofficial economy. Falling oil prices in
2008–10 and UN sanctions since 2008 have exacerbated
Iran's economic problems.

Oil and gas extraction and processing dominate the
economy, but other industries include petrochemicals,
textiles, construction materials, food processing, metal
fabrication and armaments. Agricultural production
includes wheat, rice, other grains, sugar beet and sugar
cane, fruit, nuts, cotton, dairy products, wool and
caviar.

The main trading partners are China, the UAE, South
Korea, Japan and India. Principal exports are petroleum
(80 per cent), chemical and petrochemical products, fruit
and nuts, and carpets. The main imports are industrial
raw materials and intermediate goods, capital goods,
foodstuffs, consumer goods and technical services.
GNI – US$328,593m; US$4,530 per capita (2009)
Annual average growth of GDP – 3 per cent (2010 est)
Inflation rate – 11.8 per cent (2010 est)
Population below poverty line – 18 per cent (2007 est)
Unemployment – 14.6 per cent (2010 government est)
Total external debt – US$12,840m (2010 est)

Imports – US$51,500m (2009)
Exports – US$78,100m (2009)

BALANCE OF PAYMENTS
Trade – US$34,203m surplus (2010)
Current Account – US$23,987m surplus (2008)

Trade with UK	2009	2010
Imports from UK	£374,036,961	£285,807,268
Exports to UK	£206,359,213	£194,666,672

COMMUNICATIONS
Iran's seaports include Asaluyeh, Bushehr and Abadan
(largely destroyed in the 1980–8 war with Iraq) on the
Persian Gulf and Bandar Abbas on the Strait of Hormuz.
The 850km of navigable waterways are mainly on the
river Karun and Lake Urmia. There are 172,927km of
roads, of which 125,908km are surfaced, and 8,442km
of railways. There are 319 airports and airfields; the
principal airports are at Tehran and Shiraz.

The state-owned telephone system is being modernised
and expanded to include rural as well as urban areas. The
fixed-line network has more than doubled in capacity, to
26 million users, since 2000. Mobile phone distribution
and internet use have grown dramatically; there were
52 million mobile subscribers and 32 million internet
users in 2009.

EDUCATION AND HEALTH
Primary education, between age six and 14, is compulsory
and free.
Literacy rate – 82.3 per cent (2008 est)
Gross enrolment ratio (percentage of relevant age group) –
  primary 103 per cent; secondary 83 per cent; tertiary
  36 per cent (2009 est)
Health expenditure (per capita) – US$269 (2009)
Hospital beds (per 1,000 people) – 1.4 (2004–9)

MEDIA
The relative freedom of the media has been increasingly
challenged in recent years, and since the 2009 protests
there has been a sustained crackdown on all independent
media; western journalists have been expelled from or
denied entry to the country, some domestic media
workers have been dismissed or imprisoned, and several
foreign-based radio stations have been banned. Viewing
of satellite television is widespread and generally tolerated
by the authorities, despite an official ban. The internet
is the main forum for expressing dissident opinions, but
websites and blogs are subject to government censorship.

CULTURE
Iran is rich in Islamic and pre-Islamic architecture.
Persepolis, constructed by Darius in the sixth century BC
and the capital of the Achaemenian Empire, lies 644km
south of Tehran. It was declared a UNESCO World
Heritage Site in 1979. The Persian philosopher,
astronomer and poet Omar Khayyam (1048–1131)
is best-known for his *Rubaiyat,* a series of rhyming
quatrains.

The film industry was boosted in 1998 by the
government's decision to subsidise productions. Director
Abbas Kiarostami (*b.* 1940), whose films include Palme
d'Or winner *Taste of Cherry* and *Ten,* has received much
critical acclaim, while author and filmmaker Marjane
Satrapi (*b.* 1969) received widespread acclaim for her
graphic novel and film *Persepolis.*

IRAQ

Jumhuriyat al-Iraq – Republic of Iraq

Area – 438,317 sq. km
Capital – Baghdad; population, 5,751,210 (2009 est)
Major cities – Arbil, Basra, Kirkuk, Mosul, Najaf,
Sulaymaniyah
Currency – New Iraqi dinar (NID) of 1,000 fils
Population – 29,671,605 rising at 2.45 per cent a year
(2010 est); Arab (75–80 per cent), Kurdish (15–20 per
cent) (est)
Religion – Muslim 97 per cent (of which Shia 65 per cent,
Sunni 35 per cent), Christian 3 per cent
(predominantly Chaldean Catholic) (est)
Language – Arabic (official), Kurdish (official in Kurdish
Autonomous Region), Turkoman, Assyrian, Armenian
Population density – 72 per sq. km (2009 est)
Urban population – 67 per cent (2008 est)
Median age (years) – 20.6 (2010 est)
National anthem – 'Mawtini' ['My Homeland']
National day – 14 July (Republic Day)
Life expectancy (years) – 70.25 (2010 est)
Mortality rate – 4.92 (2010 est)
Birth rate – 29.41 (2010 est)
Infant mortality rate – 43.16 (2010 est)
Death penalty – Retained
CPI score – 1.5 (2010)

CLIMATE AND TERRAIN

The north-west and south of Iraq consist of an almost
barren desert plain. The area between the Euphrates and
Tigris rivers, which run across the country from
north-west to south-east, is fertile, irrigated and heavily
cultivated. The rivers run through marshland to their
outflow in the Persian Gulf, on which Iraq has a 58km
coastline. In the north-east the land rises to the Kurdistan
mountains. Elevation extremes range from 3,611m to 0m
(Persian Gulf). The climate is mostly desert, though
colder and wetter in the mountains. Average temperatures
in Baghdad range from 10°C in January to 35°C in July.

HISTORY AND POLITICS

The Sumerians, the world's oldest civilisation, were the
first people to populate the areas around the Tigris and
Euphrates rivers. From around 3000 BC they began to
build city-states, of which Ur, Lagash and Eridu are the
earliest examples; the city-states were unified into an
empire *c.*2350 BC. In the seventh century BC the area
became part of the Assyrian Empire until this was
destroyed by the Babylonians and the Medes. Apart from
150 years of Roman rule (AD 114–266), Iraq was under
Persian rule from the mid-sixth century BC until Persia's
conquest by Arab Muslims in AD 637. The battle of

Karbala in AD 680 marked the split between Sunnis and
Shias, a decisive moment in Islamic history.

Iraq came under the control of the Ottoman Empire
from 1533 until 1916, when the Ottomans, weakened
by the First World War, ceded control to the British.
A provisional government was set up in 1920, and in
1921 the Emir Faisal was elected king of Iraq. The
monarchy was overthrown in 1958, and after a coup in
1968 Iraq came under the control of the socialist Ba'ath
Party. In 1979 Saddam Hussein became president.

Under Saddam Hussein's regime, Iraq was at war three
times: with Iran from 1980–8; in January 1991, when a
US-led alliance of NATO and Middle East countries
launched a military offensive to liberate Kuwait, which
Iraq had invaded and occupied in August 1990; and in
March 2003, when US-led forces invaded Iraq after
Saddam Hussein had for over a decade obstructed
attempts to verify the decommissioning of its weapons of
mass destruction. Saddam Hussein was captured in
December 2003, and was convicted and executed in
2006 for crimes against humanity.

Following the invasion and occupation between March
and May 2003, a coalition provisional authority became
the occupying authority in Iraq before handing over
sovereignty in June 2004 to the Iraqi interim governing
council. Foreign combat troops had been withdrawn from
the country by August 2010, although more than 50,000
support and training troops remain.

In the March 2010 legislative elections, the Iraqi
National Movement (al-Iraqiya) bloc led by former prime
minister Iyad Allawi won the most seats, but only by a
narrow margin over the State of Law (SL) bloc led by
incumbent prime minister Nouri al-Maliki. After several
months of negotiations, the al-Iraqiya, SL and Kurdistan
Alliance (KA) blocs agreed in November 2010 to form
a coalition government under Nouri al-Maliki, and this
was sworn in on 21 December. Jalal Talabani, the Kurdish
president of the interim government in 2005 and
re-elected to the office in 2006, was re-elected for a
second term in November 2010.

INTERNAL UNREST
There are about four million Kurds in north-east Iraq, in
areas adjoining the predominantly Kurdish areas in Iran
and Turkey. Iraq's Kurdish nationalists have demanded an
autonomous homeland, Kurdistan, since the 1960s, and
turned to militant tactics in the 1970s. Their demands
were opposed by Saddam Hussein's regime with great
brutality. An uprising after the Gulf War (1991) was
suppressed by Iraqi troops, prompting the creation of
UN safe havens which enabled the Kurds to set up a
semi-autonomous region in the north. An air exclusion
zone was also established, but there was further conflict
with Iraqi forces and between the two main Kurdish
parties in the 1990s. During the war in 2003, Kurdish
fighters fought alongside US troops in the north, taking
control of the northern cities and establishing an
administration in the area, which is now autonomous.
The boundary of the autonomous area has yet to be
defined, and its precise location will decide control of
Kirkuk and of oilfields in the region; this issue is the cause
of tension between the central and regional governments,
and of some intercommunal violence between Arabs and
Kurds in the area.

The Shias in southern Iraq also rebelled after the Gulf
War and were brutally suppressed. The UN established an
air exclusion zone over southern Iraq in 1992 to protect
the population, but persecution continued until 2003.

After May 2003, there was insurgent activity throughout the country, particularly in the Baghdad area, the predominantly Sunni-populated towns in the centre and west of the country, and in and around Mosul. Initially the targets were foreign troops, Iraqi military and police, and foreign aid and reconstruction workers, but from early 2005 the attacks became increasingly sectarian in nature. The level of violence has dropped since 2007 because of the US military 'surge', a ceasefire by one of the main militias, the Mahdi Army, from August 2007, and a key Sunni militia, the Awakening movement, turning against al-Qaida. There was an upsurge of violence in 2008 as the government mounted offensives against militias in Basra, Mosul and parts of Baghdad, and another upsurge in 2009–10 in the run-up to the legislative election and in the months following its inconclusive result. The approximate number of deaths as at December 2010 was: Iraqi civilians 99,000–108,000; US troops 4,400; and other coalition troops 318.

POLITICAL SYSTEM
Under the 2005 constitution, the president is elected by the legislature for a four-year term, renewable once. The president nominates the prime minister, subject to the approval of the legislature. The unicameral Council of Representatives *(Majlis al-Nuwab)* has 325 members (increased from 275 at the 2010 election), of whom 82 (formerly 69) must be women and 15 from minorities; members are directly elected for a four-year term.

HEAD OF STATE
President, Jalal Talabani, *elected* 6 April 2005, *re-elected* 22 April 2006, November 2010
Vice-Presidents, Tariq al-Hashimi; Khodeir al-Khaozai

SELECTED GOVERNMENT MEMBERS *as at June 2011*
Prime Minister, Defence (interim), Interior (interim), Nouri Jawad al-Maliki
Deputy Prime Ministers, Saleh Mutlaq; Hussain al-Shahristani; Roj Nouri Shawis
Foreign Affairs, Hoshyar al-Zebari

EMBASSY OF THE REPUBLIC OF IRAQ
3 Elvaston Place, London SW7 5QH
T 020-7590 9220 W www.iraqembassy.org.uk
Chargé d'affaires, Abdulmuhaimen al-Oraibi

BRITISH EMBASSY
International Zone, Baghdad
T (+964) 790 192 6280 E britembbaghdad@fco.gov.uk
W http://ukiniraq.fco.gov.uk
Ambassador Extraordinary and Plenipotentiary, HE Michael Aron, CMG, LVO, *apptd* 2011

BRITISH COUNCIL
c/o British Embassy, International Zone, Baghdad *(post should be sent to Amman, Jordan office)*
T (+962) 790 191 1971 W www.britishcouncil.org/iraq
Director, Brendan McSharry

DEFENCE
Iraq's armed forces were officially disbanded by the coalition provisional authority in May 2003. Since then, new Iraqi security forces have been recruited and trained by coalition troops. The army has 212 main battle tanks, 434 armoured infantry fighting vehicles and 1,479 armoured personnel carriers. The navy has over 38 patrol and coastal combatant vessels, based at Umm Qasr.

Military budget – US$4,900m (2010)
Military personnel – 245,782: army 238,010, navy 2,605, air force 5,167, Ministry of Interior forces 413,613

ECONOMY AND TRADE
The economy suffered three decades of state intervention, mismanagement, corruption, militarisation, war and international sanctions as well as the looting, insurgency and sabotage that followed the 2003 Allied invasion. With the improvement in the security situation, economic activity has increased, the institutions required to implement economic policy are being put in place and a debt reduction programme has been arranged. However, regulatory restrictions, inadequate infrastructure and corruption hamper economic development, and unemployment remains high (over 15 per cent).

Oil is the main resource and export, and production has returned to pre-2003 levels. Other industries include chemicals, textiles, construction materials, food processing and metal fabrication.

The main trading partners are the USA (28 per cent of exports), Turkey (25 per cent of imports), Syria and India. Principal exports are crude oil (84 per cent), other crude materials, food and livestock. The main imports are food, medicine and manufactured goods.
GNI – US$61,838m; US$2,210 per capita (2009)
Annual average growth of GDP – 5.5 per cent (2010 est)
Inflation rate – 4.2 per cent (2010 est)
Population below poverty line – 25 per cent (2008 est)
Total external debt – US$52,580m (2010 est)

BALANCE OF PAYMENTS
Trade – US$19,077m surplus (2010)
Current Account – US$13,886m surplus (2008)

Trade with UK	2009	2010
Imports from UK	£163,433,684	£194,430,226
Exports to UK	£620,704	£2,190,965

COMMUNICATIONS
The transport infrastructure was severely damaged during the wars in 1991 and 2003, and subsequent security problems have slowed reconstruction. Key bridges, airports and ports, including the main seaport at Basra, have been repaired and reopened. The main international airport is at Baghdad; the national carrier, Iraqi Airways, was dissolved by the government in 2010 in an attempt to end a dispute with Kuwait Airways over reparations claimed for the alleged theft of planes and spare parts during Iraq's invasion of the country in 1990. There are 44,900km of roads and 2,272km of railways; train services between Baghdad and Basra resumed in 2008. The 5,279km of waterways are primarily on the Tigris and Euphrates rivers.

The telephone system was badly disrupted in 2003 but is being repaired with greater capacity. Mobile phone services are expanding rapidly. There were 1.1 million fixed lines in use, 20 million mobile phone subscribers and 326,000 internet users in 2009.

EDUCATION AND HEALTH
Since 2003 the country's education system has been reviewed, and over 2,500 schools have been refurbished. Primary education is compulsory.
Literacy rate – 74.1 per cent (2008 est)
Gross enrolment ratio (percentage of relevant age group) – primary 103 per cent; secondary 51 per cent (2007 est)

Health expenditure (per capita) – US$98 (2009)
Hospital beds (per 1,000 people) – 1.3 (2004–9)

MEDIA

Once strictly controlled, the media has begun to flourish since 2003, although dozens of media workers have been killed in the insurgency and by coalition military actions. However, regulations introduced in 2009 require media workers to obtain work permits and introduced US$5,000 (around £3,000) licence fees for all broadcast media, measures that raised concern about the government's attitude to media freedom. There are more than 100 newspapers and periodicals, many with an ethnic or religious affiliation, and private radio and television stations have also begun to thrive. International broadcasts from Dubai, Iran, the USA and Europe are widely available. The television and radio stations set up by the coalition provisional authority now form part of the publicly funded Iraqi Public Broadcasting Service. Satellite television is very popular, attracting around 70 per cent of Iraqi viewers. In the autonomous Kurdish areas, rival factions operate their own media outlets.

IRELAND

Eire – Ireland

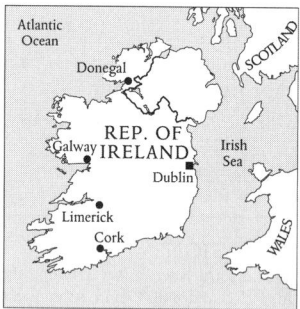

Area – 70,273 sq. km
Capital – Dublin *(Baile Átha Cliath)*; population, 1,084,160 (2009 est)
Major cities – Cork (Corcaigh), Galway (Gaillimh), Limerick (Liumneach), Swords (Sord Cholm Cille), Waterford (Port Láirge)
Currency – Euro (€) of 100 cents
Population – 4,622,917 rising at 1.01 per cent a year (2010 est)
Religion – Christian (Roman Catholic 87 per cent, Anglican 3 per cent, Presbyterian 1 per cent), Muslim 1 per cent (est)
Language – English, Irish (Gaelic) (both official)
Population density – 65 per sq. km (2009)
Urban population – 61 per cent (2008 est)
Median age (years) – 34.5 (2010 est)
National anthem – 'Amhran na bhFiann' ['The Soldier's Song']
National day – 17 March (St Patrick's Day)
Life expectancy (years) – 80.07 (2010 est)
Mortality rate – 6.3 (2010 est)
Birth rate – 16.37 (2010 est)
Infant mortality rate – 3.89 (2010 est)
Death penalty – Abolished for all crimes (since 1990)
CPI score – 8 (2010)

CLIMATE AND TERRAIN

The greatest length of the island of Ireland is 486km, from Torr Head in the north-east to Mizen Head in the south-west, and the greatest breadth is 280km, from Dundrum Bay in the east to Annagh Head in the west. Northern Ireland, in the north-east, is part of the UK. The republic has a central plain broken by hills and numerous lakes and bogs. It is surrounded by low mountains, including the Wicklow, Knockmealdown, Galty and Boggeragh mountains, and drained by the principal river, the Shannon (386km), which flows into the Atlantic Ocean. On the north coast of Achill Island (Co. Mayo) are the highest cliffs in the British Isles, 609m above sea level. Elevation extremes range from 1,041m (Carrauntoohil, Co. Kerry) to 0m (Irish Sea).

HISTORY AND POLITICS

Settled by the Celts around 300 BC, Ireland developed a distinct culture that remained largely intact until Christianity was introduced in the fifth century AD, after which Christian Ireland became a centre of learning and high culture. Viking raiders began sustained attacks *c*.800 and established settlements from the mid-ninth century. In the 12th century, Anglo-Norman barons, invited to Ireland by a Gaelic king seeking allies, brought much of the south under their own control, and Henry II of England declared himself Lord of Ireland in 1171. The island was unified under English control during Elizabeth I's reign. From the early 17th century, England began to promote the settlement of Protestant Scots in the north-eastern kingdom of Ulster, the last stronghold of Celtic power. This policy produced a long-standing antagonism between the north's Protestant and Roman Catholic populations.

In the mid-17th century, widespread support in Ireland for the royalist side in the English Civil War prompted bloody reprisals from Oliver Cromwell, who reasserted English control of Ireland in 1649–50. Irish support for the deposed Catholic king James II was defeated by William III at the Battle of the Boyne (1690) and penal laws passed in 1695 suppressed Catholic wealth and power. Popular discontent in the late 18th century and a rebellion in 1798 led to the abolition of the Irish parliament by the Act of Union (1800), which united Britain and Ireland. Simultaneously, Catholic opposition to English rule became increasingly organised with the formation of the Catholic Association, but agitation for home rule failed until 1912, when legislation was passed but did not come into effect because of the First World War.

By 1916, demands in some quarters had shifted from home rule to independence from Britain, and a rebellion (the 'Easter Rising') broke out in Dublin. It was repressed by the British but inspired Irish nationalists to contest the 1918 elections and, on gaining a majority of the Irish seats, to declare Irish independence. Britain's attempt to suppress the nationalists by force led to the Anglo-Irish War (1919–21), which was concluded by a treaty giving Ireland internal self-government as the Irish Free State, with dominion status within the Commonwealth, but leaving as part of the UK the six predominantly Protestant counties in the north-east. Opposition to the partition by some nationalists developed into civil war in 1922–3. In 1937, the Irish Free State declared itself independent and sovereign, and in 1948 it left the Commonwealth and became a republic.

The status of Northern Ireland remained divisive, with the partition unacknowledged by the Irish constitution of 1937. The Anglo-Irish agreement in 1985 gave the Irish government a consultative role in the government of Northern Ireland, and in 1993 the Downing Street declaration set out a joint Anglo-Irish peace proposal to end the conflict in the north. The Irish government was involved in the negotiation of the 1998 Good Friday agreement; its proposals, including Irish recognition of the partition and the right of the north to self-determination, were approved in a referendum by 94 per cent of voters in the republic.

Ireland joined the EC in 1973 and the eurozone in 1999.

The 1997 presidential election was won by Mary McAleese, and she was confirmed in office unopposed in 2004. The coalition government of the Fianna Fail, Progressive Democrats and Green Party lost the early election called in February 2011 because of the country's economic crisis. The opposition Fine Gail (FG) won the most seats but without a majority, and formed a coalition government with the Labour Party; the FG leader Enda Kenny was elected prime minister. A presidential election is due in October 2011.

POLITICAL SYSTEM
Under the 1937 constitution, the president *(Uachtaran na Eireann)* is directly elected for a seven-year term, renewable once. The bicameral National Parliament *(Oireachtas)* consists of the House of Representatives *(Dail Eireann)* and the senate *(Seanad Eireann)*. The *Dail* has 166 members, elected for a five-year term by proportional representation. The *Seanad* has 60 members, who serve a five-year term; of these, 11 are nominated by the prime minister *(Taoiseach)* and 49 are elected, six by the universities and 43 from panels of candidates representing various sectoral interests.

The *Taoiseach* is appointed by the president on the nomination of the *Dail,* while other members of the government are appointed by the president on the nomination of the *Taoiseach* with the previous approval of the *Dail.* The *Taoiseach* appoints a member of the government to be the deputy prime minister *(Tanaiste).*

HEAD OF STATE
President, Mary McAleese, *elected* 30 October 1997, *confirmed in office* 1 October 2004

SELECTED GOVERNMENT MEMBERS *as at June 2011*
Taoiseach (Prime Minister), Enda Kenny
Tanaiste (Deputy PM), Foreign Affairs, Eamon Gilmore
Defence, Alan Shatter
Finance, Michael Noonan

EMBASSY OF IRELAND
17 Grosvenor Place, London SW1X 7HR
T 020-7235 2171 W www.embassyofireland.co.uk
Ambassador Extraordinary and Plenipotentiary, HE Bobby McDonagh, *apptd* 2009

BRITISH EMBASSY
29 Merrion Road, Ballsbridge, Dublin 4
T (+353) (1) 205 3700 W britishembassyinireland.fco.gov.uk
Ambassador Extraordinary and Plenipotentiary, HE Julian King, CMG, *apptd* 2009

BRITISH COUNCIL
Newmount House, 22/24 Lower Mount Street, Dublin 2
T (+353) (1) 676 4088 W www.britishcouncil.org/ireland
Director, Matt Burney

DEFENCE
The army has 67 armoured personnel carriers. The navy has 8 patrol and coastal combatant vessels at 2 bases. The air force has 6 multi-role helicopters.
Military budget – US$1,200m (2010)
Military personnel – 10,460: army 8,500, navy 1,110, air force 850

ECONOMY AND TRADE
Since the 1980s Ireland's economy has been transformed from a mainly agricultural to a modern, export-led economy that experienced strong growth from the mid-1990s. But an over-inflated property sector and high levels of personal debt left the economy exposed in the 2008 global financial crisis, causing it to contract rapidly and go into a deep recession which put severe pressure on the financial system and government finances. Stabilisation of the financial system pushed the budget deficit to nearly 32 per cent of GDP in 2010, despite austerity budgets in 2009 and 2010, and in November 2010 the government agreed loan packages with the IMF and EU to avoid defaulting on its sovereign debt.

Agriculture now accounts for 2 per cent of GDP and 5 per cent of employment; services contribute 70 per cent and industry 29 per cent of GDP, and the sectors account for 76 per cent and 20 per cent of employment respectively. Major industries include mining, pharmaceuticals, chemicals, computer hardware and software, food and drink production, and tourism. Although the Kinsale gas field off the south coast meets some of Ireland's gas needs, and hydroelectric power is generated from the Shannon barrage and other schemes, the country is a net importer of energy.

The main trading partners are other EU countries and the USA. Principal exports are machinery, computers, chemicals, pharmaceuticals, livestock and livestock products. The main imports are data processing equipment, other machinery, chemicals, petroleum and petroleum products, textiles and clothing.
GNI – US$184,447m; US$44,280 per capita (2009)
Annual average growth of GDP – –0.6 per cent (2010 est)
Inflation rate – –1.5 per cent (2010 est)
Population below poverty line – 4.2 per cent (2008 est)
Unemployment – 13.7 per cent (2010 est)
Total external debt – US$2,131,000m (2010)
Imports – US$62,400m (2009)
Exports – US$115,900m (2009)

BALANCE OF PAYMENTS
Trade – US$59,292m surplus (2010)
Current Account – US$6,705m deficit (2009)

Trade with UK	2009	2010
Imports from UK	£15,295,838,653	£16,316,524,067
Exports to UK	£12,246,224,617	£12,814,052,101

COMMUNICATIONS
Ireland has 96,036km of roads and 3,237km of railways. There are over 950km of waterways, although these are used only by leisure craft. The main ports are Cork, Dun Laoghaire, Galway, Limerick and Waterford. The principal airport is at Dublin, with others at Shannon, Waterford, Cork, Killarney, Galway and Knock. There were 2 million fixed telephone lines in use, 5 million mobile subscribers and 3 million internet users in 2009.

EDUCATION AND HEALTH

Primary education is directed by the state, with the exception of several private primary schools. Education is compulsory until age 16.

Gross enrolment ratio (percentage of relevant age group) – primary 105 per cent; secondary 115 per cent; tertiary 58 per cent (2008 est)
Health expenditure (per capita) – US$4,952 (2009)
Hospital beds (per 1,000 people) – 5.2 (2004–9)

MEDIA

Irish broadcasting is regulated by a commission appointed by the Department of Communications. The main radio and television broadcaster is the state-run Raidio Telefis Eireann (RTE), whose competitors include a handful of Irish commercial stations and British terrestrial and satellite services. There are three national newspapers: the *Irish Times, Irish Independent* and *Irish Examiner*.

CULTURE

Given its size, Ireland has a disproportionately rich literary history, having produced four Nobel prize-winners: poets W. B. Yeats (1865–1939) and Seamus Heaney (b. 1939), dramatist George Bernard Shaw (1856–1950), and novelist, poet and playwright Samuel Beckett (1906–89). Other great writers include Jonathan Swift (1667–1745), Bram Stoker (1847–1912), Oscar Wilde (1854–1900) and James Joyce (1882–1941).

Traditional forms of sport and music remain popular. Hurling and Gaelic football are passionately supported, as are rugby and football. Similarly, musicians adopting and adapting traditional music, such as the Pogues, Clannad and Enya (b. 1961), have achieved international success, alongside rock groups U2 and Thin Lizzy and boybands Westlife and Boyzone.

ISRAEL AND PALESTINIAN TERRITORIES

Medinat Yisra'el/Dawlat Isra'il – State of Israel

Area – 20,072 sq. km (includes Jerusalem and the Golan Heights)
Capital – The legislature and most government departments are in Jerusalem; population 767,634 (2009 est). A resolution proclaiming Jerusalem as the capital of Israel was adopted by the *Knesset* in 1950. It is not, however, recognised as the capital by the UN because East Jerusalem is part of the Occupied Territories captured in 1967; the UN and international law continues to consider the pre-1950 capital Tel Aviv (population, 392,500) to be the capital

Major cities – Haifa; Rishon Le'Zion
Currency – New Israeli Shekel (NIS) of 100 agora
Population – 7,353,985 rising at 1.63 per cent a year (2010 est); includes about 508,600 settlers in the occupied areas. Since independence, Israel has had a policy of granting an immigration visa to every Jew who expresses a desire to settle in the country; between 1948 and 2009, over 3 million immigrants entered Israel from over 100 different countries
Religion – Jewish 76 per cent (of which secular 44 per cent, 'traditional religious' or 'traditional non-religious' 39 per cent, Orthodox 10 per cent, *Haredi* 7 per cent), Muslim 16.5 per cent (predominantly Sunni; Druze 2 per cent), Christian 2 per cent (predominantly Eastern Orthodox) (est)
Language – Hebrew, Arabic (both official), English
Population density – 344 per sq. km (2009)
Urban population – 92 per cent (2008 est)
Median age (years) – 29.3 (2010 est)
National anthem – 'Hatikvah' ['The Hope']
National day – fifth day of Jewish month of Iyar (anniversary of Independence Day, 1948); falls on 25 April in 2012
Life expectancy (years) – 80.86 (2010 est)
Mortality rate – 5.45 (2010 est)
Birth rate – 19.51 (2010 est)
Infant mortality rate – 4.17 (2010 est)
Death penalty – Retained for certain crimes (last used 1962)
CPI score – 6.1 (2010)

CLIMATE AND TERRAIN

Israel comprises the partly forested hill country of Galilee and parts of Judea and Samaria, the coastal plain from the Gaza Strip to north of Acre (including the plain of Esdraelon running from Haifa Bay to the south-east); the Negev, a triangular rocky desert in the south; and parts of the Jordan valley, including the Hula region, Lake Tiberias and the south-western part of the Dead Sea. Elevation extremes range from 1,208m (Har Meron) at the highest point to –408m (Dead Sea) at the lowest, which is the Earth's deepest depression. The climate is temperate, with hotter, drier conditions in the south and east. Average temperatures in Tel Aviv range from 14°C in January to 27°C in August.

HISTORY AND POLITICS

Regarded by Jews as their homeland since the Israelite settlement in Old Testament times, Palestine was conquered by the Babylonians, the Greeks and the Romans between the sixth and first centuries BC, beginning the diaspora. Conquered by Muslim Arabs in the seventh century AD, the area was contested between Muslims and Christians during the Crusades before becoming part of the Ottoman Empire in the 16th century.

Zionist settlement in Palestine began in the 1880s and the British declared support for a Jewish homeland there in 1917 after capturing much of the Middle East from the Ottoman Empire during the First World War. Britain administered the area under a League of Nations mandate from 1918 to 1948, during which period Jewish immigration from Europe was encouraged, but this resulted in tension with the Arab population of Palestine, who had also been promised recognition of an Arab state by the British.

After the Second World War, the British mandate became increasingly untenable and it withdrew in 1948.

The UN voted to partition Palestine, creating a Jewish and an Arab state, but the proposal was rejected by the Arabs, prompting the Jews to announce the creation of the independent State of Israel on 14 May 1948. This led to a ten-month war, the first of a series of conflicts between Israel and neighbouring Arab states. Further conflict occurred in 1956, when Israel attacked Egypt's Suez Canal zone; in 1967 (the Six-Day War) when Israel gained control of the Gaza Strip, the Sinai peninsula, the West Bank and east Jerusalem, and the Golan Heights in Syria (the 'Occupied Territories'); in 1973, when Egypt and Syria attempted to regain their lost territory; and in 1982, when Israel invaded Lebanon to drive Palestinian guerrillas out of Beirut, occupying a buffer zone in the south until 2000. Southern Lebanon was the scene of further conflict in 2006, when Israeli forces attempted to dislodge Hezbollah guerrillas. The 1978 Camp David talks led to a peace treaty with Egypt in 1979, as a result of which Israel withdrew from Sinai. A peace treaty was signed with Jordan in 1994.

Israel has also experienced decades of internal violence by Palestinians seeking to recover land and property lost in 1948, and to end Israeli occupation of the territories taken in 1967. The Palestine Liberation Organisation (PLO), under Yasser Arafat, began a guerrilla war and terrorist campaign in the 1960s. A more widespread popular uprising *(intifada)* in the Gaza Strip and West Bank began in 1987 and lasted until 1993, when talks between Israel and the PLO resulted in the Oslo accords, which set out interim self-government arrangements for Palestinian areas until a final settlement was reached. Implementation began with the establishment of the Palestinian Autonomous Areas in 1994 and their extension in 1995. The security situation deteriorated again from the mid-1990s, with further violence evoking an increasingly hard line from a new Israeli government already critical of the peace accords. Implementation of the Oslo accords stalled and negotiations on outstanding issues reached deadlock. A second *intifada* began in 2000, and in 2002 Israel began building a security wall between Jewish and Palestinian areas despite international protests at this *de facto* partitioning of the country.

In 2003, the USA, Russia, the EU and the UN proposed a 'road map' for peace which envisioned a two-state solution to the conflict, but little progress was made until 2004. The Israeli government fulfilled a key undertaking – the evacuation and dismantling of Jewish settlements in, and military disengagement from, the Gaza Strip in 2005 – but refused to negotiate with the militant Palestinian government elected in 2006. After a Palestinian power struggle in 2007 led to the creation of rival administrations in Gaza and the West Bank, Israel resumed talks with the West Bank administration headed by President Abbas, but it has continued its tight blockade of Gaza and its retaliation to attacks from the territory. The Israeli military invasion of Gaza in December 2008 caused talks to be broken off. They were revived briefly in 2010 before foundering on the government's failure to renew a ban on construction of Jewish settlements in the West Bank.

The 2007 presidential election was won by Shimon Peres. In September 2008, Tzipi Livni was elected head of the governing Kadima party but her attempts to form a new coalition were unsuccessful and an election was held in February 2009. Although Kadima won 28 seats to Likud's 27 seats, Likud succeeded in forming a coalition government with the Labour party and three smaller parties under Benjamin Netanyahu; the government took office in March 2009.

POLITICAL SYSTEM
There is no written constitution; most constitutional provision is set out in the basic law on government. The head of state is the president, elected by the legislature for a seven-year term, which is not renewable. The unicameral *Knesset* has 120 members elected by proportional representation for a four-year term. The prime minister is responsible to the *Knesset,* and appoints the cabinet, subject to the approval of the *Knesset.*

HEAD OF STATE
President, Shimon Peres, *elected* 13 June 2007, *sworn in* 15 July 2007

SELECTED GOVERNMENT MEMBERS *as at June 2011*
Prime Minister, Benjamin Netanyahu
Vice Prime Ministers, Silvan Shalom; Moshe Ya'alon
Deputy Prime Ministers, Ehud Barak *(Defence);* Avigdor Liberman *(Foreign Affairs);* Dan Meridor; Eliyahu Yishai *(Interior)*
Finance, Yuval Steinitz

EMBASSY OF ISRAEL
2 Palace Green, London W8 4QB
T 020-7957 9500 E info@london.mfa.gov.il
W http://london.mfa.gov.il
Ambassador Extraordinary and Plenipotentiary, HE Ron Prosor, *apptd* 2007

BRITISH EMBASSY
1 Ben Yehuda Street, Migdalor Building, 15th Floor, Tel Aviv 63801
T (+972) (3) 725 1222 E webmaster.telaviv@fco.gov.uk
W http://ukinisrael.fco.gov.uk
Ambassador Extraordinary and Plenipotentiary, HE Matthew Gould, MBE, *apptd* 2010

BRITISH COUNCIL
PO Box 3302, Beit HaCrystal, 12 Hahilazon Street, Ramat Gan 52136
T (+972) (3) 611 3600 W www.britishcouncil.org/israel
Director, Simon Kay

DEFENCE
Israel is believed to have a nuclear capability of around 200 warheads, which could be delivered by aircraft or *Jericho* I and II missiles. The army has 3,501 main battle tanks and over 10,484 armoured personnel carriers. The navy has 3 submarines and 57 patrol and coastal vessels at 4 bases. The air force has 460 combat aircraft and 81 armed helicopters.
Military expenditure – US$15,600m (2010)
Military personnel – 176,500: army 133,000, navy 9,500, air force 34,000; paramilitary 8,050
Conscription duration – 24–48 months (Jews and Druze only; Christians, Circassians and Muslims may volunteer)

ECONOMY AND TRADE
Israel has a technically advanced market economy, having developed its agriculture and industry intensively since the 1970s despite limited natural resources. After a short recession in the early 2000s, structural reforms and tighter fiscal control were implemented, resulting in steady growth from 2003 to 2007, increased foreign

investment and a rising demand for exports. Despite the high level of external debt, the economy proved resilient in the global downturn, although it contracted slightly in 2008–9. Its debt and deficits are covered by foreign aid and loans; the USA is the main source of economic and military aid and is Israel's main creditor, owed about half of its external debt.

Israel has developed a strong technology sector, central to which are the aviation, electronics, biotechnology, communications and software industries. Other important industries include timber and paper, mineral and metal products, cement, chemicals, plastics, textiles, diamond cutting and tourism, which is reviving. The country is also an important producer of citrus fruits, vegetables, cotton, beef, poultry and dairy products. Service industries account for 65 per cent of GDP, industry for 32.6 per cent and agriculture for 2.4 per cent.

The main trading partners are the USA (35 per cent of exports), Belgium, other EU states and China. Principal exports are high-technology machinery and equipment, software, cut diamonds, agricultural products, chemicals, textiles and clothing. The main imports are raw materials, military equipment, investment goods, rough diamonds, fuels, grain and consumer goods.

GNI – US$190,808m; US$25,790 per capita (2009)
Annual average growth of GDP – 3.4 per cent (2010 est)
Inflation rate – 2.6 per cent (2010 est)
Population below poverty line – 23.6 per cent (2007; defined as less than US$7.30 per day)
Unemployment – 6.4 per cent (2010 est)
Total external debt – US$89,680m (2010)
Imports – US$49,300m (2009)
Exports – US$47,900m (2009)

BALANCE OF PAYMENTS
Trade – US$5,091m deficit (2009)
Current Account – US$7,191m surplus (2009)

Trade with UK	2009	2010
Imports from UK	£1,098,885,933	£1,333,199,223
Exports to UK	£974,263,067	£1,465,322,511

COMMUNICATIONS
Israel State Railways operates a network of 975km, serving the main cities and towns. There are 18,290km of roads, including 146km of motorway. A major road-building programme has been under way in the West Bank since 1992. The chief seaports are Haifa and Ashdod on the Mediterranean, and Eilat on the Red Sea; Acre has an anchorage for small vessels. There are 48 airports and airfields; the chief international airport is Ben Gurion, between Tel Aviv and Jerusalem. Israel's flag-carrier is *El Al* airlines. The highly developed telephone system provides services for 3.2 million fixed-line users, 9 million mobile phone subscribers and 4.5 million internet users.

EDUCATION AND HEALTH
Education is compulsory between the ages of five and 16 and is free.
Literacy rate – 97.1 per cent (2008 est)
Gross enrolment ratio (percentage of relevant age group) – primary 111 per cent; secondary 90 per cent; tertiary 60 per cent (2008 est)
Health expenditure (per capita) – US$1,966 (2009)
Hospital beds (per 1,000 people) – 5.8 (2004–9)

MEDIA AND CULTURE
The Israeli Broadcasting Authority (IBA) is a public broadcaster operating television and radio services funded largely by a licence fee. It competes with two main terrestrial commercial channels and a number of satellite and cable stations. The IBA's radio stations have faced commercial competition since 1995; there are also a large number of unlicensed radio stations. There are five national daily newspapers, all privately owned.

In Palestinian areas, the Palestinian Broadcasting Corporation runs television and radio services in competition with dozens of domestic and foreign private stations. There are two private daily newspapers, one affiliated with Hamas, and one published by the Palestinian National Authority. Palestinian media workers face intimidation and violence at the hands of both the Israeli military and Palestinian groups. Self-censorship is common.

Jerusalem has a vast number of historic sites, including the Church of the Holy Sepulchre, sacred to Christians, and the al-Aqsa Mosque, which stands on the Temple Mount. The Israel Museum in the city houses the Dead Sea Scrolls.

PALESTINIAN AUTONOMOUS AREAS

Area – The total area is 6,231 sq. km. The area which is fully autonomous is 412 sq. km, of which the Gaza Strip is 352 sq. km and the Jericho enclave 60 sq. km
Capital – Although Palestinians claim East Jerusalem as their capital, the administrative capital was established in 1994 in Gaza City; population 479,400 (2005 est); since 2007 the president and transitional government have been located in Ramallah, on the West Bank; population, 69,479 (2009 est)
Major towns – Jabalia, Khan Yunis, Rafah in the Gaza Strip; Hebron, Jericho, Nablus and Ramallah on the West Bank
Population – 4,119,083 (2003 est)
Religion – Muslim 98 per cent (predominantly Sunni); small Jewish and Christian minorities (est)
Flag – Three horizontal stripes of black, white, green with a red triangle based on the hoist (the PLO flag)
National anthem – 'Fidai, Fidai' ['Freedom Fighter, Freedom Fighter']
Death penalty – Retained
Literacy rate – 93.8 per cent (2007 est)

HISTORY AND POLITICS
Since 1967 the West Bank and Gaza Strip have been under Israeli occupation and until 1994 were administered by the Israeli ministry of defence. Frustration at continued Israeli occupation led to a popular uprising *(intifada)* from 1987 until the mid 1990s, when talks between Israel and the Palestinian Liberation Organisation (PLO) resulted in the Oslo accords (1993–5), which set out interim self-government arrangements for Palestinian areas until a final settlement was reached; the 1993 provisions were intended to be for a five-year interim period during which the final status of the West Bank, Gaza and Jerusalem was to be resolved.

The Gaza Strip and the town of Jericho on the West Bank were handed over to the Palestinian National Authority (PNA) in 1994, and six West Bank towns and most of Hebron in 1995. The final status talks opened in 1996, but stalled in the late 1990s and broke down in 2001. Efforts to restart negotiations were hindered by the election of Israeli governments critical of the peace accords, and the outbreak of the second *intifada* in 2000.

In 2003, the USA, Russia, the EU and the UN proposed the 'road map' peace plan, a staged process leading to the establishment of an autonomous Palestinian state by 2005, which also sought political reforms in the PNA. Although endorsed by most parties, implementation of the peace plan made little progress because of the continuing *intifada*, internal power struggles within the Palestinian administration and the refusal of Israel and the USA to negotiate with the Palestinian president Yasser Arafat. This stalemate was broken only by the death of Arafat in 2004 and the election of a moderate as his successor. Talks with Israel resumed but the peace process continued to be jeopardised by the Palestinian authorities' inability to rein in the violence of extremists, and it stalled in early 2006 with the victory of the Islamist group Hamas in the Palestinian legislative election; Hamas refused to renounce violence, to recognise Israel's right to exist or to abide by existing peace agreements with Israel, which led international donors to cut off funding, causing increasingly severe hardship, especially in Gaza.

The 2005 presidential election was won by the Fatah candidate Mahmoud Abbas. In the 2006 legislative election, the Hamas movement, regarded by many countries as a terrorist organisation, won the most seats and formed the new government. Relations between Hamas and the more moderate Fatah, always tense, often became violent in 2006–7 and in June 2007 descended into a near civil war that left Hamas in control of the Gaza Strip and Fatah in control of the West Bank areas. In June 2007, President Abbas declared a state of emergency and dissolved the unity government appointed in March 2007, subsequently appointing a new, transitional government. Hamas politicians rejected the dissolution of the unity government and called for further talks. Talks in 2009 were unsuccessful and the 2010 elections were postponed, with the mandates of the president and parliament being extended. Fresh talks in spring 2011 led to an accord, signed in May 2011, under which a unity government will be formed until elections are held.

In the Hamas-controlled Gaza Strip, confrontation with Israel escalated from 2007 and resulted in an Israeli aerial bombardment and military invasion from December 2008 to January 2009. The Israeli blockade of Gaza was tightened further, and the population of Gaza experienced extreme hardship until Egypt opened its border in May 2011. Talks between President Abbas and the Israeli government resumed in 2007, but were broken off in early 2008 because of Israel's invasion of Gaza. Talks resumed briefly in 2010 but broke down after the Israeli government allowed Jewish settlement in the West Bank to continue.

POLITICAL SYSTEM

The Interim Agreement of 1995 invested the Palestinian Authority with executive, legislative and judicial authority, but not sovereignty, in the autonomous areas.

The executive president is directly elected for a five-year term. The unicameral Palestinian Legislative Council (*Majlis al-Tashri'i*) has one seat reserved for the president and 132 seats for members elected from party lists for a five-year term. The president appoints the prime minister, who appoints the council of ministers, which must be approved by the legislature.

SELECTED GOVERNMENT MEMBERS *as at June 2011*
President, Mahmoud Abbas, *elected* 9 January 2005
Prime Minister, Finance, Salam Khaled Abdallah Fayyad
Interior, Sa'id Abu Ali
Foreign Affairs, Riyad Najib Abd-al-Rahman al-Maliki

PALESTINIAN GENERAL DELEGATION
5 Galena Road, London W6 0LT
T 020-8563 0008 W www.palestiniangd.org.uk
General Delegate, Prof. Manuel Hassassian

BRITISH CONSULATE-GENERAL
PO Box 19690, 19 Nashashibi Street, Sheikh Jarrah Quarter, East Jerusalem 97200
T (+972) (2) 541 4100 W http://ukinjerusalem.fco.gov.uk
Consul-General, Sir Vincent Fean, KCVO, *apptd* 2010

BRITISH COUNCIL
PO Box 19136, 31 Nablus Road, East Jerusalem 97200
T (+972) (2) 626 7111 W www.britishcouncil.org/ps
Director, Sandra Hamrouni

ECONOMY AND TRADE

The *intifada*, and Israeli security restrictions in response to it, have damaged infrastructure and severely constrained economic activity in the Palestinian areas and external trade since 2000. Incomes had dropped and poverty risen sharply even before 2006, when the policies of the new Hamas government led to an embargo by international funding providers, and Israel stopped remitting customs dues collected on behalf of the Palestinian Authority. Emergency aid, provided through channels that bypass the Hamas government, was resumed in late 2006. The effects were and remain most severe in Gaza, where the population is dependent on food aid. On the West Bank, some Israeli restrictions have been eased since 2007, and the president's economic and structural reforms since 2008, underpinned by foreign aid donors, have stimulated economic development.

Most economic activity consists of small family businesses engaged in farming, quarrying and small-scale manufacturing of construction materials and textiles, metal goods, handicrafts and agricultural processing. The main exports are stone, fruit, olives, vegetables and flowers, and the main trading partners are Israel, Jordan and Egypt.

Inflation rate – 9.9 per cent (2009 est)
Population below poverty line – West Bank 46 per cent (2007 est); Gaza Strip 70 per cent (2009 est)

Trade with UK	2009	2010
Imports from UK	£1,670,663	£1,622,039
Exports to UK	£656,319	£884,571

ITALY

Repubblica Italiana – Italian Republic

Area – 301,340 sq. km

Capital – Rome; population, 3,357,470 (2009 est).
The 'Eternal City' was founded, according to legend, by Romulus in 753 BC. It was the centre of the Latin civilisation and capital of the Roman republic and empire

Major cities – Bari, Bologna, Florence, Genoa, Milan, Naples, Turin, Venice, Verona. The chief town of Sicily is Palermo, and of Sardinia is Cagliari

Currency – Euro (€) of 100 cents

Population – 58,090,681 falling at 0.08 per cent a year (2010 est)

Religion – Christian (Roman Catholic 87 per cent) (est)

Language – Italian (official), German, French, Slovene

Population density – 205 per sq. km (2009)

Urban population – 68 per cent (2008 est)

Median age (years) – 43.7 (2010 est)

National anthem – 'L'Inno di Mameli' ['Mameli's Hymn']

National day – 2 June (Republic Day)

Life expectancy (years) – 80.33 (2010 est)

Mortality rate – 10.83 (2010 est)

Birth rate – 8.01 (2010 est)

Infant mortality rate – 5.41 (2010 est)

Death penalty – Abolished for all crimes (since 1994)

CPI score – 3.9 (2010)

CLIMATE AND TERRAIN

Italy consists of a peninsula, the islands of Sicily, Sardinia, Elba and about 70 smaller islands. The smaller islands include Pantelleria, the Pelagian islands, the Aeolian islands, Capri, the Flegrean islands, the Pontine archipelago, the Tremiti islands and the Tuscan archipelago. Most of the islands are mountainous.

The peninsula is also largely mountainous, but between the spine of the Apennines and the eastern coastline are two large fertile plains: Emilia-Romagna in the north and Apulia in the south. Italy is divided from France and Switzerland by the Alps, and from Austria and Slovenia by both the Alps and the Dolomites. Three volcanoes, Vesuvius, Etna and Stromboli, are still active. Elevation extremes range from 4,748m (Mt Bianco di Courmayeur) at the highest point to 0m (Mediterranean Sea) at the lowest. At the foot of the Alps lie the great lakes of Como, Maggiore and Garda. The chief rivers are the Po (651km) and the Adige, flowing through the northern plain to the Adriatic Sea, and the Arno (Florentine plain) and the Tiber (flowing through Rome to Ostia), which flow to the west coast. The climate is Mediterranean, with warm dry summers and mild winters.

HISTORY AND POLITICS

In pre-Roman times, the Italian peninsula was inhabited by the Etruscans in the north, the Latins in the centre and Greeks in the south, but by the third century BC most of it was part of the Roman Empire. At the height of its power, the Roman Empire included parts of western Europe, Asia Minor and north Africa. Conquered and settled by a variety of invaders after the fall of Rome, the peninsula developed into a number of competing city states. These, with their powerful and wealthy merchant classes, became the locations (and provided the capital) for the Renaissance. The country was divided between Austria, the Papal States, Naples, Sardinia and four duchies when Italian nationalists began to agitate for a unified Italy in the 19th century. The *Risorgimento* from 1848 united the northern states, culminating in the declaration of the Kingdom of Italy in 1861; unification was completed with the conquest of the Papal States in 1870.

In 1923, the Fascist leader Benito Mussolini seized power and promised a firm rule to end political instability. He committed Italy to an alliance with Nazi Germany and thus led Italy into the Second World War on the Axis side. The Allied invasion of Sicily in 1943 led to Mussolini's deposition; he was killed by partisans in April 1945. Italy became a republic in 1946 after voters narrowly approved the abolition of the monarchy in a referendum.

A post-war economic boom lasted until the late 1970s, when high inflation and unemployment occurred. This was a time of serious civil unrest, with unions opposed to often corrupt governments, and extreme right- and left-wing groups conducting violent campaigns. In the early 1990s, there was a drive to reform the political establishment after links were exposed between the government and organised crime; many politicians were arrested. In 1993, the electoral system was changed from proportional representation to majority voting in 75 per cent of the seats in an attempt to remedy the political instability that had resulted in 45 governments in 47 years. Although governments have continued to be coalitions, those of the past ten years have generally lasted longer. Corruption in public administration and business remains a problem.

Italy was a founding member of the EEC in 1957 and of the eurozone in 1999.

The 2006 presidential election was won, after four rounds of voting, by Giorgio Napolitano. In the 2008 legislative election, the People of Freedom party (PdL), with the support of the Northern League and the Movement for Autonomy, achieved a majority in both chambers. The PdL and Northern League formed a coalition government under PdL leader Silvio Berlusconi (prime minister 1994, 2001–6, 2008–), but the coalition lost its legislative majority in 2010 after a split in the PdL.

POLITICAL SYSTEM

The 1948 constitution has been amended several times, notably in 2001 to provide for greater autonomy for the 20 regions in tax, education and environment matters. The president, who must be over 50 years of age, is elected for a seven-year term by an electoral college consisting of both chambers of the legislature and 58 regional representatives. The bicameral *Parlamento* comprises a 630-member Chamber of Deputies and a senate with 315 members directly elected on a regional basis and a variable number of life senators, who are past presidents and senators appointed by incumbent presidents. Elected members of both chambers serve a five-year term.

HEAD OF STATE
President, Giorgio Napolitano, *elected* 11 May 2006, *took office* 15 May 2006

SELECTED GOVERNMENT MEMBERS *as at June 2011*
Prime Minister, Silvio Berlusconi
Foreign Affairs, Franco Frattini
Defence, Ignazio La Russa
Economy and Finance, Giulio Tremonti
Interior, Roberto Maroni

ITALIAN EMBASSY
14 Three Kings Yard, Davies Street, London W1K 4EH
T 020-7312 2200 E ambasciata.londra@esteri.it
W www.amblondra.esteri.it
Ambassador Extraordinary and Plenipotentiary, HE Alain Economides *apptd* 2010

BRITISH EMBASSY
Via XX Settembre 80a, I-00187 Rome
T (+39) (6) 4220 0001 W http://ukinitaly.fco.gov.uk
Ambassador Extraordinary and Plenipotentiary, HE Christopher Prentice, CMG, *apptd* 2011

BRITISH COUNCIL
Via di San Sebastianello 16, 00187 Rome
T (+39) (6) 478 141 W www.britishcouncil.org/italy
Director, Christine Melia

DEFENCE
The army has 320 main battle tanks, 243 armoured infantry fighting vehicles and 2,398 armoured personnel carriers. The navy has 6 submarines, 2 aircraft carriers, 4 destroyers, 12 frigates, 22 patrol and coastal vessels, 16 combat aircraft and 41 armed helicopters. The air force has 252 combat aircraft.
Military budget – US$20,500m (2010)
Military personnel – 184,609: army 107,500, navy 34,000, air force 43,109; paramilitary 142,330

ECONOMY AND TRADE
Economically, Italy is divided between a prosperous and industrially developed north and a largely agricultural and welfare-dependent south that has high unemployment levels. There is a large unofficial economy that is estimated to be worth 15 per cent of GDP, but measures to tackle this and wider structural reforms have made slow progress because of political opposition and sluggish economic performance. The growth rate has been low in recent years, and the global economic downturn caused a recession in 2008–9. A budget deficit that is above the 3 per cent eurozone limit and public debt of over 115 per cent of GDP has left the government struggling to service its debt.

Tourism is the largest industry. Other major industries include precision machinery, iron and steel, chemicals, food processing, textiles, motor vehicles, fashion clothing, footwear, ceramics and electrical goods. The services sector contributes 73.3 per cent of GDP, industry 24.9 per cent and agriculture 1.8 per cent. The main trading partners are other EU states, especially Germany and France. Principal exports are the products of the main industries, plus food, beverages, minerals and non-ferrous metals. The main imports are engineering and energy products, industrial raw materials and transport equipment.

GNI – US$2,076,253m; US$35,110 per capita (2009)
Annual average growth of GDP – 1.1 per cent (2010 est)
Inflation rate – 1.4 per cent (2010 est)
Unemployment – 8.4 per cent (2010 est)
Total external debt – US$2,223,000m (2010 est)
Imports – US$413,800m (2009)
Exports – US$406,200m (2009)

BALANCE OF PAYMENTS
Trade – US$36,575m deficit (2010)
Current Account – US$71,270m deficit (2009)

Trade with UK	2009	2010
Imports from UK	£8,251,001,265	£8,761,376,789
Exports to UK	£12,324,551,575	£14,188,652,849

COMMUNICATIONS
A 6,700km network of motorways *(autostrade)* covers the country but there are 487,700km of roads in total. There are 20,254km of railways; the main railway system is run by the state-owned *Ferrovia dello Stato.* In 2001, Italy and France agreed plans to build a 52km rail tunnel through the Alps as part of a high-speed rail link between Turin and Lyon; commissioning of the project is scheduled for 2012. Alitalia, Italy's state-owned international and domestic airline, went bankrupt in 2008, but was restructured and relaunched in 2009 under private ownership. There are 132 airports and airfields, the major ones being at Rome, Milan, Naples and Venice, Palermo and Catania (Sicily) and Cagliari (Sardinia). The main seaports are Naples, Genoa, Livorno, Trieste, Venice, Palermo and Catania. In 2009, there were 21.3 million fixed telephone lines in use, 90.6 million mobile phone subscribers and 29.2 million internet users.

EDUCATION AND HEALTH
Education is free and compulsory between the ages of six and 16. Pupils who obtain a middle school certificate may seek admission to any senior secondary school, which may be a lyceum with a classical or scientific or artistic bias, or an institute directed at technology, trade or industry, or teacher training. Courses at the lyceums and technical institutes usually last five years and success in the final examination qualifies students for admission to university. The universities at Bologna, Modena, Parma and Padua were established in the 12th century.
Literacy rate – 98.9 per cent (2008 est)
Gross enrolment ratio (percentage of relevant age group) – primary 103 per cent; secondary 101 per cent; tertiary 67 per cent (2008 est)
Health expenditure (per capita) – US$3,328 (2009)
Hospital beds (per 1,000 people) – 3.7 (2004–9)

MEDIA
Rai is Italy's public radio and television broadcaster and competes with a number of private television broadcasters, the leading one being Mediaset, part of the media empire of prime minister Silvio Berlusconi. News Corporation's Sky Italia has a virtual monopoly of the cable subscriptions market. There are around 2,500 commercial radio stations. The press is highly regionalised, although there are five national dailies, including *La Stampa* and *La Repubblica,* but readership is generally low, with television the primary source of news. In its 2010 Press Freedom Index, Reporters Without Borders expressed concern at the concentration of media ownership and the government's questionable treatment of journalists.

CULTURE

Florence, the capital of Tuscany, was the 'cradle' of the Renaissance in the 14th to 16th centuries; many of the greatest names in Italian art flourished there, including Donatello (1386–1466), Botticelli (1445–1510), Leonardo da Vinci (1452–1519) and Michelangelo (1475–1564), often under the patronage of the Medici family. Other significant artists include Titian (c.1490–1576), Caravaggio (1571–1610) and Modigliani (1884–1920).

Italy's wealth of composers includes Monteverdi (1567–1643), whose *Orfeo* (1607) is the oldest opera still regularly performed, Vivaldi (1678–1741), Verdi (1813–1901) and Puccini (1858–1924).

Dante Alighieri (1265–1321) and Boccaccio (1313–75) were two of the earliest Europeans to write in the vernacular. The works of the poet Petrarch (1304–74), politician Niccoló Machiavelli (1469–1527) and diplomat Baldassare Castiglione (1478–1529) strongly influenced other European writers. Notable modern writers include Primo Levi (1919–1987), Italo Calvino (1923–1985), Dario Fo (*b.* 1926), winner of the Nobel prize for literature in 1997, and Umberto Eco (*b.* 1932).

Italian cinema has produced world-renowned auteurs such as Luchino Visconti (1906–76), Federico Fellini (1920–93) and Michelangelo Antonioni (1912–2007). Director Sergio Leone (1929–89) and composer Ennio Morricone (*b.* 1928) are famed for their work on spaghetti westerns.

Football is the most popular sport and the country's national team has won the World Cup four times. Formula 1 motor racing also attracts significant interest and Ferrari has won more world championships than any other constructor.

JAMAICA

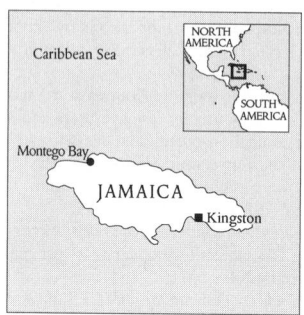

Area – 10,991 sq. km
Capital – Kingston; population, 579,642 (2009 est)
Major towns – Montego Bay, Portmore, Spanish Town
Currency – Jamaican dollar (J$) of 100 cents
Population – 2,847,232 rising at 0.75 per cent a year (2010 est)
Religion – Christian (Protestant 55 per cent, Roman Catholic 2 per cent, other 8 per cent), Rastafarian 1 per cent (est)
Language – English (official), Jamaican patois
Population density – 249 per sq. km (2009)
Urban population – 53 per cent (2008 est)
Median age (years) – 23.9 (2010 est)
National anthem – 'Jamaica, Land We Love'
National day – 6 August (Independence Day)
Life expectancy (years) – 73.48 (2010 est)

Mortality rate – 6.48 (2010 est)
Birth rate – 19.47 (2010 est)
Infant mortality rate – 14.91 (2010 est)
HIV/AIDS adult prevalence – 1.7 per cent (2009 est)
Death penalty – Retained
CPI score – 3.3 (2010)

CLIMATE AND TERRAIN

An island in the Caribbean Sea, south of Cuba and west of Hispaniola, Jamaica is mostly mountainous and forested, with a narrow coastal plain. Elevation extremes range from 2,256m (Blue Mountain Peak) at the highest point to 0m (Caribbean Sea) at the lowest. The climate is tropical, although more temperate inland. The average temperature in Jamaica is 27°C.

HISTORY AND POLITICS

Jamaica was visited by Columbus in 1494 and settled by the Spanish from 1509. Captured by the British in 1655, it became a crown colony in 1865. Jamaica became internally self-governing in 1959 and independent in 1962.

Post-independence politics has been dominated by the conservative Jamaican Labour Party (JLP) and social-democratic People's National Party (PNP). Relations between the two parties, often fraught, degenerated in the 1970s into violence that marred elections and political life for some years. Despite the current political stability, there is still widespread lawlessness, which now is often connected to drug-trafficking.

In the 2007 legislative election, the PNP, which had been in power since 1989, was narrowly defeated by the JLP, which won 33 of the 60 seats. The JLP formed a government under Bruce Golding.

POLITICAL SYSTEM
Under the 1962 constitution, the head of state is Queen Elizabeth II, represented locally by a governor-general. The bicameral parliament consists of the House of Representatives, with 60 directly elected members, and the senate of 21 appointed members, 13 nominated by the prime minister and eight by the leader of the opposition; both chambers serve five-year terms. The prime minister is the leader of the majority party in the elected chamber.
Governor-General, HE Patrick Allen, GCMG, *apptd* 2009

SELECTED GOVERNMENT MEMBERS *as at June 2011*
Prime Minister, Defence, Bruce Golding
Deputy Prime Minister, Foreign Affairs, Kenneth Baugh
Finance and Public Service, Audley Shaw
National Security, Dwight Nelson

JAMAICAN HIGH COMMISSION
1–2 Prince Consort Road, London SW7 2BZ
T 020-7823 9911 E jamhigh@jhcuk.com W http://jhcuk.org
High Commissioner, HE Anthony Johnson, *apptd* 2010

BRITISH HIGH COMMISSION
PO Box 575, 28 Trafalgar Road, Kingston 10
T (+1) (876) 510 0700 W http://ukinjamaica.fco.gov.uk
High Commissioner, HE Howard Drake, *apptd* 2010

BRITISH COUNCIL
c/o British High Commission
T (+1) (876) 929 6915 W www.britishcouncil.org/jamaica
Manager, Pauline Samuels

DEFENCE
The army has 4 armoured personnel carriers. The coastguard has 11 patrol and coastal combatant vessels at 3 bases.

Military expenditure – US$62m (2009)
Military personnel – 2,830: army 2,500, coastguard 190, air force 140

ECONOMY AND TRADE
The economy is weak owing to high interest rates, increased foreign competition, high unemployment, growing internal and external debt, and storm damage in 2004, 2007 and 2008. It depends on foreign aid and remittances from expatriates; remittances were worth nearly 20 per cent of GDP but declined to about 15 per cent after the global downturn began. This hit the economy badly, and IMF support was needed in 2010. Economic growth is hindered by the high level of violent crime and corruption. Tourism, the main foreign exchange earner, remains strong, though the bauxite/alumina industry (the main industry after tourism) suffered in the downturn.

The economy is dominated by the service sector, which makes up 64.6 per cent of GDP; industry accounts for 29.7 per cent, and agriculture for 5.7 per cent. Industries include alumina and bauxite extraction, processing agricultural produce and light manufacturing.

The main trading partners are the USA, Trinidad and Tobago, Canada, Venezuela and the UK. Principal exports are alumina, bauxite, sugar, bananas, rum, coffee, yams, beverages, chemicals and clothing. The main imports are food, consumer goods, industrial supplies, fuel, and parts and accessories for capital goods.

GNI – US$11,428m; US$4,590 per capita (2009)
Annual average growth of GDP – −0.8 per cent (2010 est)
Inflation rate – 13 per cent (2010 est)
Population below poverty line – 14.8 per cent (2003 est)
Unemployment – 12.9 per cent (2010 est)
Total external debt – US$12,660m (2010 est)
Imports – US$5,100m (2009)
Exports – US$1,200m (2009)

BALANCE OF PAYMENTS
Trade – US$3,418m deficit (2010)
Current Account – US$2,534m deficit (2008)

Trade with UK	2009	2010
Imports from UK	£46,186,968	£68,426,475
Exports to UK	£93,090,564	£47,715,892

COMMUNICATIONS
There are several harbours, Kingston being the main seaport. The principal airports are at Kingston and Montego Bay. The island has 21,552km of roads, of which 15,937km are surfaced. The rail network is no longer in use. The number of fixed telephone lines has declined as mobile phone usage has grown; mobile phone density was over 110 per cent in 2009.

EDUCATION AND HEALTH
In 2010 the Inter-American Development Bank provided US$45m in funding to enable the government to make improvements to the education system and expand compulsory schooling from age 16 to 18.

Literacy rate – 86.4 per cent (2008 est)
Gross enrolment ratio (percentage of relevant age group) – primary 93 per cent; secondary 91 per cent; tertiary 24 per cent (2008 est)
Health expenditure (per capita) – US$231 (2009)
Hospital beds (per 1,000 people) – 1.7 (2004–9)

MEDIA
The state broadcaster was privatised in 1997 and now operates as Television Jamaica Ltd. It competes with one commercial and one religious broadcaster, and several local cable channels. There are a large number of commercial radio stations and four privately owned newspapers. The press operates independently and freely criticises the establishment.

CULTURE
Jamaica is widely regarded as the birthplace of reggae, and is also the home of ska, dub and dancehall. Significant musicians include reggae pioneer Bob Marley (1945–81), Jimmy Cliff (*b.* 1948) and Desmond Dekker (1941–2006). Closely connected to reggae is the Rastafari religious movement, which originated in the 1930s among descendants of slaves brought from Africa.

Major literary figures include the poets Claude McKay (1890–1948), a leading voice of the Harlem Renaissance, and Louis Simpson (*b.* 1923), who won the Pulitzer prize in 1964 after emigrating to the USA.

Jamaica has produced a number of notable sports figures, including the cricketer Michael Holding (*b.* 1954) and the sprinters Asafa Powell (*b.* 1982) and Usain Bolt (*b.* 1986).

JAPAN

Nihon-koku / Nippon-koku – Japan

Area – 377,915 sq. km
Capital – Tokyo; population, 36,506,600 (2009 est)
Major cities – Fukuoka, Hiroshima, Kawasaki, Kobe, Kyoto (the ancient capital), Nagoya, Osaka, Saitama, Sapporo, Yokohama
Currency – Yen of 100 sen
Population – 126,804,433 falling at 0.24 per cent a year (2010 est)
Religion – Shinto 82 per cent, Buddhist 70 per cent, Christian 2 per cent (est); much of the population adheres to more than one religion, most commonly combining Shinto and Buddhist beliefs
Language – Japanese (official)
Population density – 350 per sq. km (2009)
Urban population – 66 per cent (2008 est)
Median age (years) – 44.6 (2010 est)
National anthem – 'Kimi ga Yo' ['May Your Reign Last Forever']

National day – 23 December (Birthday of Emperor
  Akihito)
Life expectancy (years) – 82.17 (2010 est)
Mortality rate – 9.83 (2010 est)
Birth rate – 7.41 (2010 est)
Infant mortality rate – 2.79 (2010 est)
Death penalty – Retained
CPI score – 7.8 (2010)

CLIMATE AND TERRAIN

Japan consists of four large islands: Honshu (or
Mainland), Shikoku, Kyushu and Hokkaido, and many
smaller islands. Typically, the islands have coastal plains
and wooded, mountainous interiors; 67 per cent of
Japan's land area is forested. The mountains running
across the mainland from the Sea of Japan to the Pacific
Ocean include a number of volcanoes, mainly extinct or
dormant. Elevation extremes range from 3,776m (Mt Fuji)
at the highest point to −4m (Hachiro-gata) at the lowest.
The climate varies from temperate in the north to tropical
in the south. Average temperatures in Tokyo range from
4°C in January to 27°C in August.

The islands are located at the intersection of three
tectonic plates and are prone to seismic activity; 20 per
cent of the world's major earthquakes occur in this area.
A magnitude-9 earthquake and the ensuing tsunami
devastated the north-east of Honshu in March 2011 (*see
also* Events of the Year).

HISTORY AND POLITICS

A centralised state had been established in what is now
Japan by the fifth century AD. In the 12th century, the
country was plunged into centuries of rivalry and conflict
between different *samurai* (feudal warrior class) families,
who were subdued and ruled by successive dynasties of
shoguns (military overlords) nominally appointed by the
emperor. Imperial control was re-established in 1868 after
long periods of civil warfare.

Contact with the West was severely restricted until the
19th century, when the visit of a US naval officer,
Commodore Perry, led to the Japanese opening their ports
to foreign trade. Industrialisation followed and Japan
adopted a Western-style constitution in 1889. Policies
became more outward-looking and, in the case of foreign
policy, more aggressive, with successful wars against
imperial China (1894–5) and Russia (1904–5), and the
annexation of Korea in 1910.

A period of intense nationalism in the 1920s was
accompanied by a rise in militarism, leading to Japan's
invasion of China in 1931 and a pact with Germany and
Italy in 1940. Japan entered the Second World War in
1941 with an attack on the US naval base at Pearl Harbor,
Hawaii, and occupied British, French and Dutch colonial
possessions in south-east Asia in 1941–2. Pushed back
by Allied forces in 1943–5, Japan surrendered after
atomic bombs were dropped on Hiroshima and Nagasaki
in 1945. Political, social and economic reforms were
introduced during the post-war Allied occupation; Japan's
independence was restored in 1952.

The Liberal Democrat Party (LDP) has dominated
post-war politics, holding power continuously from 1955
to 1993, and then – usually as the main party in coalition
governments – from 1994 to 2009. In 2007, it lost
control of the upper house of the legislature to the
Democratic Party of Japan (DPJ), and the DPJ won an
overwhelming majority of seats in elections to the lower
house of the legislature in 2009. The DPJ formed a
coalition government under DPJ leader Yukio Hatoyama.

Hatoyama resigned in June 2010 and was replaced as
party leader and prime minister by Naoto Kan. The DPJ
coalition lost their majority in the upper house after the
2010 elections.

POLITICAL SYSTEM

The 1947 constitution established Japan as a
constitutional monarchy with a hereditary emperor as
head of state. The bicameral Diet comprises the House
of Representatives (the lower house) and the House of
Councillors. The House of Representatives has 480
members directly elected for a four-year term, including
180 by proportional representation. The House of
Councillors has 242 members, including 96 elected by
proportional representation, who serve six-year terms,
with half elected every three years; unlike the lower
house, it cannot be dissolved by the prime minister. The
prime minister is formally elected by the House of
Representatives and appoints the cabinet.

HEAD OF STATE

HIM The Emperor of Japan, Akihito, *born* 23 December
  1933, *succeeded* 8 January 1989, *enthroned* 12
  November 1990
Heir, HRH Crown Prince Naruhito Hironomiya, *born*
  23 February 1960

SELECTED GOVERNMENT MEMBERS *as at June 2011*
Prime Minister, Naoto Kan
Finance, Yoshihiko Noda
Foreign Affairs, Takeaki Matsumoto
Defence, Toshimi Kitazawa
Internal Affairs, Kazuhiro Haraguchi

EMBASSY OF JAPAN
101–104 Piccadilly, London W1J 7JT
T 020-7465 6500 E info@ld.mofa.go.jp
W www.uk.emb-japan.go.jp
Ambassador Extraordinary and Plenipotentiary, HE Keiichi
  Hayashi, *apptd* 2011

BRITISH EMBASSY
No. 1 Ichiban-cho, Chiyoda-ku, Tokyo 102–8381
T (+81) (3) 5211 1100 W http://ukinjapan.fco.gov.uk
Ambassador Extraordinary and Plenipotentiary, HE David
  Warren, *apptd* 2008

BRITISH COUNCIL
1–2 Kagurazaka, Shinjuku-ku, Tokyo 162–0825
T (+81) (3) 3235 8031 W www.britishcouncil.org/japan
Director, Jason James

DEFENCE

The constitution prohibits the maintenance of armed
forces, although internal security forces were created in
the 1950s and their mission was extended in 1954 to
include the defence of Japan against aggression.
In the 1990s, legislation was passed permitting limited
participation by the armed forces in UN peacekeeping
missions and allowing them to enter foreign conflicts in
order to rescue Japanese nationals. A revision to the USA–
Japan defence cooperation guidelines agreed in 1997
permits Japan to play a supporting role in US military
operations in areas surrounding Japan; Japanese troops
were also deployed in Iraq to assist with post-war
reconstruction between 2003 and 2006.

The Ground Self-Defence Force (GSDF) has 850 main
battle tanks, 780 armoured personnel carriers, 70

armoured infantry fighting vehicles and 185 armed helicopters. The Maritime Self-Defence Force (MSDF) has 18 submarines, 1 aircraft carrier, 30 destroyers, 16 frigates, 6 patrol and coastal vessels, 95 combat aircraft and 93 armed helicopters at five bases. The Air Self-Defence Force (ASDF) has 374 combat aircraft.

Military budget – US$52,800m (2010)

Military personnel – 247,746: GSDF 151,641, MSDF 45,518, ASDF 47,123, central staff 3,464; paramilitary 12,636

ECONOMY AND TRADE

Japan has the third-largest economy in the world after the USA and China. Its rapid post-war economic growth, based largely on car and consumer electronics manufacturing, experienced a marked contraction from 1990. Exacerbated by the 1997 Asian economic crisis, the recession lasted 14 years, causing unprecedented levels of bankruptcy, unemployment and homelessness and a huge public debt (estimated at 192 per cent of GDP in 2009). Reforms introduced from 2001, particularly to the corporate and public sectors, improved economic growth from 2002 to 2007, but the economy went into recession again in 2008 owing to the global downturn. Government stimulus packages and an increase in global demand spurred the start of a recovery from late 2009, but the drop in production and cost of reconstruction following the 2011 earthquake and tsunami are expected to reverse this.

High-technology industries remain the mainstay of the economy, producing vehicles, electronic equipment, machine tools, steel and other metals, ships, chemicals, textiles and processed food. Financial services is also a major sector, supplying a global market. Agriculture is constrained by the mountainous terrain but intensive cultivation produces high yields, and there is a large fishing industry. The service sector contributes 75.9 per cent of GDP, industry 23 per cent and agriculture 1.1 per cent.

The main trading partners are China, the USA, other Pacific Rim countries and the Gulf states. Principal exports include transport equipment, motor vehicles, semiconductors, electrical machinery and chemicals. The main imports are machinery and equipment, fuels, foodstuffs, chemicals, textiles and raw materials.

GNI – US$5,228,305m; US$38,080 per capita (2009)

Annual average growth of GDP – 3 per cent (2010 est)

Inflation rate – −0.9 per cent (2010 est)

Unemployment – 5.2 per cent (2010 est)

Total external debt – US$2,246,000m (2010)

Imports – US$550,600m (2009)

Exports – US$580,800m (2009)

BALANCE OF PAYMENTS

Trade – US$77,278m surplus (2010)

Current Account – US$141,656m surplus (2009)

Trade with UK	2009	2010
Imports from UK	£3,372,530,776	£3,328,979,042
Exports to UK	£7,247,201,664	£8,624,970,671

COMMUNICATIONS

Japan has a large merchant fleet, with 673 ships of over 1,000 tonnes in 2010. The main seaports are Tokyo, Osaka, Nagoya, Yokohama, Kobe and Kawasaki. There are 176 airports and airfields; the principal airports include Haneda (Tokyo), Narita, Kansai and Chubu. There are 26,435km of railway track and 1,203,777km of roads. *Shinkansen* (bullet train) tracks are currently being extended. The Seikan rail tunnel and the Seto Ohashi rail bridge link the four major islands. In 2009, there were 44.3 million fixed telephone lines in use, 114.9 million mobile phone subscribers and 99.1 million internet users.

EDUCATION AND HEALTH

Elementary education is free, and compulsory at elementary level (six-year course) and lower secondary (three-year course).

Gross enrolment ratio (percentage of relevant age group) – primary 102 per cent; secondary 101 per cent; tertiary 58 per cent (2008 est)

Health expenditure (per capita) – US$3,321 (2009)

Hospital beds (per 1,000 people) – 13.8 (2004–9)

MEDIA

A public broadcaster, NHK, provides radio and television services; satellite and cable television is widespread and digital broadcasting is expanding. Around 80 per cent of the population reads a daily newspaper, creating huge markets for publications such as *Asahi Shimbun, Nikkei Net* and the English-language title *The Japan Times.*

CULTURE

The popularity of technology in Japan has not obliterated traditional culture, instead creating a mixture of the old and new. Traditional woodblock printing and imported Western cartoons have been combined into 'manga', a form of comic book illustration. Animated manga, known as 'anime', are broadcast on television, included in computer games and have spawned a number of internationally successful films, most notably *Spirited Away* (2002) directed by Hayao Miyazaki (*b.* 1941), the first anime film to win an Academy Award. Akira Kurosawa (1910–98), awarded an Oscar for Lifetime Achievement, directed *Rashomon* (1950), *Seven Samurai* (1954) and many other films. Notable contemporary authors include Kenzaburo Oe (*b.* 1935) and Haruki Murakami (*b.* 1949).

Imported sports such as football and baseball are popular. The country co-hosted the 2002 football World Cup with South Korea, and the national baseball league has existed since 1936. However, sumo remains the quintessential Japanese sport. Its roots are lost, but references to its earlier name, Sumai, exist in texts from the eighth century.

JORDAN

Al-Mamlakah al-Urduniyah al-Hashimiyah – Hashemite Kingdom of Jordan

Area – 89,342 sq. km
Capital – Amman; population, 1,087,910 (2009 est)
Major cities – Al Aqaba, Az Zarqa, Irbid
Currency – Jordanian dinar (JD) of 10 dirhams
Population – 6,407,085 rising at 2.16 per cent a year
(2010 est); Arab (98 per cent), Circassian (1 per cent),
Armenian (1 per cent) (est)
Religion – Muslim (Sunni 95 per cent), Christian 2 per
cent (est)
Language – Arabic (official), English
Population density – 67 per sq. km (2009)
Urban population – 78 per cent (2008 est)
Median age (years) – 21.8 (2010 est)
National anthem – 'As-Salam al-Malaki al-Urdoni' ['Long
Live the King']
National day – 25 May (Independence Day)
Life expectancy (years) – 79.92 (2010 est)
Mortality rate – 2.66 (2010 est)
Birth rate – 27.06 (2010 est)
Infant mortality rate – 17.03 (2010 est)
Death penalty – Retained
CPI score – 4.7 (2010)

CLIMATE AND TERRAIN

Most of the country is a desert plateau, with the valley of
the River Jordan and the Dead Sea in the west marking
the border with Israel. The Jordan Valley and its extension
from the Dead Sea to the Gulf of Aqaba are part of the
Great Rift Valley in Africa. The only hills lie in the south,
along the edge of the Great Rift Valley, although there is
a hilly outcrop in the centre of the desert. Elevation
extremes range from 1,854m (Jabal Umm al Dami) at the
highest point to –408m (Dead Sea) at the lowest. The
climate is arid, but with a rainy season in the west from
November to April. Summers are very hot, and
temperatures in the Jordan Valley have been known to
reach 49°C. Winters can be cold, with frost and snow on
the plateau.

HISTORY AND POLITICS

The area was part of the Roman Empire and subsequently
of the Byzantine Empire. It came under Arab control in
the seventh century, and in the 16th century became part
of the Ottoman Empire until the latter's collapse in 1918.
The emirate of Transjordan was created in 1921 and
administered by the British under a League of Nations
mandate. When the mandate ended in 1946, Transjordan
became independent as the Hashemite Kingdom of
Jordan.

During the first Arab–Israeli War of 1948, Jordan
seized the West Bank and part of Jerusalem, but these
areas were recaptured by Israel in the Six Day War of
1967, resulting in an influx of Palestinian refugees into
Jordan; these refugees and their descendants now
constitute the majority of the Jordanian population.
Jordan attempted to expel Palestinian guerrillas from the
West Bank in 1970–1, causing a brief civil war. Jordan
recognised the Palestinian Liberation Organisation (PLO)
as the sole representative of the Palestinian people in the
Occupied Territories in 1974, but severed links with the
PLO and expelled its personnel in 1986. Jordan formally
renounced sovereignty over the West Bank and East
Jerusalem in 1999, having signed a peace agreement with
Israel in 1994.

The economy declined in the 1980s and internal
stability became increasingly precarious. Riots in 1989
forced the government to initiate a process of political,
social and economic reform. The country's first free

elections under universal suffrage took place in 1989, and
a ban on political parties was lifted in 1992. Real power,
however, effectively rests with the king, with parliament
amending or approving legislation that originates with
the monarch and his government. Although support for
Islamist parties has grown, the system favours people's
tribal loyalties over their religious affiliation;
consequently there has been little constitutionally
expressed opposition to the peace treaty with Israel or the
close ties with the USA, both generally unpopular.

The legislature was dissolved halfway through its term
in November 2009. After the legislative election in
November 2010, over 85 per cent of seats were won by
pro-government candidates; the announcement of this
result led to rioting. Since January 2011, Jordan has
experienced demonstrations similar to those elsewhere in
the Arab world, with protestors demanding political
reform, lower food prices and measures to tackle
unemployment. The king dismissed the government in
February 2011 and appointed a new prime minister,
Marouf Bakhit.

POLITICAL SYSTEM

The 1952 constitution provides for a monarchy with a
hereditary king as head of state. The bicameral National
Assembly comprises a House of Deputies and a senate or
House of Notables. The House of Deputies has 120
members (increased from 110 members in 2010), directly
elected for a four-year term; 12 seats (increased from six
seats in 2010) are now reserved for women. The senate
has 55 members, who are appointed by the king for a
four-year term. The king appoints the prime minister, who
chooses the council of ministers.

HEAD OF STATE

HM The King of Jordan, Abdullah II, *born* 30 January
1962, *succeeded* 7 February 1999
Crown Prince, Hamzeh ibn al-Hussein, *born* 29 March
1982

SELECTED GOVERNMENT MEMBERS *as at June 2011*
Prime Minister, Defence, Marouf Bakhit
Deputy Prime Minister, Interior, Sa'ad Hayel Srour
Finance, Mohammad Abu Hammour
Foreign Affairs, Nasser Judah

EMBASSY OF THE HASHEMITE KINGDOM OF JORDAN
6 Upper Phillimore Gardens, London W8 7HA
T 020-7937 3685 E london@fm.gov.jo
W www.jordanembassy.org.uk
Ambassador Extraordinary and Plenipotentiary, HE Dr Alia
Hatoug-Bouran, *apptd* 2006

BRITISH EMBASSY
PO Box 87, Abdoun, Amman 11118
T (+962) (6) 590 9200 E amman.enquiries@fco.gov.uk
W http://ukinjordan.fco.gov.uk
Ambassador Extraordinary and Plenipotentiary, HE Peter
Millett, *apptd* 2011

BRITISH COUNCIL
PO Box 634, Rainbow Street, First Circle, Jebel Amman, Amman
11118
T (+962) (6) 460 3420 W www.britishcouncil.org/jordan
Director, Marc Jessel

DEFENCE

The army has 1,044 main battle tanks, 1,391 armoured
personnel carriers and 303 armoured infantry fighting

vehicles. The navy has 7 patrol and coastal vessels at its base at Aqaba. The air force has 102 combat aircraft and 25 armed helicopters.

Military budget – US$2,530m (2010)
Military personnel – 100,500: army 88,000, navy 500, air force 12,000; paramilitary 10,000

ECONOMY AND TRADE

Jordan's economic development has been hindered by its lack of natural resources, influxes of refugees from the West Bank in 1967 and Iraq since 2003, and the impact of conflict on its trade with Israel and Iraq. High levels of poverty, unemployment and government debt are long-term problems. Since 1999, King Abdullah has implemented economic reforms, and these measures have increased productivity and exports, begun to attract foreign direct investment, and won agreement to debt rescheduling from international donors. Even so, the economy is still dependent on foreign aid, of which the USA is the largest provider, and a drop in this aid in 2009 exacerbated the effects of the global downturn on the already struggling economy.

Jordan has no oil reserves of its own and few water resources. Since 2003, several Gulf states have temporarily extended aid to Jordan in order to compensate for the loss of its usual oil supplies from Iraq. The country also imports natural gas, but aims to become a net exporter of electricity via its national grid's links with those of Syria and Egypt. It is currently considering nuclear power generation to ensure an adequate future supply. Jordan has also begun joint ventures with Israel and Syria to guarantee water supplies.

The service sector, including tourism, accounts for 66.2 per cent of GDP. Industry generates 30.3 per cent, from activities that include garment manufacturing, fertilisers, potash and phosphate mining, pharmaceuticals, oil refining, cement, inorganic chemicals and light manufacturing. Agriculture, which accounts for 3.4 per cent of GDP, produces citrus and stone fruits, tomatoes, cucumbers, olives, sheep, poultry and dairy products.

The main export markets are the USA, Iraq, India and Saudi Arabia, and the main sources of imports are Saudi Arabia, China, the USA, Germany and Egypt. Principal exports are clothing, fertilisers, potash, phosphates, vegetables and pharmaceuticals. The main imports are crude oil, machinery, transport equipment, iron and cereals.

GNI – US$25,703m; US$3,980 per capita (2009)
Annual average growth of GDP – 3.2 per cent (2010 est)
Inflation rate – 4.4 per cent (2010 est)
Unemployment – 13.4 per cent (2010 est)
Total external debt – US$5,522m (2010 est)
Imports – US$14,500m (2009)
Exports – US$6,500m (2009)

BALANCE OF PAYMENTS
Trade – US$8,017m deficit (2010)
Current Account – US$1,276m deficit (2009)

Trade with UK	2009	2010
Imports from UK	£245,401,706	£222,755,820
Exports to UK	£15,156,160	£19,976,041

COMMUNICATIONS

Jordan has 7,891km of roads; Amman is linked to Jordan's seaport at Aqaba, the Saudi Arabian port of Jeddah and the Syrian and Iraqi capitals by roads which

are of considerable importance in the overland trade of the Middle East. The 507km of rail track comprises two sections of the former Hejaz Railway: one passenger line between Amman and Daraa in Syria, and the other carrying phosphate rock from the mines of al-Hasa and al-Abiad to Aqaba. There are 18 airports and airfields; the principal airports are at Amman and Aqaba.

The telephone system is modern and growing, but fixed-line subscriptions are declining as mobile phone use grows. There were 6 million mobile phone subscribers, 501,000 fixed lines in use and 1.6 million internet users in 2009.

EDUCATION AND HEALTH

Literacy rate – 91.1 per cent (2008 est)
Gross enrolment ratio (percentage of relevant age group) – primary 97 per cent; secondary 88 per cent; tertiary 41 per cent (2008 est)
Health expenditure (per capita) – US$336 (2009; includes contributions from the UN Relief and Works Agency for Palestinian refugees)
Hospital beds (per 1,000 people) – 1.8 (2004–9)

MEDIA

There is strict media censorship, and scrutiny extends to internet usage. Jordan Radio and Television, the state-run broadcaster, operates three terrestrial television channels and a satellite channel as well as radio services in Arabic, English and French. A number of private radio stations also operate, and international broadcasts are available in the capital and the north.

KAZAKHSTAN

Qazaqstan Respublikasy – Republic of Kazakhstan

Area – 2,724,900 sq. km
Capital – Astana (previously known as Akmola and Tselinograd); population, 649,818 (2009 est)
Major cities – Almaty (the former capital), Oskemen, Pavlodar, Qaraghandy, Semey, Shymkent, Taraz
Currency – Tenge of 100 tiyn
Population – 15,460,484 rising at 0.4 per cent a year (2010 est); Kazakh (53.4 per cent), Russian (30 per cent), Ukrainian (3.7 per cent), Uzbek (2.5 per cent), German (2.4 per cent), Tatar (1.7 per cent), Uygur (1.4 per cent) (est). The Russian population is concentrated in the north of the country, where it forms a significant majority, and in Almaty
Religion – Muslim 65 per cent (predominantly Sunni), Christian 31 per cent (mostly Russian Orthodox) (est)
Language – Kazakh, Russian (both official)

Population density – 6 per sq. km (2009)
Urban population – 58 per cent (2008 est)
Median age (years) – 29.9 (2010 est)
National anthem – 'Menin Qazaqstanym' ['My
    Kazakhstan']
National day – 16 December (Independence Day)
Life expectancy (years) – 68.19 (2010 est)
Mortality rate – 9.39 (2010 est)
Birth rate – 16.66 (2010 est)
Infant mortality rate – 24.93 (2010 est)
Death penalty – Retained for certain crimes
CPI score – 2.9 (2010)
Gross enrolment ratio (percentage of relevant age group) –
    primary 108 per cent; secondary 99 per cent; tertiary
    41 per cent (2009 est)
Literacy rate – 99.6 per cent (2008 est)
Health expenditure (per capita) – US$330 (2009)
Hospital beds (per 1,000 people) – 7.6 (2004–9)

CLIMATE AND TERRAIN
Landlocked Kazakhstan stretches from the basin of the
river Volga and the Caspian Sea in the west to the Altai
and Tien Shan mountains in the east. The terrain consists
of arid steppes and semi-deserts, flat in the west, hilly in
the east and mountainous in the south-east. Elevation
extremes range from 6,995m (Khan Tangiri Shyngy) at
the highest point to −132m (Vpadina Kaundy) at the
lowest. The country contains the northern part of the Aral
Sea in the south-west, and Lake Balkhash and Lake
Zaysan in the east. The climate is continental, and while
arid in much of the country, it can be Siberian in the
north. Average yearly temperatures in Astana range from
−16°C in January to 22°C in July.

HISTORY AND POLITICS
Kazakhstan was inhabited by nomadic tribes before being
invaded by Genghis Khan and incorporated into his
empire in 1218. After this empire disintegrated, feudal
towns emerged based on large oases and the nomadic
tribes formed federations led by khans. The towns
affiliated in the late 15th century and established a
Kazakh state which engaged in almost continuous warfare
with the marauding khanates on its southern border. After
turning to Russia for protection in the 1730s, the Kazakh
khanates were formally incorporated into the Russian
Empire in the early 19th century.

The 1917 Bolshevik revolution in Russia was followed
by civil war in Kazakhstan, which became an autonomous
republic within the USSR in 1920 and a full union
republic in 1936. Kazakhstan suffered severely under
Stalin's policies of agricultural collectivisation and
'sedentarisation', which forced nomadic tribes to become
farmers; around 1.5 million people died of famine or
disease. Later Soviet rule saw the country used as a test site
for nuclear weapons.

Growing nationalism in the 1980s and a reformist
leader led to economic and cultural reforms in 1989 and a
declaration of sovereignty in 1990. Kazakhstan declared
its independence in December 1991, and became a
founding member of the Commonwealth of Independent
States. It entered an economic, social and military union
with Kyrgyzstan and Uzbekistan in 1994, and an
economic and military pact with Russia in 1995, when it
achieved nuclear-free status. It agreed in 2009 to form
a customs union with Belarus and Russia from 2010.
Despite economic reforms and considerable foreign
investment since the 1990s, the country has serious

economic, social and environmental problems, while its
international standing is tarnished by political illiberalism
and corruption.

Nursultan Nazarbayev, the reformist communist leader
of 1989, became head of state in 1990 and was re-elected
in 1991, 1999, 2005 and 2011; the April 2011 election,
in which he received 95 per cent of the vote, was
criticised by international observers. A 2007
constitutional reform allows him to serve for an unlimited
number of terms. He has been criticised for concentrating
power in the presidency and suppressing political and
media freedom.

In 2006, three pro-government parties merged with
Nazarbayev's Fatherland Republican Party (Otan), which
subsequently changed its name to Nur-Otan. Nur-Otan
won every seat in the lower legislative chamber in the
2007 legislative elections, which observers said were
better conducted than the 2004 elections but still did not
meet international standards of fairness.

POLITICAL SYSTEM
The president is directly elected; in 2007 the constitution
was amended to reduce the presidential term from seven
to five years, renewable once, although President
Nazarbayev is exempt from this restriction. The bicameral
Parlament is composed of the assembly *(Majlis)* and the
senate. The assembly has 107 members, 98 directly
elected on a single constituency basis and nine seats
reserved for ethnic groups; all serve a five-year term. The
senate has 47 members, of whom 32 are indirectly elected
and 15 are appointed for a six-year term, with half elected
every three years. The president appoints the prime
minister and other senior ministers.

HEAD OF STATE
President, Nursultan Nazarbayev, *elected* 1 December
    1991, *confirmed in office by referendum* 1995, *re-elected*
    1999, 2005, 2011

SELECTED GOVERNMENT MEMBERS *as at June 2011*
Prime Minister, Karim Massimov
First Deputy Prime Minister, Umirzak Shukeev
Deputy Prime Minister, Aset Isekeshev
Defence, Adilbek Dzhaksybekov
Foreign Affairs, Yerzhan Kazykhanov
Internal Affairs, Kalmukhanbet Kasymov
Finance, Bolat Zhamishev

EMBASSY OF THE REPUBLIC OF KAZAKHSTAN
33 Thurloe Square, London SW7 2SD
T 020-7581 4646 E london@kazembassy.org.uk
W www.kazembassy.org.uk
Ambassador Extraordinary and Plenipotentiary, HE Kairat
    Abusseitov, *apptd* 2008

BRITISH EMBASSY
62 Kosmonavtov Street, Astana
T (+7) (717) 255 6200 E ukinkz@fco.gov.uk
W http://ukinkz.fco.gov.uk
Ambassador Extraordinary and Plenipotentiary, HE David
    Moran, *apptd* 2009

BRITISH COUNCIL
97 Zholdabeskov Street, Samal -2, Samal Towers, Block A -2,
11th Floor, Almaty 050051
T (+7) (727) 244 4144 W www.britishcouncil.org/kazakhstan
Director, Lena Milosevic

DEFENCE

The CIS mutual defence treaty of 1993, to which Kazakhstan is a signatory, retains a common air defence force, and Kazakh forces also take part in the CIS peacekeeping force on the Tajikistan–Afghanistan border. An agreement signed with Russia in 1995 provides for eventual reunification of the two states' armed forces. By 1996, all nuclear warheads had been returned to Russia, although Kazakhstan retained 48 SS-18 intercontinental ballistic missiles. Kazakhstan participates in the NATO partnership for peace programme.

The army has 980 main battle tanks, 370 armoured personnel carriers and 1,520 armoured infantry fighting vehicles. The navy has 17 patrol and coastal combatant vessels. The Caspian Sea Flotilla, which Kazakhstan shares with Russia and Turkmenistan, operates under Russian command. The air force has 162 combat aircraft and over 40 armed helicopters.

Military budget – US$1,120m (2010)
Military personnel – 49,000: army 30,000, navy 3,000, air force 12,000, MoD 4,000; paramilitary 31,500
Conscription duration – 24 months

ECONOMY AND TRADE

Economic reforms and privatisation in the 1990s enabled GDP to grow by at least 8 per cent a year from 2002 to 2007, although lower commodity prices and banking sector problems caused the economy to contract briefly in 2008–9. Growth has largely been achieved through exploitation of vast oil and natural gas reserves, particularly since the opening of export pipelines to Black Sea ports (in 2001) and China (2005), and Kazakhstan's use of the Azerbaijan–Turkey pipeline (from 2008); the country is also part of a four-country consortium developing another pipeline to China. As a result of the boom, the government has eliminated the budget deficit, but it is also trying to stimulate growth in other industries to reduce dependency on oil. A fund was set up in 2001 to manage state finances and protect the economy from volatile oil prices. Despite these revenues, poverty remains widespread.

Other mineral resources are considerable and there is a significant mining industry exploiting coal, iron ore, manganese, chrome, lead, zinc, copper, titanium, bauxite, silver, gold, phosphate and uranium deposits. A large and well-developed agricultural sector produces grain, wool, cotton and livestock as cash crops. The main industries are mineral extraction and processing and machine-building, especially agricultural machinery and electric motors. Services contribute 51.8 per cent of GDP, industry 42.8 per cent and agriculture 5.4 per cent, although agriculture employs 28 per cent of the workforce.

The main trading partners are China, Russia, Germany and other European states. Principal exports are oil and oil products (59 per cent), ferrous metals, chemicals, machinery, grain, wool, meat and coal. The main imports are machinery and equipment, metal products and foodstuffs.

GNI – US$103,414m; US$6,920 per capita (2009)
Annual average growth of GDP – 4.9 per cent (2010 est)
Inflation rate – 6.7 per cent (2010 est)
Population below poverty line – 12.1 per cent (2008 est)
Unemployment – 5.5 per cent (2010 est)
Total external debt – US$94,440m (2010 est)
Imports – US$28,400m (2009)
Exports – US$43,200m (2009)

BALANCE OF PAYMENTS
Trade – US$29,015m surplus (2010)
Current Account – US$6,279m surplus (2008)

Trade with UK	2009	2010
Imports from UK	£260,089,846	£236,998,846
Exports to UK	£202,700,953	£137,614,164

COMMUNICATIONS

Because of Kazakhstan's size, long-distance internal travel is usually by air, and the country has 97 airports and airfields; the principal airports are at Astana, Almaty and Atyrau. There are extensive rail and road networks (15,079km of railways and 93,612km of roads), although the roads are concentrated in the more populous east. There are important ports on the Caspian and Aral seas which permit international trade (albeit significantly reduced on the diminished Aral sea), while the Syr Darya and Irtysh rivers provide 4,000km of navigable waterways.

Improvement of the antiquated telephone system is a government development priority. Fixed-line services are being extended and density is now around 25 per 100 people. Mobile phone services have grown rapidly and were about 100 per 100 people by 2008. There were 5.2 million internet users in 2009.

MEDIA

There are several public television broadcasters, as well as a few private stations. Both sectors provide some Russian-language programmes. There is a public radio broadcaster as well as private stations. The state controls printing presses, and many of the roughly 1,000 newspapers are government-backed; these and their private-sector counterparts publish in Kazakh and Russian. Although freedom of the press is protected by the constitution, opposition and privately owned media are subject to censorship and harassment; insulting the president or government officials is a criminal offence.

KENYA

Jamhuri ya Kenya – Republic of Kenya

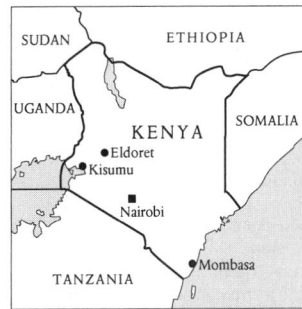

Area – 580,367 sq. km
Capital – Nairobi; population, 3,375,460 (2009 est)
Major cities – Eldoret, Kisumu, Mombasa, Nakuru
Currency – Kenyan shilling (Ksh) of 100 cents
Population – 40,046,566 rising at 2.59 per cent a year (2010 est); Kikuyu (17 per cent), Luhya (13 per cent), Kalenjin (12 per cent), Luo (10 per cent), Kamba (10 per cent), Kisii (6 per cent), Mijikenda (5 per cent), Meru (4 per cent) (2009)

Religion – Christian 82 per cent (Protestant 47 per cent, Roman Catholic 23 per cent), Muslim 11 per cent, traditional 1.6 per cent (2009)

Language – English, Swahili (both official), indigenous languages

Population density – 70 per sq. km (2009)

Urban population – 22 per cent (2008 est)

Median age (years) – 18.8 (2010 est)

National anthem – 'Ee Mungu Nguvu Yetu' ['Oh God of All Creation']

National day – 12 December (Independence Day)

Life expectancy (years) – 58.82 (2010 est)

Mortality rate – 9.26 (2010 est)

Birth rate – 35.14 (2010 est)

Infant mortality rate – 53.49 (2010 est)

HIV/AIDS adult prevalence – 6.3 per cent (2009 est)

Death penalty – Retained (not used since 1987)

CPI score – 2.1 (2010)

CLIMATE AND TERRAIN

The coastal plain and semi-desert plains in the east rise to mountainous highlands in the centre and west that are divided by the Great Rift Valley. Elevation extremes range from 5,199m (Mt Kenya) at the highest point to 0m (Indian Ocean) at the lowest. The country includes part of Lake Victoria in the south-west and most of Lake Turkana (Rudolph) in the north. Kenya is an equatorial country; the climate is tropical on the coast and arid in the interior, tempered by altitude. The average temperature is 18°C.

HISTORY AND POLITICS

Fossils of early hominids found in the Lake Turkana region suggest that the area was inhabited some 2.6 million years ago. Arabs and Persians settled on the Kenyan coast from the eighth century AD. The Portuguese gained control of coastal areas in the 16th century but Arab overlordship was reasserted in the 18th century.

European exploration of the interior began in the 19th century and in 1895, Kenya became part of Britain's East African Protectorate, becoming a colony in 1920. Demands for internal self-government by white settlers were rejected in 1923, but from 1944 a nationalist group, the Kenya African Union (KAU), was founded to campaign for African rights. The Mau Mau rebellion of 1952–6, intended to drive white settlers from African tribal lands, resulted in a state of emergency that lasted until 1960, when preparations for majority African rule began. Kenya became independent in 1963, and a republic in 1964. President Jomo Kenyatta's death in 1978 brought Daniel arap Moi to power, and he remained president until 2002, when he was barred from standing for re-election.

Kenya was a one-party state ruled by the Kenya African National Union (KANU) between 1964 and 1991. A multiparty system was reintroduced after violent agitation and international pressure in the early 1990s but KANU maintained its grip on power until the 2002 elections, which were won by the National Rainbow Coalition (NARC). Despite the NARC's anti-corruption electoral platform, once in government it made little headway against endemic corruption, and government ministers were implicated in corruption scandals in 2005 and 2006. It is estimated that up to US$1,000m (£650m) of official funds were misappropriated in 2002–7, and some aid donors suspended funding to pressurise the government into addressing the problem.

After decades of stability, intercommunal violence and conflict over land and water rights have become more frequent since the 1990s, exacerbated by a rural food crisis since 2004 following persistent drought and crop failures. In 2009 the president declared the food crisis a national disaster and asked for international food aid.

The 2007 legislative elections were won by the Orange Democratic Movement (ODM), led by Raila Odinga. The announcement that President Kibaki had won the simultaneous presidential election was greeted with accusations of electoral fraud by the opposition and triggered weeks of serious rioting; this developed into ethnic violence that left over 1,000 dead and 600,000 displaced. After international mediation, a power-sharing agreement was signed in February 2008; under this, Kibaki remained president and the post of prime minister was created for Raila Odinga. A coalition government was formed and took office in April. Disputes between the two coalition parties have slowed down government business and the implementation of reforms.

POLITICAL SYSTEM

The 2010 constitution reduced the powers of the presidency, provided for a second legislative chamber and devolved some powers to the provinces.

The president is directly elected for a five-year term, renewable once. The unicameral National Assembly, the *Bunge,* has 224 members, of whom 210 are directly elected for a five-year term, 12 are nominated by the president, and two, the attorney-general and the speaker, are *ex-officio* members. From the next elections the National Assembly will have 290 members, and a 94-member senate will become the upper legislative chamber.

HEAD OF STATE

President, C-in-C of the Armed Forces, Mwai Kibaki, *elected* 27 December 2002, *took office* 30 December 2002, *re-elected* 2007

Vice-President, Home Affairs, Stephen Musyoka

SELECTED GOVERNMENT MEMBERS *as at June 2011*

Prime Minister, Raila Odinga

Deputy Prime Ministers, Uhuru Kenyatta *(Finance);* Wycliffe Mudavadi

Foreign Affairs (acting), George Saitoti

Defence, Yussuf Haji

KENYA HIGH COMMISSION

45 Portland Place, London W1B 1AS

T 020-7636 2371 W www.kenyahighcommission.net

High Commissioner, HE Ephraim Ngare, *apptd* 2009

BRITISH HIGH COMMISSION

PO Box 30465, Upper Hill Road, 00100 Nairobi

T (+254) (20) 284 4000 W http://ukinkenya.fco.gov.uk

High Commissioner, HE Robert Macaire, *apptd* 2008

BRITISH COUNCIL

PO Box 40751, 00100 Nairobi

T (+254) (20) 283 6000 W www.britishcouncil.org.uk/africa

Director, Alison Coutts

DEFENCE

The army has 188 main battle tanks and 94 armoured personnel carriers. The navy has 5 patrol and coastal combatant vessels based at Mombasa. The air force has 42 combat aircraft and over 39 multi-role helicopters.

Military budget – US$720m (2010)
Military personnel – 24,120: army 20,000, navy 1,620,
air force 2,500; paramilitary 5,000

ECONOMY AND TRADE

Kenya acts as a regional trade and finance hub for its landlocked neighbours. However, its own economy is weak owing to endemic corruption, low commodity prices, low investor confidence and the frequent suspension of international aid because of successive governments' failure to tackle corruption. These problems are exacerbated by occasional severe droughts, and in 2008–9 the economy contracted owing to post-election violence and the global downturn, which reduced tourism, exports and expatriates' remittances. There are high budget and trade deficits, a huge foreign debt, widespread unemployment and extreme poverty, with 50 per cent of the population living below the poverty line.

The country is overwhelmingly agricultural, with 75 per cent of the population engaged in agricultural and horticultural production; this sector contributes 22 per cent of GDP. The world's third largest producer of tea, Kenya also grows coffee, maize, wheat, sugar cane, fruit and vegetables. Natural resources include gold, limestone, soda ash, salt, rubies, garnets and hydroelectric power, which makes it self-sufficient in energy.

The industrial sector has grown over the past two decades, developing a manufacturing base in consumer goods (such as textiles) and agricultural products (such as dehydrated vegetables), as well as oil refining, commercial ship repair and the production of steel, aluminium, lead and cement. Tourism is an important source of income. Industry contributes 16 per cent to GDP and the service sector 62 per cent.

The main export markets are the UK, the Netherlands, Uganda, Tanzania, the USA and Pakistan, while imports come mainly from India, China, the UAE and South Africa. Principal exports are tea, horticultural products, coffee, petroleum products, fish and cement. The main imports are machinery and transport equipment, petroleum products, vehicles, iron and steel, resins and plastics.
GNI – US$29,311m; US$760 per capita (2009)
Annual average growth of GDP – 4 per cent (2010 est)
Inflation rate – 4.2 per cent (2010 est)
Unemployment – 40 per cent (2008 est)
Total external debt – US$7,935m (2010 est)
Imports – US$10,200m (2009)
Exports – US$4,500m (2009)

BALANCE OF PAYMENTS
Trade – US$6,563m deficit (2010)
Current Account – US$2,106m deficit (2008)

Trade with UK	2009	2010
Imports from UK	£261,536,671	£256,303,027
Exports to UK	£333,889,381	£323,299,834

COMMUNICATIONS

The Kenya Railways Corporation operates 2,066km of railways, and there are 160,866km of roads. The principal seaport is Mombasa, while Kisumu on Lake Victoria also provides transport and trade. There are 191 airports and airfields; the international airports are at Nairobi, Mombasa and Eldoret.

The telephone system is limited in extent. Mobile phone distribution has grown rapidly and there were 50 subscribers per 100 people in 2009. There were 3.9 million internet users in 2009.

EDUCATION AND HEALTH

The state provides eight years of free primary education. A free secondary education programme was initiated in 2008.
Literacy rate – 73.6 per cent (2008 est)
Gross enrolment ratio (percentage of relevant age group) – primary 113 per cent; secondary 59 per cent (2008 est); tertiary 4 per cent (2009 est)
HIV/AIDS adult prevalence – 6.7 per cent (2003 est)
Health expenditure – US$33 per capita (2009)
Hospital beds (per 1,000 people) – 1.4 (2004–9)

MEDIA

Kenya has a diverse and liberal media, but government action against media outlets has caused alarm in recent years, and legislation introduced in 2009 gave the government powers to control some content on security grounds. Most people rely on broadcast media, especially radio, for news; some radio stations have begun broadcasting in local languages. The state-run Kenya Broadcasting Corporation (KBC) competes with a range of commercial television and radio stations. There are three main daily newspapers representing a range of political views; two are published in English and one in Swahili.

KIRIBATI

Republic of Kiribati

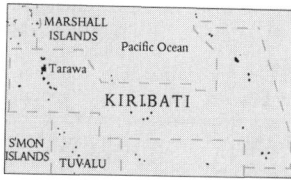

Area – 811 sq. km
Capital – Tarawa, on Bairiki; population, 42,925 (2009 est)
Currency – Australian dollar ($A) of 100 cents
Population – 99,482 rising at 1.27 per cent a year (2010 est); Micronesian (98.8 per cent) (2000)
Religion – Christian (Roman Catholic 55 per cent, Protestant 36 per cent, Mormon 3 per cent, Seventh-day Adventist 2 per cent), Baha'i 2 per cent (est)
Language – English, Kiribati (Gilbertese) (both official)
Population density – 121 per sq. km (2009)
Urban population – 44 per cent (2008 est)
Median age (years) – 22.2 (2010 est)
National anthem – 'Teirake Kaini Kiribati' ['Stand up, Kiribati']
National day – 12 July (Independence Day)
Life expectancy (years) – 64.03 (2010 est)
Mortality rate – 7.48 (2010 est)
Birth rate – 23.06 (2010 est)
Infant mortality rate – 40.13 (2010 est)
Death penalty – Abolished for all crimes (since 1979)
CPI score – 3.2 (2010)

CLIMATE AND TERRAIN

Kiribati (pronounced Kiri-bas) comprises 32 atolls and one island. About 20 are inhabited: Banaba island; the Kiribati (Gilbert) group (17); the Rawaki (Phoenix) Islands (8); and some of the Line Islands (11), including

Kiritimati (Christmas Island). They are situated in the southern central Pacific Ocean, crossed by the Equator; the area was also crossed by the international date line until 1995, when the government unilaterally moved the date line eastwards so that the whole country shared the same day. Few of the atolls are more than 800m wide or more than 3m high, making the the country particularly vulnerable to rising sea levels. The highest point is 81m (on Banaba) and the lowest is 0m (Pacific Ocean). The climate is tropical.

HISTORY AND POLITICS
The islands were settled by Austronesian-speaking peoples in the first millennium BC and Samoans, Fijians and Tongans migrated there in the 11th to 14th centuries. British settlers arrived in the islands in the early 19th century. In 1892, the Gilbert (Kiribati) and Ellice (Tuvalu) Islands were proclaimed a British protectorate and in 1916 became a British colony which subsequently incorporated the Line Islands and Phoenix Islands. During the Second World War, Banaba and the Gilbert islands were occupied by the Japanese and were the scene of fierce fighting between Japanese and US troops. Some of the Line Islands were used for British nuclear weapons tests in the 1950s and 1960s. In 1975, the territories separated and the Gilbert, Phoenix and Line Islands became independent as the Republic of Kiribati in 1979.

Open-cast phosphate mining left Banaba unfit for human habitation and the population was evacuated in 1945, to be relocated to a northern island of Fiji. Overcrowding and lack of infrastructure have caused more general environmental degradation, especially in urban areas. However, the main problem is the rise in the sea level due to global warming; salination is already contaminating water supplies and agricultural land, causing villages to be relocated, and Kiribati is expected to be the first state to lose land territory. The government is seeking permanent refugee status for its citizens in neighbouring countries.

Following the 2007 legislative elections, the Pillars of Truth grouping was the largest in the legislature, although still fewer in number than the other independent members. The incumbent president, Anote Tong, was re-elected in the 2007 presidential election. Legislative and presidential elections are due in late 2011.

POLITICAL SYSTEM
Under the 1979 constitution, the executive president is directly elected for a four-year term, with a maximum of three terms; presidential candidates are selected by and from members of the legislature. The unicameral legislature, the House of Assembly, has 46 members: 44 members directly elected for a four-year term, an appointed representative of the Banaban community in Fiji, and the attorney-general. There are no formal political parties but since the 1980s some associations of politicians formed for elections have proved durable enough to be given names.

HEAD OF STATE
President, Foreign Affairs, Anote Tong, *elected* 4 July 2003, *sworn in* 6 July 2003, *re-elected* 2007
Vice-President, Teima Onorio

SELECTED GOVERNMENT MEMBERS *as at June 2011*
Internal Affairs, Kouraiti Beniato
Finance, Natan Teewe

KIRIBATI HIGH COMMISSION
c/o Office of the President, PO Box 68, Bairiki, Tarawa, Kiribati
High Commissioner (acting), Makurita Baaro

BRITISH HIGH COMMISSIONER
HE Mac McLachlan, MBE, *apptd* 2009, resident at Suva, Fiji

ECONOMY AND TRADE
Since the phosphate deposits on Banaba ran out in 1979, the economy has been weak, dependent on coconuts, fish and tourism (over 20 per cent of GDP) as the main economic activities; development is hampered by remoteness, poor transport connections and the lack of funding, infrastructure and skills. Additional revenue comes from international aid (over 20 per cent of GDP), the sale of fishing licences, remittances from expatriates and monies from the trust fund established with phosphate mining revenues. A financial sector is being developed. The main trading partners are Pacific Rim countries. The principal exports are copra (62 per cent), coconuts, seaweed and fish. The principal imports are foodstuffs, machinery and transport equipment, manufactured goods and fuel.
GNI – US$174m; US$1,830 per capita (2009)
Annual average growth of GDP – 1.5 per cent (2010)
Inflation rate – 0.2 per cent (2007 est)

BALANCE OF PAYMENTS
Trade – US$39m deficit (2010)
Current Account – US$5m deficit (2009 est)

Trade with UK	2009	2010
Imports from UK	£1,230,700	£148,995
Exports to UK	£163,609	£18,111

COMMUNICATIONS
Air communication exists between most of the islands and is operated by the state-owned Air Kiribati; Coral Sun Airways, founded in 2009, provides additional services between the Gilbert Islands. There are 19 airports and airfields on the islands; the main international airport is on Tarawa, while another on Kiritimati operates regular services to Fiji and Hawaii. Inter-island shipping is operated by the state-owned Shipping Corporation of Kiribati. The main seaport is Betio, on Tarawa. There are no railways, and only 670km of roads.

The telephone system provides good national and international services. Mobile phones are not widespread.

MEDIA
Kiribati has no domestic television, so radio forms the islands' main source of communication. There are two weekly newspapers, one state-owned and one private.

KOREA

Independent kingdoms and city states in the Korean peninsula were united by the Buddhist Silla dynasty in AD 668. The Silla were succeeded by the Koryo dynasty in 935 and the Yi dynasty from 1395 to 1910, during which period Korea became a vassal of China, and Confucianism replaced Buddhism. Contact with outside cultures was discouraged by successive Korean rulers until 1876, when Japan forced the country to open up to foreign trade. Japan, China and Russia subsequently competed for influence, with Japan emerging as the dominant state, formally annexing Korea in 1910.

Japanese rule ended with its Second World War defeat in 1945, when Korea was divided along the 38th parallel by the occupying armies of liberation: US troops in the south and Soviet troops in the north. The Republic of Korea was founded in the south on 15 August 1948, following a general election and the adoption of a constitution. The Democratic People's Republic of Korea was established in the north on 9 September 1948; a Supreme People's Soviet was elected and a Soviet-style constitution was adopted.

UN plans to reunify the country after nationwide elections in 1950 were defied by North Korea. After elections in the south, South Korea declared its independence, which prompted its invasion by North Korea. A multinational UN force, with a large US contingent, intervened and pushed the North Korean troops back almost to the Chinese frontier. This brought China into the war in support of North Korea and their combined forces pushed back the UN troops, occupying Seoul. A UN counter-attack retook all territory south of the 38th parallel by the time an armistice was signed in 1953; a demilitarised border zone was established. The war devastated the entire peninsula, particularly North Korea, and left over 2 million people dead.

Talks between North and South Korea have taken place since the 1970s, although they were intermittent until 2000, when a summit ended with a joint declaration on normalisation measures; at a second summit in 2007 both sides agreed on the need for a peace treaty and expansion of economic cooperation. However, relations since 2002 have been complicated by international condemnation of North Korea's nuclear programme and the erratic nature of North Korea's attitude towards relations with South Korea, alternating between detente and aggression. Its attitude deteriorated steadily from early 2009, and inter-Korean relations reached a nadir in 2010 after South Korea accused North Korea of sinking a South Korean warship in March 2010 and imposed financial and trade sanctions; North Korea repudiated the accusation and severed all ties with South Korea, but in September 2010 accepted aid from the South and proposed reunions for families divided by the North/South partitioning.

DEMOCRATIC PEOPLE'S REPUBLIC OF KOREA

Choson-minjujuui-inmin-konghwaguk – Democratic People's Republic of Korea

Area – 120,538 sq. km
Capital – Pyongyang; population, 2,827,640 (2009 est)
Major cities – Chongjin, Hamhung-Hungnam, Nampo

Currency – Won of 100 chon
Population – 22,757,275 rising at 0.39 per cent a year (2010 est)
Religion – Religious activity is almost non-existent outside government-sponsored religious groups, although many believers are thought to worship in private. Historically, the main religions were Buddhism and Confucianism; Buddhism, Christianity and Chondo (a syncretic religion) are officially recognised
Language – Korean (official)
Population density – 199 per sq. km (2009)
Urban population – 63 per cent (2008 est)
Median age (years) – 33.9 (2010 est)
National anthem – 'Aegukka' ['The Patriotic Song']
National day – 9 September (Founding of the Democratic People's Republic of Korea, 1948)
Life expectancy (years) – 64.13 (2010 est)
Mortality rate – 10.6 (2010 est)
Birth rate – 14.58 (2010 est)
Infant mortality rate – 50.15 (2010 est)
Death penalty – Retained
Health expenditure (per capita) – $22 (2007)

CLIMATE AND TERRAIN

The republic occupies the northern half of the Korean peninsula. The land rises from coastal plains in the west to mountains and hills that occupy 80 per cent of the land area. Elevation extremes range from 2,744m (Paektu-san) at the highest point to 0m (Sea of Japan) at the lowest. The climate is temperate, though more extreme than in South Korea. Average temperatures in Pyongyang range from −8°C in January, to 25°C in July and August.

HISTORY AND POLITICS

After the Korean war ended in 1953, Kim Il-sung continued the process of Soviet-style reform begun in 1946. He also developed *Juche* (self-reliance), an ideology demanding total economic independence. North Korea pursued an isolationist foreign policy for several decades, only signing a mutual assistance treaty with China in 1961 and improving relations with the USSR in 1985. It established diplomatic contacts with South Korea and Japan in 1990, raising hopes that it was abandoning its isolationism, but it remains a secretive, closed country under rigid state control.

This situation has had serious consequences domestically and internationally. The economy has suffered a long decline, and a series of natural disasters in the 1990s caused severe famine, obliging the government to request international aid. It is estimated that three million people have died since the 1990s as a result of the acute food shortages, which continue despite international food and fuel aid. International relations over the past two decades have been marked by alternating bouts of tension and detente, especially over the country's nuclear development programme (*see* below).

Kim Il-sung died in 1994. His son Kim Jong-il became chairman of the National Defence Commission, designated as the highest post of the state, and general secretary of the Korean Workers' Party in 1997. The most recent elections to the Supreme People's Assembly took place in April 2009, and the assembly re-elected Kim Jong-il to his post. In September 2010 the Korean Workers' Party congress (the first for 44 years) renewed the top party leadership; Kim Jong-il's third son, Kim Jong-un, was appointed to senior political and military posts, suggesting that he has been designated as his father's successor.

INTERNATIONAL RELATIONS

North Korea's relations with other countries have been erratic over the past 20 years, largely owing to its nuclear ambitions and international reaction to these. It first agreed to freeze its nuclear development programme in return for fuel and development aid in 1994, only to restart the programme in 2002, claiming that other parties to the agreement had reneged on it. This pattern of confrontation, negotiation and non-compliance has been repeated several times, with the regime using the discontinuation of its nuclear and missile development programmes to bargain for aid from international agencies and regional powers. Six-nation talks to resolve the nuclear issues began in 2003 after North Korea withdrew from the Nuclear Non-proliferation Treaty, but North Korea has never fully complied with any of the agreements concluded at the talks. The consequent suspension of aid by other nations, and UN censure and sanctions after North Korea test-fired ballistic missiles and nuclear devices in 2006 and 2009, have been interpreted as acts of aggression by North Korea and met with a bellicose response from the regime.

POLITICAL SYSTEM

The communist Korean Workers' Party, founded in 1946 by Kim Il-sung, is the only permitted political party. However, political control and leadership is maintained by the cult of personality created by Kim Il-sung and continued by his son and successor Kim Jong-il.

The 1972 constitution was amended in 1998 to designate leading state posts; it made Kim Il-sung the Eternal President and the chairmanship of the National Defence Commission (NDC), held by Kim Jong-il, the highest post in the state, while providing that the chairman of the Presidium of the Supreme People's Assembly would represent the state on formal occasions. A further amendment in 2009 named the NDC chairman as the 'supreme leader of the state'; it also removed all references to communism, and established the *songun* principle of military responsibility for all internal affairs.

There is a unicameral legislature, the Supreme People's Assembly, which has 687 members directly elected from a single list of candidates for a five-year term. The assembly elects a presidium and the premier, appointing the government on the recommendation of the premier. The Central People's Committee, which is also elected by the assembly, directs the administrative council (government), which implements the policy formulated by the committee.

HEAD OF STATE

Eternal President, Kim Il-sung (deceased)
Chair of the National Defence Commission, Kim Jong-il
Chair of the Presidium of the Supreme People's Assembly, Kim Yong-nam

SELECTED GOVERNMENT MEMBERS *as at June 2011*

Premier, Choe Yong-rim
Deputy Premiers, Ro Tu-chol; Jon Ha-chol; Thae Jong-su; Han Kwang-bok; Kang Nung-su; Jo Pyong-ju; Kim Rak-hui; Kang Sok-ju; Ri Thae-nam
Finance, Pak Su-gil
Foreign Affairs, Pak Ui-chun

EMBASSY OF THE DEMOCRATIC PEOPLE'S REPUBLIC OF KOREA

73 Gunnersbury Avenue, London W5 4LP
T 020-8992 4965 E dprkrepmission@yahoo.co.uk

Ambassador Extraordinary and Plenipotentiary, HE Ja Song-nam, *apptd* 2007

BRITISH EMBASSY

Munsu Dong, Pyongyang
T (+850) (2) 381 7980 k
Ambassador Extraordinary and Plenipotentiary, HE Karen Wolstenholme, *apptd* 2011

DEFENCE

The army has over 3,500 main battle tanks and 2,500 armoured personnel carriers. The navy has 70 submarines, 3 frigates and 383 patrol and coastal vessels at 15 bases. The air force has 620 combat aircraft and 20 armed helicopters.

Military expenditure – US$4,380m (2009 est)
Military personnel – 1,190,000: army 1,020,000, navy 60,000, air force 110,000; paramilitary 189,000
Conscription duration – 3–12 years

ECONOMY AND TRADE

Although North Korea is rich in natural resources and had developed a heavy industry base in the first half of the 20th century, the economy is stagnant after decades of mismanagement, underinvestment and low export levels, and the diversion of resources to military expenditure. Its long decline was compounded by the loss of Soviet support from 1991. A redenomination of its currency in 2009 wiped out many people's savings, disrupted the nascent private sector, triggered rapid inflation and was met with unprecedented public protests that lasted some weeks. South Korea's imposition of sanctions in 2010 put the economy under even greater pressure.

Industrial output is centred on mining, steel, chemicals and machine building, but antiquated machinery and fuel shortages have limited output to a fraction of pre-1990 levels. Agriculture is in an equally parlous state, as collective farming, lack of arable land and chronic shortages of fertilisers and agricultural machinery prevent the country from producing enough to feed its population. It has been dependent on massive amounts of food aid since the mid-1990s to avert a repeat of the 1995 famine, but chronic malnutrition is widespread. A relaxation of restrictions on private farming and markets in 2003 was partially rescinded in 2005 and a centralised rationing system was reinstated. South Korean assistance in developing infrastructure, industry, the Kaesong Industrial Zone and tourism has been limited by North Korea's restrictions, and was reduced or suspended when South Korea imposed sanctions on the North in 2010.

The main trading partners are China and South Korea. Principal exports are minerals, metallurgical products, armaments, textiles, and agricultural and fish products. The main imports are petroleum, coal, machinery and equipment, textiles and grain.

Annual average growth of GDP – −0.9 per cent (2009 est)
Imports – US$431m (2002)
Exports – US$298m (2002)

BALANCE OF PAYMENTS

Trade – US$3,787m deficit (2010)
Current Account – US$82m deficit (2002)

Trade with UK	2009	2010
Imports from UK	£115,938	£56,557
Exports to UK	£911,478	£1,601,064

COMMUNICATIONS

North Korea has 5,242km of railways and 25,554km of roads, although few are surfaced. There are some 2,250km of waterways but these are navigable only by small craft. The main seaports are Chongjin, Nampo and Wonsan. There are 79 airports and airfields; the principal airport is at Pyongyang.

MEDIA

There are no independent media outlets in North Korea. All televisions and radios are pre-tuned to government stations and the four national newspapers are all government organs. Foreign and dissident radio stations are jammed and anyone found listening to foreign broadcasts is harshly punished. In 2010 Reporters Without Borders rated the country as second-worst in the world for press freedom.

REPUBLIC OF KOREA

Taehan-min'guk – Republic of Korea

Area – 99,720 sq. km
Capital – Seoul; population, 9,777,720 (2009 est)
Major cities – Busan, Daegu, Daejon, Gwangju, Incheon, Koyang, Songnam, Suwon,
Currency – Won of 100 jeon
Population – 48,636,068 rising at 0.26 per cent a year (2010 est)
Religion – Christian (Protestant 18 per cent, Roman Catholic 11 per cent), Buddhist 23 per cent (predominantly the Jogye order of the Seon (Zen) school) (est)
Language – Korean (official), English
Population density – 503 per sq. km (2009)
Urban population – 81 per cent (2008 est)
Median age (years) – 37.9 (2010 est)
National anthem – 'Aegukka' ['The Patriotic Song']
National day – 15 August (Liberation Day)
Life expectancy (years) – 78.81 (2010 est)
Mortality rate – 6.15 (2010 est)
Birth rate – 8.72 (2010 est)
Infant mortality rate – 4.24 (2010 est)
Death penalty – Retained (not used since 1997)
CPI score – 5.4 (2010)

CLIMATE AND TERRAIN

The country occupies the southern part of the mountainous Korean peninsula, with highlands and mountains accounting for around 70 per cent of the land area. Elevation extremes range from 1,950m (Halla-san) at the highest point to 0m (Sea of Japan) at the lowest.

The climate is temperate, although winters are very cold for the latitude. Average temperatures in Seoul range from −5°C in January to 26°C in August. The rainy season lasts from June to September.

HISTORY AND POLITICS

From 1948, South Korea experienced over 40 years of mostly authoritarian, often military, rule and great industrial development. Syngman Rhee, president from 1948, resigned in 1960 in the face of popular protests at corruption and electoral fraud. A military coup in 1961 brought General Park Chung-hee to power and he instigated a programme of industrial development; by the time of his assassination in 1979 Korea was a leading shipbuilding nation and producer of electronic goods.

Following riots against the interim government, General Chun Do-hwan assumed power in 1980 after martial law was declared. Pro-democracy agitation in the mid-1980s led to constitutional changes in 1987 and the first multiparty legislative elections in 1988, but despite the anti-corruption campaign of the new democratically elected president Roh Tae-woo, politics continued to be plagued by allegations of corruption and fraud, and was subject to military influence. The first civilian president and the first wholly civilian government since 1961 were appointed in 1993. Kim Dae-jung's inauguration as president in 1998 saw the adoption of the 'sunshine policy' of engagement with North Korea.

The 2007 presidential election was won by Lee Myung-bak, the Grand National Party (GNP) candidate. In the 2008 legislative election, the GNP won a majority of seats in the legislature. Lee Myung-bak's government reversed the 'sunshine policy' in 2008, and imposed sanctions on North Korea in 2010, blaming North Korea for the sinking of one of its warships in March 2010.

POLITICAL SYSTEM

A new constitution was adopted when the Sixth Republic was inaugurated in 1988. Under this, the president is directly elected for a five-year term, which is not renewable. He appoints the prime minister with the approval of the legislature, and members of the state council (cabinet) on the recommendation of the prime minister. The president is also empowered to take wide-ranging measures in an emergency, including the declaration of martial law, but must obtain the agreement of the legislature. The unicameral National Assembly has 299 members who are directly elected for a four-year term.

HEAD OF STATE

President, Lee Myung-bak, *elected* 19 December 2007, *sworn in* 25 February 2008

SELECTED GOVERNMENT MEMBERS *as at June 2011*

Prime Minister, Kim Hwang-sik
Finance, Bahk Jae-wan
Defence, Gen. Kim Kwan-jin
Foreign Affairs, Kim Sung-hwan
Justice, Lee Kwi-nam

EMBASSY OF THE REPUBLIC OF KOREA
60 Buckingham Gate, London SW1E 6AJ
T 020-7227 5500 E koreanembinuk@mofat.go.kr
W http://gbr.mofat.go.kr
Ambassador Extraordinary and Plenipotentiary, HE Choo Kyu-ho, *apptd* 2010

BRITISH EMBASSY

Taepyeongno 40, 4 Jeong-dong, Jung-gu, Seoul 100-120
T (+82) (2) 3210 5500 E enquiry.seoul@fco.gov.uk
W http://ukinrok.fco.gov.uk
Ambassador Extraordinary and Plenipotentiary, HE Scott
  Wightman, CMG, *apptd* 2011

BRITISH COUNCIL

4F Hungkuk Life Insurance Building, 226 Shinmunro 1-ga,
Jongro-gu, Seoul 110-786
T (+82) (2) 3702 0600 W www.britishcouncil.org/korea
Director, Roland Davies

DEFENCE

The army has 2,414 main battle tanks, 2,780 armoured personnel carriers, over 100 armoured infantry fighting vehicles and 60 armed helicopters. The navy has 23 submarines, 1 cruiser, 6 destroyers, 12 frigates, 111 patrol and coastal vessels, 8 combat aircraft, 24 armed helicopters and 100 main battle tanks. There are 8 naval bases. The air force has 490 combat aircraft.
Military budget – US$25,400m (2010)
Military personnel – 655,000: army 522,000, navy
  68,000, air force 65,000; paramilitary 4,500
Conscription duration – 26 months

ECONOMY AND TRADE

Industrialisation from the 1960s transformed South Korea from a predominantly agrarian country into one of the Asian 'miracle' economies by the 1980s. Initially based on shipbuilding and electrical goods, production shifted towards electronics and IT goods in the 1980s. By 1997 South Korea was the world's eleventh-largest economy, with an annual GDP growth rate of 8 per cent. However, the dominating conglomerates *(chaebols)* were experiencing difficulties which, exacerbated by the Asian financial crisis in 1997, caused a number to collapse in the late 1990s and the economy to contract sharply. Corporate and financial reforms were introduced and GDP growth resumed, on a more modest scale, from the early 2000s. The global downturn in 2008 caused another brief contraction in 2009 but the economy recovered strongly in 2010.

Services contribute 57.6 per cent to GDP, industry 39.4 per cent and agriculture 3 per cent. Major manufacturing industries include electronics, tele-communications, motor vehicles, chemicals, shipbuilding and steel. Tourism is of growing importance.

The main trading partners are China, Japan and the USA. Principal exports are semiconductors, tele-communications equipment, motor vehicles, computers, steel, ships and petrochemicals. The main imports are machinery, electronics and electronic equipment, oil, steel, transport equipment, organic chemicals and plastics.
GNI – US$836,893m; US$19,830 per capita (2009)
Annual average growth of GDP – 6.1 per cent (2010 est)
Inflation rate – 3 per cent (2010 est)
Population below poverty line – 15 per cent (2006 est)
Unemployment – 3.7 per cent (2010 est)
Total external debt – US$370,100m (2010 est)
Imports – US$322,800m (2009)
Exports – US$361,600m (2009)

BALANCE OF PAYMENTS

Trade – US$41,847m surplus (2010)
Current Account – US$42,668m surplus (2009)

Trade with UK	2009	2010
Imports from UK	£2,025,098,462	£2,204,852,690
Exports to UK	£2,474,153,942	£2,436,034,094

COMMUNICATIONS

There are 3,381km of railway in commercial operation, of which 1,843km are electrified. A high-speed railway line is being constructed between Seoul and Busan, and between Cheongwong county and Gwangju; there are plans to extend the service across the country by 2020. There are 103,029km of roads, of which 3,367km are motorways. There are 116 airports and airfields, including international airports at Seoul (Kimpo), Kimhae (near Busan), Daegu, Cheju city and Incheon. Busan, Incheon and Pohang are the major ports, although development and operations at Incheon are hampered by tidal variations of 9–10m.

Modern telecommunications systems served 19.2 million fixed-line users, 47.9 million mobile phone subscribers and 39.4 million internet users in 2009.

EDUCATION AND HEALTH

Primary education is free and compulsory for nine years from the age of six. Secondary and higher education is extensive, with the option of middle school to age 15 and high school to age 18.
Gross enrolment ratio (percentage of relevant age group) –
  primary 105 per cent; secondary 97 per cent; tertiary
  98 per cent (2008 est)
Health expenditure (per capita) – US$1,108 (2009)
Hospital beds (per 1,000 people) – 12.3 (2004–9)

MEDIA

Korea has a number of public radio and television broadcasters, including Korea Broadcasting System (KBS) and Munhwa Broadcasting Corporation (MBC), as well as a diversified commercial sector. There is a high rate of subscription to cable and satellite services. Newspaper readership is very high and a number of dailies, many of which are owned by industrial conglomerates, are in English.

KOSOVO

Republika e Kosoves – Republic of Kosovo

Area – 10,887 sq. km
Capital – Pristina; population 500,000 (2009 est)
Major towns – Kosovska Mitrovica; Pec; Prizren
Currency – Euro (€) of 100 cents; the Serbian dinar is also
  in circulation

Population – 1,815,048 (2010 est); Albanian (92 per cent), Serb (6 per cent); small Bosniak, Turk, Ashkali, Egyptian, Roma and Gorani minorities (2008 est)
Religion – Muslim, Christian (Serbian Orthodox, Roman Catholic, Protestant)
Language – Albanian, Serbian (both official), Bosnian, Turkish, Romani
Population density – 166 per sq. km (2009)
Median age (years) – 26.3 (2010 est)
National anthem – 'Europe'
National day – 17 February (Independence Day)
CPI score – 2.8 (2010)

CLIMATE AND TERRAIN

The landlocked country has a hilly central region which divides plains in the east and west. Mountains lie along the borders with Albania, Macedonia and Montenegro, and along much of the border with Serbia. Elevation extremes range from 2,656m (Gjeravica) to 297m (Drini i Bardhe river). The main rivers are the Drini i Bardhe in the west and the Iberi in the north. The climate is continental.

HISTORY AND POLITICS

Kosovo was at the centre of the medieval kingdom of Serbia and was the location of the Serbian defeat by the Ottoman Turks in 1389 that led to the kingdom becoming part of the Ottoman Empire; the resonances of these events underlie Serbia's refusal to countenance the independence of what it views as the heartland of its nation. Kosovo was under Ottoman rule from 1389 until 1913, when Serbia regained control following the First Balkan War. As a province of Serbia, Kosovo became part of the Kingdom of Serbs, Croats and Slovenes (subsequently Yugoslavia) in 1918.

Under Ottoman rule, migration gradually altered the population's ethnicity, and Albanians had become the dominant ethnic group by the end of the 19th century. After the Second World War, the Yugoslav federal government made Kosovo an autonomous republic within Serbia, granting autonomy almost equivalent to that of one of the constituent republics in 1974. The Serbian republican government stripped the province of its autonomy in 1989 and progressively excluded the Albanian majority from public life, suppressing their culture. The Kosovans' decisive vote in a 1991 referendum for independence from both Serbia and Yugoslavia was declared illegal by the Serbian government, which tightened its control further.

An insurgency by the Kosovan Liberation Army (KLA) from the mid 1990s provoked Serbian military reprisals that from 1998 developed into systematic ethnic cleansing. Over 800,000 people sought refuge in Albania, Macedonia or Montenegro, and over 500,000 were internally displaced. NATO intervened in March 1999, and Serbia accepted a peace plan in June 1999 and withdrew its forces. The UN then placed Kosovo under transitional administration, establishing autonomous democratic institutions to which it gradually devolved administrative responsibilities.

UN-sponsored talks on Kosovo's future (2005–7) failed to make any progress, and on 17 February 2008 the Kosovan government unilaterally declared independence from Serbia. The UN completed its hand-over of administrative powers in June 2008; that month the Serb minority set up its own assembly in Mitrovica, which has been a flashpoint for intercommunal tension. The UN's interim administration mission remains in Kosovo to maintain stability and protect the Serb minority, along with the EU (police and rule of law mission) and the International Civilian Office, headed by the EU's special representative.

Kosovo's declaration of independence had been recognised by 76 countries by June 2011, but not by the UN, which referred consideration of its legality to the International Court of Justice in 2008; the ICJ ruled in 2010 that the declaration was not illegal. Serbia refuses to accept the declaration, but began direct talks with Kosovo in March 2011 to try to resolve the dispute.

In the 2010–11 legislative elections, the Democratic Party of Kosovo, led by Hashim Thaci, remained the largest party in the legislature, but without a majority. It formed a coalition government with six smaller parties, under the leadership of Mr Thaci, in February 2011. Behgjet Pacolli was elected president unopposed in February 2011, but the constitutional court declared the election unconstitutional; Atifete Jahjaga was elected president in April 2011.

POLITICAL SYSTEM

Under the 2008 constitution, the president is elected by the legislature for a five-year term and can be re-elected once. The unicameral legislature, the Assembly of Kosovo, has 120 members, elected for a four-year term; 100 seats have directly elected members, ten seats are reserved for Serbs and ten for other minorities. The majority party or coalition nominates the prime minister, who is appointed by the president. Both the prime minister and the government must be approved by the legislature.

HEAD OF STATE
President, Atifete Jahjaga, *elected* 7 April 2011

SELECTED GOVERNMENT MEMBERS *as at June 2011*
Prime Minister, Hashim Thaci
First Deputy Prime Minister, Behgjet Pacolli
Deputy Prime Ministers, Bujar Bukoshi; Mimoza Kusari-Lila; Slobodan Petrovic; Edita Tahiri
Finance, Bedri Hamza
Foreign Affairs, Enver Hoxhaj

EMBASSY OF THE REPUBLIC OF KOSOVO
100 Pall Mall, London SW1 5NQ
T 020-7659 6140 E embassy.uk@ks-gov.net
Ambassador Extraordinary and Plenipotentiary, HE Dr Muhamet Hamiti, *apptd* 2009

BRITISH EMBASSY
Ismail Qemali 6, Arberi, Dragodan, Pristina
T (+381) 3825 4700 E britishembassy.pristina@fco.gov.uk
W http://ukinkosovo.fco.gov.uk
Ambassador Extraordinary and Plenipotentiary, HE Ian Cameron Cliff, OBE, *apptd* 2011

BRITISH COUNCIL
Perandori Justinian 6, Qyteza Pejton, 10000 Pristina
T (+381) 3824 3292 W www.britishcouncil.org/kosovo
Director, Arjeta Emra

ECONOMY AND TRADE

Under UN administration Kosovo began the transition to a market economy, and over half of state-owned businesses have been privatised. However, income levels are the lowest in Europe, and the economy is dependent on international and foreign aid and the remittances of expatriates, worth about 7.5 per cent and 14 per cent of

GDP respectively. Agriculture is close to subsistence level and inefficient; industrial output has declined because of insufficient investment and an unemployment level of over 40 per cent encourages emigration. International agencies and foreign governments are working with the Kosovan government to stimulate economic growth, attract investment and reduce unemployment.

Natural resources include lignite, lead, zinc, nickel, chrome, magnesium, kaolin and bauxite, and the mainstay of the economy is mining and the production of construction materials. Production is held back by ageing equipment and inadequacies in the power sector, although these are being addressed. Agriculture contributes 12.9 per cent of GDP, while employing 24 per cent of the workforce, industry contributes 22.6 per cent and services 64.5 per cent.

Kosovo joined the Central Europe Free Trade Area (CEFTA) in 2006, and its members are the main markets for exports of minerals and processed metal products, scrap metals, leather goods, machinery and appliances. Imports of foodstuffs, wood, fuels, chemicals, machinery and electrical equipment come mainly from EU and neighbouring countries.

GNI – US$5,619m; US$3,240 per capita (2009)
Inflation rate – 5.3 per cent (2007 est)
Population below poverty line – 35 per cent (2007 est)
Unemployment – 45 per cent (2009 est)

Trade with UK	2009	2010
Imports from UK	£4,568,632	£3,007,379
Exports to UK	£133,999	£528,922

MEDIA

Television is the primary source of news; services are provided by two private stations and the public broadcaster Kosovo Radio-Television (RTK). The European Broadcasting Union, which originally set up RTK in 1999, has accused the Kosovan government of eroding the broadcaster's editorial independence since 2008. There are over 80 licensed radio stations, and six daily newspapers selling to a limited readership; the largest of these is *Koha Ditore*. Kosovo had 377,000 internet users in 2008.

KUWAIT

Dawlat al-Kuwayt – State of Kuwait

Area – 17,818 sq. km
Capital – Kuwait City (Al Kuwayt); population, 2,229,990 (2009 est)
Currency – Kuwaiti dinar (KD) of 1,000 fils

Population – 2,789,132 rising at 3.5 per cent a year (2010 est); Kuwaiti (45 per cent), other Arab (35 per cent), South Asian (9 per cent), Iranian (4 per cent) (est)
Religion – Of citizens, Muslim (Sunni 70 per cent, the remainder predominantly Shia) (est); Christian, Hindu and Parsi minorities, mostly expatriates
Language – Arabic (official), English
Population density – 157 per sq. km (2009)
Urban population – 98 per cent (2008 est)
Median age (years) – 26.4 (2010 est)
National anthem – 'Al-Nasheed al-Watani' ['National Anthem']
National day – 25 February
Life expectancy (years) – 77.89 (2010 est)
Mortality rate – 2.29 (2010 est)
Birth rate – 21.64 (2010 est)
Infant mortality rate – 8.75 (2010 est)
Death penalty – Retained
CPI score – 4.5 (2010)

CLIMATE AND TERRAIN

Kuwait is an almost entirely flat desert plain, with elevation extremes ranging from 306m at the highest point to 0m (Persian Gulf) at the lowest. Its territory includes the island of Bubiyan and others at the head of the Persian Gulf. The climate is arid, with little rainfall but high levels of humidity. Average temperatures range from 13°C in January to 37°C in July.

HISTORY AND POLITICS

The area was under the nominal control of the Ottoman Empire from the late 16th century, but in 1756 an autonomous sheikhdom was founded that has been ruled by the al-Sabah family ever since. Kuwait entered into a treaty of friendship with Britain in 1899, in order to protect itself from Ottoman and Saudi domination, and it became a British protectorate in 1914. The borders with Saudi Arabia and Iraq were agreed between 1922 and 1933. Full independence was achieved in 1961, although Britain retained a military presence in the country until 1971.

An attempted Iraqi invasion shortly after independence in 1961 was discouraged by British troops in the Gulf. However, in August 1990 Iraq invaded and occupied Kuwait, proclaiming it a province of Iraq. In 1991, a short military campaign by a US-led alliance expelled the Iraqi forces, although there were further Iraqi incursions in 1993 before Iraq renounced its claim and recognised the new UN-demarcated border in 1994. Extensive damage was caused to the country's infrastructure and environment during the Iraqi occupation and the liberation campaign, and reconstruction was a priority throughout the 1990s. In 2003, Kuwait was a base for forces involved in the Iraq War, and it remains an important transit route for military and civilian traffic into and out of Iraq.

In recent years, there have been clashes between security forces and militant Islamists, some of whom are alleged to have links to al-Qaida.

Although Kuwait was the first Arab country in the Gulf to have an elected legislature, this was suspended from 1977–81, 1986–92 and in 1999. Since 1999 it has sat regularly, and its assertiveness has caused clashes with the government; two elections were held in 12 months in 2008–9 owing to its efforts to subject the government to parliamentary scrutiny. After the May 2009 election, Islamists remained the largest bloc but liberals gained an additional seat, and four women were elected. Pro-reform demonstrations took place in spring 2011.

POLITICAL SYSTEM

The 1962 constitution was amended in 2005 to extend the franchise to women. The head of state is the emir, chosen from among the ruling family. He exercises executive power through the council of ministers; in 2003, the post of prime minister was separated from the role of heir to the throne for the first time. The unicameral National Assembly has 50 members directly elected for a four-year term. There are no political parties.

The country is divided into six governorates: Capital, Hawalli, Al-Ahmadi, Al-Jahrah, Al-Farwaniya and Mubarak Al-Kabeer.

HEAD OF STATE

HH The Emir of Kuwait, Sheikh Sabah al-Ahmad al-Jaber al-Sabah, *born* 1929, *acceded* 29 January 2006
Crown Prince, HH Shekh Nawaf al-Ahmad al-Jaber al-Sabah

SELECTED GOVERNMENT MEMBERS *as at June 2011*
Prime Minister, Sheikh Nasser al-Muhammad al-Ahmad al-Sabah
First Deputy Prime Minister, Defence, Sheikh Jaber al-Mubarak al-Hamad al-Sabah
Deputy Prime Minister, Sheikh Mohammad Sabah al-Salem al-Sabah *(Foreign Affairs)*
Interior, Sheikh Ahmad al-Hamoud al-Sabah
Finance, Mustafa Jasim al-Shimali

EMBASSY OF THE STATE OF KUWAIT
2 Albert Gate, London SW1X 7JU
T 020-7590 3400 **E** kuwait@dircon.co.uk
Ambassador Extraordinary and Plenipotentiary, HE Khaled al-Duwaisan, GCVO, *apptd* 1993

BRITISH EMBASSY
PO Box 2, Arabian Gulf Street, Safat 13001
T (+965) 2259 4320 **W** http://ukinkuwait.fco.gov.uk
Ambassador Extraordinary and Plenipotentiary, HE Frank Baker, OBE, *apptd* 2010

BRITISH COUNCIL
PO Box 345, 2 Al Arabi Street, Block 2, Mansouriya, Safat 13004
T (+965) 251 5512 **W** www.britishcouncil.org/me
Director (acting), Michael White

DEFENCE

The army has 293 main battle tanks, 321 armoured personnel carriers and up to 450 armoured infantry fighting vehicles. The navy has 10 patrol and coastal vessels, based at Ras al-Qalaya. The air force has 50 combat aircraft and 25 armed helicopters.
Military budget – US$3,910m (2010)
Military personnel – 15,500: army 11,000, navy 2,000, air force 2,500; paramilitary 7,100

ECONOMY AND TRADE

Oil was discovered in 1938 and the development of the oil industry after 1945 transformed the country from one of the poorest in the world to one of the richest. Petroleum accounts for 95 per cent of export revenues and 95 per cent of government income. Income from foreign reserves and investment is also high, cushioning the economy from the effects of dependency on oil. Economic reform is slow owing to the tensions between the government and legislature, but a development plan passed in 2011 aims to diversify the economy, attract more investment and stimulate the private sector.

The climate and terrain limit agriculture and, with the exception of fish, all food is imported; the primary sector contributes only 0.3 per cent of GDP. Services account for 51.6 per cent of GDP and industry for 48.1 per cent. Apart from the oil and petrochemical industries, activities include the production of cement and construction materials, shipbuilding and repair, water desalination and food processing. Immigrant labour, mainly from Pakistan, India and Iran, makes up about 60 per cent of the 2 million-strong workforce.

The main export markets are Japan, South Korea, India, Taiwan, the USA and China, and the main sources of imports are the USA, China, Germany and Japan. Principal exports are oil and refined products, and fertilisers. The main imports are food, construction materials, vehicles and vehicle parts, and clothing.
GNI – US$127,141m; US$43,930 per capita (2007)
Annual average growth of GDP – 3.2 per cent (2010 est)
Inflation rate – 3.8 per cent (2010 est)
Unemployment – 2.2 per cent (2004 est)
Total external debt – US$56,810m (2010 est)
Imports – US$17,900m (2009)
Exports – US$50,300m (2009)

BALANCE OF PAYMENTS
Trade – US$41,936m surplus (2010)
Current Account – US$64,470m surplus (2008)

Trade with UK	2009	2010
Imports from UK	£451,182,053	£530,434,798
Exports to UK	£676,784,764	£958,351,509

COMMUNICATIONS

Kuwait has 5,749km of roads, most of which are surfaced, but no railway or internal waterways. There are seven airports and airstrips; the international airport is at Kuwait City. The main seaports are Ash Shu'aybah, Ash Shuwaykh, Mina' 'Abd Allah, Mina' al Ahmadi and Mina' Sa'ud.

Modern telephone systems provided 553,000 fixed lines, 3.9 million mobile phone subscribers and 1.1 million internet users in 2009.

EDUCATION AND HEALTH

Education is free and compulsory from six to 14 years.
Literacy rate – 94.5 per cent (2008 est)
Gross enrolment ratio (percentage of relevant age group) – primary 95 per cent; secondary 90 per cent (2009 est)
Health expenditure (per capita) – US$1,416 (2009)
Hospital beds (per 1,000 people) – 1.8 (2004–9)

MEDIA

Newspaper publishers require a government licence and some topics are subject to government censorship. Even so, Kuwaiti newspapers are far more outspoken in their coverage of politics than newspapers in neighbouring Arab nations. State-run radio and television broadcasters compete with commercial stations; satellite television is also widely watched.

KYRGYZSTAN

Kyrgyz Respublikasy – Kyrgyz Republic

Area – 199,951 sq. km
Capital – Bishkek; population, 854,001 (2009 est)
Major city – Osh
Currency – Som of 100 tyiyn
Population – 5,508,626 rising at 1.41 per cent a year
   (2010 est); Kyrgyz (64.9 per cent), Uzbek (13.8 per
   cent), Russian (12.5 per cent), Dungan (1.1 per cent),
   Ukrainian (1 per cent), Uygur (1 per cent) (est)
Religion – Muslim 75 per cent (predominantly Sunni),
   Christian (Russian Orthodox 20 per cent) (est)
Language – Kyrgyz, Russian (both official), Uzbek,
   Dungun
Population density – 28 per sq. km (2009)
Urban population – 36 per cent (2008 est)
Median age (years) – 24.7 (2010 est)
National anthem – 'Kyrgyz Respublikasynyn Mamlekettik
   Gimni' ['National Anthem of the Kyrgyz Republic']
National day – 31 August (Independence Day)
Life expectancy (years) – 69.74 (2010 est)
Mortality rate – 6.85 (2010 est)
Birth rate – 23.58 (2010 est)
Infant mortality rate – 30.25 (2010 est)
Death penalty – Abolished for all crimes (since 2007)
CPI score – 2.0 (2010)
Gross enrolment ratio (percentage of relevant age group) –
   primary 95 per cent; secondary 84 per cent; tertiary 51
   per cent (2009 est)
Literacy rate – 99.3 per cent (2008 est)
Health expenditure (per capita) – US$57 (2009)
Hospital beds (per 1,000 people) – 5.1 (2004–9)

CLIMATE AND TERRAIN

Kyrgyzstan is a landlocked and mountainous country
lying in the Tien Shan mountain range, with the Pamir
mountains in the extreme south. Elevations range from
7,439m (Jengish Chokusu) at the highest point to 132m
(Kara-Darya) at the lowest, though most of the country
lies at over 1,000m. The principal rivers are the Naryn
and the Chu, and the vast Issyk-Kul lake lies in the
north-east. The climate is continental but with
temperatures and humidity moderated by the altitude;
typical temperatures in the valleys range from as low as
−14°C in January to 27°C in July. Rainfall is low for the
altitude, owing to Kyrgyzstan's distance from the sea and
the rain-shadow effect of the Himalayan and Pamir
ranges.

HISTORY AND POLITICS

After periods under Turkic, Mongol and Chinese rule, the
Kyrgyz became part of the Russian Empire in the 1860s

and 1870s. After the October 1917 revolution in Russia,
the area became part of the Turkestan autonomous
republic within the USSR until 1924, when the Kirgiz
Autonomous Region was formed. Soviet rule brought
land reforms in the 1920s that resulted in the settlement
of many of the nomadic Kyrgyz. Kyrgyzstan became an
autonomous republic in 1926 and a constituent republic
of the USSR in 1936.

Reform in the USSR in the 1980s provoked an upsurge
in nationalism in Kyrgyzstan and agitation for
independence. Following the attempted coup in Moscow
in 1991, Kyrgyzstan became an independent republic and
joined the Commonwealth of Independent States.

Since independence, there has been tension between
the Kyrgyz and ethnic Uzbeks, concentrated around
Osh, and between the Kyrgyz and Dungans (ethnic
Chinese) near Bishkek. These tensions have flared into
intercommunal violence on occasions. There have also
been clashes between security forces and militant
Islamists, active near the border with Tajikistan.

Askar Akayev, a pro-reform Communist, was president
from 1990 until he was deposed in March 2005 in a
popular uprising over alleged electoral fraud; the uprising
was also fuelled by years of unrest over the dire economic
situation, corruption, nepotism and crime. The opposition
leader Kurmanbek Bakiyev was elected president in July
2005 but his tenure was undermined by the same
problems as his predecessor's, as well as a power struggle
with the legislature over the extent of presidential powers.

President Bakiyev, re-elected in 2009, was forced
from office in April 2010 after attempts to suppress
anti-government demonstrations left over 80 protesters
dead. An interim government was formed, headed by
Roza Otunbayeva, as crime and civil disruption grew.
Intercommunal violence between Kyrgyz and Uzbeks
erupted in the Osh area in June 2010 and spread to
Jalalabad. Elections were scheduled for October 2010,
but the violence caused the presidential election to be
postponed for a year; however, a referendum was held in
June 2010 which approved a draft constitution granting
greater powers to parliament at the expense of the
president. The 2010 legislative election was indecisive,
the four main parties winning roughly the same number
of seats each. Two, the Social Democratic Party and
Respublika, formed a coalition government with the
Homeland party and took office in December. The
presidential election is scheduled for late 2011.

POLITICAL SYSTEM

Under the 2010 constitution, the president will be
directly elected for a six-year term, which is not
renewable. The unicameral Supreme Council has 120
members directly elected for a five-year term. The largest
party in the legislature nominates the prime minister, and
the president appoints the cabinet; the appointments are
subject to the approval of the Supreme Council.

HEAD OF STATE
Interim President, Roza Otunbayeva, *sworn in* 3 July 2010

SELECTED GOVERNMENT MEMBERS *as at June 2011*
Prime Minister, Almazbek Atambayev
Vice Prime Ministers, Shamil Atahanov; Ibragim Junusov;
   Jantoro Satybaldiyev
Foreign Affairs, Ruslan Kazakbayev
Internal Affairs, Zarylbek Rysaliev
Defence, Maj.-Gen. Abibilla Kudayberdiyev

United Kingdom & Ireland

ATLANTIC OCEAN

North Sea

Shetland Islands
Lerwick

Fair Isle

Orkney Islands
Kirkwall

Pentland Firth
Thurso *Duncansby Head*
Wick

Cape Wrath

North West Highlands

Outer Hebrides
Lewis
Stornoway
Ullapool
Harris
N. Uist
Dornoch
Dingwall
Elgin
Fraserburgh
Peterhead

SCOTLAND
Cairngorms
Ben Macdhui 1309
Aberdeen
Stonehaven

S. Uist
Portree
Kyle of Lochalsh
Skye
Loch Ness
Inverness
Spey

Malaig
Fort William
Ben Nevis 1343
Grampian Mts.

Mull
Oban
Perth
Dundee
St. Andrews
Fife Ness

Loch Lomond
Stirling
Kirkcaldy
Firth of Forth

Islay
Greenock
Dunfermline
Falkirk
Paisley
Glasgow
Edinburgh
Berwick-upon-Tweed

Kintyre
Arran
Kilmarnock
Peebles
Galashiels
Tweed
Jedburgh
Alnwick

Ayr
Nith
Southern Uplands
Cheviot Hills

Malin Head

Bloody Foreland
Londonderry
Coleraine
Dumfries
Tyne
Blyth
Newcastle upon Tyne

Malinmore Head
Donegal
Strabane
Ballymena
Larne
Stranraer
Wigtown
Kirkcudbright
Carlisle
Consett
Durham
Sunderland

Donegal Bay
Omagh
Lough Neagh
NORTHERN
Belfast
Bangor
Penrith
Wear
Darlington
Hartlepool
Middlesbrough

Ballina
Enniskillen
Lough Erne
Portadown
Strangford Lough
IRELAND
Lurgan
Armagh
Downpatrick
Solway Firth
Workington
Lake District
Keswick
Scarborough

Sligo
Carrick on Shannon
Cavan
Mourne Mts.
Newry
Isle of Man
Douglas
Kendal
Windermere
Bridlington

Clew Bay
Castlebar
Westport
Longford
Dundalk
Barrow-in-Furness
Lancaster
Harrogate
York
Kingston upon Hull

Mask
Roscommon
Navan
Drogheda
Irish Sea
Blackpool
Preston
Bradford
Leeds
Spurn Head
Grimsby

Corrib
Athlone
Mullingar
Liverpool
Manchester
Sheffield

Clifden
Galway
Tullamore
Liffey
Dublin
Anglesey
Holyhead
Birkenhead
Peak District
Chesterfield
Lincoln
Skegness

Galway Bay
Ballinasloe
Port Laoise
Dun Laoghaire
Llandudno
Denbigh
Chester
Crewe
Nottingham
Boston
The Wash
Cromer

Milltown Malbay
Ennis
Shannon
Kildare
Bray
Caernarfon
Dee
Stoke-on-Trent
Derby
Grantham
Kings Lynn
Norfolk Broads
Great Yarmouth

Kilrush
Limerick
Kilkenny
Wicklow Mts.
Wicklow
Snowdon 1085
Wrexham
Shrewsbury
Leicester
Peterborough
Norwich
Waveney

Tralee
Tipperary
Carlow
Arklow
Dolgellau
Montgomery
Wolverhampton
Coventry
Northampton
Cambridge
Ipswich
Harwich

Valentia
Killarney
Mallow
Clonmel
Enniscorthy
Wexford
Cardigan Bay
Aberystwyth
Llandrindod Wells
Birmingham
Rugby
Bedford
Luton
The Naze

Dingle
Suir
Waterford
Rosslare
Teifi
Worcester
Cotswolds
Oxford
LONDON
Colchester

Kenmare
Youghal
Dungarvan
Mine Head
St. George's Channel
Cardigan
Fishguard
Carmarthen
Gloucester
Chiltern Hills
Southend-on-Sea
Margate

Bantry
Cork
St. David's Head
Milford Haven
Llanelli
Ebbw Vale
Bristol
Swindon
Reading
Maidstone
Canterbury

Cape Clear
Swansea
Port Talbot
Newport
Bath
Salisbury Plain
Guildford
Dover
Strait of Dover
Folkestone
Calais

Cardiff
Avon
Salisbury
Winchester
The Weald
Hastings

Bristol Channel
Barnstaple
Exmoor
Taunton
Southampton
Brighton
Boulogne

Hartland Point
Bude
Yeovil
Poole
Isle of Wight
Portsmouth
Le Touquet

Exeter
Bournemouth

Dartmoor
Tavistock
Weymouth
Portland Bill

Bodmin
Torquay
English Channel
Abbeville
Dieppe

Truro
Plymouth
Start Point

Penzance
Land's End
Falmouth
Lizard Point

Isles of Scilly
Alderney
Cherbourg
Baie de la Seine
FRANCE
Le Havre
Rouen

Guernsey
Sark
Caen
Seine

Jersey
Collines de Normandie

0   25   50   75   100 Miles
0   50   100   150 Kms

Conical Orthomorphic Projection

© Oxford Cartographers, 97319
+44 (0)1865 882 884
E & OE

Europe

ICELAND

Reykjavik

Arctic Circle

Norwegian Sea

0 100 200 300 400 Miles
0 100 200 300 400 500 600 Kms

Conical Orthomorphic Projection

© Oxford Cartographers, 97319
+44 (0)1865 882 884
E & OE

Faeroe Is.
(Denmark)

Shetland Is.

Tromsø

Bodø

N
O
R
W
A
Y

S
W
E
D
E
N

Trondheim

Bergen

Stavanger

Kristiansand

Oslo

Gothenburg

Ge

Uppsala
Vasteras
Stockholm
Orebro
Norrkopi
Linkoping
Jonkoping

ATLANTIC

OCEAN

Hebrides

Orkney Is.

North Sea

Skagerrak

Alborg

Arhus

Helsingborg

DENMARK

Copenhagen

Odense

Malmo

Bornhol
(Den.)

Inverness

Aberdeen

Dundee

Glasgow

Edinburgh

UNITED

KINGDOM

Newcastle
upon Tyne

Londonderry

Belfast

Galway

Dublin

REP. OF
IRELAND

Cork

Liverpool

Leeds

Manchester

Sheffield

Stoke-
on-Trent

Birmingham

Norwich

Swansea

Cardiff

Bristol

London

Plymouth

Southampton

Amsterdam

NETHERLANDS

Rotterdam

Antwerp

Brussels

Lille

Kiel

Rostock

Koszalin

Hamburg

Bremen

Osnabrück

Hanover

Munster

Dortmund

Düsseldorf

Cologne

BELGIUM

GERMANY

Essen

Leipzig

Dresden

Chemnitz

Wroclaw

Szczecin

Elbe

Berlin

P

Pozr

Wroclav

English Channel

Cherbourg

Le Havre

Amiens

Caen

Rouen

Seine

Rennes

Paris

Brest

Nantes

Loire

Orléans

Reims

LUX.

Luxembourg

Frankfurt

Metz

Mannheim

Strasbourg

Nancy

Stuttgart

Nuremberg

Regensburg

Plzeň

Prague

CZECH RE

Brno

Bay of

Biscay

La Coruña

Vigo

Gijón

Bilbao

León

Pamplona

San Sebastian

Burgos

Bordeaux

Limoges

Clermont-
Ferrand

Dijon

Tours

FRANCE

Nîmes

Montpellier

Toulouse

Lyon

Grenoble

Mt. Blanc
4808

Geneva

Zurich

Bern

SWITZERLAND

LIECH.

Innsbruck

AUSTRIA

Salzburg

Vienna

Munich

Bratislav

Danube

Graz

S

SLOV.

Marib

Ljubljana

Zagre

Trento

Verona

Trieste

Rijeka

CROATIA

Banja
Luka

Oporto

Douro

Coimbra

PORTUGAL

Amadora
Lisbon
Setubal

Tagus

Badajoz

Valladolid

Zaragoza

Salamanca

Madrid

SPAIN

Lerida

ANDORRA

Pyrenees

Barcelona

Valencia

Balearic Is.
(Sp.)

Palma

Mallorca

Córdoba

Seville

Granada

Murcia

Cartagena

Huelva

Faro

Cadiz

Málaga

Almeria

Tangier

Gibraltar(U.K.)

Ceuta(Sp.)

Tétouan

Rabat

Fès

Meknès

Casablanca

MOROCCO

Mountains

Atlas

Melilla(Sp.)

Oran

Sidi Bel Abbès

Oujda

Blida

Algiers

Bejaia

Constantine

ALGERIA

Skikda

Annaba

Aryanah

Tunis

TUNISIA

Sousse

Sfax

Corsica
(Fr.)

Ajaccio

Sardinia
(It.)

Sassari

Cagliari

Mediterranean

Turin

Po

Milan

Parma

Genoa

Bologne

Nice

MONACO

Marseille

La Spezia

Livorno

Florence

SAN
MARINO

Apennines

Ancona

Rome

ITALY

Pescara

Naples

Salerno

Palermo

Messina

Sicily

Reggi
Calab

Syracus

Valletta

MALTA

Split

Adriati

Foggi

Bar

Rhône

Rhine

Adige

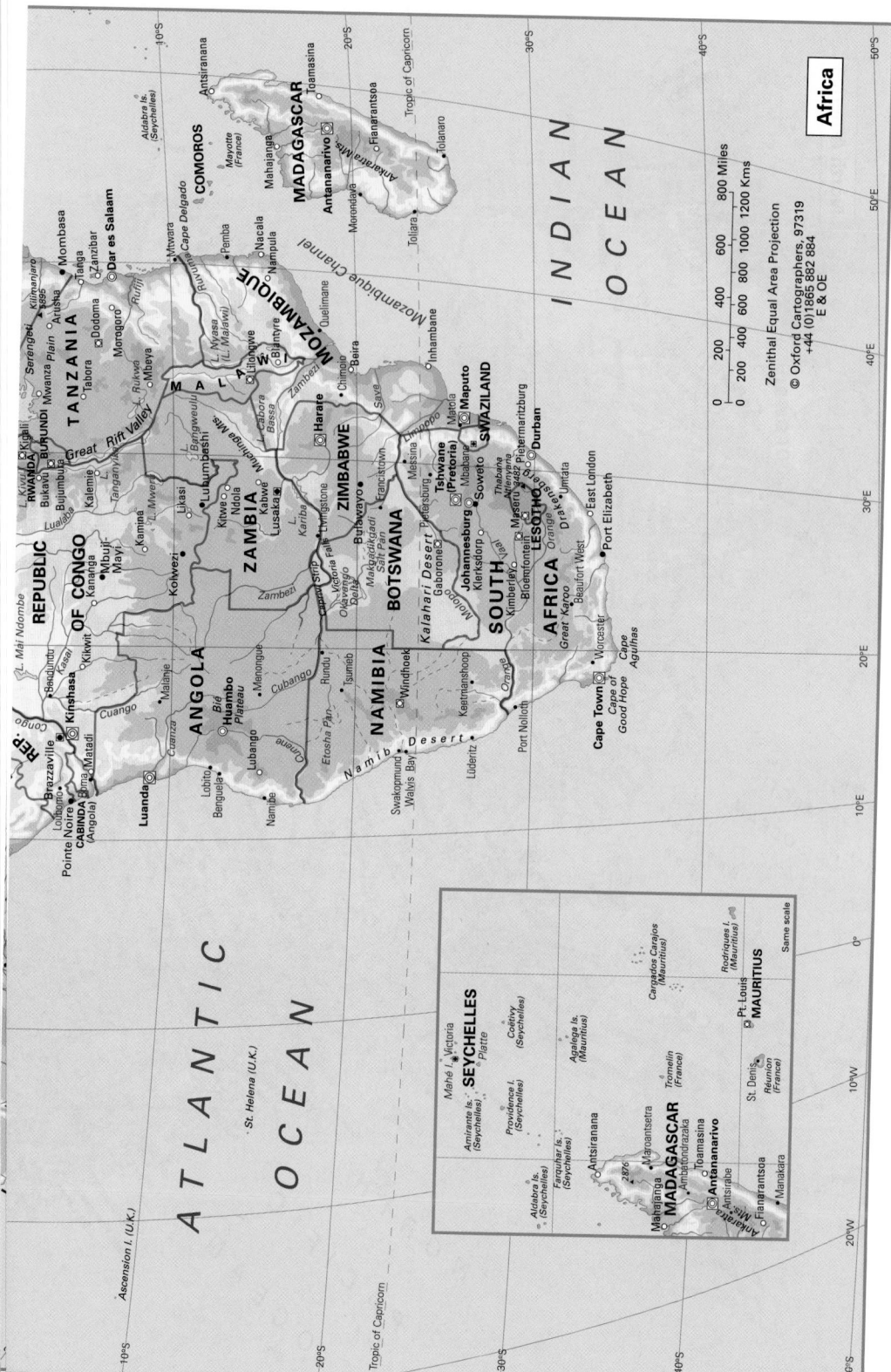

Africa

ATLANTIC OCEAN

INDIAN OCEAN

Ascension I. (U.K.)

St. Helena (U.K.)

Tropic of Capricorn

REP.

CONGO

Brazzaville
Pointe Noire
Loubomo
Boma Matadi
Kinshasa

REPUBLIC OF CONGO

L. Mai Ndombe

Bandundu
Kikwit
Kwilu
Kasai

Kananga
Mbuji-Mayi

Kamina
Kolwezi
Likasi
Lubumbashi
Kipushi
Kolwe
Kikwit

RWANDA
BURUNDI
Kigali
Bukavu
Bujumbula

L. Kivu

Serengeti
Mwanza Plain
Kilimanjaro 5895
Arusha
Moshi
Tanga
Zanzibar
Dar es Salaam
Mombasa

TANZANIA

Dodoma
Tabora
Mbeya

Great Rift Valley
L. Tanganyika
L. Rukwa
L. Mweru

Kalemie

COMOROS

Aldabra Is. (Seychelles)
Mayotte (France)

Antsiranana
Mahajanga
Toamasina

MADAGASCAR

Ankaratra Mts.
Antananarivo
Morondava
Fianarantsoa
Toliara
Tolanaro

ZAMBIA

Ndola
Kitwe
Kabwe
Lusaka

L. Bangweulu
Muchinga Mts.
L. Nyasa (L. Malawi)
L. Cabora Bassa

MALAWI
Lilongwe
Blantyre

MOZAMBIQUE

Ruvuma
Rufiji
Mtwara
Pemba
Nacala
Nampula
Quelimane
Beira
Inhambane

Cape Delgado

Mozambique Channel

ANGOLA

Luanda
Lobito
Benguela
Lubango
Namibe

Bié Plateau
Huambo
Menongue

Cuanza
Cuango
Cubango

ZIMBABWE
Harare
Bulawayo

Zambezi
Victoria Falls
Kariba
Kafue
Christgstone
Francistown

NAMIBIA
Windhoek
Swakopmund
Walvis Bay
Lüderitz
Keetmanshoop
Tsumeb
Rundu

Etosha Pan
Okavango Delta
Makgadikgadi Salt Pan

Namib Desert

Kalahari Desert

BOTSWANA
Gaborone

Orange
Molopo

SWAZILAND
Mbabane

SOUTH AFRICA

Pretoria
Tshwane
Johannesburg
Soweto
Kimberley
Kierksdorp
Bloemfontein
Beaufort West
Worcester
Cape Town
Cape of Good Hope
Cape Agulhas
Port Nolloth
Port Elizabeth
East London

LESOTHO
Maseru

Drakensberg
Thabana Ntlenyana 3482
Ladysmith
Pietermaritzburg
Durban

Messina
Umtata

Great Karoo

INDIAN OCEAN

Maputo

Zenithal Equal Area Projection

0   200   400   600   800 Miles
0   200 400 600 800 1000 1200 Kms

© Oxford Cartographers, 97319
+44 (0)1865 882 884
E & OE

SEYCHELLES
Mahé I. Victoria
Platte
Aminante Is. (Seychelles)
Coëtivy (Seychelles)
Providence I. (Seychelles)
Farquhar Is. (Seychelles)
Aldabra Is. (Seychelles)

Agalega Is. (Mauritius)
Tromelin (France)
Cargados Carajos (Mauritius)
Rodrigues I. (Mauritius)
Pt. Louis
MAURITIUS
Réunion (France)
St. Denis

MADAGASCAR
Antsiranana
Mahajanga
Maroantsetra
Ambatondrazaka
Toamasina
Antananarivo
2876
Antsirabe
Fianarantsoa
Manakara

Tropic of Capricorn

Same scale

Northern Asia

Faeroe Is.
(Denmark)

70°N   0°   10°E   20°E   30°E   40°E   60°E   80

Spitsbergen

Svalbard
(Norway)

A R C T I C

Arctic Circle

Franz Josef Land

Bergen
Oslo
Trondheim
Tromsø
Narvik
Tana

North
Cape

Barents Sea

Novaya Zemlya

Kara
Sea

Gulf of Ob

Dudinka

N O R W A Y
S W E D E N
Uppsala
Stockholm

Umeå
Lapland
Luleå

Kalakaksha Peninsula

Murmansk

Kola
Peninsula

Vorkuta

Nadym

Stockholm
Uppsala

Gulf of Bothnia

F I N L A N D

Tampere
Vaasa
Helsinki
Venta
Espoo
Gulf of Tallinn

White
Sea

Sverodvinsk

Arkhangel'sk

Pechora

Pechora

Ob'

Baltic Sea

ESTONIA
Tallinn
Tartu

Ladoga
Onega
Petrozavodsk

N. Dvina

Pechora

West

Yenisey

LATVIA
Riga
Pskov

Novgorod
Velikiye
Luki

St. Petersburg

Cherepovets
Vologda

Kotlas

Syktyvkar

M
o
u
n
t
a
i
n
s

Ukhta

Pechora

Tobol'sk

Khanty-
Mansiysk

Surgut

S i b e r i a n

Nizhnevartovsk

LITH.
Vilnius

Vitebsk
Daugavpils

Yaroslavl'
Volga (Tver')

Kostroma

Ivanovo
Tver'

Kirov
(Vyatka)

Bereznyki

Serov

U
R
A
L

Nizhniy
Tagil

Tyumen'

BELARUS
Minsk

Smolensk
Tula

Moscow

Ryazan'
Kaluga

Vladimir
Nizhniy
Novgorod
Cheboksary

Glazov

Perm
Kungur

Yekaterinburg

Kamensk-
Ural'skiy

Plain

S

Gomel'
Bryansk

Orel

Arzamas

Kazan'

Izhevsk

Tobol'sk

Ishim

Chernigov

Kursk
Belgorod

Lipetsk
Tambov

Saransk

Simbirsk
Naberezhnyye
Chelny

Sarapul

Zlatoust

Kurgan

Omsk

Tomsk

Anzhero-Sudzhensk

KHARKOV
Kharkov

Voronezh
Penza

Syzran
Tol'yatti

Ufa

Troitsk

Chelyabinsk

Kuybyshev

Kemerov

UKRAINE

Borisoglebsk

Balakhovo
Samara

Magnitogorsk

Kostanay

Petropavlovsk

Novosibirsk

Leninsk-
Kuznetskiy

Luhansk

Kamyshin

Saratov
Engel's
Orenburg

Rudnyy

Kokshetau

Novokuznetsk

Donetsk
Rostov

Volgograd

Volga

Ural'sk

Orsk

Astana

Pavlodar

Barnaul

Biysk

Elista
Stavropol'

Ural

Caspian Lowlands

Aqtobe

Atyrau

L. Tengiz

Irtysh

Rubtsovsk

Armavir

Vladikavkaz
Grozny

Makhachkala

Astrakhan

Caucasus Mts.

GEO.
Tbilisi
Gyandzha
AZERBAIJAN
40°N
Baku

Aksu
Ust-Urt
Plateau

K i r g h i z   S t e p p e

K A Z A K H S T A N

Qaraghandy

Zhezkazgan

Kazakh
Uplands

Semey

Oskemen

L. Zaysan

Altay

Sumqayit

C a s p i a n   S e a

Kara
Bogaz
Gol

Turkmenbashi

Aral
Sea
Aral'sk

Balkhash

Tacheng

Karamay

Dzungarian Bas
(Junggar Pendi

Ardabil
Rasht

UZBEKISTAN

Nukus
Dashhowuz

Syr-Dar'ya

Kyzyl-Orda

Lake
Balkhash

Taldy-Kurgan

Dzungarian Bas
Yining
Kuytun
Shihe

Kara
Elburz Mts.
Qazvin

Gorgan

Karakum Desert

Kyzylkum
Desert

Shymkent

Taraz

Almaty

Urumqi

TURKMENISTAN

Semnan
Ashgabat

Bukhara

Navoi

Turkmenabat
(Charjou)

Mary

Samarkand

Dzhizak

Tashkent

Namangan

Fergana

Bishkek

KYRGYZSTAN

Pik Pobedy
7439

Issyk
Kul'

Yining

Korla

Tien

Tehran

Qom
Esfahan

Dasht-e Kavir

IRAN

60°E

Amu Dar'ya

Dushanbe

Khujand

TAJIKISTAN

70°E

Kashi

Aksu

80°E

Tarim He

Bosten
Hu

S h a n

100°E 120°E 140°E 150°E 160°E 170°E 70°N 180° Bering Sea

0   100   200   300   400   500 Miles
0 100 200 300 400 500 600 700 800 Kms
Conical Orthomorphic Projection
© Oxford Cartographers, 97319
+44 (0)1865 882 884
E & OE

Arctic Circle

Wrangel I.

Anadyr Range

Bedr

Anadyr

Koryak Range

O C E A N

Severnaya Zemlya

Taymyr Pen.

L. Taymyr

Laptev Sea

New Siberia Is.

Lyakhov Is.

Tiksi

East Siberian

Indigirka

Cherskogo Range

Yana

Kolymna

Kolyma Mts.

60°N

Verkhoyansk Range

Central

Oienek

Lena

Magadan

Dzhugdzhur Range

Sea of Okhotsk

Vilyuy

Yakutsk

Okhotsk

Siberian

Plateau

Noril'sk

Lower Tunguska

Lena

Olekminsk

Lensk

A

Sakhalin

Aleksandrovsk
Sakhalinsky

50°N

S I

Nyurngri

Aldan

Stanovoy Mts.

Komsomol'sk
na-Amure

Amur

Sikhote-Alin Mts.

Lesosibirsk

Angara

Ust Ilimsk

Tynda

Skovorodino

Amur

Skovorodino

Birobidzhan

Khabarovsk

Achinsk   Kansk Tayshek
Krasnoyarsk

Ust-Kut

Séverobaikal'sk

Balogorsk

Blagoveshchensk

Yichum

Shuangyashan

Bratsk

Tulun

Chita

Sretensk

Bei'an

Hegang

Quitaihe

Jiamusi

Jixi

Mudanjiang

Sayan Mts.

Usol'ye-
Sibirskoye

Lake Baikal

Yablonovyy Mts.

Hailar

Daqing

Qiqihar

Harbin

Ussuriysk

Abakan   Angarsk

Irkutsk

Ulan-
Ude

Manzhouli

Baicheng

Jilin

Vladivostok

Chongjin

Kyzyl

Hovsgol
Nuur

Darhan

Ulanhot

Liaoyuan

Yanji

Uvs Nuur

Ondorhaan

Changchun

Tongliao

Siping

Fushun

DEM. PEOPLE'S
REP. OF KOREA

Hangayan Mts.

Saynshand

INNER MONGOLIA

Chifeng

Shenyang

Anshan

Pyongyang

Seoul

Altai Range

Hovd

Altay

MONGOLIA

Chengde

Fuxin

Jinzhou

Korea
Bay

Inchon

REP. OF
KOREA

Turpan
urpan Depression

Hami

Gobi Desert

Linhe

Baotou

Hohhot

Zhang-
jiakou

Jining

Datong

Beijing
(Peking)

Tangshan

Dalian

Yantai

Weihai

Kwangju

He (Yellow)

Baoding

Tianjin

Cangzhou Bo Hai

90°E

Lop Nur

Wuhai

Shizuishan

C   H   I   N

100°E

Taiyuan

Yuci

Handan

Shijiazhuang

110°E

Dezhou

Jinan

Zibo

Weifang

Qingdao

120°E

Yellow
Sea

ROMANIA
Odesa
UKRAINE
Bucharest
Kherson
Mariupol'
Rostov
Volgograd
KAZA
Emba
Shumen
Dobrich
Constanta
Simferopol'
Kerch
Sea of
Azov
Krasnodar
Armavir
Elista
Caspian Lowlands
Atyrau
Aral'sk
Kirghiz
BULGARIA
Varna
Burgas
Sevastopol'
Novorossiysk
Stavropol'
Astrakhan
Plovdiv
Edirne
Sudak
Tuapse
Maykop
RUSSIA
Black Sea
Istanbul
Bakirkoy
Bosporus
Zonguldak
Ereğli
Sochi
Caucasus Mts.
Sukhumi
Grozny
Cherkessk
Aksu
Caspian Sea
Ust-Urt
Pateau
Aral
Sea
Kyzyl-Orda
Bursa
Kocaeli
Sakarya
Karabuk
Sinop
Samsun
Abkhazia
Elbrus
5642
Vladikavkaz
Makhachkala
UZBEKISTAN
Balikesir
Eskisehir
Ordu
Trabzon
Batumi
S.Ossetia
GEORGIA
Derbent
Nukus
Kyzylkur
Desert
Manisa
Ankara
Kirikkale
Corum
Pontine Mountains
Tbilisi
ARMENIA
AZERBAIJAN
Kara-
Bogaz-
Gol
Dashhowuz
Urgench
Izmir
Usak
Yozgat
Sivas
Euphrates
Erzurum
Yerevan
Sumqayit
Baku
Turkmenbashi
Bukhara
Aydin
Kayseri
Mt.Ararat
5123
AZER.
Neftdag
Ashgabat
Karakum Desert
Amu Dar'ya
Denizli
Isparta
TURKEY
Elazig
L.Van
Khoy
Marand
Araks
Turkmenabat
(Charjou)
Antalya
Konya
Malatya
Diyarbakir
Van
Tabriz
Ardabil
Rasht
TURKMENISTAN
Mary
Taurus Mts.
Adana
Osmaniye
Kahramanmaras
Batman
Orumiyeh
Urmia
Maragheh
Zanjan
Gonbad
Bojnurd
Neyshabur
Meymaneh
Mashhad
Icel
Hatay
Gaziantep
Al Qamishli
Mahabad
Paropamisus
CYPRUS
Nicosia
Sanliurfa
Al Ladhiqiyah
Raqqah
Mosul
Arbil
Sulaymaniyah
Qazvin
Karaj
Tehran
Elburz Mts.
5671
Damavand
Gorgan
Emamrud
Sabzevar
Birjand
Herat
AFGHA
Limassol
Hamah
Dayr az Zawr
SYRIA
Kirkuk
Sanandaj
Qom
Semnan
Dasht-e Kavir
Mediterranean
Sea
Tripoli
LEBANON
Hims
Damascus
Bakhtaran
(Kermanshah)
Hamadan
Arak
Kashan
Beirut
Zahle
Syrian
Desert
Kazimiyah
Ilam
Borujerd
Khorramabad
Yazd
Dasht-e Lut
Zabul
Farah
Alexandria
Haifa
Irbid
Baghdad
Hilla
Dezful
Esfahan
Kerman
Tel Aviv
ISRAEL
Az Zarqa
Karbala
Najaf
IRAQ
Ahvaz
Zagros Mts.
IRAN
Bam
Zahedan
Cairo
Jerusalem
Amman
Dead
Sea
Al Amorrah
Nasiriyah
Euphrates
Basra
Abadan
Rafsanjan
Sirjan
Nok Kundi
El Giza
GAZA
Port Said
Ismailia
Suez
JORDAN
Elat
Aqaba
Nafud
Jahra
Kuwait
Bushehr
Borazjan
Shiraz
Jahrom
Hajjiabad
Bandar-e Abbas
BALOC
EGYPT
El Minya
Asyut
Sinai
Sharm el Sheikh
Tabuk
KUWAIT
The Gulf
Dammam
Siahan R.
Suez Canal
Ha'il
Dhahran
BAHRAIN
Al Khasab
Ras al Khaimah
Sharjah
OMAN
Chabahar
Gwadar
Al Wajh
Buraydah
Manamah
QATAR
Dubai
Makran
Turbat
Luxor
Kom Ombo
Eastern
Desert
Al Jawf
SAUDI
Anaid
Al Hufuf
Doha
Harad
Abu Dhabi
Al Ain
Sohar
Ar Rustaq
Sumail
Muscat
Sur
Aswan
Tropic of Cancer
Lake
Nasser
Halaib
Yanbu
Medina
Riyadh
Hasa
UNITED ARAB
EMIRATES
Nizwa
Ibra
Red
Sea
Mecca
At Taif
ARABIA
OMAN
Masirah
Port Sudan
Jeddah
Nubian
Desert
Asiir
Rub' al Khali
Masirah
SUDAN
Atbara
Ed Damer
Abha
Dhufar
Arab
Atbara
ERITREA
Kassala
Agordat
Asmara
Dahlak
Arch.
Farasan
Is.
Najran
Jizan
Sa'dah
Hajar
Sana'a
Hadhramaut
Halaaniyat Is.
Salalah
Se
Gedaref
Massawa
Socotra
(Yemen)
Ras Dashen
4620
Gonder
L.Tana
Bahir Dar
Hodeida
Qamar
Ibb
Ta'izz
Mukalla
YEMEN
Assab
Blue Nile
Dikhil
DJIBOUTI
Djibouti
Aden
Gulf of Aden
Boosaaso
Cape
Caseyr
ETHIOPIA
Addis
Ababa
Dire Dawa
Harer
Berbera
0   100   200   300   400 Miles
0 100 200 300 400 500 600 Kms
Nazret
Jima
Ethiopian
Highlands
Burao
Hargeysa
SOMALIA
Garoowe
Conical Orthomorphic Projection

© Oxford Cartographers, 97319
+44 (0)1865 882 884
E & OE
Awasa
Ogaden
INDIA
KENYA
Shebele
Juba
Genale

Middle East & South Asia

Taymyr Peninsula
North Siberian Plain
Arctic Circle

Laptev Sea
New Siberia Islands
Laptev Strait
East Siberian Sea

70°N

Chukchi Sea

Anadyr Range

Gulf of Anadyr

Verkhoyansk Range

Yakutsk

R U S S I A

60°N

Kolyma Range

Koryak Range

Bering Strait

Shelekhov Bay

Magadan

S i b e r i a

Kolyma

Strabanya Range

Kamchatka

Bering Sea

Alas

Irkutsk

Sea of Okhotsk

Petropavlovsk-Kamchatskiy

50°N

Komsomolsk-na-Amure

Sakhalin

A l e u t i a n   I s.
(USA)

Ulaanbaatar

Khabarovsk

Yuzhno-Sakhalinsk

MONGOLIA

Qiqihar

Harbin

Vladivostok

Sapporo

Hokkaido

Kuril Islands

International Date Line

N O R

Chifeng

Fuxin

Inner Mongolia

Shenyang

Chongjin

Sea of Japan

40°N

Beijing
(Peking)

DEM. PEOPLE'S
REP. OF KOREA

Pyongyang

Honshu

JAPAN

P A C I

Tianjin

Dalian

Seoul

Lanzhou

Yantai

Qingdao

Inchon

REP. OF
KOREA

Pusan

Tokyo

C H I N A

Yellow Sea

Mokp'o

Osaka

Midway Is.
(USA)

Xi'an

Zhengzhou

Nanjing

Chengdu

Wuhan

Shanghai

30°N

Yibin

*Chang Jiang
(Yangtze)*

Nanchang

*East China
Sea*

Kunming

Ganzhou

Fuzhou

Guilin

*Ryukyu Is.
(Japan)*

P A C I

Liuchow

Guangzhou
(Canton)

Fuzhou

Taipei

TAIWAN

Hanoi

Hong Kong

Kaohsiung

Haiphong

*Philippine
Sea*

O C E

Haikou

Hainan

Vientiane

Hue

THAILAND

Da Nang

Luzon

Northern
Mariana
Islands
(USA)

Bangkok

Manila

CAMBODIA

Phnom
Penh

Ho Chi
Minh City
(Saigon)

PHILIPPINES

Guam(U.S.A.)

MARSHALL
ISLANDS

Mindanao

Butuan

MICRONESIA

*South China
Sea*

Kota Kinabalu

Zamboanga

Davao

George Town

BRUNEI

PALAU

Caroline   Islands

KIRIBATI

Kuala Lumpur

MALAYSIA

Bandar
Seri
Begawan

Celebes

Putrajaya

Singapore

Manado

NAURU

Pakanbaru

Borneo

Sulawesi
(Celebes)

Pontianak

*Maluku
(Moluccas)*

Palembang

Balikpapan

Banjarmasin

Puncak Jaya
5029 m

New Ireland

I N D O N E S I A

New Guinea

Jakarta

Java Sea

Banda Sea

PAPUA
NEW GUINEA

SOLOMON
ISLANDS

Bandung

Surabaya

Flores   Sea

Yogyakarta

Dili

Arafura Sea

Pt. Moresby

TUVALU

EAST TIMOR

Honiara

I N D I A N

Timor

*Timor
Sea*

C. York

Arnhem
Land

Cape
York
Peninsula

Gulf of
Carpentaria

VANUATU

American
Samoa
(USA)

Wallis & Futuna
(Fr.)

SAMOA

Apia

Kimberley
Plateau

*Coral
Sea*

Port
Vila

FIJI

Suva

TONGA

O C E A N

*Great
Sandy Desert*

Barkly Tableland

New
Caledonia
(Fr.)

Townsville

Great Barrier Reef

Nuku'alofa

Tropic of Capricorn

Macdonnell Ranges

*Great
Artesian
Basin*

A U S T R A L I A

Brisbane

Great Victoria Desert

Perth

Nullarbor Plain

*Great
Dividing Range*

Sydney

C. Leeuwin

*Great
Australian Bight*

Adelaide

Canberra

Mt. Kosciuszko
2230

Tasman Sea

North
Cape

Auckland

North Island

Melbourne

NEW

*Bass
Strait*

ZEALAND

Wellington

Tasmania

Aoraki
(Mt. Cook)
3754

South Island

Hobart

Christchurch

C. Providence

Dunedin

Pacific

World Physical

World Political

Modified Gall Projection
Equatorial Scale 1:166,000,000
© Oxford Cartographers, 97319
+44 (0)1865 882 884
E & OE

Alb. Albania
Ar. Armenia
Aust. Austria
Azer. Azerbaijan
Bh. Bhutan
B&H Bosnia-Hercegovina
Brn. Brunei
Cam. Cambodia
Cam. Cameroon
Cen. Af. Rep. Central African Republic
Cro. Croatia
Cyp. Cyprus
Cz.Rep. Czech Republic
Dom. Rep. Dominican Republic

Eq. Gui. Equatorial Guinea
Es. Estonia
Ger. Germany
Gui. Guinea
Isr. Israel
Jor. Jordan
Ko. Kosovo
Kyrg. Kyrgyzstan
La. Latvia
Leb. Lebanon
Li. Lithuania
Lux. Luxembourg
Ma. F.Y.R. Macedonia
Mal. Malawi
Mo. Montenegro
Mol. Moldova

Neth. Netherlands
Q. Qatar
Rus. Russia
SL. Sierra Leone
Slok. Slovakia
Slo. Slovenia
Serb. Serbia
Sur. Suriname
Sw. Switzerland
Taj. Tajikistan
Thai. Thailand
T. Togo
Turk. Turkmenistan
UAE United Arab Emirates
UK United Kingdom
Zim. Zimbabwe

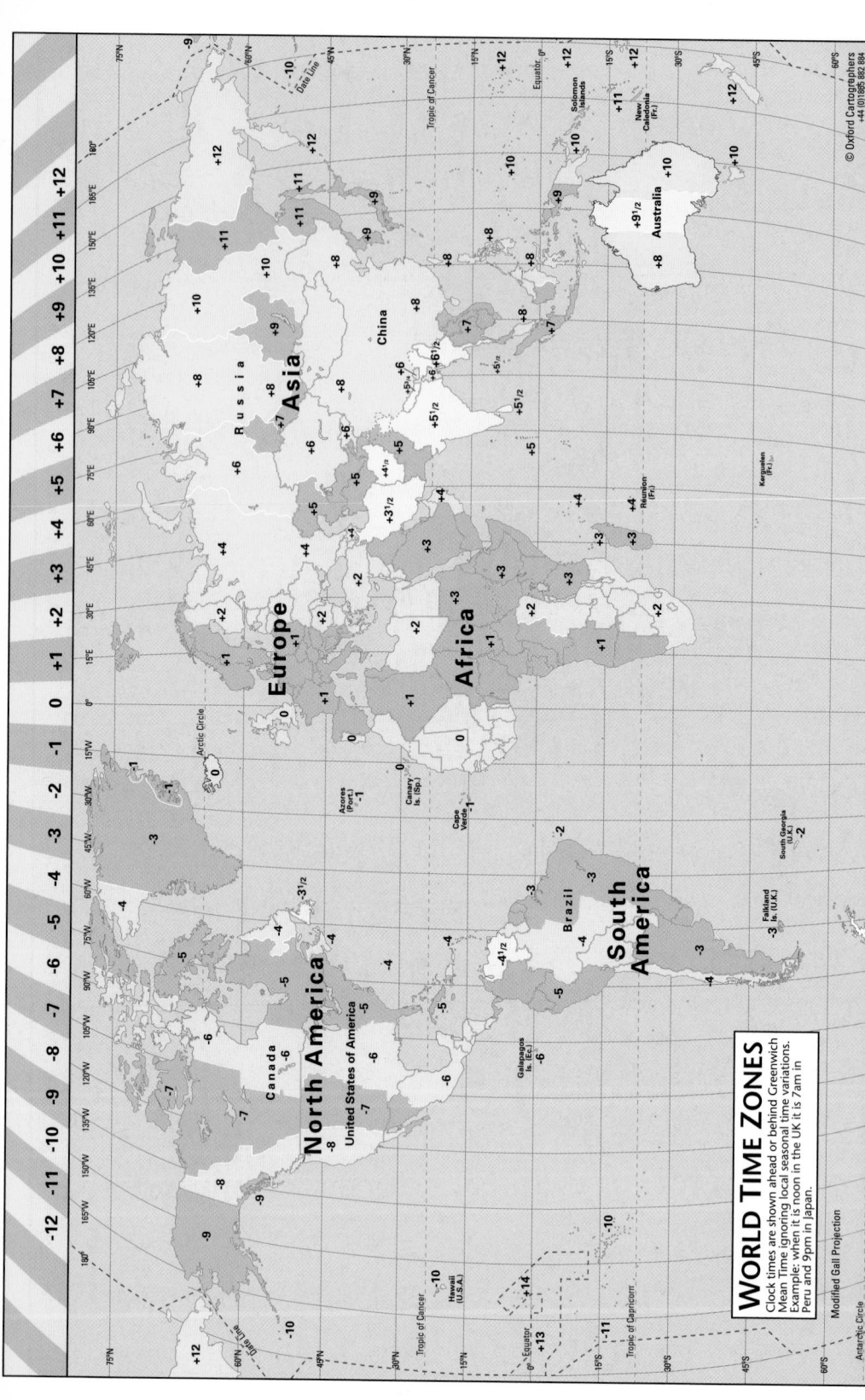

WORLD TIME ZONES

Clock times are shown ahead or behind Greenwich Mean Time ignoring local seasonal time variations. Example: when it is noon in the UK it is 7am in Peru and 9pm in Japan.

Modified Gall Projection

© Oxford Cartographers
+44 (0)1865 882 884

FLAGS OF THE WORLD

The following four pages show the national flag of each country, as it is used for international purposes. In some cases this means that the state flag is shown. Where this is the case the country name is marked (†).

 AFGHANISTAN

 ALBANIA

 ALGERIA

 ANDORRA

 ANGOLA

 ANTIGUA AND BARBUDA

 ARGENTINA

 ARMENIA

 AUSTRALIA

 AUSTRIA

 AZERBAIJAN

THE BAHAMAS

 BAHRAIN

 BANGLADESH

 BARBADOS

 BELARUS

 BELGIUM

 BELIZE

 BENIN

 BHUTAN

 BOLIVIA†

 BOSNIA AND HERCEGOVINA

 BOTSWANA

 BRAZIL

 BRUNEI

 BULGARIA

 BURKINA FASO

 BURUNDI

 CAMBODIA

 CAMEROON

 CANADA

 CAPE VERDE

  CENTRAL AFRICAN REPUBLIC

 CHAD

 CHILE

 CHINA

COLOMBIA

 THE COMOROS

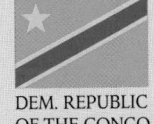 DEM. REPUBLIC OF THE CONGO

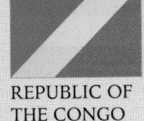 REPUBLIC OF THE CONGO

COSTA RICA

  CÔTE D'IVOIRE

 CROATIA

CUBA

CYPRUS

CZECH REPUBLIC

DENMARK

DJIBOUTI

 DOMINICA

 DOMINICAN REPUBLIC

EAST TIMOR

 ECUADOR

 EGYPT

 EL SALVADOR

 EQUATORIAL GUINEA

 ERITREA

 ESTONIA

 ETHIOPIA

 FIJI

 FINLAND

 FRANCE

 GABON

 THE GAMBIA

 GEORGIA

 GERMANY

 GHANA

 GREECE

 GRENADA

 GUATEMALA

 GUINEA

 GUINEA-BISSAU

 GUYANA

 HAITI†

 HONDURAS

 HUNGARY

 ICELAND

 INDIA

 INDONESIA

 IRAN

 IRAQ

 IRELAND

 ISRAEL

 ITALY

 JAMAICA

 JAPAN

 JORDAN

 KAZAKHSTAN

 KENYA

 KIRIBATI

 DEM. PEOPLE'S REPUBLIC OF KOREA

 REPUBLIC OF KOREA

 KOSOVO

 KUWAIT

 KYRGYZSTAN

 LAOS

LATVIA

LEBANON

LESOTHO

LIBERIA

LIBYA (NTC)

LIECHTENSTEIN

LITHUANIA

LUXEMBOURG

MACEDONIA

MADAGASCAR

MALAWI

MALAYSIA

MALDIVES

MALI

MALTA

MARSHALL
ISLANDS

MAURITANIA

MAURITIUS

MEXICO

FEDERATED STATES
OF MICRONESIA

MOLDOVA

MONACO

MONGOLIA

MONTENEGRO

MOROCCO

MOZAMBIQUE

MYANMAR

NAMIBIA

NAURU

NEPAL

THE
NETHERLANDS

NEW ZEALAND

NICARAGUA

NIGER

NIGERIA

NORWAY

OMAN

PAKISTAN

PALAU

PANAMA

PAPUA NEW
GUINEA

PARAGUAY

PERU

THE PHILIPPINES

POLAND

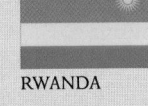
PORTUGAL

QATAR

ROMANIA

RUSSIAN
FEDERATION

RWANDA

ST CHRISTOPHER
AND NEVIS

ST LUCIA

ST VINCENT AND
THE GRENADINES

SAMOA

SAN MARINO†

SAO TOME AND
PRINCIPE

SAUDI ARABIA

SENEGAL

SERBIA†

SEYCHELLES

SIERRA LEONE

SINGAPORE

SLOVAKIA

SLOVENIA

SOLOMON ISLANDS

SOMALIA

SOUTH AFRICA

SOUTH SUDAN

SPAIN

SRI LANKA

SUDAN

SURINAME

SWAZILAND

SWEDEN

SWITZERLAND

SYRIA

TAIWAN

TAJIKISTAN

TANZANIA

THAILAND

TOGO

TONGA

TRINIDAD AND
TOBAGO

TUNISIA

TURKEY

TURKMENISTAN

TUVALU

UGANDA

UKRAINE

UNITED ARAB
EMIRATES

UNITED KINGDOM

UNITED STATES OF
AMERICA

URUGUAY

UZBEKISTAN

VANUATU

VATICAN CITY
STATE

VENEZUELA

VIETNAM

YEMEN

ZAMBIA

ZIMBABWE

SCOTTISH PARLIAMENT ELECTION 2011

Orkney & Shetland

Na h-Eileanan an Iar

Caithness, Sutherland & Ross

Banffshire & Buchan Coast

Moray

Aberdeenshire East

Inverness & Nairn

Aberdeenshire West

Skye, Lochaber & Badenoch

Angus North & Mearns

Perthshire North

Argyll & Bute

Perthshire South & Kinross-shire

Stirling

North East Fife

East Lothian

Midlothian South, Tweeddale & Lauderdale

Clydesdale

Carrick, Cumnock & Doon Valley

Ettrick, Roxburgh & Berwickshire

Dumfriesshire

Galloway & West Dumfries

CONSTITUENCIES

1 Aberdeen Central	19 East Kilbride
2 Aberdeen Donside	20 Eastwood
3 Aberdeen South & North Kincardine	21 Falkirk East
4 Airdrie & Shotts	22 Falkirk West
5 Almond Valley	23 Greenock & Inverclyde
6 Angus South	24 Hamilton, Larkhall & Stonehouse
7 Ayr	25 Kilmarnock & Irvine Valley
8 Clackmannanshire & Dunblane	26 Kirkcaldy
9 Clydebank & Milngavie	27 Linlithgow
10 Coatbridge & Chryston	28 Mid Fife & Glenrothes
11 Cowdenbeath	29 Midlothian North & Musselburgh
12 Cumbernauld & Kilsyth	30 Motherwell & Wishaw
13 Cunninghame North	31 Paisley
14 Cunninghame South	32 Renfrewshire North & West
15 Dumbarton	33 Renfrewshire South
16 Dundee City East	34 Rutherglen
17 Dundee City West	35 Strathkelvin & Bearsden
18 Dunfermline	36 Uddingston & Bellshill

Glasgow
1 Glasgow Anniesland
2 Glasgow Cathcart
3 Glasgow Kelvin
4 Glasgow Maryhill & Springburn
5 Glasgow Pollok
6 Glasgow Provan
7 Glasgow Shettleston
8 Glasgow Southside

Edinburgh
1 Edinburgh Central
2 Edinburgh Eastern
3 Edinburgh Northern & Leith
4 Edinburgh Pentlands
5 Edinburgh Southern
6 Edinburgh Western

MAJORITY
per cent

	<8	8–20	>20		<8	8–20	>20	
Labour				Liberal Democrat				
Conservative				SNP				

Voters are given two ballot papers; the first is used to vote for a candidate to become an MSP representing the voter's constituency; the second is used to vote for a party (or independent candidate) representing a region. Each region can elect a total of seven candidates, known as 'additional members'. *See* Regional Government, Scotland for further information.

REGIONS

1 Central Scotland
2 Glasgow
3 Highlands & Islands
4 Lothian
5 Mid Scotland & Fife
6 North East Scotland
7 South Scotland
8 West Scotland

- Labour
- Conservative
- Liberal Democrat
- SNP
- Green
- Independent

KEY
3

Three additional members from the Labour Party's list have been elected to that region

NATIONAL ASSEMBLY FOR WALES ELECTION 2011

CONSTITUENCIES

1 Vale of Clwyd
2 Alyn & Deeside
3 Wrexham
4 Swansea West
5 Swansea East
6 Aberavon
7 Bridgend
8 Ogmore
9 Rhondda
10 Pontypridd
11 Cynon Valley
12 Merthyr Tydfil & Rhymney
13 Caerphilly
14 Islwyn
15 Blaenau Gwent
16 Torfaen
17 Newport East
18 Newport West
19 Cardiff North
20 Cardiff West
21 Cardiff Central
22 Cardiff South & Penarth

MAJORITY
per cent

<8 8–20 >20

Labour

Conservative

Liberal Democrat

Plaid Cymru

REGIONS

1 South Wales Central
2 South Wales East
3 South Wales West
4 Wales Mid & West
5 Wales North

Labour

Conservative

Liberal Democrat

Plaid Cymru

Voters are given two ballot papers; the first is used to vote for a candidate to become an assembly member representing the voter's constituency; the second is used to vote for a party (or independent candidate) representing a region. Each region can elect a total of four candidates, known as 'additional members'. *See* Regional Government, Wales for further information.

KEY

2 Two additional members have been elected from the Conservative Party's list to represent that region

Map labels: Aberconwy, Ynys Mon, Arfon, Delyn, Clwyd West, Clwyd South, Dwyfor Meirionnydd, Montgomeryshire, Brecon & Radnorshire, Ceredigion, Preseli Pembrokeshire, Carmarthen East & Dinefwr, Monmouth, Carmarthen West & Pembrokeshire South, Llanelli, Neath, Gower, Vale of Glamorgan

NORTHERN IRELAND ASSEMBLY ELECTION 2011

Voters are given one ballot paper, on which they list the candidates in order of preference. Six candidates from each of the 18 constituencies are elected to become members of the Northern Ireland Assembly. *See* Regional Government, Northern Ireland for further information.

DUP   UUP   Other

Sinn Fein   Alliance

SDLP   Green

1 North Antrim 3 1 1 1
2 East Antrim 3 1 1 1
3 South Antrim 3 1 1 1
4 Belfast North 3 2 1
5 Belfast West 5 1
6 Belfast South 1 1 2 1 1
7 Belfast East 3 1 2
8 North Down 3 1 1 1
9 Strangford 3 2 1

10 Lagan Valley 4 1 1
11 Upper Bann 2 1 1 2
12 South Down 1 2 2 1
13 Newry & Armagh 1 3 1 1
14 Fermanagh & South Tyrone 2 3 1
15 West Tyrone 1 3 1 1
16 Mid Ulster 1 3 1 1
17 East Londonderry 3 1 1 1
18 Foyle 1 2 3

KEY
1 One member of the UUP has been elected to represent that constituency

ACCESS TO CLEAN WATER
By percentage of population

100 per cent

90 – 99 per cent

70 – 89 per cent

50 – 69 per cent

30 – 49 per cent

No information available

Source: The World Bank,
World Development Indicators 2011

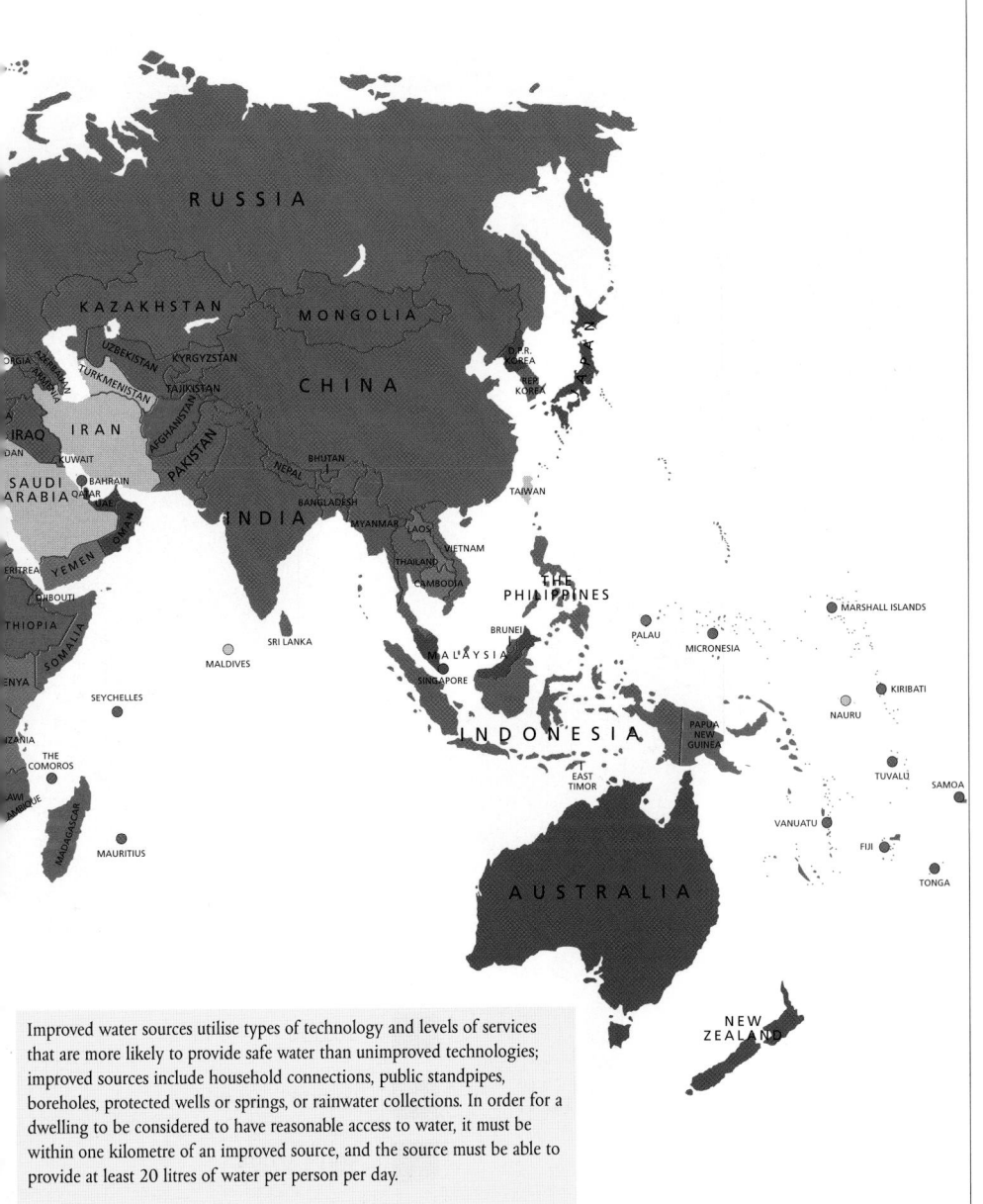

RUSSIA

KAZAKHSTAN

MONGOLIA

UZBEKISTAN   KYRGYZSTAN

TURKMENISTAN   TAJIKISTAN

CHINA

AFGHANISTAN

D.P.R.
KOREA

REP.
KOREA

IRAQ   IRAN

DAN   KUWAIT

BAHRAIN

PAKISTAN

NEPAL   BHUTAN

BANGLADESH

TAIWAN

SAUDI   QATAR
ARABIA   UAE

INDIA   MYANMAR   LAOS

VIETNAM

THAILAND

CAMBODIA

THE
PHILIPPINES

MARSHALL ISLANDS

ERITREA   YEMEN   OMAN

DJIBOUTI

THIOPIA   SOMALIA

SRI LANKA

MALDIVES

BRUNEI

MALAYSIA

SINGAPORE

PALAU

MICRONESIA

NAURU

KIRIBATI

ENYA   SEYCHELLES

INDONESIA   PAPUA
NEW
GUINEA

IZANIA   THE
COMOROS   EAST
TIMOR   TUVALU   SAMOA

AMI
AMBIQUE   MADAGASCAR

MAURITIUS

VANUATU   FIJI   TONGA

AUSTRALIA

NEW
ZEALAND

Improved water sources utilise types of technology and levels of services
that are more likely to provide safe water than unimproved technologies;
improved sources include household connections, public standpipes,
boreholes, protected wells or springs, or rainwater collections. In order for a
dwelling to be considered to have reasonable access to water, it must be
within one kilometre of an improved source, and the source must be able to
provide at least 20 litres of water per person per day.

Unimproved sources include vendors, tanker trucks, and unprotected wells
and springs. One of the UN's eight Millennium Development Goals is to
halve by 2015 the number of people without access to an improved water
source.

GNI
in US dollars

50,000 – 60,000

40,000 – 49,999

30,000 – 39,999

20,000 – 29,999

10,000 – 19,999

500 – 9,999

0 – 499

No information available

Source: The World Bank,
World Development Indicators 2011

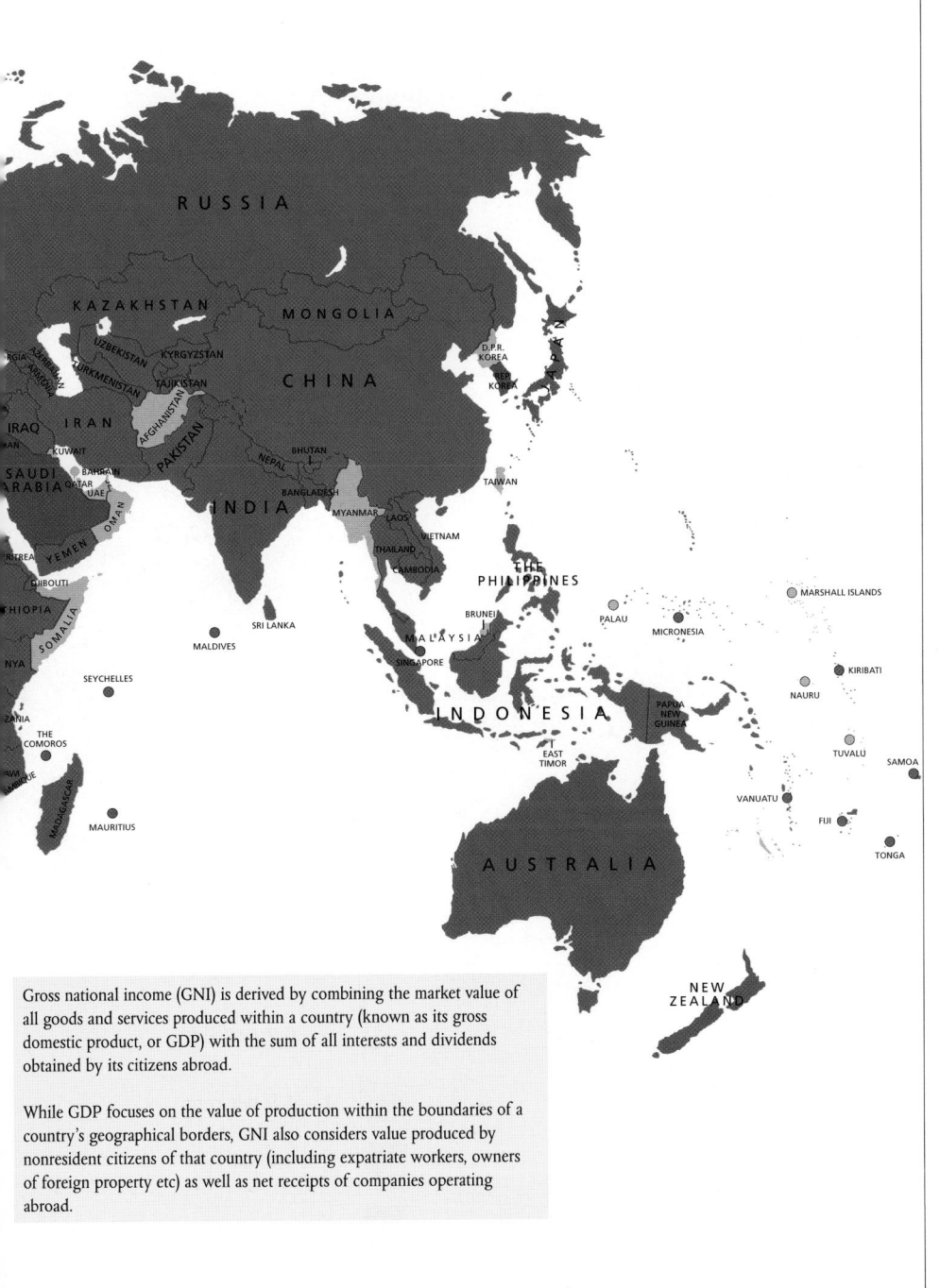

Gross national income (GNI) is derived by combining the market value of all goods and services produced within a country (known as its gross domestic product, or GDP) with the sum of all interests and dividends obtained by its citizens abroad.

While GDP focuses on the value of production within the boundaries of a country's geographical borders, GNI also considers value produced by nonresident citizens of that country (including expatriate workers, owners of foreign property etc) as well as net receipts of companies operating abroad.

POPULATION GROWTH RATES

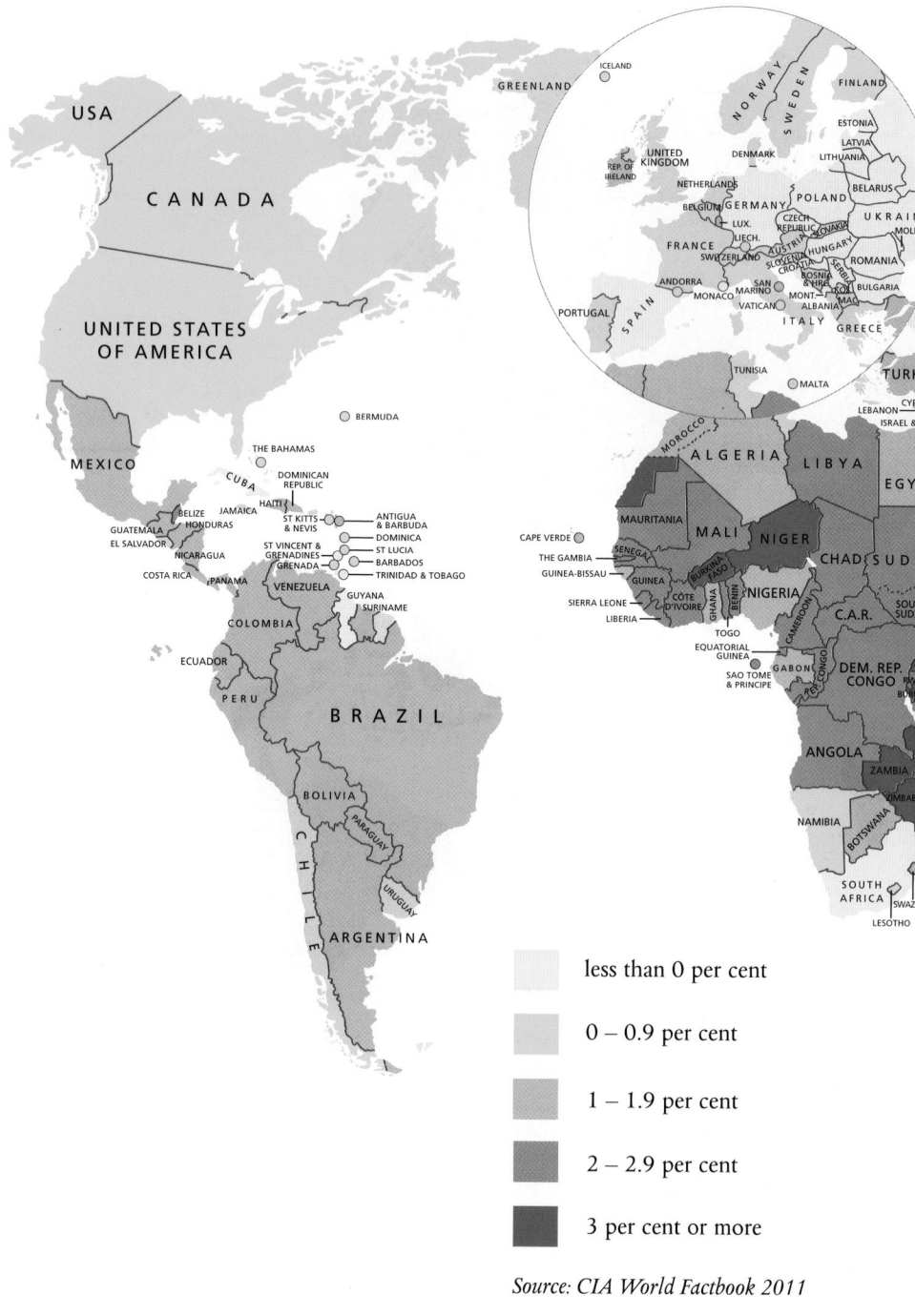

Legend:

- less than 0 per cent
- 0 – 0.9 per cent
- 1 – 1.9 per cent
- 2 – 2.9 per cent
- 3 per cent or more

Source: CIA World Factbook 2011

A review of population growth rates in the Countries of the World section shows that 167 of 194 countries had larger populations in 2011 than in 2010. The global population is continuing to grow, albeit more slowly than in the 1970s and 1980s. About one tenth of the world's population now lives in countries with a negative population growth rate, ie where the population is shrinking because fewer than one child is born per death.

In the Mediterranean and eastern Europe, declining populations are thought to be due to a combination of falling fertility rates and rising standards of living. For developed countries with industrialised economies, the effects of a fall in population growth can be far-reaching – leading to labour shortages, a decline in economic growth and a greater burden on social security systems.

BALANCE OF PAYMENTS
Trade – US$101m deficit (2010)
Current Account – US$921m deficit (2009)

Trade with UK	2009	2010
Imports from UK	£1,167,766	£3,397,668
Exports to UK	£44,067,567	£50,352,371

COMMUNICATIONS

The road network has been improved and expanded significantly since the 1990s, benefiting from substantial government investment and international funding; it is currently 36,831km in extent, although most of it remains unpaved. The Friendship Bridge over the Mekong river connects Laos with Thailand, and links up road routes from Singapore to China. A rail track across the bridge was opened in 2009, linking the Thai and Laotian rail systems. There are around 4,600km of navigable waterways, principally on the Mekong and its tributaries, although some are not navigable in the dry season. There are 41 airports and airfields; the principal airports are at Vientiane and Luang Prabang.

The telephone system is poor and limited in extent but services are improving. Mobile phone distribution is growing rapidly and subscribers numbered 3.2 million in 2009, compared to 132,200 fixed lines. There were 300,000 internet users in 2009.

MEDIA

All media outlets are strictly controlled by the government, which owns all newspapers and the radio and television broadcasting networks. Slandering the state, distorting party policies and spreading false rumours are all criminal offences. The internet remains uncensored.

LATVIA

Latvijas Republika – *Republic of Latvia*

Area – 64,589 sq. km
Capital – Riga; population, 710,637 (2009 est)
Major cities – Daugavpils, Jelgava, Liepaja
Currency – Lats of 100 santims
Population – 2,217,969 falling at 0.6 per cent a year (2010 est); Latvian (59.3 per cent), Russian (27.8 per cent), Belarusian (3.6 per cent), Ukrainian (2.5 per cent), Polish (2.4 per cent), Lithuanian (1.3 per cent) (2009 est)
Religion – Christian (Roman Catholic 23 per cent, Lutheran 20 per cent, Orthodox 17 per cent) (est)
Language – Latvian (official), Russian, Lithuanian
Population density – 36 per sq. km (2009)

Urban population – 68 per cent (2008 est)
Median age (years) – 40.4 (2010 est)
National anthem – 'Dievs, Sveti Latviju' ['God Bless Latvia']
National day – 18 November (Independence Day)
Life expectancy (years) – 72.42 (2010 est)
Mortality rate – 13.6 (2010 est)
Birth rate – 9.9 (2010 est)
Infant mortality rate – 8.59 (2010 est)
Death penalty – Retained for certain crimes (last used 1996)
CPI score – 4.3 (2010)

CLIMATE AND TERRAIN

Latvia is a flat, low-lying country on the eastern shore of the Baltic Sea, with low hills and many lakes in the south-east. Elevation extremes range from 312m (Gaizinkalns) at the highest point to 0m (Baltic Sea) at the lowest. The climate is temperate, and average temperatures in Riga range from −5°C in January and February to 17°C in July.

HISTORY AND POLITICS

Conquered and Christianised in the 13th century by the Teutonic Knights, Latvia was successively under Polish, Lithuanian and Swedish rule in the 16th and 17th centuries until it was incorporated into the Russian Empire in 1721. Under partial German occupation during the First World War, it declared its independence in 1918 and successfully defended this against the Bolsheviks in 1918–20. A dictatorship was established in 1934 following a period of political instability and economic depression. The USSR invaded and annexed Latvia in 1940, and regained control in 1944 after ousting the German forces that had invaded in 1941. Latvia suffered huge civilian losses during the Second World War, including the destruction of its large Jewish community. Many more Latvians died after the war in purges and deportations ordered by Stalin.

Agitation by nationalist groups grew from the mid-1980s. In May 1990 the legislature declared independence, and reiterated this in August 1991 following the failed coup in Moscow, when the country's independence was internationally recognised. The last Russian troops left in 1994 but a large Russian minority remains and there are intercommunal tensions. Latvia joined NATO and the EU in 2004.

In the legislative election in October 2010 the governing coaliton, made up of the Unity bloc and the Green and Farmers' Union (ZZS), won a small majority of seats, and Valdis Dombrovskis, prime minister since 2009, formed a new coalition government. Andris Berzins was elected president in June 2011 after his nomination by five members of the ZZS.

POLITICAL SYSTEM

The 1922 constitution was restored in 1993. The head of state is a president, who is elected by the legislature for a four-year term which may be renewed once. The president appoints the prime minister, who appoints the cabinet subject to approval by the legislature. The unicameral *Saeima* has 100 deputies who are directly elected for a four-year term.

HEAD OF STATE

President, Andris Berzins, *elected* 2 June 2011, *sworn in* 8 July 2011

SELECTED GOVERNMENT MEMBERS *as at June 2011*
Prime Minister, Valdis Dombrovskis
Deputy Prime Minister, Defence, Artis Pabriks
Finance, Andris Vilks
Foreign Affairs, Girts Valdis Kristovskis
Interior (acting), Aigars Stokenbergs

EMBASSY OF THE REPUBLIC OF LATVIA
45 Nottingham Place, London W1U 5LY
T 020-7312 0041 E embassy.uk@mfa.gov.lv
W www.london.mfa.gov.lv
Ambassador Extraordinary and Plenipotentiary, HE Eduards
Stiprais, *apptd* 2009

BRITISH EMBASSY
5 J. Alunana Street, Riga 1010
T (+371) 6777 4700 E british.embassy@apollo.lv
W http://ukinlatvia.fco.gov.uk
Ambassador Extraordinary and Plenipotentiary, HE Andrew
Soper, *apptd* 2010

BRITISH COUNCIL
5A-2 Blaumana Street, Riga 1011
T (+371) 6728 1730 W www.britishcouncil.org/latvia
Director, Dace Melbarde

DEFENCE
The army has 3 main battle tanks, the navy has 10 patrol
and coastal vessels and the air force has 4 multi-role
helicopters. Latvia, Lithuania and Estonia operate a joint
naval unit, BALTRON, which is located at 5 naval bases:
Liepaja, Riga, Ventspils, Tallinn and Klaipeda.
Military budget – US$250m (2010)
Military personnel – 5,745: army 1,058, navy 587, air
force 319, joint staff 3,202, National Guard 579

ECONOMY AND TRADE
The country made the transition from a planned to a
market economy in the decade after independence,
although a few large enterprises remain in state
ownership. The economy grew rapidly from 2004 to
2007, but was severely affected by the global economic
downturn because of its large current account deficit and
private-sector debt. The economy contracted by 20 per
cent in 2008–9 and was slow to return to growth. The
IMF, the World Bank and the EU provided aid in 2008–9
to avoid devaluation of the lat in return for a 40 per cent
cut in public spending.
The economy has shifted towards service industries
since independence. Services, especially transit services
and banking, is the largest sector, contributing 75.2 per
cent of GDP. Industry contributes 25.8 per cent of GDP
and includes food processing and the manufacture of
processed wood products, textiles, processed metals,
pharmaceuticals, rail transport vehicles, synthetic fibres
and electronics. The agricultural sector accounts for 4.2
per cent of GDP, employs 12 per cent of the workforce
and specialises in rearing livestock, dairy farming and
crops including grain, rapeseed, potatoes and other
vegetables.
The main trading partners are other EU states and
Russia. Principal exports are food products, timber and
wood products, metals, machinery and equipment, and
textiles. The main imports are machinery and equipment,
consumer goods, chemicals, fuel and vehicles.
GNI – US$28,066m; US$12,390 per capita (2009)
Annual average growth of GDP – –1.8 per cent (2010 est)
Inflation rate – –1.2 per cent (2010 est)

Unemployment – 19.1 per cent (2010 est)
Total external debt – US$37,280m (2010 est)
Imports – US$9,100m (2009)
Exports – US$7,000m (2009)

BALANCE OF PAYMENTS
Trade – US$2,212m deficit (2010)
Current Account – US$2,477m deficit (2009)

Trade with UK	2009	2010
Imports from UK	£107,503,162	£162,221,871
Exports to UK	£278,150,219	£386,085,481

COMMUNICATIONS
Latvia has 2,239km of railway track and 73,074km of
roads, although over 80 per cent of these are unpaved.
There are two major ports, Riga and Ventspils, and the
main airports are at Riga, Ventspils and Liepaja.
The telecommunications sector has become
increasingly competitive since 2003. Fixed-line use is
declining as mobile services expand. In 2009, there were
644,000 fixed lines in use, 2.2 million mobile phone
subscribers and 1.5 million internet users.

EDUCATION AND HEALTH
Education is compulsory from the age of seven until 16
years, after which there is the option for a further three
years of either secondary or vocational study.
Literacy rate – 99.8 per cent (2008 est)
Gross enrolment ratio (percentage of relevant age group) –
primary 98 per cent; secondary 98 per cent; tertiary 69
per cent (2008 est)
Health expenditure (per capita) – US$750 (2009)
Hospital beds (per 1,000 people) – 6.4 (2004–9)

MEDIA
There are around 140 newspapers in circulation,
including many in Russian. Television and radio output is
provided by public service broadcasters and a number of
commercial stations. Latvian versions of the main Russian
networks are also available. Press freedom, although
generally good, has recently been undermined by
instances of violence against journalists.

LEBANON

Al-Jumhuriyah al-Lubnaniyah – Lebanese Republic

Area – 10,400 sq. km
Capital – Beirut (Bayrut); population, 1,909,410
(2009 est)
Major cities – Sidon, Tripoli (Tarabulus)

Currency – Lebanese pound (L£) of 100 piastres
Population – 4,125,247 rising at 0.62 per cent a year
  (2010 est); Arab (95 per cent), Armenian (4 per cent)
  (est)
Religion – Muslim 59 per cent (Sunni 27 per cent, Shia 27
  per cent, Druze 5 per cent), Christian 41 per cent
  (Maronite 21 per cent, Greek Orthodox 8 per cent,
  Greek Catholic 5, other 7 per cent) (est)
Language – Arabic (official), French, English, Armenian
Population density – 413 per sq. km (2009)
Urban population – 87 per cent (2008 est)
Median age (years) – 29.4 (2010 est)
National anthem – 'Lebanese National Anthem'
National day – 22 November (Independence Day)
Life expectancy (years) – 74.79 (2010 est)
Mortality rate – 6.46 (2010 est)
Birth rate – 15.1 (2010 est)
Infant mortality rate – 16.4 (2010 est)
Death penalty – Retained
CPI score – 2.5 (2010)

CLIMATE AND TERRAIN

A narrow plain along the Mediterranean Sea coast is
backed by the Lebanon Mountains, along which the
Anti-Lebanon range runs parallel, forming the border
with Syria. Between the two ranges lies the fertile Bekaa
valley, the northern extremity of Africa's Great Rift Valley.
Elevations range from 3,088m (Qurnat as Sawda') at the
highest point to 0m (Mediterranean Sea) at the lowest.
The climate is Mediterranean, although the mountains
usually receive snow in winter. Average temperatures in
Beirut are 14°C in January and February and 27°C
in August.

HISTORY AND POLITICS

Lebanon was part of the Phoenician Empire from the fifth
century BC until the first century AD, when it came under
Roman rule and Christianity began to spread. Islam was
introduced by Arabs in the seventh century AD, and the
Druze faith was developed by local Muslims in the 11th
century. The area was contested between Muslims and
Christians during the Crusades before becoming part of
the Ottoman Empire in the 16th century. Following the
empire's collapse at the end of the First World War,
Lebanon became a French-administered mandated
territory, achieving independence in 1943 with a
constitution that enshrined power-sharing by all the
country's religions.

The complicated system of government established by
the constitution created tensions between Christians and
Muslims that in 1975 erupted into a 16-year civil war that
pitted a coalition of Christian groups against Druze and
Muslim militias. The conflict drew in the Palestine
Liberation Organisation (PLO), then based in Beirut;
Syrian forces, at the request of the Lebanese government,
to restore order; and Israel, which invaded in 1978 and
1982 in response to PLO guerrilla raids on Israel, and
forced the PLO to withdraw from Lebanon in 1982. By
1985, the country was close to partition as rival political
and religious factions sought to gain control.

An Arab League-sponsored ceasefire came into effect in
1989 and a peace plan, the Ta'if accord, proposed
revisions to the constitution that would reduce Christian
Maronite dominance. This was rejected by some Christian
factions and fighting continued until this opposition was
crushed by Syrian forces. A fragile peace was achieved in
1991, and elections in 1992 were peaceful, although they
were boycotted by some Christian parties.

Southern Lebanon was the only area in which conflict
was not ended by the accord. In the buffer zones
established by Israel in 1985, clashes continued
throughout the 1990s between occupying Israeli troops,
or the Israeli-backed South Lebanon Army (SLA), and the
Hezbollah militia, supported by Syria and Iran. Although
the SLA collapsed after Israel withdrew its forces in 2000,
Hezbollah's control of the south continued to be accepted
by the Lebanese government. In July 2006, Hezbollah's
capture of Israeli soldiers in a cross-border raid sparked a
month of intense fighting with Israel that killed or
displaced thousands and severely damaged infrastructure.
A fragile peace on the border was restored with the
deployment of UN peacekeeping forces and Lebanese
troops from August; it was the first deployment of
government forces on the southern border in decades,
although Hezbollah still controls much of the south. The
government extended its control in the north of the
country in 2007, taking over a militia-controlled refugee
camp after a four-month siege.

Syria's influence remains pervasive, even though it was
obliged to end its 29-year military presence in 2005 after
huge protest rallies brought down the pro-Syria
government following the assassination of former prime
minister Rafik Hariri, for which Syria was blamed.
Since 2005, Lebanese politics has been dominated by a
power struggle between pro- and anti-Syria factions and
militias. After pro-Syria ministers resigned from the
predominantly anti-Syria coalition government in
November 2006, pro-Syria factions pursued a greater role
in politics through popular protests and a legislative
boycott that left the state moribund for months.

The failure to agree on a successor to President Emile
Lahoud after his term of office ended in November 2007
created a political vacuum that led to a rise in factional
violence. After rival political leaders concluded the Doha
agreement in May 2008, a neutral candidate, General
Michel Suleiman, the head of the armed forces, was
elected president. In the 2009 legislative election, the
governing anti-Syria '14 March' coalition won 68 seats,
the opposition '8 March' bloc won 57 and independents
aligned with the '14 March' coalition won three seats.
After months of negotiation the '14 March' leader Saad
Hariri formed a national unity government which took
office in November 2009. This government collapsed in
January 2011 with the withdrawal of pro-Syria parties,
and although Najib Mikati was elected prime
minister-designate later that month, it took until June
to form a new coalition government; this comprised 18
ministers nominated by Hezbollah and its allies, and 11
nominated by either the president, the prime minister or
the Druze leader.

POLITICAL SYSTEM

The constitution dates from 1926 but has been heavily
amended, most significantly in 1943, when the National
Covenant set out the division of power between the
religious communities, and in 1990 to incorporate
the provisions of the Ta'if accord. By convention, the
presidency is held by a Maronite Christian, the prime
minister is a Sunni Muslim and the speaker is a Shia Muslim.

The president is elected by the legislature for a six-year
term, which is not renewable. The unicameral National
Assembly has 128 members, directly elected for a
four-year term; seats are divided equally between
Christians and Muslims, whose quotas are subdivided by
confession according to the distribution formalised in the
2008 election law. The prime minister is appointed by the
president following consultation with the legislature.

HEAD OF STATE
President, Gen. Michel Suleiman, *elected* 25 May 2008,
  sworn in 26 May 2008

SELECTED GOVERNMENT MEMBERS *as at July 2011*
Prime Minister, Mohammad Najib Mikati
Deputy Prime Minister, Samir Mokbel
Finance, Mohammad Safadi
Foreign Affairs, Adnan Mansour
Interior, Marwan Charbel

EMBASSY OF LEBANON
21 Palace Gardens Mews, London W8 4RA
T 020-7229 7265 E info@lebaneseembassy.org.uk
W www.lebaneseembassy.org.uk
Ambassador Extraordinary and Plenipotentiary, HE Inaam
  Osseiran, *apptd* 2007

BRITISH EMBASSY
PO Box 11-471, Armies Street, Zkak al-Blat, Serail Hill, Beirut
Centre-Ville, Beirut
T (+961) (1) 960 800 W http://ukinlebanon.fco.gov.uk
Ambassador Extraordinary and Plenipotentiary, HE Frances
  Guy, *apptd* 2006

BRITISH COUNCIL
Berytech Technology and Health, Sodeco Street, Damascus
Road, 2064 1509 Beirut
T (+961) (1) 428 900 W www.britishcouncil.org/lebanon
Director, Barbara Hewitt

DEFENCE
The army has 326 main battle tanks and 1,240 armoured
personnel carriers. The navy has 11 patrol and coastal
vessels at 2 bases. The air force has 7 combat aircraft and
9 multi-role helicopters.
Military budget – US$1,160m (2010)
Military personnel – 59,100: army 57,000, navy 1,100,
  air force 1,000; paramilitary 20,000; Hezbollah
  military force 2,000 (est)

ECONOMY AND TRADE
The civil war seriously damaged Lebanon's economy and
infrastructure, as well as its role as an entrepôt and
financial services centre for the region. Reconstruction
was almost complete when the Israeli attacks in 2006
caused an estimated US$3.6bn (£2.1bn) of infrastructure
damage. Recovery was hindered by internal instability,
which also postponed the introduction of the economic
reforms that were a condition of international funding for
reconstruction. Economic growth began anew in 2008,
and remained relatively robust in 2009 despite the global
economic downturn.

The service sector contributes 79 per cent of GDP,
largely through banking and tourism, which are the two
main economic activities. Industry accounts for 15.9 per
cent, through food processing, wine production and the
manufacture of jewellery, cement, textiles, mineral and
chemical products, timber and furniture, oil refining and
metal fabrication. Agriculture contributes 5.1 per cent of
GDP, producing fruit, vegetables, tobacco and livestock.

The main export markets are Switzerland, the UAE,
Iraq, Saudi Arabia and Syria, while imports come mainly
from the USA, the EU, China and Turkey. Principal
exports include jewellery, base metals, chemicals,
consumer goods, fruit, vegetables, tobacco and
construction materials. The main imports are petroleum

products, cars, medicines, clothing, meat, livestock and
consumer goods.
GNI – US$35,405m; US$8,060 per capita (2009)
Annual average growth of GDP – 7.2 per cent (2010 est)
Inflation rate – 3.7 per cent (2010 est)
Unemployment – 9.2 per cent (2007 est)
Total external debt – US$34,570m (2010 est)
Imports – US$16,200m (2009)
Exports – US$3,600m (2009)

BALANCE OF PAYMENTS
Trade – US$15,382m deficit (2010)
Current Account – US$3,398m deficit (2008)

Trade with UK	2009	2010
Imports from UK	£341,594,282	£398,796,927
Exports to UK	£28,181,513	£33,388,595

COMMUNICATIONS
There are 6,970km of roads, though many are in poor
repair. The 401km railway system, much of it unusable
following the civil war, was rendered completely
inoperable by the 2006 attacks. There are seven airports
and airfields, including the international airport at Beirut.
The principal seaports are Beirut and Tripoli.

The telephone system was repaired after the civil war
but planned privatisation has been held back by political
tensions. In 2009, there were 750,000 fixed lines in
use, 1.5 million mobile phone subscribers and 1 million
internet users.

EDUCATION AND HEALTH
There are nine years of compulsory education.
Literacy rate – 89.6 per cent (2008 est)
Gross enrolment ratio (percentage of relevant age group) –
  primary 103 per cent; secondary 82 per cent; tertiary
  53 per cent (2009 est)
Health expenditure (per capita) – US$663 (2009)
Hospital beds (per 1,000 people) – 3.5 (2004–9)

MEDIA
Lebanon was the first Arab country to permit private radio
and television stations; broadcast media reflect the
country's pluralism. There are a number of daily
newspapers in circulation, including French- and English-
language publications. Tele-Liban is the state-run
broadcaster and competes with several commercial
stations, including pro-Hezbollah al-Manar TV and the
market-leading Lebanese Broadcasting Corporation and
Future TV.

LESOTHO

Kingdom of Lesotho

Area – 30,355 sq. km
Capital – Maseru; population, 220,012 (2009 est)
Currency – Loti (M) of 100 lisente. The South African
    rand is also legal tender
Population – 1,919,552 rising at 0.28 per cent a year
    (2010 est); Sotho (99.7 per cent) (est)
Religion – Christian 80 per cent, indigenous religions
    20 per cent (est). Many Christians also follow
    indigenous beliefs
Language – English, Sesotho (both official), Zulu, Xhosa
Population density – 68 per sq. km (2009)
Urban population – 25 per cent (2008 est)
Median age (years) – 22.6 (2010 est)
National anthem – 'Lesotho Fatse la Bontata Rona'
    ['Lesotho, Land of Our Fathers']
National day – 4 October (Independence Day)
Life expectancy – 50.67 (2010 est)
Mortality rate – 15.71 (2010 est)
Birth rate – 27.17 (2010 est)
Infant mortality rate – 56.42 (2010 est)
HIV/AIDS adult prevalence – 23.6 per cent (2009 est)
Death penalty – Retained
CPI score – 3.5 (2010)
Military expenditure – US$54m (2009)
Military personnel – army 2,000 (est)

CLIMATE AND TERRAIN

Lesotho is a landlocked country encircled by South Africa.
It consists of a highland plateau with mountains in the
east. The lower land in the west contains most of the
arable land and 70 per cent of the population. Elevation
extremes range from 3,482m (Thabana Ntlenyana) at the
highest point to 1,400m (the junction of the Orange and
Makhaleng rivers) at the lowest. As 80 per cent of the
country lies above 1,800m, the climate is temperate, with
snow in the highlands in winter. Temperatures in Maseru
(1,528m altitude) average 21°C in January and 8°C
in July.

HISTORY AND POLITICS

The area was organised into a single territory by
Moshoeshoe the Great from the 1820s as the Sotho
people came under pressure from both the expanding
Zulu nation and the Boers. In 1868, after fighting two
wars with the Boers, Moshoeshoe sought protection from
the British government, and Basutoland became first a
British territory (1868), and then a crown colony (1884).
    The country gained independence in 1966 as the
kingdom of Lesotho, under Moshoeshoe II and with
Chief Lebua Jonathan as prime minister. The
post-independence period has been one of political
instability, with a number of coups, mutinies and periods
of civil unrest as rival political parties, army factions and
the royal family competed for power. Chief Jonathan was
overthrown in a military coup in 1986; military rule
ended with multiparty elections in 1993, although civil
unrest followed the ousting of the military rulers, and
democratic rule was restored in 1994. The 1998 elections
were also followed by severe disturbances, which were
quelled by an intervention force from neighbouring
countries at the government's request. The situation has
been more stable since an interim political authority
reviewed and modified the electoral system in time for the
2002 election. King Moshoeshoe II, deposed in 1990,
was reinstated in 1995 but died in 1996; he was
succeeded by King Letsie III, who had been king during
his father's exile.

In the 2007 legislative election, the Lesotho Congress
for Democracy retained its majority, with 61 seats, and
formed a new government.

POLITICAL SYSTEM

Under the 1993 constitution, subsequently amended, the
head of state is a hereditary monarch, with ceremonial
duties but no executive or legislative powers. The
bicameral parliament comprises the National Assembly,
with 120 members elected for a five-year term, one-third
by proportional representation, and the senate, whose 33
members comprise 22 principal chiefs and 11 members
nominated by the king. The prime minister is the leader of
the majority party in the legislature and appoints the
council of ministers.

HEAD OF STATE
HM The King of Lesotho, King Letsie III, *acceded*
    7 February 1996, *crowned* 31 October 1997

SELECTED GOVERNMENT MEMBERS *as at July 2011*
Prime Minister, Defence, Bethuel Pakalitha Mosisili
Deputy Prime Minister, Home Affairs, Archibald Lesao
    Lehohla
Finance, Timothy Thahane
Foreign Affairs, Mohlabi Tsekoa

HIGH COMMISSION OF THE KINGDOM OF LESOTHO
7 Chesham Place, London SW1X 8HN
T 020-7235 5686 E lhc@lesotholondon.org.uk
W www.lesotholondon.org.uk
High Commissioner, HE HRH Prince Seeiso Bereng Seeiso,
    apptd 2005

BRITISH HIGH COMMISSION
High Commissioner, HE Dr Nicola Brewer, *apptd* 2009,
    resident at Pretoria (Tshwane), South Africa

ECONOMY AND TRADE

The country is one of the poorest in the world, with
49 per cent of the population living below the poverty
line. With few natural resources apart from water, the
main sources of government revenue are customs dues
from the South African customs union and, since 1998,
the export of water and electricity to South Africa from
the hydroelectric facilities created by the Lesotho
Highlands Water Project. The economic situation
worsened in the early 2000s with the severe droughts
since 2001 and the declining demand for mineworkers in
South Africa (once 35 per cent of the male workforce),
which reduced income from remittances. This decline has
been partially compensated for by the resumption of
diamond mining in 2003, and the development of a small
manufacturing base processing agricultural products,
producing textiles and assembling garments, and of
tourism, especially in the highlands. Even so, nearly half
of the population is unemployed.
    The economy has always been dependent on
subsistence agriculture, which engages 86 per cent of the
population, although productivity has declined in recent
years because of drought, soil erosion and loss of labour
as farmers succumb to HIV/AIDS; nearly a quarter of the
workforce is infected with the disease.
    The main market for exports is the USA (59 per cent)
and Belgium (37 per cent); imports come mainly from
China (26 per cent), Taiwan, Hong Kong and South
Korea. Principal exports are clothing, footwear, road
vehicles, wool and mohair, food and livestock. The main
imports are food, construction materials, vehicles,
machinery, medicines and petroleum products.

GNI – US$1,934m; US$980 per capita (2009)
Annual average growth of GDP – 3.5 per cent (2010 est)
Inflation rate – 6.1 per cent (2010 est)
Unemployment – 45 per cent (2002)
Total external debt – US$647m (2010 est)
Imports – US$1,900m (2009)
Exports – US$700m (2009)

BALANCE OF PAYMENTS
Trade – US$1,351m deficit (2010)
Current Account – US$152m surplus (2008)

Trade with UK	2009	2010
Imports from UK	£1,943,182	£1,333,230
Exports to UK	£1,652,169	£1,354,317

COMMUNICATIONS
Most travel is by foot or by air, as there is little transport infrastructure other than to link the main towns to each other and to South Africa, and to access the highland hydroelectric facilities. Of the 7,091km of roads, 1,404km are surfaced. There are 26 airports and airfields; the international airport is at Maseru.

The telephone system is rudimentary but expanding. Mobile phone distribution is growing rapidly; density was over 30 per 100 people in 2009, almost exclusively in urban areas.

EDUCATION AND HEALTH
Literacy rate – 82.2 per cent (2008 est)
Gross enrolment ratio (percentage of relevant age group) –
    primary 104 per cent; secondary 45 per cent (2009 est)
Health expenditure (per capita) – US$70 (2009)
Hospital beds (per 1,000 people) – 1.3 (2004–9)

MEDIA
Lesotho has a mixture of state-run and private media. Radio is the most important medium and reforms in 1998 allowed the establishment of a number of commercial stations, although only the state-run Radio Lesotho has national coverage. Lesotho Television, also run by the state, is the only television station, but South African broadcasts can be received. The press publishes a range of weekly papers in both Sesotho and English. Government officials often use defamation laws against the media.

LIBERIA

Republic of Liberia

Area – 111,369 sq. km
Capital – Monrovia; population, 882,464 (2009 est)
Currency – Liberian dollar (L$) of 100 cents

Population – 3,685,076 rising at 2.78 per cent a year (2010 est); Kpelle (20.3 per cent), Bassa (13.4 per cent), Grebo (10 per cent), Gio (8 per cent), Mano (7.9 per cent), Kru (6 per cent), Loma (5.1 per cent), Kissi (4.8 per cent), Gola (4.4 per cent) (2008)
Religion – Christian 86 per cent, Muslim 12 per cent (est). Many Christians and Muslims also practise elements of indigenous religious beliefs
Language – English (official), about 20 ethnic languages
Population density – 41 per sq. km (2009)
Urban population – 60 per cent (2008 est)
Median age (years) – 18.4 (2010 est)
National anthem – 'All Hail, Liberia, Hail!'
National day – 26 July (Independence Day)
Life expectancy (years) – 56.58 (2010 est)
Mortality rate – 10.88 (2010 est)
Birth rate – 38.14 (2010 est)
Infant mortality rate – 76.43 (2010 est)
HIV/AIDS adult prevalence – 1.5 per cent (2009 est)
Death penalty – Retained (not used since 2000)
CPI score – 3.3 (2010)
Military budget – US$1.6m (2009)
Military personnel – 2,050: army 2,000, coast guard 50
Literacy rate – 56.7 per cent (2008 est)
Gross enrolment ratio (percentage of relevant age group) –
    primary 91 per cent (2008 est)
Health expenditure (per capita) – US$29 (2009)
Hospital beds (per 1,000 people) – 0.7 (2004–9)

CLIMATE AND TERRAIN
Liberia lies on the west African coast, just north of the equator. There are forested highlands and grassy plateaux in the interior and swampy plains on the coast, where several rivers enter the ocean. Elevation extremes range from 1,380m (Mt Wuteve) at the highest point to 0m (Atlantic Ocean) at the lowest. The climate is tropical, with very high rainfall.

HISTORY AND POLITICS
The land was purchased by the American Colonisation Society in 1821 and turned into a settlement for liberated black slaves from the USA, gaining recognition as an independent state in 1847.

In the first century of statehood, politics was dominated by the True Whig Party of the Americo-Liberian minority. Political stability ended in 1980 when a coup installed a military government under Samuel Doe. When civilian rule was restored in 1985, Doe became president, but his regime's arbitrary, corrupt rule combined with an economic collapse led to a revolt in 1989 by Charles Taylor's National Patriotic Forces of Liberia (NPFL) and the Armed Forces of Liberia (AFL). The country descended into a civil war that, apart from a respite in 1996–9, lasted until 2003. Around 250,000 people were killed and thousands were displaced. Following mediation by a number of African and European countries, all factions in the conflict signed a peace agreement in 2003 and a UN peacekeeping force was deployed. The disarming of militias was completed in 2005, and a truth and reconciliation commission was set up in 2006 and reported in 2009.

After a period of transitional government, presidential and legislative elections were held in late 2005. In the legislative election, the Congress for Democratic Change (CDC) won the most seats but without an overall majority. The Unity Party leader Ellen Johnson-Sirleaf was elected president in the second round of voting and took office in January 2006, nominating a new government that included members of two smaller parties and some independents. Presidential and legislative elections are scheduled for 11 October 2011, although elections could be moved to 8 November depending on the outcome of a referendum on constitutional changes in August.

POLITICAL SYSTEM

Under the 1986 constitution, the head of state is an executive president who is directly elected for a six-year term, renewable once. There is a bicameral National Assembly, consisting of the House of Representatives, with 64 members directly elected for a six-year term, and a senate, with 30 members (two from each of the 15 counties) normally elected for a nine-year term, although half of the current senate will serve for only six years. The president appoints the cabinet, which must be approved by the legislature.

HEAD OF STATE

President, Ellen Johnson-Sirleaf, *elected* 8 November 2005, *sworn in* 16 January 2006
Vice-President, Joseph N. Boakai

SELECTED GOVERNMENT MEMBERS, *as at July 2011*
Defence, Brownie Samukai
Finance, Augustine Nganguan
Foreign Affairs, Toga Gayewea McIntosh
Internal Affairs, Harrison Kahnweah

EMBASSY OF THE REPUBLIC OF LIBERIA
23 Fitzroy Square, London W1T 6EW
T 020-7388 5489 E info@embassyofliberia.org.uk
W www.embassyofliberia.org.uk
Ambassador Extraordinary and Plenipotentiary, HE Wesley M. Johnson, *apptd* 2007

BRITISH AMBASSADOR
HE Ian Hughes, *apptd* 2009, resident at Freetown, Sierra Leone

ECONOMY AND TRADE

The civil war devastated an economy already weakened by government mismanagement and corruption, and drove those with expertise and capital into exile. Since the war ended, foreign aid has been received to finance reconstruction, conditional on the adoption of anti-corruption measures, and economic activity has revived. Growth since 2006 has been driven by donor aid and exports, particularly of rubber and, since UN sanctions were lifted in 2006 and 2007 respectively, timber and diamonds. The country also benefited from substantial debt relief in 2010.

Liberia benefits from reliable water resources, with the potential to generate hydroelectric power, and a climate suited to agriculture. Agriculture was the main economic activity during the civil war but its contribution to GDP and its share of the labour market has declined as the industrial and service sectors have revived. Industry centres on the processing of rubber and palm oil, forestry and mining (diamonds, iron ore).

The main export markets are EU countries, South Africa and India, while imports come mainly from South Korea, Singapore, Japan and China. Principal exports are rubber, timber, iron, diamonds, cocoa and coffee. The main imports are fuels, chemicals, machinery, transport equipment, manufactured goods and foodstuffs.

GNI – US$645m; US$160 per capita (2009)
Annual average growth of GDP – 6 per cent (2010 est)

Inflation rate – 11.2 per cent (2007 est)
Total external debt – US$3,200m (2005 est)

BALANCE OF PAYMENTS
Trade - US$15,277 deficit (2010)
Current Account – US$491m deficit (2008)

Trade with UK	2009	2010
Imports from UK	£15,228,146	£10,129,879
Exports to UK	£3,428,448	£5,082,750

COMMUNICATIONS

The main seaports are Monrovia and Buchanan, and there is a merchant fleet of 2,512 ships of over 1,000 tonnes, including 2,356 foreign-owned ships registered in Liberia. There are 10,600km of roads, of which only 657km are surfaced. Owing to war damage, little of the 429km of railway track is operational, although reconstruction is underway. There are 29 airports and airfields; the international airports, Robertsfield and Spriggs Payne, are at Monrovia.

Telephone services are limited and confined mostly to Monrovia. Mobile phone coverage extends services to other towns and rural areas, and subscriptions have grown rapidly, with density reaching 25 per 100 people in 2009.

MEDIA

Following renovation of its infrastructure, the state broadcaster's radio service provides national coverage. There are a growing number of community radio stations, often supported by international agencies or churches, plus three private television stations and a number of privately owned newspapers, both daily and weekly.

LIBYA

Al-Jumahiriyah al-Arabiyah al-Libiyah ash Shabiyah al-Ishtirakiyah al-Uzma – Great Socialist People's Libyan Arab Jamahiriya

Area – 1,759,540 sq. km
Capital – Tripoli (Tarabulus); population, 1,095,110 (2009 est)
Major cities – al-Hums, az-Zawiyah, Benghazi, Misratah, Tarhunah, Zuwarah
Currency – Libyan dinar (LD) of 1,000 dirhams
Population – 6,461,454 rising at 2.12 per cent a year (2010 est); Arab–Berber (97 per cent), with some Tuareg in the south-west
Religion – Sunni Muslim 97 per cent, Christian (Coptic 1 per cent) (est)
Language – Arabic (official), Italian, English
Population density – 4 per sq. km (2009)

Urban population – 78 per cent (2008 est)
Median age (years) – 24.2 (2010 est)
National anthem – 'Allahu Akbar' ['God is Greatest']
National day – 1 September (Revolution Day)
Life expectancy (years) – 77.47 (2010 est)
Mortality rate – 3.4 (2010 est)
Birth rate – 24.58 (2010 est)
Infant mortality rate – 20.87 (2010 est)
Death penalty – Retained
CPI score – 2.2 (2010)

CLIMATE AND TERRAIN

Apart from hills on the north-west and north-east coasts and in the far south, the country is made up of plains and plateaux, with some depressions; 90 per cent is desert or semi-desert. Elevation extremes range from 2,267m (Bikku Bitti) at the highest point to –47m (Sabkhat Ghuzayyil) at the lowest. The climate is Mediterranean on the coast, and arid desert in the interior. Average temperatures in Tripoli range from 12°C in January to 27°C in July and August.

HISTORY AND POLITICS

Libya comprises the three ancient regions of Tripolitania, Cyrenaica and Phazzania (Fezzan). Tripolitania was settled by the Phoenicians in the seventh century BC, then became the eastern part of the kingdom of Carthage. Cyrenaica was colonised by the Greeks in the fourth century BC. All three regions became provinces of the Roman Empire in the first century BC, and subsequently were under the control of the Byzantine Empire until conquered by Arabs in the seventh century AD, when Islam was introduced.

Libya was part of the Ottoman Empire from the mid-16th century until 1911, when the country was conquered and colonised by Italy. Libya suffered heavy fighting in the Second World War, then came under British and French control until 24 December 1951, when it achieved independence as the Kingdom of Libya through a UN resolution.

The discovery of oil in 1959 made the country wealthy but created social discord. In 1969 the king was deposed in a military coup led by Col. Muammar al-Gaddafi and a Revolutionary Command Council was installed that proclaimed the country a republic. Economic activity, including the oil industry, was nationalised in the 1970s.

Col. Gaddafi developed a brand of Islamic socialism and sought to promote pan-Arab unity and Islam abroad. This led Libya to support militant and revolutionary groups and to become involved in international terrorism. Relationships with Western governments became increasingly strained, bringing US military reprisals for terrorist activities in the 1980s and UN sanctions from 1992 after Libya refused to extradite two men suspected of the 1988 bombing of a Pan Am aircraft over Lockerbie, Scotland. Sanctions were suspended in 1999 after the suspects were handed over for trial, and were lifted in 2003 after Libya admitted responsibility for the bombing and paid compensation. From 2003, Col. Gaddafi made further moves to end Libya's isolation and normalise relations with the West, such as abandoning its development of weapons of mass destruction.

Protests against Gaddafi's regime began in February 2011 in Benghazi and spread rapidly to other cities, including Tripoli. Government forces attempted to reimpose order as protesters advanced westward along the coast seizing control of Benghazi and other eastern cities. To protect civilians from government air attacks, in March the UN authorised an air exclusion zone over Libya, maintained by NATO, which has carried out air strikes on government forces and command centres. Fighting continued throughout the country, especially in the east, where some military leaders and units have defected to the rebels, and around the rebel enclave of Misrath in the west. In March 2011, a National Transitional Council (NTC) was set up by the rebels and has established contacts with foreign governments; a number of government ministers and diplomats have resigned or defected overseas. On 27 June 2011 the International Criminal Court issued a warrant for the arrest of Gaddafi, his son Saif and a key political aide, for crimes against humanity. On 22 August rebel fighters advanced into Tripoli, occupying the city's Green Square. Additionally, the rebel fighters claimed to have captured two of Gaddafi's sons (including Saif) alive. At the time of going to press, the USA and a large majority of UN states recognise the NTC as the legitimate government of Libya, while the whereabouts of Col. Gaddafi remain unknown.

POLITICAL SYSTEM

Under the 1977 constitution, the head of state is the 'Leader of the Revolution', Col. Muammar al-Gaddafi, who is in effect an absolute ruler. The General People's Congress, which has 760 members appointed by local 'basic people's congresses' for a three-year term, is formally responsible for policy-making and passing laws. It appoints the General People's Committee, which exercises executive power; the secretary-general of the General People's Committee is in effect the prime minister. The General People's Congress also has its own administrative secretariat. The Arab Socialist Union is the only legal political party. The NTC announced its own draft constitution in August 2011.

HEAD OF STATE *
Leader of the Revolution, Col. Muammar al-Gaddafi

SELECTED GOVERNMENT MEMBERS *as at July 2011*
Secretary-General of the General People's Congress,
   Muhammad Abul-Qasim al-Zwai
Secretary-General of the General People's Committee
   (Prime Minister), Al-Baghdadi Ali al-Mahmudi
Secretary, Economy, Muhammad al-Huwayj
Secretary, Finance, Abd-al-Hafiz Mahmud al-Zulaytini
Secretary, Foreign Liaison, Abdul Ati al-Obeidi

NATIONAL TRANSITIONAL COUNCIL * *as at August 2011*
Chair, Mustafa Abdel Jalil
Chair of the Executive Committee, Mahmoud Jibril

THE PEOPLE'S BUREAU OF THE GREAT SOCIALIST
PEOPLE'S LIBYAN ARAB JAMAHIRIYA
61–62 Ennismore Gardens, London SW7 1NH
T 020-7589 6120 E protocol_01@libyanpeoplesbureau.org.uk
W www.libyan-embassy.co.uk
Ambassador Extraordinary and Plenipotentiary, HE Omar
   R. Jelban, *apptd* 2010

BRITISH EMBASSY
PO Box 4206, Sharia Uahran 1, Tripoli
T (+218) (21) 340 3644 E tripoli.press@fco.gov.uk
W http://ukinlibya.fco.gov.uk
Ambassador Extraordinary and Plenipotentiary, HE Richard
   Northern, MBE, *apptd* 2010

* At the time of going to press the NTC was not confirmed as the
official government of Libya.

BRITISH COUNCIL
PO Box 6797, Casablanca Street, Siyahia, Tripoli
T (+218) (21) 484 3164 W www.britishcouncil.org/libya
Director, Cherry Gough

DEFENCE

The army has 800 main battle tanks, over 1,000 armoured infantry fighting vehicles and 945 armoured personnel carriers. The navy has 2 submarines, 2 frigates, 16 patrol and coastal vessels, and 7 helicopters at 4 major bases. The air force has 394 combat aircraft and 35 armed helicopters.

Military expenditure – US$1,710m (2009 est)
Military personnel – 76,000: army 50,000, navy 8,000, air force 18,000
Conscription duration – 12 to 24 months (selective)

ECONOMY AND TRADE

Normalisation of international relations stimulated economic liberalisation and the start of a slow transition towards a more market-orientated economy, as well as attracting more foreign direct investment.

The state-controlled oil industry dominates the economy, accounting for 95 per cent of export earnings and about 25 per cent of GDP; as the population is small, this gives the country a relatively high per capita GDP, although the benefits are not felt by much of the population. The considerable oil and natural gas reserves are relatively undeveloped, and further exploration has been licensed in recent years in auctions open to foreign companies. Attempts to diversify the economy have led to expansion of the manufacturing and construction sectors, which together account for more than 20 per cent of GDP, to include the production of petrochemicals, iron, steel and aluminium in addition to food processing. Owing to the terrain and climate, agriculture is a small sector, contributing only 2.6 per cent of GDP; Libya imports about 75 per cent of its food.

The main trading partners are Italy, Germany, other EU countries and China. Principal exports are crude oil, refined petroleum products, natural gas and chemicals. The main imports are machinery, semi-finished goods, food, transport equipment and consumer products.

GNI – US$61,985m; US$12,020 per capita (2009)
Annual average growth of GDP – 3.3 per cent (2010 est)
Inflation rate – 3 per cent (2010 est)
Population below poverty line – 7.4 per cent (2005 est)
Unemployment – 30 per cent (2004 est)
Total external debt – US$6,378m (2010 est)
Imports – US$10,200m (2009)
Exports – US$35,300m (2009)

BALANCE OF PAYMENTS
Trade – US$33,705m surplus (2010)
Current Account – US$36,601m surplus (2008)

Trade with UK	2009	2010
Imports from UK	£427,093,243	£377,241,478
Exports to UK	£817,340,993	£1,253,812,362

COMMUNICATIONS

There are 100,024km of roads; the coastal road running from the Tunisian frontier through Tripoli, Benghazi and Tubruq to the Egyptian border, serves the main population centres. Main roads also link the provincial centres, and the oil-producing areas of the south with the coastal towns. Libya has had no railway services since

1965. There are 137 airports and airfields; the principal airports are at Tripoli, Benghazi and Sebha. The main seaports are Benghazi, Tripoli and Tubruq.

Combined fixed-line and mobile phone density was 100 per 100 people in 2008, with 1 million fixed lines, 5 million mobile phone subscribers and 354,000 internet users.

EDUCATION AND HEALTH

There are six years of primary education and six of secondary, nine of which are compulsory.

Literacy rate – 87.3 per cent (2008 est)
Gross enrolment ratio (percentage of relevant age group) – primary 110 per cent; secondary 93 per cent (2008 est)
Health expenditure (per capita) – US$417 (2009)
Hospital beds (per 1,000 people) – 3.7 (2004–9)

MEDIA

Until the popular uprising in February 2011, the state maintained strict control over the media; the press was entirely state-run and the international publications that were available were censored by authorities. New media outlets critical of the regime – including newspapers, websites, radio stations and a Qatar-based satellite television channel – have since proliferated. The state-run Libyan Jamahiriyah Broadcasting Corporation continues to operate television and radio services and pan-Arab satellite television is available.

LIECHTENSTEIN

Fürstentum Liechtenstein – Principality of Liechtenstein

Area – 160 sq. km
Capital – Vaduz; population, 5,151 (2009 est)
Major town – Schaan
Currency – Swiss franc of 100 rappen (or centimes)
Population – 35,002 rising at 0.68 per cent a year (2010 est)
Religion – Christian (Roman Catholic 78 per cent, Protestant 8 per cent, Orthodox 1 per cent), Muslim 5 per cent (2000)
Language – German (official), Alemannic (dialect)
Population density – 224 per sq. km (2009)
Median age (years) – 41.4 (2010 est)
National anthem – 'Oben am Jungen Rhein' ['High Above the Young Rhine']
National day – 15 August (Feast of the Assumption)
Life expectancy (years) – 80.19 (2010 est)
Mortality rate – 7.49 (2010 est)
Birth rate – 9.69 (2010 est)
Infant mortality rate – 4.2 (2010 est)
Death penalty – Abolished for all crimes (since 1987)

CLIMATE AND TERRAIN
Liechtenstein is a small, mountainous landlocked principality in the Alps. The land falls in the west, in the valley of the river Rhine, which forms the western border. Elevation extremes range from 2,599m (Grauspitz) at the highest point to 430m (Ruggeller Riet) at the lowest. The climate is continental, with heavy snowfall in winter; average temperatures in the lowlands range from 4°C in January to 20°C in July.

HISTORY AND POLITICS
Although there was a sovereign state within the present boundaries from the 14th century, the present state of Liechtenstein was formed from the lordships of Schellenberg and Vaduz in 1719. Part of the Holy Roman Empire, the principality became a member of the Confederation of the Rhine that succeeded the Empire in 1806, and then of the German Confederation from 1815 until 1866. It was the only German principality to remain outside the German Empire formed in 1871. The country abolished its armed forces and declared permanent neutrality in 1868. The country's neutrality was not violated in either of the world wars.

Economic decline in the years following the First World War led Liechtenstein to adopt the Swiss currency in 1921 and to enter into a Swiss customs union in 1923. The country became extremely prosperous as an international finance centre after the Second World War. Since 2000 it has tightened its laws to prevent money laundering, and since 2008 it has started to meet international financial transparency standards.

Governments in the 20th and 21st centuries have been formed by the two main parties, the northern-based Progressive Citizens' Party (FBP) and the southern-based Fatherland Union (VU). Usually they have formed a coalition government, although the FBP formed a single-party government from 2001 to 2005. However, the government's power is limited by that of the monarchy, whose powers over the government and judiciary were increased by a 2003 referendum. Prince Hans Adam II remains head of state but in 2004 he handed over day-to-day responsibility for government to his son, Prince Alois.

The VU won an overall majority in the 2009 election. The coalition government formed with the FBP in 2005 continued, although the premiership passed from the FBP to the VU's Klaus Tschütscher.

POLITICAL SYSTEM
Under the 1921 constitution, Liechtenstein is a constitutional monarchy, with the hereditary prince as head of state. The unicameral legislature, the *Landtag*, has 25 members directly elected for a four-year term. The cabinet is appointed by the prince on the advice of the *Landtag* and consists of the head of government and four ministers.

HEAD OF STATE
HSH The Prince of Liechtenstein, Hans Adam II, *born* 14 February 1945, *succeeded* 13 November 1989
Heir, HSH Prince Alois, *born* 11 June 1968

SELECTED GOVERNMENT MEMBERS *as at June 2011*
Head of Government, Finance, Klaus Tschütscher
Deputy Head of Government, Economy, Martin Meyer
Foreign Affairs, Aurelia Frick
Home Affairs, Hugo Quaderer
Health, Social Affairs, Renate Müssner

BRITISH AMBASSADOR
HE Sarah Gillett, CMG, MVO, resident at Bern, Switzerland

ECONOMY AND TRADE
Liechtenstein has a prosperous, highly industrialised and diversified economy. Its mainstay is the financial services sector, which, with other service industries such as tourism, employs over half of the workforce. A light industrial base produces electronics, metal manufactures, dental products, ceramics, pharmaceuticals, food products, precision instruments and optical instruments, and employs 43.5 per cent of the workforce. Over half the workforce commutes daily from Austria, Switzerland and Germany.

Liechtenstein became a member of the European Free Trade Association in 1991, and of the European Economic Area in 1995. Most of its trade is with EU countries and Switzerland. The principal exports are its industrial products. The main imports are agricultural products, industrial raw materials, energy, machinery, metal goods, textiles, foodstuffs and vehicles.

GNI – US$4,817m; US$136,630 per capita (2009)
Annual average growth of GDP – 3.1 per cent (2007 est)
Inflation rate – 0.5 per cent (2009)
Unemployment – 1.5 per cent (2007)

Trade with UK	2009	2010
Imports from UK	£5,413,380	£24,297,711
Exports to UK	£17,569,273	£13,139,570

COMMUNICATIONS
Liechtenstein has no airports and only 380km of roads, 28km of waterways, and 9km of rail track which is part of the Austrian system connecting Austria and Switzerland. In 2009, there were 19,600 fixed telephone lines in use, 35,000 mobile phone subscribers and 23,000 internet users.

Liechtenstein relies on foreign and satellite broadcasters for television and radio services. Circulation for its two newspapers, *Liechtenstein Volksblatt* and *Liechtensteiner Vaterland,* is under 10,000.

LITHUANIA

Lietuvos Respublika – Republic of Lithuania

Area – 65,300 sq. km
Capital – Vilnius; population, 545,970 (2009 est)
Major cities – Kaunas, Klaipeda
Currency – Litas of 100 centas, pegged to the euro

Population – 3,545,319 falling at 0.28 per cent a year (2010 est); Lithuanian (84 per cent), Polish (6.1 per cent), Russian (4.9 per cent), Belarusian (1.1 per cent) (2009 est)
Religion – Christian (Roman Catholic 80 per cent, Orthodox 5 per cent, Lutheran 1 per cent) (est)
Language – Lithuanian (official), Russian, Polish
Population density – 53 per sq. km (2009)
Urban population – 67 per cent (2008 est)
Median age (years) – 39.7 (2010 est)
National anthem – 'Tautiska Giesme' ['National Song']
National day – 16 February (Independence Day)
Life expectancy (years) – 75.12 (2010 est)
Mortality rate – 11.25 (2010 est)
Birth rate – 9.21 (2010 est)
Infant mortality rate – 6.37 (2010 est)
Death penalty – Abolished for all crimes (since 1998)
CPI score – 5 (2010)

CLIMATE AND TERRAIN
Lithuania is a low-lying country with low hills in the west and south-east. It contains around 6,000 lakes and lagoons – over 2,800 of them sizeable – mostly lying in the east, although the Courland lagoon on the west coast is a major feature. Elevation extremes range from 294m (Aukstojas Hill) to 0m (Baltic Sea). The climate is mainly continental, and average temperatures range from −11°C in January to 23°C in July.

HISTORY AND POLITICS
Lithuania became a nation in the 13th century. It remained pagan for far longer than the rest of Europe, only becoming fully Christian in the 15th century when the Samogitians and the Aukstaitiai, the two main ethnic groups in the region, were converted. In the 14th century, a grand duchy was formed that stretched from the Baltic to the Black Sea and eastwards almost as far as Moscow. It confederated with Poland in the 16th century, before coming under Russian rule in 1795. The country joined Poland in rebelling against Russian domination twice in the 19th century.
Occupied by Germany during the First World War, Lithuania declared its independence in 1918 and successfully defended its autonomy against the Bolsheviks in 1918–19. However, the province and city of Vilnius were occupied by the newly independent Poland from 1920 until 1939. The USSR invaded and annexed Lithuania in 1940, but the country revolted in 1941 and briefly established its own government before being invaded and occupied by the Germans in their 1941 offensive against the USSR. Around 210,000 Lithuanians, mainly Jews, were killed during the German occupation. Soviet troops ousted the Germans in 1944 and re-established Soviet control, against which Lithuanians carried on a guerrilla war until 1952.
Growing nationalist sentiment led to the formation of the pro-democracy *Sajudis* ('The Movement') in 1988 to campaign for greater autonomy. A unilateral declaration of independence in 1990 was blocked by the USSR but following the failed coup in Moscow in 1991, Lithuania declared its independence a second time, and this was internationally recognised. The last Russian troops left the country in 1993. Lithuania joined NATO and the EU in 2004.
In the 2008 legislative elections, the Homeland Union–Lithuanian Christian Democrats became the largest party but without a majority. Its leader, Andrius Kubilius, became prime minister at the head of a four-party coalition government. The 2009 presidential election was won by Dalia Grybauskaite, who became the country's first female president.

POLITICAL SYSTEM
Under the 1992 constitution, the head of state is a president, who is directly elected for a five-year term, renewable once. The unicameral *Seimas* has 141 members who are directly elected for a four-year term; 71 members are elected in first-past-the-post constituencies and 70 by proportional representation. The prime minister is appointed by the president with the approval of the *Seimas*, and ministers are appointed upon the recommendation of the prime minister.

HEAD OF STATE
President, Dalia Grybauskaite, *elected* 17 May 2009, *sworn in* 12 July 2009

SELECTED GOVERNMENT MEMBERS *as at July 2011*
Prime Minister, Andrius Kubilius
Defence, Rasa Jukneviciene
Foreign Affairs, Audronius Azubalis
Interior, Raimundas Palaitis
Finance, Ingrida Simonyte

EMBASSY OF THE REPUBLIC OF LITHUANIA
84 Gloucester Place, London W1U 6AU
T 020-7486 6401 E amb.uk@urm.lt
W www.lithuanianembassy.co.uk
Ambassador Extraordinary and Plenipotentiary, HE Oskaras Jusys, *apptd* 2009

BRITISH EMBASSY
2 Antakalnio, Vilnius 10308
T (+370) (5) 246 2900 W http://ukinlithuania.fco.gov.uk
Ambassador Extraordinary and Plenipotentiary, HE Simon Butt, *apptd* 2008

BRITISH COUNCIL
4 Jogailos, Vilnius 01116
T (+370) (5) 264 4890 W www.britishcouncil.org/lithuania
Country Manager, Dr Arturas Vasilauskas

DEFENCE
The army has 187 armoured personnel carriers; the navy has 4 patrol and coastal vessels based at Klaipeda; the air force has 7 aircraft and 9 helicopters. Operates joint naval unit BALTRON (*see* Latvia: Defence).
Military budget – US$323m (2010)
Military personnel – 10,640: army 8,200, navy 530, air force 980, joint staff 1,804; paramilitary 14,600
Conscription duration – 12 months

ECONOMY AND TRADE
Lithuania's transition to a market economy is nearly complete, with the private sector now accounting for about 80 per cent GDP. The transition initially caused a recession, but the economy recovered and grew steadily from 2004 to 2008 before being plunged into a deep recession by the global economic downturn. Although recovery remains slow, drastic government cuts in public spending and the halving of imports in 2009 restored the current account deficit, which had soared to 15 per cent of GDP in 2007–8, to a surplus. The government is working vigorously to develop foreign investment and export markets.

The economy is diverse, and industries include metal-cutting machine tools, electric motors, domestic appliances, oil refining, shipbuilding, furniture making, textiles and amber extraction and jewellery making. Industry contributes 27.6 per cent to GDP, services 68.2 per cent and agriculture 4.3 per cent.

The main trading partners are Russia and other EU countries. Principal exports are mineral products, machinery and equipment, chemicals, textiles, foodstuffs and plastics. The main imports are mineral products, machinery, transport equipment, chemicals, textiles, clothing and metals.

GNI – US$37,203m; US$11,410 per capita (2009)
Annual average growth of GDP – 0.4 per cent (2010 est)
Inflation rate – 0.9 per cent (2010 est)
Population below poverty line – 4 per cent (2003)
Unemployment – 16 per cent (2010 est)
Total external debt – US$27,600m (2010 est)
Imports – US$18,300m (2009)
Exports – US$16,500m (2009)

BALANCE OF PAYMENTS
Trade – US$2,564m deficit (2010)
Current Account – US$1,423m surplus (2009)

Trade with UK	2009	2010
Imports from UK	£165,998,761	£221,071,227
Exports to UK	£363,318,524	£548,490,845

COMMUNICATIONS
There are 81,030km of roads, and a railway system of 1,767km linking the major towns with Vilnius and Klaipeda, the main seaport. The 81 airports and airfields include major airports at Vilnius, Kaunas and Palanga.

The telephone system is being modernised, although fixed-line use is declining as mobile phone services expand. By 2008 mobile phone density had reached 140 per 100 people, while fixed-line density had dropped to 22 per 100 people.

EDUCATION AND HEALTH
Education is free and compulsory from seven to 16 years, with the system comprising primary school (four years), lower secondary school (six years) and upper secondary education (two years). The language of instruction is predominantly Lithuanian, but there are also Russian and Polish schools. Vilnius University, founded in 1579, is one of the oldest in eastern Europe.

Literacy rate – 99.7 per cent (2008 est)
Gross enrolment ratio (percentage of relevant age group) – primary 96 per cent; secondary 99 per cent; tertiary 77 per cent (2008 est)
Health expenditure (per capita) – US$730 (2009)
Hospital beds (per 1,000 people) – 6.8 (2004–9)

MEDIA
The media operate independently of the state and are free to criticise the government, although politicians have attempted to influence the editorial policies of the public-service broadcaster. It operates several radio and television networks, in competition with a number of thriving commercial stations. There are around ten major national newspapers available, in Lithuanian, Russian, Polish and English.

LUXEMBOURG

Groussherzogtom Lëtzebuerg / Grand-Duché de Luxembourg / Großherzogtum Luxembourg – Grand Duchy of Luxembourg

Area – 2,586 sq. km
Capital – Luxembourg; population, 89,814 (2009 est)
Major towns – Esch-sur-Alzette, Dudelange
Currency – Euro (€) of 100 cents
Population – 497,538 rising at 1.16 per cent a year (2010 est); Luxembourger (63.1 per cent), Portuguese (13.3 per cent), French (4.5 per cent), Italian (4.3 per cent), German (2.3 per cent), other EU 7.3 per cent (2000)
Religion – Christian (Roman Catholic 90 per cent, Orthodox 1 per cent), Muslim 2 per cent (est)
Language – Luxembourgish, French, German (all official)
Population density – 192 per sq. km (2009)
Urban population – 82 per cent (2008 est)
Median age (years) – 39.3 (2010 est)
National anthem – 'Ons Heemecht' ['Our Homeland']
National day – 23 June (official birthday of Grand Duchess Charlotte)
Life expectancy (years) – 79.48 (2010 est)
Mortality rate – 8.46 (2010 est)
Birth rate – 11.7 (2010 est)
Infant mortality rate – 4.49 (2010 est)
Death penalty – Abolished for all crimes (since 1979)
CPI score – 8.5 (2010)
Military expenditure – US$249m (2009)
Military personnel – army 900; paramilitary 612
Health expenditure (per capita) – US$8,183 (2009)

CLIMATE AND TERRAIN
A landlocked grand duchy, Luxembourg has the forested plateau of the Ardennes in the north, forming part of the Natural Germano-Luxembourg Park which extends east into Germany. The south of the country is mainly fertile farmland, and in the east is the wine-growing region of the Moselle valley. Elevation extremes range from 559m (Buurgplaatz) to 133m (Moselle river). The climate is modified continental, and average temperatures in Luxembourg city range from 1°C in January to 18°C in July.

HISTORY AND POLITICS
The area was part of the Roman Empire and then became part of the Frankish Empire in the fifth century AD. It became autonomous within the Holy Roman Empire under Siegfried, Count of Ardennes, and was given the status of a duchy in 1354. Controlled by a succession of European powers after 1437 (when the House of Luxembourg died out), it was made a grand duchy under Dutch rule after the Napoleonic wars. Much of

Luxembourg joined the Belgians in their revolt against the Netherlands in 1830; in 1838 the western, French-speaking region was assigned to Belgium, and the remainder became an independent grand duchy in 1839. The treaty of London in 1867 confirmed its independence and neutrality. Occupation by Germany in both world wars prompted Luxembourg to give up its neutrality and it was a founding member of NATO in 1949.

Luxembourg entered into economic union with Belgium in 1921 and joined the Benelux economic union in 1948. It was a founder member of the EEC in 1958 and joined the eurozone in 1999.

The Christian Social Party (CSV) has held power almost continuously since the First World War, usually as the main partner in coalition governments. It remained the largest party in the legislature after the 2009 election, but without an overall majority. A new coalition government was formed under the leadership of Jean-Claude Juncker of the CSV, who has been prime minister since 1995.

POLITICAL SYSTEM
Under the 1868 constitution, the head of state is a hereditary grand duke, whose role is now largely ceremonial. The unicameral legislature, the Chamber of Deputies, has 60 members directly elected for a five-year term. There is also a Council of State, which has 21 members nominated by the grand duke; this acts as the supreme administrative tribunal and has some legislative functions. The prime minister is appointed by the grand duke on the basis of the election results and appoints the cabinet.

HEAD OF STATE
HRH *The Grand Duke of Luxembourg*, Grand Duke Henri, *born* 16 April 1955; *succeeded* 7 October 2000
Heir, HRH Prince Guillaume, *born* 11 November 1981

SELECTED GOVERNMENT MEMBERS *as at July 2011*
Prime Minister, Jean-Claude Juncker
Deputy Prime Minister, Foreign Affairs, Jean Asselborn
Interior, Jean-Marie Halsdorf
Finance, Luc Frieden

EMBASSY OF LUXEMBOURG
27 Wilton Crescent, London SW1X 8SD
T 020-7235 6961 E londres.amb@mae.etat.lu
W http://londres.mae.lu
Ambassador Extraordinary and Plenipotentiary, HE Hubert Wurth, *apptd* 2007

BRITISH EMBASSY
5 Boulevard Joseph II, L-1840, Luxembourg
T (+352) 229 864 W http://ukinluxembourg.fco.gov.uk
Ambassador Extraordinary and Plenipotentiary, HE Hon. Alice Walpole, *apptd* 2011

ECONOMY AND TRADE
The economy is stable, with steady growth, low unemployment and low inflation providing an exceptionally high standard of living. The government offset the contraction in the economy in 2008–9 with economic stimulus measures, which led to a budget deficit in 2009 but growth resumed in 2010. Banking and financial services are the dominant sector, contributing 28 per cent of GDP. Steel production used to dominate the industrial sector, but this has diversified to include IT, telecommunications, freight transport, food processing,

chemicals, metal products and engineering. Tourism is also important. The small agricultural sector consists mainly of family-owned farms. Services account for 86 per cent of GDP, industry for 13.6 per cent and agriculture for 0.4 per cent. Over 50 per cent of the workforce commutes daily from France, Belgium and Germany.

The main trading partners are other EU countries and China. Principal exports are the products of industrial activities. The main imports are minerals, metals, foodstuffs and quality consumer goods.

GNI – US$37,182m; US$76,710 per capita (2009)
Annual average growth of GDP – 3.2 per cent (2010 est)
Inflation rate – 2.1 per cent (2010 est)
Unemployment – 5.5 per cent (2010 est)
Total external debt – US$1,892,000m (2010 est)
Imports – US$24,300m (2009)
Exports – US$12,800m (2009)

BALANCE OF PAYMENTS
Trade – US$12,841m deficit (2010)
Current Account – US$2,968m surplus (2009)

Trade with UK	2009	2010
Imports from UK	£188,721,475	£235,072,289
Exports to UK	£608,032,838	£567,886,054

COMMUNICATIONS
Luxembourg has one airport. There are 5,227km of roads (including 147km of motorways), and 275km of railways. The Moselle river provides 37km of navigable waterway. In 2009 there were 273,600 fixed telephone lines in use, 719,000 mobile phone users and 424,500 internet users.

MEDIA
Despite its size, Luxembourg has a significant international media presence, providing pan-European television and radio broadcasting through media groups such as RTL. Luxembourg is also the headquarters of the Société Européenne des Satellites (SES), which operates the Astra satellite fleet, Europe's largest satellite operation. Newspapers publish mostly in French and German; popular national dailies include *Luxemburger Wort* and *Tageblatt*.

MACEDONIA

Republika Makedonija – Republic of Macedonia

Area – 25,713 sq. km
Capital – Skopje; population, 480,383 (2009 est)
Major city – Kumanovo
Currency – Denar of 100 deni

Population – 2,072,086 rising at 0.26 per cent a year (2010 est); Macedonian (64.2 per cent), Albanian (25.2 per cent), Turkish (3.9 per cent), Roma (2.7 per cent), Serb (1.8 per cent) (2002)
Religion – Christian (Orthodox 65 per cent), Muslim 32 per cent (est)
Language – Macedonian, Albanian (both official), Turkish, Romani, Serbian (each official in different regions)
Population density – 81 per sq. km (2009)
Urban population – 67 per cent (2008 est)
Median age (years) – 35.4 (2010 est)
National anthem – 'Denes Nad Makedonija' ['Today Over Macedonia']
National day – 8 September (Independence Day)
Life expectancy (years) – 74.92 (2010 est)
Mortality rate – 8.87 (2010 est)
Birth rate – 11.92 (2010 est)
Infant mortality rate – 8.76 (2010 est)
Death penalty – Abolished for all crimes (since 1991)
CPI score – 4.1 (2010)
Conscription duration – Six months
Literacy rate – 97.1 per cent (2008 est)
Gross enrolment ratio (percentage of relevant age group) – primary 88 per cent; secondary 84 per cent; tertiary 40 per cent (2008 est)
Health expenditure (per capita) – US$314 (2009)
Hospital beds (per 1,000 people) – 4.6 (2004–9)

CLIMATE AND TERRAIN

The landlocked country is a mountainous plateau divided by deep river valleys and basins, including the valleys of the Vardar river and its tributaries. Elevation extremes range from 2,764m (Golem Korab) at the highest point to 50m (Vardar river) at the lowest. Lakes Ohrid and Prespa straddle the border with Albania, and Lake Doiran the border with Greece. The climate is continental, with average temperatures in Skopje ranging from 1°C in January to 23°C in August.

HISTORY AND POLITICS

The area of present-day Macedonia was part of the ancient Macedonian kingdom, which also included northern Greece and south-west Bulgaria, in the fourth century BC. Macedonia became a province of the Roman Empire in the second century BC, coming under the control of the Byzantine Empire from the fourth century AD. Slav peoples settled the area in the seventh century and mixed with the Greek, Illyrian, Thracian, Scythian and Turkish peoples.

From the ninth to the 14th centuries the area was under the rule successively of the Bulgars, Byzantium and the Serbs, and became part of the Ottoman Empire in the late 14th century. Following the Balkan wars of 1912 and 1913 the region was divided between Bulgaria, Serbia and Greece. After the First World War, the Serbian part was awarded to the newly created state that became Yugoslavia. During the Second World War, this area was occupied by Bulgaria from 1941 to 1944, and after liberation became a republic within the communist Federal Republic of Yugoslavia.

Nationalist sentiment grew throughout the 1980s, and in 1991 Macedonia declared its independence, which Yugoslavia recognised in 1992. International recognition was initially delayed by Greece's objections to the republic's name (Greece claims that its region of Macedonia is the only one entitled to the name), but the country joined the UN in 1993 as the Former Yugoslav Republic of Macedonia; Greece recognised it under this name and lifted its trade blockade in 1995, but in 2008 blocked the republic's membership of NATO.

Throughout the 1990s there was tension and sporadic violence with the large ethnic Albanian minority, aggrieved at their lack of civil rights. Instability in neighbouring Kosovo spilled over into Macedonia in 2001, sparking a two-month uprising by ethnic Albanian separatists. Peace talks facilitated by international bodies resulted in the Ohrid framework agreement, giving Albanians greater recognition within Macedonia and making Albanian an official language.

The 2009 presidential election was won in the second round by the VMRO-DPMNE candidate, Gjorge Ivanov. In the legislative election in June 2011, the governing Better Macedonia alliance, led by the VMRO-DPMNE, remained the largest bloc but lost the overall majority it had after the 2006 election; Nikola Gruevski of the VMRO-DPMNE remained prime minister of the coalition government.

POLITICAL SYSTEM

The 1991 constitution was amended in 2001 to incorporate provisions of the Ohrid agreement relating to ethnic Albanian rights, and several times since, most notably in 2004 to give ethnic Albanians greater local autonomy in areas where they predominate.

The head of state is a president, who is directly elected for a five-year term. The unicameral legislature, the *Sobranie,* has 120 members directly elected for a four-year term. The prime minister is appointed by the president. Government ministers are elected by the assembly but are not members of it.

HEAD OF STATE
President, Gjorge Ivanov, *elected* 5 April 2009, *sworn in* 12 May 2009

SELECTED GOVERNMENT MEMBERS *as at July 2011*
Prime Minister, Nikola Gruevski
Deputy Prime Ministers, Zoran Stavrevski *(Finance);* Vladimir Pesevski *(Economy);* Abdulakim Ademi; Vasko Naumovski
Foreign Affairs, Antonio Milososki
Interior, Gordana Jankulovska
Defence, Zoran Konjanovski

EMBASSY OF THE REPUBLIC OF MACEDONIA
Suites 2.1/2.2, Buckingham Court, 75–83 Buckingham Gate, London SW1E 6PE
T 020-7976 0535 E info@macedonianembassy.org.uk
W www.macedonianembassy.org.uk
Ambassador Extraordinary and Plenipotentiary, HE Marija Efremova, *apptd* 2008

BRITISH EMBASSY
Salvador Aljende 73, Skopje 1000
T (+389) (2) 329 9299 E britishembassyskopje@fco.gov.uk
W http://ukinmacedonia.fco.gov.uk
Ambassador Extraordinary and Plenipotentiary, HE Christopher Yvon, *apptd* 2010

BRITISH COUNCIL
PO Box 562, Bulevar Goce Delcev 6, 1000 Skopje
T (+389) (2) 313 5035 W www.britishcouncil.org/macedonia
Director, Les Dangerfield, resident at Zagreb, Croatia

DEFENCE

The army has 31 main battle tanks, 11 armoured infantry fighting vehicles and 201 armoured personnel carriers.

The marine wing has 2 patrol and coastal combatant vessels. The air wing has 14 armed helicopters.

Military budget – US$140m (2010)
Military personnel – joint operational command 8,000

ECONOMY AND TRADE
Macedonia was the least developed republic in the former Yugoslavia before 1991, and economic growth was initially hindered by the trade embargo by Greece (1993–5) and the 2001 ethnic Albanian uprising. Economic growth was steady from 2003 to 2008, although the economy contracted briefly in 2009 owing to the global downturn. Unemployment remains a major problem, although official figures may be overstated because of the size of the grey economy, estimated to be worth more than 20 per cent of GDP. The country remains poor, with over a quarter of the population living below the poverty line.

Services produce 69.2 per cent of GDP, industry 22.1 per cent and agriculture 8.7 per cent. The main crops are grapes, tobacco, vegetables, fruit and dairy products. Food processing and winemaking are major industries, along with textiles, chemicals, iron, steel, cement, energy and pharmaceuticals. The main trading partners are Germany, Greece, Bulgaria, Italy, and other Balkan and EU states. Principal exports are food, wine, tobacco, textiles, manufactured goods, iron and steel. The main imports are machinery and equipment, cars, chemicals, fuels and food.

GNI – US$8,990m; US$4,400 per capita (2009)
Annual average growth of GDP – 1.5 per cent (2010 est)
Inflation rate – 1.5 per cent (2010 est)
Population below poverty line – 28.7 per cent (2008)
Unemployment – 33.1 per cent (2010 est)
Total external debt – US$5,520m (2010 est)
Imports – US$5,000m (2009)
Exports – US$2,700m (2009)

BALANCE OF PAYMENTS
Trade – US$2,043m deficit (2010)
Current Account – US$673m deficit (2008)

Trade with UK	2009	2010
Imports from UK	£30,222,307	–
Exports to UK	£26,607,177	£34,412,775

COMMUNICATIONS
Macedonia has 13,736km of roads, and 699km of railways, of which 234km are electrified. The principal airports are at Skopje and Ohrid, and there are a further 12 airports and airfields around the country.

Fixed-line telephone connections are declining as mobile phones become more widespread. There were 442,000 fixed lines in use, 1.9 million mobile phone subscribers and 1 million internet users in 2009.

MEDIA
The three channels of the state-run television service compete with a growing number of commercial stations although many local broadcasters struggle financially. There are 12 major daily and weekly press publications, reflecting a range of views; media outlets are often divided along ethnic lines. The partially government-owned *Nova Makedonija* is the leading newspaper.

MADAGASCAR

*Repoblikan'i Madagasikara / République de Madagascar –
Republic of Madagascar*

Area – 587,041 sq. km
Capital – Antananarivo; population, 1,815,690 (2009 est)
Major cities – Antsirabe, Fianarantsoa, Mahajanga, Toamasina
Currency – Ariary (MGA) of five iraimbilanja
Population – 21,281,844 rising at 2.99 per cent a year (2010 est); the people are of mixed Malayo-Indonesian, Arab and African origin. There are sizeable French, Chinese and Indian communities
Religion – Christian 50 per cent, Muslim 10 per cent (est). A large minority also follow traditional indigenous religions
Language – Malagasy, French, English (all official)
Population density – 34 per sq. km (2009)
Urban population – 29 per cent (2008 est)
Median age (years) – 18.1 (2010 est)
National anthem – 'Ry Tanindraza nay malala ô' ['Oh, Our Beloved Fatherland']
National day – 26 June (Independence Day)
Life expectancy (years) – 63.26 (2010 est)
Mortality rate – 7.97 (2010 est)
Birth rate – 37.89 (2010 est)
Infant mortality rate – 52.84 (2010 est)
Death penalty – Retained (no known use since 1958)
CPI score – 2.6 (2010)

CLIMATE AND TERRAIN
Madagascar, the fourth-largest island in the world, lies 386km off the south-east coast of Africa, from which it is separated by the Mozambique Channel. Coastal plains rise to a central plateau and mountains indented with river valleys. Elevation extremes range from 2,876m (Maromokotro) to 0m (Indian Ocean). Because of its isolation, most mammals and plants and half of its bird species are unique to the island. However, this biological diversity is threatened by deforestation and soil erosion.

The climate is tropical on the coast, temperate in the interior and arid in the south. Average temperatures in Antananarivo range from 15°C in July to 21°C in February. Madagascar is subject to tropical cyclones, which cause flooding and wind damage, particularly on the coast.

HISTORY AND POLITICS
The island was settled by peoples from south-east Asia and east Africa from around the first century AD. Although first visited by Europeans c.1500, local kingdoms ruled until the early 19th century, when the Merina kingdom conquered the island. France made the island a protectorate in 1895 after the last indigenous

resistance was defeated. During the Second World War, the British invaded in order to replace the pro-Vichy government with a Free French government. At the end of the war Madagascar was returned to France, which suppressed a nationalist uprising in 1947–8. Nationalist agitation continued throughout the 1950s and resulted in independence in 1960.

The military took control in 1972 following civil disturbances, and in 1975 martial law was imposed after a coup. A Marxist one-party state was created with Lt-Cdr Didier Ratsiraka as president. Marxism was abandoned in 1980 and, following a decade of pro-democracy agitation, a new constitution introduced parliamentary democracy in 1992.

Didier Ratsiraka was defeated in the 1993 presidential elections but returned to office in 1997 after winning the 1996 election. He refused to accept his defeat in the 2001 presidential election and the six-month struggle between his supporters and those of Marc Ravalomanana, the successful candidate, brought the country close to civil war until, in July 2002, Ratsiraka went into exile and his supporters surrendered. President Ravalomanana was re-elected in 2006 and his I Love Madagascar party (TIM) retained its large majority in the 2007 legislative election.

A power struggle between President Ravalomanana and opposition leader Andry Rajoelina began in December 2008. Following an army mutiny and Ravalomanana's resignation, Rajoelina assumed power in March 2009 with the backing of the military and the high court, but the takeover provoked continued demonstrations and widespread international condemnation. Although the four main political parties agreed transitional government arrangements in August and November 2009, disputes between the four have created political deadlock and delayed elections originally scheduled for 2010. A referendum approved a new constitution in November 2010; elections were expected in September 2011.

POLITICAL SYSTEM

Under the 2010 constitution, the president is directly elected and serves a five-year term, renewable once; the minimum age requirement for presidential candidates was lowered in 2010. The legislature is bicameral, comprising the National Assembly, which has 127 members directly elected for a four-year term, and the senate, which has 100 members, of whom two-thirds are appointed by the regional assemblies and one-third by the president; they serve a four-year term. The 258-member Congress of Transition and 65-member Higher Transition Council set up under 2009 agreements remain in office until elections give effect to the 2010 constitution.

HEAD OF STATE

President, Andry Rajoelina, *took office* 21 March 2009
Co-presidents, Emmanuel Rakotovahiny; Fetison Rakoto Andrianirina; Rajemison Rakotomaharo

SELECTED GOVERNMENT MEMBERS *as at July 2011*
Prime Minister, Col. Albert Camille Vital
Foreign Affairs, Yvette Sylla
Armed Forces, Gen. Andre Lucien Rakotoarimasy
Finance, Hery Rajaonarimampianina

EMBASSY OF THE REPUBLIC OF MADAGASCAR
4 Avenue Raphael, 75016 Paris, France
T (33) (1) 4504 6211 **E** info@ambassade-madagascar.fr
W http://ambassade-madagascar.fr/site
Ambassador Extraordinary and Plenipotentiary, vacant

BRITISH AMBASSADOR
HE Nick Leake, *apptd* 2010, resident in Port Louis, Mauritius

DEFENCE

The army has 12 light tanks and around 30 armoured personnel carriers. The navy has 7 patrol and coastal combatant vessels at 5 bases. The gendarmerie has 5 patrol and coastal combatant vessels.

Military budget – US$56m (2010)
Military personnel – 13,500: army 12,500, navy 500, air force 500; paramilitary 8,100
Conscription duration – 18 months (including civil purposes)

ECONOMY AND TRADE

Economic liberalisation and privatisation since the mid-1990s have resulted in slow but steady growth, although the political disturbances in 2002 and 2009–10, and cyclone devastation in 2000 and 2004, have been serious setbacks. President Ravalomanana's reforms and anti-corruption measures attracted increased international aid, and in 2004 half of the country's foreign debt was written off, but aid has been suspended and investment and government spending have slowed since 2009. Poverty remains endemic and unemployment high.

Agriculture, fishing and forestry are the mainstays of the economy, accounting for 26.5 per cent of GDP and employing 80 per cent of the workforce. The main cash crops include coffee, vanilla, fish, sugar cane, cocoa, cloves and pepper. The industrial sector contributes 16.7 per cent of GDP, through mining (chromite, graphite, sapphires), processing meat, fish and other agricultural products, manufacturing (textiles, paper, cement, chemicals), car assembly and oil refining. Tourism is of growing importance but visitor numbers halved in 2009.

The main trading partners are France, the USA, China and Thailand. Principal exports are agricultural products, textiles, chromite and petroleum products. The main imports are capital goods, petroleum, consumer goods and food.

GNI – US$8,498m; US$430 per capita (2009)
Annual average growth of GDP – 1.5 per cent (2010 est)
Inflation rate – 8.1 per cent (2010 est)
Population below poverty line – 50 per cent (2004 est)
Total external debt – US$2,973m (2010 est)
Imports – US$2,900m (2009)
Exports – US$1,200m (2009)

BALANCE OF PAYMENTS
Trade – US$1,355m deficit (2010)
Current Account – US$1,939m deficit (2008)

Trade with UK	2009	2010
Imports from UK	£13,099,073	£12,593,169
Exports to UK	£28,231,815	£29,422,501

COMMUNICATIONS

The main seaports are Toamasina, Antsiranana, Mahajanga and Toliara. There are 84 airports and airfields, of which the major airports are at Antananarivo and Mahajanga. Surface transport is by the 65,663km of roads and 854km of railways.

In 2009 there were 181,000 fixed telephone lines in use, 5.9 million mobile phone subscribers and 320,000 internet users.

EDUCATION AND HEALTH

Education is free and compulsory for nine years, but attendance is variable. Five years of primary education are followed by four years of lower and a possible three years of upper secondary education.

Literacy rate – 70.7 per cent (2008 est)
Gross enrolment ratio (percentage of relevant age group) – primary 160 per cent; secondary 32 per cent; tertiary 4 per cent (2009 est)
Health expenditure (per capita) – US$18 (2009)
Hospital beds (per 1,000 people) – 0.3 (2004–9)

MEDIA

State-run television and radio are the only networks with national coverage but there are hundreds of private local television and radio stations; many of the radio stations are owned by politicians. Numerous news publications print a diverse range of opinions. The freedom and independence of the press has been protected by law since 1990.

MALAWI

Dziko la Malawi – Republic of Malawi

Area – 118,484 sq. km
Capital – Lilongwe; population, 820,802 (2009 est)
Major cities – Blantyre, the commercial and industrial centre; Mzuzu; Zomba, the former capital
Currency – Kwacha (K) of 100 tambala
Population – 15,447,500 rising at 2.76 per cent a year (2010 est); about nine ethnic groups, of which the largest are Chewa and Angoni (Nguni)
Religion – Christian 80 per cent, Muslim 13 per cent (predominantly Sunni) (est)
Language – Chichewa, English (both official), Chiyao, Chitumbuka
Population density – 162 per sq. km (2009)
Urban population – 19 per cent (2008 est)
Median age (years) – 17.1 (2010 est)
National anthem – 'Mlungu dalitsani Malawi' ['Oh God Bless Our Land of Malawi']
National day – 6 July (Independence Day)
Life expectancy (years) – 50.92 (2010 est)
Mortality rate – 13.69 (2010 est)
Birth rate – 41.28 (2010 est)
Infant mortality rate – 83.5 (2010 est)
HIV/AIDS adult prevalence – 11 per cent (2009 est)
Death penalty – Retained (not used since 1992)
CPI score – 3.4 (2010)

CLIMATE AND TERRAIN

The landlocked state lies along the western and southern shores of Lake Malawi (Nyasa). The northern and central regions are plateaux with rolling terrain, while the south is mainly hills and mountains. Elevation extremes range from 3,002m (Sapitwa) to 37m (junction of Shire river and Mozambique border). The climate is subtropical, with a wet season from November to April; average temperatures in Blantyre range from 19°C in June and July to 26°C in November.

HISTORY AND POLITICS

Until contact was made with European missionaries in the 19th century, Malawi was dominated by a succession of powerful tribes that included the Maravi, the Yao and the Nguni. The missionaries campaigned for official intervention to end the east-coast slave trade, which had begun in the early 19th century, and in 1891 Britain established the Nyasaland and District Protectorate over the area. Renamed the British Central Africa Protectorate in 1893, it became the British colony of Nyasaland in 1907. The country was joined with Northern and Southern Rhodesia (now Zambia and Zimbabwe) between 1953 and 1963. It became independent, as Malawi, in 1964, with Dr Hastings Banda as prime minister.

In 1966, the country became a one-party state ruled by the Malawi Congress Party (MCP) and Dr Banda became president, declaring himself president for life in 1971. In the early 1990s, increasing pro-democracy agitation and international pressure forced Banda to introduce multiparty democracy in 1994.

In the 2004 legislative election, the MCP became the largest party with 60 seats, but without an overall majority. The simultaneous presidential election was won by the United Democratic Front (UDF) candidate Bingu wa Mutharika, who appointed a coalition government made up of the UDF and smaller parties.

In 2005, President Mutharika resigned from the UDF over the hostility of the party and his predecessor, Bakili Muluzi, to his anti-corruption campaign and founded a new party, the Democratic Progressive Party (DPP). The president's uncompromising anti-corruption stance involved him in a power struggle with Muluzi and the vice-president Cassim Chilumpha that disrupted legislative business in 2006; several senior politicians, including Muluzi and Chilumpha, have been arrested since 2006 on corruption or treason charges. President Mutharika was re-elected in 2009, and the simultaneous legislative election was won by the DPP.

POLITICAL SYSTEM
Under the 1995 constitution, the executive president is directly elected for a five-year term, renewable once. The unicameral National Assembly consists of 193 members, who are directly elected for a five-year term.

HEAD OF STATE
President, Defence, Bingu wa Mutharika, *elected* 20 May 2004, *re-elected* 2009
Vice-president, Joyce Banda

SELECTED GOVERNMENT MEMBERS *as at July 2011*
Finance, Ken Kandodo
Foreign Affairs, Etta Banda
Home Affairs, Aaron Sangala

HIGH COMMISSION OF THE REPUBLIC OF MALAWI
36 John Street, London WC1N 2AT
T 020-7421 6010 E malawihighcommission@btconnect.com
W www.malawihighcommission.co.uk
High Commissioner (acting), HE Flossie Gomile-Chidyaonga, *apptd* 2006

BRITISH HIGH COMMISSION
PO Box 30042, Lingadzi House, Lilongwe 3
T (+265) (1) 772 400 E bhclilongwe@fco.gov.uk
W http://ukinmalawi.fco.gov.uk
High Commissioner, HE Fergus Cochrane-Dyet, *apptd*
2009

BRITISH COUNCIL
PO Box 30222, Plot No. 13/20 City Centre, Lilongwe 3
T (+265) (1) 773 244 W www.britishcouncil.org/africa
Director, Julian Baker

DEFENCE

The maritime wing has 1 patrol and coastal combatant
vessel at Monkey Bay (Lake Nyasa).
Military expenditure – US$51m (2009 est)
Military personnel – 5,300: army 5,300; paramilitary
1,500

ECONOMY AND TRADE

Malawi is one of the poorest countries in Africa. It has few
natural resources and its agricultural land is under pressure
because of population growth. It also experienced years
of mismanagement under earlier governments, and
corruption remains a problem despite the government's
determination to eliminate it. These factors, and the
vulnerability of agricultural production to both drought
and severe flooding, make the country heavily dependent
on food and economic aid from international agencies and
donor nations, although this reliance has been gradually
declining since the economy started to grow in 2007.
Debt relief and tighter fiscal control reduced public debt
from over 200 per cent of GDP to 49 per cent by 2008,
although this rose to 58 per cent in 2009 as foreign
exchange earnings and investment fell.

The economy is primarily agricultural, with 85 per cent
of the workforce engaged in agriculture, which accounts
for 33.4 per cent of GDP and 90 per cent of export
revenue. Tobacco is the most important cash crop,
providing over half of export earnings, along with tea,
sugar, cotton, coffee and peanuts. The main industrial
activities are agricultural processing, sawmill products,
cement and consumer goods, now supplemented by
mining uranium, of which exports began in 2009.

The main export markets are Germany, Egypt, South
Africa, Egypt, Zimbabwe and the USA; imports come
mainly from South Africa (40 per cent), China, India and
France. Apart from tobacco and other agricultural
products, wood products and clothing are principal
exports. The main imports are food, fuels,
semi-manufactures, consumer goods and transport
equipment.
GNI – US$4,656m; US$290 per capita (2009)
Annual average growth of GDP – 6.5 per cent (2010 est)
Inflation rate – 8 per cent (2010 est)
Population below poverty line – 53 per cent (2004)
Total external debt – US$1,213m (2010 est)
Imports – US$1,600m (2009)
Exports – US$1,000m (2009)

BALANCE OF PAYMENTS
Trade – US$664m deficit (2010)
Current Account – US$360m deficit (2009)

Trade with UK	2009	2010
Imports from UK	£24,248,446	£17,464,719
Exports to UK	£23,777,442	£26,105,969

COMMUNICATIONS

Much internal transport is by water; there are 700km of
navigable waterways on Lake Malawi (Nyasa) and the
river Shire. Malawi is a partner with Zambia and
Mozambique in the Shire-Zambezi Waterway Project,
which aims to create a commercially viable link between
the landlocked countries and the Indian Ocean coast; a
river port is being developed at Nsanje. There are already
rail links with the coast through Mozambique; these were
severed during Mozambique's civil war but the route to
Nacala reopened in 2002. There are 797km of railways,
including a line linking the Zambian town of Chipata to
the Indian Ocean coast at Nacala in Mozambique. There
are 15,451km of roads, of which 6,956km are surfaced.
The main airports are at Blantyre and Lilongwe, with
30 smaller airports and airstrips around the country.

Fixed-line telephone density is about 2 per 100 people.
Mobile phone services are expanding but coverage is
limited to urban areas; density was about 15 per 100
people in 2008.

EDUCATION AND HEALTH

The government is responsible for primary and secondary
schools, technical education and primary teacher training.
Literacy rate – 72.7 per cent (2008 est)
Gross enrolment ratio (percentage of relevant age group) –
primary 113 per cent; secondary 28 per cent; tertiary
0.5 per cent (2007 est)
Health expenditure (per capita) – US$19 (2009)
Hospital beds (per 1,000 people) – 1.1 (2004–9)

MEDIA

There are four national newspapers, two of which are
dailies; the press operates freely, although the government
has used libel laws to exert pressure on journalists. Radio
is the main source of information, provided by the
state-run Malawi Broadcasting Corporation and a number
of private stations. Television was introduced in 1999; the
only provider is state-run Television Malawi.

MALAYSIA

Area – 329,847 sq. km
Capital – Kuala Lumpur; population, 1,493,500 (2009
est); Putrajaya is the administrative capital
Major cities – Ampang Jaya, Ipoh, Johor Bahru, Klang,
Kota Kinabalu, Kuching, Petaling Jaya, Shah Alam,
Subang Jaya
Currency – Malaysian ringgit (RM) of 100 sen; also
known as Malaysian dollar
Population – 28,274,729 rising at 1.61 per cent a year
(2010 est); Malay (50.4 per cent), Chinese (23.7 per
cent), indigenous (11 per cent), Indian (7.1 per cent)
(2004 est)
Religion – Muslim 60 per cent (predominantly Shafi'i, a
school of Sunni Islam), Buddhist 19 per cent, Christian
9 per cent, Hindu 6 per cent, Chinese traditional
religions 3 per cent (est)
Language – Bahasa Malaysia (Malay) (official), English,
Cantonese, Mandarin, Tamil, Telugu, Malayalam,
Punjabi, Thai, Iban, Kadazan
Population density – 84 per sq. km (2009)
Urban population – 70 per cent (2008 est)
Median age (years) – 26.5 (2010 est)
National anthem – 'Negaraku' ['My Country']
National day – 31 August (Malaysia Day)
Life expectancy (years) – 73.55 (2010 est)

Mortality rate – 4.92 (2010 est)
Birth rate – 21.41 (2010 est)
Infant mortality rate – 15.5 (2010 est)
Death penalty – Retained
CPI score – 4.4 (2010)

CLIMATE AND TERRAIN

Malaysia comprises the 11 states of peninsular Malaya plus the states of Sabah and Sarawak on the island of Borneo. The Malay peninsula, which extends from the isthmus of Kra to the Singapore Strait, is a plain with two highland areas in the north. The Malaysian part of Borneo is mostly high plateau, rising to mountains in western Sabah and eastern Sarawak, while Sarawak also has lower-lying land along the coast and in the Rajang valley; both states are densely forested. Elevation extremes range from 4,100m (Gunung Kinabalu, Sabah) at the highest point to 0m (Indian Ocean) at the lowest. The climate is tropical, experiencing the south-west monsoon from May to September and the north-east monsoon from November to March. Temperatures in Kuala Lumpur range between 22°C and 33°C all year round.

HISTORY AND POLITICS

Malaysia formed part of the Srivijaya Empire from the ninth to the 14th century. From the 16th century, the Portuguese, Dutch and British vied for control in the region. The British possessions of Singapore, Penang and Malacca were formed in 1826 into the Straits Settlement, which became a crown colony in 1867. British protection was extended over four Malay states, which federated in 1896, and protection treaties were agreed with several other states between 1885 and 1930. Following occupation by the Japanese from 1941 to 1945, the United Malays National Organisation (UMNO) was founded in 1946 to oppose the postwar political settlement, which extended equal rights to the Chinese and Indian minorities; its opposition led to an insurgency (the Emergency) by the Chinese-led Malayan Communist Party from 1948 to 1955. The nine peninsular states were federated as the Federation of Malaya in 1948. The Federation of Malaya became independent in 1957, and in 1963 it combined with Singapore, Sarawak and Sabah to form the Federation of Malaysia; Singapore withdrew from the federation in 1965.

UMNO has dominated post-independence politics, initially as the governing party and since 1971 as the dominant partner in the *Barisan Nasional* (National Front) coalition governments. Mahathir bin Muhammad became prime minister in 1981 and his 22-year tenure of office saw increasingly authoritarian rule, particularly as opposition to Malay dominance of political life grew in the 1980s and 1990s. There is considerable tension between the ethnic groups in Malaysia; Malay resentment of the large Chinese minority's economic dominance led to the adoption in 1971 of policies that favour ethnic Malays in education and employment, although the Chinese remain the wealthiest section of society. In recent years there has been intercommunal violence between ethnic Indians (the poorest group) and Malays.

The *Barisan Nasional* coalition won the 2008 legislative election, but with a majority reduced from 198 to 140 seats after a significant swing to the opposition parties. Abdullah Ahmed Badawi, prime minister since 2003, stood down in 2009 and was replaced as leader of UMNO and prime minister by his deputy, Najib Tun Abdul Razak.

POLITICAL SYSTEM

The 1957 constitution provides for a federal government and a degree of autonomy for the state governments. The supreme head of state *(Yang di-Pertuan Agong)* is elected by the nine hereditary rulers of the peninsular states from among their number and serves a five-year term.

The federal *Parlimen* has two houses, the House of Representatives and the senate. The former is the lower house and has 222 members, directly elected for a five-year term. The senate has 70 members who serve a three-year term; the legislative assembly of each state elects two members, and 44 are nominated by the head of state.

Each of the 13 states has its own constitution, which must not be inconsistent with the federal constitution. The Malay rulers are either chosen or succeed to their position in accordance with the custom of their particular state; in other states of Malaysia, choice of the head of state is at the discretion of the *Yang di-Pertuan Agong* after consultation with the chief minister of the state. The ruler or governor acts on the advice of an executive council appointed on the advice of the chief minister and a single-chamber legislative assembly. The legislative assemblies are elected on the same basis as the lower chamber of the federal legislature.

HEAD OF STATE

Supreme Head of State, HM Sultan Mizan Zainal Abidin ibni al-Marhum Sultan Mahmud, *sworn in* 13 December 2006
Deputy Head of State, Abdul Halim Mu'adzam Shah

SELECTED GOVERNMENT MEMBERS *as at July 2011*
Prime Minister, Finance, Najib Tun Abdul Razak
Deputy Prime Minister, Muhyiddin bin Mohamed Yasin
Foreign Affairs, Anifah Aman
Home Affairs, Hishammuddin Tun Hussein
Defence, Ahmad Zahid Hamidi

MALAYSIAN HIGH COMMISSION
45 Belgrave Square, London SW1X 8QT
T 020-7919 0263 E jimlondon@btconnect.com
W www.jimlondon.net
High Commissioner, HE Datuk Zakaria Sulong, *apptd* 2010

BRITISH HIGH COMMISSION
PO Box 11030, 185 Jalan Ampang, 50450 Kuala Lumpur
T (+60) (3) 2170 2200 W http://ukinmalaysia.fco.gov.uk
High Commissioner, HE Simon Featherstone, *apptd* 2010

BRITISH COUNCIL
Ground Floor, West Block, Wisma Selangor Dredging,
142 C Jalan Ampang, 50450 Kuala Lumpur
T (+60) (3) 2723 7900 W www.britishcouncil.org/malaysia
Director, Mandy Johnson

DEFENCE

The army has 48 main battle tanks, 44 armoured infantry fighting vehicles and 731 armoured personnel carriers. The navy has 2 submarines, 8 frigates, 37 patrol and coastal combat vessels and 6 armed helicopters at 7 bases. The air force has 82 combat aircraft and 17 multi-role helicopters.

Military budget – US$2,810m (2010)
Military personnel – 109,000: army 80,000, navy 14,000, air force 15,000; paramilitary 24,600

ECONOMY AND TRADE

The economy has grown vigorously since the 1970s, transforming the country into a diversified emerging economy. The government's goal is to achieve developed nation status by 2020. To this end, it has encouraged investment in high technology industries, medical technology and pharmaceuticals, and growth as a regional financial hub, especially for Islamic finance. Growth has largely been driven by export-orientated manufacturing, dependence on which the government aims to reduce.

The agricultural sector produces the raw materials for its highly developed industries. Industrial production includes rubber manufacturing, palm oil processing, pharmaceuticals, medical technology, electronics, tin mining and smelting, and logging and timber processing; in addition, oil is produced in Sabah and Sarawak, and refined in Sarawak. Tourism is a major industry. The services sector contributes 49.3 per cent of GDP, industry 41.6 per cent and agriculture 9.1 per cent.

The main trading partners are China, Singapore, the USA, Japan and other south-east Asian countries. Principal exports are electronic equipment, petroleum and liquefied natural gas, timber and wood products, palm oil, rubber, textiles and chemicals. The main imports are electronics, machinery, petroleum products, plastics, vehicles, iron and steel products, and chemicals.

GNI – US$188,934m; US$7,350 per capita (2009)
Annual average growth of GDP – 7.1 per cent (2010 est)
Inflation rate – 1.8 per cent (2010 est)
Unemployment – 3.5 per cent (2010 est)
Total external debt – US$62,820m (2010 est)
Imports – US$123,700m (2009)
Exports – US$157,500m (2009)

BALANCE OF PAYMENTS
Trade – US$32,378m surplus (2010)
Current Account – US$38,854m surplus (2008)

Trade with UK	2009	2010
Imports from UK	£1,039,740,854	£1,229,730,172
Exports to UK	£1,564,206,200	£1,875,724,207

COMMUNICATIONS

There are six main seaports in peninsular Malaysia, plus Kota Kinabalu (Sabah) and Kuching (Sarawak), and a merchant fleet of 321 ships of more than 1,000 tonnes. The Strait of Malacca and the South China Sea are busy shipping lanes with high risks of piracy and armed robbery. There are 98,721km of roads, 7,200km of navigable waterways and, in peninsular Malaysia, 1,849km of railways. The main international airports are at Kuala Lumpur, Kota Kinabalu, Kuching and Penang, with over 115 smaller airports and airfields around the country.

In 2009, there were 4.3 million fixed telephone lines in use, 30.4 million mobile phone subscribers and 15.3 million internet users.

EDUCATION AND HEALTH

There are six years of compulsory education.
Literacy rate – 92.2 per cent (2008 est)
Gross enrolment ratio (percentage of relevant age group) – primary 95 per cent; secondary 69 per cent; tertiary 36 per cent (2008 est)
Health expenditure (per capita) – US$336 (2009)
Hospital beds (per 1,000 people) – 1.8 (2004–9)

MEDIA

The government operates extremely strict censorship of all media outlets; content may be censored on security, political or moral grounds. Newspapers must annually renew their licences, which can be suspended or revoked by the home affairs minister. Controversial political websites and blogs risk government harassment and prosecution, although plans to install a national filter were abandoned.

The four main national daily newspapers are in English: *The Star, Business Times, New Straits Times* and *The Malay Mail.* The state-run Radio Television Malaysia provides services in competition with commercial operators, which broadcast in Malay, Tamil, Chinese and English.

MALDIVES

Dhivehi Raajjeyge Jumhooriyyaa – Republic of Maldives

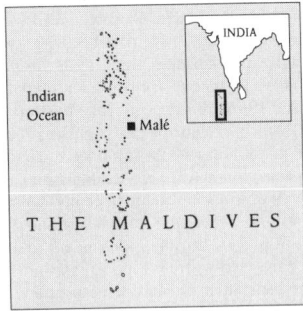

Area – 298 sq. km
Capital – Malé; population, 120,215 (2009 est)
Currency – Rufiyaa of 100 laarees
Population – 395,650 falling at 0.18 per cent a year (2010 est)
Religion – Sunni Muslim; public practice of other religions is illegal
Language – Dhivehi (official), English
Population density – 1,031 per sq. km (2009)

Urban population – 38 per cent (2008 est)
Median age (years) – 25.9 (2010 est)
National anthem – 'Gaumee Salaam' ['National Salute']
National day – 26 July (Independence Day)
Life expectancy (years) – 74.21 (2010 est)
Mortality rate – 3.68 (2010 est)
Birth rate – 14.5 (2010 est)
Infant mortality rate – 28.47 (2010 est)
Death penalty – Retained (no known use since 1952)
CPI Score – 2.3 (2010)
Literacy rate – 97.1 per cent (2008 est)

CLIMATE AND TERRAIN

The republic is an archipelago of atolls in the Indian Ocean, 643km to the south-west of Sri Lanka. There are about 1,190 coral islands grouped into 26 clusters of atolls, about 200 of which are inhabited. The islands are all flat and low-lying; none is more than 2.4m above sea level, making them vulnerable to rising sea levels caused by climate change. The climate is tropical, affected by the dry north-east monsoon (January–March) and the wet south-west monsoon (May–November).

HISTORY AND POLITICS

The Maldives were an independent sultanate from the mid-12th century. The sultan was overthrown by the Portuguese in 1558 but they were driven out in 1573 and the sultanate was re-established. In 1645, the islands became a dependency of Ceylon, which was under Dutch and then British rule. In 1887 they became an internally self-governing British protectorate. Independence was achieved in 1965, and in 1968 the Maldives became a republic under President Ibrahim Nasir.

The autocratic Nasir retired in 1978 and was succeeded by Maumoon Abdul Gayoom. His 30-year tenure, although equally autocratic, maintained political stability and allowed economic development. However, unprecedented violence during anti-government demonstrations in 2003 and 2004 led to the legalising of political parties in 2005 and the introduction of a new constitution in 2008. The 2004 Indian Ocean tsunami devastated the islands, destroying many homes and tourist resorts.

The first multi-party presidential election in 2008 was won in the second round by Mohamed Nasheed, the candidate of the Maldivian Democratic Party (MDP). In the first multi-party legislative elections in 2009, the People's Party, led by former president Maumoon Abdul Gayoom, won only two more seats than the MDP but through alliances with smaller parties secured control of the legislature. The president appointed a coalition government dominated by the MDP.

POLITICAL SYSTEM

Under the 2008 constitution, the executive president is directly elected for a five-year term, renewable once. The unicameral People's Assembly *(Majlis)* has 77 members, who are directly elected for a five-year term.

HEAD OF STATE
President, Mohamed Nasheed, *elected* 29 October 2008, *sworn in* 11 November 2008
Vice-President, Mohamed Waheed Hassan Manik

SELECTED GOVERNMENT MEMBERS *as at July 2011*
Defence, Thalhath Ibrahim Kaleyfaanu
Foreign Affairs, Ahmed Naseem
Finance, Ahmed Inaz
Home Affairs, Hassan Afeef

HIGH COMMISSION OF THE REPUBLIC OF MALDIVES
22 Nottingham Place, London W1U 5NJ
T 020-7224 2135 E info@maldiveshighcommission.org
W www.maldiveshighcommission.org
High Commissioner, HE Dr Farahanaz Faizal, *apptd* 2009

BRITISH HIGH COMMISSIONER
HE John Rankin, *apptd* 2011, resident at Colombo, Sri Lanka

ECONOMY AND TRADE

Political stability and economic liberalisation have produced steady economic growth since the 1980s, except in 2005 owing to the devastation caused by the 2004 tsunami, and 2009, when tourist numbers and exports fell owing to the global economic downturn. Balance of payments difficulties forced the government to seek IMF standby funding in 2009. The economy is heavily dependent on tourism, which accounts for 28 per cent of GDP and 60 per cent of foreign exchange receipts. Import duties and tourism-related taxes provide over 90 per cent of government tax revenue. Fishing is the second largest activity, accounting for around 6 per cent of GDP. Agriculture and manufacturing are constrained by a shortage of cultivatable land and domestic labour, and so most food is imported. Industry is concentrated on clothing manufacture, fish processing, boat-building and handicrafts, contributing 16.9 per cent to GDP.

The main export markets are Thailand, EU countries and Sri Lanka. The only significant export is fish. Imports include petroleum products, ships, food and clothing, and are provided mainly by Singapore, the UAE, India and Malaysia.

GNI – US$1,412m; US$3,970 per capita (2009)
Annual average growth of GDP – 3.4 per cent (2010 est)
Inflation rate – 7.3 per cent (2009 est)
Population below poverty line – 16 per cent (2008)
Unemployment – 14.4 per cent (2006 est)
Total external debt – US$589m (2009 est)
Imports – US$1,000m (2009)
Exports – US$100m (2009)

BALANCE OF PAYMENTS
Trade – US$1,011m deficit (2010)
Current Account – US$648m deficit (2008)

Trade with UK	2009	2010
Imports from UK	£6,311,596	£6,431,774
Exports to UK	£10,550,276	£9,150,170

COMMUNICATIONS

None of the islands is more than 13 sq. km in area. The larger islands have some roads. Transport between islands is by water or air; the country has five airports, two of which now handle international traffic following the upgrade of Gan airport. The main port is Malé. Telephone services are available on all the inhabited islands and mobile phone distribution has expanded rapidly, reaching a density of over 100 per 100 people.

MEDIA

The government operates Television Maldives and Voice of Maldives, the main television and radio stations. Private stations are few because of the prohibitive cost of licences. Two of the three daily newspapers include English-language sections. Government officials retain the power to close media outlets, and journalists largely practise self-censorship. President Nasheed pledged in 2009 to liberalise media laws to establish greater press freedom and competition.

MALI

République de Mali – Republic of Mali

Area – 1,240,192 sq. km
Capital – Bamako; population, 1,627,580 (2009 est)
Major cities – Kayes, Mopti, Ségou, Sikasso
Currency – Franc CFA of 100 centimes
Population – 13,796,354 rising at 2.61 per cent a year
   (2010 est); Mandé (50 per cent), Fulani (17 per cent),
   Voltaic (12 per cent), Songhai (6 per cent), Tuareg
   and Moor (10 per cent) (est); about 10 per cent are
   nomadic
Religion – Muslim 90 per cent (predominantly Sunni),
   indigenous beliefs 9 per cent, Christian 1 per cent
   (predominantly Roman Catholic) (est)
Language – French (official), Bambara, other African
   languages
Population density – 11 per sq. km (2009)
Urban population – 32 per cent (2008 est)
Median age (years) – 16.2 (2010 est)
National anthem – 'Pour l'Afrique et Pour Toi, Mali'
   ['For Africa and For You, Mali']
National day – 22 September (Independence Day)
Life expectancy – 52.17 (2010 est)
Mortality rate – 14.64 (2010 est)
Birth rate – 46.09 (2010 est)
Infant mortality rate – 113.66 (2010 est)
HIV / AIDS adult prevalence – 1 per cent (2009 est)
Death penalty – Retained (not used since 1980)
CPI score – 2.7 (2010)

CLIMATE AND TERRAIN
The landlocked state in west Africa is mainly savannah in
the south and desert plains in the north, with some hills in
the north-east; over 60 per cent is desert or semi-desert.
The centre is drained by the Niger river and the
south-west by the Senegal river. Elevation extremes range
from 1,155m (Hombori Tondo) at the highest point to
23m (Senegal river) at the lowest. The climate is
subtropical in the south with a rainy season from June
to November, and arid in the north. Average temperatures
in Bamako range from 24°C in January and December to
32°C in April and May.

HISTORY AND POLITICS
Mali was successively part of the empire of the Malinke
people from the 13th to 15th centuries, and of the
Songhai Empire in the 15th to 16th centuries. With the
fall of the Songhai Empire, it was divided between the
Tuareg and the Fulani and Bambara kingdoms, and then
the Tukolor and Samori kingdoms. It was conquered by
the French in 1880–95 and became a French colony.

In 1959, it formed the Federation of Mali with Senegal
before becoming a separate independent state in 1960
under a one-party socialist regime.

In 1968, a military coup led by Lt. Moussa Traoré
resulted in 23 years of oppressive military rule. Traoré was
ousted as president in 1991 in a military coup led by Gen.
Amadou Toumani Touré. Multiparty elections were held
in 1992, returning the country to civilian government.

A degree of decentralisation was introduced in 1999,
partly in response to rebellions in the north by the over
land and cultural rights. Another rebellion in 2006 by
Tuareg seeking greater autonomy for their region was
settled within a few months, but a more militant faction
carried on an insurrection from 2007 to 2009, when the
rebels disarmed and returned to negotiations.

Amadou Toumani Touré, standing as an independent
candidate, won the 2002 presidential elections, and was
re-elected in 2007 in the first round of voting. In the
2007 legislative elections, the Alliance for Democracy in
Mali (ADEMA), which had dominated government
coalitions since 1992, won the largest number of seats,
and the three-party Alliance for Democracy and Progress
coalition (of which ADEMA is a part) retained its overall
majority. Modibo Sidibé resigned as prime minister in
March 2011 and was replaced by Cissé Mariam Kaidama
Sidibé, Mali's first female prime minister.

POLITICAL SYSTEM
Under the 1992 constitution, the president is directly
elected for a five-year term, which is renewable once. The
unicameral National Assembly has 160 members, 147
directly elected for a maximum of two terms and 13 to
represent Malians abroad; all serve a five-year term.
The president appoints the prime minister, who appoints
the cabinet.

HEAD OF STATE
President, Amadou Toumani Touré, *elected* 12 May 2002,
   took office 8 June 2002, *re-elected* 2007

SELECTED GOVERNMENT MEMBERS *as at July 2011*
Prime Minister, Cissé Mariam Kaidama Sidibé
Defence, Natié Pleah
Economy and Finance, Lassine Bouaré
Foreign Affairs, Soumeylou Boubèye Maïga

EMBASSY OF THE REPUBLIC OF MALI
Avenue Molière 487, 1050 Brussels, Belgium
T (+32) (2) 345 7432 E info@amba-mali.be
W www.amba-mali.be
Ambassador Extraordinary and Plenipotentiary, HE Ibrahim
   Bocar Ba, *apptd* 2003

BRITISH AMBASSADOR
British Embassy Liaison Office, Enceinte de l'Ambassade du
Canada, Route de Koulikoro, Hippodrome, BP 2069, Bamako
T (+223) 2021 3412
HE Nicholas Griffiths, *apptd* 2010

DEFENCE
The army has 33 main battle tanks and 84 armoured
personnel carriers. The navy has 3 patrol and coastal
combatant vessels at 4 bases. The air force has 14 combat-
capable aircraft and 6 armed helicopters.
Military budget – US$208m (2010)
Military personnel – 7,350: army 7,350; paramilitary
   4,800; militia 3,000

ECONOMY AND TRADE

Mali is one of the world's poorest countries, with over 30 per cent of the population living below the poverty line. Economic reform since the mid-1990s has produced steady growth, but Mali is heavily dependent on foreign aid and remittances from expatriates. A huge foreign debt has been reduced to a more manageable size by debt cancellation and rescheduling.

The economy is based primarily on subsistence farming and animal husbandry, which contribute 45 per cent of GDP and occupy 80 per cent of the population. Gold, phosphate and iron-ore mining, and cotton and food processing are the main activities in Mali's industrial sector, which accounts for 17 per cent of GDP. Export of hydroelectric power is expected to contribute to future earnings.

The main export markets are China and Thailand; imports come mainly from Senegal, France and Côte d'Ivoire. Principal exports are cotton, gold and livestock. The main imports are fuel, machinery and equipment, construction materials, foodstuffs and textiles.

GNI – US$8,996m; US$680 per capita (2009)
Annual average growth of GDP – 5.2 per cent (2010 est)
Inflation rate – 2.5 per cent (2007 est)
Population below poverty line – 36.1 per cent (2005 est)
Unemployment – 30 per cent (2004 est)
Total external debt – US$2,800m (2002)
Imports – US$2,600m (2009)
Exports – US$2,100m (2009)

BALANCE OF PAYMENTS
Trade – US$533m deficit (2010)
Current Account – US$695m deficit (2008)

Trade with UK	2009	2010
Imports from UK	£6,260,260	£6,442,897
Exports to UK	£426,312	£509,098

COMMUNICATIONS

Mali has 18,709km of roads, 593km of railway line and 1,800km of waterways. The road network is being extended to connect Mali with all adjacent countries, and its railway is linked to Senegal. Bamako is the centre of the transport network and the main shipping point for freight, with links to ports in Côte d'Ivoire (where civil war has disrupted trade routes), Guinea and Senegal. The main port is Koulikoro on the river Niger, and the principal airport is at Bamako.

The telephone system is limited in extent and services are unreliable, though improving. In 2008, fixed-line density was less than one per 100 people, while mobile phone density was nearly 30 per 100 people.

EDUCATION AND HEALTH

There are nine years of free, compulsory education beginning at age seven.

Literacy rate – 26.2 per cent (2008 est)
Gross enrolment ratio (percentage of relevant age group) – primary 95 per cent; secondary 38 per cent; tertiary 6 per cent (2009 est)
Health expenditure (per capita) – US$38 (2009)
Hospital beds (per 1,000 people) – 0.6 (2004–9)

MEDIA AND CULTURE

The media is among the freest in Africa. Slander laws that might restrict comment on public officials are rarely invoked. The print media consists of around 40 privately owned newspapers, and there are about 50 private television and radio stations. The state operates its own daily newspaper and a radio and television broadcast network.

The music of Mali has become increasingly popular internationally in the last decade, and has absorbed some Western influences. Important names include guitarist Ali Farka Toure (1939–2006), kora player Toumani Diabaté (b. 1965), duo Amadou and Mariam, and Tuareg group Tinariwen.

MALTA

Repubblika ta' Malta – Republic of Malta

Area – 316 sq. km
Capital – Valletta; population, 199,283 (2009 est)
Major towns – Birkirkara, Mosta, Qormi, Saint Paul's Bay (San Pawl il-Bahar)
Currency – Euro (€) of 100 cents
Population – 406,771 rising at 0.39 per cent a year (2010 est)
Religion – Christian (Roman Catholic 95 per cent), Muslim 2 per cent (est)
Language – Maltese, English (both official)
Population density – 1,297 per sq. km (2009)
Urban population – 94 per cent (2008 est)
Median age (years) – 39.7 (2010 est)
National anthem – 'L-Innu Malti' ['Hymn of Malta']
National day – 21 September (Independence Day)
Life expectancy (years) – 79.59 (2010 est)
Mortality rate – 8.49 (2010 est)
Birth rate – 10.38 (2010 est)
Infant mortality rate – 3.72 (2010 est)
Death penalty – Abolished for all crimes (since 2000)
CPI score – 5.6 (2010)

CLIMATE AND TERRAIN

Malta is an archipelago of six islands in the Mediterranean Sea; Malta, Gozo and Comino are the largest. The island of Malta has a coastal plain in the north-east, rising to low hills in the south-west. Elevation extremes range from 253m (Ta'Dmejrek) at the highest point to 0m (Mediterranean Sea) at the lowest. Average temperatures in Valetta range from 12°C in January to 27°C in August.

HISTORY AND POLITICS

The islands were ruled successively by the Phoenicians, Greeks, Carthaginians, Romans, Arabs, Spanish and the Sovereign Military Order of Malta (known as the Knights of St John), which held them from 1530 until a French invasion in 1798. Liberated from French rule with British naval support in 1800, the island of Malta became a British colony in 1814, and was developed into a substantial naval base and dockyard. Malta was strategically important in both world wars, but particularly the second, when it was blockaded and subjected to aerial bombardment for five months. Its resistance led to the people of Malta being awarded the George Cross, the UK's highest award for civilian bravery, in 1942.

Malta gained its independence in 1964 and became a republic in 1974. In the 1970s it developed close links with communist and Arab states, but more pro-European and pro-US policies were adopted after the election of the Nationalist Party in 1987. Malta became a member of the EU in 2004, and adopted the euro in 2008. Since joining the EU, Malta has experienced a marked increase in illegal immigration from northern Africa.

The Nationalist Party was returned to power in the 2008 legislative election with a modest overall majority. George Abela, the only nominee, was elected president in 2009.

POLITICAL SYSTEM

Under the 1974 constitution, the president is elected by the legislature for a five-year term, renewable once. The unicameral legislature, the House of Representatives, has 69 members directly elected for a five-year term; if a party wins the majority of votes in a general election without winning a majority of seats, new seats are created until that party holds a majority of one seat. The prime minister is appointed by the president and nominates the other ministers.

HEAD OF STATE
President, George Abela, *elected* 12 January 2009, *took office* 4 April 2009

SELECTED GOVERNMENT MEMBERS *as at July 2011*
Prime Minister, Defence, Lawrence Gonzi
Deputy Prime Minister, Foreign Affairs, Tonio Borg
Home Affairs, Carmelo Mifsud Bonnici
Finance and Economy, Tonio Fenech

MALTA HIGH COMMISSION
Malta House, 36–38 Piccadilly, London W1J 0LE
T 020-7292 4800 E maltahighcommission.london@gov.mt
W www.foreign.gov.mt
High Commissioner, HE Joseph Zammit Tabona, *apptd* 2009

BRITISH HIGH COMMISSION
Whitehall Mansions, Ta' Xbiex Seafront, Ta' Xbiex XBX 1026
T (+356) 2323 0000 W http://ukinmalta.fco.gov.uk
High Commissioner, HE Louise Stanton, *apptd* 2009

BRITISH COUNCIL
Exchange Buildings, Republic Street, Valletta VLT 1117
T (+356) 2122 6377 W www.britishcouncil.org/malta
Country Manager (acting), Ingrid Eomois

DEFENCE

The Maritime Squadron has 8 patrol and coastal combatant vessels.
Military budget – US$57m (2010)
Military personnel – armed forces 1,954

ECONOMY AND TRADE

The mainstay of the economy for over a century was the dockyard, and shipbuilding and ship repairs remain

significant industries, but since the 1980s Malta has developed into a tourist destination, financial services centre and freight trans-shipment point. Tourism is now the main source of income, followed by foreign trade and manufacturing, especially of electronics and pharmaceuticals. All were adversely affected by the global downturn in 2009, but the economy began to recover in 2010. The service sector accounts for 80.9 per cent of GDP, industry for 17.2 per cent and agriculture for 1.9 per cent; Malta produces only about 20 per cent of its food requirements.

The main trading partners are other EU states, Singapore, Hong Kong and China. Principal exports are electrical machinery, mechanical appliances, fish and shellfish, and printed material. The main imports are mineral fuels and oil, machinery, aircraft and other transport equipment, semi-manufactured goods, food, beverages and tobacco.

GNI – US$7,459m; US$18,360 per capita (2009)
Annual average growth of GDP – 2 per cent (2010 est)
Inflation rate – 1.7 per cent (2010 est)
Unemployment – 7 per cent (2009)
Total external debt – US$41,020m (2010 est)
Imports – US$3,800m (2009)
Exports – US$2,200m (2009)

BALANCE OF PAYMENTS
Trade – US$1,691m deficit (2010)
Current Account – US$453m deficit (2008)

Trade with UK	2009	2010
Imports from UK	£377,432,592	£384,141,058
Exports to UK	£104,440,464	£158,447,044

COMMUNICATIONS

The main ports are Marsaxlokk (Malta's freeport) and Valletta; there is a large merchant fleet of 1,571 ships of over 1,000 tonnes. Ferry services run to the islands. There are 2,227km of roads, but no railways. The only airport is outside Valletta.

In 2009, there were 252,700 fixed lines in use, 422,100 mobile phone subscribers and 240,600 internet users.

EDUCATION

Education is free at all levels and compulsory between the ages of five and 16.
Literacy rate – 92.4 per cent (2008 est)
Gross enrolment ratio (percentage of relevant age group) – primary 99 per cent; secondary 100 per cent; tertiary 32 per cent (2008 est)

MEDIA

Radio broadcasting began in the 1930s, partly to counter fascist broadcasts from Italy. There are public-service radio and television broadcasters, as well as a thriving private sector; Italian television channels are popular, as are cable and satellite services. The main private broadcasters, like the major newspapers, tend to be owned by or have strong affiliations with political parties; the Roman Catholic Church operates a radio station and a weekly newspaper, albeit with a limited circulation. Most newspapers are published in Maltese or English.

MARSHALL ISLANDS

Republic of the Marshall Islands

Area – 181 sq. km (plus 11,673 sq. km of lagoon waters)
Capital – Majuro; population, 29,601 (2009 est)
Major towns – Ebeye, Rita
Currency – US dollar (US$) of 100 cents
Population – 65,859 rising at 2.02 per cent a year
  (2010 est); mainly Micronesian. About 70 per cent
  of the population lives on Majuro and Kwajalein
Religion – Christian (Protestant 83 per cent, Roman
  Catholic 8 per cent, Mormon 8 per cent, Seventh-day
  Adventist 1 per cent), Baha'i 1 per cent
Language – Marshallese, English (both official)
Population density – 339 per sq. km (2009)
Urban population – 71 per cent (2008 est)
Median age (years) – 21.5 (2010 est)
National anthem – 'Forever Marshall Islands'
National day – 1 May (Constitution Day)
Life expectancy (years) – 71.48 (2010 est)
Mortality rate – 4.42 (2010 est)
Birth rate – 29.94 (2010 est)
Infant mortality rate – 24.57 (2010 est)
Death penalty – Abolished for all crimes (since 1986)

CLIMATE AND TERRAIN

The republic consists of two chains of 29 atolls, five islands and over 1,000 islets in the western Pacific Ocean. All of the islands are low-lying (the highest point is 10m) and vulnerable to rising sea levels, which could submerge them by the mid-21st century. The climate is tropical, with a wet season from June to November.

HISTORY AND POLITICS

The Marshall Islands were first claimed by Spain in 1592 but were left largely undisturbed. Subsequently they were seized by Germany and formally became a protectorate in 1886. Japan took control of the islands in 1914 on behalf of the Allied powers and administered them from 1920 until 1944, when they were captured by US forces. In 1947 the islands became part of the UN Trust Territory of the Pacific Islands, administered by the USA. Between 1946 and 1958, US nuclear weapons were tested on Bikini and Enewetak atolls. Enewetak has been partially decontaminated but Bikini is uninhabitable; the USA paid compensation to the test victims in the 1980s but the government is seeking further compensation to cover the medical care of radiation victims and rectify environmental damage.

The islands became internally self-governing in 1979, and US administration ended in 1986, when a compact of free association between the Republic of the Marshall Islands and the USA came into effect. Under this agreement, the USA recognised the republic as a sovereign and independent state but retained responsibility for external security and defence as well as giving financial help. UN trust territory status was terminated in 1990 and full independence was granted in December 1990. A renegotiated compact with the USA was signed in 2003. The USA retains control of the Kwajalein atoll, where it has a military base and missile tracking station.

In the 2007 legislative election, the Our Islands (AKA) grouping won the largest number of seats. Litokwa Tomeing was elected president in 2008 but lost a vote of confidence in 2009. Jurelang Zedkaia was elected to succeed him. Legislative elections are due in late 2011.

POLITICAL SYSTEM

Under the 1979 constitution, the executive president is elected by the legislature from among its members to serve a four-year term. The unicameral legislature, the *Nitijela*, has 33 members, directly elected for a four-year term. There are no formal political parties, although groupings of like-minded independents have emerged in recent years. There is also a 12-member Council of Chiefs *(Iroij)* which has a consultative and advisory role.

HEAD OF STATE
President, Jurelang Zedkaia, *elected* 26 October 2009, *sworn in* 1 November 2009

SELECTED GOVERNMENT MEMBERS *as at July 2011*
Finance, Jack Ading
Foreign Affairs, John Silk
Internal Affairs, Norman Matthew

BRITISH AMBASSADOR
HE Stephen Lillie, *apptd* 2009, resident at Manila, the Philippines

ECONOMY AND TRADE

The islands have few natural resources, apart from possible seabed mineral deposits, and the economy is dependent on aid from the USA, supplemented by ship registration fees and the sale of fishing licences. Most islanders live by subsistence farming and fishing, with coconuts, breadfruit and fish the main commercial crops. A small-scale industrial sector produces copra and handicrafts and processes tuna. Tourism is being encouraged but has declined recently which, with a similar decline in fishing licence sales, has limited economic growth. The government is the largest employer. The main trading partners are Japan, the USA, New Zealand, Australia, China and Taiwan. Principal exports are copra and coconut products, handicrafts and fish. Main imports include food and fuel.

GNI – US$183m; US$3,060 per capita (2009)
Annual average growth of GDP – –0.3 per cent (2008 est)
Inflation rate – 12.9 per cent (2008 est)
Unemployment – 36 per cent (2006 est)
Total external debt – $87m (2008 est)

Trade with UK	2009	2010
Imports from UK	£25,899,697	£176,642
Exports to UK	£288,594	£617,890

COMMUNICATIONS

Air transport provides the main means of internal travel, and there are 15 airports and airfields throughout the islands, with internal and international flights operated by Air Marshall Islands and Continental Airlines. Majuro is the main airport as well as the main port, with a merchant fleet of 1,381 ships of over 1,000 tonnes, 1,284 of which are foreign-owned. There are 2,028km of surfaced roads. There is a modern telephone network on the major islands and atolls. Mobile phone distribution is less than a quarter of fixed-line density. Access to the internet is expensive and speeds are slow; around 3 per cent of the population are regular users.

MEDIA

There are state-owned and private broadcasters, with some areas also able to receive US forces' radio and television broadcasts; cable services carry US channels. A government-owned monthly gazette publishes official information, but leaves political coverage to the privately owned weekly newspaper *Marshall Islands Journal*, published in English and Marshallese.

MAURITANIA

Al-Jumhuriyah al-Islamiyah al-Muritaniyah – Islamic Republic of Mauritania

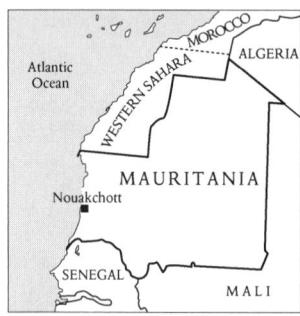

Area – 1,030,700 sq. km
Capital – Nouakchott; population, 708,789 (2009 est)
Major towns – Atar, Kaedi, Kiffa, Nouadhibou, Rosso
Currency – Ouguiya (UM) of 5 khoums
Population – 3,205,060 rising at 2.37 per cent a year (2010 est)
Religion – Muslim 99 per cent (almost entirely Sunni) (est)
Language – Arabic (official), Pulaar, Soninke, Wolof, French
Population density – 3 per sq. km (2009)
Urban population – 41 per cent (2008 est)
Median age (years) – 19.3 (2010 est)
National anthem – 'National Anthem of Mauritania'
National day – 28 November (Independence Day)
Life expectancy (years) – 60.75 (2010 est)
Mortality rate – 9 (2010 est)
Birth rate – 33.67 (2010 est)
Infant mortality rate – 61.94 (2010 est)
Death penalty – Retained (not used since 1987)
CPI score – 2.3 (2010)
Literacy rate – 56.4 per cent (2008 est)
Gross enrolment ratio (percentage of relevant age group) – primary 102 per cent; secondary 25 per cent; tertiary 4 per cent (2007 est)
Health expenditure (per capita) – US$22 (2009)
Hospital beds (per 1,000 people) – 0.4 (2004–9)

CLIMATE AND TERRAIN
About 60 per cent of the country is covered by the plains of the Sahara Desert, with some hills in the centre. The terrain is arid, apart from in the Senegal river valley on the southern border; most of the population lives there or on the coast at Nouakchott and Nouadhibou. Elevation extremes range from Kediet Ijill (915m) to −5m (Sebkhet Te-n-Dghamcha). There is a desert climate; the north of the country is virtually rainless, while the south receives some unreliable rainfall between June and October. Humidity can be high in the wet season, especially on the coast. Average temperatures in Nouakchott range from 21°C in January to 29°C in September.

HISTORY AND POLITICS
Eastern Mauritania was part of the Ghana Empire and then the Muslim Almoravid and Almohad empires from the 11th to the 13th century. The area became part of the

French West Africa protectorate in 1903 and then a colony in 1920. The country became independent as the Islamic Republic of Mauritania on 28 November 1960.

Mauritania has experienced several military coups and periods of military rule since independence. The 1984 coup brought to power Col. Maaouya ould Sid Ahmed Taya, who restored civilian rule in 1992 with multi-party elections in which he was elected president. President Taya was deposed in a military coup in 2005 and after a period of transitional government, elections were held in late 2006 and early 2007.

The 2007 presidential election was won by Sidi ould Cheikh Abdallahi. In 2008 President Abdallahi was overthrown in a military coup after attempting to sack four military leaders. Democracy was restored with the 2009 presidential election; this was won by General Mohamed ould Abdelaziz, who had led the 2008 coup, with 52 per cent of the vote. A legislative election is scheduled for October 2011.

POLITICAL SYSTEM
The 1991 constitution was amended in 2007 to reduce the term of the president, who is directly elected, to five years, renewable once. The bicameral legislature comprises the National Assembly (the lower house) and the senate. The National Assembly has 95 members who are directly elected for a five-year term. The senate has 56 members (including three representing Mauritanians abroad), who are indirectly elected for a six-year term; one-third is elected every two years.

HEAD OF STATE
President, Gen. Mohamed ould Abdelaziz, *elected* 18 July 2009, *sworn in* 5 August 2009

SELECTED GOVERNMENT MEMBERS *as at July 2011*
Prime Minister, Moulaye ould Mohamed Laghdhaf
Finance, Amedi Camara
Foreign Affairs, Hamadi ould Baba ould Hamadi
Interior, Mohamed ould Boilil
Defence, Ahmedou ould Idey ould Mohamed Radhi

EMBASSY OF THE ISLAMIC REPUBLIC OF MAURITANIA
5 rue de Montevideo, Paris 75116, France
T (+33) 4504 8354
Ambassador Extraordinary and Plenipotentiary, vacant

BRITISH AMBASSADOR
HE Timothy Morris, *apptd* 2008, resident at Rabat, Morocco

DEFENCE
The army has 35 main battle tanks and 25 armoured personnel carriers. The navy has 12 patrol and coastal combatant vessels at 2 bases.
Military expenditure – US$115m (2009)
Military personnel – 15,870: army 15,000, navy 620, air force 250; paramilitary 5,000
Conscription duration – 24 months

ECONOMY AND TRADE
Mauritania is one of the poorer countries in the region, with 40 per cent of the population living below the poverty line and unemployment at 30 per cent. Past economic mismanagement and droughts created a huge foreign debt, although the country has benefited from debt cancellation since 2000.

Natural resources include iron ore, copper, gold, gypsum, oil (off-shore production began in 2006) and rich fishing waters, although the latter are threatened by over-exploitation. Agriculture and animal husbandry, mainly at subsistence level, are the mainstay of the economy, accounting for 12.5 per cent of GDP and engaging 50 per cent of the population. The main industries are fish processing, oil production and refining, and mining.

The main trading partners are China, EU countries and Japan. Principal exports are iron ore (nearly 40 per cent), fish and fish products, gold, copper and oil. The main imports are machinery, petroleum products, capital goods, food and consumer goods.

GNI – US$3,041m; US$990 per capita (2009)
Annual average growth of GDP – 5 per cent (2010 est)
Inflation rate – 7.3 per cent (2007 est)
Population below poverty line – 40 per cent (2004 est)
Unemployment – 30 per cent (2008 est)

BALANCE OF PAYMENTS
Trade – US$173m deficit (2010)
Current Account – US$557m deficit (2008)

Trade with UK	2009	2010
Imports from UK	£10,149,138	£43,649,828
Exports to UK	£273,829	£154,320

COMMUNICATIONS
The main seaports are Nouakchott and Nouadhibou. The 728km of railway track runs from iron mines in the north to Nouadhibou. There are 11,066km of roads, ferry services on the Senegal river and 28 airports and airfields. The telephone system is limited but improvements are being made. Mobile phone distribution is growing rapidly, with a density of 70 per 100 people, compared to 2 per 100 people for fixed lines.

MEDIA
Television and radio services are state-owned, but a 2010 liberalisation law opened the broadcasting sector to private operators. Most newspapers are privately owned; there are commercial and state-run dailies in both French and Arabic. A law forbids content that undermines Islam or threatens national security.

MAURITIUS

Republic of Mauritius

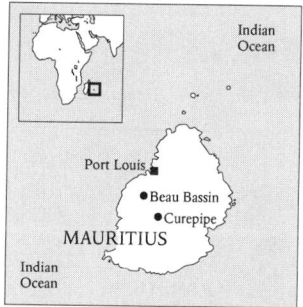

Area – 2,040 sq. km (includes Rodrigues and other islands)
Capital – Port Louis; population, 149,286 (2009 est)
Major towns – Beau Bassin-Rose Hill, Curepipe, Quatre Bornes, Vacoas-Phoenix

Currency – Mauritius rupee of 100 cents
Population – 1,294,104 rising at 0.75 per cent a year (2010 est); Indo-Mauritian (68 per cent), Creole (27 per cent), Sino-Mauritian (3 per cent), Franco-Mauritian (2 per cent) (est)
Religion – Hindu 48 per cent, Christian 33 per cent (of which Roman Catholic 73 per cent), Muslim 17 per cent (of which Sunni 90 per cent) (est)
Language – English (official), Creole, French, Bhojpuri
Population density – 628 per sq. km (2009)
Urban population – 42 per cent (2008 est)
Median age (years) – 32.3 (2010 est)
National anthem – 'Motherland'
National day – 12 March (Independence Day)
Life expectancy (years) – 74.25 (2010 est)
Mortality rate – 6.63 (2010 est)
Birth rate – 14.17 (2010 est)
Infant mortality rate – 11.85 (2010 est)
HIV/AIDS adult prevalence – 1 per cent (2009 est)
Death penalty – Abolished for all crimes (since 1995)
CPI score – 5.4 (2010)

CLIMATE AND TERRAIN
The republic is an island group in the Indian Ocean, approximately 885km east of Madagascar. The volcanic island of Mauritius rises from narrow coastal plains to a central plateau ringed by mountains. Elevation extremes range from 828m (Mt Piton) at the highest point to 0m (Indian Ocean) at the lowest. The island of Rodrigues, formerly a dependency but now part of Mauritius, is about 563km east of Mauritius, with an area of 108km; the population is 37,837 (2010). The islands of Agalega and St Brandon are dependencies of Mauritius; their total population is 289 (2010).

There is a tropical climate, modified by south-east trade winds, with little variation in temperature throughout the year. The cyclone season (December–April) brings rain but cyclones usually miss the islands.

HISTORY AND POLITICS
The islands were first visited in the tenth century, but were settled only after 1638 by the Dutch, who introduced sugar cane cultivation; the colonists withdrew in 1710. A decade later they were replaced by the French, who established plantations that were worked by African slaves. In 1814 Mauritius was ceded to the British, who had occupied it in 1810. The British abolished slavery in 1834 and imported indentured Indian and Chinese labourers to work on the plantations. Independence was achieved on 12 March 1968 and the state became a republic in 1992.

The Militant Socialist Movement (MSM) under Sir Aneerood Jugnauth held power from 1983 until 1995, and then returned to power in 2000 in coalition with the Mauritian Militant Movement (MMM). Jugnauth stood down as party leader and prime minister in 2003; he was elected president later that year and again in 2008. The MSM-MMM coalition lost the 2005 election to the opposition Socialist Alliance, which included the Mauritius Labour Party (MPT) led by Navinchandra Ramgoolam, who became prime minister. The MPT-led Alliance of the Future, now also including the MSM, won the 2010 legislative election.

POLITICAL SYSTEM
The 1968 constitution was amended in 1992 to introduce a republican form of government, and in 2001 to give the island of Rodrigues a degree of autonomy.

The president is elected by the legislature for a five-year term, renewable once. The unicameral National Assembly has 62 elected members (including two representing Rodrigues) and eight appointed members, all of whom serve a five-year term; the electoral commission allocates the appointed seats on a 'best loser' basis to give more equitable representation to ethnic minorities. The prime minister is the leader of the majority party in the legislature.

Rodrigues has had an 18-member regional assembly, a chief commissioner and a chief executive since 2002.

HEAD OF STATE
President, Sir Anerood Jugnauth, *took office* 7 October 2003, *re-elected* 2008
Vice-President, Monique Ohsan-Bellepeau

SELECTED GOVERNMENT MEMBERS *as at July 2011*
Prime Minister, Defence, Interior, Navinchandra Ramgoolam
Deputy Prime Minister, Ahmed Rashid Beebeejaun
Vice Prime Ministers, Pravind Kumar Jugnauth *(Finance and Economic Development)*; Charles Duval
Foreign Affairs, Arvin Boolell

MAURITIUS HIGH COMMISSION
32–33 Elvaston Place, London SW7 5NW
T 020-7581 0294 E londonmhc@btinternet.com
High Commissioner, HE Abhimanu Kundasamy, *apptd* 2005

BRITISH HIGH COMMISSION
PO Box 1063, Les Cascades Building, Edith Cavell Street, Port Louis
T (+230) 202 9400 E bhc@bow.intnet.mu
W http://ukinmauritius.fco.gov.uk
High Commissioner, HE Nick Leake, *apptd* 2010

BRITISH COUNCIL
PO Box 111, Royal Road, Rose Hill
T (+230) 403 0200 W www.britishcouncil.org/africa
Director, Dawn Long

DEFENCE
The army has 2 armoured infantry fighting vehicles and 16 armoured personnel carriers. The coast guard has 5 patrol and coastal combatant vessels.
Military budget – US$41m (2009)
Military personnel – none active; paramilitary 2,000

ECONOMY AND TRADE
Since independence Mauritius has developed from an economy dependent on agriculture to one with prospering tourist, manufacturing (primarily of textiles and garments) and financial sectors. Although sugar remains an important commodity (sugar cane is grown on 90 per cent of cultivated land and produces 15 per cent of export earnings), both the sugar and textile industries are beginning to decline. Diversification into fish processing, information and communications technology, hospitality and property development is being encouraged. The services sector accounts for 70.5 per cent of GDP, industry for 24.6 per cent and agriculture for 4.8 per cent.

The main trading partners are France, the UK and India. Principal exports are clothing, textiles, sugar, cut flowers, molasses and fish. The main imports are manufactured goods, capital equipment, food, fuels and chemicals.

GNI – US$8,874m; US$7,250 per capita (2009)
Annual average growth of GDP – 3.6 per cent (2010 est)
Inflation rate – 2.9 per cent (2010 est)
Population below poverty line – 8 per cent (2006 est)
Unemployment – 7.5 per cent (2010 est)
Total external debt – US$5,043m (2010 est)
Imports – US$3,700m (2009)
Exports – US$1,900m (2009)

BALANCE OF PAYMENTS
Trade – US$1,870m deficit (2010)
Current Account – US$971m deficit (2008)

Trade with UK	2009	2010
Imports from UK	£53,141,951	£58,809,581
Exports to UK	£320,955,141	£241,969,049

COMMUNICATIONS
Port Louis handles the bulk of the island's external trade. The international airport is located near Plaisance. The 2,066km of roads are all surfaced. There are no railways. The telephone system offers a good service; mobile phone distribution has risen rapidly, reaching a density of 85 per 100 people in 2009, compared to a steady 30 per 100 people for fixed telephone lines.

EDUCATION AND HEALTH
Twelve years of education are free and compulsory. Primary education lasts from ages five to ten, and secondary lasts seven years thereafter.
Literacy rate – 87.8 per cent (2008 est)
Gross enrolment ratio (percentage of relevant age group) – primary 99 per cent; secondary 88 per cent; tertiary 26 per cent (2008 est)
Health expenditure (per capita) – US$383 (2009)
Hospital beds (per 1,000 people) – 3.3 (2004–9)

MEDIA
Freedom of expression is guaranteed by the constitution and a number of daily newspapers and weekly publications offer a range of political viewpoints in several languages. The state-owned Mauritius Broadcasting Corporation runs television and radio services funded through advertising and a licence fee. Private radio stations were introduced in 2002 and satellite television is available, including international broadcasts.

MEXICO

Estados Unidos Mexicanos – United Mexican States

Area – 1,964,375 sq. km
Capital – Mexico City; population, 19,318,500
(2009 est)
Major cities – Ciudad Juárez, Guadalajara, León,
Monterrey, Puebla, Tijuana
Currency – Peso of 100 centavos
Population – 112,468,855 rising at 1.12 per cent a year
(2010 est)
Religion – Christian (Roman Catholic 88 per cent) (est)
Language – Spanish (official), 66 Mayan, Nahuatl and
other regional languages
Population density – 55 per sq. km (2009)
Urban population – 77 per cent (2008 est)
Median age (years) – 26.7 (2010 est)
National anthem – 'Himno Nacional Mexicano' ['Mexican
National Anthem']
National day – 16 September (Independence Day)
Life expectancy (years) – 76.26 (2010 est)
Mortality rate – 4.83 (2010 est)
Birth rate – 19.39 (2010 est)
Infant mortality rate – 17.84 (2010 est)
Death penalty – Abolished for all crimes (since 2005)
CPI score – 3.1 (2010)

CLIMATE AND TERRAIN

The Rio Grande river forms the eastern part of the border
with the USA. South of this, coastal plains rise to a central
plateau which lies between two spines of high mountains,
the Western and the Eastern Sierra Madre, running from
the north-west to south-east. The mountains include
volcanoes such as Popocatepetl, and in the south are
covered with dense jungle. The Yucatán peninsula in the
south-east is low-lying, and marshy on the coast. The
narrow Baja California peninsula, separated from the rest
of the country by the Gulf of California, has a range of
hills running along it. Elevation extremes range from
5,700m (Volcan Pico de Orizaba) to −10m (Laguna
Salada). The north has a desert climate, while the south is
tropical. The temperature in Mexico City can be as low as
5°C in January and up to 27°C in April.

HISTORY AND POLITICS

Mexico was the centre of Mesoamerican civilisations for
over 2,500 years: the Olmecs (*c.*1200–600 BC), based on
the Mexican Gulf Coast; the Zapotecs (*c.*300 BC to 300
AD) in the Oaxaca valley; the Mayas (*c.*300–900 AD) in
southern Mexico and the Yucatán peninsula; the Mixtecs
(*c.*800–1300) in the Oaxaca valley; and the Toltecs
(*c.*900–1170) in central Mexico and the Yucatán
peninsula. The Aztecs, who came to the region in the
13th century, ruled until their civilisation fell to the
Spanish under Hernán Cortés in 1519–21. In the first
century of Spanish occupation, the indigenous population
fell from around 21 million to one million, largely
through lack of resistance to European diseases. As the
viceroyalty of New Spain, Mexico remained under
Spanish rule until the 19th century.

After an unsuccessful revolt in 1810 and a protracted
struggle, independence was declared in 1821 and a
federal republic was instituted in 1824. Mexico suffered
extreme instability, civil war and invasion throughout
much of the 19th century. War with the USA in 1836 and
1846–8 led to the loss of about one-third of its territory.
There was civil war from 1858–61 and, in 1862–7, war
with Britain, France and Spain after Mexico suspended
interest payments on its foreign debt. Porfirio Díaz
ruled as a dictator between 1876 and 1911, until his
repressive regime was overthrown in a revolution that

introduced radical land and labour reforms, but instability
continued.

The National Revolutionary Party, founded in 1929,
came to dominate political life. Renamed the Institutional
Revolutionary Party (PRI) in 1946, it formed a succession
of authoritarian governments. Although unrest was not
eliminated under its regime, the 1960s saw rapid
industrialisation and the 1970s an oil-fuelled economic
boom. Falling oil prices led to a serious financial crisis in
1982 and Mexico defaulted on its debt. Economic
difficulties were eased in the 1990s with the introduction
of reforms and free trade agreements.

These reforms led to a degree of social upheaval.
Fearing for the status of the already marginalised
indigenous peoples, the Zapatista National Liberation
Front (EZLN) led revolts in the south of the country in
1994 and 1995. Although violence tailed off in the late
1990s, civil campaigning continued, culminating in a
mass march on Mexico City in 2001 in support of a bill of
indigenous rights. The bill was enacted later that year but
the Zapatistas claimed its provisions had been watered
down and vowed to continue their campaign.

The government faces problems with corruption and
violent crime, much of which is drug-related. Mexico is a
major producer of illegal drugs as well as the main staging
post for South American drugs trafficked into the USA.
Rivalry between drugs cartels, their resistance to the
government's drug-eradication and anti-trafficking
programmes, and the army's tactics in pursuit of these
programmes have led to a marked rise in violence since
2006, with intimidation and corruption used to suborn
law enforcement.

The PRI's political dominance ended at the 1997
election, when it lost its absolute majority in the lower
house of the legislature, although it continued in
government until 2000 and was again in power from
2003 until 2006. The 2006 presidential election was
won by Felipe Calderón of the Partido Accion Nacional
(PAN); Lopez Obrador, Calderón's closest rival, refused to
accept the result, alleging voting irregularities, and his
supporters staged mass protests for several months. In the
2006 legislative election, PAN became the largest party in
both houses of Congress, but lost its majority in the lower
chamber to the PRI in the 2009 legislative elections.

POLITICAL SYSTEM
Under the 1917 constitution, the federal republic consists
of 31 states and the federal capital. The head of state is an
executive president, directly elected for a single six-year
term. The bicameral legislature is the Congress of the
Union: the lower house, the Chamber of Deputies, has
500 members, directly elected for a three-year term, and
the senate has 128 members, directly elected for a six-year
term. The president appoints the cabinet.

Each of the states has its own constitution and is
administered by a governor, elected for a six-year term,
and a state chamber of deputies, elected for a three-year
term.

HEAD OF STATE
President, Felipe Calderón, *elected* 2 July 2006, *sworn in*
1 December 2006

SELECTED GOVERNMENT MEMBERS *as at July 2011*
Defence, Gen. Guillermo Galván Galván
Economy, Bruno Ferrari García de Alba
Foreign Affairs, Patricia Espinosa Cantellano
Interior, José Francisco Blake Mora

EMBASSY OF MEXICO
16 St George Street, London W1S 1FD
T 020-7499 8586 W http://portal.sre.gob.mx/reinounidoeng
Ambassador Extraordinary and Plenipotentiary, HE
    Eduardo Medina-Mora, *apptd* 2010

BRITISH EMBASSY
Río Lerma 71, Col. Cuauhtémoc, 06500 Mexico City
T (+52) (55) 5242 8500 E ukinmexico@fco.gov.uk
W http://ukinmexico.fco.gov.uk
Ambassador Extraordinary and Plenipotentiary, HE Judith
    Macgregor, LVO, *apptd* 2009

BRITISH COUNCIL
Lope de Vega 316, Col. Chapultepec Morales, 11570 Mexico
City
T (+52) (55) 5263 1900 W www.britishcouncil.org/mexico
Director, Christopher Rawlings

DEFENCE

The army has 709 armoured personnel carriers. The
navy has 7 frigates, 119 patrol and coastal vessels, and
7 combat aircraft. There are 18 naval bases. The air
force has 76 combat aircraft and 31 multi-role
helicopters.
Military budget – US$4,600m (2010)
Military personnel – 280,250: army 212,000, navy
    56,500, air force 11,750; paramilitary 51,500

ECONOMY AND TRADE

Mexico had a relatively closed economy until the
mid-1980s, but increased trade and domestic
liberalisation in the 1990s stimulated economic growth
and development, particularly in the industrial sector.
However, although it has free trade agreements with
over 50 countries, covering 90 per cent of its trade, its
economy is still closely tied to that of the USA and
experienced a deep recession in 2009 as the global
downturn affected its main export market. Despite recent
growth and its oil, natural gas and mineral resources,
Mexico remains a poor country; over 12 million Mexicans
work overseas, predominantly in the USA, and much of
the remaining population, especially in poor and rural
areas, is dependent on their remittances, which are a major
source of foreign exchange revenue. President Calderón
has prioritised job creation and poverty reduction
measures, which have had opposition support.

Agriculture is diverse and productive; major crops
include maize, wheat, soya beans, rice, beans, cotton,
coffee, fruit, tomatoes, beef, poultry and dairy products.
Agriculture accounts for 4.2 per cent of GDP and 13.7
per cent of employment. The main industries include
production of food, beverages, tobacco, chemicals, iron
and steel, textiles, clothing, motor vehicles, consumer
durables, oil production, mining and tourism. Tourism is
now the fourth-largest revenue earner. The services sector
accounts for 62.5 per cent of GDP and industry for
33.3 per cent.

The main trading partner is the USA (80.5 per cent of
exports; 48 per cent of imports). Canada is the other main
export market, and China the other main source of
imports. Principal exports include manufactured goods,
oil and oil products, silver, fruit, vegetables, coffee and
cotton. The main imports include metal-working
machines, steel mill products, agricultural machinery,
electrical equipment, car parts for assembly, vehicle repair
parts, aircraft and aircraft parts.

GNI – US$860,248m; US$8,960 per capita (2009)
Annual average growth of GDP – 5 per cent (2010 est)
Inflation rate – 4.1 per cent (2010 est)
Population below poverty line – 18.2 per cent (2008)
Unemployment – 5.6 per cent (2010 est)
Total external debt – US$212,500m (2010 est)
Imports – US$246,100m (2009)
Exports – US$229,700m (2009)

BALANCE OF PAYMENTS
Trade – US$3,121m deficit (2010)
Current Account – US$5,238m deficit (2009)

Trade with UK	2009	2010
Imports from UK	£720,656,134	£919,218,074
Exports to UK	£1,096,027,463	£1,477,738,521

COMMUNICATIONS

Veracruz, Tampico and Coatzacoalcos are the chief
seaports on the east coast, and Guaymas, Mazatlán, Lázaro
Cárdenas and Salina Cruz on the Pacific. There are
17,166km of railways. There are 366,095km of roads, of
which 132,289km are surfaced, and 2,900km of
navigable rivers and coastal canals. The main international
airport is at Mexico City, with nearly 60 others around
the country.

The fixed-line telephone network is limited in scope,
with a density of less than 20 per 100 people, while
mobile phone distribution has grown rapidly, reaching 75
per 100 people in 2009. In 2009 there were 31 million
internet users.

EDUCATION AND HEALTH

Education is compulsory in Mexico for ten years from
age six, although attainment varies among states. The
country's largest university is the National Autonomous
University of Mexico, situated in Mexico City.
Literacy rate – 92.8 per cent (2008 est)
Gross enrolment ratio (percentage of relevant age group) –
    primary 114 per cent; secondary 90 per cent;
    tertiary 27 per cent (2008 est)
Health expenditure (per capita) – US$515 (2009)
Hospital beds (per 1,000 people) – 1.6 (2004–9)

MEDIA

The Televisa group used to dominate Mexican
broadcasting but now competes with other television
channels and a huge number of independent radio
stations. Some northern radio stations broadcast to
Mexicans working in the USA. There are six national
daily newspapers, representing a variety of political
opinions. The murder, kidnap and intimidation of
journalists has risen markedly since the government's
offensive against drug cartels began in 2006.

CULTURE

The dominant figures in Mexican art are husband and
wife Diego Rivera (1886–1957) and Frida Kahlo
(1907–1954). In literature, essayist and poet Octavio Paz
(1914–98) won the Nobel prize in 1990, while Carlos
Fuentes (*b.* 1928) is a respected political commentator and
novelist.

As in other Latin American countries, football has a
huge following, and the country has hosted the World
Cup twice, in 1970 and 1986. Bullfighting is also very
popular and Mexico City is home to the largest ring in the
world, Plaza Mexico, which seats 40,000.

FEDERATED STATES OF MICRONESIA

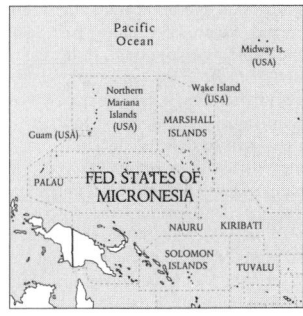

Area – 702 sq. km

Capital – Palikir, on Pohnpei; population, 6,941 (2009 est)

Major town – Weno

Currency – US dollar (US$) of 100 cents

Population – 107,154 falling at 0.28 per cent a year (2010 est); Chuukese (48.8 per cent), Pohnpeian (24.2 per cent), Kosraean (6.2 per cent), Yapese (5.2 per cent), Yap outer islands (4.5 per cent), Polynesian (1.5 per cent) (2000)

Religion – Christian (Roman Catholic 53 per cent, Protestant 41 per cent, Seventh-day Adventist 1 per cent) (2000); proportions vary greatly between the states

Language – English (official), Chuukese, Kosrean, Pohnpeian, Yapese, Ulithian, Woleaian, Nukuoro, Kapingamarangi

Population density – 158 per sq. km (2009)

Urban population – 22 per cent (2008 est)

Median age (years) – 22.4 (2010 est)

National anthem – 'Patriots of Micronesia'

National day – 10 May (Constitution Day)

Life expectancy (years) – 71.23 (2010 est)

Mortality rate – 4.4 (2010 est)

Birth rate – 22.57 (2010 est)

Infant mortality rate – 25.2 (2010 est)

Death penalty – Abolished for all crimes (since 1986)

CLIMATE AND TERRAIN

The republic consists of four major island groups totalling over 600 mountainous volcanic islands and low-lying atolls, extending over 2,900 sq. km of the western Pacific Ocean. Elevation extremes range from 791m (Dolohmwar) to 0m (Pacific Ocean). The climate is tropical, with only slight seasonal variations in temperatures; there is a stormy season between July and November. The islands are vulnerable to the effects of global warming, particularly an increase in the frequency and intensity of cyclones in the region.

HISTORY AND POLITICS

Inhabited since around 4,000 BC by migrants from the Philippines and Indonesia, Micronesia experienced contact with Europeans from the 1520s, and the islands were colonised by Spain from the 16th century. German encroachment in the 1870s and 1880s was resisted until 1899, when Germany purchased the islands from Spain. The islands were occupied by Japan on behalf of the Allies during the First World War, and administered as a League of Nations mandated territory by Japan from 1920 until the Japanese defeat in the Second World War. In 1947 the islands became part of the UN Trust Territory of the Pacific, administered by the USA.

A constitution was adopted in 1979 and the islands became independent in 1986 under a compact of free association with the USA, by which the USA retains responsibility for defence and provides substantial financial aid; a renegotiated agreement came into force in 2004. The UN trusteeship was formally terminated in 1990.

Emmanuel ('Manny') Mori was elected president in 2007, and he was re-elected in May 2011 following the legislative election in March.

POLITICAL SYSTEM

The 1979 constitution established a federal republic of four states: Chuuk, Kosrae, Pohnpei and Yap. The federal head of state is an executive president, who is elected by the federal legislature for a four-year term. The unicameral congress has 14 members, ten senators directly elected for a two-year term and four senators 'at large' (one from each state) elected for a four-year term; the president and vice-president must be selected from among the 'at large' senators. The federal cabinet is appointed by the president and approved by the congress. There are no formal political parties.

Each state has its own constitution, legislature and government.

HEAD OF STATE

President, Emmanuel Mori, *elected* 11 May 2007, *re-elected* 2011

Vice-President, Alik L. Alik

SELECTED GOVERNMENT MEMBERS *as at July 2011*

Finance, Finley S. Perman

Foreign Affairs, Lorin S. Robert

Attorney-General, Maketo Robert

BRITISH AMBASSADOR

HE Stephen Lillie, *apptd* 2009, resident at Manila, the Philippines

ECONOMY AND TRADE

Micronesia has few natural resources apart from phosphate, which is not exploited, and is highly dependent on aid from the USA, which constitutes over a quarter of GDP. The main economic activities are subsistence farming and fishing, which account for nearly 30 per cent of GDP, but both are threatened by climate change and over-fishing. The islands' remoteness and lack of facilities has constrained the development of tourism, the main industry; other industries include construction, fish processing, specialised aquaculture and handicrafts. Two-thirds of the workforce is employed by the government. The main trading partners are the USA and Japan. Principal exports are fish, garments, bananas and black pepper. The main imports are food, manufactured goods and machinery.

GNI – US$287m; US$2,500 per capita (2009)

Annual average growth of GDP – 0.3 per cent (2005 est)

Inflation rate – 2.2 per cent (2005)

Total external debt – US$60.8m (2005 est)

Trade with UK	2009	2010
Imports from UK	£38,903	£110,595
Exports to UK	£509,065	£35,643

COMMUNICATIONS

Most transport is by air or sea. There are six airports and airfields, with major airports on the four main islands, and the main seaports are Colonia (Yap), Kolonia (Pohnpei), Lele and Moen. There are 240km of roads, 42km of which are paved. The islands are all connected to the telephone system. Fixed-line use has declined as mobile phone subscriptions have increased.

MEDIA

There are no daily newspapers; the federal government produces a fortnightly information bulletin and state governments produce weekly news publications. State governments and one of the churches operate radio and cable television stations; around 95 per cent of television programming is imported.

MOLDOVA

Republica Moldova – Republic of Moldova

Area – 33,851 sq. km
Capital – Chisinau; population, 650,043 (2009 est)
Major towns – Balti, Tighina, Tiraspol
Currency – Moldovan leu (plural lei) of 100 bani
Population – 4,317,483 falling at 0.07 per cent a year (2010 est): Moldovan/Romanian (78.2 per cent), Ukrainian (8.4 per cent), Russian (5.8 per cent), Gagauz (4.4 per cent), Bulgarian (1.9 per cent) (2004)
Religion – Christian (Orthodox 96 per cent: predominantly Moldovan Orthodox; minority Bessarabian Church) (est)
Language – Moldovan (official; linguistically identical to Romanian), Russian, Gagauz
Population density – 110 per sq. km (2009)
Urban population – 42 per cent (2008 est)
Median age (years) – 35 (2010 est)
National anthem – 'Limba Noastra' ['Our Language']
National day – 27 August (Independence Day)
Life expectancy (years) – 71.09 (2010 est)
Mortality rate – 10.76 (2010 est)
Birth rate – 11.16 (2010 est)
Infant mortality rate – 12.77 (2010 est)
Death penalty – Abolished for all crimes (since 1995)
CPI score – 2.9 (2010)

CLIMATE AND TERRAIN

The landlocked country consists of rolling steppe lying mostly between the Prut and Dniester rivers. Elevation extremes range from 430m (Dealul Bulanesti) at the highest point to 2m (river Dniester) at the lowest. The climate is continental, and average temperatures in Chisinau range from −3°C in January to 21°C in July.

HISTORY AND POLITICS

Part of the Roman province of Dacia from AD 106, the area, subsequently known as Bessarabia, experienced centuries of invasion and occupation after the fall of the Roman Empire before becoming part of a larger independent Moldovan kingdom from the mid-14th century. Between the 16th and early 19th century, possession of the territory was disputed between various countries, but mainly the Ottoman and Russian empires. Bessarabia was granted to Russia in 1812.

After the Russian revolution in 1917, Bessarabia declared independence and then became a province of Romania in 1918. Romania was forced to return Bessarabia to the USSR in 1940 and it was incorporated with a small strip of land on the east bank of the river Dniester to form the Moldavian Soviet Socialist Republic. This was retaken by Romania in 1941 but recaptured by Soviet forces in 1944.

Moldovan nationalism grew in the late 1980s and the parliament asserted its political and economic sovereignty in 1990, declaring independence and joining the Commonwealth of Independent States in 1991 after the collapse of the USSR. A referendum in 1994 endorsed independence rather than unification with Romania or Russia.

The governments in the first decade after independence were made up of moderate reformists, but their ineffectiveness led to a resurgence in support for the Communist Party of Moldova (PCM), which won the majority of seats in the 1998, 2001, 2005, 2009 (April and July) and 2010 legislative elections, forming the government from 2005 to 2009. Attempts to elect a president have been unsuccessful since 2009, triggering three legislative elections in two years, but after each of the 2009 and 2010 elections neither the PCM nor the pro-Western coalition of parties that has formed the government since 2009 had a large enough majority to elect their own presidential candidate. A referendum in September 2010 on whether future presidents should be directly elected by the electorate had too small a turnout to be valid. Although the PCM won most seats in the legislative election in November 2010, the four-party pro-Western coalition government continued in office; neither bloc was able to elect its candidate as president, but the leader of the Democratic Party of Moldova was elected as speaker and as acting president.

SECESSION
Moldovan nationalism in the late 1980s and possible reunification with Romania alarmed the republic's Russian and Ukrainian ethnic minorities in the Transdniestria region (east of the Dniester) and the Gagauz (Turkish-speaking Christians) in the south-west. Both areas declared independence unilaterally in 1990, though this was not recognised. Both regions were granted a special status by the 1994 constitution, and the Gagauz have since exercised a degree of autonomy over their political, economic and cultural affairs.

A stalemate has developed over the status of Transdniestria. Fighting between separatists and government forces in 1991 was followed by a ceasefire in 1992, maintained by Russian peacekeeping troops. Despite talks sponsored by the OSCE, EU, Russia and Ukraine since the late 1990s, no political settlement has been reached, and Russia and the Transdniestrian authorities have failed to comply with agreements to withdraw Russian troops, arms and ammunition. The area has adopted symbols of nationhood but isolation because of its unresolved status has weakened its economy and internal security.

POLITICAL SYSTEM
The 1997 constitution was amended in 2000 to increase the powers of the legislature and the executive. The head of state is a president who is elected by the legislature by a three-fifths majority for a four-year term, renewable once. The unicameral legislature, the *Parlamentul*, has 101 members, who are directly elected for a four-year term. The prime minister and government are nominated by the president.

HEAD OF STATE
Acting President, Marian Lupu, *took office* 30 December 2010

SELECTED GOVERNMENT MEMBERS *as at July 2011*
Prime Minister, Vlad Filat
Deputy Prime Ministers, Eugen Carpov; Valeriu Lazar *(Economy);* Iurie Leanca *(External Affairs);* Mihai Moldovanu
Defence, Vitalie Marinuta
Finance, Veaceslav Negruta
Internal Affairs, Alexei Roibu

EMBASSY OF THE REPUBLIC OF MOLDOVA
5 Dolphin Square, Edensor Road, London W4 2ST
T 020-8995 6818 **E** embassy.london@mfa.md
W www.britania.mfa.gov.md
Ambassador Extraordinary and Plenipotentiary, vacant

BRITISH EMBASSY
18 Nicolae Iorga Str., Chisinau MD-2012
T (+373) 222 225902 **W** http://ukinmoldova.fco.gov.uk
Ambassador Extraordinary and Plenipotentiary, HE Keith Shannon, *apptd* 2009

DEFENCE
The army has 44 armoured infantry fighting vehicles and 164 armoured personnel carriers.
Military budget – US$16m (2010)
Military personnel – 5,354: army 3,231, air force 826, logistic support 1,297; paramilitary 2,379
Conscription duration – 12 months

ECONOMY AND TRADE
Moldova is one of the poorest countries in Europe, despite moves towards a market economy since independence. With few natural resources and most industry lying in the breakaway Transdniestria region, the economy is dependent on agriculture and remittances from expatriate workers. An estimated 25 per cent of the workforce was employed abroad but many returned because of the global downturn; the reduction in remittances and rise in unemployment increased Moldova's economic difficulties, and it required IMF support in 2009 and 2010.

The agricultural sector accounts for 16.3 per cent of GDP. Principal crops include vegetables, fruit, wine, grain, sugar beet, sunflower seed, tobacco, beef and milk. Major industrial activities include food processing and production of sugar, vegetable oil, agricultural machinery, foundry equipment, domestic appliances, footwear and textiles. Industry accounts for 20.1 per cent of GDP and services for 63.6 per cent.

The main trading partners are Russia, Romania, Italy, Ukraine and Germany. Principal exports are foodstuffs, textiles and machinery. The main imports are mineral products and fuel, machinery and equipment, chemicals and textiles.
GNI – US$5,708m; US$1,560 per capita (2009)
Annual average growth of GDP – 3.1 per cent (2010 est)
Inflation rate – 7.3 per cent (2010 est)
Population below poverty line – 29.5 per cent (2005)
Unemployment – 3.4 per cent (2010 est)
Total external debt – US$4,146m (2010)
Imports – US$3,300m (2009)
Exports – US$1,300m (2009)

BALANCE OF PAYMENTS
Trade – US$2,273m deficit (2010)
Current Account – US$987m deficit (2008)

Trade with UK	2009	2010
Imports from UK	£29,738,710	£42,673,547
Exports to UK	£28,232,116	£40,265,726

COMMUNICATIONS
Moldova has 9,343km of roads and 1,190km of railways. There are 11 airports and airstrips; the principal airport is at Chisinau. There are 558km of navigable waterways on the Prut, Dniester and Danube rivers; access to the Black Sea via the Danube has been agreed with Ukraine.

The antiquated telephone system is being modernised, but service is poor outside the capital. In 2009 there were 1.1 million fixed telephone lines in use, 2.7 million mobile phone subscribers and 1.3 million internet users.

EDUCATION AND HEALTH
Literacy rate – 99.3 per cent (2008 est)
Gross enrolment ratio (percentage of relevant age group) – primary 94 per cent; secondary 88 per cent; tertiary 38 per cent (2009 est)
Health expenditure (per capita) – US$181 (2009)
Hospital beds (per 1,000 people) – 6.1 (2004–9)

MEDIA
Freedom of media expression is guaranteed by the constitution, but laws exist prohibiting defamation of the state. There are four main newspapers, and Moldovan editions of Russian papers are also popular. State-run television and radio stations compete with a number of commercial operators, and broadcasts from Russia and Romania are widely available. The breakaway Transdniestria region operates its own television and radio stations.

MONACO

Principauté de Monaco – Principality of Monaco

Area – 2 sq. km
Capital – Monaco
Major town – Monte Carlo
Currency – Euro (€) of 100 cents
Population – 30,586 falling at 0.18 per cent a year
(2010 est); French (47 per cent), Monegasque
(16 per cent), Italian (16 per cent) (est)
Religion – Christian (predominantly Roman Catholic)
Language – French (official), English, Italian,
Monegasque
Population density – 16,406 per sq. km (2009)
Urban population – 100 per cent (2008 est)
Median age (years) – 48.9 (2010 est)
National anthem – 'Hymne Monégasque' ['Hymn of
Monaco']
National day – 19 November (St Rainier's Day)
Life expectancy (years) – 89.78 (2010 est)
Mortality rate – 8.01 (2010 est)
Birth rate – 7.03 (2010 est)
Infant mortality rate – 1.78 (2010 est)
Death penalty – Abolished for all crimes (since
1962)

CLIMATE AND TERRAIN
Monaco lies on 4kms of steep, rugged Mediterranean
coastline. It has been expanded by 0.3 sq. km with land
reclaimed from the sea by infilling. Elevation extremes
range from 140m (Mt Agel) at the highest point to 0m
(Mediterranean Sea) at the lowest. The climate is
Mediterranean, with average temperatures ranging from
10°C in January to 24°C in August.

HISTORY AND POLITICS
Monaco has been ruled by the Grimaldi family since the
13th century. Monarchical France recognised Monaco's
independence in the 15th century, but Revolutionary
France annexed it in 1793. Although the prince was
restored to power in 1814, Monaco did not regain its
independence until 1861. It was occupied by the Italians
and subsequently by the Germans in the Second World
War. The principality's foreign relations and security have
been aligned to those of France since 1861 by various
treaties; the terms were changed in 2005 to allow Monaco
greater control over its foreign relations and internal
administration.

POLITICAL SYSTEM
The 1962 constitution was amended in 2002 to allow the
throne to pass in the female line in the absence of male
heirs. Legislative power is held jointly by the prince and a
24-member National Council, which is directly elected
for a five-year term. Executive power is exercised by the
prince and a six-member Council of Government, headed
by a minister of state who is nominated by the prince and
approved by the French government. The judicial code is
based on that of France.
    In the 2008 legislative election, the Union for Monaco
(UPM) retained its 21 seats, an overwhelming majority, in
the legislature. Michel Roger replaced Jean-Paul Proust as
head of the government in March 2010.

HEAD OF STATE
HSH The Prince of Monaco, Prince Albert II
(Alexandre Louis Pierre), *born* 14 March 1958,
succeeded 6 April 2005
Heir, HSH Princess Caroline von Hannover, *born*
23 January 1957

SELECTED GOVERNMENT MEMBERS *as at July 2011*
Minister of State, Michel Roger
Finance and Economy, Marco Piccinini
Interior, Paul Masseron
Foreign Affairs, Franck Biancheri

EMBASSY OF THE PRINCIPALITY OF MONACO
7 Upper Grosvenor Street, London W1K 2LX
T 020-7318 1083 **E** embassy.uk@gouv.mc
W www.monaco-embassy-uk.gouv.mc
Ambassador Extraordinary and Plenipotentiary, Evelyne
Genta, *apptd* 2010

BRITISH CONSULATE-GENERAL
PO Box 265, 33 Boulevard Princesse Charlotte, 98005 Monaco
T (+377) 9350 9954
Hon. Consul-General, Sir Peter Westmacott, KCMG, LVO,
apptd 2007, resident in Marseille, France

ECONOMY AND TRADE
The economy has diversified away from its historic
dependence on tourism and gambling, and over half its
revenue now comes from financial services, retail, real
estate, construction and light industry (chemicals,
pharmaceuticals, cosmetics, medical devices, plastics,
electronics). A large floating jetty, installed in 2002, has
extended the harbour facilities, doubling the port's
capacity to handle cruise ships. As the state collects no
taxes from individuals and little from businesses, it has
become a tax haven for wealthy expatriates and foreign
companies. The state retains monopolies in a number of
sectors, including tobacco, the telephone network and the
postal service. Since 1963 Monaco has been in a customs
union with France, and through this it participates in the
EU market. Over half its trade is with EU countries,
particularly Italy.
GNI – US$6,109m; US$197,590 per capita (2009)
Unemployment – 0 per cent (2005 est)

MEDIA
Radio Monte-Carlo started broadcasting to France in the
1960s and Italy in the 1970s and now has significant
FM networks in both countries. Monaco has one
television station, and hosts the international Monte
Carlo Television Festival each year. Monaco has no daily
newspapers, but the principality's news is covered by the
French press.

MONGOLIA

Mongol Uls – Mongolia

Area – 1,564,116 sq. km
Capital – Ulaanbaatar; population, 948,719 (2009 est)
Major towns – Darhan, Erdenet
Currency – Tugrik of 100 mongo
Population – 3,086,918 rising at 1.5 per cent a year
    (2010 est); Mongol (94.9 per cent), Turkic (5 per cent)
    (2000 est)
Religion – Buddhist 90 per cent (predominantly Tibetan
    school of Mahayana), Muslim 5 per cent, Christian
    4 per cent (mostly Protestant) (est)
Language – Khalkha Mongol (official), Turkic, Russian
Population density – 2 per sq. km (2009)
Urban population – 57 per cent (2008 est)
Median age (years) – 25.8 (2010 est)
National anthem – 'Mongol ulsiin toriin duulal' ['National
    Anthem of Mongolia']
National day – 11 July (Revolution Day)
Life expectancy (years) – 67.98 (2010 est)
Mortality rate – 6.08 (2010 est)
Birth rate – 21.03 (2010 est)
Infant mortality rate – 38.56 (2010 est)
Death penalty – Retained
CPI score – 2.7 (2010)
Literacy rate – 97.2 per cent (2008 est)
Gross enrolment ratio (percentage of relevant age group) –
    primary 110 per cent; secondary 92 per cent;
    tertiary 53 per cent (2009 est)
Health expenditure (per capita) – US$74 (2009)
Hospital beds (per 1,000 people) – 5.9 (2004–9)

CLIMATE AND TERRAIN

The eastern part of landlocked Mongolia lies on a
semi-desert plateau, with steppes rising to the Mongolian
Altai and Hangai mountain ranges in the west. The Gobi
desert covers the southern third of the country. Elevation
extremes range from 4,374m (Nayramadlin Orgil) to
560m (Hoh Nuur). The country has long, cold winters,
which quickly turn into short and warm summers. The
wet season runs from June to September. Average
temperatures in Ulaanbaatar range from −28°C in
December to 16°C in July.

HISTORY AND POLITICS

The nomadic tribes of Mongolia, mostly Turks and
Uygurs, were united in the early 13th century by Genghis
Khan, forming the nucleus of a Mongol empire that
reached its zenith under Kublai Khan, Genghis's
grandson, when it stretched from Hungary to China and
as far south as Vietnam. After Kublai's death in 1294, the
empire declined. Many of the khanates formed under
Genghis survived as increasingly independent petty
kingdoms, but Mongolia itself was conquered by China in
the late 17th century and became the provinces of Inner
and Outer Mongolia.

When imperial rule in China collapsed in 1911, Outer
Mongolia declared itself an independent monarchy under
a Buddhist lama king. Chinese rule was reasserted in
1915, but in 1921 Mongolian revolutionaries, supported
by the Soviets, overthrew Chinese rule and the Mongolian
People's Revolutionary Party (MPRP) formed a
government. When the king died in 1924, the monarchy
was abolished and the ensuing republic introduced
communist-inspired defeudalisation and collectivisation
programmes and suppressed Buddhism. With the
assistance of Soviet troops, Mongolia resisted Japanese
attacks in the late 1930s, and after the Second World War
Mongolia seemed likely to remain under Soviet control,

but in a 1946 UN plebiscite the people voted for
independence.

Mongolia became more open to external contacts from
the mid-1980s and, influenced by events in eastern
Europe, a popular campaign for political and economic
reform led to the first multi-party elections in 1990 and a
massive privatisation programme, which began in 1991.
The MPRP, which had eschewed communism, continued
to dominate political life until 1996, when an alliance of
nationalists and social democrats was elected to power.
The alliance became the subject of corruption scandals
and its transition to a market economy caused widespread
social disruption and poverty. The MPRP returned to
power in the 2001 election, having already regained the
presidency in 1997, but since the 2004 election it has not
held an outright majority in the legislature and has
remained in power as part of coalition governments.

In the 2008 legislative election the MPRP won 46
seats and the Democratic Party (DP) 27 seats; the
showing of smaller parties was poorer than expected,
leading to allegations of electoral fraud that provoked
protests so violent that a four-day state of emergency was
declared. The MPRP formed a coalition government with
the DP, and Sanjaa Bayar continued as prime minister.
The 2009 presidential election was won by the DP
candidate, Tsakhiagiin Elbegdorj (prime minister 1998,
2006–8). Sanjaa Bayar resigned as prime minister in
October 2009 and was replaced by Sukhbaataryn
Batbold.

POLITICAL SYSTEM

The 1992 constitution was amended in 2000 to give the
president the right to dissolve the legislature if it is unable
to reach agreement on appointing a prime minister. The
president is directly elected for a four-year term, which is
renewable. The unicameral State Great Hural has 76
members who are directly elected for a four-year term. The
prime minister is elected by the legislature and
appoints the cabinet.

HEAD OF STATE

President, Tsakhiagiin Elbegdorj, *elected* 24 May 2009,
    sworn in 18 June 2009

SELECTED GOVERNMENT MEMBERS *as at June 2011*
Prime Minister, Sukhbaataryn Batbold
First Deputy Prime Minister, Noroviin Altanhuyag
Defence, Luvsanvandan Bold
Finance, Sangajabyn Bayartsogt
Foreign Affairs, Gombojav Zandanshatar
Justice and Internal Affairs, Tsendiin Nyamdorj

EMBASSY OF MONGOLIA

7–8 Kensington Court, London W8 5DL
T 020-7937 0150 E office@embassyofmongolia.co.uk
W www.embassyofmongolia.co.uk
Ambassador Extraordinary and Plenipotentiary, HE Bulgaa
    Altangerel, *apptd* 2008

BRITISH EMBASSY

Peace Avenue 30, Bayanzurkh District, Ulaanbaatar 13381
T (+976) (11) 458 133 W http://ukinmongolia.fco.gov.uk
Ambassador Extraordinary and Plenipotentiary, HE
    Thorhilda Abbott-Watt, *apptd* 2011

DEFENCE

The army has 370 main battle tanks, 150 armoured
personnel carriers and 310 armoured infantry fighting

vehicles. The air force has 9 aircraft and 11 armed helicopters.

Military expenditure – US$38m (2009 est)
Military personnel – 10,000: army 8,900, air force 800, construction troops 300; paramilitary 7,200
Conscription duration – 12 months

ECONOMY AND TRADE

The economy suffered during the transition to a market economy but recovered to show strong growth in recent years. This had faltered before the global downturn began; in 2008 declining commodity prices and export demand and soaring inflation caused difficulties that forced the government to seek an IMF loan in spring 2009. Mongolia has attracted foreign investment, particularly in mining, agricultural processing and infrastructure, although administrative corruption, dependency on imported energy supplies (mostly from Russia) and the vulnerability of the agrarian sector to climate extremes continue to hinder growth. Over a third of the population lives below the poverty line.

Deposits of copper, coal, molybdenum, fluorspar, tin, tungsten, uranium, gold and oil are being exploited; copper and gold sales are major drivers of recent economic growth. The agrarian sector, which makes up 15 per cent of GDP, engages 34 per cent of the workforce in agriculture and herding. The main products are grains, vegetables, forage crops, sheep, goats and other livestock. The main industries are construction, mining, processing animal products, and the production of oil, food and beverages, cashmere and natural yarns.

The main export market is China (78 per cent); the main import providers are China (36 per cent) and Russia (31 per cent). Principal exports are copper, clothing, livestock, animal products, cashmere, wool, hides, fluorspar, metals and coal. The main imports are machinery and equipment, fuels, cars, foodstuffs, industrial consumer goods, chemicals and construction materials.

GNI – US$3,968m; US$1,630 per capita (2009)
Annual average growth of GDP – 7 per cent (2010)
Inflation rate – 4.2 per cent (2009 est)
Population below poverty line – 36.1 per cent (2004)
Unemployment – 2.8 per cent (2008)
Total external debt – US$1,860m (2009)
Imports – US$2,100m (2009)
Exports – US$1,900m (2009)

BALANCE OF PAYMENTS
Trade – US$379m deficit (2010)
Current Account – US$722m deficit (2008)

Trade with UK	2009	2010
Imports from UK	£4,166,984	£11,096,576
Exports to UK	£16,834,135	£40,149,166

COMMUNICATIONS

Mongolia has 1,908km of railways and 49,249km of roads, although only about six per cent of the roads are surfaced. The main airport is at Ulaanbaatar; there are 45 other airports and airfields around the country. The lakes and main rivers are navigable in the summer months but ice-bound in winter; Lake Hovsgol near the Russian border is the only waterway currently in commercial operation. International trade is via Russia and China.

The telephone system is improving but fixed-line density is very low. In 2009 there were 189,000 fixed

telephone lines in use, 2.2 million mobile phone subscribers and 330,000 internet users.

MEDIA

There are 16 daily newspapers, including *Onoodor,* which has the biggest circulation, and *Unen* (Truth), the organ of the MPRP and the country's oldest newspaper. In 2005 the state-run radio and television service was transformed into a public-service broadcaster, and now competes with a number of private operators; access to satellite television is growing. Radio is a key medium because of the nomadic lifestyle of some of the population; Mongolian Radio is the sole broadcaster with a country-wide reach.

MONTENEGRO

Crna Gora – Montenegro

Area – 13,812 sq. km
Capital – Podgorica; population, 143,853 (2009 est)
Major cities – Cetinje (historic and cultural capital), Niksic
Currency – Euro (€) of 100 cents
Population – 666,730 falling at 0.78 per cent a year (2010 est); Montenegrin (43 per cent), Serbian (32 per cent), Bosniak (8 per cent), Albanian (5 per cent) (2003)
Religion – Christian (Orthodox 74 per cent, Roman Catholic 4 per cent), Muslim 18 per cent (est)
Language – Montenegrin (a version of Serbo-Croat) (official), Serbian, Bosnian, Albanian, Croatian
Population density – 46 per sq. km (2009)
Urban population – 60 per cent (2008 est)
Median age (years) – 37.2 (2010 est)
National anthem – 'Oj, Svijetla Majska Zoro' ['O, Bright Dawn of May']
National day – 13 July (Statehood Day)
Life expectancy (years) – 74.73 (2005 est)
Mortality rate – 8.76 (2010 est)
Birth rate – 11.09 (2010 est)
Infant mortality rate – 12.89 (2005 est)
Death penalty – Abolished for all crimes (since 2002)
CPI score – 3.7 (2010)
Literacy rate – 96.4 per cent (2008 est)

CLIMATE AND TERRAIN

The terrain is mountainous in the north and centre of the country, intersected by deep canyons and river valleys, and falls to a narrow plain on the highly indented Adriatic coast. About 40 per cent of the country is forested. Elevation extremes range from 2,522m (Bobotov Kuk) to 0m (Adriatic Sea). The main rivers are the Piva (Drina), the Tara and the Lim. Lake Skadarsko straddles the border with Albania. The climate is Mediterranean on the coast, but more continental inland. Average temperatures in Podgorica range from 5°C in January to 26°C in July.

HISTORY AND POLITICS
The area was part of the Roman province of Illyria, and then was settled by Slavs in the seventh century. In the late 12th century it was incorporated into the medieval kingdom of Serbia and so became part of the Ottoman Empire after Serbia's defeat by the Turks in 1389. When Serbia became independent in 1878, Montenegro followed and remained an independent monarchy until the end of the First World War. In 1918, Montenegro joined with Serbia and the former Austro-Hungarian provinces of Slovenia, Croatia and Bosnia-Hercegovina to form the Kingdom of Serbs, Croats and Slovenes, which was renamed Yugoslavia in 1929. Yugoslavia was occupied by Axis forces in 1941, and after liberation it reformed as a communist federal republic in 1945. When the federation disintegrated in 1991, Serbia and Montenegro formed the Federal Republic of Yugoslavia, declared on 27 April 1992.

Montenegro's desire for independence led in 2002 to an EU-brokered agreement between the leaders of Serbia, Montenegro and the Federal Republic of Yugoslavia that restructured the republic into a union of two semi-independent states, named Serbia and Montenegro, with effect from March 2003. The agreement provided for the two republics to hold referendums on whether to retain or end the union after a minimum of three years. In a referendum held in Montenegro on 21 May 2006, 55.5 per cent voted in favour of independence, which was declared on 3 June and acknowledged by Serbia on 5 June. Montenegro joined the UN in June 2006, and formally applied for EU membership in 2008.

In the 2008 presidential election, President Vujanovic was returned for a second term. In the 2009 legislative election, the Coalition for a European Montenegro again won the most seats, and Milo Djukanovic's three-party coalition government continued in office. Djukanovic resigned in December 2010 and was replaced by the finance minister, Igor Luksic.

POLITICAL SYSTEM
Under the 2007 constitution, the president is directly elected for a five-year term, which is renewable once. The unicameral Assembly of the Republic of Montenegro has 81 members directly elected for a four-year term; five members are elected from the ethnic Albanian community. The prime minister appoints the cabinet, subject to the approval of the assembly.

HEAD OF STATE
President, Filip Vujanovic, *elected* 11 May 2003, *re-elected* 6 April 2008

SELECTED GOVERNMENT MEMBERS *as at July 2011*
Prime Minister, Igor Luksic
Deputy Prime Ministers, Vujica Lazovic; Dusko Markovic
Foreign Affairs, Milan Rocen
Defence, Boro Vucinic

EMBASSY OF MONTENEGRO
18 Callcott Street, London W8 7SU
T 020-7727 6007 E unitedkingdom@mfa.gov.me
Ambassador Extraordinary and Plenipotentiary, HE Ljubisa Stankovic, *apptd* 2011

BRITISH EMBASSY
Ulcinjska 8, Gorica C, 81000 Podgorica
T (+382) (20) 618 010 E podgorica@britishembassy.co.me
W http://ukinmontenegro.fco.gov.uk
Ambassador Extraordinary and Plenipotentiary, HE Catherine Knight-Sands, *apptd* 2009

DEFENCE
The army has 8 armoured personnel carriers. The navy has 2 submarines and 5 patrol and coastal combatant vessels located at Bar.
Military budget – US$35m (2010)
Military personnel – 3,127: army 2,500, navy 401, air force 226; paramilitary 10,100

ECONOMY AND TRADE
Montenegro achieved fiscal autonomy from the Yugoslav federation in the 1990s, managing its own budget, collecting customs tariffs on its own account, maintaining its own central bank and adopting the euro. However, it faced the same problems as Serbia – slow growth, foreign debt, lack of foreign investment, high unemployment, corruption and organised crime – as well as having more limited health and education facilities, and a poor administrative capacity. Since independence, it has pursued international integration, prioritising in particular its bid for EU membership. It has privatised its aluminium industry and financial sector, and is attracting direct foreign investment in its growing tourism industry. The economy contracted sharply during the global downturn and has not yet begun to recover.

The main agricultural products are tobacco, fruit and vegetables. Major industrial activities include production of steel, aluminium and consumer goods, processing of agricultural products and tourism. The main trading partners are EU and other Balkan countries.
GNI – US$4,149m; US$6,650 per capita (2009)
Annual average growth of GDP – –1.8 per cent (2010 est)
Inflation rate – 3.4 per cent (2007)
Population below poverty line – 7 per cent (2007 est)
Unemployment – 14.7 per cent (2007 est)
Total external debt – US$650m (2006)

BALANCE OF PAYMENTS
Trade – US$1,215m deficit (2010)
Current Account – US$2,382m deficit (2008)

Trade with UK	2009	2010
Imports from UK	£4,821,909	£5,440,180
Exports to UK	£1,971,387	£3,109,165

COMMUNICATIONS
There is 250km of rail track, part of the European system linking the Adriatic port of Bar with Belgrade, via Podgorica. The 7,624km of roads include major routes linking Podgorica and the coastal ports with the hinterland and neighbouring countries. There are five airports, including international airports at Podgorica and Tivat. Modernised telecommunications systems provided services to 366,600 fixed-line subscribers, 752,000 mobile phone subscribers and 280,000 internet users in 2009.

MEDIA
Freedom of the press is guaranteed, though observers have reported continuing political influence over editorial policies. Overseas donors and organisations have

contributed funds to stimulate media growth, and there are now dozens of private radio and television stations; these vie for a limited pool of advertising revenue. There are also state-funded television and radio broadcasters.

MOROCCO

Al-Mamlakah al-Maghribiyah – Kingdom of Morocco

Area – 446,550 sq. km
Capital – Rabat; population, 1,769,590 (2009 est)
Major cities – Agadir, Casablanca, Fez, Marrakesh, Meknès, Tangier
Currency – Dirham (DH) of 100 centimes
Population – 31,627,428 rising at 1.08 per cent a year (2010 est); Arab–Berber (99.1 per cent) (est)
Religion – Muslim 99 per cent (predominantly Sunni), Christian 1 per cent (est)
Language – Arabic (official), French, Berber dialects
Population density – 72 per sq. km (2009)
Urban population – 56 per cent (2008 est)
Median age (years) – 26.5 (2010 est)
National anthem – 'Hymne Chérifien' ['Hymn of the Sharif']
National day – 30 July (Coronation Day)
Life expectancy (years) – 75.69 (2010 est)
Mortality rate – 4.74 (2010 est)
Birth rate – 19.4 (2010 est)
Infant mortality rate – 28.61 (2010 est)
Death penalty – Retained (not used since 1993)
CPI score – 3.4 (2010)

CLIMATE AND TERRAIN

Fertile coastal plains in the west rise to a mountainous centre, with ranges, including the Atlas range, running north-east to south-west. The Rif mountains lie along the northern, Mediterranean coast. Elevation extremes range from 4,165m (Jebel Toubkal) at the highest point to −55m (Sebkha Tah) at the lowest. The climate is Mediterranean, becoming more extreme in the interior. Average temperatures in Rabat range from 13°C in January to 22°C in July and August, although summer temperatures in the desert can reach over 40°C.

HISTORY AND POLITICS

From the tenth century BC, the northern coast was settled by the Phoenicians. Morocco was part of the Roman Empire from the first century AD until it was invaded by first the Vandals and then the Visigoths in the fifth and sixth centuries. Arab conquest of the area began in the seventh century but Morocco was independent from about the ninth century, successfully resisting inclusion in the Ottoman Empire in the 16th century. The current

Alawite dynasty was founded in the mid-17th century. Morocco remained isolated until the mid-19th century, when the country opened up to European trade. The subsequent growth in Spanish and French influence resulted in its partition into two protectorates from 1912. In the Second World War, Morocco was a base for the Allied offensives that drove German forces out of North Africa.

Nationalist campaigning for independence began in the 1940s. French and Spanish forces withdrew in 1956, leaving Morocco independent under Sultan Mohammed V, who adopted the title of king in 1957; the coastal towns of Ceuta and Melilla remain under Spanish control. King Hassan II, who ruled from 1961 to 1999, annexed the mineral-rich Western Sahara region in 1975.

Since the accession of King Mohammed VI in 1999, Morocco has been moving away from absolute monarchy, increasing civil liberties and addressing human rights issues. Pro-reform demonstrations in spring 2011 led to a referendum in July in which an overwhelming majority voted in favour of constitutional changes that would make the prime minister, rather than the king, the head of government.

In the 2007 legislative election the Independence Party (Istiqlal), one of the parties in the coalition government, became the largest party but without an outright majority. Its leader, Abbas el Fassi, was appointed prime minister and formed a coalition government that includes five parties and a number of independents.

POLITICAL SYSTEM

The 1992 constitution was amended in 1996 to introduce a bicameral legislature. The head of state is a hereditary constitutional monarch. The king appoints the prime minister, who appoints the members of the council of ministers. There is a bicameral legislature; the lower house, the House of Representatives *(Majlis al-Nuwab)* has 325 members who are directly elected for a five-year term. The House of Councillors *(Majlis al-Mustasharin)* has 270 members, elected by local councils, professional organisations and the 'salaried classes'; one-third of its members is elected every three years, to serve a nine-year term.

HEAD OF STATE

HM The King of Morocco, King Mohammed VI (Sidi Mohammed Ben Hassan), *born* 21 August 1963, *acceded* 23 July 1999, *crowned* 30 July 1999
Heir, HRH Crown Prince Moulay Hassan, *born* 2003

SELECTED GOVERNMENT MEMBERS *as at July 2011*
Prime Minister, Abbas el-Fassi
Economy and Finance, Salaheddine Mezouar
Foreign Affairs, Taieb Fassi Fihri
Interior, Taib Cherkaoui

EMBASSY OF THE KINGDOM OF MOROCCO
49 Queen's Gate Gardens, London SW7 5NE
T 020-7581 5001 E ambalondres@maec.gov.ma
W www.moroccanembassylondon.org.uk
Ambassador Extraordinary and Plenipotentiary, HH Princess Lalla Joumala Aaoui, *apptd* 2009

BRITISH EMBASSY
28 Avenue SAR Sidi Mohammed, Souissi 10105 (BP45), Rabat
T (+212) (0) 537 633 333 W http://ukinmorocco.fco.gov.uk
Ambassador Extraordinary and Plenipotentiary, HE Timothy Morris, *apptd* 2008

BRITISH COUNCIL
11 Allal ben Abdellah, 5ème étage, BP 427, Rabat
T (+212) (0) 537 218 130 W www.britishcouncil.org/morocco
Director, Martin Rose

DEFENCE

The army has 380 main battle tanks, 70 armoured infantry fighting vehicles and 765 armoured personnel carriers. The navy has 2 frigates and 39 patrol and coastal combatant vessels at five bases. The air force has 89 combat aircraft and 19 multi-role helicopters.

Military budget – US$3,190m (2010)
Military personnel – 195,800: army 175,000, navy 7,800, air force 13,000; paramilitary 50,000
Conscription duration – 18 months

ECONOMY AND TRADE

Economic liberalisation since 1999 has attracted foreign direct investment, and the industrial and service sectors are being developed. Despite steady growth, Morocco remains a poor country, with unemployment averaging 10 per cent, though it is often nearer 20 per cent in urban areas, and in 2005 the king launched a poverty-alleviation programme. The remittances of expatriate workers are crucial to the domestic economy but these, along with tourism and export demand, declined in 2008–9 owing to the global downturn; recovery is slow because of dependence on the sluggish European market.

The large agrarian sector generates 17.1 per cent of GDP and engages 44.6 per cent of the workforce, producing cereals, citrus fruits, vegetables, wine, olives and livestock. It faces environmental problems such as desertification and soil erosion. Another major sector is the exploitation of mineral reserves, especially phosphate. Other industries include food processing, textiles, leather goods, construction and tourism, which the government is working to expand. Industry accounts for 31.6 per cent of GDP and services for 44.6 per cent.

The main trading partners are EU countries, especially France and Spain. Principal exports are clothing, textiles, electrical components, inorganic chemicals, transistors, crude minerals, fertilisers, petroleum products, fruit and vegetables. The main imports are crude petroleum, fabrics, telecommunications equipment, wheat, gas and electricity.

GNI – US$89,489m; US$2,770 per capita (2009; includes Western Sahara)
Annual average growth of GDP – 4.2 per cent (2010 est)
Inflation rate – 2.5 per cent (2010 est)
Population below poverty line – 15 per cent (2007 est)
Unemployment – 9.8 per cent (2010 est)
Total external debt – US$22,690m (2010 est)
Imports – US$32,800m (2009)
Exports – US$13,700m (2009)

BALANCE OF PAYMENTS
Trade – US$18,025m deficit (2010)
Current Account – US$4,568m deficit (2009)

Trade with UK	2009	2010
Imports from UK	£298,857,855	£527,085,424
Exports to UK	£311,811,054	£318,839,858

COMMUNICATIONS

There are 2,067km of railways linking the major towns and 57,625km of roads; a 35,664km network of surfaced roads connects the main towns. The main ports are Tangier, Casablanca and Agadir, on the Atlantic coast.

The principal airports are at Rabat, Agadir, Casablanca and Marrakesh; Royal Air Maroc is the national airline.

There is a modern telephone system, but fixed-line density is only about 10 per 100 people, compared to mobile phone density of 75 per 100 people in 2009.

EDUCATION AND HEALTH

Education is compulsory between the ages of six and 15. There are government primary, secondary and technical schools; at Fez there is a theological university.

Literacy rate – 56.5 per cent (2008 est)
Gross enrolment ratio (percentage of relevant age group) – primary 107 per cent; secondary 56 per cent; tertiary 11 per cent (2007 est)
Health expenditure (per capita) – US$156 (2009)
Hospital beds (per 1,000 people) – 1.1 (2004–9)

MEDIA

Journalists practise a degree of self-censorship to avoid sensitive subjects such as the king, Islam and Western Sahara; bloggers are similarly careful. The private press, though, have recently begun reporting allegations of high-level corruption. The government owns Radio-Television Marocaine and has a stake in 2M, the other main television network. Private radio and television services are expanding, however, and satellite television is widely accessed. There are a number of daily newspapers, including one that is state-owned.

WESTERN SAHARA

Al-Jumhuriyya al-'Arabiyya as-Sahrawiyya ad-Dimuqratiyya – Sahrawi Arab Democratic Republic
Area – 266,000 sq. km. Neighbours: Morocco (north), Algeria (north-east), Mauritania (east and south)
Population – 507,160 (2011 est)
Administrative centre – El-Aaiun (Laayoune); population, 200,000 (2007 est)
Religion – Muslim (99 per cent) (est)
Language – Arabic, Hassaniyya Arabic, Spanish
Flag – Three horizontal stripes of black, white and green with a red crescent and a five-pointed star in the centre and a red triangle based on the hoist

Western Sahara came under Spanish rule in 1884, and became a province in 1934. Following Spain's withdrawal in 1976, Morocco and Mauritania annexed the territory and divided it between them. The Polisario Front declared the Western Sahara's independence as the Sahrawi Arab Democratic Republic in 1976, and began a guerrilla war to win the territory, setting up a government in exile. In 1979, Mauritania withdrew from its part of the territory, which was annexed by Morocco. Fighting between Polisario and Moroccan forces continued at varying levels of intensity until 1991, when a UN-brokered ceasefire came into effect.

The 1991 ceasefire was established following both sides' agreement in 1988 to UN proposals for a peace settlement, which included holding a referendum on the future status of Western Sahara. But the precise terms of the referendum have proved a sticking point and an impasse was reached that has still not been overcome despite further negotiations in 2001–4; Polisario agreed to a referendum offering the options of independence, semi-autonomy or integration for Western Sahara, but Morocco is only prepared to accept semi-autonomy or integration. The UN suspended the process of preparing for the referendum in 1996 because of disagreements over voter registration; the ceasefire remains in place. Talks have taken place intermittently since 2007 but have made no progress.

MOZAMBIQUE

República de Moçambique – Republic of Mozambique

Area – 799,380 sq. km
Capital – Maputo; population, 1,589,060 (2009 est)
Major cities – Beira, Chimoio, Nacala, Nampula
Currency – New metical (MT) of 100 centavos
Population – 22,061,451 rising at 1.8 per cent a year (2010 est)
Religion – Christian (Roman Catholic 24 per cent, Protestant 22 per cent), Muslim 20 per cent (est); many Christians and Muslims incorporate indigenous practices into their worship
Language – Portuguese (official), Emakhuwa, Xichangana, Elomwe, Cisena, Echuwabo
Population density – 29 per sq. km (2009)
Urban population – 37 per cent (2008 est)
Median age (years) – 17.5 (2010 est)
National anthem – 'Patria Amada' ['Beloved Fatherland']
National day – 25 June (Independence Day)
Life expectancy (years) – 41.37 (2010 est)
Mortality rate – 19.83 (2010 est)
Birth rate – 37.8 (2010 est)
Infant mortality rate – 103.82 (2010 est)
HIV/AIDS adult prevalence – 11.5 per cent (2009 est)
Death penalty – Abolished for all crimes (since 1990)
CPI score – 2.7 (2010)
Literacy rate – 45.0 per cent (2008 est)
Gross enrolment ratio (percentage of relevant age group) – primary 114 per cent; secondary 23 per cent (2009 est)
Health expenditure (per capita) – US$25 (2009)
Hospital beds (per 1,000 people) – 0.8 (2004–9)

CLIMATE AND TERRAIN
Coastal plains rise to plateaux in the centre and west, with mountains on the western borders. Elevation extremes range from 2,436m (Mt Binga) at the highest point to 0m (Indian Ocean) at the lowest. A number of rivers run from the western highlands to the Indian Ocean coast, including the Zambezi, Limpopo, Save and Ruvuma. The climate is tropical, with average temperatures in Maputo ranging from 19°C in June and July to 26°C in January and February.

HISTORY AND POLITICS
Between the first and fourth centuries Mozambique was settled by Bantu peoples. Trade with India and the Arabian peninsula grew and migrants from both these regions settled in the coastal areas. From the 16th century the Portuguese established settlements on the coast and along the Zambezi, trading in gold, ivory, spices and slaves, and in the late 19th century they succeeded in conquering the interior. The area was administered as part of Portuguese India from 1751, becoming a separate colony in the late 19th century and an overseas province of Portugal in 1951. Concessions to private companies that had operated as *de facto* rulers over much of the country were ended in 1930.

The *Frente de Libertacao de Mocambique* (Frelimo) was founded in 1962 to fight for independence, and a ten-year guerrilla war against Portuguese forces began in 1964. Independence was achieved in 1975, when a one-party socialist republic was set up. Opposition to this was led from 1977 by the *Resistencia Nacional de Mocambique* (Renamo) and a brutal civil war broke out that lasted until 1992. Mozambique joined the Commonwealth in 1995; although it had never been under British rule, it has close relationships and a shared experience with its neighbours, all former British colonies. Reconstruction of the economy and infrastructure progressed quickly after the civil war, although a series of natural catastrophes since 2000 have been major setbacks. Additional problems are the large number of remaining landmines, and the high number of people living with HIV/AIDS.

In 1990 Frelimo abandoned Marxist-Leninism and ended one-party rule, introducing a multiparty system. The first elections under the new constitution were held in 1994 and won by Frelimo. Frelimo retained power in the 1999, 2004 and 2009 elections, prompting allegations of vote-rigging by Renamo, though monitors believe that any irregularities were minor. In the 2009 elections President Guebuza, of Frelimo, was re-elected, and Frelimo retained its overall majority in the legislature.

POLITICAL SYSTEM
Under the 2004 constitution, the executive president is directly elected for a five-year term, renewable once. The unicameral Assembly of the Republic has 250 members, who are directly elected for a five-year term. The president appoints the prime minister and the council of ministers.

HEAD OF STATE
President, Armando Guebuza, *elected* 22 December 2004, *sworn in* 2 February 2005, *re-elected* 2009

SELECTED GOVERNMENT MEMBERS *as at July 2011*
Prime Minister, Aires Bonifacio Ali
Foreign Affairs, Oldemiro Baloi
Interior, Ricardo Alberto Mondlane
Finance, Manuel Chang
Defence, Filipe Nhussi

HIGH COMMISSION FOR THE REPUBLIC OF MOZAMBIQUE
21 Fitzroy Square, London W1T 6EL
T 020-7383 3800 E sectorconsular@mozambiquehc.co.uk
W www.mozambiquehighcommission.org.uk
High Commissioner, HE Antonio Gumende, *apptd* 2002

BRITISH HIGH COMMISSION
PO Box 55, Av. Vladimir I Lenine 310, Maputo
T (+258) (21) 356 000 E bhcgeneral@gmail.com
W http://ukinmozambique.fco.gov.uk
High Commissioner, HE Anthony Shaun Cleary, *apptd* 2010

BRITISH COUNCIL
2nd Floor, Hollard Building, 269 Av. Sociedade e Goegrafia, Maputo
T (+258) (21) 355 000 W www.britishcouncil.org/africa
Director (acting), David Pardoe

DEFENCE
The army has over 60 main battle tanks, 40 armoured infantry fighting vehicles and 271 armoured personnel carriers. The air force has 2 armed helicopters.
Military expenditure – US$84m (2009)
Military personnel – 11,200: army 10,000, navy 200, air force 1,000
Conscription duration – 24 months

ECONOMY AND TRADE
Political stability and economic liberalisation have attracted foreign direct investment and donor support, and achieved economic growth despite setbacks from devastating flooding (2000, 2001, 2007, 2008, 2010), droughts (2002, 2003, 2009, 2010) and an earthquake (2006). But the country remains dependent on foreign aid with 70 per cent of the population living below the poverty line. The huge foreign debt has been reduced to a more manageable size by debt cancellation and rescheduling, but there is a substantial ongoing trade imbalance.

Agriculture and forestry are the mainstay of the economy, accounting for 28.8 per cent of GDP and engaging about 80 per cent of the workforce; shellfish, cashew nuts, cotton, sugar, citrus fruits and timber are important exports. There are considerable oil, gas, mineral and hydroelectric power resources, which are increasingly being exploited. Industries include aluminium extraction and smelting, food processing, production of beverages, chemicals, petroleum products and textiles. There are plans to expand titanium extraction and processing, and garment-manufacturing. Industry generates 26 per cent of GDP and services 45.2 per cent. The country also benefits from trade with its landlocked neighbours.

The main trading partners are South Africa and the Netherlands. Principal exports are aluminium, agricultural products, timber and electricity. The main imports are machinery, vehicles, fuel, chemicals, metal products, foodstuffs and textiles.

GNI – US$9,696m; US$440 per capita (2009)
Annual average growth of GDP – 8.3 per cent (2010 est)
Inflation rate – 13.5 per cent (2010 est)
Population below poverty line – 70 per cent (2001 est)
Total external debt – US$4,990m (2010 est)
Imports – US$3,800m (2009)

BALANCE OF PAYMENTS
Trade – US$2,536m deficit (2010)
Current Account – US$1,179m deficit (2008)

Trade with UK	2009	2010
Imports from UK	£15,452,864	£32,361,833
Exports to UK	£45,235,005	£70,057,928

COMMUNICATIONS
The main seaports are Maputo, Beira and Nacala; these also handle trade for landlocked neighbouring countries, to which they are linked by rail. A new rail link to South Africa has been commissioned, and there are plans to develop new rail and road links to Malawi, Zambia and Botswana. There are currently 4,787km of railways. Of the 30,400km of roads, only 5,685km is surfaced.

The 460km of navigable waterways are on Cahora Bassa Lake and the lower reaches of the Zambezi; the Shire-Zambezi Waterway Project is developing a commercial waterway link with Malawi and Zambia. The principal airports are at Maputo and Beira, with 104 smaller airports and airstrips around the country.

The telephone system is efficient but there is limited fixed-line availability. Mobile phone distribution has grown rapidly. There were 82,000 fixed lines in use, 5.9 million mobile phone subscribers and 614,000 internet users in 2009.

MEDIA
Freedom of speech is guaranteed in the constitution, but criminal libel laws remain in place. There are two daily newspapers – one state-owned and one private – and several weekly publications, although these have little influence outside urban areas because of low literacy levels. Radio is the main news medium for most people, with services provided by the state broadcaster, several private stations, and dozens of community and local radio stations funded by UNESCO and the government. State and privately owned television services, including Portuguese and Brazilian channels, compete for a mainly urban audience.

MYANMAR

Pyidaungzu Myanma Naingngandaw – Republic of the Union of Myanmar

Area – 676,578 sq. km
Capital – Naypyitaw; population, 992,379 (2009 est)
Major cities – Bago, Mandalay, Mawlamyine (Moulmein), Pathein (Bassein), Yangon (Rangoon)
Currency – Kyat (K) of 100 pyas
Population – 53,414,374 rising at 1.1 per cent a year (2010 est); Burman (68 per cent), Shan (9 per cent), Karen (7 per cent), Rakhine (4 per cent), Chinese (3 per cent), Indian (2 per cent), Mon (2 per cent) (est)
Religion – Buddhist 90 per cent (predominantly Theravada), Christian 4 per cent, Muslim 4 per cent (est). Other estimates put the proportion of Muslims as high as 10 per cent
Language – Burmese (official), numerous ethnic languages
Population density – 77 per sq. km (2009)
Urban population – 33 per cent (2008 est)
Median age (years) – 26.5 (2009 est)
National anthem – 'Kaba Ma Kyei' ['Till the End of the World, Myanmar']
National day – 4 January (Independence Day)
Life expectancy (years) – 64.52 (2010 est)
Mortality rate – 8.23 (2010 est)

Birth rate – 19.49 (2010 est)
Infant mortality rate – 50.76 (2010 est)
Death penalty – Retained (not used since the 1980s)
CPI score – 1.4 (2010)

CLIMATE AND TERRAIN

Central lowlands are ringed by mountains in the west, north (part of the foothills of the Himalayas) and east. The eastern range extends down the Kra isthmus that Myanmar shares with Thailand, forming a natural border. Elevation extremes in Myanmar range from 5,881m (Hkakabo Razi) to 0m (Andaman Sea). The lowlands are drained by the Irrawaddy river and its chief tributary, the Chindwin, and the eastern mountains by the Salween. The Irrawaddy has a large delta on the Andaman coast. The climate is tropical, with a wet season from May to September. Average temperatures in Mandalay, representative of the interior lowlands, range from 20°C in January to 32°C in April, although temperatures in the interior can reach 44°C in May.

HISTORY AND POLITICS

Myanmar (also known as Burma) was first unified in the 11th century by King Anawrahta, who adopted Theravada Buddhism; his successors ruled the area until an invasion by the Mongols under Kublai Khan in 1287. The country was reunified in the 15th century but was weakened by internal dissension and wars with Siam (Thailand). King Alaunghpaya reunited the nation in the 18th century. In the first half of the 19th century, border disputes with British India spiralled into a series of wars. Following the third Anglo-Burmese war, Burma was annexed as part of British India in 1885. It became a self-governing protectorate in 1937, and was occupied by the Japanese during the Second World War. Following liberation by British troops and Burmese nationalists, the country gained independence as the Union of Burma in 1948.

Following a left-wing military coup in 1962, the economy was nationalised, and in 1974 a one-party socialist republic was formally established. Following a coup in 1988, all existing state institutions were replaced by the State Law and Order Council (SLORC), martial law was imposed and the country's name was changed to Myanmar; the SLORC was replaced by the State Peace and Development Council (SPDC) in 1997.

Pro-democracy forces, notably the National League for Democracy (NLD) under Aung San Suu Kyi, opposed military rule. In 1990 the NLD won a landslide victory in the first multiparty elections for 30 years, but the military ignored the election results and continued to rule by diktat, suppressing and persecuting pro-democracy campaigners. Aung San Suu Kyi was under house arrest for 15 of the 21 years from 1989 to 2010.

A new constitution was put to a referendum in 2008; the government claimed that 92 per cent of the 99 per cent turnout voted in favour. In preparation for legislative elections in late 2010, several electoral laws were introduced in March 2010; these excluded many political activists, such as Aung San Suu Kyi, from participation in the elections, set restrictive conditions for party registration, and tightly regulated campaigning and funding; the NLD announced a boycott of the elections. Several members of the government resigned their military commissions to contest the elections as civilians, registering a new political party, the Union Solidarity and Development Party (USDP).

In November 2010, the USDP won 259 of the seats in the lower chamber and 129 of the seats in the upper chamber in elections that opposition groups claimed were fraudulent and that were condemned internationally as a sham. The new legislature convened in January 2011, electing prime minister Thein Sein as president in February 2011. A new, nominally civilian government was sworn in on 30 March, and the dissolution of the SPDC was announced.

INSURGENCIES

Since independence in 1948 there have been various insurgencies, mostly by ethnic groups. These have included the Kachin, Kayin (Karen), Karenni, Wa, Shan, Mon, Arakan Chin and Kokang ethnic minorities. Since 1992, 18 ethnic groups have signed ceasefire agreements; the government is accused of breaking four of these since the November 2010 election. Some groups have achieved a degree of autonomy in their region; others have splintered, creating intra-ethnic tension. The country's ethnic minorities are believed to bear the brunt of the government's human rights abuses; military offensives against insurgents have displaced over half a million people.

POLITICAL SYSTEM

Under the 2010 constitution, the head of state is a president elected by the legislature for a five-year term, renewable once. The president is also head of government and appoints ministers with the approval of the legislature. The bicameral People's Assembly comprises the 440-member House of Representatives, the lower chamber, and the 224-member House of Nationalities. In each chamber, 25 per cent of seats are reserved for the military and the rest are directly elected; both chambers serve a five-year term. Constitutional changes require approval by a 75 per cent majority.

HEAD OF STATE
President, Chair of National Defence and Security Council,
   Lt.-Gen. (retd) Thein Sein
Vice-presidents, Gen. (retd) Thura Tin Aung Myint Oo;
   Sai Mauk Kham

SELECTED GOVERNMENT MEMBERS *as at July 2011*
Finance and Revenue, Gen. Hla Htun
Foreign Affairs, Gen. (retd) Wunna Maung Lwin
Home Affairs, Lt.-Gen. Ko Ko
Defence, Maj.-Gen. (retd) Hla Min

EMBASSY OF THE UNION OF MYANMAR
19A Charles Street, London W1X 8ER
T 020-7499 4340 E melondon@btconnect.com
Ambassador Extraordinary and Plenipotentiary, HE U Kyaw
   Myo Htut, *apptd* 2011

BRITISH EMBASSY
PO Box 638, 80 Strand Road, Yangon
T (+95) (1) 380 322 E be.rangoon@fco.gov.uk
W http://ukinburma.fco.gov.uk
Ambassador Extraordinary and Plenipotentiary, HE Andrew
   Heyn, *apptd* 2009

BRITISH COUNCIL
PO Box 638, 78 Kanna Road, Yangon
T (+95) (1) 254 658/256 290 W www.britishcouncil.org/burma
Director, Alan Smart

DEFENCE

The army has 150 main battle tanks and 325 armoured personnel carriers. The navy has 70 patrol and coastal combatant vessels at 6 bases. The air force has 136 combat aircraft.

Military budget – US$1,900m (2009 est)
Military personnel – 406,000: army 375,000, navy 16,000, air force 15,000; paramilitary 107,250

ECONOMY AND TRADE

Myanmar has fertile soil and an abundance of natural resources such as natural gas (it is Asia's largest exporter), timber (it is the world's largest exporter of teak), precious gems (jade, pearls, rubies and sapphires) and oil, but the economy is characterised by mismanagement and corruption. The country has become increasingly poverty-stricken under military rule and around a third of the population lives below the poverty line. The economy suffers from unpredictable policies, market distortions and inadequate commercial, transport and energy infrastructure. The regime's repressiveness has lost it development aid and attracted economic and trade sanctions since the 1990s. There is a large grey economy and considerable unofficial cross-border trade.

Agriculture is the dominant economic activity, accounting for 43.2 per cent of GDP and engaging 70 per cent of the workforce; the most important export crops are rice, pulses, beans and fish. Cyclone Nargis in 2008 flooded large tracts of arable land in the Irrawaddy delta, killed livestock and destroyed fishing boats; official obstructiveness towards or diversion of international relief has slowed the pace of recovery. The main industries are forestry, mining and oil and gas extraction, and these have attracted some foreign investment; manufacturing and services are struggling, and the then growing tourist industry declined dramatically after the violent suppression of demonstrations in 2007. Industry contributes 20 per cent of GDP and services 36.8 per cent.

The main trading partners are Thailand (47 per cent of exports; 26 per cent of imports), China (33 per cent of imports), Singapore and India. Principal exports are natural gas, wood products, agricultural produce, clothing and gems. The main imports are fabric, petroleum products, fertiliser, plastics, machinery, transport equipment, construction materials, crude oil and food.

Annual average growth of GDP – 3.1 per cent (2010 est)
Inflation rate – 9.6 per cent (2010 est)
Population below poverty line – 32.7 per cent (2007 est)
Unemployment – 5.7 per cent (2010 est)
Total external debt – US$7,145m (2010 est)
Imports – US$4,400m (2009)
Exports – US$6,700m (2009)

BALANCE OF PAYMENTS
Trade – US$1,505m surplus (2010)
Current Account – US$697m deficit (2008)

COMMUNICATIONS

The 12,800km of navigable waterways include the Irrawaddy and Chindwin rivers; the main stream of the Irrawaddy is navigable for 1,440km and carries most of the country's traffic. The chief seaports are Yangon (Rangoon), Mawlamyine (Moulmein) and Akyab (Sittwe).

The railway network of 5,031km covers most of the country. There are 27,000km of roads. The main airports are at Yangon and Mandalay.

The telephone system is rudimentary and domestic services are poor. Mobile phone services are more efficient than fixed lines and growing more quickly, with 502,000 mobile phones in 2009, compared to 812,000 fixed lines.

EDUCATION AND HEALTH

Literacy rate – 89.9 per cent (2008 est)
Gross enrolment ratio (percentage of relevant age group) – primary 115 per cent; secondary 49 per cent; tertiary 11 per cent (2007 est)
Health expenditure (per capita) – US$12 (2009)
Hospital beds (per 1,000 people) – 0.6 (2004–9)

MEDIA

The government controls and censors all media, including the four national newspapers, four television stations and the internet. Editors and journalists are answerable to the military authorities, ensuring that self-censorship is widespread. Democratic Voice of Burma, an opposition radio station broadcasting via short-wave from Norway, and foreign services such as the BBC and Voice of America, are key sources of information for the population.

NAMIBIA

Republic of Namibia

Area – 824,292 sq. km
Capital – Windhoek; population, 341,722 (2009 est)
Major towns – Rundu, Walvis Bay
Currency – Namibian dollar of 100 cents, at parity with South African rand
Population – 2,128,471 rising at 0.91 per cent a year (2010 est); Ovambo (50 per cent), Kavangos (9 per cent), Herero (7 per cent), Damara (7 per cent), Nama (5 per cent), Caprivian (4 per cent), San (Bushmen) (3 per cent), Baster (2 per cent) (est)
Religion – Christian 90 per cent (predominantly Lutheran, Roman Catholic and Anglican); Muslim, Baha'i, Jewish and Buddhist minorities.. Many of the remainder practise indigenous religions
Language – English (official), Afrikaans (lingua franca), German, Oshiwambo, Herero, Nama, other indigenous languages
Population density – 3 per sq. km (2009)
Urban population – 37 per cent (2008 est)
Median age (years) – 21.4 (2010 est)
National anthem – 'Namibia, Land of the Brave'
National day – 21 March (Independence Day)
Life expectancy (years) – 51.95 (2010 est)

Mortality rate – 12.97 (2010 est)
Birth rate – 21.82 (2010 est)
Infant mortality rate – 45.52 (2010 est)
HIV/AIDS adult prevalence – 13.1 per cent (2009 est)
Death penalty – Abolished for all crimes (since 1990)
CPI score – 4.4 (2010)
Literacy rate – 88.3 per cent (2008 est)
Gross enrolment ratio (percentage of relevant age group) – primary 112 per cent; secondary 66 per cent; tertiary 9 per cent (2008 est)
Health expenditure (per capita) – US$258 (2009)
Hospital beds (per 1,000 people) – 2.7 (2004–9)

CLIMATE AND TERRAIN
The Namib desert runs along the Atlantic coast and is separated by a line of hills and high veldt from the Kalahari desert in the interior. Elevation extremes range from 2,606m (Konigstein) to 0m (Atlantic Ocean). Major rivers include the Orange, which forms the southern border with South Africa, and the Zambezi, which runs through the Caprivi Strip in the extreme north-east of the country. The climate is arid in the west and semi-arid in the centre and north-east; rainfall is sparse and droughts are frequent. The coast is cooler and frequently foggy. Average temperatures in Windhoek range from 6°C in July to 30°C in December.

HISTORY AND POLITICS
Pre-colonial Namibia was inhabited by San and then by Bantu tribes. It was annexed by Germany in 1884 and named South West Africa. Indigenous uprisings against colonial settlement in the early 20th century were brutally suppressed, with some tribes suffering severe losses; the Herero and Nama were nearly wiped out. The territory was occupied by South Africa on behalf of the Allies in 1915 and after the First World War it became a League of Nations mandated territory, administered by South Africa.

The arrangement continued under the UN after the Second World War, but South Africa exceeded its mandate by effectively annexing the country, extending representation in the South Africa parliament to the white population in 1949, and applying apartheid in 1966. These actions were taken despite the UN's refusal to permit the country's incorporation into South Africa in 1946 and its termination of the mandate in 1966. In 1968, the UN changed the country's name to Namibia, and the South West Africa People's Organisation (SWAPO), which had campaigned for racial equality and independence since 1960, began a guerrilla war against South Africa.

South Africa's peace talks with Angola in 1988 led to agreement on independence for Namibia, and this was achieved on 21 March 1990; South Africa's Walvis Bay enclave was returned to Namibia in 1994.

The country has enjoyed stability since independence, apart from a brief period of secessionist violence in the Caprivi Strip in the late 1990s. In recent years there has been agitation for an acceleration of land reform, and the government programme moved from voluntary sales to expropriation of white-owned farms in 2005. The country's main problems arise from the demographic, economic and social impact of the high level of HIV/AIDS infection among the population.

SWAPO has been the dominant party since independence, holding the presidency and commanding a parliamentary majority without interruption. The 2004 presidential election was won by Hifikepunye Pohamba,
who was re-elected in November 2009. In the 2009 legislative elections, SWAPO retained its majority in both legislative chambers.

POLITICAL SYSTEM
Under the 1990 constitution, the executive president is directly elected for a five-year term, renewable once. There is a bicameral parliament consisting of a National Assembly, with 72 members directly elected for a five-year term and up to six additional non-voting members appointed by the president, and a National Council, whose 26 members are elected by the regional councils from among their own members for a six-year term; the latter's main function is to review and consider legislation from the lower chamber. The president appoints the prime minister and the other ministers.

HEAD OF STATE
President, Hifikepunye Pohamba, *elected* 16 November 2004, *sworn in* 21 March 2005, *re-elected* 2009

SELECTED GOVERNMENT MEMBERS *as at June 2011*
Prime Minister, Nahas Angula
Deputy Prime Minister, Marco Hausiku
Defence, Maj.-Gen. Charles Namoloh
Finance, Saara Kuugongelwa-Amathila
Foreign Affairs, Utoni Nujoma
Home Affairs, Rosalia Nghidinwa

HIGH COMMISSION FOR THE REPUBLIC OF NAMIBIA
6 Chandos Street, London W1G 9LU
T 020-7636 6244 **E** info@namibiahc.org.uk
W www.namibiahc.org.uk
High Commissioner, HE George Mbanga Liswaniso, *apptd* 2006

BRITISH HIGH COMMISSION
PO Box 22202, 116 Robert Mugabe Avenue, Windhoek
T (+264) (61) 274 800 **E** general.windhoek@fco.gov.uk
W http://ukinnamibia.fco.gov.uk
High Commissioner, HE Marianne Young, *apptd* 2011

BRITISH COUNCIL
PO Box 13392, 116 Robert Mugabe Avenue, Windhoek
T (+264) (61) 226 776 **W** www.britishcouncil.org/africa
Director, Ronnie Micallef

DEFENCE
The army has 60 armoured personnel carriers. The navy has 8 patrol and coastal combatant vessels at a base at Walvis Bay. The air force has 24 combat aircraft and 2 armed helicopters.
Military budget – US$408m (2010)
Military personnel – 9,200: army 9,000, navy 200; paramilitary 6,000

ECONOMY AND TRADE
Namibia is a poor country, with about half of the population living below the poverty line. Its arid terrain limits agriculture, but the emphasis on environmental protection (enshrined in the constitution) is helping the development of tourism. The country has rich mineral deposits; extraction of these is the main industrial activity and minerals account for over 50 per cent of foreign exchange earnings. This leaves the economy vulnerable to global price fluctuations, and the government is encouraging foreign investment to help diversification. Other industries process the products of the farming and

fisheries sectors. Agriculture operates mostly at subsistence level, accounting for 9 per cent of GDP but engaging two-thirds of the population.

The main trading partners are South Africa, the UK, Angola, Spain, Japan and China. Principal exports are diamonds, copper, gold, zinc, lead, uranium, cattle, processed fish and skins. The main imports are foodstuffs (particularly grain), petroleum products and fuel, machinery and equipment, and chemicals.

GNI – US$9,174m; US$4,270 per capita (2009)
Annual average growth of GDP – 4.1 per cent (2010 est)
Inflation rate – 4.6 per cent (2010 est)
Population below poverty line – 55.8 per cent (2005 est)
Unemployment – 51.2 per cent (2008 est)
Total external debt – US$2,373m (2010 est)
Imports – US$5,000m (2009)
Exports – US$3,300m (2009)

BALANCE OF PAYMENTS
Trade – US$2,239m deficit (2010)
Current Account – US$241m surplus (2008)

Trade with UK	2009	2010
Imports from UK	£22,710,996	£18,550,162
Exports to UK	£113,679,751	£275,810,567

COMMUNICATIONS
Namibia has 2,626km of railways and 64,189km of roads; a road bridge across the Zambezi links Namibia with Zambia, encouraging regional trade. The main airports are at Windhoek and Odangwa, with over 120 smaller airports and airfields around the country. The two main seaports are Walvis Bay and Luderitz.

Telephone services are good in both urban and rural areas. Fixed-line subscriptions have declined slightly, while mobile subscriptions have grown rapidly; combined density is about 65 per 100 people.

MEDIA
Freedom of the press is guaranteed by the constitution and government interference in reportage is rare. There are seven major newspapers, published in English, German, Afrikaans and Oshiwambo. The state-administered Namibian Broadcasting Corporation operates alongside a private television network and around 20 private and community radio stations.

NAURU

Republic of Nauru

Area – 21 sq. km
Capital – Yaren District (unofficial)
Currency – Australian dollar ($A) of 100 cents

Population – 9,267 rising at 0.59 per cent a year (2010 est); Nauruan (58 per cent), other Pacific Islander (26 per cent), Chinese (8 per cent), European (8 per cent) (est)
Religion – Christian (Protestant 46 per cent, Roman Catholic 33 per cent) (2002)
Language – Nauruan (official), English
Population density – 609.9 per sq. km (2004 est)
Urban population – 100 per cent (2008 est)
Median age (years) – 23.8 (2010 est)
National anthem – 'Nauru Bwiema' ('Song of Nauru')
National day – 31 January (Independence Day)
Life expectancy (years) – 64.99 (2010 est)
Mortality rate – 6.15 (2010 est)
Birth rate – 28.16 (2010 est)
Infant mortality rate – 8.81 (2010 est)
Death penalty – Retained (not used since 1968)

CLIMATE AND TERRAIN
Nauru is a low-lying island in the southern Pacific Ocean, 42km south of the equator and 4,000km north-east of Sydney, Australia. There is a fertile coastal plain but about 60 per cent of the land area consists of the central plateau, formed of phosphate, which has been extensively mined. The plateau rim is the highest point, at 61m; the lowest is 0m at sea level. The climate is tropical, with a rainy season from November to February.

HISTORY AND POLITICS
Nauru was first settled by Polynesian and Melanesian groups. The first Europeans to visit the island were British whalers in 1798 and by 1888 Nauru was annexed by Germany. At the outbreak of the First World War, Nauru was occupied by Australia, which continued to administer the island under a League of Nations mandate from 1920. The island was occupied by the Japanese in 1942–3, but in 1947 UN trusteeship status superseded the mandate and Nauru continued to be administered by Australia until it became independent on 31 January 1968.

A financial crisis since 2003 has caused some political instability, with five changes of president between January and August 2003 and two different presidents in 2004. A more stable period during Ludwig Scotty's second presidency (2004–7) saw the introduction of austerity measures and public sector reform, but Scotty lost a vote of confidence in December 2007 and was replaced by Marcus Stephen. The 2008 legislative election succeeded in breaking a parliamentary deadlock over the budget, but by early 2010 a realignment of political allegiances had produced another stalemate. Despite elections in April and June 2010 the legislature remained evenly split and unable to elect a new speaker or president for some months. President Stephen was re-elected in November, without recourse to a proposed constitutional change to end the deadlock.

POLITICAL SYSTEM
Under the 1968 constitution, the executive president is elected by the legislature from among its members for a three-year term. The unicameral parliament has 18 members, who are directly elected for a three-year term. The president appoints the cabinet. Although there are active political parties, most parliamentary candidates stand as independents.

HEAD OF STATE
President, Internal Affairs Marcus Stephen, *elected* 19 December 2007, *re-elected* 29 April 2008, 1 November 2010

SELECTED GOVERNMENT MEMBERS *as at June 2011*
Finance, Foreign Affairs, Kieren Keke
Justice, Mathew Batsiua
Commerce, Industry and Environment, Frederic Pitcher

HONORARY CONSULATE
Romshed Courtyard, Underriver, Sevenoaks, Kent TN15 0SD
T 01732-746061 E nauru@weald.co.uk
Honorary Consul, Martin Weston

BRITISH HIGH COMMISSIONER
HE Malcolm McLachlan, MBE, *apptd* 2009, resident at
Suva, Fiji

ECONOMY AND TRADE
Phosphate is the only resource and its extraction is the
sole industry, but reserves will be exhausted before the
mid-21st century. Profits derived from the mining
industry were invested in trust funds to provide for the
post-mining future, but heavy spending from the funds
has left the country virtually bankrupt, causing it to
default on loans and have assets seized in 2004. Nauru
accommodated asylum seekers for Australia between
2001 and 2008, but the loss of this revenue has left the
economy dependent on international aid (principally from
Australia) and revenue from the sale of fishing licences.
Diversification efforts include offshore banking and
small-scale tourism.
   The main trading partners are Australia and New
Zealand. The only export is phosphate. All food, fuel,
manufactured goods, machinery and construction
materials have to be imported.
Unemployment – 90 per cent (2004 est)
Total external debt – US$33.3m (2004 est)

Trade with UK	2009	2010
Imports from UK	£36,844	£220,576
Exports to UK	£31,636	£2,928

EDUCATION AND MEDIA
Education is free of charge and compulsory between the
ages of six and 17.
   Nauru has no daily press but there are three weekly or
fortnightly publications. A government-owned radio
service broadcasts material from the BBC and Radio
Australia, and the government-owned Nauru Television
broadcasts programmes from New Zealand.

NEPAL

*Sanghiya Loktantrik Ganatantra Nepal – Federal Democratic
Republic of Nepal*

Area – 147,181 sq. km
Capital – Kathmandu; population, 989,730 (2009 est)
Major cities – Biratnagar, Lalitpur, Pokhara
Currency – Nepalese rupee of 100 paisa
Population – 28,951,852 rising at 1.42 per cent a year
   (2010 est); Chhettri (15.5 per cent), Brahman-Hill
   (12.5 per cent), Magar (7 per cent), Tharu (6.6 per
   cent), Tamang (5.5 per cent), Newar (5.4 per cent),
   Kami (3.9 per cent), Yadav (3.9 per cent) (2001)
Religion – Hindu 80 per cent, Buddhist 9 per cent,
   Muslim 4 per cent (predominantly Sunni), Christian
   2 per cent (est)
Language – Nepali (official), English, Maithali, Bhojpuri,
   Tharu, Tamang, Newar, Magar, Awadhi
Population density – 205 per sq. km (2009)
Urban population – 17 per cent (2008 est)
Median age (years) – 21.2 (2010 est)
National anthem – 'Sayaun Thunga Phool Ka' ['Hundreds
   of Flowers']
Life expectancy (years) – 65.81 (2010 est)
Mortality rate – 6.89 (2010 est)
Birth rate – 22.43 (2010 est)
Infant mortality rate – 46 (2010 est)
Death penalty – Abolished for all crimes (since 1997)
CPI score – 2.2 (2010)

CLIMATE AND TERRAIN
The north of landlocked Nepal lies in the Himalayas, with
the snowline at about 4,880m. The terrain descends from
the mountains through a hilly central region with fertile
valleys to the southern plains, the Terai, that lie in the
valley of the Ganges. Elevation extremes range from
8,850m (Mt Everest), to 70m (Kanchan Kalan). The
climate varies from subtropical in the south to much
cooler with severe winters in the north. Average
temperatures in Kathmandu range from 1°C in January to
30-°C in May. The rainy season lasts from June to
September.

HISTORY AND POLITICS
Modern Nepal was formed from a number of small states
that were conquered and unified in the 18th century by
the Gurkha ruler Prithvi Naryan Shah. After war with the
British in 1815–16, Nepal became a British-dependent
buffer state; its independence was formally recognised in
1923.
   Power was seized by Jung Bahdur in 1846. He
assumed the title Rana and his family became hereditary
chief ministers, reducing the monarchy to a purely
ceremonial role and keeping the country isolated. In
1950–1, the Ranas were overthrown and the monarchy
was restored to power. Apart from 1959–60, when a
parliamentary system of government was in place, the
kings ruled as absolute monarchs until 1990, when a new
constitution was introduced that made the country a
constitutional monarchy and multiparty parliamentary
democracy.
   However, factionalism led to frequent changes of
government, causing political and social instability, which
was exacerbated from 1996 by a Maoist insurgency led by
the Nepal Communist Party. The insurgency began in the
west and quickly spread, despite the government's often
brutal attempts at suppression, and by 2006 the
insurgents controlled 80 per cent of the country.
   King Gyanendra's assumption of direct rule in 2005
led politicians to ally themselves with the Maoists to
achieve the restoration of democracy, and in April 2006

the king reinstated the legislature after three months of violent pro-democracy protests. In November 2006 a peace accord was signed with the Maoists, who then participated in the interim legislature set up in January 2007 and the multiparty government that took office in April.

Elections to the constituent assembly took place in April 2008, and candidates of the Communist Party of Nepal–Maoists (CPN-M) won the most seats. At its first meeting on 28 May 2008, the assembly declared the country a republic and abolished the monarchy. The assembly elected Ram Baran Yadav of the Nepali Congress party as the country's first president in July, and in August the CPN-M leader, Pushpa Kamal Dahal ('Prachanda'), was elected prime minister and formed a six-party coalition government. The prime minister and deputy prime minister resigned in May 2009 after a disagreement with the president, and Madhav Kumar Nepal, of the Marxist-Leninist Communists (CPN-UML), was appointed prime minister and appointed a new coalition government. This excluded the CPN-M, and the political stalemate that ensued crippled the government and threatened to undermine the peace process. Mr Nepal resigned in June 2010 and Jhalanath Khanal, leader of the CPN-UML, was elected prime minister in February 2011.

POLITICAL SYSTEM

The 2007 interim constitution is in force until a new constitution is drafted by the constituent assembly and is approved. The monarchy was abolished in May 2008 and the country declared a republic. The head of state is the president, who was elected by the constituent assembly. The interim legislature was replaced in May 2008 by a constituent assembly with 601 members, 240 directly elected, 335 elected by proportional representation and 26 appointed by the council of ministers. In May 2010 the assembly voted to extend its original term, which had expired, by an additional year, as it had failed to draft a new constitution. The prime minister is appointed by consensus among the political parties or elected by a two-thirds majority of the assembly. The council of ministers is responsible to the legislature.

HEAD OF STATE

President, Ram Baran Yadav, *elected* 21 July 2008, *sworn in* 23 July 2008
Vice-President, Paramananda Jha

SELECTED GOVERNMENT MEMBERS *as at July 2011*
Chair of the Council of Ministers, Jhalanath Khanal
Finance, Bharat Adhikari
Defence, Bishnu Paudel
Home Affairs, Krishna Mahara

EMBASSY OF NEPAL

12A Kensington Palace Gardens, London W8 4QU
T 020-7229 1594 E eon@nepembassy.org.uk
W www.nepembassy.org.uk
Ambassador Extraordinary and Plenipotentiary,
HE Dr Suresh Chandra Chalise, *apptd* 2010

BRITISH EMBASSY

PO Box 106, Lainchaur, Kathmandu
T (+977) (1) 441 0583 E bekathmandu@fco.gov.uk
W http://ukinnepal.fco.gov.uk
Ambassador Extraordinary and Plenipotentiary,
HE John Tucknott, MBE, *apptd* 2010

BRITISH COUNCIL

PO Box 640, Lainchaur, Kathmandu
T (+977) (1) 4410 798 W www.britishcouncil.org/nepal
Country Manager, Paula Middleton

DEFENCE

The army has 40 armoured personnel carriers.
Military budget – US$245m (2010)
Military personnel – 95,753: army 95,753; paramilitary 62,000

ECONOMY AND TRADE

The country is one of the poorest in Asia, and the economy is dependent on foreign aid and trade with India. The major foreign exchange earners are tourism, the main industry, and expatriates' remittances; both suffered a delayed effect of the global economic downturn in 2010. Tourism and hydroelectric power have potential for development, although this might compound growing environmental problems.

Agriculture is the main economic sector, generating 33 per cent of GDP and engaging about 75 per cent of the workforce; principal crops are pulses, rice, maize, wheat, sugar cane, jute, root crops, milk and meat. Industries other than tourism include carpets, textiles, cigarettes, cement and bricks, and the processing of rice, jute, sugar and oilseed. Industry accounts for 15 per cent of GDP and services for 52 per cent.

The main export markets are India (58 per cent), the USA, Bangladesh and Germany; the main import providers are India (52 per cent) and China. Principal exports are clothing, pulses, carpets, textiles, juice, pashmina and jute goods. The main imports are petroleum products, machinery and equipment, gold, electrical goods and medicine.

GNI – US$12,829m; US$440 per capita (2009)
Annual average growth of GDP – 3.5 per cent (2010 est)
Inflation rate – 8.6 per cent (2010 est)
Population below poverty line – 24.7 per cent (2008)
Unemployment – 46 per cent (2008)
Total external debt – US$4,500m (2009 est)
Imports – US$3,700m (2009)
Exports – US$900m (2009)

BALANCE OF PAYMENTS

Trade – US$3,010m deficit (2010)
Current Account – US$536m surplus (2009)

Trade with UK	2009	2010
Imports from UK	£6,328,011	£9,163,924
Exports to UK	£12,373,916	£13,376,550

COMMUNICATIONS

There is a total of 17,282km of roads, of which over half are surfaced. A major highway runs the length of the country through the Terai, linking the main lowland centres and extending into the hills to Kathmandu and Pokhara. Other highways connect Kathmandu with India and Tibet. There are 59km of railways. The principal airport is at Kathmandu, and there are over 40 smaller airports and airfields around the country.

The telephone system is extensive but fixed-line services are poor; mobile phone distribution is expanding rapidly. In 2009 there were 820,500 fixed telephone lines in use, 7.6 million mobile phone subscribers and 577,800 internet users.   •

EDUCATION AND HEALTH

Literacy rate – 57.8 per cent (2008 est)
Gross enrolment ratio (percentage of relevant age group) –
primary 124 per cent; secondary 43 per cent (2008 est)
Health expenditure (per capita) – US$25 (2009)
Hospital beds (per 1,000 people) – 5.0 (2004–9)

MEDIA

The draconian media laws introduced during the insurgency have been eased since 2006 but remain strict; journalists operating in the Terai region can face death threats and physical attacks from armed groups. Private television and radio stations operate alongside government-run networks. The two semi-official newspapers have the widest circulations of the dailies.

THE NETHERLANDS

Koninkrijk der Nederlanden – Kingdom of the Netherlands

Area – 41,543 sq. km
Capital – Amsterdam; population, 1,043,700 (2009 est)
Seat of government – The Hague (Den Haag or, in full,
's-Gravenhage), population 629,185 (2009 est)
Major cities – Almere, Eindhoven, Rotterdam, Tilburg,
Utrecht
Currency – Euro (€) of 100 cents
Population – 16,783,092 rising at 0.39 per cent a year
(2010 est); Dutch (80.7 per cent), Indonesian (2.4 per
cent), Turkish (2.2 per cent), Surinamese (2 per cent),
Moroccan (2 per cent) (2008 est)
Religion – Christian 50 per cent (Roman Catholic 30 per
cent, Protestant 20 per cent), Muslim 6 per cent (2006)
Language – Dutch, Frisian (both official); English is widely
spoken
Population density – 490 per sq. km (2009)
Urban population – 82 per cent (2008 est)
Median age (years) – 40.8 (2010 est)
National anthem – 'Het Wilhelmus' ['The William']
National day – 30 April (Queen's Day)
Life expectancy (years) – 79.55 (2010 est)
Mortality rate – 8.78 (2010 est)
Birth rate – 10.3 (2010 est)
Infant mortality rate – 4.66 (2010 est)
Death penalty – Abolished for all crimes (since 1982)
CPI score – 8.8 (2010)

CLIMATE AND TERRAIN

The Netherlands is a low-lying country; about a quarter is below sea level, making it susceptible to flooding despite the coastal defences and a network of dykes and canals. Its land area has been extended over the centuries by land reclamation (polders), found especially in the west around

the huge freshwater lake of Yssel, created in the 1930s by damming the Zuider Zee. The country is crossed by three major European rivers, the Rhine, Maas (Meuse) and Scheldt, whose estuaries are in the south-west. Mount Scenery (862m), on the Caribbean island of Saba, is considered the highest point of the Kingdom of the Netherlands. Elevation extremes in the Netherlands itself range from 322m (Vaalserberg) to −7m (Zuidplaspolder). The climate is temperate, with average temperatures in De Bilt ranging from −1°C in January to 22°C in July.

HISTORY AND POLITICS

The area was part of the Frankish Empire by the eighth century and subsequently of Middle Francia. From the 10th century, the various counties, dioceses and mercantile towns became virtually independent states owing fealty to various overlords, including the Holy Roman Emperor. In the 15th century these came under the rule of the dukes of Burgundy and then of the Habsburgs from 1477, passing to the Spanish branch of the Habsburgs in 1555. The northern provinces, led by William, Prince of Orange, rebelled against Spanish rule in 1568. The war of independence ended with the seven northern provinces forming the Union of Utrecht in 1579, and in 1581 independence was declared; the United Provinces were formally recognised as an independent republic in 1648.

The 17th century was a golden age in which the Dutch led the world in trade, art and science, founding colonies in the East and West Indies. Commercial and colonial rivalries led to three wars with Britain in the late 17th century, and resisting French attempts at domination exhausted the country in the 18th century. In 1795, French revolutionary armies overran the country and it remained under French rule until 1813. In 1815, the northern and southern provinces were reunited into one kingdom, with the hereditary *stadtholder* of the northern provinces becoming King William I of the Netherlands and grand duke of Luxembourg. The southern provinces seceded to form Belgium in 1830 and the Duchy of Luxembourg was made an independent state in 1867. The Netherlands was neutral during the First World War, but during the Second World War the country was invaded and occupied by Germany from 1940 until 1945.

The post-war period was marked by economic expansion, the construction of a liberal welfare state and decolonisation. The Netherlands formed the Benelux economic union with Belgium and Luxembourg in 1948, was a founder member of the EEC in 1958 and joined the eurozone in 1999.

Although it is a stable democracy, one party has rarely commanded a sufficient parliamentary majority to govern alone in the post-war period; governments have usually been coalitions of two or more parties. The collapse of a coalition of the Christian Democratic Alliance (CDA), the Labour Party (PvdA) and the Christian Union (CU) in February 2010 led to an election in June in which the People's Party for Freedom and Democracy (VVD) won 31 seats to the PvdA's 30 and CDA's 21. The VVD formed a minority government with the CDA and is dependent on the support of the Freedom Party (24 seats) to pass legislation.

POLITICAL SYSTEM

The kingdom consists of four autonomous elements: the Netherlands (European and Caribbean Netherlands), Aruba, Curacao and St Maarten. Under the 1983 constitution, the head of state is a hereditary constitutional monarch. The States-General *(Staten-Generaal)* consists of the First Chamber *(Eerste Kamer)* of 75 members, elected for a four-year term by the Provincial States; and the Second Chamber *(Tweede Kamer)* of 150 members, directly elected for a four-year term. The head of government is the prime minister, who is responsible to the legislature.

HEAD OF STATE
HM The Queen of the Netherlands, Queen Beatrix
  Wilhelmina Armgard, KG, GCVO, *born* 31 January
  1938; *succeeded* 30 April 1980
Heir, HRH Prince Willem Alexander, *born* 27 April 1967

SELECTED GOVERNMENT MEMBERS *as at July 2011*
Prime Minister, Mark Rutte
Deputy Prime Minister, Maxime Verhagen
Defence, Hans Hillen
Foreign Affairs, Uri Rosenthal
Finance, Jan Kees de Jager

ROYAL NETHERLANDS EMBASSY
38 Hyde Park Gate, London SW7 5DP
T 020-7590 3200 E london@netherlands-embassy.org.uk
W www.netherlands-embassy.org.uk
Ambassador Extraordinary and Plenipotentiary,
  HE Pieter Waldeck, *apptd* 2007

BRITISH EMBASSY
Lange Voorhout 10, The Hague, 2514 ED
T (+31) (70) 427 0427 E ukinnl@fco.gov.uk
W http://ukinnl.fco.gov.uk
Ambassador Extraordinary and Plenipotentiary,
  HE Paul Arkwright, *apptd* 2009

BRITISH COUNCIL
Weteringschans 85A, Amsterdam, 1017 RZ
T (+31) (20) 550 6060 W www.britishcouncil.org/netherlands
Director, Martin Hope

DEFENCE
The army has 44 main battle tanks, 151 armoured infantry fighting vehicles and 16 armoured personnel carriers. The navy has 4 submarines, 4 destroyers, and 2 frigates at 2 bases. The air force has 72 combat aircraft and 29 armed helicopters.
Military budget – US$11,300m (2010)
Military personnel – 37,368: army 20,836, navy 8,502,
  air force 8,030, military constabulary 5,911

ECONOMY AND TRADE
The Netherlands has a highly industrialised and diversified market economy, and is a major European transportation hub. The economy depends heavily on foreign trade and financial services, and contracted sharply in 2009 as exports fell by almost 25 per cent in the global economic downturn. The government nationalised two banks to stabilise the financial sector and introduced stimulus measures, creating a budget deficit.

The highly mechanised agricultural sector employs only 2 per cent of the workforce but output supplies the food processing industries and the export as well as the domestic market. Flower bulbs and cut flowers are a major contributor to this sector, as is the fishing industry. The industrial sector contributes 24.9 per cent of GDP; major industries include food processing, and the manufacture

of metal and engineering products, electrical machinery and equipment, chemicals, oil refining, construction and micro-electronics. The service industries represent 72.4 per cent of the economy. Other EU countries, China and the USA account for most overseas trade. Principal exports are machinery and equipment, chemicals, fuels and foodstuffs. The main imports are machinery and transport equipment, chemicals, fuels, foodstuffs and clothing.
GNI – US$773,940m; US$48,460 per capita (2009)
Annual average growth of GDP – 1.7 per cent (2010 est)
Inflation rate – 1.1 per cent (2010 est)
Population below poverty line – 10.5 per cent (2005)
Unemployment – 5.5 per cent (2010 est)
Total external debt – US$3,733,000m (2009 est)
Imports – US$384,700m (2009)
Exports – US$431,800m (2009)

BALANCE OF PAYMENTS
Trade – US$51,293m surplus (2010)
Current Account – US$41,652m surplus (2009)

Trade with UK	2009	2010
Imports from UK	£17,380,275,200	£20,565,717,098
Exports to UK	£21,226,934,388	£26,097,522,275

COMMUNICATIONS
The main seaport is Rotterdam, although there are a number of other ports on river estuaries or linked to the coast by the canals; 6,214km of inland waterways, including canals, are navigable by ships of up to 50 tonnes. The large merchant fleet includes 706 ships of over 1,000 tonnes. There are 136,827,km of roads and 2,900km of railways, of which 2,195km are electrified. The principal airports are at Amsterdam, Rotterdam, Eindhoven and Maastricht, with a further 23 smaller airports and airfields around the country.

There is a modern telephone system and a very high density of mobile phone ownership. In 2009 there were 7.3 million fixed telephone lines in use, 21.2 mobile phone subscribers and 14.8 million internet users.

EDUCATION AND HEALTH
Thirteen years of compulsory primary and secondary education are provided by denominational and state schools. The principal universities are at Leiden, Utrecht, Groningen, Amsterdam, Nijmegen, Maastricht and Rotterdam.
Gross enrolment ratio (percentage of relevant age group) –
  primary 107 per cent; secondary 121 per cent; tertiary
  61 per cent (2008 est)
Health expenditure (per capita) – US$5,164 (2009)
Hospital beds (per 1,000 people) – 4.3 (2004–9)

MEDIA
Ownership of the five national newspapers is highly concentrated. A competitive broadcasting sector includes Nederlandse Omroep Stichting (NOS), which oversees the country's public television networks and radio stations, and a large number of commercial stations. Public broadcasters are statutorily obliged to allocate airtime to different political, religious or other interest groups according to the number of members each has. Freedom of the press is guaranteed by the constitution.

CULTURE

The Netherlands has produced many major artists, particularly during the golden age between 1580 and 1700; these include Rembrandt (1606–69) and Vermeer (1632–75), and later figures such as Vincent van Gogh (1853–90), Piet Mondrian (1872–1944) and M. C. Escher (1898–1972). Other notables are mathematician and physicist Christiaan Huygens (1629–95), who made the first pendulum clock, and philosopher Baruch Spinoza (1632–77).

OVERSEAS TERRITORIES

The Kingdom of the Netherlands consists of four autonomous elements: the Netherlands (European and Caribbean Netherlands), Aruba, Curacao and St Maarten; the latter two were part of the Netherlands Antilles until its dissolution on 10 October 2010. The other three islands of the Netherlands Antilles, the 'Caribbean Netherlands', comprising Bonaire, St Eustatius and Saba, are now autonomous special municipalities of the Netherlands.

ARUBA
Area – 193 sq. km
Capital – Oranjestad; population, 33,112 (2009 est)
Major town – Sint Nicolaas
Currency – Aruban guilder/florin of 100 cents
Population – 106,113 rising at 1.43 per cent a year (2011 est)
Language – Dutch (official), Papiamento, Spanish, English
National Day – 18 March (Flag Day)

The Caribbean island was colonised by the Dutch in the 17th century. It was part of the Netherlands Antilles until 1986, when it became a separate, autonomous territory. The Dutch government is responsible for external affairs and represented by a resident governor. Internal government is in the hands of the prime minister and council of ministers, who are responsible to the 21-member unicameral legislature (*Staten*), directly elected for a four-year term.

The principal economic activities are tourism and offshore financial services.
Governor, Fredis Refunjol, *apptd* 2004
Prime Minister, Mike Eman, *elected* 2009

CURACAO
Area – 444 sq. km
Capital – Willemstad; population, 123,355 (2009 est)
Currency – Netherlands Antilles guilder of 100 cents; to be replaced by the Caribbean guilder in January 2012
Population – 142,180 (2010 est)
Language – Dutch (official), Papiamento, English, Spanish

The island was colonised by the Dutch in the 17th century and was part of the Netherlands Antilles from 1954 until 10 October 2010, when it became a separate, autonomous territory. The Dutch government is responsible for external affairs and represented by a resident governor. Internal affairs are in the hands of a prime minister and council of ministers, who are responsible to the 21-member unicameral legislature (*Staten*), which serves a four-year term.

The principal economic activities are tourism, oil refining and offshore financial services.
Governor, Gen. Frits Goedgedrag, *apptd* 2002
Prime Minister, Gerrit Schotte, *elected* 2010

ST MAARTEN
Area – 34 sq. km
Capital – Philipsburg
Currency – Netherlands Antilles guilder of 100 cents; to be replaced by the Caribbean guilder in January 2012
Population – 37,429 (2010)
Language – Dutch, English (official), Spanish, Creole

The territory forms the southern part of the island of St Martin in the Caribbean; the north is French territory. Possession of the island was disputed between the Dutch and the Spanish until 1648, when the Spanish relinquished it to the Dutch and French, who divided it between them. The Dutch territory was part of the Netherlands Antilles from 1954 until 10 October 2010, when it became a separate, autonomous territory. The Dutch government is responsible for external affairs and represented by a governor. Internal affairs are in the hands of a prime minister and council of ministers, who are responsible to the 15-member unicameral legislature (*Staten*), which serves a four-year term.

The principal economic activities are tourism and sugar production.
Governor, Eugene Holiday, *apptd 2010*
Prime Minister, Sarah Westcott-Williams, *apptd 2010*

NEW ZEALAND

Aotearoa – New Zealand

Area – 267,710 sq. km (includes outlying islands)
Capital – Wellington; population, 391,201 (2009 est)
Major cities – Auckland, Christchurch, Dunedin, Hamilton, Manakau, North Shore, Tauranga, Waitakere
Currency – New Zealand dollar (NZ$) of 100 cents
Population – 4,252,277 rising at 0.9 per cent a year (2010 est); European (56.8 per cent), mixed (9.7 per cent), Asian (8 per cent), Maori (7.4 per cent), Pacific Islander (4.6 per cent) (2006)
Religion – Christian (Anglican 14 per cent, other Protestant 16 per cent, Roman Catholic 13 per cent, other 10 per cent), Hindu 2 per cent, Buddhist 1 per cent, other 2 per cent (2006)
Language – English, Maori, New Zealand Sign Language (all official)
Population density – 16 per sq. km (2009)
Urban population – 87 per cent (2008 est)
Median age (years) – 36.8 (2010 est)
National anthem – 'God Defend New Zealand'/'God Save the Queen'
National day – 6 February (Waitangi Day)
Life expectancy (years) – 80.48 (2010 est)
Mortality rate – 7.1 (2010 est)

Birth rate – 13.81 (2010 est)
Infant mortality rate – 4.85 (2010 est)
Death penalty – Abolished for all crimes (since 1989)
CPI score – 9.3 (2010)

CLIMATE AND TERRAIN

New Zealand consists of North Island, South Island and neighbouring coastal islands such as Stewart Island, and outlying islands that include the Chatham, Kermadec, Three Kings, Bounty, Antipodes, Snares, Auckland and Campbell groups in the South Pacific Ocean. The two larger islands, North Island and South Island, are separated by the relatively narrow Cook Strait. The island groups are much smaller and more widely dispersed.

Much of the North and South Islands is mountainous. The North Island mountains include several volcanoes, three of which are active. The principal range is the Southern Alps, extending the entire length of the South Island to the west of the Canterbury Plains. There are geysers and hot springs in the Rotorua district and glaciers in the Southern Alps. Elevation extremes range from 3,754m (Aoraki/Mt Cook) to 0m (Pacific Ocean). The climate is temperate, though with marked regional variations; average temperatures in Christchurch (South Island) range from 5°C in July to 20°C in January. The country is subject to seismic activity; a major earthquake devastated Christchurch in February 2011.

HISTORY AND POLITICS

Settled by Polynesian tribes, the ancestors of the Maori, from about the tenth century, New Zealand was sighted by the Dutch navigator Abel Tasman in 1642 but he did not land. The British explorer James Cook surveyed the coastline in 1769, the year in which the islands were claimed by the British. The Maori accepted British sovereignty in 1840, under the treaty of Waitangi, in return for land rights and the rights of British subjects. Large-scale European immigration and the 1860s gold rush led to encroachment by settlers and 'land wars' with the Maori in 1860 and 1872; Maori resistance was defeated but concessions such as parliamentary representation were won. A tribunal was set up in 1975 to consider grievances caused by breaches of the Waitangi treaty, and in the 1990s the Maori were compensated for land lost to European settlers.

New Zealand was administered as part of Britain's New South Wales colony until 1841, when it became a separate colony. In 1907 it was granted dominion status; in 1931 the Statute of Westminster tacitly acknowledged its independence, which was formally confirmed in 1947.

New Zealand forces took part in the Boer War, both world wars, the Korean War and the Vietnam War. Since the UK's entry into the EEC in 1973, the focus of New Zealand's foreign and trade policies has shifted to Asia and the Pacific region.

Post-war politics has been dominated by the National Party and the Labour Party, either forming governments on their own or in coalition with smaller parties; coalitions have been the norm since a proportional representation voting system was introduced in 1993. In the 2008 legislative election, the National Party won the most seats but without an overall majority, and formed a coalition government with the support of three smaller parties. A legislative election is scheduled for 26 November 2011.

POLITICAL SYSTEM

There is no written constitution. The head of state is Queen Elizabeth II, represented by the governor-general, who is appointed on the advice of the New Zealand government. The unicameral House of Representatives currently has 122 members (usually 120), elected for a three-year term; there are 70 members from single-member constituencies, which include seven Maori constituencies, and 52 (usually 50) allocated from party lists; if a party wins a significantly larger proportion of constituency seats relative to their party list vote, this can result in an 'overhang' of extra seats. The prime minister and the cabinet are appointed by the governor-general on the advice of the legislature.

GOVERNOR-GENERAL
Governor-General, HE Anand Satyanand, *sworn in* August 2006

SELECTED GOVERNMENT MEMBERS *as at June 2011*
Prime Minister, John Key
Deputy Prime Minister, Finance, Bill English
Defence, Wayne Mapp
Internal Affairs, Nathan Guy
Foreign Affairs, Murray McCully

NEW ZEALAND HIGH COMMISSION
New Zealand House, 80 Haymarket, London SW1Y 4TQ
T 020-7930 8422 E email@newzealandhc.org.uk
W www.nzembassy.com/uk
High Commissioner, HE Derek Leask, *apptd* 2008

BRITISH HIGH COMMISSION
PO Box 1812, 44 Hill Street, Wellington 6011
T (+64) (4) 924 2888 E consularmail.wellington@fco.gov.uk
W http://ukinnewzealand.fco.gov.uk
High Commissioner, HE Victoria Treadell, MVO *apptd* 2010

BRITISH COUNCIL
PO Box 91488, Victoria Street West, Auckland 1142
T (+64) (9) 302 3560 W www.britishcouncil.org/nz
Director, Ingrid Leary

DEFENCE

With Australia and the USA, New Zealand formed the ANZUS Pacific military security treaty in 1951, but its non-nuclear military policy led to disagreements with USA and France in 1985, and in 1986 the USA suspended its ANZUS obligations towards New Zealand.

The army has 105 armoured infantry fighting vehicles. The navy has 2 frigates and 6 patrol and coastal vessels based at Auckland. The air force has 6 combat aircraft.
Military budget – US$1,590m (2010)
Military personnel – 9,673: army 4,905, navy 2,161, air force 2,607

ECONOMY AND TRADE

Since the 1980s industrial and service sectors have developed to complement the large, efficient agricultural sector. Growth has been driven by trade, particularly in agricultural products, but various factors had pushed the economy into recession in 2008 before the global downturn. Government stimulus measures were introduced to cushion the effects of the recession in 2009, after which a fragile recovery began.

The agricultural sector contributes 4.6 per cent of GDP, employs 7 per cent of the workforce and provides 70–80 per cent of exports. The main products are dairy products, meat, cereals, pulses, fruit, vegetables, wool and fish. The major industries are food processing, wood and paper products, textiles, machinery, transport equipment, financial services, mining, and tourism, which is overtaking agriculture as the main source of foreign exchange revenue. Non-metallic minerals such as coal, limestone and dolomite are heavily exploited, and gold and iron production is economically important. Natural gas deposits in offshore and onshore fields are used for electricity generation, though a significant amount of the country's energy is derived from sustainable sources such as hydroelectric power. Industry contributes 24 per cent of GDP and services 71.4 per cent.

The main trading partners are Australia, China, the USA and Japan. Principal exports are dairy products, meat, wood, wood products, fish and machinery. The main imports are machinery and equipment, vehicles and aircraft, petroleum, electronics, textiles and plastics.
GNI – US$121,436m; US$28,810 per capita (2009)
Annual average growth of GDP – 2.1 per cent (2010 est)
Inflation rate – 2.6 per cent (2010 est)
Unemployment – 6.5 per cent (2010 est)
Total external debt – US$64,330m (2010 est)
Imports – US$25,600m (2009)
Exports – US$24,900m (2009)

BALANCE OF PAYMENTS
Trade – US$745m surplus (2010)
Current Account – US$3,565m deficit (2009)

Trade with UK*	2009	2010
Imports from UK	£327,480,741	£390,760,955
Exports to UK	£744,805,957	£766,875,068

* Includes Tokelau, Cook Islands and Niue

COMMUNICATIONS
The railway system was renationalised in 2008, and is now operated by the New Zealand Railways Corporation; there are 4,128km of railway track. There are 93,911km of roads, of which about 65 per cent are surfaced. The principal airports are at Auckland, Wellington (North Island), Christchurch and Dunedin (South Island) and there are over 110 smaller airports and airfields around the country; the government holds a 75.5 per cent stake in Air New Zealand. Tauranga, Christchurch, New Plymouth, Auckland and Napier are the main seaports.

In 2009 the telephone system provided 1.8 million fixed lines, and there were 4.7 million mobile phone subscribers and 3.4 million internet users.

EDUCATION AND HEALTH
Education is free of charge and compulsory between the ages of 5 and 16.
Gross enrolment ratio (percentage of relevant age group) – primary 101 per cent; secondary 119 per cent; tertiary 78 per cent (2008 est)
Health expenditure (per capita) – US$2,634 (2009)
Hospital beds (per 1,000 people) – 6.2 (2002–7)

MEDIA AND CULTURE
The broadcasting sector was deregulated in 1988. Two public television networks compete with three major private networks. The public radio broadcaster operates one international and three domestic stations, and there are a large number of private radio stations, including a Maori-language broadcaster. There are three main national daily papers.

The first Maori settlers brought the art form *Whakapapa,* a type of oral genealogy, to the islands. Notable cultural figures include the writer Katherine Mansfield (1888–1923), poet Sam Hunt (*b.* 1946), filmmakers Jane Campion (*b.* 1954) and Peter Jackson (*b.* 1961), opera singer Kiri Te Kanawa (*b.* 1944), and musical comedy duo Flight of the Conchords.

TERRITORIES

TOKELAU
Area – 12 sq. km
Population – 1,384 (2011 est)

Tokelau consists of three atolls, Fakaofo, Nukunonu and Atafu, in the southern Pacific Ocean. Formerly part of Britain's Gilbert and Ellice Islands colony, Tokelau was transferred to New Zealand administration in 1926 and proclaimed part of New Zealand in 1949.

The territory is self-administering, but has rejected greater autonomy in two referendums (2006 and 2007). The Council for the Ongoing Government (cabinet) comprises three *Faipule* (village leaders) and three *Pulenuku* (village mayors), one from each atoll; the position of *Ulu-o-Tokelau* (leader) is rotated among the three *Faipule* members annually. The *General Fono,* which has 20 members elected for a three-year term, has legislative powers. Each atoll has a *Taupulega* (council of elders).

The economy is dependent on New Zealand budgetary aid, with some revenue derived from remittances and the sale of fishing rights, stamps, coins and the use of its internet suffix. The main activities are subsistence farming, copra production and handicrafts.
Administrator, Jonathan Kings, *apptd* 2011

THE ROSS DEPENDENCY
New Zealand has administrative responsibility for the Ross Dependency. This is defined as all the Antarctic islands and territories between 160° E. and 150° W. longitude which are situated south of the 60° S. parallel, including Edward VII Land and portions of Victoria Land (*see also* The North and South Poles).

ASSOCIATED STATES

COOK ISLANDS
Area – 237 sq. km
Population – 11,124 (2011 est)
Capital – Avarua, on Rarotonga

The Cook Islands consist of 15 volcanic islands and coral atolls in the southern Pacific Ocean. A former British protectorate, since 1965 the islands have been self-governing in free association with New Zealand.

Queen Elizabeth II has a representative on the islands, and the New Zealand government is represented by a high commissioner. There is a 24-member legislative assembly, and the House of Ariki, made up of 15 traditional leaders who advise on traditional matters. Executive power is exercised by a prime minister and a cabinet responsible to the legislature.

The main economic activities are tourism, agriculture (especially tropical fruits), fruit processing, fishing, garment manufacturing, handicrafts and pearl-farming; black pearls are the main export.

HM Representative, Sir Frederick Goodwin, KBE, *apptd*
   2001
Prime Minister, Henry Puna *apptd* 2010

NIUE
Area – 260 sq. km
Population – 1,311 (2011 est)
Capital – Alofi; population, 547 (2009 est)

Although part of the Cook Islands group, Niue was
administered separately after 1903. Since 1974 the island
has been self-governing in free association with New
Zealand.

A New Zealand high commissioner represents both the
Queen and the New Zealand government. There is a
20-member legislative assembly; executive power is
exercised by a prime minister and a three-member cabinet
drawn from the assembly's members.

The principal economic activities are agriculture,
fishing, tourism, handicrafts, food processing and the sale
of postage stamps and the use of its internet suffix.

New Zealand High Commissioner, Mark Blumsky, *apptd*
   2011
Premier, Toke Talagi

NICARAGUA

República de Nicaragua – Republic of Nicaragua

Area – 130,370 sq. km
Capital – Managua; population, 934,156 (2009 est)
Major cities – Chinandega, Estelí, León, Masaya, Tipitapa
Currency – Córdoba (C$) of 100 centavos
Population – 5,995,928 rising at 1.74 per cent a year
   (2010 est)
Religion – Christian (Roman Catholic 56 per cent,
   Protestant 25 per cent) (est)
Language – Spanish (official), English, Miskito
Population density – 48 per sq. km (2009)
Urban population – 57 per cent (2008 est)
Median age (years) – 22.5 (2010 est)
National anthem – 'Salve a ti, Nicaragua' ['Hail to You,
   Nicaragua']
National day – 15 September (Independence Day)
Life expectancy (years) – 71.78 (2010 est)
Mortality rate – 4.28 (2010 est)
Birth rate – 22.77 (2010 est)
Infant mortality rate – 24.16 (2010 est)
Death penalty – Abolished for all crimes (since 1979)
CPI score – 2.5 (2010)

CLIMATE AND TERRAIN
The narrow Pacific coastal plain is broken by active
volcanoes and lakes Managua and Nicaragua. A

mountainous central region separates it from the broad
Atlantic coastal plain, which constitutes 60 per cent of the
country and is covered by tropical rainforest. Elevation
extremes range from 2,438m (Mogoton) to 0m (Pacific
Ocean). The climate is generally tropical on the plains but
cooler at altitude; average temperatures in Managua range
from 32°C in April and May to 23°C in January. The
country is subject to frequent earthquakes.

HISTORY AND POLITICS
The area was settled by tribes from Mexico and
Mesoamerica from the ninth century AD. Spanish
colonisation began in 1523 but in the 17th and 18th
centuries the British were the dominant presence on the
Caribbean coast, with the Spanish controlling the Pacific
plain. Independence from Spain was achieved in 1821
and the area was initially incorporated into Mexico. In
1823 it became part of a Central American federation of
former Spanish provinces but seceded and became fully
independent in 1838. British control of the Caribbean
coast was ceded to Nicaragua in 1860.

In 1893, General José Santos Zelaya established a
dictatorship that lasted until 1909, when he was
overthrown by US troops. General Anastasio Somoza
established a dictatorship in 1938 and ruled until his
assassination in 1956, when he was succeeded as
president by his sons Luis (1956–67) and Anastasio
(1967–79). After 44 years in power, the family was
overthrown in 1979 in a popular revolt led by the *Frente
Sandinista de Liberacíon Nacional* (FSLN), popularly known
as the Sandinistas.

The Sandinistas' socialist government redistributed
land and promoted education and health services, but was
opposed by US-backed right-wing guerrillas (the
Contras). The civil war lasted from 1982 until 1990
(although there was a ceasefire from 1988), when the
Sandinistas were unexpectedly defeated in elections by a
coalition of opposition parties.

From 1990 to 2006, governments were liberal or
liberal-dominated coalitions, keeping the FSLN from
power even though it was often the largest party in the
legislature. However, in the 2006 presidential and
legislative elections, the FSLN candidate, Daniel Ortega
(president 1984–90), was elected president and the FSLN
became the largest party in the assembly. Presidential and
legislative elections are scheduled for 6 November 2011.

POLITICAL SYSTEM
The 1987 constitution was amended in 1995 to reduce
the presidential term; this was effectively overturned in
2009 when the Supreme Court lifted the ban on a
president serving two consecutive terms. The executive
president is directly elected for a five-year term, which
may be renewed only once. The unicameral National
Assembly has 90 members directly elected for a five-year
term; unsuccessful presidential and vice-presidential
candidates may be awarded a seat if they receive more
than the average percentage of the vote in each electoral
district. The cabinet is appointed by the president.

HEAD OF STATE
President, Daniel Ortega, *elected* 5 November 2006,
   sworn in 10 January 2007
Vice-President, Jaime Morales

SELECTED GOVERNMENT MEMBERS *as at July 2011*
Defence, Ruth Tapia Roa
Finance, Alberto Guevara

Foreign Affairs, Samuel Santos
Interior, Ana Isabel Morales Mazún

EMBASSY OF NICARAGUA
Suite 31, Vicarage House, 58–60 Kensington Church Street, London W8 4DP
T 020-7938 2373 E emb.ofnicaragua@virgin.net
Ambassador Extraordinary and Plenipotentiary, HE Carlos Argüello-Gomez, *apptd* 2010

BRITISH AMBASSADOR
Ambassador Extraordinary and Plenipotentiary, HE Tom Kennedy, LVO, resident at San José, Costa Rica

DEFENCE
The army has 62 main battle tanks and 166 armoured personnel carriers. The navy has 7 patrol and coastal vessels at 3 bases. The air force has 7 aircraft and 16 helicopters.
Military budget – US$38m (2010)
Military personnel – 12,000: army 10,000, navy 800, air force 1,200
Conscription duration – 18–36 months (voluntary)

ECONOMY AND TRADE
Progress towards economic recovery and reconstruction after the civil war was reversed in 1998 by Hurricane Mitch, which left 20 per cent of the population homeless. Economic growth since has been slow, and the economy contracted in 2009 as the global downturn reduced key commodity prices, export demand and remittances (worth almost 15 per cent of GDP). Although almost 80 per cent of debt was cancelled in 2004 and 2006, the government is dependent on foreign aid and nearly half the population lives below the poverty line.

Agriculture is the mainstay of the economy, accounting for 17.6 per cent of GDP and 28 per cent of employment. The main commercial crops are coffee, beef, shellfish, tobacco, sugar and peanuts. Industry includes food and timber processing, mining, the manufacture of chemicals, machinery, metal products, textiles, clothing and footwear, oil refining and tourism. Industry contributes 26.5 per cent of GDP and services 56 per cent.

The main trading partners are the USA and other Central and South American countries. Principal exports are the main commercial crops and gold. The main imports are consumer goods, machinery and equipment, raw materials and petroleum products.
GNI – US$5,905m; US$1,000 per capita (2009)
Annual average growth of GDP – 2.8 per cent (2010 est)
Inflation rate – 4.7 per cent (2010 est)
Population below poverty line – 48 per cent (2005)
Unemployment – 8 per cent (2010 est)
Total external debt – US$4,030m (2010 est)
Imports – US$3,400m (2009)
Exports – US$1,400m (2009)

BALANCE OF PAYMENTS
Trade – US$2,334m deficit (2010)
Current Account – US$925m deficit (2009)

Trade with UK	2009	2010
Imports from UK	£2,352,093	£4,494,208
Exports to UK	£11,176,819	£13,619,936

COMMUNICATIONS
The Inter-American Highway runs between Nicaragua's Honduran and Costa Rican borders, and the Inter-Oceanic Highway runs from Corinto on the Pacific coast via Managua to Rama, where there is a natural waterway to Bluefields on the Caribbean. There are 19,137km of roads. The main airport is at Managua, and there are a further 142 airports and airfields around the country. The chief ports are Corinto (Pacific) and Bluefields and El Bluff (Caribbean). There are 2,220km of inland waterways, mostly on lakes Managua and Nicaragua, and Lake Nicaragua is the chief element in a 2006 proposal to construct a canal linking the Pacific and Caribbean coasts.

The telephone system is being expanded and upgraded with the help of foreign investment. Fixed-line density was about 5 per 100 people and mobile density was 55 per 100 people in 2009.

EDUCATION AND HEALTH
Literacy rate – 78.0 per cent (2008 est)
Gross enrolment ratio (percentage of relevant age group) – primary 117 per cent; secondary 68 per cent (2008 est)
Health expenditure (per capita) – US$105 (2009)
Hospital beds (per 1,000 people) – 0.9 (2004–9)

MEDIA
There are three daily newspapers. Several commercial networks provide television services, and there are a large number of radio stations.

NIGER

République du Niger – Republic of Niger

Area – 1,267,000 sq. km
Capital – Niamey; population, 1,004,200 (2009 est)
Major cities – Maradi, Zinder
Currency – Franc CFA of 100 centimes
Population – 15,878,271 rising at 3.66 per cent a year (2010 est); Hausa (55.4 per cent), Djerma (21 per cent), Tuareg (9.3 per cent), Fulani (8.5 per cent), Kanouri Manga (4.7 per cent) (2001)
Religion – Muslim 98 per cent (of which Sunni 95 per cent, Shia 5 per cent), Christian 2 per cent (est)
Language – French (official), Arabic, Hausa, Djerma
Population density – 12 per sq. km (2009)
Urban population – 16 per cent (2008 est)
Median age (years) – 15.2 (2010 est)
National anthem – 'La Nigérienne' ['Song of Niger']
National day – 18 December (Republic Day)
Life expectancy (years) – 52.99 (2010 est)
Mortality rate – 14.47 (2010 est)

Birth rate – 51.08 (2010 est)
Infant mortality rate – 114.5 (2010 est)
Death penalty – Retained (no known use since 1976)
CPI score – 2.6 (2010)
Literacy rate – 28.7 per cent (2008 est)
Gross enrolment ratio (percentage of relevant age group) –
    primary 62 per cent; secondary 12 per cent; tertiary
    1 per cent (2009 est)
Health expenditure (per capita) – US$21 (2009)
Hospital beds (per 1,000 people) – 0.3 (2004–9)

CLIMATE AND TERRAIN

A landlocked state, the country is mostly desert, with low
hills in the north and savannah in the south. Elevation
extremes range from 2,022m (Mt Idoukal-n-Taghes/
Bagzane) to 200m (river Niger). The Niger valley in the
south-west is the only well-watered area. There is a desert
climate, except in the extreme south which is sub-tropical.
Average temperatures in Niamey range from 14°C in
January to 42°C in April.

HISTORY AND POLITICS

The area was divided between several kingdoms formed
by different tribes (Tuareg, Songhai, Hausa, Fulani) from
the tenth to 19th centuries. French colonial expansion
from the 1880s brought the whole area under its control
in 1898 and in 1904 it became part of French West
Africa. The country became autonomous in 1958 and
achieved full independence in 1960.

The first president introduced a one-party regime,
which continued under the military government installed
after a coup in 1974. Following popular agitation, civilian
government was reintroduced in 1989, other parties were
legalised in 1990, and multi-party elections held in 1993.
This political liberalisation was reversed following a
military coup in 1996 led by Brig. Ibrahim Barre
Mainassara. He was assassinated in 1999 by the military,
who restored political pluralism.

From 1990 there was a rebellion in the north by
Tuareg seeking greater social equality and political
representation. Peace agreements with rebel groups in
1995 and 1997 brought calm until 2007, when a new
rebel group emerged, seeking greater autonomy and
access to mining revenue; this group signed a ceasefire
with the government in 2009.

After seeking to increase his powers in 2009, President
Mamadou Tandja (first elected in 1999) was deposed in
February 2010 by the military, which in March 2010
appointed a transitional government. A referendum on a
new constitution was held in October 2010, and
presidential and legislative elections were held in January
2011. The Nigerien Party for Democracy and Socialism
won the most seats, but without a majority. The party's
leader, Mahamadou Issoufou, was elected president in the
second round of voting in March.

POLITICAL SYSTEM

The 2010 constitution reduced the president's powers
and restored the limit on presidential terms. The executive
president is directly elected for a five-year term, renewable
once. The unicameral National Assembly has 113
members directly elected for a five-year term. The prime
minister is appointed by the president.

HEAD OF STATE

President, Mahamadou Issoufou, *elected* 12 March 2011,
    took office 7 April 2011

SELECTED GOVERNMENT MEMBERS *as at July 2011*
Prime Minister, Brigi Rafini
Finance, Ouhoumoudou Mahamadou
Foreign Affairs, Bazoum Mohamed
Interior, Abdou Labo
Defence, Karidjo Mahamadou

EMBASSY OF THE REPUBLIC OF NIGER
154 rue de Longchamp, 75116 Paris, France
T (+33) (1) 4504 8060
Ambassador Extraordinary and Plenipotentiary,
    HE Adamou Seydou, *apptd* 2003

BRITISH AMBASSADOR
HE Peter Jones, *apptd* 2011, resident at Accra, Ghana

DEFENCE

The army has 22 armoured personnel carriers.
Military expenditure – US$51m (2009 est)
Military personnel – 5,300: army 5,200, air force 100;
    paramilitary 5,400
Conscription duration – 24 months (selective)

ECONOMY AND TRADE

Niger is one of the poorest countries in the world, with
the majority of the population living below the poverty
line. Economic progress has been hampered by political
instability, recurrent droughts (most recently in 2004–5
and 2009–10), desertification, over-grazing and rapid
population growth, leaving the country dependent on
foreign aid, which makes up over half of government
revenue. Its huge foreign debt burden was much reduced
by debt relief and cancellation in 2000 and 2005.

The mainstay of the economy is subsistence agriculture
and herding, which account for 39 per cent of GDP and
engage 90 per cent of the population; the main cash crops
are cowpeas, cotton, vegetables, cereals and livestock. The
most significant export is uranium, making the economy
vulnerable to fluctuations in global prices; efforts are
being made to diversify into exploitation of other mineral
resources, including gold and oil. The other industries
include processing agricultural products and
manufacturing cement, bricks, soap, textiles and
chemicals. Industry contributes 17 per cent of GDP and
services 44 per cent.

The main trading partners are France (53 per cent of
exports), Nigeria, the USA and China. Principal exports
are uranium ore, livestock, cowpeas and onions. The main
imports are foodstuffs, machinery, vehicles and parts,
petroleum and cereals.

GNI – US$5,281m; US$340 per capita (2009)
Annual average growth of GDP – 3.5 per cent (2010 est)
Inflation rate – 0.1 per cent (2007 est)
Total external debt – US$2,100m (2003 est)
Imports – US$1,600m (2009)
Exports – US$900m (2009)

BALANCE OF PAYMENTS
Trade – US$736m deficit (2010)
Current Account – US$713m deficit (2008)

Trade with UK	2009	2010
Imports from UK	£3,837,710	£2,831,069
Exports to UK	£300,916	£121,229

COMMUNICATIONS

Niger has no railways. Of the 18,949km of roads, less than 4,000km are surfaced. The river Niger is navigable between September and March for 300km from Niamey to the Benin frontier. The principal airport is at Niamey and there are a further 26 airports and airfields.

The telephone system is limited in extent and concentrated mainly in the more densely populated south-west. Although mobile phone distribution has grown rapidly, the combined density of fixed-line and mobile phones is less than 20 per 100 people.

MEDIA

Media freedom has improved since 1999. Although the state-run television and radio services still dominate broadcasting, private stations, particularly radio stations, are proliferating. Radio is the most important form of communication, owing to low levels of literacy. There are two major newspapers, consisting of the state-run *Le Sahel* and the weekly *Le Republican*.

NIGERIA

Federal Republic of Nigeria

Area – 923,768 sq. km
Capital – Abuja (since 1991); population, 1,857,230 (2009 est)
Major cities – Aba, Benin City, Ibadan, Ilorin, Kaduna, Kano, Lagos (the former capital), Maiduguri, Port Harcourt, Zaria
Currency – Naira (N) of 100 kobo
Population – 152,217,341 rising at 1.97 per cent a year (2010 est); Hausa and Fulani (29 per cent), Yoruba (21 per cent), Igbo (18 per cent), Ijaw (10 per cent), Kanuri (4 per cent), Ibibio (3.5 per cent), Tiv (2.5 per cent) (est)
Religion – Muslim 50 per cent (predominantly Sunni), Christian 40 per cent, indigenous beliefs 10 per cent (est); many Christians and Muslims also follow indigenous beliefs
Language – English (official), Hausa, Yoruba, Igbo, Fula, over 500 other languages
Population density – 170 per sq. km (2009)
Urban population – 48 per cent (2008 est)
Median age (years) – 19.1 (2010 est)
National anthem – 'Arise O Compatriots, Nigeria's Call Obey'
National day – 1 October (Independence Day)
Life expectancy (years) – 47.24 (2010 est)
Mortality rate – 16.31 (2010 est)
Birth rate – 36.07 (2010 est)
Infant mortality rate – 92.99 (2010 est)

HIV / AIDS adult prevalence – 3.6 per cent (2009 est)
Death penalty – Retained
CPI score – 2.4 (2010)

CLIMATE AND TERRAIN

The north is arid savannah and semi-desert plains, which rise to central hills and plateaux. There are mountains along the south-eastern border, but the south is generally low-lying and covered in tropical rainforest, with mangrove swamps along the coast and hills in the south-east. Elevation extremes range from 2,419m (Chappal Waddi) to 0m (Atlantic Ocean). The river Niger flows across the country from the north-west to the south coast, where it forms a broad delta on the Gulf of Guinea. The climate is equatorial in the south, tropical in the centre and arid in the north. The north has one rainy season (June to September), while the south has two (March–July, September–October); average temperatures in Lagos range between 21°C and 33°C all year round.

HISTORY AND POLITICS

Nigeria was at the centre of the Nok culture from 500 BC to AD 200. Various kingdoms flourished in the area in medieval times, and Islam was introduced to the north in the 13th century. The Oyo Empire was dominant in the south in the 17th century and the Muslim Sokoto Empire in the north in the 19th century. European traders had arrived on the coast in the 15th century and participated in the gold and slave trades. After Britain abolished slavery, several other powers attempted to exploit the slave trade in Nigeria, which led Britain to annex Lagos in 1861. Britain established protectorates over adjacent territories in stages during the late 19th century, amalgamating the whole area of modern Nigeria into a single political and administrative unit in 1914. The country became a federation in 1954, and increasing degrees of internal self-government were introduced until the country became independent in 1960.

Independence unleashed ethnic and regional tensions, and there were two military coups in 1966; the first coup was Igbo-led and provoked an anti-Igbo counter-coup from the north. The following year, three eastern states seceded and set up the Igbo state of Biafra, sparking a civil war. The conflict lasted until 1970, when Biafra surrendered and was reunited with Nigeria; despite an international relief effort, bombing and famine killed around one million people.

In the 30 years after 1967 there were several military coups and the governments during most of the period were military or military-dominated. Some of the regimes made efforts to reintroduce civilian government, legalise political parties and restore democracy, but invariably suspended these when the results were unfavourable to them. The most recent restoration of civilian rule was in 1999, following presidential and legislative elections.

Ethnic and regional tensions have been more openly and violently expressed since 1999, including calls for secession by various groups. The main source of tension is the religious divide between the predominantly Muslim north, where Shariah law has been introduced in 12 states, and the predominantly Christian south. There have been sporadic violent clashes in which thousands have died, leading to internal migration of Christians from the north. The latest trouble spot is the Niger delta, where activists have been demanding greater local control over oil revenues since the 1990s, but these campaigns have been overshadowed since 2003 by the activities of armed militants, who have attacked oil installations and kidnapped foreign oil workers, while trade in stolen oil has fuelled violence and corruption in the region. In a two-month government amnesty for militants in 2009, many surrendered their weapons.

The People's Democratic Party (PDP) has dominated politics since 1999, and retained its majority in both legislative chambers in the 2007 and 2011 elections. President Goodluck Jonathan, elected as vice-president in 2007, succeeded to the presidency after the death of President Yar'Adua in May 2010, and was elected president in the first round of voting in April 2011.

POLITICAL SYSTEM
The country is a federal democratic republic. Under the 1999 constitution, the executive president is directly elected for a four-year term, renewable only once. The president appoints the federal executive council, which must be approved by the senate. The bicameral National Assembly comprises the 360-member House of Representatives and the 109-member senate, both elected for a four-year term.

HEAD OF STATE
President, Goodluck Jonathan, *sworn in* 6 May 2010, *elected* 16 April 2011
Vice-President, Namadi Sambo

SELECTED GOVERNMENT MEMBERS *as at July 2011*
Defence, Haliru Mohammed
Finance, Olusegun Olutoyin Aganga
Foreign Affairs, Olugbenga Ashiru
Internal Affairs, Abba Moro

HIGH COMMISSION FOR THE FEDERAL REPUBLIC OF NIGERIA
Nigeria House, 9 Northumberland Avenue, London WC2N 5BX
T 020-7839 1244 E hc@nigeriahc.org.uk
W www.nigeriahc.org.uk
High Commissioner, HE Dr Dalhatu S. Tafida, *apptd* 2008

BRITISH HIGH COMMISSION
Dangote House, Aguiyi Ironsi Street, Wuse, Abuja
T (+234) (9) 462 3200 E information.abuja@fco.gov.uk
W http://ukinnigeria.fco.gov.uk
High Commissioner, HE Andrew Lloyd, *apptd* 2011

BRITISH COUNCIL
Plot 3645, IBB Way, Maitama, PMB 550, Garki, Abuja
T (+234) (9) 4137 8707 W www.britishcouncil.org/africa
Director, Peter Upton

FEDERAL STRUCTURE
The federal republic is divided into 36 states and the Federal Capital Territory: Abia, Adamawa, Akwa Ibom, Anambra, Bauchi, Bayelsa, Benue, Borno, Cross River, Delta, Ebonyi, Edo, Ekiti, Enugu, Gombe, Imo, Jigawa, Kaduna, Kano, Katsina, Kebbi, Kogi, Kwara, Lagos, Nassarawa, Niger, Ogun, Ondo, Osun, Oyo, Plateau, Rivers, Sokoto, Taraba, Yobe and Zamfara. Each state has an elected governor and legislature.

DEFENCE
The army has 276 main battle tanks, 157 light tanks and over 484 armoured personnel carriers. The navy has 1 frigate and 20 patrol and coastal vessels at 5 bases. The air force has 78 combat aircraft and 9 armed helicopters.
Military budget – US$1,550m (2010)
Military personnel – 80,000: army 62,000, navy 8,000, air force 10,000; paramilitaries 82,000

ECONOMY AND TRADE
Nigeria is the leading sub-Saharan oil producer, enjoying an oil boom in the 1970s and recently benefiting again from high oil prices. However, mismanagement and corruption, which dissipated the profits of the 1970s boom, mean that the majority of the population has yet to derive much benefit, and nearly three-quarters live below the poverty line. Past governments also failed to diversify the economy away from its dependence on oil, which accounts for 80 per cent of government revenue and 95 per cent of foreign exchange earnings. However, since 2008 economic reforms have been introduced to improve fiscal and monetary management, curb inflation and address regional agitation for wider distribution of oil revenues. Factors such as security and inadequate infrastructure remain obstacles to growth, but infrastructure improvements are a priority, especially in electricity supply and roads. Recent high oil revenues and debt relief or cancellation have freed Nigeria from much of its large foreign debt.

The mainstay of the economy is agriculture, mostly at subsistence level, which generates 31.9 per cent of GDP and engages 70 per cent of the labour force. The main crops include cocoa, peanuts, cotton, palm oil, maize, rice, sorghum, millet and rubber. However, agricultural output has failed to keep pace with rapid population growth, changing Nigeria from a net food exporter to a food importer. Industrial activities include oil and natural gas production, mining (coal, tin, columbite), processing agricultural products, textiles, cement and other construction materials and footwear. Industry contributes 32.9 per cent of GDP and services 35.2 per cent.

The main trading partners are the USA (34 per cent of exports), China, India, Brazil and the EU. Principal exports are oil and oil products, cocoa and rubber. The main imports are machinery, chemicals, transport equipment, manufactured goods, food and live animals.
GNI – US$162,901m; US$1,190 per capita (2009)
Annual average growth of GDP – 6.8 per cent (2010 est)
Inflation rate – 13.9 per cent (2010 est)
Population below poverty line – 70 per cent (2007 est)
Unemployment – 4.9 per cent (2007 est)
Total external debt – US$11,020m (2010 est)
Imports – US$39,000m (2009)
Exports – US$31,000m (2004)

BALANCE OF PAYMENTS
Trade – US$31,023m surplus (2010)
Current Account – US$42,261m surplus (2008)

Trade with UK	2009	2010
Imports from UK	£1,235,385,393	£1,367,745,985
Exports to UK	£621,229,035	£796,614,837

EDUCATION AND HEALTH
Literacy rate – 73.0 per cent (2008 est)
Gross enrolment ratio (percentage of relevant age group) – primary 93 per cent; secondary 30 per cent (2007 est)
Health expenditure (per capita) – US$69 (2009)
Hospital beds (per 1,000 people) – 0.5 (2004–9)

COMMUNICATIONS
Internal long-distance travel is mostly by air; there are 54 airports and airfields, including the principal airports at Lagos, Abuja, Kano and Port Harcourt. The Nigerian railway network, which is controlled by the Nigerian

Railway Corporation, has 3,505km of track. There are 193,200km of roads, and 8,600km of waterways, mostly on the Niger and Benue rivers; some parts of the Niger delta are only accessible by water. The main seaports are Lagos, Port Harcourt, Warri and Calabar. There is a high risk of piracy of shipping in the Niger delta and the Gulf of Guinea.

Both the fixed-line and mobile phone telephone networks are expanding quickly, although fixed-line density was still only 1 per 100 people in 2009, while mobile phone density had reached 50 per 100 people. There were also 43.9 million internet users.

MEDIA

State-run television and radio broadcasters provide national and regional services. All 36 states run their own radio stations and most also provide television. State services operate alongside a large number of private and commercial networks. Radio provides Nigerians with their main access to the media, as television viewing is concentrated in urban areas. There are over 100 national and local newspapers and periodicals.

CULTURE

Significant writers include Chinua Achebe (b. 1930), whose novel *Things Fall Apart* (1958) has been translated into 50 languages, the Nobel prize winner Wole Soyinka (b. 1934) and Ken Saro-Wiwa (1941–1995), whose political activism resulted in his death at the hands of the military government.

'Nollywood' is the colloquial name for the Nigerian film industry, which produces an estimated 2,000 films a year. Most go straight to low-priced DVD or VCD, and outsell Hollywood blockbusters in many parts of Africa.

Fela Kuti (1938–97) is Nigeria's most famous musician. He pioneered Afrobeat, a style combining traditional Yoruba rhythms with jazz and funk. The movement became inextricably linked with Kuti's personal politics, which saw him embrace black power, campaign against suppression of human rights in Africa, and mount two unsuccessful runs for the Nigerian presidency.

NORWAY

Kongeriket Norge – Kingdom of Norway

Area – 386,220 sq. km, of which Svalbard and Jan Mayen have a combined area of 62,418 sq. km
Capital – Oslo; population, 874,695 (2009 est)
Major cities – Bergen, Stavanger, Trondheim
Currency – Krone of 100 ore

Population – 4,676,305 rising at 0.33 per cent per year (2010 est)
Religion – Christian (Lutheran 79 per cent, other Protestant 4 per cent, Roman Catholic 1 per cent), Muslim 2 per cent (est)
Language – Bokmal and Nynorsk Norwegian (both official), Finnish, Sami (official in six municipalities)
Population density – 16 per sq. km (2009)
Urban population – 77 per cent (2008 est)
Median age (years) – 39.7 (2010 est)
National anthem – 'Ja, Vi Elsker Dette Landet' ['Yes, We Love This Country']
National day – 17 May (Constitution Day)
Life expectancy (years) – 80.08 (2010 est)
Mortality rate – 9.26 (2010 est)
Birth rate – 10.9 (2010 est)
Infant mortality rate – 3.55 (2010 est)
Death penalty – Abolished for all crimes (since 1979)
CPI score – 8.6 (2010)

CLIMATE AND TERRAIN

The terrain is mostly mountainous, with elevated, barren plateaux separated by deep, narrow valleys; the north is arctic tundra. The coastline is deeply indented with numerous fjords and fringed with thousands of rocky islands and islets; Geirangerfjord and Naeroyfjord are UNESCO World Heritage Sites. Elevation extremes range from 2,469m (Galdhopiggen) to 0m (Norwegian Sea).

Nearly half of the country lies north of the Arctic Circle, and at North Cape the sun does not appear to set between about 14 May and 29 July, causing the phenomenon known as the midnight sun; conversely, there is no apparent sunrise from about 18 November to 24 January. The climate is temperate on the coast but colder and wetter inland; average temperatures in Oslo range from −7°C in January to 22°C in July, but winter temperatures in parts of the north can drop to −40°C.

HISTORY AND POLITICS

Norway became a unified country under the rule of King Harald Fairhair in c.900 but dissolved after his death and was reunified by Olav II in c.1016–28. Canute brought Norway under Danish rule in 1028 but the throne reverted on his death to Magnus I. When the royal house died out in the 14th century, the Danish monarch was the nearest heir and in 1397 Norway, Denmark and Sweden were united under a single monarch in the Kalmar Union. Sweden seceded from the union in 1523, but Norway continued to be ruled by the Danish crown until 1814, when it was ceded to Sweden.

Although internal self-government was established in 1814, growing tension over constraints on the Norwegian government led to the union being dissolved, and Norway became independent in 1905. The first king of the newly independent country was a Danish prince, who took the throne as King Haakon VII.

The country was neutral in the First World War, but in the Second World War Norway was invaded and occupied by Germany from 1940 until 1945. Norway joined NATO in 1949 and was a founder member of the European Free Trade Association in 1960. Membership of the EU was rejected in referendums in 1972 and 1994.

After 1945, governments pursued policies of economic planning and an extensive welfare state. The Labour Party dominated politics from the 1930s to the early 1980s, governing either on its own or in coalition with smaller parties. It was returned to power in 2005 after winning a majority of seats in the legislative election, forming a coalition government with the Socialist Left and Centre parties. In the 2009 legislative election the governing coalition was returned with a one-seat majority.

POLITICAL SYSTEM

Norway is a constitutional monarchy with a hereditary monarch as head of state. Under the 1814 constitution, the unicameral *Storting* has 169 members who are directly elected for a four-year term; a 2007 constitutional amendment abolished a bicameral division within the *Storting*, which took effect from the 2009 election. The prime minister, who is responsible to parliament, appoints the cabinet.

HEAD OF STATE

HM The King of Norway, King Harald V, KG, GCVO, born 21 February 1937; *succeeded* 17 January 1991
Heir, HRH Crown Prince Haakon Magnus, *born* 20 July 1973

SELECTED GOVERNMENT MEMBERS *as at July 2011*

Prime Minister, Jens Stoltenberg
Defence, Grete Faremo
Finance, Sigbjorn Johnsen
Foreign Affairs, Jonas Gahr Store

ROYAL NORWEGIAN EMBASSY

25 Belgrave Square, London SW1X 8QD
T 020-7591 5500 **E** emb.london@mfa.no
W www.norway.org.uk
Ambassador Extraordinary and Plenipotentiary,
  HE Kim Traavik, *apptd* 2010

BRITISH EMBASSY

Thomas Heftyesgate 8, 0264 Oslo
T (+47) 2313 2700 **E** britemb@online.no
W http://ukinnorway.fco.gov.uk
Ambassador Extraordinary and Plenipotentiary,
  HE Jane Owen, *apptd* 2010

BRITISH COUNCIL

Storgaten 10 B, 0155 Oslo
T (+47) (22) 396 190 **W** www.britishcouncil.org/norway
Director, Karoline Tellum

DEFENCE

The army has 72 main battle tanks, 104 armoured infantry fighting vehicles and 390 armoured personnel carriers. The navy has 6 submarines, 5 destroyers and 6 patrol and coastal vessels at two bases. The air force has 63 combat aircraft.
Military budget – US$5,770m (2010)
Military personnel – 26,450: army 8,900, navy 3,750, air force 5,550, home guard 500, central support 7,750
Conscription duration – 12 months plus refresher training

ECONOMY AND TRADE

Norway's prosperity depends primarily upon oil and gas extraction, which accounts for nearly half of exports, and its fisheries. Oil production is declining, but exploration for oil and gas in the Barents Sea, and other areas that are becoming more accessible as the Arctic ice cap retreats, is ongoing. Norway has planned for the time when reserves are exhausted by investing revenue from this sector in a government fund. The state retains a majority share in key enterprises, including the oil industry.

The nature of the terrain restricts agriculture, which generates 2.1 per cent of GDP. The main industries apart from oil and gas are fishing, forestry, food processing, shipbuilding, pulp and paper products, metals, chemicals, mining and textiles. Shipping freight services are also significant, with Norwegian companies controlling over 5 per cent of the world's shipping fleet by tonnage. Industry contributes 40.1 per cent of GDP and services 57.8 per cent.

The main trading partners are EU countries, the USA and China. Principal exports are oil and petroleum products, machinery and equipment, metals, chemicals, ships and fish. The main imports are machinery and equipment, chemicals, metals and foodstuffs.
GNI – US$376,360m; US$84,640 per capita (2009)
Annual average growth of GDP – 1.5 per cent (2010 est)
Inflation rate – 2.4 per cent (2010 est)
Unemployment – 3.7 per cent (2010 est)
Total external debt – US$2,232,000m (2010)
Imports – US$68,500m (2009)
Exports – US$120,700m (2009)

BALANCE OF PAYMENTS

Trade – US$54,785m surplus (2010)
Current Account – US$83,825m surplus (2008)

Trade with UK	2009	2010
Imports from UK	£2,692,075,673	£2,982,853,211
Exports to UK	£14,777,830,846	£19,223,317,249

COMMUNICATIONS

There are 4,169km of railways and 92,946km of roads. The rail network stops at Bodo, just north of the Arctic Circle, and there are few roads in the far north, to which the main means of transport is by sea; the state ferry service operates between Bergen and Kirkenes carrying freight, vehicles and passengers. There are 98 airports and airfields, including the principal airports at Oslo, Bergen, Stavanger and Trondheim. The main ports are Oslo, Bergen, Kristiansand, Tonsberg, Stavanger and Narvik, and there is a large merchant fleet, with 632 ships of over 1,000 tonnes registered in Norway and 940 registered abroad.

The fixed-line telephone system serves all parts of the country and mobile phone distribution has grown rapidly. In 2009 there were 1.9 millon fixed lines in use, 5.3 million mobile phone subscribers and 4.4 million internet users.

EDUCATION AND HEALTH

Education from six to 16 is free and compulsory in the basic schools, and free from 16 to 19 years. The majority of pupils receive post-compulsory schooling at upper secondary schools, universities, and regional and specialist colleges.
Gross enrolment ratio (percentage of relevant age group) –
  primary 99 per cent; secondary 112 per cent; tertiary 73 per cent (2008 est)
Health expenditure (per capita) – US$7,662 (2009)
Hospital beds (per 1,000 people) – 3.5 (2004–9)

MEDIA AND CULTURE

The public broadcaster NRK operates radio and television channels, in competition with a number of commercial rivals. Newspaper readership is high given the size of the population, with one weekly and five daily national newspapers.

Celebrated cultural figures include the artist Edvard Munch (1863–1944), responsible for one of the world's most recognisable paintings, *The Scream* (1893); writer Knut Hamsun (1859–1952), winner of the Nobel prize in 1920; dramatist Henrik Ibsen (1828–1906); the composer Edvard Grieg (1843–1907) and the 1980s pop group A-ha, which has sold over 30 million albums worldwide.

TERRITORIES

SVALBARD
Area – 62,045 sq. km
Population – 2,019 (2011 est); Norwegian 55 per cent, Russian and Ukrainian 44 per cent

The Svalbard archipelago consists of Spitsbergen, North East Land, the Wiche Islands, Barents Island, Edge Island, Prince Charles Foreland, Hope Island and Bear Island. It lies north of the Arctic Circle, and glaciers and snow cover around 60 per cent of the area, although the west coast is ice-free for about half the year. Some 65 per cent of the Svalbard archipelago is protected to ensure biodiversity; there are seven national parks, six large nature reserves, 15 bird sanctuaries and one geotopic protected area. A global seed repository has been established on Spitsbergen. Norway's sovereignty was recognised by treaty in 1920 but the other signatories were granted equal rights to exploit mineral deposits, although this right is now only exercised by Russia. The territory is administered by a governor, who is responsible to the Ministry of Justice and Police. The main economic activities are coal mining, tourism, and research and education.

JAN MAYEN ISLAND
Area – 377 sq. km
Population – the only residents are the staff of the radio and meteorological stations

The island is barren, volcanic and partially covered by glaciers, with no exploitable natural resources. It lies in the North Atlantic Ocean about 950 km west of Norway and is home to the Beerenberg volcano, the northernmost active volcano on earth. It was annexed by Norway in 1922 and integrated into the kingdom in 1930; since 1995 it has been administered by the governor of Nordland county.

NORWEGIAN ANTARCTIC TERRITORY
The Norwegian Antarctic Territory consists of Queen Maud Land, Bouvet Island and Peter the First Island. Claimed in 1938, Queen Maud Land is a sector of the Antarctic continent which extends from 45° E. to 20° E. Peter the First Island was formally claimed in 1931 and is the only claimed area covered under the Antarctic treaty that is not part of the main land mass. Bouvet Island was claimed in 1930 (*see also* The North and South Poles).

OMAN

Saltanat Uman – Sultanate of Oman

Area – 309,500 sq. km
Capital – Muscat (Masqat); population, 634,074 (2009 est)
Major cities – Ibri, Salalah, Suhar, as-Suwayq
Currency – Rial Omani (OR) of 1,000 baisas
Population – 2,967,717 rising at 2 per cent a year (2010 est)
Religion – Muslim (predominantly Ibadhi; Shia 5 per cent) (est), with Hindu, Buddhist, Sikh, Baha'i and Christian minorities. Islam is the official religion
Language – Arabic (official), English, Baluchi, Urdu
Population density – 9 per sq. km (2009)
Urban population – 72 per cent (2008 est)
Median age (years) – 23.9 (2010 est)
National anthem – 'Nashid as-Salaam as-Sultani' ['The Sultan's Anthem']
National day – 18 November (Birthday of Sultan Qaboos, 1940)
Life expectancy (years) – 73.97 (2010 est)
Mortality rate – 3.47 (2010 est)
Birth rate – 23.9 (2010 est)
Infant mortality rate – 16 (2010 est)
Death penalty – Retained
CPI score – 5.3 (2010)

CLIMATE AND TERRAIN
Oman lies at the south-eastern corner of the Arabian peninsula and includes territory at the tip of the Musandam peninsula, which is separated from the rest of the country by the UAE. There are mountains in the north and the south-west of the country, divided by high desert plateau; over 80 per cent of the country is desert. The plateau descends to a fertile plain on the Arabian Sea coast. Elevation extremes range from 2,980m (Jabal Shams) to 0m (Arabian Sea). The climate is arid, with high temperatures and humidity throughout the year; temperatures are lower on the coast, but the high humidity often makes coastal areas the most inhospitable. Average temperatures in Muscat range from 19°C in January to 38°C in June.

HISTORY AND POLITICS
Oman began to build an empire in the Middle East from the eighth century AD and remained largely unchallenged until the arrival in 1506 of the Portuguese, who were ousted in 1650. An independent sultanate was established in 1749 by the founder of the dynasty that still rules the country. By the early 19th century, Omani rule extended to the east African coast and parts of Persia and Balochistan (in modern Pakistan). The kingdom came

under British influence from the late 19th century until 1951.

The country was divided from 1913, with religious leaders in control of the interior and the sultan of the coastal regions. The interior's attempts to assert its independence led to clashes in the 1950s, but by 1959 the sultan had established control over the whole country. An insurrection in the south by left-wing rebels supported by South Yemen began in 1965 and was defeated with British military assistance in 1975. The discovery and subsequent exploitation of oil in the mid-1960s led to the steady economic transformation of Oman, and in 1970 the sultan was overthrown in a bloodless coup by his son, Sultan Qaboos bin Said al-Said, who initiated a modernisation programme.

The country is still essentially an absolute monarchy, although a degree of political liberalisation has occurred in the past 20 years and the 1996 Basic Statute sets out the development of the political and legal systems; the first direct election to the consultative council was held in 2000 and the first by universal adult suffrage in 2003. In the 2007 election, 38 members were returned and 46 new members were elected, all as independents. Pro-reform demonstrations occurred in spring 2011.

POLITICAL SYSTEM

In 1996 the sultan issued a Basic Statute that is in effect a constitution; it established a succession mechanism, codified the system of government and set up a bicameral legislature. At present, legislation is proposed by the sultan and passed by decree. The sultan is advised by the bicameral Council of Oman, comprising the Consultative Council *(Majlis al-Shura)*, which has 84 members directly elected for a four-year term, and the Council of State *(Majlis al-Dawlah)*, which has 59 members appointed by the sultan for a four-year term. The Consultative Council has the right to review legislation, question ministers and make policy proposals. The Council of State is intended to facilitate 'constructive cooperation between the government and the citizens'. There are no political parties.

HEAD OF STATE

HM The Sultan of Oman, Prime Minister, Sultan Qaboos bin Said al-Said, *succeeded following a coup,* 23 July 1970

SELECTED GOVERNMENT MEMBERS *as at June 2011*
Deputy Prime Minister, Fahd bin Mamud al-Said
Defence, Badr bin Saud bin Hareb al-Busaidi
Foreign Affairs, Yusuf bin Alawi bin Abdullah
Interior, Saud bin Ibrahim al-Busaidi
Economy, Ahmed bin Abdul Nabi Makki

EMBASSY OF THE SULTANATE OF OMAN
167 Queen's Gate, London SW7 5HE
T 020-7225 0001
Ambassador Extraordinary and Plenipotentiary,
HE Abdul Aziz al-Hinai, *apptd* 2009

BRITISH EMBASSY
PO Box 185, Mina al-Fahal, 116 Muscat
T (+968) (24) 609 000 E enquiries.muscat@fco.gov.uk
W http://ukinoman.fco.gov.uk
Ambassador Extraordinary and Plenipotentiary,
HE Noel Guckian, *apptd* 2005

BRITISH COUNCIL
PO Box 73, Road One, Madinat al-Sultan, Qaboos West, 115 Muscat
T (+968) (24) 681 000 W www.britishcouncil.org/me
Director, Paul Doubleday

DEFENCE

The army has 117 main battle tanks and 206 armoured personnel carriers. The navy has 11 patrol and coastal vessels at 6 bases. The air force has 54 combat aircraft.
Military budget – US$4,020m (2009)
Military personnel – 42,600: army 25,000, navy 4,200, air force 5,000, Royal Household 6,400, foreign forces 2,000; paramilitary 4,400

ECONOMY AND TRADE

Although its production is more modest than other Gulf states, oil and gas are the mainstay of Oman's economy and account for nearly 80 per cent of government revenue. Oil reserves are dwindling and development plans centre on diversification, industrialisation and privatisation, with the aim of reducing the oil sector's contribution to GDP to 9 per cent by 2020. Industrial development is focused on natural gas production, metal manufacturing, petrochemicals and trans-shipment ports, with plans also to develop tourism and communication technology industries. Improved training, especially in IT and business skills, is intended to enable the local population to replace expatriate workers. The global economic crisis has slowed development.

Agriculture and fishing account for 1.4 per cent of GDP, producing dates, limes, bananas, alfalfa and vegetables as well as fish. The main industries apart from oil and natural gas extraction are oil refining, liquefied natural gas production, construction and production of cement, copper, steel, chemicals and optic fibre. Industry accounts for 48.2 per cent of GDP and services for 50.3 per cent.

The main trading partners are the UAE, China, Japan and South Korea. Principal exports are petroleum, re-exports, fish, metals and textiles. The main imports are machinery and transport equipment, manufactured goods, food and livestock.

GNI – US$58,086m; US$17,890 per capita (2008)
Annual average growth of GDP – 3.6 per cent (2010 est)
Inflation rate – 4 per cent (2010 est)
Unemployment – 15 per cent (2004 est)
Total external debt – US$8,829m (2010 est)
Imports – US$17,900m (2009)
Exports – US$28,100m (2009)

BALANCE OF PAYMENTS
Trade – US$14,047m surplus (2010)
Current Account – US$5,469m surplus (2008)

Trade with UK	2009	2010
Imports from UK	£349,956,037	£414,196,854
Exports to UK	£86,355,954	£95,828,801

COMMUNICATIONS

There are 53,430km of roads, of which 23,223km are surfaced; there are no railways. The main airports are at Muscat and Salalah, with 128 other airports and airfields around the country. The main ports are Salalah and Port Qaboos at Mutrah, which has eight deep-water berths.

The modern telephone system served 300,100 fixed-line subscribers, 4 million mobile phone subscribers and 1.5 million internet users in 2009.

EDUCATION AND HEALTH

Literacy rate – 85.0 per cent (2008 est)
Gross enrolment ratio (percentage of relevant age group) – primary 84 per cent; secondary 91 per cent; tertiary 26 per cent (2009 est)
Health expenditure (per capita) – US$497 (2009)
Hospital beds (per 1,000 people) – 1.9 (2004–9)

MEDIA

The first private radio station launched in 2007, ending a government monopoly on television and radio broadcasting. Satellite dishes are permitted, so stations from neighbouring Saudi Arabia, the UAE and Yemen can be received. There are a large number of newspapers, including four national dailies. The press can be subject to political and cultural censorship by the government.

PAKISTAN

Jamhuryat Islami Pakistan – Islamic Republic of Pakistan

Area – 796,095 sq. km
Capital – Islamabad; population, 832,002 (2009 est)
Major cities – Faisalabad, Gujranwala, Hyderabad, Karachi, Lahore, Multan, Peshawar, Quetta, Rawalpindi
Currency – Pakistan rupee of 100 paisa
Population – 184,404,791 rising at 1.59 per cent a year (2010 est); Punjabi (44.7 per cent), Pashtun (15.4 per cent), Sindhi (14.1 per cent), Sariaki (8.4 per cent), Muhajirs (7.6 per cent), Balochi (3.6 per cent) (est)
Religion – Muslim 95 per cent (predominantly Sunni) (est); small Christian and Hindu minorities; Islam is the state religion
Language – Urdu, English (both official), Punjabi, Sindhi, Siraiki, Pashto, Balochi, Hindko, Brahui, Burushaski
Population density – 220 per sq. km (2009)
Urban population – 36 per cent (2008 est)
Median age (years) – 21.2 (2010 est)
National anthem – 'Qaumi Tarana' ['National Anthem']
National day – 23 March (Republic Day)
Life expectancy (years) – 65.63 (2010 est)
Mortality rate – 7.06 (2010 est)
Birth rate – 25.3 (2010 est)
Infant mortality rate – 65.32 (2010 est)
Death penalty – Retained
CPI score – 2.3 (2010)

CLIMATE AND TERRAIN

The arid Thar desert in the east gives way to the fertile Indus valley in the centre of the country. The terrain then rises to the Makran, Kirthar and Sulaiman mountain ranges in the west and the Karakoram and Himalayan ranges in the north. Elevation extremes range from

8,611m (K2) to 0m (Indian Ocean). The climate varies greatly across the country. For most areas, the rainy season runs from July to September and is accompanied by very high humidity. Average temperatures in Lahore range from 12°C in January to 33°C in June. Pakistan is prone to earthquakes, the most recent in 2005 and 2008, and flooding; following heavy monsoon rains in 2010 the entire length of the Indus valley was flooded, displacing millions of people.

HISTORY AND POLITICS

Islam was introduced to the area from the eighth century onwards. From the 12th century, the territory formed part of successive empires covering northern India, including the Delhi sultanate and the Mughal Empire, and came under British control by the mid-19th century, forming part of the territory of British India.

Unable to agree with the Hindu-dominated Indian National Congress on the terms under which Muslim religious and political rights would be protected in an independent Indian state, in 1940 Mohammad Ali Jinnah, leader of the All-India Muslim League, and other Muslim leaders endorsed the Lahore resolution, which called for a separate state for Muslims. The predominantly Muslim areas of British India were partitioned at independence in 1947, forming the state of Pakistan. This state comprised West Pakistan (now Pakistan) and East Pakistan, the Muslim areas of Bengal, which became the independent state of Bangladesh in 1971 following a short civil war. Pakistan became a republic in 1956.

Since 1958 Pakistan has alternated between military and civilian rule. The first military regime was replaced by civilian government under Zulfiqar Ali Bhutto (1971–7), who was overthrown by General Zia ul-Haq (1977–88). Civilian governments under Benazir Bhutto and Nawaz Sharif (1988–99) proved unstable, with several rapid changes of government amid allegations of corruption. In 1999 a military coup brought General Pervez Musharraf to power. He restored civilian government in 2002, but controversially only resigned his army post and became a civilian president in 2007; he resigned as president in August 2008 to avoid impeachment proceedings.

In September 2001 President Musharraf aligned Pakistan with the West in its 'war on terror', providing support to the Allies in the Afghan war. This policy angered Islamic militants, who have carried out terrorist attacks in the major cities. Attacks intensified after the killing of the al-Qaida leader Osama bin Laden in Pakistan in May 2011.

The legislative elections originally scheduled for January 2008 were postponed to February after the assassination of Benazir Bhutto in December 2007. The two main opposition parties, Bhutto's Pakistan People's Party (PPP) and the Pakistan Muslim League–Nawaz Sharif (PML-N), won the most seats and formed a coalition government with two smaller parties; the PML-N withdrew from the coalition government in August 2008. The presidential election in September 2008 was won by Asif Ali Zadari, the widower of Benazir Bhutto. Two smaller parties withdrew from the coalition government in December 2010, and a new PPP-led coalition was formed in February 2011. In April, the Pakistan Muslim League–Quaid-e-Azam party joined the coalition.

INSURGENCIES

Balochistan, Punjab and Sindh provinces have all been affected since the 1980s by conflict between Shia and

Sunni fundamentalists. Balochistan and, since the early 1990s, Sindh (especially Karachi) have experienced violence by armed militants seeking greater autonomy for each province.

Civil order has always been harder to maintain in the North-West Frontier Province and the federally administered tribal areas than in the rest of the country. These areas became havens for the Taliban and al-Qaida fleeing Afghanistan after 2001 and for like-minded Pakistani militants, who became entrenched along the Afghan border, radicalising and destabilising increasingly wide areas. Government military and security forces are struggling to maintain control in over half of these areas. The government conceded the imposition of Shariah law in the Swat valley as part of a cease-fire agreement with the Taliban in early 2009, but when the Taliban attempted to extend their influence further into the country, the army began a counter-insurgency offensive to retake the area in April 2009, subsequently moving against the Taliban in other strongholds such as South Waziristan. These offensives led to an increase in militants' attacks in the major cities, while by 2010 the Taliban began to reassert its influence in some of the areas cleared by the army offensives in 2009.

FOREIGN RELATIONS

Since partition, sovereignty over the predominantly Muslim state of Jammu and Kashmir has been disputed between Pakistan and India. A short war in 1947–8 resulted in the state being partitioned between the two countries; its status remains unresolved, despite further outbreaks of war in 1965 and 1971, low-level conflict for control of the Siachen glacier since 1985 and occasional increases in military exchanges, most recently in 1999–2002 and 2003. Tension was exacerbated by Pakistan's support of the Muslim insurgency in the Indian part of the state, which began in the 1980s, and by both countries' acquisition of nuclear weapons. Moves towards a peaceful settlement began in 2003, when diplomatic missions were reopened and the resumption of transport links was initiated. Formal diplomatic talks began in 2004 and have achieved several accords intended to reduce tension between the two countries, although the status of Kashmir has yet to be addressed. Talks were temporarily suspended by the Indian government after the Mumbai terrorist attacks in 2008, but resumed in 2010.

International concern was raised in 2004 by disclosures that Pakistan has sold its nuclear technology to other countries.

POLITICAL SYSTEM

Pakistan is a federal republic. The 1973 constitution has been suspended and restored several times, amended in 1985, 2002 and 2003, and in 2010 was reinstated in its original form, returning some of the president's powers to the prime minister.

The president is elected by the legislature for a five-year term. The parliament *(Majlis as-Shura)* comprises a lower house, the National Assembly and the senate. The National Assembly has 342 members, of whom 60 are women and ten are elected by non-Muslim minorities; members serve a five-year term. The senate has 100 members, 88 elected by provincial assemblies, eight chosen by tribal agencies and four elected by the National Assembly; they serve a six-year term, with half elected every three years. The prime minister is nominated by and is responsible to the legislature.

There are four provinces: Balochistan, Khyber Pukhtoonkhwa (formerly North-West Frontier Province), Punjab and Sindh. Each has a provincial assembly and government. In addition, there are the Federally Administered Tribal Areas and the Islamabad Capital Territory.

HEAD OF STATE
President, Asif Ali Zardari, *elected* 6 September 2008, *sworn in* 9 September 2008

SELECTED GOVERNMENT MEMBERS *as at June 2011*
Prime Minister, Yusuf Raza Gilani
Defence, Chaudhry Ahmed Mukhtar
Foreign Affairs, Hina Khar
Finance, Abdul Hafiz Sheikh
Interior, Rehman Malik

HIGH COMMISSION FOR THE ISLAMIC REPUBLIC OF PAKISTAN
34–36 Lowndes Square, London SW1X 9JN
T 020-7664 9204 W www.phclondon.org
High Commissioner, HE Wajid Shamsul Hasan, *apptd* 2008

BRITISH HIGH COMMISSION
PO Box 1122, Diplomatic Enclave, Ramna 5, Islamabad
T (+92) (51) 282 2000 E consularenquiries.karachi@fco.gov.uk
W http://ukinpakistan.fco.gov.uk
High Commissioner, HE Adam Thomson, CMG, *apptd* 2010

BRITISH COUNCIL
PO Box 1135, Islamabad
T (+92) (51) 283 3133 W www.britishcouncil.org/pakistan
Director, David Martin

DEFENCE

The army has over 2,386 main battle tanks, 1,266 armoured personnel carriers and 26 armed helicopters. The navy has 8 submarines, 9 frigates, 10 patrol and coastal vessels, 7 combat aircraft and 6 armed helicopters at three bases. The air force has 426 combat aircraft and 19 helicopters.
Military budget – US$5,200m (2010)
Military personnel – 617,000: army 550,000, navy 22,000, air force 45,000; paramilitary 304,000

ECONOMY AND TRADE

Decades of political instability, inefficiency, corruption and high military expenditure have left Pakistan a poor and underdeveloped country. In the 2000s economic reforms, international aid and greater foreign investment produced steady growth of 5–8 per cent a year until 2008, notably in the industrial and service sectors, and reduced poverty levels by 10 per cent between 2001 and 2007. However, slower growth in 2008 caused budget and fiscal deficits that forced Pakistan to seek IMF assistance; inflation, already a persistant problem, rose to 20.3 per cent in 2008 and remains high. These problems were exacerbated by the 2010 floods, which left millions homeless, destroyed crops and damaged infrastructure. A large proportion of the country's labour force works abroad, especially in the Middle East, providing valuable remittances but also causing use of child labour within Pakistan.

Agriculture employs 43 per cent of the workforce, producing cotton, wheat, rice, sugar cane, fruit, vegetables, milk, meat and eggs, and contributing 21.8 per cent of GDP. Significant manufacturing industries include textiles and clothing, food processing, pharmaceuticals, construction materials, paper products, fertiliser and seafood. Industry accounts for 23.6 per cent of GDP and services for 54.6 per cent.

The main trading partners are the UAE, the USA, China, Saudi Arabia and Afghanistan. Principal exports are textiles (clothing, bed linen, cotton cloth and yarn), rice, leather goods, sports goods, chemicals, carpets and rugs. The main imports are petroleum, petroleum products, machinery, plastics, transport equipment, edible oils, paper, iron, steel and tea.

GNI – US$166,370m; US$1,000 per capita (2009)
Annual average growth of GDP – 2.7 per cent (2010 est)
Inflation rate – 13.4 per cent (2010 est)
Population below poverty line – 24 per cent (2005–6 est)
Unemployment – 15 per cent (2010 est)
Total external debt – US$57,210m (2010 est)
Imports – US$31,600m (2009)
Exports – US$17,500m (2009)

BALANCE OF PAYMENTS
Trade – US$16,309m deficit (2010)
Current Account – US$13,874m deficit (2008)

Trade with UK	2009	2010
Imports from UK	£461,208,391	£442,345,621
Exports to UK	£643,510,372	£745,966,440

COMMUNICATIONS
There are 260,760km of roads and 7,791 of railways. The principal airports are at Karachi, Islamabad, Lahore, Peshawar and Sialkot. Pakistan International Airlines operates domestic air services between the principal cities as well as international services. The main seaports are Karachi and Port Muhammad bin Qasim. A deepwater port at Gwadar in Balochistan, funded and constructed by China, became fully functional in 2008, and there are numerous plans to further develop the city as a regional energy and transport hub.

Recent investment has resulted in dramatic improvements in the fixed-line and mobile telephone infrastructure. Since 2000, fixed-line availability has risen gradually but mobile phone distribution has rocketed; in 2009 there were 4.05 million fixed lines in use, while mobile phone subscribers numbered 103 million. In 2009 there were 20.4 million internet users.

EDUCATION AND HEALTH
Education is free to upper secondary level.
Literacy rate – 54.2 per cent (2008 est)
Gross enrolment ratio (percentage of relevant age group) – primary 85 per cent; secondary 33 per cent; tertiary 6 per cent (2009 est)
Health expenditure (per capita) – US$23 (2009)
Hospital beds (per 1,000 people) – 0.6 (2004–9)

MEDIA
There are eight national daily newspapers, and the state-owned broadcaster, Pakistan Television Corporation Ltd, competes with around 50 private channels. The government has granted licences for a number of satellite television and radio stations since 2004. A number of unlicensed broadcasters are believed to exist in the north of the country.

PALAU

Beluu er a Belau – Republic of Palau

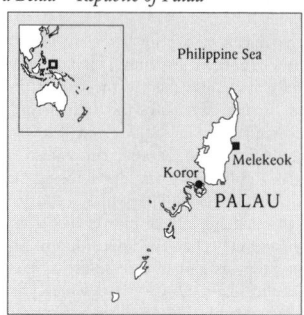

Area – 459 sq. km
Capital – Melekeok, on Babeldaob; population, 566 (2009 est)
Major town – Koror
Currency – US dollar (US$) of 100 cents
Population – 20,879 rising at 0.37 per cent a year (2010 est); Palauan (69.9 per cent), Filipino (15.3 per cent), Chinese (4.9 per cent) (2000)
Religion – Christian (Roman Catholic 42 per cent, Protestant 25 per cent, Seventh-day Adventist 5 per cent), Modekngei 9 per cent (2000). Modekngei is unique to Palau and combines elements of animism and Christian beliefs
Language – Palauan (official in most islands), English (official in all islands), Tobi, Sonsorolese, Angaur (official in respective islands), Japanese (official in Angaur), Filipino, Chinese
Population density – 44 per sq. km (2009)
Urban population – 80 per cent (2008 est)
Median age (years) – 32.4 (2010 est)
National anthem – 'Belau rekid' ['Our Palau']
National day – 9 July (Constitution Day)
Life expectancy (years) – 71.51 (2010 est)
Mortality rate – 7.81 (2010 est)
Birth rate – 10.68 (2010 est)
Infant mortality rate – 12.78 (2010 est)
Death penalty – Abolished for all crimes (since 1994)
Literacy rate – 91.9 per cent (2008 est)

CLIMATE AND TERRAIN
The republic consists of six island groups in the western Pacific Ocean; these comprise eight large islands and over 300 smaller islands or islets that are either volcanic and mountainous or coral and low-lying. Elevation extremes range from 242m (Mt Ngerchelchuus) to 0m (Pacific Ocean). The climate is tropical, with a wet season from May to November. Average daily temperatures are an almost constant 27°C.

HISTORY AND POLITICS
Palau has been inhabited since the first millennium BC. In the 19th century, Spain and Germany vied for possession until 1889, when Spain sold the islands to Germany, which exploited the phosphate deposits and developed coconut plantations. Japan occupied the islands on behalf of the Allies in 1914 and administered them after the First World War under a League of Nations mandate. Japanese forces were ousted by US troops during the Second World War.

In 1947 the islands became part of the UN Trust Territory of the Pacific, administered by the USA. In 1982 a compact of free association was signed with the USA under which the USA retained responsibility for defence and foreign policy in return for providing economic aid; the compact was ratified in 1993 and entered into force when Palau became independent on 1 October 1994.

The latest presidential and legislative elections were held in 2008; Johnson Toribiong was elected president.

POLITICAL SYSTEM
Under the 1981 constitution, the executive president is directly elected for a four-year term, renewable once. The president appoints the cabinet. The bicameral National Congress comprises the House of Delegates, which has 16 members (one from each state), and the 13-member senate; members of both chambers stand for election as independents, and serve a four-year term. A council of indigenous chiefs, composed of the paramount chief from each of the 16 states, acts as an advisory body to the president on matters concerning traditional law and customs.

Each of the 16 constituent states has its own governor and legislature.

HEAD OF STATE
President, Johnson Toribiong, *elected* 4 November 2008, *inaugurated* 15 January 2009
Vice-President, Finance, Kerai Mariur

SELECTED GOVERNMENT MEMBERS *as at July 2011*
Industry and Commerce, Jackson Ngiraingas
Minister of State, Victor Yano

BRITISH AMBASSADOR
HE Stephen Lillie, *apptd* 2009, resident at Manila, the Philippines

ECONOMY AND TRADE
The economy is reliant on economic aid from the USA and the government is keen to diversify. Tourism is now the main industry, catering for over 80,000 people a year, but the government is limiting development to protect the environment. The other main industries are handicrafts, construction and garment manufacturing. Subsistence agriculture and fishing remain important, engaging 20 per cent of the workforce and producing crops such as coconuts, copra, cassava and sweet potatoes as well as fish. Revenue is also derived from the sale of licences to foreign fishing fleets.

The main trading partners are the USA, Japan, Taiwan, Singapore and South Korea. Principal exports are shellfish, tuna, copra and clothing. The main imports are machinery and equipment, fuels, metals and foodstuffs.
GNI – US$127m; US$6,220 per capita (2009)
Annual average growth of GDP – 5.5 per cent (2005 est)
Inflation rate – 2.7 per cent (2005 est)
Unemployment – 4.2 per cent (2005 est)

Trade with UK	2009	2010
Imports from UK	£5,500	£108,816
Exports to UK	–	–

COMMUNICATIONS
There are 61km of roads, but no railways. There are three airports, on Koror, Peleliu and Angaur, which receive international flights from Guam, Japan, the Philippines and Taiwan. Koror is also the main seaport. Telecommunications systems are widely available, with about 100 per 100 people subscribing to either fixed-line or mobile phone services.

MEDIA
There is no television station in Palau, but most households can receive US and satellite television via cable. Radio broadcasting is provided by one government and two private stations, and there are three weekly news publications.

PANAMA

República de Panamá – Republic of Panama

Area – 75,420 sq. km
Capital – Panama City; population, 1,346,260 (2009 est)
Major cities – Colón, Davíd
Currency – Balboa of 100 centésimos; at parity with the US dollar, which is used as paper currency. Both Panamanian and US coins are used
Population – 3,410,676 rising at 1.46 per cent a year (2010 est)
Religion – Christian (Roman Catholic 75 per cent, Protestant 15 per cent) (est)
Language – Spanish (official), English
Population density – 46 per sq. km (2009)
Urban population – 73 per cent (2008 est)
Median age (years) – 27.2 (2010 est)
National anthem – 'Himno Istmeño' ['Hymn of the Isthmus']
National day – 3 November (Independence Day)
Life expectancy (years) – 77.61 (2010 est)
Mortality rate – 4.62 (2010 est)
Birth rate – 19.71 (2010 est)
Infant mortality rate – 11.97 (2010 est)
Death penalty – Abolished for all crimes (since 1922)
CPI score – 3.6 (2010)

CLIMATE AND TERRAIN
Panama lies on the isthmus connecting North and South America. A mountain range runs along the centre, falling to coastal plains on both coasts. There is dense tropical rainforest in the east. Elevation extremes range from 3,475m (Volcan Baru) to 0m (Pacific Ocean). The climate is tropical, with a prolonged wet season from May to January. Average temperatures are relatively constant throughout the year, and range between 22°C and 32°C.

HISTORY AND POLITICS
Panama was visited by Spanish explorers from 1502, and in 1519 became part of the Viceroyalty of New Andalucia, later New Grenada. It became a strategically important centre of trade. When it gained its

independence from Spain in 1821, Panama joined the confederacy of Gran Colombia (comprising Colombia, Venezuela, Ecuador, Peru and Bolivia). The confederacy split up in 1830 and Panama became part of Colombia until 1903, when it achieved its independence.

In the 1880s, the French attempted to construct a canal across Panama to link the Atlantic and Pacific oceans. In 1903 the USA bought the rights to build the canal, which was completed in 1914 and opened in 1919. The USA was also given control of the canal and land to either side of it, known as the Canal Zone, in perpetuity but, under a 1977 agreement, sovereignty over the Canal Zone was transferred to Panama in 2000.

Panama was under the military rule of General Omar Torrijos from 1968 until his death in 1981. In 1983, General Manuel Noriega seized power and instigated a period of military rule, supported by the USA until 1987. An internal coup to unseat Noriega was unsuccessful in 1988, but in 1989 US forces invaded and deposed him. Noriega surrendered in 1990 and was tried and sentenced in the USA on drug-trafficking and money-laundering charges in 1992.

The 2009 presidential election was won by Ricardo Martinelli of the Democratic Change party. In the simultaneous legislative election, the governing *Partido Revolucionario Democrática* (PRD) was again the individual party with the most seats, but the combined seats of the four-party Alliance for Change coalition led by Martinelli constituted a majority.

POLITICAL SYSTEM

Under the 1972 constitution, as amended in 1983, the executive president is directly elected for a five-year term, which is not renewable. The unicameral National Assembly has 71 members, who are directly elected for a five-year term. The president, who is responsible to the legislature, appoints the cabinet.

HEAD OF STATE

President, Ricardo Martinelli, *elected* 3 May 2009, *sworn in* 1 July 2009

First Vice-President, Foreign Affairs, Juan Carlos Varela

SELECTED GOVERNMENT MEMBERS *as at July 2011*
Interior, Roxana Mendez
Economy and Finance, Alberto Vallarino Clement

EMBASSY OF PANAMA
40 Hertford Street, London W1J 7SH
T 020-7493 4646 E panama1@btconnect.com
Ambassador Extraordinary and Plenipotentiary,
  HE Gilberto Arias, *apptd* 2009

BRITISH EMBASSY
PO Box 0816–07946, Torre MMG, Calle 53, Marbella, Panama City 1
T (+507) 269 0866 E britemb@cwpanama.net.pa
W http://ukinpanama.fco.gov.uk
Ambassador Extraordinary and Plenipotentiary, HE Michael Holloway, OBE, *apptd* 2011

DEFENCE

Panama abolished its armed forces in 1991. The National Maritime Service has 18 patrol and coastal combatant vessels at 3 bases.
Military budget – US$230m (2010)
Military personnel – none active; paramilitary 12,000

ECONOMY AND TRADE

The economy is based on a large service sector and has experienced steady growth in recent years, although this slowed in 2009 because of the global economic downturn. However, the distribution of wealth is uneven, and about one-quarter of the population lives below the poverty line.

The service sector accounts for 77.6 per cent of GDP, derived from the operation of the Panama Canal and the Colón free trade zone, financial services, container ports, ship registry and tourism. Enlargement of the canal to take more and larger vessels began in 2007 and is scheduled for completion in 2014. Industry, which contributes 16.6 per cent of GDP, includes construction, brewing, sugar refining and the manufacture of cement and other construction materials. Agriculture, which accounts for 5.8 per cent of GDP, is centred on bananas, rice, maize, coffee, sugar cane, vegetables, livestock and shrimp.

The main trading partners are Japan, the USA, Singapore, South Korea, EU countries and China. Principal exports are bananas, shrimp, sugar, coffee and clothing. The main imports are capital goods, foodstuffs, consumer goods and chemicals.

GNI – US$23,059m; US$6,570 per capita (2009)
Annual average growth of GDP – 5.1 per cent (2010 est)
Inflation rate – 3.3 per cent (2010 est)
Population below poverty line – 28.6 per cent (2006 est)
Unemployment – 4.4 per cent (2010 est)
Total external debt – US$13,850m (2010 est)
Imports – US$7,800m (2009)
Exports – US$900m (2009)

BALANCE OF PAYMENTS

Trade – US$8,100m deficit (2010)
Current Account – US$12m deficit (2009)

Trade with UK	2009	2010
Imports from UK	£117,258,733	£169,746,784
Exports to UK	£13,937,526	£18,209,303

COMMUNICATIONS

The Panama Canal connects the Pacific and Atlantic oceans, significantly shortening sea journeys between the two. Each year the canal handles over 14,000 transits, containing around 300 million tonnes (net) of cargo; this is about 5 per cent of world trade and over 40 per cent of trade between Asia and the east coast of the USA. The chief ports are Colón, Cristóbal and Balboa, at either end of the canal. Because of its role as a ship registry, there were 6,379 Panamanian- and 5,244 foreign-owned ships of over 1,000 tonnes registered under its flag in 2010.

Apart from the 82km of the canal, there are over 700km of navigable waterways. These are supplemented by 76km of railways and 12,000km of roads. There are 118 airports and airfields; the principal airport is at Panama City.

Modern telephone systems served 537,100 fixed-line subscribers, 5.7 million mobile phone subscribers and 960,000 internet users in 2009.

EDUCATION AND HEALTH

There are nine years of compulsory education.
Literacy rate – 93.6 per cent (2008 est)
Gross enrolment ratio (percentage of relevant age group) –
  primary 111 per cent; secondary 71 per cent; tertiary 45 per cent (2008 est)

Health expenditure (per capita) – US$591 (2009)
Hospital beds (per 1,000 people) – 2.2 (2004–9)

MEDIA
The freedom of the media has improved markedly in recent years owing to the repeal of restrictive legislation in 2005. Broadcasting is dominated by the private sector, and there are several television networks and about 100 radio stations. *La Prensa, Panama News* and *El Siglo* are among the leading newspapers.

PAPUA NEW GUINEA

Gau Hedinarai ai Papua-Matamata Guinea – Independent State of Papua New Guinea

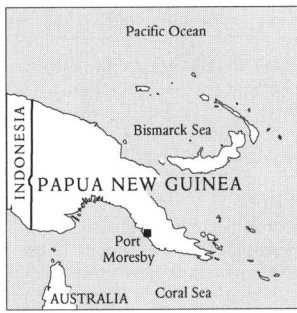

Area – 462,840 sq. km
Capital – Port Moresby; population, 313,593 (2009 est)
Major town – Lae
Currency – Kina (K) of 100 toea
Population – 6,064,515 rising at 2.03 per cent a year (2010 est)
Religion – Christian (Protestant 69 per cent, Roman Catholic 27 per cent), indigenous beliefs and other 4 per cent (2000); Christian beliefs are often combined with elements of indigenous beliefs
Language – English, Tok Pisin, Hiri Motu (all official), Motu; 860 indigenous languages are spoken, representing over 10 per cent of the world total
Population density – 15 per sq. km (2009)
Urban population – 12 per cent (2008 est)
Median age (years) – 21.6 (2010 est)
National anthem – 'O Arise, All You Sons'
National day – 16 September (Independence Day)
Life expectancy (years) – 65.99 (2010 est)
Mortality rate – 6.62 (2010 est)
Birth rate – 26.95 (2010 est)
Infant mortality rate – 44.59 (2010 est)
HIV/AIDS adult prevalence rate – 1.4 per cent (2007 est)
Death penalty – Retained (not used since 1950)
CPI score – 2.1 (2010)

CLIMATE AND TERRAIN
Papua New Guinea lies in the south-western Pacific Ocean and consists of the eastern half of the island of New Guinea, the islands of Bougainville, New Britain and New Ireland, the Admiralty Islands, the D'Entrecasteaux Islands and the Louisiade archipelago. A range of densely forested mountains runs across the centre of the Papuan part of New Guinea, descending to coastal plains and swamps, and coral reefs. Elevation extremes range from 4,509m (Mt Wilhelm) to 0m (Pacific Ocean). There are a number of active volcanoes and the country is subject to frequent eruptions and earthquakes. Over 50 per cent of the country is forested, and 20 per cent is permanently or seasonally flooded. The climate is tropical and subject to the north-west monsoon (December–March) and south-east monsoon (May–October).

HISTORY AND POLITICS
New Guinea was visited by Europeans from the 16th century, before being colonised in the 19th century. The Dutch incorporated the western part of the island (now Papua province, Indonesia) into the Dutch East Indies in 1828. In 1884–6, Britain and Germany divided the east of the island. A British protectorate was proclaimed over south-eastern New Guinea and the adjacent islands, which were annexed outright in 1888 and placed under Australian administration in 1906. The north-east was claimed by Germany in 1884 and became a colony in 1899. This was occupied by Australia in the First World War, and both the British territory and the German-mandated territory were administered by Australia from 1920 until 1942. The territories were occupied by Japan between 1942 and 1945. After the Second World War the territories were combined as a UN trust territory and administered by Australia before becoming self-governing in 1973 and independent on 16 September 1975.

Separatism on Bougainville island led to nine years of conflict (1989–98) in which an estimated 20,000 people died. A peace agreement in 2001 provided for autonomy for the island and guaranteed a referendum on independence 10 to 15 years after the election of an autonomous government. The first autonomous government was elected in 2005.

Border areas are sometimes affected by the overspill from fighting between separatists and Indonesian forces in the Indonesian province of Papua. Thousands of refugees from this conflict live in camps along the border.

Factionalism and shifting alliances have caused political instability since independence, and a proportional representation element was introduced into the voting system in 2007 to try to increase the stability of governments. Following the 2007 legislative election, the coalition led by National Alliance Party (NAP) remained the largest party in parliament, and the NAP leader Sir Michael Somare was elected prime minister for the fourth time, forming a new coalition government. Somare was convicted of financial irregularities in March 2011, was suspended for 14 days and has been on indefinite medical leave since; deputy prime minister Sam Abal is acting prime minister.

POLITICAL SYSTEM
The 1975 constitution was amended in 1998 to grant greater autonomy to Bougainville, and in March 2010 to expand the maximum number of cabinet ministers from 28 to 31. The head of state is Queen Elizabeth II, represented by a governor-general who is elected by the legislature for a six-year term. The unicameral National Parliament has 109 members, 20 from provincial electorates and the remainder from open electorates, who are directly elected for a five-year term. The prime minister is nominated by the legislature and appointed by the governor-general.

Governor-General, Michael Ogio, *sworn in* 25 February 2011

SELECTED GOVERNMENT MEMBERS *as at July 2011*
Prime Minister, Sir Michael Somare

Acting Prime Minister, Deputy Prime Minister, Sam Abal
Foreign Affairs, Ano Pala

PAPUA NEW GUINEA HIGH COMMISSION
14 Waterloo Place, London SW1Y 4AR
T 020-7930 0922 E info@png.org.uk
W www.pnghighcomm.org.uk
High Commissioner, HE Winnie Kiap, *apptd* 2011

BRITISH HIGH COMMISSION
Sec 411 Lot 1 & 2, Kiroki Street, Waigani, Port Moresby
T (+675) 325 1677 E ukinpng@datec.net.pg
W http://ukinpng.fco.gov.uk
High Commissioner, HE Jacqueline Barson, *apptd* 2010

DEFENCE
The Maritime Element has 4 patrol and coastal combatant vessels at four bases.
Military budget – US$43m (2010)
Military personnel – 3,100: army 2,500, air force 200, Maritime Element 400

ECONOMY AND TRADE
Political instability, corruption, a weak economy and high unemployment and crime levels had brought the country to the brink of economic and social collapse in 2004. The economy has grown since, owing to higher commodity prices and tight control of the national budget, but the country remains poor and underdeveloped. It is dependent on foreign aid, mostly from Australia, which accounts for nearly 20 per cent of the budget, but foreign investment in oil and liquid natural gas extraction since 2004 is expected to boost future economic growth.

Only about 1 per cent of the land area is suitable for commercial crops. About 85 per cent of the population practises subsistence farming, including some tribes in the interior so isolated that their economy is unmonetised. Mineral deposits, including copper, gold, silver, nickel, oil and natural gas, are abundant and constitute the main sources of revenue, although exploitation is hampered by the terrain and poor infrastructure. The main industries are mining, oil extraction and refining, forestry, processing of agricultural and forestry products, construction and tourism. Industry contributes 36 per cent of GDP and services 32 per cent.

The main trading partners are Australia, China, Japan and Singapore. Principal exports are oil, gold, copper ore, logs, palm oil, coffee, cocoa and shellfish. The main imports are machinery and transport equipment, manufactured goods, food, fuels and chemicals.
GNI – US$7,833m; US$1,180 per capita (2009)
Annual average growth of GDP – 6.2 per cent (2010 est)
Inflation rate – 6.8 per cent (2010 est)
Population below poverty line – 37 per cent (2002 est)
Unemployment – 1.8 per cent (2004 est)
Total external debt – US$1,548m (2010 est)
Imports – US$3,500m (2009)
Exports – US$4,500m (2009)

BALANCE OF PAYMENTS
Trade – US$2,215m surplus (2010)
Current Account – US$805m surplus (2008)

Trade with UK	2009	2010
Imports from UK	£14,088,206	£25,026,287
Exports to UK	£54,000,192	£56,304,815

COMMUNICATIONS
Dense forest in the interior means that most internal travel is by air or water. There are 11,000km of inland waterways and 9,349km of roads, of which about a third are surfaced; the most important road links Lae with the populous highlands. There are 562 airports and airstrips, the principal airports being at Port Moresby, Lae and Rabaul. Air Niugini operates regular flights internally and throughout the region. The main seaports are Port Moresby, Lae and Madang on New Guinea and Kimbe and Rabaul on New Britain. Several shipping companies operate cargo services world-wide, but cargo and passenger services between the main ports and outports are very limited.

Telephone services are minimal; combined density of fixed lines and mobile phones has risen since 2005, but only to 15 per 100 people, as mobile phone ownership in particular has grown rapidly.

EDUCATION AND HEALTH
Literacy rate – 58.2 per cent (2008 est)
Gross enrolment ratio (percentage of relevant age group) – primary 55 per cent (2008 est)
Health expenditure (per capita) – US$37 (2009)

MEDIA
Radio is the most important medium owing to the widely scattered population and low literacy levels. There are state-run and private radio and television broadcasters, although television coverage is limited to Port Moresby and regional capitals. There are two foreign-owned daily newspapers and a number of weekly publications.

PARAGUAY

República del Paraguay – Republic of Paraguay

Area – 406,752 sq. km
Capital – Asunción; population, 1,977,340 (2009 est)
Major cities – Ciudad del Este, Lambaré, Limpio, Ñemby
Currency – Guaraní (Gs) of 100 céntimos
Population – 6,375,830 rising at 1.31 per cent a year (2010 est)
Religion – Christian (Roman Catholic 90 per cent, Protestant 6 per cent) (est)
Language – Spanish, Guaraní (both official)
Population density – 16 per sq. km (2009)
Urban population – 60 per cent (2008 est)
Median age (years) – 24.9 (2010 est)
National anthem – 'Paraguayos, República o Muerte' ['Paraguayans, the Republic or Death']
National day – 15 May (Independence Day)
Life expectancy (years) – 75.99 (2010 est)

Mortality rate – 4.55 (2010 est)
Birth rate – 17.73 (2010 est)
Infant mortality rate – 23.83 (2010 est)
Death penalty – Abolished for all crimes (since 1992)
CPI score – 2.2 (2010)

CLIMATE AND TERRAIN

The landlocked country is divided by the river Paraguay into two distinct regions. The area east of the Paraguay is a fertile, grassy plateau where most of the population lives. The area to the west, the Gran Chaco, consists of a grassy and occasionally marshy plain that extends into neighbouring countries. Elevation extremes range from 842m (Cerro Pero) to 46m (the junction of the Paraguay and Paraná rivers). The climate varies from subtropical to temperate, with higher rainfall in the east and semi-arid conditions in the west. Average temperatures in Asunción range from 14°C in July to 35°C in January.

HISTORY AND POLITICS

Spanish colonisation of Paraguay began in the early 16th century and Asunción was founded in 1537. Paraguay became independent from Spain in 1811 under the dictator José Gaspar Rodriguez de Francia, who ruled until his death in 1840. His successors instigated a period of reform and modernisation which ended in 1865–70 with the catastrophic War of the Triple Alliance against Brazil, Uruguay and Argentina over access to the sea. The war resulted in the loss of over half the population as well as 150,000 sq. km of territory, and initiated a period of political instability that lasted until 1912. In the Chaco War of 1932–5, Paraguay gained territory in the west from Bolivia.

Political instability and conflict in the late 1940s ended with a coup in 1954 in which General Alfredo Stroessner seized power. His rule was autocratic and increasingly repressive, marked by corruption and human rights abuses. He was ousted in a coup in 1989 that paved the way for free multiparty elections to the presidency and legislature in 1993. These were won by the National Republican Association-Colorado Party (ANR-PC) and its presidential candidate, and the ANR-PC won all subsequent elections until 2008. Instability has prevailed since the 1990s, however, with the assassination of a vice-president, an attempted coup, widespread corruption and the growth of drug-trafficking, money-laundering and organised crime.

The 2008 presidential election was won by Fernando Lugo of the Patriotic Alliance for Change coalition (APC), the first president from outside the ANR-PC in 61 years. In the simultaneous legislative election, the ANR-PC remained the largest single party in both legislative chambers but the APC coalition held a greater number of seats.

POLITICAL SYSTEM

Under the 1992 constitution, the executive president is directly elected for a five-year term, which is not renewable. The bicameral Congress consists of a 45-member senate and an 80-member Chamber of Deputies, both directly elected for a five-year term. The president, who is responsible to the legislature, appoints the council of ministers.

HEAD OF STATE

President, Fernando Lugo, *elected* 20 April 2008, *sworn in* 15 August 2008
Vice-President, Federico Franco

SELECTED GOVERNMENT MEMBERS *as at July 2011*

Defence, Gen. (retd) Cecilio Perez Bordon
Foreign Affairs, Hector Lacognata
Interior, Rafael Filizzola

EMBASSY OF THE REPUBLIC OF PARAGUAY

3rd Floor, 344 Kensington High Street, London W14 8NS
T 020-7610 4180 E embapar@btconnect.com
W www.paraguayembassy.co.uk
Ambassador Extraordinary and Plenipotentiary,
HE Miguel Solano López, *apptd* 2009

BRITISH AMBASSADOR

HE Shan Morgan, *apptd* 2008, resident in Buenos Aires, Argentina

DEFENCE

The army has 5 main battle tanks and 30 armoured personnel carriers. The navy has 20 patrol and coastal combatant vessels at 3 bases. The air force has 6 combat aircraft.

Military budget – US$142m (2010)
Military personnel – 10,650: army 7,600, navy 1,950, air force 1,100; paramilitary 14,800
Conscription duration – 12–24 months

ECONOMY AND TRADE

Economic reforms, a condition of IMF loans in 2002, helped the economy expand rapidly from 2003 to 2008. The economy started to slow in 2008, when drought reduced production of key exports, and went into recession in 2009, when the global downturn reduced export demand and commodity prices. Although growth resumed in 2010, in the longer term it is hampered by political instability, corruption, national and foreign debt, inadequate infrastructure and high crime levels. A large unofficial economy exists. Nearly one-fifth of the population lives below the poverty line, although this rate is higher in the cities because of migration from the countryside of families made landless by the commercialisation of agriculture and forest clearances.

The country has few mineral resources although exploration for oil and gas is under way. The economy is largely agricultural, much of it at subsistence level. Agricultural production, which accounts for 21.8 per cent of GDP and engages 26.5 per cent of the workforce, is centred on cotton, sugar cane, soya beans, maize, wheat, tobacco, cassava, fruit, vegetables and livestock products. The main industries are sugar refining, forestry, manufacturing (cement, textiles, beverages, wood products, steel) and hydro-electric power generation. Industry accounts for 18.2 per cent of GDP and services for 60.1 per cent.

The main trading partners are Brazil, China, Argentina, Uruguay and Chile. Principal exports are soya beans, feed, cotton, meat, edible oils, electricity, timber and leather. The main imports are road vehicles, consumer goods, tobacco and petroleum products.

GNI – US$13,951m; US$2,250 per capita (2009)
Annual average growth of GDP – 6.5 per cent (2010 est)
Inflation rate – 4.2 per cent (2010 est)
Population below poverty line – 19.4 per cent (2008 est)
Unemployment – 6.9 per cent (2010 est)
Total external debt – US$4,346m (2010 est)
Imports – US$6,900m (2009)
Exports – US$3,200m (2009)

BALANCE OF PAYMENTS
Trade – US$5,280m deficit (2010)
Current Account – US$412m deficit (2008)

Trade with UK	2009	2010
Imports from UK	£17,778,619	£28,290,991
Exports to UK	£3,092,625	£10,173,276

COMMUNICATIONS
Although landlocked, Paraguay has 3,100km of navigable waterways on its rivers. Direct shipping services operate between Asunción and Europe and the USA, and river steamer services provide internal transport. There are 29,500km of roads, including connections with Sao Paulo and Buenos Aires, but many are impassable in severe weather. Paraguay has 36km of railways. There are 15 airports, including the principal airport at Asunción, and around 785 airfields and airstrips around the country.

The fixed-line telephone system is not extensive so mobile phone distribution has risen rapidly. In 2009 there were 387,300 fixed lines in use, 5.6 million mobile phone subscribers and 1.1 million internet users.

EDUCATION AND HEALTH
Basic education is free and compulsory for nine years.
Literacy rate – 94.6 per cent (2008 est)
Gross enrolment ratio (percentage of relevant age group) – primary 105 per cent; secondary 66 per cent; tertiary 29 per cent (2007 est)
Health expenditure (per capita) – US$159 (2009)
Hospital beds (per 1,000 people) – 1.3 (2004–9)

MEDIA
The media operates freely, although journalists investigating politically sensitive issues can experience harassment. Most of the media is privately owned, but there is a state-run national radio station. There has been a proliferation of unlicensed radio stations close to the Argentinian and Brazilian borders.

PERU

República del Perú – Republic of Peru

Area – 1,285,216 sq. km
Capital – Lima; population (including Callao), 8,769,350 (2009 est)
Major cities – Arequipa, Chiclayo, Iquitos, Piura, Trujillo
Currency – New sol of 100 centimos
Population – 29,907,003 rising at 1.19 per cent a year (2010 est)

Religion – Christian (Roman Catholic 81 per cent, Protestant 13 per cent) (2007 est)
Language – Spanish, Quechua (both official), Aymara, other Amerindian languages
Population density – 23 per sq. km (2009)
Urban population – 71 per cent (2008 est)
Median age (years) – 26.4 (2010 est)
National anthem – 'Somos libres, seámoslo siempre' ['We Are Free, Let Us Remain So Forever']
National day – 28 July (Independence Day)
Life expectancy (years) – 71.03 (2010 est)
Mortality rate – 6.13 (2010 est)
Birth rate – 19 (2010 est)
Infant mortality rate – 27.74 (2010 est)
Death penalty – Retained for certain crimes (last used 1979)
CPI score – 3.5 (2010)

CLIMATE AND TERRAIN
Peru has three main regions: the Costa, the coastal desert plain west of the Andes; the Sierra (mountain range) of the Andes, which runs parallel to the Pacific coast; and the Montaña (or Selva), a vast area of jungle stretching from the eastern foothills of the Andes to the country's eastern and north-eastern borders. Elevation extremes range from 6,768m (Nevado Huascaran) to 0m (Pacific Ocean). The climate is arid in the west, temperate in the mountains and tropical in the east. Occasionally, due to the El Niño weather system, the northern districts experience a period of higher temperatures accompanied by torrential rain. Average temperatures in Lima range from 14°C from June to October to 27°C in February.

HISTORY AND POLITICS
The Inca Empire centred on Cuzco superseded earlier civilisations in Peru and flourished from the 13th to the 15th century, when the empire reached its zenith before falling to Spanish conquistadores led by Francisco Pizarro in 1532–3. The territory formed the Viceroyalty of Peru and its gold and silver mines made Peru the principal source of wealth in Spain's American empire. After 1810, Peru became the centre of Spanish colonial government as its other colonies rebelled. Although Peru declared independence in 1821, this was achieved only with the final defeat of Spanish forces in 1824.

Peru entered into several border disputes with its neighbours in the 19th and 20th centuries, including the Pacific War (1879–83) in which it lost three southern coastal provinces to Chile. A border dispute with Ecuador was renewed in 1981, leading to a short, inconclusive war in 1995, but was resolved in 1998 following adjudication. A border dispute with Chile ended in 1999 with the implementation of accords first agreed in 1929.

Following independence, Peru alternated between periods of military dictatorship and democratic rule. The most recent return to democracy, in 1980, has not brought greater political stability or improved economic and social equality. Two left-wing insurgencies, by the Maoist *Sendero Luminoso* (Shining Path) and the *Movimento Revolucionario Tupac Amaru* (MRTA), began in the 1980s. The activities of the *Sendero Luminoso* in particular destabilised the government and the economy; the conflict caused about 69,000 deaths and saw human rights abuses by both the security forces and the guerrillas. By the late 1990s both insurgencies had been overcome, although a few Maoists remain active. The conflict has left a legacy of criminal violence, much of it related to drug production and trafficking.

Alberto Fujimori, elected president in 1990 on a platform of economic reform, subverted democratic institutions in Peru during his decade in power, suspending the legislature for three years, sacking judges and imposing order through an 'emergency national reconstruction government'. He fled to Japan in 2000 to escape corruption charges, but was extradited and convicted in 2007 of abuse of power and in 2009 of human rights abuses.

In the 2011 legislative election, the Peru Wins alliance won the most seats but without a majority. The presidential election was won in the second round in June 2011 by the Peruvian Nationalist Party candidate Ollanta Humala.

POLITICAL SYSTEM
Under the 1993 constitution, the executive president is directly elected for a five-year term, renewable once. The unicameral legislature, the Congress of the Republic, has 120 members, directly elected for a five-year term. The president, who is responsible to the legislature, appoints the council of ministers.

HEAD OF STATE
President, Ollanta Humala, *elected* 5 June 2011, *sworn in* 28 July 2011
Vice-Presidents, Luis Giampietri Rojas; Lourdes Mendoza del Solar

SELECTED GOVERNMENT MEMBERS *as at July 2011*
President of Council of Ministers, Rosario Fernandez Figueroa
Defence, Jaime Thorne León
Economy and Finance, Ismael Benavides Ferreyros
Foreign Affairs, José Antonio García Belaunde
Interior, Gen. Miguel Hidalgo

EMBASSY OF PERU
52 Sloane Street, London SW1X 9SP
T 020-7235 1917 E postmaster@peruembassy-uk.com
W www.peruembassy-uk.com
Ambassador Extraordinary and Plenipotentiary,
HE Hernan Couturier-Mariategui, *apptd* 2008

BRITISH EMBASSY
PO Box 854, Torre Parque Mar (Piso 22), Avenida José Larco 1301, Lima
T (+51) (1) 617 3000 E belima@fco.gov.uk
W http://ukinperu.fco.gov.uk
Ambassador Extraordinary and Plenipotentiary,
HE James Dauris, *apptd* 2010

DEFENCE
The army has 240 main battle tanks and 299 armoured personnel carriers. The navy has 6 submarines, 1 cruiser, 8 frigates, 14 patrol and coastal combatant vessels and 3 armed helicopters at 7 bases. The air force has 78 combat aircraft and 16 armed helicopters.
Military budget – US$1,110m (2010)
Military personnel – 115,000: army 74,000, navy 24,000, air force 17,000; paramilitary 77,000

ECONOMY AND TRADE
The economy has grown steadily since 2002, driven by increased agricultural, fisheries and mining exports, major infrastructure developments and tourism. Poverty remains widespread, but the benefits of economic growth are starting to be felt in the poorer regions and the poverty rate has declined by 19 per cent since 2002. Economic growth slowed in the global downturn, owing to reduced demand for exports and lower commodity prices, but recovered strongly in 2010.

Mineral resources, including copper, gold, silver, zinc, oil and natural gas, are abundant, and extracting and refining these is the mainstay of the economy, although this makes it vulnerable to global price fluctuations. Other industries include steel and metal fabrication, fishing and fish processing, textiles and clothes manufacture and food processing. Agriculture is centred on asparagus, coffee, cocoa, cotton, sugar cane, rice, cereals, vegetables, fruit, coca, medicinal plants, meat and dairy products. Services contribute 55 per cent to GDP, industry 35 per cent and agriculture 10 per cent.

The main trading partners are the USA, China, Switzerland, Japan, other South American countries and Canada. Principal exports are copper, gold, zinc, tin, crude oil and petroleum products, natural gas, coffee, vegetables and fruit. The main imports are oil and petroleum products, chemicals, plastics, machinery, vehicles, telecommunications equipment, iron and steel, and food.

GNI – US$122,566m; US$4,200 per capita (2009)
Annual average growth of GDP – 7.8 per cent (2010 est)
Inflation rate – 1.8 per cent (2010 est)
Population below poverty line – 34.8 per cent (2009 est)
Unemployment – 6.7 per cent (2010 est)
Total external debt – US$33,290m (2010 est)
Imports – US$20,900m (2009)
Exports – US$26,900m (2009)

BALANCE OF PAYMENTS
Trade – US$6,750m surplus (2010)
Current Account – US$248m surplus (2009)

Trade with UK	2009	2010
Imports from UK	£77,558,604	£119,231,578
Exports to UK	£171,220,047	£221,149,418

COMMUNICATIONS
Government economic stimulus packages in 2009–10 largely focused on infrastructure projects. There are 102,887km of roads, including sections of two transnational highways: the east-west Andean Highway, linking the Pacific and Atlantic coasts, and the north–south Pan-American Highway running along the Pacific coast. The state-run railways have 2,020km of track, and 8,800km of inland waterways are navigable, on tributaries of the Amazon and Lake Titicaca. The main seaports are Callao and Matarani. There are over 210 airports and airstrips, including the international airport at Lima.

The fixed-line telephone system is reasonable but limited, with a density of about 10 per 100 people. Mobile phone subscriptions have grown rapidly, to about 85 per 100 people by 2009. There were 9 million internet users in 2009.

EDUCATION AND HEALTH
Education is free and compulsory for 11 years.
Literacy rate – 89.6 per cent (2008 est)
Gross enrolment ratio (percentage of relevant age group) –
primary 109 per cent; secondary 89 per cent (2008 est)
Health expenditure (per capita) – US$201 (2009)
Hospital beds (per 1,000 people) – 1.5 (2004–9)

MEDIA
Media freedom has greatly improved since 2000, but coverage of corruption, drug-trafficking or guerrilla activities has attracted violence against the media. The major broadcasters and newspapers are privately run, with the state-run radio and television stations having relatively small audiences. There are several television networks, six national daily newspapers and a host of commercial radio broadcasters.

THE PHILIPPINES

Republika ng Pilipinas – Republic of the Philippines

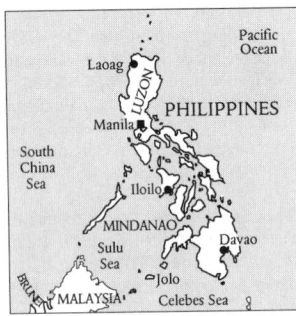

Area – 300,000 sq. km
Capital – Manila; population (Metro Manila, including Quezon City), 11,449,200 (2009 est)
Major cities – Bacolod, Cagayan de Oro, Cebu, Davao, General Santos (Dadiangas), Iloilo, Zamboanga
Currency – Philippine peso (P) of 100 centavos
Population – 99,900,177 rising at 1.93 per cent a year (2010 est); Tagalog (28.1 per cent), Cebuano (13.1 per cent), Ilocano (9 per cent), Bisaya (7.6 per cent), Hiligaynon Ilonggo (7.5 per cent), Bikol (6 per cent), Waray (3.4 per cent) (2000)
Religion – Christian (Roman Catholic 81 per cent, other 12 per cent), Muslim 5 per cent (predominantly Sunni) (est)
Language – Filipino (based on Tagalog), English (both official), Tagalog, Cebuano, Ilocano, Hiligaynon, Bicol, Waray, Pampango, Pangasinan
Population density – 308 per sq. km (2009)
Urban population – 65 per cent (2008 est)
Median age (years) – 22.7 (2010 est)
National anthem – 'Lupang Hinirang' ['Chosen Land']
National day – 12 June (Independence Day)
Life expectancy (years) – 71.38 (2010 est)
Mortality rate – 5.06 (2010 est)
Birth rate – 25.68 (2010 est)
Infant mortality rate – 19.94 (2010 est)
Death penalty – Abolished for all crimes (since 2006)
CPI score – 2.4 (2010)

CLIMATE AND TERRAIN
The Philippines comprises over 7,100 islands in the western Pacific Ocean. The principal islands are Luzon, Mindanao, Mindoro, Samar, Negros, Palawan, Panay and Leyte; other groups include the Sulu islands, Babuyanes and Batanes, Calamian and Kalayaan islands. The islands mostly have mountainous interiors and narrow coastal plains. The mountain ranges are volcanic, and some volcanoes are still active. Elevation extremes range from 2,954m (Mt Apo) to 0m (Philippine Sea). The climate is tropical, with relatively constant temperatures throughout the year which in Manila vary between averages of 22°C in January and February and 34°C in May and June, when the humidity is particularly oppressive. The country is affected by the monsoons, which cause the rainy season between July and October. During this period the country is also susceptible to typhoons, which frequently cause widespread damage and loss of life.

HISTORY AND POLITICS
The Philippine islands were settled first by Malays, then by Chinese, Indonesian and Arab traders. Islam was introduced in the 14th century and became the dominant religion in the south. The islands were discovered by Spain and then settled from 1565 by the Spanish, who introduced Roman Catholicism. Colonial rule lasted until 1898, when Spain ceded the colony to the USA following the Spanish-American War. The country became internally self-governing in 1935, was occupied by Japan from 1942 to 1944, and achieved independence from the USA in 1946.

Ferdinand Marcos was elected president in 1965, imposing martial law in 1972. His regime became increasingly repressive, corrupt and violent, and when he falsified election results in 1986 to prevent Corazon Aquino from taking office as president, a popular uprising forced him to flee the country. Aquino survived political unrest and ten attempted military coups to introduce a new constitution and entrench democratic politics.

Fidel Ramos, Aquino's successor in 1992, built on her work, raised the country's international profile and instigated peace talks with insurgents (*see* below). Joseph Estrada, elected president in 1998, was overthrown in 2001 in a popular uprising; his term was completed by Vice-President Gloria Arroyo. President Arroyo retained the presidency in the 2004 presidential election, but her popularity plummeted and her anti-corruption measures and economic reforms were undermined by corruption scandals and impeachment attempts.

The 2010 presidential election was won by Benigno ('Noynoy') Aquino III, son of former president Corazon Aquino.

INSURGENCY
A communist insurgency by the New People's Army (NPA) began in the late 1960s. The NPA is based in Mindanao but has groups in rural areas throughout the country. Peace talks between the government and the NPA's political front, the National Democratic Front, stalled in 2004 but were resumed in early 2011.

There has been a Muslim (Moro) insurgency in the southern islands, particularly Mindanao, since the 1970s. The Moro National Liberation Front (MNLF) concluded a peace agreement with the government in 1996 that ended its insurgency and established the Autonomous Region of Muslim Mindanao (ARMM). The Moro Islamic Liberation Front (MILF) agreed a ceasefire with the government in 2003, but negotiations over a Muslim 'homeland' broke down in 2008; a resumption of violence in 2009 displaced over 300,000 people until another ceasefire was agreed and peace talks resumed in late 2009.

The radical Muslim separatist group Abu Sayyaf, based on Jolo and Basilan, is viewed as a terrorist organisation and the government refuses to negotiate with it. It has links with Jamaah Islamiyah, the group responsible for the Bali bombings, and possibly with al-Qaida. Since 2001 it has carried out a series of violent kidnappings and bombings, but military operations since 2006 have depleted its numbers and its leadership.

POLITICAL SYSTEM

Under the 1987 constitution, the executive president is directly elected for a six-year term, which is not renewable. There is a bicameral Congress. The lower house, the House of Representatives, has 286–8 members, of whom 231 are directly elected and the rest appointed from party and minority group lists; all serve a three-year term. The senate has 24 members directly elected for a six-year term, with half re-elected every three years.

The Autonomous Region of Muslim Mindanao comprises the provinces of Lanao del Sur and Maguindanao on Mindanao and the island provinces of Sulu, Tawi-Tawi and Basilan. It has a 24-member regional assembly and a governor.

HEAD OF STATE

President, Benigno ('Noynoy') Aquino III, *elected* 10 May 2010, *sworn in* 30 June 2010
Vice-President, Jejomar Binay

SELECTED GOVERNMENT MEMBERS *as at June 2011*

Finance, Cesar Purisima
Trade and Industry, Gregory Domingo
Foreign Affairs, Albert del Rosario
Defence, Voltaire Gazmin

EMBASSY OF THE REPUBLIC OF THE PHILIPPINES

6–8 Suffolk Street, London SW1Y 4HG
T 020-7937 1600 E embassy@philemb.co.uk
W http://philemb.org.uk
Ambassador Extraordinary and Plenipotentiary,
HE Antonio Lagdameo, *apptd* 2009

BRITISH EMBASSY

120 Upper McKinley Road, McKinley Hill, Taguig City 1634, Manila
T (+63) (2) 858 2200 E ukinthephilippines@fco.gov.uk
W http://ukinthephilippines.fco.gov.uk
Ambassador Extraordinary and Plenipotentiary,
HE Stephen Lillie, *apptd* 2009

BRITISH COUNCIL

10th Floor, Taipan Place, F Ortigas Jr Road, Ortigas Centre, Pasig City 1605
T (+63) (2) 914 1011 W www.britishcouncil.org/philippines
Director, Amanda Burrell

DEFENCE

The army has 36 armoured infantry fighting vehicles and 293 armoured personnel carriers. The navy has 1 frigate and 65 patrol and coastal vessels at 3 bases. The air force has 34 combat aircraft and 20 multi-role helicopters.
Military budget – US$2,130m (2010)
Military personnel – 125,000: army 86,000, navy 24,000, air force 15,000; paramilitary 40,500

ECONOMY AND TRADE

The economy has been one of the best-performing in the region since 2002, owing to growth in exports, agricultural output and the service industries. Despite this, poverty has increased as economic expansion struggles to offset the high rate of population growth, and nearly a third of the population lives below the poverty line. Remittances from the millions of Filipinos working abroad are vital, accounting for about 10 per cent of GNP,

and helped to cushion the economy in 2009 from the effects of the global downturn, which briefly slowed the rate of growth.

Major industries include electronics assembly, manufacture of clothing, footwear, pharmaceuticals, chemicals and wood products, food processing, oil refining and fishing. The large agricultural sector employs 33 per cent of the workforce, producing sugar cane, coconuts, rice, maize, tropical fruits and livestock products. Agriculture accounts for 13.9 per cent of GDP, industry for 31.3 per cent and services for 54.8 per cent.

The main trading partners are the USA, Japan, China, Singapore, other Asian states and the EU. Principal exports are semiconductors and electronic products, transport equipment, clothing, copper products, petroleum products, coconut oil and fruit. The main imports are electronic products, fuels, machinery and transport equipment, iron and steel, fabrics, grains, chemicals and plastics.

GNI – US$161,127m; US$1,790 per capita (2009)
Annual average growth of GDP – 6.7 per cent (2010 est)
Inflation rate – 4.2 per cent (2010 est)
Population below poverty line – 32.9 per cent (2006 est)
Unemployment – 7.5 per cent (2010 est)
Total external debt – US$61,850m (2010 est)
Imports – US$45,700m (2009)
Exports – US$38,300m (2009)

BALANCE OF PAYMENTS

Trade – US$1,388m deficit (2010)
Current Account – US$8,552m surplus (2009)

Trade with UK	2009	2010
Imports from UK	£257,939,907	£285,673,790
Exports to UK	£690,258,821	£674,036,683

COMMUNICATIONS

There are about 213,151km of roads, and Philippine National Railway operates 995km of railways. The main ports are Manila (Luzon), Cebu, Davao, and Cagayan de Oro and Nasipit (Mindanao), and there are over 420 smaller ports. The South China Sea is an area with a high risk of piracy against shipping. There are 254 airports and airfields, including international airports at Manila, Cebu and Davao City.

There is a good telephone system, and mobile phone distribution has grown rapidly. There were 6.7 million fixed lines in use and 92.2 million mobile phone subscribers in 2010, and 8.2 million internet users in 2009.

EDUCATION AND HEALTH

There are seven years of free and compulsory primary education, followed by three years of free but non-compulsory secondary education.
Literacy rate – 93.5 per cent (2008 est)
Gross enrolment ratio (percentage of relevant age group) – primary 110 per cent; secondary 82 per cent; tertiary 29 per cent (2008 est)
Health expenditure (per capita) – US$67 (2009)
Hospital beds (per 1,000 people) – 0.5 (2004–9)

MEDIA

The media is independent and lively, but journalists are frequently subjected to intimidation and violence, especially in the southern islands. The government-owned IBC television network competes with two commercial broadcasters. There are over 700 radio stations and four main national newspapers, including the *Daily Tribune* and *Malaya*.

POLAND

Rzeczpospolita Polska – Republic of Poland

Area – 312,685 sq. km
Capital – Warsaw; population, 1,709,560 (2009 est)
Major cities – Bydgoszcz, Gdansk, Katowice, Krakow, Lodz, Lublin, Poznan, Szczecin, Wroclaw
Currency – Zloty of 100 groszy
Population – 38,463,689 falling at 0.05 per cent a year (2010 est)
Religion – Christian (Roman Catholic 94 per cent, other 5 per cent) (est)
Language – Polish (official)
Population density – 125 per sq. km (2009)
Urban population – 61 per cent (2008 est)
Median age (years) – 38.2 (2010 est)
National anthem – 'Mazurek Dabrowskiego' ['Dabrowski's Mazurka']
National day – 3 May (Constitution Day)
Life expectancy (years) – 75.85 (2010 est)
Mortality rate – 10.1 (2010 est)
Birth rate – 10.04 (2010 est)
Infant mortality rate – 6.66 (2010 est)
Death penalty – Abolished for all crimes (since 1997)
CPI score – 5.3 (2010)

CLIMATE AND TERRAIN
Poland lies mostly in a great plain crossed by the Oder, Neisse and Vistula rivers. The land rises to the Carpathian, Tatra and Sudeten mountains along the southern border. Elevation extremes range from 2,499m (Rysy) to −2m (Raczki Elblaskie). The climate is continental, and average temperatures in Warsaw range from −6°C in January to 24°C in July.

HISTORY AND POLITICS
Poland emerged as an independent kingdom in the ninth century and reached the height of its power under the Jagiellon dynasty, founded in 1386 by a dynastic marriage that united Poland and Lithuania. This commonwealth, which at its zenith stretched from the Baltic to the Black Sea, was weakened by attacks by its neighbours, and in 1772, 1793 and 1795 its territory was partitioned between Russia, Prussia and Austria. The congress of Vienna (1814–5) created the semi-independent Congress Kingdom of Poland, but this was subsequently incorporated into the Russian Empire.

Poland regained its independence after the First World War under the terms of the treaty of Versailles. The Second World War began with the German invasion of western Poland on 1 September 1939; on 17 September, Soviet forces invaded eastern Poland, and on 21 September Germany and the USSR declared that Poland had ceased to exist. Germany occupied the rest of Poland in 1941 when it launched its offensive against the USSR. The USSR aligned with the Allies, and the country was liberated by Soviet forces in 1944–5. After the war, its boundaries were redrawn. Eastern Poland was ceded to the USSR but the country gained German territory in Silesia along the Oder and Neisse rivers, effectively shifting the state 240km westwards.

The post-war coalition government was Soviet-influenced and in 1947 a communist republic was proclaimed. Nationalisation and agricultural collectivisation programmes were introduced and the Roman Catholic Church was persecuted. In 1980, following a strike at the Gdansk shipyard prompted by economic crisis and popular discontent, a mass movement for civil and national rights coalesced around the newly formed independent trade union Solidarity. The following year, the Communist government declared martial law, driving Solidarity underground. Economic decline and continuing unrest in the 1980s eventually resulted in talks in 1989 that led to multiparty elections later that year; the Communists lost power and Solidarity helped to form a coalition government.

The post-communist governments introduced economic reforms from 1990 but the transition to a market economy caused unemployment and a sharp drop in living standards. Popular discontent and a fragmented parliament led to a succession of short-lived governments. Poland joined NATO in 1999 and the EU in 2004.

In an early election in 2007, the liberal Civic Platform (PO) won most of the seats in both chambers, although without an outright majority in the lower house. The PO formed a coalition government with the Polish Popular Party and independents, under the PO leader Donald Tusk. President Lech Kaczynski, elected in 2005, was killed in a plane crash in Russia in April 2010; his successor, acting president Bronislaw Komorowski of the PO, was elected in July.

POLITICAL SYSTEM
Under the 1997 constitution, the head of state is the president, who is directly elected for a five-year term, renewable once. The president nominates the prime minister and has the right to be consulted over the appointment of the foreign, defence and interior ministers. The National Assembly is bicameral; the lower house, the Diet *(Sejm)*, has 460 members elected by proportional representation for a four-year term. The senate has 100 members elected on a provincial basis for a four-year term.

HEAD OF STATE
President, Bronislaw Komorowski, *elected* 4 July 2010, *sworn in* 6 August 2010

SELECTED GOVERNMENT MEMBERS *as at July 2011*
Prime Minister, Donald Tusk
Deputy Prime Minister, Economy, Waldemar Pawlak
Defence, Bogdan Klich
Foreign Affairs, Radoslaw Sikorski
Finance, Jan Vincent-Rostowski
Interior, Jerzy Miller

EMBASSY OF THE REPUBLIC OF POLAND
47 Portland Place, London W1B 1JH
T 020-7291 3520 E london@msz.gov.pl
W http://london.polemb.net
Ambassador Extraordinary and Plenipotentiary,
HE Barbara Tuge-Erecinska, *apptd* 2006

BRITISH EMBASSY
ul. Kawalerii 12, 00-468 Warsaw
T (+48) (22) 311 0000 E info@britishembassy.pl
W http://ukinpoland.fco.gov.uk
Ambassador Extraordinary and Plenipotentiary,
HE Ric Todd, *apptd* 2007

BRITISH COUNCIL
Al. Jerozolimskie 59, 00-697 Warsaw
T (+48) (22) 695 5900 W www.britishcouncil.org/poland
Director, Tony O'Brien

DEFENCE

The army has 946 main battle tanks, 1,536 armoured infantry fighting vehicles, 40 armoured personnel carriers and 31 armed helicopters. The navy has 5 submarines, 2 frigates, 6 patrol and coastal vessels, and 12 armed helicopters at 5 bases. The air force has 125 combat aircraft.

Military budget – US$8,3500m (2010)
Military personnel – 100,000: army 47,300, navy 8,000, air force 17,500, Special Forces 1,650, joint staff 25,550; paramilitary 21,400

ECONOMY AND TRADE

Poland's successful transition to a market economy in the 1990s came at the cost of high levels of public debt, unemployment and inflation, which were reduced by subsequent governments. The economy has grown steadily since 1992 and particularly since accession to the EU in 2004, avoiding recession in 2008–9. Further economic development is hindered by inefficiency, rigidity and low-level corruption, although the Tusk government is committed to further privatisation and restructuring public finances.

Poland has vast mineral resources, especially coal, and nearly half its area is fertile arable land. The large agricultural sector has been modernised but remains inefficient; it employs 17 per cent of the workforce but contributes only 4 per cent of GDP. The main crops are vegetables, fruit, wheat, meat, eggs and dairy products. The main industries are machine-building, iron and steel production, coal-mining, chemicals, shipbuilding, food processing, glass, beverages and textiles. Industry accounts for 29.2 per cent of GDP.

The main trading partners are other EU countries (especially Germany) and Russia. Principal exports include machinery and vehicles, manufactured and semi-manufactured goods, food and livestock. The main imports are machinery and vehicles, semi-manufactured goods, chemicals, minerals, fuels and lubricants.

GNI – US$416,141m; US$12,260 per capita (2009)
Annual average growth of GDP – 3.3 per cent (2010 est)
Inflation rate – 2.4 per cent (2010 est)
Population below poverty line – 17 per cent (2003 est)
Unemployment – 11.8 per cent (2010 est)
Total external debt – US$252,900m (2010 est)
Imports – US$145,800m (2009)
Exports – US$133,600m (2009)

BALANCE OF PAYMENTS

Trade – US$8,434m deficit (2010)
Current Account – US$26,909m deficit (2008)

Trade with UK	2009	2010
Imports from UK	£2,691,400,545	£3,665,850,931
Exports to UK	£4,611,074,117	£5,929,319,644

COMMUNICATIONS

The country has a total of 19,428km of railways, 423,997km of roads, and 3,997km of navigable rivers and canals. Over 120 airports and airfields are in use; the principal airports are at Warsaw, Krakow, Katowice and Wroclaw. The principal seaports are Gdansk, Gdynia, Swinoujscie and Szczecin.

The fixed-line telephone system is being modernised but progress has been slow, whereas mobile phone distribution has grown very rapidly and fixed-line subscriptions are now falling. In 2009 there were 9.5 million fixed lines in use, 44.5 million mobile phone subscribers and 22.4 million internet users.

EDUCATION AND HEALTH

Elementary education (ages seven to 15) is free and compulsory. Secondary education is also free, but optional.

Literacy rate – 99.3 per cent (2008 est)
Gross enrolment ratio (percentage of relevant age group) – primary 97 per cent; secondary 100 per cent; tertiary 69 per cent (2008 est)
Health expenditure (per capita) – US$804 (2009)
Hospital beds (per 1,000 people) – 6.6 (2004–9)

MEDIA

Freedom of speech is generally respected, although laws against criticism of the political system are still in force. The broadcasting market is the largest in eastern and central Europe. State-owned television (TVP) still has the largest national audience share for its output, although there are competitive commercial and subscription services. State-owned radio reaches just over half the population and there are more than 200 other commercial local and regional stations on air. Poland has over 300 newspapers, most of them local or regional, but less than a third of Poles read any newspaper.

CULTURE

Major writers include Nobel Prize winners Henryk Sienkiewicz (1846–1916), Wladyslaw Stanislaw Reymont (1867–1925), Czeslaw Milosz (1911–2004), Wislawa Szymborska (*b.* 1923), and journalist Ryszard Kapuscinski (1932–2007). The great English-language novelist Joseph Conrad (or Jozef Korzeniowski, 1857–1924) was born in Poland.

Other notable cultural figures include the pianist and composer Frédéric Chopin (1810–49); film directors Krzysztof Kieslowski (1941–96) and Academy Award winner Roman Polanski (*b.* 1933); astronomer Nicolaus Copernicus (1473–1543), who formulated the first heliocentric theory of the solar system, and scientist Marie Curie (1867–1934), who became the first woman to win a Nobel Prize, in recognition for her work in physics (1903) and chemistry (1911).

PORTUGAL

República Portuguesa – Portuguese Republic

Area – 92,090 sq. km
Capital – Lisbon; population, 2,808,190 (2009 est)
Major cities – Oporto
Currency – Euro (€) of 100 cents
Population – 10,735,765 rising at 0.24 per cent a year (2010 est)
Religion – Christian (Roman Catholic 84 per cent, other 2 per cent) (est)
Language – Portuguese, Mirandese (both official)
Population density – 116 per sq. km (2009)
Urban population – 59 per cent (2008 est)
Median age (years) – 39.7 (2010 est)
National anthem – 'A Portuguesa' ['The Portuguese Song']
National day – 10 June (Portugal Day)
Life expectancy (years) – 78.38 (2010 est)
Mortality rate – 10.74 (2010 est)
Birth rate – 10.12 (2010 est)
Infant mortality rate – 4.72 (2010 est)
Death penalty – Abolished for all crimes (since 1976)
CPI score – 6 (2010)

CLIMATE AND TERRAIN
The terrain is mountainous north of the river Tagus, with rolling hills and plains in the south. Elevation extremes range from 2,351m (Ponta do Pico, Azores) to 0m (Atlantic Ocean). Forests of pine, cork oak and eucalyptus cover about 38 per cent of the country. The climate is temperate, with average temperatures in Lisbon ranging from 8°C in January to 28°C in August.

HISTORY AND POLITICS
Part of the Roman Empire from the second century BC, the country was overrun by Vandals and Visigoths in the fifth century AD. The Visigoths were ousted by Muslims from north Africa in the eighth century, but Christian reconquest began in the tenth century and an independent Christian kingdom was established in the 12th century.

Portuguese navigators led the 15th-century European age of exploration and the country soon became a major commercial and colonial power, its empire expanding to include Brazil, parts of China and large areas of Africa. In 1807 Portugal was invaded by Napoleonic France and then became the base from which Allied forces liberated Portugal and Spain in the Peninsular War. The 19th century was politically turbulent, with power struggles between conservative and liberal politicians and between different factions of the royal family. In 1910 an armed uprising in Lisbon drove King Manuel II into exile and a republic was declared.

A period of political instability ensued until the military intervened in 1926. The constitution of 1933 gave formal expression to the authoritarian *Estado Novo* (New State) introduced by Dr Antonio Salazar, prime minister from 1932 until 1968. Marcello Caetano succeeded Salazar in 1968 but the regime's failure to liberalise at home or to conclude wars in the African colonies resulted in the government's overthrow in a military coup in 1974. Great political turmoil followed in 1974–5, a period in which most of the country's colonies gained their independence. Elections in 1976 stabilised the situation and full civilian government was restored in 1982. Portugal joined the EEC in 1986 and adopted the euro in 2002.

The 2006 presidential election was won by the Social Democrat candidate Anibal Cavaco Silva (prime minister 1985–95), and he was re-elected in January 2011. The Socialist Party government, in power since 2005 but as a minority government since the 2009 election, resigned after its austerity programme was defeated in March 2011. In the legislative election in June, the Social Democratic Party (PSD) won the most seats but not an overall majority, and formed a coalition with the Democratic and Social Centre-People's Party and independents under the PSD leader Pedro Passos Coelho.

POLITICAL SYSTEM
Under the 1976 constitution, amended in 1982 and 1989, the head of state is a president who is directly elected for a five-year term, renewable once. The unicameral Assembly of the Republic has 230 members, directly elected by proportional representation for a four-year term. The prime minister, appointed by the president, is usually the leader of the largest party in the assembly.

HEAD OF STATE
President of the Republic, Anibal Cavaco Silva, *elected* 22 January 2006, *sworn in* 9 March 2006, *re-elected* 2011

SELECTED GOVERNMENT MEMBERS *as at July 2011*
Prime Minister, Pedro Passos Coelho
Foreign Affairs, Paulo Portas
Interior, Miguel Macedo
Finance, Vitor Gaspar
Defence, José Pedro Aguiar Branco

EMBASSY OF PORTUGAL
11 Belgrave Square, London SW1X 8PP
T 020-7235 5331 **E** london@portembassy.co.uk
Ambassador Extraordinary and Plenipotentiary,
HE Joao de Vallera, *apptd* 2011

BRITISH EMBASSY
Rua de Sao Bernardo 33, 1249-082 Lisbon
T (+351) (21) 392 4000 **E** ppa.lisbon@fco.gov.uk
W http://ukinportugal.fco.gov.uk
Ambassador Extraordinary and Plenipotentiary,
HE Jill Gallard, *apptd* 2011

BRITISH COUNCIL
Rua Luis Fernandes 1–3, 1249-062 Lisbon
T (+351) (21) 321 4500 **W** www.britishcouncil.org/portugal
Director, Gill Caldicott

DEFENCE
The army has 225 main battle tanks and 473 armoured personnel carriers. The navy has 1 submarine, 5 frigates

and 24 patrol and coastal vessels at 6 bases. The air force has 70 combat aircraft.

Military budget – US$3,190m (2010)

Military personnel – 43,340: army 26,700, navy 10,540, air force 7,100; paramilitary 47,700

ECONOMY AND TRADE

Portugal's economy was transformed after it joined the EU in 1986 into a diversified and increasingly service-based economy. The rapid growth of the 1990s slowed in 2001–8, and the global downturn pushed the economy into recession in 2009. Despite government austerity measures, a budget deficit treble the eurozone limit led to the country's credit rating being downgraded in 2010 amid concerns about the country's ability to service its sovereign debt; in April 2011 the government obtained EU financial support.

Nearly 12 per cent of the workforce is engaged in agriculture, contributing 2.6 per cent of GDP. The chief products are grain, fruit and vegetables, livestock, fish, dairy products and timber and cork from the forests. The main industries are tourism, manufacturing (textiles, footwear, cork, pulp and paper, chemicals, motor vehicle components), metalworking, wine-making, oil refining, and shipbuilding and repair. Natural resources are being exploited to generate electricity from hydroelectric and solar sources to reduce dependence on imported fuel and energy. Industry accounts for 23 per cent of GDP and services for 74.5 per cent.

The main trading partners are other EU countries, particularly Spain and Angola. Principal exports are agricultural products, food, wine, oil products, wood products, other industrial products, machinery and tools. The main imports include agricultural products, chemicals, vehicles, optical and precision instruments, computer and IT components.

GNI – US$225,064m; US$21,910 per capita (2009)

Annual average growth of GDP – 1 per cent (2010 est)

Inflation rate – 1.1 per cent (2010 est)

Population below poverty line – 18 per cent (2006 est)

Unemployment – 10.7 per cent (2010 est)

Total external debt – US$497,800m (2010)

Imports – US$69,900m (2009)

Exports – US$43,400m (2009)

BALANCE OF PAYMENTS

Trade – US$26,656m deficit (2010)

Current Account – US$22,915m deficit (2009)

Trade with UK	2009	2010
Imports from UK	£1,488,712,934	£1,770,801,944
Exports to UK	£1,392,390,660	£1,720,545,975

COMMUNICATIONS

There are 3,319km of railways, of which 1,436km are electrified, and 82,900km of roads. There are 65 airports and airfields, including international airports at Lisbon, Oporto, Faro, Santa Maria (Azores) and Funchal (Madeira). The main ports are Aveiro, Figueira da Foz, Leixoes, Lisbon, Setubal and Sines.

Modern telephone systems served 4 million fixed-line subscribers, 15 million mobile phone subscribers and 5 million internet users in 2009.

EDUCATION AND HEALTH

Education is free and compulsory for nine years from the age of six. Secondary education is mainly conducted in state general unified schools, lyceums, technical and professional schools and private schools. There are also military, naval, polytechnic and other specialist schools. The university at Coimbra was founded in 1290.

Literacy rate – 95.2 per cent (2008 est)

Gross enrolment ratio (percentage of relevant age group) – primary 115 per cent; secondary 104 per cent; tertiary 60 per cent (2008 est)

Health expenditure (per capita) – US$2,410 (2009)

Hospital beds (per 1,000 people) – 3.4 (2004–9)

MEDIA

The monopoly of the public broadcaster RTP ended in 1992, and commercial stations now dominate the market. Public radio networks are operated by RTP, while the Roman Catholic Church owns Radio Renascenca. There are about 300 other local and regional commercial radio stations. Principal national newspapers include the daily titles *Diario de Noticias, Publico, Correio da Manha* and *Jornal de Noticias.*

AUTONOMOUS REGIONS

Madeira and the Azores are both autonomous regions, each with its own locally elected assembly and government.

MADEIRA is a group of islands in the Atlantic Ocean about 990km south-west of Lisbon, and consists of Madeira, Porto Santo and three uninhabited islands. Total area is 801 sq. km; population, 247,399 (2009 est). Funchal on Madeira, the largest island, is the capital.

THE AZORES is an archipelago of nine islands in the Atlantic Ocean 1,400–1,800km west of Lisbon, and consists of Flores, Corvo, Terceira, Sao Jorge, Pico, Faial, Graciosa, Sao Miguel and Santa Maria. Total area is 2,322 sq. km; population, 245,374 (2009 est). Ponta Delgada, on Sao Miguel, is the capital.

QATAR

Dawlat Qatar – State of Qatar

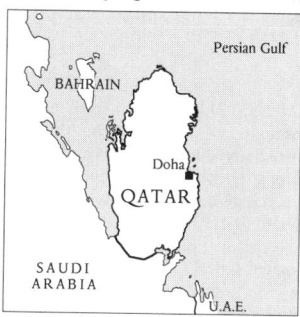

Area – 11,586 sq. km

Capital – Doha; population, 426,617 (2009 est)

Major cities – Ar Rayyan, Al Wakrah

Currency – Qatar riyal of 100 dirhams

Population – 840,926 rising at 0.87 per cent a year (2010 est); Arab (40 per cent), Indian (18 per cent), Pakistani (18 per cent), Iranian (10 per cent) (est)

Religion – Muslim 77 per cent (predominantly Sunni), Christian 8 per cent, other 14 per cent (2004)

Language – Arabic (official), English

Population density – 122 per sq. km (2009)

Urban population – 96 per cent (2008 est)

Median age (years) – 30.8 (2010 est)
National anthem – 'As-Salam al-Amiri' ['The Peace of the Amir']
National day – 18 December
Life expectancy (years) – 75.51 (2010 est)
Mortality rate – 2.44 (2010 est)
Birth rate – 15.54 (2010 est)
Infant mortality rate – 12.24 (2010 est)
Death penalty – Retained
CPI score – 7.7 (2010)
Literacy rate – 93.1 per cent (2008 est)

CLIMATE AND TERRAIN

Qatar occupies a peninsula in the Persian Gulf and is mostly a low-lying desert plain, with sand dunes in the south. Elevation extremes range from 103m (Qurayn Abu al-Bawl) to 0m (Persian Gulf). The country has a desert climate, with low rainfall and average temperatures ranging from 13°C in January to 42°C in July. Humidity along the coast often reaches 90 per cent in summer.

HISTORY AND POLITICS

Towns on the Qatari coast developed into important trading centres from the 18th century. Persian rule of the area ended in the mid-18th century and after a period of conflict, the peninsula became a dependency of Bahrain in the 1850s. A revolt against Bahraini rule in the 1860s was suppressed, but Britain intervened in 1867, recognising the dependency as a separate entity. Nominally under the rule of the Ottoman Empire from 1871 until the outbreak of the First World War, Qatar became a British protectorate in 1916, when the al-Thani family was recognised as the ruling house. It became independent in 1971.

In 1972 Sheikh Ahmad was overthrown by the crown prince and prime minister, Sheikh Khalifa. Sheikh Khalifa was overthrown in 1995 by his son and heir, Sheikh Hamad, who has since introduced liberal reforms. Municipal elections, the first democratic polls since independence, were held in 1999. A referendum in 2003 approved a new constitution, which came into force in 2005. Elections to the partially elected consultative council established by the constitution have yet to take place.

POLITICAL SYSTEM
A new constitution came into force in 2005. The head of state is a hereditary absolute monarch, the amir. There is no legislature at present, although the 2005 constitution provides for a legislative council with 45 members, 30 directly elected and 15 appointed by the amir, and this will have legislative powers. At present there is an advisory council with 35 members appointed by the amir. There are no political parties. Women have been permitted to vote and stand for election since 1999.

HEAD OF STATE
HH Amir of Qatar, Defence, Sheikh Hamad bin Khalifa al-Thani, KCMG, *assumed power* 27 June 1995
Crown Prince, HH Sheikh Tamim bin Hamad al-Thani

SELECTED GOVERNMENT MEMBERS *as at June 2011*
Prime Minister, Foreign Affairs, HH Sheikh Hamad bin Jassem bin Jabr al-Thani
Deputy Prime Minister, Abdullah bin Hamad al-Attiyah
Internal Affairs, Sheikh Abdulla bin Khalid al-Thani
Economy and Finance, Yousef bin Hussain Kamal

EMBASSY OF THE STATE OF QATAR
1 South Audley Street, London W1K 1NB
T 020-7493 2200 E london@mofa.gov.qa
W www.qatarembassy.info
Ambassador Extraordinary and Plenipotentiary, HE Khalid Rashid al-Hamoudi al-Mansouri, *apptd* 2005

BRITISH EMBASSY
PO Box 3, Doha
T (+974) 496 2000 E embassy.qatar@fco.gov.uk
W http://ukinqatar.fco.gov.uk
Ambassador Extraordinary and Plenipotentiary, John Hawkins, *apptd* 2008

BRITISH COUNCIL
PO Box 2992, 93 Al Sadd Street, Doha
T (+974) 425 1888 W www.britishcouncil.org/me-qatar
Director, Simon Winetroube

DEFENCE

The army has 30 main battle tanks, 226 armoured personnel carriers and 40 armoured infantry fighting vehicles. The navy has 21 patrol and coastal combatant vessels at 2 bases. The air force has 18 combat aircraft and 43 helicopters.
Military expenditure – US$2,500m (2009)
Military personnel – 11,800: army 8,500, navy 1,800, air force 1,500

ECONOMY AND TRADE

The economy is based largely on the production of oil and gas, which account for more than 50 per cent of GDP, about 85 per cent of export earnings and 70 per cent of government revenues. The state-owned Qatar General Petroleum Corporation controls the industry, and is responsible for oil production onshore and offshore. There has been substantial foreign investment in exploitation of Qatar's large gasfields, and the country is now the world's leading exporter of liquefied natural gas.

Other industries include oil refining, production of ammonia, fertilisers, petrochemicals, steel and cement, and ship repairing. Industry contributes 78.8 per cent of GDP, services 21.1 per cent and agriculture, which is constrained by the terrain and climate, just 0.1 per cent. The economy depends on foreign workers, who outnumber the indigenous population.

The main export markets are Japan, South Korea and Singapore; the chief sources of imports are the USA, EU states, South Korea and Japan. Principal exports are liquefied natural gas, petroleum products, fertilisers and steel. The main imports are machinery and transport equipment, food and chemicals.
Annual average growth of GDP – 19.4 per cent (2010 est)
Inflation rate – 1.1 per cent (2010 est)
Unemployment – 0.5 per cent (2010 est)
Total external debt – US$71,380m (2010 est)
Imports – US$22,500m (2009)
Exports – US$41,500m (2009)

BALANCE OF PAYMENTS
Trade – US$37,756m surplus (2010)
Current Account – US$13,797m surplus (2009)

Trade with UK	2009	2010
Imports from UK	£777,811,991	£990,362,856
Exports to UK	£704,661,834	£2,165,745,117

COMMUNICATIONS

At present, Qatar has 7,790km of roads and six airports, but no railways. Prospective transport plans include the construction in the next decade of a passenger and freight rail network, starting with a rapid transit system in the Doha area, and of a road and rail causeway linking the country with Bahrain. Doha is the principal airport, and also the main seaport. Gulf Air and Qatar Airways provide regular international air services.

Modern telecommunications systems served 285,300 fixed lines, 2.5 million mobile phone subscribers and 563,800 internet users in 2009.

MEDIA

Qatar officially ended media censorship in 1995 and since then the press has essentially been free from government interference, although some self-censorship is practised. Al Jazeera, a government-owned news and current affairs satellite television channel launched in 1996, has become one of the most important broadcasters in the Middle East; it launched an English-language channel in 2006. Domestic television and radio are exclusively state-run. The leading newspapers are privately owned, though many have links to the royal family or other leading figures.

ROMANIA

Area – 238,391 sq. km
Capital – Bucharest; population, 1,933,200 (2009 est)
Major cities – Brasov, Cluj-Napoca, Constanta, Craiova, Galati, Iasi, Timisoara
Currency – New leu (plural lei) of 100 bani
Population – 21,959,278 falling at 0.25 per cent a year (2010 est); Romanian (89.5 per cent), Hungarian (6.6 per cent), Roma (2.5 per cent) (2002); small minority of Sasi (Transylvanian Saxons)
Religion – Christian (Orthodox 87 per cent, Protestant 7 per cent, Roman Catholic 5 per cent, Greek Catholic 1 per cent) (2002); small Muslim and Jewish minorities
Language – Romanian (official), Hungarian, Romani, German
Population density – 93 per sq. km (2009)
Urban population – 54 per cent (2008 est)
Median age (years) – 38.4 (2010 est)
National anthem – 'Desteapta-te, Romane' ['Awake Thee, Romanian']
National day – 1 December (Unification Day)
Life expectancy (years) – 73.74 (2010 est)
Mortality rate – 11.78 (2010 est)
Birth rate – 9.58 (2010 est)
Infant mortality rate – 11.32 (2010 est)

Death penalty – Abolished for all crimes (since 1989)
CPI score – 3.7 (2010)

CLIMATE AND TERRAIN

The Carpathian mountain range runs south from the Ukrainian border into the centre of the country and then turns west (the Transylvanian Alps) and north. The mountains enclose the central Transylvanian plateau and divide it from the southern Wallachian plain, part of the basin of the river Danube, which runs along most of the southern border, and the eastern Moldavian plateau, through which the river Siret runs, and the Black Sea coast. The mountains are thickly forested. Elevation extremes range from 2,544m (Moldoveanu) to 0m (Black Sea). The climate is continental, with average temperatures in Bucharest ranging from −6°C in January to 30°C in July and August.

HISTORY AND POLITICS

Romania was incorporated into the Roman Empire as Dacia in the early part of the second century AD but was abandoned 150 years later when the Romans were driven out by the Goths. After centuries of rule by invading and often disparate tribal forces, the principalities of Moldavia and Wallachia came under the suzerainty of the Ottoman Empire from the 16th century to the late 19th century, when they united in 1862 and became the independent kingdom of Romania in 1881. Transylvania was successively under Hungarian, Ottoman and Austrian rule until after the First World War, in which Romania joined with the Allies; the post-war peace settlement awarded Transylvania, Bukovina and Bessarabia to Romania.

In 1940 Romania was forced to cede territory to the USSR and Hungary, and power was seized by the Romanian fascists, who took the country into the Second World War on the Axis side. When its leaders were overthrown in 1944, Romania changed sides. It was occupied in 1945 by Soviet forces and a communist-dominated government was installed. In 1947 King Michael abdicated, the monarchy was abolished and Romania became a communist republic. In 1965 Nicolae Ceausescu became leader of the Romanian Communist Party and pursued a foreign policy increasingly independent of the USSR, forming relationships with China and several western countries. Ceausescu's regime was brutal and corrupt, and when the rest of eastern Europe threw off communist rule in 1989, violent suppression of reformers provoked an uprising in December 1989 that deposed and executed the dictator and his wife.

Although Romania became a multiparty democracy in 1991, governments continued to be dominated by former communists until 1996. Popular unrest and demonstrations have persisted throughout the post-communist period, as much of the population has yet to benefit greatly from the transition to a market economy. Romania joined NATO in 2004 and the EU in 2007.

Traian Basescu, the candidate of a coalition of the Democratic and National Liberal parties, won the 2004 presidential election and was re-elected in 2009. In the 2008 legislative election, an alliance of the Social Democratic Party (PSD) and the Conservative Party (PC) remained the largest bloc, although the Democratic Liberal Party (PD-L) was the largest party. The PD-L formed a coalition government with the PSD under Emil Boc. The PSD withdrew from the coalition in October 2009, leaving a minority government which resigned after losing a vote of confidence. After failed attempts to form a government by other candidates, Emil Boc was reappointed prime minister in December 2009 at the head of a coalition of the PD-L, the Democratic Union of Hungarians in Romania and several independents.

POLITICAL SYSTEM

The 1991 constitution was amended in 2003 to bring it into line with EU requirements. The president is directly elected for a five-year term, renewable once. The bicameral parliament comprises the Chamber of Deputies with 334 seats, of which 18 are reserved for ethnic minorities, and the senate with 137 seats. Both houses are directly elected for a four-year term by proportional representation. The prime minister is appointed by the president.

HEAD OF STATE

President of the Republic, Traian Basescu, *elected* 12 December 2004, *re-elected* 2009

SELECTED GOVERNMENT MEMBERS *as at July 2011*
Prime Minister, Emil Boc
Deputy Prime Minister, Bela Marko
Interior, Traian Igas
Defence, Gabriel Oprea
Economy, Ioan Ariton
Finance, Gheorghe Ialomitianu
Foreign Affairs, Teodor Baconschi

EMBASSY OF ROMANIA
Arundel House, 4 Palace Green, London W8 4QD
T 020-7937 9666 E roemb@roemb.co.uk
W www.londra.mae.ro
Ambassador Extraordinary and Plenipotentiary,
HE Dr Ion Jinga, *apptd* 2008

BRITISH EMBASSY
24 Strada Jules Michelet, 010463 Bucharest
T (+40) (21) 201 7200 E Press.Bucharest@fco.gov.uk
W http://ukinromania.fco.gov.uk
Ambassador Extraordinary and Plenipotentiary,
HE Martin Harris, *apptd* 2010

BRITISH COUNCIL
Calea Dorobantilor 14, 010572 Bucharest
T (+40) (21) 307 9600 W www.britishcouncil.org/romania
Director, Dr Nigel Townson

DEFENCE

The army has 345 main battle tanks, 1,616 armoured personnel carriers and 20 armoured infantry fighting vehicles. The navy has 3 destroyers and 21 patrol and coastal vessels at 4 bases. The air force has 70 combat aircraft.

Under an agreement signed in 2005, the USA is allowed to use military bases in Romania.
Military budget – US$2,140m (2010)
Military personnel – 71,745: army 42,500, navy 7,345, air force 8,400, joint staff 13,500; paramilitary 79,900

ECONOMY AND TRADE

Transition to a market economy made sluggish progress until 2000, accelerating after 2004 in order to meet the requirements for EU accession. Although the economy grew steadily from 2000 to 2008, it was from a low base and the effects only recently started to have an impact on the country's widespread poverty. The economy contracted sharply in 2009 owing to the global downturn, and the government sought IMF and EU

funding in spring 2009, but political volatility in late 2009 delayed the implementation of measures to address the economic problems. The effect of the austerity measures have delayed recovery from the recession.

Agriculture remains inefficient, employing about 30 per cent of the workforce but contributing only 12.8 per cent of GDP. The principal crops are grains, sugar beet, sunflower seeds, vegetables and livestock products. Vines and fruit are grown, and extensive forests support an important timber industry. There are reserves of natural gas and oil, but Romania is a net importer of fossil fuels, although it exports electricity. Mineral deposits, including coal, iron ore, bauxite, chromium and uranium support a mining industry. Other industries include manufacturing, electrical and light machinery and car assembly, metallurgy, food processing and oil refining.

The main trading partners are EU states (especially Italy and Germany), Turkey and China. Principal exports include machinery and equipment, textiles, footwear, metals and metal products, minerals and fuels, chemicals and agricultural products. The main imports are machines and equipment, fuels, minerals, chemicals, textiles, base metals and agricultural products.

GNI – US$164,073m; US$8,330 per capita (2009)
Annual average growth of GDP – −1.9 per cent (2010 est)
Inflation rate – 6 per cent (2010 est)
Population below poverty line – 25 per cent (2005 est)
Unemployment – 8.2 per cent (2010 est)
Total external debt – US$108,900m (2010 est)
Imports – US$54,300m (2009)
Exports – US$40,600m (2009)

BALANCE OF PAYMENTS
Trade – US$12,502m deficit (2010)
Current Account – US$7,104m deficit (2009)

Trade with UK	2009	2010
Imports from UK	£661,622,700	£756,794,798
Exports to UK	£758,103,995	£1,195,170,284

COMMUNICATIONS

There are 10,784km of railways, over one-third of which are electrified. There are 66,000km of surfaced roads, of which 321km are motorway. Navigable waterways include 1,599km on the river Danube and its tributaries and 132km of canals, principally linking the Danube to the Black Sea. The main ports are Braila, Constanta, Galati and Tulcea. The main airports are at Bucharest and Timisoara.

Liberalisation of telecommunications in 2003 has led to rapid growth, especially in mobile phone use. In 2009 there were 5.3 million fixed lines in use, 25.4 million mobile phone subscribers and 7.8 million internet users.

EDUCATION AND HEALTH

Primary and secondary education is free and compulsory for ten years.
Literacy rate – 97.6 per cent (2008 est)
Gross enrolment ratio (percentage of relevant age group) – primary 100 per cent; secondary 92 per cent; tertiary 66 per cent (2008 est)
Health expenditure (per capita) – US$408 (2009)
Hospital beds (per 1,000 people) – 6.5 (2004–9)

MEDIA

State-owned broadcasters operate two television and four national radio networks. There is a thriving private television sector and over 100 private radio stations.

Cable, satellite and subscription television is becoming more widespread. There are five main daily newspapers.

RUSSIA

Rossiyskaya Federatsiya – Russian Federation

Area – 17,098,242 sq. km. Includes the Kalingrad exclave, between Lithuania and Poland. Neighbours: Norway, Finland, Estonia, Latvia, Belarus, Ukraine (west), Georgia, Azerbaijan, Kazakhstan, China, Mongolia, North Korea (south)

Capital – Moscow; population, 10,522,900 (2009 est). Founded in around 1147, it became the centre of the rising Moscow principality and in the 15th century the capital of the whole of Russia (Muscovy). In 1703 Peter the Great transferred the capital to St Petersburg, but Moscow became the capital again in 1918

Major cities – Chelyabinsk, Kazan, Nizhniy Novgorod (Gorky 1932–90), Novosibirsk (Novonikolayevsk until 1926), Omsk, Perm, Rostov, St Petersburg (Petrograd 1914–24; Leningrad 1924–91), Samara (Kuibyshev 1935–90), Ufa, Volgograd (Stalingrad 1925–61), Yekaterinburg (Sverdlovsk 1924–91)

Currency – Rouble of 100 kopeks

Population – 139,390,205 falling at 0.47 per cent a year (2010 est); Russian (79.8 per cent), Tatar (3.8 per cent), Ukrainian (2 per cent), Bashkir (1.2 per cent), Chuvash (1.1 per cent), and a further 150 nationalities (2002)

Religion – Christian (Russian Orthodox 70 per cent, other 2 per cent), Muslim 10 per cent, Buddhist 1 per cent (est); small Jewish minority

Language – Russian (official); many minority languages

Population density – 9 per sq. km (2009)

Urban population – 73 per cent (2008 est)

Median age (years) – 38.5 (2010 est)

National anthem – 'Gosudarstvenny Gimn Rossiyskoy Federatsii' ['State Anthem of the Russian Federation']

National day – 12 June (Russia Day)

Life expectancy (years) – 66.16 (2010 est)

Mortality rate – 16.04 (2010 est)

Birth rate – 11.11 (2010 est)

Infant mortality rate – 10.32 (2010 est)

HIV/AIDS adult prevalence – 1 per cent (2009 est)

Death penalty – Retained (not used since 1999)

CPI score – 2.1 (2010)

CLIMATE AND TERRAIN

Russia includes the easternmost areas of Europe and the whole of northern Asia. It lies mostly on plains which extend eastwards to the Ural mountains and then from the Urals to the Yenesei river. To the east of the Yenesei are plateaux, with lowlands in northern Siberia. Mountainous areas lie along the southern borders, in eastern Siberia and the Kamchatka peninsula. The terrain varies from the tundra of the Arctic region, through the taiga (the largest zone) of the north and centre, to the grassy plains (steppe) between the forests and the mountains. Elevation extremes range from 5,633m (Mt El'brus, Caucasus) to −28m (Caspian Sea). Russia has the longest Arctic coastline in the world (over 27,000km); it also has Baltic, Black Sea and Pacific coastlines.

The most important rivers are the Volga, the Northern Dvina, the Neva, the Don and the Kuban in the European part, and in the Asiatic part the Ob, the Irtysh, the Yenisei, the Lena, the Amur and, further north, the Khatanga, Olenek, Yana, Indigirka and Kolyma in eastern Siberia is the deepest lake in the world. Part of the Caspian Sea lies within Russia.

The climate is mostly continental, but varies with latitude and terrain from arctic conditions in the north to subtropical in the far east and on the Black Sea coast. Average temperatures in Moscow range from −14°C in January and February to 24°C in July. Rainfall is low to moderate in most of the country.

HISTORY AND POLITICS

Russia was settled by many ethnic groups, including Slavs, Turks and Bulgars in the third to seventh centuries AD, and in the 13th century came under the overlordship of the Mongols. In the 15th century the grand duke of Muscovy threw off Mongol overlordship and began a process of unification and territorial expansion continued by his successors. Internal disorder and war with neighbouring countries held back Russian development until the reign of Peter I (The Great) (1682–1725), who introduced Western ideas of government, modernised the army and founded the navy. Under Catherine II (The Great) (1762–96) Russia extended its territory further. Russian expansion in Asia led to a war with Japan in 1904–5 that ended in an unexpected defeat. Protests about the conduct of the war developed into a revolution in 1905 which, though suppressed, forced the tsar to establish Russia's first parliament *(Duma)*.

The *Duma's* powers were limited and it was unable to ameliorate the tsarist regime's endemic misgovernment or the conditions of the increasingly militant urban working class. During the First World War discontent caused by autocratic rule, the poor military conduct of the war and wartime privation led to revolution in March 1917. The tsar abdicated and a power struggle ensued between the provisional government and the Bolshevik Party. This led to a second revolution in November 1917 in which the Bolsheviks, led by Vladimir Lenin (1870–1924), seized power.

Civil war between 'red' Bolshevik forces and 'white' monarchist and anti-communist forces, the latter supported by foreign powers, lasted until the end of 1922. During the civil war, Russia was declared a Soviet republic and other Soviet republics were formed in Ukraine, Belorussia and Transcaucasia. These four republics merged to form the Union of Soviet Socialist Republics (USSR) on 30 December 1922.

During the 1930s Joseph Stalin (1879–1953) introduced a policy of rapid industrialisation under a series of five-year plans, brought all sectors of industry under government control, abolished private ownership and enforced the collectivisation of agriculture, causing severe famine. Many ethnic minority groups suffered under Stalin's regime and it is estimated that up to 1.5 million people were deported to the gulags of Siberia and the central Asian republics. After being attacked by Nazi Germany in 1941, the USSR joined the Second World War on the side of the Allies. In 1944–5 Soviet forces liberated much of eastern Europe and the post-war communist regimes in these countries were closely tied to the Soviet government.

The post-war period was dominated for 40 years by the Cold War with the West, especially the USA, prompting massive expenditure on the military-industrial sector and the provision of aid to developing countries as a means of extending Soviet influence. Tight political and economic control was maintained over the countries in the Soviet bloc, including military intervention in support of communist regimes in Europe and Afghanistan.

Mikhail Gorbachev became Soviet leader in 1985 and introduced the policies of *perestroika* (restructuring) and *glasnost* (openness) in order to revamp the economy, which had stagnated since the 1970s, to root out corruption and inefficiency, and to end the Cold War. The retreat from total control by the Communist Party unleashed ethnic and nationalist tensions.

Following the defeat of an attempted coup by hardline communists in August 1991, effective political power was in the hands of the leaders of the constituent republics, especially President Yeltsin of Russia, and the USSR began to break up as the constituent republics declared their independence. The USSR formally ceased to exist on 31 December 1991. The Russian Federation took over the USSR's seat at the UN in December 1991, was recognised as an independent state by the EC and USA in January 1992, and joined the G7 group of industrialised countries in 1996.

The presidency of Vladimir Putin (2000–8) saw an increasing degree of centralisation, the partial renationalisation of industry (especially oil and gas), the re-assertion of state control over the media, and an increasingly authoritarian stance on democracy and an aggressive approach to relations with former Soviet states.

In the 2007 legislative elections, the pro-Putin United Russia party increased its large majority in the *Duma*, and President Putin won a parliamentary seat. This enabled him to be appointed chair of the council of ministers in 2008 after his successor as president, Dmitry Medvedev, took office. President Medvedev is widely regarded as a figurehead, with Putin continuing to wield the most political power and to determine government policy. A legislative election is scheduled for 4 December 2011, followed by a presidential election in 2012.

INSURGENCIES
Chechnya occupies an area that is strategically important to Russia because routes from central Russia to the Black

Sea and Caspian Sea, and oil and gas pipelines from neighbouring countries, pass through it. The republic declared itself independent in 1991 but its attempts to assert its independence led to two wars with the federal government. The first of these, in 1994–6, resulted in the signing of the Khasavyurt accords. After the peace broke down and Russia invaded Chechnya again in 1999, President Putin refused negotiations and imposed direct rule from Moscow in 2000. Rebels continued with terrorist attacks, although these have decreased since 2007. Russia announced the end of counter-terrorism operations in Chechnya in 2009, but has had to reinstate these in some areas where rebels remain active.

The conflict in Chechnya has destabilised the whole of the northern Caucasus, especially Ingushetia and Dagestan, where violence has increased in recent years. The violence has also affected other parts of Russia, where extremists linked to Chechen separatists have carried out suicide bombings and attacks such as the Moscow theatre siege in 2002, the Beslan school siege in 2004, and the bombing of Moscow's metro system in 2010.

POLITICAL SYSTEM
The 1993 constitution introduced multiparty democracy and enshrines various human rights and civil liberties; amendments in 2008 extended the terms of office for the presidency and the State Duma from the next elections. The head of state is a president, who is directly elected for a four-year term (at present; six years from 2012), renewable once consecutively. The bicameral Federal Assembly comprises the State Duma (lower house) of 450 members, all elected by proportional representation for a four-year term (at present; five years from 2011), and the Council of the Federation, which has 166 members (two from each member of the federation), appointed for terms of varying lengths. The president appoints the chairman of the council of ministers (prime minister), subject to the approval of the legislature, but is also entitled to chair sessions of the council.

HEAD OF STATE
President, Dmitry Medvedev, *elected* 2 March 2008, *took office* 7 May 2008

SELECTED GOVERNMENT MEMBERS *as at July 2011*
Prime Minister, Vladimir Putin
First Deputy Chairs, Igor Shuvalov; Viktor Zubkov
Deputy Chairs, Alexei Kudrin *(Finance)*; Sergei Ivanov; Aleksandr Khloponin; Dmitri Kozak; Igor Sechin; Igor Shuvalov; Aleksandr Zhukov
Foreign Affairs, Sergei Lavrov
Interior, Rashid Nurgaliyev
Defence, Anatoly Serdyukov

EMBASSY OF THE RUSSIAN FEDERATION
6–7 Kensington Palace Gardens, London W8 4QX
T 020-7229 6412 E info@rusemb.org.uk
W www.rusemb.org.uk
Ambassador Extraordinary and Plenipotentiary,
HE Alexander Yakovenko, *apptd* 2011

BRITISH EMBASSY
Smolenskaya Naberezhnaya 10, 121099 Moscow
T (+7) (495) 956 7200 E moscow@britishembassy.ru
W http://ukinrussia.fco.gov.uk
Ambassador Extraordinary and Plenipotentiary,
HE Dame Anne Pringle, DCMG, *apptd* 2008

BRITISH COUNCIL
Ulitsa Nikoloyamskaya 1, 109189 Moscow
T (+7) (495) 287 1800 W www.britishcouncil.org.ru
Director, Paul de Quincey

FEDERAL STRUCTURE

Following the break-up of the USSR in 1991, a new federal treaty was signed in 1992 between the central government and the autonomous republics of the Russian Federation. Tatarstan and Bashkortostan signed the treaty in 1994 after securing considerable legislative and economic autonomy.

The Russian Federation comprises 46 *oblasti* (regions), 9 *krai* (autonomous territories), 21 *respubliki* (autonomous republics), 4 *okrugi* (autonomous areas), two cities with federal status (Moscow and St Petersburg) and one autonomous Jewish *oblast*, Yevrey. The *oblasti* are Amur, Arkhangelsk, Astrakhan, Belgorod, Bryansk, Chelyabinsk, Irkutsk, Ivanovo, Kaliningrad, Kaluga, Kemerovo, Kirov, Kostroma, Kurgan, Kursk, Leningrad, Lipetsk, Magadan, Moscow, Murmansk, Nizhny Novgorod, Novgorod, Novosibirsk, Omsk, Orenburg, Orel, Penza, Pskov, Rostov, Ryazan, Sakhalin, Samara, Saratov, Smolensk, Sverdlovsk, Tambov, Tomsk, Tula, Tver, Tyumen, Ulyanovsk, Vladimir, Volgograd, Vologda, Voronezh and Yaroslavl. The *krai* are Altai, Kamchatka, Khabarovsk, Krasnodar, Krasnoyarsk, Perm, Primorski, Stavropol and Zabaykalsk. The *respubliki* are Adygeia, Altai, Bashkortostan, Buryatia, Chechnya, Chuvashia, Dagestan, Ingushetia, Kabardino-Balkaria, Kalmykiya, Karachayevo-Cherkessia, Karelia, Khakassia, Komi, Mari-El, Mordovia, North Ossetia, Sakha, Tatarstan, Tuva and Udmurtia. The *okrugi* are Chukotka, Khanty-Mansi, Nenets and Yamalo-Nenets.

DEFENCE

Since the demise of the USSR, Russia's armed forces have been considerably reduced. Major army reform is ongoing, including a large-scale structural reorganisation, shorter conscription periods, the civilianisation of military posts and staff cuts in the defence ministry.

A CIS collective security treaty enables Russia to station troops in Armenia, Belarus, Kazakhstan, Kyrgyzstan and Tajikistan. The Black Sea fleet was divided between Russian and Ukraine under an agreement signed in 1997. In April 2010, the Strategic Arms Reduction Treaty (START) was renewed by president Medvedev and US president Obama; the bilateral treaty, originally drafted in 1991, is an agreement between the two states to continue to significantly reduce the number of operational strategic nuclear weapons.

The Strategic Deterrent Forces have 14 nuclear-powered ballistic missile submarines and 430 intercontinental ballistic missiles equipped with some 1,605 nuclear warheads. Russia also has 79 long-range strike aircraft capable of carrying strategic missiles.

The army has over 2,800 main battle tanks, 9,700 armoured personnel carriers and 7,360 armoured infantry fighting vehicles. The navy has 67 submarines, 1 aircraft carrier, 6 cruisers, 18 destroyers, 7 frigates, 78 patrol and coastal vessels, 276 combat aircraft and 101 armed helicopters. The air force has 1,604 combat aircraft.

Russia deploys forces in Armenia (3,214), Georgia (7,000), Moldova (1,500 est) and Tajikistan (5,000).
Military budget – US$41,400m (2010)
Military personnel – 1,046,000: Strategic Deterrent Forces 80,000, army 360,000, airborne 35,000, navy

161,000, air force 160,000, command and support 250,000; paramilitary 449,000
Conscription duration – 12 months

ECONOMY AND TRADE

Under the Soviet regime, an essentially agrarian economy in 1917 was transformed by the early 1960s into the second-greatest industrial power in the world. However, by the early 1970s the concentration of resources on the military-industrial complex had caused stagnation in the civilian economy. Economic reforms were introduced by President Gorbachev, including the legalisation of small private businesses, the reduction of state control over the economy, and denationalisation and privatisation. Mass privatisation of state industries began in 1992, and 80 per cent of the economy had been privatised by 1996. The largest and most economically significant industries, oil and gas, were partially renationalised from 2004.

The transition to a market economy caused severe economic crises in 1993 and 1998, but from 1999 to 2008 the economy sustained growth averaging 7 per cent a year, and unemployment and poverty declined. Average incomes grew by more than 10 per cent a year from 2002, and the middle class has expanded. Banking and fiscal reforms stimulated foreign investment, although political and economic uncertainties, corruption, excessive red tape and a lack of trust in institutions continue to inhibit growth. Other problems include the economy's vulnerability to fluctuations in global prices of key commodities and a dilapidated infrastructure. Some of these factors exacerbated the impact on Russia of the global financial crisis in autumn 2008, when a sharp fall in oil prices coincided with turmoil in the banking system and a 70 per cent drop in the stock market. Despite US$200bn in government aid to the financial sector, credit and confidence problems, a severe drop in production and rising unemployment caused a sharp contraction in the economy until late 2009.

Russia has some of the world's richest natural resources, especially mineral deposits and timber. The recent growth in the economy is founded on the exploitation and export of its oil and natural gas reserves. Russia is now the world's leading exporter of hydrocarbons and the leading supplier to European countries and China, a position that has led the country into disputes with some of its neighbours; Ukraine, Georgia and Belarus have all had gas supplies cut for short periods during price negotiations. Oil and natural gas account for 70 per cent of exports, 45 per cent of federal budget revenue and over 25 per cent of GDP. Economic diversification, especially into high technology sectors, is a government priority.

Mining (coal, iron ore, aluminium and other non-ferrous metals) and oil and natural gas extraction are concentrated in the region south of Moscow, the Volga valley, the northern Caucasus, the Urals, Siberia and the far east and north. Russia is also keen to exploit the shrinking of the Arctic ice-cap to prospect for previously inaccessible deposits under the Arctic Sea. Moscow and St Petersburg are still the two largest industrial centres, but new industrial areas have been developed in the Urals, the Kuznetsk basin, Siberia and the far east. The main industries are extracting and processing oil, gas and minerals, forestry, all forms of machine building (including transport, communications, agricultural, construction, and power generating and transmitting equipment), defence industries, shipbuilding, medical and scientific instruments, consumer durables, textiles, food processing and handicrafts.

The vast area and the great variety in climatic conditions are reflected in the structure of agriculture. In the far north, only reindeer breeding, hunting and fishing are possible; further south, forestry is combined with grain growing. In the southern half of the forest zone and in the adjacent forest-steppe zone, the acreage under grain crops is larger and agriculture more complex. The southern part of the Western Siberian plain is an important grain-growing and stock-breeding area. In the extreme south, cotton is cultivated. Vine, tobacco and other southern crops are grown on the Black Sea shore of the Caucasus.

The service sector is the largest, accounting for 62 per cent of GDP and employing 58.1 per cent of the workforce; industry contributes 33.8 per cent of GDP and employs 31.9 per cent; and agriculture accounts for 4.2 per cent of GDP and 10 per cent of employment.

Russia's main trading partners are EU countries (especially Germany), China, Ukraine, the USA and Turkey. Principal exports are oil and petroleum products, natural gas, metals, timber and wood products, chemicals, manufactured goods, military vehicles and defence equipment. The main imports are machinery, vehicles, pharmaceutical products, plastics, semi-finished metal products, meat, fruits and nuts, optical and medical equipment, iron and steel.

GNI – US$1,192,411m; US$9,340 per capita (2009)
Annual average growth of GDP – 3.8 per cent (2010 est)
Inflation rate – 6.7 per cent (2010 est)
Population below poverty line – 13.1 per cent (2009)
Unemployment – 7.6 per cent (2010 est)
Total external debt – US$482,200m (2010 est)
Imports – US$211,000m (2009)
Exports – US$303,400m (2009)

BALANCE OF PAYMENTS
Trade – US$150,621m surplus (2010)
Current Account – US$102,400m surplus (2008)

Trade with UK	2009	2010
Imports from UK	£2,286,399,343	£3,450,871,453
Exports to UK	£4,515,161,446	£5,286,091,964

COMMUNICATIONS

Because of the vast distances, the terrain and the harsh winter climate, the main means of internal long-distance travel are by air or the Trans-Siberian railway. Neither the rail nor the road systems are well-developed countrywide; both are concentrated in the more densely populated European areas and the Urals. There are 1,213 airports and airfields, although only 593 have surfaced runways. The principal international airports are at Moscow, St Petersburg and Novosibirsk, and the main national carriers are Aeroflot and S7 Airlines. The railways are state-run, with 87,157km of the network used for passenger transport and 30,000km by industry. There are 982,000km of roads, 776,000km of which are surfaced.

The most important ports include Kaliningrad on the Baltic Sea and Novorossiysk on the Black Sea. Two of the three northern ports, St Petersburg and Arkhangelsk, are icebound during winter; only Murmansk is accessible. Several ports have been built along the Arctic Sea route between Murmansk and Vladivostok and are in regular use in summer. The far eastern port of Vladivostok, Russia's Pacific naval base, is kept open by icebreakers all the year round. There is a large merchant fleet of 1,097 ships of 1,000 tonnes and over, with a further 443 ships registered in other countries.

There are 102,000km of waterways. The great rivers of European Russia flow outwards from the centre, linking all parts of the plains with the chief ports. They are supplemented by a 72,000km system of canals which provides a through route between the White Sea and Baltic Sea in the north and the Black Sea, Caspian Sea and the Sea of Azov in the south; the most notable are the White Sea–Baltic Canal, the Moscow–Volga Canal and the Volga–Don Canal.

The telecommunications infrastructure is expanding and modernising, although less quickly for fixed lines than for mobile phones, and rural services are still inadequate. There were 44.8 million fixed lines in use, 230.5 million mobile phone subscribers and 40.8 million internet users in 2009.

EDUCATION AND HEALTH

There are 11 years of compulsory education: nine at basic school level and a further two at senior secondary level. Higher education is provided by public and private accredited higher education institutions.

Literacy rate – 99.5 per cent (2008 est)
Gross enrolment ratio (percentage of relevant age group) – primary 97 per cent; secondary 85 per cent; tertiary 77 per cent (2008 est)
Health expenditure (per capita) – US$475 (2009)
Hospital beds (per 1,000 people) – 9.7 (2004–9)

MEDIA

Broadcasting is dominated by the Russian State Television and Radio Broadcasting Company (VGTRK) and stations part-owned by the government or whose owners have close ties to it. Most of the country's 400 newspapers are privately owned but some of the most influential titles are owned by companies closely linked to the government. This has reduced editorial independence, and journalists are subject to harassment, intimidation and assault for coverage of sensitive subjects such as human rights or corruption.

CULTURE

Russian is a Slavonic language and is written in the Cyrillic script.

Russian literature consisted mainly of *byliny* (folk songs), epic songs, chronicles and works of moral theology before the 19th century, when poetry reached its zenith with Alexander Pushkin (1799–1837) and Mikhail Lermontov (1814–41), while the dramatist and short-story writer Anton Chekhov (1860–1904) achieved acclaim throughout Europe for plays such as *The Three Sisters* and *The Cherry Orchard*. Novelists Nikolai Gogol (1809–52), Ivan Turgenev (1818–83), Fyodor Dostoyevsky (1821–81) and Leo Tolstoy (1828–1910) created masterpieces such as *Dead Souls, Fathers and Sons, Crime and Punishment* and *War and Peace* respectively. In the 20th century, Anna Akhmatova (1888–1966), Boris Pasternak (1890–1960), Mikhail Bulgakov (1891–1940), Vladimir Nabokov (1899–1977) and Nobel laureate Alexander Solzhenitsyn (1918–2008) have been especially acclaimed.

In classical music, Mikhail Glinka (1804–57) was an innovator to match Pushkin, while those following him include Mussorgsky (1839–81), Tchaikovsky (1840–93) – arguably the most internationally successful Russian composer, whose ballet music includes *Swan Lake* and *The Nutcracker* – Rimsky-Korsakov (1844–1908), Rachmaninov (1873–1943), Stravinsky (1882–1971), Prokofiev (1891–1953) and Shostakovich (1906–75).

Directors Sergei Eisenstein (1898–1948), Andrei Tarkovsky (1932–86) and Nikita Mikhalkov (b. 1945) are celebrated figures in Russian cinema.

RWANDA

Republika y'u Rwanda/République du Rwanda – Republic of Rwanda

Area – 26,338 sq. km
Capital – Kigali; population, 908,705 (2009 est)
Major towns – Butare; Gisenyi; Gitarama; Ruhengeri
Currency – Rwanda franc of 100 centimes
Population – 11,055,976 rising at 2.82 per cent a year (2010 est); Hutu (84 per cent), Tutsi (15 per cent), Twa (1 per cent) (est)
Religion – Christian (Roman Catholic 57 per cent, Seventh-day Adventist 11 per cent, other Protestant 26 per cent), Muslim 5 per cent, indigenous beliefs 0.1 per cent (est)
Language – Kinyarwanda, French, English (all official), Swahili
Population density – 405 per sq. km (2009)
Urban population – 18 per cent (2008 est)
Median age (years) – 18.6 (2010 est)
National anthem – 'Rwanda nziza' ['Beautiful Rwanda']
National day – 1 July (Independence Day)
Life expectancy (years) – 57.46 (2010 est)
Mortality rate – 10.19 (2010 est)
Birth rate – 37.26 (2010 est)
Infant mortality rate – 65.57 (2010 est)
HIV/AIDS adult prevalence – 2.9 per cent (2009 est)
Death penalty – Abolished for all crimes (since 2007)
CPI score – 4 (2010)
Literacy rate – 64.9 per cent (2008 est)
Gross enrolment ratio (percentage of relevant age group) – primary 151 per cent; secondary 27 per cent; tertiary 5 per cent (2009 est)
Health expenditure (per capita) – US$48 (2009)
Hospital beds (per 1,000 people) – 1.6 (2004–9)

CLIMATE AND TERRAIN

Landlocked Rwanda's terrain is mostly savannah uplands and mountains, including the volcanic Virunga range in the north-west. Elevation extremes range from 4,519m (Volcan Karisimbi) to 950m (river Rusizi). Rwanda's western border runs through Lake Kivu. The climate is temperate, with a wet season from October to May. Average daily temperatures in Rubona range between 14°C and 27°C throughout the year.

HISTORY AND POLITICS

Rwanda was settled by Hutu peoples from the tenth century. From the 14th century, they came under the dominance of Tutsi migrants, who became the rulers of a centralised kingdom established in the 15th century. This historic dominance of the majority Hutus by the minority Tutsis underlies the modern conflict between the two ethnic groups.

Rwanda became part of German East Africa in 1899 and was occupied by Belgium when the First World War broke out. After the war, it became a mandated territory administered by Belgium. In 1959 the Hutu population rebelled against Tutsi domination, overthrowing the king and causing thousands of Tutsis to flee the country. Rwanda became a republic in 1961, and independence was achieved in 1962 under a Hutu president. He was overthrown in 1973 in a military coup led by Maj.-Gen. Juvenal Habyarimana, whose National Revolutionary Development Movement (MRND) was the only legal party until 1991.

Armed Tutsi exiles in Uganda made repeated attempts to invade Rwanda in the 1960s and 1970s, but were defeated by the predominantly Hutu army. Continued conflict left thousands dead over a period of 30 years. These exiles and opponents of the MRND regime formed the Tutsi-led Rwandan Patriotic Front (FPR) in 1985. The FPR invaded the country in 1990, and a cycle of rebel incursions and military reprisals, mostly against Tutsis, continued until the Arusha peace accords were concluded in 1993.

In April 1994, the assassination of President Habyarimana triggered a massacre of the Tutsi minority and moderate Hutus by the army and youth militia *(interahamwe)*; about 1 million people were killed in three months and millions more fled to neighbouring countries. The FPR's forces mobilised to end the bloodshed and took control of the country, causing defeated forces (exFAR/I) and over two million Hutus to flee, mostly to Zaire (now the Democratic Republic of the Congo). In July 1994 the FPR established a broad-based government of national unity in which moderate Hutus held the presidency and premiership and the FPR took eight of the 22 seats. An International Criminal Tribunal for Rwanda was established in 1995 to bring to trial those directly responsible for the 1994 genocide.

Incursions by exFAR/I continued in the west, drawing Rwanda into the civil war in the Democratic Republic of the Congo from 1996 until 2002, and the Congolese border areas remain volatile. Internally, reconciliation efforts and political reforms since 1994 have been more successful in achieving social stability, although the FPR is regarded as authoritarian, suppressing political opposition. Rwanda joined the Commonwealth in 2009.

The FPR won the 2003 legislative elections and retained an overall majority in the 2008 election, continuing in government in coalition with six other parties and a number of independent members. The FPR leader Paul Kagame was elected president in 2003, and was re-elected in 2010.

POLITICAL SYSTEM

Under the 2003 constitution, the president is directly elected for a seven-year term, renewable once. The bicameral parliament consists of the Chamber of Deputies (the lower house) and the senate. The Chamber of Deputies has 80 members, of whom 53 are directly elected, 24 are women members elected by the provinces, two represent youth organisations and one represents organisations of disabled people; all serve a five-year term. The senate has 26 members indirectly elected for an eight-year term. Political parties are barred from organising on an ethnic, regional or religious basis.

In 2006 the 12 provinces were replaced by five provinces: North, East, South, West and Kigali, with the aim of creating more ethnically diverse administrative areas.

HEAD OF STATE
President, Maj-Gen. Paul Kagame, *appointed* 17 April 2000, *sworn in* 22 April 2000, *elected* 25 August 2003, *re-elected* 2010

SELECTED GOVERNMENT MEMBERS *as at July 2011*
Prime Minister, Bernard Makuza
Defence, Gen. James Kabarebe
Finance and Economic Planning, John Rwangombwa
Foreign Affairs, Louise Mushikiwabo

HIGH COMMISSION OF THE REPUBLIC OF RWANDA
120–122 Seymour Place, London W1H 1NR
T 020-7224 9832 E uk@ambarwanda.org.uk
W www.ambarwanda.org.uk
High Commissioner, Ernest Rwamucyo, *apptd* 2010

BRITISH HIGH COMMISSION
Parcelle No. 1131, Blvd de l'Umuganda, Kacyira-Sud,
BP 576 Kigali
T (+250) 0252 585 771 E embassy.kigali@fco.gov.uk
W http://ukinrwanda.fco.gov.uk
High Commissioner, HE Benedict Llewellyn-Jones, OBE, *apptd* 2011

DEFENCE
The army has 24 main battle tanks, over 35 armoured infantry fighting vehicles and 56 armoured personnel carriers. The air force has at least 5 armed helicopters.
Military budget – US$75m (2010)
Military personnel – 33,000: army 32,000, air force 1,000; paramilitary 2,000

ECONOMY AND TRADE
Rwanda is the most densely populated country in Africa, with few natural resources and minimal industry. Over half the population lives below the poverty line and economic growth, especially in food production, struggles to keep up with population growth. It is dependent on international aid but the demands of its high foreign debt have been reduced by debt relief. Regional instability, inadequate transport links with other countries and energy shortages hamper development, although electricity supply is expected to become more reliable when methane from Lake Kivu starts to be tapped.

Around 90 per cent of the population is engaged in agriculture, which is mainly at subsistence level and contributes 42.1 per cent of GDP. The main industries are mining, processing agricultural products, small-scale manufacturing and tourism, which is now the main foreign exchange earner.

The main trading partners are Kenya, Uganda, Democratic Republic of Congo, China and Belgium. The main exports are coffee, tea, hides and tin ore. The principal imports are foodstuffs, machinery and equipment, steel, petroleum products and construction materials.
GNI – US$5,179m; US$490 per capita (2009)
Annual average growth of GDP – 6 per cent (2010 est)

Inflation rate – 6.4 per cent (2010 est)
Total external debt – US$1,400m (2004 est)
Imports – US$1,200m (2009)
Exports – US$200m (2009)

BALANCE OF PAYMENTS
Trade – US$1,247m deficit (2010)
Current Account – US$230m deficit (2008)

Trade with UK	2009	2010
Imports from UK	£9,292,599	£7,290,913
Exports to UK	£4,370,667	£5,349,242

COMMUNICATIONS
Rwanda has received considerable foreign aid to upgrade its transport infrastructure since 1994. The main internal transport system is the 14,000km road network, which links with those of neighbouring countries to provide access to Kenyan and Tanzanian ports. There are no railways, although the Tanzanian president Jakaya Kikwete has confirmed the country is seeking funding for a rail link with Burundi and Rwanda. Lake Kivu is navigable by shallow boats, and provides access, but no regular services, to the Democratic Republic of the Congo. The principal airport is at Kigali.

The limited fixed-line telephone system mostly serves government and business, and mobile phone distribution has grown rapidly. There were 33,000 fixed lines in use, 2.4 million mobile phone subscribers and 450,000 internet users in 2009.

MEDIA
The broadcast media is mainly state-owned, and the state-run Radio Rwanda has the largest audience. Private radio stations have opened since 2004, and the BBC World Service, Voice of America and Deutsche Welle all broadcast in Kigali. Television is mostly confined to urban areas. There are a growing number of newspapers, but they are subject to government restrictions and harassment, and generally exercise self-censorship. The country's restrictive media laws and the government's strained relationship with print media was demonstrated in the run up to the presidential elections in 2010, when 30 media organisations were suspended.

ST KITTS AND NEVIS

Federation of St Christopher and Nevis (Federation of St Kitts and Nevis)

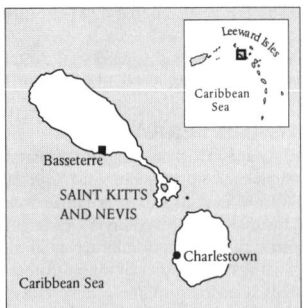

Area – 261 sq. km
Capital – Basseterre; population, 12,847 (2009 est)
Major town – Charlestown, the chief town of Nevis

Currency – East Caribbean dollar (EC$) of 100 cents
Population – 49,898 rising at 0.84 per cent a year (2010 est)
Religion – Christian (Anglican 50 per cent, Roman Catholic 25 per cent) (est)
Language – English (official)
Population density – 191 per sq. km (2009)
Urban population – 32 per cent (2008 est)
Median age (years) – 31.5 (2010 est)
National anthem – 'Oh Land of Beauty!'
National day – 19 September (Independence Day)
Life expectancy (years) – 74.37 (2010 est)
Mortality rate – 7.11 (2010 est)
Birth rate – 14.23 (2010 est)
Infant mortality rate – 9.9 (2010 est)
Death penalty – Retained (last used 2008)
Literacy rate – 97.8 per cent (2008 est)

CLIMATE AND TERRAIN
The volcanic islands of St Kitts (St Christopher) (168 sq. km) and Nevis (93 sq. km) are part of the Leeward group in the eastern Caribbean Sea. The centre of St Kitts is forest-clad and mountainous, with the Great Salt Pond occupying the tip of its southern peninsula; elevation extremes range from 1,156m (Mt Liamuiga) to 0m (Caribbean Sea). Nevis, separated from the southern tip of St Kitts by a strait 3km wide, is dominated by Nevis Peak (985m). The climate is tropical, moderated by north-east trade winds, and a wet season occurs from May to September. The islands are in the hurricane belt.

HISTORY AND POLITICS
The islands were inhabited by Carib, or Kalinago, people when discovered in 1493 by Christopher Columbus, who gave St Christopher its name. Colonisation by the British began in 1623–4, when St Kitts became the first British colony in the West Indies, and French settlement began shortly after. The island was held jointly from 1628 to 1713, although there were skirmishes between the British and French settlers in the 17th century; France dropped its claims after 1783. Nevis was settled by the British from 1628. The two islands were part of the Leeward Islands colony from 1871 to 1956, and then of the West Indies Federation from 1958 to 1962. They achieved internal self-government in 1967 and became independent in September 1983.

A separatist movement was formed on Nevis in 1970. A referendum on the issue in 1998 resulted in a 61.8 per cent vote in favour of secession, which fell short of the two-thirds majority required.

The Labour Party, which has been in power since 1995, retained its overall majority in the 2010 legislative election, and began its fourth term of office under Denzil Douglas.

POLITICAL SYSTEM
Under the 1983 constitution, the head of state is Queen Elizabeth II, represented by a governor-general appointed on the advice of the prime minister. The unicameral National Assembly has 15 members: 11 directly elected for a five-year term, a speaker, and three appointed by the governor-general on the advice of the prime minister and the leader of the opposition. The prime minister, who is responsible to the legislature, and the cabinet are appointed by the governor-general.

Nevis is responsible for its own internal affairs. It has an eight-member Nevis Island assembly and is governed by the Nevis Island administration, headed by the premier.

Governor-General, HE Sir Cuthbert Sebastian, GCMG, OBE, *apptd* 1996

SELECTED GOVERNMENT MEMBERS *as at July 2011*
Prime Minister, Finance, Denzil Douglas
Deputy Prime Minister, Foreign Affairs, National Security, Sam Condor

HIGH COMMISSION FOR ST KITTS AND NEVIS
10 Kensington Court, London W8 5DL
T 020-7937 9718 E info@sknhc.co.uk
High Commissioner, HE Kevin Isaacs, *apptd* 2011

BRITISH HIGH COMMISSIONER
HE Paul Brummell, *apptd* 2009, resident at Bridgetown, Barbados

ECONOMY AND TRADE
The sugar industry was the mainstay of the economy for over 300 years but was closed down in 2005 after decades of operating at a loss. Tourism (the chief source of foreign exchange revenue), offshore financial services and manufacturing, especially distilling, food processing, clothing and electronics, are being developed, although all, especially tourism, have suffered in the global downturn. Services now account for 71 per cent of GDP, industry for 26 per cent and agriculture for 3 per cent. The economy of Nevis relies on farming, but a sea-island cotton industry is being developed for export. The economy is restricted by one of the world's highest public debt burdens (estimated at 185 per cent of GDP in 2009) and the country remains vulnerable to costly damage from natural disasters and shifts in tourism demand.

The main trading partners are the USA and Trinidad and Tobago. Principal exports are machinery, food, electronic equipment, beverages and tobacco. The main imports are machinery, manufactured goods, food and fuels.

GNI – US$512m; US$10,150 per capita (2009)
Annual average growth of GDP – –1.5 per cent (2010 est)
Inflation rate – 4.5 per cent (2007 est)
Total external debt – US$314m (2004 est)

BALANCE OF PAYMENTS
Trade – US$185m deficit (2010)
Current Account – US$195m deficit (2008)

Trade with UK	2009	2010
Imports from UK	£7,693,108	£5,249,278
Exports to UK	£223,704	£340,719

COMMUNICATIONS
The islands have a total of 383km of roads, of which 163km are surfaced, and 50km of narrow-gauge railways on St Kitts. Basseterre is a port of registry and has deep-water harbour facilities. There are regular ferries between Basseterre and Charlestown. There are two airports; that on St Kitts can take most large jet aircraft, and Nevis' airport can take small aircraft and has night-time landing facilities. There were 20,500 fixed lines in use, 83,000 mobile phone subscribers and 17,000 internet users in 2009.

MEDIA
The government-owned broadcaster ZIZ operates national television and radio networks. Cable television

services are also available, and there are several private radio stations. *The Sun* is the sole daily newspaper and is privately owned.

ST LUCIA

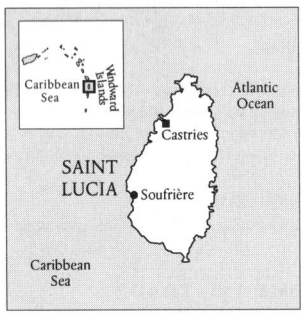

Area – 616 sq. km
Capital – Castries; population, 15,395 (2009 est)
Currency – East Caribbean dollar (EC$) of 100 cents
Population – 160,922 rising at 0.4 per cent a year (2010 est)
Religion – Christian (Roman Catholic 67 per cent, Protestant 18 per cent, other 5 per cent), Rastafarian 2 per cent (est); small Muslim minority
Language – English (official), French patois
Population density – 282 per sq. km (2009)
Urban population – 28 per cent (2008 est)
Median age (years) – 30.3 (2010 est)
National anthem – 'Sons and Daughters of Saint Lucia'
National day – 22 February (Independence Day)
Life expectancy (years) – 76.65 (2010 est)
Mortality rate – 6.9 (2010 est)
Birth rate – 14.81 (2010 est)
Infant mortality rate – 13.07 (2010 est)
Death penalty – Retained
CPI score – 7 (2009)
Literacy rate – 94.8 per cent (2008 est)

CLIMATE AND TERRAIN

St Lucia is the second-largest island in the Windward group. The interior is mountainous and densely forested, with elevation extremes ranging from 950m (Mt Gimie) to 0m (Caribbean Sea). The area around the volcanic peaks of Gros Piton and Petit Piton is a UNESCO World Heritage Site. The climate is tropical, moderated by trade winds and with a wet season from July to November. The island is in the hurricane belt.

HISTORY AND POLITICS

The original Arawak settlers were superseded by Caribs by AD 800. The island was sighted by Columbus in 1502 and European settlement began in the 1550s. Control was disputed between France and Britain from the mid-17th century until 1814, when the island was ceded to Britain. It achieved internal self-government in 1967 and became independent in 1979. Violent crime and a gang culture have grown in recent years, largely as a result of drug-trafficking.

The St Lucia Labour Party, in power since 1997, lost the 2006 general election to the United Workers Party, which formed a government under Sir John Compton; he died in September 2007 and Stephenson King became prime minister.

POLITICAL SYSTEM

Under the 1979 constitution, the head of state is Queen Elizabeth II, represented by a governor-general appointed on the advice of the prime minister. The bicameral parliament consists of the house of assembly and the senate. The senate has 11 members, six nominated by the government, three by the opposition and two by the governor-general. The House of Assembly has 17 elected members and an appointed speaker who serve a five-year term. The prime minister, who is responsible to the legislature, and the cabinet are appointed by the governor-general.

Governor-General, HE Dame Pearlette Louisy, *apptd* 1997

SELECTED GOVERNMENT MEMBERS *as at July 2011*
Prime Minister, Finance, Economy, Stephenson King
Home Affairs, George Guy Mayers
External Affairs, Rufus Bousquet
Attorney-General, Nicholas Frederick

HIGH COMMISSION FOR ST LUCIA
1 Collingham Gardens, London SW5 0HW
T 020-7370 7123 E enquiries@stluciahcuk.org
W www.stluciahcuk.org
High Commissioner, HE Eldridge Stephens, OBE, *apptd* 2008

BRITISH HIGH COMMISSIONER
HE Paul Brummell, *apptd* 2009, resident at Bridgetown, Barbados

ECONOMY AND TRADE

The economy was dependent on bananas (which still account for about 41 per cent of export earnings), but has diversified since preferential access to EU markets ended in 1999. Tourism and offshore financial services have been developed, and the manufacturing sector is the most diverse in the Caribbean, processing agricultural products, assembling electronic components and producing clothing, beverages and corrugated cardboard boxes. Services now account for 80 per cent of GDP, industry for 15 per cent and agriculture for 5 per cent. The economy contracted in the global downturn as tourist numbers fell.

The main trading partners are Brazil, Spain and the UK. Principal exports are bananas, clothing, cocoa, vegetables, fruit and coconut oil. The main imports are food, manufactured goods, machinery and transport equipment, chemicals and fuels.

GNI – US$873m; US$5,190 per capita (2009)
Annual average growth of GDP – 1.1 per cent (2010 est)
Inflation rate – 1.9 per cent (2007 est)
Unemployment – 20 per cent (2003 est)
Total external debt – US$257m (2004 est)
Imports – US$500m (2009)
Exports – US$200m (2009)

BALANCE OF PAYMENTS
Trade – US$290m deficit (2010)
Current Account – US$306m deficit (2008)

Trade with UK	2009	2010
Imports from UK	£14,978,913	£15,171,017
Exports to UK	£19,077,675	£14,007,147

COMMUNICATIONS

St Lucia has around 1,200km of roads and two airports, at Castries and Vieux Fort. Castries also has a deep-water harbour. Modern telecommunications systems provided services to 41,000 fixed lines and 142,900 internet subscribers in 2009.

MEDIA
The television and radio broadcasters are privately owned, other than one government-owned radio network which broadcasts in English and Creole. The island has two main newspapers, *The Star* and *The Voice*, both published three times a week.

ST VINCENT AND THE GRENADINES

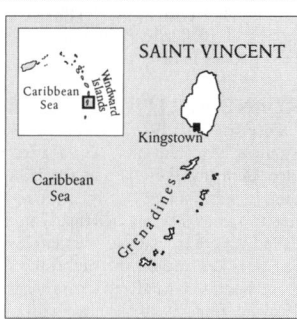

Area – 389 sq. km
Capital – Kingstown; population, 28,199 (2009 est)
Currency – East Caribbean dollar (EC $) of 100 cents
Population – 104,217 falling at 0.34 per cent a year (2010 est)
Religion – Christian (Anglican 47 per cent, Methodist 28 per cent, Roman Catholic 13 per cent), other (includes Hindu, Seventh-Day Adventist and Rastafarian) 12 per cent
Language – English (official), French patois
Population density – 280 per sq. km (2009)
Urban population – 47 per cent (2008 est)
Median age (years) – 29.5 (2010 est)
National anthem – 'St Vincent, Land So Beautiful'
National day – 27 October (Independence Day)
Life expectancy (years) – 73.9 (2010 est)
Mortality rate – 6.94 (2010 est)
Birth rate – 14.89 (2010 est)
Infant mortality rate – 14.7 (2010 est)
Death penalty – Retained
CPI score – 6.4 (2009)
Literacy rate – 88.1 per cent (2008 est)

CLIMATE AND TERRAIN
The state, which lies in the Windward group, consists of St Vincent and the 32 small islands and cays of the northern Grenadines, a chain stretching 64km across the eastern Caribbean Sea between St Vincent and Grenada. St Vincent itself is a mountainous and densely forested volcanic island. The Grenadines, of which the largest are Bequia, Canouan, Mayreau, Mustique and Union Island, are low-lying coral islands. Elevation extremes range from 1,234m (La Soufriére volcano, St Vincent) to 0m (Caribbean Sea). The climate is tropical, with a rainy season from May to November. The islands lie in the hurricane belt.

HISTORY AND POLITICS
Settled successively by the Ciboney people, the Arawaks and the Caribs, St Vincent was sighted by Christopher Columbus in 1498 but resisted European settlement longer than other Caribbean islands. Although granted by Charles I to the Earl of Carlisle in 1627, control was disputed between the British and the French until the islands were ceded to Britain in 1783. A Black Carib uprising in 1795–7 resulted in thousands of Black Caribs being deported. Internal self-government was granted in 1969, and independence as St Vincent and the Grenadines was achieved in 1979.

An early election in 2001 was won decisively by the opposition Unity Labour Party (ULP), which was returned for a second term in 2005 and narrowly retained its majority at the 2010 election. A referendum in 2009 rejected a draft constitution which proposed to replace the monarchy with a republic.

POLITICAL SYSTEM
Under the 1979 constitution, the head of state is Queen Elizabeth II, represented by a governor-general appointed on the advice of the prime minister. The unicameral House of Assembly has 21 members: 15 directly elected for a five-year term and six senators appointed by the governor-general (four on the advice of the government and two on the advice of the opposition). The prime minister, who is responsible to the legislature, and the cabinet are appointed by the governor-general.
Governor-General, Sir Frederick Ballantyne, GCMG, apptd 2002

SELECTED GOVERNMENT MEMBERS *as at July 2011*
Prime Minister, Finance, Economy, National Security, Ralph Gonsalves
Deputy Prime Minister, Girlyn Miguel

HIGH COMMISSION FOR ST VINCENT AND THE GRENADINES
10 Kensington Court, London W8 5DL
T 020-7565 2874 E svghighcom@clara.co.uk
High Commissioner, HE Cenio E. Lewis, apptd 2001

BRITISH HIGH COMMISSIONER
HE Paul Brummell, apptd 2009, resident at Bridgetown, Barbados

ECONOMY AND TRADE
The economy was based on bananas (which still account for over a third of exports) but since 1999, when preferential access to EU markets ended, efforts have been made to diversify. Tourism (the development of which has been hampered by drug-related crime), manufacturing and offshore banking services have all expanded, although the economy contracted in 2009 owing to the global downturn. Services now account for 64 per cent of GDP, industry for 26 per cent and agriculture for 10 per cent.

The main export markets are Greece and Poland. Imports come mostly from Singapore, Trinidad and Tobago, and the USA. Principal exports are bananas, vegetables, starch and tennis racquets. The main imports are foodstuffs, machinery and equipment, chemicals, fertilisers, minerals and fuel.
GNI – US$562m; US$5,130 per capita (2009)
Annual average growth of GDP – 0.5 per cent (2010 est)
Inflation rate – 0.8 per cent (2009 est)
Total external debt – US$479m (2010 est)
Imports – US$4300m (2009)
Exports – US$50m (2007)

BALANCE OF PAYMENTS
Trade – US$306m deficit (2010)
Current Account – US$217m deficit (2008)

Trade with UK	2009	2010
Imports from UK	£9,933,460	£9,598,582
Exports to UK	£4,666,003	£2,792,768

COMMUNICATIONS
The islands have around 829km of roads, of which 580km are surfaced. The main harbour is at Kingstown, which is a port of registry for shipping. There is a large merchant marine of 444 ships of over 1,000 tonnes; 382 ships are foreign-owned. There are six airports; although none can accommodate international flights at present, an international airport is under construction and scheduled for completion in 2013. There are modern telecommunications systems.

MEDIA
The press is privately owned, and its freedom is guaranteed by the constitution. There is one daily newpaper, *The Herald,* and several other weekly titles. There are several private radio stations and a national radio service which is partly government-funded. Television broadcasting is operated by the St Vincent and the Grenadines Broadcasting Corporation.

SAMOA

Malo Sa'oloto Tuto'atasi o Samoa – Independent State of Samoa

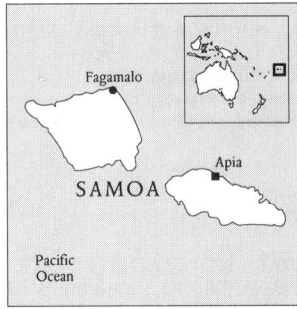

Area – 2,831 sq. km
Capital – Apia, on Upolu; population, 36,433 (2009 est)
Currency – Tala (S$) of 100 sene
Population – 192,001 rising at 0.61 per cent a year (2010 est); Samoan (Polynesian) (92.6 per cent) (2001); the population also includes Euronesians, Chinese and Europeans
Religion – Christian (Congregational 34 per cent, Roman Catholic 19 per cent, Methodist 14 per cent, Mormon 13 per cent, other 15 per cent); small Baha'i minority (2006)
Language – Samoan (official), English
Population density – 63 per sq. km (2009)
Urban population – 23 per cent (2008 est)
Median age (years) – 21.8 (2010 est)
National anthem – 'The Banner of Freedom'
National day – 1 June (Independence Day)
Life expectancy (years) – 72.13 (2010 est)
Mortality rate – 5.36 (2010 est)
Birth rate – 22.92 (2010 est)

Infant mortality rate – 23.21 (2010 est)
Death penalty – Abolished for all crimes (since 2004)
CPI score – 4.1 (2010)
Literacy rate – 98.7 per cent (2008 est)

CLIMATE AND TERRAIN
Samoa consists of the islands of Savai'i, Upolu, Apolima, Manono, Fanuatapu, Namua, Nu'utele, Nu'ulua and Nu'usafe'e in the south Pacific Ocean. All the islands are volcanic in origin, with narrow coastal plains and mountainous, densely forested interiors. Elevation extremes range from 1,857m (Mauga Silisili, Savai'i) to 0m (Pacific Ocean). The climate is tropical, with a wet season from November to April. Temperatures average between 23°C and 30°C all year round. The islands are vulnerable to cyclones and tsunamis.

HISTORY AND POLITICS
Inhabited since *c.*1000 BC, Samoa was visited by European traders, explorers and missionaries from the 18th century. Germany, the UK and the USA disputed control of the islands until 1899, when the nine western islands (Western Samoa) became a German colony and the eastern islands American Samoa. Western Samoa was occupied by New Zealand on the outbreak of the First World War and became a mandated territory administered by New Zealand from 1920. Internal self-government was granted in 1959, and Western Samoa became independent on 1 June 1962. The state was treated as a member country of the Commonwealth until its formal admission in 1970. In 1997 the state dropped 'Western' from its name.

Former prime minister Tuiatua Tupua Tamasese Efi was elected head of state in June 2007, following his predecessor's death the previous month. The Human Rights Protection Party, which has been in power since 1981, remained the largest party in the legislature after the March 2011 election; it won 28 seats, the Tautua Samoa Party won 13 seats and independents won eight.

POLITICAL SYSTEM
Under the 1962 constitution, the head of state is elected and has functions analogous to those of a constitutional monarch. Initially an office held for life, the monarch is now elected by the legislature for a five-year term. The unicameral legislative assembly *(Fono)* has 49 members elected for a five-year term; only members of the *Matai* (elected clan leaders) may stand for election. The prime minister is appointed by the monarch on the recommendation of the legislature and appoints cabinet.

HEAD OF STATE
Head of State, Tuiatua Tupua Tamasese Efi, *elected* 16 June 2007, *sworn in* 20 June 2007

SELECTED GOVERNMENT MEMBERS *as at July 2011*
Prime Minister, Foreign Affairs, Tuilaepa Sailele Malielegaoi
Deputy Prime Minister, Fonotoe Nuafesili Pierre Lauofo
Finance, Faumuina Tiatia Liugua

EMBASSY OF SAMOA
20 avenue de l'Oree, 1000 Brussels, Belgium
T (+32) (2) 660 8454 E samoanembassy@skynet.be
High Commissioner, HE Tuala Falani Chan Tung, *apptd* 2006

BRITISH HIGH COMMISSIONER
HE Victoria Treadell, MVO *apptd* 2010, resident at Wellington, New Zealand

ECONOMY AND TRADE

The economy is underdeveloped but has grown steadily in the past decade, diversifying away from its traditional dependence on fishing, agriculture (which is vulnerable to cyclones), remittances from migrant workers (worth about 25 per cent of GDP) and international aid. Agriculture and fishing generates 11.6 per cent of GDP, employing about two-thirds of the labour force and supplying about 90 per cent of exports. Manufacturing is branching out from small-scale processing of agricultural products into light manufacturing (particularly of motor vehicle components), and offshore financial services are being developed. Tourism has grown rapidly and accounts for about 25 per cent of GDP. The economy has contracted since 2008, as remittances and tourism fell during the global downturn, and a tsunami in 2009 caused severe damage.

The main trading partners are American Samoa, Australia, New Zealand, Fiji and China. Principal exports are fish, coconut oil and cream, copra, taro, vehicle parts, garments and beer. The main imports are machinery and equipment, industrial supplies and foodstuffs.

GNI – US$481m; US$2,840 per capita (2009)
Annual average growth of GDP – –2 per cent (2010 est)
Inflation rate – 6 per cent (2007 est)
Total external debt – US$177m (2004 est)
Imports – US$200m (2009)
Exports – US$15m (2007)

BALANCE OF PAYMENTS
Trade – US$250m deficit (2010)
Current Account – US$11m deficit (2009)

Trade with UK	2009	2010
Imports from UK	£394,389	£1,585,930
Exports to UK	£547,564	£457,320

COMMUNICATIONS

There are 2,337km of roads, of which 332km are surfaced. Upolu contains the harbours of Apia and Mulifanua, and Savai'i the harbour of Salelologa. There are four airports, including an international airport 35km west of Apia on Upolu. Transport systems were severely damaged by a tsunami in 2009.

Telecommunications systems serve about 95 per cent of the country, with a combined fixed-line and mobile phone density of 85 per 100 people.

MEDIA

There are two daily papers, one weekly title and one fortnightly. The press is generally free to report as it chooses, although the *Samoa Observer* has been sued by the government for reporting on alleged corruption. The state-run Samoa Broadcasting Corporation operates television and radio networks, competing with a small number of privately owned television and radio stations.

SAN MARINO

Repubblica di San Marino – Republic of San Marino

Area – 61 sq. km
Capital – San Marino; population, 4,389 (2009 est)
Currency – Euro (€) of 100 cents
Population – 31,477 rising at 1.11 per cent a year (2010 est)
Religion – Christian (Roman Catholic 90 per cent) (est)
Language – Italian (official)
Population density – 524 per sq. km (2009)
Urban population – 94 per cent (2008 est)
Median age (years) – 42.1 (2010 est)
National anthem – 'Inno Nazionale della Repubblica' ['National Anthem of the Republic']
National day – 3 September (Republic Day)
Life expectancy (years) – 82.95 (2010 est)
Mortality rate – 7.75 (2010 est)
Birth rate – 9.18 (2010 est)
Infant mortality rate – 4.79 (2010 est)
Death penalty – Abolished for all crimes (since 1865)

CLIMATE AND TERRAIN

A landlocked enclave in central Italy, the republic lies in the foothills of the Apennines, 20km from the Adriatic Sea. Elevation extremes range from 755m (Mt Titano) to 55m (Torrente Ausa). The climate is Mediterranean, with an average annual rainfall of 762mm.

HISTORY AND POLITICS

The republic is said to have been founded in the fourth century by a Christian stonecutter seeking refuge from religious persecution. By the 12th century a self-governing commune was established, and a parliamentary constitution was adopted in 1600. The republic resisted papal claims and those of neighbouring dukedoms from the 15th to 18th centuries, and the papacy recognised its independence in 1631. In 1862 it signed a treaty with the newly united kingdom of Italy which recognised its integrity and sovereignty and accorded it the protection of Italy. San Marino became a member of the UN in 1992.

Following the 2006 legislative election, the Christian Democratic Party (PDCS) remained the largest party in the legislature, but a coalition government was formed by the Party of Socialists and Democrats (PSD), United Left and Popular Alliance (AP) parties. A split in the government in 2008 led to an early election that resulted in the Pact for San Marino coalition (of the PDCS, AP, Freedom List and Union of Moderates) winning the most seats and forming a new coalition government.

POLITICAL SYSTEM

The 1600 constitution has been amended several times. The joint heads of state are two captains-regent who are elected at six-monthly intervals (March and September) by the legislature, taking office the month after the election. Executive power is vested in the captains-regent and the Congress of State (cabinet), which is also elected by the legislature. The unicameral legislature, the Great and General Council, has 60 members, who are directly elected for a five-year term.

HEADS OF STATE *as at July 2011*
Captains-Regent, Maria Luisa Berti; Filippo Tamagnini

SELECTED GOVERNMENT MEMBERS *as at July 2011*
Finance, Gabriele Gatti
Foreign Affairs, Antonella Mularoni
Internal Affairs, Valeria Ciavatta

EMBASSY OF THE REPUBLIC OF SAN MARINO
c/o Consulate of the Republic of San Marino, Flat 51, 162 Sloane Street, London SW1X 9BS
T 020-7823 4762 E dipartimentoaffariesteri@pa.sm

Ambassador Extraordinary and Plenipotentiary, HE Countess Marina Meneghetti de Camillo, *apptd* 2002, resident at Rome, Italy

BRITISH AMBASSADOR
HE Christopher Prentice, CMG, *apptd* 2011, resident at Rome, Italy

ECONOMY AND TRADE

Tourism and banking are the basis of the economy, and the service sector contributes 60.7 per cent of GDP. In 2009, investment outflows following Italy's tax amnesty, a money-laundering scandal at its largest bank and the global downturn contributed to a deep recession and growing budget deficit. The government is working to improve standards of financial transparency.

The principal agricultural products are grains, grapes, olives, cheeses and hides. The main industries apart from tourism and banking are quarrying, forestry, winemaking and the manufacture of clothing, electronics and ceramics. Sales of postage stamps and coins also generate significant revenue. San Marino is in a customs union with the EU.
GNI – US$1,681m; US$50,670 per capita (2008)
Annual average growth of GDP – −13 per cent (2009 est)
Inflation rate – −3.5 per cent (2008 est)
Unemployment – 3.1 per cent (2008 est)

Trade with UK	2009	2010
Imports from UK	£10,009,227	£6,898,352
Exports to UK	£4,014,480	£4,432,783

MEDIA

San Marino has a state-run broadcaster, which provides radio and television services. The two daily newspapers are *La Tribuna Sammarinese* and *San Marino Oggi.*

SAO TOME AND PRINCIPE

Republica Democratica de Sao Tome e Principe – Democratic Republic of Sao Tome and Principe

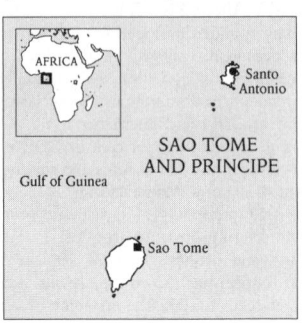

Area – 964 sq. km
Capital – Sao Tome; population, 59,851 (2009 est)
Currency – Dobra of 100 centimos
Population – 175,808 rising at 2.11 per cent a year (2010 est)
Religion – Christian (Roman Catholic 85 per cent, Protestant 12 per cent), Muslim 2 per cent (est)
Language – Portuguese (official), Creole dialects
Population density – 170 per sq. km (2009)
Urban population – 610 per cent (2008 est)
Median age (years) – 17.5 (2010 est)
National anthem – 'Independencia total' ['Total Independence']
National day – 12 July (Independence Day)
Life expectancy (years) – 62.73 (2010 est)
Mortality rate – 8.45 (2010 est)
Birth rate – 39.09 (2010 est)
Infant mortality rate – 54.64 (2010 est)
Death penalty – Abolished for all crimes (since 1990)
CPI score – 3.0 (2010)
Literacy rate – 88.4 per cent (2008 est)

CLIMATE AND TERRAIN

The republic consists of the islands of Sao Tome, Principe and several uninhabited islets off the west coast of Africa. The islands, which are volcanic in origin, are mountainous and thickly forested. Elevation extremes range from 2,024m (Pico de Sao Tome) to 0m (Atlantic Ocean). The climate is tropical, with a wet season from October to May. Average daily temperatures are between 21°C and 31°C all year round.

HISTORY AND POLITICS

The uninhabited islands were discovered by the Portuguese between 1469 and 1472, and settlement began in 1493. Plantations were established that became important producers of sugar cane, cocoa and coffee. Agitation against Portuguese rule began in the late 1950s. The islands gained independence from Portugal in 1975 and became a one-party state under the rule of the Movement for the Liberation of Sao Tome and Principe (MLSTP). The government nationalised the plantations and formed close links with the communist bloc. These were scaled down in the 1980s as the economy deteriorated, and in 1990 the MLSTP abandoned Marxism and introduced political pluralism and economic liberalisation. The first multiparty elections were held in 1991. Democracy has brought a degree of political instability, and tensions have been heightened recently by disagreements over the exploitation of offshore oil reserves.

President Fradique de Menezes was re-elected at the 2006 presidential election. In the 2010 legislative election, the opposition Independent Democratic Action (ADI) party became the largest party in the legislature, but without a majority, and formed a government with a number of independent members under the ADI leader Patrice Trovoada (prime minister February–May 2008). A presidential election was scheduled for 17 July 2011.

POLITICAL SYSTEM
Under the 1990 constitution, the president is directly elected for a five-year term, renewable once. The unicameral National Assembly has 55 members, directly elected for a four-year term. The prime minister is appointed by the president and nominates the cabinet.

Since 1995 Príncipe has been internally self-governing, with an eight-member regional council.

HEAD OF STATE
President, Fradique de Menezes, *elected* 29 July 2001, *sworn in* 3 September 2001, *re-elected* 2006

SELECTED GOVERNMENT MEMBERS *as at July 2011*
Prime Minister, Patrice Trovoada
Defence, Elsa Teixeira Pinto
Finance, Angela Viegas Santiago
Foreign Affairs, Carlos Alberto Pires Tiny

EMBASSY OF SAO TOME AND PRINCIPE
175 avenue de Tervuren, 1150 Brussels, Belgium
T (+32) (2) 734 8966 E ambassade@saotomeprincipe.be
Ambassador Extraordinary and Plenipotentiary,
  HE Armindo de Brito Fernandes, *apptd* 2011

BRITISH AMBASSADOR
HE Richard Wildash, *apptd* 2010, resident at Luanda, Angola

ECONOMY AND TRADE
The economy has benefited from cancellation of about 90 per cent of the country's external debt over the past decade. It is largely dependent on cocoa, but tourism is being encouraged in an attempt to diversify. A major economic shift will begin with the start of oil production from offshore reserves in the Gulf of Guinea. The fields are being developed jointly with Nigeria, and Sao Tome and Principe will receive 40 per cent of the revenue. Most of the population is engaged in subsistence farming and fishing.

The principal export markets are the UK (33 per cent), the Netherlands (27 per cent) and Belgium (21 per cent), and the main source of imports is Portugal (56 per cent). Principal exports are cocoa (80 per cent), copra, coffee and palm oil. The main imports are machinery and electrical equipment, foodstuffs and petroleum products.
GNI – US$194m; US$1,130 per capita (2009)
Annual average growth of GDP – 6 per cent (2010 est)
Inflation rate – 13 per cent (2010 est)
Population below poverty line – 54 per cent (2004 est)
Total external debt – US$318m (2002 est)

BALANCE OF PAYMENTS
Trade – US$101m deficit (2010)
Current Account – US$88m deficit (2008)

Trade with UK	2009	2010
Imports from UK	£147,050	£229,917
Exports to UK	£10,964	£102,538

COMMUNICATIONS
There are 320km of roads, 218km of which are surfaced but in poor condition. There are two airports, and the ports are Santo Antonio, on Principe, and Sao Tome. The telephone system supported 7,800 fixed lines, 64,000 mobile phone users and 26,700 internet users in 2009.

MEDIA
Freedom of expression is generally respected. The islands' only radio and television stations are state-run, but opposition parties are given free air time. There are three privately owned newspapers and one published by the government.

SAUDI ARABIA

Al-Mamlakah al-Arabiyah as Suudiyah – Kingdom of Saudi Arabia

Area – 2,149,690 sq. km
Capital – Riyadh (Ar-Riyadh); population, 4,725,270 (2009 est)
Major cities – Ad Dammam, Jeddah, Mecca, Medina, Tabuk, At Ta'if
Currency – Saudi riyal (SR) of 100 halalas
Population – 25,731,776 rising at 1.55 per cent a year (2010 est); includes some 5,576,076 non-nationals (2010 est)
Religion – Muslim (Sunni 85 per cent, predominantly Wahhabi; Shia 10 per cent) (est). Public practice of other religions is forbidden
Language – Arabic (official)
Population density – 13 per sq. km (2009)
Urban population – 82 per cent (2008 est)
Median age (years) – 24.9 (2010 est)
National anthem – 'As-Salaam al Malaki' ['The Royal Salute']
National day – 23 September (Unification Day)
Life expectancy (years) – 73.87 (2010 est)
Mortality rate – 3.34 (2010 est)
Birth rate – 19.43 (2010 est)
Infant mortality rate – 16.73 (2010 est)
Death penalty – Retained
CPI score – 4.7 (2010)

CLIMATE AND TERRAIN
Saudi Arabia comprises about 80 per cent of the Arabian peninsula. The Hejaz region (north-west) runs along the northern Red Sea coast to the Asir and contains the holy

cities of Mecca and Medina. The mountainous Asir (south-west) and the coastal plain of the Tihama lie along the southern Red Sea coast from the Hejaz to the border with Yemen. The Nejd plateau extends over the centre, including the Nafud and Dahna deserts. The Hasa (east) is low-lying and largely desert. The Empty Quarter (south) is the world's largest sand desert. Elevation extremes range from 3,133m (Jabal Sawda) to 0m (Persian Gulf). There is a desert climate, with extremes of temperature in the interior; coastal areas are more temperate but extremely humid. Average temperatures in Riyadh range from 3°C in January to 45°C in July.

HISTORY AND POLITICS

The Arabian peninsula was the birthplace of the Muslim faith in the seventh century and the base from which the religion and a Muslim empire expanded, eventually stretching from India to Spain. When this empire declined in the 12th century, Arabia became isolated and internally divided. The rise of the al-Saud family began in the 18th century, when it united the Nejd in support of the Wahhabi religious movement. The modern state was the culmination of a 30-year campaign by Abd-al Aziz al-Saud (often known as Ibn Saud) to unite the four tribal regions of the Hejaz, Asir, Najd and Hasa; the Kingdom of Saudi Arabia was proclaimed on 23 September 1932.

The ruling family preserved stability for many years by suppressing dissent and resisting calls for greater democracy, with some of its actions raising international concerns over human rights abuses. Internal tension grew in the 1990s because of the continuing presence of foreign, particularly US, troops in the country after the 1991 Gulf War; troops, and foreign nationals became terrorist targets. Despite the troops' redeployment to Qatar in early 2003, the frequency of attacks increased following the start of the Iraq War in 2003 and included Saudi as well as foreign victims. Some dissident groups are believed to have links with al-Qaida. Since 2003 demand for political reform has grown and become more militant. In 2005, the country's first nationwide elections were held for half the seats on municipal councils, with voting by universal male suffrage.

King Abdullah acceded to the throne after the death of his half-brother King Fahd in 2005.

POLITICAL SYSTEM

There is no written constitution; constitutional practice is provided for by articles of government based on the Qur'an and the teachings and sayings of the Prophet Muhammad *(Sunnah)* and issued by royal decree.

Saudi Arabia is a hereditary monarchy. The king is head of government and appoints the council of ministers (established in 1953), whose term of office was fixed in 1993 at four years.

There is no legislature; the Consultative Council *(Majlis-al-Shura)* debates policy, proposes legislation in certain areas and makes recommendations to the king. The council's 150 members are appointed by the king and serve a four-year term. Its decisions are taken by majority vote. There are no political parties.

Each of the 13 provinces has a governor appointed by the king and a council of prominent local citizens to advise the governor on local government, budgetary and planning issues.

HEAD OF STATE

The King of Saudi Arabia, Custodian of the Two Holy Mosques, Prime Minister, King Abdullah bin Abdul Aziz al-Saud, *born* 1923, *succeeded* 2 August 2005

HRH Crown Prince, Deputy Prime Minister, Defence, Prince Sultan bin Abdul Aziz al-Saud

SELECTED GOVERNMENT MEMBERS *as at July 2011*
Interior, HRH Prince Nayef bin Abdul Aziz al-Saud
Finance, Ibrahim bin Abdel Aziz al-Assaf
Foreign Affairs, HRH Prince Saud al-Faisal bin Abdul Aziz al-Saud
Economy, Khaled bin Mohammad al-Qussaibi

ROYAL EMBASSY OF SAUDI ARABIA
30 Charles Street, London W1J 5DZ
T 020-7917 3000 E ukemb@mofa.gov.sa
W www.saudiembassy.org.uk
Ambassador Extraordinary and Plenipotentiary, HE HRH Prince Mohamed bin Nawaf bin Abdul Aziz al-Saud, *apptd* 2005

BRITISH EMBASSY
PO Box 94351, Diplomatic Quarter, Riyadh 11693
T (+966) (1) 488 0077 E PressOffice.Riyadh@fco.gov.uk
W http://ukinsaudiarabia.fco.gov.uk
Ambassador Extraordinary and Plenipotentiary, HE Sir Tom Phillips, KCMG, *apptd* 2010

BRITISH COUNCIL
PO Box 58012, C-14, 3rd Floor, Al-Fazari Square, Diplomatic Quarter, Riyadh 11594
T (+966) (1) 483 1818
W www.britishcouncil.org/me-saudiarabia
Director, Adrian Chardwick

DEFENCE

The army has 565 main battle tanks, 1,840 armoured personnel carriers, 780 armoured infantry fighting vehicles and 12 armed helicopters. The navy has 3 destroyers, 4 frigates, 30 patrol and coastal vessels, and 34 multi-role helicopters at 7 bases. The air force has 349 combat aircraft.

Military budget – US$45,240m (2010)
Military personnel – 233,500: army 75,000, navy 13,500, air force 20,000, Air Defence Force 16,000, Industrial Security Force 9,000, National Guard 100,000; paramilitary 15,500

ECONOMY AND TRADE

The economy is based on oil extraction and processing, but since 1970 the government has used five-year development plans to encourage diversification, and the non-oil sector now accounts for over half of GDP. The 2000–5 and 2005–9 development plans encouraged the growth of the private sector (now responsible for about 40 per cent of GDP) and an increase in the proportion of Saudi Arabian citizens in the workforce (about 80 per cent of workers are foreign nationals). The 2005–9 plan focused on the development of mineral industries, housing and transport schemes, petrochemical plants, electricity generation, water supplies and desalination, telecommunications and ports. The 2010–14 plan aims to increase natural gas production and to promote the growth of small- and medium-sized businesses, partly through further privatisation; it also partially opened the Saudi stock market to foreign investors.

Oil extraction since the 1940s has brought great wealth. Saudi Arabia has the largest proven reserves of oil in the world (about 20 per cent of the world total) and the fifth-largest reserves of recoverable gas. Depending on world prices, the oil and gas industry contributes around

45 per cent of GDP and about 80 per cent of government revenue.

The main industries apart from oil extraction and refining include production of petrochemicals, ammonia, industrial gases, caustic soda, cement, fertiliser, plastics and metals, commercial ship and aircraft repair and construction. Industry accounts for 61.9 per cent of GDP and the service sector for 35.4 per cent. Agriculture contributes 2.7 per cent but is limited by the terrain, although productivity has been increased by extensive irrigation, desalination and the use of aquifers. The main products are grains, fruit, meat and dairy products.

The main trading partners are the USA, China, Japan and South Korea. Oil and petroleum products constitute 90 per cent of exports. The principal imports are machinery and equipment, foodstuffs, chemicals, motor vehicles and textiles.

GNI – US$384,379m; US$17,210 per capita (2009)
Annual average growth of GDP – 3.8 per cent (2010 est)
Inflation rate – 5.7 per cent (2010 est)
Unemployment rate – 10.8 per cent (among males only) (2010 est)
Total external debt – US$82,920m (2010 est)
Imports – US$89,500m (2009)
Exports – US$188,500m (2009)

BALANCE OF PAYMENTS
Trade – US$144,201m surplus (2010)
Current Account – US$20,478m surplus (2009)

Trade with UK	2009	2010
Imports from UK	£2,648,095,106	£3,076,566,521
Exports to UK	£555,991,836	£424,447,489

COMMUNICATIONS
The main cargo ports are Jeddah on the Red Sea coast and Dammam on the Gulf coast. The main oil port (the world's largest) is Ras Tanura. There are 1,378km of railways, operated by the state-run Saudi Railway Organisation, which link Riyadh with the Gulf ports; there are plans to build a railway from Jeddah to Dammam. The road network totals 221,372km (of which 47,529km are surfaced), including a 3,891km motorway system connecting all the cities and main towns. The 25km-long King Fahd Causeway connects the Eastern Province to Bahrain. There are 217 airports and airfields; the three international airports are at Riyadh, Jeddah (serving Mecca) and Dammam.

Modern telecommunications systems provided services to 4.2 million fixed telephone lines, 44.9 million mobile phone subscribers and 9.7 million internet users in 2009.

EDUCATION AND HEALTH
With the exception of a few schools for expatriate children, all schools are supervised by the government and are segregated. There is great emphasis on vocational training, provided at literacy and artisan skill training centres and more advanced industrial, commercial and agricultural education institutes. The King Abdullah University of Science and Technology, a graduate-level research university and the first mixed-sex campus in Saudi Arabia, opened in 2009.

Literacy rate – 85.6 per cent (2008 est)
Gross enrolment ratio (percentage of relevant age group) – primary 99 per cent; secondary 97 per cent; tertiary 33 per cent (2009 est)
Health expenditure (per capita) – US$714 (2009)
Hospital beds (per 1,000 people) – 2.2 (2004–9)

MEDIA AND CULTURE
Saudi Arabia's media is one of the most tightly controlled in the Middle East. Criticism of the government and royal family and the questioning of religious doctrine are not tolerated.

The only television and radio networks are operated by the state-run Broadcasting Service of the Kingdom of Saudi Arabia (BSKSA). Private radio and TV stations are not permitted, but there is a big market for pan-Arab services from satellite and subscription-based broadcasters. Although not necessarily state-run, Saudi newspapers normally follow the lead of the state-run press agency. Pan-Arab newspapers are also available but are censored. The government uses security systems to block websites with content it deems unsuitable.

Saudi culture revolves around Islam – it was the birthplace of the religion and two of Islam's holiest sites are situated in the country. Mecca was the Prophet Muhammad's birthplace and contains the Great Mosque, within which is the *Ka'abah* or sacred shrine of the Muslim religion. This is the focus of the annual *Hajj* ('pilgrimage'). Medina ('city of light'), some 300km north of Mecca, is celebrated as the first city to embrace Islam and as the burial place of the Prophet.

SENEGAL

République du Sénégal – Republic of Senegal

Area – 196,722 sq. km
Capital – Dakar; population, 2,776,700 (2009 est)
Major cities – Kaolack, Mbour, Saint-Louis, Thiès, Ziguinchor
Currency – Franc CFA of 100 centimes
Population – 12,323,252 rising at 2.58 per cent a year (2010 est); Wolof (43.3 per cent), Fulani (23.8 per cent), Serer (14.7 per cent), Jola (3.7 per cent), Mandinka (3 per cent), Soninke (1.1 per cent), European and Lebanese (1 per cent) (est)
Religion – Muslim 94 per cent, Christian 4 per cent (est). Most incorporate indigenous beliefs into their worship
Language – French (official), Wolof, Fula, Jola, Mandinka
Population density – 65 per sq. km (2009)
Urban population – 42 per cent (2008 est)
Median age (years) – 17.9 (2010 est)
National anthem – 'Pincez Tous vos Koras, Frappez les Balafons' ['All Pluck Your Koras, Strike the Balafons']
National day – 4 April (Independence Day)
Life expectancy (years) – 59.38 (2010 est)
Mortality rate – 9.49 (2010 est)
Birth rate – 37.27 (2010 est)
Infant mortality rate – 57.7 (2010 est)
Death penalty – Abolished for all crimes (since 2004)
CPI score – 2.9 (2010)

CLIMATE AND TERRAIN
The terrain is generally low and rolling, with plains rising to hills in the south-east. There is desert in the north, savannah in the centre and tropical forest in the south. Elevation extremes range from 581m (near Nepen Diakha) to 0m (Atlantic Ocean). There are three rivers: the Senegal on the northern border; and the Gambia and the Casamance in the south. The climate is tropical, with a wet season from June to September. Average temperatures in Dakar range from 17°C in February to 30°C from July to October.

HISTORY AND POLITICS
Senegal was part of the Mali Empire in the 14th to 15th centuries. The first European visitors were the Portuguese in 1445. The French established a fort at Saint-Louis in 1659 and European traders exported slaves, ivory, gold and other commodities from there in the 17th and 18th centuries. The interior was colonised by the French in the mid-19th century and the territory became part of French West Africa in 1902. It became an autonomous state in 1958 and achieved independence as part of the Federation of Mali in June 1960, seceding to form the Republic of Senegal in August 1960. From 1966 to 1978, the country was a one-party state under the rule of the Senegalese Progressive Union (UPS), which changed its name to the Socialist Party (PS) in 1976.

In the early 1980s a separatist insurgency led by the Movement of Democratic Forces of Casamance (MFDC) began in the impoverished Casamance region south of the river Gambia. A 2001 peace agreement was not implemented because of splits and leadership changes among the separatists. Further splits have prevented the full implementation of a 2004 peace agreement, as some separatist factions remain active, and clashes continue between government troops and rebels.

The Socialist Party's 40 years of political domination ended in 2000 with the election of Abdoulaye Wade, leader of the Senegalese Democratic Party (PDS), as president. The 2001 legislative election was won by an alliance of 40 parties, the *Sopi* (Change) coalition, led by the PDS; the PS retained only ten seats. President Wade was re-elected in the first round of the 2007 presidential election. The *Sopi* coalition retained its majority in the 2007 legislative elections, which were boycotted by 12 opposition parties.

POLITICAL SYSTEM
The 2001 constitution was amended in 2007 to re-establish the senate as the upper chamber of a bicameral legislature. The executive president is directly elected for a seven-year term, renewable once. The bicameral *Parlement* comprises the National Assembly, the lower chamber, which has 150 members directly elected for a five-year term; and the senate, which has 100 members, 35 indirectly elected and 65 appointed by the president, for a five-year term. The president appoints the prime minister, who nominates the other ministers.

HEAD OF STATE
President, Abdoulaye Wade, *elected* 19 March 2000, *sworn in* 1 April 2000, *re-elected* 2007

SELECTED GOVERNMENT MEMBERS *as at July 2011*
Prime Minister, Souleymane Ndene Ndiaye
Finance and Economy, Abdoulaye Diop
Interior, Ousmane Ngom
Foreign Affairs, Madicke Niang

EMBASSY OF THE REPUBLIC OF SENEGAL
39 Marloes Road, London W8 6LA
T 020-7938 4048 E senegalembassy@hotmail.co.uk
W www.senegalembassy.com
Ambassador Extraordinary and Plenipotentiary,
   HE Abdou Sourang, *apptd* 2007

BRITISH EMBASSY
PO Box 6025, 20 rue du Docteur Guillet, Dakar
T (+221) 823 7392 E britemb@orange.sn
W http://ukinsenegal.fco.gov.uk
Ambassador Extraordinary and Plenipotentiary,
   HE Robert Marshall, *apptd* 2011

BRITISH COUNCIL
Rue AAB-68, Amitie Zone A&B, BP 6232, Dakar
T (+221) 869 2700 W www.britishcouncil.org/africa
Director, Eric Lawrie

DEFENCE
The army has over 36 armoured personnel carriers. The navy has 10 patrol and coastal combatant vessels at 2 bases. The air force has 1 combat capable aircraft and 2 armed helicopters.
Military budget – US$199m (2010)
Military personnel – 13,620: army 11,900, navy 950, air force 770; paramilitary 5,000
Conscription duration – 24 months (selective)

ECONOMY AND TRADE
Despite steady growth since the mid-1990s and the cancellation of two-thirds of its foreign debt in recent years, Senegal remains poor; over half live below the poverty line, and unemployment is over 40 per cent. The country is heavily dependent on foreign aid and remittances from expatriate workers, but infrastructure projects and the development of the textiles, information technology, telecommunications services and tourism industries are government priorities.

Agriculture and fishing are the mainstays of the economy, engaging 77.5 per cent of the workforce and contributing 14.9 per cent of GDP. The main industries are food and fish processing, mining (phosphate, iron, zircon, gold), oil refining, the production of fertiliser and construction materials, ship construction and repair, and tourism. Industry accounts for 21.4 per cent of GDP and services for 63.6 per cent.

The main trading partners are France, Mali, other EU countries, India and China. The principal exports are fish, groundnuts, petroleum products, phosphates and cotton. Principal imports are food, beverages, capital goods and fuels.
GNI – US$12,778m; US$1,040 per capita (2009)
Annual average growth of GDP – 3.9 per cent (2010 est)
Inflation rate – 1.2 per cent (2010 est)
Unemployment – 48 per cent (2007 est)
Total external debt – US$3,885m (2010 est)
Imports – US$4,500m (2009)
Exports – US$1,900m (2009)

BALANCE OF PAYMENTS
Trade – US$2,258m deficit (2010)
Current Account – US$1,908m deficit (2008)

Trade with UK	2009	2010
Imports from UK	£272,538,289	£509,129,398
Exports to UK	£9,574,339	£13,669,558

COMMUNICATIONS

Senegal has a road network of some 13,576km, of which 3,972km are surfaced. Overseas donors are providing funds for road-building programmes in the north and the south. There are also 906km of railways and 1,000km of navigable waterways, mainly on the Senegal, Saloum and Casamance rivers. Dakar is the main port and the location of the principal airport; the seaport facilities are being modernised and a second international airport near Dakar is planned. The national carrier, Air Senegal, collapsed in 2009; a new carrier, Senegal Airlines, began operations in partnership with the Dubai-based Emirates Airlines in January 2011.

The telephone system is good although not extensive. In 2009 there were 279,000 fixed lines in use, 6.9 million mobile phone subscribers and 1.8 million internet users.

EDUCATION AND HEALTH

Literacy rate – 41.9 per cent (2008 est)
Gross enrolment ratio (percentage of relevant age group) – primary 84 per cent; secondary 30 per cent; tertiary 8 per cent (2008 est)
Health expenditure (per capita) – US$59 (2009)
Hospital beds (per 1,000 people) – 0.3 (2004–9)

MEDIA

The longstanding tradition of press freedom has been undermined since 2008 by state intimidation. The state-run broadcaster operates the only free television channels and the main national and regional radio networks. There are many private radio stations, and subscription-based television is available. There are five major daily newspapers, one of which is state-owned.

SERBIA

Republika Srbija – Republic of Serbia

Area – 77,474 sq. km
Capital – Belgrade; population, 1,115,380 (2009 est)
Major cities – Kragujevac, Nis, Novi Sad
Currency – Serbian dinar of 100 paras
Population – 7,344,847 falling at 0.47 per year (2010 est); Serb (82.9 per cent), Hungarian (3.9 per cent), Bosniak (1.8 per cent), Roma (1.4 per cent), Yugoslav (1.1 per cent), Montenegrin (0.9 per cent) (2002)
Religion – Christian (Serbian Orthodox 84 per cent, Roman Catholic 5 per cent, Protestant 2 per cent), Muslim 5 per cent (est)
Language – Serbian (official), Hungarian, Romanian, Slovak, Ukrainian, Croatian (all official in different regions), Bosnian, Romani
Population density – 83 per sq. km (2009)
Urban population – 52 per cent (2008 est)
Median age (years) – 41.1 (2010 est)
National anthem – 'Boze Pravde' ['God of Justice']
National day – 15 February (Constitution Day)
Life expectancy (years) – 74.09 (2010 est)
Mortality rate – 13.89 (2010 est)
Birth rate – 9.2 (2010 est)
Infant mortality rate – 6.65 (2010 est)
Death penalty – Abolished for all crimes (since 2002)
CPI score – 3.5 (2010)
Literacy rate – 96.4 per cent (2008 est)
Gross enrolment ratio (percentage of relevant age group) – primary 98 per cent; secondary 91 per cent; tertiary 50 per cent (2009 est)
Health expenditure (per capita) – US$419 (2009)
Hospital beds (per 1,000 people) – 5.4 (2004–9)

CLIMATE AND TERRAIN

The landlocked country is mountainous in the south, while the north is dominated by the low-lying plains of the Danube and its major tributaries, the Sava, the Tisa and the Morava. Its highest point is 2,169m (Midzor) and its lowest is 35m (the confluence of the Danube and Timok rivers). The climate is continental; average temperatures in Belgrade range from −3°C in January to 28°C in July.

HISTORY AND POLITICS

The medieval kingdom of Serbia emerged in the 12th century to form a large and prosperous state in the Balkans. Defeat by the Turks in 1389 led to almost 500 years of Turkish rule. After gaining increasing autonomy within the Ottoman Empire from 1815, Serbia became fully independent in 1878 and a kingdom in 1881. At the end of the First World War Serbia joined with the former Austro-Hungarian provinces of Slovenia, Croatia and Bosnia and Hercegovina and the kingdom of Montenegro to form the Kingdom of Serbs, Croats and Slovenes, renamed Yugoslavia in 1929. Yugoslavia was occupied and partitioned by the Axis powers in 1941 and reformed after liberation in 1945 as a communist federal republic. When the federation disintegrated in 1991–2, Serbia and Montenegro were left to form the rump Federal Republic of Yugoslavia (FRY), which was declared on 27 April 1992.

Serbia under Slobodan Milosevic (president 1989–96) opposed the break-up of the federation and supported various military efforts, ultimately unsuccessful, to unite ethnic Serbs in neighbouring republics into a 'Greater Serbia'. Milosevic dominated Serbian and federal politics in the 1990s, becoming president of the FRY in 1997. His corrupt and repressive regime ended when he lost the 2000 federal presidential election; he was arrested in 2001 and extradited to the UN International Criminal Tribunal for the Former Yugoslavia, where he died in 2006 during his trial.

In 2003 the Federal Republic of Yugoslavia was restructured into a union of Serbia and Montenegro, each with semi-independent status. Montenegro voted to become independent in May 2006 and the union was dissolved in June, with Serbia succeeding to the union's membership of international bodies. The Serbian province of Kosovo unilaterally declared its independence in 2008 after nine years under UN administration.

Boris Tadic, leader of the Democratic Party (DS), was elected president in 2004; he was re-elected in 2008. After the 2007 legislative election, a coalition government was formed by the DS, the Democratic Party of Serbia

(DSS) and two smaller parties. This government resigned in March 2008, after only ten months in office, because of disagreements between the coalition partners over policy towards the EU following Kosovo's declaration of independence. In elections held in May, the For a European Serbia coalition, led by the DS, won the most seats but without an overall majority. It formed a coalition government with the Socialist Party.

POLITICAL SYSTEM

Under the 2006 constitution, the president is directly elected for a five-year term, renewable once. The unicameral National Assembly has 250 members, directly elected for a four-year term. The prime minister is appointed by the president.

HEAD OF STATE

President, Boris Tadic, *elected* 27 June 2004, *took office* 11 July 2004, *re-elected* 2008

SELECTED GOVERNMENT MEMBERS *as at July 2011*
Prime Minister, Mirko Cvetkovic
Deputy Prime Ministers, Verica Kalanovic; Ivica Dacic; Bozidar Djelic; Jovan Krkobabic
Economy, Nebojsa Ciric
Foreign Affairs, Vuk Jeremic
Defence, Dragan Sutanovac

EMBASSY OF THE REPUBLIC OF SERBIA
28 Belgrave Square, London SW1X 8QB
T 020-7235 9049 E london@serbianembassy.org.uk
W http://serbianembassy.org.uk
Ambassador Extraordinary and Plenipotentiary, Dejan Popovic, *apptd* 2008

BRITISH EMBASSY
Resavska 46, 11000 Belgrade
T (+381) (11) 264 5055 E belgrade.man@fco.gov.uk
W http://ukinserbia.fco.gov.uk
Ambassador Extraordinary and Plenipotentiary, HE Michael Davenport, LVO, *apptd* 2011

BRITISH COUNCIL
Terazije 8/1, 11000 Belgrade
T (+381) (11) 302 3800 W www.britishcouncil.org/serbia
Director, Andrew Glass

DEFENCE

The army has 212 main battle tanks, 39 armoured personnel carriers and 323 armoured infantry fighting vehicles. The air force has 83 combat aircraft.
Military budget – US$918m (2010)
Military personnel – 29,125: army 12,260, air force and air defence 4,262, training command 6,212, MoD 6,391
Conscription duration – abolished in 2011

ECONOMY AND TRADE

Economic mismanagement, UN sanctions in the 1990s and damage to infrastructure and industry from NATO bombing in 1999 had reduced the economy to about 40 per cent of its 1990 size by 2000. Since 2000, governments have pursued economic reforms and international reintegration, obtained international support for economic restructuring, and rescheduled payments or received debt relief on much of its foreign debt. Progress has been intermittent, but most of the economy is now privatised. Economic growth averaged 6 per cent until 2008, but the economy was severely affected by the global downturn, which brought credit constraints, a fall in foreign investment and manufacturing output, a sharp drop in export demand and reduced remittances from expatriate workers. The government sought IMF support in 2008 as the budget and trade deficits grew. Serbia submitted a formal application for EU membership in 2009.

Agriculture accounts for 12.6 per cent of GDP and employs 23.9 per cent of the workforce. The main agricultural products are wheat, maize, sugar beet, sunflowers, fruit, meat and milk. Industry includes food processing and production of base metals, furniture, machinery, chemicals, sugar, tyres, clothing and pharmaceuticals. Industry contributes 21.9 per cent of GDP and services 65.5 per cent.

The main trading partners are Russia, the EU and neighbouring states. Principal exports are iron and steel, rubber, clothing, wheat, fruit, vegetables and non-ferrous metals.
GNI – US$42,274m; US$6,000 per capita (2009)
Annual average growth of GDP – 1.8 per cent (2010 est)
Inflation rate – 4.9 per cent (2010 est)
Population below poverty line – 7.9 per cent (2008 est)
Unemployment – 17.2 per cent (2010 est)
Total external debt – US$32,310m (2010 est)

BALANCE OF PAYMENTS
Trade – US$8,448m deficit (2010)
Current Account – US$8,646m deficit (2008)

Trade with UK	2009	2010
Imports from UK	£94,010,676	£87,904,834
Exports to UK	£65,505,305	£83,128,195

COMMUNICATIONS

Serbia has 36,884km of roads, around 31,938km of which are surfaced. There are also 3,379km of railways, linking Belgrade directly to Athens, Bucharest, Budapest, Istanbul, Ljubljana, Munich, Skopje, Sofia, Thessaloniki, Vienna and Zagreb. There are 587km of navigable waterways on the Danube and Sava rivers; the principal ports include Belgrade and Novi Sad on the Danube. The main international airport is at Belgrade.

Modernisation of the telephone system is progressing, although rural services are not as good as those in urban areas. There were 3.1 million fixed lines in use, 9.9 million mobile phone subscribers and 4.1 million internet users in 2009.

MEDIA

The ousting of Milosevic allowed the media much greater freedom and outlets subsequently proliferated. A media regulatory system is in operation and issues licences to the hundreds of private-sector radio and television broadcasters. The state-funded national broadcaster RTS aims to develop into a public service, and state-funded local and regional media outlets are to be privatised. Newspapers include the dailies *Danas, Blik,* and *Politika,* and the weeklies *Vreme* and *NIN.*

SEYCHELLES

République des Seychelles/Repiblik Sesel – Republic of Seychelles

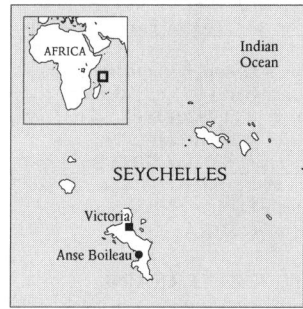

Area – 455 sq. km
Capital – Victoria, on Mahé; population, 26,001 (2009 est)
Currency – Seychelles rupee of 100 cents
Population – 88,340 rising at 0.97 per cent a year (2010 est)
Religion – Christian 93 per cent (Roman Catholic 82 per cent, Anglican 6 per cent), Hindu 2 per cent, Muslim 1 per cent (2002)
Language – English, French, Creole (all official)
Population density – 191 per sq. km (2009)
Urban population – 54 per cent (2008 est)
Median age (years) – 32 (2010 est)
National anthem – 'Koste Seselwa' ['Seychellois Unite']
National day – 18 June (Constitution Day)
Life expectancy (years) – 73.28 (2010 est)
Mortality rate – 6.92 (2010 est)
Birth rate – 15.53 (2010 est)
Infant mortality rate – 11.97 (2010 est)
Death penalty – Abolished for all crimes (since 1993)
CPI score – 4.8 (2010)
Literacy rate – 91.8 per cent (2008 est)

CLIMATE AND TERRAIN

Seychelles consists of 115 islands spread over 643,737 sq. km of the south-west Indian Ocean, north of Madagascar. There is a relatively compact granitic group of 32 islands, with high hills and mountains, of which Mahé is the largest and most populated (about 90 per cent of the population lives on Mahé), and an outlying coralline group, for the most part only slightly above sea-level. Elevation extremes range from 905m (Morne Seychellois) to 0m (Indian Ocean). The climate is tropical, with average temperatures between 24°C and 31°C throughout the year, and a wet season from November to March.

HISTORY AND POLITICS

The uninhabited islands were proclaimed French territory in 1756, but settlement of the Mahé group began only in 1770. The group was a dependency of Mauritius, and was ceded to Britain with Mauritius in 1814. In 1903 these islands, together with the coralline group, were formed into a colony separate from Mauritius. On 29 June 1976, the islands became an independent republic.

Following a coup d'état in 1977, when France-Albert René became president, Seychelles became a one-party state ruled by the Seychelles People's Progressive Front (SPPF) in 1979. Opposition parties were permitted from

1991 and in 1993 President René reintroduced a multiparty constitution. Power has remained with the SPPF under the pluralist system, although opposition parties are beginning to achieve a greater share of the vote.

President René stepped down in mid-term in 2004 and the rest of his term was served by the vice-president, James Michel, who was elected president in 2006 and re-elected in May 2011. In the 2007 legislative election, the SPPF retained its overall majority.

POLITICAL SYSTEM

Under the 1993 constitution, the executive president is directly elected for a five-year term, with a maximum of three consecutive terms. The unicameral National Assembly has up to 34 members: 23 directly elected by constituencies and up to 11 allocated by proportional representation; members serve a five-year term. The council of ministers is appointed by the president.

HEAD OF STATE
President, Defence, James Michel, *assumed office* 14 April 2004, *elected* July 2006, *re-elected* 2011
Vice-President, Finance, Danny Faure

SELECTED GOVERNMENT MEMBERS *as at July 2011*
Foreign Affairs, Jean-Paul Adam
Home Affairs, Joel Morgan

SEYCHELLES HIGH COMMISSION
4th Floor, 111 Baker Street, London W1U 6RR
T 020-7935 7770 E consulate@seychelles-gov.net
W www.seychelles-gov.net
High Commissioner, HE Patrick Pillay, *apptd* 2010

BRITISH HIGH COMMISSION
PO Box 161, Oliaji Trade Centre, Victoria, Mahé
T (+248) 283 666 E bhcvictoria@fco.gov.uk
W http://ukinseychelles.fco.gov.uk
High Commissioner, HE Matthew Forbes, OBE, *apptd* 2009

DEFENCE

The coast guard has 5 patrol and coastal combatant vessels at a base at Port Victoria.
Military budget – US$7m (2010)
Military personnel – 200: army 200; paramilitary 450

ECONOMY AND TRADE

Seychelles prospered after independence owing to the development of tuna fishing and tourism, which employs about 30 per cent of the workforce. The economy struggled in 2008–9 owing to external debt, high deficits, food and oil price rises and a reduction in foreign exchange earnings after tourism declined in the global economic downturn, but recovered in 2010.

Agriculture, small-scale manufacturing and offshore financial services are being developed to diversify the economy. Apart from fishing and tourism, the main industries involve processing fish, coconuts and vanilla, producing coir rope, furniture and beverages, boat-building and printing.

The main trading partners are EU countries, Saudi Arabia and South Africa. The principal exports are canned tuna, frozen fish, cinnamon bark, copra and re-exports of petroleum products. The principal imports are machinery and equipment, foodstuffs, petroleum products and chemicals.

GNI – US$655m; US$8,480 per capita (2009)
Annual average growth of GDP – 3.5 per cent (2010 est)
Inflation rate – –2.2 per cent (2010 est)
Unemployment rate – 2 per cent (2006 est)
Total external debt – US$1,374m (2009 est)
Imports – US$900m (2009)
Exports – US$400m (2009)

BALANCE OF PAYMENTS
Trade – US$498m deficit (2010)
Current Account – US$412m deficit (2008)

Trade with UK	2009	2010
Imports from UK	£18,854,915	£21,240,368
Exports to UK	£64,511,611	£45,835,878

COMMUNICATIONS
There are around 458km of roads, most of which are surfaced. The main port is Victoria, and ferries run regularly between Mahé, Praslin and La Digue. Some 14 airports, eight with surfaced runways, serve the islands; the principal airport is at Mahé.

The telephone system serves all the islands. There were 22,100 fixed lines in use and 92,300 mobile phone subscribers in 2009, and 32,000 internet users in 2008.

MEDIA
Although the media has operated more freely since one-party rule was abolished in 1993, the only terrestrial radio and television stations and the sole daily newspaper are controlled by the government. There is no privately owned broadcasting sector because of prohibitive broadcasting licence fees, and libel laws have been used against private and pro-opposition newspapers. Cable and satellite television and international radio stations are available.

SIERRA LEONE

Republic of Sierra Leone

Area – 71,740 sq. km
Capital – Freetown; population, 875,432 (2009 est)
Major towns – Bo, Kenema
Currency – Leone (Le) of 100 cents
Population – 5,245,695 rising at 2.22 per cent a year (2010 est); 20 ethnic groups, of which the largest are the Temne (35 per cent), Mende (31 per cent), Limba (8 per cent) and Kono (5 per cent), Krio (Creole) 2 per cent (2004)
Religion – Muslim 77 per cent, Christian 21 per cent, indigenous and other beliefs 2 per cent (predominantly animist) (est)

Language – English (official), Krio (Creole; lingua franca), Mende (in the south), Temne (in the north)
Population density – 80 per sq. km (2009)
Urban population – 38 per cent (2008 est)
Median age (years) – 19 (2010 est)
National anthem – 'High We Exalt Thee, Realm of the Free'
National day – 27 April (Independence Day)
Life expectancy (years) – 55.69 (2010 est)
Mortality rate – 11.97 (2010 est)
Birth rate – 38.79 (2010 est)
Infant mortality rate – 80.16 (2010 est)
HIV/AIDS adult prevalence – 1.6 per cent (2009 est)
Death penalty – Retained
CPI score – 2.4 (2010)

CLIMATE AND TERRAIN
The land rises from mangrove swamps along the coast, to low-lying wooded country, and then to a mountainous plateau in the east. Elevation extremes range from 1,948m (Loma Mansa) to 0m (Atlantic Ocean). The climate is tropical, with a rainy season from May to November; rainfall peaks in July and August, and is particularly heavy on the coast. Average temperatures range from 22°C to 31°C throughout the year.

HISTORY AND POLITICS
Coastal trading posts were established by the Portuguese in the 15th century and the British in the 17th century. In 1787 British philanthropists and abolitionists established a settlement for repatriated former slaves from Britain and its colonies on the Freetown peninsula. In 1808 the settlement was declared a crown colony and became the main base in west Africa for enforcing the 1807 Act outlawing the slave trade. In 1896 a protectorate was declared over the hinterland. The Freetown colony and the protectorate were united in 1951, and in 1961 Sierra Leone became independent.

The country became a republic in 1971 and a one-party state in 1978. Transition to a multiparty democracy began in 1991 but was aborted by a military coup in 1992. Civilian rule was restored with the 1996 elections. Another coup in May 1997 was short-lived, and the government was reinstated in March 1998 with the assistance of ECOWAS troops.

The transition to multiparty and civilian rule was complicated by the civil war with the Revolutionary United Front (RUF), which began in 1991. Fighting continued until 2001, when a lasting ceasefire was agreed, and the war was declared over in 2002. An estimated 50,000 people were killed, 30,000 mutilated and a third of the population displaced between 1991 and 2002. A truth and reconciliation commission and a UN-supported war crimes tribunal were set up in 2002.

The 2007 presidential election was won by Ernest Bai Koroma, the All People's Congress (APC) candidate, in the second round. The APC won a majority of seats in the simultaneous legislative election, defeating the Sierra Leone People's Party, which had been in power since 2002.

POLITICAL SYSTEM
Under the 1991 constitution, the executive president is directly elected for a five-year term, renewable once. The unicameral parliament has 124 members: 112 directly elected for a five-year term and 12 indirectly elected to represent the 12 provincial districts. The president, who

is responsible to the legislature, appoints and chairs the cabinet.

HEAD OF STATE
President, Ernest Bai Koroma, *elected* 18 September 2007
Vice-President, Samuel Sam-Sumana

SELECTED GOVERNMENT MEMBERS *as at July 2011*
Finance, Samura Kamara
Foreign Affairs, Joseph B. Dauda
Internal Affairs, Musa Tarawali
Defence, Maj. (retd) Paolo Conteh

SIERRA LEONE HIGH COMMISSION
41 Eagle Street, London WC1R 4TL
T 020-7404 0140 E info@slhc-uk.org.uk
W www.slhc-uk.org.uk
High Commissioner, HE Edward Turay, *apptd* 2010

BRITISH HIGH COMMISSION
6 Spur Road, Freetown
T (+232) (22) 232 961
E freetown.general.enquiries@fco.gov.uk
W http://ukinsierraleone.fco.gov.uk
High Commissioner, HE Ian Hughes, *apptd* 2009

BRITISH COUNCIL
PO Box 124, Tower Hill, Freetown
T (+232) (22) 222 223 W www.britishcouncil.org/africa
Director, Louisa Waddingham

DEFENCE
The process of disarming the country's various factions after the civil war was completed in 2004. The army took over full responsibility for internal security in December 2005 when the UN peacekeeping forces left. The navy has 1 patrol and coastal combatant vessel at a base in Freetown.
Military budget – US$13m (2010)
Military personnel – 10,500: Joint Staff 10,500

ECONOMY AND TRADE
The country was devastated by a decade of civil war, and unemployment increased with the demobilisation of former combatants. Economic activity has grown since the end of the war but the country remains extremely poor, dependent on foreign aid and expatriates' remittances. It benefited from having around 90 per cent of its foreign debt written off in 2006.

There are significant mineral deposits and agricultural and fishery resources, although the lack of infrastructure hampers development. Diamonds account for about half of export earnings, but nearly 50 per cent of GDP is generated by agriculture, much of which is at subsistence level. Industry consists mainly of mining (diamonds, rutile, bauxite), processing agricultural products, light manufacturing for the domestic market, oil refining and ship repair.

The main export market is Belgium (27 per cent) and the USA; the chief import suppliers are South Africa, China, the USA and Côte d'Ivoire. Principal exports are diamonds, rutile, cocoa, coffee and fish. The main imports are foodstuffs, machinery and equipment, fuels and lubricants, and chemicals.
GNI – US$1,901m; US$340 per capita (2009)
Annual average growth of GDP – 5.2 per cent (2010 est)
Inflation rate – 11.7 per cent (2007 est)
Population below poverty line – 70.2 per cent (2004)

Total external debt – US$1,610m (2003 est)
Imports – US$500m (2009)
Exports – US$200m (2009)

BALANCE OF PAYMENTS
Trade – US$285m deficit (2010)
Current Account – US$228m deficit (2008)

Trade with UK	2009	2010
Imports from UK	£20,731,223	£39,584,948
Exports to UK	£11,216,500	£8,722,137

COMMUNICATIONS
The railway system was phased out in 1974, but an extensive 11,300km road network has been developed since, although only 904km are surfaced. A bridge over the Mano river links Sierra Leone with Liberia. There is an international airport at Freetown and eight airfields around the country. Freetown, which has one of the world's largest natural harbours, is the main port and there are smaller ports at Pepel, Bonthe and Niti.

The fixed-line telephone system is poor and mobile phone distribution is growing rapidly. There were about 32,800 fixed lines in use, 1.2 million mobile phone subscriptions and 14,900 internet users in 2009.

EDUCATION AND HEALTH
School attendance has improved considerably since the civil war ended. The public University of Sierra Leone incorporates several campuses in Freetown, and Njala University was constituted in Bo in 2005; there are a number of other technical and teacher-training institutes throughout the country.
Literacy rate – 39.2 per cent (2008 est)
Gross enrolment ratio (percentage of relevant age group) –
primary 158 per cent; secondary 35 per cent (2007 est)
Health expenditure (per capita) – US$44 (2009 est)
Hospital beds (per 1,000 people) – 0.4 (2004–9)

MEDIA
Media freedom is limited by the government's use of libel laws to restrict coverage of politically sensitive issues. Broadcasters also have to contend with unreliable electricity supplies and a lack of advertising revenue. The national broadcaster operates televison and radio networks, alongside one privately owned television station and dozens of radio stations, including a UN network. Dozens of privately run newspapers are published in Freetown, despite low literacy levels.

SINGAPORE

*Xinjiapo   Gongheguo / Republik   Singapura / Cinkappur
Kutiyaracu – Republic of Singapore*

Area – 697 sq. km
Capital – Singapore
Currency – Singapore dollar (S$) of 100 cents
Population – 4,701,069 rising at 0.86 per cent a year
  (2010 est); Chinese (76.8 per cent), Malay (13.9 per
  cent), Indian (7.9 per cent) (2000)
Religion – Buddhist 42 per cent, Muslim 15 per cent
  (predominantly Sunni), Christian 15 per cent, Taoist 8
  per cent, Hindu 4 per cent (est)
Language – Mandarin, English, Malay, Tamil (all official),
  Hokkien, Cantonese, Teochew
Population density – 7,125 per sq. km (2009)
Urban population – 100 per cent (2008 est)
Median age (years) – 39.6 (2010 est)
National anthem – 'Majulah Singapura' ['Onward,
  Singapore']
National day – 9 August (Independence, 1965)
Life expectancy (years) – 82.06 (2010 est)
Mortality rate – 4.8 (2010 est)
Birth rate – 8.65 (2010 est)
Infant mortality rate – 2.32 (2010 est)
Death penalty – Retained
CPI score – 9.3 (2010)
Literacy rate – 94.7 per cent (2008 est)
Gross enrolment ratio (percentage of relevant age group) –
  primary 78 per cent; secondary 63 per cent (2006 est)
Health expenditure (per capita) – US$1,501 (2009)
Hospital beds (per 1,000 people) – 3.1 (2004–9)

CLIMATE AND TERRAIN

Singapore consists of the island of Singapore and 63 islets
situated off the southern extremity of the Malay
peninsula, from which it is separated by the Straits of
Johor. The land rises from the shore to a low, undulating
central plateau. Elevation extremes range from 166m
(Bukit Timah) to 0m (Singapore Strait). The state is just
north of the Equator and the climate is tropical, subject to
monsoons in June to September and December to March.
The average temperature is 27°C, and there is frequent
rain and high humidity.

HISTORY AND POLITICS

Singapore, a trading site since the 13th century, was
established as a British trading post by Sir Stamford
Raffles in 1819 and was ceded to Britain in perpetuity in
1824. In 1826 it was incorporated with Penang and
Malacca to form the Straits Settlements and they became a
crown colony in 1867. Singapore became the commercial
and financial hub of south-east Asia in the 19th century,
and the principal British military base in the Far East in
the 1920s. In 1942, during the Second World War, it fell
to Japanese forces. Liberated in 1945, it became a separate
colony in 1946, and internal self-government was
introduced in 1959. It became part of the Federation of
Malaysia in 1963, before withdrawing to become an
independent sovereign state in 1965.

Although Singapore is a multiparty state, the People's
Action Party (PAP) has dominated politics since 1959;
opposition candidates were elected to parliament for the
first time in 1981. The PAP leader Lee Kuan Yew was
prime minister from 1959 until he retired in 1990; he
remained a cabinet minister until 2011.

Sellapan Rama Nathan was elected president in 1999
and was declared re-elected in 2005, although no election
was held on either occasion as he was the sole eligible
candidate. In the 2011 general election, the PAP retained
its large majority with 81 seats, but opposition parties
won an unprecedented six seats. Lee Hsien Loong, the son

of Lee Kuan Yew, continued in office as prime minister, a
post he has held since 2004. A presidential election was
due in August 2011.

POLITICAL SYSTEM

The 1959 constitution was amended in 1965 to end the
affiliation with Malaysia and make Singapore a republic,
and in 1991 to make the presidency directly elected. The
president is directly elected for a six-year term, which is
renewable. The president appoints the prime minister and,
on his advice, the members of the cabinet. There is a
unicameral parliament with 87 directly elected members
and up to nine extra members from opposition parties
(NCMPs) (currently three), depending on their share of
the vote; all members serve a five-year term. Up to nine
members can also be nominated by the government for a
two-year term (NMPs) to bring the opposition numbers
up to 18.

HEAD OF STATE

President, Sellapan Rama Nathan, *took office* 1 September
  1999, *re-elected* 2005

SELECTED GOVERNMENT MEMBERS *as at July 2011*

Prime Minister, Lee Hsien Loong
Deputy Prime Minister, Rear-Adm. Teo Chee Hean *(Home
  Affairs)*
Foreign Affairs, K. Shanmugam
Finance, Tharman Shanmugaratnam

HIGH COMMISSION FOR THE REPUBLIC OF SINGAPORE

9 Wilton Crescent, London SW1X 8SP
T 020-7235 8315 E singhc_lon@sgmfa.gov.sg
W www.mfa.gov.sg/london
High Commissioner, HE Michael Eng Cheng Teo,
  apptd 2002

BRITISH HIGH COMMISSION

100 Tanglin Road, Singapore 247919
T (+65) 6424 4200 E commercial.singapore@fco.gov.uk
W http://ukinsingapore.fco.gov.uk
High Commissioner, HE Antony Phillipson, *apptd* 2011

BRITISH COUNCIL

30 Napier Road, Singapore 258509
T (+65) 6473 1111 W www.britishcouncil.org/sg
Director, Mark Howard

DEFENCE

The army has 196 main battle tanks, over 1,280 armoured
personnel carriers and 272 armoured infantry fighting
vehicles. The navy has 5 submarines, 6 frigates and 35
patrol and coastal combatant vessels at 2 bases. The air
force has 148 combat aircraft and 11 armed helicopters.
Military budget – US$8,340m (2010)
Military personnel – 72,500; army 50,000, navy 9,000,
  air force 13,500; paramilitary 75,100
Conscription duration – 24 months

ECONOMY AND TRADE

Historically based on trade in raw materials from
surrounding countries and on entrepot trade in finished
products, the economy industrialised rapidly after
independence and diversified, becoming a regional
financial and technology centre and a tourist destination.
Economic growth has rarely flagged since 1965; although

the global economic downturn pushed the economy into recession in 2008, it recovered strongly in 2010.

Agriculture is limited and contributes little to GDP. Industries include manufacturing (especially consumer electronics, information technology products, biomedical sciences, pharmaceuticals and chemicals), engineering, oil refining, rubber processing, food processing and ship repair; industry contributes 27.2 per cent of GDP. The service sector (financial and business services, entrepot trade, tourism) accounts for 72.8 per cent of GDP and employs 70 per cent of the workforce.

The main trading partners are the USA, Malaysia, China, Indonesia, Japan and Hong Kong. Principal exports are machinery and equipment (especially electronic), consumer goods, pharmaceuticals and other chemicals and mineral fuels. The main imports are machinery and equipment, mineral fuels, chemicals, food and consumer goods.

GNI – US$179,170m; US$37,220 per capita (2009)
Annual average growth of GDP – 14.6 per cent (2010 est)
Inflation rate – 2.6 per cent (2010 est)
Unemployment – 2.3 per cent (2010 est)
Total external debt – US$21,660m (2010 est)
Imports – US$245,800m (2009)
Exports – US$269,800m (2009)

BALANCE OF PAYMENTS
Trade – US$41,155m surplus (2010)
Current Account – US$33,838m surplus (2008)

Trade with UK	2009	2010
Imports from UK	£2,846,943,615	£3,313,867,465
Exports to UK	£2,422,103,565	£2,876,405,069

COMMUNICATIONS
There are 3,356km of roads, all surfaced, and 30km of railway and an extensive light rail system on the island. The road system is connected to the Malaysian network via a 1.1km causeway and a road bridge across the Straits of Johor; the causeway also carries a rail link to Malaysia. Singapore is one of the largest and busiest seaports in the world, although there is a high risk of piracy in the South China Sea. It has a large merchant fleet of 1,422 ships of over 1,000 tonnes, with 327 registered in other countries, while 850 foreign-owned ships are registered in Singapore. There is one international airport, at Changi; Singapore Airlines is the national carrier.

The modern telecommunications systems provided services to 1.8 million fixed-line users, 6.6 million mobile phone subscribers and 3.2 million internet users in 2009.

MEDIA
Singapore's media is tightly regulated by the government. Private satellite dishes are illegal and internet access is controlled, although the government sees the country as a digital media pioneer and plans to create thousands of new jobs in this sector. Broadcasting is dominated by MediaCorp, owned by a state investment agency. Singapore Press Holdings, which has close links to the ruling party, has a virtual monopoly on the newspaper industry, and publishes 17 newspapers.

SLOVAKIA

Slovenska Republika – Slovak Republic

Area – 49,035 sq. km
Capital – Bratislava; population, 428,003 (2009 est)
Major city – Kosice
Currency – Euro (€) of 100 cents
Population – 5,470,306 rising at 0.13 per cent a year
  (2010 est); Slovak (85.8 per cent), Hungarian (9.7 per
  cent), Roma (1.7 per cent), Ruthenian/Ukrainian (1 per
  cent) (2001)
Religion – Christian (Roman Catholic 69 per cent,
  Lutheran 7 per cent, other 8 per cent) (2001)
Language – Slovak (official), Hungarian, Romani,
  Ukrainian
Population density – 113 per sq. km (2009)
Urban population – 56 per cent (2008 est)
Median age (years) – 37.3 (2010 est)
National anthem – 'Nad Tatrou sa blyska' ['Lightning Over
  the Tatras']
National day – 1 September (Constitution Day)
Life expectancy (years) – 75.62 (2010 est)
Mortality rate – 9.56 (2010 est)
Birth rate – 10.55 (2010 est)
Infant mortality rate – 6.71 (2010 est)
Death penalty – Abolished for all crimes (since 1990)
CPI score – 4.3 (2010)
Gross enrolment ratio (percentage of relevant age group) –
  primary 103 per cent; secondary 92 per cent; tertiary
  54 per cent (2008 est)
Health expenditure (per capita) – US$1,373 (2009)
Hospital beds (per 1,000 people) – 6.6 (2004–9)

CLIMATE AND TERRAIN
Slovakia is landlocked and mountainous, lying in the western Carpathian range which includes the Tatra and Beskid mountains to the north. The mountains fall to plains in the south-east and south-west; the latter is the plain of the river Danube and its tributary the Vah, which rises in the Tatras. Elevation extremes range from 2,655m (Gerlachovsky stit) to 94m (Bodrog river). The climate is temperate, with warm humid summers and cold dry winters. Average temperatures in Kosice range from −7°C in January to 26°C in July.

HISTORY AND POLITICS
The area was part of the kingdom of Greater Moravia in the ninth century, became part of the Magyar kingdom of Hungary in the tenth century and, with Hungary, came under Austrian Habsburg rule from the 16th century. After the dissolution of the Austro-Hungarian Empire in 1918, Slovakia became part of Czechoslovakia.

Following the German annexation of Czechoslovakia in 1938–9, Slovakia became a nominally independent fascist state but was exploited as part of the German war effort. After an abortive uprising in 1944, Slovakia was liberated by Soviet forces in 1945 and returned to Czechoslovakia, where a communist regime assumed power in 1948. Following the collapse of communist rule in 1989, Slovak separatism gained ground and the Czech and Slovak republics negotiated the dissolution of the federation into two sovereign states in 1992. Dissolution took effect on 1 January 1993.

The Movement for a Democratic Slovakia (HZDS) dominated the coalition governments that held office in the 1990s, pursuing populist nationalist policies. It was ousted at the 1998 election by an alliance of liberals, centrists, left-wingers and ethnic Hungarians, which formed a coalition government that was re-elected in 2002. This government introduced the constitutional and economic reforms necessary to meet the requirements for EU membership. Slovakia joined NATO and the EU in 2004, and the eurozone in 2009.

The 2004 presidential election was won by Ivan Gasparovic; he was re-elected in 2009. After the 2006 legislative election, the centre-left Direction–Social Democracy party (Smer-SD) became the largest party in the legislature, but without a majority, and formed a three-party coalition government. Smer-SD remained the largest party after the 2010 legislative election, but four centre-right parties held a majority of seats and formed a coalition government headed by Iveta Radicova of the Slovak Democratic and Christian Union-Democratic Party.

POLITICAL SYSTEM
The 1993 constitution has been amended several times, most recently in 1999 to allow direct elections to the presidency. The president is directly elected for a five-year term, renewable once. The unicameral National Council has 150 members, who are directly elected for a four-year term by proportional representation. The prime minister, who is appointed by the president, nominates the cabinet.

HEAD OF STATE
President, Ivan Gasparovic, *elected* 17 April 2004, *sworn in* 15 June 2004, *re-elected* 2009

SELECTED GOVERNMENT MEMBERS *as at July 2011*
Prime Minister, Iveta Radicova
Deputy Prime Ministers, Ivan Miklos *(Finance);* Rudolf Chmel; Jan Figel
Defence, Lubomir Galko
Foreign Affairs, Mikulas Dzurinda
Interior, Daniel Lipsic

EMBASSY OF THE SLOVAK REPUBLIC
25 Kensington Palace Gardens, London W8 4QY
T 020-7313 6470 E emb.london@mzv.sk
W www.slovakembassy.co.uk
Ambassador Extraordinary and Plenipotentiary, Miroslav Wlachovsky, *apptd* 2011

BRITISH EMBASSY
Panska 16, Bratislava 811 01
T (+421) (2) 5998 2000 E bebra@internet.sk
W http://ukinslovakia.fco.gov.uk
Ambassador Extraordinary and Plenipotentiary, HE Michael Roberts, *apptd* 2007

BRITISH COUNCIL
PO Box 68, Panska 17, 814 99 Bratislava
T (+421) (2) 5443 1074 W www.britishcouncil.org/slovakia
Director, Andrew Spells

DEFENCE
The army has 245 main battle tanks, 132 armoured personnel carriers and 383 armoured infantry fighting vehicles. The air force has 22 combat aircraft and 16 armed helicopters.
Military budget – US$1,090m (2010)
Military personnel – 16,531: army 7,322, air force 4,190, central staff 1,462, support and training 3,557
Conscription duration – 6 months

ECONOMY AND TRADE
Slovakia has nearly completed the transition from a centrally planned to a free-market economy, following structural reforms and privatisation begun after 1998. As a result, foreign investment has risen, especially in the vehicle and electronics industries, and GDP grew steadily in 2000–8. The economy contracted in 2009 because of the global economic downturn, recovering in 2010.

Natural resources include brown coal and lignite, natural gas, oil, iron ore, copper and manganese. Major industries include production of metal and metal products, food and beverages, fuel and energy (electricity, gas, coke, oil and nuclear), chemicals and synthetic fibres, machinery, paper and printing, ceramics, transport vehicles, textiles and electrical and optical equipment. Industry accounts for 35.6 per cent of GDP, services 61.8 per cent and agriculture 2.7 per cent.

The main trading partners are other EU countries (especially Germany and the Czech Republic) and Russia. Principal exports are machinery and electrical equipment (36 per cent), vehicles (21 per cent), base metals, chemicals, minerals and plastics. The main imports are machinery and transport equipment, mineral products, vehicles, base metals, chemicals and plastics.
GNI – US$84,690m; US$16,130 per capita (2009)
Annual average growth of GDP – 4 per cent (2010 est)
Inflation rate – 1.2 per cent (2010 est)
Unemployment – 12.5 per cent (2010 est)
Total external debt – US$59,330m (2010 est)
Imports – US$54,500m (2009)
Exports – US$55,200m (2009)

BALANCE OF PAYMENTS
Trade – US$200m surplus (2010)
Current Account – US$6,220m deficit (2008)

Trade with UK	2009	2010
Imports from UK	£365,615,310	£451,164,856
Exports to UK	£1,537,626,411	£1,610,662,647

COMMUNICATIONS
Slovakia has a total of 43,761km of roads, including 384km of motorways. There are 3,622km of railways, and 172km of navigable waterways on the river Danube. The main Danube ports are Bratislava and Komarno, and the principal airport is at Bratislava.

The modern telecommunications system has expanded rapidly in recent years, especially for mobile phones. In 2009 there were 1 million fixed telephone lines in use, 5.5 million mobile phone subscribers and 4 million internet users.

MEDIA
The public broadcasters, Slovak TV and Slovak Radio, operate national networks in competition with private companies; Slovak TV has lost much of its audience share to privately owned TV Markiza since 1990, and there are now over 20 private radio stations. Cable and satellite television channels are also popular. The major daily newspapers are all privately owned. The press operates freely, although there is concern about the use of defamation laws against journalists.

SLOVENIA

Republika Slovenija – Republic of Slovenia

Area – 20,273 sq. km
Capital – Ljubljana; population, 260,092 (2009 est)
Major city – Maribor
Currency – Euro (€) of 100 cents
Population – 2,003,136 falling at 0.14 per cent a year
   (2010 est); Slovene (83.1 per cent), Serb (2 per cent),
   Croat (1.8 per cent), Bosniak (1.1 per cent) (2002)
Religion – Christian (Roman Catholic 58 per cent,
   Orthodox 2 per cent), Muslim 2 per cent (2002)
Language – Slovene (official), Serbo-Croat; Hungarian and
   Italian are also official in designated municipalities
Population density – 101 per sq. km (2009)
Urban population – 48 per cent (2008 est)
Median age (years) – 42.1 (2010 est)
National anthem – 'Zdravljica' ['A Toast']
National day – 25 June (Statehood Day)
Life expectancy (years) – 77.12 (2010 est)
Mortality rate – 10.74 (2010 est)
Birth rate – 8.92 (2010 est)
Infant mortality rate – 4.21 (2010 est)
Death penalty – Abolished for all crimes (since 1989)
CPI score – 6.4 (2010)

CLIMATE AND TERRAIN
The Alps cover 42 per cent of the country, towards the north, and the south lies on the high Karst plateau. The only low-lying areas are the Pannonian plain in the east and north-east, and the short (47km) narrow coastal belt on the Adriatic Sea. Elevation extremes range from 2,864m (Triglav) to 0m (Adriatic Sea). The climate is continental in most of the country but Mediterranean on the coast. Average temperatures in Ljubljana range from −7°C in January to 27°C in July.

HISTORY AND POLITICS
Settled by Slovenes in the sixth century, the area was later ruled by Slavs, Franks and Hungarians before coming under the control of the Austrian Habsburg dynasty in the

14th century. Following the collapse of the Austro-Hungarian Empire in 1918, Slovenia became part of the Kingdom of the Serbs, Croats and Slovenes (later Yugoslavia). German forces invaded Yugoslavia in 1941 and Slovenia was divided between Germany, Italy and Hungary. In 1945 it was reformed as a constituent part of the communist federal republic of Yugoslavia. After a dispute with Italy and nine years of international administration, the Adriatic coast and hinterland were returned to Slovenia in 1954, while Italy retained Trieste.

The first multiparty elections, held in April 1990, were won by the pro-independence 'Demos' coalition. In a referendum in December 1990, 88 per cent of the electorate voted for independence, which was declared on 25 June 1991. A ten-day war with the Yugoslav National Army followed before the army withdrew under the terms of an EU-brokered ceasefire. Slovenia became a member of NATO and the EU in 2004, and joined the eurozone in 2007.

The Liberal Democracy of Slovenia party (LDS) was the major party in every government from 1991 to 2004. The 2007 presidential election was won by an independent candidate, Danilo Turk. Following the 2008 legislative election, the Social Democrats (SD) formed a coalition government with three other parties (including the LDS) and several independents.

POLITICAL SYSTEM
Under the 1991 constitution, the president is directly elected for a five-year term. The unicameral National Assembly has 90 members directly elected for a four-year term. The National Council, which has 40 members indirectly elected for a five-year term, has an advisory role. The prime minister, who is nominated by the president and elected by the legislature, appoints the cabinet.

HEAD OF STATE
President, Danilo Turk, *elected* 11 November 2007;
  sworn in 22 December 2007

SELECTED GOVERNMENT MEMBERS *as at July 2011*
Prime Minister, Borut Pahor
Defence, Ljubica Jelusic
Finance, Franc Krizanic
Foreign Affairs, Samuel Zbogar
Internal Affairs, Katarina Kresal

EMBASSY OF THE REPUBLIC OF SLOVENIA
10 Little College Street, London SW1P 3SH
T 020-7222 5700 E vlo@gov.si W http://london.embassy.si
Ambassador Extraordinary and Plenipotentiary,
  HE Iztok Jarc, *apptd* 2009

BRITISH EMBASSY
4th Floor, Trg Republike 3, 1000 Ljubljana
T (+386) (1) 200 3910 E info@british-embassy.si
W http://ukinslovenia.fco.gov.uk
Ambassador Extraordinary and Plenipotentiary,
  HE Andrew Page, *apptd* 2009

BRITISH COUNCIL
Tivoli Center, Tivolska 30, 1000 Ljubljana
T (+386) (1) 300 2030 W www.britishcouncil.org/slovenia
Director, James Hampson

DEFENCE
The army has 45 main battle tanks and 112 armoured personnel carriers. The army's Maritime Element has 1 patrol and coastal combatant vessel.

Military budget – US$672m (2010)
Military personnel – army 7,600; paramilitary 4,500

ECONOMY AND TRADE
Always the most prosperous republic of the former Yugoslavia, Slovenia's transition to a market economy was smoothed by good infrastructure and a well-educated workforce, and it has successfully re-orientated its exports towards Western markets. Much of the economy remains in state ownership and taxes are high, deterring foreign investment and inhibiting its international competitiveness. The economy contracted sharply in 2009 owing to the global downturn; it started to recover in 2010, although unemployment rose to 10 per cent.

Agriculture contributes 2.4 per cent of GDP, industry 31 per cent and the service sector 66.6 per cent. The main agricultural products are potatoes, hops, wheat, sugar beet, maize, grapes and livestock. Industries include mining and mineral processing (iron ore, aluminium, lead, zinc), electronics (including for military purposes), vehicles, electric power equipment, wood products, textiles, chemicals and machine tools.

The main trading partners are other EU countries (particularly Germany and Italy) and Croatia. Principal exports are manufactured goods, machinery and transport equipment, chemicals and food. These items, along with fuels and lubricants, are also the main imports.

GNI – US$47,286m; US$23,520 per capita (2009)
Annual average growth of GDP – 1 per cent (2010 est)
Inflation rate – 2.1 per cent (2010 est)
Population below the poverty line – 12.3 per cent (2008 est)
Unemployment – 10.6 per cent (2010 est)
Total external debt – US$51,570m (2010 est)
Imports – US$23,800m (2009)
Exports – US$22,300m (2009)

BALANCE OF PAYMENTS
Trade – US$1,867m deficit (2010)
Current Account – US$3,365m deficit (2008)

Trade with UK	2009	2010
Imports from UK	£171,575,270	£211,990,082
Exports to UK	£246,102,212	£354,381,123

COMMUNICATIONS
There are 38,925km of roads and 1,228km of railways, of which 503km are electrified. Major international road and rail routes cross the country. There are 16 airports and airfields, with international airports at Ljubljana, Maribor and Portoroz. Koper is the main port, receiving shipments from landlocked central European countries.

In 2009 there were 1 million fixed telephone lines in use, 2.1 million mobile phone subscribers and 1.3 million internet users.

EDUCATION AND HEALTH
Education is free and compulsory between the ages of six and 15.

Literacy rate – 99.7 per cent (2008 est)
Gross enrolment ratio (percentage of relevant age group) – primary 97 per cent; secondary 97 per cent; tertiary 87 per cent (2008 est)
Health expenditure (per capita) – US$2,175 (2009)
Hospital beds (per 1,000 people) – 4.7 (2004–9)

MEDIA
Slovenia saw a rapid development of its media market after the fall of communism. The main newspapers are privately owned, and the broadcasting sector is a mix of public and private ownership. The television market is mainly shared between the public service, RTV Slovenia, and the private stations Pop TV and Kanal A. About two-thirds of households are connected to cable or satellite.

SOLOMON ISLANDS

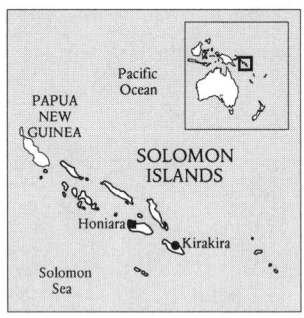

Area – 28,896 sq. km
Capital – Honiara, on Guadalcanal; population, 71,921 (2009 est)
Currency – Solomon Islands dollar (SI$) of 100 cents
Population – 559,198 rising at 2.27 per cent a year (2010 est); Melanesian (94.5 per cent), Polynesian (3 per cent), Micronesian (1.2 per cent) (est)
Religion – Christian (Anglican 33 per cent, Roman Catholic 19 per cent, Pentecostal 17 per cent, Seventh-day Adventist 11 per cent, Methodist 10 per cent, Christian Fellowship Church 2 per cent), animist 5 per cent (est)
Language – English (official), Melanesian Pidgin (lingua franca); around 120 indigenous languages exist
Population density – 19 per sq. km (2009)
Urban population – 18 per cent (2008 est)
Median age (years) – 20.6 (2010 est)
National anthem – 'God Save Our Solomon Islands'
National day – 7 July (Independence Day)
Life expectancy (years) – 73.94 (2010 est)
Mortality rate – 3.96 (2010 est)
Birth rate – 28.6 (2010 est)
Infant mortality rate – 18.41 (2010 est)
Death penalty – Abolished for all crimes (since 1966)
CPI score – 2.8 (2010)
Literacy rate – 76.6 per cent (2008 est)

CLIMATE AND TERRAIN
Forming a scattered archipelago of mountainous islands and low-lying coral atolls in the south-west Pacific Ocean, the Solomon Islands stretch about 1,448km in a south-easterly direction from the Shortland Islands to the Santa Cruz islands. The six biggest islands are Choiseul, New Georgia, Santa Isabel, Guadalcanal, Malaita and Makira (San Cristobal). They are characterised by thickly forested mountain ranges intersected by deep, narrow valleys. Elevation extremes range from 2,310m (Mt Popomanaseu) to 0m (Pacific Ocean). The climate is tropical, with little variation in temperature, and a wet season between November and April. The islands are prone to seismic activity and tsunamis.

HISTORY AND POLITICS

The islands were discovered by the Spanish in 1568 and visited by Europeans intermittently for about 300 years. Following the arrival of missionaries and traders, Britain declared a protectorate in 1893 over the southern islands; the northern islands were ceded to Britain by Germany in 1899. Some of the islands were occupied by the Japanese in 1942, and recaptured by Allied forces in 1943–5 after fierce fighting, especially on Guadalcanal. After the Second World War, campaigns began for self-government, which was achieved in 1976; independence followed in 1978.

Ethnic tension on Guadalcanal between the indigenous Isatabus and migrants from the island of Malaita escalated from 1998 into conflict between militant factions. Despite a fragile peace following a ceasefire agreement signed in October 2000, and elections in 2001, lawlessness and corruption pervaded the country. This was exacerbated by worsening economic and social problems as the government struggled to maintain law and order and provide essential services. In June 2003 the government requested assistance from neighbouring countries and an Australian-led regional assistance mission was deployed. It restored public order and disarmed the militias by late 2003, and has since worked to restore stable government and revive the economy.

In the August 2010 legislative election, independents won over the half the seats, but the largest party was the Solomon Islands Democratic Party (SIDP), with 14 seats. The SIDP leader, Danny Philip, was elected prime minister and appointed a government which included a number of members of the previous administration.

POLITICAL SYSTEM

Under the 1978 constitution, the Solomon Islands is a constitutional monarchy. The head of state is Queen Elizabeth II, represented by a governor-general, who is chosen by the legislature. The unicameral National Parliament has 50 members who are directly elected for a four-year term. The prime minister is elected by the legislature from among its members, and nominates the cabinet, which is formally appointed by the governor-general.

Governor-General, Frank Kabui, *apptd* 2009

SELECTED GOVERNMENT MEMBERS *as at July 2011*
Prime Minister, Danny Philip
Deputy Prime Minister, Home Affairs, Manasseh Maelanga
Finance, Gordon Darcy Lilo
Foreign Affairs, Peter Shanel Agovaka

HIGH COMMISSION FOR THE SOLOMON ISLANDS
17 Avenue Edouard Lacombe, 1040 Brussels, Belgium
T (+32) (2) 732 7085 E siembassy@compuserve.com
High Commissioner, HE Joseph Ma'ahanua, *apptd* 2006

BRITISH HIGH COMMISSION
PO Box 676, Telekom House, Mendana Avenue, Honiara
T (+677) 21705 E bhc@solomon.com.sb
W http://ukinsolomonislands.fco.gov.uk
High Commissioner, HE Timothy Smart, *apptd* 2008

ECONOMY AND TRADE

The civil unrest of 1998–2003 left the country virtually bankrupt but the restoration of law and order enabled the economy to recover until its modest but steady growth was curtailed by the global downturn and natural disasters in 2009 and 2010. The country's greater dependency since 2003 on foreign aid, principally from Australia, increased as the downturn reduced government revenues.

Agriculture, much at subsistence level, is the largest economic sector, accounting for over 40 per cent of GDP and engaging 75 per cent of the population. Abundant mineral resources are largely undeveloped, although there are plans to reopen a major gold mine. The main industries are fishing, mining, forestry and processing agricultural products; industry contributes 11 per cent of GDP.

The main export market is China (57 per cent); most imports come from Singapore and Australia. Principal exports are timber, fish, copra, palm oil and cocoa. The main imports are food, machinery and equipment, manufactured goods, fuels and chemicals.

GNI – US$480m; US$910 per capita (2009)
Annual average growth of GDP – 2.8 per cent (2010 est)
Inflation rate – 6.3 per cent (2007 est)
Total external debt – US$166m (2004 est)
Imports – US$200m (2009)
Exports – US$200m (2009)

BALANCE OF PAYMENTS
Trade – US$76m deficit (2010)
Current Account – US$106m deficit (2008)

Trade with UK	2009	2010
Imports from UK	£3,329,959	£327,633
Exports to UK	£561,185	£1,316,662

COMMUNICATIONS

There are 1,360km of roads, of which only 33km are surfaced. The main ports are Honiara and Yandina. There are 36 airports and airfields, the main one being at Honiara. Solomon Airlines operates international services to other Pacific states and Australia. Air Niugini flies from Papua New Guinea to Honiara.

Telephone services are limited; in 2009 there were 8,200 fixed telephone lines in use, 30,000 mobile phone subscribers and 10,000 internet users.

MEDIA

The Solomon Islands Broadcasting Corporation (SIBC) operates public radio services, and there are two commercial stations. One Television provides television programmes, and external satellite services can be received. Low literacy levels mean that SIBC has greater influence than the press, which consists of one daily, two weekly and two monthly newspapers. Australia and Taiwan have donated funds and equipment to develop the domestic media, and press freedom and security have improved since 2003.

SOMALIA

Jamhuuriyada Demuqraadiga Soomaaliyeed – Somalia

Area – 637,657 sq. km
Capital – Mogadishu; population, 1,352,800 (2009 est)
Major cities – Baidoa, Berbera, Burao, Hargeisa, Kismayu
Currency – Somali shilling of 100 cents; other currencies are also in circulation
Population – 10,112,453 rising at 2.81 per cent a year (2010 est)
Religion – Muslim (predominantly Sunni, including Sunni forms of Sufism); small Christian minority
Language – Somali (official), Arabic, Italian, English
Population density – 15 per sq. km (2009)
Urban population – 37 per cent (2008 est)
Median age (years) – 17.6 (2010 est)
National anthem – 'Somaliyaay toosoo' ['Somalia, Wake Up']
National day – 1 July (Foundation Day)
Life expectancy (years) – 50 (2010 est)
Mortality rate – 15.24 (2010 est)
Birth rate – 43.33 (2010 est)
Infant mortality rate – 107.42 (2010 est)
Death penalty – Retained
CPI score – 1.1 (2010)
Gross enrolment ratio (percentage of relevant age group) – primary 33 per cent; secondary 8 per cent (2007 est)

CLIMATE AND TERRAIN

The country is mostly an arid and flat or undulating plateau, rising to hills in the north. Elevation extremes range from 2,416m (Shimbiris) to 0m (Indian Ocean). The climate is tropical, influenced by the north-east and south-west monsoons. Rainfall is greater in the south than the north, but is low and irregular throughout the country, leading to frequent droughts. Average temperatures in Mogadishu are between 23°C and 32°C throughout the year.

HISTORY AND POLITICS

From the eighth century onwards Arab settlers introduced Islam and established coastal trading towns that developed into sultanates. European contact began in the early 16th century, with Italian, French and British interest intensifying after the Suez Canal opened in 1869. Protectorates were established in the north by the British (1887) and in the centre and the south by the Italians (1889–1905). Italian Somalia was returned to Italian administration as a UN Trust Territory in 1950. The two protectorates became independent and merged to form the United Republic of Somalia in July 1960.

In 1969 the armed forces seized power in a coup led by Maj.-Gen. Muhammad Siad Barre, and established a

socialist Islamic regime which became a one-party state in 1979. Insurrection in the north began in 1978, and by 1988 opposition to the government had developed into a civil war, the rebels toppling the Said Barre regime in 1991. Attempts to establish a new central government failed as political and clan rivalries split the former rebels. The situation degenerated into civil war between rival 'warlords' and the state effectively disintegrated; in the 2000s, the fighting has also involved militant Islamic groups, some with links to al-Qaida. Local administrations headed by traditional, religious or business leaders have developed in most areas.

Attempts to re-establish a central government were unsuccessful until 2004, when two years of peace talks concluded with the establishment of a transitional federal legislature and president in 2004 and a transitional federal government in 2005. The federal government's attempts to assert its authority, supported between 2007 and January 2009 by Ethiopian armed forces, led to an upsurge in violence as its forces were resisted by Islamist militias loyal to the Union of Islamic Courts and opponents of Ethiopian 'occupation'.

Most of the Alliance for the Re-liberation of Somalia (ARS), formed in 2007 to resist the Ethiopian presence in Somalia, agreed a ceasefire with the government in 2008 in return for Ethiopian withdrawal, and subsequently joined the legislature and government. More hard-line Islamist insurgents, in particular the al-Shabaab militia, continue to oppose the government and have regained control of much of the south of the country. Although the transitional government has been located in Mogadishu since early 2009, its control of the capital is partial, tenuous and constantly challenged. Piracy in the Gulf of Aden and the Indian Ocean became a major problem in early 2008; hijackings off the coast of Somalia accounted for 92 percent of all ship seizures in 2010.

Abdullahi Yusuf Ahmed, elected president in 2004, resigned in December 2008, and the legislature elected the ARS leader Sheikh Sharif Ahmed as president.

SECESSION

The northern-based Somali National Movement (SNM) took control of the north-west (the former British Somaliland protectorate) after Siad Barre's deposition, and in May 1991 declared unilateral independence as the 'Republic of Somaliland'. It has its own political system, government institutions and currency, supported by revenue from expatriates' remittances, customs duties from the port at Berbera and livestock exports. The leaders of the regime have refused to take part in the peace process since 1999 and have not signed the 2004 peace agreement; they are seeking international recognition of Somaliland's independence.

The north-east of the country proclaimed its autonomy as the region of Puntland in 1998. Puntland seeks participation in a federal Somalia rather than independence. Its leaders have taken part in the peace process, signing the 2004 peace agreement; its former leader, Col. Abdullahi Yusuf Ahmed, was federal president from 2004 to 2008. Since 2005 the area has been the hub of piracy in the region, especially the Gulf of Aden.

There has been sporadic fighting between Somaliland and Puntland over Somaliland's Sool and Sanaag regions, which Puntland claims on ethnic grounds.

POLITICAL SYSTEM

Somalia has been without an effective central government since 1991. The 2004 peace agreement established transitional federal institutions (TFIs) in 2005 with a five-year mandate to draw up a constitution and hold elections; their mandate was extended for two years in 2009 and for three years in 2011. The TFIs include the Transitional Federal Assembly, which originally had 275 seats but was expanded to 450 seats in 2009 to include 200 ARS members and a further 75 representatives of civil society. The assembly elects the president and approves the appointment of ministers to the transitional federal government.

HEAD OF STATE
President, Sheikh Sharif Ahmed, *sworn in* 31 January 2009

SELECTED GOVERNMENT MEMBERS *as at July 2011*
Prime Minister, Abdiweli Mohamed Ali
Deputy Prime Ministers, Hussein Arab Isse *(Defence)*;
   Mohamed Mohamud Ibrahim *(Foreign Affairs)*
Internal Affairs, Abdisamed Mohamud Sheikh Hassan

DEFENCE
There have been no national armed forces since 1991, despite attempts at re-establishment by the transitional government. Somaliland and Puntland have their own militias with limited amounts of equipment.

ECONOMY AND TRADE
The lack of central government has prevented broad-based economic development or assistance from international donors. About 60 per cent of the population lives below the poverty line, and many are dependent on remittances from relatives abroad. Natural resources are not exploited and industry is virtually non-existent but the lack of regulation has led to a thriving and relatively sophisticated entrepreneurial economy, especially in livestock, remittance/money transfer services (in the absence of a banking sector) and telecommunications. Infrastructure has been developed by commercial concerns, with businesses building small airfields and using natural harbours for overseas trade, and the three main telecommunications companies jointly funding internet infrastructure. The main factor inhibiting trade is the lack of a functional central bank.

Agriculture, primarily livestock-raising by nomads or semi-nomads, is the most important economic sector. It accounts for about 65 per cent of GDP and over half of export earnings, but is vulnerable to drought.

The main export markets are the UAE and Yemen; imports come mainly from Djibouti. Principal exports are livestock, bananas, hides, fish, charcoal and scrap metal. The main imports are manufactured goods, petroleum products, foodstuffs, construction materials and qat.
Annual average growth of GDP – 2.6 per cent (2010 est)
Total external debt – US$3,000m (2001 est)

BALANCE OF PAYMENTS
Trade – US$684 deficit (2010)

Trade with UK	2009	2010
Imports from UK	£1,147,049	£1,868,768
Exports to UK	£14,720	£4,599

COMMUNICATIONS
The main ports are Mogadishu, Kismayu and Merca in the south, and Berbera (in Somaliland) in the north, although these have all been damaged by war. There is a high risk of piracy and armed robbery of shipping in the Gulf of Aden and the Indian Ocean; since 2008 there have been coordinated international efforts against Somali pirates threatening international shipping in the region. The international airports are at Mogadishu and Hargeisa (in Somaliland). There are international flights to Kenya and the UAE.

Little of the public telephone system has survived the civil wars, but mobile phone services are available in most major population centres. There were 100,000 fixed lines in use, 641,000 mobile phone subscribers and 106,000 internet users in 2009.

MEDIA
Many new print and broadcast outlets emerged after Siad Barre was ousted in 1991, but most were tied to one of the country's warring factions. Recent years have seen the emergence of stronger regional media, particularly in radio, but broadcasters and journalists operate in a dangerous environment which limits their ability to report freely and objectively. Many Somalis rely on foreign broadcasts for news and information.

SOUTH AFRICA

Republic of South Africa

Area – 1,219,090 sq. km
Capital – The seat of government is Pretoria (Tshwane): population, 1,403,880 (2009 est); the seat of the legislature is Cape Town: population, 3,352,890 (2009 est); and the seat of the judiciary is Bloemfontein: population, 436,356 (2009 est)
Major cities – Durban, Johannesburg, Port Elizabeth
Currency – Rand (R) of 100 cents
Population – 49,109,107 falling at 0.05 per cent a year (2010 est)
Religion – Christian 80 per cent (African Independent Churches 26 per cent, other 54 per cent); small minorities of Muslims, Hindus, Jews and Buddhists (est). Many combine Christian and indigenous beliefs
Language – Afrikaans, English, isiNdebele, isiXhosa, isiZulu, Sepedi, Sesotho, Setswana, siSwati, Tshivenda, Xitsonga (all official); the most widely spoken are isiZulu, isiXhosa and Afrikaans, but English is the lingua franca
Population density – 41 per sq. km (2009)
Urban population – 61 per cent (2008 est)
Median age (years) – 24.7 (2010 est)

National anthems – 'Nkosi Sikelel' iAfrika' ['God Bless Africa'], incorporating 'Die Stem van Suid Afrika' ['The Call of South Africa']
National day – 27 April (Freedom Day)
Life expectancy (years) – 49.2 (2010 est)
Mortality rate – 16.99 (2010 est)
Birth rate – 19.61 (2010 est)
Infant mortality rate – 43.78 (2010 est)
HIV/AIDS adult prevalence – 17.8 per cent (2009 est)
Death penalty – Abolished for all crimes (since 1997)
CPI score – 4.5 (2010)

CLIMATE AND TERRAIN
South Africa occupies the southernmost part of the African continent, with the exception of Lesotho and Swaziland. Its territory includes Prince Edward and Marion Islands, 1,920km to the south-east of Cape Town. The narrow coastal plain is separated by a mountainous escarpment, including the Drakensberg range, from a high inland plateau (the Great Karoo and the Highveld), an area of semi-arid scrubland in the west merging into grasslands or savannah in the centre and east. Elevation extremes range from 3,408m (Njesuthi) to 0m (Atlantic Ocean). The main rivers are the Orange and the Limpopo and their tributaries. The country lies at the convergence of the Atlantic and Indian oceans, and the climate is influenced by the cold Benguela current along the west coast and the warm Agulhas current along the east, as well as by the altitude of the interior. These influences cause cooler, drier conditions in the west and almost subtropical warmth and rainfall in the east. Average temperatures in Pretoria (Tshwane) range from 3°C in July to 28°C in December.

HISTORY AND POLITICS
Hunter-gatherers, the San (Bushmen) and Khoikhoi, inhabited southern Africa from c.8000 BC. By the eighth century AD, Bantu-speaking peoples had arrived from the north and settled. The Portuguese navigator Bartolomeu Días charted the coast in 1488 and the Dutch founded the colony of the Cape of Good Hope in 1652. The British occupied the Cape in 1795 after Revolutionary France had conquered the Netherlands, and the colony was ceded to Britain in 1806. From 1836 the Boers (descendants of Dutch settlers) migrated north-east in the Great Trek to escape British rule, and founded the republic of Natal in 1839; the British annexed Natal in 1844, made it a colony in 1856 and added Zululand to it in 1897 after victory in the Zulu wars. The Boer republics of Transvaal (founded 1852) and Orange Free State (founded 1854) became British colonies in 1902 after the Boer Wars of 1880–1 and 1899–1902. The four self-governing colonies were united in 1910 to form the Union of South Africa, with dominion status. It became a sovereign state within the Commonwealth in 1931. South Africa left the Commonwealth and became a republic on 31 May 1961, largely as a result of international condemnation of the Sharpeville massacre (1960), in which 67 protesters were killed by police.

The National Party came to power in 1948 and intensified racial segregation through its policy of apartheid ('separateness'), which it pursued until 1991. As a result, South Africa's social and political structure came to be based on racial segregation, with separate institutions and facilities for different racial groups. The African National Congress (ANC) and other opposition groups mounted a civil disobedience campaign, following which most opposition groups were banned. Internal

opposition continued, with strikes and violence in the 1980s leading to the declaration of a state of emergency in 1985. Internationally, the country became isolated as economic and cultural sanctions were imposed.

In 1984, a new constitution extended the franchise to mixed race and Asian people, but the progressive dismantling of apartheid began with the desegregation of public facilities in 1989. This was followed by the lifting of the bans on the ANC and other anti-apartheid groups, the release from prison of ANC leader Nelson Mandela (1990) and the effective abolition of the laws implementing apartheid in 1991. Negotiations between the government of F. W. de Klerk, the ANC and other political and civil groups reached agreement in 1991 on the establishment of an interracial administration and the formation of a five-year coalition government following multiracial elections. In 1993 the franchise was extended to all adults, and elections took place in April 1994. The ANC won a majority in both legislative chambers, and Nelson Mandela was elected president. South Africa rejoined the Commonwealth and took its UN seat again in 1994.

High levels of HIV/AIDS infection, a very high crime rate, social disruption and lack of education resulting from apartheid are serious problems. There has also been growing discontent in recent years at the lack of progress in reducing poverty since the end of apartheid. Despite these problems, South Africa is widely regarded as the dominant political, economic and diplomatic force in the region.

The ANC has won all the legislative elections since 1994, but is increasingly racked by internal tensions and tainted by corruption allegations. In April 2009 its majority in the National Assembly was reduced by 13 seats and it lost one of the provincial assemblies as two of the opposition parties began to challenge its dominance. In May 2009, Jacob Zuma of the ANC was elected president.

POLITICAL SYSTEM
Under the 1997 constitution, the executive president is elected by the National Assembly for a five-year term, renewable once. The president, who is responsible to the legislature, appoints the cabinet. The bicameral parliament consists of the National Assembly, the lower house, and the National Council of Provinces. The National Assembly has 400 members directly elected by proportional representation for a five-year term. The National Council of Provinces has 90 members, ten for each province, selected by the provincial legislatures for a five-year term.

South Africa is divided into nine provinces: Eastern Cape, Free State, Gauteng, KwaZulu-Natal, Limpopo, Mpumalanga, Northern Cape, North-West, and Western Cape. Each province has its own premier, legislature and constitution.

HEAD OF STATE
President, Jacob Zuma, *elected* 6 May 2009, *sworn in* 9 May 2009
Deputy President, Kgalema Motlanthe

SELECTED GOVERNMENT MEMBERS *as at July 2011*
Defence, Lindiwe Nonceba Sisulu
Finance, Pravin Gordhan
Foreign Affairs, Maite Nkoana-Mashabane
Home Affairs, Nkosazana Dlamini-Zuma

SOUTH AFRICAN HIGH COMMISSION
South Africa House, Trafalgar Square, London WC2N 5DP
T 020-7451 7299 W www.southafricahouseuk.com
High Commissioner, HE Dr Zola Skweyiya, apptd 2009

BRITISH HIGH COMMISSION
255 Hill Street, Arcadia 0002, Pretoria (Tshwane)
T (+27) (12) 405 2400 E media.pretoria@fco.gov.uk
W http://ukinsouthafrica.fco.gov.uk
High Commissioner, HE Dr Dame Nicola Brewer, DCMG,
apptd 2009

BRITISH COUNCIL
275 Jan Smuts Avenue, Dunkeld Corner, Dunkeld West 2196
T (+27) (11) 560 9300 W www.britishcouncil.org/africa
Director, David Cordingley

DEFENCE
The South African National Defence Force (SANDF) was
created in 1994 from the merger of the South African
Defence Forces (SADF), the Umkhonto we Sizwe (MK)
armed wing of the ANC, the Azanian People's Liberation
Army (APLA) of the Pan Africanist Congress of Azania,
and the defence forces of the four former 'independent'
homelands.

The army has 34 main battle tanks, 810 armoured
personnel carriers and 534 armoured infantry fighting
vehicles. The navy has 3 submarines, 4 frigates and 5
patrol and coastal vessels at 4 bases. The air force has 39
combat aircraft and 11 armed helicopters.

Military budget – US$4,150m (2010)
Military personnel – 62,082: army 37,141, navy 6,244,
air force 10,653, Military Health Service 8,044

ECONOMY AND TRADE
The economy varies between the sophisticated and
well-developed, based on manufacturing, mining and
financial services; the living eked out by the very poor,
mostly through subsistence agriculture; and a large
informal sector. Growth was strong until 2008, when the
global economic downturn caused a contraction in the
economy owing to falling commodity prices and export
demand from which slow recovery is being made.
State-owned enterprises are being used to create jobs and
raise incomes. However, unemployment remains high and
poverty widespread (about half the population lives below
the poverty line), and productivity and trade are
constrained by outdated infrastructure in some sectors;
power cuts have been frequent since 2007 because of the
unreliability of the electricity supply.

Agriculture, forestry and fishing account for 3 per cent
of GDP and employ 9 per cent of the workforce. Principal
crops are maize, wheat, sugar cane, fruit and vegetables.
Livestock farming and cotton and viticulture are also
widespread.

The largest industry is mining; South Africa is the
world's largest producer of gold, platinum and chromium,
as well as producing diamonds, manganese, coal, copper,
iron ore, tin, uranium and titanium. Other industries
include car assembly, metalworking, food processing, ship
repair and production of machinery, textiles, iron and
steel, chemicals and fertiliser; manufacturing is
concentrated most heavily around Johannesburg, Pretoria
(Tshwane) and the major ports. Tourism is a significant
industry, with over nine million visitors in 2007, and
South Africa is a major transit point for its landlocked
neighbours. Industry contributes 31.2 per cent of GDP
and services 65.8 per cent.

Fossil-fuel based electricity generation is being
supplemented by nuclear power; one nuclear power
station is in operation and others are planned. South
Africa exports electricity through its electricity grid
connections to all states in southern Africa. Water
resources are inadequate to meet demand, so water is
imported from the highlands of Lesotho.

The main trading partners are China, Germany, the
USA and Japan. Principal exports are gold, diamonds,
platinum, other metals and minerals, and machinery and
equipment. Principal imports are machinery and
equipment, chemicals, petroleum products, scientific
instruments and foodstuffs.

GNI – US$279,023m; US$5,760 per capita (2009)
Annual average growth of GDP – 3 per cent (2010 est)
Inflation rate – 4.5 per cent (2010 est)
Unemployment – 23.3 per cent (2010 est)
Total external debt – US$80,520m (2010 est)
Imports – US$73,200m (2009)
Exports – US$62,600m (2009)

BALANCE OF PAYMENTS
Trade – US$1,715m surplus (2010)
Current Account – US$19,593m deficit (2008)

Trade with UK	2009	2010
Imports from UK	£2,153,771,710	£3,015,164,053
Exports to UK	£7,333,406,607	£6,025,605,168

COMMUNICATIONS
The country has 20,192km of railways, including the
high-speed Gautrain which links Johannesburg's main
international airport with its commercial district and will
eventually connect with Pretoria. There are 362,100km
of roads, of which 73,500km are surfaced, and over 578
airports and airfields, with international airports at
Johannesburg, Durban and Cape Town. South African
Airways operates international services worldwide and it
is the principal operator of domestic flights. Durban is the
largest seaport. Other major ports are Cape Town, Port
Elizabeth, East London, Saldanha, Mossel Bay and
Richards Bay.

The telephone system is the most developed in Africa,
and there is a very high level of mobile phone ownership.
There were 4.3 million fixed lines in use, 46.4 million
mobile phone subscribers and 4.4 million internet users in
2009.

EDUCATION AND HEALTH
Education is compulsory between the ages of seven and
15. It is provided by the state and organised into three
levels: general education and training, further education
and training, and higher education. The nine provincial
legislatures manage education facilities, subject to a
national policy framework.

Literacy rate – 88.4 per cent (2008 est)
Gross enrolment ratio (percentage of relevant age group) –
primary 101 per cent; secondary 94 per cent (2009 est)
Health expenditure (per capita) – US$485 (2009)
Hospital beds (per 1,000 people) – 2.8 (2004–9)

MEDIA AND CULTURE
South Africa's media industry is the largest and most
influential in Africa. The South African Broadcasting
Corporation (SABC) is a major, state-owned television
and radio broadcaster, and there is a thriving private
sector, with widespread take-up of cable and satellite

television and a large number of radio stations since deregulation in 1996. *The Star* is Johannesburg's oldest daily newspaper, while the *Sunday Times* is the longest running weekly title; *Beeld* is a popular Afrikaans daily title. Press freedom is generally respected, with little evidence of repressive measures against journalists.

South Africa is home to a diversity of cultures, and black cultures such as Zulu, Xhosa and Ndebele are experiencing a revival after their suppression during the apartheid years. Celebrated figures include the writers Nadine Gordimer (*b.* 1923) and J. M. Coetzee (*b.* 1940), winners of the Nobel prize for literature in 1991 and 2003 respectively. The Nobel peace prize was won by Archbishop Desmond Tutu (*b.* 1931) in 1984, and shared by Nelson Mandela (*b.* 1918) and F. W. de Klerk (*b.* 1936) in 1993.

SPAIN

Reino de España – Kingdom of Spain

Area – 505,370 sq. km
Capital – Madrid; population, 5,762,050 (2009 est)
Major cities – Barcelona, Bilbao, Las Palmas (Gran Canaria), Málaga, Murcia, Palma (Majorca), Seville, Valencia, Zaragoza
Currency – Euro (€) of 100 cents
Population – 46,505,963 rising at 0.49 per cent a year (2010 est)
Religion – Christian (Roman Catholic 73 per cent) (est)
Language – Castilian (Spanish) (official), Catalan, Galician, Basque (all are official in certain regions)
Population density – 92 per sq. km (2009)
Urban population – 77 per cent (2008 est)
Median age (years) – 40.1 (2010 est)
National anthem – 'La Marcha Real' ['The Royal March']
National day – 12 October
Life expectancy (years) – 81.07 (2010 est)
Mortality rate – 8.72 (2010 est)
Birth rate – 10.91 (2010 est)
Infant mortality rate – 3.42 (2010 est)
Death penalty – Abolished for all crimes (since 1995)
CPI score – 6.1 (2010)

CLIMATE AND TERRAIN
Spain occupies over 80 per cent of the Iberian peninsula, and includes two archipelagos and territories on or just off the Moroccan coast. The interior consists of an elevated plateau surrounded and traversed by mountain ranges: the Pyrenees on the border with France, the Cantabrian Mountains (north-west), the Sierra de Guadarrama, Sierra Morena, Montes de Toledo (centre) and the Sierra Nevada (south). Elevation extremes range from 3,718m (Pico de

Teide, Tenerife, Canary Islands) to 0m (Mediterranean Sea). The principal rivers are the Duero, the Tajo (Tagus), the Guadiana, the Guadalquivir, the Ebro and the Miño. The climate is Mediterranean in the southern and eastern coastal areas, and temperate further inland and at altitude. Average temperatures in Madrid range from 0°C in January to 33°C in July.

HISTORY AND POLITICS
The Romans conquered the Iberian peninsula in the second century BC. It was overrun by Vandals and Visigoths in the fifth century AD, and invaded and occupied by Muslims from Africa in the eighth century. Christians in the north formed small kingdoms which had reconquered the peninsula by 1492. Spain's modern form derives from the dynastic union of the kingdoms of Castile and Aragón in 1479. In the 16th century, Spain's exploration and colonisation of the New World made it one of the richest and most powerful nations in Europe, with an empire that covered most of central and southern America. However, a succession of costly wars and revolts in the 17th and 18th centuries saw this empire go into steady decline. Its central and southern American possessions declared independence in the early 19th century, and most other overseas possessions had been lost by 1900.

The restoration of the Bourbon monarchy after the Napoleonic occupation of 1808–14 initiated over a century of political instability, with power struggles between conservative and liberal factions in royal, political and military circles. The dictatorship of Gen. Primo de Rivera (1923–30) ended with the exiling of King Alfonso XIII and the declaration of the Second Republic in 1931. Left-wing victory in the 1936 election led to an army revolt in Spanish Morocco that spread throughout Spain, developing into a civil war that lasted until 1939. Gen. Francisco Franco, who had led the right-wing Nationalist forces in the civil war, became president and ruled the country until his death in 1975. His death was followed, according to his wishes, by the restoration of the monarchy, and Prince Juan Carlos of Bourbon (grandson of Alfonso XIII) became head of state as King Juan Carlos I. The first free election was held in 1977, and a referendum in 1978 endorsed a democratic constitution.

Spain joined NATO in 1982 and the EEC in 1986, becoming a member of the euro zone in 1999.

The Spanish Socialist Workers' Party (PSOE) won an unexpected victory in the 2004 election, held three days after the bombing of commuter trains in Madrid by a group linked to al-Qaida. In the 2008 legislative elections the PSOE increased its seats, remaining the largest party in the Congress of Deputies but without a majority; the main opposition party, the Popular Party, won the most seats in the senate. José Luis Rodríguez Zapatero continued as prime minister at the head of a minority PSOE government, which has the support of five small parties.

INSURGENCIES
The Basque separatist organisation ETA (*Euzkadi ta Azkatasuna* – Basque Nation and Liberty), formed in 1959, has carried out a terrorist campaign of bombings, shootings and kidnappings since 1961 in an attempt to gain independence for the Basque country. ETA rejected regional autonomy for the Basque country in 1979 as insufficient and continued its campaign, but has been

greatly weakened since the early 1990s by increased cooperation between Spanish security forces and their European counterparts. *Herri Batasuna,* regarded as ETA's political wing, was banned in 2003. ETA has announced a number of ceasefires since 1998, during some of which it has held talks with the government or political parties, but no progress has been made towards a political settlement that it considers acceptable; in January 2011 it declared a permanent ceasefire.

POLITICAL SYSTEM

The 1978 constitution has been amended at various times to devolve powers to the 19 autonomous regions. The head of state is a hereditary constitutional monarch. There is a bicameral legislature, the *Cortes Generales,* comprising a 350-member Congress of Deputies directly elected for a four-year term, and a senate with 264 members, 208 directly elected and 56 appointed by the assemblies of the autonomous regions, for a four-year term.

There are 19 autonomous regions: Andalucía, Aragón, Asturias, Balearic Islands, the Basque Country, Canary Islands, Cantabria, Castilla-La Mancha, Castilla y León, Catalonia, Ceuta, Extremadura, Galicia, La Rioja, Madrid, Melilla, Murcia, Navarra and Valencia. Each has its own elected legislature and government. In 2006 a referendum endorsed the *Cortes'* approval of greater autonomy for Catalonia.

HEAD OF STATE

HM The King of Spain, King Juan Carlos I de Borbón, KG, GCVO, *born* 5 January 1938, *acceded to the throne* 22 November 1975
Heir, HRH The Prince of the Asturias (Prince Felipe Juan Pablo Alfonso y Todos los Santos), *born* 30 January 1968

SELECTED GOVERNMENT MEMBERS *as at July 2011*
Prime Minister, José Luis Rodríguez Zapatero
Vice President for Economy and Finance, Elena Salgado Mendez
Foreign Affairs, Trinidad Jimenez Garcia-Herrera
Interior, Antonio Camacho
Defence, Carmen Chacon Piqueras

EMBASSY OF SPAIN

39 Chesham Place, London SW1X 8SB
T 020-7235 5555 **E** emb.londres@maec.es
W www.mae.es/embajadas/londres/es/home
Ambassador Extraordinary and Plenipotentiary,
HE Carles Casajuana Palet, *apptd* 2008

BRITISH EMBASSY

Torre Espacio, Paseo de la Castellana 259D, 28046 Madrid
T (+34) (91) 714 6300 **W** http://ukinspain.fco.gov.uk
Ambassador Extraordinary and Plenipotentiary,
HE Giles Paxman, LVO, *apptd* 2009

BRITISH COUNCIL

Paseo del General Martínez, Campos 31, E-28010 Madrid
T (+34) (91) 337 3500 **W** www.britishcouncil.org/spain
Director, Rod Pryde

DEFENCE

The army has 447 main battle tanks, 144 armoured infantry fighting vehicles and 1,997 armoured personnel carriers. The navy has 4 submarines, 1 aircraft carrier, 4 destroyers, 6 frigates, 24 patrol and coastal vessels, 24

combat aircraft and 20 armed helicopters at 6 bases. The air force has 179 combat aircraft.
Military budget – US$10,200m (2010)
Military personnel – 142,212: army 78,121, navy 21,606, air force 21,172, joint staff 21,313; paramilitary 80,210

ECONOMY AND TRADE

Conservatism and isolation held back economic development until the mid-20th century, but the economy improved from the 1950s with industrialisation and the development of tourism. The mixed capitalist economy showed above-average growth, stimulated by liberalisation, privatisation and deregulation, from the mid-1990s until 2007. In 2008 it entered a severe recession because of the global economic downturn. This pushed unemployment to 20 per cent in 2010 (from 8 per cent in 2007). The downturn in construction and the property market left many banks struggling in 2010, and rising public-sector debt led to Spain's international credit rating being downgraded; the government introduced austerity measures in response but concern continues over the impact on the eurozone of Spain's sovereign debt.

The generally fertile country produces grains, vegetables, olives, sugar beets, citrus and other fruits, meat and dairy products. Viticulture is widespread. Spain also has one of Europe's largest fishing industries. The agricultural sector contributes 2.9 per cent of GDP and employs 4.2 per cent of the workforce. Abundant mineral resources include coal, iron ore, copper, zinc, lead, uranium and tungsten. Metal extraction and the manufacture of metal products, including steel, are major industries. A diverse industrial sector includes manufacturing (principally textiles, clothing, footwear, beverages, chemicals, cars, machine tools, clay products, pharmaceuticals and medical equipment), food processing, shipbuilding and tourism. The tourist industry usually caters for over 52 million visitors a year, but it has been hit by the recession. Industry accounts for 25.5 per cent of GDP and the service sector for 71.6 per cent.

The main trading partners are other EU countries, especially France and Germany. Principal exports include machinery, vehicles, foodstuffs, pharmaceuticals, medicines and other consumer goods. The main imports are machinery and equipment, fuels, chemicals, semi-finished goods, foodstuffs, consumer goods, and measuring and medical equipment.
GNI – US$1,430,230m; US$32,120 per capita (2009)
Annual average growth of GDP – –0.4 per cent (2010 est)
Inflation rate – 1.3 per cent (2010 est)
Population below the poverty line – 19.8 per cent (2005)
Unemployment – 20 per cent (2010 est)
Total external debt – US$2,166,000m (2010 est)
Imports – US$290,700m (2009)
Exports – US$220,800m (2009)

BALANCE OF PAYMENTS

Trade – US$69,269m deficit (2010)
Current Account – US$74,136m deficit (2009)

Trade with UK	2009	2010
Imports from UK	£8,952,783,708	£9,630,415,364
Exports to UK	£9,134,372,285	£9,973,111,067

COMMUNICATIONS

Spain has a total of 681,298km of roads, all of which are surfaced (including 15,152km of motorways). Railways total 15,293km, and there are 1,000km of navigable inland waterways. The main ports are Algeciras, Alicante, Barcelona, Bilbao, Cádiz, Santander and Valencia, and Las Palmas in the Canary Islands. The principal airports are at Madrid, Barcelona, Alicante, Málaga, Valencia and Bilbao, and there are over 145 other airports and airfields around the country.

The modern telecommunications systems provided services to 20 million fixed-line subscribers, 51 million mobile phone subscribers and 28.1 million internet users in 2009.

EDUCATION AND HEALTH

Education is free from age six to 18, and compulsory to the age of 16. Private schools (about 30 per cent of primary and 60 per cent of secondary schools) have to fulfil certain criteria to receive government maintenance grants. There are 73 universities, the oldest of which, Salamanca, was founded in 1218. Other historic foundations are Valladolid (1346), Barcelona (1430), Zaragoza (1474), Santiago (1495), Valencia (1500), Seville (1505) and Madrid (1508).

Literacy rate – 97.9 per cent (2008 est)
Gross enrolment ratio (percentage of relevant age group) – primary 107 per cent; secondary 120 per cent; tertiary 71 per cent (2008 est)
Health expenditure (per capita) – US$3,075 (2009)
Hospital beds (per 1,000 people) – 3.2 (2004–9)

MEDIA

Broadcasting has expanded in recent years, with cable, satellite and digital services growing steadily. Public radio and television services are run by RadioTelevision Espanola (RTVE), which is funded by advertising and state subsidies. Many private radio and TV stations operate at both national and regional levels. There are four Madrid-based daily newspapers and another two based in Barcelona. Popular titles include *El Mundo*, *ABC*, *El País* and *El Periodico de Catalunya*.

CULTURE

Spain's literature is one of the oldest in the world. The *Poem of the Cid*, the earliest of Spain's heroic works, was written *c*.1140. The outstanding writers of Spain's Golden Age are Miguel de Cervantes (1547–1616), Lope de Vega (1562–1635) and Pedro Calderón de la Barca (1600–81). The Nobel prize for literature has been awarded to five Spanish authors: J. Echegaray (1832–1916), J. Benavente (1866–1954), Juan Ramón Jiménez (1881–1958), Vicente Aleixandre (1898–1984) and Camilo José Cela (1916–2002). Federico Garciá Lorca (1898–1936) is the most esteemed modern dramatist.

Spain's long tradition in fine art includes the work of El Greco (1541–1614), Velázquez (1599–1660), Goya (1746–1828), Picasso (1881–1973), Miró (1893–1983) and Salvador Dalí (1904–89).

ISLANDS AND ENCLAVES

THE BALEARIC ISLES form an archipelago off the east coast of Spain. There are four large islands (Majorca/Mallorca, Minorca, Ibiza and Formentera) and seven smaller ones (Aire, Aucanada, Botafoch, Cabrera, Dragonera, Pinto and El Rey). Area 4,992 sq. km; population 1,106,049 (2010 est). The archipelago forms a province of Spain. The capital is Palma, on Majorca.

THE CANARY ISLANDS are an archipelago in the Atlantic off the African coast, consisting of seven islands and six islets. Area 7,447 sq. km; population 2,118,519 (2010 est). The Canary Islands form two provinces of Spain: Las Palmas, comprising Gran Canaria, Lanzarote, Fuerteventura and six islets, with the seat of administration at Las Palmas, in Gran Canaria; and Santa Cruz de Tenerife, comprising Tenerife, La Palma, La Gomera and El Hierro, with the seat of administration at Santa Cruz, in Tenerife.

ISLA DE FAISANES is an uninhabited Franco-Spanish condominium, at the mouth of the Bidassoa in La Higuera bay.

CEUTA is a fortified post on the Moroccan coast, opposite Gibraltar. Area 19 sq. km; population 80,579 (2010 est). Ceuta is an autonomous city of Spain.

MELILLA is a town on a rocky promontory of the Moroccan coast, connected with the mainland by a narrow isthmus. Area 13 sq. km; population 76,034 (2010 est). Melilla is an autonomous city of Spain.

OVERSEAS TERRITORIES

The following territories, which are Spanish settlements on the Moroccan seaboard, come under direct Spanish administration. They are uninhabited other than by military personnel.

PENON DE ALHUCEMAS is a bay including six islands.
PENON DE LA GOMERA (or Peñón de Velez) is a fortified rocky islet.
THE CHAFFARINAS (or Zaffarines) is a group of three islands near the Algerian frontier.

SRI LANKA

Shri Lamka Prajatantrika Samajaya di Janarajaya/Ilankai Jananayaka Choshalichak Kutiyarachu – Democratic Socialist Republic of Sri Lanka

Area – 65,610 sq. km
Capital – Colombo; population, 681,484 (2009 est), Sri Jayewardenepura Kotte; population, 123,090 (2009 est) is the administrative capital
Major cities – Dehiwala-Mount Lavinia, Jaffna, Kalmunai, Kandy, Moratuwa, Negombo, Trincomalee, Vavuniya
Currency – Sri Lankan rupee of 100 cents
Population – 21,513,990 rising at 0.86 per cent a year (2010 est); Sinhalese (73.8 per cent), Sri Lankan Moor (7.2 per cent), Indian Tamil (4.6 per cent), Sri Lankan Tamil (3.9 per cent) (2001 est; excludes predominantly Tamil areas then held by rebels)
Religion – Buddhist 70 per cent (predominantly Theravada), Hindu 15 per cent, Christian 8 per cent (predominantly Roman Catholic), Muslim 7 per cent (predominantly Sunni) (est)

Language – Sinhala (official), Tamil, English
Population density – 324 per sq. km (2009)
Urban population – 15 per cent (2008 est)
Median age (years) – 31.3 (2010 est)
National anthem – 'Sri Lanka Matha' ['Mother Sri Lanka']
National day – 4 February (Independence Day)
Life expectancy (years) – 75.3 (2010 est)
Mortality rate – 6.2 (2010 est)
Birth rate – 15.88 (2010 est)
Infant mortality rate – 18.14 (2010 est)
Death penalty – Retained (not used since 1976)
CPI score – 3.2 (2010)
Literacy rate – 90.8 per cent (2008 est)
Gross enrolment ratio (percentage of relevant age group) –
    primary 97 per cent (2009 est)
Health expenditure (per capita) – US$84 (2009)
Hospital beds (per 1,000 people) – 3.1 (2004–9)

CLIMATE AND TERRAIN

Sri Lanka (formerly Ceylon) is an island in the Indian Ocean, separated from India by the narrow Palk Strait. The land is low-lying in the north and along the coasts, rising to a central massif with hills and mountains in the south and centre. Forests, jungle and scrub cover the greater part of the island. In areas over 600m above sea level, grasslands *(patanas* or *talawas)* are found. Elevation extremes range from 2,524m (Pidurutalagala) to 0m (Indian Ocean). The climate is tropical with little seasonal variation in conditions and humidity, which often reaches around 90 per cent. The island experiences the south-west monsoon from May to September and the north-east monsoon from October to January.

HISTORY AND POLITICS

Modern Sri Lanka is a product of its history of settlement, which began with the arrival of the Sinhalese in the sixth century BC. They settled in the north, but gradually moved southwards under pressure from Tamil invasions from southern India, which began in the third century BC. These Tamils settled in the northern and eastern coastal areas. The Portuguese landed in the early 16th century and established control over most of the island by 1618. These territories were conquered by the Dutch in 1658 and held until 1798, when they were ceded to the British, becoming a British crown colony in 1802. With the annexation of the kingdom of Kandy in 1815, all Ceylon came under British rule. Plantation agriculture flourished, and in the mid-19th century large numbers of predominantly Tamil indentured labourers were brought over from southern India. Ceylon achieved independence in 1948. In 1972 it became a republic and the country was renamed Sri Lanka ('Resplendent Island'). Politics has been dominated since 1948 by the United National Party (UNP) and the Sri Lanka Freedom Party (SLFP); the latter formed the United People's Freedom Alliance (UPFA) with the People's Liberation Front (JVP) in 2004.

Tension between the Buddhist Sinhalese majority and the Hindu Tamil minority dates from the early 20th century, and intensified after policies discriminating against Tamils were introduced following independence. Separatist movements developed in the 1970s to campaign for an independent Tamil state in the north and east of the island, and in 1983 the Liberation Tigers of Tamil Eelam (LTTE) began a guerrilla war against government forces for control of these areas. Although fighting tended to be confined to the north, especially the Jaffna peninsula, terrorist attacks occurred throughout the island. The LTTE captured territory in the north and along the east coast between the early 1990s and the mid 2000s, holding almost a third of the island by 2005. After the 2002 ceasefire broke down in 2006 amid escalating violence, government forces mounted major offensives, recapturing the eastern province in 2007 and the north between January 2008 and May 2009, when the LTTE forces were finally defeated. The conflict is estimated to have left 70,000 dead and displaced over 1 million people. International concern was expressed over allegations of war crimes against civilians trapped in the conflict zone in the final stages of the civil war.

The 2005 presidential election was won by the SLFP leader Mahinda Rajapakse, and he was re-elected in an early election in January 2010. The legislative election in April 2010 was won by the SLFP-led UPFA, with an increased majority.

POLITICAL SYSTEM

The 1978 constitution was amended in 1983 to ban parties advocating separatism, in 1987 to create provincial councils, and in 2010 to remove the limit on presidential terms. The executive president is directly elected for a six-year term, which may be renewed. The unicameral parliament has 225 members directly elected by proportional representation for a six-year term. The president appoints the prime minister and cabinet.

Elected councils were set up in the nine provinces in 1987 in an attempt to defuse ethnic tensions. The Northern and Eastern provinces were merged into one from 1988 to 2006.

HEAD OF STATE

President; Defence; Finance, Mahinda Rajapakse,
    elected 17 November 2005, *re-elected* 2010

SELECTED GOVERNMENT MEMBERS *as at July 2011*
Prime Minister, Dissanayake Jayaratne
Home Affairs, John Seneviratne
Foreign Affairs, G. L. Peiris

HIGH COMMISSION OF THE DEMOCRATIC SOCIALIST
REPUBLIC OF SRI LANKA
13 Hyde Park Gardens, London W2 2LU
T 020-7262 1841 E mail@slhc-london.co.uk
W http://www.srilankahighcommission.co.uk
High Commissioner, HE Pakeer Mohideen Amza *(acting)*,
    apptd 2011

BRITISH HIGH COMMISSION
389 Bauddhaloka Mawatha, Colombo 7
T (+94) (11) 539 0639 E bhctrade@slt.lk
W http://ukinsrilanka.fco.gov.uk
High Commissioner, HE John Rankin, *apptd* 2011

BRITISH COUNCIL
PO Box 753, 49 Alfred House Gardens, Colombo 3
T (+94) (1) 1258 1171 W www.britishcouncil.org/srilanka
Director, Tony Reilly

DEFENCE

The army has 62 main battle tanks, 217 armoured personnel carriers and 62 armoured infantry fighting vehicles. The navy has 134 patrol and coastal vessels at 5 bases. The air force has 23 combat aircraft and 13 armed helicopters.

Military budget – US$1,440m (2010)
Military personnel – 160,900: army 117,900, navy
    15,000, air force 28,000; paramilitary 62,200

ECONOMY AND TRADE

Despite the 26-year civil war and the 2004 Indian Ocean tsunami, which destroyed tourist resorts and the fishing industry, the economy saw sustained growth throughout the 2000s. The 2008–9 global downturn affected productivity only slightly, but high government debt and budget deficits obliged the government to seek an IMF loan. Reconstruction in the east and north is expected to stimulate economic growth. The once predominantly agricultural economy has become increasingly industrialised and diversified, with service industries such as tourism now making the greatest contribution to GDP. Remittances from expatriate workers are also economically significant.

Agriculture still accounts for 12.6 per cent of GDP and over 32 per cent of employment. The main crops are rice, sugar cane, grains, pulses, oilseed, spices, vegetables, fruit, tea, rubber, coconuts, livestock products and fish. Manufacturing is based on processing the main cash crops of rubber, tea, coconuts, tobacco and other commodities, and production of textiles, clothing, beverages and cement; other industries include oil refining and mining gemstones. Service industries such as telecommunications, banking and insurance, information technology services and tourism are also important; the tourist industry usually caters for over 400,000 visitors a year. The service sector accounts for 57.6 per cent of GDP and industry for 29.8 per cent.

The main trading partners are India, the USA, China, the UK and Singapore. Principal exports are textiles and clothing, tea, rubber manufactures, spices, diamonds, emeralds, rubies, coconut products and fish. The main imports are oil, textile fabrics, machinery and transport equipment, building materials, mineral products and foodstuffs.

GNI – US$41,494m; US$1,990 per capita (2009)
Annual average growth of GDP – 6.9 per cent (2010 est)
Inflation rate – 5.6 per cent (2010 est)
Unemployment – 5.4 per cent (2010 est)
Population below poverty line – 23 per cent (2008 est)
Total external debt – US$17,970m (2009 est)
Imports – US$9,900m (2009)
Exports – US$7,400m (2009)

BALANCE OF PAYMENTS
Trade – US$6,425m deficit (2010)
Current Account – US$3,719m deficit (2008)

Trade with UK	2009	2010
Imports from UK	£119,788,834	£129,526,294
Exports to UK	£688,221,062	£681,028,624

COMMUNICATIONS

There are 91,907km of roads. The rail network is government-run and there are 1,449km of track. Colombo is the main port although the first phase of a deep-water container port opened in 2010 at Hambantota, largely financed by China. The principal airport is Bandaranaike International, to the north of the capital.

Fixed-line telephone services now extend to most of the country, and mobile phone distribution is expanding rapidly. There were 3.5 million fixed lines in use and 15.9 million mobile phone users in 2010, and 1.8 million internet users in 2009.

MEDIA

Many of the main media outlets are state-owned, including two major television stations, the radio networks operated by the Sri Lanka Broadcasting Corporation and several newspapers. There are also privately owned broadcast media and newspapers. Outlets tend to be divided on ethnic lines, and services are provided in Sinhala, Tamil and English. The private media debate political issues and criticise the government, but often face harassment, intimidation and violence for doing so.

SUDAN

Jumhuriyat as-Sudan – Republic of the Sudan

Area – 2,505,813 sq. km
Capital – Khartoum; population, 5,021,390 (2009 est)
Major cities – Kassala, Kusti, Nyala, El Obeid, Port Sudan
Currency – Sudanese pound (SDP) of 100 piastres
Population – 43,939,598 rising at 2.5 per cent a year (2010 est); Arab and Nubian peoples populate the north and centre, with Nilotic and black African peoples in the south
Religion – Muslim 60 per cent (predominantly Sunni; in north), indigenous beliefs 10 per cent (est); Christian minority (5 per cent) mostly in south and Khartoum; many animists also follow Christian practices
Language – Arabic, English (both official), Nubian, Ta Bedawie
Population density – 18 per sq. km (2009)
Urban population – 43 per cent (2008 est)
Median age (years) – 18.4 (2010 est)
National anthem – 'Nahnu Jund Allah Jund Al-Watan' ['We Are the Army of God and of Our Land']
National day – 1 January (Independence Day)
Life expectancy (years) – 54.21 (2010 est)
Mortality rate – 11.66 (2010 est)
Birth rate – 36.58 (2010 est)
Infant mortality rate – 72.39 (2010 est)
HIV/AIDS adult prevalence – 1.1 per cent (2009 est)
Death penalty – Retained
CPI score – 1.6 (2010)
NB Data include South Sudan

CLIMATE AND TERRAIN

Sudan is predominantly desert; the Libyan Desert in the west is separated from the rocky Nubian Desert in the east by the fertile valley of the Nile and its tributaries. There are mountains in the west and the south, and along the Red Sea coast. Elevation extremes range from 3,187m (Kinyeti, South Sudan) to 0m (Red Sea). The climate is arid on the desert plains, tropical in the south, and cooler at altitude. There is a rainy season from April to October. Average temperatures in Khartoum range from 16°C in January to 42°C in May.

HISTORY AND POLITICS

Parts of northern Sudan were included in the Egyptian Empire from 1900 BC and the Nubian Empire from the sixth century BC. The country was converted to Coptic Christianity in the sixth century AD, and Islam was introduced in the seventh century by Arab invaders, but did not become widespread until the 15th century. From the eighth century onwards, northern Sudan was conquered and occupied by several Arab and Arab-African powers. The south remained independent. Egypt established its control over the north in the early 19th century. The Mahdi revolt in the 1880s led to a joint Anglo-Egyptian campaign to subdue the country, and it was administered as an Anglo-Egyptian condominium from 1899. On 19 December 1955 the Sudanese legislature declared Sudan an independent sovereign state, and on 1 January 1956 a republic was proclaimed.

Tensions between the dominant Arab, Muslim north and the black African, Christian and animist south have dominated the post-independence period. The first civil war in the south began in 1955 and lasted until 1972, when the south was given greater autonomy. A second civil war broke out in 1983, largely because of attempts to impose Shari'ah law on the whole country.

The civil wars caused years of political instability in the country as a whole, resulting in several coups, and Sudan spent much of the period between 1958 and 2005 under military or one-party rule. Following a 2004 peace agreement, a new constitution was approved in 2005, under which the president and vice-president were sworn in, and a power-sharing government took office.

The first multiparty presidential and legislative elections for 24 years were held in 2010. President al-Bashir was re-elected as national president and his National Congress Party won an overall majority nationally amid allegations of vote-rigging and intimidation.

INSURGENCIES

In the western region of Darfur, tension between nomadic Arab livestock herders and black African farmers over land and grazing rights led to a rise in intercommunal violence in the 1990s. Between 2002 and 2009 black African rebels protesting at marginalisation were ruthlessly suppressed by government forces, often operating through Arab militia *(Janjaweed)* which carried out mass executions and forcible depopulation. The government resisted international pressure to disarm the militias, and obstructed the deployment of peacekeeping troops and the work of aid agencies inside Darfur.

Incursions into neighbouring countries to attack refugees there destabilised the region. Two of the main rebel groups signed peace agreements with the government, one in 2006 and the other in 2009, although violence by smaller rebel groups and banditry continues. An estimated 300,000 have died from violence, starvation or disease since 2003, and 2.7 million people have been internally displaced or become refugees in Chad and the Central African Republic. The International Criminal Court issued a warrant for the arrest of President al-Bashir for war crimes and crimes against humanity in 2009, and for genocide in 2010.

POLITICAL SYSTEM

Under the 2005 constitution, the executive president is directly elected for a five-year term, renewable once. The bicameral National Legislature comprises a National Assembly with 450 members, including 112 seats reserved for women, directly elected for a five-year term, and a Council of States with two members from each of the 25 states. The president appoints the cabinet.

NB South Sudanese members were to withdraw from the Sudan legislature when the south became independent.

HEAD OF STATE

President, Prime Minister, Field Marshal Omar al-Bashir, *seized power* 1989, *elected* 1996, *re-elected* 2000, *sworn in under new constitution* 9 July 2005, *re-elected* 2010
Vice-President, Ali Osman Mohammed Taha

SELECTED GOVERNMENT MEMBERS *as at July 2011*
Defence, Lt.-Gen. Abdel-Rahim Hussein
Finance, Ali Mahmoud Abdul-Rasoul
Foreign Affairs, Ali Ahmed Karti
Interior, Ibrahim Mohamed Hamid

EMBASSY OF THE REPUBLIC OF THE SUDAN
3 Cleveland Row, London SW1A 1DD
T 020-7839 8080 E admin@sudanembassy.co.uk
W www.sudan-embassy.co.uk
Ambassador Extraordinary and Plenipotentiary, Abdullahi Hamad Ali Alazreg, *apptd* 2011

BRITISH EMBASSY
PO Box 801, Off Sharia Al Baladiya, Khartoum East
T (+249) (1) 8377 7105 E amged.mohamed@fco.gov.uk
W http://ukinsudan.fco.gov.uk
Ambassador Extraordinary and Plenipotentiary, HE Nicholas Kay, CMG, *apptd* 2010

BRITISH COUNCIL
PO Box 1253, 14 Abu Sinn Street, Khartoum Central
T (+249) 183 780817 W www.britishcouncil.org/africa
Director, Richard Weyers

DEFENCE

The army has 360 main battle tanks, 419 armoured personnel carriers and 75 armoured infantry fighting vehicles. The navy has 4 patrol and coastal combatant vessels at 3 bases. The air force has 84 combat aircraft and 31 armed helicopters.

Military expenditure – US$696m (2009 est)
Military personnel – 109,300: army 105,000, navy 1,300, air force 3,000; paramilitary 17,500
Conscription duration – 24 months

ECONOMY AND TRADE

Since 1997 Sudan has worked with the IMF to implement economic reforms which, despite the country's political instability and vulnerability to drought, have stabilised the economy. In 1999 Sudan began exporting oil, and increases in oil and agricultural production, light industry and exports have resulted in steady growth in GDP in recent years. However, many of the oilfields lie in the south and control is disputed with South Sudan.

Agriculture, much at subsistence level, provides employment for around 80 per cent of the workforce and contributes 32.1 per cent of GDP. Mechanised and traditional agriculture is practised in areas with sufficient rainfall and irrigation. The principal crops include cotton, groundnuts, sorghum, millet, wheat, gum arabic, sugar cane, tropical fruits and livestock. Industry consists of oil extraction and refining, cotton ginning, manufacture of textiles, cement, edible oils, sugar, soap, shoes, pharmaceuticals, armaments and vehicle assembly. Industry contributes 29 per cent of GDP and services 38.9 per cent.

The main trading partners are China, Japan and India. Principal exports are oil and petroleum products, cotton, sesame, livestock, groundnuts, gum arabic and sugar. The main imports are foodstuffs, manufactured goods, refinery and transport equipment, medicines, chemicals, textiles and wheat.

GNI – US$49,255m; US$1,220 per capita (2009)
Annual average growth of GDP – 5.2 per cent (2010 est)
Inflation rate – 11.8 per cent (2010 est)
Population below poverty line – 40 per cent (2004 est)
Unemployment – 18.7 per cent (2002 est)
Total external debt – US$37,980m (2010 est)
Imports – US$8,200m (2009)
Exports – US$7,800m (2009)

BALANCE OF PAYMENTS
Trade – US$1,827m surplus (2010)
Current Account – US$5,229m deficit (2008)

Trade with UK	2009	2010
Imports from UK	£122,925,450	£138,248,418
Exports to UK	£17,821,590	£11,021,070

COMMUNICATIONS
Large areas of the country lack basic infrastructure, which has been a focus of development since the late 1990s. The railway network is about 5,980km in length. There are 11,900km of roads, of which 4,320km are surfaced, and there are over 4,000km of navigable waterways, including 1,700km on the White and Blue Nile rivers. Port Sudan, on the Red Sea, is the main seaport. The principal airport is at Khartoum, and there are over 100 other airports and airfields. Sudan Airways provides domestic and international flights.

The fixed-line telephone system is being upgraded; mobile phone services are growing rapidly. In 2009 there were 370,000 fixed lines in use, 15.3 million mobile phone subscribers and 4.2 million internet users.

EDUCATION AND HEALTH
Education is free for most children, and compulsory for eight years; six years of primary education is followed by at least two years of secondary education. There are three types of secondary school: general, academic and vocational. The primary language of instruction is Arabic.
Literacy rate – 60.9 per cent (2008 est)
Gross enrolment ratio (percentage of relevant age group) –
   primary 74 per cent; secondary 38 per cent (2009 est)
Health expenditure (per capita) – US$95 (2009)
Hospital beds (per 1,000 people) – 0.7 (2004–9)

MEDIA
Radio and television are controlled by the government, and news reports are scrutinised by a military censor. There are no wholly privately owned television stations. It is possible to access foreign broadcasts via satellite television and international radio stations. There are several privately owned newspapers but their freedom of expression is limited. A number of broadcasters and

newspapers operate in the country's south, some with foreign funding.

SOUTH SUDAN
The Republic of South Sudan

Area – c.644,629 sq. km
Capital – Juba
Major cities – Malakal, Wau
Currency – Sudanese pound (SDP) of 100 piastres
Population – 9–11 million; mainly Nilotic and black African peoples, of which the largest group is the Dinka
Religion – Christian, animist; many animists also follow Christian practices
Language – English (official), Arabic, indigenous languages
National Day – 9 July (Independence day)

HISTORY AND POLITICS
The history of the area is largely unrecorded until the early 19th century, as natural barriers prevented the invasions and occupations affecting northern Sudan. In the 19th century, Egypt attempted to extend its influence into the region but the south was only joined with the north with the arrival of the British in the late 19th century, becoming part of a joint Anglo-Egyptian condominium from 1899. Following the independence of Sudan in 1955, tensions between the dominant Arab, Muslim north and the black African, Christian and animist south led to civil war from 1955 to 1972, and again in 1983. A peace process began in 2000 and the parties to it – the government, the Sudan People's Liberation Army/Movement (SPLA/M) and the southern National Democratic Alliance – finalised a peace agreement in 2004. Under this, the southern parties joined a national unity government, a largely autonomous administration was set up in the south in October 2005 and a referendum on independence for the south was held after six years.

In the referendum in January 2011, the south voted overwhelmingly to separate from the north. In the run up to independence on 9 July, disputes led to a deteriorating security situation in border areas, particularly over control of the oil-rich territory of Abyei. A separate referendum in Abyei on whether to join northern or southern Sudan has been postponed indefinitely because of the conflict, while South Kurdufan and Blue Nile states are to hold 'popular consultations' on their status.

POLITICAL SYSTEM
The transitional constitution, which came into force at independence, will remain in force until a permanent constitution is adopted. It provides for the current president of the government of South Sudan to become president of the independent republic, and for the South Sudan Legislative Assembly to be reconstituted as a bicameral National Legislature. This will consist of the National Legislative Assembly (comprising the current South Sudan Legislative Assembly, plus South Sudanese members of Sudan's National Assembly) and the Council of States (comprising South Sudanese members of Sudan's Council of States, plus 20 representatives appointed by the president). The president and legislature will serve a four-year term.

The republic has 10 states, each with a legislative assembly and executive.

HEAD OF STATE
President, Salva Kiir Mayardit, *sworn in under draft constitution* 9 July 2011
Vice-President, Riek Machar Teny

SELECTED GOVERNMENT MINISTERS *as at July 2011*
Foreign Affairs, Deng Alor Kuol
Internal Affairs, Maj.-Gen. Gier Chuang Aluong
Finance, David Deng Athorbei
Education, Michael Milli Hussein

SURINAME

Republiek Suriname – Republic of Suriname

Area – 163,820 sq. km
Capital – Paramaribo; population, 259,343 (2009 est)
Major towns – Lelydorp, Nieuw Nickerie
Currency – Suriname dollar of 100 cents
Population – 486,618 rising at 1.11 per cent a year (2010 est); Hindustani (37 per cent), Creole (31 per cent), Javanese (15 per cent), Maroons (10 per cent), Amerindian (2 per cent), Chinese (2 per cent) (est)
Religion – Christian 48 per cent, Hindu 27 per cent, Muslim 20 per cent (predominantly Sunni), indigenous beliefs 5 per cent (est)
Language – Dutch (official), English, Surinamese (Sranang Tongo), Caribbean Hindustani (a dialect of Hindi), Javanese
Population density – 3 per sq. km (2009)
Urban population – 75 per cent (2008 est)
Median age (years) – 28.3 (2010 est)
National anthem – 'God zij met ons Suriname' ['God Be With Our Suriname']
National day – 25 November (Independence Day)
Life expectancy (years) – 73.98 (2010 est)
Mortality rate – 5.53 (2010 est)
Birth rate – 16.61 (2010 est)
Infant mortality rate – 18.19 (2010 est)
HIV/AIDS adult prevalence – 1 per cent (2009 est)
Death penalty – Retained (not used since 1982)
CPI score – 3.7 (2009)
Literacy rate – 90.6 per cent (2008 est)

CLIMATE AND TERRAIN
The narrow, swampy coastal plain is home to about 90 per cent of the population. From the coastal belt, the land rises to a hilly interior covered by tropical rainforest and savannah; the rainforest contains a great diversity of flora and fauna. Elevation extremes range from 1,230m (Juliana Top) to −2m (coastal plain). The land is drained by several rivers, some of which have been dammed to create large artificial lakes used to generate hydro-electric power. The climate is tropical, moderated by the north-east trade winds. There are two wet seasons, from April to August and November to February.

HISTORY AND POLITICS
Although visited and claimed by Spanish explorers in 1593, early European settlements all failed. A British colony was founded in 1651 but this was ceded to the Dutch in 1667. Dutch rule was interrupted by British occupation during the French Revolutionary and Napoleonic wars, but was restored in 1816. The colony, known as Dutch Guiana, became autonomous in 1954, and achieved independence in 1975 as Suriname. At independence, about 40 per cent of the population emigrated to the Netherlands.

The early years of independence were politically unstable, with a period of military rule under Desi Bouterse following a coup in 1980. Democratic, civilian rule was restored with elections in 1987, but the military overthrew the government in 1990 in a coup engineered by Bouterse. Democratic elections in 1991 were won by the New Front for Democracy and Development alliance, led by Ronald Venetiaan, who became president. President Venetiaan introduced an unpopular austerity programme, which improved the economy but lost him the 1996 election.

Ronald Venetiaan was elected president again in 2000, and again introduced an austerity programme to tackle dire economic conditions; he was re-elected in 2005. After the 2010 legislative election, the Mega Combination bloc, dominated by Desi Bouterse's National Democratic Party, held the most seats in the legislature, and agreed with the A Combination bloc to form a coalition government. Desi Bouterse was subsequently elected president by parliament.

POLITICAL SYSTEM
Under the 1987 constitution, the executive president is elected for a five-year term by a two-thirds majority in the legislature or, if the required majority cannot be achieved, by a specially convened United Peoples' Assembly including district and local council representatives. The vice-president is elected in the same way. The unicameral National Assembly has 51 members directly elected for a five-year term. The council of ministers is appointed by the president and chaired by the vice-president.

HEAD OF STATE
President, Desi Bouterse, *elected* 19 July 2010, *sworn in* 12 August 2010
Vice-President, Robert Ameerali

SELECTED GOVERNMENT MEMBERS *as at July 2011*
Defence, Lamuré Latour
Finance, Adelien Wijnerman
Foreign Affairs, Winston Lackin
Internal Affairs, Soewarto Moestadja

HONORARY CONSULATE OF THE REPUBLIC OF SURINAME
127 Pier House, 31 Cheyne Walk, London SW3 5HN
T 07768-196 326 E ajethu@honoraryconsul.info
W www.honoraryconsul.info
Honorary consul, Amwedhkar Jethu

BRITISH AMBASSADOR
HE Andrew Ayre, *apptd* 2011, resident at Georgetown, Guyana

DEFENCE

The army has 15 armoured personnel carriers. The navy has 8 patrol and coastal combatant vessels at a base in Paramaribo. The air force has 4 combat capable aircraft.

Military budget – US$49m (2010)
Military personnel – 1,840: army 1,400, navy 240, air force 200

ECONOMY AND TRADE

Former president Venetiaan introduced policies that contained rampant inflation and other economic problems, and produced steady growth for a few years before the global downturn, which caused the economy to contract owing to reduced global prices for key commodities. The mainstays of the economy are mining, especially bauxite and gold, and oil and alumina production; these account for 85 per cent of exports and 25 per cent of government revenue, making the economy vulnerable to global price fluctuations. Bauxite reserves are declining, but oil production is increasing from existing offshore fields and onshore exploration has begun. Other industries include forestry, food processing and fishing. Industry accounts for 24.4 per cent of GDP and services for 64.8 per cent. Agriculture employs only 8 per cent of the population but produces 10.8 per cent of GDP.

The main trading partners are the USA, Canada, the Netherlands, Belgium and Trinidad and Tobago. Principal exports are alumina, gold, crude oil, timber, fish and shrimps, rice and bananas. The main imports are capital equipment, petroleum, foodstuffs, cotton and consumer goods.

GNI – US$2,738m; US$4,760 per capita (2008)
Annual average growth of GDP – 3.5 per cent (2010 est)
Inflation rate – 6.4 per cent (2007 est)
Unemployment – 9.5 per cent (2004 est)
Total external debt – US$504.3m (2005 est)
Imports – US$500m (2009)
Exports – US$500m (2009)

BALANCE OF PAYMENTS
Trade – US$381m surplus (2010)
Current Account – US$121m surplus (2008)

Trade with UK	2009	2010
Imports from UK	£11,224,629	£9,895,612
Exports to UK	£2,979,890	£493,686

COMMUNICATIONS

There are 4,300km of roads in total, of which approximately one-quarter is surfaced. There are no railways. The 1,200km of waterways provide the most effective means of travel in the interior. The main seaport is Paramaribo. There are 51 airports and airfields; the principal airport is at Paramaribo.

The telephone system is good and mobile phone services have expanded rapidly. Combined fixed-line and mobile density is now about 175 per 100 people.

MEDIA

State-owned broadcast media offer a range of views, and operate alongside commercial radio and television stations. The two daily newspapers, *De West* and *De Ware Tijd*, are privately owned. The government upholds freedom of expression.

SWAZILAND

Umbuso weSwatini – Kingdom of Swaziland

Area – 17,364 sq. km
Capital – Mbabane; population, 73,815 (2009 est). Lobamba is the legislative capital
Major town – Manzini
Currency – Lilangeni (E; plural *Emalangeni*) of 100 cents; the Lilangeni has a par value with the South African rand, which is also in circulation
Population – 1,354,051 rising at 1.21 per cent a year (2010 est)
Religion – Christian (Zionist 40 per cent, Roman Catholic 20 per cent), Muslim 10 per cent, other 30 per cent
Language – English, siSwati (both official)
Population density – 69 per sq. km (2009)
Urban population – 25 per cent (2008 est)
Median age (years) – 20.1 (2010 est)
National anthem – 'Nkulunkulu Mnikati wetibusiso temaSwati' ['Oh God, Bestower of Blessings on the Swazi']
National day – 6 September (Independence Day)
Life expectancy (years) – 47.97 (2010 est)
Mortality rate – 14.99 (2010 est)
Birth rate – 27.12 (2010 est)
Infant mortality rate – 66.71 (2010 est)
HIV/AIDS adult prevalence – 25.9 per cent (2009 est)
Death penalty – Retained (not used since 1983)
CPI score – 3.2 (2010)
Literacy rate – 79.6 per cent (2008 est)
Gross enrolment ratio (percentage of relevant age group) – primary 108 per cent; secondary 53 per cent (2007 est)
Health expenditure (per capita) – US$156 (2009)
Hospital beds (per 1,000 people) – 2.1 (2004–9)

CLIMATE AND TERRAIN

The main regions of the landlocked country are: the densely forested and mountainous Highveld along the western border, with an average altitude of 1,219m; the Middleveld, a mixed farming area which averages about 609m in altitude, and the Lowveld, which was mainly scrubland until the introduction of sugar cane plantations, in the centre; and the Lubombo ridge, along the eastern edge of the Lowveld. Elevation extremes range from 1,862m (Emlembe) to 21m (Great Usutu river). Four rivers, the Komati, Usutu, Mbuluzi and Ngwavuma, flow from west to east.

The climate varies; the Highveld is humid and temperate, the Middleveld and Lubombo are subtropical, and the Lowveld is tropical and semi-arid. Average temperatures in Mbabane, in the Highveld, range from 5°C in June to 25°C in January and December.

HISTORY AND POLITICS

The Swazi people are believed to have arrived in the area in the 16th century, and by the mid-17th century had developed a strong kingdom three times the size of the present country. This became a protectorate of the Boer republic of the Transvaal in 1884, and subsequently of Britain. The Kingdom of Swaziland became independent in 1968.

In 1973 King Sobhuza II suspended the constitution, banned political parties and assumed absolute power. The parliamentary system was replaced by traditional tribal communities *(tinkhundla)*. Sobhuza II died in 1982, and was succeeded by a son who was a minor. The regency between 1982 and 1986 led to power struggles within the royal family, but the real power passed to the Dlamini clan, which continues to dominate the government.

Demands for democratisation of the constitution have grown over the past 20 years, with the campaigning of political movements and trade unions supported by popular demonstrations, general strikes and blockades of the border with South Africa.

Swaziland has the highest levels of HIV/AIDS infection in the world, and as a consequence faces serious demographic, economic and social problems.

POLITICAL SYSTEM

The 2005 constitution retains the executive powers of the king; it appears to permit political parties while maintaining the ban on their members standing for election. The head of state is a hereditary king who is effectively an absolute monarch who rules by decree. There is a bicameral parliament comprising a 30-member senate and a 65-member House of Assembly; members of both serve a five-year term. Each of the country's 55 administrative districts *(tinkhundla)* directly elects one member to the House of Assembly and the king appoints ten members; the new constitution increases these to 60 elected and 15 appointed members. The members of the House of Assembly elect ten of their own number to the senate and a further 20 senators are appointed by the king.

HEAD OF STATE

HM The King of Swaziland, King Mswati III, crowned 25 April 1986

SELECTED GOVERNMENT MEMBERS *as at July 2011*
Prime Minister, Barnabas Sibusiso Dlamini
Deputy Prime Minister, Themba Masuku
Finance, Majozi Sithole
Foreign Affairs, Lutfo Dlamini
Home Affairs, Chief Mgwagwa Gamedze

KINGDOM OF SWAZILAND HIGH COMMISSION
20 Buckingham Gate, London SW1E 6LB
T 020-7630 6611 E enquiries@swaziland.org.uk
High Commissioner, HE Dumsile Sukati, *apptd* 2011

BRITISH HIGH COMMISSIONER
HE Dr Nicola Brewer, *apptd 2009,* resident at Pretoria (Tshwane), South Africa

ECONOMY AND TRADE

The country is very poor, with over two-thirds of the population living below the poverty line. Customs dues from the South African Customs Union and remittances from expatriates working in South Africa are a vital supplement to the domestic economy; customs revenue dropped sharply in the global downturn and the government applied for international financial assistance.

Subsistence agriculture occupies about 70 per cent of the population and contributes 8.6 per cent of GDP. Sugar cane, cotton, citrus fruits and pineapples are the main cash crops and the basis of industries producing sugar, canned fruit and soft drink concentrates. Coal mining has become less important since the 1980s with diversification into manufacturing such products as textiles, clothing, wood pulp and refrigerators. However, a shift in global trading concessions devastated the clothing industry in 2005, leaving thousands unemployed, and has affected the sugar industry, although this has adapted. Industry contributes 42 per cent of GDP and services 49.4 per cent.

South Africa accounts for about 60 per cent of exports and over 90 per cent of imports. Principal exports are the products of agriculture and manufacturing. The main imports are vehicles, machinery, transport equipment, foodstuffs, petroleum products and chemicals.

GNI – US$2,874m; US$2,470 per capita (2009)
Annual average growth of GDP – 2 per cent (2010 est)
Inflation rate – 5 per cent (2010 est)
Population below poverty line – 69 per cent (2006)
Unemployment – 40 per cent (2006 est)
Total external debt – US$497m (2010 est)
Imports – US$1,500m (2009)
Exports – US$1,500m (2009)

BALANCE OF PAYMENTS
Trade – US$28m deficit (2010)
Current Account – US$187m deficit (2009)

Trade with UK	2009	2010
Imports from UK	£6,082,510	£5,245,896
Exports to UK	£15,049,505	£12,864,098

COMMUNICATIONS

The railway network is 301km long and connects with the Mozambique port of Maputo and the South African railway to Richards Bay and Durban. There are 3,594km of roads, of which 1,078km are surfaced. There is an international airport at Manzini, which is expected to be replaced by the new Sikhuphe International Airport by late 2011. Swaziland Airlink, in association with South African Airlink, provides scheduled air services to southern and eastern Africa.

Although modern, the fixed-line telephone system is not extensive and mobile phone services have grown rapidly. There were 44,000 fixed lines in use, 656,000 mobile phone subscribers and 90,100 internet users in 2009.

MEDIA

The media is under tight government control. State-run broadcasters provide the only television and radio channels, apart from an American evangelical Christian radio station which uses local transmitters to broadcast regionally. One daily newspaper supports the government, the other carries little political content.

SWEDEN

Konungariket Sverige – Kingdom of Sweden

Area – 450,295 sq. km
Capital – Stockholm; population, 1,278,820 (2009 est)
Major cities – Gothenburg, Malmo, Uppsala
Currency – Swedish krona of 100 ore
Population – 9,074,055 rising at 0.16 per cent a year
  (2010 est)
Religion – Christian (Lutheran 71 per cent, other
  Protestant 4 per cent), Muslim 5 per cent (est)
Language – Swedish (official), Finnish, Sami dialects,
  Meankieli, Romani, Yiddish (all official national
  minority languages)
Population density – 23 per sq. km (2009)
Urban population – 85 per cent (2008 est)
Median age (years) – 41.7 (2010 est)
National anthem – 'Du Gamla, Du Fria' ['Thou Ancient,
  Thou Freeborn']
National day – 6 June (Flag Day)
Life expectancy (years) – 80.97 (2010 est)
Mortality rate – 10.2 (2010 est)
Birth rate – 10.14 (2010 est)
Infant mortality rate – 2.74 (2010 est)
Death penalty – Abolished for all crimes (since 1972)
CPI score – 9.2 (2010)

CLIMATE AND TERRAIN

The terrain is mostly flat or rolling lowlands in the south
and along the east coast, with mountains in the west.
Elevation extremes range from 2,111m (Kebnekaise) to
−2.4m (reclaimed bay of Lake Hammarsjon). There are
many lakes, including Vanern, Vattern, Malaren and
Hjalmaren in the south, and over 20,000 islands off the
coast near Stockholm. The climate is temperate in the
south and subarctic in the north; average temperatures in
Stockholm range from −5°C in January to 22°C in July.

HISTORY AND POLITICS

Sweden takes its name from the Svear people who were
the dominant population in the east from *c.*500 AD, while
the Goths inhabited the west. A kingdom had emerged
from a gradual union of the two peoples by *c.*1000,
although the south and west remained under Danish rule
until the 17th century. During the Viking expansion
(*c.*700–1000), the Swedes colonised the eastern Baltic,
Finland and Russia; Finland was incorporated into the
kingdom in the 12th century. The Union of Kalmar
(1397) brought Sweden and Norway under Danish rule.
Sweden regained its independence following a rebellion
by noblemen in 1523 which resulted in the election of
Gustav I to the Swedish throne.
  Sweden's power reached its zenith in the 17th century

under Gustav II. The Danes were driven out of southern
Sweden, the Baltic coast of Russia was seized and the
Swedish army pushed into Germany after vanquishing the
Catholic League. Swedish power waned with its defeat in
the Great Northern War (1700–21). Finland was lost to
Russia in 1809. Norway was ceded to Sweden by the
congress of Vienna (1814–15) but gained its
independence in 1905.
  Sweden remained neutral during both world wars.
Post-war politics has been dominated by Social
Democrat-led coalitions which established a mixed
economy and a generous welfare state between 1946 and
1969. Right-wing and centrist parties have held power in
1976–82, 1991–4 and since 2006. Sweden joined the
EU in 1995, but the government decided against
membership of the eurozone in 1997, a decision
confirmed by referendum in 2003.
  After the 2010 general election, the Social Democrats
remained the largest single party in the legislature but
with fewer seats than the four-party Alliance for Sweden
coalition government (comprising the Moderate Party,
Centre Party, Liberal People's Party and Christian
Democrats) that had been in government since the 2006
election. The Alliance for Sweden coalition continued in
office as a minority government.

POLITICAL SYSTEM

Sweden is a hereditary constitutional monarchy. The
1975 constitution was amended in 1979 to vest the
succession in the monarch's eldest child irrespective of
sex. The unicameral legislature, the *Riksdag*, has 349
members directly elected by proportional representation
for a four-year term. The prime minister appoints the
council of ministers.
  Sweden is divided into 21 counties *(lan)* and 290
municipalities *(kommun)*.

HEAD OF STATE

HM The King of Sweden, King Carl XVI Gustaf, KG,
  born 30 April 1946, *succeeded* 15 September 1973
Heir, HRH Crown Princess Victoria Ingrid Alice Desiree,
  Duchess of Vastergotland, *born* 14 July 1977

SELECTED GOVERNMENT MEMBERS *as at July 2011*
Prime Minister, Fredrik Reinfeldt
Deputy Prime Minister, Jan Bjorklund
Defence, Sten Tolgfors
Finance, Anders Borg
Foreign Affairs, Carl Bildt

EMBASSY OF SWEDEN
11 Montagu Place, London W1H 2AL
T 020-7917 6400 E ambassaden.london@foreign.ministry.se
W www.swedenabroad.com/london
Ambassador Extraordinary and Plenipotentiary,
  HE Nicola Clase, *apptd* 2010

BRITISH EMBASSY
PO Box 27819, Skarpogatan 6–8, 115 93 Stockholm
T (+46) (8) 671 3000 E info@britishembassy.se
W http://ukinsweden.fco.gov.uk
Ambassador Extraordinary and Plenipotentiary,
  HE Paul Johnston, *apptd* 2011

BRITISH COUNCIL
c/o British Embassy
T (+46) (8) 671 3110 W www.britishcouncil.org/sweden
Country Manager, Elin Svensson

DEFENCE

The army has 280 main battle tanks, 489 armoured personnel carriers and 354 armoured infantry fighting vehicles. The navy has 6 submarines and 19 patrol and coastal vessels at 2 bases. The air force has 130 combat aircraft.

Sweden has a policy of non-alignment in peace and neutrality in war, and has declined to become a member of NATO.

Military budget – US$5,540m (2010)

Military personnel – 21,070: army 7,332, navy 3,423, air force 3,770; paramilitary 800; voluntary auxiliary organisations 30,000

Conscription – abolished from July 2010

ECONOMY AND TRADE

Sweden developed from an agricultural to an industrial economy in the early 20th century. The prosperity that had funded the generous welfare state after 1946 ended in the early 1990s, when Sweden experienced a deep recession. It recovered to experience strong growth before briefly entering recession again in 2008–9 as a result of the global downturn.

The main, export-orientated industries are engineering and high-tech manufacturing, mining and forestry. Forests cover over half the total land area and sustain the timber, finished wood products, pulp and paper milling industries. Mineral resources include iron ore, lead, zinc, sulphur, granite, marble, precious and heavy metals (the latter not exploited) and extensive deposits of low-grade uranium ore. The engineering sector provides 50 per cent of output and exports, particularly specialised machinery and systems such as electrical and electronic equipment and armaments, and motor vehicles and aircraft; other industries produce pharmaceuticals, plastics and chemicals.

Sweden has no significant resources of hydrocarbon fuels and relies upon imported gas and coal for 50 per cent of its energy needs and hydroelectricity for about 15 per cent. In 2009 the government reversed its previous policy of phasing out nuclear power. Less than 10 per cent of the land area is farmland and only 1.1 per cent of the labour force is employed in farming. Agriculture contributes 1.7 per cent of GDP, industry 26.1 per cent and services 72.2 per cent.

The main trading partners are other EU states, Norway and the USA. Principal exports include machinery, vehicles, paper products, pulp and wood, iron and steel products, and chemicals. The main imports are machinery, oil and petroleum products, chemicals, vehicles, iron and steel, foodstuffs and clothing.

GNI – US$413,384m; US$48,840 per capita (2009)

Annual average growth of GDP – 4.1 per cent (2010 est)

Inflation rate – 1.4 per cent (2010 est)

Unemployment – 8.3 per cent (2010 est)

Total external debt – US$853,300m (2010)

Imports – US$120,100m (2009)

Exports – US$131,300m (2009)

BALANCE OF PAYMENTS

Trade – US$9,802m surplus (2010)

Current Account – US$37,279m surplus (2008)

Trade with UK	2009	2010
Imports from UK	£4,106,945,098	£5,372,739,533
Exports to UK	£5,359,370,008	£6,532,167,636

COMMUNICATIONS

The railway network is 11,633km in length. There are 572,900km of roads, including 1,900km of motorways. There are also 2,052km of waterways, navigable for small steamers and barges. The main ports are Gothenburg, Helsingborg, Malmo and Stockholm. The principal airports are at Malmo, Gothenburg, Lulea, Malmo and Umea. Scandinavian Airlines provides international and domestic flights, and domestic flights are also provided by Malmo Aviation. The Oresund Bridge connects Sweden to Denmark.

The modern telecommunications systems provided services to 5.1 million fixed-line subscribers, 11.4 million mobile phone subscribers and 8.4 million internet users in 2009.

EDUCATION AND HEALTH

The state education system provides nine years of free and compulsory schooling from the age of seven to 16 in the comprehensive elementary schools. A majority of pupils continue into further education of three years' duration in the upper secondary schools, and a unified higher education system administered in six regional areas containing one of the universities: Uppsala (founded 1477); Lund (1668); Stockholm (1878); Gothenburg (1887); Umea (1963) and Linkoping (1967).

Gross enrolment ratio (percentage of relevant age group) – primary 95 per cent; secondary 103 per cent; tertiary 71 per cent (2008 est)

Health expenditure (per capita) – US$4,252 (2009)

MEDIA

Public television is run by Sveriges Television (SVT). There are a number of commercial stations and around two-thirds of households have cable or satellite television. Commercial radio began in 1993, and some of the main stations now have near-national networks, in competition with public broadcaster Sveriges Radio. The country is among the world's top consumers of newspapers and the government provides subsidies to newspapers regardless of their political affiliation. There are four Stockholm-based daily newspapers, one based in Gothenburg and one in Malmo.

CULTURE

Several Swedish writers have become globally successful, among them crime-fiction writers Henning Mankel (*b.* 1948) and Stieg Larsson (1954–2004), and Astrid Lindgren (1907–2002), the creator of *Pippi Longstocking*. A number of Swedes have received Academy awards, including directors Ingmar Bergman (1918–2007), and Lasse Hallstrom (*b.* 1946) and actors Greta Garbo (1905–90) and Ingrid Bergman (1915–82). ABBA is the country's best-known musical export and has sold over 370 million albums; founders Bjorn Ulvaeus and Benny Andersson also had international hits with the stage musicals *Mamma Mia!* and *Chess*. In science, astronomer Anders Celsius (1701–44) devised the eponymous temperature scale, and the chemist and industrialist Alfred Nobel (1833–96) invented dynamite and founded the Nobel prizes.

SWITZERLAND

Schweizerische Eidgenossenschaft/Confédération suisse/ Confederazione Svizzera/Confederaziun svizra – Swiss Confederation

Area – 41,277 sq. km
Capital – Bern; population, 345,720 (2009 est)
Major cities – Basel, Geneva, Lausanne, Zurich
Currency – Swiss franc of 100 rappen (or centimes)
Population – 7,623,438 rising at 0.22 per cent a year
    (2010 est); German (65 per cent), French (18 per cent),
    Italian (10 per cent), Romansch (1 per cent) (est)
Religion – Christian (Roman Catholic 42 per cent,
    Protestant 35 per cent, Orthodox 2 per cent), Muslim 4
    per cent (majority Sunni) (2000)
Language – German, French, Italian, Romansch
    (all official), Serbo-Croatian, Albanian, Portuguese,
    Spanish, English
Population density – 193 per sq. km (2009)
Urban population – 73 per cent (2008 est)
Median age (years) – 41.3 (2010 est)
National anthem – 'Schweizerpsalm'/'Cantique
    suisse'/'Salmo svizzero'/'Psalm svizzer' ['Swiss Psalm']
National day – 1 August (Confederation Day)
Life expectancy (years) – 80.97 (2010 est)
Mortality rate – 8.65 (2010 est)
Birth rate – 9.56 (2010 est)
Infant mortality rate – 4.12 (2010 est)
Death penalty – Abolished for all crimes (since 1992)
CPI score – 8.7 (2010)

CLIMATE AND TERRAIN

Landlocked Switzerland is the most mountainous country in Europe. The central plateau of rolling hills, plains and over 1,500 lakes is enclosed by mountains. The Jura mountains lie in the north-west and the Alps, which cover two-thirds of the country, occupy the south and east. Elevation extremes range from 4,634m (Dufourspitze, Alps) to 195m (Lake Maggiore). Lakes Neuchâtel, Lucerne and Zurich lie wholly within the country, but Lake Maggiore is shared with Italy, Lake Geneva with France and Lake Constance with Germany and Austria. The Rhine, Rhône and Inn rivers all rise in the Alps. The climate is temperate, with conditions that vary with altitude. Average temperatures in Zurich range from –4°C in January to 23°C in July.

HISTORY AND POLITICS

The area was conquered by the Romans in 58 BC and then overrun by Germanic tribes in the fourth century AD. It was a province of the medieval Holy Roman Empire from 1033. The Swiss confederation began in 1291 as a defensive alliance of three cantons to protect their

autonomy, and expanded during the following centuries, becoming independent of the Habsburgs in the 14th century. Its independence was recognised by the Treaty of Westphalia in 1648. French revolutionary forces captured Switzerland in 1789 and named it the Helvetic Republic. Independence was restored in 1814, and the congress of Vienna (1815) joined Geneva, Neuchatel and Valais to the confederation and recognised the country's perpetual neutrality in international affairs. A new constitution was adopted in 1848 which replaced the loose confederation of cantons with a federal state and enhanced the powers of the central government.

Many policy decisions are submitted to national referendums. Although the federal government has pursued a policy of gradual integration with the EU and applied for membership in 1992, referendums have rejected membership of the European Economic Area (1992), approved bilateral trade agreements with the EU (2000), and rejected EU membership (2001).

Proportional representation, introduced in 1919, resulted in coalition governments throughout the 20th and into the 21st century. Apart from a 12-month period in 2007–8, since 1959 the federal government has been a coalition of four parties: the Swiss People's Party (SVP), the Social Democratic Party, the Christian Democratic People's Party and the Radical Democratic Party. Following the 2007 legislative election, the SVP remained the largest party in the legislature, although it withdrew from the coalition government for a year from December 2007 after one of its ministers was voted out of office. A legislative election is scheduled for 23 October 2011.

POLITICAL SYSTEM

Under the 1998 constitution, the head of state is a president elected annually (along with the vice-president) for a one-year term by the federal legislature from the members of the Federal Council; consecutive terms may not be served. The bicameral legislature, the Federal Assembly, has two chambers: the National Council has 200 members, directly elected for a four-year term; the Council of States has 46 members (two from each canton and one from each half-canton) directly elected within each canton for a four-year term.

Executive power is in the hands of a Federal Council of seven members, elected for a four-year term by the Federal Assembly after every legislative election. The Federal Council is chaired by the president. Not more than one person from the same canton may be elected a member of the Council; however, there is a tradition that Italian- and French-speaking areas should between them be represented on the council by at least two members.

Any citizen able to obtain 100,000 voters' signatures in support of holding a referendum on a given issue can initiate a national referendum.

SELECTED GOVERNMENT MEMBERS *as at July 2011*
President of the Swiss Confederation, Micheline Calmy-Rey
Vice-President, Finance, Eveline Widmer-Schlumpf
Defence, Ueli Maurer
Public Economy, Johann Schneider-Ammann
Interior, Didier Burkhalter

EMBASSY OF SWITZERLAND
16–18 Montagu Place, London W1H 2BQ
T 020-7616 6000 E lon.vertretung@eda.admin.ch
W www.eda.admin.ch/london

Ambassador Extraordinary and Plenipotentiary,
HE Anton Thalmann, *apptd* 2010

BRITISH EMBASSY
Thunstrasse 50, 3005 Bern
T (+41) (31) 359 7700 E info@britishembassy.ch
W http://ukinswitzerland.fco.gov.uk
Ambassador Extraordinary and Plenipotentiary,
HE Sarah Gillett, CMG, MVO, *apptd* 2009

BRITISH COUNCIL
PO Box 532, Sennweg 2, 3000 Bern 9
T (+41) (31) 301 1473 W www.britishcouncil.org/switzerland
Director, Caroline Morrissey, MBE

CONFEDERAL STRUCTURE

There are 23 cantons, three of which are subdivided, making 20 cantons and six half-cantons, or 26 in all. Each canton and half-canton has its own government and a substantial degree of autonomy. The main language in 19 of the cantons is German; in the others it is French (*) or Italian (†).

The confederation consists of: Aargau, Appenzell-Ausserrhoden, Appenzell-Innerrhoden, Basel-Country, Basel-Town, Bern, *Fribourg, *Geneva, Glarus, Graubünden/Grischun, *Jura, Lucerne, *Neuchatel, Nidwalden, Obwalden, St Gallen, Schaffhausen, Schwyz, Solothurn, Thurgau, †Ticino, Uri, *Valais, *Vaud, Zug and Zurich.

DEFENCE

The army has 344 main battle tanks, 346 armoured personnel carriers and 154 armoured infantry fighting vehicles. The air force has 87 combat aircraft.
Military budget – US$4,570m (2010)
Military personnel – 25,620: joint 3,711 active, 21,909 conscripts
Conscription duration – 18 weeks, then 3-week refresher courses

ECONOMY AND TRADE

Switzerland has a prosperous and stable market economy with low unemployment and a highly skilled labour force. Its prosperity is based on banking, financial services and export-orientated industrial manufacturing. The economy went into recession in 2009 owing to slower export demand and the impact on the banking sector during the 2008 global financial crisis; the largest bank required government support. Although not an EU member, Switzerland has brought many practices in line with the EU's to maintain its competitiveness, and it is currently adopting OECD standards on tax administration and transparency.

Agriculture is practised in the mountain valleys and the central plateau, where grains, fruits and vegetables are grown. Dairy farming and stock-raising are also important. The industrial sector is noted for precision, electrical and mechanical engineering, pharmaceuticals, chemicals, telecommunications, food processing and packaging, and graphics. Banking, insurance and tourism are the major service industries. Agriculture contributes 1.3 per cent of GDP, industry 27.5 per cent and services 71.2 per cent.

The main trading partners are EU countries (especially Germany) and the USA. Principal exports are machinery, chemicals, metals, watches and agricultural products. The main imports are machinery, chemicals, vehicles, metals, agricultural products and textiles.

GNI – US$512,338m; US$65,430 per capita (2009)
Annual average growth of GDP – 2.8 per cent (2010 est)
Inflation rate – 0.7 per cent (2010 est)
Unemployment – 3.9 per cent (2010 est)
Population below poverty line – 7.4 per cent (2009 est)
Total external debt – US$1,190,000m (2010 est)
Imports – US$147,500m (2009)
Exports – US$166,200m (2009)

BALANCE OF PAYMENTS
Trade – US$18,865m surplus (2010)
Current Account – US$11,947m surplus (2008)

Trade with UK	2009	2010
Imports from UK	£5,057,072,305	£11,110,540,359
Exports to UK	£10,268,943,761	£7,498,280,114

COMMUNICATIONS

There are 71,454km of roads, including 1,790km of motorways. Railway track totals 4,876km, almost all of which is electrified. Transnational Alpine routes are served by all-weather road and rail tunnels. The Rhine carries commercial shipping on the 65km stretch from Basel-Rheinfelden and Schaffhausen-Bodensee, and there are 12 navigable lakes. The principal airports are at Zurich, Basel, Bern and Geneva.

Modern telecommunications systems provided services to 4.6 million fixed-line subscribers, 9.2 million mobile phone subscribers and 6.1 million internet users in 2009.

EDUCATION AND HEALTH

Education is controlled by cantonal and communal authorities and is free and compulsory from ages seven to 16. Special schools make a feature of commercial and technical instruction. Major universities include Basel (founded 1460), Bern (1834), Fribourg (1889), Geneva (1873), Lausanne (1890), Zurich (1832) and Neuchatel (1909), the technical universities of Lausanne and Zurich and the economics university of St Gall.
Gross enrolment ratio (percentage of relevant age group) – primary 103 per cent; secondary 96 per cent; tertiary 49 per cent (2008 est)
Health expenditure (per capita) – US$7,141 (2009)
Hospital beds (per 1,000 people) – 5.3 (2004–9)

MEDIA AND CULTURE

The public-service Swiss Broadcasting Corporation (SRG/SSR), which is funded mainly through licence fees, dominates broadcasting; it operates seven television networks and 18 radio stations, broadcasting in all of the country's official languages. Private radio and television stations operate at regional level, and television stations from France, Germany and Italy are widely available through multi-channel cable and satellite television. The press has full editorial freedom. Newspapers tend to be regional, reflecting linguistic divisions: there are two German-language dailies based in Zurich, two French-language dailies in Geneva and an Italian-language daily in Lugano.

Important cultural figures include the writer and philosopher Jean-Jacques Rousseau (1712–78), the psychoanalyst Carl Jung (1875–1961), the poet Carl Spitteler (1845–1924), who won the Nobel prize for literature in 1919, and the writer and founder of modern structural linguistics Ferdinand de Saussure (1857–1913).

SYRIA

Al-Jumhuriyah al-Arabiyah assSuriyah – Syrian Arab Republic

Area – 185,180 sq. km
Capital – Damascus; population, 2,527,260 (2009 est)
Major cities – Aleppo (Halab), Hama (Hamah), Homs (Hims), Latakia (Al Ladhiqiyah)
Currency – Syrian pound (S£) of 100 piastres
Population – 22,198,110 rising at 1.95 per cent a year (2010 est)
Religion – Muslim (Sunni 74 per cent, Druze 3 per cent; other 13 per cent, including Alawite sect), Christian 10 per cent (of which Greek Orthodox is the largest denomination) (est)
Language – Arabic (official), Kurdish, Armenian, Aramaic, Circassian, French
Population density – 115 per sq. km (2009)
Urban population – 54 per cent (2008 est)
Median age (years) – 21.5 (2010 est)
National anthem – 'Homat el Diyar' ['Guardians of the Homeland']
National day – 17 April (Independence Day)
Life expectancy (years) – 74.46 (2010 est)
Mortality rate – 3.7 (2010 est)
Birth rate – 24.44 (2010 est)
Infant mortality rate – 16.14 (2010 est)
Death penalty – Retained
CPI score – 2.5 (2010)

CLIMATE AND TERRAIN

There is a narrow coastal plain and ranges of mountains in the west, and the fertile basin of the river Euphrates in the north-east. The centre and south of the interior consist of semi-arid and desert plateaus. Elevation extremes range from 2,814m (Mt Hermon) to −200m (unnamed location near Lake Tiberias). There is a desert climate in much of the country, moderated by altitude in the mountains, and a Mediterranean climate on the coast. Average temperatures in Damascus range from 2°C in January to 37°C in August.

HISTORY AND POLITICS

The area was successively part of the Phoenician, Persian, Roman and Byzantine empires. It was conquered by Muslim Arabs in the seventh century, and by the Turks in the 11th century. The location of many battles during the medieval Crusades, Syria became part of the Ottoman Empire in 1516. Following the empire's collapse after the First World War, Syria became a mandated territory in 1920, administered by France with the mandated territory of Lebanon as 'Greater Lebanon'. It became independent in 1946 when French forces withdrew. Syria

formed part of the United Arab Republic with Egypt from 1958 to 1961, when it seceded. It was involved in the Arab-Israeli wars in 1948, 1967 and 1973, losing the Golan Heights to Israel in 1967.

Syrian intervention in Lebanon began in 1976, its military presence influencing politics there after the civil war ended. Forces remained until 2005, when they were withdrawn in response to massive popular protests in Lebanon and intense international pressure following the assassination of former Lebanese prime minister Rafik Hariri. Following the withdrawal, many western states continued to accuse Syria of supporting and arming Lebanese militants. Syrian relations with the West have also been strained in recent years by its support for Iraqi insurgents and Palestinian militants, and suspicions that it was attempting to develop weapons of mass destruction. Since the mid 2000s, the country has moved to end its isolation, re-engage with peace processes in the Middle East, and improve relations with the USA and EU states.

The Arab Socialist Renaissance (Ba'ath) Party has been the ruling party since 1963. Hafez al-Assad seized power in a coup in 1970 and was elected president in 1971. He remained president until his death in 2000, when he was succeeded by his son, Bashar al-Assad, who was re-elected unopposed in 2007. Following the 2007 legislative election, the Ba'ath Party and its allies retained a large majority in the legislature. Pro-democracy protests spread to all the major cities since early 2011 despite violent military crackdowns by the government that have killed hundreds and displaced thousands of people; the repression has attracted international condemnation and sanctions. *See also* Events of the Year.

POLITICAL SYSTEM

The 1973 constitution declares that the Arab Socialist Renaissance (Ba'ath) Party is the leading party in the state and society. The executive president is elected for a seven-year term by the legislature and confirmed in office by a national referendum. The president appoints the council of ministers. The unicameral People's Council *(Majlis al-Sha'ab)* has 250 members directly elected for a four-year term. The only candidates permitted to stand in elections are those from the Ba'ath Party, parties allied with it or independents.

HEAD OF STATE
President, Lt-Gen. Bashar al-Assad, *elected* 27 June 2000, *confirmed by referendum* 10 July 2000, *re-elected* 2007
Vice-Presidents, Farouk al-Shara; Najah al-Attar

SELECTED GOVERNMENT MEMBERS *as at July 2011*
Prime Minister, Adel Safar
Defence, Lt.-Gen. Ali Habib Mahmud
Finance, Mohammad al-Jleilati
Foreign Affairs, Walid al-Muallem
Interior, Brig.-Gen. Mohammad Ibrahim al-Shaar

EMBASSY OF THE SYRIAN ARAB REPUBLIC
8 Belgrave Square, London SW1X 8PH
T 020-7245 9012 W www.syremb.com
Ambassador Extraordinary and Plenipotentiary,
HE Sami Khiyami, *apptd* 2004

BRITISH EMBASSY
PO Box 37, Kotob Building, Mohammad Kurd Ali Street, Malki, Damascus
T (+963) (11) 339 1513

E british.embassy.damascus@fco.gov.uk
W http://ukinsyria.fco.gov.uk
Ambassador Extraordinary and Plenipotentiary,
HE Simon Collis *apptd* 2007

BRITISH COUNCIL

PO Box 33105, Maysaloun Street, Shalaan, Damascus
T (+963) (11) 331 0631 W www.britishcouncil.org/syria
Director, Elizabeth White

DEFENCE

The army has 4,950 main battle tanks, 1,500 armoured personnel carriers and up to 2,450 armoured infantry fighting vehicles. The navy has 32 patrol and coastal vessels and 13 armed helicopters at 3 bases. The air force has 555 combat aircraft and 36 armed helicopters.
Military budget – US$1,890m (2010)
Military personnel – 295,000: army 220,000, navy 5,000, air force 30,000, air defence 40,000; paramilitary 108,000
Conscription duration – 30 months

ECONOMY AND TRADE

The economy is state-controlled and predominantly state-owned, although recent modest economic reforms have included some privatisation and the reduction of state subsidies; a stock exchange opened in 2009. Oil and agriculture account for nearly half of GDP, but other activities, such as financial services, telecommunications, tourism and non-oil industry and trade, are becoming increasingly important. Gas is produced for domestic use, and phosphate is mined and processed; other non-oil industry includes the manufacture of textiles, processed food, beverages, tobacco and cement, and car assembly. Agriculture contributes 17.6 per cent of GDP, industry 26.8 per cent and services 55.6 per cent.

The main export markets are Iraq, Lebanon, Germany and Italy; imports come chiefly from Saudi Arabia, China, Turkey and Egypt. Principal exports are crude oil, minerals, petroleum products, fruit and vegetables, cotton fibre, textiles, clothing, meat, livestock and wheat. The main imports are machinery and transport equipment, electric power machinery, food and livestock, metals and metal products, chemicals, plastics, yarn and paper.
GNI – US$50,910m; US$2,410 per capita (2009)
Annual average growth of GDP – 4 per cent (2010 est)
Inflation rate – 5.9 per cent (2010 est)
Population below poverty line – 11.9 per cent (2006 est)
Unemployment – 8.3 per cent (2010 est)
Total external debt – US$7,682m (2010 est)
Imports – US$16,300m (2009)
Exports – US$10,400m (2009)

BALANCE OF PAYMENTS

Trade – US$4,709m deficit (2010)
Current Account – US$1,942m deficit (2008)

Trade with UK	2009	2010
Imports from UK	£147,147,184	£132,954,421
Exports to UK	£69,937,869	£17,009,001

COMMUNICATIONS

There are 2,052km of railways, which link with the networks of neighbouring countries. The country has 97,401km of roads, 19,490km of which are surfaced. The principal airports are at Aleppo and Damascus; internal air services operate between all major cities. The main port is Latakia.

Telecommunications systems are being improved and networks are growing rapidly. In 2009 there were 3.9 million fixed telephone lines in use, 9.7 million mobile phone subscribers and 4.5 million internet users.

EDUCATION AND HEALTH

Education is under state control. Elementary education is free at state schools and is compulsory from the age of seven. Upper secondary education is not compulsory and is free only at state schools. There are universities at Damascus, Halab, Tishrin and Hims.
Literacy rate – 83.7 per cent (2008 est)
Gross enrolment ratio (percentage of relevant age group) – primary 122 per cent; secondary 75 per cent (2009 est)
Health expenditure (per capita) – US$72 (2009)
Hospital beds (per 1,000 people) – 1.5 (2004–9)

MEDIA

The only domestic television network and the main radio channels and newspapers are owned and controlled by the government or the Ba'ath party. There has been a cautious easing of controls since 2000; private publications were licensed, as were private radio stations in 2005, and satellite receivers are now permitted so many viewers have access to foreign television broadcasts. However, news broadcasting remains the monopoly of the state-controlled media, and foreign and domestic media output and the internet are censored.

TAIWAN

T'ai-wan – Taiwan (Republic of China)

Area – 35,980 sq. km
Capital – Taipei; population, 2,646,474 (2001 est)
Major cities – Kaohsiung, Taichung, Tainan
Currency – New Taiwan dollar (NT$) of 100 cents
Population – 23,024,956 rising at 0.21 per cent a year (2010 est); Han Chinese 98 per cent (Holo 70 per cent, Hakka 14 per cent), indigenous (2 per cent) (est)
Religion – Buddhist 35 per cent, Taoist 33 per cent, Christian 2 per cent (est). Many combine Buddhism and Taoism, and may also practise Chinese folk beliefs. About 3 per cent belong to the Falun Gong spiritual movement
Language – Mandarin (official), Taiwanese (Min-Nan), Hakka dialects
Population density – 618 per sq. km (2001)
Median age – 37 (2010 est)
National anthem – 'San Min Chu I' ['Three Principles of the People']
National day – 10 October (Republic Day)
Life expectancy (years) – 78.15 (2010 est)

Mortality rate – 6.87 (2010 est)
Birth rate – 8.97 (2010 est)
Infant mortality rate – 5.26 (2010 est)
Death penalty – Retained (last used 2011)
CPI score – 5.8 (2010)

CLIMATE AND TERRAIN

The island of Taiwan (formerly Formosa) lies 145km east of the Chinese mainland. Mountains run the length of the island, covering over half the terrain, with lowlands in the west. Elevation extremes range from 3,952m (Yu Shan) to 0m (South China Sea). Taiwan shares the tropical monsoon climate of southern China, with large seasonal variations in temperature, dry winters and wet summers. The typhoon season lasts from May to November, with particularly high humidity between July and September. Average temperatures in Taipei range from 12°C in January and February and 33°C in July.

Territories include the Penghu (Pescadores) islands (80.47 sq. km), some 56km west of Taiwan, as well as Kinmen (Quemoy) (109 sq. km) and Matsu (7 sq. km), which are only a few kilometres from mainland China.

HISTORY AND POLITICS

Settled by Chinese from about the 12th century, the island was annexed by China in the 17th century, and ceded to Japan in 1895 at the end of the Sino-Japanese War. It was returned to China after Japan's defeat in the Second World War. The Kuomintang (KMT) government, led by Gen. Chiang Kai-shek, withdrew to Taiwan in 1949 after being defeated by the communists in mainland China. The territory remained under Chiang Kai-shek's presidency until his death in 1975. He was succeeded as president by his son, Gen. Chiang Ching-kuo, who ruled until his death in 1988. Martial law was lifted in 1987 after 38 years. In 1991 the Taiwanese government declared an end to the state of war with China, officially recognising the People's Republic of China for the first time, and ended emergency measures that had frozen political life in Taiwan since 1949.

Democratisation of the authoritarian one-party state began in the 1980s and led to the first multiparty elections in 1992. The 'Senior Parliamentarians' who had retained their seats since being elected on the mainland in 1948 were forcibly retired in 1991–2. From this point, power shifted away from the mainlanders to the native Taiwanese, and 50 years of KMT rule ended when the Democratic Progressive Party (DPP), which favours self-determination, won the presidency in 2000 and the 2001 legislative election.

The DPP retained the presidency and continued in government after the 2004 elections. However, in the 2008 elections the KMT returned to power, winning a majority of seats in the legislature, and the KMT candidate, Ma Ying-jeou, was elected president. Premier Liu Chao-shiuan and his cabinet resigned in September 2009 over the poor response to Typhoon Morakot in the preceding month; a new government was formed under Wu Den-yih.

FOREIGN RELATIONS

Most nations acknowledge the position of the Chinese government that Taiwan is a province of the People's Republic of China, and as a result Taiwan has formal diplomatic relations with only 23 countries and no seat at the UN. China has sanctioned the use of force to prevent Taiwan declaring itself independent.

Contacts between Taiwan and China began in the 1980s and have led to a gradual relaxation of restrictions on direct economic, trade and transport links, and on travel and tourism. Since the KMT returned to power in 2008, Taiwan has sought greater economic cooperation and integration with China.

POLITICAL SYSTEM

The 1947 constitution (which originally applied to the whole of China) has been amended a number of times since 1991. In 2004 an amendment provided for future proposed constitutional changes to be put to a referendum instead of the National Assembly (formerly the upper house of the legislature), which was disbanded under 2005 provisions that also reduced the number of legislative seats with effect from the 2008 election.

The president is directly elected for a four-year term, renewable once. The unicameral Legislative Yuan has 113 members: 73 directly elected, 34 elected proportionately by party and six elected by indigenous peoples in two constituencies; all serve a four-year term. The president appoints the premier and, on the premier's advice, the cabinet.

HEAD OF STATE
President, Ma Ying-jeou, *elected* 22 March 2008
Vice-President, Vincent Siew

SELECTED GOVERNMENT MEMBERS *as at July 2011*
Premier, Wu Den-yih
Defence, Kao Hua-chu
Economy, Shih Yen-shiang
Foreign Affairs, Timothy Yang Chin-tien
Interior, Jiang Yi-huah

BRITISH COUNCIL
2F-1, 106 XinYi Rd, Sec. 5, Taipei 110
T (+886) (2) 8722 1000 W www.britishcouncil.org/taiwan
Director, Alison Devine

DEFENCE

The army has over 926 main battle tanks, 950 armoured personnel carriers, 225 armoured infantry fighting vehicles, 62 armed helicopters and 39 multi-role helicopters. The navy has 4 submarines, 4 cruisers, 22 frigates, 73 patrol and coastal vessels, 32 combat aircraft and 20 armed helicopters at 5 bases. The air force has 477 combat aircraft.

Military budget – US$9,300m (2010)
Military personnel – 290,000: army 200,000, navy 45,000, air force 45,000; paramilitary 17,000
Conscription duration – 12 months

ECONOMY AND TRADE

Since the 1950s Taiwan has transformed itself from a mainly agricultural country into a highly developed industrial economy. This transition was driven by exports. There has been a gradual shift away from state domination of the economy, with a reduction in government influence on investment and foreign trade, and privatisation in the financial and industrial sectors. Taiwan's export markets suffered severely in the global economic downturn and the economy contracted sharply in 2008–9, but it recovered strongly in 2010.

Only a quarter of the land area is suitable for agriculture but the soil is very fertile, producing rice, corn, vegetables, fruit, tea, flowers, meat and dairy products. The industrial base includes electronics, communications and information technology products, oil refining, armaments, chemicals, textiles, iron and steel, machinery, cement, food processing, vehicles, consumer goods, pharmaceuticals and fishing. Agriculture contributes 1.4 per cent of GDP, industry 31.1 per cent and services 67.5 per cent.

The main trading partners are China (28 per cent of exports), Japan (20 per cent of imports), the USA and Hong Kong. Principal exports are electronic and computer equipment, flat panels, machinery, metals, textiles, plastics, chemicals and precision instruments. The main imports are electronic and electrical equipment, machinery, crude oil and precision instruments.

Average annual growth of GDP – 8.3 per cent (2010 est)
Inflation rate – 1.3 per cent (2010 est)
Population below poverty line – 1.08 per cent (2008 est)
Unemployment – 5.2 per cent (2010 est)
Total external debt – US$91,410m (2010 est)
Imports – US$174,600m (2009)
Exports – US$203,700m (2009)

BALANCE OF PAYMENTS
Trade – US$23,364m surplus (2010)
Current Account – US$42,572m surplus (2009)

Trade with UK	2009	2010
Imports from UK	£754,577,469	£1,049,063,249
Exports to UK	£2,400,413,264	£3,027,826,270

COMMUNICATIONS
Taiwan has 1,580km of railways and a total road network of 41,475km, most of which is surfaced (including 720km of motorways). The main ports are Keelung, Kaohsiung and Taichung, and there are international airports at Taoyuan (near Taipei), Kaohsiung and Taichung. There are internal flights between the major cities.

Digital telecommunications systems provided services to 14.6 million fixed-line telephone subscribers, 27 million mobile phone subscribers and 16.1 million internet users in 2009.

MEDIA
The media is among the most liberal and competitive in Asia. There are some 350 newspapers, all of which are privately owned and reflect a wide range of views. The broadcast media, especially television, has a high level of ownership by the government, the military and political parties. Both terrestrial and cable television services operate, and cable subscription is the highest in the region. There are over 170 radio stations.

TAJIKISTAN

Jumhurii Tojikiston – Republic of Tajikistan

Area – 143,100 sq. km
Capital – Dushanbe; population, 703,939 (2009 est)
Major towns – Khujand, Kulob
Currency – Somoni of 100 dirams
Population – 7,487,489 rising at 1.85 per cent a year (2010 est); Tajik (79.9 per cent), Uzbek (15.3 per cent), Russian (1.1 per cent), Kyrgyz (1.1 per cent) (2000)
Religion – Muslim 97 per cent (of which Sunni 96 per cent, Shia 4 per cent), Christian 2 per cent (predominantly Russian Orthodox) (est)
Language – Tajik (official), Russian
Population density – 50 per sq. km (2009)
Urban population – 26 per cent (2008 est)
Median age (years) – 22.2 (2010 est)
National anthem – 'Surudi Milli' ['National Anthem']
National day – 9 September (Independence Day)
Life expectancy (years) – 65.68 (2010 est)
Mortality rate – 6.72 (2010 est)
Birth rate – 26.49 (2010 est)
Infant mortality rate – 39.78 (2010 est)
Death penalty – Retained (not used since 2004)
CPI score – 2.1 (2010)
Literacy rate – 99.7 per cent (2008 est)
Gross enrolment ratio (percentage of relevant age group) – primary 102 per cent; secondary 84 per cent; tertiary 20 per cent (2008 est)
Health expenditure (per capita) – US$38 (2009)
Hospital beds (per 1,000 people) – 5.4 (2004–9)

CLIMATE AND TERRAIN
The landlocked country is mountainous, with the Pamir highlands in the east and the high ridges of the Pamir-Altai ranges in the centre. More than half of the country lies above 3,000m. Elevation extremes range from 7,495m (Qullai Ismoili Somoni) to 300m (Syr Darya river). The main rivers are the Syr Darya, flowing through the Fergana valley in the north, and the Amu Darya and its tributaries in the west and south. Most of the population lives on the fertile plains formed by these rivers. The climate is continental, with average temperatures in central areas of −2°C in January and 25°C in July.

HISTORY AND POLITICS
The area that is now Tajikistan was conquered by Alexander the Great in the fourth century BC and remained under Greek and Greco-Persian rule for 200 years, until the kingdom of Kushan was established throughout the Bactria region.

Tajikistan was invaded by Muslim Arabs in the eighth century AD, and Islam was the prevalent religion by the time of the Samanid Persian conquest in the ninth century. From the ninth to the 16th century, the region was ruled by a succession of Turkic, Mongol and Uzbek states, and remained under the control of various feudal principalities until the 19th century. In 1868, the northern part was subsumed within the Russian Empire, while the south was annexed by the Bukhara khanate. At the time of the Russian revolution in 1917 the Central Asian territories attempted to establish their independence, but Bolshevik power was consolidated in the north by April 1918, and in the rest of Tajikistan by 1920. In 1924 the Tajikistan Autonomous Soviet Socialist Republic was formed as part of the Uzbek Republic, before Tajikistan was given full republican status within the USSR in 1929.

Tajikistan declared its independence on 9 September 1991. In 1992, anti-government demonstrations escalated into a five-year civil war between government forces and Islamic and pro-democracy groups. A peace accord signed in 1997 was implemented by 2000. Political assassinations and bombings occurred after the end of the civil war, but the level of violence has dropped since 2002.

Former communists have dominated politics since 1991 and power is concentrated in the president's hands. Opposition parties are weak and face harassment; a number of opposition leaders have been arrested on criminal charges, moves that their supporters claim are politically motivated.

President Rakhmon has served as head of state since 1992, and was re-elected for a third term in 2006. The 2010 legislative elections were won by the incumbent (former communist) People's Democratic Party of Tajikistan (HDKT) with an overwhelming majority, although international observers considered the polls flawed.

POLITICAL SYSTEM
The 1994 constitution was amended in 1999 and 2003, following referendums, to introduce changes to the presidential term of office and the legislative structure. The executive president is directly elected for a single seven-year term, although the 2003 amendment permits the current incumbent to stand for two further terms. The bicameral parliament consists of the Assembly of Representatives *(Majlisi Namoyandogan)*, which has 63 members directly elected for a five-year term, and the National Assembly *(Majlisi Milli)*, which has 33 members, 25 elected by five regional assemblies and eight appointed by the president, to serve a five-year term. Administratively, Tajikistan is divided into two provinces and the Gorno-Badakhshan autonomous region.

HEAD OF STATE
President, Emomali Rakhmon, *elected by Supreme Soviet*
   19 November 1992, *elected* 6 November 1994,
   re-elected 1999, 2006

SELECTED GOVERNMENT MEMBERS *as at July 2011*
Prime Minister, Akil Akilov
First Deputy Prime Minister, Asadullo Ghulomov
Deputy Prime Ministers, Murodali Alimardonov *(Economy)*;
   Ruqiya Qurbonova
Defence, Col.-Gen. Sherali Khayrulloyev
Finance, Safarali Najmiddinov
Foreign Affairs, Hamrokhon Zarifi
Internal Affairs, Abdurahim Qahhorov

EMBASSY OF THE REPUBLIC OF TAJIKISTAN
Grove House, 27 Hammersmith Grove, London W6 0NE
T 020-8834 1003 E info@tajembassy.ork.uk
W www.tajembassy.org.uk
Ambassador Extraordinary and Plenipotentiary,
   HE Erkin Kasymov, *apptd* 2008

BRITISH EMBASSY
65 Mirzo Tursunzade Street, Dushanbe 734002
T (+992) 372 42221 E dushanbe.reception@fco.gov.uk
W http://ukintajikistan.fco.gov.uk
Ambassador Extraordinary and Plenipotentiary,
   HE Trevor Moore, *apptd* 2009

DEFENCE
The army has 37 main battle tanks, 23 armoured infantry fighting vehicles and 23 armoured personnel carriers. The air force has 4 armed helicopters.

Military budget – US$84m (2010)
Military personnel – 8,800: army 7,300, air force 1,500;
   paramilitary 7,500
Conscription duration – 24 months

ECONOMY AND TRADE
Since the civil war, there has been steady economic growth but the economy remains fragile owing to the inconsistent implementation of structural reforms, corruption, poor industrial and transport infrastructure, energy shortages and high foreign debt. The country has benefited from debt cancellation, and is receiving substantial aid, primarily to develop industrial and transport infrastructure. However, over 50 per cent of the population lives below the poverty line and many are dependent on remittances. The global downturn reduced the value of remittances and export commodity prices in 2009.

Agriculture is the major sector of the economy, accounting for 19.2 per cent of GDP but 50 per cent of employment. Cattle-raising and cotton-growing predominate; other crops are grain, fruit, grapes and vegetables. Abundant mineral deposits are not fully exploited. Industry consists of aluminium and hydro-electric power production, mining (zinc and lead) and production of cement and vegetable oil. The sector contributes 22.6 per cent of GDP and employs 12.8 per cent of the workforce.

The main trading partners are Russia, China, Turkey and Uzbekistan. Principal exports are aluminium, electricity, cotton, fruit, vegetable oil and textiles. The main imports are petroleum products, aluminium oxide, machinery and equipment, and foodstuffs.
GNI – US$4,912m; US$700 per capita (2009)
Annual average growth of GDP – 5.5 per cent (2010 est)
Inflation rate – 5.8 per cent (2010 est)
Population below poverty line – 53 per cent (2009 est)
Unemployment – 2.2 per cent (2009 est)
Total external debt – US$1,997m (2010 est)

BALANCE OF PAYMENTS
Trade – US$1,931m deficit (2010)
Current Account – US$394m deficit (2008)

Trade with UK	2009	2010
Imports from UK	£5,045,511	£1,290,667
Exports to UK	£29,740	£43,313

COMMUNICATIONS
Infrastructure development is a government priority, with China supporting a road-building programme and the USA funding a bridge linking Tajikistan with Afghanistan. There are 680km of railway and 27,767km of roads; many roads, including the main highways, are only open in the summer months. About 200km of the river Vakhsh is navigable. The main airport is at Dushanbe, and there are 25 other airports and airfields around the country.

Telecommunications systems are expanding and being modernised. There were 290,000 fixed telephone lines in use, 4.9 million mobile phone subscribers and 700,000 internet users in 2009.

MEDIA
The government retains tight control over the media: state-run radio and television stations dominate broadcasting, newspapers must be registered and the authorities control the printing presses. Independent

journalists frequently come under government pressure. The private broadcasting sector has about 15 active television stations and 10 radio stations. There are more than 200 newspapers, some government-owned and others linked to political parties.

TANZANIA

Jamhuri ya Muungano wa Tanzania – United Republic of Tanzania

Area – 947,300 sq. km
Capital – Dodoma; population, 200,447 (2009 est)
Major cities – Arusha, Dar es Salaam, Mbeya, Mwanza, Zanzibar
Currency – Tanzanian shilling of 100 cents
Population – 41,892,895 rising at 2.03 per cent a year (2010 est); over 130 African ethnic groups on the mainland; Arab, African and mixed race on Zanzibar
Religion – mainland: Christian 62 per cent, Muslim 35 per cent (of which Sunni 80 per cent, Shia 20 per cent), other 3 per cent; Zanzibar: Muslim 98 per cent (est)
Language – Swahili, English (both official), Arabic (especially on Zanzibar)
Population density – 49 per sq. km (2009)
Urban population – 25 per cent (2008 est)
Median age (years) – 18.3 (2010 est)
National anthem – 'Mungu ibariki Afrika' ['God Bless Africa']
National day – 26 April (Union Day)
Life expectancy (years) – 52.49 (2010 est)
Mortality rate – 12.31 (2010 est)
Birth rate – 33.44 (2010 est)
Infant mortality rate – 68.13 (2010 est)
HIV/AIDS adult prevalence – 5.6 per cent (2009 est)
Death penalty – Retained (not used since 1995)
CPI score – 2.7 (2010)

CLIMATE AND TERRAIN
Tanzania comprises the former Tanganyika, on the mainland of east Africa, and the islands of Zanzibar, Pemba and Mafia. Most of the country lies on the central African plateau, from which rise mountains that run across the centre of the country from north-east to south-west. Peaks include Mt Kilimanjaro (5,895m), the highest point on the continent of Africa, and Mt Meru (4,564m). The lowest point is 0m (Indian Ocean). The land falls to plains in the south-east and along the coast, and to swamps in the west. Large areas of lakes Victoria, Tanganyika and Malawi (Nyasa) lie on the northern and western borders, and there are smaller lakes in the north-east and south-west. The Serengeti National Park covers an area of 9,656 sq. km in the north of the country. The climate is

tropical, modified by altitude, with a rainy season from November to April except in coastal regions, which get most rain between March and May; rainfall is sporadic in the interior but more reliable and heavier on the coast.

HISTORY AND POLITICS
The area was settled by Bantu people from the fifth century AD, and city states developed along the coast from the eighth century, trading with Arab, Indian and Persian merchants. Portuguese explorers arrived in the 15th century, and in the 16th century the Portuguese conquered Zanzibar, periodically controlling the coastal states on the mainland. They were ousted from Zanzibar in 1699 by Arabs from Oman, and Oman exercised overlordship over the east African coast from Zanzibar until 1861, when the sultanates of Oman and Zanzibar were separated. The sultanate of Zanzibar became a British protectorate in 1890 and Germany established the colony of German East Africa on the mainland in the 1890s. After the First World War, Tanganyika became a mandated territory under British administration, and achieved independence on 9 December 1961. It became a republic in 1962. Zanzibar became independent as a constitutional monarchy on 10 December 1963. The sultan was overthrown in a revolution in 1964 and Zanzibar united with Tanganyika on 26 April 1964; the new country was formally named the United Republic of Tanzania in October 1964.

The country was a one-party state from 1965 to 1992 under the Revolutionary Party of Tanzania (CCM). The constitution was amended in 1992 to allow multiparty politics, with the stipulation that all parties must be active in both the mainland and Zanzibar, and that parties must not be formed on regional, religious, tribal or racial grounds. The first multiparty elections were held in 1995 and were won by the CCM, which has continued to dominate politics.

In the 2010 national elections, Jakaya Kikwete was re-elected president, and the CCM retained its overwhelming majority in the legislature. In Zanzibar's simultaneous 2010 presidential and legislative elections, the CCM candidate Ali Mohamed Shein was elected president, and the CCM retained a narrow majority in the legislature.

POLITICAL SYSTEM
The 1977 constitution was amended in 1992 to introduce multiparty elections, and in 2000 to allow the president to nominate up to ten members of parliament. The executive president is directly elected for a five-year term, renewable once. The president is always from Tanganyika and the vice-president is always from Zanzibar. The unicameral National Assembly *(Bunge)* has 357 members: 239 directly elected, 102 seats reserved for women, ten appointed by the president, five chosen by Zanzibar's legislature, and the speaker. All serve a five-year term. The *Bunge* enacts laws that apply to the whole of Tanzania and laws that apply only to the mainland; laws that apply specifically to Zanzibar are enacted by the island's own legislature, the 50-member House of Representatives. Zanzibar also has its own directly elected president (who is a member of the Union government) and legislature.

HEAD OF STATE
President of the United Republic, Jakaya Kikwete, *elected* 14 December 2005, *took office* 21 December 2005, *re-elected* 2010

Vice-President, Mohammed Gharib Bilal
President of Zanzibar, Ali Mohamed Shein

SELECTED GOVERNMENT MEMBERS *as at July 2011*
Prime Minister, Mizengo Pinda
Defence, Hussein Mwinyi
Finance, Mustapha Mkullo
Foreign Affairs, Bernard Membe
Home Affairs, Shamsi Vuai Nahoda

HIGH COMMISSION FOR THE UNITED REPUBLIC OF
TANZANIA
3 Stratford Place, London W1C 1AS
T 020-7569 1470 E tanzarep@tanzania-online.gov.uk
W www.tanzania-online.gov.uk
High Commissioner (acting), HE Peter Kallaghe,
   apptd 2011

BRITISH HIGH COMMISSION
PO Box 9200, Umoja House, Garden Avenue, Dar es Salaam
T (+255) (22) 211 0101 E bhc.dar@dar.mail.fco.gov.uk
W http://ukintanzania.fco.gov.uk
High Commissioner, HE Diane Corner, *apptd* 2009

BRITISH COUNCIL
PO Box 9100, Samora Avenue/Ohio Street, Dar es Salaam
T (+255) (22) 211 6574 W www.britishcouncil.org/africa
Director, Sally Robinson

DEFENCE

The army has 45 main battle tanks and 14 armoured
personnel carriers. The navy has 8 patrol and coastal
combatant vessels at 3 bases. The air force has 25 combat
capable aircraft.
Military expenditure – US$247m (2009 est)
Military personnel – 27,000: army 23,000, navy 1,000,
   air force 3,000; paramilitary 1,400
Conscription duration – 24 months (including civil duties)

ECONOMY AND TRADE

State control has been dismantled gradually since the
mid-1980s. Liberalisation and modernisation policies,
supported by the World Bank, IMF and aid donors, have
increased private-sector growth and investment, and
produced steady GDP growth in recent years. However,
around one-third of the population still lives below the
poverty line.

Agriculture is the mainstay of the economy, accounting
for 42 per cent of GDP, about 80 per cent of employment
and 85 per cent of exports. It provides coffee, tea, cotton,
pyrethrum, cashew nuts, grains, fruit and vegetables as
well as the raw materials for industries producing sugar,
beer, cigarettes and sisal twine. Zanzibar and Pemba
produce cloves and clove oil, and coconuts and their
derivatives. Increased output of minerals (chiefly
diamonds, gold and iron) has driven recent economic
growth, and salt, soda ash, cement, petroleum products,
footwear, clothing, wood products and fertiliser are also
produced. Tourism is a major source of revenue, especially
for Zanzibar. Industry accounts for 18 per cent of GDP
and services for 40 per cent.

The main trading partners are India, China, Japan, the
UAE and South Africa. Principal exports are gold, coffee,
cashew nuts, manufactures (especially clothing) and
cotton. The main imports are consumer goods, machinery
and transport equipment, industrial raw materials and
crude oil.

GNI – US$21,385m; US$500 per capita (2009;
   mainland Tanzania only)
Annual average growth of GDP – 6.4 per cent (2010 est)
Inflation rate – 7.2 per cent (2010 est)
Total external debt – US$7,576m (2010 est)
Imports – US$6,300m (2009)
Exports – US$2,400m (2009)

BALANCE OF PAYMENTS
Trade – US$4,169m deficit (2010)
Current Account – US$2,012m deficit (2008)

Trade with UK	2009	2010
Imports from UK	£96,851,813	£118,239,379
Exports to UK	£18,580,295	£21,576,268

COMMUNICATIONS

There are 78,890km of roads, only 4,741km of which are
surfaced. The 3,689km of railways connect Dar es Salaam
with Zambia, northern Tanzania and Kenya, and lakes
Tanganyika and Victoria. The three great lakes in the
north and east are the main trade routes with
neighbouring countries, via ports at Mwanza, Musoma,
Bukoba (Lake Victoria) and Kigoma (Lake Tanganyika).
The main seaports are Dar es Salaam, Tanga, Mtwara,
Zanzibar, Mkoani and Wete (Pemba); international
shipping faces a high risk of piracy in the Indian Ocean.
Coastal shipping services connect the mainland to
Zanzibar, and lake services operate on Lake Tanganyika
and Lake Malawi (Nyasa). The principal international
airports are at Dar es Salaam, Kilimanjaro and Zanzibar.

The fixed-line telephone system is being modernised;
mobile phone distribution has grown rapidly. There were
173,552 fixed lines and 17.7 million mobile phone
subscribers in 2010, and 678,000 internet users in 2009.

EDUCATION AND HEALTH

Education is compulsory for seven years. The teaching
medium is Swahili but the government is making efforts
to improve English standards in secondary and higher
education.
Literacy rate – 72.6 per cent (2008 est)
Gross enrolment ratio (percentage of relevant age group) –
   primary 105 per cent; secondary 27 per cent (2009 est)
Health expenditure (per capita) – US$25 (2009)
Hospital beds (per 1,000 people) – 1.1 (2004–9)

MEDIA

The mainland has a liberal media environment, with
privately owned broadcasters and newspapers operating
alongside the state-run media. Radio has long been the
dominant medium and private stations are prevalent in
urban areas, but audiences have turned increasingly to
television, which was launched only in 1994.

Zanzibar has a less liberal media policy and there are
no private broadcasters or newspapers on the island,
although locals can access mainland media.

THAILAND

Ratcha Anachak Thai – Kingdom of Thailand

Area – 513,120 sq. km
Capital – Bangkok (Krung Thep); population, 6,901,690 (2009 est)
Major cities – Chon Buri, Nonthaburi, Samut Prakan, Udon Thani
Currency – Baht of 100 satang
Population – 67,089,500 rising at 0.65 per cent a year (2010 est); Thai, including Lao (75 per cent), Chinese (14 per cent) (est)
Religion – Buddhist 94 per cent (predominantly Theravada), Muslim 5 per cent (predominantly Sunni) (est); many Buddhists also incorporate Brahmin-Hindu and animist practices
Language – Thai (official), English
Population density – 133 per sq. km (2009)
Urban population – 33 per cent (2008 est)
Median age (years) – 34 (2010 est)
National anthem – 'Phleng Chat' ['National Song']
National day – 5 December (Birthday of the King)
Life expectancy (years) – 75.02 (2010 est)
Mortality rate – 6.47 (2010 est)
Birth rate – 13.01 (2010 est)
Infant mortality rate – 16.71 (2010 est)
HIV/AIDS adult prevalence – 1.3 per cent (2009 est)
Death penalty – Retained (last used 2009)
CPI score – 3.5 (2010)

CLIMATE AND TERRAIN

Thailand is divided geographically into four regions: the north is mountainous and forested; to the north-east is the semi-arid Korat plateau; the centre is a fertile plain lying in the Chao Phraya basin; and the south is the narrow, mountainous isthmus of Kra. Extremes of elevation range from 2,576m (Doi Inthanon) to 0m (Gulf of Thailand). The principal rivers are the Chao Phraya and its tributaries in the central plains and the Mekong on the north and eastern borders. The climate is tropical, with a monsoon season from June to October and high humidity.

HISTORY AND POLITICS

The Thai nation was founded in the 13th century and expanded in the following centuries at the expense of the declining Khmer Empire. Although trade with China, Japan and Europe developed in the 17th century, in 1699 an isolationist policy was adopted. Burma invaded in the 18th century, leaving the country in a state of anarchy until reunification in 1782 under the first king of the present Chakri dynasty. From the late 19th century, Thailand (then known as Siam) opened up to European contact and trade under a series of modernising kings who reformed the country's administration and commerce. It was the only country in the region to avoid colonisation by a European power.

Following a revolution in 1932, Thailand became a constitutional monarchy with parliamentary government. It was occupied by Japan from 1941 until 1945, after which it was under military or military-controlled governments for most of the following 50 years. In 1992, mass demonstrations in Bangkok forced from power the military-aligned government that had won the 1992 election. Civilian rule was restored until 2006, when the military staged a coup against the government led by Thaksin Shinawatra.

The military handed over to a civilian government after the 2007 legislative election, but political volatility has continued, with mass demonstrations and sit-ins in Bangkok by the anti-Thaksin People's Alliance for Democracy (PAD) or 'yellow shirts', or the pro-Thaksin United Front for Democracy against Dictatorship (UDD) or 'red shirts', and clashes between the two. The PAD demonstrated against the six-party coalition government headed by the pro-Thaksin People Power Party (PPP), which was formed after the 2007 election. The PPP and its two main coalition partners were ordered to dissolve in 2008 after being found guilty of electoral fraud, and the government was replaced by a seven-party coalition led by the Democratic Party. This government faced 18 months of protests by the UDD, culminating in the violent dispersal of its supporters in May 2010 after a two-month occupation of central Bangkok. In the legislative election in July 2011, the For Thai party (PTP), a successor party to the PPP, won an overall majority and its leader, Yingluck Shinawatra (sister of Thaksin Shinawatra), formed a coalition government with four smaller parties.

INSURGENCY

The Muslim minority is concentrated in the isthmus of Kra. A separatist campaign in the region began in the 1970s but died down in the 1980s. Violence was renewed in 2004 and has since claimed over 3,000 lives.

FOREIGN RELATIONS

Sovereignty over border territory around the Hindu temple complex at Preah Vihear has been disputed with Cambodia for over a century. Although the temple complex was awarded to Cambodia in 1962, the status of adjacent territory remains unsettled. Tensions increased in 2008, when Cambodia had the temple listed as a UNESCO World Heritage Site, and there has been frequent sporadic fighting in the area between the countries' troops.

POLITICAL SYSTEM

Thailand is a constitutional monarchy with a hereditary monarch as head of state. The 2007 constitution provides for a bicameral National Assembly comprising a 500-member House of Representatives, elected for a four-year term, and a senate with 150 members: 76 elected members (one from each province) and 74 members appointed by a selection committee; senators serve a six-year term. The prime minister is appointed by the king and approved by and responsible to the House of Representatives.

HEAD OF STATE

HM The King of Thailand, King Bhumibol Adulyadej (Rama IX), *born* 5 December 1927, *succeeded* 9 June 1946

Heir, HRH Crown Prince Maha Vajiralongkorn,
   born 28 July 1952

SELECTED GOVERNMENT MEMBERS *as at July 2011*
Prime Minister, Yingluck Shinawatra
Deputy Prime Ministers, Yongyuth Wichaidit; Charlerm
   Yubamrung; Police Gen. Kowit Watana
Defence, Yuthasak Sasiprapha
Finance, Thirachai Phuvanatnaranubala
Foreign Affairs, Surapong Towichukchaikul

ROYAL THAI EMBASSY
29–30 Queen's Gate, London SW7 5JB
T 020-7589 2944 E csinfo@thaiembassy.org.uk
W www.thaiembassyuk.org.uk
Ambassador Extraordinary and Plenipotentiary,
   HE Kitti Wasinondh, *apptd* 2007

BRITISH EMBASSY
14 Wireless Road, Bangkok 10330
T (+662) 305 8333 E info.bangkok@fco.gov.uk
W http://ukinthailand.fco.gov.uk
Ambassador Extraordinary and Plenipotentiary,
   HE Asif Ahmad, *apptd* 2010

BRITISH COUNCIL
254 Chulalongkorn Soi 64, Siam Square, Phayathai Road,
Pathumwan, Bangkok 10330
T (+662) 652 5678 W www.britishcouncil.org/thailand
Director, Chris Gibson

DEFENCE
The army has 283 main battle tanks, 950 armoured
personnel carriers and 5 armed helicopters. The navy has
1 aircraft carrier, 10 frigates, 82 patrol and coastal vessels,
39 combat aircraft and 8 armed helicopters at 5 bases.
The air force has 165 combat aircraft.
Military budget – US$4,810m (2010)
Military personnel – 305,860: army 190,000, navy
   69,860, air force 46,000; paramilitary 113,700
Conscription duration – 24 months

ECONOMY AND TRADE
Thailand was transformed from an agricultural to an
export-orientated industrial economy in the last quarter
of the 20th century, sustaining steady growth after its
quick recovery from the 1997 economic crisis. The 2008
global economic downturn caused the export-dependent
economy to contract sharply, but it made a strong
recovery in 2010.
   The agricultural sector generates 10.4 per cent of GDP
and employs 42 per cent of the workforce. The main
crops are rice, cassava, rubber, maize, sugar cane, coconuts
and soya beans. In recent years fishing and livestock
production have grown in importance. There are reserves
of natural gas, lignite, tin, tungsten and lead.
   The main industry is tourism, which has been the chief
foreign exchange earner since the 1980s. Other industries
include textiles and clothing, agricultural processing,
beverages, tobacco, cement, mining and light
manufacturing (jewellery, electrical appliances, computers
and parts), furniture, plastics and cars and vehicle parts.
Industry contributes 45.6 per cent of GDP and services
44 per cent.
   The main trading partners are Japan, China, the USA
and Malaysia. Principal exports are textiles and footwear,
fish products, rice, rubber, jewellery, cars, computers and

electrical appliances. The main imports are capital goods,
intermediate goods and raw materials, consumer goods
and fuels.
GNI – US$251,964m; US$3,760 per capita (2009)
Annual average growth of GDP – 7.6 per cent (2010 est)
Inflation rate – 3.3 per cent (2010 est)
Population below poverty line – 9.6 per cent (2006 est)
Unemployment – 1.2 per cent (2010 est)
Total external debt – US$82,500m (2010 est)
Imports – US$134,800m (2009)
Exports – US$152,100m (2009)

BALANCE OF PAYMENTS
Trade – US$10,784m surplus (2010)
Current Account – US$20,291m surplus (2009)

Trade with UK	2009	2010
Imports from UK	£884,910,336	£1,508,795,014
Exports to UK	£2,119,317,894	£2,393,659,088

COMMUNICATIONS
There are 180,053km of roads, almost all of which are
surfaced, and 4,071km of railways. Bangkok is the main
international airport, though airports at Chiang Mai,
Phuket and Hat Yai also receive international flights.
The main ports are Bangkok and Sattahip, and there
are 3,701km of inland waterways navigable by small
boats.
   A competitive telecommunications sector has seen a
rapid growth in mobile phone take-up. In 2009 there
were 7 million fixed lines in use, 83 million mobile phone
subscribers and 17.5 million internet users.

EDUCATION AND HEALTH
Primary and lower secondary education is compulsory
and free, and upper secondary education is free in
government schools. Private universities and colleges are
playing an increasing role in higher education.
Literacy rate – 94.4 per cent (2008 est)
Gross enrolment ratio (percentage of relevant age group) –
   primary 91 per cent; secondary 76 per cent; tertiary
   45 per cent (2009 est)
Health expenditure (per capita) – US$168 (2009)

MEDIA
Nearly all the national terrestrial television networks
and many of the radio networks are controlled by the
government and the military, although media reforms
are being introduced to reduce military interest and allow
the private sector more involvement. Although free to
criticise policy and expose abuses of power, the media
tends towards self-censorship regarding the monarchy,
military and judiciary. Newspapers are largely privately
run, with popular titles including *Bangkok Post* and
Thairath.

TIMOR-LESTE

Republika Demokratika Timor Lorosa'e/Republica Democratica de Timor-Leste – Democratic Republic of Timor-Leste

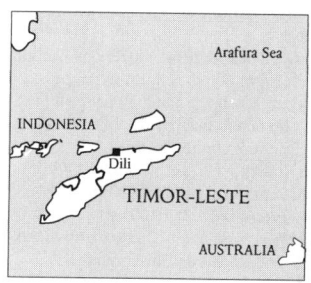

Area – 14,874 sq. km. Includes the enclave of Oecussi
Capital – Dili; population, 166,441 (2009 est)
Major towns – Baucau, Dare, Los Palos, Maliana, Pantemakassar (Oecussi)
Currency – US dollar (US$) of 100 cents
Population – 1,154,625 rising at 2 per cent a year (2010 est)
Religion – Christian (Roman Catholic 98 per cent, Protestant 1 per cent), Muslim 1 per cent (est)
Language – Tetum, Portuguese (both official), Indonesian, English, around 16 indigenous languages
Population density – 76 per sq. km (2009)
Urban population – 27 per cent (2008 est)
Median age (years) – 22.2 (2010 est)
National anthem – 'Patria' ['Fatherland']
National day – 28 November (Independence Day)
Life expectancy – 67.61 (2010 est)
Mortality rate – 5.93 (2010 est)
Birth rate – 25.93 (2010 est)
Infant mortality rate – 39.32 (2010 est)
Death penalty – Abolished for all crimes (since 1999)
CPI score – 2.5 (2010)
Military personnel – 1,332: army 1,250, naval element 82
Literacy rate – 50.1 per cent (2008 est)
Gross enrolment ratio (percentage of relevant age group) – primary 113 per cent (2009 est); secondary 51 per cent; tertiary 15 per cent (2009 est)
Health expenditure (per capita) – US$73 (2009)

CLIMATE AND TERRAIN

The republic comprises the eastern half of the island of Timor, plus the enclave of Oecussi, which lies on the northern coast, separated from the rest of the country by the Indonesian province of West Timor. The island, about 296km long and 72km wide, lies at the eastern end of the Malay archipelago and is the largest of the Lesser Sunda Islands. The interior is covered in forests and mountains. Elevation extremes range from 2,963m (Mt Tatamailau) to 0m (Timor Sea). The climate is tropical.

HISTORY AND POLITICS

The island was settled in prehistoric times by peoples from other parts of the region. It was discovered by the Portuguese *c.*1515 and, after disputes over possession between the Portuguese and the Dutch, was partitioned between the two. The eastern part of the island was a Portuguese colony from 1702 until 1975, apart from three years of Japanese occupation during the Second World War. Portuguese rule collapsed following the 1974 coup in Portugal, and a power struggle between

pro-independence parties led to a brief civil war. The Revolutionary Front for an Independent East Timor (Fretilin) emerged as the strongest party, and unilaterally declared Portuguese Timor independent in November 1975. However, Indonesia used the civil war as a pretext to invade in December 1975, and annexed East Timor as its 27th province in July 1976. By 1979, most of East Timor was under Indonesia's control, although Fretilin continued to engage in guerrilla warfare until the 1990s. The UN never recognised the annexation.

Following the fall of the Suharto regime in Indonesia, a plebiscite was held in August 1999 offering the population autonomy within Indonesia or independence; in a turnout of 98.5 per cent, 78.5 per cent voted for independence. This result provoked violence by supporters of integration into Indonesia and Indonesian troops, who murdered hundreds of people and devastated towns. UN peacekeeping troops were deployed in September 1999, and the UN set up a transitional administration. East Timor became independent as the Democratic Republic of Timor-Leste on 20 May 2002.

The UN mission left in 2005 when its peacekeeping duties ended. International troops returned in May 2006 to re-establish law and order after clashes between demonstrating ex-soldiers and the authorities had escalated into wider, factional violence. A non-military UN peacekeeping mission was set up in August 2006. Instability continued, with violent protests in August 2007 over the appointment of Xanana Gusmao as prime minister, and attacks on the president and prime minister by renegade soldiers in February 2008.

The 2007 presidential election was won in the second round by Jose Ramos-Horta (prime minister 2006–7). In the 2007 legislative election, Fretilin won the largest number of seats, but without an overall majority. Negotiations with the National Congress for Timorese Reconstruction (CNRT) over forming a coalition failed, and instead the CNRT formed a coalition government with smaller parties under its leader, Xanana Gusmao (president 2002–7).

POLITICAL SYSTEM

The 2002 constitution established a parliamentary democracy. The president is directly elected for a five-year term, renewable once. The unicameral National Parliament has 65 members, directly elected for a five-year term. The council of ministers is nominated by the prime minister, who is appointed by the president.

HEAD OF STATE
President, Jose Ramos-Horta, *elected* 9 May 2007, *took office* 20 May 2007

SELECTED GOVERNMENT MEMBERS *as at July 2011*
Prime Minister, Defence, Xanana Gusmao
Deputy Prime Minister, Jose Luis Guterres
Finance, Emilia Pires
Foreign Affairs, Zacarias da Costa

BRITISH EMBASSY
Ambassador Extraordinary and Plenipotentiary, HE Martin Hatfull, *apptd* 2008, resident at Jakarta, Indonesia

ECONOMY AND TRADE

An internationally funded programme in 2002–5 achieved substantial reconstruction of the infrastructure destroyed in the 1999 post-referendum violence, but the civil unrest of 2006 caused further damage and disrupted economic activity. Economic growth since independence is largely owing to the exploitation of offshore oil and gas deposits, which has boosted government revenue but has had little impact on unemployment levels; there are no domestic production facilities so oil and gas are piped to Australia for processing. High levels of poverty and unemployment, weak civil administration, a low skills base and inadequate infrastructure all hinder development, although increased government spending in 2009–10 was focused on basic infrastructure.

Services contribute 55 per cent of GDP, industry 12.8 per cent, and agriculture 32.2 per cent, although it engages 90 per cent of the population. The main commercial crops are coffee, timber, rice, maize, vegetables, tropical fruits and vanilla. There are some light manufacturing industries and quarrying. The main trading partners are Australia, Indonesia and EU countries. Principal exports are coffee, oil, natural gas, sandalwood and marble. The main imports are food, fuels and machinery.

GNI – US$2,915m; US$2,460 per capita (2008)
Annual average growth of GDP – 8 per cent (2010 est)
Inflation rate – 7.8 per cent (2007 est)
Population below poverty line – 42 per cent (2003 est)
Unemployment – 20 per cent (2006 est)

BALANCE OF PAYMENTS
Current Account – US$1,177m surplus (2007)

Trade with UK	2009	2010
Imports from UK	£171,338	£131,473
Exports to UK	£23,196	£328,510

COMMUNICATIONS
There are no railways or waterways, and Dili is the only port. There is one major road, which links the main townships along the northern coast. There are 6,040km of roads in total, 2,600km of which are surfaced. There are six airports and airfields; the only international airport is at Dili. The telephone system is rudimentary and largely limited to urban areas.

MEDIA
There are national public radio and television services and a number of community radio stations, many of which receive funding and support from international organisations. Public radio covers around 90 per cent of the country, but access to television broadcasts is largely limited to the capital. Three newspapers are published daily.

TOGO

République togolaise – Togolese Republic

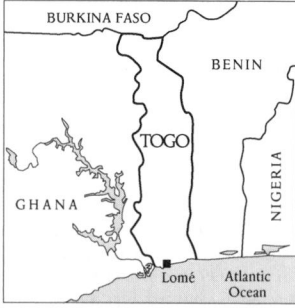

Area – 56,785 sq. km
Capital – Lomé; population, 1,592,630 (2009 est)
Major cities – Atakpamé, Kara, Sokodé
Currency – Franc CFA of 100 centimes
Population – 6,587,239 rising at 2.77 per cent a year (2010 est); 37 tribes, largest of which are Ewe, Mina and Kabre.
Religion – Christian 48 per cent (Roman Catholic 28 per cent, Protestant 10 per cent, other 10 per cent), animist 33 per cent, Muslim (Sunni) 14 per cent (est)
Language – French (official), Ewe, Mina (in the south), Kabye, Dagomba (in the north)
Population density – 122 per sq. km (2009)
Urban population – 42 per cent (2008 est)
Median age (years) – 19.2 (2010 est)
National anthem – 'Salut à toi, pays de nos aïeux' ['Hail to Thee, Land of Our Forefathers']
National day – 27 April (Independence Day)
Life expectancy (years) – 62.25 (2010 est)
Mortality rate – 8.15 (2010 est)
Birth rate – 35.88 (2010 est)
Infant mortality rate – 53.23 (2010 est)
HIV/AIDS adult prevalence – 3.2 per cent (2009 est)
Death penalty – Abolished for all crimes (since 2009)
CPI score – 2.4 (2010)
Literacy rate – 53.2 per cent (2008 est)
Gross enrolment ratio (percentage of relevant age group) – primary 105 per cent; secondary 41 per cent; tertiary 5 per cent (2007 est)
Health expenditure (per capita) – US$29 (2009)
Hospital beds (per 1,000 people) – 0.9 (2004–9)

CLIMATE AND TERRAIN
From hills in the centre of the country, the terrain declines to savannah in the north and in the south to a plateau that leads to a coastal plain with marshes and lagoons. Elevation extremes range from 986m (Mt Agou) to 0m (Atlantic Ocean). The climate in the south is tropical with two wet seasons (March to July and September to November). In the north it is semi-arid with one wet season (May to September). The average temperature in Lomé is 27°C all year round.

HISTORY AND POLITICS
Germany established a protectorate, Togoland, over the area in 1884, and this was occupied on the outbreak of the First World War by Britain and France. The country was divided between Britain and France as a League of Nations mandate after the war and the mandate was renewed by the UN in 1946. In 1957, following a plebiscite, British Togoland integrated with Ghana when it became independent. French Togoland achieved independence as the Republic of Togo in 1960.

There was a military coup in 1963 led by Gnassingbé Eyadéma, who installed a civilian president. In 1967 Eyadéma overthrew the government and became president himself, introducing a one-party state under his *Rassemblement du peuple togolais* (RPT). Violent demonstrations in 1990 forced the government to introduce a multiparty constitution in 1992. Eyadéma and the RPT were returned to power in the first multiparty elections in 1993 and in two subsequent elections. The regime continued its brutal suppression of opposition, particularly before and after elections.

After President Eyadéma's death in February 2005, the military attempted to install his son, Faure Gnassingbé, as president but this attracted domestic and international condemnation. Gnassingbé resigned as acting president, only to be elected to the presidency in April 2005. Following reconciliation talks in 2006, the government and opposition leaders signed an accord providing for the participation of opposition parties in a transitional government, and a national unity government was appointed until a legislative election was held in 2007. The election, the first without an opposition boycott for two decades, was nevertheless won by the RPT, which retained its majority; the polls were declared free and fair by observers. President Gnassingbé was re-elected in March 2010.

POLITICAL SYSTEM

Under the 1992 constitution, the president is directly elected for a five-year term. The unicameral National Assembly has 81 members, who are directly elected for a five-year term. The prime minister is appointed by the president and appoints the cabinet in consultation with the president.

HEAD OF STATE

President, Defence, Faure Gnassingbé, *elected* 24 April 2005, *sworn in* 4 May 2005, *re-elected* 2010

SELECTED GOVERNMENT MEMBERS *as at July 2011*

Prime Minister, Gilbert Houngbo
Economy and Finance, Adji Otheth Ayassor
Foreign Affairs, Eliot Ohin

EMBASSY OF THE REPUBLIC OF TOGO

8 rue Alfred Roll, 75017 Paris, France
T (+33) (1) 4380 1213
Ambassador Extraordinary and Plenipotentiary,
HE Calixte Batossie Madjoulba, *apptd* 2011

BRITISH AMBASSADOR

HE Peter Jones, *apptd* 2011, resident at Accra, Ghana

DEFENCE

The army has 2 main battle tanks, 20 armoured infantry fighting vehicles and 30 armoured personnel carriers. The navy has 2 patrol and coastal combatant vessels at a base at Lomé. The air force has 10 combat capable aircraft.
Military budget – US$67m (2009 est)
Military personnel – 8,550: army 8,100, navy 200, air force 250; paramilitary 750
Conscription duration – 24 months (selective)

ECONOMY AND TRADE

Progress on economic reform, intended to attract foreign investment and balance the budget, is slow, lacking impetus on privatisation and financial transparency. Resumption of aid to Togo, mostly suspended in the 1990s because of its human rights record, has increased since the 2007 election, and the country had 95 per cent of its external debt written off in 2010. Growth is hampered by declining productivity and underinvestment.

The economy is predominantly based on agriculture, accounting for 47.4 per cent of GDP, engaging 65 per cent of the workforce and providing most of the country's exports as well as the raw materials for industry. Industrial activity centres on phosphate mining, agricultural processing and manufacture of cement, handicrafts, textiles and beverages. Industry accounts for 25.4 per cent of GDP and 5 per cent of employment.

The main export markets are Germany, Ghana, Burkina Faso and India; imports come mainly from China (37 per cent) and EU states. Principal exports are re-exports,

cotton, phosphates, coffee and cocoa. The main imports are machinery and equipment, foodstuffs and petroleum products.
GNI – US$2,850m; US$440 per capita (2009)
Annual average growth of GDP – 3.3 per cent (2010 est)
Inflation rate – 2.6 per cent (2010 est)
Total external debt – US$1,573m (2008 est)
Imports – US$1,400m (2009)
Exports – US$800m (2009)

BALANCE OF PAYMENTS

Trade – US$661m deficit (2010)
Current Account – US$214m deficit (2008)

Trade with UK	2009	2010
Imports from UK	£19,288,453	£19,557,847
Exports to UK	£801,143	£691,916

COMMUNICATIONS

Togo has 7,520km of roads, of which approximately one-third is surfaced. There are 568km of railways. The chief waterway is the Mono river, depending on rainfall, and the main ports are Lomé and Kpeme. The principal airport is at Lomé.

The telephone system served 179,000 fixed telephone lines, 2.2 million mobile phone subscribers and 356,000 internet users in 2009.

MEDIA

The government owns the main national television and radio stations, one of the three daily newspapers and, in association with the ruling RPT party, some of the private radio stations. Privately owned media outlets have increased since the 1990s but often have limited finances. Freedom of expression is not respected; journalists can be subject to harassment, and broadcasting stations and presses to arbitrary closure.

TONGA

Pule'anga Tonga – Kingdom of Tonga

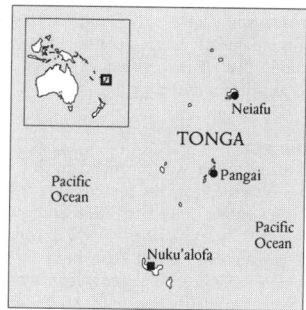

Area – 747 sq. km
Capital – Nuku'alofa, on Tongatapu; population, 24,260 (2009 est)
Currency – Pa'anga (T$) of 100 seniti
Population – 122,580 rising at 1.28 per cent a year (2010 est)
Religion – Christian (Free Wesleyan 37 per cent, Mormon 17 per cent, Roman Catholic 16 per cent, Free Church 11 per cent, other 16 per cent) (2006); small Baha'i, Muslim, Hindu and Buddhist minorities
Language – English, Tongan (both official)

Population density – 144 per sq. km (2009)
Urban population – 25 per cent (2008 est)
Median age (years) – 22.7 (2010 est)
National anthem – 'Koe Fasi Oe Tu'i Oe Otu Tonga' ['Song of the King of the Tonga Islands']
National day – 4 June (Emancipation Day)
Life expectancy (years) – 71.03 (2010 est)
Mortality rate – 4.95 (2010 est)
Birth rate – 17.78 (2010 est)
Infant mortality rate – 11.28 (2010 est)
Death penalty – Retained (not used since 1982)
CPI score – 3 (2010)
Literacy rate – 99.2 per cent (2008 est)

CLIMATE AND TERRAIN

Tonga comprises over 170 islands in three groups, situated in the south Pacific Ocean some 724km east-south-east of Fiji. Most of the islands are of coral formation, but some are volcanic (Tofua, Kao and Niuafo'ou or 'Tin Can' Island). Elevation extremes range from 1,033m (on Kao Island) to 0m (Pacific Ocean). The climate is tropical, moderated by trade winds, with an average temperature of 26°C all year round.

HISTORY AND POLITICS

The islands were settled by Polynesians from *c.*1000 AD. They were visited by European explorers from the 17th century. The country was reunited in 1845 after a civil war, and a modern constitution adopted in 1875. Tonga became a British protectorate in 1900, and regained full independence on 4 June 1970.

A pro-democracy movement began in 1992 and gathered momentum throughout the 1990s, with the first political party being established in 1994. Following consultation on political and constitutional reform in 2005 and negotiations in 2007, a political reform commission reported in 2009, recommending reducing the monarchy to a ceremonial role and introducing a popularly elected legislature. These constitutional changes took effect with the 2010 legislative election.

In the 2010 legislative election, the Democratic Party of the Friendly Islands (DPFI), a breakaway faction of the pro-reform Human Rights and Democracy Movement, won 12 of the popularly elected seats, and independents the remaining five. The legislature elected a noble, Tu'ivakano, as prime minister.

POLITICAL SYSTEM
The 1875 constitution was amended in 2003 to give greater powers to the king; the present king relinquished some of his executive powers in 2008 and most of the remainder in 2010, when new constitutional arrangements came into effect. The head of state is a hereditary monarch whose role is now largely ceremonial. The unicameral Legislative Assembly *(Fale Alea)* has 26 members: nine hereditary nobles elected by their peers, and 17 popularly elected representatives who serve a three-year term. The 14-member privy council acts as a cabinet. The prime minister is elected by the legislature.

HEAD OF STATE
HM *The King of Tonga,* King (Siaosi) George Tupou V, *born* 4 May 1948, *acceded* 11 September 2006, *crowned* 1 August 2008
Heir, HRH Crown Prince Tupouto'a Lavaka, *born* 12 July 1959

SELECTED GOVERNMENT MEMBERS *as at July 2011*
Prime Minister, Foreign Affairs, Defence, Lord Tu'ivakano
Deputy Prime Minister, Samiu Vaipulu
Finance, Sunia Fili

TONGA HIGH COMMISSION
36 Molyneux Street, London W1H 6AB
T 020-7724 5828 E fetu@btinternet.com
High Commissioner, HE Dr Sione Ngongo Kioa, *apptd* 2006

BRITISH HIGH COMMISSIONER
HE Malcolm McLachlan, MBE, resident at Suva, Fiji, *apptd* 2009

ECONOMY AND TRADE

There are few natural resources and the country is dependent on foreign aid and remittances from Tongans working abroad. The government is encouraging the development of a private sector and committing increased funds towards education and health. Unemployment is high.

The main economic activities are agriculture, fishing and tourism, which is the second-largest source of foreign exchange revenue after remittances. The main crops are squashes, coconuts, bananas, vanilla beans, cocoa, coffee, ginger and black pepper. Fish is an important staple food. A small light industry sector processes agricultural produce.

The main export markets are Hong Kong, the USA and Japan; imports come chiefly from Fiji and New Zealand. Principal exports are squashes, fish, vanilla beans and root crops. The main imports are foodstuffs, machinery and transport equipment, fuels and chemicals.

GNI – US$318m; US$3,260 per capita (2009)
Annual average growth of GDP – 0.3 per cent (2010 est)
Inflation rate – 5.9 per cent (2007 est)
Population below poverty line – 24 per cent (FY2003/2004 est)
Unemployment – 13 per cent (2004 est)
Total external debt – US$80.7m (2004 est)
Imports – US$200m (2009)
Exports – US$80m (2007)

BALANCE OF PAYMENTS
Trade – US$156m deficit (2010)
Current Account – US$39m deficit (2008)

Trade with UK	2009	2010
Imports from UK	£664,587	£421,202
Exports to UK	£88,838	£28,926

COMMUNICATIONS

There are 680km of roads in Tonga, 184km of which are surfaced. Its principal port is Nuku'alofa. There are six airfields on the islands; one has a surfaced runway.

Competition between providers has stimulated rapid expansion of telecommunications services; by 2009 the combined fixed-line and mobile phone density was about 70 per 100 people.

MEDIA

A 2003 constitutional amendment increased state control of the media. The weekly newspaper, *Tonga Chronicle,* and the Tonga Broadcasting Commission, which operates television and radio stations, are both state-run. The privately owned *Times of Tonga* newspaper is published from New Zealand. There are a number of private television and radio stations.

TRINIDAD AND TOBAGO

Republic of Trinidad and Tobago

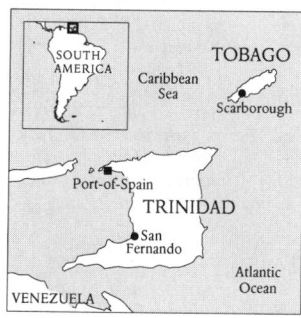

Area – 5,128 sq. km
Capital – Port of Spain, on Trinidad; population, 57,351 (2009 est)
Major towns – Chaguanas, San Fernando, Scarborough (Tobago)
Currency – Trinidad and Tobago dollar (T$) of 100 cents
Population – 1,228,691 falling at 0.09 per cent a year (2010 est)
Religion – Christian 58 per cent (Roman Catholic 26 per cent, Protestant 26 per cent, other 6 per cent), Hindu 22 per cent, Muslim 6 per cent (2000)
Language – English (official), Caribbean Hindustani (a dialect of Hindi), French, Spanish, Chinese
Population density – 261 per sq. km (2009)
Urban population – 13 per cent (2008 est)
Median age (years) – 32.6 (2010 est)
National anthem – 'Forged from the Love of Liberty'
National day – 31 August (Independence Day)
Life expectancy (years) – 71.09 (2010 est)
Mortality rate – 8.21 (2010 est)
Birth rate – 14.37 (2010 est)
Infant mortality rate – 28.9 (2010 est)
HIV/AIDS adult prevalence – 1.5 per cent (2009 est)
Death penalty – Retained (last used 1999)
CPI score – 3.6 (2010)

CLIMATE AND TERRAIN

Trinidad, the most southerly of the West Indian islands, lies 11km off the north coast of Venezuela. The island is mostly flat, with low mountains, the Northern Range, across almost its entire northern width and some low hills in the centre. Elevation extremes range from 940m (Mt Aripo) to 0m (Caribbean Sea). Pitch Lake, on the south-west coast, is the world's largest natural source of asphalt.

Tobago lies 30km north-east of Trinidad. The island has a range of hills, Main Ridge, running along its length; the highest point is 549m. Several islands, of which Chacachacare, Huevos, Monos and Gaspar Grande are the most important, lie west of Corozal Point, the north-west extremity of Trinidad.

The climate is tropical, with a wet season from June to December. Temperatures are constant all year round.

HISTORY AND POLITICS

Trinidad is believed to be the oldest site of human habitation in the Caribbean archipelago, with excavated human remains dating back 7,200 years. The islands were home to a number of indigenous peoples, including the Nepuyo, Yaio and Caribs.

Trinidad and Tobago were discovered by Columbus in 1498. Trinidad was colonised in 1532 by Spain, capitulated to the British in 1797, and was ceded to Britain in 1802. Tobago was colonised by the Dutch from the 1630s but subsequently changed hands numerous times until it was ceded to Britain by France in 1814. The two islands were amalgamated into a single British colony in 1889. Internal self-government was granted in 1959 and independence was attained in 1962; the country became a republic in 1976. Although politically stable, the republic has experienced growing levels of drug- and gang-related violence since the 1990s.

The People's National Movement (PNM) has dominated post-independence politics, only out of office in 1986–91, 1995–2001, and since May 2010. The PNM won the 2009 election for the Tobago legislature, but lost the early general election in 2010 to the People's Partnership coalition, which took office under Kamla Persad-Bissessar, the country's first female prime minister. President Richards, first elected in 2003, was declared re-elected in 2008, when he was the only candidate for the presidency.

POLITICAL SYSTEM

Under the 1976 constitution, the president is elected for a five-year term by an electoral college consisting of both houses of the legislature. The bicameral parliament comprises the House of Representatives and the senate. The former has 41 members directly elected for a five-year term. The senate has 31 members, of whom 16 are appointed on the advice of the prime minister, six on the advice of the leader of the opposition and nine at the discretion of the president, to serve a five-year term.

Since 1980 Tobago has had internal self-government through its House of Assembly, which has 16 members, 12 directly elected and four appointed, who serve a four-year term.

HEAD OF STATE
President, George Maxwell Richards, *elected* 14 February 2003, *took office* 17 March 2003, *re-elected* 2008

SELECTED GOVERNMENT MEMBERS *as at July 2011*
Prime Minister, Kamla Persad-Bissessar
Attorney-General, Anand Ramlogan
Finance, Winston Dookeran
Foreign Affairs, Surujrattan Rambuchan
National Security, Brig. John Sandy

HIGH COMMISSIONER OF THE REPUBLIC OF TRINIDAD AND TOBAGO
42 Belgrave Square, London SW1X 8NT
T 020-7245 9351 W www.tthighcommission.co.uk
High Commissioner, HE Garvin Nicholas, *apptd* 2011

BRITISH HIGH COMMISSION
PO Box 778, 19 St Clair Avenue, St Clair, Port of Spain
T (+868) 350 0444 W http://ukintt.fco.gov.uk
High Commissioner, HE Arthur Snell, *apptd* 2011

BRITISH COUNCIL
c/o British High Commission
T (+868) 628 0565 W www.britishcouncil.org/tt.
Manager, Jasbinder Birk

DEFENCE
The coastguard has 20 patrol and coastal combatant vessels at 5 bases.
Military budget – US$172m (2010)
Military personnel – 4,063: army 3,000, coastguard 1,063

ECONOMY AND TRADE
The country is the most prosperous in the Caribbean, owing largely to its oil and natural gas reserves, but the government has encouraged diversification into petrochemicals, aluminium, plastics, financial services and tourism to reduce its dependence on the energy sector. After years of steady growth, the economy contracted briefly in 2009 as export demand and oil prices fell.

The agricultural sector is small, accounting for 0.5 per cent of GDP and 4 per cent of employment; the main products are cocoa, rice, citrus fruits, coffee, vegetables and poultry. Sugar production has declined since 2003 when the state-owned sugar company was closed. Apart from oil and gas extraction and processing, the main industries are tourism, food processing, production of chemicals, steel products, cement, beverages and cotton textiles.

The main trading partners are the USA (42.2 per cent of exports; 32.6 per cent of imports), Jamaica, Colombia and Venezuela. Principal exports are oil and petroleum products, liquified natural gas, chemicals, steel products, beverages, cereals and cereal products, sugar, cocoa, coffee, citrus fruits, vegetables and flowers. The main imports are fuels, lubricants, machinery, transport equipment, manufactured goods, food, chemicals and livestock.

GNI – US$20,705m; US$16,700 per capita (2009)
Annual average growth of GDP – 2.1 per cent (2010 est)
Inflation rate – 11.3 per cent (2010 est)
Population below poverty line – 17 per cent (2007 est)
Unemployment – 6.4 per cent (2010 est)
Total external debt – US$4,303m (2010 est)
Imports – US$7,100m (2009)
Exports – US$12,100m (2009)

BALANCE OF PAYMENTS
Trade – US$3,236m surplus (2010)
Current Account – US$8,775m surplus (2008)

Trade with UK	2009	2010
Imports from UK	£105,938,549	£100,723,801
Exports to UK	£334,214,157	£298,144,338

COMMUNICATIONS
The two islands have about 8,320km of roads, of which about half are surfaced. The three main ports are Scarborough (Tobago), Port of Spain and Point Lisas, where new industries powered by local natural gas are located. The international airport is at Port of Spain on Trinidad, and Tobago is served by Crown Point airport.

Modern telecommunications systems provided services to 315,000 fixed-line subscribers, 2 million mobile phone subscribers and 593,000 internet users in 2009.

EDUCATION AND HEALTH
Education is free at all state-owned and government-assisted denominational schools, and at certain faculties

at the University of the West Indies. Attendance is compulsory for children aged six to 12 years, after which attendance at free secondary schools is determined by success in the secondary school entrance examination at 11 years.
Literacy rate – 98.8 per cent (2008 est)
Gross enrolment ratio (percentage of relevant age group) – primary 103 per cent; secondary 89 per cent (2008 est)
Health expenditure (per capita) – US$1,069 (2009)
Hospital beds (per 1,000 people) – 2.5 (2004–9)

MEDIA
There are both private and state-owned media organisations. Private television and radio stations predominate and the freedom of the press is constitutionally protected. *Newsday* and *Trinidad Guardian* are popular newspapers.

TUNISIA

Al-Jumhuriyah at-Tunisiyah – Tunisian Republic

Area – 163,610 sq. km
Capital – Tunis; population, 758,729 (2009 est)
Major cities – Aryanah, Sfax
Currency – Tunisian dinar of 1,000 millimes
Population – 10,589,025 rising at 0.97 per cent a year (2010 est)
Religion – Muslim 99 per cent (predominantly Sunni; Shia less than 1 per cent) (est); small minorities of Christians and Jews. Sunni Islam is the official religion
Language – Arabic (official), French
Population density – 67 per sq. km (2009)
Urban population – 67 per cent (2008 est)
Median age (years) – 29.7 (2010 est)
National anthem – 'Humat al-Hima' ['Defenders of the Homeland']
National day – 20 March (Independence Day)
Life expectancy (years) – 75.99 (2010 est)
Mortality rate – 5.24 (2010 est)
Birth rate – 15.31 (2010 est)
Infant mortality rate – 21.75 (2010 est)
Death penalty – Retained (not used since 1991)
CPI score – 4.3 (2010)

CLIMATE AND TERRAIN
A central plain rises to mountains in the north, and in the semi-arid south merges into the Sahara desert. There are salt lakes in the west. Elevation extremes range from 1,544m (Jebel ech Chambi) to −17m (Shatt al Gharsah). The northern and coastal regions have a Mediterranean climate, while there is a desert climate in the south. Average temperatures in Tunis range from 7°C in January to 32°C in August.

HISTORY AND POLITICS

The area was ruled successively by the Phoenicians, Carthaginians, Romans, Byzantines and Arabs before becoming a largely autonomous part of the Ottoman Empire in the 16th century. In the 19th century French influence grew and it was formally declared a French protectorate in 1883. It was briefly occupied by Germany during the Second World War (1942–3), and became independent as a monarchy under the bey in 1956. In 1957 the bey was deposed and the country became a republic under one-party rule with Habib Bourguiba as president.

There was a growing demand throughout the 1970s for the legalisation of other political parties and the government's resistance to these led to serious unrest. Multiparty legislative elections were held in 1981, but the ruling party, the Constitutional Democratic Rally (RCD), retained its grip on power until 2011. Although proclaimed president for life in 1975, President Bourguiba was deposed in 1987 on the grounds of senility by the prime minister Zine el-Abidine Ben Ali. Ben Ali was subsequently elected president in unopposed elections in 1989 and 1994, and in multiparty elections in 1999, 2004 and 2009.

Ben Ali's authoritarian regime maintained tight constraints on the political opposition, with electoral laws and media access weighted in favour of the RCD. However, nationwide protests over unemployment and political restrictions from December 2010 forced Ben Ali to leave office and flee the country in January 2011, and the RCD was dissolved by the courts in March 2011. The speaker of the Chamber of Deputies, Fouad Mebazaa, was appointed interim president and a government of national unity was formed. Elections to a constituent assembly to rewrite the constitution were scheduled for July, before being put back to October 2011.

POLITICAL SYSTEM

Under the 2002 constitution, the executive president is directly elected for a five-year term. The parliament *(Barlaman)* comprises the Chamber of Deputies *(Majlis al-Nuwaab)*, with 214 members directly elected for a five-year term, and the Chamber of Councillors *(Majlis al-Mustasharin)*, which has 126 members (85 elected by municipal councils, professional organisations and trade unions, and 41 appointed by the president), who serve a six-year term, with half elected every three years.

HEAD OF STATE

Interim President, Fouad Mebazaa, *took office* 15 January 2011

SELECTED GOVERNMENT MEMBERS *as at July 2011*

Prime Minister, Beji Caid Essebsi
Defence, Abdel Zbidi
Finance, Jalloul Ayed
Foreign Affairs, Mouldi Kefi
Interior, Habib Essid

EMBASSY OF TUNISIA

29 Prince's Gate, London SW7 1QG
T 020-7584 8117 E london@tunisianembassy.co.uk
Ambassador Extraordinary and Plenipotentiary,
HE Hatem Atallah, *apptd* 2010

BRITISH EMBASSY

Rue du Lac Windemere, Les Berges du Lac, 1053 Tunis
T (+216) (71) 108 700 E british.embassy@planet.tn
W http://ukintunisia.fco.gov.uk
Ambassador Extraordinary and Plenipotentiary,
HE Chris O'Connor, *apptd* 2008

BRITISH COUNCIL

87 Avenue Mohamed V, 1002 Tunis Belvédère
T (+216) 7184 8588 W www.britishcouncil.org/tunisia
Director, Eunice Crook

DEFENCE

The army has 84 main battle tanks and 268 armoured personnel carriers. The navy has 25 patrol and coastal combatant vessels at 3 bases. The air force has 27 combat aircraft.

Military expenditure – US$532m (2009)
Military personnel – 35,800: army 27,000, navy 4,800, air force 4,000; paramilitary 12,000
Conscription duration – 12 months (selective)

ECONOMY AND TRADE

The economy is diverse and an increasing proportion is in private ownership, with further liberalisation planned. Growth was steady from the late 1990s until 2008, although the economy contracted in 2009 as export demand dropped. Poverty levels have been reduced but unemployment remains a problem.

Agriculture and fisheries account for 10.6 per cent of GDP; the main products are olives, grain, tomatoes, citrus fruits, sugar beets, dates, almonds, meat and dairy products. The main industries are oil production, mining (principally phosphates and iron ore), tourism, processing agricultural products and manufacture of textiles, footwear and beverages. Tourism is the chief foreign exchange earner.

The main trading partners are EU countries, especially France and Italy. Principal exports are clothing, semi-finished goods and textiles, agricultural products, mechanical goods, phosphates and chemicals, hydrocarbons and electrical equipment. The main imports are textiles, machinery and equipment, hydrocarbons, chemicals and foodstuffs.

GNI – US$37,328m; US$3,720 per capita (2009)
Annual average growth of GDP – 3.4 per cent (2010 est)
Inflation rate – 4.5 per cent (2010 est)
Population below poverty line – 3.8 per cent (2005 est)
Unemployment – 14 per cent (2010 est)
Total external debt – US$18,760m (2010 est)
Imports – US$19,100m (2009)
Exports – US$14,400m (2009)

BALANCE OF PAYMENTS

Trade – US$5,791m deficit (2010)
Current Account – US$620m deficit (2006)

Trade with UK	2009	2010
Imports from UK	£152,643,422	£202,102,779
Exports to UK	£351,221,362	£624,665,751

COMMUNICATIONS

Tunisia has 19,232km of roads, over 12,655km of which are surfaced. There are 2,165km of railways. The main ports include Bizerte, Sfax and Rades. The principal airports are at Tunis, Monastir and Djerba.

The telephone system is being upgraded and expanded, and mobile and internet subscriptions are growing rapidly. In 2009 there were 1.3 million fixed lines in use, 9.8 million mobile phone subscribers and 3.5 million internet users.

EDUCATION AND HEALTH
There are 11 years of free and compulsory education.
Literacy rate – 78.5 per cent (2008 est)
Gross enrolment ratio (percentage of relevant age group) – primary 107 per cent; secondary 92 per cent; tertiary 34 per cent (2008 est)
Health expenditure (per capita) – US$240 (2009)
Hospital beds (per 1,000 people) – 2.1 (2004–9)

MEDIA
The media was tightly controlled by the Ben Ali regime using a network of censors, imposing harsh penalties for breaching press codes and blocking websites. The fall of the regime has allowed the media to operate more freely since early 2011. Most alternatives to the state-run television networks are satellite channels broadcasting pan-Arab programmes.

TURKEY

Turkiye Cumhuriyeti – Republic of Turkey

Area – 783,562 sq. km
Capital – Ankara (Angora), in Asia; population, 3,845,610 (2009 est)
Major cities – Adana, Antalya, Bursa, Gaziantep, Istanbul, Izmir, Konya
Currency – New Turkish lira (TL) of 100 kurus
Population – 77,804,122 rising at 1.27 per cent a year (2010 est); Turkish (70–75 per cent), Kurdish (18 per cent) (2008 est)
Religion – Muslim 99 per cent (predominantly Hanafi, a school of Sunni Islam; a large minority are Alevi, a Shia sect); small Christian and Jewish minorities (est)
Language – Turkish (official), Kurdish, Dimli, Azeri, Kabardian
Population density – 97 per sq. km (2009)
Urban population – 69 per cent (2008 est)
Median age (years) – 28.1 (2010 est)
National anthem – 'Istiklal Marsi' ['The Independence March']
National day – 29 October (Republic Day)
Life expectancy (years) – 72.23 (2010 est)
Mortality rate – 6.1 (2010 est)
Birth rate – 18.28 (2010 est)
Infant mortality rate – 24.84 (2010 est)
Death penalty – Abolished for all crimes (since 2004)
CPI score – 4.4 (2010)

CLIMATE AND TERRAIN
Turkey in Europe consists of the relatively low-lying area of Eastern Thrace, including the cities of Istanbul and Edirne, and is separated from Asia by the Bosporus at Istanbul and by the Sea of Marmara and the Dardanelles (a strait about 64km in length, with a width varying from 1.6km to 6.4km).

Turkey in Asia comprises the whole of Asia Minor or Anatolia. Western Anatolia consists of a high central plateau with narrow coastal plains fringed by mountains in the north and south. Eastern Anatolia is mountainous, the land falling to a plateau between the mountains and the Syrian border. Elevation extremes range from 5,166m (Mt Ararat) to 0m (Mediterranean Sea). The Euphrates and Tigris rivers rise in the eastern mountains, which also contain many lakes, including Lake Van. Anatolia is prone to earthquakes.

The climate is temperate, but more extreme in the interior. Average temperatures in Ankara range from −4°C in January to 30°C in August.

HISTORY AND POLITICS
Asia Minor was part of the empire of Alexander the Great and then of the Roman and Byzantine empires, coming under Turkish rule in the 11th century. The Ottoman Empire was founded in the 13th century and reached its zenith in the 16th century, its rule encompassing much of western Asia, northern Africa and south-eastern Europe. In the 17th century it began a steady decline, and after defeat in the First World War the empire's remaining territory was partitioned. Following a nationalist revolt and the expulsion of foreign forces, the sultanate was abolished and Turkey was proclaimed a republic on 29 October 1923, under Gazi Mustafa Kemal (later known as Kemal Ataturk), who was elected president. Policies of secularism, rapid modernisation, economic development and neutrality were introduced. Turkey was neutral for much of the Second World War, but joined the Allies in 1945.

Since 1945 there has been a multiparty system but political deadlock, economic problems and civil unrest or terrorism have led to military intervention to restore stability in 1960, 1971, 1980 and 1997.

Turkey joined NATO in 1952. It became a candidate for EU membership in 1999 and subsequently introduced constitutional, economic and human and civil rights reforms to meet the preconditions for membership negotiations. The EU accession process began in 2005 but impetus has flagged since 2007.

Tension between secularists and Islamists has grown in recent years, particularly since the Islamic-based Justice and Development Party (AKP), led by Recep Tayyip Erdogan, came to power in 2002. Seculists' concerns about the AKP's agenda caused a four-month political crisis in 2007, preventing the election of a new president and leading outgoing President Sezer to refuse approval of constitutional amendments. The impasse was ended by early legislative elections in July 2007, in which the AKP won a greatly increased majority. In August the AKP candidate, Abdullah Gul, was elected president in the third round of voting. The AKP retained its overall majority in the legislative election in June 2011.

INSURGENCIES
Turkey's 12 million Kurds are the majority population in the south-east of the country, and have sought greater political and cultural rights for many years. The Kurdistan Workers' Party (PKK) has fought a guerrilla war for an

ethnic homeland in the south-east since 1984 and has been blamed for bombings in other parts of Turkey. Conflict on the Turkey–Iraq border has caused tension in relations with Iraq, especially in 2008 after Turkish military incursions into the autonomous Kurdish area in northern Iraq, where PKK fighters have taken refuge. The government started to seek a political solution to the violence in 2009, introducing measures to increase Kurdish language rights and reduce the military presence in the south-east.

A number of bombings attributed to Muslim extremists occurred in Istanbul in 2003 and 2004.

POLITICAL SYSTEM
The 1982 constitution has been amended several times, mostly recently in 2010; the 2010 amendments increase parliamentary control over the judiciary and the military. The current president was elected by the legislature for a single seven-year term; from 2014, the president will be directly elected for a four-year term, renewable once. The unicameral Turkish Grand National Assembly has 550 members who were directly elected for a four-year term. The prime minister is appointed by the president and appoints the cabinet.

HEAD OF STATE
President, Abdullah Gul, *elected* 27 August 2007

SELECTED GOVERNMENT MEMBERS *as at July 2011*
Prime Minister, Recep Tayyip Erdogan
Deputy Prime Ministers, Besir Atalay; Ali Babacan;
    Bulent Arinc; Bekir Bozdag
Finance, Mehmet Simsek
Foreign Affairs, Ahmet Davutoglu
Interior, Idris Naim Sahin

EMBASSY OF THE REPUBLIC OF TURKEY
43 Belgrave Square, London SW1X 8PA
T 020-7393 0202 E turkemb.london@mfa.gov.tr
W www.londra.be.mfa.gov.tr
Ambassador Extraordinary and Plenipotentiary,
    HE Unal Cevikoz, *apptd* 2010

BRITISH EMBASSY
Sehit Ersan Caddesi 46/A, Cankaya, Ankara
T (+90) (312) 455 3344 E britembinf@turk.net
W http://ukinturkey.fco.gov.uk
Ambassador Extraordinary and Plenipotentiary,
    HE David Reddaway, CMG, MBE, *apptd* 2009

BRITISH COUNCIL
Karum Is Merkezi, D Blok 430 Kat 5, Kavalklidere, Ankara
T (+90) (312) 455 3600 W www.britishcouncil.org.tr
Director, Margaret Jack

DEFENCE
The army has 4,503 main battle tanks, 3,643 armoured personnel carriers, 650 armoured infantry fighting vehicles and 37 armed helicopters. The navy has 14 submarines, 17 frigates, 52 patrol and coastal vessels and 10 armed helicopters at 12 bases. The air force has 426 combat aircraft. Since its invasion of Cyprus in 1974, Turkey has maintained forces in the north of the island and at present has about 36,000 personnel stationed there.

As a member of NATO, Turkey is host to the Sixth Allied Tactical Air Force Headquarters. Some 1,560 US European Command personnel are based mainly at Incirlik in southern Turkey.
Military budget – US$10,500m (2010)
Military personnel – 510,600: army 402,000, navy 48,600, air force 60,000; paramilitary 102,200
Conscription duration – 15 months

ECONOMY AND TRADE
The economy combines modern industry and commerce with a traditional agriculture sector. The private sector is growing steadily following large-scale privatisations of basic industry, banking, transport and communications. Financial and fiscal reforms from 2002 achieved growth averaging over 5 per cent a year from 2005 to 2007, although large current account and trade deficits remain.

The agricultural sector accounts for 8.8 per cent of GDP and employs 29.5 per cent of the workforce. The principal crops are tobacco, cotton, grain, olives, sugar beets, pulses, nuts, citrus and other fruits, and livestock products. A diverse industrial sector is dominated by textiles and clothing (which employ one-third of the industrial workforce), food processing, vehicle assembly, electronics, mining, iron and steel, oil, construction, timber and paper. Turkey is also a destination and a transit route for oil and gas from central Asian countries. Tourism is a major industry and source of foreign revenue. Industry contributes 25.7 per cent of GDP and services 65.5 per cent.

The main trading partners are EU countries (especially Germany), Russia, China and the USA. Principal exports are clothing, foodstuffs, textiles, metal manufactures and transport equipment. The main imports are machinery, chemicals, semi-finished manufactures, fuels and transport equipment.
GNI – US$606,932m; US$8,720 per capita (2009)
Annual average growth of GDP – 7.3 per cent (2010 est)
Inflation rate – 8.7 per cent (2010 est)
Population below poverty line – 17.11 per cent (2008 est)
Unemployment – 12.4 per cent (2010 est)
Total external debt – US$270,700m (2010)
Imports – US$140,900m (2009)
Exports – US$102,100m (2009)

BALANCE OF PAYMENTS
Trade – US$71,598m deficit (2010)
Current Account – US$13,853m deficit (2009)

Trade with UK	2009	2010
Imports from UK	£2,252,092,566	£3,665,850,931
Exports to UK	£3,935,699,827	£4,832,536,063

COMMUNICATIONS
Turkey has nearly 352,046km of roads, of which about 313,151km are surfaced. There are 8,699km of railways, and 1,200km of navigable waterways. The principal ports are Istanbul (Europe) and Izmir (Asia). There is a large merchant fleet of 645 ships of 1,000 tonnes or over. The principal airports are at Istanbul and Ankara.

Telecommunications systems are being modernised and expanded, especially the mobile phone network. There were 16.5 million fixed lines in use, 62.8 million mobile phone subscribers and 27.2 million internet users in 2009.

EDUCATION AND HEALTH
Education is free, secular and compulsory from the ages of six to 14. There are elementary, secondary and vocational schools.

Literacy rate – 88.7 per cent (2008 est)
Gross enrolment ratio (percentage of relevant age group) – primary 99 per cent; secondary 82 per cent; tertiary 38 per cent (2008 est)
Health expenditure (per capita) – US$571 (2009)
Hospital beds (per 1,000 people) – 2.4 (2004–9)

MEDIA

Media freedom has increased since 1999 as many restrictions have been lifted to comply with EU accession requirements. However, journalists remain subject to harassment and prosecution, and broadcasters to suspension of services for airing sensitive issues. Turkey has one state television and radio broadcaster, TRT, over 300 private television channels and more than 1,000 private radio stations. TRT has begun to broadcast Kurdish-language programmes, to conform with EU criteria on minority rights. There are around 40 national daily newspapers, including *Hurriyet, Milliyet* and *Cumhuriyet,* and the English-language *Hurriyet Daily News.*

CULTURE

Turkey is rich in archaeological remains, including Ephesus, a religious and cultural centre in Greek and Roman times, and an important centre of early Christianity; Troy, the Homeric city of Ilium; and a wealth of sites from the Roman, Byzantine, early Christian and Ottoman periods. Ankara (then called Ancyra) was the capital of the Roman province of *Galatia Prima,* and a marble temple (now in ruins), dedicated to Augustus, contains the *Monumentum (Marmor) Ancyranum,* inscribed with a record of the reign of Augustus Caesar.

The Roman city of Byzantium was selected by Constantine the Great as the capital of the eastern Roman Empire in AD 328 and was renamed Constantinople after the emperor's death. Now Istanbul, it contains the celebrated church of St Sophia, which, after becoming a mosque, was made a museum in 1934, and Topkapi, the former palace of the Ottoman sultans. In 2006 author Orhan Pamuk (*b.* 1952) became the first Turkish Nobel laureate.

TURKMENISTAN

Area – 488,100 sq. km
Capital – Ashgabat; population, 637,238 (2009 est)
Major cities – Dashhowuz, Turkmenabat
Currency – Manat of 100 tennesi
Population – 4,940,916 rising at 1.14 per cent a year (2010 est); Turkmen (85 per cent), Uzbek (5 per cent), Russian (4 per cent) (2003 est)

Religion – Muslim 89 per cent (majority Sunni), Christian 9 per cent (mainly Orthodox) (est)
Language – Turkmen (official), Russian, Uzbek
Population density – 11 per sq. km (2009)
Urban population – 49 per cent (2008 est)
Median age (years) – 24.8 (2010 est)
National anthem – 'Garassyz, Bitarap, Turkmenistanyn Dowlet Gimni' ['National Anthem of Independent Neutral Turkmenistan']
National day – 27 October (Independence Day, 1991)
Life expectancy (years) – 68.2 (2010 est)
Mortality rate – 6.27 (2010 est)
Birth rate – 19.62 (2010 est)
Infant mortality rate – 43.84 (2010 est)
Death penalty – Abolished for all crimes (since 1999)
CPI score – 1.6 (2010)
Literacy rate – 99.5 per cent (2008 est)
Health expenditure (per capita) – US$77 (2009)
Hospital beds (per 1,000 people) – 4.1 (2004–9)

CLIMATE AND TERRAIN

Over 80 per cent of the country is taken up by the Kara Kum (Black Sands) desert. There are mountains in the south and along the Iranian border, and areas below sea level along the edges of the Caspian Sea. Elevation extremes range from 3,139m (Gora Ayribaba) to −81m (Lake Akchanaya, although Lake Sarygamysh sometimes has a lower elevation because of fluctuations in its water level). There is a subtropical desert climate. Average temperatures in Ashgabat range from −4°C in January to 36°C in July.

HISTORY AND POLITICS

Turkmenistan was conquered successively by the Persians, Greeks (under Alexander the Great), Parthians, Arabs and Mongols from the sixth century BC. From the early 19th century until 1886 Turkmenistan was gradually incorporated into the Russian Empire. A Turkmen revolt against Russian rule in 1916 brought a period of autonomy until 1921, when Soviet control over Turkmenistan was established and it became an Autonomous Soviet Socialist Republic. Turkmenistan became a full republic of the USSR in 1925. It declared its independence from the USSR on 27 October 1991.

Saparmurat Niyazov became leader of the Turkmen Communist Party in 1985, and was elected president in 1990, becoming president for life in 2004. His autocratic regime, through harassment and authoritarianism, prevented the development of any effective political opposition or press freedom, rejecting political pluralism in favour of a cult of personality. After President Niyazov's death in 2006, Gurbanguly Berdimuhammedov was elected president. He is introducing reforms, but the country remains in effect a one-party state under an authoritarian regime.

The Democratic Party of Turkmenistan (DP), the renamed Communist Party, is currently the only legal political party, although the president said in 2010 that other political parties might be registered. The DP held all the seats in the legislature after the 2008 elections.

POLITICAL SYSTEM
A new constitution was adopted in 2008 which encouraged multiparty politics and economic liberalisation, abolished the People's Council and increased the powers of the enlarged legislature. The executive president is directly elected for a five-year term.

The unicameral parliament *(Majlis)* has 125 members directly elected for a five-year term.

The country is divided into five provinces (Ahal, Balkan, Dashhowuz, Lebap and Mary) and the city of Ashgabat.

HEAD OF STATE
President, Chair of the Council of Ministers, Gurbanguly Berdimuhammedov, *elected* 14 February 2007

SELECTED GOVERNMENT MEMBERS *as at July 2011*
First Deputy Chair, Foreign Affairs, Rashid Meredov
Defence, Begench Gundogdiyev
Finance, Dovletgeldy Sadykov
Interior, Iskander Mulikov

EMBASSY OF TURKMENISTAN
2nd Floor, St George's House, 14–17 Wells Street, London W1T 3PD
T 020-7255 1071 E tkm-embassy-uk@btconnect.com
W www.turkmenembassy.org.uk
Ambassador Extraordinary and Plenipotentiary,
HE Yazmurad N. Seryayev, *apptd* 2003

BRITISH EMBASSY
301–308 Office Building, Four Points Ak Altin Hotel, Ashgabat
T (+993) (12) 363 462 E beasb@online.tm
W http://ukinturkmenistan.fco.gov.uk
Ambassador Extraordinary and Plenipotentiary,
HE Keith Allan, *apptd* 2010

DEFENCE
The army has 680 main battle tanks, 829 armoured personnel carriers and 942 armoured infantry fighting vehicles. The navy has 6 patrol and coastal combatant vessels. The air force has 94 combat aircraft and 10 armed helicopters.
Military budget – US$261m (2010)
Military personnel – 22,000: army 18,500, navy 500, air force 3,000
Conscription duration – 24 months

ECONOMY AND TRADE
The Niyazov regime was reluctant to adopt market reforms; his successor has introduced reforms, but most economic activity remains in state control and is inefficient. Turkmenistan has large reserves of natural gas and some oil, but exports were restricted by a lack of export routes until 2009–10, when existing pipelines to Russia and Iran were supplemented by a new gas pipeline to China and a second pipeline to Iran; a trans-Caucasian route to European markets is also under exploration. However, government misuse of the revenues from these commodities means little has been done to alleviate the widespread poverty or high level of unemployment.

Agriculture is intensive around the irrigated oases, with half the irrigated land used to grow cotton. Agriculture accounts for 10.2 per cent of GDP and 48 per cent of employment; grain and livestock are the other main products. The principal industries are gas and oil production, petroleum products, textiles (including silk) and food processing. Industry contributes 30 per cent of GDP.

The main trading partners are Ukraine, Turkey, Russia, the UAE and the EU. Principal exports are gas, crude oil, petrochemicals, textiles and cotton fibre. The main imports are machinery and equipment, chemicals and foodstuffs.

GNI – US$19,238m; US$3,420 per capita (2009)
Annual average growth of GDP – 11 per cent (2010 est)
Inflation rate – 12 per cent (2010 est)
Population below poverty line – 30 per cent (2004 est)
Unemployment – 60 per cent (2004 est)
Total external debt – US$5,000m (2009 est)

BALANCE OF PAYMENTS
Trade – US$3,137m surplus (2010)
Current Account – US$1,678m deficit (2009)

Trade with UK	2009	2010
Imports from UK	£28,513,671	£48,016,042
Exports to UK	£59,426,834	£66,955,236

COMMUNICATIONS
Turkmenistan has 58,592km of roads, 47,577km of which are surfaced, and 2,980km of railways. There are two important waterways, the Amu Darya river in the north-east and the Niyazov (formerly Kara Kum) canal running across the Kara Kum desert from the Amu Darya to the Caspian Sea, providing 1,300km of transport routes. The main port is Turkmenbashi, on the Caspian Sea, and the main airport is at Ashgabat.

Telecommunications networks are underdeveloped but are being improved slowly. There were 478,000 fixed lines in use, 1.5 million mobile phone subscribers and 80,400 internet users in 2009.

MEDIA
The government has total control of the media, monitoring output, operating printing presses, censoring foreign media output before broadcast and controlling access to the internet. There are no private broadcast media, and most newspapers are mouthpieces of state or party organisations.

TUVALU

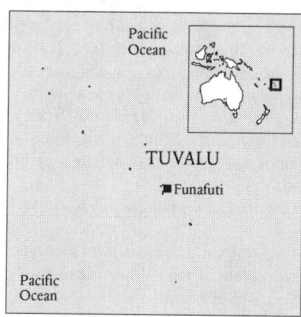

Area – 26 sq. km
Capital – Funafuti; population, 4,956 (2009 est)
Currency – The Australian dollar (A$) of 100 cents is legal tender. In addition there are Tuvalu dollar and cent coins in circulation
Population – 10,472 rising at 0.66 per cent a year (2010 est); Polynesian (96 per cent), Micronesian (4 per cent) (est)
Religion – Christian (Congregationalist 97 per cent, Seventh-day Adventist 1 per cent), Baha'i 1 per cent (est)
Language – English, Tuvaluan (both official), Samoan, Kiribati (on Nui)
Population density – 381 per sq. km (2008)

Urban population – 49 per cent (2008 est)
Median age (years) – 23.9 (2010 est)
National anthem – 'Tuvalu mo te Atua' ['Tuvalu for the Almighty']
National day – 1 October (Independence Day)
Life expectancy (years) – 64.39 (2010 est)
Mortality rate – 9.36 (2010 est)
Birth rate – 23.01 (2010 est)
Infant mortality rate – 35.52 (2010 est)
Death penalty – Abolished for all crimes (since 1978)

CLIMATE AND TERRAIN

Tuvalu comprises nine low-lying coral islands and atolls in the south-west Pacific Ocean. The highest elevation is 5m and the lowest is 0m (Pacific Ocean). The climate is tropical, with an average temperature of 26°C all year round.

HISTORY AND POLITICS

The islands were discovered by Europeans in the 18th century and, as the Ellice Islands, came under the control of the British in 1877. They formed part of the Gilbert and Ellice Islands protectorate (later a colony) from 1892, but were granted separate status from the Gilbert Islands in 1975. The islands became independent as Tuvalu on 1 October 1978. The country is seriously affected by rising sea levels, which are threatening its economic viability.

There are no political parties; allegiances are influenced by personal and island loyalties. Although politically stable as a democracy, there are frequent changes in government as support in parliament shifts. In the September 2010 legislative election the majority of incumbent members retained their seats and the legislature elected Maatia Toafa (prime minister 2004–6) as prime minister. Toafa was defeated in a confidence vote in December 2010 and was replaced by Willy Telavi.

POLITICAL SYSTEM
Under the 1978 constitution, Tuvalu is a constitutional monarchy with Queen Elizabeth II as head of state, represented by a governor-general who is appointed on the advice of the prime minister. The unicameral legislature, the Parliament of Tuvalu, has 15 members who are directly elected for a four-year term. The prime minister is elected by the legislature from among its members, and appoints the cabinet, who must be members of parliament. Local government services are provided by elected island councils.
Governor-General, HE Sir Iakoba Italeli, GCMG

SELECTED GOVERNMENT MEMBERS *as at July 2011*
Prime Minister; Home Affairs, Willy Telavi
Foreign Affairs, Apisai Ielemia
Finance, Lotoala Metia

HONORARY CONSULATE OF TUVALU
Tuvalu House, 230 Worple Road, London SW20 8RH
T 020-8879 0985 E tuvaluconsulate@netscape.net
Honorary Consul, Dr Iftikhar A. Ayaz

BRITISH HIGH COMMISSIONER
HE Malcolm McLachlan, MBE, *apptd* 2009, resident at Suva, Fiji

ECONOMY AND TRADE

The main economic activities are subsistence agriculture and fishing, although agricultural productivity is threatened by the increasing salinity of the soil as the sea

level rises; the only cash crop is coconuts. Tourism is limited by the state's remoteness. Most employment is in the public sector or abroad, often as merchant seamen; many families rely on remittances from expatriate workers. The government receives substantial annual income from a trust fund set up in 1987, and raises revenue through the sale of fishing licences, postage stamps and coins, and the leasing of its telephone code and internet suffix.

The main trading partners are Japan, the USA, New Zealand and Australia. The only exports are copra and fish. The main imports are food, livestock, fuels, machinery and manufactured goods.
Annual average growth of GDP – 3 per cent (2006 est)
Inflation rate – 3.8 per cent (2006 est)

BALANCE OF PAYMENTS
Trade – US$27m deficit (2010)

Trade with UK	2009	2010
Imports from UK	£932	£30,557
Exports to UK	—	£2,444

COMMUNICATIONS

Funafuti has an airfield, from which a service operates regularly to Fiji and Kiribati, and it is also the main port. There are 8km of roads on the islands. The telephone system provides an adequate service, with 1,700 fixed lines in use and 2,000 mobile phone subscribers in 2009, and 4,200 internet users in 2008.

MEDIA

The state-owned Tuvalu Media Corporation publishes a fortnightly newspaper and runs Radio Tuvalu, the main information source for islanders. There is no domestic television, although many islanders watch foreign programming via satellite.

UGANDA

Republic of Uganda

Area – 241,038 sq. km
Capital – Kampala; population, 1,535,060 (2009 est)
Major towns – Entebbe, Gulu, Lira
Currency – Uganda shilling of 100 cents
Population – 33,398,682 rising at 3.56 per cent a year (2010 est); Baganda (16.9 per cent), Banyakole (9.5 per cent), Basoga (8.4 per cent), Bakiga (6.9 per cent), Iteso (6.4 per cent), Langi (6.1 per cent), Acholi (4.7 per cent), Bagisu (4.6 per cent), Lugbara (4.2 per cent), Bunyoro (2.7 per cent); other 29.6 per cent (2002)

Religion – Christian 85 per cent (Roman Catholic 42 per cent, Anglican 36 per cent, other 7 per cent), Muslim 12 per cent (predominantly Sunni), indigenous beliefs 3 per cent (est); indigenous beliefs are often blended into or observed alongside Christianity or Islam
Language – English (official), Luganda, Swahili, Arabic
Population density – 166 per sq. km (2009)
Urban population – 13 per cent (2008 est)
Median age (years) – 15 (2010 est)
National anthem – 'O Uganda, Land of Beauty'
National day – 9 October (Independence Day)
Life expectancy (years) – 52.98 (2010 est)
Mortality rate – 11.9 (2010 est)
Birth rate – 47.55 (2010 est)
Infant mortality rate – 63.7 (2010 est)
HIV/AIDS adult prevalence – 6.5 per cent (2009 est)
Death penalty – Retained
CPI score – 2.5 (2010)

CLIMATE AND TERRAIN
The landlocked country lies on a high plateau with mountain ranges in the west, south-west and north-east. Elevation extremes range from 5,110m (Mt Stanley) to 621m (Lake Albert). Nearly 20 per cent of the country is covered by lakes, rivers and wetlands, and it contains about half of lakes Victoria, Edward and Albert (Mobuto), as well as lakes Kyoga, Kwania, George and Bisina (formerly Salisbury) and the course of the Nile from its outlet from Lake Victoria to the South Sudan border at Nimule. The climate is tropical, moderated by the altitude. There are two rainy seasons (March–May, October–December) in the south; the north is drier, semi-arid in places, with a single, longer rainy season.

HISTORY AND POLITICS
Indigenous people had formed several kingdoms in the area by the 14th century. External contact began in the early 19th century with Arab traders and then European explorers. A British protectorate was established over the kingdom of Buganda in 1894 and gradually extended to other territory by 1914. Uganda became independent on 9 October 1962 as a federation of the kingdoms of Ankole, Buganda, Bunyoro, Busoga and Toro.

In 1963 Uganda was proclaimed a federal republic but in 1966 prime minister Milton Obote overthrew the president, ended the federal status and became executive president. In 1971 President Obote was deposed in an army coup led by Maj.-Gen. Idi Amin, who proclaimed himself head of state. His brutal dictatorship was overthrown in 1979 with military assistance from Tanzania.

Milton Obote was re-elected president in 1980 but political instability and human rights abuses continued. He was ousted by a military coup in 1985 amid a civil war with the rebel National Resistance Army (NRA) led by Yoweri Museveni. A military council was installed but the NRA captured Kampala in January 1986, securing control of the rest of the country in the following few months. Museveni began a process of reconstruction which resulted in Uganda becoming relatively peaceful and stable, and restored a degree of prosperity.

Museveni's 'Movement' system of government, under which political parties were allowed to exist but not to contest elections, was in place from 1986 until a 2005 referendum resulted in a return to multiparty politics. In multiparty elections held in February and March 2011, President Museveni was re-elected for a fourth term in the first round of the presidential election, and the National Resistance Movement retained its overwhelming majority in parliament.

INSURGENCIES
The Lord's Resistance Army (LRA), whose aims have never been specified, began a low-level insurgency in northern Uganda in the late 1980s. Its activities have spread into north-eastern Congo (where most of the LRA is now located), southern Sudan, the Central African Republic and Kenya, despite offensives against LRA bases by Ugandan, Sudanese and Congolese forces since 2008. In Uganda, thousands have been massacred or mutilated, an estimated 20,000 children abducted to serve in its forces, and 1.7 million people displaced into camps

Terrorist attacks by Islamic extremists have begun in recent years. Some were carried out by Somalian Islamists, as African Union peacekeepers (predominantly Ugandan) have prevented them establishing complete control of the Somalian capital, but other attacks were the work of the Allied Democratic Forces, based in the Democratic Republic of Congo, which seeks to create an Islamic state in Uganda.

POLITICAL SYSTEM
The 1995 constitution was amended in 2005 to allow multiparty elections. The president is directly elected for a five-year term; the two-term limit was abolished in 2005. The unicameral parliament has 238 directly elected members and 137 (including 112 women) elected indirectly to represent particular groups; all serve a five-year term. The prime minister is appointed by the president, subject to the approval of parliament.

HEAD OF STATE
President, Yoweri Museveni, *sworn in* 29 January 1986, *elected* 9 May 1996, *re-elected* 2001, 2006, 2011
Vice-President, Edward Kiwanuka Ssekandi

SELECTED GOVERNMENT MEMBERS *as at July 2011*
Prime Minister, Amama Mbabazi
Deputy Prime Ministers, Henry Muganwa Kajura; Eriya Kategaya; Gen. Moses Ali
Defence, Crispus W. C. B. Kiyonga
Finance, Maria Kiwanuka
Foreign Affairs, Sam Kutesa

UGANDA HIGH COMMISSION
Uganda House, 58–59 Trafalgar Square, London WC2N 5DX
T 020-7839 5783 E info@ugandahighcommission.co.uk
W www.ugandahighcommission.co.uk
High Commissioner, HE Joan Rwabyomere, *apptd* 2006

BRITISH HIGH COMMISSION
PO Box 7070, 4 Windsor Loop, Kampala
T (+256) (31) 231 2000 E bhcinfo@starcom.co.ug
W http://ukinuganda.fco.gov.uk
High Commissioner, HE Martin Shearman, CVO, *apptd* 2008

BRITISH COUNCIL
PO Box 7070, Rwenzori Courts, Plot 2 and 4A, Nakasero Road, Kampala
T (+256) (41) 456 0800 W www.britishcouncil.org/africa
Director, Sital Dhillon

DEFENCE
The army has 185 main battle tanks, 31 armoured infantry fighting vehicles and 79 armoured personnel carriers. The air wing has 15 combat-capable aircraft and 10 helicopters.
Military budget – US$230m (2010)

Military personnel – 45,000: Ugandan People's Defence Force 45,000; paramilitary 1,800

ECONOMY AND TRADE

Economic reforms adopted since 1986 have produced steady economic growth, which was only slightly affected by the global downturn. However, there has been little industrialisation, so the economy is vulnerable to fluctuations in global commodity prices, especially that of coffee, its main export. Uganda's debt burden has been reduced by debt relief since 2000 but it is still dependent on foreign aid.

Agriculture is the most important economic sector, contributing 23.6 per cent of GDP and engaging about 80 per cent of the workforce. The principal crops are coffee, tea, cotton, tobacco, cassava, potatoes, maize, millet, pulses, cut flowers and livestock products. Industrial activity centres on production of sugar, tobacco, cotton textiles, cement and steel, brewing and fishing. Tourism is growing, and oil has been discovered but is not yet being exploited.

The main export markets are neighbouring countries, the UAE, the EU and Switzerland; imports come chiefly from Kenya, India, the UAE and China. Principal exports are coffee, fish and fish products, tea, cotton, cut flowers, horticultural products and gold. Electricity is exported to Kenya, Tanzania and Rwanda. The main imports are capital equipment, vehicles, petroleum, medical supplies and cereals.

GNI – US$15,711m; US$460 per capita (2009)
Annual average growth of GDP – 5.8 per cent (2010 est)
Inflation rate – 9.4 per cent (2010 est)
Total external debt – US$2,888m (2010 est)
Imports – US$4,400m (2009)
Exports – US$3,600m (2009)

BALANCE OF PAYMENTS
Trade – US$1,543m deficit (2010)
Current Account – US$469m deficit (2008)

Trade with UK	2009	2010
Imports from UK	£49,659,175	£56,592,998
Exports to UK	£9,227,960	£11,219,320

COMMUNICATIONS

There are over 1,244km of rail track, and 70,746km of roads, of which 16,272km are surfaced. Having no coast, Uganda is dependent upon rail and road links to Mombasa in Kenya and Dar es Salaam in Tanzania for much of its trade, although some of the lakes and parts of the river Nile provide navigable routes internally and to neighbouring countries. There is an international airport at Entebbe, and 45 other airports and airfields around the country.

The fixed-line telephone system is inadequate and mobile phone distribution is growing rapidly. In 2009 there were 233,500 fixed lines in use, 9.4 million mobile phone subscribers and 3.2 million internet users.

EDUCATION AND HEALTH

Education is a joint undertaking by the government, local authorities and voluntary agencies. In 1996 the Universal Primary Education programme was launched, under which four children per family are entitled to receive free primary education.

Literacy rate – 74.6 per cent (2008 est)
Gross enrolment ratio (percentage of relevant age group) –

primary 122 per cent; secondary 27 per cent; tertiary 4 per cent (2009 est)
Health expenditure (per capita) – US$43 (2009)
Hospital beds (per 1,000 people) – 0.4 (2004–9)

MEDIA

Private broadcasters have proliferated since media laws were liberalised in 1993, although they can be subject to constraints if the government perceives reporting as a threat to national security or likely to raise racial tension. They operate alongside the television and radio networks run by the public broadcaster. Radio is the most popular medium. The main newspapers include *New Vision*, which is state-owned but editorially independent.

UKRAINE

Ukrayina – Ukraine

Area – 603,550 sq. km
Capital – Kiev (Kyiv); population, 2,778,850 (2009 est)
Major cities – Dnipropetrovsk, Donetsk, Kharkiv, L'viv, Odesa, Zaporizhzhya
Currency – Hryvnia of 100 kopiykas
Population – 45,415,596 falling at 0.62 per cent a year (2010 est); Ukrainian (77.8 per cent), Russian (17.3 per cent); small Belarusian, Moldovan, Crimean Tatar, Bulgarian, Romanian, Polish, Hungarian and Greek minorities (2001)
Religion – Christian (Ukrainian Orthodox 84 per cent, Greek Catholic 8 per cent, Roman Catholic 2 per cent, Protestant 2 per cent), Muslim 1 per cent (predominantly Sunni) (est)
Language – Ukrainian (official), Russian
Population density – 79 per sq. km (2009)
Urban population – 68 per cent (2008 est)
Median age (years) – 39.7 (2010 est)
National anthem – 'Shche ne vmerla, Ukrainy' ['Ukraine's Glory Has Not Perished']
National day – 24 August (Independence Day)
Life expectancy (years) – 68.46 (2010 est)
Mortality rate – 15.7 (2010 est)
Birth rate – 9.62 (2010 est)
Infant mortality rate – 8.73 (2010 est)
HIV/AIDS adult prevalence – 1.1 per cent (2009 est)
Death penalty – Abolished for all crimes (since 1999)
CPI score – 2.4 (2010)

CLIMATE AND TERRAIN

Much of the country lies in a plain (steppe), with the Carpathian mountains in the west and mountains in the south of the Crimean peninsula. Elevation extremes range from 2,061m (Hora Hoverla) to 0m (Black Sea). The main rivers are the Dnieper, which runs through the centre of the country, the Dniester in the west, the Southern Buh and the Northern Donets (a tributary of the Don). The climate is continental, and Mediterranean in the southern Crimea. Average temperatures in Kiev range from −9°C in January to 26°C in July.

HISTORY AND POLITICS

The earliest Slavic state was formed on the river Dnieper with its capital at Kiev in the ninth century AD. The area was invaded successively by the Goths, Huns and Khazars, and then by the Tatar-Mongols in the 13th century. It came under Lithuanian rule in the 14th century, and was part of the Polish–Lithuanian Commonwealth in the 16th century. The east rebelled in 1685 and became part of Russia in the 17th century. The west became part of the Habsburg empire after 1795.

A reunified Ukraine declared its independence in 1918, but a civil war ensued which ended in 1921 with the partitioning of Ukraine between the USSR and Poland. In 1922 Ukraine became a constituent republic of the USSR. Germany invaded and occupied Ukraine from 1941 until forced to withdraw by the Red Army in 1944. Ukraine regained its western territory in the aftermath of the Second World War, and in 1954 the Crimea was transferred from Russia to Ukraine. Ukraine declared itself independent of the USSR on 24 August 1991.

In 1986 Ukraine suffered the world's worst nuclear disaster, when a reactor at the Chernobyl nuclear plant exploded. At least 10,000 people have died from radiation poisoning, the long-term health of millions more has been affected and a large area of the country is permanently contaminated.

Tensions between pro-Russian and pro-western political blocs, and divisions within the pro-western parties, have caused political instability since 2004, with two legislative elections and several changes of government. The 2007 legislative election was called after a power struggle between President Yushchenko and the prime minister, Viktor Yanukovych, produced a political impasse. Yanukovych's Party of Regions (PR) remained the largest party in the legislature but without an outright majority, and President Yushchenko's Our Ukraine–People's Self Defence Bloc (OUPSD) and the Yulia Tymoshenko Bloc (YTB) formed a coalition government headed by Yulia Tymoshenko (prime minister February–September 2005). This government collapsed in September 2008 after disagreements over its response to Russia's use of force in Georgia; an early legislative election was called for December, but was cancelled when the OUPSD and YTB joined with the Lytvyn Bloc to reconstitute the coalition government. The government resigned after losing a vote of confidence in March 2010 and was replaced by a four-party coalition led by the PR. Viktor Yanukovych was elected president in January 2010.

FOREIGN RELATIONS

In the aftermath of the USSR's disintegration in 1991, relations between Ukraine and Russia were strained by disputes over the Black Sea fleet and the status of Crimea. An agreement was reached in 1997 over the division of the fleet and Russia's lease of a naval base in Sevastopol. Disputes over Crimea have flared up intermittently, most recently in 2003 over a border in the region. The main causes of tension are the pro-Western policies pursued by some recent governments, particularly the possibility of Ukraine joining NATO, and the economic interdependence of the two countries; Ukraine is heavily dependent on Russia for gas supplies, and pipelines carrying much of Russia's gas exports to Europe pass through Ukraine. Price disputes have led to Russia suspending gas supplies on four occasions, but relations have improved since the election of President Yanukovych.

Ukraine signed a partnership and cooperation agreement with the EU in 1994 and an association agreement is under negotiation; President Yanukovych is less committed to EU membership than his predecessor. Ukraine was involved in NATO's Partnership for Peace programme in the 1990s. It applied for NATO membership during Viktor Yushchenko's presidency, but President Yanukovych's preference is for a strengthened relationship short of membership.

POLITICAL SYSTEM

The 1996 constitution was amended in 2006 to transfer some powers from the president to the legislature; the constitutional court returned these powers to the president in late 2010. The president is directly elected for a five-year term. The unicameral Supreme Council has 450 members, who are directly elected for a five-year term. The prime minister is appointed by the president, subject to the legislature's approval.

The country is divided into 24 provinces, the autonomous republic of Crimea and two municipalities (Kiev and Sevastopol) with provincial status.

HEAD OF STATE

President, Viktor Yanukovych, *elected* 7 February 2010, *sworn in* 25 February 2010

SELECTED GOVERNMENT MEMBERS *as at August 2011*

Prime Minister, Mykola Azarov
First Deputy Prime Minister, Andriy Klyuyev
Deputy Prime Ministers, Borys Kolesnikov;
  Serhiy Tyhypko
Finance, Fedir Yaroshenko
Interior, Anatoliy Mohylyov
Defence, Mykhaylo Yezhel
Foreign Affairs, Kostyantyn Hryshchenko

EMBASSY OF UKRAINE

60 Holland Park, London W11 3SJ
T 020-7727 6312 E emb_gb@mfa.gov.ua
W www.ukremb.org.uk
Ambassador Extraordinary and Plenipotentiary,
  HE Volodymyr Khandogiy, *apptd* 2010

BRITISH EMBASSY

Desyatinna 9, Kiev 01025
T (+380) (44) 490 3660 E ukembinf@gmail.com
W http://ukinukraine.fco.gov.uk
Ambassador Extraordinary and Plenipotentiary,
  HE Leigh Turner, *apptd* 2008

BRITISH COUNCIL

4/12 Vul. Hryhoriya Skovorody, Kiev 04070
T (+380) (44) 490 5600 W www.britishcouncil.org/ukraine
Director, Margaret Jack

DEFENCE

The army has 2,988 main battle tanks, 1,432 armoured personnel carriers, 3,028 armoured infantry fighting vehicles and 139 armed helicopters. The navy has 1 submarine, 1 frigate, 10 patrol and coastal vessels, 10 combat aircraft and 72 armed helicopters at 6 bases. The air force has 211 combat aircraft.

Russia has around 13,000 navy personnel at Sevastopol; Russia's lease of the naval base, agreed in 1997, was extended in 2010 to run until at least 2042.

Military budget – US$1,430m (2010)
Military personnel – 129,925: army 70,753, navy 13,932, air force 45,240; paramilitary 84,900
Conscription duration – 18–24 months

ECONOMY AND TRADE

The first decade of independence was characterised by economic mismanagement and opposition to economic restructuring. Reform began in the late 1990s and brought economic growth, with rises in output and exports and a reduction in inflation. However, the slow progress of reform has been a drag on the economy, leaving it vulnerable to external factors such as the global economic downturn; the economy contracted severely in 2009 after key commodity prices and export demand fell. The government sought IMF support in autumn 2008, but some funding has been delayed owing to political volatility.

The agricultural sector is large and productive, with over half the land under cultivation. The main crops are grain, sugar beet, sunflower seeds and vegetables; stock-raising and dairy-farming are also important. Agriculture accounts for 9.8 per cent of GDP and 16 per cent of employment. There are large deposits of coal, iron ore and other minerals. The main industrial activities are mining and metal processing, manufacture of machinery and transport equipment and chemicals, electricity generation and food processing, especially sugar. Ukraine imports three-quarters of its oil and gas, principally from Russia; supplies have been suspended on occasions by price disputes with Russia, but in 2009 the two countries signed 10-year gas supply and transit agreements.

The main trading partners are Russia (21 per cent of exports; 29 per cent of imports), China, Germany and Turkey. Principal exports are ferrous and non-ferrous metals (especially steel), fuel and petroleum products, chemicals, machinery and transport equipment, and foodstuffs. The main imports are energy (primarily gas), machinery and equipment, and chemicals.

GNI – US$111,105m; US$2,800 per capita (2009)
Annual average growth of GDP – 4.3 per cent (2010 est)
Inflation rate – 9.8 per cent (2010 est)
Population below poverty line – 35 per cent (2009)
Unemployment – 8.4 per cent (2010 est)
Total external debt – US$97,500m (2010 est)
Imports – US$45,400m (2009)
Exports – US$39,700m (2009)

BALANCE OF PAYMENTS
Trade – US$9,433m deficit (2010)
Current Account – US$12,763m deficit (2008)

Trade with UK	2009	2010
Imports from UK	£583,689,767	£442,600,929
Exports to UK	£138,742,068	£213,297,887

COMMUNICATIONS

Ukraine has a total of 169,496km of roads, 165,844km of which are surfaced. It has 21,684km of railways, and 2,185km of waterways, mostly on the river Dnieper. Its main seaports are Mariupol on the Sea of Azov, and Kherson, Mykolayiv, Odesa and Sevastopol on the Black Sea. There is a large merchant fleet of 160 ships of 1,000

tonnes and over, with a further 197 Ukrainian-owned ships registered in other countries. The principal airports are at Kiev and Odesa.

The fixed-line telephone system is being improved. In 2009 there were 13 million fixed lines in use, 55.3 million mobile phone subscribers and 7.8 million internet users.

EDUCATION AND HEALTH

Literacy rate – 99.7 per cent (2008 est)
Gross enrolment ratio (percentage of relevant age group) – primary 98 per cent; secondary 94 per cent; tertiary 79 per cent (2008 est)
Health expenditure (per capita) – US$180 (2009)
Hospital beds (per 1,000 people) – 8.7 (2004–9)

MEDIA

There are several private and state-owned television and radio networks. Ukraine has seven daily newspapers, many of which are mass-circulation publications; some publish both Ukrainian and Russian editions. Major titles include *Fakty i Kommentarii, Silski Visti* and *Segodnya*. The press asserted its independence to a much greater extent following the disputed presidential election of 2004, although concerns about media policy have been raised since president Yanukovych's election in 2010.

UNITED ARAB EMIRATES

Al-Imarat al-Arabiyah al-Muttahidah – United Arab Emirates

Area – 83,600 sq. km
Capital – Abu Dhabi; population, 666,360 (2009 est)
Major cities – Ajman, Al-Ain, Ash Shariqah, Dubai
Currency – UAE dirham (Dh) of 100 fils
Population – 4,975,593 rising at 3.56 per cent a year (2010 est); Emirati nationals 20.1 per cent, non-nationals 79.9 per cent (2005 est); of the non-nationals, about half are from South Asia and a quarter are Arab or Iranian
Religion – Muslim 76 per cent, Christian 9 per cent (est), large Hindu and Buddhist minorities; Islam is the state religion, and 90 per cent of nationals are Muslim (Sunni 85 per cent, Shia 15 per cent)
Language – Arabic (official), Persian, English, Hindi, Urdu
Population density – 55 per sq. km (2009)
Urban population – 78 per cent (2008 est)
Median age (years) – 30.2 (2010 est)
National anthem – 'Ishy Bilady' ['Long Live My Homeland']
National day – 2 December (Independence Day, 1971)
Life expectancy (years) – 76.32 (2010 est)
Mortality rate – 2.08 (2010 est)

Birth rate – 15.98 (2010 est)
Infant mortality rate – 12.3 (2010 est)
Death penalty – Retained
CPI score – 6.3 (2010)

CLIMATE AND TERRAIN
The United Arab Emirates (UAE) is situated in the south-east of the Arabian peninsula. Six of the emirates lie on the shore of the Gulf, between the Musandam peninsula in the east and the Qatar peninsula in the west, while the seventh, Fujairah, lies on the Gulf of Oman. A flat coastal plain merges into the desert of the interior, and there are mountains in the east. Elevation extremes range from 1,527m (Jabal Yibir) to 0m (Persian Gulf). There is a desert climate, although it is cooler in the mountains, with high humidity on the coast. Average temperatures in Sharjah range from 12°C in January to 39°C in August.

HISTORY AND POLITICS
The United Arab Emirates (formerly the Trucial States) is composed of seven emirates. Six of these came together as an independent state on 2 December 1971 when they ended their individual special treaty relationships with the British government, and they were joined by Ras al-Khaimah on 10 February 1972. On independence, the union government assumed full responsibility for all internal and external affairs apart from those internal matters that remain the prerogative of the individual emirates.

Sheikh Zayed of Abu Dhabi was president from independence until his death in 2004. He was succeeded as Sultan of Abu Dhabi by his son, Sheikh Khalifa, who was also elected president of the UAE. The first national elections were held in 2006, when half the members of the Federal National Council were elected by a small electoral college. A legislative election was scheduled for 24 September 2011.

POLITICAL SYSTEM
The 1971 provisional constitution, approved in 1996, was amended in 2008 to convert the Federal National Council from a consultative into a legislative body and to extend its original two-year term to 2011. Overall authority lies with the Supreme Council, comprising the hereditary rulers of the seven emirates, each of whom also governs in his own territory. The president and vice-president are elected every five years by the Supreme Council from among its members. The president appoints the prime minister and the council of ministers. The unicameral Federal National Council has 40 members, eight members each from Abu Dhabi and Dubai, six each from Sharjah and Ras al-Khaimah and four each for Fujairah, Umm al-Qaiwain and Ajman; half are elected by an electoral college and half are appointed by the rulers of each emirate.

HEAD OF STATE
President, HH Sheikh Khalifa bin Zayed al-Nahyan *(Abu Dhabi), elected* 3 November 2004, *re-elected* 2009
Vice-President, Prime Minister, Defence, HH Sheikh Mohammed bin Rashid al-Maktoum *(Dubai)*

SELECTED GOVERNMENT MEMBERS *as at August 2011*
Deputy Prime Ministers, Lt.-Gen. Sheikh Saif bin Zayed al-Nahyan *(Interior);* Sheikh Mansour bin Zayed al-Nahyan
Finance, HH Sheikh Hamdan bin Rashid al-Maktoum

Foreign Affairs, Sheikh Abdullah bin Zayed al-Nahyan
Economy, Sultan bin Saeed al-Mansouri

EMBASSY OF THE UNITED ARAB EMIRATES
30 Prince's Gate, London SW7 1PT
T 020-7581 1281 E informationuk@mofa.gov.ae
W www.uae-embassy.ae/uk
Ambassador Extraordinary and Plenipotentiary,
HE Abdul Rahman Ghanim al-Mutaiwee, *apptd* 2009

BRITISH EMBASSY
PO Box 248, Khalid bin al-Waleed Street (Street 22), Abu Dhabi
T (+971) (2) 610 1100 E chancery.abudhabi@fco.gov.uk
W http://ukinuae.fco.gov.uk
Ambassador Extraordinary and Plenipotentiary,
HE Dominic Jermey, OBE, *apptd* 2010

BRITISH COUNCIL
PO Box 46523, Villa No. 7, Al-Nasr Street, Khalidiya, Abu Dhabi
T (+971) (2) 691 0600 W www.britishcouncil.org/me-uae
Director, Richard Cotton

FEDERAL STRUCTURE
The emirates are: Abu Dhabi, Ajman, Dubai, Fujairah, Ras al-Khaimah, Sharjah and Umm al-Qaiwain. Each emirate has its own government, judicial system and penal code. Abu Dhabi has an executive council chaired by the crown prince.

DEFENCE
The army has 471 main battle tanks, 892 armoured personnel carriers and 430 armoured infantry fighting vehicles. The navy has 16 patrol and coastal vessels at 8 bases. The air force has 184 combat aircraft, and 30 armed and over 23 multi-role helicopters.
Military budget – US$7,960m (2010)
Military personnel – 51,000: army 44,000, navy 2,500, air force 4,500

ECONOMY AND TRADE
Exploitation of the territories' oil reserves began in the 1960s and transformed the UAE from poor rural principalities into modern states with a high standard of living. Oil and gas production dominate the economy, although diversification means that output now accounts for less than 25 per cent of GDP. The economy is also dependent on foreign workers, who make up about 85 per cent of the workforce, but the government aims to increase opportunities for its citizens through improved education and expansion of the private sector. The economy was badly hit by the global downturn, particularly in Dubai, which was heavily exposed when property prices crashed; its debt crisis has been alleviated by loans from federal and Abu Dhabi institutions.

Agriculture is limited by the terrain but the area under cultivation has been extended by irrigation and water desalination projects. The main products are dates, vegetables, watermelons, poultry, eggs and dairy products. Non-hydrocarbon industries include fishing, aluminium, cement, petrochemicals, fertilisers, commercial ship repair, construction materials, handicrafts, textiles, boat-building, financial services and tourism. Several free-trade zones are attracting foreign investment.

The main export markets are Japan, South Korea and India; imports come chiefly from China, India, the USA, Germany and Japan. Principal exports are crude oil (45 per cent), natural gas, re-exports, dried fish and dates. The main imports are machinery and transport equipment, chemicals and food.

GNI – US$103,500m; US$26,210 per capita (2006)
Annual average growth of GDP – 2.6 per cent (2010 est)
Inflation rate – 2.2 per cent (2010 est)
Population below poverty line – 19.5 per cent (2003)
Total external debt – US$122,700m (2010 est)
Imports – US$140,000m (2009)
Exports – US$175,000m (2009)

BALANCE OF PAYMENTS
Trade – US$70,351m surplus (2010)
Current Account – US$22,155m surplus (2008)

Trade with UK	2009	2010
Imports from UK	£4,017,082,386	£4,177,961,866
Exports to UK	£567,337,254	£937,768,948

COMMUNICATIONS
There are 4,080km of roads, all of which are surfaced, but no railway system. Jebel Ali, Khor Fakkan, Mina Zayed, Mina Rashid, Mina Saqr and Mina Khalid are the significant ports, and there is an international airport in every emirate except Ajman, where one is under construction.

Modern telecommunications systems provided services to 1.6 million fixed-line subscribers, 10.7 million mobile phone subscribers and 3.4 million internet users in 2009.

EDUCATION AND HEALTH
Education is free in state schools and compulsory from ages six to 14.
Literacy rate – 90.0 per cent (2008 est)
Gross enrolment ratio (percentage of relevant age group) –
   primary 105 per cent; secondary 95 per cent; tertiary 30 per cent (2009 est)
Health expenditure (per capita) – US$1,520 (2009)
Hospital beds (per 1,000 people) – 1.9 (2004–9)

MEDIA
Dubai is a regional media hub, home to pan-Arab satellite television channels and international media organisations such as Reuters and Sony; Abu Dhabi is establishing a similar media zone. UAE residents can receive broadcasts from a variety of domestic and pan-Arab television and radio stations, and there are a number of national daily newspapers. There are restrictions on media content, however, with censorship of foreign publications and frequent internal self-censorship. A 1988 law requires the licensing of publications and outlines acceptable subjects for coverage.

UNITED KINGDOM

United Kingdom of Great Britain and Northern Ireland

Area – 243,122 sq. km
Capital – London; population, 7,753,600 (2009)
Major cities – Birmingham, Bristol, Edinburgh, Glasgow, Leeds, Liverpool, Manchester, Sheffield
Currency – Pound sterling (£) of 100 pence
Population – 62,348,447 rising at 0.56 per cent a year (2010 est)
Religion – Christian 72 per cent (Anglican 29 per cent, Roman Catholic 10 per cent, other Protestant 14 per cent), Muslim 3 per cent, Hindu 1 per cent (est); small Jewish, Sikh and Buddhist minorities
Language – English, Welsh, Lowland Scots, Scottish Gaelic, Irish
Population density – 256 per sq. km (2009)
Urban population – 90 per cent (2008 est)
Median age (years) – 39.8 (2010 est)
National anthem – 'God Save the Queen'
Life expectancy (years) – 79.92 (2010 est)
Mortality rate – 9.33 (2010 est)
Birth rate – 12.7 (2010 est)
Infant mortality rate – 4.5 (2010 est)
Death penalty – Abolished for all crimes (since 1998)
CPI score – 7.6 (2010)

CLIMATE AND TERRAIN
The terrain of Great Britain is higher in the north and west, with low mountains and rugged hills in Scotland, northern England and Wales; the land declines towards the south and east, with its lowest points in the south-east. Northern Ireland is more low-lying, with low mountains in the north and east. The heavily indented coastline varies in height between high cliffs and sea level. Elevation extremes range from 1,343m (Ben Nevis, Scotland) to –4m (the Fens, eastern England). Although Scotland contains numerous large lochs and northern England includes an area known as the Lake District, the largest freshwater lake is Lough Neagh in Northern Ireland. The main rivers are the Thames, the Severn and the Trent in England and Wales, and the Tay in Scotland. The climate is temperate and extremes are rare, but the convergence of Atlantic, Arctic and European weather systems produces unusually changeable weather conditions. Average temperatures in London range from 2°C in January to 22°C in July.

HISTORY AND POLITICS
England, the largest of the United Kingdom's four constituent countries, was unified by the early tenth century. It experienced a period of Danish rule in the early 11th century, and then in 1066 was conquered by Duke William of Normandy. The Norman kings and their successors sought to expand their rule over the whole of Britain. Wales was conquered in the 13th century and politically united with England in 1535. English involvement in Ireland began in the 12th century and control of the whole island was finally established in Elizabeth I's reign. The succession of Elizabeth I by James VI of Scotland in 1603 united the two countries under one crown, followed by the transfer of Scottish government to Westminister by the Act of Union in 1707, creating Great Britain. Government of Ireland was transferred to Westminster in 1801, when the state became known as the United Kingdom. When the rest of Ireland became independent in 1921, the six counties of Northern Ireland chose to remain under British rule. Sectarian violence broke out in 1968 between the Protestant majority and the Roman Catholic minority over civil rights, and was continued by paramilitary forces

seeking union with the Republic of Ireland until a peace process began in the 1990s. Self-government was granted to Scotland, Wales and Northern Ireland in 1999.

In 1215, facing a revolt by the barons, King John signed Magna Carta, which attempted to define good kingship and began the country's constitutional development. The attempts of the Stuart kings to extend royal powers at the expense of Parliament in the mid 17th century led to the English Civil Wars, which established the relationship of the executive to the legislature. From the late 17th century Britain embarked on a period of massive trade expansion, emerging as a major colonial power in the 18th century with control over large territories, particularly in North America and the Indian subcontinent; 13 of the North American colonies seceded in 1776 and formed the United States of America.

Industrialisation began in Britain in the second half of the 18th century, and entered a second phase after 1830 that stimulated great economic growth and further colonial expansion throughout the 19th century. But Britain's economic and political dominance declined in the 20th century, undermined by the two world wars, the second war leaving the country close to economic collapse. Most of its colonies were granted independence between 1947 and the mid 1980s, many joining the Commonwealth. After the UK joined the European Community in 1973, its economic and diplomatic focus shifted from the Commonwealth to Europe.

The Labour government elected in 1945 pursued socialist economic and welfare policies, nationalising key industries, setting up the National Health Service and expanding the social security system. Economic decline continued until the 1980s, when it was reversed by the Conservative government led by Margaret Thatcher, the country's first woman prime minister. Her administration privatised nationalised industries, opened up welfare services to market forces and reduced the role of local government, polarising politics and public opinion. She also established a close relationship with the USA that was supportive of its foreign policy. This has been continued by her successors, most recently in the support for the US 'war on terror' and the deployment of British forces in Afghanistan since 2001, Iraq from 2003 to 2009, and in Libyan air space.

At the 2010 legislative election, the Conservative party won the most seats but without an outright majority. After negotiations with the Liberal Democrat party, a coalition government was formed under the Conservative leader, David Cameron, with the Liberal Democrat leader, Nick Clegg, as deputy prime minister.

POLITICAL SYSTEM

There is no written constitution. The head of state is a hereditary constitutional monarch. The bicameral parliament consists of the House of Commons, the lower house, and the House of Lords. The House of Commons has 650 members, directly elected for a five-year term. The House of Lords is appointed and numbers vary; in July 2011 it had 827 members, comprising 24 archbishops and bishops of the Church of England, 713 life peers and 90 hereditary peers. The prime minister is the leader of the majority party or coalition in the House of Commons.

Powers over certain internal matters were devolved in 1999 to Scotland, Wales and Northern Ireland, each of which has its own legislature and government; devolution was suspended in Northern Ireland several times between

2000 and 2007 owing to the breakdown of power-sharing arrangements.

HEAD OF STATE
HM The Queen of the United Kingdom of Great Britain and Northern Ireland, Queen Elizabeth II, *born* 21 April 1926; *succeeded* 6 February 1952; *crowned* 2 June 1953
Heir, HRH The Prince of Wales (Prince Charles Philip Arthur George), *born* 14 November 1948

SELECTED GOVERNMENT MEMBERS *as at July 2011*
Prime Minister, First Lord of the Treasury, Civil Service, David Cameron
Deputy Prime Minister, Nick Clegg
Chancellor of the Exchequer, George Osborne
Foreign and Commonwealth Affairs, William Hague
Justice, Lord Chancellor, Kenneth Clarke
Home Affairs, Theresa May
Defence, Liam Fox

DEFENCE
The army has 325 main battle tanks, over 2,059 armoured personnel carriers, 526 armoured infantry fighting vehicles and 66 armed helicopters. The navy has 11 submarines, 1 aircraft carrier, 7 destroyers, 17 frigates, 22 patrol and coastal combatant vessels, 12 combat aircraft and 113 armed helicopters at 7 bases. The air force has 334 combat aircraft and 47 multi-role helicopters.
Military budget – US$56,500m (2010)
Military personnel – 178,470: army 102,600, navy 35,480, air force 40,390

ECONOMY AND TRADE
The UK has a highly developed and technologically advanced economy that is now dominated by services and trade. It was the first industrialised nation, developing an economy in the 19th century based on heavy industry, mass manufacturing and global trade. It became less predominant as industrialisation spread to other countries, and the demands of the Second World War caused a postwar industrial decline that left the economy less efficient than many of its competitors and increasingly undercut by cheaper production in the developing world. In the 1980s, privatisation of state industries and constraints on public spending improved government finances, and primary industrial activities were increasingly replaced by service industries. After emerging from recession in the early 1990s, the economy experienced its longest-recorded period of expansion, outperforming the rest of the EU states, until 2008. The global economic downturn, tight credit and the end of the property boom caused the economy to go into recession from early 2008 until late 2009. The banking sector in particular was badly affected by the global financial crisis in 2008 and government intervention was necessary to stabilise the financial system, including nationalising or part-nationalising major banks. These measures left the government with a massive public-sector debt to service, and the new coalition government announced tight constraints on public spending from 2010.

The service sector, especially banking, insurance and business services, electronics, telecommunications and tourism, now contributes 77.1 per cent of GDP and employs 80.4 per cent of the workforce. Agriculture is intensive, highly mechanised and efficient, employing 0.9 per cent of the workforce, although contributing only 1.4 per cent of GDP. The UK has large but declining reserves of oil, gas and coal, and the country became a net importer of energy in 2005. Other industrial output is mostly of manufactured goods, including machine tools, electrical power equipment, automation and transport equipment, aircraft, ships, motor vehicles and parts, electronics and communications equipment, metals, chemicals, paper and paper products, food processing, textiles, clothing and other consumer goods.

The main trading partners are other EU countries, the USA and China. The principal exports are manufactured goods, fuels, chemicals, food, beverages and tobacco. The main imports are manufactured goods, machinery, fuels and foodstuffs.

GNI – US$2,218,056m; US$41,370 per capita (2009)
Annual average growth of GDP – 1.6 per cent (2010 est)
Inflation rate – 3.3 per cent (2010)
Population below poverty line – 14 per cent (2006 est)
Unemployment – 8 per cent (2010 est)
Total external debt – US$8,981,000m (2010)
Imports – US$484,000m (2009)
Exports – US$356,100m (2009)

BALANCE OF PAYMENTS
Trade – US$151,329m deficit (2010)
Current Account – US$28,838m deficit (2009)

COMMUNICATIONS

Traditionally a seafaring nation, the UK has a large merchant navy, with 527 ships of over 1,000 tonnes registered in the UK and 275 ships registered overseas. The main ports are at Grimsby and Immingham, London, Milford Haven, Southampton, Tees and Hartlepool, Forth, Liverpool, Felixstowe, Dover and Belfast. There is an extensive road network of 394,467km, including 3,559km of motorways. Railway passenger services are operated by 23 private companies. The network is being upgraded, and nearly a third of the 16,454km of track is now electrified. The Channel tunnel links the UK railway network to those of mainland Europe. About 3,200km of waterways are navigable, although most are used for leisure and only about 600km for commerce. There are about 144 licensed civil airports, of which Heathrow (the world's busiest international airport), Gatwick, Stansted and Manchester handle the highest volume of passengers.

Technologically advanced telecommunications systems provided services to 32.1 million fixed telephone lines, 80.3 million mobile phone subscribers and 51.4 million internet users in 2009.

EDUCATION AND HEALTH

Full-time education is compulsory between the ages of five and 16 in Great Britain and four and 16 in Northern Ireland. Education between the ages of 16 and 18 is voluntary, but under recent government legislation, will become compulsory from 2013. There are 116 universities, including the Open University, which offers distance-learning access to further and higher education.

Gross enrolment ratio (percentage of relevant age group) –
primary 106 per cent; secondary 99 per cent; tertiary 57 per cent (2008 est)
Health expenditure (per capita) – US$3,285 (2009)
Hospital beds (per 1,000 people) – 3.4 (2004–9)

MEDIA

The media is free, rarely censored and exerts considerable influence, particularly in political life. The press is mostly owned by large communications companies and therefore

financially independent of any political party, although most newspapers adopt a political stance. The British Broadcasting Corporation is a public service broadcaster with a worldwide reputation. It provides radio and television programmes, in competition with several commercial radio and television stations, including cable and satellite services. There are plans for the analogue television signal to be switched off by 2012. British libel laws, under which the burden of proof lies with the defendant, have led to an increasing number of foreign claimants filing libel suits in the UK over articles or books which would not warrant an action in their own country; the laws are currently under review.

OVERSEAS TERRITORIES

See pp 1074–1083

UNITED STATES OF AMERICA

Area – 9,826,675 sq. km
Capital – Washington, District of Columbia; population, 4,420,650 (2009 est)
Major cities – Chicago, Dallas, Houston, Los Angeles, New York, Philadelphia, Phoenix, San Antonio, San Diego, San José
Currency – US dollar (US$) of 100 cents
Population – 310,232,863 rising at 0.97 per cent a year (2010 est); white 80 per cent, black 12.9 per cent, Asian 4.4 per cent, Amerindian and Alaskan native 1 per cent, native Hawaiian and other Pacific islander 0.2 per cent; Hispanic 15.1 per cent (persons of Hispanic origin may be of any race or ethnic group) (2007 est)
Religion – Christian (Protestant 51 per cent, Roman Catholic 24 per cent, Mormon 2 per cent, other 2 per cent), Jewish 2 per cent, Buddhist 1 per cent, Muslim 1 per cent (est)
Language – English, Spanish, Hawaiian (official in Hawaii)
Population density – 34 per sq. km (2009)
Urban population – 82 per cent (2008 est)
Median age (years) – 36.8 (2010 est)
National anthem – 'The Star-Spangled Banner'
National day – 4 July (Independence Day)
Life expectancy (years) – 78.24 (2010 est)
Mortality rate – 8.38 (2010 est)
Birth rate – 13.83 (2010 est)
Infant mortality rate – 6.14 (2010 est)
Death penalty – Abolished in 16 states, District of Columbia and US insular territories
CPI score – 7.1 (2010)

CLIMATE AND TERRAIN

The coastline has a length of about 3,329km on the Atlantic Ocean, 12,268km on the Pacific, 1,705km on the Arctic, and 2,624km on the Gulf of Mexico. The principal river is the Mississippi-Missouri-Red (5,970km long), traversing the whole country from Montana to its mouth in the Gulf of Mexico. The Rocky Mountains range runs the length of the western portion of the country. West of this, bordering the Pacific coast, the Cascade Mountains and Sierra Nevada form the outer edge of a high tableland, consisting partly of stony and sandy desert and partly of grazing land and forested mountains, and including the Great Salt Lake, which extends to the Rocky Mountains. A vast central plain lies between the Rockies and the hills and low mountains of the eastern states, where large forests still exist, remnants of the forests which formerly extended over the entire Atlantic slope. Elevation extremes range from 6,194m (Mt McKinley, Alaska) to −86m (Death Valley, California). The climate varies with latitude but is mostly temperate, with semi-arid conditions on the great plains and arid in the south-west. Average temperatures in Washington DC range from −1°C from December–February to 31°C in July.

Two states are detached: Alaska and Hawaii. Alaska occupies the north-western extremity of North America, separated from the rest of the USA by the Canadian province of British Columbia. The terrain is arctic tundra with mountain ranges, and the climate is arctic. The state of Hawaii is a chain of about 20 mountainous volcanic islands in the north Pacific Ocean, of which the chief islands are Hawaii, Maui, Oahu, Kauai and Molokai. The climate is tropical.

The Pacific coast and Hawaii are prone to seismic activity. The Atlantic and Gulf of Mexico coasts frequently experience hurricanes.

HISTORY AND POLITICS

The area that is now the USA was first inhabited by nomadic hunters who probably arrived from Asia c.30,000 BC. The continent was reached by the Norse in the tenth century and explored by the Spanish after their first landfall in North America in 1513. European colonisation began in the 16th century, with Spanish settlements in the south, and British, Dutch, French, German and Swedish settlements along the eastern seaboard. In the first century of European settlement, much of the native population was killed by diseases brought by the colonists. Many black Africans were introduced as slaves to work on the plantations in the southern colonies of the continent.

By 1733 there were 13 British colonies, composed mostly of religious non-conformists who had left Britain to escape persecution. A rebellion broke out in these colonies in 1775, largely because of the colonists' objection to being taxed by, but having no representation in, the British parliament. The British government's forces were defeated with French, Spanish and Dutch assistance. The Declaration of Independence which inaugurated the United States of America was signed on 4 July 1776; Britain recognised American sovereignty in 1783. The first federal constitution was drawn up in 1787; ten amendments, termed the Bill of Rights, were added in 1791. The 13 original states of the Union ratified the constitution between 1787 and 1790. Vermont, Kentucky and Tennessee were admitted in the 1790s, but most of the states acceded in the 19th century, as the opening up of the centre and west led to the creation of new states, and European or neighbouring countries ceded or sold their territories to the USA.

The Civil War (1861–5) was fought over the issue of slavery, which was integral to the economy of the southern states but was opposed by the northern states. The Confederacy of 11 southern states (Virginia, North Carolina, South Carolina, Georgia, Alabama, Florida, Tennessee, Mississippi, Louisiana, Texas, Arkansas) seceded in 1860–1, but was defeated by the northern states.

The USA industrialised rapidly in the late 19th century. It emerged as a world economic and military superpower in the 20th century and played a decisive role in the two world wars. Its economic and military (including nuclear) supremacy has given the USA a key role in shaping the post-war world. The Cold War with the USSR, which began after the Second World War, ended in 1990.

Following terrorist attacks in New York and Washington DC on 11 September 2001, President George W. Bush declared a 'war on terror'. As part of this, the USA led multi-national forces into conflicts in Afghanistan in 2001 and Iraq in 2003; US troops remain in both countries to help stabilise internal security. Problems in the US financial sector triggered a global economic downturn in 2007; the US government has promoted international attempts to safeguard against similar events.

The 2008 presidential election was won by the Democrat candidate Barack Obama, the first African-American to hold the office. In the 2008 legislative elections, the Democrat Party retained its majorities in both houses of congress. The Democrat majority in the senate was lost in early 2010 but a narrow majority was regained at the November 2010 elections. In the 2010 elections to the House of Representatives, the Democrats lost heavily to the Republicans.

POLITICAL SYSTEM

By the constitution of 17 September 1787 (which has been amended 15 times, most recently in 1992), the government of the USA is entrusted to three separate authorities: the federal executive (the president and cabinet), the legislature (Congress, which consists of a senate and a House of Representatives) and the judicature. The president is indirectly elected by an electoral college to serve a four-year term, and may serve a maximum of two consecutive terms. If a president dies in office, the vice-president serves the remainder of his term. The president appoints the cabinet officers and all the chief officials, subject to confirmation by the senate. He makes recommendations of a general nature to Congress, and when laws are passed, he may return them to Congress with a veto. But, if a measure so vetoed is again passed by both houses by a two-thirds majority in each house, it becomes law, notwithstanding the objection of the president.

Each of the 50 states has its own executive, legislature and judiciary. In theory, they are sovereign, but in practice their autonomy is increasingly circumscribed.

PRESIDENTIAL ELECTIONS

Candidates for the presidency must be at least 35 years of age and a native citizen of the USA. The electoral college for each state is directly elected by universal adult suffrage in the November preceding the January in which the presidential term expires. The number of members of the electoral college is equal to the whole number of senators and representatives to which the state is entitled in the national congress. The electoral college for each state meets in its state in December and each member votes for a presidential candidate by ballot. The ballots are sent to

Washington, and opened on 6 January by the president of the senate in the presence of Congress. The candidate who has received a majority of the whole number of electoral votes cast is declared president for the ensuing term. If no one has a majority, then from the highest on the list (not exceeding three) the House of Representatives elects a president, the votes being taken by states, the representation from each state having one vote. A presidential term begins at noon on 20 January.

HEAD OF STATE
President, Barack Obama, *elected* 2008, *sworn in* 20 January 2009
Vice-President, Joseph Biden

SELECTED GOVERNMENT MEMBERS *as at August 2011*
Secretary of State, Hillary Clinton
Defence, Leon Panetta
Interior, Ken Salazar
Treasury, Timothy Geithner
Secretary for Homeland Security, Janet Napolitano

THE CONGRESS
Legislative power is vested in the bicameral Congress, comprising the senate and the House of Representatives. The senate has 100 members, two from each state, elected for a six-year term, with one-third elected every two years. The House of Representatives has 435 members directly elected in each state for a two-year term; a resident commissioner from Puerto Rico and a delegate each from American Samoa, the District of Columbia, Guam, the Northern Mariana Islands and the Virgin Islands serve as non-voting members of the house.

Members of the 112th congress were elected on 2 November 2010 and sworn into office on 5 January 2011. As at July 2011, the 112th congress is constituted as follows:

Senate: Democrats 51; Republicans 47; Independent 2
House of Representatives: Democrats 192; Republicans 243
President of the Senate, The Vice-President
Senate majority leader, Harry Reid *(D), Nevada*
Speaker of the House of Representatives, John Boehner *(R), Ohio*
House majority leader, Eric Cantor *(R), Virginia*

THE JUDICATURE
The federal judiciary consists of three sets of federal courts: the Supreme Court at Washington, DC, consisting of a Chief Justice and eight Associate Justices; the US court of appeals, consisting of 179 circuit judges within 12 regional circuits and one federal circuit; and the 94 US district courts served by 678 district court judges.

THE SUPREME COURT
US Supreme Court Building, Washington DC 20543
Chief Justice, John Roberts, *apptd* 2005

UNITED STATES EMBASSY
24 Grosvenor Square, London W1A 1AE
T 020-7499 9000 W www.usembassy.org.uk
Ambassador Extraordinary and Plenipotentiary,
  HE Louis B. Susman, *apptd* 2009

BRITISH EMBASSY
3100 Massachusetts Avenue NW, Washington DC 20008
T (+1) (202) 588 6500 E washi@fco.gov.uk
W http://ukinusa.fco.gov.uk
Ambassador Extraordinary and Plenipotentiary,
  Sir Nigel Sheinwald, GCMG, *apptd* 2006

BRITISH COUNCIL
c/o The British Embassy
T (+1) (202) 588 6500 W www.britishcouncil.org/usa
Director, Sharon Memis

THE STATES OF THE UNION

The USA is a federal republic consisting of 50 states and the federal District of Columbia, and also of organised territories. Of the present 50 states, 13 are original states, seven were admitted without previous organisation as territories, and 30 were admitted after such organisation.

§ The 13 original states
(D) Democratic Party; (I) Independent; (R) Republican Party

State (with date and order of admission)	Area sq. km	Population (2009 est)	Capital	Governor (end of term in office)
Alabama (AL) (1819, 22)	133,915	4,708,708	Montgomery	Robert Bentley (R), Jan. 2015
Alaska (AK) (1959, 49)	1,530,694	698,473	Juneau	Sean Parnell (R), Dec. 2014
Arizona (AZ) (1912, 48)	295,259	6,595,778	Phoenix	Jan Brewer (R), Jan. 2015
Arkansas (AR) (1836, 25)	137,754	2,889,450	Little Rock	Mike Beebe (D), Jan. 2015
California (CA) (1850, 31)	411,047	36,961,664	Sacramento	Jerry Brown (D), Jan. 2015
Colorado (CO) (1876, 38)	269,595	5,024,748	Denver	John Hickenlooper (D), Jan. 2015
Connecticut (CT) § (1788, 5)	12,997	3,518,288	Hartford	Dan Malloy (D), Jan. 2015
Delaware (DE) § (1787, 1)	5,297	885,122	Dover	Jack Markell (D), Jan. 2013
Florida (FL) (1845, 27)	151,939	18,537,969	Tallahassee	Rick Scott (R), Jan. 2015
Georgia (GA) § (1788, 4)	152,576	9,829,211	Atlanta	Nathan Deal (R), Jan. 2015
Hawaii (HI) (1959, 50)	16,760	1,295,178	Honolulu	Neil Abercrombie (D), Dec. 2014
Idaho (ID) (1890, 43)	216,430	1,545,801	Boise	C. L. (Butch) Otter (R), Jan. 2015
Illinois (IL) (1818, 21)	145,933	12,910,409	Springfield	Patrick Quinn III (D), Jan. 2015
Indiana (IN) (1816, 19)	93,719	6,423,113	Indianapolis	Mitchell E. Daniels (R), Jan. 2013
Iowa (IA) (1846, 29)	145,752	3,007,856	Des Moines	Terry Branstad (R), Jan. 2015
Kansas (KS) (1861, 34)	213,097	2,818,747	Topeka	Sam Brownback (R), Jan. 2015
Kentucky (KY) (1792, 15)	104,661	4,314,113	Frankfort	Steve Beshear (D), Dec. 2011
Louisiana (LA) (1812, 18)	123,677	4,492,076	Baton Rouge	Bobby Jindal (R), Jan. 2012
Maine (ME) (1820, 23)	86,156	1,318,301	Augusta	Paul LePage (R), Jan. 2015

Maryland (MD) § (1788, 7)	27,091	5,699,478	Annapolis	Martin O'Malley (D), Jan. 2015
Massachusetts (MA) § (1788, 6)	21,455	6,593,587	Boston	Deval Patrick (D), Jan. 2015
Michigan (MI) (1837, 26)	151,584	9,969,727	Lansing	Rick Snyder (R), Jan. 2015
Minnesota (MN) (1858, 32)	218,600	5,266,214	St Paul	Mark Dayton (D), Jan. 2015
Mississippi (MS) (1817, 20)	123,514	2,951,996	Jackson	Haley Barbour (R), Jan. 2012
Missouri (MO) (1821, 24)	180,514	5,987,580	Jefferson City	Jeremiah (Jay) Nixon (D), Jan. 2013
Montana (MT) (1889, 41)	380,848	974,989	Helena	Brian Schweitzer (D), Jan. 2013
Nebraska (NE) (1867, 37)	200,349	1,796,619	Lincoln	Dave Heineman (R), Jan. 2015
Nevada (NV) (1864, 36)	286,352	2,643,085	Carson City	Brian Sandoval (R), Jan. 2015
New Hampshire (NH) § (1788, 9)	24,033	1,324,575	Concord	John Lynch (D), Jan. 2013
New Jersey (NJ) § (1787, 3)	20,168	8,707,739	Trenton	Chris Christie (R), Jan. 2014
New Mexico (NM) (1912, 47)	314,925	2,009,671	Santa Fé	Susana Martinez (R), Jan. 2015
New York (NY) § (1788, 11)	127,189	19,541,453	Albany	Andrew Cuomo (D), Jan. 2015
North Carolina (NC) § (1789, 12)	136,412	9,380,884	Raleigh	Beverly Perdue (D), Jan. 2013
North Dakota (ND) (1889, 39)	183,117	646,844	Bismarck	Jack Dalrymple (R), Dec. 2014
Ohio (OH) (1803, 17)	107,044	11,542,645	Columbus	John Kasich (R), Jan. 2015
Oklahoma (OK) (1907, 46)	181,185	3,687,050	Oklahoma City	Mary Fallin (R), Jan. 2015
Oregon (OR) (1859, 33)	251,418	3,825,657	Salem	John Kitzhaber (D), Jan. 2015
Pennsylvania (PA) § (1787, 2)	117,347	12,604,767	Harrisburg	Tom Corbett (R), Jan. 2015
Rhode Island (RI) § (1790, 13)	3,139	1,053,209	Providence	Lincoln Chafee (I), Jan. 2015
South Carolina (SC) § (1788, 8)	80,582	4,561,242	Columbia	Nikki R. Haley (R), Jan. 2015
South Dakota (SD) (1889, 40)	199,730	812,383	Pierre	Dennis Daugaard (R), Jan. 2015
Tennessee (TN) (1796, 16)	109,153	6,296,254	Nashville	Bill Haslem (R), Jan. 2015
Texas (TX) (1845, 28)	691,027	24,782,302	Austin	Rick Perry (R), Jan. 2015
Utah (UT) (1896, 45)	219,888	2,784,572	Salt Lake City	Gary Herbert (R), Jan 2013
Vermont (VT) (1791, 14)	24,900	621,760	Montpelier	Peter Shumlin (D), Jan. 2013
Virginia (VA) § (1788, 10)	105,586	7,882,590	Richmond	Bob McDonnell (R), Jan. 2014
Washington (WA) (1889, 42)	176,479	6,664,195	Olympia	Christine Gregoire (D), Jan. 2013
West Virginia (WV) (1863, 35)	62,761	1,819,777	Charleston	Earl Ray Tomblin (D), Jan. 2013
Wisconsin (WI) (1848, 30)	145,436	5,654,774	Madison	Scott Walker (R), Jan. 2015
Wyoming (WY) (1890, 44)	253,324	544,270	Cheyenne	Matthew Mead (R), Jan. 2015
Dist. of Columbia (DC) (1791)	179	599,657	–	Vincent Gray (D), Jan. 2015 *(Mayor)*

OUTLYING TERRITORIES AND POSSESSIONS

	Area sq. km	Population (2009 est)	Capital	Governor (end of term in office)
American Samoa	199	65,628	Pago Pago	Togiola Tulafono (D), Jan. 2013
Guam	541	178,430	Hagatna	Eddie Calvo (R), Jan. 2015
Northern Mariana Islands	477	88,662	Saipan	Benigno Fitial (C), Jan. 2015
Puerto Rico	13,790	3,967,288	San Juan	Luis G. Fortuño (R), Jan. 2013
US Virgin Islands	363	109,825	Charlotte Amalie	John de Jongh Jr (D), Jan. 2015

DEFENCE

Each military department is separately organised and functions under the direction, authority and control of the Secretary of Defence (except the Coast Guard, which is part of the Department of Homeland Security created in 2002). The air force has primary responsibility for the Department of Defence space development programmes and projects. Under US strategic command the USA has 730 submarine-launched ballistic missiles, 450 laser-guided nuclear missiles *(Minuteman III)* and 95 heavy nuclear-capable bombers. There are currently 4 space-based early warning satellites in orbit and the USA operates land-based early warning systems throughout the world. The army has 5,795 main battle tanks, 6,452 armoured infantry fighting vehicles, 19,881 armoured personnel carriers and 1,239 armed helicopters.

The navy has 14 strategic submarines, 57 tactical submarines, 11 aircraft carriers, 22 cruisers, 59 destroyers, 22 frigates, 28 patrol and coastal vessels, 31 principal amphibious ships, 947 combat aircraft and 255 armed helicopters. The Marine Corps has 447 main battle tanks, 370 combat aircraft and 147 armed helicopters. The air force has 1,808 combat aircraft.

In May 2010 the Department of Defence, for the first time, disclosed the size of its nuclear arsenal, which then stood at 5,113 warheads.

Military expenditure – US$712,800m (2010)

Military personnel – 1,563,996: army 639,063, navy 336,289, Marine Corps 204,056, air force 340,990, coastguard 43,598

ECONOMY AND TRADE

The USA is one of the world's leading industrial nations, with a sophisticated market economy that saw huge growth during the 20th century. Economic development was due in part to the mechanisation of the agrarian economy, the expansion of the transport infrastructure and large amounts of relatively cheap migrant labour; more recently it has been driven by rapid advances in technology. In the late 20th century, the economy shifted emphasis from industry to services, and government involvement in the economy was steadily reduced. Until 2008, the economy experienced steady growth, with low unemployment and inflation, although there were large budget and trade deficits, high levels of personal debt and an increasingly uneven distribution of wealth.

The US sub-prime mortgage crisis in 2007 triggered a global economic downturn, and falling property prices and tight credit pushed the domestic economy into recession by mid 2008. Following the failure of several investment banks, Congress passed a US$700bn relief programme to stabilise the financial markets in October 2008, and in spring 2009 a US$787bn fiscal stimulus package and a record US$3.6 trillion budget for 2010 were approved. Despite these measures, the economy still experienced the collapse of key industries (such as vehicle manufacturing), and rising unemployment and inflation before growth restarted in late 2009 after the USA's longest and deepest recession since the 1930s; the budget and trade deficits remain very high. The USA's triple 'A' credit rating was reduced in August 2011 following a deficit reduction plan passed by Congress.

Agriculture is a major industry in the USA, with about 18 per cent of land under cultivation. Principal crops are wheat, maize, other grains, fruit, vegetables, cotton, meat and dairy products. Agriculture, fishing and forestry contribute 1.2 per cent of GDP and employ 0.7 per cent of the workforce.

Mining and extraction are important to the economy. Large quantities of coal, iron ore, phosphate rock, copper, zinc and lead are mined. About one-third of the country's oil requirements are supplied by domestic production, principally from fields in the Gulf of Mexico. Natural gas is also produced. Despite its domestic oil and natural gas resources and its electricity generating capacity, the USA is a net importer of energy.

The industrial sector is highly diversified and technologically advanced. The main manufacturing industries produce steel, vehicles, aircraft and aerospace equipment, telecommunications equipment, chemicals, electronic equipment and consumer goods, and process food. Industry contributes 22.2 per cent of GDP and services account for 76.7 per cent of GDP.

The main trading partners are Canada, China, Mexico, Japan, Germany and the UK. Principal exports are capital goods (chiefly transistors, aircraft, vehicle parts, computers, telecommunications equipment), industrial supplies (e.g. organic chemicals), consumer goods (cars, medicines) and agricultural produce (soya beans, fruit, maize). The main imports are industrial goods (especially crude oil), consumer goods (cars, clothing, medicines, furniture, toys), capital goods (computers, telecommunications equipment, vehicle parts, office machines, electric power machinery) and agricultural products.

GNI – US$14,011,000m; US$46,360 per capita (2009)
Annual average growth of GDP – 2.8 per cent (2010 est)
Inflation rate – 1.4 per cent (2010 est)
Population below poverty line – 12 per cent (2004 est)
Unemployment – 9.6 per cent (2010 est)
Total external debt – US$13,980,000m (2010)
Imports – US$1,605,300m (2009)
Exports – US$1,056,700m (2009)

BALANCE OF PAYMENTS
Trade – US$633,904m deficit (2010)
Current Account – US$417,999m deficit (2009)

Trade with UK	2009	2010
Imports from UK	£33,598,991,523	£37,436,308,922
Exports to UK	£32,100,909,704	£34,889,461,456

GDP BY INDUSTRY (2010)

	US$bn
Private industries (total)	12,696.5
Agriculture, forestry, fisheries	154.1
Mining	281.4
Construction	505.6
Manufacturing	1,717.5
Transportation and warehousing	406.5
Wholesale trade	807.7
Retail trade	862.8
Finance, insurance and real estate	3,093.7
Information	670.3

Source: Bureau of Economic Analysis, 'Value Added by Industry'

COMMUNICATIONS

There are approximately 6.5 million km of roads, with surfaced roads accounting for 67 per cent of the total. There are 224,792km of railways, and more than 41,000km of navigable internal waterways, of which 19,300km are used for commerce. The main seaports are at Baton Rouge, Corpus Christi, Hampton Roads, Houston, Long Beach, Los Angeles, Miami, New Orleans, New York, Oaklands, Plaquemines, Port Canaveral, Port Everglades, Savannah, Seattle, Tampa and Texas City. There are over 15,000 airports and airfields; nearly 200 are capable of handling international flights, but the rest cater for the high domestic demand as air travel is the main form of transport for long-distance internal journeys.

Technologically advanced systems provide multi-purpose telecommunications facilities, though fixed-line subscriptions are declining as mobile phone use grows. There were 141 million fixed-line subscribers, 286 million mobile phone subscribers and 245 million internet users in 2009.

EDUCATION AND HEALTH

All the states have compulsory school attendance laws. In general, children are obliged to attend school from seven to 16 years of age. Of the total revenue for public elementary and secondary schools in 2008, 43.5 per cent came from local governments, 48.3 per cent from state governments and 8.2 per cent from the federal government. Among the better-known universities are Harvard (founded in 1636), Yale (1701) and Princeton (1746).

Gross enrolment ratio (percentage of relevant age group) –
    primary 99 per cent; secondary 94 per cent; tertiary 83 per cent (2008 est)
Health expenditure (per capita) – US$7,410 (2009)
Hospital beds (per 1,000 people) – 3.1 (2004–9)

MEDIA

The media industry is the largest and most influential in the world, and television programming is exported around the world. Internally, television and radio are regulated by the Federal Communications Commission. The major television networks are ABC, CBS, NBC, CNN, Fox, MTV, HBO and the Public Broadcasting System, which serves around 350 local member stations and is partially funded by the government and by private grants. There are around 10,000 commercial radio stations and the National Public Radio network which has over 600 non-commercial member stations, and more than 1,500 daily newspapers, including *The Wall Street Journal*, *USA Today*, *The Washington Post* and *The New York Times*. However, a decline in advertising revenues caused the parent companies of a number of major daily newspapers to file for bankruptcy protection in 2008–9, and several others are experiencing financial difficulties. *Time*, *Newsweek* and *US News and World Report* are influential current affairs magazines, while *Rolling Stone* and *Vanity Fair* are popular entertainment titles.

CULTURE

The culture of the USA is indebted to the diverse origins of its immigrants; European, African and Latin American influences are particularly strong. Often at the forefront of modern philosophical, literary and artistic movements (such as feminism, postmodernism and postcolonialism), the USA boasts many important writers, film-makers and artists.

The best-known writers include Edgar Allan Poe (1809–49), Mark Twain (1835–1910), Henry James (1843–1916), and poets Walt Whitman (1819–92) and Emily Dickinson (1830–86) in the 19th century; William Faulkner (1897–1962), Ernest Hemingway (1899–1961), John Steinbeck (1902–68), poet Robert Frost (1874–1963) and dramatist Eugene O'Neill (1888–1953) in the early 20th century; and Saul Bellow (1915–2005), J. D. Salinger (1919–2010), John Updike (1932–2009), Philip Roth (*b.* 1933) and playwrights Arthur Miller (1915–2005) and Tennessee Williams (1911–83) among the postwar generation. African-American literature has been assimiliated into the literary canon through the works of James Baldwin (1924-87), Ralph Ellison (1913–94), Maya Angelou (*b.* 1928), Toni Morrison (*b.* 1931) and Alice Walker (*b.* 1944). David Foster Wallace (1962–2008) was one of the most acclaimed writers of recent times.

The Hollywood film industry is the most wide-reaching in the world; celebrated film-makers include Walt Disney (1901–66), Orson Welles (1915–85), Frank Capra (1897–1991), Stanley Kubrick (1928–99), Francis Ford Coppola (*b.* 1939), Martin Scorsese (*b.* 1942) and Steven Spielberg (b. 1946).

Modern art found a spiritual home on the east coast and the Guggenheim and Metropolitan museums in New York house vast collections. Renowned artists include Edward Hopper (1882–1967), Jackson Pollock (1912–56), Roy Lichtenstein (1923–97) and Andy Warhol (1928–87).

The music of the USA reflects the country's ethnic diversity, with superior recording and distribution methods ensuring that rock and roll, country, blues, jazz and hip-hop became known worldwide. Musical icons include Elvis Presley (1935–77) and Bob Dylan (*b.* 1941) in rock, Hank Williams (1923–53) and Johnny Cash (1932–2003) in country music, Leadbelly (1888–1949) and Muddy Waters (1915–83) in blues, and Louis Armstrong (1901–71), Miles Davis (1926–91) and John Coltrane (1926–67) in jazz.

US TERRITORIES ETC

US insular areas are territories that are not part of one of the 50 US states or a federal district. The US Department of the Interior's Office of Insular Affairs has jurisdiction over American Samoa, Guam, the Northern Mariana Islands, the US Virgin Islands, part of Palmyra Atoll (4 sq. km) and Wake Atoll (6.4 sq. km), the latter shared with the US army's Space and Strategic Defence Command. The US Fish and Wildlife Service has jurisdiction over Baker Island (1.5 sq. km), Howland Island (2.5 sq. km), Jarvis Island (4.2 sq. km), Johnston Atoll (2.5 sq. km,

shared with the Defence Threat Reduction Agency), Midway Atoll (5.2 sq. km), Navassa Island (7.8 sq. km), Kingman Reef and part of Palmyra Atoll. The Aleutian Islands (17,666 sq. km) form part of the Alaskan archipelago.

Four of the eight populated insular areas are represented in the House of Representatives: Puerto Rico by a resident commissioner, and American Samoa, Guam and the US Virgin Islands by one non-voting delegate each.

PUERTO RICO

Commonwealth of Puerto Rico

Area – 13,790 sq. km

Capital – San Juan; population, 2,729,980 (2009 est).
  Other major towns are: Bayamón, Carolina, Poncel

Population – 3,989,133 rising at 0.25 per cent per year (2011 est); most people are of Spanish descent. The official languages are Spanish and English

National day – 25 July (Constitution Day)

Puerto Rico (Rich Port) is an island of the Greater Antilles group in the Caribbean Sea and was discovered in 1493 by Columbus. It was a Spanish possession until 1898, when it was ceded to the USA after the Spanish–American War. Residents have been US citizens since 1917, and Puerto Rico is represented in Congress by a non-voting resident commissioner, who is directly elected for a four-year term. Under its 1952 constitution, Puerto Rico is a self-governing commonwealth. The governor is directly elected for a four-year term. The bicameral legislative assembly consists of a 27-member senate and a 51-member House of Representatives, whose members serve four-year terms. Tourism, pharmaceuticals, electronics, clothing and food processing are the main economic activities.

Governor, Luis G. Fortuño (New Progressive Party)

GUAM

Guahan – *Territory of Guam*

Area – 541.3 sq. km

Capital – Hagatna (also known as Agana); population, 149,000 (2007 est)

Population – 183,286 rising at 1.31 per cent per year (2011 est); Chamorro (37 per cent), Filipino (26 per cent), other Pacific islander (11 per cent). The official languages are Chamorro (a language of the Malayo-Polynesian family with admixtures of Spanish) and English; most Chamorro residents are bilingual

National day – first Monday in March (Discovery Day)

Guam is the largest of the Mariana Islands, in the north Pacific Ocean. A Spanish colony for centuries, it was ceded to the USA in 1898 after the Spanish–American War. Guam was occupied by the Japanese in 1941 but was recaptured by US forces in 1944. Any person born in Guam is a US citizen. Guam is represented in Congress by a non-voting delegate, who is directly elected for a two-year term. Under the Organic Act of Guam 1950, Guam has statutory powers of self-government. The governor and lieutenant-governor are directly elected for a four-year term. The 15-member unicameral legislature is directly elected every two years. The main sources of revenue are tourism (particularly from Japan) and US military spending; the military installation is one of the most strategically important US bases in the Pacific.

Governor, Eddie Calvo (R)

Trade with UK	2009	2010
Imports from UK	£1,687,254	£1,077,570
Exports to UK	£94,782	£13,646

AMERICAN SAMOA

Territory of American Samoa
Area – 199 sq. km
Capital – Pago Pago
Population – 67,242 rising at 1.21 per cent per year
    (2011 est)
National day – 17 April (Flag Day)

American Samoa consists of the islands of Tutuila, Aunu'u, Ofu, Olosega, Ta'u, Rose Island and Swains Island. The islands were discovered by Europeans in the 18th century and the USA took possession in 1900. Those born in American Samoa are US non-citizen nationals, although some have acquired citizenship through service in the US armed forces or other naturalisation procedures. American Samoa is represented in Congress by a non-voting delegate, who is directly elected for a two-year term. Under the 1966 constitution, American Samoa has a measure of self-government, with certain powers reserved to the US Secretary of the Interior. The governor and deputy governor are directly elected for a four-year term. The bicameral legislative assembly comprises a 21-member House of Representatives (one appointed member and 20 members directly elected for a two-year term) and an 18-seat senate with members elected from among the traditional chiefs for a four-year term. Tuna fishing and canning are the principal economic activities. The economy and infrastructure were severely damaged by a tsunami in 2009.
Governor, Togiola Tulafono (D)

THE UNITED STATES VIRGIN ISLANDS

Area – 1,910 sq. km
Capital – Charlotte Amalie, on St Thomas; population, 53,526 (2009 est)
Population – 109,666 falling at 0.08 per cent per year
    (2011 est)
National day – 31 March (Transfer Day)

There are three main islands, St Thomas, St Croix and St John, and about 50 small islets or cays. These constituted the Danish part of the Virgin Islands from the 17th century until purchased by the USA in 1917. Those born in the US Virgin Islands are US nationals. The Virgin Islands are represented in Congress by a non-voting representative, who is directly elected for a two-year term. Under the provisions of the Revised Organic Act of 1954, the islands have powers of self-government. The governor and lieutenant-governor are directly elected for a four-year term. The unicameral senate has 15 members directly elected for a two-year term. Tourism, oil refining and manufacturing are the main industries.
Governor, John de Jongh Jr (D)

NORTHERN MARIANA ISLANDS

Commonwealth of the Northern Mariana Islands
Area – 464 sq. km
Seat of government – Saipan
Population – 46,050 falling at 4 per cent per year
    (2011 est)
National day – 8 January (Commonwealth Day)

The USA administered the Northern Mariana Islands, a group of 14 islands in the north-west Pacific Ocean, as part of a UN trusteeship until the trusteeship agreement was terminated in 1986, when the islands became a commonwealth under US sovereignty. Those resident in 1976 or subsequently born in the islands are US citizens. The islands are represented in Congress by a non-voting representative, who is directly elected for a two-year term. Under the 1978 constitution, the islands are self-governing. The governor and lieutenant-governor are directly elected for a four-year term. The bicameral legislature comprises a 20-member House of Representatives and a nine-member senate; members are directly elected, representatives for two years and senators for four years. Tourism and manufacturing, especially of clothing, are the main industries.
Governor, Benigno Fitial (C)

URUGUAY

República Oriental del Uruguay – Oriental Republic of Uruguay

Area – 176,215 sq. km
Capital – Montevideo; population, 1,632,620 (2009 est)
Major towns – Ciudad de la Costa, Salto
Currency – Uruguayan peso of 100 centésimos
Population – 3,510,386 rising at 0.45 per cent a year
    (2010 est)
Religion – Christian 81 per cent (Roman Catholic 47 per cent) (2006)
Language – Spanish (official), Portunol or Brazilero (Portuguese-Spanish mix used along the northern border)
Population density – 19 per sq. km (2009)
Urban population – 92 per cent (2008 est)
Median age (years) – 33.7 (2010 est)
National anthem – 'Himno Nacional' ['National Anthem']
National day – 25 August (Independence Day)
Life expectancy (years) – 76.55 (2010 est)
Mortality rate – 9.06 (2010 est)
Birth rate – 13.67 (2010 est)
Infant mortality rate – 10.99 (2010 est)
Death penalty – Abolished for all crimes (since 1907)
CPI score – 6.9 (2010)

CLIMATE AND TERRAIN

The country consists mainly of undulating grassy plains, with low hills. Elevation extremes range from 514m (Cerro Catedral) to 0m (Atlantic Ocean). The principal river is the Rio Negro (with its tributary, the Yi), flowing from north-east to south-west into the Rio Uruguay; damming of the Negro has created a reservoir that is the largest artificial lake in South America. The climate is warm temperate, with occasional cold and strong winds. Average temperatures in Montevideo range from 6°C in July to 28°C in January.

HISTORY AND POLITICS

The hostility of the indigenous Charrúa Amerindians when the Rio de la Plata was first explored by the Spanish in 1516 discouraged colonisation until the 17th century. Although initially settled by the Portuguese, the *Banda Oriental*, as the territory lying on the eastern bank of the river Uruguay was then called, was disputed between the Portuguese and the Spanish until the late 18th century and then between Brazil and Argentina after Spanish rule was overthrown. Uruguay's independence was recognised in 1828 and a republic was inaugurated in 1830. In the mid-19th century there was a power struggle between the conservatives *(Blancos)* and liberals *(Colorados)* which descended into civil war. From 1904 until the 1960s the country experienced political stability and prosperity.

The period from 1962 to 1973 saw economic decline and turmoil caused by the Marxist Tupamaros guerrillas. They were crushed by a military dictatorship that held power from 1973 until 1985, when a return to civilian rule was agreed after violent anti-government protests at the regime's repressive rule and the deteriorating economy.

The Colorado and National *(Blanco)* parties now both occupy the centre ground, but their dominance of politics has been eroded by left-wing parties such as New Space and coalitions such as the Progressive Encounter-Broad Front (EP-FA). The EP-FA won outright majorities in both legislative chambers in the 2004 and the 2009 elections. The 2009 presidential election was won by the EP-FA candidate José Mujica, and he appointed an EP-FA-led coalition government.

POLITICAL SYSTEM

Under the 1997 constitution, the executive president is directly elected for a five-year term, which is not renewable. The president, who appoints the council of ministers, is responsible to the legislature. The bicameral general assembly consists of a Chamber of Representatives, with 99 members directly elected for a five-year term, and the Chamber of Senators, which has 31 members, 30 directly elected for a five-year term and the vice-president as an *ex officio* member.

The republic is divided into 19 departments, each with an elected governor and legislature.

HEAD OF STATE

President, José Mujica, *elected* 29 November 2009, *took office* 1 March 2010
Vice-President, Danilo Astori

SELECTED GOVERNMENT MEMBERS *as at August 2011*
Economy and Finance, Fernando Lorenzo
Foreign Relations, Luis Almagro
Interior, Eduardo Bonomi
Defence, Eleuterio Fernandez Huidobro

EMBASSY OF URUGUAY
125 Kensington High Street, London W8 5SF
T 020-7937 4170 **E** emburuguay@emburuguay.org.uk
Ambassador Extraordinary and Plenipotentiary,
   HE Julio Moreira Moran, *apptd* 2009

BRITISH EMBASSY
PO Box 16024, Calle Marco Bruto 1073, 11300 Montevideo
T (+598) (2) 622 3630 **E** ukinuruguay@gmail.com
W http://ukinuruguay.fco.gov.uk
Ambassador Extraordinary and Plenipotentiary,
   HE Patrick Mullee, *apptd* 2008

DEFENCE

The army has 15 main battle tanks, 176 armoured personnel carriers and 18 armoured infantry fighting vehicles. The navy has 2 frigates, 18 patrol and coastal combatant vessels and 1 combat aircraft at 5 bases. The air force has 16 combat aircraft.
Military budget – US$431m (2010)
Military personnel – 24,621: army 16,234, navy 5,403, air force 2,984; paramilitary 818

ECONOMY AND TRADE

After years of steady growth, Uruguay suffered a severe recession from 1998, largely owing to the economic problems of Brazil and Argentina, its main export markets and sources of tourists. It reduced many to poverty in what had previously been a moderately prosperous society, and over a quarter of households still lived below the poverty line in 2008. The recession culminated in a banking crisis in 2002; IMF loans, the rescheduling of foreign debt repayments and the government's emergency measures achieved a recovery and the economy grew strongly from 2004 to 2008. The 2008 global downturn slowed economic growth in 2009 as commodity prices and tourist numbers fell, but Uruguay avoided recession, mainly through increased public expenditure, and recovered in 2010.

Ranching and livestock products (beef, mutton, wool) have been the mainstay of the economy since the mid-19th century, generating the prosperity that enabled Uruguay to develop an extensive welfare system in the early 20th century, although dependence on these products leaves the economy vulnerable to price fluctuations. Other crops include rice, grains, soya beans, citrus fruits, wine grapes, linseed and sunflower seed. Agricultural produce is the basis of the food processing and beverages industries. Other industries include fishing, forestry and the manufacture of electrical machinery, transport equipment, petroleum products, textiles and chemicals. Exploited minerals include clinker, dolomite, marble and granite. Tourism and offshore financial services also contribute substantially to revenue. Agriculture contributes 9.3 per cent of GDP, industry 22.8 per cent and services 67.9 per cent.

The main trading partners are Brazil, Argentina, China and the USA. Principal exports are meat, soya beans, cellulose, rice, wheat, timber, dairy products and wool. The main imports are crude and refined oil, vehicles and vehicle parts, mobile phones and insecticide.
GNI – US$30,811m; US$9,010 per capita (2009)
Annual average growth of GDP – 7.1 per cent (2010 est)
Inflation rate – 6.8 per cent (2010 est)
Unemployment – 7.4 per cent (2010 est)
Total external debt – US$13,390m (2010 est)
Imports – US$6,200m (2009)
Exports – US$5,400m (2009)

BALANCE OF PAYMENTS
Trade – US$1,991m deficit (2010)
Current Account – US$253m deficit (2009)

Trade with UK	2009	2010
Imports from UK	£55,034,646	£76,387,381
Exports to UK	£106,535,851	£101,696,197

COMMUNICATIONS

There are 77,732km of roads, 7,743km of which are surfaced, and 1,641km of railway, of which 1,200km are operational. There are 1,600km of navigable waterways, mainly on the Uruguay and Negro rivers. A bridge across the Rio de la Plata links Uruguay and Argentina. The main ports are Montevideo and Colonia on the coast, and Fray Bentos and Paysandú on the river Uruguay. There is an international airport near Montevideo, and 57 smaller airports and airfields around the country.

Modernised telephone systems provided services to 953,000 fixed-line subscribers, 4.1 million mobile phone subscribers, and 1.4 million internet users in 2009.

EDUCATION AND HEALTH

Primary and secondary education is compulsory and free, and technical and trade schools and evening courses for adult education are state-run. The university at Montevideo was founded in 1849.

Literacy rate – 97.9 per cent (2008 est)

Gross enrolment ratio (percentage of relevant age group) – primary 114 per cent; secondary 88 per cent; tertiary 65 per cent (2008 est)

Health expenditure (per capita) – US$698 (2009)

Hospital beds (per 1,000 people) – 2.9 (2004–9)

MEDIA

The constitution enshrines freedom of expression. There are more than 100 daily and weekly newspapers, all privately owned, and more than 100 radio stations, as well as 20 television channels. The government owns one television and one radio station.

UZBEKISTAN

O'zbekiston Respublikasi – Republic of Uzbekistan

Area – 447,400 sq. km

Capital – Tashkent; population, 2,200,910 (2009 est)

Major cities – Andijan, Bukhara, Karsi, Namangan, Nukus, Samarkand

Currency – Som of 100 tiyins

Population – 27,865,738 rising at 0.94 per cent a year (2010 est); Uzbek (80 per cent), Russian (5.5 per cent), Tajik (5 per cent), Kazakh (3 per cent), Karakalpak (2.5 per cent), Tatar (1.5 per cent) (est)

Religion – Muslim 93 per cent (of which Sunni 99 per cent, Shia 1 per cent), Christian (Russian Orthodox 4 per cent) (est)

Language – Uzbek (official), Russian, Tajik

Population density – 65 per sq. km (2009)

Urban population – 37 per cent (2008 est)

Median age (years) – 25.2 (2010 est)

National anthem – 'O'zbekiston Respublikasining Davlat Madhiyasi' ['National Anthem of the Republic of Uzbekistan']

National day – 1 September (Independence Day, 1991)

Life expectancy (years) – 72.24 (2010 est)

Mortality rate – 5.29 (2010 est)

Birth rate – 17.51 (2010 est)

Infant mortality rate – 22.66 (2010 est)

Death penalty – Abolished for all crimes (since 2008)

CPI score – 1.6 (2010)

CLIMATE AND TERRAIN

Landlocked Uzbekistan has four regions: the Ustyurt plateau and Amu Darya delta in the west; the Kyzyl Kum desert east of the Aral Sea; the Tien Shan and Pamir mountains in the east and south-east; and the fertile Fergana valley in the east, crossed by the Syr Darya river. Elevation extremes range from 4,301m (Adelunga Toghi) to −12m (Sariqarnish Kuli). The country includes the southern part of the Aral Sea. There is a semi-arid desert climate, although it is colder in the mountains. Average temperatures in Tashkent range from −5°C in January to 35°C in July.

HISTORY AND POLITICS

Settlements in the south developed as important transit points on the ancient 'Silk Road' in the first century BC. Bukhara and Samarkand became two of the most important cultural and academic centres in the Islamic world after the religion was introduced in the eighth century. In the 13th century the area became part of the Mongol Empire, with Samarkand as its capital during the reign of Amir Timur (Tamerlane). As the empire declined, independent principalities emerged. The three khanates in what is now Uzbekistan, Khiva, Kokand and Bukhara, were annexed by the Russian Empire in the second half of the 19th century. In 1917 a Bolshevik revolution broke out in Tashkent and by 1921 all of Uzbekistan had been absorbed into the USSR. Under Soviet rule a massive land irrigation programme was implemented to allow the cultivation of cotton, but this also led to the drying up of the Aral Sea.

Uzbekistan declared its independence from the USSR on 1 September 1991 but post-independence political life has been dominated by the former communists. The main opposition parties, *Erk* (Freedom) and *Birlik* (Unity), were banned in 1992 and have since become inactive; other forms of opposition are suppressed and the government has been accused of human rights abuses, including the systematic use of torture. The former communist leader Islam Karimov, who came to power in 1990, was elected president in 1991 and has retained the presidency since, in unopposed elections or through the extension of his term of office in referendums. He was re-elected in 2007 for a third term, despite the constitutional restriction to two terms.

All legislative elections since independence have been won by the People's Democratic Party (the former Communist Party) or its allies. After the latest legislative election in December 2009 and January 2010, the largest party in the legislative chamber was the pro-Karimov Liberal Democratic Party; opposition parties were barred from contesting the election. Most elections have been reported by observers to be neither free nor fair and have attracted international criticism.

INSURGENCIES

The Islamic Movement of Uzbekistan (IMU), founded in 1996, has carried out armed attacks and bombings sporadically since 1999, but has little support. However, its activities have provided the government with an excuse to curtail human rights and suppress political opposition and protests, such as those in Andijan in 2005, when over 180 protesters were killed by troops.

POLITICAL SYSTEM

The 1992 constitution was amended in 2002 to create a bicameral legislature and extend the president's term of office, and in 2011 to make the prime minister responsible to the legislature. The president is directly elected; his term of office was five years, renewable only once, but was extended to seven years. The legislature, the Supreme Assembly, became bicameral after the 2004–5 elections. The Legislative Chamber has 150 members, 135 directly elected and 15 members of the Ecological Movement of Uzbekistan. The senate has 101 members, 16 appointed by the president, 84 elected by regional deputies to represent the regions and the capital, and President Karimov. Members of both houses serve a five-year term. The president appoints the cabinet, which is chaired by the prime minister.

The country is divided into 12 provinces, the autonomous republic of Karakalpakstan, and the city of Tashkent.

HEAD OF STATE

President, Islam Karimov, *elected* 29 December 1991, *elected by referendum for a five-year term* 1995, *re-elected* 2000, 2007

SELECTED GOVERNMENT MEMBERS *as at August 2011*
Prime Minister, Shavkat Mirziyaev
First Deputy Prime Minister, Finance, Rustam Azimov
Deputy Prime Ministers, Farida Akbarova; Abdulla Aripov;
  Ergash Shoismatov; Ulugbek Roziqulov;
  Botir Khodayev; Elyor Ganiev
Defence, Gen. Kabil Berdiyev
Interior, Bahodir Matlubov

EMBASSY OF THE REPUBLIC OF UZBEKISTAN
41 Holland Park, London W11 3RP
T 020-7229 7679 E info@uzbekembassy.org
W www.uzbekembassy.org
Ambassador Extraordinary and Plenipotentiary,
  HE Otabek Akbarov, *apptd* 2007

BRITISH EMBASSY
Ul. Gulyamova 67, Tashkent 100000
T (+998) (71) 120 1500 E brit@emb.uz
W http://ukinuzbekistan.fco.gov.uk
Ambassador Extraordinary and Plenipotentiary,
  HE Rupert Joy, *apptd* 2009

BRITISH COUNCIL
University of World Languages Building, 11 Mirobod St,
Tashkent 700031
T (+998) (71) 140 0660/61/62/63
W www.britishcouncil.org.uk/uzbekistan
Director, Steve McNulty

DEFENCE

The army has 340 main battle tanks, 399 armoured infantry fighting vehicles and 309 armoured personnel carriers. The air force has 135 combat capable aircraft and 29 armed helicopters.
Military budget – US$1,420m (2010)
Military personnel – 67,000: army 50,000, air force 17,000; paramilitary 20,000
Conscription duration – 12 months

ECONOMY AND TRADE

The economy remains centrally planned and control has increased in some areas, stifling economic activity. Economic growth and living standards are among the worst in the former Soviet republics, with over a quarter of the population living below the poverty line. The 2008 global downturn had little impact owing to the country's relative economic isolation.

The economy is based on intensive agricultural production, particularly of cotton, made possible by extensive irrigation schemes. Vegetables, fruit, grain and livestock are also produced. The main industries are textile manufacture, food processing, machine building, metallurgy, mining (especially for gold), oil and natural gas production and chemicals. Oil and gas exports offer potential for greater economic growth and have attracted foreign interest, notably from Russia and China, but exploitation is hampered by a lack of modern oil pipelines and basic infrastructure. Agriculture contributes 21.2 per cent of GDP, industry 32.3 per cent and services 46.4 per cent.

The main trading partners are Russia, Ukraine, China, South Korea and Kazakhstan. Principal exports are oil and natural gas, cotton, gold, mineral fertilisers, metals, textiles, food products, machinery and motor vehicles. The main imports are machinery and equipment, foodstuffs, chemicals and metals.
GNI – US$32,526m; US$1,100 per capita (2009)
Annual average growth of GDP – 8.2 per cent (2010 est)
Inflation rate – 15 per cent (2010 est)
Population below poverty line – 26 per cent (2008 est)
Unemployment – 1.1 per cent (2010 est)
Total external debt – US$4,236m (2010 est)

BALANCE OF PAYMENTS
Trade – US$1,272m surplus (2010)
Current Account – US$3,562m surplus (2008)

Trade with UK	2009	2010
Imports from UK	£43,800,986	£55,064,186
Exports to UK	£29,360,708	£47,295,974

COMMUNICATIONS

Uzbekistan has 86,496km of roads, 75,511km of which are paved. It has 3,645km of railway, and 1,100km of waterways. The principal airport is at Tashkent.

The fixed-line telephone system is antiquated and mobile phone distribution is growing rapidly. There were 1.9 million fixed lines in use, 16.4 million mobile phone subscribers and 4.7 million internet users in 2009.

EDUCATION AND HEALTH

Literacy rate – 96.9 per cent (2008 est)
Gross enrolment ratio (percentage of relevant age group) –
  primary 92 per cent; secondary 104 per cent; tertiary 10 per cent (2009 est)

Health expenditure (per capita) – US$62 (2009)
Hospital beds (per 1,000 people) – 4.8 (2004–9)

MEDIA

The government strictly controls the media and much of the population relies on foreign broadcasts. Self-censorship by journalists is common because of state harassment, and internet access to independent websites is blocked. There is a mixture of government-run and private television and radio stations. Almost all newspapers are produced by the state or by pro-government organisations.

VANUATU

Ripablik blong Vanuatu / République de Vanuatu – Republic of Vanuatu

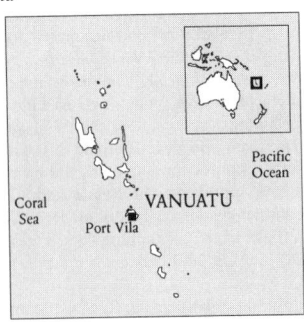

Area – 12,189 sq. km
Capital – Port Vila, on Efaté; population, 43,629 (2009 est)
Major town – Luganville, on Espiritu Santo
Currency – Vatu
Population – 221,552 rising at 1.36 per cent a year (2010 est); 98.7 per cent are Melanesian, the rest being mostly Micronesian, Polynesian and European (est)
Religion – Christian (Presbyterian 31 per cent, Anglican 13 per cent, Roman Catholic 13 per cent, Seventh-day Adventist 11 per cent, other 14 per cent), indigenous (including John Frum Movement cargo cult) 6 per cent (est)
Language – English, French, Bislama (all official); over 100 local languages exist
Population density – 20 per sq. km (2009)
Urban population – 25 per cent (2008 est)
Median age (years) – 24.6 (2010 est)
National anthem – 'Yumi, Yumi, Yumi' ['We, We, We']
National day – 30 July (Independence Day)
Life expectancy (years) – 64.33 (2010 est)
Mortality rate – 7.49 (2010 est)
Birth rate – 21.08 (2010 est)
Infant mortality rate – 48.17 (2010 est)
Death penalty – Abolished for all crimes (since 1980)
CPI score – 3.6 (2010)
Literacy rate – 78.9 per cent (2008 est)

CLIMATE AND TERRAIN

Situated in the south Pacific Ocean, Vanuatu comprises 13 large and some 70 small islands, of either coral or volcanic origin, including the Banks Islands and Torres Islands in the north. The principal islands are Vanua Lava, Espiritu Santo, Maewo, Pentecost, Ambae, Malekula, Ambrym, Epi, Efaté, Erromango, Tanna and Aneityum. Most islands are mountainous and covered with dense rainforest. Elevation extremes range from 1,877m (Tabwemasana) to 0m (Pacific Ocean). The climate varies from tropical in the north of the archipelago to subtropical in the south, and all the islands experience cyclones. Several islands have active volcanoes and seismic events are frequent.

HISTORY AND POLITICS

Some of the islands of Vanuatu have been inhabited for over 4,000 years. Europeans first visited in the early 17th century, and Captain Cook named the islands the New Hebrides in 1774. In the 19th century, the British and the French established plantations, and from 1906 jointly administered the islands as the Condominium of the New Hebrides. This became independent as the Republic of Vanuatu in 1980.

The 2009 presidential election was won by Iolu Abil in the third round of voting. Governments are formed by frequently shifting coalitions of various parties. In the 2008 legislative election, the Vanuaaku Pati won the most seats and formed a coalition government under Edward Natapei. He lost a vote of confidence in December 2010 and was replaced as prime minister by his deputy, Sato Kilman, who headed a reshuffled government. Kilman lost a vote of confidence in April 2011, and Serge Vohor of the Union of Moderate Parties was elected prime minister and formed a new coalition. However, Vohor's election was declared invalid in May, and Kilman's government was reinstated.

POLITICAL SYSTEM

Under the 1980 constitution, the head of state is a president who is elected for a five-year term by an electoral college consisting of the members of the legislature and the presidents of the six provincial governments. The unicameral parliament has 52 members, directly elected for a four-year term. The prime minister is elected by parliament from among its members, and appoints the council of ministers. The National Council of Chiefs advises on matters of custom.

HEAD OF STATE
President, Iolu Abil, *elected* 2 September 2009

SELECTED GOVERNMENT MEMBERS *at August 2011*
Prime Minister, Sato Kilman
Finance and Economic Management, Moana Carcasses Kalosil
Foreign Affairs, Alfred Carlot
Internal Affairs, George Wells

BRITISH HIGH COMMISSIONER
HE Malcolm McLachlan, MBE, *apptd* 2009, resident at Suva, Fiji

ECONOMY AND TRADE

The economy is based on small-scale agriculture and fishing; 65 per cent of the population is employed on plantations or in subsistence agriculture. Subsistence crops include yams, taro, fruit and vegetables; the principal cash crops are coconuts, cocoa and coffee. Cattle are kept on the plantations. There is a small light industrial sector producing frozen food and fish and canned meat, and processing wood. Eco-tourism and offshore financial services are of growing importance.

The main export markets are Thailand (57.7 per cent) Japan and Poland; imports come chiefly from Japan, Australia, China and Singapore. Principal exports are copra, beef, cocoa, timber, kava and coffee. The main imports are machinery and equipment, foodstuffs and fuels.

GNI – US$626m; US$2,620 per capita (2009)
Annual average growth of GDP – 4.1 per cent (2010 est)
Inflation rate – 3.9 per cent (2007 est)
Total external debt – US$81.2m (2004 est)
Imports – US$300m (2009)
Exports – US$100m (2009)

BALANCE OF PAYMENTS
Trade – US$162m deficit (2010)
Current Account – US$14m deficit (2009)

Trade with UK	2009	2010
Imports from UK	£5,016,125	£1,608,755
Exports to UK	£496,597	£488,352

COMMUNICATIONS
Vanuatu has 1,070km of roads, of which 256km are surfaced. There are no railways. The main ports are Forari, Port Vila and Santo. There are 31 airports and airfields on the islands; the main international airport is at Port Vila. Air connections and cruise ship facilities are being improved to boost tourism.

There were 7,200 fixed telephone lines, 126,500 mobile phone subscribers and 17,000 internet users in 2009.

VATICAN CITY STATE

Status Civitatis Vaticanae or Sancta Sedes / stato Della Città del Vaticano or Santa Sede – State of the Vatican city or the Holy See

ROME
(ITALY)

Vatican
Museums

St. Peter's
Basilica

St. Peter's
Square

ROME
(ITALY)

Area – 0.44 sq. km (enclave only)
Capital – Vatican City
Currency – Euro (€) of 100 cents
Population – 829 (2010 est)
Religion – Christian (Roman Catholic)
Language – Latin (official), Italian, French
National anthem – 'Inno e Marcia Pontificale' ['Pontifical Anthem and March']
National day – 19 April (election of Pope Benedict XVI, 2005)
Death penalty – Abolished for all crimes (since 1969)

HISTORY
The Vatican City State is an independent sovereign state that consists of an enclave within the city of Rome and extraterritorial areas including offices and basilicas in Rome, the pope's summer residence and the location

of Vatican Radio's transmitter. The Holy See, which comprises the pope and the departments that carry out the government of the Roman Catholic Church worldwide, has sovereign authority over the Vatican City State's territory, providing its government and diplomatic representation overseas.

The head of the Roman Catholic Church became a temporal ruler in the eighth century, holding territory in central Italy. The Papal States were annexed in 1860 by the newly unified kingdom of Italy, and Rome was captured by Italian troops in 1870–1, when the pope withdrew into the Vatican palace. In the Lateran treaties (1929), Italy recognised the pope's sovereignty over the city of the Vatican, and declared the state to be neutral and inviolable territory. The Vatican City State has special observer status at the United Nations.

The pope, the Sovereign Pontiff, is the head of state of the Vatican City, which is governed as an absolute monarchy. He is elected for life by a conclave consisting of those members of the Sacred College of Cardinals who are under the age of 80. Administration of the state is carried out by the Pontifical Commission and the Secretariat of State, which are appointed by the pope. All Vatican officials vacate their offices on the death of a pope. Pope Benedict XVI confirmed in office the president of the Pontifical Commission and the members of the Secretariat of State after his election.

Sovereign Pontiff, His Holiness Pope Benedict XVI (Joseph Ratzinger), *born* 16 April 1927, *elected* 19 April 2005, *inaugurated* 24 April 2005

SECRETARIAT OF STATE *as at July 2011*
Secretary of State, Cardinal Tarcisio Bertone
Substitute for General Affairs, Archbishop Fernando Filoni
Secretary for Relations with States, Archbishop Dominique Mamberti

PONTIFICAL COMMISSION
President, Archbishop Giovanni Lajolo

APOSTOLIC NUNCIATURE
54 Parkside, London SW19 5NE
T 020-8944 7189
Apostolic Nuncio, HE Archbishop Antonio Mennini, *apptd* 2011

BRITISH EMBASSY TO THE HOLY SEE
Via XX Settembre 80/A, 00187 Rome
T (+39) (6) 4220 4000 E holysee@fco.gov.uk
W http://ukinholysee.fco.gov.uk
Ambassador Extraordinary and Plenipotentiary,
HE Francis Campbell, *apptd* 2005

ECONOMY
The Vatican City budget is separate from that of the Holy See. The City's revenue is generated by museum admission charges and the sale of postage stamps, coins, medals, souvenirs and publications. The Holy See derives its income from investments, property, global banking and financial services and donations from Roman Catholics worldwide. The annual collections known as Peter's Pence are used for charitable and overseas aid work and disaster relief.

MEDIA AND CULTURE
Vatican Radio broadcasts worldwide in many languages, and the Vatican Information Service is the official news service.

The city is a World Heritage Site. Its architectural masterpiece, St Peter's Basilica, is famed for its domed roof and the Sistine Chapel ceiling, respectively designed and painted by Michelangelo. The Vatican museum contains a vast art collection.

VENEZUELA

República Bolivariana de Venezuela – Bolivarian Republic of Venezuela

Area – 912,050 sq. km
Capital – Caracas; population, 3,050,770 (2009 est)
Major cities – Barquisimeto, Ciudad Guayana, Maracaibo, Valencia
Currency – Bolívar fuerte (Bs. F) of 100 céntimos
Population – 27,223,228 rising at 1.52 per cent a year (2010 est)
Religion – Christian (Roman Catholic 96 per cent, Protestant 2 per cent); other 2 per cent (est)
Language – Spanish (official), several indigenous languages
Population density – 32 per sq. km (2009)
Urban population – 93 per cent (2008 est)
Median age (years) – 25.8 (2010 est)
National anthem – 'Gloria al Bravo Pueblo' ['Glory to the Brave People']
National day – 5 July (Independence Day)
Life expectancy (years) – 73.77 (2010 est)
Mortality rate – 5.14 (2010 est)
Birth rate – 20.29 (2010 est)
Infant mortality rate – 21.07 (2010 est)
Death penalty – Abolished for all crimes (since 1863)
CPI score – 2.0 (2010)

CLIMATE AND TERRAIN
The Andean mountains, of which the main range is the Sierra Nevada de Mérida, run across the north-west of the country, separating the northern coast from the central plains *(llanos)*. The Guiana Highlands occupy the south-east of the country. Elevation extremes range from 5,007m (Pico Bolivar) to 0m (Caribbean Sea). The Orinoco flows across the centre of the country to its delta on the Atlantic coast. Its upper waters are united with those of the Rio Negro (a Brazilian tributary of the Amazon) by a natural river or canal, known as the Brazo Casiquiare. The coastal lowlands contain many lagoons and lakes, including Lake Maracaibo (area 13,351 sq. km), the largest lake in South America. The climate varies from tropical to alpine, depending on altitude, and most areas experience a wet season from May to November. Average temperatures in Caracas range from 14°C in January to 27°C in April and May.

HISTORY AND POLITICS
Columbus landed on the coast in 1498, and the first Spanish settlement was established at Cumaná in 1520. Venezuela became part of the Viceroyalty of New Granada in the early 18th century. There were several revolts against Spanish colonial rule, and a declaration of independence in 1811 was followed by several years of struggle until troops led by Simón Bolivar defeated the Spanish at the battle of Carabobo in 1821. Venezuela became part of Gran Colombia (with Colombia, Ecuador and Panama), and then an independent republic in 1830 under the first of a series of *caudillos* (military leaders). The first truly democratic elections were held in 1947 but the government was overthrown by the military within months. An enduring civilian democracy was established in 1958 and introduced a period of relative political stability.

Oil revenues supported a buoyant economy in the 1970s but a price collapse in the mid-1980s led to economic difficulties and widespread poverty, causing social unrest and a number of attempted coups. Since he came to power in 1998, President Hugo Chávez's economic and social reforms and his authoritarian style have polarised domestic opinion, provoking strikes and demonstrations, an attempted military coup in 2002 and a recall referendum in 2004, which he won.

President Chávez was re-elected again in 2006. In the 2010 legislative election, the president's United Socialist Party of Venezuela and its allies won an overall majority, but lost its two-thirds majority (needed to change the constitution) as opposition parties won 67 seats.

POLITICAL SYSTEM
Under the 1999 constitution, the executive president is directly elected for a six-year term; the limit on the number of successive terms was abolished in 2009. The unicameral National Assembly has 165 members, 162 directly elected and three representing indigenous people, who serve a five-year term. The president appoints the vice-president and the council of ministers.

The country is divided into 23 states, one capital district and one federal dependency composed of 11 island groups (72 individual islands). The states have considerable autonomy and each has its own legislature and elected governor.

HEAD OF STATE
President, Col. (retd) Hugo Chávez Frías, *elected* 6 December 1998, *sworn in* 2 February 1999, *re-elected* 2000, 2006
Vice-President, Elías Jaua Milano

SELECTED GOVERNMENT MEMBERS *as at July 2011*
Interior and Justice, Tarek El Aissami
Defence, Carlos Mata Figueroa
Economy, Jorge Giordani
Foreign Relations, Nicolas Maduro

EMBASSY OF THE BOLIVARIAN REPUBLIC OF VENEZUELA
1 Cromwell Road, London SW7 2HW
T 020-7584 4206 E info@venezlon.co.uk
W www.embavenez-uk.org
Ambassador Extraordinary and Plenipotentiary,
HE Samuel Moncada, *apptd* 2007

BRITISH EMBASSY

Edificio Torre la Castellana, Piso 11, Avenida la Principal de la Castellana, Caracas 1601

T (+58) (212) 263 8411 E britishembassy@internet.ve

W http://ukinvenezuela.fco.gov.uk

Ambassador Extraordinary and Plenipotentiary,
HE Catherine Nettleton, *apptd* 2010

BRITISH COUNCIL

Torre Credicard, Piso 3, Avenida Principal El Bosque, Chacaito, Caracas

T (+58) (212) 952 9965 W www.britishcouncil.org/venezuela

Director, Peter Brown

DEFENCE

The army has 81 main battle tanks, 91 armoured personnel carriers and 10 armed helicopters. The navy has 2 submarines, 6 frigates, 6 patrol and coastal vessels and 10 combat aircraft at 10 bases. The air force has 99 combat aircraft.

Military expenditure – US$3,330m (2010)
Military personnel – 115,000: army 63,000, navy 17,500, air force 11,500, National Guard 23,000
Conscription duration – 30 months (selective)

ECONOMY AND TRADE

Much of industry is state-owned, and since President Chávez came to power an increasing proportion of the private sector, some foreign-owned, has been nationalised, including oil, electricity, financial, steel, construction and agribusiness companies. Laws passed in December 2010 will increase government control of the economy, which is struggling because of imbalances, high inflation and electricity shortages after a severe drought in 2009–10 left hydroelectric plants inoperable.

Oil and gas are the mainstays of the economy, providing over 90 per cent of exports and over 50 per cent of government revenue, but heavy dependence on them makes the economy vulnerable to global price fluctuations. The economy went into recession in 2009 owing to lower prices and the global downturn.

Other major industries are mining (coal, iron ore, bauxite, gold), production of construction materials, textiles, steel and aluminium, food processing and vehicle assembly. Industry contributes 34.9 per cent of GDP and services 61.1 per cent.

Agriculture comprises large-scale commercial farms and subsistence farming. Land distribution is uneven, but redistribution of land to the rural poor, breaking up larger estates, has begun. Agricultural products include maize, sorghum, sugar cane, rice, bananas, vegetables and coffee. There is an extensive beef and dairy farming industry. Agriculture provides 4.1 per cent of GDP and engages 13 per cent of the workforce.

The main trading partners are the USA (37.8 per cent of exports; 27.1 per cent of imports), Colombia, China and Brazil. Principal exports are oil, bauxite and aluminium, minerals, chemicals, agricultural products and basic manufactures. The main imports are agricultural products, raw materials, machinery, transport equipment and construction materials.

GNI – US$323,481m; US$10,090 per capita (2009)
Annual average growth of GDP – –2.8 per cent (2010 est)
Inflation rate – 29.8 per cent (2010 est)
Population below poverty line – 37.9 per cent (2005 est)
Unemployment – 12.1 per cent (2010 est)
Total external debt – US$55,610m (2010 est)

Imports – US$40,600m (2009)
Exports – US$57,600m (2009)

BALANCE OF PAYMENTS
Trade – US$42,591m surplus (2010)
Current Account – US$8,561m surplus (2009)

Trade with UK	2009	2010
Imports from UK	£277,360,066	£217,847,335
Exports to UK	£396,227,834	£379,821,201

COMMUNICATIONS

There are 96,155km of roads, some 32,308km of them surfaced. The 7,100km of inland waterways include 400km on the river Orinoco which, with Lake Maracaibo, is navigable by ocean-going ships. Road and river communications have made railways practically redundant, except for carrying iron ore in the south-east, although the government is expanding the network and there are now 806km of lines. The main ports are Maracaibo, Puerto Cabello and Caracas-La Guaira; there is a high risk of piracy for shipping in Venezuelan waters. There are over 400 airports and airfields, the principal airports being at Caracas and Maracaibo.

Telecommunications are being modernised and expanded. In 2009 there were 6.9 million fixed lines in use, 28.1 million mobile phone subscribers and 8.9 million internet users.

EDUCATION AND HEALTH

There are nine years of compulsory education. Under President Chávez, healthcare and education programmes have been greatly expanded.

Literacy rate – 95.2 per cent (2008 est)
Gross enrolment ratio (percentage of relevant age group) – primary 103 per cent; secondary 81 per cent; tertiary 79 per cent (2008 est)
Health expenditure (per capita) – US$686 (2009)
Hospital beds (per 1,000 people) – 1.3 (2004–9)

MEDIA

Media watchdogs have accused President Chávez of creating a climate of fear among journalists. In 2007 the terrestrial transmission licence of RCT, the country's oldest private television station and an outspoken critic of the president, was revoked by the government, and in 2009 opposition television network Globovision was heavily fined for alleged tax evasion and several dozen radio stations were closed. There are many private radio and television broadcasters in addition to the state-run networks (on which President Chávez has his own television and radio shows). There are six daily newspapers, including *El Mundo* and *El Nacional*.

VIETNAM

Cong Hoa Xa Hoi Chu Nghia Viet Nam – Socialist Republic of Vietnam

Area – 331,210 sq. km
Capital – Hanoi; population, 2,667,800 (2009 est)
Major cities – Bien Hoa, Da Nang, Haiphong, Ho Chi Minh City (Saigon)
Currency – Dong of 10 ho or 100 xu
Population – 89,571,130 rising at 1.1 per cent a year (2010 est); Kinh (85.7 per cent), Tay (1.9 per cent), Thai (1.8 per cent), Muong (1.5 per cent), Khmer (1.5 per cent), Hmong (1.2 per cent), Nung (1.1 per cent) (2009)
Religion – Buddhist 50 per cent (predominantly Mahayana), Christian (Roman Catholic 7 per cent, Protestant 1 per cent), Cao Dai 3 per cent, Hoa Hao 2 per cent (est). Cao Dai is a syncretistic religion that combines elements of several faiths. Hoa Hao is a branch of Buddhism
Language – Vietnamese (official), English, French, Chinese, Khmer; Mon-Khmer and Malayo-Polynesian are spoken in mountain areas
Population density – 281 per sq. km (2009)
Urban population – 28 per cent (2008 est)
Median age (years) – 27.4 (2010 est)
National anthem – 'Tien Quan Ca' ['Army March']
National day – 2 September (Independence Day)
Life expectancy (years) – 71.94 (2010 est)
Mortality rate – 5.97 (2010 est)
Birth rate – 17.29 (2010 est)
Infant mortality rate – 21.57 (2010 est)
Death penalty – Retained
CPI score – 2.7 (2010)

CLIMATE AND TERRAIN

The country is mostly mountainous, apart from the densely populated fertile plains around the deltas of the Hong (Red River) in the north and the Mekong in the south. Elevation extremes range from 3,144m (Fan Si Pan) to 0m (South China Sea). The climate is tropical and affected by the monsoon cycle. The wet season lasts from May to September, although the coast, being affected by typhoons and tropical storms, receives most rain between September and January.

HISTORY AND POLITICS

Independent kingdoms in Vietnam were unified in the 15th century but power became decentralised until the early 19th century, when central authority was reasserted with the assistance of France. From 1858 to 1884 France conquered Vietnam, establishing three protectorates which in 1887 became part of France's Indo-Chinese

Union with Cambodia and Laos. Vietnam was under Japanese occupation from 1940 to 1945; Vietnamese communists fought a guerrilla war of resistance against the occupiers and, controlling most of the country when the Second World War ended, declared independence.

France's attempts to reassert its control led to the Indo-China War (1946–54) which ended with France's withdrawal and an armistice dividing the country into communist North Vietnam and non-communist South Vietnam. A communist insurgency began in South Vietnam in 1957 and escalated into war between the communist north and the US-backed south. Direct military intervention by the USA began in the early 1960s but ended after talks resulted in a peace agreement in 1973. The civil war continued until the south was defeated in 1975, and North and South Vietnam were reunified in 1976 as the Socialist Republic of Vietnam.

A degree of economic liberalisation was introduced from 1986 and a new constitution in 1992 approved many economic and political reforms, but power remains with the ruling Communist Party. After a major government corruption scandal in 2006, the party leadership requested comments on its political platform; this prompted a public debate about the party's role, criticism of government and some calls for political pluralism. Subsequently, the government has continued its anti-corruption campaign but cracked down on media coverage of corruption and pro-democracy campaigners.

After the 2006 Communist Party Congress, the president and prime minister resigned to allow a younger leadership to be appointed; Nguyen Minh Triet was elected president to complete his predecessor's term of office, and he appointed Nguyen Tan Dung as prime minister. Both were re-elected to their posts in 2007, but the former lost the 2011 presidential race to Truong Tan Sang. In the May 2011 legislative election, the Communist Party and its allies held all the seats apart from four won by independent candidates.

POLITICAL SYSTEM

The 1992 constitution was amended in 2001 to allow small-scale capitalism greater freedom. The president is elected by the legislature to serve a five-year term. The unicameral National Assembly *(Quoc-Hoi)* has 500 members, who are directly elected for a five-year term. The head of government is the prime minister, who is responsible to the National Assembly, which appoints the council of ministers. However, effective power lies with the Communist Party of Vietnam. Its highest executive body is the Central Committee, elected by the national party congress held every five years. The politburo and the secretariat of the central committee, which exercise the real power, are elected at the party congress.

HEAD OF STATE
President, Truong Tan Sang, *elected* 25 July 2011
Vice-President, Nguyen Thi Doan

SELECTED GOVERNMENT MEMBERS *as at July 2011*
Prime Minister, Nguyen Tan Dung
Deputy Prime Ministers, Vu Van Ninh; Nguyen Thien Nhan; Hoang Trung Hai
Finance, Vuong Dinh Hue
Internal Affairs, Nguyen Thai BinhSon
National Defence, Gen. Phung Quang Thanh

EMBASSY OF THE SOCIALIST REPUBLIC OF VIETNAM
12–14 Victoria Road, London W8 5RD
T 020-7937 1912 E consular@vietnamembassy.org.uk
W www.vietnamembassy.org.uk
Ambassador Extraordinary and Plenipotentiary,
    HE Vu Quang Minh, *apptd* 2011

BRITISH EMBASSY
Central Building, 31 Hai Ba Trung, Hanoi
T (+84) (4) 936 0500 E behanoi02@vnn.vn
W http://ukinvietnam.fco.gov.uk
Ambassador Extraordinary and Plenipotentiary,
    HE Dr Antony Stokes, LVO, *apptd* 2010

BRITISH COUNCIL
20 Thuy Khue, Tay Ho District, Hanoi
T (+84) (4) 843 6780 W www.britishcouncil.org/vietnam
Director, Robin Rickard

DEFENCE
The army has 1,315 main battle tanks, 1,380 armoured personnel carriers and 300 armoured infantry fighting vehicles. The navy has 2 submarines and 56 patrol and coastal vessels at 7 bases. The air force has 223 combat aircraft and 26 armed helicopters.
Military budget – US$2,410m (2010)
Military personnel – 482,000: army 412,000, navy 40,000, air force 30,000; paramilitary 40,000
Conscription duration – 24–36 months

ECONOMY AND TRADE
The economy struggled for a decade after 1975 owing to the devastation of war and the imposition of a centrally planned economy. Since economic liberalisation and international integration were adopted in 1986, the economy has grown substantially, albeit from a low base, and export-driven industries are being developed. Poverty was reduced by over 40 per cent between 1993 and 2007, although more remote rural areas have yet to benefit. The global downturn reduced economic growth in 2008–9, and the economy recovered in 2010.

Agriculture's contribution is gradually shrinking, but still accounts for 20.6 per cent of GDP and employs 54 per cent of the workforce. The main industries are food processing, clothing and footwear, machine building, coal mining, steel, cement, chemical fertiliser, glass, tyres and paper, and oil and gas production from large offshore reserves. Industry now contributes 41.1 per cent of GDP and services 38.3 per cent.

The main trading partners are China, Japan, the USA and South Korea. Principal exports are clothing, footwear, fish and seafood, crude oil, electronics, wood products, rice and machinery. The main imports are machinery and equipment, petroleum products, steel products, raw materials, electronics, plastics and vehicles.
GNI – US$91,857m; US$1,000 per capita (2009)
Annual average growth of GDP – 6.8 per cent (2010 est)
Inflation rate – 11.1 per cent (2010 est)
Population below poverty line – 12.3 per cent (2009 est)
Unemployment – 6.4 per cent (2010 est)
Total external debt – US$33,450m (2010 est)
Imports – US$66,700m (2009)
Exports – US$55,800m (2009)

BALANCE OF PAYMENTS
Trade – US$12,000m deficit (2010)
Current Account – US$10,706m deficit (2008)

Trade with UK	2009	2010
Imports from UK	£209,679,762	£276,293,147
Exports to UK	£1,050,664,663	£1,236,732,020

COMMUNICATIONS
Vietnam has 171,392km of roads, 125,789km of which are unsurfaced. It has 2,347km of railways and 5,000km of navigable waterways. The main ports are Haiphong, Da Nang and Ho Chi Minh City; there is a high risk of piracy in the South China Sea. The principal airports are at Ho Chi Minh City, Hanoi and Da Nang.

Telecommunications systems are being modernised and expanded, and mobile phone distribution is growing rapidly. There were 17.4 million fixed lines in use, 98.2 million mobile phone subscribers and 23.4 million internet users in 2009.

EDUCATION AND HEALTH
Literacy rate – 90.3 per cent (2008 est)
Gross enrolment ratio (percentage of relevant age group) – primary 90 per cent; secondary 76 per cent; tertiary 16 per cent (2006 est)
Health expenditure (per capita) – US$80 (2009)
Hospital beds (per 1,000 people) – 2.9 (2004–9)

MEDIA
The government controls the media and it has closed broadcasters and jailed journalists who have reported on matters outside the narrowly defined official limits. There is one national television station and many local stations; some satellite channels are also available. The state-run radio network operates several national stations. The Communist Party and the People's Army both publish a daily newspaper and there are also newspapers published in English and French.

YEMEN

Al-Jumhuriyah al-Yamaniyah – Republic of Yemen

Area – 527,968 sq. km
Capital – Sana'a; population, 2,228,530 (2009 est)
Major cities – Aden (the former capital of South Yemen), Al Hudaydah, Ibb, Al Mukulla, Ta'izz
Currency – Riyal of 100 fils
Population – 23,495,361 rising at 2.71 per cent a year (2010 est)
Religion – Muslim (Sunni 55 per cent, Shia 45 per cent) (est)
Language – Arabic (official)
Population density – 45 per sq. km (2009)
Urban population – 31 per cent (2008 est)
Median age (years) – 17.9 (2010 est)
National anthem – 'United Republic'

National day – 22 May (Unification Day)
Life expectancy (years) – 63.36 (2010 est)
Mortality rate – 7.24 (2010 est)
Birth rate – 34.37 (2010 est)
Infant mortality rate – 56.77 (2010 est)
Death penalty – Retained
CPI score – 2.2 (2010)

CLIMATE AND TERRAIN

A mountainous region in the west and south divides the desert plains of the interior from the narrow coastal plains. Elevation extremes range from 3,666m (Jabal an Nabi Shu'ayb) to 0m (Arabian Sea). There is a desert climate, which is particularly harsh in the east, but moderated in the western mountains by the monsoon. The coast experiences high humidity and the average temperature in Aden is 29°C.

The islands of Perim and Kamaran in the Red Sea, and Suqutra in the Gulf of Aden, are Yemeni territory. The border with Saudi Arabia, except for the north-west corner, is unclear and is being delineated following an agreement between the two countries.

HISTORY AND POLITICS

Northern Yemen became part of the Ottoman Empire in the early 16th century and although it achieved some independence in the 17th century, Ottoman control was re-established in the 1870s and the area remained part of the empire until its collapse at the end of the First World War. In 1918 north Yemen became an independent kingdom under the rule of the Hamid al-Din dynasty. A revolution in 1962 overthrew the monarchy and the Yemen Arab Republic was declared. Fighting between royalists and republicans continued until 1967, when the republican regime was recognised internationally.

Aden, on the south coast, came under British rule in 1839, and a protectorate was gradually established over the sultanates of the southern hinterland in the second half of the 19th century. An armed rebellion against British rule began in 1963. After British troops withdrew in 1967, power was seized by the National Liberation Front, which established a repressive communist regime in the People's Republic of South Yemen (later renamed the People's Democratic Republic of Yemen).

The two countries united to form the Republic of Yemen on 22 May 1990. A power struggle between the former northern and southern elites led to a three-month civil war in 1994 in which a southern attempt to secede was crushed by northern government forces. Tensions remain between the north and south, where secessionist sentiment has re-emerged; southerners perceive the south to be marginalised and their resentment has led to public protests and occasional violence, countered by government offensives against armed separatists.

There was fighting in the north-west from 2004 until 2010 as government forces attempted to suppress an insurgency by the al-Houthis, a Shia sect in the predominantly Sunni country; despite a 2010 ceasefire, there have been further clashes between government and rebels forces. Yemen has also experienced a number of terrorist attacks since 2002, blamed on Islamic extremists, and since 2009 fears have arisen that al-Qaida-linked militants have been regrouping there after being forced out of Afghanistan and Pakistan.

In the 2003 legislative election, the ruling General People's Congress (GPC) won 228 seats and formed a coalition government with the Yemeni Alliance for Reform (YAR or al-Islah). The legislative election due in 2009 was postponed for two years pending constitutional reform. Lt.-Gen. Ali Abdullah Saleh, president of North Yemen from 1978 and president of the united country since 1990, faced sustained popular protests from early 2011 demanding his resignation and greater democracy. Saleh announced that he would not stand for re-election in 2013 but refused to leave office early despite international mediation attempts and the defection of senior military and political figures. The protests and government attempts to suppress them became increasingly violent; in June 2011 Saleh sought hospital treatment in Saudi Arabia for burns sustained in an attack on his compound. *See also* Events of the Year.

POLITICAL SYSTEM

The president announced in March 2011 the drafting of a new constitution transferring powers from the presidency to the legislature. Under the 1991 constitution, the president is directly elected for a seven-year term, renewable once. The unicameral House of Representatives *(Majlis al-Nowab)* has 301 members directly elected for a six-year term. In addition, there is an advisory Shura council, whose 111 members are appointed by the president. The prime minister is appointed by the president.

HEAD OF STATE
President, Field Marshal Ali Abdullah Saleh, *took office* 22 May 1990, *elected* 1 October 1994, *re-elected* 1999, 2006
Vice-President, Gen. Abd-Rabbu Mansour Hadi

SELECTED GOVERNMENT MEMBERS *as at August 2011*
Prime Minister, Ali Mohammad Mujawar
Deputy Prime Minister, Abdul-Karim Ismail al-Arhabi *(Economic Affairs)*
Foreign Affairs, Abu-Bakr Abdallah al-Qirbi
Defence, Mohammad Nasser Ahmed

EMBASSY OF THE REPUBLIC OF YEMEN
57 Cromwell Road, London SW7 2ED
T 020-7584 6607 E yemen.embassy@btconnect.com
Ambassador Extraordinary and Plenipotentiary,
  HE Abdulla Ali Al-Radhi, *apptd* 2010

BRITISH EMBASSY
PO Box 1287, 938 Thaher Himiyar Street, East Ring Road (opposite Mövenpick Hotel), Sana'a
T (+967) (1) 308 100 E britishembassysanaa@fco.gov.uk
W http://ukinyemen.fco.gov.uk
Ambassador Extraordinary and Plenipotentiary,
  HE Jonathan Wilks, *apptd* 2010

BRITISH COUNCIL
PO Box 2157, 3rd Floor, Administrative Tower, Sana'a Trade Centre, Algiers Street, Sana'a
T (+967) (1) 448 356 W www.britishcouncil.org/me-yemen
Director, Michael White

DEFENCE

The army has 790 main battle tanks, 240 armoured personnel carriers and 200 armoured infantry fighting vehicles. The navy has 20 patrol and coastal vessels at 2 bases. The air force has 79 combat aircraft and 8 armed helicopters.
Military budget – US$2,020m (2010)
Military personnel – 66,700: army 60,000, navy 1,700, air force 3,000, air defence 2,000; paramilitary 71,200
Conscription duration – 24 months

ECONOMY AND TRADE

Despite its oil industry, the mainstay of the economy, Yemen is one of the poorest countries in the Arab world. The government began an IMF restructuring programme in 2006 that aims to diversify the economy and attract foreign investment. Implementation has been hampered by popular protests, security problems internally and from piracy in nearby waters, corruption and rapid population growth. Falling oil prices nearly halved the government's revenue in 2009, although Yemen also benefited from its first exports of liquified natural gas.

Agriculture is largely of a subsistence nature, and, with herding and fishing, engages over 75 per cent of the population, contributing 8.2 per cent of GDP. Apart from oil and natural gas extraction and oil refining, industry consists of small-scale manufacturing of cotton textiles, leather goods, handicrafts, aluminium products and cement, food processing and ship repair.

The main trading partners are China, India, Thailand and the UAE. Principal exports are crude oil, coffee, dried and salted fish, and liquified natural gas. The main imports are food and livestock, machinery and equipment, and chemicals.

GNI – US$24,894m; US$1,060 per capita (2009)
Annual average growth of GDP – 5.2 per cent (2010 est)
Inflation rate – 12.2 per cent (2010 est)
Population below poverty line – 45.2 per cent (2003)
Unemployment – 35 per cent (2003 est)
Total external debt – US$7,147m (2010 est)
Imports – US$8,500m (2009)
Exports – US$5,000m (2009)

BALANCE OF PAYMENTS
Trade – US$2,994m deficit (2010)
Current Account – US$2,685m deficit (2009)

Trade with UK	2009	2010
Imports from UK	£74,609,413	£75,308,922
Exports to UK	£1,794,907	£41,185,490

COMMUNICATIONS

Yemen has 71,300km of roads, of which 6,200km are surfaced. Its main ports are at Aden, Al Hudaydah and Al-Mukalla. There is a high risk of piracy in offshore waters in the Gulf of Aden. The principal airports are at Sana'a and Aden.

Since unification a national telephone network has been created, but although mobile phone distribution is expanding rapidly, fixed-line telephone density remains low. There were 997,000 fixed lines in use, 8.3 million mobile phone users and 2.3 million internet users in 2009.

EDUCATION AND HEALTH

Literacy rate – 60.4 per cent (2008 est)
Gross enrolment ratio (percentage of relevant age group) – primary 85 per cent (2008 est); tertiary 10 per cent (2007 est)
Health expenditure (per capita) – US$64 (2009)
Hospital beds (per 1,000 people) – 0.7 (2004–9)

MEDIA

All broadcasting is state-run and administered by the Ministry of Information. Television and radio are the main means of communication owing to low levels of literacy. The government also funds some newspapers and controls most of the printing. There are four main newspapers: *Al-Thawrah, Yemen Times, Yemen Observer*

and *Al-Ayyam*. Journalists are increasingly subject to intimidation or arrest for criticism of government officials or policy.

ZAMBIA

Republic of Zambia

Area – 752,618 sq. km
Capital – Lusaka; population, 1,412,590 (2009 est)
Major cities – Kitwe, Ndola
Currency – Kwacha (K) of 100 ngwee
Population – 13,460,305 rising at 3.12 per cent a year (2010 est); over 70 ethnic groups, of which the Lozi, Bemba, Ngoni, Tonga, Luvale and Kaonde are the largest
Religion – Christian 87 per cent, Hindu and Muslim 1 per cent, other, including indigenous beliefs, 7 per cent (est)
Language – English (official), Bemba, Kaonde, Lozi, Lunda, Luvale, Nyanja, Tonga (national), over 70 other local languages
Population density – 17 per sq. km (2009)
Urban population – 35 per cent (2008 est)
Median age (years) – 16.5 (2010 est)
National anthem – 'Stand and Sing of Zambia, Proud and Free'
National day – 24 October (Independence Day)
Life expectancy (years) – 52.03 (2010 est)
Mortality rate – 12.84 (2010 est)
Birth rate – 44.63 (2010 est)
Infant mortality rate – 68.4 (2010 est)
HIV/AIDS adult prevalence – 13.5 per cent (2009 est)
Death penalty – Retained (not used since 1997)
CPI score – 3 (2010)
Literacy rate – 70.9 per cent (2008 est)
Gross enrolment ratio (percentage of relevant age group) – primary 113 per cent; secondary 49 per cent (2009 est)
Health expenditure (per capita) – US$47 (2009)
Hospital beds (per 1,000 people) – 1.9 (2004–9)

CLIMATE AND TERRAIN

Landlocked Zambia lies on a forested plateau cut through by river valleys and with higher land in the north and north-east. Elevation extremes range from 2,301m (in the Mafinga Hills) to 329m (Zambezi river). The Zambezi and its tributaries are the main rivers. Lake Bangweulu and parts of Lakes Tanganyika, Mweru and Kariba lie within its boundaries. The climate is tropical, moderated by altitude, with a rainy season from October to April.

HISTORY AND POLITICS

Most of the ethnic groups in Zambia migrated there between the 16th and the 18th centuries. Portuguese explorers arrived in the late 18th century and, with Arab traders, began slave-trading in the 19th century. The area came under British administration in 1889, was named Northern Rhodesia in 1911 and became a British protectorate in 1924. It was part of the Central African Federation with South Rhodesia (Zimbabwe) and Nyasaland (Malawi) from 1953 to 1963, when the federation was dissolved and Northern Rhodesia achieved internal self-government. It became an independent republic in 1964 under the name of Zambia.

Kenneth Kaunda of the United National Independence Party (UNIP) became president at independence and remained in power until 1991. Zambia was a one-party state ruled by the UNIP from 1972 until 1990, when pressure from opposition groups led to a new constitution, under which multiparty legislative and presidential elections were held in 1991. The UNIP and President Kaunda were defeated by the Movement for Multiparty Democracy (MMD) and its presidential candidate Frederick Chiluba.

Serious food shortages have occurred in recent years owing to floods and drought, leading to appeals for international food aid in 2001 and 2005. The country also faces serious demographic, economic and social problems because of high levels of HIV/AIDS infection.

The MMD remained the largest party in the legislature after the 2006 elections, although it commands a majority only because of the support of the appointed members of the legislature. Former vice-president Rupiah Banda was elected in 2008 to serve the remainder of the presidential term after President Levy Mwanawasa's death. Presidential and legislative elections are due in late 2011.

POLITICAL SYSTEM
Under the 1991 constitution, the executive president is directly elected for a five-year term, renewable once. The unicameral National Assembly has 158 members: 150 directly elected, up to eight nominated by the president, and a speaker; all serve a five-year term. The president appoints the cabinet.

A new constitution is under debate, although it is unclear whether it will be adopted before the 2011 elections.

HEAD OF STATE
President, Rupiah Banda, *elected* 30 October 2008, *sworn in* 2 November 2008
Vice-President, George Kunda

SELECTED GOVERNMENT MEMBERS *as at August 2011*
Home Affairs, Mkhondo Lungu
Foreign Affairs, Kabinga Pande
Finance, Situmbeko Musokotwane

HIGH COMMISSION FOR THE REPUBLIC OF ZAMBIA
Zambia House, 2 Palace Gate, London W8 5NG
T 020-7589 6655 E zhcl@btconnect.com
W www.zambiahc.org.uk
High Commissioner, HE Royson Mukwena, *apptd* 2009

BRITISH HIGH COMMISSION
PO Box 50050, 5210 Independence Avenue, 15101 Ridgeway, Lusaka
T (+260) (21) 1423 200 E lusakageneralenquiries@fco.gov.uk
W http://ukinzambia.fco.gov.uk

High Commissioners, HE Thomas Carter and HE Carolyn Davidson, *apptd* 2008

BRITISH COUNCIL
PO Box 34571, Heroes Place, Cairo Road, Lusaka
T (+260) (21) 122 8332 W www.britishcouncil.org/africa
Director, Donna McGowan

DEFENCE

The army has 30 main battle tanks and 33 armoured personnel carriers. The air force has 28 combat-capable aircraft.
Military budget – US$276m (2010)
Military personnel – 15,100: army 13,500, air 1,600; paramilitary 1,400

ECONOMY AND TRADE

The transition since the 1990s from a state-controlled to a free-market economy has improved productivity, especially in the now-privatised copper industry. Strong growth since 1996 suffered only a brief check in 2008 owing to the global economic downturn. The economy grew further in 2010 due to high copper prices and a good maize crop harvest. It is also driven in particular by mining, hydro-electric power generation, construction and tourism. Poverty remains a problem in the country, with around two-thirds of the population below the poverty line.

Copper is the main source of foreign earnings and increased demand in recent years for electronics has spurred investment and greater output. However, 85 per cent of the workforce remains engaged in agriculture, mostly at subsistence level, which accounts for 19.7 per cent of GDP. The main industries are copper and cobalt mining and processing, construction, food processing, beverages, chemicals, textiles, fertiliser and horticulture.

The main trading partners are South Africa and China. Principal exports are copper, cobalt, electricity, tobacco, cut flowers and cotton. The main imports are machinery, transport equipment, petroleum products, electricity, fertiliser, foodstuffs and clothing.
GNI – US$11,444m; US$960 per capita (2009)
Annual average growth of GDP – 7 per cent (2010 est)
Inflation rate – 8.5 per cent (2010 est)
Total external debt – US$3,495m (2010 est)
Imports – US$3,800m (2009)
Exports – US$4,200m (2009)

BALANCE OF PAYMENTS
Trade – US$2,032m surplus (2010)
Current Account – US$1,049m deficit (2008)

Trade with UK	2009	2010
Imports from UK	£41,644,455	£45,525,577
Exports to UK	£22,488,425	£30,265,442

MEDIA

The state-run Zambia National Broadcasting Association provides the only television service and dominates radio broadcasting; private radio stations provide little political content. Three of the four main newspapers are state-owned. Libel and security laws are used against journalists, and defaming the president is a criminal offence.

ZIMBABWE

Republic of Zimbabwe

Area – 390,757 sq. km

Capital – Harare; population, 1,606,260 (2009 est)

Major cities – Bulawayo, Chitungwiza, Gweru, Mutare

Currency – Zimbabwe dollar (Z$) of 100 cents; circulation suspended April 2009; US dollar, South African rand and other currencies in use

Population – 11,651,858 rising at 2.95 per cent a year (2010 est); Shona (82 per cent), Ndebele (14 per cent) (est)

Religion – Christian 70 per cent, Muslim 1 per cent (est); indigenous beliefs are widely followed, often combined with Christian beliefs

Language – English (official), Shona, Ndebele, numerous tribal dialects

Population density – 32 per sq. km (2009)

Urban population – 37 per cent (2008 est)

Median age (years) – 17.8 (2010 est)

National anthem – 'Simudzai Mureza wedu WeZimbabwe' ['Blessed be the Land of Zimbabwe']

National day – 18 April (Independence Day)

Life expectancy (years) – 47.55 (2010 est)

Mortality rate – 14.9 (2010 est)

Birth rate – 31.57 (2010 est)

Infant mortality rate – 30.9 (2010 est)

HIV/AIDS adult prevalence – 14.3 per cent (2009 est)

Death penalty – Retained

CPI score – 2.4 (2010)

CLIMATE AND TERRAIN

A landlocked country, Zimbabwe lies mainly on a high plateau with a central high veld and mountains in the east. Elevation extremes range from 2,592m (Inyangani) to 162m (confluence of the Runde and Save rivers). The climate is tropical, moderated by altitude, with a wet season from November to March. Average temperatures in Harare range from 7°C in June and July to 29°C in October.

HISTORY AND POLITICS

Organised settlement of the region began at least 20,000 years ago and a succession of Shona kingdoms ruled the area until the early 19th century; they included the builders of the Great Zimbabwe complex that gives the country its name. In the 19th century the Ndebele people occupied an area of the south (Matabeleland), and were often in dispute with the people of the north (Mashonaland). The area came under British influence from the 1880s, when the British started to exploit the mineral resources, and by 1893 the whole country was under British control. It became the British protectorate

of Southern Rhodesia in 1898, and a self-governing colony in 1923. It was part of the Central African Federation with Northern Rhodesia (Zambia) and Nyasaland (Malawi) from 1953 until 1963.

Opposition to independence under black majority rule in Southern Rhodesia prompted a unilateral declaration of independence (UDI) in 1965 by the white-dominated colonial government. International sanctions and guerrilla warfare by African nationalist groups forced the government to negotiate, and the UDI was terminated in 1979. Power was transferred to the majority population and the country became independent as the Republic of Zimbabwe in 1980.

Robert Mugabe became prime minister at independence and executive president in 1987. The political dominance of his party, the Zimbabwe African National Union-Patriotic Front (ZANU-PF), after 1987 made the country in effect a one-party state. Mugabe's regime became increasingly autocratic, brutally suppressing opposition and dissent, and rejecting international criticism of human rights and other abuses. The appropriation of white-owned farms, which began in 2000, caused an agricultural collapse that has resulted in chronic food shortages and malnutrition; distribution of international food aid is often inequitable, used by ZANU-PF to garner support.

In the 2008 legislative elections, ZANU-PF lost its majority in the lower chamber, winning 97 seats to the 99 seats of the Movement for Democratic Change (MDC); it retained its majority in the senate, with 30 seats to the MDC's 24. The MDC leader Morgan Tsvangirai won the first round of the 2008 presidential election with 47.9 per cent of the vote (President Mugabe polled 43.2 per cent), which was insufficient for outright victory. In advance of the second-round polls, ZANU-PF conducted a campaign of violence and intimidation against MDC supporters so severe that Morgan Tsvangirai withdrew from the election; although the victor by default, President Mugabe persisted with polling and won 85 per cent of the vote.

An internationally brokered power-sharing arrangement was agreed between ZANU-PF and the MDC in September 2008 and January 2009, although negotiations over the composition of the cabinet were not completed until February 2009, when Morgan Tsvangirai was sworn in as prime minister at the head of a national unity government. The new government moved to end Zimbabwe's international isolation and to seek support for its political and economic reforms, but has largely been rendered impotent by ZANU-PF's disregard for the power-sharing agreement and its continuing violence and intimidation.

POLITICAL SYSTEM

The 1980 constitution was amended in 1987, 1990, 2005 and 2007. The national unity government is an interim one until a new constitution has been approved, after which elections will take place.

The executive president is directly elected for a six-year term. The bicameral parliament comprises the House of Assembly and the senate. The former now has 214 members, 210 directly elected for a five-year term, plus (since 2009) the vice-presidents, prime minister and deputy prime minister as *ex officio* members. The senate (re-introduced in 2005) now has 100 members, who serve a five-year term: 60 elected (six from each province), five appointed by the president, ten provincial governors, 18 traditional chiefs and, since 2009, a further 11 senators were appointed, five by the president and six by the MDC.

The country is divided into eight provinces and two cities (Bulawayo and Harare) with provincial status. The provinces are: Manicaland, Mashonaland Central, Mashonaland East, Mashonaland West, Masvingo, Matabeleland North, Matabeleland South and Midlands.

HEAD OF STATE

President, Robert Mugabe, *elected* 30 December 1987, *re-elected* 1990, 1996, 2002, 2008
Vice-Presidents, John Nkomo; Joyce Mujuru

SELECTED GOVERNMENT MEMBERS *as at August 2011*

Prime Minister, Morgan Tsvangirai
Defence, Emmerson Mnangagwa
Finance, Tendai Biti
Foreign Affairs, Simbarashe Mumbengegwi
Home Affairs, Theresa Makone

EMBASSY OF THE REPUBLIC OF ZIMBABWE

Zimbabwe House, 429 Strand, London WC2R 0JR
T 020-7836 7755 E zimlondon@yahoo.co.uk
Ambassador Extraordinary and Plenipotentiary,
HE Gabriel Mharadze Machinga, *apptd* 2005

BRITISH EMBASSY

PO Box 4490, 3 Norfolk Road, Mount Pleasant, Harare
T (+263) (4) 8585 5200 E bhcinfo@zol.co.zw
W http://ukinzimbabwe.fco.gov.uk
Ambassador Extraordinary and Plenipotentiary,
HE Mark Canning, CMG, *apptd* 2009

BRITISH COUNCIL

PO Box 664, 16 Cork Road, Belgravia, Harare
T (+263) (4) 775 313-4 W www.britishcouncil.org/africa
Director, Jill Coates

DEFENCE

The army has 40 main battle tanks and 85 armoured personnel carriers. The air force has 45 combat-capable aircraft and 6 armed helicopters.
Military budget – US$98m (2010)
Military personnel – 29,000: army 25,000, air force 4,000; paramilitary 21,800

ECONOMY AND TRADE

Poor governance, and in particular the seizure of almost all the white-owned commercial farms, caused a rapid contraction in the agriculture-based economy in the decade from the late 1990s; agricultural output and GDP halved, international aid was suspended because of the government's outstanding arrears on past loans, and the migration of professional and skilled labour and high levels of HIV/AIDS infection depleted the workforce. After the national unity government took office, hyperinflation was stemmed by adopting the US dollar and the economy has grown rapidly, but unemployment remains high and poverty and dependence on food aid is widespread.

Agriculture accounted for 28 per cent of GDP in 1998 and engaged two-thirds of the workforce, but in 2010 accounted for only 19.5 per cent of GDP. The most important crops are cotton and tobacco for export and maize for domestic consumption. Other crops include wheat, coffee, sugar cane, peanuts and livestock.

The mining sector is important to the economy as a

foreign exchange earner. Almost all mineral production is exported. Gold is the most important product; others are coal, platinum, copper, nickel, tin, diamonds, iron ore and other metal and non-metal ores. Mining is now the largest industrial activity and supports a ferro-alloy industry and a steel works. Manufacturing, traditionally highly dependent on the agricultural sector for raw materials, produces wood products, cement, chemicals, fertiliser, clothing, footwear, foodstuffs and beverages; output has dropped in some industries because of transport difficulties and power rationing. Industry generates 24 per cent of GDP and services 56.5 per cent.

The main trading partners are South Africa, the Democratic Republic of Congo, Botswana and China. Principal exports are platinum, cotton, tobacco, gold, ferro-alloys, textiles and clothing. The main imports are machinery and transport equipment, other manufactures, chemicals, fuels and food.

GNI – US$5,213m; US$360 per capita (2009)
Annual average growth of GDP – 4.1 per cent (2010 est)
Inflation rate – 5 per cent (2010 est)
Population below poverty line – 68 per cent (2004)
Unemployment – 95 per cent (2009 est)
Total external debt – US$5,772m (2010 est)
Imports – US$2,900m (2009)
Exports – US$1,700m (2009)

BALANCE OF PAYMENTS

Trade – US$1,357m deficit (2010)
Current Account – US$945m deficit (2008)

Trade with UK	2009	2010
Imports from UK	£19,484,600	£29,968,973
Exports to UK	£50,681,621	£27,382,882

COMMUNICATIONS

Zimbabwe has 97,267km of roads, of which 18,481km are surfaced. There are 3,427km of railways but services have become increasingly restricted by lack of diesel and spare parts, leading to the reintroduction into service of steam locomotives. The country relies on rail connections through Mozambique and South Africa for access to seaports. The main airports are at Harare and Bulawayo.

The telephone system is badly maintained. Mobile phone distribution is growing quickly, but internet access is largely limited to Harare. In 2009 there were 385,100 fixed lines in use, 3 million mobile phone subscribers and 1.4 million internet users.

EDUCATION AND HEALTH

Education is compulsory at primary level, and the language of instruction is English.
Literacy rate – 91.7 per cent (2008 est)
Gross enrolment ratio (percentage of relevant age group) – primary 104 per cent; secondary 41 per cent (2008 est); tertiary 3 per cent (2009 est)
Hospital beds (per 1,000 people) – 3.0 (2004–9)

MEDIA

The only television and radio stations and the two main daily newspapers are state-run. The national unity government set up a commission in late 2009 to initiate media liberalisation and license new outlets. Six new newspapers began publishing in 2010, but readership is limited by high cover prices. Journalists face draconian measures, including imprisonment, for failing to register with a government body, and for publishing 'false news' critical of the government.

THE NORTH AND SOUTH POLES

THE ARCTIC

The Arctic is the region around the Earth's north pole; it includes the ice-covered Arctic Ocean, parts of Canada, the USA, Greenland, Iceland, Finland, Norway, Sweden and Russia. The area is commonly defined as lying north of the line of latitude known as the Arctic Circle (running at 66° 33′ N) or inside the 10°C July isotherm.

The climate is harsh, particularly during winter (October–March) when the Arctic receives little sunlight; the average monthly temperature in December, January and February is around −10 to −15°C, but on individual nights may fall as low as −60°C over the larger land masses. In summer, conditions are often damp and foggy although there is daylight for 24 hours a day. The average monthly temperature in high summer ranges from just above zero over permanent ice to 15°C in continental areas. The Arctic is rarely as cold as the Antarctic since there is water, not land, underneath the Arctic ice. The water is warmer than the air above it, causing heat to rise and moderate the cold.

The polar bear is the region's apex predator. Other native species include varieties of caribou, lemming, wolf, hare and fox; many bird species also migrate to tundra areas in summer. Until recently, vegetation was limited to Arctic tundra, a biome consisting of around 1,700 species of low-lying shrubs, grasses, sedges, lichens and mosses. However, the *Arctic Biodiversity Trends – 2010* report indicates that this tundra is slowly being replaced with flora typical of more southern locations, such as trees and evergreen shrubs. A comprehensive study of these issues, the *Arctic Biodiversity Assessment*, is scheduled for completion in 2013.

ARCTIC SEA ROUTES

In 1906 Norwegian explorer Roald Amundsen first successfully navigated the Northwest passage, but the shallow waterways he encountered ensured that the route held little commercial potential until recently. Similarly, the Northern Sea route (formerly the Northeast passage) linking the Atlantic and Pacific oceans around Russia's Arctic coast, was first navigated by Finnish-Swedish explorer Adolf Erik Nordenskjold in 1878–9, but thereafter only icebreakers and Russian submarines regularly traversed it.

In summer 2007, the Northwest passage was declared open and ice-free for the first time since records began in late 1978; the first commercial ship travelled through it in September 2008. In August 2008 the Northwest passage and the Northern Sea route were open simultaneously for the first time, making the Arctic circumnavigable. Two German ships became the first cargo vessels to navigate the Northern Sea route in September 2009.

CLIMATE CHANGE

The extent of ice in the Arctic has become a key measure of global climate change. The rate at which the ice melts grows exponentially: whereas the white ice reflects sunlight back into space, the darker seas absorb its heat, and the rising sea temperature melts the surrounding ice. The extent of the sea ice roughly doubles between summer and winter, typically reaching its greatest extent in March and retreating to its lowest point in September. The record low was recorded on 16 September 2007, when ice cover was 41 per cent below the 1979–2000 average September low. According to the *Catlin Arctic Survey*, the average thickness of Arctic ice-cover stood at 4.8m in 2009; just 10 per cent of this was 'multiyear' ice (ice that has survived at least 2 summers), a decrease from 30 per cent in the years 1981–2000.

NATURAL RESOURCES

The Arctic's receding ice presents opportunities for national governments to lay claim to a wealth of hydrocarbon and mineral deposits. In 2008 the US Geological Survey estimated that 20 per cent of the world's undiscovered oil and gas reserves – as much as 90 billion barrels of oil, 44 billion barrels of natural gas liquids and 1,670 trillion cubic feet of natural gas – are located within the Arctic Circle. Under the 1982 UN Convention on the Law of the Sea, no state owns the pole or the ocean surrounding it: the five countries that border the Arctic Ocean – Russia, Denmark, Norway, Canada and the USA (a non-signatory) – are limited to an economic zone of 200 nautical miles from their coastline, unless able to prove that their continental shelf extends beyond that limit. In August 2007, Russia planted a flag in the seabed below the pole, on the Lomonosov Ridge which spans much of the Arctic, and which Russia claims is an extension of the Eurasian continent and therefore part of its territory. However, Canadian and Danish geologists assert that Lomonosov is an extension of the North American continent, and therefore falls under their jurisdiction.

THE ANTARCTIC

The Antarctic is generally defined as the area lying within the Antarctic Convergence, the zone where cold northward-flowing Antarctic sea water sinks below warmer southward-flowing water. This zone fluctuates unevenly between the latitudes of 48° S and 61° S, typically extending further north in the Atlantic Ocean than in the Pacific. The continent itself lies almost entirely within the Antarctic Circle; it has an area of around 14 million sq. km, 98 per cent of which is permanently ice-covered. The average thickness of the grounded ice is 2,034m, but in places it exceeds 4,700m; it amounts to some 25.4 million cubic km, and represents around 90 per cent of the world's fresh water and 91 per cent of the world's glacier ice. Much of the sea freezes in winter, forming fast ice which breaks free of the coast in summer and drifts north as pack ice.

CLIMATE AND TERRAIN

Antarctica is the highest, coldest and driest continent on Earth, with average coastal temperatures ranging from just above freezing in the summer (December–February) to −17°C in winter. Conditions on the interior plateau are more severe, with katabatic (gravity-driven) winds and frequent cyclonic storms pushing average winter temperatures down to −65°C. The Vostok research station holds the record for the lowest surface temperature recorded on Earth at −89.6°C. Elevation extremes range from 4,897m (Vinson Massif) at the highest point to −2,540m (Bentley Subglacial Trench) at the lowest. The Transantarctic mountains bisect the continent north–south, dividing the west Antarctic ice sheet – an ice-filled marine basin – from the significantly larger and more elevated east sheet. With average precipitation of just 140mm a year, Antarctica is considered a desert.

CLIMATE CHANGE

While the recent decline in levels of ice in the Arctic has been clear and visible, concurrent changes in the Antarctic have been more complex. Despite reports of a recent thickening of the interior of the east ice sheet due to increased snowfall, studies of data produced by NASA's Grace satellite indicate that the Antarctic ice sheet as a whole has declined by more than 100 cubic km (24 cubic miles) a year since 2002, the majority of that loss having taken place in the west Antarctic.

The British Antarctic Survey has found that the west coast of the Antarctic Peninsula has become one of the fastest-warming areas on the planet, with annual mean temperatures rising by around 3°C over the past 50 years. In 2009, a group of British geophysicists found that the retreat of the Pine Island Glacier in the Western Antarctic had quadrupled between 1995 and 2006. Curiously, the temperatures recorded by the Amundsen-Scott station at the South Pole actually show a recent cooling, as do some studies of east Antarctica as a whole. The precise cause of this is unknown, but scientists have proposed that the warming of the seas in the surrounding ocean has produced more precipitation, which cools the area when it falls as snow. Greater snowfall has also been associated with an expansion of Antarctica's sea ice. The snow's additional weight appears to push existing sea ice deeper into the water, causing more of it to freeze. However, this expansion is neither uniform nor universally accepted, and a number of other studies cite a long-term and continuing decline in Antarctic sea ice since at least the 1950s.

HISTORY AND DISCOVERY

The idea of Antarctica is much older than proof of the continent's existence. The notion of *Terra Australis*, a vast southern continent which counterbalanced the northern lands of Europe, Asia and North Africa, originated with Aristotle, and was depicted on a world map as early as 1531. The supposed size of this land was gradually emended over the course of 16th-century exploration and further corrected after James Cook's circumnavigation of the globe in 1774. His journey from New Zealand to the Cape of Good Hope (via Tierra del Fuego), travelling at a high southern latitude (between 53° and 60°), confirmed that any landmass must be confined to the polar region.

The date of the first sighting of Antarctica is unclear. In 1820 three separate expeditions, from the UK, the USA and Russia, each claimed to have seen the continent within days of each other, and the argument has never been settled. The golden age of Antarctic exploration was prompted by the discovery of the magnetic North Pole in 1831, but it was not until the beginning of the 20th century that real progress was made. James Clark Ross was the first to identify the approximate location of the South Pole, but was unable to reach it. British explorers Robert Scott in 1901–4 and Ernest Shackleton in 1907–9 got closer, but it was not until Norwegian adventurer Roald Amundsen pioneered a new route, through the Axel Heiberg Glacier, that the pole was reached in December 1911. Scott's second attempt was also successful, but he arrived a month later and perished with his team on the return journey.

FLORA AND FAUNA

The only land animals to survive on the Antarctic continent are tiny invertebrates, including microscopic mites, lice, ticks, nematodes, rotifers and tardigrades. The largest land animal is the *Belgica antarctica*, a flightless midge just 2–6mm in size. The snow petrel, one of only three birds that breed exclusively in Antarctica, has been spotted at the South Pole. Large numbers of seals, penguins and other seabirds go ashore to breed in the summer; the emperor penguin is the only species that breeds ashore throughout the winter. Four species of albatross breed in South Georgia during the summer, but their numbers are in serious decline owing to the effects of longline fishing in the Southern Ocean region. Recent climate change has also affected the continent's wildlife, with the number of Adelie penguins falling significantly, as open-water species such as the chinstrap and gentoo penguins invade its Antarctic Peninsula habitat to take advantage of the warming temperatures.

By contrast, the Antarctic seas abound with life; recent expeditions identified over 700 previously unknown species. Krill, which congregates in large schools, is crucial to the ecosystem and provides a diet for migratory whales (including killer, humpback and blue whales), a number of species of seal, penguin, albatross and other, smaller birds. Each of these species is threatened by a substantial fall in recorded levels of krill since the 1970s, thought to be caused by a reduction in the sea ice which shields its larvae from predators during winter. In 2010 a group of research bodies completed the Census of Antarctic Marine Life, an inventory of over 16,000 marine species compiled from 19 expeditions; scientists estimate that 39–58 per cent of the Antarctic's marine species are yet to be described.

With almost all of the Antarctic continent permanently covered in ice, only a small number of flowering plants, ferns and club mosses survive. Most of these are found on the sub-Antarctic islands, while only two species (a grass and a pearlwort) extend south of 60° S. Antarctic vegetation is dominated by lichens and mosses, with a few liverworts, algae and fungi surviving in the cracks and pore spaces of sandstone and granite rocks.

ANTARCTIC LAW

The Antarctic treaty was signed on 1 December 1959 when 12 states (Argentina, Australia, Belgium, Chile, France, Japan, New Zealand, Norway, South Africa, the Soviet Union, the UK and the USA) pledged to promote scientific and technical cooperation unhampered by politics. The signatories agreed to establish free use of the Antarctic continent for peaceful scientific purposes; freeze all territorial claims and disputes in the Antarctic; ban all military activities in the area; and prohibit nuclear explosions and the disposal of radioactive waste. The Antarctic treaty was defined as covering areas south of latitude 60° S, excluding the high seas but including the ice shelves, and came into force in 1961. The treaty provides that any member of the UN can accede to it; it has since been signed by a further 36 states. In 1998 an extension to the treaty came into effect, placing a 50-year ban on mining, oil exploration and mineral extraction in Antarctica, and stipulating that all tourists, explorers and expeditions now require permission to enter the Antarctic from a relevant national authority. However, in recent years the region's coastal states have asserted often conflicting claims to oil- and gas-rich territory on the Antarctic sea bed. Under the terms of the UN Convention on the Law of the Sea, each nation's sovereignty over its continental shelf extends up to 350 nautical miles beyond its territorial coasts; the UN Commission on the Limits of the Continental Shelf is examining evidence submitted in support of these claims.

SCIENTIFIC RESEARCH
There are 20 nations with permanently manned research stations in Antarctica:

Country	Number of research stations
Argentina	6
Chile	5
Russian Federation	5
Australia	3
USA	3
China	2
France	2
UK	2

Brazil, Germany, India, Italy (shared with France), Japan, New Zealand, Norway, Poland, South Africa, South Korea, Ukraine and Uruguay each have a single station.

POPULATION AND TOURISM
Antarctica has no indigenous inhabitants, although the continent maintains a population of tourists, scientists and research workers which peaks in the summer months at over 4,400.

Antarctic tourism is a growth industry. The first *Lonely Planet* guide to Antarctica was published in 1996, and ship-borne cruises typically depart from Argentina, Chile and the Falkland Islands. The continent has also become a popular venue for extreme sports enthusiasts: it is now possible to sky-dive, ski, ride a motorbike and fly a helicopter across the continent, and the Vinson Massif and other peaks have become desirable destinations for mountaineers. The huts built by Scott and Shackleton are also popular attractions. The International Association of Antarctic Tour Operators recorded 6,704 tourists in the 1992–3 summer season, rising to more than 46,000 in 2007–8 and dipping to just under 37,000 in 2009–10.

In 1991 the International Association of Antarctica Tour Operators was founded with the objective of providing a self-regulating code of conduct for all operators to follow, but membership is voluntary, and fears remain regarding tourism-related environmental damage.

THE BRITISH ANTARCTIC SURVEY
The British Antarctic Survey (BAS) is part of the Natural Environment Research Council and carries out the majority of Britain's scientific research in Antarctica. Around 400 staff are employed by BAS and the organisation supports five research stations, four of which are staffed throughout the winter months. *See* the BAS website (W www.antarctica.ac.uk) for further information.

UK OVERSEAS TERRITORIES

ANGUILLA

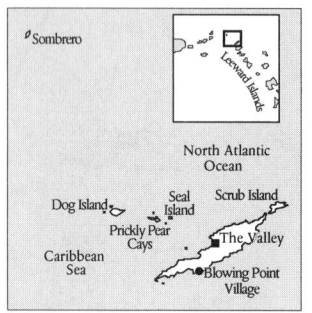

Area – 91 sq. km
Capital – The Valley; population, 1,635 (2009 est)
Currency – East Caribbean dollar (EC$) of 100 cents
Population – 14,766 rising at 2.22 per cent a year
(2010 est)
Religion – Christian (Protestant 83 per cent, Roman
Catholic 6 per cent, other denominations 2 per cent)
(est)
Language – English (official)
Population density – 150 per sq. km (2005 est)
Flag – British blue ensign with the coat of arms and
three dolphins in the fly
National day – 30 May (Anguilla Day)
Life expectancy (years) – 80.77 (2010 est)
Mortality rate – 4.09 (2010 est)
Birth rate – 13 (2010 est)
Infant mortality rate – 3.49 (2010 est)
Population below poverty line – 23 per cent (2002)

CLIMATE AND TERRAIN

Anguilla is a flat coralline island in the eastern Caribbean
and one of the most northerly of the Leeward Islands.
Elevation extremes range from 65m (Crocus Hill) at the
highest point to 0m (Caribbean Sea) at the lowest.
The climate is tropical, modified by north-east trade
winds, with temperatures ranging from 25°C to 31°C
throughout the year.

HISTORY AND POLITICS

Anguilla has been a British colony since 1650. For much
of its history it was linked administratively with St Kitts,
but three months after the Associated State of Saint
Christopher (St Kitts)-Nevis-Anguilla came into being in
1967, the Anguillans repudiated government from St
Kitts. After a period of direct rule, in 1976 Anguilla was
given a new status and separate constitution. Final
separation from St Kitts and Nevis was effected in
December 1980 and Anguilla reverted to a British
dependency.

The 1982 constitution (amended in 1990) provides for
a governor, an executive council comprising four of the
elected assembly members and two *ex-officio* members
(the attorney-general and deputy governor), and a
12-member House of Assembly, consisting of a speaker,
seven elected members, two nominated members and two

ex-officio members (the attorney-general and deputy
governor). The 2010 general election was won by the
Anguilla United Movement with four seats.
Governor, HE Alistair Harrison, CVO, *apptd* 2009
Chief Minister, Hon. Hubert Hughes

ECONOMY

The main economic activity is tourism, which has
stimulated construction. Offshore financial services,
lobster fishing and expatriates' remittances are also
important. Export earnings are mainly from sales of fish,
lobsters, livestock, salt, concrete blocks and rum.
Imports – US$200m (2009)
Exports – US$13m (2006)

BALANCE OF PAYMENTS
Trade – US$140m deficit (2010)
Current Account – US$35m deficit (2002)

Trade with UK	2008	2009
Imports from UK	£953,970	£573,321
Exports to UK	£282,169	£50,527

COMMUNICATIONS

The road network is gradually expanding but less than
half is paved. The main ports are Blowing Point ferry
terminal and Clayton J. Lloyd (formerly Wallblake)
airport, near The Valley.

BERMUDA

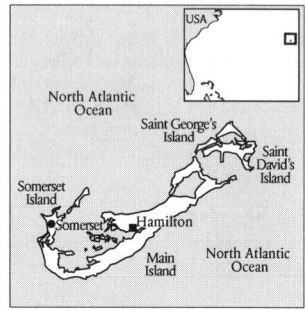

Area – 54 sq. km
Capital – Hamilton, on Main Island; population, 11,535
(2009 est)
Currency – Bermuda dollar of 100 cents
Population – 68,265 rising at 0.62 per cent a year
(2010 est)
Religion – Christian (Protestant 52 per cent, Roman
Catholic 15 per cent) (est)
Language – English (official), Portuguese
Population density – 1,288 per sq. km (2009 est)
Flag – British red ensign with the coat of the arms in
the fly
National day – 24 May (Bermuda Day)
Life expectancy (years) – 80.6 (2010 est)
Mortality rate – 7.43 (2010 est)
Birth rate – 11.47 (2010 est)
Infant mortality rate – 2.46 (2010 est)

CLIMATE AND TERRAIN

Bermuda is a group of over 130 small islands, of which about 20 are inhabited, in the North Atlantic Ocean. All the islands are volcanic in origin, with hilly interiors, surrounded by coral reefs. Elevation extremes range from 76m (Town Hill) at the highest point to 0m (Atlantic Ocean) at the lowest. The climate is subtropical, regulated by the Gulf Stream, with an average temperature of 24°C.

HISTORY AND POLITICS

Bermuda was discovered by the Spanish in 1503 but colonised by the British from the early 17th century, becoming a colony in 1684. Independence from the UK was rejected in a 1995 referendum.

Internal self-government was introduced in 1968. The governor is responsible for external affairs, defence, internal security and the police, although administrative matters for the police service have been delegated to the minister of labour, home affairs and public safety. The cabinet comprises the premier and six elected assembly members. The legislature consists of the senate of 11 appointed members and the House of Assembly with 36 members elected for a five-year term. At the 2007 election, the ruling Progressive Labour Party (PLP) retained its 22 seats and continued in office. Ewart Brown stepped down as PLP leader in 2010 and was replaced by Paula Cox.

Governor, HE Sir Richard Gozney, KCMG, *apptd* 2007
Premier, Hon. Paula Cox

ECONOMY

The economy is based on offshore financial services for international business (especially re-insurance), and tourism. Other activities include light manufacturing (re-exports of pharmaceuticals are the main export) and construction.

Trade – US$1,292m deficit (2010)

Trade with UK	2008	2009
Imports from UK	£191,142,795	£20,922,122
Exports to UK	£74,555,014	£863,642

COMMUNICATIONS

The main islands are connected by a series of bridges and causeways. There are 447km of roads, all of which are paved, and one airport, near Ferry Reach on St David's Island. The main ports are at Hamilton and St George. The telephone system is extensive, and mobile telephone distribution is widespread.

BRITISH ANTARCTIC TERRITORY

For map *see* The North and South Poles.

Area – 1,709,400 sq. km
Population – There is no indigenous population. The British Antarctic Survey maintains two permanently staffed research stations, at Halley and Rothera; one part-time (summer-only) station at Signy (South Orkney Islands); and two summer-only logistics facilities, at Fossil Bluff (Alexander Island) and Sky Blu (Eastern Ellsworth Land). Several other countries maintain research stations in the territory
Flag – British white ensign, without the cross of St George, with the territory's coat of arms in the fly

CLIMATE AND TERRAIN

The British Antarctic Territory (BAT) consists of the areas south of 60°S. latitude, between longitudes 20°W. and 80°W. The territory includes the South Orkney Islands, the South Shetland Islands, the mountainous Antarctic Peninsula and all adjacent islands, and the land mass extending to the South Pole. The highest point of the territory is 3,184m (Mt Jackson).

Only around 0.7 per cent of the territory remains ice-free, and the permanent ice sheet that covers the remainder is, in places, nearly 5km thick. The climate is polar desert with very little precipitation, and the annual average temperature at the South Pole is –48°C.

HISTORY AND POLITICS

Britain made its first territorial claim to part of the Antarctic in 1908. Since 1943, a permanent presence has been maintained which became the British Antarctic Survey (BAS) in 1962. In the same year, the territory, originally administered as a dependency of the Falkland Islands, became a UK overseas territory in its own right.

The BAT is administered by the Foreign and Commonwealth Office, and has a full suite of laws, and legal and postal administrations. All activities are governed by the Antarctic Treaty of 1961, which has the objectives of keeping Antarctica demilitarised and promoting international scientific cooperation. The territory is self-financing from income-tax revenue and the sale of postage stamps and coins.

GOVERNMENT OF THE BRITISH ANTARCTIC TERRITORY
Polar Regions Unit, Overseas Territories Directorate, Foreign and Commonwealth Office, London SW1A 2AH
T 020-7008 1921 E Lesley.Peto@fco.gov.uk
Commissioner (non-resident), Colin Roberts, *apptd* 2008
Administrator, Rob Bowman

BRITISH INDIAN OCEAN TERRITORY

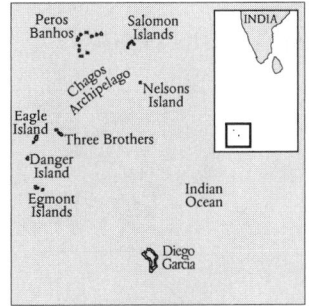

Area – 54,400 sq. km, of which 60 sq. km is land
Population – No indigenous population now lives in the archipelago; around 4,000 military personnel and civilian contract employees (2004 est) are based at the joint UK–US naval support facility on Diego Garcia
Currency – US dollar (US$) of 100 cents
Flag – Divided horizontally into blue and white wavy stripes, with the Union Flag in the canton and a crowned palm-tree over all in the fly

CLIMATE AND TERRAIN

The British Indian Ocean Territory (BIOT) comprises the Chagos Archipelago of 55 islands in six main groups, situated on the Great Chagos Bank in the Indian Ocean, about 1,900km north-east of Mauritius. The largest and most southerly of the islands is Diego Garcia, a sand cay with an area of about 44 sq. km. The main island groups are Peros Banhos (29 islands with a total land area of 6.5 sq. km) and Salamon (11 islands with a total land area of 3.2 sq. km).

The flat and low terrain rarely rises more than 2m above sea level. The climate is hot and humid, although moderated by trade winds.

HISTORY AND POLITICS

The Chagos Archipelago, originally colonised by the French, was one of the dependencies of Mauritius ceded to Britain in 1814 and was administered from Mauritius until 1965, when the BIOT was established. The islands of Farquhar, Desroches and Aldabra became part of the Seychelles when it became independent in 1976; since then the territory has consisted of the Chagos Archipelago only. Since the 1980s, successive Mauritian governments have claimed sovereignty over the islands, arguing that they were annexed illegally.

Diego Garcia is used as a joint naval support facility by Britain and the USA. The islands' former inhabitants were forcibly relocated between 1967 and 1973 to allow for the construction of the naval base, most being resettled in Mauritius and the Seychelles. Since the 1990s they have taken legal action to obtain the right to return to and settle in the islands; the first visit by former residents, a day trip, took place in 2006. In 2006, the Chagossians won a High Court case allowing them to return to the archipelago, but not to Diego Garcia. The House of Lords overturned this ruling on appeal in 2008; the outcome of a case before the European Court of Human Rights is pending. The British government unilaterally, and controversially, declared the Chagos archipelago a marine-protected area in April 2010.

Commissioner (non-resident), Colin Roberts, *apptd* 2008
Administrator, Joanne Yeadon, *apptd* 2007

BRITISH VIRGIN ISLANDS

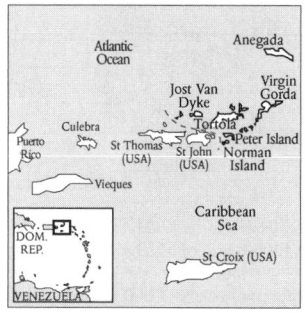

Area – 151 sq. km
Capital – Road Town, on Tortola; population, 9,384 (2009 est)
Currency – US dollar (US$) of 100 cents
Population – 24,939 rising at 1.78 per cent a year (2010 est)

Religion – Christian (Protestant 86 per cent, Roman Catholic 10 per cent) (est)
Language – English (official)
Population density – 146 per sq. km (2005)
Flag – British blue ensign with the coat of arms in the fly
National day – 1 July (Territory Day)
Life expectancy (years) – 77.45 (2010 est)
Mortality rate – 4.41 (2010 est)
Birth rate – 14.52 (2010 est)
Infant mortality rate – 14.11 (2010 est)

CLIMATE AND TERRAIN

The easternmost part of the Virgin Islands archipelago in the Caribbean Sea, the British Virgin Islands comprise Tortola, Anegada, Virgin Gorda, Jost Van Dyke and about 40 islets and cays; 16 of the islands are inhabited. Apart from Anegada, which is flat, the British Virgin Islands are hilly with coral reefs offshore. The highest point of elevation is 521m (Mt Sage, on Tortola). The climate is sub-tropical, with little variation in temperature, which typically ranges between 25°C in January and 29°C in July. The hurricane season is from June to November.

HISTORY AND POLITICS

Initially settled by Arawak Indians, the islands were named by Christopher Columbus in 1493 and colonised by the Dutch in the early 17th century. Annexed by the British in 1672, the islands were part of the Leeward Islands colony from 1872 to 1960. After a period of direct rule, a measure of self-government was introduced by the 1977 constitution and extended in 2000.

Under the 2007 constitution, the governor, appointed by the crown, retains responsibility for defence, security, external affairs and the civil service. The executive council comprises the premier, four other elected Assembly members and the attorney-general. The House of Assembly consists of a speaker, one *ex-officio* member (the attorney-general) and 13 members elected for a four-year term.

The 2007 election was won by the opposition Virgin Islands Party with ten seats.

Governor, HE Boyd McCleary, CMG, CVO, *apptd* 2010
Premier, Hon. Ralph T. O'Neal, OBE

ECONOMY

The main industries are tourism, which generates about 45 per cent of GDP, and offshore financial services. Other industries include construction and light manufacturing. The major exports are rum, fresh fish, fruit, livestock, gravel and sand. Chief imports are building materials, cars, foodstuffs and machinery.

Trade with UK	2008	2009
Imports from UK	£9,475,301	£31,380
Exports to UK	£72,695,112	£10,630,295

COMMUNICATIONS

The principal airport is on Beef Island, linked by bridge to Tortola, and there are also airfields on Anegada and Virgin Gorda. Road Harbour, at Road Town, is the main port, and ferry services connect the main islands. Many of the 200km of roads are steep and narrow.

CAYMAN ISLANDS

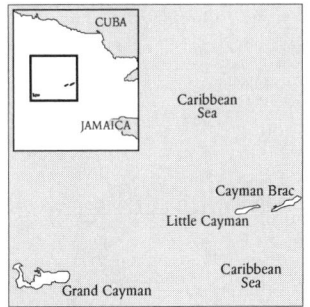

Area – 264 sq. km
Capital – George Town, on Grand Cayman; population,
   31,723 (2009 est)
Currency – Cayman Islands dollar (CI$) of 100 cents
Population – 50,209 rising at 2.34 per cent a year
   (2010 est)
Religion – Christian (Protestant 68 per cent, Roman
   Catholic 13 per cent) (est)
Language – English (official), Spanish
Population density – 229 per sq. km (2009 est)
Flag – British blue ensign with the coat of arms in
   the fly
National day – first Monday in July (Constitution Day)
Life expectancy (years) – 80.57 (2010 est)
Mortality rate – 5 (2010 est)
Birth rate – 12.29 (2010 est)
Infant mortality rate – 6.78 (2010 est)
GNI – US$43,703 per capita (2002)
Annual average growth of GDP – 1.1 per cent (2008)

CLIMATE AND TERRAIN
The Cayman Islands comprise Grand Cayman, Cayman
Brac and Little Cayman. Situated about 240km south of
Cuba, the low-lying islands are divided from Jamaica,
268km to the south-east, by the Cayman Trench, the
deepest part of the Caribbean Sea. Typical temperatures
are 20°C in January and 30°C in July. Hurricane season is
from July to November.

HISTORY AND POLITICS
The territory derives its name from the Carib word
caymanas (crocodile). The islands were ceded to Britain by
Spain in 1670, and permanent settlement began in the
1730s. A dependency of Jamaica from 1863, the islands
came under direct rule after 1962, and a measure of
self-government was granted in 1972.

The 1972 constitution (revised 1994 and 2009)
provides for a governor, a legislative assembly and a
cabinet. The governor is responsible for the police, civil
service, defence and external affairs, and chairs the
cabinet. The cabinet comprises two appointed official
members (the deputy governor and attorney-general) and
five of the assembly's elected members. The legislative
assembly has 15 members elected for a four-year term and
the two appointed official members of the cabinet, as well
as a speaker.

The election in May 2009 was won by the opposition
United Democratic Party.
Governor, HE Duncan Taylor, CBE, *apptd* 2010
Leader of Government Business, Hon. W. McKeeva Bush,
   OBE

CAYMAN ISLANDS GOVERNMENT OFFICE
6 Arlington Street, London SW1A 1RE T 020-7491 7772
W www.gov.ky

ECONOMY
The mainstays of the economy are offshore financial
services (largely owing to the absence of direct taxation)
and tourism. Government revenue is derived from fees and
duties.

Trade with UK	2008	2009
Imports from UK	£9,804,953	£10,163,692
Exports to UK	£60,312,167	£2,003,173

COMMUNICATIONS
The islands are served by airports at George Town and on
Cayman Brac and by an airfield on Little Cayman. George
Town is the main port. There are 785km of surfaced
roads.

FALKLAND ISLANDS

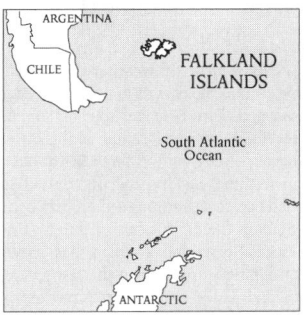

Area – 12,173 sq. km
Capital – Stanley, on East Falkland; population, 2,212
   (2009 est)
Currency – Falkland Island pound of 100 pence
Population – 3,140 rising at 0.01 per cent a year (2009
   est)
Religion – Christian 67 per cent, other 1 per cent (est)
Language – English
Flag – British blue ensign with the coat of arms centred in
   the fly
National day – 14 June (Liberation Day)

CLIMATE AND TERRAIN
The Falkland Islands consist of East Falkland (6,759 sq.
km), West Falkland (5,413 sq. km) and around 700 small
islands in the South Atlantic Ocean, about 480km from
the South American mainland. Elevation extremes range
from 705m (Mt Usbourne) at the highest point to 0m
(Atlantic Ocean) at the lowest. Average temperatures in
Stanley range from −1°C in June to 13°C in January, and
annual rainfall is low (around 600mm per year).

HISTORY AND POLITICS
The Falkland Islands have a long history of occupation by
European countries, including France, Spain and the UK,
which claimed sovereignty in 1765 and established its
first settlement in 1766.

In 1820 the Falklands were claimed for the newly
independent Argentina and a settlement was founded in
1826 but this was destroyed by the USA in 1831. In

1833 occupation was resumed by the British, and the islands were permanently colonised. Argentina continued to claim sovereignty over the islands (known to them as *las Islas Malvinas*), and invaded the islands on 2 April 1982. A British naval and military task force recaptured the islands on 14 June 1982. A small naval and military garrison remains in the islands. Argentina has reasserted its claims of sovereignty since 2007, and particularly since oil exploration began in offshore waters.

Under the 2009 constitution, the governor chairs an executive council consisting of three of the elected members of the legislative assembly and two *ex-officio* members, the chief executive and the financial secretary. The legislative assembly consists of eight members elected for a four-year term, the same two *ex-officio* members and a speaker. The last election was held in 2009; the next is to be held by November 2013. There are no political parties and all members sit as independents.

Governor, HE Nigel Haywood, CVO, *apptd* 2010
Chief Executive, Dr Tim Thorogood, *apptd* 2008

FALKLAND ISLANDS GOVERNMENT OFFICE
Falkland House, 14 Broadway, London SW1H 0BH
T 020-7222 2542 W www.falklands.gov.fk

ECONOMY

Since the establishment of a conservation and managed fishing zone around the islands in 1987, the economy has been transformed, with revenue from fishing and related activities overtaking sheep-farming as the main industry. Fishing licence fees now provide about half of government revenue, making the islands self-supporting in all but defence costs, although there has been concern since 2005 about the effect of overfishing on fish stocks. Tourism, especially wildlife tourism, has grown rapidly, with visitor numbers doubling in the last ten years.. Fish, meat, wool and hides are the principal exports. Chief imports are fuel, food and drink, construction materials and clothing.

There are believed to be substantial reserves of oil and gas offshore and the Falkland Islands government has licensed exploration for exploitable sites; exploratory drilling began in 2010 but has failed so far to find commercially exploitable reserves.

Trade with UK	2008	2009
Imports from UK	£25,307,483	£21,474,576
Exports to UK	£3,807,050	£2,635,030

COMMUNICATIONS

There is an international airport at Mt Pleasant, served by military flights to the UK (which also carry civilian passengers) and by commercial flights to Chile. The main port is Stanley Harbour, and a regular shipping service operates to the UK. The road network is gradually expanding but only roads in and around Stanley are paved, and most longer internal journeys are by light aircraft. International telecommunications are possible through a satellite link, and nearly three-quarters of all households have internet access.

GIBRALTAR

Area – 6.5 sq. km
Capital – Gibraltar
Currency – Gibraltar pound of 100 pence
Population – 28,877 rising at 0.27 per cent a year (2010 est)
Religion – Christian (Roman Catholic 78 per cent, other 10 per cent), Muslim 4 per cent, Jewish 2 per cent, Hindu 2 per cent (est)
Language – English (official), Spanish, Italian, Portuguese
Population density – 3,105 per sq. km (2009 est)
Flag – White with a red stripe along the lower edge; over all a red castle with a key hanging from its gateway
National day – 10 September
Life expectancy (years) – 78.53 (2010 est)
Mortality rate – 8.17 (2010 est)
Birth rate – 14.2 (2010 est)
Infant mortality rate – 6.82 (2010 est)

CLIMATE AND TERRAIN

Gibraltar is a rocky promontory, 426m at its highest point, that juts southwards from the south-east coast of Spain, with which it is connected by a low isthmus. It is about 32km from the coast of Africa, across the Strait of Gibraltar.

HISTORY AND POLITICS

Gibraltar was captured in 1704, during the War of the Spanish Succession, by a combined Dutch and English force, and was ceded to Britain by the treaty of Utrecht (1713). This treaty stipulates that if Britain ever relinquishes colonial rights over Gibraltar, the colony would return to Spain.

Spanish claims to the territory were a source of tension for many years, but after the overwhelming rejection of a joint sovereignty arrangement in a referendum in 2002, Spain moderated its attitude and the previously bilateral Anglo-Spanish talks about the territory became tripartite with the inclusion of Gibraltar from 2006.

Gibraltar is part of the EU (with the UK government responsible for enforcing EU directives affecting Gibraltar), but is not a full member and is exempt from the common policies on customs, commerce, agriculture, fisheries and VAT. Gibraltarians have voted in EU elections since 2004.

The 1969 constitution made provision for self-government in respect of certain domestic matters, but full internal autonomy came into effect with the 2006 constitution. This limited the governor's responsibilities to external affairs, defence, internal security and public service. The House of Assembly was restyled the Gibraltar Parliament, and may determine its own size; at present, it consists of an appointed speaker and 17 members elected for a four-year term. The government is formed by the chief minister (who is the leader of the majority party) and ministers from among the elected members of parliament.

The 2007 elections were won by the incumbent Gibraltar Social Democrats with ten seats. New elections were due by October 2011.

Governor, HE Vice-Admiral Sir Adrian Johns KBE, CBE, *apptd* 2009
Chief Minister, Hon. Peter Caruana

GOVERNMENT OF GIBRALTAR
150 Strand, London WC2R 1JA T 020-7836 0777
W www.gibraltar.gov.uk

ECONOMY
The economy is dominated by tourism (especially retail for day visitors), offshore financial services and shipping, and these three sectors account for about 85 per cent of GDP. Diversification efforts have encouraged telecommunications in particular and Gibraltar has become a centre for internet businesses, especially internet gaming. A shift from a predominantly public-sector to a private-sector economy has occurred in recent years, although government spending still has a significant impact on the local economy. The chief sources of government revenue are port dues, the rent of the crown estate in the town, and duties on consumer items (although value added tax is not applied in the territory).

GNI – US$5,000 per capita (2001)

Trade with UK	2008	2009
Imports from UK	£420,319,853	£359,370,965
Exports to UK	£17,021,036	£13,532,504

COMMUNICATIONS
Gibraltar has one international airport; commercial air links to Spain and through Spanish air space reopened in 2006. The 29km road network is all surfaced; road links to Spain reopened in the 1980s. The port services the large shipping industry, cruise liners and a regular ferry service to Tangiers (Morocco).

MONTSERRAT

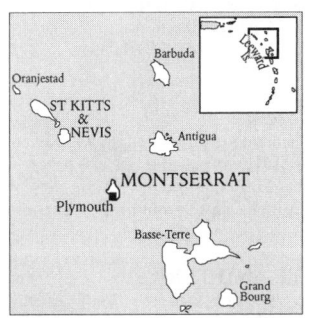

Area – 102 sq. km
Capital – Plymouth (abandoned 1997); the seat of government is now at Brades, in the north, population, 823 (2009 est); a new capital is under construction at nearby Little Bay

Currency – East Caribbean dollar (EC$) of 100 cents
Population – 5,118 rising at 0.39 per cent a year (2010 est)
Language – English (official)
Population density – 55 per sq. km (2005 est)
Flag – British blue ensign with the coat of arms in the fly
National day – Second Saturday in June (birthday of Queen Elizabeth II)
Life expectancy (years) – 72.91 (2010 est)
Mortality rate – 7.82 (2010 est)
Birth rate – 11.72 (2010 est)
Infant mortality rate – 15.8 (2010 est)

CLIMATE AND TERRAIN
Montserrat is a mountainous volcanic island in the Leeward group in the Caribbean Sea. Its lowest point of elevation is 0m (Caribbean Sea); its highest point was 914m (Chances Peak), although a lava dome in a crater in the Soufrière Hills volcano is estimated to be over 930m. Volcanic activity since 1995 has left over half of the island devastated by lava flows and ash. The climate is tropical and the average temperature is 26°C.

HISTORY AND POLITICS
Discovered by Columbus in 1493, Montserrat became a British colony in 1632. The first settlers were predominantly Irish indentured servants from St Kitts. France and Britain fought over the island during the 17th and 18th centuries but Montserrat was finally restored to Britain in 1783.

Volcanic activity by the Soufrière Hills volcano since 1995, particularly in 1996, 1997, 2003 and 2008, has left over half of the island uninhabitable, and prompted the migration of two-thirds of the population in the late 1990s. A 'special vulnerable area', to which access is restricted, covers two-thirds of the island and two maritime exclusion zones extend between 2km and 4km offshore.

The 1990 constitution was amended in 1999 after more than half of the constituencies were made uninhabitable by volcanic activity. Following modernisation talks, a new constitution was promulgated in 2010 and will come into force in September 2011. Under this, the cabinet is chaired by the governor and comprises the premier and three other elected members and two *ex-officio* members (the attorney-general and the financial secretary). The legislative assembly consists of nine members elected for a five-year term and two *ex-officio* members (as above). In the 2009 general election the Movement for Change and Prosperity won the most seats.

Governor, HE Peter A. Waterworth, *apptd* 2007
Chief Minister, Hon. Reuben Meade

GOVERNMENT OF MONTSERRAT
180–186 Kings Cross Road, London WC1X 9DE
T 020-7520 2622

ECONOMY
Continuing volcanic activity has restricted economic activity to the northern third of the island. Activity includes mining and quarrying, construction (mostly public sector), financial and professional services, and tourism. Communications improved with the opening of Gerald's airport in the north in 2005, allowing regular commercial air services to resume. There are port facilities

at Little Bay, and a ferry service to and from Antigua was reintroduced in December 2009.

Trade with UK	2008	2009
Imports from UK	£913,425	£637,817
Exports to UK	£300,844	£268,965

PITCAIRN ISLANDS

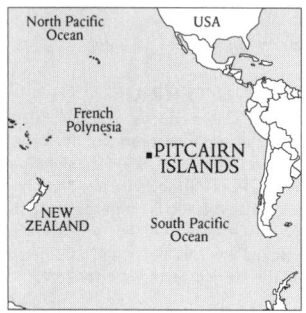

Pitcairn, Henderson, Ducie and Oeno Islands
Area – 47 sq. km
Capital – Adamstown, on Pitcairn Island
Currency – New Zealand dollar (NZ$) of 100 cents
Population – 48 (2010 est)
Religion – Seventh Day Adventist 100 per cent
Language – English, Pitkern (both official)
Flag – British blue ensign with the coat of arms in the fly
National day – Second Saturday in June (birthday of Queen Elizabeth II)

CLIMATE AND TERRAIN
Pitcairn is the chief of a group of rugged islands situated in the South Pacific Ocean, roughly midway between New Zealand and Panama. The other main islands of the group are Henderson, lying 168km north-east of Pitcairn; Oeno, lying 120km north-west; and Ducie, lying 470km east. These are uninhabited. Henderson Island is a UNESCO World Heritage Site. The climate is tropical, with average temperatures ranging from 19°C in August to 24°C in February.

HISTORY AND POLITICS
Pitcairn was settled in 1790 by mutineers from the *Bounty* and their Tahitian companions. The population was resettled on Norfolk Island in 1856 but two groups of people returned, in 1859 and 1864. It became a British settlement under the British Settlements Act 1887.

Under the 2010 constitutional arrangements, the islands are administered by the governor (usually the British High Commissioner to New Zealand), in consultation with the island council, which manages internal affairs. The commissioner liaises between the governor and the council. The island council comprises ten members: the governor; two members appointed by the governor; one member appointed by the council itself; and six, including the mayor, who are elected. The mayor is elected every three years; elections for other council members are held every year in December.
Governor (non-resident), HE Victoria Treadell, MVO, *apptd* 2010 *(British High Commissioner to New Zealand)*
Commissioner (non-resident), Leslie Jaques, *apptd* 2003
Mayor, Mike Warren

ECONOMY
The islanders live by subsistence fishing and horticulture, and the sale of honey and handicrafts, although tourism is being promoted. Apart from small fees charged for licences there are no taxes and government revenue is derived almost solely from the sale of postage stamps and .pn internet domain names, and income from investments. Since financial reserves became exhausted a few years ago the islands have received budgetary aid from the UK.

Trade with UK	2008	2009
Imports from UK	£414,052	£56,051
Exports to UK	–	£104,684

COMMUNICATIONS
There is no airfield and the only means of access is by sea; cruise and container ships stop irregularly but a regular shipping supply route to French Polynesia was established in 2006. There are 6.4km of dirt roads on the islands. A telephone system and internet access have been introduced in recent years.

ST HELENA, ASCENSION AND TRISTAN DA CUNHA

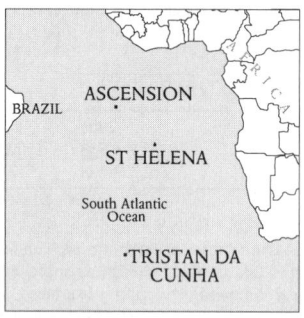

Religion – Christian (predominantly Protestant); Baha'i minority
Language – English (official)
National day – Second Saturday in June (birthday of Queen Elizabeth II)
Life expectancy (years) – 78.6 (2010 est)
Mortality rate – 6.91 (2010 est)
Birth rate – 10.95 (2010 est)
Infant mortality rate – 16.98 (2010 est)

ST HELENA
Area – 122 sq. km
Capital – Jamestown; population, 699 (2009 est)
Currency – St Helena pound (£) of 100 pence
Population – 4,000 (2010 est)
Flag – British blue ensign with the coat of arms in the fly

CLIMATE AND TERRAIN
St Helena is situated in the South Atlantic Ocean, 1,500km south of the Equator and about 1,900km west of Africa. The island is rugged and volcanic, with sheer cliffs rising to a central plateau. Mt Actaeon, at 818m, is the highest elevation. The climate is tropical but mild, tempered by trade winds, and the average temperature is about 24°C.

HISTORY AND POLITICS

St Helena is believed to have been discovered by the Portuguese navigator Joao da Nova in 1502. It was used as a port of call for vessels of all nations trading to the East until the late 19th century. It was annexed by the Dutch in 1633 but never occupied by them, and the British East India Company seized it in 1659. From 1815 to 1821 the island was lent to the British government as a place of exile for Napoléon Bonaparte, who died there on 5 May 1821, and in 1834 it was annexed to the British crown. The Zulu chief Dinizulu was exiled to the island in 1890, and up to 6,000 Boer prisoners were held there between 1900 and 1903.

Under the 2009 constitution, government is administered by a governor, advised by an executive council comprising three *ex-officio* members (the chief secretary, financial secretary and attorney-general) and five elected members of the legislative council. The legislative council consists of 12 members elected for a four-year term, the three *ex-officio* members of the executive council and a speaker.

Governor, HE Andrew Gurr, *apptd* 2007

GOVERNMENT OF ST HELENA
7 Portland Place, London W1B 1PP **T** 020-7031 0314

ECONOMY AND TRADE

St Helena's importance as a port of call on the sea routes between Europe and Africa and Asia declined after the opening of the Suez Canal. The island has few natural resources and its economy is dependent on an annual grant from the UK. The main economic activities are agriculture, the sale of fishing licences, fish processing and tourism. The only significant exports are coffee and frozen, canned and dried fish.

Trade with UK	2008	2009
Imports from UK	£10,223,739	£10,206,841
Exports to UK	£345,375	£4,430,891

COMMUNICATIONS

Access is solely by sea, provided by a regular supply ship. Jamestown is the only port. Plans for a long-promised airport were cancelled by the UK government in 2009, then revived in 2010; completion is scheduled for 2012. St Helena has 138km of roads, most of which are single track. Telecommunication services are provided via satellite links, which also enable television programmes to be received for distribution by cable. There are two local radio stations and two weekly newspapers.

ASCENSION ISLAND

Area – 88 sq. km
Capital – Georgetown; population, 560 (2003 est)
Currency – St Helena/Ascension pound (£) of 100 pence
Population – 880 (2010 est)

CLIMATE AND TERRAIN

The island is a rocky volcanic peak that lies in the South Atlantic Ocean some 1,200km north-west of St Helena. The highest point (Green Mountain, 859m) is covered with lush vegetation. It is an important breeding place for the green turtle and a number of seabird species.

HISTORY AND POLITICS

Ascension is said to have been discovered by Joao da Nova in 1501 and two years later it was visited on Ascension Day by Alphonse d'Albuquerque, who gave the island its

present name. It was uninhabited until the arrival of Napoleon in St Helena in 1815, when a small British naval garrison was stationed on the island. As HMS *Ascension* it remained under the supervision of the Board of Admiralty until 1922, when it was made a dependency of St Helena. The island was an important logistical centre in both world wars and during the Falklands conflict, and it has a continuing role as a military air base and in broadcasting, telecommunications and satellite tracking.

In 2002 new constitutional arrangements introduced a measure of self-government, and in 2009 Ascension ceased to be a dependency of St Helena. The governor, who is resident in St Helena, retains responsibility for defence, external affairs, internal security and public service. The governor, represented locally by the island administrator, chairs the island council, which consists of five elected members and two *ex-officio* members (the director of resources and the attorney-general).

Administrator, Ross Denny, *apptd* 2008

ECONOMY

Before 2002 the island was administered and financed by the main commercial users (the BBC and Cable and Wireless) and the military. With the change in governance in 2002, a fiscal regime was introduced to finance public services through taxation. This funds public services, including a school, a hospital, police and judicial services. A private sector is developing following the sale of government-owned concerns to commercial operators and the establishment of a sports fishing industry.

COMMUNICATIONS

Georgetown is the only port and there are regular scheduled shipping services, as well as regular air links to the UK and the USA by military aircraft and occasional charter flights. Ascension has 40km of roads. Telecommunication services are provided via satellite links. There is a local radio station and a weekly newspaper.

TRISTAN DA CUNHA

Area – 98 sq. km
Capital – Edinburgh of the Seven Seas
Currency – Currency is that of the UK
Population – 265 (2010 est)
Flag – British blue ensign with the coat of arms in the fly

CLIMATE AND TERRAIN

Tristan da Cunha is the chief of a group of islands in the South Atlantic Ocean which lie some 2,333km south-west of St Helena. All of the islands are volcanic and steep-sided with cliffs or narrow beaches. The highest point of elevation is 2,060m (Queen Mary's Peak) while the lowest is 0m (Atlantic Ocean). Gough and Inaccessible Islands are UNESCO World Heritage Sites.

HISTORY AND POLITICS

Tristan da Cunha was discovered in 1506 by the Portuguese navigator Tristao da Cunha. In 1760 a British naval officer visited the islands and gave his name to Nightingale Island. In 1816 the group was annexed to the British crown and a garrison was placed on Tristan da Cunha. When this force was withdrawn in 1817, four adults and two children remained at their own request and formed a settlement, which was joined in 1827 by five women from St Helena and afterwards by others from Cape Colony. Owing to its position on a major sea route the colony thrived, with an economy based on trade with passing ships, until the late 19th century, when the opening of the Suez Canal led to decline.

In 1961 a volcano, believed to have been extinct for thousands of years, erupted and the danger of further volcanic activity led to the evacuation of inhabitants to the UK until 1963.

Tristan da Cunha and Inaccessible, Nightingale and Gough Islands were dependencies of St Helena from 1938 to 2009. They are administered by the governor of St Helena through a resident administrator, who is advised by an island council. This consists of eight members elected for a three-year term, of whom one must be a woman, and three appointed members.
Administrator, Sean Burns, *apptd* 2010

ECONOMY
The island is almost financially self-sufficient; UK government aid finances training scholarships and a resident medical officer at the hospital. The main activities are crayfish fishing, fish processing, agriculture and the sale of postage stamps and coins.

COMMUNICATIONS
Communications with the outside world are by sea as there is no airport. Scheduled visits to the island are limited to about nine calls a year by fishing vessels from Cape Town and annual calls by a South African research vessel. Tristan da Cunha has 20km of roads. There is a local radio station and a newspaper.

SOUTH GEORGIA AND THE SOUTH SANDWICH ISLANDS

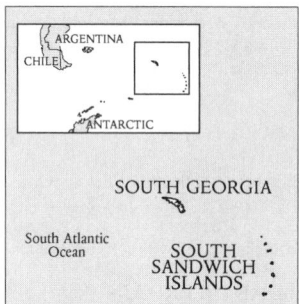

Area – 3,903 sq. km
Capital – King Edward Point (administrative centre), on South Georgia
Currency – Pound sterling
Population – There is no indigenous population. The British Antarctic Survey maintains two permanently staffed research stations, at King Edward Point and on Bird Island, to the north-west of South Georgia; in addition, there are the Government Officers at King Edward Point, and the curators of the museum at Grytviken, South Georgia
Flag – British blue ensign, with the coat of arms in the fly

CLIMATE AND TERRAIN
South Georgia lies 1,390km south-east of the Falkland Islands. Over half of the mountainous island is permanently ice-covered, with many large glaciers. The main mountain range is the Allardyce, and elevation extremes range from 2,934m (Mt Paget) at the highest

point to 0m (Atlantic Ocean) at the lowest. The South Sandwich Islands, lying about 750km miles south-east of South Georgia, are a chain of 11 uninhabited volcanic islands some 350km long. Some of the volcanoes are still active.

HISTORY AND POLITICS
South Georgia was used by whalers and sealers of many nationalities following its discovery by Captain Cook in 1775. Britain annexed South Georgia and the South Sandwich Islands in 1908 and since then they have been under continuous British occupation, apart from a brief period during the Falklands conflict in 1982; Argentina claims sovereignty over the territory. A small British army garrison was maintained on South Georgia between 1982 and 2001.

Under the present constitution, which came into effect in 1985, the commissioner is concurrently the governor of the Falkland Islands. A chief executive officer, also based in the Falklands Islands, is responsible for administration. Government officers are based in South Georgia.
Commissioner (non-resident), HE Nigel Haywood, CVO, *apptd* 2010
Senior Executive Officer (non-resident), Martin Collins

ECONOMY
A conservation and management fishing zone was established around the islands in 1993 and a licensing regime introduced for fishing vessels. Sale of fishing licences, passenger landing fees, harbour dues, and the sale of postage stamps and commemorative coins are the main sources of revenue. Tourism, especially wildlife tourism, is growing, but prior permission to land on the islands must be sought and is subject to environmental impact assessments and landing fees.

Access is possible only by sea; there are no scheduled services but cruise ships and other vessels call at South Georgia.

TURKS AND CAICOS ISLANDS

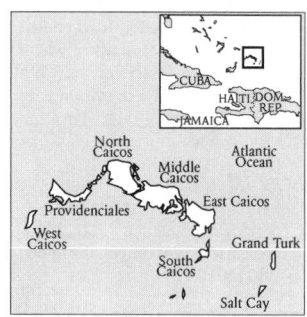

Area – 430 sq. km
Capital – Cockburn Town, on Grand Turk; population, 6,195 (2009 est)
Currency – US dollar (US$) of 100 cents
Population – 23,528 rising at 2.49 per cent a year (2010 est)
Religion – Christian (Protestant 86 per cent) (est)
Language – English (official)
Population density – 35 per sq. km (200900 est)
Flag – British blue ensign with the coat of arms in the fly

National day – 30 August (Constitution Day)
Life expectancy (years) – 75.64 (2010 est)
Mortality rate – 4.17 (2010 est)
Birth rate – 20.44 (2010 est)
Infant mortality rate – 13.43 (2010 est)

CLIMATE AND TERRAIN

The Turks and Caicos Islands lie about 80km south-east of the Bahamas, of which they are geographically an extension. There are around 40 islands and cays, of which six are permanently inhabited. The climate is marine tropical, moderated by trade winds; the average annual temperature is 27°C. Flamingo Hill on East Caicos is the highest elevation, at 48m.

HISTORY AND POLITICS

The islands changed hands several times between the French, Spanish and British between their discovery in 1512 and the arrival of the first settlers, a group of Bermudans, in the 1670s. They were administered as part of the Bahamas from 1799 until 1848, when they achieved separate colonial status, but they were administered from Jamaica between 1872 and 1962, and from the Bahamas between 1965 and 1973. Since 1973 the territory has had its own governor, and internal self-government was introduced in the 1970s.

The 2006 constitution provided for ministerial government and a partially elected legislature, with the governor retaining responsibility for defence, external affairs, internal security and the regulation of financial services. Following an inquiry into alleged political corruption in 2008–9, on 14 August 2009 the UK government suspended parts of the constitution, dismissed the House of Assembly and imposed direct rule by the governor for a period of at least two years, during which time legislative, administrative and financial reforms were to be implemented. The cabinet and legislature were replaced by an Advisory Council and an Consultative Forum, which the governor may consult.

Governor, HE Gordon Wetherell, *apptd* 2008

GOVERNMENT OF TURKS AND CAICOS ISLANDS
42 Westminster Palace Gardens, 1–7 Artillery Row, London
SW1P 1RR T 020-7222 9024

ECONOMY

The main industries are tourism, offshore financial services and fishing. The USA is the main source of tourists.

Trade with UK	2008	2009
Imports from UK	£2,317,567	£3,257,817
Exports to UK	£143,036	£2,915

COMMUNICATIONS

The principal airports are on the islands of Grand Turk and Providenciales and provide international air links. There are smaller airports on the other main islands, and regular internal air services between them. The main seaports are on Grand Turk and Providenciales. The islands also have a total of 121km of roads, 24km of which are surfaced.

THE YEAR 2010–11

The year under review covers the period from 1 August 2010 to 31 July 2011

EVENTS OF THE YEAR 2010–11

UK AFFAIRS

AUGUST 2010

8. Ken McGonigle, a British security contractor for NATO in Afghanistan, was shot dead by a prisoner who had overpowered his guards and seized their weapons. **9.** Ed Stafford, a former British army captain, became the first man to walk the entire 4,000-mile length of the Amazon river from its source to the Atlantic Ocean. **13.** The Secretary of State for Communities and Local Government, Eric Pickles, announced that the Audit Commission, the independent body that monitors the efficiency of public expenditure on local services, would be abolished by 2013. **24.** A report by the Police Ombudsman for Northern Ireland on the 1972 bombings in Claudy, which killed nine people, concluded that the government, the police and the Roman Catholic Church had colluded in protecting a priest who was the prime suspect in the attack.

SEPTEMBER 2010

6. St Comgall's Catholic primary school in Antrim, Northern Ireland, was evacuated after an eight-year-old pupil found a pipe-bomb in the playground and took it into the classroom; bomb disposal experts later confirmed that the device was viable. **14.** A report published by OFSTED stated that about 500,000 of the 1.7 million schoolchildren classed as having special educational needs had been wrongly classified; it concluded that schools were over-eager to identify children as having special needs in order to improve their inspection scores and access additional funding. **16.** Pope Benedict XVI arrived in Edinburgh at the start of a four-day state visit to Britain. The Metropolitan Police arrested six men in connection with an alleged plot to assassinate the Pope; five of the men were employed as street cleaners by Westminster City Council and were arrested at the council's depot near Baker Street. **20.** In an address to the Liberal Democrat party conference in Liverpool, the deputy prime minister, Nick Clegg, stated that the Liberal Democrats and the Conservatives would always remain separate parties but that coalition government was the only solution in the current economic climate; he argued that the impending public-sector spending cuts were essential to deal with the national deficit. **23.** Although the strategic defence and security review had yet to report, the secretary of state for defence, Liam Fox, promised that the UK would keep its nuclear deterrent capability, retain the ability to mount medium-scale operations oversees and continue with the joint strike fighter programme. The ONS published data on sexual identity for the first time, as part of the Integrated Household Survey, which is based on interviews with more than 450,000 adults; the findings indicated that 1.4 per cent of the total adult population identify themselves as gay, lesbian or bisexual. **25.** Ed Miliband was elected as the new leader of the Labour Party in a narrow victory over his older brother David. **29.** In his inaugural address as Labour leader, Ed Miliband declared to the party conference in Manchester that his 'new generation' party would regain the trust of voters, and pledged to move the party on from the 'ghosts of the past'.

OCTOBER 2010

4. At the Conservative Party conference in Birmingham, the chancellor of the exchequer, George Osborne, announced that child benefit would be discontinued from 2013 for those households with a parent paying higher-rate income tax and that the amount of benefits that could be received by any household would be capped at £500 a week. **9.** Linda Norgrove, a British aid worker who was kidnapped by the Taliban in Afghanistan's Kunar province on 26 September, died during a rescue attempt by US special forces; the results of an investigation into her death, announced on 11 October, indicated that she was killed by a grenade detonated by her rescuers. Police made 13 arrests during a demonstration in Leicester by the English Defence League and a counter-protest by the Unite Against Fascism. **11.** The inquests began at the Royal Courts of Justice into the deaths of the 52 people killed in the London underground and bus bombings in London on 7 July 2005; the inquests' remit included examining whether the emergency services' response was adequate and whether MI5 and the police could have prevented the bombings (*see* 6 May 2011). **12.** An Angolan man, Jimmy Mubenga, died on a flight to Angola while being forcibly deported from the UK by a private security firm, G4S (*see* Crimes and Legal Affairs 17 October); on 30 October G4S's contract with the government was cancelled. **19.** At the presentation of the strategic defence and security review, the prime minister, David Cameron, announced that defence spending would decrease by 8 per cent over a four-year period; cuts included the loss of 25,000 civilian jobs at the Ministry of Defence, 7,000 soldiers from the army, 5,000 naval personnel and 5,000 RAF personnel. **20.** The chancellor presented the government's spending review, which outlined £83bn worth of spending cuts to be implemented over four years in order to cut the national deficit; on average there was a 19 per cent decrease in budgets across all government departments, with a loss of around 490,000 public sector jobs, and an additional £7bn worth of cuts to social welfare benefits, but no change to plans for the NHS budget to increase every year until 2015. **21.** Three peers were suspended from the House of Lords over expenses claims; Baroness Uddin (formerly Labour) was suspended until April 2012 and told to repay £125,349, Lord Bhatia (cross-bencher), who had repaid £27,446, was suspended for eight months and Lord Paul (formerly Labour), who had repaid £41,982, was suspended for four months. **22.** A nuclear submarine, HMS *Astute*, ran aground while undergoing sea trials off the Isle of Skye; the vessel was later refloated but suffered damage from a tugboat in the process. **29.** Direct flights from Yemen to the UK were suspended after police found a suspicious package at East Midlands airport on a cargo flight bound for the USA; the package was later confirmed to be a bomb hidden in a printer cartridge, and a similar device was also discovered on a US-bound aircraft in Dubai.

NOVEMBER 2010

2. At a summit in London, the prime minister and President Sarkozy of France agreed measures for closer cooperation on defence between the UK and France. **3.** The universities minister, David Willetts, announced government plans to allow English universities to increase annual tuition fees, currently capped at £3,290 per student, up to a maximum of £9,000 from the start of the 2012–13 academic year. **5.** Phil Woolas, the Labour MP for Oldham East and Saddleworth and shadow immigration minister, was stripped of his parliamentary seat, suspended from the Labour Party and banned from standing in general and local elections or for any elected public office for three years after a specially convened election court found that he had knowingly lied about his Liberal Democrat opponent in campaign leaflets for the 2010 general election. **10.** At student protests in London over the government's plans to allow universities to increase tuition fees (*see* 3 November), 14 people, including seven police officers, were injured and 35 protestors were arrested; a breakaway group of demonstrators broke into the Conservative Party's headquarters at Millbank, vandalised the premises and threw missiles from the roof of the building. **14.** Paul and Rachel Chandler, a British couple kidnapped by Somali pirates in 2009 while sailing off the Seychelles, were released by their captors after relatives paid a ransom believed to be around £400,000. **16.** The engagement was announced of Prince William to Catherine Middleton (*see* 29 April 2011). **17.** Parts of Cornwall, especially around Lostwithiel and Mevagissey, suffered severe flooding after more than 40mm of rain fell in an hour; floodwaters up to 1.8m (6ft) deep carried away cars, forced hundreds from their homes and caused travel chaos, blocking trunk roads and cutting the county's main rail link for several hours. **23.** Train operators announced fare increases averaging 6.2 per cent from January 2011. **24.** In London, around 10,000 students took part in further protests over university tuition fees, during which two police officers were injured and 29 people were arrested; demonstrators had planned to march from Trafalgar Square to the Liberal Democrat headquarters in Cowley Street but around half of the protesters were confined by the police in Whitehall for more than four hours before being gradually released. **28–30.** Temperatures dropped as low as −18°C in some parts of the UK and the heaviest November snowfall since 1933 was recorded, leading to chaos on the roads, cancelled flights and school closures throughout the country.

DECEMBER 2010

2. The freezing weather conditions continued throughout the UK, with −21°C recorded in Altnaharra, Scotland. **9.** Thousands of protesters opposed to the rise in university tuition fees clashed with police outside the Houses of Parliament as MPs voted 323–302 in favour of raising the tuition fees' cap in England from £3,290 to £9,000 a year; protesters smashed windows at the Treasury and the supreme court and attacked the motorcade of the Prince of Wales and the Duchess of Cornwall, en route to the Royal Variety Performance. **13.** The communities secretary, Eric Pickles, announced that local authority funding (comprising central government funding, council tax, business rates and other grants) would be cut by an average of 4.4 per cent for 2011–12; the Local Government Association commented that the funding settlement would 'inevitably' mean cuts to local services. **14.** The House of Lords passed the legislation raising

university tuition fees. **18–20.** South-eastern England experienced its heaviest December snowfall in 20 years, grounding flights to and from Heathrow airport and stranding thousands of passengers. **20.** The secretary of state for transport, Philip Hammond, unveiled the detailed route of the first section (London to Birmingham) of the proposed high-speed railway between London and Manchester/Leeds. **21.** Controversial remarks by the secretary of state for business, innovation and skills, Vince Cable, about News Corporation's proposed takeover of BSkyB led the prime minister to transfer all responsibility for competition and policy issues relating to the media and telecommunications sectors immediately to the secretary for culture, media and sport (*see also* Arts and Media, 3 March).

JANUARY 2011

10. The secretary of state for health, Andrew Lansley, announced further compensation of around £130m for hundreds of people who contracted hepatitis C after being treated by the NHS with contaminated blood in the 1970s and 1980s. **11.** Eric Illsley, the Labour MP for Barnsley Central, pleaded guilty at Southwark crown court to fraudulently claiming £14,000 of parliamentary expenses; he resigned as a MP on 8 February, two days before he was sentenced to a year in prison. **12.** In an open letter to the health secretary, Andrew Lansley, and the secretary of state for work and pensions secretary, Iain Duncan Smith, 27 organisations, including MENCAP, MIND and the RNIB, urged the government to reverse its decision to abolish the disability living allowance mobility payment, arguing that the loss of this payment would effectively make severely disabled people housebound. **13.** In the Oldham East and Saddleworth by-election, the first since the general election, Debbie Abrahams held the seat for Labour, receiving 42 per cent of the vote. The Ministry of Justice announced that three prisons, Ashwell, Lancaster Castle and Morton Hall, would close by July 2011, resulting in the loss of 800 prison places. **20.** Alan Johnson resigned as shadow chancellor after only three months in the job, citing personal problems; the shadow home secretary, Ed Balls, was appointed in his place. **21.** Andy Coulson resigned as the prime minister's director of communications following continued speculation that he was aware of the widespread hacking of celebrities' and politicians' mobile phone messages by journalists at the *News of the World* during his five-year editorship of the newspaper. **31.** The Universities and Colleges Admission Service (UCAS) announced that a record number of 583,501 people had applied for a degree course starting in 2011.

FEBRUARY 2011

5. The English Defence League held a demonstration in Luton, its largest to date; Unite Against Fascism protestors again held a counter-demonstration (*see* 9 October). **6.** The speaker of the House of Commons, John Bercow, issued a written statement warning MPs over their conduct after Paul Maynard, an MP who suffers from cerebral palsy, was openly mocked in the chamber. **11.** A high court judge ruled that the scrapping of the schools-building programme, which led to over 700 projects being cancelled, was 'arbitrary and legally flawed'; the judge urged the secretary for education, Michael Gove, to reconsider. The communities secretary, Eric Pickles, approved the construction of the UK's largest biofuel power station in Bristol, overturning a decision by

Bristol City Council, which had rejected the proposals on environmental grounds. **14.** The health service ombudsman delivered a highly critical report on care for the elderly within the NHS, accusing it of 'failing to meet even the most basic standards'. **16.** The Home Office announced that migrants coming to the UK to work in jobs with annual salaries of £150,000 or more would be exempt from the annual limit on immigration. **17.** The work and pensions secretary, Iain Duncan Smith, introduced the Welfare Reform Bill, widely regarded as the most significant reshaping of the welfare state in 60 years. **22.** The education secretary outlined new guidelines for adoption intended to increase the number of children in care being placed with families; it included measures to allow white couples to adopt children from different ethnic backgrounds. **25.** The Home Office released figures showing that 237,890 immigrants were allowed to settle permanently in the UK in 2010, an increase of 22 per cent on the 2009 figure.

MARCH 2011

3. The director of the London School of Economics, Sir Howard Davies, resigned following controversy over the institution's financial links with Colonel Gaddafi's regime in Libya. **4.** A referendum was held in Wales on the extension of the Welsh Assembly's powers to pass legislation without ratification from the UK government; 63.5 per cent voted in favour. **5.** A Special Boat Service unit escorting two British diplomats to meet opponents of Colonel Gaddafi in Libya was captured and detained by rebel forces before being released the following day; on 7 March, the foreign secretary, William Hague, stated that he took full responsibility for the failed mission. **9.** The government outlined plans to ban tobacco displays from shops; from April 2012, larger retailers will be required to keep tobacco out of customers' sight, although smaller shops will have until 2015 to comply. **10.** Lord Hutton of Furness published his report on public sector pension reform; his recommendations included scrapping the current final-salary scheme for public-sector workers and increasing the pension age for members of the armed forces, the police and fire services to 60. **12.** Liberal Democrat MPs voted overwhelmingly against the coalition government's plans for a major overhaul of the NHS, embarrassing their party leadership. **13.** The Home Office announced a reduction of 270,000 in the number of jobs open to skilled migrants from outside the EU. **19.** The home secretary, Theresa May, announced that 80,000 fewer student visas will be available to international students from April 2011. **20.** Prince William embarked on a five-day tour of Australia and New Zealand to visit victims of the January floods in Australia and the February earthquake in New Zealand. **22.** The Royal Navy disclosed that nuclear reactors installed in its new submarines failed to meet safety standards and would be replaced; the debate over fitting the already controversial nuclear reactors had already caused an 18-month delay, costing an estimated £261m. **24.** University lecturers throughout the UK staged a one-day strike over pay cuts and changes to their pension scheme. **26.** Over 250,000 people marched through central London to protest at the government's programme of public service cuts; 66 people were injured during the demonstration, including 13 police officers. **28.** The MoD issued an unprecedented apology for the killing of 12-year-old Majella O'Hare in County Armagh in 1976; she was shot in the back by a paratrooper manning an army checkpoint. **29.** Thirty-eight patients who

underwent surgery at a hospital in north Wales were informed that they were at risk of contracting Creutzfeldt-Jakob disease (CJD), as the instruments used to perform their operations had not been sterilised properly following an operation on a man believed to have the disease.

APRIL 2011

1. A police constable, Ronan Kerr, was killed in Omagh, County Tyrone, by a bomb attached to his car. **4.** Documents released after lying forgotten in the Foreign and Commonwealth Office archives for 50 years revealed that British officials suppressing the Mau Mau uprising between 1952 and 1960 had subjected prisoners to sexual abuse and torture. **5.** During a brief visit to Pakistan, the prime minister pledged £650m to fund 4 million school places and 8,000 teachers. **8.** A large bomb was found in an abandoned van near Newry in Northern Ireland. **13.** The health secretary, Andrew Lansley, received a 99 per cent no-confidence vote from nurses attending the Royal College of Nursing's conference over his proposed Health and Social Care Bill. **14.** The business secretary, Vince Cable, warned that the prime minister's promise to reduce the number of immigrants into the UK was unwise and risked inflaming extremism. **20.** The Bishop of Oxford, Rt. Revd John Pritchard, detailed proposals to restrict the number of places at church schools made available to children from a Church of England background, claiming that the primary function of church schools is to serve the wider community. **22.** A new branch of the Tesco supermarket chain was seriously damaged during a riot in Bristol that was triggered by a police raid on squat housing activists opposed to the store's opening; eight police officers were injured. **29.** Prince William of Wales and Catherine Middleton were married at Westminster Abbey in a ceremony attended by 2,000 guests and watched by a worldwide audience of over 2 billion; the Queen bestowed the title of Duke of Cambridge on the prince shortly before his wedding.

MAY 2011

5. Local elections took place in 36 metropolitan boroughs, 194 district councils and 49 unitary authorities in the UK; elections to the Scottish parliament, the National Assembly for Wales and the Northern Ireland Assembly were also held, and a UK-wide referendum on whether to change the voting system from first-past-the-post to a form of proportional representation, the alternative vote (AV) system. The local election results showed that the Conservative party had gained four councils and the Labour party 26 councils, while the Liberal Democrats lost nine. In the elections to the devolved parliaments, the Scottish election produced the first single-party majority (for the SNP) in the assembly's history; in Wales the elections resulted in gains for Labour (four seats) and the Conservatives (two seats), but losses for Plaid Cymru (four seats) and the Liberal Democrats (one seat); and in Northern Ireland the election resulted in gains for the Democratic Unionists (two seats) and Sinn Fein (one seat), but losses for the Ulster Unionists and the SDLP (two seats each). In the referendum on the voting system, 67.9 per cent voted in favour of retaining the first-past-the-post system. **6.** The inquests on the victims of the 7 July 2005 bombings in London concluded; Lady Justice Hallett recorded a verdict of unlawful killing, ruled that no failings by the emergency services contributed to the victims' deaths, criticised MI5's record-keeping, said that a public inquiry into the bombings was unnecessary, and made nine recommendations for the emergency services and the authorities. **10.** David Laws, briefly the Liberal Democrat chief secretary to the Treasury in May 2010, was found to be in breach of six House of Commons rules in a report published by the Independent Parliamentary Standards Authority (IPSA); the IPSA commissioner stated that there was no evidence to suggest that Mr Laws had acted for personal financial gain. **17.** The Queen began a four-day state visit to the Republic of Ireland, the first by a British monarch in 100 years. **18.** The secretary of state for justice, Kenneth Clarke, caused controversy after suggesting to a caller in a BBC radio phone-in that there was a distinction between 'serious, proper rape' and other forms of rape; he later wrote to the caller to apologise if his comments had upset her. **23.** President Obama of the USA arrived in the UK at the start of a four-day state visit. **25.** President Obama addressed both houses of Parliament in Westminster Hall, the first president of the USA to do so.

JUNE 2011
1. The Home Office granted 161,000 asylum seekers and their dependants leave to remain in the UK as part of an operation to clear a backlog of 450,000 asylum applications. **4.** A number of well-known British academics announced plans to start a private university charging tuition fees of £18,000 a year. **8.** The Privy Council membership of the former Labour MP Elliott Morley was revoked, making Mr Morley only the second privy counsellor to be expelled from the council in 200 years. **11.** The Labour leader, Ed Miliband, was openly criticised by senior party members for failing to make an impact with voters; the results of a YouGov poll, coincidentally released the same day, showed that 41 per cent of the respondents thought that electing Mr Miliband as party leader was the wrong decision. **12.** Four Britons who had been held captive in Eritrea since December 2010 on charges of espionage and terrorism were released. **17.** In an interview with *The Times* newspaper, the education secretary, Michael Gove, claimed that the GCSE and A-level examinations system had been 'discredited', provoking anger among teachers and students' leaders. **21.** The general secretary of UNISON, the largest public-sector trade union, warned the government that there would be sustained industrial action unless the government shelved its proposals to reform public sector pensions. **26.** The defence secretary, Liam Fox, announced a radical reorganisation of the MoD, a reduction in the number of senior officers and the creation of a new joint force to integrate and oversee military intelligence and cyber-warfare. **30.** Civil servants and teachers in England and Wales staged a one-day strike over the government's proposed public-sector pension reforms. The Duke and Duchess of Cambridge began an official visit to Canada and California.

JULY 2011
4. The family of Milly Dowler (*see* Crimes and Legal Affairs 24 June) revealed that an investigator at the *News of the World* had hacked into Milly's mobile phone messages after her disappearance and deleted messages, leading her family to believe that she was still alive. A report by Martin Narey, the government's ministerial adviser on adoption, recommended a complete overhaul of the UK's adoption system. **5.** The families of other

murder victims were named as possible phone-hacking victims; major advertisers began to withdraw their advertising from the *News of the World.* **8.** The prime minister announced that there would be a public inquiry led by a judge into why the original police investigation into phone-hacking by the *News of the World* failed to uncover the extent of the problem; the prime minister also announced a separate inquiry into the effectiveness of the Press Complaints Commission. **11.** Two-thirds of the universities in England won approval to charge tuition fees of up to £9,000 from autumn 2012. **13.** There was an emergency debate in the House of Commons on the phone-hacking scandal. Lord Justice Leveson was appointed to chair the inquiry into phone-hacking. An independent review by Lord Philips of a helicopter crash on the Mull of Kintyre in 1994 which killed 29 people, including some of the UK's most senior intelligence officers, recommended that the original inquiry's finding of gross negligence by the two RAF pilots should be set aside as it was not supported by the evidence; the defence secretary apologised to the families of the two pilots for the distress caused by the original finding. **14.** Charlie Gilmour, a student at Cambridge university and the son of the Pink Floyd guitarist David Gilmour, was jailed for 16 months for offences committed during his drug-fuelled rampage, which included throwing a dustbin at a royal motorcade and swinging from the Cenotaph, at student protests in London in December 2010. **16.** Sir Paul Stephenson resigned as commissioner of the Metropolitan Police after it emerged that he had accepted hospitality arranged by Neil Wallis (*see* Crimes and Legal Affairs 14 July), who had acted as a public relations adviser to the force in 2009–10. **19.** Rupert Murdoch, the chairman and chief executive of News Corporation, and his son James, chairman of BSkyB, appeared before a parliamentary select committee to answer questions about phone-hacking at the *News of the World*; towards the end of the hearing, a protestor lunged at Rupert Murdoch and smeared him with a shaving-foam pie (*see* Crimes and Legal Affairs 29 July). **21.** Prince Andrew stepped down from his role as the UK's special representative for trade and investment; the prince had been criticised in March over his links to Jeffrey Epstein, an American billionaire who is a convicted sex offender. **30.** The Queen's eldest granddaughter, Zara Phillips, married the England rugby player Mike Tindall at Canongate Kirk, Edinburgh.

ARTS AND MEDIA

AUGUST 2010
11. Richard Desmond, the new owner of Channel Five television, announced a £20m cost-cutting drive, including job losses of over 25 per cent. **16.** The former prime minister Tony Blair announced that he would donate the proceeds from his autobiography, *A Journey,* to the Royal British Legion. **19.** Research published by the media regulator OFCOM found that people in the UK spend a daily average of seven hours and five minutes, or 45 per cent of waking hours, consuming digital media. **22.** The film director Richard Lester announced that he had donated his entire archive, covering his 40-year career in film and television, to the British Film Institute's National Archive. **28.** Robert Devereux, a former partner in the Virgin business empire, announced that he would sell more than 300 works from his art collection and use the proceeds to set up a charity supporting artists in Africa.

SEPTEMBER 2010
7. The xx were awarded the 2010 Mercury Music prize; other artists shortlisted included Paul Weller, Laura Marling, Mumford & Sons and Biffy Clyro. A previously unknown poem by Ted Hughes was published in the *New Statesman,* 12 years after his death; 'Last Letter' described the night his estranged wife Sylvia Plath committed suicide. 11. It was announced that recordings of 65 British television dramas originally broadcast between 1957 and 1970, and previously thought to be lost, had been discovered in the Library of Congress in Washington DC; they were donated to the BFI National Archive. 12. Lord Sainsbury donated £25m to the British Museum to build a new wing; it was the largest donation made to a cultural institution by a living donor since 1985. 14. The chairman of the BBC Trust, Sir Michael Lyons, announced that he would leave the post in April 2011; the controller of BBC One, Jay Hunt, announced that she would be leaving to join Channel 4. 15. The Threadneedle prize, a visual arts award established in 2008, was awarded to Patricia Cain for *Building the Riverside Museum.*

OCTOBER 2010
1. Jonathan Franzen's new novel, *Freedom,* had to be reprinted after it was discovered that an uncorrected version of the manuscript had been published by accident; the publisher, Harper Collins, offered to exchange all uncorrected copies for the new version. 2. Zaha Hadid's design for the National Museum of 21st Century Arts in Rome won the RIBA Stirling prize for architecture. 6. Seamus Heaney won the Forward prize for poetry for his collection *Human Chain,* inspired by his experiences after suffering a stroke in 2006. 11. The BBC announced that its deputy director, Mark Byford, was to be made redundant and would leave the corporation in summer 2011; Mr Byford's redundancy pay was estimated to be almost £1m. 12. Howard Jacobson won the Booker prize for his novel *The Finkler Question.* 15. Health and safety considerations forced Tate Modern to stop visitors from walking on Ai Weiwei's exhibit in the Turbine Hall featuring 100m individually created porcelain sunflower seeds, as it would create potentially harmful levels of dust. 19. The BBC agreed to freeze the licence fee for six years and to take over the funding of the World Service from the Foreign Office. 20. The budget for the Department for Culture, Media and Sport was cut by 24 per cent in the government's comprehensive spending review; Arts Council England's budget was cut by 30 per cent. 25. *The Independent* launched a 56-page tabloid spin-off, *i,* priced at 20p and intended to attract younger readers and commuters. Sony announced that it would discontinue the Walkman, first produced in 1979, owing to a lack of sales. 28. Lloyd Dorfman, the founder of Travelex, donated £10m to the National Theatre; the theatre recognised the gift by renaming its Cottesloe theatre the Dorfman.

NOVEMBER 2010
5. BBC news journalists belonging to the National Union of Journalists began a 48-hour strike in protest at proposed cuts to pensions. 11. An 18th-century Chinese vase discovered at a home in Ruislip, London, sold for £53.1m at Bainbridge's auctioneers in Ruislip; it was believed to be a record sum for any Chinese artwork sold at auction. 16. Music by The Beatles became available for download on iTunes for the first time; in the first week over 2 million tracks were downloaded. 17. The Department for Culture, Media and Sport announced the

withdrawal from 2015 of funding for seven non-national museums in the UK, including the Horniman Museum in London and the Museum of Science and Industry in Manchester. 27. Jamie Oliver became the second person after J. K. Rowling to sell more than £100m of books in Britain. 29. Ed Vaizey, a junior minister for culture, media and sport, announced that the British Film Institute would take on many of the functions of the UK Film Council after the council's abolition in July 2011. It was announced that a collection of 271 works by Pablo Picasso had been found at the home of a retired electrician in France; Mr Le Guennec said that they had been given to him in exchange for installing alarm systems at Picasso's homes.

DECEMBER 2010
2. The Dulwich Picture Gallery announced that it would mark its 200th anniversary in 2011 by displaying one masterpiece each month on loan from institutions in Europe and the USA, including paintings by Vincent van Gogh and David Hockney. 6. Susan Philipsz won the Turner prize for a sound piece, a recording of her own voice singing a Scottish lament; it was the first time in the history of the award that a sound installation had been nominated. 7. A first edition of John James Audubon's *The Birds of America* sold for £7.3m at auction, a record for a printed book. 15. Readers of *The Stage* newspaper voted Dame Judi Dench the greatest stage actor of all time. 16. Google, in collaboration with scientists at Harvard University, released a searchable database containing 5 million English language books published between 1800 and 2000, around 4 per cent of all the books ever printed; the database will be used to chart the evolution of the English language. 18. The Spoliation Advisory Panel ruled that the Courtauld Institute in London should keep *The Coronation of the Virgin* by Rubens, rejecting the claim of the family of the former owner that the former owner had been forced to sell the painting before the Nazis seized the collection in 1934. 20. The European Commission reclassified artworks by Dan Flavin and Bill Viola as light fixtures for taxation purposes; they became liable to VAT at 20 per cent, whereas sculptures are liable for VAT at 5 per cent. 22. Booktrust, the UK charity which encourages children to enjoy reading, was told that it would lose all of its annual £13m government funding; on 26 December the charity was told that funding would continue.

JANUARY 2011
5. The Costa book award category winners were announced; the novel award was won by Maggie O'Farrell for *The Hand That First Held Mine,* the first novel award by Kishwar Desai for *Witness the Night;* the biography award by Edmund de Waal for *The Hare With Amber Eyes,* the poetry award by Jo Shapcott for *Of Mutability;* and the children's book award by Jason Wallace for *Out of Shadows.* 6. A fundraising campaign successfully raised £2.7m to prevent the sale of *The Procession to Calvary,* a painting by Pieter Bruegel the Younger; it remains on display at Nostell Priory, a National Trust property near Wakefield. 11. An employment tribunal found the BBC guilty of ageism in a case brought by the 53-year-old former *Countryfile* presenter Miriam O'Reilly. 20. Liz Lochhead was appointed as Scotland's new makar, or national poet. 24. Derek Walcott won the T. S. Eliot poetry prize for his collection *White Egrets.* 25. Jo Shapcott won the overall Costa book of the year award for her poetry collection *Of Mutability.* 26. The BBC

World Service announced 650 job losses and the closure of five foreign language services following a reduction in its grant-in-aid funding from the Foreign and Commonwealth Office. **27.** The auction houses Christie's and Sotheby's both announced an increase in sales in 2010; Christie's recorded a 53 per cent increase on its 2009 sales, the highest in the company's history.

FEBRUARY 2011
1. The Google Art Project was launched, allowing users to take a virtual tour of 17 museums worldwide and view around 1,000 artworks online. **5.** Read-ins and appearances from authors such as Philip Pullman and Mark Haddon were held countrywide to protest against the planned closure of 450 libraries owing to local government funding cuts. **7.** Arianna Huffington and her business partner Kenneth Lerer sold the news website the Huffington Post, which they had set up in 2005, to AOL for $315m (£195m). Lee Horton, a former sports editor of the Sunday tabloid *The People*, was sentenced to 15 months in prison for defrauding the newspaper of over £370,000 between 2000 and 2008. **13.** At the BAFTA film awards, *The King's Speech* won seven awards, including best film, best British film and best actor (for Colin Firth); the best actress award was won by Natalie Portman for her performance in *Black Swan*. **14.** At the Grammy awards, Lady Gaga won five awards, including best pop album; Arcade Fire won album of the year for *The Suburbs*. **15.** At the Brit awards, the best British group award was won by Take That, the best British album award by Mumford and Sons for *Sigh No More*, and the best British single award by Tinie Tempah for 'Pass Out'. **23.** The writer John le Carré donated his entire literary archive, including handwritten drafts of his novels and personal correspondence, to the Bodleian Library, Oxford. **24.** The British fashion designer John Galliano was arrested after allegedly making racist and anti-semitic remarks to a couple in a Paris bar; the designer was suspended by his employer, the Dior fashion house. **28.** Following the lifting of the ban on product placement on British television (except on BBC programmes), a Nescafe coffee machine became the first product to be promoted, appearing during an episode of *This Morning* on ITV.

MARCH 2011
1. Dior sacked designer John Galliano after a video clip was posted on the internet supporting the allegation that the designer had made anti-semitic comments in a Paris bar. **3.** The secretary of state for culture, media and sport, James Hunt, gave provisional approval to News Corporation's bid to take over the 61 per cent of BSkyB that it did not already own, after the company gave assurances that it would safeguard the independence of its Sky News channel (*see* 13 July). **5.** One million books were given away in the UK and Ireland to mark the inaugural World Book Night; the copies of 25 titles were distributed by around 20,000 people at locations including pubs, hospitals and the London Underground. **7.** Pablo Picasso's painting *Nude, Green Leaves and Bust*, went on display at Tate Modern; in 2010 the painting became the most expensive work of art sold at auction, when it was purchased for $106.5m (£65.4m). **13.** At the 2011 Olivier awards, *After the Dance*, a Terence Rattigan play largely neglected for 70 years until it was staged at the National Theatre, won four awards, including best revival. **14.** Brian True-May, the producer of the *Midsomer Murders* television crime drama, was suspended from his job after he suggested that the ITV1 show was

'the last bastion of Englishness' and that there was no place on the programme for ethnic minorities. **27.** Arts Council England was criticised by a parliamentary select committee for 'spending far too much on itself' and was told to sell works from its collection for the first time; the Arts Council responded by stating the findings were out-of-date and that selling artworks was not a sensible solution.

APRIL 2011
1. In a joint online venture, 228 national and local radio stations launched the 'Radioplayer' service, which allows listeners to search for stations by postcode, genre, song title or artist. **7.** News International, the UK newspaper division of News Corporation that managed the *News of the World*, issued an unreserved apology to eight victims of phone-hacking by the newspaper and and set up a £15m fund to compensate them. **16.** The poet laureate, Carol Ann Duffy, confirmed that she had composed a poem for the wedding of Prince William and Kate Middleton called *Rings*; the poem was published on the morning of the wedding. **21.** OFCOM announced that the final of *The X Factor*, screened in December 2010, did not breach broadcasting rules for its controversial dance routines but, in an unusual move, the media regulator appeared to criticise the *Daily Mail* for publishing images 'significantly more graphic and close up' than the ITV broadcast. **22.** The actor Michael Sheen began a 72-hour performance of *The Passion* in his home town of Port Talbot; the drama involved a cast of 1,000 local people and seven choirs, and culminated in a crucifixion scene on a seafront roundabout.

MAY 2011
1. The Tate Modern announced plans to honour the Chinese artist Ai Weiwei with a five-foot-high sculpture made from 10 million of the 100 million porcelain 'seeds' in the artist's installation in the gallery's Turbine Hall in October 2010; Ai Weiwei had been detained without charge by the Chinese government since April 2011. **10.** At the Sony Radio Academy Awards, Ronnie Wood was named music radio personality of the year, Frank Skinner won the best entertainment programme prize, and TalkSport was awarded UK station of the year. **11.** The Cannes Film Festival opened with a screening of the Woody Allen film *Midnight in Paris* starring Carla Bruni, the wife of the French president. **18.** The Man Booker International Prize was awarded to Philip Roth, but only after Carmen Callil, one of the three members of the judging panel, quit because of her disagreement with the decision. **19.** The Danish director Lars von Trier was banned from the Cannes film festival for claiming to be a Nazi and stating that he sympathised with Adolf Hitler. **21.** A new sculpture gallery, the Hepworth Wakefield, was opened in Yorkshire. **22.** Daniel Rigby, considered the fourth favourite in the category, won the BAFTA best actor award for his performance as a young Eric Morecambe. **26.** Cheryl Cole was dropped as a judge of the US version of *The X Factor* less than a month after her arrival in the USA.

JUNE 2011
7. Julia Donaldson, author of more than 100 children's books, including the bestselling *The Gruffalo*, was appointed the seventh Children's Laureate. **8.** The Orange Prize for Fiction was won by Tea Obreht, a Serbian-American author and the youngest-ever winner of the prize, for *The Tiger's Wife*. **12.** At the 65th Tony

theatre awards in New York, the British play *War Horse,* adapted by Nick Stafford from a novel by Michael Morpurgo, won five awards including best play, and the British actor Mark Rylance won best actor for his role in *Jerusalem.* **16.** A BBC Trust investigation into the *Panorama* documentary 'Primark: On the Rack', screened in 2008, ruled that the documentary had broken guidelines on accuracy and fairness and that a section of the film was probably not genuine. **22.** The dissident Chinese artist Ai Weiwei was released on bail by the Chinese authorities following global condemnation of his imprisonment (*see* 1 May). **29.** Sir Terence Conran donated £17.5m to relocate the Design Museum from Shad Thames to the Commonwealth Institute building in Kensington, west London.

JULY 2011

4. Michael Portillo was appointed as the chairman of a £55m scheme to help arts and heritage organisations succeed in a struggling economy; the scheme, funded by the Heritage Lottery Fund, Arts Council England and the Department for Culture, Media and Sport, allows applicants to bid for grants of up to £5m. **6.** The 2011 BBC Samuel Johnson prize for non-fiction was won by the Dutch historian Frank Dikotter for his account of modern Chinese history in *Mao's Great Famine: The History of China's Most Devastating Catastrophe, 1958–62.* **7.** News International announced the closure of its bestselling Sunday newspaper, the 168-year-old *News of the World,* following accusations of illegal activities, including hacking the mobile phones of murder victims and their families and making payments to the police for information (*see* UK Affairs); the paper published its final edition on 10 July. **12.** The BBC revealed, in the first detailed disclosure of its highest earners' salaries, that at least seven broadcasters were paid more than £1m in 2010–11. **13.** News Corporation announced that it had withdrawn its bid to take control of BSkyB following further revelations in the *News of the World* phone-hacking scandal. **15.** Rebekah Brooks resigned as chief executive of News International, the UK division of News Corporation; she was replaced by Tom Mockridge. The eighth and final Harry Potter film, *Harry Potter and the Deathly Hallows: Part 2,* was released; it made £23m in its opening weekend, breaking UK box office records, including the biggest single-day figures. **29.** Baroness Buscombe announced that she was standing down as chair of the Press Complaints Commission after the commission was criticised over the phone-hacking scandal.

BUSINESS AND ECONOMIC AFFAIRS

AUGUST 2010

2. HSBC, the UK's biggest bank, reported pre-tax profits of £7bn for the first six months of 2010, more than double its profits for the same period in 2009. **6.** The chief executive of RBS, Steven Hester, urged the government to begin selling its 83 per cent stake in the bank after RBS announced interim pre-tax profits of £1.1bn. **11.** In its quarterly inflation report, the Bank of England downgraded its previous growth forecast for the British economy. The International Labour Organisation reported that global youth unemployment had risen to 81 million, or 13 per cent, of 620 million economically active 15–24 year-olds at the end of 2009, an increase of 7.8 million since 2007. **12.** General Motors, whose largest shareholder has been the US government since

2009 when it was restructured following bankruptcy, reported a profit of $1.3bn (£795m) for the second quarter of 2010, its largest since 2004; the company's chief executive, Ed Whitacre, announced his resignation with effect from 1 September. **13.** New competition laws came into effect which barred supermarket chains from signing deals with landlords or councils to exclude rivals from a particular area. The travel agent and tour operator Sun4U collapsed, affecting 7,000 customers. **16.** Barclays bank agreed to pay $298m (£190m) in penalties to the US government to settle two criminal charges against its dollar clearance branch in New York, which was accused of handling money transfers from five countries (Cuba, Iran, Libya, Sudan and Myanmar) with which business is prohibited under US foreign policy. **17.** The travel group Flight Options ceased trading; most of the 60,000 customers who had forward bookings with the company were thought to be covered by the Civil Aviation Authority's Air Travel Organisers' Licensing protection programme. **23.** Marks & Spencer announced the appointment of Robert Swannell, a former investment banker, as its next chairman, taking over from Sir Stuart Rose in January 2011. Research published by the Local Data Company found that over 300 of 807 former Woolworths' stores remained unoccupied since the chain went into administration in 2008. **24.** The Financial Services Authority (FSA) fined the UK division of Zurich Insurance over £2m for the loss of 46,000 customers' personal information, including credit card and identity details. **25.** BP confirmed that it no longer intended to compete for an oil exploration licence in Greenland. **26.** Asil Nadir returned to the UK after 17 years in northern Cyprus to face £34m fraud charges relating to the collapse of his Polly Peck business empire in 1990.

SEPTEMBER 2010

4. HM Revenue and Customs announced that between 2008 and 2010 nearly 6 million people in the UK had paid the wrong amount of tax through the pay-as-you-earn (PAYE) system; 4.3 million people were entitled to a rebate but 1.4 million people had underpaid by an average of £1,500. **8.** The Office for National Statistics (ONS) reported that in the period April to June 2010, the number of workless households (where all household members aged 16 and over are unemployed) had risen to a record high of 3.9 million, a fifth of all households. **15.** Addressing the Trades Union Congress (TUC) in Manchester, the governor of the Bank of England, Mervyn King, admitted that lenders and policymakers rather than workers were responsible for the banking crisis and warned that the costs of the UK's financial crisis would be borne for a generation. **19.** The trade union Unite announced that it was launching a high court action against the airline BMI, claiming that the airline was in breach of contract with its employees after failing to honour a three-year pay deal announced in 2007; the union had expected the final year of the pay deal to begin in April 2010 after the 2009–10 pay rise was suspended for one year. **20.** The Council of Mortgage Lenders reported that £11.4bn was lent to homeowners in August; this was 14 per cent less than in July, and the lowest level for August since 2000. **21.** Figures from the ONS showed that a 'payroll tax', levied on companies for each employee bonus of more than £25,000 paid between December 2009 and April 2010, raised £3.5bn in revenue for the Treasury; this was £1bn more than estimated by the Treasury in June. **22.** Figures from the Bank of England showed that yields on government ten-year bonds fell to 2.95 per cent at the end of August, their lowest level for 12 months. **31.** The Irish government announced a £39bn bailout package for its banking sector, increasing the country's budget deficit to 32 per cent of GDP.

OCTOBER 2010
1. The cost to BP of cleaning up pollution caused by the Deepwater Horizon rig explosion in the Gulf of Mexico in April 2010 reached $11.2bn (£7bn); the oil group announced that it would use assets in the region as collateral for its $20bn (£12.6bn) compensation fund. **4.** Crown Currency Exchange, a popular currency exchange website, went into administration; administrators believed the company, which was not covered by any FSA compensation scheme, owed about £20m to approximately 13,000 customers and warned customers that any currency that had been ordered but not yet delivered would not be sent to them. **5.** A former futures trader for the French bank Société Général, Jérôme Kerviel, who was caught gambling €50bn (£42bn) of the bank's money in 2008, was ordered to repay €4.9bn (£4.2bn), the net loss incurred by the bank once the account was settled, and sentenced to three years in prison for fraud and breach of trust. **12.** The US government ended the moratorium on deepwater oil-drilling in the Gulf of Mexico. **15.** The Air Transport Users Council (ATUC) reported that many airlines were denying apparently legitimate claims for compensation from passengers stranded when the ash cloud from the Eyjafjallajokull volcano in Iceland forced the closure of European airspace for six days in April 2010. **19.** China's central bank increased interest rates for the first time in three years after the World Bank warned that the flow of capital into fast-growing Asian economies could cause real estate and equity markets in the region to become overinflated. **26.** The UK's GDP increased by 0.8 per cent in the period July to September 2010.

NOVEMBER 2010
17. National Savings and Investments (NS&I) reported that deposits decreased sharply following a decision in July 2010 to stop selling its index-linked inflation-protected savings certificates; gross inflows to NS&I decreased from £5.5bn in the quarter to June 2010 to £3.6bn in the quarter to September 2010. **18.** The bi-annual economic outlook report by the Organisation for Economic Cooperation and Development (OECD) warned that house prices in many countries were still elevated despite the 2008–9 slump and that the UK and USA could face a second downturn in the market. **21.** The Irish prime minister, Brian Cowen, announced that Ireland had formally requested a financial rescue package worth €80bn–€90bn (£67bn–£75bn) from the European Union and the International Monetary Fund (IMF); EU ministers endorsed the request in order to safeguard financial stability within the eurozone. **22.** In a statement to the House of Commons, the chancellor of the exchequer, George Osborne, announced that it was in the UK's national interest to provide financial assistance to Ireland in the form of direct loans should the assistance provided by the EU and IMF package prove insufficient. **28.** The EU agreed a €85bn (£72bn) financial rescue package for Ireland; around €35bn (£30bn) would go towards stabilising the republic's banking system and the remaining €50bn (£42bn) would help with the Irish government's day-to-day expenditure.

DECEMBER 2010
3. Mitsubishi Heavy Industries announced plans to establish a wind turbine research and manufacturing base in Edinburgh after securing a £30m subsidy from the government; investment in the development will exceed £100m over five years. **4.** UK Uncut, a group campaigning against tax avoidance by big businesses, held sit-ins and protests at branches of Topshop, Boots, Vodaphone, HSBC and Barclays nationwide; the Oxford Street branch of Topshop in London was forced to close for several hours after around 200 demonstrators entered the store at 11am. **10.** The Royal Institution of Chartered Surveyors reported that home ownership in the UK dropped to 67.9 per cent in 2009, its lowest level since 1991. **13.** A report published by the Bank of England showed that the number of UK households experiencing difficulties paying essential bills had risen from 8.9 million in 2009 to 10.5 million in 2010. **14.** Around 1,200 workers at the Heinz factory in Wigan staged a 24-hour walkout after rejecting a two-year pay increase of 3.3 per cent and 3 per cent; two further 24-hour strikes were held on 21 and 29 December. **15.** ONS figures showed that 33,000 public-sector jobs were cut in the quarter to October 2010, while the number of private-sector jobs remained unchanged. **20.** BAE Systems pleaded guilty to a charge of failing to keep proper accounts in relation to payments to an adviser on the sale of a radar system to Tanzania; the following day the company was fined £500,000. **21.** The ONS reported that public sector borrowing had reached an unprecedented £23bn in November 2010 as modest rises in tax revenues failed to offset an increase in public spending.

JANUARY 2011
3. The Bank of America agreed to pay the American mortgage companies Fannie Mae and Freddie Mac a total of almost $3bn (£1.89bn) to settle claims that it had sold on bad home loans to the mortgage finance groups in 2008. **4.** The standard rate of VAT increased from 17.5 per cent to 20 per cent. **5.** The entertainment retailer HMV Group announced that 40 HMV stores and 20 Waterstone's bookshops would close following a poor Christmas trading period. The housing charity Shelter reported that 10 per cent of people in private rented accommodation and 8 per cent of mortgage borrowers had used credit cards to meet their housing costs in the year to 31 August 2010. **6.** The National Grid was fined £8m by the Office of Gas and Electricity Markets (OFGEM) for failing to report accurately roadworks at four locations in the UK between 2005 and 2008. **11.** Workers at the Heinz factory in Wigan held a fourth 24-hour strike after rejecting a revised two-year pay offer from the company (*see* 14 December). The French aeroplane manufacturer Airbus, employer of 11,000 people in the UK, announced the largest aircraft order (in terms of numbers ordered) in commercial aviation history after winning a contract to provide 180 planes to the budget Indian airline Indigo in a deal worth $15.6bn (£9.6bn). **18.** The ONS reported that the consumer prices index (CPI) increased to 3.7 per cent in December, from 3.3 per cent in November, owing to record increases in household food and transport costs. **25.** Official figures showed that GDP decreased by 0.5 per cent in the last quarter of 2010, giving an annual growth of 1.4 per cent, below the 1.8 per cent forecast. **26.** Barclays bank announced the closure of its branch-based operation selling financial products, with the loss of 1,000 jobs.

FEBRUARY 2011
1. The US pharmaceutical company Pfizer announced the closure of its high-tech research facility in Sandwich, Kent, resulting in the loss of 2,400 jobs. **2.** Barclays bank announced 285 job losses at its Barclaycard call centres; Nationwide building society revealed that it was closing ten branches, with the loss of 100 jobs. **7.** The Association of British Insurers said burst pipes caused by the cold weather accounted for £680m, or three-quarters, of the £900m claimed for property damage in December 2010. **8.** The chancellor, George Osborne, announced that the levy on profits in the banking industry would be increased from £1.7bn to £2.5bn for 2011, raising an extra £800m for the exchequer. **9.** Four of the UK's largest banks (Barclays, HSBC, Lloyds Banking Group and Royal Bank of Scotland) committed to lending more money to businesses as part of the government's 'Project Merlin' initiative; the four banks plus Santander pledged to make £190bn of credit available in 2011 (15 per cent more than in 2010), with £76bn of this going to smaller businesses. **14.** Auto Windscreens went into administration; its 1,042 employees were made redundant on 25 February after efforts to raise finance or find a buyer failed. **15.** The ONS published figures showing that consumer price index inflation increased to 4 per cent in January 2011. **22.** The FSA fined DB Mortgages, owned by Deutsche Bank, £840,000 for irresponsible lending, and demanded an additional £1.5m in redress for the lender's customers. **24.** In the Confederation of British Industry's quarterly distributive trades survey, 73 per cent of high street retailers reported that average prices were higher than 12 months previously, the highest percentage since 1991. A report from the Asda supermarket chain showed that disposable income for the average family was £174 a week, almost £10 less a week than in January 2010.

MARCH 2011
1. Barclays bank bought 1.15 million Egg credit card accounts from Citigroup for about £2bn; the Egg cardholder business will be absorbed into the bank's Barclaycard operation. **10.** Despite concerns over the rate of inflation, the Bank of England's monetary policy committee kept the bank base rate at 0.5 per cent. **14.** Southern Cross Healthcare, the UK's largest operator of residential care homes, announced that it was in danger of defaulting on its debts and was seeking to restructure rent owed to its landlords. **15.** British gas prices increased following the announcement by Royal Dutch Shell that liquefied natural gas shipments would be diverted to Japan to help ease the country's energy crisis in the wake of the 11 March earthquake and resulting devastation (*see* Asia). **16.** Figures released by the ONS showed that unemployment reached a 17-year-high in the final quarter of 2010; the number of people out of work increased by 27,000 to 2.52 million. **23.** The 2011 Budget was published; measures included a 1p per litre cut in fuel duty to be implemented from 6pm, a £630 increase in the tax-free personal allowance from April 2012, and a reduction in corporation tax from 28 per cent to 26 per cent from April 2011 and then by 1 per cent a year until 2014–15. The Budget forecast public sector borrowing of £146bn for 2011–12, revised the forecast of economic growth from 2.1 per cent (end 2010) to 1.7 per cent, and said inflation was expected to remain at 4–5 per cent. **30.** A report by the House of Lords economic affairs committee said that the 'big four' accountancy firms (Deloitte, Ernst & Young, KPMG and PwC), which dominate the market for auditing listed companies' accounts, had been complacent in their oversight of banks before the financial crisis.

APRIL 2011
1. Sport Media Group, the parent company of the *Daily Sport* and *Sunday Sport* newspapers, ceased trading, the first national newspapers to close in the UK since 1995. British Airways reported pre-tax profits of £157m, the first pre-tax profit for the airline in three years. **7.** The European Central Bank raised interest rates from 1 per cent to 1.25 per cent, the first increase since 2008. **10.** The Independent Commission on Banking released its interim report on the UK banking sector; it called for extensive reforms, including separating UK banks' retail services from their investment services. **15.** Three of the world's largest internet poker companies (PokerStars, Full Tilt Poker and Absolute Poker) were shut down and charged with money laundering, fraud and illegal gambling following an investigation by the FBI. **20.** The price of gold reached $1,500 (£915) an ounce for the first time ever. The Apple electronics and computer software company released its quarterly financial figures, revealing a 95 per cent increase in profits year-on-year; the increase was attributed mainly to the global success of the iPhone 4. **21.** BP filed a £24bn lawsuit against its Deepwater Horizon partners, including Haliburton, the oil services corporation whose cement slurry failed to seal the stricken oil well, and Cameron International, the manufacturers of the malfunctioning valve that was supposed to prevent oil leaking from a well. **29.** The European Commission announced that it was investigating 16 of the world's largest investment banks, including HSBC, Royal Bank of Scotland and Barclays, over allegations of collusion and abuse of their collective market dominance, and the contributory effect of this on the EU sovereign debt crisis. **30.** Centrica, the owner of British Gas, ceased production at its Morecambe Bay reservoir for maintenance work; the north gas field was reopened on 1 July, but the company did not reopen the south field, saying that it was not economically viable following the government's decision to increase the tax on oil and gas production from 20 per cent to 32 per cent.

MAY 2011
5. Lloyds Bank set aside £3.2bn to compensate customers who were mis-sold payment protection insurance on loans arranged after 1998. **7.** Four directors of MG Rover who received £42m in pay and pensions from the company were disqualified from holding any company directorships for a combined total of 19 years, but the investigation by the Serious Fraud Office concluded that there was insufficient evidence to pursue criminal proceedings against them. **10.** The electronics and computer software corporation, Microsoft, acquired the internet telephone company Skype for $8.5bn (£5.2bn), the biggest deal in the company's history. **17.** A National Audit Office report on progress with the National Programme for IT in the NHS project found that the £11.4bn scheme, launched in 2002 to create electronic care records for all NHS patients by 2010, would not achieve its aims, but warned that if the government abandoned the project, IT companies could claim billions of pounds in compensation. **20.** The struggling HMV retail group sold its 314-bookshop chain Waterstone's for £53m to the Russian billionaire Alexander Mamut. **22.** Following an investigation into the mobile phone company TalkTalk, the industry regulator OFCOM

concluded that the company was engaging in 'dishonest, misleading or deceptive conduct' by providing misleading information to customers; the company was given until 20 June to make the necessary improvements to its service. **25.** The chief economist of the OECD advised the UK chancellor, George Osborne, that there was 'scope for slowing the pace' of public sector cuts if UK economic growth remained sluggish. **31.** Southern Cross Healthcare announced that it would defer 30 per cent of its rent payments for four months in an attempt to remain in business.

JUNE 2011
3. The government announced that the Betfred bookmaking firm had won the auction to buy the state-owned Horserace Totalisator Board (the Tote) for £265m; of this, £90m went to the exchequer, £90m to the racing industry, £60m to pay off the Tote's debts and £25m to its pension fund. **7.** HMV Group agreed renegotiated terms with its creditors, giving the struggling retailer until September 2013 to repay its £220m loan. **8.** Southern Cross Healthcare announced that it would cut 3,000 jobs by October 2011; it also asked HM Revenue and Customs if it could defer income tax payments and VAT for up to three months. **15.** The chancellor announced his intention of selling part of the state-owned Northern Rock bank by auction before the end of 2011. **16.** The Guardian Media Group reported a £33m loss for the 2010–11 financial year. **18.** The price of gold reached $1,600 (£979) an ounce for the first time ever. **23.** Oil prices fell dramatically following the news that a number of countries would release some of their emergency stockpiles of crude oil, for only the third time since the 1970s, and sell them on the global energy market. **24.** The home furnishing store Habitat sold its brand name, its website and three of its London stores, including its flagship store on Tottenham Court Road, to Home Retail Group (owner of Argos and Homebase) for £24.5m; administrators were called in to seek a potential buyer for the remaining 30 outlets. **26.** The prime ministers of the UK and China, David Cameron and Wen Jiabao, signed a trade deal worth £1.4bn, in an agreement that will enable UK firms to expand in China's regional cities.

JULY 2011
4. Bombadier, Britain's only remaining train builder, announced that it was cutting 1,400 jobs after the government awarded a £1.5bn contract to build 1,200 new carriages to the German company Siemens. **5.** The Treasury created a loophole to allow less profitable early-stage offshore oil-drilling operations to avoid the windfall tax on North Sea oil production; after the decision was announced, the Norwegian oil company Statoil said that it would resume operations, which had been suspended since March in protest at the tax. **6.** The Crown Estate's annual report was released, showing a record profit of £230.9m in the year ending 31 March 2011, a 9.6 per cent increase on the previous year. **11.** The Payments Council announced that it was reversing its decision to abolish cheques by 2018 as a result of the sustained public outcry against the proposal. **19.** The Competition Commission rejected a final appeal from the airports' operator BAA contesting the court of appeal's 2009 ruling that had ordered the sale of Stansted Airport and either Edinburgh or Glasgow airports; the commission declared that the sale of Stansted must commence within three months. **26.** The UK fell from third to seventh in the list of worldwide destinations for

foreign direct investment, according to the United Nations Conference on Trade and Development. **27.** Centrica, the parent company of British Gas, announced profits of £1.3bn for the first half of 2011, but claimed that its proposed 18 per cent increase in domestic power prices from August 2011 was essential if the company was to break even for the second half of 2011. **29.** The Office of Fair Trading announced a six-week consultation over referring to the Competition Commission the dominance of the 'big four' accountancy firms (*see* 30 March) in the market for auditing companies listed on the stock exchange.

CRIMES AND LEGAL AFFAIRS

AUGUST 2010
1. Following a successful pilot scheme in four police areas, the child sexual offenders disclosure scheme, or Sarah's law, which allows people to find out if a person who has contact with a child is a registered sex offender, was extended to eight forces' areas; in March 2011 it was rolled out in the rest of England and Wales. **2.** Raymond Scott, an unemployed antiques dealer, was given an eight-year prison sentence for handling a stolen copy of a 17th-century First Folio of Shakespeare's plays worth about £1m. **6.** Annette Hopkins was given a suspended jail sentence and fined £27,000 after being convicted of wilful neglect over her ill-treatment and neglect of nine residents of her care home in Southampton. **18.** Two 11-year-old boys found guilty of attempting to rape an eight-year-old girl in Hayes, west London, in 2009 were given three-year supervision orders; the judge ruled that a jail sentence would not be in their best interests. **23.** The body of Gareth Williams, an MI6 officer, was found in a padlocked holdall in his flat; the cause of death remained unknown.

SEPTEMBER 2010
7. Lorraine Thorpe was sentenced to life imprisonment for the murder of her father and his friend; aged 15 when the crimes were committed, she is believed to be Britain's youngest female double murderer. **14.** The television presenter Ray Gosling was given a 90-day suspended sentence for wasting police time after claiming on a television programme that he killed his partner, who was dying of an AIDS-related illness. The singer George Michael was sentenced to eight weeks in prison, fined £1,250 and banned from driving for five years for driving while under the influence of cannabis. **16.** The co-founder of the MQM party in Pakistan, Imran Farooq, was found dead outside his home in London with stab wounds and head injuries. **19.** A victim of sexual assault was awarded £16,000 damages and received a personal apology from the director of public prosecutions, Keir Starmer, after the Crown Prosecution Service pressurised her into giving evidence without a screen, dropped her case without consulting her, and claimed the collapse of the case was partly her fault. **22.** The judge at the retrial of Abdullah Baybasin directed the jury to find him not guilty because of lack of evidence; Mr Baybasin was sentenced to 22 years in prison in 2006 for drug smuggling, blackmail and perverting the course of justice but in 2009 the court of appeal ordered a retrial after deeming the judge's summing-up in the original trial unfair. **30.** Thames Valley Police published a report on Project Champion, a surveillance project in a predominantly Muslim area of Birmingham, which found that the operation was implemented with virtually no

consultation or regard for the law; the project was abandoned in June 2010 when it was discovered that residents had been misled into believing that the cameras were being used to combat anti-social behaviour rather than for a counter-terrorism operation.

OCTOBER 2010

4. John Maden was sentenced to life imprisonment for the rape and murder of his 12-year-old niece in April 2010; Mr Maden was told he would never be released. **7.** An inquest jury ruled that the barrister Mark Saunders was lawfully killed by police marksmen following a five-hour siege in 2008, although it also criticised the police's handling of some aspects of the incident. **16.** Analysis of stop-and-search figures by the London School of Economics and the Open Society Justice Initiative found that black people in England and Wales were 26.6 times more likely to be stopped and searched by police than white people in 2008–9. **17.** Three security guards employed by the private security firm G4S were arrested in connection with the death of Jimmy Mubenga, who died on a flight to Angola as he was being forcibly deported from the UK. **20.** Prince Saud Abdulaziz bin Nasser al Saud of Saudi Arabia was sentenced to life imprisonment in the UK for the murder of his servant Bandar Abdulaziz, who was found beaten and strangled in the Landmark Hotel, London, in February 2010. As part of the government's comprehensive spending review, the secretary of state for justice, Kenneth Clarke, announced plans to cut the prison population in England and Wales by 3,000 within four years. The supreme court ruled that prenuptial agreements should have full legal status in English law; the ruling was made in a case between a German multimillionairess, Katrin Radmacher, and her French millionaire ex-husband, Nicolas Granatino, who had argued that their prenuptial agreement was not binding. **27.** A former quality control manager for the British pharmaceutical company GlaxoSmithKline, Cheryl Eckard, was awarded £61m of the settlement between the company and US regulators, believed to be the largest ever award to a whistleblower; Ms Eckard reported contamination problems at a factory in Puerto Rico from 2002 onwards, but her reports were ignored and she was dismissed in 2003. **28.** Figures released by the Home Office showed that 101,248 people were stopped and searched by police under counter-terrorism powers in the year 2009–10, but no arrests were made for terrorism-related offences.

NOVEMBER 2010

3. Roshonara Choudhry was sentenced to a minimum of 15 years in prison for the attempted murder of the MP Stephen Timms, who she stabbed at a constituency surgery in May 2010. **5.** A woman was sentenced to eight months in prison for retracting an allegation that she had been raped by her husband; the sentence was overturned by the court of appeal on 23 November and replaced with a community sentence. **12.** Frances Inglis lost an appeal against her conviction for murder in January 2010, but the court of appeal reduced her sentence from nine years to five years; in 2008 Ms Inglis killed her 22-year-old son, who was left brain-damaged by severe head injuries suffered in 2007, because she believed it would end his suffering. **15.** The junior minister for justice, Jonathan Djanogly, announced plans to reduce access to free legal advice in cases such as divorce, housing and benefits, in order to cut the number of civil law cases for which free legal advice was made available by 547,000 a year. **16.**

Muawaz Khalid and Nabeel Shafi were sentenced to life imprisonment for murdering Gurmail Singh during a robbery at his shop in West Yorkshire in February 2010; three other men received shorter jail sentences for their part in the robbery. **20.** Four men were charged with the murder of Shaleem Amar, who was found fatally injured in the back of a van following a police chase in Sunningdale, Berkshire, on 17 November. **22.** The high court ruled that MI5's evidence at the inquests into the London Underground and bus bombings on 7 July 2005 should be heard in public; the home secretary, Theresa May, had sought to have the evidence heard in private in the interests of national security (*see* UK Affairs, 11 October). **23.** The European court of human rights upheld the case of two Scottish prisoners that the UK blanket ban on prisoners' voting was illegal, in line with its 2005 ruling on the matter, and gave the UK government six months to bring UK law in line with the European human rights convention. **24.** Learco Chindamo was arrested in connection with a robbery four months after his release from prison, where he had served 14 years for the murder of headteacher Philip Lawrence in 1995.

DECEMBER 2010

3. Harpreet Aulakh was sentenced to a minimum of 28 years in prison for ordering the murder of his estranged wife Geeta, who was killed in November 2009; Sher Singh, who carried out the murder, and Jaswant Dhillon, who acted as a lookout, were both sentenced to a minimum of 22 years. **7.** Julian Assange, the founder of the WikiLeaks website, was arrested in the UK following an extradition request from Sweden, where he was accused of rape and sexual assault; he was released on bail with conditions on 16 December. A British businessman, Shrien Dewani, was arrested on a charge of conspiring to murder his wife, Anni; Mrs Dewani was shot in an alleged kidnapping while on honeymoon in South Africa in November 2010. **9.** Joji Obara was jailed for life in Japan for the abduction and mutilation of British student Lucie Blackman in Tokyo in 2000; he had been acquitted of her murder in an earlier trial. **13.** Mark Weston, acquitted of the murder of Vikki Thompson in 1996, was found guilty at his second trial on the charge after the discovery of new forensic evidence; a second trial became possible after the 'double jeopardy' rule was ended in 2005, making Mr Watson the first person in England and Wales to be convicted at a murder retrial. **15.** The director of public prosecutions announced that in future lawyers would have to seek his approval to prosecute in cases similar to that of a woman who was convicted of perverting the course of justice for retracting a rape allegation (*see* 5 November). **17.** Tony Dyce was given a whole-life sentence for the murders of Norma Richards and her two children in 1982; he was convicted after a cold case review owing to advances in DNA testing. **21.** Stephen Griffiths, a criminology student, was given a whole-life sentence for the murders of three women, Suzanne Blamires, Shelley Armitage and Susan Rushworth, who worked as prostitutes in Bradford. **22.** Eddie Gilfoyle, convicted of murdering his wife Paula in 1992, was released from prison after serving 18 years of a life sentence; Mr Gilfoyle's parole conditions prevented him having any contact with the media. **23.** At Glasgow high court, Tommy Sheridan, the former leader of the Scottish Socialist Party and MSP, was convicted of perjury in his defamation case against the *News of the World* in 2006; he was later sentenced to three years in prison. **25.** Joanna

Yeates, a landscape architect, was found dead three miles from her home in Bristol after going missing on 17 December; Ms Yeates' landlord, Christopher Jeffries, was arrested on 30 December and was later released without charge (*see* 20 January and 29 July).

JANUARY 2011

7. David Chaytor, the former MP for Bury North, was sentenced to 18 months in prison for forging documents to fraudulently claim £22,650 in parliamentary expenses. **10.** Colin Blanchard was given an indeterminate sentence, with the possibility that he might never be released, for leading a paedophile ring; he recruited four women, two of them working in a nursery, and persuaded them to abuse children. The trial of six environmental campaigners accused of plotting to take over a Nottinghamshire power station collapsed when it was discovered that one of the key activists, Mark Kennedy, was an undercover police officer at the time. Micheala McAreavey, daughter of the Tyrone Gaelic football team manager Mickey Harte, was found dead in her hotel room while on her honeymoon; three hotel workers were charged in connection with her murder on 12 January. **11.** Edward Woolard, an A-Level student, was sentenced to 32 months in jail, with half to be served in a young offenders' institution, for throwing a fire extinguisher from a roof during student protests over tuition fee increases in London in November 2010. **18.** A judge ruled that Peter and Hazelmary Bull, owners of a hotel in Cornwall, had unlawfully discriminated against civil partners Martyn Hall and Steven Preddy by refusing to allow them to share a double bed; Mr and Mrs Bull argued that their policy was due to their Christian beliefs. **20.** Police arrested Vincent Tabak for the murder of Joanna Yeates (*see* 25 December); Mr Tabak lived next door to Ms Yeates. **25.** Lord Taylor of Warwick was convicted of false accounting after fraudulently claiming over £11,000 in parliamentary expenses (*see* 31 May). **26.** Ruby Thomas and Joel Alexander were jailed for seven years and six years respectively for a homophobic attack on Ian Baynham in Trafalgar Square in 2009 which left their victim with a fractured skull; Mr Baynham later died of his injuries.

FEBRUARY 2011

1. The Home Office launched a website mapping crime throughout the UK; users were initially able to search for crimes in their street or area that had taken place in December 2010. **3.** Seventeen men received prison sentences ranging from four-and-a-half years to 15 years for armed raids on jewellery shops committed almost fortnightly over a 16-month period in 2008–9; they stole jewellery worth more than £3.5m in total. **8.** Lancashire constabulary announced that new DNA evidence proved that Joan Harrison was murdered in 1975 by Christopher Smith, who died in 2008; it had previously been thought that Ms Harrison was a victim of Peter Sutcliffe, the 'Yorkshire Ripper' who was convicted in 1981 of killing 13 women. **10.** The House of Commons overwhelmingly voted to uphold a blanket ban on voting rights for prisoners (*see* 23 November 2010); on 11 April the European Court of Human Rights gave the UK government six months to bring UK law in line with the European human rights convention. The director of public prosecutions issued guidance to ensure that victims of rape who retracted true allegations owing to coercion or violence would not be prosecuted (*see* 5 November and 15 December). **14.** Lydia Erhire became the first person

in the UK to be jailed for breaking the law preventing forced marriages; Ms Erhire was sentenced to eight months in prison for breaking a protection order taken out by her son, who was believed to be held against his will in Nigeria, although his exact whereabouts were unknown. **16.** The supreme court ruled that people included on the sex offenders' register would be able to apply to have their names removed 15 years after release from prison. **23.** Colin Hatch, sentenced to indefinite life imprisonment for the murder of a seven-year-old boy in 1994, was killed in his cell at Full Sutton prison; Damien Fowkes, a fellow inmate, was charged with his murder. **24.** A judge ruled that Julian Assange could be extradited to Sweden to face trial for rape and sexual assault (*see* 7 December); Assange announced his intention to appeal against the ruling. **28.** A former British soldier, Daniel Fitzsimons, was sentenced to 20 years in prison by an Iraqi court for the murder of two fellow security contractors; he was the first westerner to be convicted in Iraq since the 2003 invasion.

MARCH 2011

4. Allison Cox was sentenced to a year in prison for attempting to poison the businesswoman Jacqueline Gold while she was employed as a nanny by Ms Gold. **7.** Milton Woolf, a South African national, and Jacqueline Swan were sentenced to four-and-a-half years' and one year's imprisonment respectively for providing a 'no questions asked' safety deposit box service to criminals, including contract killers, drug dealers, paedophiles and people traffickers; the case resulted from the Metropolitan Police's biggest investigation into organised crime, during which £500m of assets were seized. **11.** The trial of three men accused of the murder of Daniel Morgan in 1987 collapsed after 18 months of legal arguments as the Crown Prosecution Service could not guarantee that the defence had received all relevant documents; it was the fifth inquiry into the murder to fail, and the Metropolitan Police admitted that the killers had probably avoided justice because of police corruption in the late 1980s. Qhuram Awan and Karl Ness, who provided a safe house for gunman Raoul Moat in July 2010 after he killed his ex-girlfriend and her new partner and shot a police officer, were convicted of a number of serious offences, including conspiracy to murder. **14.** The Home Office announced that jail sentences for convicted terrorists would be reduced if they provide evidence against co-conspirators. **16.** Operation Rescue, a three-year joint investigation by a number of UK police forces, successfully shut down a global paedophile network; the operation exposed over 70,000 members in the UK, USA, Australia, New Zealand and Thailand. **17.** Rajib Karim, a former British Airways employee, was sentenced to 30 years in prison after being convicted on nine terrorism charges, including plotting to blow up a passenger plane. **18.** Two brothers from Brighton, Henry and Victor Mears, who sold thousands of people tickets for what they claimed was a Lapland-inspired theme park, were sentenced to 13 months for fraud. Mohammed Hanif Khan, a Muslim cleric who had been convicted of raping a young boy, was jailed for 16 years. **22.** Christopher Grady, who deliberately drove a car containing his five-year-old daughter and six-year-old son into the River Avon in February 2010, was sentenced to life imprisonment for murder and attempted murder. **23.** Valentine Burnett was jailed for seven and a half years for rape after his DNA, which had been taken after he reported a burglary, linked him to a crime committed in

1986. **28.** Mohammed Riaz was jailed for 30 years for the murder of his brother-in-law Mahmood Ahmad in 2010; a severed thumb was all that was found of Mr Ahmad, but it was enough to lead to Mr Riaz's conviction. **29.** A wealthy financier embroiled in a libel dispute with his family over a multimillion-pound trust fund made British legal history after a super-injunction granted him anonymity, preventing his family from releasing details of their accusations on the internet.

APRIL 2011

2. Three Britons were jailed for a total of 25 years in Spain, where they had been arrested in September 2007 with £22m of cocaine in the back of their car. **3.** As part of an investigation by the Metropolitan Police into allegations of phone-hacking at the *News of the World*, the chief reporter Neville Thurlbeck and former assistant editor Ian Edmondson were arrested on suspicion of conspiring to intercept voicemail messages. John Sweeney was sentenced to life imprisonment without the possibility of parole for the murder and dismemberment of two women, whose bodies were found in canals in Rotterdam and London. **7.** Able Seaman Ryan Donovan, a Royal Navy sailor aboard the British nuclear submarine HMS *Astute*, opened fire on fellow crew members, killing one officer and seriously wounding another. **10.** Michael Kelly, who murdered his former partner and son with an axe in December 2010, was sentenced to a minimum of 30 years' imprisonment. **11.** Two members of an east London street gang, who shot dead a 16-year-old girl with a submachine gun in a bungled revenge attack, were each sentenced to a minimum of 32 years in prison. **15.** James Weatherup, a senior reporter at the *News of the World*, was arrested for illegally intercepting voicemail messages, the third *News of the World* journalist to be charged in relation to the ongoing phone-hacking scandal. **18.** Mohammed Sarwar, a teacher from Manchester who lived a double life as the leader of a cocaine-smuggling gang, was jailed for 21 years; a number of former pupils that he had recruited to the gang were also jailed. **19.** Robin Garbutt, a shopkeeper who bludgeoned his wife to death with an iron bar and then blamed the crime on a fictitious armed robber, was jailed for a minimum of 20 years for her murder. **26.** The BBC journalist Andrew Marr revealed that he had taken out a super-injunction in 2008 to prevent fellow journalists from reporting his extramarital affair. **27.** The electronics manufacturer Sony revealed that an unauthorised person had compromised the security of its Playstation network, and may have gained access to the accounts of 77 million people, including 3 million in the UK.

MAY 2011

4. A barrister, Jonathan Sumption, was appointed a justice of the supreme court, the first time since 1949 that an appointment to the highest court in the UK was made from the legal profession rather than from the judiciary. **14.** Network Rail was fined £3m for the 2002 Potter's Bar train crash in which seven people died; the rail infrastructure company had admitted breaches of safety regulations that led to the accident. **18.** The court of appeal found that there was sufficient new evidence to justify a retrial in the case of the murder of Stephen Lawrence, the black teenager stabbed by a gang of white youths in 1993. **22.** The *Sunday Herald* became the first mainstream publication to reveal the identity of a married footballer alleged to have had an affair with glamour model Imogen Thomas; the footballer had been granted a

privacy order preventing anyone from disclosing his identity, but later that day the Liberal Democrat MP John Hemming used parliamentary privilege to name Ryan Giggs as the footballer in question, only minutes after the high court ruled that the privacy order must stand to protect the footballer's family. **27.** The court of appeal ruled that Sharon Shoesmith, the former director of children's services at Haringey council, was dismissed unlawfully over the death of Peter Connelly, also known as Baby P. **31.** Lord Taylor of Warwick was sentenced to 12 months in prison after being convicted of fraudulently claiming parliamentary expenses (*see* 25 January); he was the first peer to be jailed as a result of the expenses scandal. Police in Bristol arrested four people after undercover filming by the BBC's *Panorama* programme revealed serious abuse at Winterbourne View, a care facility for people with mental illnesses.

JUNE 2011

2. A lobster fisherman and four accomplices were given jail sentences ranging from 14 years to 24 years for attempting to smuggle cocaine worth £53m in rucksacks attached to buoys off the coast of the Isle of Wight. **9.** A high court judge ruled that an autistic 21-year-old man had been kept in care unlawfully by Hillingdon council for nearly a year instead of being allowed to live with his father. **13.** Three paedophiles were jailed and a fourth was given a community sentence for running a child pornography ring that distributed millions of obscene images to subscribers in over 40 countries from a farmhouse in Lincolnshire. **16.** A juror convicted of contempt of court for communicating with a defendant via the internet, the first case of its kind in the UK, was sentenced to eight months in prison. **21.** A joint operation conducted by the Metropolitan Police and the FBI to catch a team of computer hackers targeting intelligence agencies and global corporations, including the CIA and Nintendo, led to the arrest of a 19-year-old man at his family home in Essex. **24.** Levi Bellfield, a former nightclub bouncer who was jailed for life in 2008 for murdering two young women, was sentenced to a second whole-life term for the murder of teenager Milly Dowler in 2002. **26.** An investigation revealed that motor insurance companies had been selling on their customers' personal details to claims-management companies and personal injury lawyers.

JULY 2011

1. Lord Hanningfield, a Conservative peer who fraudulently claimed nearly £14,000 in parliamentary expenses, was jailed for nine months. **7.** The Belfast court of appeal dismissed the appeal of Michael McKevitt and Liam Campbell against a court judgment that found them responsible for the Omagh bombing in 1998, and upheld the appeals of Colm Murphy and Seamus Daly, but ordered Murphy to be retried and said Daly may also face a retrial; the civil case against the four men was brought in 2009 by the families of those killed in the bombing, who were awarded £1.6m in damages. **8.** Clive Goodman, the former royal editor and reporter of the *News of the World* who served four months in prison in 2007 for phone-hacking, was arrested as part of the wider investigation into the scandal; Andy Coulson, the prime minister's former director of communications, was arrested and questioned over allegations of corruption and phone-hacking while he was editor of the *News of the World*. **14.** Neil Wallis, a former deputy editor of the *News of the World*, was arrested by officers investigating phone-hacking at the newspaper. **15.** A court ruled that 55,000 ex-coalminers could file lawsuits against their former solicitors, who had failed to secure them satisfactory compensation for health problems associated with their working conditions. **20.** Rebecca Leighton, a nurse at Stepping Hill hospital in Stockport, was charged with criminal damage with intent to endanger life following a police investigation into deaths at the hospital; five patients had died after their saline solution bags were contaminated with insulin. The high court gave permission for four Kenyan men to sue the British government for alleged torture during the Mau Mau rebellion in the 1950s. **21.** The former wife of the Russian billionaire Boris Berezovsky was awarded up to £220m in the UK's biggest divorce settlement. **29.** *The Daily Mirror* and *The Sun* were fined £50,000 and £18,000 respectively for contempt of court over articles about Christopher Jeffries, a suspect arrested by police investigating the murder of Joanna Yates (*see* 25 December), as the articles were deemed to pose a substantial risk of prejudicing any trial that Mr Jeffries might have faced; earlier, Mr Jeffries accepted an undisclosed but substantial sum in damages for libel from eight newspapers over allegations about him in their reports. Jonathan May-Bowles pleaded guilty to assaulting Rupert Murdoch at the parliamentary select committee hearing on the phone-hacking scandal.

ENVIRONMENT AND SCIENCE

AUGUST 2010

3. The Human Genetics Commission recommended that the DNA testing of children should be limited to cases where there is an immediate and compelling medical reason for the test. **4.** A US government report claimed that 75 per cent of the oil spill in the Gulf of Mexico, the worst in American history, had been cleaned up or dispersed. **5.** A 260 sq. km sheet of ice broke off the Petermann glacier on the coast of Greenland; it was the largest calving of ice to occur in the Arctic Ocean since 1962. **10.** Preliminary results of a study by medical researchers at King's College London, published in the *Journal of Neuroscience,* indicated that brain scans could be 90 per cent accurate in diagnosing people with autism by identifying structural differences in their brains. **17.** The journal *Nature Geoscience* published research which identified newly-discovered fossils as sea sponges that lived about 650 million years ago; it had previously been thought that animal life on Earth had first emerged around 635 million years ago. **25.** Research published in *Science Translational Medicine* showed that cornea implants grown from synthetic human tissue could improve the sight of patients with damaged eyes.

SEPTEMBER 2010

3. BP announced that it would take two weeks to permanently seal the Deepwater Horizon oil-well leak in the Gulf of Mexico (*see* 4 August). **19.** A joint UK and US project to create a global inventory of all known plants resulted in more than 600,000 names being deleted, as many species had been named more than once; the final species total was expected to be around 400,000. **22.** In the online journal *PLoS One,* US paleontologists reported the discovery of the fossils of two previously unknown dinosaurs, *Kosmoceratops,* which was unique in having 15 full-sized horns on its head, and *Utahceratops;* they lived 76 million years ago in the swamps that covered what is now southern Utah. **28.** A one-day science symposium

was held in London to mark the 175th anniversary of the British Geological Survey; discussions included the results of tooth analysis of male remains buried near Stonehenge in the Bronze Age which suggest that one male (the Amesbury Archer) came from the Alps and the other (the Boy with the Amber necklace) from the Mediterranean area.

OCTOBER 2010

4. The ten-year Census of Marine Life project (COML) was completed; the project added more than 16,000 species to COML databases and concluded that there are over one million species living in the oceans, less than a quarter of which have been described in scientific literature. **6.** The National Institute of Health and Clinical Excellence recommended that the availability of Aricept, Excelon and Reminyl, drugs that help delay the onset of Alzheimer's disease, should be extended to sufferers with the mild form of the disesase; in 2007 NICE had restricted the drugs to patients with moderate-stage Alzheimer's. **21.** Scientists from NASA published the results of an experiment that discovered around 155kg of water vapour and water-ice on the Moon, as well as other elements such as mercury and silver. **27.** Scientists working on the 1,000 Genomes project announced that they had successfully mapped 95 per cent of all variations in human DNA; the project aims to sequence and compare the DNA of 2,500 individuals from around the world. **28.** Astronomers carried out a 'census' of planets orbiting 166 of Earth's closest sun-like stars and used their findings to estimate that there could be 50 billion planets with a mass similar to Earth orbiting stars in the Milky Way. **29.** The Department for Environment, Food and Rural Affairs (DEFRA) announced plans to transfer woodland belonging to the Forestry Commission, a government department, to the private sector after a three-month period of public consultation; powers to enable the sale were included in the Public Bodies Bill 2010. At a UN biodiversity summit in Nagoya, Japan, ministers from nearly 200 nations agreed the Aichi targets, which aim to halve the loss of natural habitats, and adopted the Nagoya Protocol, which would share the financial benefits of the world's genetic resources with developing countries with effect from 2020. **31.** The results of an analysis led by Prof. David Nutt, a former government adviser on drugs, found that alcohol is more harmful than cocaine, cannabis or ecstasy when its effect on others is taken into account.

NOVEMBER 2010

1. A report in the journal *Proceedings of the National Academy of Sciences* described the discovery of a previously unknown way in which the immune system attacks viruses, from within an infected cell rather than from the outside. **2.** The results of a pilot study, published in the *Proceedings of the Royal Society B,* found that three blind patients who had an electronic chip implanted into their retina for three months benefited from improved sight; the participants were able to discern shapes and distinguish between colours. **16.** Game park officials in South Africa, home to 90 per cent of the world's rhinoceroses, announced that 261 of the animals had been killed by poachers in 2010, more than double the number killed in 2009. **24.** The International Tiger Forum, called by Prime Minister Putin of Russia and the head of the World Bank, Robert Zoellick, closed with nearly $330m (£208m) pledged towards the goal of doubling the number of wild tigers by 2022.

DECEMBER 2010

2. The journal *Science* published details of the discovery in a lake in Yosemite national park, USA, of a microbe that can live on arsenic, a chemical that is poisonous to other organisms. **3.** It was reported that over 700 Dartmoor ponies had been killed in 2010 to be sold to zoos as meat, as the market price for the animals had dropped. **6.** In the journal *Nature Neuroscience*, scientists reported the discovery of a 'biochemical switch' that might be able to stimulate the brain to mend nerves affected by multiple sclerosis. **7.** Prof. Peter Rothwell announced the results of a five-year study into the effects on 25,000 patients of taking a low daily dose of aspirin; the scientists found that there were 21 per cent fewer cancer-related deaths after five years among the aspirin-taking group compared with those that did not take any aspirin. **11.** At UN climate change talks in Cancun, Mexico, participating countries agreed to a goal of 'substantially reducing global emissions by 2050', although the agreement did not specify by how much emissions should be cut, and to establish a fund to enable developing countries to adapt to climate change. **21.** A palaeontologist at Bristol University, Michael Benton, announced that he and his colleagues had discovered the remains of a complete ecosystem that had survived a mass extinction event 252 million years ago; the 20,000 fossils were found on a hillside in south-west China. Doctors at the Care fertility treatment clinic in Nottingham announced that in July they had successfully performed a bone-marrow transplant on a nine-year-old girl using tissue from her baby brother, who was born after being specially selected from several IVF embryos as the perfect tissue match for his sister.

JANUARY 2011

4. The first trial began of the polypill, a daily tablet containing low doses of drugs to protect against heart attacks and strokes in those over the age of 50. Channel 4 News reported that nearly 600 women had become pregnant and a further 1,600 had suffered adverse reactions while using the Implanon contraceptive implant; the NHS had paid a total of £119,000 in compensation to nine women. **11.** The final data of the Sloan Digital Sky Survey was released; the survey produced the most detailed image of the universe to date, with half a billion objects, including galaxies, stars and nebulae, detectable in the image. **12.** Dr Stephen Kingsmore outlined a new genetic test for prospective parents that could identify whether they are likely to pass on up 600 genetic disorders to their children; trials were expected to begin in the UK in summer 2011. **20.** It was announced that surgeons had successfully performed a voice-box transplant on 52-year-old Brenda Jensen, who had been unable to speak for 11 years; the operation was the first to replace an entire vocal system. **26.** The Game and Wildlife Conservation Trust announced that it would undertake a trial cull of crows and magpies to see if this would slow the decline in the number of songbirds in the UK. **27.** The secretary of state for the environment, food and rural affairs, Caroline Spelman, launched a three-month public consultation on the ownership and management of Forestry Commission woodland; the government proposals included guarantees that protection of public access and wildlife would remain in place (*see* 29 October).

FEBRUARY 2011

1. Research was published in the journal *Nature Communications* describing the ability of a calcite prism to bend light around objects, rendering them invisible; the prism could only hide small objects, such as pins and paperclips. **2.** NASA announced the discovery of hundreds of new planets, including a solar system similar to the Earth's with at least six orbiting planets, observed by the Kepler space telescope. **6.** Scientists at Oxford University announced that they had successfully tested a flu vaccine with the potential to protect against all known strains of the illness; the vaccine targets proteins common to all flu viruses rather than those that are liable to mutate. Two probes successfully took simultaneous images of the Sun from opposite sides as part of the NASA Stereo mission, the first panoramic image of the Sun. **11.** The environment secretary announced the postponement of the sale of 40,000 hectares of public forest, the 15 per cent that was allowed to be sold by the government in any four-year public spending period, and said that criteria such as protecting public access needed to be strengthened. **16.** Three cups made from human skulls, unearthed at Cheddar Gorge in Somerset several decades ago, were examined using new techniques and were found to be around 14,700 years old. **17.** The environment secretary announced that the government was abandoning its plans to sell off Forestry Commission woodland in the face of widespread opposition to the sale from the public and the media; a petition against the plans had received over 500,000 signatures (*see* 27 January 2011).

MARCH 2011

10. The *Global Bee Colony Disorders and Other Threats to Insect Pollination* report by the UN environment programme highlighted factors such as air pollution and new, fast-spreading fungal diseases caused by globalisation as the principal reasons for the rapid worldwide decline in bee numbers. **13.** The UK Young Scientist of the Year award was won by Hannah Eastwood for her work investigating the removal of chromium from drinking water. **23.** Scientists in Japan successfully cultivated tissue from baby mice to generate sperm which was used to produce 12 live mouse pups; the experiment was described as a crucial advance towards treating male infertility. **26.** Famous landmarks around the world, such as the Sydney Opera House and Big Ben, had their electric power turned off for an hour in support of the World Wide Fund for Nature's 'Earth hour'.

APRIL 2011

14. The trial began of the GV1001 vaccine designed to prime the human immune system to kill tumour cells; the vaccine will be tested on patients with advanced pancreatic cancer to see if it makes chemotherapy more effective. **20.** The National Trust announced plans to permit badger culling on its property in order to protect cattle from tuberculosis. **21.** Multinational fossil fuel companies, including Shell and Statoil, launched a campaign to promote shale gas, a controversial form of fuel which had recently became accessible owing to a technical advance known as fracking; supporters claim the EU could save €990bn (£875bn) by 2050 by using shale gas rather than investing in renewable energy, while opponents believe that the extraction process could lead to gas leaks and water contamination.

MAY 2011

7. Scientists at CERN used the Large Hadron Collider to smash together the nuclei of lead atoms at 99.999 per cent the speed of light, generating temperatures of around 10 trillion degrees Celsius and creating what is believed to be the hottest and densest matter ever observed. **9.** Dallas Wiens, who lost almost all of his face when he touched an electric cable in 2008, unveiled his new face, the result of the USA's first full face transplant, at a press conference in Boston. **18.** After discovering the remains of six *Tarbosaurus bataar,* a cousin of the *Tyrannosaurus rex,* during a five-year expedition in the Gobi desert, a leading palaeontologist, Philip Currie, claimed that the close proximity of the fossils suggested that the dinosaurs hunted in packs rather than being solitary hunters as previously believed. **27.** A leading psychologist, Prof. Brian Butterworth of University College London, argued in the journal *Science* for the condition dyscalculia, a form of 'number blindness', to be given an equivalent status to dyslexia. **30.** European regulators approved the use in the EU of an artificial retina, Argus II, which restores some vision to people who have lost their sight because of the genetic disease retinitis pigmentosa.

JUNE 2011

2. Met Office figures showed that the spring of 2011 was the driest in England and Wales since 1893, and the warmest spring in central England according to records stretching back 352 years. **7.** A research team from the British company GW Pharmaceuticals, who developed the first licensed cannabis-based medicine, announced that it had bred new varieties of cannabis to treat conditions such as diabetes, epilepsy and Crohn's disease. **9.** The first-ever pictures showing the International Space Station fully assembled with a shuttle docked in its parking bay were released by NASA and the European Space Agency; the photographs featured the *Endeavour* shuttle on its final mission. **19.** Corporal Isaias Hernandez, a US marine who lost 70 per cent of his right thigh muscles in a mortar blast in Afghanistan, avoided amputation by undergoing a radical new therapy whereby his remaining muscles were impregnated through an extracellular matrix with a growth-promoting substance extracted from pig bladders, which prompted his damaged muscles to regenerate. **20.** Scientists developed a vaccine that cured prostate cancer in mice, with no side-effects or need for other treatment. **29.** The Forestry Commission published the Woodfuel Implementation Plan, to encourage woodland owners in England to cut down 10 million trees each year to heat homes through wood-burning stoves and boilers; in addition to being environmentally friendly, the plan stated that the thinning of the woodlands would not undermine their long-term future and would help to revive flowers such as bluebells and entice back endangered birds.

JULY 2011

11. The government's chief scientific adviser, Sir John Beddington, published a report, *International Dimensions of Climate Change,* which argued that the government should use climate-related disasters overseas to persuade voters of the need for costly environmental policies; the report also stated that individuals need to take more personal responsibility for climate change. **18.** The government asked the UK National Centre for Replacement, Refinement and Reduction of Animals in Research to reduce testing on animals through a science-led programme which would minimise animal use. **19.** The government confirmed its plans to begin culling 35,000 badgers a year from June 2012, in an attempt to reduce tuberculosis rates in cattle; the plans were opposed by the RSPCA and scientists who said that the culling might increase cases of bovine TB (*see* 20 April).

SPORT

AUGUST 2010

1. James Anderson took ten wickets in England's victory over Pakistan at Trent Bridge in the first Test match of the series. The British team finished the European Athletics Championships in Barcelona with a record tally of 19 medals, including six gold medals. **9.** Martin O'Neill resigned as manager of Aston Villa five days before the start of the new Premier League season. **11.** The England football manager, Fabio Capello, revealed that he would not select David Beckham for the national team in future, primarily owing to Beckham's age. **14.** Hampshire won the Twenty20 cricket final, despite having tied with Somerset on 173 runs, because they had lost only five wickets to their opponents' six. **15.** Andy Murray beat Roger Federer in the Toronto Masters tennis final, winning the Rogers cup for a second successive year. The German golfer Martin Kaymer won the US PGA Championship in a three-hole play-off against Bubba Watson of the USA.

SEPTEMBER 2010

1. A new rule governing the selection of Premier League football squads came into force; the rule requires each squad to consist of 25 players, at least eight of whom have spent no less than three seasons or 36 months with an English or Welsh-affiliated club. **3.** The International Cricket Council charged Pakistan's Test captain, Salman Butt, and the opening bowlers Mohammad Amir and Mohammad Asif under its anti-corruption code over alleged match-fixing incidents during the final Test match against England at Lord's. **5.** The women's England rugby team lost the World Cup final to the defending champions New Zealand. **8.** John Higgins was fined £75,000 and banned from snooker for six months after failing to report a match-fixing fraud; he was cleared of charges of accepting a bribe and agreeing to engage in corrupt conduct. **14.** Rafael Nadal beat Novak Djokovic in the final of the US Open tennis championships; he became the seventh man to win all four major tennis championships. Steph Brennan, the former physiotherapist of the Harlequins rugby union team, was struck off for his involvement in the 'Bloodgate' scandal in 2009. **16.** The former England cricket captain Andrew Flintoff retired from professional cricket after failing to recover fully from a knee operation. **19.** The chairman of the Pakistan Cricket Council, Ijaz Butt, accused the England cricket team of deliberately losing the third one-day international at Lords; he withdrew the accusation 10 days later. Ricky Hatton announced his retirement from boxing six days after entering a rehabilitation clinic for treatment for his cocaine and alcohol addiction. **22.** During preparations for the 2010 Commonwealth Games in India, a footbridge near the Jawaharlal Nehru stadium in Delhi collapsed, injuring five construction workers.

OCTOBER 2010

3. The Commonwealth Games opened in Delhi; around a dozen athletes were understood not to be competing owing to concerns over health and safety at the venues. **5.** The European team won the Ryder Cup by one point after Graeme McDowell beat Hunter Mahan in the last singles match. **7.** Danielle Brown became the first English paralympian to win a Commonwealth medal, taking gold in the women's team compound archery event. **7.** The British swimmer Rebecca Adlington won the gold medal in the 800 metres freestyle in the Commonwealth Games;

the following day she won the gold medal in the 400 metres freestyle. **13.** The Australian team fell to fifth in the Test cricket rankings after losing to India in the second Test at Bangalore, the first time Australia had dropped below England since the rankings were introduced. Tom Daley narrowly beat the Olympic gold medalist Matt Mitcham to win the gold medal in the 10m individual platform diving at the Commonwealth Games. **14.** The Commonwealth Games closed; England finished third in the medals table, winning 142 medals, 37 of which were gold. **15.** New England Sports Ventures, owners of the Boston Red Sox, bought Liverpool FC for around £300m. Ticket prices for the London 2012 Olympic Games were released; they ranged from £20 to £2,012 for a premium seat at the opening ceremony. **20.** Wayne Rooney announced that he did not intend to renew his contract with Manchester United when it expired in August 2012; two days later he signed a five-year contract with the club, doubling his wages to around £200,000 a week. FIFA suspended two members of its executive committee after allegations that they were involved in selling their votes in the 2018 and 2022 World Cup ballots on 28 October; following an investigation, the pair were banned from voting in either ballot.

NOVEMBER 2010
1. Lee Westwood became the world's number one golfer when his nearest rival in the world rankings, Martin Kaymer, finished ten shots off the lead at the Andalucia Masters; Westwood supplanted Tiger Woods, who had been number one for more than five years. **8.** Zulqarnain Haider, the Pakistan wicketkeeper, fled from Dubai to London before the final one-day international against South Africa; he claimed to have 'received threatening messages' after disobeying match-fixing instructions. **14.** Sebastian Vettel became the youngest-ever Formula One world champion after his win in the Abu Dhabi grand prix. **25.** The Australian bowler Peter Siddle claimed a hat-trick on the opening day of the first Test in the 2010–11 Ashes series at the Gabba, Brisbane.

DECEMBER 2010
2. Russia was chosen to host the 2018 FIFA World Cup after a majority vote in Zurich; England, one of three other possible hosts, received only two votes out of a possible 22. Qatar won the vote to host the 2022 FIFA World Cup. **5.** During the second Ashes match, at Adelaide, the England batsman Alastair Cook scored his 15th Test century, taking him to an England record for unbeaten runs and time spent at the crease (383 runs in 1,058 minutes). Serbia beat France to win its first Davis Cup in tennis by 3–2. **19.** Tony McCoy, the winning jockey in the 2010 Grand National on Don't Push it, won the 2010 BBC Sports Personality of the Year award.

JANUARY 2011
2. A one-minute silence was observed by fans and players at the Rangers v Celtic game to mark the 40th anniversary of the Ibrox stadium disaster in which 66 people died. **7.** England won the Ashes series 3–1 after beating Australia by an innings and 83 runs in Sydney. **8.** Roy Hodgson left Liverpool FC by mutual consent after seven months as manager; Kenny Dalglish, the former Liverpool player and manager, took charge until the end of the season. **25.** The football commentator Andy Gray was dismissed by Sky Sports following an enquiry into three occasions when he was recorded making sexist comments off-camera; another presenter, Richard Keys, resigned the following day over comments he had made

about a female linesman on 22 January. **30.** Novak Djokovic beat Andy Murray to win the men's Australian Open tennis final. **31.** Chelsea signed Fernando Torres from Liverpool for £50m, making the Spanish striker the most expensive signing by a British football club.

FEBRUARY 2011
4. England beat Wales 26–19 in the first match of the 2011 Six Nations Championship; it was the first time England had defeated Wales in Cardiff since 2003. **5.** A record 41 goals were scored in eight Premier League matches; these included Newcastle's recovery from being 4–0 down to draw with Arsenal, and Wolves ending Manchester United's unbeaten run of 24 league games. **6.** Robert Kubica, the Formula One driver for Renault, suffered arm and leg fractures in a high-speed rally crash in Italy; Renault later confirmed that Kubica's injuries were so severe that he would be unavailable for the 2011 season. **9.** Real Madrid, with revenues of €438.6m (£387.8m), topped the annual Deloitte league table of football's biggest earning teams; Manchester United, in third place, was the highest ranking of seven English teams in the top 20. **11.** The board of the Olympic Park Legacy Company voted unanimously in favour of West Ham United's bid to take over the Olympic stadium after the London 2012 Olympics; the bid was preferred to Tottenham Hotspur's proposal to knock down the stadium and build a new one. **12.** Two horses died at Newbury racecourse when they were electrocuted by underground cabling; owing to the danger posed by the cables, the last six races of the day were cancelled. **15.** Alberto Contador was cleared by the Royal Spanish Cycling Federation of knowingly using the banned drug clenbuterol after appealing against a one-year ban imposed after he tested positive in July 2010. **19.** The Malaysian cyclist Azizulhasni Awang was involved in a crash in the keirin final in Manchester which resulted in a 20cm wooden splinter piercing his calf; the 23-year-old remounted his bike to claim third place in the race. **20.** The footballer Ashley Cole accidentally shot a work-experience student with an air rifle at the Chelsea training ground; the student received medical attention on site. **27.** Birmingham City beat Arsenal 2–1 in the Carling Cup final at Wembley, winning their first major trophy since 1963. England tied with India on 338 runs in a cricket World Cup match in Bangalore; Graeme Swann hit a single off the final ball to equal the score set by India.

MARCH 2011
2. Ireland won a shock victory over England in the cricket World Cup; the match included a record-breaking innings by Kevin O'Brien, who hit a century off 50 balls. **3.** The Manchester City defender Kolo Touré was suspended after he tested positive for a specified substance, a slimming product belonging to his wife. Manchester United confirmed that Sir Alex Ferguson would not speak to the club television station MUTV after it aired an interview with the manager in which he criticised referee Martin Atkinson's credibility following a match between Manchester United and Chelsea; Ferguson was charged with improper conduct by the FA over his comments. **15.** Over 6.6 million tickets for 670 sessions at the London 2012 Olympic Games went on sale to the public. On the opening day of the Cheltenham Festival, the jockey Ruby Walsh rode three of the winning horses. **18.** The Cheltenham Gold Cup was won by Long Run, the youngest winner of the prestigious race since 1963. **19.** England won the rugby Six Nations Championship despite losing to Ireland in their final game. **20.** John

Terry was reinstated as captain of the England football team a year after being dropped from the position; the England manager, Fabio Capello, revealed that he had not discussed his decision with Rio Ferdinand, who lost the captaincy to Terry. **26.** Sri Lanka defeated England in the quarter-final stage of the cricket World Cup; the Sri Lankan openers Tillakaratne Dilshan and Upul Tharanga achieved a record 231-run partnership. **27.** In Melbourne, Sebastian Vettel finished first in the opening race of the 2011 Formula One season.

APRIL 2011
2. India won the cricket World Cup for the first time since 1983 after they defeated Sri Lanka in Mumbai; the match saw the final international appearance of Muttiah Muralitharan. **8.** The footballer Wayne Rooney received a two-game ban from the Football Association for using offensive language; the striker swore directly at a television camera after scoring a hat-trick in his club's win against West Ham United on 2 April. **9.** Ballabriggs won the Grand National at Aintree, having led the race from halfway; the field was diverted around two of the fences on the second circuit to avoid two horses which had fallen earlier in the race. **10.** Charl Schwartzel won the US Masters in Augusta; the expected winner, the Northern Ireland golfer Rory McIlroy had entered the final day with a four-stroke lead but shot 80, the highest final round since 1956. **17.** Emmanuel Mutai of Kenya finished the London Marathon in a time of two hours four minutes and forty seconds, setting a new record for the men's race; a fellow Kenyan, Mary Keitany, won the women's race. Stoke defeated Bolton in the FA Cup semi-final at Wembley to reach the cup final for the first time in the club's history. **23.** Fernando Torres scored his first goal for Chelsea in his 14th match for the club; Torres had played for a total of 732 minutes for the club without scoring. **28.** The London Organising Committee of the Olympic and Paralympic Games (LOCOG) announced that there had been 20 million applications for the 6.6 million available tickets for the 2012 games, and that 50 per cent of the 650 available sessions were over-subscribed.

MAY 2011
2. John Higgins won his fourth World Snooker Championship title when he beat Judd Trump at the Crucible Theatre, one year to the day after being suspended over alleged match-fixing (see 8 September). **5.** The England cricket captaincy was divided into three roles, with Andrew Strauss, Alastair Cook and Stuart Broad leading the Test, one-day and Twenty20 teams respectively. **9.** The Belgian cyclist Wouter Weylandt died of injuries sustained when he crashed during the third stage of the Giro d'Italia. **14.** Manchester City beat Stoke 1–0 in the FA Cup final. Manchester United won a record 19th football league title. **21.** Leinster beat Northampton Saints to win the Heineken Cup final, recovering from being 22–6 down at half-time to win 33–22. **22.** On the final day of the Premier League season, Blackpool and Birmingham joined West Ham in relegation to the Championship. Carlo Ancelotti was dismissed as manager of Chelsea after failing to win a trophy in his second season at the club. **27.** The prime minister, David Cameron, and the junior minister for sport, Hugh Robertson, backed demands for the presidential election at FIFA to be postponed because both the candidates, Sepp Blatter and Mohamed bin Hammam, were under investigation by the FIFA ethics committee over corruption allegations; bin Hammam withdrew from the

presidency contest on 29 May. **28.** Manchester United were beaten 3–1 in the Champions League final at Wembley by Barcelona, which secured their third European Cup in five years.

JUNE 2011
1. Sepp Blatter was re-elected as president of FIFA in an uncontested ballot after receiving 186 votes from the 206 delegates eligible to vote; a motion by the FA chairman, David Bernstein, to postpone the election to await the outcome of an investigation into corruption allegations involving Mr Blatter was rejected by FIFA delegates. **4.** The Queen's horse Carlton House finished third in the Derby; the race was won by Pour Moi. Li Na defeated defending champion Francesca Schiavone in the women's final of the French Open Championships, becoming the first Asian player to win a grand slam tennis tournament. **5.** Rafael Nadal beat Roger Federer in the men's final of the French Open, equalling Bjorn Borg's record of six French Open titles. **7.** Matt Prior, the England wicketkeeper, apologised to MCC members after smashing a window above their heads in an angry reaction to his dismissal by Sri Lanka in a match at Lord's; glass from the shattered window injured one spectator. **10.** John Steele resigned as chief executive of the Rugby Football Union after being criticised over the search for a new performance director for the England team. **12.** The prestigious Dauphiné Libéré cycling road race was won by Bradley Wiggins. **13.** Andy Murray beat Jo-Wilfried Tsonga to win the AEGON Championship trophy at Queen's Club, London. **19.** The 22-year-old Northern Ireland golfer Rory McIlroy won the US Open, his first major title, with an eight-shot victory, becoming the youngest champion since 1923. In football, England were eliminated from the European Under-21 Championship when they lost 2–1 to the Czech Republic despite having been in the lead until the 89th minute of the match. **22.** Andre Villas-Boas was appointed manager of Chelsea after the club's owner, Roman Abramovich, paid Porto a record £13.3 million to release him from his contract with them.

JULY 2011
1. Andy Murray lost his third successive Wimbledon semi-final when he was beaten in four sets by Rafael Nadal. **2.** David Haye lost on points to the Ukranian boxer Wladimir Klitschko in Hamburg in a title fight he hoped would unify the world heavyweight division. **3.** Novak Djokovic beat Rafael Nadal in the men's final at Wimbledon, becoming the first Serb to win the Wimbledon men's singles title; the win was Djokovic's 50th victory from 51 matches since winning the Davis Cup in December 2010. **8.** Bradley Wiggins fell and broke his collarbone in a mass pile-up during the seventh stage of the Tour de France, which was won by Mark Cavendish. **9.** The England women's football team was eliminated at the quarter-final stage of the women's World Cup after losing to France in a penalty shootout. **14.** On the first day of the 140th Open Championship at Royal St George's, the amateur golfer Tom Lewis shared the lead after he hit a five-under-par round of 65, the lowest by an amateur in the tournament's history; Lewis finished the Open as the top amateur. **17.** Darren Clarke won the Open Championship, securing his first major title and becoming the first Briton to win the Open since 1999. **24.** Mark Cavendish won the green jersey in the Tour de France, becoming the first Briton to win a classification since 1984; Cadel Evans became the first Australian recipient of the yellow jersey as he won the overall race.

INTERNATIONAL AFFAIRS

AFRICA

AUGUST 2010

1. In Sao Tome and Principe, the legislative election was won by the Independent Democratic Action party, whose leader, Patrice Trovoada, was appointed prime minister on 13 August. **2.** A number of attacks by Rwandan Hutu rebel groups in the Democratic Republic of Congo culminated in the rape of around 300 villagers; Callixte Mbarushimana, executive secretary of one of the groups implicated in the attacks, was arrested in Paris on 11 October. **4.** In a referendum in Kenya, 67 per cent of voters approved a new constitution which would introduce a bill of rights and land reform, and curb the powers of the president. **9.** In Rwanda, Paul Kagame was re-elected president with 93 per cent of the vote; only candidates allied to his ruling Rwandan Patriotic Front party were permitted to stand in the election. **18.** In South Africa, 1.3 million public sector workers began an indefinite strike over poor pay; on 1 September a pay rise of 7.5 per cent was rejected, and on 6 September the strike was suspended for further negotiations. **20.** More than half of Benin's MPs signed a petition to impeach the country's president, Thomas Yayi Boni, over claims that he was complicit in a collapsed Ponzi scheme in which 70,000 people lost money. **23.** In Somalia, the Islamist militia group al-Shabab declared war on the transitional government, beginning a series of attacks by storming a hotel in Mogadishu and killing 32 people.

SEPTEMBER 2010

1. A government announcement of price increases for bread and other basic foodstuffs sparked three days of rioting in Mozambique; on 7 September the government reversed the decision to increase prices, and on 21 September it introduced subsidies on some foodstuffs, water and electricity for poorer households. **4.** Weeks of torrential rain caused flooding in southern Sudan that displaced around 89,000 people. **7.** In Nigeria, gunmen from the Islamist sect Boko Haram stormed a prison in Bauchi, killing four people and freeing 759 prisoners. **12.** The Nigerian government announced that it had intercepted a large consignment of arms in transit from Iran to Gambia; Nigeria said that if investigations showed that there had been a breach of international law, it would report Iran to the UN security council. **15.** The UN security council voted to end the sanctions imposed on Sierra Leone in 1997, as the government was considered to have regained control of its territory and disarmed rebel forces following its civil war. **21.** Somalia's prime minister, Umar Abdirashid Ali Shermarke, resigned, claiming he was unable to agree with President Sheikh Sharif Ahmed on proposed changes to the country's constitution. **21.** The UN Office for the Coordination of Humanitarian Affairs (OCHA) announced an outbreak of 'acute massive lead poisoning' in the Zamfara state of Nigeria; OCHA estimated that the outbreak, caused by illegal gold mining, had affected 18,000 people since March 2010, including killing 200 children. **23.** Further conflict between the Islamist group al-Shabab and pro-government troops in Mogadishu left at least 22 people dead (*see* 23 August).

OCTOBER 2010

6. Birtukan Mideska, the leader of Ethiopia's largest opposition party, was released from prison after serving five years of a life sentence for treason. **17.** Flash flooding in Benin affected around two-thirds of the country, killing about 50 people and displacing 100,000.

NOVEMBER 2010

15. In Guinea, the presidential election was won by the opposition leader Alpha Condé with 52.5 per cent of the vote; the result, a surprise victory, led to two days of violence and demonstrations in the capital, in which at least four people were killed and around 30 injured. **17.** A referendum in Madagascar approved a new constitution; rebel Madagascan soldiers claimed that they had seized power and planned to dissolve the government over the lack of democracy, but President Rajoelina, who had himself seized power in March 2009, dismissed the claims, and on 21 November the rebels surrendered. **22.** The government of Gambia cut diplomatic ties with Iran and ordered Iranian officials to leave the country within 48 hours after a consignment of arms from Iran was intercepted en route to Gambia by the Nigerian authorities (*see* 12 September). **28.** The second round of the presidential election in Côte d'Ivoire, a run-off between the incumbent president Laurent Gbagbo and the opposition leader Alassane Ouattara, was held (*see* 2 December). **30.** The national news agency of Zimbabwe published a report claiming that the ruling party, Zanu-PF, had abused its land reform policy by giving commercial farms in the country's most fertile areas to influential supporters; 40 per cent of farms were found to be owned by cabinet ministers, judges and senior army officers and government officials.

DECEMBER 2010

2. Alassane Ouattara was declared the winner of the Côte d'Ivoire presidential election by the electoral commission, with 54 per cent of the vote; he was subsequently recognised as the president-elect by the UN, the African Union, the EU and the USA. **3.** The constitutional court in Côte d'Ivoire declared Laurent Gbagbo the winner of the presidential election, with 51 per cent of the vote; he was supported by the army, and Alassane Ouattara and his government spent several months besieged in an Abidjan hotel, protected by UN peacekeeping troops. **11.** The UN mission in Côte d'Ivoire ratified the electoral commission's declaration of the result of the presidential election, confirming Alassane Ouattara's victory. **15.** The International Criminal Court formally accused six of Kenya's political elite of having committed serious crimes, including rape and murder, during the country's post-election violence in 2007; the six men included cabinet ministers, the head of the civil service, a former chief of police and the deputy prime minister, Uhuru Kenyatta. **18.** In Côte d'Ivoire, Laurent Gbagbo ordered French and UN peacekeeping troops to leave the country amid mounting international pressure on him to step down following his defeat in the November presidential election. **22.** The World Bank suspended financial aid to Côte d'Ivoire because of the country's political crisis. **24.** Three bombings in the Nigerian city of Jos killed 32 people and injured 74; later the same day, the Islamist sect Boko Haram attacked two churches. The Economic Community of West African States called on Laurent Gbagbo to step down as president of Côte d'Ivoire. **31.** The EU imposed sanctions on 59 people linked to Laurent Gbagbo.

JANUARY 2011

9–15. A referendum was held in southern Sudan on independence from the north; 99.57 per cent of south

Sudanese voted in favour (*see* 9 July). **15.** The legislature of the Democratic Republic of Congo approved constitutional changes that removed a second round in presidential elections, allowing future presidents to be elected by a simple majority. **19.** The UN sent a further 2,000 peacekeeping troops to Côte d'Ivoire. **27.** David Kato, a Ugandan gay-rights activist, was murdered in his home; in October 2010 Kato had been featured on the front page of *Rolling Stone*, a homophobic Ugandan tabloid, under the headline 'Hang Them'.

FEBRUARY 2011
9. Fighting between security forces and rebels in southern Sudan left 105 dead. **18.** A presidential election was held in Uganda which was won by the incumbent president, Yoweri Museveni, who began his fourth elected term of office; opposition candidates alleged that Museveni had bribed voters and electoral officials. Thousands of demonstrators protested in Djibouti, demanding the resignation of President Ismael Omar Guelleh. **21.** A military court in the Democratic Republic of Congo convicted nine former soldiers of the rape of more than 50 women; the attacks, which occurred on 1 January in the eastern town of Fizi, occurred amid clashes between the army and local and foreign militias. At the Muslim festival of Maouloud in Mali, panic caused a stampede that left 36 dead and 65 injured. **23.** In Somalia, government offensives against the Islamist militant group al-Shabab left around 115 people dead.

MARCH 2011
6. More than 50 African Union peacekeepers were killed in Somalia in a major offensive against Islamist militants. **8.** Clashes between security forces and militia in southern Sudan's Upper Nile state left 56 dead. **10.** Laurent Gbagbo, the defeated presidential candidate in Côte d'Ivoire (*see* 28 November 2010), rejected a proposal by the African Union to end the power struggle in the country. **25.** The charity Raising Malawi, founded in 2006 by the singer Madonna and the co-director of the Kaballah centre, Michael Berg, announced that it had abandoned plans for a $15m (£9m) academy for girls in the country after the charity's board of directors was removed following serious financial mismanagement; the collapse of the project resulted in a dispute with villagers who lost land to the project. **31.** Forces loyal to Alassane Ouatarra took control of the capital of Côte d'Ivoire, meeting little resistance.

APRIL 2011
4. Forces loyal to Alassane Ouattara, the internationally recognised president-elect of Cote d'Ivoire, took control of most of the country in a lightning offensive and blockaded Laurent Gbagbo in his residence in Abidjan; French forces attacked Mr Gbagbo's positions in an attempt to destroy heavy weaponry. **8.** A presidential election was held in Djibouti; President Guelleh was re-elected with 80 per cent of the vote. **11.** Laurent Gbagbo was arrested in the presidential palace in Abidjan, after four months of post-election violence in Côte d'Ivoire that left an estimated 3,000 people dead and about a million displaced; the new president, Allassane Ouattara, announced that allegations of atrocities by both sides' forces during the conflict would be thoroughly investigated. **15.** Following an army mutiny and rioting in the capital city, President Compaoré of Burkina Faso dismissed the government of Tertius Zongo and appointed Luc Adolphe Tiao as prime minister. **16.** A

presidential election was held Nigeria; the incumbent president, Goodluck Jonathan, was declared the winner on 19 April, which sparked several days of rioting in the predominantly Muslim north, the stronghold of his main opponent, that left around 500 people dead and thousands displaced. **27.** The Ugandan opposition leader Kizza Besigye was arrested during protests at rising food and oil prices in the capital; Besigye's arrest sparked further protests in the city in which two people were killed and over 120 injured.

MAY 2011
4. Government forces in Côte d'Ivoire overcame the last pockets of pro-Gbagbo resistance in Abidjan. **6.** Alassane Ouattara was sworn in as president of Côte d'Ivoire. **17.** The international criminal tribunal for Rwanda convicted two former Rwandan officers of genocide and crimes against humanity for the murder of 800,000 people in 2004.

JUNE 2011
16. Jeremy Ratcliffe, the former head of a children's charity founded by Nelson Mandela, was found not guilty by a South African court of illegally keeping unlicensed 'blood' diamonds; Ractcliffe had been given the diamonds by the British supermodel Naomi Campbell, who had allegedly received them as a gift from the former Liberian president Charles Taylor. In southern Sudan, clashes between northern troops and southern militia continued in Southern Kordofan state.

JULY 2011
1. A referendum in Morocco approved constitutional changes proposed by the king; the changes leave the king with sole authority over security, the armed forces and religion but cede greater executive power to elected politicians. **9.** The southern part of Sudan became independent as South Sudan; on 14 July the new country became the 193rd member of the United Nations. A plane carrying 110 people crashed into dense forest in the Democratic Republic of Congo, killing 53. **20.** The UN declared a famine in two areas of Somalia, inlcuding the Bakool and Lower Shabelle regions of the country; the famine arose from the worst drought in east Africa in over 40 years. **21.** President Kibaki of Kenya set fire to five tonnes of confiscated elephant ivory, believed to be worth £10m, to draw attention to the illegal killing of elephants by ivory poachers; the president was almost burned as he lit the mound of 335 tusks. **27.** 78 people were killed after a military transport plane crashed in southern Morocco, killing 78 of the 81 people on board.

THE AMERICAS

AUGUST 2010
5. The collapse of a tunnel in a copper mine near Copiapó, Chile, trapped 33 miners 622m underground; rescuers made contact with the men on 22 August, and began to drill a borehole large enough to allow them to escape (*see* 13 October). **7.** Juan Manuel Santos Calderon was sworn in as president of Colombia. **10.** Venezuela and Colombia agreed to restore diplomatic relations, which had been broken off in July 2010 over an allegation by the Colombian government that Venezuela was harbouring FARC rebels. **23.** In Tamaulipas state, Mexico, 72 migrants from central and south America were killed by the Los Zetas drug gang. **30.** Ten per cent of Mexico's federal police officers were dismissed for failing

'trust control exams', including lie-detector and toxicology tests.

SEPTEMBER 2010
4. A poll of 892 New Yorkers found that two-thirds were opposed to the proposed construction of a Muslim community centre near the site of the World Trade Centre buildings destroyed on 11 September 2001; the centre, dubbed 'the Ground Zero mosque', had become the subject of a controversy after the *Wall Street Post* reported the proposals in May 2010. **5.** Torrential rain in Guatemala caused landslides in which 38 people were killed. **8.** Terry Jones, a Pentecostal preacher in Florida, threatened to burn 200 copies of the Qur'an in protest at the proposed 'Ground Zero mosque'; the burning, originally proposed on Facebook in July 2010, was cancelled after Interpol warned that the plan could incite violent retaliation. **13.** The Cuban government announced that it was cutting a million public sector jobs in an effort to galvanise entrepreneurship and private-sector employment. **14.** In US senate elections in Delaware and New York, candidates from the conservative Tea Party movement won surprise victories over Republican establishment favourites. **22.** The military chief of the FARC rebel faction in Colombia was killed by government forces during a bombing raid; FARC had increased its attacks on security forces since President Santos took office in August. **27.** In legislative elections in Venezuela, the Democratic Unity coalition won 65 of the 165 seats, overturning President Chávez's two-thirds majority in the National Assembly. **27.** The first of five US soldiers accused of killing unarmed Afghan civilians appeared before a military tribunal.

OCTOBER 2010
1. The Ecuadorian government declared a state of emergency after rebellious police officers blocked airports and roads in protest at austerity measures. **8.** President Obama announced that Tom Donilon, formerly a senior adviser in President Clinton's administration, would replace General James Jones as the national security adviser. **13.** All 33 Chilean miners trapped underground since August were successfully rescued in a 24-hour period using a capsule to evacuate them one at a time. **19.** A Californian judge ruled that the current 'don't ask, don't tell' policy adopted towards homosexual personnel by the US military was illegal. The presidents of Bolivia and Peru signed an accord allowing Bolivia to build a port on a strip of the Peruvian coastline; Bolivia has been landlocked since the 1879–84 War of the Pacific. **20.** A cholera epidemic began in rural Haiti; the disease spread in subsequent weeks, reaching the capital, Port-au-Prince, by 8 November. **23.** Drug cartels carried out a number of murders throughout Mexico, killing over 60 people, most of whom were civilians. **31.** The second round of the presidential election in Brazil was won by Dilma Rousseff; she became the first female president of the country when she was sworn in on 1 January 2011.

NOVEMBER 2010
2. In mid-term elections in the USA, the Republicans made significant gains in both the senate and House of Representatives, taking overall control of the House of Representatives with a 25-seat majority, while the Democrats retained control of the senate by three seats. **16.** In Haiti, a suggestion that the cholera outbreak, which had killed around 1,100 people since mid October, had been caused by a south Asian strain of the disease

carried by UN troops from Nepal led to clashes between Haitians and UN peacekeepers in northern Haiti in which two people died. **23.** A Pentagon report was published describing the progress of US operations in Afghanistan as 'patchy'; combat incidents were shown to have risen 300 per cent since 2007 and the number of Afghans who judged their security situation to be 'bad' was at its highest level since 2008. **28.** Newspapers around the world, including the *Guardian*, the *New York Times*, *Le Monde*, *El País* and *Der Spiegel*, began to publish 251,287 US embassy cables that had been posted on the WikiLeaks website; many of the documents, which dated from 1966 to February 2010, contained diplomatically sensitive material. Presidential and legislative elections were held in Haiti despite many voters lacking the identity documents that would allow them to vote and with thousands of those killed in January's earthquake still on the electoral register. **30.** The Pentagon published a poll of serving US troops showing that 70 per cent believed that having homosexuals openly serving in the military would make no detrimental difference to morale.

DECEMBER 2010
1. The online retailer Amazon stopped hosting WikiLeaks content 24 hours after being contacted by the chairman of the US senate's committee on homeland security; on 4 December, the online payment site PayPal announced that it had frozen WikiLeaks' account. **3.** Heavy rains and flooding in Venezuela left 32 people dead and around 70,000 homeless. **8.** A fire in a prison in Chile killed more than 80 inmates and critically injured 14 others. Haiti's electoral commission announced that Mirlande Manigat had come first in the first round of the presidential election, with Jude Celestin of the ruling Inite party second; the omission of the popular Michel Martelly by less than 1 per cent led to violent protests in which government buildings were set on fire and the international airport closed (*see* 3 February). **16.** The US congress approved a bill extending tax cuts for households earning over $250,000; the cuts, a legacy of the Bush administration, had been due to expire at the month. **22.** Legislation repealing the 'don't ask, don't tell' policy on homosexuals serving in the US armed forces was signed into law.

JANUARY 2011
5. The Republican John Boehner was elected speaker of the US House of Representatives. **8.** A local man opened fire on a public meeting in Tucson, Arizona, killing six people, including a federal judge and a nine-year-old girl, and injuring 13 people, including US congresswoman Gabrielle Giffords. **11–12.** Torrential rain in south-eastern Brazil caused flooding, mudslides and landslides that left over 900 dead. **16.** Jean-Claude 'Baby Doc' Duvalier, a former president of Haiti, returned to the country after 25 years in exile in France; on 18 January, criminal charges, including torture and crimes against humanity, were filed against him.

FEBRUARY 2011
3. The Haitian electoral commission announced that the candidates in the second round of the presidential election would be Mirlande Manigat and Michel Martelly, disqualifying the government-backed candidate Jude Celestin, whose original inclusion in the second round had been contested, because of irregularities (*see* 8 December). **18.** Public-sector workers in Wisconsin demonstrated against proposed changes to employment

legislation that would remove their right to negotiate on pension contributions and health insurance. The USA vetoed a UN security council resolution condemning the resumption of Jewish settlement-building in the West Bank and Jerusalem; the other 14 members voted in favour.

MARCH 2011
18. Jean-Bertrand Aristide, a former president of Haiti, returned to the country after seven years in exile. **20.** Terry Jones, a Pentecostal preacher, oversaw the burning of a copy of the Qur'an at his church in Florida (*see* 8 September 2010). The second round of the Haitian presidential election took place; Michel Martelly was declared the winner on 5 April and was sworn in as president on 14 May. **24.** A US soldier, Jeremy Morlock, was sentenced to 24 years in prison after pleading guilty to the murders of three unarmed Afghan civilians; the German magazine *Der Spiegel* had published photographs of Morlock and other soldiers posing with their victims.

APRIL 2011
9. President Obama announced US federal spending cuts of $38bn (£23bn); the cuts, mostly to public services and infrastructure projects, were passed by congress on 15 April. **11.** A UN special rapporteur on torture complained that the US government was preventing him from having an unmonitored meeting with Bradley Manning, the US soldier arrested in May 2010 on suspicion of having passed restricted material to the WikiLeaks website, amid mounting international condemnation of the conditions in which Mr Manning was being held; on 20 April Mr Manning was moved from solitary confinement at a maximum-security military prison in Virginia to a medium-security military prison in Kansas. **13.** Detectives in Mexico discovered the bodies of 116 people in a mass grave near the border with Texas; the victims were thought to be Mexican migrants killed by the Los Zetas drug cartel. **25.** The WikiLeaks website posted US military dossiers on prisoners at Guantanamo Bay which implied that some prisoners had been maltreated; it had already shared 759 classified US government files with the UK and US media. The USA experienced the first of 334 tornadoes in three days, including four tornadoes given the highest ranking on the Enhanced Fujita scale; the outbreak, the largest in US history, affected 21 states and caused 344 deaths.

MAY 2011
2. In the Canadian legislative election, the Conservative Party won 166 seats, securing prime minister Stephen Harper his first majority government; the Liberal Party had its worst ever electoral performance, winning only 34 seats, and the separatist Bloc Québécois lost its official party status. **14.** Dominique Strauss-Kahn, the French managing director of the International Monetary Fund, was arrested at John F. Kennedy airport and charged with the sexual assault and attempted rape of a chambermaid at a New York hotel earlier that day; on 18 May, Mr Strauss-Kahn resigned from his post at the IMF.

JUNE 2011
5. The second round of the presidential election took place in Peru; Ollanta Humala won a narrow victory over Keiko Fujimori and was sworn in on 28 July. In the USA, a Democratic congressman, Anthony Weiner, admitted sending sexually suggestive photographs of himself over

the internet and lying to cover up the incident; the congressman resigned from congress on 21 June. **6.** Dominique Strauss-Kahn pleaded not guilty to sexual assault and attempted rape charges at his arraignment in New York (*see* 14 May). **11.** Thousands of emails to and from Sarah Palin, the former governer of Alaska and Senator John McCain's vice-presidential running mate in 2008, were released under freedom of information laws; the emails covered a period from 2006 to 2008 before the presidential race. **23.** President Obama announced the withdrawal of 33,000 US troops from Afghanistan. **26.** New York became the sixth US state to legalise same-sex marriage. **28.** The French finance minister Christine Lagarde was appointed managing director of the IMF, becoming its first female head.

JULY 2011
2. President Chavez of Venezuela confirmed that he was being treated for cancer in Cuba. **22.** The US space shuttle Atlantis returned to Earth after a 13-day journey to the International Space Station; the shuttle's flight was the last in NASA's human spaceflight programme following President Obama's decision to restructure the agency's programme. **27.** President Humala of Peru appointed the singer Susana Baca as the country's new culture minister; the Grammy award-winning singer became Peru's first black government minister.

ASIA

AUGUST 2010
2. Violent pro-independence demonstrations in Kashmir resulted in the deaths of nine protesters, four of whom were shot by police; the protests were the culmination of six weeks of violence in the state. **3.** The assassination of a senior politician in Karachi, Pakistan, led to city-wide riots and reprisals that left 45 people dead. **6.** Ten medical charity workers, including the British doctor Karen Woo, were killed by gunmen in the Badakhshan province of Afghanistan. **7.** Heavy rainfall and flooding in China's northwestern Gansu province caused mudslides which killed over 1,400 people. **8.** The severe flooding in the Indus valley in Pakistan reached Sind and Punjab provinces; by the time the floodwaters started to recede in September, an estimated 1,781 people had died and over six million had been displaced. **13.** Myanmar's ruling junta announced that parliamentary elections, the first since 1990, would be held on 7 November. **17.** President Karzai of Afghanistan issued a decree ordering all private security firms working in the country to cease operations within four months **18.** Afghanistan's independent electoral commission announced that 938 polling stations would remain closed during the forthcoming legislative elections because of security concerns. **23.** In the Philippines, a former policeman armed with an automatic rifle hijacked a bus in Manila; a 12-hour stand-off with police ended in the death of the gunman and eight of his hostages.

SEPTEMBER 2010
13. Rioting and arson in Kashmir left 18 people dead; the violence was believed to be in response to an Iranian news report claiming that a copy of the Qur'an had been desecrated in New York on the ninth anniversary of the September 11 terrorist attacks. **16.** The UN-backed genocide tribunal in Cambodia indicted the four most senior surviving leaders of the Khmer Rouge regime on charges including genocide, torture and religious

persecution; the four denied all the charges. **18.** Legislative elections were held in Afghanistan amid sporadic violence that left 13 dead; the UN had withdrawn a third of its permanent workforce from the country three days earlier in expectation of election-related violence. **19.** Islamist gunmen opened fire on a military convoy in Tajikistan, killing 23 soldiers. **23.** Floods in the northern Indian state of Uttar Pradesh left around 20 people dead, caused two million to be evacuated and washed away more than 1,000 homes. **25.** The defence minister of Pakistan resigned after accusing the country's army of killing two Pakistani politicians, including former prime minister Benazir Bhutto. **28.** The Afghanistan government established a 68-member 'high peace council' to facilitate talks with the Taliban. **30.** Two Pakistani soldiers were killed and four injured at an outpost near the Afghan border when US helicopters mistook them for insurgents; in response, Pakistan prohibited all NATO supply vehicles from using a key border crossing.

OCTOBER 2010
6. The Pakistani Taliban began a series of attacks on NATO supply convoys, destroying over 40 vehicles stranded by the closing of a border crossing into Afghanistan (*see* 30 September); the border was reopened on 11 October after the USA apologised for the incident on 30 September. **8.** Liu Xiaobo, a Chinese human rights activist and political prisoner, was awarded the Nobel peace prize; the Chinese government condemned the decision. **10.** Kim Jong-un, the son of the ailing North Korean leader Kim Jong-il, made his first public appearance at a military parade celebrating the 65th anniversary of the ruling Workers' Party; a senior North Korean official had confirmed on 8 October that Kim Jong-un would eventually succeed his father as the country's leader. A legislative election was held in Kyrgyzstan; no party won a majority, and on 30 November a three-party coalition agreement was announced. **12.** Twenty-three senior Communist Party members sent an open letter to the Chinese premier, Wen Jiabao, calling for democratic reforms. **25.** Indonesia suffered three natural disasters within 24 hours which left over 400 dead, 300 missing and about 20,000 displaced; experts believed that a 7.7-magnitude earthquake, whose epicentre lay off Sumatra, triggered a tsunami that swept across much of the archipelago; these events were followed on 26 October by the eruption of Mount Merapi on Java.

NOVEMBER 2010
7. Legislative elections were held in Myanmar amid concerns about corruption and voter intimidation; subsequent unrest caused around 20,000 people to cross the border into Thailand. **11.** The G20 summit began in Seoul, South Korea, with discussion of collaborative solutions to the international financial crisis; the two-day summit ended with leaders agreeing on guidelines to counter global trade imbalances and the signing of the Seoul Development Consensus for Shared Growth, which emphasised the importance of public-sector investment in developing economies. **13.** The democracy campaigner and Nobel Peace laureate Aung San Suu Kyi was released from house arrest in Rangoon, Myanmar; she had spent 15 of the past 21 years under house arrest. **16.** A report published by India's auditor-general accused the former telecommunications minister, Andimuthu Raja, of having lost the Indian government around £22bn in revenue by

underselling mobile phone spectrum licences in 2008; Raja was arrested in connection with the scandal on 10 February 2011. **20.** In Afghanistan, about a quarter of the 5.6 million votes cast in September's legislative election were disqualified by the independent electoral commission after it uncovered widespread corruption; the revised results, released on 24 November, led to popular protests and further investigations. **23.** In Phnom Penh, Cambodia, a stampede broke out on a bridge at the annual Water festival; about 345 people were killed and hundreds were injured. North Korea fired around 200 artillery shells at Yeonpyeong, a South Korean island off the peninsula's west coast, killing two marines and two civilians, and injuring 20 others; South Korea returned fire with F-16 fighter jets, and on 25 November the South Korean defence minister resigned over the incident. **28.** A leaked US diplomatic cable revealed that a Chinese foreign ministry official supported the reunification of the Korean peninsula under South Korean control, a stance that differs greatly from China's official line of championing North Korea; the document, dating from 2009, was one of 250,000 leaked cables published by the WikiLeaks website.

DECEMBER 2010
5. The Atomic Energy Organisation of Iran announced that it had successfully used its first batch of refined uranium ore at a conversion plant in Isfahan; the announcement came the day before an international summit on Iran's nuclear ambitions was held in Geneva. **6.** Two suicide bombers detonated devices at a tribal meeting in north-west Pakistan, killing 50 people and injuring over 100; the meeting had been called to discuss the formation of an anti-Taliban militia. **17.** The Japanese government announced a new defence policy shifting its priorities from dealing with the threat formerly posed by Russia to the potential threat from China; troops will be redeployed to protect strategic islands whose possession is disputed with China. **23.** North Korea's armed forces minister, Kim Yong-chun, threatened to begin 'a holy war' in response to military exercises with live ammunition carried out by South Korean forces close to the border between the two countries. **25.** In north-west Pakistan, a female suicide bomber with links to the Pakistani Taliban killed 45 people as they queued outside a food aid distribution depot.

JANUARY 2011
2. One of the parties in Pakistan's coalition government left the coalition in protest at increases in taxation and oil prices; this left the government 12 seats short of a majority in the national assembly. **4.** The governor of Pakistan's Punjab province, Salman Taseer, was shot dead in Islamabad by one of his bodyguards. **12.** Flooding in Sri Lanka reached its peak; it left 27 people dead and displaced around 325,000. **14.** The prime minister of Japan, Naoto Kan, reshuffled the government to try to deal with the country's financial crisis. **15.** Over 100 people were killed and 44 injured in a stampede at a Hindu festival in the Indian state of Kerala.

FEBRUARY 2011
4. Thai and Cambodian troops exchanged fire along a disputed stretch of their common border over a four-day period, killing 11 people, injuring about 90 and displacing 21,000 villagers; the clashes were caused by the two countries' dispute over ownership of the

11th-century Preah Vihear temple, a UNESCO World Heritage site.

MARCH 2011

4. China announced a 12.7 per cent increase in its military spending in 2011–12, fuelling growing unease in other Asian countries about China's increasing military assertiveness. **10.** The Dalai Lama, Tenzin Gyatso, announced that he would retire from political life with immediate effect. **11.** An earthquake of magnitude 9.0 struck the north-east coast of Honshu, Japan's main island, shifting the island by 2.4m and the Earth's axis by 25cm; it was followed by six days of severe aftershocks and further earthquakes. The earthquake triggered a tsunami which travelled up to 10km (6 miles) inland in places, flooding a total area of about 561 sq. km (217 sq. miles) and completely destroying many coastal towns. Power systems failed at two nuclear reactors at the Fukushima nuclear power plant on Japan's east coast; the Japanese government declared a state of nuclear emergency and declared an exclusion zone of 3km (1.9 miles) around the plant. **12.** A nuclear reactor at Fukushima exploded, raising fears of a partial meltdown; the exclusion zone was extended to 20km (12.4 miles). **13.** A level-4 nuclear emergency was declared at two Fukushima nuclear reactors. There were explosions at two Fukushima nuclear reactors and an explosion and fire in a spent fuel pool. **15.** Radiation levels at the Fukushima plant reached a peak of 400 millisieverts per hour. **16.** A Pakistan court dropped murder charges against a CIA agent, Raymond Davis, after his victims' relatives accepted $1.4m (£859,000) in compensation. **17.** A leaked US diplomatic cable was published that suggested the ruling Congress party in India had attempted to buy parliamentary support in 2008; a US diplomat had been informed that a fund of 500m–600m rupees (£6.6m–18m) existed to be used for a vote of confidence in the government. **18.** A minute's silence was held in Japan exactly one week after the devastating earthquake and tsunami; an estimated 6,500 were dead, over 8,600 were missing, over 452,000 were homeless, 1m households were without water and thousands were without electricity. The Japanese nuclear safety agency raised the status of the nuclear emergency to level 5; the International Atomic Energy Agency said the situation was still grave but had not worsened for 24 hours. **20.** A gas explosion caused a coal mine to collapse in Pakistan's Balochistan province, killing 43 miners.

APRIL 2011

1. In Mazar-e-Sharif, Afghanistan, seven UN workers were murdered by protestors angered by the burning of a Qur'an by a fringe Christian group in the USA; around a dozen people died in subsequent clashes with police in Kandahar (*see* The Americas 20 March). The preliminary results of India's 2010 census showed that the country's population had grown by 181 million since 2000. **2.** Seawater off the Japanese coast near the damaged Fukushima nuclear power plant was found to be 7.5 million times the legal radiation limit; engineers succeeded in plugging a leak of radioactive fluid on 6 April. **12.** Japan's nuclear safety agency raised the alert status of the damaged Fukushima plant to level 7, the highest level possible; it was estimated that 190,000 terabecquerels of radioactive iodine had been released since 11 March and that a plume of radioactive water extended 322km (200 miles) east into the Pacific Ocean. **22.** An area 20km (12 miles) in radius around the Daiichi

nuclear power plant in Fukushima, Japan, was declared a restricted zone; the 80,000 people living in the area were evacuated. Fighting broke out again on the Thailand-Cambodia border, part of an ongoing border dispute (see 4 February); eight days of clashes left at least 16 soldiers dead, dozens wounded and displaced thousands of villagers. **25.** Nearly 500 members of the Taliban escaped from Sarpoza prison in the Afghan city of Kandahar. The UN published a report accusing both the Sri Lankan army and the Tamil Tiger separatists of war crimes during the final stages of the country's civil war in 2009; the report claimed that the army had killed up to 40,000 civilians by indiscriminate shelling of supposedly demilitarised zones. **27.** Lobsang Sangay was elected prime minister of Tibet's government-in-exile following the Dalai Lama's announcement that he was withdrawing from political life (*see* 10 March).

MAY 2011

2. The al-Qaeda leader Osama bin Laden was killed in a raid by US forces on his walled compound in the Pakistan city of Abbottabad; he had been tracked to the compound 50km (31 miles) north of Islamabad through one of his couriers, who had been under surveillance since 2002. **3.** President Nursultan Nazarbayev of Kazakhstan was re-elected with 95 per cent of the vote; the Organisation for Security and Cooperation in Europe (OSCE) criticised the poll for an absence of opposition candidates, who had boycotted the election. **13.** A double suicide-bombing in Shabqadar, Pakistan, killed at least 80 people, mostly recruits at a Frontier Corps base; the bombings, perpetrated by the Taliban, were said to be revenge attacks for the death of Osama bin Laden. **13.** In state elections in India, the Communist Party lost control of West Bengal and southern Kerala to the Trinamool Congress, part of the ruling coalition.

JUNE 2011

5. An al-Qaeda commander, Ilyas Kashmiri, was killed by a US missile strike in Pakistan; the commander, seen as a possible replacement for Osama bin Laden, was one of the five most wanted militant leaders in the country and was believed to be involved in the 2008 Mumbai massacre. **17.** Fighting broke out in northern Myanmar as government forces attempted to clear separatist militia from an area where a hydroelectric plant was to be constructed; Kachin separatist groups were opposed to the construction of the plant because of concerns over its environmental impact. **19.** President Karzai of Afghanistan officially confirmed that the USA was engaged in talks with the Taliban; insurgents attacked a police station near the presidential palace in Kabul, leaving three people dead. **26.** In Afghanistan, a suicide bomber drove a car through a clinic in Agra, killing 35 people; the Taliban denied responsibility for the attack. **27.** The Japanese government was restructured to include portfolios for post-earthquake reconstruction and nuclear issues.

JULY 2011

3. A legislative election was held in Thailand; the majority of seats were won by the For Thai Party led by Yingluck Shinawatra, sister of the ousted premier Thaksin Shinawatra, and she began to form a coalition government with four smaller parties. **10.** More than 20,000 demonstrators took to the streets of Kuala Lumpar, Malaysia in a rally protesting at the government administrative and electoral reforms; hundreds of protestors were detained as police fired tear gas in an attempt to subdue the protests. **12.** A train was derailed in Uttar Pradesh state, India, killing at least 68 people. A cargo truck crashed into a canal in south-east Bangladesh, killing 42 schoolchildren; the truck was taking the children home from a nearby football tournament. **13.** The half-brother of President Karzai of Afghanistan, Ahmed Wali Karzai, was killed by a bodyguard in Kandahar; the Taliban claimed responsibility for the assassination but officials said it was possible that Karzai was killed for tribal or drug-related reasons. **14.** A triple bomb blast during the rush-hour in Mumbai, India, killed at least 21 people; the explosion occurred in the week of the fifth anniversary of the Mumbai train blasts, which killed more than 180 commuters. **25.** A crash involving two high-speed bullet trains killed 38 people in Wenzhou City, east China; the crash became the focus of a media propaganda investigation on 28 July after it emerged that journalists had been ordered not to analyse the causes of the incident.

AUSTRALASIA AND THE PACIFIC

AUGUST 2010
21. A snap legislative election was held in Australia; it resulted in a hung parliament, as the Labour party and the Liberal–National coalition both won 72 seats; Julia Gillard continued as prime minister at the head of a Labour government after securing the support of two independent MPs.

SEPTEMBER–OCTOBER 2010
2–6 September. Heavy rainfall in south and south-eastern Australia affected Victoria most badly; the state experienced widespread flooding for about a week as the floodwaters moved down the Murray river. **4 September.** An earthquake with a magnitude of 7.1 hit New Zealand's South Island; two people were critically injured and about 100,000 buildings were damaged in Christchurch. **16 September.** A legislative election was held in Tuvalu; on 29 September, MPs elected Maatia Toafa (prime minister 2004–6) as prime minister.

NOVEMBER 2010
19. A gas explosion in a coal mine on New Zealand's South Island left 29 miners trapped underground; all 29 men are believed to have died in a second explosion on 24 November. **25.** A legislative election was held in Tonga, the first in which the majority of seats in the legislature were filled by elected representatives.

DECEMBER 2010
15. A boat carrying Iranian, Iraqi and Kurdish refugees was wrecked off the coast of the Australian territory of Christmas Island, with the loss of at least 28 people. **24.** Tropical Cyclone Tasha made landfall near Cairns in Queensland, Australia, triggering the heaviest December rainfall on record in the state; the rainfall exacerbated isolated flooding in the state since late November, causing a series of floods in towns and cities in the basins of the Fitzroy, Burnett, Condamine, Balonne and Mary rivers over the following two weeks as the floodwaters moved downstream. **28.** Flooding in southern Queensland led to mass evacuation of a number of towns.

JANUARY 2011
8–10. Heavy rainfall in Queensland raised the level of the existing floodwaters, which had started to recede, and caused flooding in previously unaffected areas, including a flash flood in Toowoomba and the Lockyer valley. **11.** The Brisbane river broke its banks, leading to the evacuation of parts of the city; the flooding peaked on 13 January. Three-quarters of the state of Queensland was declared a disaster zone, with flooding covering nearly half the state and affecting about 200,000 people and over 70 towns and cities; 35 people had died, 21 of them in Toowoomba and the Lockyer valley, and nine were missing. **12.** Several days of heavy rain began in south-eastern Australia, affecting Victoria most badly and causing flash flooding. **16.** Flooding began in Victoria, Australia, and continued to spread throughout January and early February, affecting more than 51 communities and causing two deaths. **17.** The premier of Queensland, Anna Bligh, announced a commission of inquiry into the 2010–11 Queensland floods; the commission's interim report on 1 August 2011 made 175 recommendations.

FEBRUARY 2011
3. Cyclone Yasi made landfall in Queensland, Australia, causing renewed flash flooding in Victoria and over A\$3.5bn (£2.2bn) of damage, including the destruction of 15 per cent of the country's sugar cane crop. **22.** A 6.3-magnitude earthquake in New Zealand's South Island caused 181 deaths and damaged buildings and power supplies in Christchurch.

MARCH 2011
18. Around 250 asylum seekers rioted at Australia's Christmas Island detention centre over their living conditions and the time taken to process their asylum applications.

APRIL–MAY 2011
1 April. The legislative assembly of French Polynesia passed a motion of no confidence in the government of president Gaston Tong Sang; Sang was replaced by Oscar Temaru of the Union for Democracy, who named his government on 6 April. **24 April.** The prime minister of Vanuatu, Sato Kilman, lost a confidence vote in the parliament; he was replaced the same day by Serge Vohor, the leader of the Union of Moderate Parties, who formed a new coalition government.

JUNE–JULY 2011
13 June. A 6.5-magnitude earthquake in New Zealand's South Island injured 46 people and destroyed or caused further damage to buildings in Christchurch.

EUROPE

AUGUST 2010
4. After peat and forest fires shrouded the city in smog, the concentration of carbon monoxide in Moscow reached 5.7 times its normal level; weekly fatality levels in the city doubled and many flights were grounded. **5.** The Russian government announced a ban on the export of wheat and related food items from 15 August until the end of 2010; the ban was imposed because of poor harvests following months of drought and wildfires. **29.** Islamist rebels attacked the residence of the Chechen president, Ramzan Kadyrov, in Tsentoroi; at least 19 people were killed.

SEPTEMBER 2010
5. The Basque separatist organisation ETA announced a unilateral ceasefire, although it stopped short of

surrendering its weapons or describing the ceasefire as permanent. **7.** In France, demonstrations and strikes occurred nationwide as over a million people protested against proposed changes to the pension system, including an increase in the retirement age from 60 to 62. **14.** The French senate passed legislation making it illegal for Muslim women to wear the veil in public. **15.** Russia and Norway signed a treaty dividing a long-disputed area of the Barents Sea equally between them. **18.** A legislative election was held in Sweden; the Social Democrats remained the largest single party but held fewer seats than the incumbent Alliance coalition, which formed a minority government. **22.** In Switzerland, Simonetta Sommaruga, a Social Democratic candidate, was elected to the federal council, resulting in females outnumbering males in the government for the first time. **29.** The Italian prime minister, Silvio Berlusconi, survived a confidence vote in the legislature by securing the backing of a group of rebel MPs. The European Commission gave the French government until 15 October to incorporate the EU's freedom of movement policies into its law; France had expelled around 1,000 Roma immigrants since July 2010. **31.** The Irish government announced a £39bn support package for its struggling banking sector, effectively nationalising the Anglo Irish and Allied Irish banks; the move drove up the country's budget deficit to 32 per cent of GDP, the highest in the developed world.

OCTOBER 2010

5. The Hungarian government declared a state of emergency in three counties after toxic sludge escaped from a reservoir of chemical waste at an alumina plant 161km (100 miles) south-west of Budapest, flooding nearby towns and villages and leaving seven dead and 150 injured; despite the efforts of emergency services, rivers in western Hungary were seriously polluted. **12.** Around 3 million people attended demonstrations and strikes throughout France against plans to raise the retirement age; on 20 October, President Sarkozy ordered riot police to dismantle oil depot blockades after fuel shortages sparked days of further unrest. **19.** Gunmen and suicide bombers stormed the Chechen parliament in Grozny, killing three people and injuring 17. **25.** Serbia's application to join the EU was allowed to progress to the European Commission; EU foreign ministers stressed that Serbia's accession would remain contingent upon it estabishing good relations with Kosovo. **27.** France's national assembly passed legislation raising the minimum retirement age from 60 to 62, despite two weeks of popular protests against the measure.

NOVEMBER 2010

2. Greek counter-terrorism officials in Athens uncovered a letter-bomb campaign targeting European political figures; 14 devices were detected over the subsequent two days, including one addressed to President Sarkozy of France and eight to various European embassies. **9.** In Sweden, a man was arrested in connection with a series of attacks on Malmo's immigrant population; he was thought to be responsible for at least 17 shootings, including one death, since October 2009. **12.** The French and Italian governments welcomed an influx of Christian asylum seekers from Iraq, prompted by a number of al-Qaida attacks on the Christian population of Baghdad in late October and early November. **14.** President Sarkozy reshuffled his government, replacing his foreign minister, the human-rights campaigner Bernard Kouchner, with former justice minister Michéle Alliot-Marie; the ministry of immigration and national identity, created during Sarkozy's 2007 electoral campaign, was scrapped. **19.** A two-day NATO summit began in Lisbon; its agenda included nuclear disarmament, Turkey's relations with the EU and the implementation of a £169m missile shield over Europe and North America. **24.** The Irish government announced a four-year austerity plan, including €2.8bn (£2.3bn) of cuts to welfare spending and a phased VAT increase from 21 per cent to 23 per cent by 2014, and indicated that up to 25,000 public-sector jobs could be cut. **27.** In Iceland, an election was held to elect 31 members to an assembly to write a new constitution for the country. **28.** The Irish government announced that it would receive loans totalling €85bn (£72bn) from the IMF and EU to help support its banking system (*see* 31 September); over 100,000 people had demonstrated against the proposed rescue package in Dublin the day before.

DECEMBER 2010

4. The Spanish goverment declared a 'state of alarm' after air traffic controllers staged a walk-out over working conditions that left the country's airspace closed and around 20,000 passengers grounded; martial law was applied at midday and by the evening 90 per cent of controllers had returned to work. **12.** Kosovo held its first legislative election since declaring independence in 2008; the Democratic Party remained the largest party but without an overall majority, but the electoral commission ordered a rerun of the ballot in five municipalities on 9 January after suspicions of irregularities. **13.** In Moscow, protests against immigration by around 5,000 Russian nationalists left at least two people dead and dozens injured; on 17 December, a second day of riots led to the arrest of nearly 1,000 people. **14.** The Italian prime minister, Silvio Berlusconi, narrowly survived confidence votes in both chambers of the Italian legislature; the votes were brought after scandals in his personal life and corruption allegations. **16.** A Council of Europe report on allegations of human-organ trafficking during the Kosovo war was presented to the council's legal and human rights committee; the report implicated Kosovo's prime minister, Hachim Thaci. **17.** A report on allegations of misconduct by Silvio Berlusconi was submitted to the Italian parliament. **19.** President Lukashenko of Belarus was re-elected for a fourth term with 80 per cent of the vote; around 10,000 people protested at the result, alleging corruption, and nearly 600 people, including seven opposition candidates, were arrested.

JANUARY 2011

10. The Basque separatist group ETA announced that the ceasefire it had declared in September 2010 would be permanent and open to independent verification (*see* 5 September). **13.** The Italian constitutional court ruled that the prime minister, Silvio Berlusconi, could not excuse himself from attending court hearings in the three trials he was facing because of his government duties. **14.** Italian magistrates announced that Silvio Berlusconi had been under investigation since 21 December over allegations of paying an under-age prostitute for sex and abuse of office for securing the girl's release after she had been arrested for theft in May 2010. The last of the major credit rating agencies downgraded Greece's sovereign debt from 'investment grade' to 'speculative' status. **22.** The Irish prime minister, Brian Cowen, stepped down as leader of the Fianna Fail party, despite surviving a party leadership vote and an attempt by cabinet members to oust him, in advance of the general election called for 25 February; a former foreign minister, Micheál Martin, was elected to replace Cowen on 26 January. **23.** The Green party pulled out of Ireland's coalition government, leaving a minority government under Fianna Fail in power. **24.** A suicide bomb attack at Domodedovo airport in Moscow killed 36 people and left 180 injured; on 8 February a faction of the Islamist Caucasian Front claimed responsibility.

FEBRUARY 2011

7–11. In France, thousands of legal professionals demonstrated in protest after President Sarkozy said that judges had been too lax in releasing a recidivist criminal who subsequently murdered an 18-year-old girl; during the demonstrations only urgent law cases were heard. **14.** Hundreds of thousands of Italians demonstrated in protest at the conduct of prime minister Silvio Berlusconi (*see* 14 January). **25.** In a legislative election in Ireland, Fine Gael won the most seats, but without an overall majority; on 6 March it reached an agreement on a coalition with the Labour Party.

MARCH 2011

6. In Russia, Chechnya's parliament unanimously re-elected Ramzan Kadyrov to another term as president of the republic. **10.** The Italian government approved a draft bill which would allow Italian defendants to sue judges and prosecutors for trial errors. **14.** The German government announced that it was suspending plans to extend the life of the country's nuclear power stations following the disaster at the Fukushima plant in Japan. **23.** Portugal's minority government resigned after the legislature rejected its proposed austerity measures, and a legislative election was called (*see* 5 June).

APRIL 2011

7. Portugal's outgoing government applied to the EU and IMF for a financial bailout package; the bailout, finalised in May 2011, was worth €78bn (£70.2bn) over three years. **11.** A bombing on the Minsk underground system killed 14 people and injured about 200; two men were arrested the following day. A law imposing a €150 (£132) fine on Muslim women wearing the veil in public came into force in France; minor protests in Paris were disbanded by police and the first fine was issued at 5.30pm the same day. **13.** The Italian chamber of deputies passed legislation streamlining the Italian judicial system; the law effectively halted the trial of prime minister Silvio Berlusconi for allegedly bribing his legal adviser to withhold court testimony. **15.** The International Criminal Tribunal for the Former Yugoslavia found two Croatian commanders, Ante Gotovina and Mladen Markac, guilty of war crimes committed during Croatia's war with Serbia in 1991–5; Gotovina was sentenced to 24 years in jail and Markac to 18 years. **17.** In legislative elections in Finland, the National Coalition Party, the junior partner in the outgoing coalition, became the largest party, but without an overall majority. **29.** Spain's national statistics institute published data showing that unemployment in the country had reached a record 21.3 per cent in the first quarter of 2011.

MAY 2011

11. The Danish government announced that the country would reintroduce customs controls and border checks at its frontiers with Germany and Sweden; the move came after France and Italy campaigned in late April for tighter

EU border controls because of increased migration from war-torn north Africa. There was a 24-hour strike and demonstrations in Athens in protest at austerity measures introduced by the Greek government; about 25 people were injured in clashes with riot police. Two earthquakes of around magnitude 5.0 hit the Spanish city of Lorca, killing ten people and injuring dozens. **12.** John Demjanjuk, a 91-year-old Ukrainian, was sentenced in Germany to five years in prison for his involvement in the murder of 28,060 Jews at the Sobibor concentration camp during the Second World War. **26.** The former Bosnian-Serb general Ratko Mladic, wanted for war crimes during the Bosnian war in the 1990s, was arrested in Lazareno, Serbia, after 16 years of evading arrest. **27.** Greece's government failed to win support from other parties for the budget cuts and speedy privatisation of state-owned businesses needed to obtain the release of the fifth instalment of its EU bailout package.

JUNE 2011

3. Ratko Mladic went on trial before the International Criminal Tribunal for the Former Yugoslavia in The Hague on charges of genocide, crimes against humanity and violations of the rules of war in Bosnia-Hercegovina between 1992 and 1995. **5.** In the Portuguese general election, the Social Democrats became the largest party, but without an overall majority, and two weeks later formed a coalition with a smaller party. **16.** Thousands of demonstrators protested in Athens against new austerity measures being debated by the legislature; the Greek prime minister, George Papandreou, reshuffled the government, replacing the unpopular finance minister George Papaconstantinou with Evangelos Venizelos. **21.** A passenger plane travelling from Moscow crashed in Petrozavodsk, northern Russia, killing 44 people. **28.** President Sarkozy of France announced €1bn (£884m) of investment in atomic power despite protests from anti-nuclear activists outside the country's oldest power plant in Alsace.

JULY 2011

2. Following a small civil cermony the previous day, Prince Albert II of Monaco married the former Olympic swimmer Charlene Wittstock in a religious ceremony at the Prince's Palace in Monte Carlo. **6.** In a landmark case, a Dutch appeal court ruled that the Netherlands was partly responsible for the deaths of Muslim men at Srebrenica in July 1995 after the country's forces, serving with the UN, failed to protect them in a designated UN 'safe haven'. **12.** A tourist ship sank on the Volga river, 129 km (80 miles) south of Kazan in central Russia; 128 passengers died. **21.** Goran Hadzic was arrested in northern Serbia for crimes committed during the Croatian war, after seven years on the run. **22.** Leaders of eurozone countries agreed an additional €109bn (£96bn) bailout for Greece amid fears of the sovereign debt crisis spreading to Italy and Spain. **23.** In Norway, a car-bomb explosion in Oslo and gunman's attack on young people attending a political rally on Utoya island left 77 dead and 153 injured; Anders Behring Brievik, a right-wing extremist, was arrested on Utoya island and claimed responsibility for both attacks.

MIDDLE EAST

AUGUST 2010

16. Iran's vice president announced plans to begin building ten uranium enrichment plants in 2011. **17.**

The Lebanese parliament voted in favour of lifting employment restrictions for the country's 400,000 Palestinian refugees, who gained the same employment rights as other foreigners. A suicide bomber at an army recruiting station in Baghdad killed around 60 recruits and soldiers. **25.** Bombings in seven Iraqi cities killed over 50 people. **31.** US troops formally ended combat operations in Iraq; remaining US military personnel, although still available to participate in operations led by Iraqi forces when requested, assumed non-combat roles. The Iranian newspaper *Kayhan* stated that the French president's wife, Carla Bruni-Sarkozy, 'deserved death' for her defence of an Iranian woman, Sakineh Mohammadi Ashtiani, awaiting execution by stoning after being convicted of adultery in 2006.

SEPTEMBER 2010

2. A two-day summit began in Washington DC between the Israeli prime minister, Benjamin Netanyahu, and the Palestinian president, Mahmoud Abbas, the first direct peace negotiations between Israeli and Palestinian leaders since 2008; both agreed to hold fortnightly talks thereafter, but talks were suspended on 26 September. **12.** In a referendum in Turkey, voters approved 26 reforms intended to make the constitution more democratic. **15.** Sakineh Mohammadi Ashtiani (*see* 31 August) appeared on Iranian state television to repudiate allegations that she had been tortured in prison; her lawyer, who had been denied access to his client for more than a month, suspected that Ashtiani appeared under duress. **25.** The rival Palestinian groups Hamas and Fatah announced that they had agreed to share power in order to present a united stance in future negotiations with Israel. **26.** A ten-month freeze on the construction of Jewish settlements in the West Bank ended at midnight, and building work subsequently resumed.

OCTOBER 2010

2. An aide to the Palestinian president Mahmoud Abbas stated that there would be no further talks between Israel and Palestinian leaders until settlement-building in the West Bank was suspended again (*see* 2 September). **10.** The first two of nine Iraqi civilians on trial for the killing of six British military police officers in 2003 were acquitted. **15.** The Israeli government issued new building permits for land in the West Bank. **26.** The Iraqi supreme court sentenced Tariq Aziz, deputy prime minister in Saddam Hussain's government, to death by hanging; on 17 November, President Talabani of Iraq refused to sign Aziz's execution order. **29.** Iran agreed to resume talks on its nuclear programme; negotiations on controlling its uranium enrichment programme had broken down in October 2009. **31.** A Catholic church in Baghdad was attacked during a service by gunmen from the Islamic State of Iraq jihadi group, an organisation affiliated with al-Qaeda; 58 people, most of whom were worshippers, were killed.

NOVEMBER 2010

2. Bombings in 12 predominantly Shia areas of Baghdad left 76 people dead and nearly 200 injured. **11.** Eight months after the inconclusive legislative election in Iraq, rival political blocs brokered a power-sharing deal allowing a coalition government to be formed and the legislature re-elected Jabal Talabani as president; on 25 November, Nouri al-Maliki of the State of Law bloc was formally asked to form a government. **28.** Leaked memos from US embassies in the Middle East revealed that King Abdullah of Saudi Arabia had 'frequently exhorted the US to attack Iran to put an end to its nuclear weapons programme'; the memos were among the confidential cables released by the WikiLeaks website. In the first round of the legislative election in Egypt, the incumbent National Democratic Party increased its majority from 75 per cent to 97 per cent; voter intimidation and ballot stuffing were reported at many polling stations and at least eight people were killed in election-related violence.

DECEMBER 2010

3. Fires spread throughout the Carmel forest in northern Israel; aircraft and firefighters from at least ten countries cooperated to fight the fires, which killed 42 people. **5.** The second phase of Egypt's legislative elections was boycotted by many opposition groups. **6.** A 14-year-old boy was arrested in connection with the Carmel forest fires in Israel. **8.** Peace talks intended to extend Israel's construction moratorium in the West Bank stalled after Israel turned down an incentive package from the US government; this included $3bn (£1.9bn) worth of fighter planes and promises of future diplomatic support from the UN (*see* 26 September). **15.** A suicide bomb attack at a mosque in eastern Iran by the Sunni rebel group Jundollah killed 41 people and injured more than 50. **17.** A Tunisian street vendor, Mohamed Bouazizi, committed suicide by self-immolation in Sidi Bouzid after his wares were confiscated by police; the act sparked off several weeks of civil unrest throughout the country. **20.** A 6.3-magnitude earthquake in south-east Iran left seven people dead and hundreds trapped or injured.

JANUARY 2011

1. The bombing of a Christian church in Alexandria, Egypt, killed 21 people and injured 97; the attack was later attributed to al-Qaeda. **12.** Eleven ministers belonging to Hezbollah and allied parties resigned from Lebanon's national unity government, causing the government to collapse; Hezbollah wanted the government to sever its links with the UN-backed Special Tribunal for Lebanon, tasked with investigating the assassination of the former prime minister Rafiq Hariri in 2005, and to denounce the tribunal's findings, which were expected to indict Hezbollah members for the assassination, before the release of its report. **14.** President Ben Ali of Tunisia fled the country for Saudi Arabia following weeks of anti-government protests in which 219 people had died; on 17 January an interim government headed by the prime minister, Mohammed Ghannouchi, promised free and fair elections within six months. **17.** Israel's defence minister, Ehud Barak, left the Labour party to form his own 'Independence' faction, and was joined by four other Labour members of the Knesset. **18.** The Special Tribunal for Lebanon issued a sealed indictment for the assassination of Rafiq Hariri; it was replaced with a new indictment on 6 May. A suicide bomb attack at a police recruitment station in Tikrit, Iraq, killed 65 people; the next day, two attacks in Baquba left more than 45 people dead and 74 wounded. **22.** In Istanbul, two days of negotiations between Iran and six other nations over Iran's nuclear programme reached an impasse; Iran demanded the lifting of UN sanctions against the country, while delegates from Britain, China, France, Germany, Russia and the USA demanded the suspension of Iran's nuclear enrichment programme. **25.** Popular protests began in Egypt, demanding the end of Hosni Mubarak's 30-year presidency. The Hezbollah-backed Najib Mikrati was appointed prime minister-designate of Lebanon and began trying to form a government. **31.** In Egypt, the army announced that it would not use force against the protesters.

FEBRUARY 2011

1. President Mubarak of Egypt said that he would stand down in September 2011, but this failed to placate the demonstrators and protests continued. **3.** In anti-government demonstrations in Egypt, ten people died and hundreds were injured. In Yemen, 20,000 demonstrators protested against President Ali Abdullah Saleh's 32 years in power; protests continued daily for weeks. The government of Algeria lifted its 19-year state of emergency in order to alleviate nascent anti-government sentiment in the country. **11.** After 18 days of mass protests, Hosni Mubarak stepped down as president of Egypt, handing executive power to the Supreme Council of Egyptian Armed Forces; on 13 February the Supreme Council dissolved parliament and suspended the constitution in readiness for a referendum. **13.** In Iran, activists were arrested in a government attempt to prevent planned protests. **14.** Thousands of opposition supporters demonstrated in Tehran in the largest demonstrations since the disputed presidential election in 2009. Protests continued in Bahrain. Members of the Palestinian government in the West Bank resigned after leaked documents showed that negotiators had made major concessions to Israel in 2008; the new government was asked to plan for elections in September 2011. **15.** Pro-democracy protesters took control of part of the Bahraini capital, Manama, and established a camp on the Pearl roundabout. **16.** In Benghazi, Libya, the arrest of a human-rights campaigner led to demonstrations and clashes with police in which at least two people were killed and 38 injured; military suppression and airstrikes nationwide in the three following days left around 230 people dead, prompting the resignation of many senior diplomats. **17.** Security forces destroyed the protest camp on the Pearl roundabout in Manama, Bahrain, killing three protesters and injuring hundreds; two days later protesters reclaimed the site after the army was ordered to withdraw by the crown prince. **18.** A 'day of rage' saw pro-democracy demonstrations in Bahrain, Egypt, Jordan, Kuwait, Libya, Syria and Yemen; many ended in bloodshed after security forces fired on protesters. In Iran, government supporters marched through Tehran, demanding the execution of opposition leaders. **21.** Libya's second largest city, Benghazi, on the Mediterranean coast, was captured by anti-Gaddafi rebels after days of fighting. **22.** Colonel Gaddafi appeared on television to refute rumours that he had fled to Venezuela, and ordered his forces to crush the uprising; thousands fled to the Egyptian and Tunisian borders and several oil companies suspended production. **23.** Opposition supporters took control of Misratah, in western Libya. **26.** The USA froze around $30bn (£18.45bn) of Colonel Gaddafi's assets in response to the Libyan government's crackdown on anti-government protests; France began to send aid aircraft to the rebel-held town of Benghazi.

MARCH 2011

10. Haji Yar Mohammad Karzai, a cousin of President Karzai of Afghanistan, was shot dead by NATO forces during a night raid; he had been mistaken for the father of a Taliban commander. **13.** After two weeks of intense fighting, pro-Gaddafi forces recaptured Brega from the rebels. The Israeli government approved plans to build 500 housing units in West Bank settlements. **14.**

Responding to a request from Bahrain's ruling family, Saudi Arabian troops entered Bahrain to help to quell the two-month uprising; martial law was declared the next day. **17.** The UN security council voted unanimously in favour of imposing an air exclusion zone over Libya, and authorised all measures necessary to protect civilians; two days later, NATO forces launched air and missile attacks on Libyan military facilities. **18.** President Ali Abdullah Saleh of Yemen declared a state of emergency, banning the carrying of arms by anyone, after government snipers fired on an activists' camp in Sana'a, killing 45 protesters. In Syria, security forces killed two demonstrators at a rally demanding political freedom in the southern city of Deraa. In Bahrain, the monument on the Pearl roundabout in Manama was demolished by the government. **19.** NATO carried out air strikes against pro-Gaddafi forces advancing on Benghazi. **22.** Moshe Katsav, a former president of Israel, was sentenced to seven years in prison after being convicted of rape and other sexual offences. **26.** Demonstrators protested in towns throughout Syria as unrest spread from the Deraa area; protests continued for months, particularly after prayers on Fridays, with government forces using extreme force against the demonstrators. **26.** Libyan rebels retook Ajdabiya. **27.** Libyan rebels captured Brega, Ras Lanuf, Uqayla and Bin Jawad, putting all of the oil areas in rebel hands. **30.** Libya's foreign minister, Mousa Kousa, defected to the UK.

APRIL 2011

6. Around 300 people fleeing civil unrest in north Africa died when their boat capsized south of Sicily. **7–10.** Israeli forces and Hamas fighters in Gaza exchanged air and mortar fire for three days, until leaders on both sides appealed for calm on 10 April; the clashes left 19 Palestinians dead and wounded civilians on both sides. **15.** Pro-reform demonstrations in the suburbs of Damascus, the Syrian capital, and in Deraa led to the deaths of around 90 people; at least 130 people had already been killed in weekly protests that had been gaining momentum since mid-March. **16.** Fighting in the western Libyan city of Misrata intensified, with troops loyal to Colonel Gaddafi reportedly using cluster bombs against the civilian population; by the end of April over 1,000 people had died in the city. **18.** Syrian security forces opened fire on 5,000 anti-government demonstrators in Homs, Syria's third-largest city, killing two people. **19.** The Syrian government approved the lifting of the country's 48-year state of emergency. **22.** Thousands of protestors attended pro-democracy demonstrations throughout Syria; 100 people were killed by government security forces. **23.** In Syria, 12 mourners were killed as they buried those killed during the previous day's demonstrations; two Syrian MPs resigned their seats in the legislature. **24.** Following protests by thousands of people in Sana'a, President Ali Abdullah Saleh of Yemen vowed to leave office within 30 days and hand over power to his prime minister. **30.** A NATO airstrike on targets in Tripoli, Libya, killed one of Colonel Gaddafi's sons and three of his grandchildren; western embassies throughout Tripoli were ransacked the following day.

MAY 2011

4. Leaders of the rival Palestinian groups Hamas and Fatah met for the first time in five years and agreed to form an interim national unity government; the agreement, brokered by Egypt and signed in Cairo, anticipated Palestine-wide legislative and presidential elections within a year. **10.** An EU arms embargo on Syria and sanctions against 13 government members came into force; the penalties came after nearly four months of protests in the country in which around 800 demonstrators had been killed by security forces and over 7,000 arrested. **11.** In Yemen, government forces clashed with defecting Yemeni troops during pro-democracy demonstrations, leaving 18 people dead. **12.** NATO airstrikes in Libya killed six people. **15.** Palestinian protestors clashed with Israeli troops on the Israeli border with Syria, Jordan and Lebanon; at least 12 people died and hundreds were injured.

JUNE 2011
2. After President Ali Abdullah Saleh of Yemen refused to sign an exit agreement brokered by Saudi Arabia and other Gulf states, there were running battles in the streets of Sana'a that left 41 people dead. **4.** A missile hit the president of Yemen's compound, killing three guards and a cleric. **6.** Over 100 people were killed in Syria in continuing protests against the ruling regime; the protests were triggered by the president's decision to cut off internet connections in all the major cities. Libyan rebels captured Yafran, consolidating their hold on the western mountains. Egypt's transitional government agreed a $3bn (£1.8bn) loan from the International Monetary Fund to help stabilise the country's economy; Egypt's former finance minister Youssef Boutros-Ghali was sentenced *in absentia* to 30 years in jail for profiteering and abusing state assets. **11.** In Libya, a heavy aerial bombardment of the besieged rebel enclave of Misrata by pro-Gaddafi forces left 31 rebels dead. **12.** In Turkey's general election, the incumbent Justice and Development party won over half the seats in the legislature. **17.** It was feared that the violence in Syria had spilled over into

Lebanon after clashes between Alawites and Sunnis in Tripoli. Ayman al-Zawahiri, an Egyptian militant, was declared the successor to Osama bin Laden as leader of al-Qaeda. **21.** Former president Ben Ali of Tunisia and his wife Leila were found guilty of theft *in absentia*; the couple were accused of unlawful possession of large sums of foreign currency and artefacts after they fled the country in January. **28.** The International Criminal Court issued an arrest warrant for the Libyan leader Muammar Gaddafi and his son Saif al-Islam for crimes against humanity; the Libyan government dismissed the warrants, claiming they were based on 'falsified charges'. **30.** Violent protests took place in Cairo as people expressed their dissatisfaction with Egypt's military-led transitional government; around 1,000 people were injured. The Special Tribunal for Lebanon handed sealed indictments and four arrest warrants for the assassins of Rafiq Hariri to Lebanon's state prosecutor.

JULY 2011
11. Supporters of the Syrian government stormed the French and US embassies in Damascus in protest at foreign diplomats' visits to protesters in Hama. **12.** Israel's parliament passed a law preventing its citizens from calling for cultural, academic or consumer boycotts. **15.** The USA recognised the Libyan rebels as the country's legitimate government. **28.** The mayor of Kandahar, Ghulam Haider Hamidi, was killed by a suicide bomber. **29.** The military leader of the rebel forces in Libya, Abdel Fatah Younis, was found dead outside Benghazi; the president of the Libyan National Transitional Council, Abdul Mustafa Jalil, claimed that Younis was killed by pro-Gaddafi agents en route to Benghazi from the Brega frontline, although this was later disputed by the Gaddafi regime.

OBITUARIES 2010–11

Abouna, Bishop Andreas, Chaldean Auxiliary Bishop of Baghdad (2003–10), aged 67 – *d.* 27 July 2010, *b.* 23 March 1943

Acton (4th) and Acton of Bridgnorth (life peerage, 2000), Lord, lawyer, writer and politician, aged 69 – *d.* 10 October 2010, *b.* 30 July 1941

Allison, Clive, co-founder of publishing house Allison & Busby, aged 67 – *d.* 25 July 2011, *b.* 15 June 1944

Ampthill (4th), Lord, CBE, PC, Deputy Speaker of the House of Lords (1983–2011), aged 89 – *d.* 23 April 2011, *b.* 15 October 1921

Babbitt, Milton, American composer and musical theorist, aged 94 – *d.* 29 January 2011, *b.* 10 May 1916

Baden-Powell, Lady Patience, CBE, Chief Commissioner of the Guide Association (1980–5), aged 74 – *d.* 18 December 2010, *b.* 27 October 1936

Bailey, Trevor, CBE, cricketer, aged 87 – *d.* 10 February 2011, *b.* 3 December 1923

Ballesteros, Severiano, golfer, aged 54 – *d.* 7 May 2011, *b.* 9 April 1957

Baillie, William, painter, president, Royal Scottish Academy (1990–8), aged 88 – *d.* 21 May 2011, *b.* 19 April 1923

Barry, John, film score composer, aged 77 – *d.* 30 January 2011, *b.* 3 November 1933

Bennett, Corinne, MBE, cathedral architect, aged 75 – *d.* 10 July 2010, *b.* 3 March 1955

Bingham of Cornhill, Lord, KG, PC, Master of the Rolls (1992–6), Lord Chief Justice (1996–2000) and Senior Lord of Appeal in Ordinary (2000–8), aged 76 – *d.* 11 September 2010, *b.* 13 October 1933

Blair, Lt.-Gen. Sir Chandos, KCVO, OBE, MC, GOC Scotland and Governor of Edinburgh Castle (1972–6), aged 91 – *d.* 22 January 2011, *b.* 25 February 1919

Bohley, Bärbel, artist and East German political activist: one of the founder members of the New Forum movement, aged 65 – *d.* 11 September 2010, *b.* 24 May 1945

Boston of Faversham, Lord, QC, Deputy Speaker of the House of Lords (1991–2008), aged 81 – *d.* 23 July 2011, *b.* 21 March 1930

Boxall, Tony, photographer, aged 81 – *d.* 18 December 2010, *b.* 15 December 1929

Bryan, Sir Arthur, chair of Wedgwood (1968–86), aged 87 – *d.* 11 February 2011, *b.* 4 March 1923

Burton, Raymond, CBE, clothing retailer and founder of Topshop, aged 93 – *d.* 5 February 2011, *b.* 3 November 1917

Byatt, Sir Hugh, CMG, KCVO, Ambassador to Angola (1978–81), Sao Tome and Principe (1980–1) and Portugal (1981–6), aged 83 – *d.* 16 February 2011, *b.* 27 August 1927

Carnegy of Lour, Baroness, FRSA, aged 85 – *d.* 9 November 2010, *b.* 28 March 1925

Chernomyrdin, Viktor, Prime Minister of Russia (1992–8), aged 72 – *d.* 3 November 2010, *b.* 9 April 1938

Chopping, Dr Peter, radiation oncologist and wartime medical officer, aged 93 – *d.* 16 November 2010, *b.* 4 January 1917

Clarke, Sir Ellis, GCMG, President of Trinidad and Tobago (1976–86), aged 93 – *d.* 30 December 2010, *b.* 28 December 1917

Clayton, Dame Barbara, DBE, professor of pathology, aged 88 – *d.* 11 January 2011, *b.* 2 September 1922

Cleminson, Sir James, KBE, MC, industrialist, aged 89 – *d.* 14 September 2010, *b.* 31 August 1921

Clucas, Sir Kenneth, KCB, Permanent Secretary Department of Prices and Consumer Protection (1974–9) and Department of Trade (1979–82), aged 88 – *d.* 27 August 2010, *b.* 18 November 1921

Cohen, Raymond, violinist, aged 91 – *d.* 28 January 2011, *b.* 27 July 1919

Cooper, Sir Henry, OBE, boxer (1954–71), aged 76 – *d.* 1 May 2011, *b.* 3 May 1934

Cossiga, Francesco, president of Italy (1985–92), aged 82 – *d.* 17 August 2010, *b.* 26 July 1928

Coverley, Bernadine, writer, journalist and muse of Lucian Freud, aged 68 – *d.* 24 July 2011, *b.* 4 August 1942

Crossland, Prof. Sir Bernard, FRS, mechanical engineer, aged 87 – *d.* 17 January 2011, *b.* 20 October 1923

Curtis, Tony, actor, aged 85 – *d.* 29 September 2010, *b.* 3 June 1925

Day, Corinne, photographer, aged 48 – *d.* 27 August 2010, *b.* 19 February 1962

Day, Robin, furniture designer, aged 95 – *d.* 9 November 2010, *b.* 25 May 1915

Dhrangadhara, HH Maharaja Shriraj Sahib of Halvad, KCIE, last ruling Maharaja of Halvad Dhrangadhara, India (1942–7) and the last survivng recipient of the Order of the Indian Empire, aged 87 – *d.* 1 August 2010, *b.* 3 March 1923

Dominic, Zoë, photographer, aged 90 – *d.* 11 January 2011, *b.* 4 July 1920

Elliott of Morpeth, Lord, aged 90 – *d.* 20 May 2011, *b.* 11 December 1920

Eichinger, Bernd, German film producer, aged 61 – *d.* 24 January 2011, *b.* 11 April 1949

Edwards, Blake, American film director, aged 88 – *d.* 16 December 2010, *b.* 26 July 1922

Evans, Larry, American chess grandmaster, aged 78 – *d.* 15 November 2010, *b.* 23 March 1932

Feller, Bob, American baseball pitcher, aged 92 – *d.* 15 December 2010, *b.* 3 November 1918

Fenn, Prof. John, American analytical chemist, joint winner of the Nobel Prize in Chemistry (2002), aged 93 – *d.* 12 December 2010, *b.* 15 June 1917

Foot, Philippa, philosopher, aged 90 – *d.* 3 October 2010, *b.* 3 October 1920

Freud, Lucian, OM, CH, figurative painter, aged 88 – *d.* 20 July 2011, *b.* 8 December 1922

Fyfe of Fairfield, Lord, aged 69 – *d.* 1 February 2011, *b.* 10 April 1941

Gallie, Phil, Conservative MP for Ayr (1992–7), Conservative MSP for Scotland South (1999–2007), aged 71 – *d.* 24 January 2011, *b.* 3 June 1939

Gems, Iris (Pam), playwright, aged 85 – *d.* 13 May 2011, *b.* 1 August 1925

Gibson, Robin, OBE, chief curator of the National Portrait Gallery (1994–2001), aged 66 – *d.* 9 August 2010, *b.* 3 May 1944

Gorecki, Henryk, Polish composer, aged 76 – *d.* 12 November 2010, *b.* 6 December 1933

Gorst, Sir John, Conservative MP for Hendon North (1970–97), aged 82 – *d.* 31 July 2010, *b.* 28 June 1928

Gouriet, John, right-wing political activist and joint founder of the National Association for Freedom, aged 75 – *d.* 4 September 2010, *b.* 1 June 1935

Gross, John, literary critic and editor, aged 75 – *d.* 10 January 2011, *b.* 12 March 1935

Gwynn-Jones, Sir Peter, Garter King of Arms, aged 70 – *d.* 21 August 2010, *b.* 12 March 1940

Hall, Sir Basil, KCB, MC, TD, HM Procurator General and Treasury Solicitor (1975–80), aged 98 – *d.* 2 May 2011, *b.* 2 January 1918

Hanrahan, Brian, BBC foreign correspondent, aged 61 – *d.* 20 December 2010, *b.* 22 March 1949

Harris, Rosina, solicitor and expert in copyright law who became the first female senior partner of a leading London firm, aged 89 – *d.* 29 September 2010, *b.* 30 May 1921

Hawkey, Raymond, graphic designer, aged 80 – *d.* 23 August 2010, *b.* 2 February 1930

Heselden, Jimi, OBE, inventor, entrepreneur and philanthropist who earned his fortune inventing 'concertainer' units, used as fortification walls for defence forces, aged 62 – *d.* 26 September 2010, *b.* 27 March 1948

Hickman, Ron, OBE, designer who invented the 'Workmate' portable workbench, a staple for DIY enthusiasts, aged 78 – *d.* 17 February 2011, *b.* 21 October 1932

Hofmann, Peter, German operatic tenor, aged 66 – *d.* 29 November 2010, *b.* 22 August 1944

Holmes, Andy, rower, aged 51 – *d.* 24 October 2010, *b.* 15 October 1959

Howard, Anthony, CBE, journalist and broadcaster, aged 76 – *d.* 19 December 2010, *b.* 12 February 1934

Hoyland, John, painter, aged 76 – *d.* 31 July 2011, *b.* 12 October 1934

Ibbotson, Eva, children's author, aged 85 – *d.* 20 October 2010, *b.* 21 January 1925

Irons, Andy, world champion surfer, aged 32 – *d.* 2 November 2010, *b.* 24 July 1978

Jacques, Brian, children's author, aged 71 – *d.* 5 February 2011, *b.* 15 June 1939

Jenkins, Elizabeth, novelist and biographer, aged 104 – *d.* 5 September 2010, *b.* 31 October 1905

Johnson Smith, Sir Geoffrey, BBC television journalist and Conservative MP (1959–2001), aged 86 – *d.* 12 August 2010, *b.* 16 April 1924

Johnstone, Gwyneth, painter, aged 96 – *d.* 8 December 2010, *b.* 1914

Kermode, Sir Frank, literary scholar and critic, aged 90 – *d.* 17 August 2010, *b.* 29 November 1919

King-Smith, Dick, OBE, children's aithor, aged 88 – *d.* 4 January 2011, *b.* 27 March 1922

Knowles, Wyn, editor of the BBC Radio 4 programme *Woman's Hour* (1971–83), aged 86 – *d.* 13 July 2010, *b.* 30 July 1923

Lachhiman Gurung, VC, Havildar, Gurkha rifleman decorated in Burma (1945), aged 93 – *d.* 12 December 2010, *b.* 1917

Laidlaw, Sir Christophor Laidlaw, industrialist, aged 88 – *d.* 27 November 2010, *b.* 9 August 1922

Langley, R. F., poet and teacher, aged 72 – *d.* 25 January 2011, *b.* 23 October 1938

Larsen, Bent, Danish chess grandmaster, aged 75 – *d.* 9 September 2010, *b.* 4 March 1935

Leach, Admiral of the Fleet Sir Henry, GCB, Chief of Naval Staff and First Sea Lord (1979–82), aged 87– *d.* 26 April 2011, *b.* 18 November 1923

Le Bailly, Vice-Adm. Sir Louis, KBE, CB, naval engineer, aged 95 – *d.* 3 October 2010, *b.* 18 July 1915

Livsey of Talgarth, CBE, Lord, Liberal MP (1985–8), Liberal Democrat MP (1988–92) for Brecon and Radnor; Liberal Democrat MP for Brecon and Radnorshire (1997–2001); Leader, Welsh Liberal Democrats (1988–92 and 1997–2001), aged 75 – *d.* 16 September 2010, *b.* 2 May 1935

Lofthouse, Nat, OBE, footballer, aged 85 – *d.* 15 January 2011, *b.* 27 August 1925

Lowther, Sir John, KCVO, CBE, Lord Lieutenant for Northamptonshire (1984–98), aged 87 – *d.* 11 April 2011, *b.* 17 November 1923

Lubbock, Tom, art critic and illustrator, aged 53 – *d.* 9 January 2011, *b.* 28 December 1957

Lumet, Sidney, American film director, aged 86 – *d.* 9 April 2011, *b.* 25 June 1924

McKenna, T. P., Irish actor, aged 81 – *d.* 13 February 2011, *b.* 7 September 1929

McIntosh of Haringey, Rt. Hon. Lord, Labour peer, aged 77 – *d.* 27 August 2010, *b.* 30 April 1933

Mahon, Sir (John) Denis, CH, CBE, art historian, collector and philanthropist, aged 100 – *d.* 24 April 2011, *b.* 8 November 1910

Maitland, Sir Donald, GCMG, OBE, diplomat and public servant, aged 88 – *d.* 22 August 2010, *b.* 16 August 1922

Malcolm, Mary, BBC television announcer (1948–56), aged 92 – *d.* 13 October 2010, *b.* 15 March 1918

Mantle, Rt. Revd John, Bishop of Brechin, Scottish Episcopal Church (2005–10), aged 64 – *d.* 29 November 2010, *b.* 3 April 1946

Mark, Sir Robert, GBE, QPM, Commissioner of the Metropolitan Police (1972–7), aged 93 – *d.* 30 September 2010, *b.* 13 March 1917

Marsden, Brian, astronomer, aged 73 – *d.* 18 November 2010, *b.* 5 August 1937

Marsh, Lord, PC, Labour MP for Greenwich (1959–71), chair of British Rail (1971–6), aged 83 – *d.* 29 July 2011, *b.* 14 March 1928

Matthews, Bernard, CBE, CVO, turkey farmer, aged 80 – *d.* 25 November 2010, *b.* 24 January 1930

Menke, Sally, American film editor who collaborated with director Quentin Tarantino on all of his films, aged 56 – d. 27 September 2010, b. 17 December 1953

Miller, David, OBE, Ambassador to Armenia (1995–7), aged 73 –d. 30 November 2010, b. 26 March 1937

Mills, Dame Barbara, DBE, QC, Director of Public Prosecutions (1992–8), aged 70 – d. 28 May 2011, b. 10 August 1940

Monson (11th), Lord, aged 78 – d. 12 February 2011, b. 3 May 1932

Morgan, Edwin, OBE, national poet for Scotland, aged 90 – d. 19 August 2010, b. 27 April 1920

Neal, Patricia, actor, aged 84 – d. 8 August 2010, b. 20 January 1926

Nielsen, Leslie, Canadian actor, aged 84 – d. 28 November 2010, b. 11 February 1926

Olsen, Ken, American computing pioneer, aged 84 – d. 6 February 2011, b. 20 February 1926

Onslow (7th), Earl of, aged 73 – d. 14 May 2011, b. 28 February 1938

Oppenheim, Dennis, artist, aged 72 – d. 21 January 2011, b. 6 September 1938

Oxford and Asquith (2nd), Earl of, KCMG, Governor and Commander-in-Chief Seychelles (1962–7), aged 94 – d. 16 January 2011, b. 22 April 1916

Pearson, Katie, television producer, author and columnist, aged 51 – d. 10 December 2010, b. 6 June 1959

Penn, Arthur, American film and stage director, aged 88 – d. 28 September 2010, b. 27 September 1922

Pilkington of Oxenford, Revd Canon Lord, aged 77 – d. 14 February 2011, b. 5 September 1933

Pitt, Ingrid, actor, aged 73 – d. 23 November 2010, b. 21 November 1937

Postlethwaite, Pete, OBE, actor, aged 64 – d. 2 January 2011, b. 7 February 1946

Price, Dame Margaret, soprano opera singer, aged 69 – d. 28 January 2011, b. 13 April 1941

Puddefoot, Susanne, journalist, editor of the *The Times* 'Women's Page' (1966–70), aged 75 – d. 13 September 2010, b. 3 October 1934

Radcliffe, Anthony, curator and scholar of sculpture, Keeper of Sculpture at the Victoria & Albert Museum (1979–89), aged 77 – d. 1 January 2011, b. 23 February 1933

Rafferty, Gerry, singer and songwriter, aged 63 – d. 4 January 2011, b. 16 April 1947

Rawlins, Surgeon Vice-Adm. Sir John, KBE, Medical Director-General of the Royal Navy (1977–80), aged 89 – d. 27 July 2011, b. 12 May 1922

Rayner, Claire, OBE, agony aunt, writer and broadcaster, aged 79 – d. 11 October 2010, b. 2 January 1931

Reid, Jimmy, Scottish trade unionist, aged 78 – d. 11 August 2010, b. 9 July 1932

Richards, Dean, footballer, aged 36 – d. 26 February 2011, b. 9 June 1974

Robinson, Robert, television and radio presenter, aged 83 – d. 12 August 2011, b. 17 December 1927

Rodger of Earlsferry, Lord, Lord of Appeal in Ordinary (2001–9), Justice of the Supreme Court (2009–11), aged 66 – d. 26 June 2011, b. 18 September 1944

Russell, Jane, American actor, aged 89 – d. 28 February 2011, b. 21 June 1921

Sanderson, Dr Ronald, psychiatrist, introduced the use of LSD for treatment of patients in Britain, aged 94 – d. 18 June 2010, b. 1 April 1916.

Sandage, Allan, American astronomer, aged 84 – d. 13 November 2010, b. 18 June 1926

Sayle, Murray, journalist and adventurer, aged 84 – d. 18 September 2010, b. 1 January 1926

Scott, Sir David, GCMG, British High Commissioner to Uganda (1967–70); New Zealand (1973–7) and Ambassador to South Africa (1976–9), aged 91 – d. 27 December 2010, b. 3 August 1919

Sellors, Sir Patrick, KCVO, ophthalmic surgeon and Surgeon Oculist to the Queen (1980–99), aged 76 – d. 30 September 2010, b. 11 February 1934

Sessions, Cdr. His Hon. Judge John, Judge Advocate of the Fleet (1995–2007), aged 69 – d. 16 June 2010, b. 8 January 1941

Shaw, Sir Brian, chair of the Port of London Authority (1993–2000), aged 77 – d. 5 February 2011, b. 21 March 1933

Shearing, Sir George, jazz pianist and composer, aged 91 – d. 14 February 2011, b. 13 August 1919

Smith, Bobby, footballer, aged 77 – d. 18 September 2010, b. 22 February 1933

Smith, Sir Cyril, MBE, Liberal and Liberal Democrat MP for Rochdale (1972–92), aged 82 – d. 3 September 2010, b. 28 June 1928

Soldner, Paul, American ceramic artist, aged 89 – d. 3 January 2011, b. 24 April 1921

Strabolgi (11th), Lord, aged 96 – d. 24 December 2010, b. 1 November 1914

Stack, Prunella, OBE, Keep-fit pioneer and leader of the Women's League of Health and Beauty, aged 96 – d. 30 December 2010, b. 28 July 1914

Stevens, Ted, US Republican senator for Alaska (1968–2009), aged 86 – d. 9 August 2010, b. 18 November 1923

Stevenson, Rt. Revd Kenneth, Bishop of Porstmouth (1995–2009), aged 61 – d. 11 January 2011, b. 9 November 1949

Strabolgi (11th), Lord, Labour politician, aged 96 – d. 24 December 2010, b. 1 November 1914

Sutherland, Dame Joan, OM, DBE, operatic soprano, aged 83 – d. 11 October 2010, b. 7 November 1926

Taylor, Dame Elizabeth, DBE, actor, aged 79 – d. 23 March 2011, b. 27 February 1932

Tennant, Sir Anthony, chief executive (1987–9), chair (1989–92) Guinness, aged 80 – d. 4 August 2011, b. 5 November 1930

Titmus, Fred, cricketer, aged 78 – d. 23 March 2011, b. 24 November 1932

Tree, Lady Anne, founder of the Fine Cell Work charity, aged 82 – d. 9 August 2010, b. 6 November 1927

Tulbahadur Pun, Lt. VC, decorated in Burma (1944), aged 88 – d. 20 April 2011, b. 23 March 1923

Wakefield, Sir Peter, KBE, CMG, Ambassador to Lebanon (1975–8) and Belgium (1979–82), aged 88 – d. 1 December 2010, b. 13 May 1922

Walker, Catherine, fashion designer, aged 65 – d. 23 September 2010, b. 27 June 1945

Walker, Rt. Revd Peter, Bishop of Ely (1977–89), aged 91 – d. 28 December 2010, b. 6 December 1919

Walters, Sir Roger, KBE, architect, aged 93 – d. 11 September 2010, b. 31 March 1917

Waterhouse, Sir Ronald, GBE, judge of the High Court of Justice, Family Division (1978–88), Queen's Bench Division (1988–96), aged 85 – *d.* 8 May 2011, *b.* 8 May 1926

Wilson, William, Labour MP for Coventry South (1964–74) and Coventry South-East (1974–83), aged 97 – *d.* 18 August 2010, *b.* 28 June 1913

Windlesham (3rd), Lord, CVO, PC, politician, television executive and president of Brasenose College, Oxford (1989–2002), aged 78 – *d.* 21 December 2010, *b.* 28 January 1932

Winehouse, Amy, singer-songwriter, aged 27 – *d.* 23 July 2011, *b.* 14 September 1983

Wisdom, Sir Norman, comic actor, aged 95 – *d.* 4 October 2010, *b.* 4 February 1915

Wood, John, CBE, actor, aged 81 – *d.* 6 August 2011, *b.* 5 July 1930

Yates, Peter, film director, aged 81 – *d.* 9 January 2011, *b.* 24 July 1929

York, Susannah, actor, aged 72 – *d.* 15 January 2011, *b.* 9 January 1939

ARCHAEOLOGY

Dr Nadia Durrani and Dr Neil Faulkner

BRITISH HOMINIDS GET OLDER

A dominant theme of recent work on the British Palaeolithic (or Old Stone Age) has been the way in which the dates of early hominid activity have been pushed back. Until recently, the oldest-known hominid remains in the UK were those of Swanscombe Man, found in a gravel quarry in Kent in the 1930s onwards. Dated to no earlier than 400,000 years ago, these postdated the great Anglian glaciation. All this changed in 1994 with the discovery of a hominid tibia in a gravel quarry at Boxgrove in Sussex, followed by two teeth a couple of years later. The remains all belonged to *Homo heidelbergensis* – essentially the European form of *Homo erectus*. Dated to around 500,000 years ago, they pushed back the hominid presence in Britain to a period before the great glaciation. A second sensational discovery by a team working at Pakenham in Suffolk in 2008 revealed flint tools and flakes in recently exposed coastal deposits dating to around 700,000 years ago. There were no fossils, but the tools proved the presence of tool-making hominids in the area at the time.

Now the picture has been pushed back yet further thanks to new dating evidence for deposits, containing flint tools and flakes, at another East Anglian coastal site: Happisburgh in Norfolk. Simon Parfitt of University College London has announced that 78 stone artefacts date to around 800,000 years ago, making them about 100,000 years older than any other tools yet found in Britain. The people who made these tools occupied what was then a marshy floodplain bordering one of the ancient courses of the River Thames. They shared this landscape with rhinos, hyenas and mammoths, whose fossil bones have been found at the site. They were present during a relatively warm interglacial, though temperatures were chillier than those of modern Britain (akin to those found in today's southern Scandinavia).

The new dating used a combination of methods. Palaeomagnetic dating of the sediments showed that they predated the last switch in the polarity of the Earth's magnetic field, which took place around 780,000 years ago. This was supported by analysis of the plant and animal remains, where the dating technique involves observing which species are present and which are not. As for the people who left these tools, specialists like Chris Stringer of the Natural History Museum and the Ancient Human Occupation of Britain project assume they were made by a hominid dubbed *Homo antecessor*, otherwise known mainly from sites in Spain, and an even earlier ancestor than Boxgrove's *Homo heidelbergensis*.

These are not the British Isles' only ancient residents whose dates are being pushed back in time: the same is true of the more recent Neanderthals. During extensive rescue excavations (involving no fewer than 75 trenches) in advance of major road improvements at the junction of the M25 and A2 south of the Dartford Crossing, two flint scrapers were found lying on a buried land surface. They were dated to around 100,000 years ago using a scientific technique called optically stimulated luminescence,

which allows the age of sediments to be estimated. Around this time, the only known hominids in Europe were the Neanderthals; previously, however, the oldest Neanderthal sites in Britain were those at Lynford Quarry in Norfolk and Coygan Cave in Carmarthenshire, both dating to around 60,000 years ago.

Pushing the Neanderthal presence back 40,000 years takes us to the early phases of the Devensian glaciation, when climate conditions were relatively severe. It is possible that roaming hunter-gatherer bands were tempted to migrate north-westwards across the land bridge that then linked Britain with the Continent by the movement of big game like mammoth.

Further grist to this particular academic mill comes from Dr Tom Higham, deputy director of the Oxford Radiocarbon Accelerator Unit, who has thrown open the debate about Neanderthal extinction with the claim that more accurate dating methods prove that fossils from Russia's Mezmaiskaya Cave are 10,000 years older than previously thought. This would push Neanderthal extinction back to almost 40,000 years ago, predating the arrival in Europe of us – anatomically modern humans – or *Homo sapiens*. This would absolve our species of responsibility for the extinction of the Neanderthals, as many models propose, whether by out-competing them for scarce food resources or something worse.

HOMES AND DECOR ALSO GET OLDER

Moving forward many millennia and the oldest dwelling yet found in Britain has been uncovered at Star Carr near Scarborough in North Yorkshire – a Mesolithic (Middle Stone Age) site dating between 9200 and 8500 BC. The house is represented by a circular post-built structure, some 3.5m in diameter, which may have been walled and roofed with reeds, turves or animal hides, and may also have had an internal hearth.

Star Carr is probably the most famous Mesolithic site in Britain, having been first investigated by Grahame Clark in 1949–51, when shale and amber beads were found, as well as red-deer antler head-dresses probably used in hunting ceremonies. However, no structures were uncovered in the early excavations, despite the wet peat-bog conditions and the opportunities for good preservation of organic material. The newly discovered house, at least 500 years older than the Mesolithic house discovered at Howick in Northumberland, is the result of new excavations being organised collaboratively by the universities of Manchester and York.

Work led by Nick Card of the Orkney Research Centre for Archaeology at the Ness of Brodgar has also been uncovering the remains of other prehistoric houses, this time of Neolithic (New Stone Age) date, c.3000 BC. A group of large rectangular stone buildings inside a massive enclosure at what is unquestionably a major ritual site is producing evidence that people painted their interiors with red, yellow and orange pigments made from ground-up iron oxide. Five separate painted stones have been found, some decorated with lines and chevrons similar to the patterns often found pecked or incised on stones both at this site and at many others where Neolithic rock-art has been found.

HENGES AND MOUNDS

Silbury Hill is famous as an artificially constructed mound near Avebury in Wiltshire, and is one of a complex of monuments that includes Avebury Ring and West Kennett Long Barrow. Silbury Hill is almost 40m high, extends across 2ha (5 acres), and dates from about 2490–2340 BC. It is formed of chalk and clay dug out of the surrounding landscape, and it is estimated that it would have required 15 years' work by 500 men to construct. It therefore represents an extraordinary investment of effort by Late Neolithic people. Its purpose is almost certainly ritual, perhaps providing a platform for ceremonies involving the worship of the sun and the moon.

What is new, is the discovery that Silbury Hill appears to have a little sister in the grounds of nearby Marlborough College. Long thought to be the motte of a Norman castle, the tree-covered mound turns out to date to 2400 BC. The discovery was made during conservation work by Donald Insall Associates in response to fears that the mound was being destabilised by tree-roots. Soil cores were bored into the 19m-high mound, and charcoal within samples taken from different levels was found to be of the same early date, making the whole mound broadly contemporary with nearby Silbury Hill. The mound was, in fact, reused by the Normans, but it had not, as previously believed, been built by them.

The Marlborough Mound was not the only new discovery in this extraordinary Late Neolithic landscape. Marden Henge, located between Pewsey and Devizes in Wiltshire, is an example of a 'superhenge' – along with Durrington Walls and Avebury in Wiltshire and Mount Pleasant in Dorset – its massive banks and ditches enclose an area around 10.5ha (26 acres). Marden is unique in having once contained a large mound at its centre – the Hatfield Barrow – comparable in scale to Silbury Hill. Antiquarian investigations by Sir Richard Colt Hoare (1758–1838) and William Cunnington (1754–1810) recovered animal bones, burnt wood, and 'two small parcels of burned human bones', but the excavators' tunnels caused the mound to collapse, and the landowner later levelled the site to fill in the ditch around it and sold off the surplus topsoil.

New excavations by English Heritage's Jim Leary have revealed a number of fascinating finds: a series of metalled surfaces forming a roadway from the henge entrance to the River Avon about 100m away; a mini henge-within-a-henge with an internal diameter of about 20m located at the south-western edge of the larger henge; and a well-preserved Neolithic house sitting on the henge bank, with associated middens (rubbish dumps) replete with pig bones, pottery and tools of bone and flint.

The Marden discoveries add to a growing corpus of evidence for the intensity and complexity of the ritual landscapes of Late Neolithic Wiltshire. Leary in particular is now questioning the primacy of Stonehenge. Traditionally, other sites have been seen as satellites or way stations on the route to a single main monument. Now it appears that Marden may, along with Avebury, represent a monument complex of comparable significance in its own right. 'Marden is the biggest of the henges,' says Leary, 'and the only one that has a mound and mini-henge within the larger henge enclosure.'

Meanwhile, research continues at Stonehenge itself, where a major focus recently has been the origin and meaning of the stones themselves. While not questioning the now well-established idea that the stones were transported from the Preseli Hills in South Wales, researchers from Leicester and Wales have identified a dozen different rock types and related these to precise source locations in the Hills. This has cast doubt on export southwards direct to the Bristol Channel via Milford Haven and raised the possibility that the stones made the more hazardous voyage out into the Irish Sea and around St David's Head. This adds weight to the results of Tim Darvill and Geoffrey Wainwright's ten years of fieldwork in the Preseli Hills, with its emphasis on the ritual significance of the region and therefore on the symbolism inherent in the stones – so that Stonehenge becomes, for them, 'Preseli in microcosm'. Work continues with the aim of 'adding more detail to our rapidly expanding knowledge of the people, places and rocks that gave Stonehenge its power'.

Another angle on the social world represented by these Late Neolithic monument complexes is afforded by analysis of human remains. Wessex Archaeology's Jacqueline McKinley has recently finished osteological analysis of the human remains of the 'Amesbury Archer' and the 'Boscombe Bowmen', two high-status burial groups of Beaker date (c.2400–1800 BC) from the vicinity of Stonehenge. The discovery that the 'Archer' (more likely primarily a metalworker) was disabled and walked with a limp, and that one of the 'Bowmen' had also suffered a serious leg injury, indicates that life 4,000 years ago was not a crude matter of survival of the fittest, but that rank and status could be achieved in other ways than physical prowess.

SKULLS, BRAINS AND GENOCIDE

British archaeology has had quite a grisly year. It has recently emerged, for example, that our ancestors, the *Homo sapiens* hunter-gatherers who occupied Cheddar Gorge around 14,700 years ago, had some rather questionable habits. Analysis of human skull-caps from Gough's Cave has revealed that these were deliberately modified by having all soft tissue scraped away after death and then the bones of the face and base of the skull systematically cut out. The cranial vaults, according to palaeo-anthropologist Silvia Bello of the Natural History Museum, were 'meticulously shaped into cups by retouching the broken edges ... all in all, it was a very painstaking process, given the tools available.' Was this evidence of cannibalism or merely post-mortem reuse of the skulls? Either way, it is likely that some sort of ritual appropriation of the power of the deceased is represented.

Fast-forward to the Early Bronze Age (c.2500–1500 BC) and we have another old story updated. Gristhorpe Man was a skeleton discovered inside a massive oak trunk in 1834. He was remarkably complete, strikingly tall, very well-fed, had a fine set of teeth and an impressive array of grave goods: skin wrappings, a bone fastening-pin, a bronze dagger with polished whalebone pommel, a bark or wicker vessel, a flint knife, two other flint flakes, a small wooden object, a fox metatarsal, pine marten phalanges, a horn ring and mistletoe berries.

A battery of scientific tests in the archaeological laboratories of Bradford University have confirmed the authenticity of the remains. Radiocarbon testing has produced a date of 2200–2020 BC for tooth dentine and femur samples, establishing beyond doubt that Gristhorpe Man is indeed Early Bronze Age in date. Bradford's Alan Ogden has since produced a facial reconstruction, so that visitors to the Rotunda Museum in Scarborough can meet their ancestor face-to-face as well as seeing the skeleton, the oak coffin and the grave-goods on display.

Fast-forward again to the Iron Age (*c.*750 BC–AD 43) and we have another example of ritual treatment of human remains. An Iron Age man with intact brain was unearthed during excavations at the University of York in 2008. A team of archaeologists, chemists, bio-archaeologists and neurologists have since been trying to fathom how the brain could have survived when all other soft tissue decayed. The remains have been radiocarbon-dated to between 673 and 482 BC, the man aged between 26 and 45, and the cause of death identified as being due to hanging, followed by decapitation, with the head buried separately from the body. Fractures on the second neck vertebra are consistent with traumatic spinal dislocation, and a cluster of nine horizontal cut-marks on the front of the bone indicate decapitation. The assumption is that this represents a gruesome ritual killing. It is still not entirely clear why the brain tissue survived so well.

Excavation of an Iron Age hillfort at Fin Cop in the Derbyshire Peak District has revealed disturbing evidence of the genocidal violence of Iron Age warfare. Clive Waddington's team dug two trenches across the main defensive ditch around the site and revealed a total of nine individuals. Stratigraphic evidence implies that these burials were placed in the ditch when the hillfort was abandoned, and radiocarbon dating of the remains places this at some point between 410 and 40 BC. What is particularly disturbing is that all of the bodies were of women and children, and, if the excavated sample is in any way representative, there could be hundreds of others lying in other parts of the ditch fill.

Waddington sees the discovery as a hammer-blow to currently fashionable ideas about hillforts being mere 'symbolic statements in the landscape' and prehistoric society being essentially cooperative and peaceful. 'The evidence for the violent sacking of Fin Cop, the killing of women and children and their unceremonious disposal in large numbers in the ditch, suggests a very different experience – at least in this case.' This seems confirmed by the fact that the ramparts were hastily constructed, and the ditch and a second circuit were unfinished when the site was abandoned, implying a hasty improvisation of defence in some sort of military emergency.

OLD GODS AND A NEW KING

The excavation of bullion and hoards of Late Iron Age and Roman date is throwing new light on the personalities, the deities and the troubles of this period. A metal-detectorist has unearthed the only example of a new type of Celtic coin inscribed with the name of a previously unknown king. The gold stater shows a horse and horseman on the obverse (front face) of the coin along with the inscriptions *EPPI* and *ANAREVITO*.

The *EPPI* refers to Eppillus, or 'Little Horse', a ruler of the Atrebates tribe who claimed descent from Commius, a former Celtic ally of Julius Caesar in Gaul who fled across the Channel to set up his own kingdom in West Sussex and Hampshire. Eppillus eventually proclaimed himself *Rex Calleva*, 'King of Silchester', and later took control of north and east Kent.

ANAREVITO, however, is unknown. He does not claim to be the son of Eppillus – there is no F meaning 'son' before his name – but clearly there is a close relationship. But was he a relative or a leading lieutenant, a successor or a co-ruler? We do not know. We can assume that his rule was very brief, given that his coins are clearly very scarce indeed. The discovery adds another small part to the political jigsaw puzzle of Britain immediately before the Roman Conquest.

The Celtic god Toutatis (aka Totatis and Teutates), on the other hand, has long been known. It is his and his worshippers' whereabouts in Britain that have been mysterious. Adam Daubney of the Portable Antiquities Scheme (PAS) has been plotting the location of a series of recent metal-detected finds of enigmatic finger-rings inscribed *TOT* or some other abbreviation. Such rings numbered only seven in 2001, but the development of the PAS over the last decade, with its network of archaeological finds liaison officers dedicated to recording metal-detected and other chance finds, has seen the total soar to 68 – far more than for any other deity in Roman Britain.

Dating to the second and third centuries AD, these rings show a very tight cluster in the former territory of the Corieltauvi (a region centred on modern Lincolnshire), implying that Toutatis may have been the patron deity of this particular Celtic tribe. This may, in turn, imply a link with Celtic tribal groups on the Continent from whom the leaders of the Corieltauvi were descended, since the worship of Toutatis is also well-known in parts of Gaul and beyond. The discovery is yet another in a steady stream of new insights that we owe to the systematic identification, recording and plotting of finds, mainly of metal-detected metallic artefacts, through the cooperation of the PAS and metal-detectorists.

Mithras, the Persian saviour god, is another deity worshipped in Roman Britain whose reach has been further revealed by new archaeological discoveries. One of two carved altar stones found in East Lothian has been shown to bear an inscription dedicating the monument to Mithras, extending the worship of this deity – popular especially among army officers and traders – further north than ever before. The altars were found during the redevelopment of a cricket pavilion at Musselburgh, about 5 miles east of Edinburgh. They are almost certainly related to a second century AD Roman fort at Inveresk, just under a mile away, excavated by Ian Richmond in 1946.

ROMAN HOARDS

Metal-detectorists sometimes make one-off spectacular discoveries, like the Frome Hoard in Somerset, which comprised a large ceramic container filled to the brim with what turned out to be no less than 52,000 Roman coins – the largest single Roman coin hoard ever discovered in Britain. This, too, was a PAS project, with the pot of coins shipped to the British Museum to be studied by a team led by PAS coin expert Sam Moorhead. The coins ranged in date from AD 253 to 293, including 766 coins of the rebel emperor Carausius (AD 286–293); the presence in quantity of his coins, but the absence of any of his successor, the rebel emperor Allectus, allows a tight date to be proposed for the deposition of the hoard.

Each of the 'radiate' coins forming the hoard had a buying power in today's money of around 50p, making the entire deposit worth about £25,000 – relatively speaking, a much more significant sum than it would be today. Debate rages about the purpose of such hoards, with specialists divided between those who tend to favour ritual interpretations – seeing hoards as offerings to the gods – and those who prefer utilitarian ones, seeing them as caches of valuables in troubled times.

The latter interpretation is supported by another hoard of similar date that also came to light last year. The hoard of 1,250 coins, also deposited in a ceramic container, was found on the site of Colchester's former army barracks, buried in the fill of one of the great ditches that formed the defences of the Iron Age *oppidum*. The latest coins imply deposition in AD 270 or 271, which fits a pattern of intensive hoard-deposition in the early AD 270s in coastal areas around much of southern Britain. The assumption is that these areas were vulnerable to endemic seaborne raiding at this time – making the hoards safety caches rather than ritual deposits.

The richest period of Roman hoarding was about a century later, and among the richest of all Romano-British hoards was the Hoxne Hoard from Suffolk. The haul of gold and silver artefacts found in 1992 is, in fact, one of the richest hoards ever found anywhere in the Roman Empire. Catherine Johns spent the last two decades of her career at the British Museum studying the hoard, and recently published a major monograph on the subject. The objects had been buried in a wooden chest and included 29 pieces of gold jewellery, a dozen silver vessels, nearly 100 silver spoons, about 40 other silver objects, and a cache of 14,865 gold and silver coins. The latest of the coins were minted in AD 407–408, and it is these that give the date of deposition at the very end of the Roman period.

The Hoxne Hoard is one of a series of comparable Late Roman hoards from Britain that includes those from Mildenhall, Thetford, Water Newton, Corbridge, and Traprain Law. The impression is twofold. First, that Britain contained some exceptionally rich people in the dying days of Roman rule and, second, that the security situation was dire, with the rich burying caches of precious objects and then either fleeing or perishing so that they were unable to recover them. The Hoxne Hoard is symbolic of both a golden age and an imminent dark age.

A LUMP OF RUSTY OLD IRON

Possibly the most important single archaeological discovery of the year was a single lump of rusty old iron. The object was found in the base of a 'sunken featured building', a structure commonly found on Early to Middle Anglo-Saxon settlement sites, characterised by having a floor suspended over a rectangular pit. The structure was found on a site at Lyminge in Kent being excavated by a team led by Gabor Thomas of Reading University. The artefacts associated with the iron object included jewellery, glass and pottery of seventh century AD date. The iron object proved to be a coulter, an upright blade for cutting the sod before turning by the plough-share, and one of the distinguishing features of a heavy plough.

Previously, the earliest use of such ploughs had been thought to date to the Late Anglo-Saxon period, perhaps as late as the 11th century. The advantage of the heavy plough is that it allows heavy clay soils to be cultivated and for deeply buried nutrients to be tapped to keep the land in good heart; lighter ploughs tend merely to 'scratch' the surface. The presence of an iron coulter in a seventh century deposit shows that Anglo-Saxon farmers were able to develop a fully medieval system of farming some four centuries before the Norman Conquest. The significance of this discovery in terms of labour productivity, agricultural output and population growth is impossible to exaggerate. The impact of the heavy plough on life in Britain would have been as transformative as the introduction of the steam-engine or electric power in a later period.

TV HIGHS AND BUDGETARY LOWS

Time Team, the longest-running TV archaeology series ever, broadcast its 200th programme last year. Its success is due to the clever combination of a race against time, a group of eccentric but likeable characters, a mystery to solve, the excitement of fast-paced field discovery and an unfolding narrative. None of the various attempts to replicate the *Time Team* formula in slightly modified form by other broadcasters has really succeeded, proving the perfect pitch of the original in all respects.

If *Time Team* is the popular face of British archaeology, transforming it from a rather esoteric pursuit to such an appealing subject at university that undergraduate numbers doubled in a decade, then the aforementioned Portable Antiquity Scheme is perhaps the most solid practical achievement. The PAS has created a direct link between archaeologists and thousands of amateur investigators, so as to accumulate a vast corpus of new data for analysis and research. At the same time professional rescue archaeology was booming, with development-driven, contractor-funded excavations providing employment for thousands of field archaeologists and an unending stream of new sites evaluated and recorded.

Suddenly, in the wake of the coalition government's cuts, that world has gone. Thousands of archaeologists have either lost their jobs or found it impossible to get new work when old contracts were terminated. Professional digging units have been shrunk down to core staff, and a wave of redundancies is rippling through museums, heritage agencies and university departments. The cuts are set to change the face of British archaeology as they threaten to do to every other part of British life. The future is uncertain.

ARCHITECTURE

John Hitchman

LONDON 2012 OLYMPIC PARK, STRATFORD, LONDON

The long-awaited London Olympic Games will for many people be the defining event of 2012, and much attention has focused on the enormous construction programme that has been put in place to provide the various sporting venues that will adorn the lavishly landscaped Olympic Park in East London's Lea Valley. Chief among these is the Olympic Stadium, venue for the opening and closing ceremonies, and the track and field events that lie at the core of the Olympic athletic tradition. Other high-profile venues include the Aquatics Centre for swimming and diving, the Velodrome and associated Velopark for cycling, and arenas for handball, basketball and Paralympic events, aside from the many support facilities such as the Energy Centre, the Media Centre and the Athletes' Village.

OLYMPIC STADIUM
Architect: Populous

Construction of the £500m Olympic Stadium started in May 2008 and, refreshingly for such a high-profile building, it has been completed on time and under budget. A final turf-laying ceremony on 31 March 2011 marked the end of construction in readiness for the remaining temporary works and fitting-out activities to be undertaken prior to final completion of the running track surface. In keeping with the culture of financial restraint following the global economic crisis, the new stadium provides an object lesson in economy and simplicity, in marked contrast to the extraordinary complexity and over-engineering of the 'Bird's Nest' stadium of the 2008 Beijing Games.

'Low carbon' and 'environmentally sustainable' have been important determining criteria in the design of the Games' facilities and the Stadium is witness to this – it is the lightest Olympic stadium yet in its use of steel (10,000 tonnes) and has been designed so that a substantial proportion of seating can be demounted after the Games as it reverts to legacy mode (a reconfigured football stadium). The stadium provides for 80,000 seats, arranged in an elliptical bowl, for the most part in two simple tiers, under a partially enclosing lightweight polyester fabric perimeter roof structure, around the outer edge of which are mounted 14 triangulated lighting towers, the effect of which is to give the structure the semblance of a jewelled coronet.

The stadium is contained within two branches of the River Lea, while further infrastructure constraints result in a very tight site area for the building. To avoid encroaching on these, reductions were made in the extent of public facilities, concourses, shops and food outlets to be provided within the stadium itself, with a substantial proportion housed outside in separate pods at ground level. This facilitated a much more compact and lightweight design than would otherwise have been possible. The site slopes away to the west and this has been exploited by locating athletes' changing rooms and warm-up areas, support and administration facilities,

together with drop-off areas and an Olympic Family entrance in a basement structure supporting the main circulation podium level that surrounds the stadium structure.

From the main podium level, access into the stadium is simple and direct, beneath the black-painted, inclined steel columns and trusses supporting the precast concrete tiers of the upper level seating. The stark black-and-white colour scheme of the encircling concourse is enlivened by vivid splashes of colour introduced into the free-standing toilet blocks placed between the main structural supports and through coloured glass balustrades lining the access stairs to the upper tiers. These enable exciting shafts of coloured light to filter down to the concourse and provide a subtle aid to way-finding as the colours change from zone to zone.

The lower, permanent tier of seating is formed as a concrete bowl, above which the main supporting steelwork was erected. This takes the form of 112 raking steel columns, which support the upper tier terracing. Above this, a 13m-high, white-painted tubular steel lattice compression truss circles the stadium, supported on inclined V-shaped pairs of white-painted steel columns, the resulting triangulated framing patterns defining the outward 'exoskeleton' appearance of the Games' centrepiece. The lightweight roof membrane is supported from a network of tension cables operating between the outer truss and an inner tension ring, rather in the manner of a bicycle wheel laid horizontally (with an open ring rather than a solid hub at its centre).

Leaning forward from their support points on the inner ring, triangular lighting towers are restrained by cables from the perimeter truss and tied to intermediate tripod frames springing from the inner ring of the truss. The skyline is therefore broken up by a complicated filigree of struts and cables, which contributes to the generally festive flavour of the whole concept.

OLYMPIC VELODROME
Architect: Hopkins Architects

On its formal opening in February 2011, the £90m Olympic Velodrome became the first of the Olympic Park venues to be completed. Sited at the north end of the park, it forms the centrepiece of what will be a permanent Velopark with a road circuit and BMX and mountain bike courses alongside. The design team for the Velodrome was selected in 2007 after a design competition judged by a panel that included leading architects and Olympic cycling gold medallist Sir Chris Hoy. The project has benefited from a degree of clarity surrounding its use both during the Games and in legacy mode afterwards. Consequently it will be one of the least altered of the venues when it is turned over to regular use by cycling clubs (who made valuable contributions to the briefing process) and local schools, while periodically hosting larger regional and national cycling events.

Any building housing a cycle track comes with its own particular set of design constraints and problems. Perhaps the most obvious is the characteristic geometry of the racing track, with its steeply banked curves at each end, here as steep as 47°, which have a significant impact on the layout of spectator seating. Then there are environmental issues to manage. Racing cyclists prefer a warm temperature for competition, typically between 26–28°C, as the resulting lower air density enables them to move faster through the air, albeit by fractions of a second, while spectators need to be kept cool and comfortable, particularly in hot weather and with capacity crowds in attendance, as during the Games.

A further specific and local constraint concerned the discovery on the site of a large quantity of contaminated soil. In order to minimise the cost of excavation therefore, the building was raised out of the ground by 1.6m, the extra elevation lending the building a greater presence on the site than its slim sectional profile might otherwise have commanded.

With occupancy levels likely to be relatively low once the Games have finished, the designers sought to make the building as compact and economical as possible, with a sophisticated engineering input mindful of the advanced technology of modern day racing cycles. The developed concept split the 6,000 capacity seating into upper and lower tiers, 2,500 in the lower section, 3,500 above. This enables the upper tier to be closed off for normal occupancy levels when the fewer numbers of spectators can be concentrated track-side. A dramatic double curvature roof structure spans the seating areas and track, poised over a continuous perimeter concourse with full-height glazing around the outside, affording views down onto the track and, thanks to its raised level, out over the surrounding park. The visibility of side walls and roof together give this venue a strong visual, almost sculptural, impact around the site – its form at once slim, lean, taut and elegant.

The roof structure utilises a double curvature lightweight tensioned cable net as the primary support structure and seems destined to earn the building the soubriquet 'the Pringle', its shape closely resembling that of the popular crisp. The net is built up from pairs of galvanised steel cables clamped together on a grid, the whole assembly being put together on the ground before being lifted into place and tensioned against a perimeter ring beam.

The ring beam sweeps up over the main banks of seating fronting the track straights and sweeps down around the banked curved ends of the track where just a couple of rows of seats continue around the perimeter of the track to maintain continuity and atmosphere, an important feature for competitors. The outward visible form of the roof therefore echoes the banked profile of the track inside, but its perceived axis is actually at right angles to the long axis of the track circuit, because the mass of the seating is placed fronting the main straights not at the curved ends.

The ring beam takes its support from a series of outwardly inclined steel trusses rising from a series of deep concrete columns ringing the concourse level. The trusses are extended inwards to provide support for the upper level tiers of seating and are clad on the outside with panels of profiled western red cedar boards, laid horizontally. Around the base and near the upper leading edge sets of the boards have a cut-away edge section to generate open slots that provide a passage for natural ventilation. These allow cooler air to enter at low level and warm air to be vented at the top, depending on the season and prevailing conditions.

Internally all attention is focused on the sweeping curves of the track, made from long narrow strips of pale Siberian pine, while the flat central infield preparation

area, with ramps leading up from the lower ground level, is painted a vivid swimming pool blue and glows under the natural light flooding in from the overhead roof-lights. This is an immensely successful design, combining elegant architecture and sophisticated engineering to produce a clearly thought out, efficiently detailed and memorable end product that functions as both a physical as well as symbolic, indeed iconic, expression of the sport it hosts.

TURNER CONTEMPORARY ART GALLERY, MARGATE, KENT
Architect: David Chipperfield Architects

The seaside town of Margate, facing the full might of the North Sea on the Isle of Thanet, the easternmost point on the North Kent coast, might not at first sight seem the most obvious of locations for a new international art gallery. However, the now rather faded resort has a claim to historical associations with that incomparable master of English landscape painting, J. M. W. Turner, for Turner was a frequent visitor to Margate, once enthusing to Ruskin that 'the skies over Thanet are the loveliest in Europe'. The gallery's name is reinforced by the coincidental fact that the new building sits on the spot once occupied by a long since demolished guesthouse where Turner stayed during his visits and engaged the companionship of his landlady. It is an exposed location, right on the seafront, tucked between the lifeboat station to the east and the former customs building, Droit House, overlooking the harbour to the west.

An earlier design for a new gallery, which proposed a startlingly unconventional 'blob' with its base set partly in the sea, was beset by technical problems and escalating costs that led to its eventual abandonment. The new gallery adopts a much more conventional formal response, almost industrial in flavour, and sets its face against the fury of the winter storms behind the protecting arm of the sea wall at the point where it starts its sweeping curve to embrace the harbour.

Six similarly-sized mono-pitch volumes have been loosely coalesced around a central spine of circulation, the individual shed-like components staggered in plan, thereby generating a series of small terraces around the perimeter and reducing the perceived overall size of the structure. However, what appears from a distance to be a huddle of semi-industrial sheds reveals on closer inspection an altogether higher level of craftsmanship, crisp detailing and sophisticated finishes.

The highly engineered aluminium curtain wall skin, with its grid of white, acid-etched glass rain-screen panels alternating with sections of clear glazing and thin, vertical glazing mullions, displays a level of delicacy that is in total contrast to the robust setting of the harbour walls and the forbidding expanses of open sea to the north. The detailing has had to be rigorously organised as the exposed nature of its location means that it will be lashed by the gales and battered by waves and salt spray, every junction tested to the hilt.

It was the implied and frequently actual drama of the seascapes that appealed to Turner of course, together with the distinctive quality of the light. The internal treatment of the gallery spaces has endeavoured to maintain this link with natural light and the external environment rather than develop the sealed black box concept found in many modern galleries. This has been achieved through the careful integration of high level clerestory north-lights into the mono-pitch roofs to light the gallery spaces and the treatment of other window elements as a means of focusing attention on the views of townscape and seascape.

The main gallery spaces are on the first floor where four of the mono-pitch volumes are set out in adjoining pairs and a central circulation spine provides a link between back of house offices in the single projecting volume at the east end and an education room similarly located at the west end. Where the main stair and lift rise from the ground floor reception area the spine has been expanded to form a mezzanine gallery space overlooking the void of a double-height section of the foyer on the seaward side.

At ground level a large lobby receives visitors approaching from the west via a broad set of steps onto a paved terrace and provides access on one side to a café and on the other to the main foyer, which stretches from back to front and incorporates a shop area, central reception desk and double-height display space. Full-height glazing to the outer café walls provides strong visual links back over the beach to the main promenade and out over the harbour.

The internal palette of finishes is simple and basic: white walls and either white or ribbed concrete ceilings, clear glass and polished concrete floors. The colour will no doubt come with the art, as in an installation by Daniel Buren for the opening show, which transforms the double-height rectangular foyer window into a huge circular lens focusing on the sea, bounded by alternating bright yellow stripes and reflected, ad infinitum, by flanking mirrors on the side walls.

The building was completed in April 2011 for a total cost of £17.4m and has successfully demonstrated its environmental credentials, especially with the use of natural light and ventilation, by gaining a BREEAM Very Good rating under testing by the BRE, the first gallery in the UK to do so. It remains to be seen whether the new gallery will in time lead to an improvement in the general fortunes of Margate by inspiring the sort of cultural re-awakening that has often led to a wider programme of urban renewal in other locations.

RIVERSIDE MUSEUM, GLASGOW, SCOTLAND
Architect: Zaha Hadid Architects

The latest in a series of unconventional 'silver icons' that has sprung up alongside the banks of the River Clyde in recent years has been completed, providing a new 10,000 sq. m home for Glasgow's Museum of Transport. The fancifully sculptured form, from the office of 2010 Stirling Prize-winner Zaha Hadid, occupies a prominent riverside position on a tight promontory at the point where the Rivers Clyde and Kelvin converge, downstream from Glasgow's city centre and within sight of the old Govan shipyards, with their iconic dockside cranes.

Opened to the public on 21 June 2011, the building is now home to the Transport Museum's collection of some 3,000 exhibits, which range from vintage steam locomotives, trams and buses, through to cars, cycles and a fine collection of model ships. If the total area available has not significantly increased over that provided by the former museum, and some of the exhibits are rather oddly displayed and inaccessible, perched up on individual shelves projecting from the walls like grossly oversized Dinky toys, it is nonetheless a remarkable structure and a notable addition to Glasgow's burgeoning collection of trophy buildings.

The highly unusual design features a large column-free central exhibition space that has been squeezed and moulded into a dynamic Z-shaped profile under a flowing pleated roof of considerable structural complexity. The design was declared the winner of an architectural competition held in 2004 and it is perhaps partly because of the unconventional nature of the building's form and the resulting engineering gymnastics required to realise the concept that it was 2007 before work started on site, leading to completion of the basic building at the end of 2010 prior to the fitting out of the interiors and installation of the museum's exhibits. The disarming visual simplicity of the finished product belies the challenging complexity encountered in resolving the geometry of the steel framing. In the finished building the necessary forest of steelwork is entirely hidden from public view, both inside and out.

The design concept's folding plate structure emerges in dramatic fashion on the north *(Fig. 1)* and south elevations, where the wild, zigzag eaves extend beyond the full-height, glazed end walls enclosing the exhibition space. The uneven saw-tooth profiles, slightly different on each elevation, provide an instantly memorable, if bizarre, visual image, reading like a caricature of the ubiquitous multi-ridge roof forms of the industrial buildings of the past or even as a wild graph plotting the ups and downs of some precarious enterprise.

It is unfortunate that what is arguably the finest 'elevation', the roofscape, cannot be fully appreciated from ground level, so that what was no doubt one of the main selling points of the architect's model fails to be properly readable by the visiting public. According to the designers its flowing lines and undulating forms can be taken as a metaphor for the idea of rippling waters amid the context of converging rivers. It looks stunning from above – a pleasure unfortunately afforded only to the privileged few who can take the aerial route down the Clyde.

For museum visitors, arriving on the landside across a new public square, entry to the museum is made through the north glazed elevation, into which is recessed an entrance lobby giving direct access to the exhibition space. On the west side a two-storey bank of support facilities, including offices and gallery spaces at upper level and educational spaces at ground level, follows one of the few straight sections of the external side walls. Almost immediately the lofty exhibition space swings

Fig. 1 Riverside Museum (north elevation), Zaha Hadid Architects

sharply to the left and then squeezes into another dramatic about-turn to the right before flowing out through the south-facing, glazed façade fronting the River Clyde. Visible through the clear end wall and moored alongside the newly constructed quay is the three-masted tall ship SS *Glenlee*, a potent reminder of the city's maritime heritage.

The sinuous bulging curve of the eastern elevation is occupied by a second bank of support accommodation, incorporating smaller enclosed exhibition spaces, a café with glazed river frontage and utility rooms and offices occupied by the Clyde Maritime Trust. The main exhibition space is crossed near its centre point by a single bridge connecting the upper level exhibition and gallery spaces on either side and providing visitors with a welcome and different perspective of the meandering space and folding roof planes as well as the exhibits. The workmanship and detailing throughout are immaculate, which is only right for a building that has come in at £60m, excluding fit-out costs.

ONE NEW CHANGE, CITY OF LONDON

Design architect: Ateliers Jean Nouvel
Executive architect: Sidell Gibson Architects

Any new building that dares raise its head in the immediate vicinity of St Paul's Cathedral is likely to find itself enveloped in all manner of constraints and caveats aimed at preserving the visibility and dominance of Sir Christopher Wren's masterpiece. Viewing corridors (some from miles away), sight lines and height gradients are the initial determining factors, but inevitably questions of style and material will surface, as the recent development history of this part of the city well demonstrates. It is therefore a matter of note that such an assuredly contemporary building as this has emerged to take up a place right at the foot of the famous dome.

The site is bounded to the north by Cheapside, to the east by Bread Street, to the south by Watling Street and to the west lies the boundary with the cathedral precinct, New Change. It is subject to strict limitations as to height and massing, although these were not uniform across the site, as evidenced by the contour-like lines of the height gradient mapping. The retention of an open public space was also an important requirement in the redevelopment of the site.

Jean Nouvel was the winner of a design competition organised by the developer, Land Securities, in 2003, with a proposal that responded directly to the volumetric constraints of the St Paul's grid. The architect originally likened his building to a stealth bomber, and the comparison is apt not only for the building's ability to sneak in under the radar but because the design has many of the characteristic features of the iconic warplane, not least its faceted geometry and the smooth inscrutability of its façade treatment. The brief called for 25,000 sq. m of retail and 35,000 sq. m of office space and such a volume of accommodation squeezed in under the height limits has generated a very dense development. The building opened in October 2010 after a three-year construction programme.

The retail space occupies the lower ground, ground and first floors, with offices occupying the upper five levels. At ground level the plot is subdivided into quarters by public covered shopping arcades entering from three sides and an open entry mall from the fourth side facing onto New Change, all meeting at a central fulcrum – part atrium, part open light well, rising through the height of the building. This central space connects with the lower ground level through an open void and features a pair of wall climber lifts connecting to all floor levels and the roof, where an extensive public terrace has been created.

The connection to New Change takes the form of a dramatic slash through the building's mass, opening up the central atrium core areas to an exciting view of the east end and towering dome of St Paul's. The resulting public open space therefore penetrates to the heart of the development, providing daylight and fresh air, its sides splaying out to encompass the impressive vista. The glazed façades add a further layer of visual interest by providing multi-faceted reflections of the cathedral's east end.

Further retail units are located at first floor level, where arcades extend from the central space to north and south, emerging as balcony like openings in the glazed frontages facing Cheapside and Watling Street. Long angular voids are cut into the arcade floors, like slashed openings, providing sight lines up and down. There is a racy, cutting edge feel to the general ambience, accentuated by the glass balustrades and the folded geometry of the polished ceiling finishes, though only time will tell whether the units at the ends of these arms will be a long-term commercial success.

Offices are accessed from a spacious reception area encircling the central light-well and connecting to ground level via a dedicated set of escalators from the lobby on Watling Street. From this reception area a further set of escalators provides workers with a short cut back down to the first floor shopping and catering units – no need to leave the building for lunch! However, where the treatment of the office interiors follows fairly conventional norms the same cannot be said of the external elevations.

The shifting tonality and reflectivity of the building's faceted glass skin – 6,500 sheets of glass make up the complete façade with 289 different configurations of patterning and 21 different colours – combine with the unconventional geometry of the façades to generate an intriguing and slightly alien presence in the street scene, with corners chamfered, projecting canopies diving up and down and façades leaning in and out at various angles. It is as though the building were crouching, ready at a moment's notice to morph into something altogether different. The contrast with St Paul's could not be greater and the design pushes the technology of all-glass facades arguably to its limit, given developing priorities for low-carbon, energy-efficient, sustainable construction methods.

HOLBURNE MUSEUM EXTENSION, BATH

Architect: Eric Parry Architects

The warm, honey-coloured stonework and grandly porticoed frontage of Charles Harcourt Masters' 1795, former Sydney Hotel terminates one of the finest street vistas in Georgian Bath, occupying a prominent axial position within the landscaped setting of Sydney Gardens at the north end of Great Pulteney Street. With its flanking colonnaded pavilions it acted as a gateway link between the urbanity of the city streets and the softer landscape of what were once the much more extensive pleasure gardens that today remain as a small but valuable 'green lung'.

The hotel was drastically reconfigured towards the end of the First World War by the architect Reginald

Fig. 2 Holburne Museum Extension (section), Eric Parry Architects

Blomfield to create a museum to house the substantial collection of art and artefacts assembled by a Scottish baronet, Sir William Holburne of Menstrie (once a very young mid-shipman at Trafalgar and latterly a resident of Bath). In doing so Blomfield eradicated the axial connection from street to garden by placing the main stair centrally at the rear, while making many other interior and exterior alterations.

In 2002 a design competition was organised for an extension to the museum as part of a general improvement programme. This, predictably, generated the common quandary in such exercises – whether to match the stone-based classical aesthetic of the original or to provide something contrasting and contemporary in style. In Bath such a debate can become almost intractable given the passionate advocacy in the city for the use of the local Bath stone. However, given the decidedly imposing nature of the original and the impossibility of successfully matching it today, the architects eventually managed to win the argument in favour of modernity. Consequently the museum has acquired a refreshingly contemporary addition in a crisply detailed and visually arresting style that works equally as well with its historic counterpart as its landscape setting.

The form of the new extension *(Fig. 2)* is that of a simple cubic volume arranged over three storeys, with a further basement level providing storage, servicing and archive facilities. A café occupies the ground floor while galleries fill the upper floors, the first floor managing to squeeze in a mezzanine level as it mirrors the height of the refurbished main ballroom gallery in the old museum. The simple volume is separated from the stone rear elevation of the original by a narrow linking core containing staircase and lift, which creates a re-entrant recess articulating the junction between the two.

The new stair and lift core provides a central point of access linking the new building back to the old at each floor level. This arrangement re-establishes the axial through-route of the original Sydney Hotel, a reversion

that has been made possible by the courageous and strategic decision to relocate Blomfield's staircase to one side away from its previous central position.

The external elevations feature an increasing level of solidity, enclosure and rhythmic complexity with each successive storey. The café occupies the entire ground floor and is enclosed by full-height, clear glazed screen walls providing uninterrupted 180° views out into the gardens. This transparent enclosure turns out on closer inspection to be a double-skinned wall, with a wide cavity between the skins, which continues up past the more solid enclosure of the first floor galleries and terminates at the underside of the second floor gallery, which projects forward to the plane of the outer skin.

The enclosure of the second floor gallery, by contrast, is almost completely opaque, with natural lighting provided primarily by means of roof-lights and with just one window opening placed symmetrically on the principal axis. The remaining sections of façade are clad with a series of alternating flat panels and projecting fins, fabricated out of a ceramic material with a fabulous mottled blue-green finish that strikes up a direct relationship with the natural colour palette of the surrounding gardens and mature trees. The spacing of the fins is irregular, creating a feeling of vitality and an intriguing visual complexity.

The many layered reflections, verdant colours and the overall exotic flavour of this intricate double-skinned build-up generate an immediate resonance with the museum's garden setting and demonstrate that it is not always essential to slavishly follow the heritage route in order to fit modern buildings into a historic setting. Completed in February 2011, this is a relatively modest extension in terms of size, which cost £3.5 million out of a total build cost of £6.5m and an overall project cost of £11m, but it raises the Holburne Museum to a completely new level and puts it on a par with some of the best of the country's civic museums, one of great subtlety, imagination and finesse.

AWARDS

RIBA AWARDS 2010

THE STIRLING PRIZE 2010
National Museum of XXI Century Arts (MAXXI), Rome, Italy; Zaha Hadid Architects

The Stirling shortlist
Ashmolean Museum, Oxford; Rick Mather Architects
Bateman's Row, London; Theis and Khan Architects
Christ's College School, Guildford; DSDHA
Clapham Manor Primary School, London; dRMM
Neues Museum, Berlin, Germany; David Chipperfield Architects in collaboration with Julian Harrap Architects

RIBA SPECIAL AWARDS 2010
The Manser Medal – Hunsett Mill, Norfolk; Acme
The Stephen Lawrence Prize – The Artist's House, London; Gumuchdjian Architects

BRITISH CONSTRUCTION INDUSTRY AWARDS 2010
Prime Minister's Better Public Building Award – New Stobhill Hospital, Glasgow; Reiach and Hall Architects
Major Project Award – Ropemaker Place, London; Arup Associates
Building Award – CircleBath Private Hospital, Bath; Foster + Partners

Small Building Award – Lowther Children's Centre, London; Patel Taylor
Conservation Award – Medieval & Renaissance Galleries, V&A, London; MUMA

RIAS AWARD 2010
RIAS Andrew Doolan Best Building in Scotland Award – Shettleston Housing Association Offices, Glasgow; Elder and Cannon Architects

RIBA AWARD 2011
Royal Gold Medal – Sir David Chipperfield CBE

CIVIC TRUST AWARDS 2011
Special Award for Sustainability – Medieval & Renaissance Galleries, V&A, London; MUMA
Special Award for Restoration – McManus Galleries, Dundee; Page \ Park
Special Award for Inclusive Design – The West Centre, Glasgow; Anderson Bell + Christie
Michael Middleton Award (Conservation) – Norwich Cathedral Visitors Centre; Hopkins Architects
Special Award for Community Engagement – Stonebridge Hillside Hub, London; Edward Cullinan Architects
Special Award for Scotland – The Briggait, Glasgow; Wasps Studios/Nicoll Russell Studios
National Panel Special Award – Tyne Cot Cemetery, Zonnebeke, Belgium; Govaert en Vanhoutte

ART AND CULTURE

Ossian Ward

CUTS, GIFTS AND MORE PROTESTS

A survey of 2,000 people in September 2010 commissioned by the organisers of the Threadneedle art prize found that two-thirds of respondents agreed there should be radical changes to arts funding, with one fifth suggesting that the government should not support the visual arts at all. As if on cue, round upon round of cuts were announced, beginning with chancellor George Osborne's wide-ranging spending review.

A national campaign against the proposals was launched with the help of celebrity artists such as David Shrigley and Mark Wallinger; Cornelia Parker created an image of the famous Angel of the North sculpture by Antony Gormley with one of its wings clipped, and Bob and Roberta Smith (artist Patrick Brill) made a sign that read: 'Art Gallery Closed: Sunday, Monday, Tuesday, Wednesday, Thursday. Admission £17.50'. Sir Nicholas Serota, the director of Tate, warned that the proposed baseline cut of 15 per cent across all arts organisations would lead to partial closures and severe reductions in the high quality of exhibition programming.

When Arts Council England revealed the extent of its cuts in March 2011, however, there was less bloodshed in the visual arts sector than initially feared, with many major institutions – including the South London Gallery, the Serpentine Gallery, the Photographers' Gallery and the Towner in Eastbourne – all receiving substantial increases. The losers included the Institute of Contemporary Arts (ICA) – which had its funding slashed by 42 per cent – and Museums Sheffield, which had its support stopped, along with 682 other regularly funded bodies such as Animate Projects and Artsway in the New Forest.

In November, seven museums deemed to be 'non-national', including London's Design Museum, the Geffrye Museum, the Horniman Museum and the Museum of Science and Industry in Manchester, were stripped of central government support. The Design Museum received a healthy fillip the following summer, however, thanks to a donation of around £17.5m from Sir Terence Conran, who founded its predecessor, the Boilerhouse, in the basement of the Victoria & Albert Museum (V&A) in 1982. This gift – partly to help the Design Museum move into its new Commonwealth Institute site by 2014 – brought Conran's total patronage over the years in this sector to around £50m, although it was a bittersweet 80th birthday for him as his beloved Habitat (which he set up in 1964) went into administration and he stepped down as provost of the Royal College of Art after seven years.

Individual largesse and corporate sponsorship of the arts came increasingly under the spotlight as the government suggested arts organisations should implement a new philanthropic funding model based on the examples set by wealthy donors in America. The Treasury began consultation on tax incentives, hitherto limited to donations made posthumously, which could significantly boost giving to museums and galleries. While private-sector philanthropy fell for the third year running, by a further 11 per cent – which included such high-profile corporate dropouts as UBS, which pulled its ongoing sponsorship of Tate Modern – there were also significant boons for the British Museum (£25m from Lord Sainsbury), the National Gallery (£2m from the Hintze Family) and the Serpentine Gallery (an undisclosed amount given by Dr Mortimer and Theresa Sackler for an extension designed by Zaha Hadid, to be opened in time for the start of the Olympics in 2012). Dame Vivien Clore Duffield also donated £8.2m to help build new learning centres in 11 institutions including the Whitworth Art Gallery in Manchester, the Museum of Liverpool and Kettle's Yard in Cambridge.

In December 2010, culture secretary Jeremy Hunt announced a £100m fund to help boost philanthropic activity (paid for by the Arts Council, the Department for Culture Media and Sport and the Heritage Lottery Fund) with the emphasis on building endowment funds in the American mould.

Budget cuts in arts education were met with furious demonstrations by students – including a sit-in at the National Gallery and a protest at the 2010 Turner Prize ceremony, where 30 students found sympathy with the winning artist, Susan Philipsz, as well as with master of ceremonies for the night, Sir Nicholas Serota.

Other concerted bursts of activism occurred at various museums, including Tate Britain, the British Museum and the National Portrait Gallery, which had accepted sponsorship from oil company BP. Groups called Culture Beyond Oil and Liberate Tate picketed exhibitions and evening events throughout the year spilling tar-like treacle inside or staging performances outside.

NEW MUSEUMS AND MUSEUM NEWS

Named after J. M. W. Turner, Margate's Turner Contemporary art gallery (*see also* Architecture) was opened in April 2011 by another local artist, Tracey Emin, although her homecoming exhibition is scheduled to open in 2012. The art gallery was designed by British architect David Chipperfield, who was also behind a new gallery complex for Wakefield in Yorkshire, which opened a month later: the Hepworth Wakefield pays homage to abstract sculptor Barbara Hepworth (1903–75), one of the town's best-known daughters and this country's most-famous 20th century female artist. At 1,600sq. m it is the largest purpose-built gallery constructed in the UK since the Hayward Gallery in 1968 and will be used to permanently display works from the Hepworth Estate, as well as changing shows of younger sculptors such as Eva Rothschild, whose work inaugurated the building alongside that of Dame Barbara.

Other new-build or extension projects recently or nearly completed include a history museum called M-Shed in Bristol, a new Jerwood Gallery in Hastings by HAT Projects, Bath's Holburne Museum, remodelled by Eric Parry Architects, the Museum of Liverpool by 3XN/AEW, the Royal Museum in Edinburgh by Gareth Hoskins, and FirstSite gallery in Colchester by Rafael Viñoly. These were all considered to be among the last of the predominantly publicly funded buildings destined to open in the foreseeable future, leaving question marks over other existing capital projects.

However, the V&A pushed on with its scheme to open an outpost in Dundee by 2015, approving the scheme presented by Japanese architectural firm Kengo Kuma and Associates. The V&A also appointed a new director, Martin Roth from Dresden's State Art Collections, after the surprise resignation of Sir Mark Jones in June 2011, following his announcement that he would be leaving to become master of St Cross College, Oxford.

While the British Museum continued construction on its World Conservation and Exhibitions Centre, it also won plaudits from the art-going public and industry insiders, first by being voted the nation's favourite cultural attraction for the second year in a row and then by winning the prestigious £100,000 Art Fund Prize for its groundbreaking documentary project, 'The History of the World in 100 Objects'. The British Museum also made headlines by acquiring a number of ivory treasures from the Assyrian city of Nimrud, although much of the media attention may have been because they were first discovered by none other than Agatha Christie, who reportedly cleaned them with face cream.

Expansion work continued on the so-called Tate Modern 2, while the existing Tate Modern also took on a new director, Chris Dercon, who began his post there in March 2011, having left Munich's Haus der Kunst. He pledged to set up an acquisitions committee in India and a new curatorial post was also put in place to focus on African art, paid for by a Nigerian bank. The museum was likewise happy to receive a big donation from the public art commissioning body Artangel, which left its collection to the Tate as part of the commissioning body's 20th anniversary celebrations. Tate Liverpool was less fortunate, losing long-term director Christoph Grünenberg after ten years' service, as well as an unspecified number of staff in a round of voluntary redundancies.

A delve into Tate's archive revealed the brouhaha caused by the acquisition and exposition of Carl Andre's *Equivalent VIII* in the 1970s, infamously known as 'the pile of bricks', while its holdings of beloved northern painter L. S. Lowry came under fire when notables including actor Ian McKellen joined in a chorus to have the 23 works put on show, or else sold to another institution that would dignify them more often with prolonged exhibition.

Uncharitably, Charles Saatchi's desire to hand his private collection over to the public seemed to have been temporarily rebuffed, after talks with Arts Council officials broke down. Saatchi's vision for a Museum of Contemporary Art London, or MoCA for short, was to mirror his own collecting habits by enabling the institution to buy and sell works in order to refresh the holdings intermittently. However, the practice of deaccessioning is still not allowed by the UK's Museums Association, although there were believed to be other troublesome stipulations and responsibilities with regard to the lease of Saatchi's current site in Chelsea and the ongoing custodianship of the gifted works that scuppered any possible agreement. In less serious Saatchi-related news, seven-year-old Leilah Poulain had her painting of a penguin shown at the Saatchi Gallery after beating 1,700 other contestants in an online competition.

MARKET MOVEMENTS AND ALL'S FAIR IN ART FAIRS

The UK slipped a spot in the global art sales rankings, according to the British Art Market Federation, thanks to the growing wealth of Chinese art buyers, who accounted for 23 per cent of all auction and gallery purchases (totalling around £5bn). The USA retained top spot with 34 per cent, while Britain dropped a few points to 22 per cent, although the figures prompted fears that Europe could be left way behind by the new markets emerging in the Far East.

Christie's claimed that 2010 was its best year on record, partially due to some strong Asian sales, while Sotheby's hit back at its big rival with an astonishing round of record-breaking London contemporary art auctions in June 2011, taking more than £100m in one evening, thanks mainly to a German collection featuring works by Gerhard Richter and Sigmar Polke. Christie's own post-war and contemporary summer sale raked in just under £80m, with a Francis Bacon selling for just shy of £18m on its own. Although still third in the pecking order, auctioneers Bonhams announced they would open a new £30m headquarters in London in 2013.

London's art fairs continued to expand with the addition of a small fair for contemporary work, called Sunday, timed to run in conjunction with the main autumn event, the Frieze Art Fair, while an even more niche Moving Image fair would join the swelling ranks, specialising in video art. Another relatively successful newcomer in 2010 was the French-run Pavilion of Art and Design, with 50 dealers showing decorative arts and Old Masters. This new challenger was certainly behind Frieze's decision to mount a sister event, Frieze Masters, to cater for a similar number of dealers and collectors in anything from antiques to modernist pieces, with the inaugural edition planned for late 2012. Another major announcement from Frieze was the procurement of a site for their first fair in New York, also slated for 2012. This followed hot on the heels of news that Art Basel, the world's largest fair franchise, had just taken over the new Asian fixture on the art world calendar in Hong Kong, named Art HK. Back in London, the rebranded Masterpiece fair (aimed at a more general buyer of high-end luxury goods) seemed to be gaining ground, too.

GALLERY COMINGS AND ARTIST GOINGS

The gallery scene in London moved on apace, with signs that commercial interest in art was beginning to return to its formerly frenzied, pre-recession state. New York's heavyweight Pace Gallery released news of its first UK branch opening in early 2012, which sparked stories about a possible 'art arms race' with the all-powerful Gagosian Gallery; Pace hired former Gagosian director Mollie Dent-Brocklehurst to lead its London operations. White Cube, led by Britain's most voracious dealer Jay Jopling, also refused to stand still, with its renovation of a giant warehouse in Bermondsey due to open in the last quarter of 2011.

The Lisson Gallery launched an offshoot of its own in Milan, as well as securing representation of Chinese art-star Ai Weiwei. Weiwei was newsworthy for many different reasons: his impressive installation for the Unilever Series of commissions in Tate Modern's Turbine Hall, *Sunflower Seeds*, had to be closed soon after opening due to the tiny porcelain-crafted facsimiles giving off potentially harmful dust when walked upon; and for continuing to make political waves in his home nation, where Chinese authorities variously put him under house arrest and bulldozed his freshly built studio in Shanghai, despite city leaders inviting him to break ground there in the first place. In April the artist was detained again, provoking international outrage and a global campaign to 'Free Ai Weiwei'.

Despite his imprisonment – during which Weiwei was named an honorary Royal Academician – two major London exhibitions of his work went ahead (one at Lisson, one outdoors at Somerset House). It was not until a few days before a state visit to the UK by Chinese premier Wen Jiabao that Weiwei was released, having been accused of dodging taxes in China. He was initially fined close to $1m and gagged from appearing on any forms of media for one year.

Among notable obituary notices of the year were the artists Leonora Carrington, a British-born surrealist painter who spent much time in Mexico with Frida Kahlo and others, and Cy Twombly, an American painter of the abstract expressionist generation who just happened to have opened a show only days before his death at the Dulwich Picture Gallery, where his work was coupled with that of Nicolas Poussin ('Twombly and Poussin: Arcadian Painters', 29 June–25 September 2011).

ARTIST POWER AND ART-WORLD PLAYERS

Various artists and historians weighed in on the turns of events throughout the tumultuous Arab Spring; amid calls to end looting and destruction, museums around the world united with cultural figures in Egypt against possible smuggling of objects beyond the country's borders.

Among other artists responding to contemporary events was Slovakian conceptualist Roman Ondak, who installed a replica of the Fénix 2 capsule – used to rescue 33 trapped Chilean miners in 2010 – at his show at Modern Art Oxford ('Time Capsule', 12 March–20 May 2011). Bob and Roberta Smith also channelled perhaps the biggest public-interest news story of the year – the royal wedding between Prince William and Kate Middleton – for a tongue-in-cheek pair of sculptures of the happy couple made from local rubbish.

Another previously anti-establishment figure, the cross-dressing artist Grayson Perry, was inducted as one of the 80 living Royal Academicians in March 2011, alongside the newly elected sculptor Phyllida Barlow, draughtsman Timothy Hyman and printmaker Anne Desmet. Also playing against type was the shadowy street-artist Banksy, who raised £90,000 to help free members of a Russian art collective called Voina, who had been arrested in St Petersburg for a performance aimed against the ministry of home affairs. Banksy extended his munificence to graffiti fans keen to visit the blockbuster exhibition 'Art in the Streets' at the Museum of Contemporary Art in Los Angeles, by sponsoring free tickets (usually $10) every Monday. All this affection for LA was perhaps surprising, seeing as he didn't win the Oscar for his much-fancied documentary, *Exit Through the Gift Shop*, which premiered on British television in late summer 2011.

It's not often the money-wielders of the art world get rewarded more than they do financially but Anthony d'Offay, long one of London's preeminent art gallerists, was awarded the Prince of Wales Medal for Arts Philanthropy in recognition of his sizeable gift of 725 works worth around £125m to the nation for a knock-down sum in 2008.

MORE MOVERS, SHAKERS AND GLITTERING PRIZES

The British Council named Graham Sheffield, formerly artistic director of the Barbican and CEO of the West Kowloon Cultural District in Hong Kong, as their new artistic director. The National Gallery lost two of its most talented curators: Luke Syson left for the Metropolitan Museum in New York, having only just finished securing the works for his blockbuster Leonardo Da Vinci show in London in 2011, while Xavier Bray moved across town to the Dulwich Picture Gallery. Another new face on the museum scene was Christoph Vogtherr, who replaced Rosalind Savill as director of the Wallace Collection.

One of the most keenly awaited appointments was that of the new executive director of the beleaguered ICA, which turned out be Gregor Muir, a former director of commercial gallery Hauser & Wirth and a friend to the Young British Artists (YBAs). He took up his post in January 2011, succeeding Ekow Eshun who resigned in August 2010 after finally steering the institution out of a turbulent few years of job cuts and financial mismanagement. The artist Pablo Bronstein's architecturally themed show, 'Sketches for Regency Living', became the first under Muir's tenure (9 June–25 September 2011).

The Max Mara Art Prize for Women went to Andrea Büttner while the Deutsche Börse Photography Prize went to Magnum-affiliated Jim Goldberg. The annual Turner Prize boasted a shortlist of Martin Boyce, Karla Black, George Shaw and Hilary Lloyd and was set to leave London and Tate Britain for only the second time in its history in late 2011, visiting the Baltic in Gateshead.

ART CRIME, RESTITUTION AND THE LAW

Tracey Emin was the victim of forger Jonathon Rayfern, who had previously worked with Emin's techniques. He made £26,000 by selling fake drawings and embroideries over the internet, and was jailed for 16 months.

In March 2011 Bonhams auctioned a work expressly against the wishes of the artist, Sir Anthony Caro. His monumental *Lagoon*, of 1976/7, had been 'mutilated' by the addition of metal feet, said the artist, although he might have felt that justice was done when the sculpture failed to attract any bidders on the night.

Sotheby's withdrew a controversial lot after it discovered that a 16th-century ivory mask, once the property of a Nigerian king, may well have been looted by the British army some 200 years ago. A Jewish owner who claimed he was forced to sell a Rubens painting, *The Coronation of the Virgin*, after World War II, lost his case to have the disputed picture removed from the Courtauld Institute. The Spoliation Advisory Panel believed that a deal for the work had been settled on a 'cold, financial calculation', rather than under the duress of the Nazis.

It was a case of art grime, rather than art crime, that caused consternation at the National Gallery during a particularly cold December, when visitors were found to be dragging in dangerous amounts of salt and grit used to de-ice the roads outside. A chemical compound of chloride, released into the air after prolonged trampling by visitors, was discovered to be potentially harmful for the priceless Old Master pictures hanging on the walls, especially those incorporating vermilion pigment.

The European Commission made a surprising ruling in the same month, when it declassified art works made from neon tubes by the pioneering American artist Dan Flavin, refusing their importation to the UK as sculpture (paying just the usual 5 per cent VAT due on works of art), instead suggesting they be declared as light fixtures – so liable to pay the full 20 per cent VAT. Even a Bill Viola installation was classified as projectors and wall fittings because it was decided that it did not constitute a work of art until the equipment was turned on.

One of the most successful and widely seen works of art all year was Christian Marclay's epic 24-hour video, *The Clock*. Inaugurated at White Cube in London (15 October–13 November 2010), then included in 'British Art Show 7' – which visited four venues around the country (23 October 2010–4 December 2011). The film also travelled to New York and to the Venice Biennale, where it won the prestigious Golden Lion, as voted for by a jury including film director John Waters. There was some discussion of whether Marclay's collage of snippets of Hollywood films and television images featuring clock faces and watches to tell the time throughout a 24-hour period, might not constitute copyright infringement: 'Technically it's illegal,' said the London-based artist, 'but most would consider it fair use.' Various museums competed to acquire a copy of the film, including Tate and the Museum of Modern Art in New York, while the Los Angeles County Museum of Art, the National Gallery of Canada and the Museum of Fine Arts, Boston, were among the early purchasers, paying around $500,000.

EXHIBITIONS: INDOORS, OUTDOORS AND ONLINE

Museums announced significant increases in annual attendance rates – the V&A noted a 24 per cent increase since August 2009, the National Gallery boasted 18 per cent more visitors, with the various Tate galleries also up 15 per cent. The UK institutions were found to be lagging slightly behind the numbers attracted by the Louvre in Paris – some 8.5 million annually – although the British Museum, Tate Modern and National Gallery all featured in the top five most-visited museums in the world (New York's Metropolitan Museum of Art came third).

Big temporary exhibitions of the year included an impressionism show in Scotland ('Impressionist Gardens', 31 July–17 October 2010), the V&A's latest style-driven blockbuster on the aesthetic movement of Oscar Wilde, William Morris and the pre-Raphaelites ('The Cult of Beauty', 2 April–17 July 2011), the British Museum's revelatory exhibitions on an often-ignored Eastern civilisation ('Afghanistan: Crossroads of the Ancient World', 3 March–17 July 2011) and Tate Modern's comprehensive show of 'Gauguin' (30 September 2010–16 January 2011). More contemporary offerings included the sixth Liverpool Biennial (18 September–28 November 2010), a Tracey Emin retrospective, 'Love is What You Want' at the Hayward Gallery (18 May–29 August 2011) and 'Modern British Sculpture' at the Royal Academy (22 January–7 April 2011).

In terms of public art, Nigerian-born Yinka Shonibare's *Nelson's Ship in a Bottle* continued to sit on the fourth plinth in Trafalgar Square, while the artists Elmgreen & Dragset, and Katharina Fritsch were chosen to create its replacements for 2012 and 2013 respectively. Mark Wallinger's proposal to install a giant white horse in Kent, near the new Eurostar terminal at Ebbsfleet, spiralled in costs even further, to an estimated £12m, putting the whole project in jeopardy. Plans for a similarly grandiose sculpture for completion in Northumberland by 2013, were unveiled by artist/architect Charles Jencks, whose half-mile long reclining female form was already being dubbed a future 'Goddess of the North'. Former YBA Gavin Turk completed his first ever public commission, placing an enormous 40ft-high sculpture of a rusty nail in the City of London's new shopping mall, One New Change.

Two significant websites changed the way people could access works of art online. The first came from internet search giants Google, whose Art Project placed high-resolution versions of 1,000 famous works of art from 17 leading institutions into three-dimensional museum environments, based on the Google Earth and Street View mapping software. In addition, the BBC teamed up with the Public Catalogue Foundation to create the site 'Your Paintings', where some 200,000 publicly owned paintings were uploaded, including a long-lost William Hogarth found in the offices of an archaeology team in Bristol.

BUSINESS AND FINANCE

Timothy Hindle

There was much talk during the year, among both politicians and businessmen, of rebalancing the economy. The prime minister, David Cameron, promised a 'massive rebalancing' as a means to stimulate growth. Yet it was also a year when many existing imbalances seemed to get worse, not better.

One of the most controversial was in pay. In June 2011, *The Economist* printed the headline: 'Overpaid Bosses are Back'. It was referring to top executives in the USA, but it might as well have been talking about the UK. The take-home pay of Stephen Hester, the boss of the Royal Bank of Scotland – an institution rescued and now 83 per cent owned by the taxpayer – was £7.7m, while the three best paid executives at Barclays Bank took home more than £29.3m between them for 12 months' work. Bob Diamond, Barclays' new boss, told a parliamentary committee that 'the period of remorse and apology' over bankers' bonuses was over. The bonuses, he said, 'are essential to retaining talent'. Not everyone found that they could agree with him.

These amounts, though, were as small potatoes compared with the sums accruing to the owners/ managers of Glencore International plc, the world's largest commodity trading company. When it was floated on the London Stock Exchange in May 2011, it was the biggest initial public offering (IPO) in the exchange's history, valuing the company at around $60bn (£36bn). The stake of Alex Beard, the man who headed the company's oil division, was worth $2.8bn (£1.7bn), making him, overnight, the tenth richest Briton.

The growing imbalance between the rich and poor in societies everywhere was highlighted in a report by the Organisation for Economic Cooperation and Development (OECD). Almost all its 22 member countries recorded increasing income inequality from the mid-1980s to the late 2000s. The average income of the best-paid 10 per cent of the population in OECD countries is now about nine times that of the worst-paid 10 per cent. The extent of the increase in inequality in the UK was exceeded only by that in Mexico, the USA and Israel.

The OECD was unable to supply reasons as to why labour markets are so inefficient, and continue to get more so. It was not perhaps surprising that the UK's labour unions, dormant for many years, started to flex their muscles again. In June, a number of public sector workers, including teachers, librarians and immigration officers, stayed at home in response to planned cuts to their pensions and benefits.

Another grey area of corporate ethics raised its head during the year: taxation. When Glencore became a public company, the Jersey-based organisation was revealed to have paid almost no corporation tax for years despite having made billions of pounds in profits. Barclays bank disclosed that it paid only £113m in UK corporation tax in 2009, a mere 2.5 per cent of its global pre-tax profits in that year. Meanwhile Vodafone, the Newbury-based multinational mobile phone business, restructured its global empire during the year but stalled in India, over the local tax authorities' claim that it owed $2.5bn (£1.6bn)

in capital gains tax for an offshore deal completed in 2007.

Corporate ethics and corporate profits are not irreconcilable. Employees prefer to work for companies with high ethical standards and consumers increasingly want to buy ethically produced goods and services, albeit at a premium. But the ethical 'movement' in business has been slow to take off. Until it does, the largely benevolent 'invisible hand' of Adam Smith's 'free market' will continue to seem sometimes more like an invisible sleight-of-hand, stealing from the back pockets of the poor to overpay the rich.

MONEY MAKING MONEY – SOMETIMES
The imbalance in the UK economy that most politicians have in mind when they refer to the phenomenon is the emphasis on financial services at the expense of manufacturing. It is easy to exaggerate the size of the financial sector in the UK. Financial 'intermediation' accounts for only 8 per cent of GDP while manufacturing accounts for 12.8 per cent. The latter has, however, been declining steadily from the start of this century while finance has only been on the wane since 2008.

Manufacturing gained a boost in April due to the wedding of Prince William and Kate Middleton. The festivities (and the good weather before and during them) brought shoppers out and retail sales in April increased by 1.1 per cent on a year earlier, the biggest rise since 2002. Dressmakers gained, particularly the fashion business of the late designer Alexander McQueen – which was responsible for the wedding dress itself – and Zara, a hugely successful Spanish clothing firm that produced the cornflower blue dress that the Duchess wore on the morning after the wedding, a dress that cost £49.99.

In May, the economic picture changed dramatically. Retail sales fell by 1.4 per cent, with electrical-goods vendors particularly hard hit. National retailers, such as Mothercare, Thorntons and Dixons, continued to close shops in a trend that left the nation's high streets looking ever more glum.

There was some good news for manufacturing, however, when JLR (Jaguar Land Rover, now owned by India's Tata Motors) said it intended to invest some £5bn over the next five years to upgrade its UK plant and enable it to match big rivals BMW, Mercedes Benz and Audi on quality. JLR made profits of just over £1bn in its latest financial year, a remarkable turnaround considering that Tata paid little more than that when it bought the company (from Ford) just three years earlier.

Rolls-Royce, the engine-maker and a reminder of what quality British manufacturing once was, reached a A$95m (£62m) settlement with Australian airline Qantas for an in-flight explosion involving a Rolls-Royce Trent 900 engine on one of the airline's Airbus A380 jets in November 2010. The explosion forced the plane to make an emergency landing in Singapore, and Qantas to ground all its A380s while it carried out safety checks.

BP continued with its expensive clean-up in the Gulf of Mexico. The explosion at its Deepwater Horizon rig in the Gulf of Mexico in April 2010 killed 11 people and caused some of the worst pollution ever seen. A US presidential commission reported in January that 'most of the mistakes and oversights' leading up to it 'can be traced to a single over-arching failure – a failure of management'. But none of the company's current or former managers stood up to take responsibilty.

The commission blamed BP, which managed the rig, and several of its contractors. These included Transocean, which actually owned the rig, and Halliburton which supplied the cement that did not hold. Several of the companies mentioned by the commission accepted the findings and settled with BP for their share of the damage.

BP set out to sell assets in order to help it pay the clean-up costs, amounting in the end to something north of $40bn (£25bn). It sold off a stake in an Argentinian oil company for over $7bn (£4bn) together with assets in Venezuela, Vietnam and the North Sea. Then, in February, BP became a buyer again, paying $9bn (£6bn) for a stake in the natural gas assets of India's Reliance Industries.

It was not a particularly good year for the UK's finance industry. Hedge funds found few good targets. One prominent fund, RAB Capital, considered delisting after a wave of redemptions by its investors. An organisation that in 2003 had conjured up a 1,000 per cent return on one of its funds faced the prospect of liquidation. Several hedge funds, whose managers had propped up West London's property market and Mayfair's restaurants for years, sought to relocate to Malta where they hoped life might be cheaper.

It was not a good year for private equity either; Candover, one of the UK's biggest private equity groups, wound itself up during the year after a series of disastrous investments. Meanwhile, following a long running court battle, American bank Citigroup seized music label EMI from Terra Firma Capital Partners. Terra Firma had been struggling to service loans that it had obtained from Citigroup to finance its original buy-out of EMI back in 2007. In June, Citigroup put EMI up for sale and the music group announced that it was looking for 'strategic alternatives'.

The banks too had an uncomfortable time. HSBC announced that it would scale back its operations, while Lloyds Banking Group, rescued by the government in 2009, said it would shed 15,000 jobs by 2014 and pull out of half the countries where it currently operates.

The banks came under the beady eyes of yet another commission, this one chaired by Sir John Vickers, former chief economist at the Bank of England. Vickers' two main recommendations, published in April, were:

- retail-banking operations should be legally 'ring-fenced' from investment banking
- banks should set aside 10 per cent of their capital as a buffer against harder times

Banks complained that the requirements could cost them up to £15bn a year. But in July, Chancellor of the Exchequer George Osborne put his weight behind the recommendations.

Another economic imbalance – that between richer and poorer countries within the euro zone – also caused problems during the year. Portugal followed Greece and Ireland in asking for a bail-out from richer, better balanced economies within the region sharing the common European currency. The UK breathed a sigh of relief that it had chosen to retain the pound sterling, but it was not totally immune to events in troubled euro lands elsewhere. The Irish government spent some €50bn (£44bn) trying to bail out its banks before turning abroad

for help, and its problems in particular threatened to spill across the Irish Sea.

Meanwhile the European Court of Justice threw the insurance industry into turmoil when it ruled that gender may no longer be used as a factor in determining insurance rates. Hence young women drivers, statistically half as likely to have an accident as their male counterparts, are now subject to the same premiums. At the other end of the insurance business, male pensioners, whose life expectancy is considerably less than a woman of the same age, will no longer be able to purchase more generous annuities.

SECURITY AND PRIVACY

Another delicate balance disturbed during the year was that between the right to privacy and the right to know. In the UK, the information commissioner found that Google had committed a 'significant breach' of the law by collecting data from wireless networks, while Google's 'street view' service caused Germany to demand that internet companies pay more heed to privacy concerns.

The world's favourite search engine found itself under attack on many fronts. It was forced to redirect its Chinese internet services through Hong Kong after a cyber-attack on its website there, while in America, it is to be subjected to 'privacy audits' by the Federal Trade Commission (FTC) for the next 20 years. This was in response to Google's failure to stop email addresses from being shared publicly on Buzz, its new social-networking site.

During the year, Facebook was valued at $50bn (£31bn), five times what it had been worth a mere 18 months earlier. LinkedIn, a social network for professionals, sold shares that valued it at $3.3bn (£2bn), soon after announcing its first-ever profit, while blog site Twitter, found itself valued at $8bn (£5bn). Meanwhile back in Seattle, Microsoft paid $8.5bn (£5bn) for online video-phone service Skype; 400 times Skype's operating income.

At the same time, Myspace, a social-networking site that until 2006 was more popular than Facebook, laid off half its worldwide workforce during the year. Its owner, Rupert Murdoch's News Corporation, finally managed to sell it off in a deal that valued the business at $35m (£22m) – News Corporation had paid $580m (£357m) for it in 2005, when Mr Murdoch had described Myspace as 'one of the web's hottest properties'.

FINES AND SETTLEMENTS

Banks J.P. Morgan Chase and Goldman Sachs paid fines of hundreds of millions of dollars in settlements with the Securities and Exchange Commission (SEC) for deals where they had misled investors, but they admitted no wrongdoing. Goldman Sachs was also fined £17.5m by regulators in the UK for failing to disclose that it had been under investigation for fraud in the USA.

The French bank Société Générale was fined £1.58m by the FSA, for inaccurately reporting its trades. Over a two-year period the bank managed to get around 80 per cent of them wrong.

BLOWING HOT AND COLD

Climate change was responsible for much of the rapid fluctuation in commodity prices during the year. Come rain or shine, it was much the same story. At one stage in 2010 the price of wheat rose at its fastest rate since 1973, largely because of contrasting weather patterns – excessive floods in Canada and excessive dryness in Russia and the Ukraine. The Russians put a temporary ban on all grain exports. Meanwhile floods in Pakistan, the world's fourth largest producer, pushed up the price of cotton.

The UN's index of world food prices hit a record level at the end of 2010. Sugar hit a 30-year high in November and the price of maize, a staple food for many poorer regions of the world, rose by almost 25 per cent in the first half of October alone – according to the UN's Food and Agriculture Organisation, rice, wheat and maize account for 60 per cent of the world's food energy intake.

It was not only the climate, though, that affected commodity prices. A shift in world economic power also played its part. The millions of Chinese workers who had been producing goods for western consumers for decades began to consume themselves. China overtook Japan to become the world's second largest economy and it was estimated that China was consuming around 40 per cent of the world's copper – the majority of it going into pipes in the high-rise apartment blocks that mushroomed across the country.

Political and economic uncertainty also played a part. A long-running presidential stand-off in the Côte d'Ivoire sent the price of cocoa sky-high as beans piled up in the ports of the west African country that is responsible for a third of the world's cocoa production.

In February, gold hit an all-time high of $1,445 (£889) per troy ounce. At the same time silver hit its highest price for 31 years while the price of oil rose to $115 (£71) a barrel, its highest level for several years. Political instability played its part here too – disruptions in oil-producing countries following the 'Arab Spring' and events in Libya in particular, put fear into the hearts of the markets.

THE NUCLEAR OPTION

The high price of oil sent investors yet again searching for alternatives. But the nuclear option received a heavy blow on 11 March when a devastating tsunami off the coast of Japan struck the Fukushima power plant. The subsequent nuclear leak there caused damage estimated by the World Bank at around $235bn (£145bn).

The effects of the Japanese earthquake spread far and wide. In Sunderland, Nissan closed its plant for ten days because of a shortage of essential parts from the organisation's facility in Japan.

Germany pledged very quickly to shut down all its nuclear power plants by 2022. That gave it just over a decade to find alternative sources for almost one-quarter of its energy supply. Conversely, in the UK, the government named the sites of eight new nuclear power stations that it plans to build by 2025. They are designed to replace the 25 per cent of the country's generating capacity that is scheduled to close by the end of this decade. Time will tell which was the wiser decision.

CONSERVATION

THE NATURAL ENVIRONMENT

Peter Marren

WRONG BEAVERS?

Two colonies of beavers live in the wild in the UK. One, the official introduction, is in Knapdale in western Scotland, where three families of Norwegian beavers were released in 2009. The other is along the River Tay and its tributaries where at least 20 beavers were living wild in 2010, having escaped from private collections and perhaps bred. The Knapdale beavers are the forerunners of a programme to reintroduce the animal to Britain, where it died out about 400 years ago. The animals are tagged and monitored to see how they fare and to assess their environmental impact. The Tay beavers play no part in this plan. Scottish Natural Heritage (SNH) wants to round them all up and return them to captivity. In a 'trapping trial' over winter 2010–11, it managed to catch just one beaver, which later died.

SNH claims that the beavers must be recaptured since their release was illegal, and because the animals' welfare might be at risk. Beavers are social animals and should be released only as 'bonded pairs' or families. On the Tay the beavers may be lone individuals with little prospect of ever finding a mate. They are probably of Bavarian origin, and SNH believes that they are less closely related to the extinct British race than those of Scandinavian descent. It is even possible that some of the Tay beavers may belong to the separate American species, which never occurred in Europe.

Opponents to their recapture, which include prominent naturalists, believe that SNH is under pressure from farming and fishery lobbies that are less than enthusiastic about the whole project. Sir John Lister-Kaye, an expert on beavers, believes that the Tay offers a much more favourable habitat for the animals than Knapdale. While he does not approve of the way they were introduced, he says it nonetheless offers a great opportunity to study the behaviour of beavers in the wild. If any of the animals causes problems, he would have no objection to their being trapped and returned to captivity; this is normal practice in Europe where the once endangered beaver has been successfully reintroduced to most countries which it once inhabited.

The claims and counter-claims continue. In the meantime, an attempt is being made to conciliate landowners and establish the facts by means of a working group set up to study the interactions of beavers with migratory sport fish, such as salmon and sea trout.

U-TURN ON THE WOODS

A public outcry followed the coalition government's proposal, in January 2011, to sell 15 per cent of the public forest estate in England – the maximum permissible by law in a single step. As the consultation document made clear, this was to be the first step in an effective privatisation of England's publicly owned forests and a radical change in the role of the Forestry Commission from owner to enabler. As events soon made clear, there

was very little public support for privatisation. Opposition came from MPs from all parties, as well as an online petition which accumulated over a million signatures. A letter of protest to *The Times* newspaper was signed by, among others, the Archbishop of Canterbury. The government decided to backtrack. 'If there is one clear message from this experience,' admitted the secretary of state, Caroline Spelman, 'it is that people cherish their forests and woodlands and the benefits they bring.'

At issue was the well-justified fear that private woodland owners would be less than enthusiastic about public access. While they could not close established rights of way, they could, if they chose, close car parks, dismantle picnic areas and put up unfriendly notices. The press found plenty of examples of newly sold woods where public access had been restricted by such means. Another fear was that wildlife value could be compromised, for example if a wood was apportioned into small, individually sold lots to maximise profit. While amenity bodies, such as the National Trust and the Woodland Trust, might stand to acquire woods of high value, they would require grants to manage them properly. And no charity or trust is capable of managing extensive historic forests such as the New Forest and the Forest of Dean.

One argument that might have convinced government was that the sale of woods would not necessarily result in significant savings. Throughout the EU, the fragmentation of forest ownership has led to greatly increased administrative costs, and therefore an increase in the size of the regulatory body – as the Forestry Commission was careful to point out.

The government's plans were shelved. Instead, Ms Spelman established an independent panel under the chair of the Bishop of Liverpool, with representatives from conservation and amenity bodies, including the National Trust and the Ramblers, to advise her on 'the future of forestry and woodland policy in England'. The panel, which is holding hearings across the country, will present its report in autumn 2011. One possible option is the recommendation of an integrated forest and wildlife service along the lines of the American model.

BIRDS AND BIODIVERSITY

The UN designated 2010 as the International Year of Biodiversity, 'a celebration of life on earth and the value of biodiversity'. In Britain the official yardstick of biodiversity is breeding birds, the only animals where a health check can be monitored year on year – with the help of thousands of birdwatchers. Recovery programmes are in place for many rare or declining birds, but progress is patchy. The bittern has recovered comparatively well, from only 15 'booming males' in 1993 to 82 today, thanks largely to lottery-funded reedbed creation and other donations. The cirl bunting has also increased from 352 to 862 pairs, thanks to targeted environmental stewardship measures in its limited breeding area in South Devon. Similarly targeted conservation has helped corncrake and stone curlew.

The UK is also gaining new species of breeding birds. The purple heron bred successfully for the first time in Britain at the RSPB's Dungeness Reserve in 2010. Four pairs of spoonbill produced six chicks at Holkham in Norfolk, and may be on the verge of colonising Britain. The project to reintroduce the great bustard on Salisbury Plain made further progress in 2010 with four more hatchlings, a total of 18 birds now established in the wild. Some 16 sea eagle chicks were donated by Norway to join the attempted reintroduction of this magnificent bird (one of the world's largest birds of prey) to eastern Scotland. There are already 52 breeding pairs in Scotland following its successful reintroduction in west Scotland. More contentiously, the giant eagle owl is now breeding in at least two sites in the Pennines, creating concern that it might prey on England's small and beleaguered population of hen harriers.

On the debit side, we failed to halt or even slow down the seemingly inexorable decline of many farmland birds. Once common species such as snipe, turtle dove and corn bunting are vanishing from places where they were once familiar. Skylark, linnet and yellowhammer are still widespread but their numbers are falling steadily. There is particular concern over some of our migratory songbirds, including two that are closely associated with the English spring: the cuckoo and nightingale.

HARE TODAY, GONE TOMORROW?

The mountain hare differs from the more familiar brown hare in its smaller ears and legs, and by growing a thick white coat in winter. Confined to the uplands, it is particularly common on heather moors managed for grouse. Its numbers vary naturally on a ten-year cycle, but there are signs that the animal may be in trouble. Its habitat has been reduced by afforestation and the decline of managed grouse moors. It is also vulnerable to climate change — for the hare's white coat is undoubtedly a liability when there is no snow!

A more proximate cause, for which there is growing evidence, is that the mountain hare is being over-shot. They are shot legally on unenclosed moorland between October and February. Although the meat is of no great commercial value, the hare shoot was a traditional reward for hard-working ghillies at the end of the season. Unfortunately the animals are now regarded by some estates as a serious nuisance for they carry the tick responsible for spreading the 'Louping-ill' virus fatal to young grouse chicks. A study carried out by Scottish Natural Heritage revealed that 20 per cent of hares killed on Scottish estates were not shot but snared. Believing that the mountain hare faces a bleak future on moorland estates, the Hare Preservation Trust has called for shooting to be restricted under licence.

The Irish race of the mountain hare is larger and does not turn completely white in winter; some believe it is a separate species endemic to Ireland. It too is under pressure, not so much by shooting but by competition with the brown hare. The latter was introduced to Northern Ireland by 19th century landowners, and is now common there, but the brown hare is still scarce within the Irish Republic. However, it seems to have a competitive advantage over its relative in the lowlands, possibly because it seems less susceptible to various infections. It has recently displaced its rival over much of southern Sweden. Dr Neil Reid, who has studied this effect, believes that this could easily happen in Ireland too, for there are too few extensive mountain areas to act as a refuge. He calls for urgent preventative measures to protect 'this uniquely Irish species'.

THE PARCHED SPRING

In 2011, parts of England and Wales suffered the driest spring for a century. Although water resources held up well, it was a difficult time for wildlife. Fish trapped in pools in several rivers had to be rescued and transferred elsewhere. Lapwings and other waders which depend on a supply of insects in wet grassland to feed their young experienced reduced breeding success. Swallows and house martins, which need supplies of wet mud to build their nests, likewise had a barren spring. Another vulnerable species was the natterjack toad which breeds in shallow pools, many of which dried up too soon for the tadpoles to develop. Drought is a natural phenomenon which wildlife has to come to terms with, but it is exacerbated by abstraction and land drainage.

The most easily measured effect of the drought was fire. Up to the end of June, Natural England logged 85 'damaging fires' totaling 3,045 hectares, on land of value to wildlife, nearly half of it on sites of special scientific interest (SSSIs). Among the most seriously damaged places were the Bagshot and Broadmoor Heaths on the Surrey/Berkshire border, where fires were started by vandals, and the National Trust for Scotland's Torridon Estate lost five square miles of regenerating woodland. Since many of the fires took place during the nesting season, they took a toll of breeding birds, especially heathland species such as woodlark and Dartford warbler. Perhaps the overall loser was the twite, which had the misfortune to be nesting on many of the burned-out places in the north.

BUZZING PROBLEMS

Bumblebees, already under severe pressure from loss of habitat, are threatened by a new breed of pesticide known as neo-nicotinoids. These chemicals, so-named for their resemblance to nicotine from tobacco, are cheap, effective in small doses, and harmless to birds and mammals (including ourselves). They are generally applied to the seeds of rape and other crops, and persist within the growing plant. Unfortunately the chemical seems to be equally deadly to insects, including bees, which pollinate the crop.

The evidence that wild bees are becoming victims to neo-nicotinoids is circumstantial but there is a compelling dossier of cases from other countries. A leaked memo from the US Environmental Protection Agency admitted that 'standard tests and field studies suggest potential for long-term toxic risk to honey bees and other beneficial insects'. Incidents involving the mass death of bees have led to the partial withdrawal of neo-nicotinoids in parts of Germany, France and other European countries. By contrast, the UK's position 'is the most relaxed in Europe' according to Peter Melchett, director of the Soil Association.

The charity Buglife has investigated a number of cases which, it says, links neo-nicotinoids to the death of wild bumblebees, earthworms and other beneficial invertebrates. The official position is that the pesticides 'do not pose an unacceptable risk when products are used correctly'. However, DEFRA's Chief Scientific Adviser, Bob Watson, has asked for regular research updates on impacts on 'non-target' species. It has also become a parliamentary issue after 70 MPs signed an early day motion stating their concern.

INSECTS AND LIGHT POLLUTION

Britain's night skies are brighter than ever before. From the point of view of a nocturnal flying insect, street lights, car headlamps and other bright lights form a dazzling kaleidoscope that disrupts their natural rhythms of day and night. It is estimated that a third of insects attracted to lights die as a result of collisions or from being picked off by predators such as bats. A single bright light used to illuminate a large statue in Italy attracted around 5 million moths.

Exactly how and why artificial light attracts insects has been much debated. One theory is that moths are not so much attracted as dazzled, and so unable to see beyond the light. Another, which has some physiological support, is that, because of the structure of its eye, the insect sees a black band next to the light, and it is that dark refuge, and not the light, which it is trying to reach. There is also growing evidence that some insects are also attracted to polarised light from shiny surfaces such as plastic sheeting on farm fields, shiny tarmac, car surfaces and even solar panels. Apparently they are especially attractive to flying aquatic insects, such as water beetles, which deposit their eggs on these sterile surfaces.

The great unknown is to what extent light pollution is contributing to the known decline of nocturnal insects, from moths to glow worms. Moths do not fly around modern street lights as they used to, and there is evidence that yellow sodium light may prevent moths from flying altogether; thereby the chances of them mating, feeding and laying is drastically reduced.

The charity Buglife has suggested a number of measures that could alleviate the position. Solar panels could include patterns of rough or coloured glass to reduce their reflectivity. Motion sensors could be attached to security lights enabling them to switch off when not required. Car parks could be situated away from water bodies to reduce their attraction for water insects. But, if light pollution really is to blame for the lack of moths on our windows at night, there may be no overall remedy.

POLITICS AND THE ENVIRONMENT

A radical shake-up of government 'quangos' or quasi-autonomous bodies may deprive both Natural England and the Environment Agency of their accustomed independence to speak out on issues affecting wildlife and the environment. A statement by cabinet minister Francis Maude in October 2010 promised to transfer the two into 'leaner, front line delivery bodies focused strongly on the government's ambitions for the environment and the green economy'. Both are required to reduce their running costs, work more closely with other government bodies to avoid duplication, and to implement new ways of working.

The shake-up has also resulted in the abolition of numerous other quangos, including the Sustainable Development Commission and the Royal Commission on Environmental Pollution. In addition, DEFRA secretary Caroline Spelman has released a consultative document placing economic development inside national parks on a par with conservation; wildlife observers are equally anxious about the implications of 'localism' as set out in the decentralisation and localism bill introduced into parliament in December 2010. The bill's intention to demolish state control over many aspects of life (including housing targets) and shift the balance in favour of local decision-making is feared by some to threaten a development free-for-all. Wildlife Link, an umbrella body

for 22 wildlife charities, responded with a call for a 'living landscape', a blueprint for restoring wild habitats by establishing corridors or 'nature improvement areas' with the support and help of local communities and partnerships. Inside each zone, the needs of wildlife would take priority over development.

The government's Natural Environment White Paper, published in June 2011, acknowledged the need for restoration and recovery, and committed itself to the establishment of 12 such areas. From the point of view of our wildlife bodies, this is a small step to balance the assault on Natural England's ability to advise its own government, but it was welcomed nonetheless.

KILLER SHRIMPS AND PARAKEETS

The damage caused to agriculture and horticultural interests by invasive, non-native species of plants and animals is estimated to cost £1.3bn a year. For example, the attempted eradication of the grey squirrel from Anglesey has cost £440,000 so far, and a concerted programme to get rid of the water primrose about £73,000 (against an estimated bill of £242m if nothing was done to contain its spread).

One species that made the headlines in 2010–11 was the so-called killer shrimp, *Dikerogammarus villosus*. This carnivorous creature, around 2cm long, has spread across Europe, possibly in its larval form attached to the hulls of boats. It feeds on insect larvae, baby fish and fellow shrimps, and is said to go on killing sprees, leaving most of the prey uneaten, like a fox in a henhouse. It has the potential to damage fisheries, and perhaps cause an ecological disaster by targeting the native freshwater shrimp, a keystone species in the foodwebs of clean rivers. In 2010 it was detected at Graffham Water in Cambridgeshire, and later in Cardiff Bay and a reservoir near Port Talbot in South Wales. Other water bodies in South Wales are being investigated using nets baited with cat food. One theory is that the species is hitching a ride on inflatable tyres now used for fishing in open water.

A more colourful invader is the monk parakeet, a popular cage bird with green and grey plumage, and a bright red bill. Since the mid-1990s a small suburban population has built up in the home counties, centred on the Hertfordshire town of Borehamwood. Though harmless-seeming, the birds build large communal nests which, in America, have caused problems in electricity substations when the collapsing rain-sodden structures cause local black-outs. The birds are also potential pests of orchard fruit and other crops. On these grounds DEFRA, with the endorsement of the RSPB, decided to round them all up, by trapping and shooting. Both it and another invader, the ring-necked parakeet, are classed as pests. The latter bird, which is now common around London and spreading elsewhere, stands accused of taking over the nests sites of native species such as starlings and woodpeckers. It, too, may face a cull in the coming years. The control of such birds is certainly feasible. A programme to eradicate the ruddy duck by trapping and shooting has succeeded in reducing its UK population from 4,400 birds to just 120.

HIGH-SPEED HABITAT DESTRUCTION

The government's plans for phase 2 of high-speed rail envisage a link between London and Birmingham that will reduce the journey time to just 50 minutes. There are also planned extensions to Manchester and Leeds – all at an estimated cost of £32bn. If the plan is approved, work will begin in 2015.

The Wildlife Trusts drew up a list of the cost in environmental terms. In the path of the London to Birmingham line lie over 50 ancient woods, numerous local wildlife sites and ten SSSIs. In the Chilterns, high speed rail will plough through Weedonhill, Lotts and Pipers Woods, among the best in the region, and demolish Calvert Jubilee, a former clay pit and now a quiet lake used by breeding waterfowl. In Northamptonshire it will destroy medieval parkland and limestone grassland; in Warwickshire, woodland, rich meadows and natural watercourses. In the Birmingham area a new viaduct will bisect the Park Hall nature reserve and remove access to it. In London it will run alongside Perivale Wood, one of the oldest nature reserves in the country.

The trusts also point out the dangers to wildlife of increased fragmentation and isolation from other sites. The barrier formed by the line will compromise the movement of animals, from the badger to the tiny small blue butterfly. They are sceptical of the claims made by the promoters of environmental gain. The reduction in carbon emissions, it believes, will be insignificant. The impact assessment is inadequate, and the costs take no account of mitigation and compensation measures, say the trusts.

BADGERS AND BOVINE TB

The badger is a fully protected animal that many farmers want to stamp out. The spread of bovine TB in cattle, and its link with wild badgers, is a thorny subject that successive governments have wrestled with for years. From the outset, the new coalition signalled its intention to re-examine the issue and develop 'affordable options' for a policy of badger control. In September 2010 the agriculture minister Jim Paice issued a consultation paper on his proposal to issue licences to farmers and landowners who wished to cage-trap or shoot badgers at their own expense, commenting that 'it is clear that the current approach has failed to stop the spread of this terrible disease'. His position was undermined by allegations that some farmers had been deliberately keeping cattle they knew to be infected with TB. Such infringements of the regulations would make it difficult if not impossible to bring the disease under control.

Meanwhile the Welsh government proposed to badger cull across a 'TB hotspot' of 110 square miles centred on North Pembrokeshire. The Badger Trust successfully appealed and won a reprieve after the judge ruled the proposed cull unlawful, largely on technical grounds. The minister first made it clear that his government would pursue its policy, and then, in July 2011, abruptly changed his mind and scrapped the plan. This outcome has implications for badger policy in England since the law is the same.

On 19 July, environment secretary Caroline Spelman announced her intention to cull badgers by shooting in two pilot areas in south-west England. If this is successful, farmers throughout England may be issued with licences to kill badgers as early as October 2012. She added that the government remained committed to the development of vaccines both for cattle and badgers.

In the meantime an injectable vaccine for badgers is available, which should slow the progress and severity of the disease, though it will not prevent infection. Using cage-traps, about 90 per cent of all badgers within a particular area can be vaccinated. A field trial based in another TB hotspot in Gloucestershire will run for the next five years. Outside this area, vaccination is available as a 'licensed option' for those with sufficient training and experience. The Food and Environment Research Agency (FERA) is also assessing the feasibility of vaccination via an oral bait.

BUILT HERITAGE

Matthew Saunders

MONEY MATTERS

The overarching impact of the year under review was that of the drastic cuts in public expenditure announced by the coalition government. English Heritage was told that, over a four-year period, it would face budget reductions of 32 per cent, while the national museums will lose 15 per cent. The support from the public purse for the Churches Conservation Trust is due to decrease, over the same four years, by 20 per cent. Expenditure on high-profile conservation schemes, such as planned improvements to the setting of the monoliths and a new visitor centre at Stonehenge, was dropped completely (although here the Heritage Lottery Fund stepped in with its own grant of £10m).

Elsewhere, the picture was very different. The National Trust saw an excess of income over expenditure in 2009–10 of £58.7m, 22.5 per cent better than in the preceding year, and its membership grew to a quite extraordinary 3.7 million. Sales of Lotto tickets increased, and this in combination with the restitution by the new government of the four original lottery 'good causes' to their 20 per cent shares, meant that the Heritage Lottery Fund could plan for an annual income of £300m in each of the years 2013–19. This compares with £250m in 2011–12 and only £205m in 2010–11.

The government also proroposed a drastic reduction in the number of heritage agencies. At one stage there was talk of creating a new 'Heritage Commission' that would swallow up English Heritage, the Heritage Lottery Fund and the Churches Conservation Trust. In the end all three retained their independence but it was a close-run thing. However, the Museums and Galleries Commission was abolished and its powers passed to the Arts Council and the Commission for Architecture and the Built Environment also succumbed, after losing its £3m grant from the Department for Culture, Media and Sport, but found some sort of after-life in the embrace of the Design Council, with which it was combined. One of the most unexpected, but welcome, reprieves announced in the 2011 budget was that of the Listed Places of Worship Scheme, under which historic churches and chapels can reclaim the VAT they incur on repairs up to a capped total of £12m in 2011–12, increasing to £13m in 2014–15.

ENGLISH HERITAGE

In the early summer of 2011 English Heritage launched its 'National Heritage List for England', an online database, which for the first time gave the public a definitive one-stop shop through which to access the list of listed buildings, the schedule of ancient monuments, the register of parks, gardens, battlefields and wrecks, and world heritage sites. Only conservation areas, the exclusive preserve of local authorities, were excluded. The database is accessible at: www.english-heritage.org.uk.

English Heritage also launched a major initiative on heritage crime in the form of its ambitious 'National Heritage Protection Plan' in spring 2011 and consolidated its support officers for the Places of Worship Scheme. Its annual report *Heritage Counts 2010* focused on the economy and found, *inter alia*, that over a ten-year period every £1 invested in historic attractions generated

£1.70 in additional economic activity. Its report for 2011 is due to cover industrial archaeology.

POLICY CHANGES

In terms of government policy, the principal change noted in 2010 was the publication of the planning policy statement *Planning for the Historic Environment*. The deadening bureaucracy of the title should not obscure the significance of the document. In company with the associated *Practice Guide* compiled by English Heritage, it brought together in one location the present thinking of central government on policy and practice to do with historic buildings and archaeology. But no sooner had it been accepted and digested than the new coalition government announced that all planning policy statements, on all subjects, would be succeeded by a single new inclusive document, a 'national planning policy framework'. The government also proposed a radical decentralisation of the planning system through its Localism bill. The conservation world was initially alarmed at some clauses which reduced the protection of conservation areas and listed buildings, but the offending clauses were later dropped.

In the spring of 2011 SAVE, campaigner for endangered historic buildings, won a landmark case against the government when the court of appeal ruled that the demolition of a building could be classed as 'development' and therefore needed planning permission. On a separate note, the revised order on ecclesiastical exemption (S11176/2010), published just before the election, allowed the management of listed curtilage structures around a historic church, such as mortuary chapels, lychgates and belltowers, to come under the control of the church rather than the secular authorities. It also formalised the protection of 'peculiars' such as Westminster Abbey, St George's Chapel, Windsor and Christ Church Cathedral, Oxford.

THE HERITAGE LOTTERY FUND

The Heritage Lottery Fund announced scores of grants benefiting, among others:
• Brecknock Museum, Powys, Wales (£1.9m)
• Castle Drogo, Devon (£2.5m)
• Design Museum, London (£4.95m), to allow it to be rehoused in the former Commonwealth Institute
• Dunfermline Museum, Fife, Scotland (£2.82m)
• Hexham Abbey, Northumberland (£1.89m), to provide significant new exhibition space
• House Mill, Bromley-by-Bow, Tower Hamlets, London (£2.66m)
• National Memorial Arboretum, Staffordshire (£1.5m)
• Quarr Abbey, Isle of Wight (£1m)
• Southwell Palace, Nottinghamshire (£994,300), to restore the ruins
• Swiss Garden, Old Warden, Bedfordshire (£2.38m)

BEGINNINGS AND ENDINGS

Most of the new attractions which opened during the year were Heritage Lottery Fund beneficiaries – the new Galleries of Modern London, at the Museum of London; the People's History Museum, in its new premises in Manchester; the Hull History Centre; the Plaza Super Cinema, Stockport, now in the hands of a trust; the Museum of Liverpool, at its prominent position near The Three Graces; The Hepworth (art gallery) at Wakefield; the Cumbrian Archive Centre on the outskirts of Carlisle; Strawbery Hill, Horace Walpole's 18th-century Gothic villa in outer west London; the 18th-century gardens surrounding Chiswick House; the Holburne Museum, Bath, with its uncompromising new extension to the rear; the Robert Burns Museum at Alloway; and the Watts Gallery at Compton, Surrey, built to celebrate the corpus of work by the Victorian painter, G. F. Watts.

The new Museum of Somerset opened at Taunton Castle and Ordsall Hall, Salford and the Shire Hall, Monmouth both re-opened after extensive repair works. The most expensive museum outside London since the Second World War, the Riverside at Glasgow, designed by Zaha Hadid, greeted its first visitors in June 2011 and Britain's newest cathedral, at Bury St Edmunds, Suffolk, which had received a grant of £3m from the Millennium Commission, saw the final completion of its great central tower, designed by Stephen Dykes-Bower.

Other attractions closed their doors – the Museum of Domestic Architecture at Cat Hill in Cockfosters, north London (prior to relocation at Hendon); the Topolski Gallery, celebrating the work of cartoonist Felix Topolski, on London's South Bank, and the Livesey Museum for Children in Southwark.

In terms of historic places of worship, the most serious loss in the year was the collapse and subsequent clearance of the former Brunswick Methodist Chapel of 1823 at Stockton on Tees, in Cleveland. There was a serious fire at the medieval church at Sheering in Essex, but the intention to rebuild was swiftly affirmed. The authorities at the great Catholic seminary at Ushaw in County Durham, a complex of 27 listed buildings, announced that it would close in June 2011. In addition, very significant parish churches were closed at Ufford in Huntingdonshire, Belgrave in Leicester and Brampton Abbots in Herefordshire. Plans were declared to bring back into pastoral use two longstanding redundant churches – St James, Toxteth in Liverpool and St John's, Chatham, both late Georgian in origin. St Augustine's Abbey Church at Ramsgate, where Pugin is buried and which he founded, is to become a mainstream Catholic church after the monastery announced that it was selling up. In addition, the Friends of Friendless Churches took four historic places of worship into care

There seemed good reason to suppose that one of the greatest of all bishop's palaces, Auckland Castle in County Durham, will be able to enjoy an indefinite future after Jonathan Ruffer donated £12m to prevent the sale of the sequence of 18th-century paintings contained inside by Zurburan and to underpin its more systematic opening to the public, probably under the aegis of the National Trust. Lord Rothschild promised a further £1m.

The Landmark Trust acquired four secular properties which, after conservation, will be opened as holiday lets. These included the Oxenford Gatehouse near Peper Harow in Surrey, designed in 1843 by Pugin and Belmont; and Belmont House in Lyme Regis, the late 18th-century seaside villa which belonged to Mrs Eleanor Coade, the famed manufacturer of artificial stone and, latterly, John Fowles, author of *The French Lieutenant's Woman*. The future of the Grade 1 listed Blackpool Tower and Winter Gardens seemed far more assured after Blackpool Council agreed to buy it (for £30m). The eponymous family at Lowther Castle in Cumbria (designed by Sir Robert Smirke 1806–14, and unroofed in 1957) announced ambitious plans to open to the public for the first time in 70 years.

DANCE

Bridie Macmahon

Impending funding reductions in the light of wider public sector cuts overshadowed the year for many dance companies and organisations. Arts Council England (ACE), faced with a cut of 29.6 per cent in its own budget for the period 2011–15, announced its funding decisions and a new national portfolio of arts organisations in March 2011. It had decided to pass 14.9 per cent of its funding reduction onto the budget for portfolio organisations, and to cut strategically rather than sharing the pain equally. Using a range of published criteria against which to assess all applications, and employing an open application process for the first time rather than its previous continuous funding system, ACE selected 695 organisations to fund in place of the previous 849; of the existing regularly funded organisations who applied, 206 were unsuccessful and will lose all ACE support. Each of the successful applicants was awarded what was deemed to be the level of funding appropriate to its individual circumstances and to the programme set out in the application.

For the dance world, this will mean the complete loss of funding for Ballet Black (which marked its 10th anniversary in the year under review), Dance UK, The Cholmondeleys and The Featherstonehaughs, Henri Oguike Dance Company, Woking Dance Festival and Youth Dance England. Dance Umbrella will lose 43 per cent of its funding over the period, Shobana Jeyasingh Dance Company 28.7 per cent and the Contemporary Dance Trust 20 per cent. The leading dance companies and the Royal Opera House will all lose about 15 per cent. Some choreographers and smaller contemporary companies have however received substantial increases, including Hofesh Shechter Company, Wayne McGregor/Random Dance, BalletBoyz, Balbir Singh Dance Company and Vincent Dance Theatre, and seven organisations, including the Association of Dance of the African Diaspora and the Grand Theatre in Blackpool, received funding for the first time. Support for regional dance agencies has also increased.

THE ROYAL BALLET
Against this backdrop, companies continued to perform and tour and create with considerable courage and determination. But with one eye on the future, this was not a year for taking artistic or administrative risks. This may have been part of the reasoning behind the appointment in June 2011 of Kevin O'Hare, the current administrative director of the Royal Ballet, as its new director to succeed Monica Mason on her retirement in 2012. A range of names had been cited as possible successors to Mason, but amid all the speculation the quiet insider had been largely ignored. Positive reasons for his selection are his intelligence, popularity and complete understanding of the operations, traditions, repertoire and purpose of the Royal Ballet. O'Hare was trained at the Royal Ballet School and became an admired principal dancer with Sadler's Wells Royal Ballet (now Birmingham Royal Ballet). He then trained in company management with the Royal Shakespeare Company before being appointed company manager first at

Birmingham Royal Ballet and then at the Royal Ballet. He was appointed administrative director in 2009 and has been at the heart of the organisation as it prepared for Mason's departure and made plans for the future. His appointment is therefore almost radical in its simplicity and logic; for the Royal Ballet there is indeed no place like home.

O'Hare is no dull bureaucrat, and his aim is to work with the best creative dance talents available to the company and to widen accessibility by seeing the company perform in new arenas – including the O2, where he helped to ensure that successful performances of Kenneth MacMillan's *Romeo and Juliet* were given for the first time in June 2011 to huge audiences. The Royal Ballet reached out in other ways too during the year: a number of performances were relayed live on big screens in venues across the country, and live and recorded performances were shown in many cinemas. This is an initiative that will expand in coming years, and is an excellent way of making the company's work available to wider audiences.

The company's big new work of the season, Christopher Wheeldon's *Alice's Adventures in Wonderland,* was on the other hand seen by comparatively few people since it was given only a handful of performances in spite of what must have been an enormous financial outlay. It was the Royal's first new full-length production since 1995 and so arrived loaded with attention and expectation. Visually it did not disappoint, with a stunning set and costumes by Bob Crowley and hugely effective and imaginative digital projections by Jon Driscoll and Gemma Carrington. Lewis Carroll's episodic story does not however lend itself easily to a coherent narrative structure or to serious engagement with the leading characters, and this is reflected in Wheeldon's production, which is best seen as a visual and theatrical *tour de force* rather than as a straightforward ballet. Joby Talbot's score was enjoyable and effective and Lauren Cuthbertson was perfect casting as Alice – effervescent, very English and slightly fey. What did disappoint was the choreography itself – there was a sense that Wheeldon did not have confidence in choreography in its own right as a vehicle to take the plot forward. While acknowledging the creativity, humour and spectacle of the work, it felt like an opportunity missed.

CREATIONS AND REVIVALS
The other new works of the season were by Kim Brandstrup and Wayne McGregor. Brandstrup's *Invitus Invitam* was a short, emotionally charged work based on the unwilling separation of the emperor Titus from his mistress Berenice, superbly danced by Edward Watson and Leanne Benjamin. McGregor's *Live Fire Exercise* used a digital projection of a massive (silent) explosion as the fiery backdrop to a piece for six dancers, moving in typical McGregor style – angular, unbalanced, disturbed – but with little apparent relation to the image behind them that dominated the stage. The rest of the Royal's repertoire during the season included the company premiere of Balanchine's joyful, sparkling *Ballo della Regina* and welcome revivals of a range of quality one-act works including Frederick Ashton's *Rhapsody,* proving

over time to be one of his outstanding creations, MacMillan's *The Rite of Spring*, with the sacrificial victim played this time by a male dancer (Edward Watson alternating with Steven McRae), and David Bintley's *Still Life at the Penguin Café*, last performed by the company in 1993; all showed the dancers in superb form technically and artistically.

To mark the 10th anniversary of the death of Dame Ninette de Valois, the founder of the Royal Ballet and the Royal Ballet Schools, a conference was held at the Royal Ballet School in April 2011 to explore her life and legacy. Entitled 'Adventurous Traditionalist' and chaired by Jane Pritchard, curator at the V&A, the conference comprised an exhibition, films, performances, lectures and panel discussions, and brought together dance practitioners, academics, social historians and cultural commentators in an analysis and celebration of de Valois' achievements. The conference was also a timely review of aspects of the history of the Royal Ballet as it reached its 80th anniversary in 2011.

De Valois joined Sergei Diaghilev's Ballets Russes in 1923, and both the company and the impresario himself left a profound impression on her. It had always been thought that no film footage existed of the Ballets Russes, since Diaghilev had prohibited filming of the company, but in early 2011 a member of the London Ballet Circle, Susan Eastwood, found 30 seconds of film incorrectly labelled in the Pathé Film archives which was then verified as the Ballets Russes by Jane Pritchard. The film shows a rehearsal of *Les Sylphides* in Switzerland in 1928, with dancers led by Serge Lifar. Pritchard also co-curated a major exhibition, 'Diaghilev and the Golden Age of the Ballets Russes', at the V&A in the autumn of 2010, and a season of related dance films was held at the British Film Institute to coincide with the exhibition. In the spring of 2011, Kremlin Ballet Theatre staged a season of revivals and restagings of works from the Ballets Russes repertoire at the London Coliseum, but both the quality and the authenticity of the stagings were questionable.

AGONY AND ECSTASY

One of the works staged by the Kremlin Ballet Theatre, *The Blue God*, had been controversially (re-)choreographed by Wayne Eagling, director of English National Ballet. Eagling came to prominence again in *The Agony and the Ecstasy*, a television documentary on his company shown by the BBC in the spring of 2011. Neither he nor his fellow choreographer Derek Deane, both former Royal Ballet dancers, emerged from the programme with much credit. The dancers themselves worked heroically to present performances of Eagling's new *Nutcracker*, Deane's *Swan Lake* at the Royal Albert Hall, and *Romeo and Juliet*. The *Nutcracker*, premiered in London in December 2010, was a largely successful and traditional production that will replace the company's almost universally criticised 2002 offering. Beautifully designed by Peter Farmer, this is a production that (with revisions) will stand the test of time. The leads were danced by the fascinating and unexpectedly effective new partnership of Daria Klimentová, the company's senior ballerina, and Vadim Muntagirov, its new young star. Another new work, by Van Le Ngoc and entitled *Vue de l'Autre*, was presented in March 2011, once more showcasing the talents of Klimentová and Muntagirov.

ENB also revived Rudolf Nureyev's production of *Romeo and Juliet* to mark the 50th anniversary of his defection to the West in June 1961, and mounted some interesting shorter works including a revival of Serge

Lifar's *Suite en Blanc* and rare performances (in Britain) of works by the French choreographer Roland Petit (*L'Arlésienne, Le Jeune Homme et la Mort* and *Carmen*). These performances at the London Coliseum in July 2011 turned into a tribute to Petit following his death only days before at the age of 87. The co-founder of Les Ballets des Champs-Elysées in 1945, Petit went on to direct the Ballet de Marseille for 25 years. He created scores of dramatic, finely constructed works, many starring his wife and collaborator Zizi Jeanmaire. His range embraced ballet, dance for Hollywood films and glamorous revues staged at the Casino de Paris, and he will be remembered for his great theatricality and visual flair.

Birmingham Royal Ballet also mounted a big new production for the Christmas 2010 season. This time it was *Cinderella*, choreographed by BRB director David Bintley and premiered in Birmingham in November 2010. Bintley focuses initially on the dark side of Cinderella's miserable home life, with viciously unpleasant Ugly Sisters (Skinny and Dumpy) and a malevolent stepmother (danced with relish by Marion Tait). As the story unfolds, however, there is some real poetry to be found, especially when Bintley's choreography is enhanced by John Macfarlane's beautiful designs. Elisha Willis was a gentle, endearing Cinderella and Iain Mackay a likeable prince.

In February 2011 the company returned to Hong Kong to perform Bintley's *Hobson's Choice* at the Hong Kong Arts Festival, and in May 2011 it toured Japan, fulfilling its engagements in spite of the earthquake and tsunami that had devastated the country two months earlier. It performed *The Sleeping Beauty, The Dream* and *Daphnis and Chloë* in four cities, to great acclaim. At the end of the season, the company's ballet mistress and former principal dancer Marion Tait was appointed assistant director of BRB, and principal character artist David Morse retired after 50 years with the company.

ANOTHER ALICE

Another big new production was staged in April 2011 when, only six weeks after the premiere of the Royal Ballet's *Alice*, Scottish Ballet presented its own version of the Lewis Carroll classic at the Theatre Royal, Glasgow. This production, by Scottish Ballet's director Ashley Page, was smaller but in its way just as imaginative as the grand London version. It took scenarios and characters from both *Alice in Wonderland* and *Through the Looking Glass*. In this production, Alice falls into Wonderland through the lens of Charles Dodgson's camera, and photographs of Alice taken by Dodgson are worked into the design of the ballet. Page fails, as did Wheeldon, to overcome the difficulties of translating the book into a satisfying narrative work; but there is much to admire in the choreography, the designs by Antony McDonald and the score by Robert Moran.

In November 2010, Scottish Ballet had announced that Ashley Page would step down as director in August 2012 after ten years in the post. It transpired that only a short-term extension of contract had been offered to him, and that he had decided instead to leave 'with great sadness and regret'. His tenure has seen an enormous improvement in the standard of dancing in the company, and a distinctive style has been forged based partly on his own edgy, modern but classically-based choreography.

Northern Ballet Theatre, in the meantime, appeared to re-state its direction by changing its name to Northern Ballet – a rather strange decision for a company renowned for its theatrical approach to dance and its dramatic, narrative ballets. The name change coincided with its move into a new home in Quarry Hill, Leeds, the largest purpose-built space for dance outside London, which it will share with Phoenix Dance Theatre (which celebrated its 30th anniversary in 2011). Northern Ballet mounted a new production, *Cleopatra*, in February 2011. Choreographed by its director, David Nixon, and with bold, attractive designs by Nixon and Christopher Giles to a score by Claude-Michel Schönberg, the work drew strong performances from Martha Leebolt as Cleopatra and Tobias Batley as Mark Anthony. In May 2011, the company departed from its usual repertoire to perform a well-received production of *Giselle* at the Grand Theatre, Leeds.

RAMBERT TURNS 85

Another company on the move is Rambert Dance Company, which celebrated its 85th birthday on 15 June 2011 and had by then raised £18 million of the £19.5 million required for a planned new home on the South Bank in London; work on the site was due to start in the summer of 2011. The company presented the UK premiere of German choreographer Henrietta Horn's *Cardoon Club* in October 2010, and a powerful and moving new work by Aletta Collins, *Awakenings*, to a score by Tobias Picker, in September 2010. *Awakenings* was based on the book of the same name by the neurologist Oliver Sacks, and depicted sufferers from encephalitis lethargica (sleepy sickness) rediscovering consciousness and feeling. As always the Rambert dancers, especially Jonathan Goddard, showed their great talent and commitment to the full in this work. Another successful premiere was *Monolith*, by Tim Rushton, the artistic director of Danish Dance Theatre, which was inspired by mystical energies which haunt sites of man-made gathering places.

Dance Umbrella presented its usual wide range of dance companies in the autumn of 2010, and included a retrospective of the work of the American choreographer and dancer Trisha Brown. Wayne McGregor mounted a new work for his own company, Random Dance, in November 2010: *FAR* was inspired by Roy Porter's study of the Enlightenment, *Flesh in the Age of Reason,* set to music by Vivaldi and a score by Ben Frost. In the same month, Siobhan Davies Dance launched ROTOR, an ambitious programme of performances, sound installations and artworks by award-winning artists.

In March 2011 a dance work choreographed by Javier De Frutos to music by the Pet Shop Boys premiered at Sadler's Wells Theatre. Based on a Hans Christian Andersen story, *The Most Incredible Thing* was loud and colourful but choreographically and dramatically weak. Akram Khan produced a beautiful new work, *Vertical Road,* in September 2010, to music by Nitin Sawhney and inspired by the concept of the path between the earthly and the spiritual. One of Khan's former collaborators, the great French dancer Sylvie Guillem, performed a season of works at Sadler's Wells in July 2011 that showed that at the age of 46 she has lost none of her strength or charisma. Shortly after Guillem's season, Hofesh Shechter brought the 'choreographer's cut' of his hugely successful and exciting work *Political Mother* to Sadler's Wells.

Visitors to the UK during the year included American Ballet Theatre, Alvin Ailey, Dutch National Ballet, the Bern Ballet, the Forsythe Company, and the Mariinsky Ballet in a major season at the Royal Opera House in the summer of 2011 to mark the 50th anniversary of its first performances in London. The Peter Schaufuss Company

brought Ashton's 1955 *Romeo and Juliet,* a beautiful and rarely seen small-scale version of the ballet, to the London Coliseum in July 2011, with the young Bolshoi stars Ivan Vasiliev and Natalia Osipova leading every performance.

Two great dance teachers died in the year under review – Frank Freeman, a former Royal Ballet dancer who became a highly respected and greatly loved classical ballet teacher and a fellow of the Royal Academy of Dance (RAD), died on 24 February 2011 at the age of 65; and Rachel Cameron, an Australian dancer and teacher who had been awarded the RAD's Queen Elizabeth II Coronation Award in November 2010, died on 6 March 2011 at the age of 86. A happier milestone was the celebration in October 2010 of the 100th anniversary of the first publication of the famous and influential dance magazine *The Dancing Times*.

THE PAST AND THE FUTURE

A controversial book on the history of ballet, *Apollo's Angels* by Jennifer Homans, was published in 2010. Homans is an American former dancer, and her eloquent history ended with an analysis of the current state of classical ballet that suggested that the art form, 'an art of high ideals and self-control in which proportion and grace stand for an innter truth and elevated state of being', may be in terminal decline. Her statement of the problem is persuasive; ballet is fundamentally counter-cultural in the present era. But it also fails to trust the adaptability and resilience of the art form, and the ongoing willingness of many dancers and choreographers to give their lives to learning, creating and performing in this rarefied language.

An indicator of ballet's potential appeal was given by the release in January 2011 of a new 'ballet' film. The dance world looked on with amusement and bemusement as the wider world flocked to *Black Swan,* starring Natalie Portman as an increasingly deranged ballerina given the leading role in *Swan Lake* (*see also* Film). The Royal Ballet dancer Edward Watson is quoted as saying about the film in an interview, 'it makes what we do look so naff and laughable'. It is to be hoped that more and more people will in time be given the opportunity to see real ballet at its best, including through initiatives being taken by Watson's own company, so that its great beauty and expressiveness can be more widely appreciated.

NEW PRODUCTIONS

ROYAL BALLET

Founded 1931 as the Vic-Wells Ballet
Royal Opera House, Covent Garden, London WC2E 9DD

Invitus Invitam (Kim Brandstrup), 15 October 2010. A one-act work. *Music,* François Couperin arranged by Thomas Adès; *design,* Richard Hudson. Cast led by Leanne Benjamin and Edward Watson
Alice's Adventures in Wonderland (Christopher Wheeldon), 28 February 2011. A full-length work. *Score,* Joby Talbot; *designs,* Bob Crowley; *scenario,* Nicholas Wright; *lighting design,* Natasha Katz; *projection design,* Jon Driscoll and Gemma Carrington. Cast led by Lauren Cuthbertson (Alice), Sergei Polunin, Edward Watson, Zenaida Yanowsky and Steven McRae
Live Fire Exercise (Wayne McGregor), 13 May 2011. A one-act work. *Music,* Michael Tippett; *artist,* John Gerrard. Cast, Lauren Cuthbertson, Sarah Lamb, Akane Takada, Federico Bonelli, Ricardo Cervera, Eric Underwood

BIRMINGHAM ROYAL BALLET
Founded 1946 as the Sadler's Wells Opera Ballet
Birmingham Hippodrome, Thorp Street, Birmingham B5 4AU

Cinderella (David Bintley), 24 November 2010. *Music,* Prokofiev; *design,* John Macfarlane. Cast led by Elisha Willis, Iain Mackay, Gaylene Cummerfield, Carol-Anne Millar, Marion Tait and Victoria Marr

ENGLISH NATIONAL BALLET
Founded 1950 as London Festival Ballet
Markova House, 39 Jay Mews, London SW7 2ES

The Nutcracker (Wayne Eagling, based on a concept by Toer van Schayk and Wayne Eagling), 10 December 2010. *Music,* Tchaikovsky; *design,* Peter Farmer. Cast led by Daria Klimentová, Vadim Muntagirov, Junor Souza, Fabian Reimair and James Streeter
Vue de l'autre (Van Le Ngoc), 16 March 2011. *Music,* Ludovico Einaudi; *design,* Van Le Ngoc and Wizzy Shawyer. Cast led by Daria Klimentová and Vadim Muntagirov

RAMBERT DANCE COMPANY
Founded 1926 as the Marie Rambert Dancers
94 Chiswick High Road, London W4 1SH

Awakenings (Aletta Collins), 22 September 2010. *Score,* Tobias Picker; *design,* Miriam Buether. Cast, Eryck Brahamania, Kirill Burlov, Malgorzata Dzierzon, Jonathan Goddard, Thomasin Gulgec, Gemma Nixon, Pieter Symonds and Angela Towler
Monolith (Tim Rushton), 16 February 2011. *Score,* Peteris Vasks; *design,* Charlotte Ostergaard and Tim Rushton

SCOTTISH BALLET
Founded 1956 as the Western Theatre Ballet; moved to Glasgow as Scottish Theatre Ballet 1969
Tramway, 25 Albert Drive, Glasgow G41 2PE

Still Life (Val Caniparoli), 23 September 2010. *Music,* Elena Kats-Chernin; *design,* Sandra Woodall
Alice (Ashley Page), 12 April 2011. *Score,* Robert Moran; *design,* Antony McDonald. Cast led by Sophie Martin (Alice), Erik Cavallari, Tomomi Sato, Owen Thorne, Adam Blyde, Quenby Hersh, Martina Forioso and Tama Barry

AWARDS

CRITICS' CIRCLE NATIONAL DANCE AWARDS 2010
De Valois Award for Outstanding Achievement in Dance – Alistair Spalding, chief executive and director of Sadler's Wells Theatre
Special Achievement Award – Jann Parry, biographer of Kenneth MacMillan
Dancing Times Award for Best Male Dancer – Ivan Vasiliev (Bolshoi Ballet)
Award for Best Female Dancer – Natalia Osipova (Bolshoi Ballet)
Award for Outstanding Company – Rambert Dance Company
Best Classical Choreography – Liam Scarlett for *Asphodel Meadows* (The Royal Ballet)
Best Modern Choreography – Russell Maliphant for *Afterlight*
Patron's Award – Daria Klimentová (English National Ballet)
Best Foreign Dance Company – Bolshoi Ballet
Outstanding Female Performance (Classical) – Martha Leebolt (Northern Ballet)
Outstanding Male Performance (Classical) – Vadim Muntagirov (English National Ballet)
Outstanding Female Performance (Modern) – Pieter Symonds (Rambert Dance Company)
Outstanding Male Performance (Modern) – Daniel Proietto (Russell Maliphant Company)
Jane Attenborough Dance UK Industry Award – Gill Clarke (independent dance artist)

LAURENCE OLIVIER AWARDS 2011 (DANCE)
Best New Dance Production – *Babel (words)* by Sidi Larbi Cherkaoui and Damien Jalet
Outstanding Achievement in Dance – Antony Gormley (set design for *Babel*)
Best Theatre Choreographer – Leon Baugh *(Sucker Punch)*

ROYAL ACADEMY OF DANCE QUEEN ELIZABETH II CORONATION AWARD 2010
Rachel Cameron

THE PLACE PRIZE 2011
Ben Duke and Raquel Meseguer *(It Needs Horses)*

YOUNG BRITISH DANCER OF THE YEAR 2011

2002	Anniek Soobroy	2007	Sergiy Polunin
2003	Joseph Caley	2008	William Bracewell
2004	Aaron Robison	2009	Yasmine Naghdi
2005	Ruth Bailey	2010	Francesca Hayward
2006	James Hay	2011	Anna Rose O'Sullivan

FILM

THE NUMBERS GAME

One of 2011's enduring film images didn't occur in the cinema but outdoors, when hundreds of fans gathered in London's Trafalgar Square in July for the premiere of *Harry Potter and the Deathly Hallows – Part 2*. The final of eight films based upon author J. K. Rowling's seven hugely popular books was set, at the time of writing, to break box office records in the UK and around the world. The series has seen stars Daniel Radcliffe, Emma Watson and Rupert Grint grow up before audiences' eyes over ten years and, according to the majority of critics, director David Yates provided a suitable finale.

Toy Story 3 was released just before the period under review but is worth including as it became the largest grossing film at the box office in the UK and Ireland for 2010, taking £73.8m. It relegated James Cameron's *Avatar*, which came out just before Christmas 2009, to second place, a welcome triumph for an animated film with real heart, and a well-made story to tell. If it proves to be the final send-off for Tom Hanks' Woody, Tim Allen's Buzz Lightyear and many other favourite characters, it will have been wholly deserved.

Other Hollywood revivals were less successful, notably *Wall Street: Money Never Sleeps,* the belated sequel to Oliver Stone's unforgettable 1987 take on the excesses of high finance. The original famously encapsulated the go-getting economic mores of the time, and proved to be a prescient observation on the hazardous and morally questionable new world of finance. While the opportunity was ripe for another such satire, Stone delivered instead a relationship drama, wrapped up in a paper-thin thriller plot about conspiracy, deception and murder. Released two years after the height of the global financial crisis, *Wall Street 2* lagged behind events far more earth-shattering than anything present in this lurid offering. Although Michael Douglas reprises his role as banker Gordon Gekko, the resurrection of that iconic anti-hero only disappoints.

Similarly uninspired was *Pirates of the Caribbean: On Stranger Tides,* in which Johnny Depp returns to his lucrative movie pantomime act for the fourth time. Penélope Cruz now plays the enigmatic pirate Angelica, who ropes Depp into a quest for the fountain of youth that also involves Blackbeard (played by a very aged Ian McShane). Little else of the plot is worth repeating. Poorly scripted, the fourth *Pirates* movie primarily serves as a tongue-in-cheek parody of previous episodes. As with the last outing, its excessively complicated plot tries extremely hard to be clever, but ends up hopelessly muddled. Depp's Captain Jack Sparrow is still a funny and well-performed character, but little else here shines.

Several of the more disdained films of the year flourished triumphantly at the box office. *Transformers: Dark of the Moon* was the third film in Michael Bay's saga: a franchise increasingly pilloried by critics, but which continues to generate spectacular financial returns. The series exists to showcase gigantic robots hammering away at each other, a joyless spectacle set up by inane dialogue and an incoherent plot. It is a long, messy film full of noise and chaos, but devoid of many actual thrills – the fight sequences are protracted beyond all pity for the audience.

The *Twilight* franchise is another favourite target of derision, in particular for its almost evangelical themes of abstinence and restraint, and most recent feature *Eclipse* is no different. Predecessors in the 'teen vampire' genre such as Buffy took these trademarks and wrapped them in layers of astute wit and irony. Instead, the *Twilight* films are stuffed to excess with one-dimensional characters, overly reliant on pedestrian dialogue, and somewhat cheesy special effects. But the emotions are honest, and the story of love and frustrated feelings resonates with its target demographic, so the highbrow arbiters of culture may be missing the point.

BRIDGES' TROUBLED WATERS

Perhaps the most bizarre revival this year was sci-fi thriller *Tron: Legacy,* about the inner world residing within the realms of a computer mainframe. Back in 1982, *Tron* was the first movie to embed human actors into a digital world. This sequel tries its best to live up to this reputation of pushing at the digital frontiers – with a budget estimated at more than US$200 million, it is the most beautifully rendered film since *Avatar*, replete with lavish, exotic effects of the kind filmmakers could only dream of even a few years ago. It is even more disappointing, then, that the final experience amounts to little more than a soulless parade of special effects, devoid of any real plot. The original *Tron* stars Jeff Bridges and he returns here, in a dual role as young and old avatars of his past character.

While that may have been a sentimental revisiting of a role for Bridges, he was on powerful form filling the boots of John Wayne in the Coen brothers' take on *True Grit,* based on Charles Portis' novel. Their sombre version of the film that won Wayne an Oscar in 1969 has 14-year-old Maddie Ross (a stand-out performance from Hailee Steinfeld) join forces with Bridges' ageing marshal Rooster Cogburn to track her father's killer in hostile territory. It was a fitting follow-up to *No Country for Old Men* for the Coens, although its cynicism, and Bridges' mumbled dialogue, may see it less handsomely rewarded than its illustrious predecessor.

LONG LIVE THE KING

The great crowd-pleaser – and Oscar-winner – of the year was *The King's Speech,* which had reports of audiences breaking into spontaneous applause at the close, perhaps appropriately for a film that often felt closer to a theatre piece, not least due to three outstanding central performances. Colin Firth was the stuttering King George VI, known as Bertie, whose sudden accession to the throne causes his wife Elizabeth (a supremely dry-witted Helena Bonham Carter) to seek the help of unorthodox Australian speech coach Lionel Logue (Geoffrey Rush, on sparkling form). Tom Hooper's film neatly sidestepped the monarch's politics in the run-up to the Second World War, although its release fortuitously chimed with what turned out to be a royal wedding year.

An edgier mainstream hit was *Black Swan,* director Darren Aronofsky's intense and wildly melodramatic journey through the tortured psyche of a competitive young ballerina. Natalie Portman deservedly won an Oscar for her portrayal of Nina, who finds herself competing for the attentions of French actor Vincent Cassel's artistic director with a new dancer, played by Mila Kunis. Aronofsky constantly played with audience perceptions using shifting visual effects and pumping up Tchaikovsky's majestic score as Nina finally achieves her ambition to star in *Swan Lake.* The film was notable, too, for performances from Barbara Hershey as Nina's domineering mother and a brave Winona Ryder as the lead dancer on her way out.

Another big success of the winter was *The Social Network,* a zeitgeist-riding picture adapted by Aaron Sorkin – creator of TV series *The West Wing* – from Ben Mezrich's book *The Accidental Billionaires* about the founding of social networking site Facebook. Sorkin laces the dizzying tangle of lawsuits and rivalries that emerged with scathing wit and cracking dialogue. Director David Fincher (of *Fight Club* fame) has spoken about how he deliberately used the snappy opening scene to get audiences to sit up and take notice. While Nine Inch Nails' Trent Reznor and Atticus Ross won an Oscar for their soundtrack, actor Jesse Eisenberg was unlucky not to be officially recognised for his nerdy take on Facebook's Mark Zuckerberg in a year dominated by Colin Firth as much as Christian Bale, who changed his physique for David O. Russell's *The Fighter.*

WHAT'S UP, DOCS?

The Social Network makes a superb companion piece to the year's most intriguing documentary, *Catfish,* in which filmmakers Ariel Schulman and Henry Joost purportedly follow Ariel's photographer brother Nev's burgeoning, long-distance friendship with a woman on Facebook. *Catfish* has been much debated as each dramatic escalation in the relationship seems masterfully controlled, although the question of the film's own authenticity only adds to its central premise. In many ways, it is irrelevant to the very real debates the film explores about honesty and personal identity in the digital world. The result is a compelling piece of storytelling, and a compulsively watchable study of relationships, virtual and real.

Spearheaded by the populist broadsides of Morgan Spurlock and Michael Moore, documentaries that probe the political, economic and social realities of modern life have become box-office fodder in the past decade, and examples this year were plentiful. Davis Guggenheim, the director of *An Inconvenient Truth,* gave us *Waiting for Superman,* a compelling cinematic argument for massive prison reform; in one of the movie's biggest eye-openers, Guggenheim reveals that housing a man in prison – where the film claims inner-city high-school dropouts are statistically likely to wind up – costs three times as much per year as sending them (as children) to even the most exclusive private school.

Matt Damon, a frequent campaigner for left-wing causes, lent his narration and personal PR to *Inside Job,* winner of the Academy Award for Best Feature Documentary. The film depicts with admirable and sometimes shocking clarity the escalating greed and recklessness that brought the financial system to the brink of collapse in the summer of 2008. Director Charles Ferguson speaks at length with journalists, politicians, academics and industry insiders to offer a clear picture of the crisis that rocked the world economy and global financial markets, and the vast web of special interests – linking major corporations, government and academia – that were vested in keeping us on the road to ruin.

Unravelling the web of toxic financial instruments that brought the global financial system to its knees is no easy matter, but it is told here in a lucid and compelling manner. Most startling is the observation that, despite all the political rhetoric about reforming Wall Street, almost nothing has been done. Many of the main perpetrators are still in positions of power, and some of them have key posts in Washington; as the film points out, most of the funding for Barack Obama's campaign came from the world of high finance. *Inside Job* is by no means an objective account of what has happened, but its argument is compelling enough, its picture of an industry driven to reckless risk and mania well-told, and very convincing.

Unlikely support for the boom in 3D cinema presentations came in the form of documentaries, no less, from two veteran German directors: Werner Herzog and Wim Wenders. Arthouse provocateur Herzog displayed the full wonder of the oldest artworks known to man in *Cave of Forgotten Dreams.* Granted unprecedented access to the Chauvet caves in southern France, Herzog's small team captures in 3D the magnificence of these Palaeolithic paintings of cave lions, bears and bison, some as many as 32,000 years old. The director arguably outstays his welcome with a sidetrack that betrays a reptilian fascination evident in recent feature *Bad Lieutenant,* but the leap between the two only serves to underline Herzog's fearsome intelligence and continuing relevance.

Wim Wenders' achievement in harnessing 3D for a feature-length movie dedicated to dance pioneer Pina Bausch is arguably even more impressive. Bausch died just as shooting was due to begin in 2009 and *Pina,* which includes memories of the choreographer from members of her Tanztheater Wuppertal company alongside excerpts of her celebrated productions, serves as a vivid tribute.

SMALL, BEAUTIFUL

Another arthouse hit was the French drama *Of Gods and Men,* which won the Grand Prix at the Cannes Film Festival 2010. A thoughtful and grave study of a group of isolated monks, it is a tale of how the peaceful harmony between Christians and Muslims in Algeria in the 1990s is lethally disrupted. The film, starring Lambert Wilson and Michael Lonsdale, focuses on the chain of events that led to real-life tragedy: the decay of government, the rise of extremism in that vacuum, and the monks' frightened confrontation with state officials and terrorists. What actually happened has never been satisfactorily defined, but director Xavier Beauvois teases every last drop of emotional power from the story that provides spiritual resolution for this doomed community.

Several small films drew attention, acclaim and awards this year. *Blue Valentine* was a bittersweet account of the blossoming and unravelling of love. Ryan Gosling and Michelle Williams play a working-class couple in Pennsylvania in a toxic marriage; the film intercuts scenes of the beginnings of their relationship and its painful decline. Williams, in particular, powerfully portrays the ennui that eats away at her character's feelings – frustrated by her own failed ambitions to become a doctor, she is angrily perplexed by her husband's lack of drive.

Shot on a minimal budget, Gareth Edwards' *Monsters* was quintessential post-modern sci-fi: a high-concept idea

1150   The Year 2010–11

translated into a grimy, downbeat context. Edwards' movie imagines that a probe containing seeds of alien life crash lands in Mexico, turning that entire nation into a quarantined zone. The film draws explicitly on past icons of filmmaking – namely the Conrad-inspired upriver nightmares of Francis Ford Coppola and Werner Herzog. Like *District 9*, the film is peppered with political satire – here mocking American fears of their Mexican neighbours.

The director (and son of David Bowie) Duncan Jones won plaudits for 2009's low-key existential thriller *Moon*, and he was granted an altogether bigger budget for his return to that movie's theme of split identities in *Source Code*. In this thriller version of *Groundhog Day*, a man (Jake Gyllenhaal) re-lives the eight minutes before an explosion on a mission to find the bomber of a doomed Chicago commuter train. Like 2010's *Inception*, *Source Code* is ingenious enough to make the most of its preposterous plot, and it shares that film's authoritative, iron determination to tell its story with total conviction.

The much-anticipated return of Terrence Malick may lead some cinema-goers to question the auteur's authority and determination. Malick has been celebrated since his 1973 debut, *Badlands*, starring Martin Sheen and Sissy Spacek. Since then, his measured output – including a 20-year hiatus between second feature *Days of Heaven* and 1998's *The Thin Red Line* – has only seen his reputation grow beyond all recognition. So it was little surprise his long-heralded project *The Tree of Life* scooped the most prestigious prize, the Palme d'Or, from a jury led by Robert De Niro at the Cannes Film Festival 2011. The UK release date was initially clouded in mystery but, from 8 July 2011, audiences were able to debate the merits of a film that harnessed images of the solar system and dinosaurs to the tale of three brothers growing up in 1950s Texas under the stern hand of their frustrated father, played by Brad Pitt. Themes of faith and the glory of creation were lost to many under the heavy-handed symbolism of modern-day sequences featuring a bemused, under-utilised Sean Penn as one of the grown-up boys. Malick's legacy may rest on it.

AWARDS

ACADEMY AWARDS 2011
Best Picture – *The King's Speech* (Tom Hooper)
Directing – Tom Hooper *(The King's Speech)*
Actor in a Leading Role – Colin Firth *(The King's Speech)*
Actress in a Leading Role – Natalie Portman *(Black Swan)*
Actor in a Supporting Role – Christian Bale *(The Fighter)*
Actress in a Supporting Role – Melissa Leo *(The Fighter)*
Animated Feature Film – *Toy Story 3* (Lee Unkrich)

Writing (Original Screenplay) – *The King's Speech*, by David Seidler
Writing (Adapted Screenplay) – *The Social Network*, by Aaron Sorkin
Foreign Language Film – *In a Better World* (Susanne Bier), Denmark
Documentary Feature – *Inside Job* (Charles Ferguson)

CANNES FILM FESTIVAL 2011
Palme d'Or – *The Tree of Life* (Terrence Malick)
Grand Prix – *Once Upon a Time in Anatolia* (Nuri Bilge Ceylan) and *The Kid with a Bike* (Jean-Pierre and Luc Dardenne)
Jury Prize – *Polisse* (Maiwenn)
Best Director – Nicolas Winding Refn *(Drive)*
Best Actor – Jean Dujardin *(The Artist)*
Best Actress – Kirsten Dunst *(Melancholia)*
Best Screenplay – Joseph Cedar *(Footnote)*
Caméra d'Or – *Las Acacias* (Pablo Giorgelli)
Un Certain Regard – *Arirang* (Kim Ki-Duk)

BERLIN FILM FESTIVAL 2011
Golden Bear – *A Separation* (Asghar Farhadi)
Grand Jury Prize – *The Turin Horse* (Béla Tarr)
Silver Bear for Best Director – Ulrich Kohler *(Sleeping Sickness)*

VENICE FILM FESTIVAL 2010
Golden Lion – *Somewhere* (Sofia Coppola)
Special Jury Prize – *Essential Killing* (Jerzy Skolimowski)

ORANGE BRITISH ACADEMY FILM AWARDS 2010
Best Film – The King's Speech (Tom Hooper)
Director – David Fincher *(The Social Network)*
Outstanding British Film – *The King's Speech* (Tom Hooper)
Outstanding Debut by a British Writer, Director or Producer – *Four Lions* (Chris Morris)
Original Screenplay – *The King's Speech*, by David Seidler
Adapted Screenplay – *The Social Network*, by Aaron Sorkin
Film not in the English Language – *The Girl with the Dragon Tattoo* (Niels Arden Oplev)
Animated Film – *Toy Story 3* (Lee Unkrich)
Leading Actor – Colin Firth *(The King's Speech)*
Leading Actress – Natalie Portman *(Black Swan)*
Supporting Actor – Geoffrey Rush *(The King's Speech)*
Supporting Actress – Helena Bonham Carter *(The King's Speech)*
Academy Fellowship – Christopher Lee
Outstanding British Contribution to Cinema – the *Harry Potter* films

LITERATURE

Nick Rennison

FICTION

One indisputably influential contemporary novelist is Philip Roth, whose 27th work of fiction, *Nemesis* (Jonathan Cape), was published in October 2010. In a career lasting more than half a century, Roth has won every major accolade that the US literary establishment has to offer and books like *Portnoy's Complaint* and *American Pastoral* have been acclaimed as works of genius but even he is not immune to criticism. There are those prepared to debate his claims to greatness. When he was chosen as the fourth recipient of the Man Booker International Prize in May 2011, one of the judges, Carmen Callil, withdrew in protest, claiming that 'he goes on and on and on about the same subject in almost every single book.' The prize had already attracted some controversy when John Le Carré, who appeared on the shortlist, let it be known that he did not want to be there. 'I am enormously flattered to be named as a finalist of the 2011 Man Booker International Prize,' he said in a statement issued by his agent. 'However I do not compete for literary prizes and have therefore asked for my name to be withdrawn.'

Another, less rancorous debate than the one between Callil and the admirers of Philip Roth was aroused by Man Booker's curious decision to celebrate the life of the late Beryl Bainbridge by inviting the public to vote online for a Best of Beryl winner from the five titles by her that had been shortlisted for the real Booker prize over the years. Victory went to *Master Georgie*, her novel set during the Crimean War. Some saw the award as a graceful tribute to a distinguished novelist; others considered it an unnecessary and faintly ludicrous award which she would not herself have wanted.

A new novel by Beryl Bainbridge was amongst the more eagerly anticipated fictional offerings in the period under review. Unfinished at the time of her death in July 2010, *The Girl in the Polka Dot Dress* (Little, Brown) appeared in May 2011 in a version put together by her friend and editor Brendan King from her working manuscript, in which Bainbridge took a possibly apocryphal incident that figures in conspiracy theories surrounding the assassination of Robert Kennedy in 1968. Although this last, posthumous novel was largely set in America, Bainbridge's fiction for most of her career was very English in its subjects and in its concerns. Two novels published this year attempted to anatomise the nature of Englishness in ways which she would doubtless have appreciated. *The Stranger's Child* (Picador) was Alan Hollinghurst's first novel since *The Line of Beauty* in 2004. It began in 1913 with a young, gay poet's weekend visit to the country house of a friend and then opened out into a long perspective on 20th century England. Graham Swift's *Wish You Were Here* (Picador) took the story of a man returning to the village where he grew up in order to bury his brother, a soldier killed in Iraq, and shaped it into a moving meditation on the changing nature of what it means to be English. Further ways of telling English stories were also on display in the year's fiction. Philip Hensher's *King of the Badgers* (Fourth Estate) was set in a

small coastal town in the West Country whose inhabitants are traumatised by the disappearance of a young girl and the media circus which then descends upon them. Justin Cartwright's *Other People's Money* (Bloomsbury) created comedy out of the credit crunch with its story of Julian Trevelyan-Tubal, chairman of the bank Tubal & Co, and his desperate efforts to keep the family business afloat in times of trouble. The appropriately named *At Last* (Picador) by Edward St Aubyn was the final volume in his series of darkly comic novels about sex, booze and familial dysfunction in the English aristocracy.

Historical fiction remained popular with both writers and readers alike. Amitav Ghosh's *River of Smoke* (John Murray), the second part of a historical trilogy which began with *Sea of Poppies*, followed the fortunes of three ships caught up in storms in the Indian Ocean in the year 1838. Andrew Miller's sixth novel *Pure* (Sceptre) saw a return to the 18th century, in which a young engineer in pre-revolutionary France is given the task of dismantling an ancient Parisian cemetery. As in most years, Victorian England proved a favourite destination for historical novelists. Jane Harris's *Gillespie and I* (Faber) had its elderly, unreliable narrator in the 1930s looking back on her involvement fifty years earlier with a gifted and troubled artist and his family. *Derby Day* (Chatto & Windus) by D. J. Taylor was an exceptionally clever, pastiche of a 19th century novel that had a richness of character that almost matched the works of Dickens and Thackeray on which it was modelled.

Other novelists took the present and the recent past as settings for a variety of compelling tales. Ali Smith's *There but for the* (Hamish Hamilton), with its arrestingly truncated title, was a playful and provocative story about a dinner guest who locks himself in his hosts' spare room and refuses to emerge. *Waterline* (Viking), the story of a one-time shipbuilder in the Glasgow yards and his decline into homelessness and despair, was a second novel by Ross Raisin. Anne Enright's *The Forgotten Waltz* (Jonathan Cape), a dark and funny story of love, adultery and betrayal in the days of the 'Celtic Tiger' Irish boom, was her first novel since *The Gathering* won the Man Booker Prize in 2007. Another previous winner of the Man Booker, Aravind Adiga, published his second novel to largely enthusiastic reviews. In *Last Man in Tower* (Atlantic), the differences between the old and the new India were vividly embodied in the story of the battle between a ruthless property developer and a retired schoolteacher over the future of a housing co-operative.

Voices from across the Atlantic continued to be heard with attention. Jonathan Franzen's *Freedom* (Fourth Estate) received probably more coverage than any other novel in the autumn of 2010. Most reviewers and readers loved Franzen's multi-layered story which traced the lives of liberal, middle-class Walter and Patty Berglund and their two children as they unfolded over several decades. Franzen's close friend David Foster Wallace committed suicide in September 2008 but the posthumous publication of *The Pale King* (Hamish Hamilton), a vast and varied novel constructed from more than 1,500 pages of manuscript he left behind, provided a reminder of his remarkable talent. Other American novels that attracted a slew of favourable reviews included Jennifer Egan's *A Visit from the Goon Squad* (Corsair), winner of the 2011 Pulitzer Prize for Fiction, a clever kaleidoscope of intersecting stories focused on a group of people involved in the music industry, and *Great House* (Viking) by Nicole Krauss which explored ideas of memory and loss through the lives of men and women around the world connected via their possession of an antique desk. Born in Serbia but brought up in the USA, Tea Obreht became, at the age of 25, the youngest ever winner of the Orange Prize for Fiction with her debut novel, *The Tiger's Wife* (Weidenfeld & Nicolson).

Crime fiction seemed ever more international in its flavour, even in the UK, a market notoriously resistant to novels in translation. The taste for Scandinavian murder mysteries showed no signs of disappearing. Film adaptations ensured continuing sales for Stieg Larsson's 'Millennium' trilogy. Meanwhile an old master returned in *The Troubled Man* (Harvill Secker) which was Henning Mankell's first novel in a decade about his humane and melancholic Swedish policeman Kurt Wallander. Jo Nesbo's *The Leopard* (Harvill Secker) was the seventh novel featuring his Oslo detective Inspector Harry Hole, here investigating the killings of young women who all stayed at an isolated mountain hostel on one particular night. In *An Uncertain Place* (Harvill Secker), prize-winning French crime writer Fred Vargas brought her recurring character Commissaire Adamsberg to London and then despatched him halfway across Europe in search of a vampiric killer. From Italy came the veteran Andrea Camilleri, whose book *The Track of Sand* (Mantle) was his twelfth featuring Inspector Montalbano.

Scotland was the setting for some of the best of British crime fiction. Denise Mina's *The End of the Wasp Season* (Orion) traced the links between the suicide of a disgraced millionaire banker in his Kentish garden and a young woman brutally killed in an upmarket Glasgow suburb. Also set in Glasgow, Chris Brookmyre's *Where the Bodies Are Buried* (Little, Brown) saw its central character drawn into a dirty world of gangland murders. South of the border, the husband and wife team who write under the joint name of Nicci French published *Blue Monday* (Michael Joseph), a compelling account of a child kidnapping. Irish author John Banville, writing under the pseudonym of Benjamin Black which he uses for crime fiction, published *A Death in Summer* (Mantle), set against the backdrop of 1950s Dublin.

Plugged (Headline) was the first venture into adult fiction by Eoin Colfer, best known for the 'Artemis Fowl' children's books. He set it across the Atlantic and made his narrator, Daniel McEvoy, a doorman at a seedy New Jersey club. There was no indication whether or not Colfer intends McEvoy to be an ongoing character but he would do well to consider the possibility of future books featuring him. Harlan Coben returned to Myron Bolitar, the sports agent and crime investigator who has appeared in nine previous novels, in *Live Wire* (Orion); Michael Connelly's *The Fifth Witness* (Orion) was another excursion for defense attorney Mickey Haller; and *Moonlight Mile* (Little, Brown) by Dennis Lehane provided a further case for his detectives Patrick Kenzie and Angie Gennaro. Meanwhile Jeffrey Deaver took time out from his own novels about the severely disabled detective Lincoln Rhyme but only to become the latest author to don Ian Fleming's mantle. *Carte Blanche* (Hodder) was a new James Bond story in which 007 entered the 21st century for the first time.

Finally in crime fiction, 26 bestselling writers ranging from Kathy Reichs to Peter James were each invited to contribute a chapter to *No Rest for the Dead* (Simon & Schuster). The gimmick of multiple authorship is one that has been tried in the past often enough but this latest venture made for interesting reading.

In speculative fiction, the boundaries between SF, horror and fantasy continued to blur and talented writers continued to make use of whatever elements of different genres best suited their aims. *Embassytown* (Macmillan) by the much-admired China Miéville was an exploration of the nature of language and communication wrapped in a compelling story of encounters between human beings, with their capacity for deception, and an alien race who can only speak the truth. Charles Stross's *Rule 34* (Orbit) combined cutting-edge SF and many of the motifs of crime fiction in a thought-provoking thriller about the dark possibilities of the internet's future. *Surface Detail* (Orbit) was the ninth in Iain M. Banks's loosely connected series of novels set in the interstellar society known as The Culture. South African novelist and journalist Lauren Beukes won the 2011 Arthur C. Clarke Award for *Zoo City* (Angry Robot), set in an alternative version of Johannesburg where criminals all have animal familiars attached to them. The other major British prize in the genre, the British Science Fiction Association Award, went to Ian McDonald's *The Dervish House* (Gollancz).

In fantasy literature, 2011 looked set to be dominated by the American writer George R. R. Martin. *A Dance with Dragons* (Harper Voyager), the fifth doorstop of a volume in his 'Song of Ice and Fire' series has had a rocky road to publication but its eventual appearance coincided with the broadcasting of *Game of Thrones*, the lavish TV series based on earlier books in the sequence. Homegrown fantasy fiction of note included Ben Aaronovitch's *Moon Over Soho* (Gollancz), the second in a series in which a Metropolitan police officer finds himself confronting wizards, vampires and gods of the Thames; *The Curious Case of the Clockwork Man* (Snowbooks), a steampunk adventure set in an alternative 19th century, by Mark Hodder; and Joe Abercrombie's *The Heroes* (Gollancz), set in the epic world of his earlier 'First Law' trilogy.

NON-FICTION

In non-fiction, the year was filled with substantial historical works, notable for their range of reference and their ambition. *The Great Sea* (Allen Lane) by David Abulafia was highly praised for the author's ability to mix panoramic narrative with great detail in what was subtitled 'A Human History of the Mediterranean'. *Civilization: The West and the Rest* (Allen Lane), which explored the reasons why the West came to dominate the world in recent centuries, was another of the sweeping, provocative histories for which Niall Ferguson has become well-known. *Rome* (Weidenfeld & Nicolson), by Robert Hughes, was a boisterously opinionated cultural history of the city from its legendary foundation to the present day. Another world city was the subject of Simon Sebag Montefiore's *Jerusalem* (Weidenfeld & Nicolson) which covered three millennia in the history of a place at the heart of three religions. Two 19th century wars which still have resonances in the present day were also the subjects of major works. *Crimea* (Allen Lane) by Orlando Figes looked at the 1850s war between Russia on one hand and Britain, France and the decaying Ottoman Empire on the other; Amanda Foreman's *A World on Fire* (Allen Lane) was a huge, 1,000-page plus account of the American Civil War. Both conflicts have at different times been described as the first war of the modern era and both were vividly reconstructed in the books devoted to them.

Literary biography flourished in the year and works of note in the period included Gordon Bowker's *James Joyce* (Weidenfeld & Nicolson), a new rival to Richard Ellmann's magisterial work on the Irish novelist, and Rosamund Bartlett's *Tolstoy: A Russian Life* (Profile), a brave attempt to encompass the author's tumultuous life in less than 400 pages. *Constance* (John Murray) by Franny Moyle was, in the words of its own subtitle, 'The Tragic and Scandalous Life of Mrs. Oscar Wilde'. *The Children of Lovers* (Faber) was a much more personal work — Judy Golding's touching memoir of growing up as the daughter of the author of *Lord of the Flies*.

There were plenty of books predicting what is to come as well as those anatomising what has passed. Books on the future of the internet have become significantly less gung-ho in the last year. A number of very different works cast a sceptical eye on the wilder claims of those determined to see nothing but utopia awaiting us. *The Shallows* (Atlantic) by Nicholas Carr argued that use of the internet was changing the ways we think, read and remember; Evgeny Morozov's *The Net Delusion* (Allen Lane) was an assault on the belief that new social media were reliable agents of political change in a world where the internet can just as easily be at the service of authoritarian regimes; and Eli Pariser's *The Filter Bubble* (Viking) claimed that an ever more commercialised internet is in danger of narrowing our lives rather than enriching them.

POETRY

The second half of 2010 saw the culmination of a series of events to mark the 25th anniversary of the death of Philip Larkin. A statue of the poet was unveiled at the railway station in Hull, the town where he spent much of his adult life, and *Letters to Monica* (Faber) gathered together his correspondence with Monica Jones, his long-term companion.

The year 2011 has been marked so far by cuts and resignations at two of the poetry world's most significant organisations. The Poetry Book Society, founded in the 1950s by T. S. Eliot and others, lost all its Arts Council funding in the spring, representing a severe and unanticipated threat to its future. Meanwhile, there were different kinds of problems at the Poetry Society where there was a string of resignations by members of its board. One of those who went was society president Jo Shapcott who was in the news earlier in the year for happier reasons. Her collection *Of Mutability* (Faber), elegant reflections on change and mortality, won the Costa Book of the Year award. Lanarkshire-born poet Liz Lochhead was named as the second Scots makar, or national poet, in succession to Edwin Morgan who died in August 2010. The 2010 T. S. Eliot Prize, administered by the under-threat Poetry Books Society, went to *White Egrets* (Faber), the latest book by the veteran Caribbean poet Derek Walcott; the Forward Prize was won by Seamus Heaney for *Human Chain* (Faber).

Michael Longley confirmed his status as one of the finest contemporary Irish poets with a new collection, *A Hundred Doors* (Jonathan Cape). Wendy Cope revealed the metrical skill and offbeat humour for which she is known in *Family Values* (Faber); and Jackie Kay published *Fiere* (Picador), a poetic companion work to the prose memoir *Red Dust Road*, published in 2010, in which she recounted her search for her birth parents. Sean O'Brien published

November (Picador), a volume of elegiac verse, much of it commemorating departed family and friends; and Geoffrey Hill's *Clavics* (Enitharmon) was a short sequence of poems embodying Hill's admiration for the poetry of the mid-17th century.

CHILDREN'S

This was the year in which a new champion of children's literature was announced. Julia Donaldson, author of *The Gruffalo* (Macmillan Children's), became the seventh children's laureate in June 2011. Taking over from Anthony Browne, she will hold the post until 2013.

As Donaldson began her laureateship, the prospects of children's and young adult literature looked healthy, although, looking at the lists of bestsellers, it would be easy to assume that only fantasy series stood any chance of real success in the market. There was no new novel by Stephenie Meyer and vampires were not baring their fangs in teen fiction with quite the regularity they did a few years ago, but other supernatural creatures were on hand to plug the gap. Fallen angels figured in the novels of Lauren Kate of which *Passion* (Doubleday Childrens) was the latest; *Forever* (Scholastic) was the last volume in the 'Wolves of Mercy Falls' series by Maggie Stiefvater which featured teenage werewolves; and Rick Riordan published *The Throne of Fire* (Puffin), the second of the 'Kane Chronicles' about two modern teens who learn that the gods and legendary creatures of Ancient Egypt are all too real.

Series and series' characters continued to be immensely popular. *Scorpia Rising* (Walker) was the latest novel about teenage spy Alex Rider, written by Anthony Horowitz. *Kidnap in the Caribbean* (Orion Children's) by Lauren St John was the second in the sequence of Laura Marlin mysteries, the first of which had been *Dead Man's Cove*. There were, of course, standalone novels as well which gained both enthusiastic reviews and eager readers. *Artichoke Hearts* (Macmillan Children's) by Sita Brahmachari was a first novel which won the 2011 Waterstone's Children's Book Prize; Eva Ibbotson's *One Dog and His Boy* (Marion Lloyd) was an appealing story about Fleck and Hal, the dog and the boy of the title, setting off on a journey towards freedom; and *Little Manfred* (HarperCollins Children's) was a new book by Michael Morpurgo, author of *War Horse*.

With the last film released in the summer of 2011, some might have thought that Harry Potter would be old news but the schoolboy wizard and his creator continued to make headlines. J. K. Rowling launched Pottermore, a website intended to sell e-book versions of the novels and to become a vast online community for all fans. Meanwhile, a new work by Enid Blyton was discovered in a collection of manuscripts bought by the Seven Stories children's books centre in Newcastle; *Mr. Tumpy's Caravan* was originally thought to be a version of a book published decades ago but close examination revealed that it was a completely new work.

NEWS AND FAREWELLS

Either directly or indirectly, the continuing economic downturn and government cuts had their effects on books and the book trade this year. The HMV Group, after issuing a series of profit warnings, put Waterstone's on the market in March 2011 in an attempt to improve its financial position and, two months later, sold the bookshop chain for £53m to a fund controlled by the Russian billionaire Alexander Mamut. Mamut almost immediately announced the appointment of James Daunt, the founder of the small, upmarket London chain of Daunt Books, as the new managing director of Waterstone's. Libraries were under threat throughout the country and the campaign against large-scale closures won the support of many writers and publishers. Author Philip Pullman made a particularly eloquent defence of libraries in a speech he gave to a public meeting called in January 2011 to protest against cuts in Oxfordshire. Pullman delivered a fiery polemic that became an instant hit online. Later in the year, Arts Council England did announce increases of nearly 10 per cent in its funding for literature - and this at a time when other areas of the arts were facing cutbacks.

Money could still be found to keep a rare Jane Austen manuscript in the country. Auctioned at Sotheby's in July for close to 1 million pounds, the manuscript for her unfinished novel *The Watsons* might well have gone abroad but the Bodleian Library in Oxford, with the help of the National Heritage Memorial Fund, was able to put up the money to buy it. Another literary legacy from much the same period had already stayed in Britain; a love letter by John Keats was bought in March for £96,000 by the City of London Corporation with the financial assistance of the Heritage Lottery Fund.

In June 2011, the British Library was in the news with the announcement of an agreement between the library and Google to digitise hundreds of thousands of books and pamphlets published between 1700 and 1870 held in its collections. The debate about the future of online access to the literature of the past continues. To Dame Lynne Brindley, the chief executive of the British Library, the joint project was simply a logical extension of the ambition of her predecessors to provide access to knowledge to everyone. To critics of Google it seemed one more substantial step forward in the multinational corporation's hubristic campaign to control the world's knowledge.

Of the people who died in the year, few can have had so remarkable a life as Patrick Leigh Fermor who passed away in June 2011 at the age of 96. Once described as 'a cross between Indiana Jones, James Bond and Graham Greene', Leigh Fermor had, in the course of his long life, been a linguist, travel writer, novelist, translator and war hero. He will probably be best remembered for his two travel books, *A Time of Gifts* (1977) and *Between the Woods and the Water* (1986). A third volume has been promised for a quarter of a century. The many admirers of his work will hope that some version of it will be published posthumously. Others who died in the period under review included the literary critics Sir Frank Kermode and John Gross; the Scottish poet Edwin Morgan; the historian Tony Judt; the centenarian novelist and biographer Elizabeth Jenkins whose first novel had been published in 1929 and praised by Virginia Woolf; children's author Elizabeth Beresford, creator of the Wombles of Wimbledon Common; the novelist Diana Norman who had also published historical fiction under

the name of Ariana Franklin; the historian and biographer Vincent Cronin; children's author Dick King-Smith, writer of *The Sheep-Pig*, the book on which the movie *Babe* was based; Brian Jacques, the fantasy author best known for his 'Redwall' books; crime writer H. R. F. Keating, creator of Bombay detective Inspector Ghote; Diana Wynne Jones, author of *Howl's Moving Castle* and other fantasy novels for children; the military historian Richard Holmes; the feminist SF novelist Joanna Russ; the thriller writer Craig Thomas; the playwright Pam Gems; the novelist Josephine Hart, author of *Damage*; and the novelist and book reviewer Francis King.

AWARDS

MAN BOOKER PRIZE 2010
Howard Jacobson – *The Finkler Question* (winner)

SHORTLIST
Peter Carey – *Parrot and Olivier in America*
Emma Donoghue – *Room*
Damon Galgut – *In a Strange Room*
Andrea Levy – *The Long Song*
Tom McCarthy – *C*

MAN BOOKER INTERNATIONAL PRIZE 2011
Philip Roth

COSTA BOOK AWARDS
Costa Book of the Year Award: Jo Shapcott – *Of Mutability*

CATEGORY WINNERS
Costa Novel Award: Maggie O'Farrell – *The Hand That First Held Mine*
Costa First Novel Award: Kishwar Desai – *Witness the Night*
Costa Biography Award: Edmund de Waal – *The Hare with Amber Eyes*
Costa Poetry Award: Jo Shapcott – *Of Mutability*
Costa Children's Book Award: Jason Wallace – *Out of Shadows*

ORANGE PRIZE FOR FICTION 2011
Tea Obreht – *The Tiger's Wife*

BBC SAMUEL JOHNSON PRIZE FOR NON-FICTION 2011
Frank Dikötter – *Mao's Great Famine*

CARNEGIE MEDAL IN CHILDREN'S LITERATURE 2011
Patrick Ness – *Monsters of Men*

WALTER SCOTT PRIZE FOR HISTORICAL FICTION 2011
Andrea Levy – *The Long Song*

THE MEDIA

Steve Clarke

TELEVISION

TELEVISION

The emergence of a scaled-back BBC and the attempt by Rupert Murdoch's News Corporation to tighten its grip on the UK via its pay-TV firm, BSkyB, were two opposing forces challenging the television eco-system. The media mogul fought to take total control of BSkyB and, for good measure, bought his daughter Elisabeth's London-based production firm, Shine Group, maker of such hit shows as *MasterChef*. But as the phone-hacking and police corruption scandal at the *News of the World* re-ignited in the summer of 2011, Murdoch's ambition to own BSkyB outright remained unfulfilled. In July regulator Ofcom began an investigation to assess whether News Corporation – owner of News International, *News of the World's* publisher – was a 'fit and proper' company to be the majority shareholder in BSkyB.

While in December ITV's flagship soap *Coronation Street* celebrated its 50th anniversary with a live hour-long episode, it was the unlikely vehicle of a sumptuously filmed period serial set in the closing years of the Edwardian era, *Downton Abbey*, which gave the broadcaster its biggest new drama success for years. Costume drama is generally the preserve of the BBC; the Julian Fellowes-created *Downton Abbey*, however, overshadowed the corporation's restaging of *Upstairs, Downstairs* with the result that the revival looked derivative.

A new TV sub-genre to emerge during the year was the so-called 'structured reality' show. This was most successfully executed in *The Only Way Is Essex*, which made its debut on ITV2 in October 2010. Another unlikely hit was Channel 4's *My Big Fat Gypsy Wedding*, which also proved the ability of reality TV to reinvent itself.

ROYAL RATINGS BONANZA

For many viewers the marriage of Prince William and Kate Middleton in April 2011, watched by an estimated global audience of 2 billion, was the undoubted TV event of the year. Traditionally the BBC attracts the majority of viewers for state occasions. This royal wedding was no exception, but several critics thought ITV's coverage more in tune with the times than the BBC's somewhat formal approach. Technologically, 3D TV moved a step nearer the mass market as Sky launched what it billed as 'Europe's first 3D TV channel' in October 2010.

Not for the first time, the satellite broadcaster had stolen a march on rivals. Audiences were kept waiting until the following June before the BBC climbed onboard the 3D bandwagon when it transmitted the ladies' and men's Wimbledon tennis finals in 3D.

LICENCE FEE FREEZE LEAVES BBC COLD

The coalition government's decision to force the BBC to make what some commentators claimed were the most draconian cuts for decades was the result of frenzied negotiations between media minister Jeremy Hunt and the BBC's director-general Mark Thompson.

The eventual agreement, announced on 20 October 2010, involved freezing the licence fee at its present level for six years. The BBC was also to take on the cost of running the World Service – hitherto paid for by the Foreign Office – as well as other broadcasting responsibilities. These included helping to bankroll S4C, the Welsh-language Channel 4, plus paying towards proposed new local TV news stations and a contribution towards the cost of introducing high-speed broadband across the UK.

The impact of these measures was a widespread cost-cutting programme likely to lead to the loss of 4,000 BBC jobs and trim around £700m (roughly 20 per cent of the BBC's licence fee income) from the corporation's annual budget. Opinion formers were divided over the wisdom of this economic belt tightening. Many agreed with the government that the BBC should not be immune from the austerity measures affecting the public sector in general while commercial broadcasters were glad to see the corporation being forced to make cuts after what they regarded as years of unfair competition. Others were appalled.

TORY GRANDEE APPOINTED TO RUN BBC

A further reminder that the BBC needed to adjust itself to the new atmosphere at Whitehall came in February 2011 when it was confirmed that the ex-Conservative cabinet member and the last governor of Hong Kong, Chris Patten, would succeed Michael Lyons, a one-time Labour council leader, as the BBC Trust's new chairman.

Rightly or wrongly, Jonathan Ross's reported £18m fee had been seen by much of the press as the main manifestation of the corporation's alleged profligacy. The final edition of Ross's Friday-night, BBC1 chat show was broadcast in July 2010. Ross's replacement, *The Graham Norton Show*, began four months later. Reviewers reacted favourably to the new programme, a view shared by BAFTA jury members the following spring when Norton won the prize for best entertainment performance.

DOWNTON ABBEY PROVIDES AN ESCAPE

Was it a coincidence that the aristocratic country house serial *Downton Abbey* was such a big success at precisely the time an old Etonian once again took up residence in Downing Street? Critic Mark Lawson, writing in the *Guardian*, hailed 'the return of toff TV. . . shortly after the formation of the poshest government in the country since Harold Macmillan in the 1950s.'

Featuring a starry cast led by Maggie Smith and Hugh Bonneville, *Downton Abbey* was a huge hit as ratings exceeded 10 million and brought ITV1 an unusually up-market audience. Lawson noted that posh period drama tends to thrive during grim economic times because 'viewers crave escapism'. Underneath all the trappings of upper-class Edwardian life, Lawson suspected the show was just another soap opera: 'In common with *Coronation Street* and *EastEnders*, *Downton Abbey* has a comic matriarch (Dame Maggie Smith's Dowager Countess of Grantham) and a hissable villain (Siobhan Finneran's maid O'Brien) and frequent plot-lines featuring pregnancies and sexual scandal.' The programme failed to win any trophies at either BAFTA or the Royal Television Society's programme awards.

Edgier TV drama was provided during the period 2010–11 by, among others, Channel 4. The broadcaster's

This Is England '86, written and directed by Shane Meadows, and Peter Kosminsky's depiction of Britain's role in the post-war founding of the state of Israel, *The Promise*, were two examples of how TV fiction continued to push the envelope. Vicky McClure won much praise for her role as skinhead Lol in *This Is England '86*.

Crime stories have always been one of the main ingredients in the TV mix. In this genre, a contemporary take on Sherlock Holmes, starring Benedict Cumberbatch and Martin Freeman as the great investigator and his dim sidekick, Watson, stood out. However, reviewers wondered why there were just three episodes of *Sherlock*, made by Hartswood Films for BBC1 and co-written by Steven Moffat, the screenwriter in charge of the latest batch of *Doctor Who*. A very different kind of detective show, and one that developed a cult following during the winter, was *The Killing*. This Danish import, showcased by BBC4, was admired for its naturalism and compared favourably to US shows like *The Sopranos* and *The Wire*.

Another jewel in the BBC4 crown was *The Road To Coronation Street*, made by ITV Studios as part of the programme's 50th anniversary celebrations. In the opinion of many critics the film was a perfectly realised evocation of how, against the odds, the then untried actor-turned-writer Tony Warren persuaded Granada to back what became Britain's longest-running TV soap opera.

REALITY TV REINVENTS ITSELF – IN ESSEX

The demise of *Big Brother* on Channel 4 (a new version of the show was due to make its debut on Five during the autumn of 2011) left programme makers wondering how to re-awaken audience's appetites for reality TV. In *The Only Way Is Essex* they seemed to hit upon an answer.

Described by producers Lime Pictures, the makers of teen soap *Hollyoaks*, as 'real people in modified situations, saying unscripted lines but in a structured way,' *The Only Way Is Essex* (known as *TOWIE* to its fans) rapidly became a cult hit. Viewers were able to keep up to date with the cast, characterised by their flash cars and fake tans, via real-time updates on social networking sites. Mind-stretching it wasn't, but a lot of people found the show and its youthful stars disturbingly addictive.

A measure of its success was that a rival programme, depicting a more up-market group of 'characters', soon appeared – E4's *Made In Chelsea*. Commentators detected the influence of American MTV reality shows like *The Hills* and *Jersey Shore*. The latter spawned a much-publicised British version re-located to Newcastle and inevitably titled *Geordie Shore*. The show was dismissed as 'bordering on pornographic' by local MP Chi Onwurah. 'It's exploiting those young people and exploiting our city,' she told the *Newcastle Evening Chronicle*.

My Big Fat Gypsy Wedding was another must-view programme for reality TV addicts. Some critics accused it of sneering and stereotyping, but hefty ratings of more than 8 million represented a big win for Channel 4.

In comedy, *Miranda* continued to score for BBC2. Such was its success that the show's next series, expected in 2012, will be shown on BBC1. A new comedy starring Steve Coogan and Rob Brydon, and directed by Michael Winterbottom, *The Trip*, divided audiences and critics. The long-awaited airline comedy from Matt Lucas and David Walliams, *Come Fly With Me*, in which the duo play more than a dozen characters, achieved one of the highest BBC audiences for a new comedy – more than 10 million viewers tuned in.

TV'S X FACTOR AND THE FAMILY VIEWING WATERSHED

Certain kinds of politicians and opinion formers have always liked to blame TV for society's failings. A report by Reg Bailey, chief executive of the Mothers' Union, *Letting Children Be Children*, accused broadcasters of ignoring the 9pm family viewing watershed by screening items such as raunchy dance routines in entertainment shows like ITV's *The X Factor*. 'Some parents even questioned whether the watershed still exists,' said the report, which was scathing about what it regarded as the commercialisation and sexualisaton of childhood.

In an era when internet pornography is freely available and viewers can easily time-shift programmes via devices like the Sky+ recorder, the debate over the 9pm watershed is not as straightforward as it was in the analogue age. In December 2010 press attention focused on the final of *The X Factor* and a dance sequence performed by pop sirens Christina Aguilera and Rihanna.

Some people, especially devotees of the *Daily Mail*, which campaigned against the show, considered Aguilera and Rihanna's performance to be unsuitable for family audiences. However, following almost 3,000 complaints, an investigation by media regulator Ofcom concluded that the sequence was not in breach of its codes but was 'at the very margin of acceptability'. The watchdog took the unusual step of criticising the *Daily Mail* for exposing readers to images more sexually explicit than those in the TV programme. Ofcom claimed readers who had not watched the show would have been misled into thinking it more titillating than it was.

Such publicity, of course, did *The X Factor* no harm; the final on 12 December 2010 generated a new record high as more than 17 million viewers watched. When Matt Cardle was announced as the winner, the audience peaked with 19.4 million viewers – a 60 per cent audience share.

While *The X Factor* helped ITV to a strong financial performance its relaunched breakfast time service, *Daybreak*, fronted by Adrian Chiles and Christine Bleakley, was one long headache for the broadcaster. In September 2010 the show launched with a promising 1 million viewers. By summer this had dropped to 700,000.

RADIO

We live in an age of ever-expanding media choice, but during the period 2010–11 a record proportion of the UK population listened to the radio. More than 90 per cent of people in the UK tuned in to radio on a weekly basis, according to an analysis from radio ratings body Rajar, published in May.

But inevitably, more listeners, albeit a tiny minority, were accessing their favourite shows via the internet. In this context, the launch in April of the Radioplayer, an unusual example of the BBC and commercial radio working together, may turn out to be a milestone. The service gave audiences access to more than 200 local and national stations across the country and a catch-up option. The managing director of Radioplayer, Michael Hill, hailed the initiative as a 'quiet breakthrough' for the radio industry. He added: 'Growing digital radio is a long game, but we now have two magic ingredients – a simple consistent Radioplayer with millions of users, and an industry working collaboratively on its digital future. It's a great start.'

KERSHAW AND BAKER RETURN

Two hugely talented but very different radio presenters welcomed back during the year were Andy Kershaw and

Danny Baker. Kershaw returned to Radio 3 to host Music Planet, billed as 'Radio 3's most significant and ambitious world music project ever', in January, and a companion piece to BBC1's Human Planet. Despite some initial scepticism, most reviewers were won over by his enthusiasm and obvious love and knowledge of the music.

In April Danny Baker was welcomed back to Radio London following treatment for cancer. The indefatigable Baker told listeners via Facebook: 'I intend to un-retire again. I shall return to BBC London on Monday April 18th at 3pm to give it another go. I realise this will reduce Steve Wright's overall audience figures by more than 300 but it's a tough game we're in Steve.'

FOUR JUST KEEPS ON GROWING
Radio 4's fortunes continued to thrive in 2010–11. The station achieved its biggest-ever audience of nearly 11 million listeners. The BBC attributed the rise to an unusually high number of big news stories, such as the Japanese tsunami and the events of the 'Arab Spring'. The storyline dreamed up to celebrate the 60th anniversary of The Archers, broadcast in January, also played its part when more than 5 million listeners tuned in.

Audience figures may have been in the ascendant, but BBC Radio was suffering from the cuts that were forcing the Corporation to make some tough priorities across the organisation.

There were howls of anguish from staff when it emerged that due to the new licence fee settlement the World Service would have to save £46m from its annual budget of £236.7m by the end of March 2014. While the subsequent intervention of the new BBC chair, Chris Patten, managed to squeeze another £4m from the Foreign Office, five language services – Albanian, Macedonian, Portuguese for Africa, Serbian, and English for the Caribbean – were marked for closure.

In other areas, World Service radio broadcasts in languages including Mandarin Chinese, Russian, Turkish and Vietnamese will cease, with output switching to a mix of online, mobile and, in some cases, TV distribution.

ELECTRIC PROMS UNPLUGGED
On the domestic front Radio 4's The Friday Play, Between Ourselves, The Choice and On The Ropes, a fixture of the schedules for 24 years, were all axed. Also for the chop were The Electric Proms, dropped from Radio 2 following five years of coverage. More than 1,000 hours of children's shows on digital station Radio 7, which was rebranded as Radio 4 Extra, were also cut when it emerged that the average age of Radio 7's listeners was 48.

TALKSPORT WINS POLE POSITION
In commercial radio, one of the year's biggest successes was TalkSport beating BBC Radio 3 and 4 to win UK station of the year at the Sony Radio Academy Awards after achieving a new record audience. In October the national sports station had grown its audience by 19.6 per cent year on year to 2.96 million, according to Rajar.

RONNIE WOOD IS A NEW 'FACE' ON RADIO
Among music fans of a certain vintage, Bob Dylan's Theme Time Radio Hour was probably the most talked about radio shows of the noughties. One of Dylan's occasional backing musicians, the Rolling Stone's Ronnie Wood, followed in Dylan's slipstream by also hanging up his guitar and heading for the airwaves. Wood was voted Music Radio Personality of the Year for his Friday evening series, Absolute Classic Rock, broadcast on

Absolute Radio. He beat such established radio talent as Chris Moyles, who during 2010–11 signed a new two and a half year contract with Radio 1 for a reported £1.25m.

LONDONERS FLOCK BACK TO CAPITAL
In May it emerged that 95.8 Capital was once more London's most popular radio station – for the first time since 2005. The station's audience was 2.18 million listeners a week, which translated to an audience share of 6.1 per cent. Capital's return to pole position coincided with the launch of the Capital brand to another 10 stations across the UK.

Meanwhile commentators wondered if Smooth Radio's decision to relaunch itself as what it claimed was the UK's 'first national pop station' was, in the words of Gillian Reynolds, 'very brave or a bit desperate'. The move involved amalgamating a chain of existing regional stations. Simon Bates was poached from Classic FM to host Smooth's breakfast show. Competing against Radio 2 was not for the fainthearted, but early indications were that Smooth had got off to a good start, with a record UK reach of 3.084 million listeners; an increase of 14.5 per cent.

THE PRESS

The phone-hacking affair in which News of the World journalists were alleged to have eavesdropped on voicemails left by celebrities and other public figures dogged the reputation of Britain's biggest newspaper publisher, News International, throughout the year. But new revelations in early July that the phone of murdered schoolgirl Milly Dowler had been hacked sparked a sequence of extraordinary events that may have far-reaching consequences for the British press, media regulation and the relationship between the press, the police and politicians.

THE PHONE-HACKING SCANDAL ERUPTS
At the eye of the storm was Rupert Murdoch, whose global media conglomerate, News Corporation, may never be quite the same following the events of July 2011. These began on 4 July when the Guardian revealed that not only had Milly Dowler's phone messages been intercepted, but messages left on her phone after she went missing but before her body was found, had been deleted. This gave false hope to the girl's family that their daughter was still alive, and jeopardised the police investigation into her murder.

Subsequently it emerged that victims of the London bombings in July 2005 had also been victims of phone hacking by the News of the World. The relatives of soldiers killed in Iraq and Afghanistan were revealed as other targets for having their voicemails intercepted. Public outrage was immediate.

What had once been a story only reported in detail by the liberal wing of the British media and dismissed by the mayor of London, Boris Johnson, in September 'as a load of codswallop cooked up by the Labour Party', dominated the front pages and television news bulletins for most of the first three weeks of July.

NEWS OF THE WORLD FOLDS
The first casualty of a scandal was News of the World itself, which published its final edition on 10 July. Public fury was so great that many large companies, including Ford, pulled their advertisements from the Sunday tabloid. Owners News International announced that all revenues

from the paper's last edition would be donated to charity.

By axing the paper, News International hoped to draw a line under the controversy and so start to rebuild the company's reputation. But the Murdochs, led by Rupert and his son James, a senior executive at News when it sanctioned a large payment to one of those whose phone was hacked – football official Graham Taylor – badly miscalculated the public mood.

PRIME MINISTER'S FORMER AIDE ARRESTED
One of the first of those caught up in the scandal to be arrested was Andy Coulson, the *News of the World's* former editor who, until January, served as Prime Minister David Cameron's director of communications. He was held by police on suspicion of intercepting people's voicemails and for allegedly bribing the police. Subsequently, London's two most senior police officers, Commissioner Sir Paul Stephenson, and Assistant Commissioner John Yates, resigned as allegations of police corruption and the Metropolitan Police's links with News International emerged. Rebekah Brooks, chief executive of News International and a former editor of both the *News of the World* and *The Sun*, and Les Hinton, another ex-head of News International, also resigned. Brooks, like Coulson, was also arrested. Both deny knowledge of phone-hacking at the *News of the World*. The two have been bailed until October.

Another casualty of the scandal was Murdoch's bid to own the satellite broadcaster BSkyB outright. For almost a year the mogul battled to buy the 61 per cent of BSkyB he did not already own. It was poised to be the biggest deal of his career. For months politicians and regulators negotiated with Murdoch over the bid, which would, in many experts' opinions, have given News Corporation unprecedented power in the UK media. In early July the Secretary of State for Culture, Media and Sport Jeremy Hunt was preparing to give the BSkyB bid final approval. However, public opinion forced Murdoch to withdraw his offer as politicians from all parties agreed it was no longer 'in the public interest'.

COMMONS HEARING
On July 19 Murdoch and his son James appeared before a House of Commons select committee where they were questioned by MPs on the phone-hacking scandal. An apparently contrite Murdoch described the occasion as 'the most humble day of my life'. Proceedings were interrupted when a member of the public threw a cardboard plate covered in shaving foam at the 80-year-old tycoon. Mr Murdoch's wife, Wendi Deng, watching from the public gallery, struck her husband's attacker and the hearing had to be adjourned. When it reconvened, Murdoch was asked if he would resign over the affair. He replied in the negative adding that he was the best person to clean up the mess. Throughout the session both Murdoch's denied any knowledge or responsibility for the wrong-doing at News International. Murdoch blamed the criminal acts on others he had 'trusted'.

BLAME IT ON THE BBC
The web of relationships between Murdoch, his lieutenants, politicians and the police were regarded by many commentators as having seriously undermined Britain's democracy for many decades. Others maintained this sort of talk was an over-reaction and that certain news organisations, led by the *Guardian* and the BBC, were guilty of whipping up anti-Murdoch 'hysteria'.

With a new police investigation into phone-hacking not expected to complete its work for many months, if not years, and a lengthy public inquiry into media ethics chaired by Judge Levenson, the impact of 'hackgate' will reverberate for a very long time to come. It remains to be seen if any concrete steps are taken to ensure that no other, single media organisation is allowed to accumulate as much power as Rupert Murdoch managed in a 40-year career as a British newspaper proprietor.

TWITTER DERAILS 'SUPER-INJUNCTIONS'
The issue of protecting people's privacy and press intrusion was debated by media commentators, albeit in a different context, when it came to light in the spring that several public figures had taken out so-called 'super-injunctions' preventing newspapers from revealing details of their private lives. These legal devices, or 'gagging orders', not only block the media from reporting the details of a story, but also prevent journalists from mentioning the existence of the injunction.

The increased use of 'super-injunctions,' however, became compromised after users of the social networking site Twitter identified some of the personalities who had used the law in this way to protect their privacy. The *Daily Mail* noted that Twitter had 'made a mockery of the celebrity trend for using privacy injunctions to hide their identity'. Media minister Jeremy Hunt described the situation as 'farcical' but, for the time being, ruled out introducing new privacy laws.

CIRCULATIONS
For editors worried about their newspaper's circulation the royal nuptials in April boosted sales. Estimates suggested that most national papers benefited from a 25 per cent uplift in the number of copies they sold the day following the marriage of HRH Prince William to Kate Middleton.

Significantly in 2010–11, no other UK newspaper group followed the example of *The Times* and *Sunday Times* in erecting a so-called 'pay wall' to sell online versions of their titles. In the spring it was reported that News International, publishers of *The Times* and *Sunday Times*, had signed up 79,000 digital subscribers since introducing the charges in 2010.

Earlier in the year News International reported that the number of people buying online subscriptions to the papers was 'encouraging', but the *Guardian's* media editor, Dan Sabbagh, suggested that revenue gained from online sales was less than the amount lost as a result of declining circulation of the titles' print versions, with circulations of broadsheet newspapers falling at a rate of between 6 and 8 per cent.

Arguably, it was still too early to tell if a paid-for online business model could improve the challenged business models of mainstream newspaper publishers in the age of the internet. In June the *Guardian's* editor, Alan Rusbridger, giving the Hugh Cudlipp lecture, said that 'staking the future on print' was 'truly reckless'.

However, two conspicuous success stories of the UK media year involved newspapers. In October the *Independent,* owned by Russian entrepreneur Alexander Lebedev, launched *i*, which he claimed was 'the first national quality newspaper to be launched in 25 years.' In fact, *i*, sold at the modest price of 20p and was a digested form of the *Independent,* aimed at 'lapsed readers of quality newspapers'. In its first six months, *i* achieved a circulation of 175,714 – enough to merit a Saturday edition, according to its publishers. In London, the *Evening Standard,* also owned by Lebedev, proved the sceptics wrong when it became clear that making it free to readers had put it on a path towards profitability.

THE INTERNET

Will social media eventually kill television? That was a question raised by media commentators throughout the year as social networking sites, such as Facebook and Twitter, became ever more ubiquitous. Some so-called 'cyber-utopians' claimed that the role social media played in the 'Arab Spring', which began with an uprising in Tunisia in December before spreading to Egypt, Bahrain, Syria, Yemen and eventually Libya, was crucial. Most observers agreed that these momentous events would have occurred regardless of social media networks. But there seemed little doubt that just as governments of all kinds once only had to worry about the power of the press and broadcasters, in the 21st century they have to consider the effects of internet-driven media and its ability to by-pass national borders.

YOUTUBE IS BANNED IN TUNISIAN UPRISING

During the turmoil in North Africa, Tunisia's eventually ousted leader Ben Ali – who had controlled state-run newspapers and television stations for years – closed down the video file-sharing site YouTube. Meanwhile social media platforms provided protestors with news and information from different locations within their own countries unavailable via conventional outlets, and allowed dissidents to communicate with one another. These self-styled 'citizen journalists,' who used mobile phones to film in places where traditional media could not penetrate, was used by conventional broadcasters, especially Al Jazeera.

Undoubtedly, the internet was deployed to organise protests in Egypt and elsewhere during the Arab Spring, but it was easy to exaggerate its impact in marshalling dissent. As Evgeny Morozov, a contributing editor for *Foreign Policy* magazine, observed in the *Guardian* in March: 'One reason we keep talking about the role of Twitter and Facebook is that the immediate aftermath of the Middle Eastern spring has left us so little else to talk about. . . [and thorough] political analyses of the causes of these revolutions won't be available for a few years.'

However, Labour MP Tom Watson was convinced that without social media the *News of the World* phone-hacking story would have remained largely unreported, stating, 'I think the story might not have come about had not people using social media expressed their outrage. Certainly without Facebook or Twitter a consumer boycott of the advertisers of the *News of the World* would not have been organised so quickly.' In this instance, the website Mumsnet was a key factor in campaigning against the doomed Sunday newspaper.

SENIORS JOIN THE SOCIAL MEDIA REVOLUTION

Although evidence supplied by website Inside Facebook and research company Brilliant Media showed that the number of subscribers with a Facebook account in the UK and the USA was dwindling, another piece of research from American data specialist Nielsen indicated that membership of the social network site grew 41 per cent between 2009 and 2011.

Significantly, Facebook's popularity among the over-50s was rising faster than any other age group. The trend was similar for Twitter.

In the UK during May, 26.8 million people visited Facebook, up 7 per cent on the previous year; worldwide the site had more than 750 million users. Only Google, whose British advertising revenue had surpassed that of ITV, was more popular, according to Nielsen, with 33.9 million users.

Even so Google's chair, Eric Schmidt, speaking in early June, said he had 'screwed-up' by not developing a successful social media strategy for the search giant. It remains to be seen whether the technology giant's new Google+ initiative, announced in June, will provide real competition to Facebook and echo the success of Android, the company's smart-phone platform that was the market leader by the first quarter of 2011.

GOOGLE OPENS ITS OWN LAPTOP

In May, in a direct challenge to Microsoft, Google unveiled its first 'Chromebooks', laptops that will run on its Chrome operating system. Unlike conventional computer systems which use installed software like Microsoft Word, Chrome is built around web-based applications such as Google Docs. There was scepticism over whether people would take to laptops so heavily reliant on an internet connection. Enthusiasts, however, suggested that in time technology of this type would herald the end of the traditional PC.

During the year the use of tablet devices, such as Apple's iPad, and apps, which were becoming more sophisticated, moved nearer to the mainstream. In February, News Corporation launched *The Daily*, a news app designed for iPads aimed at the American market. There was criticism that the app was not so much a newspaper, but rather a second-rate magazine. So far, no plans have been announced to launch a UK version of *The Daily*. Meanwhile in a costly setback for News Corp, the company sold social networking site MySpace for a loss after the service was outpaced by the rise of Facebook.

DIGITAL MEDIA NO LONGER A WASTE LAND

There was much praise for an app based on, of all things, T. S. Eliot's fearsomely erudite and complex poem *The Waste Land*. Published by Touch Press the poem's digital reinvention was available for £7.99. According to John Naughton, writing in *The Observer*, the app had achieved the impossible by unlocking the arcane secrets of the literary masterpiece in a way that, for him, print could never do.

The Eliot app provided the full text of the poem, alongside interactive notes to its esoteric references; a filmed performance of the entire text by Fiona Shaw (synchronised to the text); complete audio recordings of readings of the poem (also synchronised to the text) by Eliot himself, Alec Guinness, Ted Hughes and Viggo Mortensen; plus more than 35 expert video perspectives on the poem, filmed in partnership with the BBC Arena arts programme. 'Sitting there, iPad on lap, it was as though the poem had suddenly burst into life', enthused Naughton. Within hours of its release on 7 June, the app climbed to the number one position in the UK iTunes App Store book category.

During 2010–11 there was embarrassment for Sony in April after a large-scale attack by hackers forced it to shut down its PlayStation Network. In the incident the personal details of 100 million customers were made vulnerable to cyber-thieves. Putting the matter right would reportedly cost Sony $173m (£107m) plus the fall-out from the damage to the company's reputation.

MUSIC

CLASSICAL MUSIC

Leonora Dawson-Bowling

ANNIVERSARIES

The 2010–11 classical season continued Mahlerian celebrations from the previous season as the two years embraced not only the 150th anniversary of the late Romantic composer's birth (1860) but also the centenary of his death (1911). Orchestras across the country dedicated themselves to a profusion of Gustav Mahler symphony and song cycle performances. In particular, the London Philharmonic Orchestra's Mahler series at the Royal Festival Hall, conducted by Vladimir Jurowski, combined these with rarely performed Mahler orchestral arrangements of other composers' compositions.

The Mahler festivities were also in full swing at Birmingham's Symphony Hall. The City of Birmingham Symphony Orchestra took the opportunity to perform a number of Mahler's seminal works with music director Andris Nelsons at the helm and, coupled with their own chorus and the Hallé Choruses, started the cycle with Symphony No. 8 (Mahler's 'Symphony of a Thousand'), 100 years to the week of its premiere in September 1910, the last Mahler premiere during his lifetime. Antonio Pappano with the Santa Cecilia Orchestra from Rome, Valery Gergiev with the London Symphony Orchestra and the aforementioned Vladimir Jurowski with the London Philharmonic Orchestra also took the stage in Birmingham as part of the run. In true keeping with the theme of anniversaries, Sir Simon Rattle concluded the cycle with *Das Lied von der Erde* on 12 June 2011, 20 years to the day that he, as then CBSO Music Director, conducted their inaugural concert at Birmingham's then-new Symphony Hall.

Lorin Maazel and the Philharmonia Orchestra opted for the so-called 'Maazel: Mahler Cycle 2011'. This not only featured concerts of all Mahler's symphonies and four major song cycles around the UK and Europe but also a dedicated online mini-site with a blog about the concert series as well as films and articles about the man and his work.

Performances celebrating Robert Schumann's bicentenary continued to the end of 2010 and into 2011 given that he, like Mahler, had adjacent anniversaries over two years: born in 1810, he died in 1856. Highlights included a number of BBC Proms chamber concerts performed by Mark Padmore and Imogen Hooper, Toby Spence and the Nash Ensemble, Francesco Piemontesi and Meta4 over July and August 2010, and the plentiful spread of the Schumann lieder and string quartets at the Oxford Lieder Festival in October 2010. The latter featured performances from the likes of Wolfgang Holzmair and Julius Drake, Alasdair Beatson, the Doric String Quartet and a number of talented young singers and pianists from UK music colleges taking the opportunity to bring some of Schumann's lesser-known lieder to light.

Travelling back a few centuries from these relatively youthful composers, the 2010–11 season also saw many concerts ahead of the 400th anniversary of the birth of Spanish Renaissance choral composer Tomás Luis de Victoria, most noticeably The Sixteen, who took their 'Choral Pilgrimage' of Victoria's works around the major cathedrals, abbeys and churches of Britain.

Other notable anniversaries were the 300th anniversary (birth) of Wilhelm Friedemann Bach (son of J. S. Bach), 250th anniversary (birth) of Luigi Cherubini, 50th anniversary (death) of Percy Grainger and 100th anniversary (birth) of Gian Carlo Menotti.

OTHER HIGHLIGHTS

Following the success of 'The Beethoven Experience' and 'A Bach Christmas' in recent years, BBC Radio 3 opened 2011 by broadcasting 12 days of non-stop Mozart entitled 'The Genius of Mozart'. Each day ran according to a theme relating to his life or influences. The programmes played every note he ever wrote and included informative discussions of his life and works as well as the 1983 broadcast of Peter Shaffer's famous play *Amadeus* with Simon Callow in the title role. As part of this celebration, all five of the BBC's orchestras and the BBC Singers performed works by the famous composer across the country over this period. Taking up the theme, King's Place in London dedicated much of 2011 to its 'Mozart Unwrapped' 40-concert series, starting with a live broadcast by the Orchestra of the Age of Enlightenment of Mozart classics to begin the New Year and the Radio 3 Mozart fortnight.

Looking back over the first decade of the 21st century, the Royal Scottish National Orchestra brought together their 'Ten out of 10' series of concerts exploring a selection of symphonic compositions written over this period. These ranged from well-established composers such as James MacMillan, John Adams and Guillaume Connesson to those still in the throes of discovery including Esa-Pekka Salonen, better known as principal conductor of the Philharmonia Orchestra.

The BBC National Orchestra of Wales rather charmingly chose to weave the theme of 'Myth and Legend: Stories and Fables' loosely through their 2010–11 season. Principal conductor Thierry Fischer lauded the ability of music to intensify and enliven the emotive power of fables and stories. The series included Ravel's *Daphnis et Chloé*, Roussel's *Bacchus et Ariane*, along with Carl Orff's *Carmina Burana* (inspired by stories from medieval Germany), Liszt's *Mazeppa* (the chilling story of a man tied to a horse), Strauss's *Don Juan* (the story of the world's greatest lover), Berlioz' *Roméo et Juliette* symphony, Mussorgsky's *Night on a Bare Mountain* (witches meeting on a Kiev mountain) and Simon Holt's double piano concerto *Centauromachy* where the pianos depicted the opposing sides of the mythical centaur. The concept of the fantastical even stretched as far as contemporary sci-fi in John Adams' *Harmonielehre* centred around a magical oil-tanker.

Béla Bartók held the particular focus of the Philharmonia Orchestra in 2010–11. Principal conductor and artistic advisor Esa-Pekka Salonen led the orchestra and the concert-going audience through a season of concerts around the UK (and beyond) featuring the Hungarian composer's chamber works, concertos, other orchestral works and only opera as well as pieces by composers who touched and influenced him. These included Enescu, Dohnanyi, Stravinsky, Kodaly and Ligeti. Ligeti also featured along with Johann Strauss and Richard Strauss in another interesting Philharmonia project, several full screenings of Stanley Kubrick's epic film *2001: A Space Odyssey*, complete with the film score performed live to great effect by the Philharmonia Orchestra and Voices under the direction of André de Ridder.

For the 2010–11 season, the Royal Philharmonic Orchestra introduced the 'Great Classics' series. These concerts were seemingly related by being 'cult greats', each itself internally linked by themes such as 'English Classics' – some with straplines as eyebrow-raising as 'the tender, the rollicking and the sensual'. The classical cynic may blench but the enlightened may see these as first-rate performances of world-class classical music cleverly branded to appeal to a wider audience. More modern and populist still, the RPO's 'Stars and Showstoppers' series also returned to the Royal Albert Hall. The orchestra's versatile performances included 'Best of Broadway', 'Symphonic Rock' and 'Film Music Gala'.

In a similar vein, the Orchestra of the Age of Enlightenment continued their 'Nightshift' series, reaching out beyond conventional classical audiences. These concerts, billed as 'classical music: minus the rules', aimed to bring audiences classical music in a late-night, drink-in-hand atmosphere, often at venues such as east London's Village Underground, equally home to DJ club nights. Performers at these events talked concert-goers through the music and certain classical concepts, and received an excellent, positive response in return.

Alongside composer anniversaries, a number of venues, orchestras and choirs celebrated significant milestones during the 2010–11 season. The BBC Symphony Orchestra celebrated its 80th birthday in October 2010 with a concert of contemporary works to complement the centrepiece, Stravinsky's *The Rite of Spring*. The performance at the Barbican, conducted by principal guest conductor David Robertson, opened with Wagner's *Flying Dutchman* overture, which had been performed in the very first BBC SO concert.

In 2010–11, the City of Birmingham Symphony Orchestra celebrated its 90th anniversary; Sir Edward Elgar conducted the inaugural concert in November 1920 at Birmingham's Town Hall. The orchestra honoured the occasion with a concert of Elgar's own Violin Concerto, which had premiered ten years earlier in 1910, along with Strauss's suite from *Der Rosenkavalier* and – rather appropriately – an exuberant account of Haydn's Symphony No. 90.

The Wigmore Hall, where many of the most talented soloists and chamber groups have found their voice, commemorated its 110 years during the 2010–11 season. The intimate London concert hall's anniversary year played host to world-class concerts including a selection of contemporary compositions and featured performances from Daniel Barenboim, Stephen Kovacevich and Martha Argerich, Diana Damrau, Jonas Kaufmann, Jordi Savall, Andras Schiff, Andreas Scholl, the Takacs Quartet and Mitsuko Uchida. Pianist Alfred Brendel also gave a special series of lectures on the interpretation and character of classical music. The apex of the season was two gala concerts on 31 May and 1 June 2011, the 110th anniversary of the hall's opening (as the Bechstein Hall). The renowned Huddersfield Choral Society, founded in 1836, celebrated a mighty 175th season with

a number of fund-raising concerts and events culminating in a gala concert of Elgar's *The Dream of Gerontius* in June 2011.

FESTIVALS

The BBC Proms' 116th season, running from July to September 2010, brought London and the UK a delightful variety of works, genres and eras. In Mahler's anniversary year, they inevitably but wonderfully opened proceedings with his monumental 'Symphony of a Thousand' (Symphony No. 8), brought to the first-night audience by the stupendous forces of the BBC Symphony Orchestra and choirs combined with the Chorus and Orchestra of Welsh National Opera. Two other great Romantic highlights were concert performances by Plácido Domingo, Antonio Pappano and the Royal Opera of Verdi's *Simon Boccanegra*, and by Bryn Terfel and the WNO of Wagner's *Meistersinger*, presented by self-proclaimed Wagner-lover, Stephen Fry.

Audience members of a more early music persuasion were also not disappointed. All six of Bach's 'Brandenburg' concertos were performed by the English Baroque Soloists, and pianist Paul Lewis light-fingered his way round all five of Beethoven's piano concertos (after recently recording the set). A particular gem towards the end of the festival was Monteverdi's *Vespro della Beata Vergine 1610*, performed superbly by Sir John Eliot Gardiner and the Monteverdi Choir, who positioned their tenor soloists to great atmospheric effect.

At the other end of the spectrum was the Sondheim 80th birthday Prom with the great man present and a star-studded troupe performing numbers from the many shows he has written and composed in his long musical life. But Sondheim was by no means the only modern item on the Proms menu with works by Judith Weir, Thea Musgrave, Bayan Northcott, Brian Ferneyhough, John Taverner, Jonathan Harvey, Gabriel Jackson, John Adams, John Cage, Arvo Part, Mark-Anthony Turnage and a whole roster of young, budding composers.

Unusually, there were two 'Last Night of the Proms' concerts: the traditional one held on the real final night and a second concert as part of a day-long tribute to Proms founder Henry Wood, a recreation of his 'Last Night' concert 100 years earlier, a set of short popular classics and new works.

The Edinburgh International Festival brought its usual variety of international performances to the Scottish capital from 13 August to 5 September 2010. Mozart's *Idomeneo* was well received and the performance had an extra poignancy after an introductory tribute paid to conductor and honorary festival president Sir Charles Mackerras who had been due to conduct it. Other items of note among the superb range of international orchestras, chamber groups and soloists were the Kronos Quartet's concert which challenged the boundaries of the conventional string quartet, John Adams' oratorio *El Nino* depicting the nativity from Mary's perspective and the premiere of Australian Brett Dean's opera, *Bliss*.

In November 2010, the Huddersfield Contemporary Festival, the UK's largest international festival of new and experimental music, played host to some 50 events. The festival enthused audiences with works by Mauricio Kagel, Brian Ferneyhough and emerging composers Juste Janulyte, Patrick Allison, Edward Caine, Stephanie Conner, Johnny Herbert and resident composer Rebecca Saunders. From the delicate to the hyperactive, performances were abundant with sensitivity and the requisite virtuosic panache and were generally well received. The festival particularly paid tribute to John Cage and a highlight for one small audience was a performance on a late-evening train of a musical 'happening' by American Alvin Curran inspired by Cage's *3 Excursions in Search of a Lost Silence* composed 30 years earlier with a particular Bologna train in mind.

In June 2011, the Aldeburgh Festival presented its audiences with everything from Ockeghem to Pierre Boulez and Marco Stroppa. The Suffolk festival opened with Messiaen's *Et exspecto resurrectionem mortuorum*, a 30-minute fanfare for winds and percussion coupled with Mahler's *Das Lied von der Erde* from Sir Simon Rattle and the CBSO. Other highlights included a concert performance of Britten's *The Rape of Lucretia* with a first-rate line-up of soloists along with performances by old festival favourites, the versatile choir Exaudi, and the new Aldeburgh resident ensemble, the conductor-less Spira Mirabilis.

The two-week Cheltenham Festival, running from the end of June 2011, was a feast of variety. Several groups explored the theme of the festival, 'music and mathematics' in their performances. In surroundings as varied as the Cheltenham Pump Room and Tewkesbury Abbey, audiences equally enjoyed the pure tones of Stile Antico with works from Renaissance Spain, Leif Ove Andsnes' piano sonatas, larger orchestral offerings from the London Philharmonic Orchestra and the Bournemouth Symphony Orchestra, the Swingle Singers' beatbox workshop and Dame Evelyn Glennie bashing out percussive premieres. For those whose appetites were whetted by the Royal Opera House's recent production of *Anna Nicole*, Mark-Anthony Turnage's *Greek* was also not to be missed.

MOVES AND NEW APPOINTMENTS

In May 2011, American violinist Joshua Bell took up the baton as the new music director of the Academy of St Martin in the Fields, the first person to hold the title since Sir Neville Marriner, who founded the orchestra in 1958.

It was a year of change for the BBC Concert Orchestra. In August 2010, they announced the appointment of American Keith Lockhart (conductor of the Boston Pops) as their Principal Conductor and Austrian Johannes Wildner as their principal guest conductor.

In September 2010, South African conductor Gerard Korsten started his three-year term as the fifth music director of London Mozart Players 2010.

In March 2011, the BBC Philharmonic Orchestra announced that John Storgards would be their new principal guest conductor from January of the following season, succeeding Vassily Sinaisky, who in turn was announced as conductor emeritus. Storgards is continuing a concurrent role as chief conductor of the Helsinki Philharmonic Orchestra until the 2013–14 season. In September 2011, Spanish conductor Juanjo Mena took on the mantle of chief conductor for an initial three-year contract while former chief conductor Gianandrea Noseda is continuing his work with the orchestra as Conductor Laureate. In the same month, after a long and fruitful relationship, the English Chamber Orchestra appointed Colin Davis conductor emeritus.

In the choral world, The Sixteen began their new residency in Manchester as associate artists of the Bridgewater Hall from the outset of the 2010–11 season and, in January 2011, Paul Brough took up the position of principal guest conductor of the BBC Singers, a role he is sharing with existing principal guest conductor Bob Chilcott. In December 2010, the London Philharmonic

Orchestra welcomed Julian Anderson as its new composer in residence and, in June 2011, the BBC National Orchestra of Wales announced Welsh composer Mark Bowden as their new resident composer.

Soprano Dame Emma Kirkby received the Queen's Medal for Music for the year 2010, the sixth Queen's Medal for Music. In the New Year's Honours 2011, Vernon Ellis (philanthropist and chair of the English National Opera) was knighted, Felicity Palmer CBE (mezzo soprano) received a DBE, and Howard Goodall (composer and 'national ambassador for singing') and Professor John Wallace OBE (Principal of the RSAMD) both received CBEs.

COMPETITIONS

In April 2011, mezzo soprano Kitty Whately fended off competition from baritone runners-up Jonathan McGovern and Marcus Farnsworth to win the prestigious Kathleen Ferrier Award, held at the Wigmore Hall. The Accompanist's Prize went to McGovern's accompanist Timothy End.

In the same month, soprano Stefanie True clinched the first prize of the Handel Singing Competition at St George's, Hanover Square, in an all-soprano/mezzo final with her recital of arias from *Agrippina, Clori, mia bella clori* and *Saul*.

In June 2011, with entrants from all over the world and a substantial 20 finalists, soprano Valentina Nafornita, from Moldova, took away the winning prize at the Cardiff Singer of the World competition, performing a programme of Donizetti, Dvorak and Gounod.

In July 2011, at the St Albans International Organ Festival, Brit David Baskeyfield won the Interpretation Competition and Paul Goussot from France won the Improvisation Competition with an improvisation on a theme handed to the competitors 40 minutes in advance.

AWARDS

CLASSIC FM/GRAMOPHONE AWARDS 2010

Recording of the Year and Early Music – Byrd *Infelix Ego*: The Cardinall's Musick/Andrew Carwood

Artist of the Year – Joyce DiDonato

Lifetime Achievement – Alfred Brendel

Special Achievement – Brian Couzens

Young Artist of the Year – Sol Gabetta

Editor's Choice – Marin Alsop's recording of Bernstein's *Mass*

Label of the Year – Linn Records

Specialist Classical Chart Award – André Rieu

Baroque Instrumental – Vivaldi *The French Connection*: La Serenissima/Adrian Chandler

Baroque Vocal – Lotti, Zelenka, Bach Choral works: Baltasar-Neumann Chorus and Ensemble/Thomas Hengelbrock

Chamber – Beethoven Sonatas for Piano and Violin: Isabelle Faust (violin), Alexander Melnikov (piano)

Choral – Verdi *Messa da Requiem*: Soloists, Chorus and Orchestra of the Accademia Nazionale di Santa Cecilia/Antonio Pappano

Concerto – Elgar Violin Concerto: Thomas Zehetmair (violin), Hallé Orchestra/Sir Mark Elder

Contemporary – Adès *The Tempest*: Soloists, Chorus and Orchestra of the Royal Opera House, Covent Garden/Thomas Adès

DVD Documentary – *Leonard Bernstein: Reflections*: Peter Rosen

DVD Performance – Purcell *The Fairy Queen*: Soloists, OAE/William Christie

Historic Archive – Beethoven 32 Piano Sonatas, *Eroica Variations* etc: Friedrich Gulda (piano)
DVD Reissue – *Vladimir Horowitz: Complete Original Jacket Collection:* Vladimir Horowitz
Instrumental – *Volodos in Vienna:* Arcadi Volodos (piano)
Opera – Wagner *Götterdämmerung:* Soloists, Choruses, Hallé Orchestra/Sir Mark Elder
Orchestral – Dvorak *Symphonic Poems:* Czech PO/Sir Charles Mackerras
Recital – Rossini *Colbran, the Muse:* Joyce DiDonato (mezzo), Chorus and Orchestra of the Accademia Nazionale di Santa Cecilia/Eduardo Müller
Solo Vocal – Schubert *Winterreise:* Mark Padmore (tenor), Paul Lewis (piano)

BBC MUSIC MAGAZINE AWARDS 2011
Orchestral and Disc of the Year – Prokofiev *Romeo and Juliet:* London Symphony Orchestra/Valery Gergiev
Opera – Mozart *Die Zauberflöte:* Soloists, RIAS Kammerchor, Akademie für Alte Musik Berlin/René Jacobs
Choral – JS Bach Complete Motets, BWV 118, 225-230: Soloists, Bach Collegium Japan/Masaaki Suzuki
Chamber –Janacek Violin Sonata; Grieg Violin Sonata No. 2 in G, Op. 13; Franck Violin Sonata in A: Vadim Repin (violin), Nikolai Lugansky (piano)
Vocal – Schubert *Die Winterreise:* Werner Güra (tenor), Christoph Berner (piano)
Instrumental – Shostakovich 24 Preludes and Fugues, Op. 87: Alexander Melnikov (piano)
Newcomer –Janacek *In the Mists;* Schubert Piano Sonata in A minor, D784 plus works by Rachmaninov and Liszt: Ivana Gavric (piano)
Technical Excellence – Briggs *Messe pour Notre-Dame, Trinity College Service, Te Deum laudamus, O Lord, support us* etc: Choir of Trinity College, Cambridge/Stephen Layton, David Briggs (organ)
Premiere Recording – David Matthews Symphonies Nos 2 and 6: BBC National Orchestra of Wales/Jac van Steen
Best DVD – Purcell *The Fairy Queen:* Soloists, Glyndebourne Chorus, OAE/William Christie, dir. Jonathan Kent

ROYAL PHILHARMONIC SOCIETY AWARDS 2011
Audience Development – English National Opera: New audience initiatives
Chamber Music and Song – Takacs Quartet
Chamber-Scale Composition – Brian Ferneyhough: String Quartet No. 6
Concert Series and Festivals – Southbank Centre: Helmut Lachenmann Weekend
Conductor – Ivan Fischer
Creative Communication – BBC4: Opera Italia
Education – Sing Up
Ensemble – Aurora Orchestra
Instrumentalist – Leon Fleisher
Large-Scale Composition – James Dillon: *Nine Rivers*
Opera and Music Theatre – The Royal Opera: *Tannhäuser*
Singer – Susan Bickley
Young Artists – Alina Ibragimova

CLASSIC BRIT AWARDS 2011
Female Artist of the Year – Alison Balsom (trumpet)
Male Artist of the Year – Antonio Pappano (conductor)
Newcomer Award – Vilde Frang (violin)
Composer of the Year – Arvo Part (composer)
Critics' Award – Tasmin Little (violin)

Artist of the Decade – Il Divo (vocal group)
Classic FM Album of the Year – *Moonlight Serenade* by Andre Rieu (violin) and Johann Strauss Orchestra (Decca)
Outstanding Contribution to Music – John Barry (composer)

POP MUSIC

Piers Martin

ADELE'S 21
One name dominated pop music this year: Adele. The 23-year-old singer from north London, whose full name is Adele Adkins, released her second album, *21,* in January 2011, and then watched as the record books had to be rewritten. By the end of July, *21* had spent 18 weeks at number one on the UK album chart, selling more than 2.8 million copies, and became the first album of 2011 to sell 3 million copies in the US, topping the Billboard 200 chart for 12 weeks. Released with little fanfare, *21* sold 208,000 copies in its first week in the UK – the biggest-selling January release for five years – but it was Adele's acclaimed performance of the single 'Someone Like You' at the televised BRIT Awards in February that comprehensively catapulted the soulful diva into the mainstream, precipitating an 890 per cent increase in purchases of *21* on the Amazon site within an hour of the broadcast.

At one point, with the singles 'Someone Like You' and 'Rolling In The Deep' nestled in the top five, and both her albums, *21* and her 2008 debut *19,* also in the top five, Adele became the first living artist since The Beatles in 1964 to have two UK top five albums and singles at the same time. An unbroken run of 11 weeks at the top of the UK album chart meant that Adele overtook Madonna's 1990 compilation *Immaculate Collection* for the most consecutive weeks at number one by a female solo artist. The record also became the longest-running consecutive UK number one since Bob Marley & The Wailers' *Legend* in 1984, which spent 12 weeks at the top. The album's run was interrupted at the summit by the Foo Fighters' *Wasted Light,* but resumed the position the following week.

A blend of musical influences, including folk, Motown and country, coupled with Adele's personal lyrics and heartfelt delivery, gave *21* an emotional authenticity with which fans could identify. Adele herself is an unpretentious star who does not appear to crave publicity and is building a huge fan base the old-fashioned way – through the quality of her music and the power of word-of-mouth, free from flashy gimmicks and brand endorsements. Her success also added to the fortunes of one of the UK's leading independent labels, XL Recordings, which enjoyed an impressive 12 months with other big-selling albums by Radiohead, Vampire Weekend and the 2010 Mercury Music Prize winners, the xx.

RIHANNA, BEYONCÉ AND LADY GAGA
Adele led the way for a handful of powerful female artists, each of whom could reasonably claim the year as their own. New albums by Rihanna *(Loud),* Beyoncé *(4)* and Lady Gaga *(Born This Way)* performed strongly, but only Rihanna, the vivacious Barbadian R&B star, was able to keep up with Adele. *Loud* was the fifth biggest-selling UK album of 2010, while a string of singles including 'Only Girl (In The World)', 'S&M' and 'Rude Boy'

1164   The Year 2010–11

cemented her position as the queen of the one-track digital download: sales of her singles neared 2.5 million in 2010 alone, according to the British Phonographic Industry (BPI). Rihanna also featured on the UK's top-selling single of 2010, Eminem's 'Love The Way You Lie', which, though it didn't reach number one, stayed in the top ten for 14 weeks. Beyoncé held the UK top spot for a fortnight at the start of July with *4*, a week after headlining the Sunday at the Glastonbury Festival, but the album did not pack the punch the singer deserved.

Few records in recent memory have received greater levels of pre-release build-up than Lady Gaga's second album, *Born This Way*, which, almost inevitably, was unable to live up to the faintly absurd expectations placed upon it by a relentless media campaign. The New York pop icon – whose debut album, *The Fame*, was the biggest-selling album in the world in 2010 – was rarely out of the public eye this year and could regularly be seen sporting an array of outrageous costumes including, at an awards ceremony in September 2010, a dress made from raw meat.

Indeed, Gaga – real name Stefani Germanotta – became better known as an avant-garde fashion muse than a musician, and the aggressive manner with which she was paired with brands such as Starbucks, Google Chrome and the international *Metro* newspapers to promote *Born This Way* threatened to overshadow the music. Preceded by the generic Euro-pop of 'Judas' and 'Born This Way', which dealt loosely with Christianity and homosexuality respectively, the album arrived in May and sold 215,000 copies to Gaga's loyal fan base of self-styled 'little monsters' in its first week in the UK, entering the charts at number one. In the US, the record's first-week sales were 1.1 million – the highest opening week since 2005 – with Amazon MP3 selling 440,000 at 99 cents (60p). Its 662,000 downloads made it the biggest sales week on record for a digital album.

AMY WINEHOUSE

One event that threw the successes of Adele and Lady Gaga into sharp relief was the death of the British singer Amy Winehouse at the age of 27. Both paid fulsome tribute to Winehouse, who was found dead at her home in Camden, north London, on 23 July 2011. According to police, the cause of her death was unexplained, but the singer's ongoing problems with drug and alcohol abuse had been well documented; one of her biggest hits was called 'Rehab'. A commanding jazz and blues vocalist, Winehouse found huge international success with her second album, 2006's *Back To Black*, a Motown-styled modern-day soul collection produced by Mark Ronson, but struggled to cope with the pressures of fame, often cutting a tragic figure in the tabloid press. A 12-date European tour in June was cancelled following a poor first-night performance in Belgrade where Winehouse was booed offstage, apparently too intoxicated to perform. One week after the singer's death, *Back To Black* returned to the top of the UK album chart and her 2003 debut *Frank* entered at number five. A clothing collection Winehouse designed for the Fred Perry brand was also released posthumously.

TAKE THAT AND PROFIT

Boosted by the return of Robbie Williams, Take That's first album as a five-piece since their 2005 comeback, *Progress*, ended the year as 2010's best seller, shifting 1.8 million copies in just over one month. On the first day of release in November 2010, the album sold 235,000

copies, which by the end of the week had risen to 518,600 – the biggest opening week total since Oasis's *Be Here Now* in 1997, according to the BPI. With the members' ages hovering around 40, Take That found themselves labelled more accurately as a 'man band' rather than a boy band, and also discovered that their live appeal was greater than ever: when their Progress Live tour was announced in October, a record 1.1 million tickets were sold in one day. The band's eight concerts at Wembley Stadium in June and July 2011 generated £38m – to date, the largest amount for a series of concerts.

Other home-grown acts who fared well this year included Florence and the Machine and folk quartet Mumford & Sons: both made significant inroads into the US market with their respective 2009 debuts *Lungs* and *Sigh No More*. In the UK *Lungs* was 2010's tenth biggest seller, while *Sigh No More* sold over 710,000 and scooped the Brit award for best British album. Rapper-turned-soulman Plan B, aka Londoner Ben Drew, became a household name with his second album, 2010's *The Defamation Of Strickland Banks*, which sold more than a million copies, making it the sixth biggest seller of the year. Crowned best British male at the Brits, Drew also sold 800,000 singles and was the most-played artist on BBC Radio 1. At the Ivor Novello awards in May, Drew was named songwriter of the year in addition to picking up gongs for album of the year and most-performed work for his single 'She Said'.

ANOTHER SALES SLUMP

Overall, however, the music industry endured another gloomy 12 months as sales of albums in the UK fell for the sixth consecutive year, BPI figures revealed. Combined digital and physical album sales slumped 7 per cent from 128.9 million to 119.9 million, and although sales of digital albums increased by 30 per cent, this was not enough to offset the decline in CD sales. This echoed figures from the global record industry, where revenue fell by 8.4 per cent in 2010 to less than $16bn (£9.7bn). Nor could a 5 per cent growth in the global digital market balance the $1.8bn (£1.1bn) shortfall from physical sales. Illegal downloading is still the biggest thorn in the music industry's side – and the problem is growing. BPI research showed that 76 per cent of all music tracks acquired in 2010 in the UK – around 1.2 billion – were downloaded illegally, and that 23 per cent of people aged 16–54 use file-sharing to obtain music.

In light of this, the news in January 2011 that music retailer HMV Group was to close 60 UK stores in 12 months was perhaps not surprising. The move came as a result of poor Christmas sales and 'challenging trading conditions', a spokesman said. In June, the retailer announced a loss of £121.7m, which it hoped to counter by focusing on selling concert tickets and expensive headphones, the market for which is worth £150m.

Physical sales of UK singles decreased to 1.9 million in 2010, down from 2.5 million the year before, however, combined physical and digital singles sales in the UK reached a new high of 162 million. Reacting to the drop in demand for CDs as consumers moved to digital, Mercury Records, home to Elton John and Arcade Fire, announced in March that it was stopping production of all physical singles. In another pro-digital, anti-piracy shift called 'On Air, On Sale', two of the UK's biggest record companies, Sony and Universal, made singles available to buy on the same day they are released to radio stations. Previously, tracks would be given to radio stations weeks in advance in order to prepare the song for release, risking being illegally downloaded.

One devastating blow to the record industry that could not have been predicted came during the London riots in August 2011 when looters set fire to the Sony DADC distribution centre in Enfield, north London, destroying 3.2 million CDs, vinyl releases and rare boxed sets from thousands of artists. The warehouse was used by the distributor PIAS to store stock belonging to more than 150 independent labels, such as XL Recordings, Domino, Warp and Ninja Tune.

RAPPERS' DELIGHT

This year, London rapper Tinie Tempah became the runaway success of British urban music as he rose from underground credibility to mainstream pop star. The 22-year-old's debut album, *Disc-Overy*, an up-tempo mix of electro and hip-hop, sold more than 300,000 copies. He also sold over a million singles. At the Brits, Tempah, whose real name is Patrick Okogwu, won best breakthrough artist and best single for 'Pass Out', the tenth best-selling track of 2010. Okogwu's one-time touring partner, Katy B, also enjoyed a remarkable 12 months. The 22-year-old singer from Peckham, south London, made waves in the dubstep scene before breaking into the charts with 'Lights On' and 'Broken Record' – light-hearted songs about clubbing – and scoring a number two album with her debut, *On A Mission*. Katy B also collaborated with the so-called 'dubstep supergroup' Magnetic Man, a bass-heavy three-piece featuring Croydon luminaries Skream, Benga and Artwork. Amid much hot air, their self-titled debut entered the album chart top five and they swiftly became festival favourites. For a more sophisticated take on the voguish dubstep sound, some looked to young Enfield pianist James Blake, whose eponymous debut enchanted many with its sparse electronics and soulful melancholy.

X FACTOR FATIGUE?

ITV1 talent show *The X Factor* appeared to loosen its vice-like grip on pop this year, mainly because the series' 2010 winner, Matt Cardle, failed to follow his inevitable Christmas number one, 'When We Collide' – a smoochy rendition of Scottish rockers Biffy Clyro's 'Many Of Horror' – with an album. One previous *X Factor* contestant, Olly Murs, did surface with a successful self-titled album, and also found work as a TV presenter. Colourful newcomer Jessie J may not have searched for stardom via the *X Factor* route, but her determination to see her name in lights paid off when she was awarded the critics' choice Brit and was swiftly unleashed upon a public who soon got used to her lingerie-clad posturing and inanely tuneful repertoire.

One song that did capture the public's imagination, but for all the wrong reasons, was 'Friday' by US teenager Rebecca Black, the video for which became a viral hit in March 2011, with more than 167 million YouTube views. A poorly sung, banal pop tune, the song was intended as a vanity release for her daughter by Black's mother, who paid $4,000 to the label ARK Music Factory to produce the song and video. Dubbed by some critics 'the worst song ever', the video was removed from YouTube and Black used her infamy to become a minor celebrity.

DIGITAL BEATLES, PAPER RADIOHEAD

In November 2010, the coveted catalogue of songs by The Beatles was made available for digital download via Apple's iTunes store. EMI said that 450,000 albums had been bought in the first seven days and that 2 million Beatles singles were downloaded. Despite the success, only one song, 'Hey Jude', entered the top 40. Industry experts noted that the albums might have fared better in the charts if the releases had been staggered rather than placed on iTunes simultaneously.

On St Valentine's Day 2011, the Oxford art-rock band Radiohead announced that their new, eighth album, *The King of Limbs,* would be released five days later, prompting feverish speculation. The downloadable version materialised one day early, on 18 February, with the physical formats arriving in March and a special 'newspaper' edition published in May. The band and long-time collaborator, artist Stanley Donwood, produced a one-off, tabloid-size, 12-page paper called *The Universal Sigh* that was fleetingly distributed in key cities around the world. Unlike Radiohead's last groundbreaking album venture, 2007's pay-what-you-like *In Rainbows,* this record had a fixed price. Sharing its name with an old oak tree in Wiltshire's Savernake Forest, *The King of Limbs'* electronic textures and subtle rhythms made it one of the band's more obtuse efforts.

Radiohead's Britpop contemporaries, Pulp, took a leaf out of Blur's book and reformed the original line-up for a summer of lucrative festival headline shows in the UK and Europe. Ten years ago, the Sheffield five-piece, led by Jarvis Cocker, were on the wane: their last album, 2001's *We Love Life,* limped into the charts at number six, spending a mere three weeks in the top 40, and they split soon after. Absence clearly makes the heart grow fonder, though, because Pulp, always an excellent live act, were rapturously received wherever they performed.

Elsewhere, the Dorset singer-songwriter PJ Harvey released her eighth album, the fiercely political and musically inventive *Let England Shake,* to widespread acclaim, with many critics calling it her finest work. And Montreal ensemble Arcade Fire cemented their reputation as one of the world's biggest bands with a third album of romantic indie-rock, *The Suburbs.* A Brit award for best international album and a summer headline show in London's Hyde Park underlined their prowess. US rockers Kings of Leon also hosted their own show at Hyde Park, and though their October 2010-released fifth album *Come Around Sundown* was a roaring success – the 13th biggest seller in the UK in 2010 – the band's gruelling touring schedule appeared to have sapped their inspiration and caused internal rifts. By the summer of 2011, the four piece were being forced to cancel shows following tired and emotional singer Caleb Followill's erratic performances.

AWARDS
BRIT AWARDS 2011
British Male Solo Artist – Plan B
British Female Solo Artist – Laura Marling
British Group – Take That
British Single – Tinie Tempah, 'Pass Out'
British Album – Mumford & Sons, *Sigh No More*
British Breakthrough Act – Tinie Tempah
British Producer – Markus Dravs
Critics' Choice – Jessie J
International Male Solo Artist – Cee Lo Green
International Female Solo Artist – Rihanna
International Breakthrough Act – Justin Bieber
International Group – Arcade Fire
International Album – Arcade Fire, *The Suburbs*

MERCURY MUSIC PRIZE 2010
The xx, *xx*

NME AWARDS 2011
British Band – Muse
Album – Arcade Fire, *The Suburbs*
Track – Foals, 'Spanish Sahara'
Solo Artist – Laura Marling
Live Band – Biffy Clyro
New Band – Hurts
International Band – My Chemical Romance
Festival – Glastonbury
Godlike Genius – Dave Grohl

MUSIC OF BLACK ORIGIN (MOBO) AWARDS
2010
UK Act – JLS
Song – N-Dubz ft Mr Hudson, 'Playing With Fire'
Album – JLS, *JLS*
Newcomer – Tinie Tempah
Hip-Hop – Professor Green
International – Eminem
R&B – Plan B
Jazz – Empirical
Gospel – Guvna B
Reggae – Gyptian
African Act – K'Naan
Lifetime Achievement – Billy Ocean

OPERA

Elizabeth Forbes

ROYAL OPERA
The season at Covent Garden got off to a rather slow start, with the first 'new' production, (borrowed from Schwetzingen) the UK premiere of Agostino Steffani's baroque opera *Niobe, regina di Tebe,* first performed in 1688. This worthy piece of excavation did not excite a great deal of interest. Infinitely more enjoyable was Cilea's *Adriana Lecouvreur,* directed by David McVicar. With Adriana and her lover Maurizio sung by Angela Gheorghiu and Jonas Kaufmann, and Mark Elder in the pit, Cilea's colourful score was displayed to the best possible advantage.

Tannhäuser, not heard at Covent Garden since 1987, was also much to the taste of the audience. Directed by Tim Albery, Wagner's early opera brought out superlative playing from the orchestra, conducted by Semyon Bychkov and magnificent, full-throated singing from the chorus. A fine cast was headed by Johan Botha in the title role and Eva-Maria Westbroek as Elisabeth. Westbroek's next appearance could not have been more different: she sang the title role in the world premiere of Mark-Anthony Turnage's *Anna Nicole,* the true story of actress and model Anna Nicole Smith, who died aged 39 after a drug overdose. Music director Antonio Pappano conducted the brilliant score, while Richard Jones's production was hugely entertaining, with Westbroek sensational as Anna and Alan Oke notable as the 87-year-old billionaire she married.

Mark Elder returned to Covent Garden to conduct Rimsky-Korsakov's *The Tsar's Bride* – 'Verdi with vodka,' as the conductor described the opera. Paul Curran's powerful production, set in contemporary Russia, highlighted the plight of Marfa, beautifully sung by Marina Poplavskaya, caught between the might of the Tsar (invisible in the original, but with a walk-on part here) and the villain Gryaznov (Johan Reuter) who loved Marfa. A final 'new' production, originating in Santa Fe, was *Cendrillon,* Massenet's version of the Cinderella story, stylishly directed by Laurent Pelly, with Joyce DiDonato in the title role and Alice Coote an ardent lover as Prince Charming. Their duets together were gorgeous.

Some interesting revivals included McVicar's production of *Rigoletto,* which boasted Dmitri Hvorostovsky and Paolo Gavanelli in the title role, both magnificent. *Fidelio* starred Nina Stemme as Leonore; Rolando Villazón sang a romantic Werther in Massenet's opera, conducted by Pappano. Phillida Lloyd's impeccable production of Verdi's *Macbeth,* also conducted by Pappano, with Simon Keenlyside as the murderous Thane, introduced Liudmyla Monastyrska as a trumpet-voiced Lady Macbeth, while the chorus was in particularly fine form. Puccini's *Madama Butterfly,* in the Moshe Leiser and Patrice Caurier production, was chosen for the Big Screen relay in July. 24,000 people around the UK watched the performance, 10,000 of them in Trafalgar Square in London, where hundreds were turned away. Butterfly was sung by Latvian soprano Kristine Opolais, a last-minute replacement, who received rave reviews from all the critics. Tosca, Cavaradossi and Scarpia were double cast in

Jonathan Kent's staging of Puccini's opera, but the finer cast was undoubtedly Gheorghiu, Kaufmann and Bryn Terfel, all in magnificent voice.

This was Elaine Padmore's last season as director of opera at Covent Garden. She took up the post in January 2000, a month after the house had reopened after two years of reconstruction. There were severe technical problems: old productions did not fit and had to be altered, new ones were delayed or cancelled, but these problems were soon resolved. Standards began to rise and have continued to rise ever since. The core repertory of operas has been maintained while many works by forgotten or living composers have been introduced. We are going to miss Elaine Padmore very much indeed. Her successor is Kasper Holten, the young Dane who took over from her in Copenhagen in 2000.

For ROH2, the Linbury Studio Theatre played host to Music Theatre Wales, who offered the UK premiere of *In the Penal Colony* by Philip Glass and to English Touring Opera, who brought the UK premiere of Alexander Goehr's *Promised End* as well as Thomas Linley's Duenna, with libretto by R. B. Sheridan. There were two world premieres: James MacMillan's *Clemency,* based on the story of Abraham and Sarah from the book of Genesis, directed by Katie Mitchell, and Luke Bedford's *Seven Angels,* presented by the Opera Group and the Birmingham Contemporary Music Group, conducted by Nicholas Collon and directed by John Fulljames.

ENGLISH NATIONAL OPERA
English National Opera continued its policy of inviting directors from theatre and film to try their hands at opera. This worked better in some cases than others. Simon McBurney, artistic director of the theatre company Complicité, making his operatic debut, offered a stunning production of *A Dog's Heart* in the UK premiere of Alexander Raskatov's new work, in which the dog Sharik (a splendid puppet) became human after an organ transplant. Here the director's ideas matched the composer's perfectly, while the performances, especially Steven Page as the Professor, also fitted in seamlessly. Rufus Norris, another theatre director, who made his operatic debut with Mozart's *Don Giovanni,* was rather less successful, while Ian McNeil's set, the star turn of the production, overshadowed the singers.

Film director Mike Figgis chose Donizetti's *Lucrezia Borgia* for his operatic debut and resisted the idea of updating the tragedy from early 16th century, but added six 'vignettes' between scenes, filmed in Rome to illustrate Lucrezia's earlier life; though admittedly the plot of the opera is almost impenetrable, these vignettes shed very little light on it. Another film director, Terry Gilliam, made his operatic debut with Berlioz' *The Damnation of Faust* (not really an opera but a dramatic poem), which he set in the first half of the 20th century, with scenes from the 1936 Berlin Olympic Games and culminating in Auschwitz. Music director Edward Gardner encouraged the ENO chorus and orchestra to great heights.

Gardner had opened the season with a more familiar version of Goethe's drama, Gounod's *Faust,* staged in an excellent production by Canadian-American theatre director, Des McAnuff, who also set the opera in the period spanning both world wars. Toby Spence made a notable Faust. Britten's *A Midsummer Night's Dream,* directed by Christopher Alden, divided critical and popular opinion alike. There was no wood near Athens; a school courtyard made up Charles Edwards's permanent set, with the adult characters as the school staff – the headmaster was Oberon and the music mistress Tytania – while the boys were the fairies. With counter-tenor Iestyn Davies indisposed, Oberon was splendidly sung by William Towers from a stage box; out of a very strong cast, Anna Christy as Tytania, Jamie Manton as Puck and Willard White as Bottom were outstandingly good, as were chorus and orchestra under Leo Hussain.

Another new production that divided opinion was Verdi's *Simon Boccanegra,* staged by the much-admired Russian director/designer Dmitri Tcherniakov, who under-estimated the audience's ability to follow an admittedly complicated plot by flashing synopses between every scene and by making the cast over-act like characters in a silent film. Musically Gardner ensured a fine performance with Bruno Caproni good as Simon, though in the council chamber scene, set in a modern board-room, he was unable to exercise the Doge's authority. However, the great duets with Brindley Sherratt's imposing Fiesco were strongly sung.

The world premiere of Nico Muhly's *Two Boys,* with libretto by Craig Lucas, was directed by Bartlett Sher and conducted by Rumon Gamba. Concerned with the world of the internet, found by many young people more real than the outer world, the opera dealt with the elucidation by DI Anne Strawson (a sympathetic Susan Bickley) of the stabbing of the younger boy by the older Brian (a marvellous performance by tenor Nicky Spence), helped or hindered by a number of fictitious characters met in the chat room. The music, influenced by Philip Glass, John Adams and Britten, was easy to listen to, while the large cast was excellent.

Two revivals deserve mention: Janacek's *The Makropulos Case,* directed by Christopher Alden, conducted by Richard Armstrong, with Amanda Roocroft a scintillating Emilia Marty, and Nikolaus Lehnhoff's staging of *Wagner's Parsifal,* conducted by Mark Wigglesworth, in which John Tomlinson's magnificent Gurnemanz dominated the proceedings. ENO's annual appearance at the Young Vic was very successful. The staging of *The Return of Ulysses* by Australian theatre director Benedict Andrews, though set in modern times, caught exactly the mixture of ancient legend and cosy domesticity that is so striking in Monteverdi's opera. Gods mingled happily with humans; Minerva and Penelope were look-alikes in identical dresses; Tom Randle made a very fine Ulysses, while Jonathan Cohen was the stylish conductor of 13 ENO instrumentalists.

OPERA NORTH, SCOTTISH OPERA AND WELSH NATIONAL OPERA

Opera North contributed a very strong season. The first new production, Britten's *The Turn of the Screw,* was powerfully directed by Alessandro Talevi and conducted with equal force by music director Richard Farnes. As light relief, *The Merry Widow,* newly staged by Giles Havergal, provided an ideal contrast. Lehár's operetta, conducted by Wyn Davies, boasted an excellent cast, headed by Stephanie Corley as Hanna. Tim Albery's production of *Fidelio,* originally staged by Scottish Opera, set in the 21st century, clearly demonstrated the timelessness of Beethoven's opera. The conducting of Richard Armstrong and Emma Bell's Leonore were outstanding.

The UK premiere of *The Portrait* (1980), by Polish composer Mieczylaw Weinberg, was perhaps the most interesting event of Opera North's season. Based on a story by Gogol, the opera dealt with a talented artist betrayed by greed. Lightly scored and subtle in tone, the music was finely conducted by Rossen Gergov, but David Pountney's production and Dan Potra's designs weighed rather too heavily on it. The powerful drama of Janácek's *From the House of the Dead,* based on Dostoevsky's novel, was well brought out in John Fulljames' production. Farnes conducted an outstanding cast. A semi-staged concert performance of *Das Rheingold,* starting a *Ring* cycle to be completed by 2013, Wagner's bicentenary, was also conducted by Farnes. Given in Leeds Town Hall (and repeated in three other cities), this boasted a director/designer in Peter Mumford and was dramatically as well as musically enthralling.

Scottish Opera's new staging of Mozart's *Le nozze di Figaro,* conducted by music director Francesco Corti and stylishly directed by Thomas Allen, was traditional in setting and period. Harry Fehr's production of Handel's *Orlando* was utterly different, with the hero transposed from a legendary knight mad with love, to an RAF pilot in the 1940s suffering from combat fatigue. Counter tenor Tim Mead's impeccably sung and strongly acted Orlando was sensational, especially in his mad scene. *Intermezzo,* in which Richard Strauss thinly disguised himself and his wife Pauline as Robert and Christine Storch, was cleverly directed by Wolfgang Quetes and conducted by Corti with evident affection. The new production of Verdi's *Rigoletto* was critically lambasted, but the orchestral playing under conductor Tobias Ringborg was praised, as were the singers.

Welsh National Opera's new production of *Fidelio,* borrowed from Bordeaux, was not much liked. Directed and designed by Giuseppe Frigeni, with the dialogue severely cut, Beethoven's escape opera lacked dramatic power. However, music director Lothar Koenigs encouraged the WNO orchestra and chorus to make up for this deficiency. John Copley's new version of Johann Strauss's evergreen *Die Fledermaus* was much better but again the conductor, Thomas Rösner and the orchestra were the stars of the performance. Luckily Mozart's *Cosi fan tutte,* directed by Benjamin Davis and conducted by Daniele Rustioni, was very much more enjoyable. Set in a British seaside town in the 1950s, the officers were disguised as red-coats from a Butlins Camp. An excellent cast was dominated by the Don Alfonso of Neil Davies, a revival of Christopher Alden's production of Puccini's *Turandot* was also extremely enjoyable. Conducted by Koenigs with great power, the opera was equally strongly sung, especially by Anna Shafajinskaia as Turandot and Gwyn Hughes Jones as Calaf.

FESTIVALS

Glyndebourne opened with Wagner's *Die Meistersinger von Nürnberg* in a fine new production by David McVicar, set in the Biedermeier period; Gerald Finley offered an unusually youthful Hans Sachs, singing with unfailing beauty of tone and great expressiveness. Johannes Martin Kränzle as Beckmesser also sang his best, unlike some singers of the role. The London Philharmonic Orchestra played superbly under music director Vladimir Jurowski, while the augmented chorus sang with tremendous enthusiasm. It is noteworthy that Finley, as well as seven of the other 11 Mastersingers, began their careers in the Glyndebourne Chorus.

The second new production of the season was Handel's *Rinaldo*, directed by Robert Carsen, with the Orchestra of the Age of Enlightenment under Ottavio Dantone. Set in a boarding school, a small, much-bullied boy, Rinaldo, imagined the conflict between Christians and Saracens in the First Crusade. Sonia Prina was dramatically perfect as Rinaldo; Luca Pisaroni made a splendid villain as Argante, while Anett Fritsch was a touching and lyrical Almirena. Revivals included Donizetti's *L'elisir d'amore* with Danielle de Niese as Adina and Paolo Gavanelli as Dr Dulcamara; and Dvořák's *Rusalka*, with Dina Kuznetsova in the title role, conducted by Andrew Davis.

Garsington opened in its new home, a specially built pavilion on the Wormsley Estate in Buckinghamshire, with Olivia Fuchs's production of *The Magic Flute*, conducted by Martin André. In the event Mozart's music was better served than Schikaneder's text, despite Jeremy Sams' witty translation. Rossini's *Il Turco in Italia*, directed by Martin Duncan, set the action in the 1950s Italy of a Fellini film; great fun was had by all, especially Quirijn de Lang's Turk and Rebecca Nelsen's Fiorilla. The real success of the season was the UK premiere of Vivaldi's 1720 comic opera *La verità in cimento (Truth on Trial)*, in which Sultan Mamud admitted that 25 years ago he switched the baby sons of his wife and his mistress. Mayhem resulted, perfectly controlled by director David Freeman. The score was magically conducted by Laurence Cummings. From a superb cast, veteran mezzos Jean Rigby as Wife and Diana Montague as Mistress deserved the highest praise.

Grange Park opened with Verdi's *Rigoletto*, directed by Daniel Slater; set in a 1940s Los Angeles Police Department with the Duke as Chief, this was a more violent affair than Jonathan Miller's mafioso version for ENO, where the violence was mostly off-stage. Damiano Salerno made a strong Rigoletto while Toby Purser conducted the responsive English Chamber Orchestra. Wagner was new territory for Grange Park and David Fielding's staging of *Tristan und Isolde* stretched the company to its limits. Stephen Barlow conducted the ECO, while Richard Berkeley-Steele's Tristan, captain of a modern ferry boat and Alwyn Mellor's Isolde were splendidly sung.

Cheltenham staged a revival of Mark-Anthony Turnage's first opera, *Greek*, by Music Theatre of Wales, directed by Michael McCarthy, conducted by Michael Rafferty. Greek also turned up at Buxton, where the ambitious programme contained three new productions: Donizetti's *Maria de Rohan*, Handel's *Saul* and Thomas's *Mignon*. This was Andrew Greenwood's final season as artistic director at Buxton. Edinburgh offered the Vlaamse Opera's production of Rossini's *Semiramide*, conducted by Alberto Zedda, directed and designed by Nigel Lowery and the Mariinsky Opera's staging of Strauss' *Die Frau ohne Schatten*, conducted by Valery Gergiev, directed by Jonathan Kent. There were also concert performances of Massenet's *Thais* and Haydn's *Orlando paladino*.

At Longborough the emergent cycle of Wagner's *Ring* went from strength to strength with *Siegfried*. Alan Privett's endlessly inventive production made all the right dramatic points, while Anthony Negus' tight control of the excellent orchestra spun a seamless web of musical delight. Daniel Brenna made a youthful, energetic Siegfried who, having brushed aside Philip Joll's canny old Wanderer as if he were an annoying fly, hastened to awaken the radiantly voiced Brunhilde of Alwyn Mellor.

Among its usual mixture of popular and less well-known Italian operas, Holland Park offered a genuine rarity, Catalani's *La Wally*, with Gweneth-Ann Jeffers in the title role. The opera was a particular favourite of Toscanini, who conducted the US premiere in 1909.

ACE CUTS

In March 2011 the Arts Council England (ACE) announced the cuts it would be making to opera companies' funding during the next four years. Financial support for the Royal Opera House, Covent Garden, is slashed by 15 per cent, as is Opera North; Welsh National Opera loses 15 per cent of its grant from ACE for performances it gives in England; English National Opera is docked by 11 per cent, as are the Bath and Cheltenham Festivals and the Birmingham Opera Company; Scottish Opera, funded by the Scottish government, loses only 4 per cent; though Glyndebourne receives no money from ACE, Glyndebourne Touring Opera does and loses 1.6 per cent. Two smaller organisations gain: Buxton Festival by 3.8 per cent and English Touring Opera by 7 per cent.

OBITUARIES

Dame Joan Sutherland, Australian soprano, died on 10 October 2010, aged 83. She came to London in 1951 and the following year made her debut at Covent Garden as Second Lady in Mozart's *The Magic Flute*. During the next seven seasons she sang a varied repertory, including Lady Rich in Britten's *Gloriana*, Amelia in *A Masked Ball* and several other Verdi roles, the eponymous Aida, Gilda in *Rigoletto* and Desdemona in *Otello*. She also tackled several Rhine Maidens and Valkyries in Wagner's *Ring* cycle and sang Eva in *Die Meistersinger von Nürnberg*. In 1955 she created Jenifer in the premiere of Tippett's *A Midsummer Marriage* and in 1958 sang Madame Lidoine in the UK premiere of Poulenc's *The Carmelites*.

Meanwhile, Sutherland had been studying with her husband, conductor Richard Bonynge, and in 1959 took an entirely new departure, singing the tremendously florid title role in a new production by Franco Zeffirelli of Donizetti's *Lucia di Lammermoor*. Scoring an immense personal triumph, she became in demand all over the world as a bel canto singer. At Covent Garden she sang Bellini's Amina in *La sonnambula*, Elvira in *I puritani* and the title role of *Norma*; Marie in Donizetti's *La Fille du régiment* and the title roles of *Maria Stuarda* and *Lucrezia Borgia*, Handel's *Alcina*, Massenet's *Esclarmonde* and Rossini's *Semiramide*.

Swiss tenor Hugues Cuénod died on 6 December 2010, aged 108. At first a concert singer, he took to opera in the 1950s, appearing at Glyndebourne from 1951 and at Covent Garden from 1954. His roles included Sellem the Auctioneer in Stravinsky's *The Rake's Progress*, Dr Caius in Verdi's *Falstaff*, M. Triquet in Tchaikovsky's *Eugene Onegin*, Don Basilio in Mozart's *Le nozze di Figaro*, M. Taupe the Prompter in Richard Strauss' *Capriccio* and the Dancing Master in Strauss' *Ariadne auf Naxos*. He continued to sing until well into his 80s.

Robert Tear, Welsh tenor, died on 29 March 2011, aged 72. He sang with the English Opera Group, making his debut in 1963 as the Male Chorus in Britten's *The Rape of Lucretia*. In 1966 he created Misael in Britten's *Burning Fiery Furnace*. Ha sang Jaquino in Beethoven's *Fidelio* and the Simpleton in *Boris Godunov* for Welsh National Opera in 1969, then made his Covent Garden debut in 1970 as Dov in the premiere of Tippett's *The*

Knot Garden. He also created the Deserter in Henze's *We Come to the River* and Rimbaud in Tavener's *Thérèse* in 1976. Other roles included Paris in Tippett's *King Priam* and Jack in his *A Midsummer Marriage,* Lensky in *Eugene Onegin,* Matteo in Strauss' *Arabella* and Herod in his *Salome,* Froh and Loge in Wagner's *Das Rheingold* and David in his *Die Meistersinger,* Tom Rakewell in Stravinsky's *The Rake's Progress* and the title role of Handel's *Samson.* Above all he excelled in Britten, as *Peter Grimes,* Captain Vere in *Billy Budd* and Aschenbach in *Death in Venice.*

PRODUCTIONS

In the summary of company activities below, the date in parenthesis indicates the year that the current production entered their repertory.

ROYAL OPERA
Founded 1946
Royal Opera House, Covent Garden, London WC2E 9DD
W www.roh.org.uk

REPERTORY: *Così fan tutte* (1995), *Don Pasquale* (2005), *Rigoletto* (2001), *Roméo et Juliette* (1994), *Hänsel und Gretel* (2008), *Il barbiere di Siviglia* (2005), *Die Zauberflöte* (2003), *Aida* (2010), *Fidelio* (2007), *Werther* (2004), *Macbeth* (2002), *Tosca* (2006), *Peter Grimes* (2004), *Madama Butterfly* (2003)

NEW PRODUCTIONS: *Niobe, regina di Tebe* (Agostino Steffani), 23 September 2010, UK premiere. Conductor, Thomas Hengelbrock; director, Lukas Hemleb; designers, Raimund Bauer; Andrea Schmidt-Futterer. Véronique Gens (Niobe), Jacek Laszczkowski (Anfione)
Adriana Lecouvreur (Cilea), 18 November 2010. Conductor, Mark Elder; director, David McVicar; designers, Charles Edwards, Brigitte Reiffenstuel. Angela Gheorghiu (Adriana), Olga Borodina (Princesse de Bouillon), Jonas Kaufmann (Maurizio), Alessandro Corbelli (Michonnet)
Tannhäuser (Wagner), 11 December 2010. Conductor, Semyon Bychkov; director, Tim Albery; designers, Michael Levine, Jon Morrell. Johan Botha (Tannhäuser), Eva-Maria Westbroek (Elisabeth), Christian Gerhaher (Wolfram), Michaela Schuster (Venus)
Anna Nicole (Turnage), 17 February 2011, world premiere. Conductor, Antonio Pappano; director, Richard Jones; designers, Miriam Buether, Nicky Gillibrand. Eva-Maria Westbroek (Anna), Alan Oke (J. Howard Marshal II), Susan Bickley (Virgie), Gerald Finley (Stern)
The Tsar's Bride (Rimsky-Korsakov), 14 April 2011. Conductor, Mark Elder; director, Paul Curran; designer, Kevin Knight. Marina Poplavskaya (Marfa), Ekaterina Gubanova (Lyubasha), Dmitry Popov (Likov), Johan Reuter (Gryaznoy), Paata Burchuladze (Sobakin)
Cendrillon (Massenet), 5 July 2011. Conductor, Bertrand de Billy; director/costume designer, Laurent Pelly; designers, Barbara de Limburg, Jean-Jacques Delmotte. Joyce DiDonato (Cendrillon), Alice Coote (Prince Charming), Ewa Podles (Madame de la Haltière), Jean-Philippe Lafone (Pandolfe), Eglise Gutiérrez (The Fairy)

ENGLISH NATIONAL OPERA
Founded 1931
London Coliseum, St Martin's Lane, London WC2N 4BS
W www.eno.org

REPERTORY: *The Makropulos Case* (2006), *La bohème* (2009), *Parsifal* (1999), *The Mikado* (1986)

NEW PRODUCTIONS: *Faust* (Gounod), 18 September 2010. Conductor, Edward Gardner; director, Des McAnuff; designers, Robert Brill, Paul Tazewell. Toby Spence (Faust), Iain Pattterson (Mephistopheles), Melody Moore (Marguerite), Benedict Nelson (Valentine), Anna Grevelius (Siebel)
Radamisto (Handel), 7 October 2010. Conductor, Lawrence Cummings; director, David Alden; designer, Gideon Davey. Lawrence Zazzo (Radamisto), Christine Rice (Zenobia), Sophie Bevan (Polissena), Ailish Tynan (Tigrana)
Don Giovanni (Mozart), 6 November 2010. Conductor, Kirill Karabits; director, Rufus Norris; designers, Ian MacNeil, Nicky Gillibrand. Iain Paterson (Don Giovanni), Katherine Broderick (Donna Anna), Robert Murray (Don Ottavio), Sarah Redgwick (Donna Elvira), Brindley Sherratt (Leporello), Sarah Tynan (Zerlina)
A Dog's Heart (Alexander Skuratov), 20 December 2010, UK stage premiere. Conductor, Garry Walker; director, Simon McBurney; designers, Michael Levine; Christine Cunningham. Steven Page (The Professor), Leigh Melrose (Bormenthal), Peter Hoare (Shankov), Andrew Watts/Elena Vassilieva (Sharik the dog)
Lucrezia Borgia (Donizetti), 31 January 2011. Conductor, Paul Daniel; director, Mike Figgis; designers, Es Devlin, Brigitte Reiffenstuel. Claire Rutter (Lucrezia), Michael Fabiano (Gennaro), Alastair Miles (Alfonso d'Este), Elizabeth DeShong (Orsini)
The Return of Ulysses (Monteverdi), 24 March 2011 at the Young Vic. Conductor, Jonathan Cohen; director, Benedict Andrews; designer, Börkur Jónsson. Tom Randle (Ulysses), Pamela Helen Steven (Penelope), Ruby Hughes (Minerva)
The Damnation of Faust (Berlioz), 6 May 2011. Conductor, Edward Gardner; director, Terry Gilliam; designers, Hildegard Bechler, Katrina Bechtler; Peter Hoare (Faust), Christine Rice (Marguerite), Christopher Purves (Mephistopheles)
A Midsummer Night's Dream (Britten), 19 May 2011. Conductor, Leo Hussain; director, Christopher Alden; designers, Charles Edwards, Sue Wilmington. William Towers/Iestyn Davies (Oberon), Anna Christy (Tytania), Willard White (Bottom) ·
Simon Boccanegra (Verdi), 8 June 2011. Conductor, Edward Gardner; director/ designer, Dmitri Tcherniakov. Bruno Caproni (Boccanegra), Brindley Sherratt (Fiesco), Rena Harms (Amelia), Peter Auty (Adorno)
Two Boys (Nico Muhly), 24 June 2011, world premiere. Conductor, Rumon Gamba; director, Bartlett Sher; designers, Michael Yeargan, Catherine Zuber. Susan Bickley (Anne), Nicky Spence (Brian), Mary Bevan (Rebecca), Heather Shipp (Fiona)

OPERA NORTH
Founded 1978
Grand Theatre, 46 New Briggate, Leeds LS1 6NU
W www.operanorth.co.uk

REPERTORY: *The Adventures of Pinocchio* (2007)

NEW PRODUCTIONS: *The Turn of the Screw* (Britten), 2 October 2010. Conductor, Richard Farnes; director, Alessandro Talevi; designer, Madeleine Boyd. Benjamin Hulett (Quint), Elizabeth Atherton (Governess), Giselle Allen (Miss Jessel), Yvonne Howard (Mrs Grose)

The Merry Widow (Lehár), 16 October 2010. Conductor, Wyn Davies; director, Giles Havergal; designer, Leslie Travers. Stephanie Corley (Hanna Glawari), William Dazeley (Danilo), Amy Freston (Valencienne), Allan Clayton (Camille)
Carmen (Bizet), 17 January 2011. Conductor, Andreas Delfs; director, Daniel Kramer; designers, Soutra Gilmour, Gabrielle Dalton. Heather Shipp (Carmen), Peter Auty (Don José), Anne Sophie Duprels (Micaela), Kostas Smoriginas (Escamillo)
The Portrait (Mieczylaw Weinberg), 2 February 2011, UK premiere. Conductor, Rossen Gergov; director, David Pountney; designer, Dan Potra. Paul Nilon (Chartkov), Richard Burkhard (Nikita), Katherine Broderick (Lisa), Peter Savidge (Professor), Nicholas Sharratt (Lamplighter)
Fidelio (Beethoven), 14 April 2011. Conductor, Richard Armstrong; diector, Tim Albery; designer; Stewart Laing. Emma Bell (Leonore), Fflur Wyn (Marzelline), Steven Harrison (Florestan), Andrew Foster-Williams (Don Pizarro), Jeremy White (Rocco)
From the House of the Dead (Janacek), 5 May 2011. Conductor, Richard Farnes; director, John Fulljames; designer, Dick Bird. Richard Morrison (Goryanchikov), Alan Oke (Skuratov), Mark Le Brocq (Shapkin), Jeffrey Lloyd-Roberts (Filka), Robert Hayward (Shishkov)
Das Rheingold (Wagner), 18 June 2011. Conductor, Richard Farnes; director/ designer, Peter Mumford. Michael Druiett (Wotan), Yvonne Howard (Fricka), Nicholas Folwell (Alberich), Wolfgang Ablinger-Sperrhacke (Loge)
Performances were given in Leeds and on tour in Edinburgh, Newcastle, Nottingham, Salford Quays, Gateshead and Birmingham.

SCOTTISH OPERA
Founded 1962
39 Elmbank Crescent, Glasgow G2 4PT
W www.scottishopera.org.uk

REPERTORY: *The Cunning Little Vixen* (1980)

NEW PRODUCTIONS: *Le nozze di Figaro* (Mozart), 29 October 2010. Conductor, Francesco Corti; director, Thomas Allen; designer, Simon Higlett. Thomas Oliemans (Figaro), Nadine Livingston (Susanna), Roderick Williams (Count), Kate Valentine, (Countess), Ulrike Mayer (Cherubino)
Orlando (Handel), 15 February 2011. Conductor, Paul Goodwin; director, Harry Fehr; designer, Yannis Thavoris. Tim Mead (Orlando), Andrew Radley (Medoro), Claire Booth (Dorinda), Sally Silver (Angelica)
Intermezzo (Strauss), 26 March 2011. Conductor, Francesco Corti; director, Wolfgang Quetes; designer, Manfred Kaderk. Roland Wood (Robert Storch), Anita Bader (Christine Storch), Nicky Spence (Baron Lummer)
Rigoletto (Verdi), 11 May 2011. Conductor, Tobias Ringborg; director, Matthew Richardson; designer, Jon Morrell. Eddie Wade (Rigoletto), Nadine Livingston (Gilda), Edgaras Mondvidas (Duke), Louise Collett (Maddalena), Gregory Frank (Sparafucile)
Performances were given in Glasgow and on tour in Edinburgh, Aberdeen, Inverness and Belfast.

WELSH NATIONAL OPERA
Founded 1946
Wales Millennium Centre, Bute Place, Cardiff Bay CF10 5AL
W www.wno.org.uk

REPERTORY: *Die Zauberflöte* (2005), *Ariadne auf Naxos* (2004), *Il trovatore* (2003), *Turandot* (1994)

NEW PRODUCTIONS: *Fidelio* (Beethoven), 24 September 2010. Conductor, Lothar Koenigs; director/designer, Giuseppe Frigeni. Lisa Milne (Leonore), Dennis O'Neill (Florestan), Clive Bayley (Rocco), Robert Hayward (Pizarro), Elizabeth Donovan (Marzelline)
Die Fledermaus (Johann Strauss), 12 February 2011. Conductor, Thomas Rösner; director, John Copley; designer, Tim Read. Nuccia Focile (Rosalinde), Mark Stone (Eisenstein), Paul Charles Clarke (Alfred), Joanne Boag (Adele), Helen Lepalaan (Orlovsky), Alan Opie (Frank)
Così fan tutte (Mozart), 20 May 2011. Conductor, Daniele Rustioni; director, Benjamin Davis; designer, Max Jones. Camilla Roberts (Fiordiligi), Charlotte Ellett (Dorabella), Anne-Marie Gibbons (Despina), Robin Tritschler (Ferrando), Gary Griffiths (Guglielmo), Neal Davies (Don Alfonso)
Performances were given in Cardiff and on tour in Swansea, Birmingham, Bristol, Plymouth, Milton Keynes, Llandudno and Southampton.

GLYNDEBOURNE
Founded 1934
Glyndebourne, Lewes, East Sussex BN8 5UU
W www.glyndebourne.com

REPERTORY: *Don Giovanni* (2010), *L'elisir d'amore* (2007), *Rusalka* (2009), *The Turn of the Screw* (2006)

NEW PRODUCTIONS: *Die Meistersinger von Nürnberg* (Wagner), 21 May 20011. Conductor, Vladimir Jurowski; director, David McVicar; designer, Vicki Mortimer. Gerald Finley (Hans Sachs), Marco Jentzsch (Walther), Anna Gabler (Eva), Alastair Miles (Pogner), Johannes Martin Kränzle (Beckmesser)
Rinaldo (Handel), 2 July 2011. Conductor, Ottavio Dantone; director, Robert Carsen; designer, Gideon Davey. Sonia Prina (Rinaldo), Anett Fritsch (Almirena), Brenda Rae (Armida), Luca Pisarone (Argante)

GLYNDEBOURNE TOURING OPERA: *La bohème* (2000), *Don Pasquale* (2011), *Rinaldo* (2011)
Performances were given at Glyndebourne, Woking, Milton Keynes, Norwich, Plymouth, Wimbledon and Stoke on Trent.

PARLIAMENT

Patrick Robathan

The coalition government mantra for the year was 'the scale of the deficit we inherited [means that cuts are] inevitable', telling the opposition to 'ask themselves why we have to make those reductions. It is because of the incompetence and the economic inheritance that they left behind'. They had no room for complacency as by the summer recess there had been a total of 147 separate backbench revolts by government MPs, the majority coming from the 2010 intake. Speaker John Bercow helped bolster backbench scrutiny of the executive by granting a far larger number of urgent questions than ever before, thus forcing ministers to come to the House to make statements when otherwise they would not have done.

Returning after the conference recess on 11 October foreign secretary William Hague made a statement on the death of Linda Norgrove, British aid worker taken hostage in Afghanistan, who had died during the course of a rescue attempt by US forces. This was followed by a statement from the work and pensions secretary Iain Duncan Smith on details of the new work programme and plans for wider benefit reform.

On 12 October business, innovation and skills secretary Vince Cable made a statement on higher education and student finance following the publication of Lord Browne's inquiry report, recommending an increase in student fees. On 14 October minister for the cabinet office Francis Maude made a statement on public bodies reform, taking 'decisive action to restore accountability and responsibility to public life'.

On 18 October education secretary Michael Gove responded to an urgent question on the fairness premium to disadvantaged young children, pupils and students. On 19 October prime minister David Cameron made a statement on the Strategic Defence and Security Review – 'not simply a cost-saving exercise but about taking the right decisions to protect our national security in the years ahead.'

COMPREHENSIVE SPENDING REVIEW

On 20 October chancellor George Osborne revealed details of his comprehensive spending review outlining the loss of around 490,000 public sector jobs; an average 19 per cent four-year cut in departmental budgets; structural deficit to be eliminated by 2015; £7bn in additional welfare budget cuts; police funding to be cut by 4 per cent a year; retirement age to rise from 65 to 66 years by 2020; English schools budget protected; £2bn extra for social care; NHS budget in England to increase every year until 2015; regulated rail fares to increase 3 per cent above inflation; and the bank levy to be made permanent. 'Today's the day when Britain steps back from the brink, when we confront the bills from a decade of debt...We made sure we're all in this together and we've taken our country back from the brink of bankruptcy. A stronger Britain starts here'. In response, shadow chancellor Alan Johnson stated 'It's our firm belief that the rush to cut the deficit endangers the recovery and reduces

the prospects for employment in the short term and for prosperity in the longer term'.

On 26 October communities and local government minister Bob Neill answered an urgent question on proposed industrial action by firefighters in London over the bonfire period. Transport secretary Philip Hammond made a statement on investment plans for transport networks, 'in the longer term, I want such decisions on local transport priorities to be taken out of Whitehall and placed in the hands of local people'. On 27 October financial secretary to the treasury Mark Hoban responded to an urgent question on the conclusion of the taskforce on strengthening economic governance in the European Union that was presented to the European Council on 21 October. William Hague then made the first of proposed quarterly reports to the House on progress towards UK objectives in Afghanistan. On 29 October Vince Cable published a white paper, setting out the government's role in supporting locally driven growth and job creation.

On 1 November home secretary Theresa May made a statement on the airline bomb plot, following the discovery of a suspect package at East Midlands Airport onboard a UPS courier aircraft en route from Cologne to Chicago. On 2 November cabinet office minister Mark Harper answered an urgent question on prisoners' right to vote – the government accepted that there was a legal obligation, as a result of the Strasbourg judgment in the case of prisoner, John Hirst, to change the law. Defence secretary Liam Fox replied to an urgent question on the signing of two defence treaties with France, which marked a deepening of the UK–France bilateral relationship. On 3 November minister for universities and science David Willetts gave more detail of proposals for higher education funding and student finance, capping tuition fees at £9,000 per annum.

On 8 November cabinet office minister Oliver Letwin published departmental business plans, part of a programme of fundamental structural reform, that would 'change the nature of government'. On 11 November Iain Duncan Smith announced measures to secure a welfare system fit for the 21st century, 'where work always pays and is seen to pay by those who are engaged in it'. Police minister Nick Herbert made a statement on the previous day's public disorder at the National Union of Students rally.

On 15 November David Cameron reported on his visit to China and the outcome of the G20 summit in Korea where progress had been made on fiscal consolidation. Justice secretary Kenneth Clarke published two documents announcing, respectively, proposals for the reform of legal aid and civil litigation funding in England and Wales. On 16 November energy and climate change secretary Chris Huhne published the report of the Redfern inquiry, which had investigated the analysis of human tissue that was carried out in UK nuclear facilities from 1955 to 1992. Ken Clarke announced that the government had agreed a mediated settlement of the civil damages claims brought by Guantanamo Bay detainees. On 17 November Mark Hoban responded to an urgent question on the proposed financial rescue package for Ireland. On 18 November minister for equalities Lynne Featherstone responded to an urgent question on the government's intention to drop section 1 of the Equality Act 2010, which places duties on public bodies to act in respect of socio-economic disadvantage.

On 22 November David Cameron reported on the NATO summit in Lisbon, effectively three summits: a meeting of all the coalition countries involved in Afghanistan; a summit on the planned reform of NATO; and a NATO–Russia Council. George Osborne made a statement on the international financial assistance package for Ireland, 'we are doing this because it is overwhelmingly in Britain's national interest that we have a stable Irish economy and banking system'. On 23 November Theresa May made a statement on controlling migration 'focusing on tackling abuse and supporting only the most economically beneficial migrants'. On 25 November transport secretary Philip Hammond made a statement on plans for investment in rail infrastructure and rolling stock.

AUTUMN FORECAST
On 29 November George Osborne made a statement regarding the Office for Budget Responsibility's (OBR) first autumn forecast and measures being taken to support economic growth, including the new growth review and a programme of reforms to the corporate tax system. The OBR had revised its growth forecast for the year from 1.2 per cent to 1.8 per cent, but had lowered its estimate for future years. Their forecast for public sector job losses over the next four years was revised down to 330,000, but the OBR expected total unemployment to rise to a peak of just over 8 per cent in 2011 before falling again. The OBR's assessment was that there 'will be no double-dip recession', that this was to be expected following 'the deepest recession since the war, the greatest budget deficit in our peacetime history and the biggest banking crisis of our lifetimes', but that overall, Britain's economic recovery was on track, 'the economy is growing, more jobs are being created and the deficit is falling'. Alan Johnson accused the coalition of risking the UK's future prosperity with its programme of spending cuts.

On 7 December justice secretary Ken Clarke published plans to reform rehabilitation and sentencing policy designed to reduce re-offending without reducing the punishment of offenders. On 8 December pensions minister Steve Webb delivered the annual social security benefits uprating statement for 2011–12, confirming a move from the retail price index to the consumer price index as the method of uprating, resulting in an uplift of 3.1 per cent for the year in question.

UNIVERSITY TUITION FEES
Meanwhile, while violent demonstrations were taking place outside parliament, MPs inside voted to allow the level of student tuition fees to be raised to a maximum of £9,000 per annum by 323 votes to 302. In all some twenty-one Liberal Democrat MPs voted against the government's proposals alongside six Conservatives. In addition a further eight Liberal Democrat MPs abstained as did two Conservatives. Liberal Democrat MPs Mike Crockart and Jenny Willott resigned as junior ministerial aides to enable them to vote against the fees rise, as did Conservative Lee Scott. When the measure was debated in the Lords on 14 December, a Labour amendment to throw out the proposals was defeated by 283 votes

to 215. On 13 December home secretary Theresa May made a statement on the violence that had taken place in London during the demonstrations against the government's plans to increase the university tuition fee cap, 'the blame for the violence lies squarely and solely with those who carried it out'.

Communities and local government secretary Eric Pickles made the annual statement on finance for local authorities, with an average reduction of 4.4 per cent. Chris Huhne reported on the outcome of the UN climate conference in Cancun, 'a triumph for the spirit of international co-operation'. On 14 December justice minister Jonathan Djanogly announced the response to the consultation on HM Courts Service estate, with the closure of 93 magistrates' courts and 49 county courts. On 15 December the Commons passed a motion suspending three former Labour MPs (Stephen Byers, Geoff Hoon and Richard Caborn) from the House for breaking the rules of parliament over access before the election. On 16 December Chris Huhne announced a consultation on reform of the electricity market to secure 'investment in cleaner, greener power and delivering secure, affordable and low-carbon energy for decades to come'.

A COLD SNAP AND THE CHRISTMAS RECESS
On 20 December Attorney General Dominic Grieve responded to an urgent question on the ruling by the High Court that the government's temporary immigration cap announced in June was not legal: he would be laying changes to the rules to make them compliant. David Cameron reported on the outcome of the European Council meeting, which had agreed a 2.91 per cent increase in the 2011 EC budget. Transport secretary Philip Hammond made a statement on plans for the redevelopment of a national high-speed rail network, to deliver 'transformational change to the way Britain works and competes in the 21st century'. He then had to make a second statement on the severe winter weather – with December set to be the coldest on record since 1910 – reiterating that the government would take whatever action necessary to mitigate its effects. On 21 December both Houses rose for Christmas.

Returning from the Christmas recess on 10 January 2011 health secretary Andrew Lansley responded to an urgent question on the response to the current flu outbreak. He then made a statement on improvements to compensation and support for those affected by hepatitis C and HIV-infected blood in the 1990s. On 11 January George Osborne replied to an urgent question on bank bonuses confirming that he was in discussions with the banks regarding reaching a new settlement, stating that preferably 'the banks pay smaller bonuses than they would otherwise have done; are more transparent about those they do pay; make a greater contribution to local communities and regional economies; treat customers more fairly; and, above all, lend materially and verifiably more than they were planning to lend to the businesses of Britain'.

On 17 January foreign office minister David Lidington responded to an urgent question on the declaration of a state of emergency in Tunisia and assistance to British nationals. On 19 January transport minister Norman Baker published a white paper on local transport which aimed to produce a transport system that 'helps create growth in the economy and tackles climate change by cutting our carbon emissions'. His Labour shadow Maria Eagle called it 'a re-heated and re-packaged announcement'. In a debate Labour forced a vote on plans to abolish the education maintenance grant but their motion was defeated by 317 votes to 258.

Foreign secretary William Hague responded to an urgent question on cuts to the BBC World Service on 26 January – expenditure limits would be reduced by 16 per cent in real terms over the next three years. Theresa May made her statement on the outcome of Lord MacDonald of River Glaven's review of counter-terrorism and security powers, promising legislation to introduce the new regime 'in the coming weeks'.

On 31 January foreign office minister Alistair Burt made a statement on the situation in Egypt stressing that the safety of British citizens was the top priority.

HEALTH AND SOCIAL CARE BILL

This controversial bill which would disband all 151 primary care trusts and strategic health authorities, giving responsibility for commissioning to GP-led groups and by establishing HealthWatch and local health and wellbeing boards within local councils received its second reading on 31 January by 321 votes to 235. Whilst no Liberal Democrats actually voted against the bill, Andrew George abstained warning that, 'although I think that the bill is well-intentioned, I think in order for it to proceed and not to damage the NHS I believe that it needs some further major surgery during committee and report stage'. It completed its stormy committee stage on 31 March but before proceeding to report stage Andrew Lansley announced on 4 April that the government would take the opportunity of the natural break in the passage of the bill to consult further on the proposed reforms with a review on choice and competition led by Sir Stephen Bubb and an overall review led by Professor Steve Field and bring forward any amendments to improve the plan. John Healey called it 'no way to run a bill; no way to run a government; no way to run the NHS'. Mr Lansley gave his response to NHS Future Forum on 14 June, accepting the core recommendations. The bill was therefore re-committed to the committee on 28 June, which was completed on 14 July.

THE MIDDLE EAST AND NORTH AFRICA

On 14 February William Hague made a statement on recent developments in the Middle East and north Africa following his visit to the region to discuss the situation with the UK's partners, 'we cannot set the pace of this change and must respect each country's right to find its own way, but we will be a reliable friend and partner to all those looking to do so, and a staunch defender of Britain's interests in the region'. Defence secretary Liam Fox gave his assessment of progress towards UK objectives in Afghanistan, 'we have seen progress over the past few months but the need for strategic patience remains. . .There is still a great deal to do, but I believe there is also cause for cautious optimism'. On 15 February Liam Fox returned to the Commons to answer an urgent question on redundancies in the MoD with the revelation that soldiers with years of service had been informed of their redundancies by email. On 16 February Theresa May made a statement on the ruling by the supreme court that not granting those on the sex offenders register an opportunity to seek a review was a breach of their human rights. She announced that the government would shortly announce the establishment of a commission to investigate the creation of a British 'bill of rights'. After a stormy passage through the House of Lords the parliamentary voting system and constituencies bill (which provided for a referendum on the voting system for parliamentary elections on 5 May) gained royal assent.

On 17 February William Hague replied to an urgent question on the situation in Bahrain. Environment secretary Caroline Spelman then reported on her decision to end the consultation on the future of the public forest estate; to remove the clauses relating to it from the public bodies bill; and to establish a panel to consider forestry policy in England.

Returning from the short half-term recess on 28 February David Cameron updated members on developments in Libya and the Middle East, confirming that around 600 British nationals had been evacuated, and warned that military intervention by the UK may be inevitable 'we do not in any way rule out the use of military assets. We must not tolerate this regime using military force against its own people'. On 2 March Liam Fox responded to an urgent question on redundancies in the armed forces. On 3 March culture secretary Jeremy Hunt came to the House to make a later than usual statement on News Corporation's proposed bid for BSkyB, confirming that as a result of News Corporation's undertakings in lieu, he was minded not to refer the bid to the Competition Commission but would be consulting on the undertakings.

On 7 March William Hague gave a further update on developments in Libya and the Middle East – there had been further evacuations of British citizens and the Gaddafi regime had launched military counter-attacks against opposition forces.

On 14 March David Cameron reported on the outcome of the special European Council on developments in Africa, especially Libya. He also gave the government response to the earthquake and tsunami that had struck Japan.

The House of Commons held a debate on UN Security Council Resolution 1973, authorising the enforcement of a no-fly zone in Libya on 21 March, which was passed by 557 votes to 13 – one Conservative MP John Baron voted against. MPs also approved a motion freezing their salaries for the coming year.

BUDGET 2011

On 23 March Chancellor George Osborne presented his second budget, 'a budget for growth. . .to put fuel into the tank of the British economy'. The measures included:
- fuel duty cut by 1p per litre
- alcohol and tobacco duty increased to 2 per cent above inflation
- air passenger duty increase delayed by one year
- corporation tax cut by an extra 1 per cent
- financial help for first-time buyers
- direct tax rates to be linked to CPI rather than RPI from April 2012; raising £1bn a year for the treasury
- plans to merge tax and national insurance

Overall, inflation was set to remain between 4 per cent and 5 per cent in 2011, falling to 2.5 per cent in 2012. Mr Osborne was also forced to downgrade his growth forecasts. After four days of debate the Budget was passed by 327 votes to 250 on 29 March. In the divisions on various budget resolutions two Liberal Democrat MPs (Malcolm Bruce and Sir Robert Smith) voted against the extra charge being placed on North Sea oil companies and one (Greg Mulholland) against the increased rates of alcohol duty. This was the 51st rebellion by backbench Liberal Democrat MPs against coalition policies.

MORE MIDDLE EAST DEVELOPMENTS

On 23 March 15 Conservative MPs voted against a draft European Council decision to amend Article 136 of the

Lisbon Treaty, allowing the Euro countries to establish a stability mechanism: the 15th Conservative rebellion on Europe in the session. On 24 March Mark Hoban responded to an urgent question on the decision to approve a treaty change on the European financial stability mechanism following developments in Portugal without a referendum. William Hague updated MPs on actions being taken to protect civilians in Libya and other issues of concern in Syria and Yemen – Britain would be hosting an international conference to take forward the implementation of UN Security Council Resolution 1973.

On 28 March Theresa May replied to an urgent question on the violent disturbances during the TUC march in London, which saw 56 police officers and 53 members of the public hurt. David Cameron reported on developments in Libya where RAF pilots had made more than 120 sorties. Michael Gove made a statement on reform of post-16 education funding with a consultation on a fairer funding formula for all school and colleges in the sector and a more targeted support scheme to replace education maintenance allowance (EMA). On 29 March Ken Clarke made a statement on the response to Lord Justice Jackson's recommendations for reform of no win, no fee arrangements and a consultation on further overhaul of the civil justice system. On 30 March William Hague reported on the London conference on Libya. On 31 March international development minister Stephen O'Brien responded to an urgent question on the humanitarian situation in Côte d'Ivoire with the UK providing a significant emergency aid package. Ken Clarke announced the outcome of the competition to manage five prisons with three of them to be run by the private sector.

EASTER RECESS

On the Monday before rising for the Easter recess – 4 April, there were no less than five statements in the Commons. Firstly, minister for veterans Andrew Robathan replied to an urgent notice question on the details of Army and Royal Navy tranche 1 redundancies, details of which had appeared in the press at the weekend. William Hague updated members on developments in Africa (both Libya and Côte d'Ivoire) and the Middle East (Bahrain and Syria). Andrew Lansley made a statement about NHS modernisation. Northern Ireland secretary Owen Paterson then made a statement on the murder of PC Ronan Kerr in Omagh. Finally, pensions minister Steve Webb published a green paper on reform of state pensions – examining whether the existing pensions system is suitable for meeting the challenges of the future. On 5 April two urgent questions were granted: deputy prime minister Nick Clegg replied to one on the strategy to improve social mobility and foreign office minister Henry Bellingham responded to one on steps being taken to gain consular access to and secure the release of British nationals taken prisoner by the Eritrean authorities in December 2010.

On return from the Easter recess on 27 April Alistair Burt answered an urgent question on the repercussions of the escape of some 476 Taliban prisoners in Kandahar on UK soldiers. William Hague updated MPs on developments in the Middle East and North Africa, having chaired the first meeting of the Libya contact group in Doha on 13 April.

On 3 May David Cameron reported on the killing of Osama bin Laden by US forces and the consequences for the security of British people at home and abroad and for UK foreign policy. Ed Miliband wholeheartedly supported the action taken by the USA. On 4 May the clerk of the House, Malcolm Jack, announced his retirement at the end of September.

Labour forced a debate on the future of the NHS on 9 May, calling into doubt the government's handling of the reform, but the motion was defeated by 284 votes to 231 – no Liberal Democrat MP voted in support of the Labour motion *per se* but Andrew George voted in both lobbies and 19 backbench Liberal Democrat MPs did not vote. On 10 May universities minister David Willetts answered an urgent question on proposals for students to buy off-quota university places. On 12 May Liberal Democrat MP David Laws made a personal statement to the House in response to the Standards and Privileges Committee report that had recommended he face a seven-sitting-day suspension from the House for breaking a number of important rules regarding his expenses – the motion giving effect to this was passed on 16 May.

WEIGHTMAN REPORT

On 17 May Nick Clegg outlined the government's plans for House of Lords reform publishing a draft bill with a view to holding some form of elections to the upper chamber in 2015. Chris Huhne announced proposals for a fourth 'carbon budget', setting 'ambitious targets to reduce greenhouse emission in line with the advice from the independent committee on climate change' for a 50 per cent reduction from 1990 levels, with progress to be reviewed in early 2014. On 18 May Chris Huhne answered an urgent question on the implications for the UK nuclear industry of the Weightman report on events in the Fukushima nuclear site in March – 'no reason for curtailing the operation of nuclear power plants in the UK'. During the remaining stages debate on the localism bill the government encountered some backbench opposition – 21 Conservative MPs supported an amendment from John Stevenson, aiming to change the electoral system for electing mayors from the supplementary vote to first past the post and there were five minor Liberal Democrat rebellions, involving a total of six MPs.

'SUPER-INJUNCTIONS'

On 23 May Dominic Grieve responded to an urgent question on the granting and enforcement of privacy injunctions. During the debate Liberal Democrat MP John Hemming named one current case, 'with about 75,000 people having named Ryan Giggs on Twitter, it is obviously impracticable to imprison them all' and Speaker Bercow immediately took the MP to task over his comments, 'occasions such as this are occasions for raising the issues of principle involved, not seeking to flout for whatever purpose'. On 24 May defence minister Nick Harvey answered an urgent question on military deployments in Libya, stressing that no decision had been made on possible deployment of UK apache helicopters. Vince Cable published the detailed plans for a 'green investment bank' to ensure a successful transition to a low-carbon economy and the setting up of an advisory group chaired by Sir Adrian Montague.

WHITSUN RECESS

Returning after the Whitsun recess on 7 June, care services minister Paul Burstow replied to an urgent question on the decision not to hold an external independent inquiry into the abuse of vulnerable adults at Winterbourne View care home exposed by the BBC *Panorama* programme.

William Hague updated MPs on developments in the Middle East and North Africa following his visit to Benghazi. Theresa May made a statement on the review of the government's 'prevent strategy' on terrorism. On 8 June both Houses paid tribute to HRH the Duke of Edinburgh on the occasion of his ninetieth birthday. Much later than usual Theresa May came to the House to announce the details of the new national crime agency.

On 20 June Mark Hoban replied to an urgent question on HM Treasury's contingency plan in case of a default by Greece. On 21 June Ken Clarke made a statement in response to two consultations on sentencing reform and legal aid, announcing the introduction of a bill on legal aid.

On 27 June David Cameron reported on the European Council which had focused on Europe's economy, stating that he was determined 'to ensure that Britain did not have to contribute to any new Greek bail-out through the European financial stability mechanism'. Liam Fox reported on the publication of Lord Levene's review of MoD structure and management. MPs then debated the issue of House of Lords reform, which merely underlined that there was no real consensus on the issue. On 28 June Michael Gove answered an urgent question on possible school closures due to the public service workers strike called for that Thursday and his advice to parents worried about the situation. David Willetts published a higher education white paper designed to 'improve social mobility without compromising academic excellence or institutional autonomy'. On 29 June William Hague gave his regular update on developments in Africa and the Middle East: nearly 13,000 sorties had been carried out by the RAF in Libya. On 30 June Speaker Bercow announced that Robert Rogers had been appointed as the new Clerk of the House. Jeremy Hunt replied to an urgent question on News Corporation's proposed acquisition of BSkyB and the publication of the results of the consultation on the undertakings in lieu. He would consult further on a revised set of undertakings but was still minded not to refer the takeover. Police minister Nick Herbert made a statement on the high court ruling that the current arrangements for police bail were not legal – the Home Office would be introducing an emergency bill to close this anomaly. The Police (Bail & Detention) bill which ensured that time spent on bail should not count towards any maximum period of pre-charge detention completed all its Commons stages on 7 July and was dealt with in the Lords on 12 July, gaining royal assent on the same day. On 30 June George Osborne also rushed through a measure to amend spending on the Civil List before the bill (Sovereign Grant bill) had even been published – it was passed by the Commons in one day (14 July). See also Public Acts of Parliament.

PHONE-HACKING

On 5 July Labour MP Chris Bryant applied for an emergency debate on the need for a public inquiry into phone-hacking at the News of the World and the related conduct of the Metropolitan Police Service between 2006 and 2011. Given the seriousness of the issue and that he had the support of at least 40 other members Speaker Bercow unusually granted his request and ordered that there be a three hour debate the following day. On 6 July David Cameron made a statement on Afghanistan and his intention to reduce the UK force levels there to 9,000 by the end of 2012. During Chris Bryant's debate on phone-hacking Damian Green reiterated that the prime minister had announced there would be a fully independent public inquiry but it must not jeopardise any criminal investigation and so should await the outcome of the current police investigations.

On 11 July Jeremy Hunt announced that News Corporation had withdrawn their undertakings in lieu and so he would be referring their bid for BSkyB to the Competition Commission with immediate effect. On 13 July David Cameron announced that, after cross-party discussions, he had asked Lord Justice Leveson to lead a two-part inquiry into the phone-hacking scandal, one into the culture, practices and ethics of the press (to start immediately); the other into the extent of unlawful and improper conduct at the News of the World and other newspapers. Liam Fox published Lord Philip's review into the fatal Mull of Kintyre chinook helicopter crash in 1994, overturning the findings of an earlier investigation that found the pilots guilty of negligence to a gross degree. An opposition day debate on Rupert Murdoch rather lost its steam when the government eventually agreed not to oppose the motion on phone-hacking, and so the matter was not put to the vote at the end of the debate. On 14 July fisheries minister Richard Benyon answered an urgent question on the European Commission's proposed reforms of the Common Fisheries Policy, which the government welcomed. Philip Hammond made a statement on coastguard modernisation, which would see the retention of ten centres overall plus London, all operating on a 24-hour basis.

In the final week before the summer recess Theresa May made a statement on 18 July on the resignation of both Metropolitan Police Commissioner Sir Paul Stephenson and Deputy Commissioner John Yates over the phone-hacking investigation and allegations of police corruption – with agreement of the Mayor of London, Tim Godwin would stand in as acting Commissioner. Liam Fox made a statement on the next steps in implementing the strategic defence and security review involving bringing the army back from Germany, creating a better future for the reserve forces, and delivering on the commitment to agree a ten-year defence equipment budget. Communities and local government secretary Eric Pickles published a consultation on repatriating business rates to local councils. With certain Labour MPs trying to prevent former Liberal Democrat chief secretary David Laws from being elected to a committee looking into the draft Financial Services bill (something that would normally be nodded through), a motion had to be debated and voted on (passed by 273 votes to 9). In what was seen as a tit-for-tat move a Conservative backbench MP (Nick de Bois) objected to a new Labour nominee for the culture, media and sport committee (Cathy Jamieson), meaning she could not take part in the next day's session. On 19 July Caroline Spelman published the government's bovine tuberculosis eradication programme for England which would allow for licenced culling of badgers in certain areas. Outside the chamber Rupert Murdoch, his son James and the recently resigned chief executive of News International, Rebekah Brooks, gave evidence to the culture, media and sport committee. The Commons had been due to rise for the summer recess on 19 July but given the phone-hacking scandal Speaker Bercow granted Leader of the House Sir George Young's request to recall parliament for one day – 20 July. On that day David Cameron, who returned early from a planned trip to various African countries, made a statement on and answered questions on public confidence in the media and the police for two hours and nineteen minutes, before leading on a full debate on the same issue. Both Houses of Parliament then rose for the summer recess.

PARLIAMENT RECALLED
Following rioting and civil unrest across London and other cities in England, the prime minister asked Speaker Bercow to recall the House on 11 August. On that day David Cameron made a statement on the rioting which was followed by a general debate. It was the first time parliament had been recalled during the summer recess since 2002 when then Speaker Michael Martin acceded to a request from the government for MPs to debate the situation in Iraq.

PUBLIC ACTS OF PARLIAMENT

Public acts included in this list are those which received the royal assent after 26 July 2010. The date stated after each act is the date on which it came into operation. For further information *see* W www.legislation.gov.uk

Appropriation (No. 3) Act 2010 ch. 30 (29 July 2010) authorises the use of resources for the service of the year ending with 31 March 2011 and to apply certain sums out of the Consolidated Fund to the service of the year ending with 31 March 2011; to appropriate the supply authorised in this Session of Parliament for the service of the year ending with 31 March 2011; and to repeal certain Consolidated Fund and Appropriation Acts.

Finance (No. 2) Act 2010 ch. 31 (27 July 2010) grants certain duties, alters other duties, and amends the law relating to the National Debt and the Public Revenue, and makes further provision in connection with finance.

Academies Act 2010 ch. 32 (27 July 2010) enables more schools to achieve academy status and gives them the freedoms and flexibilities to continue to drive up standards.

Finance (No. 3) Act 2010 ch. 33 (16 December 2010) grants certain duties, alters other duties, and amends the law relating to the National Debt and the Public Revenue, and makes further provision in connection with finance.

Equitable Life (Payments) Act 2010 ch. 34 (16 December 2010) provides finance for payments in cases where persons have been adversely affected by maladministration in the regulation before December 2001 of the Equitable Life Assurance Society; and for connected purposes.

Local Government Act 2010 ch. 35 (16 December 2010) prevents the implementation of existing proposals made for the purposes of Part 1 of the Local Government and Public Involvement in Health Act 2007.

Savings Accounts and Health in Pregnancy Grant Act 2010 ch. 36 (16 December 2010) makes provision for eligibility for a child trust fund; repeals the Saving Gateway Accounts Act 2009; makes provision about entitlement to health in pregnancy grant; and for connected purposes.

Superannuation Act 2010 ch. 37 (16 December 2010) supports reform of the Civil Service Compensation Scheme (CSCS); makes provision for and in connection with limiting the value of the benefits which may be provided under so much of any scheme under section 1 of the Superannuation Act 1972 as provided by virtue of section 2(2) of that Act for benefits to be provided by way of compensation to or in respect of persons who suffer loss of office or employment; and makes provision about the procedure for modifying such a scheme.

Terrorist Asset-Freezing etc. Act 2010 ch. 38 (16 December 2010) makes provision for imposing financial restrictions on, and in relation to, certain persons believed or suspected to be, or have been, involved in terrorist activities; to amend Schedule 7 to the Counter-Terrorism Act 2008; and for connected purposes.

Consolidated Fund Act 2010 ch. 39 (21 December 2010) authorises the use of resources for the service of the year ending with 31 March 2011 and applies certain sums out of the Consolidated Fund to the service of the year ending with 31 March 2011; and authorises the use of resources for the year ending with 31 March 2012 and the issue of sums out of the Consolidated Fund for the year ending with 31 March 2012.

Identity Documents Act 2010 ch. 40 (21 December 2010) makes provision for and in connection with the repeal of the Identity Cards Act 2006; makes certain that identity cards ceased to be valid legal documents in Europe on 21 January 2011 and that the National Identity Register was to be destroyed within two months of the act coming into force.

Loans to Ireland Act 2010 ch. 41 (21 December 2010) makes provision in connection with the making of loans to Ireland by the United Kingdom; ensures the aggregate amount of payments made by the Treasury by way of Irish loans in the period beginning with 9 December 2010 and ending with 8 December 2015 must not exceed £3,250m.

Parliamentary Voting System and Constituencies Act 2011 ch. 1 (16 February 2011) makes provision for a referendum on the voting system for parliamentary elections and to provide for parliamentary elections to be held under the alternative vote system if a majority of those voting in the referendum are in favour of that; makes provision about the number and size of parliamentary constituencies; and for connected purposes.

Appropriation Act 2011 ch. 2 (16 March 2011) authorises the use of resources for the service of the year ending with 31 March 2010 and 31 March 2011 and to apply certain sums out of the Consolidated Fund to the service of the years ending with 31 March 2010 and 31 March 2011; and to appropriate the supply authorised in this Session of Parliament for the service of the years ending with 31 March 2010 and 31 March 2011.

National Insurance Contributions Act 2011 ch. 3 (22 March 2011) makes provision for and in connection with increasing rates of national insurance contributions and a regional secondary Class 1 contributions holiday for new businesses.

Budget Responsibility and National Audit Act 2011 ch. 4 (22 March 2011) makes provision for a Charter for Budget Responsibility and for the publication of Financial Statements and Budget Reports; to establish the office for Budget Responsibility; to make provision about the Comptroller and Auditor-General and to establish a body corporate called the National Audit Office; to amend

Schedules 5 and 7 to the Government of Wales Act 2006 in relation to the Auditor-General for Wales; and for connected purposes.

Postal Services Act 2011 ch. 5 (13 June 2011) makes provision for the restructuring of the Royal Mail group and about the Royal Mail Pension Plan; to make new provision about the regulation of postal services, including provision for a special administration regime; and for connected purposes.

Sports Grounds Safety Authority Act 2011 ch. 6 (12 July 2011) confers further powers on the Football Licensing Authority and amends its name; and for connected purposes.

Estates of Deceased Persons (Forfeiture Rule and Law of Succession) Act 2011 ch. 7 (12 July 2011) amends the law relating to the distribution of the estates of deceased persons; and for connected purposes.

Wreck Removal Convention Act 2011 ch. 8 (12 July 2011) implements the Nairobi International Convention on the Removal of Wrecks 2007.

Police (Detention and Bail) Act 2011 ch. 9 (12 July 2011) makes provision about the calculation of certain periods of time for the purposes of Part 4 of the Police and Criminal Evidence Act 1984.

Supply and Appropriation (Main Estimates) Act 2011 ch. 10 (19 July 2011) authorises the use of resources for the year ending with 31 March 2012; to authorise both the issues of sums out of the Consolidated Fund and the application of income for that year; and to appropriate the supply authorised for that year by this Act and by the Consolidated Fund Act 2010.

Finance Act 2011 ch. 11 (19 July 2011) grants certain duties, alters other duties, and amends the law relating to the National Debt and the Public Revenue, and makes further provision in connection with finance.

European Union Act 2011 ch. 12 (19 July 2011) makes provision about treaties relating to the European Union and decisions made under them, including provision implementing the Protocol signed at Brussels on 23 June 2010 amending the Protocol (No. 36) on transitional provisions annexed to the Treaty on European Union, to the Treaty on the Functioning of the European Union and to the Treaty establishing the European Atomic Energy Community; and to make provision about the means by which directly applicable or directly effective European Union law has effect on the United Kingdom.

WHITE PAPERS

This section provides an outline of a selection of white papers that have been published in the last year. For further information *see* W www.official-documents.gov.uk or www.parliament.uk. Alternatively, visit the websites of individual government departments – *see* Government Departments section.

Healthy Lives, Healthy People: Our Strategy for Public Health in England was presented to parliament by the Secretary of State for Health in November 2010. The paper sets out the government's long-term vision for the future of public health in England. These plans include ending central control, giving local government the freedom, responsibility and funding to improve public health in their area; financial incentives to reward progress on improving health and reducing health inequalities; and a new public health service – Public Health England – to replace the existing structures.

The Importance of Teaching was presented to parliament by the Secretary of State for Education in November 2010. The schools white paper sets out a radical reform programme for the schools system, freeing schools from the constraints of central government direction and placing teachers at the heart of school improvement. Based on evidence from the world's best education systems, the paper outlines the government's plans for how the prestige of the teaching profession will be raised and how the quality of initial training and continuing professional development in teaching will be improved. The paper also details new powers for teachers to improve discipline; a transformation of the school curriculum; changes to school performance tables, Ofsted inspections and governance; and a fairer funding system for the most deprived children.

Universal Credit: Welfare That Works was presented to parliament by the Secretary of State for Work and Pensions in November 2010. Building on the consultation document *21st Century Welfare*, published in July 2010, the paper sets out the government's plans to reform the welfare system by creating a single overarching 'universal credit' which will replace a number of existing benefits. The paper explains how the universal credit will be implemented to make a fairer, more affordable system, better equipped to tackle poverty, worklessness and welfare dependency. The paper promotes work and personal responsibility, outlines the need for change, and also explains how the universal credit will affect benefit recipients.

The *Giving White Paper* was presented to parliament by the Minister of State for the Cabinet Office and Paymaster General in May 2011. The white paper seeks to renew Britain's culture of philanthropy, in line with the concept of the 'Big Society', by working with charities and businesses to support modern ways for contributions to be made in a busy lifestyle. Commitments in the white paper include: over £40m of funding over two years to support volunteering by way of the Social Action Fund, Challenge Prizes and Local Infrastructure Fund; trial charity promotions on the public-service website

(W www.direct.gov.uk); the availability of government buildings to charities and voluntary groups; and the holding of a 'giving summit' to bring together charities, philanthropists, businesses, technologists and financiers to set the course for the future of giving.

Higher Education: Students at the Heart of the System was presented to parliament by the Secretary of State for Business, Innovation and Skills in June 2011. The white paper sets out policies for the reform of education first published in *Skills for Sustainable Growth* in November 2010. The reforms tackle three major issues: putting higher education on a sustainable footing; delivering better student experiences from institutions offering improved teaching, assessments, feedback and preparation for the world of work; and encouraging institutions to take more responsibility for increasing social mobility. The paper also considers a new system of post-qualification applications (PQA), meaning the university application round occurs after exam results rather than before. The paper additionally includes plans to extend tuition loans to part-time students and introduce a new national scholarship programme.

The Natural Choice: Securing the Value of Nature was presented to parliament by the Secretary of State for Environment, Food and Rural Affairs in June 2011. The paper outlines the government's vision to establish a better quality natural environment over the next 50 years. Published in response to the review *Making Space for Nature*, the white paper, the first on the natural environment in 20 years, includes initiatives such as reconnecting nature; connecting people and nature for better quality of life; and capturing and improving the value of nature.

Open Public Services was presented to parliament by the Minister for Government Policy in July 2011. The white paper sets out a comprehensive policy framework across public services. There are five key principles concerning public-service modernisation: choice – wherever possible to increase choice; decentralisation – power to be decentralised to the lowest appropriate level; diversity – public-services to be open to a range of providers; fairness – ensuring fair access to public services; and accountability – public services to be accountable to users and taxpayers.

Planning our Electric Future: a White Paper for Secure, Affordable and Low-carbon Electricity was presented to parliament by the Secretary of State for Energy and Climate Change in July 2011. Responding to the challenges of constantly increasing energy demand, the government set out key measures within the paper to attract investment, reduce the impact on consumer bills and to create a secure combination of electricity sources including gas, new nuclear, renewables, and carbon capture and storage. Major elements of the reform include a carbon price floor to provide a strong incentive to invest in low-carbon generation and the introduction of long-term contracts to provide stable financial incentives to invest in low-carbon electricity generation.

SCIENCE AND DISCOVERY

Storm Dunlop

DANGERS FROM OLD PLATES

The Tohoku earthquake that struck Japan on 11 March 2011 has caused a drastic re-evaluation of the geological behaviour at subduction zones, where one tectonic plate dives beneath another. Early research, presented at a meeting of the Seismological Society of America in April 2011, suggested that such 'megathrust' events and the highest-magnitude earthquakes may occur with old, slow-moving plates rather than younger, fast-moving plates. The ocean crust off Japan is about 140-million-years-old and the crust involved in the destructive earthquake and tsunami of 26 December 2004 in the Indian Ocean off Indonesia is about 80–90 million-years-old. This gives cause for concern that any subduction zone with ancient rocks may be subject to similar major events. Of particular concern is the apparently locked, tiny, Juan de Fuca plate on the Cascadia subduction zone in northwestern America. A megathrust here would devastate Vancouver, British Columbia, together with Seattle and Portland in Washington and Oregon.

Rupture was formerly assumed to occur normally in one direction along a fault, or to spread from the centre towards both ends. The Indonesian rupture was exceptionally long (around 1,200km) with a displacement of about 8m in places. In contrast, the area affected by the Tohoku earthquake and aftershocks was about 200km across, but rupture occurred in multiple directions, and at various locations and depths. Japan was shifted about 8m towards the east and preliminary results suggest utterly unprecedented displacements of 24m for parts of the seabed and some 60m on the fault itself.

LAND, SEA, AND NOW AIR

Atmospheric scientists from the University of Illinois at Urbana-Champaign announced in *Geophysical Research Letters* in June 2011 that they had photographed ripples in the (permanently present) airglow in the ionosphere at altitudes of approximately 250km, created by the tsunami of 11 March 2011. The tsunami's 100m-high ocean waves created atmospheric density waves that propagates upwards, creating collisions between ionized and neutral particles, with the resulting emission of light. Because of their altitude, such ionospheric ripples are detectable at great distances (around 1,000 km) so could possibly warn of an approaching tsunami.

DOING THE SPLITS

The East African Rift system is a divergent plate boundary, where the African Plate will eventually split into the large Nubian Plate and the smaller, Somali Plate. Most activity is concentrated in the Afar Triangle, the triple junction (of the East-African, Red-Sea, and Gulf-of-Aden rifts), where the incipient Nubian and Somali Plates are pulling away from the Arabian Plate. In 2005, a crack, up to 8m wide and 60km long, suddenly arose in just 10 days in the Dabbahu rift segment. It has been expanding ever since. Erta Ale, north of Dabbahu, one of the few volcanoes worldwide with a permanent lava lake, is continuously active but began a major eruption in November 2010,

with effusive lava flows. In December 2010, an associated series of earthquakes occurred 100km offshore on the Gulf of Aden Rift and on 12 June 2011, in an event possibly related, Nabro volcano, on the northern edge of the Triangle, in Eritrea, began its first eruption for at least 10,000 years. In a study published online in *Nature Geoscience* on 13 March 2011, geologists at the University of Southampton showed that the crust was being stretched rapidly, causing it to sink and also creating abrupt subsurface melting and enabling repeated lava flows to reach the surface. Much of the area is now below sea level, only divided from the ocean by a narrow section of land in Eritrea. The area offers the opportunity to study, on land, geological processes that normally occur at sea-floor spreading centres.

DRILLING TO THE CORE

In March 2011 it was announced in *Nature* by an international team of scientists that an attempt would be made to recover the deepest-ever samples of oceanic crust. Initially the Japanese vessel *Chikyu* will drill to 2km below the seafloor off Costa Rica above the Cocos Plate in the eastern Pacific, reopening a previously drilled hole that reached the zone between upper and lower oceanic crust, where basalts give way to the lower gabbros. The immediate aim is to recover the previously unsampled gabbros, but ultimately is it hoped to retrieve rocks from the Earth's mantle, effectively reviving the earlier Mohole project – named for the Mohorovicic Discontinuity between crust and mantle – initiated in 1961, but abandoned in 1966, when the US Congress withdrew funding. The mantle makes up the bulk of the Earth, with a thickness of about 2,900km from its boundary with the outer core, and is believed to consist of rocks known as peridotites. Pristine samples would be invaluable in understanding the processes taking place within the mantle, such as the slow motions responsible for plate tectonics. Even under the seafloor where the crust is thinnest, the mantle lies at depths of around 6km, so reaching it is a major undertaking, requiring new technology and new techniques.

TOP DOWN, AND BOTTOM UP

On 1 June 2011, an international team of scientists reported in *Nature* the results of an aerial survey, using ice-penetrating radar, of the East-Antarctic bedrock. These revealed the existence of deep trenches and 'fjords', indicating that growth of the Antarctic icecap – which probably started with major glaciers on the now completely hidden Gamburtsev Mountains – occurred in several pulses, gouging the fjord-like features, before the ice merged into a single sheet, now 4km deep in places.

Another international study, published online in *Science* in March 2011, revealed that vast quantities of liquid water are freezing onto the base of the ice sheet above the Gamburtsev Mountains. In places this accreted ice is hundreds of metres thick and represents as much as half of the column of ice.

IS EL NIÑO CHANGING?

In a study published in *Geophysical Research Papers* in August 2010, researchers at NASA's Jet Propulsion

Laboratory and NOAA's Pacific Marine Environmental Laboratory found that a form of El Niño, where the warmest waters occur in the central, rather than eastern, Pacific is becoming more common. The frequency of such events appears to have doubled over recent decades, with the most intense event occurring in 2009–10. Currently, long-range weather forecasting is based on El Niño producing greatest warming in the eastern Pacific, so the shift in location of the most intense heating (which has a profound effect on global weather patterns), may require significant modification of existing forecasting models, and invalidate certain predictions of future climate. It is currently uncertain whether the changes to El Niño are themselves the result of global warming.

THE EARLIEST LIFEFORM ON EARTH?
Although some workers hold that the strange chemistry of the rocks from Isua in Greenland indicates the existence of bacteria 3.8×10^9 years ago, results announced in October 2010 in *Earth and Planetary Science Letters* by an international team led by the University of Bergen offer more certain evidence of the presence of microbes at least 3.34×10^9 years ago. The trace fossils are microscopic tubules, seemingly created by microbes in basalts from the Barberton Greenstone Belt in South Africa. The material filling the tubules has been positively dated by uranium/lead isotopic dating methods.

AND THE EARLIEST LAND PLANTS?
Also in October 2010, a team from the Argentine Institute of Snow, Ice and Environmental Research published, in *New Phytologist*, the discovery of the cryptospores of five varietes of liverworts in rocks from the Sierras Subandinas, in northwestern Argentina. The rocks are dated to 473–471 million years ago, earlier than the oldest cryptospores previously known from Saudi Arabia and the Czech Republic, with ages of 463–461 million years. This suggests that the first land plants arose in the Ordovician (488–472 million years ago), or even in the late Cambrian (499–488 million years ago), and that the evolutionary step took place on the ancient Gondwana supercontinent.

DID DINOSAURS BECOME EXTINCT LATER THAN WE THOUGHT?
Not only has evidence emerged that the Chixchulub impact event occurred about 300,000 years before the Cretaceous/Tertiary (KT) extinction event, but results published in *Geology* in January 2011 by scientists from the Univesity of Alberta, establish that some hadrosaurs (plant-eating dinosaurs) apparently lived no less than 700,000 years after the impact. Although derived from a single female hadrosaur bone, using uranium/lead direct-dating techniques, the measurements appear robust. The question of whether the impact was the primary cause of the KT extinction event (and the extinction of non-avian dinosaurs in particular) or whether pockets of habitat and their dinosaur populations were not affected, remains unresolved.

IN THE DEPTHS SOMETHING STIRRED . . .
In June 2011, an international team announced in *Nature* that they had discovered three species of nematode worms in water from cracks at depths of 1.3km in two South-African gold mines. These, the deepest multicellular organisms known, survive on subsurface bacteria in the water (which is at 48°C and contains about 1 per cent of the oxygen found in surface and oceanic water). One new species has now been named *Halicephalobus mephisto*. Traces of nematode DNA were even found in water at the far greater depth of 3.6km. Radiocarbon dating shows the age of the water is 3,000–12,000 years, indicating that the worms were not carried to such depths by later mining.

THESE FEET WERE MADE FOR WALKING
A long-standing debate about the stance and gait of *Australopithecus afarensis* appears to have been resolved. Neither the famous, original 'Lucy' fossil nor the 'Kadanumu' specimen discovered much later included bones from the feet. In February 2011, *Science* carried the report by researchers from the University of Missouri and Arizona State University of the discovery at Hadar, in Ethiopia, of a metatarsal bone with a curvature that implies that the foot was fully arched, as in humans, implying true bipedal locomotion. The structure of the hands and arms, however, retains primitive characteristics, suggesting that an arboreal (climbing) lifestyle had not yet been completely abandoned.

AFRICA TO ASIA, OR ASIA TO AFRICA?
It has long been accepted that early hominids evolved in Africa and that *Homo erectus* was the first to migrate to the Near East and Asia, followed at a later date by *Homo sapiens*. Recent discoveries in Asia have cast some doubt that *H. erectus* – widely regarded as the ancestor of *H. sapiens* – did originate in East Africa. In March 2011, archaeologists from the Sharma Center for Heritage Education in Tamil Nadu, India, announced, in *Science*, the discovery of over 3,600 Acheulian tools, generally associated with *H. erectus*, at Attirampakkam. No hominid remains were found. The age of the tool-bearing layers' soil has been found to be 1.07 to 1.77 million years, and six individual tools have been buried for 1.5 million years. Previously, it had been thought that another species, *H. Heidelbergensis*, had left Africa and taken the Acheulian tool-making technology to southern Asia and Europe around 500,000 years ago. Further intriguing evidence comes with the announcement online in June 2011 in *Proceedings of the National Academy of Sciences* by a team of researchers from the University of North Texas, that tools found at Dmanisi in Georgia could be positively shown to be between 1.77 and 1.85 million years old. Such dates are equal to, or slightly earlier than, the earliest evidence for *H. erectus* in Africa. The tools came from layers below those previously found to contain 1.77-million-year-old *H. erectus* fossils, including brain cases that suggested an early form of the species. Because there are various possiblities for the way in which the *Homo* genus evolved, and its geographic location is uncertain, these findings suggest that it is distinctly possible that the *Homo* lineage originated in Asia with *H. erectus*.

HOMO SAPIENS ACQUIRED VITAL GENES FROM NEANDERTHALS AND DENISOVANS
Following the discovery of Neanderthal genes in certain, modern, non-African humans, announced in May 2010, more details have emerged of probable interbreeding between *Homo sapiens* and other species. Human leukocyte antigens (HLA) are an essential part of the immune system. They occur as some 200 genes, each of which may have hundreds of variants (alleles). This vast range of alleles allows the immune system to respond to an enormous variety of diseases and to mount a response to new challenges. When *H. sapiens* left Africa around 60,000–50,000 Before Present (BP), their HLA alleles

would have been appropriate for local diseases, not those likely to be encountered in Europe or Asia.

At a Royal Society meeting on human evolution in June 2011, Peter Parham of Stanford University in California presented results indicating that *H. sapiens* acquired HLA genes from both *Homo neanderthalensis* and from the new species (announced in March 2010 and known as Denisovans), found at the Denisova Cave in the Altai Mountains. Both of these species had lived outside Africa for perhaps 200,000 years, and thus had time to develop suitable forms of HLA. One allele, not found in modern African humans, but common in Europeans and Asians, is found in the Neanderthal genome. Another (known as HLA-A*11), is primarily found in Asians, and apparently originated in the Denisovans.

Whereas only a small fraction of the modern, non-African human genome (1–6 per cent) comes from other species, the situation with HLAs is very different. For the HLA-A alleles, in particular, the proportion derived from other hominin species increases dramatically eastwards from about 50 per cent in modern Europeans, to 72 per cent in Chinese, and 90 per cent in humans from Papua New Guinea. This suggests increasing selection of alleles for tropical diseases as *H. sapiens* migrated eastwards, whereas those moving into colder, northern climates faced fewer diseases.

TAKING A LONG LOOK AT ANTI-HYDROGEN
Although atoms of anti-hydrogen (the antimatter counterpart of hydrogen, consisting of an antiproton and a positron) were first created in 2002, in November 2010 the Alpha collaboration at CERN announced success in trapping anti-hydrogen atoms for about one-fifth of a second. In June 2011, *Nature Physics* carried their report of trapping anti-atoms for as long as 1,000 seconds; more than long enough to be able to carry out significant investigation of their properties, and determine whether antimatter obeys exactly the same laws as matter, and perhaps shedding light on why our universe consists of matter, when all theoretical considerations suggest equal amounts of matter and antimatter should have been created in the Big Bang. The team is now working to increase the number of atoms trapped (currently about 300), rather than increase their longevity.

HINTS OF THE HIGGS?
In April 2011 it was announced that the Large Hadron Collider (LHC) at CERN had reached a world-record intensity (known as integrated luminosity) for the collision of two beams of protons, each with an energy of 3.5 teravolts (3.5 TeV). The luminosity measured, and expressed as one inverse femtobarn, is equivalent to around 70 million million (70×10^{12}) collisions. In late July 2011, it was announced at the Europhysics conference that the Atlas and CMS teams at the LHC had seen interesting particle events corresponding to a mass of between 140 and 145 GeV, and also that the team working with the Tevatron synchrotron at the Fermi National Accelerator Laboratory (Fermilab) in Batavia, Illinois, had detected (at a lower level of probability) similar events around 140 GeV. It is expected that by the end of the current LHC run in 2012, confirmation or refutation of the long-sought Higgs mechanism and associated particle will have been achieved.

A MINI-BIG BANG
In another development, on 7 November 2010, the LHC was used to create collisions between lead ions, thus creating what is known as a quark-gluon plasma that closely replicates conditions during the Big Bang, some 13.7×10^9 years ago. The high temperatures (more than 10×10^{12} K) and densities achieved are designed to study the strong force, responsible for binding atomic nuclei together and producing some 98 per cent of their mass.

SO THEY'RE NOT ELLIPTICAL AFTER ALL
For many years it has been generally accepted that there was a distinct dichotomy in the nature of galaxies with two major classes: the spirals, with a considerable content of gas and dust gathered into flattened disks, and with significant new star formation; and the ellipticals, ranging from nearly spherical galaxies to greatly flattened ellipsoids, with little or no gas and dust, generally older stars, and no star formation. It was believed that the differences reflected a fundamental difference in the way in which the classes of galaxies had been formed. Examination of the nearest 260 elliptical and lenticular galaxies by the international Atlas3D survey, with results announced in July 2011 and to be published in *Monthly Notices of the Royal Astronomical Society*, investigated the rotation speed of the individual galaxies. It brought the surprising finding that some 66 per cent of the 'ellipticals' actually had a disk-like structure, and merely presented an elliptical shape because of their inclination to the line of sight. Only the 'slow rotators' were truly spheroidal in shape. This finding that the majority of galaxies have a common structure is likely to lead to a complete revision of theories of galaxy formation and evolution.

EVEN BETTER AND BRIGHTER SUPERNOVAE
Type Ia supernovae are of fundamental importance in cosmology. They were considered to have a consistent peak brightness at outburst, and could thus be used as 'standard candles' in the determination of cosmic distances. It was discrepancies between the calculated distances of Type Ia supernovae and those of their parent galaxies as determined from the readily determined redshifts (recession velocities) that first suggested that the expansion of the universe was accelerating with time, driven by what has come to be called 'dark energy' of unknown nature. These findings have since been confirmed by other observations. In January 2011, a team from the Harvard-Smithsonian Center for Astrophysics announced, at a meeting of the American Astronomical Association, that slight differences in colour, previously ascribed to intervening dust, were actually intrinsic to the supernovae. Correction for this effect will lead to more accurate distance determinations, and thus to refinements in determining the effects of dark energy. In June 2011, a team of astronomers from California Institute of Technology, led by Robert Quimby, announced in *Nature* that they had identified six supernovae that appear to form a new class. They are approximately 10 times as bright as normal Type Ia supernovae and display other distinguishing characteristics, notably a long decay time and an absence of hydrogen in their spectra. Their extreme luminosity cannot be explained by any of three known mechanisms: radioactive decay of newly formed elements, shock-wave heating prior to the stellar explosion or collision of ejecta with a surrounding hydrogen-rich shell. One suggestion for a possible mechanism is that ejecta from the supernova explosion collided with shells of hydrogen-poor, evolved elements, expelled by a high-mass pulsating progenitor at an earlier stage of evolution. Another possibility is that the explosion created a magnetar – a rapidly rotating stellar

remnant with an extremely powerful magnetic field. Strong magnetic braking could convert the rotational energy into a source that increased the luminosity. The six unusual supernovae all appeared in dwarf galaxies and, in fact, led to the galaxies being discovered. If they are unique to such galaxies, they may not affect distance-determinations with 'normal' Type Ia supernovae. If they originate in high-mass stars they probably resemble the first stars to be formed after the Big Bang, and thus illustrate conditions in the early universe.

LAUNCHED AT LAST!

In May 2011, in one of its last missions, the Space Shuttle transported the Alpha Magnetic Spectrometer (AMS) to the International Space Station (ISS). Probably the most important scientific experiment mounted on the station, the AMS is the world's most advanced cosmic-ray detector. Although cosmic rays have many origins, it should be able to detect particles that are derived from dark matter, hints of which have been seen by other experiments, notably the PAMELA experiment of 2006, but which remain unconfirmed – dark matter is believed to form 83 per cent of the matter in the universe. AMS has the unique ability to differentiate between low-mass antiparticles and high-mass 'ordinary' matter particles with the same electrical charge. The complex and expensive equipment (costing some $2bn (£1.2bn)), which took 16 years to build, was launched only after extensive lobbying by scientists and intervention by Congress, which directed NASA to extend the Shuttle programme for that purpose. Even so, sensitivity and accuracy have been sacrificed for longevity, in that a highly sophisticated cryogenic superconducting magnet, designed and manufactured in Britain, was replaced at a late stage by a conventional permanent magnet, which does not require a supply of liquid helium for cooling.

PLANETS, PLANETS, AND STILL MORE PLANETS

By mid-July 2011, 563 extrasolar planets (exoplanets) had been firmly established. In May 2011 it was announced that NASA's Kepler satellite had obtained evidence, in the first four months of data (from May to September 2009), of more than 1,200 candidate exoplanets, 408 in 170 multiple-planet systems. (Most candidates require follow-up observations or timing analysis.) Kepler detects transits, where planets cross in front of their parent star, causing a slight decrease in the light. One system, Kepler-11, described earlier in February 2011 in *Nature*, was found to contain no less than six planets. Remarkably, all were observed to transit the parent star, and thus indicated a strongly co-planar system (flatter than the Solar System itself). The planets themselves are rocky and gaseous bodies, comparable with Uranus and Neptune in size, but orbiting very close to the star.

Exoplanets may also be detected through the microlensing effect: when a planet passes in front of a star it causes a brief spike in luminosity. In May 2011, the Microlensing Observations in Astrophysics (MOA) survey, an international, Japanese-led team, using a 1.8m telescope in New Zealand, announced in *Nature* that, in a small region towards the galactic centre, they had found evidence for 10 Jupiter-sized, free-floating planets. These have presumably been ejected from their original planetary systems through catastrophic gravitational encounters with other planets or the parent star. A second microlensing group, the Optical Gravitational Lensing

Experiment (OGLE) observed many of the same events, and confirmed the MOA analysis. Although long predicted, and some candidates were known, this is the first time that such 'orphan' planets have been positively identified.

In November 2010, a team from the Max-Planck-Institut für Astronomie (MPIA) announced in *Science Express* that they had detected an exoplanet of 1.2 Jupiter masses orbiting a star known as HIP 13044, and which has an extragalactic origin. The star (and planet) belong to the Helmi stream, which once formed a dwarf galaxy that was captured and cannibalized by the Galaxy some 6 to 9×10^9 years ago.

These, and other, studies – and particularly the discovery of so many 'orphan' planets in such a small region – suggest that the formation of planets is extremely widespread and that the number of planets in the Galaxy far exceeds the total number of stars.

VERY PRECIOUS DUST

In November 2010, the Japanese Space Agency announced that the Hayabusa spaceprobe, despite many difficulties, had actually obtained dust samples from the minor planet (asteroid) Itokawa. Although the sampling mechanism did not function correctly, about 1,500 minute grains were captured and returned to Earth. The minerals identified include olivine, pagioclase and pyroxene, and although all are common on Earth, their abundances and isotopic composition prove their extraterrestrial origin. The mineral troilite, which does not occur on Earth, was also identified, and all the minerals resemble those in primitive meteorites.

The Itokawa samples are the first to be returned by a spaceprobe from a minor planet, becoming the fourth set of extraterrestrial samples returned directly to Earth, joining lunar material brought by US and Soviet missions, cometary particles collected by NASA's Stardust probe, and solar-wind particles captured by NASA's Genesis probe. Meteorites have provided other material confidently believed to have originated in the Moon, Mars, and certain minor planets, such as Vesta.

MESSAGES FROM MESSENGER

On 18 March 2011, NASA's Messenger probe finally entered Mercury orbit, after six planetary fly-bys to reduce its velocity to that of the planet. The probe has special shielding to protect it from the intense heat, and is already starting to produce unexpected results. Images show widespread lava plains that have been erupted over a significant part of the planet's history, somewhat at variance with the accepted view that the planet had formerly undergone significant contraction in diameter, which would tend to reduce volcanism. Many surface features are unlike those found on the Moon, and the elemental ratios indicate that the composition differs markedly from that of the other planets, probably indicating a variation in the distribution of elements in the original protoplanetary disk from which they formed.

Mercury is the only terrestrial planet (apart from the Earth) to have a magnetic field. The centre of the field is significantly displaced (towards the north) from the centre of the planet, creating a major disparity in the shape of the magnetosphere, with the southern polar region being strongly exposed to the impact of charged particles from the solar wind, releasing atoms (in the process known as 'sputtering') to create the planet's tenuous and fugitive atmosphere. Messenger is regularly observing the bursts of highly energetic particles, first detected in 1976 by the

Mariner 10 probe, and which are produced by some currently unknown mechanism in the magnetosphere.

TOO MUCH WATER, SO HOW DID THE MOON FORM?

New analysis of the famous 'orange soil' samples returned by the Apollo 17 mission to the Taurus-Littrow region of the Moon in December 1972, published in *Science Express* in April 2011 by a team from Brown University in Providence, Rhode Island and Case Western Reserve University in Cleveland, Ohio, revealed unexpectedly that the lunar mantle contains large quantities of water, apparently even more, in relative terms, than the Earth's mantle. This poses major problems for the generally accepted theory of the Moon's formation, in which the impact of a large (Mars-sized) body produced a ring of high-temperature debris around the Earth, from which the Moon accreted. The presence of large quantities of water argues against a high-temperature origin.

DAWN OVER VESTA

On 15 July 2011, NASA's Dawn spaceprobe entered orbit around minor planet 4 Vesta, the fourth minor planet to be discovered (in 1807) the second most massive in the Main Asteroid Belt between Mars and Jupiter, and the first to be studied in detail by an orbiter. Vesta is approximately ellipsoidal with dimensions of some 550km × 468km. It has a differentiated interior (probably with a metallic core, olivine mantle, and silicate crust) and is the source of certain meteorites recovered on Earth. Vesta has a much higher albedo (reflectivity) than other minor planets and its geological composition and structure are significant for understanding the history of the formation of the Solar System.

Launched in September 2007, Dawn has used ion propulsion, with the highest accelerations of any spacecraft (approximately 6.7km per second) to match velocity with Vesta, allowing it to be captured gravitationally, initially at a distance of approximately 16,000 km. This distance will be reduced gradually, but after one year of research, in July 2012, Dawn will leave orbit and travel to 1 Ceres, the dwarf planet that is the largest body in the Main Belt. Dawn will reach Ceres and enter orbit in 2015.

ANOTHER VIRAL DISEASE ERADICATED

In October 2010, the UN Food and Agriculture Organisation announced that rinderpest, one of the most lethal viral diseases of cattle, had been completely eliminated. Formerly prevalent in Europe, Asia, the Middle East, the Arabian Peninsula, and Africa, rinderpest becomes the second viral disease (after smallpox) to be eradicated by human intervention. Although a vaccine has been available for some time, success finally came with the development of a simple, reliable and rapid field test that could be used (together with the vaccine) even in areas of nomadic herding or civil unrest.

MOSQUITOES AND MALARIA

The fight against malaria appears to be entering a new phase, targeting the carrier mosquitoes. In July 2010, researchers from the University of Arizona, working with the Universities of Georgia and California Davis, reported in *PLoS Pathogens* that they had genetically engineered a malaria-resistant mosquito. This altered a protein, essential for cellular communication within mosquitoes and also for the development of the malarial parasite. The result was disruption of the processes, also shortening the insect's lifespan. The technique was tested against the most virulent malaria parasite, *Plasmodium falciparum*, but has not yet included the *Anopheles gambiae* species of mosquito, the most significant malaria vector in Africa.

In a separate development, in April 2011, an international team of scientists announced in *Nature* that they had successfully modified a gene in mosquitoes that was beneficial to the mosquito's cellular repair machinery, causing the gene to be reproduced in all offspring and to spread throughout the population in just a few generations. The hope is that the technique could be used to make mosquitoes target animals rather than humans, produce all-male offspring (which cannot transmit malaria) or, by combining the two methods, prevent the parasite from multiplying.

PROTECTING MAJOR CROPS

Wheat, one of the world's staple crops, is under major threat from various fungal pathogens. Two virulent strains of stem rust and stripe rust have reduced yields by as much as 40 per cent in affected areas. Variants of a strain of stem rust, Ug99, are spreading rapidly from eastern Africa towards Asian countries, and threaten to extend worldwide. A strain of yellow rust that is perhaps even more virulent is held in check only by the drought conditions currently occurring in northern and eastern Africa and is likely to erupt into prominence when rains return.

In August 2010, UK scientists, led by a team from the University of Liverpool, released draft sequences of the wheat genome, and in June 2011, an international consortium of researchers published details in *PLos Genetics* of the genome of another fungal wheat disease, leaf blotch, which typically reduces yields by up to 15 per cent. In May 2011, another international study, co-led by the US Department of Agriculture, published the genome for stem rust (and also that of poplar leaf rust) in *Proceedings of the National Academy of Sciences*. Study of leaf blotch will reveal how the fungus evades wheat's defences, knowledge of the rust genome should help to counter that threat, and details of the actual wheat genome should assist in the development of varieties having increased disease resistance, higher yields, or tolerance a wider range of environmental conditions.

Two other significant crop genomes have been sequenced. The complete genome for the cacao tree was placed in the public domain in September 2010 by an international team of researchers, giving hope that varieties suitable for differing regional conditions and offering better yields may be developed. Another international team, led by researchers from the James Hutton Institute at Dundee in Scotland, announced decoding of the full genome of the potato, the world's fourth largest crop, enabling the development of varieties with increased nutritional value, and greater disease and pest resistance.

THE STEM-CELL SAGA

Ethical issues have dogged research into the use of human embryo stem cells (heSCs), particularly in the USA. Although the Obama administration annulled the Bush administration's ban on federal funding of research with new cell lines, this was subject to an immediate legal challenge, and although a short-lived injunction banning research was overturned in April 2011, this is still subject to legal submissions by so-called 'pro-life' activists. It was hoped a viable alternative would be induced pluripotent stem cells (iPSCs), where cells such as skin cells are 'reprogrammed' to act like heSCs, capable of turning into any desired type of cell. In March 2011, however, a team from the University of California, San Diego, announced in *Nature* that various lines of human induced stem cells (hiPSCs) contained mutations, the majority of which changed certain protein functions, and could therefore cause undesirable effects, including cancer. In May 2011, the team announced that in mice, iPSCs made from their own cells were rejected by the immune system.

In July 2011, researchers at McMaster University revealed in *Cell Stem Cell* that although hPSCs have the capacity to become any of the 226 cell types in the human body, they exist as various forms, encoded by varying proteins attached to their DNA, and that these forms preferentially develop into specific cell types. Separation of the cells using the protein markers enabled the researchers to produce more blood or neural cells than if the cells were 'forced' to develop into a particular type.

Some developments with iPSCs have proved successful. In August 2010, a team from the Buck Institute for Age Research reported online in *Stem Cells* that they had used human iPSCs, derived from skin and blood cells to treat rodents afflicted with Parkinson's disease. In June 2011, researchers from Indiana University-Purdue University Indianapolis reported, also online in *Stem Cells*, that they had successfully created replacement retinal cells from samples taken from a patient with a rare form of inherited eye disease.

Successful treatments have been developed using mesenchymal stem cells, MSCs, which may be derived from various forms of tissue and which are able to differentiate into a restricted, but still useful, range of cells. The most significant development, announced in early July 2011, was possibly the creation of a completely synthetic section of trachea, successfully grafted into a patient. Scans of the diseased section was used to create a completely artificial replica. This was seeded with MSCs taken from the patient's bone marrow. In the final stage, during the operation, epithelial cells from the patient's mucosa were added, which grew into the layer normally lining the trachea. The scaffold may be tailored to be permanent or to eventually dissolve, and the overall technique is initially suitable for organs such as the trachea, ureter, or blood vessels

A paper published in *Cell Stem Cell* in July 2011, by a team from Case Western Reserve University described how MSCs play a vital part within the body in combating injury to blood vessels. Injection of MSCs into the blood stream or damaged tissue appears to have reduced damage or cured a whole range of conditions, including heart attacks, strokes, burns, and wounds. In South Korea, approval has been given for stem cells to be used experimentally to treat patients who have survived heart attacks. Scientists at the University of California have also found that MSCs produce a protein that kills certain bacteria. In July 2011, a team based at the University of Toronto, announced in *Science* that they had succeeded in isolating what are known as haematopoietic stem cells from bone marrow. The cells, which have been known to exist for many years, are able to produce all types of blood cell, including oxygen-carrying red cells and the white blood cells responsible for immunity, raising the possibility that they could be used to reconstitute every fraction of a patient's blood.

THEATRE

Matt Trueman

THE FIRST CUT IS THE DEEPEST

If a pocketful of Tony Awards proved the strength of Britain's subsidised theatre sector, it only served to make the year's arts funding cuts seem all the more wrong-headed. Not only did *War Horse*'s Broadway run pick up all five awards for which it was nominated, including Best Play and Best Direction, it was a commercial smash, announcing its 15-week run at the Vivian Beaumont Theatre would extend indefinitely. Handspring Puppet Company was also awarded a Special Tony for Outstanding Artistry. Despite initial concerns about the commercial chances of its idiosyncratic portrait of rural England, Jez Butterworth's *Jerusalem* proved a critical and commercial success. Mark Rylance nabbed the Best Actor Tony for a second time, delivering a characteristically obscure acceptance speech about walking through walls, and the play extended at the Music Box Theatre.

Both plays had involved lengthy development processes that would not have been possible without subsidy. Butterworth delivered his first draft to the Royal Court as early as 2003, while *War Horse* was devised over two years of workshops at the National Theatre.

After Chancellor of the Exchequer George Osborne announced a 29.6 per cent cut to Arts Council England's government funding in October, a total reduction of around £350m by 2014, ACE set about a strategic review. Only permitted to pass on 15 per cent cuts to frontline organisations, its own overheads will be cut by 50 per cent, having already reduced administrative costs by 21 per cent over the previous 18 months.

Six days after the Comprehensive Spending Review, ACE announced a temporary across-the-board cut of 6.9 per cent (8.7 per cent in real terms) to its regularly funded organisations, all of which would have to reapply to join the new national portfolio in early 2011. Coupled with reductions to local authorities, some of which withdrew arts funding entirely, there was a major shake up for theatre funding in England, with a number of high-profile casualties. Though general consensus deemed the process rigorous and astute, some commentators believed the overhaul had not gone far enough.

It meant a number of prominent venues and theatre companies would lose regular government subsidy altogether, among them the Riverside Studios in Hammersmith and once-legendary, now-jaded companies Shared Experience, Trestle and Forkbeard Fantasy. Faulty Optic and Third Angel, small companies that have delivered interesting, characterful work in recent years, also lost out.

In *The Guardian*, writer Nosheen Iqbal suggested that black and ethnic minority companies were the hardest hit, citing total cuts to Nitro, Britain's oldest black theatre company, and Yellow Earth Theatre, its only East Asian one. In May, Manchester's Greenroom, Britain's only performance venue led by a black artistic director, became the first venue to close after losing funding entirely. There were also heavy cuts to the black-led Talawa Theatre Company and venues specifically targeting multi-ethnic audiences, such as Rich Mix, Watermans and Yaa Asantewaa Arts and Community Centre, all in London.

While both the National and the RSC agreed to take on cuts of 14.9 per cent over four years, there were several other high-profile losers. The Soho Theatre lost 17.6 per cent of its ACE funding over the same period, while Max Stafford Clark's Out of Joint was hit with a 27.9 per cent reduction. Perhaps the most surprising was the Almeida, which was hit with a £347,626 (39 per cent) cut despite regularly producing critically acclaimed work under artistic director Michael Attenborough, the suspicion being that its potential to replace subsidy with philanthropy played some part in the decision.

However, there were large increases for the nearby Arcola Theatre (up 82.1 per cent) and the Barbican Centre (108.7 per cent). Around the country, companies engaged in innovative and contemporary theatre practice, such as Unlimited, Punchdrunk, Told by an Idiot, Quarantine and Pilot Theatre, received significant funding increases, as did the independent producing house Fuel Theatre. There were also sizeable uplifts for circus organisations and companies making work for young audiences.

Equally, a number of very worthy organisations will receive regular funding for the first time. These included Edward Hall's all-male Shakespeare outfit Propeller, physical theatre companies Gecko, dreamthinkspeak and experimental collectives Coney, Clod Ensemble and Slung Low. Bristol's burgeoning performance scene received a shot in the arm with Theatre Bristol and Tobacco Factory included for the first time. Musical theatre was also boosted by the inclusion of Perfect Pitch, an organisation devoted to developing the rare beast that is the new British musical.

NEW DIRECTIONS

The shifting sands of financing theatre went hand in hand with – perhaps even directly triggered – an unusual level of change in the personnel at leading venues and theatre companies. As the year went on, the merry-go-round of artistic directors gathered speed. There were at least 15 major personnel changes at the UK's top theatrical venues and organisations.

Arguably most prominent was Michael Grandage, who announced in October that he would leave the Donmar Warehouse at the end of 2011, after nine years as artistic director. Since taking over from Sam Mendes in 2002, Grandage has overseen a particularly fruitful period for the Covent Garden producing house, which won more than 80 awards globally during his tenure.

His successor will be Josie Rourke, who trained at the Donmar and was artistic director of the Bush Theatre from 2007. In July, that theatre revealed Madani Younis, artistic director of Bradford's Freedom Studios, would succeed Rourke.

Nicholas Kent set March 2012 as the date of his departure from Kilburn's Tricycle Theatre, citing a £350,000 shortfall in the theatre's overall funding. Kent has helmed the Tricycle for 27 years and won great critical acclaim for his political programming and pioneering of verbatim theatre as a form, leading the theatre to be christened 'the Department of Public Morality' in *The Sunday Times*.

Elsewhere in London, Steve Marmion took over from Lisa Goldman at the Soho Theatre and immediately set about revitalising the place, most drastically by converting the subterranean Indian restaurant into a new cabaret and comedy space. Carrie Cracknell and Natalie Abrahami left Notting Hill's Gate Theatre, succeeded by Bush associate Christopher Haydon. The Unicorn's artistic director of 14 years Tony Graham handed over to Purni Morell, head of the National Theatre Studio, while Vauxhall's Oval House Theatre, the Southwark Playhouse and the Camden People's Theatre also changed hands.

Outside London, new artistic regimes began at Salisbury Playhouse – Gareth Machin taking over from Philip Wilson – and the Birmingham Rep, where Roxanna Silbert replaces Rachel Kavanaugh. After 35 years at the helm, Braham Murphy, co-founder of Manchester's Royal Exchange announced his departure, Ian Brown left the West Yorkshire Playhouse and, in Scotland, the Traverse's artistic director Dominic Hill joined the Glasgow Citizens Theatre, where he succeeds Jeremy Raison. Ramin Gray took over at the Actors Touring Company from Bijan Sheibani.

SAFETY FIRST

The economic downturn also had an effect on theatre programming, much of which seemed intent on defying the financial crisis. Though in January the Society of London Theatre was able to reveal record combined box office takings of £512m, it was hard to avoid the suspicion increasingly commercially minded and conservative programming was responsible. Major dramatists and familiar titles reigned supreme and Shakespeare's best-known plays seemed to pile up, often in direct competition with one another. Though celebrity casting has long since dogged the West End, its credibility was enhanced with the impetus reverting from personalities to top performers in vast, demanding roles.

None more so than *Hamlet*, which got three major productions with a fourth, starring Michael Sheen, due at the Young Vic before the year's end. At the Sheffield Crucible, John Simm, late of *Life on Mars*, made a wiry, unpretentious prince – his Sheffield accent scuffing the poetry's polish – in Paul Miller's otherwise uninspiring staging. By contrast, Nicholas Hytner's version for the Olivier stage presented a paranoid dictatorship governed by surveillance and suspicious deaths. In a luminously clear and multi-faceted performance, Rory Kinnear showed Hamlet hardening from self-pitying student languishing in tracksuit to hardcore activist targeting a cause with zeal. The Globe, meanwhile, toured a conventional storytelling staging with recent RADA graduate Joshua McGuire *(Posh)* in the lead.

After queuing for a while, Derek Jacobi finally climbed Mount Lear for the Donmar Warehouse. On Christopher Oram's patchwork snowstorm set, Jacobi's characteristic finicky precision made for a fascinating study, subverting 'Blow winds and crack your cheeks' into a stage-whispered trance, albeit lacking the devastating emotional force that the role demands.

Kevin Spacey's *Richard III*, the third and final Bridge Project production under Sam Mendes, was similarly lacking in emotion. An all-purpose dictator, finally strung up by his feet like Mussolini, Spacey's Richard was best characterised by an egotism born of absolute disdain for others; its defining moment being his faux-grudging acceptance of the crown like an Oscar-winner feigning surprise.

On a lighter note, David Tennant and Catherine Tate sparred their way through *Much Ado About Nothing*, a summer smash at the Wyndham's Theatre that reunited a

former Dr Who with his assistant under Josie Rourke's direction. Tennant's Benedick entered on a golf buggy, later appearing in drag, while Tate's Beatrice dangled from the rafters by her ankles.

However, Shakespeare's epic royals and tumbling lovers weren't the only event productions designed to draw the crowds. In February, Oscar-winning director Danny Boyle, whose career began at the Royal Court, staged Nick Dear's sprawling adaptation of *Frankenstein*. With Jonny Lee Miller *(Trainspotting)* and Benedict Cumberbatch, a bankable name since leading the BBC's *Sherlock*, alternating the roles of Victor Frankenstein and the Creature, the Olivier production sold out well in advance. Critical consensus deemed Miller the better monster, Cumberbatch the superior doctor and Boyle's production truly spectacular.

Another of Hytner's smash hits, Richard Bean's *One Man, Two Guvnors*, transposed Goldoni's *The Servant of Two Masters* to the turf wars of 1960s Brighton. With double entendres and pratfalls galore, including a hilariously ancient waiter repeatedly toppling down a staircase, it drew a neat parallel between the conventions of commedia dell'arte and proper-end-of-the-pier stuff. *History Boys* star James Corden, whose popularity had dwindled in recent years, was perfectly cast in the harlequin role of Francis Henshall, a former skiffle band member turned overworked manservant.

After raves heralding it the funniest play since Michael Frayn's *Noises Off*, *One Man, Two Guvnors* announced a transfer to the West End, where commercial theatre seemed to reclaim some of the musical's traditional territory. Keira Knightley returned to London, leading *The Children's Hour* opposite *Mad Men* star Elisabeth Moss. Kristin Scott Thomas led Ian Rickson's revival of *Betrayal* and Ben Barnes starred in Trevor Nunn's turgid production of *Birdsong* at the Comedy Theatre.

YEAR OF THE RAT

Equally conservative was the renaissance afforded to the so-called 'well-made play', kick-started by the centenary of Terence Rattigan's birth. Such was the playwright's prominence, it often seemed as though you were never more than six feet from a Rattigan play.

The celebrations began in earnest with Thea Sharrock's deliciously taught *After the Dance* at the National, which would pick up four Olivier awards, including Best Director. In the West End, Trevor Nunn brought *Flare Path* to the Haymarket, drawing a fantastic performance from Sheridan Smith as the lively Doris, if blander ones from leads Sienna Miller and James Purefoy. At the Old Vic, Sharrock revived Rattigan's last, *Cause Célèbre*, with Anne-Marie Duff beautifully drained in the central role of the murderous unfaithful wife, Alma Rattenbury, though the production felt uncomfortably squished onto the proscenium arch stage.

Further afield, the Jermyn Street Theatre unearthed the unseen *Less than Kind*, while Maxine Peake starred in the West Yorkshire Playhouse version of *Deep Blue Sea*, which would also get a production at the Chichester Festival Theatre. The same Chichester season also contained a double bill of *The Browning Version* and David Hare's new one-act response, *South Downs*. It also marked the world premiere of Nicholas Wright's adaptation of Rattigan's screenplay *Nijinsky*.

Tennessee Williams' centenary, by contrast, passed without fuss in the UK, where the only noteworthy revival was the Young Vic's expressionist take on *The Glass Menagerie*. In a tenderly over-exaggerated production, Joe Hill-Gibbins' direction captured the warping of recollection, with cracking performances from Leo Bill as a clenched Tom and Sinead Matthews as a scratchy, brittle Laura. The Cock Tavern, meanwhile, unearthed two of Williams' lost plays, *I Never Get Dressed Until After Dark On Sundays* and *A Cavalier for Milady*, though neither proved revelatory.

The Royal Court kick-started Arnold Wesker's 80th birthday with a meticulous *Chicken Soup with Barley* that felt like historical recreation rather than purposeful drama. The critics, however, loved it.

But it wasn't only the greats that returned to fashion. Promising young director Blanche McIntyre's production of Emlyn Williams' 1950 play *Accolade* had the critics dishing out the superlatives. It centres on a high-society scandal after an acclaimed writer's past sexual encounter with a teenager comes to light on the eve of his investiture at Buckingham Palace.

BELT UNTIGHTENING

Another beneficiary of the downturn was the big-money musical. *Les Misérables* celebrated its 25th anniversary in style, attracting big names (Matt Lucas and Nick Jonas) to the West End, returning to the Barbican and staging a huge concert at the 02 Arena. Kneehigh flopped at the Gielgud with *The Umbrellas of Cherbourg*, which was replaced with *Lend Me a Tenor*, while a musical version of Patrick Swayze film *Ghost* opened at the Piccadilly Theatre. The National brought the Afrobeat Broadway hit *Fela!* to London, while the Donmar revived off-Broadway smash *The 25th Annual Putnam County Spelling Bee*.

The West End was won, however, by two new musicals. *Shrek: the Musical*, adapted from the Dreamworks animation, stormed Drury Lane, faithfully replicating the film's imagery. Stalwart supporting actor Nigel Lindsay won the chance to spend 90 minutes in the make-up chair each day, greening up alongside *Britain's Got Talent* judge Amanda Holden and ex-*EastEnders* star Nigel Harman. Harman's diminutive baddie, played on his knees with false legs, took the plaudits from largely muted, but not dismissive, reviews.

More successful – critically, if not commercially – was *Betty Blue Eyes*, George Stiles and Anthony Drewe's adaptation of *A Private Function* by Alan Bennett, starring an animatronic pig with the voice of Kylie Minogue. Set in 1947, its echoes of a familiar austerity Britain even stretched to a popular royal wedding.

The year's best show was an extraordinary musical collaboration between verbatim theatre-maker Alecky Blythe and composer Adam Cork. *London Road*, which opened at the National's Cottesloe theatre in April and extended through the summer, concerned the small Ipswich community initially devastated by their street's association with serial killer Steve Wright who, in 2006, had murdered five sex-workers.

Blythe's method, developed during plays such as *The Girlfriend Experience* and *Cruising*, is to edit 'scripts' of recorded interviews, which are relayed into the actors' ears and replicated onstage. Here, the headphones went, but the addition of music gave greater control over the material. *London Road* was an unexpectedly heartfelt, humane and, most surprising of all, uplifting piece of theatre that placed 'the people' – not victims, not perpetrators, goodies or baddies, but affected bystanders – on the National stage.

STATE OF THE NATION, STATE OF THE GLOBE

At the Royal Court, Dominic Cooke's manifesto of the middle classes continued, though it came close to tipping point. The Court's best, and most celebrated offering was *Clybourne Park* by Bruce Norris, a fiercely clever exposé of polite racism, property and hypocrisy. We see the white neighbourhood of Lorraine Hansberry's *A Raisin in the Sun* in 1959, guarding against a black family moving in, and in 2009, with the colours inverted.

Nina Raine's *Tribes* explored the insularity and self-protectionism of the liberal elite by inserting deaf protagonists into the chattering classes. Michelle Terry was astonishingly delicate as Sylvia, the new, ingratiating girlfriend of the family's youngest, converting him to the deaf community with which she is becoming increasingly jaded. Penelope Skinner gave us a rural sex farce in *The Village Bike*. E. V. Crowe took us back to boarding school with *Kin*, a fairly shallow piece that suggested a certain cynicism about young writers and the Royal Court's favourite topic.

To a boom year for young female writers, we can add Ella Hickson, whose 2008 Edinburgh Fringe hit *Precious Little Talent* was revived at the Trafalgar Studios, and the youngest of the bunch, Anya Reiss. Reiss was 17 and preparing for A-levels when her debut, *Spur of the Moment*, opened at the Royal Court Upstairs. It showed a suburban family at odds with one another when their 13-year-old daughter takes a not-unrequited shine to their university student lodger. With an unsettling premise, teetering on the brink of paedophilia, and a knack for snappy, loaded dialogue, *Spur of the Moment* picked up a number of awards. Almost a year later, Reiss followed it up with *The Acid Test*, a look at generational divergence and the question of maturity. While neither play had much in the way of barnstorming argument, Reiss writes with the same sharp-eyed observation and wit as Alan Ayckbourn, albeit in day-glo colours.

More directly political were Nina Raine's *Tiger Country*, a glimpse inside the frustrations and fault-lines of the National Health Service, and J. T. Rogers' *Blood and Gifts*, an examination of the USA's arms supplying to Afghan rebels in the 1980s that was originally part of the Tricycle's *Great Game* cycle. Theatre 503 dedicated a season of short plays to the new coalition government, brilliantly matching form and content by engendering collaborations between unlikely pairings of artists. *Theatre Uncut* responded to the government's swingeing public-sector cuts with a host of short plays by writers including Dennis Kelly, David Greig, Jack Thorne, Lucy Kirkwood and Mark Ravenhill. The headline event took place at Southwark Playhouse, with simultaneous offshoots happening in 79 other theatres from Edinburgh to Exeter in the UK and Berlin, Chicago and New York overseas.

It was, however, the environment that took centre stage. For several years commentators have bemoaned theatre's inability or unwillingness to tackle climate change, frequently citing Steve Waters' *The Contingency Plan* (Bush Theatre, 2009) as the only successful example. However, this year the floodgates opened. At the National, dramaturg Ben Power and director Bijan Sheibani coordinated a collaborative text of interweaving narratives by Moira Buffini, Matt Charman, Penelope Skinner and Jack Thorne. *Greenland* threw together a love story at the Copenhagen summit with ornithologists in the Arctic Circle using a vivid and vibrant theatricality. Deemed muddled and moralistic by critics, who reserved special praise for its awkward, life-size pantomime polar bear, it nonetheless threw up some fascinating information, albeit without much real-world impact.

Richard Bean's *The Heretic* bordered on farce. It subverted the climate-change play with a climate-change sceptic as protagonist. Though it proved a fascinating and, thanks in part to Johnny Flynn's gawky dope of an eco-student, wildly entertaining drama, it offered very little to debate, happy as it was to concoct, or at least smooth, evidence for its own purposes.

In fact, the subject's best play to date aimed at it very indirectly. *Wastwater* by Simon Stephens, also at the Court, allowed three distinct, but disjointedly connected, scenes to rub against each other. First, a foster mother bidding farewell to her emigrating son; second, newly adulterous lovers meeting for sex in a hotel room and third, the purchase of an imported child in an empty warehouse. Directed with palpable unease by Katie Mitchell and bordering on revulsion for humanity, *Wastwater* suggested climate change and our inaction over it as deep-set within our nature. It was a fascinatingly dense watch, the sort that can leave you sweating in your seat, but one marvelously misconstrued by the overnight critics seeking neatly packaged answers from plays 'about' something.

There was, in all this, a sense of looming apocalypse, which recurred onstage time and again. Another environmental piece, Mike Bartlett's brilliantly ambitious and almost unstageable *Earthquakes in London*, placed the capital teetering on the edge of disaster. The play smashed generations together, as the three daughters of a sell-out environmentalist (based on James Lovelock) find their lives rupturing with crises. Directed with flair – and yet still falling short of the text's sheer vastness – Rupert Goold's production was bright and breezy to the point of overdose. Bartlett had a phenomenal year, with his attack on baby boomer ethics, *Love, Love, Love* touring the country to rave reviews.

But the most uncomfortable vision of a dying world came in a debut play. Andrew Sheridan's *Winterlong*, which bears resemblance to work by Simon Stephens, Robert Holman and Philip Ridley, is the sort of play you squirm through. Co-winner of the Bruntswood Prize, alongside Vivienne Franzmann's schoolyard-as-warzone play *Mogadishu*, *Winterlong* presented an ashen world of paedophiles, torture, dead babies and dead animals that seemed, nonetheless, to glisten with hope. In a wasteland, it took a pile of chocolate bars dumped on the floor – their wrappers catching the light, the generosity of their purchase shining – to suggest that humanity, in spite of its capacity for horror, might be able to save itself.

Sheridan's was a devastating debut, the like of which may well be severely threatened by the scale of cuts to arts funding over the coming four years.

AWARDS

2011 LAURENCE OLIVIER AWARDS

Best Actor – Roger Allam for *Henry IV Parts I & II* at Shakespeare's Globe

Best Actress – Nancy Carroll for *After the Dance* at the National Theatre

Best Actor in a Supporting Role – Adrian Scarborough for *After the Dance* at the National Theatre

Best Actress in a Supporting Role – Michelle Terry for *Tribes* at the Royal Court

Mastercard Best New Play – *Clybourne Park* by Bruce Norris at the Royal Court

Best Revival – *After the Dance* at the National Theatre

Best Actor in a Musical – David Thaxton for *Passion* at the Donmar Warehouse

Best Actress in a Musical – Sheridan Smith for *Legally Blonde* at the Savoy

Best Performance in a Supporting Role in a Musical – Jill Halfpenny for *Legally Blonde* at the Savoy

Best New Musical – *Legally Blonde* at the Savoy

Best Musical Revival – *Into the Woods* at Regent's Park Open Air Theatre

Best New Dance Production – Eastman vzw and Royal Opera House La Monnaie's *Babel (Words)* at Sadler's Wells

Outstanding Achievement in Dance – Antony Gormley for his set design of *Babel (Words)* at Sadler's Wells

Best New Opera Production – OperaUpClose, *La Bohème* at the Soho Theatre

Outstanding Achievement in Opera – Christian Gerhaher for his performance in *Tannhäuser* at the Royal Opera House

Outstanding Achievement in an Affiliate Theatre – *Blasted* at the Lyric Hammersmith

Best Entertainment – *The Railway Children* at the Waterloo Station Theatre

Best Director – Howard Davies for *The White Guard* at the National Theatre

Best Theatre Choreographer – Leon Baugh for *Sucker Punch* at the Royal Court

XL Video Award for Best Set Design – *The White Guard* at the National Theatre, designed by Bunny Christie

Best Lighting Design – *The White Guard* at the National Theatre, designed by Neil Austin

Best Sound Design – *King Lear* at the Donmar Warehouse, designed by Adam Cork

Best Costume Design – *After the Dance* at the National Theatre, designed by Hildegard Bechtler

BBC Radio 2 Olivier Audience Award – *We Will Rock You* at the Dominion Theatre

Outstanding Achievement – Michael Codron

Special Award – Stephen Sondheim

CRITICS' CIRCLE AWARDS FOR 2010

Best Actor – David Suchet for *All My Sons* at the Apollo

Best Actress – Jenny Jules for *Ruined* at the Almeida

The John and Wendy Trewin Award for Best Shakespearean Performance – Derek Jacobi for *King Lear* at the Donmar Warehouse

The Jack Tinker Award for Most Promising Newcomer – Daniel Kaluuya for *Sucker Punch* at the Royal Court

Best New Play – *Clybourne Park* by Bruce Norris at the Royal Court

The Peter Hepple Award for Best Musical – *Matilda: The Musical* at the Courtyard Theatre, Stratford

Best Director (awarded jointly) – Michael Grandage for *King Lear* at the Donmar Warehouse and Thea Sharrock for *After the Dance* at the National Theatre

Best Designer – Bunny Christie for *The White Guard* at the National Theatre

Most Promising Playwright – Anya Reiss for *Spur of the Moment* at the Royal Court

EVENING STANDARD THEATRE AWARDS FOR 2010

Best Actor – Rory Kinnear for *Hamlet* at the National Theatre

The Natasha Richardson Award for Best Actress – Nancy Carroll for *After the Dance* at the National Theatre

The Milton Shulman Award for Outstanding Newcomer – *You Me Bum Bum Train* created by Kate Bond and Morgan Lloyd at the LEB Building

Best Play – *Clybourne Park* by Bruce Norris at the Royal Court

The Ned Sherrin Award for Best Musical – *Passion* at the Donmar Warehouse

Best Director – Howard Davies for *The White Guard* at the National Theatre and *All My Sons* at the Apollo

Best Design – Miriam Buether for *Earthquakes in London* at the National Theatre and *Sucker Punch* at the Royal Court

The Charles Wintour Award for Most Promising Playwright – Anya Reiss for *Spur of the Moment* at the Royal Court

Editor's Award for Shooting Star – Daniel Kaluuya for *Sucker Punch* at the Royal Court

The Lebedev Special Award – Sir Michael Gambon

The Moscow Art Theatre's Golden Seagull – Sir Peter Hall

WEATHER

The main features of the 12-month period ending June 2011 were the cool and wet August, the remarkable spell of cold weather and snow which lasted from late November to late December, and the extraordinarily warm and dry spring. Of these, the spring warmth was statistically the most exceptional event, but the severe period in the run-up to Christmas had the greatest impact on people's lives. The cold weather with widespread and often severe frost began on 24 November and lasted with only the briefest of breaks until 27 December. The table below gives every calendar month since 1861 with a mean central England temperature (CET) of zero or below:

Month	Year (CET, °C))
December	1874 (–0.2); 1878 (–0.3); 1890 (–0.8); 2010 (–0.5)
January	1879 (–0.7); 1881 (–1.5); 1940 (–1.4); 1963 (–2.1); 1979 (–0.4)
February	1895 (–1.8); 1947 (–1.9); 1956 (–0.2); 1963 (–0.7); 1986 (–1.1)

It was the coldest December in the CET record for 120 years, and this was widely reported in the media, but to place it in its proper historical context it should also be noted that it was the coldest individual calendar month only since February 1986, and that there were nine colder months in the last century and a half.

NEWSWORTHY EVENTS
Flooding affected parts of Northern Ireland on 6–7 September following prolonged heavy rain; at Lough Fea (Londonderry) 107mm fell during the two days. Mid-November brought gales and local flooding; the peak gust of 90mph at Capel Curig (Caernarfon) on 12 November was the highest of 2010, while short-lived floods hit south-east Cornwall on 16 November after 50–80mm of rain fell in little more than an hour. Snow fell daily during the last week of November and the first few days of December in eastern Scotland and north-east England with accumulated depths of 40–70cm by 2 December, and further heavy snow hit the central lowlands of Scotland during the morning rush hour on 6 December, resulting in gridlock on the roads, and the resignation of the Scottish transport minister.

Renewed heavy snow across southern England and the south Midlands on 18 December resulted in the closure of several airports, notably Heathrow where snow-clearing procedures were severely criticised. Flooding hit Snowdonia and the Lake District in mid-January following 267mm of rain in seven days at Honister (Cumbria), and floods returned to mid and north Wales between 3 and 7 February with Lake Vyrnwy (Montgomeryshire) collecting 237mm in five days, triggering flooding on several rivers in the area. Gale damage was also reported widely during the first week of February, with a maximum gust of 93mph at Lerwick (Shetland) on 4 February.

On 23 April the temperature reached 27.8°C at Wisley (Surrey), the highest anywhere in the UK for that particular month since 1949, while the main event in May was a severe gale in Scotland on the 23rd which left two people dead and 30,000 temporarily without electricity.

Drought orders were issued for parts of the Midlands, East Anglia and Lincolnshire in early June following the driest spring in these regions since 1893, but the rains returned almost immediately so fears of a repetition of the 1976 drought quickly faded.

THE YEAR 2010

The CET for the entire year was 8.9°C which is 1.1°C below the average for the standard reference period 1981–2010. The cold weather was mostly concentrated at the beginning and end of the year, though August, too, was notably cool. Rainfall, averaged over England and Wales, totalled 798mm over the year, which is 13 per cent below the long-term normal. The sunshine aggregate of 1,690 hours, again averaged over England and Wales, was 10 per cent above normal and the highest annual figure for five years.

TEMPERATURE

July 2010 was a warm month in southern, central and eastern parts of England with a noteworthy warm spell during the first ten days, and the temperature peaked at 31.7°C at Swanscombe in Kent on the 9th, but Wales, northwest England, Scotland and Northern Ireland had near-average temperatures. August was a cool month with temperatures typically around 1°C below the 1981–2010 average, and over much of Britain it was the coolest August since 1993. September and October enjoyed near-average temperatures, but, thanks to the severe weather which set in during the last week, November was the coldest since 1993 with the monthly temperature about 2°C below the average.

As already noted, December was an exceptional month. The lowest individual temperature recorded was –21.3°C at Altnaharra, Sutherland, on the morning of 2 December, and on 22 December the temperature failed to climb above –15.8°C, also at Altnaharra.

The cold weather relaxed immediately after Christmas, January 2011 was a near-average month, and February turned out to be the warmest for nine years. The warmth continued throughout the spring, especially during April which turned out to be the warmest April in the entire 352-year long record. June, by contrast, was the coolest over England and Wales since 1999, and in Scotland and Northern Ireland since 1991. Nevertheless, a brief hot spell late in the month produced the highest temperature anywhere in the UK for five years: 33.3°C at Olympic Park in London.

WEATHER STATISTICS 2010

	Mean Temp. °C	Diff. from normal °C	Rainfall mm	Percentage of normal	Sunshine hours	Percentage of normal
England	8.5	–1.2	798	87	1,690	110
Wales	8.1	–1.1	874	79	1,776	117
Scotland	7.8	–0.9	936	98	1,449	111
Northern Ireland	8.9	–1.0	820	92	1,697	126
UK	8.3	–1.1	826	91	1,639	113

MEAN MONTHLY TEMPERATURE (°C)

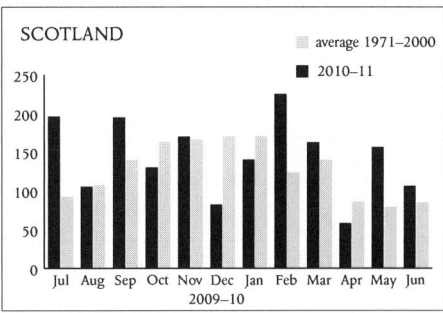

RAINFALL

July was a dry month in the Midlands, East Anglia and the South East, but exceptionally wet in northern and western parts of the UK. During August the pattern was reversed with as much as two and a half times the normal rainfall in East Anglia. During the autumn, rainfall ranged from slightly below normal in southern and eastern England to slightly above in Scotland and Northern Ireland, but October was the only drier-than-average month nationwide. During December 2010 the rainfall equivalent of the month's snows amounted to less than half of the long-term average. In January 2011; in most southern parts of the UK it was a rather wet month, but elsewhere it was generally dry. February was a wet month especially in western Scotland, north-west England and parts of Wales. Both March and April were exceptionally dry over England and Wales. May was also very dry in some eastern and midland counties of England, but it was a remarkably wet month in north-west England, Northern Ireland and Scotland. June's rainfall was rather above average in most regions with the exception of the Midlands.

MEAN MONTHLY RAINFALL (MM)

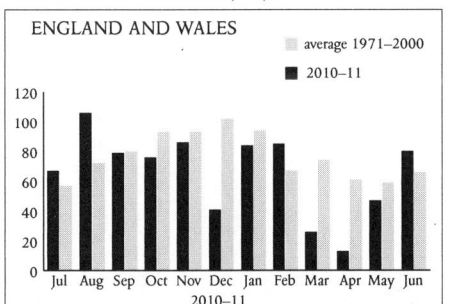

SUNSHINE

For a fourth consecutive year there was a marked sunshine deficit in most parts of the country during July and August 2010. Sunshine amounts during the three autumn months were near or rather above the long-term average, and in parts of Northern Ireland there was more sunshine in November than there had been in July. December was generally very sunny except in southern counties where it was a very dull month, while in January it was dull in the east and sunny in the west. February was a gloomy month in all parts of the UK, and in southeast England it was the dullest winter quarter since that of 1971–2 with less than half the normal amount of sunshine recorded locally. By contrast, both March and April were very sunny months, especially in East Anglia and southern England where excesses relative to the average amounted to more than 50 per cent. During May and June sunshine aggregates were generally close to, or modestly in excess of, the norm.

MONTHLY SUNSHINE (HOURS)

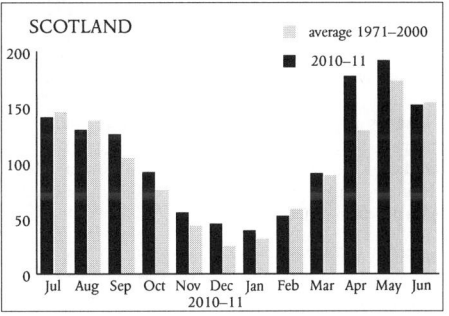

UK WEATHER STATIONS

Given below are temperature, rainfall and sunshine at selected climatological stations for July 2010 to June 2011.

Ht   height of station above mean sea-level
Temp mean monthly air temperature
Rain total monthly rainfall
Sun total monthly sunshine duration

	Ht	July 2010			August 2010			September 2010			October 2010		
	m	Temp °C	Rain mm	Sun hrs	Temp °C	Rain mm	Sun hrs	Temp °C	Rain mm	Sun hrs	Temp °C	Rain mm	Sun hrs
Stornoway	15	13.5	108	106	13.0	60	90	12.3	129	104	9.7	120	92
Aberdeen	65	14.5	108	137	13.8	44	113	12.1	91	97	9.1	61	91
Glasgow	59	15.3	155	95	14.4	89	170	13.2	185	135	9.5	119	89
Belfast	68	15.7	106	80	14.3	60	146	13.8	110	102	10.1	47	107
Durham	102	16.1	57	105	14.6	55	119	13.9	76	110	9.9	48	83
York	8	16.7	54	133	15.7	44	143	14.3	70	121	10.4	35	110
Manchester	69	16.6	69	82	14.5	117	116	13.4	90	117	9.7	74	125
Holyhead	10	15.8	127	121	15.1	32	175	14.7	93	130	11.9	91	132
Nottingham	117	17.2	37	116	15.5	81	122	14.1	67	109	10.5	52	107
Norwich	32	18.9	30	188	16.1	81	138	14.0	61	106	10.9	70	90
Birmingham	140	17.6	27	125	15.7	120	118	13.9	57	117	10.5	52	111
Cardiff	46	17.2	58	154	15.8	117	159	14.5	40	145	11.3	48	121
Bristol	42	17.9	59	153	16.3	111	151	14.7	39	148	11.2	53	121
London	137	18.1	12	163	16.3	116	112	14.3	49	105	11.0	90	89
Bournemouth	10	18.0	34	166	16.1	95	106	14.0	58	123	11.2	74	117
Camborne	86	16.1	78	118	15.5	72	155	14.7	84	145	12.1	82	148

	Ht	November 2010			December 2010			January 2011			February 2011		
	m	Temp °C	Rain mm	Sun hrs	Temp °C	Rain mm	Sun hrs	Temp °C	Rain mm	Sun hrs	Temp °C	Rain mm	Sun hrs
Stornoway	15	5.1	91	49	2.4	43	38	4.6	105	32	5.9	81	66
Aberdeen	65	4.3	92	59	0.0	61	50	3.3	43	67	4.9	89	55
Glasgow	59	4.5	121	72	−1.4	45	69	3.2	89	55	5.1	182	53
Belfast	68	4.9	106	83	−0.5	46	78	2.9	29	71	6.5	86	70
Durham	102	4.9	136	76	−0.1	58	78	3.7	32	70	5.8	56	61
York	8	5.1	67	85	−0.5	30	88	3.9	37	73	6.3	91	55
Manchester	69	4.5	64	84	−0.9	23	55	3.3	54	37	6.6	139	43
Holyhead	10	6.9	86	85	2.3	54	62	4.7	48	73	7.5	93	72
Nottingham	117	5.1	61	79	0.0	34	61	4.1	32	55	6.5	71	41
Norwich	32	5.9	73	53	0.1	22	59	4.5	60	49	6.2	39	43
Birmingham	140	5.1	53	73	−0.5	23	53	3.8	34	61	6.9	48	47
Cardiff	46	6.6	82	77	1.0	28	58	4.3	108	49	7.6	71	40
Bristol	42	6.1	58	62	0.7	24	56	4.4	82	54	7.5	52	42
London	137	5.7	39	58	0.5	31	35	4.3	93	41	6.5	56	44
Bournemouth	10	6.5	107	58	0.5	63	26	4.7	89	47	7.1	76	43
Camborne	86	7.9	164	85	4.0	48	91	5.8	103	83	8.5	90	58

	Ht	March 2011			April 2011			May 2011			June 2011		
	m	Temp °C	Rain mm	Sun hrs	Temp °C	Rain mm	Sun hrs	Temp °C	Rain mm	Sun hrs	Temp °C	Rain mm	Sun hrs
Stornoway	15	6.2	87	81	9.9	51	141	10.1	154	162	11.3	53	162
Aberdeen	65	6.2	68	124	10.3	14	182	10.5	51	185	12.4	105	140
Glasgow	59	5.7	117	88	10.4	64	172	10.7	149	154	12.3	101	141
Belfast	68	6.4	45	125	11.5	20	192	11.5	59	152	12.7	88	134
Durham	102	6.5	25	144	11.2	8	214	11.7	42	166	13.5	48	132
York	8	6.7	8	142	12.0	1	231	11.9	44	195	14.1	51	197
Manchester	69	6.5	17	138	11.4	12	197	12.1	65	136	13.4	62	159
Holyhead	10	7.0	30	168	11.3	32	210	12.3	78	175	13.3	49	221
Nottingham	117	7.1	11	124	12.1	3	186	12.5	45	169	14.5	47	178
Norwich	32	6.3	19	127	11.5	15	216	13.3	14	237	15.3	64	220
Birmingham	140	7.1	11	131	11.9	2	200	12.6	48	199	14.3	50	191
Cardiff	46	7.7	26	173	12.3	9	219	12.7	63	165	14.2	120	215
Bristol	42	7.8	13	142	12.9	4	231	13.1	37	193	14.7	95	198
London	137	7.3	14	125	13.3	3	207	13.3	25	195	15.1	104	202
Bournemouth	10	7.1	19	145	11.9	7	217	12.7	25	189	15.0	84	173
Camborne	86	7.9	26	147	11.7	18	239	12.1	35	170	13.3	75	203

METEOROLOGICAL OBSERVATIONS IN LONDON *(Hampstead Observatory)*

Maximum temperature is for the period 9am to 9pm; minimum temperature is for the period 9pm to 9am; the 'rainfall day' is the 24 hours starting at 9am on the day of entry; the 'wet hours' column counts all clock-hours during the rainfall day during which 0.2mm or more has fallen; sunshine is for the calendar day. All times are GMT.

July 2010

Day	Temperature Min °C	Max °C	Rain mm	Wet hours	Sun hours
1	13.4	25.5	0.0	0	7.7
2	18.6	25.3	0.2	1	3.1
3	15.3	25.6	0.0	0	8.2
4	12.2	23.0	0.0	0	9.0
5	12.8	23.6	0.0	0	7.2
6	11.4	22.0	0.0	0	7.3
7	13.5	22.2	0.0	0	1.7
8	16.2	26.1	0.0	0	4.9
9	14.8	30.4	0.0	0	10.8
10	16.6	29.0	0.0	0	9.8
11	16.4	26.6	0.0	0	7.4
12	16.3	22.8	1.3	4	2.7
13	13.1	20.2	0.0	0	0.2
14	15.6	20.6	3.5	6	1.0
15	13.9	19.9	2.2	3	3.3
16	12.3	21.2	0.0	0	5.6
17	12.6	20.7	0.0	0	6.4
18	11.7	24.5	0.0	0	7.2
19	14.5	28.7	0.0	0	8.3
20	17.3	27.8	0.0	0	4.6
21	16.0	24.5	0.0	0	8.7
22	13.1	22.3	0.9	3	6.0
23	13.1	19.5	0.0	0	1.0
24	13.2	24.6	0.7	2	7.1
25	14.8	25.3	0.4	2	3.0
26	16.5	23.0	0.4	1	2.8
27	15.9	23.7	0.0	0	2.5
28	13.8	24.2	0.0	0	7.2
29	12.3	21.0	0.0	0	2.3
30	11.3	21.3	2.2	3	3.4
31	16.2	24.1	0.0	0	2.8

August 2010

Day	Temperature Min °C	Max °C	Rain mm	Wet hours	Sun hours
1	13.7	23.3	0.0	0	2.8
2	14.4	22.1	0.0	0	2.8
3	11.4	21.1	0.2	1	4.7
4	13.6	19.5	5.7	3	1.8
5	10.3	21.8	0.0	0	6.4
6	11.0	19.8	3.5	2	4.0
7	15.0	21.3	5.3	3	2.2
8	12.8	23.1	0.0	0	5.7
9	13.1	24.1	6.4	4	7.7
10	13.5	17.9	7.7	8	0.5
11	10.1	21.9	0.0	0	6.7
12	12.2	19.1	0.9	3	1.5
13	11.0	18.6	6.6	8	1.8
14	11.9	18.6	3.1	3	1.3
15	12.4	22.2	0.0	0	5.6
16	11.8	24.0	0.4	2	5.5
17	13.8	19.3	7.9	3	0.2
18	11.4	21.1	1.3	1	5.1
19	11.2	20.1	0.2	1	3.5
20	15.6	19.8	0.2	1	0.3
21	18.0	21.4	0.9	3	0.5
22	16.4	21.9	28.4	12	2.4
23	15.9	19.8	3.3	1	1.4
24	10.2	19.7	0.2	1	7.1
25	10.8	17.6	22.0	12	2.6
26	12.6	19.0	15.2	20	0.1
27	10.7	16.7	0.0	0	1.3
28	9.3	19.3	0.0	0	6.3
29	10.7	17.9	2.4	2	3.8
30	8.1	19.2	0.0	0	7.2
31	8.6	19.4	0.0	0	8.5

September 2010

Day	Temperature Min °C	Max °C	Rain mm	Wet hours	Sun hours
1	9.3	20.1	0.0	0	9.8
2	10.1	20.5	0.0	0	9.0
3	11.1	21.3	0.0	0	7.2
4	10.5	19.8	0.0	0	4.6
5	12.5	18.9	0.0	0	1.7
6	12.4	18.8	13.6	11	2.0
7	12.9	19.2	0.0	0	4.2
8	13.0	17.9	5.3	3	1.3
9	11.9	19.9	0.0	0	4.2
10	12.9	19.6	0.0	0	0.4
11	15.4	20.9	0.0	0	1.0
12	10.2	19.6	0.0	0	6.2
13	10.1	17.4	0.0	0	1.9
14	13.9	18.0	4.4	7	0.0
15	8.3	16.1	0.0	0	4.1
16	10.4	17.5	0.0	0	2.5
17	6.7	15.4	0.0	0	4.5
18	5.2	17.0	0.2	1	5.5
19	10.7	16.0	0.0	0	1.1
20	13.9	20.7	0.0	0	4.9
21	10.5	21.2	0.0	0	5.4
22	11.1	22.7	0.4	1	8.3
23	13.4	16.5	9.5	6	1.2
24	10.6	12.6	1.1	3	0.2
25	4.3	13.2	0.0	0	5.0
26	6.2	13.4	3.1	7	2.1
27	9.8	14.9	0.4	2	0.2
28	12.4	15.9	1.3	4	0.2
29	13.3	16.1	12.8	10	0.0
30	7.4	15.6	0.2	0	6.0

October 2010

Day	Temperature Min °C	Max °C	Rain mm	Wet hours	Sun hours
1	11.6	15.3	13.6	10	0.0
2	9.6	15.2	28.2	11	2.4
3	11.2	17.3	4.4	7	1.9
4	12.1	15.4	0.9	3	0.0
5	10.6	16.6	13.6	7	0.3
6	12.0	17.4	0.0	0	4.4
7	9.0	17.2	0.0	0	5.4
8	14.3	20.2	0.2	1	5.5
9	13.9	16.6	0.0	0	0.3
10	12.3	18.9	0.0	0	5.6
11	9.7	17.6	0.0	0	7.6
12	9.0	14.6	0.0	0	3.9
13	8.4	11.4	0.0	0	0.0
14	8.3	10.3	0.0	0	0.0
15	8.7	12.1	0.9	3	0.2
16	5.8	12.8	0.2	1	4.5
17	4.4	12.6	0.0	0	5.1
18	3.6	14.1	0.7	2	2.5
19	6.4	12.5	6.4	6	3.7
20	1.0	8.4	0.0	0	7.1
21	−1.0	11.1	0.2	1	4.1
22	3.8	11.6	7.5	5	0.5
23	8.3	11.3	1.1	2	2.9
24	1.7	10.5	0.0	0	5.6
25	0.9	11.3	0.0	0	7.1
26	2.6	12.0	5.9	7	0.0
27	11.8	16.0	0.4	2	3.2
28	9.5	14.4	0.0	0	0.4
29	11.0	13.4	2.0	3	0.2
30	7.9	13.7	3.3	4	4.5
31	8.9	11.6	1.1	4	0.0

November 2010

Day	Temperature Min °C	Max °C	Rain mm	Wet hours	Sun hours
1	7.6	13.0	0.9	2	2.0
2	8.6	13.8	0.0	0	0.6
3	11.6	15.2	0.0	0	3.7
4	12.8	17.5	0.0	0	4.5
5	14.0	15.8	8.1	9	0.0
6	7.1	10.3	0.0	0	0.7
7	3.0	8.3	2.9	2	2.9
8	3.3	7.0	2.2	6	0.0
9	3.7	6.9	2.0	3	0.0
10	1.3	8.9	1.8	4	6.1
11	0.3	13.1	3.3	4	1.0
12	8.8	10.7	4.4	8	0.1
13	8.0	9.3	1.5	2	0.1
14	6.8	7.2	2.6	5	0.0
15	1.5	8.3	0.2	1	2.4
16	0.1	9.3	0.0	0	5.9
17	1.4	6.3	4.4	11	0.0
18	4.2	9.4	0.9	2	1.2
19	3.6	11.2	0.0	0	5.6
20	4.1	7.1	0.0	0	0.0
21	3.9	6.6	0.0	0	0.2
22	3.7	6.1	0.4	1	0.2
23	3.7	6.0	0.0	0	0.3
24	−1.3	4.5	0.0	0	4.7
25	−0.9	1.0	0.0	0	1.9
26	−3.5	3.3	0.0	0	6.7
27	−3.6	0.1	0.0	0	1.0
28	−5.8	0.3	0.0	0	5.0
29	−4.8	0.1	1.8	6	1.0
30	−1.9	−0.1	2.0	10	0.1

December 2010

Day	Temperature Min °C	Max °C	Rain mm	Wet hours	Sun hours
1	−2.3	−1.3	4.2	14	0.0
2	−2.8	−1.8	0.4	4	0.1
3	−5.5	2.6	1.2	4	0.0
4	−5.1	4.9	1.5	3	0.5
5	−0.1	4.4	0.0	0	4.8
6	−4.5	−1.7	0.2	0	0.0
7	−3.9	−0.3	0.0	0	0.7
8	−2.5	1.5	0.0	0	1.9
9	−3.6	4.1	0.0	0	5.1
10	−1.1	5.9	0.0	0	0.0
11	2.8	7.9	0.0	0	0.9
12	0.0	5.7	0.0	0	4.0
13	−1.6	4.2	1.1	4	3.0
14	−1.3	3.3	0.2	1	1.4
15	−1.8	4.5	1.3	6	0.0
16	−0.6	5.4	2.8	7	0.0
17	−5.1	−1.9	0.9	1	1.4
18	−5.7	−0.5	7.5	0	0.0
19	−5.0	−1.2	0.0	0	0.0
20	−6.1	−0.3	2.0	1	1.1
21	−5.2	0.4	0.5	6	0.0
22	−0.4	0.2	0.0	8	0.0
23	−2.4	0.8	0.0	2	0.0
24	−2.4	0.6	0.0	3	5.8
25	−3.6	−1.9	0.0	0	0.0
26	−5.7	2.5	0.0	6	5.0
27	−4.9	3.1	6.6	10	0.3
28	1.5	7.5	1.3	5	0.0
29	2.7	7.8	0.4	2	0.0
30	4.8	5.9	0.2	1	0.0
31	3.7	5.5	0.0	0	0.0

January 2011

Day	Temperature Min °C	Max °C	Rain mm	Wet hours	Sun hours
1	3.7	5.8	0.7	2	0.2
2	0.3	2.2	0.0	0	1.1
3	−1.5	2.2	0.0	0	0.7
4	1.1	3.6	0.2	1	0.7
5	2.8	6.0	1.5	7	2.3
6	3.7	4.0	13.0	11	0.0
7	0.9	9.2	14.7	13	0.3
8	8.2	9.1	0.0	0	1.4
9	0.3	6.3	0.2	1	6.3
10	0.6	7.4	9.2	8	0.7
11	4.0	6.4	7.3	7	0.4
12	2.4	11.2	1.8	6	0.0
13	10.5	12.3	3.1	6	0.0
14	10.2	10.6	6.6	3	0.0
15	6.5	10.2	0.0	0	0.0
16	9.2	11.4	10.3	8	0.7
17	7.3	7.3	19.8	13	0.0
18	2.5	6.6	0.0	0	6.3
19	−0.5	6.7	0.4	2	5.5
20	1.3	4.6	0.4	2	0.6
21	0.1	3.0	0.2	1	4.4
22	−0.4	5.2	0.4	2	0.3
23	4.3	6.2	0.4	1	0.0
24	4.4	5.9	0.2	1	0.0
25	1.8	7.1	1.1	4	0.3
26	4.9	5.7	1.3	3	0.1
27	0.0	1.6	0.0	0	0.0
28	−0.8	0.0	0.0	0	0.2
29	−1.6	0.1	0.0	0	0.0
30	−1.4	3.9	0.0	0	4.3
31	−0.3	4.5	0.0	0	1.3

February 2011

Day	Temperature Min °C	Max °C	Rain mm	Wet hours	Sun hours
1	−3.3	5.8	0.4	2	0.2
2	1.8	9.0	0.0	0	0.2
3	2.9	9.6	0.0	0	4.6
4	7.7	11.2	0.0	0	0.0
5	10.3	11.8	0.0	0	0.0
6	9.1	10.4	0.0	0	2.1
7	7.5	10.7	0.0	0	0.5
8	0.6	9.9	0.2	1	7.5
9	4.5	10.0	1.1	2	3.4
10	6.7	9.7	14.1	11	0.0
11	6.9	11.3	2.9	7	0.1
12	7.3	10.6	0.2	1	2.1
13	4.1	7.4	4.6	9	0.0
14	3.2	8.9	0.7	2	4.1
15	3.9	6.0	1.8	5	0.0
16	3.6	10.3	0.0	0	3.1
17	3.3	8.5	0.0	0	4.6
18	2.9	6.0	11.2	6	0.9
19	0.9	5.1	2.4	6	0.0
20	3.0	3.9	0.0	0	0.0
21	2.5	5.5	1.5	6	0.0
22	3.3	6.1	3.3	5	0.0
23	5.2	9.6	1.8	4	0.0
24	7.1	13.8	0.0	0	4.9
25	6.7	13.4	3.1	4	2.1
26	7.4	7.9	3.1	4	0.2
27	2.2	9.4	2.9	4	3.7
28	2.3	2.9	0.7	3	0.0

March 2011

Day	Temperature Min °C	Max °C	Rain mm	Wet hours	Sun hours
1	2.0	3.6	0.0	0	0.0
2	1.1	6.2	0.0	0	4.3
3	−1.3	3.4	0.0	0	1.6
4	−0.7	6.8	0.0	0	5.9
5	−0.6	6.5	0.2	1	1.5
6	2.4	5.2	0.0	0	2.9
7	−0.5	8.4	0.2	1	8.1
8	−0.7	11.5	0.0	0	8.2
9	2.9	10.4	0.0	0	3.2
10	4.4	12.3	0.0	0	1.8
11	3.3	10.7	0.0	0	2.3
12	6.6	12.8	0.0	0	4.7
13	7.9	9.3	1.6	3	0.4
14	1.9	11.1	0.2	1	6.2
15	5.3	11.4	0.0	0	4.7
16	6.4	8.6	0.0	0	0.0
17	2.3	9.2	0.0	0	1.1
18	4.6	5.4	6.2	6	0.0
19	−0.3	12.1	0.0	0	8.9
20	2.6	12.0	0.0	0	6.2
21	3.5	15.0	0.0	0	3.0
22	7.7	15.6	0.0	0	1.8
23	6.0	16.3	0.0	0	8.4
24	4.0	15.4	0.0	0	8.8
25	4.2	17.9	0.0	0	8.3
26	5.9	12.6	0.0	0	2.9
27	5.2	13.8	0.0	0	7.6
28	4.8	13.7	0.0	0	7.2
29	4.0	14.7	0.2	1	2.3
30	8.9	10.9	6.2	7	0.1
31	8.2	17.4	0.2	1	3.0

April 2011

Day	Temperature Min °C	Max °C	Rain mm	Wet hours	Sun hours
1	10.6	15.7	0.0	0	3.2
2	11.5	17.5	0.0	0	4.9
3	5.8	14.8	0.0	0	5.4
4	4.6	13.6	1.8	5	5.6
5	7.8	11.5	0.2	1	0.0
6	10.7	22.4	0.0	0	9.8
7	7.9	21.1	0.0	0	8.7
8	6.7	21.2	0.0	0	10.2
9	7.5	17.4	0.0	0	10.3
10	5.5	18.8	0.0	0	9.6
11	7.6	20.0	0.4	2	7.4
12	4.1	14.3	0.0	0	8.6
13	3.9	11.8	0.0	0	1.1
14	6.5	12.7	0.0	0	2.1
15	8.5	15.5	0.0	0	4.1
16	9.0	17.1	0.0	0	4.5
17	8.8	19.3	0.0	0	6.4
18	6.5	17.6	0.0	0	7.1
19	8.9	24.8	0.0	0	9.7
20	8.5	24.0	0.0	0	8.8
21	11.5	24.0	0.0	0	6.6
22	9.6	25.2	0.0	0	10.1
23	13.5	26.6	0.2	1	8.1
24	11.1	22.8	0.0	0	10.3
25	8.5	20.6	0.0	0	10.3
26	7.1	15.1	0.0	0	3.3
27	6.7	16.2	0.0	0	10.5
28	4.8	15.0	0.0	0	5.6
29	8.0	19.0	0.0	0	4.3
30	10.0	19.8	0.0	0	10.4

May 2011

Day	Temperature Min °C	Max °C	Rain mm	Wet hours	Sun hours
1	9.6	17.6	0.0	0	10.1
2	7.6	15.1	0.0	0	10.4
3	4.4	14.0	0.0	0	10.0
4	2.7	15.8	0.0	0	10.7
5	7.3	19.0	0.2	1	4.3
6	8.9	24.2	2.1	5	9.8
7	13.2	22.9	3.7	4	2.7
8	13.6	19.1	0.0	0	6.0
9	10.5	20.0	0.0	0	10.0
10	9.8	20.9	0.0	0	8.0
11	8.6	16.7	0.0	0	0.8
12	6.9	17.8	0.0	0	7.3
13	6.3	17.5	0.0	0	6.6
14	5.7	16.6	0.0	0	6.6
15	7.0	14.6	0.0	0	5.5
16	10.2	19.8	0.0	0	3.5
17	9.9	17.5	0.9	4	1.5
18	11.8	18.1	2.3	2	0.1
19	6.3	20.0	0.0	0	5.1
20	9.3	18.2	0.0	0	6.5
21	8.5	20.7	1.2	1	10.3
22	9.6	18.0	0.2	1	7.7
23	8.7	18.6	0.2	1	6.5
24	6.4	18.9	0.0	0	10.4
25	6.2	19.7	0.0	0	12.0
26	10.2	14.4	12.5	4	2.6
27	9.0	15.6	0.0	0	3.5
28	7.7	14.6	0.2	1	1.5
29	12.0	18.2	0.0	0	4.7
30	11.6	20.3	2.5	6	2.8
31	6.0	18.5	0.0	0	8.1

June 2011

Day	Temperature Min °C	Max °C	Rain mm	Wet hours	Sun hours
1	6.6	20.8	0.0	0	9.5
2	10.6	22.6	0.0	0	7.9
3	11.4	24.6	0.0	0	12.4
4	11.2	25.6	0.0	0	9.4
5	11.5	18.0	18.0	18	1.7
6	8.0	14.6	0.0	0	1.8
7	9.1	18.3	0.0	0	7.0
8	8.4	17.0	2.4	4	7.0
9	8.0	16.9	0.2	1	8.3
10	7.3	13.9	17.6	11	3.4
11	6.8	18.3	0.4	1	8.0
12	7.1	13.0	10.1	12	0.2
13	13.0	21.2	0.0	0	6.0
14	9.6	22.7	0.0	0	12.8
15	13.4	19.0	11.9	2	3.0
16	11.8	18.0	5.5	5	5.5
17	8.9	14.0	9.5	10	2.3
18	9.9	16.8	1.3	3	9.7
19	9.7	18.3	0.0	0	7.3
20	8.9	19.4	3.3	5	8.3
21	13.2	20.5	0.2	1	7.0
22	10.8	17.7	6.4	4	5.5
23	9.8	18.6	0.0	0	8.0
24	8.4	18.6	8.1	11	8.0
25	10.4	23.1	0.0	0	6.0
26	14.7	28.5	0.0	0	12.0
27	17.5	31.0	0.0	0	8.0
28	17.1	19.8	8.6	4	0.2
29	9.1	20.9	0.0	0	8.5
30	8.4	20.1	0.2	1	7.5

SPORTS RESULTS

ALPINE SKIING

WORLD CUP 2010–11

MEN
Downhill: Didier Cuche (Switzerland), 510pts
Slalom: Ivica Kostelic (Croatia), 478pts
Giant Slalom: Ted Ligety (USA), 383pts
Super Giant Slalom: Didier Cuche (Switzerland), 291pts
Overall: Ivica Kostelic (Croatia), 1,356pts

WOMEN
Downhill: Lindsey Vonn (USA), 650pts
Slalom: Marlies Schild (Austria), 680pts
Giant Slalom: Viktoria Rebensburg (Germany), 435pts
Super Giant Slalom: Lindsey Vonn (USA), 560pts
Overall: Maria Hoefl-Riesch (Germany), 1,728pts

AMERICAN FOOTBALL

AFC Championship 2010-11: Pittsburgh Steelers beat
New York Jets 24–19
NFC Championship 2010-11: Green Bay Packers beat
Chicago Bears 21–14
XLV Superbowl 2011: Green Bay Packers beat Pittsburgh
Steelers 31–25

ANGLING

BRITISH CHAMPIONSHIPS 2010
Individual: Stephen Broome
Individual (ladies): Samantha Perkins

TEAMS
First Division: Starlets AS
Second Division: Four Ashes AC
Ladies: Starlets AS

ASSOCIATION FOOTBALL

LEAGUE COMPETITIONS 2010–11

ENGLAND AND WALES
Premier League
1. Manchester United, 80pts
2. Chelsea, 71pts
3. Manchester City, 71pts
Relegated: Birmingham, Blackpool, West Ham

Championship
1. Queens Park Rangers, 88pts
2. Norwich, 84pts
Play-off winner and third promotion place: Swansea
Relegated: Preston, Sheffield United, Scunthorpe

League 1
1. Brighton, 95pts
2. Southampton, 92pts
Play-off winner and third promotion place: Peterborough
Relegated: Dagenham & Redbridge, Bristol Rovers,
Plymouth, Swindon

League 2
1. Chesterfield, 86pts
2. Bury, 81pts
3. Wycombe Wanderers, 80pts
Play-off winner and fourth promotion place: Stevenage
Borough
Relegated: Lincoln City, Stockport

Football Conference
1. Crawley Town, 105pts
Play-off winner and second promotion place: AFC
Wimbledon

Welsh Premier League
1. Bangor City, 70pts
2. The New Saints, 68pts
3. Neath, 58pts

SCOTLAND
Premier Division
1. Rangers, 93pts
2. Celtic, 92pts
Relegated: Hamilton

Division 1
1. Dunfermline, 70pts
Relegated: Cowdenbeath, Stirling Albion

Division 2
1. Livingston, 82pts
Also promoted: Ayr United
Relegated: Alloa Athletic, Peterhead

Division 3
1. Arbroath, 66pts
Play-off winner and second promotion place: Albion Rovers
Bottom: Clyde

NORTHERN IRELAND
Premier League
1. Linfield, 85pts
2. Crusaders, 74pts
3. Glentoran, 66pts

REPUBLIC OF IRELAND
Premier Division 2010: 1. Shamrock Rovers, 67pts;
2. Bohemians, 67pts; 3. Sligo Rovers, 63pts

FRANCE
Ligue 1: 1. Lille, 76pts; 2. Marseille, 68pts; 3. Lyon, 64pts

GERMANY
Bundesliga: 1. Borussia Dortmund, 75; 2. Bayer
Leverkusen, 68pts; 3. Bayern Munich, 65pts

ITALY
Serie A: 1. AC Milan, 82pts; 2. Inter Milan, 76pts;
3. Napoli, 70pts

NETHERLANDS
Eredivisie: 1. Ajax, 73pts; 2. FC Twente, 71pts; 3. PSV
Eindhoven, 69pts

SPAIN
La Liga: 1. Barcelona, 96pts; 2. Real Madrid, 92pts;
3. Valencia, 71pts

CUP COMPETITIONS 2010–11
ENGLAND
FA Cup final 2011: Manchester City beat Stoke 1–0
League Cup final 2011: Birmingham beat Arsenal 2–1
Football League Trophy final 2011: Carlisle United beat
Brentford 1–0
FA Vase final 2011: Whitley Bay beat Coalville Town 3–2
FA Trophy final 2011: Darlington beat Mansfield Town
1–0
Community Shield 2011: Manchester United beat
Manchester City 3–2

WOMEN
FA Cup final 2011: Arsenal beat Bristol Academy 2–0
Women's Super League: 1. Arsenal, 32pts; 2. Birmingham
City, 29pts; 3. Everton, 22pts
Premier League Cup final 2011: Barnet beat Nottingham
Forest 4–3 on penalties (0–0 aet)

WALES
FAW Welsh Cup final 2011: Llanelli beat Bangor City 4–1
Welsh League Cup final 2011: The New Saints beat
Llanelli 4–3

SCOTLAND
Scottish Cup final 2011: Celtic beat Motherwell 3–0
League Cup final 2011: Rangers beat Celtic 2–1

NORTHERN IRELAND
Irish Cup final 2011: Linfield beat Crusaders 2–1

EUROPE
Champions League final 2011: Barcelona beat Manchester
United 3–1
Europa League final 2011: FC Porto beat Braga 1–0

FIFA BALLON D'OR*
2010 – Lionel Messi (Argentina)
2009 – Lionel Messi (Argentina)
2008 – Cristiano Ronaldo (Portugal)
2007 – Kaká (Brazil)
2006 – Fabio Cannavaro (Italy)
2005 – Ronaldinho (Brazil)
2004 – Ronaldinho (Brazil)
2003 – Zinedine Zidane (France)
2002 – Ronaldo (Brazil)
2001 – Luís Figo (Portugal)
2000 – Zinedine Zidane (France)
1999 – Rivaldo (Brazil)
1998 – Zinedine Zidane (France)
1997 – Ronaldo (Brazil)
1996 – Ronaldo (Brazil)
1995 – George Weah (Liberia)
* Pre-2010, known as the FIFA World Player of the Year award

ATHLETICS

EUROPEAN CROSS COUNTRY CHAMPIONSHIPS
Albufeira, Portugal, 12 December 2010

SENIOR MEN (9.87km)
Individual: Sergei Lebid (Ukraine), 29min 15sec
Team: France, 33pts

U23 MEN (8.17km)
Individual: Hassan Chandi (France), 24min 11sec
Team: Ireland, 60pts

JUNIOR MEN (6.07km)
Individual: Abdelaziz Merzougui (Spain), 18min 07sec
Team: Great Britain, 62pts

SENIOR WOMEN (8.17km)
Individual: Jessica Augusto (Portugal), 26min 52sec
Team: Portugal, 19pts

U23 WOMEN (6.07km)
Individual: Meryem Erdogan (Turkey), 20min 08sec
Team: Great Britain, 47pts

JUNIOR WOMEN (3.97km)
Individual: Charlotte Purdue (Great Britain), 12min 42sec
Team: Great Britain, 23pts

UK INDOOR CHAMPIONSHIPS
Sheffield, 12–13 February 2011

MEN
60m: Dwain Chambers (Belgrave), 6.57sec
200m: Danny Talbot (Birchfield), 20.89sec
400m: Nigel Levine (Windsor), 46.76sec
800m: Joe Thomas (Cardiff), 1min 47.87sec
1,500m: Nick McCormick (Morpeth), 3min 45.30sec
3,000m: Andy Baddeley (Harrow), 7min 54.60sec
60mH: Andy Turner (Sale), 7.61sec
High jump: Tom Parsons (Birchfield), 2.31m
Pole vault: Max Eaves (Newham), 5.61m
Long jump: Ezekiel Ewulo (Woodford Green), 7.60m
Triple jump: Ben Williams (Stoke), 15.88m
Shot: Scott Rider (Birchfield), 17.96m

WOMEN
60m: Jodie Williams (Herts), 7.24sec
200m: Joice Maduaka (Woodford Green), 23.63sec
400m: Kelly Sotherton (Birchfield), 53.46sec
800m: Marilyn Okoro (Shaftesbury Barnet),
2min 04.36sec
1,500m: Stacey Smith (Gateshead), 4min 22.96sec
3,000m: Helen Clitheroe (Preston), 8min 55.26sec
60mH: Gemma Bennett (Shaftesbury Barnet), 8.22sec
High jump: Jessica Ennis (Sheffield), 1.88m
Pole vault: Holly Bleasdale (Blackburn), 4.36m
Long jump: Kelly Proper (Ireland), 6.35m
Triple jump: Laura Samuel (Leicester), 13.24m
Shot: Eden Francis (Birchfield), 15.85m

ENGLISH NATIONAL CROSS COUNTRY
CHAMPIONSHIPS
Alton Towers, 19 February 2011

SENIOR MEN
Individual: Steve Vernon (Stockport), 35min 11sec
Team: Leeds City, 188pts

JUNIOR MEN
Individual: Jonny Hay (Aldershot), 28min 17sec
Team: Shaftesbury Barnet, 99pts

SENIOR WOMEN
Individual: Louise Damen (Winchester), 23min 49sec
Team: Charnwood, 45pts

JUNIOR WOMEN
Individual: Charlotte Purdue (Aldershot), 25min 24sec
Team: Aldershot, Farnham & Dist, 8pts

EUROPEAN INDOOR CHAMPIONSHIPS
Paris, France, 4–6 March 2011

MEN
60m: Francis Obikwelu (Portugal), 6.53sec
400m: Leslie Djhone (France), 45.54sec
800m: Adam Kszczot (Poland), 1min 47.87sec
1,500m: Manuel Olmedo (Spain), 3min 41.03sec
3,000m: Mo Farah (Great Britain), 7min 53.00sec
60mH: Petr Scoboda (Czech Republic), 7.49sec
4 × 400m: France, 3min 06.17sec
High jump: Ivan Ukhov (Russia), 2.38m
Pole vault: Renaud Lavillenie (France), 6.03m
Long jump: Sebastian Bayer (Germany), 8.16m
Triple jump: Teddy Tamgho (France), 17.92m
Shot: Ralf Bartels (Germany), 21.16m
Heptathlon: Andrei Krauchanka (Belarus), 6,282pts

WOMEN
60m: Olesya Povh (Ukraine), 7.13sec
400m: Denisa Rodsolova (Czech Republic), 51.73sec
800m: Yevgeniya Zinurova (Russia), 2min 00.19sec
1,500m: Yelena Arzhakova (Russia), 4min 13.78sec
3,000m: Helen Clitheroe (Great Britain), 8min 56.66sec
60mH: Carolin Nytra Germany), 7.80sec
4 × 400m: Russia, 3min 29.34sec
High jump: Antonietta Di Martino (Italy), 2.01m
Pole vault: Anna Rogowska (Poland), 4.85m
Long jump: Darya Klishina (Russia), 6.80m
Triple jump: Simona La Mantia (Italy), 14.60m
Shot: Anna Avdeyeva (Russia), 18.70m
Pentathlon: Antoinette Nana Djimou Ida (France), 4,723pts

IAAF WORLD CROSS COUNTRY
CHAMPIONSHIPS
Punta Umbria, Spain, 20 March 2011

SENIOR MEN (12km)
Individual: Imane Merga (Ethiopia), 33min 50sec
Team: Kenya, 14pts

JUNIOR MEN (8km)
Individual: Geoffrey Kipsang Kamworor (Kenya), 22min 21sec
Team: Kenya, 20pts

SENIOR WOMEN (8km)
Individual: Vivian Cheruiyot (Kenya), 24min 58sec
Team: Kenya, 15pts

JUNIOR WOMEN (6km)
Individual: Faith Chepngetich Kipyegon (Kenya), 18min 53sec
Team: Ethiopia, 17pts

LONDON MARATHON
London, 17 April 2011

Men: Emmanuel Mutai (Kenya), 2hr 04min 40sec
Women: Mary Keitany (Kenya), 2hr 19min 19sec

EUROPEAN TEAM CHAMPIONSHIPS
Stockholm, Sweden, 18–19 June 2011

MEN
100m: Christophe Lemaitre (France), 9.95sec
200m: Christophe Lemaitre (France), 20.28sec
400m: Maksim Dyldin (Russia), 45.82sec
800m: Adam Kszczot (Poland), 1min 46.50sec
1,500m: Manuel Olmedo (Spain), 3min 38.63sec
3,000m: Juan Carlos Higuero (Spain), 8min 03.43sec
5,000m: Jesus Espana (Spain), 13min 39.25sec
3,000m St: Vincent Zouaoui-Dandrieux (France), 8min 30.85sec
110mH: Andy Turner (Great Britain), 13.42sec
400mH: Dai Greene (Great Britain), 49.21sec
4 × 100m: Great Britain, 38.60sec
4 × 400m: Russia, 3min 02.42sec
High jump: Dmytro Demyanyuk (Ukraine), 2.35m
Pole vault: Maksym Mazuryk (Ukraine), 5.72m
Long jump: Aleksandr Menkov (Russia), 8.20m
Triple jump: Fabrizio Schembri (Italy),16.95m
Shot: David Storl (Germany), 20.81m
Discus: Robert Harting (Germany), 65.63m
Hammer: Markus Esser (Germany), 79.28m
Javelin: Dmytro Kosynskyy (Ukraine), 81.29m

WOMEN
100m: Véronique Mang (France), 11.23sec
200m: Mariya Ryemyen (Ukraine), 23.10sec
400m: Antonina Yefremova (Ukraine), 51.02sec
800m: Mariya Savinova (Russia), 1min 58.75sec
1,500m: Charlene Thomas (Great Britain), 4min 06.85sec
3,000m: Olesya Syreva (Russia), 8min 53.20sec
5,000m: Dolores Checa (Spain),15min 16.89sec
3,000m St: Gulnara Galkina (Russia), 9min 31.20sec
100mH: Tatyana Dektyareva (Russia), 13.16sec
400mH: Zuzana Hejnova (Czech Republic), 53.87sec
4 × 100m: Ukraine, 42.86sec
4 × 400m: Russia, 3min 27.17sec
High jump: Emma Green (Sweden), 1.89m
Pole vault: Anna Rogowska (Poland), 4.75m
Long jump: Darya Klishina (Russia), 6.74m
Triple jump: Olha Saladukha (Ukraine), 14.85m
Shot: Nadine Kleinert (Germany), 17.81m
Discus: Kateryna Karsak (Ukraine), 63.35m
Hammer: Betty Heidler (Germany), 73.43m
Javelin: Christina Obergföll (Germany), 66.22m

Points: Russia, 385; Germany, 331.5; Ukraine, 304; Great Britain, 289; France, 284; Poland, 264; Spain, 245; Italy, 237; Belarus, 220; Czech Republic, 217; Portugal, 176.5; Sweden, 158

UK TRIALS AND CHAMPIONSHIPS
Birmingham, 29–31 July 2011

MEN
100m: Dwain Chambers (Belgrave), 10.09sec
200m: Christian Malcolm (Cardiff), 20.85sec
400m: Martyn Rooney (Croydon), 45.44sec
800m: Andrew Osagie (Harlow), 1min 46.84sec
1,500m: James Shane (Newham & Essex), 3min 36.22sec
5,000m: Mo Farah (Newham & Essex), 14min 00.72sec
10,000m: Juan Luis Barrios (Mexico), 27min 38.12sec
3,000m St: Luke Gunn (Derby), 8min 40.16sec
110mH: Lawrence Clarke (WSE Hounslow), 13.58sec
400mH: Nathan Woodward (Tamworth), 49.66sec

5,000m Walk: Tom Bosworth (Birchfield), 19min
  29.87sec
High jump: Tom Parsons (Birchfield), 2.28m
Pole vault: Steve Lewis (Newham & Essex), 5.50m
Long jump: Julian Reid (Unattached), 8.06m
Triple jump: Larry Achike (Shaftesbury Barnet), 16.83m
Shot: Carl Myerscough (Blackpool), 18.57m
Discus: Abdul Buhari (Newham & Essex), 63.32m
Hammer: Alex Smith (Sale), 73.26m
Javelin: Lee Doran (Sheffield), 78.63m
*Decathlon: Daniel Awde (Woodford Green), 7,869pts

WOMEN
100m: Jeanette Kwakye (Woodford Green), 11.23sec
200m: Anyika Onuora (Liverpool), 23.26sec
400m: Perri Shakes Drayton (Victoria Park), 51.52sec
800m: Jenny Meadows (Wigan), 2min 02.28sec
1,500m: Hannah England (Oxford), 4min 07.05sec
5,000m: Julia Bleasdale (Hillingdon), 15min 49.02sec
10,000m: Worknesh Kidane (Ethiopia), 31min 08.92sec
3,000m St: Lennie Waite (Unattached), 10min 03.18sec
100mH: Tiffany Porter (Woodford Green), 12.76sec
400mH: Perri Shakes Drayton (Victoria Park), 55.52sec
5,000m Walk: Jo Jackson (Middlesbrough), 21min
  42.32sec
High jump: Jessica Ennis (Sheffield), 1.89m
Pole vault: Holly Bleasdale (Blackburn), 4.56m
Long jump: Shara Proctor (Birchfield), 6.65m
Triple jump: Laura Samuel (Birchfield), 13.67m
Shot: Eden Francis (Birchfield), 16.73m
Discus: Jade Nicholls (Shaftesbury Barnet), 56.19m
Hammer: Sophie Hitchon (Blackburn), 67.69m
Javelin: Goldie Sayers (Belgrave), 60.57m
*Heptathlon: Gemma Weetman (Oswestry), 5,379pts

* Held at Bedford, 4–5 June 2011

WORLD CHAMPIONSHIPS
Daegu, Republic of Korea, 27 August–4 September 2011

MEN
100m: Yohan Blake (Jamaica), 9.92sec
200m: Usain Bolt (Jamaica), 19.40sec
400m: Kirani James (Grenada), 44.60sec
800m: David Rudisha (Kenya), 1min 43.91sec
1,500m: Asbel Kiprop (Kenya), 3min 35.69sec
5,000m: Mo Farah (Great Britain), 13min 23.36sec
10,000m: Ibrahim Jeilan (Ethiopia), 27min 13.81sec
Marathon: Abel Kirui (Kenya), 2 hr, 07min 38sec
3,000m St: Ezekiel Kemboi (Kenya), 8min 14.85sec
110mH: Jason Richardson (USA), 13.16sec
400mH: Dai Greene (Great Britain), 48.26sec
4 × 100m: Jamaica, 37.04sec
4 × 400m: USA, 2min 59.31sec
20km Walk: Valeriy Borchin (Russia), 1hr 19min 56sec
50km Walk: Sergey Bakulin (Russia), 3hr 41min 24 sec
High jump: Jesse Williams (USA), 2.35m
Pole vault: Pawel Wojciechowski (Poland), 5.90m
Long jump: Dwight Phillips (USA), 8.45m
Triple jump: Christian Taylor (USA), 17.96m
Shot: David Storl (Germany), 21.78m
Discus: Robert Harting (Germany), 68.97m
Hammer: Koji Murofushi (Japan), 81.24m
Javelin: Matthias de Zordo (Germany), 86.27m
Decathlon: Trey Hardee (USA), 8,607pts

WOMEN
100m: Carmelita Jeter (USA), 10.90sec

200m: Veronica Campbell-Brown (Jamaica), 22.22sec
400m: Amantle Montsho (Botswana), 49.56sec
800m: Mariya Savinova (Russia), 1min 55.87sec
1,500m: Jennifer Simpson (USA), 4min 05.40sec
5,000m: Vivian Cheruiyot (Kenya), 14min 55.36sec
10,000m: Vivian Cheruiyot (Kenya), 30min 48.98sec
Marathon: Edna Kiplagat (Kenya), 2hr 28min 43sec
3,000m St: Yuliya Zaripova (Russia), 9min 07.03sec
100mH: Sally Pearson (Australia), 12.28sec
400mH: Lashinda Demus (USA), 52.47sec
4 × 100m: USA, 41.56sec
4 × 400m: USA, 3min 18.09sec
20km Walk: Olga Kaniskina (Russia), 1hr 29min 42sec
High jump: Anna Chicherova (Russia), 2.03m
Pole vault: Fabiana Murer (Brazil), 4.85m
Long jump: Brittney Reese (USA), 6.82m
Triple jump: Olha Saladukha (Ukraine), 14.94m
Shot: Valerie Adams (New Zealand), 21.24m
Discus: Li Yanfeng (China), 66.52m
Hammer: Tatyana Lysenko (Russia), 77.13m
Javelin: Mariya Abakumova (Russia), 71.99m
Heptathlon: Tatyana Chernova (Russia), 6,880pts

BADMINTON

WORLD CHAMPIONSHIPS 2011
London, August

Men's Singles: Dan Lin (China) beat Chong Wei Lee
  (Malaysia) 2–1
Women's Singles: Yihan Wang (China) beat Shao Chieh
  Cheng (Chinese Taipei) 2–0
Men's Doubles: Yun Cai and Haifeng Fu (China) beat Sung
  Hyun Ko and Yeon Seong Yoo (South Korea) 2–0
Women's Doubles: Xiaoli Wang and Yang Wu (China) beat
  Qing Tian and Yunlei Zhao (China) 2–0
Mixed Doubles: Nan Zhang and Yunlei Zhao (China) beat
  Chris Adcock and Imogen Bankier (Great Britain) 2–0

ALL-ENGLAND CHAMPIONSHIPS 2011
Birmingham, March

Men's Singles: Chong Wei Lee (Malaysia) beat Dan Lin
  (China) 2–0
Women's Singles: Shixian Wang (China) beat Eriko Hirose
  (Japan) 2–0
Men's Doubles: Mathias Boe and Carsten Mogensen
  (Denmark) beat Kien Keat Koo and Boon Heong Tan
  (Malaysia) 2–1
Women's Doubles: Xiaoli Wang and Yang Yu (China)
  beat Mizuki Fujii and Reika Kakiiwa (Japan) 2–0
Mixed Doubles: Chen Xu and Jin Ma (China) beat Sudket
  Prapakamol and Saralee Thoungthongkam (Thailand)
  2–0

ENGLISH NATIONAL CHAMPIONSHIPS 2011
Manchester, February

Men's Singles: Rajiv Ouseph beat Carl Baxter 2–0
Women's Singles: Nicola Cerfontyne beat Sarah Walker
  2–1
Men's Doubles: Chris Langridge and Nathan Robertson
  beat Chris Adcock and Andy Ellis 2–0
Women's Doubles: Jenny Wallwork and Gabby White beat
  Mariana Agathangelou and Heather Olver 2–0
Mixed Doubles: Nathan Robertson and Jenny Wallwork
  beat Chris Adcock and Gabby White 2–1

SCOTTISH NATIONAL CHAMPIONSHIPS 2011
Perth, February

Men's Singles: Kieran Merrilees beat Gordon Hoggan 2–0
Women's Singles: Susan Egelstaff beat Linda Sloan 2–0
Men's Doubles: Jamie Neill and Keith Turnbull beat Martin
    Campbell and Angus Gilmour 2–1
Women's Doubles: Jillie Cooper and Emma Mason beat
    Imogen Bankier and Linda Sloan 2–1
Mixed Doubles: Paul Van Rietvelde and Imogen Bankier
    beat Martin Campbell and Jillie Cooper 2–0

WELSH NATIONAL CHAMPIONSHIPS 2011
Cardiff, February

Men's Singles: Daniel Font beat Martyn Lewis 2–0
Women's Singles: Sarah Thomas beat Carissa Turner 2–0
Men's Doubles: Matthew Hughes and Martyn Lewis beat
    James Phillips and Joe Morgan 2–0
Women's Doubles: Bethan Higginson and Vikki Jones beat
    Caroline Harvey and Carissa Turner 2–0
Mixed Doubles: Joe Morgan and Jo Sullivan beat Nic
    Strange and Vikki Jones 2–1

BASEBALL

American League Championship Series 2010: Texas Rangers
    beat New York Yankees 4–2
National League Championship Series 2010: San Francisco
    Giants beat Philadelphia Phillies 4–2
World Series 2010: San Francisco Giants beat Texas
    Rangers 4–1

BASKETBALL

BRITISH

MEN
BBL Play-off final 2011: Mersey Tigers beat One Health
    Sharks Sheffield 79–74
BBL Trophy final 2011: Mersey Tigers beat Guildford
    Heat 84–66
BBL Cup final 2011: One Health Sharks Sheffield beat
    Mersey Tigers 93–66
BBL Champions 2010–11: Mersey Tigers

WOMEN
EBL Division 1 2010–11: Sheffield Hatters
EBL Division 1 Play-off final 2010–11: Sheffield Hatters
    beat UWIC Archers 91–69
National Cup final 2011: Sheffield Hatters beat
    Nottingham Wildcats 87–55

USA – NATIONAL BASKETBALL LEAGUE (NBA)
Eastern Conference final 2011: Miami Heat beat Chicago
    Bulls 4–1
Western Conference final 2011: Dallas Mavericks beat
    Oklahoma City Thunder 4–1
NBA final 2011: Dallas Mavericks beat Miami Heat 4–2

BOWLS — INDOOR

WORLD CHAMPIONSHIPS 2011
Norfolk, January

Men's Singles: Paul Foster (Scotland) beat Alex Marshall
    (Scotland) 1½–½

Women's Singles: Alison Merrien (Channel Islands) beat
    Karen Murphy (Australia) 2–1
Men's Pairs: Paul Foster and Alex Marshall (Scotland)
    beat Andrew Barker and Michael Stepney (Scotland)
    2–1
Mixed Pairs: Simon Skelton and Alison Merrien
    (England/Channel Islands) beat Greg Harlow and
    Ellen Falkner (England) 2–1

BRITISH ISLES INDOOR BOWLS
CHAMPIONSHIPS 2011
Co Durham, March

Singles: Robert Grant (Scotland) beat David Corkhill
    (Ireland) 21–11
Pairs: Scotland beat Channel Islands 30–19
Triples: England beat Wales 24–10
Fours: Ireland beat Channel Islands 23–12

ENGLISH NATIONAL CHAMPIONSHIPS 2011
Nottingham, April

Singles: Greg Harlow beat Gary R Smith 21–16
Pairs: City of Ely beat Bournemouth 26–18
Triples: Torquay Utd beat Bletchley 18–10
Fours: Cumbria beat Cyphers 24–21
Liberty Trophy (Inter-County Championship) final: Norfolk
    beat Somerset 151–66
Champion of Champions (Warner Lakeside, February):
    Ashley Clipston beat Neil McKee 21–20

SCOTTISH NATIONAL CHAMPIONSHIPS 2011
Livingston, April

Pairs: Arbroath beat East Lothian 21–15
Triples: Blantyre beat Stonehaven 23–13
Fours: West Lothian beat East Lothian 22–11

BOWLS — OUTDOOR

BRITISH ISLES CHAMPIONSHIPS 2011
Edinburgh, July

Singles: Ireland beat England 21–16
Pairs: Scotland beat Jersey 22–19
Triples: Wales beat England 22–13
Fours: Wales beat Guernsey 26–9

ENGLISH NATIONAL CHAMPIONSHIPS 2011
Worthing, August

Singles: Durham A beat Warwickshire B 21–15
Pairs: Worcestershire B beat Nottinghamshire B
    23–11
Triples: Devon B beat Bedfordshire B 17–15
Fours: Berkshire A beat Somerset B 27–14
Inter-County Championship: Devon beat Berkshire
    117–106

WELSH NATIONAL CHAMPIONSHIPS 2011
Llandrindod Wells, August

Singles: Penarth beat Glyncorrwg 21–16
Pairs: Pontrhydyfen beat Parc-y-Dre 26–10
Triples: Barry Athletic beat Ely Valley 12–11
Fours: Presteigne beat Beaufort 19–11

BOXING

WORLD CHAMPIONS
as at 30 August 2011

WORLD BOXING COUNCIL (WBC)
Heavy: Vitaly Klitschko (Ukraine)
Cruiser: Krzysztof Wlodarczyk (Poland)
Light-heavy: Bernard Hopkins (USA)
Supermiddle: Carl Froch (Great Britain)
Middle: Julio Cesar Chavez Jr. (Mexico)
Superwelter: Saul Alvarez (Mexico)
Welter: Victor Ortiz (USA)
Superlight: vacant
Light: vacant
Superfeather: Takahiro Aoh (Japanese)
Feather: Jhonny Gonzalez (Mexico)
Superbantam: Toshiaki Nishioka (Japan)
Bantam: Nonito Donaire (Philippines)
Superfly: Tomas Rojas Gomez (Mexico)
Fly: Pongsaklek Wonjongkam (Thailand)
Lightfly: Adrian Hernandez (Mexico)
Straw: Kazuto Ioka (Mexico)

WORLD BOXING ASSOCIATION (WBA)
Heavy: Wladimir Klitschko (Ukraine)
Cruiser: Guillermo Jones (Panama)
Light-heavy: Beibut Shumenov (Kazakhstan)
Supermiddle: Andre Ward (USA)
Middle: Gennady Golovkin (Kazakhstan)
Superwelter: Austin Trout (USA)
Welter: Vyacheslav Senchenko (Ukraine)
Superlight: Amir Khan (Great Britain)
Light: Juan Manuel Marquez (Mexico)
Superfeather: Takashi Uchiyama (Japan)
Feather: Chris John (Indonesia)
Superbantam: Celestino Caballero (Panama)
Bantam: Anselmo Moreno (Panama)
Superfly: Hugo Cazares (Mexico)
Fly: Luis Concepcion (Panama)
Lightfly: Giovanni Segura (Mexico)
Minimum: Pornsawan Porpramook (Thailand)

WORLD BOXING ORGANISATION (WBO)
Heavy: Wladimir Klitschko (Ukraine)
Cruiser: Marco Huck (Germany)
Light-heavy: Nathan Cleverly (Great Britain)
Supermiddle: Robert Stieglitz (Germany)
Middle: vacant
Superwelter: Sergei Dzinziruk (Ukraine)
Welter: Manny Pacquiao (Puerto Rico)
Superlight: Timothy Bradley (USA)
Light: Juan Manuel Marquez (Mexico)
Superfeather: Ricky Burns (Great Britain)
Feather: Juan Manuel Lopez (Puerto Rico)
Superbantam: Wilfredo Vasquez Jr. (Puerto Rico)
Bantam: Fernando Montiel (Mexico)
Superfly: Omar Narvaez (Argentina)
Fly: Julio Cesar Miranda (Mexico)
Lightfly: Ivan Calderon (Puerto Rico)
Straw: Donnie Nietes (Philippines)

INTERNATIONAL BOXING FEDERATION (IBF)
Heavy: Wladimir Klitschko (Ukraine)
Cruiser: Steve Cunningham (USA)
Light-heavy: Tavoris Cloud (USA)
Supermiddle: Lucian Bute (Romania)
Middle: Sebastian Sylvester (Germany)

Superwelter: Cory Spinks (USA)
Welter: Dejan Zavec (Slovenia)
Superlight: Juan Urango (Colombia)
Light: vacant
Superfeather: Robert Guerrero (USA)
Feather: Cristobal Cruz (Mexico)
Super-bantam: Celestine Caballero (Panama)
Bantam: Yonnhy Perez (Colombia)
Super-fly: Simphiwe Nongqayi (South Africa)
Fly: vacant
Light-fly: Brian Viloria (Philippines)
Straw: Raul Garcia (Mexico)

BRITISH CHAMPIONS
Heavy: Tyson Fury
Cruiser: Robert Norton
Light-heavy: Tony Bellew
Super-middle: George Groves
Middle: Martin Murray
Light-middle: Prince Arron
Welter: Lee Purdy
Light-welter: Ashley Theophane
Light: Anthony Crolla
Super-feather: Gary Sykes
Feather: Stephen Smith
Super-bantam: Jason Booth
Bantam: Stuart Hall
Super-fly: Lee Haskins
Fly: Chris Edwards

CHESS

FIDE World Champion 2010: Viswanathan Anand (Sri Lanka)
British Champion 2011: Mickey Adams
British Women's Champion: Jovanka Houska

CRICKET

TEST SERIES

AUSTRALIA V ENGLAND
Brisbane (25–29 November 2010): England drew with Australia. England 260 and 517–1; Australia 481 and 107–1
Adelaide (3–7 December 2010): England beat Australia by an innings and 71 runs. England 620–5d; Australia 245 and 304
Perth (16–20 December 2010): Australia beat England by 267 runs. Australia 268 and 309; England 187 and 123
Melbourne (26–30 December 2010): England beat Australia by an innings and 157 runs. England 513; Australia 98 and 258. England retain the Ashes
Sydney (3–7 January 2011): England beat Australia by an innings and 83 runs. England 644; Australia 280 and 281

ENGLAND V SRI LANKA
Cardiff (26–30 May 2011): England beat Sri Lanka by an innings and 14 runs. England 496–5 dec; Sri Lanka 400 and 82
Lord's (3–7 June 2011): England drew with Sri Lanka. England 486 and 335–7 dec; Sri Lanka 479 and 127–3
The Rose Bowl (16–20 June 2011): England drew with Sri Lanka. England 377–8 dec; Sri Lanka 184 and 334–5

ENGLAND V INDIA
Lord's (21–25 July): England beat India by 196 runs.
England 474–8 and 269–6 dec; India 286 and 261
Trent Bridge (29 July–1 August): England beat India by
319 runs. England 221 and 544; India 288 and 158
Edgbaston (10–13 August): England beat India by an innings
and 242 runs. England 710–7; India 224 and 244
The Oval (18–22 August): England beat India by an
innings and 8 runs. England 591–6; India 300 and 283

ONE-DAY INTERNATIONALS

AUSTRALIA V ENGLAND
Melbourne (16 January 2011): Australia beat England by
6 wickets. Australia 297–4; England 294
Hobart (21 January 2011): Australia beat England by
46 runs. Australia 230; England 184
Sydney (23 January 2011): Australia beat England by
4 wickets. Australia 215–6; England 214
Adelaide (26 January 2011): England beat Australia by
21 runs. England 299–8; Australia 278–7
Brisbane (30 January 2011): Australia beat England by
51 runs. Australia 249; England 198
Sydney (2 February 2011): Australia beat England by
2 wickets. Australia 334–8; England 333–6
Perth (6 February 2011): Australia beat England by
57 runs. Australia 279–7; England 222

ENGLAND V SRI LANKA
The Oval (28 June 2011): England beat Sri Lanka by
110 runs (Duckworth-Lewis method). England 229–8;
Sri Lanka 121
Headingley (1 July 2011): Sri Lanka beat England by
69 runs. Sri Lanka 309–5; England 240
Lord's (3 July 2011): Sri Lanka beat England by 6 wickets.
Sri Lanka 249–4; England 246–7
Trent Bridge (6 July 2011): England beat Sri Lanka by
10 wickets. England 171–0; Sri Lanka 174
Old Trafford (9 July 2011): England beat Sri Lanka by
16 runs. England 268–9; Sri Lanka 252

IRELAND V ENGLAND
Dublin (25 August): England beat Ireland by 11 runs
(Duckworth-Lewis method). England 201–8; Ireland
117–8

ICC CRICKET WORLD CUP 2011
India, Sri Lanka and Bangladesh, February–April 2011

Group stage
Group A

	Matches	Won	Lost	Tied	N/R	Pts	Net RR
Pakistan	6	5	1	0	0	10	+0.758
Sri Lanka	6	4	1	0	1	9	+2.582
Australia	6	4	1	0	1	9	+1.123
New Zealand	6	4	2	0	0	8	+1.135
Zimbabwe	6	2	4	0	0	4	+0.030
Canada	6	1	5	0	0	2	−1.987
Kenya	6	0	6	0	0	0	−3.042

Group B

	Matches	Won	Lost	Tied	N/R	Pts	Net RR
South Africa	6	5	1	0	0	10	+2.026
India	6	4	1	1	0	9	+0.900
England	6	3	2	1	0	7	+0.072
West Indies	6	3	3	0	0	6	+1.066
Bangladesh	6	3	3	0	0	6	−1.361
Ireland	6	2	4	0	0	4	−0.696
Netherlands	6	0	6	0	0	0	−2.045

Quarter-finals
Mirpur (23 March 2011): Pakistan beat West Indies by
10 wickets. Pakistan 113–0; West Indies 112
Ahmedabad (24 March 2011): India beat Australia by
5 wickets. India 261–5; Australia 260–6
Mirpur (25 March 2011): New Zealand beat South Africa
by 49 runs. New Zealand 221–8; South Africa 172
Colombo (26 March 2011): Sri Lanka beat England by
10 wickets. Sri Lanka 231–0; England 229–6

Semi-finals
Colombo (29 March 2011): Sri Lanka beat New Zealand
5 wickets. Sri Lanka 220–5; New Zealand 217
Mohali (30 March 2011): India beat Pakistan by 29 runs.
India 260–9; Pakistan 231

Final
Mumbai (2 April 2011): India beat Sri Lanka by 6 wickets.
India 277–4; Sri Lanka 274–6

TWENTY20 INTERNATIONALS

AUSTRALIA V ENGLAND
Adelaide (12 January 2011): England won by 1 wicket.
England 158–9; Australia 157–4
Melbourne (14 January 2011): Australia won by 4 runs.
Australia 147–7; England 143–6

ENGLAND V SRI LANKA
Bristol (25 June 2011): Sri Lanka won by 9 wickets. Sri
Lanka 137–1; England 136–9

ENGLAND AND WALES DOMESTIC COMPETITIONS
County Championship 2010, Division 1: Nottinghamshire,
214pts; *Relegated* Kent, 151pts; Essex, 126pts –
Division 2: Sussex, 235pts; *Promoted* Worcestershire,
208pts
Clydesdale Bank 40 final 2010: Warwickshire Bears beat
Somerset by 3 wickets. Warwickshire Bears 200–7;
Somerset 199
Friends Provident Twenty20 Cup final 2011: Leicestershire
beat Somerset by 18 runs. Leicestershire 145–6;
Somerset 127–9

OTHER INTERNATIONAL DOMESTIC CHAMPIONSHIPS
Australia: Sheffield Shield final 2010–11: Tasmania beat
New South Wales by 7 wickets. Tasmania 453 and
203–3; New South Wales 440 and 215–5 dec. *Ryobi
One-Day Cup final 2010–11:* Victoria beat Tasmania by
84 runs (Duckworth-Lewis method). Victoria 194;
Tasmania 109. *KFC Twenty20 Big Bash final 2010–
11:* South Australia beat New South Wales by 8
wickets. South Australia 155–2; New South Wales
153–8
Bangladesh: National League 2010–11 final: Rajshahi
Division drew with Dhaka Division. Rajshahi Division
314 and 240–6; Dhaka Division 280 and 330 –
Rajshahi Division won on first-innings lead. *National
League One-Day final 2010–11:* Dhaka Division beat
Barisal Division by 3 wickets. Dhaka Division 222–7;
Barisal Division 221–9
India: Irani Trophy final 2010–11: Rest of India beat
Mumbai by 361 runs. Rest of India 668 and 387–3
(dec); Mumbai 274 and 420. *BCCI Corporate Trophy
2010–11:* Indian Oil Corporation XI beat India
Cements by 3 runs. Indian Oil Corporation XI 268–8;

India Cements 265. *NKP Salve Challenger Trophy 2010–11:* India Blue beat India Green by 140 runs. India Blue 287–7; India Green 147. *Deodhar Trophy 2010–11:* North Zone beat West Zone by 5 wickets. North Zone 107–5; West Zone 101. *Duleep Trophy final 2010–11:* South Zone beat North Zone by 7 wickets. South Zone 477 and 178–3; North Zone 337 and 317. *Ranji Trophy Super League 2010–11:* Rajasthan drew with Baroda. Rajasthan 394 and 341; Baroda 361 and 28–4 – Rajasthan won on first innings lead. *Syed Mushtaq Ali Trophy 2010–11:* Bengal beat Madhya Pradesh by 1 run. Bengal 142–7; Madhya Pradesh 141–8. *Vijay Hazare Trophy final 2010–11:* Jharkhand beat Gujarat by 159 runs. Jharkhand 255–8; Gujarat 96. *Indian Premier League Twenty20 final 2011:* Chennai Super Kings beat Royal Challengers Bangalore by 58 runs. Chennai Super Kings 205–5; Royal Challengers Bangalore 147–8
New Zealand: Plunket Shield 2010–11: Canterbury 41pts. *One Day Competition final 2010–11:* Auckland beat Canterbury by 6 runs. Auckland 335–6; Canterbury 329–9. *HRV Cup final 2010-11:* Auckland beat Central Districts by 4 runs. Auckland 158–8; Central Districts 154–9
Pakistan: Quaid-e-Azam Trophy final 2010–11: Habib Bank Limited beat Pakistan International Airlines by 5 wickets. Habib Bank Limited 313 and 236–5; Pakistan International Airlines 228 and 319. *Faysal Bank Pentangular Cup final 2010–11:* Sind beat Baluchistan by 4 wickets. Sind 513 and 236–6; Baluchistan 299 and 449. *Faysal Bank One-Day National Cup final 2010–11:* Habib Bank Limited beat National Bank of Pakistan by 64 runs. Habib Bank Limited 273–9; National Bank of Pakistan 209. *Faysal Bank Twenty20 Cup final 2010–11:* Lahore Lions beat Karachi Dolphins by 37 runs. Lahore Lions 221–3; Karachi Dolphins 184
South Africa: SuperSport Series 2010–11: Cape Cobras, 113.44pts. *MTN40 final 2010–11:* Knights beat Titans by 8 wickets. Knights 152–2; Titans 227 (Duckworth-Lewis method). *Standard Bank Pro20 Series final 2010–11:* Cape Cobras beat Warriors by 12 runs. Cape Cobras 166–5; Warriors 154–6. *CSA Provincial Three-Day Challenge 2010–11:* Western Province 201.56pts. *CSA Provincial One-Day Challenge 2010–11:* Western Province 49pts
Sri Lanka: Premier League Tournament 2010–11: Bloomfield Cricket and Athletic Club, 114.455pts. *Premier Limited Overs Tournament final 2010–11:* Shared title between Colts and Sinhalese – match abandoned without a ball bowled. *SLC Inter-Provincial Limited-Over Tournament final 2010–11:* Kandurata beat Basnahira by 53 runs. Kandurata 225; Basnahira 172
West Indies: WICB Cup final 2010–11: Shared title between Leeward Islands and Barbados – match tied. Leeward Islands 139; Barbados 139. *Regional Four Day Tournament 2010–11:* Jamaica beat Combined Campuses and Colleges by 8 wickets. Jamaica 225 and 15–2; Combined Campuses and Colleges 112 and 122. *Caribbean T20 final 2010-11:* Trinidad & Tobago beat Hampshire by 36 runs. Trinidad & Tobago 147–7; Hampshire 111–8
Zimbabwe: Castle Logan Cup final 2010–11: Matabeleland Tuskers beat Mountaineers by 18 runs. Matabeleland Tuskers 195 and 290; Mountaineers 239 and 228. *MetBank Pro40 final 2010–11:* Southern Rocks beat Mid West Rhinos by 8 wickets. Southern Rocks 155–2; Mid West Rhinos 151.

Stanbic Bank 20 Series final 2010–11: Matabeleland Tuskers beat Southern Rocks by 9 wickets. Matabeleland Tuskers 158–1; Southern Rocks 154–8

CURLING

MEN'S WORLD CHAMPIONSHIP 2011
Saskatchewan, Canada, April

Final: Canada beat Scotland 6–5

WOMEN'S WORLD CHAMPIONSHIP 2011
Esbjerg, Denmark, March

Final: Sweden beat Canada 7–5

CYCLING

Vuelta a España 2010: Vincenzo Nibali (Italy)
Giro d'Italia 2011: Alberto Contador (Spain)
Tour de France 2011: Cadel Evans (Australia)

WORLD ROAD RACE CHAMPIONSHIPS 2010
Geelong, Australia, September–October

MEN
Elite Time Trial: Fabian Cancellara (Switzerland)
Road Race: Thor Hushovd (Norway)

WOMEN
Elite Time Trial: Emma Pooley (Great Britain)
Road Race: Giorgia Bronzini (Italy)

BRITISH NATIONAL ROAD RACE CHAMPIONSHIPS 2011
Stamfordham, June

MEN
Road Race: Bradley Wiggins

WOMEN
Road Race: Lizzie Armitstead

WORLD TRACK CHAMPIONSHIPS 2011
Apeldoorn, Netherlands, March

MEN
Points Race: Edwin Ávila (Colombia)
Sprint: Grégory Baugé (France)
1km Time Trial: Stefan Nimke (Germany)
Individual Pursuit: Jack Bobridge (Australia)
Scratch Race: Kwok Ho Ting (Hong Kong)
Keirin: Shane Perkins (Australia)
Team Pursuit: Australia
Madison: Leigh Howard and Cameron Meyer (Australia)
Team Sprint: France
Omnium: Michael Freiberg (Australia)

WOMEN
Points Race: Tatsiana Sharakova (Belarus)
500m Time Trial: Olga Panarina (Belarus)
Individual Pursuit: Sarah Hammer (USA)
Scratch Race: Marianne Vos (Netherlands)
Keirin: Anna Meares (Australia)
Sprint: Anna Meares (Australia)
Team Sprint: Australia
Team Pursuit: Great Britain
Omnium: Tara Whitten (Canada)

DARTS

BDO World Championship 2011: Martin Adams (England) beat Dean Winstanley (England) 7–5
PDC World Championship 2010–11: Adrian Lewis (England) beat Gary Anderson (Scotland) 7–5

EQUESTRIANISM

Burghley Horse Trials 2011: William Fox-Pitt (Great Britain) on Parklane Hawk
Badminton Horse Trials 2011: Mark Todd (New Zealand) on NZB Land Vision
British Open Horse Trials 2011 (Gatcombe Park): Andrew Nicholson (New Zealand) on Nereo

ETON FIVES

Amateur Championship (Kinnaird Cup) final 2011: T. Dunbar and S. Cooley beat J. Toop and M. Wiseman 3–0
Alan Barber Cup final 2011: Old Olavians beat Old Salopians 2–1
County Championship final 2011: Hertfordshire beat Warwickshire 3–0
Schools' Championship 2011: Shrewsbury 1 beat Highgate 1 3–0
Preparatory Schools' Tournament 2011: Highgate 1 beat Highgate 2 2–1
National Ladies' Championships 2011 final: K. White and D. Redmond beat C. Cooley and M. Rees 3–0

FENCING

WORLD CHAMPIONSHIPS 2010
Paris, France, November

MEN
Individual Foil: Peter Joppich (Germany)
Individual Epée: Nikolai Novosjolov (Estonia)
Individual Sabre: Won Woo-Young (South Korea)
Team Foil: China
Team Epée: France
Team Sabre: Russia

WOMEN
Individual Foil: Elisa Di Francisca (Italy)
Individual Epée: Maureen Nisima (France)
Individual Sabre: Mariel Zagunis (USA)
Team Foil: Italy
Team Epée: Romania
Team Sabre: Russia

EUROPEAN CHAMPIONSHIPS 2011
Sheffield, United Kingdom, July

MEN
Individual Foil: Giorgio Avola (Italy)
Individual Epée: Jorg Fiedler (Germany)
Individual Sabre: Alexey Yakimenko (Russia)
Team Foil: Italy
Team Epée: France
Team Sabre: Italy

WOMEN
Individual Foil: Elisa Di Francisca (Italy)
Individual Epée: Tiffany Géroudet (Switzerland)
Individual Sabre: Olga Kharlan (Ukraine)
Team Foil: Italy
Team Epée: Romania
Team Sabre: Italy

FIGURE SKATING

WORLD CHAMPIONSHIPS 2011
Moscow, Russia, 24 April–1 May

Men: Patrick Chan (Canada)
Women: Miki Ando (Japan)
Pairs: Aliona Savchenko and Robin Szolkowy (Germany)
Ice Dance: Meryl Davis and Charlie White (USA)

EUROPEAN CHAMPIONSHIPS 2011
Bern, Switzerland, 24–30 January

Men: Florent Amodio (France)
Women: Sarah Meier (Switzerland)
Pairs: Aliona Savchenko and Robin Szolkowy (Germany)
Ice Dance: Nathalie Péchalat and Fabian Bourzat (France)

BRITISH CHAMPIONSHIPS 2011
Sheffield, 21–27 November 2010

Men: David Richardson
Women: Jenna McCorkell
Pairs: Stacey Kemp and David King
Ice Dance: Louise Walden and Owen Edwards

GOLF (MEN)

THE MAJOR CHAMPIONSHIPS 2011
US Masters (Augusta, 7–10 April): Charl Schwartzel (South Africa), 274
US Open (Congressional Country Club, 16–19 June): Rory McIlroy (Northern Ireland), 268
The Open (Royal St George's, 14–17 July): Darren Clarke (Northern Ireland), 275
US PGA Championship (Atlanta Athletic Club, 11–14 August): Keegan Bradley (USA), 272

WORLD RANKINGS
as at 28 August 2011

1. Luke Donald (England); 2. Lee Westwood (England); 3. Steve Stricker (USA); 4. Dustin Johnson (USA); 5. Martin Kaymer (Germany)

PGA EUROPEAN TOUR 2010
KLM Open (Hilversumsche, Netherlands): Martin Kaymer (Germany), 266
Austrian Open presented by Botarin (Diamond Country Club): José Manuel Lara (Spain), 271
Vivendi Cup (Golf de Joyenval, France): John Parry (England), 271
Alfred Dunhill Links Championship (St Andrews, Carnoustie and Kingsbarns, Scotland): Martin Kaymer (Germany), 271
Portugal Masters (Oceânico Victoria): Richard Green (Australia), 270
Castelló Masters Costa Azahar (Club de Campo del Mediterráneo, Spain): Matteo Manassero (Italy), 268
Andalucia Valderrama Masters (Club de Golf Valderrama, Spain): Graeme McDowell (Northern Ireland), 281
WGC–HSBC Champions (Sheshan International, China): Francesco Molinari (Italy), 269

Barclays Singapore Open (The Tanjong and the Serapong): Adam Scott (Australia), 267
UBS Hong Kong Open (Fanling): Ian Poulter (England), 258
Dubai World Championship (Jumeirah Golf Estates): Robert Karlsson (Sweden), 274

TEAM CHAMPIONSHIPS
Ryder Cup 2010 (Celtic Manor, Wales): Europe beat USA, 14½–13½

EUROPEAN TOUR RACE TO DUBAI 2010*
1. Martin Kaymer (Germany); 2. Graeme McDowell (Northern Ireland); 3. Lee Westwood (England); 4. Ian Poulter (England); 5. Francesco Molinari (Italy)
* Formerly known as the European Tour Order of Merit

PGA EUROPEAN TOUR 2011
Alfred Dunhill Championship (Leopard Creek, South Africa): Pablo Martin (Spain), 277
South African Open (Durban Country Club): Ernie Els (South Africa), 257
Africa Open (East London, South Africa): Louis Oosthuizen (South Africa), 276
Joburg Open (Royal Johannesburg and Kensington, South Africa): Charl Schwartzel (South Africa), 265
Abu Dhabi HSBC Golf Championship (Abu Dhabi): Martin Kaymer (Germany), 264
Volvo Golf Champions (Royal Golf Club, Bahrain): Paul Casey (England), 268
Commercialbank Qatar Masters (Doha): Thomas Björn (Denmark), 274
Omega Dubai Desert Classic (Emirates): Alvaro Quiros (Spain), 277
Avantha Masters (New Delhi, India): SSP Chowrasia (India), 273
WGC – Accenture Match Play Championship (Ritz-Carlton, USA): Luke Donald (England)
WGC – Cadillac Championship (Doral, USA): Nick Watney (USA), 272
Sicilian Open (Donnafugata, Italy): Raphaël Jacquelin (France), 272
Open de Andalucía (Málaga, Spain): Paul Lawrie (Scotland), 268
Trophée Hassan II (Agadir, Morocco): David Horsey (England), 274
Maybank Malaysian Open (Kuala Lumpur): Matteo Manassero (Italy), 272
Volvo China Open (Chengdu): Nicola Colsaerts (Belgium), 264
Ballantine's Championship (Blackstone, South Korea): Lee Westwood (England), 276
Open de España (Terrassa): Thomas Aiken (South Africa), 278
Iberdrola Open (Pula, Spain): Darren Clarke (Northern Ireland), 274
Volvo World Match Play Championship (Finca Cortesin, Spain): Ian Poulter (England)
Madeira Islands Open (Porto Santo Golfe, Portugal): Michael Hoey (Northern Ireland), 278
BMW PGA Championship (Wentworth, England): Luke Donald (England), 278
Saab Wales Open (Celtic Manor): Alexander Noren (Sweden), 275
BMW Italian Open (Royal Park Roveri): Robert Rock (England), 267
Saint-Omer Open (Lumbres, France): Matthew Zions (Australia), 276

BMW International Open (Munich, Germany): Pablo Larrazábal (Spain), 272
Alstom Open de France (Le Golf National): Thomas Levet (France), 277
Barclays Scottish Open (Castle Stuart): Luke Donald (England), 197 (54 holes)
Nordea Masters (Bro Hof Slot, Sweden): Alexander Noren (Sweden), 273
Irish Open (Killarney): Simon Dyson (England), 269
WGC – Bridgestone Invitational (Firestone, USA): Adam Scott (Australia), 263
Czech Open (Prosper Resort): Oliver Fisher (England), 275
Johnnie Walker Championship (Gleneagles, Scotland): Thomas Björn (Denmark), 277
Omega European Masters (Crans-sur-Sierre, Switzerland): Thomas Björn (Denmark), 264

AMATEUR CHAMPIONSHIPS 2011
British Amateur Championship (Hillside): Bryden Macphern (Australia)
English Amateur Championship (Woburn): Steven Brown
Brabazon Trophy (English Open Strokeplay), (Burnham and Berrow): Neil Raymond (England), 287
Scottish Amateur Championship (Western Gailes): David Law
Scottish Open Amateur Stroke Play Championship (Blairgowrie): Andrew Sullivan (England), 282
Welsh Amateur Championship (Aberdovey): Jason Shufflebotham
Welsh Open Stroke Play (St Pierre): Darren Wright (England), 284
Irish Amateur Open Championship (Royal Dublin): Rhys Pugh (Wales), 294
Irish Amateur Close Championship (Shannon): Paul Cutler (Ireland), 290
Lytham Trophy (Royal Lytham Golf Club): Jack Senior (England), 299
Berkshire Trophy (The Berkshire): Josh White (England), 277

GOLF (WOMEN)

THE MAJOR CHAMPIONSHIPS 2011
Kraft Nabisco Championship (Dinah Shore, USA, 31 March–3 April): Stacy Lewis (USA), 275
US Women's Open (The Broadmoor, 7–10 July): So Yeon Ryu (South Korea), 281
Wegmans LPGA Championship (Locust Hill, USA, 23–26 June): Yani Tseng (Taiwan), 269
Ricoh Women's British Open (Carnoustie, 28–31 July): Yani Tseng (Taiwan), 272

EUROPEAN LPGA TOUR 2010
UNIQA Open (Fohrenwald-Wiener Neustadt, Austria): Laura Davies (England), 205
Open de France Féminin (Paris International): Trish Johnson (England), 274
Open de España Femenino (Flamingos): Laura Davies (England), 202
Sanya Ladies Open (Yalong Bay, China): Lee-Anne Pace (South Africa), 205
Suzhou Taihu Ladies Open (Suzhou International, China): Lee-Anne Pace (South Africa), 211
Korean Ladies Masters (Haevichi): Hyun-Ji Kim (South Korea), 208
Hero Honda Women's Indian Open (DLF Golf and Country Club): Laura Davies (England), 213
Omega Dubai Ladies Masters (Emirates): Iben Tinning (Denmark), 277

EUROPEAN LPGA TOUR ORDER OF MERIT 2010
1. Lee-Anne Pace (South Africa); 2. Laura Davies (England); 3. Melissa Reid (England); 4. In-Kyung Kim (South Korea); 5. Iben Tinning (Denmark)

TEAM CHAMPIONSHIP 2009
Solheim Cup: USA beat Europe 16–12

EUROPEAN LPGA TOUR 2010
ISPS HANDA Women's Australian Open (Commonwealth): Yani Tseng (Taiwan), 276
ANZ RACV Ladies Masters (Royal Pines, Australia): Yani Tseng (Taiwan), 264
Pegasus New Zealand Women's Open (Pegasus): Kristie Smith (Australia), 276
Lalla Meryem Cup (Soleil, Morocco): Zuzana Kamasova (Slovakia), 286
Turkish Airlines Ladies Open (National Golf Club, Antalya): Christel Boeljon (Netherlands), 287
ISPS HANDA Portugal Ladies Open (Campo Real): Ashleigh Simon (South Africa), 200
UniCredit Ladies German Open (Golfpark Gut Hausen): Diana Luna (Italy), 264
Allianz Ladies Slovak Open (Gray Bear): Caroline Hedwall (Sweden), 205
Deloitte Dutch Ladies Open (Golfclub Broekpolder): Melissa Reid (England), 213
Tenerife Ladies Match Play (Golf Las Americas, Spain): Becky Brewerton (Wales)
Deutsche Bank Ladies Swiss Open (Golf Gerre Losone): Diana Luna (Italy), 203
Finnair Masters (Helsinki, Finland): Caroline Hedwall (Sweden), 202
Evian Masters (Evian-Les-Bains, France): Ai Miyazato (Japan), 273
British Open (Carnoustie): Yani Tseng (Taiwan), 272
Irish Open (Killeen Castle): Suzann Pettersen (Norway), 198
Ladies Scottish Open (Archerfield Links): Catriona Matthew (Scotland), 201

TEAM CHAMPIONSHIPS 2011
European Nations Cup (La Sella, Spain): Sweden (Sophie Gustafson and Anna Nordqvist)

AMATEUR CHAMPIONSHIPS 2011
British Open Championship (Royal Portrush): Lauren Taylor (England)
Astor Trophy (Fairhaven): Great Britain and Ireland beat New Zealand 4–3
Ladies' British Open Amateur Stroke Play Championship (Royal Ashdown Forest): Leona Maguire (Northern Ireland), 288
English Close Amateur Championship (West Sussex): Lucy Williams (England)
English Open Stroke Play Championship (Alwoodley): Charley Hull (England)
Helen Holm (Scottish Open Stroke Play Championship) (Troon): Charlotte Ellis (England), 213
Scottish Ladies Close Amateur Championship (Machrihanish): Louise Kenney
Welsh Open Stroke Play (Tenby): Charley Hull (England), 225
Welsh Close Match Play Championship (Royal St David's): Becky Harries (Wales)
Irish Open Strokeplay Championship (Elm Park): Leona Maguire (Ireland), 206
Irish Close Championship (Carlow): Danielle McVeigh

GREYHOUND RACING

2010
Williamhill.com St Leger (Wimbledon): Droopy's Bradley

2011
The Coral Regency (Hove): Blonde Fletch
Pall Mall (Oxford): Brittons Empire
Ladbrokes Golden Jacket (Crayford): Bush Paddy
Grand National (Wimbledon): Victoria Falls
The Williamhill.com Derby (Wimbledon): Taylors Sky

GYMNASTICS

WORLD ARTISTIC CHAMPIONSHIPS 2010
Rotterdam, the Netherlands, 16–24 October

MEN
Team All-around: China
Individual All-around: Kōhei Uchimura (Japan)

　Floor: Eleftherios Kosmidis (Greece)
　Pommel Horse: Krisztian Berki (Hungary)
　Still Rings: Chen Yibing (China)
　Vault: Thomas Bouhail (France)
　Parallel Bars: Feng Zhe (China)
　High Bar: Zhang Chenglong (China)

WOMEN
Team All-around: Russia
Individual All-around: Aliya Mustafina (Russia)

　Floor: Lauren Mitchell (Australia)
　Beam: Ana Porgras (Romania)
　Vault: Alicia Sacramone (USA)
　Uneven Bars: Beth Tweddle (Great Britain)

EUROPEAN ARTISTIC CHAMPIONSHIPS 2011
Berlin, Germany, 4–10 April

MEN
Individual All-around: Philipp Boy (Germany)

　Floor: Flavius Koczi (Romania)
　Pommel Horse: Krisztian Berki (Hungary)
　Still Rings: Konstantin Pluzhnikov (Russia)
　Vault: Thomas Bouhail (France)
　Parallel Bars: Marcel Nguyen (Germany)
　High Bar: Epke Zonderland (Netherlands)

WOMEN
Individual All-around: Anna Dementyeva (Russia)

　Floor: Sandra Raluca Izbaşa (Romania)
　Beam: Anna Dementyeva (Russia)
　Vault: Sandra Raluca Izbaşa (Romania)
　Uneven Bars: Beth Tweddle (Great Britain)

BRITISH CHAMPIONSHIPS 2010
Leicester, 5–7 November

Individual All-around: Daniel Purvis and Sam Hunter*

　Floor: Ruslan Panteleymonov and Daniel Purvis*
　Pommel Horse: Louis Smith
　Still Rings: Samuel Fern
　Vault: Theo Seager and Luke Folwell*
　Parallel Bars: Ruslan Pantelemonov
　High Bar: Theo Seager
* Identical scores

BRITISH WOMEN'S CHAMPIONSHIPS 2011
Liverpool, 9–10 July

Overall Champion: Hannah Whelan

  Floor: Beth Tweddle
  Beam: Danusia Francis
  Vault: Imogen Cairns
  Asymmetric Bars: Beth Tweddle

HOCKEY

MEN
England Hockey League 2010–11: Premier Division: East
  Grinstead, 45pts; *Conference East:* Southgate, 42pts;
  Conference North: University of Durham, 39pts;
  Conference West: University of Exeter, 49pts
England Hockey League Championship final 2011: Beeston
  beat East Grinstead 2–1
England Hockey League Cup final 2010–11: Beeston beat
  Doncaster 6–2
County Championship 2010–11: A Division: Yorkshire
  beat Warwickshire 3–1; B Division: Bedfordshire drew
  with Hertfordshire 3–3. Bedfordshire won 5–4 on
  penalty strokes; C Division: Gloucestershire beat
  Somerset 2–1

WOMEN
England Hockey League 2010–11: Premier Division:
  Leicester, 42pts; *Conference East:* Sevenoaks, 41pts;
  Conference North: Sutton Coldfield, 45pts; *Conference
  West:* Buckingham, 44pts
England Hockey League Championship final 2010–11:
  Reading beat Leicester 3–2
England Hockey League Cup final 2010–11: Bowdon
  Hightown beat Surbiton 4–1

HORSE RACING

NATIONAL HUNT
HENNESSY GOLD CUP
(1957) Newbury, 3 miles and about 2½ f

2007 Denman (7y), S. Thomas
2008 Madison du Berlais (7y), T. Scudamore
2009 Denman (9y), R. Walsh
2010 Diamond Harry (7y), D. Jacob

TINGLE CREEK CHASE
(1957) Sandown, 2 miles

2007 Twist Magic (5y), S. Thomas
2008 Master Minded (5y), A. P. McCoy
2009 Twist Magic (7y), R. Walsh
2010 Master Minded (7y), N. Fehily

KING GEORGE VI CHASE
(1937) Kempton, about 3 miles

2007 Kauto Star (7y), R. Walsh
2008 Kauto Star (8y), R. Walsh
2009 Kauto Star (9y), R. Walsh
2010 Long Run (6y), S. Waley-Cohen*
* Race took place on 15 January 2011, after original meeting
was postponed due to snow and frost

CHAMPION HURDLE
(1927) Cheltenham, 2 miles and about ½ f

2008 Katchit (5y), R. Thornton
2009 Punjabi (6y), B. Geraghty
2010 Binocular (6y), A. P. McCoy
2011 Hurricane Fly (7y), R. Walsh

QUEEN MOTHER CHAMPION CHASE
(1959) Cheltenham, about 2 miles

2008 Master Minded (5y), R. Walsh
2009 Master Minded (6y), R. Walsh
2010 Big Zeb (9y), B. Geraghty
2011 Sizing Europe (9y), A. E. Lynch

CHELTENHAM GOLD CUP
(1924) 3 miles and about 2½ f

2008 Denman (8y), S. Thomas
2009 Kauto Star (9y), R. Walsh
2010 Imperial Commander (9y), P. Brennan
2011 Long Run (6y), S. Waley-Cohen

GRAND NATIONAL
(1837) Liverpool, 4 miles and about 4 f

2008 Comply or Die (9y), T. Murphy
2009 Mon Mome (9y), L. Treadwell
2010 Don't Push It (10y), A. P. McCoy
2011 Ballabriggs (10y), J. Maguire

BET365 GOLD CUP
(1957) Sandown, 3 miles and about 5 f

2008 Monkerhostin (11y), R. Johnson
2009 Hennessy (8y), A. P. McCoy
2010 Church Island (11y), A. Heskin
2011 Poker De Sivola (8y), T. Murphy

STATISTICS
WINNING NATIONAL HUNT TRAINERS 2010–11

P. F. Nicholls	£2,272,084
N. J. Henderson	2,117,797
D. McCain Jr	1,252,376
P. J. Hobbs	1,078,760
D. E. Pipe	916,667
N. A. Twiston-Davies	909,087
A. King	850,473
J. O'Neill	827,349
T. Vaughan	560,474
E. Williams	555,064

WINNING NATIONAL HUNT JOCKEYS 2010–11

	1st	2nd	3rd	Unpl.	Total mts
A. P. McCoy	218	137	91	439	885
R. Johnson	151	116	110	408	785
J. Maguire	95	79	62	254	490
P. Moloney	79	76	75	301	531
P. J. Brennan	78	61	58	338	535
G. Lee	77	80	67	382	606
T. O'Brien	74	41	58	291	464
B. Hughes	65	68	60	348	541
T. Scudamore	63	84	55	354	556
A. Coleman	61	50	54	327	492

The above statistics have been provided by *Timeform*, publishers
of the *Racehorses* and *Chasers and Hurdlers* annuals

THE FLAT

THE CLASSICS

ONE THOUSAND GUINEAS

(1814) Rowley Mile, Newmarket, for three-year-old fillies

Year	Winner	Betting	Owner	Jockey	Trainer	Runners
2007	Finsceal Beo	5–4	M. A. Ryan	K. Manning	J. Bolger	21
2008	Natagora	11–4	Stefan Friborg	C-P Lemaire	P. Bary	15
2009	Ghanaati	20–1	H. Al Maktoum	R. Hills	B. Hills	19
2010	Special Duty	9–2	K. Abdulla	S. Pasquier	Mrs C. Head-Maarek	17
2011	Blue Bunting	16–1	Godolphin	F. Dettori	M. Al Zarooni	18

TWO THOUSAND GUINEAS

(1809) Rowley Mile, Newmarket, for three-year-olds

Year	Winner	Betting	Owner	Jockey	Trainer	Runners
2007	Cockney Rebel	25–1	P. Cunningham	O. Peslier	G. Huffer	24
2008	Henrythenavigator	11–1	Mrs J. Magnier	J. Murtagh	A. O'Brien	15
2009	Sea the Stars	8–1	C. Tsui	M. Kinane	M. Oxx	16
2010	Makfi	33–1	M. Offenstadt	C-P. Lemaire	M. Delzangles	19
2011	Frankel	1–2	K. Abdulla	T. Queally	Sir H. Cecil	13

THE DERBY

(1780) Epsom, 1 mile and about 4 f, for three-year-olds

The first winner was Sir Charles Bunbury's Diomed in 1780. The owners with the record number of winners are Lord Egremont, who won in 1782, 1804, 1805, 1807, 1826 (also won five Oaks); and Aga Khan III, who won in 1930, 1935, 1936, 1948, 1952. Other winning owners are: Duke of Grafton (1802, 1809, 1810, 1815); Mr J. Bowes (1835, 1843, 1852, 1853); Sir J. Hawley (1851, 1858, 1859, 1868); the 1st Duke of Westminster (1880, 1882, 1886, 1899); and Sir Victor Sassoon (1953, 1957, 1958, 1960).

The Derby was run at Newmarket in 1915–18 and 1940–5.

Year	Winner	Betting	Owner	Jockey	Trainer	Runners
2007	Authorized	5–4	Saleh Al Homeizi and Imad Al Sagar	L. Dettori	P. Chapple-Hyam	17
2008	New Approach	5–1	H. R. H. Princess Haya of Jordan	K. Manning	J. Bolger	16
2009	Sea the Stars	11–4	C. Tsui	M. Kinane	M. Oxx	12
2010	Workforce	6–1	K. Abdulla	R. Moore	M. Stoute	12
2011	Pour Moi	4–1	Mrs J. Magnier, M. Tabor and D. Smith	M. Barzalona	A. Fabre	13

THE OAKS

(1779) Epsom, 1 mile and about 4 f, for three-year-old fillies

Year	Winner	Betting	Owner	Jockey	Trainer	Runners
2007	Light Shift	13–2	Niarchos family	T. Durcan	H. Cecil	14
2008	Look Here	33–1	J. H. Richmond-Watson	S. Sanders	R. M. Beckett	16
2009	Sariska	9–4	Michael Bell	Jamie Spencer	Lady Bamford	12
2010	Snow Fairy	9–1	Anamoine Ltd.	R. Moore	E. A. L. Dunlop	15
2011	Dancing Rain	20–1	M. J. and L. A. Taylor	J. Murtagh	W. Haggas	13

ST LEGER

(1776) Doncaster, 1 mile and about 6 f, for three-year-olds (2006 run at York)

Year	Winner	Betting	Owner	Jockey	Trainer	Runners
2006	Sixties Icon	11–8	Mrs S. Roy	L. Dettori	J. Noseda	11
2007	Lucarno	7–2	G. Strawbridge	J. Fortune	J. H. M. Gosden	10
2008	Conduit	8–1	Sir Michael Stoute	L. Dettori	Ballymacoll Stud	14
2009	Mastery	14–1	Godolphin	T. Durcan	S. Bin Suroor	8
2010	Arctic Cosmos	12–1	Ms R. Hood and R. Geffen	W. Buick	J. Gosden	10

RESULTS

CAMBRIDGESHIRE HANDICAP

(1839) Newmarket, 1 mile and 1 f

2007 Pipedreamer (3y), J. Fortune
2008 Tazeez (4y), R. Hills
2009 Supaseus (6y), T. Block
2010 Credit Swap (5y), J. Crowley

PRIX DE L'ARC DE TRIOMPHE

(1920) Longchamp, Paris, 1½ miles

2007 Dylan Thomas (4y), K. Fallon
2008 Zarkava (3y), C. Soumillon
2009 Sea the Stars (3y), M. J. Kinane
2010 Workforce (3y), R. Moore

CESAREWITCH
(1839) Newmarket, 2 miles and about 2 f

2007 Leg Spinner (6y), J. Murtagh
2008 Caracciola (11yr), E. Ahern
2009 Darley Sun (3y), A. Atzeni
2010 Aaim to Prosper (6y), L-P. Beuzelin

CHAMPION STAKES
(1877) Newmarket, 1 mile and 2 f

2007 Literato (3y), C-P. Lemaire
2008 New Approach (3y), K. J. Manning
2009 Twice Over (4y), T. Queally
2010 Twice Over (5y), T. Queally

DUBAI WORLD CUP
(1996) Dubai, 1 mile and 2 f

2008 Curlin (4y), R. Albarado
2009 Well Armed (6y), A. Gryder
2010 Gloria de Campeao (7y), T. Pereira
2011 Victoire Pisa (4y), M. Dimuro

LINCOLN HANDICAP
(1965) Doncaster, 1 mile

2008 Smokey Oakey (4y), J. Quinn
2009 Expresso Star (4y), J. Fortune
2010 Penitent (4y), J. Murtagh
2011 Sweet Lightning (6y), J. Murtagh

JOCKEY CLUB STAKES
(1894) Newmarket, 1½ miles

2008 Getaway (5y), S. Pasquier
2009 Bronze Cannon (4y), J. Fortune
2010 Jukebox Jury (4y), R. Ffrench
2011 Dandina (5y), P. Mulrennan

PRIX DU JOCKEY CLUB
(1836) Chantilly, 1 mile and about 2½ f, for
   three-year-olds

2008 Vision D'Etat, I. Mendizabal
2009 Le Havre, C-P. Lemaire
2010 Lope de Vega, M. Guyon
2011 Reliable Man, G. Mosse

ASCOT GOLD CUP
(1807) Ascot, 2 miles and about 4 f

2008 Yeats (7y), J. Murtagh
2009 Yeats (8y), J. Murtagh
2010 Rite of Passage (6y), P. J. Smullen
2011 Fame and Glory (5y), J. Spencer

IRISH DERBY
(1866) Curragh, 1½ miles, for three-year-olds

2008 Frozen Fire, J. A. Heffernan
2009 Fame and Glory, J. Murtagh
2010 Cape Blanco, J. Murtagh
2011 Treasure Beach, C. O'Donoghue

ECLIPSE STAKES
(1886) Sandown, 1 mile and about 2 f
2008 Mount Nelson (4y), J. Murtagh

2009 Sea the Stars (3y), M. J. Kinane
2010 Twice Over (5y), T. Queally
2011 So You Think (5y), S. Heffernan

KING GEORGE VI AND QUEEN ELIZABETH DIAMOND
STAKES
(1952) Ascot, 1 mile and about 4 f

2008 Duke of Marmalade (4y), J. Murtagh
2009 Conduit (4y), R. Moore
2010 Harbinger (4y), O. Peslier
2011 Nathaniel (3y), W. Buick

GOODWOOD CUP
(1812) Goodwood, about 2 miles

2008 Yeats (7y), J. Murtagh
2009 Schiaparelli (6 y), L. Dettori
2010 Illustrious Blue (7y), J. Crowley
2011 Opinion Poll (5y), L. Dettori

STATISTICS
WINNING FLAT OWNERS 2010

K. Abdulla	£3,727,072
Godolphin	2,487,940
Sheikh Hamdan bin Mohammed Al Maktoum	1,410,791
Hamdan Al Maktoum	1,369,017
Cheveley Park Stud	914,552
D. Smith, Mrs J. Magnier & M. Tabor	914,544
Highclere Thoroughbred Racing	718,141
Dr Marwan Koukash	654,918
Mrs J. Magnier, M. Tabor & D. Smith	562,347
J. Abdullah	555,596

WINNING FLAT TRAINERS 2010

R. Hannon	£3,005,121
Sir M. Stoute	2,797,412
A. P. O'Brien	2,590,555
M. Johnston	2,300,865
Sir H. R. Cecil	2,116,846
R. A. Fahey	1,926,303
S. bin Suroor	1,904,985
J. H. M. Gosden	1,561,286
B. W. Hills	1,355,094
M. Jarvis	1,240,326

WINNING FLAT SIRES 2010

	Races won	Stakes
Galileo by Sadler's Wells	38	£2,401,934
Oasis Dream by Green Desert	108	1,905,350
Dansili by Danehill	77	1,816,444
King's Best by Kingmambo	59	1,400,100
Cape Cross by Green Desert	113	1,375,441
Dubawi by Dubai Millennium	94	1,309,232
Invincible Spirit by Green Desert	84	1,160,273
Danehill Dancer by Danehill	93	1,099,357
Choisir by Danehill Dancer	47	965,028
Kyllachy by Pivotal	106	925,815

WINNING FLAT JOCKEYS 2010

	1st	2nd	3rd	Unpl.	Total mts
P. Hanagan	205	139	144	726	1214
R. Hughes	192	171	123	612	1098
K. Fallon	140	96	104	480	820
R. Moore	138	139	98	409	784
L. Dettori	123	73	70	276	542
J. Fanning	120	109	95	571	895
J. Spencer	108	99	96	390	693
N. Callan	107	105	91	519	822
G. Baker	102	91	67	432	692
S. Sanders	102	80	91	486	759

The above statistics have been provided by *Timeform,* publishers
of the *Racehorses* and *Chasers and Hurdlers* annuals

ICE HOCKEY

MEN'S WORLD CHAMPIONSHIP 2011
Bratislava and Košice, Slovakia, 29 April–15 May
Final: Finland beat Sweden 6–1

WOMEN'S WORLD CHAMPIONSHIP 2011
Zurich and Winterthur, Switzerland, 16–25 April
Final: USA beat Canada 3–2

DOMESTIC COMPETITIONS
Elite League Champions 2010–11: Sheffield Steelers
Play-off Champions 2011: Nottingham Panthers
Challenge Cup final 2010–11: Nottingham Panthers beat
Belfast Giants 4–3

NATIONAL HOCKEY LEAGUE
Stanley Cup final 2010–11: Boston Bruins beat Vancouver
Canucks 4–3

JUDO

EUROPEAN CHAMPIONSHIPS 2011
Istanbul, Turkey, 21–24 April

MEN
Heavyweight (over 100kg): Teddy Riner (France)
Light-heavyweight (100kg): Amel Mekic (Bosnia and
Hercegovina)
Middleweight (90kg): Ilias Iliadis (Greece)
Welterweight (81kg): Elnur Mammadli (Azerbaijan)
Lightweight (73kg): João Pina (Portugal)
Junior Lightweight (66kg): Miklós Ungvári (Hungary)
Bantamweight (60kg): Georgii Zantaraia (Ukraine)

WOMEN
Heavyweight (over 78kg): Elena Ivashchenko (Russia)
Light-heavyweight (78kg): Audrey Tcheumeo (France)
Middleweight (70kg): Edith Bosch (Netherlands)
Welterweight (63kg): Gevrise Emane (France)
Lightweight (57kg): Sabrina Filzmoser (Austria)
Junior Lightweight (52kg): Penelope Bonna (France)
Bantamweight (48kg): Alina Dumitru (Romania)

BRITISH OPEN CHAMPIONSHIPS 2011
London, 14–15 May

MEN
Heavyweight (over 100kg): Roy Meyer (Netherlands)
Light-heavyweight (100kg): Meheddi Khaldoun (France)
Middleweight (90kg): Joakim Dvarby (Sweden)
Welter (81kg): Loic Pietri (France)
Lightweight (73kg): Miguel Romero (Spain)
Junior Lightweight (66kg): Nathon Burns (Great Britain)
Bantamweight (60kg): Sergio Pessoa (Canada)

WOMEN
Heavyweight (over 78kg): Emilie Andeol (France)
Light-heavyweight (78kg): Geraldine Mentouopou (France)
Middleweight (70kg): Kim Polling (Netherlands)
Welter (63kg): Sarah Loko (France)
Lightweight (57kg): Morgane Brunet (France)
Junior Lightweight (52kg): Delphine Delsalle (France)
Bantamweight (48kg): Ewa Konieczny (Poland)

MOTORCYCLING

MOTOGP 2010
San Marino (Misano): Dani Pedrosa (Spain), Honda
Spain (Aragon): Casey Stoner (Australia), Ducati
Japan (Motegi): Casey Stoner (Australia), Ducati
Malaysia (Sepang): Valentino Rossi (Italy), Yamaha
Australia (Phillip Island): Casey Stoner (Australia),
Ducati
Portugal (Estoril): Jorge Lorenzo (Spain), Yamaha
Spain (Valencia): Jorge Lorenzo (Spain), Yamaha
Riders' Championship 2010: 1. Jorge Lorenzo (Spain),
Yamaha, 383pts; 2. Dani Pedrosa (Spain), Honda,
245pts; 3. Valentino Rossi (Italy), Yamaha, 233pts

MOTOGP 2011
Qatar (Doha): Casey Stoner (Australia), Honda
Spain (Jerez): Jorge Lorenzo (Spain), Yamaha
Portugal (Estoril): Dani Pedrosa (Spain), Honda
France (Le Mans): Casey Stoner (Australia), Honda
Catalonia (Barcelona): Casey Stoner (Australia), Honda
Great Britain (Silverstone): Casey Stoner (Australia),
Honda
Netherlands (Assen): Ben Spies (USA), Yamaha
Italy (Mugello): Jorge Lorenzo (Spain), Yamaha
Germany (Sachsenring): Dani Pedrosa (Spain), Honda
USA (Mazda Raceway): Casey Stoner (Australia), Honda
Czech Republic (Brno): Casey Stoner (Australia), Honda
USA (Indianapolis): Casey Stoner (Australia), Honda

MOTO2 2010
San Marino (Misano): Toni Elias (Spain), Moriwaki
Spain (Aragon): Andrea Iannone (Italy), Speed Up
Japan (Motegi): Toni Elias (Spain), Moriwaki
Malaysia (Sepang): Roberto Rolfo (Italy), Suter
Australia (Phillip Island): Alex De Angelis (San Marino),
Motobi
Portugal (Estoril): Stefan Bradl (Germany), Suter
Spain (Valencia): Karel Abraham (Czech Republic), FTR
Riders' Championship 2010: 1. Toni Elias (Spain),
Moriwaki, 271pts; Julian Simon (Spain), Suter, 201pts;
Andrea Iannone (Italy), Speed Up, 199pts

MOTO2 2011
Qatar (Doha): Stefan Bradl (Germany), Kalex
Spain (Jerez): Andrea Iannone (Italy), Suter
Portugal (Estoril): Stefan Bradl (Germany), Kalex
France (Le Mans): Marc Marquez (Spain), Suter
Catalonia (Barcelona): Stefan Bradl (Germany), Kalex
Great Britain (Silverstone): Stefan Bradl (Germany), Kalex
Netherlands (Assen): Marc Marquez (Spain), Suter
Italy (Mugello): Marc Marquez (Spain), Suter
Germany (Sachsenring): Marc Marquez (Spain), Suter
Czech Republic (Brno): Andrea Iannone (Italy), Suter
USA (Indianapolis): Marc Marquez (Spain), Suter

125CC GRAND PRIX 2010
San Marino (Misano): Marc Marquez (Spain), Derbi
Spain (Aragon): Pol Espargaro (Spain), Derbi
Japan (Motegi): Marc Marquez (Spain), Derbi
Malaysia (Sepang): Marc Marquez (Spain), Derbi
Australia (Phillip Island): Marc Marquez (Spain), Derbi
Portugal (Estoril): Nicolas Terol (Spain), Aprilia
Spain (Valencia): Bradley Smith (Great Britain), Aprilia
Riders' Championship 2010: 1. Marc Marquez (Spain),
Derbi, 310pts; 2. Nicolas Terol (Spain), Aprilia,
296pts; 3. Pol Espargaro (Spain), Derbi, 281pts

125CC GRAND PRIX 2011
Qatar (Doha): Nicolas Terol (Spain), Aprilia
Spain (Jerez): Nicolas Terol (Spain), Aprilia
Portugal (Estoril): Nicolas Terol (Spain), Aprilia
France (Le Mans): Maverick Viñales (Spain), Aprilia
Catalonia (Barcelona): Nicolas Terol (Spain), Aprilia
Great Britain (Silverstone): Jonas Folger (Germany), Aprilia
Netherlands (Assen): Maverick Viñales (Spain), Aprilia
Italy (Mugello): Nicolas Terol (Spain), Aprilia
Germany (Sachsenring): Hector Faubel (Spain), Aprilia
Czech Republic (Brno): Sandro Cortese (Germany), Aprilia
USA (Indianapolis): Nicolas Terol (Spain), Aprilia

ISLE OF MAN TOURIST TROPHY 2011
Senior: John McGuinness (England), Honda
Supersport: Race 1 – Bruce Anstey (New Zealand), Honda; Race 2 – Gary Johnson (England), Honda

WORLD SUPERBIKES 2010
Germany (Nurburgring): Race 1 – Jonathan Rea (Great Britain), Honda; Race 2 – Noriyuki Haga (Japan), Yamaha
Italy (Imola): Race 1 – Carlos Checa (Spain), Ducati; Race 2 – Carlos Checa (Spain), Ducati
France (Magny Cours): Race 1 – Cal Crutchlow (Great Britain), Yamaha; Race 2 – Max Biaggi (Italy), Aprilia
Riders' World Championship 2010: 1. Max Biaggi (Italy), Aprilia, 451pts; 2. Leon Haslam (Great Britain), Suzuki, 376pts; 3. Carlos Checa (Spain), Ducati, 297pts

WORLD SUPERBIKES 2011
Australia (Phillip Island): Race 1 – Carlos Checa (Spain), Ducati; Race 2 – Carlos Checa (Spain), Ducati
Great Britain (Donington): Race 1 – Marco Melandri (Italy), Yamaha; Race 2 – Carlos Checa (Spain), Ducati
Netherlands (Assen): Race 1 – Jonathan Rea (Great Britain), Honda; Race 2 – Carlos Checa (Spain), Ducati
Italy (Monza): Race 1 – Eugene Laverty (Ireland), Yamaha; Race 2 – Eugene Laverty (Ireland), Yamaha
USA (Salt Lake City): Race 1 – Carlos Checa (Spain), Ducati; Race 2 – Carlos Checa (Spain), Ducati
San Marino (Misano): Race 1 – Carlos Checa (Spain), Ducati; Race 2 – Carlos Checa (Spain), Ducati
Spain (Aragon): Race 1 – Marco Melandri (Italy), Yamaha; Race 2 – Max Biaggi (Italy), Aprilia
Czech Republic (Brno): Race 1 – Marco Melandri (Italy), Yamaha; Race 2 – Max Biaggi (Italy), Aprilia
British (Silverstone): Race 1 – Carlos Checa (Spain), Ducati; Race 2 – Carlos Checa (Spain), Ducati

MOTOR RACING

FORMULA 1 GRAND PRIX 2010
Italian (Monza): Fernando Alonso (Spain), Ferrari
Singapore (Marina Bay): Fernando Alonso (Spain), Ferrari
Japanese (Suzuka): Sebastian Vettel (Germany), RBR-Renault
Korean (Yeongam): Fernando Alonso (Spain), Ferrari
Brazilian (Interlagos): Sebastian Vettel (Germany), RBR-Renault
Abu Dhabi (Yas Marina): Sebastian Vettel (Germany), RBR-Renault
Drivers' World Championship 2010: 1. Sebastian Vettel (Germany), RBR-Renault, 256pts; 2. Fernando Alonso (Spain), Ferrari, 252pts; 3. Mark Webber (Australia), RBR-Renault, 242pts

Constructors' World Championship 2010: 1. RBR-Renault, 498pts; 2. McLaren-Mercedes, 454pts; 3. Ferrari, 396pts

FORMULA 1 GRAND PRIX 2011
Australian (Melbourne): Sebastian Vettel (Germany), RBR-Renault
Malaysian (Sepang): Sebastian Vettel (Germany), RBR-Renault
Chinese (Shanghai): Lewis Hamilton (Great Britain), McLaren-Mercedes
Turkish (Istanbul): Sebastian Vettel (Germany), RBR-Renault
Spanish (Barcelona): Sebastian Vettel (Germany), RBR-Renault
Monaco (Monte Carlo): Sebastian Vettel (Germany), RBR-Renault
Canadian (Montreal): Jenson Button (Great Britain), McLaren-Mercedes
European (Valencia): Sebastian Vettel (Germany), RBR-Renault
British (Silverstone): Fernando Alonso (Spain), Ferrari
German (Nürburgring): Lewis Hamilton (Great Britain), McLaren-Mercedes
Hungarian (Budapest): Jenson Button (Great Britain), McLaren-Mercedes
Belgium (Spa): Sebastian Vettel (Germany), RBR-Renault

INDIANAPOLIS 500 2011
Indianapolis, USA, 29 May
Dan Wheldon (Great Britain), Bryan Herta Autosport

LE MANS 24-HOUR RACE 2011
Le Mans, France, 11–12 June
Marcel Fässler (Switzerland), André Lotterer (Germany) and Benoit Tréluyer (France), Audi

MOTOR RALLYING

WORLD RALLY CHAMPIONSHIP 2010
Japan: Sébastien Loeb (France), Citroën
France: Sébastien Loeb (France), Citroën
Spain: Sébastien Loeb (France), Citroën
Great Britain: Sébastien Loeb (France), Citroën
Drivers' World Championship 2010: 1. Sébastien Loeb (France), Citroën, 276pts; 2. Jari-Matti Latvala (Finland), Ford, 171pts; 3. Petter Solberg (Norway), Citroën, 169pts
Manufacturers' World Championship 2010: 1. Citroën, 456pts; 2. BP Ford, 337pts; 3. Citroën Junior, 217pts

WORLD RALLY CHAMPIONSHIP 2011
Sweden: Mikko Hirvonen (Finland), Ford
Mexico: Sébastien Loeb (France), Citroën
Portugal: Sébastien Ogier (France), Citroën
Jordan: Sébastien Ogier (France), Citroën
Italy: Sébastien Loeb (France), Citroën
Argentina: Sébastien Loeb (France), Citroen
Greece: Sébastien Ogier (France), Citroën
Finand: Sébastien Loeb (France), Citroen
Germany: Sébastien Ogier (France), Citroën

BRITISH RALLY CHAMPIONSHIP 2010
Yorkshire: Gwyndaf Evans (Great Britain), Subaru
Drivers' Championship 2010: 1. Keith Cronin (Ireland), Subaru, 98pts; 2. Gwyndaf Evans (Great Britain), Mitsubishi, 88pts; 3. Jason Pritchard (Great Britain), Subaru, 78pts

BRITISH RALLY CHAMPIONSHIP 2011

Rallye Sunseeker: David Bogie (Scotland), Mitsubishi
North Wales: Elfyn Evans (Wales), Ford
Pirelli International: David Bogie (Scotland), Mitsubishi
Jim Clark International: David Bogie (Scotland), Mitsubishi
Rally NI: Marty McCormack (Northern Ireland), Citroën

DAKAR RALLY RAID 2011
Argentina and Chile, 1–16 January

Motorcycle: Marc Coma (Spain), KTM
Quad: Alejandro Patronelli (Argentina), Yamaha
Car: Nasser Al-Attiyah (Qatar), Volkswagen
Truck: Vladimir Chagin (Russia), Kamaz

NETBALL

Superleague 2010–11: Hertfordshire Mavericks
Superleague Grand Final 2011: Hertfordshire Mavericks
   beat Surrey Storm 57–46

NORDIC EVENTS

BIATHLON WORLD CUP 2010–11

MEN
Overall: Tarjei B (Norway), 1110pts

WOMEN
Overall: Kaisa Mäkäräinen (Finland), 1005pts

BIATHLON WORLD CHAMPIONSHIPS 2011
Khanty-Mansiysk, Russia, 3–13 March

MIXED
Relay: Norway

NORDIC WORLD CUP 2010–11
World Cup: Jason Lamy-Chappuis (France), 894pts
Nation Cup: Austria, 2586pts

POLO

Prince of Wales Trophy 2011: El Remanso beat Aravali
   12–7
Queen's Cup final 2011: Talandracas beat Enigma 9–8
Warwickshire Cup 2011: Laird beat Black Bears 9–8
Gold Cup (British Open) final 2011: Zacara beat Les Lions
   12–11
Coronation Cup 2011: England beat Brazil 8–7

RACKETS

Noel Bruce Cup 2010: Mark Hubbard and Ben Bomford
   (Malvern) beat Charlie Danby and Alex
   Titchener-Barrett (Harrow) 4–2
Amateur Singles Championship final 2010: Alex
   Titchener-Barrett beat Will Hopton 3–0
The Foster Cup final 2010 (public schools' singles
   championship): N. Hopcroft (Wellington) beat
   R. Owen (Cheltenham) 3–0
British Professional Singles Championship final 2011: Mark
   Hubbard beat Neil Smith 3–1
British Open Singles Championship final 2011: Alex
   Titchener-Barrett beat Will Hopton 4–0
British Open Doubles Championship final 2011: James
   Coyne and Will Hopton beat George Tysoe and Mike
   Bailey

Amateur Doubles Championship 2011: G. Barker and
   A. Robinson beat T. Cockroft and A. Titchener-Barrett
   4–0
Public Schools Doubles 2011: N. Hopcroft and A. Boobyer
   (Wellington) beat R. Owen and C. Stout
   (Cheltenham) 4–3

REAL TENNIS

MEN
British Open Singles final 2010: Rob Fahey (Australia) beat
   Steve Virgona (Australia)
British Open Doubles final 2010: Steve Virgona (Australia)
   and Rob Fahey (Australia) beat Tim Chisholm (USA)
   and Conor Medlow (Great Britain)
World Doubles Championship 2011: Robert Fahey
   (Australia) and Steve Virgona (Australia) beat Ben
   Matthews (Great Britain) and Julian Snow (Great
   Britain)
Henry Leaf Cup final 2011 (public schools' old boys'
   doubles championship): Harrow beat Charterhouse
   2–1
John Prenn and Charlie Danby (Harrow) beat Adam
   Dolman and James Acheson-Gray (Charterhouse) 2–1

WOMEN
British Open Singles Championship final 2011: Claire
   Vigrass (Great Britain) beat Sarah Vigrass (Great
   Britain) 2–0
British Open Doubles Championship final 2011: K. Hird
   (Great Britain) and F. Adam (USA) beat C. Vigrass
   (Great Britain) and S. Vigrass (Great Britain) 2–1

ROWING

BRITISH CHAMPIONSHIPS 2011
Holme Pierrepont, Nottingham, 15–17 July

MEN
Single sculls: B. Crean (Agecroft), 8min 34.00sec
Double sculls: London/ISIS, 7min 48.59sec
Quadruple sculls: Leander, 7min 12.76sec
Coxless pairs: Worcester, 8min 08.23sec
Coxless fours: Molesey, 7min 22.10sec
Coxed fours: Molesey, 7min 22.10sec
Eights: Leander Club, 6min 58.30sec

WOMEN
Single sculls: F. Sanjana (Mortlake, Anglian & Alpha), 9min
   31.96sec
Double sculls: Molesey/Agecroft, 7min 27.89sec
Quadruple sculls: Nottingham, 7min 47.70sec
Coxless pairs: Aberdeen, 9min 20.65sec
Coxless fours: Sir William Borlase/St Pauls, 8min
   20.41sec
Coxed fours: City of Oxford, 8min 43.30sec
Eights: Henley/Reading University, 8min 10.07sec

HENLEY ROYAL REGATTA 2011
Grand Challenge Cup: Ruder Club Hansa von 1898 e.V.
   Dortmund (Germany) beat Molesey B. C. and Leander
   Club by 1 length
Stewards' Challenge Cup: Leander Club and Molesey B. C.
   beat Chula Vista Training Center (USA) by 2½ lengths
Queen Mother Challenge Cup: Reading University and
   Leander Club beat C. A. R. C. Mladost and R. C.
   Tresnjevka (Croatia) by 1¼ lengths

Silver Goblets and Nickalls' Challenge Cup: P. Reed and A. Triggs Hodge (Leander Club and Molesey B. C.) beat L. Carboncini and N. Mornati (Centro Nazionale di Canottaggio Piediluco, Italy) easily
Double Sculls Challenge Cup: M. Wells and R. Bateman (Leander Club) beat D. Crawshay and S. Brennan (Australian Institute of Sport, Australia) by 2½ lengths
Diamond Challenge Sculls: A. Campbell (The Tideway Scullers' School) beat N. Hudson (Australian Institute of Sport) easily
Remenham Challenge Cup: Princeton Training Center (USA) beat Leander Club and Gloucester R. C. by 1¾ lengths
Princess Grace Challenge Cup: Princeton Training Center 'B' (USA) beat Australian Institute of Sport 'B' (Australia) by 1¼ length
Princess Royal Challenge Cup: M. Knapkova (Czech Republic) beat G. L. Stone (USA) by 2½ lengths
Ladies' Challenge Plate: Berliner Ruderclub and Olympische Ruderclub Rostock (Germany) beat Leander Club 'A' by ½ length
Visitors' Challenge Cup: Leander Club and Imperial College London beat National University of Ireland and Gráinne Mhaol B. C. (Ireland) by 3 lengths
Prince of Wales Challenge Cup: Leander Club 'A' beat The Tideway Scullers School 'A' by 1 length
Thames Challenge Cup: Upper Yarra R. C. (Australia) beat Star Club by 1 length
Wyfold Challenge Cup: London R. C. 'A' beat Nottingham R.C. 'A' by 2 lengths
Britannia Challenge Cup: Banks R. C. (Australia) beat London R.C. 'A' by ¾ length
Temple Challenge Cup: University of California (USA) beat Amsterdamsche Studenten Roeivereeniging Nereus (Netherlands) by 4½ lengths
Prince Albert Challenge Cup: Harvard University 'A' (USA) beat Oxford Brookes University 'A' by 1¾ lengths
Princess Elizabeth Challenge Cup: Abingdon School beat St Andrew's School (USA) by 1¾ lengths
Fawley Challenge Cup: Sydney R.C. (Australia) beat Walton R.C. 'A' by 4 lengths

THE 157TH UNIVERSITY BOAT RACE
Putney–Mortlake, 4 miles, 1 f, 180 yd, 26 March 2011

Oxford beat Cambridge by 4 lengths; 17min 32sec
Cambridge have won 80 times, Oxford 76 and there has been one dead heat. The record time is 16min 19sec, rowed by Cambridge in 1998.

OTHER ROWING EVENTS
Wingfield Sculls 2010: Men, Alan Campbell (Tideway Scullers); *Women,* Anna Watkins (Leander Club)
Oxford Torpids 2011: Men, Christ Church; *Women,* Magdalen
Oxford Summer Eights 2011: Men, Oriel; *Women,* Balliol
Head of the River 2011: Men, Leander Club; *Women,* Leander Club

RUGBY FIVES

National Open Singles Championship final 2010: J. Toop beat W. Ellison 2–0
National Ladies' Singles Championship final 2010: C. Knowles beat K. Briedenhann 2–0
National Ladies' Doubles Championship final 2010: C. Knowles and M. Whitehead beat A. Ganguly and A. Steel 2–0

National Open Doubles Championship final 2011: H. Buchanan and R. Perry beat M. Bate and W. Ellison 2–0
National Club Championship final 2011: Old Paulines beat Manchester Youth Club 105–65
National Schools' Singles Championship final 2011: L. Thomson (Christ's Hospital) beat N. Edmonds (St. Paul's) 2–0
National Schools' Doubles Championship final 2011: Christ's Hospital I beat St. Paul's I 2–0
Varsity Match 2011: Cambridge beat Oxford 238–201

RUGBY LEAGUE

Carnegie Challenge Cup final 2011: Wigan beat Leeds 28–18
Super League Grand Final 2010: Wigan beat St. Helens 22–10
World Club Challenge 2011: St George Illawarra Dragons beat Wigan 21–15

AMATEUR COMPETITIONS 2010–11
National Conference League Premier Division Grand Final: Thatto Heath Crusaders beat Siddal 30–18
First Division Champions: Oulton Raiders
Second Division Champions: Hunslet Warriors
BARLA National Cup final: Sharlston Rovers beat Fryston 20–18
Varsity Match 2011: Oxford beat Cambridge 60–16

RUGBY UNION

SIX NATIONS' CHAMPIONSHIP 2011

4 February	Cardiff	England beat Wales 26–19
5 February	Rome	Ireland beat Italy 13–11
	Paris	France beat Scotland 34–21
12 February	London	England beat Italy 59–13
	Edinburgh	Wales beat Scotland 24–6
13 February	Dublin	France beat Ireland 25–22
26 February	Rome	Wales beat Italy 24–16
	London	England beat France 17–9
27 February	Edinburgh	Ireland beat Scotland 21–18
12 March	Rome	Italy beat France 22–21
	Cardiff	Wales beat Ireland 19–13
	London	England beat Scotland 22–16
19 March	Edinburgh	Scotland beat Italy 21–8
	Dublin	Ireland beat England 24–8
	Paris	France beat Wales 28–9

Final standings: 1. England, 8pts; 2. France, 6pts; 3. Ireland, 6pts; 4. Wales, 6pts; 5. Scotland, 2pts; 6. Italy, 2pts

EUROPEAN COMPETITIONS 2010–11
Heineken European Cup final: Leinster beat Northampton 33–22
European Challenge Cup final: Harlequins beat Stade Français 19–18

DOMESTIC COMPETITIONS 2010–11

ENGLAND
Premiership: Leicester Tigers, 78pts
Premiership final: Saracens beat Leicester Tigers 22–18
RFU Championship: Worcester Warriors, 101pts
RFU Championship final: Worcester Warriors beat Cornish Pirates 21–12 (at Penzance); Worcester Warriors beat Cornish Pirates 25–20 (at Worcester). Worcester promoted to Premiership.

National League: Division 1, London Scottish, 132pts;
   Division 2 (North), Fylde, 132pts; (South) Ealing,
   132pts
British and Irish Cup final: Bristol Rugby beat Bedford
   Blues 17–14
County Championship final (Bill Beaumont Cup):
   Lancashire beat Hertfordshire 32–23
County Shield final: Dorset & Wilts beat Surrey 43–22
County Plate final: Northumberland beat North Midlands
   31–17
129th Varsity Match: Oxford beat Cambridge 21–10

ANGLO-WELSH
LV Cup final: Gloucester beat Newcastle Falcons 34–7

CELTIC
Magners League: Munster, 79pts
Magners League final: Munster beat Leinster 19–9

SCOTLAND
Premier League: Division 1, Melrose, 46pts; *Division 2,*
   Edinburgh Academical, 47pts; *Division 3,*
   Whitecraigs, 98pts
Cup final: Ayr beat Melrose 25–21

WALES
Premiership: Pontypridd, 107pts; *National League:*
   Division 1 (East), Ebbw Vale, 89pts; (West), Bridgend,
   96pts; (North) Caernarfon, 81pts
WRU Challenge Cup final: Pontypridd beat Aberavon
   35–24

IRELAND
All Ireland League: Division 1A, Cork Constitution,
   47pts; Division 1B, Clontarf, 47pts; Division 2,
   Ballynahinch, 68pts; Division 3, City of Derry, 58pts

SHOOTING

142ND NATIONAL RIFLE ASSOCIATION
IMPERIAL MEETING
Bisley, 9–23 July 2011

Queen's Prize: D. N. Kent, 145.11 v-bulls
Grand Aggregate: D. Lloyd, 821.65 v-bulls; D. N. Kent,
   818.8 v-bulls
Prince of Wales Prize: D. N. Kent, 75.8 v-bulls
St George's Vase: D. A. Stewart, 73.5 v-bulls
All Comers' Aggregate: G. C. D. Barnett, 373.46 v-bulls
Kolapore Cup: Great Britain, 1188.176 v-bulls
Chancellor's Trophy: Cambridge University, 1149.107
   v-bulls
National Trophy: Scotland, 2075.279 v-bulls
Musketeers Cup: Exeter University, 580.61 v-bulls
County Championship Long Range: Surrey, 594.89 v-bulls
Mackinnon Challenge Cup: England, 1156.126 v-bulls
The Albert: J. M. B. Baillie-Hamilton, 222.28 v-bulls
Hopton Challenge Cup: R. J. Lygoe, 221.29 v-bulls

SNOOKER

2010–11
Shanghai Masters: Ali Carter (England) beat Jamie Burnett
   (Scotland) 10–7
World Open (Glasgow): Neil Robertson (Australia) beat
   Ronnie Sullivan (England) 5–1
UK Championship (Telford): John Higgins (Scotland) beat
   Mark Williams (Wales) 10–9

Masters (Wembley): Ding Junhui (China) beat Marco Fu
   (Hong Kong) 10–4
Welsh Open (Newport): John Higgins (Scotland) beat
   Stephen Maguire (Scotland) 9–6
German Masters (Berlin): Mark Williams (Wales) beat
   Mark Selby (England) 9–7
China Open (Beijing): Judd Trump (England) beat Mark
   Selby (England) 10–8
World Championship (Sheffield): John Higgins (Scotland)
   beat Judd Trump (England) 18–15
Australian Open (Bendigo): Stuart Bingham (England)
   beat Mark Williams (Wales) 9–8

SPEED SKATING

WORLD ALL-ROUND CHAMPIONSHIPS 2011
Calgary, Canada, 12–13 February

MEN
Gold: Ivan Skobrev (Russia); *Silver:* Håvard Bkko
   (Norway); *Bronze:* Jan Blokhuisjen (Netherlands)
500m: Shani Davis (USA), 35.08sec
1,500m: Ivan Skobrev (Russia), 1min 42.94sec
5,000m: Koen Verweij (Netherlands), 6min 12.20sec
10,000m: Ivan Skobrev (Russia), 12min 58.36sec

WOMEN
Gold: Ireen Wüst (Netherlands); *Silver:* Christine Nesbitt
   (Canada); *Bronze:* Martina Sáblíková (Czech Republic)
500m: Christine Nesbitt (Canada), 37.72sec
1,500m: Ireen Wüst (Netherlands), 1min 52.59sec
3,000m: Ireen Wüst (Netherlands), 3min 58.01sec
5,000m: Ireen Wüst (Netherlands), 6min 55.85sec

EUROPEAN ALL-ROUND CHAMPIONSHIPS 2011
Collalbo, Italy, 7–9 January

MEN
Gold: Ivan Skobrev (Russia); *Silver:* Jan Blokhuijsen
   (Netherlands); *Bronze:* Koen Verweij (Netherlands)
500m: Konrad Niedzwiedzki (Poland), 36.04sec
1,500m: Ivan Skobrev (Russia), 1min 52.52sec
5,000m: Jan Blokhuijsen (Netherlands), 6min 32.21sec
10,000m: Ivan Skobrev (Russia), 13min 39.80sec

WOMEN
Gold: Martina Sáblíková (Czech Republic); *Silver:* Ireen
   Wüst (Netherlands); *Bronze:* Marrit Leenstra
   (Netherlands)
500m: Karolina Erbanova (Czech Republic), 39.29sec
1,500m: Martina Sáblíková (Czech Republic), 2min
   00.37sec
3,000m: Martina Sáblíková (Czech Republic), 4min
   11.36sec
5,000m: Martina Sáblíková (Czech Republic), 7min
   07.78sec

WORLD SHORT TRACK CHAMPIONSHIPS 2011
Sheffield, 11–13 March

MEN
500m: Simon Cho (USA), 42.307sec
1,000m: Noh Jin-Kyu (Rep. of Korea), 1min 28.552sec
1,500m: Noh Jin-Kyu (Rep. of Korea), 2min 18.291sec
3,000m: Noh Jin-Kyu (Rep. of Korea), 4min 51.638sec
5,000m relay: Canada, 6min 52.731sec
Overall: Noh Jin-Kyu (Rep. of Korea), 102pts

WOMEN
500m: Fan Kexin (China), 44.620sec
1,000m: Cho Ha-Ri (Rep. of Korea), 1min 38.895sec
1,500m: Katherine Reutter (USA), 2min 33.978sec
3,000m: Cho Ha-Ri (Rep. of Korea), 5min 13.353sec
3,000m relay: China, 4min 16.295sec
Overall: Cho Ha-Ri (Rep. of Korea), 81pts

EUROPEAN SHORT TRACK CHAMPIONSHIPS
2011
Heerenveen, Netherlands, 14–16 January

MEN
500m: Thibaut Fauconnet (France), 42.235sec
1,000m: Thibaut Fauconnet (France), 1min 26.888sec
1,500m: Thibaut Fauconnet (France), 2min 15.920sec
3,000m: Thibaut Fauconnet (France), 4min 50.275sec
5,000m relay: Netherlands, 6min 50.818sec
Overall: Thibaut Fauconnet (France), 136pts

WOMEN
500m: Martina Valcepina (Italy), 44.847sec
1,000m: Arianna Fontana (Italy), 1min 34.588sec
1,500m: Arianna Fontana (Italy), 2min 29.292sec
3,000m: Arianna Fontana (Italy), 5min 15.742sec
3,000m relay: Netherlands, 4min 19.253sec
Overall: Arianna Fontana (Italy), 115pts

SQUASH

MEN
British Grand Prix 2010: Ramy Ashour (Egypt) beat
James Willstrop (England) 3–1
World Open 2010: Nick Matthew (England) beat James
Willstrop (England) 3–1
World Team Championship 2010: Egypt beat England 2–0
European Championship 2011: Gregory Gaultier (France)
beat Thierry Lincou (France) 3–1
European Team Championship 2011: England beat France
3–0
British National Championship 2011: Daryl Selby beat
Nick Matthew 3–2

WOMEN
World Team Championship 2010: Australia beat England
2–1
World Open 2010: Nicol David (Malaysia) beat Omneya
Abdel Kawy (Egypt) 3–0
European Championship 2011: Natalie Grinham
(Netherlands) beat Camille Serme (France) 3–1
European Team Championship 2011: England beat
Netherlands 3–0
British National Championship 2011: Laura Massaro beat
Jenny Duncalf 3–2

SWIMMING

SWIMMING AT THE 2011 WORLD AQUATICS
CHAMPIONSHIPS
Shanghai, China, 24–31 July

MEN
50m freestyle: Cesar Cielo (Brazil), 21.52sec
100m freestyle: James Magnussen (Australia), 47.63sec
200m freestyle: Ryan Lochte (USA), 1min 44.44sec
400m freestyle: Park Tae-Hwan (South Korea), 3min
42.04sec
800m freestyle: Sun Yang (China), 7min 38.57sec

1,500m freestyle: Sun Yang (China), 14min 34.14sec
4 × 100m freestyle relay: Australia, 3min 11.00sec
4 × 200m freestyle relay: USA, 7min 02.67sec
50m backstroke: Liam Tancock (Great Britain), 24.50sec
100m backstroke: Jeremy Stravius (France) and Camille
Lacourt (France), 52.76sec
200m backstroke: Ryan Lochte (USA), 1min 52.96sec
50m breaststroke: Felipe França Silva (Brazil), 27.01sec
100m breaststroke: Alexander Dale Oen (Norway),
58.71sec
200m breaststroke: Daniel Gyurta (Hungary), 2min
08.41sec
50m butterfly: Cesar Cielo (Brazil), 23.10sec
100m butterfly: Michael Phelps (USA), 50.71sec
200m butterfly: Michael Phelps (USA), 1min 53.34sec
200m individual medley: Ryan Lochte (USA), 1min
54.00sec
400m individual medley: Ryan Lochte (USA), 4min 07.13sec
4 × 100m medley relay: USA, 3min 32.06sec

WOMEN
50m freestyle: Therese Alshammar (Sweden), 24.14sec
100m freestyle: Alexsandra Gerasimenya (Belarus) and
Jeanette Ottesen (Denmark), 53.45sec
200m freestyle: Federica Pellegrini (Italy), 1min 55.58sec
400m freestyle: Federica Pellegrini (Italy), 4min 01.97sec
800m freestyle: Rebecca Adlington (Great Britain), 8min
17.51sec
1,500m freestyle: Lotte Friis (Denmark), 15min 49.59sec
4 × 100m freestyle relay: Netherlands, 3min 33.96sec
4 × 200m freestyle relay: USA, 7min 46.14sec
50m backstroke: Anastasia Zuyeva (Russia), 27.79sec
100m backstroke: Zhao Jing (China), 59.05sec
200m backstroke: Missy Franklin (USA), 2min 05.10sec
50m breaststroke: Jessica Hardy (USA), 30.19sec
100m breaststroke: Rebecca Soni (USA), 1min 05.05sec
200m breaststroke: Rebecca Soni (USA), 2min 21.47sec
50m butterfly: Inge Dekker (Netherlands), 25.71sec
100m butterfly: Dana Vollmer (USA), 56.87sec
200m butterfly: Jiao Liuyang (China), 2min 05.55sec
200m individual medley: Ye Shiwen (China), 2min 08.90sec
400m individual medley: Elizabeth Beisel (USA), 4min
31.78sec
4 × 100m medley relay: USA, 3min 52.36sec

BRITISH CHAMPIONSHIPS 2011
Manchester, 5–12 March

MEN
50m freestyle: Adam Brown (Hatfield), 22.29sec
100m freestyle: Adam Brown (Hatfield), 49.41sec
200m freestyle: Ross Davenport (Loughborough
University), 1min 48.34sec
400m freestyle: Robert Renwick (Glasgow), 3min 51.90sec
800m freestyle: Tom Allen (Swansea), 8min 00.25sec
1,500m freestyle: David Davies (Cardiff), 15min 06.44sec
50m backstroke: Liam Tancock (Loughborough
University), 24.95sec
100m backstroke: Liam Tancock (Loughborough
University), 53.44sec
200m backstroke: James Goddard (Stockport), 1min
57.08sec
50m breaststroke: Douglas Scott (East Kilbride), 28.74sec
100m breaststroke: Michael Jamieson (Edinburgh
University), 1min 01.31sec
200m breaststroke: Michael Jamieson (Edinburgh
University), 2min 10.42sec

50m butterfly: Jack Marriot (Oxford University), 24.33sec
100m butterfly: Michael Rock (Stockport), 52.70sec
200m butterfly: Michael Rock (Stockport), 1min 56.31sec
200m medley: James Goddard (Stockport), 1min 58.22sec
400m medley: Roberto Pavoni (Loughborough University), 4min 13.37sec

WOMEN
50m freestyle: Francesca Halsall (Loughborough University), 25.08sec
100m freestyle: Francesca Halsall (Loughborough University), 55.01sec
200m freestyle: Rebecca Adlington (Nova), 1min 58.90sec
400m freestyle: Rebecca Adlington (Nova), 4min 02.84sec
800m freestyle: Rebecca Adlington (Nova), 8min 20.23sec
1,500m freestyle: Keri-Anne Payne (Stockport), 16min 06.67sec
50m backstroke: Georgia Davies (Swansea), 28.67sec
100m backstroke: Gemma Spofforth (Portsmouth), 1min 00.52sec
200m backstroke: Stephanie Proud (Chester le Street), 2min 09.41sec
50m breaststroke: Kathryn Johnstone (Edinburgh University), 32.47sec
100m breaststroke: Stacey Tadd (Bath University), 1min 09.97sec
200m breaststroke: Stacey Tadd (Bath University), 2min 28.99sec
50m butterfly: Jessica Sylvester (Nova), 27.37sec
100m butterfly: Ellen Gandy (Beckenham), 57.68sec
200m butterfly: Ellen Gandy (Beckenham), 2min 06.13sec
200m medley: Hannah Miley (Garioch), 2min 12.01sec
400m medley: Hannah Miley (Garioch), 4min 39.12sec

TABLE TENNIS

WORLD CHAMPIONSHIPS 2011
Rotterdam, Netherlands, 8–15 May

Men's singles: Zhang Jike (China) beat Wang Hao (China) 4–2
Women's singles: Ding Ning (China) beat Li Xiaoxia (China) 4–2
Men's doubles: Ma Long and Xu Xin (China) beat Chen Qi and Ma Lin (China) 4–2
Women's doubles: Guo Yue and Li Xiaoxia (China) beat Ding Ning and Guo Yan (China) 4–0

TENNIS

US OPEN CHAMPIONSHIPS 2010
New York, 30 August–13 September

Men's Singles: Rafael Nadal (Spain) beat Novak Djokovic (Serbia) 6–4, 5–7, 6–4, 6–2
Women's Singles: Kim Clijsters (Belgium) beat Vera Zvonareva (Russia) 6–2, 6–1
Men's Doubles: Bob Bryan (USA) and Mike Bryan (USA) beat Rohan Bopanna (India) and Aisam-ul-Haq Qureshi (Pakistan) 7–6, 7–6
Women's Doubles: Vania King (USA) and Yaroslava Shvedova (Kazakhstan) beat Nadia Petrova (Russia) and Liezel Huber (USA) 2–6, 6–4, 7–6
Mixed Doubles: Liezel Huber (USA) and Bob Bryan (USA) beat Kveta Peschke (Czech Republic) and Aisam-ul-Haq Qureshi (Pakistan) 6–4, 6–4

AUSTRALIAN OPEN CHAMPIONSHIPS 2011
Melbourne, 17–30 January

Men's Singles: Novak Djokovic (Serbia) beat Andy Murray (Great Britain) 6–4, 6–2, 6–3
Women's Singles: Kim Clijsters (Belgium) beat Li Na (China) 3–6, 6–3, 6–3
Men's Doubles: Bob Bryan (USA) and Mike Bryan (USA) beat Mahesh Bhupathi (India) and Leander Paes (India) 6–3, 6–4
Women's Doubles: Gisela Dulko (Argentina) and Flavia Pennetta (Italy) beat Victoria Azarenka (Belarus) and Maria Kirilenko (Russia) 2–6, 7–5, 6–1
Mixed Doubles: Katarina Srebotnik (Slovenia) and Daniel Nestor (Canada) beat Chan Yung-jan (Chinese Taipei) and Paul Hanley (Australia) 6–3, 3–6, 10–7

FRENCH OPEN CHAMPIONSHIPS 2011
Paris, 22 May–5 June

Men's Singles: Rafael Nadal (Spain) beat Roger Federer (Switzerland) 7–5, 7–6, 5–7, 6–1
Women's Singles: Li Na (China) beat Francesca Schiavone (Italy) 6–4, 7–6
Men's Doubles: Max Mirnyi (Belarus) and Daniel Nestor (Canada) beat Juan Sebastian Cabal (Colombia) and Eduardo Schwank (Argentina) 7–6, 3–6, 6–4
Women's Doubles: Andrea Hlavackova (Czezh Republic) and Lucie Hradecka (Czech Republic) beat Sania Mirza (India) and Elena Vesnina (Russia) 6–4, 6–3
Mixed Doubles: Casey Dellacqua (Australia) and Scott Lipsky (USA) beat Katarina Srebotnik (Slovenia) and Nenad Zimonjic (Serbia) 7–6, 4–6, 10–7

ALL-ENGLAND CHAMPIONSHIPS 2011
Wimbledon, 20 June–3 July

Men's Singles: Novak Djokovic (Serbia) beat Rafael Nadal (Spain) 6–4, 6–1, 1–6, 6–3
Ladies' Singles: Petra Kvitova (Czech Republic) beat Maria Sharapova (Russia) 6–3, 6–4
Men's Doubles: Bob Bryan (USA) and Mike Bryan (USA) beat Robert Lindstedt (Sweden) and Horia Tecau (Romania) 6–3, 6–4, 7–6
Ladies' Doubles: Kveta Peschke (Czech Republic) and Katarina Srebotnik (Slovenia) beat Sabine Lisicki (Germany) and Samantha Stosur (Australia) 6–3, 6–1
Mixed Doubles: Jurgen Melzer (Austria) and Iveta Benesova (Czech Republic) beat Mahesh Bhupathi (India) and Elena Vesnina (Russia) 6–3, 6–2

TEAM CHAMPIONSHIPS
Davis Cup final 2010: Serbia beat France 3–2
Fed Cup final 2010: Italy beat USA 3–1

2010 (XIX) COMMONWEALTH GAMES

New Delhi, India, 3–14 October 2010

ARCHERY

MEN
Recurve Individual: Rahul Banerjee (India)
Recurve Team: Australia
Compound Individual: Duncan Busby (England)
Compound Team: England

WOMEN
Recurve Individual: Deepika Kumari (India)
Recurve Team: India
Compound Individual: Nicky Hunt (England)
Compound Team: England

ATHLETICS

MEN
100m: Lerone Clarke (Jamaica), 10.12sec
200m: Leon Baptiste (England), 20.45sec
400m: Mark Mutai (Kenya), 45.44sec
800m: Boaz Lalang (Kenya), 1min 46.60sec
1,500m: Silas Kiplagat (Kenya), 3min 41.78sec
5,000m: Moses Kipsiro (Uganda), 13min 31.25sec
10,000m: Moses Kipsiro (Uganda), 27min 57.39sec
Marathon: John Kelai (Kenya), 2hr 14min 35sec
20km Walk: Jared Tallent (Australia), 1hr 22min 18sec
3,000mSt: Richard Mateelong (Kenya), 8min 16.39sec
110mH: Andy Turner (England), 13.38sec
400mH: Dai Greene (Wales), 48.52sec
4 × 100m: England, 38.74sec
4 × 400m: Australia, 3min 03.30sec
High Jump: Donald Thomas (Bahamas), 2.32m
Pole Vault: Steve Hooker (Australia), 5.60m
Long Jump: Fabrice Lapierre (Australia), 8.30m
Triple Jump: Tosin Oke (Nigeria), 17.16m
Shot: Dylan Armstrong (Canada), 21.02m
Discus: Benn Harradine (Australia), 65.45m
Hammer: Christiaan Harmse (South Africa), 73.15m
Javelin: Jarrod Bannister (Australia), 81.71m
Decathlon: Jamie Adjetey-Nelson (Canada), 8,070pts

WOMEN
100m: Natasha Mayers (St Vincent), 11.73sec
200m: Cydonie Mothersille (Cayman Islands), 22.89sec
400m: Amantle Montsho (Botswana), 50.10sec
800m: Nancy Langat (Kenya), 2min 00.01sec
1500m: Nancy Langat (Kenya), 4min 05.26sec
5000m: Vivian Cheruiyot (Kenya), 15min 55.12sec
10,000m: Grace Momanyi (Kenya), 32min 34.11sec
Marathon: Irene Jeroctich (Kenya), 2hr 34min 32sec
20km Walk: Jo Jackson (England), 1hr 34min 22sec
3,000mSt: Milcah Chemos Cheywa (Kenya), 9min 40.96sec
100mH: Sally Pearson (Australia), 12.67sec
400mH: Muizat Ajoke Odumosu (Nigeria), 55.28sec
4 × 100m: England, 44.19sec
4 × 400m: India, 3min 27.77sec
High Jump: Nicole Forrester (Canada), 1.91m
Pole Vault: Alana Boyd (Australia), 4.40m
Long Jump: Alice Falaiye (Canada), 6.50m
Triple Jump: Trecia Smith (Jamaica), 14.19m
Shot: Valerie Adams (New Zealand), 20.47m
Discus: Krishna Poonia (India), 61.51m
Hammer: Sultana Frizell (Canada), 68.57m
Javelin: Sunette Viljoen (South Africa), 62.34m
Heptathlon: Louise Hazel (England), 6,156pts

BADMINTON

Men's Singles: Lee Chong Wei (Malaysia)
Women's Singles: Saina Nehwal (India)
Men's Doubles: Malaysia
Women's Doubles: India
Mixed Doubles: Malaysia
Team Event: Malaysia

BOXING

Light Flyweight (49kg): Patrick Barnes (N Ireland)
Flyweight (52kg): Suranjoy Singh (India)
Bantamweight (56kg): Manju Wanniarachchi (Sri Lanka)
Lightweight (60kg): Tom Stalker (England)
Light-welterweight (64kg): Manoj Kumar (India)
Welterweight (69kg): Patrick Gallagher (N Ireland)
Middleweight (75kg): Eamonn O'Kane (N Ireland)
Light-heavyweight (81kg): Callum Johnson (Scotland)
Heavyweight (91kg): Simon Vallily (England)
Super-heavyweight (91kg+): Paramjeet Samota (India)

CYCLING

MEN
Sprint: Shane Perkins (Australia)
Team Sprint: Australia
1,000m Time Trial: Scott Sunderland (Australia), 1min 01.41sec
Keirin: Josiah Ng (Malaysia)
4,000m Individual Pursuit: Jack Bobridge (Australia), 4min 17.49sec
4,000m Team Pursuit: Australia, 3min 55.42sec
20km Scratch Race: Cameron Meyer (Australia), 22min 57.64sec
Points Race: Cameron Meyer (Australia), 89pts
40km Road Time Trial: David Millar (Scotland), 47min 18.66sec
168km Road Race: Allan Davis (Australia), 3hr 49min 48sec

WOMEN
Sprint: Anna Meares (Australia)
Team Sprint: Australia
500m Time Trial: Anna Meares (Australia), 33.75sec
3,000m Individual Pursuit: Alison Shanks (New Zealand), 3min 30.87sec
10km Scratch Race: Megan Dunn (Australia), 13min 01.71sec
Points Race: Megan Dunn (Australia), 45pts
29km Road Time Trial: Tara Whitten (Canada), 38min 59.30sec
112km Road Race: Rochelle Gilmore (Australia), 2hr 49min 30sec

DIVING

MEN
1m Springboard Individual: Alexandre Despatie (Canada), 468.15pts
3m Springboard Individual: Alexandre Despatie (Canada), 513.75pts
3m Springboard Synch: Canada, 430.50pts
10m Platform Individual: Tom Daley (England), 538.35pts
10m Platform Synch: England, 439.65pts

WOMEN
1m Springboard Individual: Jennifer Abel (Canada), 301.75pts
3m Springboard Individual: Sharleen Stratton (Australia), 376.00pts
3m Springboard Synch: Canada, 318.90pts
10m Platform Individual: Pandelela Rinong Pamg (Malaysia), 371.05pts
10m Platform Synch: Australia, 335.76pts

GYMNASTICS – ARTISTIC

MEN
Team: Australia, 259.050pts
Individual All-Around: Luke Folwell (England), 85.550pts
Floor Exercises: Thomas Pichler (Australia), 14.675pts
Parallel Bars: Joshua Jefferis (Australia), 14.625pts
Horizontal Bar: Dimitris Krasias (Cyprus), 13.900pts
Pommel Horse: Prashanth Sellathurai (Australia), 15.500pts
Vault: Luke Folwell (England), 15.762pts
Rings: Samuel Offord (Australia), 14.825pts

WOMEN
Team: Australia, 163.700pts
Individual All-Around: Lauren Mitchell (Australia),
    58.200pts
Floor Exercises: Imogen Cairns (England), 14.200pts
Uneven Bars: Lauren Mitchell (Australia), 14.150pts
Beam: Lauren Mitchell (Australia), 14.475pts
Vault: Imogen Cairns (England), 13.725pts

GYMNASTICS – RHYTHMIC

WOMEN
Team: Australia, 235.775pts
Individual All-Around: Naazmi Johnston (Australia),
    100.100pts
Rope: Chrystalleni Trikomiti (Cyprus), 25.800pts
Ball: Naazmi Johnston (Australia), 25.100pts
Hoop: Elaine Koon (Malaysia), 25.300pts
Ribbon: Chrystalleni Trikomiti (Cyprus), 25.700pts

HOCKEY
 Men: Australia
 Women: Australia

LAWN BOWLS

MEN
Singles: Rob Weale (Wales)
Pairs: South Africa
Triples: South Africa

WOMEN
Singles: Natalia Melmore (England)
Pairs: England
Triples: South Africa

NETBALL
New Zealand

RUGBY 7S
New Zealand

SHOOTING

MEN
10m Air Pistol Singles: Omkar Singh (India), 681.8pts
10m Air Pistol Pairs: India, 1,163pts
10m Air Rifle Singles: Gagan Narang (India), 703.6pts
10m Air Rifle Pairs: India, 1,193pts
25m Standard Pistol Singles: Bin Gai (Singapore), 570pts
25m Standard Pistol Pairs: Singapore, 1,116pts
25m Rapid Fire Pistol Singles: Vijay Kumar (India), 787.5pts
25m Rapid Fire Pistol Pairs: India 1,162pts
25m Centre Fire Pistol Singles: Harpreet Singh (India),
    580pts
25m Centre Fire Pistol Pairs: India, 1,159pts

50m Pistol Singles: Omkar Singh (India), 653.6pts
50m Pistol Pairs: Singapore, 1,094pts
50m Rifle Prone Singles: Jonathan Hammond (Scotland),
    696.9pts
50m Rifle Prone Pairs: Scotland, 1,181pts
50m Rifle 3-Positions Singles: Gagan Narang (India),
    1,262.2pts
50m Rifle 3-Positions Pairs: India, 2,325pts
Trap Singles: Aaron Heading (England), 147pts
Trap Pairs: Australia, 198pts
Double Trap Singles: Stevan Walton (England), 190pts
Double Trap Pairs: England, 189pts
Skeet Singles: Richard Brickell (England), 144pts
Skeet Pairs: Cyprus, 194pts

WOMEN
10m Air Pistol Singles: Pei Chin Ng (Malaysia), 481.9pts
10m Air Pistol Pairs: India, 759pts
10m Air Rifle Singles: Jasmine Xiang Wei Ser (Singapore),
    501.7pts
10m Air Rifle Pairs: Malaysia, 793pts
25m Sport Pistol Singles: Anisa Sayyed (India), 786.8pts
25m Sport Pistol Pairs: India, 1,156pts
50m Rifle Prone Singles: Jen McIntosh (Scotland), 597pts
50m Rifle Prone Pairs: Scotland, 1,169pts
50m Rifle 3-Positions Singles: Alethea Sedgman (Australia),
    197pts
50m Rifle 3-Positions Pairs: Singapore, 1,149pts
Trap Singles: Anita North (England), 93pts
Trap Pairs: Australia, 93pts

OPEN
Full-Bore Rifle Singles: Parag Patel (England), 396pts
Full-Bore Rifle Pairs: New Zealand, 588pts

SQUASH
Men's Singles: Nick Matthew (England)
Men's Doubles: England
Women's Singles: Nicol David (Malaysia)
Women's Doubles: New Zealand
Mixed Doubles: Australia

SWIMMING

MEN
50m Freestyle: Brent Hayden (Canada), 22.01sec
100m Freestyle: Brent Hayden (Canada), 47.98sec
200m Freestyle: Robbie Renwick (Scotland), 1min
    47.85sec
400m Freestyle: Ryan Cochrane (Canada), 3min 48.48sec
1,500m Freestyle: Ryan Cochrane (Canada), 15min
    01.49sec
4 × 100m Freestyle: Australia, 3min 13.92sec
4 × 200m Freestyle: Australia, 7min 10.29sec
50m Backstroke: Liam Tancock (England), 24.62sec
100m Backstroke: Liam Tancock (England), 53.59sec
200m Backstroke: James Goddard (England), 1min
    55.58sec
50m Breaststroke: Cameron van der Burgh (South Africa),
    27.18sec
100m Breaststroke: Cameron van der Burgh (South Africa),
    1min 00.10sec
200m Breaststroke: Brenton Rickard (Australia), 2min
    10.89sec
50m Butterfly: Jason Dunford (Kenya), 23.35sec
100m Butterfly: Geoff Huegill (Australia), 51.69sec
200m Butterfly: Chad Guy Dertrand le Clos (South
    Africa), 1min 56.48sec

200m Individual Medley: James Goddard (England), 1min 58.10sec
400m Individual Medley: Chad le Clos (South Africa), 4min 13.25sec
4 × 100m Medley: Australia, 3min 33.15sec

WOMEN
50m Freestyle: Yolane Kukla (Australia), 24.86sec
100m Freestyle: Alicia Coutts (Australia), 54.09sec
200m Freestyle: Kylie Palmer (Australia), 1min 57.50sec
400m Freestyle: Rebecca Adlington (England), 4min 05.68sec
800m Freestyle: Rebecca Adlington (England), 8min 24.69sec
4 × 100m Freestyle: Australia, 3min 36.36sec
4 × 200m Freestyle: Australia, 7min 53.71sec
50m Backstroke: Sophie Edington (Australia), 28.00sec
100m Backstroke: Emily Seebohm (Australia), 59.79sec
200m Backstroke: Meagen Nay (Australia), 2min 07.56sec
50m Breaststroke: Leiston Pickett (Australia), 30.84sec
100m Breaststroke: Leisel Jones (Australia), 1min 05.84sec
200m Breaststroke: Leisel Jones (Australia), 2min 25.38sec
50m Butterfly: Francesca Halsall (England), 26.24sec
100m Butterfly: Alicia Coutts (Australia), 57.57sec
200m Butterfly: Jessicah Schipper (Australia), 2min 07.04sec
200m Individual Medley: Alicia Coutts (Australia), 2min 09.70sec
400m Individual Medley: Hannah Miley (Scotland), 4min 38.83sec
4 × 100m Medley: Australia, 3min 56.99sec

SYNCHRONISED SWIMMING
Women's Solo: Marie-Pier Boudreau Gagnon (Canada), 95.334pts
Women's Duet: Canada, 95.084pts

TABLE TENNIS
Men's Singles: Yang Zi (Singapore)
Women's Singles: Feng Tianwei (Singapore)
Men's Doubles: India
Women's Doubles: Singapore
Mixed Doubles: Singapore
Men's Team: Singapore
Women's Team: India

TENNIS
Men's Singles: Somdev Devvarman (India)
Women's Singles: Anastasia Rodionova (Australia)
Men's Doubles: Australia
Women's Doubles: Australia
Mixed Doubles: Scotland

WEIGHTLIFTING

MEN
56kg: Amirul Ibrahim (Malaysia), 257kg
62kg: Aricco Jumitih (Malaysia), 276kg
69kg: Ravi Kumar (India), 321kg
77kg: Yukio Peter (Nauru), 333kg
85kg: Simplice Ribouem (Australia), 333kg
94kg: Faavae Faauliuli (Samoa), 334kg
105kg: Niusila Opeloge (Samoa), 338kg
105kg+: Damon Kelly (Australia), 397kg

WOMEN
48kg: Augustina Nwaokolo (Nigeria), 175kg
53kg: Marilou Dozois Prevost (Canada), 182kg
58kg: Renu Bala Chanu Yumnam (India), 197kg
63kg: Obioma Okoli (Nigeria), 211kg
69kg: Christine Girard (Canada), 235kg
75kg: Hadiza Zakari (Nigeria), 239kg
75kg+: Ele Opeloge (Samoa), 285kg

WRESTLING – FREESTYLE

MEN
55kg: Azhar Hussain (Pakistan)
60kg: Yogeshwar Dutt (India)
66kg: Sushil Kumar (India)
74kg: Narsingh Yadav (India)
84kg: Muhammad Inam (Pakistan)
96kg: Sinvie Boltic (Nigeria)
120kg: Arjan Bhullar (Canada)

WOMEN
48kg: Carol Huynh (Canada)
51kg: Ifeoma Nwoye (Nigeria)
55kg: Geeta (India)
59kg: Alka Tomar (India)
63kg: Justine Bouchard (Canada)
67kg: Anita (India)
72kg: Ohenewa Akuffo (Canada)

WRESTLING – GRECO-ROMAN
55kg: Rajender Kumar (India)
60kg: Ravinder Singh (India)
66kg: Myroslav Dykun (England)
74kg: Sanjay (India)
84kg: Efionayi Agbonavbare (Nigeria)
96kg: Anil Kumar (India)
120kg: Ivan Popov (Australia)

SPORTS RECORDS

ATHLETICS WORLD RECORDS
As at 30 August 2011

All the world records given below have been accepted by the International Amateur Athletic Federation. Fully automatic timing to 1/100th second is mandatory up to and including 400 metres. For distances up to and including 10,000 metres, records will be accepted to 1/100th second if timed automatically, and to 1/10th if hand timing is used.

MEN

TRACK EVENTS	hr	min	sec
100m			9.58
Usain Bolt (Jamaica) 2009			
200m			19.19
Usain Bolt (Jamaica) 2009			
400m			43.18
Michael Johnson (USA) 1999			
800m		1	41.01
David Rudisha (Kenya) 2010			
1,000m		2	11.96
Noah Ngeny (Kenya) 1999			
1,500m		3	26.00
Hicham El Guerrouj (Morocco) 1998			
1 mile		3	43.13
Hicham El Guerrouj (Morocco) 1999			
2,000m		4	44.79
Hicham El Guerrouj (Morocco) 1999			
3,000m		7	20.67
Daniel Komen (Kenya) 1996			
5,000m		12	37.35
Kenenisa Bekele (Ethiopia) 2004			
10,000m		26	17.53
Kenenisa Bekele (Ethiopia) 2005			
20,000m		56	26.0
Haile Gebrselassie (Ethiopia) 2007			
21,285m	1	00	00.0
Haile Gebrselassie (Ethiopia) 2007			
25,000m	1	12	25.4
Moses Mosop (Kenya) 2011			
30,000m	1	26	47.4
Moses Mosop (Kenya) 2011			
Marathon	2	03	59
Haile Gebrselassie (Ethiopia) 2009			
110m hurdles (1.07m)			12.87
Dayron Robles (Cuba) 2008			
400m hurdles (0.97m)			46.78
Kevin Young (USA) 1992			
3,000m St		7	53.63
Saif Saeed Shaheen (Qatar) 2004			

RELAYS		min	sec
4 × 100m			37.04
Jamaica, 2011			
4 × 200m		1	18.68
USA, 1994			
4 × 400m		2	54.29
USA, 1993			
4 × 800m		7	02.43
Kenya, 2006			

		min	sec
4 × 1,500m		14	36.23
Kenya, 2009			

FIELD EVENTS	m	ft	in
High jump	2.45	8	0½
Javier Sotomayor (Cuba) 1993			
Pole vault	6.14	20	1¾
Sergei Bubka (Ukraine) 1994			
Long jump	8.95	29	4½
Mike Powell (USA) 1991			
Triple jump	18.29	60	0¼
Jonathan Edwards (GB) 1995			
Shot	23.12	75	10¼
Randy Barnes (USA) 1990			
Discus	74.08	243	0
Jürgen Schult (GDR) 1986			
Hammer	86.74	284	7
Yuriy Sedykh (USSR) 1986			
Javelin	98.48	323	1
Jan Zelezny (Czech Rep.) 1996			
Decathlon†			9,026pts
Roman Sebrle (Czech Rep.) 2001			

† Ten events comprising 100m, long jump, shot, high jump, 400m, 110m hurdles, discus, pole vault, javelin, 1,500m

WALKING (TRACK)	hr	min	sec
20,000m	1	17	25.6
Bernard Segura (Mexico) 1994			
29,572m	2	00	00.0
Maurizio Damilano (Italy) 1992			
30,000m	2	01	44.1
Maurizio Damilano (Italy) 1992			
50,000m	3	35	27.2
Yohann Diniz (France) 2011			

WOMEN

TRACK EVENTS	hr	min	sec
100m			10.49
Florence Griffith-Joyner (USA) 1988			
200m			21.34
Florence Griffith-Joyner (USA) 1988			
400m			47.60
Marita Koch (GDR) 1985			
800m		1	53.28
Jarmila Kratochvilova (Czechoslovakia) 1983			
1,500m		3	50.46
Qu Yunxia (China) 1993			
1 mile		4	12.56
Svetlana Masterkova (Russia) 1996			
3,000m		8	06.11
Wang Junxia (China) 1993			
5,000m		14	11.15
Tirunesh Dibaba (Ethiopia) 2008			
10,000m		29	31.78
Wang Junxia (China) 1993			
Marathon	2	15	25
Paula Radcliffe (GB) 2003			
100m hurdles (0.84m)			12.21
Yordanka Donkova (Bulgaria) 1988			
400m hurdles (0.76m)			52.34
Yuliya Pechonkina (Russia) 2003			
3,000m St		8	58.81
Gulnara Galkina (Russia) 2008			

RELAYS

	min	sec
4 × 100m		41.37
GDR, 1985		
4 × 200m	1	27.46
USA, 2000		
4 × 400m	3	15.17
USSR, 1988		
4 × 800m	7	50.17
USSR, 1984		

FIELD EVENTS

	m	ft	in
High jump	2.09	6	10¼
Stefka Kostadinova (Bulgaria) 1987			
Pole vault	5.06	16	7¼
Yelena Isinbayeva (Russia) 2009			
Long jump	7.52	24	8¼
Galina Chistyakova (USSR) 1988			
Triple jump	15.50	50	10¼
Inessa Kravets (Ukraine) 1995			
Shot	22.63	74	3
Natalya Lisovskaya (USSR) 1987			
Discus	76.80	252	0
Gabriele Reinsch (GDR) 1988			
Hammer	79.42	260	7
Betty Heidler (Germany) 2011			
Javelin (new implement in 1999)	72.28	237	2
Barbora Spotakova (Czech Rep.) 2008			
Heptathlon†	7,291pts		
Jackie Joyner-Kersee (USA) 1986			

† Seven events comprising 100m hurdles, shot, high jump, 200m, long jump, javelin, 800m

ATHLETICS NATIONAL (UK) RECORDS
As at 30 August 2011

Records set anywhere by athletes eligible to represent Great Britain and Northern Ireland.

MEN

TRACK EVENTS	hr	min	sec
100m			9.87
Linford Christie, 1993			
Dwain Chambers, 2002			
200m			19.87
John Regis, 1994			
400m			44.36
Iwan Thomas, 1997			
800m		1	41.73
Sebastian Coe, 1981			
1,000m		2	12.18
Sebastian Coe, 1981			
1,500m		3	29.67
Sebastian Coe, 1985			
1 mile		3	46.32
Steve Cram, 1985			
2,000m		4	51.39
Steve Cram, 1985			
3,000m		7	32.79
David Moorcroft, 1982			
5,000m		12	53.11
Mo Farah, 2011			
10,000m		26	46.57
Mo Farah, 2011			
20,000m		57	28.7
Carl Thackery, 1990			
20,855m	1	00	00.0
Carl Thackery, 1990			
25,000m	1	15	22.6
Ron Hill, 1965			
30,000m	1	31	30.4
Jim Alder, 1970			
Marathon	2	07	13
Steve Jones, 1985			
3,000mSt		8	07.96
Mark Rowland, 1988			
110m hurdles			12.91
Colin Jackson, 1993			
400m hurdles			47.82
Kriss Akabusi, 1992			

RELAYS		min	sec
4 × 100m			37.73
GB team, 1999			
4 × 200m		1	21.29
GB team, 1989			
4 × 400m		2	56.60
GB team, 1996			
4 × 800m		7	03.89
GB team, 1982			

FIELD EVENTS	m	ft	in
High jump	2.37	7	9¼
Steve Smith, 1993			
Pole vault	5.80	19	0¼
Nick Buckfield, 1998			
Long jump	8.35	27	4¾
Chris Tomlinson, 2011			
Triple jump	18.29	60	0¼
Jonathan Edwards, 1995			
Shot	21.92	71	11
Carl Myerscough, 2003			
Discus	67.63	221	10
Lawrence Okoye, 2011			
Hammer	77.54	254	5
Martin Girvan, 1984			
Javelin	91.46	300	1
Steve Backley, 1992			
Decathlon	8,847pts		
Daley Thompson, 1984			

WALKING (TRACK)	hr	min	sec
20,000m	1	23	26.5
Ian McCombie, 1990			
30,000m	2	19	18
Christopher Maddocks, 1984			
50,000m	4	05	44.6
Paul Blagg, 1990			
26,037m	2	00	00.0
Ron Wallwork, 1971			

WOMEN

TRACK EVENTS		min	sec
100m			11.05
Montell Douglas, 2008			
200m			22.10
Kathy Cook, 1984			
400m			49.43
Kathy Cook, 1984			
800m		1	56.21
Kelly Holmes, 1995			
1,500m		3	57.90
Kelly Holmes, 2004			
1 mile		4	17.57
Zola Budd, 1985			
3,000m		8	22.20
Paula Radcliffe, 2002			

		min	sec
5,000m		14	29.11
Paula Radcliffe, 2004			
10,000m		30	01.09
Paula Radcliffe, 2002			
Marathon	2	15	25
Paula Radcliffe, 2003			
100m hurdles			12.56
Tiffany Porter, 2011			
400m hurdles			52.74
Sally Gunnell, 1993			
3,000mSt		9	29.14
Helen Clitheroe, 2008			

RELAYS		min	sec
4 × 100m			42.43
GB team, 1980			
4 × 200m		1	31.57
GB team, 1977			
4 × 400m		3	22.01
GB team, 1991			
4 × 800m		8	23.8
GB team, 1971			

FIELD EVENTS	m	ft	in
High jump	1.95	6	4¾
Diana Elliott, 1982			
Susan Jones, 2001			
Jessica Ennis, 2007			
Pole vault	4.70	15	6
Holly Bleasdale, 2011			
Long jump	6.90	22	7¾
Beverley Kinch, 1983			
Triple jump	15.15	49	8½
Ashia Hansen, 1997			
Shot	19.36	63	6¼
Judy Oakes, 1988			
Discus	67.48	221	5
Margaret Ritchie, 1981			
Hammer	69.59	228	3
Sophie Hitchon, 2011			
Javelin	65.75	215	8
Goldie Sayers, 2008			
Heptathlon			6,831pts
Denise Lewis, 2000			

SWIMMING WORLD RECORDS

As at 30 August 2011

MEN	min	sec
50m freestyle		20.91
Cesar Cielo Filho (Brazil)		
100m freestyle		46.91
Cesar Cielo Filho (Brazil)		
200m freestyle	1	42.00
Paul Biedermann (Germany)		
400m freestyle	3	40.07
Paul Biedermann (Germany)		
800m freestyle	7	32.12
Zhang Lin (China)		
1,500m freestyle	14	34.14
Sun Yang (China)		
50m breaststroke		26.67
Cameron Van Der Burgh (South Africa)		
100m breaststroke		58.58
Brenton Rickard (Australia)		

	min	sec
200m breaststroke	2	07.31
Christian Sprenger (Australia)		
50m butterfly		22.43
Rafael Munoz (Spain)		
100m butterfly		49.82
Michael Phelps (USA)		
200m butterfly	1	51.51
Michael Phelps (USA)		
50m backstroke		24.04
Liam Tancock (GB)		
100m backstroke		51.94
Aaron Peirsol (USA)		
200m backstroke	1	51.92
Aaron Peirsol (USA)		
200m medley	1	54.10
Ryan Lochte (USA)		
400m medley	4	03.84
Michael Phelps (USA)		
4 × 100m freestyle relay	3	08.24
USA		
4 × 200m freestyle relay	6	58.55
USA		
4 × 100m medley relay	3	27.28
USA		

WOMEN	min	sec
50m freestyle		23.73
Britta Steffen (Germany)		
100m freestyle		52.07
Britta Steffen (Germany)		
200m freestyle	1	52.98
Federica Pellegrini (Italy)		
400m freestyle	3	59.15
Federica Pellegrini (Italy)		
800m freestyle	8	14.10
Rebecca Adlington (GB)		
1,500m freestyle	15	42.54
Kate Ziegler (USA)		
50m breaststroke		29.80
Jessica Hardy (USA)		
100m breaststroke	1	04.45
Jessica Hardy (USA)		
200m breaststroke	2	20.12
Annamay Pierse (Canada)		
50m butterfly		25.07
Therese Alshammar (Sweden)		
100m butterfly		56.06
Sarah Sjostrom (Sweden)		
200m butterfly	2	01.81
Liu Zigi (China)		
50m backstroke		27.06
Zhao Jing (China)		
100m backstroke		58.12
Gemma Spofforth (GB)		
200m backstroke	2	04.81
Kirsty Coventry (Zimbabwe)		
200m medley	2	06.15
Ariana Kukors (USA)		
400m medley	4	29.45
Stephanie Rice (Australia)		
4 × 100m freestyle relay	3	31.72
The Netherlands		
4 × 200m freestyle relay	7	42.08
China		
4 × 100m medley relay	3	52.19
China		

TIME AND SPACE

ASTRONOMY

TIME MEASUREMENT AND CALENDARS

TIDES AND TIDAL PREDICTIONS

ASTRONOMY

The following pages give astronomical data for each month of the year 2012. There are four pages of data for each month. All data are given for 0h Greenwich Mean Time (GMT), ie at the midnight at the beginning of the day named. This applies also to data for the months when British Summer Time is in operation (for dates, *see* below).

The astronomical data are given in a form suitable for observation with the naked eye or with a small telescope. These data do not attempt to replace the *Astronomical Almanac* for professional astronomers.

A fuller explanation of how to use the astronomical data is given on pages 1279–81.

CALENDAR FOR EACH MONTH

The calendar for each month comprises dates of general interest plus the dates of birth or death of well-known people. For key religious, civil and legal dates *see* page 9. For details of flag-flying days *see* page 23. For royal birthdays *see* pages 23 and 24–5. Public holidays are given in italics. *See* also pages 10 and 11.

Fuller explanations of the various calendars can be found under Time Measurement and Calendars.

The zodiacal signs through which the Sun is passing during each month are illustrated. The date of transition from one sign to the next, to the nearest hour, is given under Astronomical Phenomena.

JULIAN DATE

The Julian date on 2012 January 0.0 is 2455926.5. To find the Julian date for any other date in 2012 (at 0h GMT), add the day-of-the-year number on the extreme right of the calendar for each month to the Julian date for January 0.0.

SEASONS

The seasons are defined astronomically as follows:

Spring from the vernal equinox to the summer solstice
Summer from the summer solstice to the autumnal equinox
Autumn from the autumnal equinox to the winter solstice
Winter from the winter solstice to the vernal equinox

The time when seasons start in 2012 (to the nearest hour) are:

Northern Hemisphere

Vernal equinox	March 20d 05h GMT
Summer solstice	June 20d 23h GMT
Autumnal equinox	September 22d 15h GMT
Winter solstice	December 21d 11h GMT

Southern Hemisphere

Autumnal equinox	March 20d 05h GMT
Winter solstice	June 20d 23h GMT
Vernal equinox	September 22d 15h GMT
Summer solstice	December 21d 11h GMT

The longest day of the year, measured from sunrise to sunset, is at the summer solstice. The longest day in the United Kingdom will fall on 20 June in 2012.

The shortest day of the year is at the winter solstice. The shortest day in the United Kingdom will fall on 21 December in 2012.

The equinox is the point at which day and night are of equal length all over the world.

In popular parlance, the seasons in the northern hemisphere comprise the following months:

Spring	March, April, May
Summer	June, July, August
Autumn	September, October, November
Winter	December, January, February

BRITISH SUMMER TIME

British Summer Time is the legal time for general purposes during the period in which it is in operation (*see also* pages 1283–4). During this period, clocks are kept one hour ahead of Greenwich Mean Time. The hour of changeover is 01h Greenwich Mean Time. The duration of Summer Time in 2012 is from March 25 01h GMT to October 28 01h GMT.

JANUARY 2012

FIRST MONTH, 31 DAYS. *Janus*, god of the portal, facing two ways, past and future

1	Sunday	Giuseppe Piazzi, Italian astronomer, discovered the first asteroid, Ceres 1801	day 1
2	Monday	Construction of the Brooklyn Bridge, New York, commenced 1870	week 1 day 2
3	Tuesday	The first battery-powered watch, the Hamilton Electric 500, was released 1957	3
4	Wednesday	Sir Isaac Newton, physicist and mathematician who discovered the law of gravitation *b.* 1642	4
5	Thursday	X-rays first demonstrated by German physicist Wilhelm Konrad von Röntgen 1896	5
6	Friday	Demonstration by Samuel Morse of the first electric telegraph system 1838	6
7	Saturday	Nikola Tesla, Serbian inventor, mechanical and electrical engineer *d.* 1943	7
8	Sunday	Professor Stephen Hawking, theoretical physicist and cosmologist *b.* 1942	8
9	Monday	Jean Pierre Blanchard made first successful balloon flight in the USA 1793	week 2 day 9
10	Tuesday	London Underground railway opened, carrying 30,000 passengers on the first day 1863	10
11	Wednesday	Insulin was used to successfully treat diabetes for the first time 1922	11
12	Thursday	Jean Joseph Lenoir, inventor of the first practical internal combustion engine *b.* 1822	12
13	Friday	The Wham-O Company introduced the Pluto Platter, later to become famous as the Frisbee 1957	13
14	Saturday	Edmond Halley, Astronomer Royal after whom Halley's Comet is named *d.* 1742	14
15	Sunday	Construction completed of the Pentagon in Virginia, consisting of 17.5 miles of corridors 1943	15
16	Monday	Nylon, the 'miracle fibre', was patented by Wallace Carothers of the Dupont company 1937	week 3 day 16
17	Tuesday	Benjamin Franklin, author, statesman, inventor and scientist *b.* 1706	17
18	Wednesday	Airbus' 840-passenger A380, the world's biggest passenger jet, was unveiled in France 2005	18
19	Thursday	James Watt, inventor after whom the unit of power is named *b.* 1736	19
20	Friday	Dr Edwin 'Buzz' Aldrin, the second man to walk on the Moon *b.* 1930	20
21	Saturday	First Concorde flight carrying commercial passengers 1976	21
22	Sunday	Dr Roberta Bondar became the first Canadian woman in space 1992	22
23	Monday	Charles King, biochemist who discovered and isolated vitamin C *d.* 1988	week 4 day 23
24	Tuesday	The Macintosh 128K, the first computer built by Apple Macintosh, was released 1984	24
25	Wednesday	Robert Boyle, physicist and chemist, most widely known for Boyle's Law *b.* 1627	25
26	Thursday	The electric dental drill was patented by George F. Green of Kalamazoo, Michigan 1875	26
27	Friday	John Logie Baird, electrical engineer, gave the first public demonstration of television 1926	27
28	Saturday	The space shuttle *Challenger* exploded shortly after lift-off, killing all crew 1986	28
29	Sunday	Lewis Urry, chemical engineer who invented the alkaline and lithium battery *b.* 1927	29
30	Monday	Orville Wright, aviation pioneer and aeroplane inventor *d.* 1948	week 5 day 30
31	Tuesday	Ham, a chimp, returned safely to Earth after being sent into space 1961	31

ASTRONOMICAL PHENOMENA

d h
2 23 Jupiter in conjunction with Moon. Jupiter 5°S.
5 01 Earth at perihelion (147 million km.)
14 01 Mars in conjunction with Moon. Mars 8°N.
16 15 Saturn in conjunction with Moon. Saturn 6°N.
20 16 Sun's longitude 300° ♒
22 12 Mercury in conjunction with Moon. Mercury 5°S.
24 01 Mars at stationary point
26 10 Venus in conjunction with Moon. Venus 6°S.
30 11 Jupiter in conjunction with Moon. Jupiter 4°S.

CONSTELLATIONS
The following constellations are near the meridian at

	d	h		d	h
December	1	24	January	16	21
December	16	23	February	1	20
January	1	22	February	15	19

Draco (below the Pole), Ursa Minor (below the Pole), Camelopardalis, Perseus, Auriga, Taurus, Orion, Eridanus and Lepus

THE MOON

Phases, Apsides and Node	d	h	m
☽ First Quarter	1	06	15
○ Full Moon	9	07	30
☾ Last Quarter	16	09	08
● New Moon	23	07	39
☽ First Quarter	31	04	10

Apogee (404,618km)	2	20	17
Perigee (369,851km)	17	21	16
Apogee (404,363km)	30	17	42

MINIMA OF ALGOL

d	h	d	h	d	h
3	00.3	14	11.5	25	22.8
5	21.1	17	08.4	28	19.7
8	17.9	20	05.2	31	16.5
11	14.7	23	02.0		

Mean longitude of ascending node on January 1, 253°

THE SUN

s.d. 16′.3

Day	Right Ascension			Dec.		Equation of time		Rise 52°		Rise 56°		Transit		Set 52°		Set 56°		Sidereal time			Transit of first point of Aries		
	h	m	s	°	′	m	s	h	m	h	m	h	m	h	m	h	m	h	m	s	h	m	s
1	18	43	20	23	04	−3	05	8	08	8	31	12	03	15	59	15	36	6	40	15	17	16	54
2	18	47	45	22	59	−3	33	8	08	8	31	12	04	16	00	15	37	6	44	12	17	12	58
3	18	52	10	22	54	−4	01	8	08	8	31	12	04	16	01	15	38	6	48	09	17	09	02
4	18	56	34	22	48	−4	29	8	08	8	30	12	05	16	02	15	39	6	52	05	17	05	06
5	19	00	58	22	42	−4	56	8	07	8	30	12	05	16	03	15	41	6	56	02	17	01	11
6	19	05	21	22	35	−5	23	8	07	8	29	12	06	16	04	15	42	6	59	58	16	57	15
7	19	09	44	22	28	−5	49	8	07	8	29	12	06	16	06	15	44	7	03	55	16	53	19
8	19	14	07	22	21	−6	15	8	06	8	28	12	06	16	07	15	45	7	07	51	16	49	23
9	19	18	29	22	13	−6	41	8	06	8	27	12	07	16	08	15	47	7	11	48	16	45	27
10	19	22	50	22	04	−7	06	8	05	8	27	12	07	16	10	15	48	7	15	44	16	41	31
11	19	27	11	21	56	−7	30	8	05	8	26	12	08	16	11	15	50	7	19	41	16	37	35
12	19	31	31	21	46	−7	54	8	04	8	25	12	08	16	13	15	52	7	23	38	16	33	39
13	19	35	51	21	37	−8	17	8	03	8	24	12	08	16	14	15	53	7	27	34	16	29	43
14	19	40	10	21	27	−8	40	8	02	8	23	12	09	16	16	15	55	7	31	31	16	25	47
15	19	44	29	21	16	−9	02	8	02	8	22	12	09	16	17	15	57	7	35	27	16	21	51
16	19	48	47	21	05	−9	23	8	01	8	21	12	10	16	19	15	59	7	39	24	16	17	56
17	19	53	04	20	54	−9	44	8	00	8	20	12	10	16	20	16	01	7	43	20	16	14	00
18	19	57	21	20	42	−10	04	7	59	8	18	12	10	16	22	16	03	7	47	17	16	10	04
19	20	01	37	20	30	−10	23	7	58	8	17	12	11	16	24	16	05	7	51	14	16	06	08
20	20	05	52	20	18	−10	42	7	57	8	16	12	11	16	25	16	07	7	55	10	16	02	12
21	20	10	06	20	05	−11	00	7	56	8	14	12	11	16	27	16	09	7	59	07	15	58	16
22	20	14	20	19	51	−11	17	7	55	8	13	12	11	16	29	16	11	8	03	03	15	54	20
23	20	18	33	19	38	−11	33	7	53	8	11	12	12	16	31	16	13	8	07	00	15	50	24
24	20	22	45	19	24	−11	49	7	52	8	10	12	12	16	32	16	15	8	10	56	15	46	28
25	20	26	57	19	09	−12	04	7	51	8	08	12	12	16	34	16	17	8	14	53	15	42	32
26	20	31	08	18	55	−12	18	7	50	8	07	12	12	16	36	16	19	8	18	49	15	38	36
27	20	35	17	18	40	−12	31	7	48	8	05	12	13	16	38	16	21	8	22	46	15	34	40
28	20	39	26	18	24	−12	44	7	47	8	03	12	13	16	39	16	23	8	26	43	15	30	45
29	20	43	35	18	09	−12	56	7	45	8	01	12	13	16	41	16	25	8	30	39	15	26	49
30	20	47	42	17	53	−13	06	7	44	8	00	12	13	16	43	16	27	8	34	36	15	22	53
31	20	51	49	17	36	−13	16	7	42	7	58	12	13	16	45	16	30	8	38	32	15	18	57

DURATION OF TWILIGHT (in minutes)

Latitude	52°	56°	52°	56°	52°	56°	52°	56°
	1 January		11 January		21 January		31 January	
Civil	41	47	40	45	38	43	37	41
Nautical	84	96	82	93	80	90	78	87
Astronomical	125	141	123	138	120	134	117	130

THE NIGHT SKY

Mercury begins the year as a difficult morning object visible low above the south-eastern horizon at about the beginning of morning civil twilight. Its magnitude is then −0.4. It is getting closer to the Sun and is unlikely to be visible after the first two days of the month. Unfortunately its low declination means that observers in Scotland will not be able to see it at all.

Venus, magnitude −0.4, is a magnificent evening object in the south-western sky, and by the end of the month can still be seen for as long as 3 hours after sunset. On the evening of the 26th the thin waxing crescent Moon passes 5 degrees north of the planet.

Mars begins the year as a morning object, though by the end of the month it is becoming visible low above the eastern horizon shortly after 21h. During January its magnitude brightens from +0.2 to −0.5. Mars is moving eastwards from Leo into Virgo, reaching its first stationary point on the 24th, commencing its retrograde motion. On the morning of the 14th the waning gibbous Moon passes about 9 degrees south of the planet.

Jupiter, magnitude −2.5, is an evening object, visible in the southern sky, shortly after sunset. Jupiter is in the constellation of Aries. On the evening of the 2nd, the waxing Moon, just after First Quarter, passes 4 degrees north of the planet: there is a repeat performance on the 30th.

Saturn, magnitude +0.7, is a morning object, visible in the south-eastern sky after about 03h at the beginning of the month and 01h by the end of the month. Saturn is moving very slowly eastwards in the constellation of Virgo, and is easily located since it is less than 10 degrees west-north-west of Spica. On the 16th the waning Moon, at Last Quarter, passes 7 degrees south of the planet.

THE MOON

Day	R.A. h	R.A. m	Dec. °	Hor. Par. '	Semi-diam. '	Sun's Co-Long. °	PA of Br. Limb °	Ph. %	Age d	Rise 52° h	Rise 52° m	Rise 56° h	Rise 56° m	Transit h	Transit m	Set 52° h	Set 52° m	Set 56° h	Set 56° m
1	0	18	+ 7.3	54.5	14.8	354	246	48	7.3	11	10	11	02	18	09	0	16	0	22
2	1	04	+11.4	54.3	14.8	6	248	57	8.3	11	30	11	18	18	52	1	22	1	33
3	1	50	+15.1	54.2	14.8	18	251	66	9.3	11	53	11	38	19	37	2	28	2	43
4	2	37	+18.2	54.3	14.8	31	254	75	10.3	12	21	12	02	20	24	3	34	3	52
5	3	27	+20.6	54.6	14.9	43	257	83	11.3	12	56	12	34	21	13	4	37	4	59
6	4	19	+22.1	54.9	15.0	55	261	89	12.3	13	40	13	16	22	04	5	36	6	00
7	5	12	+22.5	55.4	15.1	67	264	95	13.3	14	33	14	10	22	57	6	29	6	53
8	6	07	+21.9	56.0	15.2	79	265	98	14.3	15	36	15	15	23	49	7	14	7	36
9	7	01	+20.0	56.5	15.4	91	241	100	15.3	16	46	16	28	—		7	51	8	10
10	7	55	+17.2	57.1	15.6	103	124	99	16.3	18	01	17	48	0	41	8	21	8	36
11	8	48	+13.3	57.6	15.7	115	117	97	17.3	19	18	19	09	1	32	8	47	8	57
12	9	40	+8.8	58.0	15.8	128	117	92	18.3	20	35	20	32	2	21	9	09	9	15
13	10	32	+3.7	58.4	15.9	140	117	85	19.3	21	54	21	55	3	10	9	30	9	32
14	11	23	−1.6	58.7	16.0	152	116	76	20.3	23	13	23	19	3	59	9	51	9	48
15	12	15	−6.8	59.0	16.1	164	115	66	21.3	—		—		4	49	10	13	10	05
16	13	08	−11.8	59.1	16.1	176	113	54	22.3	0	34	0	45	5	41	10	38	10	25
17	14	04	−16.1	59.3	16.1	188	110	43	23.3	1	54	2	10	6	35	11	07	10	50
18	15	02	−19.4	59.3	16.2	200	105	32	24.3	3	13	3	33	7	32	11	45	11	24
19	16	02	−21.6	59.2	16.1	213	101	22	25.3	4	26	4	50	8	31	12	33	12	08
20	17	03	−22.5	59.1	16.1	225	96	13	26.3	5	30	5	54	9	30	13	32	13	07
21	18	03	−21.9	58.8	16.0	237	92	7	27.3	6	21	6	44	10	29	14	40	14	18
22	19	02	−20.0	58.4	15.9	249	93	2	28.3	7	02	7	21	11	25	15	55	15	37
23	19	59	−16.9	57.8	15.8	261	121	0	29.3	7	34	7	48	12	18	17	11	16	58
24	20	52	−13.0	57.2	15.6	274	227	1	0.7	7	59	8	09	13	07	18	26	18	17
25	21	43	−8.6	56.6	15.4	286	238	3	1.7	8	20	8	26	13	54	19	39	19	35
26	22	31	−3.9	55.9	15.2	298	240	8	2.7	8	39	8	41	14	38	20	49	20	50
27	23	17	+0.9	55.4	15.1	310	242	14	3.7	8	57	8	55	15	21	21	58	22	03
28	0	03	+5.5	54.9	14.9	322	243	22	4.7	9	15	9	09	16	04	23	06	23	14
29	0	48	+9.8	54.5	14.8	334	245	30	5.7	9	35	9	25	16	47	—		—	
30	1	34	+13.7	54.3	14.8	347	248	39	6.7	9	56	9	43	17	31	0	12	0	25
31	2	21	+17.1	54.2	14.8	359	251	49	7.7	10	22	10	05	18	17	1	18	1	35

MERCURY

Day	R.A. h	R.A. m	Dec. °	Diam. "	Phase %	Transit h	Transit m	5° high 52° h	5° high 52° m	5° high 56° h	5° high 56° m
1	17	16	−22.1	6	80	10	37	7	26	7	59
3	17	28	−22.6	6	83	10	40	7	34	8	08
5	17	40	−23.0	5	85	10	45	7	41	8	17
7	17	52	−23.3	5	87	10	49	7	49	8	25
9	18	05	−23.6	5	89	10	54	7	56	8	33
11	18	17	−23.8	5	90	10	59	8	02	8	40
13	18	30	−23.9	5	92	11	04	8	08	8	47
15	18	44	−23.9	5	93	11	09	8	14	8	52
17	18	57	−23.8	5	94	11	15	8	19	8	57
19	19	10	−23.7	5	95	11	21	8	23	9	00
21	19	24	−23.5	5	96	11	26	8	26	9	03
23	19	38	−23.1	5	96	11	32	8	29	9	04
25	19	51	−22.7	5	97	11	38	8	31	9	05
27	20	05	−22.2	5	98	11	44	8	32	9	05
29	20	19	−21.6	5	98	11	50	8	33	9	04
31	20	33	−20.9	5	99	11	56	8	33	9	02

VENUS

Day	R.A. h	R.A. m	Dec. °	Diam. "	Phase %	Transit h	Transit m	5° high 52° h	5° high 52° m	5° high 56° h	5° high 56° m
1	21	07	−18.4	13	83	14	28	18	09	17	46
6	21	32	−16.5	13	82	14	32	18	27	18	07
11	21	56	−14.4	14	80	14	36	18	45	18	28
16	22	19	−12.2	14	79	14	40	19	03	18	48
21	22	41	−9.8	14	78	14	43	19	20	19	08
26	23	04	−7.3	15	76	14	45	19	36	19	27
31	23	26	−4.8	15	75	14	47	19	52	19	45

MARS

Day	R.A. h	R.A. m	Dec. °	Diam. "	Phase %	Transit h	Transit m	5° high 52° h	5° high 52° m	5° high 56° h	5° high 56° m
1	11	28	+6.6	9	92	4	47	22	44	22	42
6	11	33	+6.3	9	92	4	32	22	30	22	28
11	11	36	+6.1	10	93	4	16	22	15	22	13
16	11	39	+6.0	10	93	3	59	21	58	21	56
21	11	40	+6.0	11	94	3	40	21	39	21	38
26	11	40	+6.1	11	95	3	21	21	19	21	17
31	11	40	+6.4	12	96	3	00	20	57	20	55

SUNRISE AND SUNSET

	London 0° 05' 51° 30'		Bristol 2° 35' 51° 28'		Birmingham 1° 55' 52° 28'		Manchester 2° 15' 53° 28'		Newcastle 1° 37' 54° 59'		Glasgow 4° 14' 55° 52'		Belfast 5° 56' 54° 35'	
d	h m	h m	h m	h m	h m	h m	h m	h m	h m	h m	h m	h m	h m	h m
1	8 06	16 01	8 16	16 12	8 18	16 04	8 25	16 00	8 31	15 48	8 47	15 53	8 46	16 08
2	8 06	16 03	8 16	16 13	8 18	16 05	8 25	16 02	8 31	15 50	8 47	15 55	8 46	16 09
3	8 06	16 04	8 16	16 14	8 18	16 06	8 25	16 02	8 31	15 51	8 47	15 56	8 46	16 10
4	8 06	16 05	8 15	16 15	8 18	16 07	8 24	16 03	8 31	15 52	8 46	15 57	8 45	16 12
5	8 05	16 06	8 15	16 16	8 17	16 08	8 24	16 05	8 30	15 53	8 46	15 58	8 45	16 13
6	8 05	16 07	8 15	16 17	8 17	16 10	8 24	16 06	8 30	15 55	8 45	16 00	8 45	16 14
7	8 05	16 08	8 14	16 19	8 17	16 11	8 23	16 07	8 29	15 56	8 45	16 01	8 44	16 16
8	8 04	16 10	8 14	16 20	8 16	16 12	8 23	16 09	8 29	15 58	8 44	16 03	8 43	16 17
9	8 04	16 11	8 14	16 21	8 16	16 14	8 22	16 10	8 28	15 59	8 44	16 04	8 43	16 19
10	8 03	16 12	8 13	16 23	8 15	16 15	8 21	16 11	8 27	16 01	8 43	16 06	8 42	16 20
11	8 03	16 14	8 12	16 24	8 14	16 17	8 21	16 13	8 26	16 02	8 42	16 08	8 41	16 22
12	8 02	16 15	8 12	16 25	8 14	16 18	8 20	16 15	8 26	16 04	8 41	16 09	8 41	16 23
13	8 01	16 17	8 11	16 27	8 13	16 20	8 19	16 16	8 25	16 06	8 40	16 11	8 40	16 25
14	8 01	16 18	8 10	16 28	8 12	16 21	8 18	16 18	8 24	16 07	8 39	16 13	8 39	16 27
15	8 00	16 20	8 10	16 30	8 11	16 23	8 17	16 19	8 23	16 09	8 38	16 15	8 38	16 28
16	7 59	16 21	8 09	16 31	8 11	16 24	8 17	16 21	8 22	16 11	8 37	16 17	8 37	16 30
17	7 58	16 23	8 08	16 33	8 10	16 26	8 16	16 23	8 21	16 13	8 36	16 18	8 36	16 32
18	7 57	16 24	8 07	16 35	8 09	16 28	8 14	16 24	8 19	16 15	8 34	16 20	8 35	16 34
19	7 56	16 26	8 06	16 36	8 08	16 29	8 13	16 26	8 18	16 16	8 33	16 22	8 33	16 36
20	7 55	16 28	8 05	16 38	8 06	16 31	8 12	16 28	8 17	16 18	8 32	16 24	8 32	16 38
21	7 54	16 29	8 04	16 40	8 05	16 33	8 11	16 30	8 16	16 20	8 30	16 26	8 31	16 39
22	7 53	16 31	8 03	16 41	8 04	16 35	8 10	16 32	8 14	16 22	8 29	16 28	8 30	16 41
23	7 52	16 33	8 02	16 43	8 03	16 36	8 08	16 33	8 13	16 24	8 28	16 30	8 28	16 43
24	7 51	16 35	8 00	16 45	8 02	16 38	8 07	16 35	8 11	16 26	8 26	16 32	8 27	16 45
25	7 49	16 36	7 59	16 46	8 00	16 40	8 06	16 37	8 10	16 28	8 24	16 34	8 25	16 47
26	7 48	16 38	7 58	16 48	7 59	16 42	8 04	16 39	8 08	16 30	8 23	16 36	8 24	16 49
27	7 47	16 40	7 57	16 50	7 58	16 44	8 03	16 41	8 07	16 32	8 21	16 39	8 22	16 51
28	7 45	16 42	7 55	16 52	7 56	16 45	8 01	16 43	8 05	16 34	8 20	16 41	8 21	16 53
29	7 44	16 43	7 54	16 53	7 55	16 47	8 00	16 45	8 04	16 36	8 18	16 43	8 19	16 55
30	7 43	16 45	7 52	16 55	7 53	16 49	7 58	16 47	8 02	16 38	8 16	16 45	8 17	16 57
31	7 41	16 47	7 51	16 57	7 52	16 51	7 57	16 49	8 00	16 40	8 14	16 47	8 16	16 59

JUPITER

Day	R.A. h m	Dec. ° '	Transit h m	5° high 52° h m	56° h m
1	1 55.0	+10 28	19 12	1 36	1 41
11	1 56.4	+10 39	18 34	0 59	1 04
21	1 59.0	+10 56	17 57	0 24	0 29
31	2 02.8	+11 20	17 22	23 47	23 53

Diameters – equatorial 41" polar 39"

SATURN

Day	R.A. h m	Dec. ° '	Transit h m	5° high 52° h m	56° h m
1	13 48.6	-8 36	7 07	2 27	2 38
11	13 50.8	-8 46	6 30	1 50	2 02
21	13 52.3	-8 51	5 52	1 13	1 25
31	13 53.2	-8 54	5 14	0 35	0 46

Diameters – equatorial 17" polar 15"
Rings – major axis 39" minor axis 10"

URANUS

Day	R.A. h m	Dec. ° '	Transit h m	10° high 52° h m	56° h m
1	0 04.2	-0 20	17 21	22 13	22 06
11	0 05.1	-0 14	16 43	21 35	21 28
21	0 06.2	-0 06	16 05	20 58	20 51
31	0 07.5	+0 03	15 27	20 21	20 14

Diameter 4"

NEPTUNE

Day	R.A. h m	Dec. ° '	Transit h m	10° high 52° h m	56° h m
1	22 04.9	-12 22	15 22	19 03	18 42
11	22 06.0	-12 16	14 44	18 25	18 04
21	22 07.3	-12 09	14 06	17 48	17 27
31	22 08.6	-12 02	13 28	17 11	16 50

Diameter 2"

FEBRUARY 2012

SECOND MONTH, 28 or 29 DAYS. *Februa*, Roman festival of Purification

1	*Wednesday*	The space shuttle *Columbia* broke up as it re-entered the Earth's atmosphere 2003	day 32
2	*Thursday*	Dmitry Mendeleyev, chemist who created periodic table of elements arranged by atomic mass *d.* 1907	33
3	*Friday*	The Soviet Union's *Luna 9* became the first controlled spacecraft to land on the Moon 1966	34
4	*Saturday*	Charles Lindbergh, pilot of first one-man flight across the Atlantic *b.* 1902	35
5	*Sunday*	John Dunlop, inventor who developed and patented the first pneumatic tyre *b.* 1840	36
6	*Monday*	Alan Shepard became the first man to hit a golf ball on the Moon 1971	week 6 day 37
7	*Tuesday*	Concorde crossed the Atlantic (between New York and London) in record time 1996	38
8	*Wednesday*	The astronaut crew of the final Skylab mission returned to Earth 1974	39
9	*Thursday*	Mintonette, now known as volleyball, was invented by William G. Morgan 1895	40
10	*Friday*	Gary Kasparov, the world chess champion, lost a game to Deep Blue, an IBM computer 1996	41
11	*Saturday*	Thomas Edison, physicist whose inventions included the light bulb and phonograph *b.* 1847	42
12	*Sunday*	Albert Alexander became the first human test subject to be treated with penicillin 1941	43
13	*Monday*	France carried out its first atomic-bomb test in Algeria 1960	week 7 day 44
14	*Tuesday*	Dolly the sheep, the first mammal cloned from an adult, was euthanised due to premature ageing 2003	45
15	*Wednesday*	Galileo Galilei, mathematician and astronomer, the first man to use a telescope to study the skies *b.* 1564	46
16	*Thursday*	The Kyoto Protocol, aimed at cutting air pollution, came into force 2005	47
17	*Friday*	Christopher Latham Sholes, inventor of the first commercially successful typewriter *d.* 1890	48
18	*Saturday*	Pluto, then regarded as our solar system's ninth planet, was discovered by Clyde Tombaugh 1930	49
19	*Sunday*	Nicolaus Copernicus, astronomer who proposed the Earth and other planets revolved around the Sun *b.* 1473	50
20	*Monday*	The Soviet Union launched *Mir,* the world's biggest space station 1986	week 8 day 51
21	*Tuesday*	Jethro Tull, agriculturalist who invented a horse-drawn seed drill *d.* 1741	52
22	*Wednesday*	Heinrich Hertz, physicist after whom the unit of frequency is named *b.* 1857	53
23	*Thursday*	Passenger railway service linking Perth with Sydney (3,961 kilometres) opened 1970	54
24	*Friday*	Paris and Brussels became the first two cities to be connected by telephone link 1887	55
25	*Saturday*	Gunsmith Samuel Colt patented the first revolving barrel firearm 1836	56
26	*Sunday*	First factory for production of Volkswagen, the 'people's car', is opened by Adolf Hitler 1936	57
27	*Monday*	Ivan Petrovich Pavlov, physiologist, best known for studies of animal behaviour *d.* 1936	week 9 day 58
28	*Tuesday*	James Watson and Frances Crick announced they had determined the double-helix structure of DNA 1953	59
29	*Wednesday*	John Holland, engineer who designed the modern submarine *b.* 1840	60

ASTRONOMICAL PHENOMENA

h d
7 09 Mercury in superior conjunction
7 14 Saturn at stationary point
10 05 Mars in conjunction with Moon. Mars 9°N.
12 21 Saturn in conjunction with Moon. Saturn 6°N.
19 06 Sun's longitude 330° ⋈
19 21 Neptune in conjunction
23 01 Mercury in conjunction with Moon. Mercury 6°S.
25 19 Venus in conjunction with Moon. Venus 3°S.
27 04 Jupiter in conjunction with Moon. Jupiter 4°S.

MINIMA OF ALGOL

d	*h*	*d*	*h*	*d*	*h*
3	13.3	15	00.6	26	11.9
6	10.1	17	21.4	29	08.7
9	07.0	20	18.2		
12	03.8	23	15.1		

CONSTELLATIONS

The following constellations are near the meridian at

	d	*h*		*d*	*h*
January		24	February	15	21
January	16	23	March	1	20
February	1	22	March	16	19

Draco (below the Pole), Camelopardalis, Auriga, Taurus, Gemini, Orion, Canis Minor, Monoceros, Lepus, Canis Major and Puppis

THE MOON

Phases, Apsides and Node

		d	*h*	*m*
○	Full Moon	7	21	54
☾	Last Quarter	14	17	04
●	New Moon	21	22	35
Perigee (367,891km)		11	18	44
Apogee (404,899km)		27	14	05

Mean longitude of ascending node on February 1, 251°

THE SUN

s.d. 16′.2

Day	Right Ascension			Dec.		Equation of time		Rise 52°		56°		Transit		Set 52°		56°		Sidereal time			Transit of first point of Aries		
	h	m	s	°	′	m	s	h	m	h	m	h	m	h	m	h	m	h	m	s	h	m	s
1	20	55	54	17	20	−13	26	7	41	7	56	12	13	16	47	16	32	8	42	29	15	15	01
2	20	59	59	17	03	−13	34	7	39	7	54	12	14	16	49	16	34	8	46	25	15	11	05
3	21	04	03	16	45	−13	41	7	38	7	52	12	14	16	50	16	36	8	50	22	15	07	09
4	21	08	06	16	28	−13	48	7	36	7	50	12	14	16	52	16	38	8	54	18	15	03	13
5	21	12	09	16	10	−13	54	7	34	7	48	12	14	16	54	16	40	8	58	15	14	59	17
6	21	16	10	15	52	−13	59	7	33	7	46	12	14	16	56	16	43	9	02	12	14	55	21
7	21	20	11	15	33	−14	03	7	31	7	44	12	14	16	58	16	45	9	06	08	14	51	25
8	21	24	11	15	15	−14	06	7	29	7	42	12	14	17	00	16	47	9	10	05	14	47	30
9	21	28	10	14	56	−14	09	7	27	7	40	12	14	17	02	16	49	9	14	01	14	43	34
10	21	32	09	14	37	−14	11	7	26	7	38	12	14	17	03	16	51	9	17	58	14	39	38
11	21	36	06	14	17	−14	12	7	24	7	36	12	14	17	05	16	54	9	21	54	14	35	42
12	21	40	03	13	58	−14	12	7	22	7	33	12	14	17	07	16	56	9	25	51	14	31	46
13	21	43	59	13	38	−14	12	7	20	7	31	12	14	17	09	16	58	9	29	47	14	27	50
14	21	47	54	13	18	−14	11	7	18	7	29	12	14	17	11	17	00	9	33	44	14	23	54
15	21	51	49	12	57	−14	09	7	16	7	27	12	14	17	13	17	02	9	37	41	14	19	58
16	21	55	43	12	37	−14	06	7	14	7	24	12	14	17	15	17	05	9	41	37	14	16	02
17	21	59	36	12	16	−14	03	7	12	7	22	12	14	17	17	17	07	9	45	34	14	12	06
18	22	03	29	11	55	−13	59	7	10	7	20	12	14	17	18	17	09	9	49	30	14	08	10
19	22	07	21	11	34	−13	54	7	08	7	17	12	14	17	20	17	11	9	53	27	14	04	15
20	22	11	12	11	12	−13	49	7	06	7	15	12	14	17	22	17	13	9	57	23	14	00	19
21	22	15	02	10	51	−13	43	7	04	7	13	12	14	17	24	17	16	10	01	20	13	56	23
22	22	18	52	10	29	−13	36	7	02	7	10	12	14	17	26	17	18	10	05	16	13	52	27
23	22	22	41	10	08	−13	29	7	00	7	08	12	13	17	28	17	20	10	09	13	13	48	31
24	22	26	30	9	46	−13	21	6	58	7	05	12	13	17	29	17	22	10	13	09	13	44	35
25	22	30	18	9	23	−13	12	6	56	7	03	12	13	17	31	17	24	10	17	06	13	40	39
26	22	34	05	9	01	−13	03	6	54	7	01	12	13	17	33	17	26	10	21	03	13	36	43
27	22	37	52	8	39	−12	53	6	52	6	58	12	13	17	35	17	28	10	24	59	13	32	47
28	22	41	38	8	16	−12	43	6	49	6	56	12	13	17	37	17	31	10	28	56	13	28	51
29	22	45	24	7	54	−12	32	6	47	6	53	12	12	17	39	17	33	10	32	52	13	24	56

DURATION OF TWILIGHT (in minutes)

Latitude	52°	56°	52°	56°	52°	56°	52°	56°
	1 February		11 February		21 February		31 February	
Civil	37	41	35	39	34	38	34	37
Nautical	77	86	75	83	74	81	73	80
Astronomical	117	130	114	126	113	124	112	124

THE NIGHT SKY

Mercury passes through superior conjunction on the 7th and is thus unsuitably placed for observation until the last week of the month, when it becomes visible as an evening object very low in the western sky, at the end of evening civil twilight. During this period its magnitude fades from −1.2 to −0.8.

Venus continues to be visible as a brilliant object in the early evenings in the southwestern sky, shortly after sunset. Its magnitude is −4.1. The waxing crescent Moon passes 2 degrees north of the planet on the evening of the 25th.

Mars, its magnitude brightening from −0.6 to −1.2 as it approaches opposition early next month, is becoming visible for the greater part of the night. Its retrograde motion takes it back into the constellation of Leo. The waning gibbous Moon will be seen passing about 9 degrees south of the planet on February 9–11.

Jupiter, magnitude −2.3, continues to be visible in the south-western sky in the early part of the evening. On the 27th the waxing crescent Moon passes 3 degrees north of the planet.

Saturn, in the constellation of Virgo, continues to be visible as a morninig object in the south-eastern sky and by the end of the month should be visible by about 23h. Its magnitude is +0.5. It reaches its first stationary point on the 7th and then moves very slowly retrograde. On the 12th the waning gibbous Moon passes about 7 degrees south of the planet.

Zodiacal Light. The evening cone may be observed stretching up from the western horizon, along the ecliptic, after the end of twilight, from the 9th to the 22nd. This faint phenomenon is only visible under good conditions and in the absence of both moonlight and artificial lighting.

THE MOON

Day	R.A. *h*	R.A. *m*	Dec. °	Hor. par. ′	Semi-diam. ′	Sun's Co-Long. °	PA of Br. Limb °	Ph. %	Age *d*	Rise 52° *h*	Rise 52° *m*	Rise 56° *h*	Rise 56° *m*	Transit *h*	Transit *m*	Set 52° *h*	Set 52° *m*	Set 56° *h*	Set 56° *m*
1	3	10	+19.7	54.4	14.8	11	255	58	8.7	10	54	10	33	19	04	2	22	2	42
2	4	00	+21.5	54.7	14.9	23	259	67	9.7	11	33	11	10	19	54	3	22	3	45
3	4	53	+22.4	55.1	15.0	35	263	76	10.7	12	21	11	58	20	45	4	18	4	42
4	5	46	+22.1	55.7	15.2	47	267	84	11.7	13	20	12	57	21	37	5	06	5	29
5	6	41	+20.8	56.4	15.4	60	271	90	12.7	14	26	14	07	22	30	5	47	6	07
6	7	35	+18.3	57.1	15.6	72	272	96	13.7	15	40	15	24	23	22	6	20	6	37
7	8	29	+14.8	57.8	15.8	84	265	99	14.7	16	57	16	46	—		6	49	7	01
8	9	23	+10.5	58.5	15.9	96	184	100	15.7	18	16	18	11	0	13	7	13	7	21
9	10	16	+5.5	59.0	16.1	108	130	98	16.7	19	37	19	36	1	04	7	35	7	38
10	11	08	+0.1	59.4	16.2	120	122	94	17.7	20	58	21	02	1	54	7	57	7	55
11	12	02	−5.3	59.6	16.2	132	119	88	18.7	22	20	22	29	2	45	8	19	8	13
12	12	56	−10.4	59.6	16.2	145	116	79	19.7	23	42	23	56	3	38	8	44	8	33
13	13	51	−14.9	59.5	16.2	157	112	69	20.7	—		—		4	32	9	12	8	57
14	14	49	−18.6	59.3	16.2	169	107	58	21.7	1	01	1	20	5	28	9	47	9	27
15	15	48	−21.0	59.0	16.1	181	102	47	22.7	2	16	2	39	6	25	10	31	10	08
16	16	48	−22.2	58.7	16.0	193	97	36	23.7	3	22	3	46	7	24	11	25	11	01
17	17	48	−22.0	58.3	15.9	205	92	26	24.7	4	16	4	40	8	21	12	29	12	06
18	18	46	−20.5	57.9	15.8	217	88	17	25.7	5	00	5	20	9	17	13	40	13	20
19	19	42	−17.9	57.4	15.7	230	85	9	26.7	5	34	5	50	10	10	14	54	14	38
20	20	35	−14.3	57.0	15.5	242	85	4	27.7	6	01	6	13	10	59	16	08	15	57
21	21	26	−10.2	56.5	15.4	254	94	1	28.7	6	24	6	32	11	47	17	20	17	14
22	22	14	−5.6	56.0	15.2	266	167	0	0.1	6	44	6	48	12	32	18	32	18	30
23	23	01	−0.9	55.5	15.1	278	226	1	1.1	7	02	7	02	13	15	19	41	19	43
24	23	47	+3.8	55.0	15.0	291	236	4	2.1	7	21	7	17	13	58	20	49	20	56
25	0	33	+8.2	54.6	14.9	303	241	9	3.1	7	40	7	32	14	41	21	56	22	07
26	1	19	+12.3	54.3	14.8	315	244	15	4.1	8	01	7	49	15	25	23	02	23	17
27	2	06	+15.8	54.2	14.8	327	248	23	5.1	8	25	8	10	16	10	—		—	
28	2	54	+18.7	54.2	14.8	339	252	31	6.1	8	54	8	35	16	57	0	07	0	25
29	3	43	+20.7	54.3	14.8	352	257	40	7.1	9	30	9	08	17	45	1	08	1	30

MERCURY

Day	R.A. *h*	R.A. *m*	Dec. °	Diam. ″	Phase %	Transit *h*	Transit *m*	5° high 52° *h*	5° high 52° *m*	5° high 56° *h*	5° high 56° *m*
1	20	40	−20.5	5	99	11	59	8	33	9	01
3	20	54	−19.6	5	99	12	05	15	38	15	12
5	21	08	−18.7	5	100	12	11	15	52	15	28
7	21	22	−17.6	5	100	12	17	16	05	15	43
9	21	36	−16.5	5	100	12	23	16	20	15	59
11	21	50	−15.2	5	99	12	29	16	34	16	16
13	22	04	−13.9	5	99	12	35	16	49	16	32
15	22	17	−12.4	5	98	12	41	17	04	16	49
17	22	31	−10.9	5	96	12	47	17	19	17	06
19	22	45	−9.3	5	94	12	53	17	34	17	22
21	22	58	−7.7	5	91	12	58	17	48	17	39
23	23	11	−6.0	6	88	13	03	18	03	17	55
25	23	23	−4.3	6	83	13	08	18	16	18	10
27	23	35	−2.6	6	77	13	11	18	29	18	24
29	23	46	−0.9	6	70	13	14	18	40	18	37
31	23	56	+0.6	7	62	13	16	18	49	18	47

VENUS

Day	R.A. *h*	R.A. *m*	Dec. °	Diam. ″	Phase %	Transit *h*	Transit *m*	5° high 52° *h*	5° high 52° *m*	5° high 56° *h*	5° high 56° *m*
1	23	30	−4.3	15	74	14	48	19	55	19	49
6	23	51	−1.6	16	73	14	49	20	11	20	06
11	0	12	+1.0	16	71	14	51	20	26	20	23
16	0	33	+3.6	17	69	14	52	20	40	20	40
21	0	54	+6.2	17	67	14	53	20	54	20	56
26	1	15	+8.7	18	65	14	54	21	08	21	12
31	1	36	+11.1	19	63	14	55	21	22	21	28

MARS

Day	R.A. *h*	R.A. *m*	Dec. °	Diam. ″	Phase %	Transit *h*	Transit *m*	5° high 52° *h*	5° high 52° *m*	5° high 56° *h*	5° high 56° *m*
1	11	39	+6.4	12	96	2	56	20	52	20	50
6	11	37	+6.8	12	97	2	34	20	28	20	26
11	11	33	+7.3	13	98	2	11	20	02	19	59
16	11	29	+7.9	13	99	1	47	19	35	19	31
21	11	23	+8.6	13	99	1	21	19	05	19	02
26	11	16	+9.3	14	100	0	55	18	35	18	31
31	11	09	+10.0	14	100	0	28	18	05	18	00

SUNRISE AND SUNSET

	London 0° 05′ 51° 30′				Bristol 2° 35′ 51° 28′				Birmingham 1° 55′ 52° 28′				Manchester 2° 15′ 53° 28′				Newcastle 1° 37′ 54° 59′				Glasgow 4° 14′ 55° 52′				Belfast 5° 56′ 54° 35′			
d	h	m	h	m	h	m	h	m	h	m	h	m	h	m	h	m	h	m	h	m	h	m	h	m	h	m	h	m
1	7	40	16	49	7	49	16	59	7	50	16	53	7	55	16	51	7	58	16	42	8	12	16	49	8	14	17	01
2	7	38	16	51	7	48	17	01	7	49	16	55	7	53	16	53	7	56	16	44	8	10	16	51	8	12	17	03
3	7	36	16	52	7	46	17	02	7	47	16	57	7	52	16	55	7	55	16	46	8	09	16	54	8	10	17	05
4	7	35	16	54	7	45	17	04	7	45	16	58	7	50	16	56	7	53	16	49	8	07	16	56	8	09	17	07
5	7	33	16	56	7	43	17	06	7	44	17	00	7	48	16	58	7	51	16	51	8	05	16	58	8	07	17	09
6	7	32	16	58	7	41	17	08	7	42	17	02	7	46	17	00	7	49	16	53	8	03	17	00	8	05	17	11
7	7	30	17	00	7	40	17	10	7	40	17	04	7	44	17	02	7	47	16	55	8	01	17	02	8	03	17	14
8	7	28	17	01	7	38	17	12	7	38	17	06	7	43	17	04	7	45	16	57	7	58	17	04	8	01	17	16
9	7	26	17	03	7	36	17	13	7	36	17	08	7	41	17	06	7	43	16	59	7	56	17	07	7	59	17	18
10	7	25	17	05	7	35	17	15	7	35	17	10	7	39	17	08	7	41	17	01	7	54	17	09	7	57	17	20
11	7	23	17	07	7	33	17	17	7	33	17	12	7	37	17	10	7	39	17	03	7	52	17	11	7	55	17	22
12	7	21	17	09	7	31	17	19	7	31	17	14	7	35	17	12	7	37	17	05	7	50	17	13	7	53	17	24
13	7	19	17	11	7	29	17	21	7	29	17	16	7	33	17	14	7	35	17	08	7	48	17	15	7	51	17	26
14	7	17	17	12	7	27	17	23	7	27	17	17	7	31	17	16	7	32	17	10	7	45	17	18	7	49	17	28
15	7	15	17	14	7	25	17	24	7	25	17	19	7	29	17	18	7	30	17	12	7	43	17	20	7	46	17	30
16	7	13	17	16	7	23	17	26	7	23	17	21	7	27	17	20	7	28	17	14	7	41	17	22	7	44	17	32
17	7	12	17	18	7	21	17	28	7	21	17	23	7	25	17	22	7	26	17	16	7	39	17	24	7	42	17	34
18	7	10	17	20	7	20	17	30	7	19	17	25	7	23	17	24	7	24	17	18	7	36	17	26	7	40	17	36
19	7	08	17	22	7	18	17	32	7	17	17	27	7	20	17	26	7	21	17	20	7	34	17	28	7	38	17	38
20	7	06	17	23	7	16	17	33	7	15	17	29	7	18	17	28	7	19	17	22	7	32	17	31	7	35	17	40
21	7	04	17	25	7	14	17	35	7	13	17	31	7	16	17	30	7	17	17	24	7	29	17	33	7	33	17	42
22	7	02	17	27	7	12	17	37	7	11	17	33	7	14	17	32	7	15	17	26	7	27	17	35	7	31	17	45
23	7	00	17	29	7	09	17	39	7	09	17	34	7	12	17	34	7	12	17	28	7	25	17	37	7	29	17	47
24	6	57	17	31	7	07	17	41	7	06	17	36	7	10	17	36	7	10	17	31	7	22	17	39	7	26	17	49
25	6	55	17	32	7	05	17	42	7	04	17	38	7	07	17	38	7	08	17	33	7	20	17	41	7	24	17	51
26	6	53	17	34	7	03	17	44	7	02	17	40	7	05	17	40	7	05	17	35	7	17	17	44	7	22	17	53
27	6	51	17	36	7	01	17	46	7	00	17	42	7	03	17	42	7	03	17	37	7	15	17	46	7	19	17	55
28	6	49	17	38	6	59	17	48	6	58	17	44	7	01	17	44	7	00	17	39	7	12	17	48	7	17	17	57
29	6	47	17	39	6	57	17	50	6	56	17	46	6	58	17	46	6	58	17	41	7	10	17	50	7	15	17	59

JUPITER

Day	R.A. h	m	Dec. °	′	Transit h	m	5° high 52° h	m	56° h	m
1	2	03.3	+11	23	17	18	23	44	23	50
11	2	08.2	+11	51	16	44	23	12	23	18
21	2	14.1	+12	24	16	11	22	41	22	48
31	2	20.7	+13	01	15	38	22	12	22	19

Diameters – equatorial 37″ polar 35″

SATURN

Day	R.A. h	m	Dec. °	′	Transit h	m	5° high 52° h	m	56° h	m
1	13	53.3	−8	54	5	10	0	31	0	42
11	13	53.4	−8	52	4	31	23	48	0	03
21	13	52.9	−8	46	3	51	23	07	23	19
31	13	51.8	−8	37	3	11	22	26	22	37

Diameters – equatorial 18″ polar 16″
Rings – major axis 41″ minor axis 11″

URANUS

Day	R.A. h	m	Dec. °	′	Transit h	m	10° high 52° h	m	56° h	m
1	0	07.7	+0	04	15	23	20	17	20	10
11	0	09.3	+0	14	14	45	19	40	19	34
21	0	11.0	+0	26	14	08	19	04	18	57
31	0	13.0	+0	39	13	30	18	27	18	21

Diameter 4″

NEPTUNE

Day	R.A. h	m	Dec. °	′	Transit h	m	10° high 52° h	m	56° h	m
1	22	08.7	−12	01	13	24	17	07	16	47
11	22	10.2	−11	53	12	46	16	30	16	10
21	22	11.6	−11	45	12	08	15	53	15	33
31	22	13.1	−11	37	11	31	15	16	14	56

Diameter 2″

♓ MARCH 2012 ♈

THIRD MONTH, 31 DAYS. *Mars*, Roman god of battle

1	*Thursday*	The USA tested a hydrogen bomb in the Pacific (at the time, the biggest-ever man-made explosion) 1954 day 61	
2	*Friday*	NASA launched *Pioneer 10*, which became the first space probe to exit the solar system 1972	62
3	*Saturday*	Alexander Graham Bell, inventor of the electric telephone *b.* 1847	63
4	*Sunday*	Emile Berliner received a patent for his invention – the gramophone 1887	64

5	*Monday*	The Britannia Bridge, designed and built by Robert Stephenson, opened 1850 week 10 day 65	
6	*Tuesday*	German pharmaceutical company Friedrich Bayer & Co patented aspirin 1899	66
7	*Wednesday*	Queen Elizabeth II officially opened the Victoria Line on the London Underground 1969	67
8	*Thursday*	Abraham Darby, ironmaster who first used coke in the smelting of iron ore *d.* 1717	68
9	*Friday*	Yuri Gagarin, cosmonaut who was the first human to travel into space *b.* 1934	69
10	*Saturday*	Marcello Malpighi, regarded as the founder of microscopic anatomy *b.* 1628	70
11	*Sunday*	Cai Lun, a Chinese eunuch, revolutionised papermaking, allowing it to be mass produced AD 105	71

12	*Monday*	Sir William Henry Perkin, chemist made famous for his discovery of mauveine *b.* 1838 week 11 day 72	
13	*Tuesday*	Uranus was discovered by astronomer Sir William Herschel 1781	73
14	*Wednesday*	Albert Einstein, regarded as the father of modern physics *b.* 1879	74
15	*Thursday*	Jesse Reno, an engineer, received a patent for the first escalator – the Reno Inclined Elevator 1892	75
16	*Friday*	Georg Simon Ohm, physicist after whom the unit of electrical resistance is named *b.* 1789	76
17	*Saturday*	University of California scientists announced the discovery of a new element, californium 1950	77
18	*Sunday*	Rudolf Diesel, mechanical engineer best known for the invention of the diesel engine *b.* 1858	78

19	*Monday*	The Sydney Harbour Bridge, known locally as the 'Coathanger', was opened 1932 week 12 day 79	
20	*Tuesday*	Sir Isaac Newton, physicist and mathematician who discovered the law of universal gravitation *d.* 1727	80
21	*Wednesday*	The first driverless trains on the London Underground were demonstrated to the public 1963	81
22	*Thursday*	Robert Millikan, Nobel laureate physicist who devised the Millikan oil-drop experiment *b.* 1868	82
23	*Friday*	The USA announced plans to develop a space-based system to defend against nuclear missiles 1983	83
24	*Saturday*	Bacteriologist Robert Koch announced the discovery of mycobacterium tuberculosis 1882	84
25	*Sunday*	Astronomer Christiaan Huygens discovered Titan, the largest moon of Saturn 1655	85

26	*Monday*	Jonas Salk announces the successful test of the first safe and effective polio vaccine 1953 week 13 day 86	
27	*Tuesday*	Sir Frederick Henry Royce, car manufacturer and co-founder of the Rolls-Royce company *b.* 1863	87
28	*Wednesday*	Henri Fabre, aviator and inventor, succeeded in taking off from water in his seaplane *Le Canard* 1910	88
29	*Thursday*	John Pemberton brewed the first batch of Coca-Cola (originally used for medicinal purposes) 1886	89
30	*Friday*	Hymen Lipman registered the first patent for a lead pencil with an attached rubber 1858	90
31	*Saturday*	Robert Bunsen, chemist credited with inventing the Bunsen burner *b.* 1811	91

ASTRONOMICAL PHENOMENA
d h
3 20 Mars at opposition
5 09 Mercury at greatest elongation E. 18°
7 23 Mars in conjunction with Moon. Mars 9°N.
11 03 Saturn in conjunction with Moon. Saturn 6°N.
12 08 Mercury at stationary point
14 06 Jupiter in conjunction with Venus. Jupiter 3°S.
20 05 Sun's longitude 0° ♈
21 19 Mercury in inferior conjunction
22 12 Mercury in conjunction with Moon. Mercury 1°S.
24 18 Uranus in conjunction
25 22 Jupiter in conjunction with Moon. Jupiter 3°S.
26 19 Venus in conjunction with Moon. Venus 2°N.
27 07 Venus at greatest elongation E. 46°

MINIMA OF ALGOL
d	h	d	h	d	h
3	05.5	14	16.8	26	04.1
6	02.4	17	13.6	29	00.9
8	23.2	20	10.5	31	21.8
11	20.0	23	07.3		

CONSTELLATIONS
The following constellations are near the meridian at

	d	h		d	h
February	1	24	March	16	21
February	15	23	April	1	20
March	1	22	April	15	19

Cepheus (below the Pole), Camelopardalis, Lynx, Gemini, Cancer, Leo, Canis Minor, Hydra, Monoceros, Canis Major and Puppis

THE MOON
Phases, Apsides and Node		d	h	m
☽	First Quarter	1	01	21
○	Full Moon	8	09	39
☾	Last Quarter	15	01	25
●	New Moon	22	14	37
☽	First Quarter	30	19	41

	d	h	m
Perigee (362,383km)	10	10	08
Apogee (405,801km)	26	06	12

Mean longitude of ascending node on March 1, 250°

THE SUN

s.d. 16'.1

Day	Right Ascension			Dec.		Equation of time		Rise 52°		Rise 56°		Transit		Set 52°		Set 56°		Sidereal time			Transit of first point of Aries		
	h	m	s	°	'	m	s	h	m	h	m	h	m	h	m	h	m	h	m	s	h	m	s
1	22	49	09	−7	31	−12	20	6	45	6	51	12	12	17	40	17	35	10	36	49	13	21	00
2	22	52	54	−7	08	−12	08	6	43	6	48	12	12	17	42	17	37	10	40	45	13	17	04
3	22	56	38	−6	45	−11	56	6	41	6	46	12	12	17	44	17	39	10	44	42	13	13	08
4	23	00	22	−6	22	−11	43	6	38	6	43	12	12	17	46	17	41	10	48	38	13	09	12
5	23	04	05	−5	59	−11	30	6	36	6	40	12	11	17	47	17	43	10	52	35	13	05	16
6	23	07	47	−5	35	−11	16	6	34	6	38	12	11	17	49	17	45	10	56	32	13	01	20
7	23	11	30	−5	12	−11	02	6	32	6	35	12	11	17	51	17	48	11	00	28	12	57	24
8	23	15	12	−4	49	−10	47	6	29	6	33	12	11	17	53	17	50	11	04	25	12	53	28
9	23	18	53	−4	25	−10	32	6	27	6	30	12	10	17	55	17	52	11	08	21	12	49	32
10	23	22	34	−4	02	−10	17	6	25	6	28	12	10	17	56	17	54	11	12	18	12	45	36
11	23	26	15	−3	38	−10	01	6	23	6	25	12	10	17	58	17	56	11	16	14	12	41	41
12	23	29	56	−3	15	−9	45	6	20	6	22	12	10	18	00	17	58	11	20	11	12	37	45
13	23	33	36	−2	51	−9	29	6	18	6	20	12	09	18	02	18	00	11	24	07	12	33	49
14	23	37	16	−2	27	−9	12	6	16	6	17	12	09	18	03	18	02	11	28	04	12	29	53
15	23	40	56	−2	04	−8	55	6	13	6	15	12	09	18	05	18	04	11	32	01	12	25	57
16	23	44	36	−1	40	−8	38	6	11	6	12	12	08	18	07	18	06	11	35	57	12	22	01
17	23	48	15	−1	16	−8	21	6	09	6	09	12	08	18	09	18	08	11	39	54	12	18	05
18	23	51	54	−0	53	−8	04	6	07	6	07	12	08	18	10	18	10	11	43	50	12	14	09
19	23	55	33	−0	29	−7	47	6	04	6	04	12	08	18	12	18	12	11	47	47	12	10	13
20	23	59	12	−0	05	−7	29	6	02	6	01	12	07	18	14	18	14	11	51	43	12	06	17
21	0	02	51	+0	19	−7	11	6	00	5	59	12	07	18	15	18	17	11	55	40	12	02	21
22	0	06	30	+0	42	−6	53	5	57	5	56	12	07	18	17	18	19	11	59	36	11	58	26
23	0	10	08	+1	06	−6	35	5	55	5	53	12	06	18	19	18	21	12	03	33	11	54	30
24	0	13	47	+1	30	−6	17	5	53	5	51	12	06	18	21	18	23	12	07	30	11	50	34
25	0	17	25	+1	53	−5	59	5	50	5	48	12	06	18	22	18	25	12	11	26	11	46	38
26	0	21	04	+2	17	−5	41	5	48	5	46	12	06	18	24	18	27	12	15	23	11	42	42
27	0	24	42	+2	40	−5	23	5	46	5	43	12	05	18	26	18	29	12	19	19	11	38	46
28	0	28	21	+3	04	−5	05	5	43	5	40	12	05	18	28	18	31	12	23	16	11	34	50
29	0	31	59	+3	27	−4	47	5	41	5	38	12	05	18	29	18	33	12	27	12	11	30	54
30	0	35	38	+3	50	−4	29	5	39	5	35	12	04	18	31	18	35	12	31	09	11	26	58
31	0	39	17	+4	14	−4	11	5	36	5	32	12	04	18	33	18	37	12	35	05	11	23	02

DURATION OF TWILIGHT (in minutes)

Latitude	52°	56°	52°	56°	52°	56°	52°	56°
	1 March		11 March		21 March		31 March	
Civil	34	37	34	37	34	37	34	38
Nautical	73	80	73	80	74	81	75	84
Astronomical	112	124	113	125	115	128	120	135

THE NIGHT SKY

Mercury reaches its greatest eastern elongation (18 degrees) on the 5th and therefore is visible in the evenings for the first 10 days of the month. It may be detected low above the west-south-western horizon around the beginning of evening civil twilight. At first its magnitude is −0.8 but this has diminished to about +1.1 by the end of its period of visibility.

Venus, magnitude −4.5, reaches its greatest eastern elongation (46 degrees) on the 27th and completely dominates the southwestern sky for about 4 hours after sunset. On the 14th the planet passes 3 degrees north of Jupiter while on the evening of the 26th the waxing crescent Moon passes 2 degrees south of Venus.

Mars reaches opposition on the 3rd and is therefore visible throughout the hours of darkness. Its retrograde motion takes it back in the direction of Regulus, in Leo, though it reaches its second stationary point next month, still about 5 degrees from that star. During the month its magnitude fades from −1.2 to −0.9. The Full Moon passes about 9 degrees south of the planet on the night of the 7th–8th.

Jupiter, magnitude −2.1, is now only visible low above the south-western horizon for a short while after sunset. On the 25th the crescent Moon, only 3 days old, passes about 3 degrees north of the planet.

Saturn continues to be visible from the late evenings onwards, magnitude +0.4, in the constellation of Virgo. By the end of the month it should be visible low above the eastern horizon by about 21h as it moves towards opposition next month. During the night of the 10th–11th the waning gibbous Moon passes about 7 degrees south of the planet.

Zodiacal Light. The evening cone may be observed stretching up from the western horizon, along the ecliptic, after the end of twilight, from the 9th to the 23rd. This faint phenomenon is only visible under good conditions and in the absence of both moonlight and artificial lighting. The proximity of Venus will make detection of this faint phenomenon more difficult.

THE MOON

Day	R.A. h	R.A. m	Dec. °	Hor. par. '	Semi-diam. '	Sun's Co-Long. °	PA of Br. Limb °	Ph. %	Age d	Rise 52° h	Rise 52° m	Rise 56° h	Rise 56° m	Transit h	Transit m	Set 52° h	Set 52° m	Set 56° h	Set 56° m
1	4	34	+21.9	54.6	14.9	4	262	50	8.1	10	13	9	50	18	35	2	05	2	29
2	5	27	+22.1	55.1	15.0	16	266	59	9.1	11	06	10	43	19	26	2	56	3	19
3	6	20	+21.2	55.8	15.2	28	271	69	10.1	12	08	11	47	20	17	3	39	4	01
4	7	13	+19.2	56.6	15.4	40	275	78	11.1	13	17	12	59	21	08	4	16	4	34
5	8	07	+16.2	57.4	15.6	52	278	86	12.1	14	31	14	18	22	00	4	47	5	01
6	9	00	+12.3	58.3	15.9	65	279	92	13.1	15	49	15	41	22	51	5	13	5	23
7	9	54	+7.6	59.1	16.1	77	276	97	14.1	17	10	17	07	23	42	5	37	5	42
8	10	47	+2.3	59.8	16.3	89	250	100	15.1	18	33	18	34	—		5	59	6	00
9	11	41	-3.2	60.2	16.4	101	143	99	16.1	19	57	20	03	0	34	6	22	6	18
10	12	37	-8.5	60.5	16.5	113	123	96	17.1	21	21	21	33	1	28	6	46	6	38
11	13	34	-13.4	60.5	16.5	125	116	90	18.1	22	45	23	02	2	23	7	14	7	01
12	14	33	-17.4	60.2	16.4	137	110	82	19.1	—		—		3	20	7	48	7	30
13	15	33	-20.3	59.8	16.3	150	104	73	20.1	0	03	0	25	4	19	8	31	8	09
14	16	34	-21.8	59.2	16.1	162	98	62	21.1	1	14	1	37	5	19	9	22	8	59
15	17	34	-21.9	58.6	16.0	174	93	51	22.1	2	12	2	36	6	17	10	24	10	01
16	18	33	-20.7	58.0	15.8	186	87	40	23.1	2	59	3	20	7	13	11	32	11	12
17	19	29	-18.4	57.4	15.6	198	83	30	24.1	3	36	3	53	8	06	12	44	12	28
18	20	22	-15.1	56.8	15.5	211	80	20	25.1	4	05	4	18	8	56	13	57	13	45
19	21	13	-11.2	56.3	15.3	223	78	13	26.1	4	28	4	37	9	43	15	09	15	01
20	22	01	-6.8	55.8	15.2	235	78	7	27.1	4	49	4	54	10	28	16	19	16	16
21	22	48	-2.2	55.3	15.1	247	83	3	28.1	5	08	5	09	11	12	17	28	17	29
22	23	34	+2.4	54.9	15.0	259	102	1	29.1	5	27	5	24	11	55	18	36	18	41
23	0	19	+6.8	54.6	14.9	272	202	0	0.4	5	46	5	39	12	38	19	43	19	52
24	1	05	+11.0	54.3	14.8	284	234	2	1.4	6	06	5	56	13	21	20	49	21	03
25	1	52	+14.6	54.1	14.7	296	243	5	2.4	6	29	6	15	14	06	21	54	22	11
26	2	39	+17.7	54.0	14.7	308	250	10	3.4	6	57	6	39	14	52	22	57	23	17
27	3	28	+20.0	54.1	14.7	320	255	17	4.4	7	30	7	09	15	39	23	55	—	
28	4	19	+21.4	54.2	14.8	333	260	24	5.4	8	10	7	47	16	28	—		0	17
29	5	10	+21.9	54.6	14.9	345	265	33	6.4	8	58	8	35	17	17	0	47	1	10
30	6	02	+21.4	55.0	15.0	357	271	42	7.4	9	55	9	33	18	07	1	33	1	55
31	6	54	+19.8	55.7	15.2	9	275	52	8.4	10	59	10	40	18	57	2	11	2	31

MERCURY

Day	R.A. h	R.A. m	Dec. °	Diam. "	Phase %	Transit h	Transit m	5° high 52° h	5° high 52° m	5° high 56° h	5° high 56° m
1	23	51	-0.1	6	66	13	15	18	45	18	42
3	0	00	+1.4	7	57	13	16	18	53	18	51
5	0	08	+2.7	7	48	13	15	18	59	18	58
7	0	14	+3.9	8	39	13	13	19	01	19	02
9	0	18	+4.8	8	31	13	08	19	01	19	01
11	0	20	+5.4	9	23	13	02	18	56	18	58
13	0	20	+5.7	9	16	12	53	18	49	18	50
15	0	18	+5.7	10	10	12	43	18	38	18	39
17	0	14	+5.4	10	5	12	31	18	23	18	24
19	0	09	+4.8	11	2	12	18	18	07	18	07
21	0	03	+4.0	11	1	12	04	17	48	17	48
23	23	57	+3.0	11	1	11	50	6	09	6	10
25	23	51	+2.0	11	2	11	36	6	01	6	03
27	23	46	+0.9	11	4	11	24	5	53	5	56
29	23	42	-0.1	11	8	11	12	5	47	5	50
31	23	39	-0.9	11	11	11	01	5	40	5	45

VENUS

Day	R.A. h	R.A. m	Dec. °	Diam. "	Phase %	Transit h	Transit m	5° high 52° h	5° high 52° m	5° high 56° h	5° high 56° m
1	1	31	+10.7	18	64	14	55	21	19	21	25
6	1	52	+13.0	19	62	14	56	21	33	21	40
11	2	13	+15.3	20	59	14	56	21	45	21	55
16	2	33	+17.4	21	57	14	57	21	58	22	10
21	2	53	+19.3	22	55	14	58	22	10	22	23
26	3	14	+21.1	23	52	14	58	22	20	22	36
31	3	34	+22.7	25	49	14	59	22	30	22	48

MARS

Day	R.A. h	R.A. m	Dec. °	Diam. "	Phase %	Transit h	Transit m	5° high 52° h	5° high 52° m	5° high 56° h	5° high 56° m
1	11	11	+9.9	14	100	0	34	6	51	6	55
6	11	03	+10.6	14	100	0	07	6	27	6	32
11	10	56	+11.2	14	100	23	34	6	03	6	09
16	10	49	+11.8	14	99	23	07	5	40	5	46
21	10	42	+12.3	13	99	22	42	5	16	5	23
26	10	37	+12.6	13	98	22	17	4	53	5	00
31	10	32	+12.8	13	97	21	53	4	30	4	37

SUNRISE AND SUNSET

	London 0° 05' 51° 30'		Bristol 2° 35' 51° 28'		Birmingham 1° 55' 52° 28'		Manchester 2° 15' 53° 28'		Newcastle 1° 37' 54° 59'		Glasgow 4° 14' 55° 52'		Belfast 5° 56' 54° 35'	
d	h m	h m	h m	h m	h m	h m	h m	h m	h m	h m	h m	h m	h m	h m
1	6 45	17 41	6 55	17 51	6 53	17 47	6 56	17 47	6 56	17 43	7 07	17 52	7 12	18 01
2	6 43	17 43	6 53	17 53	6 51	17 49	6 54	17 49	6 53	17 45	7 05	17 54	7 10	18 03
3	6 40	17 45	6 50	17 55	6 49	17 51	6 51	17 51	6 51	17 47	7 02	17 56	7 07	18 05
4	6 38	17 47	6 48	17 57	6 47	17 53	6 49	17 53	6 48	17 49	7 00	17 58	7 05	18 07
5	6 36	17 48	6 46	17 58	6 44	17 55	6 47	17 55	6 46	17 51	6 57	18 00	7 03	18 09
6	6 34	17 50	6 44	18 00	6 42	17 57	6 44	17 57	6 43	17 53	6 55	18 03	7 00	18 11
7	6 32	17 52	6 42	18 02	6 40	17 58	6 42	17 59	6 41	17 55	6 52	18 05	6 58	18 13
8	6 29	17 53	6 39	18 04	6 37	18 00	6 40	18 01	6 38	17 57	6 50	18 07	6 55	18 15
9	6 27	17 55	6 37	18 05	6 35	18 02	6 37	18 03	6 36	17 59	6 47	18 09	6 53	18 17
10	6 25	17 57	6 35	18 07	6 33	18 04	6 35	18 04	6 33	18 01	6 44	18 11	6 50	18 19
11	6 23	17 59	6 33	18 09	6 31	18 06	6 32	18 06	6 31	18 03	6 42	18 13	6 48	18 20
12	6 20	18 00	6 30	18 10	6 28	18 07	6 30	18 08	6 28	18 05	6 39	18 15	6 45	18 22
13	6 18	18 02	6 28	18 12	6 26	18 09	6 28	18 10	6 26	18 07	6 37	18 17	6 43	18 24
14	6 16	18 04	6 26	18 14	6 24	18 11	6 25	18 12	6 23	18 09	6 34	18 19	6 40	18 26
15	6 14	18 06	6 24	18 16	6 21	18 13	6 23	18 14	6 21	18 11	6 31	18 21	6 38	18 28
16	6 11	18 07	6 21	18 17	6 19	18 14	6 20	18 16	6 18	18 13	6 29	18 23	6 35	18 30
17	6 09	18 09	6 19	18 19	6 17	18 16	6 18	18 17	6 16	18 15	6 26	18 25	6 33	18 32
18	6 07	18 11	6 17	18 21	6 14	18 18	6 16	18 19	6 13	18 17	6 24	18 27	6 30	18 34
19	6 05	18 12	6 15	18 22	6 12	18 20	6 13	18 21	6 11	18 19	6 21	18 29	6 28	18 36
20	6 02	18 14	6 12	18 24	6 10	18 22	6 11	18 23	6 08	18 21	6 18	18 31	6 25	18 38
21	6 00	18 16	6 10	18 26	6 07	18 23	6 08	18 25	6 05	18 23	6 16	18 33	6 23	18 40
22	5 58	18 17	6 08	18 27	6 05	18 25	6 06	18 27	6 03	18 25	6 13	18 35	6 20	18 42
23	5 55	18 19	6 05	18 29	6 02	18 27	6 03	18 29	6 00	18 27	6 10	18 38	6 18	18 44
24	5 53	18 21	6 03	18 31	6 00	18 29	6 01	18 30	5 58	18 29	6 08	18 40	6 15	18 46
25	5 51	18 22	6 01	18 32	5 58	18 30	5 59	18 32	5 55	18 31	6 05	18 42	6 13	18 48
26	5 49	18 24	5 59	18 34	5 55	18 32	5 56	18 34	5 53	18 33	6 03	18 44	6 10	18 50
27	5 46	18 26	5 56	18 36	5 53	18 34	5 54	18 36	5 50	18 34	6 00	18 46	6 08	18 51
28	5 44	18 28	5 54	18 37	5 51	18 36	5 51	18 38	5 48	18 36	5 57	18 48	6 05	18 53
29	5 42	18 29	5 52	18 39	5 48	18 37	5 49	18 40	5 45	18 38	5 55	18 50	6 03	18 55
30	5 40	18 31	5 50	18 41	5 46	18 39	5 46	18 41	5 43	18 40	5 52	18 52	6 00	18 57
31	5 37	18 33	5 47	18 43	5 44	18 41	5 44	18 43	5 40	18 42	5 49	18 54	5 58	18 59

JUPITER

Day	R.A.		Dec.		Transit		5° high	
							52°	56°
	h	m	°	'	h	m	h m	h m
1	2	20.0	+12	57	15	41	22 15	22 22
11	2	27.3	+13	35	15	09	21 46	21 54
21	2	35.3	+14	15	14	38	21 18	21 27
31	2	43.7	+14	56	14	07	20 51	21 00

Diameters – equatorial 35" polar 33"

SATURN

Day	R.A.		Dec.		Transit		5° high	
							52°	56°
	h	m	°	'	h	m	h m	h m
1	13	51.9	−8	38	3	15	22 30	22 41
11	13	50.3	−8	27	2	34	21 48	21 59
21	13	48.1	−8	13	1	52	21 05	21 16
31	13	45.6	−7	58	1	10	20 22	20 32

Diameters – equatorial 19" polar 17"
Rings – major axis 42" minor axis 11"

URANUS

Day	R.A.		Dec.		Transit		10° high	
							52°	56°
	h	m	°	'	h	m	h m	h m
1	0	12.8	+0	38	13	34	18 31	18 25
11	0	14.8	+0	51	12	57	17 55	17 49
21	0	16.9	+1	04	12	19	17 19	17 13
31	0	19.0	+1	18	11	42	16 43	16 37

Diameter 4"

NEPTUNE

Day	R.A.		Dec.		Transit		10° high	
							52°	56°
	h	m	°	'	h	m	h m	h m
1	22	12.9	−11	38	11	34	7 49	8 09
11	22	14.3	−11	30	10	56	7 10	7 30
21	22	15.7	−11	23	10	18	6 31	6 51
31	22	16.9	−11	16	9	40	5 52	6 12

Diameter 2"

APRIL 2012

FOURTH MONTH, 30 DAYS. *Aperire*, to open; Earth opens to receive seed.

1	*Sunday*	William Harvey, physician best known for his description of blood circulation *b.* 1578	day 92

2	*Monday*	Samuel Morse, inventor of Morse Code (communications system of dots and dashes) *d.* 1872	week 14 day 93
3	*Tuesday*	RAF officer David McIntyre completed the first aerial photographic survey of Mt Everest 1933	94
4	*Wednesday*	Microsoft, the computer technology corporation, was founded by Bill Gates and Paul Allen 1975	95
5	*Thursday*	Joseph Lister, surgeon and medical scientist credited as the founder of antiseptic medicine *b.* 1827	96
6	*Friday*	*Early Bird* became the first commercial communications satellite to be placed in geosynchronous orbit 1965	97
7	*Saturday*	Congreves – the original friction matches – were first sold by their inventor, John Walker 1827	98
8	*Sunday*	The steamship *Great Western*, designed by Isambard K. Brunel, made her maiden transatlantic voyage 1838	99

9	*Monday*	The space shuttle *Endeavour* was launched on an 11-day mission 1994	week 15 day 100
10	*Tuesday*	Walter Hunt, a mechanic and inventor, received a patent for the safety pin 1849	101
11	*Wednesday*	The Ryan X-13 Vertijet, the first jet to take off and land vertically, completed a full flight 1957	102
12	*Thursday*	Yuri Gagarin became the first man to travel in space; the Soviet Union declared the space race won 1961	103
13	*Friday*	Joseph Bramah, engineer and inventor best known for inventing the hydraulic press *b.* 1748	104
14	*Saturday*	Christiaan Huygens, mathematician, astronomer and physicist who invented the pendulum clock *b.* 1629	105
15	*Sunday*	Leonardo da Vinci, polymathic artist, engineer and scientist *b.*1452	106

16	*Monday*	Isaac Newton was knighted by Queen Anne at Trinity College, London 1705	week 16 day 107
17	*Tuesday*	The crew of Apollo 13 safely landed on Earth after experiencing a major malfunction while en route to the Moon 1970	108
18	*Wednesday*	Albert Einstein, physicist awarded the Nobel Prize for Physics for his theories of relativity *d.* 1955	109
19	*Thursday*	Charles Darwin, naturalist best known for his study of evolution and *On the Origin of Species d.* 1882	110
20	*Friday*	Marie Curie, physicist and chemist, isolated the radioactive element radium 1902	111
21	*Saturday*	Crew from Apollo 16 landed in the previously unexplored Descartes Highlands area of the Moon 1972	112
22	*Sunday*	James Hargreaves, carpenter and inventor, credited with inventing the spinning jenny *d.* 1778	113

23	*Monday*	Max Planck, physicist who formulated the quantum theory of radiation *b.* 1858	week 17 day 114
24	*Tuesday*	The Hubble Space Telescope was launched 1990	115
25	*Wednesday*	Construction of the 163km Suez Canal (connecting the Mediterranean with the Red Sea) began 1859	116
26	*Thursday*	Charles Richter, seismologist best known for inventing the earthquake-measuring Richter scale *b.* 1900	117
27	*Friday*	Francis Clarke and M. G. Foster received a patent for the electric hearing aid 1880	118
28	*Saturday*	Dennis Tito, a businessman, made history by becoming the first paying passenger to go into space 2001	119
29	*Sunday*	Harold Urey, scientist who was a key figure in developing the atomic bomb *b.* 1893	120

30	*Monday*	J. J. Thomson announced his discovery of the first subatomic particle, the electron 1897	week 18 day 121

ASTRONOMICAL PHENOMENA

d h
3 21 Mars in conjunction with Moon. Mars 8°N.
4 10 Mercury at stationary point
7 10 Saturn in conjunction with Moon. Saturn 6°N.
10 16 Pluto at stationary point
14 04 Mars at stationary point
15 18 Saturn at opposition
18 17 Mercury at greatest elongation W. 27°
18 19 Mercury in conjunction with Moon. Mercury 7°S.
19 16 Sun's longitude 30° ♉
22 17 Jupiter in conjunction with Moon. Jupiter 2°S.
25 04 Venus in conjuction with Moon. Venus 6°N.
30 01 Venus at greatest brilliancy

MINIMA OF ALGOL

d	h	d	h	d	h
3	18.6	15	05.9	26	17.1
6	15.4	18	02.7	29	14.0
9	12.2	20	23.5		
12	09.0	23	20.3		

CONSTELLATIONS

The following constellations are near the meridian at

	d	h		d	h
March	1	24	April	15	21
March	16	23	May	1	20
April	1	22	May	16	19

Cepheus (below the Pole), Cassiopeia (below the Pole), Ursa Major, Leo Minor, Leo, Sextans, Hydra and Crater

THE MOON

Phases, Apsides and Node	d	h	m
○ Full Moon	6	19	19
☾ Last Quarter	13	10	50
● New Moon	21	07	18
☽ First Quarter	29	09	57

Perigee (358,306km)	7	17	06
Apogee (406,429km)	22	14	03

Mean longitude of ascending node on April 1, 248°

THE SUN

s.d. 16'.0

Day	Right Ascension			Dec. +		Equation of time		Rise 52°		Rise 56°		Transit		Set 52°		Set 56°		Sidereal time			Transit of first point of Aries		
	h	m	s	°	'	m	s	h	m	h	m	h	m	h	m	h	m	h	m	s	h	m	s
1	0	42	55	4	37	−3	53	5	34	5	30	12	04	18	34	18	39	12	39	02	11	19	07
2	0	46	34	5	00	−3	35	5	32	5	27	12	03	18	36	18	41	12	42	58	11	15	11
3	0	50	13	5	23	−3	18	5	30	5	25	12	03	18	38	18	43	12	46	55	11	11	15
4	0	53	52	5	46	−3	00	5	27	5	22	12	03	18	40	18	45	12	50	52	11	07	19
5	0	57	31	6	09	−2	43	5	25	5	19	12	03	18	41	18	47	12	54	48	11	03	23
6	1	01	10	6	31	−2	26	5	23	5	17	12	02	18	43	18	49	12	58	45	10	59	27
7	1	04	50	6	54	−2	09	5	20	5	14	12	02	18	45	18	51	13	02	41	10	55	31
8	1	08	30	7	16	−1	52	5	18	5	12	12	02	18	46	18	53	13	06	38	10	51	35
9	1	12	10	7	39	−1	35	5	16	5	09	12	01	18	48	18	55	13	10	34	10	47	39
10	1	15	50	8	01	−1	19	5	14	5	06	12	01	18	50	18	57	13	14	31	10	43	43
11	1	19	31	8	23	−1	03	5	11	5	04	12	01	18	51	18	59	13	18	27	10	39	47
12	1	23	11	8	45	−0	47	5	09	5	01	12	01	18	53	19	01	13	22	24	10	35	52
13	1	26	53	9	07	−0	32	5	07	4	59	12	00	18	55	19	03	13	26	21	10	31	56
14	1	30	34	9	28	−0	17	5	05	4	56	12	00	18	57	19	05	13	30	17	10	28	00
15	1	34	16	9	50	−0	02	5	03	4	54	12	00	18	58	19	08	13	34	14	10	24	04
16	1	37	58	10	11	+0	12	5	00	4	51	12	00	19	00	19	10	13	38	10	10	20	08
17	1	41	41	10	32	+0	26	4	58	4	49	11	59	19	02	19	12	13	42	07	10	16	12
18	1	45	24	10	53	+0	39	4	56	4	46	11	59	19	03	19	14	13	46	03	10	12	16
19	1	49	08	11	14	+0	52	4	54	4	44	11	59	19	05	19	16	13	50	00	10	08	20
20	1	52	51	11	35	+1	05	4	52	4	41	11	59	19	07	19	18	13	53	56	10	04	24
21	1	56	36	11	55	+1	17	4	50	4	39	11	59	19	09	19	20	13	57	53	10	00	28
22	2	00	21	12	16	+1	29	4	48	4	36	11	58	19	10	19	22	14	01	50	9	56	32
23	2	04	06	12	36	+1	40	4	46	4	34	11	58	19	12	19	24	14	05	46	9	52	37
24	2	07	51	12	56	+1	51	4	44	4	32	11	58	19	14	19	26	14	09	43	9	48	41
25	2	11	38	13	15	+2	02	4	42	4	29	11	58	19	15	19	28	14	13	39	9	44	45
26	2	15	24	13	35	+2	12	4	40	4	27	11	58	19	17	19	30	14	17	36	9	40	49
27	2	19	11	13	54	+2	21	4	38	4	25	11	58	19	19	19	32	14	21	32	9	36	53
28	2	22	59	14	13	+2	30	4	36	4	22	11	57	19	20	19	34	14	25	29	9	32	57
29	2	26	47	14	31	+2	38	4	34	4	20	11	57	19	22	19	36	14	29	25	9	29	01
30	2	30	36	14	50	+2	46	4	32	4	18	11	57	19	24	19	38	14	33	22	9	25	05

DURATION OF TWILIGHT (in minutes)

Latitude	52°	56°	52°	56°	52°	56°	52°	56°
	1 April		11 April		21 April		31 April	
Civil	34	38	35	39	37	42	39	44
Nautical	76	84	79	89	83	96	89	106
Astronomical	120	136	127	147	137	165	152	204

THE NIGHT SKY

Mercury, despite being at greatest western elongation (27 degrees) on the 18th, is unsuitably placed for observation throughout the month.

Venus, magnitude −4.5, reaches its greatest brilliancy on the last day of the month and therefore continues to dominate the western sky in the evenings for several hours after sunset. The waxing crescent Moon will be seen passing about 6 degrees south of the planet on April 24–25.

Mars, its magnitude fading from −0.7 to 0.0 during the month, is in the constellation of Leo, reaching its second stationary point on the 14th. By the end of the month it will be too low in the west-north-western sky to be visible after about 02h. On the night of April 3–4 the waxing gibbous Moon passes about 9 degrees south of the planet.

Jupiter, magnitude −2.0, is only visible for about the first 3 weeks of April, low in the western sky after sunset. However, it may be possible to detect it on the evening of the 22nd as the thin crescent Moon passes 2 degrees north of it.

Saturn, reaches opposition on the 15th, and therefore is visible throughout the hours of darkness. It is in the constellation of Virgo, and has a magnitude of +0.2. The rings of Saturn are getting more easily visible in smaller telescopes as the minor axis is now 10 arcseconds. The Full Moon is in the vicinity of the planet on the night of April 6–7, passing 7 degrees south of it.

THE MOON

Day	R.A. h	R.A. m	Dec. °	Hor. Par. ′	Semi-diam. ′	Sun's Co-Long. °	PA of Br. Limb °	Ph. %	Age d	Rise 52° h	Rise 52° m	Rise 56° h	Rise 56° m	Transit h	Transit m	Set 52° h	Set 52° m	Set 56° h	Set 56° m
1	7	46	+17.3	56.5	15.4	21	279	62	9.4	12	09	11	54	19	47	2	44	2	59
2	8	39	+13.8	57.4	15.6	34	283	72	10.4	13	23	13	13	20	37	3	11	3	23
3	9	31	+9.5	58.3	15.9	46	285	81	11.4	14	41	14	35	21	27	3	36	3	43
4	10	23	+4.6	59.2	16.1	58	285	89	12.4	16	01	16	01	22	19	3	59	4	02
5	11	17	−0.8	60.1	16.4	70	283	95	13.4	17	25	17	29	23	12	4	21	4	20
6	12	12	−6.2	60.7	16.5	82	272	99	14.4	18	50	18	59	—		4	45	4	39
7	13	10	−11.4	61.1	16.7	94	165	100	15.4	20	16	20	31	0	07	5	12	5	01
8	14	09	−15.8	61.2	16.7	107	118	98	16.4	21	40	22	00	1	05	5	44	5	29
9	15	11	−19.2	60.9	16.6	119	108	93	17.4	22	57	23	20	2	06	6	24	6	04
10	16	14	−21.2	60.4	16.5	131	100	85	18.4	—		—		3	07	7	14	6	51
11	17	17	−21.8	59.7	16.3	143	94	76	19.4	0	03	0	26	4	08	8	15	7	51
12	18	17	−20.9	58.9	16.1	155	87	66	20.4	0	55	1	17	5	07	9	23	9	02
13	19	15	−18.8	58.1	15.8	167	82	55	21.4	1	36	1	54	6	02	10	35	10	18
14	20	10	−15.7	57.3	15.6	180	78	44	22.4	2	08	2	22	6	54	11	48	11	35
15	21	01	−11.9	56.5	15.4	192	75	34	23.4	2	33	2	43	7	42	13	00	12	52
16	21	50	−7.7	55.9	15.2	204	73	25	24.4	2	55	3	01	8	27	14	11	14	06
17	22	37	−3.2	55.3	15.1	216	73	17	25.4	3	14	3	16	9	11	15	19	15	19
18	23	22	+1.4	54.9	14.9	228	73	10	26.4	3	33	3	31	9	53	16	27	16	30
19	0	08	+5.8	54.5	14.9	241	76	5	27.4	3	51	3	46	10	36	17	33	17	41
20	0	53	+10.0	54.2	14.8	253	82	2	28.4	4	11	4	02	11	19	18	40	18	51
21	1	39	+13.7	54.1	14.7	265	112	0	29.4	4	34	4	21	12	03	19	45	20	00
22	2	27	+16.9	54.0	14.7	277	235	0	0.7	5	00	4	43	12	49	20	48	21	07
23	3	15	+19.4	54.0	14.7	290	251	3	1.7	5	31	5	11	13	36	21	48	22	09
24	4	05	+21.0	54.0	14.7	302	259	6	2.7	6	09	5	47	14	24	22	42	23	05
25	4	56	+21.7	54.2	14.8	314	265	12	3.7	6	54	6	31	15	13	23	29	23	52
26	5	48	+21.4	54.6	14.9	326	270	19	4.7	7	48	7	26	16	02	—		—	
27	6	39	+20.2	55.0	15.0	339	275	27	5.7	8	48	8	29	16	51	0	10	0	30
28	7	31	+18.0	55.6	15.1	351	280	36	6.7	9	55	9	38	17	40	0	43	1	00
29	8	22	+14.8	56.3	15.3	3	284	46	7.7	11	05	10	53	18	28	1	12	1	25
30	9	12	+10.9	57.2	15.6	15	287	56	8.7	12	19	12	11	19	16	1	37	1	46

MERCURY

Day	R.A. h	R.A. m	Dec. °	Diam. ″	Phase %	Transit h	Transit m	5° high 52° h	5° high 52° m	5° high 56° h	5° high 56° m
1	23	38	−1.3	11	13	10	57	5	38	5	42
3	23	37	−2.0	10	17	10	48	5	32	5	37
5	23	38	−2.5	10	21	10	41	5	28	5	33
7	23	39	−2.8	10	25	10	35	5	23	5	29
9	23	42	−2.9	9	29	10	31	5	19	5	25
11	23	46	−2.9	9	33	10	27	5	15	5	21
13	23	51	−2.7	9	37	10	24	5	11	5	17
15	23	57	−2.4	8	40	10	23	5	08	5	13
17	0	04	−2.0	8	44	10	21	5	04	5	09
19	0	11	−1.4	8	47	10	21	5	01	5	05
21	0	19	−0.8	8	50	10	21	4	57	5	01
23	0	27	0.0	7	53	10	22	4	54	4	57
25	0	36	+0.9	7	56	10	23	4	50	4	53
27	0	46	+1.9	7	58	10	25	4	47	4	49
29	0	56	+2.9	7	61	10	27	4	44	4	45
31	1	07	+4.0	6	64	10	30	4	41	4	41

VENUS

Day	R.A. h	R.A. m	Dec. °	Diam. ″	Phase %	Transit h	Transit m	5° high 52° h	5° high 52° m	5° high 56° h	5° high 56° m
1	3	38	+23.0	25	49	14	59	22	32	22	50
6	3	57	+24.3	26	46	14	58	22	40	23	00
11	4	16	+25.4	28	42	14	57	22	46	23	07
16	4	33	+26.3	30	39	14	55	22	49	23	12
21	4	49	+27.0	32	35	14	51	22	50	23	14
26	5	04	+27.5	35	31	14	45	22	47	23	12
31	5	16	+27.8	37	27	14	38	22	41	23	06

MARS

Day	R.A. h	R.A. m	Dec. °	Diam. ″	Phase %	Transit h	Transit m	5° high 52° h	5° high 52° m	5° high 56° h	5° high 56° m
1	10	31	+12.8	13	97	21	48	4	25	4	33
6	10	29	+12.9	12	96	21	26	4	03	4	10
11	10	27	+12.8	12	95	21	05	3	41	3	49
16	10	26	+12.6	11	94	20	45	3	20	3	27
21	10	27	+12.4	11	93	20	26	3	00	3	07
26	10	29	+12.0	10	92	20	08	2	40	2	46
31	10	32	+11.5	10	91	19	52	2	21	2	27

SUNRISE AND SUNSET

	London 0° 05'	51° 30'	Bristol 2° 35'	51° 28'	Birmingham 1° 55'	52° 28'	Manchester 2° 15'	53° 28'	Newcastle 1° 37'	54° 59'	Glasgow 4° 14'	55° 52'	Belfast 5° 56'	54° 35'
d	h m	h m	h m	h m	h m	h m	h m	h m	h m	h m	h m	h m	h m	h m
1	5 35	18 34	5 45	18 44	5 41	18 43	5 42	18 45	5 37	18 44	5 47	18 56	5 55	19 01
2	5 33	18 36	5 43	18 46	5 39	18 44	5 39	18 47	5 35	18 46	5 44	18 58	5 53	19 03
3	5 30	18 38	5 41	18 48	5 37	18 46	5 37	18 49	5 32	18 48	5 42	19 00	5 50	19 05
4	5 28	18 39	5 38	18 49	5 34	18 48	5 34	18 50	5 30	18 50	5 39	19 02	5 48	19 07
5	5 26	18 41	5 36	18 51	5 32	18 50	5 32	18 52	5 27	18 52	5 36	19 04	5 45	19 09
6	5 24	18 43	5 34	18 53	5 30	18 51	5 30	18 54	5 25	18 54	5 34	19 06	5 43	19 11
7	5 22	18 44	5 32	18 54	5 27	18 53	5 27	18 56	5 22	18 56	5 31	19 08	5 40	19 12
8	5 19	18 46	5 29	18 56	5 25	18 55	5 25	18 58	5 20	18 58	5 29	19 10	5 38	19 14
9	5 17	18 48	5 27	18 58	5 23	18 56	5 23	19 00	5 17	19 00	5 26	19 12	5 35	19 16
10	5 15	18 49	5 25	18 59	5 21	18 58	5 20	19 01	5 15	19 02	5 24	19 14	5 33	19 18
11	5 13	18 51	5 23	19 01	5 18	19 00	5 18	19 03	5 12	19 04	5 21	19 16	5 30	19 20
12	5 10	18 53	5 21	19 03	5 16	19 02	5 16	19 05	5 10	19 06	5 18	19 18	5 28	19 22
13	5 08	18 54	5 18	19 04	5 14	19 03	5 13	19 07	5 07	19 08	5 16	19 20	5 26	19 24
14	5 06	18 56	5 16	19 06	5 12	19 05	5 11	19 09	5 05	19 10	5 13	19 22	5 23	19 26
15	5 04	18 58	5 14	19 08	5 09	19 07	5 09	19 10	5 03	19 11	5 11	19 24	5 21	19 28
16	5 02	18 59	5 12	19 09	5 07	19 09	5 06	19 12	5 00	19 13	5 08	19 26	5 18	19 30
17	5 00	19 01	5 10	19 11	5 05	19 10	5 04	19 14	4 58	19 15	5 06	19 28	5 16	19 32
18	4 58	19 03	5 08	19 13	5 03	19 12	5 02	19 16	4 55	19 17	5 03	19 30	5 14	19 34
19	4 56	19 04	5 06	19 14	5 01	19 14	4 59	19 18	4 53	19 19	5 01	19 32	5 11	19 35
20	4 53	19 06	5 03	19 16	4 58	19 16	4 57	19 20	4 51	19 21	4 59	19 34	5 09	19 37
21	4 51	19 08	5 01	19 18	4 56	19 17	4 55	19 21	4 48	19 23	4 56	19 36	5 07	19 39
22	4 49	19 09	4 59	19 19	4 54	19 19	4 53	19 23	4 46	19 25	4 54	19 38	5 04	19 41
23	4 47	19 11	4 57	19 21	4 52	19 21	4 51	19 25	4 44	19 27	4 51	19 40	5 02	19 43
24	4 45	19 13	4 55	19 23	4 50	19 23	4 48	19 27	4 41	19 29	4 49	19 42	5 00	19 45
25	4 43	19 14	4 53	19 24	4 48	19 24	4 46	19 29	4 39	19 31	4 47	19 44	4 58	19 47
26	4 41	19 16	4 51	19 26	4 46	19 26	4 44	19 30	4 37	19 33	4 44	19 46	4 55	19 49
27	4 39	19 18	4 49	19 28	4 44	19 28	4 42	19 32	4 35	19 35	4 42	19 48	4 53	19 51
28	4 37	19 19	4 47	19 29	4 42	19 30	4 40	19 34	4 32	19 37	4 40	19 50	4 51	19 53
29	4 35	19 21	4 46	19 31	4 40	19 31	4 38	19 36	4 30	19 39	4 37	19 52	4 49	19 55
30	4 34	19 23	4 44	19 32	4 38	19 33	4 36	19 38	4 28	19 41	4 35	19 55	4 47	19 56

JUPITER

Day	R.A. h m	Dec. ° '	Transit h m	5° high 52° h m	56° h m
1	2 44.5	+15 00	14 04	20 48	20 58
11	2 53.4	+15 41	13 33	20 22	20 32
21	3 02.6	+16 21	13 03	19 55	20 06
31	3 12.0	+17 00	12 33	19 29	19 40

Diameters – equatorial 33" polar 31"

SATURN

Day	R.A. h m	Dec. ° '	Transit h m	5° high 52° h m	56° h m
1	13 45.3	−7 56	1 06	5 50	5 40
11	13 42.5	−7 39	0 24	5 10	5 00
21	13 39.7	−7 23	23 38	4 29	4 19
31	13 36.8	−7 07	22 56	3 48	3 39

Diameters – equatorial 19" polar 17"
Rings – major axis 43" minor axis 10"

URANUS

Day	R.A. h m	Dec. ° '	Transit h m	10° high 52° h m	56° h m
1	0 19.2	+1 19	11 38	6 38	6 43
11	0 21.2	+1 33	11 01	5 59	6 05
21	0 23.2	+1 46	10 24	5 21	5 26
31	0 25.1	+1 58	9 46	4 42	4 47

Diameter 4"

NEPTUNE

Day	R.A. h m	Dec. ° '	Transit h m	10° high 52° h m	56° h m
1	22 17.1	−11 16	9 37	5 49	6 08
11	22 18.2	−11 09	8 58	5 10	5 29
21	22 19.2	−11 04	8 20	4 31	4 50
31	22 20.0	−11 00	7 41	3 52	4 11

Diameter 2"

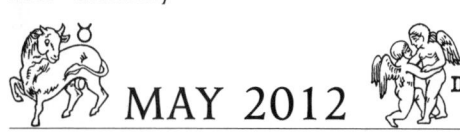

MAY 2012

FIFTH MONTH, 31 DAYS. *Maia*, goddess of growth and increase

1	*Tuesday*	The Empire State Building, at the time, the tallest skyscraper in the world, dedicated 1931	day 122
2	*Wednesday*	Sir William Bayliss, physiologist who discovered the first known hormone, secretin *b.* 1860	123
3	*Thursday*	A team of 18 doctors led by Donald Ross successfully completed the UK's first heart transplant 1968	124
4	*Friday*	Bartolomeo Cristofori, inventor of the pianoforte, precursor of the piano *b.* 1655	125
5	*Saturday*	*Ariel 3,* the first artificial satellite designed and built in Britain, was launched from the USA 1967	126
6	*Sunday*	Yale's self-detaching and attaching key-lock was patented by Linus Yale, Jr 1851	127

7	*Monday*	Edwin Land, inventor of the Polaroid camera *b.* 1909	week 19 day 128
8	*Tuesday*	The Thames Barrier was officially opened by HM Queen Elizabeth II 1984	129
9	*Wednesday*	Albert Michelson, physicist who became the first American to win the Nobel prize in sciences *d.* 1931	130
10	*Thursday*	The First Transcontinental Railroad, revolutionising transportation in the USA, was completed 1869	131
11	*Friday*	Ottmar Mergenthaler, inventor whose Linotype typesetting machine revolutionised publishing *b.* 1854	132
12	*Saturday*	Dorothy Hodgkin, biochemist whose research into chemical structures led to her 1964 Nobel prize *b.* 1910	133
13	*Sunday*	Marie Curie, Nobel prize winning physicist, became the first female professor at the Sorbonne 1906	134

14	*Monday*	H. J. Heinz, founder of the H. J. Heinz Co., producer of ketchup and other foods *d.* 1919	week 20 day 135
15	*Tuesday*	The W-1 turbojet engine, the first Allied aircraft to use jet propulsion, was tested in Britain 1941	136
16	*Wednesday*	Bouncing bombs, developed by Barnes Wallis, were used in Operation Chastise by the RAF 1943	137
17	*Thursday*	Edward Jenner, surgeon who received worldwide recognition for developing a smallpox vaccine *b.* 1749	138
18	*Friday*	Helen Sharman became the first Briton in space after answering an advert for an astronaut vacancy 1991	139
19	*Saturday*	Balamurali Ambati, aged 17 years and 294 days, graduated to become the world's youngest doctor 1995	140
20	*Sunday*	Levi Strauss and Jacob Davis received a patent to create 'waist overalls', now known as blue jeans 1873	141

21	*Monday*	Charles Lindbergh landed in Paris, completing the first solo non-stop transatlantic flight 1927	week 21 day 142
22	*Tuesday*	Apollo 10's lunar module flew within 14 miles of the Moon's surface in a rehearsal for Apollo 11 1969	143
23	*Wednesday*	Franz Mesmer, a forerunner of modern hypnotists who used to 'mesmerise' his patients *b.* 1734	144
24	*Thursday*	Samuel Morse sent the first telegraph – 'What hath God wrought!' – from Baltimore to Washington 1844	145
25	*Friday*	Igor Sikorsky, pilot and pioneer of aviation in fixed-wing aircraft and helicopters *b.* 1889	146
26	*Saturday*	Sally Ride, the first American woman to go into space (aboard the *Challenger* in 1983) *b.* 1951	147
27	*Sunday*	John Howard Northrop, biochemist whose study of enzymes led to his 1946 Nobel prize *d.* 1987	148

28	*Monday*	Two monkeys, Able and Baker, became the first living creatures to survive space flight 1959	week 22 day 149
29	*Tuesday*	Sir Humphry Davy, chemist who discovered several chemical elements, including magnesium *d.* 1829	150
30	*Wednesday*	The first hovercraft, the SR. N1 designed by Sir Christopher Cockerell, made its maiden trip 1959	151
31	*Thursday*	John Harvey Kellogg applied for a patent for 'flaked cereal', now known as Corn Flakes 1884	152

ASTRONOMICAL PHENOMENA

d h
1 08 Mars in conjunction with Moon. Mars 7°N.
4 18 Saturn in conjunction with Moon. Saturn 6°N.
13 13 Jupiter in conjunction
15 15 Venus at stationary point
20 05 Mercury in conjunction with Moon. Mercury 2°S.
20 13 Jupiter in conjunction with Moon. Jupiter 2°S.
20 15 Sun's longitude 60° ♊
21 00 Annular eclipse of Sun (see page 1278)
22 06 Jupiter in conjunction with Mercury. Jupiter 0°.4 S.
22 21 Venus in conjunction with Moon. Venus 5°N.
27 11 Mercury in superior conjunction
29 06 Mars in conjunction with Moon. Mars 6°N.

MINIMA OF ALGOL

Algol is inconveniently situated for observation during May

CONSTELLATIONS

The following constellations are near the meridian at

	d	h		d	h
April	1	24	May	16	21
April	15	23	June	1	20
May	1	22	June	15	19

Cepheus (below the Pole), Cassiopeia (below the Pole), Ursa Minor, Ursa Major, Canes Venatici, Coma Berenices, Bootes, Leo, Virgo, Crater, Corvus and Hydra

THE MOON

Phases, Apsides and Node	d	h	m
○ Full Moon	6	03	35
☾ Last Quarter	12	21	47
● New Moon	20	23	47
☽ First Quarter	28	20	16

Perigee (356,955 km)	6	03	40
Apogee (406,439 km)	19	16	28

Mean longitude of ascending node on May 1, 247°

THE SUN

Day	Right Ascension			Dec.		Equation of time		Rise 52°		Rise 56°		Transit		Set 52°		Set 56°		Sidereal time			Transit of first point of Aries		
	h	m	s	°	′	m	s	h	m	h	m	h	m	h	m	h	m	h	m	s	h	m	s
1	2	34	25	15	08	+2	54	4	30	4	15	11	57	19	25	19	40	14	37	19	9	21	09
2	2	38	14	15	26	+3	01	4	28	4	13	11	57	19	27	19	42	14	41	15	9	17	13
3	2	42	04	15	44	+3	07	4	26	4	11	11	57	19	29	19	44	14	45	12	9	13	17
4	2	45	55	16	01	+3	13	4	24	4	09	11	57	19	30	19	46	14	49	08	9	09	22
5	2	49	46	16	18	+3	18	4	22	4	07	11	57	19	32	19	48	14	53	05	9	05	26
6	2	53	38	16	35	+3	23	4	20	4	04	11	57	19	34	19	50	14	57	01	9	01	30
7	2	57	30	16	52	+3	27	4	19	4	02	11	57	19	35	19	52	15	00	58	8	57	34
8	3	01	23	17	08	+3	31	4	17	4	00	11	56	19	37	19	54	15	04	54	8	53	38
9	3	05	17	17	24	+3	34	4	15	3	58	11	56	19	39	19	56	15	08	51	8	49	42
10	3	09	11	17	40	+3	37	4	14	3	56	11	56	19	40	19	58	15	12	48	8	45	46
11	3	13	06	17	56	+3	39	4	12	3	54	11	56	19	42	20	00	15	16	44	8	41	50
12	3	17	01	18	11	+3	40	4	10	3	52	11	56	19	43	20	02	15	20	41	8	37	54
13	3	20	57	18	26	+3	41	4	09	3	50	11	56	19	45	20	04	15	24	37	8	33	58
14	3	24	53	18	40	+3	41	4	07	3	48	11	56	19	46	20	05	15	28	34	8	30	02
15	3	28	50	18	55	+3	40	4	06	3	47	11	56	19	48	20	07	15	32	30	8	26	07
16	3	32	48	19	09	+3	39	4	04	3	45	11	56	19	50	20	09	15	36	27	8	22	11
17	3	36	46	19	22	+3	38	4	03	3	43	11	56	19	51	20	11	15	40	23	8	18	15
18	3	40	45	19	35	+3	35	4	01	3	41	11	56	19	53	20	13	15	44	20	8	14	19
19	3	44	44	19	48	+3	33	4	00	3	40	11	56	19	54	20	15	15	48	17	8	10	23
20	3	48	44	20	01	+3	29	3	59	3	38	11	57	19	55	20	16	15	52	13	8	06	27
21	3	52	44	20	13	+3	25	3	57	3	36	11	57	19	57	20	18	15	56	10	8	02	31
22	3	56	45	20	25	+3	21	3	56	3	35	11	57	19	58	20	20	16	00	06	7	58	35
23	4	00	47	20	37	+3	16	3	55	3	33	11	57	20	00	20	21	16	04	03	7	54	39
24	4	04	49	20	48	+3	11	3	54	3	32	11	57	20	01	20	23	16	07	59	7	50	43
25	4	08	51	20	59	+3	05	3	52	3	30	11	57	20	02	20	25	16	11	56	7	46	47
26	4	12	54	21	09	+2	58	3	51	3	29	11	57	20	04	20	26	16	15	52	7	42	52
27	4	16	57	21	20	+2	52	3	50	3	28	11	57	20	05	20	28	16	19	49	7	38	56
28	4	21	01	21	29	+2	44	3	49	3	26	11	57	20	06	20	29	16	23	46	7	35	00
29	4	25	06	21	39	+2	36	3	48	3	25	11	57	20	07	20	31	16	27	42	7	31	04
30	4	29	10	21	48	+2	28	3	47	3	24	11	58	20	08	20	32	16	31	39	7	27	08
31	4	33	15	21	56	+2	20	3	47	3	23	11	58	20	10	20	34	16	35	35	7	23	12

DURATION OF TWILIGHT (in minutes)

Latitude	52°	56°	52°	56°	52°	56°	52°	56°
	1 May		11 May		21 May		31 May	
Civil	39	44	41	48	44	53	46	57
Nautical	89	106	97	120	106	141	115	187
Astronomical	152	204	176	TAN	TAN	TAN	TAN	TAN

THE NIGHT SKY

Mercury remains unsuitably placed for observation throughout the month.

Venus, magnitude −4.4, continues to be visible in the west-northwestern sky in the evenings after sunset. The period available for observation is decreasing day by day so that by the end of the month Venus will only be seen for a very short while after sunset. Observers with small telescopes will notice a significant change in the size and shape of the planet during the month. On the 1st it is about a quarter illuminated with a diameter of 37 arc-seconds while at the end of May it is an incredibly thin sliver, only 1% illuminated but with a diameter of 57 seconds – if it can be seen at all! On the evening of May 22nd the waxing crescent moon passes 5 degrees south of the planet.

Mars continues to be visible in the southwestern sky in the evenings, but by the end of the month it will be lost to view soon after midnight. During May its magnitude fades from 0.0 to +0.5. On the first day of the month the Moon, just past First Quarter, passes 8 degrees south of the planet: again, on the 29th, it passes 7 degrees south of the planet.

Jupiter remains too close to the Sun for observation throughout the month.

Saturn continues to be visible in the southern skies, in the constellation of Virgo, moving slowly retrograde a few degrees north of Spica. Its magnitude is +0.4. On the 4th the waxing gibbous Moon passes 7 degrees south of Saturn.

THE MOON

Day	R.A. h	R.A. m	Dec. °	Hor. Par. ′	Semi-diam. ′	Sun's Co-Long. °	PA of Bright Limb °	Ph. %	Age d	Rise 52° h	Rise 52° m	Rise 56° h	Rise 56° m	Transit h	Transit m	Set 52° h	Set 52° m	Set 56° h	Set 56° m
1	10	03	+6.4	58.1	15.8	27	289	67	9.7	13	35	13	32	20	06	1	59	2	04
2	10	55	+1.3	59.0	16.1	40	289	77	10.7	14	54	14	56	20	56	2	21	2	22
3	11	48	−3.9	59.9	16.3	52	289	86	11.7	16	17	16	24	21	49	2	44	2	40
4	12	43	−9.1	60.7	16.5	64	286	93	12.7	17	42	17	54	22	45	3	09	3	00
5	13	41	−13.9	61.2	16.7	76	281	98	13.7	19	08	19	25	23	45	3	38	3	25
6	14	43	−17.8	61.4	16.7	88	246	100	14.7	20	30	20	51	—		4	14	3	56
7	15	46	−20.5	61.3	16.7	100	105	99	15.7	21	44	22	07	0	47	5	00	4	38
8	16	51	−21.7	60.9	16.6	113	95	95	16.7	22	44	23	07	1	51	5	57	5	34
9	17	55	−21.3	60.2	16.4	125	88	88	17.7	23	32	23	51	2	53	7	05	6	42
10	18	56	−19.5	59.3	16.2	137	82	80	18.7	—		—		3	52	8	19	8	00
11	19	53	−16.6	58.4	15.9	149	77	70	19.7	0	08	0	23	4	47	9	34	9	20
12	20	47	−12.9	57.4	15.6	161	74	60	20.7	0	36	0	48	5	37	10	49	10	39
13	21	37	−8.7	56.6	15.4	174	71	49	21.7	1	00	1	07	6	25	12	01	11	55
14	22	25	−4.2	55.8	15.2	186	70	39	22.7	1	20	1	23	7	09	13	10	13	09
15	23	11	+0.3	55.2	15.0	198	69	30	23.7	1	39	1	38	7	52	14	18	14	21
16	23	57	+4.8	54.7	14.9	210	70	21	24.7	1	58	1	53	8	35	15	25	15	32
17	0	42	+9.0	54.3	14.8	222	71	14	25.7	2	17	2	09	9	18	16	31	16	42
18	1	28	+12.9	54.1	14.7	235	74	8	26.7	2	38	2	27	10	01	17	36	17	51
19	2	15	+16.2	54.0	14.7	247	77	4	27.7	3	03	2	48	10	46	18	40	18	58
20	3	03	+18.8	54.0	14.7	259	82	1	28.7	3	33	3	14	11	33	19	41	20	02
21	3	53	+20.7	54.0	14.7	271	181	0	0.1	4	08	3	47	12	21	20	38	21	00
22	4	44	+21.6	54.2	14.8	284	266	1	1.1	4	52	4	29	13	10	21	27	21	50
23	5	35	+21.6	54.4	14.8	296	272	4	2.1	5	43	5	20	13	59	22	10	22	31
24	6	27	+20.5	54.8	14.9	308	277	8	3.1	6	41	6	21	14	48	22	45	23	03
25	7	18	+18.5	55.2	15.0	320	281	14	4.1	7	46	7	28	15	37	23	15	23	30
26	8	09	+15.7	55.7	15.2	333	285	22	5.1	8	54	8	41	16	24	23	41	23	51
27	8	59	+12.0	56.3	15.4	345	288	31	6.1	10	05	9	56	17	12	—		—	
28	9	48	+7.7	57.1	15.5	357	291	41	7.1	11	19	11	14	17	59	0	04	0	10
29	10	38	+2.9	57.9	15.8	9	292	52	8.1	12	34	12	34	18	47	0	25	0	27
30	11	29	−2.1	58.7	16.0	21	292	63	9.1	13	52	13	57	19	37	0	46	0	44
31	12	22	−7.2	59.5	16.2	34	291	73	10.1	15	13	15	23	20	30	1	09	1	03

MERCURY

Day	R.A. h	R.A. m	Dec. °	Diam. ″	Phase %	Transit h	Transit m	5° high 52° h	5° high 52° m	5° high 56° h	5° high 56° m
1	1	07	+4.0	6	64	10	30	4	41	4	41
3	1	18	+5.2	6	67	10	33	4	38	4	37
5	1	29	+6.5	6	70	10	37	4	35	4	33
7	1	41	+7.8	6	73	10	41	4	32	4	29
9	1	53	+9.2	6	77	10	46	4	30	4	26
11	2	07	+10.6	6	80	10	51	4	28	4	22
13	2	20	+12.0	6	83	10	57	4	26	4	19
15	2	35	+13.5	5	86	11	04	4	25	4	17
17	2	49	+14.9	5	90	11	11	4	24	4	15
19	3	05	+16.4	5	93	11	19	4	24	4	13
21	3	21	+17.8	5	95	11	27	4	24	4	12
23	3	38	+19.2	5	98	11	37	4	26	4	12
25	3	56	+20.5	5	99	11	47	4	28	4	13
27	4	14	+21.6	5	100	11	57	4	31	4	15
29	4	33	+22.7	5	100	12	08	19	42	20	00
31	4	51	+23.6	5	98	12	19	19	58	20	17

VENUS

Day	R.A. h	R.A. m	Dec. °	Diam. ″	Phase %	Transit h	Transit m	5° high 52° h	5° high 52° m	5° high 56° h	5° high 56° m
1	5	16	+27.8	37	27	14	38	22	41	23	06
6	5	25	+27.8	41	22	14	27	22	30	22	55
11	5	31	+27.7	44	18	14	13	22	14	22	39
16	5	33	+27.3	48	13	13	54	21	52	22	16
21	5	31	+26.6	51	8	13	32	21	25	21	48
26	5	24	+25.7	54	4	13	05	20	51	21	12
31	5	13	+24.6	57	1	12	34	20	13	20	32

MARS

Day	R.A. h	R.A. m	Dec. °	Diam. ″	Phase %	Transit h	Transit m	5° high 52° h	5° high 52° m	5° high 56° h	5° high 56° m
1	10	32	+11.5	10	91	19	52	2	21	2	27
6	10	35	+10.9	10	91	19	36	2	02	2	07
11	10	40	+10.3	9	90	19	21	1	43	1	48
16	10	45	+9.6	9	90	19	06	1	25	1	30
21	10	51	+8.9	9	90	18	52	1	07	1	11
26	10	57	+8.1	8	89	18	39	0	50	0	53
31	11	04	+7.2	8	89	18	27	0	33	0	35

SUNRISE AND SUNSET

d	London 0° 05'	51° 30'	Bristol 2° 35'	51° 28'	Birmingham 1° 55'	52° 28'	Manchester 2° 15'	53° 28'	Newcastle 1° 37'	54° 59'	Glasgow 4° 14'	55° 52'	Belfast 5° 56'	54° 35'
	h m	h m	h m	h m	h m	h m	h m	h m	h m	h m	h m	h m	h m	h m
1	4 32	19 24	4 42	19 34	4 36	19 35	4 34	19 39	4 26	19 43	4 33	19 57	4 45	19 58
2	4 30	19 26	4 40	19 36	4 34	19 36	4 32	19 41	4 24	19 44	4 31	19 58	4 42	20 00
3	4 28	19 27	4 38	19 37	4 32	19 38	4 30	19 43	4 22	19 46	4 28	20 00	4 40	20 02
4	4 26	19 29	4 36	19 39	4 30	19 40	4 28	19 45	4 19	19 48	4 26	20 02	4 38	20 04
5	4 24	19 31	4 34	19 41	4 28	19 41	4 26	19 47	4 17	19 50	4 24	20 04	4 36	20 06
6	4 23	19 32	4 33	19 42	4 26	19 43	4 24	19 48	4 15	19 52	4 22	20 06	4 34	20 08
7	4 21	19 34	4 31	19 44	4 25	19 45	4 22	19 50	4 13	19 54	4 20	20 08	4 32	20 09
8	4 19	19 35	4 29	19 45	4 23	19 46	4 20	19 52	4 11	19 56	4 18	20 10	4 30	20 11
9	4 17	19 37	4 28	19 47	4 21	19 48	4 18	19 54	4 09	19 58	4 16	20 12	4 28	20 13
10	4 16	19 39	4 26	19 48	4 19	19 50	4 17	19 55	4 07	19 59	4 14	20 14	4 27	20 15
11	4 14	19 40	4 24	19 50	4 18	19 51	4 15	19 57	4 06	20 01	4 12	20 16	4 25	20 17
12	4 13	19 42	4 23	19 52	4 16	19 53	4 13	19 59	4 04	20 03	4 10	20 18	4 23	20 18
13	4 11	19 43	4 21	19 53	4 14	19 55	4 11	20 00	4 02	20 05	4 08	20 20	4 21	20 20
14	4 10	19 45	4 20	19 55	4 13	19 56	4 10	20 02	4 00	20 07	4 06	20 22	4 19	20 22
15	4 08	19 46	4 18	19 56	4 11	19 58	4 08	20 04	3 58	20 08	4 04	20 24	4 18	20 24
16	4 07	19 48	4 17	19 58	4 10	19 59	4 07	20 05	3 57	20 10	4 02	20 25	4 16	20 25
17	4 05	19 49	4 15	19 59	4 08	20 01	4 05	20 07	3 55	20 12	4 01	20 27	4 14	20 27
18	4 04	19 51	4 14	20 01	4 07	20 02	4 03	20 08	3 53	20 14	3 59	20 29	4 13	20 29
19	4 02	19 52	4 13	20 02	4 05	20 04	4 02	20 10	3 52	20 15	3 57	20 31	4 11	20 30
20	4 01	19 54	4 11	20 03	4 04	20 05	4 01	20 12	3 50	20 17	3 56	20 33	4 10	20 32
21	4 00	19 55	4 10	20 05	4 03	20 07	3 59	20 13	3 49	20 19	3 54	20 34	4 08	20 34
22	3 59	19 56	4 09	20 06	4 01	20 08	3 58	20 15	3 47	20 20	3 52	20 36	4 07	20 35
23	3 57	19 58	4 08	20 07	4 00	20 10	3 56	20 16	3 46	20 22	3 51	20 38	4 05	20 37
24	3 56	19 59	4 06	20 09	3 59	20 11	3 55	20 17	3 44	20 23	3 49	20 39	4 04	20 38
25	3 55	20 00	4 05	20 10	3 58	20 12	3 54	20 19	3 43	20 25	3 48	20 41	4 02	20 40
26	3 54	20 01	4 04	20 11	3 57	20 14	3 53	20 20	3 42	20 26	3 47	20 42	4 01	20 41
27	3 53	20 03	4 03	20 13	3 56	20 15	3 52	20 22	3 40	20 28	3 45	20 44	4 00	20 43
28	3 52	20 04	4 02	20 14	3 55	20 16	3 51	20 23	3 39	20 29	3 44	20 45	3 59	20 44
29	3 51	20 05	4 01	20 15	3 54	20 17	3 49	20 24	3 38	20 31	3 43	20 47	3 58	20 46
30	3 50	20 06	4 00	20 16	3 53	20 19	3 48	20 25	3 37	20 32	3 42	20 48	3 57	20 47
31	3 49	20 07	4 00	20 17	3 52	20 20	3 48	20 27	3 36	20 33	3 41	20 50	3 56	20 48

JUPITER

Day	R.A. h	m	Dec. °	'	Transit h	m	5° high 52° h	m	56° h	m
1	3	12.0	+17	00	12	33	5	38	5	26
11	3	21.5	+17	38	12	03	5	04	4	52
21	3	31.2	+18	14	11	34	4	31	4	19
31	3	40.8	+18	47	11	04	3	58	3	45

Diameters – equatorial 33" polar 31"

SATURN

Day	R.A. h	m	Dec. °	'	Transit h	m	5° high 52° h	m	56° h	m
1	13	36.8	−7	07	22	56	3	48	3	39
11	13	34.2	−6	53	22	14	3	08	2	58
21	13	32.0	−6	42	21	32	2	27	2	18
31	13	30.2	−6	33	20	51	1	47	1	38

Diameters – equatorial 19" polar 17"
Rings – major axis 42" minor axis 9"

URANUS

Day	R.A. h	m	Dec. °	'	Transit h	m	10° high 52° h	m	56° h	m
1	0	25.1	+1	58	9	46	4	42	4	47
11	0	26.9	+2	09	9	09	4	04	4	09
21	0	28.4	+2	18	8	31	3	25	3	30
31	0	29.8	+2	27	7	53	2	46	2	51

Diameter 4"

NEPTUNE

Day	R.A. h	m	Dec. °	'	Transit h	m	10° high 52° h	m	56° h	m
1	22	20.0	−11	00	7	41	3	52	4	11
11	22	20.6	−10	57	7	03	3	13	3	32
21	22	21.0	−10	55	6	24	2	34	2	52
31	22	21.2	−10	54	5	45	1	54	2	13

Diameter 2"

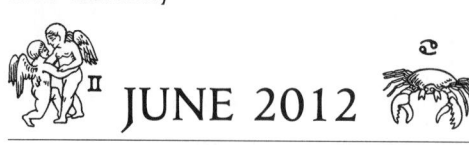

JUNE 2012

SIXTH MONTH, 30 DAYS. *Junius*, Roman *gens* (family)

1	*Friday*	Sir Frank Whittle, pilot and aviation engineer who invented the jet engine *b.* 1907	day 153
2	*Saturday*	Guglielmo Marconi secured the first patent for a system of communication by electromagnetic waves 1896	154
3	*Sunday*	Major Edward White II became the first American astronaut to complete a spacewalk 1965	155
4	*Monday*	The first shopping trolleys were introduced at a supermarket in Oklahoma City, USA 1937	week 23 day 156
5	*Tuesday*	Dr Michael Gottlieb first described the epidemic disease which was later to become known as AIDS 1981	157
6	*Wednesday*	Henry Seely received a patent for his electric flatiron 1882	158
7	*Thursday*	The first domestic videocassette recorder, the Betamax produced by Sony, went on sale in Japan 1975	159
8	*Friday*	Sir Tim Berners-Lee, computer scientist credited with inventing the world wide web *b.* 1955	160
9	*Saturday*	George Stephenson, engineer and inventor of the famous *Rocket* locomotive *b.* 1781	161
10	*Sunday*	The ballpoint pen was patented by Laslo Biro; commercial production began two years later 1943	162
11	*Monday*	Jacques-Yves Cousteau, diving innovator who co-invented the aqualung *b.* 1910	week 24 day 163
12	*Tuesday*	Carl Elsener patented the multi-function penknife, later known as the 'Swiss Army knife' 1897	164
13	*Wednesday*	Space probe *Pioneer 10*, launched in 1972, became the first man-made object to exit the solar system 1983	165
14	*Thursday*	John Logie Baird, engineer, the first person to televise pictures of objects in motion *d.* 1946	166
15	*Friday*	Benjamin Franklin demonstrated the electrical nature of lightning by flying a kite during a storm 1752	167
16	*Saturday*	US aviation pioneer Henry Berliner conducted the first manned, controlled helicopter flight 1922	168
17	*Sunday*	Charles Goodyear obtained a patent for a procedure he discovered to stop rubber melting in heat 1837	169
18	*Monday*	Waterloo Bridge was opened in London, on the second anniversary of the Battle of Waterloo 1817	week 25 day 170
19	*Tuesday*	Valentina Tereshkova returned to Earth, three days after becoming the first woman in space 1963	171
20	*Wednesday*	Sir Frederick G. Hopkins, who won the 1929 Nobel Prize for Physiology for his study of vitamins *b.* 1861	172
21	*Thursday*	The first stored-program computer, the Small-Scale Experimental Machine, ran its first program 1948	173
22	*Friday*	The Royal Greenwich Observatory, a centre for practical astronomy, was created by Royal Warrant 1675	174
23	*Saturday*	Christopher Latham Sholes, with two colleagues, received a patent for the typewriter 1868	175
24	*Sunday*	Sir Fred Hoyle, astronomer who formulated a basis for the steady-state theory of the universe *b.* 1915	176
25	*Monday*	Lucien B. Smith patented barbed wire, which was intended to enclose livestock 1867	week 26 day 177
26	*Tuesday*	Samuel Crompton, inventor of the spinning mule, which revolutionised cotton production *d.* 1827	178
27	*Wednesday*	The world's first atomic power station began producing electricity in Obninsk, Russia 1954	179
28	*Thursday*	Adolphe Sax patented the saxophone, which was a combination of a clarinet and an oboe 1846	180
29	*Friday*	The space shuttle *Atlantis* docked with *Mir* to form the largest man-made satellite to orbit Earth 1995	181
30	*Saturday*	The Prince of Wales officially opened Tower Bridge 1894	182

ASTRONOMICAL PHENOMENA

d h
1 02 Saturn in conjunction with Moon. Saturn 6°N.
1 21 Venus in conjunction with Mercury. Venus 0°.2 S.
4 11 Partial eclipse of Moon (see page 1278)
4 21 Neptune at stationary point
6 01 Venus in inferior conjunction (transit)
17 08 Jupiter in conjunction with Moon. Jupiter 1°S.
18 00 Venus in conjunction with Moon. Venus 2°S.
20 23 Sun's longitude 90° ♋
21 17 Mercury in conjunction with Moon. Mercury 6°N.
25 08 Saturn at stationary point
26 11 Mars in conjunction with Moon. Mars 5°N.
27 15 Venus at stationary point
28 08 Saturn in conjunction with Moon. Saturn 6°N.
29 15 Pluto at opposition

MINIMA OF ALGOL

Algol is inconveniently situated for observation during June

CONSTELLATIONS

The following constellations are near the meridian at

	d	*h*		*d*	*h*
May	1	24	June	15	21
May	16	23	July	1	20
June	1	22	July	16	19

Cassiopeia (below the Pole), Ursa Minor, Draco, Ursa Major, Canes Venatici, Bootes, Corona, Serpens, Virgo and Libra

THE MOON

Phases, Apsides and Node	*d*	*h*	*m*
○ Full Moon	4	11	12
☾ Last Quarter	11	10	41
● New Moon	19	15	02
☽ First Quarter	27	03	30
Perigee (358,492km)	3	13	23
Apogee (405,762km)	16	01	33

Mean longitude of ascending node on June 1, 245°

THE SUN

s.d. 15′.8

Day	Right Ascension h	m	s	Dec. °	′	Equation of time m	s	Rise 52° h	m	Rise 56° h	m	Transit h	m	Set 52° h	m	Set 56° h	m	Sidereal time h	m	s	Transit of first point of Aries h	m	s
1	4	37	21	22	05	+2	11	3	46	3	22	11	58	20	11	20	35	16	39	32	7	19	16
2	4	41	27	22	13	+2	02	3	45	3	21	11	58	20	12	20	36	16	43	28	7	15	20
3	4	45	33	22	20	+1	52	3	44	3	20	11	58	20	13	20	38	16	47	25	7	11	24
4	4	49	40	22	27	+1	42	3	44	3	19	11	58	20	14	20	39	16	51	21	7	07	28
5	4	53	47	22	34	+1	31	3	43	3	18	11	59	20	15	20	40	16	55	18	7	03	32
6	4	57	54	22	40	+1	21	3	42	3	17	11	59	20	16	20	41	16	59	15	6	59	37
7	5	02	01	22	46	+1	10	3	42	3	16	11	59	20	17	20	42	17	03	11	6	55	41
8	5	06	09	22	52	+0	58	3	41	3	16	11	59	20	17	20	43	17	07	08	6	51	45
9	5	10	17	22	57	+0	47	3	41	3	15	11	59	20	18	20	44	17	11	04	6	47	49
10	5	14	26	23	01	+0	35	3	40	3	15	12	00	20	19	20	45	17	15	01	6	43	53
11	5	18	34	23	06	+0	23	3	40	3	14	12	00	20	20	20	46	17	18	57	6	39	57
12	5	22	43	23	10	+0	11	3	40	3	14	12	00	20	20	20	46	17	22	54	6	36	01
13	5	26	52	23	13	−0	02	3	40	3	13	12	00	20	21	20	47	17	26	50	6	32	05
14	5	31	02	23	16	−0	15	3	40	3	13	12	00	20	21	20	48	17	30	47	6	28	09
15	5	35	11	23	19	−0	27	3	39	3	13	12	01	20	22	20	48	17	34	44	6	24	13
16	5	39	20	23	21	−0	40	3	39	3	13	12	01	20	22	20	49	17	38	40	6	20	17
17	5	43	30	23	23	−0	53	3	39	3	13	12	01	20	23	20	49	17	42	37	6	16	21
18	5	47	40	23	24	−1	06	3	39	3	13	12	01	20	23	20	50	17	46	33	6	12	26
19	5	51	49	23	25	−1	20	3	39	3	13	12	01	20	23	20	50	17	50	30	6	08	30
20	5	55	59	23	26	−1	33	3	40	3	13	12	02	20	24	20	50	17	54	26	6	04	34
21	6	00	09	23	26	−1	46	3	40	3	13	12	02	20	24	20	50	17	58	23	6	00	38
22	6	04	19	23	26	−1	59	3	40	3	13	12	02	20	24	20	51	18	02	19	5	56	42
23	6	08	28	23	25	−2	12	3	40	3	14	12	02	20	24	20	51	18	06	16	5	52	46
24	6	12	38	23	24	−2	25	3	41	3	14	12	03	20	24	20	51	18	10	13	5	48	50
25	6	16	47	23	23	−2	38	3	41	3	15	12	03	20	24	20	51	18	14	09	5	44	54
26	6	20	56	23	21	−2	51	3	42	3	15	12	03	20	24	20	50	18	18	06	5	40	58
27	6	25	05	23	19	−2	03	3	42	3	16	12	03	20	24	20	50	18	22	02	5	37	02
28	6	29	14	23	16	−3	15	3	43	3	16	12	03	20	24	20	50	18	25	59	5	33	06
29	6	33	23	23	13	−3	28	3	43	3	17	12	04	20	24	20	50	18	29	55	5	29	11
30	6	37	31	23	09	−3	39	3	44	3	18	12	04	20	23	20	49	18	33	52	5	25	15

DURATION OF TWILIGHT (in minutes)

Latitude	52°	56°	52°	56°	52°	56°	52°	56°
	1 June		11 June		21 June		31 June	
Civil	46	58	48	61	49	63	48	61
Nautical	116	TAN	124	TAN	127	TAN	124	TAN
Astronomical	TAN	TAN	TAN	TAN	TAN	TAN	TAN	TAN

THE NIGHT SKY

Mercury is only visible under good conditions for about 5 days around the 19th, its magnitude falling from −0.4 to +0.2 during this period. The planet may be seen very low above the west-northwestern horizon at the end of evening civil twilight. The long duration of twilight means that it is very unlikely to be seen at all from as far north as Scotland.

Venus is too close to the Sun for observation at first, but passes rapidly through inferior conjunction on the 6th. By the middle of the month it becomes visible in the east-north-eastern sky, in the early mornings for a short while before sunrise, magnitude −4.1. Venus will transit the Sun on the morning of the 6th (see page 1278 for details).

Mars continues to be visible as an evening object, passing from Leo into Virgo during the month. During this period its magnitude fades from +0.6 to +0.9. On the 26th the Moon, at First Quarter, passes 6 degrees south of the planet.

Jupiter, is now moving away from the Sun, becoming visible low in the east-northeastern sky before dawn, after the first three weeks of the month. It is moving steadily eastwards in the constellation of Taurus, magnitude −2.0. Note its proximity to the much brighter planet Venus.

Saturn, magnitude +0.6, continues to be visible in the western sky in the evenings. On the 25th it reaches its second stationary point and resumes its direct motion. Saturn is still in the constellation of Virgo. The Moon passes 7 degrees south of the planet on the morning of the 1st and again on the 28th.

Twilight. Reference to the section above shows that astronomical twilight lasts all night for a period around the summer solstice (i.e. in June and July), even in southern England. Under these conditions the sky never gets completely dark as the Sun is always less than 18 degrees below the horizon.

THE MOON

Day	R.A.		Dec.	Hor. Par.	Semi- diam.	Sun's Co- Long.	PA. of Br. Limb	Ph.	Age	Rise				Transit		Set			
										52°		56°				52°		56°	
	h	m	°	'	'	°	°	%	d	h	m	h	m	h	m	h	m	h	m
1	13	17	−12.0	60.2	16.4	46	289	83	11.1	16	37	16	51	21	26	1	35	1	24
2	14	16	−16.2	60.8	16.6	58	286	91	12.1	18	00	18	19	22	26	2	06	1	51
3	15	18	−19.4	61.1	16.7	70	282	97	13.1	19	18	19	41	23	29	2	46	2	26
4	16	22	−21.3	61.1	16.7	82	281	100	14.1	20	26	20	50	—		3	37	3	15
5	17	27	−21.6	60.8	16.6	95	82	100	15.1	21	21	21	42	0	33	4	40	4	17
6	18	30	−20.4	60.3	16.4	107	80	97	16.1	22	04	22	21	1	35	5	53	5	32
7	19	31	−17.9	59.5	16.2	119	76	91	17.1	22	36	22	50	2	33	7	11	6	54
8	20	27	−14.4	58.6	16.0	131	72	83	18.1	23	03	23	12	3	28	8	29	8	16
9	21	20	−10.2	57.6	15.7	143	69	74	19.1	23	25	23	30	4	18	9	44	9	37
10	22	10	−5.6	56.7	15.5	156	68	65	20.1	23	45	23	45	5	05	10	57	10	53
11	22	58	−1.0	55.9	15.2	168	67	55	21.1	—		—		5	49	12	07	12	08
12	23	44	+3.6	55.2	15.0	180	67	45	22.1	0	03	0	01	6	33	13	15	13	20
13	0	30	+7.9	54.7	14.9	192	68	35	23.1	0	23	0	16	7	15	14	21	14	30
14	1	16	+11.9	54.3	14.8	204	70	26	24.1	0	44	0	33	7	59	15	27	15	40
15	2	02	+15.3	54.1	14.7	217	72	18	25.1	1	07	0	53	8	43	16	31	16	48
16	2	50	+18.2	54.0	14.7	229	75	12	26.1	1	35	1	17	9	29	17	34	17	54
17	3	40	+20.3	54.1	14.7	241	78	6	27.1	2	08	1	48	10	17	18	32	18	54
18	4	30	+21.5	54.2	14.8	253	80	2	28.1	2	49	2	26	11	06	19	24	19	47
19	5	22	+21.7	54.5	14.8	266	74	0	29.1	3	37	3	15	11	55	20	09	20	31
20	6	14	+20.9	54.8	14.9	278	302	0	0.4	4	34	4	13	12	45	20	48	21	07
21	7	06	+19.1	55.2	15.0	290	289	2	1.4	5	37	5	19	13	34	21	20	21	35
22	7	57	+16.5	55.6	15.2	302	289	6	2.4	6	45	6	30	14	22	21	46	21	58
23	8	47	+13.0	56.1	15.3	315	291	11	3.4	7	56	7	45	15	10	22	10	22	18
24	9	37	+8.8	56.7	15.4	327	293	19	4.4	9	08	9	02	15	57	22	31	22	35
25	10	26	+4.2	57.3	15.6	339	294	27	5.4	10	22	10	20	16	44	22	52	22	52
26	11	16	−0.7	57.9	15.8	351	294	38	6.4	11	38	11	40	17	32	23	14	23	09
27	12	07	−5.7	58.5	15.9	4	294	48	7.4	12	55	13	03	18	22	23	37	23	28
28	13	00	−10.5	59.1	16.1	16	292	60	8.4	14	15	14	27	19	15	—		23	52
29	13	56	−14.8	59.7	16.3	28	289	71	9.4	15	36	15	53	20	12	0	05	—	
30	14	54	−18.3	60.2	16.4	40	285	81	10.4	16	54	17	15	21	11	0	40	0	22

MERCURY

Day	R.A.		Dec.	Diam.	Phase	Transit		5° high			
								52°		56°	
	h	m	°	"	%	h	m	h	m	h	m
1	5	01	+24.0	5	97	12	24	20	05	20	25
3	5	19	+24.6	5	95	12	35	20	20	20	40
5	5	38	+25.0	5	91	12	45	20	33	20	53
7	5	56	+25.3	5	87	12	55	20	44	21	05
9	6	13	+25.4	6	83	13	05	20	53	21	14
11	6	30	+25.3	6	79	13	13	21	01	21	22
13	6	46	+25.1	6	74	13	21	21	07	21	27
15	7	01	+24.7	6	70	13	28	21	11	21	31
17	7	16	+24.2	6	66	13	35	21	14	21	33
19	7	29	+23.7	6	62	13	40	21	15	21	33
21	7	42	+23.0	7	58	13	44	21	15	21	32
23	7	53	+22.3	7	55	13	48	21	14	21	30
25	8	04	+21.6	7	51	13	51	21	12	21	27
27	8	14	+20.8	7	48	13	52	21	08	21	23
29	8	23	+19.9	8	44	13	53	21	04	21	18
31	8	31	+19.1	8	41	13	53	20	59	21	12

VENUS

Day	R.A.		Dec.	Diam.	Phase	Transit		5° high			
								52°		56°	
	h	m	°	"	%	h	m	h	m	h	m
1	5	11	+24.3	57	1	12	28	4	51	4	31
6	4	58	+22.8	58	0	11	56	4	27	4	10
11	4	46	+21.3	57	1	11	24	4	05	3	49
16	4	35	+19.9	55	4	10	54	3	43	3	29
21	4	28	+18.8	52	7	10	28	3	23	3	10
26	4	25	+18.0	48	12	10	06	3	05	2	53
31	4	26	+17.5	45	17	9	47	2	49	2	37

MARS

Day	R.A.		Dec.	Diam.	Phase	Transit		5° high			
								52°		56°	
	h	m	°	"	%	h	m	h	m	h	m
1	11	06	+7.0	8	89	18	24	0	29	0	32
6	11	13	+6.1	8	89	18	12	0	12	0	14
11	11	21	+5.1	7	89	18	00	23	52	23	53
16	11	29	+4.1	7	89	17	49	23	36	23	36
21	11	38	+3.1	7	89	17	38	23	20	23	19
26	11	47	+2.0	7	89	17	27	23	03	23	01
31	11	56	+0.9	7	89	17	17	22	47	22	44

SUNRISE AND SUNSET

d	London 0° 05' h m	51° 30' h m	Bristol 2° 35' h m	51° 28' h m	Birmingham 1° 55' h m	52° 28' h m	Manchester 2° 15' h m	53° 28' h m	Newcastle 1° 37' h m	54° 59' h m	Glasgow 4° 14' h m	55° 52' h m	Belfast 5° 56' h m	54° 35' h m
1	3 49	20 08	3 59	20 18	3 51	20 21	3 47	20 28	3 35	20 35	3 39	20 51	3 55	20 49
2	3 48	20 10	3 58	20 19	3 50	20 22	3 46	20 29	3 34	20 36	3 38	20 52	3 54	20 51
3	3 47	20 11	3 57	20 20	3 49	20 23	3 45	20 30	3 33	20 37	3 38	20 54	3 53	20 52
4	3 47	20 11	3 57	20 21	3 49	20 24	3 44	20 31	3 32	20 38	3 37	20 55	3 52	20 53
5	3 46	20 12	3 56	20 22	3 48	20 25	3 44	20 32	3 31	20 39	3 36	20 56	3 51	20 54
6	3 45	20 13	3 56	20 23	3 47	20 26	3 43	20 33	3 31	20 40	3 35	20 57	3 51	20 55
7	3 45	20 14	3 55	20 24	3 47	20 27	3 42	20 34	3 30	20 41	3 34	20 58	3 50	20 56
8	3 44	20 15	3 55	20 25	3 46	20 28	3 42	20 35	3 29	20 42	3 34	20 59	3 49	20 57
9	3 44	20 16	3 54	20 26	3 46	20 29	3 41	20 36	3 29	20 43	3 33	21 00	3 49	20 58
10	3 44	20 16	3 54	20 26	3 45	20 29	3 41	20 37	3 28	20 44	3 33	21 01	3 48	20 59
11	3 43	20 17	3 53	20 27	3 45	20 30	3 40	20 37	3 28	20 45	3 32	21 02	3 48	20 59
12	3 43	20 18	3 53	20 28	3 45	20 31	3 40	20 38	3 28	20 46	3 32	21 02	3 48	21 00
13	3 43	20 18	3 53	20 28	3 45	20 31	3 40	20 39	3 27	20 46	3 31	21 03	3 47	21 01
14	3 43	20 19	3 53	20 29	3 44	20 32	3 40	20 39	3 27	20 47	3 31	21 04	3 47	21 01
15	3 43	20 19	3 53	20 29	3 44	20 32	3 40	20 40	3 27	20 47	3 31	21 04	3 47	21 02
16	3 43	20 20	3 53	20 30	3 44	20 33	3 40	20 40	3 27	20 48	3 31	21 05	3 47	21 02
17	3 42	20 20	3 53	20 30	3 44	20 33	3 39	20 41	3 27	20 48	3 31	21 05	3 47	21 03
18	3 43	20 21	3 53	20 30	3 44	20 34	3 39	20 41	3 27	20 49	3 31	21 06	3 47	21 03
19	3 43	20 21	3 53	20 31	3 44	20 34	3 40	20 41	3 27	20 49	3 31	21 06	3 47	21 03
20	3 43	20 21	3 53	20 31	3 45	20 34	3 40	20 42	3 27	20 49	3 31	21 06	3 47	21 04
21	3 43	20 21	3 53	20 31	3 45	20 34	3 40	20 42	3 27	20 49	3 31	21 06	3 47	21 04
22	3 43	20 22	3 53	20 31	3 45	20 34	3 40	20 42	3 27	20 50	3 31	21 07	3 48	21 04
23	3 44	20 22	3 54	20 31	3 45	20 35	3 41	20 42	3 28	20 50	3 32	21 07	3 48	21 04
24	3 44	20 22	3 54	20 31	3 46	20 35	3 41	20 42	3 28	20 50	3 32	21 07	3 48	21 04
25	3 44	20 22	3 55	20 31	3 46	20 35	3 41	20 42	3 29	20 50	3 33	21 07	3 49	21 04
26	3 45	20 22	3 55	20 31	3 47	20 34	3 42	20 42	3 29	20 49	3 33	21 06	3 49	21 04
27	3 45	20 21	3 55	20 31	3 47	20 34	3 42	20 42	3 30	20 49	3 34	21 06	3 50	21 04
28	3 46	20 21	3 56	20 31	3 48	20 34	3 43	20 42	3 30	20 49	3 34	21 06	3 50	21 04
29	3 46	20 21	3 57	20 31	3 48	20 34	3 44	20 41	3 31	20 49	3 35	21 06	3 51	21 03
30	3 47	20 21	3 57	20 31	3 49	20 34	3 44	20 41	3 32	20 48	3 36	21 05	3 52	21 03

JUPITER

Day	R.A. h m	Dec. ° '	Transit h m	5° high 52° h m	5° high 56° h m
1	3 41.8	+18 51	11 01	3 55	3 42
11	3 51.3	+19 21	10 31	3 22	3 09
21	4 00.6	+19 49	10 01	2 49	2 35
31	4 09.7	+20 14	9 31	2 17	2 02

Diameters – equatorial 33" polar 31"

SATURN

Day	R.A. h m	Dec. ° '	Transit h m	5° high 52° h m	5° high 56° h m
1	13 30.0	−6 33	20 47	1 43	1 34
11	13 28.8	−6 28	20 06	1 03	0 54
21	13 28.2	−6 27	19 27	0 23	0 14
31	13 28.1	−6 29	18 47	23 39	23 30

Diameters – equatorial 18" polar 16"
Rings – major axis 41" minor axis 9"

URANUS

Day	R.A. h m	Dec. ° '	Transit h m	10° high 52° h m	10° high 56° h m
1	0 29.9	+2 28	7 49	2 43	2 47
11	0 31.0	+2 34	7 11	2 04	2 08
21	0 31.8	+2 39	6 32	1 25	1 29
31	0 32.3	+2 42	5 54	0 46	0 50

Diameter 4"

NEPTUNE

Day	R.A. h m	Dec. ° '	Transit h m	10° high 52° h m	10° high 56° h m
1	22 21.2	−10 54	5 41	1 50	2 09
11	22 21.2	−10 54	5 01	1 11	1 30
21	22 21.0	−10 56	4 22	0 32	0 51
31	22 20.6	−10 58	3 42	23 48	0 11

Diameter 2"

JULY 2012

SEVENTH MONTH, 31 DAYS. *Julius* Caesar, formerly *Quintilis*, fifth month of Roman pre-Julian calendar

1	Sunday	The Wallace–Darwin theory of evolution was first published at the Linnean Society 1858	day 183
2	Monday	The first directed flight of a zeppelin was made in Germany; the *LZ-1* flew for 18 minutes 1900	week 27 day 184
3	Tuesday	André-Gustave Citroën, engineer who introduced Ford's method of car mass-production to Europe *d.* 1935	185
4	Wednesday	Marie Curie died, almost certainly due to her exposure to radiation 1934	186
5	Thursday	Dolly the sheep, the first mammal to be cloned from an adult cell, was born 1996	187
6	Friday	Louis Pasteur began the modern era of immunisation by vaccinating a boy bitten by a rabid dog 1885	188
7	Saturday	Henry Phillips received several patents for the Phillips-head screw and screwdriver 1936	189
8	Sunday	John Pemberton, pharmacist who invented Coca-Cola *b.* 1831	190
9	Monday	Elias Howe, inventor who designed and patented the first sewing machine *b.* 1819	week 28 day 191
10	Tuesday	*Telstar 1*, the first satellite to relay TV and telephone signals across the Atlantic, was launched 1962	192
11	Wednesday	US space station Skylab re-entered Earth's atmosphere and disintegrated 1979	193
12	Thursday	The Panama Canal, which cost US $347m to complete, was formally dedicated 1920	194
13	Friday	William Hedley, engineer who built the first commercially used steam locomotive, *Puffing Billy b.* 1779	195
14	Saturday	Alfred Nobel, engineer and innovator, demonstrated dynamite for the first time 1867	196
15	Sunday	Hippolyte Mège Mouriés patented margarine, which was created after a request from Napoleon III 1869	197
16	Monday	The first atom bomb was successfully tested in New Mexico, USA 1945	week 29 day 198
17	Tuesday	Georges Lemaître, astronomer and cosmologist who proposed the modern big-bang theory *b.* 1894	199
18	Wednesday	Hendrik Lorentz, physicist whose work on electromagnetic radiation inspired Albert Einstein *b.* 1853	200
19	Thursday	Chief engineer Fulgence Bienvenüe oversaw the opening of the Métropolitan subway in Paris 1900	201
20	Friday	Neil Armstrong became the first person to walk on the surface of the Moon 1969	202
21	Saturday	The 7,414 kilometre Trans-Siberian railway was completed, becoming the longest railway in the world 1904	203
22	Sunday	Gregor Mendel, pioneer in the study of heredity and regarded as the father of genetics *b.* 1822	204
23	Monday	Sir William Ramsay, chemist who discovered elements including neon and krypton *d.* 1916	week 30 day 205
24	Tuesday	Amelia Earhart, who in 1932 became the first woman to fly solo over the Atlantic *b.* 1897	206
25	Wednesday	Louise Brown, the first baby to be conceived via the method of in-vitro fertilisation, was born 1978	207
26	Thursday	Apollo 15 launched, the first mission to the Moon which used the lunar rover 1971	208
27	Friday	The de Havilland Comet, the first jet-propelled airliner, made its maiden flight 1949	209
28	Saturday	A water tricycle was pedalled across the English Channel in under eight hours by Mr Ferry 1883	210
29	Sunday	The National Aeronautics and Space Administration (NASA) was founded 1958	211
30	Monday	Henry Ford, industrialist whose Model T cars revolutionised the industry *b.* 1863	week 31 day 212
31	Tuesday	Stephanie Kwolek, inventor of Kevlar, which is used in aircraft parts and body armour *b.* 1923	213

ASTRONOMICAL PHENOMENA

d h
1 02 Mercury at greatest elongation E. 26°
5 04 Earth at aphelion (152 million km.)
12 16 Venus at greatest brilliancy
13 10 Uranus at stationary point
15 02 Mercury at stationary point
15 03 Jupiter in conjunction with Moon. Jupiter 0°.5 S.
15 15 Venus in conjunction with Moon. Venus 4°S.
20 08 Mercury in conjunction with Moon. Mercury 0°.5 N.
22 10 Sun's longitude 120° ♌
24 19 Mars in conjunction with Moon. Mars 4°N.
25 15 Saturn in conjunction with Moon. Saturn 6°N.
28 20 Mercury in inferior conjunction

MINIMA OF ALGOL

d	h	d	h	d	h
1	15.9	13	03.1	24	14.4
4	12.7	16	00.0	27	11.2
7	09.5	18	20.8	30	08.0
10	06.3	21	17.6		

CONSTELLATIONS

The following constellations are near their meridian at

	d	h		d	h
June	1	24	July	16	21
June	15	23	August	1	20
July	1	22	August	16	19

Ursa Minor, Draco, Corona, Hercules, Lyra, Serpens, Ophiuchus, Libra, Scorpius and Sagittarius

THE MOON

Phases, Apsides and Node	d	h	m
○ Full Moon	3	18	52
☾ Last Quarter	11	01	48
● New Moon	19	04	24
☽ First Quarter	26	08	56

	d	h	m
Perigee (362,384km)	1	18	10
Apogee (404,744km)	13	16	51
Perigee (367,343km)	29	08	37

Mean longitude of ascending node on July 1, 243°

THE SUN

s.d. 15′.8

Day	Right Ascension h m s	Dec. + ° ′	Equation of time m s	Rise 52° h m	Rise 56° h m	Transit h m	Set 52° h m	Set 56° h m	Sidereal time h m s	Transit of first point of Aries h m s
1	6 41 40	23 05	−3 51	3 45	3 19	12 04	20 23	20 49	18 37 48	5 21 19
2	6 45 47	23 01	−4 02	3 45	3 20	12 04	20 23	20 48	18 41 45	5 17 23
3	6 49 55	22 56	−4 13	3 46	3 20	12 04	20 22	20 48	18 45 42	5 13 27
4	6 54 02	22 51	−4 24	3 47	3 21	12 04	20 22	20 47	18 49 38	5 09 31
5	6 58 09	22 46	−4 35	3 48	3 22	12 05	20 21	20 46	18 53 35	5 05 35
6	7 02 16	22 40	−4 45	3 49	3 24	12 05	20 20	20 45	18 57 31	5 01 39
7	7 06 22	22 34	−4 54	3 50	3 25	12 05	20 20	20 45	19 01 28	4 57 43
8	7 10 28	22 27	−5 04	3 51	3 26	12 05	20 19	20 44	19 05 24	4 53 47
9	7 14 34	22 20	−5 13	3 52	3 27	12 05	20 18	20 43	19 09 21	4 49 51
10	7 18 39	22 12	−5 21	3 53	3 28	12 05	20 18	20 42	19 13 18	4 45 56
11	7 22 44	22 05	−5 30	3 54	3 30	12 06	20 17	20 41	19 17 14	4 42 00
12	7 26 48	21 56	−5 37	3 55	3 31	12 06	20 16	20 39	19 21 11	4 38 04
13	7 30 52	21 48	−5 45	3 56	3 32	12 06	20 15	20 38	19 25 07	4 34 08
14	7 34 55	21 39	−5 51	3 57	3 34	12 06	20 14	20 37	19 29 04	4 30 12
15	7 38 58	21 29	−5 58	3 58	3 35	12 06	20 13	20 36	19 33 00	4 26 16
16	7 43 00	21 20	−6 04	4 00	3 37	12 06	20 12	20 34	19 36 57	4 22 20
17	7 47 02	21 10	−6 09	4 01	3 38	12 06	20 11	20 33	19 40 53	4 18 24
18	7 51 04	20 59	−6 14	4 02	3 40	12 06	20 10	20 31	19 44 50	4 14 28
19	7 55 05	20 48	−6 18	4 03	3 42	12 06	20 08	20 30	19 48 47	4 10 32
20	7 59 05	20 37	−6 22	4 05	3 43	12 06	20 07	20 28	19 52 43	4 06 36
21	8 03 05	20 26	−6 25	4 06	3 45	12 06	20 06	20 27	19 56 40	4 02 41
22	8 07 04	20 14	−6 28	4 08	3 47	12 07	20 05	20 25	20 00 36	3 58 45
23	8 11 02	20 02	−6 30	4 09	3 48	12 07	20 03	20 24	20 04 33	3 54 49
24	8 15 00	19 49	−6 31	4 10	3 50	12 07	20 02	20 22	20 08 29	3 50 53
25	8 18 58	19 36	−6 32	4 12	3 52	12 07	20 00	20 20	20 12 26	3 46 57
26	8 22 54	19 23	−6 32	4 13	3 54	12 07	19 59	20 18	20 16 22	3 43 01
27	8 26 51	19 10	−6 32	4 15	3 55	12 07	19 57	20 16	20 20 19	3 39 05
28	8 30 46	18 56	−6 30	4 16	3 57	12 07	19 56	20 15	20 24 16	3 35 09
29	8 34 41	18 42	−6 29	4 18	3 59	12 06	19 54	20 13	20 28 12	3 31 13
30	8 38 35	18 27	−6 27	4 19	4 01	12 06	19 53	20 11	20 32 09	3 27 17
31	8 42 29	18 13	−6 24	4 21	4 03	12 06	19 51	20 09	20 36 05	3 23 21

DURATION OF TWILIGHT (in minutes)

Latitude	52°	56°	52°	56°	52°	56°	52°	56°
	1 July		11 July		21 July		31 July	
Civil	48	61	47	58	44	53	42	49
Nautical	124	TAN	117	TAN	107	146	98	123
Astronomical	TAN	TAN	TAN	TAN	TAN	TAN	182	TAN

THE NIGHT SKY

Mercury reaches greatest eastern elongation (26 degrees) on the 1st but the long duration of twilight means that it remains unsuitably placed for observation throughout the month.

Venus, magnitude −4.5, is rapidly moving away from the Sun and is visible as a morning object, dominating the eastern sky for several hours before dawn. It will attain its greatest brilliancy on the 12th. Locating Venus in daylight is a challenge for keen sighted naked-eye observers, ideally standing in shade from the Sun. A good opportunity comes within a few hours after sunrise on the 15th when Venus will be about 2 degrees to the left and 5 degrees below the waning crescent Moon.

Mars, its magnitude fading from +0.9 to +1.1 during the month, is moving steadily eastwards towards Spica, in Virgo. By the end of the month it will be too low in the western sky to be seen after 21h. On the 24th the Moon, shortly before First Quarter, passes 4 degrees south of the planet.

Jupiter, magnitude −2.1, continues to be visible as a bright morning object in the south-eastern sky. By the end of the month it is becoming visible low above the eastern horizon shortly after midnight. On the morning of the 15th the waning crescent Moon will be seen approaching Jupiter and observers in southeast England will be able to see an actual occultation of the planet between about 01h 45m and 02h 00m. Those with telescopes may be able to see the satellites Io and Europa being occulted as well. Good observing conditions are required in the ENE sky since the altitude is then only around 10 degrees.

Saturn, magnitude +0.7, continues to be visible in the evenings, low above the western horizon although by the end of the month the long evening twilight severely restricts the time available for observation before the planet sets. On the 25th, the Moon, just before First Quarter, passes 6 degrees south of the planet.

THE MOON

Day	R.A. h	R.A. m	Dec. °	Hor. Par. '	Semi-diam. '	Sun's Co-Long. °	PA. of Br. Limb °	Ph. %	Age d	Rise 52° h	Rise 52° m	Rise 56° h	Rise 56° m	Transit h	Transit m	Set 52° h	Set 52° m	Set 56° h	Set 56° m
1	15	56	−20.7	60.4	16.5	52	281	89	11.4	18	06	18	29	22	13	1	24	1	02
2	16	59	−21.7	60.5	16.5	65	278	95	12.4	19	07	19	30	23	16	2	20	1	56
3	18	03	−21.2	60.3	16.4	77	282	99	13.4	19	55	20	15	—		3	27	3	05
4	19	05	−19.2	59.9	16.3	89	34	100	14.4	20	33	20	49	0	16	4	43	4	24
5	20	04	−16.0	59.2	16.1	101	64	98	15.4	21	03	21	14	1	13	6	02	5	47
6	20	59	−12.0	58.5	15.9	113	65	93	16.4	21	28	21	34	2	06	7	20	7	10
7	21	52	−7.5	57.6	15.7	126	65	87	17.4	21	49	21	52	2	56	8	36	8	31
8	22	41	−2.8	56.8	15.5	138	64	79	18.4	22	09	22	07	3	43	9	49	9	48
9	23	29	+1.9	56.0	15.2	150	65	70	19.4	22	28	22	23	4	27	10	59	11	02
10	0	15	+6.4	55.3	15.1	162	66	61	20.4	22	49	22	40	5	11	12	07	12	15
11	1	02	+10.6	54.8	14.9	174	67	51	21.4	23	11	22	59	5	55	13	14	13	26
12	1	48	+14.3	54.4	14.8	187	70	41	22.4	23	37	23	21	6	39	14	20	14	35
13	2	36	+17.3	54.2	14.8	199	73	32	23.4	—		23	49	7	25	15	23	15	42
14	3	25	+19.6	54.2	14.8	211	76	24	24.4	0	08	—		8	12	16	23	16	44
15	4	15	+21.1	54.3	14.8	223	80	16	25.4	0	46	0	24	9	00	17	18	17	40
16	5	07	+21.7	54.5	14.9	236	83	10	26.4	1	31	1	09	9	49	18	06	18	28
17	5	59	+21.2	54.9	15.0	248	85	5	27.4	2	25	2	03	10	39	18	47	19	07
18	6	51	+19.7	55.3	15.1	260	82	2	28.4	3	27	3	07	11	29	19	22	19	39
19	7	43	+17.3	55.8	15.2	272	39	0	29.4	4	34	4	18	12	19	19	51	20	04
20	8	34	+14.0	56.3	15.3	285	309	1	0.9	5	44	5	32	13	07	20	16	20	25
21	9	25	+10.0	56.8	15.5	297	300	4	1.9	6	57	6	50	13	55	20	38	20	43
22	10	15	+5.4	57.3	15.6	309	298	9	2.9	8	11	8	08	14	43	21	00	21	00
23	11	05	+0.5	57.8	15.7	321	297	16	3.9	9	27	9	28	15	30	21	21	21	18
24	11	56	−4.5	58.2	15.9	334	296	25	4.9	10	44	10	50	16	20	21	44	21	36
25	12	48	−9.3	58.6	16.0	346	294	35	5.9	12	02	12	12	17	11	22	10	21	58
26	13	42	−13.7	59.0	16.1	358	291	46	6.9	13	21	13	36	18	05	22	41	22	25
27	14	38	−17.3	59.3	16.2	10	288	57	7.9	14	38	14	57	19	02	23	20	23	00
28	15	38	−20.0	59.6	16.2	23	283	68	8.9	15	51	16	13	20	01	—		23	47
29	16	39	−21.4	59.7	16.3	35	278	79	9.9	16	54	17	17	21	01	0	09	—	
30	17	41	−21.4	59.7	16.3	47	274	87	10.9	17	47	18	08	22	01	1	10	0	47
31	18	42	−20.0	59.5	16.2	59	271	94	11.9	18	29	18	46	22	59	2	20	2	00

MERCURY

Day	R.A. h	R.A. m	Dec. °	Diam. "	Phase %	Transit h	Transit m	5° high 52° h	5° high 52° m	5° high 56° h	5° high 56° m
1	8	31	+19.1	8	41	13	53	20	59	21	12
3	8	38	+18.3	8	37	13	52	20	53	21	05
5	8	44	+17.4	9	34	13	49	20	46	20	57
7	8	49	+16.7	9	30	13	46	20	38	20	49
9	8	52	+15.9	9	27	13	42	20	30	20	39
11	8	55	+15.2	10	23	13	36	20	20	20	30
13	8	56	+14.6	10	20	13	29	20	10	20	19
15	8	56	+14.1	10	16	13	21	19	59	20	08
17	8	55	+13.7	11	13	13	12	19	48	19	56
19	8	53	+13.4	11	10	13	01	19	36	19	44
21	8	50	+13.3	11	7	12	50	19	24	19	32
23	8	45	+13.3	11	5	12	37	19	12	19	19
25	8	40	+13.4	12	3	12	24	18	59	19	07
27	8	34	+13.6	11	1	12	11	18	47	18	55
29	8	28	+14.0	11	1	11	57	5	19	5	11
31	8	23	+14.4	11	2	11	44	5	03	4	54

VENUS

Day	R.A. h	R.A. m	Dec. °	Diam. "	Phase %	Transit h	Transit m	5° high 52° h	5° high 52° m	5° high 56° h	5° high 56° m
1	4	26	+17.5	45	17	9	47	2	49	2	37
6	4	31	+17.4	41	21	9	32	2	35	2	23
11	4	39	+17.5	38	26	9	21	2	22	2	11
16	4	49	+17.8	35	30	9	12	2	11	1	59
21	5	02	+18.2	33	34	9	05	2	02	1	50
26	5	17	+18.6	30	38	9	00	1	54	1	42
31	5	33	+19.1	28	41	9	57	1	48	1	35

MARS

Day	R.A. h	R.A. m	Dec. °	Diam. "	Phase %	Transit h	Transit m	5° high 52° h	5° high 52° m	5° high 56° h	5° high 56° m
1	11	56	+0.9	7	89	17	17	22	47	22	44
6	12	05	−0.2	6	89	17	06	22	31	22	27
11	12	15	−1.4	6	89	16	56	22	15	22	11
16	12	25	−2.6	6	89	16	47	21	59	21	54
21	12	35	−3.7	6	89	16	37	21	44	21	37
26	12	46	−4.9	6	90	16	28	21	28	21	20
31	12	57	−6.2	6	90	16	19	21	13	21	04

SUNRISE AND SUNSET

d	London 0° 05' 51° 30'		Bristol 2° 35' 51° 28'		Birmingham 1° 55' 52° 28'		Manchester 2° 15' 53° 28'		Newcastle 1° 37' 54° 59'		Glasgow 4° 14' 55° 52'		Belfast 5° 56' 54° 35'	
	h m	h m	h m	h m	h m	h m	h m	h m	h m	h m	h m	h m	h m	h m
1	3 48	20 21	3 58	20 30	3 50	20 33	3 45	20 41	3 32	20 48	3 37	21 05	3 52	21 02
2	3 48	20 20	3 59	20 30	3 50	20 33	3 46	20 40	3 33	20 47	3 37	21 04	3 53	21 02
3	3 49	20 20	3 59	20 30	3 51	20 32	3 46	20 40	3 34	20 47	3 38	21 04	3 54	21 01
4	3 50	20 19	4 00	20 29	3 52	20 32	3 47	20 39	3 35	20 46	3 39	21 03	3 55	21 01
5	3 51	20 19	4 01	20 29	3 53	20 31	3 48	20 38	3 36	20 46	3 40	21 02	3 56	21 00
6	3 52	20 18	4 02	20 28	3 54	20 31	3 49	20 38	3 37	20 45	3 41	21 01	3 57	20 59
7	3 53	20 18	4 03	20 27	3 55	20 30	3 50	20 37	3 38	20 44	3 43	21 01	3 58	20 59
8	3 54	20 17	4 04	20 27	3 56	20 29	3 51	20 36	3 39	20 43	3 44	21 00	3 59	20 58
9	3 55	20 16	4 05	20 26	3 57	20 29	3 52	20 36	3 40	20 42	3 45	20 59	4 00	20 57
10	3 56	20 15	4 06	20 25	3 58	20 28	3 53	20 35	3 42	20 41	3 46	20 58	4 01	20 56
11	3 57	20 15	4 07	20 24	3 59	20 27	3 55	20 34	3 43	20 40	3 48	20 57	4 03	20 55
12	3 58	20 14	4 08	20 23	4 00	20 26	3 56	20 33	3 44	20 39	3 49	20 55	4 04	20 54
13	3 59	20 13	4 09	20 23	4 01	20 25	3 57	20 32	3 46	20 38	3 50	20 54	4 05	20 53
14	4 00	20 12	4 10	20 22	4 02	20 24	3 58	20 31	3 47	20 37	3 52	20 53	4 07	20 52
15	4 01	20 11	4 11	20 21	4 04	20 23	4 00	20 30	3 48	20 36	3 53	20 52	4 08	20 51
16	4 02	20 10	4 13	20 20	4 05	20 22	4 01	20 28	3 50	20 34	3 55	20 50	4 09	20 49
17	4 04	20 09	4 14	20 18	4 06	20 21	4 02	20 27	3 51	20 33	3 56	20 49	4 11	20 48
18	4 05	20 08	4 15	20 17	4 07	20 20	4 04	20 26	3 53	20 32	3 58	20 48	4 12	20 47
19	4 06	20 06	4 16	20 16	4 09	20 18	4 05	20 25	3 54	20 30	3 59	20 46	4 14	20 45
20	4 07	20 05	4 18	20 15	4 10	20 17	4 07	20 23	3 56	20 29	4 01	20 45	4 15	20 44
21	4 09	20 04	4 19	20 14	4 12	20 16	4 08	20 22	3 57	20 27	4 03	20 43	4 17	20 42
22	4 10	20 03	4 20	20 12	4 13	20 14	4 09	20 21	3 59	20 26	4 04	20 41	4 18	20 41
23	4 11	20 01	4 22	20 11	4 14	20 13	4 11	20 19	4 01	20 24	4 06	20 40	4 20	20 39
24	4 13	20 00	4 23	20 10	4 16	20 12	4 12	20 18	4 02	20 23	4 08	20 38	4 22	20 38
25	4 14	19 58	4 24	20 08	4 17	20 10	4 14	20 16	4 04	20 21	4 09	20 36	4 23	20 36
26	4 16	19 57	4 26	20 07	4 19	20 09	4 16	20 14	4 05	20 19	4 11	20 34	4 25	20 35
27	4 17	19 56	4 27	20 05	4 20	20 07	4 17	20 13	4 07	20 18	4 13	20 33	4 27	20 33
28	4 19	19 54	4 29	20 04	4 22	20 05	4 19	20 11	4 09	20 16	4 15	20 31	4 28	20 31
29	4 20	19 53	4 30	20 02	4 23	20 04	4 20	20 09	4 11	20 14	4 17	20 29	4 30	20 29
30	4 22	19 51	4 32	20 01	4 25	20 02	4 22	20 08	4 12	20 12	4 18	20 27	4 32	20 28
31	4 23	19 49	4 33	19 59	4 27	20 01	4 24	20 06	4 14	20 10	4 20	20 25	4 33	20 26

JUPITER

Day	R.A. h m	Dec. ° '	Transit h m	5° high 52° h m	56° h m
1	4 09.7	+20 14	9 31	2 17	2 02
11	4 18.4	+20 36	9 00	1 44	1 29
21	4 26.7	+20 56	8 29	1 11	0 56
31	4 34.4	+21 12	7 57	0 38	0 22

Diameters – equatorial 35" polar 33"

SATURN

Day	R.A. h m	Dec. ° '	Transit h m	5° high 52° h m	56° h m
1	13 28.1	−6 29	18 47	23 39	23 30
11	13 28.7	−6 36	18 09	23 00	22 51
21	13 29.9	−6 46	17 31	22 21	22 12
31	13 31.7	−6 59	16 53	21 42	21 33

Diameters – equatorial 17" polar 15"
Rings – major axis 39" minor axis 9"

URANUS

Day	R.A. h m	Dec. ° '	Transit h m	10° high 52° h m	56° h m
1	0 32.3	+2 42	5 54	0 46	0 50
11	0 32.5	+2 43	5 14	0 07	0 11
21	0 32.5	+2 42	4 35	23 23	23 28
31	0 32.1	+2 40	3 55	22 44	22 48

Diameter 4"

NEPTUNE

Day	R.A. h m	Dec. ° '	Transit h m	10° high 52° h m	56° h m
1	22 20.6	−10 58	3 42	23 48	0 11
11	22 20.0	−11 02	3 02	23 09	23 28
21	22 19.2	−11 07	2 22	22 29	22 48
31	22 18.4	−11 12	1 42	21 50	22 09

Diameter 2"

AUGUST 2012

EIGHTH MONTH, 31 DAYS. *Augustus*, formerly *Sextilis*, sixth month of Roman pre-Julian calendar

1	Wednesday	Joseph Priestley identified a gas which he called 'dephlogisticated air' (oxygen) 1774	day 214
2	Thursday	The Tower Subway, a tunnel running beneath the River Thames, was officially opened 1870	215
3	Friday	Elisha Otis, inventor of a safety device for lifts which made high-rise buildings practical *b.* 1811	216
4	Saturday	Étienne Lenoir, who developed the first commercially successful internal combustion engine *d.* 1900	217
5	Sunday	The UK, USA and USSR signed the Nuclear Test Ban Treaty to prohibit above-ground nuclear tests 1963	218

6	Monday	Sir Alexander Fleming, bacteriologist best known for his discovery of penicillin *b.* 1881	week 32 day 219
7	Tuesday	Alan Hazeltine, inventor of the neutrodyne circuit which made commercial radio possible *b.* 1886	220
8	Wednesday	The LZ-127 *Graf Zeppelin* embarked on the first round-the-world flight by airship 1929	221
9	Thursday	Nathan Ames patented the first escalator-type idea, which he named 'revolving stairs' 1859	222
10	Friday	*Magellan*, a space probe tasked with mapping the surface of Venus, arrived at its destination 1990	223
11	Saturday	Christiaan Eijkman, physician whose part in discovering vitamins won him the 1929 Nobel prize *b.* 1858	224
12	Sunday	IBM introduced its personal computer for $1,600, which quickly came to dominate the market 1981	225

13	Monday	Johann Christoph Denner, inventor of the clarinet *b.* 1655	week 33 day 226
14	Tuesday	Enzo Ferrari, founder of the sports car manufacturer which bears his name *b.* 1898	227
15	Wednesday	M. W. Hanchett patented his invention, a dental chair with adjustable elevation and tilting options 1848	228
16	Thursday	Chemists met in Ottawa to name the element 110, which they decided to call Darmstadtium 2003	229
17	Friday	Three Americans made the first transatlantic crossing in a hot air balloon, taking six days 1978	230
18	Saturday	Astronomer Pierre Janssen discovered helium in the solar spectrum 1868	231
19	Sunday	Orville Wright, aviation pioneer who, with his brother Wilbur, invented the first aeroplane *b.* 1871	232

20	Monday	The first round-the-world telegram was sent; it read 'This message sent around the world' 1911	week 34 day 233
21	Tuesday	William Murdock, inventor and pioneer in steam power who made use of coal gas for lighting *b.* 1754	234
22	Wednesday	*Voyager 2* discovered Neptune's first complete ring, about 27,360 kilometres above its atmosphere 1989	235
23	Thursday	Bryan Allen piloted the first human-powered flight, for 1.9 kilometres, using the *Gossamer Condor* 1977	236
24	Friday	The International Astronomical Union reclassified Pluto as a dwarf planet rather than a planet 2006	237
25	Saturday	Hans Adolf Krebs, biochemist who discovered the citric acid cycle and won the 1953 Nobel prize *b.* 1900	238
26	Sunday	Electricity was first transmitted commercially, utilising power generated by Niagara Falls 1895	239

27	Monday	The world's biggest battery was connected (to supply emergency power to Fairbanks, Alaska) 2003	week 35 day 240
28	Tuesday	Paul MacCready, inventor of the first human-powered flying machines (*see* 23 August) *d.* 2007	241
29	Wednesday	The USSR tested its first atomic device, 'First Lightning', escalating nuclear arms development 1949	242
30	Thursday	Sir Ernest Rutherford, nuclear physics pioneer who achieved the 'splitting' of light atoms *b.* 1871	243
31	Friday	General Motors demonstrated the first solar-powered car, built by William Cobb, in Chicago, USA 1955	244

ASTRONOMICAL PHENOMENA

d	h	
8	06	Mercury at stationary point
11	21	Jupiter in conjunction with Moon. Jupiter 0°.1 N.
13	20	Venus in conjunction with Moon. Venus 0°.6 S.
15	09	Venus at greatest elongation W. 46°
15	11	Saturn in conjunction with Mars. Saturn 3°N.
16	03	Mercury in conjunction with Moon. Mercury 3°N.
16	12	Mercury at greatest elongation W. 19°
22	00	Saturn in conjunction with Moon. Saturn 5°N.
22	06	Mars in conjunction with Moon. Mars 2°N.
22	17	Sun's longitude 150° ♍
24	13	Neptune at opposition

MINIMA OF ALGOL

d	h	d	h	d	h
2	04.8	13	16.1	25	03.3
5	01.6	16	12.9	28	00.1
7	22.4	19	09.7	30	20.9
10	19.2	22	06.5		

CONSTELLATIONS

The following constellations are near their meridian at

	d	h		d	h
July	1	24	August	16	21
July	16	23	September	1	20
August	1	22	September	15	19

Draco, Hercules, Lyra, Cygnus, Sagitta, Ophiuchus, Serpens, Aquila and Sagittarius

THE MOON

Phases, Apsides and Node		d	h	m
○	Full Moon	2	03	27
☾	Last Quarter	9	18	55
●	New Moon	17	15	54
☽	First Quarter	24	13	54
○	Full Moon	31	13	58

Apogee (404,084km)	10	10	52
Perigee (369,764km)	23	19	23

Mean longitude of ascending node on August 1, 242°

THE SUN

s.d. 15′.8

Day	Right Ascension			Dec.		Equation of time		Rise 52°		Rise 56°		Transit		Set 52°		Set 56°		Sidereal time			Transit of first point of Aries		
	h	m	s	+ °	′	m	s	h	m	h	m	h	m	h	m	h	m	h	m	s	h	m	s
1	8	46	22	17	58	−6	20	4	22	4	05	12	06	19	49	20	07	20	40	02	3	19	25
2	8	50	14	17	43	−6	16	4	24	4	06	12	06	19	48	20	05	20	43	58	3	15	30
3	8	54	06	17	27	−6	11	4	25	4	08	12	06	19	46	20	03	20	47	55	3	11	34
4	8	57	57	17	11	−6	06	4	27	4	10	12	06	19	44	20	01	20	51	51	3	07	38
5	9	01	48	16	55	−6	00	4	29	4	12	12	06	19	42	19	58	20	55	48	3	03	42
6	9	05	38	16	38	−5	53	4	30	4	14	12	06	19	41	19	56	20	59	45	2	59	46
7	9	09	27	16	22	−5	46	4	32	4	16	12	06	19	39	19	54	21	03	41	2	55	50
8	9	13	16	16	05	−5	39	4	33	4	18	12	06	19	37	19	52	21	07	38	2	51	54
9	9	17	04	15	48	−5	30	4	35	4	20	12	05	19	35	19	50	21	11	34	2	47	58
10	9	20	52	15	30	−5	21	4	36	4	22	12	05	19	33	19	47	21	15	31	2	44	02
11	9	24	39	15	12	−5	12	4	38	4	24	12	05	19	31	19	45	21	19	27	2	40	06
12	9	28	26	14	55	−5	02	4	40	4	26	12	05	19	29	19	43	21	23	24	2	36	10
13	9	32	12	14	36	−4	52	4	41	4	28	12	05	19	27	19	41	21	27	20	2	32	15
14	9	35	58	14	18	−4	41	4	43	4	30	12	05	19	25	19	38	21	31	17	2	28	19
15	9	39	43	13	59	−4	29	4	45	4	32	12	04	19	23	19	36	21	35	14	2	24	23
16	9	43	27	13	40	−4	17	4	46	4	33	12	04	19	21	19	34	21	39	10	2	20	27
17	9	47	11	13	21	−4	05	4	48	4	35	12	04	19	19	19	31	21	43	07	2	16	31
18	9	50	55	13	02	−3	51	4	49	4	37	12	04	19	17	19	29	21	47	03	2	12	35
19	9	54	38	12	42	−3	38	4	51	4	39	12	04	19	15	19	26	21	51	00	2	08	39
20	9	58	20	12	23	−3	24	4	53	4	41	12	03	19	13	19	24	21	54	56	2	04	43
21	10	02	02	12	03	−3	09	4	54	4	43	12	03	19	11	19	21	21	58	53	2	00	47
22	10	05	44	11	43	−2	54	4	56	4	45	12	03	19	08	19	19	22	02	49	1	56	51
23	10	09	25	11	22	−2	39	4	58	4	47	12	03	19	06	19	16	22	06	46	1	52	56
24	10	13	05	11	02	−2	23	4	59	4	49	12	02	19	04	19	14	22	10	42	1	49	00
25	10	16	46	10	41	−2	06	5	01	4	51	12	02	19	02	19	11	22	14	39	1	45	04
26	10	20	25	10	20	−1	50	5	02	4	53	12	02	19	00	19	09	22	18	36	1	41	08
27	10	24	05	10	00	−1	32	5	04	4	55	12	01	18	58	19	06	22	22	32	1	37	12
28	10	27	44	9	38	−1	15	5	06	4	57	12	01	18	55	19	04	22	26	29	1	33	16
29	10	31	22	9	17	−0	57	5	07	4	59	12	01	18	53	19	01	22	30	25	1	29	20
30	10	35	00	8	56	−0	39	5	09	5	01	12	00	18	51	18	59	22	34	22	1	25	24
31	10	38	38	8	34	−0	20	5	11	5	03	12	00	18	49	18	56	22	38	18	1	21	28

DURATION OF TWILIGHT (in minutes)

Latitude	52°	56°	52°	56°	52°	56°	52°	56°
	1 August		11 August		21 August		31 August	
Civil	41	49	39	45	37	42	35	40
Nautical	97	121	90	107	84	97	79	90
Astronomical	179	TAN	154	210	139	168	128	148

THE NIGHT SKY

Mercury is at greatest western elongation (19 degrees) on the 16th and is visible as a morning object, low above the east-north-eastern horizon for about 8 days either side of the 20th. During this period its magnitude brightens from +1.1 to −1.2. On the morning of the 16th the old waning Moon passes 4 degrees south of the planet.

Venus, magnitude −4.3, reaches its greatest western elongation (46 degrees) on the 15th and thus continues to be a magnificent object in the eastern skies before dawn. On the 13th the waning crescent Moon will be seen near Venus on the mornings of the 13th and 14th.

Mars, magnitude +1.1, is coming to the end of its evening apparition after about the first 3 weeks of the month, though it could possibly be detected very low above the south-western horizon as the thin waning crescent Moon passes about 3 degrees south of the planet on August 22–23. Earlier in the month Mars passes 2 degrees north of Spica (magnitude +1.0) on the 13th,

and 3 degrees south of Saturn (magnitude +0.8) on the 15th.

Jupiter continues to be visible as a brilliant object, magnitude −2.2, in the south-eastern sky in the late evenings. On the 3rd Jupiter will be seen passing 5 degrees north of Aldebaran, in Taurus. The waning crescent Moon passes 1 degree south of the planet on the evening of the 11th.

Saturn, magnitude +0.8, is visible low above the south-western horizon for a short while in the evenings. On the 22nd the waxing crescent Moon passes 6 degrees south of the planet. Do not confuse Saturn with Mars which is very slightly fainter.

Neptune is at opposition on the 24th, in the constellation of Aquarius. It is not visible to the naked-eye since its magnitude is +7.9.

Meteors. The maximum of the famous Perseid meteor shower occurs on the 12th, though there will be interference from the waning gibbous Moon after midnight.

THE MOON

Day	R.A. h	R.A. m	Dec. °	Hor. Par. '	Semi-diam. '	Sun's Co-Long. °	PA. of Br. Limb °	Ph. %	Age d	Rise 52° h	Rise 52° m	Rise 56° h	Rise 56° m	Transit h	Transit m	Set 52° h	Set 52° m	Set 56° h	Set 56° m
1	19	41	−17.4	59.1	16.1	71	275	98	12.9	19	02	19	15	23	54	3	37	3	20
2	20	38	−13.8	58.6	16.0	84	323	100	13.9	19	29	19	38	—		4	55	4	43
3	21	31	−9.4	58.0	15.8	96	47	99	14.9	19	52	19	57	0	45	6	12	6	05
4	22	22	−4.8	57.3	15.6	108	57	96	15.9	20	13	20	14	1	33	7	27	7	24
5	23	11	0.0	56.5	15.4	120	60	90	16.9	20	33	20	30	2	20	8	39	8	41
6	23	59	+4.7	55.9	15.2	132	62	84	17.9	20	53	20	46	3	05	9	50	9	55
7	0	46	+9.0	55.3	15.1	144	65	76	18.9	21	15	21	04	3	49	10	58	11	08
8	1	33	+12.9	54.8	14.9	157	67	67	19.9	21	40	21	26	4	34	12	05	12	18
9	2	21	+16.2	54.4	14.8	169	71	58	20.9	22	09	21	51	5	19	13	09	13	26
10	3	09	+18.8	54.3	14.8	181	74	48	21.9	22	44	22	23	6	05	14	11	14	31
11	3	59	+20.5	54.3	14.8	193	78	39	22.9	23	26	23	04	6	53	15	07	15	29
12	4	50	+21.4	54.5	14.8	206	83	30	23.9	—		23	54	7	42	15	58	16	21
13	5	42	+21.3	54.8	14.9	218	87	21	24.9	0	16	—		8	31	16	43	17	03
14	6	34	+20.2	55.2	15.1	230	90	14	25.9	1	14	0	53	9	21	17	20	17	38
15	7	26	+18.1	55.8	15.2	242	92	8	26.9	2	18	2	01	10	11	17	52	18	06
16	8	18	+15.1	56.4	15.4	255	91	3	27.9	3	28	3	15	11	00	18	19	18	29
17	9	09	+11.3	57.0	15.5	267	77	1	28.9	4	41	4	32	11	49	18	43	18	49
18	10	00	+6.9	57.6	15.7	279	340	0	0.4	5	56	5	51	12	38	19	05	19	08
19	10	51	+2.0	58.2	15.8	291	308	2	1.4	7	13	7	12	13	27	19	27	19	25
20	11	43	−3.0	58.6	16.0	303	301	7	2.4	8	30	8	35	14	17	19	50	19	44
21	12	35	−8.0	58.9	16.1	316	297	14	3.4	9	49	9	58	15	08	20	16	20	05
22	13	30	−12.5	59.2	16.1	328	294	22	4.4	11	09	11	22	16	02	20	45	20	31
23	14	26	−16.4	59.3	16.1	340	289	32	5.4	12	27	12	45	16	57	21	22	21	03
24	15	24	−19.3	59.3	16.2	352	285	43	6.4	13	40	14	02	17	55	22	07	21	45
25	16	24	−21.0	59.2	16.1	5	279	55	7.4	14	46	15	09	18	54	23	03	22	40
26	17	25	−21.3	59.1	16.1	17	274	66	8.4	15	41	16	03	19	53	—		23	47
27	18	25	−20.4	58.9	16.0	29	269	76	9.4	16	26	16	45	20	50	0	08	—	
28	19	23	−18.2	58.6	16.0	41	266	85	10.4	17	01	17	16	21	44	1	20	1	02
29	20	20	−15.0	58.2	15.9	53	264	92	11.4	17	30	17	41	22	36	2	36	2	22
30	21	13	−11.0	57.8	15.7	66	266	97	12.4	17	55	18	01	23	25	3	52	3	43
31	22	04	−6.5	57.2	15.6	78	284	99	13.4	18	17	18	19	—		5	07	5	02

MERCURY

Day	R.A. h	R.A. m	Dec. °	Diam. "	Phase %	Transit h	Transit m	5° high 52° h	5° high 52° m	5° high 56° h	5° high 56° m
1	8	20	+14.7	11	2	11	37	4	55	4	47
3	8	16	+15.2	11	4	11	26	4	41	4	31
5	8	13	+15.8	10	7	11	15	4	27	4	17
7	8	12	+16.3	10	11	11	06	4	15	4	04
9	8	12	+16.8	9	16	10	59	4	04	3	53
11	8	14	+17.3	9	22	10	54	3	56	3	45
13	8	18	+17.6	8	29	10	50	3	51	3	39
15	8	24	+17.9	8	36	10	49	3	48	3	36
17	8	32	+18.0	7	43	10	49	3	47	3	35
19	8	41	+17.9	7	51	10	51	3	49	3	37
21	8	53	+17.7	7	59	10	55	3	54	3	42
23	9	05	+17.2	6	67	10	59	4	01	3	50
25	9	18	+16.6	6	75	11	05	4	10	4	00
27	9	33	+15.8	6	81	11	12	4	21	4	11
29	9	47	+14.9	6	87	11	19	4	34	4	25
31	10	02	+13.7	5	91	11	26	4	47	4	39

VENUS

Day	R.A. h	R.A. m	Dec. °	Diam. "	Phase %	Transit h	Transit m	5° high 52° h	5° high 52° m	5° high 56° h	5° high 56° m
1	5	36	+19.2	28	42	8	56	1	47	1	34
6	5	54	+19.6	26	45	8	54	1	43	1	30
11	6	13	+19.8	25	48	8	54	1	41	1	27
16	6	33	+20.0	23	50	8	54	1	41	1	26
21	6	54	+20.0	22	53	8	55	1	42	1	28
26	7	16	+19.8	21	56	8	57	1	45	1	31
31	7	38	+19.4	20	58	9	00	1	49	1	36

MARS

Day	R.A. h	R.A. m	Dec. °	Diam. "	Phase %	Transit h	Transit m	5° high 52° h	5° high 52° m	5° high 56° h	5° high 56° m
1	12	59	−6.4	6	90	16	18	21	10	21	01
6	13	10	−7.6	6	90	16	09	20	54	20	44
11	13	21	−8.8	6	90	16	01	20	39	20	28
16	13	33	−10.0	5	91	15	53	20	24	20	11
21	13	45	−11.2	5	91	15	45	20	09	19	55
26	13	57	−12.4	5	91	15	37	19	55	19	39
31	14	09	−13.6	5	91	15	30	19	40	19	23

SUNRISE AND SUNSET

	London 0° 05'	51° 30'	Bristol 2° 35'	51° 28'	Birmingham 1° 55'	52° 28'	Manchester 2° 15'	53° 28'	Newcastle 1° 37'	54° 59'	Glasgow 4° 14'	55° 52'	Belfast 5° 56'	54° 35'
d	h m	h m	h m	h m	h m	h m	h m	h m	h m	h m	h m	h m	h m	h m
1	4 25	19 48	4 35	19 58	4 28	19 59	4 25	20 04	4 16	20 08	4 22	20 23	4 35	20 24
2	4 26	19 46	4 36	19 56	4 30	19 57	4 27	20 02	4 18	20 06	4 24	20 21	4 37	20 22
3	4 28	19 44	4 38	19 54	4 31	19 55	4 29	20 01	4 20	20 04	4 26	20 19	4 39	20 20
4	4 29	19 43	4 39	19 53	4 33	19 54	4 30	19 59	4 21	20 02	4 28	20 17	4 40	20 18
5	4 31	19 41	4 41	19 51	4 34	19 52	4 32	19 57	4 23	20 00	4 30	20 15	4 42	20 16
6	4 32	19 39	4 42	19 49	4 36	19 50	4 34	19 55	4 25	19 58	4 32	20 13	4 44	20 14
7	4 34	19 37	4 44	19 47	4 38	19 48	4 35	19 53	4 27	19 56	4 33	20 10	4 46	20 12
8	4 35	19 35	4 45	19 45	4 39	19 46	4 37	19 51	4 29	19 54	4 35	20 08	4 47	20 10
9	4 37	19 34	4 47	19 43	4 41	19 44	4 39	19 49	4 30	19 52	4 37	20 06	4 49	20 08
10	4 38	19 32	4 49	19 42	4 43	19 42	4 40	19 47	4 32	19 50	4 39	20 04	4 51	20 06
11	4 40	19 30	4 50	19 40	4 44	19 40	4 42	19 45	4 34	19 48	4 41	20 02	4 53	20 04
12	4 42	19 28	4 52	19 38	4 46	19 38	4 44	19 43	4 36	19 46	4 43	19 59	4 55	20 01
13	4 43	19 26	4 53	19 36	4 48	19 36	4 46	19 41	4 38	19 43	4 45	19 57	4 57	19 59
14	4 45	19 24	4 55	19 34	4 49	19 34	4 47	19 39	4 40	19 41	4 47	19 55	4 58	19 57
15	4 46	19 22	4 56	19 32	4 51	19 32	4 49	19 36	4 42	19 39	4 49	19 52	5 00	19 55
16	4 48	19 20	4 58	19 30	4 52	19 30	4 51	19 34	4 43	19 37	4 51	19 50	5 02	19 52
17	4 50	19 18	5 00	19 28	4 54	19 28	4 53	19 32	4 45	19 34	4 53	19 48	5 04	19 50
18	4 51	19 16	5 01	19 26	4 56	19 26	4 54	19 30	4 47	19 32	4 55	19 45	5 06	19 48
19	4 53	19 14	5 03	19 24	4 57	19 24	4 56	19 28	4 49	19 30	4 57	19 43	5 08	19 46
20	4 54	19 12	5 04	19 22	4 59	19 22	4 58	19 26	4 51	19 27	4 59	19 40	5 09	19 43
21	4 56	19 10	5 06	19 20	5 01	19 19	5 00	19 23	4 53	19 25	5 01	19 38	5 11	19 41
22	4 57	19 08	5 08	19 18	5 02	19 17	5 01	19 21	4 55	19 23	5 03	19 35	5 13	19 39
23	4 59	19 06	5 09	19 15	5 04	19 15	5 03	19 19	4 57	19 20	5 05	19 33	5 15	19 36
24	5 01	19 03	5 11	19 13	5 06	19 13	5 05	19 17	4 58	19 18	5 07	19 30	5 17	19 34
25	5 02	19 01	5 12	19 11	5 07	19 11	5 07	19 14	5 00	19 15	5 08	19 28	5 19	19 32
26	5 04	18 59	5 14	19 09	5 09	19 08	5 08	19 12	5 02	19 13	5 10	19 25	5 20	19 29
27	5 05	18 57	5 16	19 07	5 11	19 06	5 10	19 10	5 04	19 10	5 12	19 23	5 22	19 27
28	5 07	18 55	5 17	19 05	5 12	19 04	5 12	19 07	5 06	19 08	5 14	19 20	5 24	19 24
29	5 09	18 53	5 19	19 02	5 14	19 02	5 13	19 05	5 08	19 05	5 16	19 18	5 26	19 22
30	5 10	18 50	5 20	19 00	5 16	18 59	5 15	19 03	5 10	19 03	5 18	19 15	5 28	19 19
31	5 12	18 48	5 22	18 58	5 17	18 57	5 17	19 00	5 11	19 01	5 20	19 13	5 30	19 17

JUPITER

Day	R.A. h m	Dec. ° '	Transit h m	5° high 52° h m	56° h m
1	4 35.1	+21 13	7 54	0 34	0 19
11	4 42.0	+21 26	7 22	0 00	23 41
21	4 48.0	+21 37	6 48	23 23	23 07
31	4 53.0	+21 45	6 14	22 47	22 31

Diameters – equatorial 37″ polar 35″

SATURN

Day	R.A. h m	Dec. ° '	Transit h m	5° high 52° h m	56° h m
1	13 31.9	−7 00	16 49	21 39	21 29
11	13 34.3	−7 16	16 12	21 00	20 50
21	13 37.1	−7 35	15 36	20 22	20 12
31	13 40.4	−7 56	15 00	19 44	19 34

Diameters – equatorial 16″ polar 15″
Rings – major axis 37″ minor axis 9″

URANUS

Day	R.A. h m	Dec. ° '	Transit h m	10° high 52° h m	56° h m
1	0 32.0	+2 39	3 51	22 40	22 44
11	0 31.4	+2 35	3 11	22 00	22 05
21	0 30.5	+2 29	2 31	21 21	21 25
31	0 29.3	+2 21	1 51	20 41	20 45

Diameter 4″

NEPTUNE

Day	R.A. h m	Dec. ° '	Transit h m	10° high 52° h m	56° h m
1	22 18.3	−11 12	1 38	21 46	22 05
11	22 17.3	−11 18	0 58	21 06	21 26
21	22 16.3	−11 24	0 17	20 26	20 46
31	22 15.2	−11 30	23 33	19 47	20 06

Diameter 2″

SEPTEMBER 2012

NINTH MONTH, 30 DAYS. *Septem* (seven), seventh month of Roman pre-Julian calendar

1	*Saturday*	A solar flare was observed for the first time by astronomer Richard Carrington 1859	day 245
2	*Sunday*	The first non-stop aeroplane flight from Europe to the USA was completed, taking 37 hours 1930	246

3	*Monday*	Carl D. Anderson, Nobel prize-winning physicist who discovered the positive electron *b.* 1905	week 36 day 247
4	*Tuesday*	The Forth Road Bridge opened (at the time, Europe's longest suspension bridge) 1964	248
5	*Wednesday*	James Glaisher and Henry Coxwell set a new altitude record when their balloon ascended 11 kilometres 1862	249
6	*Thursday*	John Derry, piloting a de Havilland DH 108, became the first Briton to break the sound barrier 1948	250
7	*Friday*	James Van Allen, physicist who discovered Earth's magnetosphere (Van Allen radiation belts) *b.* 1914	251
8	*Saturday*	Scotch tape, the first transparent adhesive tape was marketed for the first time by 3M 1930	252
9	*Sunday*	Scientists stated that the hole in the ozone layer had reached record size (28 million sq. kilometres) 2000	253

10	*Monday*	Geneticist Sir Alec Jeffreys developed the techniques required for DNA fingerprinting 1984	week 37 day 254
11	*Tuesday*	Carl Zeiss, manufacturer of high-quality optical instruments (lenses, microscopes etc) *b.* 1816	255
12	*Wednesday*	Dr Richard Gatling, inventor of the Gatling gun, the first successful machine gun *b.* 1818	256
13	*Thursday*	A rail detector car which found faults in railroad tracks was demonstrated in New York, USA 1928	257
14	*Friday*	Ivan Petrovich Pavlov, physiologist famed for his research into the 'conditioned reflex' *b.* 1849	258
15	*Saturday*	The first weather balloon used for meteorological research in the USA was released in Missouri 1904	259
16	*Sunday*	Gabriel Fahrenheit, inventor of the mercury thermometer and the eponymous temperature scale *d.* 1736	260

17	*Monday*	Thomas Etholen Selfridge became the first person to die in a powered aeroplane crash 1908	week 38 day 261
18	*Tuesday*	Léon Foucault, physicist who experimentally proved that the Earth rotates on its axis *b.* 1819	262
19	*Wednesday*	Ötzi, the mummified body of a man who lived in about 3,300 BC, was discovered in the Ötztal Alps 1991	263
20	*Thursday*	Sir James Dewar, chemist who invented the Dewar flask by creating a vacuum in a container *b.* 1842	264
21	*Friday*	*Galileo*'s eight-year mission to Jupiter ended when the probe burnt up in the planet's atmosphere 2003	265
22	*Saturday*	Michael Faraday, physicist who contributed towards the understanding of electromagnetism *b.* 1791	266
23	*Sunday*	Johan Galle discovered Neptune after using calculations predicting the planet's location 1846	267

24	*Monday*	John Young, astronaut who became the first person to make six spaceflights *b.* 1930	week 39 day 268
25	*Tuesday*	The first transfusion using human blood took place at Guy's Hospital, London 1818	269
26	*Wednesday*	Nils Bohlin, inventor of the three-point lap and shoulder seatbelt, present in most cars *d.* 2002	270
27	*Thursday*	Europe's first travelator (moving walkway) opened at Bank Underground station in London 1960	271
28	*Friday*	Dr Elizabeth Garrett Anderson became the first woman to obtain a medical qualification in Britain 1865	272
29	*Saturday*	Enrico Fermi, physicist known for his nuclear research, including on induced radioactivity *b.* 1901	273
30	*Sunday*	The world's first hydroelectric power plant was opened on the Fox River in Wisconsin, USA 1882	274

ASTRONOMICAL PHENOMENA
d h
8 11 Jupiter in conjunction with Moon. Jupiter 0°.6 N.
10 13 Mercury in superior conjunction
12 15 Venus in conjunction with Moon. Venus 4°N.
16 11 Mercury in conjunction with Moon. Mercury 6°N.
18 05 Pluto at stationary point
18 11 Saturn in conjunction with Moon. Saturn 5°N.
19 21 Mars in conjunction with Moon. Mars 0°.1 N.
22 15 Sun's longitude 180° ♎
29 07 Uranus at opposition

MINIMA OF ALGOL
d	h	d	h	d	h
2	17.7	14	05.0	25	16.2
5	14.5	17	01.8	28	13.0
8	11.4	19	22.6		
11	08.2	22	19.4		

CONSTELLATIONS
The following constellations are near their meridian at

	d	h		d	h
August	1	24	September	15	21
August	16	23	October	1	20
September	1	22	October	16	19

Draco, Cepheus, Lyra, Cygnus, Vulpecula, Sagitta, Delphinus, Equuleus, Aquila, Aquarius and Capricornus

THE MOON
Phases, Apsides and Node

		d	h	m
☾	Last Quarter	8	13	15
●	New Moon	16	02	11
☽	First Quarter	22	19	41
○	Full Moon	30	03	19

Apogee (404,256km)	7	05	58
Perigee (365,775km)	19	02	41

Mean longitude of ascending node on September 1, 240°

THE SUN

s.d. 15'.9

Day	Right Ascension			Dec.		Equation of time		Rise 52°		Rise 56°		Transit		Set 52°		Set 56°		Sidereal time			Transit of first point of Aries		
	h	m	s	°	'	m	s	h	m	h	m	h	m	h	m	h	m	h	m	s	h	m	s
1	10	42	16	+8	12	-0	01	5	12	5	05	12	00	18	46	18	54	22	42	15	1	17	32
2	10	45	53	+7	51	+0	18	5	14	5	07	12	00	18	44	18	51	22	46	11	1	13	36
3	10	49	30	+7	29	+0	38	5	15	5	09	11	59	18	42	18	48	22	50	08	1	09	41
4	10	53	07	+7	07	+0	58	5	17	5	11	11	59	18	40	18	46	22	54	05	1	05	45
5	10	56	43	+6	44	+1	18	5	19	5	13	11	59	18	37	18	43	22	58	01	1	01	49
6	11	00	20	+6	22	+1	38	5	20	5	15	11	58	18	35	18	41	23	01	58	0	57	53
7	11	03	56	+6	00	+1	58	5	22	5	17	11	58	18	33	18	38	23	05	54	0	53	57
8	11	07	32	+5	37	+2	19	5	24	5	19	11	58	18	30	18	35	23	09	51	0	50	01
9	11	11	08	+5	15	+2	40	5	25	5	20	11	57	18	28	18	33	23	13	47	0	46	05
10	11	14	43	+4	52	+3	01	5	27	5	22	11	57	18	26	18	30	23	17	44	0	42	09
11	11	18	19	+4	29	+3	22	5	28	5	24	11	56	18	23	18	27	23	21	40	0	38	13
12	11	21	54	+4	06	+3	43	5	30	5	26	11	56	18	21	18	25	23	25	37	0	34	17
13	11	25	30	+3	43	+4	04	5	32	5	28	11	56	18	19	18	22	23	29	34	0	30	21
14	11	29	05	+3	20	+4	25	5	33	5	30	11	55	18	16	18	19	23	33	30	0	26	26
15	11	32	40	+2	57	+4	47	5	35	5	32	11	55	18	14	18	17	23	37	27	0	22	30
16	11	36	15	+2	34	+5	08	5	37	5	34	11	55	18	12	18	14	23	41	23	0	18	34
17	11	39	51	+2	11	+5	29	5	38	5	36	11	54	18	09	18	11	23	45	20	0	14	38
18	11	43	26	+1	48	+5	51	5	40	5	38	11	54	18	07	18	09	23	49	16	0	10	42
19	11	47	01	+1	24	+6	12	5	42	5	40	11	54	18	05	18	06	23	53	13	0	06	46
20	11	50	36	+1	01	+6	33	5	43	5	42	11	53	18	02	18	03	23	57	09	0	02	50
																				23	58	54
21	11	54	12	+0	38	+6	54	5	45	5	44	11	53	18	00	18	01	0	01	06	23	54	58
22	11	57	47	+0	14	+7	16	5	46	5	46	11	53	17	58	17	58	0	05	03	23	51	02
23	12	01	22	-0	09	+7	37	5	48	5	48	11	52	17	55	17	55	0	08	59	23	47	07
24	12	04	58	-0	32	+7	58	5	50	5	50	11	52	17	53	17	53	0	12	56	23	43	11
25	12	08	34	-0	56	+8	18	5	51	5	52	11	52	17	51	17	50	0	16	52	23	39	15
26	12	12	10	-1	19	+8	39	5	53	5	54	11	51	17	48	17	48	0	20	49	23	35	19
27	12	15	46	-1	42	+9	00	5	55	5	56	11	51	17	46	17	45	0	24	45	23	31	23
28	12	19	22	-2	06	+9	20	5	56	5	58	11	51	17	44	17	42	0	28	42	23	27	27
29	12	22	58	-2	29	+9	40	5	58	6	00	11	50	17	41	17	40	0	32	38	23	23	31
30	12	26	35	-2	52	+10	00	6	00	6	02	11	50	17	39	17	37	0	36	35	23	19	35

DURATION OF TWILIGHT (in minutes)

Latitude	52°	56°	52°	56°	52°	56°	52°	56°
	1 September		11 September		21 September		31 September	
Civil	35	39	34	38	34	37	34	37
Nautical	79	89	76	85	74	82	73	80
Astronomical	127	147	120	136	116	129	113	125

THE NIGHT SKY

Mercury passes through superior conjunction on the 10th and is therefore unsuitably placed for observation throughout the month.

Venus, magnitude −4.1, continues to be visible as a magnificent object in the eastern sky for three hours before sunrise. The old crescent Moon passes south of the planet on the 12th.

Mars is unsuitably placed for observation during the month, and will not be seen again for the rest of the year.

Jupiter, magnitude −2.4, is moving slowly eastwards in Taurus, and by the end of the month is visible low above the eastern horizon by 21h. The Moon, at Last Quarter, passes about 1 degree south of the planet on the 8th.

Saturn has now moved closer to the Sun and will not be available for observation again until early in the New Year.

Uranus is at opposition on the 29th, in the constellation of Pisces. The planet is barely visible to the naked-eye as its magnitude is +5.7, but it is readily located with only small optical aid.

Zodiacal Light. The morning cone may be observed stretching up from the eastern horizon, along the ecliptic, before the beginning of morning twilight, from the 14th to the 27th. This faint phenomenon is only visible under good conditions and in the absence of both moonlight and artificial lighting.

THE MOON

Day	R.A. h m	Dec. °	Hor. Par. ′	Semi-diam. ′	Sun's Co-Long. °	PA. of Br. Limb °	Ph. %	Age d	Rise 52° h m	Rise 56° h m	Transit h m	Set 52° h m	Set 56° h m
1	22 54	−1.8	56.7	15.4	90	24	100	14.4	18 37	18 36	0 12	6 20	6 19
2	23 42	+2.9	56.1	15.3	102	52	98	15.4	18 58	18 52	0 57	7 31	7 35
3	0 29	+7.4	55.5	15.1	114	60	94	16.4	19 19	19 10	1 42	8 40	8 48
4	1 17	+11.4	55.0	15.0	126	64	88	17.4	19 43	19 30	2 27	9 48	10 00
5	2 05	+14.9	54.6	14.9	139	68	81	18.4	20 11	19 54	3 13	10 54	11 09
6	2 53	+17.7	54.4	14.8	151	73	73	19.4	20 43	20 24	3 59	11 57	12 16
7	3 43	+19.8	54.2	14.8	163	77	65	20.4	21 22	21 00	4 46	12 56	13 17
8	4 33	+21.0	54.3	14.8	175	82	55	21.4	22 08	21 46	5 34	13 49	14 11
9	5 24	+21.2	54.5	14.9	187	86	46	22.4	23 02	22 41	6 23	14 35	14 57
10	6 15	+20.5	54.9	15.0	200	91	36	23.4	—	23 44	7 12	15 15	15 34
11	7 07	+18.8	55.4	15.1	212	95	27	24.4	0 03	—	8 01	15 49	16 05
12	7 58	+16.2	56.1	15.3	224	98	19	25.4	1 09	0 54	8 50	16 18	16 30
13	8 50	+12.7	56.8	15.5	236	100	11	26.4	2 20	2 09	9 39	16 44	16 52
14	9 41	+8.6	57.6	15.7	249	99	6	27.4	3 34	3 28	10 28	17 07	17 11
15	10 32	+3.8	58.4	15.9	261	93	2	28.4	4 51	4 49	11 17	17 30	17 30
16	11 25	−1.2	59.0	16.1	273	38	0	29.4	6 10	6 12	12 08	17 53	17 49
17	12 18	−6.3	59.5	16.2	285	311	1	0.9	7 30	7 37	13 00	18 19	18 10
18	13 13	−11.0	59.8	16.3	298	299	5	1.9	8 51	9 03	13 55	18 48	18 35
19	14 10	−15.2	59.9	16.3	310	292	11	2.9	10 12	10 28	14 51	19 23	19 06
20	15 10	−18.4	59.9	16.3	322	286	20	3.9	11 29	11 49	15 50	20 06	19 46
21	16 10	−20.4	59.6	16.3	334	280	30	4.9	12 38	13 00	16 49	20 59	20 37
22	17 11	−21.1	59.3	16.2	346	274	41	5.9	13 37	13 59	17 48	22 02	21 40
23	18 12	−20.5	58.9	16.0	359	269	52	6.9	14 24	14 44	18 45	23 12	22 53
24	19 10	−18.6	58.4	15.9	11	264	63	7.9	15 02	15 18	19 40	—	—
25	20 06	−15.7	57.9	15.8	23	260	73	8.9	15 33	15 45	20 31	0 25	0 10
26	20 59	−11.9	57.4	15.6	35	258	82	9.9	15 58	16 06	21 20	1 39	1 29
27	21 50	−7.7	56.9	15.5	47	257	90	10.9	16 21	16 25	22 07	2 53	2 47
28	22 39	−3.2	56.4	15.4	59	258	95	11.9	16 42	16 42	22 52	4 05	4 03
29	23 27	+1.5	56.0	15.2	72	266	99	12.9	17 02	16 58	23 37	5 16	5 18
30	0 14	+5.9	55.5	15.1	84	315	100	13.9	17 23	17 16	—	6 25	6 31

MERCURY

Day	R.A. h m	Dec. °	Diam. ″	Phase %	Transit h m	5° high 52° h m	5° high 56° h m
1	10 10	+13.1	5	93	11 29	4 54	4 47
3	10 25	+11.8	5	96	11 37	5 08	5 02
5	10 40	+10.4	5	98	11 43	5 23	5 18
7	10 54	+8.9	5	99	11 50	5 37	5 33
9	11 09	+7.4	5	100	11 56	5 51	5 49
11	11 22	+5.8	5	100	12 02	17 57	17 58
13	11 36	+4.2	5	100	12 08	17 55	17 54
15	11 49	+2.6	5	99	12 13	17 52	17 50
17	12 02	+1.1	5	99	12 18	17 48	17 45
19	12 15	−0.5	5	98	12 23	17 45	17 41
21	12 27	−2.1	5	97	12 27	17 41	17 36
23	12 39	−3.6	5	96	12 31	17 37	17 30
25	12 51	−5.1	5	95	12 35	17 33	17 25
27	13 03	−6.6	5	94	12 39	17 29	17 19
29	13 14	−8.0	5	93	12 42	17 25	17 14
31	13 25	−9.4	5	91	12 46	17 20	17 08

VENUS

Day	R.A. h m	Dec. °	Diam. ″	Phase %	Transit h m	5° high 52° h m	5° high 56° h m
1	7 42	+19.3	20	58	9 00	1 50	1 37
6	8 05	+18.7	19	61	9 03	1 57	1 44
11	8 27	+17.9	18	63	9 06	2 04	1 52
16	8 50	+16.8	18	65	9 09	2 13	2 02
21	9 13	+15.6	17	67	9 12	2 23	2 14
26	9 36	+14.2	16	69	9 15	2 34	2 26
31	9 58	+12.6	16	71	9 18	2 46	2 39

MARS

Day	R.A. h m	Dec. °	Diam. ″	Phase %	Transit h m	5° high 52° h m	5° high 56° h m
1	14 12	−13.8	5	91	15 29	19 37	19 20
6	14 24	−14.9	5	92	15 22	19 23	19 05
11	14 37	−16.0	5	92	15 15	19 10	18 49
16	14 51	−17.1	5	92	15 09	18 56	18 34
21	15 04	−18.1	5	93	15 03	18 43	18 19
26	15 18	−19.1	5	93	14 57	18 30	18 05
31	15 33	−20.0	5	93	14 51	18 18	17 51

SUNRISE AND SUNSET

	London 0° 05′ | 51° 30′		Bristol 2° 35′ | 51° 28′		Birmingham 1° 55′ | 52° 28′		Manchester 2° 15′ | 53° 28′		Newcastle 1° 37′ | 54° 59′		Glasgow 4° 14′ | 55° 52′		Belfast 5° 56′ | 54° 35′	
d	h m	h m	h m	h m	h m	h m	h m	h m	h m	h m	h m	h m	h m	h m
1	5 13	18 46	5 23	18 56	5 19	18 55	5 19	18 58	5 13	18 58	5 22	19 10	5 31	19 15
2	5 15	18 44	5 25	18 54	5 21	18 52	5 20	18 55	5 15	18 56	5 24	19 08	5 33	19 12
3	5 17	18 41	5 27	18 51	5 22	18 50	5 22	18 53	5 17	18 53	5 26	19 05	5 35	19 10
4	5 18	18 39	5 28	18 49	5 24	18 48	5 24	18 51	5 19	18 51	5 28	19 02	5 37	19 07
5	5 20	18 37	5 30	18 47	5 26	18 46	5 26	18 48	5 21	18 48	5 30	19 00	5 39	19 05
6	5 21	18 35	5 31	18 45	5 27	18 43	5 27	18 46	5 23	18 45	5 32	18 57	5 41	19 02
7	5 23	18 32	5 33	18 42	5 29	18 41	5 29	18 43	5 25	18 43	5 34	18 55	5 42	19 00
8	5 25	18 30	5 35	18 40	5 31	18 39	5 31	18 41	5 26	18 40	5 36	18 52	5 44	18 57
9	5 26	18 28	5 36	18 38	5 32	18 36	5 33	18 39	5 28	18 38	5 38	18 49	5 46	18 55
10	5 28	18 26	5 38	18 35	5 34	18 34	5 34	18 36	5 30	18 35	5 40	18 47	5 48	18 52
11	5 29	18 23	5 39	18 33	5 36	18 31	5 36	18 34	5 32	18 33	5 41	18 44	5 50	18 50
12	5 31	18 21	5 41	18 31	5 37	18 29	5 38	18 31	5 34	18 30	5 43	18 41	5 52	18 47
13	5 32	18 19	5 43	18 29	5 39	18 27	5 40	18 29	5 36	18 28	5 45	18 39	5 53	18 44
14	5 34	18 16	5 44	18 26	5 41	18 24	5 41	18 26	5 38	18 25	5 47	18 36	5 55	18 42
15	5 36	18 14	5 46	18 24	5 42	18 22	5 43	18 24	5 39	18 22	5 49	18 34	5 57	18 39
16	5 37	18 12	5 47	18 22	5 44	18 20	5 45	18 21	5 41	18 20	5 51	18 31	5 59	18 37
17	5 39	18 09	5 49	18 19	5 46	18 17	5 47	18 19	5 43	18 17	5 53	18 28	6 01	18 34
18	5 40	18 07	5 51	18 17	5 47	18 15	5 48	18 17	5 45	18 15	5 55	18 26	6 02	18 32
19	5 42	18 05	5 52	18 15	5 49	18 12	5 50	18 14	5 47	18 12	5 57	18 23	6 04	18 29
20	5 44	18 03	5 54	18 13	5 51	18 10	5 52	18 12	5 49	18 10	5 59	18 20	6 06	18 27
21	5 45	18 00	5 55	18 10	5 52	18 08	5 54	18 09	5 51	18 07	6 01	18 18	6 08	18 24
22	5 47	17 58	5 57	18 08	5 54	18 05	5 55	18 07	5 52	18 04	6 03	18 15	6 10	18 22
23	5 49	17 56	5 59	18 06	5 56	18 03	5 57	18 04	5 54	18 02	6 05	18 12	6 12	18 19
24	5 50	17 53	6 00	18 03	5 57	18 01	5 59	18 02	5 56	17 59	6 07	18 10	6 14	18 17
25	5 52	17 51	6 02	18 01	5 59	17 58	6 01	17 59	5 58	17 57	6 09	18 07	6 15	18 14
26	5 53	17 49	6 03	17 59	6 01	17 56	6 02	17 57	6 00	17 54	6 11	18 04	6 17	18 12
27	5 55	17 46	6 05	17 56	6 03	17 54	6 04	17 55	6 02	17 52	6 13	18 02	6 19	18 09
28	5 57	17 44	6 07	17 54	6 04	17 51	6 06	17 52	6 04	17 49	6 15	17 59	6 21	18 06
29	5 58	17 42	6 08	17 52	6 06	17 49	6 08	17 50	6 06	17 47	6 16	17 57	6 23	18 04
30	6 00	17 40	6 10	17 50	6 08	17 46	6 09	17 47	6 08	17 44	6 18	17 54	6 25	18 01

JUPITER

Day	R.A. h m	Dec. ° ′	Transit h m	5° high 52° h m	5° high 56° h m
1	4 53.5	+21 45	6 10	22 44	22 28
11	4 57.3	+21 51	5 35	22 08	21 51
21	4 59.9	+21 54	4 58	21 31	21 14
31	5 01.1	+21 55	4 20	20 52	20 36

Diameters – equatorial 41″ polar 38″

SATURN

Day	R.A. h m	Dec. ° ′	Transit h m	5° high 52° h m	5° high 56° h m
1	13 40.7	−7 58	14 56	19 40	19 30
11	13 44.4	−8 21	14 21	19 02	18 52
21	13 48.4	−8 45	13 45	18 25	18 14
31	13 52.7	−9 10	13 10	17 48	17 36

Diameters – equatorial 16″ polar 14″
Rings – major axis 35″ minor axis 9″

URANUS

Day	R.A. h m	Dec. ° ′	Transit h m	10° high 52° h m	10° high 56° h m
1	0 29.2	+2 20	1 47	20 37	20 42
11	0 27.9	+2 12	1 06	19 57	20 02
21	0 26.5	+2 03	0 25	19 17	19 22
31	0 25.0	+1 53	23 40	18 37	18 42

Diameter 4″

NEPTUNE

Day	R.A. h m	Dec. ° ′	Transit h m	10° high 52° h m	10° high 56° h m
1	22 15.1	−11 30	23 29	3 19	3 00
11	22 14.1	−11 36	22 49	2 38	2 18
21	22 13.2	−11 41	22 08	1 58	1 37
31	22 12.3	−11 46	21 28	1 17	0 57

Diameter 2″

OCTOBER 2012

TENTH MONTH, 31 DAYS. *Octo* (eighth), eighth month of Roman pre-Julian calendar

1	*Monday*	Ford's Model T, the first assembly line car, was introduced to the US market 1908	week 40 day 275
2	*Tuesday*	Charles Darwin returned from his momentous voyage to the Pacific aboard *HMS Beagle* 1836	276
3	*Wednesday*	The UK tested its first nuclear weapon, named 'Hurricane', in Australia 1952	277
4	*Thursday*	The Soviet Union launched *Sputnik*, the first man-made satellite, which commenced the space age 1957	278
5	*Friday*	Robert Goddard, inventor and physicist credited as the father of modern rocketry *b.* 1882	279
6	*Saturday*	Benjamin Hanks received a patent for the self-winding clock 1783	280
7	*Sunday*	The Soviet space probe *Luna 3* photographed the far side of the Moon for the first time 1959	281

8	*Monday*	The Post Office Tower, then the tallest building in London, was officially opened 1965	week 41 day 282
9	*Tuesday*	The first generator at the Hoover Dam began transmitting electricity to Los Angeles 1936	283
10	*Wednesday*	Henry Cavendish, scientist who measured the density and mass of the Earth *b.* 1731	284
11	*Thursday*	Kathryn D. Sullivan, a NASA astronaut, became the first woman to walk in space 1984	285
12	*Friday*	Robert Stephenson, civil engineer who built many bridges, including the Britannia Bridge *d.* 1859	286
13	*Saturday*	At the International Meridian Conference, Greenwich was adopted as the universal meridian 1884	287
14	*Sunday*	George Eastman, founder of Kodak, received a patent for the paper-strip photographic film 1884	288

15	*Monday*	Evangelista Torricelli, physicist credited with inventing the barometer *b.* 1608	week 42 day 289
16	*Tuesday*	Samuel Franklin Cody completed the first aeroplane flight in the UK 1908	290
17	*Wednesday*	Dr Ernest Goodpasture, pathologist who developed vaccines against influenza and smallpox *b.* 1886	291
18	*Thursday*	Thomas Edison, inventor of the phonograph who held over 1,000 patents *d.* 1931	292
19	*Friday*	Auguste Lumière, pioneer of photographic equipment, including a motion-picture camera *b.* 1862	293
20	*Saturday*	The metre was redefined as the distance that light travels in a vacuum in 1/299,792,458 of a second 1983	294
21	*Sunday*	Alfred Nobel, chemist and inventor of dynamite whose funds instituted the famed annual prizes *b.* 1833	295

22	*Monday*	The Campaign for Nuclear Disarmament held its biggest ever protest against nuclear weapons 1983	week 43 day 296
23	*Tuesday*	The first modern rhinoplasty was performed by surgeon Joseph Carpue in London 1814	297
24	*Wednesday*	Concorde made its last commercial passenger flight, landing at Heathrow airport 2003	298
25	*Thursday*	The first domestic microwave oven, manufactured by the Tappan Stove Company, went on sale 1955	299
26	*Friday*	A patent was issued by Hamilton Smith for a rotary washing machine, which cycled reheated water 1858	300
27	*Saturday*	Isaac Singer, inventor whose company was the world's largest sewing machine manufacturer *b.* 1811	301
28	*Sunday*	John Wallis, mathematician credited with introducing the mathematical symbol for infinity *d.* 1703	302

29	*Monday*	John Glenn became the oldest person to go into space, aboard the shuttle *Discovery*, at 77 1998	week 44 day 303
30	*Tuesday*	Daniel Cooper patented a time clock which recorded employees' hours of work 1888	304
31	*Wednesday*	Michael Collins, astronaut who orbited the Moon in the momentous Apollo 11 mission *b.* 1930	305

ASTRONOMICAL PHENOMENA

d   h
4 13 Jupiter at stationary point
5 10 Saturn in conjunction with Mercury. Saturn 3°N.
5 21 Jupiter in conjunction with Moon. Jupiter 0°.9 N.
12 15 Venus in conjunction with Moon. Venus 6°N.
16 02 Saturn in conjunction with Moon. Saturn 4°N.
17 02 Mercury in conjunction with Moon. Mercury 1°S.
18 14 Mars in conjunction with Moon. Mars 2°S.
23 00 Sun's longitude 210° ♏
25 09 Saturn in conjunction
26 15 Mercury at greatest elongation E. 24°

MINIMA OF ALGOL

d	*h*	*d*	*h*	*d*	*h*
1	09.8	12	21.1	24	08.3
4	06.7	15	17.9	27	05.2
7	03.5	18	14.7	30	02.0
10	00.3	21	11.5		

CONSTELLATIONS
The following constellations are near their meridian at

	d	*h*		*d*	*h*
September	1	24	October	16	21
September	15	23	November	1	20
October	1	22	November	15	19

Ursa Major (below the Pole), Cepheus, Cassiopeia, Cygnus, Lacerta, Andromeda, Pegasus, Capricornus, Aquarius and Piscis Austrinus

THE MOON

Phases, Apsides and Node		*d*	*h*	*m*
☾	Last Quarter	8	07	33
●	New Moon	15	12	02
☽	First Quarter	22	03	32
○	Full Moon	29	19	49

	d	*h*	*m*
Apogee (405,128km)	5	00	37
Perigee (360,685km)	17	00	53

Mean longitude of ascending node on October 1, 238°

THE SUN

s.d. 16'.1

Day	Right Ascension			Dec.		Equation of time		Rise 52°		Rise 56°		Transit		Set 52°		Set 56°		Sidereal time			Transit of first point of Aries		
	h	m	s	°	'	m	s	h	m	h	m	h	m	h	m	h	m	h	m	s	h	m	s
1	12	30	12	3	16	+10	19	6	01	6	04	11	49	17	37	17	34	0	40	31	23	15	39
2	12	33	49	3	39	+10	39	6	03	6	06	11	49	17	34	17	32	0	44	28	23	11	43
3	12	37	27	4	02	+10	58	6	05	6	08	11	49	17	32	17	29	0	48	25	23	07	47
4	12	41	05	4	25	+11	16	6	06	6	10	11	49	17	30	17	27	0	52	21	23	03	52
5	12	44	43	4	48	+11	34	6	08	6	12	11	48	17	28	17	24	0	56	18	22	59	56
6	12	48	22	5	11	+11	52	6	10	6	14	11	48	17	25	17	21	1	00	14	22	56	00
7	12	52	01	5	34	+12	10	6	11	6	16	11	48	17	23	17	19	1	04	11	22	52	04
8	12	55	41	5	57	+12	27	6	13	6	18	11	47	17	21	17	16	1	08	07	22	48	08
9	12	59	20	6	20	+12	43	6	15	6	20	11	47	17	18	17	14	1	12	04	22	44	12
10	13	03	01	6	43	+13	00	6	17	6	22	11	47	17	16	17	11	1	16	00	22	40	16
11	13	06	42	7	05	+13	15	6	18	6	24	11	47	17	14	17	09	1	19	57	22	36	20
12	13	10	23	7	28	+13	30	6	20	6	26	11	46	17	12	17	06	1	23	54	22	32	24
13	13	14	05	7	50	+13	45	6	22	6	28	11	46	17	10	17	03	1	27	50	22	28	28
14	13	17	48	8	13	+13	59	6	23	6	30	11	46	17	07	17	01	1	31	47	22	24	32
15	13	21	31	8	35	+14	12	6	25	6	32	11	46	17	05	16	58	1	35	43	22	20	37
16	13	25	14	8	57	+14	25	6	27	6	34	11	45	17	03	16	56	1	39	40	22	16	41
17	13	28	59	9	19	+14	38	6	29	6	36	11	45	17	01	16	54	1	43	36	22	12	45
18	13	32	43	9	41	+14	50	6	31	6	38	11	45	16	59	16	51	1	47	33	22	08	49
19	13	36	29	10	03	+15	01	6	32	6	40	11	45	16	57	16	49	1	51	29	22	04	53
20	13	40	15	10	24	+15	11	6	34	6	42	11	45	16	55	16	46	1	55	26	22	00	57
21	13	44	01	10	46	+15	21	6	36	6	44	11	45	16	53	16	44	1	59	23	21	57	01
22	13	47	49	11	07	+15	30	6	38	6	46	11	44	16	50	16	41	2	03	19	21	53	05
23	13	51	37	11	28	+15	39	6	39	6	49	11	44	16	48	16	39	2	07	16	21	49	09
24	13	55	25	11	49	+15	47	6	41	6	51	11	44	16	46	16	37	2	11	12	21	45	13
25	13	59	14	12	10	+15	54	6	43	6	53	11	44	16	44	16	34	2	15	09	21	41	17
26	14	03	04	12	30	+16	01	6	45	6	55	11	44	16	42	16	32	2	19	05	21	37	22
27	14	06	55	12	51	+16	07	6	46	6	57	11	44	16	40	16	30	2	23	02	21	33	26
28	14	10	47	13	11	+16	12	6	48	6	59	11	44	16	39	16	28	2	26	58	21	29	30
29	14	14	39	13	31	+16	16	6	50	7	01	11	44	16	37	16	25	2	30	55	21	25	34
30	14	18	32	13	50	+16	20	6	52	7	03	11	44	16	35	16	23	2	34	52	21	21	38
31	14	22	25	14	10	+16	23	6	54	7	06	11	44	16	33	16	21	2	38	48	21	17	42

DURATION OF TWILIGHT (in minutes)

Latitude	52°	56°	52°	56°	52°	56°	52°	56°
	1 October		11 October		21 October		31 October	
Civil	34	37	34	37	34	38	35	39
Nautical	73	80	73	80	74	81	75	83
Astronomical	113	125	112	124	113	124	114	126

THE NIGHT SKY

Mercury, although reaching greatest eastern elongation (24 degrees) on the 26th remains unsuitably placed for observation throughout October.

Venus is still a magnificent object in the eastern sky in the early mornings for about three hours before dawn, magnitude −4.1. The planet passes only about 0.1 degrees below Regulus, closest approach being around 2 hours after sunrise on the morning of the 3rd. On the 12th the thin crescent Moon passes 6 degrees south of Venus.

Mars is unsuitably placed for observation.

Jupiter continues to be visible in the evening skies as a brilliant object, magnitude −2.6. It reaches its first stationary point on the 4th and then moves slowly retrograde in the constellation of Taurus. On the 5th the waning gibbous Moon passes about 1 degree south of the planet. The four Galilean satellites are readily observable with a small telescope or even a good pair of binoculars provided that they are held rigidly.

Saturn remains too close to the Sun for observation throughout October as it passes through conjunction on the 25th.

THE MOON

Day	R.A. h	R.A. m	Dec. °	Hor. Par. '	Semi-diam. '	Sun's Co-Long. °	PA. of Br. Limb °	Ph. %	Age d	Rise 52° h	Rise 52° m	Rise 56° h	Rise 56° m	Transit h	Transit m	Set 52° h	Set 52° m	Set 56° h	Set 56° m
1	1	02	+10.1	55.1	15.0	96	49	99	14.9	17	46	17	35	0	22	7	33	7	43
2	1	49	+13.7	54.7	14.9	108	63	97	15.9	18	13	17	58	1	07	8	40	8	54
3	2	38	+16.8	54.4	14.8	120	70	92	16.9	18	43	18	25	1	53	9	44	10	01
4	3	27	+19.0	54.2	14.8	132	76	87	17.9	19	20	18	59	2	40	10	44	11	04
5	4	17	+20.5	54.1	14.7	145	81	80	18.9	20	03	19	41	3	27	11	39	12	01
6	5	08	+21.0	54.2	14.8	157	86	72	19.9	20	53	20	32	4	16	12	28	12	50
7	5	58	+20.6	54.4	14.8	169	91	63	20.9	21	50	21	31	5	04	13	10	13	30
8	6	49	+19.3	54.8	14.9	181	95	53	21.9	22	53	22	37	5	52	13	46	14	03
9	7	40	+17.0	55.4	15.1	193	99	43	22.9	—		23	48	6	40	14	16	14	30
10	8	30	+14.0	56.1	15.3	206	102	34	23.9	0	00	—		7	28	14	43	14	53
11	9	20	+10.2	56.9	15.5	218	105	24	24.9	1	11	1	03	8	16	15	07	15	13
12	10	11	+5.7	57.8	15.8	230	106	16	25.9	2	26	2	21	9	05	15	30	15	32
13	11	02	+0.9	58.7	16.0	242	105	9	26.9	3	42	3	42	9	54	15	53	15	51
14	11	55	−4.2	59.6	16.2	254	102	3	27.9	5	02	5	07	10	46	16	18	16	11
15	12	50	−9.1	60.2	16.4	267	87	0	28.9	6	24	6	34	11	40	16	46	16	35
16	13	48	−13.6	60.6	16.5	279	309	0	0.5	7	47	8	02	12	38	17	19	17	04
17	14	48	−17.3	60.8	16.6	291	290	3	1.5	9	09	9	27	13	38	18	01	17	41
18	15	50	−19.8	60.7	16.5	303	282	9	2.5	10	24	10	45	14	39	18	52	18	30
19	16	53	−20.9	60.3	16.4	315	275	17	3.5	11	29	11	51	15	40	19	53	19	31
20	17	56	−20.6	59.7	16.3	328	269	27	4.5	12	21	12	41	16	40	21	02	20	43
21	18	56	−19.0	59.1	16.1	340	263	37	5.5	13	03	13	20	17	36	22	16	22	00
22	19	53	−16.2	58.4	15.9	352	259	48	6.5	13	36	13	49	18	28	23	30	23	19
23	20	47	−12.7	57.6	15.7	4	256	59	7.5	14	02	14	11	19	18	—		—	
24	21	38	−8.6	57.0	15.5	16	253	70	8.5	14	26	14	31	20	05	0	44	0	36
25	22	27	−4.1	56.4	15.4	29	252	79	9.5	14	47	14	48	20	50	1	55	1	52
26	23	15	+0.4	55.8	15.2	41	252	86	10.5	15	07	15	05	21	34	3	06	3	06
27	0	02	+4.8	55.4	15.1	53	253	92	11.5	15	28	15	22	22	19	4	14	4	19
28	0	49	+9.0	54.9	15.0	65	256	97	12.5	15	50	15	40	23	03	5	22	5	31
29	1	36	+12.7	54.6	14.9	77	264	99	13.5	16	15	16	02	23	49	6	29	6	41
30	2	24	+15.9	54.3	14.8	89	32	100	14.5	16	44	16	27	—		7	33	7	49
31	3	13	+18.4	54.1	14.8	102	73	99	15.5	17	19	16	59	0	35	8	35	8	54

MERCURY

Day	R.A. h	R.A. m	Dec. °	Diam. "	Phase %	Transit h	Transit m	5° high 52° h	5° high 52° m	5° high 56° h	5° high 56° m
1	13	25	−9.4	5	91	12	46	17	20	17	08
3	13	37	−10.7	5	90	12	49	17	16	17	02
5	13	48	−12.0	5	89	12	52	17	11	16	56
7	13	59	−13.3	5	87	12	56	17	07	16	50
9	14	10	−14.5	5	86	12	59	17	02	16	44
11	14	21	−15.7	5	84	13	01	16	57	16	37
13	14	31	−16.8	5	82	13	04	16	53	16	31
15	14	42	−17.8	6	80	13	07	16	49	16	25
17	14	52	−18.8	6	78	13	09	16	44	16	19
19	15	02	−19.7	6	76	13	12	16	40	16	13
21	15	12	−20.5	6	73	13	14	16	35	16	06
23	15	22	−21.3	6	70	13	15	16	31	16	00
25	15	31	−21.9	6	67	13	16	16	27	15	55
27	15	40	−22.5	7	63	13	17	16	23	15	49
29	15	48	−23.0	7	58	13	17	16	19	15	43
31	15	55	−23.3	7	53	13	15	16	15	15	38

VENUS

Day	R.A. h	R.A. m	Dec. °	Diam. "	Phase %	Transit h	Transit m	5° high 52° h	5° high 52° m	5° high 56° h	5° high 56° m
1	9	58	+12.6	16	71	9	18	2	46	2	39
6	10	21	+10.8	15	73	9	21	2	58	2	53
11	10	44	+8.9	15	74	9	24	3	11	3	07
16	11	06	+6.9	14	76	9	27	3	24	3	22
21	11	29	+4.7	14	78	9	29	3	38	3	37
26	11	51	+2.5	14	79	9	32	3	52	3	53
31	12	13	+0.3	13	81	9	35	4	06	4	10

MARS

Day	R.A. h	R.A. m	Dec. °	Diam. "	Phase %	Transit h	Transit m	5° high 52° h	5° high 52° m	5° high 56° h	5° high 56° m
1	15	33	−20.0	5	93	14	51	18	18	17	51
6	15	47	−20.8	5	94	14	46	18	07	17	37
11	16	02	−21.6	5	94	14	41	17	56	17	24
16	16	17	−22.3	5	94	14	37	17	45	17	12
21	16	33	−22.9	5	94	14	33	17	36	17	01
26	16	48	−23.4	5	95	14	29	17	27	16	50
31	17	04	−23.9	5	95	14	25	17	20	16	41

SUNRISE AND SUNSET

d	London 0° 05', 51° 30' h m	h m	Bristol 2° 35', 51° 28' h m	h m	Birmingham 1° 55', 52° 28' h m	h m	Manchester 2° 15', 53° 28' h m	h m	Newcastle 1° 37', 54° 59' h m	h m	Glasgow 4° 14', 55° 52' h m	h m	Belfast 5° 56', 54° 35' h m	h m
1	6 01	17 37	6 11	17 47	6 09	17 44	6 11	17 45	6 09	17 41	6 20	17 51	6 26	17 59
2	6 03	17 35	6 13	17 45	6 11	17 42	6 13	17 42	6 11	17 39	6 22	17 49	6 28	17 56
3	6 05	17 33	6 15	17 43	6 13	17 39	6 15	17 40	6 13	17 36	6 24	17 46	6 30	17 54
4	6 06	17 30	6 16	17 41	6 14	17 37	6 17	17 38	6 15	17 34	6 26	17 44	6 32	17 51
5	6 08	17 28	6 18	17 38	6 16	17 35	6 18	17 35	6 17	17 31	6 28	17 41	6 34	17 49
6	6 10	17 26	6 20	17 36	6 18	17 32	6 20	17 33	6 19	17 29	6 30	17 38	6 36	17 47
7	6 11	17 24	6 21	17 34	6 20	17 30	6 22	17 31	6 21	17 26	6 32	17 36	6 38	17 44
8	6 13	17 22	6 23	17 32	6 21	17 28	6 24	17 28	6 23	17 24	6 34	17 33	6 40	17 42
9	6 15	17 19	6 25	17 29	6 23	17 26	6 26	17 26	6 25	17 21	6 36	17 31	6 42	17 39
10	6 16	17 17	6 26	17 27	6 25	17 23	6 27	17 23	6 27	17 19	6 38	17 28	6 43	17 37
11	6 18	17 15	6 28	17 25	6 27	17 21	6 29	17 21	6 29	17 16	6 40	17 26	6 45	17 34
12	6 20	17 13	6 30	17 23	6 28	17 19	6 31	17 19	6 31	17 14	6 42	17 23	6 47	17 32
13	6 21	17 11	6 31	17 21	6 30	17 17	6 33	17 16	6 33	17 12	6 45	17 21	6 49	17 29
14	6 23	17 08	6 33	17 19	6 32	17 14	6 35	17 14	6 35	17 09	6 47	17 18	6 51	17 27
15	6 25	17 06	6 35	17 16	6 34	17 12	6 37	17 12	6 37	17 07	6 49	17 16	6 53	17 25
16	6 27	17 04	6 36	17 14	6 35	17 10	6 38	17 10	6 39	17 04	6 51	17 13	6 55	17 22
17	6 28	17 02	6 38	17 12	6 37	17 08	6 40	17 07	6 41	17 02	6 53	17 11	6 57	17 20
18	6 30	17 00	6 40	17 10	6 39	17 06	6 42	17 05	6 43	17 00	6 55	17 08	6 59	17 18
19	6 32	16 58	6 42	17 08	6 41	17 03	6 44	17 03	6 44	16 57	6 57	17 06	7 01	17 15
20	6 33	16 56	6 43	17 06	6 43	17 01	6 46	17 01	6 47	16 55	6 59	17 03	7 03	17 13
21	6 35	16 54	6 45	17 04	6 44	16 59	6 48	16 59	6 49	16 53	7 01	17 01	7 05	17 11
22	6 37	16 52	6 47	17 02	6 46	16 57	6 50	16 56	6 51	16 50	7 03	16 59	7 07	17 09
23	6 39	16 50	6 49	17 00	6 48	16 55	6 52	16 54	6 53	16 48	7 05	16 56	7 09	17 06
24	6 40	16 48	6 50	16 58	6 50	16 53	6 53	16 52	6 55	16 46	7 07	16 54	7 11	17 04
25	6 42	16 46	6 52	16 56	6 52	16 51	6 55	16 50	6 57	16 44	7 09	16 52	7 13	17 02
26	6 44	16 44	6 54	16 54	6 53	16 49	6 57	16 48	6 59	16 41	7 11	16 49	7 15	17 00
27	6 46	16 42	6 56	16 52	6 55	16 47	6 59	16 46	7 01	16 39	7 14	16 47	7 17	16 57
28	6 47	16 40	6 57	16 50	6 57	16 45	7 01	16 44	7 03	16 37	7 16	16 45	7 19	16 55
29	6 49	16 38	6 59	16 48	6 59	16 43	7 03	16 42	7 05	16 35	7 18	16 43	7 21	16 53
30	6 51	16 36	7 01	16 46	7 01	16 41	7 05	16 40	7 07	16 33	7 20	16 40	7 23	16 51
31	6 53	16 34	7 03	16 45	7 03	16 39	7 07	16 38	7 09	16 31	7 22	16 38	7 25	16 49

JUPITER

Day	R.A. h m	Dec. ° '	Transit h m	5° high 52° h m	5° high 56° h m
1	5 01.1	+21 55	4 20	20 52	20 36
11	5 00.9	+21 55	3 40	20 13	19 56
21	4 59.2	+21 52	2 59	19 32	19 15
31	4 56.2	+21 47	2 17	18 50	18 34

Diameters – equatorial 45″ polar 42″

SATURN

Day	R.A. h m	Dec. ° '	Transit h m	5° high 52° h m	5° high 56° h m
1	13 52.7	−9 10	13 10	17 48	17 36
11	13 57.1	−9 35	12 35	17 10	16 58
21	14 01.7	−10 00	12 01	16 33	16 20
31	14 06.3	−10 25	11 26	15 56	15 43

Diameters – equatorial 15″ polar 14″
Rings – major axis 35″ minor axis 10″

URANUS

Day	R.A. h m	Dec. ° '	Transit h m	10° high 52° h m	10° high 56° h m
1	0 25.0	+1 53	23 40	4 48	4 43
11	0 23.5	+1 44	23 00	4 07	4 01
21	0 22.1	+1 35	22 19	3 25	3 20
31	0 20.9	+1 27	21 38	2 44	2 38

Diameter 4″

NEPTUNE

Day	R.A. h m	Dec. ° '	Transit h m	10° high 52° h m	10° high 56° h m
1	22 12.3	−11 46	21 28	1 17	0 57
11	22 11.6	−11 50	20 48	0 36	0 16
21	22 11.1	−11 53	20 08	23 52	23 32
31	22 10.8	−11 55	19 29	23 12	22 52

Diameter 2″

NOVEMBER 2012

ELEVENTH MONTH, 30 DAYS. *Novem* (nine), ninth month of Roman pre-Julian calendar

1	Thursday	The USA tested the first hydrogen bomb, codenamed 'Ivy Mike', detonated in the Pacific 1952	day 306
2	Friday	Aviation pioneer Howard Hughes flew his eight-engine wooden aeroplane *Spruce Goose* for one minute 1947	307
3	Saturday	The Soviet Union launched the first living creature into space, a dog named Laika 1957	308
4	Sunday	Benjamin Palmer was granted the first patent in the USA for an artificial leg 1846	309

5	Monday	Fred Whipple, astronomer who proposed the 'dirty snowball' hypothesis for comets *b.* 1906	week 45 day 310
6	Tuesday	Adolphe Sax, musical instrument designer best known for inventing the saxophone *b.* 1814	311
7	Wednesday	Marie Curie, chemist and physicist who discovered radium and won two Nobel prizes *b.* 1867	312
8	Thursday	Wilhelm Conrad Röntgen, physicist, observed x-rays for the first time 1895	313
9	Friday	Physicist Gordon Gould wrote down the principles for his invention, the laser, but failed to patent his idea 1957	314
10	Saturday	Fred Cohen presented his creation, the computer virus, to a security seminar in the USA 1983	315
11	Sunday	Construction began on the Manchester Ship Canal, which took just over six years to complete 1887	316

12	Monday	*Voyager 1* began sending images of Saturn's rings 1.5 billion kilometres back to Earth 1980	week 46 day 317
13	Tuesday	An aeroplane spread pellets of dry ice at 4,000 metres creating artificial snow for the first time 1946	318
14	Wednesday	Edward H. White II became the first to walk in space, during the orbital flight of Gemini 4 *b.* 1930	319
15	Thursday	King Camp Gillette received a patent for his safety razor, which used disposable blades 1904	320
16	Friday	The discovery of Americium (atomic number 95) and curium (96), two new elements, was announced 1945	321
17	Saturday	Doug Engelbart, inventor and computer pioneer, was issued a patent for the computer mouse 1970	322
18	Sunday	Alan Shepard Jr, the USA's first man in space and one of 12 men to have walked on the Moon *b.* 1923	323

19	Monday	Blackfriars Bridge, designed by Robert Mylne, was opened 1769	week 47 day 324
20	Tuesday	Edwin Powell Hubble, astronomer who provided evidence of the expansion of the universe *b.* 1889	325
21	Wednesday	Two Frenchmen made the first manned hot-air balloon flight, travelling 8 kilometres in 25 minutes 1783	326
22	Thursday	Concorde began operating flights between New York and Europe with a flight time under 3.5 hours 1977	327
23	Friday	Octave Chanute, pioneer of aviation who heavily influenced Orville and Wilbur Wright *d.* 1910	328
24	Saturday	Charles Darwin's groundbreaking *On the Origin of Species* was published and sold out immediately 1859	329
25	Sunday	In the USA, Leroy Parsons established cable television 1948	330

26	Monday	John Newlands, chemist who first ordered chemical elements by their atomic weights *b.* 1837	week 48 day 331
27	Tuesday	Anders Celsius, physicist who developed the eponymous temperature scale *b.* 1701	332
28	Wednesday	Skywriting was demonstrated in the USA for the first time 1922	333
29	Thursday	The first US underground atomic bomb test, codenamed 'Uncle', was detonated 1951	334
30	Friday	A 4 kilogram meteorite hit Elizabeth Hodges after it crashed through her roof in Alabama, USA 1954	335

ASTRONOMICAL PHENOMENA

d h
2 01 Jupiter in conjunction with Moon. Jupiter 0°.9 N.
6 23 Mercury at stationary point
11 08 Neptune at stationary point
11 14 Venus in conjunction with Moon. Venus 5°N.
12 18 Saturn in conjunction with Moon. Saturn 4°N.
13 22 Total eclipse of Sun (see page 1278)
14 11 Mercury in conjunction with Moon. Mercury 1°S.
16 10 Mars in conjunction with Moon. Mars 4°S.
17 16 Mercury in inferior conjunction
21 22 Sun's longitude 240° ♐
26 23 Mercury at stationary point
27 01 Saturn in conjunction with Venus. Saturn 0°.5 N.
29 01 Jupiter in conjunction with Moon. Jupiter 0°.6 N.

MINIMA OF ALGOL

d	h	d	h	d	h
1	22.8	13	10.1	24	21.3
4	19.6	16	06.9	27	18.1
7	16.4	19	03.7	30	15.0
10	13.2	22	00.5		

CONSTELLATIONS

The following constellations are near their meridian at

	d	h		d	h
October	1	24	November	15	21
October	16	23	December	1	20
November	1	22	December	16	19

Ursa Major (below the Pole), Cepheus, Cassiopeia, Andromeda, Pegasus, Pisces, Aquarius and Cetus

THE MOON

Phases, Apsides and Node		d	h	m
☾	Last Quarter	7	00	36
●	New Moon	13	22	08
☽	First Quarter	20	14	31
○	Full Moon	28	14	46

	d	h	m
Apogee (406,030km)	1	15	18
Perigee (357,365km)	14	10	15
Apogee (406,360km)	28	19	19

Mean longitude of ascending node on November 1, 237°

THE SUN

Day	Right Ascension			Dec.		Equation of time		Rise 52°		Rise 56°		Transit		Set 52°		Set 56°		Sidereal time			Transit of first point of Aries		
	h	m	s	°	′	m	s	h	m	h	m	h	m	h	m	h	m	h	m	s	h	m	s
1	14	26	20	14	29	+16	25	6	55	7	08	11	44	16	31	16	19	2	42	45	21	13	46
2	14	30	15	14	48	+16	26	6	57	7	10	11	44	16	29	16	17	2	46	41	21	09	50
3	14	34	11	15	07	+16	26	6	59	7	12	11	44	16	27	16	14	2	50	38	21	05	54
4	14	38	08	15	26	+16	26	7	01	7	14	11	44	16	26	16	12	2	54	34	21	01	58
5	14	42	06	15	44	+16	25	7	03	7	16	11	44	16	24	16	10	2	58	31	20	58	02
6	14	46	05	16	02	+16	23	7	04	7	18	11	44	16	22	16	08	3	02	27	20	54	07
7	14	50	04	16	20	+16	20	7	06	7	20	11	44	16	20	16	06	3	06	24	20	50	11
8	14	54	05	16	37	+16	16	7	08	7	23	11	44	16	19	16	04	3	10	21	20	46	15
9	14	58	06	16	54	+16	11	7	10	7	25	11	44	16	17	16	02	3	14	17	20	42	19
10	15	02	08	17	11	+16	05	7	12	7	27	11	44	16	16	16	00	3	18	14	20	38	23
11	15	06	11	17	28	+15	59	7	13	7	29	11	44	16	14	15	59	3	22	10	20	34	27
12	15	10	15	17	44	+15	52	7	15	7	31	11	44	16	13	15	57	3	26	07	20	30	31
13	15	14	20	18	00	+15	44	7	17	7	33	11	44	16	11	15	55	3	30	03	20	26	35
14	15	18	25	18	16	+15	35	7	19	7	35	11	44	16	10	15	53	3	34	00	20	22	39
15	15	22	32	18	32	+15	25	7	20	7	37	11	45	16	08	15	51	3	37	56	20	18	43
16	15	26	39	18	47	+15	14	7	22	7	39	11	45	16	07	15	50	3	41	53	20	14	47
17	15	30	47	19	01	+15	03	7	24	7	41	11	45	16	06	15	48	3	45	50	20	10	52
18	15	34	56	19	16	+14	50	7	26	7	43	11	45	16	04	15	47	3	49	46	20	06	56
19	15	39	06	19	30	+14	37	7	27	7	45	11	45	16	03	15	45	3	53	43	20	03	00
20	15	43	16	19	44	+14	23	7	29	7	47	11	46	16	02	15	44	3	57	39	19	59	04
21	15	47	27	19	57	+14	08	7	31	7	49	11	46	16	01	15	42	4	01	36	19	55	08
22	15	51	39	20	10	+13	53	7	32	7	51	11	46	16	00	15	41	4	05	32	19	51	12
23	15	55	52	20	23	+13	37	7	34	7	53	11	47	15	59	15	39	4	09	29	19	47	16
24	16	00	06	20	35	+13	20	7	36	7	55	11	47	15	58	15	38	4	13	25	19	43	20
25	16	04	20	20	47	+13	02	7	37	7	57	11	47	15	57	15	37	4	17	22	19	39	24
26	16	08	35	20	58	+12	43	7	39	7	59	11	47	15	56	15	36	4	21	19	19	35	28
27	16	12	51	21	09	+12	24	7	40	8	01	11	48	15	55	15	35	4	25	15	19	31	32
28	16	17	08	21	20	+12	04	7	42	8	02	11	48	15	54	15	33	4	29	12	19	27	37
29	16	21	25	21	30	+11	43	7	43	8	04	11	48	15	53	15	32	4	33	08	19	23	41
30	16	25	43	21	40	+11	22	7	45	8	06	11	49	15	53	15	31	4	37	05	19	19	45

DURATION OF TWILIGHT (in minutes)

Latitude	52°	56°	52°	56°	52°	56°	52°	56°
	1 November		11 November		21 November		31 November	
Civil	36	40	37	41	38	43	40	45
Nautical	75	84	78	87	80	90	82	93
Astronomical	115	127	117	130	120	134	123	138

THE NIGHT SKY

Mercury passes through inferior conjunction on the 17th but moves rapidly away from the Sun becoming visible as a morning object for the last week of the month, its magnitude brightening from +1.2 to −0.2. It may be located low above the south-eastern horizon at the beginning of morning civil twilight, in the same area of sky as Venus and Saturn. For example on the morning of the 28th Venus and Saturn are not much farther than 1 degree apart, with Mercury some 8 degrees to the left and about 7 degrees lower in altitude.

Venus, magnitude −4.0, is still visible as a brilliant object in the south-eastern sky in the early mornings. Even at the end of the month it can still be seen as early as two hours before sunrise. On the morning of the 16th it will be seen passing about 4 degrees north of Spica, and on the morning of the 27th it passes only 0.5 degrees south of Saturn.

Mars remains unsuitably placed for observation.

Jupiter, magnitude −2.8, is now visible in the eastern sky as soon as darkness falls and remains visible for the greater part of the night. There will be two close passages of the Moon south of the planet during the month: the first one occurs during the night of the 1st–2nd, while the second one occurs during the night of the 28th–29th.

Saturn, magnitude +0.6, gradually becomes available during the middle of the month, low above the south-eastern horizon, for an hour or so before dawn, until the morning twilight inhibits observation.

THE MOON

Day	R.A. h	R.A. m	Dec. °	Hor. Par. '	Semi-diam. '	Sun's Co-Long. °	PA. of Br. Limb °	Ph. %	Age d	Rise 52° h	Rise 52° m	Rise 56° h	Rise 56° m	Transit h	Transit m	Set 52° h	Set 52° m	Set 56° h	Set 56° m
1	4	03	+20.1	54.0	14.7	114	80	96	16.5	17	59	17	38	1	23	9	32	9	53
2	4	53	+20.9	54.0	14.7	126	86	91	17.5	18	47	18	26	2	11	10	23	10	45
3	5	44	+20.7	54.1	14.7	138	91	85	18.5	19	42	19	21	2	59	11	07	11	28
4	6	34	+19.7	54.3	14.8	150	96	78	19.5	20	41	20	24	3	47	11	45	12	03
5	7	24	+17.7	54.7	14.9	162	100	70	20.5	21	46	21	32	4	34	12	17	12	32
6	8	13	+14.9	55.3	15.1	174	104	60	21.5	22	54	22	43	5	21	12	44	12	55
7	9	02	+11.5	55.9	15.2	187	107	50	22.5	—		23	58	6	08	13	08	13	16
8	9	51	+7.4	56.8	15.5	199	109	40	23.5	0	04	—		6	54	13	31	13	35
9	10	41	+2.8	57.7	15.7	211	110	30	24.5	1	17	1	15	7	42	13	53	13	53
10	11	32	−2.1	58.7	16.0	223	110	20	25.5	2	33	2	35	8	31	14	16	14	12
11	12	25	−7.0	59.6	16.2	235	109	12	26.5	3	52	3	59	9	23	14	42	14	33
12	13	21	−11.7	60.4	16.5	248	106	5	27.5	5	15	5	26	10	18	15	12	14	59
13	14	20	−15.7	61.0	16.6	260	102	1	28.5	6	38	6	54	11	17	15	50	15	32
14	15	23	−18.8	61.3	16.7	272	298	0	0.1	7	58	8	18	12	19	16	37	16	16
15	16	27	−20.6	61.3	16.7	284	275	2	1.1	9	11	9	33	13	23	17	35	17	13
16	17	32	−20.8	61.0	16.6	296	268	6	2.1	10	11	10	32	14	26	18	44	18	23
17	18	35	−19.6	60.3	16.4	309	263	14	3.1	10	59	11	17	15	26	19	59	19	42
18	19	35	−17.1	59.5	16.2	321	258	23	4.1	11	36	11	51	16	22	21	16	21	03
19	20	32	−13.7	58.7	16.0	333	254	33	5.1	12	06	12	16	17	14	22	32	22	23
20	21	25	−9.6	57.8	15.7	345	251	44	6.1	12	31	12	37	18	03	23	46	23	41
21	22	15	−5.2	56.9	15.5	357	249	54	7.1	12	53	12	55	18	49	—		—	
22	23	04	−0.6	56.2	15.3	9	249	64	8.1	13	13	13	12	19	33	0	57	0	56
23	23	51	+3.8	55.5	15.1	22	249	74	9.1	13	34	13	29	20	17	2	06	2	09
24	0	37	+8.0	55.0	15.0	34	250	82	10.1	13	55	13	46	21	01	3	13	3	21
25	1	24	+11.9	54.6	14.9	46	252	89	11.1	14	19	14	07	21	46	4	20	4	31
26	2	12	+15.2	54.3	14.8	58	254	94	12.1	14	47	14	31	22	32	5	25	5	40
27	3	00	+17.9	54.1	14.7	70	256	98	13.1	15	19	15	00	23	19	6	27	6	45
28	3	50	+19.7	54.0	14.7	82	255	100	14.1	15	57	15	37	—		7	26	7	47
29	4	40	+20.8	54.0	14.7	94	101	100	15.1	16	43	16	21	0	07	8	19	8	41
30	5	31	+20.9	54.0	14.7	107	96	98	16.1	17	35	17	14	0	55	9	06	9	27

MERCURY

Day	R.A. h	R.A. m	Dec. °	Diam. "	Phase %	Transit h	Transit m	5° high 52° h	5° high 52° m	5° high 56° h	5° high 56° m
1	15	58	−23.4	7	51	13	14	16	13	15	36
3	16	03	−23.6	8	45	13	11	16	08	15	31
5	16	06	−23.6	8	38	13	06	16	04	15	27
7	16	07	−23.4	8	31	12	59	15	59	15	23
9	16	06	−23.0	9	23	12	49	15	53	15	18
11	16	03	−22.4	9	15	12	37	15	47	15	14
13	15	56	−21.5	10	8	12	22	15	39	15	09
15	15	47	−20.5	10	3	12	05	15	31	15	04
17	15	37	−19.2	10	0	11	47	8	13	8	38
19	15	27	−17.9	10	1	11	29	7	46	8	09
21	15	18	−16.7	10	5	11	13	7	22	7	42
23	15	11	−15.8	9	12	10	59	7	01	7	21
25	15	07	−15.1	9	20	10	47	6	46	7	05
27	15	06	−14.9	8	30	10	39	6	36	6	54
29	15	07	−14.9	8	39	10	33	6	30	6	48
31	15	11	−15.1	7	48	10	30	6	28	6	47

VENUS

Day	R.A. h	R.A. m	Dec. °	Diam. "	Phase %	Transit h	Transit m	5° high 52° h	5° high 52° m	5° high 56° h	5° high 56° m
1	12	18	−0.2	13	81	9	35	4	09	4	13
6	12	40	−2.5	13	82	9	38	4	24	4	30
11	13	03	−4.8	13	83	9	41	4	40	4	47
16	13	26	−7.1	12	85	9	44	4	55	5	05
21	13	49	−9.3	12	86	9	48	5	11	5	23
26	14	13	−11.5	12	87	9	52	5	28	5	42
31	14	37	−13.6	12	88	9	56	5	45	6	01

MARS

Day	R.A. h	R.A. m	Dec. °	Diam. "	Phase %	Transit h	Transit m	5° high 52° h	5° high 52° m	5° high 56° h	5° high 56° m
1	17	07	−23.9	5	95	14	24	17	18	16	40
6	17	23	−24.2	5	95	14	21	17	12	16	32
11	17	40	−24.4	4	96	14	17	17	07	16	26
16	17	56	−24.5	4	96	14	14	17	03	16	22
21	18	13	−24.5	4	96	14	11	17	00	16	19
26	18	30	−24.4	4	96	14	08	16	59	16	18
31	18	46	−24.2	4	97	14	05	16	58	16	19

SUNRISE AND SUNSET

	London 0° 05'	51° 30'	Bristol 2° 35'	51° 28'	Birmingham 1° 55'	52° 28'	Manchester 2° 15'	53° 28'	Newcastle 1° 37'	54° 59'	Glasgow 4° 14'	55° 52'	Belfast 5° 56'	54° 35'
d	h m	h m	h m	h m	h m	h m	h m	h m	h m	h m	h m	h m	h m	h m
1	6 54	16 33	7 04	16 43	7 04	16 37	7 09	16 36	7 11	16 28	7 24	16 36	7 27	16 47
2	6 56	16 31	7 06	16 41	7 06	16 35	7 11	16 34	7 13	16 26	7 26	16 34	7 29	16 45
3	6 58	16 29	7 08	16 39	7 08	16 34	7 12	16 32	7 15	16 24	7 28	16 32	7 31	16 43
4	7 00	16 27	7 10	16 37	7 10	16 32	7 14	16 30	7 17	16 22	7 31	16 30	7 33	16 41
5	7 01	16 26	7 11	16 36	7 12	16 30	7 16	16 28	7 19	16 20	7 33	16 28	7 35	16 39
6	7 03	16 24	7 13	16 34	7 14	16 28	7 18	16 26	7 21	16 19	7 35	16 26	7 37	16 37
7	7 05	16 22	7 15	16 33	7 15	16 27	7 20	16 25	7 23	16 17	7 37	16 24	7 39	16 35
8	7 07	16 21	7 17	16 31	7 17	16 25	7 22	16 23	7 25	16 15	7 39	16 22	7 41	16 34
9	7 09	16 19	7 18	16 29	7 19	16 23	7 24	16 21	7 27	16 13	7 41	16 20	7 43	16 32
10	7 10	16 18	7 20	16 28	7 21	16 22	7 26	16 19	7 29	16 11	7 43	16 18	7 45	16 30
11	7 12	16 16	7 22	16 26	7 23	16 20	7 28	16 18	7 31	16 09	7 45	16 16	7 47	16 28
12	7 14	16 15	7 24	16 25	7 25	16 19	7 30	16 16	7 33	16 08	7 47	16 14	7 49	16 26
13	7 15	16 13	7 25	16 23	7 26	16 17	7 31	16 15	7 35	16 06	7 49	16 12	7 51	16 25
14	7 17	16 12	7 27	16 22	7 28	16 16	7 33	16 13	7 37	16 04	7 51	16 11	7 53	16 23
15	7 19	16 11	7 29	16 21	7 30	16 14	7 35	16 12	7 39	16 03	7 54	16 09	7 55	16 22
16	7 21	16 09	7 30	16 19	7 32	16 13	7 37	16 10	7 41	16 01	7 56	16 07	7 56	16 20
17	7 22	16 08	7 32	16 18	7 33	16 11	7 39	16 09	7 43	15 59	7 58	16 06	7 58	16 19
18	7 24	16 07	7 34	16 17	7 35	16 10	7 41	16 07	7 45	15 58	8 00	16 04	8 00	16 17
19	7 26	16 05	7 36	16 16	7 37	16 09	7 42	16 06	7 47	15 57	8 02	16 03	8 02	16 16
20	7 27	16 04	7 37	16 14	7 39	16 08	7 44	16 05	7 49	15 55	8 04	16 01	8 04	16 14
21	7 29	16 03	7 39	16 13	7 40	16 07	7 46	16 03	7 51	15 54	8 06	16 00	8 06	16 13
22	7 31	16 02	7 40	16 12	7 42	16 05	7 48	16 02	7 52	15 52	8 07	15 58	8 08	16 12
23	7 32	16 01	7 42	16 11	7 44	16 04	7 49	16 01	7 54	15 51	8 09	15 57	8 10	16 10
24	7 34	16 00	7 44	16 10	7 45	16 03	7 51	16 00	7 56	15 50	8 11	15 56	8 11	16 09
25	7 35	15 59	7 45	16 09	7 47	16 02	7 53	15 59	7 58	15 49	8 13	15 55	8 13	16 08
26	7 37	15 58	7 47	16 08	7 48	16 01	7 54	15 58	8 00	15 48	8 15	15 53	8 15	16 07
27	7 38	15 57	7 48	16 08	7 50	16 00	7 56	15 57	8 01	15 47	8 17	15 52	8 17	16 06
28	7 40	15 57	7 50	16 07	7 52	16 00	7 58	15 56	8 03	15 46	8 18	15 51	8 18	16 05
29	7 41	15 56	7 51	16 06	7 53	15 59	7 59	15 55	8 05	15 45	8 20	15 50	8 20	16 04
30	7 43	15 55	7 53	16 05	7 55	15 58	8 01	15 54	8 06	15 44	8 22	15 49	8 21	16 03

JUPITER

Day	R.A.		Dec.		Transit		5° high		
								52°	56°
	h	m	°	'	h	m	h m	h m	h m
1	4	55.9	+21	47	2	13	18 46	18 29	
11	4	51.6	+21	40	1	29	18 03	17 47	
21	4	46.4	+21	32	0	45	17 19	17 03	
31	4	40.7	+21	23	0	00	16 35	16 19	

Diameters – equatorial 48" polar 45"

SATURN

Day	R.A.		Dec.		Transit		5° high		
								52°	56°
	h	m	°	'	h	m	h m	h m	h m
1	14	06.8	−10	28	11	22	6 53	7 06	
11	14	11.4	−10	51	10	48	6 20	6 34	
21	14	15.9	−11	14	10	13	5 47	6 01	
31	14	20.2	−11	35	9	38	5 15	5 29	

Diameters – equatorial 15" polar 14"
Rings – major axis 35" minor axis 10"

URANUS

Day	R.A.		Dec.		Transit		10° high		
								52°	56°
	h	m	°	'	h	m	h m	h m	h m
1	0	20.8	+1	26	21	34	2 40	2 34	
11	0	19.7	+1	20	20	54	1 59	1 53	
21	0	18.9	+1	15	20	14	1 18	1 12	
31	0	18.3	+1	12	19	34	0 38	0 32	

Diameter 4"

NEPTUNE

Day	R.A.		Dec.		Transit		10° high		
								52°	56°
	h	m	°	'	h	m	h m	h m	h m
1	22	10.7	−11	55	19	25	23 08	22 48	
11	22	10.6	−11	55	18	45	22 29	22 09	
21	22	10.7	−11	55	18	06	21 50	21 29	
31	22	11.0	−11	53	17	27	21 11	20 51	

Diameter 2"

DECEMBER 2012

TWELFTH MONTH, 31 DAYS. *Decem* (ten), tenth month of Roman pre-Julian calendar

| 1 | Saturday | Workers broke through the final wall to link the Channel Tunnel between the UK and France 1990 | day 336 |
| 2 | Sunday | Barney Clark became the first recipient of a permanent artificial heart, surviving for 112 days 1982 | 337 |

3	Monday	Samuel Crompton, inventor of the spinning mule *b.* 1753	week 49 day 338
4	Tuesday	Glenn L. Martin, aviation pioneer whose bomber planes played major parts in the Second World War *d.* 1955	339
5	Wednesday	The UK's first stretch of motorway, the Preston bypass (now part of the M6), was opened 1958	340
6	Thursday	Thomas Edison completed the first sound recording when he recited 'Mary Had a Little Lamb' 1877	341
7	Friday	Apollo 17, the sixth and final US mission to land men on the Moon, launched 1972	342
8	Saturday	Harrison Brown, best known for isolating plutonium for its use in the first atomic bombs *d.* 1986	343
9	Sunday	Astronauts completed repairs on the faulty Hubble Space Telescope by correcting a faulty lens 1993	344

10	Monday	The first Nobel prizes were awarded, on the fifth anniversary of Alfred Nobel's death 1901	week 50 day 345
11	Tuesday	The first dental anaesthetic, nitrous oxide ('laughing gas'), was used for a tooth extraction 1844	346
12	Wednesday	Radio pioneer Guglielmo Marconi sent the first radio transmission across the Atlantic 1901	347
13	Thursday	Gordo, a monkey, was lost in the Atlantic due to a technical problem after a 482 kilometre space journey 1958	348
14	Friday	*Rutan Voyager*, the first plane to fly non-stop around the world without refuelling, took off 1986	349
15	Saturday	The Chernobyl nuclear plant in Ukraine was shut down, 14 years after the infamous disaster 2000	350
16	Sunday	The Underground link from Heathrow airport to central London opened 1977	351

17	Monday	Sir Francis Beaufort, creator of the eponymous scale used to measure wind speeds *d.* 1857	week 51 day 352
18	Tuesday	Sir John Alcock, pilot who, in 1919, made the first non-stop transatlantic flight *d.*1919	353
19	Wednesday	The Williamsburg Bridge opened in New York City, becoming the world's longest suspension bridge 1903	354
20	Thursday	New York's Broadway became known as the 'Great White Way' after being lit by electricity 1880	355
21	Friday	Dried human blood serum was prepared for the first time; it was later used in the Second World War 1933	356
22	Saturday	Electric lights were first used to decorate Christmas trees by Edward Johnson 1882	357
23	Sunday	Apollo 8 astronauts became the first to orbit the Moon and escape the influence of Earth's gravity 1968	358

24	Monday	James Prescott Joule, physicist after whom the unit of energy is named *b.* 1818	week 52 day 359
25	Tuesday	Scientists failed to make contact with Beagle 2, a British probe which should have landed on Mars 2003	360
26	Wednesday	Charles Babbage, pioneer of mechanical computation who proposed the difference engine *b.* 1791	361
27	Thursday	*HMS Beagle*, with Charles Darwin aboard, left Plymouth on a voyage of scientific discovery 1831	362
28	Friday	The first commercial movie screening, *Workers Leaving The Lumière Factory in Lyon*, takes place 1895	363
29	Saturday	Cosmonaut Yuri Romanenko returned to Earth having spent a record 326 days aboard *Mir* 1987	364
30	Sunday	A second full moon of the month was visible (a 'blue moon') at the same time as a total lunar eclipse 1982	365

| 31 | Monday | Donald Campbell broke the water speed record with an average 276.33mph in *Bluebird* 1964 | week 53 day 366 |

ASTRONOMICAL PHENOMENA
d h
3 02 Jupiter at opposition
4 23 Mercury at greatest elongation W. 21°
10 10 Saturn in conjunction with Moon. Saturn 4°N.
11 13 Venus in conjunction with Moon. Venus 2°N.
12 00 Mercury in conjunction with Moon. Mercury 1°N.
13 12 Uranus at stationary point
15 08 Mars in conjunction with Moon. Mars 5°S.
21 11 Sun's longitude 270° ♑
26 00 Jupiter in conjunction with Moon. Jupiter 0°.4 N.
30 14 Pluto in conjunction

MINIMA OF ALGOL

d	h	d	h	d	h
3	11.8	14	23.1	26	10.3
6	08.6	17	19.9	29	07.2
9	05.4	20	16.7		
12	02.2	23	13.5		

CONSTELLATIONS
The following constellations are near their meridian at

	d	h		d	h
November	1	24	December	16	21
November	15	23	January	1	20
December	1	22	January	16	19

Ursa Major (below the Pole), Ursa Minor (below the Pole), Cassiopeia, Andromeda, Perseus, Triangulum, Aries, Taurus, Cetus and Eridanus

THE MOON

Phases, Apsides and Node	d	h	m
☾ Last Quarter	6	15	31
● New Moon	13	08	42
☽ First Quarter	20	05	19
○ Full Moon	28	10	21
Perigee (357,071km)	12	23	07
Apogee (406,117 km)	25	21	06

Mean longitude of ascending node on December 1, 235°

THE SUN

s.d. 16'.3

Day	Right Ascension h	m	s	Dec. °	'	Equation of time m	s	Rise 52° h	m	56° h	m	Transit h	m	Set 52° h	m	56° h	m	Sidereal time h	m	s	Transit of first point of Aries h	m	s
1	16	30	01	21	50	+11	00	7	46	8	07	11	49	15	52	15	31	4	41	01	19	15	49
2	16	34	21	21	59	+10	37	7	47	8	09	11	50	15	51	15	30	4	44	58	19	11	53
3	16	38	41	22	07	+10	14	7	49	8	11	11	50	15	51	15	29	4	48	54	19	07	57
4	16	43	01	22	15	+9	50	7	50	8	12	11	50	15	50	15	28	4	52	51	19	04	01
5	16	47	22	22	23	+9	25	7	51	8	14	11	51	15	50	15	28	4	56	48	19	00	05
6	16	51	44	22	31	+9	00	7	53	8	15	11	51	15	49	15	27	5	00	44	18	56	09
7	16	56	06	22	37	+8	35	7	54	8	16	11	52	15	49	15	27	5	04	41	18	52	13
8	17	00	29	22	44	+8	09	7	55	8	18	11	52	15	49	15	26	5	08	37	18	48	17
9	17	04	52	22	50	+7	42	7	56	8	19	11	53	15	49	15	26	5	12	34	18	44	22
10	17	09	15	22	55	+7	15	7	57	8	20	11	53	15	48	15	25	5	16	30	18	40	26
11	17	13	39	23	01	+6	47	7	58	8	21	11	53	15	48	15	25	5	20	27	18	36	30
12	17	18	04	23	05	+6	19	7	59	8	23	11	54	15	48	15	25	5	24	23	18	32	34
13	17	22	29	23	09	+5	51	8	00	8	24	11	54	15	48	15	25	5	28	20	18	28	38
14	17	26	54	23	13	+5	23	8	01	8	25	11	55	15	48	15	25	5	32	17	18	24	42
15	17	31	19	23	16	+4	54	8	02	8	26	11	55	15	49	15	25	5	36	13	18	20	46
16	17	35	45	23	19	+4	25	8	03	8	26	11	56	15	49	15	25	5	40	10	18	16	50
17	17	40	11	23	21	+3	55	8	04	8	27	11	56	15	49	15	25	5	44	06	18	12	54
18	17	44	37	23	23	+3	26	8	04	8	28	11	57	15	49	15	26	5	48	03	18	08	58
19	17	49	03	23	25	+2	56	8	05	8	29	11	57	15	50	15	26	5	51	59	18	05	02
20	17	53	29	23	26	+2	26	8	05	8	29	11	58	15	50	15	26	5	55	56	18	01	07
21	17	57	56	23	26	+1	57	8	06	8	30	11	58	15	51	15	27	5	59	52	17	57	11
22	18	02	22	23	26	+1	27	8	06	8	30	11	59	15	51	15	27	6	03	49	17	53	15
23	18	06	49	23	26	+0	57	8	07	8	31	11	59	15	52	15	28	6	07	46	17	49	19
24	18	11	15	23	25	+0	27	8	07	8	31	12	00	15	52	15	29	6	11	42	17	45	23
25	18	15	41	23	23	−0	02	8	08	8	31	12	00	15	53	15	29	6	15	39	17	41	27
26	18	20	07	23	21	−0	32	8	08	8	31	12	01	15	54	15	30	6	19	35	17	37	31
27	18	24	33	23	19	−1	02	8	08	8	32	12	01	15	55	15	31	6	23	32	17	33	35
28	18	28	59	23	16	−1	31	8	08	8	32	12	02	15	56	15	32	6	27	28	17	29	39
29	18	33	25	23	13	−2	00	8	08	8	32	12	02	15	56	15	33	6	31	25	17	25	43
30	18	37	50	23	09	−2	29	8	08	8	32	12	03	15	57	15	34	6	35	21	17	21	47
31	18	42	16	23	05	−2	58	8	08	8	31	12	03	15	58	15	35	6	39	18	17	17	51

DURATION OF TWILIGHT (in minutes)

Latitude	52°	56°	52°	56°	52°	56°	52°	56°
	1 December		11 December		21 December		31 December	
Civil	40	45	41	47	41	47	41	47
Nautical	82	93	84	96	85	97	84	96
Astronomical	123	138	125	141	126	142	125	141

THE NIGHT SKY

Mercury reaches greatest western elongation (21 degrees) on the 4th and continues to be visible as a morning object during the first half of the month, low above the east-north-eastern horizon. During this period its magnitude brightens from −0.3 to −0.5.

Venus, magnitude −4.0, is still visible as a magnificent object in the south-eastern sky in the mornings before dawn. It is now moving more rapidly towards the Sun and consequently rising later and later until by the end of December observers in southern England will have to wait until shortly after 07h, while those in Scotland will have to wait until about half-an-hour before sunrise. Given favourable conditions and a clear horizon observers may be able to see a line up of three planets, a star and the Moon low above the SE-SSE horizon around 07h on the morning of the 9th. From left to right they are Mercury, Venus, Saturn, Spica, and the waning crescent Moon.

However, atmospheric extinction may make it too difficult to spot Mercury at such a low altitude.

Mars remains unsuitably placed for observation.

Jupiter, magnitude −2.8, reaches opposition on the 3rd and is therefore visible throughout the hours of darkness. On the 7th Jupiter passes 5 degrees north of Aldebaran as it moves slowly retrograde in the constellation of Taurus. During the night of the 25–26th the waxing gibbous Moon passes about 1 degree south of the planet.

Saturn, magnitude +0.6, can now be seen in the early mornings in the south-eastern quadrant of the sky after about 04h. Early in the month Saturn passes from Virgo into Libra. On the 10th the waning crescent Moon passes 5 degrees south of the planet.

Meteors. The maximum of the well known Geminid meteor shower occurs on the 13th. As there is a New Moon that day it will provide no interference.

THE MOON

Day	R.A. h	R.A. m	Dec. °	Hor. Par. '	Semi-diam. '	Sun's Co-Long. °	PA. of Br. Limb °	Ph. %	Age d	Rise 52° h	Rise 52° m	Rise 56° h	Rise 56° m	Transit h	Transit m	Set 52° h	Set 52° m	Set 56° h	Set 56° m
1	6	21	+20.0	54.2	14.8	119	99	95	17.1	18	34	18	15	1	43	9	46	10	05
2	7	11	+18.3	54.4	14.8	131	102	90	18.1	19	36	19	21	2	31	10	19	10	35
3	8	01	+15.7	54.8	14.9	143	106	84	19.1	20	42	20	30	3	18	10	48	11	00
4	8	49	+12.5	55.2	15.1	155	109	76	20.1	21	50	21	43	4	04	11	12	11	22
5	9	37	+8.6	55.8	15.2	167	111	67	21.1	23	00	22	57	4	49	11	35	11	40
6	10	25	+4.3	56.6	15.4	179	112	57	22.1	—		—		5	35	11	56	11	58
7	11	14	−0.3	57.4	15.6	192	113	46	23.1	0	13	0	13	6	22	12	18	12	16
8	12	05	−5.1	58.3	15.9	204	112	36	24.1	1	27	1	32	7	10	12	41	12	35
9	12	57	−9.7	59.2	16.1	216	111	25	25.1	2	45	2	54	8	02	13	08	12	57
10	13	53	−14.0	60.1	16.4	228	108	16	26.1	4	06	4	19	8	57	13	40	13	25
11	14	53	−17.5	60.8	16.6	240	105	8	27.1	5	26	5	45	9	57	14	21	14	02
12	15	56	−19.9	61.2	16.7	253	103	3	28.1	6	43	7	05	10	59	15	13	14	51
13	17	01	−20.9	61.4	16.7	265	115	0	29.1	7	51	8	13	12	04	16	17	15	55
14	18	06	−20.4	61.2	16.7	277	251	1	0.7	8	47	9	07	13	07	17	31	17	12
15	19	10	−18.4	60.7	16.5	289	254	4	1.7	9	31	9	48	14	07	18	51	18	35
16	20	10	−15.2	60.0	16.3	301	251	10	2.7	10	05	10	18	15	03	20	10	19	59
17	21	06	−11.2	59.1	16.1	313	249	18	3.7	10	33	10	41	15	55	21	28	21	21
18	21	59	−6.7	58.1	15.8	326	247	28	4.7	10	57	11	01	16	44	22	42	22	40
19	22	50	−2.1	57.1	15.6	338	246	38	5.7	11	19	11	19	17	30	23	54	23	56
20	23	38	+2.5	56.3	15.3	350	246	48	6.7	11	40	11	36	18	15	—		—	
21	0	25	+6.9	55.5	15.1	2	247	58	7.7	12	01	11	53	18	59	1	03	1	09
22	1	12	+10.9	54.9	15.0	14	249	67	8.7	12	24	12	13	19	44	2	10	2	20
23	1	59	+14.3	54.5	14.8	26	251	76	9.7	12	50	12	35	20	29	3	16	3	29
24	2	48	+17.2	54.2	14.8	39	254	84	10.7	13	20	13	03	21	16	4	19	4	36
25	3	37	+19.3	54.0	14.7	51	256	90	11.7	13	56	13	36	22	03	5	19	5	39
26	4	27	+20.6	54.0	14.7	63	259	95	12.7	14	39	14	18	22	52	6	15	6	36
27	5	17	+20.9	54.1	14.7	75	258	98	13.7	15	29	15	08	23	40	7	04	7	25
28	6	08	+20.4	54.2	14.8	87	238	100	14.7	16	26	16	07	—		7	46	8	06
29	6	59	+18.9	54.4	14.8	99	127	100	15.7	17	28	17	11	0	28	8	22	8	39
30	7	49	+16.5	54.7	14.9	111	115	98	16.7	18	33	18	20	1	16	8	52	9	06
31	8	38	+13.4	55.1	15.0	123	114	94	17.7	19	41	19	32	2	02	9	18	9	29

MERCURY

Day	R.A. h	R.A. m	Dec. °	Diam. "	Phase %	Transit h	Transit m	5° high 52° h	5° high 52° m	5° high 56° h	5° high 56° m
1	15	11	−15.1	7	48	10	30	6	28	6	47
3	15	17	−15.6	7	56	10	28	6	30	6	49
5	15	24	−16.2	7	62	10	27	6	33	6	54
7	15	33	−16.9	6	68	10	28	6	39	7	01
9	15	42	−17.7	6	73	10	30	6	46	7	09
11	15	52	−18.4	6	77	10	33	6	54	7	18
13	16	03	−19.2	6	81	10	36	7	03	7	29
15	16	15	−20.0	6	84	10	39	7	12	7	39
17	16	26	−20.7	5	86	10	43	7	22	7	51
19	16	38	−21.4	5	88	10	48	7	31	8	02
21	16	51	−22.0	5	90	10	52	7	41	8	14
23	17	03	−22.6	5	92	10	57	7	50	8	25
25	17	16	−23.1	5	93	11	02	8	00	8	36
27	17	29	−23.5	5	94	11	07	8	09	8	46
29	17	43	−23.9	5	95	11	13	8	17	8	56
31	17	56	−24.1	5	96	11	18	8	25	9	05

VENUS

Day	R.A. h	R.A. m	Dec. °	Diam. "	Phase %	Transit h	Transit m	5° high 52° h	5° high 52° m	5° high 56° h	5° high 56° m
1	14	37	−13.6	12	88	9	56	5	45	6	01
6	15	01	−15.5	12	89	10	01	6	02	6	21
11	15	26	−17.3	11	90	10	06	6	19	6	41
16	15	51	−18.8	11	91	10	12	6	36	7	01
21	16	17	−20.2	11	92	10	18	6	52	7	20
26	16	44	−21.3	11	93	10	25	7	08	7	38
31	17	10	−22.2	11	94	10	32	7	22	7	55

MARS

Day	R.A. h	R.A. m	Dec. °	Diam. "	Phase %	Transit h	Transit m	5° high 52° h	5° high 52° m	5° high 56° h	5° high 56° m
1	18	46	−24.2	4	97	14	05	16	58	16	19
6	19	03	−23.8	4	97	14	02	16	59	16	21
11	19	20	−23.3	4	97	13	59	17	00	16	24
16	19	37	−22.8	4	97	13	56	17	02	16	28
21	19	53	−22.1	4	97	13	53	17	05	16	33
26	20	10	−21.3	4	98	13	50	17	08	16	38
31	20	26	−20.4	4	98	13	46	17	12	16	44

SUNRISE AND SUNSET

d	London 0° 05' | 51° 30'		Bristol 2° 35' | 51° 28'		Birmingham 1° 55' | 52° 28'		Manchester 2° 15' | 53° 28'		Newcastle 1° 37' | 54° 59'		Glasgow 4° 14' | 55° 52'		Belfast 5° 56' | 54° 35'	
	h m	h m	h m	h m	h m	h m	h m	h m	h m	h m	h m	h m	h m	h m
1	7 44	15 55	7 54	16 05	7 56	15 57	8 02	15 54	8 08	15 43	8 24	15 48	8 23	16 03
2	7 45	15 54	7 55	16 04	7 57	15 57	8 04	15 53	8 09	15 42	8 25	15 48	8 25	16 02
3	7 47	15 54	7 57	16 04	7 59	15 56	8 05	15 52	8 11	15 42	8 27	15 47	8 26	16 01
4	7 48	15 53	7 58	16 03	8 00	15 56	8 07	15 52	8 12	15 41	8 28	15 46	8 27	16 00
5	7 49	15 53	7 59	16 03	8 01	15 55	8 08	15 51	8 14	15 40	8 30	15 45	8 29	16 00
6	7 51	15 52	8 00	16 02	8 03	15 55	8 09	15 51	8 15	15 40	8 31	15 45	8 30	15 59
7	7 52	15 52	8 02	16 02	8 04	15 54	8 11	15 51	8 17	15 39	8 33	15 44	8 32	15 59
8	7 53	15 52	8 03	16 02	8 05	15 54	8 12	15 50	8 18	15 39	8 34	15 44	8 33	15 59
9	7 54	15 51	8 04	16 02	8 06	15 54	8 13	15 50	8 19	15 39	8 35	15 44	8 34	15 58
10	7 55	15 51	8 05	16 01	8 07	15 54	8 14	15 50	8 20	15 38	8 36	15 43	8 35	15 58
11	7 56	15 51	8 06	16 01	8 08	15 54	8 15	15 50	8 21	15 38	8 38	15 43	8 36	15 58
12	7 57	15 51	8 07	16 01	8 09	15 54	8 16	15 49	8 23	15 38	8 39	15 43	8 37	15 58
13	7 58	15 51	8 08	16 01	8 10	15 54	8 17	15 49	8 24	15 38	8 40	15 43	8 38	15 58
14	7 59	15 51	8 09	16 02	8 11	15 54	8 18	15 50	8 25	15 38	8 41	15 43	8 39	15 58
15	8 00	15 51	8 10	16 02	8 12	15 54	8 19	15 50	8 25	15 38	8 42	15 43	8 40	15 58
16	8 01	15 52	8 10	16 02	8 13	15 54	8 20	15 50	8 26	15 38	8 42	15 43	8 41	15 58
17	8 01	15 52	8 11	16 02	8 14	15 54	8 21	15 50	8 27	15 38	8 43	15 43	8 42	15 58
18	8 02	15 52	8 12	16 02	8 14	15 55	8 21	15 50	8 28	15 39	8 44	15 43	8 43	15 58
19	8 03	15 53	8 12	16 03	8 15	15 55	8 22	15 51	8 28	15 39	8 45	15 44	8 43	15 59
20	8 03	15 53	8 13	16 03	8 16	15 55	8 22	15 51	8 29	15 39	8 45	15 44	8 44	15 59
21	8 04	15 54	8 14	16 04	8 16	15 56	8 23	15 52	8 30	15 40	8 46	15 45	8 44	16 00
22	8 04	15 54	8 14	16 04	8 17	15 56	8 24	15 52	8 30	15 40	8 46	15 45	8 45	16 00
23	8 05	15 55	8 14	16 05	8 17	15 57	8 24	15 53	8 30	15 41	8 47	15 46	8 45	16 01
24	8 05	15 55	8 15	16 05	8 17	15 58	8 24	15 53	8 31	15 42	8 47	15 46	8 46	16 01
25	8 05	15 56	8 15	16 06	8 18	15 58	8 25	15 54	8 31	15 42	8 47	15 47	8 46	16 02
26	8 06	15 57	8 15	16 07	8 18	15 59	8 25	15 55	8 31	15 43	8 48	15 48	8 46	16 03
27	8 06	15 58	8 16	16 08	8 18	16 00	8 25	15 56	8 31	15 44	8 48	15 49	8 46	16 04
28	8 06	15 58	8 16	16 09	8 18	16 01	8 25	15 57	8 32	15 45	8 48	15 50	8 46	16 05
29	8 06	15 59	8 16	16 09	8 18	16 02	8 25	15 58	8 32	15 46	8 48	15 51	8 46	16 06
30	8 06	16 00	8 16	16 10	8 18	16 03	8 25	15 59	8 31	15 47	8 48	15 52	8 46	16 07
31	8 06	16 01	8 16	16 11	8 18	16 04	8 25	16 00	8 31	15 48	8 47	15 53	8 46	16 08

JUPITER

Day	R.A.		Dec.		Transit		5° high 52°		56°	
	h	m	°	'	h	m	h	m	h	m
1	4	40.7	+21	23	0	00	7	20	7	36
11	4	34.9	+21	13	23	10	6	34	6	50
21	4	29.5	+21	03	22	26	5	48	6	04
31	4	24.9	+20	55	21	42	5	04	5	19

Diameters – equatorial 48″ polar 45″

SATURN

Day	R.A.		Dec.		Transit		5° high 52°		56°	
	h	m	°	'	h	m	h	m	h	m
1	14	20.2	−11	35	9	38	5	15	5	29
11	14	24.2	−11	54	9	03	4	41	4	56
21	14	28.0	−12	11	8	27	4	07	4	22
31	14	31.3	−12	26	7	51	3	33	3	48

Diameters – equatorial 16″ polar 14″
Rings – major axis 36″ minor axis 11″

URANUS

Day	R.A.		Dec.		Transit		10° high 52°		56°	
	h	m	°	'	h	m	h	m	h	m
1	0	18.3	+1	12	19	34	0	38	0	32
11	0	18.1	+1	10	18	55	23	54	23	49
21	0	18.2	+1	11	18	15	23	15	23	10
31	0	18.5	+1	14	17	36	22	37	22	31

Diameter 4″

NEPTUNE

Day	R.A.		Dec.		Transit		10° high 52°		56°	
	h	m	°	'	h	m	h	m	h	m
1	22	11.0	−11	53	17	27	21	11	20	51
11	22	11.6	−11	50	16	48	20	33	20	12
21	22	12.3	−11	45	16	10	19	55	19	34
31	22	13.2	−11	40	15	32	19	17	18	57

Diameter 2″

RISING AND SETTING TIMES

TABLE 1. SEMI-DIURNAL ARCS (HOUR ANGLES AT RISING/SETTING)

Dec.	Latitude 0°	10°	20°	30°	40°	45°	50°	52°	54°	56°	58°	60°	Dec.
	h m	h m	h m	h m	h m	h m	h m	h m	h m	h m	h m	h m	
0°	6 00	6 00	6 00	6 00	6 00	6 00	6 00	6 00	6 00	6 00	6 00	6 00	0°
1°	6 00	6 01	6 01	6 02	6 03	6 04	6 05	6 05	6 06	6 06	6 06	6 07	1°
2°	6 00	6 01	6 03	6 05	6 07	6 08	6 10	6 10	6 11	6 12	6 13	6 14	2°
3°	6 00	6 02	6 04	6 07	6 10	6 12	6 14	6 15	6 17	6 18	6 19	6 21	3°
4°	6 00	6 03	6 06	6 09	6 13	6 16	6 19	6 21	6 22	6 24	6 26	6 28	4°
5°	6 00	6 04	6 07	6 12	6 17	6 20	6 24	6 26	6 28	6 30	6 32	6 35	5°
6°	6 00	6 04	6 09	6 14	6 20	6 24	6 29	6 31	6 33	6 36	6 39	6 42	6°
7°	6 00	6 05	6 10	6 16	6 24	6 28	6 34	6 36	6 39	6 42	6 45	6 49	7°
8°	6 00	6 06	6 12	6 19	6 27	6 32	6 39	6 41	6 45	6 48	6 52	6 56	8°
9°	6 00	6 06	6 13	6 21	6 31	6 36	6 44	6 47	6 50	6 54	6 59	7 04	9°
10°	6 00	6 07	6 15	6 23	6 34	6 41	6 49	6 52	6 56	7 01	7 06	7 11	10°
11°	6 00	6 08	6 16	6 26	6 38	6 45	6 54	6 58	7 02	7 07	7 12	7 19	11°
12°	6 00	6 09	6 18	6 28	6 41	6 49	6 59	7 03	7 08	7 13	7 20	7 26	12°
13°	6 00	6 09	6 19	6 31	6 45	6 53	7 04	7 09	7 14	7 20	7 27	7 34	13°
14°	6 00	6 10	6 21	6 33	6 48	6 58	7 09	7 14	7 20	7 27	7 34	7 42	14°
15°	6 00	6 11	6 22	6 36	6 52	7 02	7 14	7 20	7 27	7 34	7 42	7 51	15°
16°	6 00	6 12	6 24	6 38	6 56	7 07	7 20	7 26	7 33	7 41	7 49	7 59	16°
17°	6 00	6 12	6 26	6 41	6 59	7 11	7 25	7 32	7 40	7 48	7 57	8 08	17°
18°	6 00	6 13	6 27	6 43	7 03	7 16	7 31	7 38	7 46	7 55	8 05	8 17	18°
19°	6 00	6 14	6 29	6 46	7 07	7 21	7 37	7 45	7 53	8 03	8 14	8 26	19°
20°	6 00	6 15	6 30	6 49	7 11	7 25	7 43	7 51	8 00	8 11	8 22	8 36	20°
21°	6 00	6 16	6 32	6 51	7 15	7 30	7 49	7 58	8 08	8 19	8 32	8 47	21°
22°	6 00	6 16	6 34	6 54	7 19	7 35	7 55	8 05	8 15	8 27	8 41	8 58	22°
23°	6 00	6 17	6 36	6 57	7 23	7 40	8 02	8 12	8 23	8 36	8 51	9 09	23°
24°	6 00	6 18	6 37	7 00	7 28	7 46	8 08	8 19	8 31	8 45	9 02	9 22	24°
25°	6 00	6 19	6 39	7 02	7 32	7 51	8 15	8 27	8 40	8 55	9 13	9 35	25°
26°	6 00	6 20	6 41	7 05	7 37	7 57	8 22	8 35	8 49	9 05	9 25	9 51	26°
27°	6 00	6 21	6 43	7 08	7 41	8 03	8 30	8 43	8 58	9 16	9 39	10 08	27°
28°	6 00	6 22	6 45	7 12	7 46	8 08	8 37	8 52	9 08	9 28	9 53	10 28	28°
29°	6 00	6 22	6 47	7 15	7 51	8 15	8 45	9 01	9 19	9 41	10 10	10 55	29°
30°	6 00	6 23	6 49	7 18	7 56	8 21	8 54	9 11	9 30	9 55	10 30	12 00	30°
35°	6 00	6 28	6 59	7 35	8 24	8 58	9 46	10 15	10 58	12 00	12 00	12 00	35°
40°	6 00	6 34	7 11	7 56	8 59	9 48	12 00	12 00	12 00	12 00	12 00	12 00	40°
45°	6 00	6 41	7 25	8 21	9 48	12 00	12 00	12 00	12 00	12 00	12 00	12 00	45°
50°	6 00	6 49	7 43	8 54	12 00	12 00	12 00	12 00	12 00	12 00	12 00	12 00	50°
55°	6 00	6 58	8 05	9 42	12 00	12 00	12 00	12 00	12 00	12 00	12 00	12 00	55°
60°	6 00	7 11	8 36	12 00	12 00	12 00	12 00	12 00	12 00	12 00	12 00	12 00	60°
65°	6 00	7 29	9 25	12 00	12 00	12 00	12 00	12 00	12 00	12 00	12 00	12 00	65°
70°	6 00	7 56	12 00	12 00	12 00	12 00	12 00	12 00	12 00	12 00	12 00	12 00	70°
75°	6 00	8 45	12 00	12 00	12 00	12 00	12 00	12 00	12 00	12 00	12 00	12 00	75°
80°	6 00	12 00	12 00	12 00	12 00	12 00	12 00	12 00	12 00	12 00	12 00	12 00	80°

Note: If latitude and declination are of the same sign, take out the respondent directly. If they are of opposite signs, subtract the respondent from 12h.

Table 1 gives the complete range of declinations in case any user wishes to calculate semi-diurnal arcs for bodies other than the Sun and Moon.

Example:

Lat.	Dec.	Semi-diurnal arc
+52°	+20°	7h 51m
+52°	−20°	4h 09m

TABLE 2. CORRECTION FOR REFRACTION AND SEMI-DIAMETER

	m	m	m	m	m	m	m	m	m	m	m	m	
0°	3	3	4	4	4	5	5	5	6	6	6	7	0°
10°	3	3	4	4	4	5	5	6	6	6	7	7	10°
20°	4	4	4	4	5	5	6	7	7	8	8	9	20°
25°	4	4	4	4	5	6	7	8	8	9	11	13	25°
30°	4	4	4	5	6	7	8	9	11	14	21	—	30°

SUNRISE AND SUNSET

The local mean time of sunrise or sunset may be found by obtaining the hour angle from Table 1 and applying it to the time of transit. The hour angle is negative for sunrise and positive for sunset. A small correction to the hour angle, which always has the effect of increasing it numerically, is necessary to allow for the Sun's semi-diameter (16′) and for refraction (34′); it is obtained from Table 2. The resulting local mean time may be converted into the standard time of the country by taking the difference between the longitude of the standard meridian of the country and that of the place, adding it to the local mean time if the place is west of the standard meridian, and subtracting it if the place is east.

Example– Required the New Zealand Mean Time (12h fast on GMT) of sunset on May 23 at Auckland, latitude 36° 50′ S. (or minus), longitude 11h 39m E. Taking the declination as +20°.6 (page 1245), we find

	h	*m*
New Zealand Standard Time	+ 12	00
Longitude	− 11	39
Longitudinal Correction	+ 0	21
Tabular entry for Lat. 30° and Dec. 20°, opposite signs	+ 5	11
Proportional part for 6° 50′ of Lat.	−	15
Proportional part for 0°.6 of Dec.	−	2
Correction (Table 2)	+	4
Hour angle	4	58
Sun transits (page 1245)	11	57
Longitudinal correction	+	21
New Zealand Mean Time	17	16

MOONRISE AND MOONSET

It is possible to calculate the times of moonrise and moonset using Table 1, though the method is more complicated because the apparent motion of the Moon is much more rapid and also more variable than that of the Sun.

TABLE 3. LONGITUDE CORRECTION

X	40m	45m	50m	55m	60m	65m	70m
A							
h	*m*	*m*	*m*	*m*	*m*	*m*	*m*
1	2	2	2	2	3	3	3
2	3	4	4	5	5	5	6
3	5	6	6	7	8	8	9
4	7	8	8	9	10	11	12
5	8	9	10	11	13	14	15
6	10	11	13	14	15	16	18
7	12	13	15	16	18	19	20
8	13	15	17	18	20	22	23
9	15	17	19	21	23	24	26
10	17	19	21	23	25	27	29
11	18	21	23	25	28	30	32
12	20	23	25	28	30	33	35
13	22	24	27	30	33	35	38
14	23	26	29	32	35	38	41
15	25	28	31	34	38	41	44
16	27	30	33	37	40	43	47
17	28	32	35	39	43	46	50
18	30	34	38	41	45	49	53
19	32	36	40	44	48	51	55
20	33	38	42	46	50	54	58
21	35	39	44	48	53	57	61
22	37	41	46	50	55	60	64
23	38	43	48	53	58	62	67
24	40	45	50	55	60	65	70

The parallax of the Moon, about 57′, is near to the sum of the semi-diameter and refraction but has the opposite effect on these times. It is thus convenient to neglect all three quantities in the method outlined below.

Notation

ϕ	= latitude of observer
λ	= longitude of observer (measured positively towards the west)
T_{-1}	= time of transit of Moon on previous day
T_0	= time of transit of Moon on day in question
T_1	= time of transit of Moon on following day
δ_0	= approximate declination of Moon
δ_R	= declination of Moon at moonrise
δ_S	= declination of Moon at moonset
h_0	= approximate hour angle of Moon
h_R	= hour angle of Moon at moonrise
h_S	= hour angle of Moon at moonset
t_R	= time of moonrise
t_S	= time of moonset

Method

1. With arguments ϕ, δ_0 enter Table 1 on page 1276 to determine h_0 where h_0 is negative for moonrise and positive for moonset.

2. Form approximate times from
$$t_R = T_0 + \lambda + h_0$$
$$t_S = T_0 + \lambda + h_0$$

3. Determine δ_R, δ_S for times t_R, t_S respectively.

4. Re-enter Table 1 (as above) with
   (*a*) arguments ϕ, δ_R to determine h_R
   (*b*) arguments ϕ, δ_S to determine h_S

5. Form $\quad t_R = T_0 + \lambda + h_R + AX$
$$t_S = T_0 + \lambda + h_S + AX$$

where $\quad A = (\lambda + h)$

and $\quad X = (T_0 - T_{-1})$ if $(\lambda + h)$ is negative
$\quad\quad\quad X = (T_1 - T_0)$ if $(\lambda + h)$ is positive

AX is the respondent in Table 3.

Example – To find the times (GMT) of moonrise and moonset at Vancouver ($\phi = +49°$, $\lambda = +8h 12m$) on 2012 January 19. The starting data (page 1230) are

T_{-1}	= 7h 32m
T_0	= 8h 31m
T_1	= 9h 30m
δ_0	= −22°

1. h_0 = 4h 09m
2. Approximate values
   t_R = 19d 08h 31m + 8h 12m + (−4h 09m)
   = 19d 12h 34m
   t_S = 19d 08h 31m + 8h 12m + (+4h 09m)
   = 19d 20h 52m
3. δ_R = −22°.0
   δ_S = −22°.4
4. h_R = −4h 09m
   h_S = +4h 12m
5. t_R = 19d 08h 31m + 8h 12m + (−4h 09m) + 10m
   = 19d 12h 44m
   t_S = 19d 08h 31m + 8h 12m + (+4h 09m) + 31m
   = 19d 21h 23m

To get the LMT of the phenomenon the longitude is subtracted from the GMT thus:

Moonrise = 19d 12h 44m − 8h 12m = 19d 04h 32m
Moonset = 19d 21h 23m − 8h 12m = 19d 13h 11m

ECLIPSES 2012

During 2012 there will be three eclipses, two of the Sun and one of the Moon. (Penumbral eclipses of the Moon are not mentioned in this section as they are so difficult to observe.)

1. An annular eclipse of the Sun on May 20–21 is visible as a partial eclipse from North America, the Pacific Ocean, Asia, and the north polar regions, beginning at 20h 56m and ending at 02h 49m. The track of the annular eclipse starts at 22h 06m in southeastern China, crosses southern Japan, crosses the Pacific Ocean and ends at 01h 39m in Texas, U.S.A. The maximum duration of annularity is 5m 46s.

2. A partial eclipse of the Moon on June 4 begins at 10h 00m and ends at 12h 06m. It is visible from the Americas, eastern Asia and Australasia.

3. A total eclipse of the Sun occurs on November 13–14. The partial phase is visible from Australasia, the Pacific Ocean, the extreme south of South America, and Antarctica, beginning at 20h 25m and ending at 23h 48m. The track of totality starts at 20h 35m in the extreme north of Australia, crosses the South Pacific Ocean and ends at 23h 48m off the coast of South America. The maximum duration of totality is 4m 2s.

TRANSIT

A transit of Venus occurs on June 5–6, visible from extreme western Europe, northeast Africa, north and central America, northwest of south America, Australasia and Asia. From the British Isles the beginning occurs before sunrise on June 6, which occurs at 03h 45m at Greenwich and 03h 30m at Edinburgh. For both places the interior egress occurs at 04h 37m, and exterior egress at 04h 55m. However, the Sun is still at a very low altitude (7 degrees at Greenwich and 9 degrees at Edinburgh).

POSITIONS OF STARS

The positions of heavenly bodies on the celestial sphere are defined by two co-ordinates, right ascension and declination, which are analogous to longitude and latitude on the surface of the Earth. If we imagine the plane of the terrestrial equator extended indefinitely, it will cut the celestial sphere in a great circle known as the celestial equator. Similarly the plane of the Earth's orbit, when extended, cuts in the great circle called the ecliptic. The two intersections of these circles are known as the First Point of Aries and the First Point of Libra. If from any star a perpendicular is drawn to the celestial equator, the length of this perpendicular is the star's declination. The arc, measured eastwards along the equator from the First Point of Aries to the foot of this perpendicular, is the right ascension. An alternative definition of right ascension is that it is the angle at the celestial pole (where the Earth's axis, if prolonged, would meet the sphere) between the great circles to the First Point of Aries and to the star.

The plane of the Earth's equator has a slow movement, so that our reference system for right ascension and declination is not fixed. The consequent alteration in these quantities from year to year is called precession. In right ascension it is an increase of about 3 seconds a year for equatorial stars, and larger or smaller changes in either direction for stars near the poles, depending on the right ascension of the star. In declination it varies between $+20''$ and $-20''$ according to the right ascension of the star.

A star or other body crosses the meridian when the sidereal time is equal to its right ascension. The altitude is then a maximum, and may be deduced by remembering that the altitude of the elevated pole is numerically equal to the latitude, while that of the equator at its intersection with the meridian is equal to the co-latitude, or complement of the latitude.

Thus in London (lat. 51° 30′) the meridian altitude of Sirius is found as follows:

	°	′
Altitude of equator	38	30
Declination south	16	43
Difference	21	47

The altitude of Capella (Dec. +46° 00′) at lower transit is:

	°	′
Altitude of pole	51	30
Polar distance of star	44	00
Difference	7	30

The brightness of a heavenly body is denoted by its magnitude. Omitting the exceptionally bright stars Sirius and Canopus, the twenty brightest stars are of the first magnitude, while the faintest stars visible to the naked eye are of the sixth magnitude. The magnitude scale is a precise one, as a difference of five magnitudes represents a ratio of 100 to 1 in brightness. Typical second magnitude stars are Polaris and the stars in the belt of Orion. The scale is most easily fixed in memory by comparing the stars with Norton's *Star Atlas*. The stars Sirius and Canopus and the planets Venus and Jupiter are so bright that their magnitudes are expressed by negative numbers. A small telescope will show stars down to the ninth or tenth magnitude, while stars fainter than the twentieth magnitude may be photographed by long exposures with the largest telescopes.

MEAN AND SIDEREAL TIME

The length of a sidereal day in mean time is 23h 56m 04s.09. Hence 1h MT = 1h+9^s.86 ST and 1h ST = 1h − 9^s.83 MT.

Acceleration						Retardation					
h	m	s	m	s	s	h	m	s	m	s	s
1	0	10	0	00	0	1	0	10	0	00	0
2	0	20	3	02	1	2	0	20	3	03	1
3	0	30	9	07	2	3	0	29	9	09	2
4	0	39	15	13	3	4	0	39	15	15	3
5	0	49	21	18	4	5	0	49	21	21	4
6	0	59	27	23	5	6	0	59	27	28	5
7	1	09	33	28	6	7	1	09	33	34	6
8	1	19	39	34	7	8	1	19	39	40	7
9	1	29	45	39	8	9	1	28	45	46	8
10	1	39	51	44	9	10	1	38	51	53	9
11	1	48	57	49	10	11	1	48	57	59	10
12	1	58	60	00		12	1	58	60	00	
13	2	08				13	2	08			
14	2	18				14	2	18			
15	2	28				15	2	27			
16	2	38				16	2	37			
17	2	48				17	2	47			
18	2	57				18	2	57			
19	3	07				19	3	07			
20	3	17				20	3	17			
21	3	27				21	3	26			
22	3	37				22	3	36			
23	3	47				23	3	46			
24	3	57				24	3	56			

To convert an interval of mean time to the corresponding interval of sidereal time, enter the acceleration table with the given mean time (taking the hours and the minutes and seconds separately) and add the acceleration obtained to the given mean time. To convert an interval of sidereal time to the corresponding interval of mean time, take out the retardation for the given sidereal time and subtract.

The columns for the minutes and seconds of the argument are in the form known as critical tables. To use these tables, find in the appropriate left-hand column the two entries between which the given number of minutes and seconds lies; the quantity in the right-hand column between these two entries is the required acceleration or retardation. Thus the acceleration for 11m 26s (which lies between the entries 9m 07s and 15m 13s) is 2s. If the given number of minutes and seconds is a tabular entry, the required acceleration or retardation is the entry in the right-hand column above the given tabular entry, eg the retardation for 45m 46s is 7s.

Example – Convert 14h 27m 35s from ST to MT

	h	m	s
Given ST	14	27	35
Retardation for 14h		2	18
Retardation for 27m 35s			5
Corresponding MT	14	25	12

EXPLANATION OF ASTRONOMICAL DATA

Positions of the heavenly bodies are given only to the degree of accuracy required by amateur astronomers for setting telescopes, or for plotting on celestial globes or star atlases. Where intermediate positions are required, linear interpolation may be employed.

Definitions of the terms used cannot be given here. They must be sought in astronomical literature and textbooks.

A special feature has been made of the times when the various heavenly bodies are visible in the British Isles. Since two columns, calculated for latitudes 52° and 56°, are devoted to risings and settings, the range 50° to 58° can be covered by interpolation and extrapolation. The times given in these columns are Greenwich Mean Times for the meridian of Greenwich. An observer west of this meridian must add his/her longitude (in time) and vice versa.

In accordance with the usual convention in astronomy, + and − indicate respectively north and south latitudes or declinations.

All data are, unless otherwise stated, for 0h Greenwich Mean Time (GMT), ie at the midnight at the beginning of the day named. Allowance must be made for British Summer Time during the period that this is in operation.

PAGE ONE OF EACH MONTH

The calendar for each month is explained on page 1227.

Under the heading Astronomical Phenomena will be found particulars of the more important conjunctions of the Sun, Moon and planets with each other, and also the dates of other astronomical phenomena of special interest.

Times of Minima of Algol are approximate times of the middle of the period of diminished light.

The Constellations listed each month are those that are near the meridian at the beginning of the month at 22h

local mean time. Allowance must be made for British Summer Time if necessary. The fact that any star crosses the meridian 4m earlier each night or 2h earlier each month may be used, in conjunction with the lists given each month, to find what constellations are favourably placed at any moment. The table preceding the list of constellations may be extended indefinitely at the rate just quoted.

The principal phases of the Moon are the GMTs when the difference between the longitude of the Moon and that of the Sun is 0°, 90°, 180° or 270°. The times of perigee and apogee are those when the Moon is nearest to, and farthest from, the Earth, respectively. The nodes or points of intersection of the Moon's orbit and the ecliptic make a complete retrograde circuit of the ecliptic in about 19 years. From a knowledge of the longitude of the ascending node and the inclination, whose value does not vary much from 5°, the path of the Moon among the stars may be plotted on a celestial globe or star atlas.

PAGE TWO OF EACH MONTH

The Sun's semi-diameter, in arc, is given once a month.

The right ascension and declination (Dec.) is that of the true Sun. The right ascension of the mean Sun is obtained by applying the equation of time, with the sign given, to the right ascension of the true Sun, or, more easily, by applying 12h to the Sidereal Time. The direction in which the equation of time has to be applied in different problems is a frequent source of confusion and error. Apparent Solar Time is equal to the Mean Solar Time plus the Equation of Time. For example, at 12h GMT on August 8 the Equation of Time is −5m 35s and thus at 12h Mean Time on that day the Apparent Time is 12h − 5m 35s = 11h 54m 23s.

The Greenwich Sidereal Time at 0h and the Transit of the First Point of Aries (which is really the mean time when the sidereal time is 0h) are used for converting mean time to sidereal time and vice versa.

The GMT of transit of the Sun at Greenwich may also be taken as the local mean time (LMT) of transit in any longitude. It is independent of latitude. The GMT of transit in any longitude is obtained by adding the longitude to the time given if west, and vice versa.

LIGHTING-UP TIME

The legal importance of sunrise and sunset is that the Road Vehicles Lighting Regulations 1989 (SI 1989 No. 1796) as amended, make the use of front and rear position lamps on vehicles compulsory during the period between sunset and sunrise. Headlamps on vehicles are required to be used during the hours of darkness on unlit roads, on lit roads with a speed limit exceeding 30mph, or whenever visibility is seriously reduced. The hours of darkness are defined in these regulations as the period between half an hour after sunset and half an hour before sunrise.

In all laws and regulations 'sunset' refers to the local sunset, ie the time at which the Sun sets at the place in question. This common-sense interpretation has been upheld by legal tribunals.

SUNRISE AND SUNSET

The times of sunrise and sunset are those when the Sun's upper limb, as affected by refraction, is on the true horizon of an observer at sea-level. Assuming the mean refraction to be 34′, and the Sun's semi-diameter to be 16′, the time given is that when the true zenith distance of the Sun's centre is 90°+34′+16′ or 90° 50′, or, in other words, when the depression of the Sun's centre below the true horizon is 50′. The upper limb is then 34′ below the true horizon, but is brought there by refraction. An observer on a ship might see the Sun for a minute or so longer, because of the dip of the horizon, while another viewing the sunset over hills or mountains would record an earlier time. Nevertheless, the moment when the true zenith distance of the Sun's centre is 90° 50′ is a precise time dependent only on the latitude and longitude of the place, and independent of its altitude above sea-level, the contour of its horizon, the vagaries of refraction or the small seasonal change in the Sun's semi-diameter; this moment is suitable in every way as a definition of sunset (or sunrise) for all statutory purposes.

TWILIGHT

Light reaches us before sunrise and continues to reach us for some time after sunset. The interval between darkness and sunrise or sunset and darkness is called twilight. Astronomically speaking, twilight is considered to begin or end when the Sun's centre is 18° below the horizon, as no light from the Sun can then reach the observer. As thus defined twilight may last several hours; in high latitudes at the summer solstice the depression of 18° is not reached, and twilight lasts from sunset to sunrise.

The need for some sub-division of twilight is met by dividing the gathering darkness into four stages.

(1) *Sunrise or Sunset,* defined as above
(2) *Civil twilight,* which begins or ends when the Sun's centre is 6° below the horizon. This marks the time when operations requiring daylight may commence or must cease. In England it varies from about 30 to 60 minutes after sunset and the same interval before sunrise
(3) *Nautical twilight,* which begins or ends when the Sun's centre is 12° below the horizon. This marks the time when it is, to all intents and purposes, completely dark
(4) *Astronomical twilight,* which begins or ends when the Sun's centre is 18° below the horizon. This marks theoretical perfect darkness. It is of little practical importance, especially if nautical twilight is tabulated

To assist observers the durations of civil, nautical and astronomical twilights are given at intervals of ten days. The beginning of a particular twilight is found by subtracting the duration from the time of sunrise, while the end is found by adding the duration to the time of sunset. Thus the beginning of astronomical twilight in latitude 52°, on the Greenwich meridian, on March 11 is found as 06h 23m − 113m = 04h 30m and similarly the end of civil twilight as 17h 58m +34m = 18h 32m. The letters TAN (twilight all night) are printed when twilight lasts all night.

Under the heading The Night Sky will be found notes describing the position and visibility of the planets and other phenomena.

PAGE THREE OF EACH MONTH

The Moon moves so rapidly among the stars that its position is given only to the degree of accuracy that permits linear interpolation. The right ascension (RA) and declination (Dec.) are geocentric, ie for an imaginary observer at the centre of the Earth. To an observer on the surface of the Earth the position is always different, as the altitude is always less on account of parallax, which may reach 1°.

The lunar terminator is the line separating the bright from the dark part of the Moon's disk. Apart from irregularities of the lunar surface, the terminator is elliptical, because it is a circle seen in projection. It becomes the full circle forming the limb, or edge, of the Moon at New and Full Moon. The selenographic longitude of the terminator is measured from the mean centre of the visible disk, which may differ from the visible centre by as much as 8°, because of libration.

Instead of the longitude of the terminator the Sun's selenographic co-longitude (Sun's co-long.) is tabulated. It is numerically equal to the selenographic longitude of the morning terminator, measured eastwards from the mean centre of the disk. Thus its value is approximately 270° at New Moon, 360° at First Quarter, 90° at Full Moon and 180° at Last Quarter.

The Position Angle (PA) of the Bright Limb is the position angle of the midpoint of the illuminated limb, measured eastwards from the north point on the disk. The Phase column shows the percentage of the area of the Moon's disk illuminated; this is also the illuminated percentage of the diameter at right angles to the line of cusps. The terminator is a semi-ellipse whose major axis is the line of cusps, and whose semi-minor axis is determined by the tabulated percentage; from New Moon to Full Moon the east limb is dark, and vice versa.

The times given as moonrise and moonset are those when the upper limb of the Moon is on the horizon of an observer at sea-level. The Sun's horizontal parallax (Hor. par.) is about 9″, and is negligible when considering sunrise and sunset, but that of the Moon averages about 57′. Hence the computed time represents the moment when the true zenith distance of the Moon is 90° 50′ (as for the Sun) minus the horizontal parallax. The time required for the Sun or Moon to rise or set is about four minutes (except in high latitudes).

See also page 1277 and footnote on page 1281.

The GMT of transit of the Moon over the meridian of Greenwich is given; these times are independent of latitude but must be corrected for longitude. For places in the British Isles it suffices to add the longitude if west, and vice versa. For other places a further correction is necessary because of the rapid movement of the Moon relative to the stars. The entire correction is conveniently determined by first finding the west longitude λ of the place. If the place is in west longitude, λ is the ordinary west longitude; if the place is in east longitude λ is the complement to 24h (or 360°) of the longitude and will be greater than 12h (or 180°). The correction then consists of two positive portions, namely λ and the fraction $\lambda/24$ (or $\lambda°/360$) multiplied by the difference between consecutive transits. Thus for Christchurch, New Zealand, the longitude is 11h 31m east, so $\lambda = 12$h 29m and the fraction $\lambda/24$ is 0.52. The transit on the local date 11 October 2012 is found as follows:

		d	h	m
GMT of transit at Greenwich	October 10	07	28
λ			12	29
$0.52 \times (7h\ 28m - 6h\ 40m)$				25
GMT of transit at Christchurch		10	20	22
Corr. to NZ Standard Time			12	00
Local standard time of transit	October 11	08	22

As is evident, for any given place the quantities λ and the correction to local standard time may be combined permanently, being here 24h 29m.

Positions of Mercury are given for every second day, and those of Venus and Mars for every fifth day; they may be interpolated linearly. The diameter (Diam.) is given in seconds of arc. The phase is the illuminated percentage of the disk. In the case of the inner planets this approaches 100 at superior conjunction and 0 at inferior conjunction. When the phase is less than 50 the planet is crescent-shaped or horned; for greater phases it is gibbous. In the case of the exterior planet Mars, the phase approaches 100 at conjunction and opposition, and is a minimum at the quadratures.

Since the planets cannot be seen when on the horizon, the actual times of rising and setting are not given; instead, the time when the planet has an apparent altitude of 5° has been tabulated. If the time of transit is between 00h and 12h the time refers to an altitude of 5° above the eastern horizon; if between 12h and 24h, to the western horizon. The phenomenon tabulated is the one that occurs between sunset and sunrise. The times given may be interpolated for latitude and corrected for longitude, as in the case of the Sun and Moon.

PAGE FOUR OF EACH MONTH

The GMTs of sunrise and sunset for seven cities, whose adopted positions in longitude (W.) and latitude (N.) are given immediately below the name, may be used not only for these phenomena, but also for lighting-up times (see page 1279 for a fuller explanation).

The particulars for the four outer planets resemble those for the planets on Page Three of each month, except that, under Uranus and Neptune, times when the planet is 10° high instead of 5° high are given; this is because of the inferior brightness of these planets. The diameters given for the rings of Saturn are those of the major axis (in the plane of the planet's equator) and the minor axis respectively. The former has a small seasonal change due to the slightly varying distance of the Earth from Saturn, but the latter varies from zero when the Earth passes through the ring plane every 15 years to its maximum opening half-way between these periods. The rings were last open at their widest extent (and Saturn at its brightest) in 2002; this will occur again in 2017. The Earth passed through the ring plane in 2009.

TIME

From the earliest ages, the natural division of time into recurring periods of day and night has provided the practical time-scale for the everyday activities of the human race. Indeed, if any alternative means of time measurement is adopted, it must be capable of adjustment

---

SUNRISE, SUNSET, MOONRISE AND MOONSET

The tables have been constructed for the meridian of Greenwich and for latitudes 52° and 56°. They give Greenwich Mean Time (GMT) throughout the year. To obtain the GMT of the phenomenon as seen from any other latitude and longitude in the British Isles, first interpolate or extrapolate for latitude by the usual rules of proportion. To the time thus found, the longitude (expressed in time) is to be added if west (as it usually is in Great Britain) or subtracted if east. If the longitude is expressed in degrees and minutes of arc, it must be converted to time at the rate of 1° = 4m and 15′ = 1m. A method of calculating rise and set time for other places in the world is given on page 1277.

The GMT at which the planet transits the Greenwich meridian is also given. The times of transit are to be corrected to local meridians in the usual way, as already described.

---

so as to remain in general agreement with the natural time-scale defined by the diurnal rotation of the Earth on its axis. Ideally the rotation should be measured against a fixed frame of reference; in practice it must be measured against the background provided by the celestial bodies. If the Sun is chosen as the reference point, we obtain Apparent Solar Time, which is the time indicated by a sundial. It is not a uniform time but is subject to variations which amount to as much as a quarter of an hour in each direction. Such wide variations cannot be tolerated in a practical time-scale, and this has led to the concept of Mean Solar Time in which all the days are exactly the same length and equal to the average length of the Apparent Solar Day.

The positions of the stars in the sky are specified in relation to a fictitious reference point in the sky known as the First Point of Aries (or the Vernal Equinox). It is therefore convenient to adopt this same reference point when considering the rotation of the Earth against the background of the stars. The time-scale so obtained is known as Apparent Sidereal Time.

GREENWICH MEAN TIME

The daily rotation of the Earth on its axis causes the Sun and the other heavenly bodies to appear to cross the sky from east to west. It is convenient to represent this relative motion as if the Sun really performed a daily circuit around a fixed Earth. Noon in Apparent Solar Time may then be defined as the time at which the Sun transits across the observer's meridian. In Mean Solar Time, noon is similarly defined by the meridian transit of a fictitious Mean Sun moving uniformly in the sky with the same average speed as the true Sun. Mean Solar Time observed on the meridian of the transit circle telescope of the Royal Observatory at Greenwich is called Greenwich Mean Time (GMT). The mean solar day is divided into 24 hours and, for astronomical and other scientific purposes, these are numbered 0 to 23, commencing at midnight. Civil time is usually reckoned in two periods of 12 hours, designated am (ante meridiem, ie before noon) and pm (post meridiem, ie after noon), although the 24 hour clock is increasingly being used.

UNIVERSAL TIME

Before 1925 January 1, GMT was reckoned in 24 hours commencing at noon; since that date it has been reckoned from midnight. To avoid confusion in the use of the designation GMT before and after 1925, since 1928 astronomers have tended to use the term Universal Time (UT) or Weltzeit (WZ) to denote GMT measured from Greenwich Mean Midnight.

In precision work it is necessary to take account of small variations in Universal Time. These arise from small irregularities in the rotation of the Earth. Observed astronomical time is designated UT0. Observed time corrected for the effects of the motion of the poles (giving rise to a 'wandering' in longitude) is designated UT1. There is also a seasonal fluctuation in the rate of rotation of the Earth arising from meteorological causes, often called the annual fluctuation. UT1 corrected for this effect is designated UT2 and provides a time-scale free from short-period fluctuations. It is still subject to small secular and irregular changes.

APPARENT SOLAR TIME

As mentioned above, the time shown by a sundial is called Apparent Solar Time. It differs from Mean Solar Time by an amount known as the Equation of Time, which is the total effect of two causes which make the length of the apparent solar day non-uniform. One cause of variation is that the orbit of the Earth is not a circle but an ellipse, having the Sun at one focus. As a consequence, the angular speed of the Earth in its orbit is not constant; it is greatest at the beginning of January when the Earth is nearest the Sun.

The other cause is due to the obliquity of the ecliptic; the plane of the equator (which is at right angles to the axis of rotation of the Earth) does not coincide with the ecliptic (the plane defined by the apparent annual motion of the Sun around the celestial sphere) but is inclined to it at an angle of 23° 26'. As a result, the apparent solar day is shorter than average at the equinoxes and longer at the solstices. From the combined effects of the components due to obliquity and eccentricity, the equation of time reaches its maximum values in February (−14 minutes) and early November (+16 minutes). It has a zero value on four dates during the year, and it is only on these dates (approximately April 15, June 14, September 1 and December 25) that a sundial shows Mean Solar Time.

SIDEREAL TIME
A sidereal day is the duration of a complete rotation of the Earth with reference to the First Point of Aries. The term sidereal (or 'star') time is a little misleading since the time-scale so defined is not exactly the same as that which would be defined by successive transits of a selected star, as there is a small progressive motion between the stars and the First Point of Aries due to the precession of the Earth's axis. This makes the length of the sidereal day shorter than the true period of rotation by 0.008 seconds. Superimposed on this steady precessional motion are small oscillations (nutation), giving rise to fluctuations in apparent sidereal time amounting to as much as 1.2 seconds. It is therefore customary to employ Mean Sidereal Time, from which these fluctuations have been removed. The conversion of GMT to Greenwich sidereal time (GST) may be performed by adding the value of the GST at 0h on the day in question (page two of each month) to the GMT converted to sidereal time using the table on page 1278.

Example – To find the GST at August 8d 02h 41m 11s GMT

	h	m	s
GST at 0h	21	07	38
GMT	2	41	11
Acceleration for 2h			20
Acceleration for 41m 11s			7
Sum = GST =	23	49	16

If the observer is not on the Greenwich meridian then his/her longitude, measured positively westwards from Greenwich, must be subtracted from the GST to obtain Local Sidereal Time (LST). Thus, in the above example, an observer 5h east of Greenwich, or 19h west, would find the LST as 4h 49m 16s.

EPHEMERIS TIME
An analysis of observations of the positions of the Sun, Moon and planets taken over an extended period is used in preparing ephemerides. (An ephemeris is a table giving the apparent position of a heavenly body at regular intervals of time, eg one day or ten days, and may be used to compare current observations with tabulated positions.)

Discrepancies between the positions of heavenly bodies observed over a 300-year period and their predicted positions arose because the time-scale to which the observations were related was based on the assumption that the rate of rotation of the Earth is uniform. It is now known that this rate of rotation is variable. A revised time-scale, Ephemeris Time (ET), was devised to bring the ephemerides into agreement with the observations.

The second of ET is defined in terms of the annual motion of the Earth in its orbit around the Sun (1/31556925.9747 of the tropical year for 1900 January 0d 12h ET). The precise determination of ET from astronomical observations is a lengthy process as the requisite standard of accuracy can only be achieved by averaging over a number of years.

In 1976 the International Astronomical Union adopted Terrestrial Dynamical Time (TDT), a new dynamical time-scale for general use whose scale unit is the SI second (*see* Atomic Time, below). TDT was renamed Terrestrial Time (TT) in 1991. ET is now of little more than historical interest.

TERRESTRIAL TIME
The uniform time system used in computing the ephemerides of the solar system is Terrestrial Time (TT), which has replaced ET for this purpose. Except for the most rigorous astronomical calculations, it may be assumed to be the same as ET. During 2012 the estimated difference TT − UT is about 67 seconds.

ATOMIC TIME
The fundamental standards of time and frequency must be defined in terms of a periodic motion adequately uniform, enduring and measurable. Progress has made it possible to use natural standards, such as atomic or molecular oscillations. Continuous oscillations are generated in an electrical circuit, the frequency of which is then compared or brought into coincidence with the frequency characteristic of the absorption or emission by the atoms or molecules when they change between two selected energy levels. Since the 13th General Conference on Weights and Measures in October 1967, the unit of time, the second, has been defined in the International System of units (SI) as 'the duration of 9 192 631 770 periods of the radiation corresponding to the transition between the two hyperfine levels of the ground state of the caesium-133 atom'.

In the UK, the national time scale is maintained by the National Physical Laboratory (NPL), using an ensemble of atomic clocks based on either caesium or hydrogen atoms. In addition the NPL (along with several other national laboratories) has constructed and operates a caesium fountain primary frequency standard, which utilises the cooling of caesium atoms by laser light to determine the duration of the SI second at the highest attainable level of accuracy. Caesium fountain primary standards typically achieve an accuracy of around 1 part in 1,000 000 000 000 000, which is equivalent to one second in 30 million years.

Timekeeping worldwide is based on two closely related atomic time scales that are established through international collaboration. International Atomic Time (TAI) is formed by combining the readings of more than 250 atomic clocks located in about 55 institutes and was set close to the astronomically based Universal Time (UT) near the beginning of 1958. It was formally recognised in 1971 and since 1988 January 1 has been maintained by the International Bureau of Weights and Measures

(BIPM). Civil time in almost all countries is now based on Coordinated Universal Time (UTC), which differs from TAI by an integer number of seconds and was designed to make both atomic time and UT available with accuracy appropriate for most users. On 1 January 1972 UTC was set to be exactly 10 seconds behind TAI, and since then the UTC time-scale has been adjusted by the insertion (or, in principle, omission) of leap seconds in order to keep it within ±0.9 s of UT. These leap seconds are introduced, when necessary, at the same instant throughout the world, either at the end of December or at the end of June. The last leap second occurred immediately prior to 0h UTC on 2009 January 1 and was the 24th leap second. All leap seconds so far have been positive, with 61 seconds in the final minute of the UTC month. The time 23h 59m 60s UTC is followed one second later by 0h 0m 00s of the first day of the following month. Notices concerning the insertion of leap seconds are issued by the International Earth Rotation and Reference Systems Service (IERS).

The computation of UTC is carried out monthly by the BIPM and takes place in three stages. First, a weighted average known as Echelle Atomique Libre (EAL) is calculated from all of the contributing atomic clocks. In the second stage, TAI is generated by applying small corrections, derived from the results contributed by primary frequency standards, to the scale interval of EAL to maintain its value close to that of the SI second. Finally, UTC is formed from TAI by the addition of an integer number of seconds. The results are published monthly in the BIPM Circular T in the form of offsets at 5-day intervals between UTC and the time scales of contributing organisations.

RADIO TIME-SIGNALS

UTC is made generally available through time-signals and standard frequency broadcasts such as MSF in the UK, CHU in Canada and WWV and WWVH in the USA. These are based on national time-scales that are maintained in close agreement with UTC and provide traceability to the national time-scale and to UTC. The markers of seconds in the UTC scale coincide with those of TAI.

To disseminate the national time-scale in the UK, special signals (call-sign MSF) are broadcast by the National Physical Laboratory. From 2007 April 1 the MSF service, previously broadcast from British Telecom's radio station at Rugby, has been transmitted from Anthorn radio station in Cumbria. The signals are controlled from a caesium beam atomic frequency standard and consist of a precise frequency carrier of 60 kHz which is switched off, after being on for at least half a second, to mark every second. The first second of the minute begins with a period of 500 ms with the carrier switched off, to serve as a minute marker. In the other seconds the carrier is always off for at least one tenth of a second at the start and then it carries an on-off code giving the British clock time and date, together with information identifying the start of the next minute. Changes to and from summer time are made following government announcements. Leap seconds are inserted as announced by the IERS and information provided by them on the difference between UTC and UT is also signalled. Other broadcast signals in the UK include the BBC six pips signal, the BT Timeline ('speaking clock'), the NPL telephone and internet time services for computers, and a coded time-signal on the BBC 198 kHz transmitters which is used for timing in the electricity supply industry. From 1972 January 1 the six

pips on the BBC have consisted of five short pips from second 55 to second 59 (six pips in the case of a leap second) followed by one lengthened pip, the start of which indicates the exact minute. From 1990 February 5 these signals have been controlled by the BBC with seconds markers referenced to the satellite-based US navigation system GPS (Global Positioning System) and time and day referenced to the MSF transmitter. Formerly they were generated by the Royal Greenwich Observatory. The NPL telephone and internet services are directly connected to the national time scale.

Accurate timing may also be obtained from the signals of international navigation systems such as the ground-based eLORAN, or the satellite-based American GPS or Russian GLONASS systems.

STANDARD TIME

Since 1880 the standard time in Britain has been Greenwich Mean Time (GMT); a statute that year enacted that the word 'time' when used in any legal document relating to Britain meant, unless otherwise specifically stated, the mean time of the Greenwich meridian. Greenwich was adopted as the universal meridian on 13 October 1884. A system of standard time by zones is used worldwide, standard time in each zone differing from that of the Greenwich meridian by an integral number of hours or, exceptionally, half-hours or quarter-hours, either fast or slow. The large territories of the USA and Canada are divided into zones approximately 7.5° on either side of central meridians.

Variations from the standard time of some countries occur during part of the year; they are decided annually and are usually referred to as Summer Time or Daylight Saving Time.

At the 180th meridian the time can be either 12 hours fast on Greenwich Mean Time or 12 hours slow, and a change of date occurs. The internationally recognised date or calendar line is a modification of the 180th meridian, drawn so as to include islands of any one group on the same side of the line, or for political reasons. The line is indicated by joining up the following coordinates:

Lat.	Long.	Lat.	Long.
90° S.	180°	48° N.	180°
51° S.	180°	53° N.	170° E.
45° S.	172.5° W.	65.5° N.	169° W.
15° S.	172.5° W.	68° N.	169° W.
5° S.	180°	90° N.	180°

Changes to the date line would require an international conference.

BRITISH SUMMER TIME

In 1916 an Act ordained that during a defined period of that year the legal time for general purposes in Great Britain should be one hour in advance of Greenwich Mean Time. The Summer Time Acts 1922 and 1925 defined the period during which Summer Time was to be in force, stabilising practice until the Second World War.

During the Second World War (1941–5) and in 1947 Double Summer Time (two hours in advance of Greenwich Mean Time) was used for the period in which ordinary Summer Time would have been in force. During these years clocks were also kept one hour in advance of Greenwich Mean Time in the winter. After the war, ordinary Summer Time was invoked each year from 1948–68.

Between 1968 October 27 and 1971 October 31

clocks were kept one hour ahead of Greenwich Mean Time throughout the year. This was known as British Standard Time.

The most recent legislation is the Summer Time Act 1972, which enacted that 'the period of summer time for the purposes of this Act is the period beginning at two o'clock, Greenwich Mean Time, in the morning of the day after the third Saturday in March or, if that day is Easter Day, the day after the second Saturday in March, and ending at two o'clock, Greenwich Mean Time, in the morning of the day after the fourth Saturday in October.'

The duration of Summer Time can be varied by Order in Council and in recent years alterations have been made to synchronise the period of Summer Time in Britain with that used in Europe. The rule for 1981–94 defined the period of Summer Time in the UK as from the last Sunday in March to the day following the fourth Saturday in October and the hour of changeover was altered to 01h Greenwich Mean Time.

There was no rule for the dates of Summer Time between 1995–7. Since 1998 the 9th European Parliament and Council Directive on Summer Time has harmonised the dates on which Summer Time begins and ends across member states as the last Sundays in March and October respectively. Under the directive Summer Time begins and ends at 01hr Greenwich Mean Time in each member state. Amendments to the Summer Time Act to implement the directive came into force in 2002.

The duration of Summer Time in 2012 is:
March 25 01h GMT to October 28 01h GMT

MEAN REFRACTION

Alt.		Ref.	Alt.		Ref.	Alt.		Ref.
°	′	′	°	′	′	°	′	′
1	20	21	3	12	13	7	54	6
1	30	20	3	34	12	9	27	5
1	41	19	4	00	11	11	39	4
1	52	18	4	30	10	15	00	3
2	05	17	5	06	9	20	42	2
2	19	16	5	50	8	32	20	1
2	35	15	6	44	7	62	17	0
2	52	14	7	54		90	00	
3	12							

The refraction table is in the form of a critical table (*see* page 1278).

ASTRONOMICAL CONSTANTS

Solar parallax	8″.794
Astronomical unit	149597870 km
Precession for the year 2012	50″.291
Precession in right ascension	3ˢ.075
Precession in declination	20″.043
Constant of nutation	9″.202
Constant of aberration	20″.496
Mean obliquity of ecliptic (2012)	23° 26′ 17″
Moon's equatorial hor. parallax	57′ 02″.70
Velocity of light in vacuo per second	299792.5 km
Solar motion per second	20.0 km
Equatorial radius of the Earth	6378.140 km
Polar radius of the Earth	6356.755 km

North galactic pole (IAU standard)
RA 12h 49m (1950.0). Dec.+27°.4 N.
Solar apex   RA 18h 06m Dec. +30°
Length of year (in mean solar days)

Tropical	365.24219
Sidereal	365.25636
Anomalistic (perihelion to perihelion)	365.25964
Eclipse	346.62003

Length of month (mean values)	d	h	m	s
New Moon to New	29	12	44	02.9
Sidereal	27	07	43	11.5
Anomalistic (perigee to perigee)	27	13	18	33.2

THE EARTH

The shape of the Earth is that of an oblate spheroid or solid of revolution whose meridian sections are ellipses not differing much from circles, while the sections at right angles are circles. The length of the equatorial axis is about 12,756 km, and that of the polar axis is 12,714 km. The mean density of the Earth is 5.5 times that of water, although that of the surface layer is less. The Earth and Moon revolve about their common centre of gravity in a lunar month; this centre in turn revolves round the Sun in a plane known as the ecliptic, that passes through the Sun's centre. The Earth's equator is inclined to this plane at an angle of 23.4°. This tilt is the cause of the seasons. In mid-latitudes, and when the Sun is high above the Equator, not only does the high noon altitude make the days longer, but the Sun's rays fall more directly on the Earth's surface; these effects combine to produce summer. In equatorial regions the noon altitude is large throughout the year, and there is little variation in the length of the day. In higher latitudes the noon altitude is lower, and the days in summer are appreciably longer than those in winter.

The average velocity of the Earth in its orbit is 30km a second. It makes a complete rotation on its axis in about 23h 56m of mean time, which is the sidereal day. Because of its annual revolution round the Sun, the rotation with respect to the Sun, or the solar day, is more than this by about four minutes. The extremity of the axis of rotation, or the North Pole of the Earth, is not rigidly fixed, but wanders over an area roughly 20 metres in diameter.

ELEMENTS OF THE SOLAR SYSTEM

Orb	Mean distance from Sun (Earth = 1)	km 10⁶	Sidereal period days	Synodic period days	Incl. of orbit to ecliptic ° '	Diameter km	Mass (Earth = 1)	Period of rotation on axis days
Sun	—	—	—	—	—	1,392,000	332,981	25–35*
Mercury	0.39	58	88.0	116	7 00	4,879	0.0553	58.646
Venus	0.72	108	224.7	584	3 24	12,104	0.8150	243.019r
Earth	1.00	150	365.3	—	—	12,756e	1.0000	0.997
Mars	1.52	228	687.0	780	1 51	6,794e	0.1074	1.026
Jupiter	5.20	778	4,332.6	399	1 18	142,984e / 133,708p	317.83	0.410e
Saturn	9.55	1429	10,759.2	378	2 29	120,536e / 108,728p	95.16	0.426e
Uranus	19.22	2875	30,684.6	370	0 46	51,118e	14.54	0.718r
Neptune	30.11	4504	60,191.2	367	1 46	49,528e	17.15	0.671
Pluto†	39.80	5954	91,708.2	367	17 09	2,390	0.002	6.387

e equatorial, p polar, r retrograde, * depending on latitude, † reclassified as a dwarf planet since August 2006

THE SATELLITES

Name	Star mag.	Mean distance from primary km	Sidereal period of revolution d	Name	Star mag.	Mean distance from primary km	Sidereal period of revolution d
EARTH				SATURN			
I Moon	—	384,400	27.322	VII Hyperion	14	1,481,000	21.277
				VIII Iapetus	11	3,561,300	79.330
MARS				IX Phoebe	16	12,952,000	550.48r
I Phobos	11	9,378	0.319				
II Deimos	12	23,459	1.262	URANUS			
				VI Cordelia	24	49,770	0.335
JUPITER				VII Ophelia	24	53,790	0.376
XVI Metis	17	127,960	0.295	VIII Bianca	23	59,170	0.435
XV Adrastea	19	128,980	0.298	IX Cressida	22	61,780	0.464
V Amalthea	14	181,300	0.498	X Desdemona	22	62,680	0.474
XIV Thebe	16	221,900	0.675	XI Juliet	21	64,350	0.493
I Io	5	421,600	1.769	XII Portia	21	66,090	0.513
II Europa	5	670,900	3.551	XIII Rosalind	22	66,940	0.558
III Ganymede	5	1,070,000	7.155	XIV Belinda	22	75,260	0.624
IV Callisto	6	1,883,000	16.689	XV Puck	20	86,010	0.762
XIII Leda	20	11,165,000	240.92	V Miranda	16	129,390	1.413
VI Himalia	15	11,460,000	250.57	I Ariel	14	191,020	2.520
X Lysithea	18	11,717,000	259.22	II Umbriel	15	266,300	4.144
VII Elara	17	11,741,000	259.65	III Titania	14	435,910	8.706
XII Ananke	19	21,276,000	629.77r	IV Oberon	14	583,520	13.463
XI Carme	18	23,404,000	734.17r	XVI Caliban	22	7,230,000	579.5r
VIII Pasiphae	17	23,624,000	743.68r	XX Stephano	24	8,002,000	676.5r
IX Sinope	18	23,939,000	758.90r	XVII Sycorax	21	12,179,000	1,283.4r
				XVIII Prospero	23	16,418,000	1,992.8r
SATURN				XIX Setebos	23	17,459,000	2,202.2r
XVIII Pan	20	133,583	0.575				
XV Atlas	18	137,640	0.602	NEPTUNE			
XVI Prometheus	16	139,353	0.613	III Naiad	25	48,230	0.294
XVII Pandora	16	141,700	0.629	IV Thalassa	24	50,080	0.311
XI Epimetheus	15	151,422	0.694	V Despina	23	52,530	0.335
X Janus	14	151,472	0.695	VI Galatea	22	61,950	0.429
I Mimas	13	185,520	0.942	VII Larissa	22	73,550	0.555
II Enceladus	12	238,020	1.370	VIII Proteus	20	117,650	1.122
III Tethys	10	294,660	1.888	I Triton	13	354,760	5.877
XIII Telesto	19	294,660	1.888	II Nereid	19	5,513,400	360.136
XIV Calypso	19	294,660	1.888				
IV Dione	10	377,400	2.737	PLUTO			
XII Helene	18	377,400	2.737	I Charon	17	19,600	6.387
V Rhea	10	527,040	4.518				
VI Titan	8	1,221,850	15.945				

Currently the total number of satellites of the outer planets are: Jupiter 62, Saturn 60, Uranus 27, Neptune 13, Pluto 3.

TERRESTRIAL MAGNETISM

The Earth's main magnetic field corresponds approximately to that of a very strong small bar magnet near the centre of the Earth, but with appreciable smooth spatial departures. The origin of the main field is generally ascribed to electric currents associated with fluid motions in the Earth's core. As a result not only does the main field vary in strength and direction from place to place, but also with time. Superimposed on the main field are local and regional anomalies whose magnitudes may in places approach that of the main field; these are due to the influence of mineral deposits in the Earth's crust. A small proportion of the field is of external origin, mostly associated with electric currents in the ionosphere. The configuration of the external field and the ionisation of the atmosphere depend on the incident particle and radiation flux from the Sun. There are, therefore, short-term and non-periodic as well as diurnal, 27-day, seasonal and 11-year periodic changes in the magnetic field, dependent upon the position of the Sun and the degree of solar activity.

A magnetic compass points along the horizontal component of a magnetic line of force. These lines of force converge on the 'magnetic dip-poles', the places where the Earth's magnetic field is vertical. These poles move with time, and their present approximate adopted mean positions are 85.5° N., 140.2° W. and 64.4° S., 137.1° E.

There is also a 'magnetic equator', at all points of which the vertical component of the Earth's magnetic field is zero and a magnetised needle remains horizontal. This line runs between 2° and 12° north of the geographical equator in Asia and Africa, turns sharply south off the west African coast, and crosses South America through Brazil, Bolivia and Peru; it re-crosses the geographical equator in mid-Pacific.

Reference has already been made to secular changes in the Earth's field. The following table indicates the changes in magnetic declination (or variation of the compass). Declination is the angle in the horizontal plane between the direction of true north and that in which a magnetic compass points. Similar, though much smaller, changes have occurred in 'dip' or magnetic inclination. Secular changes differ throughout the world. Although the London observations suggest a cycle with a period of several hundred years, an exact repetition is unlikely.

London			Greenwich		
1580	11°	15′ E.	1900	16°	29′ W.
1622	5°	56′ E.	1925	13°	10′ W.
1665	1°	22′ W.	1950	9°	07′ W.
1730	13°	00′ W.	1975	6°	39′ W.
1773	21°	09′ W.	1998	3°	32′ W.
1850	22°	24′ W.			

In order that up-to-date information on declination may be available, many governments publish magnetic charts on which there are lines (isogonic lines) passing through all places at which specified values of declination will be found at the date of the chart.

In the British Isles, isogonic lines now run approximately north-east to south-west. Though there are considerable local deviations due to geological causes, a rough value of magnetic declination may be obtained by assuming that at 50° N. on the meridian of Greenwich, the value in 2012 is 0° 49′ west and allowing an increase of 11′ for each degree of latitude northwards and one of 26′ for each degree of longitude westwards. For example, at 53° N., 5° W., declination will be about 0° 49′ + 33′ + 130′, ie 3° 32′ west. The average annual change at the present time is about 11′ decrease.

The number of magnetic observatories is about 180, irregularly distributed over the globe. There are three in Great Britain, run by the British Geological Survey: at Hartland, north Devon; at Eskdalemuir, Dumfries and Galloway; and at Lerwick, Shetland Islands. The following are some recent annual mean values of the magnetic elements for Hartland.

Year	Declination West ° ′	Dip or inclination ° ′	Horizontal intensity nanoTesla (nT)	Vertical intensity nT
1960	9 58.8	66 43.9	18707	43504
1965	9 30.1	66 34.0	18872	43540
1970	9 06.5	66 26.1	19033	43636
1975	8 32.3	66 17.0	19212	43733
1980	7 43.8	66 10.3	19330	43768
1985	6 56.1	66 07.9	19379	43796
1990	6 15.0	66 09.7	19539	43896
1995	5 33.2	66 07.3	19457	43951
2000	4 43.6	66 06.9	19508	44051
2005	3 56.4	66 06.0	19576	44177
2010	3 09.5	66 02.1	19670	44251

As well as navigation at sea, in the air and on land by compass the oil industry depends on the Earth's magnetic field as a directional reference. They use magnetic survey tools when drilling well-bores and require accurate estimates of the local magnetic field, taking into account the crustal and external fields.

MAGNETIC STORMS

Occasionally, sometimes with great suddenness, the Earth's magnetic field is subject for several hours to marked disturbance. During a severe storm in October 2003 the declination at Eskdalemuir changed by over 5° in six minutes. In many instances such disturbances are accompanied by widespread displays of aurorae, marked changes in the incidence of cosmic rays, an increase in the reception of 'noise' from the Sun at radio frequencies, and rapid changes in the ionosphere and induced electric currents within the Earth which adversely affect satellite operations, telecommunications and electric power transmission systems. The disturbances are caused by changes in the stream of ionised particles which emanates from the Sun and through which the Earth is continuously passing. Some of these changes are associated with visible eruptions on the Sun, usually in the region of sun-spots. There is a marked tendency for disturbances to recur after intervals of about 27 days, the apparent period of rotation of the Sun on its axis, which is consistent with the sources being located on particular areas of the Sun.

TIME MEASUREMENT AND CALENDARS

MEASUREMENTS OF TIME

Measurements of time are based on the time taken by the earth to rotate on its axis (day); by the moon to revolve around the earth (month); and by the earth to revolve around the sun (year). From these, which are not commensurable, certain average or mean intervals have been adopted for ordinary use.

THE DAY
The day begins at midnight and is divided into 24 hours of 60 minutes, each of 60 seconds. The hours are counted from midnight up to 12 noon (when the sun crosses the meridian), and these hours are designated am *(ante meridiem);* and again from noon up to 12 midnight, which hours are designated pm *(post meridiem),* except when the 24-hour reckoning is employed. The 24-hour reckoning ignores am and pm, numbering the hours 0 to 23 from midnight.

Colloquially the 24 hours are divided into day and night, day being the time while the sun is above the horizon (including the four stages of twilight defined in the Astronomy section). Day is subdivided into morning, the early part of daytime, ending at noon; afternoon, from noon to about 6pm; and evening, which may be said to extend from 6pm until midnight. Night begins at the close of astronomical twilight (*see* the Astronomy section) and extends beyond midnight to sunrise the next day.

The names of the days are derived from Old English translations or adaptations of the Roman titles.

Sunday	Sol	Sun
Monday	Luna	Moon
Tuesday	Tiw/Tyr (god of war)	Mars
Wednesday	Woden/Odin	Mercury
Thursday	Thor	Jupiter
Friday	Frigga/Freyja (goddess of love)	Venus
Saturday	Saeterne	Saturn

THE MONTH
The month in the ordinary calendar is approximately the twelfth part of a year, but the lengths of the different months vary from 28 (or 29) days to 31.

THE YEAR
The equinoctial or tropical year is the time that the earth takes to revolve around the sun from equinox to equinox, ie 365.24219 mean solar days, or 365 days 5 hours 48 minutes and 45 seconds.

The calendar year usually consists of 365 days but a year containing 366 days is called a bissextile (*see* Roman calendar) or leap year, one day being added to the month of February so that a date 'leaps over' a day of the week. In the Roman calendar the day that was repeated was the sixth day before the beginning of March, the equivalent of 24 February.

A year is a leap year if the date of the year is divisible by four without remainder, unless it is the last year of the century. The last year of a century is a leap year only if its number is divisible by 400 without remainder, eg the years 1800 and 1900 had only 365 days but the year 2000 had 366 days.

THE SOLSTICE
A solstice is the point in the tropical year at which the sun attains its greatest distance, north or south, from the Equator. In the northern hemisphere the furthest point north of the Equator marks the summer solstice and the furthest point south marks the winter solstice.

The date of the solstice varies according to locality. For example, if the summer solstice falls on 21 June late in the day by Greenwich time, that day will be the longest of the year at Greenwich though it may be by only a second, but it will fall on 22 June, local date, in Japan, and so 22 June will be the longest day there. The date of the solstice is also affected by the length of the tropical year, which is 365 days 6 hours less about 11 minutes 15 seconds. If a solstice happens late on 21 June in one year, it will be nearly 6 hours later in the next (unless the next year is a leap year), ie early on 22 June, and that will be the longest day.

This delay of the solstice does not continue because the extra day in a leap year brings it back a day in the calendar. However, because of the 11 minutes 15 seconds mentioned above, the additional day in a leap year brings the solstice back too far by 45 minutes, and the time of the solstice in the calendar is earlier, in a four-year pattern, as the century progresses. The last year of a century is in most cases not a leap year, and the omission of the extra day puts the date of the solstice later by about 6 hours. Compensation for this is made by the fourth centennial year being a leap year. The solstice has become earlier in date throughout the last century and, because the year 2000 was a leap year, the solstice will get earlier still throughout the 21st century. The date of the winter solstice, the shortest day of the year, is affected by the same factors as the longest day.

At Greenwich the sun sets at its earliest by the clock about ten days before the shortest day. The daily change in the time of sunset is due in the first place to the sun's movement southwards at this time of the year, which diminishes the interval between the sun's transit and its setting. However, the daily decrease of the Equation of Time causes the time of apparent noon to be continuously later day by day, which to some extent counteracts the first effect. The rates of the change of these two quantities are not equal or uniform; their combination causes the date of earliest sunset to be 12 or 13 December at Greenwich. In more southerly latitudes the effect of the movement of the sun is less, and the change in the time of sunset depends on that of the Equation of Time to a greater degree, and the date of earliest sunset is earlier than it is at Greenwich, eg on the Equator it is about 1 November.

THE EQUINOX
The equinox is the point at which the sun crosses the Equator and day and night are of equal length all over the world. This occurs in March and September.

DOG DAYS
The days about the heliacal rising of the Dog Star, noted from ancient times as the hottest period of the year in the northern hemisphere, are called the Dog Days. Their incidence has been variously calculated as depending on the Greater or Lesser Dog Star (Sirius or Procyon) and

their duration has been reckoned as from 30 to 54 days. A generally accepted period is from 3 July to 15 August.

CHRISTIAN CALENDAR

In the Christian chronological system the years are distinguished by cardinal numbers before or after the birth of Christ, the period being denoted by the letters BC (Before Christ) or, more rarely, AC *(Ante Christum),* and AD *(Anno Domini –* In the Year of Our Lord). The correlative dates of the epoch are the fourth year of the 194th Olympiad, the 753rd year from the foundation of Rome, AM 3761 in Jewish chronology, and the 4,714th year of the Julian period. The actual date of the birth of Christ is somewhat uncertain.

The system was introduced into Italy in the sixth century. Though first used in France in the seventh century, it was not universally established there until about the eighth century. It has been said that the system was introduced into England by St Augustine (AD 596), but it was probably not generally used until some centuries later. It was ordered to be used by the bishops at the Council of Chelsea (AD 816).

THE JULIAN CALENDAR
In the Julian calendar (adopted by the Roman Empire in 45 BC) all the centennial years were leap years, and for this reason towards the close of the 16th century there was a difference of ten days between the tropical and calendar years; the equinox fell on 11 March of the calendar, whereas at the time of the Council of Nicaea (AD 325), it had fallen on 21 March. In 1582 Pope Gregory ordained that 5 October should be called 15 October and that of the end-century years only the fourth should be a leap year.

THE GREGORIAN CALENDAR
The Gregorian calendar was adopted by Italy, France, Spain and Portugal in 1582, by Prussia, the Roman Catholic German states, Switzerland, Holland and Flanders on 1 January 1583, by Poland in 1586, Hungary in 1587, the Protestant German and Netherland states and Denmark in 1700, and by Great Britain and its Dominions (including the North American colonies) in 1752, by the omission of 11 days (3 September being reckoned as 14 September). Sweden omitted the leap day in 1700 but observed leap days in 1704 and 1708, and reverted to the Julian calendar by having two leap days in 1712; the Gregorian calendar was adopted in 1753 by the omission of 11 days (18 February being reckoned as 1 March). Japan adopted the calendar in 1872, China in 1912, Bulgaria in 1916, Turkey and Soviet Russia in 1918, Yugoslavia and Romania in 1919, and Greece in 1923.

In the same year that the change was made in England from the Julian to the Gregorian calendar, the start of the new year was also changed from 25 March to 1 January.

THE ORTHODOX CHURCHES
Some Orthodox churches still use the Julian reckoning but the majority of Greek Orthodox churches and the Romanian Orthodox Church have adopted a modified 'New Calendar', observing the Gregorian calendar for fixed feasts and the Julian for movable feasts.

The Orthodox Church year begins on 1 September. There are four fast periods and, in addition to Pascha (Easter), twelve great feasts, as well as numerous commemorations of the saints of the Old and New Testaments throughout the year.

THE DOMINICAL LETTER
The dominical letter is one of the letters A–G which are used to denote the Sundays in successive years. If the first day of the year is a Sunday the letter is A; if the second, B; the third, C; and so on. A leap year requires two letters, the first for 1 January to 29 February, the second for 1 March to 31 December.

EPIPHANY
The feast of the Epiphany, commemorating the manifestation of Christ, later became associated with the offering of gifts by the Magi. The day was of great importance from the time of the Council of Nicaea (AD 325), as the primate of Alexandria was charged at every Epiphany feast with the announcement in a letter to the churches of the date of the forthcoming Easter. The day was also of importance in Britain as it influenced dates, ecclesiastical and lay, eg Plough Monday, when work was resumed in the fields, fell on the Monday in the first full week after Epiphany.

LENT
The Teutonic word *Lent,* which denotes the fast preceding Easter, originally meant no more than the spring season; but from Anglo-Saxon times, at least, it has been used as the equivalent of the more significant Latin term *Quadragesima,* meaning the 'forty days' or, more literally, the fortieth day. Ash Wednesday is the first day of Lent, which ends at midnight before Easter Day.

PALM SUNDAY
Palm Sunday, the Sunday before Easter and the beginning of Holy Week, commemorates the triumphal entry of Christ into Jerusalem and is celebrated in Britain (when palm is not available) by branches of willow gathered for use in the decoration of churches on that day.

MAUNDY THURSDAY
Maundy Thursday is the day before Good Friday, the name itself being a corruption of *dies mandati* (day of the mandate) when Christ washed the feet of the disciples and gave them the mandate to love one another.

EASTER DAY
Easter Day is the first Sunday after the full moon which happens on, or next after, the 21st day of March; if the full moon happens on a Sunday, Easter Day is the Sunday after.

This definition is contained in an Act of Parliament (24 Geo. II c. 23) and explanation is given in the preamble to the Act that the day of full moon depends on certain tables that have been prepared. These tables are summarised in the early pages of the Book of Common Prayer. The moon referred to is not the real moon of the heavens, but a hypothetical moon on whose 'full' the date of Easter depends, and the lunations of this 'calendar' moon consist of 29 and 30 days alternately, with certain necessary modifications to make the date of its full agree as nearly as possible with that of the real moon, which is known as the Paschal Full Moon.

A FIXED EASTER
In 1928 the House of Commons agreed to a motion for the third reading of a bill proposing that Easter Day shall, in the calendar year next but one after the commencement of the Act and in all subsequent years, be the first Sunday after the second Saturday in April. Easter would thus fall on the second or third Sunday in April, ie

between 9 and 15 April (inclusive). A clause in the bill provided that before it shall come into operation, regard shall be had to any opinion expressed officially by the various Christian churches. Efforts by the World Council of Churches to secure a unanimous choice of date for Easter by its member churches have so far been unsuccessful.

ROGATION DAYS

Rogation Days are the Monday, Tuesday and Wednesday preceding Ascension Day and from the fifth century were observed as public fasts with solemn processions and supplications. The processions were discontinued as religious observances at the Reformation, but survive in the ceremony known as 'beating the parish bounds'. Rogation Sunday is the Sunday before Ascension Day.

EMBER DAYS

The Ember days occur on the Wednesday, Friday and Saturday of the same week, four times a year. Used for the ordination of clergy, these days are set aside for fasting and prayer. The weeks in which they fall are: (a) after the third Sunday in Advent, (b) before the second Sunday in Lent, (c) before Trinity Sunday and (d) after Holy Cross day.

TRINITY SUNDAY

Trinity Sunday is eight weeks after Easter Day, on the Sunday following Pentecost (Whit Sunday). Subsequent Sundays are reckoned in the Book of Common Prayer calendar of the Church of England as 'after Trinity'.

Thomas Becket (1118–70) was consecrated Archbishop of Canterbury on the Sunday after Whit Sunday and his first act was to ordain that the day of his consecration should be held as a new festival in honour of the Holy Trinity. This observance spread from Canterbury throughout the whole of Christendom.

MOVEABLE FEASTS TO THE YEAR 2035

Year	Ash Wednesday	Easter	Ascension	Pentecost (Whit Sunday)	Advent Sunday
2012	22 February	8 April	17 May	27 May	2 December
2013	13 February	31 March	9 May	19 May	1 December
2014	5 March	20 April	29 May	8 June	30 November
2015	18 February	5 April	14 May	24 May	29 November
2016	10 February	27 March	5 May	15 May	27 November
2017	1 March	16 April	25 May	4 June	3 December
2018	14 February	1 April	10 May	20 May	2 December
2019	6 March	21 April	30 May	9 June	1 December
2020	26 February	12 April	21 May	31 May	29 November
2021	17 February	4 April	13 May	23 May	28 November
2022	2 March	17 April	26 May	5 June	27 November
2023	22 February	9 April	18 May	28 May	3 December
2024	14 February	31 March	9 May	19 May	1 December
2025	5 March	20 April	29 May	8 June	30 November
2026	18 February	5 April	14 May	24 May	29 November
2027	10 February	28 March	6 May	16 May	28 November
2028	1 March	16 April	25 May	4 June	3 December
2029	14 February	1 April	10 May	20 May	2 December
2030	6 March	21 April	30 May	9 June	1 December
2031	26 February	13 April	22 May	1 June	30 November
2032	11 February	28 March	6 May	16 May	28 November
2033	2 March	17 April	26 May	5 June	27 November
2034	22 February	9 April	18 May	28 May	3 December
2035	7 February	25 March	3 May	13 May	2 December

NOTES

Ash Wednesday (first day in Lent) can fall at earliest on 4 February and at latest on 10 March

Mothering Sunday (fourth Sunday in Lent) can fall at earliest on 1 March and at latest on 4 April

Easter Day can fall at earliest on 22 March and at latest on 25 April

Ascension Day is forty days after Easter Day and can fall at earliest on 30 April and at latest on 3 June

Pentecost (Whit Sunday) is seven weeks after Easter and can fall at earliest on 10 May and at latest on 13 June

Trinity Sunday is the Sunday after Whit Sunday

Corpus Christi falls on the Thursday after Trinity Sunday

Sundays after Pentecost – there are not less than 18 and not more than 23

Advent Sunday is the Sunday nearest to 30 November

EASTER DAYS AND DOMINICAL LETTERS 1500 TO 2035

Dates up to and including 1752 are according to the Julian calendar. For dominical letters in leap years, *see* note below

		1500–1599	1600–1699	1700–1799	1800–1899	1900–1999	2000–2035
March							
d	22	1573	1668	1761	1818		
e	23	1505/16	1600	1788	1845/56	1913	2008
f	24	1611/95	1706/99	1940			
g	25	1543/54	1627/38/49	1722/33/44	1883/94	1951	2035
A	26	1559/70/81/92	1654/65/76	1749/58/69/80	1815/26/37	1967/78/89	
b	27	1502/13/24/97	1608/87/92	1785/96	1842/53/64	1910/21/32	2005/16
c	28	1529/35/40	1619/24/30	1703/14/25	1869/75/80	1937/48	2027/32
d	29	1551/62	1635/46/57	1719/30/41/52	1807/12/91	1959/64/70	
e	30	1567/78/89	1651/62/73/84	1746/55/66/77	1823/34	1902/75/86/97	
f	31	1510/21/32/83/94	1605/16/78/89	1700/71/82/93	1839/50/61/72	1907/18/29/91	2002/13/24
April							
g	1	1526/37/48	1621/32	1711/16	1804/66/77/88	1923/34/45/56	2018/29
A	2	1553/64	1643/48	1727/38	1809/20/93/99	1961/72	
b	3	1575/80/86	1659/70/81	1743/63/68/74	1825/31/36	1904/83/88/94	
c	4	1507/18/91	1602/13/75/86/97	1708/79/90	1847/58	1915/20/26/99	2010/21
d	5	1523/34/45/56	1607/18/29/40	1702/13/24/95	1801/63/74/85/96	1931/42/53	2015/26
e	6	1539/50/61/72	1634/45/56	1729/35/40/60	1806/17/28/90	1947/58/69/80	
f	7	1504/77/88	1667/72	1751/65/76	1822/33/44	1901/12/85/96	
g	8	1509/15/20/99	1604/10/83/94	1705/87/92/98	1849/55/60	1917/28	2007/12
A	9	1531/42	1615/26/37/99	1710/21/32	1871/82	1939/44/50	2023/34
b	10	1547/58/69	1631/42/53/64	1726/37/48/57	1803/14/87/98	1955/66/77	
c	11	1501/12/63/74/85/96	1658/69/80	1762/73/84	1819/30/41/52	1909/71/82/93	2004
d	12	1506/17/28	1601/12/91/96	1789	1846/57/68	1903/14/25/36/98	2009/20
e	13	1533/44	1623/28	1707/18	1800/73/79/84	1941/52	2031
f	14	1555/60/66	1639/50/61	1723/34/45/54	1805/11/16/95	1963/68/74	
g	15	1571/82/93	1655/66/77/88	1750/59/70/81	1827/38	1900/06/79/90	2001
A	16	1503/14/25/36/87/98	1609/20/82/93	1704/75/86/97	1843/54/65/76	1911/22/33/95	2006/17/28
b	17	1530/41/52	1625/36	1715/20	1808/70/81/92	1927/38/49/60	2022/33
c	18	1557/68	1647/52	1731/42/56	1802/13/24/97	1954/65/76	
d	19	1500/79/84/90	1663/74/85	1747/67/72/78	1829/35/40	1908/81/87/92	
e	20	1511/22/95	1606/17/79/90	1701/12/83/94	1851/62	1919/24/30	2003/14/25
f	21	1527/38/49	1622/33/44	1717/28	1867/78/89	1935/46/57	2019/30
g	22	1565/76	1660	1739/53/64	1810/21/32	1962/73/84	
A	23	1508	1671		1848	1905/16	2000
b	24	1519	1603/14/98	1709/91	1859		2011
c	25	1546	1641	1736	1886	1943	

No dominical letter is placed against the intercalary day 29 February, but since it is still counted as a weekday and given a name, the series of letters moves back one day every leap year after intercalation. Thus, a leap year beginning with the dominical letter C will change to a year with the dominical letter B on 1 March

HINDU CALENDAR

The Hindu calendar is a luni-solar calendar of 12 months, each containing 29 days, 12 hours. Each month is divided into a light fortnight (Shukla or Shuddha) and a dark fortnight (Krishna or Vadya) based on the waxing and waning of the moon. In most parts of India the month starts with the light fortnight, ie the day after the new moon, although in some regions it begins with the dark fortnight, ie the day after the full moon.

The new year according to the civil calendar begins on the first day of the month of Chaitra (March/April) and ends in the month of Phalgun (March). The financial new year begins on the first day of Kartik (Diwali day). For most Hindus, the first day of Chaitra and the first day of Kartik are equally important.

The 12 months – Chaitra, Vaishakh, Jyeshtha, Ashadh, Shravan, Bhadrapad, Ashvin, Kartik, Margashirsh, Paush, Magh and Phalgun – have Sanskrit names derived from 12 asterisms (constellations). There are regional variations to the names of the months but the Sanskrit names are understood throughout India.

Every lunar month that has a solar transit is termed pure *(shuddha)*. The lunar month without a solar transit is impure *(mala)* and called an intercalary month. An intercalary month occurs approximately every 32 lunar months, whenever the difference between the Hindu year of 360 lunar days (354 days 8 hours solar time) and the 365 days 6 hours of the solar year reaches the length of one Hindu lunar month (29 days 12 hours).

The leap month may be added at any point in the Hindu year. The name given to the month varies according to when it occurs but is taken from the month immediately following it. The leap month in 2012 is Bhadrapad.

The days of the week are called Raviwar (Sunday), Somawar (Monday), Mangalwar (Tuesday), Budhawar (Wednesday), Guruwar (Thursday), Shukrawar (Friday) and Shaniwar (Saturday). The names are derived from the Sanskrit names of the sun, the moon and five planets, Mars, Mercury, Jupiter, Venus and Saturn.

Most fasts and festivals are based on the lunar calendar but a few are determined by the apparent movement of the sun, eg Sankranti and Pongal (in southern India), which are celebrated on 14/15 January to mark the start of the Sun's apparent journey northwards and a change of season.

Festivals celebrated throughout India are Chaitra (the New Year), Raksha-bandhan (the renewal of the kinship bond between brothers and sisters), Navaratri (a nine-night festival dedicated to the goddess Parvati), Dasara (the victory of Rama over the demon army), Diwali (a festival of lights), Makara Sankranti, Shivaratri (dedicated to Shiva), and Holi (a spring festival). British Hindus commonly celebrate the festival of Diwali as the start of the financial new year.

Regional festivals are Durga-puja (dedicated to the goddess Durga (Parvati)), Sarasvati-puja (dedicated to the goddess Sarasvati), Ganesh Chaturthi (worship of Ganesh on the fourth day (Chaturthi) of the light half of Bhadrapad), Ramanavami (the birth festival of the god Rama) and Janmashtami (the birth festival of the god Krishna).

The main festivals celebrated in Britain are Navaratri, Dasara, Durga-puja, Diwali, Holi, Sarasvati-puja, Ganesh Chaturthi, Raksha-bandhan, Ramanavami and Janmashtami.

For dates of the main festivals in 2012, *see* page 9.

JEWISH CALENDAR

The story of the Flood in the Book of Genesis indicates the use of a calendar of some kind and that the writers recognised 30 days as the length of a lunation. However, after the diaspora, Jewish communities were left in considerable doubt as to the times of fasts and festivals. This led to the formation of the Jewish calendar as used today. It is said that this was done in AD 358 by Rabbi Hillel II, though some assert that it did not happen until much later.

The calendar is luni-solar, and is based on the lengths of the lunation and of the tropical year as found by Hipparchus (c.120 BC), which differ little from those adopted at the present day. The year AM 5772 (2011–12) is the 15th year of the 304th Metonic (Minor or Lunar) cycle of 19 years and the 4th year of the 207th Solar (or Major) cycle of 28 years since the Era of the Creation. Jews hold that the Creation occurred at the time of the autumnal equinox in the year known in the Christian calendar as 3760 BC (954 of the Julian period). The epoch or starting point of Jewish chronology corresponds to 7 October 3761 BC. At the beginning of each solar cycle, the Tekufah of Nisan (the vernal equinox) returns to the same day and to the same hour.

The hour is divided into 1,080 minims, and the month between one new moon and the next is reckoned as 29 days 12 hours 793 minims. The normal calendar year, called a regular common year, consists of 12 months of 30 days and 29 days alternately. Since 12 months such as these comprise only 354 days, in order that each of them shall not diverge greatly from an average place in the solar year, a 13th month is occasionally added after the fifth month of the civil year (which commences on the first day of the month Tishri); or as the penultimate month of the ecclesiastical year (which commences on the first day of the month Nisan). The years when this happens are called Embolismic or leap years.

Of the 19 years that form a Metonic cycle, seven are leap years; they occur at places in the cycle indicated by the numbers 3, 6, 8, 11, 14, 17 and 19, these places being chosen so that the accumulated excesses of the solar years should be as small as possible.

A Jewish year is of one of the following six types:

minimal common	353 days
regular common	354 days
full common	355 days
minimal leap	383 days
regular leap	384 days
full leap	385 days

The regular year has alternate months of 30 and 29 days. In a Full year Marcheshvan, the second month of the civil year, has 30 days instead of 29; in minimal years Kislev, the third month, has 29 instead of 30. The additional month in leap years is called Adar Sheni (Adar II) and follows the month called Adar Rishon; the usual Adar festivals are observed in Adar Sheni. In a leap year Adar I has 30 days, in all other years it has 29. None of the variations mentioned are allowed to change the number of days in the other months, which still follow the alternation of the normal 12.

These are the main features of the Jewish calendar, which must be considered permanent because as a Jewish law it cannot be altered except by a Great Sanhedrin.

The Jewish day begins between sunset and nightfall. The time used is that of the meridian of Jerusalem, which is 2h 21m in advance of Greenwich Mean Time. Rules for the beginning of sabbaths and festivals were laid down for the latitude of London in the 18th century and hours for nightfall are fixed annually by the Chief Rabbi.

JEWISH CALENDAR 5772–73
AM 5772 is a regular common year of 12 months, 51 sabbaths and 354 days. AM 5773 is a minimal common year of 12 months, 50 sabbaths and 353 days.

Month (length)	AM 5772	AM 5773
Tishri 1 (30)	29 September 2011	17 September 2012
Marcheshvan 1 (29)	29 October	17 October
Kislev 1 (30/29)	27 November	15 November
Tebet 1 (29)	27 December	14 December
Shebat 1 (30)	25 January 2012	12 January 2013
*Adar 1 (29)	24 February	
Nisan 1 (30)	24 March	
Iyar 1 (29)	23 April	
Sivan 1 (30)	22 May	
Tammuz 1 (29)	21 June	
Ab 1 (30)	20 July	
Elul 1 (29)	19 August	

* Known as Adar Rishon in leap years

JEWISH FASTS AND FESTIVALS
For dates of principal festivals in 2012, *see* page 9.

Tishri 1–2	Rosh Hashanah (New Year)
Tishri 3	*Fast of Gedaliah
Tishri 10	Yom Kippur (Day of Atonement)
Tishri 15–21	Succoth (Feast of Tabernacles)
Tishri 21	Hoshana Rabba
Tishri 22	Shemini Atseret (Solemn Assembly)
Tishri 23	Simchat Torah (Rejoicing of the Law)
Kislev 25	Hanukkah (Dedication of the Temple) begins
Tebet 10	Fast of Tebet
†Adar 13	§Fast of Esther
†Adar 14	Purim
†Adar 15	Shushan Purim
Nisan 15–22	Pesach (Passover)
Sivan 6–7	Shavuoth (Feast of Weeks)
Tammuz 17	*Fast of Tammuz
Ab 9	*Fast of Ab

* If these dates fall on the sabbath the fast is kept on the following day
† Adar Sheni in leap years
§ This fast is observed on Adar 11 (or Adar Sheni 11 in leap years) if Adar 13 falls on a sabbath

MUSLIM CALENDAR

The Muslim era is dated from the *Hijrah,* or flight of the Prophet Muhammad from Mecca to Medina, the corresponding date of which in the Julian calendar is 16 July AD 622. The lunar *hijri* calendar is used principally in Iran, Egypt, Malaysia, Pakistan, Mauritania, various Arab states and certain parts of India. Iran uses the solar hijri calendar as well as the lunar hijri calendar. The dating system was adopted about AD 639, commencing with the first day of the month Muharram.

The lunar calendar consists of 12 months of either 30 or 29 days, with the intercalation of one day at the end of the 12th month at stated intervals in each cycle of 30 years. The object of the intercalation is to reconcile the date of the first day of the month with the date of the actual new moon.

Some adherents still take the date of the evening of the first physical sighting of the crescent of the new moon as that of the first of the month. If cloud obscures the moon the present month may be extended to 30 days, after which the new month will begin automatically regardless of whether the moon has been seen. (Under religious law a month must have less than 31 days.) This means that the beginning of a new month and the date of religious festivals can vary from the published calendars.

In each cycle of 30 years, 19 years are common and contain 354 days, and 11 years are intercalary (leap years) of 355 days, the latter being called *kabish.* The mean length of the Hijrah years is 354 days 8 hours 48 minutes and the period of mean lunation is 29 days 12 hours 44 minutes.

To ascertain if a year is common or kabish, divide it by 30: the quotient gives the number of completed cycles and the remainder shows the place of the year in the current cycle. If the remainder is 2, 5, 7, 10, 13, 16, 18, 21, 24, 26 or 29, the year is kabish and consists of 355 days.

MUSLIM CALENDAR 1433–34
Hijrah 1433 (remainder 23) is a common year and Hijrah 1434 (remainder 24) is a kabish year. Calendar dates below are estimates based on calculations of moon phases.

Month (length)	1433 AH	1434 AH
Muharram 1	26 November	15 November
(30/29)	2011	2012
Safar 1 (29/30)	26 December	14 December
Rabi' I 1 (30/29)	24 January 2012	13 January 2013
Rabi' II 1 (30)	23 February	
Jumada I 1 (29)	24 March	
Jumada II 1 (30)	22 April	
Rajab 1 (30)	22 May	
Sha'ban 1 (29)	21 June	
Ramadan 1 (30)	20 July	
Shawwal 1 (29)	19 August	
Dhu'l Qa'da 1 (30)	17 September	
Dhu'l Hijjah 1 (29)	17 October	

MUSLIM FESTIVALS
Ramadan is a month of fasting for all Muslims because it is the month in which the revelation of the *Qur'an* (Koran) began. During Ramadan, Muslims abstain from food, drink and sexual pleasure from dawn until after sunset throughout the month.

The two major festivals are *Eid ul-Fitr* and *Eid ul-Adha.* Eid ul-Fitr marks the end of the Ramadan fast and is celebrated on the day after the sighting of the new moon of the following month. Eid ul-Adha, the festival of

sacrifice (also known as the great festival), celebrates the submission of the Prophet Ibrahim (Abraham) to God. Eid ul-Adha falls on the tenth day of Dhu'l-Hijjah, coinciding with the day when those on *hajj* (pilgrimage to Mecca) sacrifice animals.

Other days accorded special recognition are:

Muharram 1	New Year's Day
Muharram 10	Ashura (the day Prophet Noah left the Ark and Prophet Moses was saved from Pharoah (Sunni), the death of the Prophet's grandson Husain (Shi'ite))
Rabi'u-l-Awwal (Rabi' I) 12	Mawlid ul-Nabi (birthday of the Prophet Muhammad)
Rajab 27	Laylat ul-Isra' wa'l-Mi'raj (The Night of Journey and Ascension)
Ramadan *	Laylat ul-Qadr (Night of Power)
Dhu'l-Hijjah 10	Eid ul-Adha (Festival of Sacrifice)
* Moveable feast	

For dates of the major celebrations in 2012, *see* page 9.

SIKH CALENDAR

The Sikh calendar is a lunar calendar of 365 days divided into 12 months. The length of the months varies between 29 and 32 days.

There are no prescribed feast days and no fasting periods. The main celebrations are Baisakhi Mela (the new year and the anniversary of the founding of the Khalsa), Diwali Mela (festival of light), Hola Mohalla Mela (a spring festival held in the Punjab), and the Gurpurbs (anniversaries associated with the ten Gurus).

For dates of the major celebrations in 2012, *see* page 9.

THAI CALENDAR

Thailand adopted the Suriyakati calendar, a modified version of the Gregorian calendar, during the reign of King Rama V in 1888, using 1 April as the first day of the year. In 1940 the date of the new year was changed to 1 January. The years are counted from the beginning of the Buddhist era (BE), which is calculated to have commenced upon the death of the Lord Buddha, taken to have occurred in 543 BC, so AD 2012 is BE 2555. The Chinese system of associating years with one of twelve animals is also in use in Thailand. The Chantarakati lunar calendar is used to determine religious holidays; the new year begins on the first day of the waxing moon in November or, if there is a leap month, in December.

CIVIL AND LEGAL CALENDAR

THE HISTORICAL YEAR
Before 1752, two calendar systems were used in England. The civil or legal year began on 25 March and the historical year on 1 January. Thus the civil or legal date 24 March 1658 was the same day as the historical date 24 March 1659; a date in that portion of the year is written as 24 March 1658/9, the earlier date showing the civil or legal year.

THE NEW YEAR
In England in the seventh century, and as late as the 13th, the year was reckoned from Christmas Day, but in the 12th century the Church in England began the year with the feast of the Annunciation of the Blessed Virgin ('Lady

Day') on 25 March, and this practice was adopted generally in the 14th century. The civil or legal year in the British dominions (exclusive of Scotland) began with Lady Day until 1751. But in and since 1752 the civil year has begun with 1 January. New Year's Day in Scotland was changed from 25 March to 1 January in 1600.

Elsewhere in Europe, 1 January was adopted as the first day of the year by Venice in 1522, German states in 1544, Spain, Portugal and the Roman Catholic Netherlands in 1556, Prussia, Denmark and Sweden in 1559, France in 1564, Lorraine in 1579, the Protestant Netherlands in 1583, Russia in 1725, and Tuscany in 1751.

REGNAL YEARS

Regnal years are the years of a sovereign's reign and each begins on the anniversary of his or her accession, eg regnal year 61 of the present queen begins on 6 February 2012.

The system was used for dating Acts of Parliament until 1962. The Summer Time Act 1925, for example, is quoted as 15 and 16 Geo. V c. 64, because it became law in the parliamentary session which extended over part of both of these regnal years. Acts of a parliamentary session during which a sovereign died were usually given two year numbers, the regnal year of the deceased sovereign and the regnal year of his or her successor, eg those passed in 1952 were dated 16 Geo. VI and 1 Elizabeth II. Since 1962 Acts of Parliament have been dated by the calendar year.

QUARTER AND TERM DAYS

Holy days and saints days were the usual means in early times for setting the dates of future and recurrent appointments. The quarter days in England and Wales are the feast of the Nativity (25 December), the feast of the Annunciation (25 March), the feast of St John the Baptist (24 June) and the feast of St Michael and All Angels (29 September).

The term days in Scotland are Candlemas (the feast of the Purification), Whitsunday, Lammas (Loaf Mass) and Martinmas (St Martin's Day). These fell on 2 February, 15 May, 1 August and 11 November respectively. However, by the Term and Quarter Days (Scotland) Act 1990, the dates of the term days were changed to 28 February (Candlemas), 28 May (Whitsunday), 28 August (Lammas) and 28 November (Martinmas).

RED-LETTER DAYS

Red-letter days were originally the holy days and saints days indicated in early ecclesiastical calendars by letters printed in red ink. The days to be distinguished in this way were approved at the Council of Nicaea in AD 325.

These days still have a legal significance, as judges of the Queen's Bench Division wear scarlet robes on red-letter days falling during the law sittings. The days designated as red-letter days for this purpose are:

Holy and saints days
The Conversion of St Paul, the Purification, Ash Wednesday, the Annunciation, the Ascension, the feasts of St Mark, SS Philip and James, St Matthias, St Barnabas, St John the Baptist, St Peter, St Thomas, St James, St Luke, SS Simon and Jude, All Saints, St Andrew.

Civil calendar (for dates, see page 9)
The anniversaries of the Queen's accession, the Queen's birthday and the Queen's coronation, the Queen's official birthday, the birthday of the Duke of Edinburgh, the birthday of the Prince of Wales, St David's Day and Lord Mayor's Day.

PUBLIC HOLIDAYS

Public holidays are divided into two categories, common law and statutory. Common law holidays are holidays 'by habit and custom'; in England, Wales and Northern Ireland these are Good Friday and Christmas Day.

Statutory public holidays, known as bank holidays, were first established by the Bank Holidays Act 1871. They were, literally, days on which the banks (and other public institutions) were closed and financial obligations due on that day were payable the following day. The legislation currently governing public holidays in the UK, which is the Banking and Financial Dealings Act 1971, stipulates the days that are to be public holidays in England, Wales, Scotland and Northern Ireland.

If a public holiday falls on a Saturday or a Sunday then another day will be given in lieu, usually the following Monday. For example, Christmas Day 2011 falls on a Sunday, so Monday 26 December is a 'substitute' holiday. For dates of public holidays in 2012 and 2013, see pages 10–11. The public holidays are:

England and Wales
*New Year's Day
Good Friday
Easter Monday
*The first Monday in May
The last Monday in May
†The Queen's Diamond Jubilee
The last Monday in August
Christmas Day
Boxing Day

Scotland
New Year's Day
*2 January
Good Friday
The first Monday in May
*The last Monday in May
†The Queen's Diamond Jubilee
The first Monday in August
‡St Andrew's Day
Christmas Day
Boxing Day

Northern Ireland
*New Year's Day
Good Friday
17 March
Easter Monday
*The first Monday in May
The last Monday in May
†The Queen's Diamond Jubilee
§12 July
The last Monday in August
Christmas Day
Boxing Day

* Granted annually by royal proclamation
† 2012 only
‡ Voluntary public holiday in exchange for an existing local holiday
§ Subject to proclamation by the Secretary of State for Northern Ireland

CHRONOLOGICAL CYCLES AND ERAS

SOLAR (OR MAJOR) CYCLE
The solar cycle is a period of 28 years; in any corresponding year of each cycle the days of the week recur on the same day of the month.

METONIC (LUNAR, OR MINOR) CYCLE
In 432 BC, Meton, an Athenian astronomer, found that 235 lunations are very nearly, though not exactly, equal in duration to 19 solar years and so after 19 years the phases of the Moon recur approximately on the same days of the month. The dates of full moon in a cycle of 19 years were inscribed in figures of gold on public monuments in Athens, and the number showing the position of a year in the cycle is called the golden number of that year.

JULIAN PERIOD
The Julian period was proposed by Joseph Scaliger in 1582. The period is 7,980 Julian years, and its first year coincides with the year 4713 BC. The figure of 7,980 is the product of the number of years in the solar cycle, the Metonic cycle and the cycle of the Roman indiction (28 × 19 × 15).

ROMAN INDICTION
The Roman indiction is a period of 15 years, instituted for fiscal purposes about AD 300.

EPACT
The epact is the age of the calendar Moon, diminished by one day, on 1 January, in the ecclesiastical lunar calendar.

CHINESE CALENDAR
A lunar calendar was the sole calendar in use in China until 1911, when the government adopted the new (Gregorian) calendar for official and most business activities. The Chinese tend to follow both calendars, the lunar calendar playing an important part in personal life, eg birth celebrations, festivals, marriages; and in rural villages the lunar calendar dictates the cycle of activities, denoting the change of weather and farming activities.

The lunar calendar is used in Hong Kong, Singapore, Malaysia, Tibet and elsewhere in south-east Asia. The calendar has a cycle of 60 years. The new year begins at the first new moon after the sun enters the sign of Aquarius, ie the new year falls between 21 January and 19 February in the Gregorian calendar.

Each year in the Chinese calendar is associated with one of 12 animals: the rat, the ox, the tiger, the rabbit, the dragon, the snake, the horse, the goat or sheep, the monkey, the chicken or rooster, the dog, and the pig.

The date of the Chinese new year and the astrological sign for the years 2012–15 are:

2012	23 January	Dragon
2013	10 February	Snake
2014	31 January	Horse
2015	19 February	Goat or Sheep

COPTIC CALENDAR
In the Coptic calendar, which is used in parts of Egypt and Ethiopia, the year is made up of 12 months of 30 days each, followed, in general, by five complementary days. Every fourth year is an intercalary or leap year and in these years there are six complementary days. The intercalary year of the Coptic calendar immediately precedes the leap year of the Julian calendar. The era is that of Diocletian or the Martyrs, the origin of which is fixed at 29 August AD 284 (Julian date).

INDIAN ERAS
In addition to the Muslim reckoning, other eras are used in India. The Saka era of southern India, dating from 3 March AD 78, was declared the national calendar of the Republic of India with effect from 22 March 1957, to be used concurrently with the Gregorian calendar. As revised, the year of the new Saka era begins at the spring equinox, with five successive months of 31 days and seven of 30 days in ordinary years, and six months of each length in leap years. The year AD 2012 is 1934 of the revised Saka era.

The year AD 2012 corresponds to the following years in other eras:

Year 2069 of the Vikram Samvat era
Year 1419 of the Bengali San era
Year 1188 of the Kollam era
Year 5113 of the Kaliyuga era
Year 2555 of the Buddha Nirvana era

JAPANESE CALENDAR
The Japanese calendar is essentially the same as the Gregorian calendar, the years, months and weeks being of the same length and beginning on the same days as those of the Gregorian calendar. The numeration of the years is different, based on a system of epochs or periods, each of which begins at the accession of an emperor or other important occurrence. The method is not unlike the British system of regnal years, except that each year of a period closes on 31 December. The Japanese chronology begins about AD 650 and the three latest epochs are defined by the reigns of emperors, whose actual names are not necessarily used:

Epoch
Taisho – 1 August 1912 to 25 December 1926
Showa – 26 December 1926 to 7 January 1989
Heisei – 8 January 1989

The year Heisei 24 begins on 1 January 2012.

The months are known as First Month, Second Month, etc, First Month being equivalent to January. The days of the week are Nichiyobi (Sun-day), Getsuyobi (Moon-day), Kayobi (Fire-day), Suiyobi (Water-day), Mokuyobi (Wood-day), Kinyobi (Metal-day) and Doyobi (Earth-day).

THE MASONIC YEAR
Two dates are quoted in warrants, dispensations, etc, issued by the United Grand Lodge of England, those for the current year being expressed as *Anno Domini* 2012 – *Anno Lucis* 6012. This *Anno Lucis* (year of light) is based on the Book of Genesis 1:3, the 4,000-year difference being derived, in modified form, from *Ussher's Notation*, published in 1654, which places the Creation of the World in 4004 BC.

OLYMPIADS
Ancient Greek chronology was reckoned in Olympiads, cycles of four years corresponding with the periodic Olympic Games held on the plain of Olympia, in Elis, once every four years. The intervening years were the first, second, etc, of the Olympiad, which received the name of the victor at the Games. The first recorded Olympiad is that of Choroebus, 776 BC.

ZOROASTRIAN CALENDAR
Zoroastrians, followers of the Iranian prophet Zarathushtra (known to the Greeks as Zoroaster) are mostly to be found in Iran and in India, where they are known as Parsees.

The Zoroastrian era dates from the coronation of the last Zoroastrian Sasanian king in AD 631. The Zoroastrian calendar is divided into 12 months, each comprising 30 days, followed by five holy days of the Gathas at the end of each year to make the year consist of 365 days.

In order to synchronise the calendar with the solar year of 365 days, an extra month was intercalated once every 120 years. However, this intercalation ceased in the 12th century and the new year, which had fallen in the spring, slipped back to August. Because intercalation ceased at different times in Iran and India, there was one month's difference between the calendar followed in Iran (Kadmi calendar) and that followed by the Parsees (Shenshai calendar). In 1906 a group of Zoroastrians decided to bring the calendar back in line with the seasons again and restore the new year to 21 March each year (Fasli calendar).

The Shenshai calendar (new year in August) is mainly used by Parsees. The Fasli calendar (new year, 21 March) is mainly used by Zoroastrians living in Iran, in the Indian subcontinent, or away from Iran.

ROMAN CALENDAR

Roman historians adopted as an epoch the foundation of Rome, which is believed to have happened in the year 753 BC. The ordinal number of the years in Roman reckoning is followed by the letters AUC (ab urbe condita), so that the year 2012 is 2765 AUC (MMDCCLXV). The calendar that we know has developed from one said to have been established by Romulus using a year of 304 days divided into ten months, beginning with March. To this Numa added January and February, making the year consist of 12 months of 30 and 29 days alternately, with an additional day so that the total was 355. It is also said that Numa ordered an intercalary month of 22 or 23 days in alternate years, making 90 days in eight years, to be inserted after 23 February.

However, there is some doubt as to the origination and the details of the intercalation in the Roman calendar. It is certain that some scheme of this kind was inaugurated and not fully carried out, for in the year 46 BC Julius Caesar found that the calendar had been allowed to fall into some confusion. He sought the help of the Egyptian astronomer Sosigenes, which led to the construction and adoption (45 BC) of the Julian calendar, and, by a slight alteration, to the Gregorian calendar now in use. The year 46 BC was made to consist of 445 days and is called the Year of Confusion.

In the Roman (Julian) calendar the days of the month were counted backwards from three fixed points, or days, and an intervening day was said to be so many days before the next coming point, the first and last being counted. These three points were the Kalends, the Nones, and the Ides. Their positions in the months and the method of counting from them will be seen in the table below. The year containing 366 days was called bissextilis annus, as it had a doubled sixth day (bissextus dies) before the March Kalends on 24 February – ante diem sextum Kalendas Martias, or a.d. VI Kal. Mart.

Present days of the month	March, May, July, October have thirty-one days	January, August, December have thirty-one days		April, June, September, November have thirty days		February has twenty-eight days, and in leap year twenty-nine	
1	Kalendis	Kalendis		Kalendis		Kalendis	
2	VI	IV ⎱ ante		IV ⎱ ante		IV ⎱ ante	
3	V ⎱ ante	III ⎰ Nonas		III ⎰ Nonas		III ⎰ Nonas	
4	IV ⎰ Nonas	pridie Nonas		pridie Nonas		pridie Nonas	
5	III ⎰	Nonis		Nonis		Nonis	
6	pridie Nonas	VIII		VIII		VIII	
7	Nonis	VII		VII		VII	
8	VIII	VI ⎱ ante		VI ⎱ ante		VI ⎱ ante	
9	VII	V ⎰ Idus		V ⎰ Idus		V ⎰ Idus	
10	VI ⎱ ante	IV		IV		IV	
11	V ⎰ Idus	III		III		III	
12	IV	pridie Idus		pridie Idus		pridie Idus	
13	III	Idibus		Idibus		Idibus	
14	pridie Idus	XIX		XVIII		XVI	
15	Idibus	XVIII		XVII		XV	
16	XVII	XVII		XVI		XIV	
17	XVI	XVI		XV		XIII	
18	XV	XV		XIV		XII	
19	XIV	XIV		XIII		XI	
20	XIII	XIII		XII	ante Kalendas	X	ante Kalendas
21	XII	XII	ante Kalendas	XI	(of the month	IX	Martias
22	XI	ante Kalendas	XI	(of the month	X	following)	VIII	
23	X	(of the month	X	following)	IX		VII	
24	IX	following)	IX		VIII		*VI	
25	VIII	VIII		VII		V	
26	VII	VII		VI		IV	
27	VI	VI		V		III	
28	V	V		IV		pridie Kalendas	
29	IV	IV		III		Martias	
30	III	III		pridie Kalendas			
31	pridie Kalendas (Aprilis, Iunias, Sextilis, Novembris)	pridie Kalendas (Februarias, Septembris, Ianuarias)		(Maias, Quinctilis, Octobris, Decembris)			

* Repeated in leap year

CALENDAR FOR ANY YEAR 1780–2040

To select the correct calendar for any year between 1780 and 2040, consult the index below
*leap year

1780 N*	1813 K	1846 I	1879 G	1912 D*	1945 C	1978 A	2011 M
1781 C	1814 M	1847 K	1880 J*	1913 G	1946 E	1979 C	2012 B*
1782 E	1815 A	1848 N*	1881 M	1914 I	1947 G	1980 F*	2013 E
1783 G	1816 D*	1849 C	1882 A	1915 K	1948 J*	1981 I	2014 G
1784 J*	1817 G	1850 E	1883 C	1916 N*	1949 M	1982 K	2015 I
1785 M	1818 I	1851 G	1884 F*	1917 C	1950 A	1983 M	2016 L*
1786 A	1819 K	1852 J*	1885 I	1918 E	1951 C	1984 B*	2017 A
1787 C	1820 N*	1853 M	1886 K	1919 G	1952 F*	1985 E	2018 C
1788 F*	1821 C	1854 A	1887 M	1920 J*	1953 I	1986 G	2019 E
1789 I	1822 E	1855 C	1888 B*	1921 M	1954 K	1987 I	2020 H*
1790 K	1823 G	1856 F*	1889 E	1922 A	1955 M	1988 L*	2021 K
1791 M	1824 J*	1857 I	1890 G	1923 C	1956 B*	1989 A	2022 M
1792 B*	1825 M	1858 K	1891 I	1924 F*	1957 E	1990 C	2023 A
1793 E	1826 A	1859 M	1892 L*	1925 I	1958 G	1991 E	2024 D*
1794 G	1827 C	1860 B*	1893 A	1926 K	1959 I	1992 H*	2025 G
1795 I	1828 F*	1861 E	1894 C	1927 M	1960 L*	1993 K	2026 I
1796 L*	1829 I	1862 G	1895 E	1928 B*	1961 A	1994 M	2027 K
1797 A	1830 K	1863 I	1896 H*	1929 E	1962 C	1995 A	2028 N*
1798 C	1831 M	1864 L*	1897 K	1930 G	1963 E	1996 D*	2029 C
1799 E	1832 B*	1865 A	1898 M	1931 I	1964 H*	1997 G	2030 E
1800 G	1833 E	1866 C	1899 A	1932 L*	1965 K	1998 I	2031 G
1801 I	1834 G	1867 E	1900 C	1933 A	1966 M	1999 K	2032 J*
1802 K	1835 I	1868 H*	1901 E	1934 C	1967 A	2000 N*	2033 M
1803 M	1836 L*	1869 K	1902 G	1935 E	1968 D*	2001 C	2034 A
1804 B*	1837 A	1870 M	1903 I	1936 H*	1969 G	2002 E	2035 C
1805 E	1838 C	1871 A	1904 L*	1937 K	1970 I	2003 G	2036 F*
1806 G	1839 E	1872 D*	1905 A	1938 M	1971 K	2004 J*	2037 I
1807 I	1840 H*	1873 G	1906 C	1939 A	1972 N*	2005 M	2038 K
1808 L*	1841 K	1874 I	1907 E	1940 D*	1973 C	2006 A	2039 M
1809 A	1842 M	1875 K	1908 H*	1941 G	1974 E	2007 C	2040 B*
1810 C	1843 A	1876 N*	1909 K	1942 I	1975 G	2008 F*	
1811 E	1844 D*	1877 C	1910 M	1943 K	1976 J*	2009 I	
1812 H*	1845 G	1878 E	1911 A	1944 N*	1977 M	2010 K	

A

	January	February	March
Sun.	1 8 15 22 29	5 12 19 26	5 12 19 26
Mon.	2 9 16 23 30	6 13 20 27	6 13 20 27
Tue.	3 10 17 24 31	7 14 21 28	7 14 21 28
Wed.	4 11 18 25	1 8 15 22	1 8 15 22 29
Thur.	5 12 19 26	2 9 16 23	2 9 16 23 30
Fri.	6 13 20 27	3 10 17 24	3 10 17 24 31
Sat.	7 14 21 28	4 11 18 25	4 11 18 25

	April	May	June
Sun.	2 9 16 23 30	7 14 21 28	4 11 18 25
Mon.	3 10 17 24	1 8 15 22 29	5 12 19 26
Tue.	4 11 18 25	2 9 16 23 30	6 13 20 27
Wed.	5 12 19 26	3 10 17 24 31	7 14 21 28
Thur.	6 13 20 27	4 11 18 25	1 8 15 22 29
Fri.	7 14 21 28	5 12 19 26	2 9 16 23 30
Sat.	1 8 15 22 29	6 13 20 27	3 10 17 24

	July	August	September
Sun.	2 9 16 23 30	6 13 20 27	3 10 17 24
Mon.	3 10 17 24 31	7 14 21 28	4 11 18 25
Tue.	4 11 18 25	1 8 15 22 29	5 12 19 26
Wed.	5 12 19 26	2 9 16 23 30	6 13 20 27
Thur.	6 13 20 27	3 10 17 24 31	7 14 21 28
Fri.	7 14 21 28	4 11 18 25	1 8 15 22 29
Sat.	1 8 15 22 29	5 12 19 26	2 9 16 23 30

	October	November	December
Sun.	1 8 15 22 29	5 12 19 26	3 10 17 24 31
Mon.	2 9 16 23 30	6 13 20 27	4 11 18 25
Tue.	3 10 17 24 31	7 14 21 28	5 12 19 26
Wed.	4 11 18 25	1 8 15 22 29	6 13 20 27
Thur.	5 12 19 26	2 9 16 23 30	7 14 21 28
Fri.	6 13 20 27	3 10 17 24	1 8 15 22 29
Sat.	7 14 21 28	4 11 18 25	2 9 16 23 30

EASTER DAYS

March 26	1815, 1826, 1837, 1967, 1978, 1989
April 2	1809, 1893, 1899, 1961
April 9	1871, 1882, 1939, 1950, 2023, 2034
April 16	1786, 1797, 1843, 1854, 1865, 1911
	1922, 1933, 1995, 2006, 2017
April 23	1905

B (LEAP YEAR)

	January	February	March
Sun.	1 8 15 22 29	5 12 19 26	4 11 18 25
Mon.	2 9 16 23 30	6 13 20 27	5 12 19 26
Tue.	3 10 17 24 31	7 14 21 28	6 13 20 27
Wed.	4 11 18 25	1 8 15 22 29	7 14 21 28
Thur.	5 12 19 26	2 9 16 23	1 8 15 22 29
Fri.	6 13 20 27	3 10 17 24	2 9 16 23 30
Sat.	7 14 21 28	4 11 18 25	3 10 17 24 31

	April	May	June
Sun.	1 8 15 22 29	6 13 20 27	3 10 17 24
Mon.	2 9 16 23 30	7 14 21 28	4 11 18 25
Tue.	3 10 17 24	1 8 15 22 29	5 12 19 26
Wed.	4 11 18 25	2 9 16 23 30	6 13 20 27
Thur.	5 12 19 26	3 10 17 24 31	7 14 21 28
Fri.	6 13 20 27	4 11 18 25	1 8 15 22 29
Sat.	7 14 21 28	5 12 19 26	2 9 16 23 30

	July	August	September
Sun.	1 8 15 22 29	5 12 19 26	2 9 16 23 30
Mon.	2 9 16 23 30	6 13 20 27	3 10 17 24
Tue.	3 10 17 24 31	7 14 21 28	4 11 18 25
Wed.	4 11 18 25	1 8 15 22 29	5 12 19 26
Thur.	5 12 19 26	2 9 16 23 30	6 13 20 27
Fri.	6 13 20 27	3 10 17 24 31	7 14 21 28
Sat.	7 14 21 28	4 11 18 25	1 8 15 22 29

	October	November	December
Sun.	7 14 21 28	4 11 18 25	2 9 16 23 30
Mon.	1 8 15 22 29	5 12 19 26	3 10 17 24 31
Tue.	2 9 16 23 30	6 13 20 27	4 11 18 25
Wed.	3 10 17 24 31	7 14 21 28	5 12 19 26
Thur.	4 11 18 25	1 8 15 22 29	6 13 20 27
Fri.	5 12 19 26	2 9 16 23 30	7 14 21 28
Sat.	6 13 20 27	3 10 17 24	1 8 15 22 29

EASTER DAYS

April 1	1804, 1888, 1956, 2040
April 8	1792, 1860, 1928, 2012
April 22	1832, 1984

C

	January	February	March
Sun.	7 14 21 28	4 11 18 25	4 11 18 25
Mon.	1 8 15 22 29	5 12 19 26	5 12 19 26
Tue.	2 9 16 23 30	6 13 20 27	6 13 20 27
Wed.	3 10 17 24 31	7 14 21 28	7 14 21 28
Thur.	4 11 18 25	1 8 15 22	1 8 15 22 29
Fri.	5 12 19 26	2 9 16 23	2 9 16 23 30
Sat.	6 13 20 27	3 10 17 24	3 10 17 24 31

	April	May	June
Sun.	1 8 15 22 29	6 13 20 27	3 10 17 24
Mon.	2 9 16 23 30	7 14 21 28	4 11 18 25
Tue.	3 10 17 24	1 8 15 22 29	5 12 19 26
Wed.	4 11 18 25	2 9 16 23 30	6 13 20 27
Thur.	5 12 19 26	3 10 17 24 31	7 14 21 28
Fri.	6 13 20 27	4 11 18 25	1 8 15 22 29
Sat.	7 14 21 28	5 12 19 26	2 9 16 23 30

	July	August	September
Sun.	1 8 15 22 29	5 12 19 26	2 9 16 23 30
Mon.	2 9 16 23 30	6 13 20 27	3 10 17 24
Tue.	3 10 17 24 31	7 14 21 28	4 11 18 25
Wed.	4 11 18 25	1 8 15 22 29	5 12 19 26
Thur.	5 12 19 26	2 9 16 23 30	6 13 20 27
Fri.	6 13 20 27	3 10 17 24 31	7 14 21 28
Sat.	7 14 21 28	4 11 18 25	1 8 15 22 29

	October	November	December
Sun.	7 14 21 28	4 11 18 25	2 9 16 23 30
Mon.	1 8 15 22 29	5 12 19 26	3 10 17 24 31
Tue.	2 9 16 23 30	6 13 20 27	4 11 18 25
Wed.	3 10 17 24 31	7 14 21 28	5 12 19 26
Thur.	4 11 18 25	1 8 15 22 29	6 13 20 27
Fri.	5 12 19 26	2 9 16 23 30	7 14 21 28
Sat.	6 13 20 27	3 10 17 24	1 8 15 22 29

EASTER DAYS
March 25   1883, 1894, 1951, 2035
April 1   1866, 1877, 1923, 1934, 1945, 2018, 2029
April 8   1787, 1798, 1849, 1855, 1917, 2007
April 15   1781, 1827, 1838, 1900, 1906, 1979, 1990, 2001
April 22   1810, 1821, 1962, 1973

D (LEAP YEAR)

	January	February	March
Sun.	7 14 21 28	4 11 18 25	3 10 17 24 31
Mon.	1 8 15 22 29	5 12 19 26	4 11 18 25
Tue.	2 9 16 23 30	6 13 20 27	5 12 19 26
Wed.	3 10 17 24 31	7 14 21 28	6 13 20 27
Thur.	4 11 18 25	1 8 15 22 29	7 14 21 28
Fri.	5 12 19 26	2 9 16 23	1 8 15 22 29
Sat.	6 13 20 27	3 10 17 24	2 9 16 23 30

	April	May	June
Sun.	7 14 21 28	5 12 19 26	2 9 16 23 30
Mon.	1 8 15 22 29	6 13 20 27	3 10 17 24
Tue.	2 9 16 23 30	7 14 21 28	4 11 18 25
Wed.	3 10 17 24	1 8 15 22 29	5 12 19 26
Thur.	4 11 18 25	2 9 16 23 30	6 13 20 27
Fri.	5 12 19 26	3 10 17 24 31	7 14 21 28
Sat.	6 13 20 27	4 11 18 25	1 8 15 22 29

	July	August	September
Sun.	7 14 21 28	4 11 18 25	1 8 15 22 29
Mon.	1 8 15 22 29	5 12 19 26	2 9 16 23 30
Tue.	2 9 16 23 30	6 13 20 27	3 10 17 24
Wed.	3 10 17 24 31	7 14 21 28	4 11 18 25
Thur.	4 11 18 25	1 8 15 22 29	5 12 19 26
Fri.	5 12 19 26	2 9 16 23 30	6 13 20 27
Sat.	6 13 20 27	3 10 17 24 31	7 14 21 28

	October	November	December
Sun.	6 13 20 27	3 10 17 24	1 8 15 22 29
Mon.	7 14 21 28	4 11 18 25	2 9 16 23 30
Tue.	1 8 15 22 29	5 12 19 26	3 10 17 24 31
Wed.	2 9 16 23 30	6 13 20 27	4 11 18 25
Thur.	3 10 17 24 31	7 14 21 28	5 12 19 26
Fri.	4 11 18 25	1 8 15 22 29	6 13 20 27
Sat.	5 12 19 26	2 9 16 23 30	7 14 21 28

EASTER DAYS
March 24   1940
March 31   1872, 2024
April 7   1844, 1912, 1996
April 14   1816, 1968

E

	January	February	March
Sun.	6 13 20 27	3 10 17 24	3 10 17 24 31
Mon.	7 14 21 28	4 11 18 25	4 11 18 25
Tue.	1 8 15 22 29	5 12 19 26	5 12 19 26
Wed.	2 9 16 23 30	6 13 20 27	6 13 20 27
Thur.	3 10 17 24 31	7 14 21 28	7 14 21 28
Fri.	4 11 18 25	1 8 15 22	1 8 15 22 29
Sat.	5 12 19 26	2 9 16 23	2 9 16 23 30

	April	May	June
Sun.	7 14 21 28	5 12 19 26	2 9 16 23 30
Mon.	1 8 15 22 29	6 13 20 27	3 10 17 24
Tue.	2 9 16 23 30	7 14 21 28	4 11 18 25
Wed.	3 10 17 24	1 8 15 22 29	5 12 19 26
Thur.	4 11 18 25	2 9 16 23 30	6 13 20 27
Fri.	5 12 19 26	3 10 17 24 31	7 14 21 28
Sat.	6 13 20 27	4 11 18 25	1 8 15 22 29

	July	August	September
Sun.	7 14 21 28	4 11 18 25	1 8 15 22 29
Mon.	1 8 15 22 29	5 12 19 26	2 9 16 23 30
Tue.	2 9 16 23 30	6 13 20 27	3 10 17 24
Wed.	3 10 17 24 31	7 14 21 28	4 11 18 25
Thur.	4 11 18 25	1 8 15 22 29	5 12 19 26
Fri.	5 12 19 26	2 9 16 23 30	6 13 20 27
Sat.	6 13 20 27	3 10 17 24 31	7 14 21 28

	October	November	December
Sun.	6 13 20 27	3 10 17 24	1 8 15 22 29
Mon.	7 14 21 28	4 11 18 25	2 9 16 23 30
Tue.	1 8 15 22 29	5 12 19 26	3 10 17 24 31
Wed.	2 9 16 23 30	6 13 20 27	4 11 18 25
Thur.	3 10 17 24 31	7 14 21 28	5 12 19 26
Fri.	4 11 18 25	1 8 15 22 29	6 13 20 27
Sat.	5 12 19 26	2 9 16 23 30	7 14 21 28

EASTER DAYS
March 24   1799
March 31   1782, 1793, 1839, 1850, 1861, 1907
            1918, 1929, 1991, 2002, 2013
April 7   1822, 1833, 1901, 1985
April 14   1805, 1811, 1895, 1963, 1974
April 21   1867, 1878, 1889, 1935, 1946, 1957, 2019, 2030

F (LEAP YEAR)

	January	February	March
Sun.	6 13 20 27	3 10 17 24	2 9 16 23 30
Mon.	7 14 21 28	4 11 18 25	3 10 17 24 31
Tue.	1 8 15 22 29	5 12 19 26	4 11 18 25
Wed.	2 9 16 23 30	6 13 20 27	5 12 19 26
Thur.	3 10 17 24 31	7 14 21 28	6 13 20 27
Fri.	4 11 18 25	1 8 15 22 29	7 14 21 28
Sat.	5 12 19 26	2 9 16 23	1 8 15 22 29

	April	May	June
Sun.	6 13 20 27	4 11 18 25	1 8 15 22 29
Mon.	7 14 21 28	5 12 19 26	2 9 16 23 30
Tue.	1 8 15 22 29	6 13 20 27	3 10 17 24
Wed.	2 9 16 23 30	7 14 21 28	4 11 18 25
Thur.	3 10 17 24	1 8 15 22 29	5 12 19 26
Fri.	4 11 18 25	2 9 16 23 30	6 13 20 27
Sat.	5 12 19 26	3 10 17 24 31	7 14 21 28

	July	August	September
Sun.	6 13 20 27	3 10 17 24 31	7 14 21 28
Mon.	7 14 21 28	4 11 18 25	1 8 15 22 29
Tue.	1 8 15 22 29	5 12 19 26	2 9 16 23 30
Wed.	2 9 16 23 30	6 13 20 27	3 10 17 24
Thur.	3 10 17 24 31	7 14 21 28	4 11 18 25
Fri.	4 11 18 25	1 8 15 22 29	5 12 19 26
Sat.	5 12 19 26	2 9 16 23 30	6 13 20 27

	October	November	December
Sun.	5 12 19 26	2 9 16 23 30	7 14 21 28
Mon.	6 13 20 27	3 10 17 24	1 8 15 22 29
Tue.	7 14 21 28	4 11 18 25	2 9 16 23 30
Wed.	1 8 15 22 29	5 12 19 26	3 10 17 24 31
Thur.	2 9 16 23 30	6 13 20 27	4 11 18 25
Fri.	3 10 17 24 31	7 14 21 28	5 12 19 26
Sat.	4 11 18 25	1 8 15 22 29	6 13 20 27

EASTER DAYS
March 23   1788, 1856, 2008
April 6   1828, 1980
April 13   1884, 1952, 2036
April 20   1924

G

	January	February	March
Sun.	5 12 19 26	2 9 16 23	2 9 16 23 30
Mon.	6 13 20 27	3 10 17 24	3 10 17 24 31
Tue.	7 14 21 28	4 11 18 25	4 11 18 25
Wed.	1 8 15 22 29	5 12 19 26	5 12 19 26
Thur.	2 9 16 23 30	6 13 20 27	6 13 20 27
Fri.	3 10 17 24 31	7 14 21 28	7 14 21 28
Sat.	4 11 18 25	1 8 15 22	1 8 15 22 29

	April	May	June
Sun.	6 13 20 27	4 11 18 25	1 8 15 22 29
Mon.	7 14 21 28	5 12 19 26	2 9 16 23 30
Tue.	1 8 15 22 29	6 13 20 27	3 10 17 24
Wed.	2 9 16 23 30	7 14 21 28	4 11 18 25
Thur.	3 10 17 24	1 8 15 22 29	5 12 19 26
Fri.	4 11 18 25	2 9 16 23 30	6 13 20 27
Sat.	5 12 19 26	3 10 17 24 31	7 14 21 28

	July	August	September
Sun.	6 13 20 27	3 10 17 24 31	7 14 21 28
Mon.	7 14 21 28	4 11 18 25	1 8 15 22 29
Tue.	1 8 15 22 29	5 12 19 26	2 9 16 23 30
Wed.	2 9 16 23 30	6 13 20 27	3 10 17 24
Thur.	3 10 17 24 31	7 14 21 28	4 11 18 25
Fri.	4 11 18 25	1 8 15 22 29	5 12 19 26
Sat.	5 12 19 26	2 9 16 23 30	6 13 20 27

	October	November	December
Sun.	5 12 19 26	2 9 16 23 30	7 14 21 28
Mon.	6 13 20 27	3 10 17 24	1 8 15 22 29
Tue.	7 14 21 28	4 11 18 25	2 9 16 23 30
Wed.	1 8 15 22 29	5 12 19 26	3 10 17 24 31
Thur.	2 9 16 23 30	6 13 20 27	4 11 18 25
Fri.	3 10 17 24 31	7 14 21 28	5 12 19 26
Sat.	4 11 18 25	1 8 15 22 29	6 13 20 27

EASTER DAYS

March 23	1845, 1913
March 30	1823, 1834, 1902, 1975, 1986, 1997
April 6	1806, 1817, 1890, 1947, 1958, 1969
April 13	1800, 1873, 1879, 1941, 2031
April 20	1783, 1794, 1851, 1862, 1919, 1930, 2003, 2014, 2025

I

	January	February	March
Sun.	4 11 18 25	1 8 15 22	1 8 15 22 29
Mon.	5 12 19 26	2 9 16 23	2 9 16 23 30
Tue.	6 13 20 27	3 10 17 24	3 10 17 24 31
Wed.	7 14 21 28	4 11 18 25	4 11 18 25
Thur.	1 8 15 22 29	5 12 19 26	5 12 19 26
Fri.	2 9 16 23 30	6 13 20 27	6 13 20 27
Sat.	3 10 17 24 31	7 14 21 28	7 14 21 28

	April	May	June
Sun.	5 12 19 26	3 10 17 24 31	7 14 21 28
Mon.	6 13 20 27	4 11 18 25	1 8 15 22 29
Tue.	7 14 21 28	5 12 19 26	2 9 16 23 30
Wed.	1 8 15 22 29	6 13 20 27	3 10 17 24
Thur.	2 9 16 23 30	7 14 21 28	4 11 18 25
Fri.	3 10 17 24	1 8 15 22 29	5 12 19 26
Sat.	4 11 18 25	2 9 16 23 30	6 13 20 27

	July	August	September
Sun.	5 12 19 26	2 9 16 23 30	6 13 20 27
Mon.	6 13 20 27	3 10 17 24 31	7 14 21 28
Tue.	7 14 21 28	4 11 18 25	1 8 15 22 29
Wed.	1 8 15 22 29	5 12 19 26	2 9 16 23 30
Thur.	2 9 16 23 30	6 13 20 27	3 10 17 24
Fri.	3 10 17 24 31	7 14 21 28	4 11 18 25
Sat.	4 11 18 25	1 8 15 22 29	5 12 19 26

	October	November	December
Sun.	4 11 18 25	1 8 15 22 29	6 13 20 27
Mon.	5 12 19 26	2 9 16 23 30	7 14 21 28
Tue.	6 13 20 27	3 10 17 24	1 8 15 22 29
Wed.	7 14 21 28	4 11 18 25	2 9 16 23 30
Thur.	1 8 15 22 29	5 12 19 26	3 10 17 24 31
Fri.	2 9 16 23 30	6 13 20 27	4 11 18 25
Sat.	3 10 17 24 31	7 14 21 28	5 12 19 26

EASTER DAYS

March 22	1818
March 29	1807, 1891, 1959, 1970
April 5	1795, 1801, 1863, 1874, 1885, 1931, 1942, 1953, 2015, 2026, 2037
April 12	1789, 1846, 1857, 1903, 1914, 1925, 1998, 2009
April 19	1829, 1835, 1981, 1987

H (LEAP YEAR)

	January	February	March
Sun.	5 12 19 26	2 9 16 23	1 8 15 22 29
Mon.	6 13 20 27	3 10 17 24	2 9 16 23 30
Tue.	7 14 21 28	4 11 18 25	3 10 17 24 31
Wed.	1 8 15 22 29	5 12 19 26	4 11 18 25
Thur.	2 9 16 23 30	6 13 20 27	5 12 19 26
Fri.	3 10 17 24 31	7 14 21 28	6 13 20 27
Sat.	4 11 18 25	1 8 15 22 29	7 14 21 28

	April	May	June
Sun.	5 12 19 26	3 10 17 24 31	7 14 21 28
Mon.	6 13 20 27	4 11 18 25	1 8 15 22 29
Tue.	7 14 21 28	5 12 19 26	2 9 16 23 30
Wed.	1 8 15 22 29	6 13 20 27	3 10 17 24
Thur.	2 9 16 23 30	7 14 21 28	4 11 18 25
Fri.	3 10 17 24	1 8 15 22 29	5 12 19 26
Sat.	4 11 18 25	2 9 16 23 30	6 13 20 27

	July	August	September
Sun.	5 12 19 26	2 9 16 23 30	6 13 20 27
Mon.	6 13 20 27	3 10 17 24 31	7 14 21 28
Tue.	7 14 21 28	4 11 18 25	1 8 15 22 29
Wed.	1 8 15 22 29	5 12 19 26	2 9 16 23 30
Thur.	2 9 16 23 30	6 13 20 27	3 10 17 24
Fri.	3 10 17 24 31	7 14 21 28	4 11 18 25
Sat.	4 11 18 25	1 8 15 22 29	5 12 19 26

	October	November	December
Sun.	4 11 18 25	1 8 15 22 29	6 13 20 27
Mon.	5 12 19 26	2 9 16 23 30	7 14 21 28
Tue.	6 13 20 27	3 10 17 24	1 8 15 22 29
Wed.	7 14 21 28	4 11 18 25	2 9 16 23 30
Thur.	1 8 15 22 29	5 12 19 26	3 10 17 24 31
Fri.	2 9 16 23 30	6 13 20 27	4 11 18 25
Sat.	3 10 17 24 31	7 14 21 28	5 12 19 26

EASTER DAYS

March 29	1812, 1964
April 5	1896
April 12	1868, 1936, 2020
April 19	1840, 1908, 1992

J (LEAP YEAR)

	January	February	March
Sun.	4 11 18 25	1 8 15 22 29	7 14 21 28
Mon.	5 12 19 26	2 9 16 23	1 8 15 22 29
Tue.	6 13 20 27	3 10 17 24	2 9 16 23 30
Wed.	7 14 21 28	4 11 18 25	3 10 17 24 31
Thur.	1 8 15 22 29	5 12 19 26	4 11 18 25
Fri.	2 9 16 23 30	6 13 20 27	5 12 19 26
Sat.	3 10 17 24 31	7 14 21 28	6 13 20 27

	April	May	June
Sun.	4 11 18 25	2 9 16 23 30	6 13 20 27
Mon.	5 12 19 26	3 10 17 24 31	7 14 21 28
Tue.	6 13 20 27	4 11 18 25	1 8 15 22 29
Wed.	7 14 21 28	5 12 19 26	2 9 16 23 30
Thur.	1 8 15 22 29	6 13 20 27	3 10 17 24
Fri.	2 9 16 23 30	7 14 21 28	4 11 18 25
Sat.	3 10 17 24	1 8 15 22 29	5 12 19 26

	July	August	September
Sun.	4 11 18 25	1 8 15 22 29	5 12 19 26
Mon.	5 12 19 26	2 9 16 23 30	6 13 20 27
Tue.	6 13 20 27	3 10 17 24 31	7 14 21 28
Wed.	7 14 21 28	4 11 18 25	1 8 15 22 29
Thur.	1 8 15 22 29	5 12 19 26	2 9 16 23 30
Fri.	2 9 16 23 30	6 13 20 27	3 10 17 24
Sat.	3 10 17 24 31	7 14 21 28	4 11 18 25

	October	November	December
Sun.	3 10 17 24 31	7 14 21 28	5 12 19 26
Mon.	4 11 18 25	1 8 15 22 29	6 13 20 27
Tue.	5 12 19 26	2 9 16 23 30	7 14 21 28
Wed.	6 13 20 27	3 10 17 24	1 8 15 22 29
Thur.	7 14 21 28	4 11 18 25	2 9 16 23 30
Fri.	1 8 15 22 29	5 12 19 26	3 10 17 24 31
Sat.	2 9 16 23 30	6 13 20 27	4 11 18 25

EASTER DAYS

March 28	1880, 1948, 2032
April 4	1920
April 11	1784, 1852, 2004
April 18	1824, 1976

K

	January	February	March	April	May	June	July	August	September	October	November	December
Sun.	3 10 17 24 31	7 14 21 28	7 14 21 28	4 11 18 25	2 9 16 23 30	6 13 20 27	4 11 18 25	1 8 15 22 29	5 12 19 26	3 10 17 24 31	7 14 21 28	5 12 19 26
Mon.	4 11 18 25	1 8 15 22	1 8 15 22 29	5 12 19 26	3 10 17 24 31	7 14 21 28	5 12 19 26	2 9 16 23 30	6 13 20 27	4 11 18 25	1 8 15 22 29	6 13 20 27
Tue.	5 12 19 26	2 9 16 23	2 9 16 23 30	6 13 20 27	4 11 18 25	1 8 15 22 29	6 13 20 27	3 10 17 24 31	7 14 21 28	5 12 19 26	2 9 16 23 30	7 14 21 28
Wed.	6 13 20 27	3 10 17 24	3 10 17 24 31	7 14 21 28	5 12 19 26	2 9 16 23 30	7 14 21 28	4 11 18 25	1 8 15 22 29	6 13 20 27	3 10 17 24	1 8 15 22 29
Thur.	7 14 21 28	4 11 18 25	4 11 18 25	1 8 15 22 29	6 13 20 27	3 10 17 24	1 8 15 22 29	5 12 19 26	2 9 16 23 30	7 14 21 28	4 11 18 25	2 9 16 23 30
Fri.	1 8 15 22 29	5 12 19 26	5 12 19 26	2 9 16 23 30	7 14 21 28	4 11 18 25	2 9 16 23 30	6 13 20 27	3 10 17 24	1 8 15 22 29	5 12 19 26	3 10 17 24 31
Sat.	2 9 16 23 30	6 13 20 27	6 13 20 27	3 10 17 24	1 8 15 22 29	5 12 19 26	3 10 17 24 31	7 14 21 28	4 11 18 25	2 9 16 23 30	6 13 20 27	4 11 18 25

EASTER DAYS
March 28	1869, 1875, 1937, 2027
April 4	1790, 1847, 1858, 1915, 1926, 1999, 2010, 2021
April 11	1819, 1830, 1841, 1909, 1971, 1982, 1993
April 18	1802, 1813, 1897, 1954, 1965
April 25	1886, 1943, 2038

M

	January	February	March	April	May	June	July	August	September	October	November	December
Sun.	2 9 16 23 30	6 13 20 27	6 13 20 27	3 10 17 24	1 8 15 22 29	5 12 19 26	3 10 17 24 31	7 14 21 28	4 11 18 25	2 9 16 23 30	6 13 20 27	4 11 18 25
Mon.	3 10 17 24 31	7 14 21 28	7 14 21 28	4 11 18 25	2 9 16 23 30	6 13 20 27	4 11 18 25	1 8 15 22 29	5 12 19 26	3 10 17 24 31	7 14 21 28	5 12 19 26
Tue.	4 11 18 25	1 8 15 22	1 8 15 22 29	5 12 19 26	3 10 17 24 31	7 14 21 28	5 12 19 26	2 9 16 23 30	6 13 20 27	4 11 18 25	1 8 15 22 29	6 13 20 27
Wed.	5 12 19 26	2 9 16 23	2 9 16 23 30	6 13 20 27	4 11 18 25	1 8 15 22 29	6 13 20 27	3 10 17 24 31	7 14 21 28	5 12 19 26	2 9 16 23 30	7 14 21 28
Thur.	6 13 20 27	3 10 17 24	3 10 17 24 31	7 14 21 28	5 12 19 26	2 9 16 23 30	7 14 21 28	4 11 18 25	1 8 15 22 29	6 13 20 27	3 10 17 24	1 8 15 22 29
Fri.	7 14 21 28	4 11 18 25	4 11 18 25	1 8 15 22 29	6 13 20 27	3 10 17 24	1 8 15 22 29	5 12 19 26	2 9 16 23 30	7 14 21 28	4 11 18 25	2 9 16 23 30
Sat.	1 8 15 22 29	5 12 19 26	5 12 19 26	2 9 16 23 30	7 14 21 28	4 11 18 25	2 9 16 23 30	6 13 20 27	3 10 17 24	1 8 15 22 29	5 12 19 26	3 10 17 24 31

EASTER DAYS
March 27	1785, 1842, 1853, 1910, 1921, 2005
April 3	1825, 1831, 1983, 1994
April 10	1803, 1814, 1887, 1898, 1955, 1966, 1977, 2039
April 17	1870, 1881, 1927, 1938, 1949, 2022, 2033
April 24	1791, 1859, 2011

L (LEAP YEAR)

	January	February	March	April	May	June	July	August	September	October	November	December
Sun.	3 10 17 24 31	7 14 21 28	6 13 20 27	3 10 17 24	1 8 15 22 29	5 12 19 26	3 10 17 24 31	7 14 21 28	4 11 18 25	2 9 16 23 30	6 13 20 27	4 11 18 25
Mon.	4 11 18 25	1 8 15 22 29	7 14 21 28	4 11 18 25	2 9 16 23 30	6 13 20 27	4 11 18 25	1 8 15 22 29	5 12 19 26	3 10 17 24 31	7 14 21 28	5 12 19 26
Tue.	5 12 19 26	2 9 16 23	1 8 15 22 29	5 12 19 26	3 10 17 24 31	7 14 21 28	5 12 19 26	2 9 16 23 30	6 13 20 27	4 11 18 25	1 8 15 22 29	6 13 20 27
Wed.	6 13 20 27	3 10 17 24	2 9 16 23 30	6 13 20 27	4 11 18 25	1 8 15 22 29	6 13 20 27	3 10 17 24 31	7 14 21 28	5 12 19 26	2 9 16 23 30	7 14 21 28
Thur.	7 14 21 28	4 11 18 25	3 10 17 24 31	7 14 21 28	5 12 19 26	2 9 16 23 30	7 14 21 28	4 11 18 25	1 8 15 22 29	6 13 20 27	3 10 17 24	1 8 15 22 29
Fri.	1 8 15 22 29	5 12 19 26	4 11 18 25	1 8 15 22 29	6 13 20 27	3 10 17 24	1 8 15 22 29	5 12 19 26	2 9 16 23 30	7 14 21 28	4 11 18 25	2 9 16 23 30
Sat.	2 9 16 23 30	6 13 20 27	5 12 19 26	2 9 16 23 30	7 14 21 28	4 11 18 25	2 9 16 23 30	6 13 20 27	3 10 17 24	1 8 15 22 29	5 12 19 26	3 10 17 24 31

EASTER DAYS
March 27	1796, 1864, 1932, 2016
April 3	1836, 1904, 1988
April 17	1808, 1892, 1960

N (LEAP YEAR)

	January	February	March	April	May	June	July	August	September	October	November	December
Sun.	2 9 16 23 30	6 13 20 27	5 12 19 26	2 9 16 23 30	7 14 21 28	4 11 18 25	2 9 16 23 30	6 13 20 27	3 10 17 24	1 8 15 22 29	5 12 19 26	3 10 17 24 31
Mon.	3 10 17 24 31	7 14 21 28	6 13 20 27	3 10 17 24	1 8 15 22 29	5 12 19 26	3 10 17 24 31	7 14 21 28	4 11 18 25	2 9 16 23 30	6 13 20 27	4 11 18 25
Tue.	4 11 18 25	1 8 15 22 29	7 14 21 28	4 11 18 25	2 9 16 23 30	6 13 20 27	4 11 18 25	1 8 15 22 29	5 12 19 26	3 10 17 24 31	7 14 21 28	5 12 19 26
Wed.	5 12 19 26	2 9 16 23	1 8 15 22 29	5 12 19 26	3 10 17 24 31	7 14 21 28	5 12 19 26	2 9 16 23 30	6 13 20 27	4 11 18 25	1 8 15 22 29	6 13 20 27
Thur.	6 13 20 27	3 10 17 24	2 9 16 23 30	6 13 20 27	4 11 18 25	1 8 15 22 29	6 13 20 27	3 10 17 24 31	7 14 21 28	5 12 19 26	2 9 16 23 30	7 14 21 28
Fri.	7 14 21 28	4 11 18 25	3 10 17 24 31	7 14 21 28	5 12 19 26	2 9 16 23 30	7 14 21 28	4 11 18 25	1 8 15 22 29	6 13 20 27	3 10 17 24	1 8 15 22 29
Sat.	1 8 15 22 29	5 12 19 26	4 11 18 25	1 8 15 22 29	6 13 20 27	3 10 17 24	1 8 15 22 29	5 12 19 26	2 9 16 23 30	7 14 21 28	4 11 18 25	2 9 16 23 30

EASTER DAYS
March 26	1780
April 2	1820, 1972
April 9	1944
April 16	1876, 2028
April 23	1848, 1916, 2000

GEOLOGICAL TIME

The earth is thought to have come into existence approximately 4,600 million years ago, but for nearly half this time, the Archean era, it was uninhabited. Life is generally believed to have emerged in the succeeding Proterozoic era. The Archean and the Proterozoic eras are often together referred to as the Precambrian.

Although primitive forms of life, eg algae and bacteria, existed during the Proterozoic era, it is not until the strata of Palaeozoic rocks are reached that abundant fossilised remains appear. Since the Precambrian, there have been three great geological eras:

PALAEOZOIC ('ANCIENT LIFE')
*c.*542–*c.*251 million years ago

Cambrian – Mainly sandstones, slate and shales; limestones in Scotland. Shelled fossils and invertebrates, eg trilobites and brachiopods appear, as do the earliest known vertebrates (jawless fish)
Ordovician – Mainly shales and mudstones, eg in north Wales; limestones in Scotland. First fish
Silurian – Shales, mudstones and some limestones, found mostly in Wales and southern Scotland
Devonian – Old red sandstone, shale, limestone and slate, eg in south Wales and the West Country
Carboniferous – Coal-bearing rocks, millstone grit, limestone and shale. First traces of land-living creatures
Permian – Marls, sandstones and clays. First reptile fossils

There were two great phases of mountain building in the Palaeozoic era: the Caledonian, characterised in Britain by NE–SW lines of hills and valleys; and the later Hercynian, widespread in west Germany and adjacent areas, and in Britain exemplified in E–W lines of hills and valleys.

The end of the Palaeozoic era was marked by the extensive glaciations of the Permian period in the southern continents and the decline of amphibians. It was succeeded by an era of warm conditions.

MESOZOIC ('MIDDLE FORMS OF LIFE')
*c.*251–*c.*65.5 million years ago

Triassic – Mostly sandstone, eg in the West Midlands; primitive mammals appear
Jurassic – Mainly limestones and clays, typically displayed in the Jura mountains, and in England in a NE–SW belt from Lincolnshire and the Wash to the Severn and the Dorset coast
Cretaceous – Mainly chalk, clay and sands, eg in Kent and Sussex

Giant reptiles were dominant during the Mesozoic era, but it was at this time that marsupial mammals first appeared, as well as *Archaeopteryx lithographica,* the earliest known species of bird. Coniferous trees and flowering plants also developed during the era and, with the birds and the mammals, were the main species to survive into the Cenozoic era. The giant reptiles became extinct.

CENOZOIC ('RECENT LIFE')
from *c.*65.5 million years ago

Palaeocene ⎫ The emergence of new forms of life,
Eocene ⎭ including existing species; primate appear
Oligocene – Fossils of a few still existing species
Miocene – Fossil remains show a balance of existing and extinct species
Pliocene – Fossil remains show a majority of still existing species
Pleistocene – The majority of remains are those of still existing species
Holocene – The present, post-glacial period. Existing species only, except for a few exterminated by humans

In the last 25 million years, from the Miocene through the Pliocene periods, the Alpine-Himalayan and the circum-Pacific phases of mountain building reached their climax. During the Pleistocene period ice-sheets repeatedly locked up masses of water as land ice; its weight depressed the land, but the locking-up of the water lowered the sea level by 100–200 metres. The glaciations and interglacials of the Ice Age are difficult to date and classify, but recent scientific opinion considers the Pleistocene period to have begun approximately 1.64 million years ago. The last glacial retreat, merging into the Holocene period, was *c.* 10,000 years ago.

HUMAN DEVELOPMENT

Any consideration of the history of humans must start with the fact that all members of the human race belong to one species of animal, ie *Homo sapiens,* the definition of a species being in biological terms that all its members can interbreed. As a species of mammal it is possible to group humans with other similar types, known as the primates. Amongst these is found a sub-group, the apes, which includes, in addition to humans, the chimpanzees, gorillas, orangutans and gibbons. All lack a tail, have shoulder blades at the back, and a Y-shaped chewing pattern on the surface of their molars, as well as showing the more general primate characteristics of four incisors, a thumb which is able to touch the fingers of the same hand, and finger and toe nails instead of claws. The factors available to scientific study suggest that human beings have chimpanzees and gorillas as their nearest relatives in the animal world. However, there once lived creatures, now extinct, which were closer to modern man than the chimpanzees and gorillas, and which shared with modern man the characteristics of having flat faces (ie the absence of a pronounced muzzle), being bipedal, and possessing large brains.

The debate surrounding evidence for the oldest human ancestors is ongoing. The fossil record becomes more patchy as time stretches backward, which makes new hominid discoveries harder to confirm. The earliest putative hominin for which there is significant fossil evidence is *Ardipithecus ramidus,* for which an almost complete skeleton, dating to at least 4.4 million years ago, was discovered in the Afar Rift, Ethiopia in 1992. Analysis of the *Ardipithecus ramidus* skeleton suggests the creature had characteristics of both humans and apes; able to climb trees and walk on two feet.

The subsequent Australopithecines have left more numerous remains in south and east Africa, among which sub-groups may be detected. Living between 4.2 and 1.5 million years ago, they were relatives of modern humans in respect of the fact that they walked upright, did not have an extensive muzzle and had similar types of pre-molars. The first australopithecine remains were recognised at Taung in South Africa in 1924 and named *Australopithecus africanus,* dating between 3.3 and 2.3 million years ago. The most impressive discovery was made at Hadar, Ethiopia, in 1974 when about half a skeleton of *Australopithecus afarensis,* known as 'Lucy', was found. Some 3.2 million years ago, 'Lucy' (who is now considered to be male) certainly walked upright.

Also in east Africa, especially at Olduvai Gorge in

Tanzania, between *c.* 2.5 and 1.8 million years ago, lived a hominid group which not only walked upright, had a flat face, and a large brain case, but also made simple pebble and flake stone tools. These early pebble tool users, because of their distinctive characteristics, have been grouped as a separate sub-species, now extinct, of the genus *Homo* and are known as *Homo habilis* or 'handy man'.

The use of fire, again a human characteristic, is associated with another group of extinct hominids whose remains, about a million years old, are found in south and east Africa, China, Indonesia, north Africa and Europe. Mastery of the techniques of making fire probably helped the colonisation of the colder northern areas and in this respect the site of Vertesszollos in Hungary is of particular importance. *Homo ergaster* in Africa and *Homo erectus* in Asia are the names given to this group of fossils and they relate to a number of famous individual discoveries, eg Solo Man, Heidelberg Man, and especially Peking Man who lived at the cave site at Choukoutien which has yielded evidence of fire and burnt bone.

The well-known group the Neanderthals, or *Homo neanderthalensis,* is an extinct form of human that lived between about 350,000 and 24,000 years ago, thus spanning the last Ice Age and living alongside modern humans. The Neanderthals' ability to adapt to the cold climate on the edge of the ice-sheets is one of their characteristic features, with remains being found only in Europe, Asia and the Middle East. Complete Neanderthal skeletons were found during excavations at Tabun in Israel, together with evidence of tool-making and the use of fire. Distinguished by very large brains, it seems that Neanderthals were the first to develop recognisable social customs, especially deliberate burial rites. Why the Neanderthals became extinct is not clear but it may be connected with the climatic changes at the end of the Ice Ages, which would have seriously affected their food supplies; possibly they became too specialised for their own good.

The shin bone of Boxgrove Man found in 1993 – *Homo heidelbergensis* – and the Swanscombe skull are the best known early human fossil remains found in England. Some specialists prefer to group Swanscombe Man (or, more probably, woman) together with the Steinheim skull from Germany, seeing both as a separate sub-species. There is too little evidence as yet on which to form a final judgement.

Anatomically modern humans – *Homo sapiens sapiens* ('doubly wise man') – had evolved to our present physical condition and had colonised much of the world by about 40,000 years ago. There are many previously distinguished individual specimens, eg Cromagnon Man, the first early *Homo sapiens sapiens* of the European Upper Palaeolithic. It was such modern humans that spread to the American continent, potentially by crossing the landbridge between Siberia and Alaska and from there moved south through North America and into South America.

One of the problems for those studying human fossils is the lack in many cases of sufficient quantities of fossil bone for analysis. It is important that theories should be tested against evidence, rather than the evidence being made to fit the theory. The Piltdown hoax of 1912 (and not fully exposed until the 1970s) is a well-known example of 'fossils' being forged to fit what was seen in some quarters as the correct theory of human evolution.

The discovery of the structure of DNA in 1953 has come to have a profound effect upon the study of human evolution. For example, it was claimed in 1987 that a common ancestor of all human beings was a person who lived in Africa some 200,000 years ago, thus encouraging the 'out of Africa' theory of hominid migration from east Africa to the Middle East and then throughout the world. There is no doubt that the studies based on DNA have vast potential to elucidate further the course of human evolution.

CULTURAL DEVELOPMENT

The Eurocentric bias of early archaeologists meant that the search for a starting point for the development and transmission of cultural ideas, especially by migration, trade and warfare, concentrated unduly on Europe and the Near East. The Three Age system, whereby prehistory was divided into a Stone Age, a Bronze Age and an Iron Age, was devised by Christian Thomsen, curator of the National Museum of Denmark in the early 19th century, to facilitate the classification of the museum's collections. The descriptive adjectives referred to the materials from which the implements and weapons were made and came to be regarded as the dominant features of the societies to which they related. The refinement of the Three Age system once dominated archaeological thought and remains a generally accepted concept in the popular mind. However, it is now seen by archaeologists as an inadequate model for human development.

Common sense suggests that there were no complete breaks between one so-called Age and another, any more than contemporaries would have regarded 1485 as a complete break between medieval and modern English history. Nor can the Three Age system be applied universally. In some areas it is necessary to insert a Copper Age, while in South Africa there would seem to be no Bronze Age at all; in Australia, Old Stone Age societies survived, while in South America, New Stone Age communities exist into modern times.

The concept of the 'Neolithic revolution', associated with the domestication of plants and animals, was a development of particular importance in the human cultural pattern. It reflected change from the hunter-gatherer economies to a more settled agricultural way of life and therefore, so the argument goes, made possible the development of urban civilisation. However, it can no longer be argued that this change was an instantaneous 'revolution' – it was typically a more gradual process – or that it took place only in one area from which all development stemmed. Though it appears that the cultivation of wheat and barley was first undertaken, together with the domestication of cattle and goats/sheep, around 10,000 years ago in the Fertile Crescent (the area bounded by the rivers Tigris and Euphrates), there is evidence that sorghum was first domesticated in Africa, rice was first deliberately planted and pigs domesticated in south-east Asia, maize first cultivated in Central America and llamas first domesticated in South America. Cultural change took place independently in different parts of the world at different rates and different times.

The Neolithic period of cultural development has been difficult to date reliably because the transition to agriculture took place long before writing was invented. The development and refinement of radio-carbon dating and other scientific methods of producing absolute chronologies is enabling the cross-referencing of societies to be undertaken. It may eventually be possible to obtain a reliable chronological framework, in absolute terms of years, against which the cultural development of any particular area may be set.

GEOLOGICAL TIME

Era	Period	Epoch	Dates*	Evolutionary Stages
Cenozoic	Quarternary	Holocene	11,700 BP†–present	
		Pleistocene	2,588,000–11,700 BP	First humans
	Neogene	Pliocene	5.332–2.588 Mya ‡	Majority of still existing species
		Miocene	23.03–5.332 Mya	
	Paleogene	Oligocene	33.9–23.03 Mya	
		Eocene	55.8–33.9 Mya	} First modern mammals
		Palaeocene	65.5–55.8 Mya	
Mesozoic	Cretaceous		145.5–65.5 Mya	
	Jurassic		199.6–145.5 Mya	First birds
	Triassic		251–199.6 Mya	First mammals
Palaeozoic	Permian		299–251 Mya	First reptiles
	Carboniferous		359.2–299 Mya	First traces of land-living creatures
	Devonian		416–359.2 Mya	
	Silurian		443.7–416 Mya	
	Ordovician		488.3–443.7 Mya	First fish
	Cambrian		542–488.3 Mya	First invertebrates
Precambrian	Proterozoic		2,500–542 Mya	First primitive life forms, eg algae and bacteria
	Archaean		3,800–2,500 Mya	} Earth uninhabited
	Hadean		4,600–3,800 Mya	

* approximate †BP = Before Present ‡Mya = million years ago

TIDES AND TIDAL PREDICTIONS

TIDES

Tides are the periodic rise and fall of the sea level caused mainly by the gravitational pull, or tide raising force (TRF), of the Moon and the Sun. The Moon's TRF accounts for 70 per cent of the total; the Sun's for 30 per cent. When the Moon and the Sun are in line with the Earth they are said to be 'in conjunction' (or syzygy) and their combined TRFs are greatest. This produces the largest rise and fall of the tide, otherwise known as spring tides; they occur just after a full or new moon. The opposite effect, just after the Moon's first and last quarters, when the Sun and Moon form a right angle with the Earth, produces neap tides, with a relatively small tidal range between high water and low water.

A lunar day is about 24 hours and 50 minutes, giving two complete tidal cycles, with about 12 hours and 25 minutes between successive high waters. These are known as semi-diurnal tides and are applicable in the Atlantic Ocean and around the coasts of north-west Europe. Other parts of the world have diurnal tides, with only one high water and one low water each (lunar) day, or mixed tides which are partly diurnal and partly semi-diurnal.

Land and seabed conditions influence the tides locally. On the south coast of England, for example, double high waters occur between Swanage and Selsey Bill, and low water is much more sharply defined than high water. Tides can also be greatly affected by the Coriolis force, which is induced by the Earth's rotation and, in the northern hemisphere, tends to deflect any moving object to the right. Thus the easterly flood tidal stream in the English Channel is deflected towards the French coast causing higher high waters; on the ebb the opposite happens causing lower low waters. This, coupled with local geography, means that the mean spring range of the tide at St Malo is nearly 11m while the range on the English coast at Portland, 120 miles to the north, is a mere 2m.

Meteorological conditions also affect the tides. Prolonged strong winds and unusually high (or low) atmospheric pressure can significantly lower (or raise) the height of the tide; the wind alone can affect the predicted times of high and low water by as much as an hour. Variation of pressure by 34 millibars from the norm can cause a height difference of 0.3m. Intense minor depressions, line squalls, or other abrupt changes in the weather can cause wave oscillations known as seiches. The wave period of a seiche can vary from a few minutes to about 2 hours, with heights of up to a metre. Wick on the north-east coast of Scotland and Fishguard in south-west Wales are particularly prone to seiches.

TIDAL STREAMS

Tidal streams are the horizontal movements of water caused by the rise and fall of the tide. They normally change direction about every 6 hours. Tidal streams should not be confused with ocean currents, such as the Gulf Stream, which run indefinitely in the same direction. The rate, or set, of the stream at any particular place is proportional to the range of the tide. Thus, the rate during spring tides is greater than that at neaps. In the central English Channel the maximum spring rate is nearly 5 knots while the neap rate at the same position is just 3 knots. As with tidal heights, local geography plays a significant role in the rate of the tidal stream. For example, in the narrow waters of the Pentland Firth between mainland Scotland and the Orkney Islands, rates of 16 knots have been recorded.

The tidal stream does not necessarily turn at the same time as high or low water. In the English Channel the stream turns at approximately high and low water at Dover. However, high water at Dover is at about the same time as low water at Plymouth, and vice versa.

Around the UK, the main flood tidal stream sets eastward up the English Channel, north-east into the Bristol Channel, and north up the west coasts of Ireland and Scotland. However, the flood sets south-east through the North Channel and south into the Irish Sea, where it meets the northerly flood through St George's Channel at the Isle of Man. Off the east coasts of Scotland and England the stream sets south as far as the Thames Estuary before meeting the north-going stream from the eastern part of the Dover Strait.

DEFINITIONS

Chart Datum (CD) is the reference level from which tidal levels are predicted. **Ordnance Datum** at Newlyn is the datum of the land levelling system on mainland England, Scotland and Wales. This is the datum from which heights on UK land maps are measured. CD varies from about 5m above Ordnance Datum to about 6.5m below. **Highest Astronomical Tide (HAT)** and **Lowest Astronomical Tide (LAT)** are the highest and lowest levels of the tide that can be predicted to occur under average meteorological, and any combination of astronomical, conditions. **Duration** of the tide is the interval between low water and the next high water. It can be used to calculate the approximate time of low water when only the time of high water is known. **Mean Sea Level (MSL or ML)** is the average level of the sea's surface over a long period, normally observed over 18.6 years. The **Range** of the tide is the difference between the heights of successive high waters and low waters. It is greatest at spring tides, least at neaps. The range may be indicated by **Tidal Coefficients** which are proportional to, but not the same as, the range on a particular day. A coefficient of 95 indicates an average spring tide, while 45 is an average neap tide.

PREDICTIONS

The following data are daily predictions of the time and height of high water at London Bridge, Liverpool, Greenock and Leith. The time of the data is Greenwich Mean Time; this applies also to data for the months when British Summer Time is in operation and the hour's time difference should be added. The datum of predictions for each port shows the difference of height, in metres from Ordnance datum (Newlyn).

The tidal information for London Bridge, Liverpool, Greenock and Leith is reproduced by permission of the Controller of Her Majesty's Stationery Office and the UK Hydrographic Office. © Crown copyright. All rights reserved. The section was compiled with the assistance of Andy Du Port and Chris Stevens.

JANUARY 2012   *High Water*   GMT

	LONDON BRIDGE *Datum of Predictions 3.20m below				LIVERPOOL (Gladstone Dock) *Datum of Predictions 4.93m below				GREENOCK *Datum of Predictions 1.62m below				LEITH *Datum of Predictions 2.90m below			
	hr	ht m	hr	ht m	hr	ht m	hr	ht m	hr	ht m	hr	ht m	hr	ht m	hr	ht m
SU 1	06 25	6.2	19 00	6.1	03 54	7.7	16 19	7.9	05 16	3.1	17 32	3.3	07 54	4.6	20 11	4.6
M 2	07 13	6.0	19 52	5.8	04 50	7.4	17 19	7.5	06 03	3.0	18 23	3.1	08 47	4.4	21 08	4.5
TU 3	08 18	5.8	20 55	5.7	05 57	7.2	18 27	7.4	06 56	3.0	19 23	3.0	09 43	4.4	22 08	4.4
W 4	09 29	5.7	22 00	5.8	07 10	7.3	19 37	7.5	07 59	3.0	20 36	2.9	10 43	4.4	23 11	4.4
TH 5	10 35	5.9	23 06	6.0	08 14	7.6	20 37	7.7	09 11	3.0	21 51	3.0	11 45	4.6	—	—
F 6	11 37	6.2	—	—	09 06	8.0	21 27	8.1	10 14	3.2	22 50	3.1	00 14	4.6	12 43	4.8
SA 7	00 06	6.2	12 30	6.4	09 49	8.4	22 09	8.4	11 03	3.4	23 37	3.2	01 07	4.8	13 29	5.0
SU 8	00 56	6.5	13 15	6.7	10 27	8.7	22 48	8.7	11 44	3.5	—	—	01 51	5.0	14 10	5.2
M 9	01 40	6.6	13 56	6.8	11 04	9.0	23 25	8.9	00 19	3.2	12 20	3.6	02 30	5.2	14 47	5.4
TU 10	02 20	6.7	14 36	7.0	11 40	9.2	—	—	00 58	3.3	12 55	3.7	03 07	5.4	15 22	5.5
W 11	02 59	6.8	15 15	7.1	00 02	9.1	12 18	9.4	01 36	3.3	13 32	3.8	03 44	5.5	15 57	5.6
TH 12	03 36	6.9	15 55	7.2	00 41	9.2	12 56	9.4	02 14	3.3	14 11	3.8	04 22	5.5	16 34	5.6
F 13	04 12	6.9	16 34	7.1	01 21	9.2	13 36	9.4	02 53	3.3	14 52	3.8	05 02	5.5	17 13	5.5
SA 14	04 49	6.9	17 15	6.9	02 03	9.0	14 18	9.2	03 33	3.4	15 34	3.8	05 44	5.4	17 56	5.4
SU 15	05 29	6.8	17 59	6.7	02 47	8.8	15 05	8.9	04 14	3.3	16 17	3.7	06 30	5.2	18 43	5.3
M 16	06 12	6.6	18 48	6.5	03 37	8.4	15 59	8.6	04 57	3.2	17 04	3.6	07 21	5.0	19 39	5.1
TU 17	07 05	6.5	19 48	6.2	04 36	8.1	17 05	8.2	05 46	3.1	17 58	3.4	08 21	4.8	20 51	4.9
W 18	08 12	6.3	21 00	6.1	05 49	7.9	18 25	8.0	06 49	3.0	19 05	3.2	09 34	4.7	22 12	4.8
TH 19	09 34	6.2	22 15	6.1	07 08	7.9	19 46	8.0	08 26	3.0	20 43	3.1	10 48	4.8	23 28	4.9
F 20	10 51	6.3	23 32	6.2	08 21	8.3	20 57	8.4	09 51	3.1	22 12	3.1	11 57	4.9	—	—
SA 21	12 04	6.5	—	—	09 23	8.7	21 56	8.7	10 51	3.3	23 16	3.2	00 35	5.1	12 57	5.2
SU 22	00 39	6.5	13 05	6.8	10 16	9.1	22 46	9.0	11 41	3.5	—	—	01 33	5.3	13 48	5.4
M 23	01 33	6.7	13 56	7.0	11 02	9.4	23 30	9.2	00 09	3.3	12 27	3.6	02 21	5.5	14 33	5.6
TU 24	02 19	6.8	14 41	7.1	11 44	9.6	—	—	00 57	3.3	13 10	3.7	03 05	5.6	15 16	5.7
W 25	03 01	6.9	15 23	7.1	00 10	9.2	12 23	9.6	01 39	3.3	13 49	3.7	03 47	5.5	15 57	5.7
TH 26	03 38	7.0	16 01	7.1	00 47	9.1	12 59	9.5	02 16	3.3	14 27	3.7	04 27	5.4	16 37	5.6
F 27	04 12	7.0	16 35	6.9	01 20	8.9	13 33	9.2	02 50	3.3	15 02	3.7	05 05	5.3	17 15	5.4
SA 28	04 44	6.8	17 06	6.7	01 53	8.7	14 08	8.9	03 24	3.3	15 38	3.6	05 43	5.1	17 53	5.2
SU 29	05 16	6.7	17 36	6.4	02 27	8.4	14 44	8.5	04 00	3.3	16 14	3.4	06 21	4.9	18 32	5.0
M 30	05 47	6.4	18 09	6.2	03 04	8.0	15 26	8.0	04 37	3.2	16 53	3.3	07 03	4.6	19 17	4.7
TU 31	06 23	6.2	18 48	5.9	03 48	7.5	16 16	7.5	05 17	3.1	17 36	3.1	07 50	4.4	20 10	4.4

FEBRUARY 2012   *High Water*   GMT

	LONDON BRIDGE				LIVERPOOL (Gladstone Dock)				GREENOCK				LEITH			
W 1	07 08	5.9	19 41	5.7	04 47	7.1	17 24	7.1	06 02	3.0	18 28	2.9	08 45	4.3	21 12	4.3
TH 2	08 15	5.6	21 00	5.5	06 05	7.0	18 45	7.0	06 57	2.9	19 34	2.7	09 48	4.2	22 19	4.2
F 3	09 44	5.6	22 21	5.6	07 28	7.1	20 02	7.3	08 10	2.9	21 07	2.7	10 57	4.3	23 31	4.4
SA 4	10 58	5.9	23 33	6.0	08 34	7.6	21 02	7.7	09 36	3.0	22 28	2.9	12 07	4.6	—	—
SU 5	12 00	6.3	—	—	09 24	8.1	21 48	8.2	10 37	3.2	23 20	3.0	00 38	4.6	13 04	4.9
M 6	00 31	6.4	12 52	6.6	10 06	8.6	22 28	8.7	11 21	3.3	—	—	01 28	4.9	13 48	5.1
TU 7	01 19	6.6	13 36	6.9	10 44	9.1	23 06	9.1	00 03	3.2	11 59	3.5	02 09	5.2	14 26	5.4
W 8	02 01	6.8	14 18	7.1	11 21	9.4	23 44	9.4	00 43	3.2	12 37	3.6	02 46	5.4	15 02	5.6
TH 9	02 41	7.0	14 59	7.2	11 59	9.7	—	—	01 21	3.3	13 15	3.7	03 23	5.6	15 37	5.7
F 10	03 19	7.1	15 38	7.3	00 22	9.5	12 38	9.8	01 58	3.3	13 56	3.8	04 01	5.7	16 14	5.8
SA 11	03 56	7.2	16 18	7.2	01 02	9.5	13 18	9.7	02 35	3.4	14 37	3.8	04 40	5.7	16 54	5.8
SU 12	04 33	7.1	16 57	7.0	01 42	9.4	13 58	9.5	03 13	3.4	15 18	3.8	05 22	5.5	17 37	5.7
M 13	05 11	7.0	17 38	6.7	02 25	9.1	14 44	9.1	03 51	3.4	16 00	3.7	06 06	5.3	18 25	5.4
TU 14	05 54	6.8	18 23	6.4	03 12	8.6	15 36	8.6	04 31	3.3	16 45	3.5	06 55	5.0	19 20	5.1
W 15	06 44	6.5	19 19	6.1	04 10	8.1	16 43	8.0	05 15	3.2	17 34	3.2	07 53	4.7	20 33	4.8
TH 16	07 49	6.2	20 31	5.9	05 25	7.7	18 10	7.6	06 10	3.0	18 35	3.0	09 09	4.6	21 59	4.6
F 17	09 14	6.0	21 56	5.8	06 51	7.7	19 39	7.7	07 54	2.8	20 42	2.8	10 31	4.6	23 21	4.7
SA 18	10 40	6.1	23 24	6.0	08 11	8.0	20 54	8.1	09 40	3.0	22 17	2.9	11 47	4.8	—	—
SU 19	11 58	6.4	—	—	09 15	8.5	21 50	8.5	10 40	3.2	23 13	3.1	00 33	4.9	12 50	5.0
M 20	00 30	6.4	12 57	6.8	10 05	8.9	22 35	8.9	11 28	3.4	—	—	01 28	5.2	13 39	5.3
TU 21	01 22	6.7	13 45	7.0	10 48	9.3	23 14	9.1	00 00	3.2	12 13	3.6	02 12	5.3	14 21	5.5
W 22	02 04	6.8	14 26	7.0	11 25	9.4	23 49	9.2	00 42	3.3	12 53	3.6	02 50	5.4	14 59	5.6
TH 23	02 41	6.9	15 02	7.0	12 00	9.5	—	—	01 19	3.3	13 16	3.6	03 26	5.4	15 36	5.6
F 24	03 14	7.0	15 35	7.0	00 20	9.1	12 33	9.4	01 50	3.3	14 05	3.6	04 01	5.4	16 11	5.5
SA 25	03 45	7.1	16 04	6.9	00 51	9.0	13 04	9.2	02 21	3.3	14 38	3.5	04 34	5.3	16 46	5.4
SU 26	04 15	7.0	16 31	6.7	01 20	8.8	13 36	9.0	02 52	3.3	15 10	3.5	05 08	5.1	17 20	5.2
M 27	04 45	6.8	17 00	6.5	01 51	8.6	14 08	8.6	03 26	3.4	15 44	3.4	05 43	4.9	17 56	5.0
TU 28	05 15	6.6	17 30	6.3	02 23	8.2	14 43	8.1	04 00	3.3	16 20	3.2	06 20	4.7	18 37	4.7
W 29	05 48	6.3	18 05	6.0	02 59	7.8	15 25	7.6	04 36	3.2	17 01	3.0	07 02	4.5	19 24	4.5

MARCH 2012   *High Water*   GMT

	LONDON BRIDGE *Datum of Predictions 3.20m below				LIVERPOOL (Gladstone Dock) *Datum of Predictions 4.93m below				GREENOCK *Datum of Predictions 1.62m below				LEITH *Datum of Predictions 2.90m below			
	hr m	ht m	hr m	ht m	hr m	ht m	hr m	ht m	hr m	ht m	hr m	ht m	hr m	ht m	hr m	ht m
TH 1	06 27	6.0	18 49	5.7	03 47	7.3	16 23	7.1	05 17	3.0	17 50	2.8	07 54	4.3	20 22	4.3
F 2	07 19	5.7	19 51	5.5	04 59	6.9	17 48	6.8	06 08	2.9	18 53	2.6	08 58	4.2	21 32	4.2
SA 3	08 38	5.5	21 29	5.4	06 33	6.9	19 19	7.0	07 14	2.8	20 22	2.6	10 11	4.2	22 47	4.3
SU 4	10 14	5.7	22 54	5.8	07 53	7.4	20 28	7.5	08 42	2.8	22 02	2.8	11 27	4.4	—	—
M 5	11 24	6.2	23 58	6.3	08 50	8.0	21 19	8.2	10 00	3.0	22 56	3.0	00 00	4.5	12 31	4.7
TU 6	12 21	6.6	—	—	09 36	8.6	22 01	8.7	10 50	3.2	23 39	3.1	00 57	4.9	13 19	5.1
W 7	00 49	6.6	13 09	6.9	10 17	9.1	22 41	9.2	11 32	3.4	—	—	01 41	5.2	13 59	5.4
TH 8	01 34	6.9	13 54	7.1	10 56	9.6	23 20	9.6	00 19	3.2	12 14	3.5	02 20	5.5	14 36	5.7
F 9	02 15	7.1	14 36	7.3	11 35	9.9	23 59	9.8	00 58	3.3	12 56	3.6	02 58	5.7	15 13	5.9
SA 10	02 55	7.3	15 17	7.3	12 16	10.0	—	—	01 36	3.4	13 38	3.7	03 36	5.8	15 53	6.0
SU 11	03 34	7.4	15 57	7.2	00 40	9.8	12 58	9.9	02 13	3.4	14 21	3.8	04 17	5.8	16 35	5.9
M 12	04 14	7.4	16 37	7.0	01 21	9.6	13 41	9.6	02 51	3.5	15 03	3.7	04 59	5.6	17 21	5.7
TU 13	04 54	7.2	17 18	6.7	02 05	9.2	14 27	9.1	03 29	3.5	15 46	3.6	05 44	5.4	18 11	5.4
W 14	05 38	6.9	18 03	6.4	02 53	8.7	15 21	8.5	04 09	3.4	16 30	3.4	06 34	5.1	19 09	5.0
TH 15	06 29	6.6	18 57	6.0	03 52	8.2	16 31	7.8	04 53	3.2	17 19	3.1	07 34	4.7	20 25	4.7
F 16	07 35	6.2	20 10	5.8	05 09	7.7	17 59	7.4	05 48	2.9	18 22	2.8	08 53	4.5	21 49	4.5
SA 17	09 00	6.0	21 39	5.8	06 35	7.6	19 29	7.5	07 33	2.8	20 51	2.7	10 16	4.5	23 10	4.6
SU 18	10 26	6.1	23 05	6.0	07 54	7.9	20 41	8.0	09 20	2.9	22 05	2.9	11 32	4.7	—	—
M 19	11 42	6.5	—	—	08 57	8.4	21 33	8.4	10 19	3.2	22 56	3.0	00 20	4.8	12 34	5.0
TU 20	00 11	6.4	12 39	6.8	09 45	8.8	22 15	8.7	11 07	3.4	23 39	3.1	01 13	5.1	13 22	5.2
W 21	01 00	6.7	13 24	6.9	10 25	9.0	22 50	8.9	11 50	3.5	—	—	01 54	5.2	14 02	5.3
TH 22	01 40	6.8	14 02	6.9	11 01	9.2	23 22	9.0	00 17	3.2	12 31	3.5	02 29	5.3	14 38	5.4
F 23	02 15	6.9	14 35	6.9	11 33	9.3	23 52	9.1	00 50	3.2	13 07	3.5	03 01	5.3	15 12	5.4
SA 24	02 46	7.0	15 04	6.9	12 05	9.2	—	—	01 20	3.3	13 40	3.4	03 33	5.3	15 46	5.4
SU 25	03 16	7.1	15 31	6.9	00 21	9.0	12 36	9.1	01 49	3.3	14 11	3.4	04 05	5.2	16 19	5.3
M 26	03 46	7.1	15 59	6.8	00 51	8.9	13 07	8.9	02 21	3.4	14 43	3.3	04 36	5.1	16 53	5.2
TU 27	04 16	6.9	16 28	6.6	01 20	8.7	13 39	8.5	02 53	3.4	15 16	3.3	05 10	5.0	17 28	5.0
W 28	04 47	6.7	16 59	6.4	01 51	8.4	14 13	8.2	03 26	3.4	15 52	3.2	05 45	4.8	18 07	4.8
TH 29	05 20	6.4	17 33	6.1	02 25	8.0	14 52	7.7	04 00	3.3	16 33	3.0	06 25	4.6	18 52	4.5
F 30	05 59	6.2	18 15	5.9	03 08	7.6	15 45	7.3	04 39	3.1	17 21	2.8	07 12	4.4	19 46	4.3
SA 31	06 47	5.9	19 10	5.6	04 11	7.2	17 00	7.0	05 26	2.9	18 22	2.6	08 12	4.2	20 51	4.2

APRIL 2012   *High Water*   GMT

	LONDON BRIDGE				LIVERPOOL (Gladstone Dock)				GREENOCK				LEITH			
	hr m	ht m	hr m	ht m	hr m	ht m	hr m	ht m	hr m	ht m	hr m	ht m	hr m	ht m	hr m	ht m
SU 1	07 53	5.7	20 33	5.5	05 39	7.1	18 28	7.1	06 28	2.8	19 42	2.6	09 26	4.2	22 05	4.3
M 2	09 27	5.8	22 07	5.8	07 03	7.4	19 44	7.5	07 48	2.8	21 22	2.7	10 43	4.4	23 18	4.5
TU 3	10 43	6.2	23 17	6.2	08 07	7.9	20 41	8.2	09 12	2.9	22 22	2.9	11 49	4.7	—	—
W 4	11 44	6.6	—	—	08 59	8.6	21 28	8.8	10 12	3.2	23 08	3.1	00 19	4.9	12 42	5.1
TH 5	00 12	6.7	12 38	6.9	09 44	9.1	22 11	9.3	11 00	3.3	23 49	3.2	01 08	5.2	13 26	5.4
F 6	01 02	7.0	13 25	7.1	10 28	9.6	22 53	9.6	11 47	3.5	—	—	01 50	5.5	14 07	5.7
SA 7	01 46	7.2	14 10	7.2	11 11	9.9	23 35	9.8	00 30	3.3	12 33	3.6	02 31	5.7	14 49	5.9
SU 8	02 30	7.4	14 54	7.3	11 55	10.0	—	—	01 11	3.4	13 20	3.7	03 12	5.8	15 32	6.0
M 9	03 13	7.5	15 37	7.2	00 18	9.9	12 40	9.8	01 50	3.5	14 05	3.7	03 54	5.8	16 19	5.9
TU 10	03 55	7.5	16 19	7.0	01 03	9.7	13 27	9.5	02 30	3.6	14 50	3.6	04 39	5.7	17 08	5.7
W 11	04 39	7.3	17 02	6.7	01 49	9.3	14 16	9.0	03 10	3.5	15 35	3.5	05 27	5.4	18 01	5.4
TH 12	05 26	7.0	17 49	6.4	02 39	8.8	15 12	8.4	03 52	3.4	16 22	3.2	06 19	5.1	19 03	5.0
F 13	06 20	6.6	18 43	6.1	03 39	8.3	16 21	7.8	04 39	3.2	17 15	3.0	07 22	4.8	20 15	4.7
SA 14	07 25	6.3	19 53	5.9	04 52	7.9	17 41	7.5	05 37	3.0	18 27	2.7	08 38	4.6	21 30	4.6
SU 15	08 41	6.1	21 14	5.9	06 10	7.7	19 03	7.5	07 10	2.8	20 24	2.7	09 54	4.6	22 45	4.6
M 16	09 58	6.2	22 32	6.1	07 25	7.9	20 13	7.8	08 46	2.9	21 35	2.8	11 05	4.7	23 52	4.7
TU 17	11 12	6.4	23 38	6.4	08 27	8.2	21 05	8.2	09 48	3.1	22 25	3.0	12 06	4.9	—	—
W 18	12 10	6.6	—	—	09 16	8.5	21 46	8.5	10 38	3.3	23 07	3.1	00 45	4.9	12 55	5.0
TH 19	00 29	6.6	12 56	6.7	09 56	8.7	22 21	8.7	11 23	3.3	23 44	3.2	01 27	5.1	13 37	5.1
F 20	01 10	6.7	13 33	6.7	10 32	8.9	22 53	8.8	12 02	3.3	—	—	02 03	5.2	14 14	5.2
SA 21	01 45	6.8	14 05	6.8	11 06	9.0	23 24	8.9	00 17	3.2	12 39	3.3	02 35	5.2	14 48	5.3
SU 22	02 17	7.0	14 34	6.8	11 38	9.0	23 54	8.9	00 48	3.3	13 13	3.3	03 06	5.2	15 22	5.2
M 23	02 48	7.0	15 02	6.8	12 11	8.9	—	—	01 19	3.4	13 44	3.2	03 37	5.2	15 55	5.2
TU 24	03 19	7.0	15 32	6.8	00 24	8.8	12 43	8.7	01 51	3.5	14 17	3.2	04 09	5.2	16 30	5.1
W 25	03 51	6.9	16 03	6.6	00 55	8.7	13 16	8.5	02 23	3.5	14 52	3.2	04 43	5.1	17 06	5.0
TH 26	04 24	6.7	16 36	6.4	01 27	8.5	13 51	8.2	02 56	3.5	15 29	3.1	05 19	4.9	17 45	4.8
F 27	05 00	6.6	17 12	6.2	02 03	8.2	14 32	7.9	03 31	3.4	16 11	3.0	05 58	4.8	18 28	4.7
SA 28	05 40	6.4	17 54	6.0	02 46	7.9	15 22	7.6	04 09	3.2	16 58	2.9	06 42	4.6	19 18	4.5
SU 29	06 27	6.2	18 47	5.9	03 43	7.6	16 26	7.3	04 53	3.1	17 55	2.7	07 35	4.4	20 17	4.4
M 30	07 28	6.0	19 56	5.8	04 57	7.4	17 43	7.4	05 51	2.9	19 05	2.7	08 42	4.4	21 26	4.5

MAY 2012   *High Water*   GMT

	LONDON BRIDGE *Datum of Predictions 3.20m below*				LIVERPOOL (Gladstone Dock) *Datum of Predictions 4.93m below*				GREENOCK *Datum of Predictions 1.62m below*				LEITH *Datum of Predictions 2.90m below*			
	hr m	ht m	hr m	ht m	hr m	ht m	hr m	ht m	hr m	ht m	hr m	ht m	hr m	ht m	hr m	ht m
TU 1	08 48	6.0	21 22	5.9	06 14	7.6	18 56	7.7	07 03	2.9	20 28	2.8	09 58	4.5	22 37	4.6
W 2	10 04	6.3	22 35	6.3	07 22	8.0	19 59	8.2	08 24	3.0	21 38	2.9	11 06	4.8	23 40	4.9
TH 3	11 08	6.6	23 36	6.7	08 20	8.6	20 53	8.8	09 32	3.2	22 31	3.1	12 03	5.1	—	—
F 4	12 05	6.9	—	—	09 12	9.1	21 41	9.2	10 29	3.3	23 18	3.2	00 33	5.2	12 54	5.4
SA 5	00 30	7.0	12 58	7.1	10 01	9.5	22 28	9.6	11 21	3.5	—	—	01 20	5.5	13 41	5.7
SU 6	01 20	7.3	13 47	7.1	10 49	9.7	23 14	9.8	00 03	3.4	12 12	3.5	02 05	5.7	14 28	5.9
M 7	02 07	7.4	14 34	7.2	11 37	9.8	—	—	00 47	3.5	13 02	3.6	02 49	5.8	15 16	5.9
TU 8	02 54	7.5	15 20	7.1	00 00	9.8	12 26	9.6	01 30	3.6	13 51	3.5	03 35	5.8	16 06	5.9
W 9	03 41	7.5	16 05	7.0	00 47	9.6	13 16	9.3	02 13	3.6	14 40	3.5	04 23	5.7	16 57	5.7
TH 10	04 28	7.3	16 51	6.7	01 36	9.4	14 07	8.9	02 55	3.6	15 28	3.3	05 13	5.5	17 52	5.4
F 11	05 18	7.0	17 38	6.5	02 27	9.0	15 02	8.4	03 40	3.5	16 18	3.2	06 07	5.2	18 52	5.1
SA 12	06 10	6.7	18 30	6.3	03 24	8.5	16 02	7.9	04 27	3.3	17 12	3.0	07 08	5.0	19 56	4.8
SU 13	07 10	6.4	19 31	6.1	04 27	8.1	17 09	7.6	05 24	3.1	18 15	2.8	08 16	4.8	21 01	4.6
M 14	08 14	6.2	20 39	6.0	05 35	7.9	18 21	7.5	06 36	3.0	19 30	2.7	09 22	4.7	22 06	4.6
TU 15	09 20	6.2	21 47	6.1	06 42	7.8	19 29	7.6	07 58	2.9	20 42	2.8	10 27	4.7	23 10	4.6
W 16	10 28	6.2	22 53	6.2	07 45	8.0	20 26	7.9	09 07	3.0	21 38	2.9	11 27	4.7	—	—
TH 17	11 30	6.4	23 49	6.4	08 38	8.1	21 11	8.2	10 02	3.1	22 25	3.0	00 07	4.7	12 22	4.8
F 18	12 19	6.5	—	—	09 23	8.3	21 50	8.4	10 49	3.2	23 06	3.1	00 54	4.9	13 08	4.9
SA 19	00 35	6.6	13 01	6.6	10 03	8.5	22 24	8.6	11 32	3.2	23 44	3.2	01 33	5.0	13 48	5.0
SU 20	01 15	6.8	13 36	6.6	10 40	8.6	22 57	8.7	12 11	3.2	—	—	02 08	5.1	14 25	5.1
M 21	01 51	6.9	14 09	6.7	11 15	8.7	23 30	8.8	00 18	3.3	12 46	3.1	02 41	5.2	15 00	5.1
TU 22	02 25	6.9	14 41	6.7	11 49	8.7	—	—	00 52	3.4	13 20	3.1	03 14	5.2	15 34	5.1
W 23	02 58	6.9	15 13	6.7	00 03	8.8	12 24	8.6	01 24	3.5	13 54	3.1	03 47	5.2	16 10	5.1
TH 24	03 32	6.9	15 47	6.6	00 36	8.7	12 59	8.5	01 57	3.5	14 30	3.1	04 22	5.1	16 47	5.1
F 25	04 08	6.8	16 22	6.5	01 11	8.6	13 36	8.4	02 31	3.5	15 09	3.1	04 58	5.0	17 25	5.0
SA 26	04 46	6.7	17 00	6.4	01 48	8.4	14 17	8.2	03 07	3.5	15 52	3.0	05 36	4.9	18 08	4.9
SU 27	05 27	6.6	17 41	6.3	02 30	8.2	15 03	8.0	03 46	3.4	16 37	3.0	06 19	4.8	18 55	4.8
M 28	06 13	6.4	18 30	6.2	03 21	8.1	15 59	7.8	04 30	3.3	17 29	2.9	07 07	4.7	19 48	4.7
TU 29	07 08	6.3	19 29	6.1	04 22	7.9	17 04	7.8	05 21	3.2	18 28	2.8	08 04	4.7	20 50	4.7
W 30	08 16	6.2	20 43	6.1	05 31	8.0	18 13	7.9	06 25	3.1	19 36	2.8	09 14	4.7	21 58	4.8
TH 31	09 29	6.4	21 58	6.4	06 40	8.2	19 20	8.2	07 41	3.1	20 50	2.9	10 25	4.8	23 03	4.9

JUNE 2012   *High Water*   GMT

	LONDON BRIDGE				LIVERPOOL (Gladstone Dock)				GREENOCK				LEITH			
F 1	10 35	6.5	23 03	6.7	07 45	8.5	20 21	8.6	08 56	3.2	21 54	3.1	11 30	5.1	—	—
SA 2	11 37	6.7	—	—	08 45	8.9	21 16	9.0	10 01	3.3	22 50	3.2	00 02	5.2	12 28	5.3
SU 3	00 03	7.0	12 35	6.9	09 40	9.2	22 07	9.4	10 59	3.4	23 40	3.4	00 55	5.4	13 21	5.6
M 4	00 59	7.2	13 28	7.0	10 33	9.4	22 57	9.6	11 54	3.4	—	—	01 44	5.6	14 13	5.8
TU 5	01 50	7.4	14 18	7.0	11 25	9.5	23 46	9.7	00 28	3.5	12 48	3.4	02 32	5.7	15 04	5.8
W 6	02 41	7.4	15 07	7.1	12 16	9.4	—	—	01 14	3.6	13 41	3.4	03 20	5.8	15 54	5.8
TH 7	03 30	7.4	15 54	7.0	00 35	9.6	13 06	9.2	01 59	3.6	14 31	3.3	04 09	5.7	16 46	5.7
F 8	04 19	7.3	16 40	6.9	01 23	9.4	13 54	8.9	02 43	3.6	15 20	3.2	04 59	5.6	17 38	5.4
SA 9	05 07	7.1	17 25	6.7	02 11	9.1	14 42	8.5	03 27	3.5	16 07	3.1	05 51	5.4	18 32	5.2
SU 10	05 55	6.8	18 11	6.5	03 01	8.8	15 32	8.1	04 12	3.4	16 54	3.0	06 46	5.2	19 26	4.9
M 11	06 45	6.5	19 01	6.3	03 53	8.4	16 26	7.8	05 01	3.3	17 43	2.9	07 44	4.9	20 23	4.7
TU 12	07 38	6.3	19 58	6.2	04 50	8.0	17 27	7.5	05 56	3.1	18 34	2.8	08 42	4.7	21 20	4.5
W 13	08 35	6.1	20 59	6.1	05 51	7.7	18 32	7.4	06 58	2.9	19 29	2.8	09 41	4.6	22 18	4.5
TH 14	09 34	6.0	22 01	6.1	06 55	7.7	19 36	7.5	08 09	2.9	20 31	2.9	10 40	4.5	23 17	4.5
F 15	10 36	6.1	23 02	6.2	07 56	7.7	20 32	7.8	09 17	2.9	21 33	2.9	11 40	4.6	—	—
SA 16	11 36	6.2	23 58	6.4	08 50	7.9	21 18	8.1	10 14	3.0	22 26	3.1	00 12	4.7	12 35	4.7
SU 17	12 26	6.4	—	—	09 36	8.1	21 58	8.4	11 02	3.0	23 12	3.2	01 01	4.8	13 22	4.8
M 18	00 45	6.6	13 10	6.6	10 17	8.3	22 35	8.6	11 45	3.1	23 52	3.3	01 42	5.0	14 02	4.9
TU 19	01 28	6.8	13 49	6.7	10 54	8.5	23 10	8.7	12 23	3.1	—	—	02 19	5.1	14 39	5.1
W 20	02 06	6.8	14 26	6.7	11 30	8.6	23 45	8.8	00 27	3.4	13 00	3.1	02 54	5.2	15 15	5.2
TH 21	02 43	6.9	15 02	6.7	12 06	8.7	—	—	01 01	3.5	13 36	3.1	03 29	5.3	15 51	5.2
F 22	03 19	6.9	15 37	6.7	00 19	8.9	12 43	8.7	01 34	3.6	14 13	3.1	04 04	5.3	16 28	5.2
SA 23	03 55	7.0	16 12	6.7	00 56	8.9	13 21	8.7	02 10	3.6	14 51	3.1	04 40	5.2	17 06	5.2
SU 24	04 33	6.9	16 49	6.6	01 34	8.8	14 00	8.6	02 48	3.6	15 32	3.1	05 17	5.2	17 47	5.1
M 25	05 13	6.8	17 28	6.5	02 14	8.7	14 44	8.4	03 28	3.6	16 15	3.1	05 58	5.1	18 31	5.0
TU 26	05 57	6.6	18 12	6.4	03 00	8.5	15 33	8.2	04 10	3.5	17 01	3.1	06 42	5.0	19 21	4.9
W 27	06 46	6.5	19 03	6.3	03 52	8.4	16 30	8.1	04 57	3.4	17 51	3.0	07 34	4.9	20 17	4.8
TH 28	07 45	6.3	20 07	6.3	04 54	8.2	17 36	8.0	05 52	3.2	18 50	2.9	08 37	4.9	21 23	4.8
F 29	08 56	6.3	21 24	6.4	06 05	8.2	18 47	8.1	07 00	3.1	20 05	2.9	09 52	4.9	22 32	4.9
SA 30	10 05	6.3	22 36	6.5	07 18	8.3	19 56	8.4	08 22	3.1	21 24	3.0	11 04	5.0	23 37	5.0

JULY 2012   *High Water*   GMT

	LONDON BRIDGE *Datum of Predictions 3.20m below					LIVERPOOL (Gladstone Dock) *Datum of Predictions 4.93m below					GREENOCK *Datum of Predictions 1.62m below					LEITH *Datum of Predictions 2.90m below				
	hr	m	ht/m	hr	ht/m	hr	m	ht/m	hr	m	ht/m	hr	m	ht/m	hr	m	ht/m	hr	m	ht/m	hr	m	ht/m
SU 1	11 13	6.5	23 43	6.8	08 27	8.5	20 58	8.8	09 40	3.1	22 29	3.2	12 10	5.2	—	—
M 2	12 18	6.6	—	—	09 29	8.8	21 54	9.1	10 46	3.2	23 25	3.3	00 36	5.2	13 09	5.4
TU 3	00 44	7.0	13 16	6.8	10 25	9.1	22 46	9.4	11 45	3.3	—	—	01 29	5.5	14 03	5.6
W 4	01 40	7.2	14 08	7.0	11 17	9.3	23 35	9.6	00 15	3.5	12 40	3.3	02 19	5.6	14 53	5.7
TH 5	02 32	7.3	14 56	7.1	12 05	9.3	—	—	01 02	3.6	13 32	3.3	03 07	5.7	15 42	5.7
F 6	03 20	7.4	15 41	7.1	00 21	9.6	12 51	9.2	01 46	3.6	14 20	3.2	03 55	5.7	16 29	5.6
SA 7	04 06	7.3	16 24	7.1	01 06	9.5	13 34	9.0	02 29	3.6	15 04	3.2	04 42	5.7	17 16	5.4
SU 8	04 49	7.1	17 04	6.9	01 48	9.3	14 14	8.7	03 10	3.6	15 44	3.2	05 28	5.5	18 03	5.2
M 9	05 31	6.9	17 43	6.7	02 30	8.9	14 55	8.3	03 50	3.5	16 23	3.1	06 16	5.3	18 50	5.0
TU 10	06 11	6.6	18 23	6.5	03 13	8.5	15 38	7.9	04 31	3.4	17 03	3.1	07 04	5.0	19 38	4.7
W 11	06 54	6.3	19 09	6.2	04 00	8.1	16 29	7.6	05 14	3.2	17 45	3.0	07 55	4.8	20 28	4.5
TH 12	07 42	6.0	20 05	6.0	04 56	7.7	17 30	7.3	06 01	3.0	18 31	2.9	08 50	4.5	21 22	4.4
F 13	08 38	5.8	21 10	5.9	06 01	7.4	18 41	7.2	06 57	2.8	19 25	2.9	09 48	4.4	22 20	4.4
SA 14	09 41	5.8	22 16	5.9	07 12	7.3	19 50	7.4	08 09	2.7	20 31	2.9	10 50	4.4	23 23	4.5
SU 15	10 48	5.9	23 21	6.2	08 17	7.5	20 47	7.8	09 33	2.8	21 44	3.0	11 56	4.5	—	—
M 16	11 53	6.2	—	—	09 11	7.8	21 34	8.2	10 36	2.9	22 43	3.2	00 24	4.7	12 54	4.7
TU 17	00 17	6.4	12 45	6.5	09 56	8.2	22 14	8.5	11 24	3.0	23 28	3.3	01 15	4.9	13 40	4.9
W 18	01 06	6.7	13 30	6.7	10 35	8.4	22 51	8.8	12 05	3.0	—	—	01 57	5.1	14 19	5.1
TH 19	01 48	6.8	14 10	6.8	11 12	8.7	23 26	9.0	00 05	3.4	12 44	3.1	02 35	5.3	14 55	5.2
F 20	02 26	6.9	14 47	6.8	11 47	8.9	—	—	00 39	3.5	13 19	3.1	03 10	5.4	15 31	5.4
SA 21	03 04	7.0	15 23	6.9	00 01	9.2	12 24	9.0	01 13	3.6	13 55	3.1	03 45	5.5	16 07	5.4
SU 22	03 40	7.1	15 58	6.9	00 38	9.2	13 02	9.0	01 51	3.6	14 31	3.2	04 20	5.6	16 45	5.4
M 23	04 18	7.1	16 33	6.9	01 15	9.2	13 41	9.0	02 30	3.7	15 10	3.2	04 56	5.5	17 24	5.4
TU 24	04 56	6.9	17 10	6.8	01 55	9.1	14 22	8.8	03 10	3.7	15 50	3.2	05 36	5.4	18 07	5.3
W 25	05 36	6.7	17 51	6.7	02 37	8.9	15 07	8.5	03 51	3.6	16 32	3.2	06 20	5.3	18 54	5.1
TH 26	06 21	6.5	18 37	6.5	03 26	8.6	16 01	8.2	04 35	3.5	17 17	3.1	07 09	5.1	19 47	4.9
F 27	07 14	6.2	19 37	6.3	04 25	8.3	17 07	8.0	05 24	3.3	18 10	3.0	08 11	4.9	20 53	4.8
SA 28	08 23	6.1	20 55	6.2	05 41	8.0	18 26	7.9	06 24	3.1	19 24	2.9	09 30	4.8	22 08	4.7
SU 29	09 39	6.1	22 16	6.3	07 03	7.9	19 42	8.1	07 52	2.9	21 03	2.9	10 50	4.8	23 20	4.9
M 30	10 56	6.2	23 31	6.6	08 20	8.2	20 49	8.6	09 34	3.0	22 18	3.1	12 02	5.0	—	—
TU 31	12 09	6.5	—	—	09 25	8.6	21 47	9.0	10 46	3.1	23 15	3.4	00 25	5.1	13 04	5.3

AUGUST 2012   *High Water*   GMT

	LONDON BRIDGE					LIVERPOOL (Gladstone Dock)					GREENOCK					LEITH				
W 1	00 38	6.9	13 09	6.7	10 20	8.9	22 37	9.4	11 42	3.2	—	—	01 20	5.4	13 56	5.5
TH 2	01 34	7.1	13 59	6.9	11 07	9.2	23 22	9.6	00 03	3.5	12 33	3.2	02 08	5.6	14 42	5.6
F 3	02 22	7.3	14 43	7.1	11 50	9.3	—	—	00 49	3.6	13 19	3.2	02 53	5.7	15 25	5.7
SA 4	03 06	7.3	15 23	7.2	00 03	9.7	12 32	9.2	01 31	3.7	14 00	3.2	03 36	5.8	16 08	5.6
SU 5	03 46	7.3	16 00	7.2	00 43	9.6	13 06	9.1	02 10	3.6	14 36	3.2	04 19	5.7	16 49	5.4
M 6	04 24	7.1	16 36	7.1	01 19	9.4	13 40	8.8	02 47	3.6	15 10	3.2	05 00	5.5	17 29	5.2
TU 7	04 59	6.9	17 09	6.9	01 55	9.0	14 15	8.5	03 22	3.5	15 45	3.2	05 41	5.3	18 09	5.0
W 8	05 31	6.6	17 43	6.6	02 32	8.6	14 52	8.1	03 58	3.4	16 22	3.2	06 23	5.1	18 51	4.8
TH 9	06 04	6.3	18 20	6.3	03 12	8.1	15 35	7.7	04 35	3.2	17 01	3.1	07 08	4.8	19 38	4.6
F 10	06 41	6.0	19 04	6.0	04 02	7.6	16 31	7.3	05 17	3.0	17 45	3.0	07 59	4.5	20 30	4.4
SA 11	07 32	5.7	20 08	5.7	05 06	7.2	17 45	7.1	06 07	2.8	18 36	2.9	08 57	4.3	21 30	4.3
SU 12	08 45	5.5	21 29	5.6	06 25	7.0	19 07	7.2	07 11	2.6	19 38	2.9	10 01	4.2	22 35	4.4
M 13	10 04	5.6	22 43	5.9	07 44	7.2	20 16	7.6	08 43	2.6	20 58	2.9	11 12	4.3	23 45	4.6
TU 14	11 18	6.0	23 47	6.3	08 46	7.6	21 08	8.1	10 13	2.8	22 11	3.1	12 21	4.6	—	—
W 15	12 16	6.4	—	—	09 33	8.1	21 50	8.5	11 04	3.0	23 00	3.3	00 45	4.8	13 13	4.9
TH 16	00 39	6.6	13 04	6.7	10 13	8.5	22 27	8.9	11 45	3.1	23 39	3.4	01 31	5.1	13 54	5.1
F 17	01 23	6.9	13 46	6.8	10 49	8.9	23 03	9.2	12 23	3.1	—	—	02 10	5.3	14 31	5.4
SA 18	02 03	7.0	14 24	7.0	11 25	9.2	23 38	9.5	00 15	3.5	12 58	3.2	02 46	5.5	15 06	5.5
SU 19	02 42	7.1	15 01	7.1	12 01	9.4	—	—	00 52	3.6	13 33	3.2	03 21	5.7	15 42	5.6
M 20	03 19	7.2	15 37	7.2	00 15	9.6	12 39	9.4	01 31	3.7	14 08	3.3	03 56	5.8	16 20	5.6
TU 21	03 57	7.2	16 12	7.1	00 54	9.6	13 18	9.3	02 11	3.8	14 46	3.3	04 34	5.8	17 00	5.6
W 22	04 34	7.0	16 49	7.0	01 33	9.4	13 59	9.1	02 52	3.8	15 24	3.4	05 15	5.7	17 42	5.4
TH 23	05 13	6.7	17 30	6.8	02 16	9.1	14 44	8.7	03 33	3.7	16 05	3.3	06 00	5.5	18 29	5.2
F 24	05 56	6.4	18 16	6.6	03 05	8.7	15 38	8.3	04 15	3.5	16 49	3.2	06 52	5.2	19 23	4.9
SA 25	06 46	6.1	19 14	6.3	04 07	8.1	16 48	7.8	05 02	3.3	17 41	3.1	07 56	4.9	20 31	4.7
SU 26	07 54	5.9	20 36	6.1	05 29	7.7	18 12	7.8	06 00	3.0	18 55	2.9	09 19	4.7	21 53	4.7
M 27	09 19	5.9	22 03	6.2	06 59	7.7	19 34	8.0	07 37	2.8	20 54	2.9	10 43	4.7	23 10	4.8
TU 28	10 45	6.1	23 23	6.5	08 19	8.0	20 42	8.5	09 43	2.9	22 08	3.2	11 57	5.0	—	—
W 29	12 00	6.4	—	—	09 21	8.5	21 37	9.0	10 45	3.1	23 01	3.4	00 16	5.1	12 58	5.2
TH 30	00 29	6.9	12 57	6.8	10 10	8.9	22 23	9.4	11 34	3.2	23 48	3.6	01 10	5.4	13 45	5.4
F 31	01 22	7.1	13 43	7.0	10 52	9.1	23 03	9.6	12 17	3.3	—	—	01 54	5.6	14 26	5.5

SEPTEMBER 2012   *High Water*   GMT

	LONDON BRIDGE *Datum of Predictions 3.20m below*				LIVERPOOL (Gladstone Dock) *Datum of Predictions 4.93m below*				GREENOCK *Datum of Predictions 1.62m below*				LEITH *Datum of Predictions 2.90m below*			
	hr	ht m	hr	ht m	hr	ht m	hr	ht m	hr	ht m	hr	ht m	hr	ht m	hr	ht m
SA 1	02 06	7.2	14 23	7.1	11 29	9.3	23 40	9.6	00 31	3.6	12 57	3.3	02 35	5.7	15 04	5.6
SU 2	02 45	7.2	14 58	7.2	12 03	9.2	—	—	01 11	3.6	13 31	3.3	03 14	5.7	15 42	5.5
M 3	03 20	7.2	15 31	7.2	00 15	9.5	12 36	9.1	01 47	3.6	14 02	3.3	03 53	5.7	16 19	5.4
TU 4	03 52	7.0	16 03	7.1	00 48	9.3	13 06	8.9	02 21	3.6	14 34	3.3	04 30	5.5	16 54	5.2
W 5	04 22	6.9	16 35	7.0	01 21	9.0	13 37	8.7	02 53	3.5	15 08	3.4	05 07	5.3	17 31	5.1
TH 6	04 51	6.6	17 06	6.7	01 55	8.6	14 11	8.3	03 27	3.4	15 44	3.4	05 45	5.1	18 09	4.9
F 7	05 20	6.3	17 39	6.4	02 31	8.2	14 49	7.9	04 03	3.3	16 22	3.3	06 27	4.8	18 52	4.6
SA 8	05 52	6.0	18 17	6.0	03 14	7.7	15 37	7.4	04 42	3.1	17 04	3.1	07 15	4.5	19 43	4.4
SU 9	06 33	5.7	19 05	5.7	04 12	7.1	16 47	7.1	05 30	2.8	17 54	3.0	08 12	4.3	20 44	4.3
M 10	07 31	5.5	20 23	5.5	05 33	6.8	18 18	7.0	06 33	2.6	18 55	2.9	09 17	4.2	21 52	4.3
TU 11	09 10	5.4	21 57	5.7	07 03	7.0	19 37	7.4	08 00	2.6	20 11	2.9	10 27	4.3	23 04	4.5
W 12	10 36	5.7	23 08	6.1	08 13	7.5	20 34	8.0	09 44	2.8	21 31	3.1	11 40	4.5	—	—
TH 13	11 40	6.2	—	—	09 03	8.1	21 18	8.5	10 37	3.0	22 26	3.3	00 09	4.8	12 38	4.9
F 14	00 03	6.6	12 31	6.6	09 43	8.6	21 57	9.0	11 18	3.1	23 08	3.4	00 59	5.1	13 22	5.2
SA 15	00 51	6.9	13 14	6.9	10 21	9.1	22 34	9.4	11 56	3.2	23 48	3.6	01 40	5.4	14 01	5.5
SU 16	01 33	7.1	13 54	7.1	10 58	9.4	23 12	9.7	12 31	3.3	—	—	02 17	5.7	14 38	5.7
M 17	02 14	7.2	14 33	7.2	11 35	9.7	23 51	9.9	00 28	3.7	13 07	3.4	02 53	5.9	15 15	5.8
TU 18	02 54	7.3	15 12	7.3	12 15	9.7	—	—	01 11	3.7	13 44	3.4	03 31	6.0	15 54	5.8
W 19	03 33	7.2	15 50	7.4	00 31	9.8	12 56	9.6	01 53	3.8	14 22	3.5	04 12	5.9	16 36	5.7
TH 20	04 12	7.0	16 30	7.2	01 14	9.6	13 39	9.3	02 36	3.8	15 01	3.5	04 56	5.8	17 20	5.5
F 21	04 52	6.7	17 12	7.0	02 00	9.2	14 26	8.9	03 18	3.7	15 43	3.5	05 44	5.5	18 08	5.3
SA 22	05 35	6.4	18 01	6.7	02 52	8.6	15 23	8.4	04 01	3.5	16 28	3.3	06 40	5.2	19 04	5.0
SU 23	06 26	6.1	19 01	6.3	03 58	8.0	16 36	8.0	04 49	3.2	17 21	3.1	07 49	4.9	20 17	4.7
M 24	07 34	5.9	20 24	6.1	05 22	7.6	18 01	7.8	05 49	2.9	18 42	3.0	09 13	4.7	21 41	4.7
TU 25	09 03	5.8	21 49	6.2	06 52	7.6	19 20	8.1	07 58	2.8	20 38	3.0	10 33	4.7	22 57	4.9
W 26	10 28	6.1	23 08	6.5	08 09	8.0	20 27	8.5	09 36	2.9	21 48	3.3	11 46	5.0	—	—
TH 27	11 40	6.5	—	—	09 06	8.5	21 19	8.9	10 30	3.1	22 40	3.5	00 01	5.1	12 44	5.2
F 28	00 11	6.9	12 36	6.8	09 52	8.8	22 02	9.2	11 14	3.3	23 25	3.6	00 53	5.3	13 28	5.4
SA 29	01 02	7.1	13 20	6.9	10 30	9.1	22 40	9.4	11 53	3.3	—	—	01 36	5.5	14 06	5.5
SU 30	01 43	7.1	13 57	7.0	11 04	9.2	23 15	9.4	00 07	3.6	12 28	3.4	02 14	5.6	14 41	5.5

OCTOBER 2012   *High Water*   GMT

	LONDON BRIDGE				LIVERPOOL (Gladstone Dock)				GREENOCK				LEITH			
M 1	02 19	7.0	14 30	7.1	11 35	9.2	23 47	9.4	00 46	3.6	12 59	3.4	02 51	5.6	15 15	5.5
TU 2	02 50	7.0	15 01	7.2	12 05	9.1	—	—	01 21	3.6	13 28	3.4	03 27	5.5	15 49	5.4
W 3	03 19	7.0	15 32	7.2	00 19	9.2	12 35	9.0	01 53	3.5	14 00	3.5	04 03	5.4	16 22	5.3
TH 4	03 47	6.9	16 04	7.0	00 52	9.0	13 06	8.8	02 25	3.5	14 34	3.5	04 38	5.3	16 56	5.1
F 5	04 16	6.7	16 35	6.8	01 24	8.6	13 38	8.5	02 59	3.4	15 05	3.4	05 15	5.1	17 32	5.0
SA 6	04 45	6.4	17 07	6.5	01 59	8.2	14 13	8.1	03 35	3.3	15 46	3.4	05 55	4.9	18 13	4.8
SU 7	05 16	6.2	17 44	6.2	02 39	7.8	14 56	7.7	04 15	3.1	16 27	3.3	06 40	4.6	19 01	4.6
M 8	05 55	5.9	18 29	5.9	03 30	7.3	15 56	7.3	05 02	2.9	17 15	3.1	07 33	4.4	19 58	4.4
TU 9	06 45	5.6	19 28	5.7	04 42	7.0	17 22	7.1	06 02	2.7	18 14	3.0	08 35	4.3	21 08	4.4
W 10	07 57	5.5	20 59	5.7	06 10	7.0	18 45	7.4	07 22	2.7	19 25	3.0	09 45	4.4	22 20	4.5
TH 11	09 41	5.6	22 19	6.1	07 26	7.5	19 49	7.9	09 01	2.8	20 42	3.1	10 55	4.6	23 26	4.8
F 12	10 53	6.1	23 20	6.5	08 22	8.1	20 39	8.5	10 05	3.0	21 44	3.3	11 56	4.9	—	—
SA 13	11 49	6.6	—	—	09 08	8.7	21 23	9.1	10 46	3.2	22 34	3.5	00 20	5.1	12 46	5.3
SU 14	00 13	6.9	12 38	6.9	09 49	9.2	22 05	9.5	11 25	3.4	23 19	3.6	01 05	5.4	13 29	5.6
M 15	01 01	7.1	13 22	7.2	10 30	9.6	22 46	9.8	12 03	3.4	—	—	01 46	5.7	14 09	5.8
TU 16	01 46	7.2	14 05	7.4	11 10	9.8	23 29	10.0	00 05	3.7	12 42	3.5	02 26	5.9	14 49	5.9
W 17	02 29	7.3	14 48	7.5	11 52	9.9	—	—	00 52	3.8	13 21	3.6	03 09	6.1	15 30	5.9
TH 18	03 12	7.2	15 31	7.5	00 13	9.9	12 37	9.8	01 37	3.8	14 02	3.7	03 53	6.0	16 14	5.8
F 19	03 54	7.1	16 14	7.3	00 59	9.6	13 23	9.5	02 22	3.8	14 44	3.7	04 41	5.9	17 00	5.6
SA 20	04 36	6.8	17 00	7.1	01 49	9.2	14 13	9.1	03 07	3.7	15 27	3.6	05 33	5.6	17 51	5.4
SU 21	05 21	6.5	17 52	6.8	02 44	8.6	15 12	8.6	03 54	3.5	16 14	3.5	06 31	5.2	18 50	5.1
M 22	06 13	6.2	18 54	6.4	03 50	8.0	16 22	8.2	04 45	3.2	17 11	3.3	07 41	4.9	20 05	4.9
TU 23	07 21	6.0	20 10	6.3	05 08	7.7	17 40	8.0	05 52	2.9	18 30	3.1	09 06	4.8	21 23	4.8
W 24	08 41	6.0	21 25	6.3	06 30	7.7	18 55	8.1	07 43	2.9	20 07	3.1	10 12	4.8	22 34	4.9
TH 25	09 59	6.1	22 39	6.5	07 44	8.0	20 00	8.4	09 07	3.0	21 18	3.3	11 21	4.9	23 36	5.1
F 26	11 09	6.4	23 43	6.7	08 41	8.3	20 53	8.7	10 01	3.2	22 22	3.4	12 18	5.1	—	—
SA 27	12 05	6.6	—	—	09 26	8.6	21 37	8.9	10 44	3.3	22 58	3.5	00 29	5.2	13 04	5.2
SU 28	00 34	6.9	12 50	6.8	10 04	8.9	22 15	9.1	11 23	3.4	23 41	3.6	01 14	5.3	13 42	5.3
M 29	01 16	6.9	13 28	6.9	10 37	9.0	22 49	9.1	11 57	3.4	—	—	01 53	5.4	14 17	5.4
TU 30	01 50	6.9	14 01	7.0	11 09	9.1	23 23	9.1	00 20	3.5	12 28	3.5	02 30	5.4	14 50	5.4
W 31	02 21	6.9	14 33	7.1	11 39	9.1	23 55	9.0	00 55	3.5	12 59	3.6	03 05	5.4	15 22	5.4

NOVEMBER 2012 *High Water* GMT

	LONDON BRIDGE *Datum of Predictions 3.20m below				LIVERPOOL (Gladstone Dock) *Datum of Predictions 4.93m below				GREENOCK *Datum of Predictions 1.62m below				LEITH *Datum of Predictions 2.90m below			
	hr	ht m	hr	ht m	hr	ht m	hr	ht m	hr	ht m	hr	ht m	hr	ht m	hr	ht m
TH 1	02 49	6.9	15 05	7.1	12 10	9.0	—	—	01 28	3.5	13 32	3.7	03 39	5.3	15 54	5.3
F 2	03 18	6.9	15 37	7.0	00 28	8.9	12 41	8.9	02 01	3.4	14 06	3.7	04 14	5.2	16 28	5.2
SA 3	03 48	6.7	16 10	6.8	01 01	8.6	13 13	8.6	02 36	3.4	14 41	3.7	04 51	5.1	17 03	5.1
SU 4	04 20	6.5	16 44	6.6	01 36	8.3	13 48	8.3	03 13	3.3	15 17	3.6	05 30	4.9	17 42	4.9
M 5	04 53	6.3	17 21	6.4	02 15	8.0	14 29	8.0	03 53	3.2	15 56	3.5	06 13	4.8	18 26	4.7
TU 6	05 31	6.1	18 05	6.2	03 02	7.6	15 21	7.7	04 39	3.0	16 41	3.3	07 01	4.6	19 18	4.6
W 7	06 18	5.9	18 58	6.0	04 01	7.4	16 30	7.5	05 33	2.9	17 35	3.2	07 57	4.5	20 20	4.5
TH 8	07 17	5.8	20 08	6.0	05 15	7.3	17 48	7.6	06 41	2.8	18 40	3.1	09 02	4.5	21 32	4.6
F 9	08 39	5.8	21 30	6.1	06 30	7.6	18 57	7.9	08 03	2.9	19 53	3.2	10 11	4.7	22 40	4.8
SA 10	10 02	6.1	22 37	6.5	07 35	8.1	19 57	8.5	09 15	3.1	21 02	3.3	11 14	4.9	23 39	5.1
SU 11	11 06	6.5	23 36	6.8	08 30	8.6	20 49	9.0	10 08	3.2	22 00	3.5	12 09	5.2	—	—
M 12	12 02	6.9	—	—	09 18	9.1	21 37	9.4	10 54	3.4	22 53	3.6	00 31	5.4	12 58	5.5
TU 13	00 30	7.0	12 53	7.2	10 04	9.6	22 24	9.7	11 37	3.5	23 44	3.7	01 19	5.7	13 43	5.8
W 14	01 20	7.2	13 42	7.4	10 49	9.8	23 11	9.9	12 20	3.7	—	—	02 04	5.9	14 26	5.9
TH 15	02 08	7.2	14 29	7.5	11 35	9.9	—	—	00 34	3.7	13 03	3.7	02 51	6.0	15 11	6.0
F 16	02 54	7.2	15 16	7.5	00 00	9.8	12 22	9.9	01 24	3.7	13 47	3.8	03 39	6.0	15 57	5.9
SA 17	03 40	7.1	16 04	7.4	00 50	9.6	13 11	9.7	02 13	3.7	14 31	3.8	04 30	5.9	16 45	5.7
SU 18	04 26	6.9	16 53	7.2	01 41	9.2	14 02	9.3	03 01	3.6	15 16	3.8	05 23	5.6	17 38	5.5
M 19	05 13	6.7	17 45	6.9	02 35	8.7	14 58	8.9	03 50	3.4	16 05	3.6	06 21	5.3	18 36	5.3
TU 20	06 04	6.4	18 43	6.6	03 34	8.2	16 00	8.5	04 43	3.2	16 59	3.4	07 25	5.0	19 45	5.0
W 21	07 03	6.2	19 46	6.4	04 40	7.9	17 07	8.2	05 44	3.1	18 05	3.3	08 33	4.8	20 55	4.9
TH 22	08 10	6.1	20 51	6.3	05 51	7.7	18 15	8.1	06 57	3.0	19 22	3.2	09 39	4.8	22 00	4.9
F 23	09 19	6.1	21 58	6.3	07 03	7.8	19 22	8.1	08 15	3.0	20 36	3.2	10 44	4.8	23 02	4.9
SA 24	10 26	6.2	23 04	6.4	08 05	8.0	20 20	8.3	09 17	3.1	21 37	3.3	11 43	4.9	23 59	5.0
SU 25	11 27	6.4	—	—	08 55	8.3	21 08	8.5	10 07	3.2	22 29	3.4	12 34	5.0	—	—
M 26	00 00	6.5	12 17	6.6	09 37	8.5	21 50	8.7	10 50	3.4	23 14	3.4	00 49	5.1	13 17	5.2
TU 27	00 45	6.6	12 59	6.7	10 13	8.7	22 27	8.8	11 28	3.5	23 56	3.4	01 32	5.1	13 54	5.3
W 28	01 23	6.7	13 36	6.8	10 46	8.9	23 02	8.9	12 02	3.6	—	—	02 11	5.2	14 28	5.3
TH 29	01 56	6.7	14 11	6.9	11 19	9.0	23 36	8.9	00 33	3.4	12 36	3.7	02 46	5.2	15 01	5.4
F 30	02 27	6.8	14 44	6.9	11 51	9.0	—	—	01 08	3.4	13 10	3.7	03 20	5.3	15 33	5.3

DECEMBER 2012 *High Water* GMT

	LONDON BRIDGE				LIVERPOOL (Gladstone Dock)				GREENOCK				LEITH			
SA 1	02 59	6.8	15 17	6.9	00 10	8.8	12 23	8.9	01 42	3.4	13 43	3.8	03 55	5.2	16 07	5.3
SU 2	03 31	6.7	15 51	6.9	00 44	8.7	12 57	8.8	02 17	3.4	14 18	3.8	04 31	5.2	16 42	5.2
M 3	04 04	6.6	16 27	6.8	01 20	8.5	13 31	8.6	02 54	3.3	14 54	3.7	05 08	5.1	17 19	5.1
TU 4	04 39	6.5	17 05	6.7	01 57	8.3	14 10	8.4	03 34	3.3	15 33	3.6	05 49	5.0	17 59	5.0
W 5	05 17	6.4	17 47	6.5	02 39	8.1	14 54	8.2	04 17	3.2	16 15	3.5	06 33	4.8	18 44	4.8
TH 6	05 59	6.2	18 35	6.4	03 29	7.8	15 49	8.0	05 04	3.1	17 03	3.4	07 22	4.7	19 36	4.8
F 7	06 50	6.1	19 32	6.2	04 29	7.7	16 55	7.9	05 58	3.0	17 58	3.3	08 20	4.7	20 39	4.7
SA 8	07 53	6.0	20 45	6.2	05 38	7.7	18 06	8.0	07 04	3.0	19 05	3.3	09 26	4.7	21 53	4.8
SU 9	09 14	6.1	21 58	6.4	06 49	8.0	19 15	8.3	08 20	3.0	20 20	3.3	10 34	4.9	23 01	5.0
M 10	10 28	6.4	23 03	6.6	07 53	8.4	20 18	8.7	09 29	3.2	21 30	3.4	11 35	5.1	—	—
TU 11	11 32	6.8	—	—	08 51	8.9	21 15	9.1	10 26	3.3	22 32	3.5	00 02	5.3	12 31	5.4
W 12	00 04	6.8	12 30	7.1	09 44	9.3	22 09	9.4	11 16	3.5	23 28	3.6	00 57	5.5	13 21	5.6
TH 13	01 00	7.0	13 24	7.3	10 34	9.7	23 01	9.6	12 03	3.7	—	—	01 49	5.8	14 08	5.8
F 14	01 52	7.1	14 15	7.4	11 23	9.9	23 51	9.7	00 22	3.6	12 50	3.8	02 39	5.9	14 56	5.9
SA 15	02 42	7.1	15 06	7.5	12 11	9.9	—	—	01 15	3.6	13 36	3.9	03 28	6.0	15 43	5.9
SU 16	03 30	7.1	15 55	7.5	00 41	9.6	13 00	9.8	02 06	3.6	14 21	3.9	04 19	5.9	16 32	5.8
M 17	04 16	7.1	16 43	7.3	01 30	9.3	13 49	9.6	02 54	3.5	15 06	3.8	05 10	5.7	17 23	5.7
TU 18	05 02	6.9	17 31	7.0	02 19	8.9	14 38	9.2	03 41	3.4	15 52	3.7	06 03	5.4	18 17	5.4
W 19	05 48	6.7	18 21	6.7	03 08	8.5	15 29	8.8	04 28	3.3	16 40	3.6	06 58	5.1	19 15	5.2
TH 20	06 35	6.5	19 13	6.5	04 00	8.1	16 24	8.3	05 15	3.2	17 32	3.4	07 57	4.9	20 17	4.9
F 21	07 30	6.3	20 09	6.2	05 00	7.7	17 26	8.0	06 06	3.1	18 29	3.2	08 56	4.7	21 18	4.8
SA 22	08 31	6.1	21 07	6.1	06 06	7.5	18 32	7.8	07 02	3.0	19 36	3.1	09 56	4.6	22 19	4.7
SU 23	09 35	6.0	22 11	6.0	07 17	7.6	19 39	7.9	08 09	3.0	20 50	3.1	10 57	4.6	23 22	4.6
M 24	10 39	6.1	23 16	6.1	08 19	7.8	20 38	8.0	09 18	3.1	21 57	3.1	11 57	4.7	—	—
TU 25	11 40	6.3	—	—	09 09	8.1	21 27	8.2	10 15	3.2	22 51	3.2	00 21	4.7	12 50	4.9
W 26	00 11	6.3	12 31	6.5	09 51	8.4	22 09	8.4	11 02	3.4	23 37	3.2	01 11	4.9	13 33	5.1
TH 27	00 55	6.5	13 15	6.7	10 28	8.7	22 46	8.6	11 42	3.5	—	—	01 53	5.0	14 10	5.2
F 28	01 37	6.6	13 53	6.8	11 02	8.9	23 21	8.8	00 17	3.3	12 19	3.6	02 30	5.1	14 45	5.3
SA 29	02 13	6.7	14 29	6.8	11 35	9.0	23 55	8.8	00 54	3.3	12 52	3.7	03 04	5.2	15 18	5.4
SU 30	02 47	6.7	15 03	6.9	12 08	9.1	—	—	01 28	3.3	13 24	3.7	03 37	5.3	15 51	5.4
M 31	03 19	6.8	15 36	6.9	00 28	8.8	12 42	9.0	02 02	3.3	13 58	3.7	04 12	5.3	16 25	5.3

GENERAL REFERENCE

WEIGHTS AND MEASURES

CONVERSION TABLES

THE PERIODIC TABLE

NOBEL PRIZE WINNERS

ABBREVIATIONS

WEIGHTS AND MEASURES

SI UNITS

The Système International d'Unités (SI) is an international and coherent system of units devised to meet all known needs for measurement in science and technology. The system was adopted by the eleventh Conférence Générale des Poids et Mesures (CGPM) in 1960. A comprehensive description of the system is given in *SI The International System of Units* (HMSO). The British Standards that describe the essential features of the International System of Units are *Specifications for SI units and recommendations for the use of their multiples and certain other units* (BS ISO 1000:1992) and *Conversion factors for units* (BS 350: 2004).

The system consists of seven base units and the derived units formed as products or quotients of various powers of the base units. Together the base units and the derived units make up the coherent system of units. In the UK the SI base units, and almost all important derived units, are realised at the National Physical Laboratory and disseminated through the National Measurement Office.

BASE UNITS
Ampere (A) = unit of electric current
Candela (cd) = unit of luminous intensity
Kelvin (K) = unit of thermodynamic temperature
Kilogram (kg) = unit of mass
Metre (m) = unit of length
Mole (mol) = unit of amount of substance
Second (s) = unit of time

DERIVED UNITS
For some of the derived SI units, special names and symbols exist; those approved by the CGPM are as follows:

Becquerel (Bq) = unit of activity (of a radionuclide)
Coulomb (C) = unit of electric charge, quantity of electricity
Degree Celsius (°C) = unit of Celsius temperature
Farad (F) = unit of electric capacitance
Gray (Gy) = unit of absorbed dose, specific energy imparted, kerma, absorbed dose index
Henry (H) = unit of inductance
Hertz (Hz) = unit of frequency
Joule (J) = unit of energy, work, quantity of heat
Katal (kat) = unit of catalytic activity
Lumen (lm) = unit of luminous flux
Lux (lx) = unit of illuminance
Newton (N) = unit of force
Ohm (Ω) = unit of electric resistance
Pascal (Pa) = unit of pressure, stress
Radian (rad) = unit of plane angle
Siemens (S) = unit of electric conductance
Sievert (Sv) = unit of dose equivalent, dose equivalent index
Steradian (sr) = unit of solid angle
Tesla (T) = unit of magnetic flux density
Volt (V) = unit of electric potential, potential difference, electromotive force
Watt (W) = unit of power, radiant flux
Weber (Wb) = unit of magnetic flux

Other derived units are expressed in terms of base units. Below are some of the more commonly used derived units:

Ampere per metre (A m^{-1}) = unit of magnetic field strength
Candela per square metre (cd m^{-2}) = unit of luminance
Cubic metre (m^3) = unit of volume
Joule per kelvin (J K^{-1}) = unit of heat capacity
Joule per kilogram kelvin (J kg^{-1} K^{-1}) = unit of specific heat capacity
Kilogram per cubic metre (kg m^{-3}) = unit of density
Kilogram metre per second (kg m s^{-1}) = unit of momentum
Metre per second (m s^{-1}) = unit of velocity
Metre per second squared (m s^{-2}) = unit of acceleration
Newton per metre (N m^{-1}) = unit of surface tension
Pascal second (Pa s) = unit of dynamic viscosity
Square metre (m^2) = unit of area
Volt per metre (V m^{-1}) = unit of electric field strength
Watt per square metre (W m^{-2}) = unit of heat flux density, irradiance
Watt per metre kelvin (W m^{-1} K^{-1}) = unit of thermal conductivity

Non SI units accepted for use with the SI by the CGPM:

Minute	
Hour	measurement of time
Day	
Degree	
Minute	plane angle measurement
Second	
Hectare	measurement of area
Litre	measurement of volume
Tonne	measurement of mass

SI PREFIXES
Decimal multiples and submultiples of the SI units are indicated by SI prefixes. These are as follows:

Multiples	*Submultiples*
yotta (Y) $\times 10^{24}$	deci (d) $\times 10^{-1}$
zetta (Z) $\times 10^{21}$	centi (c) $\times 10^{-2}$
exa (E) $\times 10^{18}$	milli (m) $\times 10^{-3}$
peta (P) $\times 10^{15}$	micro (μ) $\times 10^{-6}$
tera (T) $\times 10^{12}$	nano (n) $\times 10^{-9}$
giga (G) $\times 10^9$	pico (p) $\times 10^{-12}$
mega (M) $\times 10^6$	femto (f) $\times 10^{-15}$
kilo (k) $\times 10^3$	atto (a) $\times 10^{-18}$
hecto (h) $\times 10^2$	zepto (z) $\times 10^{-21}$
deca (da) $\times 10$	yocto (y) $\times 10^{-24}$

METRIC UNITS

The metric primary standards are the metre as the unit of measurement of length, and the kilogram as the unit of measurement of mass. Other units of measurement are defined by reference to the primary standards.

MEASUREMENT OF LENGTH
Kilometre (km) = 1,000 metres
Metre (m) = the length of the path travelled by light in a vacuum during a time interval of 1/299,792,458 of a second

Decimetre (dm) = 1/10 metre
Centimetre (cm) = 1/100 metre
Millimetre (mm) = 1/1,000 metre

MEASUREMENT OF AREA
Hectare (ha) = 100 ares
Decare = 10 ares
Are (a) = 100 square metres
Square metre = a superficial area equal to that of a square
  each side of which measures one metre
Square decimetre = 1/100 square metre
Square centimetre = 1/100 square decimetre
Square millimetre = 1/100 square centimetre

MEASUREMENT OF VOLUME
Cubic metre (m³) = a volume equal to that of a cube each
  edge of which measures one metre
Cubic decimetre = 1/1,000 cubic metre
Cubic centimetre (cc) = 1/1,000 cubic decimetre
Hectolitre = 100 litres
Litre = a cubic decimetre
Decilitre = 1/10 litre
Centilitre = 1/100 litre
Millilitre = 1/1,000 litre

MEASUREMENT OF CAPACITY
Hectolitre (hl) = 100 litres
Litre (l or L) = a cubic decimetre
Decilitre (dl) = 1/10 litre
Centilitre (cl) = 1/100 litre
Millilitre (ml) = 1/1,000 litre

MEASUREMENT OF MASS OR WEIGHT
Tonne (t) = 1,000 kilograms
Kilogram (kg) = equal to the mass of the international
  prototype of the kilogram
Hectogram (hg) = 1/10 kilogram
Gram (g) = 1/1,000 kilogram
*Carat (metric) = 1/5 gram
Milligram (mg) = 1/1,000 gram

* Used only for transactions in precious stones, metals or pearls

IMPERIAL UNITS

The imperial primary standards are the yard as the unit of
measurement of length and the pound as the unit of
measurement of mass. Other units of measurement are
defined by reference to the primary standards.

MEASUREMENT OF LENGTH
Mile = 1,760 yards
Furlong = 220 yards
Chain = 22 yards
Yard (yd) = 0.9144 metre
Foot (ft or ') = 1/3 yard
Inch (in or ") = 1/36 yard

MEASUREMENT OF AREA
Square mile = 640 acres
Acre = 4,840 square yards
Rood = 1,210 square yards
Square yard (sq. yd) = a superficial area equal to that of a
  square each side of which measures one yard
Square foot (sq. ft) = 1/9 square yard
Square inch (sq. in) = 1/144 square foot

MEASUREMENT OF VOLUME
Cubic yard = a volume equal to that of a cube each edge of
  which measures one yard
Cubic foot = 1/27 cubic yard
Cubic inch = 1/1,728 cubic foot

MEASUREMENT OF CAPACITY
Bushel = 8 gallons
Peck = 2 gallons
Gallon (gal) = 4.54609 cubic decimetres
Quart (qt) = 1/4 gallon
Pint (pt) = 1/2 quart
Gill = 1/4 pint
Fluid ounce (fl oz) = 1/20 pint
Fluid drachm = 1/8 fluid ounce
Minim (min) = 1/60 fluid drachm

MEASUREMENT OF MASS OR WEIGHT
Ton = 2,240 pounds
Hundredweight (cwt) = 112 pounds
Cental = 100 pounds
Quarter = 28 pounds
Stone = 14 pounds
Pound (lb) = 0.45359 kilogram
Ounce (oz) = 1/16 pound
*Ounce troy (oz tr) = 12/175 pound
Dram (dr) = 1/16 ounce
Grain (gr) = 1/7,000 pound
Pennyweight (dwt) = 24 grains
Ounce apothecaries' = 480 grains
Drachm (Ʒ1) = 1/8 ounce apothecaries'
Scruple (℈1) = 1/3 drachm

* Used only for transactions in gold, silver or other precious
metals, and articles made therefrom

MEASUREMENT OF ELECTRICITY

Units of measurement of electricity are defined by the
Weights and Measures Act 1985 as follows:
Ampere (A) = that constant current which, if maintained
  in two straight parallel conductors of infinite length, of
  negligible circular cross-section and placed 1 metre
  apart in a vacuum, would produce between these
  conductors a force equal to 2×10^{-7} newton per metre
  of length
Ohm (Ω) = the electric resistance between two points of
  a conductor when a constant potential difference of
  1 volt, applied between the two points, produces in the
  conductor a current of 1 ampere, the conductor not
  being the seat of any electromotive force
Volt (V) = the difference of electric potential between two
  points of a conducting wire carrying a constant current
  of 1 ampere when the power dissipated between these
  points is equal to 1 watt
Watt (W) = the power which in one second gives rise to
  energy of 1 joule
Kilowatt (kW) = 1,000 watts
Megawatt (MW) = one million watts

MEASUREMENT OF SOUND

INTENSITY
Decibels (db) are used to measure the power or intensity of
sound. Decibel level is calculated on a logarithmic scale as
a ratio against a standard power; each increase of 10db on
the scale corresponds to ten times the intensity and twice
the loudness. Some examples of decibel levels are:

Silence	0db
Noise level of ordinary conversation	60db
Damage threshold for noise	90db
Noise level of typical streetworks	110db
Pain threshold for noise	130db

FREQUENCY AND PITCH

Frequency is a measure of how many waves or sound waves pass through a medium over a certain period of time. It is measured in Hertz (Hz) (*see* Derived SI Units) and a frequency of one Hz equals one wave, or one vibration every second. The typical range for human hearing is between 20Hz and 20,000Hz.

Frequency is closely linked to pitch, which indicates how high or low a sound is; a high frequency will have a high pitch, and a frequency doubled sounds an octave higher.

WATER AND LIQUOR MEASURES

1 cubic foot = 62.32 pounds
1 gallon = 10 pounds
1 cubic cm = 1 gram
1,000 cubic cm = 1 litre; 1 kilogram
1 cubic metre = 1,000 litres; 1,000 kilograms; 1 tonne
An inch of rain on the surface of an acre (43,560 sq. feet)
  = 3,630 cubic feet = 100.992 tons
Cisterns: A cistern 4 × 2.5 feet and 3 feet deep will hold brimful 186.963 gallons, weighing 1,869.63 pounds in addition to its own weight

WATER FOR SHIPS
Kilderkin = 18 gallons
Barrel = 36 gallons
Puncheon = 72 gallons
Butt = 110 gallons
Tun = 210 gallons

BOTTLES OF WINE
Traditional equivalents in standard champagne bottles:
Magnum = 2 bottles
Jeroboam = 4 bottles
Rehoboam = 6 bottles
Methuselah = 8 bottles
Salmanazar = 12 bottles
Balthazar = 16 bottles
Nebuchadnezzar = 20 bottles
A quarter of a bottle is known as a *nip*
An eighth of a bottle is known as a *baby*

ANGULAR AND CIRCULAR MEASURES

60 seconds (") = 1 minute (')
60 minutes = 1 degree (°)
90 degrees = 1 right angle or quadrant
Diameter of circle × 3.1416 = circumference
Diameter squared × 0.7854 = area of circle
Diameter squared × 3.1416 = surface of sphere
Diameter cubed × 0.523 = solidity of sphere
One degree of circumference × 57.3 = radius*
Diameter of cylinder × 3.1416; product by length or height, gives the surface
Diameter squared × 0.7854; product by length or height, gives solid content

* Or, one radian (the angle subtended at the centre of a circle by an arc of the circumference equal in length to the radius) = 57.3 degrees

MILLION, BILLION ETC

The long- and short-scale systems result in different numerical values for sums greater than a million. Many European countries use the long-scale system while the short-scale system is used by the USA and most English-speaking countries. In 1974 the UK government officially adopted the short-scale system, but the use of the terms billion and trillion in the UK can still be ambiguous.

Long-scale
Million	thousand × thousand	10^6
Billion	million × million	10^{12}
Trillion	million × billion	10^{18}
Quadrillion	million × trillion	10^{24}

Short-scale
Million	thousand × thousand	10^6
Billion	thousand × million	10^9
Trillion	million × million	10^{12}
Quadrillion	million × billion	10^{15}

NAUTICAL MEASURES

DISTANCE
Distance at sea is measured in nautical miles. The British Standard nautical mile was 6,080 feet but this measure has been obsolete since 1970 when the international nautical mile of 1,852 metres was adopted by the Hydrographic Department of the Ministry of Defence. The cable (600 feet or 100 fathoms) was a measure approximately one-tenth of a nautical mile. Such distances are now expressed in decimal parts of a sea mile or in metres.

Soundings at sea were recorded in fathoms (6 feet). Depths are now expressed in metres on Admiralty charts.

SPEED
Speed is measured in nautical miles per hour, called knots. A ship moving at the rate of 30 nautical miles per hour is said to be doing 30 knots.

Knots	Mph	Knots	Mph
1	1.1515	9	10.3636
2	2.3030	10	11.5151
3	3.4545	15	17.2727
4	4.6060	20	23.0303
5	5.7575	25	28.7878
6	6.9090	30	34.5454
7	8.0606	35	40.3030
8	9.2121	40	46.0606

TONNAGE
Under the Merchant Shipping Act 1854, the tonnage of UK-registered vessels was measured in tons of 100 cubic feet. The need for a universal method of measurement led to the adoption of the International Convention on Tonnage Measurements of Ships 1969, which measures, in cubic metres, all the internal spaces of a vessel for the gross tonnage and those of the cargo compartments for the net tonnage. The convention has applied since July 1982 to new ships, ships which needed to be remeasured because of substantial alterations, and ships whose owners requested remeasurement. On 18 July 1994 the convention became mandatory.

TEMPERATURE SCALES

The SI (International System) unit of temperature is the Kelvin (K), which is defined as the fraction 1/273.16 of the temperature of the triple point of water (ie where ice, water and water vapour are in equilibrium). The zero of the Kelvin scale is the absolute zero of temperature. The freezing point of water is 273.15K and the boiling point (as adopted in the International Temperature Scale of 1990) is 373.124K.

The Celsius scale (°C; formerly centigrade) is defined by subtracting 273.15 from the Kelvin temperature. The Fahrenheit (°F) scale is related to the Celsius scale by the relationships:

Temperature °F = (temperature °C $\times$ 1.8) + 32
Temperature °C = (temperature °F − 32) ÷ 1.8

It follows from these definitions that the freezing point of water is 0°C and 32°F. The boiling point is 99.974°C and 211.953°F.

The temperature of the human body varies from person to person and in the same person can be affected by a variety of factors. In most people body temperature varies between 36.5°C and 37.2°C (97.7–98.9°F).

Conversion between scales

°C	°F	°C	°F	°C	°F
100	212	60	140	20	68
99	210.2	59	138.2	19	66.2
98	208.4	58	136.4	18	64.4
97	206.6	57	134.6	17	62.6
96	204.8	56	132.8	16	60.8
95	203	55	131	15	59
94	201.2	54	129.2	14	57.2
93	199.4	53	127.4	13	55.4
92	197.6	52	125.6	12	53.6
91	195.8	51	123.8	11	51.8
90	194	50	122	10	50
89	192.2	49	120.2	9	48.2
88	190.4	48	118.4	8	46.4
87	188.6	47	116.6	7	44.6
86	186.8	46	114.8	6	42.8
85	185	45	113	5	41
84	183.2	44	111.2	4	39.2
83	181.4	43	109.4	3	37.4
82	179.6	42	107.6	2	35.6
81	177.8	41	105.8	1	33.8
80	176	40	104	Zero	32
79	174.2	39	102.2	−1	30.2
78	172.4	38	100.4	−2	28.4
77	170.6	37	98.6	−3	26.6
76	168.8	36	96.8	−4	24.8
75	167	35	95	−5	23
74	165.2	34	93.2	−6	21.2
73	163.4	33	91.4	−7	19.4
72	161.6	32	89.6	−8	17.6
71	159.8	31	87.8	−9	15.8
70	158	30	86	−10	14
69	156.2	29	84.2	−11	12.2
68	154.4	28	82.4	−12	10.4
67	152.6	27	80.6	−13	8.6
66	150.8	26	78.8	−14	6.8
65	149	25	77	−15	5
64	147.2	24	75.2	−16	3.2
63	145.4	23	73.4	−17	1.4
62	143.6	22	71.6	−18	0.4
61	141.8	21	69.8	−19	−2.2

DISTANCE OF THE HORIZON

The distance to the horizon can be calculated, in metric units, using the equation $D = 3.8373\sqrt{H}$ where D is the distance in kilometres and H is the height of the observer in metres, and in imperial units using the equation $D = 1.3157\sqrt{H}$ where D is the distance in miles and H is the height of the observer in feet. The resulting distances are those following a straight line from the observer to the horizon; it is not the distance along the curvature of the Earth. The difference between these two figures, however, is minimal for heights below 100km (62 miles).

Height in metres (feet)	Range in km (miles)
1.7 (5.6)*	5.0 (3.1)
5 (16)	8.6 (5.3)
10 (32.8)	12.1 (7.5)
50 (164)	27.1 (16.8)
100 (328)	38.4 (23.8)
509 (1,670)†	86.6 (53.8)
1,000 (3,281)	121.34 (75.4)
5,000 (16,404)	271.3 (168.5)
8,848 (29,028)‡	361.0 (224.2)
9,144 (30,000)§	366.9 (228.0)

* Average human height in the UK
† Height of the tallest inhabited building (Taipei 101)
‡ Height of Mt Everest
§ Height of cruising aeroplane

PAPER MEASURES

Printing paper
5 bundles = 1 bale
2 reams = 1 bundle
516 sheets = 1 ream

Writing paper
480 sheets = 1 ream
20 quires = 1 ream
24 sheets = 1 quire

INTERNATIONAL PAPER SIZES

The basis of the international series of paper sizes is a rectangle having an area of one square metre, the sides of which are in the proportion of 1:√2. The proportions 1:√2 have a geometrical relationship, the side and diagonal of any square being in this proportion. The effect of this arrangement is that if the area of the sheet of paper is doubled or halved, the shorter side and the longer side of the new sheet are still in the same proportion 1:√2. This feature is useful where photographic enlargement or reduction is used, as the proportions remain the same.

Description of the A series is by capital A followed by a figure. The basic size has the description A0 and the higher the figure following the letter, the greater is the number of sub-divisions and therefore the smaller the sheet. Half A0 is A1 and half A1 is A2. Where larger dimensions are required the A is preceded by a figure. Thus 2A0 means twice the size A0; 4A0 is four times the size of A0.

B sizes are intermediate between any two adjacent sizes of the A series. The A series is for magazines and books, B for posters, wall charts and other large items, and C for envelopes. The paper size recommended for business correspondence is A4.

ENVELOPE SIZES

Standard C series envelope sizes are designed for use with the A series of paper sizes. The DL (dimension lengthwise) format is not part of the C series, but is widely used for business letters.

A SERIES

	mm			mm
A0	841 × 1189	A6		105 × 148
A1	594 × 841	A7		74 × 105
A2	420 × 594	A8		52 × 74
A3	297 × 420	A9		37 × 52
A4	210 × 297	A10		26 × 37
A5	148 × 210			

B SERIES

	mm		mm
B0	1000 × 1414	B6	125 × 176
B1	707 × 1000	B7	88 × 125
B2	500 × 707	B8	62 × 88
B3	353 × 500	B9	44 × 62
B4	250 × 353	B10	31 × 44
B5	176 × 250		

ENVELOPE SIZES

	mm	Usage
C0	917 × 1297	A0 sheet
C1	648 × 917	A1 sheet
C2	458 × 648	A2 sheet, A1 sheet folded in half
C3	324 × 458	A3 sheet, A2 folded in half
C4	229 × 324	A4 sheet, A3 folded in half
C5	162 × 229	A5 sheet, A4 folded in half
C6	114 × 162	A5 sheet folded in half
DL	110 × 220	A4 sheet folded in thirds, A5 in half

BOOK SIZES

Traditional		Modern	
	mm		mm
Royal Quarto	250 × 320	Crown Royal	210 × 280
Demy Quarto	220 × 290	Royal	191 × 235
Crown Quarto	190 × 250	Demy	152 × 229
Royal Octavo	150 × 250	*Paperbacks*	
Demy Octavo	143 × 222	C Format	143 × 222
Large Crown		B format	129 × 198
Octavo	129 × 198	A format	111 × 175

OBSOLETE MEASURES

Length
Cubit, Digit, Ell, Finger, Hand (still in use for measurement of horses), League, Palm, Span
Capacity
Barrel, Bushel, Cask, Hogshead, Sester, Tun
Weight
Clove, Fother, Last, Mark, Nail, Sack, Tod
Area
Bovate, Carucate, Perch, Virgate, Yoke

CLOTHING SIZES

MEN'S

Item	UK	USA	Europe
Suits	36	36	46
	38	38	48
	40	40	50
	42	42	52
	44	44	54
	46	46	56
Shirts	12	12	30–31
	12½	12½	32
	13	13	33
	13½	13½	34–35
	14	14	36
	14½	14½	37
	15	15	38
	15½	15½	39–40
	16	16	41
	16½	16½	42
	17	17	43
	17½	17½	44–45
Shoes	6½	7	39
	7	7½	40
	7½	8	41
	8	8½	42
	8½	9	43
	9	9½	43
	9½	10	44
	10	10½	44
	10½	11	45

WOMEN'S

Item	UK	USA	Europe
Clothing	8	6	36
	10	8	38
	12	10	40
	14	12	42
	16	14	44
	18	16	46
	20	18	48
	22	20	50
	24	22	52
Shoes	4	5½	37
	4½	6	37
	5	6½	38
	5½	7	38
	6	7½	39
	6½	8	39
	7	8½	40
	7½	9	40
	8	9½	41

CONVERSION TABLES FOR WEIGHTS AND MEASURES

Bold figures equal units of either of the columns beside them; thus: 1 cm = 0.394 inches and 1 inch = 2.540 cm

LENGTH			AREA			VOLUME			WEIGHT (MASS)		
Centimetres		*Inches*	*Square cm*		*Square in*	*Cubic cm*		*Cubic in*	*Kilograms*		*Pounds*
2.540	**1**	0.394	6.452	**1**	0.155	16.387	**1**	0.061	0.454	**1**	2.205
5.080	**2**	0.787	12.903	**2**	0.310	32.774	**2**	0.122	0.907	**2**	4.409
7.620	**3**	1.181	19.355	**3**	0.465	49.161	**3**	0.183	1.361	**3**	6.614
10.160	**4**	1.575	25.806	**4**	0.620	65.548	**4**	0.244	1.814	**4**	8.819
12.700	**5**	1.969	32.258	**5**	0.775	81.936	**5**	0.305	2.268	**5**	11.023
15.240	**6**	2.362	38.710	**6**	0.930	98.323	**6**	0.366	2.722	**6**	13.228
17.780	**7**	2.756	45.161	**7**	1.085	114.710	**7**	0.427	3.175	**7**	15.432
20.320	**8**	3.150	51.613	**8**	1.240	131.097	**8**	0.488	3.629	**8**	17.637
22.860	**9**	3.543	58.064	**9**	1.395	147.484	**9**	0.549	4.082	**9**	19.842
25.400	**10**	3.937	64.516	**10**	1.550	163.871	**10**	0.610	4.536	**10**	22.046
50.800	**20**	7.874	129.032	**20**	3.100	327.742	**20**	1.220	9.072	**20**	44.092
76.200	**30**	11.811	193.548	**30**	4.650	491.613	**30**	1.831	13.608	**30**	66.139
101.600	**40**	15.748	258.064	**40**	6.200	655.484	**40**	2.441	18.144	**40**	88.185
127.000	**50**	19.685	322.580	**50**	7.750	819.355	**50**	3.051	22.680	**50**	110.231
152.400	**60**	23.622	387.096	**60**	9.300	983.226	**60**	3.661	27.216	**60**	132.277
177.800	**70**	27.559	451.612	**70**	10.850	1147.097	**70**	4.272	31.752	**70**	154.324
203.200	**80**	31.496	516.128	**80**	12.400	1310.968	**80**	4.882	36.287	**80**	176.370
228.600	**90**	35.433	580.644	**90**	13.950	1474.839	**90**	5.492	40.823	**90**	198.416
254.000	**100**	39.370	645.160	**100**	15.500	1638.710	**100**	6.102	45.359	**100**	220.464

Metres		*Yards*	*Square m*		*Square yd*	*Cubic m*		*Cubic yd*	*Metric tonnes*		*Tons (UK)*
0.914	**1**	1.094	0.836	**1**	1.196	0.765	**1**	1.308	1.016	**1**	0.984
1.829	**2**	2.187	1.672	**2**	2.392	1.529	**2**	2.616	2.032	**2**	1.968
2.743	**3**	3.281	2.508	**3**	3.588	2.294	**3**	3.924	3.048	**3**	2.953
3.658	**4**	4.374	3.345	**4**	4.784	3.058	**4**	5.232	4.064	**4**	3.937
4.572	**5**	5.468	4.181	**5**	5.980	3.823	**5**	6.540	5.080	**5**	4.921
5.486	**6**	6.562	5.017	**6**	7.176	4.587	**6**	7.848	6.096	**6**	5.905
6.401	**7**	7.655	5.853	**7**	8.372	5.352	**7**	9.156	7.112	**7**	6.889
7.315	**8**	8.749	6.689	**8**	9.568	6.116	**8**	10.464	8.128	**8**	7.874
8.230	**9**	9.843	7.525	**9**	10.764	6.881	**9**	11.772	9.144	**9**	8.858
9.144	**10**	10.936	8.361	**10**	11.960	7.646	**10**	13.080	10.161	**10**	9.842
18.288	**20**	21.872	16.723	**20**	23.920	15.291	**20**	26.159	20.321	**20**	19.684
27.432	**30**	32.808	25.084	**30**	35.880	22.937	**30**	39.239	30.481	**30**	29.526
36.576	**40**	43.745	33.445	**40**	47.840	30.582	**40**	52.318	40.642	**40**	39.368
45.720	**50**	54.681	41.806	**50**	59.799	38.228	**50**	65.398	50.802	**50**	49.210
54.864	**60**	65.617	50.168	**60**	71.759	45.873	**60**	78.477	60.963	**60**	59.052
64.008	**70**	76.553	58.529	**70**	83.719	53.519	**70**	91.557	71.123	**70**	68.894
73.152	**80**	87.489	66.890	**80**	95.679	61.164	**80**	104.636	81.284	**80**	78.737
82.296	**90**	98.425	75.251	**90**	107.639	68.810	**90**	117.716	91.444	**90**	88.579
91.440	**100**	109.361	83.613	**100**	119.599	76.455	**100**	130.795	101.605	**100**	98.421

Kilometres		*Miles*	*Hectares*		*Acres*	*Litres*		*Gallons*	*Metric tonnes*		*Tons (US)*
1.609	**1**	0.621	0.405	**1**	2.471	4.546	**1**	0.220	0.907	**1**	1.102
3.219	**2**	1.243	0.809	**2**	4.942	9.092	**2**	0.440	1.814	**2**	2.205
4.828	**3**	1.864	1.214	**3**	7.413	13.638	**3**	0.660	2.722	**3**	3.305
6.437	**4**	2.485	1.619	**4**	9.844	18.184	**4**	0.880	3.629	**4**	4.409
8.047	**5**	3.107	2.023	**5**	12.355	22.730	**5**	1.100	4.536	**5**	5.521
9.656	**6**	3.728	2.428	**6**	14.826	27.276	**6**	1.320	5.443	**6**	6.614
11.265	**7**	4.350	2.833	**7**	17.297	31.822	**7**	1.540	6.350	**7**	7.716
12.875	**8**	4.971	3.327	**8**	19.769	36.368	**8**	1.760	7.257	**8**	8.818
14.484	**9**	5.592	3.642	**9**	22.240	40.914	**9**	1.980	8.165	**9**	9.921
16.093	**10**	6.214	4.047	**10**	24.711	45.460	**10**	2.200	9.072	**10**	11.023
32.187	**20**	12.427	8.094	**20**	49.421	90.919	**20**	4.400	18.144	**20**	22.046
48.280	**30**	18.641	12.140	**30**	74.132	136.379	**30**	6.599	27.216	**30**	33.069
64.374	**40**	24.855	16.187	**40**	98.842	181.839	**40**	8.799	36.287	**40**	44.092
80.467	**50**	31.069	20.234	**50**	123.555	227.298	**50**	10.999	45.359	**50**	55.116
96.561	**60**	37.282	24.281	**60**	148.263	272.758	**60**	13.199	54.431	**60**	66.139
112.654	**70**	43.496	28.328	**70**	172.974	318.217	**70**	15.398	63.503	**70**	77.162
128.748	**80**	49.710	32.375	**80**	197.684	363.677	**80**	17.598	72.575	**80**	88.185
144.841	**90**	55.923	36.422	**90**	222.395	409.137	**90**	19.798	81.647	**90**	99.208
160.934	**100**	62.137	40.469	**100**	247.105	454.596	**100**	21.998	90.719	**100**	110.231

THE PERIODIC TABLE OF ELEMENTS

Key:

6 — atomic number
Carbon — name of element
C — chemical number
12.01 — atomic mass

IA Alkali metals	IIA Alkaline earth metals	IIIB	IVB	VB	VIB	VIIB	VIII	VIII	VIII	IB	IIB	IIIA	IVA	VA	VIA	VIIA	Noble gases
1 Hydrogen H 1.01																	2 Helium He 4.00
3 Lithium Li 6.94	4 Beryllium Be 9.01											5 Boron B 10.81	6 Carbon C 12.01	7 Nitrogen N 14.01	8 Oxygen O 16.00	9 Fluorine F 19.00	10 Neon Ne 20.18
11 Sodium Na 22.99	12 Magnesium Mg 24.31											13 Aluminium Al 26.98	14 Silicon Si 28.09	15 Phosphorus P 30.97	16 Sulphur S 32.07	17 Chlorine Cl 35.45	18 Argon Ar 39.95
19 Potassium K 39.10	20 Calcium Ca 40.08	21 Scandium Sc 44.96	22 Titanium Ti 47.88	23 Vanadium V 50.94	24 Chromium Cr 52.00	25 Manganese Mn 54.94	26 Iron Fe 55.85	27 Cobalt Co 58.93	28 Nickel Ni 58.69	29 Copper Cu 63.55	30 Zinc Zn 65.38	31 Gallium Ga 69.72	32 Germanium Ge 72.64	33 Arsenic As 74.92	34 Selenium Se 78.96	35 Bromine Br 79.904	36 Krypton Kr 83.80
37 Rubidium Rb 85.47	38 Strontium Sr 87.62	39 Yttrium Y 88.91	40 Zirconium Zr 91.22	41 Niobium Nb 92.91	42 Molybdenum Mo 95.96	43 Technetium Tc 97.91	44 Ruthenium Ru 101.07	45 Rhodium Rh 102.91	46 Palladium Pd 106.42	47 Silver Ag 107.87	48 Cadmium Cd 112.41	49 Indium In 114.82	50 Tin Sn 118.71	51 Antimony Sb 121.76	52 Tellurium Te 127.60	53 Iodine I 126.9045	54 Xenon Xe 131.29
55 Caesium Cs 132.91	56 Barium Ba 137.33	Lanthanide series (see below)	72 Hafnium Hf 178.49	73 Tantalum Ta 180.94	74 Tungsten W 183.85	75 Rhenium Re 186.21	76 Osmium Os 190.23	77 Iridium Ir 192.22	78 Platinum Pt 195.08	79 Gold Au 196.97	80 Mercury Hg 200.59	81 Thallium Tl 204.38	82 Lead Pb 207.2	83 Bismuth Bi 208.98	84 Polonium Po 209	85 Astatine At 210	86 Radon Rn 222
87 Francium Fr 223	88 Radium Ra 226	Actinide series (see below)	104 Rutherfordium Rf 261	105 Dubnium Db 262	106 Seaborgium Sg 266	107 Bohrium Bh 264	108 Hassium Hs 277	109 Meitnerium Mt 268	110 Darmstadtium Ds 271	111 Roentgenium Rg 272	112 Copernicium Cn 285						

Rare earth elements—Lanthanide series

57 Lanthanum La 138.91	58 Cerium Ce 140.12	59 Praseodymium Pr 140.91	60 Neodymium Nd 144.24	61 Promethium Pm 145	62 Samarium Sm 150.36	63 Europium Eu 151.96	64 Gadolinium Gd 157.25	65 Terbium Tb 158.93	66 Dysprosium Dy 162.50	67 Holmium Ho 164.93	68 Erbium Er 167.26	69 Thulium Tm 168.93	70 Ytterbium Yb 173.05	71 Lutetium Lu 174.97

Actinide series

89 Actinium Ac 227	90 Thorium Th 232.04	91 Protactinium Pa 231.04	92 Uranium U 238.03	93 Neptunium Np 237	94 Plutonium Pu 244	95 Americium Am 243	96 Curium Cm 247	97 Berkelium Bk 247	98 Californium Cf 251	99 Einsteinium Es 252	100 Fermium Fm 257	101 Mendelevium Md 258	102 Nobelium No 259	103 Lawrencium Lr 262

Transition metals

Non-metals

The periodic table arranges the elements into horizontal rows (periods) and vertical columns (groups) according to their atomic number. The elements in a group all have similar properties; across each period, atoms are electropositive (form positive ions) to the left and electronegative to the right. The earliest version of the periodic table was devised in 1869 by Dmitriy Mendeleyev, who predicted the existence of several elements from gaps in the table.

NOBEL PRIZE WINNERS

For prize winners for the years 1901–2007, *see* earlier editions of *Whitaker's Almanack*.

The Nobel Prizes are awarded each year from the income of a trust fund established by the Swedish scientist Alfred Nobel, the inventor of dynamite, who died on 10 December 1896 leaving a fortune of £1,750,000. The prizes are awarded to those who have contributed most to the common good in the domain of:

Physics – awarded by the Royal Swedish Academy of Sciences
Chemistry – awarded by the Royal Swedish Academy of Sciences
Physiology or Medicine – awarded by the Karolinska Institute
Literature – awarded by the Swedish Academy of Arts

Peace – awarded by a five-person committee elected by the Norwegian Storting
Economic Sciences (instituted 1969) – awarded by the Royal Swedish Academy of Sciences

The prizes are awarded every year on 10 December, the anniversary of Nobel's death. The first awards were made on 10 December 1901. The Trust is administered by the board of directors of the Nobel Foundation, Stockholm, consisting of five members and three deputy members. The Swedish government appoints a chair and a deputy chair, the remaining members being appointed by the awarding authorities.

The awards in the last three years have been distributed as follows:

	2008	2009	2010
Physics	Yoichiro Nambu *(USA)*, Makoto Kobayashi *(Japan)*, Toshihide Maskawa *(Japan)*	Willard S. Boyle *(Canada)*, Charles K. Kao *(China)*, George E. Smith *(USA)*	Andre Geim *(Russia)*, Konstantin Novoselov *(Russia)*
Chemistry	Osamu Shimomura *(USA)*, Martin Chalfie *(USA)*, Roger Y. Tsien *(USA)*	Venkatraman Ramakrishnan *(India)*, Thomas A. Steitz *(USA)*, Ada E. Yonath *(Israel)*	Richard F. Heck *(USA)*, Ei-ichi Negishi *(China)*, Akira Suzuki *(Japan)*
Physiology or Medicine	Harald zur Hausen *(Germany)*, François Barré-Sinoussi *(France)*, Luc Montagnier *(France)*	Elizabeth H. Blackburn *(Australia)*, Carol W. Greider *(USA)*, Jack W. Szostak *(UK)*	Robert G. Edwards *(UK)*
Literature	Jean-Marie Gustave Le Clézio *(France and Mauritius)*	Herta Müller *(Romania)*	Mario Vargas Llosa *(Peru)*
Peace	Martti Ahtisaari *(Finland)*	Barack H. Obama *(USA)*	Liu Xiaobo *(China)*
Economic Sciences	Paul Krugman *(USA)*	Elinor Ostrom *(USA)*, Oliver E. Williamson *(USA)*	Peter A. Diamond *(USA)*, Dale T. Mortensen *(USA)*, Christopher A. Pissarides *(Cyprus)*

ABBREVIATIONS AND ACRONYMS

Ψ	seaport

A

A	ampere
AA	Alcoholics Anonymous
AAA	Amateur Athletic Association
AAS	*Annual Abstract of Statistics*
ABA	Amateur Boxing Association
ABE	Association of Building Engineers
ABM	anti-ballistic missile
abr	abridged
ac	alternating current
a/c	account
AC	*(ante Christum)* before Christ
	Companion, Order of Australia
ACAS	Advisory, Conciliation and Arbitration Service
ACT	Australian Capital Territory
AD	*(anno Domini)* in the year of our Lord
ADB	Asian Development Bank
ADC	Aide-de-Camp
ADC (P)	Personal ADC to the Queen
Adj.	Adjutant
Adj. Gen.	Adjutant General
ad lib	*(ad libitum)* at pleasure
Adm.	Admiral
AE	Air Efficiency award
AEM	Air Efficiency Medal
aet	after extra time
AFC	Air Force Cross
AFM	Air Force Medal
AG	Attorney-General
AGM	air-to-ground missile
	annual general meeting
AH	*(anno Hegirae)* in the year of the Hegira
AI	artificial intelligence
AIDS	acquired immune deficiency syndrome
AIM	Alternative Investment Market
alt	altitude
am	*(ante meridiem)* before noon
AM	amplitude modulation
	(anno mundi) in the year of the world
	Assembly Member *(Wales)*
amp	amplifier
AMU	Arab Maghreb Union
ANC	African National Congress
anon	anonymous
ANZAC	Australian and New Zealand Army Corps
AO	Air Officer
	Officer, Order of Australia
AOC	Air Officer Commanding

AONB	area of outstanding natural beauty
APEC	Asia-Pacific Economic Cooperation
app	application
apptd	appointed
APR	annual percentage rate
ASA	Advertising Standards Authority
	Amateur Swimming Association
ASAP	as soon as possible
ASBO	antisocial behaviour order
ASEAN	Association of South-East Asian Nations
ASLEF	Associated Society of Locomotive Engineers and Firemen
ASLIB	Association for Information Management
ATC	Air Training Corps
AUC	*(ab urbe condita)* in the year from the foundation of Rome
	(anno urbis conditae) in the year of the founding of the city
AV	Authorised Version *(of Bible)*
AVR	Army Volunteer Reserve
AWOL	absent without (official) leave

B

b.	born
	bowled *(cricket)*
BA	Bachelor of Arts
BAA	British Airports Authority
	British Astronomical Association
BAF	British Athletics Federation
BAFTA	British Academy of Film and Television Arts
BAS	Bachelor in Agricultural Science
	British Antarctic Survey
BBA	British Bankers' Association
BBC	British Broadcasting Corporation
BBFC	British Board of Film Classification
BBSRC	Biotechnology and Biological Sciences Research Council
BC	before Christ
	borough council
	British Columbia *(Canada)*
BCH (D)	Bachelor of (Dental) Surgery
BCL	Bachelor of Civil Law
BCOM	Bachelor of Commerce
BD	Bachelor of Divinity
BDA	British Dental Association

BDS	Bachelor of Dental Surgery
BED	Bachelor of Education
BEM	British Empire Medal
BENG	Bachelor of Engineering
BFI	British Film Institute
BFPO	British Forces Post Office
BIS	Business, Innovation and Skills (Department for)
BLIT	Bachelor of Literature
BLITT	Bachelor of Letters
BM	Bachelor of Medicine
	British Museum
BMA	British Medical Association
BMI	body mass index
BMUS	Bachelor of Music
BNFL	British Nuclear Fuels
Bp	Bishop
BPHARM	Bachelor of Pharmacy
BPHIL	Bachelor of Philosophy
bpm	beats per minute
BPS	British Psychological Society
Brig.	Brigadier
BSC	Bachelor of Science
BSE	bovine spongiform encephalopathy
BSI	British Standards Institution
BST	British Summer Time
Bt.	Baronet
BTEC	Business and Technology Education Council
BTU	British thermal unit
BVMS	Bachelor of Veterinary Medicine and Surgery

C

c.	*(circa)* about
	chapter *(Public Acts)*
C	Celsius
	centigrade
C.	Conservative
CA	chartered accountant *(Scotland)*
CAA	Civil Aviation Authority
CAB	Citizens Advice Bureau
CAD	computer-aided design
Cadw	Ancient Monuments Board for Wales
Cantuar:	of Canterbury *(Archbishop)*
CAP	Common Agricultural Policy
Capt.	Captain
CARICOM	Caribbean Community and Common Market
Carliol	of Carlisle (Bishop)
CB	Companion, Order of the Bath
CBE	Commander, Order of the British Empire
CBI	Confederation of British Industry
CBSS	Council of the Baltic Sea States

CC	Chamber of Commerce
	city council
	Companion, Order of Canada
	county council
	county court
CCC	county cricket club
CCF	Combined Cadet Force
CCHEM	chartered chemist
CCTA	City Colleges for Technology and the Arts
CD	Civil Defence
	Corps Diplomatique
Cdr	Commander
Cdre	Commodore
CDS	Chief of the Defence Staff
CE	civil engineer
	Common (or Christian) Era
CEFAS	Centre for Environment, Fisheries and Aquaculture Science
CENG	chartered engineer
CEO	chief executive officer
CERN	European Organisation for Nuclear Research
Cestr:	of Chester *(Bishop)*
CET	Central European Time
	Common External Tariff
cf	*(confer)* compare
CF	Chaplain to the Forces
CFC	chlorofluorocarbon
CGC	Conspicuous Gallantry Cross
CGEOL	chartered geologist
CGI	computer-generated imagery
CGM	Conspicuous Gallantry Medal
cgs	centimetre-gramme-second *(system)*
CGS	Chief of General Staff
CH	Companion of Honour
CHB/M	Bachelor/Master of Surgery
CI	Channel Islands
	Imperial Order of the Crown of India
CIA	Central Intelligence Agency
CICA	Conference on Interaction and Confidence Building Measures in Asia
	Criminal Injuries Compensation Authority
Cicestr:	of Chichester *(Bishop)*
CID	Criminal Investigation Department
CIE	Companion, Order of the Indian Empire
C-in-C	Commander-in-Chief
CILIP	Chartered Institute of Library and Information Professionals
CIPFA	Chartered Institute of Public Finance and Accountancy

CIS	Commonwealth of Independent States
CJD	Creutzfeld-Jakob disease
CLG	Department for Communities and Local Government
CLJ	Commander, Order of St Lazarus of Jerusalem
CM	*(Chirurgiae Magister)* Master of Surgery
CMG	Companion, Order of St Michael and St George
CMEC	Child Maintenance and Enforcement Commission
CND	Campaign for Nuclear Disarmament
c/o	care of
CO	Commanding Officer
C of E	Church of England
COI	Central Office of Information
Col.	Colonel
cons.	consecrated
Cpl.	Corporal
CPM	Colonial Police Medal
CPRE	Campaign to Protect Rural England
CPS	Crown Prosecution Service
CSI	Companion, Order of the Star of India
CTC	City Technology Colleges
CVO	Commander, Royal Victorian Order

D

d	*(denarius)* penny
d.	died
DAB	Digital Audio Broadcasting
DBE	Dame Commander, Order of the British Empire
dc	direct current
DC	District of Columbia *(USA)*
	district council
DCB	Dame Commander, Order of the Bath
D CH	*(Doctor Chirurgiae)* Doctor of Surgery
DCL	Doctor of Civil Law
DCM	Distinguished Conduct Medal
DCMG	Dame Commander, Order of St Michael and St George
DCMS	Department for Culture, Media and Sport
DCVO	Dame Commander, Royal Victorian Order
DD	Doctor of Divinity
DDS	Doctor of Dental Surgery
DDT	dichlorodiphenyl trichloroethane
DECC	Department of Energy and Climate Change
del	*(delineavit)* he/she drew it
DEFRA	Department of the Environment, Food and Rural Affairs

DFC	Distinguished Flying Cross
DfE	Department for Education
DFID	Department for International Development
DFM	Distinguished Flying Medal
DfT	Department for Transport
DG	*(Dei gratia)* by the grace of God
	director-general
DIP ED	Diploma in Education
DIP HE	Diploma in Higher Education
DIPHS	Diploma of the Heraldry Society
DL	Deputy Lieutenant
DLIT	Doctor of Literature
DLITT	Doctor of Letters
DLR	Docklands Light Railway
DMUS	Doctor of Music
DNA	deoxyribonucleic acid
DNB	*Dictionary of National Biography*
do	*(ditto)* the same
DoH	Department of Health
DPH *or* DPHIL	Doctor of Philosophy
DPP	Director of Public Prosecutions
Dr	Doctor
DSC	Distinguished Service Cross
	Doctor of Science
DSM	Distinguished Service Medal
DSO	Companion, Distinguished Service Order
DTP	desktop publishing
Dunelm:	of Durham *(Bishop)*
DUP	Northern Ireland Democratic Unionist Party
DV	*(Deo volente)* God willing
DVD	digital versatile disc
DVLA	Driver and Vehicle Licensing Agency
DVT	deep vein thrombosis
DWI	Drinking Water Inspectorate
DWP	Department for Work and Pensions

E

E	east
	email
Ebor:	of York *(Archbishop)*
EBRD	European Bank for Reconstruction and Development
EC	Elizabeth Cross
	European Community
ECB	England and Wales Cricket Board
	European Central Bank
ECG	electrocardiogram
ECGD	Export Credits Guarantee Department

ECOWAS	Economic Community of West African States	
ED	Efficiency Decoration	
EEC	European Economic Community	
EEG	electroencephalogram	
EFA	European Fighter Aircraft	
EFTA	European Free Trade Association	
eg	*(exempli gratia)* for the sake of example	
EHRC	Equality and Human Rights Commission	
EIB	European Investment Bank	
EMS	European Monetary System	
EMU	European Monetary Union	
EPSRC	Engineering and Physical Sciences Research Council	
ER	*(Elizabetha Regina)* Queen Elizabeth	
ERM	exchange rate mechanism	
ERNIE	electronic random number indicator equipment	
ESA	European Space Agency	
ESRC	Economic and Social Research Council	
est	established estimate	
ETA	*(Euzkadi ta Askatasuna)* Basque separatist organisation	
et al	*(et alibi)* and elsewhere *(et alii)* and others	
etc	*(et cetera)* and the other things / and so forth	
et seq	*(et sequentia)* and the following	
EU	European Union	
EURATOM	European Atomic Energy Community	
Exon:	of Exeter *(Bishop)*	

F

f	*(forte)* loud	
F	Fahrenheit Fellow of	
FA	Football Association	
FANY	First Aid Nursing Yeomanry	
FAO	for the attention of	
FAQ	frequently asked questions	
FARC	*(Fuerzas Armadas Revolucionarias de Colombia)* Colombian rebel organisation	
FBA	Fellow, British Academy	
FBAA	Fellow, British Association of Accountants and Auditors	
FBI	Federal Bureau of Investigation	
FBS	Fellow, Botanical Society	
FBU	Fire Brigades Union	
FC	football club	
FCA	Fellow, Institute of Chartered Accountants in England and Wales	

FCCA	Fellow, Chartered Association of Certified Accountants	
FCGI	Fellow, City and Guilds of London Institute	
FCIA	Fellow, Corporation of Insurance Agents	
FCIARB	Fellow, Chartered Institute of Arbitrators	
FCIB	Fellow, Chartered Institute of Bankers Fellow, Corporation of Insurance Brokers	
FCIBSE	Fellow, Chartered Institution of Building Services Engineers	
FCII	Fellow, Chartered Insurance Institute	
FCIPS	Fellow, Chartered Institute of Purchasing and Supply	
FCIS	Fellow, Institute of Chartered Secretaries and Administrators	
FCIT	Fellow, Chartered Institute of Transport	
FCMA	Fellow, Chartered Institute of Management Accountants	
FCO	Foreign and Commonwealth Office	
FCP	Fellow, College of Preceptors	
FD	*(Fidei Defensor)* Defender of the Faith	
FE	further education	
fec	*(fecit)* made this	
ff	*(fecerunt)* made this (pl) folios following	
ff	*(fortissimo)* very loud	
FFA	Fellow, Faculty of Actuaries *(Scotland)* Fellow, Institute of Financial Accountants	
FFAS	Fellow, Faculty of Architects and Surveyors	
FFCM	Fellow, Faculty of Community Medicine	
FFPHM	Fellow, Faculty of Public Health Medicine	
FGS	Fellow, Geological Society	
FHS	Fellow, Heraldry Society	
FHSM	Fellow, Institute of Health Service Management	
FIA	Fellow, Institute of Actuaries	
FIBIOL	Fellow, Institute of Biology	
FICE	Fellow, Institution of Civil Engineers	
FICS	Fellow, Institution of Chartered Shipbrokers	
FIEE	Fellow, Institution of Electrical Engineers	
FIERE	Fellow, Institution of Electronic and Radio Engineers	
FIFA	*(Fédération Internationale de Football Association)* International Federation of Football Association	
FIM	Fellow, Institute of Metals	

FIMGT	Fellow, Institute of Management	
FIMM	Fellow, Institution of Mining and Metallurgy	
FINSTF	Fellow, Institute of Fuel	
FINSTP	Fellow, Institute of Physics	
FIQS	Fellow, Institute of Quantity Surveyors	
FIS	Fellow, Institute of Statisticians	
FJI	Fellow, Institute of Journalists	
FLS	Fellow, Linnean Society	
FM	Field Marshal frequency modulation	
FMEDSCI	Fellow, Academy of Medical Sciences	
fo	folio	
FO	Flying Officer	
FOB	free on board	
FPHS	Fellow, Philosophical Society	
FRAD	Fellow, Royal Academy of Dancing	
FRAES	Fellow, Royal Aeronautical Society	
FRAGS	Fellow, Royal Agricultural Societies	
FRAI	Fellow, Royal Anthropological Institute	
FRAM	Fellow, Royal Academy of Music	
FRAS	Fellow, Royal Asiatic Society Fellow, Royal Astronomical Society	
FRBS	Fellow, Royal Botanic Society Fellow, Royal Society of British Sculptors	
FRCA	Fellow, Royal College of Anaesthetists	
FRCGP	Fellow, Royal College of General Practitioners	
FRCM	Fellow, Royal College of Music	
FRCO	Fellow, Royal College of Organists	
FRCOG	Fellow, Royal College of Obstetricians and Gynaecologists	
FRCP	Fellow, Royal College of Physicians, London	
FRCPATH	Fellow, Royal College of Pathologists	
FRCPE *or* FRCPED	Fellow, Royal College of Physicians, Edinburgh	
FRCPI	Fellow, Royal College of Physicians, Ireland	
FRCPSYCH	Fellow, Royal College of Psychiatrists	
FRCR	Fellow, Royal College of Radiologists	
FRCS	Fellow, Royal College of Surgeons of England	
FRCSE *or* FRCSED	Fellow, Royal College of Surgeons of Edinburgh	
FRCSGLAS	Fellow, Royal College of Physicians and Surgeons of Glasgow	

FRCSI	Fellow, Royal College of Surgeons in Ireland
FRCVS	Fellow, Royal College of Veterinary Surgeons
FRECONS	Fellow, Royal Economic Society
FRENG	Fellow, Royal Academy of Engineering
FRGS	Fellow, Royal Geographical Society
FRHISTS	Fellow, Royal Historical Society
FRHS	Fellow, Royal Horticultural Society
FRIBA	Fellow, Royal Institute of British Architects
FRICS	Fellow, Royal Institution of Chartered Surveyors
FRMETS	Fellow, Royal Meteorological Society
FRMS	Fellow, Royal Microscopical Society
FRNS	Fellow, Royal Numismatic Society
FRPHARMS	Fellow, Royal Pharmaceutical Society
FRPS	Fellow, Royal Photographic Society
FRS	Fellow, Royal Society
FRSA	Fellow, Royal Society of Arts
FRSC	Fellow, Royal Society of Chemistry
FRSE	Fellow, Royal Society of Edinburgh
FRSH	Fellow, Royal Society of Health
FRSL	Fellow, Royal Society of Literature
FRTPI	Fellow, Royal Town Planning Institute
FSA	Fellow, Society of Antiquaries / Financial Services Authority / Food Standards Agency
FSS	Fellow, Royal Statistical Society
FSVA	Fellow, Incorporated Society of Valuers and Auctioneers
FT	*Financial Times*
FTI	Fellow, Textile Institute
FTII	Fellow, Chartered Institute of Taxation
FZS	Fellow, Zoological Society

G

GATT	General Agreement on Tariffs and Trade
GBE	Dame/Knight Grand Cross, Order of the British Empire
GC	George Cross
GCB	Dame/Knight Grand Cross, Order of the Bath
GCC	Gulf Cooperation Council
GCE	General Certificate of Education

GCHQ	Government Communications Headquarters
GCLJ	Knight Grand Cross, Order of St Lazarus of Jerusalem
GCMG	Dame/Knight Grand Cross, Order of St Michael and St George
GCSE	General Certificate of Secondary Education
GCSI	Knight Grand Commander, Order of the Star of India
GCVO	Dame/Knight Grand Cross, Royal Victorian Order
GDP	gross domestic product
Gen.	General
GHQ	general headquarters
GLA	Greater London Authority
GM	genetically modified / George Medal
GMB	Britain's General Union
GMT	Greenwich Mean Time
GNI	gross national income
GNVQ	General National Vocational Qualification
GOC	General Officer Commanding
GP	General Practitioner
GPS	Global Positioning System
Gp Capt.	Group Captain
GSA	Girls' Schools Association
GST	Greenwich Sidereal Time

H

HA	Health Authority
HAC	Honourable Artillery Company
HB	His Beatitude
HBM	Her/His Britannic Majesty('s) / Honorary Chaplain to the Forces
HD	High Definition *(television)*
HE	Her/His Excellency / higher education / His Eminence
HGV	heavy goods vehicle
HH	Her/His Highness / Her/His Honour / His Holiness
HIM	Her/His Imperial Majesty
HIV	human immunodeficiency virus
HJS	*(hic jacet sepultus)* here lies buried
HM	Her/His Majesty('s)
HMAS	Her/His Majesty's Australian Ship
HMC	Headmasters' and Headmistresses' Conference
HMI	Her/His Majesty's Inspector
HML	Her/His Majesty's Lieutenant

HMS	Her/His Majesty's Ship
HMSO	Her/His Majesty's Stationery Office
HNC	Higher National Certificate
HND	Higher National Diploma
Hon.	Honorary / Honourable
HP	hire purchase
HQ	headquarters
HR	human resources
HRH	Her/His Royal Highness
HRT	hormone replacement therapy
HSE	Health and Safety Executive / *(hic sepultus est)* here is buried
HSH	Her/His Serene Highness
HTML	hypertext mark-up language
HTTP	hypertext transfer protocol
HWM	high water mark

I

I	Island
IAEA	International Atomic Energy Agency
IATA	International Air Transport Association
IB	International Baccalaureate
IBF	International Boxing Federation
ibid	*(ibidem)* in the same place
IBRD	International Bank for Reconstruction and Development
ICAO	International Civil Aviation Organisation
ICC	International Cricket Council / International Criminal Court
ICJ	International Court of Justice
ICOMOS	International Council on Monuments and Sites
ICRC	International Committee of the Red Cross
ICT	Information and Communication Technology
id	*(idem)* the same
IDA	International Development Association
IDD	international direct dialling
ie	*(id est)* that is
IEA	International Energy Agency
IFA	independent financial adviser
IFAD	International Fund for Agricultural Development
IFC	International Finance Corporation
ILO	International Labour Organisation/Office

IMF	International Monetary Fund
IMO	International Maritime Organisation
inc.	incorporated
INLA	Irish National Liberation Army
in loc	*(in loco)* in its place
INRI	*(Iesus Nazarenus Rex Iudaeorum)* Jesus of Nazareth, King of the Jews
inst	*(instant)* current month
Interpol	International Criminal Police Organisation
IOC	International Olympic Committee
IoM	Isle of Man
IOU	I owe you
IoW	Isle of Wight
IP	intellectual property internet protocol
IPS	Identity and Passport Service
IPSA	Independent Parliamentary Standards Authority
iPSC	induced pluripotent stem cell
IQ	intelligence quotient
IRA	Irish Republican Army
IRB	International Rugby Board
IRC	International Rescue Committee
Is	Islands
ISA	individual savings account
ISBN	International Standard Book Number
ISO	Imperial Service Order International Organisation for Standardisation
ISP	internet service provider
ISSN	International Standard Serial Number
ITN	Independent Television News
ITU	International Telecommunication Union
ITUC	International Trade Union Confederation
ITV	Independent Television
IUCN	International Union for Conservation of Nature
IVF	in vitro fertilisation
IWC	International Whaling Commission

J

J	Judge Justice
JP	Justice of the Peace
Jr	Junior

K

| KBE | Knight Commander, Order of the British Empire |
| KCB | Knight Commander, Order of the Bath |

KCLJ	Knight Commander, Order of St Lazarus of Jerusalem
KCMG	Knight Commander, Order of St Michael and St George
KCSI	Knight Commander, Order of the Star of India
KCVO	Knight Commander, Royal Victorian Order
KG	Knight of the Garter
KGB	*(Komitet Gosudarstvennoi Bezopasnosti)* Committee of State Security *(USSR)*
kHz	kilohertz
KLJ	Knight, Order of St Lazarus of Jerusalem
KP	Knight, Order of St Patrick
KStJ	Knight, Order of St John of Jerusalem
Kt.	Knight
KT	Knight of the Thistle
kV	kilovolt
kW	kilowatt
kWh	kilowatt hour

L

Lab.	Labour
Lat.	Latitude
lbw	leg before wicket *(cricket)*
lc	lower case *(printing)*
LCD	Liquid Crystal Display
LCJ	Lord Chief Justice
LCM	least/lowest common multiple
LD	Liberal Democrat
LDS	Licentiate in Dental Surgery
LEA	Local Education Authority
LHB	Local Health Board *(Wales)*
LHD	*(Literarum Humaniorum Doctor)* Doctor of Humane Letters/Literature
Lib.	Liberal
lit	literary
Lit Hum	*(Literae Humaniores)* classics course, Oxford University
LITT D	Doctor of Letters
LJ	Lord Justice
LLB	Bachelor of Laws
LLD	Doctor of Laws
LLM	Master of Laws
loc cit	*(loco citato)* in the place cited
Londin:	of London *(Bishop)*
Long.	longitude
LS	*(loco sigilli)* place of the seal
LSC	Legal Services Commission
lsd	*(librae, solidi, denarii)* pounds, shillings and pence
LSE	London School of Economics and Political Science

LST	Local Sidereal Time
Lt	Lieutenant
LTA	Lawn Tennis Association
LTTE	Liberation Tigers of Tamil Eelam
ltd	limited *(liability)*
LVO	Lieutenant, Royal Victorian Order
LW	long wave
LWM	low water mark

M

M	Member Monsieur
m.	married
MA	Master of Arts
Maj.	Major
maj.	majority
max	maximum
MB	*(Medicinae Baccalaureus)* Bachelor of Medicine
MBA	Master of Business Administration
MBC	Metropolitan Borough Council
MBE	Member, Order of the British Empire
MBO	management buy-out
MC	Master of Ceremonies Military Cross
MCB	Muslim Council of Britain
MCC	Marylebone Cricket Club
MCH(D)	Master of (Dental) Surgery
MD	managing director Doctor of Medicine
MDC	Movement for Democratic Change (Zimbabwe)
MDS	Master of Dental Surgery
ME	Middle English myalgic encephalomyelitis
MEC	Member of Executive Council
MED	Master of Education
mega	one million times
MEP	Member of the European Parliament
Mgr	Monsignor
MI	Military Intelligence
micro	one-millionth part
milli	one-thousandth part
min	minimum minutes
MIT	Massachusetts Institute of Technology
MLA	Member of Legislative Assembly *(Northern Ireland)* Museums, Libraries and Archives Council
MLC	Member of Legislative Council
MLITT	Master of Letters
Mlle	Mademoiselle
MLR	minimum lending rate
MM	Military Medal
Mme	Madame
MMR	measles, mumps and rubella *(vaccine)*
MN	Merchant Navy
MO	Medical Officer/Orderly
MoD	Ministry of Defence

MoJ	Ministry of Justice	NT	National Theatre
MP	Member of Parliament		National Trust
	Military Police		New Testament
mph	miles per hour		Northern Territory
MPHIL	Master of Philosophy		*(Australia)*
MR	Master of the Rolls	NUJ	National Union of
MRC	Medical Research Council		Journalists
MRI	magnetic resonance	NUM	National Union of
	imaging		Mineworkers
MRSA	methicillin-resistant	NUS	National Union of
	staphylococcus aureus		Students
MS	manuscript *(pl* MSS)	NUT	National Union of
	Master of Surgery		Teachers
	multiple sclerosis	NVQ	National Vocational
MSC	Master of Science		Qualification
MSP	Member of Scottish	NZ	New Zealand
	Parliament		
MUSB/D	Bachelor/Doctor of Music		
MV	merchant vessel		
	motor vessel		
MVO	Member, Royal Victorian		
	Order		
MW	medium wave		
	megawatt		

O

OAP	old age pension(er)		
OAPEC	Organisation of Arab		
	Petroleum Exporting		
	Countries		
OAS	Organisation of American		
	States		
Ob *or* obit	died		
OBE	Officer, Order of the		
	British Empire		
OBR	Office for Budget		
	Responsibility		
OC	Officer Commanding		
OE	Old English		
	omissions excepted		
OECD	Organisation for		
	Economic Cooperation		
	and Development		
OED	*Oxford English Dictionary*		
OFCOM	Office of Communications		
OFGEM	Office of Gas and		
	Electricity Markets		
OFM	Order of Friars Minor		
	(Franciscans)		
Ofsted	Office for Standards in		
	Education, Children's		
	Services and Skills		
OFT	Office of Fair Trading		
OFWAT	Office of Water Services		
OHMS	On Her/His Majesty's		
	Service		
OIC	Organisation of the		
	Islamic Conference		
OM	Order of Merit		
ono	or near(est) offer		
ONS	Office for National		
	Statistics		
op	*(opus)* work		
OP	opposite prompt side *(of*		
	theatre)		
	Order of Preachers		
	(Dominicans)		
	out of print *(books)*		
op cit	*(opere citato)* in the work		
	cited		
OPEC	Organisation of Petroleum		
	Exporting Countries		
OPSI	Office of Public Sector		
	Information		
ORR	Office of Rail Regulation		
OS	Old Style *(calendar)*		
	Ordnance Survey		
OSA	Order of St Augustine		
OSB	Order of St Benedict		

N

N	north
n/a	not applicable
	not available
NAAFI	Navy, Army and Air Force
	Institutes
NAFTA	North American Free
	Trade Agreement
NAO	National Audit Office
NASA	National Aeronautics and
	Space Administration
NASUWT	National Association of
	Schoolmasters/Union
	of Women Teachers
NATO	North Atlantic Treaty
	Organisation
nb	*(nota bene)* note well
NCO	non-commissioned
	officer
NDPB	non-departmental public
	body
NEB	New English Bible
nem con	*(nemine contradicente)* no
	one contradicting
NERC	Natural Environment
	Research Council
nes	not elsewhere specified
NESTA	National Endowment for
	Science, Technology
	and the Arts
NFU	National Farmers' Union
NHS	National Health Service
NI	National Insurance
	Northern Ireland
no	*(numero)* number
non seq	*(non sequitur)* it does not
	follow
Norvic:	of Norwich *(Bishop)*
NP	Notary Public
NRA	National Rifle Association
NS	New Style *(calendar)*
NSPCC	National Society for the
	Prevention of Cruelty
	to Children
NSW	New South Wales
	(Australia)

OSCE	Organisation for Security
	and Cooperation in
	Europe
OStJ	Officer, Order of St John
	of Jerusalem
OT	Old Testament
OTC	Officers' Training Corps
Oxon	(of) Oxford
	Oxfordshire

P

p	page
PA	personal assistant
	Press Association
	public address (system)
PAYE	pay as you earn
PAYG	pay as you go
pc	*(per centum)* in the
	hundred
PC	personal computer
	Plaid Cymru
	Police Constable
	politically correct
	Privy Counsellor
PCB	polychlorinated biphenyl
PCT	Primary Care Trust
PDSA	People's Dispensary for
	Sick Animals
PE	physical education
Petriburg:	of Peterborough *(Bishop)*
PFI	Private Finance Initiative
PG	parental guidance
	postgraduate
PGA	Professional Golfers
	Association
PGCE	Postgraduate Certificate of
	Education
PHD	Doctor of Philosophy
PIF	Pacific Islands Forum
pl	plural
PLA	Port of London Authority
plc	public limited company
PLO	Palestine Liberation
	Organisation
pm	*(post meridiem)* after noon
PM	post mortem
	Prime Minister
PMRAFNS	Princess Mary's Royal Air
	Force Nursing Service
PO	Petty Officer
	Pilot Officer
	post office
	postal order
POW	prisoner of war
pp	pages
	(per procurationem) by
	proxy
PPS	Parliamentary Private
	Secretary
PR	proportional
	representation
	public relations
PRA	President of the Royal
	Academy
pro tem	*(pro tempore)* for the time
	being
prox	*(proximo)* next month
PRS	President of the Royal
	Society
PRSE	President of the Royal
	Society of Edinburgh

PS (*postscriptum*) postscript
psc passed staff college
PSNCR public sector net cash requirement
PSV public service vehicle
PTA Parent Teacher Association
Pte. Private
PTO please turn over

Q

QARANC Queen Alexandra's Royal Army Nursing Corps
QARNNS Queen Alexandra's Royal Naval Nursing Service
QBD Queen's Bench Division
QC Queen's Counsel
QE quantitative easing
QED (*quod erat demonstrandum*) which was to be proved
QGM Queen's Gallantry Medal
QHC Queen's Honorary Chaplain
QHDS Queen's Honorary Dental Surgeon
QHNS Queen's Honorary Nursing Sister
QHP Queen's Honorary Physician
QHS Queen's Honorary Surgeon
Qld Queensland (*Australia*)
QMG Quartermaster-General
QPM Queen's Police Medal
QS quarter sessions Queen's Scholar
QSO quasi-stellar object (*quasar*) Queen's Service Order
quango quasi-autonomous non-governmental organisation
qv (*quod vide*) which see

R

r. (*recto*) on the right-hand page
R (*Regina*) Queen (*Rex*) King
RA Royal Academy/Academician Royal Artillery
RAC Royal Armoured Corps Royal Automobile Club
RADA Royal Academy of Dramatic Art
RADC Royal Army Dental Corps
RAEC Royal Army Educational Corps
RAES Royal Aeronautical Society
RAF Royal Air Force
RAM random-access memory Royal Academy of Music
RAMC Royal Army Medical Corps
RAN Royal Australian Navy
RAOC Royal Army Ordnance Corps

RAPC Royal Army Pay Corps
RAVC Royal Army Veterinary Corps
R&B rhythm and blues
RBS Royal Bank of Scotland Royal Society of British Sculptors
RC Red Cross Roman Catholic
RCM Royal College of Music
RCN Royal College of Nursing
RCT Royal Corps of Transport
R&D research and development
RD refer to drawer (*banking*) Royal Naval and Royal Marine Forces Reserve Decoration Rural Dean
RE Religious Education Royal Engineers
REM rapid eye movement
REME Royal Electrical and Mechanical Engineers
Rep representative Republican
Rep. Republic
Revd Reverend
RFL Rugby Football League
RFU Rugby Football Union
RGS Royal Geographical Society
RHS Royal Horticultural Society
RI Royal Institute of Painters in Watercolours Royal Institution
RIBA Royal Institute of British Architects
RIP (*requiescat in pace*) may he/she rest in peace
RIR Royal Irish Regiment
RM Royal Marines
RMA Royal Military Academy
RMT National Union of Rail, Maritime and Transport Workers
RN Royal Navy
RNIB Royal National Institute of Blind People
RNID Royal National Institute for Deaf People
RNLI Royal National Lifeboat Institution
RNR Royal Naval Reserve
RNVR Royal Naval Volunteer Reserve
RNXS Royal Naval Auxiliary Service
RNZN Royal New Zealand Navy
ROC Royal Observer Corps
Roffen: of Rochester (*Bishop*)
ROI Republic of Ireland Royal Institute of Oil Painters
RoSPA Royal Society for the Prevention of Accidents
RP Received Pronunciation Royal Society of Portrait Painters
RPA Rural Payments Agency
rpm revolutions per minute
RRC Lady of Royal Red Cross

RSA Royal Scottish Academician Royal Society of Arts
RSC Royal Shakespeare Company
RSE Royal Society of Edinburgh
RSM Regimental Sergeant Major
RSPB Royal Society for the Protection of Birds
RSPCA Royal Society for the Prevention of Cruelty to Animals
RSV Revised Standard Version (*of Bible*)
RSVP (*répondez, s'il vous plaêt*) please reply
RSW Royal Scottish Society of Painters in Watercolours
Rt. Hon. Right Honourable
RTPI Royal Town Planning Institute
RUC Royal Ulster Constabulary
RV Revised Version (*of Bible*)
RWS Royal Water Colour Society
RYS Royal Yacht Squadron

S

s second (*also* sec) section (Public Acts) (*solidus*) shilling
S south
SA Salvation Army South Africa South America South Australia
SAARC South Asian Association for Regional Cooperation
SAE stamped addressed envelope
Salop Shropshire
SARS severe acute respiratory syndrome
Sarum: of Salisbury (Bishop)
SAS Special Air Service
SBS Special Boat Service
SCD Doctor of Science
SCM State Certified Midwife
SCO Shanghai Cooperation Organisation
SDLP Social Democratic and Labour Party
SEAQ Stock Exchange Automated Quotations system
sec second (*also* s)
SEN special educational needs State Enrolled Nurse
SERPS State Earnings Related Pension Scheme
SF Sinn Fein
SFO Serious Fraud Office
SHA Strategic Health Authority
SI statutory instrument (*Système International d'Unités*) International System of Units

sic	*(sic)* so written
SIDS	sudden infant death syndrome
sig	signature
	Signor
SJ	Society of Jesus *(Jesuits)*
SLD	Social and Liberal Democrats
SMP	Statutory Maternity Pay
SNP	Scottish National Party
SOCA	Serious Organised Crime Agency
SOE	Special Operations Executive
sp	*(sine prole)* without issue
Sr	Senior
	Sister *(title)*
SRO	self-regulating organisation
SS	steamship
SSC	Solicitor before Supreme Court *(Scotland)*
SSN	standard serial number
SSP	statutory sick pay
SSSI	Site of Special Scientific Interest
ST	*Social Trends*
St	Saint *(pl. SS)*
	street
STD	*(Sacrae Theologiae Doctor)* Doctor of Sacred Theology
	subscriber trunk dialling
stet	*(stet)* let it stand *(printing)*
STFC	Science and Technology Facilities Council
STI	sexually transmitted infection
stp	standard temperature and pressure
STP	*(Sacrae Theologiae Professor)* Professor of Sacred Theology
Sub Lt.	sub-lieutenant
SVQ	Scottish Vocational Qualification

T

TA	Territorial Army
TB	tuberculosis
TD	Territorial Decoration
TEFL	teaching English as a foreign language
temp	temperature
	temporary employee
TES	*Times Educational Supplement*
THES	*Times Higher Education Supplement*
TLS	*Times Literary Supplement*
TNT	trinitrotoluene *(explosive)*
trans.	translated
TRH	Their Royal Highnesses
trs	transpose *(printing)*
TT	Tourist Trophy *(motorcycle races)*
	tuberculin tested

TTP	*Tehrik-i-Taliban Pakistani* (Pakistani Taliban)
TUC	Trades Union Congress

U

U	Unionist
UAB	unitary awarding body
UAE	United Arab Emirates
uc	upper case *(printing)*
UC	Unitary Council
UCAS	Universities and Colleges Admissions Service
UCATT	Union of Construction, Allied Trades and Technicians
UCL	University College London
UCU	University and College Union
UDA	Ulster Defence Association
UDI	Unilateral Declaration of Independence
UDR	Ulster Defence Regiment
UEFA	Union of European Football Associations
UFF	Ulster Freedom Fighters
UG	undergraduate
UHF	ultra-high frequency
UKAEA	UK Atomic Energy Authority
UN	United Nations
UNESCO	United Nations Educational, Scientific and Cultural Organisation
UNHCR	United Nations High Commissioner for Refugees
UNICEF	United Nations Children's Fund
UNIDO	United Nations Industrial Development Organisation
UNPO	Unrepresented Nations and Peoples Organisation
UPU	Universal Postal Union
USB	universal serial bus
USDAW	Union of Shop, Distributive and Allied Workers
USSR	Union of Soviet Socialist Republics
UTC	coordinated universal time system *(Temps Universel Coordonné)*
UVF	Ulster Volunteer Force

V

v	*(versus)* against
v.	*(verso)* on the left-hand page
V&A	Victoria and Albert Museum
VA	Vicar Apostolic
	Victoria and Albert Order

VAD	Voluntary Aid Detachment *(nursing)*
VAT	value added tax
VC	Victoria Cross
VD	venereal disease
	Volunteer Officers' Decoration
VDU	visual display unit
Ven.	Venerable
VHF	very high frequency
VRD	Royal Naval Volunteer Reserve Officers' Decoration
VSO	Voluntary Service Overseas

W

W	website
	west
w.	widowed
WBC	World Boxing Council
WBO	World Boxing Organisation
WCC	World Council of Churches
WEA	Workers' Educational Association
WEU	Western European Union
WFTU	World Federation of Trade Unions
WHO	World Health Organisation
WI	West Indies
	Women's Institute
Winton:	of Winchester *(Bishop)*
WIPO	World Intellectual Property Organisation
WMD	weapons of mass destruction
WMO	World Meteorological Organisation
WO	Warrant Officer
WRAC	Women's Royal Army Corps
WRAF	Women's Royal Air Force
WRNS	Women's Royal Naval Service
WRVS	Women's Royal Voluntary Service
WS	Writer to the Signet
WTO	World Trade Organisation
WWW	World Wide Web

Y

YHA	Youth Hostels Association
YMCA	Young Men's Christian Association
YWCA	Young Women's Christian Association

Z

ZANU-PF	Zimbabwean African National Union – Patriotic Front

INDEX

STOP PRESS

CHANGES SINCE PAGES WENT TO PRESS

EVENTS OF THE YEAR

UK AFFAIRS

3 August. Stuart Kuttner, the former managing editor of the *News of the World*, was arrested following investigations into alleged phone-hacking at the newspaper. **6 August.** Horatio Chapple, a 17-year-old student from Salisbury, Wiltshire, was mauled to death by a polar bear on a remote Norwegian island in the Arctic Circle; the student was part of a tour run by the British Schools Exploring Society, a youth development charity based at the Royal Geographical Society in London. **7 August.** Rioting, looting and arson erupted in Tottenham, north London, following an initally peaceful protest in response to the fatal shooting of local resident Mark Duggan; rioting lasted for around four days, spreading to Birmingham, Liverpool, Manchester and Bristol: three people died and there were over 900 arrests. **11 August.** Parliament was recalled to debate the riots; it was the first time parliament had been recalled during the summer recess since 2002. **13 August.** An oil spill from the Gannet Alpha platform became one of the worst in UK waters for approximately ten years; the spill from the Royal Dutch Shell-operated platform, situated around 180km (112 miles) off the coast of Aberdeen, Scotland, was said to be pouring roughly five barrels of oil a day into the North Sea. **17 August.** Clive Goodman, the former royal correspondent of the *News of the World*, claimed that phone-hacking was 'widely discussed' at editorial meetings at the newspaper; the allegations, made in a letter addressed to News International in 2008, also claimed that hacking was carried out with 'full support' of other senior journalists. A British man was killed by a shark while snorkelling off the coast of the Seychelles; Ian Redmond, 30, from Lancashire, initially survived the attack off Anse Lazio beach on Praslin, but later died from his injuries in hospital. **19 August.** James Desborough, the former showbusiness reporter at the *News of the World*, was arrested by police officers investigating phone-hacking allegations at the newspaper; the arrest followed private investigator Glenn Mulcaire's decision to sue News International after the publisher stopped paying his legal costs.

BUSINESS AND ECONOMIC AFFAIRS

5 August. Around £50bn was wiped off the value of Britain's 100 biggest companies amid fears of the financial crises in the eurozone and USA economies.

SPORT

11 August. In cricket, England beat India in the third test at Edgbaston, Birmingham, to become the number one test cricket nation in the world. **27 August.** The 13th World Athletics Championships opened in South Korea; Great Britain's Mo Farah and Dai Greene both won gold medals in the 5,000m and 400m hurdles respectively, while Jessica Ennis, Phillips Idowu and Hannah England also picked up silver medals in their respective events.

MIDDLE EAST

1 August. Over 100 people were killed in Hama, Syria, during ongoing protests against president Bashar al-Assad's regime; the violence was condemned by the UN security council on 4 August following growing international impatience towards the Syrian regime. **3 August.** The trial of former Egyptian president Hosni Mubarak began in Cairo; the former president, removed from his post following mass protests in February, denied all charges of corruption. **8 August.** In Israel, over 300,000 people gathered on the streets of Tel Aviv and Jerusalem to protest against rising living costs and to demand social justice. **16 August.** A series of co-ordinated explosions across Iraq killed 74 people and wounded 250 people; the explosions, largely consigned to Shia Muslim areas of the country, were attributed to the al-Qaida affiliated Sunni extremist group, Islamic State of Iraq. **23 August.** Rebel forces advanced into the Libyan capital Tripoli, taking control of Col. Gaddafi's compound. **3 September.** Turkey expelled their Israeli ambassador and suspended its military agreements following Israel's refusal to apologise for its actions during a raid of a Turkish flotilla in 2010.

THE AMERICAS

2 August. In the USA, the House of Representatives voted overwhelmingly in favour of an economic package to prevent the country defaulting on debt for the first time in its history; the country's credit rating was downgraded from AAA to AA+ on 6 August following concerns over the budget deficit. **24 August.** Dominique Strauss-Kahn, former head of the International Monetary Fund, was acquitted of allegedly sexually assaulting a hotel maid in New York City in May. **25 August.** Steve Jobs, co-founder of American technology giant Apple Inc., resigned as chief executive of the company, succeeded by chief operating officer Tim Cook. **28 August.** Tropical storm Irene hit the state of New York, USA, causing 11 deaths and the evacuation of approximately 370,000 people from their homes.